2022 Higher Education Directory®

Published by

Higher Education Publications, Inc.

Edited by

Mary Pat Rodenhouse

Reston, Virginia

2022

2022 Edition

Higher Education Publications, Inc.
1801 Robert Fulton Drive, Suite 380
Reston, VA 20191-5499
(888) 349-7715
(571) 313-0478
FAX (571) 313-0526
Email: info@hepinc.com
Internet address: www.hepinc.com

Carnegie classification codes with permission from The Carnegie Foundation for the Advancement of Teaching.

Internet addresses (URL's) were originally drawn from lists maintained by Washington and Lee University and the University of North Carolina-Chapel Hill and through the annual survey sent out by Higher Education Publications, Inc.

Printed in the United States of America

ISBN-10: 0-914927-83-3; ISBN-13: 978-0-914927-83-9
ISSN 0736-0797
Library of Congress Catalogue Card Number: 83-641119
Library of Congress Cataloging-in Publication Data

HEP. . . Higher Education Directory®
Reston, VA; Higher Education Publications.
V.: 28cm
Annual
Began with issue for 1983.

A directory of accredited postsecondary, degree-granting institutions in the U.S., its possessions and territories accredited by regional, national, professional and specialized agencies recognized as accrediting bodies by the U.S. Secretary of Education and the Council for Higher Education Accreditation (CHEA) which honors recognition provided by the former Council on Postsecondary Accreditation (COPA)/Commission on Recognition of Postsecondary Accreditation (CORPA)
Description based on 2021.
Cover title: 2022 Higher Education Directory®
Spine title: 2022 Higher Education Directory® Fortieth Edition

ISSN 0736-0797 = The Higher Education Directory®.

1. Education, Higher—United States—Directories.
2. Recognized accrediting agencies and associations—United States—Directories.
3. Acronyms, explanatory notes and symbols—United States—Directories.
4. Institution changes (additions, deletions, mergers and name changes)—United States—Directories.
5. Administrative officers, titles and title codes—United States—Directories.
6. United States Department of Education offices, statewide agencies for higher education and educational associations (and consortia)—United States—Directories.
7. Religious affiliation by denomination.
8. Carnegie classification codes.
9. Statistics.
10. Universities and colleges—United States—Directories.
11. College administrators alphabetical listing, phone numbers—United States—Directories.
12. Regional, national, professional and specialized accreditation alphabetical listing—United States—Directories.
13. Institutional FICE & Unit ID Number listing—United States—Directories.
14. Institutional alphabetical listing—United States—Directories.

I. Higher Education Publications, Inc.
II. Title: Higher Education Directory®.

L901.E34 378.73-dc19 83-641119 AACR 2 MARC-S

Table of Contents

Dedication and Acknowledgments

This 40th edition of the Higher Education Directory is dedicated to Frederick F. Hafner, who founded Higher Education Publications, Inc. on September 26, 1982. He steadfastly shepherded it from the print to the digital age with fairness, integrity and pride. Mr. Hafner passed away on December 25, 2020 and is missed by the many who knew and loved him.

Thirty-nine years ago, Higher Education Publications, Inc. was formed to produce a directory to succeed the Department of Education's *Education Directory: Colleges and Universities*.

Our thanks to the thousands of people who have supplied us the necessary data contained in the directory. Over this past year we have had a response/update rate of 96% from main campuses—truly outstanding! We are most appreciative of the many subscribers who have supported us in our efforts to bring you the most accurate and current information available. And, a special thanks to all of you who suggest improvements to our directory.

The accuracy and completeness of the contents of the 2022 edition was assured by a group of editors, updating and proofing specialists including Mary Pat Rodenhouse, Jodi Mondragon, Emmy Brown, Jackie Hafner, Doris Jean and Pam Smith. Barbara Herrman handled our typesetting. Mark Schreiber managed the HigherEd Direct update system and the database.

You may be familiar with our website, but if you have not yet visited it, I encourage you to go to www.hepinc.com. The site features the latest news on higher education, accreditations and administrative changes along with many helpful resources. Also, please visit our new LinkedIn and Facebook pages. We feel that our increased Internet and social media presence will help us to continue to meet the goals we established for ourselves thirty-nine years ago—to provide you with the most authoritative, timely and accurate information on the higher education community.

Mary Pat Rodenhouse
Senior Editor

Reston, Virginia

Foreword

The 2022 edition of the *Higher Education Directory*® contains listings of accredited, degree-granting institutions of postsecondary education in the United States and its territories.

Criteria for Listing in this Directory

To be listed in this Directory, an institution must meet the following guidelines:

(1) They are degree-granting (legally authorized to offer and are offering a program of college-level studies leading toward a degree[1]);
(2) They have submitted the information required for listing; and
(3) They meet one of the following criteria for listing:
   A. The institution is accredited at the college level by an accrediting agency that is recognized by the U.S. Secretary of Education;
   B. The institution holds pre-accredited status with an accrediting agency recognized by the U.S. Secretary of Education whose recognition includes the pre-accreditation status;
   C. The institution is accredited at the college level by an accrediting agency recognized by the Council for Higher Education Accreditation (CHEA).

"College level" means a postsecondary associate, baccalaureate, post-baccalaureate, or rabbinical education program.

Verification of Accreditations

Verification of each accreditation for all institutions was done by comparing the accreditation against the current Directory (and updated lists) for each respective regional, national, professional and specialized association or agency, along with telephone calls to numerous accrediting associations whenever there was a question of accuracy. Over 20,000 accreditations were verified through September 2021.

The reader is reminded that many institutions have programs which may not be recognized by a professional or specialized association, but are considered fine programs. The institutions may or may not have sought such recognition.

General Organization of the Directory

Our approach to the organization of the material is to make the desired information readable and easy to find. There are four indexes which are cross-referenced to the main institutional listing.

A. Prologue
   1. Accrediting agencies with addresses. Regional accrediting commissions are listed alphabetically while national, professional and specialized bodies are listed alphabetically under headings showing their specialties.
   2. Acronyms used in the Directory for accrediting bodies are listed alphabetically.
   3. Explanatory notes and symbols.
   4. U.S. postal abbreviations of states.
   5. Institution changes.
   6. Administrative officers' description and job codes.
   7. U.S. Department of Education offices.
   8. Statewide agencies of higher education.
   9. Higher education associations.
   10. Consortia of institutions of higher education.
   11. Association name index.
   12. Religious affiliation by denomination.
   13. Carnegie classification codes.
   14. Statistical data.

B. College and university listings by state with institutional characteristics and administrative officers.
   1. Institution Name. If an * appears before the institution's name, it is a part of a system. A line between institutions separates two systems.
   2. Alpha Code. The first institution listed on a page is coded (A), the second (B), etc. The Administrators' index is also coded to enable the reader to locate the desired institution quickly.
   3. Address.
   4. County.
   5. FICE Identification. This was the Federal Interagency Commission on Education number originally assigned by the Department of Education. We continue to use the term FICE. However, the Department of Education in their Office of Student Financial Assistance uses OPEID, Office of Postsecondary Education Identification. OPEID consists of the first six digits of the FICE plus two more digits indicating branch campuses. Numbers beginning with 66 are for accredited institutions for which we cannot locate a FICE or OPEID number. These are identification numbers only.
   6. Telephone Number.
   7. Unit ID Number. A unique number developed by the National Center for Education Statistics (NCES) for the Education Department's IPEDS Reports.
   8. Carnegie Classification Code. (see page ***xlv***)
   9. Main FAX Number.
   10. School Calendar.
   11. URL (Universal Resource Locator).
   12. Date Established.
   13. Annual Tuition & Fees for 2020-21 school year.
   14. Fall 2020 Enrollment. Head count (not FTE) in degree programs as reported on the latest IPEDS survey.
   15. Type of Student Body.
   16. Affiliation or Control.
   17. IRS Status.
   18. Highest Degree Offered.
   19. Accreditation (see page ***vi***). **N.B. Institutional accreditation is in bold face.**
   20. Administrative and academic officers with job classification code (see page ***xxiii*** for descriptions).
   21. Non-system branch campuses. The names of these campuses are in italic type and their listings are shortened. Non-system branch campuses are listed if they are identified by the parent institutions' accrediting organization as a branch campus.

C. Index of administrators is an alphabetical listing of all the administrators with their most direct phone number and E-mail address. The page and reference letter indicate the page on which the administrator's institution listing begins.

D. Index of regional, national, professional and specialized accreditation alphabetically by state. This index standardizes and simplifies reviewing of the 146 accrediting classifications.

E. FICE number index. Numeric listing of FICE number and school.

F. Alphabetic index of institutions.

[1]The *Higher Education Directory*® lists degree-granting institutions approved by regional, national, professional or specialized accrediting agencies.

Accrediting Agencies

The following regional, national, professional and specialized accrediting agencies are recognized by the U.S. Secretary of Education or the Council for Higher Education Accreditation (CHEA). The U.S. Department of Education (USDE) dates specified are the date of initial listing as a U.S. Department of Education recognized agency, the date of the U.S. Secretary's most recent grant of renewed recognition based on the last full review of the agency by the National Advisory Committee on Institutional Quality and Integrity, and the date of the agency's next scheduled review for renewal of recognition.[1] The Council for Higher Education (CHEA) date reflects initial recognition by CHEA.

Regional Accrediting Bodies

Delaware, District of Columbia, Maryland, New Jersey, New York, Pennsylvania, Puerto Rico, Virgin Islands

Middle States Commission on Higher Education M
USDE: 1952/2017/2023 CHEA: 2013
3624 Market Street, Suite 2 West
Philadelphia, PA 19104
(267) 284-5000 Fax (215) 662-5501
Heather Perfetti, President
E-mail: info@msche.org
URL: www.msche.org

Connecticut, Maine, Massachusetts, New Hampshire, Rhode Island, Vermont

New England Commission of Higher Education EH
USDE: 1952/2017/2023 CHEA: 2013
3 Burlington Woods Drive, Suite 100
Burlington, MA 01803-4514
(781) 425-7785 Fax (781) 425-1001
Lawrence Schall, President
E-mail: info@neche.org
URL: www.neche.org

Arizona, Arkansas, Colorado, Illinois, Indiana, Iowa, Kansas, Michigan, Minnesota, Missouri, Nebraska, New Mexico, North Dakota, Ohio, Oklahoma, South Dakota, West Virginia, Wisconsin, Wyoming

Higher Learning Commission HLC
USDE: 1952/2017/2023 CHEA: 2015
230 South LaSalle Street, Suite 7-500
Chicago, IL 60604-1411
(800) 621-7440 Fax (312) 263-7462
Barbara Gellman-Danley, President
E-mail: info@hlcommission.org
URL: www.hlcommission.org

Alaska, Idaho, Montana, Nevada, Oregon, Utah, Washington

Northwest Commission on Colleges and Universities NW
USDE: 1952/2018/2023 CHEA: 2019
8060 165th Avenue, NE, Suite 200
Redmond, WA 98052
(425) 558-4224 Fax (205) 525-9848
Sonny Ramaswamy, President
E-mail: info@nwccu.org
URL: www.nwccu.org

Alabama, Florida, Georgia, Kentucky, Louisiana, Mississippi, North Carolina, South Carolina, Tennessee, Texas, Virginia

Commission on Colleges
Southern Association of Colleges and Schools SC
USDE: 1952/2019/2022 CHEA: 2015
1866 Southern Lane
Decatur, GA 30033-4097
(404) 679-4500 Fax (404) 679-4558
Belle S. Wheelan, President
E-mail: questions@sacscoc.org
URL: www.sacscoc.org

California, Hawaii, American Samoa, Guam, Commonwealth of the Northern Marianas, Federated States of Micronesia, Republic of the Marshall Islands, Republic of Palau

Senior College and University Commission
Western Association of Schools and Colleges WC
USDE: 1952/2017/2023 CHEA: 2014
1001 Marina Village Pkwy, Suite 420
Alameda, CA 94501
(510) 748-9001 Fax (510) 748-9797
Jamienne Studley, President
E-mail: wasc@wscuc.org
URL: www.wscuc.org

Accrediting Commission for Community and Junior Colleges
Western Association of Schools and Colleges WJ
USDE: 1952/2019/2024 CHEA: 2016
10 Commercial Boulevard, Suite 204
Novato, CA 94949
(415) 506-0234 Fax (415) 506-0238
Stephanie Droker, President
E-mail: accjc@accjc.org
URL: www.accjc.org

[1]U.S. Department of Education, Nationally Recognized Accrediting Agencies, www2.ed.gov/admins/finaid/accred/accreditation.html.

National, Professional and Specialized Accrediting Bodies

Acupuncture

Accreditation Commission for Acupuncture and Oriental Medicine (ACAOM)
USDE: 1988/2016/2021
8941 Aztec Drive, Suite 2
Eden Prairie, MN 55347
(952) 212-2434 Fax (952) 657-7068
Mark S. McKenzie, Executive Director
E-mail: info@acaom.org
URL: www.acaom.org

First-professional master's degree, professional master's level certificate and diploma programs and professional post-graduate doctoral programs in acupuncture and Oriental medicine, and free-standing institutions that offer such programs **ACUP**

Allied Health

Accrediting Bureau of Health Education Schools (ABHES)
USDE: 1969/2016/2021
7777 Leesburg Pike, Suite 314N
Falls Church, VA 22043
(703) 917-9503 Fax (703) 917-4109
India Y. Tips, Executive Director
E-mail: info@abhes.org
URL: www.abhes.org

Institutions specializing in allied health education **ABHES**
Specialized programs for
Medical assistant **MAAB**
Medical laboratory technician **MLTAB**
Surgical technologist **SURTEC**

Commission on Accreditation of Allied Health Education Programs (CAAHEP)
CHEA: 2001
9355 113th Street N, #7709
Seminole, FL 33775
(727) 210-2350 Fax (727) 210-2354
Kathleen Megivern, Executive Director
E-mail: mail@caahep.org
URL: www.caahep.org

The Commission on Accreditation of Allied Health Education Programs (CAAHEP) is recognized as an accrediting agency for accreditation of education for the allied health occupations. In carrying out its accreditation activities, CAAHEP cooperates with the Committees on Accreditation sponsored by various allied health and medical specialty organizations. CAAHEP is the coordinating agency for accreditation of education for the following allied health occupations:
Advanced cardiovascular sonography **ACS**
Anesthesia technologist **AT**
Anesthesiologist assistant **AA**
Art therapist **ACATE**
Assistive technology practitioner **ATECH**
Blood bank technology **BBT**
Cardiovascular technologist **CVT**
Clinical researcher **CR**
Cytotechnologist **CYTO**
Diagnostic medical sonographer **DMS**
Emergency medical technician-paramedic **EMT**
Exercise science **EXSC**
Kinesiotherapy **KIN**
Lactation consultant **LC**
Medical assistant **MAC**
Medical illustrator **MIL**
Neurodiagnostic technologist **NDT**
Orthotist/prosthetist **OPE**
Perfusionist **PERF**
Polysomnographic technologist **POLYT**
Recreation therapist **CARTE**
Surgical assistant **SURGA**
Surgical technologist **SURGT**

Anesthesia Technology

Commission on Accreditation of Allied Health Education Programs (see listing under Allied Health)
Committee on Accreditation for Anesthesia Technology Education
(612) 836-3311
Theresa Sisneros, Director Accreditation Services
E-mail: theresa@caahep.org
URL: www.caahep.org/coa-ate

Anesthesiologist Assistant

Commission on Accreditation of Allied Health Education Programs (see listing under Allied Health)
Accreditation Review Committee for the Anesthesiologist Assistant
(612) 836-3311
Jennifer Anderson Warwick, Executive Director
E-mail: arc-aa@arc-aa.org
URL: www.caahep.org/arc-aa

Post-baccalaureate programs for anesthesiologist assistant **AA**

Art

Commission on Accreditation
National Association of Schools of Art and Design (NASAD)
USDE: 1966/2017/2023
11250 Roger Bacon Drive, Suite 21
Reston, VA 20190
(703) 437-0700 Fax (703) 437-6312
Karen P. Moynahan, Executive Director
E-mail: info@arts-accredit.org
URL: nasad.arts-accredit.org

Institutions and departments within institutions offering degree and non-degree granting programs in art/design and art/design-related programs **ART**

Art Therapy

Commission on Accreditation of Allied Health Education Programs (see listing under Allied Health)
Accreditation Council for Art Therapy Education (ACATE)
4875 Eisenhower Avenue, Suite 240
Alexandria, VA 22304
(724) 830-1140
Ron Hunt, Coordinator
E-mail: acatecouncil@gmail.com

Programs for the art therapist **ACATE**

Assistive Technology

Commission on Accreditation of Allied Health Education Programs (see listing under Allied Health)
Committee on Accreditation for Rehabilitation Engineering and Assistive Technology Education (CoA-RATE)
2025 M Street NW, Suite 800
Washington, DC 20036
(202) 367-1121
Andrea Van Hook, Executive Director
E-mail: execoffice@resna.org

Programs for the assistive technology practitioner **ATECH**

Athletic Training

Commission on Accreditation of Athletic Training Education (CAATE)
CHEA: 2014
2001 K Street NW, 3rd Floor North
Washington, DC 20006
(512) 733-9700
Dale West, Executive Director
E-mail: support@caate.net
URL: www.caate.net

Programs for athletic training **CAATE**

Audiology

Accreditation Commission for Audiology Education
CHEA: 2012
11480 Commerce Park Drive, Suite 220
Reston, VA 20191
(703) 226-1056
Andrew Stafford, Director of Professional Standards and Credentialing
E-mail: info@acaeaccred.org
URL: www.acaeaccred.org

Programs leading to the Doctor of Audiology degree **ACAE**

Council on Academic Accreditation in Audiology and Speech Language Pathology
American Speech-Language-Hearing Association (ASHA)
USDE: 1967/2021/2026 CHEA: 2003
2200 Research Boulevard
Rockville, MD 20850-3289
(301) 296-5700 Fax (301) 296-8570
Kimberlee Moore, Director of Accreditation
E-mail: accreditation@asha.org
URL: caa.asha.org

Doctoral degree programs in audiology **AUD**

Aviation

Aviation Accreditation Board International
CHEA: 2013
115 South 8th Street, Suite 102
Opelika, AL 36801
(334) 748-9359 Fax (334) 748-9360
Guy Smith, President
E-mail: ceci@aabi.aero
URL: www.aabi.aero

Non-engineering programs for aviation **AAB**

Behavior Analysis

Accreditation Board
Association for Behavior Analysis International
CHEA: 2021
550 W. Centre Avenue
Portage, MI 49024
(269) 402-9310
Jenna Mrljak, ABAI Education Manager
E-mail: abaiaccreditation@abainternational.org
URL: https://accreditation.abainternational.org

Programs in behavior analysis **ABAI**

Bible College Education

Commission on Accreditation
Association for Biblical Higher Education (ABHE)
USDE: 1952/2017/2022 CHEA: 2001
5850 T. G. Lee Boulevard, Suite 130
Orlando, FL 32822
(407) 207-0808 Fax (407) 207-0840
Lisa Beatty, Director, Commission on Accreditation
E-mail: coa@abhe.org
URL: www.abhe.org

Bible colleges and programs offering undergraduate and graduate programs **BI**

Blood Bank Technology

Commission on Accreditation of Allied Health Education Programs (see listing under Allied Health)
AABB
Committee on Accreditation of Specialists in Blood Bank Technology Schools

4550 Montgomery Avenue, Suite 700 North Tower
Bethesda, MD 20814
(301) 907-6977 Fax (301) 907-6895
Meredith Eller, Director of Accreditation and Quality
E-mail: accreditation@aabb.org
URL: www.aabb.org

Programs for blood bank technologist **BBT**

Business

Accrediting Council for Independent Colleges and Schools (ACICS)
USDE: 1956/2016/2021
1350 Eye Street NW, Suite 560
Washington, DC 20005
(202) 336-6780 Fax (202) 789-1747
Michelle Edwards, President/CEO
E-mail: info@acics.org
URL: www.acics.org

Institutions offering certificates/diplomas, associate, baccalaureate and master's degree programs to educate students for professional, technical, or occupational careers **ACICS**

Accreditation Council for Business Schools and Programs (ACBSP)
CHEA: 2001
11520 West 119th Street
Overland Park, KS 66213
(913) 339-9356 Fax (913) 339-6226
Jeffrey Alderman, President/CEO
E-mail: info@acbsp.org
URL: www.acbsp.org

Business administration, management, accounting and related business fields **ACBSP**

International Accreditation Council for Business Education
CHEA: 2011
11960 Quivira Road, Suite 300
Overland, KS 66213
(913) 631-3009 Fax (913) 631-9154
Phyllis Okrepkie, President
E-mail: iacbe@iacbe.org
URL: www.iacbe.org

Undergraduate and graduate level business programs in institutions that grant associates, bachelor's and/or graduate degrees **IACBE**

Cardiac Sonography

Commission on Accreditation of Allied Health Education Programs (see listing under Allied Health)
Committee on Accreditation for Advanced Cardiovascular Sonography (COA-ACS)
2530 Meridian Parkway, Suite 450
Durham, NC 27713
Mary Alice Dilday
(919) 465-9020
E-mail: coaacs@gmail.com

Programs for advanced cardiovascular sonography **ACS**

Cardiovascular Technology

Commission on Accreditation of Allied Health Education Programs (see listing under Allied Health)
Joint Review Committee on Education in Cardiovascular Technology (JRC-CVT)
1449 Hill Street
Whitinsville, MA 01588-1032
(978) 456-5594 Fax (727) 210-2354
Jackie Long-Goding, Executive Director
E-mail: office@jrccvt.org
URL: www.jrccvt.org

Programs for cardiovascular technology **CVT**

Chiropractic

The Council on Chiropractic Education (CCE)
USDE: 1974/2019/2022 CHEA: 2005
10105 E. Via Linda, Suite 103 PMB 3642
Scottsdale, AZ 85258
(480) 443-8877 Fax (480) 483-7333
Craig S. Little, President
E-mail: cce@cce-usa.org
URL: www.cce-usa.org

Programs leading to and institutions offering the Doctorate of Chiropractic (D.C.) degree **CHIRO**

Christian Studies Education

Accreditation Commission
Transnational Association of Christian Colleges and Schools (TRACS)
USDE: 1991/2018/2021 CHEA: 2001
15935 Forest Road
Forest, VA 24551
(434) 525-9539 Fax (434) 616-2638
Timothy Eaton, President
E-mail: info@tracs.org
URL: www.tracs.org

Christian liberal arts institutions which offer certificates/diplomas and associate, baccalaureate and graduate degrees **TRACS**

Clinical Laboratory Sciences

National Accrediting Agency for Clinical Laboratory Sciences (NAACLS)
CHEA: 2002
5600 North River Road, Suite 720
Rosemont, IL 60018
(773) 714-8880 Fax (773) 714-8886
Dianne M. Cearlock, Chief Executive Officer
E-mail: info@naacls.org
URL: www.naacls.org

Programs for:
- cytogenetic technologist **CGTECH**
- diagnostic molecular scientist **DMOLS**
- histologic technician/technologist **HT**
- medical laboratory technician **MLTAD**
- medical technologist/laboratory scientist **MT**
- pathologists' assistant **PA**

Clinical Pastoral Education

Accreditation Commission
Association for Clinical Pastoral Education, Inc. (ACPEI)
USDE: 1969/2017/2022
55 Ivan Allen Jr. Boulevard, Suite 835
Atlanta, GA 30308
(404) 320-1472 Fax (404) 320-0849
Trace Haythorn, Executive Director/CEO
E-mail: acpe@acpe.edu
URL: www.acpe.edu

Basic, advanced and supervisory clinical pastoral education programs **PAST**

Clinical Research

Commission on Accreditation of Allied Health Education Programs (see listing under Allied Health)
Committee on Accreditation of Academic Programs in Clinical Research (CAAPCR)
(734) 604-1989
Stephen A. Sonstein, Chair
E-mail: ssonstein@gmail.com

Academic programs in clinical research **CR**

Construction Education

American Council for Construction Education (ACCE)
CHEA: 2001
300 Decker Drive
Irving, TX 75062
(972) 600-8800
Steve Nellis, President/CEO
E-mail: acce@acce-hq.org
URL: www.acce-hq.org

Associate, baccalaureate and master's degree programs **CONST**

Continuing Education

Accrediting Council for Continuing Education and Training (ACCET)
USDE: 1978/2018/2024
1722 N Street NW
Washington, DC 20036
(202) 955-1113 Fax (202) 955-1118
Christopher Lambert, Executive Director
E-mail: info@accet.org
URL: www.accet.org

Institutions offering noncollegiate continuing education and institutions offering occupational associate degree programs **CNCE**

Cosmetology

National Accrediting Commission of Career Arts and Sciences (NACCAS)
USDE: 1970/2021/2026
3015 Colvin Street
Alexandria, VA 22314
(703) 600-7600 Fax (703) 379-2200
Darin M. Wallace, Executive Director
E-mail: webinfo@naccas.org
URL: www.naccas.org

Postsecondary schools and departments of cosmetology arts and sciences and massage therapy **COSME**

Counseling and Related Educational Programs

Council for Accreditation of Counseling and Related Educational Programs (CACREP)
CHEA: 2002
500 Montgomery Street, Suite 350
Alexandria, VA 22314
(703) 535-5990 Fax (703) 739-6209
M. Sylvia Fernandez, President and CEO
E-mail: cacrep@cacrep.org
URL: www.cacrep.org

Programs in counseling and its specialties **CACREP**

Masters in Psychology and Counseling Accrediation Council
CHEA: 2021
595 New Loudon Road, #265
Latham, New York 12110
(518) 764-7581
Pat O'Connor, Executive Director
E-mail: mpcaced@gmail.com
URL: http://mpcacaccreditation.org

Programs in counseling and psychological services **MPCAC**

Culinary Arts

Accrediting Commission
American Culinary Federation
CHEA: 2004
6816 Southpoint Pkwy, Suite 400
Jacksonville, FL 33216
(904) 824-4468 Fax (904) 940-0741
Heidi Cramb, Executive Director
E-mail: acf@acfchefs.net
URL: www.acfchefs.org

Programs in culinary arts which award certificates, diplomas or associate degrees and bachelor degree programs in culinary management **ACFEI**

Cytotechnology

Commission on Accreditation of Allied Health Education Programs (see listing under Allied Health)
Cytotechnology Programs Review Committee
American Society of Cytopathology
100 West 10th Street, Suite 605
Wilmington, DE 19801
(302) 543-6583 Fax (302) 543-6597
Elizabeth Jenkins, Executive Director
E-mail: asc@cytopathology.org
URL: www.cytopathology.org

Programs for the cytotechnologist **CYTO**

Dance

Commission on Accreditation
National Association of Schools of Dance (NASD)
USDE: 1983/2019/2024
11250 Roger Bacon Drive, Suite 21
Reston, VA 20190
(703) 437-0700 Fax (703) 437-6312
Karen P. Moynahan, Executive Director
E-mail: info@arts-accredit.org
URL: nasd.arts-accredit.org

Institutions and departments within institutions offering degree and non-degree-granting programs in dance and dance-related disciplines **DANCE**

Dental and Dental Auxiliary Programs

Commission on Dental Accreditation
American Dental Association (ADA)
USDE: 1952/2017/2022
211 East Chicago Avenue, Suite 1900
Chicago, IL 60611
(800) 621-6108 Fax (312) 440-2915
Sherin Tooks, Director
E-mail: tookss@ada.org
URL: www.ada.org/coda

Programs leading to:
- D.D.S. or D.M.D. degree, advanced general dentistry and specialty programs **DENT**
- Dental hygiene **DH**
- Dental assisting **DA**
- Dental laboratory technology **DT**
- Dental therapy **DTH**

Diagnostic Medical Sonography

Commission on Accreditation of Allied Health Education Programs (see listing under Allied Health)
Joint Review Committee on Education in Diagnostic Medical Sonography
6021 University Boulevard, Suite 500
Ellicot City, MD 21043-6090
(443) 973-3251 Fax (866) 738-3444
Gerry Magat, Executive Director
E-mail: mail@jrcdms.org
URL: www.jrcdms.org

Programs for the diagnostic medical sonographer **DMS**

Dietetics

Accreditation Council for Education in Nutrition and Dietetics
Academy of Nutrition and Dietetics
USDE: 1974/2017/2023
120 South Riverside Plaza, Suite 2190
Chicago, IL 60606-6995
(312) 899-0040 Fax (312) 899-4817
Rayane AbuSabha, Executive Director
E-mail: acend@eatright.org
URL: www.eatrightpro.org/acend

Coordinated programs in dietetics **DIETC**
Didactic programs **DIETD**
Post-baccalaureate internships **DIETI**
Dietetic technician programs **DIETT**

Distance Education and Training

Distance Education Accrediting Commission
USDE: 1959/2017/2022 CHEA: 2001
1101 17th Street NW, Suite 808
Washington, DC 20036
(202) 234-5100 Fax (202) 332-1386
Leah K. Matthews, Executive Director
E-mail: info@deac.org
URL: www.deac.org

Distance education institutions including associate, baccalaureate, master's, and doctoral degree-granting programs primarily through the distance learning method **DEAC** (formerly DETC)

Emergency Medical Services

Commission on Accreditation for Allied Health Programs (see listing under Allied Health)
Committee on Accreditation of Educational Programs for the Emergency Medical Services Professions
8301 Lakeview Parkway, Suite 111-312
Rowlett, TX 75088
(214) 703-8445 Fax (214) 703-8992
George Hatch Jr., Executive Director
E-mail: george@coaemsp.org
URL: www.coaemsp.org

Programs for the emergency medical technician-paramedic **EMT**

English Language

Commission on English Language Program Accreditation (CEA)
USDE: 2003/2018/2022
1001 North Fairfax Drive, Suite 630
Alexandria, VA 22314
(703) 665-3400 Fax (703) 519-2071
Heidi Vellenga, Executive Director
E-mail: info@cea-accredit.org
URL: www.cea-accredit.org

English language programs **CEA**

Exercise Sciences

Commission on Accreditation of Allied Health Education Programs (see listing under Allied Health)
Committee on Accreditation for the Exercise Sciences
401 W. Michigan Street
Indianapolis, IN 46202
(317) 777-1135 Fax (317) 634-7817
William Coale, Director
E-mail: wcoale@acsm.org
URL: www.coaes.org

Programs for exercise science and related departments **EXSC**

Family and Consumer Sciences

Council for Accreditation
American Association of Family and Consumer Sciences (AAFCS)
CHEA: 2001
107 S. West Street, #816
Alexandria, VA 22314
(703) 706-4600 Fax (703) 636-7648
Nancy Bock, Executive Director
E-mail: accreditation@aafcs.org
URL: www.aafcs.org

Baccalaureate programs in family and consumer sciences **AAFCS**

Fire and Emergency

International Fire Service Accreditation Congress
CHEA: 2011
1723 West Tyler Avenue
Oklahoma State University
Stillwater, OK 74078
(405) 744-8303 Fax (405) 744-7377
Jillian Conaghan, Manager
E-mail: admin@ifsac.org
URL: www.ifsac.org

Fire and emergency related programs **IFSAC**

Forensic Science

Forensic Science Educational Program Accreditation Commission
American Academy of Forensic Sciences (AAFS)
CHEA: 2012
410 North 21st Street
Colorado Springs, CO 80904
(719) 636-1100 Fax (719) 636-1993
Nancy J. Jackson, Director of Development and Accreditation
E-mail: info@aafs.org
URL: www.aafs.org

Bachelor or master's degree programs in forensic science **FEPAC**

Funeral Service Education

Committee on Accreditation
American Board of Funeral Service Education (ABFSE)
USDE: 1972/2021/2026 CHEA: 2001
992 Mantua Pike, Suite 108
Woodbury Heights, NJ 08097
(816) 233-3747 Fax (856) 579-7354
Robert C. Smith III, Executive Director
E-mail: exdir@abfse.org
URL: www.abfse.org

Institutions and programs awarding diplomas, associate and bachelor's degrees in funeral service or mortuary science **FUSER**

Health Informatics and Information Management

Commission on Accreditation for Health Informatics and Information Management Education (CAHIIM)
CHEA: 2012
200 East Randolph Street, Suite 5100
Chicago, IL 60601
(312) 235-3255
Angela Kennedy, Chief Executive Officer
E-mail: info@cahiim.org
URL: www.cahiim.org

Associate and baccalaureate degree programs in health information management and master's degree programs in health informatics and health information management **CAHIIM**

Healthcare Management

Commission on Accreditation of Healthcare Management Education (CAHME)
CHEA: 2003
PO Box 911
Spring House, PA 19477
(301) 298-1820
Anthony Stanowski, President and CEO
E-mail: info@cahme.org
URL: www.cahme.org

Graduate programs in healthcare management **HSA**

Human Services

Council for Standards in Human Services Education (CSHSE)
CHEA: 2014
3337 Duke Street
Alexandria, VA 22314
(571) 257-3959
Yvonne Chase, President
E-mail: info@cshse.org
URL: www.cshse.org

Human services educational programs **CSHSE**

Industrial Technology

The Association of Technology, Management, and Applied Engineering
CHEA: 2002
14141 46th Street North Unit #1203
Clearwater, FL 33762
(919) 635-8335 Fax (919) 779-5642
Dean Bartles, Executive Director
E-mail: admin@atmae.org
URL: www.atmae.org

Technology, applied technology, engineering technology and technology-related programs at the associate, baccalaureate and master's degree level **NAIT**

Interior Design

Council for Interior Design Accreditation (CIDA)
CHEA: 2013
206 Grandville Avenue, Suite 350
Grand Rapids, MI 49503
(616) 458-0400 Fax (616) 458-0460
Holly Mattson, Executive Director
E-mail: info@accredit-id.org
URL: www.accredit-id.org

Professional degree level programs (master's and baccalaureate degrees) **CIDA**

Jewish Studies

Association of Institutions of Jewish Studies (AIJS)
USDE: 2015/2021/2026
500 West Kennedy Boulevard
Lakewood, NJ 08701
(732) 363-7330 Fax (732) 415-8198
Doniel Ginsberg, President
E-mail: info@theaijs.com
URL: theaijs.com

Postsecondary institutions of Jewish studies **AIJS**

Journalism and Mass Communications

Accrediting Committee
Accrediting Council on Education in Journalism and Mass Communications (ACEJMC)
CHEA: 2002
University of Mississippi
201 Bishop Hall, PO Box 1848
University, MS 38677
(662) 915-5504
Patricia Thompson, Executive Director
E-mail: pthomps1@olemiss.edu
URL: www.acejmc.org

Units within institutions offering professional baccalaureate and master's degree programs in journalism and mass communications **JOUR**

Kinesiotherapy

Commission on Accreditation of Allied Health Education Programs (see listing under Allied Health)
Committee on Accreditation of Education Programs for Kinesiotherapy
118 College Drive #5142
Hattiesburg, MS 39406-0002
(601) 266-5371
Jerry W. Purvis, Coord COPSKT
E-mail: kinesiotherapy.ao@gmail.com

Kinesiotherapy programs **KIN**

Lactation Education

Commission on Accreditation of Allied Health Education Programs (see listing under Allied Health)
Lactation Education Accreditation and Approval Review Committee (LEAARC)
110 Horizon Drive, Suite 210
Raleigh, NC 27615
(984) 500-5902
Jackie Long-Goding, Executive Director
E-mail: office@LEAARC.org
URL: www.leaarc.org

Landscape Architecture

Landscape Architectural Accreditation Board
American Society of Landscape Architects (ASLA)
CHEA: 2003
636 Eye Street, NW
Washington, DC 20001-3736
(202) 898-2444 Fax (202) 898-1185
Kristopher Pritchard, Director Accreditation and Education
E-mail: info@asla.org
URL: www.asla.org

Baccalaureate and master's programs leading to the first professional degree **LSAR**

Law

Council of the Section of Legal Education and Admissions to the Bar
American Bar Association (ABA)
USDE: 1952/2018/2021
321 North Clark Street, 19th Floor
Chicago, IL 60654-7598
(312) 988-6738 Fax (312) 988-5681
William E. Adams, Managing Director of Accreditation and Legal Education
E-mail: legaled@americanbar.org
URL: www.americanbar.org/groups/legal_education

Programs in legal education; professional schools of law **LAW**

Library and Information Studies

Committee on Accreditation
American Library Association (ALA)
CHEA: 2013
225 North Michigan Avenue, Suite 1300
Chicago, IL 60611-2795
(312) 280-2432 Fax (312) 280-2433
Karen O'Brien, Director of Accreditation
E-mail: accred@ala.org
URL: www.ala.org/accreditation

Master's programs in library and information studies **LIB**

Marriage and Family Therapy

Commission on Accreditation for Marriage and Family Therapy Education
American Association for Marriage and Family Therapy (AAMFT)
CHEA: 2003
112 South Alfred Street
Alexandria, VA 22314-3061
(703) 253-0448 Fax (703) 253-0508
Jill Fogolin, Director of Accreditation
E-mail: coa@aamft.org
URL: www.coamfte.org

Clinical training programs at the master's, doctorate and post-graduate levels **MFCD**

Massage Therapy

Commission on Massage Therapy Accreditation
USDE: 2002/2021/2022
900 Commonwealth Place, Suite 200-331
Virginia Beach, VA 23464
(202) 888-6790 Fax (202) 888-6787
Dawn Hogue, Executive Director
E-mail: info@comta.org
URL: www.comta.org

Institutions that award postsecondary certificates, diplomas, and associate degrees in the practice of massage therapy, bodywork, aesthetics/esthetics and skin care **COMTA**

Medical Assistant Education

(see listing under Allied Health)
Accrediting Bureau of Health Education Schools (ABHES)

Medical assistant programs **MAAB**

Commission on Accreditation of Allied Health Education Programs (see listing under Allied Health)
Medical Assisting Education Review Board
20 North Wacker Drive, Suite 1575
Chicago, IL 60606-2963
(312) 392-0155
Sarah R. Marino, Executive Director
E-mail: maerb@maerb.org
URL: www.maerb.org

One and two year medical assistant programs **MAC**

Medical Illustrator Education

Commission on Accreditation of Allied Health Education Programs (see listing under Allied Health)
Accreditation Review Committee for the Medical Illustrator
Shelley Wall, Chair, ARC-MI
E-mail: swall@utoronto.ca
URL: www.ami.org

Programs for medical illustrator **MIL**

Medical Laboratory Technician Education

(see listing under Allied Health)
Accrediting Bureau of Health Education Schools (ABHES)

Schools and programs for the medical laboratory technician **MLTAB**

(see listing under Clinical Laboratory Sciences)
National Accrediting Agency for Clinical Laboratory Sciences (NAACLS)

Programs for medical laboratory technician **MLTAD**

Medical Physics

Commission on Accreditation of Medical Physics Education Programs, Inc.
CHEA: 2017
1631 Prince Street
Alexandria, VA 22314
(571) 298-1239 Fax (571) 298-1301
Michael McNitt-Gray, President
E-mail: campep_admin@campep.org
URL: www.campep.org

Medical physics programs **CAMPEP**

Medical Technology

(see listing under Clinical Laboratory Sciences)
National Accrediting Agency for Clinical Laboratory Sciences (NAACLS)

Programs for medical technologist/laboratory scientist **MT**

Medicine

Liaison Committee on Medical Education (LCME)
USDE: 1952/2018/2023
The LCME is administered in odd-numbered years, beginning each July 1, by:
American Medical Association (AMA)
330 North Wabash Avenue, Suite 39300
Chicago, IL 60611
(312) 464-4933
Barbara Barzansky, LCME Co-Secretary
E-mail: barbara.barzansky@ama-assn.org
URL: www.lcme.org

The LCME is administered in even-numbered years, beginning each July 1, by:
Association of American Medical Colleges (AAMC)
655 K Street NW, Suite 100
Washington, DC 20001-2399
(202) 826-0596
Veronica Catanese, LCME Co-Secretary
E-mail: vcatanese@aamc.org
URL: www.aamc.org

Programs leading to the M.D. degree **MED**

Midwifery Education

Midwifery Education Accreditation Council (MEAC)
USDE: 2001/2021/2026
850 Mt. Pleasant Avenue
Ann Arbor, MI 48103
(360) 466-2080 Fax (480) 907-2936
Trixi Packmohr, Executive Director
E-mail: info@meacschools.org
URL: www.meacschools.org

Accreditation of direct-entry midwifery educational institutions and programs conferring degrees and certificates **MEAC**

Montessori Teacher Education

Montessori Accreditation Council for Teacher Education (MACTE)
USDE: 1995/2021/2026
420 Park Street
Charlottesville, VA 22902
(434) 202-7793
Rebecca Pelton, President
E-mail: info@macte.org
URL: www.macte.org

Montessori teacher-education programs and institutions **MACTE**

Music

Commission on Accreditation
National Association of Schools of Music (NASM)
USDE: 1952/2019/2024
11250 Roger Bacon Drive, Suite 21
Reston, VA 20190
(703) 437-0700 Fax (703) 437-6312
Karen P. Moynahan, Executive Director
E-mail: info@arts-accredit.org
URL: nasm.arts-accredit.org

Institutions and departments within institutions offering degree and non-degree-granting programs in music and music-related disciplines **MUS**

Naturopathic Medical Education

Council on Naturopathic Medical Education (CNME)
USDE: 2003/2021/2026
PO Box 178
Great Barrington, MA 01230
(413) 528-8877
Daniel Seitz, Executive Director
E-mail: council@cnme.org
URL: www.cnme.org

Naturopathic doctoral education programs **NATUR**

Neurodiagnostic Technology

Commission on Accreditation of Allied Health Education Programs (see listing under Allied Health)
Committee on Accreditation for Education in Neurodiagnostic Technology
1449 Hill Street
Whitinsville, MA 01588
(978) 338-6300 Fax (978) 832-2638
Jackie Long-Goding, Executive Director
E-mail: office@coa-ndt.org
URL: www.coa-ndt.org

Programs for the electroneurodiagnostic technologist **NDT**

Nuclear Medicine Technology

Joint Review Committee on Educational Programs in Nuclear Medicine Technology
CHEA: 2013
820 West Danforth Road, #B1
Edmund, OK 73003
(405) 285-0546 Fax (405) 285-0579
Jan Winn, Executive Director
E-mail: mail@jrcnmt.org
URL: www.jrcnmt.org

Programs for the nuclear medicine technologist **NMT**

Nurse Anesthetists

Council on Accreditation of Nurse Anesthesia Educational Programs
USDE: 1955/2018/2023 CHEA: 2011
222 South Prospect Avenue
Park Ridge, IL 60068-4001
(847) 655-1160 Fax (847) 692-7137
Francis Gerbasi, Chief Executive Officer
E-mail: accreditation@coacrna.org
URL: www.coacrna.org

Nurse anesthesia educational institutions and programs at the post-master's certificate, master's and doctoral degree levels **ANEST**

Nurse-Midwifery

Accreditation Commission for Midwifery Education
USDE: 1982/2017/2023
8403 Colesville Road, Suite 1230
Silver Spring, MD 20910
(240) 485-1803 Fax (240) 485-1818
Angela Smith, Executive Director
E-mail: acme@acnm.org
URL: www.midwife.org/accreditation

Pre-certification, basic certificate and master's degree nurse-midwifery educational programs **MIDWF**

Nursing

Commission on Collegiate Nursing Education (CCNE)
USDE: 2000/2018/2023
655 K Street NW, Suite 750
Washington, DC 20001
(202) 887-6791 Fax (202) 887-8476
Jennifer Butlin, Executive Director
E-mail: jbutlin@ccneaccreditation.org
URL: www.aacnnursing.org/ccne

Baccalaureate and higher degree nursing education **NURSE**

Accreditation Commission for Education in Nursing
USDE: 1952/2017/2023 CHEA: 2011
3390 Peachtree Road NE, Suite 1400
Atlanta, GA 30326
(404) 975-5000 Fax (404) 975-5020
Marsal P. Stoll, CEO
E-mail: info@acenursing.org
URL: www.acenursing.org

Programs in:
- Practical nursing (certificate) **PNUR**
- Diploma nurse education **DNUR**
- Associate degree **ADNUR**
- Baccalaureate and higher degree nurse education **NUR**

Occupational Education

Council on Occupational Education (COE)
USDE: 1969/2016/2021
7840 Roswell Road, Bldg 300, Suite 325
Atlanta, GA 30350
(770) 396-3898 Fax (770) 396-3790
Gary Puckett, President/Executive Director
E-mail: info@council.org
URL: www.council.org

Occupational/vocational institutions that grant certificates or diplomas and the applied associate degree in specific career and technical education **COE**

Occupational Therapy

Accreditation Council for Occupational Therapy Education
American Occupational Therapy Association
USDE: 1952/2017/2022 CHEA: 2013
6116 Executive Boulevard, Suite 200
North Bethesda, MD 20852-4929
(301) 652-6611
Teresa Brininger, Director of Accreditation
E-mail: accred@aota.org
URL: www.acoteonline.org

Occupational therapy programs **OT**
Occupational therapy assistant programs **OTA**

Opticianry

Commission on Opticianry Accreditation
CHEA: 2010
PO Box 592
Canton, NY 13617
(703) 468-0566
Debra White, Director of Accreditation
E-mail: director@COAccreditation.com
URL: www.coaccreditation.com

Two-year opticianry degree programs **OPD**

Optometry

Accreditation Council on Optometric Education
American Optometric Association (AOA)
USDE: 1952/2017/2023 CHEA: 2012
243 North Lindbergh Boulevard
St. Louis, MO 63141
(314) 991-4100 Fax (314) 991-4101
Stephanie Puljak, ACOE Director
E-mail: accredit@aoa.org
URL: www.theacoe.org

Programs in:
- First professional **OPT**
- Optometric residency **OPTR**
- Optometric technology **OPTT**

Orthotic and Prosthetic Education

Commission on Accreditation of Allied Health Education Programs (see listing under Allied Health)
National Commission on Orthotic and Prosthetic Education (NCOPE)

330 John Carlyle Street, Suite 200
Alexandria, VA 22314
(703) 836-7114 Fax (703) 890-2425
Robin C. Seabrook, Executive Director
E-mail: info@ncope.org
URL: www.ncope.org

Programs for orthotic and prosthetic education **OPE**

Osteopathic Medicine

Commission on Osteopathic College Accreditation
American Osteopathic Association
USDE: 1952/2018/2021
Department of Education
142 East Ontario Street
Chicago, IL 60611-2864
(312) 202-8124 Fax (312) 202-8200
Jed Brinton, Secretary, COCA
E-mail: predoc@osteopathic.org
URL: www.osteopathic.org/accreditation

Programs leading to and institutions offering the D.O. (Doctor of Osteopathy/Osteopathic Medicine) degree **OSTEO**

Perfusion

Commission on Accreditation of Allied Health Education Programs (see listing under Allied Health)
Accreditation Committee - Perfusion Education (AC-PE)
519 West Ridge Road
Littleton, CO 80120
(303) 794-6283
Linda Cantu, Executive Director
E-mail: office@ac-pe.org
URL: www.ac-pe.org

Programs for the perfusionist **PERF**

Pharmacy

Accreditation Council for Pharmacy Education (ACPE)
USDE: 1952/2017/2022 CHEA: 2004
190 South LaSalle Street, Suite 2850
Chicago, IL 60603
(312) 664-3575 Fax (866) 228-2631
Janet P. Engle, Executive Director
E-mail: info@acpe-accredit.org
URL: www.acpe-accredit.org

Professional degree programs in pharmacy **PHAR**

Physical Therapy

Commission on Accreditation in Physical Therapy Education
American Physical Therapy Association (APTA)
USDE: 1977/2017/2023 CHEA: 2012
3030 Potomac Avenue, Suite 100
Alexandria, VA 22305
(703) 706-3245 Fax (703) 684-7343
Mary Romanello, Director of Accreditation
E-mail: accreditation@apta.org
URL: www.capteonline.org

Professional programs for the physical therapist **PTA**
Programs for the physical therapist assistant **PTAA**

Physician Assistant

Accreditation Review Commission on Education for the Physician Assistant (ARC-PA)
CHEA: 2004
3325 Paddocks Pkwy, Suite 345
Suwanee, GA 30024
(770) 476-1224 Fax (770) 476-1738
Sharon Luke, Executive Director
E-mail: AccreditationServices@arc-pa.org
URL: www.arc-pa.org

Programs for the physician assistant **ARCPA**

Planning (City and Regional)

Planning Accreditation Board
CHEA: 2013
2334 West Lawrence Avenue, Suite 209
Chicago, IL 60625
(773) 334-7200
Jesmarie Johnson, Executive Director
E-mail: jjohnson@planningaccreditationboard.org
URL: www.planningaccreditationboard.org

Bachelor and master's level programs in planning **PLNG**

Podiatry

Council on Podiatric Medical Education
American Podiatric Medical Association (APMA)
USDE: 1952/2016/2022 CHEA: 2004
9312 Old Georgetown Road
Bethesda, MD 20814-1621
(301) 581-9200 Fax (301) 571-4903
Heather Stagliano, Director
E-mail: cpmestaff@cpme.org
URL: www.cpme.org

Colleges and programs of podiatric medicine, including first professional and doctorate degree programs **POD**

Polysomnographic Technology

Commission on Accreditation of Allied Health Education Programs (see listing under Allied Health)
Committee on Accreditation for Polysomnographic Technologist Education
1711 Frank Avenue
New Bern, NC 28560
(252) 626-3238
Karen Monarchy Rowe, Executive Director
E-mail: karenmonarchy@suddenlink.net
URL: coapsg.org

Programs for polysomnographic technology **POLYT**

Psychology

Psychological Clinical Science Accreditation System (PCSAS)
CHEA: 2012
1800 Massachusetts Avenue NW, Suite 402
Washington, DC 20036-1218
(301) 455-8046
Alan G. Kraut, Executive Director
E-mail: akraut@pcsas.org
URL: www.pcsas.org

Psychological clinical science doctoral training programs **PCSAS**

Commission on Accreditation
American Psychological Association (APA)
USDE: 1970/2018/2021 CHEA: 2013
750 First Street NE
Washington, DC 20002-4242
(202) 336-5979 Fax (202) 336-5978
Jacqueline Remondet Wall, Director, Office of Program Consultation and Accreditation
E-mail: apaaccred@apa.org
URL: www.apa.org/ed/accreditation

Doctoral programs in:
- Clinical psychology **CLPSY**
- Counseling psychology **COPSY**
- Combined professional-scientific psychology **PSPSY**
- School psychology **SCPSY**
- Doctoral internship program in health service psychology **IPSY**
- Post-doctoral residency in health service psychology **PDPSY**

Public Affairs and Administration

Commission on Peer Review and Accreditation
Network of Schools of Public Policy, Affairs and Administration (NASPAA)
CHEA: 2004
1029 Vermont Avenue, NW, Suite 1100
Washington, DC 20005
(202) 628-8965 Fax (202) 626-4978
Martha Bohrt, Chief Accreditation Officer
E-mail: copra@naspaa.org
URL: www.naspaa.org

Master's degree programs in public affairs, public policy and administration **SPAA**

Public Health

Council on Education for Public Health (CEPH)
USDE: 1974/2019/2024
1010 Wayne Avenue, Suite 220
Silver Spring, MD 20910-5600
(202) 789-1050
Laura Rasar King, Executive Director
E-mail: lking@ceph.org
URL: www.ceph.org

Baccalaureate and graduate level programs in schools of public health and public health programs outside of schools of public health **PH**

Rabbinical and Talmudic Education

Accreditation Commission
Association of Advanced Rabbinical and Talmudic Schools (AARTS)
USDE: 1974/2018/2023 CHEA: 2011
11 Broadway, Suite 405
New York, NY 10004
(212) 363-1991 Fax (212) 533-5335
Bernard Fryshman, Interim Executive Director
E-mail: office@aarts-schools.org

Advanced rabbinical and Talmudic schools **RABN**

Radiologic Technology

Joint Review Committee on Education in Radiologic Technology
USDE: 1957/2016/2022 CHEA: 2004
20 North Wacker Drive, Suite 2850
Chicago, IL 60606-3182
(312) 704-5300 Fax (312) 704-5304
Leslie F. Winter, Chief Executive Officer
E-mail: mail@jrcert.org
URL: www.jrcert.org

Programs for:
- Magnetic resonance **RADMAG**
- Medical dosimetry **RADDOS**
- Radiographer **RAD**
- Radiation therapist technologist **RTT**

Recreation, Park and Leisure Studies

Council on Accreditation of Parks, Recreation, Tourism and Related Professions
CHEA: 2003
1401 Marvin Road NE, Suite 307 #172
Lacey, WA 98516
(360) 205-2096 Fax (360) 453-7893
Shelley Dahle, COAPRT Programs Manager
E-mail: coaprt@accreditationcouncil.org
URL: www.accreditationcouncil.org

Baccalaureate degree programs in recreation, park resources and leisure studies **CAPRT**

Recreation Therapy

Commission on Accreditation of Allied Health Education Programs (see listing under Allied Health)
Committee on Accreditation of Recreational Therapy Education (CARTE)

520 Wakara Way
Salt Lake City, UT 84108
(801) 213-6993
Rhonda Nelson, Chair
E-mail: rhonda.nelson@hsc.utah.edu

Recreational therapy education programs **CARTE**

Respiratory Care

Commission on Accreditation for Respiratory Care (CoARC)
CHEA: 2012
264 Precision Boulevard
Telford, TN 37690
(817) 283-2835 Fax (817) 354-8519
Thomas Smalling, CEO
E-mail: tom@coarc.com
URL: www.coarc.com

Degree programs in respiratory care **COARC**
Certificate programs in polysomnography **COARCP**

Social Work

Commission on Accreditation
Council on Social Work Education (CSWE)
CHEA: 2003
333 John Carlyle Street, Suite 400
Alexandria, VA 22314
(703) 683-8080 Fax (703) 683-8099
Darla Spence Coffey, President/CEO
E-mail: info@cswe.org
URL: www.cswe.org

Baccalaureate and master's degree programs **SW**

Speech-Language Pathology

Council on Academic Accreditation in Audiology and Speech Language Pathology
American Speech-Language-Hearing Association (ASHA)
USDE: 1967/2021/2026 CHEA: 2003
2200 Research Boulevard
Rockville, MD 20850-3289
(301) 296-5700 Fax (301) 296-8570
Kimberlee Moore, Director of Accreditation
E-mail: accreditation@asha.org
URL: caa.asha.org

Master's in speech-language pathology **SP**

Sports Management

Commission on Sports Management Accreditation
CHEA: 2018
2236 Water Blossom Lane
Fort Collins, CO 80526
(202) 329-1189
Heather Alderman, Executive Director
E-mail: cosma@cosmaweb.org
URL: www.cosmaweb.org

Sports management degree programs **COSMA**

Surgical Assisting and Technology

(see listing under Allied Health)
Accrediting Bureau of Health Education Schools (ABHES)

Surgical technologist programs **SURTEC**

Commission on Accreditation of Allied Health Education Programs (see listing under Allied Health)
Accreditation Review Council on Education in Surgical Technology and Surgical Assisting
19751 East Mainstreet, Suite 339
Parker, CO 80138
(303) 694-9262 Fax (303) 741-3655
Ron Kruzel, Executive Director
E-mail: info@arcstsa.org
URL: www.arcstsa.org

Programs for the surgical technologist **SURGT**
Programs for the surgical assistant **SURGA**

Teacher Education

Association for Advancing Quality in Educator Preparation
CHEA: 2021
P.O. Box 7511
Fairfax Station, VA 22039
(301) 276-5106
Mark LaCelle-Peterson, President & CEO
E-mail: aaqep@aaqep.org
URL: aaqep.org

Programs that prepare professional educators **AAQEP**

Council for the Accreditation of Educator Preparation
CHEA: 2014
1140 19th Street NW, Suite 400
Washington, DC 20036
(202) 223-0077 Fax (202) 296-6620
Christopher Koch, President
E-mail: caep@caepnet.org
URL: caepnet.org

Educator preparation programs **CAEP**
NCATE Educator preparation program **CAEPN**
TEAC Education preparation program **CAEPT**

National Association for the Education of Young Children
CHEA: 2021
1401 H Street NW, Suite 600
Washington, DC 20005
(202) 232-8777 Fax (202) 328-1846
Rhian Evans Allvin, Chief Executive Officer
E-mail: info@naeyc.org
URL: https://www.naeyc.org/accreditation

Degree programs in early childhood education **NAEYC**

Theatre

Commission on Accreditation
National Association of Schools of Theatre (NAST)
USDE: 1982/2019/2024
11250 Roger Bacon Drive, Suite 21
Reston, VA 20190
(703) 437-0700 Fax (703) 437-6312
Karen P. Moynahan, Executive Director
E-mail: info@arts-accredit.org
URL: nast.arts-accredit.org

Institutions and departments within institutions offering degree granting and non-degree-granting programs in theatre and theatre-related disciplines **THEA**

Theology

The Commission on Accrediting
The Association of Theological Schools (ATS)
USDE: 1952/2016/2021 CHEA: 2012
10 Summit Park Drive
Pittsburgh, PA 15275-1110
(412) 788-6505 Fax (412) 788-6510
Frank Yamada, Executive Director
E-mail: yamada@ats.edu
URL: www.ats.edu

Freestanding schools, as well as schools or programs affiliated with larger institutions, offering graduate professional education for ministry and graduate study of theology **THEOL**

Trade and Technical Education

Accrediting Commission of Career Schools and Colleges (ACCSC)
USDE: 1967/2016/2021
2101 Wilson Boulevard, Suite 302
Arlington, VA 22201
(703) 247-4212 Fax (703) 247-4533
Michale McComis, Executive Director
E-mail: info@accsc.org
URL: www.accsc.org

Private, postsecondary degree-granting and non-degree-granting institutions that are predominantly organized to educate students for trade, occupational or technical careers **ACCSC**

Veterinary Medicine

Council on Education
American Veterinary Medical Association (AVMA)
USDE: 1952/2018/2024 CHEA: 2012
1931 North Meacham Road, Suite 100
Schaumburg, IL 60173
(800) 248-2862 Fax (847) 925-1329
Karen Martens Brandt, Director Education and Research
E-mail: kbrandt@avma.org
URL: www.avma.org

Colleges of veterinary medicine offering programs leading to a D.V.M./D.M.V. professional degree **VET**

Other

New York State Board of Regents Commission of Education
USDE: 1952/2017/2023
State Education Department
The University of the State of New York
89 Washington Avenue, Room 110 EB
Albany, NY 12234
(518) 474-5844 Fax (518) 473-4909
Betty A. Rosa, Interim Commissioner of Education
E-mail: commissioner@nysed.edu
URL: www.nysed.gov

Degree-granting institutions of higher education in New York that designate the agency as their sole or primary nationally recognized accrediting agency for purposes of establishing eligibility to participate in Higher Education Act programs **NY**

Accrediting Agencies Recognized for their Pre-accreditation Categories[1]

Under the terms of the Higher Education Act and other Federal legislation providing funding assistance to postsecondary education, an institution or program is eligible to apply for participation in certain Federal programs if, in addition to meeting other statutory requirements, it is accredited by a nationally recognized accrediting agency—or if it is an institution with respect to which the U.S. Secretary of Education has determined that there is satisfactory assurance the institution or program will meet the accreditation standards of such agency or association within a reasonable time. An institution or program may establish satisfactory assurance of accreditation by acquiring pre-accreditation status with a nationally recognized accrediting agency which has been recognized by the U.S. Secretary of Education for the award of such status. According to the Criteria for Nationally Recognized Accrediting Agencies, if an accrediting agency has developed a pre-accreditation status, it must demonstrate that it applies criteria and follows procedures that are appropriately related to those used to award accreditation status. The criteria for recognition also requires an agency's standards for pre-accreditation to permit an institution or program to hold pre-accreditation no more than five years.

The following is a list of accrediting agencies recognized by the U.S. Secretary of Education for their pre-accreditation categories and the categories which are recognized.

Regional Institution Accrediting Bodies

Middle States Commission on Higher Education:
Candidate for Accreditation

New England Commission of Higher Education:
Candidate for Accreditation

Higher Learning Commission: *Candidate for Accreditation*

Northwest Commission on Colleges and Universities:
Candidate for Accreditation

Southern Association of Colleges and Schools
Commission on Colleges: *Candidate for Accreditation*

Western Association of Schools and Colleges
Accrediting Commission for Community and Junior Colleges: *Candidate for Accreditation*

Western Association of Schools and Colleges
Senior College and University Commission: *Candidate for Accreditation*

National, Institutional and Specialized Accrediting Bodies

Academy of Nutrition and Dietetics
Accreditation Council for Education in Nutrition and Dietetics: *Pre-accreditation*

Accreditation Commission for Acupuncture and Oriental Medicine: *Pre-accreditation, Candidate for Accreditation*

Accreditation Commission for Midwifery Education: *Pre-accreditation*

Accreditation Council for Pharmacy Education: *Candidate, Pre-candidate*

American Optometric Association
Accreditation Council on Optometric Education: *Preliminary Approval* (for professional degree programs); *Candidacy Pending* (for optometric residency programs in Veterans Administration facilities)

American Osteopathic Association
Commission on Osteopathic College Accreditation: *Provisional Accreditation*

American Physical Therapy Association
Commission on Accreditation in Physical Therapy Education: *Candidate for Accreditation*

American Podiatric Medical Association
Council on Podiatric Medical Education: *Candidate for Accreditation*

American Psychological Association
Commission on Accreditation: *Preaccreditation (doctoral internship and postdoctoral residency programs only)*

American Speech-Language-Hearing Association
Council on Academic Accreditation in Audiology and Speech Language Pathology: *Candidate for Accreditation*

American Veterinary Medical Association
Council on Education: *Reasonable Assurance of Accreditation*

Association for Biblical Higher Education
Commission on Accreditation: *Candidate for Accreditation*

Association of Advanced Rabbinical and Talmudic Schools
Accreditation Commission: *Correspondent, Candidate for Accreditation*

The Association of Theological Schools
The Commission on Accrediting: *Candidate for Accredited Membership*

Council on Education for Public Health: *Pre-accreditation*

Council on Naturopathic Medical Education: *Pre-accreditation*

Council on Occupational Education: *Candidate for Accreditation*

Midwifery Education Accreditation Council: *Pre-accreditation*

Transnational Association of Christian Colleges and Schools
Accreditation Commission: *Candidate for Accreditation*

[1]U.S. Department of Education, Nationally Recognized Accrediting Agencies and Associations, www2.ed.gov/admins/finaid/accred/accreditation_pg8.html.

Abbreviations, Explanatory Notes and Symbols

Abbreviations

Listed below are the abbreviations used in this Directory for the recognized regional accrediting commissions and the recognized national, professional and specialized accrediting bodies. Addresses for these associations can be found under our listing of Accrediting Agencies beginning on page viii.

The recognized regional accrediting commissions are indicated throughout this Directory by the following abbreviations:

EH New England Commission of Higher Education

HLC Higher Learning Commission, North Central Association

M Middle States Commission on Higher Education

NW Northwest Commission on Colleges and Universities

SC Southern Association of Colleges and Schools, Commission on Colleges

WC Western Association of Schools and Colleges, Senior College and University Commission

WJ Western Association of Schools and Colleges, The Accrediting Commission for Community and Junior Colleges

National, professional and specialized accrediting agencies and associations are listed below. Wherever possible, degree levels are shown by the following symbols: (C) diploma/certificate; (A) associate; (B) baccalaureate; (M) master's; (S) beyond master's but less than doctorate; (FP) first professional; (D) doctorate.

AA Commission on Accreditation of Allied Health Education Programs: anesthesiologist assistant (M)

AAB Aviation Accreditation Board International: aviation (A,B,M,D)

AAFCS American Association of Family and Consumer Sciences: family and consumer sciences (B)

AAQEP Association for Advancing Quality in Educator Preparation: professional educators (C,B,M)

ABAI Association for Behavior Analysis International Accreditation Board: behavior analysis (M,D)

ABHES Accrediting Bureau of Health Education Schools: allied health (C,A,B,M)

ACAE Accreditation Commission for Audiology Education: audiology (D)

ACATE Commission on Accreditation of Allied Health Education Programs: art therapy (M)

ACBSP Accreditation Council for Business Schools and Programs: business administration, management, accounting and related business fields (A,B,M,D)

ACCSC Accrediting Commission of Career Schools and Colleges: occupational, trade and technical education (C,A,B,M)

ACFEI American Culinary Federation, Inc.: culinary arts and culinary management (C,A,B)

ACICS Accrediting Council for Independent Colleges and Schools: business and business-related programs (C,A,B,M)

ACS Commission on Accreditation of Allied Health Education Programs: advanced cardiovascular sonography (C)

ACUP Accreditation Commission for Acupuncture and Oriental Medicine: acupuncture (C,M,D)

ADNUR Accreditation Commission for Education in Nursing: nursing (A)

AIJS Association of Institutions of Jewish Studies: Jewish studies (C,A,B)

ANEST Council on Accreditation of Nurse Anesthesia Educational Programs: nurse anesthesia (C,M,D)

ARCPA Accreditation Review Commission on Education for the Physician Assistant: physician assisting programs (A,B,M)

ART National Association of Schools of Art and Design: art and design (C,A,B,M,D)

AT Commission on Accreditation of Allied Health Education Programs: anesthesia technology (A)

ATECH Commission on Accreditation of Allied Health Education Programs: assistive technology (C,M)

AUD American Speech-Language-Hearing Association: audiology (D)

BBT Commission on Accreditation of Allied Health Education Programs: blood bank technology (C,M)

BI Association for Biblical Higher Education: bible college education (C,A,B,M,FP,D)

CAATE Commission on Accreditation of Athletic Training Education: athletic training (B,M,D)

CACREP Council for Accreditation of Counseling & Related Education programs: counseling and its specialties (M,D)

CAEP Council for the Accreditation of Educator Preparation: teacher education (B,M,D)

CAEPN Council for the Accreditation of Educator Preparation: teacher education (B,M,D)

CAEPT Council for the Accreditation of Educator Preparation: teacher education (B,M,D)

CAHIIM Commission on Accreditation for Health Informatics and Information Management Education: health information management and health informatics (A,B,M)

CAMPEP Commission on Accreditation of Medical Physics Education Programs, Inc.: medical physics (C,M,D)

CAPRT Council on Accreditation of Parks, Recreation, Tourism and Related Professions: recreation, park resources, and leisure studies (B)

CARTE Commission on Accreditation of Recreational Therapy Education: recreational therapy (B,M)

CEA Commission on English Language Program Accreditation: english language (C)

CGTECH National Accrediting Agency for Clinical Laboratory Sciences: cytogenetic technologist (B)

CHIRO Council on Chiropractic Education: chiropractic education (FP,D)

CIDA Council for Interior Design Accreditation: interior design (B,M)

CLPSY American Psychological Association: clinical psychology (D)

CNCE Accrediting Council for Continuing Education and Training: continuing education (C,A)

COARC Commission on Accreditation for Respiratory Care: respiratory care (A,B,M)

COARCP Commission on Accreditation for Respiratory Care: polysomnography (C)

COE Council on Occupational Education: occupational, trade, and technical education (C,A)

COMTA Commission on Massage Therapy Accreditation: massage therapy, bodywork, aesthetics/esthetics and skin care (C,A)

CONST American Council for Construction Education: construction education (A,B,M)

COPSY American Psychological Association: counseling psychology (D)

COSMA Commission on Sports Management: sports management (B,M,D)

COSME National Accrediting Commission of Career Arts and Sciences: cosmetology and massage therapy (C)

CR Commission on Accreditation of Allied Health Education Programs: clinical researcher (C,A,M)

CSHSE Council for Standards in Human Services Education: human services (A,B,M)

CVT Commission on Accreditation of Allied Health Education Programs: cardiovascular technology (C,A,B)

CYTO Commission on Accreditation of Allied Health Education Programs: cytotechnology (C,B,M)

DA American Dental Association: dental assisting (C,A)

DANCE National Association of Schools of Dance: dance (C,A,B,M,D)

DEAC Distance Education and Accrediting Commission: home study schools (A,B,M,D)

DENT American Dental Association: dentistry (FP,D)

DH American Dental Association: dental hygiene (C,A,B,M)

DIETC Academy of Nutrition and Dietetics: coordinated dietetics programs (B,M,D)

DIETD Academy of Nutrition and Dietetics: didactic dietetics programs (B,M)

DIETI Academy of Nutrition and Dietetics: dietetic post-baccalaureate internships

DIETT Academy of Nutrition and Dietetics: dietetic technician (A)

DMOLS National Accrediting Agency for Clinical Laboratory Sciences: diagnostic molecular scientist (C,B,M)

DMS Commission on Accreditation of Allied Health Education Programs: diagnostic medical sonography (C,A,B,M)

DNUR Accreditation Commission for Education in Nursing: nursing (C)

DT American Dental Association: dental laboratory technology (C,A)

DTH American Dental Association: dental therapy (A)

EMT Commission on Accreditation of Allied Health Education Programs: emergency medical technician-paramedic (C,A,B)

EXSC Commission on Accreditation of Allied Health Education Programs: exercise science (C,A,B,M)

FEPAC American Academy of Forensic Sciences: forensic science (B,M)

FUSER American Board of Funeral Service Education: funeral service education (C,A,B)

HSA Commission on Accreditation of Healthcare Management Education: healthcare management (M)

HT National Accrediting Agency for Clinical Laboratory Sciences: histologic technology (C,A,B)

IACBE International Accreditation Council for Business Education: business programs, accounting and business related (A,B,M,D)

IFSAC International Fire Service Accreditation Congress Degree Assembly: fire and emergency related programs (A,B,M)

IPSY American Psychological Association: doctoral internships in health service psychology

JOUR Accrediting Council on Education for Journalism and Mass Communications: journalism and mass communications (B,M)

KIN Commission on Accreditation of Allied Health Education Programs: kinesiotherapy (B)

LAW American Bar Association: law (FP,D)

LC Commission on Accreditation of Allied Health Programs: lactation consultant (C,A,B,M)

LIB American Library Association: library and information studies (M)

LSAR American Society for Landscape Architects: landscape architecture (B,M)

MAAB Accrediting Bureau of Health Education Schools: medical assisting (C,A)

MAC Commission on Accreditation of Allied Health Education Programs: medical assisting (C,A)

MACTE Montessori Accreditation Council for Teacher Education: Montessori teacher education (C)

MEAC Midwifery Education Accreditation Council: midwifery education (C, A,B,M,D)

MED Liaison Committee on Medical Education: medicine (FP,D)

MFCD American Association for Marriage and Family Therapy: marriage and family therapy (M,D)

MIDWF Accreditation Commission for Midwifery Education: nurse midwifery (C,M,D)

MIL Commission on Accreditation of Allied Health Education Programs: medical illustrator (M)

MLTAB Accrediting Bureau of Health Education Schools: medical laboratory technician (C,A)

MLTAD National Accrediting Agency for Clinical Laboratory Sciences: medical laboratory technician (C,A)

MPCAC Masters in Psychology and Counseling Accreditation Council: counseling and psychology (M)

MT National Accrediting Agency for Clinical Laboratory Sciences: medical technology/laboratory scientist (C,B)

MUS National Association of Schools of Music: music (C,A,B,M,D)

NAEYC National Association for the Education of Young Children: early childhood education (A,B,M)

NAIT The Association of Technology, Management, and Applied Engineering: technology, applied technology, engineering technology and technology-related programs (A,B,M)

NATUR Council on Naturopathic Medical Education: naturopathic medical education (FP,D)

NDT Commission on Accreditation of Allied Health Education Programs: neurodiagnostic technology (C,A)

NMT Joint Review Committee on Educational Programs in Nuclear Medicine Technology: nuclear medicine technology (C,A,B,M)

NUR Accreditation Commission for Education in Nursing: nursing (B,M,D)

NURSE Commission on Collegiate Nursing Education: nursing (C,B,M,D)

NY New York State Board of Regents:
Degree-granting institutions of higher education in New York that designate the agency as their sole or primary nationally recognized accrediting agency for purposes of establishing elibility to participate in Higher Education Act programs

OPD Commission on Opticianry Accreditation: opticianry (A)

OPE Commission on Accreditation of Allied Health Education Programs: orthotics and prosthetics (C,B,M)

OPT American Optometric Association: optometry (FP,D)

OPTR American Optometric Association: optometric residency programs

OPTT American Optometric Association: optometric technician (C)

OSTEO American Osteopathic Association, Office of Osteopathic Education: osteopathic medicine (FP,D)

OT American Occupational Therapy Association: occupational therapy (M,D)

OTA American Occupational Therapy Association: occupational therapy assistant (A,B)

PA National Accrediting Agency for Clinical Laboratory Sciences: pathologist's assistant (C,M)

PAST Association for Clinical Pastoral Education: clinical pastoral education

PCSAS Psychological Clinical Science Accreditation System: psychological clinical science (D)

PDPSY American Psychological Association: post-doctorate residency in health service psychology

PERF Commission on Accreditation of Allied Health Education Programs: perfusionist (C,B,M)

PH Council on Education for Public Health: public health (B,M,D)

PHAR Accreditation Council for Pharmacy Education: pharmacy (FP,D)

PLNG Planning Accreditation Board: certified planning (B,M)

PNUR Accreditation Commission for Education in Nursing: practical nursing (C)

POD American Podiatric Medical Association: podiatry (FP,D)

POLYT Commission on Accreditation of Allied Health Education Programs: polysomnographic technologist education (C,A)

PSPSY American Psychological Association: combined professional-scientific psychology (D)

PTA American Physical Therapy Association: physical therapy (D)

PTAA American Physical Therapy Association: physical therapy assistant (A)

RABN Association of Advanced Rabbinical and Talmudic Schools: rabbinical and Talmudic education (A,B,M,D)

RAD Joint Review Committee on Education in Radiologic Technology: radiography (C,A,B)

RADDOS Joint Review Committee on Education in Radiologic Technology: medical dosimetry (C,B,M)

RADMAG Joint Review Committee on Education in Radiologic Technology: magnetic resonance (C,A,B)

RTT Joint Review Committee on Education in Radiologic Technology: radiation therapy (C,A,B,M)

SCPSY American Psychological Association: school psychology (D)

SP American Speech-Language-Hearing Association: speech-language pathology (M)

SPAA Network of Schools of Public Policy, Affairs and Administration: public affairs and administration (M)

SURGA Commission on Accreditation of Allied Health Education Programs: surgical assistant (C,A)

SURGT Commission on Accreditation of Allied Health Education Programs: surgical technology (C,A)

SURTEC Accrediting Bureau of Health Education Schools: surgical technology (C,A)

SW Council on Social Work Education: social work (B,M)

THEA National Association of Schools of Theatre: theatre (C,A,B,M,D)

THEOL Association of Theological Schools: theology (M,FP,D)

TRACS Transnational Association of Christian Colleges and Schools: christian studies education (C,A,B,M,D)

VET American Veterinary Medical Association: veterinary medicine (FP,D)

Explanatory Notes and Symbols

Associate degree: includes junior colleges, community colleges, technical institutes, and schools offering at least a two-year program of college-level studies, either leading to an associate degree wholly or principally creditable toward a baccalaureate degree.

Baccalaureate: includes those institutions offering programs of studies leading to the customary bachelor of arts or bachelor of science degrees.

First professional degree: includes those institutions that offer the academic requirements for selected professions based on programs that require at least two academic years of previous college work for entrance and a total of at least six years of college work for completion.

Master's: includes those institutions offering the customary first graduate degree, master of arts or master of science degree in the liberal arts and sciences, or the next degree in the same field after the first professional degree.

Beyond master's but less than doctorate: includes those institutions offering "postgraduate pre-doctoral degrees".

Graduate non-degree granting: includes institutions offering work beyond the bachelor's level but not conferring degrees. In some instances the degrees are conferred by cooperating institutions.

Doctorate: includes those institutions offering a Ph.D. or its equivalent in any field.

Postdoctoral research only: includes institutions operating solely for the purpose of research at the postdoctoral level.

First Talmudic/Rabbinic degree: undergraduate degree granted by accredited Rabbinical schools. The schools in New York "using this designation do not imply that the 'First Talmudic/Rabbinic Degree' is equivalent to any secular academic degree recognized by the Board of Regents".*

Second Talmudic/Rabbinic degree: graduate degree granted by accredited Rabbinical schools. The schools in New York "using this designation do not imply that the 'Second Talmudic/Rabbinic Degree' is equivalent to any secular academic degree recognized by the Board of Regents".*

Special 5yr Faith Based: undergraduate degree granted by accredited faith-based school that requires 5 years of study to complete.

---

*The University of the State of New York, The State Education Department, Albany, New York, letter August 17, 1983.

Symbols

* The institution is part of a system.

Used preceding any of the acronyms for the accrediting agencies the following symbols indicate that:

The accrediting agency has stated publicly that the institution or program is preliminary or provisionally accredited, accredited with some reservations, or approved on probation.

@ The institution or program has attained a pre-accredited status.

& The institution is covered under the regional accreditation of the parent institution.

U.S. Postal Abbreviation of States and Territories

Alabama	AL
Alaska	AK
American Samoa	AS
Arizona	AZ
Arkansas	AR
California	CA
Colorado	CO
Connecticut	CT
Delaware	DE
District of Columbia	DC
Florida	FL
Georgia	GA
Guam	GU
Hawaii	HI
Idaho	ID
Illinois	IL
Indiana	IN
Iowa	IA
Kansas	KS
Kentucky	KY
Louisiana	LA
Maine	ME
Maryland	MD
Marshall Islands	MH
Massachusetts	MA
Michigan	MI
Micronesia	FM
Minnesota	MN
Mississippi	MS
Missouri	MO
Montana	MT
Nebraska	NE
Nevada	NV
New Hampshire	NH
New Jersey	NJ
New Mexico	NM
New York	NY
North Carolina	NC
North Dakota	ND
Northern Marianas	MP
Ohio	OH
Oklahoma	OK
Oregon	OR
Palau	PW
Pennsylvania	PA
Puerto Rico	PR
Rhode Island	RI
South Carolina	SC
South Dakota	SD
Tennessee	TN
Texas	TX
Utah	UT
Vermont	VT
Virgin Islands	VI
Virginia	VA
Washington	WA
West Virginia	WV
Wisconsin	WI
Wyoming	WY

Institution Changes

FICE/ID Number

Institutions and Offices Added

Alaska

Alaska Christian College	041386

Arkansas

Jackson Theological Seminary	667411

California

California University - Silicon Valley	667207
Grace University	667422
Hayfield University	667415
Healthcare Career College	041327
The Lee Strasberg Theatre Institute	667413
The Los Angeles Performing Arts Conservatory	667412
Trident University International	041279
Virscend University	667414

Colorado

CollegeAmerica Colorado Springs	666293

Florida

Med-Life Institute-Naples	667220

Georgia

Hudson Taylor University	667416
Morris Brown College	667423

Illinois

Chicago College of Oriental Medicine	667406

Louisiana

Bridges Christian College	667417
Delta College of Arts & Technology	025383
WorldQuant University	667408

Massachusetts

Sattler College	667410

Missouri

Carver Baptist Bible College, Institute & Theological Seminary	667418

New Hampshire

Upper Valley Educators Institute	034373

New Jersey

Hackensack Meridian School of Medicine	042933

New Mexico

Southwest University of Naprapathic Medicine	667420

FICE/ID Number

New York

Yeshiva of Kasho	043017

Oregon

American Denturist College	667421

South Carolina

Southeastern College	035554
Southeastern College	037464

Tennessee

The Institute for G.O.D.	667419

Texas

Southwest School of Art	667407

Virginia

Washington Theological Seminary	667424

Washington

Great Northern University	667409

Institutions and Offices Dropped

Alabama

Judson College *(Closed)*	001023

Arizona

Brighton College *(No longer accredited by DEAC)*	666710
CollegeAmerica-Flagstaff *(No longer accredited by ACCSC)*	031203
CollegeAmerica-Phoenix *(Branch of main campus that is no longer accredited by ACCSC)*	666017
Han University of Traditional Medicine *(No longer accredited by ACUP)*	041193
Southwest University of Visual Arts *(Closed)*	024915

California

California College San Diego *(Closed)*	021108
California College San Diego *(Closed)*	770551
Dell'Arte International School of Physical Theatre *(No longer offer a degree)*	030256
FIDM/Fashion Institute of Design & Merchandising-San Diego *(Closed)*	666005
FIDM/Fashion Institute of Design and Merchandising-San Francisco *(Closed)*	013041

Institution Changes

	FICE/ID Number
John F. Kennedy University *(Closed)*	004484
Los Angeles ORT College *(No longer accredited)*	025703
Sierra States University *(Closed)*	667325
Yuin University *(Closed)*	667351

Florida

American College for Medical Careers *(Closed)*	004666
Gordon-Conwell Theological Seminary-Jacksonville *(No longer a branch campus)*	770111

Georgia

Brown College of Court Reporting *(Closed)*	020609

Hawaii

Babel University Professional School of Translation *(No longer accredited by DEAC)*	666350

Idaho

Stevens-Henager College-Boise *(Closed)*	666329

Illinois

Lindenwood University Belleville Campus *(No longer a branch campus)*	770322
Realtor University *(Closed)*	667270

Maryland

Ana G. Mendez University Capital Area Campus *(Closed)*	770924

Massachusetts

Becker College *(Closed)*	002123

Minnesota

CenterPoint Massage and Shiatsu Therapy School & Clinic *(Closed)*	041488

Nebraska

Creative Center *(Closed)*	031643

New Mexico

Southwest University of Visual Arts *(Closed)*	666524

New York

	FICE/ID Number
Bard High School Early College Manhattan *(No longer a branch campus)*	770114
Bard High School Early College Queens *(No longer a branch campus)*	770115
Christ the King Seminary *(Closed)*	002822
Christie's Education, New York *(No longer accredited by NY)*	036654
Concordia College *(Closed)*	002709
Elmira Business Institute *(Closed)*	009043

Oklahoma

Oklahoma Wesleyan University Tulsa Campus *(Closed)*	770378

Puerto Rico

Liberty Junior College *(No longer accredited by ABHES)*	041316
Monteclaro: Escuela de Hoteleria y Artes Culinarias *(Closed)*	034143

South Carolina

Forrest College *(No longer accredited by ACICS)*	004924

Texas

Dallas Nursing Institute *(No longer accredited by ABHES)*	034165

Utah

Independence University *(Closed)*	022061
Stevens-Henager College *(Closed)*	003674
Stevens-Henager College *(Closed)*	666038

Vermont

New England Culinary Institute *(Closed)*	022540

Merged Institutions

Colorado

American Sentinel University *into*	041277
Post University	001401

Delaware

Wesley College *into*	001433
Delaware State University	001428

Indiana

Ancilla College *into*	001784
Marian University	001821

New York

Touro College Bay Shore *into*	770145
Touro College Jacob D. Fuchsberg Law Center	770148

FICE/ID Number

Oregon

Pacific Northwest College of Art *into* 003207
Willamette University 003227

Texas

Austin Graduate School of Theology *into* 023628
Lipscomb University 003486
The University of Texas Health Science Center at Tyler *into* 667206
University of Texas at Tyler 011163

Virginia

Radford University Carilion *into* 006622
Radford University 003732

Wisconsin

Wisconsin Indianhead Technical College-Rice Lake Campus *into* 770465
Northwood Technical College 011824

Name Changes

Arizona

from: Ottawa University Arizona 666066
to: Ottawa University Phoenix, AZ
from: Ottawa University Surprise 770982
to: Ottawa University Surprise, AZ
from: The School of Architecture at Taliesin 025332
to: The School of Architecture

California

from: Ashford University 001881
to: University of Arizona Global Campus
from: Brandman University 041618
to: University Massachusetts Global
from: Chicago School of Professional Psychology-Irvine Campus 770492
to: Chicago School of Professional Psychology-Anaheim Campus
from: Cogswell University of Silicon Valley 001177
to: University of Silicon Valley
from: Fashion Institute of Design and Merchandising-Orange County 666004
to: FIDM/Fashion Institute of Design and Merchandising-Orange County
from: Methodist Theological Seminary in America 667133
to: Henry Appenzeller University
from: San Joaquin Valley College-Fresno Aviation Campus 666009
to: San Joaquin Valley College-Fresno Trades Education Center
from: Studio School 770969
to: Hussian College (formerly known as Studio School)
from: Weimar Institute 667302
to: Weimar University

Colorado

from: Western State Colorado University 001372
to: Western Colorado University

FICE/ID Number

Connecticut

from: Goodwin College 022449
to: Goodwin University

District of Columbia

from: TEACH-NOW Graduate School of Education 667305
to: Moreland University

Florida

from: North Florida Community College 001508
to: North Florida College

Georgia

from: Pacific Institute of Technology 667239
to: Pacific College of Technology
from: Piedmont College 001588
to: Piedmont University

Illinois

from: Resurrection University 006250
to: Oak Point University

Iowa

from: Hamilton Technical College 012064
to: Orion Technical College

Kansas

from: Ottawa University Kansas City 666083
to: Ottawa University Overland Park, KS

Louisiana

from: Northwest Louisiana Technical College Natchitoches Campus 021602
to: Central Louisiana Technical Community College Natchitoches Campus

Maine

from: Beal College 005204
to: Beal University

Massachusetts

from: University of Massachusetts Medical School 009756
to: UMass Chan Medical School

Michigan

from: Davenport University Midland 770270
to: Davenport University Great Lakes Bay Campus - Midland

Missouri

from: St. Louis College of Pharmacy 002504
to: University of Health Sciences and Pharmacy in St. Louis
from: Washington University in St. Louis-School of Medicine 770329
to: Washington University School of Medicine in St. Louis

Institution Changes

FICE/ID Number

Nebraska

from: North Platte Community College-North Campus — 770338
to: Mid-Plains Community College North Platte - North Campus

Nevada

from: Sierra Nevada College — 009192
to: Sierra Nevada University

New Jersey

from: Middlesex County College — 002615
to: Middlesex College

New York

from: Cold Spring Harbor Laboratory/Watson School of Biological Sciences — 034563
to: Cold Spring Harbor Laboratory, School of Biological Sciences

from: Medaille College Rochester Branch Campus — 770140
to: Medaille College Rochester Campus

from: New York Chiropractic College — 012277
to: Northeast College of Health Sciences

from: St. Paul's School of Nursing — 012364
to: Saint Paul's School of Nursing-Queens

North Carolina

from: Davidson County Community College — 002919
to: Davidson-Davie Community College

from: Grace College of Divinity — 041737
to: Manna University

Ohio

from: Clark State Community College — 004852
to: Clark State College

from: Miami University Hamilton Campus — 003079
to: Miami University Regionals

from: Ohio University Zanesville Branch — 003108
to: Ohio University Zanesville

Oklahoma

from: Oklahoma State University Center for Health Sciences College of Osteopathic — 011282
to: Oklahoma State University Center for Health Sciences

Oregon

from: Mount Angel Seminary — 003203
to: Mount Angel Abbey & Seminary

Pennsylvania

from: Montgomery County Community College West Campus — 770162
to: Montgomery County Community College Pottstown Campus

from: Northampton Community College Monroe County Branch Campus — 770164
to: Northampton Community College Monroe Campus

from: YTI Career Institute — 770588
to: YTI Career Institute / Lancaster

FICE/ID Number

Rhode Island

from: University of Rhode Island Graduate School of Oceanography — 770129
to: University of Rhode Island Narragansett Bay Campus

South Dakota

from: Mitchell Technical Institute — 008284
to: Mitchell Technical College

from: Western Dakota Technical Institute — 010170
to: Western Dakota Technical College

Tennessee

from: Baptist College of Health Sciences — 034403
to: Baptist Health Sciences University

from: Martin Methodist College — 003504
to: The University of Tennessee Southern

Utah

from: Broadview University — 011166
to: Broadview College

from: New Charter University — 041292
to: Bottega University

Virginia

from: Bethel College — 041538
to: Ascent College

from: Medical Careers Institute — 022472
to: ECPI University-Newport News

from: Protestant Episcopal Theological Seminary in Virginia — 003731
to: Virginia Theological Seminary

West Virginia

from: New River Technical College Mercer County Campus — 770469
to: New River Community and Technical College Mercer County Campus

from: New River Technical College Nicholas County Campus — 770470
to: New River Community and Technical College Nicholas County Campus

Wisconsin

from: Ottawa University Wisconsin — 666084
to: Ottawa University Brookfield, WI

from: University of Wisconsin Washington County — 770462
to: University of Wisconsin-Milwaukee at Washington County

from: University of Wisconsin Waukesha — 770460
to: University of Wisconsin-Milwaukee at Waukesha

from: Wisconsin Indianhead Technical College — 011824
to: Northwood Technical College

from: Wisconsin Indianhead Technical College-Ashland Campus — 770463
to: Northwood Technical College-Ashland Campus

from: Wisconsin Indianhead Technical College-New Richmond Campus — 770464
to: Northwood Technical College-New Richmond Campus

from: Wisconsin Indianhead Technical College-Superior Campus — 770466
to: Northwood Technical College-Superior Campus

Codes and Descriptions of Administrative Officers

We have modified the Manpower Codes used in the *Higher Education Directory* to better reflect the organizational structures of colleges and universities. Codes are now grouped by major organizational division—Executive, Academic, External Affairs, Fiscal Affairs, Institutional Affairs, Information Technology, and Student Affairs. Some codes have been redefined and several have been added. New and modified codes are marked by an asterisk (*).

Executive

(01) **Chief Executive Officer (President/Chancellor)** - Directs all affairs and operations of a higher education institution.

(02) **Chief Executive Officer Within a System (President/ Chancellor)** - Directs all affairs and operations of a campus or an institution which is part of a university-wide system.

(03) **Executive Vice President** - Responsible for all or most functions and operations of an institution under the direction of the Chief Executive Officer.

(100) **Chief of Staff** - Senior non-secretarial staff assistant to the President/Chancellor. Manages administration and operations of the Office of the President.

(00)* **Chairman of the Board** - Directs the operations of the institution's Board of Directors.

(101) **Secretary of the Institution/Board of Governors** - Responsible for liaison between the Board and the institution. Maintains governance and official Board records.

(125)* **President/Chancellor Emeritus** - A past chief executive currently holding an advisory or honorary position at the institution.

(17) **Chief of Health Care Professions** - Senior administrator of academic health care programs, hospitals, clinic or affiliated healthcare programs.

(12) **Director of Branch Campus** - Official who is in charge of a branch campus.

(04) **Administrative Assistant to the President** - Senior administrative assistant to the Chief Executive Officer.

(41) **Athletic Director** - Manages intramural and intercollegiate programs including employment, scheduling, promotion, maintenance and related functions.

Academic Affairs

(05) **Chief Academic Officer** - Directs the academic program of the institution. Typically includes academic planning, teaching, research, extensions and coordination of interdepartmental affairs. May include Provost.

(20) **Associate Academic Officer** - Responsible for many of the functions and operations under the direction of the Chief Academic Officer.

(08) **Chief Library Officer** - Directs the activities of all institutional libraries.

Dean or Director. Serves as the principal administrator for the institutional program indicated:

(47) **Agriculture**
(76) **Allied Health Sciences**
(48) **Architecture/Interior Design**
(49) **Art and Sciences**
(50) **Business**
(77) **Computer and Information Science**
(51) **Continuing Education**
(78) **Cooperative Education**
(52) **Dentistry**
(53) **Education**
(54) **Engineering**
(55) **Evening/Adult Programs**
(56) **Extension**
(59) **Family and Consumer Sciences**
(57) **Fine Arts**
(97) **General Studies**
(80) **Government/Public Affairs**
(58) **Graduate Programs**
(92) **Honors Program**
(79) **Humanities**
(60) **Journalism/Communications**
(61) **Law**
(62) **Library Services**
(81) **Mathematics/Sciences**
(63) **Medicine**
(64) **Music**
(65) **Natural Resources**
(66) **Nursing**
(75) **Occupational Education**
(106) **Online Education/E-learning**
(67) **Pharmacy**
(68) **Physical Education**
(82) **Political Science/International Affairs**
(107) **Professional Programs**
(69) **Public Health**
(83) **Social and Behavioral Sciences**
(70) **Social Work**
(87) **Summer Session/School**
(72) **Technology**
(73) **Theology**
(74) **Veterinary Medicine**
(94) **Women's Studies**

External Affairs

(111)* **Director of Institutional Advancement** - Responsible for the comprehensive plan to ensure ongoing growth in public awareness of an institution and its strategic goals.

(30) **Director of Development** - Organizes and directs programs connected with the fund raising activities of the institution. May include Advancement.

(110)* **Associate Advancement/Development Officer** - Assists and supports the Chief Advancement/Development Officer.

(29) **Director of Alumni Relations** - Coordinates alumni activities between the institution and the alumni.

(44) **Director Annual Giving** - Operates the annual giving from all supporters of the institutions.

(112)* **Director Planned Giving/Major Gifts** - Identifies, cultivates and solicits planned and major gifts for ongoing financial support.

(102) **Director of Foundation/Corporate Relations** - Directs institution's efforts in the area of soliciting grants and gifts from foundations and corporations.

(26) **Chief Public Relations/Marketing/Communications Officer** - Directs public relations program. May include alumni relations, publication, marketing and development.

(27) **Associate Public Relations/Marketing/Communications Officer** - Assists and reports to the Chief Public Relations/Marketing/ Communications Officer.

(31) **Chief Community Relations Officer** - Directs the educational (usually non-credit), cultural and recreational services to the community.

(103) **Director of Workforce Development** - Directs the institution's efforts in course development and instruction for students and the community in skills necessary to gain employment.

Fiscal Affairs

(10) **Chief Financial/Business Officer** - Directs business and financial affairs including accounting, purchasing, investments, auxiliary enterprises and related business matters.

(21) **Associate Financial/Business Officer** - Assists and reports to the Chief Business Officer. May include Controller.

(45) **Chief Institutional Planning Officer** - Directs the long-range planning and the allocation of the institution's resources.

(115)* **Chief Investment Officer** - Responsible for the oversight of the endowment and other financial assets of the college.

(25) **Chief Contract and Grants Administrator** - Conducts administrative activities in connection with contracts and grants.

(109) **Chief Auxiliary Services Officer** - Responsible for management and operations of college support services including food service, bookstore, vending, student union, and printing.

(114)* **Chief Budget Administrator** - Responsible for preparation and management of institutional budgets.

(113)* **Bursar** - Responsible for the overall operations of student financial services including billing, receivables and cashiering functions.

(96) **Director of Purchasing** - Coordinates purchasing of goods and services.

(116)* **Audit Officer** - Responsible for independent assessment of the effectiveness of internal administrative accounting controls and helps ensure conformance with managerial policies.

(40) **Director of Bookstore** - Responsible for the operation of the bookstore including purchasing, advertising, sales, employment, inventory and related functions.

Institutional Affairs

(11) **Chief of Operations/Administration** - Responsible for administrative functions that are generally non-academic and non-financial.

(117)* **Chief Risk Management Officer** - Responsible for the oversight of the college's risk management programs including emergency and crisis response management, operational risk, technology and cyber risks, insurance and facility vulnerability, and threat assessment.

(15) **Chief Human Resources Officer** - Administers the institution's personnel policies and programs for staff or faculty and staff.

(16) **Associate Human Resources Officer** - Assists and reports to the Chief Human Resources Officer.

(118)* **Director Employee Benefits** - Manages the college's compensation and benefit programs, policies and procedures.

(09) **Director of Institutional Research** - Conducts research and studies on the institution including design of studies, data collection, analysis and reporting.

(46) **Chief Research Officer** - Initiates and directs research in using the facilities and personnel in new areas of academic and scientific exploration.

(108) **Director of Institutional Assessment** - Facilitates and directs institution-wide assessment activities for academic programs and non-academic departments.

(22) **Director of Affirmative Action/Equal Opportunity** - Responsible for the institution's program relating to affirmative action and equal opportunity.

(28) **Director of Diversity** - Responsible for the institution's diversity programs.

(43) **Director of Legal Services (General Counsel)** - Salaried staff person responsible for advising on legal rights, obligations and related matters.

(19) **Director of Security/Safety** - Manages campus police. Responsible for security programs, training, traffic and parking regulations.

(18) **Chief Facilities/Physical Plant Officer** - Responsible for the construction, rehabilitation and maintenance of buildings and grounds.

(86) **Director of Government Relations** - Coordinates institution's relations with local, state, and federal government.

Information Technology (IT)

(13) **Chief Information Technology Officer (CIO)** - Responsible for oversight of IT infrastructure and support, computation and communication infrastructure and services, and administrative information systems across the institution.

(14) **Associate Information Technology Officer** - Assists and reports to the Chief Information Officer.

(24) **Director of Educational Media** - Responsible for audio-visual services and multi-media learning devices.

(90) **Director of Academic Computing** - Responsible for operation and coordination of the institution's various academic computer facilities and labs.

(91) **Director of Administrative Computing** - Responsible for operation of the institution's administrative computing facility.

(105) **Director of Web Services** - Directs the development, operations and content of the institution's web sites.

(119)* **Director of IT Security** - Responsible for technology security in order to protect information and prevent unauthorized access.

(120)* **Director of Online/E-learning Platform** - Coordinates all aspects of institution's online learning platforms.

Student Affairs

(32) **Chief Student Affairs/Student Life Officer** - Responsible for the direction of student life programs including counseling and testing, housing, placement, student union, relationships with student organizations and related functions.

(35) **Associate Student Affairs/Student Life Officer** - Assists Chief Student Life Officer in the non-academic student life activities.

(84) **Director of Enrollment Management** - Plans, develops, and implements strategies to sustain enrollment. Supervises administration of all admissions and financial aid operations.

(07) **Director of Admissions** - Responsible for the recruitment, selection and admission of students.

(123)* **Director of Graduate Admissions** - Responsible for the recruitment, selection and admission of graduate students.

(06) **Registrar** - Responsible for student registration, scheduling of classes, examinations and classroom facilities, student records and related matters.

(37) **Director of Student Financial Aid** - Directs the administration of all forms of student aid.

(39) **Director Resident Life/Student Housing** - Manages student housing operations.

(36) **Director of Student Placement** - Directs the operation of the student placement office to provide career counseling and job placement services to undergraduates, graduates and alumni.

(38) **Director of Student Counseling** - Directs non-academic counseling and testing for students including referral to outside agencies.

(121)* **Director of Student Success/Academic Advising** - assists students in the development and ongoing achievement of their educational goals through academic support and planning.

(124)* **Director of Student Retention** - Develops and evaluates programs and initiatives to improve student retention, engagement and transition.

(89) **Director of First Year Experience** - Works with academic and students affairs to facilitate freshman engagement, learning, transition and integration into the college community.

(93) **Director of Minority Education/Students** - Develops and supports the overall success of students, particularly those from underrepresented minority groups.

(23) **Director of Health Services** - Directs the operation of clinics, medical staff and other programs which provide institutional health services.

(42) **Chaplain/Director Campus Ministry** - Plans, directs the pastoral ministry and religious activities.

(85) **Director of Foreign Students** - Directs student life activities solely concerned with foreign students.

(104) **Director of Study Abroad** - Coordinates and advises students and faculty on academic studies conducted internationally.

(33) **Dean of Men** - Directs student life activities solely concerned with male students.

(34) **Dean of Women** - Directs student life activities solely concerned with female students.

(122)* **Director of Greek Life** - Responsible for all aspects of fraternity and sorority life on campus.

Other

(88) Use this code for those titles that do not fit the above positions.

United States Department of Education Offices

Dr. Miguel Cardona **(A)**
Secretary of Education
United States Department of Education
400 Maryland Avenue, SW
Washington, DC 20202
(202) 401-3000
FAX: (202) 260-7867
URL: www.ed.gov

Mr. James Kvaal **(B)**
Under Secretary of Education
Office of the Under Secretary
United States Department of Education
400 Maryland Avenue, SW
Room 7E307
Washington, DC 20202
(202) 453-7333
URL: sites.ed.gov/ous/

Annmarie Weisman **(C)**
Dpty Asst Secretary for Policy/Planning/Innovation
Office of Postsecondary Education
United States Department of Education
400 Maryland Avenue, SW
Room 293-01
Washington, DC 20202
(202) 453-6712
E-MAIL: annmarie.weisman@ed.gov
URL: www2.ed.gov/about/offices/list/ope/ppi.html

George Alan Smith Ed.D. **(D)**
Executive Director
National Advisory Committee on Institutional Quality & Integrity
Office of Postsecondary Education
United States Department of Education
400 Maryland Avenue, SW
Room 271-03
Washington, DC 20202
(202) 453-7757
E-MAIL: george.alan.smith@ed.gov
URL: https://sites.ed.gov/naciqi

Herman Bounds Jr., Ed.S. **(E)**
Director
Accreditation Group
Office of Post Secondary Education
U.S. Department of Education
400 Maryland Avenue, SW
Room 270-01
Washington, DC 20202
(202) 453-7615
E-MAIL: herman.bounds@ed.gov
URL: www.ed.gov/accreditation?src=rn

Ms. Peggy Carr **(F)**
Commissioner
National Center for Education Statistics
550 12th Street, SW
Room 4061
Washington, DC 20202
(202) 245-6168
E-MAIL: peggy.carr@ed.gov
URL: www.nces.ed.gov

Statewide Agencies of Higher Education

ALABAMA

Alabama Commission on Higher Education **(G)**
PO Box 302000
Montgomery, AL 36130-2000
(334) 242-1998
Dr. Jim Purcell
Executive Director
E-MAIL: jim.purcell@ache.edu
URL: www.ache.edu

Alabama Community College System **(H)**
PO Box 302130
Montgomery, AL 36130-2130
(334) 293-4524
FAX: (334) 293-4504
Jimmy H. Baker
Chancellor
E-MAIL: jimmy.baker@accs.edu
URL: www.accs.edu

ALASKA

Alaska Commission on Postsecondary Education **(I)**
PO Box 110505
Juneau, AK 99811-0505
(907) 465-6740
FAX: (907) 465-5316
Ms. Sana Efird
Executive Director
E-MAIL: eed.acpe-execdirector@alaska.gov
URL: www.acpe.alaska.gov

ARIZONA

Arizona Board of Regents **(J)**
2700 North Central Avenue
Suite 400
Phoenix, AZ 85004
(602) 229-2505
FAX: (602) 229-2555
Mr. John Arnold
Executive Director
E-MAIL: john.arnold@azregents.edu
URL: www.azregents.edu

Arizona Commission for Postsecondary Education **(K)**
1740 W. Adams
Suite 3009
Phoenix, AZ 85007
(602) 542-7230
FAX: (602) 258-2483
Daniel Helm
Interim Executive Director
E-MAIL: acpe@azhighered.gov
URL: highered.az.gov

ARKANSAS

Arkansas Division of Higher Education **(L)**
423 Main Street
Suite 400
Little Rock, AR 72201
(501) 371-2030
FAX: (501) 371-2003
Dr. Maria Markham
Director
E-MAIL: maria.markham@adhe.edu
URL: www.adhe.edu

CALIFORNIA

California Community Colleges Chancellor's Office **(M)**
1102 Q Street
Suite 4400
Sacramento, CA 95811
(916) 445-8752
FAX: (916) 322-4783
Mr. Eloy Ortiz Oakley
Chancellor
E-MAIL: eoakley@cccco.edu
URL: www.cccco.edu

COLORADO

Colorado Department of Higher Education **(N)**
1600 Broadway
Suite 2200
Denver, CO 80202
(303) 862-3001
FAX: (303) 996-1329
Dr. Angie Paccione
Executive Director
E-MAIL: questions@dhe.state.co.us
URL: highered.colorado.gov

Colorado Community College System **(O)**
9101 East Lowry Boulevard
Denver, CO 80230-6011
(720) 858-2424
FAX: (303) 620-4043
Joseph Garcia
Chancellor
E-MAIL: chancellor@cccs.edu
URL: www.cccs.edu

CONNECTICUT

Board of Regents for Higher Education Connecticut State Colleges & Universities **(P)**
61 Woodland Street
Hartford, CT 06105
(860) 723-0011
FAX: (860) 723-0009
Terrence Cheng
President
E-MAIL: tcheng@commnet.edu
URL: www.ct.edu/regents/

Office of Higher Education **(Q)**
450 Columbus Boulevard
Suite 707
Hartford, CT 06103
(860) 947-1801
Mr. Timothy D. Larson
Executive Director
E-MAIL: timothy.d.larson@ct.gov
URL: www.ctohe.org

DELAWARE

Delaware Department of Education Higher Education Office **(R)**
401 Federal Street
Dover, DE 19901
(302) 735-4120
FAX: (302) 739-5894
Shana Payne
Director
E-MAIL: dheo@doe.k12.de.us
URL: www.delawarestudentsuccess.org

Delaware Technical Community College **(S)**
PO Box 897
Dover, DE 19903
(302) 857-1667
Dr. Mark T. Brainard
President
E-MAIL: brainard@dtcc.edu
URL: www.dtcc.edu

DISTRICT OF COLUMBIA

Office of the State Superintendent of Education Government of the District of Columbia **(T)**
1050 First Street, NE
Washington, DC 20002
(202) 272-6436
FAX: (202) 727-2019
Dr. Christina Grant
State Superintendent of Education
E-MAIL: christina.grant@dc.gov
URL: www.osse.dc.gov

District of Columbia Higher Education Licensure Commission **(U)**
1050 1st Street, NE
5th Floor
Washington, DC 20002
(202) 481-3951
FAX: (202) 741-0229
Mrs. Angela Lee
Executive Director
E-MAIL: osse.elcmail@dc.gov
URL: helc.osse.dc.gov

FLORIDA

Board of Governors State University System of Florida **(V)**
325 West Gaines Street
Suite 1614
Tallahassee, FL 32399-0400
(850) 245-0466
FAX: (850) 245-9685
Mr. Marshall M. Criser III
Chancellor
E-MAIL: chancellor@flbog.edu
URL: www.flbog.edu

Florida Department of Education Division of Florida Colleges **(W)**
325 West Gaines Street
Suite 1244 Turlington Building
Tallahassee, FL 32399
(850) 245-0407
Ms. Kathryn S. Hebda
Chancellor
E-MAIL: chancellorfcs@fldoe.org
URL: www.fldoe.org/schools/higher-ed/fl-college-system/

GEORGIA

Board of Regents of the University System of Georgia **(X)**
270 Washington Street, SW
Atlanta, GA 30334
(404) 962-3049
Dr. Steve Wrigley
Chancellor
E-MAIL: chancellor@usg.edu
URL: www.usg.edu/regents/

HAWAII

University of Hawaii Board of Regents **(Y)**
2444 Dole Street
Bachman Hall, Room 209
Honolulu, HI 96822
(808) 956-8213
FAX: (808) 956-5156
Mr. Randy Moore
Chair
E-MAIL: bor@hawaii.edu
URL: www.hawaii.edu/offices/bor/

IDAHO

Idaho State Board of Education **(Z)**
PO Box 83720
Boise, ID 83720-0037
(208) 332-1571
FAX: (208) 334-2632
Mr. Matt Freeman
Executive Director
E-MAIL: matt.freeman@osbe.idaho.gov
URL: www.boardofed.idaho.gov

Statewide Agencies of Higher Education

ILLINOIS

Illinois Board of Higher Education (A)
1 N. Old State Capitol Plaza
Suite 333
Springfield, IL 62701-1377
(217) 782-2551
FAX: (888) 261-2881
Ms. Ginger Ostro
Executive Director
E-MAIL: chase@ibhe.org
URL: www.ibhe.org

Illinois Community College Board (B)
401 East Capitol Avenue
Springfield, IL 62701
(217) 785-0123
FAX: (217) 524-4981
Dr. Brian Durham
Executive Director
E-MAIL: brian.durham@illinois.gov
URL: www2.iccb.org/iccb/

INDIANA

Indiana Commission for Higher Education (C)
101 West Ohio Street
Suite 300
Indianapolis, IN 46204
(317) 464-4400
FAX: (317) 464-4410
Mrs. Teresa Lubbers
Commissioner for Higher Education
E-MAIL: tlubbers@che.in.gov
URL: www.in.gov/che/

IOWA

Board of Regents, State of Iowa (D)
11260 Aurora Avenue
Urbandale, IA 50322-7905
(515) 281-3934
FAX: (515) 281-6420
Mr. Mark J. Braun
Executive Director
E-MAIL: mark.braun@iowaregents.edu
URL: www.iowaregents.edu

Iowa College Student Aid Commission (E)
475 SW 5th Street
Suite D
Des Moines, IA 50309
(515) 725-3410
FAX: (515) 725-3401
Dr. Mark Wiederspan
Executive Director
E-MAIL: mark.wiederspan@iowa.gov
URL: www.iowacollegeaid.gov

Iowa Department of Education Division of Community Colleges and Workforce Preparation (F)
400 East 14th Street
Des Moines, IA 50319-0146
(515) 281-8260
FAX: (515) 242-5988
Jeremy Varner
Administrator
E-MAIL: jeremy.varner@iowa.gov
URL: www.educateiowa.gov

KANSAS

Kansas Board of Regents (G)
1000 SW Jackson Street
Suite 520
Topeka, KS 66612-1368
(785) 430-4240
FAX: (785) 430-4233
Dr. Blake Flanders
President and CEO
E-MAIL: bflanders@ksbor.org
URL: www.kansasregents.org

Kansas Legislative Research Department (H)
Room 68 West, State Capitol Building
300 SW 10th Avenue
Topeka, KS 66612-1504
(785) 296-3181
Mr. J. G. Scott
Director
E-MAIL: kslegres@klrd.ks.gov
URL: www.kslegres.org

KENTUCKY

Kentucky Council on Postsecondary Education (I)
100 Airport Road
Third Floor
Frankfort, KY 40601
(502) 892-3001 or (502) 573-1555
FAX: (502) 573-1535
Dr. Aaron Thompson
President
E-MAIL: aaron.thompson@ky.gov
URL: cpe.ky.gov

Kentucky Community & Technical College System (J)
300 North Main Street
Versailles, KY 40383
(859) 256-3132
FAX: (859) 256-3116
Dr. Paul Czarapata
President
E-MAIL: president@kctcs.edu
URL: www.kctcs.edu

LOUISIANA

Louisiana Board of Regents (K)
1201 N. Third Street
Suite 6-200
Baton Rouge, LA 70802
(225) 342-4253
FAX: (225) 342-9318
Dr. Kim Hunter Reed
Commissioner of Higher Education
E-MAIL: emily.skaikay@laregents.edu
URL: regents.la.gov

Louisiana Department of Education (L)
PO Box 94064
Baton Rouge, LA 70804-9064
(225) 342-3607
FAX: (225) 342-7316
Dr. Cade Brumley
State Superintendent of Education
E-MAIL: cade.brumley@la.gov
URL: www.louisianabelieves.com

MAINE

Maine Department of Education Higher Education and Educator Support Services (M)
23 State House Station
Augusta, ME 04333-0023
(207) 624-6620
FAX: (207) 624-6700
Ms. Pender Makin
Commissioner of Education
E-MAIL: commish.doe@maine.gov
URL: www.maine.gov/doe/

MARYLAND

Maryland Higher Education Commission (N)
6 North Liberty Street, 10th Floor
Baltimore, MD 21201
(410) 767-3300
FAX: (410) 332-0250
Dr. James D. Fielder
Secretary of Higher Education
E-MAIL: james.fielder@maryland.gov
URL: www.mhec.maryland.gov

MASSACHUSETTS

Massachusetts Department of Higher Education (O)
One Ashburton Place
Room 1401
Boston, MA 02108
(617) 994-6901
FAX: (617) 727-6656
Mr. Carlos Santiago
Commissioner
E-MAIL: commissioner@dhe.mass.edu
URL: www.mass.edu

MICHIGAN

Michigan Department of Labor and Economic Opportunity, Proprietary/Post Secondary Schools (P)
201 N. Washington Square
Lansing, MI 48913
(517) 930-9135
Vern Westendorf
State Administrative Manager
E-MAIL: westendorfv@michigan.gov
URL: www.michigan.gov/pss

Michigan Workforce Development (Q)
201 North Washington Square
Victor Office Center, 3rd Floor
Lansing, MI 48913
(517) 335-5858
FAX: (517) 241-9810
URL: www.michigan.gov/wda

MINNESOTA

Minnesota Office of Higher Education (R)
1450 Energy Park Drive
Suite 350
St. Paul, MN 55108-5227
(651) 642-0567
FAX: (651) 642-0675
Mr. Dennis W. Olsen Jr.
Commissioner
E-MAIL: info.ohe@state.mn.us
URL: www.ohe.state.mn.us

Minnesota State Colleges and Universities (S)
30 7th Street East
Suite 350
St. Paul, MN 55101-7804
(651) 201-1696
Dr. Devinder Malhotra
Chancellor
E-MAIL: chancellor@minnstate.edu
URL: www.minnstate.edu

MISSISSIPPI

Mississippi Board of Trustees of State Institutions of Higher Learning (T)
3825 Ridgewood Road
Jackson, MS 39211
(601) 432-6198
FAX: (601) 432-6972
Dr. Alfred Rankins Jr.
Commissioner of Higher Education
E-MAIL: commissioner@ihl.state.ms.us
URL: www.mississippi.edu/ihl/

Mississippi Community College Board (U)
3825 Ridgewood Drive
Jackson, MS 39211
(601) 432-6734
FAX: (601) 432-6480
Mr. Kell Smith
Executive Director
E-MAIL: ksmith@mccb.edu
URL: www.mccb.edu

MISSOURI

Coordinating Board for Higher Education Missouri Department of Higher Education (V)
PO Box 1469
Jefferson City, MO 65101
(573) 751-2361
FAX: (573) 751-6635
Ms. Zora Mulligan
Commissioner of Higher Education
E-MAIL: info@dhewd.mo.gov
URL: dhewd.mo.gov/cbhe/

MONTANA

Office of the Commissioner of Higher Education (W)
PO Box 203201
Helena, MT 59620-3201
(406) 449-9125
FAX: (406) 449-9171
Mr. Clayton Christian
Commissioner
E-MAIL: cchristian@montana.edu
URL: www.mus.edu/che

NEBRASKA

Nebraska's Coordinating Commission for Postsecondary Education (X)
PO Box 95005
Lincoln, NE 68509-5005
(402) 471-2847
Dr. Michael Baumgartner
Executive Director
E-MAIL: mike.baumgartner@nebraska.gov
URL: ccpe.nebraska.gov

NEW HAMPSHIRE

New Hampshire Department of Education Division of Educator Support and Higher Education Higher Education Commission (Y)
101 Pleasant Street
Concord, NH 03301
(603) 271-2408
Mr. Stephen Appleby
Director
E-MAIL: stephen.m.appleby@doe.nh.gov
URL: www.education.nh.gov/who-we-are/higher-education-commission

Community College System of New Hampshire (Z)
26 College Drive
Concord, NH 03301
(603) 230-3501
FAX: (603) 271-2725
Dr. Mark Rubinstein
Interim Chancellor
E-MAIL: mrubinstein@ccsnh.edu
URL: www.ccsnh.edu

NEW JERSEY

State of New Jersey Office of the Secretary of Higher Education (a)
1 John Fitch Plaza, 10th Floor
PO Box 542
Trenton, NJ 08625-0542
(609) 292-8052
FAX: (609) 292-7225
Dr. Brian Bridges
Secretary of Higher Education
E-MAIL: brian.bridges@oshe.nj.gov
URL: nj.gov/highereducation/

NEW MEXICO

New Mexico Higher Education Department (b)
2044 Galisteo Street
Suite 4
Santa Fe, NM 87505
(505) 476-8400
FAX: (505) 476-8454
Ms. Stephanie Rodriguez
Cabinet Secretary
E-MAIL: exec.admin@state.nm.us
URL: www.hed.state.nm.us

NEW YORK

New York State Education Department (c)
89 Washington Avenue
Room 111
Albany, NY 12234
(518) 474-5844
Dr. Betty A. Rosa
Commissioner
E-MAIL: commissioner@nysed.gov
URL: www.nysed.gov

Community Colleges and the Education Pipeline (d)
The State University of New York
353 Broadway, Room T9
Albany, NY 12246
(518) 320-1276
Johanna Duncan-Poitier
Senior Vice Chancellor
E-MAIL: johanna.duncan-poitier@suny.edu
URL: www.suny.edu/powerofsuny/educationpipeline/

New York State Education Department Office of Higher Education (A)
89 Washington Avenue
Room 975
Albany, NY 12234
(518) 486-3633
Mr. William Murphy
Deputy Commissioner
E-MAIL: hedepcom@nysed.gov
URL: highered.nysed.gov

NORTH CAROLINA

The University of North Carolina System (B)
910 Raleigh Road
Chapel Hill, NC 27514
(919) 962-4622
Mr. Peter Hans
President
E-MAIL: president@northcarolina.edu
URL: www.northcarolina.edu

North Carolina Community Colleges (C)
200 West Jones Street
Raleigh, NC 27603
(919) 807-6950
Mr. Thomas Stith III
President
E-MAIL: stitht@nccommunitycolleges.edu
URL: www.nccommunitycolleges.edu

NORTH DAKOTA

North Dakota State Board of Higher Education (D)
600 East Boulevard Avenue, Dept 215
State Capitol, 10th Floor
Bismarck, ND 58505-0230
(701) 328-2960
FAX: (701) 328-2961
Mr. Nick Hacker
Board Chair
E-MAIL: nicholas.hacker@ndus.edu
URL: www.ndus.edu/board

OHIO

Ohio Department of Higher Education (E)
25 South Front Street
Columbus, OH 43215
(614) 466-6000
FAX: (614) 466-5866
Mr. Randy Gardner
Chancellor
E-MAIL: chancellor@highered.ohio.gov
URL: www.ohiohighered.org

OKLAHOMA

Oklahoma State Regents for Higher Education (F)
655 Research Parkway
Suite 200
Oklahoma City, OK 73104
(405) 225-9100
FAX: (405) 225-9235
Dr. Glen D. Johnson
Chancellor
E-MAIL: chancellorjohnson@osrhe.edu
URL: www.okhighered.org

OREGON

Higher Education Coordinating Commission (G)
3225 25th Street SE
Salem, OR 97302
(503) 378-5690
Ben Cannon
Executive Director
E-MAIL: info.hecc@hecc.oregon.gov
URL: www.oregon.gov/HigherEd

Oregon Higher Education Coordinating Commission Office of Community Colleges and Workforce Development (H)
3225 25th Street SE
Salem, OR 97302
(503) 947-2428
Donna Lewelling
Director
E-MAIL: donna.j.lewelling@hecc.oregon.gov
URL: www.oregon.gov/highered/about/pages/office-ccwd.aspx

PENNSYLVANIA

Pennsylvania Department of Education Office of Postsecondary and Higher Education (I)
333 Market Street
12th Floor
Harrisburg, PA 17126-0333
(717) 772-3737
FAX: (717) 772-3622
Tanya I. Garcia Ph.D.
Deputy Secretary
E-MAIL: tagarcia@pa.gov
URL: www.education.pa.gov/postsecondary-adult/pages/default.aspx

Pennsylvania Department of Education Liaison to Postsecondary and Higher Education Institutions (J)
333 Market Street
12th Floor
Harrisburg, PA 17126-0333
(717) 783-6786
FAX: (717) 772-3622
Ms. Lynette Kuhn
Division Chief - Higher Education, Access & Equity
E-MAIL: lykuhn@pa.gov
URL: www.education.pa.gov

RHODE ISLAND

Rhode Island Office of the Postsecondary Commissioner (K)
560 Jefferson Boulevard
Suite 200
Warwick, RI 02886
(401) 736-1100
Dr. Shannon Gilkey
Commissioner on Postsecondary Education
E-MAIL: media@riopc.edu
URL: riopc.edu

Community College of Rhode Island (L)
400 East Avenue
Warwick, RI 02886
(401) 825-2188
FAX: (401) 825-2166
Dr. Meghan Hughes
President
E-MAIL: meghanhughes@ccri.edu
URL: www.ccri.edu

SOUTH CAROLINA

South Carolina Commission on Higher Education (M)
1122 Lady Street
Suite 300
Columbia, SC 29201
(803) 737-2155
Dr. Rusty L. Monhollon
President and Executive Director
E-MAIL: rmonhollon@che.sc.gov
URL: www.che.sc.gov

South Carolina State Board for Technical and Comprehensive Education (N)
111 Executive Center Drive
Columbia, SC 29210
(803) 896-5280
Dr. Tim Hardee
System President
E-MAIL: andrewsl@sctechsystem.edu
URL: www.sctechsystem.edu

SOUTH DAKOTA

South Dakota Board of Regents (O)
306 East Capitol Avenue
Suite 200
Pierre, SD 57501
(605) 773-3455
FAX: (605) 773-5320
Brian L. Maher
Executive Director and Chief Executive Officer
E-MAIL: info@sdbor.edu
URL: sdbor.edu

South Dakota Department of Education (P)
Office of the Secretary
800 Governors Drive
Pierre, SD 57501-2291
(605) 773-5669
FAX: (605) 773-6139
Ms. Tiffany Sanderson
Secretary of Education
E-MAIL: doe@state.sd.us
URL: www.doe.sd.gov

TENNESSEE

Tennessee Higher Education Commission (Q)
312 Rosa Parks Avenue
9th Floor
Nashville, TN 37243
(615) 741-7562
Ms. Emily House
Executive Director
E-MAIL: victoria.harpool@tn.gov
URL: www.tn.gov/thec/

Tennessee Board of Regents (R)
1 Bridgestone Park
Nashville, TN 37214
(615) 365-1505
FAX: (615) 366-3903
Dr. Jothany Blackwood
Vice Chancellor for Academic Affairs
E-MAIL: jothany.blackwood@tbr.edu
URL: www.tbr.edu/board/tennessee-board-regents

University of Tennessee Board of Trustees (S)
813 Andy Holt Tower
Knoxville, TN 37996-0170
(865) 974-8886
FAX: (865) 974-0100
Ms. Cynthia Moore
Secretary/Special Counsel to the Board of Trustees
E-MAIL: cynthia.moore@tennessee.edu
URL: trustees.tennessee.edu

TEXAS

Texas Higher Education Coordinating Board (T)
PO Box 12788
Austin, TX 78711-2788
(512) 427-6101
FAX: (512) 427-6127
Harrison Keller
Commissioner of Higher Education
E-MAIL: commissioner@highered.texas.gov
URL: www.highered.texas.gov

Texas Higher Education Coordinating Board Division of College Readiness and Success (U)
PO Box 12788
Austin, TX 78711-2788
(512) 427-6247
FAX: (512) 427-6444
Jerel Booker J.D.
Assistant Commissioner
E-MAIL: jerel.booker@highered.texas.gov
URL: www.highered.texas.gov

UTAH

Utah System of Higher Education State Board of Regents (V)
60 South 400 West
Salt Lake City, UT 84101-1284
(801) 321-7200
Mr. David Woolstenhulme
Commissioner of Higher Education
E-MAIL: dwoolstenhulme@ushe.edu
URL: www.ushe.edu

VERMONT

Vermont Agency of Education (W)
1 National Life Drive
Davis 5
Montpelier, VT 05620-2501
(802) 828-1130
FAX: (802) 828-6430
Mr. Brad James
Education Finance Manager
E-MAIL: brad.james@vermont.gov
URL: www.education.vermont.gov

VIRGINIA

State Council of Higher Education for Virginia (X)
101 North 14th Street
James Monroe Building, 10th Floor
Richmond, VA 23219
(804) 225-2600
Mr. Peter Blake
Director
E-MAIL: peterblake@schev.edu
URL: www.schev.edu

Virginia's Community Colleges (Y)
300 Arboretum Place
Suite 200
Richmond, VA 23236
(804) 819-4903
Dr. Glenn DuBois
Chancellor
E-MAIL: gdubois@vccs.edu
URL: www.vccs.edu

WASHINGTON

Washington Student Achievement Council (Z)
917 Lakeridge Way SW
Olympia, WA 98502
(360) 753-7800
Mr. Michael P. Meotti
Executive Director
E-MAIL: info@wsac.wa.gov
URL: www.wsac.wa.gov

Washington State Board for Community and Technical Colleges (a)
PO Box 42495
Olympia, WA 98504-2495
(360) 704-4355
FAX: (360) 704-4415
Jan Yoshiwara
Executive Director
E-MAIL: jyoshiwara@sbctc.edu
URL: www.sbctc.edu

WEST VIRGINIA

West Virginia Higher Education Policy Commission (b)
1018 Kanawha Boulevard, East
Suite 700
Charleston, WV 25301-2800
(304) 558-0699
FAX: (304) 558-1011
Dr. Sarah Armstrong Tucker
Chancellor
E-MAIL: sarah.tucker@wvhepc.edu
URL: www.wvhepc.edu

WISCONSIN

State of Wisconsin Higher Educational Aids Board (c)
PO Box 7885
Madison, WI 53707-7885
(608) 267-2206
FAX: (608) 267-2808
Dr. Connie Hutchison
Executive Secretary
E-MAIL: connie.hutchinson@wi.gov
URL: heab.wi.gov

Wisconsin Technical College System (d)
PO Box 7874
Madison, WI 53707-7874
(608) 267-9066
FAX: (608) 266-1285
Dr. Morna K. Foy
President
E-MAIL: president@wtcsystem.edu
URL: www.wtcsystem.edu

WYOMING

Wyoming Community College Commission (e)
2300 Capitol Avenue
5th Floor, Suite B
Cheyenne, WY 82002
(307) 777-7763
Dr. Sandy Caldwell
Executive Director
E-MAIL: sandra.caldwell@wyo.gov
URL: communitycolleges.wy.edu

AMERICAN SAMOA

Board of Higher Education (American Samoa) American Samoa Community College (f)
PO Box 2609
Pago Pago, AS 96799
(684) 699-9155
E-MAIL: info@amsamoa.edu
URL: www.amsamoa.edu

Statewide Agencies of Higher Education

FEDERATED STATES OF MICRONESIA

Board of Regents College of Micronesia-FSM **(A)**
PO Box 159
Kolonia Pohnpei, FM 96941
(691) 320-2480
Suzanne L. Gallen
Chairwoman
E-MAIL: national@comfsm.fm
URL: www.comfsm.fm

PUERTO RICO

Puerto Rico Council on Education **(B)**
PO Box 9023271
San Juan, PR 00902-3271
(787) 722-2121, ext. 3800
Mr. Edward Moreno Alonso
Chairman Board of Education
URL: www.ce.pr.gov

Higher Education Associations

AACSB International (A)
777 South Harbour Island Boulevard
Suite 750
Tampa, FL 33602-5730
(813) 769-6500
Ms. Caryn L. Beck-Dudley
President and Chief Executive Officer
E-MAIL: mediarelations@aacsb.edu
URL: www.aacsb.edu

AASA, The School Superintendents Association (B)
1615 Duke Street
Alexandria, VA 22314
(703) 528-0700
FAX: (703) 841-1543
Dr. Daniel A. Domenech
Executive Director
E-MAIL: ddomenech@aasa.org
URL: www.aasa.org

AAUW (C)
1310 L Street, NW
Suite 1000
Washington, DC 20005
(202) 785-7700
Kimberly Churches
Chief Executive Officer
E-MAIL: executive@aauw.org
URL: www.aauw.org

ABET (D)
415 North Charles Street
Baltimore, MD 21201
(410) 347-7700
Michael K. J. Milligan PhD,PE,CAE
Executive Director and CEO
E-MAIL: comms@abet.org
URL: www.abet.org

Academy of Legal Studies in Business (E)
Western Carolina University
College of Business
Forsyth Hall
Cullowhee, NC 28723
(513) 255-6950
Mr. Daniel Herron
Executive Secretary
E-MAIL: herron3653@gmail.com
URL: www.alsb.org

Academy of Nutrition and Dietetics Accreditation Council for Education in Nutrition and Dietetics (ACEND) (F)
120 South Riverside Plaza
Suite 2190
Chicago, IL 60606-6995
(312) 899-0040, ext. 5400
FAX: (312) 899-4817
Dr. Rayane AbuSabha
Executive Director
E-MAIL: acend@eatright.org
URL: www.eatrightpro.org/acend

Accreditation Commission for Acupuncture and Herbal Medicine (ACAHM) (G)
8941 Aztec Drive
Suite 2
Eden Prairie, MN 55347
(952) 212-2434
Mr. Mark McKenzie
Executive Director
E-MAIL: mark.mckenzie@acahm.org
URL: www.acahm.org

Accreditation Commission for Education in Nursing (ACEN) (H)
3390 Peachtree Road, NE
Suite 1400
Atlanta, GA 30326
(404) 975-5000
Dr. Marsal Stoll
CEO
E-MAIL: mstoll@acenursing.org
URL: www.acenursing.org

Accreditation Commission for Midwifery Education (ACME) (I)
8403 Colesville Road
Suite 1230
Silver Spring, MD 20910
(240) 485-1803
Angela Smith
Executive Director
E-MAIL: asmith@acnm.org
URL: www.midwife.org/Accreditation

Accreditation Committee - Perfusion Education (J)
519 W. Ridge Road
Littleton, CO 80120
(303) 794-6283
Ms. Theresa Sisneros
Executive Director
E-MAIL: office@ac-pe.org
URL: www.ac-pe.org

Accreditation Council for Business Schools and Programs (K)
11520 West 119th Street
Overland Park, KS 66213
(913) 339-9356
Mr. Jeffrey Alderman
President & CEO
E-MAIL: info@acbsp.org
URL: www.acbsp.org

Accreditation Council for Pharmacy Education (L)
190 S. LaSalle Street
Suite 2850
Chicago, IL 60603
(312) 664-3575
FAX: (866) 228-2631
Janet P. Engle, PharmD PhD (Hon)
Executive Director
E-MAIL: jengle@acpe-accredit.org
URL: www.acpe-accredit.org

Accreditation Review Commission on Education for the Physician Assistant (ARC-PA) (M)
3325 Paddocks Parkway
Suite 345
Suwanee, GA 30024
(770) 476-1224
FAX: (770) 476-1738
Ms. Sharon Luke
Executive Director
E-MAIL: sharonluke@arc-pa.org
URL: www.arc-pa.org

Accreditation Review Committee for the Anesthesiologist Assistant (N)
,
(612) 836-3311
Ms. Jennifer Anderson Warwick
Executive Director
E-MAIL: arc-aa@arc-aa.org
URL: www.caahep.org/arc-aa

Accreditation Review Committee for the Medical Illustrator (O)
University of Toronto
312 Health Sciences Complex
3359 Mississauga Road North
Mississauga, ON L5L 1CS
(905) 569-4265
Ms. Shelley Wall
ARC-MI Chair
E-MAIL: s.wall@utoronto.ca
URL: www.caahep.org/arc-mi

Accreditation Review Council on Education in Surgical Technology and Surgical Assisting (P)
19751 E. Main Street
Parker, CO 80138
(303) 694-9262
Mr. Ron Kruzel
Executive Director
E-MAIL: info@arcstsa.org
URL: www.arcstsa.org

Accrediting Bureau of Health Education Schools (ABHES) (Q)
7777 Leesburg Pike
Suite 314 North
Falls Church, VA 22043
(703) 917-9503
FAX: (703) 917-4109
India Y. Tips
Executive Director
E-MAIL: itips@abhes.org
URL: www.abhes.org

Accrediting Commission for Community and Junior Colleges Western Association of Schools and Colleges (R)
10 Commercial Boulevard
Suite 204
Novato, CA 94949
(415) 506-0234
FAX: (415) 506-0238
Dr. Stephanie Droker
President
E-MAIL: accjc@accjc.org
URL: accjc.org

Accrediting Commission of Career Schools and Colleges (S)
2101 Wilson Boulevard
Suite 302
Arlington, VA 22201
(703) 247-4212
FAX: (703) 247-4533
Dr. Michale McComis
Executive Director
E-MAIL: mccomis@accsc.org
URL: www.accsc.org

Accrediting Council for Continuing Education & Training (ACCET) (T)
1722 N Street, NW
Washington, DC 20036
(202) 955-1113
Mr. Christopher D. Lambert
Executive Director
E-MAIL: info@accet.org
URL: www.accet.org

Accrediting Council for Independent Colleges and Schools (U)
1350 Eye Street, NW
Suite 560
Washington, DC 20005
(202) 336-6780
FAX: (202) 789-1747
Ms. Michelle Edwards
President & CEO
E-MAIL: medwards@acics.org
URL: www.acics.org

Accrediting Council on Education in Journalism and Mass Communications (V)
University of Mississippi
201 Bishop Hall
University, MS 38677
(662) 915-5504
Patricia Thompson
ACEJMC Executive Director
E-MAIL: pthomps1@olemiss.edu
URL: www.acejmc.org

ACPE: The Standard in Spiritual Care & Education (W)
55 Ivan Allen Jr. Boulevard
Suite 835
Atlanta, GA 30308
(404) 320-1472
FAX: (404) 320-0849
Trace Haythorn Ph.D
Executive Director/CEO
E-MAIL: acpe@acpe.edu
URL: www.acpe.edu

ACT, Inc. (X)
500 ACT Drive
Box 168
Iowa City, IA 52243-0168
(319) 337-1000
Ms. Janet Godwin
Interim CEO and Chief Operating Officer
URL: www.act.org

AEF: The Association of National Advertisers (ANA) Educational Foundation (Y)
155 E. 44th Street
4th Floor
New York, NY 10017
(212) 986-8060
Mr. Gordon McLean
President
E-MAIL: gm@aef.com
URL: aef.com

American Academy for Liberal Education (AALE) (Z)
Washington, DC 20016
(202) 389-6550
Mary Ann Powers
Executive Director
E-MAIL: aaleinfo@aale.org
URL: www.aale.org

American Anthropological Association (a)
2300 Clarendon Boulevard
Suite 1301
Arlington, VA 22201
(703) 528-1902
FAX: (703) 528-3546
Dr. Edward Liebow
Executive Director
E-MAIL: eliebow@americananthro.org
URL: www.americananthro.org

American Association for Adult and Continuing Education (AAACE) (b)
2900 Delk Road
Suite 700, PMB 321
Marietta, GA 30067
(678) 809-4120
FAX: (404) 393-9506
Terry Dougherty CMP
Managing Director
E-MAIL: terry@aaace.org
URL: www.aaace.org

American Association for Employment in Education (c)
PO Box 510
Sycamore, IL 60178
(614) 485-1111
FAX: (360) 244-7802
Mr. Tim Neubert
Executive Director
E-MAIL: execdir@aaee.org
URL: www.aaee.org

American Association for Marriage and Family Therapy Commission on Accreditation for Marriage and Family Therapy Education (d)
112 South Alfred Street
Alexandria, VA 22314-3061
(703) 253-0448
FAX: (703) 253-0508
Ms. Jill Fogolin
Director of Accreditation
E-MAIL: jfogolin@aamft.org
URL: www.coamfte.org

American Association for Women in Community Colleges (AAWCC) (e)
PO Box 175
Lansdowne, PA 19050
Dr. Monica Umphrey
President
E-MAIL: info@aawccnatl.org
URL: www.aawccnatl.org

American Association of Blood Banks Committee on Accreditation of Specialist in Blood Banking Technology Schools (f)
4550 Montgomery Avenue
Suite 700 North Tower
Bethesda, MD 20814
(301) 215-6540
Ms. Melanie Sloan
Staff Liaison Accreditation and Quality
E-MAIL: msloan@aabb.org
URL: www.caahep.org/CoA-SBBT

American Association of Colleges for Teacher Education (g)
1602 L Street, NW
Suite 601
Washington, DC 20036
(202) 293-2450
FAX: (202) 457-8095
Dr. Lynn M. Gangone
President & Chief Executive Officer
E-MAIL: smonroe@aacte.org
URL: www.aacte.org

American Association of Colleges of Nursing (h)
655 K Street, NW
Suite 750
Washington, DC 20001-2399
(202) 463-6930
FAX: (202) 785-8320
Dr. Deborah Trautman
President & Chief Executive Officer
E-MAIL: dtrautman@aacnnursing.org
URL: www.aacnnursing.org

American Association of Colleges of Osteopathic Medicine (i)
7700 Old Georgetown Road
Suite 250
Bethesda, MD 20814
(301) 968-4100
FAX: (301) 968-4101
Dr. Robert Cain DO
President and CEO
E-MAIL: president@aacom.org
URL: www.aacom.org

American Association of Collegiate Registrars and Admissions Officers (AACRAO) (A)
1108 16th Street, NW
Suite 400
Washington, DC 20036
(202) 293-9161
FAX: (202) 872-8857
Ms. Melanie Gottlieb
Interim Executive Director
E-MAIL: gottliebm@aacrao.org
URL: www.aacrao.org

American Association of Community Colleges (B)
1 Dupont Circle, NW
Suite 700
Washington, DC 20036
(202) 728-0200, ext. 235
FAX: (202) 833-2467
Dr. Walter G. Bumphus
President/CEO
E-MAIL: wbumphus@aacc.nche.edu
URL: www.aacc.nche.edu

American Association of Family and Consumer Sciences (AAFCS) (C)
107 S. West Street, #816
Alexandria, VA 22314
(703) 706-4602
FAX: (703) 636-7648
Lori A. Myers PhD, CFCS
Sr Director, Credentialing, Education & Research
E-MAIL: lmyers@aafcs.org
URL: www.aafcs.org

American Association of Medical Assistants (D)
20 North Wacker Drive
Suite 1575
Chicago, IL 60606
(312) 899-1500
FAX: (312) 899-1259
Mr. Donald A. Balasa J.D., MBA
Chief Executive Officer
E-MAIL: dbalasa@aama-ntl.org
URL: aama-ntl.org

American Association of Physics Teachers (E)
One Physics Ellipse
College Park, MD 20740-3845
(301) 209-3311
FAX: (301) 209-0845
Dr. Beth A. Cunningham
Executive Officer
E-MAIL: eo@aapt.org
URL: www.aapt.org

American Association of Presidents of Independent Colleges and Universities (F)
PO Box 7070
Provo, UT 84602-7070
(801) 422-4648
Mr. Joshua Figueira
Executive Director
E-MAIL: director@aapicu.org
URL: www.aapicu.org

American Association of State Colleges and Universities (G)
1717 Rhode Island Avenue, NW
Suite 700
Washington, DC 20036
(202) 293-7070
FAX: (202) 296-5819
Dr. Mildred Garcia
President
E-MAIL: presg@aascu.org
URL: www.aascu.org

American Association of Teachers of Slavic and East European Languages (H)
University of Southern California
3501 Trousdale Parkway
THH 255L
Los Angeles, CA 90089-4353
(213) 740-2734
Dr. Elizabeth Durst
Executive Director
E-MAIL: aatseel@usc.edu
URL: www.aatseel.org

American Association of University Professors (I)
1133 19th Street, NW
Suite 200
Washington, DC 20036
(202) 737-5900
FAX: (202) 737-5526
Dr. Julie Schmid
Executive Director
E-MAIL: aaup@aaup.org
URL: www.aaup.org

American Bar Association Section of Legal Education and Admissions to the Bar (J)
321 North Clark Street
21st Floor
Chicago, IL 60654
(312) 988-6746
Mr. William E. Adams
Managing Director Accreditation & Legal Education
E-MAIL: legaled@americanbar.org
URL: www.americanbar.org/groups/legal_education

American Board of Funeral Service Education Committee on Accreditation (K)
992 Mantua Pike
Suite 108
Woodbury Heights, NJ 08097
(816) 233-3747
FAX: (856) 579-7354
Robert C. Smith III
Executive Director
E-MAIL: exdir@abfse.org
URL: www.abfse.org

American Catholic Philosophical Association (L)
University of St. Thomas
Center for Thomistic Studies
3800 Montrose Boulevard
Houston, TX 77006
(713) 942-3483
FAX: (713) 525-6964
Dr. Brian Carl
Secretary
E-MAIL: acpa@stthom.edu
URL: www.acpaweb.org

American Chemical Society Approval Program Office (M)
1155 Sixteenth Street, NW
Washington, DC 20036
(202) 872-4589
FAX: (202) 872-6066
E-MAIL: cpt@acs.org
URL: www.acs.org/acsapprovalprogram

American College of Nurse-Midwives (N)
8403 Colesville Road
Suite 1230
Silver Spring, MD 20910
(240) 485-1800
FAX: (240) 485-1818
Ms. Katrina Holland
Chief Executive Officer
E-MAIL: info@acnm.org
URL: www.midwife.org

American College Personnel Association (ACPA) (O)
1 Dupont Circle, NW
Suite 300
Washington, DC 20036-1188
(202) 835-2272
FAX: (202) 827-0601
Mr. Chris Moody
Executive Director
E-MAIL: info@acpa.nche.edu
URL: www.myacpa.org

American Collegiate Retailing Association (P)
Montclair State University
Department of Marketing, SB 592A
1 Normal Avenue
Montclair, NJ 07043
(973) 655-7935
Dr. Patrali Chatterjee
President
E-MAIL: chatterjeep@montclair.edu
URL: www.acraretail.org

American Conference of Academic Deans (ACAD) (Q)
14460 Falls of Neuse Road
Suite 149-279
Raleigh, NC 27614
(202) 281-5115
Ms. Laura A. Matthias
Executive Director
E-MAIL: info@acad.org
URL: www.acad.org

American Council for Construction Education (R)
300 Decker Drive
Suite 330
Irving, TX 75062
(972) 600-8800
Mr. Steve Nellis
President/CEO
E-MAIL: steve.nellis@acce-hq.org
URL: www.acce-hq.org

American Council of Trustees and Alumni (S)
1730 M Street, NW
Suite 600
Washington, DC 20036-4525
(202) 467-6787
FAX: (202) 467-6784
Dr. Michael B. Poliakoff
President
E-MAIL: info@goacta.org
URL: www.goacta.org

American Council on Education (T)
1 Dupont Circle, NW
Washington, DC 20036
(202) 939-9300
Ted Mitchell
President
E-MAIL: president@acenet.edu
URL: www.acenet.edu

American Counseling Association (U)
6101 Stevenson Avenue
Suite 600
Alexandria, VA 22304
(800) 347-6647, ext. 231
FAX: (800) 473-2329
Mr. Richard Yep CAE, FASAE
Chief Executive Officer
E-MAIL: ryep@counseling.org
URL: www.counseling.org

American Culinary Federation Education Foundation Accrediting Commission (V)
6816 Southpoint Parkway
Suite 400
Jacksonville, FL 32216
(904) 824-4468
FAX: (904) 940-0741
Director of Education & Programs
E-MAIL: acf@acfchefs.net
URL: www.acfchefs.org

American Educational Research Association (W)
1430 K Street, NW
Suite 1200
Washington, DC 20005
(202) 238-3200
FAX: (202) 238-3250
Dr. Felice J. Levine
Executive Director
E-MAIL: flevine@aera.net
URL: www.aera.net

American Forensic Association (X)
PO Box 67021
Chestnut Hill, MA 02467-0001
(313) 577-2953
Dr. Kelly Young
President
E-MAIL: kelly.young@wayne.edu
URL: www.americanforensicassoc.org

American Institute of Architecture Students (Y)
1735 New York Avenue, NW
3rd Floor
Washington, DC 20006
(202) 808-0075
Ms. Ashley Ash
Interim Executive Director
E-MAIL: mailbox@aias.org
URL: www.aias.org

American Library Association Office for Accreditation (Z)
225 N. Michigan Avenue
Suite 1300
Chicago, IL 60601
(312) 280-2434
Karen O'Brien
Director, Office for Accreditation
E-MAIL: accred@ala.org
URL: www.ala.org/accreditation

American Mathematical Association of Two Year Colleges (a)
Southwest Tennessee Community College
5983 Macon Cove
Memphis, TN 38134
(901) 333-5643
FAX: (901) 333-5651
Anne Dudley
Executive Director
E-MAIL: adudley@amatyc.org
URL: www.amatyc.org

American Occupational Therapy Association Accreditation Council for Occupational Therapy Education (ACOTE) (b)
6116 Executive Boulevard
Suite 200
North Bethesda, MD 20852-4929
(301) 652-6611 Ext. 2981
FAX: (240) 762-5140
Dr. Teresa Brininger
Director of Accreditation
E-MAIL: accred@aota.org
URL: acoteonline.org

American Optometric Association Accreditation Council on Optometric Education (c)
243 North Lindbergh Boulevard
Floor 1
St. Louis, MO 63141
(314) 991-4100
FAX: (314) 991-4101
Director
E-MAIL: accredit@aoa.org
URL: www.theacoe.org

American Osteopathic Association (d)
Commission on Osteopathic College Accreditation
142 East Ontario Street
Chicago, IL 60611-2864
(312) 202-8124
Jed Brinton JD
Secretary
E-MAIL: jbrinton@osteopathic.org
URL: osteopathic.org/accreditation

American Physical Therapy Association (e)
3030 Potomac Avenue
Suite 100
Alexandria, VA 22305-3085
(703) 684-2782
Mr. Justin Moore
Chief Executive Officer
E-MAIL: dorisellmore@apta.org
URL: www.apta.org

American Political Science Association (f)
1527 New Hampshire Avenue, NW
Washington, DC 20036
(202) 483-2512
FAX: (202) 483-2657
Dr. Steven Rathgeb Smith
Executive Director
E-MAIL: apsa@apsanet.org
URL: www.apsanet.org

American Psychological Association Office of Program Consultation & Accreditation (g)
750 First Street, NE
Washington, DC 20002-4242
(202) 336-5979
FAX: (202) 336-5978
Dr. Jacqueline Remondet Wall
Director
E-MAIL: apaaccred@apa.org
URL: accreditation.apa.org

American Real Estate and Urban Economics Association (h)
c/o Travelink
404 BNA Drive, Suite 650
Nashville, TN 37217
(800) 242-0528
FAX: (615) 367-0012
E-MAIL: areuea@travelink.com
URL: www.areuea.org

American Society for Engineering Education (A)
1818 N Street, NW
Suite 600
Washington, DC 20036
(202) 331-3545
FAX: (202) 265-8504
Dr. Norman L. Fortenberry
Executive Director
E-MAIL: n.fortenberry@asee.org
URL: www.asee.org

American Society for Microbiology (B)
1752 N Street, NW
Washington, DC 20036
(202) 942-9264
Ms. Irene Hulede
Director, Education
E-MAIL: education@asmusa.org
URL: www.asm.org

American Society for Microbiology Subcommittee on Postgraduate Educational Programs (C)
1752 N Street, NW
Washington, DC 20036-2804
(202) 942-9281
Ms. Sue Williams
Program Coordinator
E-MAIL: certification@asmusa.org
URL: www.asm.org/fellowships/cpep/

American Speech-Language-Hearing Association (ASHA) (D)
2200 Research Boulevard
Rockville, MD 20850
(301) 296-5700
Dr. Arlene A. Pietranton
Chief Executive Officer
E-MAIL: apietranton@asha.org
URL: www.asha.org

American Student Government Association (E)
412 NW 16th Avenue
Suite 4
Gainesville, FL 32601-4203
(352) 373-6907
FAX: (352) 373-8120
Mr. Butch Oxendine Jr.
Executive Director
E-MAIL: butch@asgaonline.com
URL: www.asgahome.org

American Veterinary Medical Association (F)
1931 North Meacham Road
Suite 100
Schaumburg, IL 60173
(800) 248-2862
FAX: (847) 925-1329
Dr. Karen Martens Brandt
Director Education and Research
E-MAIL: kbrandt@avma.org
URL: www.avma.org

APPA-Leadership in Educational Facilities (G)
PO Box 29
Alexandria, VA 22313-0029
(703) 684-1446
E. Lander Medlin
President & CEO
E-MAIL: lander@appa.org
URL: www.appa.org

Association for Asian Studies (H)
825 Victors Way
Suite 310
Ann Arbor, MI 48108
(734) 665-2490
FAX: (734) 665-3801
Ms. Hilary Finchum-Sung
Executive Director
E-MAIL: hvfinchum@asianstudies.org
URL: www.asianstudies.org

Association for Biblical Higher Education Commission on Accreditation (I)
5850 T.G. Lee Boulevard
Suite 130
Orlando, FL 32822
(407) 207-0808
FAX: (407) 207-0840
Dr. Lisa L. Beatty
Director, Commission on Accreditation
E-MAIL: lisa.beatty@abhe.org
URL: www.abhe.org

Association for Business Communication (J)
P.O. Box 304
Natural Bridge Sta, VA 24579-0304
(540) 231-1939
Dr. Jim Dubinsky
Executive Director
E-MAIL: exec_director@businesscommunication.org
URL: www.businesscommunication.org

Association for Business Simulation and Experiential Learning (K)
Lander University
College of Business
320 Stanley Avenue
Greenwood, SC 29649
(864) 388-8232
FAX: (864) 388-8020
Dr. Mick Fekula
VP/Executive Director
E-MAIL: mfekula@lander.edu
URL: www.absel.org

Association for Chaplaincy and Spiritual Life in Higher Education (L)
,
(203) 432-8751
Maytal Saltiel
President
E-MAIL: maytal.saltiel@yale.edu
URL: www.acslhe.org

Association for Collaborative Leadership (ACL) (M)
5329 Fayette Avenue
Madison, WI 53713
(608) 571-7096
E-MAIL: admin@national-acl.org
URL: www.national-acl.org

Association for Continuing Higher Education (N)
2900 Delk Road
Suite 700, PMB 321
Marietta, GA 30067
(423) 251-5100
Dr. Tina Marie Coolidge
President
E-MAIL: admin@acheinc.org
URL: www.acheinc.org

Association for Education and Rehabilitation of the Blind and Visually Impaired AER Accreditation Program (O)
5680 King Centre Drive
Suite 600
Alexandria, VA 22315
(703) 671-4500
Mr. Mark Richert
Interim Executive Director
E-MAIL: accreditation@aerbvi.org
URL: www.aerbvi.org

Association for Education in Journalism and Mass Communication (P)
234 Outlet Pointe Boulevard
Suite A
Columbia, SC 29210-5667
(803) 798-0271
FAX: (803) 772-3509
Ms. Amanda Caldwell
Interim Executive Director
E-MAIL: amanda@aejmc.org
URL: www.aejmc.org

Association for General and Liberal Studies (Q)
428 5th Street
Columbus, IN 47201
(812) 376-7468
Ms. Joyce Lucke
Executive Director
E-MAIL: execdir@agls.org
URL: www.agls.org

Association for Information Systems (R)
PO Box 2712
Atlanta, GA 30301-2712
(404) 413-7445
Mr. Matthew Nelson
Associate Executive Director
E-MAIL: matt@aisnet.org
URL: aisnet.org

Association for Institutional Research (S)
P.O. Box 13739
Tallahassee, FL 32317
(850) 385-4155
FAX: (850) 385-5180
Dr. Christine M. Keller
Executive Director & CEO
E-MAIL: ckeller@airweb.org
URL: www.airweb.org

Association for Library and Information Science Education (ALISE) (T)
4 Lan Drive
Suite 310
Westford, MA 01886
(978) 674-6190
FAX: (978) 250-1117
Ms. Cambria Happ
Executive Director
E-MAIL: office@alise.org
URL: www.alise.org

Association for Prevention Teaching and Research (U)
1001 Connecticut Avenue, NW
Suite 610
Washington, DC 20036
(202) 463-0550
FAX: (202) 463-0555
Ms. Allison L. Lewis
Executive Director
E-MAIL: info@aptrweb.org
URL: www.aptrweb.org

Association for the Study of Higher Education (ASHE) (V)
4505 South Maryland Parkway
Box 453068 CEB141
Las Vegas, NV 89154-3068
(702) 895-2737
Dr. Jason P. Guilbeau
Executive Director
E-MAIL: office@ashe.ws
URL: www.ashe.ws

Association for Theatre in Higher Education (ATHE) (W)
PO Box 922
Santa Cruz, CA 95061
(628) 222-4088
Ms. Aimee Zygmonski
Executive Director
E-MAIL: info@athe.org
URL: www.athe.org

Association of Advanced Rabbinical and Talmudic Schools Accreditation Commission (X)
11 Broadway
Suite 405
New York, NY 10004
(212) 363-1991
FAX: (212) 533-5335
Dr. Bernard Fryshman
Interim Executive Director
E-MAIL: office@aarts-schools.org

Association of American Colleges & Universities (Y)
1818 R Street, NW
Washington, DC 20009
(202) 387-3760
Dr. Lynn Pasquerella
President
E-MAIL: commish@aacu.org
URL: www.aacu.org

Association of American Law Schools (Z)
1614 20th Street, NW
Washington, DC 20009-1001
(202) 296-8851
FAX: (202) 296-8869
Ms. Judith Areen
Executive Director
E-MAIL: info@aals.org
URL: www.aals.org

Association of American Medical Colleges (a)
655 K Street, NW
Suite 100
Washington, DC 20001-2399
(202) 828-0460
Dr. David J. Skorton
President/CEO
E-MAIL: aamcpresident@aamc.org
URL: www.aamc.org

Association of American Universities (b)
1200 New York Avenue, NW
Suite 550
Washington, DC 20005
(202) 408-7500
FAX: (202) 408-8184
Dr. Barbara R. Snyder
President
E-MAIL: leah.norton@aau.edu
URL: www.aau.edu

Association of Catholic Colleges and Universities (c)
1 Dupont Circle, NW
Suite 650
Washington, DC 20036
(202) 457-0650
FAX: (202) 728-0977
Rev. Dennis H. Holtschneider C.M.,Ph.D.
President
E-MAIL: skerr-porcari@accunet.org
URL: www.accunet.org

Association of College and University Housing Officers-International (d)
1445 Summit Street
Columbus, OH 43201-2105
(614) 292-0099
FAX: (614) 292-3205
Ms. Mary DeNiro
CEO/Executive Director
E-MAIL: office@acuho-i.org
URL: www.acuho-i.org

Association of College Unions International (ACUI) (e)
One City Centre, Suite 200
120 West Seventh Street
Bloomington, IN 47404-3839
(812) 245-2284
Dr. John Taylor
Chief Executive Officer
E-MAIL: acui@acui.org
URL: www.acui.org

Association of Collegiate Conference and Events Directors-International (ACCED-I) (f)
1001-A East Harmony Road
#516
Fort Collins, CO 80525
(970) 449-4960, ext. 4
FAX: (970) 449-4965
Ms. Karen Nedbal
Executive Director
E-MAIL: karen@acced-i.org
URL: www.acced-i.org

Association of Collegiate Schools of Architecture (g)
1735 New York Avenue, NW
Suite 300
Washington, DC 20006
(202) 785-2324
Michael Monti Ph.D.
Executive Director
E-MAIL: mmonti@acsa-arch.org
URL: www.acsa-arch.org

Association of Collegiate Schools of Planning (h)
c/o Donna Dodd, Executive Director
2910 Kerry Forest Parkway, D4-206
Tallahassee, FL 32309
(850) 385-2054
Dr. Marlon Boarnet
President
E-MAIL: presidentsoffice@acsp.org
URL: www.acsp.org

Association of Community College Trustees (i)
1101 17th Street NW
Suite 300
Washington, DC 20036
(202) 775-4667
Jee Hang Lee
President and CEO
E-MAIL: president@acct.org
URL: www.acct.org

Association of Departments of English (j)
85 Broad Street
Suite 500
New York, NY 10004-2434
(646) 576-5136
Mr. Stephen Olsen
Interim Director
E-MAIL: solsen@mla.org
URL: ade.mla.org

Higher Education Associations

Association of Departments of Foreign Languages (A)
85 Broad Street
Suite 500
New York, NY 10004-2434
(646) 576-5153
FAX: (646) 576-5160
Dr. Lydia B. Tang
Associate Director
E-MAIL: ltang@mla.org
URL: www.adfl.mla.org

Association of Governing Boards of Universities and Colleges (B)
1133 20th Street, NW
Suite 300
Washington, DC 20036
(202) 296-8400
FAX: (202) 223-7053
Mr. Henry V. Stoever
President and CEO
E-MAIL: hwoelk@agb.org
URL: www.agb.org

Association of Graduate Liberal Studies Programs (C)
c/o Rice University
6100 Main Street, MS-550
Houston, TX 77005
(713) 348-6118
Mr. Christopher Pastore
President
E-MAIL: info@aglsp.org
URL: www.aglsp.org

Association of International Education Administrators-AIEA (D)
811 Ninth Street
Suite 215
Durham, NC 27705
(919) 893-4980
Dr. Darla K. Deardorff
Executive Director
E-MAIL: info@aieaworld.org
URL: www.aieaworld.org

Association of Jesuit Colleges and Universities (E)
1 Dupont Circle, NW
Suite 405
Washington, DC 20036
(202) 862-9893
Rev. Michael J. Garanzini S.J.
President
E-MAIL: info@ajcunet.edu
URL: www.ajcunet.edu

Association of Military Colleges and Schools of the United States (F)
Arnold, MD
(703) 272-8406
Ray Rottman
Executive Director
E-MAIL: amcsus1@gmail.com
URL: www.amcsus.org

Association of Performing Arts Professionals (G)
919 18th Street, NW
Suite 650
Washington, DC 20006
(202) 207-3844
FAX: (202) 833-1543
Ms. Lisa Richards Toney
President and CEO
E-MAIL: executiveoffice@apap365.org
URL: www.apap365.org

Association of Practical Theology (H)
,
(303) 765-3139
Kathrine Turpin
President
E-MAIL: kturpin@iliff.edu
URL: www.practicaltheology.org

Association of Presbyterian Colleges and Universities (I)
c/o Agnes Scott College
Box 1102
141 E. College Avenue
Decatur, GA 30030
(470) 443-1948
Mr. Jeff Arnold
Executive Director
E-MAIL: jeff.arnold@presbyteriancolleges.org
URL: www.presbyteriancolleges.org

Association of Public and Land-Grant Universities (J)
1220 L Street, NW
Suite 1000
Washington, DC 20005
(202) 478-6040
FAX: (202) 478-6046
Mr. Peter McPherson
President
E-MAIL: pmcpherson@aplu.org
URL: www.aplu.org

Association of Research Libraries (K)
21 Dupont Circle, NW
Suite 800
Washington, DC 20036
(202) 296-2296
FAX: (202) 872-0884
Mary Lee Kennedy
Executive Director
E-MAIL: mkennedy@arl.org
URL: arl.org

Association of Schools Advancing Health Professions (L)
122 C Street, NW
Suite 200
Washington, DC 20001-2109
(202) 237-6481
Mr. John Colbert
Executive Director
E-MAIL: john@asahp.org
URL: www.asahp.org

Association of Specialized and Professional Accreditors (M)
3023 N. Clark Street
#317
Chicago, IL 60657
(773) 857-7900
Mr. Joseph Vibert
Executive Director
E-MAIL: jvibert@aspa-usa.org
URL: aspa-usa.org

Association of Teacher Educators (N)
PO Box 793
Manassas, VA 20113
(703) 659-1708
Alisa Chapman
Executive Director
E-MAIL: achapman@ate1.org
URL: www.ate1.org

The Association of Technology, Management, and Applied Engineering (ATMAE) (O)
486 Cornell Road
Blairsville, PA 15717
(919) 635-8335
Dean Bartles Ph.D.
Executive Director
E-MAIL: admin@atmae.org
URL: www.atmae.org

Association of Theological Schools in the United States and Canada The Commission on Accrediting (P)
10 Summit Park Drive
Pittsburgh, PA 15275-1110
(412) 788-6505
FAX: (412) 788-6510
Dr. Frank M. Yamada
Executive Director
E-MAIL: yamada@ats.edu
URL: www.ats.edu

Association of University Presses (Q)
1412 Broadway
Suite 2135
New York, NY 10018
(212) 989-1010
FAX: (212) 989-0275
Peter M. Berkery Jr.
Executive Director
E-MAIL: pberkery@aupresses.org
URL: www.aupresses.org

Association of University Programs in Health Administration (R)
1730 M Street, NW
Suite 407
Washington, DC 20036
(202) 763-7283
Daniel Gentry Ph.D., MHA
President & CEO
E-MAIL: aupha@aupha.org
URL: www.aupha.org

Association of University Research Parks (S)
9070 South Rita Road
Suite 1750
Tucson, AZ 85747
(520) 529-2521
Mr. Brian Darmody
Chief Executive Officer
E-MAIL: info@aurp.net
URL: www.aurp.net

Aviation Accreditation Board International (T)
115 S. 8th Street
Suite 102
Opelika, AL 36801
(334) 748-9359
FAX: (334) 748-9360
Guy Smith Ph.D.
President
E-MAIL: victoria@aabi.aero
URL: www.aabi.aero

Big Ten Academic Alliance (U)
1819 South Neil Street
Suite D
Champaign, IL 61820-7271
(217) 244-9849
FAX: (217) 244-7127
Ms. Kara McKinn
Coordinator Communications
E-MAIL: kara.mckinn@btaa.org
URL: btaa.org

Broadcast Education Association (V)
1 M Street, SE
Washington, DC 20003
(202) 602-0584
FAX: (202) 609-9940
Ms. Heather Birks
Executive Director
E-MAIL: heather@beaweb.org
URL: www.beaweb.org

Career Education Colleges & Universities (W)
1530 Wilson Boulevard
Suite 1050
Arlington, VA 22209
(571) 970-3941
FAX: (866) 363-2181
Dr. Jason Altmire
President and CEO
E-MAIL: president@career.org
URL: www.career.org

Carnegie Foundation for the Advancement of Teaching (X)
51 Vista Lane
Stanford, CA 94305
(650) 566-5100
FAX: (650) 326-0278
Dr. Timothy Knowles
President
URL: www.carnegiefoundation.org

College and University Professional Association for Human Resources (CUPA-HR) (Y)
1811 Commons Point Drive
Knoxville, TN 37932
(877) 287-2474
FAX: (865) 637-7674
Mr. Andy Brantley
President & Chief Executive Officer
E-MAIL: memberservice@cupahr.org
URL: cupahr.org

College Art Association (Z)
50 Broadway
21st Floor
New York, NY 10004
(212) 691-1051
FAX: (212) 627-2381
Ms. Meme Omogbai
Executive Director
E-MAIL: nyoffice@collegeart.org
URL: www.collegeart.org

The College Board (a)
250 Vesey Street
New York, NY 10281
(212) 713-8000
Mr. Jeremy Singer
President
URL: www.collegeboard.org

College English Association (b)
1100 E. Fifth Street
Anderson, IN 46012
(765) 641-4424
Mr. Scott Borders
Executive Director
E-MAIL: cea.english@gmail.com
URL: cea-web.org

College Media Association (c)
355 Lexington Avenue
15th Floor
New York, NY 10017
(212) 297-2195
Meredith Taylor
Executive Director
E-MAIL: mltaylor@kellencompany.com
URL: www.collegemedia.org

Columbia Scholastic Press Association (d)
Columbia University
90 Morningside Drive
Suite B01
New York, NY 10027
(212) 854-9400
Mr. Edmund J. Sullivan
Executive Director
E-MAIL: cspa@columbia.edu
URL: www.cspa.columbia.edu

Commission on Accreditation for Health Informatics and Information Management Education (CAHIIM) (e)
200 E. Randolph Street
Suite 5100
Chicago, IL 60601
(312) 235-3255
Dr. Angela Kennedy
Chief Executive Officer
E-MAIL: info@cahiim.org
URL: www.cahiim.org

Commission on Accreditation of Allied Health Education Programs (f)
9355 - 113th Street N. #7709
Seminole, FL 33775
(727) 210-2350
FAX: (727) 210-2354
Kathleen Megivern J.D.
Executive Director
E-MAIL: megivern@caahep.org
URL: www.caahep.org

Commission on Accreditation of Healthcare Management Education (CAHME) (g)
PO Box 911
Spring House, PA 19477
(301) 298-1825
Dr. Anthony Stanowski
President & CEO
E-MAIL: astanowski@cahme.org
URL: cahme.org

Commission on Collegiate Nursing Education (CCNE) (h)
655 K Street NW
Suite 750
Washington, DC 20001
(202) 887-6791
FAX: (202) 887-8476
Dr. Jennifer Butlin
Executive Director
E-MAIL: jbutlin@ccneaccreditation.org
URL: www.ccneaccreditation.org

Commission on Dental Accreditation (i)
211 East Chicago Avenue
Suite 1900
Chicago, IL 60611
(312) 440-4653
Dr. Sherin Tooks
Director
E-MAIL: tooks@ada.org
URL: ada.org/en/coda

Commission on English Language Program Accreditation (CEA) (j)
1001 North Fairfax Street
Suite 630
Alexandria, VA 22314
(703) 665-3400
Dr. Heidi E. Vellenga
Executive Director
E-MAIL: hvellenga@cea-accredit.org
URL: www.cea-accredit.org

The Commission on Independent Colleges and Universities (CICU) in New York (A)
17 Elk Street
Albany, NY 12207
(518) 436-4781
Ms. Lola W. Brabham
President
E-MAIL: info@cicu.org
URL: www.cicu.org

Commission on Massage Therapy Accreditation (B)
900 Commonwealth Place
Suite 200-331
Virginia Beach, VA 23464
(202) 888-6790
FAX: (202) 888-6787
Ms. Dawn Hogue
Executive Director
E-MAIL: dhogue@comta.org
URL: www.comta.org

Commission on Opticianry Accreditation (C)
PO Box 592
Canton, NY 13617
(703) 468-0566
Mrs. Debra White
Director of Accreditation
E-MAIL: director@coaccreditation.com
URL: www.coaccreditation.com

Committee on Accreditation for Education in Neurodiagnostic Technology (D)
1449 Hill Street
Whitinsville, MA 01588
(978) 338-6300
FAX: (978) 832-2638
Dr. Jackie Long-Goding PhD,RRTNPS
Executive Director
E-MAIL: office@coa-ndt.org
URL: www.coa-ndt.org

Committee on Accreditation of Education Programs for Kinesiotherapy (CoA-KT) (E)
University of Southern Mississippi
118 College Drive #5122
Hattiesburg, MS 39406-0002
(601) 266-5371
Jerry W. Purvis
E-MAIL: jerry.purvis@usm.edu
URL: www.caahep.org/about-caahep/committees-on-accreditation/kine

Committee on Accreditation for the Exercise Sciences (F)
401 West Michigan Street
Indianapolis, IN 46202
(317) 777-1135
FAX: (317) 634-7817
Mr. William Coale
Director
E-MAIL: wcoale@coaes.org
URL: www.coaes.org

Committee on Accreditation for Polysomnographic Technologist Education (G)
1711 Frank Avenue
New Bern, NC 28560
(252) 626-3238
Ms. Karen Monarchy Rowe
Executive Director
E-MAIL: karenmonarchy@suddenlink.net
URL: caahep.org/about-caahep/committees-on-accreditation/polysomn

Committee on Accreditation of Educational Programs for the Emergency Medical Services Professions (H)
8301 Lakeview Parkway
Suite 111-312
Rowlett, TX 75088
(214) 703-8445, ext. 112
FAX: (214) 703-8992
Dr. George W. Hatch Jr.
Executive Director
E-MAIL: george@coaemsp.org
URL: www.coaemsp.org

Conference on College Composition and Communication (I)
340 N. Neil Street #104
Champaign, IL 61820
(877) 369-6283
Dr. David F. Green
Secretary
E-MAIL: cccc@ncte.org
URL: https://cccc.ncte.org/

Council for Accreditation of Counseling and Related Educational Programs (CACREP) (J)
500 Montgomery Street
Suite 350
Alexandria, VA 22314
(703) 535-5990
Dr. M. Sylvia Fernandez
President and CEO
E-MAIL: cacrep@cacrep.org
URL: www.cacrep.org

Council for Adult and Experiential Learning (K)
10 W. Market Street
Suite 1100
Indianapolis, IN 46204
(312) 499-2600
Ms. Jeannie McCarron
Senior Director, Member Engagemenet
E-MAIL: jmccarron@cael.org
URL: www.cael.org

Council for Advancement and Support of Education (L)
1201 Eye Street, NW
Suite 530A
Washington, DC 20005
(202) 328-2273
FAX: (202) 387-4973
Ms. Sue Cunningham
President and CEO
E-MAIL: president@case.org
URL: www.case.org

Council for Agricultural Science and Technology (CAST) (M)
4420 West Lincoln Way
Ames, IA 50014-3447
(515) 292-2125
Mr. Kent G. Schescke
Executive Vice President
E-MAIL: cast@cast-science.org
URL: www.cast-science.org

Council for Aid to Education (N)
1732 1st Avenue
#21535
New York, NY 10128
(212) 661-5800
Dr. Robert Yayac
President & CEO
E-MAIL: info@cae.org
URL: www.cae.org

Council for Christian Colleges & Universities (O)
321 8th Street, NE
Washington, DC 20002-6107
(202) 546-8713
Shirley V. Hoogstra J.D.
President
E-MAIL: council@cccu.org
URL: www.cccu.org

Council for Economic Education (P)
122 East 42nd Street
Suite 1012
New York, NY 10168
(212) 730-7007
FAX: (212) 730-1793
Ms. Nan Morrison
President and CEO
E-MAIL: njmorrison@councilforeconed.org
URL: www.councilforeconed.org

Council for Higher Education Accreditation (Q)
1 Dupont Circle, NW
Suite 510
Washington, DC 20036
(202) 955-6126
FAX: (202) 955-6129
Dr. Cynthia Jackson-Hammond
President
E-MAIL: chea@chea.org
URL: chea.org

Council for Interior Design Accreditation (CIDA) (formerly FIDER) (R)
206 Grandville Avenue
Suite 350
Grand Rapids, MI 49503-4014
(616) 970-6668
Ms. Holly Mattson
Executive Director
E-MAIL: info@accredit-id.org
URL: www.accredit-id.org

Council for Research in Music Education (S)
University of Illinois at Urbana-Champaign
School of Music
1114 W. Nevada
Urbana, IL 61801
(217) 244-6310
Dr. Janet R. Barrett
Editor
E-MAIL: janetbar@illinois.edu
URL: bcrme.press.illinois.edu

Council for the Accreditation of Educator Preparation (T)
1140 19th Street, NW
Suite 400
Washington, DC 20036
(202) 223-0077
Mr. Christopher Koch
President
E-MAIL: caep@caepnet.org
URL: www.caepnet.org

Council for the Advancement of Standards in Higher Education (U)
2598 E. Sunrise Boulevard
Suite 2014
Fort Lauderdale, FL 33304
(800) 889-7270
Ms. Doreen Murner
Executive Director
E-MAIL: executive_director@cas.edu
URL: www.cas.edu

Council of Colleges of Acupuncture and Herbal Medicine (CCAHM) (V)
1501 Sulgrave Avenue
Suite 301
Baltimore, MD 21209
(410) 464-6041
FAX: (410) 464-6042
Ms. Roberta Herman MBA, CAE
Executive Director
E-MAIL: rherman@ccahm.org
URL: www.ccahm.org

Council of Colleges of Arts & Sciences (W)
,
(952) 641-3037
Amber Elaine Cox MSW
Executive Director
E-MAIL: connect@ccas.net
URL: www.ccas.net

Council of Graduate Schools (X)
1 Dupont Circle, NW
Suite 230
Washington, DC 20036-1146
(202) 223-3791
FAX: (202) 331-7157
Dr. Suzanne Ortega
President
E-MAIL: president@cgs.nche.edu
URL: www.cgsnet.org

Council of Independent Colleges (Y)
1 Dupont Circle, NW
Suite 320
Washington, DC 20036-1142
(202) 466-7230
Dr. Marjorie Hass
President
E-MAIL: cic@cic.nche.edu
URL: www.cic.edu

The Council of Writing Program Administrators (Z)
,
(765) 973-8637
Dr. Kelly Blewett
Secretary
E-MAIL: cwpasecretary@gmail.com
URL: www.wpacouncil.org

Council on Academic Accreditation in Audiology and Speech-Language Pathology American Speech-Language-Hearing Association (a)
2200 Research Boulevard #310
Rockville, MD 20850
(301) 296-5796
Ms. Kimberlee Moore
Director of Accreditation
E-MAIL: accreditation@asha.org
URL: caa.asha.org

Council on Accreditation of Nurse Anesthesia Educational Programs (COA) (b)
222 South Prospect Avenue
Park Ridge, IL 60068-4001
(847) 655-1160
Francis Gerbasi Ph.D., CRN
Chief Executive Officer
E-MAIL: fgerbasi@coacrna.org
URL: www.coacrna.org

Council on Accreditation for Two-Year Colleges (c)
200 South 14th Street
Parsons, KS 67357
(620) 820-1223
FAX: (620) 421-0921
Dr. George Knox
Executive Director
E-MAIL: meganf@labette.edu
URL: www.catyc.com

Council on Accreditation of Parks, Recreation, Tourism and Related Professions (COAPRT) (d)
1401 Marvin Road NE
Suite 307, #172
Lacey, WA 98516
(360) 205-2096
FAX: (360) 453-7893
Shelley Dahle
Program Manager
E-MAIL: copart@accreditationcouncil.org
URL: www.accreditationcouncil.org

Council on Chiropractic Education (e)
10105 E. Via Linda
Suite 103, PMB 3642
Scottsdale, AZ 85258
(480) 443-8877
Craig S. Little Ed.D.
President
E-MAIL: cce@cce-usa.org
URL: www.cce-usa.org

Council on Education for Public Health (f)
1010 Wayne Avenue
Suite 220
Silver Spring, MD 20910
(202) 789-1050
Dr. Laura Rasar King
Executive Director
E-MAIL: lking@ceph.org
URL: www.ceph.org

Council on Governmental Relations (g)
1200 New York Avenue, NW
Suite 460
Washington, DC 20005
(202) 289-6655
FAX: (202) 289-6698
Ms. Wendy Streitz
President
E-MAIL: wstreitz@cogr.edu
URL: www.cogr.edu

Council on Higher Education Solutions for Adults (CHESA) (h)
303 W. Burleson Street
Marshall, TX 75670
(903) 472-2762
FAX: (903) 471-8675
Dr. Tracy Andrus Sr.
President/CEO
E-MAIL: tandrus26@gmail.com

Council on Naturopathic Medical Education (i)
PO Box 178
Great Barrington, MA 01230
(413) 528-8877
Dr. Daniel Seitz J.D., Ed.D
Executive Director
E-MAIL: danseitz@cnme.org
URL: www.cnme.org

Council on Occupational Education (j)
7840 Roswell Road
Building 300, Suite 325
Atlanta, GA 30350
(800) 917-2081
FAX: (770) 396-3790
Dr. Gary Puckett
President/Executive Director
E-MAIL: gary.puckett@council.org
URL: www.council.org

Higher Education Associations

Council on Podiatric Medical Education (A)
9312 Old Georgetown Road
Bethesda, MD 20814
(301) 581-9200
FAX: (301) 571-4903
Dr. Heather M. Stagliano
Director
E-MAIL: hmstagliano@cpme.org
URL: cpme.org

Council on Social Work Education (B)
333 John Carlyle Street
Suite 400
Alexandria, VA 22314
(703) 519-2048
Dr. Tanya Smith Brice
VP of Education
E-MAIL: tbrice@cswe.org
URL: www.cswe.org

Council on Undergraduate Research (C)
267 Kentlands Boulevard #4021
Gaithersburg, MD 20878
(202) 783-4810
FAX: (202) 783-4811
Mrs. Lindsay L. Currie
Executive Officer
E-MAIL: lcurrie@cur.org
URL: www.cur.org

CSAB, Inc. (D)
417 Terrace Way
Towson, MD 21204-3725
(410) 339-5456
Ms. Liz Glazer
Executive Director
E-MAIL: lglazer@csab.org
URL: www.csab.org

Cultural Vistas (E)
1250 H Street, NW
Suite 300
Washington, DC 20005
(212) 497-3500
Ms. Jennifer Clinton
President & CEO
E-MAIL: info@culturalvistas.org
URL: www.culturalvistas.org

Cytotechnology Programs Review Committee (CPRC) (F)
100 W. 10th Street
Suite 603
Wilmington, DE 19801
(302) 660-4944
Mr. Melvin Limson
Director, Programs and Development
E-MAIL: mlimson@apcprods.org
URL: www.caahep.org/about-caahep/committees-on-accreditation/cyto

Decision Sciences Institute (G)
University of Houston
C.T. Bauer College of Business
4750 Calhoun Road, Suite 325A
Houston, TX 77204-6021
(713) 743-4815
Ms. Vivian Landrum
Executive Director
E-MAIL: info@decisionsciences.org
URL: decisionsciences.org

Distance Education Accrediting Commission (H)
1101 17th Street, NW
Suite 808
Washington, DC 20036
(202) 234-5100
Dr. Leah K. Matthews
Executive Director
E-MAIL: info@deac.org
URL: www.deac.org

Education Commission of the States (I)
700 Broadway
Suite 810
Denver, CO 80203-3442
(303) 299-3600
Mr. Jeremy Anderson
President
E-MAIL: ecs@ecs.org
URL: www.ecs.org

Education Development Center (J)
43 Foundry Avenue
Waltham, MA 02453-8313
(617) 969-7100
FAX: (617) 969-5979
Mr. David Offensend
President and CEO
E-MAIL: contact@edc.org
URL: www.edc.org

EDUCAUSE (K)
4845 Pearl East Circle
Suite 118, PMB 43761
Boulder, CO 80301-6112
(303) 449-4430
FAX: (303) 440-0461
John O'Brien Ph.D.
President and CEO
E-MAIL: info@educause.edu
URL: www.educause.edu

Financial Management Association International (L)
University of South Florida
Muma College of Business
4202 East Fowler Avenue, BSN 3403
Tampa, FL 33620-5500
(813) 974-2084
FAX: (813) 974-3318
Ms. Michelle Lui
Executive Director
E-MAIL: fma@coba.usf.edu
URL: www.fma.org

Friends Association for Higher Education (M)
1501 Cherry Street
Philadelphia, PA 19102
(215) 241-7116
E-MAIL: fahe@quaker.org
URL: www.quakerfahe.com

The Gerontological Society of America (N)
1220 L Street, NW
Suite 901
Washington, DC 20005-4001
(202) 587-2821
Mr. James Appleby
CEO
E-MAIL: geron@geron.org
URL: www.geron.org

H. Wiley Hitchcock Institute for Studies in American Music (O)
Brooklyn College, CUNY
2900 Bedford Avenue
Brooklyn, NY 11210-2889
(718) 951-5655
Stephanie Jensen-Moulton
Director
E-MAIL: hisam@brooklyn.cuny.edu
URL: www.hisam.org

HEATH Resource Center at the National Youth Transitions Center The George Washington University Graduate School of Education & Human Development (P)
2134 G Street, NW
Suite 308
Washington, DC 20052-0001
E-MAIL: askheath@gwu.edu
URL: www.heath.gwu.edu

Higher Education Resource Services (HERS) (Q)
1901 East Asbury Avenue
Suite 220
Denver, CO 80208
(303) 871-6866
FAX: (303) 871-6766
Dr. Gloria Thomas
President
E-MAIL: gthomas@hersnetwork.org
URL: www.hersnetwork.org

Higher Learning Commission (R)
230 South LaSalle Street
Suite 7-500
Chicago, IL 60604-1411
(312) 263-0456 / (800) 621-7440
FAX: (312) 263-7462
Dr. Barbara Gellman-Danley
President
E-MAIL: info@hlcommission.org
URL: hlcommission.org

Hispanic Association of Colleges and Universities (S)
8415 Datapoint Drive
Suite 400
San Antonio, TX 78229
(210) 692-3805
FAX: (210) 692-0823
Dr. Antonio R. Flores
President and CEO
E-MAIL: hacu@hacu.net
URL: www.hacu.net

IACLEA (International Association of Campus Law Enforcement Administrators) (T)
PO Box 825345
Philadelphia, PA 19182-5345
(855) 442-2532
Mr. John Bernhards
Executive Director
E-MAIL: jbernhards@iaclea.org
URL: www.iaclea.org

The Institute for Higher Education Policy (U)
1825 K Street, NW
Suite 720
Washington, DC 20006
(202) 861-8223
FAX: (202) 861-9307
Mamie Voight
Interim President
E-MAIL: mvoight@ihep.org
URL: www.ihep.org

Institute of International Education Council for International Exchange of Scholars (V)
1400 K Street, NW
Suite 700
Washington, DC 20005
(202) 686-4000
FAX: (202) 686-4029
E-MAIL: scholars@iie.org
URL: www.cies.org

International Accreditation Council for Business Education (W)
11960 Quivira Road
Suite 300
Overland Park, KS 66213
(913) 631-3009
FAX: (913) 631-9154
Dr. Phyllis Okrepkie
President
E-MAIL: iacbe@iacbe.org
URL: www.iacbe.org

International Association of Baptist Colleges and Universities (X)
Dallas Baptist University
3000 Mountain Creek Parkway
Dallas, TX 75211
(214) 333-5186
Mrs. Ashley Hill
Executive Director
E-MAIL: ashleyhill@baptistschools.org
URL: www.baptistschools.org

International Communication Association (Y)
1500 21st Street, NW
Washington, DC 20036
(202) 955-1444
FAX: (202) 955-1448
Ms. Laura Sawyer
Executive Director
E-MAIL: lsawyer@icahdq.org
URL: www.icahdq.org

International Council on Education for Teaching (Z)
5201 University Boulevard
PLG 301
Laredo, TX 78041
(956) 326-2420
FAX: (956) 326-2419
James O'Meara
President
E-MAIL: president@icet4u.org
URL: www.icet4u.org

International Fire Service Accreditation Congress (a)
1723 W. Tyler Avenue
Stillwater, OK 74078
(405) 744-8303
FAX: (405) 744-7377
Director
E-MAIL: admin@ifsac.org
URL: ifsac.org

Joint Review Committee on Education in Cardiovascular Technology (JRC-CVT) (b)
1449 Hill Street
Whitinsville, MA 01588-1032
(978) 456-5594
FAX: (727) 210-2354
Ms. Jackie Long-Goding
Executive Director
E-MAIL: office@jrccvt.org
URL: www.jrccvt.org

Joint Review Committee on Education in Diagnostic Medical Sonography (c)
6021 University Boulevard
Suite 500
Ellicott City, MD 21043
(443) 973-3251
FAX: (866) 738-3444
Mr. Gerry Magat MS
Executive Director
E-MAIL: mail@jrcdms.org
URL: www.jrcdms.org

Joint Review Committee on Education in Radiologic Technology (d)
20 North Wacker Drive
Suite 2850
Chicago, IL 60606-3182
(312) 704-5300
FAX: (312) 704-5304
Leslie F. Winter
Chief Executive Officer
E-MAIL: lwinter@jrcert.org
URL: www.jrcert.org

Joint Review Committee on Educational Programs in Nuclear Medicine Technology (e)
820 West Danforth Road
Suite B1
Edmond, OK 73003
(405) 285-0546
FAX: (405) 285-0579
Ms. Jan M. Winn
Executive Director
E-MAIL: mail@jrcnmt.org
URL: jrcnmt.org

Journalism Association of Community Colleges (f)
c/o CNPA Services, Inc.
2701 K Street
Sacramento, CA 95816-5131
(916) 288-6021
FAX: (916) 288-6002
Mr. Joe Wirt
Administrator
E-MAIL: joe@cnpa.com
URL: jacconline.org

Landscape Architectural Accreditation Board of the American Society of Landscape Architects (g)
636 Eye Street, NW
Washington, DC 20001-3736
(202) 216-2359
FAX: (202) 898-1185
Mr. Kristopher Pritchard
Accreditation & Education Director
E-MAIL: kpritchard@asla.org
URL: asla.org/laab

Laspau (h)
25 Mount Auburn Street
Suite 200
Cambridge, MA 02138-6095
(617) 495-5255
FAX: (617) 495-8990
Ms. Angelica Natera
Executive Director
E-MAIL: angelica_natera@harvard.edu
URL: www.laspau.harvard.edu

Law School Admission Council (i)
662 Penn Street
Newtown, PA 18940
(215) 968-1162
Ms. Kellye Testy
President and CEO
E-MAIL: fwilliams@lsac.org
URL: www.lsac.org

Liaison Committee on Medical Education (LCME) American Medical Association (j)
330 North Wabash Avenue
Suite 39300
Chicago, IL 60611-5885
(312) 464-4933
Barbara Barzansky Ph.D.,MHPE
LCME Co-Secretary
E-MAIL: barbara.barzansky@ama-assn.org
URL: www.lcme.org

Linguistic Society of America (A)
522 21st Street, NW
Suite 120
Washington, DC 20006-5012
(202) 835-1714
FAX: (202) 835-1717
Ms. Alyson Reed
Executive Director
E-MAIL: lsa@lsadc.org
URL: www.linguisticsociety.org

Literacy Research Association, Inc. (B)
PO Box 3105
LaGrange, GA 30241
(706) 443-1334
FAX: (706) 883-8215
Mr. VJ Mayor
Executive Director
E-MAIL: vjmayor@asginfo.net
URL: www.LiteracyResearchAssociation.org

Lutheran Educational Conference of North America (C)
5915 S. Remington Place
Suite 100
Sioux Falls, SD 57108
(605) 271-9894
Mr. Kenneth Gaschk
E-MAIL: ken.gaschk@cuw.edu
URL: www.lutherancolleges.org

Marketing EDGE (D)
500 7th Avenue
8th Floor
New York, NY 10018
(212) 790-1512
Terri L. Bartlett
President
E-MAIL: admin@marketingedge.org
URL: www.marketingedge.org

Medical Assisting Education Review Board (E)
20 N. Wacker Drive
Suite 1575
Chicago, IL 60606-2963
(312) 392-0155
FAX: (312) 899-1259
Mr. Jim Hardman
Assistant Director of Accreditation
E-MAIL: jhardman@maerb.org
URL: www.maerb.org

Middle States Commission on Higher Education (F)
3624 Market Street
Suite 2 West
Philadelphia, PA 19104-2680
(267) 284-5025
FAX: (215) 662-5501
Dr. Heather F. Perfetti
President
E-MAIL: president@msche.org
URL: www.msche.org

Midwest Association of Colleges and Employers (G)
1101 North Delaware Street
Indianapolis, IN 46202
(866) 606-1316
E-MAIL: admin@mwace.org
URL: www.mwace.org

Midwestern Higher Education Compact (MHEC) (H)
105 Fifth Avenue South
Suite 450
Minneapolis, MN 55401
(612) 677-2777
FAX: (612) 767-3353
Ms. Susan G. Heegaard
President
E-MAIL: susanh@mhec.org
URL: www.mhec.org

Midwifery Education Accreditation Council (MEAC) (I)
850 Mt. Pleasant Avenue
Ann Arbor, MI 48103
(360) 466-2080, ext. 0
Ms. Beatrix Packmohr
Executive Director
E-MAIL: info@meacschools.org
URL: www.meacschools.org

Modern Language Association (J)
85 Broad Street
Suite 500
New York, NY 10004-2434
(646) 576-5000
FAX: (646) 458-0030
Dr. Paula M. Krebs
Executive Director
E-MAIL: execdirector@mla.org
URL: mla.org

Montessori Accreditation Council for Teacher Education (MACTE) (K)
420 Park Street
Charlottesville, VA 22902
(434) 202-7793
Dr. Rebecca Pelton
President
E-MAIL: rebecca@macte.org
URL: www.macte.org

NACADA: The Global Community for Academic Advising (L)
Kansas State University
2323 Anderson Avenue
Suite 225
Manhattan, KS 66502-2912
(785) 532-5717
FAX: (785) 532-7732
Ms. Melinda Anderson
Executive Director
E-MAIL: nacada@ksu.edu
URL: www.nacada.ksu.edu

NACAS (M)
435 Merchant Walk Square
Suite 300-139
Charlottesville, VA 22902
(434) 245-8425
FAX: (434) 245-8453
Mr. Matt Marcial
CEO
E-MAIL: info@nacas.org
URL: www.nacas.org

NASPA-Student Affairs Administrators in Higher Education (N)
111 K Street, NE
10th Floor
Washington, DC 20002-4409
(202) 265-7500
Dr. Kevin Kruger
President
E-MAIL: office@naspa.org
URL: www.naspa.org

The National Academy of Education (O)
500 5th Street, NW
Washington, DC 20001
(202) 334-2341
Mr. Gregory White
Executive Director
E-MAIL: info@naeducation.org
URL: www.naeducation.org

National Academy of Kinesiology (P)
2001 Juniper Drive
Mahomet, IL 61853
(217) 800-1156
FAX: (217) 590-0528
Ms. Kim Scott
Business Manager
E-MAIL: staff@nationalacademyofkinesiology.org
URL: nationalacademyofkinesiology.org

National Accrediting Agency for Clinical Laboratory Sciences (Q)
5600 North River Road
Suite 720
Rosemont, IL 60018
(773) 714-8880
FAX: (773) 714-8886
Dianne M. Cearlock Ph.D.
CEO
E-MAIL: dcearlock@naacls.org
URL: www.naacls.org

National Accrediting Commission of Career Arts & Sciences (R)
3015 Colvin Street
Alexandria, VA 22314
(703) 600-7600
Tony Mirando M.S., D.C.
Executive Director
E-MAIL: amirando@naccas.org
URL: www.naccas.org

National Association for College Admission Counseling (S)
1050 North Highland Street
Suite 400
Arlington, VA 22201
(703) 836-2222
FAX: (703) 243-9375
Angel B. Perez
Chief Executive Officer
E-MAIL: ceo@nacacnet.org
URL: www.nacacnet.org

National Association for Equal Opportunity in Higher Education (T)
110 Maryland Avenue, NE
Suite 509
Washington, DC 20002
(202) 552-3300
FAX: (202) 552-3330
Lezli Baskerville Esquire
President & CEO
E-MAIL: lbaskerville@nafeo.org
URL: www.nafeonation.org

National Association for the Legal Support of Alternative Schools (U)
18520 N.W. 67th Avenue #188
Miami, FL 33015
(800) 456-7784
Mrs. Chau Trinh
Institutional Representative
E-MAIL: educate@nalsas.org
URL: www.nalsas.org

National Association for Practical Nurse Education and Service, Inc. (V)
2071 N. Bechtle Avenue
PMB 307
Springfield, OH 45504
(703) 933-1003
FAX: (703) 940-4089
Ann Bauer LPN
President
E-MAIL: president@napnes.org
URL: www.napnes.org

National Association of Agricultural Educators (W)
One Paragon Centre
2525 Harrodsburg Road
Suite 200
Lexington, KY 40504-3358
(859) 967-2892
Alissa Smith
Executive Director
E-MAIL: asmith.naae@uky.edu
URL: www.naae.org

National Association of College and University Attorneys (X)
1 Dupont Circle, NW
Suite 620
Washington, DC 20036
(202) 833-8390
Ona Alston Dosunmu
President & CEO
E-MAIL: odosunmu@nacua.org
URL: www.nacua.org

National Association of College and University Business Officers (Y)
1110 Vermont Avenue, NW
Suite 800
Washington, DC 20005
(202) 861-2500
FAX: (202) 861-2583
Ms. Susan W. Johnston
President
E-MAIL: susan.johnston@nacubo.org
URL: nacubo.org

The National Association of College & University Food Services (Z)
1515 Turf Lane
Suite 100
East Lansing, MI 48823
(517) 332-2494
FAX: (517) 332-8144
E-MAIL: membership@nacufs.org
URL: www.nacufs.org

National Association of College Stores (a)
500 East Lorain Street
Oberlin, OH 44074
(440) 775-7777
FAX: (440) 775-4769
Mr. Ed Schlichenmayer
Chief Executive Officer
E-MAIL: info@nacs.org
URL: www.nacs.org

National Association of College Wind and Percussion Instructors (b)
Station 6670
Montevallo, AL 35115
(940) 898-2588
Ms. Danielle Woolery
President
E-MAIL: dwoolery@twu.edu
URL: www.nacwpi.org

National Association of Colleges and Employers (c)
62 Highland Avenue
Bethlehem, PA 18017-9481
(610) 868-1421
FAX: (610) 868-0208
Mr. Shawn VanDerziel
Executive Director
E-MAIL: svanderziel@nacedweb.org
URL: www.naceweb.org

National Association of Correctional Education Standards and Accreditation (NACESA) (d)
303 W. Burleson Street
Marshall, TX 75670
(903) 472-2762
FAX: (903) 471-8675
Dr. Tracy L. Andrus Sr.
E-MAIL: tandrus26@gmail.com

National Association of Educational Procurement (e)
7918 Jones Branch Drive
Suite 300
McLean, VA 22102-3345
(443) 281-9901
Ms. Krista Ferrell
Executive Director
E-MAIL: kferrell@naepnet.org
URL: www.naepnet.org

National Association of Independent Colleges and Universities (f)
1025 Connecticut Avenue, NW
Suite 700
Washington, DC 20036-5405
(202) 785-8866
FAX: (202) 835-0003
Dr. Barbara Mistick
President
E-MAIL: geninfo@naicu.edu
URL: naicu.edu

National Association of Schools of Art and Design (g)
11250 Roger Bacon Drive
Suite 21
Reston, VA 20190
(703) 437-0700
FAX: (703) 437-6312
Karen P. Moynahan
Executive Director
E-MAIL: info@arts-accredit.org
URL: nasad.arts-accredit.org

National Association of Schools of Dance (h)
11250 Roger Bacon Drive
Suite 21
Reston, VA 20190
(703) 437-0700
FAX: (703) 437-6312
Karen P. Moynahan
Executive Director
E-MAIL: info@arts-accredit.org
URL: nasd.arts-accredit.org

National Association of Schools of Music (i)
11250 Roger Bacon Drive
Suite 21
Reston, VA 20190
(703) 437-0700
FAX: (703) 437-6312
Karen P. Moynahan
Executive Director
E-MAIL: info@arts-accredit.org
URL: nasm.arts-accredit.org

National Association of Schools of Theatre (j)
11250 Roger Bacon Drive
Suite 21
Reston, VA 20190
(703) 437-0700
FAX: (703) 437-6312
Karen P. Moynahan
Executive Director
E-MAIL: info@arts-accredit.org
URL: nast.arts-accredit.org

National Association of State Directors of Teacher Education and Certification (A)
1629 K Street, NW
Suite 300
Washington, DC 20006
(202) 204-2208
Dr. Phillip S. Rogers
Executive Director
E-MAIL: philrogers@nasdtec.org
URL: www.nasdtec.net

National Association of Student Financial Aid Administrators (B)
1801 Pennsylvania Avenue, NW
Suite 850
Washington, DC 20006-3606
(202) 785-0453
FAX: (202) 785-1487
Mr. Justin Draeger
President
E-MAIL: info@nasfaa.org
URL: www.nasfaa.org

National Association of System Heads (C)
3300 Metzerott Road
Adelphi, MD 20783
(301) 445-2780
Rebecca Martin
Executive Director
E-MAIL: rmartin@nash-dc.org
URL: www.nashonline.org

National Catholic Educational Association (D)
407 Bicksler Square SE
Leesburg, VA 20175-3773
(571) 257-0010
FAX: (703) 243-0025
Mr. Lincoln Snyder
President/CEO
E-MAIL: lsnyder@ncea.org
URL: www.ncea.org

National Coalition for Campus Children's Centers (E)
188 Front Street
Suite 116-104
Franklin, TN 37064
(615) 614-3723
Ms. Tonya Palla
Executive Director
E-MAIL: tonyap@campuschildren.org
URL: www.campuschildren.org

National Collegiate Athletic Association (F)
PO Box 6222
Indianapolis, IN 46206-6222
(317) 917-6222
Mr. Tom Paskus
Principal Academic Research Scientist
E-MAIL: research@ncaa.org
URL: www.ncaa.org

National Commission on Orthotic and Prosthetic Education (NCOPE) (G)
330 John Carlyle Street
Suite 200
Alexandria, VA 22314
(703) 836-7114 x 225
FAX: (703) 890-2425
Ms. Robin Seabrook
Executive Director
E-MAIL: rseabrook@ncope.org
URL: www.ncope.org

National Communication Association (H)
1765 N Street, NW
Washington, DC 20036
(202) 464-4622
FAX: (202) 464-4600
Linda Taliaferro
Interim Executive Director
E-MAIL: ltaliaferro@natcom.org
URL: www.natcom.org

National Council for Continuing Education and Training (I)
9526 Argyle Forest Boulevard
Suite B2-322
Jacksonville, FL 32222
(904) 466-9466
Mr. Ed Harper
Acting Executive Director
E-MAIL: nccet@nccet.org
URL: www.nccet.org

National Council of Instructional Administrators (NCIA) Dept of Educational Administration (J)
141 Teachers College Hall
PO Box 880360
University of Nebraska - Lincoln
Lincoln, NE 68588-0360
(402) 472-3726
FAX: (402) 472-4300
Katherine Wesley
Executive Director
E-MAIL: kwesley4@unl.edu
URL: cehs.unl.edu/ncia/

National Council of University Research Administrators (K)
1015 18th Street, NW
Suite 901
Washington, DC 20036
(202) 466-3894
FAX: (202) 223-5573
Kathleen M. Larmett
Executive Director
E-MAIL: info@ncura.edu
URL: www.ncura.edu

National Education Association (L)
1201 16th Street, NW
Suite 810
Washington, DC 20036
(202) 833-4000
FAX: (202) 822-7974
Ms. Kim A. Anderson
Executive Director
E-MAIL: mboyd@nea.org
URL: www.nea.org/he

National Forensic Association (M)
Illinois State University
School of Communication
Campus Box 4480
Normal, IL 61790-4480
(309) 438-8447
FAX: (309) 438-3048
Prof. Megan Koch
President
E-MAIL: mkoch@ilstu.edu
URL: sites.google.com/site/nationalforensicsassociation/

National Institute for Learning Outcomes Assessment (N)
University of Illinois at Urbana-Champaign
CRC, 51 Gerty Drive, Room 127
Champaign, IL 61821
(217) 244-2155
Dr. Gianina Baker
Acting Director
E-MAIL: niloa@education.illinois.edu
URL: www.learningoutcomeassessment.org

National League for Nursing (O)
The Watergate Building, 8th Floor
2600 Virginia Avenue, NW
Washington, DC 20037
(800) 669-1656
Dr. Beverly Malone
President & Chief Executive Officer
E-MAIL: oceo@nln.org
URL: www.nln.org

National Rural Education Association (P)
615 McCallie Avenue
Hunter Hall 205
Chattanooga, TN 37421
(423) 425-4539
Dr. Allen Pratt
Executive Director
E-MAIL: allen-pratt@utc.edu
URL: www.nrea.net

National Society for Experiential Education (Q)
c/o Talley Management Group, Inc.
19 Mantua Road
Mt. Royal, NJ 08061
(856) 423-3427
FAX: (856) 423-3420
Haley Brust
Executive Director
E-MAIL: nsee@talley.com
URL: www.nsee.org

National Writing Project (R)
2120 University Avenue
University of California
Berkeley, CA 94704
(510) 679-2424
Elyse Eidman-Aadahl
Executive Director
E-MAIL: nwp@nwp.org
URL: www.nwp.org

Network of Schools of Public Policy, Affairs, and Administration (S)
1029 Vermont Avenue, NW
Suite 1100
Washington, DC 20005
(202) 628-8965
Ms. Angel Wright-Lanier
Executive Director
E-MAIL: naspaa@naspaa.org
URL: www.naspaa.org

New England Commission of Higher Education (NECHE) (T)
3 Burlington Woods Drive
Suite 100
Burlington, MA 01803-4514
(781) 425-7785
FAX: (781) 425-1001
Dr. Lawrence M. Schall
President
E-MAIL: info@neche.org
URL: www.neche.org

New England Board of Higher Education (U)
45 Temple Place
Boston, MA 02111
(617) 533-9519
Dr. Michael K. Thomas
President and CEO
E-MAIL: presidentsoffice@nebhe.org
URL: www.nebhe.org

North American Association of Summer Sessions (V)
North Carolina State University
2016 Harris Hall
Campus Box 7302
Raleigh, NC 27695-7302
(919) 515-2261
E-MAIL: naass@naass.org
URL: www.naass.org

Northwest Commission on Colleges and Universities (W)
8060 165th Avenue, NE
Suite 100
Redmond, WA 98052
(425) 558-4224
FAX: (205) 525-9848
Dr. Sonny Ramaswamy
President
E-MAIL: sonny@nwccu.org
URL: www.nwccu.org

Planning Accreditation Board (X)
2334 W. Lawrence Avenue
Suite 209
Chicago, IL 60625
(773) 334-7200
Ms. Jesmarie Soto Johnson
Executive Director
E-MAIL: jjohnson@planningaccreditationboard.org
URL: www.planningaccreditationboard.org

Quality Education for Minorities (QEM) Network (Y)
1818 N Street, NW
Suite 350
Washington, DC 20036
(202) 659-1818
Dr. Erin Lynch
President
E-MAIL: elynch@qem.org
URL: www.qem.org

Society for College and University Planning (Z)
1330 Eisenhower Place
Ann Arbor, MI 48108
(734) 669-3270
Mike Moss CAE
President
E-MAIL: info@scup.org
URL: www.scup.org

Society for Slovene Studies (a)
148 Russsell Street #3
Worcester, MA 01609
Ms. Kristina Helena Reardon
Secretary
E-MAIL: kristina.reardon@gmail.com
URL: www.slovenestudies.com

The Society for the Future of Higher Education (b)
c/o Western Kentucky University
1906 College Heights Boulevard
#8020
Bowling Green, KY 42101-1041
(270) 745-2907
FAX: (270) 745-5374
Ms. Vivienne Felix
Executive Director
E-MAIL: society@svhe.org
URL: sfhe.us

Society of American Foresters (c)
2121 K Street, NW
Suite 315
Washington, DC 20037
(866) 897-8720
FAX: (202) 938-3911
Mr. Terry Baker
Chief Executive Officer
E-MAIL: membership@safnet.org
URL: www.eforester.org

Society of Professors of Education (d)
University of West Georgia
College of Education
Dept of LAI
1601 Maple Street
Carrollton, GA 30118-5160
(678) 839-6132
Dr. Robert C. Morris
Secretary-Treasurer
E-MAIL: rmorris@westga.edu
URL: societyofprofessorsofeducation.wordpress.com

Southeastern Universities Research Association (e)
1201 New York Avenue, NW
Suite 430
Washington, DC 20005
(202) 408-7872
FAX: (202) 408-8250
Mr. Scott Hartranft
Interim President & CEO
E-MAIL: shartranft@sura.org
URL: www.sura.org

Southern Association for College Student Affairs (f)
Clemson University
211B Old Main
Clemson, SC 29634-0707
(864) 656-5100
Dr. Tony W. Cawthan
Executive Director
E-MAIL: cawthat@clemson.edu
URL: www.sacsa.org

Southern Association of Colleges and Schools Commission on Colleges (g)
1866 Southern Lane
Decatur, GA 30033-4097
(404) 679-4512
Dr. Belle S. Wheelan
President
E-MAIL: bwheelan@sacscoc.org
URL: sacscoc.org

Southern States Communication Association (h)
University of Tennessee at Knoxville
293 Communications
1345 Circle Park Drive
Knoxville, TN 37996-0324
(423) 425-4633
FAX: (423) 756-5559
Mr. John Haas
Executive Director
E-MAIL: director@ssca.net
URL: www.ssca.net

State Higher Education Executive Officers (i)
3035 Center Green Drive
Suite 100
Boulder, CO 80301-2205
(303) 541-1600
FAX: (303) 541-1639
Dr. Robert Anderson
President
E-MAIL: randerson@sheeo.org
URL: www.sheeo.org

Tennessee Independent Colleges and Universities Association (A)
555 Marriott Drive
Suite 315
Nashville, TN 37214
(615) 242-6400
Dr. Claude O. Pressnell Jr.
President
E-MAIL: pressnell@ticua.org
URL: www.ticua.org

Transnational Association of Christian Colleges and Schools (TRACS) (B)
15935 Forest Road
Forest, VA 24551
(434) 525-9539
Dr. Timothy W. Eaton
President
E-MAIL: info@tracs.org
URL: www.tracs.org

The Tuition Exchange (C)
3 Bethesda Metro Center
Suite 700
Bethesda, MD 20814
(301) 941-1827
FAX: (301) 657-9776
Mr. Robert D. Shorb
Executive Director/CEO
E-MAIL: rshorb@tuitionexchange.org
URL: www.tuitionexchange.org

UNCF (D)
1805 7th Street NW
Washington, DC 20001
(800) 331-2244
Dr. Michael Lomax
President & CEO
E-MAIL: lori.bonnette@uncf.org
URL: www.uncf.org

University Aviation Association (E)
8092 Memphis Avenue
Suite 132
Memphis, TN 38053
(901) 563-0505
Ms. Dawn E. Vinson
Executive Director
E-MAIL: hello@uaa.aero
URL: www.uaa.aero

University Film and Video Association (F)
960 War Eagle Drive S
Colorado Springs, CO 80919
(646) 498-1182
Ms. Christina Lane
President
E-MAIL: home@ufva.org
URL: www.ufva.org

University Photographers' Association of America (G)
P.O. Box 433
Clalfon, NJ 07830-0433
(908) 335-0157
Mr. Glenn Carpenter
UPAA President
E-MAIL: carpenter@morainevalley.edu
URL: www.upaa.org

University Professional & Continuing Education Association (UPCEA) (H)
One Dupont Circle, NW
Suite 330
Washington, DC 20036
(202) 659-3130
FAX: (202) 785-0374
Dr. Robert Hansen
CEO
E-MAIL: rhansen@upcea.edu
URL: upcea.edu

University Risk Management and Insurance Association, Inc. (I)
PO Box 1027
Bloomington, IN 47402
(812) 727-7130
FAX: (812) 727-7129
Ms. Jenny Whittington
Executive Director
E-MAIL: urmia@urmia.org
URL: www.urmia.org

Urban Affairs Association (J)
c/o Urban Studies Program
University of Wisconsin-Milwaukee
PO Box 413
Milwaukee, WI 53201-0413
(414) 229-3025
Dr. Margaret Wilder
UAA Executive Director
E-MAIL: info@uaamail.org
URL: www.urbanaffairsassociation.org

WASC Senior College and University Commission (K)
1001 Marina Village Parkway
Suite 402
Alameda, CA 94501
(510) 748-9001
FAX: (510) 748-9797
Ms. Jamienne S. Studley
President
E-MAIL: kmatarrese@wscuc.org
URL: www.wscuc.org

Western Interstate Commission for Higher Education (L)
3035 Center Green Drive
Suite 200
Boulder, CO 80301-2204
(303) 541-0201
Dr. Demaree K. Michelau
President
E-MAIL: dmichelau@wiche.edu
URL: www.wiche.edu

Consortia of Institutions of Higher Education

Alabama Association of Independent Colleges and Universities (A)
4266 Lomac Street
Montgomery, AL 36106
(334) 356-2220
FAX: (334) 356-2202
Paul M. Hankins
President
E-MAIL: hankinsp@knology.net
URL: www.aaicu.net

Arkansas' Independent Colleges and Universities (B)
PO Box 300
Little Rock, AR 72203
(501) 378-0843
FAX: (501) 374-1523
Mr. Andy Goodman
President
E-MAIL: agoodman@arkindcolleges.org
URL: www.arkindcolleges.org

Associated Colleges of the Midwest (C)
180 N. Michigan Avenue
Suite 2020
Chicago, IL 60601
(312) 263-5000
FAX: (312) 263-5879
Ms. Sonya Malunda
President
E-MAIL: acm@acm.edu
URL: www.acm.edu

Association of Independent California Colleges and Universities (D)
1121 L Street
Suite 802
Sacramento, CA 95814
(916) 446-7626
Ms. Kristen F. Soares
President
E-MAIL: aiccu@aiccu.edu
URL: www.aiccu.edu

Association of Independent Colleges and Universities in Massachusetts (E)
5 Brighton Street
Belmont, MA 02478
(617) 742-5147
Mr. Bob McCarron
President
E-MAIL: rob.mccarron@aicum.org
URL: www.aicum.org

Association of Independent Colleges and Universities of Ohio (F)
41 South High Street
Suite 1690
Columbus, OH 43215
(614) 228-2196
FAX: (614) 228-8406
Mr. C. Todd Jones
President & General Counsel
E-MAIL: tjones@aicuo.edu
URL: www.aicuo.edu

Association of Independent Colleges and Universities of Pennsylvania (G)
101 North Front Street
Harrisburg, PA 17101-1404
(717) 232-8649
FAX: (717) 233-8574
Thomas P. Foley J.D.
President
E-MAIL: foley@aicup.org
URL: www.aicup.org

Association of Independent Colleges and Universities of Rhode Island (H)
50 Park Row West
Suite 100
Providence, RI 02903
(401) 272-8270
Mr. Daniel Egan
President
E-MAIL: degan@aicuri.org
URL: www.aicuri.org

Association of Independent Colleges of Art & Design (I)
236 Hope Street
Providence, RI 02906
(401) 270-5991
FAX: (401) 270-5993
Ms. Deborah Obalil
President & Executive Director
E-MAIL: deborah@aicad.org
URL: aicad.org

Association of Independent Kentucky Colleges and Universities (J)
484 Chenault Road
Frankfort, KY 40601
(502) 695-5007
Dr. OJ Oleka
President
E-MAIL: info@aikcu.org
URL: www.aikcu.org

Association of Vermont Independent Colleges (K)
PO Box 254
Montpelier, VT 05601
(802) 828-8826
Susan Stitely
President
E-MAIL: sstitely@vermont-icolleges.org
URL: vermont-icolleges.org

Atlanta Regional Council for Higher Education (L)
141 E. College Avenue
Box 1084
Decatur, GA 30030
(404) 471-6422
Ms. Tracey Brantley
Executive Director
E-MAIL: tbrantley@atlantahighered.org
URL: www.atlantahighered.org

Boston Theological Interreligious Consortium (M)
PO Box 391069
Cambridge, MA 02139
(207) 370-5275
Stephanie Edwards PhD
Executive Director
E-MAIL: edwards@bostontheological.org
URL: www.bostontheological.org

CCUMC (Consortium of College & University Media Centers) (N)
201 E. Main Street
Suite 1405
Lexington, KY 40507
(859) 514-9185
Kristy Howard
Executive Director
E-MAIL: ccumc@ccumc.org
URL: ccumc.org

Central Pennsylvania Consortium (O)
c/o Franklin & Marshall College
PO Box 3003
Lancaster, PA 17604-3003
(717) 358-4282
FAX: (717) 358-4455
Ms. Kathryn Missildine
Executive Assistant
E-MAIL: kathy.missildine@fandm.edu
URL: www.centralpennsylvaniaconsortium.org

CHESLA, Connecticut Higher Education Supplemental Loan Authority (P)
10 Columbus Boulevard
7th Floor
Hartford, CT 06106-1978
(860) 761-8453
Ms. Jeanette W. Weldon
Executive Director
E-MAIL: jweldon@chesla.org
URL: www.chesla.org

Christian College Consortium (Q)
1020 Hesli Hill Court
Shoreview, MN 55126-1408
(651) 636-2182
Dr. James H. Barnes III
President
E-MAIL: j-barnes@bethel.edu
URL: www.ccconsortium.org

Community College Futures Assembly (R)
Bellwether College Consortium
Alamo Colleges District
2222 N. Alamo Street
San Antonio, TX 78215
(210) 485-0836
Ms. Rose Martinez
E-MAIL: martinez1702@alamo.edu
URL: www.bellwethercollegeconsortium.com

The Consortium for Graduate Study in Management (S)
229 Chesterfield Business Parkway
Chesterfield, MO 63005
(636) 681-5553
FAX: (636) 681-5499
Mr. Peter J. Aranda III
Executive Director and CEO
E-MAIL: recruiting@cgsm.org
URL: www.cgsm.org

Consortium of Universities of the Washington Metropolitan Area (T)
1020 19th Street, NW
Suite 500
Washington, DC 20036
(202) 331-8080
Dr. Andrew Flagel
President & CEO
E-MAIL: aflagel@consortium.org
URL: www.consortium.org

Consortium on Financing Higher Education (U)
1 Main Street
Suite 1210
Cambridge, MA 02142
(617) 253-5030
Ms. Janet L. Rapelye
President
E-MAIL: cofhe-info@mit.edu
URL: web.mit.edu/cofhe/

Cooperating Raleigh Colleges (V)
William Peace University
15 E. Peace Street
Raleigh, NC 27604
(919) 346-6169
Ms. Maura DiColla
Director
E-MAIL: director@crcraleighcolleges.org
URL: www.crcraleighcolleges.org

Council of Independent Colleges in Virginia (W)
PO Box 1005
Bedford, VA 24523
(540) 586-0606
FAX: (540) 586-2630
Mr. Robert B. Lambeth Jr.
President
E-MAIL: lambeth@cicv.org
URL: www.cicv.org

Council of Presidents (X)
410 Eleventh Avenue, SE
Suite 101
Olympia, WA 98501
(360) 292-4100
Mr. Paul Francis
Executive Director
E-MAIL: pfrancis@councilofpresidents.org
URL: www.councilofpresidents.org

Federation of Independent Illinois Colleges and Universities (Y)
1123 South Second Street
Springfield, IL 62704
(217) 789-1400
Mr. David W. Tretter
President
E-MAIL: davetretter@federationedu.org
URL: www.federationedu.org

Five College Consortium (Z)
97 Spring Street
Amherst, MA 01002
(413) 542-4009
FAX: (413) 542-4028
Dr. Sarah K. A. Pfatteicher
Executive Director
E-MAIL: fciexecdirector@fivecolleges.edu
URL: www.fivecolleges.edu

Georgia Independent College Association (a)
50 Hurt Plaza SE
Suite 655
Atlanta, GA 30303
(404) 233-5433
Ms. Jenna Colvin
President
E-MAIL: jcolvin@georgacolleges.org
URL: www.georgiacolleges.org

Graduate Theological Foundation (b)
116 E. Sheridan Avenue
Suite 207
Oklahoma City, OK 73104
(800) 423-5983
FAX: (405) 653-9435
Paul J. Kirbas DMin, PhD
President
E-MAIL: provost@gtfeducation.org
URL: www.gtfeducation.org

Great Lakes Colleges Association (c)
535 West William
Suite 301
Ann Arbor, MI 48103
(734) 661-2350
FAX: (734) 661-2349
Dr. Michael (Mickey) McDonald
President
E-MAIL: smith@glca.org
URL: www.glca.org

Greater Cincinnati Collegiate Connection (d)
Union Institute & University
2090 Florence Avenue
Cincinnati, OH 45206
(859) 392-2428
Ms. Janet Piccirillo
Executive Director
E-MAIL: janet.piccirillo@myunion.edu
URL: www.gccollegiateconnection.org

Hartford Consortium for Higher Education (e)
349 Main Street
2nd Floor
Hartford, CT 06108
Mr. Greg Haddad
Coordinator of Operations & External Relations
E-MAIL: ghaddad@metrohartford.com
URL: www.hartfordconsortium.org

Higher Education Consortium for Urban Affairs, Inc. (HECUA) (f)
2233 University Avenue West
Suite 210
St. Paul, MN 55114
(651) 287-3300
FAX: (651) 659-9421
Ms. Ariella Tilsen
Interim Executive Director
E-MAIL: hecua@hecua.org
URL: www.hecua.org

Higher Education Consortium of Metropolitan St. Louis (g)
734 West Port Plaza
Suite 273
St. Louis, MO 63146
(314) 985-8833
FAX: (314) 985-8835
Ms. Cassandra M. Pinkston
Chief Executive Officer
E-MAIL: cpinkston@hecstl.org
URL: www.hecstl.org

Higher Education Data Sharing (HEDS) Consortium (h)
Wabash College
Trippet Hall
410 West Wabash Avenue
Crawfordsville, IN 47933
(765) 361-6331
Charles Blaich
Director
E-MAIL: kmcdorman@hedsconsortium.org
URL: www.hedsconsortium.org

Independent Colleges and Universities of Missouri (i)
PO Box 1865
Jefferson City, MO 65102-1865
(573) 635-9160
FAX: (573) 635-6258
Mr. William A. Gamble
Executive Director
E-MAIL: bill@molobby.com
URL: independentcollegesanduniversitiesofmo.com

Independent Colleges and Universities of New Jersey (j)
142 West State Street
Trenton, NJ 08608
(609) 218-5026
FAX: (609) 498-0055
Steve Reynolds
President and CEO
E-MAIL: sreynolds@njcolleges.org
URL: www.njcolleges.org

Independent Colleges and Universities of Texas, Inc. (A)
1303 San Antonio Street
Suite 820
Austin, TX 78701
(512) 472-9522
FAX: (512) 472-2371
Dr. Steven Johnson
President
E-MAIL: steven.johnson@icut.org
URL: icut.org

Independent Colleges of Indiana (B)
30 S. Meridian Street
Suite 800
Indianapolis, IN 46204
(317) 236-6090
Dr. David W. Wantz
President and CEO
E-MAIL: dwantz@icindiana.org
URL: www.icindiana.org

Independent Colleges of Washington (C)
600 Stewart Street
Suite 600
Seattle, WA 98101
(206) 623-4494
Terri Standish-Kuon Ph.D.
President & CEO
E-MAIL: info@icwashington.org
URL: www.icwashington.org

Inter-University Consortium for Political and Social Research (ICPSR) (D)
The University of Michigan
Institute for Social Research
PO Box 1248
Ann Arbor, MI 48106-1248
(734) 615-8400
Dr. Margaret Levenstein
Director
E-MAIL: maggiel@umich.edu
URL: www.icpsr.umich.edu

Inter-University Council of Ohio (IUC) (E)
10 West Broad Street
Suite 450
Columbus, OH 43215
(614) 464-1266
FAX: (614) 464-9281
Ms. Cindy McQuade
Vice President of Operations
E-MAIL: mcquade.2@osu.edu
URL: www.iuc-ohio.org

Iowa Association of Community College Trustees (F)
855 East Court Avenue
Des Moines, IA 50309
(515) 282-4692
FAX: (515) 282-3743
Ms. Emily Shields
Executive Director
E-MAIL: ejshields@iacct.com
URL: www.iacct.com

Iowa Association of Independent Colleges and Universities (G)
3775 EP True Parkway #253
West Des Moines, IA 50265
(515) 282-3175
Mr. Gary Steinke
President
E-MAIL: president@iaicu.org
URL: www.iowaprivatecolleges.org

Kansas Independent College Association (H)
700 South Kansas Avenue
Suite 622
Topeka, KS 66603
(785) 235-9877
Mr. Matthew E. Lindsey
President
E-MAIL: matt@kscolleges.org
URL: www.kscolleges.org

Lehigh Valley Association of Independent Colleges (I)
1309 Main Street
Bethlehem, PA 18018
(610) 625-7888
Diane Dimitroff
Executive Director
E-MAIL: dimitroffd@lvaic.org
URL: www.lvaic.org

Louisiana Association of Independent Colleges and Universities (J)
PO Box 3332
Baton Rouge, LA 70821
(225) 389-9885
Dr. Kenya L. Messer
President
E-MAIL: kmesser@laicu.org
URL: www.laicu.org

Maryland Independent College and University Association (K)
140 South Street
Annapolis, MD 21401
(410) 269-0306
Ms. Sara Fidler
President
E-MAIL: sfidler@micua.org
URL: www.micua.org

Massachusetts Education & Career Opportunities Inc (L)
484 Main Street
Suite 500
Worcester, MA 01608
(508) 754-6829
FAX: (508) 797-0069
Mr. Mark Bilotta
CEO
E-MAIL: mbilotta@massedco.org
URL: www.massedco.org

Michigan Independent Colleges & Universities (M)
120 N. Washington Square
Suite 950
Lansing, MI 48933
(517) 372-9160
Robert LeFevre
President
E-MAIL: rlefevre@micolleges.org
URL: www.micolleges.org

Minnesota Private College Council, Inc. (N)
445 Minnesota Street
Suite 500
St. Paul, MN 55101-2903
(651) 228-9061
FAX: (651) 228-0379
E-MAIL: colleges@mnprivatecolleges.org
URL: www.mnprivatecolleges.org

National Student Exchange (O)
2613 Northridge Parkway
Suite 106
Ames, IA 50010
(515) 450-5529
Dr. Debra Sanborn
President
E-MAIL: info@nse.org
URL: nse.org

New England Faculty Development Consortium (P)
108 Bromfeld Road
Somerville, MA 02144
(617) 627-4007
Annie Soisson Ed.D
President
E-MAIL: annie.soisson@tufts.edu
URL: www.nefdc.org

New Hampshire College & University Council (Q)
2 Pillsbury Street
Suite 302
Concord, NH 03301
(603) 225-4199
Dr. Debby Scire
President and CEO
E-MAIL: scire@compactnh.org
URL: www.nhcuc.org

New Jersey Association of State Colleges and Universities (R)
150 West State Street
Trenton, NJ 08608
(609) 989-1100
Mr. Eugene Lepore
Executive Director
E-MAIL: elepore@njascu.org
URL: www.njascu.org

New Jersey Council of County Colleges (S)
330 West State Street
Trenton, NJ 08618
(609) 392-3434
Dr. Aaron Fichtner
President
E-MAIL: afichtner@njccc.org
URL: www.njccc.org

New Orleans Educational Telecommunications Consortium (T)
2045 Lakeshore Drive
Suite 541
New Orleans, LA 70122
(504) 524-0350
E-MAIL: noetc@noetc.org
URL: www.noetc.org

North Carolina Independent Colleges and Universities (U)
530 North Blount Street
Raleigh, NC 27604
(919) 832-5817
FAX: (919) 833-0794
Dr. A. Hope Williams
President
E-MAIL: williams@ncicu.org
URL: www.ncicu.org

North Dakota Independent College Fund (V)
University of Mary
7500 University Drive
Bismarck, ND 58504
(701) 355-8329
FAX: (701) 255-7687
Mr. Jeff Beauchamp
Executive Director
E-MAIL: jrbeauchamp@umary.edu

Northeast Consortium of Colleges and Universities in Massachusetts (NECCUM) (W)
c/o Office of the President
Northern Essex Community College
100 Elliott Street
Haverhill, MA 01830
(978) 556-3719
Ms. Michelle Sunday
E-MAIL: msunday@necc.mass.edu
URL: uml.edu/registrar/policies-and-procedures/neccum.aspx

Oak Ridge Associated Universities (X)
MS-22
PO Box 117
Oak Ridge, TN 37831-0117
(865) 576-3300
FAX: (865) 576-3816
Mr. Andy Page
President and CEO
E-MAIL: andy.page@orau.org
URL: www.orau.org

Oklahoma Independent Colleges and Universities (Y)
PO Box 57148
Oklahoma City, OK 73157-7148
(405) 371-1780
Lesa Smaligo
Executive Director
E-MAIL: lesa@oicu.org
URL: www.oicu.org

Oregon Alliance of Independent Colleges & Universities (Z)
8125 SW Tualatin Sherwood Road
Suite 200
Tualatin, OR 97062
(503) 342-0004
Mr. Brent Wilder
President
E-MAIL: info@oaicu.org
URL: oaicu.org

Pennsylvania's State System of Higher Education Foundation, Inc. (a)
2986 North Second Street
Harrisburg, PA 17110
FAX: (717) 720-7082
Ms. Cynthia Pritchard
President/CEO
E-MAIL: cpritchard@thepafoundation.org
URL: www.thepafoundation.org

Pittsburgh Council on Higher Education (b)
201 Wood Street
Pittsburgh, PA 15222
(412) 657-8105
Ms. Karina Chavez
Executive Director
E-MAIL: kchavez@pointpark.edu
URL: www.pche-pa.org

Quad-Cities Graduate Study Center (c)
WIU - QC Campus
3300 River Drive
Moline, IL 61265
(309) 762-9481, x62274
Shirley Moore
E-MAIL: shirley@gradcenter.org
URL: www.gradcenter.org

Second Nature (d)
18 Tremont Street
Suite 608
Boston, MA 02108
(617) 722-0036
FAX: (617) 259-1734
Dr. Timothy Carter
President
E-MAIL: info@secondnature.org
URL: www.secondnature.org

South Carolina Independent Colleges & Universities, Inc. (e)
PO Box 12007
Columbia, SC 29211
(803) 799-7122
FAX: (803) 254-7504
Dr. Jeffrey Perez
President & CEO
E-MAIL: jeff@scicu.org
URL: www.scicu.org

South Metropolitan Higher Education Consortium (f)
202 S. Halsted Street
Chicago Heights, IL 60411
(708) 709-3764
Ms. Allessandra Kummelehne
Executive Director
E-MAIL: akummelehne@prairiestate.edu
URL: southmetroed.org

Southern Regional Education Board (g)
592 Tenth Street, NW
Atlanta, GA 30318-5776
(404) 875-9211
FAX: (404) 872-1477
Dr. Stephen L. Pruitt
President
E-MAIL: stephen.pruitt@sreb.org
URL: www.sreb.org

Strategic Ohio Council for Higher Education (SOCHE) (h)
3155 Research Boulevard
Suite 204
Dayton, OH 45420
(937) 258-8890
FAX: (937) 258-8899
Dr. Cassie Barlow
President
E-MAIL: cassie.barlow@soche.org
URL: www.soche.org

Texas International Education Consortium (i)
1103 West 24th Street
Austin, TX 78705
(512) 477-9283
FAX: (512) 322-0592
Robin Lerner
President & CEO
E-MAIL: info@tiec.org
URL: www.tiec.org

Tuition Plan Consortium/Private College 529 Plan (j)
,
(314) 727-0900
Mr. Robert Cole
President & CEO
E-MAIL: robert@pc529.com
URL: www.privatecollege529.com

The Virginia College Fund (k)
1015 E. Main Street
Richmond, VA 23219
(804) 355-3271
FAX: (804) 355-3271
Mr. Carthan F. Currin III
President
E-MAIL: office@thevcf.org
URL: www.thevcf.org

Virginia Tidewater Consortium for Higher Education (l)
4900 Powhatan Avenue
Norfolk, VA 23529-0293
(757) 683-3183
FAX: (757) 683-4515
Dr. Lawrence G. Dotolo
President
E-MAIL: lgdotolo@aol.com
URL: www.vtc.odu.edu

Consortia of Institutions of Higher Education

Washington Theological Consortium (A)
415 Michigan Avenue, NE
Suite 105
Washington, DC 20017
(202) 832-2675
FAX: (202) 526-0818
Dr. Larry Golemon
Executive Director
E-MAIL: wtc@washtheocon.org
URL: washtheocon.org

West Virginia Independent Colleges & Universities (B)
c/o Three Point Strategies, LLC
PO Box 7058
Charleston, WV 25356
(304) 814-9348
Mr. Ben Beakes
Executive Director
E-MAIL: wvicu@wvicu.org
URL: www.wvicu.org

Wisconsin Association of Independent Colleges and Universities (C)
122 West Washington Avenue
Suite 700
Madison, WI 53703-2723
(608) 256-7761
FAX: (608) 256-7065
Dr. Rolf Wegenke
President
E-MAIL: mail@waicu.org
URL: www.waicu.org

The Work Colleges Consortium (D)
CPO 2163
Berea, KY 40404
(859) 985-3156
Ms. Robin Taffler
Executive Director
E-MAIL: info@workcolleges.org
URL: www.workcolleges.org

NAME INDEX

US Department of Education Offices, Statewide Agencies of Higher Education, Higher Education Associations, Consortia of Institutions of Higher Education

Institutions By Religious Affiliation

African Methodist Episcopal
- Allen University ... SC
- Edward Waters College ... FL
- Jackson Theological Seminary ... AR
- Paul Quinn College ... TX
- Payne Theological Seminary ... OH
- Shorter College ... AR
- Wilberforce University ... OH

African Methodist Episcopal Zion Church
- Clinton College ... SC
- Hood Theological Seminary ... NC
- Livingstone College ... NC

American Baptist
- Alderson Broaddus University ... WV
- Bacone College ... OK
- Berkeley School of Theology ... CA
- Eastern University ... PA
- Franklin College of Indiana ... IN
- Judson University ... IL
- Linfield University ... OR
- Northern Seminary ... IL
- Ottawa University ... KS
- University of Sioux Falls ... SD

Assemblies Of God Church
- Ascent College ... VA
- Assemblies of God Theological Seminary MO
- Bridges Christian College ... LA
- Evangel University ... MO
- Global University ... MO
- Lumbee River Christian College ... NC
- North Central University ... MN
- Northpoint Bible College ... MA
- Northwest University ... WA
- Southeastern University ... FL
- Southwestern Assemblies of God University ... TX
- Trinity Bible College & Graduate School . ND
- University of Valley Forge ... PA
- Vanguard University of Southern California ... CA

Baptist
- American Baptist College ... TN
- Arkansas Baptist College ... AR
- Arlington Baptist University ... TX
- Baptist Bible College ... MO
- Baptist Missionary Association Theological Seminary ... TX
- Baptist University of the Americas ... TX
- Baylor University ... TX
- Bethel University ... MN
- Bluefield College ... VA
- Boston Baptist College ... MA
- Brewton-Parker College ... GA
- Campbell University ... NC
- Campbellsville University ... KY
- Cedarville University ... OH
- Central Baptist College ... AR
- Central Baptist Theological Seminary ... KS
- Central Baptist Theological Seminary of Minneapolis ... MN
- Chowan University ... NC
- Clarks Summit University ... PA
- Dallas Baptist University ... TX
- East Texas Baptist University ... TX
- Gardner-Webb University ... NC
- Hardin-Simmons University ... TX
- Howard Payne University ... TX
- Huntsville Bible College ... AL
- International Baptist College and Seminary ... AZ
- Jacksonville College ... TX
- Maple Springs Baptist Bible College & Seminary ... MD
- Missouri Baptist University ... MO
- Morris College ... SC
- Oakland City University ... IN
- Selma University ... AL
- Shaw University ... NC
- Shorter University ... GA
- Simmons College of Kentucky ... KY
- Southeastern Baptist College ... MS
- The Crown College of the Bible ... TN
- The John Leland Center for Theological Studies ... VA
- Trinity Baptist College ... FL
- Truett McConnell University ... GA
- University of the Cumberlands ... KY
- Veritas Baptist College ... IN
- Virginia Beach Theological Seminary ... VA
- Virginia Union University ... VA
- West Coast Baptist College ... CA

Brethren Church
- Ashland University ... OH

Christian Church (Disciples Of Christ)
- Barton College ... NC
- Bethany College ... WV
- Bushnell University ... OR
- Chapman University ... CA
- Christian Theological Seminary ... IN
- Columbia College ... MO
- Culver-Stockton College ... MO
- Eureka College ... IL
- Jarvis Christian College ... TX
- Lexington Theological Seminary ... KY
- Midway University ... KY
- Phillips Theological Seminary ... OK
- Texas Christian University ... TX
- Transylvania University ... KY
- University of Lynchburg ... VA
- William Woods University ... MO

Christian Churches And Churches of Christ
- Boise Bible College ... ID
- Central Christian College of the Bible ... MO
- Dallas Christian College ... TX
- Great Lakes Christian College ... MI
- Johnson University ... TN
- Kentucky Christian University ... KY
- Lincoln Christian University ... IL
- Manhattan Christian College ... KS
- Point University ... GA
- Saint Louis Christian College ... MO

Christian Methodist Episcopal
- Lane College ... TN
- Miles College ... AL
- Texas College ... TX

Christian Reformed Church
- Calvin Theological Seminary ... MI
- Calvin University ... MI
- Dordt University ... IA

Church Of Christ
- Pepperdine University ... CA

Church Of God
- Anderson University ... IN
- Lee University ... TN
- Mid-America Christian University ... OK
- Pentecostal Theological Seminary ... TN
- The University of Findlay ... OH
- Universidad Teologica Del Caribe ... PR
- Warner Pacific University ... OR
- Warner University ... FL

Church of God in Christ
- All Saints Bible College ... TN

Church of New Jerusalem
- Bryn Athyn College of the New Church ... PA

Church Of The Brethren
- Bethany Theological Seminary ... IN
- Bridgewater College ... VA
- Manchester University ... IN
- McPherson College ... KS

Church Of The Nazarene
- Eastern Nazarene College ... MA
- MidAmerica Nazarene University ... KS
- Mount Vernon Nazarene University ... OH
- Nazarene Bible College ... CO
- Nazarene Theological Seminary ... MO
- Northwest Nazarene University ... ID
- Olivet Nazarene University ... IL
- Point Loma Nazarene University ... CA
- Southern Nazarene University ... OK
- Trevecca Nazarene University ... TN

Churches Of Christ
- Abilene Christian University ... TX
- Amridge University ... AL
- Crowley's Ridge College ... AR
- Faulkner University ... AL
- Freed-Hardeman University ... TN
- Harding University Main Campus ... AR
- Heritage Christian University ... AL
- Lipscomb University ... TN
- Lubbock Christian University ... TX
- Mid-Atlantic Christian University ... NC
- Ohio Valley University ... WV
- Southwestern Christian College ... TX
- York College ... NE

Cumberland Presbyterian
- Bethel University ... TN
- Memphis Theological Seminary ... TN

Evangelical Congregational Church
- Evangelical Theological Seminary ... PA

Evangelical Covenant Church Of America
- North Park University ... IL

Evangelical Free Church Of America
- Trinity International University ... IL

Evangelical Lutheran Church In America
- Augsburg University ... MN
- Augustana College ... IL
- Augustana University ... SD
- Bethany College ... KS
- California Lutheran University ... CA
- Capital University ... OH
- Carthage College ... WI
- Concordia College ... MN
- Finlandia University ... MI
- Gettysburg College ... PA
- Grand View University ... IA
- Gustavus Adolphus College ... MN
- Lenoir-Rhyne University ... NC
- Luther College ... IA
- Luther Seminary ... MN
- Lutheran School of Theology at Chicago IL
- Midland University ... NE
- Muhlenberg College ... PA
- Newberry College ... SC
- Pacific Lutheran University ... WA
- Roanoke College ... VA
- St. Olaf College ... MN
- Susquehanna University ... PA
- Texas Lutheran University ... TX
- Thiel College ... PA
- United Lutheran Seminary ... PA
- Wartburg College ... IA
- Wartburg Theological Seminary ... IA
- Wittenberg University ... OH

Evangelical Lutheran Synod
- Bethany Lutheran College ... MN

Free Methodist
- Central Christian College of Kansas ... KS
- Greenville University ... IL
- Seattle Pacific University ... WA
- Spring Arbor University ... MI

Free Will Baptist
- California Christian College ... CA
- Randall University ... OK
- Southeastern Free Will Baptist College ... NC
- Welch College ... TN

Friends
- Earlham College and Earlham School of Religion ... IN
- George Fox University ... OR
- Guilford College ... NC
- Malone University ... OH
- William Penn University ... IA
- Wilmington College ... OH

Greek Orthodox
- Hellenic College-Holy Cross Greek Orthodox School of Theology ... MA

Interdenominational
- Athens College of Ministry ... GA
- Bethany Global University ... MN
- Christian Witness Theological Seminary . CA
- Denver Seminary ... CO
- Evangelical Seminary of Puerto Rico ... PR
- Faith International University ... WA
- God's Bible School and College ... OH
- Haven University ... CA
- Interdenominational Theological Center .. GA
- Kentucky Mountain Bible College ... KY
- Messiah University ... PA
- Oak Hills Christian College ... MN
- Palm Beach Atlantic University ... FL
- Phoenix Seminary ... AZ
- Rocky Mountain College ... MT
- South Florida Bible College ... FL
- The King's University ... TX
- Union Bible College ... IN
- Wesley Biblical Seminary ... MS

Jewish
- Academy for Jewish Religion ... NY
- Academy for Jewish Religion, California . CA
- Bais Medrash Ateres Shlomo ... NY
- Hebrew Union College-Jewish Institute of Religion ... NY
- Mechon L'Hoyroa ... NY
- New York Medical College ... NY
- Reconstructionist Rabbinical College ... PA
- Women's Institute of Torah Seminary ... MD

Latter-day Saints
- Brigham Young University ... UT
- Brigham Young University Hawaii ... HI
- Brigham Young University-Idaho ... ID
- Ensign College ... UT

Lutheran
- Valparaiso University ... IN

Lutheran Church - Missouri Synod
- Concordia Seminary ... MO
- Concordia Theological Seminary ... IN
- Concordia University ... NE
- Concordia University Chicago ... IL
- Concordia University Irvine ... CA
- Concordia University Texas ... TX
- Concordia University Wisconsin ... WI
- Concordia University, St. Paul ... MN

Mennonite Brethren Church
- Fresno Pacific University ... CA
- Tabor College ... KS

Mennonite Church
- Anabaptist Mennonite Biblical Seminary .. IN
- Bethel College ... KS
- Bluffton University ... OH
- Eastern Mennonite University ... VA
- Goshen College ... IN
- Grace College and Seminary ... IN
- Hesston College ... KS
- Rosedale Bible College ... OH

Missionary Church
- Bethel University ... IN

Moravian Church
- Moravian College ... PA
- Salem College ... NC

Multiple Protestant Denominations
- Huston-Tillotson University ... TX
- LeMoyne-Owen College ... TN
- Paine College ... GA

Non-denominational
- Belmont University ... TN
- California Victor University ... CA
- Carolina College of Biblical Studies ... NC
- Cedar Crest College ... PA
- China Evangelical Seminary North America ... CA
- Georgetown College ... KY
- Grace University ... CA
- Grove City College ... PA
- Heartland Christian College ... MO
- Montreat College ... NC
- North American University ... TX
- Pacific Bible College ... OR
- Providence Christian College ... CA
- Regional Christian University ... TX
- Sattler College ... MA
- Shepherds Theological Seminary ... NC
- Southern Bible Institute and College ... TX
- The Bible Seminary ... TX
- University of Fort Lauderdale ... FL
- Washington University of Virginia ... VA
- Williamson College ... TN

North American Baptist
- Sioux Falls Seminary ... SD

Original Free Will Baptist Church
- University of Mount Olive ... NC

Other Protestant
- Beulah Heights University ... GA
- Manna University ... NC
- Ohio Christian University ... OH

Pentecostal Church of God
- Messenger College ... TX

Universidad Pentecostal Mizpa ... PR

Pentecostal Holiness Church

Emmanuel College ... GA
Southwestern Christian University ... OK

Pentecostal/Charismatic Non-Denominational

Urshan College and Urshan Graduate School of Theology ... MO

Presbyterian

Sterling College ... KS
Whitworth University ... WA

Presbyterian Church (U.S.A.)

Agnes Scott College ... GA
Austin College ... TX
Austin Presbyterian Theological Seminary ... TX
Belhaven University ... MS
Blackburn College ... IL
Bloomfield College ... NJ
Buena Vista University ... IA
Carroll University ... WI
Columbia Theological Seminary ... GA
Davis & Elkins College ... WV
Eckerd College ... FL
Grace Mission University ... CA
Hampden-Sydney College ... VA
Hanover College ... IN
Hastings College ... NE
King University ... TN
Lees-McRae College ... NC
Louisville Presbyterian Theological Seminary ... KY
Lyon College ... AR
Macalester College ... MN
Mary Baldwin University ... VA
McCormick Theological Seminary ... IL
Millikin University ... IL
Missouri Valley College ... MO
Monmouth College ... IL
Muskingum University ... OH
Pittsburgh Theological Seminary ... PA
Presbyterian College ... SC
Princeton Theological Seminary ... NJ
Queens University of Charlotte ... NC
Rhodes College ... TN
Schreiner University ... TX
Stillman College ... AL
Tusculum University ... TN
Union Presbyterian Seminary ... VA
University of Dubuque ... IA
University of Jamestown ... ND
University of Pikeville ... KY
University of the Ozarks ... AR
Warren Wilson College ... NC
Waynesburg University ... PA
Westminster College ... PA
William Peace University ... NC
Wilson College ... PA

Presbyterian Church In America

Covenant College ... GA
Covenant Theological Seminary ... MO
Presbyterian Theological Seminary in America ... CA
Reformed University ... GA
Virginia Christian University ... VA
Washington Theological Seminary ... VA

Protestant Episcopal

Bexley Seabury ... IL
Church Divinity School of the Pacific ... CA
General Theological Seminary ... NY
Nashotah House ... WI
Saint Augustine's University ... NC
Seminary of the Southwest ... TX
Sewanee: The University of the South ... TN
Trinity Episcopal School for Ministry ... PA
Virginia Theological Seminary ... VA
Voorhees College ... SC

Reformed Church In America

Central College ... IA
Hope College ... MI
New Brunswick Theological Seminary ... NJ
Northwestern College ... IA
Western Theological Seminary ... MI

Reformed Episcopal Church

Reformed Episcopal Seminary ... PA

Reformed Presbyterian Church

Evangelia University ... CA
Geneva College ... PA
Reformed Presbyterian Theological Seminary ... PA

Roman Catholic

Alvernia University ... PA
Anna Maria College ... MA
Aquinas College ... MI
Aquinas College ... TN
Aquinas Institute of Theology ... MO
Assumption College for Sisters ... NJ
Assumption University ... MA
Athenaeum of Ohio ... OH
Augustine Institute ... CO
Ave Maria School of Law ... FL
Avila University ... MO
Barry University ... FL
Belmont Abbey College ... NC
Benedictine College ... KS
Benedictine University ... IL
Boston College ... MA
Brescia University ... KY
Briar Cliff University ... IA
Cabrini University ... PA
Caldwell University ... NJ
Calumet College of Saint Joseph ... IN
Canisius College ... NY
Cardinal Stritch University ... WI
Carlow University ... PA
Carroll College ... MT
Catholic Theological Union ... IL
Chestnut Hill College ... PA
Christendom College ... VA
Christian Brothers University ... TN
Clarke University ... IA
College of Our Lady of the Elms ... MA
College of Saint Benedict ... MN
College of Saint Mary ... NE
College of the Holy Cross ... MA
Conception Seminary College ... MO
Creighton University ... NE
DePaul University ... IL
DeSales University ... PA
Divine Word College ... IA
Dominican School of Philosophy and Theology ... CA
Dominican University ... IL
Donnelly College ... KS
Duquesne University ... PA
Edgewood College ... WI
Emmanuel College ... MA
Fairfield University ... CT
Felician University ... NJ
Fontbonne University ... MO
Franciscan Missionaries of Our Lady University ... LA
Franciscan University of Steubenville ... OH
Gannon University ... PA
Georgetown University ... DC
Georgian Court University ... NJ
Gonzaga University ... WA
Gwynedd Mercy University ... PA
Holy Apostles College and Seminary ... CT
Holy Cross College ... IN
Holy Family University ... PA
Immaculata University ... PA
John Carroll University ... OH
Kenrick-Glennon Seminary, Kenrick School of Theology ... MO
King's College ... PA
La Roche University ... PA
La Salle University ... PA
Laboure College ... MA
Lewis University ... IL
Loras College ... IA
Lourdes University ... OH
Loyola Marymount University ... CA
Loyola University Chicago ... IL
Loyola University Maryland ... MD
Loyola University New Orleans ... LA
Madonna University ... MI
Magdalen College of the Liberal Arts ... NH
Marian University ... IN
Marian University ... WI
Marquette University ... WI
Marymount California University ... CA
Marymount University ... VA
Marywood University ... PA
Mercy College of Health Sciences ... IA
Mercy College of Ohio ... OH
Mercyhurst University ... PA
Merrimack College ... MA
Misericordia University ... PA
Mount Angel Abbey & Seminary ... OR
Mount Carmel College of Nursing ... OH
Mount Marty University ... SD
Mount Mary University ... WI
Mount Mercy University ... IA
Mount Saint Mary's University ... CA
Mount St. Joseph University ... OH
Mount St. Mary's University ... MD
Neumann University ... PA
Newman University ... KS
Niagara University ... NY
Notre Dame College ... OH
Notre Dame of Maryland University ... MD
Notre Dame Seminary, Graduate School of Theology ... LA
Oblate School of Theology ... TX
Ohio Dominican University ... OH
Our Lady of the Lake University ... TX
Pontifical College Josephinum ... OH
Pontifical Faculty of the Immaculate Conception at the Dominican House of Studies ... DC
Pontifical John Paul II Institute for Studies on Marriage and Family ... DC
Pope St. John XXIII National Seminary ... MA
Presentation College ... SD
Providence College ... RI
Quincy University ... IL
Regis University ... CO
Rivier University ... NH
Rockhurst University ... MO
Rosemont College ... PA
Sacred Heart Major Seminary ... MI
Sacred Heart Seminary and School of Theology ... WI
Saint Anselm College ... NH
Saint Anthony College of Nursing ... IL
Saint Bernard's School of Theology & Ministry ... NY
Saint Charles Borromeo Seminary ... PA
Saint Elizabeth University ... NJ
Saint Francis Medical Center College of Nursing ... IL
Saint Francis University ... PA
Saint Gregory the Great Seminary ... NE
Saint John's Seminary ... CA
Saint John's Seminary ... MA
Saint John's University ... MN
Saint Joseph Seminary College ... LA
Saint Joseph's College of Maine ... ME
Saint Joseph's Seminary ... NY
Saint Joseph's University ... PA
Saint Leo University ... FL
Saint Louis University ... MO
Saint Martin's University ... WA
Saint Mary Seminary and Graduate School of Theology ... OH
Saint Mary's College ... IN
Saint Mary's College of California ... CA
Saint Mary's Seminary and University ... MD
Saint Mary's University of Minnesota ... MN
Saint Mary-of-the-Woods College ... IN
Saint Meinrad School of Theology ... IN
Saint Michael's College ... VT
Saint Norbert College ... WI
Saint Patrick's Seminary & University ... CA
Saint Peter's University ... NJ
Saint Vincent College ... PA
Saint Vincent Seminary ... PA
Saint Xavier University ... IL
Salve Regina University ... RI
Seattle University ... WA
Seton Hall University ... NJ
Seton Hill University ... PA
Siena Heights University ... MI
Spring Hill College ... AL
SS. Cyril and Methodius Seminary ... MI
St. Ambrose University ... IA
St. Bonaventure University ... NY
St. Catherine University ... MN
St. John Vianney College Seminary ... FL
St. John Vianney Theological Seminary ... CO
St. John's University ... NY
St. Joseph School of Nursing ... NH
St. Mary's University ... TX
St. Thomas University ... FL
St. Vincent De Paul Regional Seminary ... FL
Stonehill College ... MA
The Catholic University of America ... DC
The College of Saint Scholastica ... MN
The Pontifical Catholic University of Puerto Rico ... PR
The University of Scranton ... PA
Thomas More University ... KY
Trinity Washington University ... DC
Universidad Central de Bayamon ... PR
University of Dallas ... TX
University of Dayton ... OH
University of Detroit Mercy ... MI
University of Holy Cross ... LA
University of Mary ... ND
University of Notre Dame ... IN
University of Providence ... MT
University of Saint Francis ... IN
University of Saint Joseph ... CT
University of Saint Mary ... KS
University of Saint Mary of the Lake-Mundelein Seminary ... IL
University of Saint Thomas ... MN
University of San Diego ... CA
University of San Francisco ... CA
University of St. Francis ... IL
University of St. Thomas ... TX
University of the Incarnate Word ... TX
University of the Sacred Heart ... PR
Ursuline College ... OH
Villanova University ... PA
Viterbo University ... WI
Walsh University ... OH
Wheeling University ... WV
Wyoming Catholic College ... WY
Xavier University ... OH
Xavier University of Louisiana ... LA

Russian Orthodox

Holy Trinity Orthodox Seminary ... NY

Seventh-day Adventist

AdventHealth University ... FL
Andrews University ... MI
Kettering College ... OH
La Sierra University ... CA
Loma Linda University ... CA
Oakwood University ... AL
Pacific Union College ... CA
Southern Adventist University ... TN
Southwestern Adventist University ... TX
Union College ... NE
Universidad Adventista de las Antillas ... PR
Walla Walla University ... WA
Washington Adventist University ... MD

Southern Baptist

B.H. Carroll Theological Institute ... TX
Blue Mountain College ... MS
California Baptist University ... CA
Carson-Newman University ... TN
Charleston Southern University ... SC
Clear Creek Baptist Bible College ... KY
Gateway Seminary ... CA
Hannibal-LaGrange University ... MO
Houston Baptist University ... TX
Louisiana College ... LA
Midwestern Baptist Theological Seminary ... MO
Mississippi College ... MS
New Orleans Baptist Theological Seminary ... LA
North Greenville University ... SC
Oklahoma Baptist University ... OK
Ouachita Baptist University ... AR
Samford University ... AL
Southeastern Baptist Theological Seminary ... NC
Southwest Baptist University ... MO
Southwestern Baptist Theological Seminary ... TX
The Baptist College of Florida ... FL
The Southern Baptist Theological Seminary ... KY
Union University ... TN
University of Mary Hardin-Baylor ... TX
University of Mobile ... AL
Wayland Baptist University ... TX
William Carey University ... MS
Williams Baptist University ... AR
Wingate University ... NC

The Christian And Missionary Alliance

Crown College ... MN
Nyack College ... NY
Simpson University ... CA
Toccoa Falls College ... GA

Unification Church

Unification Theological Seminary ... NY

Unitarian Universalist

Meadville Lombard Theological School ... IL
Starr King School for the Ministry ... CA

United Brethren Church

Huntington University ... IN

United Church Of Christ

Catawba College ... NC
Chicago Theological Seminary ... IL
Doane University ... NE
Eden Theological Seminary ... MO
Elmhurst University ... IL
Heidelberg University ... OH
Lakeland University ... WI
Lancaster Theological Seminary ... PA
Northland College ... WI
Piedmont University ... GA
The Defiance College ... OH
Tougaloo College ... MS
United Theological Seminary of the Twin Cities ... MN

United Methodist

Adrian College ... MI
Albion College ... MI
Albright College ... PA
Allegheny College ... PA

American University .... DC
Andrew College .... GA
Baker University .... KS
Bennett College .... NC
Bethune Cookman University .... FL
Birmingham-Southern College .... AL
Brevard College .... NC
Centenary College of Louisiana .... LA
Central Methodist University .... MO
Claflin University .... SC
Claremont School of Theology .... CA
Clark Atlanta University .... GA
Columbia College .... SC
Cornell College .... IA
Dakota Wesleyan University .... SD
DePauw University .... IN
Dillard University .... LA
Emory & Henry College .... VA
Emory University .... GA
Ferrum College .... VA
Florida Southern College .... FL
Garrett-Evangelical Theological Seminary IL
Greensboro College .... NC
Hamline University .... MN
Hendrix College .... AR
High Point University .... NC
Huntingdon College .... AL
Iliff School of Theology .... CO
Iowa Wesleyan University .... IA
Kansas Wesleyan University .... KS
Kentucky Wesleyan College .... KY
LaGrange College .... GA
Lebanon Valley College .... PA
Lindsey Wilson College .... KY
Louisburg College .... NC
Lycoming College .... PA
McKendree University IL
McMurry University .... TX
Methodist Theological School in Ohio ..... OH
Methodist University .... NC
Millsaps College .... MS
Morningside College .... IA
Nebraska Wesleyan University .... NE
North Carolina Wesleyan College .... NC
North Central College IL
Ohio Northern University .... OH
Ohio Wesleyan University .... OH
Oklahoma City University .... OK
Otterbein University .... OH
Pfeiffer University .... NC
Philander Smith College .... AR
Randolph-Macon College .... VA
Reinhardt University .... GA
Rust College .... MS
Saint Paul School of Theology .... KS
Shenandoah University .... VA
Simpson College .... IA
Southwestern College .... KS
Southwestern University .... TX
Spartanburg Methodist College .... SC
Tennessee Wesleyan University .... TN
Texas Wesleyan University .... TX
Union College .... KY
United Theological Seminary .... OH
University of Evansville .... IN
University of Indianapolis .... IN
Virginia Wesleyan University .... VA
Wesley Theological Seminary .... DC
Wesleyan College .... GA
West Virginia Wesleyan College .... WV
Wiley College .... TX
Wofford College .... SC
Young Harris College .... GA

Wesleyan Church

Allegheny Wesleyan College .... OH
Houghton College .... NY
Indiana Wesleyan University .... IN
Oklahoma Wesleyan University .... OK
Southern Wesleyan University .... SC

Wisconsin Evangelical Lutheran Synod

Martin Luther College .... MN

Carnegie Classification Code Definitions*

The *Higher Education Directory®* lists the updated 2018 Carnegie Classifications. Due to space limitation, the *Higher Education Directory®* only lists the basic classification—which was substantially revised in 2018. These new codes are listed below:

Associate's Colleges: Institutions at which the highest level degree awarded is an associate's degree. The institutions are sorted into nine categories based on the intersection of two factors: disciplinary focus (transfer, career & technical or mixed) and dominant student type (traditional, nontraditional or mixed). Excludes Special Focus Institutions and Tribal Colleges.

Assoc/HT-High Trad: Associate's Colleges: High Transfer-High Traditional
Assoc/HT-Mix Trad/Non: Associate's Colleges: High Transfer-Mixed Traditional/Nontraditional
Assoc/HT-High Non: Associate's Colleges: High Transfer-High Nontraditional
Assoc/MT-VT-High Trad: Associate's Colleges: Mixed Transfer/Career & Technical-High Traditional
Assoc/MT-VT-Mix Trad/Non: Associate's Colleges: Mixed Transfer/Career & Technical-Mixed Traditional/Nontraditional
Assoc/MT-VT-High Non: Associate's Colleges: Mixed Transfer/Career & Technical-High Nontraditional
Assoc/HVT-High Trad: Associate's Colleges: High Career & Technical-High Traditional
Assoc/HVT-Mix Trad/Non: Associate's Colleges: High Career & Technical-Mixed Traditional/Nontraditional
Assoc/HVT-High Non: Associate's Colleges: High Career & Technical-High Nontraditional

Baccalaureate/Associate's Colleges. Includes four-year colleges (by virtue of having at least one baccalaureate degree program) that conferred more than 50 percent of degrees at the associate's level. Excludes Special Focus Institutions, Tribal Colleges, and institutions that have sufficient masterÖs or doctoral degrees to fall into those categories.

Bac/Assoc-Assoc Dom: Baccalaureate/Associate's Colleges: Associate's Dominant
Bac/Assoc-Mixed: Baccalaureate/Associate's Colleges: Mixed Baccalaureate/Associate's

Baccalaureate Colleges. Includes institutions where baccalaureate or higher degrees represent at least 50 percent of all degrees but where fewer than 50 master's degrees or 20 doctoral degrees were awarded during the update year. (Some institutions above the master's degree threshold are also included; see Methodology) Excludes Special Focus Institutions and Tribal Colleges.

Bac-A&S: Baccalaureate Colleges: Arts & Sciences Focus
Bac-Diverse: Baccalaureate Colleges: Diverse Fields

Master's Colleges and Universities. Generally includes institutions that awarded at least 50 master's degrees and fewer than 20 doctoral degrees during the update year (with occasional exceptions; see Methodology). Excludes Special Focus Institutions and Tribal Colleges.

Masters/L: Master's Colleges & Universities: Larger Programs
Masters/M: Master's Colleges & Universities: Medium Programs
Masters/S: Master's Colleges & Universities: Small Programs

Doctoral Universities. Includes institutions that awarded at least 20 research/scholarship doctoral degrees during the update year (this does not include professional practice doctoral-level degrees, such as the JD, MD, PharmD, DPT, etc.). Excludes Special Focus Institutions and Tribal Colleges.

DU-Highest: Doctoral Universities: Very High Research Activity
DU-Higher: Doctoral Universities: High Research Activity
DU-Mod: Doctoral/Professional Universities: Moderate Research Activity

Special Focus Institutions, Two-year. Institutions where a high concentration of degrees is in a single field or set of related fields. Excludes Tribal Colleges.

Spec 2-yr-Health: Special Focus Two-Year: Health Professions
Spec 2-yr-Tech: Special Focus Two-Year: Technical Professions
Spec 2-yr-A&S: Special Focus Two-Year: Arts & Design
Spec 2-yr-Other: Special Focus Two-Year: Other Fields

Special Focus Institutions, Four-year. Institutions where a high concentration of degrees is in a single field or set of related fields. Excludes Tribal Colleges.

Spec-4-yr-Faith: Special Focus Four-Year: Faith-Related Institutions
Spec-4-yr-Med: Special Focus Four-Year: Medical Schools & Centers
Spec-4-yr-Other Health: Special Focus Four-Year: Other Health Professions Schools
Spec-4-yr-Eng: Special Focus Four-Year: Engineering Schools
Spec-4-yr-Other Tech: Special Focus Four-Year: Other Technology-Related Schools
Spec-4-yr-Bus: Special Focus Four-Year: Business & Management Schools
Spec-4-yr-Arts: Special Focus Four-Year: Arts, Music & Design Schools
Spec-4-yr-Law: Special Focus Four-Year: Law Schools
Spec-4-yr-Other: Special Focus Four-Year: Other Special Focus Institutions

Tribal Colleges. Colleges and universities that are members of the American Indian Higher Education Consortium, as identified in IPEDS Institutional Characteristics.

Tribal: Tribal Colleges

---

*All data provided by Carnegie Classification of Institutions of Higher Education by Indiana University Center for Postsecondary Research. For more detailed information on the revised Carnegie Codes, please visit http://carnegieclassifications.iu.edu/. Basic Classification methodology can be found at http://carnegieclassifications.iu.edu/methodology/basic.php.

Statistics

Institutions of Higher Education by Control, Level and State

STATE	TWO YEAR		FOUR YEAR		TOTAL		SYSTEM OFFICE	GRAND TOTAL
	PRIVATE	PUBLIC	PRIVATE	PUBLIC	PRIVATE	PUBLIC		
AL	1	24	19	15	20	39	2	61
AK	2	0	3	3	5	3	1	9
AZ	6	19	23	4	29	23	1	53
AR	3	22	15	12	18	34	2	54
CA	43	103	269	50	312	153	28	493
CO	12	7	21	22	33	29	2	64
CT	0	12	18	7	18	19	1	38
DE	1	0	2	3	3	3	0	6
DC	1	0	17	3	18	3	0	21
FL	31	1	78	39	109	40	1	150
GA	7	23	42	26	49	49	1	99
HI	2	6	5	4	7	10	2	19
ID	0	3	7	5	7	8	0	15
IL	10	47	82	12	92	59	6	157
IN	6	1	43	15	49	16	2	67
IA	0	18	38	3	38	21	3	62
KS	1	25	24	9	25	34	0	59
KY	3	16	30	8	33	24	1	58
LA	5	16	14	17	19	33	4	56
ME	1	7	14	7	15	14	2	31
MD	1	16	21	16	22	32	1	55
MA	2	16	71	14	73	30	2	105
MI	3	23	42	21	45	44	1	90
MN	4	30	40	11	44	41	3	88
MS	0	15	10	9	10	24	0	34
MO	9	17	60	13	69	30	3	102
MT	6	5	7	6	13	11	1	25
NE	6	7	15	7	21	14	2	37
NV	3	1	3	6	6	7	1	14
NH	1	7	10	4	11	11	2	24
NJ	4	18	40	13	44	31	0	75
NM	0	13	9	8	9	21	0	30
NY	23	36	188	44	211	80	6	297
NC	1	58	51	17	52	75	2	129
ND	1	4	7	7	8	11	1	20
OH	17	18	72	21	89	39	0	128
OK	5	12	14	15	19	27	0	46
OR	2	17	24	8	26	25	0	51
PA	35	17	112	20	147	37	1	185
RI	0	1	9	3	9	4	0	13
SC	2	18	25	15	27	33	0	60
SD	0	5	11	6	11	11	1	23
TN	8	13	49	10	57	23	2	82
TX	24	43	83	66	107	109	8	224
UT	1	1	13	7	14	8	1	23
VT	1	1	10	4	11	5	1	17
VA	12	24	56	17	68	41	1	110
WA	3	5	24	34	27	39	2	68
WV	5	8	13	11	18	19	2	39
WI	1	16	30	13	31	29	2	62
WY	1	4	1	4	2	8	0	10
AS	0	0	0	1	0	1	0	1
GU	0	1	1	1	1	2	0	3
MH	0	1	0	0	0	1	0	1
MP	0	0	0	1	0	1	0	1
PR	4	0	41	14	45	14	3	62
FM	0	1	0	0	0	1	0	1
PW	0	1	0	0	0	1	0	1
VI	0	0	0	1	0	1	0	1
Total	**320**	**823**	**1926**	**732**	**2246**	**1555**	**108**	**3909**

Figures do not include 1,091 additional branch campuses.

50 Largest Universities by Fall 2019 Enrollment

Institution	Enrollment
1. Western Governors University	147866
2. Southern New Hampshire University	134345
3. Grand Canyon University	103427
4. Liberty University	93349
5. Arizona State University	74795
6. University of Central Florida	71881
7. Texas A & M University	70418
8. The Ohio State University Main Campus	61369
9. Florida International University	58836
10. University of Maryland Global Campus	58526
11. University of Florida	53372
12. New York University	52775
13. University of Illinois Urbana-Champaign	52679
14. University of Minnesota	52017
15. University of South Florida	50626
16. University of Texas at Austin	50476
17. Rutgers University - New Brunswick	50411
18. American Public University System	50047
19. Michigan State University	49695
20. Walden University	49695
21. University of Washington	48149
22. The University of Texas at Arlington	48072
23. University of Michigan-Ann Arbor	47907
24. University of Houston	47090
25. Purdue University Main Campus	46655
26. University of Southern California	46287
27. University of Arizona	45601
28. University of Wisconsin-Madison	44640
29. University of California-Los Angeles	44589
30. Brigham Young University-Idaho	44481
31. University of the People	43722
32. Florida State University	43569
33. Indiana University	43064
34. University of California-Berkeley	42327
35. California State University-Fullerton	42051
36. Kennesaw State University	41181
37. University of North Texas	40953
38. Utah Valley University	40936
39. University of Cincinnati Main Campus	40826
40. University of Maryland College Park	40709
41. California State University-Northridge	40381
42. Texas Tech University	40322
43. California State University-Long Beach	40069
44. University of California-San Diego	39576
45. University of Georgia	39147
46. University of California-Davis	39074
47. Capella University	38930
48. George Mason University	38541
49. The University of Alabama	37840
50. Texas State University	37812

Institutions by Control and Tuition Range

Tuition	Public*	Private	Total
0 - 1,000	80	732	812
1,001 - 2,000	129	1	130
2,001 - 4,000	267	17	284
4,001 - 6,000	426	38	464
6,001 - 8,000	219	67	286
8,001 - 10,000	208	78	286
Over 10,000	226	1313	1539
Total	**1555**	**2246**	**3801**

* Figures for Public Institutions are In-State Tuitions

Universities, Colleges and Schools

by State*

*Includes the District of Columbia and, separately, U.S. Service Schools, American Samoa, Federated States of Micronesia, Guam, Marshall Islands, Northern Marianas, Palau, Puerto Rico, and Virgin Islands.

ALABAMA

Alabama Agricultural and Mechanical University (A)

4900 Meridian Street, Normal AL 35762-1357
County: Madison FICE Identification: 001002
Unit ID: 100654
Telephone: (256) 372-5230 Carnegie Class: Masters/L
FAX Number: (256) 372-5244 Calendar System: Semester
URL: www.aamu.edu
Established: 1875 Annual Undergrad Tuition & Fees (In-State): $10,024
Enrollment: 5,977 Coed
Affiliation or Control: State IRS Status: 501(c)3
Highest Offering: Doctorate
Accreditation: SC, AAFCS, CAEP, DIETD, PLNG, SP, SW

01 President .... Dr. Andrew HUGINE, JR.
03 Executive VP/COO .... Vacant
05 Provost/VP Academic Affairs .... Dr. Daniel K. WIMS
10 Vice President Business & Finance .... Vacant
111 VP Mktg/Comm/Advancement .... Dr. Archie TUCKER
32 Vice President Student Affairs .... Dr. Gary CROSBY
46 Interim VP Inst Rsrch/Spons Pgms .... Dr. James WALKE
88 Special Assistant to the President .... Dr. Malinda SWOOPE
114 AVP Budget & Planning .... Mr. Gregory JACKSON
84 AVP of Enrollment Mgmt .... Vacant
13 Int Chief Information Officer .... Ms. Kylie NASH
21 AVP Finance/Comptroller .... Dr. Lynda BATISTE
15 Director Human Resources .... Dr. Jarrett WALTON
18 Dir Facilities and Admin Services .... Mr. Brian SHIPP
06 Registrar .... Ms. Brenda K. WILLIAMS
30 Director of Development .... Ms. Reba JASMIN
41 Director of Athletics .... Mr. Bryan HICKS
35 Director of Student Activities .... Ms. Diann ANDERSON
37 Director of Financial Aid .... Mr. Darryl JACKSON
23 Dir Student Health & Counseling .... Mr. Micah GRIFFIN
36 Dir Career Development Services .... Ms. Yvette CLAYTON
09 Dir Institutional Research .... Dr. James WALKE
26 Director Marketing & PR .... Mr. Jerome SAINTJONES
39 Dir of Residential Housing .... Ms. Karla MILLER
19 Chief of Police .... Mr. Nadis CARLISLE
08 Director Learning Resources Center .... Dr. Annie PAYTON
96 Director of Purchasing .... Mr. Timothy THORNTON
58 Dean Graduate School/AVP Acad Affs .... Dr. Derrek DUNN
47 Dean Col Agricultural/Life/Nat Sci .... Dr. Lloyd WALKER
53 Dean College of Education .... Dr. Lena WALTON
54 Dean College of Engineering .... Dr. Chance GLENN
50 Dean Col of Business/Pub Affs .... Dr. Del SMITH
49 Interim Dean University College .... Vacant
04 Executive Assistant to President .... Dr. Brittany A. HOLLOMAN
102 Dir Foundation/Corporate Relations .... Dr. Allen VITAL
29 Director Alumni Relations .... Mrs. Sandra STUBBS
43 Dir Legal Services/General Counsel .... Mrs. Angela DEBRO
45 Chief Institutional Planning .... Dr. Archie TUCKER
07 Director of Admissions .... Mr. Dwayne GREEN
86 Director Government Relations .... Ms. Roslyn CREWS

Alabama College of Osteopathic Medicine (B)

445 Health Sciences Boulevard, Dothan AL 36303
County: Houston Identification: 667138
Unit ID: 483975
Telephone: (334) 699-2266 Carnegie Class: Spec-4-yr-Med
FAX Number: N/A Calendar System: Semester
URL: www.acom.edu
Established: 2011 Annual Graduate Tuition & Fees: N/A
Enrollment: 705 Coed
Affiliation or Control: Independent Non-Profit IRS Status: 501(c)3
Highest Offering: First Professional Degree; No Undergraduates
Accreditation: OSTEO

01 President .... Rick SUTTON
05 Dean/CAO .... James C. JONES
10 Chief Financial Officer .... Derek MILLER
09 VP of Institutional Effectiveness .... Carmen LEWIS
32 Assoc Dean Student Services .... Phillip REYNOLDS
84 Exec Dir Enrollment Management .... Tara RYALS
06 Registrar .... Yasmine HILL
07 Dir of Admissions & Enrollment .... Linda GOODSON
37 Director Student Financial Aid .... Travis COBB
29 Director Alumni Affairs .... Audrey BAWCUM
26 Dir of Communications & Marketing .... Sarah SENN
19 Director Security/Safety .... MaryAnn MAY
102 Director Foundation/Corporate Rels .... Amy BUNTING
08 Chief Library Officer .... Lisa ENNIS
15 Chief Human Resources Officer .... Kevin BROYLES
25 Chief Contract and Grants Administr .... Audrey VASAUSKAS

*Alabama Community College System (C)

135 South Union Street, Montgomery AL 36104-4340
County: Montgomery Identification: 667303
Telephone: (334) 293-4500 Carnegie Class: N/A
FAX Number: (334) 293-4504
URL: www.accs.cc

01 Chancellor .... Mr. Jimmy H. BAKER
05 VC Instruction/Research/Development .... Dr. Vicky OHLSON
10 VC Admin/Financial Services .... Mr. Bryan HELMS
32 VC Student Success .... Mr. Olivier CHARLES
100 Chief of Staff & VC SDSA .... Ms. Susan Y. PRICE
15 Director Human Resources .... Ms. Nikita T. PAYNE

*Bevill State Community College (D)

1411 Indiana Avenue, Jasper AL 35501
County: Walker FICE Identification: 005733
Unit ID: 102429
Telephone: (205) 387-0511 Carnegie Class: Assoc/HVT-Mix Trad/Non
FAX Number: (205) 387-5192 Calendar System: Semester
URL: www.bscc.edu
Established: 1965 Annual Undergrad Tuition & Fees (In-State): $5,214
Enrollment: 3,204 Coed
Affiliation or Control: State IRS Status: 501(c)3
Highest Offering: Associate Degree
Accreditation: SC, ADNUR, EMT, PNUR, SURGT

02 President .... Dr. Joel HAGOOD
05 VP Instructional/Student Services .... Dr. Leslie HARTLEY
26 Dir of Public Relations/ Advancement .... Ms. Tana COLLINS-ALLRED
10 Vice Pres Administration/Finance .... Mr. John SKALNIK
32 Dean of Students .... Ms. Melissa STOWE
15 Director of Human Resources .... Ms. Mary KINARD
18 Director of Facilities & Security .... Mr. Randy STULTS
121 Dean of Student Success/Athletics .... Mr. Max WEAVER
76 Director of Health Sciences .... Ms. Reitha CABANISS
103 Dean Workforce Solutions/Econ Dev .... Mr. Al MOORE
25 Dir IE/Research & Grants .... Dr. Russell HOWTON

*Bishop State Community College (E)

351 N Broad Street, Mobile AL 36603-5898
County: Mobile FICE Identification: 001030
Unit ID: 102030
Telephone: (251) 405-7000 Carnegie Class: Assoc/HVT-Mix Trad/Non
FAX Number: N/A Calendar System: Semester
URL: www.bishop.edu
Established: 1965 Annual Undergrad Tuition & Fees (In-State): $4,860
Enrollment: 2,176 Coed
Affiliation or Control: State IRS Status: 501(c)3
Highest Offering: Associate Degree
Accreditation: SC, ACBSP, ACFEI, ADNUR, CAHIIM, PNUR, PTAA

02 President .... Dr. Reggie SYKES
03 Executive Vice President .... Dr. Lawrence BRANDYBURG
05 Dean of Instruction .... Mr. Roderick MCSWAIN
76 Dean of Health Sciences .... Dr. Dolly HORTON
103 Dean of Workforce Development .... Mr. David FELTON
32 Chief Student Affairs Officer .... Dr. Katheryne PAVEY
10 Dean of Business/Finance .... Mrs. Lois GWINN
20 Associate Academic Dean .... Mr. Theodore LABAY
20 Associate Dean of Instruction .... Dr. Andrea AGNEW
06 Registrar .... Mr. Philip URBANEK
15 Director of Human Resources .... Mrs. Kenya PARISH-ONUKWULI
111 Director Institutional Advancement .... Mrs. Sherrica HUNT
18 Director of Physical Plant .... Mr. Kenneth HOLDER
26 Director of Public Relations .... Ms. Courtney STEELE
09 Dir of Institutional Research .... Mr. Claude BUMPERS
37 Mgr Student Fin Aid/Veterans Svcs .... Dr. Gail BEGGS
13 Chief Info Technology Officer .... Mr. Lee THRASHER
19 Director Security/Safety .... Chief Lloyd WASHINGTON
41 Athletic Director .... Mr. Trenton EAGER

*Calhoun Community College (F)

PO Box 2216, Decatur AL 35609-2216
County: Limestone FICE Identification: 001013
Unit ID: 101514
Telephone: (256) 306-2500 Carnegie Class: Assoc/HT-Mix Trad/Non
FAX Number: (256) 306-2877 Calendar System: Semester
URL: www.calhoun.edu
Established: 1963 Annual Undergrad Tuition & Fees (In-State): $4,940
Enrollment: 8,278 Coed
Affiliation or Control: State IRS Status: 501(c)3
Highest Offering: Associate Degree
Accreditation: SC, ADNUR, DA, DH, EMT, MLTAD, NAEYC, PNUR, PTAA, SURGT

02 Interim President .... Dr. Jimmy HODGES
05 VP Academic Affairs .... Vacant
32 Vice President of Student Services .... Dr. Patricia WILSON
10 Dean of Business & Finance .... Mr. Jason MORGAN
07 Director Admiss/Records/Registrar .... Ms. Alanna THOMPSON
08 Director of Library Services .... Mr. James LOYD
13 Director Information Systems .... Mr. Nathan TYLER
26 Director of PR & CETV .... Mr. Wes TORAIN
12 Dean of Research Park Campus .... Mr. Mark BRANON
18 Exec Director of Physical Plant .... Mr. Bruce CAUSEY
09 Dean Planning/Research & Grants .... Dr. Debra HENDERSHOT
103 Director Workforce Solutions .... Mr. Houston BLACKWOOD
76 Dean Health Sciences .... Mr. Bret MCGILL
81 Dean Math/Natural Sciences .... Mr. Rodney ALFORD
79 Dean Humanities & Social Sciences .... Dr. Donna ESTILL
15 Director Human Resources & Payroll .... Mrs. Kim GAINES
19 Director Public Safety .... Mr. Kevin DAVENPORT
36 Director of Career Services & Co-op .... Mrs. Kelli MORRIS
37 Director Student Financial Aid .... Mrs. Janett SPENCER
04 Secretary to President .... Ms. Belinda NOE
41 Athletic Director .... Dr. Nancy KEENUM
27 Asst Director of PR & CETV .... Ms. Sherika ATTIPOE
51 Interim Director of Adult Education .... Ms. Mindi RUSSELL
72 Dean of Technologies .... Mr. John HOLLEY
50 Dean of Business and CIS .... Dr. James PAYNE
30 Director of Development .... Ms. Johnette DAVIS
84 Director Enrollment Management .... Ms. Beth WOOD
96 Director of Purchasing .... Ms. Vanessa LOONEY

*Central Alabama Community College (G)

1675 Cherokee Road, Alexander City AL 35010
County: Tallapoosa FICE Identification: 001007
Unit ID: 100760
Telephone: (256) 234-6346 Carnegie Class: Assoc/HT-Mix Trad/Non
FAX Number: (256) 234-0384 Calendar System: Semester
URL: www.cacc.edu
Established: 1963 Annual Undergrad Tuition & Fees (In-State): $4,930
Enrollment: 1,546 Coed
Affiliation or Control: State IRS Status: 501(c)3
Highest Offering: Associate Degree
Accreditation: SC, ADNUR

02 President .... Mr. Jeff LYNN
10 Dean of Financial Services .... Ms. Lisa SAWYER
05 Int Dean Instruction/Academic Pgms .... Dr. Bryan JOHNSON
32 Dean of Students .... Ms. Jerri CARROLL
35 Associate Dean of Student Services .... Vacant
09 Assoc Dean of Inst Effect/Compl .... Ms. Cindy ENTREKIN
76 Associate Dean of Health Science .... Dr. Jennifer STEELE
08 Librarian .... Ms. Denita OLIVER
06 Records Manager .... Vacant
26 Public Relations Officer .... Mr. Brett PRITCHARD
13 Chief Information Officer .... Mr. Rickey CREEL
37 Director Student Financial Aid .... Ms. Stephanie MILLER
04 Administrative Asst to President .... Ms. Lisa FORNWALT
15 Exec Director of Human Resources .... Ms. Tina SHAW
103 Dean Workforce/Econ Development .... Mr. Michael BARNETTE

*Chattahoochee Valley Community College (H)

2602 College Drive, Phenix City AL 36869-7960
County: Russell FICE Identification: 012182
Unit ID: 101028
Telephone: (334) 291-4900 Carnegie Class: Assoc/HT-High Trad
FAX Number: (334) 291-4944 Calendar System: Semester
URL: www.cv.edu
Established: 1973 Annual Undergrad Tuition & Fees (In-State): $4,920
Enrollment: 1,399 Coed
Affiliation or Control: State IRS Status: 501(c)3
Highest Offering: Associate Degree
Accreditation: SC, ADNUR, MAAB, PNUR

02 President .... Ms. Jacqueline SCREWS
05 Dean of Instruction .... Dr. Chantae CALHOUN
04 Administrative Asst to President .... Ms. Terrah BOISCLAIR
32 Dean of Students and Campus Service .... Dr. Sherri TAYLOR
10 Dean of Financial Affairs .... Mr. Dexter JACKSON
15 Director of Human Resources .... Ms. Robin JONES
45 Director of Strategic Initiatives .... Dr. RoseMary WATKINS
103 Assoc Dean of Workforce Development . Dr. Shirley ARMSTRONG
35 Assoc Dean of Student Development .... Mrs. Vickie WILLIAMS
41 Director of Athletics .... Mr. Adam THOMAS
07 Director of Admissions/Registrar .... Ms. Sanquita ALEXANDER
37 Director of Financial Aid .... Ms. Susan BRYANT
13 Director of Information Systems .... Mr. Jody NOLES
26 Marketing & Media Coordinator .... Ms. Myya ROBINSON
60 Chair of English and Communication .... Ms. Samantha VANCE
57 Chair of Fine Arts .... Dr. William BYRD
50 Chair of Business and Computer Info .... Dr. Beth MULLIN
66 Chair of Health Sciences .... Dr. Bridgett JACKSON
81 Chair of Mathematics .... Ms. Mary JOHNSON
81 Chair of Science .... Ms. Merry CUERVO
72 Director of Applied Technology .... Mr. Clint LANGLEY
19 Director of Public Safety .... Mr. Kenneth HARRISON
51 Director of Adult Education .... Dr. Darren DEAN
08 Director Learning Resources Center .... Ms. Elizabeth BRADSHER
18 Director Facilities & Maintenance .... Vacant

*Coastal Alabama Community College (I)

1900 Highway 31 S, Bay Minette AL 36507-2698
County: Baldwin FICE Identification: 001060
Unit ID: 101161
Telephone: (251) 580-2100 Carnegie Class: Assoc/MT-VT-Mix Trad/Non
FAX Number: (251) 580-2253 Calendar System: Semester
URL: www.coastalalabama.edu
Established: 1965 Annual Undergrad Tuition & Fees (In-State): $4,860
Enrollment: 6,653 Coed
Affiliation or Control: State IRS Status: 501(c)3
Highest Offering: Associate Degree
Accreditation: SC, ACFEI, ADNUR, DA, EMT, PNUR, SURGT

02 President .... Dr. Craig POUNCEY
10 Chief Financial Officer .... Ms. Jessica DAVIS
103 Dean of Workforce Development .... Dr. Josh DUPLANTIS
32 Dean of Student Services .... Mr. Vinson BRADLEY

05 Dean of Academic Instruction ....Ms. Mary Beth LANCASTER
86 Dean of External Funding ....Dr. Melinda BYRD-MURPHY
13 Dean of Information Technology ....Mr. Brian STRICKLAND
66 Dean of Nursing & Allied Health ....Ms. Jean GRAHAM
75 Dean of Career Technology ....Ms. Linda GRANT
18 Dean of Operations & Maintenance ....Mr. Mickey STOKES
106 Director of Distance Education ....Ms. Ann STRICKLAND
06 Registrar ....Ms. Beth BRYARS
37 Director of Financial Aid ....Dr. Jim THEEUWES
108 Dir of Institutional Effectiveness ....Ms. Lindsay HUTCHERSON
19 Chief of College Police ....Mr. Jonathan DAVIDSON
15 Human Resources Coordinator ....Ms. Katlyn RICE

*Enterprise State Community College (A)

PO Box 1300, Enterprise AL 36331-1300
County: Coffee FICE Identification: 001015
Unit ID: 101143
Telephone: (334) 347-2623 Carnegie Class: Assoc/MT-VT-Mix Trad/Non
FAX Number: (334) 393-6223 Calendar System: Semester
URL: www.escc.edu
Established: 1963 Annual Undergrad Tuition & Fees (In-State): $4,960
Enrollment: 1,808 Coed
Affiliation or Control: State IRS Status: 501(c)3
Highest Offering: Associate Degree
Accreditation: SC

02 Chief Executive Officer/President ....Mr. Matt RODGERS
05 Exec Vice Pres/Dean of Instruction ....Mr. Daniel LONG
32 Dean of Students ....Ms. Kassie MATHIS
10 Dir of Financial Services ....Ms. Paula HELMS
37 Director of Financial Aid ....Mr. Kevin AMMONS
26 Dir Marketing & Media Relations ....Mr. Stephen SCHMIDT
04 Administrative Asst to President ....Ms. Jennifer ADAMS
06 Registrar ....Ms. Jennifer OLSEN
102 Dir Foundation/Community Relations ....Ms. Chellye STUMP
103 Dir Workforce Devel & Adult Educ ....Ms. Leigh SHIVER
13 Director of Information Technology ....Mr. Jason TRULL
15 Human Resources Coordinator ....Ms. Jessica LUNSFORD
18 Plant Supervisor ....Mr. Michael HELMS
121 Director Counseling/Student Success ....Ms. Dava FOSTER
105 Director Web Services ....Mr. Stephen SCHMIDT
108 Director Inst Effectiveness & Plng ....Mr. Andrew DAVIS
19 Campus Police Chief ....Mr. Jeff SPENCE
88 Aviation Division Director ....Col. Stanley SMITH
121 Director of Student Support Service ....Mr. Michael HARRISON
31 Instructional Res & Cmty Educ Dir .....Ms. Ann KELLEY-SPENCE
41 Athletic Director ....Mr. Jermaine WILLIAMS

*Gadsden State Community College (B)

1001 George Wallace Dr, PO Box 227,
Gadsden AL 35902-0227
County: Etowah FICE Identification: 001017
Unit ID: 101240
Telephone: (256) 549-8200 Carnegie Class: Assoc/HVT-High Trad
FAX Number: N/A Calendar System: Semester
URL: www.gadsdenstate.edu
Established: 1925 Annual Undergrad Tuition & Fees (In-State): $3,936
Enrollment: 3,993 Coed
Affiliation or Control: State IRS Status: 501(c)3
Highest Offering: Associate Degree
Accreditation: SC, ADNUR, COMTA, DMS, EMT, MLTAD, NAEYC, PNUR, RAD

02 President ....Dr. Kathy MURPHY
10 Dean Financial/Administrative Svcs ....Dr. Kevin MCFRY
84 Dean Enrollment & Retention ....Dr. Aletta WILLIAMSON
72 Dean Tech Educ/Workforce Devel ....Mr. Alan SMITH
76 Dean Health Sciences ....Dr. Kenneth KIRKLAND
05 Dean of Academic Programs/Services .Dr. Leslie WORTHINGTON
108 Dean of Institutional Effectiveness ....Ms. Pam JOHNSON
32 Director of Student Life ....Mr. Matthew BURTTRAM
51 Director of Adult Education ....Mr. Johnny BAKER
26 Director Public Relations/Marketing ......Ms. Jackie EDMONDSON
18 Director Physical Plant ....Mr. Stewart DAVIS
21 Director of Financial Services ....Ms. Jacqueline CLARK
43 Director of Legal Affairs/Title IX ....Ms. Michele BRADFORD
15 Director Human Resources ....Ms. Kim S. COBB
41 Athletic Director ....Mr. Mike CANCILLA
124 Assoc Dean Enrollment & Retention ....Ms. Kelley H. PEARCE
37 Director of Financial Aid ....Ms. Kelly D'EATH
06 Registrar ....Ms. Laura SWANN
13 Chief Information Officer ....Mr. Alan WALLACE

*George C. Wallace Community College - Dothan (C)

1141 Wallace Drive, Dothan AL 36303-9234
County: Dale FICE Identification: 001018
Unit ID: 101286
Telephone: (334) 983-3521 Carnegie Class: Assoc/HVT-High Trad
FAX Number: (334) 983-6066 Calendar System: Semester
URL: www.wallace.edu
Established: 1947 Annual Undergrad Tuition & Fees (In-State): $4,800
Enrollment: 3,681 Coed
Affiliation or Control: State IRS Status: 501(c)3
Highest Offering: Associate Degree
Accreditation: SC, ADNUR, COARC, EMT, MAC, PNUR, PTAA, RAD, SURGT

02 President ....Dr. Linda C. YOUNG
30 VP/Dean Institutional Svcs/Cmty Dev ....Dr. Ashli WILKINS
32 Act Dean Student Affs/Sparks Campus ....Mr. Mickey BAKER
05 Dean of Instructional Affairs ....Ms. Leslie REEDER
10 Dean of Business Affairs ....Mr. Marc NICHOLAS
07 Director Admissions/Registrar ....Mr. Keith SAULSBERRY
08 Dir Learning Resources Ctrs System ....Mr. A. P. HOFFMAN
37 Director of Financial Aid ....Mr. Anthony JOUVENAS
13 Director ITS ....Mr. Patrick ADKINSON
15 Director of Human Resources ....Ms. Brooke STRICKLAND
09 Dir Institutional Effectiveness ....Ms. Mandy SESSIONS
40 Bookstore Manager ....Mr. Jeremy JAMES
21 Director of Accounting & Finance ....Ms. Heather JOHNSON-WALKER
26 Dir Public Relations & Marketing ....Ms. Taylor WHEELER
41 Athletic Director ....Mr. Mackey SASSER

*George Corley Wallace State Community College - Selma (D)

PO Box 2530, 3000 Earl Goodwin Pkwy,
Selma AL 36702-2530
County: Dallas FICE Identification: 005699
Unit ID: 101301
Telephone: (334) 876-9227 Carnegie Class: Assoc/MT-VT-Mix Trad/Non
FAX Number: (334) 876-9250 Calendar System: Semester
URL: www.wccs.edu
Established: 1963 Annual Undergrad Tuition & Fees (In-State): $4,560
Enrollment: 1,316 Coed
Affiliation or Control: State IRS Status: 501(c)3
Highest Offering: Associate Degree
Accreditation: SC, ACBSP, ADNUR, PNUR

02 President ....Dr. James M. MITCHELL
05 Dean of Instruction ....Dr. Tammie BRIGGS
20 Asst Dean of Instruction ....Mr. Raji GOURDINE
10 Dean of Business & Finance ....Dr. Rosa SPENCER
32 Dean of Students/Exec to President ....Dr. Donitha GRIFFIN
08 Librarian ....Ms. Minnie CARSTARPHEN
76 Director of Health Science ....Dr. Pearlie MILLER
37 Financial Aid Director ....Ms. Anessa KIDD
07 Director of Admissions/Counselor ....Mr. Lonzy CLIFTON
09 Asst Dean of Institutional Effect ....Mrs. Veronica BROWN
26 Director of Community Relations ....Vacant
19 Public Safety Coordinator ....Mr. Charles DYSART
41 Athletic Director ....Mr. Marcus HANNAH
18 Director of Facilities & Safety ....Mr. Keith JACKSON
15 Human Resources Coordinator ....Ms. Colleen DIXON

*J.F. Drake State Community and Technical College (E)

3421 Meridian Street N, Huntsville AL 35811-1584
County: Madison FICE Identification: 005260
Unit ID: 101462
Telephone: (256) 539-8161 Carnegie Class: Assoc/HVT-High Trad
FAX Number: (256) 539-6439 Calendar System: Semester
URL: www.drakestate.edu
Established: 1961 Annual Undergrad Tuition & Fees (In-State): $4,830
Enrollment: 825 Coed
Affiliation or Control: State IRS Status: 501(c)3
Highest Offering: Associate Degree
Accreditation: SC, PNUR

02 President ....Dr. Patricia SIMS
05 Dean of Instruction ....Dr. Carolyn HENDERSON
10 Director of Fiscal Affairs ....Mr. Akeem ALEXANDER
103 Director of Workforce Development ....Mr. Robert GRISSIM
07 Director of Admissions/ Registrar ....Dr. Monica SUDEALL-HAWKINS
15 Human Resource Specialist ....Mrs. Katie CHANCE
13 Coordinator of IT Services ....Mr. Glenn HARBIN
08 Director of Library Services ....Ms. Carla CLIFT
37 Director Student Financial Aid ....Ms. Jennifer O'LINGER
26 Director of Public Relations ....Ms. Jennifer MALONE
121 Student Success Specialist ....Ms. Tiffany GREEN
108 Dir of Institutional Effectiveness ....Ms. Lesley SHOTTS
32 Dean of Student Services ....Dr. Nicole BELL
18 Director of Operations ....Mr. Bruce BULLUCK
04 Admin Assistant to the President ....Ms. Terell JACKSON
36 Coordinator of Placement ....Ms. Karen RAY

*J.F. Ingram State Technical College (F)

PO Box 220350, Deatsville AL 36022-0350
County: Elmore FICE Identification: 030025
Unit ID: 101471
Telephone: (334) 285-5177 Carnegie Class: Assoc/HVT-Mix Trad/Non
FAX Number: (334) 285-5328 Calendar System: Semester
URL: www.istc.edu
Established: 1965 Annual Undergrad Tuition & Fees (In-State): $5,472
Enrollment: 399 Coed
Affiliation or Control: State IRS Status: 501(c)3
Highest Offering: Associate Degree
Accreditation: COE

02 President ....Mrs. Annette FUNDERBURK
05 Dean of Instruction ....Dr. William YOUNG
11 Dean of Administration ....Dr. Brannon LENTZ
32 Dean of Students/Support Svcs ....Mrs. Rosie EDWARDS
20 Associate Dean of Instruction ....Dr. Julliana PROBST
35 Student Services Director ....Mrs. Leah DARTY
15 Human Resources Coordinator ....Ms. Andrea RICHARDSON
88 Re-Entry/Counseling Programs Coord ....Mr. Rick VEST
10 Business Office Director ....Mrs. Amelia FOX
04 Administrative Asst to President ....Ms. Samantha ROSE

*Jefferson State Community College (G)

2601 Carson Road, Birmingham AL 35215-3098
County: Jefferson FICE Identification: 001022
Unit ID: 101505
Telephone: (205) 853-1200 Carnegie Class: Assoc/HVT-Mix Trad/Non
FAX Number: (205) 853-8505 Calendar System: Semester
URL: www.jeffersonstate.edu
Established: 1963 Annual Undergrad Tuition & Fees (In-State): $5,850
Enrollment: 8,526 Coed
Affiliation or Control: State IRS Status: 501(c)3
Highest Offering: Associate Degree
Accreditation: SC, ACBSP, ACFEI, ADNUR, #COARC, CONST, EMT, FUSER, MLTAD, NAEYC, PTAA, RAD

02 President ....Mr. Keith A. BROWN
32 Vice President for Student Affairs ....Dr. Phillip M. HOBBS
05 VP for Academic Affairs ....Ms. Danielle COBURN
30 Dean Campus Development/Campus Svcs ....Vacant
10 Chief Financial Officer ....Mr. David MORRIS
97 Assoc Dean Transf Gen Stds Shelby ....Ms. Liesl W. HARRIS
97 Assoc Dn Transf Gen Stds Jefferson ....Dr. Aliakbar R. YAZDI
106 Assoc Dean Distance/Dev Education ....Mr. Alan B. DAVIS
103 Dir Center for Workforce Education ....Ms. Leah M. BIGBEE
13 Chief Information Officer ....Mr. Colin EUBANKS
37 Assoc Director Financial Aid ....Ms. Morgan CHANDLER
18 Director Maintenance ....Mr. Perry HARRIS
08 Director of Learning Resources ....Ms. Barbara GOSS
36 Director Career/Learning Services ....Dr. Tamara PAYNE
84 Associate Dean Enrollment Services ....Dr. Lillian OWENS
15 Director Human Resources ....Mrs. Debbie BOONE
26 Director Media Relations ....Mr. David BOBO
96 Purchasing Coordinator ....Ms. Ann CIMALORE
19 Director Safety & Security ....Mr. Mark BAILEY
09 Dean Institutional Effectiveness ....Ms. Amanda E. KIN
04 Administrative Asst to President ....Ms. Janie STARNES
25 Director Resource Development ....Ms. Kelli CREAMER
86 Assoc Dean Economic Development .... Mr. Guin ROBINSON
20 Dean of Instruction ....Mr. Brian GORDON
72 Assoc Dean for Technical Programs ....Mrs. Deana GOODWINE
76 Assoc Dean of Health-Related Pgms ....Dr. Vanessa LEBLANC
51 Director Adult Education ....Ms. Tierra WRIGHT
88 Director of Articulation ....Mr. Adam GOODMAN

*Lawson State Community College (H)

3060 Wilson Road, SW, Birmingham AL 35221-1798
County: Jefferson FICE Identification: 001059
Unit ID: 101569
Telephone: (205) 925-2515 Carnegie Class: Assoc/MT-VT-High Trad
FAX Number: (205) 925-3716 Calendar System: Semester
URL: www.lawsonstate.edu
Established: 1949 Annual Undergrad Tuition & Fees (In-State): $4,860
Enrollment: 2,823 Coed
Affiliation or Control: State IRS Status: 501(c)3
Highest Offering: Associate Degree
Accreditation: SC, ACBSP, ADNUR, DA, PNUR

02 President ....Dr. Cynthia T. ANTHONY
05 Vice Pres of Instructional Services ....Dr. Bruce CRAWFORD
10 Vice Pres Admin & Fiscal Services ....Ms. Sharon CREWS
32 Interim Dean of Students ....Mr. Darren ALLEN
117 Dir Fin Services/Risk Assessment ....Dr. Craig D. LAWRENCE
20 Academic Dean ....Dr. Sherri DAVIS
21 Director of Accounting ....Ms. Monique SILAS
50 Assoc Dean Business/Info Tech ....Dr. Alice MILTON
49 Assoc Dean Lib Arts/Col Trans Pgms ....Dr. Karl PRUITT
76 Assoc Dean of Health Professions ....Dr. Sherika DERICO
75 Dean of Career Tech Programs ....Dr. Robert GUNTER
35 Asst Dean of Student Life ....Mr. Darren ALLEN
07 Director of Admissions ....Mr. Dorian WALUYN
08 Librarian ....Ms. Julie KENNEDY
37 Director Student Financial Aid ....Ms. Cassandra HOLLINS
15 Director of Human Resources ....Ms. Elma BELL
26 Director of Public Relations ....Mrs. Geri ALBRIGHT
18 Director of Facilities ....Mr. Chad YANCY
19 Director Safety/Security ....Mr. James BLANTON
13 Director Information Mgmt Systems ....Mr. James MANKOWICH
41 Athletic Director ....Mr. Carlton RICE
06 Registrar ....Ms. Lori CHISEM
38 Coordinator Student Counseling ....Dr. Renee HERNDON
09 Coordinator of Data Management ....Mrs. Jamie GLASS
106 Dir Online Education/E-learning ....Dr. Kesha JAMES
25 Director of Title III ....Dr. Myrtes D. GREEN
103 Asst Dean Workforce Development ....Mr. Tommy HOBBS
88 Assist Dean Career Tech Programs ....Ms. Nancy WILSON

*Lurleen B. Wallace Community College (I)

PO Drawer 1418, 1000 Dannelly Blvd,
Andalusia AL 36420-1224
County: Covington FICE Identification: 008988
Unit ID: 101602

Telephone: (334) 222-6591 Carnegie Class: Assoc/MT-VT-Mix Trad/Non
FAX Number: (334) 881-2300 Calendar System: Semester
URL: www.lbwcc.edu
Established: 1969 Annual Undergrad Tuition & Fees (In-State): $4,860
Enrollment: 1,666 Coed
Affiliation or Control: State IRS Status: 501(c)3
Highest Offering: Associate Degree
Accreditation: SC, ADNUR, DMS, EMT, PTAA

02 President .... Dr. Brock KELLEY
04 Administrative Asst to President .... Ms. Cindy GREEN
10 CFO and Senior Personnel Officer .... Ms. Lisa CARNLEY
05 Dean of Instruction .... Dr. Shannon LEVITZKE
32 Dean of Student Affairs .... Mr. Jason JESSIE
12 Dean of the Greenville Campus .... Ms. Peige JOSEY
103 Dean Workforce Dev & Strategic Int .... Ms. Jennifer HALL
111 Director Institutional Advancement .... Ms. Chrissie DUFFY
09 Assoc Dean Inst Effect & Quality .... Dr. Kristina ANDERSON
15 Human Resources Coordinator .... Ms. Ashley WILLIAMSON
18 Dir College Facilities/Maintenance .... Mr. Tim JONES
07 Director Admissions & Records .... Ms. Jan RILEY
41 Athletic Director .... Mr. Steve HELMS
08 Director of Learning Resources .... Mr. Hugh CARTER
37 Director of Financial Aid .... Ms. Donna BASS
26 Public Info Officer/Dir Marketing .... Ms. Maggie JONES

*Marion Military Institute (A)

1101 Washington Street, Marion AL 36756-3213
County: Perry FICE Identification: 001026
Unit ID: 101648
Telephone: (800) 664-1842 Carnegie Class: Assoc/HT-High Trad
FAX Number: (334) 683-2380 Calendar System: Semester
URL: www.marionmilitary.edu
Established: 1842 Annual Undergrad Tuition & Fees (In-State): $9,418
Enrollment: 401 Coed
Affiliation or Control: State IRS Status: 501(c)3
Highest Offering: Associate Degree
Accreditation: SC

02 President .... Col. David J. MOLLAHAN
10 Comptroller .... Mrs. Jada L. HARRISON
05 Chief Academic Officer .... Mr. David IVEY
32 VP Student Affairs/Commandant .... Col. Ed PASSMORE
111 VP for Institutional Advancement .... Mrs. Suzanne MCKEE
41 Director of Athletics .... Dr. Michelle IVEY
84 Director of Enrollment Management .... Mrs. Brittany CRAWFORD
29 Director of Alumni and Comm Affairs .... Mrs. Dawn CURTIS
88 ROTC Professor of Military Science .... MG. Juan MARTINEZ
09 Director of Institutional Research .... Mr. Logan LOGAN
06 Registrar .... Vacant
15 Dir Human Resources/Compliance .... Ms. Carmon P. FIELDS
37 Director of Financial Aid .... Ms. Jacqueline WILSON
08 Director Service Academy Program .... LTC. Thomas BOWEN
18 Director of Facilities .... SCPO. Robert D. SUMLIN
17 Director of Health Services .... Mrs. Rene SUMLIN
20 Chief Instructional Officer .... Mrs. Camie JONES

*Northeast Alabama Community College (B)

PO Box 159, 138 Alabama Highway 35,
Rainsville AL 35986-0159
County: DeKalb/Jackson FICE Identification: 001031
Unit ID: 101897
Telephone: (256) 638-4418 Carnegie Class: Assoc/MT-VT-Mix Trad/Non
FAX Number: (256) 638-3052 Calendar System: Semester
URL: www.nacc.edu
Established: 1963 Annual Undergrad Tuition & Fees (In-State): $4,860
Enrollment: 2,530 Coed
Affiliation or Control: State IRS Status: 501(c)3
Highest Offering: Associate Degree
Accreditation: SC, ADNUR, EMT, PNUR

02 President .... Dr. J. David CAMPBELL
05 Vice Pres/Dean of Instruction .... Mr. Chad GORHAM
56 Director Extended Day/Distance Educ .... Mr. Chad GORHAM
32 Dean of Student Services .... Ms. Sherie GRACE
10 Dean of Admin Services .... Mr. Rodney BONE
37 Director of Financial Aid .... Mr. Kip WILLIAMSON
103 Dir Workforce Devel/Skills Training .... Mr. Mike KENNAMER
26 Director of Promotions & Marketing .... Ms. Meg NIPPERS
45 Dir Inst Planning & Assessment .... Mr. Brad DUDLEY
18 Chief Facilities/Physical Plant .... Mr. Kent JONES
06 Registrar/Chief Bus Ofcr/Dir Purch .... Mr. Rodney BONE
30 Development Director .... Ms. Heather RICE
19 Director of Police/Security .... Mr. Van MCALPIN
04 Executive Asst to President .... Ms. Brenda STRINGER
08 Dir Learning Resource Ctr/Library .... Mrs. Julia EVERETT
15 Human Resources Director .... Mrs. Lynde MANN
29 Event Planning/Alumni Relations .... Ms. Chasley BELLOMY
72 Director of Educational Technology .... Ms. Patricia COMBS
41 Athletic Director .... Mr. Chad GORHAM

*Northwest - Shoals Community College (C)

800 George Wallace Boulevard,
Muscle Shoals AL 35661-3205
County: Colbert FICE Identification: 005697
Unit ID: 101736
Telephone: (256) 331-5200 Carnegie Class: Assoc/MT-VT-Mix Trad/Non
FAX Number: (256) 331-5222 Calendar System: Semester
URL: www.nwscc.edu
Established: 1963 Annual Undergrad Tuition & Fees (In-State): $4,831
Enrollment: 3,360 Coed
Affiliation or Control: State IRS Status: 501(c)3
Highest Offering: Associate Degree
Accreditation: SC, ADNUR, EMT, MAC, PNUR

02 President .... Dr. Glenda COLAGROSS
108 Assoc Dean Inst Effect/Advancement .... Mr. John MCINTOSH
05 Assoc Dean Academic Programs .... Dr. Timmy JAMES
37 Director of Financial Aid .... Ms. Lisa LILLEY
32 Assistant Dean of Student Services .... Dr. Crystal REED
11 Asst Dean College Services .... Mr. Tom CARTER
15 Human Resources Coordinator .... Ms. Tia STONE
13 Director of Management Info Systems .... Mr. Alan MITCHELL
07 Director of Admissions/Registrar .... Ms. Tracy RABY
76 Assoc Dean Health Studies .... Ms. Rose JONES
55 Director of Adult Educ and RTW .... Ms. Tara BRANSCOME
04 Administrative Asst to President .... Ms. Teresa HARRISON
26 Public Information Officer .... Mr. Trent RANDOLPH
35 Exec Director Student Services .... Ms. Brittany JONES
25 Exec Dir Grants Dev/Strategic Prtnr .... Ms. Leslie TOMLINSON
10 Dean of Finance .... Ms. Dawnelle ROBINSON
09 Director of Institutional Research .... Ms. Angie STONE

*Reid State Technical College (D)

PO Box 588, 100 Hwy 83, Evergreen AL 36401-0588
County: Conecuh FICE Identification: 005692
Unit ID: 101994
Telephone: (251) 578-1313 Carnegie Class: Assoc/HVT-Mix Trad/Non
FAX Number: (251) 578-5355 Calendar System: Semester
URL: www.rstc.edu
Established: 1966 Annual Undergrad Tuition & Fees (In-State): $4,920
Enrollment: 279 Coed
Affiliation or Control: State IRS Status: 501(c)3
Highest Offering: Associate Degree
Accreditation: COE

02 President/Dean of Instruction .... Dr. Coretta BOYKIN
32 Dean of Students .... Dr. Tangela PURIFOY
09 Asst Dean for Institutional Effect .... Vacant
37 Director Financial Aid .... Ms. Christy GOODWIN
15 Director of Human Resources .... Ms. Brenda JACKSON
07 Admissions & Records Coord .... Ms. Natalie RAY
10 Director of Accounting .... Ms. Jenelle SMITH
06 Registrar .... Ms. Vickie NICHOLSON
19 Campus Police Officer .... Mr. James WILKINS

*Shelton State Community College (E)

9500 Old Greensboro Road, Tuscaloosa AL 35405-8522
County: Tuscaloosa FICE Identification: 005691
Unit ID: 102067
Telephone: (205) 391-2211 Carnegie Class: Assoc/HVT-High Trad
FAX Number: (205) 391-2426 Calendar System: Semester
URL: www.sheltonstate.edu
Established: 1953 Annual Undergrad Tuition & Fees (In-State): $4,560
Enrollment: 3,743 Coed
Affiliation or Control: State IRS Status: 501(c)3
Highest Offering: Associate Degree
Accreditation: SC, ADNUR, CAHIIM, COARC, PNUR

02 President .... Mr. Brad NEWMAN
10 Comptroller Business Services .... Mrs. Ann BRACKNELL
32 Dean of Student Services .... Mrs. Amanda HARBISON
13 Assoc Dean of Technology .... Mr. Grant COCKRELL
12 Dean Fredd Campus/Title III .... Mr. Ronald RANGE
35 Assoc Dean of Student Services .... Dr. Byron ABSTON
76 Allied Health Assistant Dean .... Ms. Gladys HILL
37 Director of Financial Aid .... Ms. Nicole ELAM
04 Executive Asst to the President .... Ms. Channing H. MARLOWE
07 Director of Admissions/Registrar .... Mrs. Fannie BATES-REESE
08 Asst Director Library Services .... Ms. Kelly GRIFFITH
55 Director Adult Education .... Ms. Kristen BOBO
15 Director of Human Resources .... Mr. Kevin DAVIS
14 Assoc Dean of Technical Services .... Mr. Claude LAKE
04 Administrative Asst to President .... Mrs. Ann H. TINSLEY
09 Dir Institutional Effective/Rsrch .... Dr. Louis SHEDD
106 Instructional Tech and eLearning .... Mr. John ALEXANDER
106 Business Ofc Mgmt/Technology .... Mr. Robert PRESSLEY
26 Dir of Media Communication .... Ms. Lisa WALDROP
105 Assoc Dean of Info/Tech Services .... Mr. Claude LAKE
102 Foundation .... Ms. Kimberly CHAMBLESS
25 Director of Grants .... Dr. Jonathan KOH
41 Athletic Director .... Ms. Cara CROSSLIN
88 Director of Advising .... Ms. Sophia EVERETT

*Snead State Community College (F)

PO Box 734, Boaz AL 35957-0734
County: Marshall FICE Identification: 001038
Unit ID: 102076
Telephone: (256) 593-5120 Carnegie Class: Assoc/HT-Mix Trad/Non
FAX Number: N/A Calendar System: Semester
URL: www.snead.edu
Established: 1898 Annual Undergrad Tuition & Fees (In-State): $5,344
Enrollment: 2,006 Coed
Affiliation or Control: State IRS Status: Exempt
Highest Offering: Associate Degree
Accreditation: #SC, ADNUR

02 President .... Dr. Joe WHITMORE
32 Vice President for Student Services .... Mr. Jason CANNON
10 Interim Chief Financial Officer .... Ms. Tina SIMONS
13 Acting Chief IT Officer .... Mr. Don RODEN
26 Director of Marketing/PR .... Ms. Shelley SMITH
88 Coordinator of Testing/Secondary Ed .... Ms. Tonya SHIELDS
05 Interim VP for Acad Affairs/CAO .... Mr. Vann SCOTT
106 Associate Dean Online Learning .... Mr. Michael GIBSON
81 Science Division Director .... Ms. Deborah RHODEN
79 Humanities/Languages Div Director .... Dr. Cynthia DENHAM
83 Social Sc/Business/Off Adm Div Dir .... Dr. Meredith JACKSON
81 Mathematics Division Director .... Dr. Cheri COLVIN
57 Fine Arts Division Director .... Dr. Barbara HUDSON
103 Director Workforce Development .... Ms. Teresa WALKER
76 Interim Director Health Sciences .... Dr. Lisa BROCK
41 Athletic Director .... Mr. Mark RICHARD
08 Head Librarian .... Mr. John MILLER
15 Director of Human Resources .... Ms. Amanda GUNNELS
18 Director of Physical Plant .... Mr. Steve WILLIAMS
07 Director of Admissions/Recruitment .... Ms. Tristin CALLAHAN
19 Director Security/Safety .... Mr. Paul GORE
29 Director Alumni Relations .... Ms. Shelley SMITH
102 Foundation Coordinator .... Ms. Kelli CONLEY
37 Director of Financial Aid .... Ms. Amanda CHILDRESS
04 Executive Asst to President .... Ms. Kelli CONLEY

*Southern Union State Community College (G)

PO Box 1000, Wadley AL 36276-1000
County: Randolph FICE Identification: 001040
Unit ID: 251260
Telephone: (256) 395-2211 Carnegie Class: Assoc/MT-VT-High Trad
FAX Number: (256) 395-2215 Calendar System: Semester
URL: www.suscc.edu
Established: 1922 Annual Undergrad Tuition & Fees (In-State): $4,860
Enrollment: 3,950 Coed
Affiliation or Control: State IRS Status: 501(c)3
Highest Offering: Associate Degree
Accreditation: SC, ADNUR, EMT, @PTAA, RAD, SURGT

02 President .... Mr. Todd SHACKETT
05 Dean of Academics .... Dr. Linda NORTH
32 Dean Student Development .... Mr. Gary BRANCH
35 Associate Dean of Students .... Ms. Derika GRIFFIN
20 Assoc Dean of Instruction .... Mr. Steve SPRATLIN
72 Dean of Technical Educ/Wrkfce Dev .... Dr. Darin BALDWIN
06 Registrar .... Ms. Amber LOVELACE
10 VP of Financial & Admin Services .... Mr. Ben JORDAN
04 Assistant to the President .... Ms. Alison OSBORN
09 Assoc Dean of Inst Research .... Mr. Eddie PIGG
13 Director of MIS .... Vacant
15 Director of Human Resources .... Ms. Sandra HUGHLEY
31 Director of Media Relations .... Ms. Shondae BROWN
37 Director Student Financial Aid .... Ms. Melissa TODD
45 Assoc Dean of Inst Effectiveness .... Ms. Robin BROWN
19 Chief of Campus Police .... Mr. Jimmy HOLMES
84 Director Enrollment Management .... Dr. Christopher FRANKLIN

*Trenholm State Community College (H)

PO Box 10048, Montgomery AL 36108
County: Montgomery FICE Identification: 005734
Unit ID: 102313
Telephone: (334) 420-4200 Carnegie Class: Assoc/HVT-High Trad
FAX Number: (334) 420-4206 Calendar System: Semester
URL: www.trenholmstate.edu
Established: 1963 Annual Undergrad Tuition & Fees (In-State): $4,770
Enrollment: 1,526 Coed
Affiliation or Control: State IRS Status: Exempt
Highest Offering: Associate Degree
Accreditation: SC, ACFEI, #COARC, DA, DMS, EMT, MAC, PNUR, RAD

02 Acting President .... Dr. Kemba CHAMBERS
10 Dean of Finance/Admin Svcs .... Vacant
05 Exec VP of Instructional Services .... Vacant
30 Dean of Development .... Dr. Suresh C. KAUSHIK
32 Dean of Students .... Ms. Theresa MAYS
20 Dean of Instruction .... Dr. Nakia ROBINSON
103 Dean of Workforce Development .... Mr. Danny PERRY
76 Associate Dean of Health Svcs .... Dr. Tracie CARTER
13 Director of IT .... Vacant
09 Dir of Institutional Effectiveness .... Dr. Mimi JOHNSON
18 Director Physical Plant .... Mr. Robert ALLEN
37 Director Student Financial Aid .... Ms. Betty EDWARDS
06 Registrar .... Dr. Tennie S. MCBRYDE
84 Director of Enrollment Management .... Ms. Valerie ALLEN-PORTERFIELD
08 Head Librarian .... Mr. Paul BLACKMON
26 Public Information Officer .... Ms. Angela HURST
15 Director of Human Resources .... Dr. Pam ROLLINS
51 Dir Title III/Marketing/Cont Educ .... Ms. Carol WILLIAMS
36 Coordinator Job Placement .... Ms. Shawanda WALKER
04 Administrative Asst to President .... Mrs. Shearese G. GRANT

*Wallace State Community College - Hanceville (I)

PO Box 2000, 801 Main Street, NW,
Hanceville AL 35077-2000
County: Cullman FICE Identification: 007871
Unit ID: 101295

Telephone: (256) 352-8000 Carnegie Class: Assoc/HVT-High Trad
FAX Number: (256) 352-8228 Calendar System: Semester
URL: www.wallacestate.edu
Established: 1966 Annual Undergrad Tuition & Fees (In-State): $4,860
Enrollment: 4,763 Coed
Affiliation or Control: State IRS Status: 501(c)3
Highest Offering: Associate Degree
Accreditation: SC, ACBSP, ACFEI, ADNUR, CAHIIM, COARC, DA, DH, DMS, EMT, MAC, MLTAD, NAEYC, OTA, PNUR, POLYT, PTAA, RAD

02 President .... Dr. Vicki KAROLEWICS
10 Dean of Finance & Admin Svcs .... Mary H. INGRAM
05 Dean of Academic Affairs .... Dr. Beth BOWNES-JOHNSON
72 Dean of Applied Technologies .... Wes RAKESTRAW
76 Vice President for Learning .... Lisa GERMAN
32 Vice President for Students .... Dr. Ryan SMITH
84 Asst Dean Enrollment Management .... Jennifer HILL
121 Director of Advising .... Whit RICE
109 Auxiliary Director .... Mark BOLIN
08 Head Librarian .... Lisa HULLETT
37 Director of Financial Aid .... Becky GRAVES
55 Extended Day Program Director .... Wayne MANORD
15 Director of Human Resources .... Alyce FLANIGAN
111 VP for Advancement and Innovation .... Suzanne HARBIN
18 Director of Physical Plant .... Billy ROSE
26 Director Communications/Marketing .... Kristen HOLMES
06 Registrar .... Jennifer TWITTY
09 Coordinator of Inst Research .... Mattie HUDSON
103 Director Workforce Development .... Jamie BLACKMON
13 Chief Information Technology Ofcr .... Brian ALLEN
41 Athletic Director .... Paul BAILEY

Alabama State University (A)

915 S Jackson Street, Montgomery AL 36101-0271
County: Montgomery FICE Identification: 001005
Unit ID: 100724
Telephone: (334) 229-4100 Carnegie Class: Masters/M
FAX Number: (334) 834-6861 Calendar System: Semester
URL: www.alasu.edu
Established: 1867 Annual Undergrad Tuition & Fees (In-State): $11,068
Enrollment: 4,072 Coed
Affiliation or Control: State IRS Status: 501(c)3
Highest Offering: Doctorate
Accreditation: SC, ACBSP, ART, CACREP, CAEPN, CAHIIM, MUS, OPE, OT, PTA, SW, THEA

01 President .... Dr. Quinton T. ROSS, JR.
05 Provost/Vice Pres Academic Affs .... Dr. Carl PETTIS
10 Int Vice Pres Business & Finance .... Mr. William HOPPER
13 Director Technology Services .... Mr. Larry COBB
111 Vice Pres Institutional Advance .... Ms. Lois RUSSELL
15 Director Human Resources .... Mr. Derrick CARR
20 Assoc Provost Academic Affairs .... Dr. Kennedy WEKESA
32 Int Vice Pres Student Affairs .... Dr. Kevin ROLLE
18 Vice Pres Facilities Mgt/Operations .... Mr. Donald DOTSON
45 Assoc Vice Pres Inst Effectiveness .... Dr. Christine THOMAS
35 Int Asst Vice Pres Student Affairs .... Dr. Lynwood WHITTEN
21 Int Comptroller/AVP Business & Fin .... Mrs. Alondrea J. PRITCHETT
108 Dir Acad Planning & Evaluation .... Vacant
09 Director Institutional Research .... Dr. Bryn BAKOYEMA
88 Coord Quality Enhancement Planning .... Dr. Rolanda HORN
08 Dean Libraries/Learning Resource .... Dr. Janice FRANKLIN
07 Director Admissions/Recruitment .... Mr. Freddie WILLIAMS
37 Financial Aid Director .... Ms. Robyn SIDDELL
36 Director Career Services .... Dr. Sabrina CROWDER
50 Dean College Business Admin .... Dr. Kamal HINGORANI
89 Dean University College .... Dr. Evelyn HODGE
53 Dean College of Education .... Dr. Nicole STRANGE-MARTIN
64 Dean Visual & Performing Arts .... Dr. Wendy COLEMAN
58 Dean Graduate Studies .... Dr. Caterina BRISTOL
81 Dean College of Sci Math & Tech .... Dr. Audrey NAPIER
49 Int Dean Liberal Arts/Social Sci .... Dr. Kathaleen AMENDE
76 Dean College Health Sciences .... Dr. Charlene PORTEE
51 Director Continuing Education .... Vacant
29 Director Alumni Relations .... Mr. Cromwell HANDY
23 Sr Director Health Services .... Dr. Joyce LLOYD-DAVIS
19 Depty Director of Public Safety .... Mr. Kevin KENDRICK
38 Dir Counseling & Development Svcs .... Mr. Chris JOHNS
39 Dir Housing/Residential Life .... Ms. Rakesia HINES
41 Director of Athletics .... Ms. Jennifer WILLIAMS
25 Director Research & Sponsored Pgms .... Mr. Pernell JENKINS
96 Director of Procurement .... Ms. Patricia THOMAS
101 Board Liaison .... Mrs. Danielle KENNEDY-JONES
106 Dir Online Education/E-learning .... Dr. Patrice GLENN-JONES
43 General Counsel .... Mr. Kenneth THOMAS
06 Registrar .... Ms. Marie MCNEAR
26 Chief Public Relations/Marketing .... Mr. Kenneth MULLINAX
28 Dir of Diversity/International Affs .... Mr. Linwood WHITTEN
100 Chief of Staff .... Dr. Kevin A. ROLLE
102 Exec Dir Institutional Advancement .... Mrs. Jennifer ANDERSON
84 Director Enrollment Management .... Mr. Freddie WILLIAMS

Amridge University (B)

1200 Taylor Road, Montgomery AL 36117-3553
County: Montgomery FICE Identification: 025034
Unit ID: 100690
Telephone: (800) 351-4040 Carnegie Class: Masters/S
FAX Number: (334) 387-3878 Calendar System: Semester
URL: www.amridgeuniversity.edu
Established: 1967 Annual Undergrad Tuition & Fees: $6,950
Enrollment: 775 Coed
Affiliation or Control: Churches Of Christ IRS Status: 501(c)3
Highest Offering: Doctorate
Accreditation: SC

01 President .... Dr. Michael C. TURNER
05 Academic Vice President/Dean .... Dr. Lee TAYLOR
32 VP of Student Affairs & Technology .... Mrs. Laina T. COSTANZA
06 Registrar .... Mrs. Elaine P. TARENCE
08 Director Learning Resources .... Vacant
10 Controller .... Dr. Anita L. CROSBY
113 Bursar .... Mrs. B. P. TURNER
37 Financial Aid Director .... Ms. Starr PEACOCK
13 System Admin Network Operations .... Mr. Jack TEMPLE
18 Maintenance .... Mr. Robert SHIRLEY
24 Coordinator of Network Opers .... Mr. Thomas PATTERSON
38 Director of Student Counseling .... Vacant
73 Chair School of Theology .... Dr. Rodney CLOUD
50 Chair Col of Business & Ldrshp .... Dr. Kenyetta MCCURTY
97 Dean of College of General Studies .... Vacant
15 Human Resources Coordinator .... Mrs. Patsy MORETZ
08 Head Librarian .... Mr. Terence SHERIDAN
84 Enrollment Coordinator .... Mr. Brooks HOUSLEY

Athens State University (C)

300 N Beaty Street, Athens AL 35611-1902
County: Limestone FICE Identification: 001008
Unit ID: 100812
Telephone: (256) 233-8100 Carnegie Class: Bac-Diverse
FAX Number: (256) 216-3324 Calendar System: Semester
URL: www.athens.edu
Established: 1822 Annual Undergrad Tuition & Fees (In-State): N/A
Enrollment: 2,867 Coed
Affiliation or Control: State IRS Status: 501(c)3
Highest Offering: Master's
Accreditation: SC, ACBSP, CAEPN

01 President .... Dr. Philip K. WAY
05 Provost/VP for Academic Affairs .... Dr. Catherine WEHLBURG
88 Senior Executive to the President .... Dr. Kim LAFEVOR
32 VP Enroll/Student Support Svcs .... Ms. Sarah MCABEE
84 Asst VP for Enrollment Mgmt .... Dr. Rick BARTH
10 Vice President Financial Affairs .... Mr. Mike MCCOY
21 Business Manager/Asst VP Finance .... Mr. Jonathan CRAFT
111 Vice Pres for University Advance .... Dr. Keith FERGUSON
103 VP Corporate & Community Relations .... Dr. Joe DELAP
08 Director of Libraries .... Vacant
50 Dean College of Business .... Mr. Gary VALCANA
53 Dean College of Education .... Dr. Lee VARTANIAN
49 Dean College of Arts & Sciences .... Dr. Stephen SPENCER
36 Dir of Career Development Center .... Dr. Michael RADDEN
37 Dir of Student Financial Services .... Mr. Mitchell BAZZEL
06 Registrar .... Dr. Greg HOLLIDAY
07 Chief of Records .... Ms. Teresa SUIT
29 Dir Alumni Affairs/Major Gifts .... Ms. Rachel O'SULLIVAN
30 AVP University Development .... Mr. David BROWN
26 Director of Printing & Public Rels .... Mr. Chris LATHAM
09 Director of Institutional Research .... Mr. Jeffrey GUENTHER
18 Director of Physical Plant .... Mr. Kerry WARREN
15 Director of Human Resources .... Mr. Jeff POWERS
51 Director of Ctr for Lifelong Lrng .... Mr. Andrew DOLLAR
121 Sr Director of Student Success Ctr .... Mr. Derrek SMITH
28 Dir Student Inclusion Initiatives .... Mr. Richard COLLIE
04 Administrative Asst to President .... Vacant
101 Secretary of the Institution/Board .... Mrs. Jackie GOOCH
13 Chief Info Technology Officer .... Ms. Belinda KRIGEL
19 Chief of Security/Safety .... Mr. Jerry CRABTREE

Auburn University (D)

Auburn AL 36849
County: Lee FICE Identification: 001009
Unit ID: 100858
Telephone: (334) 844-4000 Carnegie Class: DU-Highest
FAX Number: N/A Calendar System: Semester
URL: www.auburn.edu
Established: 1856 Annual Undergrad Tuition & Fees (In-State): $11,796
Enrollment: 30,737 Coed
Affiliation or Control: State IRS Status: 501(c)3
Highest Offering: Doctorate
Accreditation: SC, AAB, ART, AUD, CACREP, CAEPN, CIDA, CLPSY, CONST, COPSY, DIETD, @DIETI, IPSY, JOUR, LSAR, MFCD, MUS, NURSE, PHAR, PLNG, SP, SPAA, SW, THEA, VET

01 President .... Dr. Jay GOGUE
03 Executive Vice President .... Lt Gen. Ronald L. BURGESS
05 Provost/Senior VP Academic Affairs .... Dr. Bill C. HARDGRAVE
29 VP Alumni Affairs .... Ms. Gretchen R. VANVALKENBURG
10 VP Business & Finance & CFO .... Ms. Kelli D. SHOMAKER
111 Senior VP for Advancement .... Mr. John MORRIS
32 Senior VP Student Affairs .... Dr. Bobby R. WOODARD
84 Vice Pres Enrollment Services .... Ms. Joffery GAYMON
46 Vice Pres Research .... Dr. James WEYHENMEYER
101 Secretary to Board of Trustees .... Mr. Jon G. WAGGONER
43 General Counsel .... Ms. Jaime S. HAMMER
13 VP & Chief Information Officer .... Mr. James O'CONNOR
78 Dir AL Cooperative Extension Sys .... Dr. Mike PHILLIPS
41 Director of Athletics .... Mr. C. Allen GREENE
86 Exec Director Governmental Affairs .... Mr. Jared WHITE
26 Exec Director Public Affairs .... Dr. Jennifer ADAMS
116 AVP Internal Audit/Compl & Privacy .... Mr. M. Kevin ROBINSON
19 Exec Director Risk Mgmt & Safety .... Mr. Chris O'GWYNN
27 Assistant VP Univ Comm & Mktg .... Mr. Mike CLARDY, JR.
88 Univ Ombudsperson .... Mr. Kevin COONROD
20 Associate Provost .... Dr. Emmett WINN
20 Associate Provost .... Dr. Norman GODWIN
88 Asst VP Strat Initiatives & Comm .... Ms. Julie HUFF
28 Assoc Prov/VP Inclus & Diversity .... Dr. Taffye BENSON-CLAYTON
25 Assistant VP Research .... Ms. Martha M. TAYLOR
35 Associate VP Student Affairs .... Dr. Lady D. COX
39 Assoc VP Campus Living .... Dr. Bryan RUSH
121 Director of University Advising .... Dr. Ruthanna SPIERS
31 VP University Outreach .... Dr. Royrickers COOK
85 Asst Provost Intl Programs .... Dr. Andrew R. GILLESPIE
18 Associate VP Facilities .... Mr. Daniel P. KING
15 Associate VP Human Resources .... Ms. Karla S. MCCORMICK
21 Assoc VP Financial Svcs/Controller .... Ms. Amy K. DOUGLAS
96 Dir Procurement & Business Svcs .... Ms. Missty KENNEDY
37 Exec Dir Student Financial Svcs .... Mr. Michael C. REYNOLDS
22 Director Affirmative Action/EEO .... Ms. Kelley G. TAYLOR
108 Director Academic Assessment .... Dr. Katie BOYD
09 Director Institutional Research .... Dr. Matthew CAMPBELL
88 Acting Director University Writing .... Dr. Christopher BASGIER
120 Director Teaching & Learning Center .... Dr. Asim ALI
88 Exec Dir Performing Arts Center .... Mr. Christopher J. HEACOX
39 Dir Univ Housing/Residence Life .... Dr. Kevin J. HOULT
36 Director Career Center .... Vacant
38 Director Student Counseling Svcs .... Dr. Doug HANKES
117 Director Security/Safety .... Mr. Kelvin KING
40 Director University Bookstore .... Ms. Catherine LEE
06 University Registrar .... Ms. Karen BATTYE
47 Dean Agriculture & Dir AAES .... Dr. Paul M. PATTERSON
48 Dean Architecture/Design/Construct .... Dr. Vini NATHAN
50 Dean Business .... Dr. Annette L. RANFT
53 Dean Education .... Dr. Jeffrey FAIRBROTHER
54 Dean Engineering .... Dr. Christopher B. ROBERTS
65 Dean Forestry/Wildlife Sci .... Dr. Janaki R. ALAVALAPATI
59 Dean Human Sciences .... Dr. Susan G. HUBBARD
49 Dean Liberal Arts .... Dr. Joseph AISTRUP
66 Dean Nursing .... Dr. Gregg NEWSCHWANDER
67 Dean Pharmacy .... Dr. Richard A. HANSEN
81 Dean Sciences & Mathematics .... Dr. Nicholas J. GIORDANO
74 Dean Veterinary Medicine .... Dr. Calvin M. JOHNSON
58 Dean Graduate School .... Dr. George FLOWERS
08 Dean University Libraries .... Dr. Shali L. ZHANG
04 Administrative Asst to President .... Ms. Janie A. BOLES
07 Assoc Director of Admissions .... Ms. Allison SAGGUS
104 Director of Auburn Abroad .... Ms. Deborah WEISS
30 Director of Development .... Ms. Tara JONES
44 Director of Annual Giving .... Mr. Ryan A. KING
114 Asst VP Budgets & Business Opers .... Mr. Bryan ELMORE

Auburn University at Montgomery (E)

PO Box 244024, Montgomery AL 36124-4023
County: Montgomery FICE Identification: 008310
Unit ID: 100830
Telephone: (334) 244-3000 Carnegie Class: Masters/L
FAX Number: (334) 244-3762 Calendar System: Semester
URL: www.aum.edu
Established: 1967 Annual Undergrad Tuition & Fees (In-State): $8,860
Enrollment: 5,212 Coed
Affiliation or Control: State IRS Status: 501(c)3
Highest Offering: Doctorate
Accreditation: SC, CACREP, CAEP, MT, NURSE, SPAA

01 Chancellor .... Dr. Carl A. STOCKTON
05 Provost/Sr Vice Chancellor .... Dr. Mrinal VARMA
10 Vice Chanc Financial & Admin Svcs .... Mr. Scott PARSONS
58 Assoc Provost Grad Studies/Faculty .... Dr. Matthew RAGLAND
20 Assoc Provost Undergraduate Studies .... Dr. Joy CLARK
84 Assoc Provost Enrollment .... Dr. Sameer PANDE
41 Athletic Director .... Ms. Jessie ROSA
85 Director of Global Initiatives .... Mr. Ayush TANEJA
15 Chief HR Officer .... Ms. Leslie MEADOWS
08 Dean of Library .... Mr. Phill JOHNSON
07 Director of Admissions/Recruiting .... Mr. Ronnie MCKINNEY
37 Sr Director of Financial Aid .... Mr. Anthony RICHEY
109 Chief Campus Services Officer .... Mr. Daryl MORRIS
39 Dir Housing & Residence Life .... Ms. Iyisha HAMPTON
13 Chief Information Officer .... Mr. Tobias MENSE
32 Dean of Students .... Dr. Leon HIGDON
19 Director of Police Operations .... Ms. Brenda MITCHELL
06 Registrar .... Ms. Holly BENSON
36 Director Career Development .... Mr. Bradley ROBBINS
26 Director of Communications .... Mr. Troy JOHNSON
25 Mgr Research Compl/Spons Programs .... Ms. Debra TOMBLIN
50 Dean of College of Business .... Dr. Ross DICKENS
53 Dean of College of Education .... Dr. Sheila AUSTIN
83 Dean Col Liberal Arts/Social Sci .... Dr. Andrew MCMICHAEL
66 Dean of Nursing/Health Sci .... Dr. Jean LEUNER
23 Dir of Counseling and Health Svcs .... Ms. Greta CHAMBLESS
81 Dean College of Sciences .... Dr. Douglas LEAMAN
04 Executive Admin Asst to Chancellor .... Ms. Robin FORESTER
88 Special Asst/Collab Part/Dist Educ .... Dr. Shanta VARMA
29 Dir of Alumni Relations .... Ms. Valerie RANKIN
22 Director Disability Services .... Ms. Tamara MASSEY-GARRETT

Birmingham-Southern College (F)

900 Arkadelphia Road, Birmingham AL 35254-0001
County: Jefferson FICE Identification: 001012
Unit ID: 100937
Telephone: (205) 226-4600 Carnegie Class: Bac-A&S
FAX Number: (205) 226-4627 Calendar System: 4/1/4
URL: www.bsc.edu
Established: 1856 Annual Undergrad Tuition & Fees: $18,900
Enrollment: 1,129 Coed

Affiliation or Control: United Methodist IRS Status: 501(c)3
Highest Offering: Baccalaureate
Accreditation: SC, MUS

01 President .... Mr. Daniel COLEMAN
05 VP Academic Affairs/Provost .... Dr. Brad CASKEY
10 Int VP Finance/CFO .... Mr. Lane ESTES
11 VP Administration/Chief Oper Ofcr .... Mr. Lane ESTES
111 VP Advancement and Communications .... Ms. Virginia G. LOFTIN
13 VP Information Technology .... Mr. Anthony HAMBEY
32 VP Student Development .... Dr. David EBERHARDT
84 VP Enrollment Management .... Mr. Trent GILBERT
20 Assoc Provost .... Dr. Tim SMITH
20 Assistant Provost .... Ms. Martha Ann STEVENSON
06 Registrar .... Ms. Amy SMITH
42 Chaplain .... Rev. Julie HOLLY
29 Director Alumni Engagement .... Ms. Jennifer WATERS
23 Director of Health Services .... Ms. Yvette SPENCER
88 Asst to the VP Admin/Finance .... Mr. Chuck EVANS
26 Director of Communications .... Ms. Amy ABEYTA
08 Director of the Library .... Ms. Tiffany NORRIS
18 Director of Facilities & Events .... Mr. Travis PRINCE
15 Assoc VP/Director Human Resources .... Ms. Susan KINNEY
38 Director of Counseling .... Ms. Cara BLAKES
41 Athletic Director .... Ms. Kyndall WATERS
19 Chief of Campus Police .... Mr. Jeff HARRIS
111 Director Advancement Services .... Ms. Kimberly BURNETT
28 Dir Student Diversity & Inclusion .... Vacant
68 Dir Physical Fitness & Recreation .... Mr. Mike ROBINSON
88 Director of Leadership Studies .... Dr. Kent ANDERSEN
88 Director of Service Learning .... Ms. Kristin HARPER
104 Assoc Dir of International Programs .... Ms. Anne LEDVINA
40 Bookstore Manager .... Ms. Melissa FOSTER
96 Purchasing Manager .... Mr. Tim WILDING
30 Director Development .... Ms. Kimberly WOLFE
44 Director Development-Annual Giving .... Ms. Mercedes BUCHANAN
112 Director Donor Relations .... Ms. Daphne POWELL
25 Director Grants & Special Projects .... Dr. Joe CHANDLER
39 Associate Dean of Students .... Mr. David MILLER
04 Assistant to the President .... Ms. Brooke BOWLES
07 Director of Admissions .... Ms. Amanda HARDIE
100 Chief of Staff .... Ms. Ying LIN
36 Director Student Placement .... Vacant

Columbia Southern University (A)

21982 University Lane, Orange Beach AL 36561-3845
County: Baldwin FICE Identification: 041215
Unit ID: 450933
Telephone: (251) 981-3771 Carnegie Class: DU-Mod
FAX Number: (251) 981-3815 Calendar System: Other
URL: www.columbiasouthern.edu
Established: 1993 Annual Undergrad Tuition & Fees: $5,775
Enrollment: 18,533 Coed
Affiliation or Control: Proprietary IRS Status: Proprietary
Highest Offering: Doctorate
Accreditation: DEAC

01 President .... Mr. Ken STYRON
05 Provost and Chief Academic Officer .... Mrs. Janell GIBSON
100 Chief of Staff .... Mrs. Chelsea HOFFMAN
26 Chief Marketing Officer .... Mr. Eric MCHANEY
13 Chief Information Officer .... Mr. Scott OSWALD
10 Chief Financial Officer .... Mr. Pat TROUP
88 VP Business Development/Mil Init .... Mr. Rick COOPER
15 VP of Human Resources/Train & Dev .... Mrs. Sue BUTTS
20 Vice Provost Academic Affairs .... Dr. Misti KILL
49 Dean Col Arts & Sciences/Asst Prov .... Dr. Sonya ROGERS
117 Dean College Safety/Emergency Svc .... Dr. Misti KILL
50 Dean College of Business/Asst Prov .... Dr. Elwin JONES
111 VP of University Relations .... Mrs. Caroline WALTERS
88 Assistant Provost Special Programs .... Dr. Joe MANJONE
88 Vice Prov Inst Effect/Plng/Compl .... Dr. Khalilah BURTON
88 Special Assistant to President .... Dr. Barry GOLDSTEIN
88 Assoc VP of Business Intelligence .... Mr. Ed WITHERINGTON
14 Assoc VP of Information Technology .... Mr. Charles MIMS
32 Vice Provost for Student Affairs .... Dr. Lee BARNETT
21 Associate VP of Finance .... Mr. Craig TAYLOR
20 Dean Faculty Devel Svcs & Support .... Dr. John WILLEY
08 Dean of Library .... Ms. Jennifer STEINFORD
24 Dir of Instructional Design & Tech .... Mrs. Dayna FULLER
27 Dir of Marketing Research & Service .... Mr. Beau VIGNES
29 Dir of Community & Alumni Relations .... Mrs. Vicki BARNES
40 Director of Bookstore Operations .... Mr. David BARNES
09 Dir of Inst Research & Assessment .... Mrs. Cherea SCHELLHASE
06 Registrar .... Mrs. Rachel FARRIS
37 Director of Financial Aid .... Mrs. Marie WILLIAMS
86 Dir of State Auth & TIX Coordinator .... Mrs. Alexis HARRIS
07 Director of Admissions .... Mrs. Cindy CHIRIBAO
35 Director of Student Support Center .... Mr. Justin BOYKIN
88 Director of Success Center .... Mrs. Wendy TROUP
88 Dir Student Resolution and Conflict .... Mr. Austin HANES
121 Int Dir Acad Advising/Student Supp .... Dr. Tamara MOURAS
88 Director of Military Outreach .... Dr. Ernie ROSADO
88 Director of Veteran Initiatives .... Mr. Andrew ROMAN
16 Director of Human Resources .... Mrs. Danielle BURGE
108 Dir Acad Assessment & Data Analysis .... Dr. John HOPE
88 Asst Prov Curriculum Planning & Acc .... Ms. Sonya KOPP
88 Director of Corporate Outreach .... Ms. Sherri TWITTY
102 Director of Corporate Relations .... Mr. Tony ATCHLEY
51 Director of Continuing Education .... Ms. Nickie COOPER
88 Program Manager Vietnam .... Mr. Quang TRONG TRAN
113 Director of Student Accounts .... Mr. Aaron COLLINS
114 Int Dir of Administrative Operation .... Ms. Erica GRANT

36 Director of Career Services .... Mr. Keith CULLEN
88 Director of Academic Supp Services .... Mrs. Rachel IVERSON
18 Director of Maintenance .... Mr. Blain SNYDER
04 Manager Office of the President .... Mrs. Carmen DANIEL
19 Manager Security and Reception .... Mr. Mike JOHNS
91 Director of Technical Support .... Mrs. Pam GOUGH
88 Director of Software Development .... Mr. Jamie BARROWS
88 Director of Network Operations .... Mr. Jamie ANDREWS
88 Vice Prov Educational Supp & Svcs .... Dr. Pam NORTHRUP

Edward Via College of Osteopathic Medicine-Auburn Campus (B)

910 S. Donahue Drive, Auburn AL 36832
Telephone: (334) 442-4000 Identification: 770965
Accreditation: &OSTEO

† Branch campus of Edward Via College of Osteopathic Medicine, Blacksburg, VA

Faulkner University (C)

5345 Atlanta Highway, Montgomery AL 36109-3398
County: Montgomery FICE Identification: 001003
Unit ID: 101189
Telephone: (334) 272-5820 Carnegie Class: Masters/M
FAX Number: (334) 386-7107 Calendar System: Semester
URL: www.faulkner.edu
Established: 1942 Annual Undergrad Tuition & Fees: $22,990
Enrollment: 2,961 Coed
Affiliation or Control: Churches Of Christ IRS Status: 501(c)3
Highest Offering: Doctorate
Accreditation: SC, #ARCPA, CAEP, IACBE, LAW, @PTA, @SP, THEOL

01 President .... Dr. Michael D. WILLIAMS
00 Chancellor .... Dr. Billy D. HILYER
05 Vice President Academic Affairs .... Dr. Dave RAMPERSAD
10 Vice President Financial Services .... Mr. Joseph VICKERY
32 Vice President Student Services .... Dr. Jean-Noel THOMPSON
84 Vice President Enrollment Mgmt .... Mr. Mark HUNT
15 Vice President Human Resources .... Mrs. Renee DAVIS-KEPHART
111 Vice President Advancement .... Dr. John TYSON
43 General Counsel .... Dr. Gerald JONES
61 Dean Jones School of Law .... Dr. Charles CAMPBELL
49 Dean College Arts & Sciences .... Dr. Jeffrey ARRINGTON
50 Dean College Business/Exec Educ .... Dr. Dave KHADANGA
73 Dean College of Biblical Studies .... Vacant
53 Dean College of Education .... Dr. Leslie COWELL
76 Dean College of Health Sciences .... Dr. Leah FULLMAN
21 Associate Vice President of Finance .... Mr. Jamie HORN
110 Assoc Vice President Advancement .... Mr. Billy CAMP
61 Assoc Dean Academics Jones Law .... Dr. Michael DEBOER
06 Registrar .... Mr. Don REYNOLDS
37 Director Student Financial Aid .... Ms. Linda PYNES
12 Director Mobile Center .... Dr. Chris COKER
12 Director Birmingham Center .... Mrs. Karen BRUCE
12 Director Huntsville Center .... Mr. Bryan COLLINS
41 Athletic Director .... Mr. Hal WYNN
08 Director of Libraries .... Mrs. Angela MOORE
104 Director of Study Abroad .... Dr. Terry EDWARDS
26 Director of University Marketing .... Mr. Patrick GREGORY
07 Director of Admissions .... Mr. Mike HORN
121 Director Student Success .... Mrs. Michelle OTWELL
92 Director of Honors Program .... Dr. Andrew JACOBS
35 Dean of Students .... Ms. Candace CAIN
36 Director Career Services .... Mrs. Marie OTTINGER
38 Director Counseling Center .... Mrs. Michelle BOND
04 Exec Assistant to the President .... Mrs. Beverly TOLLIVER
19 Director Security/Safety .... Mr. David FOWLER
39 Director Student Housing .... Ms. Keri ALFORD
106 Director Faulkner University Online .... Mrs. Tiffany CANTRELL
09 Director of Institutional Research .... Mrs. Breanna YARBROUGH
29 Director Alumni Affairs .... Mr. Joey WIGINTON

Fortis Institute (D)

100 London Parkway Suite 150, Birmingham AL 35211
County: Jefferson Identification: 666683
Unit ID: 455628
Telephone: (205) 940-7800 Carnegie Class: Spec 2-yr-Health
FAX Number: (205) 942-6708 Calendar System: Other
URL: www.fortisinstitute.edu
Established: 2008 Annual Undergrad Tuition & Fees: $13,649
Enrollment: 551 Coed
Affiliation or Control: Proprietary IRS Status: Proprietary
Highest Offering: Associate Degree
Accreditation: ABHES, DH, MLTAD

01 Campus President .... Mr. Khaled SAKALLA
05 Academic Dean .... Ms. Patricia A. CUNNINGHAM
37 Director of Financial Aid .... Ms. Angela MCFADDEN
06 Senior Registrar .... Vacant
07 Director of Admissions .... Ms. Jesse JOHNSON

Heritage Christian University (E)

PO Box HCU, Florence AL 35630-0050
County: Lauderdale FICE Identification: 021997
Unit ID: 101453
Telephone: (256) 766-6610 Carnegie Class: Spec-4-yr-Faith
FAX Number: (256) 767-7887 Calendar System: Semester
URL: www.hcu.edu
Established: 1968 Annual Undergrad Tuition & Fees: $11,532
Enrollment: 110 Coed
Affiliation or Control: Churches Of Christ IRS Status: 501(c)3
Highest Offering: Master's
Accreditation: BI

01 President .... Dr. Kirk BROTHERS
05 VP of Academic Affairs/Dean .... Dr. Michael D. JACKSON
10 Sr Vice Pres Administration .... Mr. Pat MOON
111 Vice President of Advancement .... Mr. Robert YOUNGBLOOD
32 Vice Pres Student Services .... Mr. Travis HARMON
110 Assoc VP of Advancement .... Mr. J.T HARRISON
33 Dean of Men .... Dr. Ed GALLAGHER
34 Dean of Women .... Dr. Rosemary SNODGRASS
58 Director of Graduate Programs .... Dr. Jeremy BARRIER
06 Registrar .... Mr. Nathan B. DAILY
08 Librarian .... Miss Jamie S. COX
78 Director of Field Education .... Mr. Brad MCKINNON
07 Director of Admissions .... Mrs. Rebecca HARRISON
106 Director Distance Learning .... Ms. Autumn RICHARDSON
09 Dir of Institutional Effectiveness .... Mr. Monte TATOM
13 Web Communications and Tech Manager .. Mr. Justin CONNOLLY
26 Director Marketing & Events .... Ms. Brittany VANDER MAAS
37 Director of Financial Aid .... Mrs. Mechelle THOMPSON

Herzing University (F)

280 W Valley Avenue, Birmingham AL 35209-4816
Telephone: (205) 916-2800 FICE Identification: 010193
Accreditation: &HLC, EMT

† Regional accreditation is carried under the parent institution in Madison, WI.

Huntingdon College (G)

1500 East Fairview Avenue, Montgomery AL 36106-2148
County: Montgomery FICE Identification: 001019
Unit ID: 101435
Telephone: (334) 833-4497 Carnegie Class: Bac-Diverse
FAX Number: (334) 833-4347 Calendar System: Semester
URL: www.huntingdon.edu
Established: 1854 Annual Undergrad Tuition & Fees: $27,900
Enrollment: 920 Coed
Affiliation or Control: United Methodist IRS Status: 501(c)3
Highest Offering: Master's
Accreditation: SC, MUS

01 President .... Rev. J. Cameron WEST
10 Treasurer & SVP for IE/Plng & Admin .... Mr. Jay A. DORMAN
30 SVP for Student & Inst Development .... Mr. Anthony J. LEIGH
05 Chief Academic Officer .... Dr. Thomas PERRIN
07 VP for Admission .... Ms. Stephanie HICKS
09 VP Inst Research & Accreditation .... Dr. Sidney J. STUBBS
13 VP for Technology .... Dr. Anneliese H. SPAETH
26 VP Communications & Marketing .... Ms. Suellen S. OFE
20 Associate Dean of Faculty .... Dr. Sarah C. SOURS
04 Exec Asst to President/Corp Secy .... Ms. Sandra B. KELSER
21 Chief Accountant .... Ms. Emily WELLS
19 Chief of Security .... Mr. Michael S. WARD
06 Registrar .... Dr. Sidney J. STUBBS
15 AVP Human Resources/Risk Mgmt .... Dr. Christopher CLARK
21 AVP Finance Svcs & Reporting .... Ms. Belinda G. DUETT
41 Director of Athletics .... Mr. Eric LEVANDA
08 Director Houghton Memorial Library .... Mr. Eric A. KIDWELL
121 Dir Staton Ctr for Lrng Enrichment .... Ms. Maryann M. BECK
18 VP Auxiliary Services .... Ms. Laura DUNCAN
37 Director of Financial Aid .... Ms. Brittany DAVIS
36 Dir of Center for Career & Vocation .... Ms. Sherry Leigh FARQUHAR
38 Director of Counseling Services .... Dr. Latonya GRAHAM
35 Director of Student Activities .... Ms. Staci-Jo PALEK
42 Chaplain .... Rev. Rhett BUTLER
40 Bookstore Manager .... Ms. Nancy JACKSON
23 Director of Institutional Health .... Ms. Nyree CONVILLE

Huntsville Bible College (H)

906 Oakwood Avenue NW, Huntsville AL 35811-1632
County: Madison FICE Identification: 038943
Unit ID: 449348
Telephone: (256) 469-7536 Carnegie Class: Spec-4-yr-Faith
FAX Number: (256) 469-7549 Calendar System: Semester
URL: https://huntsvillebiblecollege.org/
Established: 1986 Annual Undergrad Tuition & Fees: $4,560
Enrollment: 114 Coed
Affiliation or Control: Baptist IRS Status: 501(c)3
Highest Offering: Doctorate
Accreditation: BI

01 President .... Dr. John L. CLAY
05 Dean of Academics/Instruction .... Rev. Chantaye KNOTTS
07 Admissions Officer .... Ms. Vernita CHANDLER
10 Chief Financial Officer .... Ms. Jacqueline ROBINSON
111 Advancement Officer .... Ms. Eloise MCNEALEY
58 Dean of Graduate Studies .... Dr. Mitchell WALKER
20 Dean of Distant Learning .... Rev. Trevor CRENSHAW
32 Director of Student Services .... Ms. Linda FLETCHER
08 Director of Library Media .... Ms. Victoria RICHARDSON
08 Librarian .... Ms. Carla CLIFT
37 Financial Aid Ofcr/Title IX Coord .... Ms. Doris LACEY
04 Administrative Assistant .... Ms. Cindy SMITH

Jacksonville State University (A)

700 Pelham Road N, Jacksonville AL 36265-1602
County: Calhoun FICE Identification: 001020
Unit ID: 101480
Telephone: (256) 782-5881 Carnegie Class: Masters/L
FAX Number: (256) 782-5888 Calendar System: Semester
URL: www.jsu.edu
Established: 1883 Annual Undergrad Tuition & Fees (In-State): $11,120
Enrollment: 9,238 Coed
Affiliation or Control: State IRS Status: 501(c)3
Highest Offering: Doctorate
Accreditation: SC, AAFCS, ABAI, ART, CACREP, CAEP, #COARC, DIETD, #JOUR, MUS, NAIT, NURSE, SPAA, SW, THEA

01 President .... Dr. Don C. KILLINGSWORTH
05 Provost/Sr VP Academic Affairs .... Dr. Christie SHELTON
10 Sr VP Finance & Administration .... Mr. Jim BRIGHAM
111 Acting VP University Advancement .... Dr. Emily MESSER
32 VP Student Affairs .... Mr. Terry CASEY
84 VP of Enrollment Management .... Dr. Emily W. MESSER
121 Vice Provost Student Success .... Dr. Tim KING
13 VP Information Technology .... Mr. Vinson HOUSTON
116 Chief Internal Auditor .... Mr. Nelson CLARK
15 Director Human Resources .... Ms. Tammy MCCAIN
43 Legal Counsel .... Mr. Greg HARLEY
41 Director Athletics .... Mr. Greg SEITZ
20 Vice Provost .... Dr. Joe WALSH
57 Dean School of Arts & Hum .... Dr. Staci L. STONE
81 Dean School of Science .... Dr. Timothy LINDBLOM
76 Dean School Health Prof & Wellness ... Dr. Tracey D. MATTHEWS
53 Dean School of Education .... Dr. Kimberly WHITE
50 Dean School of Business & Industry .... Dr. Steven MCCLUNG
83 Dean School Human Svc & Soc Science .... Dr. Mary NEWTON
08 Dean Library Services .... Mr. John-Bauer GRAHAM
88 Associate Vice Provost .... Ms. Lisa M. WILLIAMS
06 Registrar .... Ms. Emily WHITE
21 University Controller .... Ms. Anastasia RODRIGUEZ
109 Exec Dir Business Svcs .... Mr. Jim BRIGHAM
30 Exec Dir University Development .... Mr. William NASH
39 Director Residence Life .... Ms. Rochelle SMITH
39 Dir Univ Housing Operations .... Ms. Brooke LYON
85 Dir International Programs .... Ms. Chandni KHADKA
09 Sr Dir Inst Research/Effectiveness .... Ms. Kim PRESSON
29 Director of Alumni Relations .... Ms. Kaci OGLE
37 Director Financial Aid .... Ms. Jessica WIGGINS
18 Dir Capital Planning/Facilities .... Mr. David THOMPSON
36 Career Placement Coordinator .... Ms. Rebecca E. TURNER
38 Dir Counseling/Disability Sppt Svcs .... Ms. Julie NIX
96 Procurement/Fixed Assets .... Ms. Denise HUNT
26 Chief Marketing/Comm Officer .... Mr. Tim GARNER
19 Director Public Safety .... Mr. Michael BARTON
22 Coordinator Title IX .... Ms. Jennifer ARGO
04 Admin Assistant to the President ...... Ms. Catherine H. CHAPPELL
106 Director Online Education/E-learnin .... Mr. Chris CASEY
07 Director of Admissions .... Ms. Lauren FINDLEY
105 University Webmaster .... Mr. Chris NEWSOME
28 Director of Diversity .... Ms. Charlcie P. VANN
86 Director Government Relations .... Ms. Leigha CAUTHEN

Miles College (B)

5500 Myron Massey Boulevard, Fairfield AL 35064-2621
County: Jefferson FICE Identification: 001028
Unit ID: 101675
Telephone: (205) 929-1000 Carnegie Class: Bac-Diverse
FAX Number: (205) 929-1453 Calendar System: Semester
URL: www.miles.edu
Established: 1898 Annual Undergrad Tuition & Fees: $12,714
Enrollment: 1,440 Coed
Affiliation or Control: Christian Methodist Episcopal IRS Status: 501(c)3
Highest Offering: Baccalaureate
Accreditation: SC, ACBSP, CAEPN, SW

01 President .... Ms. Bobbie KNIGHT
05 Provost/Sr VP Academic Affairs .... Dr. Jarralynne AGEE
10 Sr VP Finance/Business Admin .... Ms. Diana KNIGHTON
111 VP Institutional Advancement .... Mr. Arthur J. BRIGATI
42 Dean of Chapel/VP Stdnt Life/Engage .... Rev. Larry BATIE
84 VP Enrollment Mgmt/Chief Innov Ofcr .. Mr. Michael A. JOHNSON
32 Dean of Students/Alumni Affairs .... Mr. Charles STALLWORTH
100 Chief of Staff .... Mr. Kenneth COACHMAN
06 College Registrar .... Vacant
41 Athletic Director .... Mr. Reginald RUFFIN
106 Dean of Online Education .... Dr. Vidal ADADEVOH
15 Director Human Resources .... Vacant
18 Director Building Operations .... Mr. Richard WILLIS
37 Asst Director Financial Aid .... Ms. Nakia BELSER

Oakwood University (C)

7000 Adventist Boulevard, NW, Huntsville AL 35896-0003
County: Madison FICE Identification: 001033
Unit ID: 101912
Telephone: (256) 726-7000 Carnegie Class: Bac-Diverse
FAX Number: N/A Calendar System: Semester
URL: www.oakwood.edu
Established: 1896 Annual Undergrad Tuition & Fees: $19,990
Enrollment: 1,374 Coed
Affiliation or Control: Seventh-day Adventist IRS Status: 501(c)3
Highest Offering: Master's
Accreditation: SC, ACBSP, CAEPN, DIETD, DIETI, NUR, SW, THEOL

01 President/CEO .... Dr. Leslie POLLARD
05 Interim Provost .... Dr. James MBYIRUKIRA
10 Vice President Financial Admin .... Ms. Sabrina COTTON
32 VP Student Life & Mission .... Dr. David RICHARDSON
46 VP QAResearch & Faculty Development .... Dr. Prudence L. POLLARD
84 VP Enrollment Svcs/Retention .... Dr. Karen BENN MARSHALL
111 Exec Dir Advancement/Development .... Mrs. Cheri WILSON
20 Asst VP Academic Administration .... Vacant
21 Asst VP Financial Admin/Controller .... Mrs. Gail CALDWELL
35 Asst VP Student Life & Mission .... Ms. Adrienne MATTHEWS
13 Chief Info Technology Officer (CIO) .... Vacant
15 Int Exec Dir of Empl Svcs/Human Res .... Mrs. Sylvia GERMANY
25 Contracts .... Ms. Cheryl SULLIVAN
26 Director Public Relations .... Vacant
07 Director Recruitment & Admissions .... Mr. Lewis JONES
37 Director Financial Aid .... Mrs. Julain GUNN CLARKE
06 Registrar .... Ms. Traci MOORE
39 Residence Life Coordinator-Men .... Mr. Woodrow VAUGHN
39 Resident Life Coordinator-Women .... Ms. Linda ANDERSON
08 Director Library Services .... Mrs. Heather RODRIGUEZ JAMES
18 Director Physical Plant .... Mr. Handel FRASER
19 Director Security .... Mr. Melvin HARRIS
38 Dir Counseling & Health Services .... Vacant
51 Dir Adult & Continuing Education .... Mrs. Ellengold GOODRIDGE
121 Dean for Student Success .... Vacant
50 Dean Business & Info Systems .... Dr. Theodore BROWN
53 Dean Education .... Dr. James MBYIRUKIRA
76 Chair Allied Health .... Dr. Andrew YOUNG
88 Chair English & Foreign Languages .... Dr. Benson PRIGG
64 Chair Music .... Dr. Jason FERDINAND
81 Chair Biological Sciences .... Dr. Elaine VANTERPOOL
88 Dean Chemistry .... Vacant
66 Chair Nursing .... Dr. Dorothy FORDE
68 Chair Health & Human Sciences .... Dr. Andrew YOUNG
70 Chair Social Work .... Dr. Shalunda SHERROD
73 Dean Religion & Theology .... Dr. R Clifford JONES
77 Chair Math & Computer Science .... Dr. Lisa JAMES
82 Chair History & Political Science .... Dr. Samuel LONDON
83 Chair Psychology .... Dr. Martin HODNETT
60 Chair Communication .... Dr. Rennae ELLIOTT

Remington College, Mobile Campus (D)

4368 Downtowner Loop South, Mobile AL 36609
County: Mobile FICE Identification: 026055
Unit ID: 366535
Telephone: (251) 343-8200 Carnegie Class: Spec-4-yr-Other Tech
FAX Number: (251) 343-0577 Calendar System: Quarter
URL: www.remingtoncollege.edu
Established: 1986 Annual Undergrad Tuition & Fees: $17,148
Enrollment: 248 Coed
Affiliation or Control: Independent Non-Profit IRS Status: 501(c)3
Highest Offering: Baccalaureate
Accreditation: ACCSC

01 Director of Campus Administration .... Tekia ROCKER
05 Dean .... Tekia ROCKER
07 Director of Admissions .... Tasha CARTER
06 Registrar/Retention .... Don SCHERMERHORN
32 Student Success Coordinator .... Jayne HARRIS

Samford University (E)

800 Lakeshore Drive, Birmingham AL 35229-0001
County: Jefferson FICE Identification: 001036
Unit ID: 102049
Telephone: (205) 726-2011 Carnegie Class: DU-Mod
FAX Number: (205) 726-2171 Calendar System: Semester
URL: www.samford.edu
Established: 1841 Annual Undergrad Tuition & Fees: $34,198
Enrollment: 5,729 Coed
Affiliation or Control: Southern Baptist IRS Status: 501(c)3
Highest Offering: Doctorate
Accreditation: SC, ANEST, #ARCPA, @AUD, CAEP, CIDA, DIETD, DIETI, LAW, MUS, NURSE, PHAR, PTA, SP, SW, THEA, THEOL

01 President .... Dr. Beck A. TAYLOR
125 President Emeritus .... Dr. Andrew WESTMORELAND
100 Assistant to the President .... Dr. Michael D. MORGAN
41 Athletic Director .... Mr. Martin NEWTON
04 Exec Assistant to the President .... Ms. Darlene KUHN
05 Provost .... Dr. Michael HARDIN
20 Sr Associate Provost .... Dr. Marci S. JOHNS
28 Assistant Provost Diversity .... Dr. Denise GREGORY
88 Asst Provost Faculty Success .... Dr. P J HUGHES
88 Director of University Fellows .... Dr. Todd KRULAK
06 Registrar .... Mr. Jeremy DIXON
08 Dean of University Library .... Dr. Kimmetha D. HERNDON
76 Dean of Health Professions .... Dr. Alan JUNG
49 Dean Howard College Arts/Sciences .... Mr. Tim HALL
50 Dean Brock School of Business .... Dr. Chad M. CARSON
73 Dean Beeson School of Divinity .... Dr. Douglas A. SWEENEY
53 Dean OB School of Education .... Dr. Anna MCEWAN
61 Dean Cumberland School of Law .... Mr. Henry C. STRICKLAND
57 Dean School of the Arts .... Dr. Joseph HOPKINS
66 Dean School of Nursing .... Dr. Melondia R. CARTER
69 Int Dean of Public Health .... Dr. Melissa LUMPKIN
67 Dean School of Pharmacy .... Dr. Michael A. CROUCH
111 Vice President of Advancement .... Mr. W. Randall PITTMAN
26 VP for Marketing and Communication .... Dr. Betsy B. HOLLOWAY
30 Asst VP Univ Adv & Exec Dir Devel .... Mr. Douglas WILSON
27 Executive Director Marketing .... Ms. Jessica BLACK
110 Sr Dir of Philanthropic Engagement .... Ms. Rhonda WHITE
29 Director Alumni Programs .... Ms. Casey RAMEY
27 Executive Dir Broadcast Media .... Mr. Brad RADICE
112 Director Gift and Estate Planning .... Mr. Gene HOWARD
10 Exec VP Business/Financial Affairs .... Mr. Harry B. BROCK, III
115 Sr AVP Business & Financial Affairs .... Ms. Lisa IMBRAGULIO
18 Assoc VP Operations .... Mr. Jeff POLECHEK
21 Controller .... Mr. Mike DARWIN
45 Chief Strategy Officer .... Mr. Colin M. COYNE
25 Chief Contract/Grants Administrator .... Ms. Linnea MINNEMA
114 Dir of Budget & Financial Planning .... Mr. Matt DEFORE
88 Dir Event Management .... Ms. Allison BRYMER
88 Dir Strat & Appl Analysis .... Dr. Randolph HORN
109 Director of Business Services .... Mr. Wade WALKER
43 General Counsel .... Mr. W. Clark WATSON
15 Asst VP & Dir of Human Resources .... Mr. Joel WINDHAM
19 Director Public Safety .... Dr. Tommy TAYLOR
09 Director of Institutional Research .... Mr. Toner EVANS
13 Chief Information Officer .... Ms. Debi WHITCOMB
90 Director Learning Applications .... Mr. Chad OWENS
32 Vice President for Student Affairs .... Dr. Phil KIMREY
35 Asst VP Student Affairs .... Dr. Garry L. ATKINS
84 Asst VP for Enrollment Mgmt .... Mr. Jason BLACK
39 Asst VP Campus & Residential Life .... Ms. Lauren M. TAYLOR
124 Asst VP for Student Development .... Ms. April ROBINSON
07 Director of Admissions .... Mr. David PRESLEY
38 Director Student Counseling .... Mr. Richard YOAKUM
37 Dir of Student Financial Services .... Mr. Lane M. SMITH
36 Director Student Placement .... Ms. Dora DITCHFIELD
104 Director Global Engagement .... Ms. Lauren DOSS
88 Director Parent Programs .... Ms. Susan DOYLE
105 Exec Dir Web/Digital Marketing .... Mr. Todd COTTON

Selma University (F)

1501 Lapsley Street, Selma AL 36701-5232
County: Dallas FICE Identification: 001037
Unit ID: 102058
Telephone: (334) 872-2533 Carnegie Class: Spec-4-yr-Faith
FAX Number: (334) 872-7746 Calendar System: Semester
URL: www.selmauniversity.edu
Established: 1878 Annual Undergrad Tuition & Fees: N/A
Enrollment: N/A Coed
Affiliation or Control: Baptist IRS Status: 501(c)3
Highest Offering: Master's
Accreditation: #BI

01 President .... Dr. Stanford ANGION
05 Chief Academic Officer .... Dr. Cheryl WASHINGTON
32 Vice Pres Student Affairs .... Vacant
10 Int Chief Financial Officer .... Uletor NIX
06 Registrar .... Ms. Marion HARRIS
100 Chief of Staff/Compliance Officer .... Mr. James E. BURRELL

South University (G)

5355 Vaughn Road, Montgomery AL 36116-1120
Telephone: (334) 395-8800 FICE Identification: 004463
Accreditation: &SC, ACBSP, MAC, NURSE, PTAA

† Regional accreditation is carried under the parent institution in Savannah, GA.

Spring Hill College (H)

4000 Dauphin Street, Mobile AL 36608-1791
County: Mobile FICE Identification: 001041
Unit ID: 102234
Telephone: (251) 380-4000 Carnegie Class: Bac-A&S
FAX Number: (251) 460-2182 Calendar System: Semester
URL: www.shc.edu
Established: 1830 Annual Undergrad Tuition & Fees: $41,868
Enrollment: 1,191 Coed
Affiliation or Control: Roman Catholic IRS Status: 501(c)3
Highest Offering: Master's
Accreditation: SC, NURSE

01 President .... Dr. Joseph LEE
05 Interim Co-Provost .... Dr. Steve ALMQUIST
05 Interim Co-Provost .... Dr. Lisa HAGER
10 Vice President Finance/Accounting .... Vacant
30 Acting VP Alumni Relations/Devel .... Dr. Racheal BANKS
32 Vice Pres Student Affairs .... Mr. Kevin ABEL
13 Director of IT .... Mr. Christopher HUGHES
20 Associate Provost .... Vacant
21 Treasury Manager .... Ms. Heidi BUTLER
37 Director of Financial Aid .... Dr. Karleen HOWARD
06 Registrar .... Ms. Linnea BATTLES
121 Director Student Advising Services .... Mr. Michael COZART
29 Director of Alumni Relations .... Mrs. Ashley WEBSTER
15 Director of Personnel .... Ms. Patricia A. DAVIS
07 Director of Admissions .... Mr. Patrick SPRAGUE
19 Director of Public Safety/Security .... Mr. Kevin ANDERSON
38 Director of Counseling Services .... Ms. Shivani BHAKTA
42 Director of Campus Ministry .... Ms. Colleen LEE
41 Director Athletics & Recreation .... Mr. Joseph NILAND, JR.
31 Dir Foley Community Service Center .... Vacant
26 Dir Communications/Instl Marketing .... Mrs. Cathy HELEAN
27 Communications Officer .... Mr. Fletcher DEVERY
36 Director of Career Services .... Ms. Jordan COCKRELL
40 Bookstore Manager .... Vacant

08 Director of Library .... Mr. Bret HEIM
39 Dir Resident Life/Student Housing .... Ms. Holly BANNING
44 Director Annual Giving .... Mr. Cris SMITH, JR.

Stillman College (A)

3601 Stillman Boulevard, Tuscaloosa AL 35401
County: Tuscaloosa FICE Identification: 001044
Unit ID: 102270
Telephone: (205) 366-8817 Carnegie Class: Bac-A&S
FAX Number: N/A Calendar System: Semester
URL: www.stillman.edu
Established: 1876 Annual Undergrad Tuition & Fees: $11,322
Enrollment: 712 Coed
Affiliation or Control: Presbyterian Church (U.S.A.) IRS Status: 501(c)3
Highest Offering: Baccalaureate
Accreditation: SC, CAEPN, IACBE

01 President .... Dr. Cynthia WARRICK
03 Executive Vice President .... Mr. Derrick C. GILMORE
05 Provost/VP Academic Affairs .... Dr. Mark MCCORMICK
10 Chief Financial Officer .... Mr. Chavis PAULK
108 VP Institutional Effectiveness .... Dr. Victoria BOMAN
111 VP Institutional Advancement .... Ms. Luanne BAKER
32 Vice President for Students Affairs .... Rev. Tyshawn GARDNER
31 Director Community Relations .... Mr. Mason BONNER
13 Director of Info Tech .... Vacant
26 VP Strategic Initiatives .... Mrs. RaSheda WORKMAN
29 Director Alumni Affairs .... Ms. Jean WILSON-SYKES
18 Senior Director Campus Services .... Mr. Phillip CUNNINGHAM
53 Dean of Education .... Dr. James GRAY
49 Dean of Arts & Sciences .... Dr. Norman GOLAR
50 Dean School of Business .... Mr. Isaac MCCOY
08 Dean of Library .... Ms. Evelyn KING
37 Director of Financial Aid .... Mr. Kenneth WILSON
23 Dir Student Development/Health Svcs .... Vacant
13 Director of Info Technology .... Mr. Michael HUBBARD
85 Director of Intl Student Affairs .... Mr. Kyris BROWN
19 Chief of Campus Police .... Ms. Carla LONGMIRE
41 Athletic Director .... Mr. Kenyon ALSTON
15 Director Human Resources .... Ms. LaKeya GOINS
42 College Chaplain .... Dr. Joseph SCRIVNER
101 Board Liaison .... Ms. RaSheda WORKMAN
04 Executive Asst to President .... Ms. Markedia WELLS
35 Dean of Student Life .... Mr. Marcus KENNEDY
06 Registrar .... Mrs. Greta EUBANKS
106 Director of Online Education .... Ms. Kristi GARRETT
30 Director of Development .... Mr. Tyler DAVIDSON
124 Dean of Retention and Placement .... Ms. Tasha WASHINGTON
84 Director Enrollment Management .... Mrs. Valarie WILSON

Talladega College (B)

627 W. Battle Street, Talladega AL 35160-2354
County: Talladega FICE Identification: 001046
Unit ID: 102298
Telephone: (256) 761-6212 Carnegie Class: Bac-A&S
FAX Number: (256) 761-8680 Calendar System: Semester
URL: www.talladega.edu
Established: 1867 Annual Undergrad Tuition & Fees: $13,866
Enrollment: 1,156 Coed
Affiliation or Control: Independent Non-Profit IRS Status: 501(c)3
Highest Offering: Master's
Accreditation: SC, SW

01 President .... Dr. Billy C. HAWKINS
05 Provost/VP for Academic Affairs .... Dr. Lisa LONG
10 VP Finance & Administration/CFO .... Vacant
32 Vice President Student Affairs .... Dr. Jeffrey BURGIN
111 VP Institutional Advancement .... Dr. Kristie KENNEY
18 Director Facilities Management .... Mr. Thomas GANCHUK
37 Director Financial Aid .... Ms. Amanda HEADEN
07 Director of Admissions .... Mr. Joel SWAN
09 Int Director Institutional Research .... Dr. Syed RAZA
35 Interim VP Student Affairs .... Mr. Michael BROWN
41 Athletic Director .... Mr. Kevin HEROD
08 Librarian/Director .... Vacant
13 Interim IT Director .... Ms. Norda THREATT
36 Director of Career Placement .... Ms. Sherissa GAITOR
19 Chief Campus Police .... Ms. Shajuana DENNARD
50 Dean Div Administration & Business .... Dr. Jonathan ELIMIMIAN
79 Dean Div Humanities/Fine Arts .... Dr. Angela WALKER
81 Dean Div of Natural Sci/Math .... Dr. Alison BROWN
83 Dean Div EWJ Social Sciences/Educ .... Dr. Rebecca MCKAY
21 Senior Associate Vice President .... Mr. Bruce SMITH
23 Health Services on Campus .... Ms. Stanmetrica CURRY
25 Title III Coor/Grants Administrator .... Dr. Charles SMITH
29 Director Alumni Relations .... Mr. Anthony JONES
06 Registrar .... Ms. Barbra SMITH
38 Director Office of Counseling/ADA .... Mr. Michael BROWN
104 Director Study Abroad .... Vacant
15 Human Resources Manager .... Mrs. Brenda RHODEN
26 Director of Public Relations .... Ms. Pasiley BOSTON
39 Director of Housing and Residence .... Ms. Candace GARRETT
124 Director of Special Events/Protocol .... Mr. Anthony JONES
04 Admin Assistant to the President .... Mrs. Nadine BALLARD

Troy University (C)

University Avenue, Troy AL 36082-0001
County: Pike FICE Identification: 001047
Unit ID: 102368
Telephone: (334) 670-3100 Carnegie Class: Masters/L
FAX Number: (334) 670-3774 Calendar System: Semester
URL: www.troy.edu
Established: 1887 Annual Undergrad Tuition & Fees (In-State): $8,908
Enrollment: 16,497 Coed
Affiliation or Control: State IRS Status: 501(c)3
Highest Offering: Doctorate
Accreditation: SC, ACBSP, ADNUR, CAATE, CACREP, CAEP, COSMA, MUS, NUR, SW

01 Chancellor .... Dr. Jack HAWKINS, JR.
05 Sr Vice Chanc for Academic Affairs .... Dr. Lance TATUM
32 Sr Vice Chanc Student Svcs/Admin .... Mr. Sohail AGBOATWALA
111 Sr Vice Chanc Advance/External Affs .... Gen. Walter GIVHAN
10 Sr VC for Fin Affs & Online Educ .... Dr. James BOOKOUT
15 Assoc VC for Human Resources .... MS. Ashley ENGLISH
12 Vice Chancellor Troy Dothan .... Dr. Don JEFFREY
12 Vice Chancellor Troy Phenix City .... Dr. Dionne ROSSER-MIMS
12 Vice Chanc Troy Montgomery .... Mr. Ray WHITE
35 Assoc Dean of Student Svcs Dothan .... Ms. Sandra HENRY
20 Asst Dean of Academics .... Vacant
53 Assoc Dean Col of Education .... Dr. Fred FIGLIANO
49 CAS Campus Coordinator Montgomery .... Mr. Martin OLLIFF
49 CAS Campus Coordinator Dothan .... Dr. Robert VILARDI
30 Assoc Vice Chanc for Development .... Ms. Rebecca WATSON
37 Assoc VC for Financial Aid .... Ms. Angela JOHNSON
20 Associate Provost for Academics .... Dr. Lee VARDAMAN
26 Chief Marketing Officer .... Ms. Samantha JOHNSON
21 Assoc Vice Chanc/Controller .... Ms. Tara DONALDSON
06 Registrar .... Ms. Vickie MILES
84 Assoc VC for Enrollment Management .... Mr. Buddy STARLING
08 Dean Library Services .... Dr. Chris SHAFFER
13 Chief Technology Officer .... Dr. Greg PRICE
27 Director University Relations .... Mr. Matthew CLOWER
29 Director Alumni Affairs .... Ms. Faith W. WARD
36 Coordinator Career Services .... Ms. Lauren COLE
18 Director Facilities/Physical Plant .... Vacant
60 Interim Director of Journalism .... Dr. Amanda DIGGS
04 Exec Assistant to the Chancellor .... Mr. Tom DAVIS
38 University Counselor .... Ms. Fran SCHEEL
123 Director of Graduate Admissions .... Vacant
88 Associate Controller .... Ms. Brenda JOHNS
09 Senior Director of IRPE .... Mr. Ronnie CREEL
86 Director of Governmental Relations .... Mr. Marcus PARAMORE
44 Director of Annual Giving .... Ms. Meredith WELCH
25 Director Sponsored Programs .... Ms. Judy FULMER
08 Int Dir of Library Svcs Troy Dothan .... Mr. Martin OLLIFF
08 Dir of Lib Svcs Troy Montgomery .... Mr. Jeff SIMPSON
20 Dean Undergrad Pgms/Assoc Provost .... Dr. Hal FULMER
35 Dean of Student Svcs Troy Campus .... Mr. Herbert REEVES
49 Dean Arts & Sciences .... Dr. Steven TAYLOR
50 Dean Business .... Dr. Judson EDWARDS
53 Dean Education .... Dr. Kerry PALMER
58 Assoc Provost/Dean Graduate Pgms .... Dr. Mary TEMPLETON
76 Dean Health/Human Services .... Dr. John GARNER
57 Dean Communication/Fine Arts .... Dr. Larry BLOCHER
35 Assoc Dean Student Svcs Troy Mont .... Dr. James SMITH
39 Director Student Housing .... Mr. Herbert REEVES
41 Sr Vice Chanc for Athletics .... Mr. Brent JONES
85 Assoc Dean Intl Student Services .... Ms. Maria FRIGGE
105 Director Web Services .... Mr. John LESTER
108 Director Institutional Assessment .... Ms. Wendy BROYLES
19 Chief of University Police .... Mr. George BEAUDRY
104 Study Abroad Coordinator .... Ms. Sarah MCKENZIE
96 Director of Procurement & Asset Mgt .... Ms. April JOHNSON

Tuskegee University (D)

1200 W. Montgomery Road, Tuskegee Inst. AL 36088
County: Macon FICE Identification: 001050
Unit ID: 102377
Telephone: (334) 727-8011 Carnegie Class: Masters/M
FAX Number: (334) 727-5276 Calendar System: Semester
URL: www.tuskegee.edu
Established: 1881 Annual Undergrad Tuition & Fees: $22,614
Enrollment: 2,747 Coed
Affiliation or Control: Independent Non-Profit IRS Status: 501(c)3
Highest Offering: Doctorate
Accreditation: SC, CAEPN, CONST, DIETD, NUR, OT, SW, VET

01 Interim President .... Dr. Charlotte P. MORRIS
05 Provost/SVP Academic Affairs .... Dr. Heshmat AGLAN, JR.
10 Exec Vice Pres Finance/CFO .... Ms. Kimberly LEWIS
46 Vice Pres Research/Dean Grad Stdnts .... Dr. Shaik JEELANI
18 Vice Pres Facilities/Construction .... Vacant
32 Vice Pres Student Affairs .... Dr. Kimberly M. SCOTT
15 Chief Human Resources Officer .... Vacant
43 VP External Affairs/General Counsel .... Vacant
26 Sr Dir Comm/Public Rels/Mktg .... Mr. Michael TULLIER
101 Exec Asst to Pres/Secy to the Board .... Mrs. Chandra CHAMBLISS
13 Chief Information Officer .... Ms. Bernice GREEN
114 Asst Vice Pres Budget & Planning .... Vacant
20 Asst Provost .... Dr. Tamara FLOYD-SMITH
47 Dean of CAENS .... Dr. Walter A. HILL
09 AVP Institutional Research .... Dr. Kellei BISHOP -SAMUELS
53 Dean School of Education .... Dr. Carlton E. MORRIS
50 Dean Col Business/Info Sciences .... Dr. Kia KOONG
54 Dean College of Engineering .... Dr. Heshmat AGLAN
66 Dean Sch Nursing/Allied Health .... Dr. Constance HENDRICKS
35 Dean of Student Life .... Ms. Tameka ANGOLA HARPER
42 Dean of the Chapel .... Dr. Gregory S. GRAY
08 Director of Library Services .... Mrs. Juanita ROBERTS
30 Director of Development .... Ms. Krystal FLOYD
29 Alumni Affairs Director .... Ms. Kimberly HOLLAND
102 Dir Corp/Foundation Relations .... Vacant
51 Int Assoc Prov Cont Educ/Extension .... Dr. Ntam BAHARANYI
36 Asst Career Development/Placement .... Ms. Chantel BOYD
113 Asst Bursar .... Ms. Stacie HENDERSON
37 Director of Financial Aid .... Mr. Advergus D. JAMES, JR.
18 Project Mgr Sodexho/Physical Plant .... Mr. Tony WARD
91 Director of Applications Support .... Ms. Jamie REYNOLDS
06 Registrar .... Dr. Elaine BROMFIELD
96 Director of Purchasing .... Ms. Cassandra PARKER
48 Interim Dean School of Architecture .... Mr. Roderick FLUKER
74 Dean College of Veterinary Medicine .... Dr. Rubye PERRY
49 Dean College of Arts and Sciences .. Dr. Channapatana PRAKASH
88 Dean National Center Bioethics .... Dr. Reuben WARREN
07 Director of Admissions .... Mr. Donovan COLEY
100 Chief of Staff .... Dr. Shirley FRIAR
104 Director Study Abroad .... Dr. Rhonda COLLIER
11 Chief of Operations .... Dr. Charles SMITH
19 Director Security/Safety .... Chief Patrick MARDIS
38 Coordinator Student Counseling .... Mrs. Ardelia M. LUNN
39 Director Housing & Residence Life .... Mr. William SAMUEL, SR.
41 Athletic Director .... Mr. Willie SLATER

United States Sports Academy (E)

One Academy Drive, Daphne AL 36526-7055
County: Baldwin FICE Identification: 021706
Unit ID: 102395
Telephone: (251) 626-3303 Carnegie Class: Spec-4-yr-Other
FAX Number: (251) 621-2527 Calendar System: Semester
URL: www.ussa.edu
Established: 1972 Annual Undergrad Tuition & Fees: N/A
Enrollment: 338 Coed
Affiliation or Control: Independent Non-Profit IRS Status: 501(c)3
Highest Offering: Doctorate
Accreditation: SC

01 President & CEO .... Dr. Thomas J. ROSANDICH
05 Provost .... Dr. Tomi WAHLSTROM
10 Director of Admin & Finance .... Ms. Gayla JACKSON
26 Director of Communications .... Mr. Eric MANN
88 Chair of Sports Management .... Dr. Brandon SPRADLEY
58 Director of Doctoral Studies .... Dr. Fred CROMARTIE
88 Chair of Sports Coaching .... Dr. Roch KING
88 Director Rec Mgmt & Sports Studies .... Dr. Sandra GERINGER
68 Dir of Sports Exercise Science .... Mr. Robert HERRON
06 Registrar .... Ms. Robin STEPHENS
08 Director of Library/Archivist .... Dr. Vandy PACETTI-DONELSON
18 Building and Grounds .... Mr. Ed SWANN
13 Chief Info Technology Officer .... Mr. Anthony FRANKLIN
105 Director Web Services .... Mr. Corey BLAKE
15 Chief Human Resources Officer .... Ms. Marina KAZANJIAN
37 Director Student Financial Aid .... Ms. Tiffany CLANTON
120 Director of Instructional Design .... Ms. Holly PARK

*University of Alabama System Office (F)

500 University Boulevard East, Tuscaloosa AL 35401
County: Tuscaloosa FICE Identification: 008004
Unit ID: 100733
Telephone: (205) 348-5861 Carnegie Class: N/A
FAX Number: (205) 348-9788
URL: www.uasystem.ua.edu

01 Chancellor .... Mr. Finis E. ST. JOHN, IV
43 General Counsel/Sr Vice Chancellor .... Mr. Sid J. TRANT
05 Sr VC Academic/Student Affairs .... Dr. Tonjanita JOHNSON
10 SVC Finance/Administration .... Dr. Dana S. KEITH
26 Director of System Communications .... Mrs. Lynn L. COLE
86 Sr Vice Chanc for External Affairs .... Mr. Clay M. RYAN
15 Dir Sys Benefits/Human Res Svcs .... Mr. John GARNER
86 Director of External Affairs .... Mr. Charlie M. TAYLOR
19 Director of System Security .... Mr. Steve ANDERSON
101 Secretary of the Board of Trustees .... Mr. Mark D. FOLEY
116 Chief Audit Officer .... Mr. Chip BIVINS

*The University of Alabama (G)

801 University Boulevard, Tuscaloosa AL 35487
County: Tuscaloosa FICE Identification: 001051
Unit ID: 100751
Telephone: (205) 348-6010 Carnegie Class: DU-Highest
FAX Number: N/A Calendar System: Semester
URL: www.ua.edu
Established: 1831 Annual Undergrad Tuition & Fees (In-State): $11,620
Enrollment: 37,840 Coed
Affiliation or Control: State IRS Status: 501(c)3
Highest Offering: Doctorate
Accreditation: SC, ART, CAATE, CACREP, CAEPN, CEA, CIDA, CLPSY, DANCE, DIETC, DIETD, JOUR, LAW, LIB, MUS, NAEYC, NURSE, SP, SPAA, SW, THEA

02 President .... Dr. Stuart R. BELL
100 Chief Administrative Officer .... Mr. Chad TINDOL
05 Executive Vice President & Provost .... Dr. James DALTON
28 VP for Diversity/Equity & Inclusion .... Dr. G. Christine TAYLOR
10 Vice Pres for Financial Affairs .... Mr. Matt FAJACK
111 Vice Pres for Advancement .... Mr. Robert 'Bob' PIERCE
32 Vice Pres for Student Life .... Dr. Myron L. POPE
88 Vice Pres for Community Affairs .... Dr. Samory T. PRUITT
26 Interim VP Strategic Communications .... Mr. Ryan BRADLEY
46 Vice President for Research .... Dr. Russell J. MUMPER
13 Vice Provost/Chief Information Ofcr .... Dr. John MCGOWAN
18 Assoc VP Facilities/Grounds .... Col. Duane LAMB

18 Sr Assoc VP Campus Development ..... Mr. Tim LEOPARD
19 Assoc VP Public Safety ..... Dr. Ralph CLAYTON
21 Assoc Provost for Financial Affairs ..... Mr. Jordan JOHNSON
20 Sr Assoc Provost Academic Affairs ..... Dr. Luoheng HAN
20 Assoc Provost Academic Affairs ..... Dr. Patty SOBECKY
15 Assoc VP Human Resources ..... Ms. Nancy H. WHITTAKER
21 Assoc Vice President for Finance ..... Ms. Julie SHELTON
21 Asst Vice Pres Finance & Operations ..... Ms. Cheryl MOWDY
27 Assoc VP Communications ..... Ms. Monica WATTS
88 Assoc VP Marketing & Brand Strategy ..... Mr. Ryan BRADLEY
29 Director of Alumni Affairs ..... Mr. Calvin BROWN
85 Assoc Provost Internatl Educ ..... Dr. Teresa WISE
06 University Registrar ..... Dr. Kenneth H. FOSHEE
09 Director Inst Research/Assessment ..... Dr. Lorne KUFFEL
36 Int Exec Director Career Center ..... Dr. Schernavia HALL
84 Assoc VP Enrollment Mgmt ..... Mr. Matthew MCLENDON
22 Exec Dir Institutional Compliance ..... Dr. Marcy HUEY
37 Director of Student Financial Aid ..... Ms. Helen ALLEN
39 Exec Director Housing/Res Cmty ..... Mr. Matthew KERCH
40 Asst VP Enterprise Operations ..... Ms. Teresa SHREVE
41 Athletic Director ..... Mr. Greg BYRNE
43 Chief University Counsel ..... Mr. Robin JONES
08 Dean of University Libraries ..... Dr. Donald GILSTRAP
49 Dean of Arts & Sciences ..... Dr. Joseph P. MESSINA
50 Dean Culverhouse Col of Business ..... Dr. Kay M. PALAN
51 Dean Col of Cont Studies ..... Dr. Jonathon HALBESLEBEN
53 Dean College of Education ..... Dr. Peter HLEBOWITSH
54 Dean College of Engineering ..... Dr. Charles L. KARR
58 Assoc Provost/Dean Graduate School ..... Dr. Susan CARVALHO
59 Dean Human Environmental Sciences ..... Dr. Stuart USDAN
60 Dean Col of Communication/Info Sci ..... Dr. Mark NELSON
61 Dean School of Law ..... Dr. Mark E. BRANDON
62 Dir Sch of Library/Info Studies ..... Dr. James ELMBORG
38 Manager Stdnt Support Svcs-Trio Pgm ..Ms. Wendy L. COGBURN
96 Purchasing Manager ..... Mr. Lane COX
76 Dean Cmty Health Sciences ..... Dr. Ricky FRIEND
66 Dean Capstone College of Nursing ..... Dr. Suzanne S. PREVOST
70 Int Dean School of Social Work ..... Dr. Lesley REID
92 Dean of Honors College ..... Dr. Tara WILLIAMS
94 Dir Women & Gender Resource Ctr ..... Ms. Elle SHAABAN-MAGANA

*University of Alabama at Birmingham (A)

1720 2nd Avenue South, Birmingham AL 35294-0001
County: Jefferson
FICE Identification: 001052
Unit ID: 100663
Telephone: (205) 934-4011
Carnegie Class: DU-Highest
FAX Number: N/A
Calendar System: Semester
URL: www.uab.edu
Established: 1969
Annual Undergrad Tuition & Fees (In-State): $8,568
Enrollment: 22,563
Coed
Affiliation or Control: State
IRS Status: 501(c)3
Highest Offering: Doctorate
Accreditation: SC, ANEST, ARCPA, ART, CACREP, CAEPN, CAHIIM, CAMPEP, CEA, CLPSY, DENT, @DIETC, DIETI, FEPAC, HSA, IPSY, MED, MT, MUS, NMT, NURSE, OPT, OPTR, OT, PAST, PH, PTA, SPAA, SW, THEA

02 President ..... Dr. Ray L. WATTS
05 Sr VP Academic Affairs & Provost ..... Dr. Pam BENOIT
10 Sr VP Financial Affairs/Admin ..... Dr. Brian BURNETT
17 CEO UAB Health System ..... Dr. Will FERNIANY
111 Vice Pres Advancement ..... Mr. Thomas I. BRANNAN
13 Vice Pres Info Technology/CIO ..... Dr. Curtis A. CARVER, JR.
28 Vice Pres for Equity & Diversity ..... Dr. Paulette P. DILWORTH
46 Vice Pres for Research ..... Dr. Chris BROWN
63 Sr VP/Dean School of Medicine ..... Dr. Selwyn M. VICKERS
20 Sr VProv Student/Faculty Success ..... Vacant
32 Vice Pres Student Affairs ..... Dr. John R. JONES, III
43 University Counsel ..... Mr. W. John DANIEL
49 Dean College of Arts & Sciences ..... Dr. Kecia M. THOMAS
50 Dean School of Business ..... Dr. Eric JACK
52 Dean School of Dentistry ..... Dr. Russell TAICHMAN
53 Interim Dean School of Education ..... Dr. Michelle A. ROBINSON
54 Dean School of Engineering ..... Dr. Jeffrey W. HOLMES
76 Dean Sch of Health Professions ..... Dr. Andrew J. BUTLER
66 Dean School of Nursing ..... Dr. Doreen C. HARPER
88 Dean School of Optometry ..... Dr. Kelly NICHOLS
69 Dean School of Public Health ..... Dr. Paul ERWIN
58 Dean Graduate School ..... Dr. Lori L. MCMAHON
18 Sr Facilities Officer ..... Mr. Greg PARSONS
29 Asst VP Alumni Affairs ..... Dr. Jennifer R. BRELAND
110 Assoc Vice Pres Development ..... Ms. Rebecca J. GORDON
26 Assoc VP Strategic Comm & CCO ..... Mr. Jim BAKKEN
105 AVP Digital Strategy & Marketing ..... Ms. Rosie O'BEIRNE
84 Vice Provost Enrollment Management ..... Dr. Bradley BARNES
21 Chief Financial Officer ..... Ms. Stephanie B. MULLINS
08 Dean of Libraries ..... Ms. Kasia J. GONNERMAN
41 Director of Athletics ..... Mr. Mark T. INGRAM
15 Chief Human Resources Officer ..... Ms. Alesia M. JONES
09 Vice Provost Inst Effectiveness ..... Ms. Eva LEWIS
19 Assoc VP Public Safety/Chief Police ..... Mr. Anthony B. PURCELL
07 Exec Dir Admisson/Financial Assist ..... Mr. Tyler M. PETERSON
37 Director of Financial Aid ..... Ms. Helen M. MCINTYRE
06 University Registrar ..... Ms. Cynthia TERRY
39 Exec Dir Student Housing & Dining ..... Mr. Marc BOOKER
36 Director Career Services ..... Mr. Brandon WRIGHT
38 Asst VP Student Dev/Health & Well ..... Dr. Rebecca KENNEDY
04 Executive Asst to President ..... Ms. Kay D. KIRK
106 Assoc Provost Academic Learning ..... Dr. Pamela E. PAUSTIAN
96 Director of Purchasing ..... Mr. Ron COLLINS
101 Board Liaison ..... Ms. Kirsten N. BURDICK

*University of Alabama in Huntsville (B)

301 Sparkman Drive, Huntsville AL 35899-1911
County: Madison
FICE Identification: 001055
Unit ID: 100706
Telephone: (256) 824-1000
Carnegie Class: DU-Higher
FAX Number: (256) 824-6073
Calendar System: Semester
URL: www.uah.edu
Established: 1950
Annual Undergrad Tuition & Fees (In-State): $11,338
Enrollment: 9,999
Coed
Affiliation or Control: State
IRS Status: 501(c)3
Highest Offering: Doctorate
Accreditation: SC, ART, CAEP, MUS, NURSE

02 President ..... Dr. Darren DAWSON
05 Provost & Exec VP Academic Affairs ..... Vacant
10 VP Finance & Administration ..... Mr. Todd BARRE
41 Director of Athletics ..... Dr. Cade SMITH
43 Chief University Counsel ..... Mr. Michael HUFF
32 VP of Student Affairs ..... Dr. Kristi MOTTER
100 Chief of Staff/Dir Community Rels ..... Vacant
46 VP Research/Economic Development ..... Dr. Thomas M. KOSHUT
46 VP for Research ..... Dr. Robert LINDQUIST
11 Assoc VP Finance & Business Svcs ..... Mr. Robert LEONARD
13 CIO ..... Mr. Malcolm RICE
20 Assoc Prov UG Studies/Inst Effect ..... Vacant
114 Associate VP Budgets & Fin Planning ..... Mr. Chih LOO
26 Director of Marketing/Communication ..... Ms. Elizabeth GIBISCH
15 Assoc VP Human Resources ..... Ms. Laurel LONG
116 Director Internal Audit ..... Ms. Tharanee M. RAVINDRAN
85 Dir International Engagement ..... Vacant
25 AVP Contracts & Grants ..... Ms. Gloria GREENE
88 Director Institute for Science Educ ..... Dr. James A. MILLER
08 Director Library ..... Dr. David P. MOORE
79 Dean Arts/Humanities/Soc Science ..... Dr. Sean LANE
81 Dean College of Science ..... Dr. Rainer STEINWANDT
50 Dean College Business Admin ..... Dr. Jason GREENE
51 Dean Prof & Cont Studies ..... Vacant
54 Dean College of Engineering ..... Dr. Shankar MAHALINGAM
58 Dean Graduate Studies ..... Vacant
66 Dean College of Nursing ..... Vacant
53 Dean Education ..... Dr. Beth QUICK
88 Dir of Cybersecurity Research & Edu ..... Mr. Tommy MORRIS
37 Director Financial Aid ..... Mr. Patrick JAMES
23 Dir Faculty & Staff Clinic ..... Ms. Louise O'KEEFE
19 Chief of Police ..... Mr. Brian COZBY
06 Registrar ..... Ms. Janet WALLER
07 Director Admissions ..... Ms. Peggy MASTERS
29 VP Alumni Rels/Univ Advancement ..... Ms. Mallie HALE
110 Director Advancement Services ..... Ms. Marcie T. EPPLING
23 Director Student Health Services ..... Vacant
88 Director ITSC ..... Dr. Sara J. GRAVES
88 Dir Small Business Develop Center ..... Mr. Foster PERRY
102 Asst Dir Corp & Foundation Gifts ..... Ms. Katie S. THURSTON
96 Director of Procurement ..... Mr. Terence HALEY
88 Director Library Computer Systems ..... Mr. Jack DROST
90 Manager Academic Technology ..... Mr. John THYGERSON
88 Director Research Institute ..... Dr. Steven MESSERVY
88 Director CMSA ..... Dr. Sara GRAVES
88 Director Ctr for Applied Optics ..... Dr. Robert LINDQUIST
88 Dir Ctr Mgmt & Econ Research ..... Mr. Nic LOYD
88 Director Propulsion Research Center ..... Dr. Robert FREDERICK
88 Dir Ctr Space Plasma/Aeronautic Res ..... Dr. Gary ZANK
88 Director Earth Systems Science Ctr ..... Dr. John R. CHRISTY
88 Dir University Ctr & Charger Union ..... Mr. William M. HALL
91 Director Enterprise Apps & IAM ..... Mr. Malcolm RICE
104 Director Global Studies Program ..... Dr. David JOHNSON
92 Dean of the Honors College ..... Dr. William WILKERSON

University of Mobile (C)

5735 College Parkway, Mobile AL 36613-2842
County: Mobile
FICE Identification: 001029
Unit ID: 101693
Telephone: (251) 675-5990
Carnegie Class: Bac-Diverse
FAX Number: N/A
Calendar System: Semester
URL: www.umobile.edu
Established: 1961
Annual Undergrad Tuition & Fees: $24,310
Enrollment: 2,016
Coed
Affiliation or Control: Southern Baptist
IRS Status: 501(c)3
Highest Offering: Doctorate
Accreditation: SC, ACBSP, ANEST, MUS, NURSE

00 Chairman of the Board of Trustees ..... Mr. Fred WILSON
01 President ..... Dr. Lonnie BURNETT
05 VP for Academic Affairs ..... Dr. Todd GREER
10 VP for Business & Financial Affairs ..... Dr. Melvin SANSOM
111 VP for Advancement ..... Dr. Bruce EARNEST
84 VP Enrollment & Student Life ..... Mrs. Charity WITTNER
26 VP for Marketing/Public Relations ..... Mrs. Lesa MOORE
21 Associate VP for Business Affairs ..... Ms. Carol CAMP
37 Assoc VP for Financial Aid ..... Ms. Marie BATSON
20 Asst VP for Academic Administration ..... Dr. Pamela BUCHANAN MILLER
27 Asst VP for Campus Communications ..... Mrs. Kathy L. DEAN
41 Int Director of Intercol Athletics ..... Dr. Melvin SANSOM
07 Director for Admissions/Enrollment ..... Mrs. Hali GIVENS
09 Senior Dir for Inst Research ..... Mrs. Kim LEOUSIS
08 Director for Library Services ..... Mr. Jeffrey D. CALAMETTI
15 Director for Human Resources ..... Mrs. Diane BLACK
50 Dean School of Business ..... Dr. Kathy DUNNING
53 Dean School of Education ..... Dr. Debra CHANCEY
66 Dean School of Nursing ..... Dr. Sarah BARNES-WITHERSPOON
57 Dean AL School of the Arts ..... Dr. Al MILLER
85 Dean Office for Global Engagement ..... Dr. Doug WILSON
88 Dean School of Health & Sports Sci ..... Dr. Lori DELONG
49 Assoc Dean College of Arts/Sciences ..... Dr. Matthew DOWNS
29 Dir of Alumni Programs ..... Mrs. Allie RATCLIFF
121 Exec Dir for Student Success ..... Mrs. Shirley SUTTERFIELD
06 Registrar ..... Ms. Eileen GARDNER
13 Director of Information Technology ..... Ms. Larkisha WINBUSH
89 Asst Dir for 1st Year Experience ..... Mrs. Shanoa REED
19 Dir of Campus Opers & Risk Mgmt ..... Ms. Vicki BURGIN
102 Exec Director of UM Foundation ..... Mr. Brian BOYLE
32 Dean of Students ..... Mr. Greg JOHNSON
04 Admin Assistant to the President ..... Mrs. Barbara GREENE

University of Montevallo (D)

Station 6001, Montevallo AL 35115-6001
County: Shelby
FICE Identification: 001004
Unit ID: 101709
Telephone: (205) 665-6000
Carnegie Class: Masters/M
FAX Number: N/A
Calendar System: Semester
URL: www.montevallo.edu
Established: 1896
Annual Undergrad Tuition & Fees (In-State): $13,710
Enrollment: 2,600
Coed
Affiliation or Control: State
IRS Status: 501(c)3
Highest Offering: Beyond Master's But Less Than Doctorate
Accreditation: SC, AAFCS, ART, CACREP, CAEPN, DIETC, MUS, SP, SW, THEA

01 President ..... Dr. John W. STEWART, III
05 Provost and VP Academic Affairs ..... Dr. Mary Beth ARMSTRONG
32 VP Student Affairs/Enrollment Mgmt ..... Dr. Tammi DAHLE
11 VP Administration/CIO ..... Ms. Kristalyn SCOTT LEE
18 Director Physical Plant ..... Mr. Cody JONES
35 Dir Student Conduct/Dean Stdnt Affs ..... Mr. Tony WYDELL MILLER
06 Registrar ..... Ms. Amanda FOX
08 Director Carmichael Library ..... Dr. Charlotte FORD
07 Director Admissions ..... Ms. Audrey CRAWFORD
37 Dir of Student Financial Services ..... Ms. Nikki BRADBURY
38 Director Counseling Services/Center ..... Mr. Joshua MILLER
19 Chief of Police ..... Mr. Tim ALEXANDER
39 Dir Housing & Residence Life ..... Mr. John DENSON
41 Director Athletics ..... Mr. Mark RICHARD
15 Director of HR and Risk Management ..... Ms. Barbara FORREST
51 Dir of Regional Inservice Center ..... Mr. Dwight JINRIGHT
09 Director of Institutional Research ..... Ms. Kris MASCETTI
49 Dean College Arts & Sciences ..... Dr. Ruth TRUSS
50 Dean College of Business ..... Dr. Stephen CRAFT
53 Dean College of Education ..... Dr. Courtney BENTLEY
57 Dean College of Fine Arts ..... Dr. Steven PETERS

University of North Alabama (E)

One Harrison Plaza, Florence AL 35632-0001
County: Lauderdale
FICE Identification: 001016
Unit ID: 101879
Telephone: (256) 765-4100
Carnegie Class: Masters/L
FAX Number: (256) 765-4644
Calendar System: Semester
URL: www.una.edu
Established: 1830
Annual Undergrad Tuition & Fees (In-State): $10,620
Enrollment: 8,086
Coed
Affiliation or Control: State
IRS Status: 501(c)3
Highest Offering: Doctorate
Accreditation: SC, ART, CACREP, CAEP, CAEPN, CIDA, JOUR, MUS, NURSE, SW

01 President ..... Dr. Kenneth D. KITTS
05 Provost & EVP Academic Affairs ..... Dr. Ross C. ALEXANDER
85 Senior Vice Provost Intl Affairs ..... Dr. Chunsheng ZHANG
10 VP Business/Financial Affs ..... Mr. Evan THORNTON
32 VP Student Affairs ..... Dr. Kimberly A. GREENWAY
111 Vice President Advancement ..... Mr. Kevin R. HASLAM
21 Assoc VP Business/Financial Affs ..... Ms. Cindy H. CONLON
28 VP Diversity/Equity & Inclusion ..... Mr. Ron K. PATTERSON
49 Dean College of Arts & Sciences ..... Dr. Sara Lynn BAIRD
50 Dean College of Business ..... Dr. Gregory A. CARNES
53 Dean Col Education/Human Sciences ..... Dr. Katie KINNEY
66 Dean Anderson College of Nursing ..... Dr. Vicki G. PIERCE
88 Director University Events ..... Dr. Kevin JACQUES
41 Interim Director of Athletics ..... Mr. Kevin HASLAM
43 General Counsel ..... Ms. Amber FITE-MORGAN
21 Controller ..... Mr. Mike NELSON
37 Director Student Financial Aid ..... Ms. Shauna JAMES
15 Asst VP for Human Resources ..... Ms. Catherine D. WHITE
13 Exec Dir Info Technology Services ..... Mr. Ethan HUMPHRES
26 Dir Univ Communications & Mktg ..... Ms. Michelle EUBANKS
18 Dir Facilities Admin & Planning ..... Mr. Kevin HUDSON
19 Interim Chief of University Police ..... Mr. Les JACKSON
23 Exec Dir Health and Well-Being ..... Ms. Teresa U. DAWSON
07 Director of Admissions ..... Ms. Julie Y. TAYLOR
09 Director of Institutional Research ..... Dr. Molly MATHIS
29 Director Alumni Relations ..... Mr. Bishop ALEXANDER
36 Director Career Center ..... Ms. Melissa T. MEDLIN
06 Interim Registrar ..... Mr. Mitch POWELL
38 Clinical Mgr Stdnt Counseling ..... Ms. Carmen RICHTER
40 Manager University Bookstore ..... Mr. Griffin HITE
04 Administrative Asst to President ..... Ms. Regina B. SHERRILL
89 Dir First Year Experience ..... Ms. Tammy RHODES
25 Dir Grants/Sponsored Programs ..... Mr. Nathan WILLINGHAM
08 University Librarian ..... Mr. Derek MALONE

39 Director Housing & Resident Life ... Ms. Jennifer SUTTON
86 Director Government Relations ... Mr. Jason A. COCHRAN

University of South Alabama (A)

307 University Boulevard, N, Mobile AL 36688-0002
County: Mobile FICE Identification: 001057
Unit ID: 102094
Telephone: (251) 460-6111 Carnegie Class: DU-Higher
FAX Number: (251) 461-1537 Calendar System: Semester
URL: www.southalabama.edu
Established: 1963 Annual Undergrad Tuition & Fees (In-State): $8,396
Enrollment: 14,224 Coed
Affiliation or Control: State IRS Status: 501(c)3
Highest Offering: Doctorate
Accreditation: **SC**, ARCPA, AUD, CACREP, CAEP, EMT, MED, MUS, NURSE, OT, PSPSY, PTA, RAD, RTT, SP, SW

01 Acting President ... Dr. John SMITH
03 Executive Vice President ... Vacant
05 Int Provost & SVP Academic Affairs ... Dr. Andrea KENT
20 Exec Vice Provost Academic Affairs ... Dr. Charles GUEST
63 VP Med Affairs/Dean COM ... Dr. John MARYMONT
10 VP Financial Affairs & Admin ... Mr. Scott WELDON
30 VP Developmental/Alumni Relations ... Ms. Margaret SULLIVAN
46 VP for Research & Economic Dev ... Ms. Lynne CHRONISTER
43 General Counsel ... Ms. Kristen DUKES
58 AVP Academic Affs/Dean Grad Sch ... Dr. J. Harold PARDUE
121 Assoc VP Academic Success ... Dr. Nicole CARR
84 Int Assoc VP Enrollment Services ... Mr. Salvadore LIBERTO
108 Assoc VP IE/Dir Inst Assessment ... Dr. Angela COLEMAN
13 Asst VP & Dir Info Tech Svcs ... Mr. Chris CANNON
15 Asst VP Human Resources ... Mr. Gerald GATTIS
86 Exec Director Government Relations ... Mr. Nicholas LAWKIS
32 VP Student Affairs/Dean of Students ... Dr. Michael MITCHELL
88 Director of Assessment ... Dr. Cara BRASWELL
26 VP Marketing/Communication ... Mr. Michael HASKINS
41 Director Athletics ... Dr. Joel ERDMANN
07 Director Admissions ... Ms. Norma TANNER
88 Director Immigration ... Ms. Regina GEORGE
09 Exec Dir IR/Planning & Analysis ... Dr. Gordon MILLS, JR.
06 Registrar ... Dr. Kelly OSTERBIND
29 Director Alumni Relations ... Ms. Karen EDWARDS
19 Chief of Police ... Mr. Zeke AULL, JR.
37 Director of Financial Aid ... Ms. Shannan WHITE
36 Director Career Services ... Ms. Bevley GREEN
12 Director USA Baldwin County ... Dr. Cynthia WILSON
18 Assoc VP/Director Facilities Mgmt ... Mr. Randy MOON
38 Director Student Counseling/Testing ... Dr. John FRIEND
28 Interim Chief Diversity Officer ... Dr. Joel BILLINGSLEY
96 Purchasing Manager ... Mr. Robert BROWN
54 Dean College of Engineering ... Dr. John USHER
51 Assoc VP Global USA ... Dr. Richard CARTER
49 Dean Arts & Sciences ... Dr. Andrzej WIERZBICKI
08 Exec Dir University Libraries ... Ms. Lorene FLANDERS
50 Interim Dean College of Business ... Dr. Alvin WILLIAMS
53 Interim Dean Educ & Prof Studies ... Dr. John KOVALESKI
66 Dean College of Nursing ... Dr. Heather HALL
76 Interim Dean Allied Health ... Dr. Susan GORDON-HICKEY
77 Dean School of Computing ... Dr. Alec YASINSAC
39 Assoc VP Auxiliary Services/Housing ... Dr. Chris CLEVELAND
04 Executive Asst to President ... Ms. Suzanne GOINS
101 Executive Asst Board Affairs ... Ms. Monica EZELL
104 Director Study Abroad ... Dr. Bri ARD
105 Asst Director Online Communication ... Mr. Ian HARBAUGH
22 HR Manager Benefits/EEO ... Ms. Yamayra BETLER
25 Mgr Grants & Contracts Acctg ... Mr. Lindsey SHEFFIELD
44 Assoc Dir Strategic Annual Campaign ... Ms. Tracy COLEMAN

The University of West Alabama (B)

100 US-11, Livingston, AL 35470, Livingston AL 35470
County: Sumter FICE Identification: 001024
Unit ID: 101587
Telephone: (205) 652-3400 Carnegie Class: Masters/L
FAX Number: (205) 652-3718 Calendar System: Semester
URL: www.uwa.edu
Established: 1835 Annual Undergrad Tuition & Fees (In-State): $10,990
Enrollment: 5,734 Coed
Affiliation or Control: State IRS Status: 501(c)3
Highest Offering: Doctorate
Accreditation: **SC**, ACBSP, ADNUR, CAATE, CAEPN

01 President ... Dr. Ken TUCKER
05 Provost ... Dr. Tim EDWARDS
10 Vice Pres Financial Affairs ... Mr. Lawson EDMONDS
111 Vice Pres Institutional Advancement ... Mr. Chris THOMASON
32 Vice President for Student Affairs ... Mr. Richard HESTER
49 Dean of Liberal Arts ... Dr. Mark DAVIS
50 Dean of Business & Technology ... Dr. Aliquippa ALLEN
53 Dean College of Education ... Dr. Jan MILLER
81 Dean of Natural Science/Math ... Dr. John MCCALL
58 Dean of Graduate Studies ... Dr. B.J KIMBROUGH
51 Dean Continuing Education ... Dr. Tina N. JONES
106 Dean Online Programs ... Dr. Jan MILLER
66 Chairperson of Nursing ... Dr. Mary HANKS
08 Director of Library ... Dr. Neil SNIDER
09 Dir Institutional Effectiveness ... Mrs. Angel JOWERS
41 Athletic Director ... Mr. Kent PARTRIDGE
35 Director of Student Life ... Mr. Byron THETFORD
06 Registrar ... Mrs. Susan SPARKMAN
37 Director Student Financial Aid ... Mr. Steve SMITH
13 Director Information Systems ... Mr. Michael PRATT
18 Director of Physical Plant ... Mr. Bobby TRUELOVE
109 Director of Auxiliary Services ... Ms. Willie JONES
36 Director Career Services/Placement ... Ms. Tammy S. WHITE
29 Director Alumni Relations ... Mrs. Katie BEARD
86 Director Government Relations ... Mr. Tom TARTT
07 Int Dir of Undergraduate Recruiting ... Mrs. Libba BAKER
96 Director of Purchasing ... Mrs. Janie WOOLDRIDGE
89 Director Freshmen Studies ... Dr. James GENTSCH
92 Director Honors Program ... Dr. Lesa SHAUL
15 Director Personnel Services ... Mrs. Brenda KILLOUGH
30 Director of Development ... Mr. Chris THOMASON
20 Associate Academic Officer ... Mrs. Angel JOWERS
26 Chief Public Relations Officer ... Ms. Betsy COMPTON
19 Director of Security/Safety ... Mr. Jeff MANUEL
103 Director Economic Development ... Mrs. Allison BRANTLEY
105 Director of Web Services ... Mr. Mike PRATT
101 Secretary Board of Trustees ... Ms. Toni TERRY
28 Director of Diversity ... Dr. B. J KIMBROUGH
85 Director of Foreign Students ... Dr. Mark DAVIS

ALASKA

Alaska Bible College (C)

248 East Elmwood Avenue, Palmer AK 99645
County: Matanuska-Susitna FICE Identification: 008843
Unit ID: 102580
Telephone: (907) 745-3201 Carnegie Class: Spec-4-yr-Faith
FAX Number: (907) 745-3210 Calendar System: Semester
URL: www.akbible.edu
Established: 1966 Annual Undergrad Tuition & Fees: $9,700
Enrollment: 40 Coed
Affiliation or Control: Independent Non-Profit IRS Status: 501(c)3
Highest Offering: Baccalaureate
Accreditation: **BI**

01 President ... Mr. David LEY
05 Vice Pres Academic Affairs ... Dr. Ben OLSON
32 Vice Pres Student Development ... Dr. Dan JARRELL
10 Vice Pres Business Admin ... Mr. Matthew COTE
42 Chaplain/Dir of Christian Ministry ... Mr. Justin ARCHULETTA
06 Registrar ... Vacant
08 Library Director ... Ms. Noel MAXWELL
07 Director of Admissions ... Mr. Josiah RICHARDSON
37 Director Financial Aid ... Ms. Christy COTE
26 Director of Communications ... Vacant
35 Dean of Students ... Vacant

Alaska Christian College (D)

35109 Royal Place, Soldotna AK 99669-9755
FICE Identification: 041386
Unit ID: 442523
Telephone: (907) 260-7422 Carnegie Class: Spec 2-yr-Other
FAX Number: (907) 260-6722 Calendar System: Semester
URL: alaskacc.edu
Established: 2001 Annual Undergrad Tuition & Fees: $8,414
Enrollment: N/A Coed
Affiliation or Control: Independent Non-Profit IRS Status: 501(c)3
Highest Offering: Associate Degree
Accreditation: **BI**

01 President ... Dr. Keith J. HAMILTON
03 Executive Vice President ... Mr. Jeff SEIMERS
11 Vice President of Operations ... Mr. Sean OFFBECK
111 Vice President of Advancement ... Mr. Eric JOHNSON
05 Vice President Academic Affairs ... Ms. Lindsey HALLAM
06 Registrar ... Ms. Brittany WILLIAMS
32 Director of Student Life ... Mr. Jacob HOEKSTRA
07 Director of Admissions ... Mr. Jeffrey SMITH
13 Director of IT Services ... Mr. David WILEY
15 Finance & Human Resources Director ... Ms. April WEBER
37 Director of Financial Aid ... Ms. Krista PITSCH
18 Director of Facilities ... Mr. Harvey LUNDQUIST

Alaska Career College (E)

1415 E. Tudor Road, Anchorage AK 99507-1033
County: Anchorage FICE Identification: 025410
Unit ID: 103501
Telephone: (907) 563-7575 Carnegie Class: Spec 2-yr-Other
FAX Number: (907) 563-8330 Calendar System: Other
URL: www.alaskacareercollege.edu
Established: 1985 Annual Undergrad Tuition & Fees: N/A
Enrollment: 412 Coed
Affiliation or Control: Proprietary IRS Status: Proprietary
Highest Offering: Associate Degree
Accreditation: **ACCSC**

01 Director ... Ms. Linda STURE
36 Director of Career Services ... Mr. Chaz ALEXANDER
10 Chief Financial/Business Officer ... Ms. Jennifer DEITZ
18 Chief Facilities/Physical Plant Ofc ... Ms. Donna BLEVINS
37 Director Student Financial Aid ... Ms. Monica MATLOCK

Alaska Pacific University (F)

4101 University Drive, Anchorage AK 99508-4672
County: Anchorage FICE Identification: 001061
Unit ID: 102669
Telephone: (907) 561-1266 Carnegie Class: Masters/S
FAX Number: (907) 562-4276 Calendar System: Semester
URL: www.alaskapacific.edu
Established: 1957 Annual Undergrad Tuition & Fees: $20,760
Enrollment: 493 Coed
Affiliation or Control: Independent Non-Profit IRS Status: 501(c)3
Highest Offering: Doctorate
Accreditation: **NW**, CAEPN, IACBE

01 Interim President ... Dr. Hilton HALLOCK
04 Executive Assistant to President ... Ms. Debbie J. ROLL
05 Acting Academic Dean ... Dr. Stephanie MORGAN
10 Chief Financial Officer ... Ms. Sheila KING
32 Dean of Students ... Mr. Ben HAHN
06 Registrar ... Ms. Michelle WHEELER
07 Director of Admissions ... Ms. Toni RILEY
109 Director of Auxiliary Services ... Mr. Brian MCDERMOTT
37 Director of Financial Aid ... Mr. Scott GRAVES
18 Director Facilities Management ... Ms. Kathy MINCKS
13 Director Information Technology ... Mr. Kent ENGLISH
111 Chief Advancement Officer ... Ms. Laurie EVANS-DINNEEN
42 Chaplain ... Mr. Brian ANDERSON
15 Director Human Resources ... Ms. Kathleen WYRICK
29 Alumni/Donor Relations ... Mr. Christopher DEEN
117 Compliance/Risk Officer ... Mr. Robert MEYER
38 Dir of Career/Counseling/Disability ... Vacant
39 Dir Campus Life/Student Housing ... Mr. Chandler STROUP
26 Director of Marketing/Communication ... Mr. Elias ROJAS

Charter College (G)

2221 E Northern Lights Blvd, #120,
Anchorage AK 99508-4157
Telephone: (907) 277-1000 Identification: 770822
Accreditation: **ABHES**, ADNUR

† Branch campus of Charter College, Vancouver, WA

Ilisagvik College (H)

PO Box 749, Barrow AK 99723
County: North Slope Borough FICE Identification: 034613
Unit ID: 434584
Telephone: (907) 852-3333 Carnegie Class: Tribal
FAX Number: (907) 852-3003 Calendar System: Semester
URL: www.ilisagvik.edu
Established: 1996 Annual Undergrad Tuition & Fees: $4,780
Enrollment: 232 Coed
Affiliation or Control: Independent Non-Profit IRS Status: 501(c)3
Highest Offering: Baccalaureate
Accreditation: **NW**, DTH

01 President ... Mrs. Justina WILHELM
11 Dean of Administration ... Mrs. Heather DINGMAN
06 Registrar ... Ms. Stephanie MORALES
05 Dean of Academic Affairs ... Ms. Birgit MEANY
15 Exec Director of Human Resources ... Ms. Robyn BURKE
18 Chief Facilities/Physical Plant ... Mr. Tom CARAWAY
111 Exec Dir Institutional Advancement ... Mrs. Caitlin WALLS
32 Dean of Students ... Mr. Hal HAYNES, JR.
37 Director Student Financial Aid ... Mrs. Nancy GRANT
08 Chief Library Officer ... Ms. Teressa WILLIAMS
10 Chief Financial Officer ... Ms. Ann Marie CLARK
101 Executive Assistant/Board Secretary ... Mrs. Nicole EVANS
13 IT Manager ... Mr. Anton EDWARDSON
04 Exec Assistant to the President ... Ms. Clarissa PELIA

*University of Alaska System (I)

2025 Yukon Drive, Suite 202, Fairbanks AK 99775-5000
County: Fairbanks FICE Identification: 008005
Unit ID: 103529
Telephone: (907) 450-8000 Carnegie Class: N/A
FAX Number: (907) 450-8012
URL: www.alaska.edu

01 Interim President ... Ms. Pat PITNEY
26 Vice President for Univ Relations ... Ms. Michelle RIZK
05 VP for Academics/Students/Research ... Dr. Paul LAYER
10 Chief Finance Officer/Controller ... Mr. Myron DOSCH
46 Chief Strategy/Planning/Budget Ofcr ... Ms. Michelle RIZK
09 AVP Data Strategy & Inst Research ... Ms. Gwendolyn GRUENIG
86 Assoc VP Public Affairs ... Ms. Robbie GRAHAM
43 General Counsel ... Mr. Matthew COOPER
15 Acting Chief HR Officer ... Mr. David BISHKO
13 Interim Chief Information Tech Ofcr ... Mr. John BOUCHER
101 Exec Officer Board of Regents ... Ms. Brandi BERG

*University of Alaska Anchorage (J)

3211 Providence Drive, Anchorage AK 99508-8000
County: Anchorage FICE Identification: 011462
Unit ID: 102553
Telephone: (907) 786-1800 Carnegie Class: Masters/L
FAX Number: (907) 786-4888 Calendar System: Semester
URL: www.uaa.alaska.edu
Established: 1954 Annual Undergrad Tuition & Fees (In-State): $8,622
Enrollment: 11,953 Coed
Affiliation or Control: State IRS Status: 501(c)3
Highest Offering: Doctorate
Accreditation: **NW**, ACFEI, ADNUR, ART, CAEPN, CLPSY, CONST, CSHSE, DA, DH, DIETC, DIETD, DIETI, EMT, MAC, MT, MUS, NAEYC, NUR, NURSE, PH, PTAA, SURGT, SW

02 Chancellor ... Sean PARNELL
05 Provost ... Denise RUNGE
10 Interim Vice Chanc Admin Services ... Bill JACOB
84 Assoc Vice Chanc Enroll Svcs ... Lora VOLDEN
111 Vice Chanc University Advancement ... Megan OLSON
32 Vice Chancellor Student Affairs ... Bruce SCHULTZ
20 Vice Provost Undergrad Acad Affairs ... Susan KALINA
46 Assoc Vice Chancellor for Research ... Aaron DOTSON
13 Interim CIO/Assoc Vice Chanc ITS ... Benjamin SHIER
18 Assoc VC Facilities/Campus Svcs ... Kim MAHONEY
29 Asst Vice Chanc Alumni Relations ... Tanya PONT
121 Dir Acad/Multicultural Success ... Sara CALDWELL-KAN
35 Dean of Students ... Ben MORTON
37 Financial Aid Director ... Shauna GRANT
09 Director Institutional Research ... Daniel CAMPBELL
15 Chief Human Resources Officer ... Steven J. PATIN
85 Director Multicultural Center ... Vacant
26 Director of Philanthropy ... Brian IBSEN
35 Director Student Life & Leadership ... Zak CLARK
07 Interim Exec Director of Admissions ... Craig MEAD
41 Director Athletics ... Greg MYFORD
06 University Registrar ... Lindsey CHADWELL
08 Dean Consortium Library ... Stephen ROLLINS
63 Director WWAMI Biomedical Program ... Jane SHELBY
38 Director Student Health & Counsel ... Mary WOODRING
50 Dean Business & Public Policy ... John NOFSINGER
51 Dean Cmty & Tech College ... Raymond WEBER
76 Int Dean College of Health ... Andre ROSAY
54 Dean College of Engineering ... Kenrick MOCK
49 Dean College Arts & Sciences ... Jenny MCNULTY
92 Dean Honors College ... Claudia LAMPMAN
39 Exec Director Campus Services ... David WEAVER
28 Chief Diversity Officer ... Jennifer BOOZ

*University of Alaska Fairbanks (A)

505 South Chandlar Drive, Fairbanks AK 99775
County: Fairbanks North Star Borough FICE Identification: 001063
Unit ID: 102614
Telephone: (907) 474-7500 Carnegie Class: DU-Higher
FAX Number: (907) 474-5379 Calendar System: Semester
URL: www.uaf.edu
Established: 1917 Annual Undergrad Tuition & Fees (In-State): $7,176
Enrollment: 6,813 Coed
Affiliation or Control: State IRS Status: 501(c)3
Highest Offering: Doctorate
Accreditation: **NW**, CACREP, CAEP, CAEPN, EMT, MAC, NAEYC, SW

02 Chancellor ... Dr. Daniel M. WHITE
05 Provost ... Dr. Anupma PRAKASH
11 Vice Chancellor Administrative Svcs ... Ms. Julie QUEEN
18 Assoc Vice Chancellor Facilities ... Ms. Kellie FRITZE
32 Vice Chancellor Student Affairs ... Ms. Alexis KNABE
46 Vice Chancellor Research ... Dr. Nettie LA BELLE-HAMER
10 AVC for Financial Services ... Ms. Amanda WALL
30 Director of Development ... Ms. Morgan DULIAN
58 Director Graduate School ... Dr. Richard COLLINS
81 Dean Col of Natural Science/Math ... Dr. Kinchel DORNER
35 Assoc Vice Chanc for Student Life ... Mr. Alexis KNABE
31 VC Rural/Cmty & Native Educ ... Dr. Charlene STERN
12 Dean UAF Comm & Tech College ... Ms. Michele STALDER
88 Dean Col Fisheries & Ocean Sciences ... Dr. Bradley MORAN
50 Dean School of Management ... Dr. Mark HERRMANN
54 Dean Col of Engineering & Mines ... Dr. William SCHNABEL
88 Dir Intl Arctic Research Center ... Dr. Hajo EICKEN
88 Dir Institute of Arctic Biology ... Dr. Diane O'BRIEN
54 Int Dir Inst Northern Engineering ... Dr. David BARNES
15 Chief Human Resources Officer ... Mr. David BISHKO
19 Chief of Police ... Ms. Kathleen CATRON
37 Director Financial Aid ... Ms. Deanna L. DIERINGER
41 Director Athletics ... Dr. Brock ANUNDSON
35 Dean of Students ... Ms. Kaydee VAN FLEIN
56 Vice Provost for Extension/Outreach ... Dr. Pete PINNEY
109 Director of Aux/Recharge/Cntrct Ops ... Vacant
85 Director International Programs ... Ms. Joanna CRUZAN
88 Fire Chief ... Mr. Forrest KUIPER
88 Dir Institute of Marine Science ... Dr. Terry WHITLEDGE
49 Dean College of Liberal Arts ... Dr. Ellen LOPEZ
53 Director School of Education ... Dr. Amy VINLOVE
12 Director Bristol Bay Campus ... Ms. Sarah ANDREW
12 Dir Chukchi Campus ... Ms. Stacey GLASER
12 Dir Interior Alaska Campus ... Mr. Byron BLUEHORSE
12 Director Kuskokwim Campus ... Ms. Linda KURDA
12 Director Northwest Campus ... Ms. Barbara AMAROK
28 Director of Diversity & EO ... Ms. Margo GRIFFITH
23 Director Health and Counseling ... Dr. B.J ALDRICH
29 Exec Director Alumni Association ... Ms. Theresa BAKKER
06 Registrar ... Mr. Mike EARNEST
88 Director Geophysical Institute ... Dr. Robert MCCOY
21 Director Business Operations ... Ms. Briana WALTERS
121 Director Academic Advising Center ... Ms. Linda M. HAPSMITH
92 Director Honors Program ... Dr. Alex HIRSCH
09 Dir Planning/Analysis/Inst Research ... Vacant
111 Director University Advancement ... Ms. Samara TABER
08 Director of Libraries ... Ms. Karen JENSEN
88 Dir UA Museum of the North ... Dr. Patrick DRUCKENMILLER
13 Chief Info Technology Officer ... Ms. Martha MASON
22 Director for Disability Services ... Ms. Amber CAGWIN
96 Dir of Procurement & Contract Svcs ... Mr. John HEBARD
88 Director Wood Center Student Union ... Ms. Cody ROGERS
97 Vice Provost/Dean Gen Studies ... Dr. Alex FITTS
04 Assistant to the Chancellor ... Ms. Jeannie PHILLIPS
106 Executive Director for E-learning ... Dr. Owen GUTHRIE
07 Director Admissions ... Ms. Anna GAGNE-HAWES

*University of Alaska Southeast (B)

11066 Auke Lake Way, Juneau AK 99801
County: Juneau FICE Identification: 001065
Unit ID: 102632
Telephone: (907) 796-6100 Carnegie Class: Masters/M
FAX Number: N/A Calendar System: Semester
URL: www.uas.alaska.edu
Established: 1956 Annual Undergrad Tuition & Fees (In-State): $6,960
Enrollment: 2,070 Coed
Affiliation or Control: State IRS Status: 501(c)3
Highest Offering: Master's
Accreditation: **NW**, #ACBSP, CAEP, CAHIIM, MAC

02 Chancellor ... Dr. Karen CAREY
05 Interim Provost ... Dr. Maren HAAVIG
84 VC Enrollment Mgmt & Stdnt Affs ... Ms. Lori KLEIN
75 Exec Dean of Career/Tech Educ ... Mr. Pete TRAXLER
46 Vice Provost for Research ... Dr. Maren HAAVIG
11 Vice Chanc Administration ... Mr. Michael CIRI
12 Sitka Campus Director ... Mr. Paul KRAFT
12 Ketchikan Campus Director ... Dr. Priscilla SCHULTE
49 Dean of Arts & Sciences ... Ms. Carin SILKAITIS
53 Int Director School of Education ... Ms. Mary Lou MADDEN
37 Financial Aid Director ... Ms. Janelle COOK
26 Exec Asst to Chanc/Public Rels Ofcr ... Ms. Keni CAMPBELL
06 Registrar ... Ms. Trisha LEE
09 Dir Institutional Effectiveness ... Ms. Kristen HANDLEY
10 Dir Business Operations ... Mr. Jon LASINSKI
15 Chief Human Resources Officer ... Mr. David BISHKO
18 Director Facilities Services ... Mr. Nathan LEIGH
08 Dean Library Services ... Ms. Elise TOMLINSON
13 Director Information/Technology ... Mr. Michael CIRI
30 Dir Development/Alumni Relations ... Ms. Lynne JOHNSON
21 Chief Budget Officer ... Ms. Julie VIGIL
22 Dep Dir Equity/Compliance/TIX ... Mr. Ryan WARK
32 Dean Students & Campus Life ... Ms. Jackie WILSON
88 Dir of PITAAS/AVC AK Native Pgms ... Ms. Ronalda CADIENTE-BROWN
88 Dir of AK Coastal Rainforest Center ... Mr. Jason FELDMAN
07 Dir of Admissions/Recruitment ... Ms. Lori KLEIN
105 Web Coordinator ... Mr. Colin OSTERHOUT
96 Procurement Services Manager ... Mr. Richard HITCHCOCK

*Prince William Sound Community College (C)

PO Box 97, 303 Lowe Street, Valdez AK 99686-0097
Telephone: (907) 834-1600 Identification: 666659
Accreditation: **&NW**

† Branch campus of University of Alaska Anchorage, Anchorage, AK

ARIZONA

Acacia University (D)

7665 South Research Drive, Tempe AZ 85284-1812
County: Maricopa Identification: 667017
Telephone: (480) 428-6034 Carnegie Class: Not Classified
FAX Number: (480) 428-6033 Calendar System: Other
URL: www.acacia.edu
Established: 2003 Annual Undergrad Tuition & Fees: N/A
Enrollment: N/A Coed
Affiliation or Control: Proprietary IRS Status: Proprietary
Highest Offering: Doctorate
Accreditation: **DEAC**

01 President ... Mr. Tim MOMAN
05 Provost/Executive Vice President ... Dr. Marilynn D. HENLEY
13 Vice President of Technology ... Mr. Michael TURICO

American InterContinental University (E)

2200 E. Germann Rd, Chandler AZ 85286
County: Maricopa FICE Identification: 021136
Unit ID: 445027
Telephone: (877) 701-3800 Carnegie Class: Masters/L
FAX Number: N/A Calendar System: Quarter
URL: www.aiuniv.edu
Established: 1970 Annual Undergrad Tuition & Fees: $11,646
Enrollment: 15,415 Coed
Affiliation or Control: Proprietary IRS Status: Proprietary
Highest Offering: Master's
Accreditation: **HLC**, AAQEP, ACBSP

01 President ... Mr. John KLINE
05 Provost & Chief Academic Officer ... Dr. Ruki JAYARAMAN
07 VP of Admissions ... Mrs. Trisha GANGER
32 VP of Strategic Student Operations ... Mr. Jeffrey SONNENBERG
88 VP Program Management ... Ms. April MIGEL
10 VP of Univ Policy/Administration ... Mr. Daniel SESSIONS
11 VP of Campus Operations ... Ms. Julia LEEMAN
09 VP Educational Alliances & IRC ... Mr. Walid KAAKOUSH
12 Campus Director-Atlanta ... Ms. Sharon SMITH
12 Campus Director-Houston ... Vacant

Arizona Christian University (F)

1 W. Firestorm Way, Glendale AZ 85306
County: Maricopa FICE Identification: 007113
Unit ID: 105899
Telephone: (602) 489-5300 Carnegie Class: Bac-Diverse
FAX Number: (602) 404-2159 Calendar System: Semester
URL: www.arizonachristian.edu
Established: 1960 Annual Undergrad Tuition & Fees: $29,250
Enrollment: 925 Coed
Affiliation or Control: Independent Non-Profit IRS Status: 501(c)3
Highest Offering: Baccalaureate
Accreditation: **HLC**

01 President ... Mr. Len MUNSIL
05 Provost & Executive Vice President ... Dr. Steve ADAMSON
20 Dean of Academic Affairs ... Dr. Edward CLAVELL
06 Registrar ... Mrs. Tracy MARTIN
84 Vice President of Enrollment ... Mr. Jeff RUTTER
106 Director of Online Students ... Mrs. Tiffany THOMAS
111 VP of University Engagement ... Mr. James GRIFFITHS
32 Dean of Students ... Dr. Jared BLACK
10 Chief Financial Officer ... Ms. Robin KLUNG
41 Director of Athletics ... Dr. Peter DRYER
18 Sr Director of Campus Operations ... Mr. Jon CLINE
21 Controller ... Mrs. Kelly BULLOCK
37 Director of Financial Aid ... Mrs. Kelsey HJERPE
13 Director of Information Technology ... Mr. John PETEET
08 Head Librarian ... Mr. Robert OLIVERIO
19 Chief of Campus Safety ... Mr. John HOEBEE
39 Director of Resident Life ... Mr. Alan BOELTER
04 Asst to President & Provost/COO ... Mrs. Julie ROSEN
84 Director of Enrollment Management ... Vacant
38 Director of Counseling Services ... Mrs. Melissa INGRAHAM
121 Director of Academic Services ... Mrs. Brenda SPEAR
09 AVP of Institutional Effectiveness ... Ms. Ruthann NSUBUGA
29 Alumni Engagement Specialist ... Mr. Tim REED
30 Director of University Engagement ... Mrs. Allison PETEET

Arizona College (G)

4425 W Olive Avenue, Suite 300,
Glendale AZ 85302-3851
Telephone: (602) 222-9300 FICE Identification: 031150
Accreditation: **ABHES**

Arizona College-Mesa (H)

163 N. Dobson Road, Mesa AZ 85201
Telephone: (855) 706-8382 Identification: 770514
Accreditation: **ABHES**

Arizona School of Acupuncture and Oriental Medicine (I)

2856 E Fort Lowell Rd., Tucson AZ 85716
County: Pima FICE Identification: 036955
Unit ID: 446039
Telephone: (520) 795-0787 Carnegie Class: Spec-4-yr-Other Health
FAX Number: (877) 222-4606 Calendar System: Quarter
URL: www.asaom.edu
Established: 1996 Annual Graduate Tuition & Fees: N/A
Enrollment: 13 Coed
Affiliation or Control: Proprietary IRS Status: Proprietary
Highest Offering: Master's; No Undergraduates
Accreditation: **ACUP**

00 Owner ... Mr. Jonathan HU
01 President ... Mr. Joshua HANNUM
05 Academic Dean ... Dr. Kara MICHALSEN
37 Director of Financial Programs ... Ms. Susan WAGNER
07 Admissions Officer ... Mr. Frank HARRIS
06 Registrar ... Ms. Haley HALL
63 Dean of Clinical Education ... Mr. Nathan ANDERSON

Arizona State University (J)

300 E. University Drive, Tempe AZ 85281
County: Maricopa FICE Identification: 001081
Unit ID: 104151
Telephone: (855) 278-5080 Carnegie Class: DU-Highest
FAX Number: N/A Calendar System: Semester
URL: www.asu.edu
Established: 1885 Annual Undergrad Tuition & Fees (In-State): $11,338
Enrollment: 74,795 Coed
Affiliation or Control: State IRS Status: 501(c)3
Highest Offering: Doctorate
Accreditation: **HLC**, AAB, ART, AUD, CAPRT, CIDA, CLPSY, CONST, COPSY, CR, DIETD, DIETI, IPSY, JOUR, LAW, LSAR, MT, MUS, NURSE, PCSAS, PLNG, SP, SPAA, SW

01 President ... Dr. Michael M. CROW
05 Exec VP & University Provost ... Dr. Nancy GONZALES
10 Exec Vice President/Treasurer & CFO ... Dr. Morgan R. OLSEN
101 Sr Vice Pres/Sec of the University ... Dr. Christine K. WILKINSON
102 CEO ASU Foundation ... Gretchen E. BUHLIG
43 Sr Vice President & General Counsel ... José A. CARDENAS
32 Sr VP Educ Outreach & Student Svcs ... Dr. James A. RUND
84 VP Enrollment Svcs/Admissions ... Kent R. HOPKINS
41 Vice President University Athletics ... Raymond ANDERSON
13 Chief Information Officer ... Dr. Lev GONICK
15 VP & Chief Human Resources Ofc ... Kevin J. SALCIDO
100 Sr VP Univ Affairs/Chief of Staff ... James O'BRIEN
106 Dean Ed Initiatives/CEO EdPlus ... Dr. Philip R. REGIER
49 Dean Liberal Arts & Sciences ... Dr. Patrick J. KENNEY
50 Int Dean W P Carey School Business ... Dr. Amy OSTROM

54 Dean Fulton Schools of Engineering .... Dr. Kyle SQUIRES
53 Dean Mary Lou Fulton Teachers Col .... Dr. Carole G. BASILE
92 VP/Dean Barrett The Honors College .... Dr. Mark JACOBS
12 VP/Dean New College Int Arts & Sci .... Dr. Todd R. SANDRIN
57 Dean Herberger Inst for Design/Arts .... Dr. Steven J. TEPPER
60 Dean Sch Journalism/Mass Comm .... Battinto BATTS, JR.
61 Dean College of Law .... Douglas J. SYLVESTER
66 Dean Col Nursing/Health Innovation .... Dr. Judith F. KARSHMER
47 Dean College of Global Futures .... Dr. Christopher G. BOONE
20 Vice Provost Undergrad Education .... Dr. Frederick C. COREY
76 Dean Health Solutions .... Dr. Deborah L. HELITZER
80 Int Dean Col Public Svc & Cmty Sol .... Dr. Cynthia LIETZ
08 University Librarian .... Dr. James O'DONNELL
107 Dn/Dir Thunderbird Sch Global Mgmt .... Dr. Sanjeev KHAGRAM
88 Dean Col Integr Science & Arts .... Dr. Joanna GRABSKI
58 VP/Dean Graduate College .... Dr. Elizabeth A. WENTZ
79 Dean of Humanities .... Dr. Jeffrey J. COHEN
81 Dean of Natural Sciences .... Dr. Kenro KUSUMI
83 Dean of Social Sciences .... Dr. Pardis MAHDAVI
97 VP/Dean University College .... Dr. Sukhwant JHAJ
46 Exec VP Knowledge Enterprise .... Dr. Sally C. MORTON
45 Senior VP & University Planner .... Richard H. STANLEY
88 VP & Vice Provost Global Futures .... Dr. Peter SCHLOSSER
88 VP of Cultural Affairs .... Colleen JENNINGS-ROGGENSACK
26 VP & Chief Marketing Officer .... Ann TOCA
32 VP Student Services .... Dr. Joanne VOGEL
86 VP of Government Affairs .... Matt SALMON
27 VP Media Relations/Strategic Comm .... Katie PAQUET
88 VP for Inclusion and Comm Eng .... Dr. Tiffany Ana LOPEZ

Arizona Western College (A)

2020 South Avenue 8E, Yuma AZ 85365
County: Yuma FICE Identification: 001071
Unit ID: 104160
Telephone: (928) 317-6000 Carnegie Class: Assoc/HT-High Trad
FAX Number: N/A Calendar System: Semester
URL: www.azwestern.edu
Established: 1963 Annual Undergrad Tuition & Fees (In-District): $2,840
Enrollment: 6,487 Coed
Affiliation or Control: State/Local IRS Status: Exempt
Highest Offering: Associate Degree
Accreditation: HLC, ADNUR, EMT, RAD

01 President .... Dr. Daniel P. CORR
05 Vice President Learning Services .... Dr. Diane CARRASCO-JAQUEZ
10 Acting VP Finance/Administration .... Ms. Michelle LANDIS
111 Vice President of Advancement .... Ms. Lori STOFFT
25 Director of Grants .... Ms. Lorraine DISCHINGER
51 Assoc Dean of Continuing Educ .... Mrs. Maria AGUIRRE
32 Vice President for Student Services .... Mr. Bryan E. DOAK
75 AVP Workforce Dev & Tech Educ .... Ms. Reetika DHAWAN
84 Associate Dean of Enrollment Svcs .... Ms. Ana ENGLISH
35 Associate Dean of Campus Life .... Ms. Nikki HAGE
21 Dir Financial Services/Controller .... Mrs. Michelle LANDIS
15 Chief Human Resources Officer .... Ms. Karen M. JOHNSON
96 Dir Purchasing & Auxiliary Services .... Ms. Margaret HAYES
18 Director of District Operations .... Mr. Steve ECKERT
13 Chief Information Officer .... Vacant
08 Director of Library Services .... Ms. Angie CREEL
41 Director of Athletics .... Mr. Jerry SMITH
19 Chief of Police .... Mr. Stephen SUHO
28 Dir Diversity/Inclusion/Access .... Ms. Laura SANDIGO
12 Associate Dean La Paz County Svcs .... Ms. Kathy OCAMPO
12 Assoc Dean for South Yuma County .... Ms. Susanna ZAMBRANO
37 Director of Financial Aid .... Ms. Ana ENGLISH
85 Coord of International Student .... Ms. Aybuke KEEHN
106 Associate Dean for Distance Educ .... Mrs. Jana MOORE
88 Director of Testing Services .... Mrs. Leticia MARTINEZ
105 Webmaster II .... Mr. Damien BATES
100 Chief of Staff .... Mrs. Ashley HERRINGTON
36 Director Career/Advisement Services .... Mr. James R. HUTCHISON
101 Executive Assistant to the District .... Mrs. Ashley HERRINGTON

Benedictine University Mesa (B)

225 East Main Street, Mesa AZ 85201
Telephone: (602) 888-5000 Identification: 770068
Accreditation: &HLC

† Branch campus of Benedictine University, Lisle, IL

Brookline College (C)

2445 West Dunlap Avenue, Suite 100, Phoenix AZ 85021
County: Maricopa FICE Identification: 022188
Unit ID: 104090
Telephone: (602) 242-6265 Carnegie Class: Spec-4-yr-Other Health
FAX Number: (602) 973-2572 Calendar System: Other
URL: www.brooklinecollege.edu
Established: 1979 Annual Undergrad Tuition & Fees: N/A
Enrollment: 1,552 Coed
Affiliation or Control: Proprietary IRS Status: Proprietary
Highest Offering: Baccalaureate
Accreditation: ABHES, MLTAD, MT, NURSE, PTAA

01 Campus Director .... Mr. Glen THARP
05 Director or Education .... Dr. Lenora SPICER

Brookline College (D)

1140 South Priest Drive, Tempe AZ 85281
Telephone: (480) 545-8755 Identification: 666403
Accreditation: ABHES, SURTEC

† Branch campus of Brookline College, Phoenix, AZ.

Brookline College (E)

5441 E 22nd Street, Suite 125, Tucson AZ 85711-5444
Telephone: (520) 748-9799 Identification: 666402
Accreditation: ABHES, SURTEC

† Branch campus of Brookline College, Phoeniz, AZ.

Bryan University (F)

350 West Washington Street, Ste 100, Tempe AZ 85281
County: Maricopa FICE Identification: 007164
Unit ID: 110219
Telephone: (602) 384-2555 Carnegie Class: Spec-4-yr-Other Health
FAX Number: (888) 458-0447 Calendar System: Quarter
URL: www.bryanuniversity.edu
Established: 1940 Annual Undergrad Tuition & Fees: $11,755
Enrollment: 1,350 Coed
Affiliation or Control: Proprietary IRS Status: Proprietary
Highest Offering: Master's
Accreditation: ACCSC, CAHIIM

01 President/COO .... Mr. Eric EVANS
03 Executive Vice President .... Mr. Dimitrios KRIARAS
05 Exec Dir Undergraduate Studies .... Mr. Nicholas KEELING
10 Chief Financial Officer .... Mr. David ROGERS
06 Registrar .... Ms. Hope BEJARANO
37 VP of Student Finance .... Ms. Roxane ROMERO
32 Dean of Students .... Dr. Dylan MATSUMORI

Carrington College - Mesa (G)

1001 W Southern Avenue, Suite 130, Mesa AZ 85210
Telephone: (480) 212-1600 FICE Identification: 023352
Accreditation: &WJ, ADNUR, DH, MAAB, #PTAA

† Regional accreditation is carried under the parent institution in Sacramento, CA.

Carrington College - Phoenix East (H)

2149 W Dunlap Avenue, Suite 103, Phoenix AZ 85021
Telephone: (602) 427-0660 Identification: 666248
Accreditation: &WJ, COARC

† Regional accreditation is carried under the parent institution in Sacramento, CA.

Carrington College - Phoenix North (I)

8503 N 27th Avenue, Phoenix AZ 85051
Telephone: (602) 393-5900 FICE Identification: 021006
Accreditation: &WJ, ADNUR, MAAB

† Regional accreditation is carried under the parent institution in Sacramento, CA.

Carrington College - Tucson (J)

201 N. Bonita Avenue, Suite 101, Tucson AZ 85745
Telephone: (520) 888-5885 FICE Identification: 030898
Accreditation: &WJ, ADNUR, MAAB

† Regional accreditation is carried under the parent institution in Sacramento, CA.

Central Arizona College (K)

8470 N Overfield Road, Coolidge AZ 85128-9779
County: Pinal FICE Identification: 007283
Unit ID: 104346
Telephone: (520) 494-5111 Carnegie Class: Assoc/HT-Mix Trad/Non
FAX Number: (520) 494-5008 Calendar System: Semester
URL: www.centralaz.edu
Established: 1961 Annual Undergrad Tuition & Fees (In-District): $2,580
Enrollment: 4,076 Coed
Affiliation or Control: Local IRS Status: 501(c)3
Highest Offering: Associate Degree
Accreditation: HLC, ADNUR, CAHIIM, DIETT, EMT, MAC, MLTAD, NAEYC, RAD

01 President .... Dr. Jacquelyn ELLIOTT
05 VP Academic Affairs .... Dr. Mary K. GILLILAND
32 VP Student Services .... Dr. Jenni CARDENAS
107 Academic Dean .... Dr. Tina BERRY
49 Academic Dean .... Vacant
103 Academic Dean .... Dr. Jani ATTEBERY
81 Academic Dean .... Mr. Jeff BUNKELMANN
10 VP/CFO Business Affairs .... Mr. Chris WODKA
15 VP Talent Development/Legal Affairs .... Ms. Brandi BAIN
08 Director Library Services .... Ms. Adriana SAAVEDRA
37 Director of Financial Aid .... Ms. Elisa JUAREZ
41 Athletic Director .... Vacant
39 Director of Residence Life .... Ms. Rosemary RAMIREZ
18 Exec Director of Facilities .... Vacant
96 Director of Purchasing .... Mr. Mark SALAZ
06 Registrar/Int Dean of Enrollment .... Ms. Veronica DURAN
07 Director of Admissions/Recruitment .... Vacant
21 Exec Dir Accounting Svc/Comptroller .... Ms. Luisa OTT
30 Director Institutional Development .... Ms. Margaret DOOLEY

35 Dean of Student Life .... Vacant
04 Exec Asst to President & Gov Board .... Ms. Mary Lou HERNANDEZ
13 Chief Info Technology Officer (CIO) .... Mr. Cameron SANDERS
19 Chief of Police .... Mr. Gregory L. ROBERTS
26 Exec Dir PR & Marketing .... Ms. Angela ASKEY
09 Exec Dir Inst Effectiveness .... Mr. Dustin MARONEY
25 Director Resource Development .... Mr. Hugo STEINCAMP
121 Director of Advising .... Mr. Derek SHANK

Chamberlain University-Phoenix (L)

2149 West Dunlap Avenue, Phoenix AZ 85021
Telephone: (602) 331-2720 Identification: 770502
Accreditation: &HLC, NURSE

† Branch campus of Chamberlain University-Addison, Addison, IL

Cochise College (M)

901 N Colombo Avenue, Sierra Vista AZ 85635-2317
County: Cochise FICE Identification: 001072
Unit ID: 104425
Telephone: (800) 966-7943 Carnegie Class: Assoc/HVT-High Non
FAX Number: (520) 417-4006 Calendar System: Semester
URL: www.cochise.edu
Established: 1964 Annual Undergrad Tuition & Fees (In-District): $2,184
Enrollment: 3,327 Coed
Affiliation or Control: State/Local IRS Status: 170(c)1
Highest Offering: Associate Degree
Accreditation: HLC

01 Chief Executive Officer/President .... Dr. James D. ROTTWEILER
04 Executive Asst to President .... Ms. Crystal WHEELER
05 Executive VP/Provost .... Dr. Verlyn FICK
11 VP Administration .... Dr. Wendy DAVIS
15 Executive Director Human Resources .... Mr. Wick LEWIS
13 Chief Information Officer .... Mr. David LUNA
102 Exec Dir Foundation & Ext Relations .... Ms. Denise HOYOS
18 Dir Maintenance & Operations .... Mr. James BARROWS
06 Registrar .... Mr. Jason THOMPSON
49 Dean Liberal Arts .... Dr. Eric BROOKS
81 Dean Math and Sciences .... Dr. Thomas GUETZLOFF
76 Dean Nursing/Allied Health .... Ms. Beth HILL
50 Dean Business and Technology .... Dr. Rod FLANIGAN
56 Dean Outreach .... Ms. Barbara RICHARDSON
32 Executive Dean Student Services .... Vacant
121 Assistant Dean Academic Support .... Dr. Karen DALE
84 Asst Dean Enroll Mgmt & Marketing .... Ms. Robyn MARTIN
103 Asst Dean Workforce Development .... Mr. Karl GRIFFOR
08 Director Library Services .... Ms. Karly SCARBROUGH
96 Director Procurement Services .... Mr. Jeff MOUNTJOY
39 Director Residential & Student Life .... Mr. Martin CRICHLOW
117 Director Risk Management .... Mr. Shane VAN BIBBER
37 Director Student Financial Aid .... Ms. Karen EMMER
38 Director Counseling and Advising .... Ms. Nanette ROMO
88 Dir TRIO Student Support Services .... Ms. Gabriela AMAVIZCA
22 Director Disability Support Service .... Ms. Maria SUAREZ
66 Director Nursing .... Ms. Melesa ASHLINE
88 Director Aviation Programs .... Ms. Belinda BURNETT
55 Director Adult Education .... Mr. Brad DALE
88 Director Small Business Dev Center .... Mr. Mark SCHMITT
51 Ctr for Lifelong Learning Manager .... Ms. Ana SMITH
88 Assistant Dean Military Programs .... Mr. Matt COPPI
113 Director of Business Office .... Ms. Sally APARICIO
25 Director Grants Management .... Ms. Celia JENKINS
90 Director Tech Support Services .... Vacant
119 Dir Tech Infrastructure & Security .... Vacant
21 Director Finance/Controller .... Ms. Debra CRAIG
88 Director EMS Program .... Ms. Kelly JUVERA
31 Director of Community Relations .... Ms. Jennifer WANTZ
41 Director of Athletics .... Mr. Guy MEYER

Cochise College (N)

4190 W. Highway 80, Douglas AZ 85607-6190
Telephone: (800) 966-7943 Identification: 770004
Accreditation: &HLC, ADNUR, EMT

Coconino Community College (O)

2800 S Lone Tree Road, Flagstaff AZ 86005
County: Coconino FICE Identification: 031004
Unit ID: 404426
Telephone: (928) 527-1222 Carnegie Class: Assoc/HT-High Non
FAX Number: (928) 226-4105 Calendar System: Semester
URL: www.coconino.edu
Established: 1991 Annual Undergrad Tuition & Fees (In-State): $3,119
Enrollment: 3,289 Coed
Affiliation or Control: State IRS Status: 501(c)3
Highest Offering: Associate Degree
Accreditation: HLC

01 President .... Dr. Colleen A. SMITH
30 Chief Development Officer .... Ms. Dianna SANCHEZ
05 Provost .... Dr. J. Nathaniel SOUTHERLAND
10 Executive Vice Pres/CFO .... Ms. Jami VAN ESS
32 Dean of Student Affairs .... Mr. Tony WILLIAMS
75 Dean of Career & Technical Educ .... Ms. Lisa BLANK
49 Dean of Arts & Sciences .... Dr. Kimberly BATTY-HERBERT
15 Exec Director for Human Resources .... Mr. Dietrich SAUER
09 Dir Institutional Research/Assess .... Mr. Michael MERICA
37 Director for Financial Aid/Vet Aff .... Mr. Robert VOYTEK

06 Registrar .... Ms. Robin JARECKI
04 Assistant to the President .... Ms. April SANDOVAL

Coconino County Community College Flagstaff Fourth Street Innovation Center (A)

3000 N Fourth Street, Flagstaff AZ 86004
Telephone: (928) 526-7600 Identification: 770005
Accreditation: &HLC

Cummings Gaduate Institute for Behavioral Health Studies (B)

16515 South 40th Street Ste 143, Phoenix AZ 85048
County: Maricopa Identification: 667376
Telephone: (480) 285-1761 Carnegie Class: Not Classified
FAX Number: N/A Calendar System: Quarter
URL: https://cgi.edu/
Established: 2015 Annual Graduate Tuition & Fees: N/A
Enrollment: N/A Coed
Affiliation or Control: Independent Non-Profit IRS Status: 501(c)3
Highest Offering: Doctorate; No Undergraduates
Accreditation: DEAC

01 President/CEO .... Dr. Cara ENGLISH
05 Dir Instruction Electronic Campus .... Lori CHRISTIANSON
11 Director of Operations .... Amanda HARRISON
26 Director of Marketing .... Melissa MCGURGAN
06 Registrar/Enrollment Coordinator .... Vicki HAYES
10 Controller/Office Manager .... Denice LANGE
51 Director of Continuing Education .... Dr. Alicia INIGUEZ

DeVry University - Phoenix Campus (C)

2149 W Dunlap Avenue, Phoenix AZ 85021
Telephone: (602) 749-7301 FICE Identification: 008322
Accreditation: &HLC, ACBSP

† Regional accreditation is carried under the parent institution in Downers Grove, IL.

Diné College (D)

One Circle Drive, Tsaile AZ 86556-9998
County: Apache FICE Identification: 008246
Unit ID: 105297
Telephone: (928) 724-6671 Carnegie Class: Tribal
FAX Number: (928) 724-3327 Calendar System: Semester
URL: www.dinecollege.edu
Established: 1968 Annual Undergrad Tuition & Fees (In-District): $1,410
Enrollment: 1,369 Coed
Affiliation or Control: Local IRS Status: 501(c)3
Highest Offering: Baccalaureate
Accreditation: HLC

01 President .... Dr. Charles ROESSEL
10 Vice Pres Finance/Administration .... Ms. Bo LEWIS
32 Vice Pres of Student Affairs .... Ms. Glennita HASKEY
05 Provost .... Dr. Geraldine GARRITY
86 Vice Pres External Affairs/PR .... Ms. Marie R. NEZ
06 Registrar .... Ms. Louise LITZIN
37 Financial Aid Officer .... Mr. Nolan S. BEGAYE
15 Dir Department of Human Resources .... Mr. Merle DAYZIE
18 Supt Maintenance Operations .... Mr. Leon JACKSON
21 Controller .... Ms. Raychelle LEONARD
46 Dir Inst Grants/Sponsored Projects .... Ms. Amanda MCNEILL

Dunlap-Stone University (E)

19820 North 7th Street, Suite 100, Phoenix AZ 85024
County: Maricopa Identification: 666315
Telephone: (602) 648-5750 Carnegie Class: Not Classified
FAX Number: (602) 648-5755 Calendar System: Other
URL: www.dunlap-stone.edu
Established: 1995 Annual Undergrad Tuition & Fees: N/A
Enrollment: N/A Coed
Affiliation or Control: Proprietary IRS Status: Proprietary
Highest Offering: Master's
Accreditation: DEAC

00 Chancellor .... Dr. Donald N. BURTON
01 President/Chief Academic Officer .... Mrs. Caulyne BARRON

Eastern Arizona College (F)

615 N Stadium Avenue, Thatcher AZ 85552-0769
County: Graham FICE Identification: 001073
Unit ID: 104577
Telephone: (928) 428-8233 Carnegie Class: Assoc/MT-VT-High Non
FAX Number: (928) 428-2578 Calendar System: Semester
URL: www.eac.edu
Established: 1888 Annual Undergrad Tuition & Fees (In-District): $2,700
Enrollment: 4,392 Coed
Affiliation or Control: State/Local IRS Status: 501(c)3
Highest Offering: Associate Degree
Accreditation: HLC, ADNUR, EMT

01 President .... Mr. Todd HAYNIE
05 Vice President of Academics .... Dr. Susan WOOD
11 Vice President of Administration .... Mr. Heston WELKER
13 Chief Information Officer .... Mr. Thomas THOMPSON
20 Dean of Instruction .... Dr. Phil MCBRIDE
20 Dean of Curriculum and Instruction .... Dr. Janice LAWHORN
32 Dean of Students .... Dr. Gary SORENSEN
06 Registrar .... Ms. Heather AUGENSTEIN
35 Dean of Student Services .... Mr. Kenny SMITH
12 Director of Discovery Park Campus .... Mr. Paul ANGER
21 Director Fiscal Control/Controller .... Mr. Troy AINSWORTH
37 Director of Financial Aid .... Mrs. Sharon MONTOYA
108 Director of Accreditation .... Mrs. Shannon SEBALLOS
08 Director of Library Services .... Mrs. Tammy POWERS
26 Dir of Marketing & Public Relations .... Mr. Kris MCBRIDE
18 Director of Physical Resources .... Mr. Jeremy HUGHES
102 Executive Director EAC Foundation .... Mr. David UDALL
35 Director of Student Life .... Mr. Danny BATTRAW
41 Athletic Director .... Mr. James BAGNALL
15 Director Admin Support/HR .... Mrs. Lydia NEWKIRK
04 Exec Asst to the President and DGB .... Mrs. Jodi KEIM
86 Special Asst Government Relations .... Mr. Keith ALEXANDER

Eastern Arizona College Gila Pueblo Campus (G)

8274 Six Shooter Canyon,PO Box 2656, Globe AZ 85502
Telephone: (928) 425-8481 Identification: 770008
Accreditation: &HLC

Eastern Arizona College Payson Campus (H)

201 North Mud Springs Rd,PO Box 359, Payson AZ 85547
Telephone: (928) 468-8039 Identification: 770009
Accreditation: &HLC

Embry-Riddle Aeronautical University-Prescott Campus (I)

3700 Willow Creek Road, Prescott AZ 86301-3270
Telephone: (800) 888-3728 FICE Identification: 021047
Accreditation: &SC, AAB, ACBSP

† Regional accreditation is carried under the parent institution in Daytona Beach, FL.

Grand Canyon University (J)

3300 W Camelback Road, Phoenix AZ 85017-3030
County: Maricopa FICE Identification: 001074
Unit ID: 104717
Telephone: (602) 639-7500 Carnegie Class: DU-Mod
FAX Number: N/A Calendar System: Semester
URL: www.gcu.edu
Established: 1949 Annual Undergrad Tuition & Fees: $17,800
Enrollment: 103,427 Coed
Affiliation or Control: Independent Non-Profit IRS Status: 501(c)3
Highest Offering: Doctorate
Accreditation: HLC, AAQEP, ACBSP, CAATE, NURSE, @SW, THEOL

01 President/Chief Executive Officer .... Mr. Brian MUELLER
05 Provost .... Dr. Hank RADDA
10 Vice Pres Business/Finance .... Ms. Junette WEST
11 Chief Administrative Officer .... Mr. Brian ROBERTS
13 Chief Information Officer .... Mr. Joseph MILDENHALL
43 General Counsel .... Mr. Brian ROBERTS
20 Exec VP Academic Affairs/Registrar .... Dr. Jennifer LECH
26 Exec Vice Pres of Marketing .... Ms. Christel MOSBY
41 Vice President of Athletics .... Ms. Jamie BOGGS
32 VP Student Svcs/Dean of Students .... Dr. Tim GRIFFIN
121 Vice Pres Student Success .... Dr. Joe VERES
110 Vice President Advancement .... Dr. T. Kale GOBER
37 Vice Pres Student Financial Aid .... Ms. Trish LEONARD
50 Dean Colangelo College Business .... Dr. Randy GIBB
53 Dean College of Education .... Dr. Kimberly LAPRADE
66 Dean College Nursing/Hlth Care Prof .... Dr. Lisa SMITH
49 Dean College Sci/Engineering/Tech .... Dr. K. Mark WOODEN
58 Dean College Doctoral Studies .... Dr. Michael BERGER
57 Dean of Fine Arts and Production .... Mr. Claude PENSIS
73 Dean College of Theology .... Dr. Jason HILES
79 Dean College Human/Social Science .... Dr. Sherman ELLIOTT

Harrison Middleton University (K)

3345 South Rural Road, Tempe AZ 85282-5404
County: Maricopa Identification: 666169
Telephone: (877) 248-6724 Carnegie Class: Not Classified
FAX Number: (800) 762-1622 Calendar System: Other
URL: www.hmu.edu
Established: 1998 Annual Graduate Tuition & Fees: N/A
Enrollment: N/A Coed
Affiliation or Control: Proprietary IRS Status: Proprietary
Highest Offering: Doctorate; No Undergraduates
Accreditation: DEAC

01 President .... Dr. Joseph COULSON
05 Exec Vice Pres of Education/CEO .... Mr. Michael CURD
51 VP/Dean Continuing Education .... Ms. Rebecca FISHER
09 Vice Pres of Accreditation .... Ms. Lauren GUTHRIE
06 Registrar .... Ms. Lauren GUTHRIE

Indian Bible College (L)

2237 E. Cedar Avenue, Flagstaff AZ 86004
County: Coconino Identification: 667317
Telephone: (928) 774-3890 Carnegie Class: Not Classified
FAX Number: (928) 774-2655 Calendar System: Semester
URL: www.indianbible.org
Established: 1958 Annual Undergrad Tuition & Fees: N/A
Enrollment: N/A Coed
Affiliation or Control: Independent Non-Profit IRS Status: 501(c)3
Highest Offering: Baccalaureate
Accreditation: BI

01 President .... Dr. Jason KOPPEN
32 EVP/Dean of Students .... Mr. Clint ROSS
05 Academic Dean .... Mr. Gene STEVENSON
07 Director Admissions .... Mr. Daniel ESPLIN
08 Librarian .... Ms. Deedra DALLAS

International Baptist College and Seminary (M)

2211 W Germann Road, Chandler AZ 85286
County: Maricopa FICE Identification: 033473
Unit ID: 436614
Telephone: (480) 245-7903 Carnegie Class: Spec-4-yr-Faith
FAX Number: (480) 245-7909 Calendar System: Semester
URL: www.ibcs.edu
Established: 1980 Annual Undergrad Tuition & Fees: $12,900
Enrollment: 78 Coed
Affiliation or Control: Baptist IRS Status: 501(c)3
Highest Offering: Doctorate
Accreditation: TRACS

00 Chancellor .... Vacant
01 President .... Pastor Nathan M. MESTLER
32 Dean of Students .... Dr. Kristopher ENDEAN
05 Acting Chief Academic Officer .... Pastor Nathan M. MESTLER
10 Chief Financial Officer .... Mr. Matt EBERLE
20 Seminary Dean .... Dr. David SHUMATE
30 Chief Development/Advancement .... Vacant
07 Director of Admissions .... Pastor Scott OLSON
09 Director of Inst Effectiveness .... Mrs. Rebecca M. STERTZBACH
08 Media Center Director .... Mr. Lee WILL
34 Dean of Women .... Mrs. Marcia L. GAMMON
06 Registrar .... Miss Brittany MOFFITT
37 Financial Aid Administrator .... Mrs. Eliza MAYORAL
04 Exec Asst to President/Office Mgr .... Mrs. Rebecca M. STERTZBACH

*Maricopa County Community College District Office (N)

2411 W 14th Street, Tempe AZ 85281-6941
County: Maricopa FICE Identification: 001075
Unit ID: 105136
Telephone: (480) 731-8000 Carnegie Class: N/A
FAX Number: (480) 731-8850
URL: www.maricopa.edu

01 Interim Chancellor .... Dr. Steven R. GONZALES
05 Interim VC & Provost .... Dr. Eric LESHINSKIE
102 President/CEO Foundation .... Mr. Brian F. SPICKER
15 Chief Human Resources Officer .... Ms. Georgetta KELLY
13 Vice Chancellor Information Tech .... Dr. Mark KOAN
103 Chief Workforce/Econ Dev Officer .... Ms. Darcy RENFRO
09 Assoc VC Inst Strategy/Rsrch/Effect .... Mr. Matthew ASHCRAFT

*Chandler-Gilbert Community College (O)

2626 E Pecos Road, Chandler AZ 85225-2499
County: Maricopa FICE Identification: 030722
Unit ID: 364025
Telephone: (480) 732-7000 Carnegie Class: Assoc/HT-High Non
FAX Number: (480) 732-7090 Calendar System: Semester
URL: www.cgc.maricopa.edu
Established: 1992 Annual Undergrad Tuition & Fees (In-District): $2,070
Enrollment: 13,395 Coed
Affiliation or Control: State/Local IRS Status: 501(c)3
Highest Offering: Associate Degree
Accreditation: HLC, ADNUR

02 College President .... Dr. Gregory PETERSON
04 Administrative Asst to President .... Ms. Susan D. AROZ
05 Vice President Academic Affairs .... Dr. William GUERRIERO
32 VP Student Affairs .... Ms. Veronica HIPOLITO
11 VP Administrative Services .... Mr. Bradley S. KENDREX
49 Dean of Arts and Sciences .... Mr. Chris SCHNICK
20 Dean of Instruction .... Ms. Gabriela ROSU
31 Assoc VP of Community Affairs .... Ms. Jenna KAHL
10 Assoc VP of Business Operations .... Ms. Bernadette LA MAZZA
84 Dean of Enrollment Services .... Dr. Felicia RAMIREZ-PEREZ
88 Dean of Student Development .... Dr. Anne SUZUKI
07 Director Admissions .... Ms. Linda SHAW
09 Director Planning & Research .... Ms. Theresa WONG
36 Dir Career/Education Planning Svcs .... Vacant
85 Director International Educ Program .... Ms. Annie A. JIMENEZ
22 Dir Disability Resources & Svcs .... Ms. Dawn GRUICHICH
18 Interim Facilities Director .... Mr. Josh DODDROE
35 Director Student Life & Leadership .... Mr. Michael GREENE
41 Athletic Director .... Mr. Edward YEAGER
19 College Police Commander .... Mr. Charles MOUNT
37 Director Financial Aid .... Mr. Timothy WOLSEY
88 Director Learning Center .... Ms. Eva R. FALLETTA
88 Director Early Outreach Programs .... Mr. Lambert YAZZIE

88 Director Instr Tech & Course Prod ... Mr. Jeremy TUTTY
66 Division Chair Nursing ... Ms. Karen FLANIGAN
13 Int Dir Computer Labs/Instr Svcs ... Ms. Sonya BRIESKE
113 Manager College Cashiers Office ... Ms. Julie WRIGHT
15 Senior Human Resource Manager ... Ms. Mika A. DAVIS

*Estrella Mountain Community College (A)

3000 N Dysart Road, Avondale AZ 85392
County: Maricopa
FICE Identification: 031563
Unit ID: 384333
Telephone: (623) 935-8000
Carnegie Class: Assoc/HT-Mix Trad/Non
FAX Number: (623) 935-8008
Calendar System: Semester
URL: www.estrellamountain.edu
Established: 1990
Annual Undergrad Tuition & Fees (In-District): $2,070
Enrollment: 8,768
Coed
Affiliation or Control: State/Local
IRS Status: 501(c)3
Highest Offering: Associate Degree
Accreditation: HLC, ADNUR

02 President ... Dr. Rey RIVERA
11 Vice President Admin Services ... Dr. Heather WEBER
32 Vice President Student Affairs ... Dr. Patricia CARDENAS-ADAME
05 Int Vice Pres of Academic Affairs ... Dr. Kathleen IUDICELLO
20 Dean of Academic Affairs ... Dr. Sylvia ORR
35 Dean of Student Services ... Ms. Laura DULGAR
09 Dean Planning/Rsrch/Effectiveness ... Dr. Rene G. WILLEKENS
08 Division Chair Information Resource ... Mr. Terry A. MEYER
18 Director Facilities Planning/Devel ... Mr. Randy L. NAUGHTON
13 Associate Vice President IT ... Mr. Chad GALLIGAN
35 Dir Student Svcs Admissions/Records ... Mr. Ralph CAMPBELL
10 Fiscal Director ... Ms. Leda JOHNSON
102 Dir Corp Foundation Rels/Dev Ops ... Mr. Jonathan P. ROBLES
37 Director Student Services ... Ms. Rosanna SHORT
114 Fiscal Director Budget ... Ms. Maggie CASTILLO
15 Director Human Resources ... Mr. Teofilo FERRER

*GateWay Community College (B)

108 N 40th Street, Phoenix AZ 85034-1795
County: Maricopa
FICE Identification: 008303
Unit ID: 105145
Telephone: (602) 286-8000
Carnegie Class: Assoc/HVT-Mix Trad/Non
FAX Number: (602) 286-8072
Calendar System: Semester
URL: www.gatewaycc.edu/
Established: 1968
Annual Undergrad Tuition & Fees (In-District): $2,070
Enrollment: 4,670
Coed
Affiliation or Control: State/Local
IRS Status: 501(c)3
Highest Offering: Associate Degree
Accreditation: HLC, ADNUR, COARC, DMS, MAC, NDT, NMT, OTA, POLYT, PTAA, RAD, SURGT

02 Interim President ... Dr. Amy DIAZ
05 Int Vice Pres Academic Affairs ... Ms. Stephanie POLLIARD
32 Int Vice Pres Student Affairs ... Ms. Kristina SCOTT
11 Vice President Administrative Svcs ... Mr. Tony ASTI
09 AVP Institutional Effectiveness ... Ms. Cathy HERNANDEZ
114 College Budget Analyst ... Ms. Janet BOSE
10 Director Fiscal Services ... Ms. Cecilia SOTO
13 AVP Information Tech/Facilities ... Mr. Jose CANDANEDO
26 Director Marketing/Public Relations ... Ms. Christine LAMBRAKIS
111 AVP External Affairs ... Ms. Kristin GUBSER
37 Director Student Financial Aid ... Ms. Suzanne RINGLE
15 Human Resources Supervisor ... Ms. Francine VASQUEZ
06 Registrar/Dir Enrollment Svcs ... Ms. Kristie FOK

*Glendale Community College (C)

6000 W Olive Avenue, Glendale AZ 85302-3006
County: Maricopa
FICE Identification: 001076
Unit ID: 104708
Telephone: (623) 845-3000
Carnegie Class: Assoc/HT-Mix Trad/Non
FAX Number: (623) 845-3329
Calendar System: Semester
URL: www.gccaz.edu
Established: 1965
Annual Undergrad Tuition & Fees (In-District): $2,070
Enrollment: 14,374
Coed
Affiliation or Control: State/Local
IRS Status: 170(c)1
Highest Offering: Associate Degree
Accreditation: HLC, ADNUR, EMT

02 President ... Dr. Teresa LEYBA-RUIZ
05 VP Academic Affairs ... Mr. Scott SCHULZ
32 VP Student Affairs ... Ms. Monica CASTAÑEDA
11 Int VP Admin Services & CIO ... Ms. Augustine ERPELDING
108 Assoc VP Inst Effectiveness ... Dr. Alka ARORA SINGH
20 Dean of Academic Affairs ... Dr. Fernando CAMOU
20 Interim Dean of Academic Affairs ... Dr. Susan CAMPBELL
20 Sr AVP of Academic Affairs ... Dr. Lorelei CARVAJAL
84 Dean Enrollment Services ... Vacant
35 Dean Student Life ... Ms. Genesis TOOLE
12 Dean of Academic Affs/GCC North ... Mr. Charles JEFFERY
37 Director Financial Aid ... Ms. Annette LINDERS
18 Director Facilities ... Mr. Al GONZALES
10 Director College Business Services ... Ms. Kim GOLIS
26 Dir Sales Mktg & Public Rels ... Mr. John HECKENLAIBLE
45 Dir Institutional Effectiveness ... Mr. Kerry MITCHELL
15 Dir College Employee Svcs ... Ms. June S. FESSENDEN
30 Director of Development ... Ms. Frances MATEO
13 Director College Technology Svcs ... Mr. Isaiah WASHINGTON
38 Dept Chair Counseling ... Mr. Paul ROMO
08 Dept Chair Library ... Mr. Frank TORRES
19 Police Commander ... Ms. Debra PALOK
04 Admin Coordinator to College Pres ... Ms. Esmeralda M. ACOSTA
41 Athletic Director ... Mr. Peter OLISZCZAK
79 Dept Chair Art & Humanities ... Mr. Brendan REGAN
81 Dept Chair Biology ... Ms. Karen CONZELMAN
50 Dept Chair Business & Info Tech ... Ms. Rachelle HALL
81 Dept Chair Chemistry ... Ms. Debbie LEEDY
79 Dept Chair Comm & World Languages ... Dr. Pam JORAANSTAD
60 Dept Chair Eng/Reading/Journalism ... Mr. David MILLER
68 Dept Chair Fitness & Wellness ... Ms. Lisa LEWIS
77 Dept Chair Math/Computer Science ... Mr. Chris MILLER
66 Dept Chair Nursing ... Dr. Susan MAYER
57 Dept Chair Performing Arts ... Mr. Donald SMITH
73 Dept Chair Phil/Religious Stds ... Mr. Peter LUPU
81 Dept Chair Physical Sciences ... Mr. David RAFFAELLE
83 Dept Chair Psychology ... Dr. Julie MORRISON
88 Dept Chair Public Safety Sciences ... Mr. Chris COUGHLIN
83 Dept Chair Social Sciences ... Mr. Dean WHEELER
72 Dept Chair Tech & Consumer Sciences ... Ms. Angela JORDAN
88 Dept Chair Automotives ... Mr. Jay COVEY

*Mesa Community College (D)

1833 W Southern Avenue, Mesa AZ 85202-4866
County: Maricopa
FICE Identification: 001077
Unit ID: 105154
Telephone: (480) 461-7000
Carnegie Class: Assoc/HT-Mix Trad/Non
FAX Number: N/A
Calendar System: Semester
URL: www.mesacc.edu/
Established: 1965
Annual Undergrad Tuition & Fees (In-District): $2,070
Enrollment: 16,948
Coed
Affiliation or Control: State/Local
IRS Status: 501(c)3
Highest Offering: Associate Degree
Accreditation: HLC, ADNUR, DH, EMT

02 Interim President ... Dr. Lori BERQUAM
05 Sr Assoc VP Academic Affairs ... Dr. Nora REYES
32 Sr Assoc VP Student Affairs ... Mrs. Carmen NEWLAND
11 Int Vice Pres Admin Services ... Mr. Bradley KENDREX
13 VP Information Technology ... Vacant
09 Assoc VP Inst Effectiveness ... Mr. Dennis MITCHELL
111 AVP Institutional Advancement ... Mrs. Marcy SNITZER
20 Dean of Instruction ... Mr. Michael VOSS
20 Interim Dean of Instruction ... Dr. Miguel LUCAS
20 Dean of Instruction ... Ms. Carol ACHS
84 Dean Enrollment Services ... Ms. Patricia PEPPIN
30 Chief Development Officer ... Mr. Christos CHRONIS
37 Dir Financial Aid/Scholarships ... Ms. Patricia PEPPIN
19 Police Commander ... Mr. Steve LIEBER
25 Senior Grants Officer ... Dr. Kenichi MARUYAMA
29 Director Alumni Relations ... Ms. Marcy SNITZER
41 Athletic Director ... Mr. John MULHERN
18 Director of Facilities ... Mr. Steve AZEVEDO
07 Supv Admiss/Registration/Records ... Vacant
06 Registrar ... Mr. Jeffrey RHOADS
15 Chief Human Resources Officer ... Mr. Garrett SMITH

*Paradise Valley Community College (E)

18401 N 32nd Street, Phoenix AZ 85032-1210
County: Maricopa
FICE Identification: 026236
Unit ID: 364016
Telephone: (602) 787-6500
Carnegie Class: Assoc/HT-Mix Trad/Non
FAX Number: (602) 787-6625
Calendar System: Semester
URL: www.paradisevalley.edu
Established: 1985
Annual Undergrad Tuition & Fees (In-District): $2,070
Enrollment: 6,575
Coed
Affiliation or Control: State/Local
IRS Status: 501(c)3
Highest Offering: Associate Degree
Accreditation: HLC, ADNUR, DIETT, EMT, NAEYC

02 President ... Dr. Paul DALE
05 Vice President of Academic Affairs ... Dr. Doug BERRY
11 VP Administrative Services ... Mr. Herman GONZALEZ
32 Vice President of Student Affairs ... Dr. Jana SCHWARTZ
20 Dean of Academic Affairs ... Dr. Jamie MARTIN
84 Dean Admin Affs/Enrollment Services ... Dr. Jen MILLER
15 Director Personnel Services ... Dr. Kimberlin GLENN
10 Director Fiscal Services ... Vacant
18 Chief Facilities/Physical Plant ... Mr. Bob GARCIA
37 Director Student Financial Aid ... Ms. Katharine JOHNSON
38 Director Student Counseling ... Dr. James RUBIN
06 Registrar ... Mr. Frank AMPARO
36 Director Student Placement ... Ms. Norma CHANDLER
26 Dir of Marketing/Public Relations ... Ms. Tina MILLER
09 Dir Institutional Research/Effect ... Dr. Jeff HOYT
19 Director Security/Safety ... Mr. Scott MEEK
41 Athletic Director ... Ms. Christina HUNDLEY
30 Director of Development ... Vacant

*Phoenix College (F)

1202 W Thomas Road, Phoenix AZ 85013-4234
County: Maricopa
FICE Identification: 001078
Unit ID: 105428
Telephone: (602) 285-7777
Carnegie Class: Assoc/MT-VT-Mix Trad/Non
FAX Number: (602) 285-7700
Calendar System: Semester
URL: www.pc.maricopa.edu
Established: 1920
Annual Undergrad Tuition & Fees (In-District): $2,070
Enrollment: 9,538
Coed
Affiliation or Control: State/Local
IRS Status: 501(c)3
Highest Offering: Associate Degree
Accreditation: HLC, ADNUR, CAHIIM, DA, DH, EMT, HT, MLTAD

02 Interim President ... Dr. Clyne NAMUO
05 VP of Academic Affairs ... Dr. Kimberly BRITT
32 Vice Pres of Student Affairs ... Dr. Heather KRUSE
11 VP Administrative Services ... Mr. Paul DEROSE
15 Chief Human Resources Officer ... Ms. Barbara CHERNER
13 Chief Information Ofcr/AVP IT ... Mr. Paul ROSS
10 Assoc VP Business/Finance ... Ms. Angela GENNA
20 Dean of Academic Affairs ... Mr. Wilbert NELSON
35 Dean of Student Affairs ... Ms. Julie VOLLER
07 Dir Admissions/Registration/Records ... Ms. Brenda STARCK
37 Director Financial Aid ... Ms. Cynthia RAMOS
30 Development Director ... Ms. Deborah SPOTTS
09 Dir Inst Plng/Rsrch/Effectiveness ... Mr. Eugene YE
18 Director of Facilities ... Mr. Douglas MCCARTHY
19 Director of College Safety ... Mr. Matt VERTHEIN
41 Athletic Director ... Ms. Kristine KINCAID
84 Director Advisement/Enrollment ... Ms. Felicia RAMIREZ-PEREZ
88 Int Director Student Leadership ... Ms. Diana MARTINEZ
88 Int Dean Industry/Public Service ... Ms. Maria REYES
26 PR Marketing Manager ... Ms. Erika KEENAN
88 Sr Program Analyst ... Ms. Kimberly ANDERSON
04 Senior Administrative Specialist ... Ms. Briana JORDAN
08 Department Chair Library ... Ms. Christine MOORE
121 Department Chair Counseling ... Mr. Robert VILLEGAS GOLD

*Rio Salado College (G)

2323 W 14th Street, Tempe AZ 85281-6950
County: Maricopa
FICE Identification: 021775
Unit ID: 105668
Telephone: (480) 517-8000
Carnegie Class: Assoc/HVT-High Non
FAX Number: (480) 377-4719
Calendar System: Semester
URL: www.riosalado.edu
Established: 1978
Annual Undergrad Tuition & Fees (In-District): $2,070
Enrollment: 17,362
Coed
Affiliation or Control: State/Local
IRS Status: 501(c)3
Highest Offering: Associate Degree
Accreditation: HLC, DH

02 Interim President ... Ms. Kate SMITH
05 Int Vice President Academic Affairs ... Mr. Rick KEMP
10 Vice Pres Administrative Svcs ... Ms. Michelle GATES
32 Vice Pres Student Affairs ... Mr. Greg PEREIRA
12 Int Vice Pres Maricopa Corp College ... Ms. Patricia O'BRIEN
13 Vice President Information Services ... Mr. David O'SHEA
15 AVP Administrative & Employee Svcs ... Ms. Maria BELLINO
20 Dean of Instruction ... Mr. Rick KEMP
20 Dean Instruction Tech & Support ... Vacant
20 Dean of Instruction ... Ms. Karol SCHMIDT
84 Dean Stdnt Affs/Enrollment Mgmt ... Ms. Rachelle CLARKE
88 Assoc Dean Instruction and Support ... Ms. Earnestine HARRISON
31 Interim Dean Instruction & Cmty Dev ... Ms. Heather TYLER
88 Assoc Dean Judicial Affairs ... Vacant
21 Fiscal Director Business Svcs ... Mr. Anthony DISCALA
37 Director of Financial Aid ... Ms. Nanci REGEHR
09 Assoc Dean Institutional Research ... Mr. Dustin MARONEY
06 Dir Registration/Records/Admission ... Ms. Laurel REDMAN
18 Director of Facilities ... Mr. Richard OROS
19 Commander of Public Safety ... Mr. John PORVAZNIK
16 Human Resources Director ... Ms. Anna FLORES
08 Library Faculty Co-Chair ... Ms. Karen DOCHERTY
08 Library Faculty Co-Chair ... Ms. Sarah STOHR
04 Admin Coordinator to President ... Ms. Kevyn MILLER

*Scottsdale Community College (H)

9000 E Chaparral, Scottsdale AZ 85256-2626
County: Maricopa
FICE Identification: 008304
Unit ID: 105747
Telephone: (480) 423-6000
Carnegie Class: Assoc/HT-High Non
FAX Number: (480) 423-6200
Calendar System: Semester
URL: www.scottsdalecc.edu
Established: 1970
Annual Undergrad Tuition & Fees (In-District): $2,070
Enrollment: 7,634
Coed
Affiliation or Control: State/Local
IRS Status: 501(c)3
Highest Offering: Associate Degree
Accreditation: HLC, ACFEI, ADNUR

02 Interim President ... Ms. Chris M. HAINES
32 Vice Pres Student Affairs ... Dr. Donna YOUNG
05 Interim Vice Pres Academic Affairs ... Dr. Eddie LAMPEREZ
11 Vice Pres Administrative Services ... Ms. Colleen O'NEILL
13 AVP ITS/College CTO ... Mr. Vargha MOHEBBI
20 Interim Dean of Instruction ... Dr. Lucas MESSER
35 Dean of Student Affairs ... Ms. Larissa TRAIN
84 Dean of Enrollment Services ... Ms. Yolanda ESPINOZA
07 Director of Admissions ... Ms. Laura KRUEGER
09 Dir of Institutional Research/Plng ... Dr. Laurie COHEN
08 Director of Library Services ... Vacant
37 Director Financial Aid/Placement ... Ms. Stacie BECK
18 AVP Facilities Mgmt ... Mr. Tony MIELE
19 Director of College Safety ... Mr. Arlyn WALZ
41 Athletic Director ... Mr. Michael MCNALLY
121 Director Student Advisement ... Mr. Darryl GREELEY
04 Administrative Asst to President ... Ms. Donna COLE
10 Chief Business Officer ... Ms. Mirna ROSAS
15 Director Personnel Services ... Vacant

* South Mountain Community College (A)

7050 S 24th Street, Phoenix AZ 85042-5806
County: Maricopa FICE Identification: 021466
Unit ID: 105792
Telephone: (602) 243-8000 Carnegie Class: Assoc/HT-Mix Trad/Non
FAX Number: (602) 243-8329 Calendar System: Semester
URL: www.southmountaincc.edu
Established: 1979 Annual Undergrad Tuition & Fees (In-District): $2,070
Enrollment: 3,497 Coed
Affiliation or Control: State/Local IRS Status: 501(c)3
Highest Offering: Associate Degree
Accreditation: HLC

02 President .... Dr. Shari L. OLSON-NIKUNEN
05 Interim Vice Pres of Learning .... Ms. Bernice PORTERVINT
11 Vice Pres Administrative Svcs .... Dr. Janet L. ORTEGA
32 Vice Pres Student Affairs .... Dr. Osaro O. IGHODARO
09 Dean Research/Plng & Development .... Ms. Damita A. KALOOSTIAN
20 Dean Academic Affairs .... Ms. Bernice PORTERVINT
84 Dean Enrollment Services .... Mr. Guy H. GOODMAN
37 Director Financial Aid .... Vacant
07 Director of Admission & Records .... Ms. Jean C. WATERMOLEN
10 Director College Business Services .... Mr. Mark W. MCCAIN
18 Interim Director of Facilities .... Mr. David S. BANNENBERG
15 Human Resources Director .... Ms. Judy K. BELSHER
07 Coordinator Recruitment .... Vacant
41 Athletic Director .... Mr. Todd B. EASTIN

* *Chandler-Gilbert Community College-Williams Campus* (B)

7360 E Tahoe Avenue, Mesa AZ 85212-0908
Telephone: (480) 988-8000 Identification: 770178
Accreditation: &HLC, FUSER

* *Glendale Community College North* (C)

5727 W Happy Valley Road, Phoenix AZ 85310
Telephone: (623) 845-4000 Identification: 770179
Accreditation: &HLC

* *Mesa Community College at Red Mountain* (D)

7110 East McKellips Road, Mesa AZ 85207
Telephone: (480) 654-7200 Identification: 770180
Accreditation: &HLC

Midwestern University (E)

19555 N 59th Avenue, Glendale AZ 85308
Telephone: (623) 572-3400 Identification: 666001
Accreditation: &HLC, ANEST, ARCPA, CLPSY, DENT, OPT, OPTR, OSTEO, OT, PERF, PHAR, POD, PTA, SP, VET

† Regional accreditation is carried under the parent institution in Downers Grove, IL.

Mohave Community College (F)

1971 E. Jagerson Avenue, Kingman AZ 86409-1238
County: Mohave FICE Identification: 011864
Unit ID: 105206
Telephone: (866) 664-2832 Carnegie Class: Assoc/MT-VT-Mix Trad/Non
FAX Number: (928) 757-0836 Calendar System: Semester
URL: www.mohave.edu
Established: 1971 Annual Undergrad Tuition & Fees (In-District): $2,112
Enrollment: 3,654 Coed
Affiliation or Control: State/Local IRS Status: 501(c)3
Highest Offering: Associate Degree
Accreditation: HLC, ADNUR, DH, EMT, PTAA, RAD, SURGT

01 President .... Dr. Stacy S. KLIPPENSTEIN
03 Executive Vice President .... Dr. Tim CULVER
11 Vice Pres of Administrative Svcs .... Ms. Jennifer DIXON
32 Vice Pres Student & Cmty Engagement .... Dr. Tramaine RAUSAW
84 Dean of Enrollment and Student Svcs .... Ms. Ana MASTERSON
111 Chief Advancement Officer .... Mr. Shawn BRISTLE
13 Chief Information Officer .... Mr. Mark VANPELT
26 Chief Public Relations Officer .... Mr. James JARMAN
15 Chief Human Resources Officer .... Ms. Jennifer PICARD
12 Campus Dean Bullhead City .... Dr. Carolyn HAMBLIN
12 Campus Dean Lake Havasu .... Dr. Maria AYON
12 Campus Dean Neal Kingman .... Dr. Tramaine RAUSAW
12 Campus Dean North Mohave .... Mr. John CAWLEY
76 Dean of Health Professions .... Dr. Liliya TISHCHENKO
97 Dean General Education & Transfer .... Ms. Lucinda LEUGERS
103 Dean of Workforce & Partnerships .... Dr. Kirk LACY
18 Director of Facilities Managment .... Mr. Don MONTGOMERY
09 Director of Institutional Research .... Mr. Matt BUTCHER
04 Administrative Asst to President .... Ms. Amy CURLEY

National Paralegal College (G)

717 East Maryland Avenue, Phoenix AZ 85014-1561
County: Maricopa FICE Identification: 041574
Unit ID: 461023
Telephone: (800) 371-6105 Carnegie Class: Spec-4-yr-Other
FAX Number: (866) 347-2744 Calendar System: Other
URL: nationalparalegal.edu
Established: 2003 Annual Undergrad Tuition & Fees: $7,995
Enrollment: 693 Coed
Affiliation or Control: Proprietary IRS Status: Proprietary
Highest Offering: Master's
Accreditation: DEAC

01 President/CEO .... Avi KATZ
05 Dean/Director Education/CAO .... Stephen HAAS
13 Chief Technology Officer .... David COHEN
07 Director of Admissions .... Dana LUKSENBURG
37 Director Student Financial Aid .... Lisa PIMBER

Northern Arizona University (H)

South San Francisco Street, Flagstaff AZ 86011-0001
County: Coconino FICE Identification: 001082
Unit ID: 105330
Telephone: (928) 523-9011 Carnegie Class: DU-Higher
FAX Number: (928) 523-1848 Calendar System: Semester
URL: www.nau.edu
Established: 1899 Annual Undergrad Tuition & Fees (In-State): $11,896
Enrollment: 29,566 Coed
Affiliation or Control: State IRS Status: 501(c)3
Highest Offering: Doctorate
Accreditation: HLC, ACBSP, ARCPA, CAATE, CACREP, CAEP, CAPRT, CIDA, CONST, DH, @DIETC, DIETD, EXSC, MUS, NURSE, OT, PSPSY, PTA, SP, SW, THEA

01 President .... Dr. Jose Luis CRUZ RIVERA
100 Int Executive VP & Chief of Staff .... Mr. Josh MACKEY
05 Int Provost & VP Academic Affairs .... Dr. Karen PUGLIESI
09 VP Finance/Inst Plng & Analysis .... Mr. Bjorn FLUGSTAD
10 VP Capital Planning & Campus Ops .... Dr. Daniel T. OKOLI
46 Int Vice President for Research .... Dr. Jason WILDER
86 VP External Affairs & Partnerships .... Ms. Christy FARLEY
41 VP Intercollegiate Athletics .... Ms. Mike MARLOW
88 VP of Native American Initiatives .... Dr. Chad S. HAMILL
88 Exec Dir Inst for Tribal Env Prof .... Dr. AnnMarie CHISCHILLY
88 Exec Dir Native Amer Cultural Ctr .... Dr. Ora MAREK-MARTINEZ
43 General Counsel .... Ms. Michelle G. PARKER
88 Vice Provost Academic Personnel .... Dr. Astrid KLOCKE
13 Chief Information Officer .... Dr. Steven C. BURRELL
32 Int VP Student Affairs .... Dr. Margot SALTONSTALL
12 Assoc VP/Campus Exec Officer - Yuma .... Dr. Michael J. SABATH
15 Chief Human Resources Officer .... Mr. Josh MACKEY
21 Associate VP Comptrollers Office .... Ms. Wendy A. SWARTZ
85 Assoc VP Center for Intl Education .... Mr. Daniel PALM
108 Chief Institutional Data Officer .... Ms. Laura A. JONES
111 Assoc VP for Advancement .... Ms. Bonnie BAKER
29 Director Alumni Engagement .... Ms. Stephanie SMITH
08 Dean/University Librarian .... Dr. Cynthia A. CHILDREY
53 Dean College of Education .... Dr. Ramona N. MELLOTT
54 Dean College Eng/Forestry/Nat Sci .... Vacant
50 Dean WA Franke College of Business .... Dr. Ashok SUBRAMANIAN
83 Dean Col Social/Behavioral Sciences .... Dr. John MASSERINI
76 Int Dean Col of Health/Human Svcs .... Dr. Roger BOUNDS
06 University Registrar .... Mr. Gordon WISCHMEIER
19 Chief of Police .... Ms. Missy FRESHOUR
22 Assoc VP Equity and Access Office .... Ms. Pamela HEINONEN
23 Asst VP Campus Health Services .... Ms. Julie A. RYAN
39 Interim Dir Housing/Residence Life .... Ms. Carolyn BURRELL
36 Dir Gateway Student Success Center .... Ms. Monica S. BAI
07 Director of Admissions .... Mr. Chad A. EICKHOFF
96 Assoc VP Contracts/Purch/Risk Mgmt .... Ms. Becky E. MCGAUGH
88 Assistant to the President ECMR .... Ms. Kim A. OTT
104 Director Center for Intl Education .... Ms. Angelina PALUMBO
37 Director Financial Aid .... Ms. Amanda CORNELIUS
16 Director Human Resource Programs .... Ms. Cynthia A. CHILCOAT
64 Director School of Music .... Mr. Todd SULLIVAN
94 Director Women and Gender Studies .... Ms. Sanjam AHLUWALIA
58 Dean Graduate College .... Dr. Maribeth WATWOOD
14 Director Information Tech Services .... Mr. Don CARTER
121 Exec Dir University Advising .... Ms. Terri L. HAYES
108 VProvost Curric/Assessment & Accred .... Dr. Laurie DICKSON
88 Int Associate VP Research .... Dr. Andrew KOPPISCH
106 Assoc VP NAU Online .... Ms. Gina K. VANCE
88 Assoc VP for Government Affairs .... Ms. Katy YANEZ
88 Assoc VP Educational Partnerships .... Ms. Kathrine H. YEAGER
25 Asst VP Sponsored Projects .... Ms. Stacia LEVY
88 Asst VP Research Compliance .... Dr. David M. FAGUY

Northern Arizona University Yuma Branch Campus (I)

2020 S Avenue 8E, Yuma AZ 85365
Telephone: (928) 317-6450 Identification: 770011
Accreditation: &HLC, SW

Northland Pioneer College (J)

PO Box 610, Holbrook AZ 86025-0610
County: Navajo FICE Identification: 011862
Unit ID: 105349
Telephone: (928) 524-7311 Carnegie Class: Assoc/HVT-High Non
FAX Number: (928) 524-7312 Calendar System: Semester
URL: www.npc.edu
Established: 1973 Annual Undergrad Tuition & Fees (In-State): $2,428
Enrollment: 2,700 Coed
Affiliation or Control: State IRS Status: 501(c)3
Highest Offering: Associate Degree
Accreditation: HLC, ADNUR, EMT

01 College President .... Dr. Chato HAZELBAKER
101 Secretary of the Institution/Board .... Mr. John Paul HEMPSEY
05 VP Learning & Student Services .... Dr. Mike SOLOMONSON
10 VP for Administrative Services .... Ms. Maderia ELLISON
13 Director Information Services (CIO) .... Mr. Henry ESTES
49 Dean of Arts & Sciences .... Mr. Rickey JACKSON
103 Dean of Career/Technical Education .... Ms. Peggy BELKNAP
66 Nursing & Allied Health Director .... Ms. Ruth ZIMMERMAN
53 Dean of Education/College/Career Pr .... Ms. Gail CAMPBELL
106 Dean of Instructional Innovation .... Dr. Wei MA
15 Human Resources Director .... Ms. Lynda ANDERSON-CASEY
84 Director of Enrollment Services .... Mr. Jeremy RAISOR
06 Assistant Registrar .... Ms. Deena GILLESPIE
32 Director of Student Services .... Mr. Josh ROGERS
18 Director of Facilities and Vehicles .... Mr. David HUISH
26 Dir of Marketing/Public Relations .... Ms. Ann HESS
09 Director of Institutional Effective .... Dr. Judy YIP-REYES
88 Director Small Business Development .... Mr. Richard CHANICK
19 Director of Public Safety Education .... Mr. Jon WISNER
102 Prgm Director NPC Friends & Family .... Ms. Betsyann WILSON
37 Manager of Financial Aid Operations .... Ms. Marletha BALOO
21 Controller .... Ms. Amber HILL
08 Director of Library Services .... Ms. Shannon MOTTER
96 Procurement Manager .... Mr. Robert JOHNSON
07 Coordinator of High School Programs .... Ms. Karen ZIMMERMAN
25 Grant Accountant .... Ms. Donna SOSEMAN

Ottawa University Phoenix, AZ (K)

9414 North 25th Avenue, Phoenix AZ 85021
Telephone: (602) 371-1188 Identification: 666066
Accreditation: &HLC

† Regional accreditation is carried under the parent institution in Ottawa, KS.

Ottawa University Surprise, AZ (L)

15950 N. Civic Center Plaza, Surprise AZ 85374
Telephone: (855) 546-1342 Identification: 770982
Accreditation: &HLC

† Regional accreditation is carried under the parent institution in Ottawa, KS.

The Paralegal Institute at Brighton College (M)

8777 E. Via de Ventura, Suite 300, Scottsdale AZ 85258
County: Maricopa FICE Identification: 030737
Telephone: (602) 212-0501 Carnegie Class: Not Classified
FAX Number: (602) 212-0502 Calendar System: Other
URL: www.theparalegalinstitute.edu
Established: 1974 Annual Undergrad Tuition & Fees: N/A
Enrollment: N/A Coed
Affiliation or Control: Proprietary IRS Status: Proprietary
Highest Offering: Associate Degree
Accreditation: DEAC

01 Corporate President .... Paul ZAGNONI
05 Vice President Academic Affairs .... Gilda RADA
32 Director of Student Services .... Sean DIXON

Penn Foster College (N)

14300 N Northsight Blvd, Suite 125, Scottsdale AZ 85260-3673
County: Maricopa FICE Identification: 004049
Unit ID: 211486
Telephone: (480) 947-6644 Carnegie Class: Not Classified
FAX Number: N/A Calendar System: Other
URL: www.pennfoster.edu
Established: 1974 Annual Undergrad Tuition & Fees: N/A
Enrollment: N/A Coed
Affiliation or Control: Proprietary IRS Status: Proprietary
Highest Offering: Baccalaureate
Accreditation: DEAC

01 Chief Executive Officer .... Mr. Frank BRITT
05 Vice Pres Education/Academic Dean .... Ms. Lisa RUTSKY
10 Chief Financial Officer .... Mr. Thomas BLESSO
11 Chief Operating Officer .... Ms. Dara WARN
26 Chief Marketing Officer .... Ms. Cindy STARR
07 Vice Pres Admissions .... Vacant
13 SVP/Chief Technology Officer .... Mr. Nial MCLOUGHLIN
21 VP Corp Controller .... Mr. Thomas WISHARD
32 SVP Student Success .... Mr. Mark SLAYTON
43 General Counsel .... Ms. Heather MCALLISTER
15 SVP People/Human Resources .... Mr. Joshua BUDWAY

Phoenix Institute of Herbal Medicine and Acupuncture (O)

301 E Bethany Home Road, Ste A-100, Phoenix AZ 85012-1275
County: Maricopa FICE Identification: 036175
Unit ID: 447698
Telephone: (602) 274-1885 Carnegie Class: Spec-4-yr-Other Health
FAX Number: (602) 274-1895 Calendar System: Semester
URL: www.pihma.edu
Established: 1996 Annual Graduate Tuition & Fees: N/A
Enrollment: 132 Coed
Affiliation or Control: Proprietary IRS Status: Proprietary

Highest Offering: Master's; No Undergraduates
Accreditation: ACUP

01 President ... Ms. Catherine NIEMIEC
05 Chief Academic Officer ... Ms. Debbie MAJOR
07 Admissions ... Ms. Lisa DUNN
06 Registrar ... Ms. Judy DRAYER
30 Regulatory/Inst Development Ofcr ... Mr. Jonathan LINDSEY

Phoenix Seminary (A)

7901 E. Shea Boulevard, Scottsdale AZ 85260-5510
County: Maricopa FICE Identification: 034784
Unit ID: 381459
Telephone: (602) 850-8000 Carnegie Class: Spec-4-yr-Faith
FAX Number: (602) 850-8080 Calendar System: Semester
URL: www.ps.edu
Established: 1988 Annual Graduate Tuition & Fees: N/A
Enrollment: 260 Coed
Affiliation or Control: Interdenominational IRS Status: 501(c)3
Highest Offering: Doctorate; No Undergraduates
Accreditation: HLC, THEOL

01 President ... Dr. Brian ARNOLD
00 Chancellor ... Dr. Darryl L. DELHOUSAYE
05 Provost ... Dr. J. Michael THIGPEN
32 Vice President Student Development ... Vacant
20 Asst Dean Academic Services ... Ms. Roma ROYER
06 Registrar ... Mrs. Merry STENSON
84 Dir Enrollment & Student Services ... Mr. Kody GIBSON
10 Comptroller ... Mrs. Deborah ARNITZ
08 Director of Library Services ... Mr. Doug OLBERT
35 Dean of Students ... Dr. Joshua ANDERSON
15 Human Resources Director ... Ms. Nancy STOCKING

Pima Community College (B)

4905 East Broadway Boulevard, Tucson AZ 85709-1005
County: Pima FICE Identification: 007266
Unit ID: 105525
Telephone: (520) 206-4500 Carnegie Class: Assoc/HT-High Trad
FAX Number: (520) 206-4535 Calendar System: Semester
URL: www.pima.edu
Established: 1966 Annual Undergrad Tuition & Fees (In-District): $2,250
Enrollment: 15,544 Coed
Affiliation or Control: State/Local IRS Status: 501(c)3
Highest Offering: Associate Degree
Accreditation: HLC, ADNUR, COARC, DA, DH, DT, EMT, MLTAD, NAEYC, RAD

01 Chancellor ... Mr. Lee D. LAMBERT
05 Provost/Chief Academic Ofcr ... Dr. Dolores DURAN-CERDA
10 Exec Vice Chanc for Finance & Admin ... Dr. David BEA
12 President of Campuses ... Dr. David DORE
26 Interim VC External Relations ... Mr. Phillip BURDICK
43 College General Counsel ... Mr. Jeffrey SILVYN
100 Chief of Staff ... Mr. Thomas DAVIS
15 Chief HR Officer ... Ms. Carleen THOMPSON
88 Vice Chanc Academic Excellence ... Dr. Morgan PHILLIPS
20 Vice Chanc Educational Services ... Dr. Bruce MOSES
09 VC Strategy/Analytics & Research ... Dr. Nicola RICHMOND
32 Acting VC Student Experience ... Dr. Irene ROBLES-LOPEZ
18 Asst Vice Chancellor Facilities ... Vacant
21 Asst Vice Chanc Finance ... Mr. Daniel SOZA
13 Acting Asst VC Information Tech ... Mr. Jack SATTERFIELD
86 Exec Dir Media & Govt Rels ... Ms. Elizabeth HOWELL
19 Acting Exec Dir College Police ... Ms. Michelle NIEUWENHUIS
37 Exec Director of Financial Aid ... Ms. Norma NAVARRO-CASTELLANOS
28 Ex Dir Diversity/Equity & Inclusion ... Ms. Hilda LADNER
76 Dean of Allied Health Programs ... Mr. James CRAIG
96 Director of Procurement ... Mr. Terry ROBINSON
07 Director Admissions & Registrar ... Mr. Michael TULINO
103 VP Workforce Development ... Dr. Ian ROARK
41 Athletic Director ... Mr. Jim MONACO

Pima Community College Community Campus (C)

401 North Bonita Avenue, Tucson AZ 85709
Telephone: (520) 206-3933 Identification: 770016
Accreditation: &HLC

Pima Community College Desert Vista Campus (D)

5901 South Calle Santa Cruz, Tucson AZ 85709
Telephone: (520) 206-5101 Identification: 770017
Accreditation: &HLC, SURGT

Pima Community College Downtown Campus (E)

1255 North Stone Avenue, Tucson AZ 85709-3000
Telephone: (520) 206-7171 Identification: 770018
Accreditation: &HLC

Pima Community College East Campus (F)

8181 East Irvington Road, Tucson AZ 85709
Telephone: (520) 206-7000 Identification: 770019
Accreditation: &HLC

Pima Community College Northwest Campus (G)

7600 North Shannon Road, Tucson AZ 85709-7200
Telephone: (520) 206-2200 Identification: 770020
Accreditation: &HLC

Pima Community College West Campus (H)

2202 West Anklam Road, Tucson AZ 85709-0001
Telephone: (520) 206-6600 Identification: 770021
Accreditation: &HLC

Pima Medical Institute-East Valley (I)

2160 S Power Road, Mesa AZ 85209
Telephone: (480) 898-9898 Identification: 770515
Accreditation: ABHES

Pima Medical Institute-Mesa (J)

957 S Dobson Road, Mesa AZ 85202-2903
Telephone: (480) 644-0267 FICE Identification: 011570
Accreditation: ABHES, COARC, EMT, OTA, PTAA

Pima Medical Institute-Tucson (K)

2121 N Craycroft Road, Bldg 1, Tucson AZ 85712
County: Pima FICE Identification: 022171
Unit ID: 105534
Telephone: (520) 326-1600 Carnegie Class: Spec-4-yr-Other Health
FAX Number: (520) 326-4125 Calendar System: Other
URL: www.pmi.edu
Established: 1972 Annual Undergrad Tuition & Fees: N/A
Enrollment: 1,970 Coed
Affiliation or Control: Proprietary IRS Status: Proprietary
Highest Offering: Baccalaureate
Accreditation: ABHES, COARC, NURSE, OTA, PTAA

01 Campus Director ... Mr. Dale BERG

Prescott College (L)

220 Grove Avenue, Prescott AZ 86301-2912
County: Yavapai FICE Identification: 020653
Unit ID: 105589
Telephone: (928) 350-2100 Carnegie Class: Masters/S
FAX Number: (928) 776-5137 Calendar System: Semester
URL: www.prescott.edu
Established: 1966 Annual Undergrad Tuition & Fees: $33,669
Enrollment: 970 Coed
Affiliation or Control: Independent Non-Profit IRS Status: 501(c)3
Highest Offering: Doctorate
Accreditation: HLC, CACREP

01 President ... Mr. John FLICKER
05 Executive Vice President & Provost ... Dr. Paul BURKHARDT
10 Chief Financial Officer ... Ms. Andrea JAECKEL
84 Dean Enrollment Management ... Ms. Pamela DELANY
111 Chief Advancement Ofcr/Alumni Rels ... Ms. Marie SMITH
32 Chief Student Affairs Officer ... Ms. Kristine PREZIOSI
124 Director of Student Retention ... Ms. Jerri BROWN
06 Registrar ... Ms. Aimee WALKER
07 Director of Admissions ... Ms. Chorissa BUTLER
09 Director of Institutional Research ... Ms. Jerri BROWN
15 Director of Human Resources ... Ms. Susan KRAUSE
39 Housing Director ... Ms. Megan LETCHWORTH
18 Director of Facilities ... Mr. Brad SINN
08 Dir of Library/Learning Commons ... Ms. Zoe CARAS
13 Dir Information Technology Services ... Vacant
29 Director of Alumni Relations ... Ms. Marie SMITH
20 Associate Dean for Instruction ... Ms. Erin LOTZ

The Refrigeration School (M)

4210 E Washington Street, Phoenix AZ 85034-1816
County: Maricopa FICE Identification: 011689
Unit ID: 105659
Telephone: (602) 275-7133 Carnegie Class: Spec 2-yr-Tech
FAX Number: (602) 267-4805 Calendar System: Other
URL: www.refrigerationschool.com
Established: 1965 Annual Undergrad Tuition & Fees: N/A
Enrollment: 897 Coed
Affiliation or Control: Proprietary IRS Status: Proprietary
Highest Offering: Associate Degree
Accreditation: ACCSC

01 Campus President ... Mr. David EAKER
32 Director of Student Services ... Ms. Susan CONNELLY
07 Director of Admissions ... Mr. John PALUMBO
06 Registrar ... Ms. Clare WEISENBERGER
36 Director Student Placement ... Ms. Jessica ALONZO

The School of Architecture (N)

6433 E. Doubletree Ranch Rd, Paradise Valley AZ 85253
County: Maricopa FICE Identification: 025332
Unit ID: 104665
Telephone: (480) 750-4470 Carnegie Class: Spec-4-yr-Arts
FAX Number: N/A Calendar System: Other
URL: www.theschoolofarchitecture.edu
Established: 1932 Annual Undergrad Tuition & Fees: N/A
Enrollment: 10 Coed
Affiliation or Control: Independent Non-Profit IRS Status: 501(c)3
Highest Offering: Master's
Accreditation: HLC

01 Acting President ... Dr. Chris LASCH
05 Dean ... Ms. Stephanie LIN
08 Director of Libraries ... Vacant
07 Dir Admissions/Student Services ... Ms. Sandra L. PIERRE
10 Chief Financial Officer ... Ms. Nicole HOLLENBECK
30 Director of Development ... Ms. Alexandra MOQUAY
39 Residence Academic Manager ... Vacant
06 Registrar ... Ms. Sandra L. PIERRE

Sessions College for Professional Design (O)

51 W. Third Street, Suite E-301, Tempe AZ 85281
County: Maricopa FICE Identification: 042176
Unit ID: 475839
Telephone: (480) 212-1704 Carnegie Class: Spec 2-yr-A&S
FAX Number: (480) 212-1705 Calendar System: Semester
URL: www.sessions.edu
Established: 1997 Annual Undergrad Tuition & Fees: $10,740
Enrollment: 197 Coed
Affiliation or Control: Proprietary IRS Status: Proprietary
Highest Offering: Baccalaureate
Accreditation: DEAC

00 CEO ... Ms. Doris GRANATOWSKI
01 President ... Mr. Gordon DRUMMOND
03 Executive Vice President ... Mr. Louis J. SCHILT
11 Chief Operating Officer/Dir Tech ... Mr. Jason WOLLARD
10 Chief Financial Officer ... Ms. Carole Anne BAILO
32 Sr Dir Student Services/Acad Pgms ... Mr. Tyler DRAKE
05 Director of Education ... Dr. Meryl EPSTEIN
07 Sr Dir Admissions ... Ms. Kimberly O'HANION
37 Dir Financial Aid ... Ms. Debra RICHARDS

Sonoran Desert Institute (P)

1555 W University Drive, Suite 103, Tempe AZ 85281
County: Maricopa Identification: 667057
Unit ID: 488077
Telephone: (480) 314-2102 Carnegie Class: Spec 2-yr-Tech
FAX Number: (480) 314-2138 Calendar System: Semester
URL: www.sdi.edu
Established: 2000 Annual Undergrad Tuition & Fees: $10,630
Enrollment: 2,709 Coed
Affiliation or Control: Proprietary IRS Status: Proprietary
Highest Offering: Associate Degree
Accreditation: DEAC

01 President ... Traci LEE
05 Vice Pres Academic Affairs ... Mike OLSON
10 Vice Pres Finance ... Marc PROCHELLO
07 Director of Admissions ... Jason LARSON

Southwest College of Naturopathic Medicine & Health Sciences (Q)

2140 E Broadway Road, Tempe AZ 85282-1751
County: Maricopa FICE Identification: 031070
Unit ID: 420246
Telephone: (480) 858-9100 Carnegie Class: Spec-4-yr-Other Health
FAX Number: (480) 858-9116 Calendar System: Quarter
URL: www.scnm.edu
Established: 1993 Annual Graduate Tuition & Fees: N/A
Enrollment: 509 Coed
Affiliation or Control: Independent Non-Profit IRS Status: 501(c)3
Highest Offering: First Professional Degree; No Undergraduates
Accreditation: HLC, NATUR

01 President/Chief Executive Officer ... Paul A. MITTMAN
05 Vice President of Academic Affairs ... Garrett THOMPSON
10 Vice Pres Finance & Administration ... Edward PODOL
32 Vice President Student Affairs ... Melissa WINQUIST
13 Chief Information Officer ... Vacant
04 Executive Asst to President ... Tracy LINDBERGH
06 Registrar ... Brian MCCARTHY
07 Director of Admissions ... Gina KAEGI
08 Head Librarian ... Sally HARVEY
103 Dir Workforce/Career Development ... Joanna HAGAN
108 Director Institutional Assessment ... Tammy ARAGON

Southwest Institute of Healing Arts (R)

1538 E. Southern Ave, Tempe AZ 85282
County: Maricopa FICE Identification: 035933
Unit ID: 442879
Telephone: (480) 994-9244 Carnegie Class: Spec 2-yr-Health
FAX Number: (480) 994-3228 Calendar System: Other
URL: www.swiha.edu
Established: 1992 Annual Undergrad Tuition & Fees: N/A
Enrollment: 846 Coed
Affiliation or Control: Proprietary IRS Status: Proprietary
Highest Offering: Associate Degree
Accreditation: CNCE

01 President/Founder .... Mrs. KC MILLER
11 Chief Exec Director SWIHA .... Ms. Pam BROWN
05 Dean of Education .... Ms. Shelley TOM
32 Dean of Student Services .... Dr. Bradley BOUTE
10 Dir Finance & Human Res/Controller .... Ms. Salisha TAMANDL
35 Associate Dean of Student Services .... Mrs. Angelica DIAZ
106 Associate Dean Online Student Svcs .... Ms. Bernadett BILACH
37 Director of Financial Aid .... Ms. Amber IMES

Tohono O'odham Community College (A)

PO Box 3129, Sells AZ 85634-3129
County: Pima FICE Identification: 037844
Unit ID: 442781
Telephone: (520) 383-8401 Carnegie Class: Tribal
FAX Number: (520) 383-0029 Calendar System: Semester
URL: www.tocc.edu
Established: 1998 Annual Undergrad Tuition & Fees: $932
Enrollment: 843 Coed
Affiliation or Control: Tribal Control IRS Status: 501(c)3
Highest Offering: Associate Degree
Accreditation: HLC

01 President .... Dr. Paul ROBERTSON
05 Academic Dean .... Dr. Curtis PETERSON
10 Int Vice Pres of Finance .... Ms. Joann MIGUEL
32 Dean of Student Services .... Ms. Naomi TOM
75 Acad Chair Occupational Pgms .... Mr. George MIGUEL
97 Acad Chair for General Education .... Dr. Mario MONTES-HELU
06 Registrar .... Ms. Chandra CLAW
08 College Librarian .... Ms. Ofelia ZEPEDA
37 Financial Aid Officer .... Ms. Novia JAMES
30 Controller .... Mr. Michael MAINUS
15 Director Human Resources .... Ms. Stacy OWSLEY
09 Institutional Effectiveness Dir .... Mr. Blaine ANTONE

Universal Technical Institute (B)

10695 W Pierce Street, Avondale AZ 85323-7946
County: Maricopa FICE Identification: 008221
Unit ID: 106041
Telephone: (623) 245-4600 Carnegie Class: Spec 2-yr-Tech
FAX Number: (623) 245-4601 Calendar System: Other
URL: www.uti.edu
Established: 1965 Annual Undergrad Tuition & Fees: N/A
Enrollment: 1,845 Coed
Affiliation or Control: Proprietary IRS Status: Proprietary
Highest Offering: Associate Degree
Accreditation: ACCSC

01 Campus President .... Mr. Adrian CORDOVA
11 Director of Operations .... Mr. Patrick BENNETT
32 Director Student Experience .... Ms. Lindsay KINGSLEY
07 Director Campus Admissions .... Ms. Theresa EMEHISER
36 Director of Graduate Employment .... Ms. Cheryl RADKE

University of Advancing Technology (C)

2625 W Baseline Road, Tempe AZ 85283-1056
County: Maricopa FICE Identification: 025590
Unit ID: 363934
Telephone: (602) 383-8228 Carnegie Class: Spec-4-yr-Other Tech
FAX Number: (602) 383-8250 Calendar System: Other
URL: www.uat.edu
Established: 1983 Annual Undergrad Tuition & Fees: $18,378
Enrollment: 836 Coed
Affiliation or Control: Proprietary IRS Status: Proprietary
Highest Offering: Master's
Accreditation: HLC

01 President .... Mr. Jason PISTILLO
05 Provost .... Mr. Dave BOLMAN
26 VP Marketing & Technology .... Ms. Valerie CIMAROSSA
11 Chief Operating Officer .... Mrs. Karla ARAGON-JOYCE
32 Dean of Students/Academic Operation .... Ms. Brandi BEALS
07 Dean of Recruitment and Development .... Ms. Megan BENSON
10 Senior Controller .... Ms. Jodi ROBINSON
113 Bursar .... Ms. Renee GRAUBERGER
06 Registrar .... Ms. Jenna BROCCHINI
37 Director of Financial Aid .... Ms. Elizabeth EASTIN
04 Executive Assistant .... Ms. Christine ROGERS
06 Registrar .... Ms. Katie KEISTNER

University of Arizona (D)

1200 E University Boulevard, Tucson AZ 85721-0001
County: Pima FICE Identification: 001083
Unit ID: 104179
Telephone: (520) 621-2211 Carnegie Class: DU-Highest
FAX Number: (520) 621-9323 Calendar System: Semester
URL: www.arizona.edu
Established: 1885 Annual Undergrad Tuition & Fees (In-State): $12,716
Enrollment: 45,601 Coed
Affiliation or Control: State IRS Status: Exempt
Highest Offering: Doctorate
Accreditation: HLC, ANEST, ART, AUD, CACREP, CAMPEP, CEA, CLPSY, DANCE, DIETC, DIETD, IPSY, JOUR, LAW, LIB, LSAR, MED, MUS, NURSE, PCSAS, PERF, PH, PHAR, PLNG, SCPSY, SP, SPAA, THEA, #VET

01 President .... Dr. Robert C. ROBBINS
05 SVP/Provost/Chief Academic Ofcr .... Dr. Liesl FOLKS
10 Sr VP Business Affairs & CFO .... Ms. Lisa RULNEY
17 Sr VP Health Sciences .... Dr. Michael DAKE
32 VP Stdnt Affs/Enr Mgmt/Dean Admiss .... Dr. Kasandra K. URQUIDEZ
45 VP Strategic Initiatives .... Dr. Jane HUNTER
43 SVP Legal Affairs/General Counsel .... Dr. Laura T. JOHNSON
101 SVP/Sr Assoc to the Pres/Sec Univ .... Dr. Jon DUDAS
85 VP Global Initiatives .... Dr. Brent WHITE
88 VP Global Environmental Futures .... Dr. Joaquin RUIZ
11 VP University Planning/Design/Ops .... Mr. Robert R. SMITH
15 VP/Chief Human Resources Officer .... Ms. Helena RODRIGUES
106 AVP Digital Learning Initiatives .... Ms. Melody BUCKNER
26 VP Communications .... Ms. Holly JENSEN
47 VP/Dn Agri/Life/Veterinary Science .... Dr. Shane C. BURGESS
20 Sr Vice Provost Academic Affairs .... Dr. Gail D. BURD
86 VP Government/Cmty Relations .... Mr. Steve VOELLER
45 Senior VP Research and Innovation .... Dr. Elizabeth R. CANTWELL
88 Director Bio5 Institute .... Dr. Jennifer K. BARTON
88 Sr Advisor Health Sci/Cmty Engage .... Dr. Sally J. REEL
23 Assoc Chair Clinical Affairs .... Dr. Ann MATHIAS
09 Assoc VP Institutional Analysis .... Mr. James S. FLORIAN
88 Assoc VP Tech Parks Arizona .... Ms. Carol A. STEWART
108 Assoc Vice Prov Instruct/Assessment .... Dr. Lisa K. ELFRING
88 Assoc VP Research .... Mr. Neal R. ARMSTRONG
21 VP Financial Services .... Ms. Nicole SALAZAR
13 CIO/Director UITS .... Mr. Barry BRUMMUND
21 Assoc VP Finance Administration .... Ms. Marilyn TAYLOR
84 Asst VP Enroll Mgmt Operations .... Dr. Arezu CORELLA
18 Asst VP Plng/Design & Construction .... Mr. Peter DOURLEIN
88 Asst VP Tribal Relations .... Ms. Karen F. BEGAY
114 VP/Chief Budget Officer .... Mr. Garth PERRY
18 Asst VP Facilities Management .... Mr. Christopher M. KOPACH
117 Chief Risk Ofcr/Risk Mgmt/Safety .... Mr. Steven C. HOLLAND
88 Asst VP Govt Affairs .... Mr. Ethan R. ORR
08 Dean of University Libraries .... Mr. Shan C. SUTTON
83 Dean Social/Behavioral Science .... Dr. John P. JONES
35 Vice Prov Campus Life/Dean Students .... Ms. Kendal H. WASHINGTON WHITE
92 Dean Honors College .... Dr. Terry L. HUNT
48 Dean Col Arch/Plng/Landscape Arch .... Dr. Nancy POLLOCK-ELLWAND
53 Dean Education .... Dr. Bruce JOHNSON
58 Vice Prov/Dean Graduate College .... Dr. Andrew H. CARNIE
61 Dean James E Rogers College of Law .... Dr. Marc L. MILLER
66 Dean College of Nursing .... Dr. Ida M. MOORE
12 Interim Dean UA South .... Dr. Linda DENNO
79 Dean College of Humanities .... Dr. Alain-Philippe DURAND
57 VP/Dean Fine Arts .... Dr. Andrew SCHULZ
54 Dean College of Engineering .... Dr. David HAHN
50 Dean Eller College of Management .... Dr. Paulo GOES
69 Dean College of Public Health .... Dr. Iman A. HAKIM
74 Dean College of Veterinary Medicine .... Dr. Julie FUNK
63 Dean College of Med-Phoenix Campus .... Dr. Guy L. REED
63 Dean College of Medicine-Tucson .... Dr. Michael ABECASSIS
81 Dean College of Optical Sciences .... Dr. Thomas L. KOCH
67 Dean College of Pharmacy .... Dr. Rick SCHNELLMAN
22 Int AVP Diversity/Inclusion .... Ms. Kristen KLOTZ
40 Int AVP Business Affs/Auxiliary Svc .... Ms. Debby L. SHIVELY
23 Int Co-Exec Director Campus Health .... Dr. David B. SALAFSKY
23 Int Co-Exec Director Campus Health .... Dr. Michael STILSON
88 Exec Dir Analytics/Inst Rsrch .... Mr. Ravneet CHADHA
96 Dir Procurement & Contract Services .... Mr. Edward D. NASSER
25 Director Sponsored Proj/Services .... Mr. Paul SANDOVAL
37 Exec Dir Scholarships/Fin Aid .... Mr. Art YOUNG
41 VP/Director of Athletics .... Mr. Dave HEEKE
06 Registrar .... Mr. Alex UNDERWOOD
104 Exec Director Study Abroad .... Ms. Harmony R. DEFAZIO

The University of Arizona College of Applied Science & Technology (E)

1140 N Colombo Avenue, Sierra Vista AZ 85635
Telephone: (520) 458-8278 Identification: 770024
Accreditation: &HLC

University of Arizona Phoenix Biomedical Campus (F)

550 E Van Buren Street, Phoenix AZ 85004
Telephone: (602) 827-2002 Identification: 770023
Accreditation: &HLC, MED, PHAR

University of Phoenix (G)

4035 S Riverpoint Pkwy, Phoenix AZ 85040
County: Maricopa FICE Identification: 020988
Unit ID: 484613
Telephone: (480) 557-2000 Carnegie Class: DU-Mod
FAX Number: N/A Calendar System: Other
URL: www.phoenix.edu
Established: 1976 Annual Undergrad Tuition & Fees: $9,552
Enrollment: 89,763 Coed
Affiliation or Control: Proprietary IRS Status: Proprietary
Highest Offering: Doctorate
Accreditation: HLC, ACBSP, CACREP, HSA, NURSE, @SW

01 President University of Phoenix .... Mr. Peter COHEN
04 Assistant to the President .... Ms. Cindy WHIPPO
05 Chief Academic Officer/Provost .... Dr. John WOODS
10 Chief Financial Officer .... Mr. Chris LYNNE
45 Chief Strategy & Customer Officer .... Ms. Ruth VELORIA
11 Chief Operating Officer .... Mr. Raghu KRISHNAIAH
26 SVP/Chief Marketing Officer .... Mr. Steven GROSS
13 Chief Information Officer .... Mr. Jamie SMITH
15 Chief Human Resources .... Ms. Cheryl NAUMANN
20 Vice Prov Sch of Advanced Studies .... Dr. Hinrich EYLERS
20 Vice Provost Colleges .... Ms. Doris SAVRON
84 SVP Enrollment Services .... Mr. Brett ROMNEY
21 VP Financial Services .... Mr. Bronson LEDBETTER
43 SVP & General Counsel .... Mr. Srini MEDI
06 Registrar .... Ms. Audra MCQUARIE
19 Director Security/Safety .... Mr. Steve LINDSEY
09 Director of Institutional Research .... Mrs. Lisa MITCHELL
101 Secretary of the Institution/Board .... Ms. Kim KAUFFMAN
106 Director Online Education .... Mr. Hal D. MORGAN
28 Director of Diversity .... Ms. Saray LOPEZ
29 Director Alumni Affairs .... Mr. Chris G. CELAURO
37 Director Student Financial Aid .... Ms. Stacy TUCKER
86 SVP Government Relations .... Mr. Eric RIZZO
96 Director of Purchasing .... Mrs. Marty DALLAS

University of Phoenix Southern Arizona Campus (H)

300 S Craycroft Road, Tucson AZ 85711-4574
Telephone: (520) 881-6512 Identification: 770236
Accreditation: &HLC, ACBSP

† No longer accepting campus-based students.

West Coast Ultrasound Institute (I)

3110 North Central Ave, Suite L-100, Phoenix AZ 85012
Telephone: (602) 954-3834 Identification: 770550
Accreditation: ACCSC

† Branch campus of West Coast Ultrasound Institute, Beverly Hills, CA

Yavapai College (J)

1100 E Sheldon Street, Prescott AZ 86301-3297
County: Yavapai FICE Identification: 001079
Unit ID: 106148
Telephone: (928) 445-7300 Carnegie Class: Assoc/MT-VT-High Non
FAX Number: (928) 777-3154 Calendar System: Semester
URL: www.yc.edu
Established: 1966 Annual Undergrad Tuition & Fees (In-District): $2,600
Enrollment: 6,009 Coed
Affiliation or Control: Local IRS Status: 501(c)3
Highest Offering: Associate Degree
Accreditation: HLC, ADNUR, EMT, IFSAC, RAD

01 President .... Dr. Lisa RHINE
05 Vice Pres of Academic Affairs .... Dr. Diane RYAN
10 Vice Pres Finance/Admin Svcs .... Dr. Clint EWELL
26 VP Community Relations .... Mr. Rodney JENKINS
20 Dean for Comp Tech & Instr Support .... Ms. Stacey HILTON
12 Dean Verde Valley Campus & Sedona .... Dr. Tina REDD
75 Dean Career Technical Education .... Mr. John MORGAN
76 Dean Sci/Health/Public Safety .... Mr. Scott FARNSWORTH
79 Dir of Performing Arts Center .... Dr. Craig RALSTON
32 VP Student Development .... Ms. Tania SHELDAHL
27 Director of Marketing/Public Info .... Mr. Tyler RUMSEY
35 Assoc VP Student Development .... Ms. Diana DOWLING
09 Dir Inst Effectiveness & Research .... Dr. Tom HUGHES
15 Chief Human Resources Officer .... Dr. Emily WEINACKER
19 Chief of Police .... Mr. Tyran PAYNE
21 Dir of Business Svcs & Controller .... Mr. Frank D'ANGELO
18 Director for Facilities .... Mr. David LAURENCE
13 Chief Information Officer .... Mr. Patrick BURNS
06 Registrar .... Ms. Sheila JARRELL
96 Director of Purchasing .... Mr. Ryan BOUWHUIS
04 Exec Asst to President .... Ms. Yvonne MARTINEZ-SANDOVAL
07 Director of Admissions .... Ms. Wendy PRESENT
29 Director of Dev/Alumni Affairs .... Ms. Kammie KOBYELSKI
102 Exec Dir YC Foundation .... Ms. Mary TALOSI
37 Director Student Financial Aid .... Mr. Raymond CEO

Yavapai College Verde Valley Campus (K)

601 Black Hills Drive, Clarkdale AZ 86324
Telephone: (928) 634-7501 Identification: 770029
Accreditation: &HLC

ARKANSAS

Arkansas Baptist College (L)

1600 Dr. Martin Luther King Drive, Little Rock AR 72202-6099
County: Pulaski FICE Identification: 001087
Unit ID: 106306
Telephone: (501) 420-1200 Carnegie Class: Bac/Assoc-Mixed
FAX Number: (501) 414-0861 Calendar System: Semester
URL: www.arkansasbaptist.edu
Established: 1884 Annual Undergrad Tuition & Fees: $8,760
Enrollment: 468 Coed
Affiliation or Control: Baptist IRS Status: 501(c)3
Highest Offering: Baccalaureate
Accreditation: #HLC

01 President .... Dr. Carlos R. CLARK
05 VP for Academic & Student Affairs .... Dr. Tracey MOORE
10 VP for Business & Finance/CFO .... Ms. Camesha YOUNG
04 President's Executive Assistant .... Ms. Patsy BIGGS
21 Comptroller .... Vacant
111 VP for Institutional Advancement .... Mr. Jeff SELLERS
32 Dean of Student Affairs .... Dr. Vicki WILLIAMS
37 Director of Financial Aid .... Mr. Lloyd DIXON
100 Chief of Staff .... Ms. Shae BEARDEN
09 Dir of Institutional Research .... Ms. LaTrice SMALL
88 Ombudsman .... Dr. Vicki WILLIAMS
08 Director of Library/Media Services .... Ms. Jacqueline ELDRIDGE
26 Dir of Marketing .... Vacant
19 Director of Campus Safety .... Mr. Claiborn DURHAM
18 Director Facilities & Maintenance .... Mr. Larry THOMPSON
06 Registrar .... Ms. Delores VOLIBER
13 Director of Information Technology .... Vacant
15 Human Resources Director .... Mrs. Pamela BRIMLEY
41 Director of Athletics .... Mr. Bill INGRAM
39 Director Resident Life/Housing .... Vacant
07 Int Dir of Admissions & Recruitment .... Ms. Pamela CONARD
28 Dir Title III/Sponsored Programs .... Vacant

Arkansas Colleges of Health Education (A)

7000 Chad Colley Boulevard, Fort Smith AR 72916
County: Sebastian FICE Identification: 042568
Unit ID: 488527
Telephone: (479) 308-2200 Carnegie Class: Not Classified
FAX Number: (479) 308-2766 Calendar System: Semester
URL: https://acheedu.org/
Established: 2017 Annual Graduate Tuition & Fees: N/A
Enrollment: 678 Coed
Affiliation or Control: Independent Non-Profit IRS Status: 501(c)3
Highest Offering: Doctorate; No Undergraduates
Accreditation: HLC, OSTEO, @PTA

01 President & CEO .... Kyle D. PARKER
05 Vice Provost & VPAA .... Dr. Elizabeth MCCLAIN
100 Senior Executive Assistant .... Dr. Benny L. GOODEN
10 VP & CFO .... Dennis BAUER
45 VP & COO .... Les SMITH
13 VP & CTO .... Joel WEBB
63 Dean DO Program .... Dr. Rance MCCLAIN
63 Associate Dean Clinical Medicine .... Dr. John SEALEY
63 Assoc Dean Biomedicine .... Dr. Ross LONGLEY
20 Assoc Dean Academic Affairs .... Dr. Melissa EFURD
32 Assistant Dean Student Affairs .... Laurel MCINTOSH
58 Dean Physical Therapy .... Dr. Teressa BROWN
58 Dean Occupational Therapy .... Dr. Jennifer MOORE
58 Dean Physicians Assistant .... Dr. Henry LEMKE
58 Program Dir MSB .... Dr. Kenneth HENSLEY
29 Chair of External Alumni Relations .... Dr. Ray E. STOWERS
108 Director of Data Analytics .... Dr. Ashley GERHARDSON
08 Director of Library Services .... Zahra KAMAREI
38 Director of Mental Wellness .... Vacant
30 Director of Development .... Jackie KRUTSCH
19 Chief of Police .... Levi RISLEY
18 Director of Building & Grounds .... Eric BURNS
35 Director of Student Services .... Amanda EVENSON
06 Registrar .... Shawna MASON
37 Director of Financial Aid .... Glenna GILLIAM
07 Director of Admissions .... Kelly DEWITT
121 Academic Success Counselor .... Vacant
15 Assoc VP of Human Resources .... Barbara JETTON
16 Human Resources Manager .... Sheila BENTLEY
26 Exec Dir Marketing/Communications .... Susan DEVERO
96 Director of Procurement .... Dianna JORDAN

Arkansas Northeastern College (B)

2501 S Division Street, Blytheville AR 72315-5111
County: Mississippi FICE Identification: 012860
Unit ID: 107327
Telephone: (870) 762-1020 Carnegie Class: Assoc/HVT-High Non
FAX Number: (870) 763-3704 Calendar System: Semester
URL: www.anc.edu
Established: 1974 Annual Undergrad Tuition & Fees (In-District): $2,654
Enrollment: 1,358 Coed
Affiliation or Control: State/Local IRS Status: 501(c)3
Highest Offering: Associate Degree
Accreditation: HLC, DA, EMT

01 President .... Dr. James SHEMWELL
05 VP for Instruction/CAO .... Dr. Keith MCCLANAHAN
03 Executive Vice President .... Mrs. June WALTERS
10 Vice President for Administration .... Mr. Don RAY
13 VP Information Technology .... Mr. James W. MCCLAIN
103 VP Workforce/Economic Development .... Mr. Gene BENNETT
31 VP for Community Relations .... Dr. Blanchie HUNT
32 VP for Student Services .... Dr. Chris HEIGLE
26 Assoc VP for Dev/College Relations .... Ms. Rachel GIFFORD
21 Assoc Vice President for Finance .... Ms. Pacey BOWENS
66 Dean Nursing/Allied Hlth/PE/Rec .... Mrs. Brenda HOLIFIELD
49 Dean for Arts and Sciences .... Mr. Ryan PERKINS
36 Dean Advisement/Placement .... Dr. Bridget SHEMWELL
75 Dean for Allied Technologies .... Dr. Jamie FRAKES
32 Director for Student Services .... Mrs. Courtney FISHER
31 Coordinator Community Education .... Ms. Mary Ann GARREN
08 Director of College Library/AV .... Ms. Karen ELLIS
37 Director Financial Aid .... Mrs. Mindy WALKER

14 Associate Dean MITS .... Mr. James ODOM
21 Controller .... Ms. Kim MARSHALL
15 Human Resources & ADA Coordinator .... Mrs. Tabatha HAMPTON
18 Director Physical Plant and Grounds .... Mr. Scott CREECY
88 Director Talent Search/Educ Opp Ctr .... Mrs. Tonya HARRIS
35 Director Student Support Services .... Ms. Lisa MCGHEE
04 Assistant to Board/President .... Ms. Marlene BANKS
06 Registrar .... Mrs. Rosemary LOWE
27 Media Director .... Mr. James HARTLEY

*Arkansas State University System (C)

501 Woodlane Drive, Suite 600, Little Rock AR 72201
County: Pulaski Identification: 666187
Telephone: (501) 660-1000 Carnegie Class: N/A
FAX Number: (501) 660-1010
URL: www.asusystem.edu

01 President .... Dr. Charles L. WELCH
04 Exec Assistant to the President .... Ms. Pam KAIL
10 Executive Vice President Finance .... Ms. Julie BATES
86 Vice Pres Governmental Relations .... Mr. Shane BROADWAY
26 Vice Pres Strategic Comm/Econ Dev .... Mr. Jeff HANKINS
43 Legal Counsel .... Mr. Brad PHELPS
09 VP for Strategic Research .... Mr. Eric ATCHISON
102 President ASU System Foundation .... Mr. Philip JACKSON
15 Assoc Vice President Benefits .... Dr. LeAnne PERKINS
116 Internal Auditor .... Ms. Jo LUNBECK
13 Chief Info Technology Officer .... Mr. Henry TORRES

*Arkansas State University-Beebe (D)

PO Box 1000, Beebe AR 72012-1000
County: White FICE Identification: 001091
Unit ID: 106449
Telephone: (501) 882-3600 Carnegie Class: Assoc/MT-VT-Mix Trad/Non
FAX Number: (501) 882-8970 Calendar System: Semester
URL: www.asub.edu
Established: 1927 Annual Undergrad Tuition & Fees (In-State): $2,928
Enrollment: 2,982 Coed
Affiliation or Control: State IRS Status: 501(c)3
Highest Offering: Associate Degree
Accreditation: HLC, EMT, MLTAD, NAIT

02 Chancellor .... Dr. Jennifer METHVIN
100 Executive Assistant to Chancellor .... Ms. Melanie KIIHNL
05 Vice Chanc of Academics/CAO .... Dr. Jason GOODNER
12 Campus Ops Mgr ASU-Heber Springs .... Mr. Cody MCMICHAEL
12 Campus Operations Mgr ASU-Searcy .... Ms. LaShanda OWENS
10 Vice Chanc Finance/Admin/CFO .... Dr. Roger MOORE
13 VC Information Technology Services .... Mr. Leon LEWIS, JR.
32 Vice Chanc Student Services/CSSO .... Dr. David MAYES
111 Assoc VC Advancement .... Ms. Rose Mary JACKSON
15 Director Human Resources .... Ms. Teri ROPER
14 Director of End User Assessment .... Ms. Danya UTLEY
35 Dean Student Affairs .... Mr. Zack TUCKER
26 Director of Marketing/PR .... Mr. Keith MOORE
06 University Registrar .... Vacant
08 Library Director .... Ms. Tracy D. SMITH
19 Police Commander .... Mr. James J. MARTIN
18 Director of Physical Plant .... Mr. Mark HASTINGS
37 Director Student Financial Aid .... Ms. Angela JONES
09 Assoc VC of Institutional Research .... Ms. Katie VAUGHN
21 Controller .... Ms. Kathy WARD
72 Director of Allied Health .... Mr. Joseph SCOTT
106 Director of Distance Learning .... Ms. Stephanie UNGERANK
96 Executive Director Procurement .... Ms. Robin LANCASTER
12 Campus Operations Mgr LRAFB .... Ms. LaShanda OWENS
07 Director of Admissions .... Mr. Tyler BITTLE
31 Community Relations .... Ms. Jennifer GEORGE
105 Webmaster .... Vacant
88 Coord Concurrent Enrollment .... Ms. Ashley HANKINS
121 Director of Advising & Learning .... Ms. Catherine BURTON

*Arkansas State University-Jonesboro (E)

PO Box 600, State University AR 72467
County: Craighead FICE Identification: 001090
Unit ID: 106458
Telephone: (870) 972-2100 Carnegie Class: DU-Higher
FAX Number: (870) 972-3465 Calendar System: Semester
URL: www.astate.edu
Established: 1909 Annual Undergrad Tuition & Fees (In-State): $7,315
Enrollment: 13,106 Coed
Affiliation or Control: State IRS Status: 501(c)3
Highest Offering: Doctorate
Accreditation: HLC, ADNUR, ANEST, ART, CAATE, CACREP, CAEP, CAEPN, CEA, COSMA, DIETC, DMS, EMT, JOUR, MLTAD, MT, MUS, NUR, OT, OTA, PTA, PTAA, RAD, RADMAG, RTT, SP, SPAA, SW, THEA

02 Chancellor .... Dr. Kelly DAMPHOUSSE
05 Provost & Exec VC Acad Affairs .... Dr. Alan UTTER
10 Exec VC Finance & Administration .... Dr. Len T. FREY
84 Vice Chancellor Enrollment Mgmt .... Dr. Thillainatarajan SIVAKUMARAN
111 Vice Chancellor Univ Advancement .... Dr. Erika CHUDY
28 VC for Diversity/Community Engage .... Dr. Lonnie WILLIAMS
41 VC of Intercollegiate Athletics .... Mr. Tom BOWEN
32 VC of Student Affairs .... Dr. Martha SPACK
20 Sr Assoc Vice Chancellor AAR .... Dr. Karen WHEELER
21 Assoc Vice Chancellor Finance .... Dr. Russ HANNAH

114 Asst Vice Chanc Budget .... Ms. Donna MCMILLIN
15 Asst VC Human Resources .... Ms. Lori WINN
46 Vice Provost for Research & Tech .... Dr. Thomas RISCH
13 Asst Vice Chanc/CIO .... Mr. Henry TORRES
18 Asst Vice Chancellor Facilities .... Mr. David HANDWORK
88 Asst Vice Chanc Enrollment Services .... Mr. Terry FINNEY
108 Asst VC Institutional Effectiveness .... Dr. Fen YU
85 Exec Dir Global Engage/Outreach .... Dr. Thilla SIVAKUMARAN
06 Director of Records/Registration .... Ms. Tracy FINCH
07 Director of Admissions .... Ms. Pamela BOWIE
39 Director of Residence Life .... Ms. Natalie ESKEW
19 Chief University Police .... Mr. Randy MARTIN
22 Co-Director of Disability Services .... Ms. Dominique WHITE
22 Co-Director of Disability Services .... Mr. Blake WALKER
36 Director Career Services .... Ms. Tiffany JOHNSON
38 Director Counseling Center .... Dr. Phil HESTAND
29 Exec Dir Alumni Relations .... Ms. Lindsay BURNETT
26 Chief Communications Officer .... Dr. Bill SMITH
27 Director of Media Relations/Comm .... Mr. Tom MOORE
88 Dir of Digital Creative Services .... Mr. Todd CLARK
96 Dir Procurement & Travel Svcs .... Ms. Lisa GLASCO
04 Admin Assistant to the Chancellor .... Ms. Julie WYATT
08 Dir Library .... Mr. Jeff BAILEY
47 Dean College Agriculture/Technology .... Dr. Mickey LATOUR
81 Dean College Sciences & Math .... Dr. Lynn BOYD
50 Dean College of Business .... Dr. Melody LO
53 Dean Col of Educ & Behavioral Sci .... Dr. Mary Jane BRADLEY
60 Dean Liberal Arts & Communication .... Dr. Carl CATES
66 Dean College of Nursing Health Prof .... Dr. Susan N. HANRAHAN
97 Assoc VC Undergraduate Studies .... Dr. Jill SIMONS
58 Dean of Graduate School .... Dr. Cherisse JONES-BRANCH
54 Dean College of Engineering .... Dr. Abhijit BHATTACHARYYA
88 Asst for Administration for Provost .... Ms. Jeannie COSSEY

*Arkansas State University Mid-South (F)

2000 W Broadway Avenue,
West Memphis AR 72301-3829
County: Crittenden FICE Identification: 023482
Unit ID: 107318
Telephone: (870) 733-6722 Carnegie Class: Assoc/HT-High Non
FAX Number: (870) 733-6799 Calendar System: Semester
URL: www.asumidsouth.edu
Established: 1992 Annual Undergrad Tuition & Fees (In-District): $3,226
Enrollment: 1,203 Coed
Affiliation or Control: State/Local IRS Status: 501(c)3
Highest Offering: Associate Degree
Accreditation: HLC, COARC

02 Chancellor .... Dr. Debra WEST
05 Vice Chanc Learning/Instruction .... Mr. Jeff GRAY
10 Vice Chanc Finance & Administration .... Ms. JaNan ABERNATHY
111 Vice Chanc Inst Advancement .... Ms. Diane HAMPTON
32 Vice Chanc Student Affairs .... Mr. Jeremy REECE
103 Interim AVC Workforce Education .... Dr. Callie DUNAVIN
21 AVC Finance .... Ms. Emilee SIDES
20 Acting AVC General Education .... Mr. Mark MCCLELLAN
37 Director of Financial Aid .... Ms. Crystal BURGER
08 Director of Library/Media Center .... Ms. Brandi KATTERJOHN
06 Registrar .... Ms. Leslie ANDERSON
15 Director of Human Resources .... Ms. Lisa HAGGARD
18 Director Facilities/Physical Plant .... Mr. Ed COOK
84 AVC Enrollment Management .... Mr. John EASLEY
13 AVC for Information Systems Tech .... Mr. Ernesto MUNIZ
09 AVC Institutional Research .... Dr. Michael LEJMAN
121 Dir of Learning Success Center .... Ms. Stephanie KREHL
04 Administrative Asst to Chancellor .... Ms. Claudia OHNECK
19 Director Public Safety .... Mr. Ross PROCTOR
25 Chief Contracts/Grants Admin .... Ms. Sherri REID
41 Athletic Director .... Mr. Chris PARKER
30 Director of Development .... Ms. Debbie YEN
96 Business Manager .... Ms. Wendy CRAWFORD

*Arkansas State University-Mountain Home (G)

1600 S College Street, Mountain Home AR 72653-5326
County: Baxter Identification: 666311
Unit ID: 420538
Telephone: (870) 508-6100 Carnegie Class: Assoc/MT-VT-Mix Trad/Non
FAX Number: (870) 508-6287 Calendar System: Semester
URL: www.asumh.edu
Established: 1995 Annual Undergrad Tuition & Fees (In-District): $2,904
Enrollment: 1,271 Coed
Affiliation or Control: State/Local IRS Status: 501(c)3
Highest Offering: Associate Degree
Accreditation: HLC, EMT, PTAA

02 Chancellor .... Dr. Robin MYERS
05 Provost/Vice Chanc Academic Affairs .... Dr. Tamara DANIEL
10 VC Operations/Dir Career Pthwys .... Ms. Laura YARBROUGH
18 Chief Facilities/Physical Plant .... Mr. Nickey L. ROBBINS
26 Assoc Vice Chanc Marketing/Comm .... Mrs. Christy C. KEIRN
32 Assoc Vice Chanc of Students .... Mr. William KIMBRIEL
37 Director Student Financial Aid .... Mr. Clay BERRY
08 Director of Library .... Ms. Tina BRADLEY
09 Dir of Inst Research/Effectiveness .... Mr. David CULLIPHER
07 Admissions Coordinator .... Ms. Stephanie BEAVER
04 Exec Assistant to the President .... Ms. Mary DOUGLAS
103 Director Workforce Development .... Ms. Janel COTTER

13 Chief Information Technology Office .... Ms. Tamya STALLINGS
30 Director of Development .... Ms. Mollie MORGAN
15 Int Coordinator Human Resources .... Ms. Lindsey POWERS

*Arkansas State University-Newport (A)

7648 Victory Boulevard, Newport AR 72112-8912
County: Jackson Identification: 666153
Unit ID: 440402
Telephone: (870) 512-7800 Carnegie Class: Assoc/MT-VT-High Non
FAX Number: (870) 512-7807 Calendar System: Semester
URL: www.asun.edu
Established: 2001 Annual Undergrad Tuition & Fees (In-State): $2,856
Enrollment: 1,941 Coed
Affiliation or Control: State IRS Status: Exempt
Highest Offering: Associate Degree
Accreditation: HLC, SURGT

02 Chancellor .... Dr. Johnny M. MOORE
100 Chief of Staff .... Ms. Kristen SMITH
05 Vice Chancellor Academic Affairs .... Dr. Holly SMITH
10 Vice Chancellor Finance & Admin .... Mr. Adam ADAIR
32 Vice Chancellor Student Affairs .... Dr. Ashley BUCHMAN
103 Vice Chancellor Econ/Workforce Dev .... Mr. Jeff BOOKOUT
30 VC Leadership/Community Engagement .... Mr. Ike WHEELER
121 Dean of Student Success/Registrar .... Dr. Allen MOONEYHAN
72 Dean for Applied Science .... Mr. Robert BURGESS
97 Dean for General Education .... Mr. Joseph CAMPBELL
84 Dean of Enrollment Services .... Ms. Candace GROSS
88 Dean Leadership/Org Development .... Dr. Veronica MANNING
13 Director of IT Services .... Ms. Debbie KEYTON
15 Director Human Resources .... Ms. Sara MOSS
06 Assistant Registrar .... Ms. Phyllis WORTHINGTON
18 Director of Physical Plant .... Mr. Brian PETTIE
21 Controller .... Ms. Monika PHILLIPS
37 Director Financial Aid .... Ms. Stacey DUNLAP
09 Director of Institutional Research .... Ms. Christy MANN
19 Chief of Police .... Mr. Johnathan TUBBS
96 Director of Procurement .... Ms. Lee WEBB
66 Dean of Nursing/Allied Health .... Dr. Typhanie MYERS
36 Director of Career Pathways .... Ms. Cheryl CROSS
75 Director of Adult Education .... Mr. John KELLY
26 Director Marketing & Communications .... Mr. Jeremy SHIRLEY
111 Advancement Officer .... Ms. Teriann TURNER

*Arkansas State University-Three Rivers (B)

One College Circle, Malvern AR 72104-0816
County: Hot Spring FICE Identification: 009976
Unit ID: 107521
Telephone: (501) 337-5000 Carnegie Class: Assoc/HVT-High Non
FAX Number: N/A Calendar System: Semester
URL: www.asutr.edu
Established: 1969 Annual Undergrad Tuition & Fees (In-State): $3,458
Enrollment: 1,243 Coed
Affiliation or Control: State IRS Status: 501(c)3
Highest Offering: Associate Degree
Accreditation: HLC

01 Chancellor .... Dr. Steve ROOK
04 Executive Asst to Chancellor .... Ms. Mitzi OVERTURF
05 Vice Chancellor Academic Affairs .... Mr. Pat SIMMS
32 Vice Chancellor Student Affairs .... Dr. Kim ARMSTRONG
10 Vice Chancellor Finance & Admin .... Mr. James WHITE
111 AVC College Advancement .... Ms. Amber CHILDERS
108 AVC Planning & Assessment .... Ms. Carla CRUTCHFIELD
13 AVC Information Technology .... Mr. Jacob BLAND
20 Dean of Learning .... Ms. Tricia BAAR
76 Dean of Health Sciences .... Ms. Melinda SANDERS
51 Director Adult Education .... Ms. Casson BROCK
08 Director Learning Resources .... Ms. Allison MALONE
36 Director Career Center .... Ms. Kim ROBERSON
92 Director Honors College .... Ms. Tricia BAAR
88 Director Concurrent Enrollment .... Ms. Tara BRATTON
37 Director Financial Aid .... Ms. Angela SEXTON
36 Director Career Pathways .... Ms. Johnnie MITCHELL
88 Dir TRIO Student Support Services .... Ms. Vergina SMITH-JOACHIM
21 Controller .... Ms. Anita MARTIN
15 Director Human Resources .... Ms. Janet HUNT
103 Director Workforce Development .... Mr. Mason ROBINSON
18 Maintenance Supervisor .... Mr. Danny COTTRELL
07 Director of Admissions .... Ms. Keesha JOHNSON

Arkansas Tech University (C)

1509 North Boulder Avenue, Russellville AR 72801-2222
County: Pope FICE Identification: 001089
Unit ID: 106467
Telephone: (479) 968-0389 Carnegie Class: Masters/L
FAX Number: (479) 964-0522 Calendar System: Semester
URL: www.atu.edu
Established: 1909 Annual Undergrad Tuition & Fees (In-State): $7,668
Enrollment: 10,829 Coed
Affiliation or Control: State IRS Status: 501(c)3
Highest Offering: Doctorate
Accreditation: HLC, ART, CAEP, CAHIIM, CAPRT, MAC, MUS, NUR, PTAA

01 President .... Dr. Robin E. BOWEN
10 Interim VP Administration/Finance .... Dr. Linda BIRKNER
05 EVP Academic Affairs/Provost .... Dr. Barbara J. JOHNSON
32 Vice President Student Svcs .... Dr. Keegan NICHOLS
111 Vice President Advancement .... Mr. Jason GEIKEN
84 AVP Enrollment Management .... Dr. C. Blake BEDSOLE
12 Chancellor Ozark Campus .... Mr. Bruce SIKES
43 Associate VP & Counsel to President .Mr. Thomas PENNINGTON
20 Assoc VP Academic Affairs .... Vacant
110 Associate VP for Development .... Mr. Bryan FISHER
121 Asst VP Student Success .... Vacant
35 Assoc VP Student Affairs/Title IX .... Ms. Amy PENNINGTON
35 Chief Student Officer Ozark Campus .... Mr. Richard HARRIS
20 Chief Academic Officer Ozark Campus .... Ms. Sheila JACOBS
100 Chief of Staff .... Dr. Mary GUNTER
06 Registrar .... Ms. Tammy WEAVER
21 Controller .... Ms. Suzanne MCCALL
21 Assistant VP Admin & Finance .... Dr. Linda BIRKNER
08 Director of Library .... Mr. Brent ETZEL
86 Director Government Relations .... Ms. Ashley GOLLEHER
114 Director of Budget .... Ms. Sandra CHEFFER
09 Director of Institutional Research .... Mr. Wyatt WATSON
13 Director Information Systems/CIO .... Mr. Ken WESTER
113 Director of Student Accounts .... Ms. Angela CROW
15 Director of Human Resources .... Ms. Christina STOLARZ
37 Director Student Financial Aid .... Ms. Niki SCHWARTZ
29 Director Alumni Relations .... Mr. Kelly DAVIS
85 Assoc Dean International Students .... Mr. Yasushi ONODERA
18 Director of Physical Plant Services .... Mr. Brian LASEY
96 Director of Purchasing .... Ms. Jessica HOLLOWAY
92 Director of Honors Program .... Dr. Jan JENKINS
22 Director Affirmative Action .... Ms. Christina STOLARZ
108 Dir Assessment/Inst Effectiveness .... Dr. Christine AUSTIN
105 Webmaster .... Ms. Tera SIMPSON
19 Director Public Safety .... Mr. Josh MCMILLIAN
26 Director of University Relations .... Mr. Sam STRASNER
36 Director of Career Services .... Ms. Amanda JOHNSON
44 Director Annual Giving Programs .... Ms. Caroline VINING
07 Director of Admissions .... Ms. Jessica BROCK
41 Interim Athletic Director .... Ms. Abby DAVIS
88 Director of Prospect Research .... Ms. Pam COOPER
112 Director of Gift Planning .... Ms. Peggy MITCHELL-FERRIS
53 Dean College of Education .... Dr. Linda BEAN
49 Dean Col Arts & Humanities .... Dr. Jeffrey CASS
50 Dean College of Business .... Dr. K. Russell JONES
54 Dn Col Engineering & Applied Sci .... Dr. Judy CEZEAUX
81 Dean College of Natural & Health Sc .... Dr. Jeff ROBERTSON
106 Interim Dean College of eTech .... Dr. Jeff AULGUR
58 Dean of Graduate College .... Dr. Richard SCHOEPHOERSTER
28 Asst Dean Diversity & Inclusion .... Dr. Naquindra BROOKS
38 Assoc Dean Student Student Wellness .... Ms. Kristy DAVIS
39 Associate Dean Residence Life .... Mr. Delton GORDON
04 Admin Assistant to the President .... Ms. Jennifer FLEMING

Arkansas Tech University-Ozark Campus (D)

1700 Helberg Lane, Ozark AR 72949
Telephone: (479) 667-2117 Identification: 770003
Accreditation: &HLC, ADNUR, CAHIIM, CSHSE, CVT, EMT, OTA

Baptist Health College Little Rock (E)

11900 Colonel Glenn Rd, Ste 1000, Little Rock AR 72210
County: Pulaski FICE Identification: 031052
Unit ID: 106546
Telephone: (501) 202-6200 Carnegie Class: Spec 2-yr-Health
FAX Number: N/A Calendar System: Semester
URL: www.bhclr.edu
Established: 1921 Annual Undergrad Tuition & Fees: $11,750
Enrollment: 661 Coed
Affiliation or Control: Independent Non-Profit IRS Status: 501(c)3
Highest Offering: Associate Degree
Accreditation: ABHES, ADNUR, MT, NMT, OTA, PNUR, POLYT, RAD, SURTEC

01 Chancellor .... Dr. Judy PILE
66 Dean of Nursing .... Laura HAMILTON
06 Registrar .... Kristin WADDELL
37 Financial Aid Administrator .... Natalie MARTIN
10 Coordinator Campus/Financial Svcs .... Dr. Jamie CLARK

Black River Technical College (F)

PO Box 468/1410 Hwy 304 East,
Pocahontas AR 72455-0468
County: Randolph FICE Identification: 020522
Unit ID: 106625
Telephone: (870) 248-4000 Carnegie Class: Assoc/MT-VT-High Trad
FAX Number: (870) 248-4100 Calendar System: Semester
URL: www.blackrivertech.org
Established: 1991 Annual Undergrad Tuition & Fees (In-State): $4,118
Enrollment: 1,350 Coed
Affiliation or Control: State IRS Status: 501(c)3
Highest Offering: Associate Degree
Accreditation: HLC, COARC, EMT

01 President .... Dr. Martin EGGENSPERGER
05 VP for Academics .... Dr. Brad BAINE
32 VP for Student Affairs .... Mr. Jason SMITH
111 VP for Institutional Advancement .... Mrs. Karen LIEBHABER
10 VP for Finance and Administration .... Mrs. Rhonda STONE
37 Director of Financial Aid .... Mrs. Brandi CHESTER
06 Registrar .... Mrs. Kimberly BIGGER
04 Administrative Asst to President .... Mrs. Janna GUTHREY
106 Dir Online Education/E-learning .... Mrs. Regina MOORE
15 Director Personnel Services .... Mrs. Julie EDINGTON
19 Director Security/Safety .... Mr. Tony SAYLORS
96 Director of Purchasing .... Mrs. Janice HARVEY
13 Chief Info Technology Officer (CIO) .... Mr. Mike GREENE
18 Chief Facilities/Physical Plant .... Mr. Trent INGRAM
09 Director of Institutional Research .... Mrs. Shana SARTAIN
07 Director of Admissions .... Mrs. Angie FRENCH
50 Dean or Director Business .... Mr. Phillip DICKSON
53 Dean or Director Education .... Mrs. Donna STATLER
08 Library Director .... Mr. Mark WARNICK
35 Director of Student Development .... Mr. Neal HARWELL

Bryan University (G)

3704 West Walnut Street, Rogers AR 72756-1825
Telephone: (479) 899-6644 Identification: 666252
Accreditation: ACICS

† Branch campus of Bryan University, Springfield, MO.

Central Baptist College (H)

1501 College Avenue, Conway AR 72034-6470
County: Faulkner FICE Identification: 001093
Unit ID: 106713
Telephone: (501) 329-6872 Carnegie Class: Bac-Diverse
FAX Number: (501) 329-2941 Calendar System: Semester
URL: www.cbc.edu
Established: 1952 Annual Undergrad Tuition & Fees: $17,100
Enrollment: 604 Coed
Affiliation or Control: Baptist IRS Status: 501(c)3
Highest Offering: Baccalaureate
Accreditation: HLC, CAEP

01 President .... Mr. Terry KIMBROW
04 Admin Asst to President .... Mrs. Peggy PILLOW
05 VP for Academic Affairs .... Dr. Gary MCALLISTER
10 VP for Finance .... Mr. Paul CHERRY
111 VP for Advancement .... Vacant
84 VP for Enrollment Mgmt .... Mr. Ryan JOHNSON
32 Coordinator of Student Services .... Mrs. Marieca ASHWORTH
06 Registrar .... Mrs. Stacy JORDAN
07 Director of Admissions .... Mr. Justin MOORE
07 Director Nontraditional Enrollment .... Ms. Claudette HOLT
106 Director of Online Studies .... Mr. Steve ELDER
19 Dean of Students/Campus Security .... Mr. Chris MITCHELL
08 Library Director .... Mrs. Rachel WHITTINGHAM
26 Director of Public Relations .... Mrs. Jessica FAULKNER
37 Director of Financial Aid .... Mrs. Tonya HAMMONTREE
09 Institutional Research Analyst .... Mrs. Gwenda WILLIAMS
41 Athletic Director .... Mr. Lyle MIDDLETON
15 Director of Human Resources .... Ms. Mechelle CARGILE
29 Director of Alumni Engagement .... Mrs. Jessica FAULKNER
88 Military Relations Counselor .... Mr. Patrick JACOB
18 Director of Physical Plant .... Mr. Byron BAKER

Champion Christian College (I)

600 Garland Ave, Hot Springs AR 71913
County: Garland Identification: 667324
Telephone: (501) 623-2272 Carnegie Class: Not Classified
FAX Number: (501) 623-4262 Calendar System: Semester
URL: championchristiancollege.com
Established: 2005 Annual Undergrad Tuition & Fees: N/A
Enrollment: N/A Coed
Affiliation or Control: Independent Non-Profit IRS Status: 501(c)3
Highest Offering: Baccalaureate
Accreditation: TRACS

01 President .... Dr. Eric CAPACI
03 Executive Vice President .... Dr. Jeremy HORTON
05 Vice President of Academic Affairs .... Mr. Elsen PORTUGAL
32 VP Student Affairs/Dir Admissions .... Mr. Josiah CAPACI
06 Registrar .... Mr. Kevin CONNOR
10 Vice President of Finance .... Mrs. Marcia THOMAS

Crowley's Ridge College (J)

100 College Drive, Paragould AR 72450-9775
County: Greene FICE Identification: 001095
Unit ID: 106810
Telephone: (870) 236-6901 Carnegie Class: Bac-Diverse
FAX Number: (870) 236-7748 Calendar System: Semester
URL: www.crc.edu
Established: 1964 Annual Undergrad Tuition & Fees: $15,100
Enrollment: 192 Coed
Affiliation or Control: Churches Of Christ IRS Status: 501(c)3
Highest Offering: Baccalaureate
Accreditation: HLC, CAEP

01 President .... Dr. Richard JOHNSON
05 Vice President for Academic Affairs .... Dr. Brian DAVIS
32 Vice President for Student Affairs .... Mr. Brian DAVIS
111 Chief Financial Officer .... Mr. Tony BUNCH
06 Registrar .... Mrs. Treka CLARK
37 Director Student Financial Services .... Mrs. Shelly BEASLEY
26 Director Public Relations/Marketing .... Mr. Matthew EMERY
07 Director Admissions .... Mr. Chris HUGHES
08 Director Learning Center .... Mrs. Darah WATSON
10 Business Office Manager .... Mrs. Sonia JOHNSON
13 Director of Inst Technology .... Mr. Larry JOHNSON

15 Director of Human Services ... Mr. Tony BUNCH
11 Director of Campus Operations ... Mr. Craig CUPP

East Arkansas Community College (A)

1700 Newcastle Road, Forrest City AR 72335-2204
County: Saint Francis FICE Identification: 012260
Unit ID: 106883
Telephone: (870) 633-4480 Carnegie Class: Assoc/HT-High Non
FAX Number: (870) 633-7222 Calendar System: Semester
URL: www.eacc.edu
Established: 1974 Annual Undergrad Tuition & Fees (In-District): $3,225
Enrollment: 934 Coed
Affiliation or Control: State/Local IRS Status: Exempt
Highest Offering: Associate Degree
Accreditation: HLC, EMT

01 President ... Dr. Cathie CLINE
05 VP Transfer Educ/Student Success ... Mrs. Michelle WILSON
10 Vice President for Finance ... Mr. Tanner MCKNIGHT
75 VP Vocational/Occup/Tech Education ... Mr. Robert P. SUMMERS
37 Director Student Financial Aid ... Vacant
08 Director Library Services ... Mrs. Paige LAWS
26 Exec Dir of PR/Community Programs ... Mrs. Lindsay MIDKIFF
15 Human Resources ... Vacant
96 Purchasing Specialist ... Mrs. Lisa SILER
31 Director of Community Education ... Mrs. Logan BRASFIELD
121 Director of Advising & Counseling ... Mr. Errin JAMES
97 Dean of General Education ... Vacant
32 Dean of Student Services ... Mrs. Samantha SHARP
78 Dean of Vocational Education ... Mr. Chris NELSON
102 Director Foundation/Corporate Rels ... Mrs. Niki JONES
103 Director Workforce Development ... Mrs. Heather MCBRIDE
09 Director of Institutional Research ... Mrs. Roni HORTON
13 Director of Computer Services ... Mr. Ed ADAMS
06 Registrar ... Mr. Alvin COLEMAN, III

Ecclesia College (B)

9653 Nations Drive, Springdale AR 72762-8159
County: Benton FICE Identification: 038553
Unit ID: 446233
Telephone: (479) 248-7236 Carnegie Class: Spec-4-yr-Faith
FAX Number: (479) 248-1455 Calendar System: Semester
URL: www.ecollege.edu
Established: 1975 Annual Undergrad Tuition & Fees: $15,950
Enrollment: 193 Coed
Affiliation or Control: Independent Non-Profit IRS Status: 501(c)3
Highest Offering: Master's
Accreditation: BI

01 President ... Mr. Michael A. NOVAK
00 Chancellor ... Ms. R. Inez PARIS
05 Academic Dean ... Ms. Donna BROWN
10 Chief Financial Officer ... Ms. Melissa K. RICKS
32 Dean of Students ... Ms. Elizabeth NEWLUN
106 Academic Dean EC Online ... Dr. Ben PASCUT
111 Director of Advancement ... Mr. Michael A. NOVAK
37 Director Student Financial Aid ... Mr. Don PRESTON
41 Athletic Director ... Vacant
06 Registrar ... Ms. Amanda VINCENT
08 Head Librarian ... Mrs. Angela CRISS
103 Dean of Work ... Ms. Elizabeth NEWLUN
84 Director of Enrollment ... Mr. Chad E. HOWARD

Harding University Main Campus (C)

915 E. Market Avenue, Searcy AR 72149-5615
County: White FICE Identification: 001097
Unit ID: 107044
Telephone: (501) 279-4000 Carnegie Class: DU-Mod
FAX Number: (501) 279-4600 Calendar System: Semester
URL: www.harding.edu
Established: 1924 Annual Undergrad Tuition & Fees: $21,540
Enrollment: 4,617 Coed
Affiliation or Control: Churches Of Christ IRS Status: 501(c)3
Highest Offering: Doctorate
Accreditation: HLC, ACBSP, ARCPA, CACREP, CAEP, CIDA, @DIETC, DIETD, MUS, NURSE, PHAR, PTA, SP, SW

01 Acting President ... Dr. David BURKS
03 Executive Vice President ... Dr. David COLLINS
05 Provost ... Dr. Marty SPEARS
10 Vice President Finance ... Mrs. Tammy HALL
30 Vice President Advancement ... Dr. Bryan BURKS
13 VP Information Systems & Technology ... Mr. Keith CRONK
41 Athletic Director ... Mr. Jeff MORGAN
29 Director of Alumni Relations ... Mrs. Heather KEMPER
88 Dean College of Bible & Ministry ... Dr. Monte COX
92 Dean of Honors College ... Dr. Kevin KEHL
50 Dean College of Business ... Dr. Al FRAZIER
53 Dean College of Education ... Dr. Donny LEE
66 Dean College of Nursing ... Dr. Susan KEHL
79 Dean College of Arts & Humanities ... Dr. Warren CASEY
81 Dean College of Sciences ... Dr. Zane GASTINEAU
76 Dean College of Allied Health ... Dr. Mike MCGALLIARD
104 Exec Dir of International Programs ... Dr. Audra PLEASANT
84 Asst VP Enrollment Management ... Mr. David HALL
21 Senior Finance Officer ... Mr. Tim JONES
32 Asst VP Student Life/Dean Students ... Mr. Zach NEAL
88 Asst VP of IS&T ... Mr. Mike CHALENBURG
06 Registrar ... Mr. Tod MARTIN
38 Director of Counseling ... Dr. Lew MOORE
19 Director Security/Safety ... Mr. Craig RUSSELL
26 VP of Communication/Enrollment ... Mrs. Candice MOORE
37 Director Student Financial Aid ... Dr. Jonathan ROBERTS
58 Director of Graduate Studies ... Vacant
08 Librarian ... Mrs. Jean WALDROP
18 Chief Facilities/Physical Plant ... Mr. Danny DERAMUS
15 Asst Vice Pres Human Resources ... Mr. David ROSS
36 Director Student Placement ... Vacant
09 Director of Institutional Research ... Mr. Dustin HOWELL
96 Purchasing Coordinator ... Mrs. Karen CARPER
35 Assistant Dean of Students ... Mr. Marcus THOMAS
35 Assistant Dean of Students ... Mrs. Kara ABSTON
35 Assistant Dean of Students ... Mrs. Ranan HESTER
35 Assistant Dean of Students ... Mr. Logan LIGHT
28 Director of Diversity ... Mr. Andrew BRAXTER
39 Director Student Housing ... Mrs. Kathy ALLEN
07 Senior Director of Admissions ... Mr. Scott HANNIGAN

Henderson State University (D)

1100 Henderson Street, Arkadelphia AR 71999-0001
County: Clark FICE Identification: 001098
Unit ID: 107071
Telephone: (870) 230-5000 Carnegie Class: Masters/M
FAX Number: (870) 230-5144 Calendar System: Semester
URL: www.hsu.edu
Established: 1890 Annual Undergrad Tuition & Fees (In-State): $7,392
Enrollment: 3,163 Coed
Affiliation or Control: State IRS Status: 501(c)3
Highest Offering: Beyond Master's But Less Than Doctorate
Accreditation: HLC, ART, CACREP, CAEP, CAEPN, DIETD, MUS, NURSE

01 Interim Chancellor ... Dr. Jim BORSIG
04 Admin Assistant to the Chancellor ... Ms. Flora E. WEEKS
05 Int Provost/VC Academic Affairs ... Mr. James HUNT
10 VC Finance & Administration ... Ms. Rita FLEMING
32 VC Student Affs & Student Success ... Dr. Brad PATTERSON
111 Interim VC Advancement ... Ms. Tina HALL
43 General Counsel ... Ms. Elaine KNEEBONE
35 Asst VC Student Engagement ... Dr. Veronikha SALAZAR
39 Asst VC Housing/Community Standard ... Dr. Nicole LAIRD
13 AVC Computer/Comm Svcs & CIO ... Vacant
41 Director Athletics ... Mr. Shawn JONES
26 Exec Director of Marketing/Comm ... Ms. Tina HALL
49 Dean Ellis Col Arts/Sciences ... Dr. Angela BOSWELL
50 Dean of School of Business ... Dr. Marc MILLER
53 Dean Teachers College Henderson ... Dr. Celya TAYLOR
58 Vice Provost/Dean of Grad School ... Dr. Kenneth TAYLOR
06 Assoc Provost/Registrar ... Dr. Elwyn MARTIN
08 Interim Director Huie Library ... Ms. Lacy WOLFE
15 Director of Human Resources ... Ms. Loretta BRANTLEY
19 Director of University Police ... Mr. Jonathan CAMPBELL
38 Dir Student Health/Counseling Ctr ... Ms. Renee WALLS
07 Assoc Provost Enrollment/Admissions ... Ms. Ashlee DIXON
37 Director of Financial Aid ... Ms. Lisa SMITH
92 Director of Honors College ... Dr. C. Drew SMITH
96 Director of Purchasing ... Vacant
72 Dir Academic Tech & Help Desk ... Ms. Jennifer HOLBROOK
09 Director of Institutional Research ... Ms. Ginger OTWELL
29 Director Alumni Engagement ... Ms. Leah SEXTON

Hendrix College (E)

1600 Washington Avenue, Conway AR 72032-3080
County: Faulkner FICE Identification: 001099
Unit ID: 107080
Telephone: (501) 329-6811 Carnegie Class: Bac-A&S
FAX Number: (501) 450-1200 Calendar System: Semester
URL: www.hendrix.edu
Established: 1876 Annual Undergrad Tuition & Fees: $49,490
Enrollment: 1,077 Coed
Affiliation or Control: United Methodist IRS Status: 501(c)3
Highest Offering: Master's
Accreditation: HLC

01 President ... Mr. W. Ellis ARNOLD, III
04 Executive Assistant to President ... Ms. Donna PLEMMONS
05 Provost ... Dr. Terri BONEBRIGHT
26 Vice Pres Marketing Communications ... Mr. Rob O'CONNOR
10 Executive Vice President & CFO ... Mr. Tom SIEBENMORGEN
84 VP Enrollment/Dir Admissions ... Mr. Ryan CASSELL
15 Vice Pres for Human Resources ... Ms. Vicki LYNN
18 VP Operations/Facilities ... Ms. Sharron RUSSELL
32 Exec VP Student Affs/Dean of Stdnts ... Mr. Jim WILTGEN, JR.
27 Assoc VP Marketing Communications ... Ms. Amy FORBUS
06 Registrar ... Ms. Brenda ADAMS
08 Director of Libraries ... Ms. Britt Anne MURPHY
13 VP Technology/Chief Info Officer ... Mr. Sam NICHOLS
29 Director Alumni Relations ... Ms. Pamela OWEN
41 Director of Athletics ... Ms. Amy WEAVER
37 Director of Financial Aid ... Ms. Kristina BURFORD
79 Area Head/Humanities ... Dr. Rod MILLER
81 Area Head/Natural Sciences ... Dr. Ann WRIGHT
83 Area Head/Social Sciences ... Dr. Todd BERRYMAN
42 Chaplain ... Rev. Ellen ALSTON
20 Associate Academic Officer ... Dr. David SUTHERLAND
21 Associate Business Officer ... Mr. Shawn MATHIS
36 Director Career Services ... Ms. Leigh LASSITER-COUNTS
38 Director Student Counseling ... Ms. Mary Anne SIEBERT
09 Director of Institutional Research ... Vacant
28 Int VP for Diversity & Inclusion ... Ms. Kesha BAOUA

Jackson Theological Seminary (F)

520 North Locust Street, North Little Rock AR 72114
County: Pulaski Identification: 667411
Telephone: (501) 429-8395 Carnegie Class: Not Classified
FAX Number: (501) 375-0306 Calendar System: Semester
URL: www.jtseminary.org
Established: 1886 Annual Undergrad Tuition & Fees: N/A
Enrollment: N/A Coed
Affiliation or Control: African Methodist Episcopal IRS Status: 501(c)3
Highest Offering: Master's
Accreditation: @TRACS

01 President & CEO ... Rev. Cecil L. WILLIAMS, JR.

Jefferson Regional Medical Center School of Nursing (G)

1600 W. 40th Avenue, Pine Bluff AR 71603
County: Jefferson FICE Identification: 023308
Unit ID: 107123
Telephone: (870) 541-7858 Carnegie Class: Not Classified
FAX Number: (870) 541-7807 Calendar System: Semester
URL: www.jrmc.org
Established: 1981 Annual Undergrad Tuition & Fees: N/A
Enrollment: 55 Coed
Affiliation or Control: Independent Non-Profit IRS Status: 501(c)3
Highest Offering: Associate Degree
Accreditation: ABHES, PAST

01 President & CEO ... Brian THOMAS
05 Vice Pres/Chief Academic Officer ... Bryan JACKSON
10 Vice Pres/Chief Financial Officer ... Jeremy JEFFREY

John Brown University (H)

2000 W University Street, Siloam Springs AR 72761-2121
County: Benton FICE Identification: 001100
Unit ID: 107141
Telephone: (479) 524-9500 Carnegie Class: Masters/M
FAX Number: (479) 524-7278 Calendar System: Semester
URL: www.jbu.edu
Established: 1919 Annual Undergrad Tuition & Fees: $28,288
Enrollment: 2,343 Coed
Affiliation or Control: Independent Non-Profit IRS Status: 501(c)3
Highest Offering: Master's
Accreditation: HLC, ACBSP, CAEP, CONST, NURSE

01 President ... Dr. Charles POLLARD
10 Vice Pres Finance & Administration ... Dr. Kim HADLEY
84 Vice Pres Enrollment Management ... Mr. Donald W. CRANDALL
111 Vice Pres of University Advancement ... Dr. Jim KRALL
32 Vice Pres for Student Development ... Dr. Stephen T. BEERS
05 VP Academic Affairs/Dean of Faculty ... Dr. Ed ERICSON, III
42 Campus Pastor/Assoc Dean of Stdnts ... Vacant
06 Registrar ... Dr. Rebecca WEIMER
21 Controller ... Mr. Tom PERRY
13 Chief Information Systems Ofcr ... Mr. Paul NAST
18 Director of Facilities Services ... Mr. Steve BRANKLE
112 Director of Planned Giving ... Mr. Eric GREENHAW
08 Director of Library ... Ms. Taylor VANLANDINGHAM
85 Director International Programs ... Mr. Bill STEVENSON
29 Director of Alumni/Parent Relations ... Mr. Brad EDWARDS
37 Director of Financial Aid ... Mr. David BURNEY
07 JBU Online Recruiting ... Vacant
41 Athletic Director ... Ms. Robyn DAUGHERTY
04 Administrative Asst to President ... Ms. Kory J. DALE
09 Director of Institutional Research ... Mrs. Lynette DUNCAN
15 Chief Human Resources Officer ... Mrs. Amy FISHER
19 Director Security/Safety ... Mr. Scott WANZER
26 Director University Communications ... Ms. Julie GUMM
39 Director Residence Life ... Dr. Andre BROQUARD
108 Director Institutional Assessment ... Dr. Robert NORWOOD

Lyon College (I)

PO Box 2317, Batesville AR 72503-2317
County: Independence FICE Identification: 001088
Unit ID: 106342
Telephone: (870) 307-7000 Carnegie Class: Bac-A&S
FAX Number: (870) 307-7001 Calendar System: Semester
URL: https://www.lyon.edu/
Established: 1872 Annual Undergrad Tuition & Fees: $29,415
Enrollment: 665 Coed
Affiliation or Control: Presbyterian Church (U.S.A.) IRS Status: 501(c)3
Highest Offering: Baccalaureate
Accreditation: HLC, CAEP

01 Interim President ... Dr. Melissa P. TAVERNER
05 Provost ... Dr. Melissa P. TAVERNER
100 Chief of Staff/EVP Enrollment Svcs ... Mr. Matthew CRISMAN
32 VP Student Life & Dean of Students ... Mr. Lai-Monte HUNTER
111 Vice President of Advancement ... Dr. David HUTCHISON
89 Dean of First Year Studies ... Dr. Anthony K. GRAFTON
10 Interim VP for Business & Finance ... Mr. Joseph D. BOTANA, II
08 Director Library ... Dr. Robert KRAPOHL
110 Executive Dir of Advancement ... Mrs. Gina GARRETT
07 Dean of Admission ... Mr. Thomas NEWTON
37 Executive Director of Financial Aid ... Mr. Tommy TUCKER
36 Director Career Development ... Vacant
13 Director Information Services ... Vacant

26 Executive Dir of Communication Mrs. Madeline PYLE
41 Director of Athletics Mr. Kevin JENKINS
42 Chaplain Rev. Margaret ALSUP
53 Director of Teacher Education Dr. Kim CROSBY
38 Director Student Counseling Ms. Diane ELLIS
40 Director Bookstore Vacant
08 Head Librarian Vacant
23 Director of Health Services Mrs. Haley HAILE
18 Chief Facilities/Physical Plant Mr. Brett RAY
20 Associate Academic Officer Dr. Anthony GRAFTON
06 Registrar Mrs. Tami HALL
44 Director Annual Giving Mrs. Jill MOBLEY
09 Director of Institutional Research Mr. Andrew ENGLISH
15 Director of Human Resources Ms. Rebecca VARELA
29 Director of Alumni Affairs Mrs. Cindy BARBER

National Park College (A)

101 College Drive,
Hot Springs National Park AR 71913-9174
County: Garland FICE Identification: 012105
Unit ID: 106980
Telephone: (501) 760-4222 Carnegie Class: Assoc/HVT-High Trad
FAX Number: (501) 760-4100 Calendar System: Semester
URL: www.np.edu
Established: 1973 Annual Undergrad Tuition & Fees (In-District): $5,000
Enrollment: 1,912 Coed
Affiliation or Control: State/Local IRS Status: 501(c)3
Highest Offering: Associate Degree
Accreditation: **HLC**, ACBSP, ADNUR, CAHIIM, COARC, EMT, MLTAD, RAD

01 President Dr. John HOGAN
05 Vice Pres Academic Affairs Dr. Wade DERDEN
10 Vice Pres Finance & Admin Mr. Steve TRUSTY
32 VP Student Affairs/Enrollment Mgmt Dr. Jerry THOMAS
26 Vice Pres External Relations Ms. Darla THURBER
13 Chief Info Technology Officer Mr. Blake BUTLER
103 VP Workforce/Strategic Initiatives Ms. Kelli EMBRY
15 Assoc Vice Pres Human Resources Ms. Janet BREWER
35 Dean of Students Mr. John TUCKER
07 Dean of Enrollment Services Mr. Jason HUDNELL
09 Director Institutional Research Mr. Chris COBLE
08 Director of Library Services Ms. Lynn VALETUTTI
37 Director of Financial Aid Ms. Lisa HOPPER
102 Executive Director of Foundation Ms. Nicole HERNDON
06 Registrar Mr. Scott POST
04 Exec Assistant to the President Ms. Jill HOULIHAN
18 Director Physical Plant Mr. Brad HOPPER

North Arkansas College (B)

1515 Pioneer Drive, Harrison AR 72601-5599
County: Boone FICE Identification: 012261
Unit ID: 107460
Telephone: (870) 743-3000 Carnegie Class: Assoc/MT-VT-High Trad
FAX Number: (870) 391-3250 Calendar System: Semester
URL: www.northark.edu
Established: 1974 Annual Undergrad Tuition & Fees (In-District): $3,840
Enrollment: 1,604 Coed
Affiliation or Control: State/Local IRS Status: 501(c)3
Highest Offering: Associate Degree
Accreditation: **HLC**, ACBSP, ADNUR, EMT, MLTAD, RAD, SURGT

01 President Dr. Randy ESTERS
05 VP of Academic/Student Affairs Dr. Rick MASSENGALE
10 Vice Pres Finance & Administration Mr. Richard STIPE
111 Vice Pres Institutional Advancement Dr. Rodney ARNOLD
04 Executive Assistant to President Mrs. Joetta ADAMS
49 Dean Arts & Science/Business & IT Dr. Laura BERRY
66 Dean Nursing/Allied Hlth/Tech Pgms Dr. Josephine KERSHAW
103 Dean of Outreach & Workforce Dev Mrs. Nell BONDS
08 Student Resource Coordinator Mrs. Sharla HELLEN
108 Dir Institutional Effectiveness Mrs. Amanda KILBOURN
32 Dean of Student Success Mrs. Tavonda BROWN
41 Athletic Director Mr. Bobby HOWARD
15 Director Human Resources Mrs. Kris GREENING
18 Chief Facilities/Physical Plant Mr. Kevin SOMERS
96 Director of Purchasing Mrs. Shari HOLT
37 Director Student Financial Aid Mrs. Jennifer HADDOCK
06 Registrar Mrs. Charla JENNINGS
07 Director of Admissions Mrs. Charla JENNINGS
26 Director of Public Relations Mrs. Micki SOMERS
31 Asst Dir of Community Education Ms. Sarah BING

NorthWest Arkansas Community College (C)

1 College Drive, Bentonville AR 72712-5091
County: Benton FICE Identification: 030633
Unit ID: 367459
Telephone: (479) 986-4000 Carnegie Class: Assoc/HT-Mix Trad/Non
FAX Number: (479) 619-4118 Calendar System: Semester
URL: www.nwacc.edu
Established: 1989 Annual Undergrad Tuition & Fees (In-District): $4,096
Enrollment: 7,411 Coed
Affiliation or Control: State/Local IRS Status: 501(c)3
Highest Offering: Associate Degree
Accreditation: **HLC**, ACBSP, ACFEI, ADNUR, CAHIIM, COARC, EMT, IFSAC, PTAA

01 President Dr. Evelyn E. JORGENSON
10 VP of Finance & Administration Mr. Al MASSRI
05 Vice Pres for Learning/CAO Dr. Ricky TOMPKINS
32 VP of Student Services Dr. Todd KITCHEN
36 VP of Career & Workforce Education Mr. Tim CORNELIUS
103 Dean of Workforce Education Dr. Megan BOLINDER
13 AVP IT/Chief Information Officer Mr. Jason DEGN
11 AVP of Finance & Administration Ms. Gulizar BAGGSON
56 AVP of Washington Co Programs Ms. Brenda GREEN
88 Dir Retail & Supplier Education Ms. Teresa WARREN
11 Executive Director of Operations Mr. Jack THOMPSON
51 Dean of Adult Education Mr. Ben ALDAMA
35 Dean of Students Ms. Dale MONTGOMERY
30 Executive Director of Development Ms. Liz ANDERSON
20 Assoc VP Learning Dr. Diana JOHNSON
26 Exec Dir Cmty/Govt Rels/Marketing Mr. Grant HODGES
21 Controller Ms. Courtney WALKER
06 Registrar Mr. Jeff LEBERT
15 Int Exec Director Human Resources Ms. Beverly HILL
106 Assoc Dean of Distance Learning Dr. Kate BURKES
88 Director of Learning Resources Ms. Gwen DOBBS
84 Dir Enrollment Services Ms. Beverly GRAU
37 Director Student Financial Aid Ms. Michelle CORDELL
121 Exec Director of Student Success Mr. Eric VEST
109 Dir Food Services/Event Management Ms. Diane BOSS
88 Executive Director of Brightwater Mr. Marshall SHAFKOWITZ
09 Director of Institutional Research Ms. Kim PURDY
18 Director of Physical Plant Mr. Jim NELSON
77 Dean for Bus/Computer Information Dr. Christine DAVIS
76 Dean of Health Professions Mr. Mark WALLENMEYER
04 Exec Asst to President & BOT Ms. Lindsey WHITE
22 Exec Dir Policy/Risk & Comp Ms. Teresa TAYLOR
84 AVP of Student Services Mr. Justin WHITE
19 Interim Director of Public Safety Mr. Cecil WHITE
104 Director Global Intl Programs Mr. Jeremy YOUMANS

Ouachita Baptist University (D)

410 Ouachita Street, Arkadelphia AR 71998-0001
County: Clark FICE Identification: 001102
Unit ID: 107512
Telephone: (870) 245-5000 Carnegie Class: Bac-Diverse
FAX Number: (870) 245-5500 Calendar System: Semester
URL: www.obu.edu
Established: 1886 Annual Undergrad Tuition & Fees: $29,120
Enrollment: 1,704 Coed
Affiliation or Control: Southern Baptist IRS Status: 501(c)3
Highest Offering: Master's
Accreditation: **HLC**, CAEP, DIETD, @DIETI, MUS, NUR

01 President Dr. Ben R. SELLS
111 Vice Pres Institutional Advancement Dr. Keldon HENLEY
100 Chief of Staff Dr. Keldon HENLEY
05 Vice President Academic Affairs Dr. Stan POOLE
10 Chief Financial Officer Mr. Jason TOLBERT
32 Vice Pres for Student Development Dr. Wesley KLUCK
30 Vice President for Development Mrs. Terry G. PEEPLES
26 Asst to Pres for Comm/Mktg Mrs. Brooke ZIMNY
07 Director of Admissions Counseling Mrs. Lori MOTL
09 Director of Institutional Research Dr. Deborah ROOT
15 Director of Human Resources Mrs. Sherri PHELPS
18 Chief Facilities/Physical Plant Mr. John HARDMAN
29 Director of Alumni Relations Mr. Jon MERRYMAN
35 Dean of Students Mr. Rickey ROGERS
20 Assoc Vice Pres Academic Affairs Dr. Doug REED
36 Director of Career Services Mrs. Rachel ROBERTS
38 University Counselor Mr. Dan JARBOE
08 Librarian Dr. Ray GRANADE
06 Registrar/Director of Admissions Mrs. Susan ATKINSON
37 Acting AVP Student Financial Svcs Mrs. Karen MATROS
92 Director Honors Program Dr. Barbara PEMBERTON
13 Chief Information Officer Mr. Bill PHELPS
39 Director of Housing Ms. Caitlin HETZEL
41 Athletic Director Mr. David SHARP
43 University Counsel Mr. Bryan MCKINNEY
21 Director of Business Services Mrs. Kristi CLAY
40 Bookstore Manager Mrs. Jennifer FORTHMAN
57 Dean of School of Fine Arts Dr. Gary GERBER
50 Dean of the School of Business Mr. Bryan MCKINNEY
53 Dean Sch of Interdisciplinary Stds Dr. Stan POOLE
73 Dean School of Christian Studies Dr. Jeremy GREER
79 Dean School of Humanities & Educ Dr. Jeff ROOT
81 Dean School of Natural Sciences Dr. Tim KNIGHT
83 Dean School of Social Sciences Dr. Randall WIGHT
101 Secretary of the Institution/Board Mrs. Tracey KNIGHT
108 Director Institutional Assessment Dr. Deborah ROOT
19 Director Security/Safety Mr. Jeff CROW
04 Executive Asst to the President Mrs. Tracey KNIGHT
104 VP Cmty/Intercultural Engagement Dr. Lewis SHEPHERD
106 Asst to Pres for Grad/Prof Studies Dr. Monica HARDIN

Ozarka College (E)

218 College Drive, Melbourne AR 72556
County: Izard FICE Identification: 020870
Unit ID: 107549
Telephone: (870) 368-2300 Carnegie Class: Assoc/HVT-Mix Trad/Non
FAX Number: (870) 368-2091 Calendar System: Semester
URL: www.ozarka.edu
Established: 1991 Annual Undergrad Tuition & Fees (In-State): $3,004
Enrollment: 1,033 Coed
Affiliation or Control: State IRS Status: 501(c)3
Highest Offering: Associate Degree
Accreditation: **HLC**, ACFEI

01 President Dr. Richard L. DAWE
05 Vice President of Academic Affairs Dr. Chris LORCH
10 Exec Vice Pres of Finance/Admin Mrs. Tina WHEELIS
32 Vice Pres of Student Services Mrs. Zeda WILKERSON
111 Vice President of Advancement Dr. Joshua WILSON
45 Director of Planning/Spec Projects Ms. Kim WILSON
13 Chief Information Officer Mr. Scott PINKSTON
04 Assistant to the President Ms. Amy ESQUIVEL
30 Director of Advancement Mrs. Suellen DAVIDSON
29 Development Officer/Dir Alumni Rels Vacant
37 Director of Financial Aid Ms. Kay ADKINS
07 Director of Admissions Ms. Erika CAMPBELL
06 Registrar Vacant
26 Dir Public Relations/Marketing Ms. Katie NORRIS
15 Director of Human Resources Ms. Deedra STEED
21 Business Manager Mrs. Amber RUSH

Philander Smith College (F)

900 W. Daisy L. Gatson Bates Drive,
Little Rock AR 72202-3799
County: Pulaski FICE Identification: 001103
Unit ID: 107600
Telephone: (501) 375-9845 Carnegie Class: Bac-Diverse
FAX Number: (501) 370-5277 Calendar System: Semester
URL: www.philander.edu
Established: 1877 Annual Undergrad Tuition & Fees: $13,014
Enrollment: 799 Coed
Affiliation or Control: United Methodist IRS Status: 501(c)3
Highest Offering: Baccalaureate
Accreditation: **HLC**, ACBSP, CAEP, SW

01 President Dr. Roderick L. SMOTHERS, SR.
04 Senior Exec Assistant to President Mrs. Anita L. HATLEY
03 Executive Vice President Dr. Darnell WILLIAMS
05 Interim VP of Academic Affairs Dr. Shannon CLOWNEY-JOHNSON
32 VP of Student Affs/Enrollment Mgmt Dr. Gregory HUDSON
111 VP Institutional Advancement Mr. Charles KING
10 VP of Fiscal Affairs Mrs. Willie HUGHEY
108 Director Inst Effectiveness Dr. Laza RAZAFIMANJATO
06 Registrar Ms. Bertha OWENS
42 Chaplain/Dean of Religious Life Rev. Ronnie MILLER-YOW
35 Dean of Students Ms. Rhonda LOVELACE
15 Exec Director of Human Resources Vacant
37 Director of Financial Aid Mr. Kevin BARNES
18 Director of Physical Plant Mr. Robert YOUNG
26 Director Marketing/Public Relations Mrs. Jenelle PRIMM
88 Executive Director of WISE -P3 Mr. Glenn SERGEANT, SR.
07 Interim Director of Admissions Mr. Yohannis JOB
08 Director of the Library Mrs. Kathy ANDERSON
29 Director of Alumni Relations Mrs. Brenda HATTON-FICKLIN
41 Interim Athletic Director Mr. Brandon GREENWOOD
13 Chief Information Officer Mr. Brian CLAY
09 Director of Institutional Research Ms. Beverly RICHARDSON
19 Chief of Security Mr. Arthur WILLIAMS
51 Dir of Continuing Education (PSMI) Dr. Cedric STONE
88 Kendall Mission Center Director Dr. Cynthia BURROUGHS
40 Bookstore Manager Mr. Alvin HARRIS
17 Campus Nurse Ms. Regina STEWARD
88 Dean of Campus Culture Mr. Ronnie MILLER-YOW
49 Div Chair Natural/Physical Sciences Dr. Samar SWAID
50 Div Chair of Business/Economics Dr. Cedric STONE
53 Div Chair of Education Dr. Charity SMITH
79 Div Chair Humanities Dr. Lia STEELE-MARCELL
83 Div Chair Social Sciences Dr. Daniel EGBE
38 Director of Counseling Services Ms. LaTisha JACKSON
39 Director of Housing and Res Life Mr. Paul CRAWFORD
101 Secretary of the Institution/Board Mr. David L. LEWIS
105 Web Services Ms. Carmen BRADFORD
22 Director of Social Justice Mrs. Tamika EDWARDS
36 Director Student Engagement Dr. Vernita BOWENS

Shorter College (G)

604 Locust Street, North Little Rock AR 72114
County: Pulaski FICE Identification: 001105
Unit ID: 107840
Telephone: (501) 374-6305 Carnegie Class: Assoc/HT-Mix Trad/Non
FAX Number: (501) 374-9333 Calendar System: Semester
URL: www.shortercollege.edu
Established: 1886 Annual Undergrad Tuition & Fees: $5,596
Enrollment: 223 Coed
Affiliation or Control: African Methodist Episcopal IRS Status: 501(c)3
Highest Offering: Associate Degree
Accreditation: **TRACS**

01 President Dr. O. Jerome GREEN
10 Chief Financial Officer Mr. George MACKEY
05 Dean Academic/Student Affairs Dr. Hansen STEWART
07 Director of Admissions Ms. Arnella HAYES-CARTER
15 Chief Human Resources Officer Ms. Cordelia MITCHELL
18 Chief Facilities/Phys Plant Ofcr Mr. Nathan ALEXANDER
32 Assoc Dean Student/Academic Affairs Mr. Demetrius GILBERT
29 Director Alumni Affairs Ms. Paula PUMPHREY
36 Director Student Placement Vacant
37 Director Student Financial Aid Ms. Audra HINTON
84 Director Enrollment Management Ms. Audra HINTON
35 Associate Student Affairs Officer Ms. Mary WILLIAMS
06 Registrar Mr. Roderick DUNN
20 Associate Academic Officer Ms. Yvette WIMBERLY

South Arkansas Community College (A)

300 S West Avenue, PO Box 7010,
El Dorado AR 71731-7010
County: Union FICE Identification: 020746
Unit ID: 107974
Telephone: (870) 862-8131 Carnegie Class: Assoc/MT-VT-Mix Trad/Non
FAX Number: (870) 864-7190 Calendar System: Semester
URL: www.southark.edu
Established: 1992 Annual Undergrad Tuition & Fees (In-State): $3,012
Enrollment: 1,253 Coed
Affiliation or Control: State IRS Status: 501(c)3
Highest Offering: Associate Degree
Accreditation: HLC, EMT, OTA, PTAA, RAD, SURGT

01 President ... Dr. Bentley WALLACE
05 VP for Academic Affairs ... Dr. Stephanie TULLY-DARTEZ
32 Vice Pres for Student Services ... Dr. Derek MOORE
10 VP for Finance & Administration ... Mr. Carey TUCKER
13 Chief Info Ofcr/AVP Administration ... Dr. Tim KIRK
26 Dir Marketing & Public Relations ... Mr. Heath WALDROP
84 Director of Enrollment Services ... Vacant
08 Director Library Media Center ... Mr. Philip SHACKELFORD
37 Director of Financial Aid ... Ms. Veronda TATUM
04 Executive Asst to the President ... Ms. Kathy MODICA
15 Human Resources Director ... Mr. Bill FOWLER
18 Director of Physical Plant ... Vacant
30 Dir of Foundation/External Funding ... Ms. Cynthia REYNA
96 Director of Procurement/Budget ... Ms. Ann SOUTHALL
103 Dean Workforce & Continuing Educ ... Mr. Brooks WALTHALL
49 Dean Arts and Sciences ... Dr. James YATES
76 Dean Health Sciences ... Ms. Caroline HAMMOND
121 Dean Student Success ... Mr. Timothy R. JOHNSON

Southeast Arkansas College (B)

1900 Hazel Street, Pine Bluff AR 71603-3900
County: Jefferson FICE Identification: 005707
Unit ID: 107637
Telephone: (870) 543-5900 Carnegie Class: Assoc/HT-High Trad
FAX Number: (870) 850-8636 Calendar System: Semester
URL: www.seark.edu
Established: 1991 Annual Undergrad Tuition & Fees (In-State): $3,855
Enrollment: 1,113 Coed
Affiliation or Control: State IRS Status: 501(c)3
Highest Offering: Associate Degree
Accreditation: HLC, ADNUR, COARC, EMT, RAD, SURGT

01 President ... Dr. Steven BLOOMBERG
05 Vice President Academic Affairs ... Vacant
32 Vice President Student Affairs ... Ms. Lozanne CALHOUN
10 Vice President Fiscal Affairs ... Ms. Debbie WALLACE
21 Controller ... Mr. Steve BALLARD
13 Director of Technology Services ... Ms. JoAnn DUPRA
06 Registrar/Director of Admissions ... Ms. Sherri ROBERTS
15 Human Resources ... Ms. Jocelyn POTTER
18 Chief Facilities/Physical Plant ... Mr. Jabe THROWER
37 Director Student Financial Aid ... Ms. Donna COX
04 Administrative Asst to President ... Ms. Wanda GRIMMETT
08 Director of Library ... Ms. Kim WILLIAMS
105 Webmaster ... Vacant
97 Dean General Studies ... Ms. Tracy HARRELL
66 Dean Nursing & Allied Health ... Ms. Joyce SCOTT
103 Dean Technical Studies/Wkforce Dev ... Ms. Lyric SEYMORE
09 Director of Institutional Research ... Ms. Phylesia DAVIS
30 Director of Development ... Ms. Barbara DUNN
36 Dir Workforce/Career Development ... Mr. Jeff PULLIAM
121 Director of Advising & Retention ... Mr. Gene WHITE
106 Coord Online Education/E-learning ... Ms. Meagan COATS

Southern Arkansas University (C)

100 E University Street, Magnolia AR 71753-5000
County: Columbia FICE Identification: 001107
Unit ID: 107983
Telephone: (870) 235-4000 Carnegie Class: Masters/L
FAX Number: (870) 235-5005 Calendar System: Semester
URL: www.saumag.edu
Established: 1909 Annual Undergrad Tuition & Fees (In-State): $9,080
Enrollment: 4,432 Coed
Affiliation or Control: State IRS Status: 501(c)3
Highest Offering: Doctorate
Accreditation: HLC, #CAATE, CAEP, NUR, SW

01 President ... Dr. Trey BERRY
05 Provost/Vice Pres Academic Affairs ... Dr. David LANOUE
11 VP Administration/General Counsel ... Mr. Roger W. GILES
32 Vice President Student Affairs ... Dr. Donna Y. ALLEN
18 Director of Facilities ... Mr. Robert NASH
10 Vice President for Finance ... Ms. Shawana REED
30 Asst Vice President for Development ... Mr. Josh KEE
49 Dean Col Liberal & Performing Arts ... Dr. Helmut LANGERBEIN
50 Dean College of Business ... Dr. Robin SRONCE
53 Dean College of Education ... Dr. Kim K. BLOSS
81 Dean College of Science & Eng ... Dr. Abdel BACHRI
58 Dean School of Graduate Studies ... Dr. Kim K. BLOSS
06 Registrar ... Ms. Marisa GRIPPO
84 Dean Enrollment Services ... Ms. Sarah E. JENNINGS
35 Associate Dean of Students ... Mr. Carey BAKER
08 Director of Library ... Dr. Del G. DUKE
13 Director Info Technology Services ... Mr. Mike A. ARGO
38 Director Counsel/Testing Center ... Ms. DeAnna TRACY
39 Dean of Housing ... Ms. Sandra E. MARTIN
29 Director of Alumni Affairs ... Ms. Megan MCCURDY
110 Director of Development ... Ms. Macy BRASWELL
37 Director of Financial Aid ... Ms. Marcela C. MCRAE-BRUNSON
51 Director of Continuing Education ... Mrs. Caroline WALLER
41 Director of Athletics ... Mr. Steve BROWNING
121 Director Student Support Services ... Mrs. Stephanie MANNING
36 Director of Placement Services ... Vacant
28 Assoc Dean Multicultural Affairs ... Mr. Cledis D. STUART
27 Assoc Dir Communications Center ... Vacant
04 Asst to President ... Ms. LaTricia DAVIS
09 Director of Institutional Research ... Ms. Christine PACHECO
86 Director Government Relations ... Mrs. Sheryl EDWARDS
102 Director Foundation ... Ms. Macy BRASWELL
15 Human Resources Manager ... Ms. Tammy SIMS

Southern Arkansas University Tech (D)

P.O. Box 3499, 6415 Spellman Road, Camden AR 71711
County: Calhoun FICE Identification: 007738
Unit ID: 107992
Telephone: (870) 574-4500 Carnegie Class: Assoc/HVT-High Non
FAX Number: (870) 574-4520 Calendar System: Semester
URL: www.sautech.edu
Established: 1967 Annual Undergrad Tuition & Fees (In-State): $4,571
Enrollment: 769 Coed
Affiliation or Control: State IRS Status: 501(c)3
Highest Offering: Associate Degree
Accreditation: HLC

01 Chancellor ... Dr. Jason MORRISON
10 VC for Finance & Administration ... Mrs. Gaye MANNING
05 VC for Academics & Planning ... Dr. Valerie WILSON
32 VC for Student Services ... Dr. Edward RICE
26 Dir Communications/Public Relations ... Mrs. Kim COKER
09 Dir Inst Effectiveness & Research ... Mrs. Rita GIVENS
84 Dean of Enrollment Services ... Mrs. Jenny SANDERS
103 Director of Career Pathways ... Ms. LaTonya REED
36 Director of Career Academy ... Mrs. Rachel GASTON
107 Director AETA & Workforce Education ... Mr. Randy HARPER
88 Director of AFTA ... Mrs. Rachel NIX
13 Dir Info Tech & Telephone Services ... Mrs. Laura JOHNSON
37 Director of Financial Aid ... Mrs. Connie RILEY
18 Director of Physical Plant ... Mr. Carl RAMSAY
35 Director of Student Life ... Mr. Courtney HAYGOOD
06 Registrar ... Mr. Wayne BANKS
08 Director Rocket Success Ctr/Library ... Ms. Kyra JERRY
04 Assistant to the Chancellor ... Vacant
15 Director Human Resources ... Mrs. Olivia CLACK
21 Controller ... Mr. Dale TOMMEY
96 Buyer ... Mrs. Angela FRY
51 Director of Adult Education ... Mrs. Barbara HAMILTON
19 Director Security/Safety ... Mr. Jud MITCHELL
41 Athletic Director ... Mrs. Amy DIEHL
07 Director of Admissions ... Mrs. Jenny SANDERS
108 Director Institutional Assessment ... Vacant

*University of Arkansas System Office (E)

2404 N University Avenue, Little Rock AR 72207-3608
County: Pulaski FICE Identification: 008008
Unit ID: 108056
Telephone: (501) 686-2500 Carnegie Class: N/A
FAX Number: (501) 686-2507
URL: www.uasys.edu

01 President ... Dr. Donald R. BOBBITT
04 Assistant to the President ... Ms. Angela HUDSON
05 Vice President Academic Affairs ... Dr. Michael K. MOORE
26 Vice President University Relations ... Ms. Melissa RUST
47 Vice President Agriculture ... Dr. Mark J. COCHRAN
10 Chief Financial Officer ... Ms. Gina TERRY
43 General Counsel ... Mrs. JoAnn MAXEY
116 Chief Audit Executive ... Mrs. Laura CHEAK
30 Vice President Planning & Devel ... Mr. Christopher THOMASON
13 Chief Information Officer ... Mr. Steven FULKERSON
27 Director of Communications ... Mr. Nate HINKEL
15 AVP Benefits/Risk Management Svcs ... Mr. Steve WOOD
27 Sr Dir Policy & Public Affairs ... Mr. Ben BEAUMONT
114 Associate VP Finance ... Mrs. Chaundra HALL

*University of Arkansas Main Campus (F)

1125 W. Maple St., Fayetteville AR 72701-1201
County: Washington FICE Identification: 001108
Unit ID: 106397
Telephone: (479) 575-3836 Carnegie Class: DU-Highest
FAX Number: (479) 575-2361 Calendar System: Semester
URL: www.uark.edu
Established: 1871 Annual Undergrad Tuition & Fees (In-State): $9,384
Enrollment: 27,562 Coed
Affiliation or Control: State IRS Status: 501(c)3
Highest Offering: Doctorate
Accreditation: HLC, ART, CAATE, CACREP, CAEP, CIDA, CLPSY, DIETD, IPSY, JOUR, LAW, LSAR, MUS, NURSE, PH, SP, SW, THEA

02 Interim Chancellor ... Mr. Charles F. ROBINSON
04 Executive Asst to the Chancellor ... Ms. Sally Ann ADAMS
05 Int Provost/VC Academic Affairs ... Dr. Terry MARTIN
10 Vice Chanc Finance & Admin ... Ms. Ann BORDELON
111 Vice Chanc for Advancement ... Mr. Mark POWER
86 Vice Chanc Governmental Relations ... Mr. Randy MASSANELLI
45 Vice Provost Planning ... Ms. Colleen BRINEY
46 Int Vice Provost Research/Econ Dev ... Mr. David SNOW
32 Assoc Vice Chanc & Dean of Students ... Ms. Melissa HARWOOD-ROM
84 Vice Prov Enrol Mgt/Dean Admissions ... Dr. Suzanne MCCRAY
100 Assoc Vice Chanc and Chief of Staff ... Ms. Laura JACOBS
25 AVC Research & Sponsored Pgms ... Ms. Jennifer TAYLOR
15 Assoc Vice Chanc Human Resources ... Ms. Debbie MCLOUD
18 Assoc Vice Chanc Facilities Mgmt ... Mr. Scott TURLEY
21 Director of Business Services ... Ms. Tina M. LESTER
26 Assoc Vice Chanc University Rels ... Mr. Mark RUSHING
08 Dean of Libraries ... Vacant
49 Dean of Arts & Sciences ... Dr. Todd G. SHIELDS
50 Dean Sam Walton College of Business ... Dr. Matthew WALLER
47 Dean of Agriculture ... Dr. Deacue FIELDS
53 Dean Education/Health Professions ... Dr. Brian T. PRIMACK
48 Dean of Architecture ... Mr. Peter MACKEITH
58 Dean of Graduate School ... Dr. Pat KOSKI
54 Dean of Engineering ... Dr. Kim NEEDY
92 Dean Honors College ... Dr. Lynda COON
61 Dean of the Law School ... Ms. Margaret MCCABE
29 Assoc Vice Chanc for Alumni ... Ms. Brandy A. COX
22 Director of Equal Opportunity ... Ms. Danielle L. WOOD-WILLIAMS
07 Assoc Vice Prov Enroll/Dean Admiss ... Ms. Wendy D. STOUFFER
38 Dir of Counseling/Psych Services ... Dr. Josette CLINE
19 Director University Police ... Mr. Steve GAHAGANS
36 Exec Dir of Career Devel Center ... Ms. Angela S. WILLIAMS
13 Assoc Vice Chanc for Info Tech ... Mr. Steve KROGULL
06 Interim Registrar ... Mr. Gary GUNDERMAN
96 Director of Purchasing ... Ms. Becky MCCOY
123 Director Graduate & Intl Admissions ... Ms. Patricia GAMBOA
37 Director of Financial Aid ... Mr. Phillip Andrew BLEVINS
09 Dir Institutional Research & Assess ... Mr. Gary GUNDERMAN
102 Sr Dir Ofc Corporate & Found Rels ... Ms. Cherie RACHEL
104 Director Study Abroad ... Ms. Sarah L. MALLOY
41 Athletic Director ... Mr. Hunter YURACHEK
44 Director Annual Giving ... Ms. Lizzie JOHNSON

*University of Arkansas at Fort Smith (G)

PO Box 3649, Fort Smith AR 72913-3649
County: Sebastian FICE Identification: 001110
Unit ID: 108092
Telephone: (479) 788-7000 Carnegie Class: Bac-Diverse
FAX Number: (479) 788-7003 Calendar System: Semester
URL: www.uafs.edu
Established: 1928 Annual Undergrad Tuition & Fees (In-District): $5,754
Enrollment: 5,887 Coed
Affiliation or Control: State/Local IRS Status: 501(c)3
Highest Offering: Master's
Accreditation: HLC, ART, CAEP, DH, DMS, MUS, NAIT, NURSE, RAD, SURGT, SW

02 Chancellor ... Dr. Terisa C. RILEY
05 Provost/Vice Chanc Academic Affairs ... Dr. Georgia HALE
111 Vice Chancellor Univ Advancement ... Mr. Blake RICKMAN
10 Vice Chanc Finance & Administration ... Vacant
32 Vice Chancellor Student Affairs ... Dr. Lee KREHBIEL
58 Assoc Provost/Dir of Grad Studies ... Dr. Margaret TANNER
31 Assoc VC Campus/Cmty Events ... Mr. Stacey JONES
86 Director Govt & Univ Relations ... Dr. Ken WARDEN
20 Asst to Provost/Dir Dev Educ ... Vacant
100 Chief of Staff ... Mrs. Jennifer BELT
76 Int Dean Col of Hlth Educ & Hum Sci ... Dr. Lynn KORVICK
50 Dean College of Business & Industry ... Dr. Latisha SETTLAGE
49 Dean Col of Arts & Sciences ... Dr. Paul HANKINS
15 Dir Human Resources/EEO Officer ... Mrs. Mandy KEYES
12 Interim Dir Western AR Tech Ctr ... Dr. Andrea SLATON
107 Dir of Student Professional Dev Ctr ... Vacant
45 Asst Provost Inst Effectiveness ... Dr. John JONES
88 Director of Instructional Support ... Dr. Tara MISHRA
08 Director of Library Services ... Ms. Anne LIEBST
39 Director of Student Housing ... Ms. Beth EPPINGER
37 Director of Financial Aid ... Ms. Karen JEFFERS
07 Director of Admissions ... Mr. Andy JOHNSON
121 Director of Advisement ... Ms. Julie MOSLEY
06 Registrar ... Mr. Wayne WOMACK
85 Dir of International Relations ... Mr. Nicolas PATTILLO
26 Dir Marketing/Communications ... Mr. Chris KELLY
41 Director of Athletics ... Mr. Curtis JANZ
96 Director of Procurement Services ... Ms. Rhonda CATON
27 Assoc Director of Strategic Comm ... Ms. Rachel PUTMAN
18 Int Director of Plant Operations ... Mr. Alvin CAMPBELL
103 Dir CBPD/Family Enterprise Ctr ... Vacant
13 Director Technology Services ... Mr. Terry MEADOWS
19 Dir Chief of University Police ... Mr. Ray OTTMAN
29 Director of Alumni Affairs ... Vacant
112 Director of Planned Giving ... Ms. Anne THOMAS
36 Asst Director Career Services ... Mr. Jeff ADAMS
53 Executive Director Education ... Dr. Monica RILEY

*University of Arkansas at Little Rock (A)

2801 S University Avenue, Little Rock AR 72204-1099
County: Pulaski FICE Identification: 001101
Unit ID: 106245
Telephone: (501) 916-3000 Carnegie Class: DU-Higher
FAX Number: (501) 916-3915 Calendar System: Semester
URL: www.ualr.edu
Established: 1927 Annual Undergrad Tuition & Fees (In-State): $8,366
Enrollment: 8,899 Coed
Affiliation or Control: State IRS Status: 501(c)3
Highest Offering: Doctorate
Accreditation: HLC, ADNUR, ART, CACREP, CAEP, CAEPN, CAMPEP, CONST, DENT, LAW, MUS, NUR, SPAA, SW, THEA

02 Chancellor .... Dr. Christina S. DRALE
05 Executive Vice Chancellor & Provost .... Dr. Ann BAIN
32 Vice Chancellor for Student Affairs .... Dr. William C. DECKER
10 Vice Chanc Finance & Administration .... Mr. Gerald J. GANZ
111 Vice Chancellor Advancement .... Mr. Christian O'NEAL
41 Director of Athletics .... Mr. George L. LEE
86 Vice Chancellor University Affairs .... Ms. Joni C. LEE
13 Associate Vice Chancellor & CIO .... Dr. Thomas BUNTON
06 Registrar .... Ms. Malissa MATHIS
15 Assoc VC of Human Resources .... Ms. LaTonda WILLIAMS
26 Dir Marketing & Brand Development .... Mr. Jeff HARMON
09 Assoc Provost & Chief Data Officer .... Dr. William C. DECKER
37 Director Financial Aid .... Mr. Jonathan B. COLEMAN
07 Director of Admissions .... Ms. Chelsea B. WARD
88 Assoc Prov for UALR Collect and Arc .... Dr. Deborah J. BALDWIN
19 Chief of Police .... Ms. Regina W. CARTER
25 Director Research & Sponsored Pgm .... Ms. Tammie L. CASH

*University of Arkansas for Medical Sciences (B)

4301 W Markham, Little Rock AR 72205-7199
County: Pulaski FICE Identification: 001109
Unit ID: 106263
Telephone: (501) 686-7000 Carnegie Class: Spec-4-yr-Med
FAX Number: (501) 686-5905 Calendar System: Semester
URL: www.uams.edu
Established: 1879 Annual Undergrad Tuition & Fees (In-State): N/A
Enrollment: 2,907 Coed
Affiliation or Control: State IRS Status: 501(c)3
Highest Offering: Doctorate
Accreditation: HLC, ANEST, ARCPA, AUD, COARC, CYTO, DH, DIETI, DMS, HSA, IPSY, MED, MT, NMT, NURSE, PH, PHAR, PTA, RAD, SP

02 Chancellor .... Dr. Cam PATTERSON
05 Provost and CAO .... Dr. Stephanie F. GARDNER
10 Vice Chancellor Finance & CFO .... Ms. Amanda GEORGE
26 Vice Chanc Communications/Marketing ..... Ms. Leslie W. TAYLOR
111 VC Institutional Advancement .... Ms. Angela WIMMER
11 Assoc Vice Chanc Campus Operations .... Mr. Brian COTTEN
28 VC Diversity/Equity & Inclusion .... Dr. Brian E. GITTENS
09 Vice Chancelor for Research .... Dr. Shuk-Mei HO
13 Assoc VC IT/CIO .... Mr. Michael D. GREER
08 Library Director .... Ms. Lisa SMITH
15 Vice Chancellor for HR/Chief HR Off .... Dr. Danielle LOMBARD-SIMS
20 Asst Provost Teaching Lrng Support .... Dr. Steve E. BOONE
32 Assoc Provost Students & Admin .... Dr. Kristen STERBA
37 Director Financial Services .... Ms. Gloria KEMP
63 Dean College of Medicine .... Dr. Christopher T. WESTFALL
76 Dean College of Health Professions .... Dr. Susan LONG
66 Dean College of Nursing .... Dr. Patricia COWAN
67 Dean College of Pharmacy .... Dr. Cindy STOWE
58 Dean of the Graduate School .... Dr. Robert E. MCGEHEE, JR.
69 Dean College of Public Health .... Dr. Mark WILLIAMS
06 Dir Enrollment Svcs/Chief Registrar ..... Mr. Clinton D. EVERHART
39 Dir Campus Life/Stdnt Support Svcs .... Ms. Cheri D. GOFORTH
100 Chief of Staff .... Ms. Amy WENGER

† Tuition figure is for Medical School. Other school's tuitions vary widely.

*University of Arkansas at Monticello (C)

346 University Drive, Monticello AR 71656-3596
County: Drew FICE Identification: 001085
Unit ID: 106485
Telephone: (870) 367-1020 Carnegie Class: Masters/M
FAX Number: (870) 460-1321 Calendar System: Semester
URL: www.uamont.edu
Established: 1909 Annual Undergrad Tuition & Fees (In-State): $7,909
Enrollment: 2,645 Coed
Affiliation or Control: State IRS Status: 501(c)3
Highest Offering: Master's
Accreditation: HLC, CAEPN, EMT, MUS, SW

02 Chancellor .... Dr. Peggy DOSS
05 VC for Academic Affairs .... Ms. Crystal HALLEY
111 VC for Advancement .... Mr. Jeff WEAVER
32 VC for Student Engagement .... Dr. Moses GOLDMON
10 VC for Finance and Administration .... Mr. Alex BECKER
12 VC for UAM College of Tech-Crossett .... Ms. Linda RUSHING
12 VC for UAM College of Tech-McGehee .... Mr. Bob WARE
04 Assistant to the Chancellor .... Ms. Christy PACE
45 Exec Dir of Budget Mgmt .... Ms. Debbie GASAWAY
13 Chief Information Officer .... Ms. Anissa ROSS
86 Director of Government Relations .... Dr. John DAVIS
35 Dean of Students .... Mr. Michael DAVILA
07 Director of Admissions .... Ms. Mary WHITING
19 Director of University Police .... Mr. John KIDWELL
22 Dir Affirmative Action/EEO .... Ms. Sage LOYD
41 Director of Athletics .... Mr. Padraic MCMEEL
38 Director of Counseling/Testing .... Ms. Roberta THOMAS
37 Director of Financial Aid .... Mr. Brad FULLER
29 Director Alumni Affairs .... Mr. Jay HUGHES
08 Director of Library .... Mr. Daniel BOICE
26 Director of Marketing/Public Rels .... Ms. Ember DAVIS
18 Director of Physical Plant .... Mr. Rusty RIPPEE
96 Director of Purchasing .... Ms. Gay PACE
06 Registrar .... Ms. Sylvia MILLER
39 Director of Housing .... Vacant
15 Human Resources Manager .... Ms. Jennifer HARGIS

*University of Arkansas at Pine Bluff (D)

1200 N University Drive, Pine Bluff AR 71601-2799
County: Jefferson FICE Identification: 001086
Unit ID: 106412
Telephone: (870) 575-8000 Carnegie Class: Bac-Diverse
FAX Number: (870) 543-8009 Calendar System: Semester
URL: www.uapb.edu
Established: 1873 Annual Undergrad Tuition & Fees (In-State): $8,248
Enrollment: 2,668 Coed
Affiliation or Control: State IRS Status: 501(c)3
Highest Offering: Doctorate
Accreditation: HLC, AAFCS, ACBSP, ART, CAEP, MUS, NAIT, NURSE, SW

02 Chancellor .... Dr. Laurence B. ALEXANDER
05 Vice Chanc Academic Affairs .... Dr. Robert CARR
10 Vice Chanc Finance & Admin .... Dr. Carla M. MARTIN
32 Vice Chancellor Student Affairs .... Mr. Elbert BENNETT
45 Vice Chanc Research/Innovation .... Dr. Mansour MORTAZAVI
84 VC Enrollment Mgmt/Stdnt Success .... Dr. Braque TALLEY
100 Chief of Staff .... Mrs. Janet BROILES
41 VC/Director of Athletics .... Mr. Chris ROBINSON
15 Director of Human Resources .... Ms. Latisha SMITH
13 Director of Technical Services .... Mrs. Willette TOTTEN
09 Director of Institutional Research .... Mrs. Margaret W. TAYLOR
06 Registrar .... Ms. Kimberly YON
29 Director of Alumni Affairs .... Mr. John KUYKENDALL
08 Head Librarian .... Mr. Edward FONTENETTE
103 Dir Workforce/Career Development .... Mrs. Shirley CHERRY
108 Director Institutional Assessment .... Dr. Steve LOCHMANN
37 Director Student Financial Aid .... Mrs. Janice KEARNEY
22 Dir Affirmative Action/EEO .... Vacant
88 Director of Recruitment .... Ms. Donna RYLES
07 Director of Admissions .... Ms. Donna RYLES
18 Director Facilities/Physical Plant .... Mr. William HALIBURTON
19 Director Security/Safety .... Chief Maxcie THOMAS
30 Director of Development .... Dr. Margaret J. MARTIN-HALL
50 Dean Sch of Business & Management ... Mr. Lawrence AWOPETU
53 Dean School of Education .... Vacant
96 Director of Purchasing .... Mrs. Wauntia TROTTER
104 Director Study Abroad .... Dr. Pamela MOORE
38 Director Student Counseling .... Ms. Joyce VAUGHN
39 Int Assoc Dean Residential Services .... Mr. Ralph OWENS
86 Director Government Relations .... Mr. John KUYKENDALL

*University of Arkansas System eVersity (E)

2402 N. University Avenue, Little Rock AR 72207
County: Pulaski Identification: 667336
Telephone: (844) 837-7489 Carnegie Class: Not Classified
FAX Number: N/A Calendar System: Other
URL: eversity.edu
Established: 2014 Annual Undergrad Tuition & Fees (In-State): N/A
Enrollment: N/A Coed
Affiliation or Control: State IRS Status: 501(c)3
Highest Offering: Baccalaureate
Accreditation: DEAC

05 Chief Academic & Operating Officer .... Dr. Michael K. MOORE
32 Director of Student Experience .... Adam DAVIS
37 Director of Financial Aid .... Alexandra TUBBS
13 Director of Technology .... Jay PARKER
06 Dir Student Onboarding/Registrar .... Steven HOWELL
26 Director of Marketing .... Dan SHISLER
27 Director of Communications .... Nate HINKEL

*Cossatot Community College of the University of Arkansas (F)

183 College Drive, De Queen AR 71832
County: Sevier FICE Identification: 022209
Unit ID: 106795
Telephone: (870) 584-4471 Carnegie Class: Assoc/MT-VT-High Non
FAX Number: N/A Calendar System: Semester
URL: www.cccua.edu
Established: 1991 Annual Undergrad Tuition & Fees (In-District): $3,960
Enrollment: 1,386 Coed
Affiliation or Control: State/Local IRS Status: 501(c)3
Highest Offering: Associate Degree
Accreditation: HLC, ACBSP, OTA, PTAA

02 Chancellor .... Dr. Steve COLE
05 Vice Chancellor of Academics .... Dr. Ashley AYLETT
45 VC of Planning and Facilities .... Mr. Mike KINKADE
10 Vice Chancellor Business/Finance .... Mrs. Charlotte JOHNSON
32 Director of Student Services .... Mrs. Suzanne WARD
37 Director Student Financial Aid .... Mrs. Denise HAMMOND
06 Registrar .... Mrs. Jocelin GALVEZ
103 Dir of Public Svc/Workforce Dev .... Mrs. Tammy COLEMAN
12 Director of Ashdown Campus .... Mr. Barrett REED
15 Director of Human Resources .... Ms. Kelly PLUNK
13 Director of Technology .... Mr. Tony HARGROVE
30 Director of Development .... Mr. Dustin ROBERTS
04 Executive Assistant to Chancellor .... Ms. Wendy GARCIA
09 Director of Institutional Research .... Mrs. Tommi COBB

*Phillips Community College of the University of Arkansas (G)

PO Box 785, Helena AR 72342-0785
County: Phillips FICE Identification: 001104
Unit ID: 107619
Telephone: (870) 338-6474 Carnegie Class: Assoc/MT-VT-High Non
FAX Number: (870) 338-7542 Calendar System: Semester
URL: www.pccua.edu
Established: 1965 Annual Undergrad Tuition & Fees (In-District): $3,410
Enrollment: 1,093 Coed
Affiliation or Control: State/Local IRS Status: 501(c)3
Highest Offering: Associate Degree
Accreditation: HLC, ACBSP, ADNUR, MLTAD

02 Chancellor .... Dr. G. Keith PINCHBACK
05 Vice Chancellor for Instruction .... Dr. Deborah KING
10 Vice Chanc Finance & Administration .... Mr. Stan SULLIVANT
32 Vice Chanc Student Svcs .... Dr. Kimberley JOHNSON
30 Vice Chanc Col Advancement/Res Dev .... Mrs. Rhonda ST. COLUMBIA
12 Vice Chancellor Arkansas County .... Mrs. Kim KIRBY
84 Director Enrollment Management .... Mr. Von DANIELS
13 Director IT .... Mr. Lee WILLIAMS
37 Director Financial Aid .... Ms. Barbra STEVENSON
15 Director Human Resources .... Ms. Ella JAMES

*University of Arkansas Community College at Batesville (H)

2005 White Drive, PO Box 3350,
Batesville AR 72503-3350
County: Independence FICE Identification: 020735
Unit ID: 106999
Telephone: (870) 612-2000 Carnegie Class: Assoc/HVT-High Trad
FAX Number: (870) 793-4988 Calendar System: Semester
URL: www.uaccb.edu
Established: 1975 Annual Undergrad Tuition & Fees (In-District): $2,862
Enrollment: 1,224 Coed
Affiliation or Control: State/Local IRS Status: 501(c)3
Highest Offering: Associate Degree
Accreditation: HLC, ADNUR, EMT

02 Chancellor .... Vacant
04 Assistant to the Chancellor .... Ms. Jodie HIGHTOWER
05 Vice Chancellor for Academics .... Dr. Brian SHONK
32 Vice Chanc Student Affairs .... Mr. Zach PERRINE
10 Vice Chancellor Finance and Admin .... Ms. Mandy WALKER
88 Executive Dir of Special Projects .... Dr. Anne AUSTIN
49 Chair Div of Arts & Humanities .... Mr. Doug MUSE
50 Chair Div Business/Tech/Public Svc .... Ms. Jeanette YOUNGBLOOD
76 Chair Div Nursing/Allied Health .... Ms. Marietta CANDLER
81 Chair Div of Math and Science .... Mr. Douglas MUSE
75 Dir of Career and Tech Educ .... Mr. Zachery HARBER
09 Dir of Institutional Research .... Dr. Deltha SHARP
07 Director of Admissions .... Ms. Meagan AKINS
13 Director Information Services .... Vacant
06 Dir Student Information/Registrar .... Ms. Casey BROMLEY
37 Director of Financial Aid .... Ms. Kristen CROSS
111 Director of Advancement .... Ms. Kim WHITTEN
18 Director of Maintenance .... Mr. Heath WOOLDRIDGE
36 Director Student Development .... Ms. Louise HUGHES
103 Dir of Workforce and Career Svcs .... Vacant
08 Director Library .... Mr. Jay STRICKLAND
21 Business Office Manager .... Ms. Jennifer SINELE
15 Human Resources Coordinator .... Ms. Julie JOHNSON
96 Purchasing Agent .... Ms. Peggy JACKSON
40 Bookstore Manager .... Ms. Luanne BARBER

*University of Arkansas Community College Hope-Texarkana (I)

PO Box 140, 2500 S Main Street, Hope AR 71802-0140
County: Hempstead FICE Identification: 005732
Unit ID: 107725
Telephone: (870) 777-5722 Carnegie Class: Assoc/MT-VT-High Trad
FAX Number: (870) 777-5957 Calendar System: Semester
URL: https://www.uaht.edu/
Established: 1991 Annual Undergrad Tuition & Fees (In-State): $3,250
Enrollment: 1,211 Coed
Affiliation or Control: State IRS Status: 501(c)3
Highest Offering: Associate Degree
Accreditation: HLC, EMT, FUSER

02 Chancellor ....Dr. Christine HOLT
32 Vice Chanc Student Services ....Mr. Brian BERRY
05 Vice Chancellor for Academics ....Ms. Laura CLARK
10 Vice Chancellor for Finance ....Ms. Cindy LANCE
35 Dean of Students ....Mr. Christopher SMITH
108 Dean of Institutional Effectiveness ....Mr. John HOLLIS
111 Dir of Institutional Advancement ....Ms. Anna POWELL
88 Director of Hempstead Hall ....Ms. Amanda LANCE
13 Chief Info Technology Officer (CIO) ....Mr. Chuck JORDAN
06 Registrar ....Ms. Diana DAVIDSON
15 Human Resources Officer ....Ms. Kathryn HOPKINS

*University of Arkansas Community College at Morrilton (A)

1537 University Boulevard, Morrilton AR 72110-9601
County: Conway FICE Identification: 005245
Unit ID: 107585
Telephone: (501) 354-2465 Carnegie Class: Assoc/MT-VT-High Trad
FAX Number: (501) 977-2044 Calendar System: Semester
URL: www.uaccm.edu
Established: 1961 Annual Undergrad Tuition & Fees (In-State): $3,456
Enrollment: 1,836 Coed
Affiliation or Control: State IRS Status: 501(c)3
Highest Offering: Associate Degree
Accreditation: HLC, NAEYC

12 Chancellor ....Ms. Lisa WILLENBERG
05 Vice Chancellor for Academics ....Dr. Richard COUNTS
10 Vice Chancellor for Finance ....Mr. Jeff MULLEN
32 Vice Chancellor Student Services ....Mr. Darren JONES
09 Director of Institutional Research ....Vacant
08 Librarian ....Ms. Kristen COOKE
06 Registrar ....Ms. Linda HOLLAND
37 Financial Aid Director ....Ms. Jennifer WILLIAMS
26 Dir Marketing & Public Relations ....Ms. Mary CLARK
13 Director of Information Tech ....Mr. Steve WALLACE
18 Director of the Physical Plant ....Mr. C. Allen HOLLOWAY
07 Director of Admissions ....Ms. Rachel MULLINS
103 Coord Workforce Develop/Cmty Educ ....Ms. Jessica ROHLMAN
15 Director Personnel Services ....Ms. Judy SANDERS
30 Chief Development ....Ms. Anne CADLE
38 Director Student Counseling ....Mr. Cody DAVIS
96 Director of Purchasing ....Ms. Anna HALBROOK

*University of Arkansas - Pulaski Technical College (B)

3000 W Scenic Drive, North Little Rock AR 72118-3399
County: Pulaski FICE Identification: 020753
Unit ID: 107664
Telephone: (501) 812-2200 Carnegie Class: Assoc/HT-High Trad
FAX Number: (501) 771-2844 Calendar System: Semester
URL: www.uaptc.edu
Established: 1991 Annual Undergrad Tuition & Fees (In-State): $5,670
Enrollment: 4,810 Coed
Affiliation or Control: State IRS Status: 501(c)3
Highest Offering: Associate Degree
Accreditation: HLC, ACFEI, COARC, DA, EMT, NAEYC, OTA, SURGT

02 Chancellor ....Dr. Margaret ELLIBEE
05 Provost ....Vacant
10 Vice Chancellor for Finance ....Ms. Charlette MOORE
111 Vice Chancellor for Advancement ....Vacant
103 Director of Workforce/Comm Educ ....Ms. Sharon CANTRELL
32 Dean of Student Affairs ....Mr. Mason CAMPBELL
84 Dean of Admissions/Financial Aid ....Dr. John LEWIS
07 Director of Admissions ....Ms. Kyanna BEARD
08 Library Director ....Ms. Wendy DAVIS
18 Director of Physical Plant ....Mr. Bryan RUSHER
09 Inst Reporting & Research Coord ....Ms. Jennifer BLAYLOCK
96 Director of Purchasing ....Ms. Emily FISHER
13 Director of Information Services ....Mr. Robert DURHAM
15 Director of Human Resources ....Ms. Regina FOSSETTE
04 Assistant to the President ....Ms. Tena CARRIGAN
37 Director of Financial Aid ....Ms. Lori TAYLOR
26 Director Public Relations/Marketing ....Mr. Tim JONES
72 Dean Technical/Professional Studies ....Vacant
81 Dean Science/Math/Allied Health ....Dr. Marcio BRYANT HOWE
57 Dean Fine Arts/Humanities/Social Sc ....Dr. Christy OBERSTE
06 Registrar ....Dr. Ana HUNT
19 Director Security/Safety ....Mr. Mark STAFFORD
29 Director Alumni Affairs ....Ms. Adora CURRY

*University of Arkansas Rich Mountain (C)

1100 College Drive, Mena AR 71953-2500
County: Polk FICE Identification: 021111
Unit ID: 107743
Telephone: (479) 394-7622 Carnegie Class: Assoc/MT-VT-High Non
FAX Number: (479) 394-7295 Calendar System: Semester
URL: www.uarichmountain.edu
Established: 1983 Annual Undergrad Tuition & Fees (In-District): $3,408
Enrollment: 798 Coed
Affiliation or Control: State/Local IRS Status: 501(c)3
Highest Offering: Associate Degree
Accreditation: HLC

02 Chancellor ....Dr. Phillip WILSON
05 Vice Chancellor Academic Affairs ....Dr. Krystal THRAILKILL
32 VC Student Affairs/Registrar ....Mr. Chad FIELDING
10 Vice Chancellor Administration/CFO ....Mr. Morris BOYDSTUN
13 Chief Information Officer ....Mr. Chris MASTERS
08 Director Library Services ....Ms. Brenda MINER
37 Financial Aid Director ....Ms. Mary STANDERFER
30 Director Business Outreach ....Ms. LeAnn DILBECK
18 Associate Director Physical Plant ....Mr. Mike BECK
97 Director Adult Basic Education ....Mr. Joel BUSH
15 Director of Human Resources ....Ms. Amy LUDWIG
07 Director of Admissions ....Ms. Wendy MCDANIEL
21 Controller ....Ms. Patricia HALL
26 Dir Marketing/Community Relations ....Ms. LeAnn DILBECK
04 Executive Asst to Chancellor ....Ms. Yanel RIOS
88 Student Union Manager ....Mr. Jason WOOD
09 Coordinator Institutional Research ....Ms. Tammy ODOM
114 Budget Analysis Coordinator ....Ms. Amy LUDWIG
18 Constructions/Grounds Supervisor ....Mr. David DILBECK

*Phillips Community College of the University of Arkansas-DeWitt (D)

1210 Rice Belt Avenue, DeWitt AR 72042
Telephone: (870) 946-3506 Identification: 770174
Accreditation: &HLC

*Phillips Community College of the University of Arkansas-Stuttgart (E)

2807 Hwy 165 South, Stuttgart AR 72160-2408
Telephone: (870) 673-4201 Identification: 770175
Accreditation: &HLC

*University of Arkansas at Monticello College of Technology-Crossett (F)

1326 Highway 52 W, Crossett AR 71635
Telephone: (870) 364-6414 Identification: 770176
Accreditation: &HLC

*University of Arkansas at Monticello College of Technology-McGehee (G)

PO Box 747, McGehee AR 71654
Telephone: (870) 222-5360 Identification: 770177
Accreditation: &HLC

University of Central Arkansas (H)

201 Donaghey Avenue, Conway AR 72035-0001
County: Faulkner FICE Identification: 001092
Unit ID: 106704
Telephone: (501) 450-5000 Carnegie Class: DU-Mod
FAX Number: (501) 450-5003 Calendar System: Semester
URL: uca.edu
Established: 1907 Annual Undergrad Tuition & Fees (In-State): $9,338
Enrollment: 10,335 Coed
Affiliation or Control: State IRS Status: 501(c)3
Highest Offering: Doctorate
Accreditation: HLC, ART, #CAATE, CAEP, CIDA, COPSY, DIETD, DIETI, MUS, NURSE, OT, PTA, SCPSY, SP, THEA

01 President ....Dr. Houston D. DAVIS
05 Provost/Exec VP Academic Affairs ....Dr. Patricia S. POULTER
10 VP Finance/Administration ....Ms. Diane D. NEWTON
32 VP Student Affairs ....Dr. Robin WILLIAMSON
43 General Counsel ....Mr. Warren READNOUR
22 Asc Gen Counsel/Compliance Officer ....Mr. Adam ROSE
26 Director of Media Relations ....Ms. Fredricka SHARKEY
111 VP for University Advancement ....Dr. Mary LACKIE
41 Athletic Director ....Dr. Brad TEAGUE
15 AVP Human Resources & Risk Mgmt ....Ms. Britni ELDER
100 Chief of Staff ....Ms. Amy WHITEHEAD
86 Director Gvt/External Relations ....Mr. Jeremy GILLAM
21 Controller ....Mr. Jeremy BRUNER
108 Assoc Provost Inst Effectiveness ....Dr. Jonathan A. GLENN
20 Associate Provost Academic Success ....Dr. Kurt A. BONIECKI
84 AVP Enrollment Management ....Dr. Kevin P. THOMAS
85 AVP Intl Education/Engagement ....Dr. Phillip BAILEY
58 Dean of Graduate School ....Dr. Angela BARLOW
50 Dean College of Business ....Dr. Michael HARGIS
53 Dean College of Education ....Dr. Victoria GROVES-SCOTT
76 Dean Col Health/Behavioral Science ....Dr. Nancy REESE
49 Dean Col Arts/Humanities/Soc Sci ....Dr. Thomas WILLIAMS
81 Dean Col Natural Sci/Math ....Dr. Steve ADDISON
35 Dean of Students ....Ms. Kelly OWENS
92 Dean of Honors College ....Dr. Patricia SMITH
07 Director of Admissions ....Ms. Courtney BRYANT
08 Library Director ....Mr. R. Dean COVINGTON
06 Registrar ....Ms. Vicky SUMMERS
09 Director Institutional Research ....Ms. Amber L. HALL
13 Chief Information Officer ....Mr. Trevor SEIFERT
37 Director Student Financial Aid ....Ms. Cheryl C. LYONS
36 Dir Career Svcs/Cooperative Educ ....Dr. Kathy CLAYBORN
19 Chief University Police ....Mr. John MERGUIE
38 Director Counseling Center ....Dr. Susan SOBEL
39 AVP Housing & Residence Life ....Dr. Stephanie H. MCBRAYER
29 Director of Alumni Services ....Ms. Alison TAYLOR
116 Director Internal Audits ....Ms. Pamela L. MASSEY
18 AVP Physical Plant ....Mr. Larry D. LAWRENCE
96 Director of Purchasing ....Ms. Cassandra MCCUIEN-SMITH
113 Director Student Accounts ....Ms. Sandra OTT

University of the Ozarks (I)

415 College Avenue, Clarksville AR 72830-2880
County: Johnson FICE Identification: 001094
Unit ID: 107558
Telephone: (479) 979-1000 Carnegie Class: Bac-Diverse
FAX Number: (479) 979-1355 Calendar System: Semester
URL: www.ozarks.edu
Established: 1834 Annual Undergrad Tuition & Fees: $25,950
Enrollment: 836 Coed
Affiliation or Control: Presbyterian Church (U.S.A.) IRS Status: 501(c)3
Highest Offering: Baccalaureate
Accreditation: HLC, CAEP

01 President ....Mr. Richard L. DUNSWORTH
05 Provost ....Vacant
10 VP for Finance & Administration ....Ms. Gloria ARCIA
26 Interim VP Marketing & Enrollment ....Ms. Amy LLOYD
07 Assistant Director of Admission ....Mr. Joseph HUGHES
42 Chaplain ....Rev. Jeremy WILHEMI
06 Registrar ....Ms. Monica FRIZZELL
08 Librarian ....Mr. Stuart P. STELZER
36 Director of Career Services ....Ms. Andrea COOPER
29 Director Alumni Affairs ....Mr. Justin MCCORMICK
41 Athletic Director ....Mr. Jimmy CLARK
27 Dir University/Public Relations ....Mr. Larry A. ISCH
111 VP of Advancement ....Ms. Lori A. MCBEE
88 Director Jones Learning Center ....Ms. Dody PELTS
09 Director of Institutional Research ....Ms. Cara FLINN
13 Director of Information Technology ....Ms. Vickie ALSTON
32 Dean of Students ....Ms. Teri THOMAS
81 Dean Div of Mathematics & Sciences ....Dr. Joel HAGAMAN
79 Dean Div Humanities & Fine Arts ....Dr. David DAILY
15 Human Resources Manager ....Ms. Karen SCHLUTERMAN
19 Director Security/Safety ....Mr. Larry GRAHAM
21 Controller ....Mr. Albert LEDING
18 Chief Facilities/Physical Plant ....Mr. Donny FROST
37 Dir of Student Financial Services ....Ms. Kim MADDOX
30 Director of Development ....Mr. Brian HENDERSON
04 Admin Assistant to the President ....Ms. Connie BOOTY
83 Dean Div of Social Sciences ....Dr. Christina SCOTT
38 Director Student Counseling ....Ms. Kaethe HOEHLING

Williams Baptist University (J)

60 W. Fulbright Avenue, Walnut Ridge AR 72476
County: Lawrence FICE Identification: 001106
Unit ID: 107877
Telephone: (870) 886-6741 Carnegie Class: Bac-A&S
FAX Number: (870) 886-3924 Calendar System: Semester
URL: www.williamsbu.edu
Established: 1941 Annual Undergrad Tuition & Fees: $18,500
Enrollment: 618 Coed
Affiliation or Control: Southern Baptist IRS Status: 501(c)3
Highest Offering: Master's
Accreditation: HLC, CAEPN

01 President ....Dr. Stan NORMAN
05 Provost & EVP Campus Life ....Dr. Marvin SCHOENECKE
111 VP for University Advancement/COO ....Dr. Tim HUDDLESTON
13 VP Creative Services & Technology ....Dr. Brett COOPER
84 AVP for Enrollment Management ....Dr. Andrew WATSON
32 Dean of Students ....Ms. Amber N. GRADY
06 Registrar ....Ms. Tracy HENDERSON
04 Administrative Asst to President ....Ms. Shannon TOLSON
08 Director Library Services ....Mrs. Jennifer MATHIS
37 Director Student Financial Aid ....Dr. Andrew WATSON
124 Director Advising/Retention ....Mrs. Tonya BOLTON
42 AVP Acad Affs/Dir Campus Ministries ....Dr. Rhyne PUTMAN
18 Director Physical Plant ....Mr. Tony CONLEY
113 Bursar ....Mr. Aaron ANDREWS
14 Director Information Technologies ....Mr. Blake MCGINNIS
41 Athletic Director ....Mr. Jeff RIDER

CALIFORNIA

Abraham Lincoln University (K)

100 W Broadway, Suite 600, Glendale CA 91210
County: Los Angeles Identification: 667049
Unit ID: 488031
Telephone: (213) 252-5100 Carnegie Class: Spec-4-yr-Law
FAX Number: N/A Calendar System: Semester
URL: www.alu.edu
Established: 1996 Annual Undergrad Tuition & Fees: $6,400
Enrollment: 265 Coed
Affiliation or Control: Proprietary IRS Status: Proprietary
Highest Offering: First Professional Degree
Accreditation: DEAC

01 President & CEO ....Dr. Leslie GARGIULO
61 Vice President/Dean School of Law ....Ms. Jessica K. PARK
05 Chief Academic Officer ....Dr. Robert ABEL, JR.
11 Chief Operations Officer ....Mr. Donald GARGIULO
20 Academic Program Coordinator ....Mr. Andrew CHO
06 Registrar ....Mr. Mark WILLS
07 Director of Admissions ....Vacant
37 Financial Aid Administrator ....Ms. Kelli Jo MALAGON
13 Director of Technology ....Mr. Michael YAP
108 Assoc Dean Academic Operations ....Ms. Bernadette M. AGATON
32 Student Services Coordinator ....Ms. Kylie O'BRIEN

121 Assoc Dean Academic Success ....Ms. Lydia G. LIBERIO
88 Operations Coordinator ....Ms. Lidby LOPEZ

Academy for Jewish Religion, California (A)

1270 S Alfred Street, PO Box 351297,
Los Angeles CA 90035
County: Los Angeles FICE Identification: 041555
Unit ID: 457271
Telephone: (213) 884-4133 Carnegie Class: Spec-4-yr-Faith
FAX Number: N/A Calendar System: Semester
URL: www.ajrca.edu
Established: 2001 Annual Graduate Tuition & Fees: N/A
Enrollment: 61 Coed
Affiliation or Control: Jewish IRS Status: 501(c)3
Highest Offering: Master's; No Undergraduates
Accreditation: WC

01 President ....Rabbi Mel GOTTLIEB
05 VP/Dean of Chaplaincy School ....Rabbi Rochelle ROBINS
88 Dean of Cantorial School ....Rabbi Sam RADWINE
73 Dean of Rabbinical School ....Rabbi Tal SESSLER
58 Dean of MJS Program ....Cantor Jonathan FRIEDMANN
21 Controller ....Ms. Grace MAKOW
11 Director of Administration ....Ms. Lauren GOLDNER
10 Chief Financial Officer ....Dr. Alvin MARTIN
07 Director of Admissions/Recruitment ....Ms. Robin FEDERMAN
06 Coordinator Registration/Operations ....Ms. Elea FRIEDMAN
36 Director of Internships/Placement ....Rabbi Faith TESSLER
09 Director of Institutional Research ....Cantor Jonathan FRIEDMANN
37 Director Student Financial Aid ....Ms. Lauren GOLDNER

Academy of Art University (B)

79 New Montgomery Street,
San Francisco CA 94105-3410
County: San Francisco FICE Identification: 007531
Unit ID: 108232
Telephone: (415) 274-2200 Carnegie Class: Masters/L
FAX Number: (415) 274-8665 Calendar System: Semester
URL: www.academyart.edu
Established: 1929 Annual Undergrad Tuition & Fees: $24,664
Enrollment: 8,928 Coed
Affiliation or Control: Proprietary IRS Status: Proprietary
Highest Offering: Master's
Accreditation: WC, ART, CIDA

01 President ....Dr. Elisa STEPHENS
05 Chief Academic Officer ....Ms. Sue ROWLEY

Academy of Chinese Culture and Health Sciences (C)

1600 Broadway Street, Suite 200, Oakland CA 94612
County: Alameda FICE Identification: 032883
Unit ID: 108269
Telephone: (510) 763-7787 Carnegie Class: Spec-4-yr-Other Health
FAX Number: (510) 834-8646 Calendar System: Other
URL: www.acchs.edu
Established: 1982 Annual Undergrad Tuition & Fees: N/A
Enrollment: 97 Coed
Affiliation or Control: Independent Non-Profit IRS Status: 501(c)3
Highest Offering: Doctorate; No Lower Division
Accreditation: ACUP

01 Acting President ....Mr. Andres BELLA
03 Vice President ....Dr. Rong Yuan ZHAO
11 Vice President of Administration ....Ms. Julie WANG
05 Director of Education ....Zheng-jie KUO
06 Registrar ....Ms. Jessica DANG

Acupuncture and Integrative Medicine College-Berkeley (D)

2550 Shattuck Avenue, Berkeley CA 94704-2724
County: Alameda FICE Identification: 033274
Unit ID: 384306
Telephone: (510) 666-8248 Carnegie Class: Spec-4-yr-Other Health
FAX Number: (510) 666-0111 Calendar System: Trimester
URL: www.aimc.edu
Established: 1990 Annual Undergrad Tuition & Fees: N/A
Enrollment: 99 Coed
Affiliation or Control: Independent Non-Profit IRS Status: 501(c)3
Highest Offering: Doctorate; No Lower Division
Accreditation: ACUP

01 President ....Mr. Yasuo TANAKA
05 DAIM Director ....Dr. Thomas SIEMANN
17 Acting Clinic Dean ....Mr. Joseph DAVIS
06 Registrar ....Ms. Shirlin DUDONIS
20 Director of Academic Administration ....Ms. Annie CHI-WEI YU
08 Head Librarian ....Ms. Patricia WARD
32 Director of Student Services ....Ms. Robbyn KAWAGUCHI
10 Accounting Director ....Ms. Shirlin DUDONIS

Advanced College (E)

13180 Paramount Boulevard, South Gate CA 90280-7956
County: Los Angeles FICE Identification: 037863
Unit ID: 444343
Telephone: (562) 408-6969 Carnegie Class: Spec 2-yr-Health
FAX Number: (562) 408-0471 Calendar System: Other
URL: www.advancedcollege.edu
Established: 1999 Annual Undergrad Tuition & Fees: N/A
Enrollment: 59 Coed
Affiliation or Control: Proprietary IRS Status: Proprietary
Highest Offering: Associate Degree
Accreditation: COE

01 Chief Executive Officer ....Mr. Amin VOHRA
37 Director Financial Aid ....Mr. Roberto QUINONES
05 Chief Academic Officer ....Mr. Ghazanfar MAHMOOD
11 Vice President ....Mr. Bharpur SINGH
108 Compliance Officer ....Ms. Rumaana R. KHAN
06 Registrar ....Ms. Kaoru ITO

Agape College of Business and Science (F)

1313 P Street, Fresno CA 93721
County: Fresno Identification: 667362
Telephone: (559) 486-1166 Carnegie Class: Not Classified
FAX Number: N/A Calendar System: Quarter
URL: www.acbscollege.org/
Established: 2006 Annual Undergrad Tuition & Fees: N/A
Enrollment: N/A Coed
Affiliation or Control: Independent Non-Profit IRS Status: 501(c)3
Highest Offering: Associate Degree
Accreditation: ACICS

01 CEO/Chief Operating Officer ....Dr. Linda SCOTT
05 Chief Academic Officer ....Dr. Linda SCOTT
20 Dean of Schools ....Ms. Diana PADILLA

Alder Graduate School of Education (G)

2946 Broadway St., Ste B, Redwood City CA 94062
County: San Mateo Identification: 667356
Telephone: (650) 362-3997 Carnegie Class: Not Classified
FAX Number: N/A Calendar System: Semester
URL: aldergse.edu
Established: 2010 Annual Graduate Tuition & Fees: N/A
Enrollment: N/A Coed
Affiliation or Control: Independent Non-Profit IRS Status: 501(c)3
Highest Offering: Master's; No Undergraduates
Accreditation: WC

01 CEO/President ....Heather KIRKPATRICK
11 Chief Operating Officer ....Nimmi CHILAMKURTI
10 Chief Financial Officer ....Erik BROWN
05 Dean ....Shayna SULLIVAN
08 Instructional Research Librarian ....Leila ROD-WELCH
32 Director of Student Services ....Ivan A. IBARRA MORA

Alhambra Medical University (H)

2215 West Mission Road, Suite 280, Alhambra CA 91803
County: Los Angeles Identification: 667052
Unit ID: 487995
Telephone: (626) 289-7719 Carnegie Class: Spec-4-yr-Other Health
FAX Number: (626) 289-8641 Calendar System: Quarter
URL: www.amuedu.com
Established: 2005 Annual Graduate Tuition & Fees: N/A
Enrollment: 154 Coed
Affiliation or Control: Proprietary IRS Status: Proprietary
Highest Offering: Master's; No Undergraduates
Accreditation: ACUP

01 President ....Dr. Eric TUCKMAN
05 Academic Vice President ....Dr. David LEE
23 Director of University Clinic ....Elizabeth JIN
32 Dean of Students ....Megan HAH
07 Director of Admissions ....Qing MA
06 University Registrar ....Xiaoting DING
37 Financial Aid Director ....Luke CHEN

Allan Hancock College (I)

800 S College Drive, Santa Maria CA 93454-6399
County: Santa Barbara FICE Identification: 001111
Unit ID: 108807
Telephone: (805) 922-6966 Carnegie Class: Assoc/HT-Mix Trad/Non
FAX Number: (805) 347-9896 Calendar System: Semester
URL: www.hancockcollege.edu
Established: 1920 Annual Undergrad Tuition & Fees (In-District): $1,188
Enrollment: 10,248 Coed
Affiliation or Control: State/Local IRS Status: 501(c)3
Highest Offering: Associate Degree
Accreditation: WJ

01 Superintendent/President ....Dr. Kevin G. WALTHERS
04 Executive Asst to President ....Ms. Carmen S. CAMACHO
10 Assoc Supt/VP Finance/Admin ....Mr. Eric D. SMITH
05 Assoc Supt/VP Academic Affairs ....Dr. Robert CURRY
32 Assoc Supt/VP Student Services ....Dr. Nohemy ORNELAS
108 Vice Pres Inst Effectiveness ....Dr. Paul MURPHY
15 Director Human Resources ....Mr. Ruben RAMIREZ
35 Dean Student Services ....Ms. Mary DOMINGUEZ
38 Dean Counseling & Matriculation ....Ms. Yvonne TENIENTE
20 Dean Academic Affairs ....Dr. Sean ABEL
20 Dean Academic Affairs ....Dr. Sofia RAMIREZ-GELPI
20 Dean Academic Affairs ....Ms. Margaret LAU
20 Dean Academic Affairs ....Mr. Rick RANTZ
20 Dean Academic Affairs ....Dr. Mary PATRICK
41 Assoc Dean Kines/Rec/Athletics ....Ms. Kim ENSING
88 Assoc Dean Law Enforcement ....Mr. Mitch MCCANN
111 Exec Director College Advancement ....Dr. Jon HOOTEN
88 Artistic Director PCPA ....Mr. Mark BOOHER
13 Dir Information Technology ....Dr. Andy SPECHT
21 Director Business Services ....Ms. Laura BECKER
07 Director Admissions & Records ....Vacant
37 Director Student Financial Aid ....Ms. Mary DOMINGUEZ
26 Dir Public Affairs/Publications ....Ms. Lauren MILBOURNE
78 Dir Cooperative Work Experience ....Mr. Thomas LAMICA
124 Director EOPS & Special Outreach ......Ms. Vanessa DOMINGUEZ
18 Director Plant Services ....Vacant
19 District Police Chief ....Ms. Catherine FARLEY
88 Director Cal-SOAP ....Ms. Diana PEREZ
25 Director Institutional Grants ....Dr. LeeAnne MCNULTY
88 Counselor/Coordinator MESA ....Ms. Christine REED
88 Managing Director PCPA ....Ms. Jennifer SCHWARTZ
88 Dir Environmental Training Center ......Ms. Holly NOLAN-CHAVEZ
88 Director Special Projects ....Ms. Marina WASHBURN
88 Director Children's Center ....Ms. Maria SUAREZ
88 Dir LAP/Stdt Hlth/Veteran's Success ....Dr. Stephanie CROSBY
88 Director Public Safety ....Mr. David WHITHAM
88 Dir Student Activities & Outreach ....Ms. Stephanie ROBB
16 Asst Dir Human Resources ....Ms. Janeal BLUE

*Alliant International University President's Office (J)

1475 66th Street, Emeryville CA 94608
County: San Francisco Identification: 666132
Telephone: (415) 955-2100 Carnegie Class: N/A
FAX Number: (414) 955-2062
URL: www.alliant.edu

01 President ....Mr. Andy VAUGHN
05 Provost/SVP Academic Affairs ....Dr. Tracy HELLER
30 Sr Vice Pres Development/Inclusion ....Dr. Mary OLING-SISAY
11 Sr Vice President of Operations ....Ms. Amy KWIATKOWSKI
10 Interim Chief Financial Officer ....Mr. Christoph WINTER
06 Registrar ....Mr. Paul WELCH
15 Interim Human Resources Director ......Ms. Melissa ROTHMEYER
13 VP/Int Chief Information Officer ....Mr. John JENNINGS
32 Vice President of Student Services ....Ms. Amber ECKERT

*Alliant International University-San Diego (K)

10455 Pomerado Road, San Diego CA 92131-1799
County: San Diego FICE Identification: 011117
Unit ID: 110468
Telephone: (858) 635-4000 Carnegie Class: DU-Mod
FAX Number: (858) 693-8562 Calendar System: Semester
URL: www.alliant.edu
Established: 1952 Annual Undergrad Tuition & Fees: $13,680
Enrollment: 3,429 Coed
Affiliation or Control: Independent Non-Profit IRS Status: 501(c)3
Highest Offering: Doctorate
Accreditation: WC, ACBSP, CLPSY, MFCD

12 Campus Director ....Mr. Jose HERNANDEZ
05 Provost/Vice Pres Academic Affairs ....Dr. Tracy HELLER
32 VP Student Services ....Ms. Amber ECKERT

*Alliant International University-Fresno (L)

5130 E Clinton Way, Fresno CA 93727-2014
Telephone: (559) 456-2777 FICE Identification: 001158
Accreditation: &WC, CLPSY, MFCD

*Alliant International University-Irvine (M)

2855 Michelle Drive, Suite 300, Irvine CA 92606
Telephone: (949) 812-7440 Identification: 666157
Accreditation: &WC, MFCD

*Alliant International University-Los Angeles (N)

1000 S Fremont Avenue, Unit 5,
Alhambra CA 91803-1360
Telephone: (626) 284-2777 FICE Identification: 010013
Accreditation: &WC, CLPSY, MFCD

*Alliant International University-San Francisco (O)

1475 66th Street, Emeryville CA 94608
Telephone: (415) 955-2100 FICE Identification: 011881
Accreditation: &WC, CLPSY, MFCD

AMDA College and Conservatory of the Performing Arts (P)

6305 Yucca Street, Los Angeles CA 90028
County: Los Angeles Identification: 666721
Telephone: (323) 469-3300 Carnegie Class: Not Classified
FAX Number: (323) 469-1448 Calendar System: Semester
URL: www.amda.edu

Established: 1964 Annual Undergrad Tuition & Fees: N/A
Enrollment: N/A Coed
Affiliation or Control: Independent Non-Profit IRS Status: 501(c)3
Highest Offering: Master's
Accreditation: @WC, THEA

01 President/Artistic Director .... David MARTIN
05 Director of Education .... Barry FINKEL
10 Chief Financial Officer .... David SILVERAMN
07 Director Of Admissions .... Joseph SIRIANO
37 Associate Director of Financial Aid .... Jillian DOYLE
20 Director of Education Services .... Cynthia MOJ
32 Director of Student Services .... Debra WALSH

American Academy of Dramatic Arts, Los Angeles Campus (A)

1336 N La Brea Avenue, Hollywood CA 90028-7504
Telephone: (323) 464-2777 FICE Identification: 021069
Accreditation: &M, THEA

† Regional accreditation is carried under the parent institution in New York, NY.

American Career College-Los Angeles (B)

4021 Rosewood Avenue, Los Angeles CA 90004
County: Los Angeles FICE Identification: 022418
Unit ID: 109040
Telephone: (323) 668-7555 Carnegie Class: Spec 2-yr-Health
FAX Number: (322) 953-3654 Calendar System: Other
URL: www.americancareercollege.edu
Established: 1978 Annual Undergrad Tuition & Fees: N/A
Enrollment: 1,751 Coed
Affiliation or Control: Proprietary IRS Status: Proprietary
Highest Offering: Associate Degree
Accreditation: ABHES, SURTEC

01 Executive Director .... Ms. Lani TOWNSEND
05 Director of Education .... Mr. Jamison WALLINGTON

American Career College-Ontario (C)

3130 East Sedona Court, Ontario CA 91764
County: San Bernardino FICE Identification: 039713
Unit ID: 447768
Telephone: (909) 218-3253 Carnegie Class: Spec 2-yr-Health
FAX Number: (909) 218-3340 Calendar System: Other
URL: www.americancareercollege.edu
Established: 2006 Annual Undergrad Tuition & Fees: N/A
Enrollment: 1,435 Coed
Affiliation or Control: Proprietary IRS Status: Proprietary
Highest Offering: Associate Degree
Accreditation: ABHES, COARC

01 Executive Director .... Ms. Rita TOTTEN
05 Director of Education .... Mr. Tom BUSTAMANTE, JR.

American Career College-Orange County (D)

1200 North Magnolia Ave, Anaheim CA 92801
Telephone: (714) 763-9066 Identification: 667073
Accreditation: ABHES, COARC, OTA, PTAA, SURTEC

American Conservatory Theater (E)

415 Geary Street, San Francisco CA 94102
County: San Francisco FICE Identification: 020992
Unit ID: 109086
Telephone: (415) 439-2350 Carnegie Class: Spec-4-yr-Arts
FAX Number: (415) 834-3210 Calendar System: Semester
URL: www.act-sf.org
Established: 1969 Annual Graduate Tuition & Fees: $30,800
Enrollment: 30 Coed
Affiliation or Control: Independent Non-Profit IRS Status: 501(c)3
Highest Offering: Master's; No Undergraduates
Accreditation: WC

01 Executive Director .... Jennifer BIELSTEIN
64 Conservatory Director .... Peter J. KUO
57 Artistic Director .... Pam MACKINNON
05 Director of Academic Affairs .... Jack SHARRAR
10 Finance Director .... Jim SIVORI
30 Director Development .... Caitlin QUINN
37 Director of Financial Aid .... Jerry LOPEZ
26 Int Director Marketing .... Syche PHILLIPS
15 Dir Human Resources/EDI .... Amanda ROCCUZZO

America Evangelical University (F)

1204 W. 163rd Street, Gardena CA 90247
County: Los Angeles Identification: 667090
Unit ID: 490081
Telephone: (323) 643-0301 Carnegie Class: Spec-4-yr-Faith
FAX Number: (323) 643-0302 Calendar System: Semester
URL: www.aeu.edu
Established: 2001 Annual Undergrad Tuition & Fees: $6,250
Enrollment: 165 Coed
Affiliation or Control: Independent Non-Profit IRS Status: 501(c)3
Highest Offering: Doctorate
Accreditation: BI

01 President/CEO .... Dr. Sanghoon LEE
05 Int Vice President for Academics .... Dr. Sanghoon LEE
32 Dean of Stdnts/Spiritual Formation .... Young WOON LEE
45 Director of Planning .... Brian KIM
11 Vice Pres for Administration .... Rev. Sung Ho CHO
20 Academic Dean .... Mark YOON
30 Chief Development Officer .... Vacant
08 Director of Library .... Dr. Duck YOUNG WON
06 Registrar .... Miwon LEE
07 Director of Admissions .... Miwon LEE
37 Director Financial Aid .... Isaac JEON

American Film Institute Conservatory (G)

2021 N Western Avenue, Los Angeles CA 90027-1657
County: Los Angeles FICE Identification: 022220
Unit ID: 108870
Telephone: (323) 856-7600 Carnegie Class: Spec-4-yr-Arts
FAX Number: (323) 467-4578 Calendar System: Semester
URL: www.afi.com
Established: 1969 Annual Graduate Tuition & Fees: N/A
Enrollment: 337 Coed
Affiliation or Control: Independent Non-Profit IRS Status: 501(c)3
Highest Offering: Master's; No Undergraduates
Accreditation: WC

01 Director American Film Institute .... Mr. Bob GAZZALE
05 Dean AFI Conservatory/EVP .... Ms. Susan RUSKIN
10 Chief Financial Officer .... Mr. Lang FREDRICKSON
111 Chief Advancement Officer .... Mr. Tom WEST
15 Chief Resources Officer .... Ms. Roschoune FRANKLIN
26 Chief Communications Officer .... Ms. Juli GOODWIN
11 Vice Dean of Administration .... Ms. Yvette JUSSEAUME
20 Vice Dean of Academic Affairs .... Mr. Tom ENGFER
88 Manager Thesis Production .... Ms. Susan DRETZKA
88 Assoc Dean Productions Svcs .... Ms. Betsy POLLOCK
32 Director Fellow Affairs .... Vacant
57 Artistic Director .... Mr. James L. BROOKS
06 Registrar .... Ms. Carmela CHANEY
37 Financial Aid Director .... Ms. Trina RODLER
08 Librarian .... Mr. Robert VAUGHN
13 Director Information Technology .... Mr. Scott BLY
113 Bursar .... Ms. Jasmin CARROLL

American Graduate University (H)

733 N Dodsworth Avenue, Covina CA 91724-2408
County: Los Angeles Identification: 666982
Telephone: (626) 966-4576 Carnegie Class: Not Classified
FAX Number: (626) 915-1709 Calendar System: Other
URL: www.agu.edu
Established: 1969 Annual Graduate Tuition & Fees: N/A
Enrollment: N/A Coed
Affiliation or Control: Proprietary IRS Status: Proprietary
Highest Offering: Master's; No Undergraduates
Accreditation: DEAC

01 President .... Mr. Paul R. MCDONALD
06 Registrar & Vice President .... Ms. Debbie MCDONALD
05 Director Academic Affairs .... Mr. Paul R. MCDONALD
07 Dir Admissions/Student Achievement .... Ms. Laurie MEJIA
32 Dir Student Svcs/Student Support .... Ms. Rachel RUIZ
26 Director of Marketing .... Mr. Neil GRIFFIN

American Jewish University (I)

15600 Mulholland Drive, Los Angeles CA 90077-1599
County: Los Angeles FICE Identification: 002741
Unit ID: 116846
Telephone: (310) 476-9777 Carnegie Class: Bac-A&S
FAX Number: (310) 471-1278 Calendar System: Semester
URL: www.aju.edu
Established: 1947 Annual Undergrad Tuition & Fees: $32,404
Enrollment: 93 Coed
Affiliation or Control: Independent Non-Profit IRS Status: 501(c)3
Highest Offering: Master's
Accreditation: WC

01 President .... Dr. Jeffrey HERBST
05 Chief Academic Officer .... Dr. Robbie TOTTEN
10 VP Finance/Administration/CFO .... Mr. Adrian BREITFELD
111 Vice Pres Advancement/Chf Dev Ofcr .. Ms. Catherine SCHNEIDER
15 Director of Human Resources .... Ms. Kathy SPIRA

American Medical Sciences Center (J)

225 West Broadway, Ste 115, Glendale CA 91204
County: Los Angeles FICE Identification: 041597
Unit ID: 461263
Telephone: (818) 240-6900 Carnegie Class: Not Classified
FAX Number: (818) 240-6902 Calendar System: Semester
URL: amsc.edu
Established: 1996 Annual Undergrad Tuition & Fees: N/A
Enrollment: 52 Coed
Affiliation or Control: Proprietary IRS Status: Proprietary
Highest Offering: Baccalaureate
Accreditation: ABHES

01 Director .... Mr. Vardan KARAGEZIAN

American University of Armenia (K)

1000 Broadway, Suite 280, Oakland CA 94607
County: Alameda Identification: 666013
Telephone: (510) 925-4282 Carnegie Class: Not Classified
FAX Number: (510) 925-4283 Calendar System: Semester
URL: www.aua.am
Established: 1991 Annual Undergrad Tuition & Fees: N/A
Enrollment: N/A Coed
Affiliation or Control: Independent Non-Profit IRS Status: 501(c)3
Highest Offering: Master's
Accreditation: WC

01 President .... Dr. Karin MARKIDES
05 Interim Provost .... Dr. Brian ELLISON
11 Vice President Operations .... Ashot GHAZARYAN
10 Vice President of Finance .... Gevorg GOYUNYAN
30 VP Development .... Gaiane KHACHATRIAN
06 Associate Registrar .... Chaghig ARZROUNI-CHAHINIAN
26 Public Relations Coordinator .... Vacant
07 Dir Admissions/Recruit/Intl Stdnts .... Arina ZOHRABIAN
09 Institutional Research Manager .... Vacant
08 Head Librarian .... Satenik AVAKIAN
101 Secretary of the Institution/Board .... Caren MEGHREBLIAN
15 Director Personnel Services .... Arina BEKCHIAN
29 Director Alumni Relations .... Narine PETROSYAN
13 Dir Information/Communications Tech .... Berj GATRJYAN
50 Dean of Business and Economics .... Eric VAN GENDEREN
69 Dean of Public Health .... Varduhi PETROSYAN

American University of Health Sciences (L)

1600 E Hill Street, Building #1, Signal Hill CA 90755
County: Los Angeles FICE Identification: 032253
Unit ID: 433004
Telephone: (562) 988-2278 Carnegie Class: Spec-4-yr-Other Health
FAX Number: (562) 988-1791 Calendar System: Quarter
URL: www.auhs.edu
Established: 1994 Annual Undergrad Tuition & Fees: $23,329
Enrollment: 408 Coed
Affiliation or Control: Proprietary IRS Status: Proprietary
Highest Offering: Doctorate
Accreditation: WC, NURSE, @PHAR, TRACS

01 President .... Dr. Caroll RYAN
05 Provost .... Dr. Marilyn UVERO
10 Chief Financial/Business Officer .... Sandy SARGE
06 Registrar .... Alma PINEDA
07 Director of Admissions .... Maria MALOLES
09 Director of Institutional Research .... Thomas VESSELLA
13 Chief Information Technology Office .... Don JAYATHILAKE
32 Chief Student Affairs/Student Life ..... Genevieve (Ivy) JAVALUYAS
08 Librarian .... June KIM
26 Director of Marketing .... Ara ZHANG
04 Admin Assistant to the President .... Cynthia CHAMBERS
37 Director Student Financial Aid .... Venus CRUZ

Anaheim University (M)

1240 S State College Blvd, Ste 110,
Anaheim CA 92806-5152
County: Orange Identification: 666651
Telephone: (714) 772-3330 Carnegie Class: Not Classified
FAX Number: (714) 772-3331 Calendar System: Other
URL: www.anaheim.edu
Established: 1996 Annual Graduate Tuition & Fees: N/A
Enrollment: N/A Coed
Affiliation or Control: Proprietary IRS Status: Proprietary
Highest Offering: Doctorate; No Undergraduates
Accreditation: DEAC

01 President .... Dr. Andrew E. HONEYCUTT
05 Vice President Academic Affairs .... Dr. Rod ELLIS
11 Vice Pres Administrative Affairs .... Ms. Kate STRAUSS
106 Dir Online Learning/Development .... Mr. David BRACEY
06 Registrar .... Ms. Elizabeth MAYS

Angeles College (N)

3440 Wilshire Boulevard, Suite 310,
Los Angeles CA 90010
County: Los Angeles FICE Identification: 041604
Unit ID: 457299
Telephone: (213) 487-2211 Carnegie Class: Spec-4-yr-Other Health
FAX Number: (213) 487-2299 Calendar System: Semester
URL: www.angelescollege.edu
Established: 2004 Annual Undergrad Tuition & Fees: N/A
Enrollment: 303 Coed
Affiliation or Control: Proprietary IRS Status: Proprietary
Highest Offering: Baccalaureate
Accreditation: ABHES, NURSE

01 CEO/School Director .... Ms. Teresa KRAUSE

Angeles College-City of Industry (O)

17595 Almahurst Street, Suite 101-3,
City of Industry CA 91748
Telephone: (626) 965-5566 Identification: 770518
Accreditation: ABHES

Antelope Valley College (A)

3041 W Avenue K, Lancaster CA 93536-5426
County: Los Angeles FICE Identification: 001113
Unit ID: 109350
Telephone: (661) 722-6300 Carnegie Class: Bac/Assoc-Assoc Dom
FAX Number: (661) 722-6333 Calendar System: Semester
URL: www.avc.edu
Established: 1929 Annual Undergrad Tuition & Fees (In-District): $1,124
Enrollment: 12,057 Coed
Affiliation or Control: State/Local IRS Status: 501(c)3
Highest Offering: Baccalaureate
Accreditation: WJ, COARC, RAD

01 President/Superintendent .... Mr. Edward T. KNUDSON
05 VP Academic Affairs .... Ms. Isabelle SABER
32 VP Student Services .... Dr. Erin E. VINES
15 Vice President Human Resources .... Vacant
84 Dean Enrollment Services .... Ms. LaDonna TRIMBLE
35 Dean of Student Life .... Dr. Jill ZIMMERMAN
10 Exec Dir Fiscal/Financial Svcs .... Ms. Sarah MILLER
22 Dir Ofc Students with Disabilities .... Dr. Louis LUCERO
26 Exec Dir Marketing/Public Info .... Ms. Betsy SANCHEZ
18 Exec Director Facilities Services .... Mrs. Dawn MCINTOSH
13 Exec Dir Information Technology .... Mr. Rick SHAW
111 Exec Dir Inst Advance & Foundation .... Ms. Dianne KNIPPEL
09 Director Inst Research & Planning .... Dr. Meeta GOEL
37 Director Financial Aid .... Ms. Nichelle WILLIAMS
76 Dean Health & Safety Science .... Mr. Gregory BORMANN
79 Dean Arts & Humanities .... Ms. Kathryn MITCHELL
83 Dean Soc & Beh Sci/Bus/Comp Stds .... Mr. Duane RUMSEY
38 Dean Counseling & Matriculation .... Ms. Rashitta BROWN-ELIZE
72 Dean Career Technical Education .... Dr. Maria CLINTON
81 Dean of Math/Science & Engineering .... Dr. Christos VALIOTOS

Art Center College of Design (B)

1700 Lida Street, Pasadena CA 91103-1999
County: Los Angeles FICE Identification: 001116
Unit ID: 109651
Telephone: (626) 396-2200 Carnegie Class: Spec-4-yr-Arts
FAX Number: N/A Calendar System: Semester
URL: www.artcenter.edu
Established: 1930 Annual Undergrad Tuition & Fees: $46,486
Enrollment: 2,182 Coed
Affiliation or Control: Independent Non-Profit IRS Status: 501(c)3
Highest Offering: Master's
Accreditation: WC, ART

01 President .... Dr. Lorne M. BUCHMAN
10 Chief Financial & Admin Officer .... Mr. Rich HALUSCHAK
05 Provost .... Ms. Karen HOFMANN
30 Sr Vice Pres Development .... Ms. Emily LASKIN
07 SVP Admissions/Enrollment Mgmt .... Mr. Tom STERN
88 VP Exhibitions/Director ARW Gallery .... Mr. Steve NOWLIN
13 VP Information Technology .... Ms. Theresa ZIX
26 VP Marketing & Communication .... Mr. Jered GOLD
15 Vice Pres Human Resources .... Ms. Lisa M. SANCHEZ
28 Vice President & Diversity Officer .... Dr. Aaron BRUCE
18 VP Facilities/Campus Planning .... Mr. Rollin HOMER
88 VP Professional Dev/Industry Engage .... Ms. Kristine BOWNE
32 Associate Provost Student Affairs .... Mr. Ray QUIROLGICO
08 College Librarian & Managing Dir .... Mr. Mario ASCENCIO
21 Controller .... Ms. Lina DEASE
37 Managing Director Financial Aid .... Ms. Cheryl GILLIES
06 Registrar/Director of Enrollment .... Mr. Greg YAMAMOTO
09 Director of Institutional Research .... Ms. Esmeralda NAVA
20 Director Academic Affairs .... Ms. Leslie JOHNSON
102 Sr Dir Foundation/Govt Relations .... Mr. Darryl MORI
36 Director of Career Development .... Ms. Amanda RAJOTTE
96 Director of Purchasing .... Ms. Monica MATSUO
19 Director Campus Security .... Mr. Jim FINCH
29 Director Alumni Affairs .... Ms. Keiko DOI

Asher College (C)

1215 Howe Street, Suite 101, Sacramento CA 95825
County: Sacramento FICE Identification: 040573
Unit ID: 447777
Telephone: (916) 900-2850 Carnegie Class: Assoc/HVT-High Trad
FAX Number: (916) 649-9700 Calendar System: Other
URL: www.asher.edu
Established: 1998 Annual Undergrad Tuition & Fees: N/A
Enrollment: 748 Coed
Affiliation or Control: Proprietary IRS Status: Proprietary
Highest Offering: Associate Degree
Accreditation: CNCE

01 President .... David VICE
12 Campus Director Sacramento .... Linda FREEMAN
12 Campus Director Las Vegas .... Anne BUZAK
12 Campus Director Dallas .... Josh PAULSEN
88 Director of Compliance .... Kathryn JOHNSON
26 Director of Marketing .... Kim GASPER
37 Director Student Financial Aid .... Elona OWENS

ATA College (D)

1810 Gillespie Way, Suite 104, El Cajon CA 92020-1234
County: San Diego FICE Identification: 035324
Unit ID: 444361
Telephone: (619) 596-2766 Carnegie Class: Spec 2-yr-Tech
FAX Number: (619) 596-4526 Calendar System: Other
URL: www.atacollege.edu
Established: 2000 Annual Undergrad Tuition & Fees: N/A
Enrollment: 83 Coed
Affiliation or Control: Proprietary IRS Status: Proprietary
Highest Offering: Associate Degree
Accreditation: #COE

01 President/CEO .... Henry MARENTES
11 Vice President of Operations .... Valerie PHILLIPS
88 Director of Compliance .... Nick FLEETWOOD
07 Director of Admissions .... Vacant
05 Director of Education .... James R. KYLE
06 Registrar .... Dionne SIMPSON
37 Financial Aid Officer .... Dionne SIMPSON
36 Career & College Advisor .... Ashley BARRETT

ATI College (E)

15141 Whittier Blvd, Ste 420, Whittier CA 90603
County: Los Angeles FICE Identification: 037404
Unit ID: 444325
Telephone: (562) 864-0506 Carnegie Class: Not Classified
FAX Number: (562) 864-7806 Calendar System: Semester
URL: www.ati.edu
Established: 1998 Annual Undergrad Tuition & Fees: N/A
Enrollment: 83 Coed
Affiliation or Control: Proprietary IRS Status: Proprietary
Highest Offering: Baccalaureate
Accreditation: ACCSC

01 CEO/President .... Dr. Katherine CHO

Azusa Pacific University (F)

901 E Alosta Avenue, Azusa CA 91702-7000
County: Los Angeles FICE Identification: 001117
Unit ID: 109785
Telephone: (626) 969-3434 Carnegie Class: DU-Higher
FAX Number: (626) 969-7180 Calendar System: Semester
URL: www.apu.edu
Established: 1899 Annual Undergrad Tuition & Fees: $41,410
Enrollment: 9,006 Coed
Affiliation or Control: Independent Non-Profit IRS Status: 501(c)3
Highest Offering: Doctorate
Accreditation: WC, ART, CAATE, CAEPN, CLPSY, IACBE, MUS, NURSE, PTA, SW, THEOL

01 President .... Dr. Paul W. FERGUSON
05 Provost .... Dr. Rukshan FERNANDO
26 Exec Vice Pres External Affairs .... Mr. David E. BIXBY
32 Vice Pres for Student Affairs .... Dr. Shino SIMONS
10 Vice President Finance/Business/CFO .... Ms. Alanna CAJTHAML
43 General Counsel .... Mr. Chris JENNINGS
13 Vice President Admin/CIO .... Dr. Don DAVIS
84 VP Enrollment Management .... Dr. Heather PETRIDIS
20 Vice Provost Undergraduate Programs .... Dr. Vicky BOWDEN
35 AVP Student Life/Chief Judicial Ofc .... Mr. Willie HAMLETT
27 VP University Relations .... Dr. David PECK
49 Int Dean Col Liberal Arts/Sciences .... Dr. Denise EDWARDS-NEFF
83 Dean School Behav/Applied Sciences .... Dr. Robert WELSH
50 Int Dean School of Business Mgmt .... Dr. Roxanne HELM-STEVENS
53 Dean School of Education .... Dr. Anita HENCK
73 Dean Haggard School of Theology .... Dr. Robert DUKE
64 Dean College of of the Arts/Music .... Dr. Stephen JOHNSON
66 Dean School of Nursing .... Dr. Aja LESH
92 Dean Honors College .... Dr. David WEEKS
15 Vice President Human Resources .... Ms. Paola MARTINEZ
111 VP University Advancement .... Mr. Corbin HOORNBEEK
42 Campus Pastor .... Dr. Woody MOORWOOD
06 Associate Registrar-Undergraduate .... Ms. Mona MIKHAIL
41 Director Athletics .... Mr. Gary PINE
38 Director Counseling Center .... Dr. Bill FIALA
37 AVP for UG Academic Financial Svcs .... Mr. Jon KRIMMEL
36 Director Career Services .... Mr. AJ ZIMMERMAN
28 VP/Chief Diversity Officer .... Dr. Keith E. HALL

Barstow Community College District (G)

2700 Barstow Road, Barstow CA 92311-6699
County: San Bernardino FICE Identification: 001119
Unit ID: 109907
Telephone: (760) 252-2411 Carnegie Class: Assoc/HVT-High Trad
FAX Number: (760) 252-1875 Calendar System: Semester
URL: www.barstow.edu
Established: 1959 Annual Undergrad Tuition & Fees (In-District): $1,104
Enrollment: 2,444 Coed
Affiliation or Control: State/Local IRS Status: 170(c)1
Highest Offering: Associate Degree
Accreditation: WJ

01 Superintendent/President .... Dr. Eva BAGG
04 Exec Assistant to the President .... Ms. Michelle HENDERSON
10 Vice President Admin Services .... Vacant
05 Vice Pres Academic Affairs .... Mr. Tim BOTENGAN
32 Vice Pres Student Services .... Mr. Herbert L. ENGLISH, JR.
15 Vice President of Human Resources .... Ms. Jennifer BURCHETT
20 Dean of Instruction OL & LSS .... Vacant
103 Dean Workforce & Econ Dev .... Ms. Sandi THOMAS
09 Dir Research Dev & Planning .... Ms. Lisa HOLMES
41 Athletic Director .... Mr. Mynor MENDOZA
26 Dir of Public Rels/Comm & Marketing .... Ms. Amanda SIMPSON
18 Director Maintenance & Operations .... Mr. Richard HERNANDEZ
21 Director Fiscal Services .... Ms. Pattie GRANADOS
91 Director of Information Technology .... Mr. Bryce PRUTSOS
84 Dean Enrollment Management & Svcs .... Ms. Heather MINEHART
35 Director Student Life & Dev .... Ms. Joann GARCIA
25 Director CTE Grants .... Mr. James LEE
88 Director Military Programs .... Mr. Robbie EVANS
88 Director Special Pgms & Svcs .... Ms. Christina CALDERON
16 Dir HR Org Dev & Process Imp .... Ms. Kim YOUNG
88 Civic Center & Event Manager .... Mr. Ed WILL
90 Dir Guided Path/Equity & Achvmt .... Ms. Melissa MEADOWS
13 Dir Inst Tech & OL Svcs .... Vacant
91 Dir Learning Support Svcs .... Mr. Bryan ASDEL
88 Dir Adult Educ Consortium .... Ms. Elean RIVERA
51 Dir Adult Educ & Basic Skills .... Mr. Elias VALENCIA
114 Budget Analyst .... Ms. Terri WALKER

Bergin University of Canine Studies (H)

10201 Old Redwood Highway, Penngrove CA 94951
County: Sonoma FICE Identification: 041763
Unit ID: 461643
Telephone: (707) 545-3647 Carnegie Class: Spec-4-yr-Other
FAX Number: N/A Calendar System: Semester
URL: www.berginu.edu
Established: 1991 Annual Undergrad Tuition & Fees: N/A
Enrollment: 51 Coed
Affiliation or Control: Independent Non-Profit IRS Status: 501(c)3
Highest Offering: Master's
Accreditation: ACICS

01 President & Director of Education .... Dr. Bonita M. BERGIN
05 Chief Academic Officer .... Rebecca RICHARDSON
10 Chief Operating Officer .... Denise GREGERSEN
07 Director of Admissions Services .... Connie VAN GUILDER
06 Registrar .... Denise GREGERSEN
18 Facilities/Physical Plant Manager .... Eric JENSEN

Berkeley School of Theology (I)

2606 Dwight Way, Berkeley CA 94704-3097
County: Alameda FICE Identification: 001120
Unit ID: 108861
Telephone: (510) 841-1905 Carnegie Class: Spec-4-yr-Faith
FAX Number: (510) 841-2446 Calendar System: Semester
URL: https://www.bst.edu/
Established: 1871 Annual Graduate Tuition & Fees: N/A
Enrollment: 42 Coed
Affiliation or Control: American Baptist IRS Status: 501(c)3
Highest Offering: Doctorate; No Undergraduates
Accreditation: THEOL

01 President .... Dr. James E. BRENNEMAN
05 VP of Academics/Dean of Faculty .... Dr. LeAnn SNOW FLESHER
10 Vice Pres/Chief Financial Officer .... Ms. Yvonne WATSON
111 Vice Pres Institutional Advancement .... Dr. Lori D. SPEARS
32 Director of Student Services .... Ms. Kat A. CROSWELL
07 Director of Admissions .... Mr. Niger WOODRUFF
06 Registrar .... Ms. Kat A. CROSWELL
04 Executive Asst to President .... Mr. Sam FIELDER

Bethesda University of California (J)

730 N Euclid Street, Anaheim CA 92801-4115
County: Orange FICE Identification: 032663
Unit ID: 110060
Telephone: (714) 517-1945 Carnegie Class: Spec-4-yr-Faith
FAX Number: (714) 683-1440 Calendar System: Semester
URL: www.buc.edu
Established: 1976 Annual Undergrad Tuition & Fees: $6,580
Enrollment: 399 Coed
Affiliation or Control: Independent Non-Profit IRS Status: 501(c)3
Highest Offering: Doctorate
Accreditation: BI, TRACS

01 President .... Dr. Seung Je Jeremiah CHO
10 Vice President/Chief Financial Ofcr .... Dr. Esther CHO
05 Chief Academic Officer .... Dr. Hyo In KIM
32 Chair of Student Affairs .... Prof. Hyun Bo SIM
06 Registrar/Academic Officer .... Ms. Seonhee OH
08 Librarian .... Ms. Rachel HWANG
07 Admissions Officer .... Ms. Jane CHIANG
37 Financial Aid Officer .... Ms. Yae Lee SHIN

Beverly Hills Design Institute (K)

8484 Wilshire Boulevard, Suite 730,
Beverly Hills CA 90211-3235
County: Los Angeles FICE Identification: 041855
Unit ID: 475635
Telephone: (310) 360-8888 Carnegie Class: Spec-4-yr-Arts
FAX Number: (310) 857-6974 Calendar System: Quarter
URL: www.bhdi.edu
Established: 2005 Annual Undergrad Tuition & Fees: $23,220
Enrollment: 14 Coed
Affiliation or Control: Proprietary IRS Status: Proprietary
Highest Offering: Baccalaureate
Accreditation: ACICS

01 CEO ... Sonia ETE
05 Chief Academic Officer ... Douglas SPESERT
10 CFO/COO/Dir HR ... Thierry ETE
07 Director of Admissions/Career Svcs ... Brittany WISE
08 Director of Library ... Frida DICARLO

Biola University (A)

13800 Biola Avenue, La Mirada CA 90639-0001
County: Los Angeles FICE Identification: 001122
Unit ID: 110097
Telephone: (562) 903-6000 Carnegie Class: DU-Mod
FAX Number: (562) 903-4748 Calendar System: Semester
URL: www.biola.edu
Established: 1908 Annual Undergrad Tuition & Fees: $43,512
Enrollment: 5,815 Coed
Affiliation or Control: Independent Non-Profit IRS Status: 501(c)3
Highest Offering: Doctorate
Accreditation: WC, ACBSP, ART, CLPSY, IPSY, MUS, NURSE, SP, THEOL

01 President ... Dr. Barry H. COREY
05 Provost/Sr Vice President ... Dr. Deborah TAYLOR
10 EVP Univ Operations & Finance ... Mr. Michael PIERCE
111 EVP Transformation & Advancement ... Dr. Adam MORRIS
26 VP Enrollment/Marketing & Comms ... Vacant
32 VP Student Development ... Dr. Andre STEPHENS
20 Sr Assoc Provost ... Dr. Clark CAMPBELL
84 Assoc VP University Enrollment ... Vacant
73 Dean Talbot School Theology ... Dr. Clinton E. ARNOLD
83 Dean Rosemead School Psychology ... Dr. Doug DAUGHERTY
88 Dean Cook Sch Intercultural Studies ... Vacant
53 Dean School of Education ... Dr. June HETZEL
50 Dean Crowell School of Business ... Dr. Gary LINDBLAD
81 Dean of Science/Tech & Health ... Dr. Matthew ROUSE
82 Dean Cinema & Media Arts ... Mr. Tom HALLEEN
57 Dean of Fine Arts & Comm ... Dr. Todd GUY
79 Dean of Humanities/Social Sciences ... Dr. Melissa SCHUBERT
97 Dean of Core Curriculum ... Dr. Cherry MCCABE
08 Dean of the Library ... Dr. Gregg GEARY
42 Dean of Spiritual Development ... Dr. Todd PICKETT
06 University Registrar ... Ms. Cassandra HEATH
15 Chief Human Resources Officer ... Dr. Dave GRANT
110 Senior Director of Advancement ... Dr. Richard BEE
21 Assoc VP of Finance ... Mr. Gordon HUMMEL
37 Sr Director Financial Aid ... Vacant
19 Assoc VP/Chief of Campus Safety ... Mr. John O. OJEISEKHOBA
13 Chief Information Officer ... Mr. Steven R. EARLE
36 Dir Career Development & Success ... Ms. Tiffany LEE
41 Sr Director of Athletics ... Dr. Bethany MILLER
40 Manager Bookstore ... Ms. Melissa CASTELLANO
18 Assoc VP of Facility and Aux Ops ... Mr. Brian PHILLIPS
27 Assoc VP of University Marketing ... Mr. Brian MILLER
38 Director Counseling Center ... Dr. Melanie TAYLOR
96 Purchasing Manager ... Mrs. Breanna KLETT
106 Chief Education Technology Officer ... Mrs. Susan ISHII
43 University Legal Counsel ... Ms. Paula T. VICTOR
09 Director of University Analytics ... Vacant
28 Chief Diversity Officer ... Ms. Tamra MALONE
29 Sr Director Alumni ... Vacant
100 Chief of Staff ... Mr. Brian J. SHOOK
108 Assoc Prov of Acad Effectiveness ... Dr. Tamara ANDERSON

The Broad Center for the Management of School Systems (B)

2121 Avenue of the Stars, Ste 3000,
Los Angeles CA 90067
County: Los Angeles Identification: 667228
Telephone: (310) 954-5080 Carnegie Class: Not Classified
FAX Number: N/A Calendar System: Other
URL: www.broadcenter.org
Established: Annual Graduate Tuition & Fees: N/A
Enrollment: N/A Coed
Affiliation or Control: Independent Non-Profit IRS Status: 501(c)3
Highest Offering: Master's; No Undergraduates
Accreditation: WC

01 Executive Director ... Becca BRACY KNIGHT
26 Director Communications/Marketing ... Angela THOMPSON
07 Senior Director Recruitment ... Erin KELLER

Butte College (C)

3536 Butte Campus Drive, Oroville CA 95965-8399
County: Butte FICE Identification: 008073
Unit ID: 110246
Telephone: (530) 895-2511 Carnegie Class: Assoc/HVT-High Trad
FAX Number: (530) 895-2345 Calendar System: Semester
URL: www.butte.edu
Established: 1966 Annual Undergrad Tuition & Fees (In-District): $1,368
Enrollment: 9,335 Coed
Affiliation or Control: State/Local IRS Status: 501(c)3
Highest Offering: Associate Degree
Accreditation: WJ, COARC, EMT

01 Superintendent/President ... Dr. Samia YAQUB
05 Vice Pres Instruction ... Ms. Virginia GULEFF
10 VP for Administration/CBO ... Mr. Andrew SULESKI
45 VP Institutional Effectiveness ... Mr. Gregory STOUP
32 Vice President Student Services ... Mr. Peter GITAU
20 Dean for Instruction ... Ms. Kam BULL
20 Dean for Instruction ... Dr. Carrie MONLUX
20 Dean for Instruction ... Ms. Denise ADAMS
20 Dean for Instruction ... Ms. Teresa DOYLE
37 Director Financial Aid/Vet Svcs ... Ms. Tammera SHINAR
35 Dean Student Services ... Mr. Clinton SLAUGHTER
35 Dean Student Services ... Mr. Brad ZUNIGA
15 Exec Director Human Resources ... Mr. Chris LITTLE
18 Dir Facilities Planning/Management ... Ms. Kim JONES
09 Director of Institutional Research ... Mr. Brian MURPHY
07 Director Admissions/Records ... Ms. Monica BOYES
103 Exec Dir Econ Workforce Development ... Ms. Linda ZORN
111 Director Institutional Advancement ... Ms. Lisa DELABY
41 Director Athletics/Kinesiology ... Mr. Craig RIGSBEE
13 Chief Technology Officer ... Vacant
21 Director Business Services ... Mr. Jim NICHOLAS
38 Coordinator of Counseling ... Ms. Debbie REYNOLDS
109 Director Auxiliary Services ... Mr. Steve DEMAGGIO
22 Director Student Equity ... Ms. Monica BROWN
100 Exec Asst to President & Board ... Ms. Shannon M. MCCOLLUM
108 Director Assessment ... Mr. Eric HOILAND
19 Chief of Police ... Mr. Casey CARLSON

Cabrillo College (D)

6500 Soquel Drive, Aptos CA 95003-3194
County: Santa Cruz FICE Identification: 001124
Unit ID: 110334
Telephone: (831) 479-6100 Carnegie Class: Assoc/HT-High Trad
FAX Number: (831) 479-6425 Calendar System: Semester
URL: www.cabrillo.edu
Established: 1959 Annual Undergrad Tuition & Fees (In-District): $1,270
Enrollment: 9,792 Coed
Affiliation or Control: State/Local IRS Status: 501(c)3
Highest Offering: Associate Degree
Accreditation: WJ, DH, RAD

01 Superintendent/President ... Dr. Matthew WETSTEIN
04 Executive Assistant ... Mrs. Ronnette SMITHCAMP
05 Vice Pres Instruction ... Dr. Paul DE LA CERDA
11 VP Administrative Svcs ... Dr. Bradley OLIN
32 Vice Pres Student Svcs ... Ms. Amy LEHMAN
15 Vice Pres Human Resources ... Ms. Angela HOYT
13 Director Information Technology ... Ms. Spring ANDREWS
07 Director of Admissions/Records ... Mr. David CASTILLO
96 Dir Purchasing/Contracts/Risk Mgmt ... Mr. Michael ROBINS
26 Director Marketing & Communications ... Mrs. Kristin FABOS
10 Director Business Services ... Ms. Delana MILLER
31 Dir Community and Contract Ed ... Mr. Scott JOHNSON
18 Dir Planning & Facilities ... Mr. Jon SALISBURY
25 Dir Grants Development ... Ms. Carrie MULCAIRE
22 Dir Student Equity and Success ... Dr. Kofi AKINJIDE
121 Dir Student Resource and Support ... Ms. Karen REYES
08 Director Library ... Vacant
88 Dir Small Business Development Ctr ... Mr. Brandon NAPOLI
09 Dean Research/Planning/Inst Effect ... Mr. Terrence WILLETT
35 Dean Student Services ... Mrs. Michelle DONOHUE
38 Dean Counseling/Educ Support ... Mrs. Amy LEHMAN
102 Exec Dir Cabrillo Col Foundation ... Mrs. Eileen HILL
40 Bookstore Manager ... Ms. Linda CULLENS
37 Director Financial Aid ... Ms. Tootie TZIMBAL
103 Dean CTE & Workforce Development ... Ms. Gerlinde BRADY
106 Dean Online Education/E-learning ... Mrs. Rachel MAYO

Cal Northern School of Law (E)

1395 Ridgewood Drive, Ste 100, Chico CA 95973
County: Butte Identification: 667331
Telephone: (530) 891-6900 Carnegie Class: Not Classified
FAX Number: (530) 891-3429 Calendar System: Semester
URL: www.calnorthern.edu
Established: 1992 Annual Undergrad Tuition & Fees: N/A
Enrollment: N/A Coed
Affiliation or Control: Proprietary IRS Status: Proprietary
Highest Offering: First Professional Degree
Accreditation: WC

01 Dean and President ... Sandra BOOKS
09 Director of Institutional Research ... Martha WILSON
32 Dean of Students ... Douglas JACOBS

California Arts University (F)

4100 W. Commonwealth Ave #101, Fullerton CA 92833
County: Orange Identification: 667348
Telephone: (714) 222-1110 Carnegie Class: Not Classified
FAX Number: (714) 907-1511 Calendar System: Semester
URL: https://www.cauniv.edu/
Established: Annual Undergrad Tuition & Fees: N/A
Enrollment: N/A Coed
Affiliation or Control: Independent Non-Profit IRS Status: 501(c)3
Highest Offering: Doctorate
Accreditation: TRACS

01 President ... Dr. Sae KWANG CHUNG
05 Academic Dean ... Dr. Don LEE
06 Registrar ... Joy CHUNG
10 Business Manager ... Joel CHUNG
32 Student Dean/MA Program Director ... Dr. Hojun LEE

California Baptist University (G)

8432 Magnolia Avenue, Riverside CA 92504-3297
County: Riverside FICE Identification: 001125
Unit ID: 110361
Telephone: (951) 689-5771 Carnegie Class: Masters/L
FAX Number: N/A Calendar System: Semester
URL: www.calbaptist.edu
Established: 1950 Annual Undergrad Tuition & Fees: $36,340
Enrollment: 11,317 Coed
Affiliation or Control: Southern Baptist IRS Status: 501(c)3
Highest Offering: Doctorate
Accreditation: WC, ACBSP, ARCPA, CAATE, CONST, MUS, NURSE, PH, PTAA, RAD, SP, SW

01 President ... Dr. Ronald L. ELLIS
04 Admin Asst to the President ... Ms. Janie ARMENTROUT
10 VP for Finance & Administration ... Mr. Mark HOWE
05 VP for Academic Affairs/Provost ... Dr. Charles SANDS
84 VP Enrollment & Student Services ... Mr. Kent DACUS
111 VP for University Advancement ... Mr. Paul J. ELDRIDGE
26 VP for Marketing & Communication ... Vacant
43 VP and General Counsel ... Mr. Adam BURTON
106 VP for Online & Prof Studies ... Ms. Pamela DALY
88 VP for Global Initiatives ... Dr. Larry LINAMEN
15 Director of Human Resources ... Ms. Julie FRESQUEZ
18 Director Facilities/Planning Svcs ... Vacant
21 Director of Financial Services ... Mr. Calvin SPARKMAN
21 Director of Accounting ... Ms. Jackie STILWELL
37 Director of Financial Aid ... Mr. Joshua MOREY
40 Director of Campus Store Operations ... Mr. Greg REARDON
88 Director of Conferences & Events ... Mr. Coreylon POLK
27 Director of Marketing ... Mr. Jacob M. ROBERTSON
105 Sr Web Services Manager ... Mr. Daniel AKERS
32 Dean of Students ... Mr. Anthony LAMMONS
07 Dean of Admissions ... Mr. Taylor NEECE
41 Director of Athletics ... Mr. Tyler MARIUCCI
42 Dean Spiritual Life/Campus Pastor ... Mr. John MONTGOMERY
19 Interim Director of Safety Services ... Mr. Mark VANMETER
39 Dir Residence Life & Housing Svcs ... Mr. Daron HUBBERT
36 Sr Director Career Services ... Mr. Mike BISHOP
110 Assoc VP University Advancement ... Vacant
44 Coordinator of Donor Stewardship ... Mr. Jordan MARTINEZ
29 Sr Dir Alumni/Parent/Donor Engage ... Mr. Joshua MOSS
85 Dean of International Programs ... Mr. Bryan DAVIS
13 Assoc VP of Technology ... Dr. Tran HONG
106 Assoc VP Academics Online/Prof Stds ... Dr. Dirk DAVIS
11 Assoc Provost for Administration ... Dr. Tracy WARD
20 Director Faculty Development ... Dr. Ted MURCRAY
108 Assoc Prov for Educ Effectiveness ... Dr. Elizabeth MORRIS
06 University Registrar ... Mr. Rich SIMPSON
08 Director of Library ... Dr. Steve EMERSON
90 Dir of Instructional Technology ... Mr. Keith CASTILLO
121 Dean of Student Success ... Dr. Jeffrey BARNES
09 Director of Institutional Research ... Dr. Brian NIEMEIER
48 Dean College of Architecture ... Mr. Mark A. ROBERSON
49 Dean College of Arts & Sciences ... Dr. Lisa HERNANDEZ
50 Dean School of Business ... Dr. Tim GRAMLING
53 Dean School of Education ... Dr. Robin DUNCAN
54 Dean College of Engineering ... Dr. Phil VAN HAASTER
64 Dean School of Music ... Dr. Joseph BOLIN
66 Dean College of Nursing ... Dr. Karen BRADLEY
73 Dean School of Christian Ministries ... Dr. Chris MORGAN
83 Dean Col Behavioral & Social Sci ... Dr. Jacqueline GUSTAFSON
76 Dean College of Health Science ... Dr. David PEARSON
124 Director of Academic Engagements ... Mr. Garrett ENGLISH
110 Sr Director of Development ... Ms. Kim CUNNINGHAM
30 Director of Development ... Mr. Joshua DUNAJ
30 Director of Development ... Mr. Curt JARBOE
30 Director of Development ... Mr. Eric LANE

California Career College (H)

7003 Owensmouth Avenue, Canoga Park CA 91303
County: Los Angeles FICE Identification: 039745
Unit ID: 447713
Telephone: (818) 710-1310 Carnegie Class: Spec 2-yr-Health
FAX Number: (818) 710-1329 Calendar System: Semester
URL: www.californiacareercollege.edu
Established: 2001 Annual Undergrad Tuition & Fees: N/A
Enrollment: 159 Coed
Affiliation or Control: Proprietary IRS Status: Proprietary
Highest Offering: Associate Degree
Accreditation: ABHES

01 President ... Haleh NAIMI
05 ADN Director ... Susan NAIMI
07 Admissions Coordinator ... Armenohy TELIME

California Christian College (I)

5364 E. Belmont Avenue, Fresno CA 93727
County: Fresno FICE Identification: 008844
Unit ID: 110918
Telephone: (559) 251-4215 Carnegie Class: Spec-4-yr-Faith
FAX Number: (559) 385-2329 Calendar System: Semester
URL: www.calchristiancollege.edu
Established: 1955 Annual Undergrad Tuition & Fees: $10,050
Enrollment: 13 Coed
Affiliation or Control: Free Will Baptist IRS Status: 501(c)3
Highest Offering: Baccalaureate
Accreditation: TRACS

01 President ... Dr. Timothy M. POWELL
05 Vice Pres of Academic Affairs ... Mrs. Joanna FELTS
06 Registrar ... Mrs. Makenzie ZUERCHER
10 Chief Financial Officer ... Mrs. Pam DELL'OLIO

09 Dir Institutional Effectiveness .... Ms. Jennifer WALLEY
08 Head Librarian .... Mrs. Nanne SINGH
37 Student Finance Manager .... Ms. Melinda SCROGGINS
07 Admissions/Recruitment Counselor .... Mr. Manuel MARAVILLA
32 Dean of Students .... Mr. Trent WALLEY
15 Human Resources Manager .... Ms. Pam DELL'OLIO

California Coast University (A)

925 N. Spurgeon Street, Santa Ana CA 92701-3515
County: Orange FICE Identification: 041276
Telephone: (714) 547-9625 Carnegie Class: Not Classified
FAX Number: (714) 547-5777 Calendar System: Other
URL: www.calcoast.edu
Established: 1973 Annual Undergrad Tuition & Fees: N/A
Enrollment: N/A Coed
Affiliation or Control: Proprietary IRS Status: Proprietary
Highest Offering: Doctorate
Accreditation: DEAC

01 President .... Dr. Thomas M. NEAL
03 Executive Vice President .... Ms. Shelly MARQUARDT
32 Vice Pres of Student Affairs/CAO .... Dr. Murl TUCKER
05 Director of Academic Affairs .... Mr. Douglas PETRIKAT
06 Registrar .... Ms. Angela CENINA
13 Dir Management Information Systems .... Ms. Jojo SOBERANO

California College of the Arts (B)

1111 Eighth Street, San Francisco CA 94107-2247
County: San Francisco FICE Identification: 001127
Unit ID: 110370
Telephone: (415) 703-9500 Carnegie Class: Spec-4-yr-Arts
FAX Number: (510) 655-3541 Calendar System: Semester
URL: www.cca.edu
Established: 1907 Annual Undergrad Tuition & Fees: $51,137
Enrollment: 1,612 Coed
Affiliation or Control: Independent Non-Profit IRS Status: 501(c)3
Highest Offering: Master's
Accreditation: WC, ART

01 President .... Mr. Stephen BEAL
05 Provost .... Ms. Tammy Rae CARLAND
10 CFO/Sr VP Finance & Administration .... Mr. Ed PROHASKA
111 Sr Vice President of Advancement .... Ms. Susan AVILA
45 VP of Institutional Planning .... Vacant
84 Vice Pres of Enrollment Svcs .... Mr. Scott CLINE
26 Vice Pres Marketing/Comm Strategy .... Ms. Ann WIENS
32 Vice President Student Affairs .... Mr. George SEDANO
15 Vice President Human Resources .... Vacant
20 Associate Provost .... Ms. Julianne KIRGIS
36 Director Career Development .... Dr. Diana CHAVEZ
06 Registrar .... Ms. Yun CHRISTENSON
37 Interim Director Financial Aid ...Ms. Samantha DURANT DANCEL
29 Sr Mgr Alumni/Parent Engagement .... Ms. Lisa JONAS
13 CIO/Sr VP Operations .... Ms. Mara HANCOCK
07 Director Undergrad Admissions .... Ms. Shiraz CHAVAN
38 Director Student Counseling .... Vacant
88 Director Campus Planning .... Mr. David MECKEL
18 VP for Operations/Capital Projects .... Mr. Leigh SATA
123 Director Graduate Admissions .... Mr. David MURRAY
09 Director of Institutional Research .... Ms. Jennifer JURAS
96 Manager of Purchasing .... Ms. Jackie CRADDOCK
04 Asst to the President & Board .... Ms. Tayler HARRIMAN
08 Assoc VP of Libraries .... Ms. Annemarie HAAR
104 Dir International Programs .... Ms. Jessica MCMILLAN
19 Director Public Safety .... Mr. Abe LEAL
28 Coordinator Diversity & Inclusion .... Ms. Michelle CERAMI
35 Assoc Dir Student Life .... Ms. Janeece HAYES
44 Assistant Annual Giving .... Mr. Nathan BECKA
101 Special Asst & Board Liaison .... Ms. Adriana LOBOVITS
102 Director Leadership Giving .... Ms. Carleigh MCDONALD
105 Dir Content & Creative Strategy .... Ms. Stephanie SMITH
108 Assoc Provost Accreditation & Curr .... Ms. Dominick TRACY
86 Sr Dir of Inst Partnerships .... Ms. Karen WEBER
90 Assoc Dir Academic Computing .... Ms. Torreya CUMMINGS
91 Sr Dir Web & Infrastructure .... Mr. Eli COCHRAN
41 Athletic Director .... Vacant

California College of Music (C)

42 S. Catalina Avenue, Pasadena CA 91106
County: Los Angeles Identification: 667402
Telephone: (626) 577-1751 Carnegie Class: Not Classified
FAX Number: (626) 577-1765 Calendar System: Quarter
URL: www.ccmla.edu
Established: 1999 Annual Undergrad Tuition & Fees: N/A
Enrollment: N/A Coed
Affiliation or Control: Proprietary IRS Status: Proprietary
Highest Offering: Associate Degree
Accreditation: MUS

01 President/CEO .... Michelle T. ISHII

California Health Sciences University (D)

120 N. Clovis Ave, Clovis CA 93612
County: Fresno Identification: 667218
Unit ID: 488572
Telephone: (559) 325-3600 Carnegie Class: Not Classified
FAX Number: (559) 473-1487 Calendar System: Semester
URL: https://chsu.edu/
Established: 2012 Annual Graduate Tuition & Fees: N/A
Enrollment: 243 Coed
Affiliation or Control: Proprietary IRS Status: Proprietary
Highest Offering: Doctorate; No Undergraduates
Accreditation: WC, @OSTEO

01 President .... Florence DUNN
04 Executive Asst to President .... Kathleen HAEBERLE
05 COP Dean/Chief Academic Officer .... Dr. Mark OKAMOTO
09 Dir Inst Assessmnt/Effectiveness/IR .... Vacant
11 VP Operations/Facilities .... Jimmy DUNN
10 Deputy Chief Financial Officer .... Tanya BOHORQUEZ
13 Exec Dir of Info Technology .... John BRIAR
32 Asst Dean of Student Affairs COP .... Dr. Anitha SHENNOY
32 Asst Dean of Student Affairs COM .... Susan ELY
06 Registrar .... Janine DRAGNA
07 Director of Admissions .... Leslie WILLIAMS
26 VP Marketing/Communications .... Richele KLEISER
08 Librarian .... Joanne MUELLENBACH
37 Director Student Financial Aid .... Kevin HOOVER
15 VP of Human Resources .... Carlita ROMERO-BEGLEY
19 Director Security/Safety .... Timothy BOS
25 Director of Sponsored Programs .... Karin CHAO-BUSHOVEN
30 Fund Development Manager .... Chandler JAMESON
101 Secretary of the Institution/Board .... Kathleen HAEBERLE
18 Chief Facilities/Physical Plnt Ofcr .... James DUNN
28 Director of Diversity .... Carlita ROMERO-BEGLEY

California Institute for Human Science (E)

701 Garden View Court, Encinitas CA 92024
County: San Diego Identification: 667342
Telephone: (760) 634-1771 Carnegie Class: Not Classified
FAX Number: N/A Calendar System: Quarter
URL: www.cihs.edu
Established: 1992 Annual Undergrad Tuition & Fees: N/A
Enrollment: N/A Coed
Affiliation or Control: Independent Non-Profit IRS Status: 501(c)3
Highest Offering: Doctorate
Accreditation: @WC

01 President .... Dr. Thomas BROPHY
05 Dean of Academic Affairs .... Dr. William HOWE
07 Dean Admission/Enrollment Planning .... Dr. Joel PILCO
32 Dean of Student Life .... Dr. Nick BUSTOS
10 CFO/Financial Controller/Bursar .... Ms. Tamiko VOROS
31 Director Community Events .... Dr. Ji Hyang PADMA

California Institute of Advanced Management (F)

1000 S. Fremont Avenue, #45, A10, Alhambra CA 91803
County: Los Angeles FICE Identification: 042506
Unit ID: 487649
Telephone: (626) 350-1500 Carnegie Class: Spec-4-yr-Bus
FAX Number: (626) 350-1515 Calendar System: Other
URL: www.ciam.edu
Established: Annual Graduate Tuition & Fees: N/A
Enrollment: 209 Coed
Affiliation or Control: Independent Non-Profit IRS Status: 501(c)3
Highest Offering: Master's; No Undergraduates
Accreditation: WC

01 President/CEO/COO .... Ms. Jennie TA
05 Vice Pres Academic Affairs/Provost .... Dr. Juan GARCIA
10 Chief Financial Officer .... Mr. Salil SHARMA
43 General Counsel .... Mr. Kien TIET
06 Registrar .... Ms. Samantha SCOTT
07 Director of Admissions/Recruitment .... Mr. Stephen JACOB
32 Dir Student Affairs .... Dr. Jinny OH

California Institute of the Arts (G)

24700 McBean Parkway, Valencia CA 91355-2397
County: Los Angeles FICE Identification: 001132
Unit ID: 111081
Telephone: (661) 255-1050 Carnegie Class: Spec-4-yr-Arts
FAX Number: (661) 254-8352 Calendar System: Semester
URL: www.calarts.edu
Established: 1961 Annual Undergrad Tuition & Fees: $53,466
Enrollment: 1,166 Coed
Affiliation or Control: Independent Non-Profit IRS Status: 501(c)3
Highest Offering: Doctorate
Accreditation: WC, DANCE

01 President .... Ravi S. RAJAN
05 Provost/SVP Academic Affairs .... Tracie COSTANTINO
10 Senior VP Finance/CFO .... Vacant
111 Senior VP Advancement .... Vacant
21 Assoc Vice President and Controller .... Karla TALAVERA
15 Assoc Vice Pres Human Resources .... Vacant
18 Assoc VP Facilities .... Jesse SMITH
32 VP Student Experience .... Brian HARLAN
84 VP Enrollment .... Vacant
28 Institute Diversity Officer .... Eva GRAHAM
08 Institute Librarian .... Joan JOCSON-SINGH
57 Dean School of Art .... Thomas LAWSON
64 Dean Herb Alpert School of Music .... David ROSENBOOM
88 Dean School of Critical Studies .... Amanda BEECH
88 Dean Sharon D Lund School of Dance .... Dimitri CHAMBLAS
88 Dean School Film & Video .... Abigail SEVERENCE
88 Dean School of Theater .... Travis PRESTON
26 Executive Director Communications .... Vacant
07 Exec Director Admissions/Enrollment .... Steve CASTLES
37 Director of Financial Aid .... Vacant
29 Director Alumni & Family Engagement .... Harmony FREDERICK
22 Title IX/Dir Cmty Rights/Respons .... Dionne SIMMONS
13 VP Institute Technology/CTO .... Allan CHEN
101 Dir of Governance & Board Relations .... Kiara BROWN
43 Director of Legal Affairs .... Vacant
100 Chief of Staff .... Chebon MARSHALL

California Institute of Arts & Technology (H)

2820 Camino Del Rio South, Ste 100,
San Diego CA 92108
County: San Diego Identification: 667289
Unit ID: 490285
Telephone: (877) 559-3621 Carnegie Class: Not Classified
FAX Number: N/A Calendar System: Other
URL: www.ciat.edu
Established: 2008 Annual Undergrad Tuition & Fees: $15,390
Enrollment: 332 Coed
Affiliation or Control: Proprietary IRS Status: Proprietary
Highest Offering: Associate Degree
Accreditation: CNCE

01 President .... Jamie DOYLE
05 Dean of Education .... Melissa KINGSTON
11 Vice President for Compliance .... Claire PARK
06 Registrar .... Ed BRANCHEAU
07 Director of Admissions .... Kirsten BARRERA
13 IT Manager .... Bashar QOPI

California Institute of Integral Studies (I)

1453 Mission Street, 4th Floor,
San Francisco CA 94103-2557
County: San Francisco FICE Identification: 012154
Unit ID: 110316
Telephone: (415) 575-6100 Carnegie Class: DU-Mod
FAX Number: (415) 575-1264 Calendar System: Semester
URL: www.ciis.edu
Established: 1968 Annual Undergrad Tuition & Fees: N/A
Enrollment: 1,530 Coed
Affiliation or Control: Independent Non-Profit IRS Status: 501(c)3
Highest Offering: Doctorate
Accreditation: WC, ACUP

01 President .... Dr. Judie G. WEXLER
05 Provost .... Dr. Liz BEAVEN
10 Controller .... Ms. Tina O'GRADY
111 Vice President of Advancement .... Ms. Jillian ELLIOT
32 Dean of Students .... Ms. Yunny YIP
100 Chief of Staff .... Dr. Richard BUGGS
20 Associate Provost .... Ms. Michelle ENG
07 Director of Admissions .... Ms. Ellen DURST
06 Registrar .... Mr. Dan GURLER
26 Director of Communications .... Ms. Lisa DENENMARK
37 Financial Aid Coordinator .... Ms. Jennifer GRUCZELAK
18 Associate Director of Operations .... Ms. Monica MUNJAL
04 Administrative Asst to President .... Ms. Susan SORIANO
09 Director of Institutional Research .... Ms. Lael FON
28 Director of Diversity .... Ms. Rachel BRYANT
15 Human Resources Supervisor .... Mr. Robert CROUCH

California Institute of Technology (J)

1200 E California Boulevard, Pasadena CA 91125-0001
County: Los Angeles FICE Identification: 001131
Unit ID: 110404
Telephone: (626) 395-6811 Carnegie Class: DU-Highest
FAX Number: (626) 795-1547 Calendar System: Trimester
URL: www.caltech.edu
Established: 1891 Annual Undergrad Tuition & Fees: $56,862
Enrollment: 2,240 Coed
Affiliation or Control: Independent Non-Profit IRS Status: 501(c)3
Highest Offering: Doctorate
Accreditation: WC

01 President .... Dr. Thomas F. ROSENBAUM
101 Board Secretary .... Ms. Cathy A. LIGHT
05 Provost .... Dr. David A. TIRRELL
88 Vice President/Director JPL .... Dr. Michael WATKINS
10 VP of Admin/Chief Financial Officer .... Ms. Margo STEURBAUT
21 AVP for Finance & Treasurer .... Ms. Sharon E. PATTERSON
111 VP for Advancement & Alumni Rels ..... Mr. Dexter F. BAILEY, JR.
45 VP for Strategy Implementation .... Dr. Diana JERGOVIC
32 Vice President Student Affairs .... Dr. Kevin M. GILMARTIN
43 General Counsel .... Ms. Jennifer T. LUM
04 Exec Asst to the Pres/Asst Sec BOT .... Ms. Carol SCHUIL
28 AVP of DEI & Assessment ..... Dr. Lindsey E. MALCOM-PIQUEUX
20 Vice Provost .... Dr. Cindy A. WEINSTEIN
20 Vice Provost .... Dr. Kaushik BHATTACHARYA
15 Assoc Vice Pres Human Resources .... Ms. Julia M. MCCALLIN
110 Assoc Vice President Development .... Ms. Michelle R. CLARK
112 AVP for Campaigns .... Ms. Diane M. BINNEY
44 Asst VP Engagement & Annual Program .... Ms. Theresa A. DAVIS

86 External Relations Officer .... Mr. Ken HARGREAVES
26 Chief Strat Communications Officer .... Ms. Shayna CHABNER
81 Chair Biology & Biological Engr Div ...... Dr. Richard M. MURRAY
81 Chair Chemistry & Chemical Engr Div .... Dr. Dennis A. DOUGHERTY
54 Chair Engr & Applied Science Div .... Dr. Harry A. ATWATER
65 Chair Geology/Planet Science Div .... Dr. John P. GROTZINGER
79 Chair Humanities/Social Science Div .... Dr. Jean-Laurent ROSENTHAL
81 Chair Physics/Math/Astro Division .... Dr. Fiona HARRISON
06 Registrar .... Ms. Christy SALINAS
84 AVP Stdnt Affs/Enroll/Career Svcs .... Mr. Jarrid WHITNEY
08 University Librarian .... Ms. Kara M. WHATLEY
13 Chief Information Officer .... Mr. Jin CHANG
18 Interim AVP for Facilities .... Mr. John S. ONDERDONK
18 Sr Director Facilities Mgmt .... Mr. Christopher MCALARY
19 Chief of Campus Sec & Parking .... Vacant
16 Exec Director of Human Resources .... Ms. Tara KRUCKEBERG
23 Director Health Services .... Dr. John Y. TSAI
25 Assoc VP of Research Admin .... Dr. Richard P. SELIGMAN
117 Assoc VP Audit Svcs & Inst Comp .... Ms. Pamela D. KOYZIS
29 AVP Alumni Rels/Exec Dir Alum Assn .... Mr. Ralph AMOS
37 Acting Director Financial Aid .... Ms. Malina A. CHANG
109 AVP for Student Affairs Operations .... Mr. Dimitris SAKELLARIOU
35 AVP Stdnt Affs & Residential Exper .... Ms. Felicia HUNT
36 Director Career Development .... Ms. Claire C. RALPH
40 Manager Bookstore .... Ms. Karyn SEIXAS
41 Dir Athletics & Physical Education .... Ms. Betsy MITCHELL
58 Dean of Graduate Studies .... Vacant
85 Assoc Dir International Student Pgm ...... Ms. Laura FLOWER KIM
96 Dir Purchasing & Payment Services .... Ms. Tina LOWENTHAL
102 Director Foundation Relations .... Ms. Nelly KHIDEKEL
104 Dir Fellowshp Advising/Study Abroad ..... Ms. Lauren B. STOLPER
38 Director Counseling Center .... Ms. Jennifer HOWES
09 Sr Institutional Research Analyst .... Dr. Lindsey E. MALCOM-PIQUEUX
39 Director Student Housing .... Ms. Maria A. KATSAS
28 Chief Diversity Officer .... Dr. Cindy A. WEINSTEIN

California Intercontinental University (A)

17310 Red Hill Ave, Ste 200, Irvine CA 92614

County: Orange — Identification: 666670
Unit ID: 485546
Telephone: (866) 687-2258 — Carnegie Class: Spec-4-yr-Bus
FAX Number: (949) 861-9431 — Calendar System: Other
URL: www.caluniversity.edu
Established: 2003 — Annual Undergrad Tuition & Fees: $10,805
Enrollment: 537 — Coed
Affiliation or Control: Proprietary — IRS Status: Proprietary
Highest Offering: Doctorate
Accreditation: DEAC

01 Campus President .... Mr. Richard MADRIGAL
06 Dir Academic Admin/Registrar .... Ms. Gina BORELLI
05 Dean of Academics .... Dr. Robert NEELY
07 Director of Admissions .... Mr. Mike CRUZ
10 Chief Financial/Business Officer .... Ms. Robyn FOURNIER
11 Director of Operations .... Mr. David RODRIGUEZ

California Jazz Conservatory (B)

2087 Addison Street, Berkeley CA 94704

County: Alameda — Identification: 667217
Unit ID: 486488
Telephone: (510) 845-5373 — Carnegie Class: Spec-4-yr-Arts
FAX Number: (510) 841-5373 — Calendar System: Semester
URL: www.cjc.edu
Established: 2009 — Annual Undergrad Tuition & Fees: $21,100
Enrollment: 35 — Coed
Affiliation or Control: Independent Non-Profit — IRS Status: 501(c)3
Highest Offering: Master's
Accreditation: MUS

01 President .... Susan MUSCARELLA
05 Dean of Instruction .... Jeff DENSON
64 Director Jazz School at CJC .... Rob EWING
11 Director of Operation .... Max HODES
08 Head Librarian .... Jayn PETTINGILL
06 Registrar .... Jesse RIMLER
37 Director of Financial Aid .... Karen SHEPHERD
26 Director of Marketing/Public Rels .... Paul FINGEROTE
10 Business Manager .... Bill ARON

California Lutheran University (C)

60 W Olsen Road, Thousand Oaks CA 91360-2787

County: Ventura — FICE Identification: 001133
Unit ID: 110413
Telephone: (805) 492-2411 — Carnegie Class: Masters/L
FAX Number: (805) 493-3513 — Calendar System: Semester
URL: www.callutheran.edu
Established: 1959 — Annual Undergrad Tuition & Fees: $45,982
Enrollment: 4,027 — Coed
Affiliation or Control: Evangelical Lutheran Church In America
IRS Status: 501(c)3
Highest Offering: Doctorate
Accreditation: WC, ACBSP, CLPSY, THEOL

01 President .... Dr. Lori E. VARLOTTA
05 Provost/Vice Pres Academic Affairs .... Dr. Leanne NEILSON
111 Vice Pres University Advancement .. Dr. Regina BIDDINGS-MURO
10 Vice Pres Admin/Finance/Treasurer .... Ms. Karen DAVIS
32 Vice Pres Stdnt Life/Dean of Stdnts .... Ms. Melinda ROPER
84 VP Enrollment Mgmt/Student Success .... Dr. Matthew WARD
13 Chief Information Officer .... Mr. Zareh MARSELIAN
18 Assoc Vice Pres Facilities .... Mr. Ryan VAN OMMEREN
100 Chief of Staff .... Ms. Angela FENTIMAN
49 Dean College Arts & Sciences .... Dr. Jessica LAVARIEGA MONFORTI
53 Dean of School of Education .... Dr. Michael HILLIS
50 Dean of School of Management .... Dr. Gerhard APFELTHALER
83 Dean Grad School of Psychology .... Dr. Rick HOLIGROCKI
15 Asst VP for Human Resources .... Ms. Patricia PARHAM
06 Assoc Prov Academic Svcs/Registrar .... Ms. Maria KOHNKE
42 University Pastor .... Rev. Hazel SALIZAR-DAVIDSON
42 Vice President Mission and Identity .... Rev. Melissa MAXWELL-DOHERTY
41 Director of Athletics .... Dr. Daniel KUNTZ
107 Dean Sch for Profess/Cont Studies .... Dr. Lisa BUONO
36 Director of Career Services .... Ms. Cindy LEWIS
114 Exec Dir Budget/Financial Planning .... Mr. John CARRIGAN
29 Dir Alumni and Family Relations .... Ms. Rachel RONNING LINDGREN
38 Director Counseling Services .... Dr. Elisabeth TURNER
19 Director Security/Safety .... Mr. David HILKE
07 Dean of Undergrad Admissions .... Mr. Michael ELGARICO
09 Assoc Provost Educ Effectiveness .... Dr. Taiwo ANDE
37 Director of Financial Aid .... Mr. Jerry MCKEEN
104 Asst Director Ofc of Educ Abroad .... Ms. Annelise ANDRADE
39 Asst Dean of Stdnts/Dir of Res Life .... Dr. Christine PAUL
23 Director of Health Services .... Ms. Kerri LAUCHNER
101 Sec/Exec Asst of Institution/Board .... Ms. Rian CURLEY
44 Sr Director Annual Giving .... Ms. Michelle SPURGEON

California Miramar University (D)

3550 Camino Del Rio N. Suite 208, San Diego CA 92108

County: San Diego — Identification: 666713
Unit ID: 480781
Telephone: (858) 653-3000 — Carnegie Class: Spec-4-yr-Bus
FAX Number: (858) 653-6786 — Calendar System: Other
URL: www.calmu.edu
Established: 2005 — Annual Undergrad Tuition & Fees: $9,994
Enrollment: 174 — Coed
Affiliation or Control: Proprietary — IRS Status: Proprietary
Highest Offering: Doctorate
Accreditation: DEAC

01 President/CEO .... Bryan WALKER
05 Dean Academic Affairs .... Bijan ZAYER
10 Chief Financial Officer .... Jack THRIFT
07 International Admissions Director .... Carol KULIS
06 Registrar .... Marcelo DIFINI
37 Director Student Financial Aid .... Dune TRINN
41 Athletic Director .... Chris SHADE
13 Chief Information Officer .... Farnaz GORJIAN

California Northstate University (E)

9700 West Taron Dr, Elk Grove CA 95757

County: Sacramento — Identification: 667020
Telephone: (916) 686-7400 — Carnegie Class: Not Classified
FAX Number: (916) 686-8143 — Calendar System: Semester
URL: www.cnsu.edu
Established: 2008 — Annual Undergrad Tuition & Fees: N/A
Enrollment: N/A — Coed
Affiliation or Control: Independent Non-Profit — IRS Status: 501(c)3
Highest Offering: Doctorate
Accreditation: WC, CLPSY, DENT, #MED, PHAR

01 President .... Dr. Alvin CHEUNG
05 VP Academic Affairs .... Dr. Catherine YANG
63 VP Med Affs/Dean Col of Medicine .... Dr. Joseph SILVA
10 VP of Finance/CFO .... Ms. Shoua XIONG
11 VP of University Operations .... Dr. Mike LEE
108 VP of Inst Rsrch/Quality/Assessment .... Dr. Karen MCCLENDON
32 VP for Admissions & Student Service .... Dr. Xiaodong FENG
43 Legal Counsel .... Ms. Dina RAGAB
67 Dean of Pharmacy .... Dr. Xiaodong FENG
08 Director of Library Resources .... Mr. Scott MINOR
06 Registrar .... Ms. Michelle WALKER
07 Asst Dean Admissions/Student Affs .... Dr. Darilyn FALCK
76 Dean of Health Sciences .... Dr. Heather BROWN

California Preparatory College (F)

1250 E. Cooley Drive, Colton CA 92324

County: San Bernardino — Identification: 667398
Telephone: (909) 370-4800 — Carnegie Class: Not Classified
FAX Number: N/A — Calendar System: Semester
URL: www.calprepcollege.com
Established: 2007 — Annual Undergrad Tuition & Fees: N/A
Enrollment: N/A — Coed
Affiliation or Control: Independent Non-Profit — IRS Status: 501(c)3
Highest Offering: Associate Degree
Accreditation: WJ

01 President/CEO .... Gene EDELBACH
05 Academic Vice President .... Dr. Jamie BIRD
32 Assoc Vice Pres for Student Life .... Manual ALAMO, JR.

California Southern University (G)

3330 Harbor Boulevard, Costa Mesa CA 92626

County: Orange — Identification: 666770
Telephone: (800) 477-2254 — Carnegie Class: Not Classified
FAX Number: (714) 480-0834 — Calendar System: Semester
URL: www.calsouthern.edu
Established: 1978 — Annual Undergrad Tuition & Fees: N/A
Enrollment: N/A — Coed
Affiliation or Control: Proprietary — IRS Status: Proprietary
Highest Offering: Doctorate
Accreditation: WC, ACBSP, NURSE

01 President .... Dr. Glenn ROQUEMORE
03 Executive Vice President .... Brett O'ROURKE
100 VP/Chief of Staff .... Amanda STEED
04 Exec Assistant to the President .... Edie STILWELL
15 VP/Chief Human Resources Officer .... Mrs. Perla NGUYEN
05 VP Instruction .... Dr. Bonita NICKLE
10 VP/Chief Financial Officer .... Manila PILLAI
84 VP Enrollment Management .... Sam QASEM
06 Registrar .... Vacant
08 Librarian .... Dr. Bernadette CHANETSA
09 Director of IRAD .... Dr. Chris TSENG
13 IT Director .... Thila MENON
26 Marketing Director .... Colin MAXWELL
50 Dean Business & Management .... Dr. Jim RIEGER
83 Dean Behavioral Sciences .... Vacant
61 Dean Law .... Ellie SHEFI
66 Dept Chair Nursing .... Johanna BRUNER

*The California State University System Office (H)

401 Golden Shore, Long Beach CA 90802-4210

County: Los Angeles — FICE Identification: 001136
Unit ID: 110501
Telephone: (562) 951-4000 — Carnegie Class: N/A
FAX Number: (562) 951-4986
URL: www.calstate.edu

01 Chancellor .... Dr. Joseph I. CASTRO
05 Int Exec VC Acad/Stdnt Affairs .... Dr. Fred E. WOOD
10 Executive Vice Chancellor & CFO .... Mr. Steve RELYEA
15 Vice Chancellor Human Resources .... Ms. Evelyn NAZARIO
111 Vice Chanc Univ Rel/Advancement .... Mr. Larry SALINAS
43 Exec Vice Chanc/General Counsel .... Mr. Andrew JONES
116 Vice Chanc & Chief Audit Officer .... Mr. Vlad MARINESCU
100 Chief of Staff .... Ms. Michelle KISS
26 AVC Strategic Comm/Public Affairs .... Ms. Patti WAID
88 Senior Advisor to Chancellor .... Mr. Jai SOOKPRASERT

*California Polytechnic State University-San Luis Obispo (I)

1 Grand Avenue, San Luis Obispo CA 93407-9000

County: San Luis Obispo — FICE Identification: 001143
Unit ID: 110422
Telephone: (805) 756-1111 — Carnegie Class: Masters/L
FAX Number: (805) 756-5400 — Calendar System: Quarter
URL: www.calpoly.edu
Established: 1901 — Annual Undergrad Tuition & Fees (In-State): $10,071
Enrollment: 22,440 — Coed
Affiliation or Control: State — IRS Status: 501(c)3
Highest Offering: Master's
Accreditation: WC, ART, CAPRT, CONST, DIETD, DIETI, LSAR, MUS, PLNG

02 President .... Dr. Jeffrey D. ARMSTRONG
100 AVP & Chief of Staff .... Ms. Jessica DARIN
05 Provost .... Dr. Cynthia JACKSON-ELMOORE
32 Vice President Student Affairs .... Dr. Keith HUMPHREY
10 Senior Vice Pres Admin & Finance .... Ms. Cynthia VILLA
58 Vice Provost Intl/Grad & Ext Educ .... Vacant
41 Athletic Director .... Mr. Don OBERHELMAN
13 Vice President ITS & CIO .... Mr. Bill BRITTON
88 CEO Cal Poly Corporation .... Mr. Cody VANDORN
46 VP Research & Economic Dev .... Vacant
21 Associate Vice Pres Financial Svcs .... Ms. Angela KRAETSCH
26 Chief Communications Officer .... Mr. Chris MURPHY
18 AVP Fac Mgmt & Development .... Mr. Mike MCCORMICK
39 AVP Stdnt Affs/Exec Dir of UH .... Dr. Jo CAMPBELL
15 Int Exec Dir HR & Acad Personnel .... Dr. Al LIDDICOAT
20 Assoc Vice Provost Acad Affairs .... Dr. Bruno GIBERTI
07 Interim VP Enrollment & Strategy .... Mr. Terrance HARRIS
84 Interim Dir Enrollment Plng & Mgmt ..... Dr. Joseph BORZELLINO
88 Dir Ctr Teaching/Learning & Tech .... Mr. Patrick O'SULLIVAN
29 Assoc VP Alumni Outreach .... Vacant
19 Asst VP Pub Safety/Chf of Police .... Chief George HUGHES
06 University Registrar .... Mr. Cem SUNATA
28 Interim VP Diversity & Inclusion .... Dr. Denise ISOM
22 Director Equal Opp/Title IX Coord .... Ms. Maren HUFTON
23 AVP Health & Well Being .... Dr. Tina HADAWAY-MELLIS
38 Director of Counseling Services .... Dr. Andrea LAWSON
35 ASI Executive Director .... Ms. Michelle CRAWFORD
14 Deputy Chief Information Officer .... Mr. Ryan MATTESON
35 Dean of Students .... Dr. Joy M. PEDERSEN
103 AVP Corp Engagement & Industry .... Mr. Jim DUNNING
47 Dean Agriculture/Food & Env Sci .... Dr. Andrew THULIN
48 Dean Architect/Environmental Design .... Ms. Christine THEODOROPOULOS
50 Dean College of Business .... Dr. Damon FLEMMING
54 Dean College of Engineering .... Dr. Amy FLEISCHER

49 Dean College of Liberal Arts ... Dr. Philip J. WILLIAMS
81 Dean Science & Mathematics ... Dr. Dean WENDT
08 Dean of Library Services ... Ms. Adriana POPESCU
58 Interim Dean of Graduate Educ ... Dr. Elizabeth LOWHAM
53 Director School of Education ... Dr. J. Kevin TAYLOR
96 Asst VP Strat Business Sup Svcs ... Mr. Dru ZACHMEYER
37 Exec Director Fin Aid/Scholarship ... Ms. Gerrie HATTEN
36 Exec Director Career Services ... Ms. Eileen C. BUECHER
09 Exec Director Inst Research ... Mr. Mauricio SAAVEDRA
121 Asst Vice Prov Univ Advising ... Ms. Beth MERRITT MILLER
104 Asst Vice Provost Intl Programs ... Ms. Caroline VANDERKAR
92 Director Honors Program ... Dr. Jasna JOVANOVIC
04 Executive Asst to President ... Ms. Monica MOLINA
25 AVP for Research Admin ... Ms. Amy VELASCO
86 Director of Government Relations ... Mr. Justin WELLNER
108 Director Academic Assessment ... Dr. Michael NGUYEN
108 Dir Stdt Affs Assessment & Rsrch ... Dr. Kevin GRANT
44 Director Cmp Engage & Annual Giving ... Mr. Chris MCBRIDE
30 Interim VP for Univ Development ... Ms. Jessica L. DARIN

*California State Polytechnic University-Pomona (A)

3801 W Temple Avenue, Pomona CA 91768-2557
County: Los Angeles — FICE Identification: 001144
Unit ID: 110529
Telephone: (909) 869-7659 — Carnegie Class: Masters/L
FAX Number: (909) 869-4535 — Calendar System: Semester
URL: www.cpp.edu
Established: 1938 — Annual Undergrad Tuition & Fees (In-State): $7,438
Enrollment: 30,014 — Coed
Affiliation or Control: State — IRS Status: 501(c)3
Highest Offering: Master's
Accreditation: WC, ART, CEA, CIDA, DIETD, DIETI, LSAR, MUS, NAEYC, PLNG, SPAA

02 President ... Dr. Soraya M. COLEY
05 Provost/VP Academic Affairs ... Dr. Sylvia A. ALVA
32 VP Student Affairs ... Ms. Christina GONZALES
111 VP University Advancement ... Mr. Daniel MONTPLAISIR
10 VP Administration and Finance/CFO ... Ms. Ysabel D. TRINIDAD
20 Assoc Provost Academic Planning ... Vacant
18 Sr AVP Facilities Planning & Mgmt ... Mr. Aaron KLEMM
35 AVP & Dean of Students ... Dr. Jonathan GRADY
84 Sr AVP Enrollment Services ... Ms. Jessica M. WAGONER
88 Exec Asst to the Provost ... Ms. Diane R. GONZALEZ
46 AVP Research/Innovation/Econ Dev ... Dr. Craig LAMUNYON
26 Sr AVP for Strategic Communication ... Mr. Amon RAPPAPORT
21 Assoc VP Finance/Admin Svcs ... Mr. Joseph SIMONESCHI
35 Interim AVP Student Affairs ... Dr. Megan M. STANG
31 Pres Assoc Cmty/Campus Partnership ... Dr. Reginald S. BLAYLOCK
13 Vice President IT & CIO ... Mr. John W. MCGUTHRY
09 Exec Dir Inst Rsrch/Plng/Analytics ... Ms. Jeanette G. BAEZ
15 AVP for Employee Org/Dev/Advance ... Ms. Kimberly ALLAIN
100 Chief of Staff ... Ms. Nicole A. HAWKES
04 Director of Administration ... Ms. Francine M. RAMIREZ
47 Interim Dean College of Agriculture ... Dr. Martin SANCHO-MADRIZ
49 Dean Col Letters/Arts/Soc Sci ... Dr. Iris S. LEVINE
50 Dean Col of Business Admin ... Dr. Erik ROLLAND
54 Dean College of Engineering ... Dr. Alison A. BASKI
48 Int Dean Col Environmental Design ... Dr. Lauren W. BRICKER
88 Dean Collins College of Hosp Mgmt ... Dr. Lea R. DOPSON
81 Dean College of Science ... Dr. Alison BASKI
53 Int Dean Col Educ/Integrat Studies ... Dr. Iris S. LEVINE
30 Assoc VP for Development ... Mr. Douglas NELSON
08 Dean University Library ... Ms. Pat HAWTHORNE
41 Director of Athletics ... Mr. Brian R. SWANSON
86 Asst VP for Govt & External Affairs ... Ms. Frances TEVES
19 Interim Chief of Police ... Mr. Scott VANSCOY
88 Exec Dir Acad Rsrch & Acad Resource ... Ms. Lisa M. ROTUNNI
37 Dir Financial Aid/Scholarships ... Ms. Jeannette L. PHILLIPS
06 Registrar ... Mr. Daniel A. PARKS
96 Asst VP & Chief Procurement Officer ... Mr. Steven KIM
88 Asst VP Outreach & Educ Partnernshp ... Mr. Ronald WHITENHILL
106 Int Dean College of Extended Univ ... Dr. Erik ROLLAND
28 Pres Assoc Inclus Excell/Diversity ... Vacant
29 Exec Dir Alumni/External Affairs ... Ms. Melissa RIORDAN
39 Int Exec Dir & Dir Residence Life ... Mr. Reyes LUNA

*California State University-Bakersfield (B)

9001 Stockdale Highway, Bakersfield CA 93311-1022
County: Kern — FICE Identification: 007993
Unit ID: 110486
Telephone: (661) 654-2782 — Carnegie Class: Masters/L
FAX Number: (661) 654-3194 — Calendar System: Semester
URL: www.csub.edu
Established: 1965 — Annual Undergrad Tuition & Fees (In-State): $7,498
Enrollment: 11,745 — Coed
Affiliation or Control: State — IRS Status: 501(c)3
Highest Offering: Doctorate
Accreditation: WC, MUS, NURSE, SPAA, SW

02 President ... Dr. Lynnette ZELEZNY
100 Chief of Staff to the President ... Vacant
04 Admin Asst to the President ... Ms. Valerie STROM
05 Provost/VP Academic Affairs ... Dr. Vernon HARPER
10 Vice Pres Business/Admin Services ... Mr. Thom DAVIS
32 Vice President Student Affairs ... Dr. Thomas WALLACE
111 VP University Advancement ... Mr. Victor MARTIN
20 Associate VP Academic Affairs ... Dr. Debbie BOSCHINI
84 Assoc VP Enrollment Mgmt ... Dr. Dwayne CANTRELL
20 Assoc VP for Academic Programs ... Dr. Debra JACKSON
85 Director of International Students ... Ms. Sonia SILVA
15 AVP Human Res/Administrative Svcs ... Ms. Lori BLODORN
13 AVP & Chief Information Officer ... Mr. Faust GORHAM
88 Spec Asst to Provost Academic Aff ... Ms. Leslie WILLIAMS
21 Controller ... Ms. Queen KING
114 Univ Budget Director ... Ms. Natasha HAYES
18 Asst VP Facilities Planning/Constr ... Mr. Hasit PANCHAL
09 Int Asst VP Inst Rsrch/Plng/Assess ... Ms. Monica MALHOTRA
25 Assoc Vice Pres Grants/Resources ... Dr. Imeh EBONG
124 Assoc VP Student Affairs & Services ... Dr. Markel QUARLES
12 Interim Dean CSUB Antelope Valley ... Dr. Doreen ANDERSON-FACILE
50 Interim Dean Business/Public Admin ... Dr. John STARK
83 Dean Social Sciences/Education ... Dr. James RODRIGUEZ
79 Dean Arts & Humanities ... Dr. Robert FRAKES
81 Int Dean Natural Sciences/Math/Eng ... Dr. Todd MCBRIDE
56 Dean Extended Educ/Global Outreach ... Dr. Mark NOVAK
104 Director International Success ... Ms. Yuri SAKAMAKI
88 Dir of Acad Opers & Support ... Ms. Lisa ZUZARTE
08 Interim Dean University Library ... Ms. Sandra BOZARTH
06 Registrar ... Ms. Jennifer MCCUNE
07 Director Admissions & Records ... Mr. Ben PERLADO
29 Director Alumni Relations ... Ms. Sarah HENDRICK
41 Director Athletics ... Dr. Kenneth (Ziggy) SIEGFRIED
36 Dir for Career Educ/Cmty Engagement ... Ms. Katrina GILMORE
96 Asst VP for Business Services ... Mr. Michael CHAVEZ
38 Counseling Center ... Ms. Janet MILLAR
37 Director Financial Aid ... Mr. Chad MORRIS
92 Director CSUB Honors Program ... Dr. Jacquelyn KEGLEY
39 Director Housing & Residential Life ... Ms. Crystal BECKS
117 Director Safety/Risk/Sustainability ... Mr. Tim RIDLEY
22 Dir Svcs Students w/Disabilities ... Ms. Janice CLAUSEN
23 Assoc Dir Student Health Services ... Ms. Erika DELAMAR
30 Director of Development ... Mr. Heath NIEMEYER
88 Director Outreach Services ... Mr. Darius RIGGINS
19 Chief University Police ... Chief Marty WILLIAMSON
109 Director of Food Services ... Mr. Owen SMITH
18 Manager Facilities Operations ... Mr. Justin BERHOW
40 Bookstore Manager ... Mr. Richard SALCEDO
26 Director of Marketing & Comm ... Dr. Esra HASHEM
28 Chief Diversity Ofcr & Pres Asst ... Ms. Claudia CATOTA
44 Director Annual Giving/Stewardship ... Mr. Daniel RODELA
04 Asst to the President ... Ms. Ana SANTOS
22 Dir Equity/Inclusion/Compliance ... Mr. Marcus BROWN
102 Dir Corporate & Foundation Rels ... Ms. Lourdes NILON
43 University Counsel ... Mr. Ronnie GOMEZ

*California State University Channel Islands (C)

1 University Drive, Camarillo CA 93012-8599
County: Ventura — FICE Identification: 039803
Unit ID: 441937
Telephone: (805) 437-8400 — Carnegie Class: Masters/M
FAX Number: (805) 437-8414 — Calendar System: Semester
URL: www.csuci.edu
Established: 2002 — Annual Undergrad Tuition & Fees (In-District): $6,802
Enrollment: 7,446 — Coed
Affiliation or Control: State/Local — IRS Status: 501(c)3
Highest Offering: Master's
Accreditation: WC, ACBSP, NURSE

02 Interim President ... Dr. Richard YAO
05 Provost ... Dr. Mitch AVILA
32 Interim VP Student Affairs ... Ms. Toni DEBONI
111 VP University Advancement ... Ms. Nichole IPACH
100 Interim Chief of Staff ... Dr. Kaia TOLLEFSON
49 Dean of School of Arts & Sciences ... Dr. Vandana KOHLI
50 Int Dean MVS School of Bus & Econ ... Dr. Susan ANDRZEJEWSKI
84 Associate VP Enrollment Management ... Mr. Hung D. DANG
53 Dean of School of Education ... Dr. Brian SEVIER
25 Director Sponsored Programs ... Mr. Scott PEREZ
104 Assoc VP/Dean International Program ... Dr. Osman OZTURGUT
08 Dean of Library ... Ms. Alicia VIRTUE
88 Chief Academic Budget Officer ... Mr. Kirk R. ENGLAND
20 Assoc VP Academic Programs ... Dr. Jennifer E. PERRY
88 Assoc Vice Provost Innovation ... Ms. Jill LEAFSTEDT
121 Assoc Vice Provost Student Success ... Dr. Amanda M. QUINTERO
88 University Ombuds Officer ... Mr. Mark PATTERSON
38 Director Counseling & Psychological ... Ms. Kirsten G. OLSON
15 Interim Assistant VP Administrative ... Ms. Laurie NICHOLS
86 Sr Dir Community & Govt Relations ... Ms. Celina ZACARIAS
30 Director of University Development ... Mr. Richard S. LEROY
110 Dir Advancement Operations ... Mr. Christopher ABE
88 Dir University Events & Spec Pgms ... Ms. Alisaa BLOUGH
29 Dir Development/Alumni Engagement ... Dr. Amanda CARPENTER
112 Director Planned & Major Gifts ... Ms. Grace G. ROBINSON
44 Dir Annual Giving & Special Gifts ... Ms. Eva C. GOMEZ
19 Chief of Police ... Mr. Michael MORRIS
22 Int Title IX Administrative Sp ... Ms. Renee FUENTES
116 University Internal Auditor ... Ms. Penny MATTHEWS
35 Associate VP & Dean of Students ... Ms. Toni DEBONI
39 AVP Housing/Residential Educ & ASI ... Ms. Cindy DERRICO
88 Exec Dir Admin & Strategic Ops ... Ms. Dorothy R. AYER
06 Associate Registrar ... Ms. Colleen FOREST
07 AVP/Dir of Admissions & Records ... Ms. Ginger REYES
108 Assoc VP for SA/ROISS ... Dr. Charles E. OSIRIS
26 Exec Dir Communication & Marketing ... Ms. Nancy GILL
37 Dir Financial Aid & Scholarships ... Ms. Sunshine GARCIA
18 AVP Facilities Services ... Mr. Thomas M. HUNT
114 University Budget Officer ... Ms. Barbara A. REX
13 Chief Information Officer ... Mr. James AUGUST
88 Director Strategic Operations ... Mr. Nathan E. BOWDEN
04 Presidential Aide ... Ms. Alanna TREJO

*California State University-Chico (D)

400 W First Street, Chico CA 95929-0001
County: Butte — FICE Identification: 001146
Unit ID: 110538
Telephone: (530) 898-6116 — Carnegie Class: Masters/L
FAX Number: (530) 898-6824 — Calendar System: Semester
URL: www.csuchico.edu
Established: 1887 — Annual Undergrad Tuition & Fees (In-State): $7,864
Enrollment: 16,746 — Coed
Affiliation or Control: State — IRS Status: 501(c)3
Highest Offering: Master's
Accreditation: WC, ART, CAPRT, CONST, DIETD, DIETI, JOUR, NAIT, NURSE, SP, SPAA, SW, THEA

02 President ... Dr. Gayle E. HUTCHINSON
100 Chief of Staff ... Dr. Brooke F. BANKS
05 Provost/Vice Pres Academic Affairs ... Dr. Debra S. LARSON
10 Assoc Vice Pres Financial Services ... Ms. Stacie CORONA
32 AVP Student Affairs/Dean Students ... Ms. Sandy K. PARSONS
111 Vice Pres University Advancement ... Mr. Ahmad BOURA
45 Vice Prov Planning/Res Allocation ... Vacant
46 Assoc Vice Pres Research ... Vacant
84 Assoc Vice Pres Enroll Management ... Mr. Jerry P. ROSS
13 Acting Vice Prov Info Resources/CIO ... Mr. Andy MILLER
21 Assoc VP Financial Svcs/Univ Budget ... Ms. Stacie CORONA
15 Assoc Vice Pres Human Resources ... Ms. Sheryl WOODWARD
16 Int Assoc Vice Pres OAPL ... Ms. Evanne O'DONNELL
47 Dean College of Agriculture ... Dr. John A. UNRUH
51 Dean Continuing Education ... Ms. Clare VAN NESS
72 Dean Col Engr/Comp Sci/Const Mgmt ... Ms. Melody STAPLETON
83 Dean Col Behavior & Social Sci ... Dr. Eddie VELA
50 Dean College of Business ... Mr. Terence LAU
79 Int Dean College Humanities ... Ms. Tracy BUTTS
81 Dean College Natural Sciences ... Dr. David M. HASSENZAHL
60 Dean Coll Communication & Educ ... Dr. Angela TRETHEWEY
20 Dean Undergraduate Education ... Ms. Kate MCCARTHY
58 Dean Graduate Studies ... Dr. Sharon A. BARRIOS
08 Dean Library ... Dr. Patrick A. NEWELL
26 Director Univ Public Engagement ... Mr. Stephen B. CUMMINS
29 Director Alumni Relations ... Mr. Jay R. FRIEDMAN
09 Interim Director Inst Research ... Mr. Thomas C. ROSENOW
06 University Registrar ... Mr. Michael C. DILLS-ALLEN
07 Director of Admissions ... Vacant
36 Director Career Center ... Ms. Megan ODOM
37 Director Financial Aid/Scholarships ... Mr. Dan REED
18 Assoc VP Facilities Mgmt Svcs ... Mr. Michael A. GUZZI
96 Director of Procurement ... Ms. Sara RUMIANO
92 Director Univ Honors Program ... Mr. John MAHONEY
35 Int Dir Stdnt Conduct/Rights/Respon ... Ms. Emily N. PEART
28 Director of Diversity and Inclusion ... Mr. Tray ROBINSON
04 Executive Asst to President ... Mr. Michael JOHNSTON
104 Int Assoc VP International Educ ... Ms. Sara TRECHTER
25 Int CEO Research Foundation ... Mr. David M. HASSENZAHL
109 Exec Director Associated Students ... Mr. David BUCKLEY
23 Director Student Health Center ... Ms. Juanita D. MOTTLEY
38 Assoc Director Counseling ... Dr. Juni BANERJEE-STEVENS
39 Director University Housing ... Ms. Connie HUYCK
41 Athletic Director ... Ms. Anita S. BARKER
53 Director School of Education ... Ms. Rebecca JUSTESON
19 Chief of Police ... Mr. John REID
22 Director of Labor Relations ... Mr. Dylan SAAKE
30 Director of Development ... Ms. Daria BOOTH
43 University Counsel ... Ms. Sasha DANNA
44 Asst Director Annual Giving ... Mr. Allen K. LUNDE

*California State University-Dominguez Hills (E)

1000 E Victoria Street, Carson CA 90747-0005
County: Los Angeles — FICE Identification: 001141
Unit ID: 110547
Telephone: (310) 243-3696 — Carnegie Class: Masters/L
FAX Number: N/A — Calendar System: Semester
URL: www.csudh.edu
Established: 1960 — Annual Undergrad Tuition & Fees (In-State): $6,941
Enrollment: 18,687 — Coed
Affiliation or Control: State — IRS Status: 501(c)3
Highest Offering: Master's
Accreditation: WC, MT, MUS, NURSE, OPE, OT, SPAA, SW, THEA

02 President ... Dr. Thomas A. PARHAM
05 Provost/VP Academic Affairs ... Dr. Michael SPAGNA
10 VP Administration/Finance ... Ms. Deborah WALLACE
32 Vice President Student Affairs ... Dr. William FRANKLIN
111 VP Univ Advancement ... Mr. Scott BARRETT
13 VP/Chief Information Officer ... Mr. Chris MANRIQUEZ
35 AVP Stdnt Life/Dean of Stdnts ... Mr. Matthew SMITH
84 AVP Enrollment Management ... Dr. Deborah BRANDON
100 Chief of Staff ... Ms. Deborah ROBERSON
15 Int AVP Human Resources ... Ms. Monica PONCE
07 Interim Director of Admissions ... Ms. Christina RIOS
37 Associate Dir of Financial Aid ... Ms. Angela PROVENCIO
06 University Registrar ... Mr. John HILL
04 Senior Exec Asst & Operations Admin ... Ms. Susan SANDERS
41 Athletic Director ... Ms. Dena FREEMAN-PATTON

*California State University-East Bay (A)

25800 Carlos Bee Boulevard, Hayward CA 94542-3001
County: Alameda FICE Identification: 001138
Unit ID: 110574
Telephone: (510) 885-3000 Carnegie Class: Masters/L
FAX Number: N/A Calendar System: Semester
URL: www.csueastbay.edu
Established: 1957 Annual Undergrad Tuition & Fees (In-State): $6,890
Enrollment: 16,253 Coed
Affiliation or Control: State IRS Status: 501(c)3
Highest Offering: Doctorate
Accreditation: WC, MUS, NURSE, SP, SW

02 President .... Dr. Cathy SANDEEN
05 Provost/VP Academic Affairs .... Dr. Kimberly GREER
10 Vice Pres Admin & Finance .... Ms. Debbie CHAW
111 Vice President Univ Advancement .... Mr. William JOHNSON
32 Vice Pres Student Affairs .... Dr. Suzanne ESPINOZA
15 AVP Human Resources/Payroll Svcs .... Mr. Andre JOHNSON
84 Interim AVP Enrollment Management .... Ms. Angela SCHNEIDER
18 AVP Facilities Devel & Operations .... Ms. Winnie KWOFIE
28 University Diversity Officer .... Ms. Kimberly BAKER-FLOWERS
100 Chief of Staff .... Mr. Derek AITKEN
49 Dean Col of Ltrs/Arts/Soc Sci .... Dr. Wendy NG
50 Interim Dean Col of Business/Econ .... Dr. Nancy MANGOLD
53 Dean Col of Educ/Allied Stds .... Dr. Robert WILLIAMS
81 Dean College of Science .... Dr. Jason SINGLEY
08 Dean of Libraries .... Dr. John WENZLER
13 CIO .... Dr. Jake HORNSBY
06 Interim Registrar .... Ms. Karen MUCCI
19 Chief University Police Department .... Mr. Mark FLORES
37 Director Student Financial Aid .... Ms. Sonia JETHANI
39 Dir Student Housing/Resident Life .... Mr. Mark ALMEIDA
41 Athletic Director .... Vacant
43 Director Legal Services .... Ms. Shawna MCKEEVER
96 Director Procurement Services .... Mr. Jon MEWIN

*California State University-Fresno (B)

5200 N. Barton Avenue, Fresno CA 93740-8027
County: Fresno FICE Identification: 001147
Unit ID: 110556
Telephone: (559) 278-4240 Carnegie Class: DU-Mod
FAX Number: (559) 278-4715 Calendar System: Semester
URL: www.csufresno.edu
Established: 1911 Annual Undergrad Tuition & Fees (In-State): $6,643
Enrollment: 25,497 Coed
Affiliation or Control: State IRS Status: 501(c)3
Highest Offering: Doctorate
Accreditation: WC, ART, CACREP, CAEPN, CAPRT, CIDA, CONST, DIETD, DIETI, MUS, NAIT, NURSE, PH, PTA, SP, SPAA, SW, THEA

02 President .... Dr. Saul JIMENEZ-SANDOVAL
05 Provost/VP Academic Affairs .... Dr. Xuanning FU
10 VP Administration/CFO .... Dr. Deborah ADISHIAN-ASTONE
111 Vice Pres University Advancement .... Ms. Paula CASTADIO
32 VP Student Affs/Enroll Mgmt .... Dr. Carolyn COON
100 Chief of Staff .... Ms. Diana RALLS
43 General Counsel .... Mr. Darryl HAMM
26 Int Dir University Communications .... Ms. Shirley ARMBRUSTER
09 Int Dir Institutional Effectiveness .... Dr. Matthew ZIVOT
15 AVP for Human Resources .... Ms. Marylou MENDOZA-MILLER
30 Assoc VP University Development .... Ms. Caty PEREZ
18 Associate Vice President Facilities .... Ms. Tinnah MEDINA
84 Assoc Vice Pres Enrollment Mgmt .... Ms. Malisa LEE
13 Chief Information Officer .... Vacant
51 Dean/AVP Continuing/Global Educ .... Dr. Scott MOORE
47 Int Dean Agricultural Science/Tech .... Dr. Dennis L. NEF
79 Int Dean of Arts & Humanities .... Dr. Honora CHAPMAN
50 Int Dean Craig School of Business .... Dr. Julie OLSON-BUCHANAN
53 Dean of Kremen School of Education .... Dr. Randy YERRICK
54 Dean of Engineering .... Dr. Ramakrishna NUNNA
76 Dean of Health/Human Services .... Dr. Denise SEABERT
83 Int Dean of Social Sciences .... Dr. Jeffrey CUMMINS
81 Dean of Science & Mathematics .... Dr. Christopher G. MEYER
08 Dean of Library Services .... Ms. Delritta HORNBUCKLE
58 Dean Research/Graduate Studies .... Dr. James MARSHALL
86 Exec Dir Governmental Relations .... Vacant
23 AVP of Student Health .... Dr. Janell MORILLO
19 Chief Police .... Mr. James WATSON
41 Director of Athletics .... Mr. Terrance TUMEY
37 Director of Financial Aid .... Ms. Kelly RUSSELL
29 Executive Director Alumni Relations .... Ms. Jacquelyn GLASENER
36 Int Dir Career Development Center .... Ms. Mary WILLIS
39 Director Univ Courtyard (Housing) .... Ms. Erin BOELE
96 Dir Procurement & Support Services .... Mr. Brian COTHAM
07 Director of Admissions/Recruitment .... Mr. Phong YANG
35 Assoc Dean Student Involvement .... Mr. Colin STEWART
40 Bookstore Director .... Mr. Curt PARKINSON
06 Registrar .... Ms. Laura YAGER
44 Director Annual Giving .... Ms. Patricia O'CONNOR
90 Director Academic Computing .... Dr. Brent AUERNHEIMER
38 Director Student Counseling .... Dr. Malia SHERMAN

*California State University-Fullerton (C)

PO Box 34080, 800 N State Col Blvd, Fullerton CA 92831-3547
County: Orange FICE Identification: 001137
Unit ID: 110565
Telephone: (657) 278-2011 Carnegie Class: Masters/L
FAX Number: (657) 278-2649 Calendar System: Semester
URL: www.fullerton.edu
Established: 1957 Annual Undergrad Tuition & Fees (In-State): $6,953
Enrollment: 42,051 Coed
Affiliation or Control: State IRS Status: 501(c)3
Highest Offering: Doctorate
Accreditation: WC, ANEST, ART, CAATE, CACREP, CAEPN, CSHSE, DANCE, IPSY, JOUR, MIDWF, MUS, NURSE, PH, SP, SPAA, SW, THEA

02 President .... Mr. Framroze (Fram) VIRJEE
100 Chief of Staff .... Ms. Danielle GARCIA
05 Provost & VP Academic Affairs .... Dr. Carolyn THOMAS
10 VP Admin & Finance/CFO .... Mr. Ron COLEY
32 Vice President of Student Affairs .... Dr. Tonantzin OSEGUERA
111 VP University Advancement .... Mr. Greg SAKS
13 VP Info Tech/Chief Info Ofcr .... Mr. Amir DABIRIAN
15 VP of HR/Diversity & Inclusion .... Dr. David FORGUES
88 VP of Budget for Student Affairs .... Mr. Robert SCIALDONE
16 COO HR/Diversity & Inclusion .... Ms. Tara GARCIA
43 University Counsel .... Ms. Catherine BARRAD
110 Assoc VP University Advancement .... Mr. Todd FRANDSEN
35 AVP Student Affairs .... Dr. Martha ENCISO
35 AVP Student Affairs .... Dr. Elizabeth ZAVALA-ACEVEZ
58 AVP Academic Programs .... Dr. Mark FILOWITZ
26 AVP Strategic Communications .... Ms. Ellen TREANOR
121 AVP Student Success .... Vacant
28 AVP Diversity/Inclusion/Equity Pgms .... Mrs. Bobbie PORTER
25 AVP Research and Sponsored Projects .... Dr. Binod TIWARI
12 AVP South County Ops/Initiatives .... Dr. Steve WALK
86 AVP Govt/ Community Relations .... Ms. Elva RUBALCAVA
16 AVP Human Resource Services .... Ms. Phenicia MCCULLOUGH
45 AVP for Resource Planning/ Budget .... Ms. Laleh GRAYLEE
88 Chief of Operations Stdnt Affs .... Ms. Chalea FORGUES
18 AVP Capital Planning/Fac Mgt .... Dr. Ali IZADIAN
29 AVP Alumni Relations .... Mr. Bill COLE
109 Exec Dir/CEO Auxiliary Svcs Corp .... Mr. Chuck KISSEL
08 Dean of the Library .... Dr. Emily BONNEY
07 Director of Admissions .... Vacant
36 Director Career Center .... Ms. Jennifer MOJARRO
40 Director Titan Shops .... Ms. Kimberly BALL
19 Chief University Police .... Mr. Raymund AGUIRRE
37 Int Director Financial Aid .... Ms. Jessica BARCO
41 Director of Athletics .... Mr. James DONOVAN
96 Sr Director Contracts & Procurement .... Mr. Nelson NAGAI
35 Dean of Students .... Dr. Vincent VIGIL
94 Director Women's Center/Re-Entry .... Dr. Alyssa AVILA
88 Director Educational Partnerships .... Ms. Adriana BADILLO
39 Director Housing .... Mr. Larry MARTIN
89 Dir Univ Outreach/New Stdnt Pgm .... Ms. Colleen A. MCDONOUGH
88 Dir Athletic Academic Services .... Ms. Meredith BASIL
88 Dir Center for Internship/Com Eng .... Ms. Dawn MACY
88 Dir Student Academic Services .... Dr. Rochelle WOODS
88 Dir Veteran Student Services .... Mr. Cameron COOK
38 Dir Counseling/Psych Svcs .... Mrs. Jaime SHEEHAN
14 AVP IT/Infrastructure Services .... Mr. Berhanu TADESSE
90 AVP IT/Academic Technology Svcs .... Mr. Willie PENG
51 AVP Extension/International Pgms .... Mr. Joe SHAPIRO
79 Dean Humanities/Social Sciences .... Dr. Sheryl FONTAINE
81 Dean Natural Sciences & Math .... Dr. Marie JOHNSON
50 Dean Mihaylo Col Business/Econ .... Mr. Sridhar SUNDARAM
83 Dean Health/Human Development .... Dr. Cindy GREENBERG
57 Dean College of the Arts .... Mr. Dale MERRILL
53 Dean College of Education .... Dr. Lisa KIRTMAN
54 Dean Col Engineering & Comp Sci .... Dr. Susamma BARUA
60 Dean College of Communications .... Dr. Bey-Ling SHA
22 Title IX Coordinator .... Ms. Sarah BAUER
88 ASI Executive Director .... Dr. Dave EDWARDS
117 Executive Director Risk Mgmt .... Mr. Weili LU
88 Exec Dir Labor/Employee Relations .... Ms. Michelle TAPPER
88 University Controller .... Mr. Steven YIM
114 Dir of Acct Services & Fin Report .... Ms. Lynn GANAC
88 Director of Accounts Payable .... Ms. Mary Ann TORRES
113 Dir of Student Financial Services .... Ms. Pearl BOELTER
18 Director of Physical Plant .... Mr. Leonardo LOPEZ
88 Director of Construction .... Mr. Sarabdayal SINGH
88 Director of Planning and Design .... Mr. Emil ZORDILLA
88 Dir of Parking and Transportation .... Ms. Kristen JASKO
116 Dir of Audit Svcs & Coordination .... Ms. Cindy MERIDA
09 AVP Institutional Effectiveness .... Dr. Su SWARAT
20 COO Academic Affairs .... Ms. Erinn BANKS
88 Exec Dir Academic Fin & Space Mgmt .... Ms. Alyssa ADAMSON
88 AVP Faculty Support Services .... Dr. Kristin STANG
04 Presidential Assistant .... Mrs. Sandra QUINTERO
06 Registrar .... Mr. Rob BODEEN
102 Director Foundation/Corporate Rels .... Ms. Lauren SIEVEN
104 Director Study Abroad .... Mr. Jack HOBSON
105 Director Web Services .... Mr. Mishu VU
106 Dir of Online Education/E-learning .... Ms. Shelli WYNANTS
30 Director of Development .... Mr. Todd FRANDSEN
112 Director Planned Giving .... Mr. Hart ROUSSEL

*California State University-Long Beach (D)

1250 Bellflower Boulevard, Long Beach CA 90840
County: Los Angeles FICE Identification: 001139
Unit ID: 110583
Telephone: (562) 985-4111 Carnegie Class: Masters/L
FAX Number: (562) 985-5419 Calendar System: Semester
URL: www.csulb.edu
Established: 1949 Annual Undergrad Tuition & Fees (In-State): $6,834
Enrollment: 40,069 Coed
Affiliation or Control: State IRS Status: 501(c)3
Highest Offering: Doctorate
Accreditation: WC, AAFCS, ART, CAATE, CAPRT, CEA, CONST, DANCE, DIETD, DIETI, HSA, IPSY, JOUR, MUS, NURSE, PH, PTA, SP, SPAA, SW, THEA

02 President .... Dr. Jane C. CONOLEY
05 Provost/Sr Vice Pres Academic Affs .... Dr. Karyn SCISSUM GUNN
11 Vice Pres Administration/Finance .... Mr. Scott APEL
13 VP/Chief Information Officer .... Dr. Min YAO
32 VP Student Affairs .... Dr. Beth LESEN
30 Vice Pres Univ Rels/Development .... Ms. Michele CESCA
100 Interim Chief of Staff .... Dr. Mark WILEY
10 Assoc VP Financial Management .... Ms. Tracey RICHARDSON
20 Assoc VP Undergraduate Studies .... Dr. Kerry JOHNSON
35 Assoc Vice Pres Student Affairs .... Dr. Mary Ann TAKEMOTO
82 AVP/Dean College Prof & Intl Educ .... Dr. Jeet JOSHEE
18 AVP Physical Plng/Facilities Mgt .... Mr. Tony MALAGRINO
58 Vice Provost/Dean Grad Studies .... Dr. Jody CORMACK
20 Vice Provost Academic Planning .... Dr. Dhushy SATHIANATHAN
46 Assoc Vice Pres University Research .... Dr. Simon KIM
15 AVP Human Resource Mgmt .... Ms. Nancy TORRES
91 Assoc VP Academic Technology .... Dr. Shariq AHMED
09 Director Institutional Research .... Dr. Mahmoud ALBAWANEH
84 Asst VP Enrollment Services .... Ms. Donna GREEN
14 Assoc VP Information Technology .... Ms. Janet FOSTER
76 Dean College Health/Human Svcs .... Dr. Monica LOUNSBERY
50 Dean College of Business .... Dr. Michael SOLT
53 Dean College of Education .... Dr. Shireen PAVRI
54 Dean College of Engineering .... Dr. Jinny RHEE
57 Dean College of the Arts .... Dr. Robin BARGAR
81 Dean College Natural Sciences/Math .... Dr. Curtis BENNETT
49 Dean College of Liberal Arts .... Dr. David WALLACE
51 Dean College Continuing/Prof Ed .... Dr. Jeet JOSHEE
08 Dean Library .... Mr. Roman KOCHAN
06 University Registrar .... Ms. Donna GREEN
39 Executive Dir Housing & Res Life .... Mr. Corry COLONNA
16 Dir Staff Human Resources .... Mr. Neil IACONO
41 Director Athletics .... Mr. Andy FEE
07 Director of Admissions .... Mr. Andrew WRIGHT
36 Dir Career Development Ctr .... Ms. Erin BOOTH-CARO
23 Co-Director Health Services .... Ms. Angela GIRARD
23 Co-Director Health Services .... Dr. Kimberly FODRAN
19 Chief University Police .... Mr. Fernando SOLORZANO
38 Director Counseling/Psych Svcs .... Dr. Bong JOO
37 Director Financial Aid .... Mr. Nicolas VALDIVIA
25 Senior Director Sponsored Programs .... Ms. Maria REYES
102 Chief Op Ofcr/Rsrch Foundation .... Dr. Brian NOWLIN
28 Director of Equity & Diversity .... Ms. Larisa HAMADA
96 Director Procurement & Contracts .... Ms. Malia KINIMAKA
109 Interim General Mgr/49er Shops .... Mr. Robert DEWIT
104 Director Education Abroad .... Ms. Sharon OLSON
44 Director of Gift Planning .... Ms. Sireth TORRES
26 AVP of University Relations .... Mr. Christopher REESE
114 Assoc VP Budget & Univ Svcs .... Ms. Kara PERKINS
88 Asst VP Administrative Services .... Ms. Mishelle LAWS
20 Assoc VP Faculty Affairs .... Dr. Kirsty FLEMING
04 Deputy Chief of Staff .... Ms. Coleen FOLLOWELL
108 Director Program Review/Assessment .... Dr. Sharlene SAYEGH
22 Dir Affirmative Action/EEO .... Ms. Larisa HAMADA
26 AVP Strategic Communications .... Mr. Jeff COOK
116 Audit Liaison .... Mr. Gene WOHLGEZOGEN
105 Director Web Services .... Mr. Jesse SANTANA
86 Director Govt/Community Relations .... Ms. Ricki BURGENER
29 Director Alumni Engagement .... Ms. Noemi GUEVARA

*California State University-Los Angeles (E)

5151 State University Drive, Los Angeles CA 90032-8530
County: Los Angeles FICE Identification: 001140
Unit ID: 110592
Telephone: (323) 343-3000 Carnegie Class: Masters/L
FAX Number: (323) 343-2670 Calendar System: Semester
URL: www.calstatela.edu
Established: 1947 Annual Undergrad Tuition & Fees (In-State): $6,781
Enrollment: 26,745 Coed
Affiliation or Control: State IRS Status: 501(c)3
Highest Offering: Doctorate
Accreditation: WC, ABAI, ART, CACREP, DIETD, MT, MUS, NURSE, SP, SPAA, SW

02 President .... Dr. William A. COVINO
11 Exec VP and Chief Operating Officer .... Dr. Jose A. GOMEZ
05 Provost/Vice Pres Academic Affairs .... Dr. Jose Luis ALVARADO
10 VP Administration & CFO .... Ms. Lisa M. CHAVEZ
32 Vice President Student Life .... Dr. Nancy WADA-MCKEE
13 Int Chief Information Officer .... Mr. Alexander HARWOOD
44 Vice Pres University Advancement .... Dr. Janet S. DIAL
84 Int Vice Provost Enrollment Svcs .... Dr. Margaret GARCIA
28 VP Equity/Diversity/Inclusion .... Dr. Octavio VILLALPANDO

21 Assoc VP Financial Services .... Dr. Joyce WILLIAMS
35 Int AVP Student Life/Dean Students .... Mr. Aaron BURGESS
111 Assoc VP University Advancement .... Mr. Robert AVALOS
46 AVP Research .... Dr. Jeffrey UNDERWOOD
29 Exec Director Alumni Relations .... Ms. Maria UBAGO
26 Exec Dir Comm/Public Affairs .... Mr. Robert LOPEZ
41 Exec Dir Intercollegiate Athletics .... Dr. Daryl J. GROSS
83 Dean Natural & Social Sciences .... Dr. Pamela SCOTT-JOHNSON
88 Assoc Dean Natural/Social Sciences .... Dr. Kaven SUBRAHMANYAM
08 Dean of the University Library .... Mr. Carlos RODRIGUEZ
88 Assoc Dean of the Univ Library .... Ms. Marla PEPPERS
06 University Registrar .... Mr. Christopher COBB
58 Dean Graduate Studies .... Dr. Karin A. ELLIOT BROWN
09 Asst VP Institutional Research .... Dr. Sunny MOON
36 Dir Career Placement & Planning .... Mr. Jonathan CHOY
37 Director Student Financial Services .... Ms. Tamie NGUYEN
23 Director Health Center .... Dr. Monica JAZZABI
39 Dir Housing Svcs/Residence Life .... Mr. Leonard EDMOND
22 Director Equal Opportunity Pgm .... Vacant
18 AVP Fac/Plng/Design & Construct .... Ms. Barbara QUEEN
19 Chief of Police .... Mr. Larry BOHANNON
15 AVP Human Resources Management .... Ms. Susie VARELA
85 Director Intl Programs & Services .... Vacant
43 University Counsel .... Mr. Victor I. KING
07 Director Admissions & Recruitment .... Mr. Vince LOPEZ
96 Director Procurement & Contracts .... Mr. Thomas JOHNSON
28 Dir HR Equity/Div/Pol/Procedures .... Ms. Aundreia M. CAMERON
40 General Manager Bookstore .... Ms. Elaine REED
20 Assoc Dean Undergrad Studies .... Dr. Margaret GARCIA
49 Dean Arts & Letters .... Dr. Linda ESSIG
88 Int Associate Dean Arts/Letters .... Dr. Kevin BAASKE
54 Dean Engr/Computer Science/Tech .... Dr. Emily ALLEN
77 Assoc Dean Engr/Comp Sci/Tech .... Dr. Jianyu (Jane) DONG
107 Dean Col of Profess/Global Studies .... Dr. Harkmore LEE
88 Assoc Dean of Administration/PaGE .... Vacant
76 Dean Health & Human Services .... Dr. Ronald VOGEL
88 Assoc Dean Health & Human Svcs .... Dr. Evaon WONG-KIM
53 Dean Charter Col of Education .... Dr. Cheryl L. NEY
88 Assoc Dean Charter Col of Education .... Dr. Diane FAZZI
88 Assoc Dean of Pgms/Acad Innovation .... Ms. Regina CASH
50 Int Dean Business & Economics .... Dr. Tyrone JACKSON
88 Associate Dean Business & Economics .... Dr. Angela YOUNG
97 Dean Undergraduate Studies .... Dr. Michelle HAWLEY
92 Interim Director Honors College .... Dr. Rennie SCHOEPFLIN

† Grants Joint Doctoral degree in cooperation with the University of California-Los Angeles.

*CSU Maritime Academy (A)

200 Maritime Academy Drive, Vallejo CA 94590-0644
County: Solano FICE Identification: 001134
Unit ID: 111188
Telephone: (707) 654-1000 Carnegie Class: Bac-Diverse
FAX Number: (707) 654-1001 Calendar System: Semester
URL: www.csum.edu
Established: 1929 Annual Undergrad Tuition & Fees (In-State): $7,160
Enrollment: 952 Coed
Affiliation or Control: State IRS Status: 501(c)3
Highest Offering: Master's
Accreditation: WC, IACBE

02 President .... RADM. Thomas A. CROPPER, USMS
05 Provost/VP Academic Affairs .... Dr. Lori SCHROEDER
10 VP of Administration/Finance .... Mr. Franz LOZANO
32 VP of Student Affairs .... Ms. Kathleen MCMAHON
111 VP of University Advancement .... Mr. Robert ARP
15 AVP of Human Resources/Diversity .... Mr. Michael MARTIN
13 Chief Information Officer .... Ms. Julianne TOLSON
100 Chief of Staff/AVP Univ Affairs .... Vacant
88 Master of Training Ship .... Capt. Samuel R. PECOTA
20 Associate Vice Provost .... Dr. Graham BENTON
112 Senior Development Officer .... Ms. Linda SOLOW BOUWER
06 Registrar .... Ms. Julia L. ODOM
08 Dean of Library .... Ms. Michele VAN HOECK
07 Director of Admissions .... Vacant
37 Director of Financial Aid .... Ms. Priscilla MUHA
109 AVP Enterprise Services .... Mr. Mark GOODRICH
88 Director of SEAS .... Ms. Vineeta DHILLON
35 Dean of Students .... Mr. James DALSKE
18 AVP Facilities Management .... Mr. Audun AABERG
19 Chief of Police Services .... Chief Donny GORDON
21 University Controller .... Mr. Rabi JOSEPH
41 Director of Athletics .... Ms. Karen YODER
40 Bookstore Manager .... Mr. Andre JIMENEZ
96 Director of Purchasing .... Ms. Lorrie DINEEN-THACKERAY
09 Director of Institutional Research .... Mr. Gary MOSER
29 Director of Alumni Relations .... Ms. Theresa COSGROVE
101 Asst Director University Affairs .... Ms. Jennifer HEMBREE
114 Budget Director .... Mr. Andrew SOM
117 Director of Risk Management .... Ms. Marianne SPOTORNO
36 Director Career Services .... Ms. Wendy HIGGINS
23 Chief Medical Officer .... Ms. Rebecca MILLER

*California State University-Monterey Bay (B)

100 Campus Center, Seaside CA 93955-8000
County: Monterey FICE Identification: 032603
Unit ID: 409698
Telephone: (831) 582-3000 Carnegie Class: Masters/M
FAX Number: (831) 582-3783 Calendar System: Semester
URL: www.csumb.edu
Established: 1994 Annual Undergrad Tuition & Fees (In-State): $7,147
Enrollment: 7,409 Coed
Affiliation or Control: State IRS Status: 501(c)3
Highest Offering: Master's
Accreditation: WC, #ARCPA, IPSY, NURSE, @SP, SW

02 President .... Dr. Eduardo M. OCHOA
05 Provost .... Dr. Katherine KANTARDJIEFF
10 Vice Pres Admin & Finance/CFO .... Dr. Glen NELSON
30 Vice Pres University Development .... Ms. Barbara ZAPPAS
32 VP Student Affairs & Enroll Service .... Dr. John FRAIRE
45 VP for Strategic Initiatives .... Dr. Lawrence SAMUELS
86 Director of Governmental Affairs .... Ms. Nicole HOLLINGSWORTH
35 Dean of Students/AVP Student Affs .... Dr. Leslie WILLIAMS
21 Assoc Vice President for Finance .... Mr. Stephen MACKEY
28 AVP for Inclusive Excellence .... Dr. Brian CORPENING
108 AVP Institutional Effectiveness .... Dr. Dan SHAPIRO
15 AVP for University Personnel .... Ms. Natalie KING
06 Registrar .... Ms. Sandra NAFFZIGER
13 Chief Information Officer .... Dr. Chip LENNO
16 Director Employee & Labor Relations .... Ms. Melanie CHAVEZ
37 Director Financial Aid .... Ms. Angeles FUENTES
19 Chief of Police .... Chief Earl LAWSON
18 AVP Facilities Services & Operation .... Mr. Marcel FORTE
07 Director of Admissions .... Ms. Kimberly GUANZON
29 Director Alumni Relations .... Ms. Annie WARR
41 Athletic Director .... Mr. Kirby GARRY
96 Director of Purchasing .... Vacant

*California State University-Northridge (C)

18111 Nordhoff Street, Northridge CA 91330-0001
County: Los Angeles FICE Identification: 001153
Unit ID: 110608
Telephone: (818) 677-1200 Carnegie Class: Masters/L
FAX Number: N/A Calendar System: Semester
URL: www.csun.edu
Established: 1958 Annual Undergrad Tuition & Fees (In-State): $7,017
Enrollment: 40,381 Coed
Affiliation or Control: State IRS Status: 501(c)3
Highest Offering: Doctorate
Accreditation: WC, AAFCS, ART, #CAATE, CAPRT, CIDA, CONST, DIETD, DIETI, HSA, IPSY, JOUR, MFCD, MUS, NURSE, PH, PTA, RAD, SP, SW, THEA

02 President .... Dr. Erika D. BECK
05 Provost/Vice Pres Academic Affairs .... Dr. Mary Beth WALKER
10 Vice President Admin Finance/CFO .... Mr. Colin DONAHUE
32 VP Student Affairs/Dean of Students .... Dr. William WATKINS
111 Int VP Univ Advancement/Found Pres .... Dr. Thor STEINGRABER
13 Vice President IT/CIO .... Ms. Hilary BAKER
88 Exec Director University Corp .... Mr. Rick EVANS
20 Vice Provost Academic Affairs .... Dr. Matthew CAHN
100 Chief of Staff .... Ms. Genevieve EVANS TAYLOR
18 Assoc VP Facilities Dev/Operations .... Mr. Ken ROSENTHAL
58 Assoc VP Graduate Studies .... Dr. Amy LEVIN
21 Interim Assoc VP Financial Services .... Mr. John VEATCH
15 Assoc VP of Human Resources .... Ms. Kristina DE LA VEGA
29 Asst Vice Pres Alumni Relations .... Ms. Shellie HADVINA
26 Assoc VP of Mktg/Comm .... Mr. Jeffrey NOBLITT
121 Assoc VP for Student Success .... Dr. Melanie BOCANEGRA
91 Assoc VP of Acad Resources/Planning .... Ms. Diane S. STEPHENS
07 Director of Admissions and Records .... Mr. David R. DUFAULT-HUNTER
08 Dean University Library .... Dr. Mark STOVER
51 Dean College of Extended Learning .... Dr. Joyce A. FEUCHT-HAVIAR
79 Int Dean College of Humanities .... Dr. Jackie E. STALLCUP
50 Dean College Business/Economics .... Dr. Chandra SUBRAMANIAM
53 Dean College of Education .... Dr. Shari A. TARVER-BEHRING
57 Dean College Arts/Media/Comm .... Mr. Dan HOSKEN
83 Dean Col Social/Behavioral Sci .... Dr. Yan Dominic SEARCY
76 Dean Col Health/Human Development .... Dr. Farrell WEBB
81 Dean College Science & Math .... Dr. Jerry STINNER
54 Dean College Engr/Computer Sci .... Dr. Houssam TOUTANJI
09 Sr Dir Institutional Research .... Dr. Janet S. OH
37 Director Financial Aid/Scholarships .... Ms. Linda M. BRIGNONI
38 Director Univ Counseling Services .... Dr. Julie L. PEARCE
36 Director Career Center .... Ms. Ann N. MOREY
25 Dir Research/Graduate Studies .... Ms. Hedy L. CARPENTER
18 Senior Dir Physical Plant Mgmt .... Mr. Jason WANG
19 Director of Police Services .... Chief Gregory MURPHY
22 Director of Equity/Diversity .... Mr. Barrett MORRIS
86 AVP Government/Community Relations .... Mr. Rafael DE LA ROSA
23 Director Student Health Center .... Dr. Linda REID-CHASSIAKOS
39 Dir of Stdnt Housing/Resident Life .... Ms. Claire DAVIS
41 Dir of Intercollegiate Athletics .... Mr. Michael IZZI
35 Dir Student Involvement/Development .... Mr. Patrick BAILEY
92 Dir General Education Honors Pgm .... Dr. Beth A. WIGHTMAN
96 Manager Purchasing .... Ms. Deborah FLUGUM
06 Registrar .... Mr. Todd WOLFE
28 Chief Div Ofcr/Title IX Coordinator .... Ms. Natalie L. MASON-KINSEY
04 Exec Assistant to the President .... Ms. Elbi MAGANA
11 Dir of Administrative Operations .... Mr. Randy REYMALDO

*California State University-Sacramento (D)

6000 J Street, Sacramento CA 95819-2694
County: Sacramento FICE Identification: 001150
Unit ID: 110617
Telephone: (916) 278-6011 Carnegie Class: Masters/L
FAX Number: (916) 278-6664 Calendar System: Semester
URL: www.csus.edu
Established: 1947 Annual Undergrad Tuition & Fees (In-State): $7,418
Enrollment: 32,293 Coed
Affiliation or Control: State IRS Status: 501(c)3
Highest Offering: Doctorate
Accreditation: WC, ART, @AUD, CACREP, CAPRT, CONST, DIETD, DIETI, EMT, MUS, NURSE, PTA, SP, SW, THEA

02 President .... Dr. Robert S. NELSEN
05 Provost & VP Academic Affairs .... Dr. Steve PEREZ
111 VP University Advancement .... Dr. Lisa CARDOZA
32 VP Student Affairs .... Dr. Edward MILLS
13 VP & Chief Information Officer .... Dr. Mark HENDRICKS
10 VP Admin & CFO .... Mr. Jonathan BOWMAN
15 Sr AVP Human Resources Management .... Ms. Machelle MARTIN
26 Assoc VP Public Affairs/Advocacy .... Mr. Nathan DIETRICH
46 AVP Research Innovation & Econ Dev .... Dr. Yvonne HARRIS
20 Interim Vice Provost .... Dr. Christine M. MILLER
30 AVP University Development .... Ms. Tracy LATINO-NEWMAN
18 Assoc Vice Pres Facilities Mgmt .... Dr. Justin REGINATO
84 AVP Enrollment & Student Svcs .... Dr. Steven M. SALCIDO
27 Senior Assoc VP Univ Communications .... Ms. Jeannie WONG
35 AVP Stdnt Affs/Engage/Dean Students .... Mr. Bill MACRISS
21 Assoc VP Financial Svcs .... Ms. Gina CURRY
07 Dir Outreach & Admissions .... Mr. Brian HENLEY
08 Library Dean .... Ms. Amy KAUTZMAN
29 Assoc VP Alumni Relations .... Ms. Jennifer BARBER
19 Chief of Police .... Mr. Chet MADISON, JR.
39 Dir of Strategic Initiatives .... Mr. Michael SPEROS
41 Director of Athletics .... Dr. Mark ORR
37 Director Financial Aid/Scholarships .... Ms. Anita KERMES
22 Director of Equal Opportunity .... Mr. William BISHOP
40 Bookstore Director .... Ms. Pam PARSONS
100 Interim Chief of Staff .... Dr. Sarah BILLINGSLEY
06 University Registrar .... Ms. Danielle AMBROSE
85 AVP for International Affairs .... Dr. Paul HOFMANN
23 AVP Student Health & Counseling Svc .... Dr. Joy STEWART-JAMES
96 Sr Dir/Chief Procurement Officer .... Ms. Nicole LACK
97 Dean Undergraduate Studies .... Dr. James GERMAN
49 Dean College of Arts & Letters .... Dr. Sheree MEYER
50 Dean College of Business Admin .... Dr. William CORDEIRO
53 Dean College of Education .... Dr. Alexander SIDORKIN
54 Int Dean Col of Engr/Computer Sci .... Dr. Kevan SHAFIZADEH
76 Int Dean College Health/Human Svcs .... Dr. Mary MAGUIRE
81 Dean Col of Natural Science/Math .... Dr. Lisa HAMMERSLEY
51 Dean College Continuing Educ .... Dr. Jenni MURPHY
83 Dean Col Soc Sci/Interdisc Stds .... Dr. Dianne HYSON
58 Dean Graduate Studies .... Dr. Chevelle NEWSOME
28 Int VP for Inclusive Excellence .... Dr. Melinda WILSON RAMEY
113 University Bursar .... Ms. Elena LARSON
112 Exec Dir Advance Stewardship .... Ms. Lisa WOODARD-MINK
44 Exec Dir Annual Giving .... Ms. Sharon TAKEDA
88 Exec Dir Ctr Innov/Entrepreneurship .... Mr. Cameron LAW
90 AVP Academic Technology .... Dr. Peggy KAY

*California State University-San Bernardino (E)

5500 University Parkway, San Bernardino CA 92407-2393
County: San Bernardino FICE Identification: 001142
Unit ID: 110510
Telephone: (909) 537-5000 Carnegie Class: Masters/L
FAX Number: N/A Calendar System: Quarter
URL: www.csusb.edu
Established: 1960 Annual Undergrad Tuition & Fees (In-State): $6,952
Enrollment: 19,689 Coed
Affiliation or Control: State IRS Status: 501(c)3
Highest Offering: Doctorate
Accreditation: WC, ART, CACREP, DIETD, MUS, NURSE, PH, SPAA, SW, THEA

02 President .... Dr. Tomas MORALES
05 Provost/VP Academic Affairs .... Dr. Shari MCMAHAN
10 Vice Pres Administration/Finance .... Dr. Doug FREER
111 Vice Pres University Advancement .... Mr. Robert NAVA
13 Vice Pres ITS/CIO .... Dr. Samuel SUDHAKAR
28 Co-Chief Diversity Officer .... Mr. Alex NAJERA
28 Co-Chief Diversity Officer .... Dr. Seval YILDIRIM
11 AVP of Operations/Administration .... Ms. Monica ALEJANDRE
29 AVP Alumni/Govt & Comm Relations .... Ms. Pamela LANGFORD
20 Dep/Assoc Provost Academic Programs .... Dr. Clare WEBER
46 Assoc Provost Research .... Dr. Dorota HUIZINGA
20 Dean/AVP Undergraduate Studies .... Dr. Leslie DAVIDSON-BOYD
21 Assoc VP Finance .... Mr. M. Monir AHMED
15 Assoc VP Human Resources .... Vacant
121 Assoc VP Stdnt Success/Educ Equity .... Ms. Olivia ROSAS
32 AVP Student Svcs/Dean of Students .... Dr. Daria GRAHAM
14 Assoc VP ITS .... Mr. Gerard AU
26 Assoc VP Strategic Communications .... Mr. Bob TENCZAR
88 Assoc Provost Faculty Affairs & Dev .... Dr. Seval YILDIRIM
22 Director Title IX & Gender Equity .... Ms. Cristina ALVAREZ
06 Int Director University Registrar .... Ms. Amy BRACEROS
07 Director of Outreach .... Ms. Tiffany BONNER
23 Interim Director Health Center .... Dr. Carolyn O'KEEFE
08 University Librarian .... Mr. Cesar CABALLERO
37 Director Financial Aid .... Ms. Diana MINOR
39 Assoc Dir Housing/Residential Life .... Ms. Holly ALLAR
18 Assoc VP Facilities Management .... Ms. Jennifer SORENSON
41 Director Athletics .... Mr. Shawn FARRELL
92 Director University Honors Program .... Dr. David MARSHALL
56 Dean Col of Extended Learning .... Dr. Tatiana KARMANOVA
83 Dean Col Social/Behavioral Sciences .... Dr. Rafik MOHAMED
53 Dean College of Education .... Dr. Chinaka DOMNWACHUKWU
50 Dean College of Business .... Dr. Lawrence D. ROSE

58	Dean Graduate Studies	Dr. Dorota HUIZINGA
12	Dean CSUSB Palm Desert	Dr. Jake ZHU
100	Chief of Staff	Ms. Julie M. LAPPIN
102	Sr Dir Foundation/Corp Rels	Ms. Annya DIXON
44	Operations Manager Annual Giving	Ms. Carolina VAN ZEE
104	Study Abroad Coordinator	Ms. Amy CHIEN
104	Study Abroad Coordinator	Mr. Emilio RODRIGUEZ
09	Chief Data Officer	Ms. Muriel LOPEZ-WAGNER
29	Director Alumni Affairs	Ms. Crystal WYMER-LUCERO
104	Director of Education Abroad	Dr. Sonja LIND
04	Admin Assistant to the President	Ms. Katherine HARTLEY
106	Dean of E-learning	Dr. Tatiana KARMANOVA
19	Chief of Police	Ms. Nina JAMSEN

*California State University-San Marcos (A)

333 S Twin Oaks Valley Road,
San Marcos CA 92096-0001

County: San Diego | FICE Identification: 030113 | Unit ID: 366711
Telephone: (760) 750-4000 | Carnegie Class: Masters/L
FAX Number: (760) 750-4030 | Calendar System: Semester
URL: www.csusm.edu
Established: 1989 | Annual Undergrad Tuition & Fees (In-State): $7,712
Enrollment: 16,367 | Coed
Affiliation or Control: State | IRS Status: 501(c)3
Highest Offering: Doctorate
Accreditation: WC, IPSY, NURSE, PH, SP, SW

02	President	Dr. Ellen J. NEUFELDT
04	Presidential Aide	Ms. Viviana GARCIA
10	Int VP Finance/Admin Svcs & CFO	Mr. Leon WYDEN
05	Provost/VP Academic Affairs	Dr. Carl KEMNITZ
32	Vice President of Student Affairs	Dr. Lorena CHECA
111	Interim VP University Advancement	Ms. Jessica BERGER
20	Dean Academic Programs	Dr. Regina EISENBACH
45	Vice Prov Plng/Acad Resources	Dr. Mary OLING-SISAY
84	Assoc Vice Pres Enrollment Mgmt	Mr. Scott HAGG
15	Assoc VP Human Resource/Equal Oppty	Ms. Erika GRAVETT
49	Int Dn Col Hum Arts/Behav & Soc Sci	Dr. Elizabeth MATTHEWS
50	Int Dean Col Business Admin	Dr. Bennett CHERRY
53	Dean Col Educ/Hlth/Human Svcs	Dr. Jennifer OSTERGREN
08	Dean of Library Services	Dr. Jennifer FABBI
81	Int Dean Col of Sci/Tech/Engr/Math	Dr. Jackie TRISCHMAN
56	Int Dean of Extended Studies	Ms. Brooke JUDKINS
13	Dean Instructional/Info Technology	Mr. Kevin MORNINGSTAR
06	Registrar	Ms. Lisa MEDINA
07	Dir Admissions & Univ Registrar	Ms. Lisa MEDINA
100	Chief of Staff	Ms. Sarah VILLARREAL
21	AVP Business and Fin Svcs	Mr. Clint ROBERTS
29	Director Alumni/Parent Relations	Ms. Lori BROCKETT
96	Assoc VP Procurement/Support Svcs	Ms. Bella NEWBERG
121	Director Undergraduate Advising	Mr. David MCMARTIN
09	Dir Inst Planning & Analysis	Mr. Jeffrey MARKS
104	Executive Director Global Education	Mr. Robert CAROLIN
18	AVP Facilities Dev & Mgmt	Mr. Mark NORITA
19	Chief Univ Police Department	Mr. Lamine SECKA
22	AVP Inclusive Excellence	Dr. Aswad ALLEN
26	Chief Communications Officer	Ms. Margaret CHANTUNG
39	Director Student Housing	Mr. Malik ISMAIL
41	Athletic Director	Ms. Jennifer MILO
88	AVP Faculty Affairs	Ms. Michelle HUNT
44	Director Annual Programs	Mr. Sean BRINER
86	Director Government Relations	Mrs. Christine LEE
108	Director Institutional Assessment	Mr. Jeffrey MARKS

† Grants Joint Doctoral degree in cooperation with the University of California-San Diego.

*California State University-Stanislaus (B)

1 University Circle, Turlock CA 95382-0299

County: Stanislaus | FICE Identification: 001157 | Unit ID: 110495
Telephone: (209) 667-3122 | Carnegie Class: Masters/L
FAX Number: N/A | Calendar System: Semester
URL: www.csustan.edu
Established: 1957 | Annual Undergrad Tuition & Fees (In-State): $7,584
Enrollment: 11,163 | Coed
Affiliation or Control: State | IRS Status: 170(c)1
Highest Offering: Doctorate
Accreditation: WC, ART, MUS, NURSE, SPAA, SW, THEA

02	President	Dr. Ellen JUNN
05	Provost/VP Academic Affairs	Dr. Kimberly GREER
06	Registrar	Ms. Lisa M. BERNARDO
10	VP Business/Finance/CFO	Ms. Christene JAMES
32	VP Student Affairs	Dr. Christine ERICKSON
111	VP University Advancement	Dr. Michele LAHTI
84	VP Strategic Plng/Enroll Mgmt/Innov	Dr. Gitanjali KAUL
15	Sr AVP HR/EO/Compliance	Ms. Julie JOHNSON
100	Dir Presidential Initiatives	Ms. Neisha RHODES
79	Dean College Arts/Humanities & SS	Dr. James A. TUEDIO
50	Dean College of Business Admin	Dr. Thomas GOMEZ-ARIAS
53	Dean College of Education	Dr. Oddmund R. MYHRE
81	Dean College of Science	Dr. David EVANS
08	Dean Library Services	Mr. Ron RODRIGUEZ
106	Dean Stockton Center	Dr. Faimous HARRISON
51	Dean Extended Education	Dr. Helene CAUDILL
07	Dir Admissions & Outreach	Mr. Miguel PULIDO
41	Director Athletics	Mr. Terry DONOVAN
35	AVP Student Affs/Dean of Students	Dr. Heather DUNN CARLTON
21	Assoc VP Financial Services	Ms. Regan LINDERMAN
13	Chief Information Officer	Mr. Rafael ESPINOSA
18	Assoc VP Facilities Services	Ms. Melody MAFFEI
26	Sr AVP Comm & Public Affairs	Dr. Rosalee RUSH
19	Chief of Police	Mr. Clint STRODE
09	Director of Institutional Research	Vacant
103	Director Career Development	Ms. Julie SEDLEMEYER
28	Director of Diversity Center	Ms. Carolina ALFARO
38	Director Student Counseling	Vacant
39	Dir Resident Life/Student Housing	Ms. Renee GIANNINI
29	Director Alumni Affairs	Ms. Karlha DAVIES
30	Director of Development	Mr. Jeff PORTO, JR.
44	Director Annual Giving	Ms. Sandra SANTINI
04	Admin Assistant to the President	Ms. Naraith LOPEZ
37	Director Student Financial Aid	Ms. Belinda GARCIA
104	Director Study Abroad	Ms. Brittany FENTRESS

*Humboldt State University (C)

1 Harpst Street, Arcata CA 95521-8222

County: Humboldt | FICE Identification: 001149 | Unit ID: 115755
Telephone: (707) 826-3011 | Carnegie Class: Masters/M
FAX Number: (707) 826-5555 | Calendar System: Semester
URL: www.humboldt.edu
Established: 1913 | Annual Undergrad Tuition & Fees (In-State): $7,858
Enrollment: 6,612 | Coed
Affiliation or Control: State | IRS Status: 501(c)3
Highest Offering: Master's
Accreditation: WC, ART, IACBE, MUS, SW

02	President	Dr. Tom JACKSON, JR.
100	Chief of Staff	Ms. Sherie GORDON
05	Provost/VP Academic Affairs	Dr. Jenn CAPPS
20	Vice Prov Acad Pgms/Undergrad Stds	Vacant
32	VP Enrollment Mgmt/Student Affairs	Dr. Jason MERIWETHER
10	Vice Pres Admin & Finance	Mr. Shahrooz ROOHPARVAR
111	VP of University Advancement	Mr. Frank WHITLATCH
15	AVP Human Resources	Vacant
88	AVP Development	Ms. Deborah RICE
26	Sr Communication Officer	Ms. Aileen YOO
18	Planning Director Facilities Mgmt	Mr. Michael FISHER
84	Director of Enrollment Management	Vacant
114	Director University Budget Office	Ms. Amber BLAKESLEE
88	Director of Academic Resources	Vacant
06	Registrar	Mr. Clint REBIK
07	Director of Admissions	Mr. Pedro MARTINEZ
08	Dean of Library	Dr. Cyril OBERLANDER
44	Director of Annual Giving	Mr. Travis WILLIAMS
19	Chief of University Police	Mr. Anthony MORGAN
41	Athletic Director	Mr. Cooper JONES
39	AVP Student Affairs & Housing	Dr. Stephen ST. ONGE
13	Chief Information Officer	Ms. Bethany RIZZARDI
36	Director Career Devel Center	Ms. Kathy THORNHILL
28	Diversity Officer	Dr. Elavie NDURA
46	Executive Director Sponsored Pgms	Ms. Kacie FLYNN
104	Study Abroad Coordinator	Ms. Megan MEFFORD
35	Dean of Students	Dr. Eboni TURNBOW
37	Director Student Financial Aid	Ms. Peggy METZGER
96	Director of Contracts & Procurement	Ms. Tawny FLEMING
90	Director ITS User Support	Mr. Breck ROBINSON
09	Director Institutional Research	Mr. Michael S. LE
23	Director Health/Counseling	Vacant
38	Director Counseling & Psych Svcs	Dr. Jennifer SANFORD
56	Dean of eLearning & Ext Education	Dr. Cyril OBERLANDER
79	Dean Col Arts/Humanities/Soc Sci	Dr. Lisa BOND-MAUPIN
107	Dean College Professional Studies	Dr. Shawna YOUNG
65	Dean Col Natural Resources/Science	Dr. Eric RIGGS
21	Controller	Ms. Lynne SANDSTROM
06	Registrar eLearning & Ext Educ	Vacant
105	Web Manager	Mr. Matt HODGSON
29	Alumni Relations Outreach	Ms. Stephanie LANE
04	Administrative Asst to President	Ms. Paula PETERSEN
117	Dir of Risk Management & Safety	Ms. Cris KOCZERA
16	AVP Faculty Affairs	Dr. Simone ALOISIO

*San Diego State University (D)

5500 Campanile Drive, San Diego CA 92182-8000

County: San Diego | FICE Identification: 001151 | Unit ID: 122409
Telephone: (619) 594-5200 | Carnegie Class: DU-Higher
FAX Number: (619) 594-8894 | Calendar System: Semester
URL: www.sdsu.edu
Established: 1897 | Annual Undergrad Tuition & Fees (In-State): $7,720
Enrollment: 36,334 | Coed
Affiliation or Control: State | IRS Status: 501(c)3
Highest Offering: Doctorate
Accreditation: WC, ART, AUD, CAATE, CACREP, CAMPEP, CIDA, CLPSY, DIETD, HSA, JOUR, MFCD, NURSE, PH, PLNG, PTA, SP, SPAA, SW, THEA

02	President	Dr. Adela DE LA TORRE
05	Provost	Dr. Hector OCHOA
10	Int VP/CFO Business Affairs	Ms. Agnes WONG NICKERSON
32	Vice Pres for Student Affairs	Dr. J. Luke WOOD
30	VP Univ Relations & Development	Ms. Adrienne VARGAS
46	Interim VP for Research	Dr. Hala MADANAT
20	Assoc Vice Pres Academic Affairs	Dr. Radmila PRISLIN
88	Assoc VP Real Estate Planning & Dev	Mr. Robert SCHULZ
21	Int Assoc VP Financial Operations	Ms. Crystal LITTLE
15	Associate VP Administration	Ms. Jessica RENTTO
85	Int Associate VP for Global Affairs	Dr. Christina ALFARO
26	AVP/Chief Comm Officer	Dr. La Monica EVERETT-HAYNES
35	Int Assoc VP for Student Affairs	Ms. Rashmi PRABA
35	Assoc VP for Student Affairs	Dr. Andrea DOOLEY
35	Assoc VP for Student Affairs	Dr. Antionette MARBRAY
35	Assoc VP for Student Affairs	Dr. Randy TIMM
88	Asst VP Special Projects	Mr. James S. HERRICK
100	Chief of Staff President's Office	Ms. Brittany SANTOS-DERIEG
84	Int Assoc VP Enrollment Management	Ms. Sandra TEMORES
38	Director Counseling/Psych Services	Dr. Jennifer RIKARD
08	Int Dean Library/Information Access	Mr. Patrick MCCARTHY
110	Int Associate VP for Development	Ms. Mary DARLING
88	AVP & Exec Director Rsrch Found	Ms. Michele GOETZ
51	Dean SDSU World Campus	Dr. Radhika SESHAN
58	Assoc Dean Graduate & Rsrch Affairs	Dr. Edmund BALSDON
49	Assoc VP AA/Student Achievement	Dr. Norah SHULTZ
79	Dean of College Arts & Letters	Dr. Monica CASPER
81	Dean of College of Sciences	Dr. Jeffrey ROBERTS
54	Interim Dean College of Engineering	Dr. Eugene OLEVSKY
50	Int Dean Fowler College of Business	Dr. Bruce REINIG
76	Dean College Health/Human Svcs	Dr. Steven P. HOOKER
53	Dean of College of Education	Dr. Y. Barry CHUNG
12	Dean of Imperial Valley Campus	Dr. Gregorio PONCE
57	Dean Prof Studies/Fine Arts	Dr. Peggy SHANNON
117	Director of Emergency Services	Ms. Kayli SINGER
28	CDO/AVP Faculty Diversity & Incl	Dr. J. Luke WOOD
06	Registrar	Vacant
07	Director of Admissions	Ms. Sabrina CORTELL
36	Executive Director Career Services	Dr. James TARBOX
39	Director Office of Housing Admin	Ms. Cynthia CERVANTES
40	Assoc VP & CEO Aztec Shops	Mr. Todd SUMMER
41	Director Intercollegiate Athletics	Mr. John David WICKER
85	Dir International Student Center	Mr. Noah HANSEN
88	Director Environ Health & Safety	Mr. Terry GEE
13	Chief Tech Officer/Interim CIO	Mr. Rick NORNHOLM
09	Dir Analytic Studies/Inst Research	Ms. Jeanne STRONACH
86	Dir Govt & Comm Relations	Ms. Rachel GREGG
96	Director Procurement Mgmt	Ms. Tami FORD
21	University Controller	Ms. Beth WARREM
18	Director of Facilities Services	Mr. John FERRIS
22	Dir Educational Opportunity Program	Ms. Miriam CASTANON
37	Dir Financial Aid & Scholarships	Ms. Rose PASENELLI
88	Ombudsman	Mr. Darrell HESS
39	Director of Residential Education	Dr. Kara BAUER
121	Dir Student Ability Success Ctr	Dr. Pamela STARR
88	Sr Director Enterprise Tech Svcs	Mr. Rick NORNHOLM
29	Asst VP Alumni Engagement	Mr. Jim HERRICK
04	Executive Asst to the President	Mr. Luis MURILLO

*San Francisco State University (E)

1600 Holloway Avenue, San Francisco CA 94132-1740

County: San Francisco | FICE Identification: 001154 | Unit ID: 122597
Telephone: (415) 338-1111 | Carnegie Class: Masters/L
FAX Number: (415) 338-2514 | Calendar System: Semester
URL: www.sfsu.edu
Established: 1899 | Annual Undergrad Tuition & Fees (In-State): $7,006
Enrollment: 27,349 | Coed
Affiliation or Control: State | IRS Status: 501(c)3
Highest Offering: Doctorate
Accreditation: WC, AAFCS, ART, CACREP, CAPRT, DIETD, DIETI, JOUR, MT, MUS, NURSE, PH, PTA, SP, SPAA, SW, THEA

02	President	Dr. Lynn MAHONEY
05	Provost & VP Academic Affairs	Dr. Jennifer SUMMIT
111	Vice Pres University Advancement	Mr. Jeffrey JACKANICZ
32	VP Student Affairs/Enroll Mgmt	Dr. Jamillah MOORE
20	Vice Provost Academic Resources	Dr. Dwayne BANKS
46	Assoc VP Research Sponsored Pgms	Mr. Michael SCOTT
20	Assoc VP Academic Affairs Operation	Dr. Brian BEATTY
10	AVP Business Operations	Mr. Jay ORENDORFF
85	Interim AVP International Education	Dr. Marilyn JACKSON
13	AVP Information Technology Services	Mr. Nish MALIK
84	Senior AVP Enrollment Management	Dr. Maria MARTINEZ
15	Assoc VP Human Resources	Ms. Ingrid WILLIAMS
35	Assoc VP Student Affairs	Mr. Gene CHELBERG
100	Chief of Staff	Ms. Noriko LIM-TEPPER
53	Dean College Education	Dr. Cynthia GRUTZIK
88	Dean College Ethnic Studies	Dr. Amy SUEYOSHI
51	AVP/Dean of CELIA	Dr. Angie LIPSCHUETZ
69	Dean Col Health & Soc Science	Dr. Alvin ALVAREZ
79	Dean Col Lib Sci & Creative Arts	Dr. Andrew HARRIS
88	AVP Faculty Affairs & Prof Dev	Dr. Carleen MANDOLFO
58	Dean Graduate Studies	Dr. Sophie CLAVIER
97	Dean Undergraduate Education	Dr. Lori Beth WAY
102	Int President SF State Foundation	Ms. Venesia THOMPSON-RAMSAY
08	University Librarian	Ms. Deborah C. MASTERS
90	Director Academic Technology	Dr. Maggie BEERS
117	Risk Manager	Mr. Michael BEATTY
39	Director Resident Life	Mr. David ROURKE
28	Int Dir Diversity/Student Equity	Mr. Christian LOZANO CUELLAR
07	Director Undergraduate Admissions	Mr. Fernando PENA
38	Director Counseling & Psych Svcs	Dr. Stephen CHEN
22	Dir Education Opportunity Program	Mr. Oscar M. GARDEA
19	Chief of Police/AVP Public Safety	Chief Reginald PARSON
88	Dir Environmental Health & Safety	Mr. Marc MAJEWSKI
109	AVP Facilities Services	Mr. Frank FASANO
04	Deputy Chief of Staff	Ms. Leshia CLAUDIO
06	Registrar	Ms. Margo LANDY
37	Asst Dir Student Financial Aid	Mr. Charles B. GATES

41 Director of Athletics ....Ms. Stephanie E. SHRIEVE-HAWKINS
86 Director Government/Cmty Relations ....Vacant

† Grants additional Doctoral degrees in cooperation with the UC-Berkeley and UC-San Francisco.

*San Jose State University (A)

One Washington Square, San Jose CA 95192-0001
County: Santa Clara — FICE Identification: 001155
Unit ID: 122755
Telephone: (408) 924-1000 — Carnegie Class: Masters/L
FAX Number: (408) 924-1018 — Calendar System: Semester
URL: www.sjsu.edu
Established: 1857 — Annual Undergrad Tuition & Fees (In-State): $7,852
Enrollment: 36,208 — Coed
Affiliation or Control: State — IRS Status: 501(c)3
Highest Offering: Doctorate
Accreditation: WC, ART, @AUD, CAATE, CAPRT, CEA, DANCE, DIETD, DIETI, IPSY, JOUR, LIB, MT, MUS, NAIT, NURSE, OT, PH, PLNG, SP, SPAA, SW, THEA

02 President ....Dr. Mary PAPAZIAN
05 Provost/Sr Vice Pres Acad Affs ....Dr. Vincent DEL CASINO
10 VP Administration & Finance/CFO ....Mr. Charles FAAS
32 Vice President Student Affairs ....Mr. Patrick K. DAY
13 VP Information Technology/CIO ....Mr. Bob LIM
100 VP Strategy/Chief of Staff ....Ms. Lisa MILLORA
09 Assoc VP Research ....Dr. Pamela STACKS
20 Sr Assoc VP Grad/Undergrad Programs ....Dr. Thalia ANAGNOS
21 Assoc VP Finance ....Ms. Marna GENES
18 Assoc VP for Facilities/Operations ....Vacant
15 Senior AVP University Personnel ....Ms. Joanne WRIGHT
26 AVP Strategic Comm/Public Affairs ....Vacant
29 AVP Alumni Engagement and Giving ....Mr. Brian BATES
35 Int AVP Student Services ....Ms. Catherine VOSS PLAXTON
22 Chief Diversity Officer ....Dr. Kathleen WONG (LAU)
51 Dean Col of Intl/Extended Studies ....Dr. Ruth HUARD
84 Int Sr AVP Enrollment Mgmt ....Ms. Coleetta MCELROY
08 Int Dean University Library ....Ms. Ann AGEE
28 Sr Dir Equal Opport/Employee Rels ....Ms. Julie PAISANT
06 University Registrar ....Ms. Marian YAO
41 Director Intercollegiate Athletics ....Ms. Marie TUITE
07 Dir Undergrad Admissions/Outreach ....Ms. Deanna GONZALES
40 B&N Asst Dir Spartan Bookstore ....Ms. Lisa TOWNS
38 Dir Counseling/Psychological Svcs ....Mr. Kell FUJIMOTO
37 Assoc Dir Fin Aid/Scholarships ....Ms. Carolyn GUEL
39 Dir University Housing Services ....Mr. Kevin KINNEY
50 Dean Lucas Col/Grad Sch of Business ....Dr. Dan MOSHAVI
53 Dean Connie L Lurie Col of Educ ....Dr. Heather LATTIMER
54 Dean Charles W Davidson Col of Eng ....Dr. Sheryl EHRMAN
79 Dean Col of Humanities and the Arts ....Dr. Shannon MILLER
81 Dean College of Science ....Dr. Michael KAUFMAN
83 Dean College Social Sciences ....Dr. Walt JACOBS
04 Presidential Aide ....Ms. Zaynna TELLO

*Sonoma State University (B)

1801 E Cotati Avenue, Rohnert Park CA 94928-3609
County: Sonoma — FICE Identification: 001156
Unit ID: 123572
Telephone: (707) 664-2880 — Carnegie Class: Masters/L
FAX Number: (707) 664-2505 — Calendar System: Semester
URL: www.sonoma.edu
Established: 1960 — Annual Undergrad Tuition & Fees (In-State): $7,952
Enrollment: 8,018 — Coed
Affiliation or Control: State — IRS Status: 501(c)3
Highest Offering: Master's
Accreditation: WC, ART, CACREP, MUS, NURSE

02 President ....Dr. Judy SAKAKI
05 Provost/VP Academic Affairs ....Ms. Karen MORANSKI
10 Int VP Administration/Finance/CFO ....Mr. Stan NOSEK
111 Vice President for Advancement ....Mr. Mario PEREZ
32 Vice President for Student Affairs .... Mr. Wm. Gregory SAWYER
20 Assoc VP for Faculty Affairs ....Dr. Deborah ROBERTS
18 Chief Planning Officer ....Mr. Christopher DINNO
100 Chief of Staff/AVP Strat Initiative ......Ms. Jerlena GRIFFIN-DESTA
88 Assoc VP for Admin & Finance .... Mr. Neil MARKLEY
08 Dean of Library ....Ms. Karen SCHNEIDER
79 Dean School of Arts & Humanities .... Dr. Hollis ROBBINS
50 Dean School of Business/Economic ....Vacant
81 Dean School Science & Technology ....Ms. Elisabeth WADE
83 Dean of Social Sciences ....Ms. Tori CARLETON
26 Public Rels/Govt Relations Officer ....Dr. Robert EYLER
06 Sr Dir Records/University Registrar ....Mr. Sean JOHNSON
38 Dir of Counseling/Psych Services ....Dr. Laura WILLIAMS
37 Director of Financial Aid ....Ms. F. Shanon LITTLE
88 Dir of Dev for Intercol Athletics ....Mr. Jose HILLA
19 Chief of Police ....Mr. Nader OWEIS
21 Director Seawolf Services ....Ms. Elizabeth O'BRIEN
07 Director of Admissions ....Ms. Natalie KALOGIANNIS
84 Sr AVP Strategic Enrollment ....Mr. Elias LOPEZ
29 Dir Advancement Svcs & Stewardship ....Ms. Laurie OGG
15 AVP for Administration/Finance/HR ....Mr. Jeffrey BANKS
96 Managing Dir for Purchasing ....Ms. Jenifer BARNETT
28 AVP Strategic Initiatives/Diversity ....Ms. Janelle ROSSI
30 Director of Development ....Mr. Stephen ARNESON

California University of Management and Sciences (C)

1126 North Brookhurst St, Suite 200, Anaheim CA 92801
County: Orange — FICE Identification: 041331
Unit ID: 460075
Telephone: (714) 533-3946 — Carnegie Class: Masters/M
FAX Number: (714) 533-7778 — Calendar System: Quarter
URL: www.calums.edu
Established: 1998 — Annual Undergrad Tuition & Fees: N/A
Enrollment: N/A — Coed
Affiliation or Control: Independent Non-Profit — IRS Status: 501(c)3
Highest Offering: Master's
Accreditation: ACICS

01 President ....Jessica M. MERTZ
10 Finance Officer ....Hongjun AHN
05 Academic Dean ....Sasha SAFARZADEH
11 Dean of Administration ....Yukari NISHIOKA
07 Admissions Officer ....CJ JOHNS
32 Student Services Advisor ....Kholood JADALLA
08 Librarian ....Lionnel YAMENTOU
06 Registrar ....Hongjun AHN
85 International Student Advisor ....Yukari NISHIOKA
15 Personnel Mgr ....Jessica MERTZ

California University of Science and Medicine (D)

1501 Violet Street, Colton CA 92324
County: San Bernardino — Identification: 667343
Telephone: (909) 580-9661 — Carnegie Class: Not Classified
FAX Number: (909) 424-0345 — Calendar System: Semester
URL: https://www.cusm.org/
Established: 2015 — Annual Graduate Tuition & Fees: N/A
Enrollment: N/A — Coed
Affiliation or Control: Independent Non-Profit — IRS Status: 501(c)3
Highest Offering: Doctorate; No Undergraduates
Accreditation: @WC, #MED

01 President/Dean ....Dr. Paul LYONS
05 Vice Pres of Medical Affairs ....Dr. Robert SUSKIND
10 Chief Financial/Operating Officer ....Mr. Moe ABOUFARES
13 Chief Information Officer ....Mr. Nasser SALOMON
63 Sr Assoc Dean Medical Education ....Dr. Gordon GREEN
32 Sr Assoc Dean Student Affs/Admiss ....Dr. Peter EVELAND

California University - Silicon Valley (E)

441 De Guigne Drive #201, Sunnyvale CA 94085
County: Santa Clara — Identification: 667207
Telephone: (408) 532-5567 — Carnegie Class: Not Classified
FAX Number: N/A — Calendar System: Trimester
URL: www.cusv.us
Established: 2013 — Annual Graduate Tuition & Fees: N/A
Enrollment: N/A — Coed
Affiliation or Control: Independent Non-Profit — IRS Status: 501(c)3
Highest Offering: Master's; No Undergraduates
Accreditation: @ACUP

01 President ....Philip YANG
05 Academic Dean ....Cynthia MA

California Victor University (F)

708 W. Holt Avenue, Pomona CA 91768
County: Los Angeles — Identification: 667386
Telephone: (909) 671-4038 — Carnegie Class: Not Classified
FAX Number: (909) 671-4086 — Calendar System: Semester
URL: cavictorun.org
Established: 2010 — Annual Graduate Tuition & Fees: N/A
Enrollment: N/A — Coed
Affiliation or Control: Non-denominational — IRS Status: 501(c)3
Highest Offering: Master's; No Undergraduates
Accreditation: TRACS

01 President ....Dr. Benjamin HONG
05 Provost ....Dr. Sung W. KIM
32 Dean of Student Affairs ....Dr. Suk Young KIM

California Western School of Law (G)

225 Cedar Street, San Diego CA 92101-3046
County: San Diego — FICE Identification: 013103
Unit ID: 111391
Telephone: (619) 239-0391 — Carnegie Class: Spec-4-yr-Law
FAX Number: (619) 525-7092 — Calendar System: Trimester
URL: www.cwsl.edu
Established: 1924 — Annual Graduate Tuition & Fees: N/A
Enrollment: 796 — Coed
Affiliation or Control: Independent Non-Profit — IRS Status: 501(c)3
Highest Offering: First Professional Degree; No Undergraduates
Accreditation: @WC, LAW

01 President & Dean ....Dean Sean M. SCOTT
05 Vice Dean ....Dean Hannah BRENNER JOHNSON
46 Assoc Dean Research/Faculty Devel ....Prof. Catherine HARDEE
88 Assoc Dean of Exper Learning .... Prof. James COOPER
32 Asst Dean Students/Diversity Svcs ....Ms. Susan GARRETT FINSTER
36 Assistant Dean Career Services .... Ms. Courtney MIKLUSAK
37 Director Financial Aid ....Mr. William KAHLER
18 Exec Dir Facilities Management .... Ms. Jolie L. CARTIER
08 Assoc Dean Law Library/Info Res ....Prof. Philip T. GRAGG
10 Chief Financial Officer ....Ms. Cindy BERTRAND
07 Asst Dean Admiss/Fin Aid/Diversity ....Mr. Jorge GARCIA
06 Registrar ....Mr. Jerome THOMPSON
26 Chief Marketing Officer ....Mr. Chris VAN NOSTRAND
15 VP Administration ....Mr. Dave BLAKE
111 VP Institutional Advancement ....Ms. Dani DAWSON
100 Chief of Staff ....Mr. Christopher E. BAIDOO
108 Assoc Dean Assessment/Teaching ....Prof. Kenneth S. KLEIN

Calvary Chapel University (H)

8344 Clairemont Mesa Blvd, Ste 100, San Diego CA 92111
County: San Diego — Identification: 667372
Telephone: (954) 453-9228 — Carnegie Class: Not Classified
FAX Number: N/A — Calendar System: Other
URL: calvarychapeluniversity.com
Established: 2005 — Annual Undergrad Tuition & Fees: N/A
Enrollment: N/A — Coed
Affiliation or Control: Independent Non-Profit — IRS Status: 501(c)3
Highest Offering: Master's
Accreditation: TRACS

01 President ....Dr. F. Chapin MARSH, III
05 Chief Academic Officer .... Dr. Kathy MORALES
10 Chief Operating Officer ....Ms. Laura NUNES
07 Director of Admissions ....Ms. Pamela PRINCE

Carnegie Mellon University Silicon Valley Campus (I)

PO Box 98, Moffett Field CA 94035
Telephone: (650) 335-2810 — Identification: 770149
Accreditation: &M

† Branch campus of Carnegie Mellon University, Pittsburgh, PA

Caroline University (J)

3660 Wilshire Blvd, Ste 320, Los Angeles CA 90010
County: Los Angeles — Identification: 667387
Telephone: (213) 246-4174 — Carnegie Class: Not Classified
FAX Number: (213) 487-9199 — Calendar System: Semester
URL: www.carolineuniversity.org
Established: 2016 — Annual Graduate Tuition & Fees: N/A
Enrollment: N/A — Coed
Affiliation or Control: Independent Non-Profit — IRS Status: 501(c)3
Highest Offering: Doctorate; No Undergraduates
Accreditation: TRACS

01 President ....Dr. James LEE

*Carrington College - Administrative Office (K)

8909 Folsom Boulevard, Sacramento CA 95826
County: Sacramento — Identification: 666086
Telephone: (916) 361-5100 — Carnegie Class: N/A
FAX Number: (916) 381-1809
URL: www.carrington.edu

01 President Carrington Colleges .... Mr. Mitch CHARLES
05 Provost/Vice Pres Academic Affairs ....Mr. Ravinder DAYAL
11 Regional VP of Operations ....Mr. Michael COMO
84 Sr Director Enrollment Services ....Mr. Dan SIMON
10 Sr Dir Finance & Infrastructure ....Vacant
15 AVP/Director of Human Resources ....Ms. Lea MARSHALL

*Carrington College - Sacramento (L)

8909 Folsom Boulevard, Sacramento CA 95826
County: Sacramento — FICE Identification: 009748
Unit ID: 125532
Telephone: (916) 361-1660 — Carnegie Class: Spec 2-yr-Health
FAX Number: (916) 361-6666 — Calendar System: Other
URL: www.carrington.edu
Established: 1983 — Annual Undergrad Tuition & Fees: N/A
Enrollment: 1,709 — Coed
Affiliation or Control: Proprietary — IRS Status: Proprietary
Highest Offering: Associate Degree
Accreditation: WJ, DH, MAC

02 Campus Director ....Cynthia BRYSON
121 Student Success Center Manager ....Becky CARDWELL

Carrington College - Citrus Heights (M)

7301 Greenback Lane, Suite A, Citrus Heights CA 95621
Telephone: (916) 722-8200 — Identification: 667042
Accreditation: &WJ, MAC

† Regional accreditation is carried under the parent institution in Sacramento, CA.

Carrington College - Pleasant Hill (N)

380 Civic Drive, Suite 300, Pleasant Hill CA 94523
Telephone: (925) 609-6650 — Identification: 666043
Accreditation: &WJ, COARC, MAC, PTAA

† Regional accreditation is carried under the parent institution in Sacramento, CA.

* Carrington College - Pomona (A)

901 Corporate Center Drive, #300, Pomona CA 91768
Telephone: (909) 868-5834 Identification: 770506
Accreditation: &WJ

† Regional accreditation is carried under the parent institution in Sacramento, CA.

* Carrington College - San Jose (B)

5883 Rue Ferrari, Suite 125, San Jose CA 95138
Telephone: (408) 960-0161 Identification: 666042
Accreditation: &WJ, DH, MAC, SURGT

† Regional accreditation is carried under the parent institution in Sacramento, CA.

* Carrington College - San Leandro (C)

15555 E 14th Street, Suite 500, San Leandro CA 94578
Telephone: (510) 276-3888 Identification: 666751
Accreditation: &WJ, MAC

† Regional accreditation is carried under the parent institution in Sacramento, CA.

* Carrington College - Stockton (D)

1313 W Robinhood Drive, Suite B, Stockton CA 95207
Telephone: (209) 956-1240 Identification: 666140
Accreditation: &WJ, MAC

† Regional accreditation is carried under the parent institution in Sacramento, CA.

Casa Loma College-Van Nuys (E)

6725 Kester Avenue, Van Nuys CA 91405
County: Los Angeles FICE Identification: 006731
Unit ID: 111638
Telephone: (818) 785-2726 Carnegie Class: Spec 2-yr-Health
FAX Number: (818) 785-2191 Calendar System: Other
URL: www.casalomacollege.edu
Established: 1966 Annual Undergrad Tuition & Fees: N/A
Enrollment: 164 Coed
Affiliation or Control: Independent Non-Profit IRS Status: 501(c)3
Highest Offering: Baccalaureate
Accreditation: ABHES, PTAA

01 President .... Mr. Greg MALONE
05 Dean of Education .... Dr. Stephanie SHELBURNE
06 Registrar .... Ms. Kimberly DUNCAN
32 Director of Student Affairs .... Mr. Nicholas WALSH-DAVIS
37 Director Student Financial Aid .... Mr. George MCPHATTER
08 Head Librarian .... Ms. Jennifer MEYER
13 Chief Info Technology Officer .... Mr. Cyrill REISER
15 Chief Human Resources Officer .... Ms. Veronica PANTOJA

CBD College (F)

3699 Wilshire Boulevard, 4th Floor,
Los Angeles CA 90010
County: Los Angeles FICE Identification: 032503
Unit ID: 439367
Telephone: (213) 427-2200 Carnegie Class: Spec 2-yr-Health
FAX Number: (213) 427-9278 Calendar System: Other
URL: www.cbd.edu
Established: 1982 Annual Undergrad Tuition & Fees: N/A
Enrollment: 974 Coed
Affiliation or Control: Independent Non-Profit IRS Status: 501(c)3
Highest Offering: Baccalaureate
Accreditation: ABHES, DMS, OTA, PTAA, SURTEC

01 President .... Mr. Alan HESHEL
05 Chief Academic Officer .... Randall SANSOM
10 Chief Operating Officer .... Patricia KOUROPOVA
106 Online Dean of Education .... Chanel MARTINEZ
32 Dir Student Affairs/Career Services .... Ivan REYNOSO
07 Director of Admissions .... Jim HAYES
37 Director of Financial Aid .... Michael RENDON-THOFSON
13 Chief Technology Officer .... Randall SANSOM

Cedars-Sinai Graduate School of Biomedical Sciences (G)

8700 Beverly Boulevard, Los Angeles CA 90048
County: Los Angeles Identification: 667071
Telephone: (310) 423-8294 Carnegie Class: Not Classified
FAX Number: N/A Calendar System: Trimester
URL: www.cedars-sinai.org/education/graduate-school.html
Established: 1902 Annual Graduate Tuition & Fees: N/A
Enrollment: N/A Coed
Affiliation or Control: Independent Non-Profit IRS Status: 501(c)3
Highest Offering: Doctorate; No Undergraduates
Accreditation: WC

01 President/CEO .... Mr. Thomas PRISELAC
03 Executive Vice President .... Dr. John JENRETTE
05 Dean/Exec Vice Pres Academic Affs .... Dr. Shlomo MELMED
10 Exec Vice Pres Finance/CFO .... Mr. Edward PRUNCHUNAS

Cerritos College (H)

11110 Alondra Boulevard, Norwalk CA 90650-6298
County: Los Angeles FICE Identification: 001161
Unit ID: 111887
Telephone: (562) 860-2451 Carnegie Class: Assoc/MT-VT-High Trad
FAX Number: (562) 467-5005 Calendar System: Semester
URL: www.cerritos.edu
Established: 1955 Annual Undergrad Tuition & Fees (In-District): $1,404
Enrollment: 20,406 Coed
Affiliation or Control: State/Local IRS Status: 501(c)3
Highest Offering: Associate Degree
Accreditation: WJ, ADNUR, DA, DH, PTAA

01 President .... Dr. Jose L. FIERRO
04 Executive Assistant .... Ms. Andrea WITTIG
05 Vice President Academic Affairs .... Mr. Rick MIRANDA
10 Vice President Business Services .... Mr. Felipe LOPEZ
32 Vice President Student Services .... Dr. Dilcie D. PEREZ
15 Vice President Human Resources .. Dr. Adriana FLORES-CHURCH
20 Dean Acad Affs/Strategic Init .... Dr. Linda CLOWERS
84 Dean Enrollment Services .... Ms. Yvette TAFOYA
38 Dean of Counseling Services .... Dr. Rosa PRADO
86 Dir College/Govt Rels & Pub Affs .... Ms. Miya WALKER
88 Int Dean Stdnt Access/Wellness Svcs .... Ms. Victoria LUGO
121 Dean Student Equity & Success .... Mr. Lui AMADOR
50 Dean Business/Humanities/SS .... Ms. Rachel MASON
57 Dean Fine Arts/Communications .... Dr. Gary PRITCHARD
76 Dean Health Occupations .... Ms. Sandra MARKS
88 Dean Academic Success .... Ms. Shawna BASKETTE
49 Dean Liberal Arts .... Dr. Frank MIXSON
68 Dean Health/PE/Dance/Athl .... Dr. Rory NATIVIDAD
54 Dean Sci/Engineering/Math .... Mr. Andrew VINES
72 Dean Technology .... Dr. Yannick REAL
13 Director Information Technology .... Mr. Patrick O'DONNELL
21 Director of Fiscal Services .... Mr. Noorali DELAWALLA
35 Dean of Student Services .... Dr. Elizabeth MILLER
36 Dir of Career/Assessment Services .... Ms. Theresa LOPEZ
18 Director Physical Plant & Const Svc .... Mr. Anthony PARKER
102 Exec Dir Foundation/Inst Advance .... Ms. Carol KRUMBACH
103 Director Community Advancement .... Ms. Bellegran GOMEZ
96 Dir Purchasing/Contract Admin .... Mr. Mark LOGAN
16 Director Human Resources/Risk Mgmt .... Ms. Nancy BUVINGER
19 Chief of Campus Police .... Mr. Don MUELLER
51 Assoc Dn Adult Educ/Diversity Pgms .... Ms. Graciela VASQUEZ
31 Temp Director Community Education .... Ms. Graciela VASQUEZ
88 Director Child Development Center .... Ms. Debra WARD
88 Operations Manager .... Mr. Carlos SERNA
88 Payroll Manager .... Ms. Deanna HART
114 Budget Manager .... Mr. Conrad SELORIO
14 Manager Information Technology .... Mr. Javier BANUELOS
23 Assoc Dean Student Health Wellness .... Dr. Hillary MENNELLA
88 Director of Student Program Svcs .... Ms. Norma RODRIGUEZ
09 Dir Inst Effect/Research & Planning .... Dr. Amber HROCH
88 Sector Nvg Adv Trans Tech Projects .... Ms. Jannet MALIG
28 Dir Diver/Compliance/Title IX Coord .. Dr. Lauren ELAN HELSPER
88 EOPS Assistant Director .... Dr. Patricia ROBBINS SMITH
89 Dir Educational Partnerships & Pgm .... Ms. Colleen MCKINLEY
88 Dual Enrollment Manager .... Ms. Carla YORKE
88 Accounting Manager .... Ms. Kathy BURGOS
88 Facilities Manager .... Mr. Shannon KAVENEY
29 Director Alumni Relations .... Mr. Matthew HARMS
30 Senior Development Officer .... Vacant
37 Financial Aid Asst Director .... Ms. Jaime QUIROZ
06 Asst Dir Admissions/Records .... Ms. Sonia GONZALEZ
41 Athletic Director .... Ms. Maria V. CASTRO
88 Case Manager Basic Needs .... Ms. Pamela SEPULVEDA
88 Mgr Partnershp Adult Acad/Career Ed .... Ms. Sherryl CARTER
88 Captain Campus Police Services .... Mr. Wayne REHNELT

* Chabot-Las Positas Community College District (I)

7600 Dublin Blvd., 3rd Flr., Dublin CA 94568
County: Alameda Identification: 666925
Telephone: (925) 485-5208 Carnegie Class: N/A
FAX Number: (925) 485-5256
URL: www.clpccd.org

01 Chancellor .... Mr. Ronald GERHARD
10 Vice Chanc Business Svcs .... Mr. Jonah NICHOLAS
05 Vice Chanc Educational Svcs .... Ms. Theresa FLEISCHER ROWLAND
15 Vice Chanc Human Resource Svcs .... Mr. Wyman FONG
18 Vice Chanc Facilities/Bond Program .... Mr. Owen LETCHER
13 Chief Technology Officer .... Mr. Bruce GRIFFIN

* Chabot College (J)

25555 Hesperian Boulevard, Hayward CA 94545-2400
County: Alameda FICE Identification: 001162
Unit ID: 111920
Telephone: (510) 723-6600 Carnegie Class: Assoc/HT-High Trad
FAX Number: (510) 782-9315 Calendar System: Semester
URL: www.chabotcollege.edu
Established: 1961 Annual Undergrad Tuition & Fees (In-District): $1,150
Enrollment: 11,922 Coed
Affiliation or Control: State/Local IRS Status: 501(c)3
Highest Offering: Associate Degree
Accreditation: WJ, ART, DH, MAC, MUS, NAEYC

02 President .... Dr. Susan S. SPERLING
05 VP Academic Services .... Dr. Stacy THOMPSON
32 Vice President Student Services .... Dr. Matthew KRITSCHER
11 Vice Pres Administrative Services .... Mr. Dale WAGONER
10 Actg Chief Financial Officer .... Mr. Dale WAGONER
04 Exec Asst to the College President .... Ms. Kirti REDDY
08 Librarian .... Vacant
38 Dean Counseling .... Ms. Debra TRIGG
41 Dean Health/PE/Athletics .... Mr. Kevin KRAMER
07 Dir Admissions & Records/Registrar .... Mrs. Paulette LINO
37 Director of Financial Aid .... Mrs. Kathryn MEDINA
19 Director Safety & Security .... Vacant
09 Int Dir Institutional Effectiveness .... Vacant
15 Director Human Resources .... Dr. Wyman FONG
18 Chief Facilities/Physical Plant .... Mr. Walter BELVINS
111 Exec Director Inst Advancement .... Ms. Yvonne WU CRAIG
35 Dir Student Life/Student Services .... Mr. Arnold PAGUIO
96 Manager Purchasing/Warehouse Svcs .... Ms. Marie HAMPTON

* Las Positas College (K)

3000 Campus Hill Drive, Livermore CA 94551-7623
County: Alameda FICE Identification: 030357
Unit ID: 366401
Telephone: (925) 424-1000 Carnegie Class: Assoc/HT-High Trad
FAX Number: (925) 443-0742 Calendar System: Semester
URL: www.laspositascollege.edu
Established: 1975 Annual Undergrad Tuition & Fees (In-District): $1,168
Enrollment: 8,005 Coed
Affiliation or Control: State/Local IRS Status: 501(c)3
Highest Offering: Associate Degree
Accreditation: WJ, EMT

02 President .... Dr. Dyrell W. FOSTER
05 Vice President Academic Svcs .... Dr. Kristina WHALEN
32 Vice President Student Svcs .... Vacant
11 Vice President Admin Services .... Ms. Anette RAICHBART
04 Exec Assistant to the President .... Ms. Sheri MOORE
35 Dean of Student Services .... Ms. Elizabeth DAVID
49 Dean Arts & Humanities .... Ms. Amy MATTERN
81 Dean Math/Science/Eng/Public Safety .... Dr. Nan HO
69 Dn Pub Saf/Adv Mfg/Trans/Hlth/Kin .... Mr. Erick BELL
50 Dn Business/Soc Sci/Lrng Resources .... Mr. Stuart MCELDERRY
84 Dean of Enrollment Services .... Ms. Tamica WARD
45 Director of Research & Planning .... Mr. Rajinder SAMRA
37 Financial Aid/Veterans Assistance .... Ms. Andi SCHREIBMAN
19 Campus Safety Supervisor .... Mr. Sean PRATHER
08 Head Librarian .... Dr. Tina INZERILLA
102 Executive Director LPC Foundation .... Mr. Kenneth COOPER
41 Athletic Director .... Mr. James GIACOMAZZI
10 Associate Business Officer .... Ms. Sui SONG
18 Project Planner/Manager Facilities .... Ms. Ann KROLL
06 Registrar .... Vacant
88 Project Manager CTE .... Ms. Vicki SHIPMAN
88 Director Child Development Center .... Ms. Angela LOPEZ

Chaffey College (L)

5885 Haven Avenue, Rancho Cucamonga CA 91737-3002
County: San Bernardino FICE Identification: 001163
Unit ID: 111939
Telephone: (909) 652-6000 Carnegie Class: Assoc/HT-High Trad
FAX Number: (909) 652-6006 Calendar System: Semester
URL: www.chaffey.edu
Established: 1883 Annual Undergrad Tuition & Fees (In-State): $1,180
Enrollment: 20,025 Coed
Affiliation or Control: State IRS Status: 501(c)3
Highest Offering: Associate Degree
Accreditation: WJ, ADNUR, DA, RAD

01 Superintendent/President .... Dr. Henry D. SHANNON
11 Assoc Supt Administrative Affairs .... Ms. Melanie SIDDIQI
10 Assoc Supt Bus Svcs/Econ Dev .... Ms. Lisa BAILEY
05 Assoc Supt Instruction/Inst Effect .... Ms. Laura HOPE
32 Interim VP Student Services .... Ms. Alisha ROSAS
09 Dean Inst Research/Research Dev .... Mr. Jim FILLPOT
29 Director Alumni Relations .... Ms. Janeth RODRIGUEZ
85 Director International Students .... Vacant
35 Dean Student Life .... Mr. Christopher BRUNELLE
07 Admin Admissions/Records .... Ms. Kathy LUCERO
21 Exec Director Business Services .... Ms. Kim ERICKSON
88 Director Technical Services .... Mr. Michael FINK
88 Director Childrens Center .... Ms. Birgit MONKS
23 Director Student Health Services .... Ms. Katherine PEEK
37 Director Financial Aid .... Ms. Patricia BOPKO
109 Director Auxiliary Services .... Vacant
22 Exec Dir Equity/Outreach/Comm .... Ms. Alisha ROSAS
114 Exec Dir Budgeting & Fiscal Svc .... Ms. Anita UNDERCOFFER
88 Director Museum Gallery .... Ms. Rebecca TRAWICK
18 Manager Facilities Development .... Ms. Sarah RILEY
12 Dean Chino Campus .... Dr. Teresa HULL
88 Dean Visual Performing Arts .... Dr. Jason CHEVALIER
50 Dean Business & Applied Tech .... Ms. Joy HAERENS
81 Dean Mathematics & Science .... Mr. Theodore YOUNGLOVE
83 Dean Social/Behavioral Sciences .... Dr. Corene SCHWARTZ
79 Dean Language Arts .... Mr. Anthony DISALVO
38 Dean Counseling & Matriculation .... Ms. Amy NEVAREZ
12 Dean Fontana Campus .... Dr. Yolanda FRIDAY
76 Dean Health Sciences .... Ms. Sherrie LOEWEN
04 Exec Assistant Supt/Pres Office .... Ms. Julie SANCHEZ
41 Director Athletics .... Dr. Timi BROWN
86 Manager Government Relations .... Ms. Lorena CORONA
15 Director Human Resources .... Ms. Susan HARDIE
102 Executive Director Foundation .... Ms. Lisa NASHUA

Chamberlain University-Sacramento (A)

10971 Sun Center Drive, Rancho Cordova CA 95670
Telephone: (916) 330-3410 Identification: 770978
Accreditation: &HLC, NURSE

† Branch campus of Chamberlain University-Addison, Addison, IL

Chapman University (B)

One University Drive, Orange CA 92866-1099
County: Orange FICE Identification: 001164
Unit ID: 111948
Telephone: (714) 997-6815 Carnegie Class: DU-Higher
FAX Number: (714) 997-6713 Calendar System: 4/1/4
URL: www.chapman.edu
Established: 1861 Annual Undergrad Tuition & Fees: $57,214
Enrollment: 9,761 Coed
Affiliation or Control: Christian Church (Disciples Of Christ)
IRS Status: 501(c)3
Highest Offering: Doctorate
Accreditation: WC, ARCPA, CAEP, DANCE, LAW, MFCD, MUS, PHAR, PTA, SP, THEA

01 President .... Dr. Daniele C. STRUPPA
05 Exec VP/Provost & CAO .... Dr. Norma BOUCHARD
03 Executive Vice President & COO .... Mr. Harold W. HEWITT, JR.
111 Exec VP University Advancement .... Ms. Sheryl BOURGEOIS
32 VP & Dean of Students .... Dr. Jerry PRICE
84 VP/Dean Enrollment Management .... Mr. Michael PELLY
20 Assoc Provost of Academic Admin .... Dr. Lawrence BROWN
09 Vice Provost Inst Eff & Fac Affairs .... Mr. Joseph SLOWENSKY
49 Dean Wilkinson Col Hum/Soc Sci .... Dr. Jennifer KEENE
61 Dean School of Law .... Dr. Matthew J. PARLOW
50 Dean School Business/Economics .... Dr. Thomas TURK
67 Dean School of Pharmacy .... Dr. Ronald JORDAN
121 Director of Academic Advising .... Mr. Roberto CORONEL
53 Int Dean College of Educ Studies .... Dr. Roxanne GREITZ MILLER
57 Dean College of Film/Media Arts .... Mr. Stephen GALLOWAY
57 Dean College of Performing Arts .... Dr. Guilio ONGARO
83 Dean Col Health/Behavioral Sciences .... Dr. Janeen M. HILL
81 Int Dean College of Science/Tech .... Dr. Jason K. KELLER
54 Dean School of Engineering .... Dr. L. Andrew LYON
57 Dean/Artistic Dir Center for Arts .... Dr. William HALL
104 Director Ctr for Global Education .... Ms. Kristin BEAVERS
97 Vice Provost Undergrad Education .... Dr. Nina LENOIR
45 VP Campus Planning & Design .... Ms. Collette CREPPELL
15 Vice President/CHRO .... Mr. Brian POWELL
43 Assoc Vice Pres of Legal Affairs .... Ms. Janine DUMONTELLE
10 Assoc Vice President & Controller .... Mr. Behzad BINESH
07 Asst VP of Undergrad Admissions .... Ms. Marcela MEJIA MARTINEZ
20 Assistant Provost .... Ms. Iris GERBASI
26 VP of Strategic Marketing .... Ms. Jamie CEMAN
18 VP Facilities .... Mr. Rick TURNER
27 Director Public Relations .... Ms. Amy STEVENS
08 Interim Dean of Library .... Dr. Kevin ROSS
29 Asst VP Strategic Engagement/Dev .... Ms. Kim GREENHALL
13 VP/Chief Information Officer .... Ms. Helen NORRIS
31 VP of Community Relations .... Ms. Alisa DRISCOLL
09 Director of Institutional Research .... Dr. Marisol ARREDONDO SAMSON
06 Registrar .... Ms. Jan MCCUEN
46 VP Research & Sponsored Pgms Admin .. Dr. Thomas PIECHOTA
28 Dir of Diversity/Equity/Inclusion .... Dr. Reginald C. STEWART
37 Director Undergrad Financial Aid .... Mr. David CARNEVALE
85 Coord International Student Svcs .... Ms. Junko TAKADA
19 Chief of Public Safety .... Mr. Randy BURBA
39 Director Residence Life .... Mr. David SUNDBY
41 Athletic Director .... Mr. Terry BOESEL
42 Dean of the Chapel .... Dr. Gail STEARNS
04 Associate to the President .... Dr. Christina MARSHALL
88 Exec Assistant to the Provost .... Ms. Shehani REEDER
23 Director Student Health Services .... Ms. Jacqueline DEATS
35 Asst Dean of Student Engagement .... Dr. Chris HUTCHISON
36 VP Career & Professional Dev .... Ms. Jo Etta BANDY
38 Dir Psychological Counseling Svcs .... Dr. Andrew KAMI
96 Director Purchasing .... Mr. Adey OYENUGA
04 Executive Asst to the President .... Ms. Erika CURIEL
58 Vice Provost for Graduate Educ .... Dr. Roxanne GREITZ MILLER
102 Dir Corporate/Foundation Relations .... Mr. Mike STRINGER
44 Asst VP Legacy Planning .... Mr. David MOORE
90 Dir Educational Tech Services .... Dr. Jana REMY
105 Webmaster .... Mr. Ramiro LANDEROS
25 Dir of Sponsored Projects Svcs .... Ms. Jill BORLAND

Charles R. Drew University of Medicine & Science (C)

1731 E 120th Street, Los Angeles CA 90059-3025
County: Los Angeles FICE Identification: 010365
Unit ID: 111966
Telephone: (323) 563-4800 Carnegie Class: Spec-4-yr-Other Health
FAX Number: (323) 563-5987 Calendar System: Semester
URL: www.cdrewu.edu
Established: 1966 Annual Undergrad Tuition & Fees: $14,002
Enrollment: 872 Coed
Affiliation or Control: Independent Non-Profit IRS Status: 501(c)3
Highest Offering: Master's
Accreditation: WC, ARCPA, NURSE, PH, RAD

01 President & CEO .... Dr. David M. CARLISLE
05 EVP Academic Affairs/Provost .... Dr. Steve O. MICHAEL
100 Chief of Staff .... Vacant
45 VP Research & Health Affairs .... Dr. Jadutt VADGAMA
111 SVP Advancement & Operations .... Ms. Angela L. MINNIEFIELD
10 VP Finance/Chief Business Officer .... Mr. Carl MCLANEY
15 Int Chief Human Resources Ofcr .... Mr. Elias MUNOZ
63 Dean College of Medicine .... Dr. Deborah PROTHROW-STITH
66 Dean School of Nursing .... Dr. Diane BRECKENRIDGE
76 Dean College of Science & Health .... Dr. Hector BALCAZAR
20 Asst Provost Faculty Affairs .... Dr. William SHAY
32 Dean Student Affairs .... Vacant
20 Sr Assoc Dean Academic Affairs .... Dr. Ronald A. EDELSTEIN
09 Dir Inst Research & Effectiveness .... Mr. Richard W. LINDSTROM
21 Chief Financial Officer .... Ms. Elizabeth BASKERVILLE
08 Director Health Sciences Library .... Ms. Darlene PARKER-KELLY
06 Registrar .... Ms. Raquel MUNOZ
84 Director of Enrollment Management .... Ms. Vanessa RIGGINS
13 Chief Information Officer .... Mr. Aaron WEATHERSBY

Charter College-Oxnard (D)

2000 Outlet Center Drive, Suite 150, Oxnard CA 93036
Telephone: (805) 973-1240 Identification: 666675
Accreditation: ABHES

† Branch campus of Charter College, Vancouver, WA

Chicago School of Professional Psychology (E)

707 Wilshire Blvd. Suite 600, Los Angeles CA 90017
County: Los Angeles FICE Identification: 021553
Unit ID: 455664
Telephone: (213) 615-2700 Carnegie Class: Spec-4-yr-Other Health
FAX Number: (213) 615-7274 Calendar System: Semester
URL: www.thechicagoschool.edu
Established: 2008 Annual Undergrad Tuition & Fees: $12,524
Enrollment: 3,131 Coed
Affiliation or Control: Independent Non-Profit IRS Status: 501(c)3
Highest Offering: Doctorate
Accreditation: WC, CLPSY

01 President .... Dr. Michele NEALON
05 Vice Pres AA/Chief Academic Officer .... Dr. Ted SCHOLZ
10 Sr Director of Business Operations .... Mr. Chris JACKSON
32 Dean for Student Success .... Ms. Jennifer STRIPE PORTILLO
15 Vice Pres Human Resources .... Dr. David IWANE
11 Chief Operating Officer .... Dr. Michael FALOTICO
111 Director Inst Advancement .... Mr. Anthony MACK
26 Director of Communications .... Mr. Victor ABALOS
04 Administrative Asst to President .... Ms. Adriana KLEIMAN
06 National Registrar .... Ms. Jennifer STROBEL
08 University Librarian .... Mr. David SIBLEY
100 Chief of Staff .... Ms. Shari MIKOS
101 Secretary of the Institution/Board .... Ms. Patti TYRA
19 Director of Facilities .... Mr. Brian LA BELLE
37 Regional Assoc Director of Fin Aid .... Mr. Seph RODRIGUEZ
09 Director of Institutional Research .... Mr. Kevin MCPHERSON
108 Dir Institutional Effectiveness .... Ms. Virginia QUINONEZ
07 AVP of Admissions .... Ms. Christina SHADE

Chicago School of Professional Psychology-Anaheim Campus (F)

2400 E Katella Avenue, Suite 1200, Anaheim CA 92806
Telephone: (914) 922-9600 Identification: 770492
Accreditation: &WC, CLPSY

China Evangelical Seminary North America (G)

1520 W. Cameron Avenue Ste 275,
West Covina CA 91790
County: Los Angeles Identification: 667256
Telephone: (626) 917-9482 Carnegie Class: Not Classified
FAX Number: (626) 851-1371 Calendar System: Quarter
URL: www.cesna.edu
Established: 2007 Annual Graduate Tuition & Fees: N/A
Enrollment: N/A Coed
Affiliation or Control: Non-denominational IRS Status: 501(c)3
Highest Offering: Doctorate; No Undergraduates
Accreditation: THEOL

01 President .... Dr. Katheryn LEUNG
05 Academic Dean .... Dr. Raymond HSU
11 Chief of Administration .... Rev. Hokeung C. CHAN
30 Chief Development/Advancement .... Dr. Tina LIU
37 Director Student Financial Aid .... Dr. Chun M. FONG
08 Chief Library Officer .... Dr. Jean WU
13 Chief Info Technology Ofcr (CIO) .... Dr. Frank LIU

Christian Witness Theological Seminary (H)

1975 Concourse Drive, San Jose CA 95131
County: Santa Clara Identification: 667255
Telephone: (408) 433-2280 Carnegie Class: Not Classified
FAX Number: (408) 433-9855 Calendar System: Other
URL: www.cwts.edu
Established: 1978 Annual Graduate Tuition & Fees: N/A
Enrollment: N/A Coed
Affiliation or Control: Interdenominational IRS Status: 501(c)3
Highest Offering: Doctorate; No Undergraduates
Accreditation: THEOL

01 President .... RevDr. Jeffrey LU
11 Vice President Administration .... Rev. James IP
05 Academic Dean .... RevDr. Luke TSAI
07 Admissions Dir/Dean Student Affairs .... Dr. Peter TIE
32 Dean of Students/Dir Field Educ .... Dr. Jacob CHEUNG-SUN TSANG

Church Divinity School of the Pacific (I)

2451 Ridge Road, Berkeley CA 94709-1217
County: Alameda FICE Identification: 001165
Unit ID: 112127
Telephone: (510) 204-0700 Carnegie Class: Spec-4-yr-Faith
FAX Number: N/A Calendar System: Semester
URL: www.cdsp.edu
Established: 1893 Annual Graduate Tuition & Fees: N/A
Enrollment: 71 Coed
Affiliation or Control: Protestant Episcopal IRS Status: 501(c)3
Highest Offering: Doctorate; No Undergraduates
Accreditation: THEOL

01 President & Dean .... Rev Dr. W. Mark RICHARDSON
11 Vice President & COO .... Rev. John DWYER
05 Dean Academic Affairs .... Rev Dr. Ruth MEYERS
32 Dean of Students .... Rev. Spencer HATCHER
06 Registrar .... Ms. Mary MCCHESNEY-YOUNG
123 Director of Recruitment .... Rev. Andrew HYBL
10 Manager of Operations .... Ms. Alissa FENCSIK
37 Director of Financial Aid .... Ms. Mary MCCHESENEY-YOUNG
04 Executive Assistant .... Ms. Ayanna DAVIS

Citrus College (J)

1000 W Foothill Boulevard, Glendora CA 91741-1899
County: Los Angeles FICE Identification: 001166
Unit ID: 112172
Telephone: (626) 963-0323 Carnegie Class: Assoc/HT-High Trad
FAX Number: (626) 914-8618 Calendar System: Semester
URL: www.citruscollege.edu
Established: 1915 Annual Undergrad Tuition & Fees (In-District): $1,194
Enrollment: 11,863 Coed
Affiliation or Control: State/Local IRS Status: 501(c)3
Highest Offering: Associate Degree
Accreditation: WJ, DA

01 Superintendent/President .... Dr. Greg SCHULZ
05 Vice President Academic Affairs .... Dr. Joumana MCGOWAN
32 Vice President Student Services .... Dr. Richard RAMS
10 Vice Pres Finance/Admin Services .... Ms. Claudette E. DAIN
07 Dean Enrollment Services .... Dr. Gerald SEQUEIRA
51 Dean Career/Tech & Cont Educ .... Mr. Michael WANGLER
38 Dean of Counseling .... Dr. Nicole SMITH
15 Director Human Resources .... Dr. Robert L. SAMMIS
102 Director Foundation .... Ms. Christina M. GARCIA
35 Dean of Students .... Dr. Maryann TOLANO-LEVEQUE
18 Director Facilities & Construction .... Mr. Fred DIAMOND
09 Director of Institutional Research .... Dr. Lan HAO
06 Registrar .... Ms. Cynthia ARRIETA
37 Director Financial Aid .... Mr. Stephen FAHEY
21 Director of Fiscal Services .... Mr. Wade ELLIS
28 Manager HR/Staff Diversity .... Ms. Brenda FINK
13 Chief Information Services Officer .... Mr. Robert HUGHES
19 Director of Campus Safety .... Mr. Benjamin MACIAS
83 Dean Social/Behavioral Sciences/DE .... Dr. Dana HESTER
41 Dean Kinesiology/Athletics/Health .... Mr. Junior DOMINGO
79 Dean Language Arts & Library .... Dr. Gina HOGAN
65 Dean Natural/Physical Sci & Health .... Dr. Eric RABITOY
57 Dean Visual & Performing Arts .... Mr. John VAUGHAN
81 Dean Math & Business .... Ms. Victoria DOMINGUEZ
22 Director EOPS CARE CalWORKS .... Ms. Sarah GONZALES-TAPIA
25 Dir Grants/Development Oversight .... Dr. Marianne SMITH
101 Secretary of the Institution/Board .... Ms. Christine A. LINK
109 Director of Business Services .... Mr. Shawn JONES
26 Exec Dir of Cmty & External Rels .... Ms. Melissa UTSUKI
88 Director Haugh Performing Arts Ctr .... Ms. Tiina MITTLER
76 Director Health Sciences .... Ms. Salima ALLAHBACHAYO
121 Director Student Support Svcs .... Ms. Jessica LOPEZ-JIMINEZ
40 Enterprise Services Manager .... Mr. Eric MAGALLON

City College of San Francisco (K)

50 Frida Kahlo Way, E200, San Francisco CA 94112
County: San Francisco FICE Identification: 001167
Unit ID: 112190
Telephone: (415) 239-3000 Carnegie Class: Assoc/MT-VT-Mix Trad/Non
FAX Number: (415) 239-3919 Calendar System: Semester
URL: www.ccsf.edu
Established: 1935 Annual Undergrad Tuition & Fees (In-District): $1,165
Enrollment: 19,707 Coed
Affiliation or Control: State/Local IRS Status: 501(c)3
Highest Offering: Associate Degree
Accreditation: WJ, ACFEI, CAHIIM, DA, EMT, MAC, RAD

01 Interim Chancellor .... Dr. Rajen VURDIEN
11 Sr Vice Chanc Admin/Stdnt Affs .... Ms. Dianna GONZALES
05 Sr Vice Chancellor Academic Affairs .... Mr. Thomas BOEGEL
10 Vice Chancellor Finance/Admin & CFO .... Mr. John AL-AMIN
108 Dean of Institutional Effectiveness .... Dr. Pam MERY

12 Dean Civic Center Campus ....Dr. Geisce LY
12 Dean Southeast Campus ....Ms. Ilona MCGRIFF
12 Int Dean Mission Campus ....Ms. Gregoria CAHILL
12 Dean Downtown/Business School ....Dr. Geisce LY
32 Vice Chanc of Student Affairs ....Dr. Elizabeth CORIA
37 Dean Financial Aid/Student Success .Mr. Guillermo VILLANUEVA
07 Dean Admissions & Records ....Vacant
20 Assoc Vice Chanc of Instruction ....Ms. Edith KAEUPER
103 Int Dean Workforce Development ....Mr. John HALPIN
15 Assoc Vice Chanc Human Resources ....Ms. Clara STARR
121 Dean Student Support Services ....Ms. Lidia JENKINS
22 Assoc Dean Student Equity ......Ms. Tessa HENDERSON-BROWN
12 Dean Chinatown/Contract & Cont Ed ....Ms. Kit DAI
57 Dean Sch of Visual/Performing Arts ....Vacant
83 Dean Behavioral/Social Sci ....Ms. Jill YEE
81 Dean Science/Math/Technology/Engr ....Mr. David YEE
68 Dean J Adams Campus/Sch Hlth Educ ....Vacant
30 Assoc Vice Chanc Institutional Dev ....Ms. Kristin CHARLES
13 Technical Operations Manager ....Mr. Tim RYAN
16 Int Director Employee Relations ....Ms. Cassandra LAWSON
18 Director Buildings/Grounds ....Mr. Jimmy KIRK
96 Dean of Purchasing ....Mr. Garth KWIECIEN
19 Chief of Police/Public Safety ....Vacant
22 ADA Compliance Officer ....Dr. Leilani BATTISTE
25 Int Dean Grants/EAP ....Ms. Wendy MILLER
06 Assoc Dean Admission & Records ....Ms. Monika LIU
101 Liaison to the Board of Trustees ....Ms. Linda SHAW
41 Athletic Director ....Mr. Harold BROWN
43 Dir Legal Services/General Counsel ....Mr. Steven BRUCKMAN
26 Director of External Affairs ....Vacant
04 Assistant to the Chancellor ....Ms. Grace ESTEBAN
08 Chief Library Officer ....Dr. Donna REED
100 Chief of Staff ....Ms. Leslie MILLOY
106 Dean Online Education/E-learning ....Ms. Cynthia DEWAR

City of Hope (A)

1500 East Duarte Road, Duarte CA 91010-3000
County: Los Angeles FICE Identification: 035924
Unit ID: 441238
Telephone: (626) 256-4673 Carnegie Class: Spec-4-yr-Other Health
FAX Number: (626) 301-8105 Calendar System: Semester
URL: www.cityofhope.org
Established: 1994 Annual Graduate Tuition & Fees: N/A
Enrollment: 90 Coed
Affiliation or Control: Independent Non-Profit IRS Status: 501(c)3
Highest Offering: Doctorate; No Undergraduates
Accreditation: WC, RTT

01 President/CEO ....Robert STONE
05 Provost/Chief Scientific Officer ....Dr. Steven T. ROSEN
11 Interim Chief Operating Officer ....Vince JENSEN
10 Chief Financial Officer ....Jennifer PARKHURST
26 Sr VP & Chief Marketing/Comm Ofcr ....Gulden MESARA
28 Sr VP/Chief Diversity Officer ....Angela L. TALTON
43 General Counsel/Secretary ....Gregory SCHETINA
15 Chief Human Resource Officer ....Kety DURON
58 Dean of Graduate School ....Dr. John J. ROSSI
06 Registrar ....Tracy KURZY
07 Director of Admissions ....Stephanie PATTERSON
08 Head Librarian ....Andrea LYNCH

*The Claremont College Services (B)

101 South Mills Avenue, Claremont CA 91711-5053
County: Los Angeles Identification: 666003
Telephone: (909) 621-8026 Carnegie Class: N/A
FAX Number: (909) 621-8517
URL: https://services.claremont.edu

01 Chief Executive Officer ....Mr. Stig LANESSKOG
10 Vice President of Financial Affairs ....Mr. Steven HOLLEY
32 Vice President of Student Affairs ..Ms. Janet SMITH DICKERSON
10 AVP Financial Services/Controller ....Ms. Mia ALONZO
26 Director of Communications ....Ms. Laura MUNA-LANDA
19 Asst Vice Pres Campus Safety ....Mr. Stan SKIPWORTH
13 Chief Information Officer ....Mr. Chuck THOMPSON
101 Sec to Board/AVP Comm Relations ....Mr. Colin TUDOR
08 Dean TCC Library ....Ms. Janet BISHOP
15 Director Human Resources ....Ms. Crystal ROSETTI

*Claremont Graduate University (C)

150 E 10th Street, Claremont CA 91711-5909
County: Los Angeles FICE Identification: 001169
Unit ID: 112251
Telephone: (909) 621-8000 Carnegie Class: DU-Higher
FAX Number: (909) 621-8390 Calendar System: Semester
URL: www.cgu.edu
Established: 1925 Annual Graduate Tuition & Fees: N/A
Enrollment: 1,949 Coed
Affiliation or Control: Independent Non-Profit IRS Status: 501(c)3
Highest Offering: Doctorate; No Undergraduates
Accreditation: WC, PH

02 President ....Dr. Len JESSUP
04 Exec Asst to the President ....Ms. Cindy BIERMAN
05 Exec Vice President and Provost ....Dr. Patricia EASTON
45 VP Strategic Initiatives ....Dr. Diane CHASE
10 VP Finance/Admin/Treasurer ....Ms. Leslie NEGRITTO
30 VP Development/External Relations ....Ms. Kristen ANDERSEN-DALEY
26 VP Marketing & Communications ....Ms. Cynthia BAKER
84 Asst VP Enroll/Dean of Admissions ....Mr. Timothy COUNCIL
46 Assoc Provost for Research ....Dr. Andrew CONWAY
20 Assoc Provost for Acad Affairs ....Vacant
108 AVP Institutional Effectiveness ....Dr. Teresa SHAW
15 Assoc VP for Human Resources ....Vacant
47 Botany Center ....Dr. Lucinda MCDADE
50 Drucker-Ito Grad School of Mgt ....Dr. Katharina PICK
83 Behavioral & Organizational Sci ....Dr. Michelle BLIGH
69 Community & Global Health ....Dr. Jay ORR
53 Educational Studies ....Dr. DeLacy GANLEY
77 Center for Information Science ....Dr. Lorne OLFMAN
81 Mathematical Sciences Institute ....Dr. Allon PERCUS
82 Politics & Economics ....Dr. Michelle BLIGH
73 Arts and Humanities ....Dr. Lori Anne FERRELL
09 Institutional Research Officer ....Dr. Yumi HUANG
08 Library Dean ....Dr. Janet BISHOP
19 Director of Campus Safety ....Mr. Stan SKIPWORTH
21 Assoc VP Finance/Admin ....Mr. Ryan CALLAHAN
29 Director of Alumni Engagement ....Ms. Rachel JIMENEZ
32 Asst VP Stdnt Affs/Dean of Students ....Ms. Quamina CARTER
36 Director of Career Development ....Dr. Christine KELLY
37 Director Student Financial Aid ....Ms. Kristal GAMMA
85 Director of International Students ....Dr. Ariel CARPENTER
06 Registrar ....Vacant
18 Director of Facilities ....Mr. Michael VILLEGAS
90 AVP Tech & Info Systems ....Mr. Manoj CHITRE
91 Dir of Enterprise Infrastructure ....Mr. Nasir HAKEEM
106 Dir Online Education/E-learning ....Vacant

*Claremont McKenna College (D)

500 E 9th Street, Claremont CA 91711-6400
County: Los Angeles FICE Identification: 001170
Unit ID: 112260
Telephone: (909) 621-8111 Carnegie Class: Bac-A&S
FAX Number: (909) 621-8790 Calendar System: Semester
URL: www.claremontmckenna.edu
Established: 1946 Annual Undergrad Tuition & Fees: $56,475
Enrollment: 1,264 Coed
Affiliation or Control: Independent Non-Profit IRS Status: 501(c)3
Highest Offering: Master's
Accreditation: WC

02 President and CEO ....Hiram E. CHODOSH
05 VP Academic Affs/Dean Faculty ....Peter UVIN
111 Vice President for Advancement ....Michelle CHAMBERLAIN
10 Vice Pres of Business and COO ....Coreen RODGERS
11 VP for Planning and Administration ....Matthew G. BIBBENS
32 Vice President of Student Affairs ....Sharon BASSO
115 Vice Pres/Chief Investment Officer ....James J. FLOYD
29 Asst Vice Pres Alumni/Parent Rels ....Evan RUTTER
07 Assoc Vice President for Admissions ....Jennifer SANDOVAL DANCS
26 Assoc VP Public Affs/Communications ....Vacant
13 Assoc VP/Chief Technology Officer ....Cynthia HUMES
92 Dean of Robert Day Scholars Program ...Michelle CHAMBERLAIN
06 Registrar/Dir Institutional Rsrch ....Elizabeth MORGAN
15 Director of Human Resources ....Andrea GALE
104 Director of Off-Campus Study ....Kristen MALLORY
41 Director of Athletics ....Erica PERKINS JASPER
04 Special Assistant to the President ....Cheryl M. AGUILAR
18 AVP Facilities Mgt/Capital Projects ....Larry BURIK

*Claremont School of Theology (E)

1325 N College Avenue, Claremont CA 91711-3199
County: Los Angeles FICE Identification: 001288
Unit ID: 124283
Telephone: (909) 447-2500 Carnegie Class: Spec-4-yr-Faith
FAX Number: (909) 626-7062 Calendar System: Semester
URL: www.cst.edu
Established: 1885 Annual Graduate Tuition & Fees: N/A
Enrollment: 287 Coed
Affiliation or Control: United Methodist IRS Status: 501(c)3
Highest Offering: Doctorate; No Undergraduates
Accreditation: WC, THEOL

02 President ....Dr. Jeffrey KUAN
04 Exec Assistant to the President ....Ms. Maria Lise IANNUZZI
10 Chief Financial Officer ....Mr. David ROBYDEK
05 Acting VP Academic Affairs & Dean ....Dr. Andrew DREITCER
88 Vice President for Intl Relations ....Dr. JongOh LEE
20 Associate Dean ....Vacant
08 Dean of Library & Info Services ....Vacant
32 Interim Dean Students & Disability ....Dr. Clemette HASKINS
26 Interim VP Communications .Rev. Steve HORSWILL-JOHNSTON
27 Director of Communications ....Ms. Kendra FREDRICKSON-LAOUINI
30 Director Donor Stewardship/Database ....Mr. Dmitri POTEMKIN
07 Dir Admissions/Enrollment/Fin Svcs ....Ms. Tomeka JACOBS
06 Registrar ....Ms. Sansu WOODMANCY
78 Director of Field Education ....Ms. Barbara NIXON
28 Campus Diversity Officer ....Vacant

*Keck Graduate Institute (F)

535 Watson Drive, Claremont CA 91711-4817
County: Los Angeles FICE Identification: 038533
Unit ID: 440031
Telephone: (909) 607-7855 Carnegie Class: Masters/S
FAX Number: (909) 607-8086 Calendar System: Semester
URL: www.kgi.edu
Established: 1997 Annual Graduate Tuition & Fees: N/A
Enrollment: 631 Coed
Affiliation or Control: Independent Non-Profit IRS Status: 501(c)3
Highest Offering: Doctorate; No Undergraduates
Accreditation: WC, PHAR

00 Board Chair ....James WIDERGREN
02 President/CEO ....Dr. Sheldon M. SCHUSTER
04 Exec Asst to Pres & Secy BOT ....Patricia ROBIDOUX
05 Chief Academic Officer ....Vacant
11 VP & Chief Operating Officer ....Dr. Kelly ESPERIAS
10 VP for Finance & Operations ....Michael JONES
06 Registrar & Dir Student Info Mgmt ....Melissa S. BROWN
32 Dean of Students ....Dr. Cynthia MARTINEZ
88 Dean School of Applied Life Science ....Dr. Martin ZDANOWICZ
67 Dean Sch of Pharmacy & Health Sci ....Dr. Martin ZDANOWICZ
46 Dean of Research ....Larry GRILL
123 Dean of Admissions/Financial Aid ....Sofia TORO
35 Director Student & Campus Life ....Andrea MOZQUEDA
21 Asst VP Finance & Business Svcs ....David CARTER
15 Asst VP Human Resources ....Cheryl MERRITT
16 Manager Human Resources ....Michelle VEGA
18 Asst VP Campus Operations ....Mark BENNETT
37 Director Financial Aid ....Maryville TUZON
09 Director of Institutional Research ....Vacant
110 Assoc VP Institutional Development ....Sharlene RISDON-JACKSON
88 Sr Director Inst Development ....Juliet NUSBAUM
25 Dir Sponsored Research Services ....Kirsten TORGUSON
26 Sr Dir Marketing & Communications ....Ivan ALBER
120 Dir Instructional Design & Dev ....George BRADFORD
13 Director IT ....Mark BENNETT
07 Director of Admissions ....Sofia TORO
102 Sr Dir Corporate Partnerships ....Shannon BRAUN

Claremont Lincoln Univeristy (G)

150 West 1st Street, Claremont CA 91711
County: Los Angeles Identification: 667215
Unit ID: 488387
Telephone: (909) 667-4411 Carnegie Class: Spec-4-yr-Bus
FAX Number: (909) 399-3443 Calendar System: Quarter
URL: claremontlincoln.edu
Established: 2011 Annual Graduate Tuition & Fees: N/A
Enrollment: 300 Coed
Affiliation or Control: Independent Non-Profit IRS Status: 501(c)3
Highest Offering: Master's; No Undergraduates
Accreditation: WC

01 CEO/President ....Dr. Lynn PRIDDY
11 EVP/Chief Operating Officer ....Mr. Joseph SALLUSTIO
05 VP for Academic Affairs/CAO ....Dr. Joanna BAUER
32 Dean of Student Svcs/Registrar ....Ms. Karen KRAKER
20 Dean of Academic Affairs ....Dr. Nita EVANS
111 VP for University Advancement ....Vacant
10 Chief Financial Officer ....Ms. Linda RABITOY
35 Student Services Advisor ....Ms. Clair BACA
04 Executive Asst to President ....Ms. Judy MORAVITZ
30 Director of Development ....Ms. Sara GERTLER
15 Dir Admin Svcs/Chief HR Ofcr ....Ms. Nancy BARNES
37 Director Student Financial Aid ....Mr. Cesar PEREZ

CNI College (H)

1610 East St. Andrew Place, Santa Ana CA 92705
County: Orange FICE Identification: 032423
Unit ID: 433013
Telephone: (714) 437-9697 Carnegie Class: Spec-4-yr-Other Health
FAX Number: (714) 437-9356 Calendar System: Other
URL: www.cnicollege.edu
Established: 1994 Annual Undergrad Tuition & Fees: N/A
Enrollment: 522 Coed
Affiliation or Control: Proprietary IRS Status: Proprietary
Highest Offering: Baccalaureate
Accreditation: ABHES, NURSE, SURTEC

01 President ....Mr. James BUFFINGTON

*Coast Community College District Administration Offices (I)

1370 Adams Avenue, Costa Mesa CA 92626-5429
County: Orange FICE Identification: 008711
Unit ID: 112376
Telephone: (714) 438-4600 Carnegie Class: N/A
FAX Number: (714) 438-4882
URL: www.cccd.edu

01 Chancellor ....Dr. John WEISPFENNING
10 Vice Chancellor Finance & Adm Svcs ....Dr. Andrew DUNN
05 Vice Chanc Educ Svcs & Technology ....Dr. Andreea SERBAN
15 Vice Chanc Human Resources ....Dr. Marco BAEZA
26 Dir Public Affairs/Marketing ....Mr. Erik FALLIS
96 Director of Purchasing ....Mr. John ERIKSEN

*Coastline Community College (J)

11460 Warner Avenue, Fountain Valley CA 92708-2597
County: Orange FICE Identification: 020635
Unit ID: 112385
Telephone: (714) 546-7600 Carnegie Class: Assoc/HT-Mix Trad/Non
FAX Number: (714) 241-6277 Calendar System: Semester
URL: www.coastline.edu
Established: 1976 Annual Undergrad Tuition & Fees (In-District): $1,160

Enrollment: 8,826 Coed
Affiliation or Control: State/Local IRS Status: 501(c)3
Highest Offering: Associate Degree
Accreditation: WJ

02 President ... Dr. Loretta P. ADRIAN
05 Vice Pres of Instruction ... Vacant
10 VP of Administrative Services ... Ms. Christine NGUYEN
32 Vice Pres Student Services ... Dr. Kate MUELLER
38 Dean Counseling/Matriculation ... Dr. Bruce KEELER
106 Assoc Dean of Distance Learning ... Mr. Bob NASH
12 Dean of Instruction Newport Beach ... Dr. Tom NEAL
12 Dean Instruct Tech Ed Garden Grove ... Dr. Nancy JONES
12 Dean Instruction Le Jao/Westminster ... Dr. Dana EMERSON
20 Dean Innovative Learning ... Dr. Shelly BLAIR
26 Director Public Relations/Marketing ... Ms. Dawn WILLSON
07 Director of Admissions/Records ... Ms. Jennifer MCDONALD
18 Director Maintenance & Operations ... Mr. Randy FLINT
21 Director Business Services ... Mr. Derek BUI
102 Exec Director College Foundation ... Ms. Mariam KHOSRAVANI
09 Dean Research/Plng/Effectiveness ... Dr. Aeron ZENTNER
24 Director of Electronic Media ... Ms. Judy GARVEY
15 Director of Personnel Services ... Ms. Renate DAVES
13 Director of Information Technology ... Mr. Dave THOMPSON
04 Admin Assistant to the President ... Vacant
19 Director Security/Safety ... Mr. Mike COLVER

*Golden West College (A)

15744 Golden West Street,
Huntington Beach CA 92647-2748
County: Orange FICE Identification: 001206
Unit ID: 115126
Telephone: (714) 892-7711 Carnegie Class: Assoc/HT-High Trad
FAX Number: (714) 895-8243 Calendar System: Semester
URL: www.goldenwestcollege.edu
Established: 1966 Annual Undergrad Tuition & Fees (In-District): $1,186
Enrollment: 11,396 Coed
Affiliation or Control: State/Local IRS Status: Exempt
Highest Offering: Associate Degree
Accreditation: WJ, ADNUR

02 President ... Mr. Tim MCGRATH
05 Vice Pres Instruction ... Ms. Meridith RANDALL
32 Vice Pres Student Services ... Dr. Claudia LEE
11 Vice Pres Admin Services ... Ms. Janet M. HOULIHAN
38 Dean Counseling ... Dr. Robyn BRAMMER
50 Executive Dean Business & Career Ed ... Mr. Christopher WHITESIDE
81 Interim Dean Math & Science ... Mr. Rick HICKS
49 Dean Arts & Letters ... Dr. David D. HUDSON
66 Dir School of Nursing ... Vacant
23 Director Student Health Center ... Dr. Judy CHENG
09 Dean Research/Plng/Inst Effect ... Dr. Kay NGUYEN
61 Dean Criminal Justice ... Mr. Ron LOWENBERG
35 Dean of Students & Library ... Ms. Carla MARTINEZ
84 Dean Enrollment Services ... Ms. Christina RYAN RODRIGUEZ
83 Dean Social Sci/Kines/Lrng Res ... Dr. Alex MIRANDA
15 Director Human Resources ... Ms. Leslie PICAZO
22 Dir DSPS ... Dr. Chad BOWMAN
10 Director Fiscal Services ... Mr. Paul WISNER
102 Director Foundation ... Mr. Bruce BERMAN
88 Coord Scholarships & Spec Events ... Ms. Valerie A. VENEGAS
07 Director of Admissions/Records ... Ms. Jennifer L. ORTBERG
37 Director of Financial Aid ... Ms. Adrienne BURTON
18 Director Maintenance & Operations ... Mr. Joseph B. DOWLING
41 Athletic Director ... Mr. Danny JOHNSON
04 Admin Asst to the President ... Ms. Diana RETES
19 Dir Public Safety/Emerg Prep ... Mr. Jon ARNOLD
35 Dir Student Life & Leadership Dev ... Mr. Frank CIRIONI
26 Dir Marketing & Public Relations ... Ms. Pam BRASHEAR
104 Dir of Global & Cultural Programs ... Ms. Melissa LYON
90 Dir Academic & User Support Svcs ... Mr. Kevin HARRISON
106 Dir Online Instruction ... Mr. Jorge ASCENCIO
31 Dir Community Educ & Swapmeet ... Vacant
88 Dir Guided Pathways/Dual Enroll ... Mr. Matt VALERIUS
88 Dir EOP&S ... Ms. Natalie TIMPSON

*Orange Coast College (B)

2701 Fairview Road, POB 5005, Costa Mesa CA 92626
County: Orange FICE Identification: 001250
Unit ID: 120342
Telephone: (714) 432-5072 Carnegie Class: Assoc/HT-High Trad
FAX Number: N/A Calendar System: Semester
URL: www.orangecoastcollege.edu
Established: 1947 Annual Undergrad Tuition & Fees (In-District): $1,188
Enrollment: 18,125 Coed
Affiliation or Control: State/Local IRS Status: 501(c)3
Highest Offering: Associate Degree
Accreditation: WJ, ACFEI, COARC, CVT, DA, DIETT, DMS, NDT, POLYT, RAD

02 President ... Dr. Angelica SUAREZ
05 Vice President of Instruction ... Ms. Michelle GRIMES-HILLMAN
32 Vice President Student Services ... Dr. Madjid NIROUMAND
10 Director of Fiscal Services ... Ms. Rachel KUBIK
11 Vice President Admin Services ... Dr. Richard PAGEL
84 Director Enrollment Services ... Mr. Efren GALVAN
38 Dean of Counseling ... Dr. Renee DE LONG
32 Dean of Students ... Dr. Derek VERGARA
22 Associate Dean Title IX ... Ms. Shannon QUIHUIZ
35 Director Student Life ... Mr. Michael MORVICE
26 Director Marketing & PR ... Mr. Juan GUTIERREZ
111 Exec Dir Institutional Advancement ... Mr. Douglas BENNETT
09 Admin Dir Research/Planning/IE ... Ms. Sheri STERNER
15 Director HR & Staff Development ... Ms. Rebecca MORGAN
07 Manager Enrollment Services ... Ms. Richelle PENALBA
18 Director Maintenance & Operations ... Vacant
37 Director Financial Aid ... Ms. Tanisha BRADFIELD
13 Interim Dir Information Technology ... Mr. Kevin HARRISON
23 Director Student Health Services ... Ms. Kelly DALY
88 Director Children's Center ... Ms. Patricia MENDOZA
41 Dean Kinesiology & Athletics ... Dr. Michael SUTLIFF
72 Dean of Technology ... Dr. Daniel SHRADER
50 Dean of Business & Computer Science ... Ms. Lisa KNUPPEL
83 Dean of Social & Behavioral Science ... Dr. Kevin HENSON
49 Dean of Literature & Languages ... Dr. Michael MANDELKERN
81 Dean of Math & Sciences ... Dr. Tara GIBLIN
88 Dean Consumer Health & Sciences ... Mr. Rodney FOSTER
57 Dean of Visual & Performing Arts ... Ms. Larissa NAZARENKO
25 Director CTE/Grants ... Ms. Lisa KNUPPEL
19 Interim Director Campus Security ... Mr. James RUDY
40 Manager Bookstore ... Mr. Todd MURPHY
85 Assoc Dean Global Engagement Ctr ... Mr. Nathan JENSEN
121 Dean Student Success & Student Svcs ... Mr. Stephen TAMANAHA
04 Executive Asst to President ... Ms. Thuy NGUYEN
08 Dean Library & Learning Support ... Mr. John TAYLOR
88 Director Maritime Center ... Ms. Sarah HIRSCH
22 Director Disabled Student Services ... Mr. Brian STOCKERT

The Colburn School (C)

200 S Grand Avenue, Los Angeles CA 90012-3007
County: Los Angeles Identification: 666233
Telephone: (213) 621-2200 Carnegie Class: Not Classified
FAX Number: (213) 621-2110 Calendar System: Semester
URL: www.colburnschool.edu
Established: 2003 Annual Undergrad Tuition & Fees: N/A
Enrollment: N/A Coed
Affiliation or Control: Independent Non-Profit IRS Status: 501(c)3
Highest Offering: Master's
Accreditation: MUS

01 President & CEO ... Mr. Sel KARDAN
05 Provost ... Dr. Adrian DALY
26 Vice President Communications ... Ms. Jennifer KALLEND
111 Vice President Advancement ... Ms. Annie WICKERT
15 Vice President Administration ... Ms. Linda CORMIER
10 Chief Financial Officer ... Ms. Maeesha MERCHANT

† Full room, board, and tuition are provided to accepted students through the school's endowment.

College of the Canyons (D)

26455 Rockwell Canyon Road,
Santa Clarita CA 91355-1899
County: Los Angeles FICE Identification: 008903
Unit ID: 111461
Telephone: (661) 259-7800 Carnegie Class: Assoc/HT-Mix Trad/Non
FAX Number: (661) 259-8302 Calendar System: Semester
URL: www.canyons.edu
Established: 1967 Annual Undergrad Tuition & Fees (In-District): $1,156
Enrollment: 20,573 Coed
Affiliation or Control: State/Local IRS Status: 501(c)3
Highest Offering: Associate Degree
Accreditation: WJ, MLTAD

01 Chancellor SCCCD & President COC ... Dr. Dianne G. VAN HOOK
03 Dep Chanc/Chief Diversity & Equity ... Dr. Diane FIERO
05 Asst Supt/VP Instruction ... Mr. Omar TORRES
10 Asst Supt/VP Business Services ... Ms. Sharlene COLEAL
15 Int Asst Supt/VP HR ... Dr. Rian MEDLIN
32 Asst Supt/VP Student Services ... Dr. Jasmine RUYS
18 Asst Supt/VP Facil Plng Op/Const ... Mr. Jim SCHRAGE
13 Asst Supt/VP Technology & Univ Ops ... Dr. James TEMPLE
103 VP Econ & Workforce Development ... Mr. Jeffrey FORREST
26 VP Public Info/Advoc/Ext Relations ... Mr. Eric HARNISH
12 VP Canyon County & Grants ... Dr. Ryan THEULE
21 Assoc VP Business Services ... Mr. Jason HINKLE
35 Assoc VP Student Services ... Mr. Michael JOSLIN
45 Assoc VP Inst Research & Planning ... Dr. Daylene MEUSCHKE
20 Assoc VP Instruction ... Mr. Paul WICKLINE
51 Dean Acad Innovation & Cont Ed ... Ms. Diane AVERY
69 Dean Health Prof & Public Safety ... Ms. Kathy BAKHIT
85 Dean Intl Affairs/Global Engagement ... Dr. Jia-Yi CHENG-LEVINE
50 Dean Sch Applied Tech/Int Dean Bus ... Ms. Nadia COTTI
106 Dean Educ Tech/Lrng Res/Dist Educ ... Mr. James GLAPA-GROSSKLAG
81 Dean Math/Science & Engineering ... Ms. Ann HAMILTON
75 Dean Career and Technical Educ ... Ms. Harriet HAPPEL
79 Dean Schs of Human/Social/Beh Sci ... Mr. Andy MCCUTCHEON
109 Dean Campus Services & Ops (CCC) ... Mr. Anthony MICHAELIDES
68 Dean Ph Educ/Kinesiology/Athletics ... Mr. Steve RUYS
57 Dean Vis & Perf Arts/Dir of PAC ... Ms. Jennifer SMOLOS
37 Assoc Dean Student Financial Aid ... Mr. Tom BILBRUCK
07 Assoc Dean Admiss/Records/Veterans ... Mr. Steve ERWIN
88 Assoc Dean Lrng Resources/Dir TLC ... Ms. Mojdeh MAHN
96 Exec Dir Contracts Proc/Risk Mgmt ... Ms. April GRAHAM
88 Exec Dir Small Bus Devel Center ... Ms. Catherine GROOMS
14 Exec Dir Infrastructure & Info Sec ... Mr. Hsiawen HULL
88 Exec Director Employee Training ... Mr. John MILBURN
102 Executive Director Foundation ... Ms. Michelle REY
105 Exec Dir Enterprise Applications ... Ms. Lisa SAWYER
88 Regional Dir Employer Engagement ... Mr. Michael BASTINE
88 Regional Dir Employer Engagement ... Ms. Paula HODGE
88 Dir EOPS/CARE/CalWORKS/RISE ... Ms. Cyndi BENDEZU PALOMINO
113 Director Student Business Office ... Ms. Kathleen BENZ
16 Director Human Resource Programs ... Ms. Maria CALDERON
88 Dir Prof Devel/Univ Ctr Operations ... Ms. Leslie CARR
88 Director Payroll ... Mr. Roy CASTILLO
88 Director Fiscal Services ... Ms. Balbir CHANDI
88 Director Grants Development ... Ms. Amber COLE
35 Dir Campus Life & Student Activity ... Ms. Kelly DAPP
88 Director Noncredit Enrollment Svcs ... Ms. Lisa FERRER PAVIK
88 MESA Program Director ... Ms. Amy FOOTE
31 Director of Community Relations ... Ms. Jasmine FOSTER
30 Director of Development ... Ms. Rane FRANKLIN
88 Director Academic Accommodations ... Ms. Terri GOLDSTEIN
27 Managing Dir District Comm ... Mr. John GREEN
88 Director Intl Services and Programs ... Mr. Tim HONADEL
88 Dir Volunteer & Stdnt Employment ... Mr. Yasser ISSA
88 Director Art Galleries ... Ms. Pamela LEWIS
84 Int Director Enrollment Support ... Mr. Alberto LOPEZ
23 Director Student Health & Wellness ... Ms. Mary MANUEL
28 Director Diversity and Inclusion ... Mr. Flavio MEDINA-MARTIN
88 Director Facilities ... Mr. Jason MUNOZ
88 Director Public Relations & Sports ... Mr. Jesse MUNOZ
41 Athletic Director ... Mr. Chad PETERS
19 Director Campus Safety ... Mr. Robert SADEH
25 Dir Grant/Categorical Accounting ... Ms. Carolyn SHAW
120 Interim Director Online Learning ... Ms. Joy SHOEMATE
124 Dir Outreach & School Relations ... Ms. Kari SOFFA
88 Director Veterans Resource Ctr ... Mr. Renard THOMAS
88 Dir Advertising/Social Media ... Ms. Wendy TRUJILLO
88 Dir Business Partnership/Work Engag ... Mr. Justin WALLACE
88 Director Civic Center ... Mr. Robin WILLIAMS
04 Special Assistant to the Chancellor ... Ms. Kristina HANCOCK

College of the Desert (E)

43-500 Monterey Avenue, Palm Desert CA 92260-9399
County: Riverside FICE Identification: 001182
Unit ID: 113573
Telephone: (760) 346-8041 Carnegie Class: Assoc/HT-High Trad
FAX Number: (760) 341-8678 Calendar System: Semester
URL: www.collegeofthedesert.edu
Established: 1958 Annual Undergrad Tuition & Fees (In-District): $1,383
Enrollment: 10,932 Coed
Affiliation or Control: State/Local IRS Status: 501(c)3
Highest Offering: Associate Degree
Accreditation: WJ

01 Interim Superintendent/President ... Mr. Jeff BAKER
05 VP Instruction & Student Services ... Dr. Annebelle NERY
10 Vice President Admin Services ... Mr. John RAMONT
15 Interim VP Human Resources ... Dr. Mark ZACOVIC
111 Int Exec Dir Inst Advancement ... Ms. Jessica ENDERS
102 Exec Dir of Foundation ... Ms. Catherine ABBOTT
13 Exec Dir Educational Technology ... Mr. Stuart DAVIS
18 Director of Maintenance/Operations ... Mr. Brandon TOEPFER
37 Director Financial Aid ... Ms. Kristen MILLIGAN
21 Director Fiscal Services ... Mr. Tony CARRILLO
06 Director Admissions and Records ... Ms. Cindy JUAREZ
09 Director Institutional Research ... Dr. Daniel MARTINEZ
12 Director Education Centers East ... Vacant
12 Director Education Centers West ... Mr. Scott ADKINS
19 Dir Pub Safety Dept/Emergency Prep ... Mr. Tim NAKAMURA
16 Director Human Resources ... Ms. Andrea STAEHLE
83 Dean of Social Science and Arts ... Ms. Sara BUTLER
04 Exec Admin Assistant to President ... Ms. Julia BREYER
08 Dir of Library & Learning Resources ... Vacant
79 Dean of Communication & Humanities ... Mr. Dean PAPAS
88 Exec Director Bond & Facilities ... Mr. John WHITE
25 Director Institutional Grants ... Ms. Caroline MALONEY
35 Int Associate Dean Student Services ... Mr. Carlos MALDONADO
38 Dean Counseling Services ... Ms. Amanda PHILLIPS
20 Int Associate Dean of Instruction ... Mr. Gary PLUNKETT
50 Dean Applied Sciences and Business ... Dr. Douglas BENOIT
76 Int Dean Health Sci & Education ... Dr. Courtney DOUSSETT
84 Dean Enrollment Services ... Dr. Oscar ESPINOZA-PARRA
81 Dean of Math and Science ... Mr. Steven HOLMAN
26 Public Information Officer ... Ms. Marion CHAMPION

College of Exercise Science, International Sports Sciences Association, LLC (F)

1015 Mark Avenue, Carpinteria CA 93013-2912
County: Santa Barbara FICE Identification: 042434
Unit ID: 485519
Telephone: (800) 650-4772 Carnegie Class: Spec 2-yr-Other
FAX Number: N/A Calendar System: Quarter
URL: https://college.issaonline.edu
Established: 1988 Annual Undergrad Tuition & Fees: $10,107
Enrollment: 431 Coed
Affiliation or Control: Proprietary IRS Status: Proprietary
Highest Offering: Master's
Accreditation: DEAC

01 President ... Alex HOFFMANN
05 Academic Dean/CAO ... Alex HOFFMANN
06 Registrar ... Holly HIGGINS

College of Marin (A)

835 College Avenue, Kentfield CA 94904-2590
County: Marin FICE Identification: 001178
Unit ID: 118347
Telephone: (415) 457-8811 Carnegie Class: Assoc/MT-VT-Mix Trad/Non
FAX Number: (415) 456-6017 Calendar System: Semester
URL: www.marin.edu
Established: 1926 Annual Undergrad Tuition & Fees (In-District): $1,494
Enrollment: 4,509 Coed
Affiliation or Control: State/Local IRS Status: 501(c)3
Highest Offering: Associate Degree
Accreditation: WJ, DA

01 Superintendent/President ... Dr. David W. COON
32 Asst Supt/VP Stdnt Learning/Success ... Mr. Jonathan ELDRIDGE
10 Asst Supt/VP Ops & Admin Svcs ... Mr. Greg NELSON
05 Asst VP of Instruction ... Ms. Cari TORRES-BENAVIDES
15 Manager Employee & Labor Relations ... Ms. Connie LEHUA
84 Dean Enrollment Services ... Mr. Jon HORINEK
103 Dean Workforce Dev & Career Educ ... Ms. Alina R. VARONA
81 Dean Math/Sciences ... Dr. Carol HERNANDEZ
49 Dean Arts & Humanities ... Vacant
21 Director Fiscal Services ... Ms. Peggy ISOZAKI
09 Exec Dir Plng/Research/Inst Plng ... Vacant
37 Asst Dean Enroll/Financial Aid ... Vacant
18 Dir Facil Planning & M&O ... Mr. Klaus CHRISTIANSEN
13 CIO & Director of IT ... Mr. Patrick EKOUE TOTOU
35 Dir Student Activities/Advocacy ... Ms. Sadika SULAIMAN HARA
19 Chief of Police ... Mr. Jeff MAROZICK
68 Dir Kinesiology & Athletics ... Mr. Ryan BYRNE
76 Dean Health Sciences ... Vacant
51 Dir Cmty/Lifelong/Intl Education ... Ms. Carol HILDEBRAND
22 Dir Student Accessibility Services ... Ms. Stormy C. MILLER
111 Director of Advancement ... Mr. Keith M. ROSENTHAL
26 Dir Marketing & Communications ... Ms. Nicole CRUZ
04 Exec Asst to Pres/Board ... Ms. Micol A. BENET
121 Dean Educational Success Programs ... Ms. Tonya HERSCH
43 General Counsel ... Ms. Mia ROBERTSHAW
88 Dir Child Development/Early Edu ... Ms. Corinna CALICA
08 Director of Library Services ... Vacant

College of the Sequoias (B)

915 S Mooney Boulevard, Visalia CA 93277-2234
County: Tulare FICE Identification: 001186
Unit ID: 123217
Telephone: (559) 730-3700 Carnegie Class: Assoc/HT-High Trad
FAX Number: (559) 730-3894 Calendar System: Semester
URL: www.cos.edu
Established: 1925 Annual Undergrad Tuition & Fees (In-District): $1,394
Enrollment: 12,571 Coed
Affiliation or Control: State/Local IRS Status: 501(c)3
Highest Offering: Associate Degree
Accreditation: WJ, PTAA

01 Superintendent/President ... Mr. Brent CALVIN
05 Vice President Academic Services ... Dr. Jennifer VEGA-LA SERNA
11 Vice President Administrative Svcs ... Mr. Ron BALLASTEROS-PEREZ
32 Vice President Student Services ... Ms. Jessica MORRISON
35 Dean Student Services ... Mr. Juan VAZQUEZ
35 Dean Student Services ... Ms. Michele BROCK
35 Dean Student Services ... Ms. Jenny SAE CHAO
12 Provost Tulare Center ... Dr. Louann WALDNER
12 Provost Hanford Center ... Dr. Kristin ROBINSON
81 Dean Science/Math/Eng ... Mr. Francisco BANUELOS
88 Dean Educ Support Services ... Ms. Angela SANCHEZ
49 Dean Arts & Letters ... Mr. Richard LUBBEN
50 Dean Business/Soc Sci/CFS ... Dr. Jesse WILCOXSON
09 Dean of Research ... Dr. Dali OZTURK
15 Dean Human Resources/Legal Affairs ... Mr. John BRATSCH
103 Dean CTE/Workforce Dev ... Dr. Jonna SCHENGEL
18 Dean Facilities ... Mr. Byron WOODS
13 Dean Info Technology ... Mr. Glen PROFETA
102 Exec Director Foundation ... Mr. Tim FOSTER
66 Dir Nursing/Allied Health ... Ms. Belen KERSTEN
08 Dir Library/Learning Resources ... Ms. Mai Soua LEE
88 Dir EOPS/CARE/NextUp ... Mr. Adrian BELTRAN
06 Registrar/Admissions Coordinator ... Ms. Velia RODRIGUEZ
41 Associate Dean/Athletic Director ... Mr. Brent DAVIS
19 Chief District Police ... Mr. Kevin MIZNER
37 Director Financial Aid ... Mr. David LOVERIN
40 Bookstore Manager ... Mr. Charles SLAGHT
88 Dir Access & Ability Center ... Ms. Lyndsi LITTEN
23 Director Health Center ... Ms. Joan DANIELS
88 Dir Foster Care/Independent Living ... Ms. Miriam SALLAM
35 Dir Student Activities/Affairs ... Ms. Debbie DOUGLASS
121 Director Student Success ... Ms. Elise GARCIA
26 Dir Marketing & PR ... Ms. Lauren FISHBACK
04 Executive Asst to President ... Ms. Meghan TIERCE
114 Dir Budgets & Categorical Accts ... Ms. Leangela MILLER-HERNANDEZ
10 Chief Accounting Officer ... Ms. Linda MCCAULEY
106 Coord Distance Education ... Vacant
88 Dir Dual Enrollment ... Mr. Brandon HILDRETH
88 Coord Outcomes/Assessment ... Dr. Sarah HARRIS
109 Manager Food Services ... Mr. Zachary PATTERSON

College of the Siskiyous (C)

800 College Avenue, Weed CA 96094-2899
County: Siskiyou FICE Identification: 001187
Unit ID: 123484
Telephone: (530) 938-5555 Carnegie Class: Assoc/HVT-High Non
FAX Number: (530) 938-5506 Calendar System: Semester
URL: www.siskiyous.edu
Established: 1957 Annual Undergrad Tuition & Fees (In-District): $1,496
Enrollment: 1,276 Coed
Affiliation or Control: State/Local IRS Status: 501(c)3
Highest Offering: Associate Degree
Accreditation: WJ, EMT

01 Superintendent/President ... Dr. Stephen SCHOONMAKER
10 Vice President Administrative Svcs ... Ms. Darlene MELBY
05 Vice President Instruction ... Dr. Char PERLES
32 Vice President Student Services ... Ms. Melissa GREEN
09 Int Dean Research & Evaluation ... Mr. Nathan REXFORD
41 Assoc Dean Instruction/Dir Athletic ... Mr. Charles ROCHE
75 Dean Career & Technical Education ... Vacant
07 Director Admissions & Records ... Ms. Meghan WITHERELL
15 Assoc Vice Pres Human Resources ... Ms. Theresa RICHMOND
18 Director Facilities ... Ms. Veronica RIVERA
111 Dir of Institutional Advancement ... Vacant
39 Director Student Housing ... Dr. Doug HAUGEN
26 Dir Comm Relations/Foundation ... Ms. Dawnie SLABAUGH
103 Director of Workforce Development ... Mr. Mark KLEVER
35 Director of Student Life ... Dr. Doug HAUGEN
36 Assoc Dean Student Success Programs ... Ms. Valerie ROBERTS

Columbia College Hollywood (D)

18618 Oxnard Street, Tarzana CA 91356-1411
County: Los Angeles FICE Identification: 021102
Unit ID: 112570
Telephone: (800) 785-0585 Carnegie Class: Spec-4-yr-Arts
FAX Number: (818) 345-9053 Calendar System: Quarter
URL: www.columbiacollege.edu
Established: 1952 Annual Undergrad Tuition & Fees: $26,175
Enrollment: 760 Coed
Affiliation or Control: Independent Non-Profit IRS Status: 501(c)3
Highest Offering: Baccalaureate
Accreditation: WC

01 President/CEO ... Mr. Bill SMITH
10 Chief Financial Officer ... Mr. Greg BUBLITZ
26 Director of Marketing ... Ms. Casey SULLIVAN
84 Vice Pres Enrollment Services ... Ms. Wendi FRANCZYK
05 CAO/Dean of Academic Affairs ... Mr. David CARTER
11 VP Operations ... Mr. Patrick OLMSTEAD
32 VP Student Affairs ... Ms. Kelly PARKER
108 VP Institutional Effectiveness ... Ms. Lex SANDERSON
06 Registrar ... Ms. Ingrid ELIAS
36 Sr Dir Career Dev & Alumni Affairs ... Ms. Kelley LEWIS
37 Director Financial Aid ... Dr. Jason CUPP
121 Director of Student Success ... Ms. Jessica JOHNSON-MILLS
15 Director of Human Resources ... Ms. Rena WRIGHT
07 Assoc Director Admissions ... Mr. Lee HUGHES
13 Manager of IT and Production Svcs ... Mr. Stephen DELELLO
18 Facilities Manager ... Mr. Johnny MENDOZA

Community Christian College (E)

1174 Nevada Street, 2nd Floor, Redlands CA 92374
County: San Bernardino FICE Identification: 038744
Unit ID: 446163
Telephone: (909) 794-1084 Carnegie Class: Assoc/HT-High Trad
FAX Number: (909) 794-1093 Calendar System: Quarter
URL: www.cccollege.edu
Established: 1995 Annual Undergrad Tuition & Fees: $9,750
Enrollment: 490 Coed
Affiliation or Control: Independent Non-Profit IRS Status: 501(c)3
Highest Offering: Associate Degree
Accreditation: TRACS

01 President ... Mr. Brian CARROLL
05 Vice Pres of Academic Affairs ... Dr. Robert GEE
10 Vice Pres Finance/Operations ... Mr. Richard DURANT
43 Corporate Counsel ... Mr. Robert ZIPRICK
32 Director of Student Services ... Vacant

Compton College (F)

1111 E Artesia Boulevard, Compton CA 90221-5393
County: Los Angeles FICE Identification: 001188
Unit ID: 112686
Telephone: (310) 900-1600 Carnegie Class: Assoc/MT-VT-Mix Trad/Non
FAX Number: N/A Calendar System: Semester
URL: www.compton.edu
Established: 1927 Annual Undergrad Tuition & Fees (In-State): $1,142
Enrollment: 4,612 Coed
Affiliation or Control: State IRS Status: 501(c)3
Highest Offering: Associate Degree
Accreditation: WJ

01 President/CEO ... Dr. Keith CURRY
05 Vice Pres Academic Affairs ... Ms. Sheri BERGER
32 Acting Vice Pres Student Services ... Mr. Henry GEE
10 Vice Pres Administrative Svcs ... Mr. Abdul NASSER
15 Vice President Human Resources ... Mrs. Rachelle SASSER
76 Dean Health/Human Services ... Ms. Wanda MORRIS
41 Dir Student Development/Athletics ... Mr. Andree PACHECO
08 Director Learning Resources ... Vacant
88 Director CalWORKs & DSPS ... Ms. Michelle GARCIA
22 Director EOP & S/CARE ... Ms. Christine ALDRICH
108 Director Institutional Effectivenes ... Ms. Lauren SOSENKO
37 Director Financial Aid ... Mr. Keith COBB
88 Dir Educational Partnerships ... Ms. Nelly ALVARADO
21 Director Fiscal Affairs ... Mr. Ruben JAMES
18 Chief Facilities Officer ... Ms. Linda OWENS
13 Chief Technology Officer ... Mr. Andrei YERMAKOV
07 Director Admissions & Records ... Ms. Richette BELL
06 Interim Assoc Registrar ... Mr. Brian DEAN
28 Dir Diversity/Compliance/Title IX ... Ms. Tina KUPERMAN
38 Dean Stdnt Counseling/Guided Pthwys ... Mr. Cesar JIMENEZ
96 Dir Purchasing/Auxilliary Svcs ... Mr. Reuben JAMES

† Regional accreditation is carried under the parent institution in Torrance, CA.

Concorde Career College (G)

12951 S. Euclid Street, Suite 101,
Garden Grove CA 92840-1451
County: Orange FICE Identification: 008071
Unit ID: 123679
Telephone: (714) 703-1900 Carnegie Class: Spec 2-yr-Health
FAX Number: (714) 530-8421 Calendar System: Semester
URL: concorde.edu/campus/garden-grove-california
Established: 1960 Annual Undergrad Tuition & Fees: N/A
Enrollment: 603 Coed
Affiliation or Control: Proprietary IRS Status: Proprietary
Highest Offering: Associate Degree
Accreditation: ACCSC, COARC, DH, PTAA

01 Campus President ... Ms. Lisa RHODES

Concorde Career College (H)

12412 Victory Boulevard, North Hollywood CA 91606-3134
County: Los Angeles FICE Identification: 007607
Unit ID: 124937
Telephone: (818) 766-8151 Carnegie Class: Spec 2-yr-Health
FAX Number: (818) 766-1587 Calendar System: Quarter
URL: https://www.concorde.edu/campus/north-hollywood-california
Established: 1955 Annual Undergrad Tuition & Fees: N/A
Enrollment: 613 Coed
Affiliation or Control: Proprietary IRS Status: Proprietary
Highest Offering: Associate Degree
Accreditation: ACCSC, COARC, PTAA

01 Campus President ... Garo GHAZARIAN
05 Academic Dean ... Walter GUVARA
07 Director of Admissions ... Allan GUECO
37 Director Student Financial Aid ... Cynthia STEIN

Concorde Career College (I)

201 E Airport Drive, San Bernadino CA 92408
County: San Bernardino FICE Identification: 008537
Unit ID: 124706
Telephone: (909) 884-8891 Carnegie Class: Spec 2-yr-Health
FAX Number: (909) 884-1831 Calendar System: Semester
URL: https://www.concorde.edu/campus/san-bernardino-california
Established: 1970 Annual Undergrad Tuition & Fees: N/A
Enrollment: 638 Coed
Affiliation or Control: Proprietary IRS Status: Proprietary
Highest Offering: Associate Degree
Accreditation: ACCSC, COARC, DH, NDT, POLYT, SURGT

01 Campus President ... Tracy WEST
07 Director of Admissions ... Sonia NAVARRO

Concorde Career College (J)

4393 Imperial Avenue, Suite 100,
San Diego CA 92113-1962
County: San Diego FICE Identification: 007930
Unit ID: 120661
Telephone: (619) 688-0800 Carnegie Class: Spec 2-yr-Health
FAX Number: (619) 220-4177 Calendar System: Other
URL: https://www.concorde.edu/campus/san-diego-california
Established: 1966 Annual Undergrad Tuition & Fees: N/A
Enrollment: 733 Coed
Affiliation or Control: Proprietary IRS Status: Proprietary
Highest Offering: Associate Degree
Accreditation: ACCSC, DH, PTAA, SURGT

01 Campus President ... Ms. Rachel SAFFEL
32 Director of Student Affairs ... Mr. Bill KILBY
07 Director of Admissions ... Ms. Renee CODNER

Concordia University Irvine (K)

1530 Concordia West, Irvine CA 92612-3299
County: Orange FICE Identification: 020705
Unit ID: 112075
Telephone: (949) 854-8002 Carnegie Class: Masters/L
FAX Number: (949) 214-3520 Calendar System: Semester
URL: www.cui.edu
Established: 1972 Annual Undergrad Tuition & Fees: $38,000
Enrollment: 4,071 Coed
Affiliation or Control: Lutheran Church - Missouri Synod
IRS Status: 501(c)3
Highest Offering: Doctorate
Accreditation: WC, CACREP, IACBE, MUS, NURSE

01 President ... Dr. Michael A. THOMAS
88 Vice Pres/Spec Asst to President ... Dr. Peter SENKBEIL
05 SVP/Provost ... RevDr. Scott ASHMON
111 Exec VP Advancement/Mktg/Comm ... Mr. Timothy J. JAEGER
10 Exec VP/Chief Financial Officer ... Mr. Kevin TILDEN
20 Assoc Provost ... Vacant
49 Dean School of Arts & Sciences ... Dr. Brett TAYLOR
50 Dean of Business ... Mr. George WRIGHT
107 Dean School of Professional Studies ... Mr. Mike SHURANCE
53 Dean School of Education ... Dr. Kent SCHLICHTEMEIER
73 Dean Christ College ... RevDr. Steven P. MUELLER
06 Registrar ... Ms. Dessa SOPER
09 Director of Institutional Research ... Mrs. Deborah LEE
32 VP Student Affairs/Dean of Students ... Mrs. Megan BOUSLAUGH
07 Director of Undergrad Admissions ... Vacant
123 Sr Director of Graduate Admissions ... Mr. Justin MOSCHINA
37 Director of Financial Aid ... Ms. Lori MCDONALD
113 Bursar ... Mr. Edgar LOPEZ
43 VP of Legal Affairs/General Counsel . Mr. Ronald VAN BLARCOM
15 AVP of Human Resources ... Mrs. Melinda MARTINEZ
08 Director of Library Services ... Ms. Laura GUZMAN
41 Athletic Director ... Ms. Crystal ROSENTHAL
35 Assoc Dean of Students ... Ms. Kristy FOWLER
19 Director Security/Safety ... Mr. Steven RODRIGUEZ
29 Exec Director of Alumni Relations ... Mr. Michael BERGLER
24 Senior Director of Faculty Training ... Prof. John RANDALL
36 Director of Career Services ... Mrs. Victoria JAFFEE
13 Director of IT Services ... Mr. Chris HARRIS
28 Director of Inclusion/Diversity ... Dr. Terilyn WALKER
106 Exec Dir Innov Instruction & eLrng ... Dr. Jason NEBEN

*Contra Costa Community College District Office (A)

500 Court Street, Martinez CA 94553-1278
County: Contra Costa FICE Identification: 001189
Unit ID: 112817
Telephone: (925) 229-1000 Carnegie Class: N/A
FAX Number: (925) 370-2019
URL: www.4cd.edu

01 Chancellor ... Dr. Bryan REECE
05 Exec VC Education and Technology ... Ms. Mojdeh MEHDIZADEH
11 Exec VC Administrative Svcs ... Mr. Eugene HUFF
20 AVC Educational Svcs ... Ms. Kelly SCHELIN
18 VC Facilities Plng/Construction ... Ms. Ines ZILDZIC
10 AVC/Chief Financial Officer ... Mr. Jonah NICHOLAS
15 AVC/Chief HR Officer ... Mr. Dio SHIPP

*Contra Costa College (B)

2600 Mission Bell Drive, San Pablo CA 94806-3195
County: Contra Costa FICE Identification: 001190
Unit ID: 112826
Telephone: (510) 235-7800 Carnegie Class: Assoc/MT-VT-Mix Trad/Non
FAX Number: N/A Calendar System: Semester
URL: www.contracosta.edu
Established: 1948 Annual Undergrad Tuition & Fees (In-District): $1,312
Enrollment: 6,249 Coed
Affiliation or Control: State/Local IRS Status: 501(c)3
Highest Offering: Associate Degree
Accreditation: WJ

02 President ... Dr. Tia ROBINSON-COOPER
06 Vice Pres of Student Services-Inter ... Jason CIFRA
05 Vice Pres of Instruction ... Dr. Kimberly R. ROGERS
10 Vice Pres of Business & Admin Svcs ... Dr. Tim HARRISON
108 Dean Inst Effectiveness & Equity ... Dr. Mayra PADILLA
26 Director of Marketing/Media Design ... Mr. Larry WOMACK
30 Dir Foundation/College Advancement ... Ms. Sara MARCELLINO
20 Senior Dean of Instruction ... Vacant
49 Dean Liberal Arts ... Mr. Jason BERNER
76 Interim Dean AACE ... Ms. Sandra MOORE
83 Dean of NSAS ... Ms. René SPORER
32 Dean of Student Services ... Mr. Dennis FRANCO
84 Dean of Enrollment Services ... Mr. Rod SANTOS
103 Dean of Economic & Workforce Dev ... Mr. Evan DECKER
07 Director Admissions & Records ... Mr. Cole MOYER
41 Athletics Director ... Mr. John WADE
09 Director of Institutional Research ... Vacant
18 Buildings & Grounds Manager ... Mr. Bruce KING
88 Custodial Manager ... Mr. William TANDONGFOR
21 Business Services Supervisor ... Mr. Nick DIMITRI
37 Financial Aid Supervisor ... Ms. Monica RODRIGUEZ
04 Senior Exec Asst to the President ... Ms. Joy BRUCELAS

*Diablo Valley College (C)

321 Golf Club Road, Pleasant Hill CA 94523-1544
County: Contra Costa FICE Identification: 001191
Unit ID: 113634
Telephone: (925) 685-1230 Carnegie Class: Assoc/HT-High Trad
FAX Number: (925) 685-1551 Calendar System: Semester
URL: www.dvc.edu
Established: 1949 Annual Undergrad Tuition & Fees (In-District): $1,312
Enrollment: 18,693 Coed
Affiliation or Control: State/Local IRS Status: 501(c)3
Highest Offering: Associate Degree
Accreditation: WJ, ACFEI, DA, DH

02 President ... Ms. Susan LAMB
05 Int Vice President Instruction ... Ms. Kim SCHENK
32 Vice President Student Services ... Dr. Vicki FERGUSON
10 Vice Pres Business & Admin Svcs ... Mr. Todd HAMPTON
20 Int Sr Dean Curriculum & Instr ... Ms. Nikki MOULTRIE
84 Dean Outreach/Enroll Mgt/Matric ... Vacant
12 Senior Dean San Ramon Campus ... Ms. Kenyetta TRIBBLE
41 Dean of Health/Athletic Director ... Ms. Christine WORSLEY
08 Dean Library/Ed Tech & Lrng Support ... Mr. Rick ROBISON
26 Dir Marketing and Media Design ... Ms. Brandy HOWARD
57 Dean Arts and Communication ... Ms. Janette FUNARO
81 Dean Sciences ... Mr. Joe GORGA
83 Dean Social Science ... Mr. Obed VAZQUEZ
50 Dean Math and Engineering ... Ms. Despina PRAPAVESSI
06 Registrar/Admissions ... Mr. Gabriel HARVEN
35 Dean Student Support Services ... Ms. Emily STONE
09 Int Dean IE/ALO ... Ms. Lindsay KONG
102 Director of College Advancement ... Mr. Jim BLAIR
103 Sr Dean Career & Community Partners ... Ms. Beth ARMAN
88 Dean English & Equity Pedagogy ... Mr. James NOEL
28 Dean of Student Engagement & Equity .. Ms. Rosa ARMENDARIZ
50 Dean Business ... Mr. Charlie SHI

*Los Medanos College (D)

2700 E Leland Road, Pittsburg CA 94565-5197
County: Contra Costa FICE Identification: 010340
Unit ID: 117894
Telephone: (925) 439-2181 Carnegie Class: Assoc/HT-High Trad
FAX Number: (925) 427-1599 Calendar System: Semester
URL: www.losmedanos.edu
Established: 1973 Annual Undergrad Tuition & Fees (In-District): $1,312
Enrollment: 8,521 Coed
Affiliation or Control: State/Local IRS Status: 501(c)3
Highest Offering: Associate Degree
Accreditation: WJ

02 President ... Dr. Bob KRATOCHVIL
04 Senior Executive Assistant ... Ms. Jennifer ADAMS
05 VP of Instruction ... Ms. Natalie HANNUM
32 VP of Student Services ... Dr. Tanisha MAXWELL
10 VP Business & Admin Services ... Dr. Carlos MONTOYA
45 Sr Dean Plng & Inst Effectiveness ... Dr. Chialin HSIEH
28 Dean of Equity & Inclusion ... Dr. Sabrina T. KWIST
81 Dean of Instruction ... Mr. Ryan PEDERSEN
75 Dean of Instruction ... Dr. Kristin LIMA
79 Dean of Instruction ... Vacant
38 Dean Counseling & Student Support ... Mr. Jeffrey BENFORD
121 Dean of Student Success ... Mr. David BELMAN
06 Dir Admissions & Records ... Ms. Rikki HALL
36 Director Transfer & Career Services ... Ms. Rachel ANICETTI
124 Dir Student Success/Retention Pgms ... Ms. Carla MOLINA
88 Director Early Childhood Lab School ... Ms. Angela FANTUZZI
35 Dir Student Life & Intl Student Pgm ... Ms. Teresea ARCHAGA
88 Asst Dir EOPS/CARE ... Mr. Steven FREEMAN, JR.
88 Outreach/Assessment Svcs Mgr ... Ms. Maryam PORTILLO
40 Bookstore Manager ... Mr. Robert ESTRADA
22 Manager Disability Support Services ... Ms. Virginia RICHARDS
103 Pgm Mgr Workforce & Econ Dev ... Mr. Bill BANKHEAD
88 Custodial Manager ... Mr. Frank ICHIGAYA
21 Business Services Supervisor ... Mr. Jinpa THARCHIN
18 Dir Maintenance & Operations ... Vacant
37 Financial Aid Supervisor ... Vacant
88 Office of Instruction Supervisor ... Ms. Eileen VALENZUELA
111 Dir College Advancement ... Dr. Trinh NGUYEN
26 Dir Marketing & Media Design ... Vacant
41 Athletic Director ... Mr. Richard VILLEGAS
19 Police Services ... Lt. Ryan HUDDLESTON

Copper Mountain College (E)

6162 Rotary Way, Box 1398, Joshua Tree CA 92252-6102
County: San Bernardino FICE Identification: 035424
Unit ID: 395362
Telephone: (760) 366-3791 Carnegie Class: Assoc/MT-VT-High Trad
FAX Number: (760) 366-5255 Calendar System: Semester
URL: www.cmccd.edu
Established: 1999 Annual Undergrad Tuition & Fees (In-District): $1,112
Enrollment: 1,539 Coed
Affiliation or Control: State/Local IRS Status: 170(c)1
Highest Offering: Associate Degree
Accreditation: WJ

01 Superintendent/President ... Dr. Daren OTTEN
05 VP of Academic Affairs/CIO ... Dr. Melynie SCHIEL
49 Dean of Arts & Sciences ... Vacant
32 VP of Student Services/CSSO ... Ms. Jane ABELL
15 Chief Human Resources Ofcr ... Ms. Bonnie BILGER
18 Director of Facilities & Operations ... Mr. Kevin COLE
102 Executive Director of Foundation ... Ms. Sandy SMITH
10 Chief Business Officer ... Ms. Meredith PLUMMER
35 Dean of Student Services ... Ms. Jennifer SPARLING
108 Dean of Institutional Effectiveness ... Ms. Alma CORREA
66 Coordinator for Nursing Programs ... Ms. Dawn PAGE
13 Director of Information Systems ... Mr. Steve KEMP
26 Public Relations & Event Specialist ... Ms. Jolie ALPIN
04 Executive Asst to the President ... Ms. Crisandra KAUFFMANN
07 Admissions & Records Specialist ... Ms. Maria CRUZ
08 Library Coordinator ... Mr. Derek MONYPENY
41 Athletic Director ... Mr. Ken SIMONDS

Cuesta College (F)

PO Box 8106, San Luis Obispo CA 93403-8106
County: San Luis Obispo FICE Identification: 001192
Unit ID: 113193
Telephone: (805) 546-3100 Carnegie Class: Assoc/HT-Mix Trad/Non
FAX Number: N/A Calendar System: Semester
URL: www.cuesta.edu
Established: 1963 Annual Undergrad Tuition & Fees (In-District): $1,338
Enrollment: 10,093 Coed
Affiliation or Control: State/Local IRS Status: 501(c)3
Highest Offering: Associate Degree
Accreditation: WJ, EMT

01 Superintendent/President ... Dr. Jill STEARNS
05 VP/Asst Supt Instruction ... Dr. Jason CURTIS
10 VP/Asst Supt Administrative Svcs ... Mr. Dan TROY
32 VP/Asst Supt Stdnt Success/Supp Pgm ... Dr. Elizabeth CORIA
15 Vice Pres Human Resource/Labor Rels . Ms. Melissa RICHERSON
35 Dean Stdnt Success/Support Pgm ... Dr. Maria ESCOBEDO
35 Dean Stdnt Success/Support Pgm ... Dr. Genevieve SIWABESSY
79 Dean of Instruct Arts/Hum/Math/Sci ... Ms. Madeline MEDEIROS
103 Dean of Instruct Hlth/Workforce/Kin ... Dr. John CASCAMO
09 Dean of Instruction IR & Cmty Engag ... Dr. Ryan CARTNAL
111 Exec Dir Found/Inst Advancement ... Ms. Shannon HILL
13 Exec Dir Information Technology ... Mr. Keith STEARNS
35 Coordinator Student Life/Leadership ... Dr. Anthony GUTIERREZ
66 Director of Nursing ... Ms. Marcia SCOTT
19 Chief of Police/College Safety ... Mr. David MILLARD
41 Director of Athletics ... Mr. Robert MARIUCCI
18 Director of Facilities Services ... Mr. Brian MCALISTER
84 Director Outreach/Enrollment Svcs ... Dr. Jeffery ALEXANDER
37 Assoc Dean Financial Aid & Records ... Ms. Zhrinna MCDONALD
31 Dir Workforce/Econ Devel Cmty Pgm ... Dr. Matthew GREEN
23 Director of Health Services ... Ms. Nicole JOHNSON
21 Director Fiscal Services ... Mr. Chris GREEN
102 Director of Philanthropy ... Ms. Michelle HANAFIAH
88 Director Foundation Fiscal Services ... Mr. Richard CAMARILLO
25 Director of Grant Development ... Vacant
04 Executive Asst to President ... Mr. Todd FREDERICK
04 Executive Asst to President ... Ms. Cindy DILBECK

The Culinary Institute of America at Greystone (G)

2555 Main Street, Saint Helena CA 94574-9504
Telephone: (707) 967-1100 Identification: 666260
Accreditation: &M

† Regional accreditation is carried under the parent institution in Hyde Park, NY.

Daybreak University (H)

1818 S. Western Ave #207, Los Angeles CA 90006
County: Los Angeles Identification: 667392
Telephone: (310) 739-0132 Carnegie Class: Not Classified
FAX Number: (270) 714-0317 Calendar System: Quarter
URL: www.daybreak.edu
Established: Annual Graduate Tuition & Fees: N/A
Enrollment: N/A Coed
Affiliation or Control: Independent Non-Profit IRS Status: 501(c)3
Highest Offering: Doctorate; No Undergraduates
Accreditation: TRACS

01 President ... Dr. Jea EUN OH
05 Academic Dean ... Dr. Hye JIN KIM
10 Business Manager/CFO ... Ms. Kathy Y. KANG
32 Director of Student Services ... Ms. Kyunghee BAEK
07 Director of Admisions/Registrar ... Ms. Grace J. LEE

Deep Springs College (I)

HC 72 Box 45001, Via Dyer, NV 89010-9803
County: Inyo FICE Identification: 001194
Telephone: (760) 872-2000 Carnegie Class: Not Classified
FAX Number: N/A Calendar System: Other
URL: www.deepsprings.edu
Established: 1917 Annual Undergrad Tuition & Fees: $0
Enrollment: N/A Coed
Affiliation or Control: Independent Non-Profit IRS Status: 501(c)3
Highest Offering: Associate Degree
Accreditation: WJ

01 President ... Ms. Sue DARLINGTON
05 Academic Dean ... Mr. Ryan DERBY-TALBOT
88 Ranch Manager ... Mr. Tim GIPSON
30 Director of Operations ... Mr. Padraic MACLEISH
30 Development Director ... Mr. John DEWIS
88 Chef/BH Manager ... Mr. Brian SHULSE
88 Assistant Ranch Manager ... Mr. Skyar FAVIER
04 Office Manager ... Mr. Steve TURNER

† A scholarship covers the costs of tuition, room, and board for every student.

Design Institute of San Diego (J)

8555 Commerce Avenue, San Diego CA 92121-2685
County: San Diego FICE Identification: 022980
Unit ID: 113582
Telephone: (858) 566-1200 Carnegie Class: Spec-4-yr-Arts
FAX Number: (858) 566-2711 Calendar System: Semester
URL: www.disd.edu
Established: 1977 Annual Undergrad Tuition & Fees: $25,649
Enrollment: 130 Coed
Affiliation or Control: Proprietary IRS Status: Proprietary
Highest Offering: Master's

Accreditation: WC, CIDA

01 CEO .... Ms. Margot DOUCETTE
11 Director of Operations .... Ms. Jessyca HOUCHINS
10 Chief Financial Officer .... Mr. Dennis DOUCETTE
05 Director of Academics .... Ms. Natalia WORDEN
07 Admissions .... Ms. Savanna MCDEDE
37 Financial Aid Director .... Ms. Jackie GLORIA
32 Director of Student Services .... Ms. Molly DISHMAN
08 Library Director .... Ms. Lisa SCHATTMAN
06 Registrar .... Ms. Tracy GULINO
36 Career Advisor .... Mr. Crandon GUSTAFSON

Dharma Realm Buddhist University (A)

4951 Bodhi Way, Ukiah CA 95482

County: Sacramento | Identification: 667334
Telephone: (707) 621-7000 | Carnegie Class: Not Classified
FAX Number: N/A | Calendar System: Semester
URL: www.drbu.org
Established: 1976 | Annual Undergrad Tuition & Fees: N/A
Enrollment: N/A | Coed
Affiliation or Control: Independent Non-Profit | IRS Status: 501(c)3
Highest Offering: Master's
Accreditation: WC

01 President .... Susan ROUNDS
10 VP Finance & Admin/Provost .... Douglas POWERS
05 Dean of Academics .... Martin VERHOEVEN
32 Dean of Students .... Heng LIANG

Dominican School of Philosophy and Theology (B)

2301 Vine Street, Berkeley CA 94708-1816

County: Alameda | FICE Identification: 001296
Unit ID: 113704
Telephone: (510) 849-2030 | Carnegie Class: Spec-4-yr-Faith
FAX Number: (510) 849-1372 | Calendar System: Semester
URL: www.dspt.edu
Established: 1932 | Annual Undergrad Tuition & Fees: N/A
Enrollment: 72 | Coed
Affiliation or Control: Roman Catholic | IRS Status: 501(c)3
Highest Offering: Master's
Accreditation: WC, THEOL

01 President .... Fr. Peter ROGERS
05 Academic Dean .... Rev. Christopher M. RENZ
10 Vice Pres Finance/Administration .... Mr. Ian BROOKS
07 Director of Admissions/Recruitment .... Mr. Aaron ANDERSON
06 Registrar/Student Services .... Ms. Leslie BORQUEZ
26 Director of Communications .... Ms. Heidi MCKENNA
30 Director of Development .... Mr. Marc ROVETTI
09 Director of Institutional Research .... Rev. Christopher RENZ
100 Chief of Staff .... Mr. Chris OWENS

Dominican University of California (C)

50 Acacia Avenue, San Rafael CA 94901-2298

County: Marin | FICE Identification: 001196
Unit ID: 113698
Telephone: (415) 457-4440 | Carnegie Class: Masters/M
FAX Number: N/A | Calendar System: Semester
URL: www.dominican.edu
Established: 1890 | Annual Undergrad Tuition & Fees: $47,910
Enrollment: 1,837 | Coed
Affiliation or Control: Independent Non-Profit | IRS Status: 501(c)3
Highest Offering: Doctorate
Accreditation: WC, #ARCPA, ART, NURSE, OT

01 President .... Dr. Nicola PITCHFORD
05 VP Academic Affairs/Dean of Faculty .... Ms. Mojgan BEHMAND
10 Int VP Finance and Administration .... Mr. Robert HITE
32 Dean of Student Affairs .... Dr. Paul RACCANELLO
84 Int Vice Pres Enrollment/Marketing .... Mr. Brandon BOULTER
111 VP for Advancement & Public Affairs .... Ms. Marly NORRIS
20 AVP Academic Affairs/Dean Dom Exp .... Vacant
06 AVP Academic Svcs/Univ Registrar .... Ms. Colette GALIANI
29 AVP Alumni Engagement/Annual Fund .... Ms. Jessica JORDAN
27 Executive Director Communications .... Ms. Sarah GARDNER
04 Exec Assistant President's Office .... Ms. Sandy PEARSON
101 Special Asst to Pres/Board Sec .... Ms. Jennifer KRENGEL
49 Dean Sch Liberal Arts & Education .... Dr. Gigi GOKCEK
50 Dean Barowsky School of Business .... Dr. Yung-Jae LEE
81 Dean Sch Health/Natural Science .... Dr. Ruth RAMSEY
18 Executive Director Facilities Svcs .... Mr. John HASHIZUME
08 University Librarian .... Mr. Gary GORKA
09 Director of Institutional Research .... Dr. Yu-Ti HUANG
37 Director Financial Aid .... Ms. Zelotes SMITH
07 Director Undergrad Admissions .... Ms. Maria GENTILE
15 Director Human Resources .... Mr. Jesse ANDREWS
121 Sr Director Integrative Coaching .... Ms. Naomi ELVOVE
92 Director Honors Program .... Ms. Lynn SONDAG
38 Director Univ Counseling Services .... Dr. Diane SUFFRIDGE
85 Sr Intl Officer & GEO Director .... Dr. Kati BELL
41 Director of Athletics & Rec Sports .... Ms. Amy HENKELMAN
102 Dir Foundation/Corp/Govt Relations .... Ms. Lenice SMITH
30 Director of Development .... Ms. Tracy STEMPEL HOGEN

Dongguk University Los Angeles (D)

440 Shatto Place, 2nd floor, Los Angeles CA 90020

County: Los Angeles | FICE Identification: 031095
Unit ID: 122117
Telephone: (213) 487-0110 | Carnegie Class: Spec-4-yr-Other Health
FAX Number: (213) 487-0527 | Calendar System: Quarter
URL: www.dula.edu
Established: 1979 | Annual Undergrad Tuition & Fees: N/A
Enrollment: 158 | Coed
Affiliation or Control: Independent Non-Profit | IRS Status: 501(c)3
Highest Offering: Master's; No Lower Division
Accreditation: ACUP

01 President .... Dr. Seung Deok LEE
05 Dean of Academic Affairs .... Dr. Yae CHANG
10 Chief Operating Officer/Finance Mgr .... John JEON
32 Director of Student Affairs .... Dr. Adrianus Hilman WONG
37 Director Financial Aid .... Vacant
07 Director of Admissions .... Chan Ho KIM
04 Office Manager .... Eun Young LEE
06 Registrar/Program Director .... Minji KIM
18 Facilities Manager .... Emilio LOPEZ
15 Human Resources Admin .... John JEON

El Camino College (E)

16007 Crenshaw Boulevard, Torrance CA 90506-0002

County: Los Angeles | FICE Identification: 001197
Unit ID: 113980
Telephone: (310) 660-3593 | Carnegie Class: Assoc/HT-High Trad
FAX Number: (310) 660-7798 | Calendar System: Semester
URL: www.elcamino.edu
Established: 1947 | Annual Undergrad Tuition & Fees (In-District): $1,144
Enrollment: 20,418 | Coed
Affiliation or Control: State/Local | IRS Status: 501(c)3
Highest Offering: Associate Degree
Accreditation: WJ, COARC, RAD

01 President .... Dr. Brenda A. THAMES
05 Interim VP Academic Affairs .... Dr. Jaquelyn SIMS
10 Interim VP Administrative Services .... Ms. Ann TOMLINSON
32 Vice Pres Student Services .... Mr. Ross MIYASHIRO
15 Vice Pres of Human Resources .... Ms. Jane MIYASHIRO
111 Dean Community Advancement .... Mr. Jose ANAYA
72 Dean Industry & Technology .... Mr. David GONZALES
81 Dean Mathematics .... Dr. Marlow LEMONS
50 Dean of Business .... Dr. Virginia RAPP
83 Dean Behavioral & Social Science .... Dr. Chris GOLD
68 Int Dean Health Science & Athletics .... Mr. Russel SERR
57 Dean Fine Arts .... Dr. Berkeley PRICE
76 Dean Natural Sciences .... Dr. Amy GRANT
79 Dean Humanities .... Ms. Debra BRECKHEIMER
08 Dean Library & Learning Resources .... Dr. Crystle MARTIN
121 Dean Counseling & Student Success .... Dr. Dipte PALEL
121 Dean of Student Support Services .... Ms. Idania REYES
84 Dean of Enrollment Services .... Mr. Robin DREIZLER
88 Director Special Resource Center .... Mr. Gary GRECO
13 Chief Technology Officer .... Mr. Loic AUDUSSEAU
26 Exec Dir Marketing/Communications .... Ms. Ann O'BRIEN
106 Coordinator Distance Education .... Dr. Moses WOLFENSTEIN
88 Director Public Safety .... Chief Jeffrey BAUMUNK
66 Director of Nursing .... Vacant
86 Public Info & Government Relations .... Ms. Kerri WEBB
102 Executive Director Foundation .... Ms. Andrea SALA
96 Dir Procurement & Risk Management .... Vacant
40 Director of Bookstore .... Ms. Julie BOURLIER
19 Chief of Campus Police .... Mr. Michael TREVIS
18 Exec Dir Facilities Planning/Svcs .... Mr. Jorge GUTIERREZ
35 Director of Student Development .... Dr. Gregory TOYA
37 Director Student Financial Aid .... Vacant
06 Registrar .... Ms. Lillian JUSTICE
09 Dir Institutional Research/Planning .... Ms. Viviana UNDA
28 Dir Title IX/Diversity & Inclusion .... Dr. Jayne ISHIKAWA
21 Business Manager .... Mr. Jeffrey HINSHAW
103 Director Career Education .... Ms. Adriana ESTRADA
25 Grants Development & Management .... Ms. Roberta BECKA
41 Interim Athletic Director .... Mr. Jeff MIERA
04 Executive Asst to President .... Ms. Rose MAHOWALD

Emperor's College of Traditional Oriental Medicine (F)

1807-B Wilshire Boulevard, Santa Monica CA 90403-5678

County: Los Angeles | FICE Identification: 026090
Unit ID: 114114
Telephone: (310) 453-8300 | Carnegie Class: Spec-4-yr-Other Health
FAX Number: (310) 829-3838 | Calendar System: Quarter
URL: www.emperors.edu
Established: 1983 | Annual Undergrad Tuition & Fees: N/A
Enrollment: 228 | Coed
Affiliation or Control: Proprietary | IRS Status: Proprietary
Highest Offering: Doctorate
Accreditation: ACUP

01 Chief Executive Officer/President .... Yun KIM
05 Academic Dean .... Jacques MORAMARCO
63 Dean of Clinical Education .... Robert NEWMAN
11 Chief Operations Officer .... George PARK

Empire College (G)

3035 Cleveland Avenue, Santa Rosa CA 95403-2100

County: Sonoma | FICE Identification: 009032
Unit ID: 114123
Telephone: (707) 546-4000 | Carnegie Class: Bac/Assoc-Mixed
FAX Number: (707) 546-4058 | Calendar System: Other
URL: www.empcol.edu
Established: 1961 | Annual Undergrad Tuition & Fees: N/A
Enrollment: 241 | Coed
Affiliation or Control: Proprietary | IRS Status: Proprietary
Highest Offering: Master's
Accreditation: ACICS

01 President .... Mr. Roy HURD
26 Vice Pres Marketing/Administration .... Mrs. Sherie HURD

Epic Bible College & Graduate School (H)

4330 Auburn Boulevard, Sacramento CA 95841

County: Sacramento | FICE Identification: 034033
Unit ID: 124487
Telephone: (916) 348-4689 | Carnegie Class: Spec-4-yr-Faith
FAX Number: (916) 468-0866 | Calendar System: Trimester
URL: www.EPIC.edu
Established: 1974 | Annual Undergrad Tuition & Fees: $9,689
Enrollment: 170 | Coed
Affiliation or Control: Independent Non-Profit | IRS Status: 501(c)3
Highest Offering: Doctorate
Accreditation: TRACS

01 President/CEO .... Dr. Ronald W. HARDEN
05 Vice President of Academics .... Dr. Greg L. HARTLEY
58 Director Graduate Studies .... Dr. Gene MAYNARD
73 Chair of Worship Arts .... Rev. Lane OLSON
08 Director Learning Resource .... Rev. Deborah MCCONKEY
37 Director of Financial Services .... Ms. Kandi MCGODMAN
06 Director of Records/Office Manager .... Mrs. Monida SLUPIK
106 Director of Online Program .... Rev. John GALLEGOS
26 Director Enrollment/Marketing .... Rev. Daniel HARDEN

Eternity Bible College (I)

2136 Winifred Street, Simi Valley CA 93063

County: Ventura | Identification: 667045
Telephone: (805) 581-1233 | Carnegie Class: Not Classified
FAX Number: (805) 581-1245 | Calendar System: Semester
URL: www.eternitybiblecollege.com
Established: 2004 | Annual Undergrad Tuition & Fees: N/A
Enrollment: N/A | Coed
Affiliation or Control: Independent Non-Profit | IRS Status: 501(c)3
Highest Offering: Baccalaureate
Accreditation: BI

01 President .... Spencer MACCUISH
05 Academic Dean .... Joshua WALKER
32 Dean of Students .... Chris KOTTRE
07 Director of Admissions .... Mary Beth DRAGOUN
10 Registrar/Finance Manager .... Ryan MCGLADDERY
35 Dir Student Life/Exec Asst .... Nicole MCGLADDERY

Evangelia University (J)

2660 West Woodland Drive, Suite 200, Anaheim CA 92801-2650

County: Orange | Identification: 666640
Telephone: (714) 527-0691 | Carnegie Class: Not Classified
FAX Number: (714) 527-0693 | Calendar System: Other
URL: www.evangelia.edu
Established: 1999 | Annual Undergrad Tuition & Fees: N/A
Enrollment: N/A | Coed
Affiliation or Control: Reformed Presbyterian Church | IRS Status: 501(c)3
Highest Offering: Doctorate
Accreditation: TRACS

01 President/CEO .... Dr. Sung Soo KIM
03 Vice President .... Dr. David CHO
05 Dean of Academic Affairs .... Dr. Soonhae KANG
11 Dean Admin/Chief Operating Officer .... Ki Won HAN
32 Dean of Student Affairs .... Ki Won HAN
10 Chief Financial Officer .... Dr. Chang Ho SON
06 Registrar/Foreign Student Advisor .... Charley LEE
08 Librarian .... Su Chung CHAY
106 Director of Distance Education .... Soonhae KANG

Ezra University (K)

2064 Marengo Street, Suite 200, Los Angeles CA 90033

County: Los Angeles | Identification: 667316
Telephone: (323) 221-1024 | Carnegie Class: Not Classified
FAX Number: (323) 221-1025 | Calendar System: Quarter
URL: www.ezrauniversity.org
Established: 1997 | Annual Undergrad Tuition & Fees: N/A
Enrollment: N/A | Coed
Affiliation or Control: Independent Non-Profit | IRS Status: 501(c)3
Highest Offering: Master's
Accreditation: @BI

01 President .... Dr. John PYEON
05 Dean of Academics .... Dr. L. Arik GREENBERG

Feather River College (A)

570 Golden Eagle Avenue, Quincy CA 95971-9124
County: Plumas FICE Identification: 008597
Unit ID: 114433
Telephone: (530) 283-0202 Carnegie Class: Bac/Assoc-Assoc Dom
FAX Number: (530) 283-3757 Calendar System: Semester
URL: www.frc.edu
Established: 1968 Annual Undergrad Tuition & Fees (In-District): $1,465
Enrollment: 1,821 Coed
Affiliation or Control: State/Local IRS Status: 501(c)3
Highest Offering: Baccalaureate
Accreditation: WJ

01 Superintendent/President .... Dr. Kevin TRUTNA
10 Vice President Business Services .... Mr. John IVES
05 Vice President Instruction/CIO .... Dr. Derek LERCH
32 Vice President Student Services .... Ms. Carlie MCCARTHY
20 Assistant Dean of Instruction .... Dr. Kim BEATON
15 Director Human Resources/EEO .... Mr. David BURRIS
18 Director of Facilities/CTO .... Mr. Nick BOYD
07 Registrar/Dir of Admissions .... Ms. Gretchen BAUMGARTNER
37 Director Student Financial Aid .... Mr. Andre VAN DER VELDEN
96 Purchasing Agent .... Ms. Tamara CLINE
04 Administrative Asst to President .... Ms. Cynthia HALL
09 Director of Institutional Research .... Vacant

FIDM/Fashion Institute of Design and Merchandising-Los Angeles (B)

919 S Grand Avenue, Los Angeles CA 90015-1421
County: Los Angeles FICE Identification: 011112
Unit ID: 114354
Telephone: (213) 624-1200 Carnegie Class: Spec-4-yr-Arts
FAX Number: (213) 624-9354 Calendar System: Quarter
URL: www.fidm.edu
Established: 1969 Annual Undergrad Tuition & Fees: $32,645
Enrollment: 1,886 Coed
Affiliation or Control: Proprietary IRS Status: Proprietary
Highest Offering: Master's
Accreditation: WC, ART

01 President .... Ms. Tonian HOHBERG
10 Vice President/Treasurer .... Ms. Tess STOLZER
26 Vice President Marketing/Admission .... Ms. Belinda HARDING
05 Vice President Education .... Ms. Barbara BUNDY
108 Dean of Accreditation .... Ms. Lisa SCHOENING
08 Director of the Idea Center .... Ms. Debbie SCHUVER
06 Registrar .... Mr. Michael GILBERT
37 Director Financial Aid .... Mr. Chris JENNINGS
27 Director Public Rels/Publicity .... Ms. Shirley WILSON
38 Personal Counselor .... Ms. Jessica CATTANI
96 Director College Services .... Ms. Ella VAN NORT
13 Director IT Technical Services .... Ms. Saima LATIF
15 Exec Director Human Resources .... Ms. Kim WETZEL
04 Executive Asst to President .... Ms. Megan NOWAK
104 Director International Affairs .... Ms. Sarah REPETTO
105 Director Web Mktg Ops/Publications .... Mr. Michael KAMINSKI
18 Director of FIDM Facilities .... Mr. John (Buddy) BOLOGNONE
19 Director of Security .... Mr. Todd J. ANDERSON
22 Title IX Coordinator .... Ms. Kim WETZEL
29 Director Alumni Relations .... Mr. Kevin KEELE
32 Manager Student Activities .... Ms. Angela LEAVITT
53 Dean of Education .... Ms. Sheryl RABINOVICH
90 Director Academic Computing .... Ms. Cheryl BENSMILLER

FIDM/Fashion Institute of Design and Merchandising-Orange County (C)

17590 Gillette Avenue, Irvine CA 92614-5610
Telephone: (888) 974-3436 Identification: 666004
Accreditation: &WC, ART

† Regional accreditation is carried under the parent institution in Los Angeles, CA.

Fielding Graduate University (D)

2020 De La Vina Street, Santa Barbara CA 93105-3538
County: Santa Barbara FICE Identification: 020961
Unit ID: 114549
Telephone: (800) 340-1099 Carnegie Class: DU-Mod
FAX Number: (805) 687-9793 Calendar System: Trimester
URL: www.fielding.edu
Established: 1974 Annual Graduate Tuition & Fees: N/A
Enrollment: 1,071 Coed
Affiliation or Control: Independent Non-Profit IRS Status: 501(c)3
Highest Offering: Doctorate; No Undergraduates
Accreditation: WC, CLPSY

01 President .... Dr. Katrina S. ROGERS
04 Exec Asst to President .... Mr. Bryan LOPES
03 Distinguished Sr Advisor to Pres .... Dr. Orlando L. TAYLOR
10 VP and Chief Financial Officer .... Ms. Prema WINDOKUN
05 Provost & Senior VP .... Dr. Raj PARIKH
15 Director of Human Resources .... Mr. Dino FERRARE
06 Registrar/Dir of Curriculum Svcs .... Ms. Bridget BRADY
29 Director of Alumni Relations .... Ms. Hilary MOLINA
28 Chief Diversity Officer .... Vacant
07 Director of Admissions .... Ms. Erica FICHTER
09 Director of Institutional Research .... Ms. Marine DUMAS

Five Branches University, Graduate School of Traditional Chinese Medicine (E)

1885 Lundy Avenue, Suite 108, San Jose CA 95131
County: Santa Clara Identification: 667008
Telephone: (408) 260-0208 Carnegie Class: Not Classified
FAX Number: (408) 261-3166 Calendar System: Trimester
URL: www.fivebranches.edu
Established: 2005 Annual Undergrad Tuition & Fees: N/A
Enrollment: N/A Coed
Affiliation or Control: Proprietary IRS Status: Proprietary
Highest Offering: Doctorate; No Lower Division
Accreditation: ACUP

01 President/CEO .... Ron ZAIDMAN
05 VP Academic Affairs .... Joanna ZHAO
10 VP Finance .... Liana CHEN
13 VP Operations .... Gina HUANG
06 Registrar .... Ling ZHANG
58 Director of Doctoral Program .... Robyn GRIEVE
26 Director of Marketing .... Sean ZAIDMAN
37 Director of Financial Aid .... Daryl CULLEN
58 Associate Director Doctoral Program .... Debbie CHENG
84 Director of Enrollment .... Alex HU
56 Extension Program Admin .... Lykos YANG
23 Clinic Manager .... Joyce HE
08 Library & Facility Manager .... Songsong GAO
20 Associate Academic Dean .... Nick HANCOCK

Five Branches University, Graduate School of Traditional Chinese Medicine (F)

200 7th Avenue, Santa Cruz CA 95062-4669
County: Santa Cruz FICE Identification: 031313
Unit ID: 114585
Telephone: (831) 476-9424 Carnegie Class: Spec-4-yr-Other Health
FAX Number: (831) 476-8928 Calendar System: Trimester
URL: www.fivebranches.edu
Established: 1984 Annual Undergrad Tuition & Fees: N/A
Enrollment: 349 Coed
Affiliation or Control: Proprietary IRS Status: Proprietary
Highest Offering: Doctorate; No Lower Division
Accreditation: ACUP

01 President & CEO .... Ron ZAIDMAN
05 Vice President & Dean .... Joanna ZHAO
11 Vice President Operations .... Gina HUANG
10 Vice President Finance & Accounting .... Liana CHEN
26 Dir of Marketing & Communications .... Sean ZAIDMAN
08 Librarian .... Jim EMDY
06 Registrar San Jose .... Ling ZHANG
32 Director Student Services .... Andrea CARVALHO
07 Admissions Director .... Eleonor MENDELSON
37 Director Student Financial Aid .... Daryl CULLEN
56 Director Extension Programs .... Fay DENNIS
07 Director Bridge Program Admissions .... Tom DICKLIN

*Foothill-De Anza Community College District System Office (G)

12345 El Monte Road, Los Altos Hills CA 94022-4597
County: Santa Clara FICE Identification: 009020
Unit ID: 114831
Telephone: (650) 949-6100 Carnegie Class: N/A
FAX Number: (650) 941-6289
URL: www.fhda.edu

01 Chancellor .... Dr. Judy C. MINER
10 Vice Chancellor Business Services .... Ms. Susan CHEU
15 Vice Chancellor Human Resources .... Ms. Dorene NOVOTNY
13 Vice Chancellor Technology .... Mr. Joseph MOREAU
09 Exec Dir of Inst Research/Planning .... Mr. David ULATE
19 Chief of Police .... Mr. Daniel ACOSTA
26 Coordinator District Communication .... Ms. Becky BARTINDALE
102 Exec Dir Foundation .... Mr. Dennis CIMA
96 Director of Purchasing .... Ms. Maria CONTRERAS-TANORI

*De Anza College (H)

21250 Stevens Creek Boulevard, Cupertino CA 95014-5793
County: Santa Clara FICE Identification: 004480
Unit ID: 113333
Telephone: (408) 864-5678 Carnegie Class: Assoc/HVT-High Trad
FAX Number: (408) 864-8238 Calendar System: Quarter
URL: www.deanza.edu
Established: 1967 Annual Undergrad Tuition & Fees (In-District): $1,561
Enrollment: 18,649 Coed
Affiliation or Control: State/Local IRS Status: 501(c)3
Highest Offering: Associate Degree
Accreditation: WJ, MLTAD, NAEYC

02 President .... Dr. Lloyd HOLMES
05 Vice Pres of Instruction .... Ms. Christina G. ESPINOSA-PIEB
32 VP of Student Services .... Dr. Rob MIESO
10 VP Administrative Services .... Ms. Pam GREY
20 Assoc Vice Pres Instruction .... Vacant
26 AVP Communications & External Rel .... Ms. Marisa SPATAFORE
35 Dean Student Development/EOPS .... Dr. Michele LEBLEU BURNS
38 Dean Counseling & Matriculation .... Ms. Laureen BALDUCCI
84 Dean Enrollment Services .... Ms. Nazy GALOYAN
37 Director Student Financial Aid .... Ms. Lisa MANDY
21 Director Fiscal Services .... Mr. Martin VALERA
18 Assoc Vice Pres College Operations .... Vacant
102 Exec Director Foundation .... Mr. Dennis CIMA
28 Dean Equity & Engagement .... Ms. Alicia CORTEZ
36 Supervisor Student Placement .... Ms. Casie WHEAT
09 Institutional Researcher .... Dr. Mallory NEWELL
06 Supervisor Admissions and Records .... Mr. Barry JOHNSON
04 Executive Assistant to President .... Ms. Nathaly AGUILAR
08 Head Librarian .... Mr. Tom DOLEN
13 Chief Info Technology Officer (CIO) .... Mr. Joe MOREAU
41 Athletic Director .... Mr. Kulwant SINGH
50 Dean Business/Comp Sys/Applied Tech .... Mr. Moaty FAYEK
15 Human Resources Technician .... Ms. Kit PERALES

*Foothill College (I)

12345 El Monte Road, Los Altos Hills CA 94022-4599
County: Santa Clara FICE Identification: 001199
Unit ID: 114716
Telephone: (650) 949-7777 Carnegie Class: Bac/Assoc-Assoc Dom
FAX Number: (650) 949-7375 Calendar System: Quarter
URL: www.foothill.edu
Established: 1957 Annual Undergrad Tuition & Fees (In-District): $1,563
Enrollment: 14,605 Coed
Affiliation or Control: State/Local IRS Status: 501(c)3
Highest Offering: Baccalaureate
Accreditation: WJ, COARC, DA, DH, DMS, EMT, RAD

02 President .... Ms. Thuy NGUYEN
04 Assistant to the President .... Ms. Veronica CASAS HERNANDEZ
10 VP Finance & Admin Services .... Mr. Bret WATSON
05 Exec VP Instruction & Inst Research .... Dr. Kristy LISLE
20 Int Associate VP Instruction .... Mr. Paul STARER
20 Assoc Vice Pres Instruction .... Mr. Kurt HUEG
32 Associate VP Student Services .... Dr. Laurie SCOLARI
21 Associate VP Finance & Admin Svcs .... Mr. Bret WATSON
35 Dean Student Affairs & Activities .... Ms. Leticia MALDONADO
38 Dean Counseling & Special Programs .... Mr. Roosevelt CHARLES
28 Dean EOPS .... Ms. April HENDERSON
12 Campus Director Sunnyvale Center .... Mr. Craig GAWLICK
88 Dean Disabled Stdnt Svcs/Vet Pgms .... Ms. Neelam AGARWAL
40 Director Bookstore .... Mr. Romeo PAULE
84 Dean Enrollment Services .... Mr. Anthony CERVANTES
37 Director Financial Aid .... Mr. Kevin HARRAL
22 Dean of Equity Programs .... Dr. Melissa CERVANTES
23 Director Health Services .... Vacant
76 Dean Biology & Health Sciences .... Mr. Ram SUBRAMANIAM
106 Dean Foothill Online Learning .... Ms. Lene WHITLEY-PUTZ
57 Actg Dean Fine Arts/Communications .... Ms. Debbie LEE
79 Dean Language Arts & LRC .... Ms. Valerie FONG
81 Dean Physical Sci/Math & Engr .... Mr. Ram SUBRAMANIAM
09 Supervisor Institutional Research .... Ms. Ajani BYRD
41 Athletic Director .... Mr. Mike TEIJEIRO
103 Associate VP Workforce .... Ms. Teresa ONG

Franciscan School of Theology (J)

5998 Alcala Park, San Diego CA 92110
County: San Diego FICE Identification: 011792
Unit ID: 114734
Telephone: (619) 574-5800 Carnegie Class: Spec-4-yr-Faith
FAX Number: (619) 849-8431 Calendar System: Semester
URL: www.fst.edu
Established: 1968 Annual Graduate Tuition & Fees: N/A
Enrollment: 57 Coed
Affiliation or Control: Independent Non-Profit IRS Status: 501(c)3
Highest Offering: Master's; No Undergraduates
Accreditation: WC, THEOL

01 President .... Fr. Garrett GALVIN
10 VP Finance/Business Operations .... Ms. Kimberly RENNA
05 Vice President for Academic Affairs .... Sr. Juliet MOUSSEAU
07 Assoc Dir Admissions/Recruitment .... Ms. Christine AVELLA
30 Director of Development .... Ms. Andrea DELUCIA
32 Director of Student Services .... Sr. Kathy FLOOD
26 Marketing/Recruitment Coord .... Ms. Gigi BETANCOURT
110 Development Coordinator .... Ms. Mitchelle GREENLEE
04 Executive Assistant to President .... Ms. Sharmeen ENAYAT
20 Coordinator for AA & Student Svs .... Mr. Jose CONTRERAS, JR.
84 Asst Vice President for Enrollment .... Mr. Daniel STONE

Fremont College (K)

18000 Studebaker Road, Suite 900A, Cerritos CA 90703
County: Los Angeles FICE Identification: 030399
Unit ID: 372073
Telephone: (562) 809-5100 Carnegie Class: Bac/Assoc-Mixed
FAX Number: (562) 809-7100 Calendar System: Other
URL: https://fremont.edu
Established: 1985 Annual Undergrad Tuition & Fees: N/A
Enrollment: 180 Coed
Affiliation or Control: Proprietary IRS Status: Proprietary
Highest Offering: Master's
Accreditation: ACCSC

01 Campus Director .... Tony WONG
06 Registrar .... Joyce BOYLAN

07 Director of Admissions & Marketing ..... Brian RAMAGE
08 Librarian ..... Alison QUIRION
10 Business Office/Database Specialist ..... Phillip WANG
32 Director of Student Affairs ..... Amy VARGAS
36 Director of Career Development ..... Amber CRUZ
37 Director of Financial Aid ..... Israel RODRIGUEZ

Fresno Pacific University (A)

1717 S Chestnut Avenue, Fresno CA 93702-4798
County: Fresno FICE Identification: 001253
Unit ID: 114813
Telephone: (559) 453-2000 Carnegie Class: Masters/L
FAX Number: (559) 453-2007 Calendar System: Semester
URL: www.fresno.edu
Established: 1944 Annual Undergrad Tuition & Fees: $33,452
Enrollment: 3,995 Coed
Affiliation or Control: Mennonite Brethren Church IRS Status: 501(c)3
Highest Offering: Master's
Accreditation: WC, NURSE, SW, THEOL

01 President ..... Dr. Joseph JONES
05 Provost/Senior VP Academic Affairs ..... Dr. D. Gayle COPELAND
10 Vice President Finance ..... Mr. Robert LIPPERT
26 Exec Dir of Public Relations ..... Mrs. Rebecca BRADLEY
11 Vice Pres of Operations ..... Vacant
84 Vice Pres Enrollment Mgmt ..... Mr. Jon ENDICOTT
111 VP for Advancement/Exec Dir Found ..... Mr. Donald GRIFFITH
32 Vice President Campus Life ..... Mr. Dale SCULLY
73 VP & Dean of the Seminary ..... Dr. Valerie REMPEL
50 Dean School of Business ..... Dr. Katie FLEENER
79 Dean Sch of Human/Rel/Soc Sci ..... Dr. Ron HERMS
53 Dean School of Education ..... Dr. Gary GRAMENZ
78 Dean School of Natural Sciences ..... Dr. Tara SIRVENT
08 Director of Library ..... Mr. Kevin ENNS-REMPEL
36 Director of Career Resource Center ..... Ms. Rose WINN
15 Human Resources Director ..... Mr. Jordan SHARP
29 Director Alumni Development ..... Ms. Ali SENA
37 Dir Student Financial Services ..... Mr. David RICHARDS
41 Athletic Director ..... Mr. Morgan WALKER
19 Chief of Campus Safety ..... Mr. Javier CAMPOS
26 Chief Public Rels Ofcr/Dir Pubs ..... Mr. Wayne STEFFEN
104 Dir International Pgms/Svcs Ofc ..... Ms. Angela MUNEZ
07 Director of Admissions ..... Mrs. Krista BROOKS
18 Facilities Manager ..... Mr. Gary METCALF
04 Executive Asst to President ..... Ms. Gwenevera E. BURKS
102 Dir Foundation/Corporate Relations ..... Mr. Mark DEFFENBACHER
112 Dir of Found Dev & Legacy Gifts ..... Mr. Steven REDEKOP
09 Director of Institutional Research ..... Ms. Lisa FOSTER
13 CIO ITS ..... Mr. James LONG
105 Director Web Services ..... Mr. Justin GABLE
39 Asst Dean Stdnt Dev/Title IX Coord ..... Ms. Pam SCHOCK
106 Director Center for Online Learning ..... Dr. Henrietta SIEMENS
86 Director Government Relations ..... Mr. Donald NORMAN
06 Registrar ..... Ms. Danielle JEFFRESS
108 Director Institutional Assessment ..... Ms. Candi ALEXANDER
25 Chief Contract and Grants Administr ..... Ms. Amy LAWRENCE
28 Director of Diversity ..... Ms. Patty SALINAS

Fuller Theological Seminary (B)

135 N Oakland Avenue, Pasadena CA 91182-1780
County: Los Angeles FICE Identification: 001200
Unit ID: 114840
Telephone: (626) 584-5200 Carnegie Class: Spec-4-yr-Faith
FAX Number: (626) 795-8767 Calendar System: Quarter
URL: www.fuller.edu
Established: 1947 Annual Graduate Tuition & Fees: N/A
Enrollment: 2,277 Coed
Affiliation or Control: Independent Non-Profit IRS Status: 501(c)3
Highest Offering: Doctorate; No Undergraduates
Accreditation: WC, CLPSY, THEOL

01 President ..... Dr. Mark A. LABBERTON
05 CAO ..... Dr. Alexis ABERNETHY
102 Chief of Philanthropy ..... Vacant
10 Chief Financial Officer ..... Mr. Ray ASAD
26 Co-Chief Communications & Branding ..... Ms. Kathryn SANGSLAND
26 Co-Chief Communications & Branding ..... Ms. Dana VANVALIN
88 Chief of Leadership Formation ..... Dr. Kara POWELL
73 Dean School of Mission & Theology ..... Dr. Amos YONG
83 Dean School of Psychology ..... Dr. Ted COSSE
13 Chief of Technology ..... Mr. Jeff HARWELL
88 Assoc Dean Doctor of Ministry Pgm ..... Dr. Kurt FREDRICKSON
15 Chief of HR & Org Development ..... Mrs. Bernadette (BJ) O'HALLORAN
32 Chief Student Engagement/Success ..... Mr. Marcus SUN
07 Exec Director Admissions ..... Mr. Max WEDEL
106 Chief of Teaching and Learning ..... Mr. Tommy LISTER
43 Chief Counsel ..... Mr. Lance GRIFFIN
108 Accreditation Liaison Officer ..... Dr. Dave L. SCOTT
09 Director of Institutional Research ..... Dr. Dave SCOTT
06 Registrar ..... Mrs. Andrea EDIN
11 Chief Operating Officer ..... Dr. Ted COSSE
39 Manager of Housing Services ..... Ms. Lavina SEAWRIGHT
04 Assistant to President ..... Mrs. Mandy MACINTOSH
18 Facilities Director ..... Mr. Nathan MERRITT
109 Director of Auxiliary Services ..... Mrs. Jeanne HANDOJO
85 Dir Student Affs/International Svcs ..... Mr. Matthew JIN
37 Actg Dir Student Financial Svcs ..... Ms. Theresa COWAN
08 Director of the DAH Library ..... Ms. Daniell WHITTINGTON
29 Exec Director Alumni Engagement ..... Ms. Lily TSAU

Galaxy Medical College (C)

6400 Laurel Canyon Blvd, St 270,
North Hollywood CA 91606
County: Los Angeles FICE Identification: 041596
Unit ID: 461254
Telephone: (818) 509-9970 Carnegie Class: Not Classified
FAX Number: (818) 509-9935 Calendar System: Semester
URL: www.galaxymedicalcollege.edu
Established: 2003 Annual Undergrad Tuition & Fees: N/A
Enrollment: 41 Coed
Affiliation or Control: Proprietary IRS Status: Proprietary
Highest Offering: Associate Degree
Accreditation: ABHES

01 School Director ..... Ms. Agun Anna KHACHATRYAN

Gateway Seminary (D)

3210 E. Guasti Rd, Ontario CA 91761-8642
County: San Bernadino FICE Identification: 001204
Telephone: (909) 687-1800 Carnegie Class: Not Classified
FAX Number: N/A Calendar System: Semester
URL: www.gs.edu
Established: 1944 Annual Graduate Tuition & Fees: N/A
Enrollment: N/A Coed
Affiliation or Control: Southern Baptist IRS Status: 501(c)3
Highest Offering: Doctorate; No Undergraduates
Accreditation: WC, THEOL

01 President ..... Dr. Jeff IORG
111 Vice Pres Advancement ..... Dr. Jeff JONES
05 Vice President Academic Affairs ..... Dr. Alex STEWART
32 VP Enroll/Student Svcs/Dean Stdnts ..... Dr. Adam GROZA
10 VP Business Services ..... Mr. Ray TONG
21 Controller ..... Mr. Harry WEAVER
06 Registrar ..... Ms. Deena CARTER
08 Director of Library Services ..... Dr. Jonathan MCCORMICK
12 Director PNW Campus ..... Dr. Mark BRADLEY
12 Director Arizona Campus ..... Dr. Dallas BIVINS
12 Director Rocky Mountain Campus ..... Dr. Steve VETETO
13 Director Information Technology ..... Mr. Steve POLCYN
15 Director Personnel Services ..... Ms. Jennifer PALMER
18 Chief Facilities/Physical Plant ..... Mr. Manny GUERRERO
30 Director of Development ..... Mr. Tyler SANDERS
84 Director Enrollment Management ..... Mr. Cameron SCHWEITZER
32 Director of Student Life ..... Mr. Shane TANIGAWA
20 VP Educational Effectiveness ..... Dr. D. Michael MARTIN
108 VP Institutional Effectiveness ..... Mr. Tom HIXSON

Gavilan College (E)

5055 Santa Teresa Boulevard, Gilroy CA 95020-9599
County: Santa Clara FICE Identification: 001202
Unit ID: 114938
Telephone: (408) 848-4800 Carnegie Class: Assoc/MT-VT-High Trad
FAX Number: (408) 848-4801 Calendar System: Semester
URL: www.gavilan.edu
Established: 1919 Annual Undergrad Tuition & Fees (In-District): $1,166
Enrollment: 4,494 Coed
Affiliation or Control: State/Local IRS Status: 501(c)3
Highest Offering: Associate Degree
Accreditation: WJ

01 Superintendent/President ..... Dr. Kathleen A. ROSE
05 Vice Pres Academic Affairs ..... Ms. Denee PESCARMONA
11 Vice Pres Administrative Services ..... Mr. Graciano MENDOZA
32 Int Vice Pres Student Services ..... Ms. Denee PESCARMONA
10 Business Svcs Supervisor ..... Ms. Michelle ANAYA
07 Dir of Admiss/Records & Registrar ..... Ms. Candice WHITNEY
29 Dir Alumni Affs/Foundation Coord ..... Ms. Jan BERNSTEIN CHARGIN
08 Head Librarian ..... Dr. Douglas ACHTERMAN
84 Interim Dean Enrollment Services ..... Ms. Veronica MARTINEZ
88 Interim Dean Foundational Skills ..... Dr. Randy BROWN
15 Dir Human Resources/Labor Relations ..... Ms. Lucy ALVAREZ
18 Director of Facilities/Maintenance ..... Mr. Jeff GOPP
13 Director Information Technology ..... Mr. Kyle BILLUPS
26 Director Public Information ..... Ms. Jan BERNSTEIN-CHARGIN
23 Student Health Nurse ..... Vacant
23 Dean Kinesiology and Athletics ..... Mr. Ron HANNON
40 Manager Bookstore ..... Ms. Laura HOLVERTON
49 Dean Arts/Humanities/Social Sci ..... Vacant
75 Associate Dean Career Education ..... Ms. Susan SWEENEY
96 Purchasing Specialist ..... Vacant
04 Admin Assistant to the President ..... Ms. Debra BRITT-PETTY
09 Dir Institutional Research/Planning ..... Ms. Sydney LAROSE
37 Dir Student Financial Aid ..... Ms. Marina MARTINEZ
38 Student Counseling ..... Ms. Celia MARQUEZ

Glendale Career College (F)

240 N. Brand Blvd, Lower Level, Glendale CA 91203
County: Los Angeles FICE Identification: 023385
Unit ID: 115010
Telephone: (818) 243-1131 Carnegie Class: Spec 2-yr-Health
FAX Number: (818) 243-6028 Calendar System: Semester
URL: www.glendalecareer.com
Established: 1946 Annual Undergrad Tuition & Fees: N/A
Enrollment: 632 Coed
Affiliation or Control: Proprietary IRS Status: Proprietary
Highest Offering: Baccalaureate
Accreditation: ABHES, NURSE, SURGT, SURTEC

01 Executive Director ..... Irma PIRONE

Glendale Community College (G)

1500 N Verdugo Road, Glendale CA 91208-2894
County: Los Angeles FICE Identification: 001203
Unit ID: 115001
Telephone: (818) 240-1000 Carnegie Class: Assoc/MT-VT-High Trad
FAX Number: (818) 549-9436 Calendar System: Semester
URL: www.glendale.edu
Established: 1927 Annual Undergrad Tuition & Fees (In-District): $1,175
Enrollment: 12,973 Coed
Affiliation or Control: State/Local IRS Status: 501(c)3
Highest Offering: Associate Degree
Accreditation: WJ

01 Superintendent/President ..... Dr. David VIAR
11 Exec Vice Pres Administrative Svcs ..... Dr. Anthony CULPEPPER
05 Vice Pres Instructional Services ..... Dr. Michael RITTERBROWN
32 Vice President Student Services ..... Dr. Paul SCHLOSSMAN
51 Admin Dean Continuing/Cmty Educ ..... Dr. Alfred RAMIREZ
15 VP Human Resources ..... Ms. Victoria SIMMONS
45 Dean Research/Planning/Grants ..... Dr. Edward KARPP
07 Director Admissions & Records ..... Ms. Michelle MORA
20 Dean Instructional Services ..... Ms. Agnes EGUARAS
103 Dean Workforce Development ..... Ms. Jan SWINTON
32 Dean Student Affairs ..... Ms. Tzoler OUKAYAN
35 Dean of Student Services ..... Vacant
37 Assoc Dean Stdnt Financial Aid Svcs ..... Dr. Christina TANGALAKIS
10 Director Business Services ..... Ms. Susan COURTEY
102 Exec Director College Foundation ..... Ms. Lisa BROOKS
41 Assoc Dean Athletics ..... Mr. Chris CICUTO
103 Int Assoc Dn Career Educ/Wkfrc Dev ..... Mr. Federico SAUCEDO
31 Assoc Dean Cont/Community Education ..... Dr. Ramona BARRIO-SOTILLO

Gnomon (H)

1015 N. Cahuenga Blvd, Los Angeles CA 90038
County: Los Angeles FICE Identification: 040764
Unit ID: 449384
Telephone: (323) 466-6663 Carnegie Class: Not Classified
FAX Number: (323) 466-6710 Calendar System: Quarter
URL: www.gnomon.edu
Established: 1997 Annual Undergrad Tuition & Fees: $31,554
Enrollment: 575 Coed
Affiliation or Control: Proprietary IRS Status: Proprietary
Highest Offering: Baccalaureate
Accreditation: ACCSC

01 President ..... Alex ALVAREZ
11 Vice President/Chief Admin Officer ..... Darrin KRUMWEIDE
84 Executive Director Enrollment ..... Brian BRADFORD
06 Registrar ..... Tina OLVERA

Golden Gate University (I)

536 Mission Street, San Francisco CA 94105-2968
County: San Francisco FICE Identification: 001205
Unit ID: 115083
Telephone: (415) 442-7000 Carnegie Class: Masters/L
FAX Number: N/A Calendar System: Trimester
URL: www.ggu.edu
Established: 1901 Annual Undergrad Tuition & Fees: N/A
Enrollment: 2,472 Coed
Affiliation or Control: Independent Non-Profit IRS Status: 501(c)3
Highest Offering: Doctorate
Accreditation: WC, LAW

01 President ..... Dr. David J. FIKE
05 VP of Academic Affairs ..... Ms. Barbara H. KARLIN
10 Interim Chief Financial Officer ..... Mr. Brad MITCHELL
30 Int Dir Development/Alumni Rels ..... Mr. Chris SORENSON
61 Dean School of Law ..... Mr. Colin CRAWFORD
50 Dean School of Business ..... Dr. Gordon SWARTZ
58 Dean Graduate Programs ..... Ms. Amy MCLELLAN
106 Director E-Learning ..... Mr. Doug GEIER
32 Dean of Students & Student Affairs ..... Ms. Kayla KRUPNICK-WALSH
08 Director University Library ..... Mr. James KRUSLING
08 Associate Dean Law Library ..... Mr. Michael DAW
06 University Registrar ..... Mr. Steven LIND
13 Director Information Technology ..... Mr. Daniel FORTSON
27 Director of Marketing ..... Mr. Ryan BADOWSKI
09 Dir Financial Planning/Analysis ..... Mr. Sathyapal MENON
18 Director Business Svcs/Facilities ..... Mr. Mike KOPERSKI
21 Controller ..... Ms. Grace LEE
37 Director Student Financial Aid ..... Ms. Gabriela DE LA VEGA
108 Director Institutional Assessment ..... Ms. Lisa KRAMER
15 Head Human Resources ..... Ms. S. Jamila BUCKNER
97 Int Dean School Undergrad Studies ..... Mr. Nate HINERMAN

Grace Mission University (J)

1645 West Valencia Drive, Fullerton CA 92833-3860
County: Orange Identification: 666642
Unit ID: 481058
Telephone: (714) 525-0088 Carnegie Class: Spec-4-yr-Faith
FAX Number: (714) 525-0089 Calendar System: Semester
URL: www.gm.edu
Established: 1995 Annual Undergrad Tuition & Fees: $3,120

Enrollment: 234 Coed
Affiliation or Control: Presbyterian Church (U.S.A.) IRS Status: 501(c)3
Highest Offering: Doctorate
Accreditation: BI, THEOL, TRACS

01 President & CEO ... Dr. Kyunam CHOI
05 Academic Dean ... Dr. Hyunwan KIM
10 Chief Financial Officer ... Mr. Seongyul BAEK
32 Dean of Student Affairs ... Dr. Byounggu LEE
11 Dir Administration/Financial Aid ... Mr. James KOO
06 Registrar ... Ms. Min LEE
08 Librarian ... Ms. EunJa SEO
07 Director of Admissions ... Ms. Meesun LEE
30 Director of Development ... Mrs. Suok RHIE
26 Director of Public Relations ... Dr. Changsoo LEE
37 Director of Financial Aid ... Mr. James KOO

Grace University (A)

1560 Brookhollow Dr., Suite 209, Santa Ana CA 92705
County: Orange Identification: 667422
Telephone: (714) 486-2318 Carnegie Class: Not Classified
FAX Number: N/A Calendar System: Quarter
URL: www.graceuniv.org
Established: Annual Undergrad Tuition & Fees: N/A
Enrollment: N/A Coed
Affiliation or Control: Non-denominational IRS Status: 501(c)3
Highest Offering: Baccalaureate
Accreditation: @TRACS

01 President ... John CHARITY

Graduate Theological Union (B)

2400 Ridge Road, Berkeley CA 94709-1212
County: Alameda FICE Identification: 001207
Unit ID: 115214
Telephone: (510) 649-2400 Carnegie Class: Spec-4-yr-Faith
FAX Number: (510) 649-1417 Calendar System: Semester
URL: www.gtu.edu
Established: 1962 Annual Graduate Tuition & Fees: N/A
Enrollment: 213 Coed
Affiliation or Control: Independent Non-Profit IRS Status: 501(c)3
Highest Offering: Doctorate; No Undergraduates
Accreditation: WC, THEOL

01 President ... Dr. Uriah Y. KIM
05 Int Dean/Vice Pres Academic Affairs ... Dr. Elizabeth S. PENA
10 VP Finance & Administration/CFO ... Ms. Ellen PETERSON
111 Vice President for Advancement ... Ms. Alison MUNDY
26 VP Marketing & Enrollment ... Ms. Sephora MARKSON
07 Admissions Associate ... Ms. Kelly COLWELL
32 Director of Student Life ... Ms. Chaitanya MOTUPALLI
08 Library Director ... Mr. Clay-Edward DIXON
06 Consortia Registrar ... Mr. John SEAL
18 Building & Grounds Engineer ... Mr. Curtis OSBORNE
15 Director of Human Resources ... Ms. Deborah WALKER
37 Sr Director of Financial Aid ... Ms. Denise MORITA
04 Exec Assistant to President ... Ms. Melissa HADDICK
35 Assoc Dean of Students ... Ms. Wendy ARCE

*Grossmont-Cuyamaca Community College District (C)

8800 Grossmont College Drive, El Cajon CA 92020-1799
County: San Diego FICE Identification: 007006
Unit ID: 115287
Telephone: (619) 644-7010 Carnegie Class: N/A
FAX Number: (619) 644-7936
URL: www.gcccd.edu

01 Chancellor ... Dr. Lynn NEAULT
10 Int Vice Chanc Business Services ... Ms. Sahar ABUSHABAN
15 Vice Chanc Human Resources ... Mr. Tim CORCORAN

*Cuyamaca College (D)

900 Rancho San Diego Parkway, El Cajon CA 92019-4304
County: San Diego FICE Identification: 021113
Unit ID: 113218
Telephone: (619) 660-4000 Carnegie Class: Assoc/HT-Mix Trad/Non
FAX Number: (619) 660-4399 Calendar System: Semester
URL: www.cuyamaca.edu
Established: 1978 Annual Undergrad Tuition & Fees (In-District): $1,340
Enrollment: 8,720 Coed
Affiliation or Control: State/Local IRS Status: 501(c)3
Highest Offering: Associate Degree
Accreditation: WJ

02 President ... Dr. Julianna BARNES
05 Int Vice President Instruction ... Ms. Alicia MUNOZ
32 Vice Pres Student Services ... Ms. Jessica ROBINSON
11 Int Vice Pres Admin Services ... Ms. Nicole SALGADO
81 Int Dean of Math/Sci/Engineering ... Ms. Kim DUDZIK
79 Int Dean of Arts/Human/Social Sci ... Dr. Lauren HALSTED
72 Dean of Career Technical Education ... Mr. Larry MCLEMORE
08 Int Dean Learning/Tech Resources ... Ms. Jodi REED
41 Dean Athletics/Kines/Health Educ ... Dr. Cuauhtemoc CARBONI
35 Dean Student Affairs ... Dr. Lauren VAKNIN
38 Dean Counseling Services ... Ms. Nicole JONES
37 Director of Financial Aid ... Mr. Ray REYES
07 Director Admissions & Records ... Mr. Gregory VEGA
18 Director Facilities ... Mr. Francisco GONZALEZ
04 Executive Asst to President ... Ms. Valeri WILSON
09 Sr Dean Inst Effectiv/Succ/Equity ... Ms. Brianna HAYS
26 Director College & Cmty Relations ... Ms. Christianne PENUNURI
10 Int Business Svcs Supervisor ... Mr. Michael ERICKSON

*Grossmont College (E)

8800 Grossmont College Drive, El Cajon CA 92020-1799
County: San Diego FICE Identification: 001208
Unit ID: 115296
Telephone: (619) 644-7000 Carnegie Class: Assoc/HT-High Trad
FAX Number: (619) 644-7922 Calendar System: Semester
URL: www.grossmont.edu
Established: 1961 Annual Undergrad Tuition & Fees (In-District): $1,332
Enrollment: 15,426 Coed
Affiliation or Control: State/Local IRS Status: 501(c)3
Highest Offering: Associate Degree
Accreditation: WJ, ADNUR, CEA, COARC, CVT, OTA

02 President ... Ms. Denise WHISENHUNT
05 Vice Pres of Academic Affairs ... Dr. Marshall FULBRIGHT
32 Vice Pres Student Services ... Dr. Marsha GABLE
07 Dean Admissions/Records/Fin Aid ... Mr. Aaron STARCK
38 Dean Counseling Svcs ... Ms. Martha CLAVELLE
72 Dean Career & Technical Workforce ... Mr. Javier AYALA
81 Int Dean Math/Natural Sci/Phys Educ ... Mr. Shawn HICKS
60 Int Dean Arts/Languages/Comm ... Mr. Joel CASTELLAW
79 Dean English/Social & Behav Sci ... Mr. Agustin ALBARRAN
08 Dean of Learning Resources ... Mr. Eric KLEIN
35 Dean Student Affairs ... Ms. Sara VARGHESE
09 Assoc Vice Chanc Inst Research ... Vacant
10 Chief Business Officer ... Mr. Bill MCGREEVY
18 Chief Facilities/Physical Plant ... Mr. Loren HOLMQUIST
26 Int Chief Public Relations Officer ... Mr. David OGUL
36 Director Student Placement ... Ms. Renee NASORI
37 Director Student Financial Aid ... Mr. Michael COPENHAVER
96 Director of Purchasing ... Mr. Nahid RAZI
04 Executive Assistant to President ... Ms. Bernadette BLACK

Gurnick Academy of Medical Arts (F)

2121 S. El Camino Real Bldg C200, San Mateo CA 94403
County: San Mateo FICE Identification: 041698
Unit ID: 459213
Telephone: (650) 685-6616 Carnegie Class: Spec-4-yr-Other Health
FAX Number: (650) 685-6640 Calendar System: Other
URL: www.gurnick.edu
Established: 2004 Annual Undergrad Tuition & Fees: N/A
Enrollment: 2,462 Coed
Affiliation or Control: Proprietary IRS Status: Proprietary
Highest Offering: Associate Degree
Accreditation: ABHES, DMS, PTAA, RAD

01 CEO ... Konstantin GOURJI
12 Campus Director ... Fred FARIDIAN
11 Chief Operating Officer ... Burke MALIN
05 Chief Academic Officer ... Larisa REVZINA

Hartnell College (G)

411 Central Avenue, Salinas CA 93901-1697
County: Monterey FICE Identification: 001209
Unit ID: 115393
Telephone: (831) 755-6700 Carnegie Class: Assoc/HT-High Trad
FAX Number: (831) 755-6751 Calendar System: Semester
URL: www.hartnell.edu
Established: 1920 Annual Undergrad Tuition & Fees (In-District): $1,400
Enrollment: 8,673 Coed
Affiliation or Control: State/Local IRS Status: 501(c)3
Highest Offering: Associate Degree
Accreditation: WJ, ADNUR, #COARC, PNUR

01 Int Superintendent/President ... Dr. Raul RODRIGUEZ
32 VP Student Affairs ... Dr. Romero JALOMO
10 VP Administrative Services ... Mr. Steven CROW
13 VP Information & Tech Systems ... Mr. David PHILLIPS
05 VP Academic Affairs ... Dr. Cathryn WILKINSON
111 VP Advancement/Development ... Ms. Jackie CRUZ
15 VP Human Resources/EEO ... Mr. Lyle ENGELDINER
21 Controller ... Mr. David TECHAIRA
18 Exec Dir Constr/Facilities Mgmt ... Mr. Joseph REYES
20 Dean Academic Aff Programs/Support .. Dr. Sachiko MATSUNAGA
81 Dean Academic Affs Math/Science ... Ms. Shannon BLISS
35 Director of Student Life ... Mr. Augustine NEVAREZ
26 Director of Communications ... Mr. Scott FAUST
22 Dir of Student Affairs/EOPS ... Mr. Paul CASEY
66 Dean Academic Affairs/Nursing ... Ms. Debra KACZMAR
83 Dean Acad Affs Soc/Fine Lang Arts ... Ms. Joy COWDEN
20 Dean South County Educ Programs ... Mr. Mostafa GHOUS
04 Senior Executive Assistant ... Ms. Lucille SERRANO
84 Dean of Student Affairs/Enrol Svcs ... Ms. Maria CEJA
09 Director of Institutional Research ... Dr. Matthew TRENGOVE
101 Secretary of the Institution/Board ... Ms. Lucille SERRANO
121 Dean of Student Affs Stdnt Success ... Ms. Carla JOHNSON
41 Director Athletics ... Mr. Daniel TERESA
45 Dean Inst Planning and Effective ... Dr. Brian LOFMAN
103 Dir Workforce/Career Development ... Ms. Sharon ALBERT
19 Dir Public Safety/Emergency Mgmt ... Mr. Daniel SCOTT

Harvey Mudd College (H)

301 Platt Boulevard, Claremont CA 91711-5990
County: Los Angeles FICE Identification: 001171
Unit ID: 115409
Telephone: (909) 621-8000 Carnegie Class: Bac-A&S
FAX Number: (909) 621-8360 Calendar System: Semester
URL: www.hmc.edu
Established: 1955 Annual Undergrad Tuition & Fees: $58,660
Enrollment: 854 Coed
Affiliation or Control: Independent Non-Profit IRS Status: 501(c)3
Highest Offering: Baccalaureate
Accreditation: WC

01 President ... Dr. Maria M. KLAWE
111 Vice President Advancement ... Mr. Hieu NGUYEN
10 Vice President Admin/Fin/Treasurer ... Dr. Andrew R. DORANTES
05 VP Acad Affairs/Dean of the Faculty ... Dr. Lisa M. SULLIVAN
07 Vice Pres Admissions/Financial Aid ... Ms. Thyra BRIGGS
32 Int VP Student Affs/Dean Students ... Dr. Marco VALENZUELA
13 VP/CIO ... Mr. Joseph VAUGHAN
15 Senior Director for Human Resources ... Ms. Dana NAGENGAST
18 Senior Director of Plant Operations ... Mr. Daniel MADRIGAL
28 Assoc Dean Institutional Diversity ... Dr. Jennifer ALANIS
06 Registrar ... Mr. Mark ASHLEY
26 Chief Communications Officer ... Mr. Tim HUSSEY
29 Director of Alumni Relations ... Ms. Jennifer GREEN
37 Director of Student Financial Aid ... Ms. Gilma LOPEZ
101 Director of Pres Ofc/Secy to Board ... Ms. Karen ANGEMI
100 Chief of Staff ... Ms. Karen ANGEMI
09 AVP for Institutional Research ... Dr. Laura PALUCKI BLAKE
104 Director Study Abroad ... Ms. Rhonda CHILES
30 AVP for Development ... Vacant
86 Senior Director Corporate Relations ... Ms. Colleen COXE

Haven University (I)

12761 South Euclid Street, Garden Grove CA 92840
County: Orange Identification: 667307
Telephone: (714) 592-7878 Carnegie Class: Not Classified
FAX Number: (714) 636-1725 Calendar System: Semester
URL: haven.edu
Established: 1969 Annual Undergrad Tuition & Fees: N/A
Enrollment: N/A Coed
Affiliation or Control: Interdenominational IRS Status: 501(c)3
Highest Offering: Doctorate
Accreditation: TRACS

01 President ... Dr. Kang Won LEE
10 Dean of Administration ... Dr. Brian K. TROTT
05 Dean of Academic Affairs ... Dr. Joshua SMITH
32 Actg Dean of Student Services ... Dr. Brian TROTT
07 Director of Admissions/Records ... Dr. Linda TROTT

† Previously California Graduate School of Theology 2019

Hawthorn University (J)

475 Hungry Gulch Rd, Ste C, Whitethorn CA 95589
County: Humboldt Identification: 667358
Telephone: (707) 986-4153 Carnegie Class: Not Classified
FAX Number: N/A Calendar System: Quarter
URL: www.hawthornuniversity.org
Established: 2002 Annual Graduate Tuition & Fees: N/A
Enrollment: N/A Coed
Affiliation or Control: Independent Non-Profit IRS Status: 501(c)3
Highest Offering: Doctorate; No Undergraduates
Accreditation: DEAC

01 President/Chief Academic Officer ... Dr. Dorothy GERMANO
03 Executive Vice President ... Beth MAIZES
05 Education Director ... Dr. Janet LUDWIG

Hayfield University (K)

2495 Orangethorpe Avenue, Fullerton CA 92831
County: Orange Identification: 667415
Telephone: (714) 738-1461 Carnegie Class: Not Classified
FAX Number: (714) 738-1440 Calendar System: Semester
URL: www.hayfieldun.org
Established: 1995 Annual Undergrad Tuition & Fees: N/A
Enrollment: N/A Coed
Affiliation or Control: Independent Non-Profit IRS Status: 501(c)3
Highest Offering: Master's
Accreditation: @BI

Healthcare Career College (L)

8527 Alondra Boulevard, Suite 128, Paramount CA 90723
County: Los Angeles FICE Identification: 041327
Unit ID: 450960
Telephone: (562) 804-1239 Carnegie Class: Not Classified
FAX Number: N/A Calendar System: Other
URL: www.healthcarecareercollege.edu
Established: 1998 Annual Undergrad Tuition & Fees: N/A
Enrollment: N/A Coed
Affiliation or Control: Proprietary IRS Status: Proprietary
Highest Offering: Associate Degree
Accreditation: COE

Henry Appenzeller University (A)

1325 N College Avenue, #106, Claremont CA 91711

County: Orange | Identification: 667133
Telephone: (213) 386-0080 | Carnegie Class: Not Classified
FAX Number: (213) 386-5229 | Calendar System: Semester
URL: mtsamerica.edu/
Established: 1880 | Annual Undergrad Tuition & Fees: N/A
Enrollment: N/A | Coed
Affiliation or Control: Independent Non-Profit | IRS Status: 501(c)3
Highest Offering: Master's
Accreditation: BI

01 President .... Rev. David LIM

High Desert Medical College (B)

701 West Avenue K, Ste 123, Lancaster CA 93534

County: Los Angeles | FICE Identification: 042281
Unit ID: 484002
Telephone: (661) 940-9300 | Carnegie Class: Not Classified
FAX Number: (661) 940-7319 | Calendar System: Semester
URL: www.hdmc.edu
Established: 2002 | Annual Undergrad Tuition & Fees: N/A
Enrollment: 1,016 | Coed
Affiliation or Control: Proprietary | IRS Status: Proprietary
Highest Offering: Associate Degree
Accreditation: CNCE

01 President/CEO .... LeeAnn ROHMANN

High Tech High Graduate School of Education (C)

2150 Cushing Road, San Diego CA 92106

County: San Diego | Identification: 667118
Unit ID: 485403
Telephone: (619) 398-4902 | Carnegie Class: Spec-4-yr-Other
FAX Number: (619) 758-1960 | Calendar System: Other
URL: https://hthgse.edu
Established: 2007 | Annual Graduate Tuition & Fees: N/A
Enrollment: 76 | Coed
Affiliation or Control: Independent Non-Profit | IRS Status: 501(c)3
Highest Offering: Master's; No Undergraduates
Accreditation: WC

01 President .... Ben DALEY
05 Dean .... Kelly WILSON
32 Director Student Affairs .... Hayley MURUGESAN

HIS University (D)

1245 West 6th Street, Corona CA 92882

County: Riverside | Identification: 667388
Telephone: (951) 372-8080 | Carnegie Class: Not Classified
FAX Number: (951) 372-8070 | Calendar System: Semester
URL: www.hisuniversity.edu
Established: 2004 | Annual Undergrad Tuition & Fees: N/A
Enrollment: N/A | Coed
Affiliation or Control: Independent Non-Profit | IRS Status: 501(c)3
Highest Offering: Doctorate
Accreditation: TRACS

01 President/CEO .... Dr. Eun Soon YANG
05 Chief Academic Officer .... Dr. Donna BROWN
11 Chief Operations Officer .... Dr. Boo Un OH
10 Chief Finance Officer .... Dr. Jean YOO
06 Registrar/Admin Assistant .... Ms. Kathleen BAXTER

Holy Names University (E)

3500 Mountain Boulevard, Oakland CA 94619-1699

County: Alameda | FICE Identification: 001183
Unit ID: 115728
Telephone: (510) 436-1000 | Carnegie Class: Masters/M
FAX Number: (510) 436-1199 | Calendar System: Semester
URL: www.hnu.edu
Established: 1868 | Annual Undergrad Tuition & Fees: $40,904
Enrollment: 1,014 | Coed
Affiliation or Control: Independent Non-Profit | IRS Status: 501(c)3
Highest Offering: Master's
Accreditation: WC, NURSE

01 President .... Mr. Michael GROENER
05 Provost/VP for Academic Affairs .... Dr. Kimberly BOWERS
10 VP for Finance/Admin .... Mr. Rob KINNARD
32 VP for Student Affairs .... Ms. Laura LYNDON
84 VP for Enrollment Mgmt .... Ms. Elizabeth O'BRIEN
111 VP for University Advancement .... Ms. Mary BOIVIN-MCGHEE
88 VP for Mission Integration .... Sr. Carol SELLMAN
18 VP for Facilities & Events .... Mr. Luis GUERRA
06 Registrar .... Mr. Stephen STICKA
08 Director of Library Services .... Ms. Sylvia CONTRERAS
37 Director Financial Aid .... Ms. Rose STADLER
42 Co-Director of Campus Ministry .... Ms. Jenny GIRARD-MALLEY
42 Co-Director of Campus Ministry .... Fr. Sal RAGUSA
41 Director of Athletics .... Ms. Debbie SNELL
26 University Communications Manager .... Ms. Stephanie SILVA
13 Director Information Technology .... Mr. Jay CASTILLO
15 Director Human Resources .... Ms. Patricia BARTON
04 Executive Asst to President .... Ms. Vicki TOM
09 Exec Dir of Institutional Research .... Mr. John HOFMANN
39 Interim Director Residence Life .... Ms. Angeline BANEZ
29 Director Alumni/Donor Relations .... Ms. Kelsey LINDQUIST
100 Chief of Staff .... Mr. John HOFMANN
102 Dir Foundation/Corporate Relations .... Mr. Stefan AMRINE
19 Campus Safety Director .... Mr. Joe QUINN

Homestead Schools (F)

23800 Hawthorne Blvd, Suite 200, Torrance CA 90505

County: Los Angeles | FICE Identification: 041497
Unit ID: 457086
Telephone: (310) 791-9975 | Carnegie Class: Spec-4-yr-Other Health
FAX Number: N/A | Calendar System: Other
URL: homesteadschools.com
Established: 2007 | Annual Undergrad Tuition & Fees: N/A
Enrollment: 129 | Coed
Affiliation or Control: Independent Non-Profit | IRS Status: 501(c)3
Highest Offering: Master's
Accreditation: ABHES, NURSE

01 President/CEO .... Mr. Vijay FADIA

Hope International University (G)

2500 E Nutwood Avenue, Fullerton CA 92831-3104

County: Orange | FICE Identification: 001252
Unit ID: 120537
Telephone: (714) 879-3901 | Carnegie Class: Masters/M
FAX Number: (714) 681-7451 | Calendar System: 4/1/4
URL: www.hiu.edu
Established: 1928 | Annual Undergrad Tuition & Fees: $34,450
Enrollment: 1,201 | Coed
Affiliation or Control: Independent Non-Profit | IRS Status: 501(c)3
Highest Offering: Master's
Accreditation: WC, BI, IACBE, MFCD

01 President .... Dr. Paul H. ALEXANDER
04 Exec Asst to the President .... Mrs. Sandy PRINTY
05 Vice President for Academic Affairs .... Dr. Steve EDGINGTON
49 Dean College of Arts and Sciences .... Dr. Steve EDGINGTON
50 Dean College of Business & Mgmt .... Dr. Lydia KNOPP
53 Dean College of Education .... Dr. Douglas S. DOMENE
88 Dean Col of Ministry & Bible Stds .... Dr. Timothy DALLY
83 Dean College of Psych & Counseling .... Dr. Laura L. STEELE
09 Director of Institutional Research .... Dr. Hector GALANO
08 Librarian .... Mrs. Robin HARTMAN
06 Registrar .... Mr. Ron ARCHER
10 Vice President for Business/Finance .... Mr. Tom MCGLINCHEY
37 Director Student Financial Services .... Mrs. Shannon O'SHIELDS
15 Director of Human Resources .... Ms. Ellen NIALIS
13 Director of Information Technology .... Mr. Darrell C. JONES
18 Director of Campus Facilities .... Mr. Steve MULLINS
111 Vice Pres Institutional Advancement .... Mr. Michael MULRYAN
26 Chief Public Relations Officer .... Mr. Michael MULRYAN
32 Vice President for Student Affairs .... Dr. Mark COMEAUX
41 Athletic Director .... Mr. John G. TUREK
42 Director Campus Ministry .... Mr. Joey ROSS
85 Director of International Students .... Mrs. Judy E. KIM
38 Director Student Counseling .... Dr. Laura L. STEELE
36 Director of Career Development .... Mrs. Stacey GERHART
84 Vice Pres for Enrollment Management .... Mrs. Teresa L. SMITH
07 Director Undergraduate Admissions .... Mr. Michael CRUZ
106 Dir Learning Technology .... Ms. Micah N. ALSTON
108 Director Institutional Assessment .... Mr. Andrew PAINE

Horizon University (H)

2040 S. Brea Canyon Rd, Ste 100,
Diamond Bar CA 91765

County: Los Angeles | Identification: 667360
Telephone: (909) 895-7138 | Carnegie Class: Not Classified
FAX Number: (909) 895-7143 | Calendar System: Quarter
URL: www.huca.edu
Established: 2007 | Annual Undergrad Tuition & Fees: N/A
Enrollment: N/A | Coed
Affiliation or Control: Independent Non-Profit | IRS Status: 501(c)3
Highest Offering: Master's
Accreditation: TRACS

01 President .... Henry KHOR
05 Director of Academics .... Abraham OH
06 Registrar .... Jerry CUI
07 Director of Admissions .... Aron KIM
10 Chief Financial/Business Officer .... Michael YANG
11 Director of Operations .... Benjamin STARKEY
32 Director of Student Services .... Qi DENG

Humphreys University (I)

6650 Inglewood Street, Stockton CA 95207-3896

County: San Joaquin | FICE Identification: 001212
Unit ID: 115773
Telephone: (209) 478-0800 | Carnegie Class: Bac-Diverse
FAX Number: (209) 478-8721 | Calendar System: Quarter
URL: www.humphreys.edu
Established: 1896 | Annual Undergrad Tuition & Fees: $14,580
Enrollment: 401 | Coed
Affiliation or Control: Independent Non-Profit | IRS Status: 501(c)3
Highest Offering: First Professional Degree
Accreditation: WC

01 President .... Dr. Robert G. HUMPHREYS, JR.
05 Dn Instruction/Dir Arts & Sciences .... Ms. Cynthia BECERRA
11 Director of Administrative Services .... Ms. Carrie CASTILLON
58 Dean of Graduate Studies .... Dr. Jess BONDS
61 Dean Law School .... Mr. Matthew REYNOLDS
09 Dean of Institutional Research .... Dr. Lisa KOOREN
06 Registrar .... Ms. Maria GARCIA-MILLER
07 Director of Admissions .... Ms. Santa E. LOPEZ
37 Director Student Financial Aid .... Ms. Rita FRANCO

Hussian College (formerly known as Studio School) (J)

1201 West 5th St., Ste F10, Los Angeles CA 90017

Telephone: (800) 762-1993 | Identification: 770969
Accreditation: ACCSC

† Branch campus of Hussian School of Art, Philadelphia, PA

Imperial Valley College (K)

380 E Aten Road, Imperial CA 92251-0158

County: Imperial | FICE Identification: 001214
Unit ID: 115861
Telephone: (760) 352-8320 | Carnegie Class: Assoc/MT-VT-High Trad
FAX Number: (760) 355-2663 | Calendar System: Semester
URL: www.imperial.edu
Established: 1922 | Annual Undergrad Tuition & Fees (In-District): $1,126
Enrollment: 7,123 | Coed
Affiliation or Control: Local | IRS Status: 501(c)3
Highest Offering: Associate Degree
Accreditation: WJ, EMT

01 Superintendent/President .... Dr. Martha O. GARCIA
05 Vice President Academic Services .... Dr. Christina TAFOYA
32 VP for Student Services/Equity .... Dr. Lennor JOHNSON
10 VP Administrative Services .... Vacant
15 Chief Human Resources Officer .... Mr. Clint C. DOUGHERTY
103 Dean Economic & Workforce Develop .... Mr. Efrain SILVA
76 Dean of Health & Public Safety .... Ms. Gail WARNER
49 Dean Arts/Letters/Learning Svcs .... Mrs. Betsy LANE
84 Dean Student Affs/Enroll Svcs .... Mr. James DALSKE
35 Dean Student Svcs/Special Proj .... Dr. Henry COVARRUBIAS
07 Director of Admissions and Records .... Mrs. Vikki CARR
37 Director of Financial Aid .... Ms. Lisa SEALS
09 Dir Institutional Research .... Mr. Jose CARRILLO
59 Dir Child/Family/Consumer Sciences .... Ms. Rebecca GREEN
26 Comm & Govt Relations Officer .... Ms. Elizabeth ESPINOZA
13 Chief Technology Officer .... Mr. Jeff ENZ
81 Dean of Math/Sciences .... Mr. David DRURY
102 Exec Director Foundation .... Mr. Rod SMART
18 Dir Facilities Planning/Construct .... Mr. Javier LUNA

Institute for Business and Technology (L)

2400 Walsh Avenue, Santa Clara CA 95051

County: Santa Clara | FICE Identification: 021283
Unit ID: 115931
Telephone: (408) 727-1060 | Carnegie Class: Spec 2-yr-Health
FAX Number: N/A | Calendar System: Semester
URL: www.ibttech.com
Established: 1965 | Annual Undergrad Tuition & Fees: N/A
Enrollment: 579 | Coed
Affiliation or Control: Proprietary | IRS Status: Proprietary
Highest Offering: Associate Degree
Accreditation: ACCSC

01 President/CEO .... Peter MIKHAIL
05 Director of Education .... Fred WIEHE
11 Chief Operating Officer .... Sally MIKHAIL BEMIS
06 Registrar .... Nicole TELLY
36 Director of Career Services .... Deidre THOMPSON

Institute of Buddhist Studies (M)

2140 Durant Avenue, Berkeley CA 94704

County: Alameda | Identification: 667312
Unit ID: 489335
Telephone: (510) 809-1444 | Carnegie Class: Not Classified
FAX Number: N/A | Calendar System: Semester
URL: www.shin-ibs.edu
Established: 1949 | Annual Graduate Tuition & Fees: N/A
Enrollment: 27 | Coed
Affiliation or Control: Independent Non-Profit | IRS Status: 501(c)3
Highest Offering: Master's; No Undergraduates
Accreditation: WC

00 Chancellor .... Rev. Kodo UMEZU
01 President & Vice Pres Academic Affs .... RevDr. David MATSUMOTO
30 Vice Pres Development .... Rev.Dr. Seigen YAMAOKA
32 Dean of Students .... Dr. Scott MITCHELL
10 Director of Finance .... Ms. Linda SHIOZAKI
06 Registrar .... Ms. Helen TAGAWA

Institute of Technology (N)

564 West Herndon Avenue, Clovis CA 93612

County: Fresno | FICE Identification: 030675
Unit ID: 431141
Telephone: (559) 297-4500 | Carnegie Class: Assoc/HVT-High Trad
FAX Number: (559) 297-5822 | Calendar System: Semester

URL: www.iot.edu
Established: Annual Undergrad Tuition & Fees: N/A
Enrollment: 1,279 Coed
Affiliation or Control: Proprietary IRS Status: Proprietary
Highest Offering: Associate Degree
Accreditation: ACCSC, ACFEI, PTAA

01 President .... Ron GARDNER
05 Director of Education .... Carol SMITH
66 Director of Nursing .... Paula RICHARDS
32 Director of Student Services .... Melinda WOOD
07 Director of Admissions .... Marissa MARZAN
06 Registrar .... Maria VALDEZ
37 Director of Financial Aid .... Sandi PUGH
36 Director of Career Services .... Tim KEARN
08 Librarian .... Laura HABERSTICH
18 Facilities Coordinator .... Tony LEON

Institute of Technology (A)

5601 Stoddard Road, Modesto CA 95356
Telephone: (209) 572-7800 Identification: 770554
Accreditation: ACCSC, ACFEI

Intercoast College (B)

2235 East Garvey Ave North, West Covina CA 91791
County: Los Angelos FICE Identification: 025594
Unit ID: 366289
Telephone: (626) 337-6800 Carnegie Class: Spec 2-yr-Health
FAX Number: N/A Calendar System: Other
URL: www.intercoast.edu
Established: 1985 Annual Undergrad Tuition & Fees: N/A
Enrollment: 20 Coed
Affiliation or Control: Proprietary IRS Status: Proprietary
Highest Offering: Associate Degree
Accreditation: CNCE

00 President .... Geeta A. BROWN
01 Campus President .... Christopher RUSH
106 Director Online Education .... James CHEEKS
07 Director of Admissions .... Joel MEDRANO

Interior Designers Institute (C)

1061 Camelback Road, Newport Beach CA 92660-3228
County: Orange FICE Identification: 025203
Unit ID: 116226
Telephone: (949) 675-4451 Carnegie Class: Spec-4-yr-Arts
FAX Number: (949) 759-0667 Calendar System: Quarter
URL: www.idi.edu
Established: 1984 Annual Undergrad Tuition & Fees: $20,250
Enrollment: 144 Coed
Affiliation or Control: Proprietary IRS Status: Proprietary
Highest Offering: Master's
Accreditation: ACCSC, CIDA

01 Executive Director .... Ms. Judy DEATON
10 Controller .... Ms. Shanen FOYE
07 Director of Admissions .... Ms. Judy DEATON

International American University (D)

3440 Wilshire Blvd #1000, Los Angeles CA 90010
County: Los Angeles Identification: 667389
Telephone: (213) 262-3939 Carnegie Class: Not Classified
FAX Number: (213) 262-5758 Calendar System: Other
URL: www.iaula.edu
Established: Annual Undergrad Tuition & Fees: N/A
Enrollment: N/A Coed
Affiliation or Control: Independent Non-Profit IRS Status: 501(c)3
Highest Offering: Doctorate
Accreditation: TRACS

01 CEO .... Ryan DOAN
05 Chief Academic Officer .... Dr. Richard H. GAYER
32 Assoc Director Student Services .... Susan TAN
10 Chief Financial Officer .... Jay CHUNG
15 Assoc Director Human Resources .... Sue KIM
06 Registrar .... Md OSMAN

International Reformed University and Seminary (E)

125 S. Vermont Avenue, Los Angeles CA 90004
County: Los Angeles Identification: 667132
Telephone: (213) 381-0081 Carnegie Class: Not Classified
FAX Number: (213) 381-0010 Calendar System: Semester
URL: www.irus.edu
Established: 1977 Annual Undergrad Tuition & Fees: N/A
Enrollment: N/A Coed
Affiliation or Control: Independent Non-Profit IRS Status: 501(c)3
Highest Offering: Doctorate
Accreditation: BI

01 President .... Dr. Hun Sung PARK
05 Academic Dean .... Dr. Paul Kitae PARK
32 Dean of Students .... Dr. Kwang Hoon LEE
11 Dean of Administrative Services .... Dr. Joha OH
108 Director of Assessment & Planning .... Dr. Yumee RAH
08 Librarian .... Ms. Hannah LEE
20 Director of Teaching & Learning Tec .... Ms. Hala SUN

International Technological University (F)

2010 El Camino Real, #852, Santa Clara CA 95050
County: Santa Clara Identification: 667070
Unit ID: 443128
Telephone: (888) 488-4968 Carnegie Class: Masters/L
FAX Number: (408) 331-1026 Calendar System: Trimester
URL: www.itu.edu
Established: 1994 Annual Graduate Tuition & Fees: N/A
Enrollment: 299 Coed
Affiliation or Control: Independent Non-Profit IRS Status: 501(c)3
Highest Offering: Doctorate; No Undergraduates
Accreditation: WC, ACBSP

01 President and CEO .... Yau-Gene CHAN
03 Exec Vice President/Special Advisor .... Dr. Gerald CORY
05 Provost .... Dr. Eric TAO
10 Chief Financial Officer .... Dr. Amal MOUGHARBEL
13 Chief Technology Officer .... Dr. Mamoun SAMAHA
32 Director Student Affairs .... Joe MAZARES
06 Registrar .... Evelyn PADUA-ANDREWS
08 Head Librarian .... Marion HAYES
101 Dir University Affs/Board Liaison .... Angie LO
26 Exec Dir Marketing/Enrollment Mgmt .... Micah THOMAS
15 Director Human Resources .... Leslie ANDERSON
85 Dir International Student Office .... Amy CHAUNG
07 Director of Admissions .... Suman BHARGAVA

International Theological Seminary (G)

540 E Vine Avenue, West Covina CA 91790
County: Los Angeles Identification: 666360
Unit ID: 396985
Telephone: (626) 448-0023 Carnegie Class: Not Classified
FAX Number: (626) 350-6343 Calendar System: Quarter
URL: www.itsla.edu
Established: 1982 Annual Undergrad Tuition & Fees: N/A
Enrollment: N/A Coed
Affiliation or Control: Independent Non-Profit IRS Status: 501(c)3
Highest Offering: Doctorate
Accreditation: THEOL

01 President .... Dr. James S. LEE
05 Vice Pres for Academic Affairs .... Dr. Priscilla ADOYO
10 Vice Pres of Operation/Finance .... Rev. Paul Zhaohui YANG
32 Dean of Students .... Dr. Premkumar DHARMARAJ
06 Registrar .... Ms. Letty CHEN
08 Librarian .... Ms. Susan LIU
04 Asst to President/Communication Dir .... Ms. Ei MEREN ACIERTO

John Paul the Great Catholic University (H)

220 West Grand Avenue, Escondido CA 92025
County: San Diego FICE Identification: 041937
Unit ID: 462354
Telephone: (858) 653-6740 Carnegie Class: Bac-Diverse
FAX Number: (858) 653-3791 Calendar System: Quarter
URL: www.jpcatholic.com
Established: 2003 Annual Undergrad Tuition & Fees: $27,100
Enrollment: 274 Coed
Affiliation or Control: Independent Non-Profit IRS Status: 501(c)3
Highest Offering: Master's
Accreditation: WC

01 President/Chief Academic Officer .... Dr. Derry CONNOLLY
05 Chief Academic Officer .... Bob KEITH
10 Chief Finance Officer/COO .... Kevin MAZIERE
30 Chief Development Officer .... Steve WISE
11 VP for Administration .... Lidy CONNOLLY
07 VP of Admissions .... Martin HAROLD
15 VP for Human Resources .... Anna VELASCO
32 Dean of Students .... Jonathan SPERLING
37 Director of Financial Aid .... Lisa WILLIAMS
06 Registrar .... Nick HEYE
42 Director Campus Ministry .... Austin SCHNEIDER
08 Librarian .... Melanie QUINN
26 AVP for Marketing & Admissions .... Joe HOUDE

Kaiser Permanente Bernard J Tyson School of Medicine (I)

98 S. Los Robles Avenue, Pasadena CA 91101
County: Los Angeles Identification: 667404
Telephone: (888) 576-3348 Carnegie Class: Not Classified
FAX Number: N/A Calendar System: Semester
URL: www.medschool.kp.org
Established: 2016 Annual Graduate Tuition & Fees: N/A
Enrollment: N/A Coed
Affiliation or Control: Independent Non-Profit IRS Status: 501(c)3
Highest Offering: First Professional Degree; No Undergraduates
Accreditation: #MED

01 Founding Dean & CEO .... Dr. Mark A. SCHUSTER
10 SVP Administration/Finance .... Walter HARRIS
05 Sr Assoc Dean Academic/Cmty Affairs .... Dr. Maureen T. CONNELLY
32 Sr Assoc Dean Student Affairs .... Dr. Anne EACKER

Kaiser Permanente School of Allied Health Sciences (J)

938 Marina Way South, Richmond CA 94804
County: Contra Costa Identification: 667152
Telephone: (510) 231-5000 Carnegie Class: Not Classified
FAX Number: (510) 231-5001 Calendar System: Quarter
URL: www.kpsahs.edu
Established: 1989 Annual Undergrad Tuition & Fees: N/A
Enrollment: N/A Coed
Affiliation or Control: Proprietary IRS Status: Proprietary
Highest Offering: Master's
Accreditation: WC, DMS, NMT, RAD

01 Medical Director .... Dr. C. Darryl JONES
05 Dean of Academic Affairs/CAO .... John ROTH
10 Assoc Director of Finance/CFO .... Pamela PRESSLEY
11 Regional School Administrator/CEO .... James FITZGIBBON
09 Dir Assessment/Inst Research .... Bert CHRISTENSEN
04 Admin Assistant to the President .... Diana K. JACKSON

*Kern Community College District (K)

2100 Chester Avenue, Bakersfield CA 93301-4099
County: Kern FICE Identification: 006994
Unit ID: 436313
Telephone: (661) 336-5100 Carnegie Class: N/A
FAX Number: (661) 336-5134
URL: www.kccd.edu

01 Chancellor .... Ms. Sonya CHRISTIAN
05 Vice Chanc Educational Services .... Mr. John MEANS
15 Int Vice Chanc Human Resources .... Ms. Dena RHOADES
10 Chief Financial Officer .... Ms. Deborah MARTIN
13 Chief Technology Officer .... Mr. Gary MOSER
43 General Counsel .... Mr. Christopher HINE
103 Exec Dir Econ/Workforce Development .... Mr. David TEASDALE

*Bakersfield College (L)

1801 Panorama Drive, Bakersfield CA 93305-1299
County: Kern FICE Identification: 001118
Unit ID: 109819
Telephone: (661) 395-4011 Carnegie Class: Bac/Assoc-Assoc Dom
FAX Number: (661) 395-4241 Calendar System: Semester
URL: www.bakersfieldcollege.edu
Established: 1913 Annual Undergrad Tuition & Fees (In-District): $1,418
Enrollment: 24,903 Coed
Affiliation or Control: State/Local IRS Status: 501(c)3
Highest Offering: Baccalaureate
Accreditation: WJ, CAHIIM, EMT, RAD

02 President .... Dr. Sonya CHRISTIAN
05 Vice President Instruction .... Ms. Billie Jo RICE
10 VP Finance & Administrative Svcs .... Mr. Mike GIACOMINI
32 Vice Pres Student Affairs .... Dr. Zavareh DADABHOY
09 Dean Institutional Effectiveness .... Mr. Craig HAYWARD
20 Dean of Instruction .... Dr. Rich MCCROW
66 Dean of Instruction .... Ms. Andrea THORSON
81 Dean of Instruction .... Dr. Stephen WALLER
20 Dean of Instruction .... Dr. Emmanuel MOURTZANOS
30 Int Exec Dir Foundation/Development .... Ms. Liz ROZELL
18 Dir Facilities/Maintenance/Ops .... Mr. Bill POTTER
12 Director Delano Center .... Mr. Abel GUZMAN
37 Director Financial Aid .... Ms. Jennifer ACHAN
84 Director Enrollment Services .... Ms. Michelle PENA
26 Dir Communication/Cmty Relations .... Ms. Norma ROJAS-MORA
13 Director Information Technology .... Mr. Todd COSTON
41 Director of Athletics .... Ms. Sandi TAYLOR
15 Interim Human Resources Manager .... Ms. Amalia CALDERON

*Cerro Coso Community College (M)

3000 College Heights Boulevard,
Ridgecrest CA 93555-7777
County: Kern FICE Identification: 010111
Unit ID: 111896
Telephone: (760) 384-6100 Carnegie Class: Assoc/HT-Mix Trad/Non
FAX Number: (760) 375-4776 Calendar System: Semester
URL: www.cerrocoso.edu
Established: 1973 Annual Undergrad Tuition & Fees (In-District): $1,382
Enrollment: 5,159 Coed
Affiliation or Control: State/Local IRS Status: 501(c)3
Highest Offering: Associate Degree
Accreditation: WJ

02 President .... Dr. Sean C. HANCOCK
05 Vice President Instruction .... Dr. Corey MARVIN
10 Vice Pres Finance/Admin Services .... Ms. Lisa COUCH
32 Vice President of Student Services .... Ms. Heather OSTASH
20 Dean of Instruction .... Mr. Chad HOUCK
12 Dir Eastern Sierra College Center .... Ms. Deanna CAMPBELL
12 Dir of East Kern/Kern River Valley .... Ms. Lisa STEPHENS
75 Dean Career Technical Education .... Vacant
38 Dir of Counseling Svcs/SSSP .... Ms. Christine SMALL
07 Dir Admiss/Records/VA/Fin Aid .... Mr. William BLOOM

15 Manager Human Resources ..... Ms. Resa HESS
88 Program Mgr Child Development Ctr ..... Ms. Jessica KRALL
26 Dir Public Relations/Inst Advance ..... Ms. Natalie DORRELL
13 Director Information Technology ..... Mr. Michael CAMPBELL
35 Director Outreach Services ..... Ms. Katie BACHMAN
106 Director Distance Education ..... Ms. Rebecca PANG
04 Administrative Asst to President ..... Ms. Jennifer CURTIS
41 Athletic Director ..... Mr. John MCHENRY
18 Dir Maintenance/Operations ..... Mr. Cody PAUXTIS
19 Director Security/Safety ..... Mr. Kevin KING

*Porterville College (A)

100 E College Avenue, Porterville CA 93257-6058
County: Tulare FICE Identification: 001268
Unit ID: 121363
Telephone: (559) 791-2200 Carnegie Class: Assoc/HVT-High Trad
FAX Number: (559) 784-4779 Calendar System: Semester
URL: www.portervillecollege.edu
Established: 1927 Annual Undergrad Tuition & Fees (In-District): $1,409
Enrollment: 3,964 Coed
Affiliation or Control: State/Local IRS Status: 501(c)3
Highest Offering: Associate Degree
Accreditation: WJ

02 President ..... Dr. Claudia HABIB
04 Administrative Asst to President ..... Mrs. Felisa HANNAH
05 Vice President Instruction ..... Dr. Thad RUSSELL
10 Vice Pres Finance & Admin Services ..... Dr. Arlitha WILLIAMS-HARMON
32 Vice President Student Services ..... Ms. Primavera ARVIZU
20 Int Dean Instruction ..... Dr. Michelle MILLER-GALAZ
20 Int Dean Instruction ..... Mr. Joseph CASCIO
121 Dean Student Success and Counseling ..... Mrs. Erin WINGFIELD
37 Director Financial Aid ..... Mrs. Tiffany HAYNES
76 Assoc Dean Health Careers ..... Ms. Kim BEHRENS
18 Director Maintenance & Operations ..... Mr. John WORD
102 Exec Director PC Foundation ..... Ms. Ramona CHIAPA
84 Director Enrollment Services ..... Vacant
09 Director Institutional Research ..... Mr. Michael CARLEY
13 Director Information Technology ..... Mr. Jay NAVARRETTE
35 Director Student Services ..... Mr. Frank RAMIREZ
08 Librarian ..... Mr. Chris EBERT
41 Int Athletic Director ..... Mr. Gerred LINK
21 Accounting Manager ..... Mr. Kevin KERWIN
26 Manager Communications & Marketing ..... Mr. Roger PEREZ
105 Web Content Editor ..... Mr. Kevin OTT
15 Int Human Resources Manager ..... Ms. Johanna FISHER
19 Manager Campus Safety & Security ..... Mr. Todd DEARMORE

Kernel University (B)

905 S. Euclid Street #213, Fullerton CA 92833
County: Orange Identification: 667308
Telephone: (714) 995-9988 Carnegie Class: Not Classified
FAX Number: (714) 995-9989 Calendar System: Semester
URL: www.kernel.edu
Established: 1995 Annual Undergrad Tuition & Fees: N/A
Enrollment: N/A Coed
Affiliation or Control: Independent Non-Profit IRS Status: 501(c)3
Highest Offering: Doctorate
Accreditation: TRACS

01 President ..... Matthew D. WOO
05 Academic Dean ..... Byung-Dal KUM
10 Chief Financial Officer ..... Trangthithuy LE
07 Director Admissions & Registrar ..... Timothy KING
32 Director of Student Services ..... Priscilla M. WOO

La Sierra University (C)

4500 Riverwalk Parkway, Riverside CA 92505
County: Riverside FICE Identification: 001215
Unit ID: 117627
Telephone: (951) 785-2000 Carnegie Class: Masters/M
FAX Number: (951) 785-2901 Calendar System: Quarter
URL: www.lasierra.edu
Established: 1922 Annual Undergrad Tuition & Fees: $35,208
Enrollment: 1,993 Coed
Affiliation or Control: Seventh-day Adventist IRS Status: 501(c)3
Highest Offering: Doctorate
Accreditation: WC, MUS, SW, THEOL

01 President ..... Dr. Joy A. FEHR
05 Provost ..... Dr. April SUMMITT
10 Vice President for Finance ..... Mr. David GERIGUIS
32 Vice President for Student Life ..... Ms. Yamilet BAZAN
111 Vice Pres Advancement/Univ Rels ..... Mr. Norman YERGEN
84 Int Vice Pres Enrollment Services ..... Mr. Wayne DUNBAR
26 VP Communication/Integrated Mktg ..... Dr. Marilyn THOMSEN
21 Associate Vice President Finance ..... Ms. Pamela CHRISPENS
20 Associate Provost ..... Ms. Cindy PARKHURST
49 Dean College Arts/Sciences ..... Vacant
50 Dean School of Business ..... Dr. John THOMAS
53 Dean School of Education ..... Dr. Chang-Ho JI
73 Dean School of Divinity ..... Dr Friedbert NINOW
35 Dean of Student Life ..... Ms. Marjorie ROBINSON
102 Exec Director University Foundation ..... Mr. Larry GERATY
55 Director Adult Evening Program ..... Ms. Nancy DITTEMORE
29 Alumni Director ..... Ms. Julie NARDUCCI
15 Director Human Resources ..... Ms. Dell Jean VAN FOSSEN
08 Director Library ..... Ms. Kitty SIMMONS

37 Director Student Financial Services ..... Ms. Esther KINZER
42 Director Campus Ministries ..... Mr. Samuel E. LEONOR, JR.
13 Director Information Technology ..... Mr. Geoff INGRAM
09 Director of Institutional Research ..... Ms. Jan LONG
18 Director Physical Plant ..... Mr. Al VALDEZ
38 Director Counseling Center ..... Ms. Debra WRIGHT
92 Director Honors Program ..... Dr. Douglas R. CLARK
07 Director of Admissions/Registrar ..... Vacant
36 Career Advisor ..... Mr. William PENICK
41 Athletic Director ..... Mr. Javier KRUMM

Laguna College of Art & Design (D)

2222 Laguna Canyon Road,
Laguna Beach CA 92651-1136
County: Orange FICE Identification: 023305
Unit ID: 117168
Telephone: (949) 376-6000 Carnegie Class: Spec-4-yr-Arts
FAX Number: (949) 376-6009 Calendar System: Semester
URL: www.lcad.edu
Established: 1961 Annual Undergrad Tuition & Fees: $32,600
Enrollment: 782 Coed
Affiliation or Control: Independent Non-Profit IRS Status: 501(c)3
Highest Offering: Master's
Accreditation: WC, ART

01 President ..... Dr. Jonathan BURKE
05 Provost/COO ..... Dr. Helene GARRISON
111 Vice Pres of College Advancement ..... Mr. Dominic MUMOLO
84 Vice Pres Enrollment Management ..... Mr. Christopher BROWN
10 Chief Financial Officer ..... Mr. Jim GODEK
32 Director of Student Life ..... Ms. Amanda FRENCH
06 Registrar ..... Ms. Laura PATRICK
08 Library Director ..... Ms. Viet VU
04 Exec Assistant to the President ..... Ms. Jeni RICHARDS
37 Sr Financial Aid Counselor ..... Mr. Reginald WEST, JR.
09 Director of Institutional Research ..... Ms. Laura PATRICK
15 Director Human Resources ..... Ms. Caroline CARLSON
13 Chief Information Officer ..... Mr. Matt MORTON
18 Director Facilities/Physical Plant ..... Mr. Mark DAY
26 Dir of Marketing/Communications ..... Mr. Marc LYNCHESKI

Lake Tahoe Community College (E)

1 College Drive, South Lake Tahoe CA 96150-4524
County: El Dorado FICE Identification: 012907
Unit ID: 117195
Telephone: (530) 541-4660 Carnegie Class: Assoc/MT-VT-High Non
FAX Number: (530) 541-7852 Calendar System: Quarter
URL: www.ltcc.edu
Established: 1975 Annual Undergrad Tuition & Fees (In-District): $1,131
Enrollment: 2,332 Coed
Affiliation or Control: State/Local IRS Status: 501(c)3
Highest Offering: Associate Degree
Accreditation: WJ

01 Superintendent/President ..... Mr. Jeff DEFRANCO
04 Executive Assistant to President ..... Ms. Lisa SHAFER
05 VP Academic Affairs ..... Dr. Michelle RISDON
10 Vice Pres Administrative Svcs ..... Ms. Russi EGAN
103 Dean of Workforce Development/Inst ..... Mr. Brad DEEDS
32 VP Student Services ..... Ms. Michelle BATISTA
20 Dean of Instruction ..... Ms. Ali BISSONNETTE
08 Director of Library ..... Ms. Melanie CHU
13 Director Information Tech Svcs ..... Mr. Dave BURBA
84 Director Enrollment Services ..... Mr. Steve BERRY
21 Director of Fiscal Services ..... Mr. Ryan PHILPOTT
15 Director of Human Resources ..... Ms. Shelley HANSEN
18 Int Dir of Facilities/Operations ..... Mr. Felix CHAGOYA
88 Dir Child Development Programs ..... Ms. Leslie AMATO
37 Director Financial Aid ..... Ms. Naomi FOLLETT
09 Dir of Institutional Effectiveness ..... Dr. Elizabeth BALINT
26 Dir Marketing/Communications ..... Ms. Diane LEWIS
102 Foundation Director ..... Ms. Nancy HARRISON
40 Bookstore Manager ..... Mr. Trevor OSTENDORF
96 Purchasing Agent ..... Ms. Heather CADE
41 Athletic Director ..... Mr. Steve BERRY
28 Director of Equity ..... Ms. Laura SALINAS

Lassen Community College (F)

PO Box 3000, 478-200 Highway 139,
Susanville CA 96130-3000
County: Lassen FICE Identification: 001217
Unit ID: 117274
Telephone: (530) 257-6181 Carnegie Class: Assoc/HT-Mix Trad/Non
FAX Number: (530) 251-8872 Calendar System: Semester
URL: www.lassencollege.edu
Established: 1925 Annual Undergrad Tuition & Fees (In-District): $1,127
Enrollment: 1,821 Coed
Affiliation or Control: State/Local IRS Status: 501(c)3
Highest Offering: Associate Degree
Accreditation: WJ

01 Superintendent/President ..... Dr. Trevor D. ALBERTSON
04 Assistant to President ..... Ms. Julie L. JOHNSTON
20 Interim Dean of Instruction-CIO ..... Ms. Carie CAMACHO
20 Interim Dean of Instruction-CTE ..... Ms. Roxanna HAYNES
11 Interim VP Administrative Services ..... Mr. David CORLEY
32 Interim VP Student Services ..... Ms. Brady REED
35 Interim Assoc Dean Student Services ..... Mr. Davis MURPHY

21 Director Fiscal Services ..... Ms. Marguerite LEWMAN
121 Assoc Dean Student Success/Equity ..... Vacant
08 Librarian ..... Ms. Shar MURPHY
13 Director Technology ..... Mr. David CORLEY
35 Director Student Life ..... Mr. Francis BEAUJON
41 Athletic Director ..... Mr. Glen YONAN
18 Director Facilities/Operations ..... Mr. Gregory COLLINS
15 Director Human Resources ..... Ms. Vickie RAMSEY
09 Director of Institutional Research ..... Dr. Randall JOSLIN
30 Director of Development/Alumni Rels ..... Ms. Nicole KELLEY

Latin American Bible Institute (G)

14209 E. Lomitas Avenue, La Puente CA 91746
County: Los Angeles Identification: 667319
Telephone: (626) 968-1328 Carnegie Class: Not Classified
FAX Number: (626) 961-7253 Calendar System: Semester
URL: www.labi.edu
Established: 1926 Annual Undergrad Tuition & Fees: N/A
Enrollment: N/A Coed
Affiliation or Control: Independent Non-Profit IRS Status: 501(c)3
Highest Offering: Baccalaureate
Accreditation: BI

01 President ..... Dr. Marty HARRIS
05 Provost/Dean of Academic Affairs ..... Mr. Nehemias ROMERO
10 Chief Financial Officer ..... Ms. Gabriela MORA-ALVAREZ
32 Dean of Students ..... Ms. Yvette ROBLES
06 Registrar ..... Ms. Berenice VALENCIA
08 Librarian ..... Mr. Steve VALDEZ
18 Office/Facilities Manager ..... Ms. Erika RAMIREZ

Laurus College (H)

81 Higuera Street, Ste 110, San Luis Obispo CA 93401
County: San Luis Obispo FICE Identification: 041414
Unit ID: 454786
Telephone: (805) 267-1690 Carnegie Class: Assoc/HVT-High Trad
FAX Number: (805) 352-1307 Calendar System: Quarter
URL: www.lauruscollege.edu
Established: 2006 Annual Undergrad Tuition & Fees: N/A
Enrollment: 897 Coed
Affiliation or Control: Proprietary IRS Status: Proprietary
Highest Offering: Baccalaureate
Accreditation: ACICS, DEAC

00 President/CEO ..... Mr. James REDMOND
01 School Chancellor ..... Mr. Jeff REDMOND
32 Vice Pres Student Programs ..... Ms. Cecilia MORTELA
37 Director Financial Aid ..... Mr. Tim REDMOND
06 Registrar ..... Mr. Brendan COYLE
05 Director of Education ..... Ms. Melanie BRYANT

Learnet Academy (I)

3251 W. 6th Street, 2nd Floor, Los Angeles CA 90020
County: Los Angeles Identification: 667223
Unit ID: 483221
Telephone: (213) 387-4242 Carnegie Class: Spec 2-yr-Other
FAX Number: (213) 387-5365 Calendar System: Other
URL: www.learnet.edu
Established: 1993 Annual Undergrad Tuition & Fees: N/A
Enrollment: 72 Coed
Affiliation or Control: Proprietary IRS Status: Proprietary
Highest Offering: Associate Degree
Accreditation: ACCSC, CEA

01 Executive Director ..... Ms. Tia SHIN
05 Education Director ..... Mr. Agasi ASLANYAN

The Lee Strasberg Theatre Institute (J)

7936 Santa Monica Blvd, Los Angeles CA 90046
County: Los Angeles Identification: 667413
Telephone: (323) 650-7777 Carnegie Class: Not Classified
FAX Number: (323) 650-7770 Calendar System: Quarter
URL: strasberg.edu
Established: 1969 Annual Undergrad Tuition & Fees: N/A
Enrollment: N/A Coed
Affiliation or Control: Proprietary IRS Status: Proprietary
Highest Offering: Associate Degree
Accreditation: THEA

01 President ..... Victoria KANE

Life Chiropractic College West (K)

25001 Industrial Boulevard, Hayward CA 94545-2801
County: Alameda FICE Identification: 022285
Unit ID: 117520
Telephone: (510) 780-4500 Carnegie Class: Spec-4-yr-Other Health
FAX Number: (510) 780-4525 Calendar System: Quarter
URL: www.lifewest.edu
Established: 1976 Annual Undergrad Tuition & Fees: N/A
Enrollment: 598 Coed
Affiliation or Control: Independent Non-Profit IRS Status: 501(c)3
Highest Offering: First Professional Degree; No Lower Division
Accreditation: WC, CHIRO

01 President .... Dr. Ron OBERSTEIN
03 Executive Vice President .... Dr. Anatole BOGATSKI
17 Vice President Clinical Operations .... Dr. Scott DONALDSON
05 Vice President of Academic Affairs .... Dr. Pardeep KULLAR
111 VP Institutional Advancement .... Dr. Mark ZIEGLER
10 Controller .... Angelito TOLENTINO
46 Director of Research .... Dr. Monica SMITH
51 Director of Continuing Education .... Dr. Laurie ISENBERG
08 Library Director .... Barbara DELLI GATTI
29 Director Alumni Relations .... Vacant
37 Director Financial Aid .... Brenda JOHNSON
06 Registrar .... Maria LOPEZ
15 Director Human Resources .... Tarsha ADDISON
32 Student Life Manager .... Danielle LORTA
40 Bookstore Manager .... Michael BALDWIN
41 Athletic Director .... Adriaan FERRIS
84 Director of Enrollment .... Dr. Jennifer BOSCO
30 Director of Development .... Thomas HYLAND
108 Director of Assessment & Education .... Dr. Scott KERLIN
04 Executive Assistant to President .... Sharon SETO
07 Director of Admissions .... Marc MARTIN
18 Chf Facilities/Physical Plant Ofcr .... Michael BALDWIN
26 Director of Marketing .... Alana HOPE
121 Academic Counselor .... Lori PINO
28 Diversity & Inclusion Officer .... Dr. Annette WALKER
43 General Counsel .... Antoinette MCGILL

Life Pacific University (A)

1100 W. Covina Boulevard, San Dimas CA 91773-3298

County: Los Angeles — FICE Identification: 022706
Unit ID: 117104

Telephone: (909) 599-5433 — Carnegie Class: Bac-Diverse
FAX Number: (909) 599-6690 — Calendar System: Semester
URL: www.lifepacific.edu
Established: 1923 — Annual Undergrad Tuition & Fees: $17,434
Enrollment: 604 — Coed
Affiliation or Control: Other — IRS Status: 501(c)3
Highest Offering: Master's
Accreditation: WC, BI

01 President .... Ms. Angie RICHEY
04 Exec Assistant to the President .... Mrs. Shellie DRISCOLL
05 Vice President Academic Affairs .... Dr. Daniel RUARTE
84 Director Enrollment Management .... Mr. Matthew TAPP
32 Assoc VP of Student Development .... Mr. George BOSTANIC
10 CFO .... Mr. Bob JOHANSEN
08 Librarian .... Mr. Gary MERRIMAN
06 Registrar .... Mrs. Amber BURNETT
18 Director of Facilities .... Mr. Rick MEYER
37 Director of Financial Aid .... Mrs. Luci PEREZ
09 Dean Institutional Effectiveness .... Mr. Brian TOMHAVE
15 Human Resources Director .... Ms. Heidi BONADIE
39 Director Residence Life .... Mrs. Maria MCCRACKEN
41 Athletic Director .... Mr. Tim COOK
13 IT Administrator (CIO) .... Mr. Marlon ESTELLA
111 Chief Development/Advancement .... Mrs. Lynnette LOZOYA

Lincoln Law School of Sacramento (B)

3140 J Street, Sacramento CA 95816

County: Sacramento — Identification: 667379
Telephone: (916) 446-1275 — Carnegie Class: Not Classified
FAX Number: N/A — Calendar System: Semester
URL: www.lincolnlaw.edu
Established: 1969 — Annual Graduate Tuition & Fees: N/A
Enrollment: N/A — Coed
Affiliation or Control: Proprietary — IRS Status: Proprietary
Highest Offering: First Professional Degree; No Undergraduates
Accreditation: WC

01 Chief Executive Officer .... James SMOLICH

Lincoln University (C)

401 15th Street, Oakland CA 94612-2801

County: Alameda — FICE Identification: 006975
Unit ID: 117557

Telephone: (510) 628-8010 — Carnegie Class: Spec-4-yr-Bus
FAX Number: (510) 628-8012 — Calendar System: Semester
URL: www.lincolnuca.edu
Established: 1919 — Annual Undergrad Tuition & Fees: $11,390
Enrollment: 371 — Coed
Affiliation or Control: Independent Non-Profit — IRS Status: 501(c)3
Highest Offering: Doctorate
Accreditation: WC, IACBE

01 President .... Dr. Mikhail BRODSKY
05 Provost/Chief Academic Officer .... Dr. Marc SLAVIN
11 Administrative Vice President .... Dr. Michael GUERRA
10 Chief Financial Officer/CIO .... Mr. Albert LOH
32 Dean of Students .... Mr. William HESS
07 Director of Admissions & Records .... Ms. Peggy AU
08 Head Librarian .... Ms. Nicole Y. MARSH
35 Director of Student Services .... Ms. Ana Maria GOWER
41 Director of Athletics Program .... Mr. Desmond GUMBS
13 Director of Computer Laboratory .... Mr. Shakil SHRESTHA
06 Registrar .... Ms. Maggie HUA
108 Dir of Accreditation/Compliance .... Dr. Harpal DHILLON
09 Institutional Research Coordinator .... Dr. Igor HIMELFARB

37 Director Student Financial Aid .... Ms. Wendy VASQUEZ
18 Campus Property Manager .... Mr. Mikk TEEVEER

Logos Evangelical Seminary (D)

9358 Telstar Avenue, El Monte CA 91731-2816

County: Los Angeles — FICE Identification: 039454
Unit ID: 397553

Telephone: (626) 571-5110 — Carnegie Class: Not Classified
FAX Number: N/A — Calendar System: Semester
URL: www.logos-seminary.edu
Established: 1989 — Annual Graduate Tuition & Fees: N/A
Enrollment: N/A — Coed
Affiliation or Control: Other — IRS Status: 501(c)3
Highest Offering: Doctorate; No Undergraduates
Accreditation: WC, THEOL

01 President .... Dr. James HWANG
05 Academic Dean .... Dr. Chloe SUN
111 Director of Advancement .... Rev. Mark SHEN
10 Director Finance/Administration .... Mr. James TSAI
32 Dean of Students .... Rev. Samuel LIU
12 Director Logos Training Institute .... Vacant
04 Executive Asst to President .... Ms. Kathleen LIN
08 Head Librarian .... Ms. Shelley SII
09 Institutional Research Specialist .... Ms. Becky PERNG

Loma Linda University (E)

11139 Anderson Street, Loma Linda CA 92350

County: San Bernardino — FICE Identification: 001218
Unit ID: 117636

Telephone: (909) 558-1000 — Carnegie Class: Spec-4-yr-Med
FAX Number: (909) 558-0242 — Calendar System: Quarter
URL: www.llu.edu
Established: 1905 — Annual Undergrad Tuition & Fees: N/A
Enrollment: 4,468 — Coed
Affiliation or Control: Seventh-day Adventist — IRS Status: 501(c)3
Highest Offering: Doctorate
Accreditation: WC, ANEST, ARCPA, CAHIIM, CAMPEP, CLPSY, COARC, CVT, CYTO, DENT, DH, DIETC, DMS, IPSY, MAC, MED, MFCD, MT, NMT, NURSE, OPE, OT, PA, PAST, PH, PHAR, PTA, PTAA, RAD, RADDOS, RTT, SP, SW

01 President .... Dr. Richard H. HART
05 Provost .... Dr. Ronald L. CARTER
10 Sr Vice President Financial Affairs .... Mr. Rodney NEAL
30 Sr Vice President Advancement .... Mrs. Rachelle BUSSELL
13 Vice President Information Systems .... Dr. David P. HARRIS
84 VP Student Experience .... Vacant
46 VP for Research Affairs .... Dr. Michael SAMARDZIJA
15 VP Human Resource Management .... Vacant
63 Dean of Medicine .... Dr. Tamara THOMAS
52 Dean of Dentistry .... Dr. Robert HANDYSIDES
69 Dean of Public Health .... Dr. Helen Hopp MARSHAK
66 Dean of Nursing .... Dr. Elizabeth (Becky) BOSSERT
76 Dean of Allied Health Professions .... Dr. Craig R. JACKSON
67 Dean School of Pharmacy .... Dr. Michael D. HOGUE
83 Dean School of Behavioral Health .... Dr. Beverly J. BUCKLES
73 Dean School of Religion .... Dr. Leo RANZOLIN
58 Int Exec Dir Faculty Grad Studies .... Dr. Ronald L. CARTER
06 Director of Records .... Ms. Erin SEHEULT
08 Director University Libraries .... Ms. Shanalee TAMARES
38 Director of Counseling .... Dr. William G. MURDOCH
43 General Legal Counsel .... Mr. Kent A. HANSEN
33 Dean of Men .... Mr. John NAFIE
34 Dean of Women .... Ms. Lynette BATES
37 Director Student Financial Aid .... Ms. Verdell SCHAEFER
09 Dir Educational Effectiveness .... Dr. Marilyn EGGERS
18 Director Campus Engineering .... Mr. Randy STEVENS
96 Director of Purchasing .... Mr. Tim HICKMAN
40 Campus Bookstore Manager .... Ms. Arlene ALVAREZ
42 Campus Chaplain .... Pastor Terry SWENSON

Long Beach City College (F)

4901 E Carson Street, Long Beach CA 90808-1780

County: Los Angeles — FICE Identification: 001219
Unit ID: 117645

Telephone: (562) 938-4111 — Carnegie Class: Assoc/MT-VT-High Trad
FAX Number: (562) 938-4118 — Calendar System: Other
URL: www.lbcc.edu
Established: 1927 — Annual Undergrad Tuition & Fees (In-District): $1,556
Enrollment: 23,147 — Coed
Affiliation or Control: State/Local — IRS Status: 501(c)3
Highest Offering: Associate Degree
Accreditation: WJ, ADNUR

01 Interim Superintendent/President .... Dr. Mike MUN~OZ
05 Vice Pres Academic Affairs .... Dr. Lee DOUGLAS
10 Vice Pres Business Services .... Marlene DRINKWINE
32 Int Vice Pres Student Support Svcs .... Dr. Noel CORRAL
15 Vice Pres Human Resources .... Dr. Loy NASHUA
13 Int Chief Info Systems Officer .... Robert CARMAN
16 Assoc VP Human Resources .... Kristin OLSON
84 Interim Dean Enrollment Services .... Yvonne GUTIERREZ-SANDOVAL
111 CEO College Advancement & Econ Dev .... Sheneui WEBER
75 Dean Career & Technical Education .... Gene CARBONARO
38 Int Dean Counseling/Stdnt Supp Svcs .... Javier VILLASENOR
20 Interim Dean Academic Affairs .... Kenna HILLMAN
22 Dean of Student Equity .... Sonia DE LA TORRE-INIGUEZ
60 Dean Language Arts & Comms .... Nicole GLICK

35 Dean Student Affairs .... Alisia KIRKWOOD
81 Dean of Science & Math .... Moises GUTIERREZ
76 Dean of Health Sci & Kinesiology .... Dr. Paul CREASON
09 Dean Inst Effectiveness .... Dr. Heather Van VOLKINBURG
83 Dean Social Sciences & Arts .... Elisabeth ORR
102 Exec Director Foundation .... Paul KAMINSKI
26 Exec Dir Public Affairs & Marketing .... Joshua CASTELLANOS
20 Int Assoc Dean Academic Services .... Brent GILMORE
100 Int Dir of the President's Office .... Nevon WATSON
96 Director Business Support Svcs .... Bob RAPOZA
21 Director Fiscal Services & Payroll .... John THOMPSON
37 Director Financial Aid .... Jason AVILA
41 Int Dean of Kinesiology & Athletics .... Randy TOTORP
103 Director Workforce Development .... Melissa INFUSINO
04 Int Exec Asst to the President .... Lauren ZALE
101 Interim Board Secretary .... M'Shelle REECE
105 Deputy Director Network Services .... Mark GUIDAS
106 Assoc Dean Online Lrng/Educ Tech .... Hussam KASHOU
108 Director Inst Effectiveness .... Jennifer HOLMGREN
90 Dep Dir Acad Comp/Multimedia Svcs .... Tim HEFFERN

Los Angeles Academy of Figurative Art (G)

16926 Saticoy Street, Van Nuys CA 91406

County: Los Angeles — Identification: 667231
Unit ID: 490124

Telephone: (818) 708-9232 — Carnegie Class: Spec-4-yr-Arts
FAX Number: (818) 474-8679 — Calendar System: Quarter
URL: www.laafa.edu
Established: 2002 — Annual Undergrad Tuition & Fees: $32,093
Enrollment: 5 — Coed
Affiliation or Control: Proprietary — IRS Status: Proprietary
Highest Offering: Baccalaureate
Accreditation: ART

01 President .... Maryam STORM

Los Angeles College of Music (H)

300 South Fair Oaks Avenue, Pasadena CA 91105

County: Los Angeles — FICE Identification: 038684
Unit ID: 446385

Telephone: (626) 568-8850 — Carnegie Class: Spec-4-yr-Arts
FAX Number: (626) 568-8854 — Calendar System: Quarter
URL: www.lacm.edu
Established: 1996 — Annual Undergrad Tuition & Fees: $25,650
Enrollment: 249 — Coed
Affiliation or Control: Proprietary — IRS Status: Proprietary
Highest Offering: Baccalaureate
Accreditation: MUS

01 President .... Charles T. AYLESBURY
03 Executive Vice President .... Erin WORKMAN
06 Registrar .... Jorge OJEDA
05 Dean of Academics .... Daniel WALKER
37 Director of Financial Aid .... Bertha CHAVEZ
07 Director of Admissions .... Emilio RODRIGUEZ
10 Controller .... Kristin BARRIOS

*Los Angeles Community College District Office (I)

770 Wilshire Boulevard, Los Angeles CA 90017

County: Los Angeles — FICE Identification: 001221
Unit ID: 117681

Telephone: (213) 891-2000 — Carnegie Class: N/A
FAX Number: N/A
URL: www.laccd.edu

01 Chancellor .... Dr. Francisco C. RODRIGUEZ
05 VC Educ Pgms/Inst Effectiveness .... Dr. Ryan M. CORNNER
43 General Counsel .... Mr. Jeffrey M. PRIETO
10 Chief Financial Officer/Treasurer .... Mr. Jeannette L. GORDON
15 Acting VC Human Resources .... Dr. Mercedes GUTIERREZ
18 Chief Facilities Executive .... Dr. Rueben C. SMITH
20 Deputy Chancellor .... Dr. Melinda A. NISH
103 Int VC Workforce Resource Devel .... Vacant

*East Los Angeles College (J)

1301 Avenida Cesar Chavez,
Monterey Park CA 91754-6001

County: Los Angeles — FICE Identification: 022260
Unit ID: 113856

Telephone: (323) 265-8650 — Carnegie Class: Assoc/MT-VT-Mix Trad/Non
FAX Number: (323) 265-8763 — Calendar System: Semester
URL: www.elac.edu
Established: 1945 — Annual Undergrad Tuition & Fees (In-District): $1,238
Enrollment: 33,397 — Coed
Affiliation or Control: State/Local — IRS Status: Exempt
Highest Offering: Associate Degree
Accreditation: WJ, CAHIIM, COARC

02 President .... Dr. Alberto J. ROMAN
05 VP Academic Affairs .... Mr. Ruben ARENAS
11 VP Administrative Services .... Ms. Myeshia ARMSTRONG
32 VP Student Services .... Dr. Miguel DUENAS
81 Dean STEM .... Dr. Djuradj BABIC
103 Acting Dean Cont Educ/Workforce Dev .... Dr. Laura CANTU

07 Dean Student Services ... Ms. Danelle FALLERT
88 Dean Student Services ... Dr. Sonia LOPEZ
121 Dean Student Services ... Ms. Paulina PALOMINO
120 Dean Academic Affairs ... Ms. Gina CHELSTROM
89 Dean Student Services ... Dr. Vanessa OCHOA
88 Dean Student Services ... Ms. Grace HERNANDEZ
88 Dean Language Arts ... Mr. James KENNY
57 Dean Visual Arts/Dance/Athletics ... Ms. Ming-huei LAM
83 Dean Social Sciences ... Ms. Kerrin MCMAHAN
88 Assoc Vice President Admin Svcs ... Mr. Nghi NGHIEM
88 Dean Perform Arts & Design ... Mr. Alfonso RIOS
76 Dean Health & Human Svcs ... Ms. Angelica TOLEDO
51 Dean Continuing Education ... Dr. Juan URDIALES
09 Interim Dean Inst Effectiveness ... Ms. Laura CRUZ-ATRIAN
10 College Financial Administrator ... Mr. Hao XIE
26 Public Information Officer ... Mr. Kevin JIMENEZ
15 Chief Human Resources Officer ... Ms. Maria ESTRADA
40 Bookstore Supervisor ... Mr. Miguel PEREZ
41 Athletic Director ... Mr. Bobby GODINEZ
08 Library Dept Chair ... Ms. Chonhee RHIM
88 Director Child Development Center ... Ms. Marcia CAGIGAS
04 Exec Assistant to the President ... Ms. Kristen M. VAN HALA
06 Registrar ... Ms. Anna SALAZAR
19 Director Security/Safety ... Mr. Don RUBIO
37 Director Student Financial Aid ... Ms. Lindy FONG
18 Director of College Facilities ... Mr. Jose VILLARREAL

*Los Angeles City College (A)

855 N Vermont Avenue, Los Angeles CA 90029-9990
County: Los Angeles FICE Identification: 001223
Unit ID: 117788
Telephone: (323) 953-4000 Carnegie Class: Assoc/HT-Mix Trad/Non
FAX Number: (323) 953-4013 Calendar System: Semester
URL: www.lacitycollege.edu
Established: 1929 Annual Undergrad Tuition & Fees (In-District): $1,238
Enrollment: 14,800 Coed
Affiliation or Control: Local IRS Status: 501(c)3
Highest Offering: Associate Degree
Accreditation: WJ, DT, RAD

02 President ... Dr. Mary GALLAGHER
05 Vice President Academic Affairs ... Dr. James LANCASTER
10 Vice President Administrative Svcs ... Vacant
32 Actg VP of Student Services ... Mr. Alen ANDRIASSIAN
88 VP Economic Soc Mobil & Innovation ... Ms. Marcy DRUMMOND
15 AVP Administrative Svcs/Personnel ... Mr. Michael PASCUAL
20 Dean of Academic Affairs ... Dr. Thelma DAY
103 Dean of Workforce Development ... Dr. Armando RIVERA-FIGUEROA
09 Dean of Institutional Effectiveness ... Dr. Anna BADALYAN
124 Dean of EOPS ... Dr. Saadia PORCHE
37 Dean Financial Aid ... Dr. Saadia PORCHE
35 Actg Dean Office of Student Life ... Ms. Armineh DEREGHSIAN
40 Bookstore Manager ... Ms. Christi O'CONNOR
85 Dean of International Students ... Dr. Darren GROSCH
66 Nursing Department Chair ... Dr. Christiana BASKARAN
38 Counseling Chairperson ... Mr. Edward SONG
18 Facilities Director ... Mr. Kahlil HARRINGTON
04 Executive Assistant to President ... Ms. Lillian T. JOHNSON

*Los Angeles Harbor College (B)

1111 Figueroa Place, Wilmington CA 90744-2397
County: Los Angeles FICE Identification: 001224
Unit ID: 117690
Telephone: (310) 233-4000 Carnegie Class: Assoc/HT-Mix Trad/Non
FAX Number: (310) 233-4660 Calendar System: Semester
URL: www.lahc.edu
Established: 1949 Annual Undergrad Tuition & Fees (In-District): $1,238
Enrollment: 8,101 Coed
Affiliation or Control: State/Local IRS Status: 501(c)3
Highest Offering: Associate Degree
Accreditation: WJ, ADNUR

02 President ... Dr. Luis DORADO
04 Executive Assistant to President ... Ms. Sylvia FILES
05 Vice Pres Academic Affairs ... Dr. Bobbi VILLALOBOS
10 Vice Pres Administrative Services ... Dr. Reagan ROMALI
32 Vice Pres Student Services ... Dr. Nicole ALBO-LOPEZ
21 Assoc Vice Pres Administrative Svcs ... Vacant
09 Dean of Institutional Effectiveness ... Dr. Edward PAI
20 Dean of Academic Affairs ... Dr. Chelvi SUBRAMANIAM
35 Dean Student Services ... Mr. Tiffany SERGIO
22 Dean Student Svcs/Acting Dean EWD ... Ms. Mercy YANEZ
35 Dean of Student Services ... Mrs. Dawn REID
20 Dean Acad Affs/Non-credit & Cmty Ed ... Ms. Priscilla LOPEZ
83 Div Chair Behavioral/Social Sci ... Mr. Son NGUYEN
50 Division Chairperson Business ... Ms. Wendy HOFFMAN
60 Div Chairperson Communications ... Ms. Ann WARREN
57 Div Chair Humanities/Fine Arts ... Mr. Juan BAEZ
81 Div Chairperson Math/Phys Science ... Ms. Farah SADDIGH
76 Div Chairperson Health Sciences ... Mrs. Lynn YAMAKAWA
68 Div Chairperson Physical Education ... Mr. Nabeel M. BARAKAT
59 Div Chair Sci/Family Consumer Stds ... Dr. Basil IBE
08 Division Chairperson Library ... Mr. Jonathan LEE
38 Division Chairperson Counseling ... Ms. Sara RUBIO
41 Athletic Director ... Mr. Dean DOWTY
37 Director Student Financial Aid ... Vacant
18 Facilities Manager ... Mr. Alex NELSON
13 Manager Information Technology ... Vacant
31 Community Services Manager ... Ms. Darin COSTA
85 International Student Program ... Ms. Jessica CRUZ

15 Payroll & Personnel Supervisor ... Ms. Hsin (Gina) PENG
88 Assoc Dean of STEM Pathways ... Ms. Mercy YANEZ
102 Foundation Development Officer ... Mr. Peter BOSTIC
06 Registrar ... Ms. Ruby GUERRERO
26 Chief Public Relations Officer ... Mr. Peter BOSTIC

*Los Angeles Mission College (C)

13356 Eldridge Avenue, Sylmar CA 91342-3244
County: Los Angeles FICE Identification: 012550
Unit ID: 117867
Telephone: (818) 364-7600 Carnegie Class: Assoc/HT-High Trad
FAX Number: (818) 364-7826 Calendar System: Semester
URL: www.lamission.edu
Established: 1975 Annual Undergrad Tuition & Fees (In-District): $1,238
Enrollment: 9,451 Coed
Affiliation or Control: State/Local IRS Status: 501(c)3
Highest Offering: Associate Degree
Accreditation: WJ

02 President ... Dr. Armida ORNELAS
05 Vice President Academic Affairs ... Dr. Kimberly E. MANNER
11 Vice President Administrative Svcs ... Mr. Robert PARKER
32 Vice President of Student Services ... Dr. Larry L. RESENDEZ
20 Acting Dean of Academic Affairs ... Ms. Kelly ENOS
35 Dean of Student Services ... Ms. Ludi VILLEGAS-VIDAL
88 Dean of CTE ... Ms. Marla ULIANA
35 Dean of Student Services ... Mr. Carlos R. GONZALEZ
09 Dean of Institutional Effectiveness ... Dr. Sarah L. MASTER
20 Dean of Academic Affairs ... Ms. Madelline HERNANDEZ
26 Chief Public Relations Officer ... Mr. Alejandro GUZMAN
88 Director Child Development Center ... Ms. Diane STEIN
41 Athletic Director ... Vacant
08 Head Librarian ... Mr. David GARZA
38 Counseling Chairperson ... Ms. Christine KOURINIAN
37 Financial Aid Manager ... Mr. Dennis J. SCHROEDER
18 Facilities/Physical Plant Manager ... Mr. Andrew GOOD
88 EOP & S/Care Director ... Ms. Ludi VILLEGAS-VIDAL
04 Executive Asst to President ... Ms. Oliva AYALA
10 Chief Business Officer ... Mr. Jerry HUANG
102 Dir Foundation/Corporate Relations ... Ms. Sheri RUIZ
15 Personnel Services Assistant ... Mr. Pio CASTILLO
07 Director of Admissions/Records ... Ms. Martha RIOS
36 Director Student Placement ... Ms. Wendy RIVERA
84 Director Enrollment Management ... Dr. Kimberly E. MANNER
96 Director of Purchasing ... Ms. Isabel RUIZ-MORENO
13 Chief Info Technology Officer (CIO) ... Mr. Mark HENDERSON

*Los Angeles Pierce College (D)

6201 Winnetka Avenue, Woodland Hills CA 91371-0001
County: Los Angeles FICE Identification: 001226
Unit ID: 117706
Telephone: (818) 710-4100 Carnegie Class: Assoc/HT-High Trad
FAX Number: N/A Calendar System: Semester
URL: www.piercecollege.edu
Established: 1947 Annual Undergrad Tuition & Fees (In-District): $1,238
Enrollment: 17,521 Coed
Affiliation or Control: State/Local IRS Status: 501(c)3
Highest Offering: Associate Degree
Accreditation: WJ

02 President ... Dr. Alexis MONTEVIRGEN
05 Int Vice President Academic Affairs ... Dr. Donna-Mae VILLANUEVA
11 Vice President Administrative Svcs ... Mr. Rolf SCHLEICHER
32 Vice President Student Services ... Dr. Earic DIXON-PETERS
10 Assoc Vice President Admin Services ... Mr. Bruce ROSKY
08 Chair Library ... Ms. Lauren SASLOW
38 Chair Counseling ... Ms. Alyce MILLER
20 Dean of Academic Affairs ... Dr. Donna-Mae VILLANUEVA
20 Dean of Academic Affairs ... Ms. Mary Anne GAVARRA-OH
20 Dean of Academic Affairs ... Ms. Susan RHI-KLEINERT
20 Dean of Academic Affairs ... Ms. Sharon DALMAGE
37 Director of Financial Aid ... Ms. Anafe ROBINSON
108 Dean Institutional Effectiveness ... Mr. Amari WILLIAMS
26 Public Information Officer ... Ms. Doreen CLAY
18 Director of College Facilities ... Mr. Paul NIEMAN
106 Dir Online Education/E-learning ... Ms. Wendy BASS KEER
121 Dean of Student Success ... Dr. Kalynda WEBBER MCLEAN
35 Dean Student Services ... Mr. William MARMOLEJO
06 Registrar ... Ms. Lorena LOPEZ
35 Dean of Student Services & Equity ... Dr. Genice SARCEDO-MAGRUDER
124 Dean of Student Engagement ... Mr. Juan Carlos ASTORGA

*Los Angeles Southwest College (E)

1600 W Imperial Highway, Los Angeles CA 90047-4899
County: Los Angeles FICE Identification: 007047
Unit ID: 117715
Telephone: (323) 241-5225 Carnegie Class: Assoc/HT-Mix Trad/Non
FAX Number: (323) 241-5220 Calendar System: Semester
URL: www.lasc.edu
Established: 1967 Annual Undergrad Tuition & Fees (In-District): $1,238
Enrollment: 5,216 Coed
Affiliation or Control: State/Local IRS Status: 501(c)3
Highest Offering: Associate Degree
Accreditation: WJ

02 President ... Dr. Seher AWAN
05 Vice President Academic Affairs ... Dr. Lawrence BRADFORD
32 Vice President Student Services ... Dr. Howard IRVIN

10 Vice President Admin Services ... Mr. Daniel B. HALL
111 Dean Institutional Advancement ... Mr. Jose Alfred GALLEGOS
103 Dean Career/Technical Education ... Vacant
20 Dean Academic Affairs ... Dr. Tangelia ALFRED
20 Dean Academic Affairs ... Dr. Kristi BLACKBURN
35 Dean Student Services ... Dr. Ralph DAVIS
88 Dean Special Programs & Services ... Ms. Jeanette MAGEE
55 Dean Adult Non-credit/Cont Educ ... Ms. Laura PEREZ
38 Chairperson Counseling ... Dr. Katrin WILSON
08 Chairperson Library ... Ms. Parissa SAMAIE
06 Registrar ... Vacant
18 Director of Facilities ... Mr. Preston MORTLEY
13 Regional Mgr College Tech Svcs ... Mr. Kirk YAMAMOTO
37 Financial Aid Manager ... Ms. Muniece BRUTON
26 College Public Relations Manager ... Mr. Ben DEMERS
04 Executive Assistant/Confidential ... Ms. Chauncine R. STEWART

*Los Angeles Trade-Technical College (F)

400 W Washington Boulevard,
Los Angeles CA 90015-4108
County: Los Angeles FICE Identification: 001227
Unit ID: 117724
Telephone: (213) 763-7000 Carnegie Class: Assoc/HVT-Mix Trad/Non
FAX Number: (213) 763-5393 Calendar System: Semester
URL: www.lattc.edu
Established: 1925 Annual Undergrad Tuition & Fees (In-District): $1,238
Enrollment: 11,285 Coed
Affiliation or Control: State/Local IRS Status: 501(c)3
Highest Offering: Associate Degree
Accreditation: WJ, ACFEI

02 President ... Dr. Katrina VANDERWOUDE
11 VP Administrative Services ... Mr. Harry ZIOGAS
05 Int Vice President Academic Affairs ... Dr. Rick HODGE
32 Int Vice Pres Student Affairs ... Dr. Henan JOOF
20 Dean Academic Affairs & Workforce ... Mr. Vincent JACKSON
20 Dean Academic Affairs & Workforce ... Ms. Cynthia MORLEY-MOWER
20 Dean Academic Affairs & Workforce ... Dr. Ann HAMILTON
20 Dean Academic Affairs & Workforce ... Dr. Arineh ARZOUMANIAN
35 Dean Student Services ... Dr. Henan JOOF
26 Public Relations Manager ... Mr. David YSAIS
13 Mgr Information Technology ... Mr. Sang BAIK

*Los Angeles Valley College (G)

5800 Fulton Avenue, Valley Glen CA 91401-4096
County: Los Angeles FICE Identification: 001228
Unit ID: 117733
Telephone: (818) 947-2600 Carnegie Class: Assoc/HT-High Trad
FAX Number: N/A Calendar System: Semester
URL: www.lavc.edu
Established: 1949 Annual Undergrad Tuition & Fees (In-District): $1,238
Enrollment: 15,957 Coed
Affiliation or Control: State/Local IRS Status: 501(c)3
Highest Offering: Associate Degree
Accreditation: WJ, ADNUR, COARC

02 President ... Dr. Barry C. GRIBBONS
05 Vice President Academic Affairs ... Ms. Karen DAAR
10 Vice President Admin Services ... Mr. Mike C. LEE
32 Vice President Student Services ... Mr. Florentino MANZANO
11 Associate VP Administrative Svcs ... Ms. Sarah SONG
20 Dean Academic Affairs ... Dr. Douglas MARRIOTT
20 Dean Academic Affairs ... Dr. Laurie NALEPA
20 Dean Academic Affairs ... Dr. Deborah A. DICESARE
20 Dean Academic Affairs ... Dr. Matthew JORDAN
20 Dean Academic Affairs ... Mr. Jermain PIPKINS
09 Dean Institutional Effectiveness ... Ms. Michelle R. FOWLES
35 Dean Student Life ... Dr. Elizabeth NEGRETE
88 Dean of Special Programs ... Dr. Sherri RODRIGUEZ
121 Dean Student Success & Support Svcs ... Dr. Sorangel HERNANDEZ
88 Associate Dean SSP ... Mr. David M. GREEN
35 Associate Dean Student Services ... Ms. Annie G. REED
35 Associate Dean Student Services ... Dr. Llanet MARTIN
102 Executive Director LAVC Foundation ... Mr. Raul V. CASTILLO
41 Athletic Director ... Mr. Jim FENWICK
18 Director College Facilities ... Vacant
40 College Store Manager ... Ms. Mary JOHN
26 Public Relations Manager ... Ms. Jennifer C. BORUCKI
31 Community Services Manager ... Mr. Michael B. ATKIN
13 Regional Manager College Tech Svcs ... Mr. Mark HENDERSON
37 Financial Aid Manager ... Mr. Vernon D. BRIDGES
21 College Fiscal Administrator ... Mr. Robert MEDINA
06 Registrar ... Ms. Ashley DUNN
04 Executive Assistant ... Ms. Tanya A. SIRKIN

*West Los Angeles College (H)

9000 Overland Avenue, Culver City CA 90230-5002
County: Los Angeles FICE Identification: 008596
Unit ID: 125471
Telephone: (310) 287-4200 Carnegie Class: Bac/Assoc-Assoc Dom
FAX Number: (310) 841-0396 Calendar System: Semester
URL: www.wlac.edu
Established: 1969 Annual Undergrad Tuition & Fees (In-District): $1,238
Enrollment: 11,417 Coed
Affiliation or Control: State/Local IRS Status: 501(c)3
Highest Offering: Baccalaureate

Accreditation: WJ, DH

02 President ... Dr. James M. LIMBAUGH
05 VP Academic Affairs ... Dr. Jeffrey D. ARCHIBALD
11 VP Administrative Svcs ... Ms. Silvia BARAJAS
32 VP Student Services ... Dr. Roberto O. GONZALEZ
97 Dean General Education & Transfer ... Dr. Walter JONES
20 Dean Academic Affairs ... Dr. Mary-Jo APIGO
88 Dean of Apprenticeship ... Ms. Tiffany MILLER
51 Dean Adult & Cont Education ... Dr. Allison TOM-MIURA
76 Dean of Health Sciences ... Ms. Carmen DONES
20 Dean Teaching & Learning ... Vacant
09 Dean Institutional Effectiveness ... Dr. Patricia QUINONES
22 Dean Student Services/Equity ... Mr. Angel VIRAMONTES
84 Dean Student Svcs/Enrollment ... Mr. Michael GOLTERMANN
35 Dean Student Svcs ... Ms. Angeles ABRAHAM
35 Dean Student Svcs ... Ms. Edna CORDOVA-CHAVARRY
35 Dean Student Svcs TRIO ... Dr. Celena ALCALA-BURKHARDT
41 Athletic Director ... Vacant
40 College Enterprise Manager ... Vacant
10 Chief Financial Administrator ... Ms. Rasel MENENDEZ
18 Facilities Manager ... Mr. Dean FELTON
37 Financial Aid Manager ... Mr. Glenn SCHENK
13 Manager Info System ... Mr. Tak FUJII
88 Operations Manager ... Mr. Bruce HICKS
19 Sheriff/Deputy ... Mr. Roberto GONZALEZ
88 Academic Senate President ... Dr. Patricia ZUK
26 Dir Advertising/Mktg/Public Rels ... Ms. Michelle LONG-COFFEE
102 Executive Director WLAC Foundation . Ms. Etelvina DE LA TORRE
08 Library Chair ... Ms. Susan TRUJILLO

Los Angeles County College of Nursing and Allied Health (A)

1237 North Mission Road, Los Angeles CA 90033-1083
County: Los Angeles — FICE Identification: 006165
Unit ID: 117803
Telephone: (323) 409-5911 — Carnegie Class: Spec 2-yr-Health
FAX Number: (323) 226-6343 — Calendar System: Semester
URL: dhs.lacounty.gov/wps/portal/dhs/conah/
Established: 1895 — Annual Undergrad Tuition & Fees (In-District): N/A
Enrollment: 200 — Coed
Affiliation or Control: Local — IRS Status: 501(c)3
Highest Offering: Associate Degree
Accreditation: WJ

01 Provost/Administrator ... Ms. Vivian BRANCHICK
05 Dean Education/Consulting Services ... Dr. Tammy BLASS
66 Dean School of Nursing ... Ms. Mildred GONZALES
32 Dean Col Operations/Student Svcs ... Ms. Sarah C. GRANGER
108 Dean Institutional Effectiveness ... Ms. Herminia HONDA
37 Director of Financial Aid ... Ms. Sarah GRANGER
38 Director Advisement/Counseling ... Ms. Maria CABALLERO
13 College Information Officer ... Mr. Visna KIENG
76 Dir Allied Healtlh Cont Education ... Ms. Irene DE LA TORRE

Los Angeles Film School (B)

6363 Sunset Boulevard, Hollywood CA 90028
County: Los Angeles — FICE Identification: 040373
Unit ID: 436429
Telephone: (323) 860-0789 — Carnegie Class: Spec-4-yr-Arts
FAX Number: (323) 646-0770 — Calendar System: Other
URL: www.lafilm.edu
Established: 1999 — Annual Undergrad Tuition & Fees: N/A
Enrollment: 5,669 — Coed
Affiliation or Control: Proprietary — IRS Status: Proprietary
Highest Offering: Baccalaureate
Accreditation: ACCSC

01 President ... Ms. Tammy ELLIOTT
05 Chief Academic Officer ... Vacant
06 Registrar ... Ms. Andrea NOTO
07 Director of Admissions ... Ms. Ernesta MENSAH
08 Chief Library Officer ... Ms. Georgina GARCIA-CAMPOS
10 Chief Financial/Business Officer ... Ms. Pamela PAYAWAL
13 Chief Information Technology Office ... Mr. Iyob ARIA
15 Chief Human Resources Officer ... Ms. Judy NIMOY
18 Chief Facilities/Physical Plant Ofc ... Ms. Elizabeth MCDONALD
29 Director Alumni Affairs ... Mr. Joseph BYRON
36 Director Student Placement ... Ms. Angelia BIBB-SANDERS
37 Director Student Financial Aid ... Mr. Dustin WEIR
26 Chief Public Relations/Marketing ... Mr. James WINSTEAD
38 Director Student Counseling ... Ms. Yacine NDAO
88 Compliance Officer ... Mr. Mark DEBACCO

Los Angeles Pacific College (C)

3325 Wilshire Boulevard, Ste 550,
Los Angeles CA 90010-1758
County: Los Angeles — Identification: 667143
Telephone: (213) 384-2318 — Carnegie Class: Not Classified
FAX Number: (213) 384-0419 — Calendar System: Semester
URL: www.lapacific.net
Established: 1989 — Annual Undergrad Tuition & Fees: N/A
Enrollment: N/A — Coed
Affiliation or Control: Proprietary — IRS Status: Proprietary
Highest Offering: Associate Degree
Accreditation: COE, CEA

01 President/Student Services Coord ... Ms. Mary YOON
10 Controller/Academic Director ... Mr. Ho Sung YOON

Los Angeles Pacific University (D)

300 N. Lone Hill Ave #200, San Dimas CA 91773
County: Los Angeles — FICE Identification: 042788
Unit ID: 474863
Telephone: (858) 527-2768 — Carnegie Class: Masters/S
FAX Number: (626) 276-7034 — Calendar System: Semester
URL: www.lapu.edu
Established: 2014 — Annual Undergrad Tuition & Fees: $10,800
Enrollment: 2,036 — Coed
Affiliation or Control: Independent Non-Profit — IRS Status: 501(c)3
Highest Offering: Master's
Accreditation: WC

01 President ... Dr. John REYNOLDS
11 Executive Vice Pres/COO ... Dr. Frank ROJAS
05 Vice Pres/Chief Academic Officer ... Dr. Wayne HERMAN

† Affiliated with Azusa Pacific University.

The Los Angeles Performing Arts Conservatory (E)

14004-08 Third Street Promenade,
Santa Monica CA 90401
County: Los Angeles — Identification: 667412
Telephone: (310) 656-8070 — Carnegie Class: Not Classified
FAX Number: (310) 656-8069 — Calendar System: Quarter
URL: www.laconservatory.com
Established: — Annual Undergrad Tuition & Fees: N/A
Enrollment: N/A — Coed
Affiliation or Control: Proprietary — IRS Status: Proprietary
Highest Offering: Associate Degree
Accreditation: THEA

01 Founder & CEO ... Natalia LAZARUS

*Los Rios Community College District Office (F)

1919 Spanos Court, Sacramento CA 95825-3981
County: Sacramento — FICE Identification: 001231
Unit ID: 117900
Telephone: (916) 568-3021 — Carnegie Class: N/A
FAX Number: (916) 561-0574
URL: www.losrios.edu

01 Chancellor ... Dr. Brian KING
04 Chancellor's Executive Officer ... Ms. Jennifer DELUCCHI
10 Vice Chancellor Finance/Admin ... Mr. Mario RODRIGUEZ
05 Vice Chancellor Education/Tech ... Dr. Jamey NYE
30 Assoc Vice Chanc Resource Dev ... Ms. Paula ALLISON
26 Assoc Vice Chanc Comm/Media Rels ... Mr. Gabe ROSS
18 Assoc Vice Chanc Facilities Mgmt ... Mr. Pablo MANZO
15 Assoc Vice Chanc Human Resources ... Mr. Jake KNAPP
13 Assoc Vice Chanc IT ... Ms. Tamara ARMSTRONG
20 Assoc Vice Chanc Instruction ... Vacant
32 Int Dir Educ Svcs/Student Success ... Ms. Hannah BLODGETT
37 Director Financial Aid ... Mr. Roy BECKHORN
96 Director General Services ... Ms. Anita SINGH
09 Director Institutional Research ... Ms. Betty GLYER-CULVER

*American River College (G)

4700 College Oak Drive, Sacramento CA 95841-4286
County: Sacramento — FICE Identification: 001232
Unit ID: 109208
Telephone: (916) 484-8011 — Carnegie Class: Assoc/MT-VT-High Trad
FAX Number: (916) 484-8674 — Calendar System: Semester
URL: www.arc.losrios.edu
Established: 1955 — Annual Undergrad Tuition & Fees (In-District): $1,288
Enrollment: 25,422 — Coed
Affiliation or Control: State/Local — IRS Status: 501(c)3
Highest Offering: Associate Degree
Accreditation: WJ, COARC, EMT, FUSER

02 President ... Ms. Melanie DIXON
10 Vice President Admin Services ... Ms. Koue VANG
05 Vice President Instruction ... Dr. Frank KOBAYASHI
32 Vice President Student Services ... Dr. Jeff STEPHENSON
20 Assoc VP Instruction ... Dr. Kate JAQUES
84 Assoc VP Instruction/Enrollment Mgt ... Dr. Kale BRADEN
35 Assoc VP Student Services ... Mr. Chad FUNK
103 Assoc VP Workforce Development ... Dr. Derrick BOOTH
57 Dean Fine & Applied Arts ... Ms. Angela MILANO
07 Dean Enrollment Services ... Mr. Parrish GEARY
83 Dean Behavioral/Social Science ... Dr. Kathy SORENSEN
88 Dean English ... Mr. Doug HERNDON
79 Dean Humanities ... Ms. Diana HICKS
68 Int Dean Kinesiology/Athletics ... Ms. Kat SULLIVAN-TORREZ
81 Dean Mathematics ... Mr. Adam WINDHAM
56 Int Dean McClellan Center ... Ms. Charissa GORRE
35 Dean Student Services ... Ms. Kolleen OSTGAARD
09 Dean Inst Effectiveness/Innovation ... Dr. Adam KARP
66 Dean Health & Education ... Ms. Jan DELAPP
54 Int Dean Science/Engineering ... Mr. Narinedat MADRAMOOTOO
56 Dean Natomas Center ... Mr. Roger DAVIDSON
22 Dean Library/Learning Resource Ctr ... Dr. Joshua MOON JOHNSON
50 Dean Business/Computer Science ... Ms. Kirsten CORBIN
72 Dean Technical Education ... Mr. Gary AGUILAR

04 Administrative Asst to President ... Ms. Sue MCCOY
11 Director Administrative Services ... Ms. Cheryl SEARS
26 Public Information Officer ... Mr. Scott CROW
37 Financial Aid Supervisor ... Ms. Robin GALLOWGLAS
88 Dean DE/Virtual Ed Center ... Vacant
75 Dean Career Ed & Workforce Dev ... Ms. Raquel ARATA
38 Dean Counseling ... Ms. Nisha BECKHORN
124 Int Dean Student Engage/Completion ... Mr. Eric HANDY

*Cosumnes River College (H)

8401 Center Parkway, Sacramento CA 95823-5799
County: Sacramento — FICE Identification: 007536
Unit ID: 113096
Telephone: (916) 691-7344 — Carnegie Class: Assoc/HT-High Trad
FAX Number: (916) 691-7375 — Calendar System: Semester
URL: www.crc.losrios.edu
Established: 1970 — Annual Undergrad Tuition & Fees (In-District): $1,288
Enrollment: 14,667 — Coed
Affiliation or Control: State/Local — IRS Status: 501(c)3
Highest Offering: Associate Degree
Accreditation: WJ, CAHIIM, DMS, MAC

02 President ... Dr. Edward C. BUSH
04 Admin Assistant to the President ... Ms. Rachel LARSEN
26 Public Information Officer ... Ms. Kristie WEST
05 VP Instruction & Student Learning ... Dr. Robert MONTANEZ
09 VP Inst Equity/Research/Planning ... Dr. Claire OLIVEROS
10 VP Admin Services & Student Support ... Ms. Theresa TENA
32 AVP Student Services ... Mr. Tadael EMIRU
103 AVP Econ/Strong Workforce Devel ... Ms. Kimberley HARRELL
20 AVP Instruction/Student Learning ... Dr. Michael LAWLOR
81 Int Dean Science/Math/Engineering ... Ms. Banafsheh (Bani) AMINI
79 Dean GP&Grants/Eng & Lang Studies .. Dr. Alexander CASARENO
88 Int Dean of Auto/Const Tech/EGC ... Mr. Robert JOHNSON
13 Dean Library and Technology Service ... Mr. Stephen MCGLOUGHLIN
83 Int Dean Social/Behavioral Science ... Dr. Emilie MITCHELL
38 Int Dean Couns & Student Services ... Ms. Hong PHAM
50 Dean Business & Computer Science ... Mr. Joel POWELL
68 Dean Hlth/Human Svcs/Dir of Athl ... Mr. Collin PREGLIASCO
84 Int Dean Student Svcs/Enroll Mgmt ... Ms. Joann RAMIREZ
60 Dean Arts/Media & Entertainment ... Mr. Brian RICKEL
108 Int Dean Inst Effectiveness ... Ms. Sabrina SENCIL
47 Dn Ag/Food/Nat Res/Hlth Hm Svc ... Ms. Dana WASSMER
81 Int Assoc Dean Sci/Math/Engineer ... Ms. Camille MORENO
40 Director College Store ... Ms. Maria HYDE
88 Director TRIO/Upward Bound ... Mr. Raul PASAMONTE
18 Dir Administrative Services ... Mr. Christopher RAINES
88 Dir Academic/Stdnt Supp Projects ... Dr. Tyler ROLLINS
88 Director HSI CASA ... Ms. Gladis SANCHEZ
88 Director TRIO SSS ... Ms. Ethny STEWART
89 Director First Year Experience ... Vacant
06 Registrar/Admissions & Records ... Mr. Richard ANDREWS

*Folsom Lake College (I)

10 College Parkway, Folsom CA 95630-6798
County: Sacramento — FICE Identification: 038713
Unit ID: 444219
Telephone: (916) 608-6500 — Carnegie Class: Assoc/HT-High Trad
FAX Number: N/A — Calendar System: Semester
URL: www.flc.losrios.edu
Established: 2004 — Annual Undergrad Tuition & Fees (In-District): $1,288
Enrollment: 9,542 — Coed
Affiliation or Control: State/Local — IRS Status: 501(c)3
Highest Offering: Associate Degree
Accreditation: WJ, MLTAD

02 President ... Dr. Whitney YAMAMURA
11 Vice Pres Administration ... Augustine CHAVEZ
05 Vice President Instruction ... Dr. Monica PACTOL
32 Vice President Student Services ... Sonia ORTIZ-MERCADO
12 Int Dean of Instruction RCC ... Carlos LOPEZ
12 Int Dean of Instruction EDC ... Dr. Mari PESHON MCGARRY
81 Dean Instruction BLIT/MSE ... Greg MCCORMAC
57 Dean of Instruction VAPA/LALI ... Dr. Francis FLETCHER
68 Dean of Instruction KHAN ... Matthew WRIGHT
72 Dean of Instruction CTE ... Victoria MARYATT
09 Int Dean Planning & Research ... Brian ROBINSON
35 Int Dean of Student Success ... Dr. Molly SENECAL
18 Director of Administrative Services ... Melissa WILLIAMS
10 Business Services Supervisor ... Joany HARMAN
26 Communications/Public Info Ofcr ... Kristy HART
30 Director Donor Relations ... Michele STEINER
37 Financial Aid Supervisor ... Ali PADASH
07 Admissions & Records Supervisor ... Christine WURZER
40 College Store Manager ... Rob MULLIGAN
04 Assistant to the President ... Lindsey CAMPBELL

*Sacramento City College (J)

3835 Freeport Boulevard, Sacramento CA 95822-1386
County: Sacramento — FICE Identification: 001233
Unit ID: 122180
Telephone: (916) 558-2111 — Carnegie Class: Assoc/MT-VT-High Trad
FAX Number: (916) 558-2449 — Calendar System: Semester
URL: www.scc.losrios.edu
Established: 1916 — Annual Undergrad Tuition & Fees (In-State): $1,288
Enrollment: 20,027 — Coed
Affiliation or Control: State Related — IRS Status: 501(c)3
Highest Offering: Associate Degree

Accreditation: WJ, ADNUR, DA, DH, OTA, #PTAA

02 President .... Mr. Michael GUTIERREZ
05 Vice Pres of Instruction .... Dr. Albert GARCIA
10 Vice Pres Administrative Services .... Ms. Carrie BRAY
32 Vice Pres Student Services .... Dr. Davin BROWN
20 Associate Vice Pres Instruction .... Ms. Gabriel MEEHAN
20 Associate Vice Pres Instruction .... Ms. Ginny MCREYNOLDS
13 Dean Information Technology .... Mr. Kirk SOSA
37 Dean Financial Aid/Student Svcs .... Dr. Miguel MOLINA
46 Dean Planning/Research/Development .... Vacant
08 Dean Learning Resources .... Mr. Kevin FLASH
121 Dean Counseling/Student Success .... Dr. Andre COLEMAN
40 Director College Store .... Ms. Maria HYDE
66 Director Nursing .... Ms. Carel MOUNTAIN
18 Director College Operations .... Ms. Margaret LEDNICKY
30 Director of Donor Relations .... Vacant
26 Comm & Public Information Officer .... Ms. Kaitlyn COLLIGNON
76 Dean Science & Allied Health .... Mr. James COLLINS
50 Dean Business .... Dr. Deborah SAKS
79 Dean Humanities/Fine Arts .... Mr. Chris IWATA
79 Interim Dean Languages/Literature .... Ms. Robin IKEGAMI
72 Dean Advanced Technology .... Ms. Donnetta WEBB
68 Dean PE/Health/Athletics .... Mr. Mitchell L. CAMPBELL
81 Dean Statistics/Math/Engineering .... Dr. Daniel STYER
83 Dean Behavioral/Social Science .... Ms. Kasey GARDNER
56 Dean Davis Center .... Vacant
56 Int Dean West Sacramento Ctr .... Dr. Ashu MISHRA
06 Records & Admissions Officer .... Ms. Kim GOFF
04 Administrative Asst to President .... Ms. Pamela MORRISON
88 Director HSI-SAGE .... Vacant

Loyola Marymount University (A)

1 LMU Drive, Los Angeles CA 90045-2659
County: Los Angeles FICE Identification: 011649
Unit ID: 117946
Telephone: (310) 338-2700 Carnegie Class: DU-Higher
FAX Number: N/A Calendar System: Semester
URL: www.lmu.edu
Established: 1911 Annual Undergrad Tuition & Fees: $52,977
Enrollment: 9,686 Coed
Affiliation or Control: Roman Catholic IRS Status: 501(c)3
Highest Offering: Doctorate
Accreditation: WC, CAEP, CAEPN, DANCE, LAW, MUS, THEA, THEOL

01 President .... Dr. Timothy L. SNYDER
00 Chancellor .... Fr. Robert WALSH, SJ
05 Exec Vice President & Provost .... Dr. Thomas POON
42 VP for Mission & Ministry .... Dr. John SEBASTIAN
20 Vice Provost for Academic Affairs .... Dr. David A. SAPP
84 Vice Provost Enrollment Management .... Dr. Maureen WEATHERALL
85 Vice Prov Global-Local Initiatives .... Dr. Roberta ESPINOZA
10 Sr Vice Pres/Chief Financial Ofcr .... Mr. Thomas O. FLEMING
111 Interim SVP University Advancement .... Ms. Kristi WADE
32 Sr Vice Pres for Student Affairs .... Dr. Elena M. BOVE
11 EVP & Chief Administrative Officer .... Ms. Lynne B. SCARBORO
13 VP for Information Technology Svcs .... Mr. Patrick FRONTIERA
35 VP Student Affairs/Dean Students .... Dr. Terri MANGIONE
15 Vice President for Human Resources .... Ms. Rebecca CHANDLER
18 VP for Construction and Planning .... Mr. Timothy HAWORTH
11 Vice President of Campus Operations .... Mr. Michael WONG
26 SVP Marketing/Communications .... Mr. John KIRALLA
28 VP Intercultural Affairs .... Dr. Jennifer ABE
36 Assoc Provost Career & Professional .... Mr. Branden GRIMMETT
20 Assoc Provost Undergraduate Educ .... Fr. José BADENES
106 Asc Prov Rsrch/Prof Dev/Online Lrng .... Dr. Kathleen WEAVER
109 Sr Dir Auxiliary/Business Services .... Mr. Andrew O'REILLY
100 Special Asst to President/COS .... Dr. John M. PARRISH
08 Dean University Library .... Ms. Kristine BRANCOLINI
06 University Registrar .... Dr. Jennifer SILVERMAN
61 SVP/Dean Loyola Law School .... Mr. Michael WATERSTONE
49 Dean College Liberal Arts .... Dr. Robbin D. CRABTREE
53 Dean Sch of Education .... Dr. Michelle D. YOUNG
50 Dean College of Business Admin .... Dr. Dayle SMITH
57 Dean Communication & Fine Arts .... Dr. Bryant K. ALEXANDER
54 Dean College of Science & Engineer .... Dr. Tina CHOE
88 Dean School of Film/Television .... Ms. Peggy RAJSKI
30 Sr Dir Development/Gift Planning .... Vacant
07 Asst Vice Prov Undergrad Admissions .... Mr. Matthew X. FISSINGER
37 Associate Director of Financial Aid .... Ms. Darlene WILSON
41 Athletics Director .... Mr. Craig PINTENS
27 Social Media Manager .... Ms. Shelbey GALLIHER
09 Sr Dir Inst Rsrch/Decision Support .... Ms. Christine CHAVEZ
108 Sr Dir Educ Effectiveness/Assessmnt .... Dr. Rebecca HONG
29 Executive Director of Alumni Rels .... Ms. Lisa FARLAND
23 Director of Student Health Services .... Ms. Katherine ARCE
104 Director Study Abroad .... Dr. Lisa LOBERG
25 Dir Research & Sponsored Projects .... Vacant
90 Director of Educational Technology .... Ms. Crista COPP
04 Executive Asst to President .... Ms. Debbie CAVANAGH
04 Admin Specialist to Ofc of the Pres .... Ms. Rosa CALDERON
102 Exec Dir Corp/Foundation Relations .... Ms. Michelle PLASSE
19 Chief of Public Safety .... Mr. Danny MARTINEZ
22 EEO Officer and Title IX Coord .... Ms. Sara TRIVEDI
39 Director Student Housing .... Mr. Steven NYGAARD
43 General Counsel .... Mr. Harold A. BRIDGES
04 Admin Specialist to Ofc of the Pres .... Ms. Sheila WEISENBERGER
38 Dir Student Psychological Services .... Ms. Kristin LINDEN

Marshall B. Ketchum University (B)

2575 Yorba Linda Boulevard, Fullerton CA 92831-1615
County: Orange FICE Identification: 001230
Unit ID: 123943
Telephone: (714) 449-7451 Carnegie Class: Spec-4-yr-Other Health
FAX Number: N/A Calendar System: Quarter
URL: www.ketchum.edu
Established: 1904 Annual Graduate Tuition & Fees: N/A
Enrollment: 738 Coed
Affiliation or Control: Independent Non-Profit IRS Status: 501(c)3
Highest Offering: Doctorate; No Undergraduates
Accreditation: WC, ARCPA, OPT, OPTR, PHAR

01 President .... Dr. Kevin L. ALEXANDER
111 Vice Pres University Advancement .... Ms. Joan RUBIO
100 Sr Vice President & Chief of Staff .... Dr. Julie A. SCHORNACK
32 Vice President for Student Affairs .... Dr. Carmen N. BARNHARDT
15 Vice Pres Human Resources .... Ms. Gail S. DEUTSCH
10 Senior Vice Pres Admin & Finance .... Mr. Frank SCOTTI
05 VP Educ Effectiveness/Academic Affs .... Dr. Judy ORTIZ
18 Director of Campus Operations .... Mr. Gregory SMITH
51 Director of Continuing Education .... Ms. Bonnie DELLATORRE
13 Director of Information Technology .... Mr. Samuel YOUNG
08 Director of Library Services .... Mr. Scott JOHNSON
23 Director of Special Clinic Programs .... Ms. Michele WHITECAVAGE
26 Director Marketing/Communications .... Ms. Erin HALES
88 Dean of Optometry .... Dr. Jennifer COYLE
67 Dean of Pharmacy .... Dr. Edward FISHER
88 Director PA Program .... Ms. Allison MOLLET
108 Dir Institutional Effectiveness .... Dr. Ajoy KOOMER
04 Executive Asst to the President .... Ms. Carole JOLLY
23 Assoc Dean Clinics .... Dr. Mark E. NAKANO
24 Director of Multi-Media Services .... Mr. Matt BRENEMAN
00 Chairman of the Board of Trustees .... Mr. Rick S. PRICE II
31 Director of Community Relations .... Mr. Wayne HEIDLE
109 Auxiliary Services Manager .... Ms. Debra WOODS
06 Associate Registrar .... Ms. Lisa CASSIDY
19 Director Campus Safety/Security .... Mr. Craig COOPER
38 Director Univ Student Counseling .... Ms. Alyse KIRSCHEN
30 Director of Development .... Ms. Ruby FOSTER
21 Controller .... Ms. Lori JACKLIN
114 Sr Dir Financial Reporting & Budget .... Ms. Kim ELLEN
85 Dir Registration/Intl Student Svcs .... Ms. Lauren KIM
37 Director of Financial Aid .... Mr. Nicholas NOVELLO
35 Director University Student Affairs .... Mr. Karlos SANTOS-COY
113 Director of Student Accounts .... Ms. Arlene VILLARUZ

Marymount California University (C)

30800 Palos Verdes Drive E,
Rancho Palos Verdes CA 90275-6299
County: Los Angeles FICE Identification: 010474
Unit ID: 118541
Telephone: (310) 377-5501 Carnegie Class: Bac-A&S
FAX Number: (310) 377-6223 Calendar System: Semester
URL: www.marymountcalifornia.edu
Established: 1932 Annual Undergrad Tuition & Fees: $36,908
Enrollment: 582 Coed
Affiliation or Control: Roman Catholic IRS Status: 501(c)3
Highest Offering: Master's
Accreditation: WC

01 President .... Dr. Brian MARCOTTE
10 Interim Chief Financial Officer .... Ms. Debora YAVAS
05 Provost/EVP Academic Affairs .... Dr. Ariane SCHAUER
30 Dean Institutional Development .... Mr. Ruben BARAJAS
84 Vice President Enrollment Mgmt .... Ms. Robyn JONES
32 Dean of Students .... Dr. Ryan ALCANTARA
20 Associate Academic Officer .... Ms. Susie MARTIN
08 Librarian .... Vacant
37 Director of Student Financial Svcs .... Ms. Nataly DE LA PENA
15 Dir Human Res & Risk Mgmt/Title IX .... Ms. Karen THORDARSON
18 Chief Facilities/Physical Plant .... Mr. Marc BROWN
26 Chief Public Relations Officer .... Vacant
29 Director Alumni Relations .... Vacant
36 Director Student Placement .... Mr. Maury HILLSTROM
38 Director Student Counseling .... Ms. Osmara REYES-OSARIO
96 Director of Purchasing .... Mr. Monte SCHMEISER
06 Registrar .... Ms. Paula AVERY
35 Dir Student Life & Engagement .... Vacant
09 Director of Institutional Research .... Mr. Michael SEMENOFF
21 Associate Business Officer .... Ms. Debra YAVAS
04 Administrative Asst to President .... Ms. Kimberly RAMSEY
19 Director Security/Safety .... Ms. Naja JAMES
39 Director Student Housing .... Mr. Chad FEHR
41 Athletic Director .... Ms. Courtney THOMSEN
104 Director Study Abroad .... Mr. Ryan O'CONNELL
105 Director Web Services .... Mr. Maury HILLSTROM
13 Chief Info Technology Officer .... Mr. Monte SCHMEISER
101 Secretary of the Institution/Board .... Ms. Kimberly RAMSAY
07 Director of Admissions .... Ms. Silje DEUERLIEN

The Master's University & Seminary (D)

21726 Placerita Canyon Road,
Santa Clarita CA 91321-1200
County: Los Angeles FICE Identification: 001220
Unit ID: 117751
Telephone: (661) 259-3540 Carnegie Class: Masters/M
FAX Number: N/A Calendar System: Semester
URL: www.masters.edu
Established: 1927 Annual Undergrad Tuition & Fees: $28,740
Enrollment: 2,449 Coed
Affiliation or Control: Independent Non-Profit IRS Status: 501(c)3
Highest Offering: Doctorate
Accreditation: WC, MUS

01 Int President .... Dr. Abner CHOU
125 Chancellor Emeritus .... Dr. John MACARTHUR
03 Executive Vice President .... Dr. John STEAD
05 Provost/Dean Online Learning .... Dr. Mitch HOPEWELL
58 Executive Vice President Seminary .... Dr. Nathan BUSENITZ
10 CFO/VP of Administration .... Mr. Todd KOSTJUK
84 VP/Chief Enroll & Marketing Ofcr .... Mr. Dariu DUMITRU
13 VP/Chief Information Officer .... Mr. Paul SEDY
30 Vice President of Development .... Mr. Luke CHERRY
09 Director of Institutional Research .... Mr. John MILTON
26 Chief Communications Officer .... Mr. Corey WILLIAMS
32 VP of Student Life/Campus Minister .... Rev. Harry WALLS
06 Registrar .... Mr. Don GILMORE
08 Director Library Services .... Mr. John STONE
41 Athletic Director .... Mr. Kelvin STARR
37 Director Financial Aid .... Mr. Kenneth PIESTER
29 Director Alumni Affairs .... Mr. AJ WORK
85 International Students Advisor .... Mr. Josh ENGLISH
04 Administrative Asst to President .... Ms. Allison PARI
15 Director of Human Resources .... Ms. Kim WILSON
19 Director Security/Safety .... Mr. Bryan KORTCAMP
50 Dean Business .... Mr. Dwight HAM
53 Dean Education .... Dr. Jordan MORTON

† The Master's Seminary is located at 13248 Roscoe Boulevard, Sun Valley, CA 91352.

Mayfield College (E)

35-325 Date Palm Drive, Suite 101,
Cathedral City CA 92234
County: Riverside FICE Identification: 041156
Unit ID: 454698
Telephone: (760) 328-5554 Carnegie Class: Spec 2-yr-Tech
FAX Number: (760) 328-5357 Calendar System: Semester
URL: www.mayfieldcollege.org
Established: 1997 Annual Undergrad Tuition & Fees: N/A
Enrollment: 310 Coed
Affiliation or Control: Proprietary IRS Status: Proprietary
Highest Offering: Associate Degree
Accreditation: COE

01 Campus President .... Kevin HA

Mendocino College (F)

1000 Hensley Creek Road, Ukiah CA 95482-7821
County: Mendocino FICE Identification: 011672
Unit ID: 118684
Telephone: (707) 468-3000 Carnegie Class: Assoc/MT-VT-Mix Trad/Non
FAX Number: (707) 468-3120 Calendar System: Semester
URL: www.mendocino.edu
Established: 1973 Annual Undergrad Tuition & Fees (In-District): $1,426
Enrollment: 3,338 Coed
Affiliation or Control: State/Local IRS Status: 501(c)3
Highest Offering: Associate Degree
Accreditation: WJ, @PTAA

01 Superintendent/President .... Mr. Timothy KARAS
11 Vice Pres Admin Services .... Ms. Eileen CICHOCKI
05 Vice Pres Academic Affairs .... Ms. Debra POLAK
32 Vice Pres Student Services .... Mr. Ulises VELASCO
08 Head Librarian .... Mr. Robert PARMENTER
20 Dean of Instruction .... Ms. Rebecca MONTES
75 Dean Applied Academics .... Mr. Dennis ASELTYNE
38 Dean of Counseling/Student Programs .... Mr. Antonio LOPEZ
10 Director Fiscal Services .... Mr. Joe ATHERTON
15 Director Human Resources .... Ms. Nicole MARIN
18 Director of Facilities .... Mr. MacAdam LOJOWSKY
26 Director Communications & Cmty Rels .... Ms. Janelle BIRD
41 Director of Athletics .... Mr. Matthew GORDON
13 Director Information Technology .... Mr. David JOHNSTON
09 Director of Institutional Research .... Ms. Minerva FLORES
07 Director Admissions/Registrar .... Ms. Anastasia SIMPSON-LOGG
37 Director of Financial Aid .... Ms. Yuliana SANDOVAL
04 Administrative Asst to President .... Ms. Mary LAMB
12 Director of Lake Center .... Ms. Monica FLORES
102 Exec Dir Mendocino Col Foundation .... Vacant
88 MESA/Stem Success Director .... Mr. Eric HOEFLER
12 Dean of Centers .... Dr. Amanda XU

Menlo College (G)

1000 El Camino Real, Atherton CA 94027-4301
County: San Mateo FICE Identification: 001236
Unit ID: 118693
Telephone: (800) 556-3656 Carnegie Class: Spec-4-yr-Bus
FAX Number: (650) 543-4085 Calendar System: Semester
URL: www.menlo.edu
Established: 1927 Annual Undergrad Tuition & Fees: $45,860
Enrollment: 826 Coed
Affiliation or Control: Independent Non-Profit IRS Status: 501(c)3
Highest Offering: Baccalaureate
Accreditation: WC

00 Board Chair .... Mr. Micah KANE

01 President ... Mr. Steven A. WEINER
05 Provost ... Mr. Grande H. LUM
41 VP Enrollment & Athletics ... Mr. Keith SPATARO
121 VP Student Success ... Dr. Angela SCHMIEDE
50 Dean for Business ... Dr. Mouwafac SIDAOUI
49 Dean for Arts & Sciences ... Dr. Melissa MICHELSON
21 Dir Finance & Business Affairs ... Ms. Rita YON
13 Director Information Technology ... Mr. Minh HUYNH
84 Dean of Enrollment Mgmt ... Ms. Priscila DESOUZA
08 Dean Library Services ... Ms. Valeria MOLTENI
32 Dean of Student Affairs ... Dr. LT REASE MILES
09 Director IR & Assessment ... Dr. Kristina POWERS
29 Sr Dir Alumni Engagement & Dev ... Dr. Laura KOO
15 Director of Human Resources ... Ms. Lina WOO
18 Director Facilities & Operations ... Mr. Robert TALBOTT
88 Director Internship Program ... Mr. Dylan HOULE
06 Registrar ... Ms. Cristine RABAGO
11 Director of Operations ... Ms. Linda TEUTSCHEL
07 Director of Admissions ... Mr. Rey PENATE
19 Director Security/Safety ... Mr. Taylor HENKEL
38 Director Student Counseling ... Dr. Jake KELMAN
39 Dir Resident Life/Student Housing ... Mr. Taylor HENKEL

Merced College (A)

3600 M Street, Merced CA 95348-2898

County: Merced — FICE Identification: 001237
Unit ID: 118718
Telephone: (209) 384-6000 — Carnegie Class: Assoc/MT-VT-High Trad
FAX Number: (209) 384-6043 — Calendar System: Semester
URL: www.mccd.edu
Established: 1962 — Annual Undergrad Tuition & Fees (In-District): $1,180
Enrollment: 10,645 — Coed
Affiliation or Control: State/Local — IRS Status: 501(c)3
Highest Offering: Associate Degree
Accreditation: WJ, DMS, RAD

01 President ... Mr. Chris VITELLI
04 Executive Assistant to President ... Ms. Krystal POLLINGER
05 VP of Instruction ... Ms. Melissa MOCK
32 VP of Student Services ... Mr. Michael MCCANDLESS
10 VP Administrative Services ... Mr. Joseph ALLISON
13 AVP of ITS ... Mr. Arlis BORTNER
12 Dean Los Banos Campus ... Ms. Jessina MORAN
111 AVP of External Relations ... Ms. Jill CUNNINGHAM
45 Dean Institutional Effectiveness ... Ms. Dee SIGISMOND
15 AVP of Human Resources ... Ms. Kelly AVILA
81 Dean Science/Math/Engineering ... Dr. Douglas KAIN
79 Acting Dean English & Humanities ... Mr. Travis HICKS
75 Dean Career Technical Education ... Vacant
50 Acting Dean Business/Workforce Dev ... Dr. Caroline DAWSON
83 Dean Social Sci/Fine & Perf Arts ... Mr. John ALBANO
22 Acting Dean Student Equity/Success ... Mr. Joe SERENA
26 Chief Public Relations Officer ... Ms. Jill CUNNINGHAM
06 Registrar & Dir Financial Aid ... Mrs. Traci VEYL
07 Dir Admissions & Records ... Ms. Sherry ELMS
41 Athletic Director ... Mr. Steve CASSADY
96 Director of Purchasing ... Mr. Charles HERGENRAEDER

Meridian University (B)

47 Sixth Street, Petaluma CA 94952

County: Sonoma — Identification: 667300
Telephone: (707) 765-1836 — Carnegie Class: Not Classified
FAX Number: (707) 765-2351 — Calendar System: Other
URL: www.meridianuniversity.edu
Established: 1993 — Annual Graduate Tuition & Fees: N/A
Enrollment: N/A — Coed
Affiliation or Control: Proprietary — IRS Status: Proprietary
Highest Offering: Doctorate; No Undergraduates
Accreditation: WC

00 Chancellor ... Dr. Jean HOUSTON
01 CEO ... Dr. Aftab OMER
05 Vice President Academic Affairs ... Dr. Melissa SCHWARTZ
10 Dir Administration/CFO ... Mr. Rob GALL

Merit University (C)

3699 Wilshire Blvd., Ste 970, Los Angeles CA 90010

County: Los Angeles — Identification: 667293
Telephone: (213) 325-2760 — Carnegie Class: Not Classified
FAX Number: N/A — Calendar System: Quarter
URL: www.meritu.edu
Established: 2014 — Annual Graduate Tuition & Fees: N/A
Enrollment: N/A — Coed
Affiliation or Control: Proprietary — IRS Status: Proprietary
Highest Offering: Master's; No Undergraduates
Accreditation: ACICS

01 President ... Dr. Min KIM
06 Registrar ... Namy CHAH

Middlebury Institute of International Studies at Monterey (D)

460 Pierce Street, Monterey CA 93940-2691

Telephone: (831) 647-4100 — FICE Identification: 001241
Accreditation: &EH, CEA

† Regional accrediation is carried under parent institution Middlebury College, VT.

Mills College (E)

5000 MacArthur Boulevard, Oakland CA 94613-1301

County: Alameda — FICE Identification: 001238
Unit ID: 113888
Telephone: (510) 430-2255 — Carnegie Class: Masters/M
FAX Number: (510) 430-2256 — Calendar System: Semester
URL: www.mills.edu
Established: 1852 — Annual Undergrad Tuition & Fees: $30,770
Enrollment: 961 — Female
Affiliation or Control: Independent Non-Profit — IRS Status: 501(c)3
Highest Offering: Doctorate
Accreditation: WC

01 President ... Ms. Elizabeth L. HILLMAN
05 Int Provost/VP Academic Affairs ... Ms. Patricia HARDAWAY
10 VP Finance/Administration/Treasurer ... Ms. Maria CAMMARATA
88 VP Strategic Comm/Operations ... Ms. Renee JADUSHLEVER
111 AVP for Inst Advancement ... Ms. Nikole ADAMS
84 VP for Enrollment & Marketing ... Dr. Audrey TANNER
20 Associate Provost ... Dr. Maggie HUNTER
08 Director of Library ... Ms. Janice E. BRAUN
32 VP Student Life/Dean of Students ... Dr. Chicora MARTIN
07 Assoc VP Enroll/Financial Services ... Ms. Robynne LOFTON
09 Dir Plng/Analytics/Effectiveness ... Mr. Michael FLEMING
18 AVP of Operations ... Ms. Linda ZITZNER
38 Dir Counseling/Psych Svcs ... Dr. Aviva WILCOX
41 Director of Athletics/PE/Recreation ... Ms. Allie LITTLEFOX
04 Senior Exec Asst to the Pres ... Ms. Carrie M. HALL
06 Registrar ... Mr. Cole MOYER
102 Dir Corporate & Foundation Rels ... Ms. Dyana CURRERI-ERMATINGER
15 Chief Human Resources Officer ... Ms. Kamala GREEN
19 Director of Public Safety ... Vacant
37 AVP Enrollment/Stdnt Financial Aid ... Ms. Cora MANUEL

MiraCosta College (F)

One Barnard Drive, Oceanside CA 92056-3899

County: San Diego — FICE Identification: 001239
Unit ID: 118912
Telephone: (760) 757-2121 — Carnegie Class: Bac/Assoc-Assoc Dom
FAX Number: (760) 795-6609 — Calendar System: Semester
URL: www.miracosta.edu
Established: 1934 — Annual Undergrad Tuition & Fees (In-District): $1,152
Enrollment: 12,645 — Coed
Affiliation or Control: State/Local — IRS Status 501(c)3
Highest Offering: Baccalaureate
Accreditation: WJ

01 Superintendent/President ... Dr. Sunita COOKE
101 Exec Asst to Pres/Sec to BOT ... Ms. Julie BOLLERUD
04 Exec Assistant to Supt/President ... Ms. Jeanne KOSCHWANEZ
05 Vice President Instructional Svcs ... Vacant
32 Vice President Student Svcs ... Dr. Alketa WOJCIK
11 Vice President Administrative Svcs ... Mr. Tim FLOOD
15 Vice President Human Resources ... Mr. Charles NG
79 Dean Letters/Humanities/Comm ... Ms. Dana SMITH
08 Int Dean Library/Academic Info Svcs ... Dr. Scott CONRAD
38 Dean Counseling/Student Devel ... Dr. Wendy STEWART
07 Dean Admissions/Student Support ... Mr. Freddy RAMIREZ
51 Dean Continuing/Community Education ... Dr. John MAKEVICH
49 Dean Arts/Intl Languages ... Mr. Jonathan FOHRMAN
81 Dean Math/Sciences ... Mr. Mike FINO
75 Dean Career/Technical Education ... Dr. Al TACCONE
10 Director Fiscal Services ... Ms. Katie WHITE
88 Director Small Business Dev Ctr ... Mr. Sudershan SHAUNAK
103 Dir Community Educ/Workforce Dev ... Ms. Linda KUROKAWA
06 Registrar ... Ms. Jane SPARKS
09 Dean Research/Plng/Inst Effective ... Ms. Chris TAMAN
26 Dir Public Rels/Marketing/Comm ... Dr. Kristen HUYCK
111 VP Institutional Advancement ... Vacant
18 Director Facilities ... Mr. Tom MACIAS
37 Director Financial Aid ... Mr. Michael DEAR
117 District Risk Management Officer ... Vacant
113 Dir Cashiering Svcs/Student Accts ... Ms. Jo FERRIS
16 Director Human Resources ... Vacant
36 Director Career Center ... Ms. Dorna DAVIS
88 Faculty Director/Counselor ... Ms. Lise FLOCKEN
96 Director Purchasing/Material Mgmt ... Ms. Mina HERNANDEZ
124 Director Retention Services ... Dr. Edward POEHLERT
19 Director Campus Police ... Vacant
106 Director Online Education ... Dr. James JULIUS

Monterey Peninsula College (G)

980 Fremont Street, Monterey CA 93940-4799

County: Monterey — FICE Identification: 001242
Unit ID: 119067
Telephone: (831) 646-4000 — Carnegie Class: Assoc/HT-Mix Trad/Non
FAX Number: (831) 655-2627 — Calendar System: Semester
URL: www.mpc.edu
Established: 1947 — Annual Undergrad Tuition & Fees (In-District): $1,178
Enrollment: 7,154 — Coed
Affiliation or Control: State/Local — IRS Status: 501(c)3
Highest Offering: Associate Degree
Accreditation: WJ, ADNUR

01 Superintendent/President ... Dr. David MARTIN
05 VP of Academic Affairs ... Dr. Jon KNOLLE
11 VP Administrative Services ... Mr. Steve HAIGLER
32 VP of Student Services ... Mr. Laurence WALKER

20 Dean of Instruction ... Dr. Vincent VAN JOOLEN
20 Dean of Instruction ... Ms. Diane BOYNTON
20 Dean of Instruction ... Ms. Judith CUTTING
35 Interim Dean of Student Services ... Dr. LaKisha BRADLEY
45 Dean of PRIE ... Vacant
10 Controller ... Vacant
15 Acting Chief Human Resources Office ... Ms. Kayla VALENTINE
09 Director of Institutional Research ... Dr. Rosaleen RYAN
07 Director of Admissions & Records ... Ms. Nicole DUNNE
08 Director of Library ... Mr. Jeffery SUNDQUIST
37 Student Financial Services Director ... Vacant
41 Athletic Director/Dean of SS ... Ms. Wendy BATES
18 Facilities Operations Supervisor ... Mr. Pete OLSEN
96 Purchasing Agent ... Mr. Kevin HASKIN
19 Director of Security ... Vacant
04 Admin Assistant to the President ... Ms. Shawn ANDERSON
101 Secretary of the Institution/Board ... Ms. JoRene FINNELL
102 VP Advancement/MPC Foundation ... Ms. Rebecca MICHAEL
13 Director Information Systems ... Mr. Michael MIDKIFF
26 Dir Marketing & Communications ... Ms. Kristin DARKEN
22 Director Affirm Action/Equal Opp ... Mrs. Kayla VALENTINE

Mount Madonna Institute (H)

445 Summit Road, Watsonville CA 95076

County: Santa Cruz — Identification: 667380
Telephone: (408) 847-4060 — Carnegie Class: Not Classified
FAX Number: N/A — Calendar System: Semester
URL: www.mountmadonnainstitute.org
Established: 2006 — Annual Undergrad Tuition & Fees: N/A
Enrollment: N/A — Coed
Affiliation or Control: Independent Non-Profit — IRS Status: 501(c)3
Highest Offering: Master's
Accreditation: WC

01 President ... Kathleen SAVITA BROWNFIELD
05 Interim Provost ... Dr. Mary M. SOMERVILLE
10 Chief Financial Officer ... Shanti CRUDDAS

Mount Saint Mary's University (I)

12001 Chalon Road, Los Angeles CA 90049-1599

County: Los Angeles — FICE Identification: 001243
Unit ID: 119173
Telephone: (310) 954-4000 — Carnegie Class: Masters/L
FAX Number: (310) 954-4379 — Calendar System: Semester
URL: www.msmu.edu
Established: 1925 — Annual Undergrad Tuition & Fees: $44,474
Enrollment: 2,745 — Female
Affiliation or Control: Roman Catholic — IRS Status: 501(c)3
Highest Offering: Doctorate
Accreditation: WC, ACBSP, NURSE, PTA

01 President ... Dr. Ann MCELANEY-JOHNSON
05 Provost ... Dr. Robert J. PERRINS
111 Vice Pres Institutional Advancement ... Dr. Stephanie CUBBA
10 Vice Pres Administration & Finance ... Ms. Debra MARTIN
13 VP Strategic Initiatives ... Vacant
32 Vice President Student Affairs ... Dr. Linda MCMURDOCK
84 VP Enrollment Management ... Ms. Susan DILENO
20 Associate Provost & ALO ... Dr. Michele STARKEY
09 Dir Inst Planning/Research ... Ms. Maria NARVAEZ
58 Graduate Dean ... Dr. Robert J. PERRINS
55 Dean of Weekend College ... Ms. Suzanne WILLIAMS
88 Asst VP Enrollment Management ... Mr. Dean KILGOUR
06 Registrar ... Ms. Rocio DELEON
26 Director Communications/Marketing ... Ms. Debbie REAM
15 Director of Human Resources ... Ms. Dana LOPEZ
18 Director of Facilities Mgmt ... Mr. Edwin TORRES
37 Director of Student Financing ... Ms. La Royce HOUSLEY
08 Director of MSMU Libraries ... Ms. Danielle SALOMON
28 Assoc VP Diversity and Inclusion ... Vacant
29 Director Alumni Relations ... Mr. Tom ARTEAGA
38 Director Student Counseling ... Dr. Susan SALEM
07 Director of Admissions ... Ms. Erika YAMASAKI
36 Director Career Services ... Ms. Kimberly TERRILL
04 Administrative Asst to President ... Ms. Lucille VILLEGAS
19 Director Security/Safety ... Vacant
35 Dean of Student Life ... Ms. Jessica CUEVAS
44 Director Individual Giving ... Ms. Maria SOLANO
104 Study Away Coordinator ... Vacant
105 Web Manager ... Vacant
106 Int Dir Online Education/E-learning ... Mr. Chris TSANG
39 Director of Residence Life ... Ms. Michelle SALDANA
102 Director of Institutional Giving ... Ms. Megan UEBELACKER
30 Director of Development ... Mr. Kevin A. BARRY
41 Athletic Director ... Mr. Mark SPELLMIRE
50 Dept Chair Business Administration ... Dr. Michelle FRENCH-HOLLOWAY
53 Dept Chair Education ... Dr. Carol JOHNSTON

Mt. San Antonio College (J)

1100 N Grand, Walnut CA 91789-1399

County: Los Angeles — FICE Identification: 001245
Unit ID: 119164
Telephone: (909) 274-7500 — Carnegie Class: Assoc/MT-VT-High Trad
FAX Number: N/A — Calendar System: Semester
URL: www.mtsac.edu
Established: 1946 — Annual Undergrad Tuition & Fees (In-District): $1,350
Enrollment: 28,393 — Coed
Affiliation or Control: State/Local — IRS Status: 501(c)3
Highest Offering: Associate Degree

Accreditation: WJ, COARC, EMT, HT, RAD

01 President/CEO ... Dr. William T. SCROGGINS
05 Vice President Instruction ... Ms. Kelly FOWLER
10 Vice President Administrative Svcs ... Mr. Morris J. RODRIGUE
32 Vice President Student Services ... Dr. Audrey YAMAGATA-NOJI
15 Vice President Human Resources ... Vacant
20 AVP Instruction ... Dr. Meghan CHEN
08 Dean Library/Learning Resources ... Vacant
35 Assoc VP Student Services ... Mr. Tom MAUCH
51 Provost School of Continuing Educ ... Dr. Madelyn ARBALLO
13 Chief Technology Officer/Info Tech ... Mr. Anthony MOORE
84 Dean Enrollment Management ... Dr. George BRADSHAW
21 AVP Administrative Services ... Mr. Doug JENSON
102 Executive Director of Foundation ... Mr. Bill LAMBERT
37 Director Financial Aid ... Ms. Jenny PHU
117 Director Risk Management ... Ms. Duetta LANGEVIN
46 Director Grants ... Ms. Adrienne PRICE
26 Director Marketing/Communications ... Ms. Uyen MAI
09 Dir Research/Inst Effectiveness ... Ms. Patricia QUINONES
18 Exec Dir Facilities/Planning/Mgt ... Mr. Gary NELLESEN
35 Director Student Life ... Ms. Andrea SIMS
96 Director Purchasing/Printing/Mail ... Ms. Teresa PATTERSON
50 Dean Business ... Ms. Jennifer GALBRAITH
68 Dean Kinesiology/Athletics/Dance ... Mr. Joe JENNUM
79 Dean Humanities/Social Sciences ... Dr. Karelyn HOOVER
72 Dean Tech/Health Science ... Mr. Sam AGDASI
65 Dean Natural Sciences ... Mr. Matthew JUDD
57 Dean Arts ... Mr. Mark LOWENTROUT
51 Dean School of Cont Education ... Ms. Tammi PEARSON
04 Exec Asst to President & BOT ... Ms. Carol NELSON
38 Dean of Counseling ... Mr. Francisco DORAME

Mt. San Jacinto College (A)

1499 N State Street, San Jacinto CA 92583-2399

County: Riverside — FICE Identification: 001246
Unit ID: 119216
Telephone: (951) 487-6752 — Carnegie Class: Assoc/MT-VT-High Trad
FAX Number: (951) 654-9712 — Calendar System: Semester
URL: www.msjc.edu
Established: 1962 — Annual Undergrad Tuition & Fees (In-District): $1,406
Enrollment: 13,988 — Coed
Affiliation or Control: State/Local — IRS Status: 501(c)3
Highest Offering: Associate Degree
Accreditation: WJ, DMS

01 Superintendent/President ... Dr. Roger W. SCHULTZ
04 Executive Assistant to President ... Ms. Kristen GRIMES
05 VP of Instruction ... Dr. Jeremy BROWN
32 Interim VP of Student Svcs ... Ms. Rebecca TEAGUE
10 VP of Business Svcs ... Ms. Beth GOMEZ
15 VP of Human Resources ... Ms. Jeannine STOKES
84 VP of Inst Effect/Enrollmnt Mgmt ... Mr. Brandon MOORE
20 Provost of Instruction ... Ms. Joyce JOHNSON
79 Dean of Academic Programs MVC ... Ms. Rickianne RYCRAFT
97 Dean of Academic Programs SJC ... Dr. Alma RAMIREZ
72 Dean of Instruction Comp/Tech ... Mr. Micah ORLOFF
103 Dean Career Education MVC ... Dr. Marilyn HARVEY
103 Dean Career Education SJC ... Mr. Von LAWSON
81 Dean of Academic Programs MVC ... Mr. Marc DONNHAUSER
21 Int Dean of Admin Svcs/Controller ... Ms. Gail JENSEN
13 Dean of Information Technology ... Mr. Brian ORLAUSKI
18 Dean of Facilities Plng/Cap Constr ... Mr. Todd FRANCO
35 Interim Dean of Student Svcs ... Ms. Barbara FOUNTAIN
41 Dean of Phys Ed & Athletics ... Mr. Patrick SPRINGER
45 Exec Dean Institutional Planning ... Ms. Rebecca TEAGUE
108 Dean Institutional Effectiveness ... Dr. Carlos TOVARES
26 Public Information Officer ... Ms. Karin MARRIOTT
37 Dean of Student Svcs ... Ms. Dolores SMITH
66 Assoc Dean of Nursing/Allied Hlth ... Ms. Hope FARQUHARSON
121 Assoc Dean of Instructional Svcs ... Ms. Cheri NAISH
18 Dir Maintenance & Operations MVC ... Mr. Brian TWITTY
09 Assoc Dean of Inst Research ... Mr. Nikilos (Nik) MESARIS
07 Int Director of Enrollment Svcs ... Ms. Elizabeth MASCARO
19 Director of Campus Safety ... Mr. David PASEMAN
96 Dir of Procurement & General Svcs ... Ms. Tamara CUNNINGHAM

Mount Tamalpais College (B)

PO Box 492, San Quentin CA 94964

County: Marin — Identification: 667400
Telephone: (415) 455-8088 — Carnegie Class: Not Classified
FAX Number: N/A — Calendar System: Semester
URL: www.mttamcollege.org
Established: 1996 — Annual Undergrad Tuition & Fees: N/A
Enrollment: N/A — Male
Affiliation or Control: Independent Non-Profit — IRS Status: 501(c)3
Highest Offering: Associate Degree
Accreditation: @WJ

01 President ... Jody LEWEN
05 Chief Academic Officer ... Amy JAMGOCHIAN
32 Director of Student Affairs ... David DURAND

MTI College (C)

5221 Madison Avenue, Sacramento CA 95841-3037

County: Sacramento — FICE Identification: 012912
Unit ID: 118198
Telephone: (916) 339-1500 — Carnegie Class: Assoc/HVT-High Trad
FAX Number: (916) 339-0305 — Calendar System: Quarter
URL: mticollege.edu
Established: 1965 — Annual Undergrad Tuition & Fees: N/A
Enrollment: 495 — Coed
Affiliation or Control: Proprietary — IRS Status: Proprietary
Highest Offering: Associate Degree
Accreditation: WJ

01 President ... Mr. Michael A. ZIMMERMAN
10 Vice Pres/Chief Financial Officer ... Mr. David W. ALLEN
11 Campus Director ... Mr. Lawrence RICHMAN

Musicians Institute (D)

6752 Hollywood Boulevard, Hollywood CA 90028

County: Los Angeles — FICE Identification: 021618
Unit ID: 119270
Telephone: (323) 462-1384 — Carnegie Class: Spec-4-yr-Arts
FAX Number: (323) 462-1575 — Calendar System: Quarter
URL: www.mi.edu
Established: 1977 — Annual Undergrad Tuition & Fees: $24,795
Enrollment: 714 — Coed
Affiliation or Control: Proprietary — IRS Status: Proprietary
Highest Offering: Master's
Accreditation: MUS

01 President/CEO ... Mr. Todd BERHORST
05 Chief Academic Officer ... Dr. Rachel YOON
10 Chief Financial/Business Officer ... Mr. Kengo KIDO
108 Director of Compliance ... Vacant
06 Mgr Registrar Services ... Mr. Shaun VIETEN
13 Director of Information Technology ... Mr. Tim METZ
37 Director Student Financial Aid ... Mr. Michael HONG
07 Sr Director of Admissions ... Mr. Jose HERNANDEZ

Napa Valley College (E)

2277 Napa-Vallejo Highway, Napa CA 94558-6236

County: Napa — FICE Identification: 001247
Unit ID: 119331
Telephone: (707) 256-7000 — Carnegie Class: Assoc/MT-VT-High Trad
FAX Number: (707) 253-3015 — Calendar System: Semester
URL: www.napavalley.edu
Established: 1942 — Annual Undergrad Tuition & Fees (In-District): $1,150
Enrollment: 4,931 — Coed
Affiliation or Control: State/Local — IRS Status: 501(c)3
Highest Offering: Associate Degree
Accreditation: WJ, COARC, EMT

01 Superintendent/President ... Dr. Ronald D. KRAFT
05 Int Vice President Instruction ... Ms. Faye SMYLE
10 Vice Pres Admin Svcs/Asst Supt ... Mr. Robert PARKER
32 Vice Pres Student Svcs/Asst Supt ... Mr. Oscar DE HARO
38 Dean Counseling Svcs/Stdnt Success ... Mr. Howard WILLIS
20 Dean of Instruction ... Ms. Maria VILLAGOMEZ
37 Dean Fin Aid/EOPS/Pre-Col TRIO Pgms ... Ms. Patricia MORGAN
103 Dean Career Tech Educ/Workforce Dev ... Ms. Miraglia GREGORY
13 Dean Institutional Technology ... Mr. Eric HOUCK
09 Dean Research Plng/Instl Effect ... Dr. Robyn WORNALL
36 Dean Counselor/WA III ... Mr. Howard WILLIS
04 Exec Asst to the President ... Ms. Kathy WRIGHT
07 Assoc Dean Admissions/Records ... Ms. Jessica ERICKSON
15 Exec Director Human Resources ... Ms. Charo ALBARRAN
26 Public Relations Officer ... Ms. Holly KRASSNER DAWSON
18 Director Facilities ... Mr. Matt CHRISTENSEN
19 Director College Police ... Mr. Kenneth L. ARNOLD
84 Enrollment Management ... Mr. Erik SHEARER
88 Coordinator Trans Center ... Ms. Marci SANCHEZ
28 Director of Equity & Inclusivity ... Dr. Craig ALIMO
111 Director Inst Advancement ... Ms. Carolee CATTOLICA
96 Business Services Asst/Purchasing ... Ms. Solange KADA
23 Director Student Health Services ... Ms. Nancy TAMARISK

National Career College (F)

14355 Roscoe Boulevard, Panorama City CA 91402

County: Los Angeles — FICE Identification: 041460
Unit ID: 455868
Telephone: (818) 988-2300 — Carnegie Class: Spec 2-yr-Health
FAX Number: (818) 988-9944 — Calendar System: Semester
URL: www.nccusa.edu
Established: 2005 — Annual Undergrad Tuition & Fees: N/A
Enrollment: 293 — Coed
Affiliation or Control: Proprietary — IRS Status: Proprietary
Highest Offering: Associate Degree
Accreditation: ABHES

01 Campus President ... Dr. Wazkein BARBERIAN
11 Chief Operating Officer ... Sam KSACHIKIAN
10 Director Finance/Compliance ... Anna TOVMASYAN

National Polytechnic College (G)

4105 South Street, Lakewood CA 90712

County: Los Angeles — FICE Identification: 039104
Unit ID: 447759
Telephone: (888) 243-2493 — Carnegie Class: Not Classified
FAX Number: (888) 640-7732 — Calendar System: Semester
URL: www.npcollege.edu
Established: 1996 — Annual Undergrad Tuition & Fees: N/A
Enrollment: 185 — Coed
Affiliation or Control: Proprietary — IRS Status: Proprietary
Highest Offering: Associate Degree
Accreditation: ACCSC

01 CEO and President ... Dariush (David) MADDAHI

National Test Pilot School (H)

PO Box 658, Mojave CA 93502-0658

County: Kern — Identification: 667009
Telephone: (661) 824-2977 — Carnegie Class: Not Classified
FAX Number: (661) 824-2943 — Calendar System: Semester
URL: www.ntps.edu
Established: 1981 — Annual Graduate Tuition & Fees: N/A
Enrollment: N/A — Coed
Affiliation or Control: Independent Non-Profit — IRS Status: 501(c)3
Highest Offering: Master's; No Undergraduates
Accreditation: WC

01 President/CEO ... Dr. Al L. PETERSON
05 Chief Academic Officer ... Mr. Ilan ARUSH
11 COO/Head of Training ... Mr. James BROWN
54 Director NFTI ... Mr. Marco LOTTERIO
13 Chief of Systems Academics ... Mr. Tom DREILICH
88 Chief of FW P&FQ Academics ... Dr. Gabriele DI FRANCESCO
88 Chief of RW P&FQ Academics ... Mr. Ilan ARUSH
88 Chief FW Test Pilot Instructor ... Mr. Andy EDGELL
88 Chief RW Test Pilot Instructor ... Mr. Stefan HANEKOM
06 Registrar/Student Services Rep ... Ms. Kayla CHAMNESS
10 Business Manager ... Ms. Joyce CAMIN

National University (I)

11355 N Torrey Pines Road, La Jolla CA 92037

County: San Diego — FICE Identification: 011460
Unit ID: 119605
Telephone: (858) 642-8000 — Carnegie Class: Masters/L
FAX Number: (858) 642-8714 — Calendar System: Other
URL: www.nu.edu
Established: 1971 — Annual Undergrad Tuition & Fees: $13,320
Enrollment: 18,070 — Coed
Affiliation or Control: Independent Non-Profit — IRS Status: 501(c)3
Highest Offering: Doctorate
Accreditation: WC, ANEST, CAEPN, IACBE, NURSE, PH, RTT

00 Chancellor ... Dr. Michael R. CUNNINGHAM
01 University President ... Dr. David ANDREWS
05 EVP/Provost ... Dr. Gangaram SINGH

New York Film Academy, Los Angeles (J)

3300 Riverside Drive, Burbank CA 91505

County: Burbank — FICE Identification: 041188
Unit ID: 461148
Telephone: (818) 333-3558 — Carnegie Class: Spec-4-yr-Arts
FAX Number: (818) 333-3557 — Calendar System: Semester
URL: www.nyfa.edu
Established: 2006 — Annual Undergrad Tuition & Fees: $33,834
Enrollment: 1,271 — Coed
Affiliation or Control: Proprietary — IRS Status: Proprietary
Highest Offering: Master's
Accreditation: WC, ART

01 Dean of the College ... Mr. Dan MACKLER
03 Executive Vice President ... Mr. David KLEIN
05 Dean of Faculty ... Mr. Nunzio DEFILIPPIS
32 Dean of Students ... Dr. Susan ASHE
10 Chief Financial Officer ... Mr. Kirk LENGA
06 Registrar ... Mr. Vince VOSKANIAN
07 Director of Admissions ... Vacant
08 Head Librarian ... Mr. Josh MOORMON
39 Housing Coordinator ... Ms. Sarah MARPLES

NewSchool of Architecture and Design (K)

1249 F Street, San Diego CA 92101-6634

County: San Diego — FICE Identification: 030439
Unit ID: 119775
Telephone: (619) 684-8800 — Carnegie Class: Spec-4-yr-Arts
FAX Number: (619) 684-8880 — Calendar System: Quarter
URL: www.newschoolarch.edu
Established: 1980 — Annual Undergrad Tuition & Fees: $29,427
Enrollment: 455 — Coed
Affiliation or Control: Proprietary — IRS Status: Proprietary
Highest Offering: Master's
Accreditation: WC

01 Interim President ... Dr. Tom CLAWSON
05 Chief Academic Officer ... Dr. Tom CLAWSON
32 Dean Division of Student Affairs ... Vacant
48 Dean School of Design ... Dr. Elena PACENTI
48 Head of Architecture ... Mr. Len ZEGARSKI

Nobel University (L)

505 Shatto Place #300, Los Angeles CA 90020

County: Los Angeles — Identification: 667274
Telephone: (213) 382-1136 — Carnegie Class: Not Classified
FAX Number: (213) 382-1187 — Calendar System: Semester
URL: nobeluniversity.edu
Established: 2000 — Annual Undergrad Tuition & Fees: N/A
Enrollment: N/A — Coed
Affiliation or Control: Proprietary — IRS Status: Proprietary
Highest Offering: Master's

Accreditation: **ACICS**

01 President .... Chong S. **KIM**
05 Chief Academic Officer/Provost .... Michael **KAHLER**

*North Orange County Community College District (A)

1830 W Romneya Drive, Anaheim CA 92801-1819
County: Orange — FICE Identification: 009742
Unit ID: 120023
Telephone: (714) 808-4500 — Carnegie Class: N/A
FAX Number: (714) 808-4791
URL: www.nocccd.edu

01 Interim Chancellor .... Mr. Fred **WILLIAMS**
10 Vice Chanc Finance/Facilities .... Mr. Fred **WILLIAMS**
15 Vice Chancellor Human Resources .... Ms. Irma **RAMOS**
05 Vice Chanc Educational Svcs/Tech .... Dr. Cherry **LI-BUGG**
26 Director Public/Government Affairs .... Ms. Kai **STEARNS MOORE**
04 Exec Admin Aide to Chancellor .... Ms. Alba **RECINOS**
22 Dist Director Diversity/Compliance .... Mr. Arturo **OCAMPO**

*Cypress College (B)

9200 Valley View, Cypress CA 90630-5897
County: Orange — FICE Identification: 001193
Unit ID: 113236
Telephone: (714) 484-7000 — Carnegie Class: Bac/Assoc-Assoc Dom
FAX Number: (714) 527-8238 — Calendar System: Semester
URL: www.cypresscollege.edu
Established: 1966 — Annual Undergrad Tuition & Fees (In-District): $1,146
Enrollment: 15,325 — Coed
Affiliation or Control: State/Local — IRS Status: 501(c)3
Highest Offering: Baccalaureate
Accreditation: **WJ**, ADNUR, CAHIIM, DA, DH, DMS, FUSER, RAD

02 President .... Dr. JoAnna **SCHILLING**
05 Int Vice Pres Instruction .... Dr. Kathleen **REILAND**
32 Vice President Student Services .... Dr. Paul **DE DIOS**
10 Vice Pres Administrative Services .... Mr. Alex **PORTER**
08 Dean Library/Learning Resource Ctr .... Dr. Treisa **CASSENS**
79 Dean Language Arts .... Mr. Eldon **YOUNG**
121 Dean Counseling/Student Dev .... Dr. Troy **DAVIS**
06 Registrar .... Mr. David **BOOZE**
26 Director Campus Communications .... Mr. Marc **POSNER**
102 Exec Dir Foundation/Community Rels .... Mr. Howard **KUMMERMAN**
32 Dean Student Support Services .... Mr. Paul **DE DIOS**
90 Manager Systems Technology Svcs .... Mr. Peter **MAHARAJ**
37 Director Financial Aid .... Mr. Korey **LINDLEY**
09 Int Dir Institutional Research/Plng .... Ms. Eileen **HADDAD**
18 Director Physical Plant/Facilities .... Mr. Philip **FLEMING**
19 Director Campus Safety .... Mr. Ralph **WEBB**
04 Exec Assistant to President .... Ms. Kristi **VALDEZ**
68 Dean Physical Education/Kinesiology .... Dr. Richard **RAMS**
57 Dean Fine Arts .... Dr. Katy **REALISTA**
50 Dean Business/CIS .... Mr. Henry **HUA**
83 Dean Social Sciences .... Ms. Lisa **GAETJE**
53 Int Dean Science Engineering & Math .... Dr. David **VAKIL**
76 Int Dean Health Sciences .... Mr. Stephen **SCHOONMAKER**
75 Dean Career Technical Education .... Dr. Kathleen **REILAND**
113 Campus Accounting Manager .... Ms. Dao **DO**
22 Director EOPS .... Ms. AnnMarie **RUELAS**

*Fullerton College (C)

321 E Chapman Avenue, Fullerton CA 92832-2095
County: Orange — FICE Identification: 001201
Unit ID: 114859
Telephone: (714) 992-7000 — Carnegie Class: Assoc/HT-High Trad
FAX Number: (714) 992-9930 — Calendar System: Semester
URL: www.fullcoll.edu
Established: 1913 — Annual Undergrad Tuition & Fees (In-District): $1,154
Enrollment: 21,427 — Coed
Affiliation or Control: State/Local — IRS Status: 501(c)3
Highest Offering: Associate Degree
Accreditation: **WJ**

02 President .... Dr. Greg **SCHULZ**
05 Vice President Instruction .... Dr. Jose Ramon **NUNEZ**
32 Vice Pres Student Services .... Dr. Gilbert **CONTRERAS**
11 Vice Pres Administrative Svcs .... Mr. Rodrigo **GARCIA**
50 Interim Dean Business & CIS .... Mr. Carlos **AYON**
57 Dean Fine Arts .... Mr. John **TEBAY**
79 Dean Humanities .... Mr. Dan **WILLOUGHBY**
77 Dean Math/Computer Science .... Mr. Mark **GREENHALGH**
65 Dean Natural Sciences .... Dr. Richard **HARTMANN**
68 Dean Physical Education .... Dr. David **GROSSMAN**
83 Dean Social Sciences .... Dr. Jorge **GAMBOA**
72 Dean Technology & Engr .... Mr. Kenneth **STARKMAN**
37 Director of Financial Aid .... Mr. Greg **RYAN**
23 Interim Director Health Services .... Mr. Dana **TIMMERMANS**
18 Dir Facilities/Physical Plant .... Mr. Larry **LARA**
40 Director of Bookstore .... Mr. Nick **KARVIA**
35 Director Student Activities .... Ms. Naomi **ABESAMIS**
06 Registrar .... Ms. Rena **MARTINEZ STLUKA**
19 Director Campus Safety .... Mr. Steve **SELBY**
38 Dean Counseling/Student Development .... Dr. Jennifer **LABOUNTY**
08 Dean Library (LLR & ISPS) .... Dr. Dani **WILSON**
07 Dean Admissions & Records .... Mr. Albert **ABUTIN**
90 Academic Computing Technologies .... Mr. Co **HO**

09 Director Inst Research & Planning .... Vacant
88 Director Cadena Transfer Center .... Ms. Cecilia **ARRIAZA**
26 Director Campus Communications .... Ms. Lisa **MCPHERON**
04 Exec Assistant to the President .... Ms. Jean **FOSTER**
121 Dean Student Support Services .... Dr. Elaine **LIPIZ GONZALEZ**
15 Personnel Services Specialist .... Ms. Liz **LEDEZMA RENTERIA**

Northcentral University (D)

11355 North Torrey Pines Road, La Jolla CA 92037
County: San Diego — FICE Identification: 038133
Unit ID: 444130
Telephone: (866) 776-0331 — Carnegie Class: DU-Mod
FAX Number: (844) 851-5889 — Calendar System: Other
URL: www.ncu.edu
Established: 1996 — Annual Undergrad Tuition & Fees: N/A
Enrollment: 12,471 — Coed
Affiliation or Control: Independent Non-Profit — IRS Status: 501(c)3
Highest Offering: Doctorate
Accreditation: **WC**, ACBSP, MFCD, @SW

01 President .... Dr. David **HARPOOL**
05 Provost/Chief Academic Officer .... Dr. John **LANEAR**
10 Chief Finance Officer .... Mr. Jamie **NICKEL**
37 VP Student and Financial Services .... Dr. Ian **COOPER**
07 VP Enrollment .... Mr. Ken **BOUTELLE**
15 VP Human Resources .... Ms. Angie **WALKER**
13 Chief Technology Learning Officer .... Dr. Colin **MARLAIRE**
26 VP Communications/Advancement .... Ms. Molly **GUTTERUD**
43 General Counsel .... Dr. David **HARPOOL**
50 Dean School of Business .... Dr. Tammi **COOPER**
53 Dean School of Education .... Dr. Andy **RIGGLE**
76 Dean School of Health Sciences .... Dr. Laurie **SHANDERSON**
83 Dean Sch of Social/Behavioral Sci .... Dr. James **BILLINGS**
72 Dean School of Technology .... Dr. Robert **SAPP**
09 Director Institutional Research .... Vacant
108 Director Institutional Assessment .... Dr. Heather **HUSSEY**
06 University Registrar .... Ms. Jennifer **RACER**
08 Director of Library Services .... Ms. Amanda **ZIEGLER**

Northern California Bible College (E)

4439 Stonebridge Dr, Ste 210, Pleasanton CA 94588
County: Alameda — Identification: 667349
Telephone: (925) 846-6464 — Carnegie Class: Not Classified
FAX Number: N/A — Calendar System: Quarter
URL: www.ncbc.net
Established: 1971 — Annual Undergrad Tuition & Fees: N/A
Enrollment: N/A — Coed
Affiliation or Control: Independent Non-Profit — IRS Status: 501(c)3
Highest Offering: Baccalaureate
Accreditation: **TRACS**

01 President .... David G. **SELL**
05 Chief Academic Officer/Dean .... Dr. Ray **ROBLES**

Northwestern Polytechnic University (F)

47671 Westinghouse Drive, Fremont CA 94539-7474
County: Alameda — Identification: 666759
Unit ID: 120166
Telephone: (510) 592-9688 — Carnegie Class: Not Classified
FAX Number: (510) 657-8975 — Calendar System: Trimester
URL: www.npu.edu
Established: 1984 — Annual Undergrad Tuition & Fees: $8,720
Enrollment: 33 — Coed
Affiliation or Control: Independent Non-Profit — IRS Status: 501(c)3
Highest Offering: Master's
Accreditation: **WC**, CEA

01 President .... Mr. Peter **HSIEH**
03 Executive Vice President .... Mr. Paul **CHOI**
05 Chief Academic Officer .... Ms. Nelly **MANGAROVA**
10 Chief Financial Officer .... Ms. Anne **SUTARDJI**
43 General Transactions & Corp Counsel .... Mr. Mark **SCHULTZ**
07 Dir of Admissions/Special Projects .... Ms. Monica **SINHA**
06 Registrar/Sr Academic Advisor .... Vacant
54 Dean of School of Engineering .... Dr. Thawi **IWAGOSHI**
50 Dean of School of Business .... Mr. James **CONNOR**
18 Director of Facilities .... Mr. Jose **MARTINEZ**

Notre Dame de Namur University (G)

1500 Ralston Avenue, Belmont CA 94002-1908
County: San Mateo — FICE Identification: 001179
Unit ID: 120184
Telephone: (650) 508-3500 — Carnegie Class: Masters/M
FAX Number: (650) 508-3477 — Calendar System: Semester
URL: www.ndnu.edu
Established: 1851 — Annual Undergrad Tuition & Fees: N/A
Enrollment: 585 — Coed
Affiliation or Control: Independent Non-Profit — IRS Status: 501(c)3
Highest Offering: Doctorate
Accreditation: **WC**, ACBSP

01 Interim President .... Dr. Daniel J. **CAREY**
05 VP Acad Affs/Chief Academic Ofcr .... Dr. Greg **WHITE**
10 Vice Pres Finance & Administration .... Ms. Emiko **YAMADA**
111 Int Director for Advancement .... Ms. Nicole **NIELSON**
53 Dean Education/Psychology .... Dr. Caryl **HODGES**
37 Director Financial Aid .... Mr. I. **CHEN**
08 Int Director Library Services .... Ms. Carmen **MARTINEZ**
13 Director Office of Information Tech .... Mr. Merle **MASON**
18 Director Facilities .... Ms. Jessica **FRESQUEZ**
20 Associate Provost .... Mr. Greg **WHITE**
21 Controller .... Ms. Emiko **YAMADA**
04 Exec Assistant to the President .... Ms. Deirdre **SARGENT**

Oak Valley College (H)

2759 Ayala Dr, Rialto CA 92324
County: San Bernardino — Identification: 667381
Telephone: (909) 554-3814 — Carnegie Class: Not Classified
FAX Number: N/A — Calendar System: Trimester
URL: www.oakvalleycollege.org
Established: 2016 — Annual Undergrad Tuition & Fees: N/A
Enrollment: N/A — Coed
Affiliation or Control: Independent Non-Profit — IRS Status: 501(c)3
Highest Offering: Baccalaureate
Accreditation: **@WC**

01 President .... Eric **BLUM**
10 Vice Pres Administration/Enrollment .... Melanie **CLOW**
05 Dean/Chief Academic Officer .... Afarah **BOARD**
32 Manager Student/Faculty Services .... Megan **HERING**

Occidental College (I)

1600 Campus Road, Los Angeles CA 90041-3314
County: Los Angeles — FICE Identification: 001249
Unit ID: 120254
Telephone: (323) 259-2500 — Carnegie Class: Bac-A&S
FAX Number: (323) 259-2958 — Calendar System: Semester
URL: www.oxy.edu
Established: 1887 — Annual Undergrad Tuition & Fees: $56,576
Enrollment: 1,839 — Coed
Affiliation or Control: Independent Non-Profit — IRS Status: 501(c)3
Highest Offering: Master's
Accreditation: **WC**

01 President .... Dr. Harry J. **ELAM, JR.**
05 VP Academic Affairs/Dean of College .... Dr. Wendy F. **STERNBERG**
10 Vice Pres/Chief Operating Officer .... Mr. Amos **HIMMELSTEIN**
07 VP Enrollment/Dean of Admission .... Mr. Vincent **CUSEO**
111 Vice Pres Inst Advancement .... Mr. Charlie **CARDILLO**
32 VP Student Affairs/Dean of Students .... Mr. Rob **FLOT**
26 VP Marketing/Communications .... Mr. Marty **SHARKEY**
43 General Counsel .... Mr. Jon **MCNUTT**
100 Chief of Staff .... Ms. Kimberly **URIBE**
41 Athletic Dir/VP Student Affairs .... Ms. Shanda **NESS**
18 Assoc VP for Facilities Management .... Mr. Christopher **REYES**
84 Interim VP of Enrollment .... Ms. Maricela **LIMAS MARTINEZ**
13 VP ITS/Chief Technology Officer .... Mr. James **UHRICH**
36 Exec Director Career Services .... Ms. Jamila J. **CHAMBERS**
04 Exec Assistant to President .... Ms. Rocio M. **RAMOS**
08 Library Director .... Dr. Kevin **MULROY**
29 Director Alumni/Parent Engagement .... Ms. Helena C. **LAZARO**
37 Director of Financial Aid .... Ms. Cheryl Lynn **REINSCHMIDT**
15 AVP of Human Resources .... Mr. Randy **GLAZER**
27 Director of Communications .... Mr. Jim **TRANQUADA**
09 Director of Institutional Research .... Ms. Jaclyn A. **CAMERON**
19 Director of Campus Safety .... Mr. Rick **TANKSLEY**
101 Secretary of the Institution/Board .... Ms. Marsha **SCHNIRRING**

Ohlone College (J)

43600 Mission Boulevard, Fremont CA 94539-0390
County: Alameda — FICE Identification: 004481
Unit ID: 120290
Telephone: (510) 659-6000 — Carnegie Class: Assoc/HVT-Mix Trad/Non
FAX Number: N/A — Calendar System: Semester
URL: www.ohlone.edu
Established: 1966 — Annual Undergrad Tuition & Fees (In-District): $1,196
Enrollment: 9,060 — Coed
Affiliation or Control: State/Local — IRS Status: 501(c)3
Highest Offering: Associate Degree
Accreditation: **WJ**, ADNUR, COARC, PTAA

01 President/Superintendent .... Dr. Eric **BISHOP**
05 Exec VP Academic Affairs/Dpty Supt .... Dr. Anthony **DISALVO**
10 Vice Pres Administrative Services .... Dr. Chris **DELA ROSA**
32 Vice President Student Services .... Mr. Milton **LANG**
15 Vice Pres Human Resources .... Ms. Shairon **ZINGSHEIM**
13 Assoc Vice Pres Information Tech .... Dr. Chris **DELA ROSA**
101 Asst to Pres/Board of Trustees .... Ms. Shelby **FOSTER**
08 Dean Business & Career Tech Educ .... Ms. Lesley **BUEHLER**
38 Dean Counseling/Student Support .... Dr. Andree **THOMAS**
09 Exec Dean Institutional Research .... Mr. Michael **BOWMAN**
07 Dean Admissions/Records .... Mr. Michael **LEIB**
28 Exec Dean Equity/Campus Diversity .... Ms. Melissa **CERVANTES**
83 Dean Social Science .... Dr. Ghada **AL-MASRI**
76 Dean Health Sciences .... Mr. Robert **GABRIEL**
83 Dean Language/Comm/Academic Success .... Mr. Mark **LIEU**
81 Dean Science/Engineering/Math .... Ms. Lori **SILVERMAN**
88 Interim Dean Deaf Studies .... Mr. Robert **GABRIEL**
68 Dean Kinesiology/Athl/Brdcstg/Arts .... Mr. Chris **WARDEN**
102 Executive Director Foundation .... Mr. Binh **NGUYEN**
35 Director EOPS/Student Services .... Ms. Nancy **NAVARRO-LECA**
21 Exec Director Business Services .... Mr. Farhad **SABIT**
26 Exec Dir Communications/Public Rels .... Mr. Binh **NGUYEN**
19 Chief Campus Police Services .... Mr. John **WORLEY**
18 Director of Facilities .... Mr. Oscar **GUILLEN**

37 Director Financial Aid .... Vacant
96 Dir Purchasing/Auxiliary Services .... Mr. Alex LEBEDEFF
104 Director International Programs .... Ms. Kristina RADKE
88 Director Curriculum & Scheduling .... Ms. Kimberly ROBBIE
04 Assistant to President/Supt .... Mr. Edgar HERNANDEZ

Oikos University (A)

7901 Oakport St, Ste 3000, Oakland CA 94621
County: Alameda — Identification: 667212
Telephone: (510) 639-7879 — Carnegie Class: Not Classified
FAX Number: (510) 639-7810 — Calendar System: Semester
URL: www.oikos.edu
Established: 2004 — Annual Undergrad Tuition & Fees: N/A
Enrollment: N/A — Coed
Affiliation or Control: Independent Non-Profit — IRS Status: 501(c)3
Highest Offering: Doctorate
Accreditation: **TRACS**

01 President .... Dr. Jongin KIM
05 Dean of Academics .... Dr. Ki Wook MIN
32 Director of Students .... Dr. Dongjin LEE
10 Chief Financial Officer .... Ms. Myungsoon YOON

Olivet University (B)

36401 Tripp Flats Road, Anza CA 92539
County: San Francisco — Identification: 666176
Telephone: (951) 763-0500 — Carnegie Class: Not Classified
FAX Number: (415) 371-0003 — Calendar System: Quarter
URL: www.olivetuniversity.edu
Established: 1992 — Annual Undergrad Tuition & Fees: N/A
Enrollment: N/A — Coed
Affiliation or Control: Independent Non-Profit — IRS Status: 501(c)3
Highest Offering: Doctorate
Accreditation: **#BI**

01 University President .... Dr. Matthias GEBHARDT
05 Dean of Academic Affairs .... Dr. Tracy DAVIS
32 Dean of Students .... Dr. Julia TZENG
10 Chief Financial Officer .... Mr. Barnabas JUNG
11 Chief Operating Officer/Chaplain .... Dr. Walker TZENG

Otis College of Art and Design (C)

9045 Lincoln Boulevard, Los Angeles CA 90045-3550
County: Los Angeles — FICE Identification: 001251
Unit ID: 120403
Telephone: (310) 665-6800 — Carnegie Class: Spec-4-yr-Arts
FAX Number: (310) 665-6805 — Calendar System: Semester
URL: www.otis.edu
Established: 1918 — Annual Undergrad Tuition & Fees: $49,680
Enrollment: 1,073 — Coed
Affiliation or Control: Independent Non-Profit — IRS Status: 501(c)3
Highest Offering: Master's
Accreditation: **WC**, ART

00 Chair Board of Trustees .... Ms. Mei-Lee NEY
01 President .... Mr. Charles HIRSCHHORN
05 Provost .... Ms. Jiseon Lee ISBARA
13 VP of IT and Operations .... Mr. Ankush MAHINDRA
10 VP of Financial Services/CFO .... Mr. Ankush MAHINDRA
32 VP of Campus Life .... Dr. Laura KIRALLA
15 VP of Human Resources/Risk Mgmt .... Ms. Karen HILL
26 VP of Communications and Marketing .... Mr. Lawrence ALDAVA
111 VP of Institutional Advancement .... Mr. Patrick MAHANY
35 Dean of Student Affairs .... Dr. Nick NEGRETE
56 Dean of Extension .... Mr. Mark MANROSE
84 Dean of Enrollment Mgmt .... Dr. Samuel KIM
06 Registrar .... Ms. Anna MANZANO
18 Chief Facilities/Operation Officer .... Mr. Claude NICA
37 Director Student Fin Services .... Ms. Natasha KOBRINSKY
09 Dir Inst Research & Effectiveness .... Dr. Angila ROMIOUS
14 Director Technology Infrastructure .... Mr. Matthew BALLARD
108 Asst Provost Assessment & Accred .... Ms. Joanne MITCHELL
28 Asst Dean of Stdnt Affs/Title IX .... Dr. Carol BRANCH
19 Chief Safety and Security Officer .... Mr. Rick GONZALEZ
101 Board Relations Mgr .... Ms. Doniell PETERS
04 Sr Exec Asst to President .... Ms. Renee JONES
23 Director Student Health & Wellness .... Dr. Julie SPENCER
39 Director Housing & Res Life .... Ms. Morgan BROWN
29 Director Alumni Relations .... Ms. Hazel MANDUJANO

Pacific College (D)

3160 Redhill Avenue, Costa Mesa CA 92626-3402
County: Orange — FICE Identification: 032993
Unit ID: 422695
Telephone: (800) 867-2243 — Carnegie Class: Spec-4-yr-Other Health
FAX Number: (714) 662-1702 — Calendar System: Semester
URL: www.pacific-college.edu
Established: 1993 — Annual Undergrad Tuition & Fees: N/A
Enrollment: 249 — Coed
Affiliation or Control: Proprietary — IRS Status: Proprietary
Highest Offering: Master's
Accreditation: **WC**, NURSE

01 President .... Mr. William L. NELSON
03 Vice President Instruction .... Ms. Donna WOO
11 Chief Financial/Operating Ofcr .... Ms. Sandy SARGE

Pacific College of Health and Science (E)

7445 Mission Valley Road, #104,
San Diego CA 92108-4408
County: San Diego — FICE Identification: 030277
Unit ID: 378576
Telephone: (619) 574-6909 — Carnegie Class: Spec-4-yr-Other Health
FAX Number: (619) 574-6641 — Calendar System: Trimester
URL: https://www.pacificcollege.edu
Established: 1986 — Annual Undergrad Tuition & Fees: $9,791
Enrollment: 967 — Coed
Affiliation or Control: Proprietary — IRS Status: Proprietary
Highest Offering: Doctorate
Accreditation: **WC**, ACUP

01 President .... Mr. Jack MILLER
05 Vice Pres of Academic Affairs .... Ms. Stacy GOMES
10 Chief Operating Officer .... Mr. Malcolm YOUNGREN
37 Vice Pres of Financial Aid .... Ms. Beatrice SMITH
26 Vice President Marketing .... Ms. Nathalie TUROTTE
12 Director NY Campus .... Mr. Malcolm YOUNGREN
12 Director CH Campus .... Mr. Dave FRECH
07 Vice President Admissions .... Ms. April PANIAGUA
12 Director SD Campus .... Ms. Teri POWERS
06 Registrar .... Mr. Nayeli CORONA
23 Director of Clinical Services .... Ms. Leng TANG-RITCHIE
08 Head Librarian .... Ms. Patricia BENEFIEL
13 Information Technology Director .... Mr. Greg RUSSO
88 Pacific Symposium .... Ms. Candace UNGER
29 Director Alumni Affairs .... Ms. Cynthia NEIPRIS

Pacific Oaks College (F)

45 West Eureka Street, Pasadena CA 91103
County: Los Angeles — FICE Identification: 001255
Unit ID: 120768
Telephone: (626) 529-8500 — Carnegie Class: Spec-4-yr-Other
FAX Number: N/A — Calendar System: Semester
URL: www.pacificoaks.edu
Established: 1945 — Annual Undergrad Tuition & Fees: $11,692
Enrollment: 1,238 — Coed
Affiliation or Control: Independent Non-Profit — IRS Status: 501(c)3
Highest Offering: Master's
Accreditation: **WC**, @SW

01 President .... Dr. Jack PADUNTIN
05 Vice Pres Academic Affairs .... Dr. Bree COOK
32 Dean of Students .... Ms. Victoria LUGO
15 AVP Human Resources/Title IX Coord .... Ms. Jane SAWYER
10 AVP Financial/Admin Operations .... Ms. Yug Fon CHIQUITO
35 Dir Ctr Stdnt Achievemt/Res/Enrich .... Ms. Pat MEDA
07 Assoc Vice President Admissions .... Mr. Michael PATTON
04 Dir President's Ofc/Sec to Cabinet .... Ms. Carrie ZALKIND
12 Campus Dean San Jose .... Dr. Marcia BANKIRER
53 Int Dean School of Education .... Mr. Jerell HILL
88 Assoc Dean School of CFP .... Dr. Rebecca ROJAS
83 Dean School of Human Development .... Dr. Terry WEBSTER
88 Exec Director Children's School .... Mr. Robert BOYMAN
111 Dir Advancement/External Affairs .... Ms. Johanna ATIENZA
06 Registrar .... Ms. M'isha STARKS

Pacific School of Religion (G)

1798 Scenic Avenue, Berkeley CA 94709-1323
County: Alameda — FICE Identification: 001256
Unit ID: 120795
Telephone: (510) 849-8200 — Carnegie Class: Spec-4-yr-Faith
FAX Number: (510) 845-8948 — Calendar System: Semester
URL: www.psr.edu
Established: 1866 — Annual Graduate Tuition & Fees: N/A
Enrollment: 100 — Coed
Affiliation or Control: Independent Non-Profit — IRS Status: 501(c)3
Highest Offering: Doctorate; No Undergraduates
Accreditation: **WC**, THEOL

01 President .... Rev. David VASQUEZ-LEVY
05 Vice Pres Academic Affairs/Dean .... Dr. Susan ABRAHAM
30 Vice Pres Development .... Mr. Jeffrey FISCHER-SMITH
26 Vice Pres Marketing/Enrollment .... Mr. Murry EVANS
10 Vice Pres Finance/Administration .... Ms. Natasha LEE
06 Asst Dean Academic Pgms/Registrar .... Ms. Lyndsey REED
07 Dir Admissions/Financial Aid Ofcr .... Mr. Keaton ANDREAS
32 Dir Community Life/Spiritual Care .... Rev. Ann JEFFERSON

Pacific States University (H)

3424 Wilshire Boulevard, 12th Floor,
Los Angeles CA 90010
County: Los Angeles — FICE Identification: 031633
Unit ID: 120838
Telephone: (323) 731-2383 — Carnegie Class: Spec-4-yr-Bus
FAX Number: (323) 731-7276 — Calendar System: Quarter
URL: www.psuca.edu
Established: 1928 — Annual Undergrad Tuition & Fees: $12,960
Enrollment: 26 — Coed
Affiliation or Control: Independent Non-Profit — IRS Status: 501(c)3
Highest Offering: Master's
Accreditation: **ACCSC**

01 Interim President .... Mr. Matthew SHIN
05 Dean Academic Affairs .... Dr. Heidi CROCKER
10 Asst Dean Finance/General Affairs .... Miss Rosy LIM
37 Financial Aid .... Mr. Moonsik KIM
26 Assoc Dean Public Rels/Student Affs .... Ms. Sarah MIN
13 Dir General & Technology Svcs/MIS .... Mr. Kuang Kai LU
08 University Librarian .... Ms. Aurora AREVALO
07 Dir of Admissions .... Ms. Maawiya AYEVA
32 Dir Student Services/Int Registrar .... Vacant

Pacific Union College (I)

1 Angwin Avenue, Angwin CA 94508-9797
County: Napa — FICE Identification: 001258
Unit ID: 120865
Telephone: (707) 965-6311 — Carnegie Class: Bac-Diverse
FAX Number: (707) 965-6390 — Calendar System: Quarter
URL: www.puc.edu
Established: 1882 — Annual Undergrad Tuition & Fees: $32,016
Enrollment: 959 — Coed
Affiliation or Control: Seventh-day Adventist — IRS Status: 501(c)3
Highest Offering: Master's
Accreditation: **WC**, ADNUR, ART, IACBE, MUS, NUR, SW

01 President .... Dr. Ralph TRECARTIN, JR.
05 Academic Dean/VP for Academic Admin .... Mr. Milbert MARIANO
10 VP for Financial Administration .... Mr. Brandon C. PARKER
32 Int VP for Student Life .... Mr. J.R ROGERS
84 VP for Enroll/Marketing/Comm .... Mr. Gene EDELBACH
111 VP for Alumni & Advancement .... Ms. Kellie LIND
08 Director of Library Services .... Mr. Patrick BENNER
37 Director Student Financial Services .... Mr. Frederick WHITESIDE
13 Director of Information Technology .... Mr. David RAI
06 Registrar .... Ms. Susan WALTERS
15 Director of Human Resources .... Mr. Stacy NELSON
114 Director Budgets & Fiscal Services .... Vacant
38 Director Counseling Center .... Mr. Michael JEFFERSON
18 Chief of Facilities Management .... Mr. Dale WITHERS
20 AVP for Academic Administration .... Dr. Lindsay MORTON
07 Admissions Counselor .... Mr. Lewis GOVEA
09 Director of Institutional Research .... Mr. Serhii KALYNOVSKYI

Pacifica Graduate Institute (J)

249 Lambert Road, Carpinteria CA 93013-3019
County: Carpinteria — FICE Identification: 031268
Unit ID: 115746
Telephone: (805) 969-3626 — Carnegie Class: Spec-4-yr-Other Health
FAX Number: (805) 565-1932 — Calendar System: Quarter
URL: www.pacifica.edu
Established: 1974 — Annual Graduate Tuition & Fees: N/A
Enrollment: 856 — Coed
Affiliation or Control: Proprietary — IRS Status: Proprietary
Highest Offering: Doctorate; No Undergraduates
Accreditation: **WC**

01 President/CEO .... Dr. Joseph CAMBRAY
05 Provost/ALO/VP Academic Affairs .... Dr. Peter ROJCEWICZ
10 Chief Financial Officer .... Mr. Larry BYER
43 General Counsel .... Mr. Marvin RICHARDS
84 Sr Director of Enrollment Mgmt .... Ms. Rica TORIBIO
37 Director of Financial Aid .... Ms. Tracie TEAGUE
20 CoDir of Academic Affs/Student Svcs .... Ms. Lauren LASTRA
20 CoDir of Academic Affs/Student Svcs .... Mr. Nicholas SABATINO
06 Registrar .... Ms. Francine MATAS
15 Director of Human Resources .... Ms. Norma MESA
39 Director of Guest Services .... Ms. Heather SLADE
29 Director of Alumni Relations .... Ms. Dianne TRAVIS-TEAGUE
13 Director of Information Technology .... Mr. Tim FRITZ
14 Director of Information Systems .... Mr. Griff JONES
19 Dir of Facilities/Safety/Security .... Mr. Adam BROWN
105 Director of Marketing/Webmaster .... Mr. John ZIEGLER
09 Director of Institutional Research .... Dr. Bill BILLET

Palmer College of Chiropractic, West Campus (K)

90 E Tasman Drive, San Jose CA 95134-1617
Telephone: (408) 944-6000 — FICE Identification: 021849
Accreditation: **&HLC**, &CHIRO

† Regional accreditation is carried under the parent institution in Davenport, IA.

Palo Alto University (L)

1791 Arastradero Road, Palo Alto CA 94304
County: San Mateo — FICE Identification: 021383
Unit ID: 120698
Telephone: (800) 818-6136 — Carnegie Class: Spec-4-yr-Other Health
FAX Number: (650) 433-3888 — Calendar System: Quarter
URL: www.paloaltou.edu
Established: 1975 — Annual Undergrad Tuition & Fees: N/A
Enrollment: 1,163 — Coed
Affiliation or Control: Independent Non-Profit — IRS Status: 501(c)3
Highest Offering: Doctorate
Accreditation: **WC**, CACREP, CLPSY

01 President .... Dr. Maureen O'CONNOR
108 VP for Institutional Effectiveness .... Dr. James BRECKENRIDGE
05 Interim VP for Academic Affairs .... Dr. Risa DICKSON
10 VP for Business Affairs & CFO .... Dr. June KLEIN

26 VP for External Affairs ... Ms. Camille WATSON
107 VP for Continuing & Prof Studies ... Dr. Patricia ZAPF
32 Dean of Students ... Mr. Thom SHEPARD
101 Dir of Board/President Operations ... Ms. Melanie MORRISON
30 Director of Development ... Ms. Anne FARRAH
21 Assistant Controller ... Ms. Maya RAMAKRISHNAN
15 Sr Human Resource Manager ... Ms. Holly LINDLEY
07 Asst VP for Admissions ... Ms. Alaina DUNN
27 Director of External Affairs ... Ms. Rebecca LEVY
13 Chief Information Officer ... Mr. Fei YING
37 Director of Financial Aid ... Ms. Jessica AYRES
06 Director of Registration ... Ms. Nora MARQUEZ
17 Director of Gronowski Center ... Dr. Sandra MACIAS
09 Director of Institutional Research ... Ms. Jennifer LEHNER
08 Librarian & Dir Academic Tech ... Mr. Scott HINES
113 Billing Supervisor ... Ms. Anna LITSITSA
83 Dept Chair Counseling ... Dr. William SNOW
83 Dept Chair Psychology ... Dr. Kimberly BALSAM

Palo Verde College (A)

One College Drive, Blythe CA 92225-9561
County: Riverside FICE Identification: 001259
Unit ID: 120953
Telephone: (760) 921-5500 Carnegie Class: Assoc/HT-Mix Trad/Non
FAX Number: (760) 921-5590 Calendar System: Semester
URL: www.paloverde.edu
Established: 1947 Annual Undergrad Tuition & Fees (In-District): $1,288
Enrollment: 3,854 Coed
Affiliation or Control: State/Local IRS Status: 501(c)3
Highest Offering: Associate Degree
Accreditation: WJ

01 Superintendent/President ... Dr. Donald WALLACE
05 Int VP Instructional/Student Svcs ... Mr. William SMITH
15 Assoc Vice Pres Human Resources/EEO ... Ms. Cecilia GARCIA
04 Executive Asst to Supt/President ... Ms. Denise HUNT
66 Int Assoc Dean Nursing/Allied Hlth ... Dr. Theresa BECKER
32 Dean Instruction/Student Services ... Mr. Biju RAMAN
08 Librarian ... Ms. June TURNER
07 Director of Admissions and Records ... Ms. Shelley HAMILTON
88 Site Supervisor of Child Dev Center ... Ms. Raquel BURTON
09 Director of Institutional Research ... Mr. Adam HOUSTON
18 Director Facilities and Operations ... Mr. Mario HALE
13 Director of Information Technology ... Mr. Eric EGAN
35 Mgr of Student Life/Development ... Ms. Staci LEE
10 Vice Pres Administrative Svcs ... Ms. Stephanie SLAGAN
106 Assoc Dean Correspondence Educ ... Ms. Maria KEHL
37 Acting Director of Financial Aid ... Ms. German DE LA PENA
101 Exec Asst to Supt/President/Board ... Ms. Carrie MULLION
102 Executive Director Foundation ... Ms. Stephanie SLAGAN
41 Director of Athletics ... Mr. Ryan COPPLE
38 Associate Dean of Counseling ... Ms. Irma GONZALEZ

Palomar College (B)

1140 W Mission Road, San Marcos CA 92069-1487
County: San Diego FICE Identification: 001260
Unit ID: 120971
Telephone: (760) 744-1150 Carnegie Class: Assoc/MT-VT-High Trad
FAX Number: (760) 744-8123 Calendar System: Semester
URL: www.palomar.edu
Established: 1946 Annual Undergrad Tuition & Fees (In-District): $1,344
Enrollment: 21,141 Coed
Affiliation or Control: State/Local IRS Status: 501(c)3
Highest Offering: Associate Degree
Accreditation: WJ, ADNUR, DA, EMT

01 Actg Superintendent/President ... Dr. Jack KAHN
05 Int Asst Supt/Vice Pres Instruction ... Ms. Shayla SIVERT
32 Asst Supt/VP Student Services ... Dr. Vikash LAKHANI
10 Asst Supt/VP Finance/Admn Svcs ... Ms. Ambur BORTH
15 Asst Supt/VP Human Resources ... Mr. David MONTOYA
04 Exec Assistant to the President ... Ms. Debra DOERFLER
79 Dean Languages & Literature ... Dr. Fabienne CHAUDERLOT
81 Dean Math/Science & Engineering ... Ms. Patricia MENCHACA
38 Dean Counseling Services ... Ms. Leslie SALAS
75 Dean Career/Tech/Extended Educ ... Dr. Susan WYCHE
50 Dean Arts/Media/Bus & Comp Sci ... Mr. Justin SMILEY
83 Dean Social/Behavioral Sciences ... Vacant
13 Director Info Systems & Services ... Mr. Michael DAY
84 Director Enrollment Svcs/Admissions ... Dr. Kendyl MAGNUSON
09 Sr Director Institutional Research ... Ms. Michelle BARTON
18 Director of Facilities ... Mr. Chris MILLER
35 Director Student Affairs ... Ms. Sherry TITUS
37 Director Student Financial Aid ... Ms. Adriana LEE
26 Int Dir Comm/Mktg/Public Affairs ... Ms. Julie LANTHIER-BANDY
102 Executive Director for Foundation ... Ms. Stacy RUNGAITIS
19 Chief of Police ... Mr. Chris MOORE
23 Director Health Services ... Dr. Patrick SAVAIANO
41 Director Athletics ... Mr. Daniel LYNDS

Pardee RAND Graduate School of Policy Studies (C)

1776 Main Street, Santa Monica CA 90407-2138
County: Los Angeles FICE Identification: 010441
Unit ID: 121628
Telephone: (310) 393-0411 Carnegie Class: Spec-4-yr-Other
FAX Number: (310) 451-6978 Calendar System: Quarter
URL: www.prgs.edu
Established: 1970 Annual Graduate Tuition & Fees: N/A
Enrollment: 123 Coed
Affiliation or Control: Independent Non-Profit IRS Status: 501(c)3
Highest Offering: Doctorate; No Undergraduates
Accreditation: WC

01 Dean/RAND VP Innovation ... Dr. Susan MARQUIS
05 Associate Dean ... Ms. Rachel SWANGER
06 Registrar ... Mr. Alex DUKE
07 Asst Dean Admissions ... Ms. Stefanie HOWARD
20 Asst Dean for Academic Affairs ... Ms. Angel O'MAHONEY

Pasadena City College (D)

1570 E Colorado Boulevard, Pasadena CA 91106-2041
County: Los Angeles FICE Identification: 001261
Unit ID: 121044
Telephone: (626) 585-7123 Carnegie Class: Assoc/HT-High Trad
FAX Number: (626) 585-7910 Calendar System: Semester
URL: www.pasadena.edu
Established: 1924 Annual Undergrad Tuition & Fees (In-District): $1,212
Enrollment: 25,034 Coed
Affiliation or Control: State/Local IRS Status: 501(c)3
Highest Offering: Associate Degree
Accreditation: WJ, DA, DH, DT, MAC, RAD

01 Superintendent-President ... Dr. Erika A. ENDRIJONAS
05 Vice President Instruction ... Dr. Laura RAMIREZ
10 VP Business & Administrative Svcs ... Ms. Candace JONES
32 Vice President Student Services ... Dr. Cynthia OLIVO
15 Vice President Human Resources ... Mr. Bob BLIZINSKI
09 Exec Dir Inst Research/Planning ... Ms. Crystal KOLLROSS
56 Director Extension ... Ms. Elaine CHAPMAN
121 Dean Counseling & Student Success ... Mr. Armando DURAN
88 Dean Special Services ... Dr. Ketmani KOUANCHAO
84 Dir Admissions/Records/Enrollment ... Ms. Arlene REED
37 Director Financial Aid ... Vacant
13 Associate VP Info Tech Services ... Ms. Candace JONES
26 Special Asst to Pres-Strat Comm/Mkt ... Mr. Alex BOEKELHEIDE
04 Exec Asst to President ... Ms. Armine GALUKYAN
19 Chief Police & Safety Services ... Mr. Steven MATCHAN
35 Dean Student Life ... Ms. Rebecca COBB
96 Director of Purchasing & Contracts ... Mr. George CHIDIAC
101 Secretary of the Institution/Board ... Ms. Mary THOMPSON
102 Executive Director Foundation ... Ms. Bobbi ABRAM
103 Exec Director Workforce Development ... Ms. Salvatrice CUMMO
28 Director Equity ... Vacant
21 Exec Director Fiscal Services ... Ms. Chedva WEINGART
41 Athletic Director ... Mr. Tony BARBONE

Pathways College (E)

320 N. Halstead Street, Pasadena CA 91107
County: Los Angeles Identification: 667396
Telephone: (888) 532-7282 Carnegie Class: Not Classified
FAX Number: N/A Calendar System: Trimester
URL: www.pathwayscollege.org
Established: 2015 Annual Undergrad Tuition & Fees: N/A
Enrollment: N/A Coed
Affiliation or Control: Independent Non-Profit IRS Status: 501(c)3
Highest Offering: Baccalaureate
Accreditation: @WC

01 Chancellor ... John HALL, SR.
05 Chief Academic Officer ... Melinda LESTER

PCI College (F)

17215 Studebaker Rd Ste 310, Cerritos CA 90703
County: Los Angeles FICE Identification: 034793
Unit ID: 439871
Telephone: (562) 916-5055 Carnegie Class: Spec 2-yr-Health
FAX Number: (562) 916-5057 Calendar System: Semester
URL: www.pci-ed.com
Established: 1996 Annual Undergrad Tuition & Fees: N/A
Enrollment: 140 Coed
Affiliation or Control: Proprietary IRS Status: Proprietary
Highest Offering: Baccalaureate
Accreditation: ACCSC

01 CFO ... Ray KHAN

Pepperdine University (G)

24255 Pacific Coast Highway, Malibu CA 90263-0001
County: Los Angeles FICE Identification: 010149
Unit ID: 121150
Telephone: (310) 506-4000 Carnegie Class: DU-Mod
FAX Number: (310) 506-4861 Calendar System: Semester
URL: www.pepperdine.edu
Established: 1937 Annual Undergrad Tuition & Fees: $58,002
Enrollment: 9,554 Coed
Affiliation or Control: Church Of Christ IRS Status: 501(c)3
Highest Offering: Doctorate
Accreditation: WC, CLPSY, DIETD, LAW, MUS

01 President ... Mr. James A. GASH
100 Chief of Staff ... Mr. Daniel DEWALT
45 Sr VP for Strategic Implementation ... Mr. Tim PERRIN
03 Executive Vice President ... Mr. Gary A. HANSON
04 Exec Assistant to the President ... Mrs. Cynthia PAVELL
05 Provost ... Dr. Rick MARRS
10 Chief Financial Officer ... Mr. Greg RAMIREZ
111 VP Advancement ... Ms. Lauren COSENTINO
115 Senior Vice President Investments ... Mr. Jeff PIPPIN
43 General Counsel ... Mr. Marc P. GOODMAN
11 Sr VP of Administration & COO ... Mr. Phil E. PHILLIPS
21 Chief Business Officer ... Ms. Nicolle TAYLOR
13 Chief Information Officer ... Mr. Jonathan SEE
26 Chief Marketing Officer ... Mr. Matt MIDURA
06 Assoc VP & University Registrar ... Mr. Hung V. LE
104 Dean of International Programs ... Ms. Beth LAUX
84 Dean of Admission/Enrollment Mgmt ... Dr. Kristy COLLINS
32 VP of Student Affairs ... Dr. Connie HORTON
08 Dean of Libraries ... Mr. Mark S. ROOSA
61 Dean of the Caruso School of Law ... Mr. Paul CARON
50 Dean Graziadio Business School ... Dr. Deryck VAN RENSBURG
53 Dean of Graduate School Educ/Psych ... Dr. Helen E. WILLIAMS
49 Dean of Seaver College ... Dr. Michael E. FELTNER
80 Dean of School of Public Policy ... Mr. Pete PETERSON
42 University Chaplain ... Ms. Sara BARTON
46 Vice Provost for Research and Strat ... Dr. Lee KATS
108 Assoc Provost Inst Effectiveness ... Dr. Seta KHAJARIAN
29 Vice Chanc Engagement & Mass Appeal ... Mr. Dave JOHNSON
15 Assoc VP Human Resources Officer ... Mr. Sean Mike PHILLIPS
88 Director of Ministry Outreach ... Mr. Michael COPE
39 Director of Housing Operations ... Dr. Robin GORE
88 Managing Dir Center for the Arts ... Ms. Rebecca CARSON
85 Dir Intl Student Services ... Ms. Brooke CUTLER
27 Assoc VP IM Communications ... Mr. Matthew MIDURA
23 Interim Dir Student Health Svcs ... Ms. Rebecca ROLDAN
36 Assoc Dean of Students/Career Ctr ... Mr. Brad D. DUDLEY
41 Director of Athletics ... Dr. Steven POTTS
88 Assoc VP Planning/Opers/Construct ... Mr. Lance BRIDGESMITH
18 Director Facilities Services ... Ms. Carly MISCHKE
86 Dir Government/Regulatory Affairs ... Mr. Ricky ELDRIDGE
37 Dir of Seaver Financial Assistance ... Mrs. Janet LOCKHART
09 Director of Institutional Research ... Ms. Jazmine ZANE
112 Exec Dir Estate and Gift Planning ... Mr. Curt PORTZEL
22 Director Disability Services ... Ms. Sandra HARRISON
116 Senior Assurance Associate ... Ms. Carla ANDERSON
102 Dir Corporate/Foundation Relations ... Ms. Sheila D. KING
28 Assoc VP & Title IX Coordinator ... Ms. LaShonda COLEMAN
44 Director Pepperdine Fund ... Ms. Cynthia WARE
101 Secretary of the Institution/Board ... Mrs. Joan DEMPSTER
96 Purchasing Manager ... Ms. Vanessa HIGHSMITH
07 Director of Admissions ... Vacant
103 Director Career and Coaching ... Ms. Marla PONTRELLI
105 Director Digital Marketing ... Mr. Mauricio ACEVEDO
106 Associate Provost E-learning ... Dr. David SMITH
25 Assistant Provost for Research ... Mrs. Katy CARR
30 Director of Development ... Mrs. Kimberly BARKIS
38 Director Counseling Center ... Dr. Nivla FITZPATRICK

*Peralta Community Colleges District Office (H)

333 E Eighth Street, Oakland CA 94606-2889
County: Alameda FICE Identification: 001265
Unit ID: 121178
Telephone: (510) 466-7200 Carnegie Class: N/A
FAX Number: (510) 835-4078
URL: www.peralta.edu

01 Interim Chancellor ... Dr. Carla WALTER
05 Vice Chancellor of Academic Affairs ... Dr. Siri BROWN
10 Actg VC Finance/Administration ... Mr. Adil AHMED
15 Int Vice Chanc HR/Employee Rels ... Ms. Chanelle WHITTAKER
26 Int Exec Dir Public Info/Comm/Media ... Mr. Mark JOHNSON

*Berkeley City College (I)

2050 Center Street, Berkeley CA 94704-1183
County: Alameda FICE Identification: 022427
Unit ID: 125170
Telephone: (510) 981-2800 Carnegie Class: Assoc/HT-Mix Trad/Non
FAX Number: (510) 841-7333 Calendar System: Semester
URL: www.berkeleycitycollege.edu
Established: 1974 Annual Undergrad Tuition & Fees (In-District): $1,167
Enrollment: 6,097 Coed
Affiliation or Control: State/Local IRS Status: 501(c)3
Highest Offering: Associate Degree
Accreditation: #WJ

02 President ... Dr. Angelica GARCIA
05 Vice President Instruction ... Ms. Kuniko HAY
32 Vice President Student Services ... Dr. Stacey SHEARS
81 Int Dean Math/Sci/Business/AppTech ... Dr. Joya CHAVARIN
49 Dean Liberal Arts/Social Sciences ... Ms. Lisa R. COOK
35 Dean Student Support Services ... Ms. Brenda JOHNSON
10 Director Business Services & Admin ... Ms. Shirley SLAUGHTER
121 Assoc Dean Educational Success ... Mr. Martin DE MUCHA FLORES
27 Public Information Officer ... Dr. Felicia L. BRIDGES
15 Acting Vice Chancellor HR ... Dr. Ronald MCKINLEY
18 Acting Vice Chancellor General Svcs ... Msr. Atheria SMITH
21 Supervisor Business Services ... Mr. John PANG
09 Sr Research Analyst ... Dr. Phoumy SAYAVONG
04 Executive Assistant to President ... Ms. Cynthia REESE
84 Coordinator Enrollment Services ... Ms. Gail PENDLETON
37 Financial Aid Officer ... Ms. Loan NGUYEN

*College of Alameda (A)

555 Ralph Appezzato Memorial Pkwy,
Alameda CA 94501-2109
County: Alameda FICE Identification: 006720
Unit ID: 108667
Telephone: (510) 522-7221 Carnegie Class: Assoc/HT-Mix Trad/Non
FAX Number: (510) 337-0619 Calendar System: Semester
URL: www.alameda.peralta.edu
Established: 1968 Annual Undergrad Tuition & Fees (In-District): $1,167
Enrollment: 5,107 Coed
Affiliation or Control: State/Local IRS Status: 501(c)3
Highest Offering: Associate Degree
Accreditation: #WJ, DA

02 President Dr. Nathaniel JONES, III
05 Actg Vice President of Instruction Dr. Diana BAJRAMI
32 Vice President of Student Svcs Ms. Tina VASCONCELLOS
26 Chief Public Relations Officer Vacant
20 Acting Dean of STEAM Mr. Silvester HENDERSON
88 Dean Special Programs Vacant
84 Dean Enrollment Services Dr. Amy LEE
49 Dean Liberal Studies/Language Arts Ms. Lilia CELHAY
103 Dean Career/Workforce Education Ms. Eva JENNINGS
121 Assoc Dean of Educational Success Ms. Paula ARMSTEAD
10 Dir Business & Administrative Svcs Ms. Chungwai CHUM
07 Admissions & Records Specialist Ms. Marcean BRYANT
35 Director of Campus Life Vacant
09 Director College Research/Planning Ms. Dominique BENAVIDES

*Laney College (B)

900 Fallon Street, Oakland CA 94607-4893
County: Alameda FICE Identification: 001266
Unit ID: 117247
Telephone: (510) 834-5740 Carnegie Class: Assoc/MT-VT-Mix Trad/Non
FAX Number: N/A Calendar System: Semester
URL: laney.edu
Established: 1953 Annual Undergrad Tuition & Fees (In-District): $1,167
Enrollment: 9,225 Coed
Affiliation or Control: State/Local IRS Status: 501(c)3
Highest Offering: Associate Degree
Accreditation: #WJ

02 President Dr. Rudy BESIKOF
05 Vice President of Instruction Dr. Rebecca OPSATA
32 Vice Pres Student Services Vacant
10 Vice Pres Administrative Services Dr. Derek PINTO
75 Dean Career & Technical Educ Ms. Alejandria TOMAS
84 Dean Enrollment Services Dr. Mildred LEWIS
79 Dean Humanities/Social Science Dr. Mark FIELDS
49 Dean Liberal Arts Ms. Elizabeth (Beth) MAHER
81 Dean Mathematics and Science Mr. Angel FUENTES
35 Dean Student Services Ms. Diane T. CHANG
121 Assoc Dean Educational Success Mr. Gary ALBURY
04 Executive Assistant to President Ms. Maisha JAMESON
18 Director of Facilities & Operations Ms. Amy MARSHALL
35 Dir Student Activities/Campus Life Ms. Atiya RASHADA
13 Director IT Mr. Rupinder BHATIA
88 Director Gateway to College Pgm Mr. William R. OCHOA
88 Director of AANAPISI Mr. David LEE
88 Director of BEST Center Vacant
41 Director Athletics Mr. John BEAM
109 Food Services Manager Mr. Neil BURMENKO
08 Head Librarian Ms. Evelyn LORD
37 Director of Financial Aid Ms. Jennifer MA

*Merritt College (C)

12500 Campus Drive, Oakland CA 94619-3196
County: Alameda FICE Identification: 001267
Unit ID: 118772
Telephone: (510) 531-4911 Carnegie Class: Assoc/HVT-Mix Trad/Non
FAX Number: (510) 436-2405 Calendar System: Semester
URL: www.merritt.edu
Established: 1953 Annual Undergrad Tuition & Fees (In-District): $1,167
Enrollment: 6,261 Coed
Affiliation or Control: State/Local IRS Status: 501(c)3
Highest Offering: Associate Degree
Accreditation: #WJ, DIETT, HT, RAD

02 President Dr. David JOHNSON
05 Vice President of Instruction Ms. Denise RICHARDSON
32 Vice President of Student Services Dr. Lilia CHAVEZ
10 VP of Business/Admin Services Mr. Garth KWIECIEN
96 Vice Chancellor of General Services Dr. Sadiq IKHARO
15 Vice Chancellor for Human Resources Ms. Trudy LARGENT
20 Vice Chanc Educational Services Dr. Michael ORKIN
13 Assoc VC of Information Technology Mr. Calvin MADLOCK
25 Dean Special Programs & Grants Dr. Lilia CHAVEZ
26 Exec Dir Marketing/Public Rels/Comm Mr. Jeffrey HEYMAN
08 Library Director Ms. Adoria WILLIAMS
06 Registrar Ms. Susana DE LA TORRE
35 Dir Student Activities/Campus Life Ms. Doris HANKINS
09 Director Research & Planning Mr. Nathan PELLEGRIN
101 Board Clerk Ms. Brenda MARTINEZ
102 Interim Exec Dir Foundation Ms. Kaia BURKETT
18 Facilities Director/Physical Plant Ms. Tara MARRERO
37 Director Financial Aid Svcs Vacant

Pima Medical Institute-Chula Vista (D)

780 Bay Boulevard, Suite 101,
Chula Vista CA 91910-5261
Telephone: (619) 425-3200 Identification: 666272
Accreditation: ABHES, SURTEC

† Branch campus of Pima Medical Institute, Tucson, AZ.

Pitzer College (E)

1050 N Mills Avenue, Claremont CA 91711-6110
County: Los Angeles FICE Identification: 001172
Unit ID: 121257
Telephone: (909) 621-8198 Carnegie Class: Bac-A&S
FAX Number: N/A Calendar System: Semester
URL: www.pitzer.edu
Established: 1963 Annual Undergrad Tuition & Fees: $55,878
Enrollment: 922 Coed
Affiliation or Control: Independent Non-Profit IRS Status: 501(c)3
Highest Offering: Baccalaureate
Accreditation: WC

01 President Dr. Melvin L. OLIVER
05 Vice Pres Acad Affs/Dean of Faculty Dr. Allen OMOTO
100 Chief of Staff Vacant
10 Chief Operating Ofcr/Treasurer Ms. Laura TROENDLE
111 VP Col Advancement/Communications Ms. Kimberly SHINER
07 VP Admissions/Financial Aid Ms. Yvonne BERUMEN
32 Vice Pres Student Affairs Ms. Sandra VASQUEZ
26 VP Strategic Initiatives/Cmty Rels Mr. Jim MARCHANT
30 Assoc Director of Development Ms. Teresa FLORES ROBERTS
20 Associate Dean of Faculty Mr. Phil ZUCKERMAN
20 Associate Dean of Faculty Ms. Susan PHILLIPS
06 Registrar Ms. Eva PETERS
37 Director Financial Aid Ms. Kara MOORE
09 Director of Institutional Research Mr. Marco Antonio CRUZ
15 AVP Human Resources and Payroll Ms. Deanna CABALLERO
18 Asst VP Facilities Ms. Patrice LANGEVIN
21 AVP Finance Ms. Pamela MADER
36 Director Career Services Mr. Brad THARPE
29 Director Alumni/Family Relations Mr. Brandon KYLE
101 Sr Exec Asst/Secretary to the Board Ms. Melanie LACY SORENSON

Platt College (F)

1000 S Fremont Avenue, Bldg A10 S,
Alhambra CA 91803-8845
County: Los Angeles FICE Identification: 030627
Unit ID: 260789
Telephone: (626) 300-5444 Carnegie Class: Spec-4-yr-Other Health
FAX Number: (626) 457-8295 Calendar System: Other
URL: www.plattcollege.edu
Established: 1987 Annual Undergrad Tuition & Fees: $14,354
Enrollment: 717 Coed
Affiliation or Control: Proprietary IRS Status: Proprietary
Highest Offering: Baccalaureate
Accreditation: ACCSC, COARC

01 President Mr. Christopher BECKER
06 Registrar Ms. Cathy WOLFE
07 Director of Admissions Mr. Steven BROYLES

Platt College (G)

3700 Inland Empire Blvd, Ste 400, Ontario CA 91764-4906
Telephone: (909) 941-9410 Identification: 666056
Accreditation: ACCSC, COARC

† Branch campus of Platt College, Ahambra, CA.

Platt College (H)

6465 Sycamore Canyon Blvd, Ste 100,
Riverside CA 92507
Telephone: (951) 572-4300 Identification: 770561
Accreditation: ACCSC

Platt College (I)

6250 El Cajon Boulevard, San Diego CA 92115-3919
County: San Diego FICE Identification: 023043
Unit ID: 121275
Telephone: (619) 265-0107 Carnegie Class: Spec-4-yr-Arts
FAX Number: (619) 265-8655 Calendar System: Other
URL: www.platt.edu
Established: 1980 Annual Undergrad Tuition & Fees: $17,235
Enrollment: 96 Coed
Affiliation or Control: Proprietary IRS Status: Proprietary
Highest Offering: Baccalaureate
Accreditation: ACCSC

00 Chairman Mr. Robert D. LEIKER
01 President Mrs. Meg LEIKER
03 Vice President Mr. Alfred MEDRO
10 Chief Business Officer Ms. Marianne TAXTER
05 Director of Education Mr. Julio FRIZZA-POMPA

Point Loma Nazarene University (J)

3900 Lomaland Drive, San Diego CA 92106-2899
County: San Diego FICE Identification: 001262
Unit ID: 121309
Telephone: (619) 849-2200 Carnegie Class: Masters/L
FAX Number: (619) 849-2579 Calendar System: Semester
URL: www.pointloma.edu
Established: 1902 Annual Undergrad Tuition & Fees: $38,300
Enrollment: 4,616 Coed
Affiliation or Control: Church Of The Nazarene IRS Status: 501(c)3
Highest Offering: Doctorate
Accreditation: WC, ACBSP, #ARCPA, CAATE, DIETD, EMT, MUS, NURSE, SW

01 President Dr. Bob BROWER
05 Provost/Chief Academic Officer Dr. Kerry FULCHER
10 VP Finance & CFO Mr. Joe LALUZERNE
32 VP Student Life & Formation Dr. Mary PAUL
111 Vice President Univ Advancement Ms. Kelly SMITH
13 Vice President University Services Dr. Jeff BOLSTER
15 Assoc VP for Human Resources Ms. Samara TIMMS
58 AVP Grad & Post-Trad Pgm Enrollment Ms. Jamie BROWNLEE
28 AVP Stdnt Dev/Chief Diversity Ofcr Vacant
114 Assoc VP Accounting/Finance Ms. Janet CAPRARIO
84 Assoc VP Enrollment & Retention Dr. Scott SHOEMAKER
20 Vice Prov Academic Administration Dr. Holly IRWIN
108 Vice Prov Assessment & IE Dr. Karen LEE
35 Dean of Students Dr. Jake GILBERTSON
13 Chief Information Officer Mr. Corey FLING
09 Dir Institutional Research Mr. Brent GOODMAN
12 Interim Director of Wesleyan Center Dr. Sam POWELL
18 Director of Campus Facilities Mr. Dan TORO
103 Executive Dir Strengths & Vocation Ms. Rebecca SMITH
88 Exec Dir of Enrollment Mgmt Ms. Jeanne COCHRAN
86 Dir Public Affairs Ms. Jill MONROE
42 Ld Con for Mission Res & Pst Rel Dr. Ron BENEFIEL
88 Director of Community Ministries Ms. Dana HOJSACK
88 Director of Worship Arts Mr. George WILLIAMSON
49 Dean of the Colleges Dr. Jim DAICHENDT
83 Dean College of Social Sciences Vacant
07 Director Undergraduate Admissions Ms. Shannon HUTCHISON-CARAVEO
08 Director of Ryan Library Dr. Denise NELSON
56 Dean Extended Learning Dr. Dave PHILLIPS
06 Registrar Mr. John GUNTHER
88 Director of Records Ms. Cheryl GAUGHAN
26 Assoc Vice Pres for Marketing Ms. Sharon AYALA
121 Assoc Dean Stdnt Success/Wellness Vacant
19 Director of Public Safety Mr. Mark RYAN
29 Director of Alumni Relations Ms. Kendall LUCAS
40 Bookstore Manager Mrs. Anya SELNER TAN
85 Dir Multicultural/Intl Stdnt Svcs Mr. Sam KWAPONG
41 Athletic Director Mr. Ethan HAMILTON
88 Director of Nicholson Commons Mr. Milton KARAHADIAN
104 Director Study Abroad Program Vacant
36 Dir of Career Services Mr. Nick WOLF
106 Dir Online Education/E-learning Vacant
39 Asst Dir Student Housing Ms. Molly PETERSEN
110 Exec Dir Advancement Operations Ms. Christina GARDNER
50 Dean of Business Mr. Dan BOTHE
53 Dean of Education Ms. Deb ERICKSON
101 Secretary of the Board Dr. Joe WATKINS
44 Director Annual/Planned Giving Mr. William BURFITT
37 Director Student Financial Services Ms. Molly PORTER

Pomona College (K)

550 N College Avenue, #206, Claremont CA 91711-6301
County: Los Angeles FICE Identification: 001173
Unit ID: 121345
Telephone: (909) 621-8000 Carnegie Class: Bac-A&S
FAX Number: (909) 621-8403 Calendar System: Semester
URL: www.pomona.edu
Established: 1887 Annual Undergrad Tuition & Fees: $54,774
Enrollment: 1,475 Coed
Affiliation or Control: Independent Non-Profit IRS Status: 501(c)3
Highest Offering: Baccalaureate
Accreditation: WC

01 President Dr. G. Gabrielle STARR
05 Vice President/Dean of College Dr. Robert GAINES
13 Interim Chief Information Officer Ms. Janet RUSSELL
10 Vice President/Treasurer Mr. Robert GOLDBERG
111 VP Institutional Advancement Ms. Maria WATSON
32 Vice President/Dean of Students Ms. Avis HINKSON
07 VP of Admissions & Financial Aid Mr. Seth ALLEN
26 Sr Director News/Strategic Content Mr. Mark KENDALL
100 Chief of Staff Ms. Christine CIAMBRIELLO
06 Registrar Ms. Erin Michelle COLLINS
27 Director Public Relations Vacant
29 Asst VP Alumni & Parent Engagement Ms. Alisa FISHBACH
37 Director Financial Aid Ms. Robin THOMPSON
36 Dir Career Development Ofc Ms. Hazel RAJA
15 Director Human Resources Ms. Brenda RUSHFORTH
41 Athletic Director Ms. Miriam MERRILL
44 Director Annual Giving Ms. Lucy TAKAHASHI
21 Assoc Treasurer/Controller Ms. Mary Lou WOODS
09 Director of Institutional Research Dr. Jennifer RACHFORD
18 Chief Facilities/Physical Plant Mr. Robert ROBINSON
115 Chief Investment Officer Mr. David WALLACE

Presbyterian Theological Seminary in America (A)

15605 Carmenita Road, Santa Fe Springs CA 90670
County: Los Angeles FICE Identification: 041228
Unit ID: 490045
Telephone: (562) 926-1023 Carnegie Class: Spec-4-yr-Faith
FAX Number: (562) 926-1025 Calendar System: Semester
URL: www.ptsa.edu
Established: 1977 Annual Undergrad Tuition & Fees: $7,935
Enrollment: 171 Coed
Affiliation or Control: Presbyterian Church In America IRS Status: 501(c)3
Highest Offering: First Professional Degree
Accreditation: BI, THEOL

01 President .... Dr. Sang Meyng LEE
05 Dean of Academic Affairs/CAO .... Rev. Rubin KIM
10 Chief Financial Officer .... Rev. Myung Chul LEE
32 Dean of Student Affairs .... Vacant
37 Director of Financial Aid .... Mrs. Sunny KIM
08 Librarian .... Ms. Dou Ho IM
21 Managing Treasurer/Accountant .... Mrs. Judy KIM
06 Registrar .... Mrs. Kyu Hae LEE
106 Dir Online Education/E-learning .... Mr. Jang Hoon WOO
13 IT Director .... Mr. Chul Heon JUNG

Presidio Graduate School (B)

649 Mission Street, Suite 500, San Francisco CA 94105
County: San Francisco Identification: 667150
Unit ID: 486433
Telephone: (415) 561-6555 Carnegie Class: Masters/S
FAX Number: (415) 561-6483 Calendar System: Semester
URL: www.presidio.edu
Established: 2003 Annual Graduate Tuition & Fees: N/A
Enrollment: 152 Coed
Affiliation or Control: Independent Non-Profit IRS Status: 501(c)3
Highest Offering: Master's; No Undergraduates
Accreditation: WC

01 President .... Elizabeth MAW
05 Academic Dean/CAO .... Dr. Maggie WINSLOW
10 CFO/Vice Pres of Operations .... Vacant
32 VP Student Affairs/Enrollment/COO .... Dr. Diana ASAAD
07 AVP of Admissions .... Dr. Amanda OPPERMAN

Professional Golfers Career College (C)

26109 Ynez Road, Temecula CA 92591-6013
County: Riverside FICE Identification: 033673
Unit ID: 437750
Telephone: (951) 719-2994 Carnegie Class: Spec 2-yr-Other
FAX Number: (951) 719-1643 Calendar System: Semester
URL: www.golfcollege.edu
Established: 1990 Annual Undergrad Tuition & Fees: $16,844
Enrollment: 86 Coed
Affiliation or Control: Proprietary IRS Status: Proprietary
Highest Offering: Associate Degree
Accreditation: CNCE

01 President .... Dr. Tim SOMERVILLE
10 Chief Financial Officer .... Sandi SOMERVILLE

Providence Christian College (D)

464 East Walnut Street, Pasadena CA 91101
County: Los Angeles FICE Identification: 041539
Unit ID: 455770
Telephone: (866) 323-0233 Carnegie Class: Bac-A&S
FAX Number: (626) 696-4040 Calendar System: Semester
URL: www.providencecc.edu
Established: 2002 Annual Undergrad Tuition & Fees: $33,396
Enrollment: 121 Coed
Affiliation or Control: Non-denominational IRS Status: 501(c)3
Highest Offering: Baccalaureate
Accreditation: WC

01 President .... Vacant
05 Vice Pres Academic Affairs .... Dr. David CORBIN
10 Vice Pres Finance & Operations .... Dawn DIRKSEN
111 Vice Pres Advancement .... Michael KILEDJIAN
84 Vice Pres Enrollment .... Pete HAMSTRA
06 Registrar .... Patty TSAI
29 Alumni Relations Manager .... Sevanna RICHMOND
32 Director Student Life .... Geoff SHAW

*Rancho Santiago Community College District (E)

2323 N. Broadway, Santa Ana CA 92706-1640
County: Orange FICE Identification: 006991
Unit ID: 438665
Telephone: (714) 480-7300 Carnegie Class: N/A
FAX Number: (714) 796-3915
URL: www.rsccd.edu

01 Chancellor .... Mr. Marvin MARTINEZ
10 VC Business & Fiscal Svcs .... Ms. Iris INGRAM
05 Vice Chanc Educational Svcs .... Mr. Enrique PEREZ
15 Vice Chanc Human Resources .... Mr. Cheng Yu HOU
13 Asst Vice Chanc Info Tech Svcs .... Mr. Jesse GONZALEZ
19 Chief District Safety & Security .... Mr. Ralph WEBB
04 Exec Asst to the Chancellor .... Ms. Debra GERARD

*Santa Ana College (F)

1530 W 17th Street, Santa Ana CA 92706-3398
County: Orange FICE Identification: 001284
Unit ID: 121619
Telephone: (714) 564-6000 Carnegie Class: Bac/Assoc-Assoc Dom
FAX Number: (714) 564-6379 Calendar System: Semester
URL: www.sac.edu
Established: 1915 Annual Undergrad Tuition & Fees (In-District): $1,160
Enrollment: 20,118 Coed
Affiliation or Control: State/Local IRS Status: 501(c)3
Highest Offering: Baccalaureate
Accreditation: WJ, ADNUR, OTA

02 Interim President .... Dr. Marilyn FLORES
05 Vice President Academic Affairs .... Dr. Jeffrey N. LAMB
10 Vice Chanc Business Svcs .... Iris I. INGRAM
51 Vice President Continuing Educ .... Dr. James KENNEDY
32 Vice Pres Student Services .... Dr. Vaniethia HUBBARD
11 Vice Pres Administrative Services .... Dr. Bart HOFFMAN
07 Dean of Enrollment Services .... Mark LIANG
06 Interim Registrar .... Hung NGUYEN
35 Interim Assoc Dean Student Dev .... Dr. Brenda ESTRADA
38 Dean Counseling .... Dr. Maria DELA CRUZ
37 Assoc Dean of Financial Aid .... Robert MANSON
111 Exec Director College Advancement .... Christina ROMERO
18 Interim Director Phys Plant/Facil .... Robert WARD
50 Dean Business Division .... Madeline GRANT
41 Dean Kinesiology & Athletics .... Dr. R. Douglas MANNING
57 Dean Fine & Performing Arts .... Dr. Kellori DOWER
79 Dean Humanities/Social Sciences .... Vacant
81 Dean Science/Math/Health Sci .... Dr. Saeid EIDGAHY
103 Dir Career Education/Workforce Dev .... Kimberly MATHEWS
56 Associate Dean EOPS .... Vacant
88 Associate Dean DSPS .... Dr. Veronica OFORLEA
04 Assistant to the President .... Leisa SCHUMACHER
26 Interim Public Information Officer .... Dalilah DAVALOZ
09 Director of College Research .... Vacant
35 Assistant Dean Student Services .... Teresa MERCADO-COTA
35 Dean Student Affairs .... Alicia KRUIZENGA
20 Dean Academic Affairs .... Dr. Fernando ORTIZ
88 Associate Dean Counseling .... Dr. Armando SOTO
41 Athletic Director .... Mary HEGARTY
66 Int Assoc Dean Health Sci/Nursing .... Mary STECKLER
109 Director Auxiliary Services .... Jennie ADAMS
72 Dean Human Svcs & Technology .... Dr. Larisa SERGEYEVA

*Santiago Canyon College (G)

8045 E Chapman Avenue, Orange CA 92869-4512
County: Orange FICE Identification: 036957
Unit ID: 399212
Telephone: (714) 628-4900 Carnegie Class: Assoc/HT-High Trad
FAX Number: (714) 628-4723 Calendar System: Semester
URL: www.sccollege.edu
Established: 1997 Annual Undergrad Tuition & Fees (In-District): $1,156
Enrollment: 9,003 Coed
Affiliation or Control: State/Local IRS Status: 501(c)3
Highest Offering: Associate Degree
Accreditation: WJ

02 President .... Dr. Pamela RALSTON
04 Assistant to the President .... Ms. Esther ODEGARD
32 Int Vice President Student Services .... Mr. Jose VARGAS
05 Int Vice President Academic Affairs .... Mr. Martin STRINGER
51 Vice President Continuing Educ .... Dr. James KENNEDY
10 Vice Pres Administrative Services .... Dr. Arleen SATELE
38 Dean Counseling .... Dr. Jennifer COTO
41 Int Dean Math & Sci/Athletic Dir .... Dr. Denise BAILEY
79 Int Dean Arts/Humanities/Social Sci .... Dr. Joanne ARMSTRONG
50 Dean Business/Career Educ .... Ms. Elizabeth ARTEAGA
108 Dean Institutional Effectiveness .... Mr. Aaron VOELCKER
20 Int Dean Instruct/Student Services .... Mr. Joseph ALONZO
84 Int Dean Enrollment Support Svcs .... Dr. Loretta JORDAN
20 Assistant Dean DSPS .... Ms. Starr AVEDESIAN
07 Asst Dean of Admissions & Records .... Mr. Tuyen NGUYEN
37 Asst Dean Fin Aid/Scholarships .... Ms. Sheena TRAN
18 Facilities Manager .... Mr. Chuck WALES

Reach Institute for School Leadership (H)

1221 Preservation Park Way, Ste 100, Oakland CA 94612
County: Alameda Identification: 667313
Telephone: (510) 501-5075 Carnegie Class: Not Classified
FAX Number: (510) 868-2215 Calendar System: Semester
URL: www.reachinst.org
Established: 2007 Annual Undergrad Tuition & Fees: N/A
Enrollment: N/A Coed
Affiliation or Control: Independent Non-Profit IRS Status: 501(c)3
Highest Offering: Master's
Accreditation: WC

01 Executive Director .... Ben SANDERS
11 Associate Director .... Jonna JUSTINIANO
05 Chief Academic Officer .... Liz BAHAN
32 Induction Student Services Mgr .... Ellen MACDONALD

Redwoods Community College District (I)

7351 Tompkins Hill Road, Eureka CA 95501-9300
County: Humboldt FICE Identification: 001185
Unit ID: 121707
Telephone: (707) 476-4100 Carnegie Class: Assoc/HVT-High Trad
FAX Number: (707) 476-4400 Calendar System: Semester
URL: https://www.redwoods.edu/
Established: 1964 Annual Undergrad Tuition & Fees (In-District): $1,147
Enrollment: 3,891 Coed
Affiliation or Control: State/Local IRS Status: 501(c)3
Highest Offering: Associate Degree
Accreditation: WJ, DA, EMT

01 President/Superintendent .... Dr. Keith FLAMER
05 VP of Instruction .... Ms. Kerry MAYER
04 Exec Assistant to the President .... Ms. Cynthia PETRUSHA
10 VP Administrative Services .... Ms. Julia MORRISON
32 Int VP Student Services .... Mr. Clinton SLAUGHTER
103 Director Workforce & Community Educ .... Ms. Pru RATLIFF
12 Director Del Norte Campus .... Mr. Rory JOHNSON
84 Dean of Enrollment Services .... Ms. Rianne CONNOR
88 Director of Special Programs .... Dr. Kintay JOHNSON
22 Director Disabled Student Pgm Svcs .... Vacant
18 Director Maintenance & Operations .... Mr. Steve MCKENZIE
102 Exec Dir of Foundation/Col Advance .... Mr. Marty COELHO
08 Director Library Svcs/Acad Support .... Vacant
19 Director of Public Safety .... Ms. Kristy SEHER
88 Director Administration of Justice .... Mr. Mike PERKINS
41 Director of PE & Athletics .... Mr. Bob BROWN
09 Director Institutional Research .... Mr. Paul CHOWN
26 Career Outreach & Marketing Manager .... Ms. Molly BLAKEMORE

Regan Career Institute (J)

11350 Valley Blvd, El Monte CA 91731
County: Los Angeles FICE Identification: 042554
Unit ID: 490197
Telephone: (626) 455-0312 Carnegie Class: Not Classified
FAX Number: (626) 455-0316 Calendar System: Other
URL: www.rci.edu
Established: 2004 Annual Undergrad Tuition & Fees: N/A
Enrollment: 41 Coed
Affiliation or Control: Proprietary IRS Status: Proprietary
Highest Offering: Associate Degree
Accreditation: ABHES

01 CEO .... Regan YU
11 Managing Director .... Julian LEE

Reiss-Davis Graduate Center (K)

3200 Motor Avenue, Los Angeles CA 90034
County: Los Angeles Identification: 667332
Telephone: (310) 204-1666 Carnegie Class: Not Classified
FAX Number: N/A Calendar System: Other
URL: www.reissdavis.org
Established: 1976 Annual Graduate Tuition & Fees: N/A
Enrollment: N/A Coed
Affiliation or Control: Independent Non-Profit IRS Status: 501(c)3
Highest Offering: Doctorate; No Undergraduates
Accreditation: WC

01 Chancellor & Director .... Dr. James A. INCORVAIA
11 Director of Operations .... Lourdes BROWN
05 Provost .... Dr. Halyna KORNUTA
09 Institutional Research Analyst .... Dr. Karen JAMES
06 Registrar .... Mila JOVICIC
20 Academic Dean .... Dr. Jens SCHMIDT

Rio Hondo College (L)

3600 Workman Mill Road, Whittier CA 90601-1699
County: Los Angeles FICE Identification: 001269
Unit ID: 121886
Telephone: (562) 692-0921 Carnegie Class: Bac/Assoc-Assoc Dom
FAX Number: (562) 699-7386 Calendar System: Semester
URL: www.riohondo.edu
Established: 1960 Annual Undergrad Tuition & Fees (In-District): $1,360
Enrollment: 15,692 Coed
Affiliation or Control: State/Local IRS Status: 501(c)3
Highest Offering: Baccalaureate
Accreditation: WJ, NAIT

01 Interim Superintendent/President .... Ms. Teresa DREYFUSS
05 Vice Pres Academic Svcs .... Dr. Don MILLER
10 Vice President Finance/Business .... Mr. Stephen KIBUI
32 Vice President Student Services .... Dr. Earick DIXON-PETERS
86 Dir Govt & Community Relations .... Dr. Russell CASTANEDA-CALLEROS
15 Int Exec Director Human Resources .... Ms. Cynthia NUNEZ
26 Dir Marketing & Communications .... Ms. Ruthie RETANA
35 Dir Student Life & Leadership .... Ms. Shaina PHILLIPS
06 Dir Admin & Records/Registrar .... Ms. Leigh UNGER
38 Dean Counseling .... Ms. Lisa CHAVEZ
102 Int Exec Dir RHC Foundation .... Mr. Henry GEE
37 Dir Financial Aid & Veteran Svcs .... Mr. Donald GORDON

18 Director of Facilities .... Mr. Mario GASPAR
96 Director of Purchasing .... Mr. Felix G. SARAO
04 Admin Assistant to President .... Ms. Renee D. GALLEGOS
09 Dean Inst Research & Plng .... Dr. Caroline DURDELLA
20 Dean Educational Centers .... Ms. Yolanda EMERSON
41 Athletic Director .... Ms. Yolanda EMERSON
50 Dean Business .... Ms. Gita RUNKLE

*Riverside Community College District (A)

3801 Market Street, Riverside CA 92501
County: Riverside Identification: 667039
Telephone: (951) 222-8000 Carnegie Class: N/A
FAX Number: (951) 682-5339
URL: www.rccd.edu

01 Chancellor .... Dr. Wolde-Ab ISAAC
05 Int VC Educ Svcs/Strategic Planning .... Dr. Jeannie KIM
10 VC Business & Financial Svcs .... Mr. Aaron BROWN
15 Int VC Diversity & Human Resources .... Ms. Trinda BEST
111 VC Institutional Advancement .... Ms. Rebeccah GOLDWARE
12 President Moreno Valley College .... Dr. Robin STEINBACK
12 President Norco College .... Dr. Monica GREEN
12 President Riverside City College .... Dr. Gregory ANDERSON

*Moreno Valley College (B)

16130 Lasselle Street, Moreno Valley CA 92551
County: Riverside FICE Identification: 041735
Unit ID: 460394
Telephone: (951) 571-6100 Carnegie Class: Assoc/HT-Mix Trad/Non
FAX Number: N/A Calendar System: Semester
URL: www.mvc.edu
Established: 2010 Annual Undergrad Tuition & Fees (In-District): $1,420
Enrollment: 9,158 Coed
Affiliation or Control: State/Local IRS Status: 501(c)3
Highest Offering: Associate Degree
Accreditation: WJ, DA, DH, EMT

02 President .... Dr. Robin L. STEINBACK
05 Vice Pres Academic Affairs .... Mr. Carlos LOPEZ
10 Int Vice Pres Business Services .... Mr. Majd ASKAR
32 Vice Pres of Student Services .... Mr. Christopher SWEETEN
20 Dean of Instruction .... Mrs. Anna Marie AMEZQUITA
121 Int Assoc Dean Academic Support .... Mr. Tom VITZELIO
84 Director Enrollment Services .... Ms. Jamie CLIFTON
37 Director Student Financial Services .... Ms. Sandra MARTINEZ
18 Director of Facilities .... Mr. Ron KIRKPATRICK
35 Interim Dean Student Services .... Mr. Chris BASS
38 Dean Student Svcs & Counseling .... Dr. Michael Paul WONG
22 Dean Grants/Stdnt Equity Initiative .... Dr. Andrew SANCHEZ
89 Director First Year Experience .... Mr. Ed ALVAREZ
13 Manager Tech Support Services .... Mr. Julio CUZ
23 Director Health Services .... Ms. Tracy BENNETT
25 Dean Grants & Business Services .... Mrs. Mary Ann DOHERTY
88 Dean of Instruction Public Safety .... Mr. Phillip RAWLINGS
75 Dean CTE .... Mrs. Melody GRAVEEN
81 Director STEM Innovation .... Mr. Donnell LAYNE
88 Director TRIO Programs .... Mrs. Micki GRAYSON
109 Assistant Manager Food Services .... Ms. Julie HLEBASKO
28 Director Disability Support Svcs .... Dr. Lawanda HALL
88 Asst Dir Student Financial Services .... Mr. Carlos PONCE
88 Makerspace Project Supervisor .... Mr. Jason KENNEDY
88 Asst Director Upward Bound .... Ms. Angel ORTA-PEREZ
04 Executive Admin Asst to the Pres .... Ms. Eden ANDOM
108 Dean Institutional Effectiveness .... Mr. Jacob KEVARI
88 Early Childhood Educ Manager .... Mrs. Sandra RIVAS
88 Apprenticeship Director .... Mrs. Jennifer MCDANIEL
88 Director Middle College High School .... Mr. Julio GONZALEZ

*Norco College (C)

2001 Third Street, Norco CA 92860
County: Riverside FICE Identification: 041761
Unit ID: 460464
Telephone: (951) 372-7000 Carnegie Class: Assoc/HT-Mix Trad/Non
FAX Number: N/A Calendar System: Semester
URL: www.norcocollege.edu
Established: 2010 Annual Undergrad Tuition & Fees (In-District): $1,420
Enrollment: 10,261 Coed
Affiliation or Control: State/Local IRS Status: 501(c)3
Highest Offering: Associate Degree
Accreditation: WJ

02 President .... Dr. Monica GREEN
05 Vice Pres Academic Affairs .... Dr. Samuel LEE
32 Vice Pres Student Services .... Dr. Kaneesha TARRANT
10 Vice Pres Business Services .... Dr. Michael COLLINS
45 Vice Pres Planning and Development .... Dr. Kevin FLEMING
04 Executive Asst to President .... Ms. Denise TERRAZAS
84 Dean Enrollment Services .... Mr. Mark DEASIS
09 Dean Institutional Effectiveness .... Dr. Greg AYCOCK
13 Dean Technology/Learning Resources .... Mr. Damon NANCE
18 Director Facilities .... Mr. Steven MARSHALL
25 Dean Grants/Stdnt Equity Initiative .... Dr. Gustavo OCEGUERA
37 Director Student Financial Services .... Dr. Maria GONZALEZ
20 Dean Instruction .... Dr. Jason PARKS
20 Interim Dean Instruction .... Dr. Melissa BADER

*Riverside City College (D)

4800 Magnolia Avenue, Riverside CA 92506
County: Riverside FICE Identification: 001270
Unit ID: 121901
Telephone: (951) 222-8000 Carnegie Class: Assoc/HT-High Trad
FAX Number: (951) 222-8036 Calendar System: Semester
URL: www.rcc.edu
Established: 1916 Annual Undergrad Tuition & Fees (In-District): $1,420
Enrollment: 20,080 Coed
Affiliation or Control: State/Local IRS Status: 501(c)3
Highest Offering: Associate Degree
Accreditation: WJ, ACBSP, ADNUR

02 President .... Dr. Gregory ANDERSON
05 Vice Pres Academic Affairs .... Dr. Carol FARRAR
10 VP Business Services .... Dr. Raymond WEST
32 Vice President Student Services .... Dr. FeRita CARTER
66 Dean School of Nursing .... Dr. Tammy VANT HUL
83 Dean Instruction Hum/Soc Sci .... Dr. Kristi WOODS
04 Exec Asst to the President .... Ms. Heidi GONSIER
75 Interim VP Planning & Dev .... Ms. Kristine DIMEMMO
121 Director Academic Support .... Ms. Inez MOORE
84 Dean Enrollment Services .... Ms. Kyla O'CONNOR
35 Dean Student Services .... Dr. Thomas CRUZ-SOTO
41 Director Athletics .... Mr. James WOOLDRIDGE
23 Director Health Services .... Ms. Renee MARTIN THORNTON
19 Sergeant Safety & Police .... Mr. Robert KLEVENO

Sacramento Ultrasound Institute (E)

2233 Watt Avenue #150, Sacramento CA 95825
County: Sacramento Identification: 667264
Unit ID: 490160
Telephone: (916) 877-7977 Carnegie Class: Not Classified
FAX Number: (916) 481-4032 Calendar System: Other
URL: www.sui.edu
Established: 2002 Annual Undergrad Tuition & Fees: N/A
Enrollment: 28 Coed
Affiliation or Control: Proprietary IRS Status: Proprietary
Highest Offering: Associate Degree
Accreditation: ABHES

01 President/CEO .... Mrs. Sima DERMISHYAN

SAE Expression College (F)

6601 Shellmound Street, Emeryville CA 94608-1021
County: Alameda FICE Identification: 039733
Unit ID: 447458
Telephone: (510) 654-2934 Carnegie Class: Spec-4-yr-Arts
FAX Number: (510) 658-3414 Calendar System: Semester
URL: www.sae.edu
Established: 1999 Annual Undergrad Tuition & Fees: $23,399
Enrollment: 182 Coed
Affiliation or Control: Proprietary IRS Status: Proprietary
Highest Offering: Baccalaureate
Accreditation: ACCSC

05 Director of Education .... Mr. Chris COLATOS
07 Admissions Manager .... Ms. Miok KIM

Saint John's Seminary (G)

5012 Seminary Road, Camarillo CA 93012-2500
County: Ventura FICE Identification: 001299
Unit ID: 123855
Telephone: (805) 482-2755 Carnegie Class: Spec-4-yr-Faith
FAX Number: (805) 482-3470 Calendar System: Semester
URL: www.stjohnsem.edu
Established: 1939 Annual Graduate Tuition & Fees: N/A
Enrollment: N/A Male
Affiliation or Control: Roman Catholic IRS Status: 501(c)3
Highest Offering: Master's; No Undergraduates
Accreditation: WC, THEOL

01 Rector/President .... Rev. Marco A. DURAZO
03 Executive Vice President .... Rev. Slawomir SZKREDKA
05 Academic Dean .... Rev. John O'BRIEN
07 Director of Admissions .... Rev. Thinh PHAM
06 Registrar .... Mr. Brian CAMPOS
04 Administrative Asst to President .... Ms. Maria GAETA
10 Director of Finance .... Mr. Michael COLLINS
15 Director Personnel Services .... Ms. Mary BISSINGER
18 Chief Facilities/Physical Plant .... Mr. Greg JULIUS
30 Chief Development/Advancement .... Ms. Linda CHABOLLA
32 Chief Student Affairs/Student Life .... Rev. Raymond MARQUEZ
96 Director of Purchasing .... Ms. Delia GALICIA
08 Chief Library Officer .... Dr. Victoria BRENNAN

St. Luke University (H)

1460 E. Holt Ave., Suite 72, Pomona CA 91767
County: Los Angeles Identification: 667299
Telephone: (909) 623-0302 Carnegie Class: Not Classified
FAX Number: (909) 623-0480 Calendar System: Semester
URL: www.sluedu.us
Established: 2004 Annual Undergrad Tuition & Fees: N/A
Enrollment: N/A Coed
Affiliation or Control: Independent Non-Profit IRS Status: 501(c)3
Highest Offering: Doctorate
Accreditation: TRACS

01 Founder/President .... Rev. Young D. KIM
05 Chief Academic Officer .... Dr. Kyung Hwan KIM
10 Chief Financial Officer .... Mr. David KIM
11 Director of Administration .... Ms. Jung KIM
32 Director Student Affairs .... Rev. Taehoon LEE
06 Registrar .... Kun KWAK
08 Librarian .... Ricky STROBEL

Saint Mary's College of California (I)

1928 Saint Mary's Road, Moraga CA 94556-2744
County: Contra Costa FICE Identification: 001302
Unit ID: 123554
Telephone: (925) 631-4000 Carnegie Class: Masters/L
FAX Number: (925) 376-8497 Calendar System: 4/1/4
URL: www.stmarys-ca.edu
Established: 1863 Annual Undergrad Tuition & Fees: $50,660
Enrollment: 3,439 Coed
Affiliation or Control: Roman Catholic IRS Status: 501(c)3
Highest Offering: Doctorate
Accreditation: WC

01 President .... Mr. Richard G. PLUMB
10 VP for Finance & Administration .... Ms. Susan H. COLLINS
05 Interim Provost/SVP Acad Affairs .... Dr. Corey COOK
20 VP Academic Programs/Planning .... Dr. Corey COOK
20 Interim VP Student Academics .... Dr. Aeleah SOINE
88 Interim Dean of Core .... Dr. Steve MILLER
111 VP for Advancement .... Mr. Patrick CAREW
32 Vice President for Student Life .... Dr. Anthony GARRISON
26 Asst VP College Communication .... Vacant
88 Vice President for Mission .... Dr. Frances SWEENEY
84 Vice Pres Enrollment/Communications .... Dr. Michael BESEDA
20 Associate Prov Acad Affairs/CDO .... Dr. Kathy LITTLES
43 General Counsel .... Mr. Larry NUTI
53 Dean School of Education .... Dr. Carol Ann GITTENS
81 Dean School of Science .... Dr. Roy WENSLEY
49 Dean School Liberal Arts .... Dr. Sheila HUGHES
35 Dean of Students .... Dr. Evette CASTILLO CLARK
08 Dean Library & Academic Resources .... Ms. Lauren MACDONALD
42 Director Mission & Ministry .... Ms. Karin MCCLELLAND
15 Associate VP Human Resources .... Ms. Laurie PANIAN
29 Sr Director of Alumni Engagement .... Ms. Courtney LOHMANN
50 Dean School of Bus Admin/Economics .... Dr. Elizabeth DAVIS
06 Registrar .... Ms. Tracey DONALDSON
35 Associate Dean of Students .... Mr. Jim SCIUTO
37 Director of Financial Aid .... Vacant
88 Director of Kinesiology .... Dr. Claire WILLIAMS
57 Director MFA in Creative Writing .... Dr. Matthew ZAPRUDER
102 Dir Corporate & Foundation Rels .... Mr. Bill OLDS
13 Chief Technology Officer .... Mr. Francisco CHAVEZ
19 Director of Public Safety .... Mr. Hampton CANTRELL
38 Director of Counseling Center .... Ms. Dai L. TO
41 VP for Intercollegiate Athletics .... Mr. Michael J. MATOSO
88 Museum Administrator .... Mr. John SCHNEIDER
88 Director of January Term Program .... Dr. Aaron SACHOWITZ
18 Director of Facilities .... Mr. Michael VIOLA
88 Director of Project Management .... Ms. Sarah SPERON
46 Director of Office of Research .... Ms. Elizabeth GALLAGHER
36 Dir of Career Devel Center .... Ms. Beverly MCLEAN
23 Medical Director Health & Wellness .... Ms. Rachel SNOWDEN
86 Director Community & Govt Relations .... Vacant
94 Director Women's Resource Ctr .... Ms. Sharon SOBOTTA
88 Director of CILSA .... Dr. Jennifer PIGZA
88 Assistant Director of CILSA .... Vacant
21 Controller .... Ms. Jeanne DEMATTEO
104 Director Ctr International Programs .... Vacant
121 Dir Student Engage & Academic Svcs .... Mr. Michael HOFFSHIRE
09 Director of Institutional Research .... Ms. Carlissa JACKSON
89 Dir New Student/Family Programs .... Ms. Jennifer HERZOG
96 Purchasing/Buyer .... Mr. Joe ROSA
39 Director Student Housing .... Mr. Marcus WEEMES
04 Executive Asst to President .... Dr. David FORD
07 Dean of Admissions .... Ms. Sherie GILMORE-CLEVELAND

Saint Patrick's Seminary & University (J)

320 Middlefield Road, Menlo Park CA 94025-3596
County: San Mateo FICE Identification: 010074
Telephone: (650) 325-5621 Carnegie Class: Not Classified
FAX Number: (650) 323-5447 Calendar System: Semester
URL: www.stpsu.edu
Established: 1898 Annual Undergrad Tuition & Fees: N/A
Enrollment: N/A Male
Affiliation or Control: Roman Catholic IRS Status: 501(c)3
Highest Offering: Master's
Accreditation: WC, THEOL

01 Int President-Rector/Vice Chanc .... Fr. Mark DOHERTY
03 Vice Rector .... Rev. Anthony STOEPPEL
05 Academic Dean .... Dr. Anthony LILLES
10 Director of Operations .... Mr. Richard DIZON
08 Library Director .... Mr. Matthew HOROWITZ
06 Registrar .... Mr. Manvinder (Vinay) SHAHI
07 Director of Admissions .... Ms. Grace LAXAMANA
15 Human Resources Assistant .... Ms. Maryan ALVAREZ

Saint Photios Orthodox Theological Seminary (A)

510 Collier Way, Etna CA 96027-9578

County: Siskiyou Identification: 667366
Telephone: (530) 467-3544 Carnegie Class: Not Classified
FAX Number: (530) 638-4456 Calendar System: Semester
URL: www.spots.edu
Established: 2015 Annual Undergrad Tuition & Fees: N/A
Enrollment: N/A Coed
Affiliation or Control: Independent Non-Profit IRS Status: 501(c)3
Highest Offering: Master's
Accreditation: BI

01 Rector .... M Rev. Bishop AUXENTIOS
05 Dean .... V Rev. Archimandrite PATAPIOS
06 Registrar .... Ms. Gabrielle ASGARIAN
26 Communications & Development Dir .... Mr. Alexei BUSHUNOW
08 Librarian .... Ms. Esther SCHENONE
10 Treasurer .... Schemamonk CHRYSOSTOMOS
32 Director of Student Services .... Schemanun KYPRIANE
13 Information Technology Director .... Schemamonk VLASIE
42 Director of Spiritual Life .... V Rev. Archimandrite GREGORY

The Salvation Army College for Officer Training at Crestmont (B)

30840 Hawthorne Boulevard,
Rancho Palos Verdes CA 90275-5301

County: Los Angeles FICE Identification: 036954
Telephone: (310) 265-6132 Carnegie Class: Not Classified
FAX Number: N/A Calendar System: Quarter
URL: www.crestmont.edu
Established: 1878 Annual Undergrad Tuition & Fees: N/A
Enrollment: N/A Coed
Affiliation or Control: Other IRS Status: 501(c)3
Highest Offering: Associate Degree
Accreditation: WJ

01 Training Principal .... Major Nigel CROSS
03 Assistant Training Principal .... Major Amy REARDON
05 Director of Education .... Major Stacy CROSS
10 Director of Business Administration .... Major Premek KRAMERIUS
04 Exec Secretary to Trng Principal .... Ms. Patricia EVANS
09 Director of Institutional Research .... Dr. Duncan SUTTON
15 Director of Personnel .... Major Charity KRAMERIUS

Samuel Merritt University (C)

3100 Telegraph Avenue, Oakland CA 94609

County: Alameda FICE Identification: 007012
Unit ID: 122296
Telephone: (800) 607-6377 Carnegie Class: Spec-4-yr-Other Health
FAX Number: (510) 869-6525 Calendar System: Semester
URL: www.samuelmerritt.edu
Established: 1909 Annual Undergrad Tuition & Fees: N/A
Enrollment: 2,050 Coed
Affiliation or Control: Independent Non-Profit IRS Status: 501(c)3
Highest Offering: Doctorate
Accreditation: WC, ANEST, ARCPA, NURSE, OT, POD, PTA

01 President .... Dr. Ching-Hua WANG
05 Academic Vice President/Provost .... Dr. Fred BALDINI
10 Vice Pres Finance/Admin/CFO .... Mr. Gregory GINGRAS
32 Acting Vice Pres of Student Affairs .... Mr. Timothy CRANFORD
111 Vice Pres Advancement/Communication .... Mr. Al FRISONE
20 Asst Academic Vice President .... Dr. Celeste VILLANUEVA
20 Asst Academic Vice President .... Dr. Michael NEGRETE
04 Assistant to the President .... Ms. Carrie ARNETT
66 Dean & Professor of Nursing .... Dr. Lorna KENDRICK
88 Chair Dept Physical Therapy .... Dr. Nicole CHRISTENSEN
88 Chair Dept Occupational Therapy .... Dr. Kate HAYNER
88 Chair ABSN Program .... Ms. Marianne BIANGONE
88 Chair Physician Assistant Program .... Dr. Michael DEROSA
07 Dean Admission .... Mr. Timothy CRANFORD
15 Exec Director Human Resources .... Ms. Eva HILLIARD
26 Director of Communications .... Mr. Jim MUYO
09 Director Institutional Research .... Ms. Nandini DASGUPTA
06 Registrar .... Ms. Anne SCHER
08 Library Director .... Ms. Hai-Thom SOTA
37 Director Financial Aid .... Mr. Tyler PRUETT
88 Chair Family Nurse Practitioner Pgm .... Ms. Rhonda RAMIREZ
18 Facilities Manager .... Mr. Timothy PARKER
35 Asst Director Student Services .... Ms. Kathryn WARD
12 Site Manager Sacramento .... Ms. Marianne BIANGONE
13 Dir of Information Technology Svcs .... Mr. Marcus WALTON
100 Chief of Staff .... Ms. Emily PRIETO-TSEREGOUNIS
102 Exec Dir Corporate/Foundation Rels .... Ms. Cyndi WEINGARD
108 Director Institutional Assessment .... Ms. Leslie WASSON
19 Univ Safety & Security Specialist .... Mr. Trevor FLANARY
44 Director Annual Giving .... Ms. Jenna INGALLS

*San Bernardino Community College District (D)

550 E Hospitality Lane, Suite 200,
San Bernardino CA 92408

County: San Bernardino Identification: 667040
Telephone: (909) 388-6900 Carnegie Class: N/A
FAX Number: (909) 387-1102
URL: www.sbccd.org

01 Interim Chancellor .... Jose TORRES
10 Int Vice Chanc Business/Fiscal Svcs .... James BUYSSE
15 Vice Chanc Human Resources .... Kristina HANNON
111 Assoc VC Economic Development .... Richard GALOPE
13 Chief Technology Officer .... Luke BIXLER
32 Dean Student Svcs/Development .... Joe CABRALES

*Crafton Hills College (E)

11711 Sand Canyon Road, Yucaipa CA 92399-1799

County: San Bernardino FICE Identification: 009272
Unit ID: 113111
Telephone: (909) 794-2161 Carnegie Class: Assoc/MT-VT-High Trad
FAX Number: (909) 794-0423 Calendar System: Semester
URL: www.craftonhills.edu
Established: 1972 Annual Undergrad Tuition & Fees (In-District): $1,178
Enrollment: 6,012 Coed
Affiliation or Control: State/Local IRS Status: 501(c)3
Highest Offering: Associate Degree
Accreditation: WJ, COARC, EMT

02 President .... Dr. Kevin HORAN
05 Vice Pres of Instruction .... Dr. Keith WURTZ
11 Vice President Administrative Svcs .... Mr. Mike STRONG
32 Vice President Student Services .... Dr. Delmy MONTENEGRO-SPENCER
35 Dean Stdnt Svcs/Stdnt Development .... Mr. Joe CABRALES
83 Dean Social/Info/Natural Science .... Dr. Van MUSE
49 Dean Letters/Arts/Math .... Dr. Kay WEISS
36 Dean Career Educ & Human Devel .... Mr. Daniel WORD
38 Dean Student Services/Counseling .... Mr. Mauro PENA
09 Dean Inst Effect/Research/Planning .... Dr. Giovanni SOSA
111 Director Institutional Advancement .... Ms. Michelle RIGGS
124 Director EOPS/CARE .... Dr. Rejoice CHAVIRA
37 Director Financial Aid .... Mr. John W. MUSKAVITCH
35 Director Student Life .... Dr. Ericka PADDOCK
18 Director Facilities .... Mr. Larry COOK
13 Director Technology Services .... Ms. Melissa OSHMAN
07 Director Admissions & Records .... Mr. Larry AYCOCK
04 Executive Asst to President .... Mrs. Cyndie ST. JEAN

*San Bernardino Valley College (F)

701 S Mt. Vernon Avenue,
San Bernardino CA 92410-2798

County: San Bernardino FICE Identification: 001272
Unit ID: 123527
Telephone: (909) 384-4400 Carnegie Class: Assoc/MT-VT-High Trad
FAX Number: N/A Calendar System: Semester
URL: www.valleycollege.edu
Established: 1926 Annual Undergrad Tuition & Fees (In-District): $1,328
Enrollment: 12,206 Coed
Affiliation or Control: State/Local IRS Status: 501(c)3
Highest Offering: Associate Degree
Accreditation: WJ, ADNUR

02 President .... Ms. Diana Z. RODRIGUEZ
11 VP Administrative Services .... Mr. Scott STARK
05 VP Instruction .... Dr. Dina HUMBLE
32 VP Student Services .... Dr. Scott THAYER
121 Dean Acad Success & Learning Svcs .... Ms. Patricia QUACH
72 Dn Applied Tech/Trans/Cul Arts .... Ms. Vanessa THOMAS
79 Dean Arts & Humanities .... Ms. Leticia HECTOR
88 Dean Counseling/Matriculation .... Mr. Marco COTA
50 Dean Math/Bus/Computer Tech .... Dr. Stephanie LEWIS
09 Int Dean Research/Plng/Inst Effect .... Dr. Joanna OXENDINE
81 Interim Dean of Science .... Dr. John STANSKAS
83 Dean SS/Human Development & PE .... Dr. Wallace JOHNSON
22 Dean Student Equity & Success .... Ms. Carmen RODRIGUEZ
66 Int Assoc Dean Hlth Sci/Div Nursing .... Ms. Yolanda SIMENTAL
07 Director Admissions/Records .... Ms. April DALE-CARTER
68 Director Athletics .... Mr. Dave RUBIO
88 Director Child Development .... Mr. Mark MERJIL
30 Int Director Development .... Mr. Michael LAYNE
28 Director DSP&S .... Mr. Larry BRUNSON, JR.
124 Director EOP&S/CARE .... Ms. Joanne HINOJOSA
18 Director Facilities M&O .... Mr. Robert JENKINS
37 Director Financial Aid .... Mr. Sam TREJO
89 Director First Year Experience .... Ms. Sharaf WILLIAMS
25 Dir Grant Development/Mgmt .... Vacant
08 Dir Library/Learning Support Svcs .... Mr. Ron HASTINGS
26 Director Marketing Creative Svcs/PA .... Mr. Paul BRATULIN
88 Director Police Academies .... Mr. Paul DENNIS
35 Director Student Life .... Dr. Raymond CARLOS
13 Director Campus Technology Services .... Mr. Rick HRDLICKA
103 Mgr CalWORKS/Workforce Dev .... Ms. Shalita TILLMAN
51 AEBG Administrator .... Dr. Emma DIAZ
88 Supervisor Custodial .... Mr. Albert CAMACHO
88 Supervisor Food Services .... Mr. Erik MORDEN
88 Supervisor Maintenance & Grounds .... Mr. Kevin GRISHOW

San Diego Christian College (G)

200 Riverview Parkway, Santee CA 92071

County: San Diego FICE Identification: 012031
Unit ID: 112084
Telephone: (619) 201-8700 Carnegie Class: Bac-Diverse
FAX Number: (619) 201-8749 Calendar System: Semester
URL: www.sdcc.edu
Established: 1970 Annual Undergrad Tuition & Fees: $33,312
Enrollment: 512 Coed
Affiliation or Control: Independent Non-Profit IRS Status: 501(c)3
Highest Offering: Master's
Accreditation: WC

01 President .... Dr. Kevin CORSINI
04 Exec Assistant to the President .... Ms. Kelly BUCHANAN
10 Chief Financial Officer .... Mr. Allen GARRETT
05 Int VP for Academics .... Dr. Katina EVANS
30 VP of Development .... Mr. Jim BODOR
11 VP of Operations .... Mr. Matt ZEALAND
32 Dean of Students .... Vacant
37 Sr Director of Financial Services .... Ms. Rina CAMPBELL
35 Director of Student Life .... Mr. Isaac DEAL
06 Registrar .... Vacant
07 Sr Dir of Recruitment & Outreach .... Ms. Kelly BUCHANAN
42 Director of Spiritual Life .... Mr. Steve JENKINS
15 Human Resources Specialist .... Ms. Kendra CHAMBERLAIN
08 Director of Library Services .... Mr. Matt OWEN
29 Manager of Alumni/Donor Relations .... Mr. Jim BODOR
09 Dean of Assessment and Planning .... Mrs. Lundie CARSTENSEN
41 Asst Athletic Director .... Mr. Nick FORTINI
23 Director of Health Services .... Mrs. Malia JENKINS
28 Director of Diversity .... Mr. Fred BLACKBURN
13 Chief Information Technology Ofcr .... Mr. Matt OWEN
45 Chief Institutional Planning Ofcr .... Mr. Bill CRAWFORD

*San Diego Community College District Administrative Offices (H)

3375 Camino Del Rio South, San Diego CA 92108-3883

County: San Diego FICE Identification: 008895
Unit ID: 122320
Telephone: (619) 388-6500 Carnegie Class: N/A
FAX Number: (619) 388-6913
URL: www.sdccd.edu

01 Chancellor .... Dr. Carlos O. TURNER CORTEZ
10 Exec Vice Chanc Business Tech Svcs .... Dr. Bonnie Ann DOWD
05 Vice Chanc Educational Services .... Dr. Susan TOPHAM
15 Vice Chancellor Human Resources .... Mr. Gregory A. SMITH
18 Vice Chanc Facilities Management .... Mr. Christopher MANIS
26 Director Comm & Public Relations .... Mr. Jack BERESFORD
04 Exec Assistant to the Chancellor .... Ms. Margaret LAMB
13 Chief Info Technology Officer .... Dr. Peter S. MAHARAJ
19 Chief of Police .... Mr. Joseph RAMOS
101 Board Recording Secretary .... Ms. Amanda FICKEN-DAVIS
106 Dean Online & Distributed Education .... Mr. Brian WESTON
30 Development Coordinator .... Ms. Lisa COLE-JONES
45 Chief Institutional Planning Office .... Ms. Natalia CORDOBA-VELASQUEZ
43 Director Legal Services .... Mr. Ljubisa KOSTIC

*San Diego City College (I)

1313 Park Boulevard, San Diego CA 92101-4787

County: San Diego FICE Identification: 001273
Unit ID: 122339
Telephone: (619) 388-3400 Carnegie Class: Assoc/HT-Mix Trad/Non
FAX Number: (619) 388-3063 Calendar System: Semester
URL: www.sdcity.edu
Established: 1914 Annual Undergrad Tuition & Fees (In-District): $1,144
Enrollment: 14,865 Coed
Affiliation or Control: State/Local IRS Status: 501(c)3
Highest Offering: Associate Degree
Accreditation: WJ, ADNUR

02 President .... Dr. Ricky SHABAZZ
04 Executive Asst to President .... Ms. Erin FLANAGAN
10 Vice Pres Administrative Services .... Dr. John PARKER
05 Vice Pres of Instruction .... Ms. Matilda CHAVEZ
32 Acting VP of Student Services .... Mr. Marciano PEREZ, JR.
68 Int Dean Health/Exercise Science .... Mr. Randy BARNES
83 Dean Behav & Soc Sci/Consumer Stds .... Ms. Lori ERRECA
08 Dean Information/Learning Tech .... Mr. Robbi EWELL
79 Dean School of Arts/Humanities .... Ms. Jeanie TYLER
50 Dean Sch Business/Info Tech .... Ms. Rose LAMURAGLIA
124 Dean Student Dev/Matriculation .... Dr. Nesha SAVAGE
35 Dean of Student Affairs .... Mr. Marciano PEREZ
41 Acting Dean Athletics .... Mr. Aaron DETTY
54 Act Dean Engr/Tech/Math/Sci/Nursing .... Dr. Leticia LOPEZ
28 Dean of Student Equity .... Mr. Roberto VALADEZ
22 Affirmative Action Officer .... Mr. Edwin HIEL
40 Bookstore Supervisor .... Ms. DeeDee PORTER
26 Public Information Officer .... Mr. Cesar GUMAPAS
88 Pgm Mgr Disabled Student Services .... Ms. Brianne KENNEDY
37 Director Financial Aid .... Vacant
121 Director EOPS/CARE/CalWORKS .... Ms. Beverly WARREN
56 Director Off-Campus Programs .... Ms. Catherine SCHAFER
18 Chief Facilities/Physical Plant .... Mr. Derrall CHANDLER
07 Admissions & Records Supervisor .... Ms. Megan SOTO

*San Diego Mesa College (J)

7250 Mesa College Drive, San Diego CA 92111-4998

County: San Diego FICE Identification: 001275
Unit ID: 122375
Telephone: (619) 388-2721 Carnegie Class: Bac/Assoc-Assoc Dom
FAX Number: (619) 388-2929 Calendar System: Semester
URL: www.sdmesa.edu
Established: 1962 Annual Undergrad Tuition & Fees (In-District): $1,144
Enrollment: 20,693 Coed
Affiliation or Control: State/Local IRS Status: 501(c)3
Highest Offering: Baccalaureate
Accreditation: WJ, CAHIIM, DA, PTAA, RAD

02 President .... Dr. Pamela T. LUSTER
05 Vice President Instruction .... Dr. Isabel O'CONNOR
32 Vice Pres Student Services .... Dr. Ashanti HANDS
10 Vice Pres Administrative Services .... Mr. Lorenze LEGASPI
121 Dean Student Development .... Ms. Aileen CRAKES
79 Dean Arts & Languages .... Ms. Leslie SHIMAZAKI
76 Dean Health Sciences/Public Svc .... Dr. Tina RECALDE
81 Dean School Math/Natural Sciences .... Dr. Paloma VARGAS
50 Dean Sch Business Technology .... Vacant
08 Dean Lrng Res/Academic Support .... Dr. Andrew MACNEILL
68 Dean PE/Health Educ/Athletics Dir .... Dr. Ryan SHUMAKER
79 Dean of Humanities .... Ms. Linda HENSLEY
83 Actg Dn Social/Behav Sci/Mult Stds .... Dr. Pearl LY
35 Dean Student Affairs .... Ms. Victoria MILLER
93 Dean of Student Success/Equity .... Mr. Larry MAXEY
108 Dean Institutional Effectiveness .... Vacant
09 Assoc Dean Research & Planning .... Dr. Bridget HERRIN
72 Assoc Dean Career Technical Educ .... Ms. Monica ROMERO
26 Public Information Officer .... Ms. Jennifer KEARNS
37 Financial Aid Officer .... Ms. Gilda MALDONADO
07 Student Svcs Supervisor Admission .... Ms. Ivonne ALVAREZ
04 Exec Asst to the President .... Ms. Sara Beth CAIN

*San Diego Miramar College (A)

10440 Black Mountain Road, San Diego CA 92126-2999
County: San Diego FICE Identification: 011820
Unit ID: 122384
Telephone: (619) 388-7800 Carnegie Class: Assoc/MT-VT-Mix Trad/Non
FAX Number: (619) 388-7901 Calendar System: Semester
URL: www.sdmiramar.edu
Established: 1969 Annual Undergrad Tuition & Fees (In-District): $1,144
Enrollment: 13,408 Coed
Affiliation or Control: State/Local IRS Status: 501(c)3
Highest Offering: Associate Degree
Accreditation: WJ, ACBSP, MLTAD

02 President .... Dr. Wesley LUNDBURG
05 Vice President Instruction .... Dr. Michael ODU
32 Vice President Student Services .... Mr. Adrian GONZALES
10 Vice President Admin Services .... Mr. Brett BELL
49 Dean Liberal Arts .... Dr. Lou ASCIONE
50 Dean Business/Tech/Workforce Init .... Mr. Jesse LOPEZ
81 Dean Math/Bio/Exer/Phys Sci .... Dr. Linda WOODS
19 Acting Dean Public Safety .... Dr. Linda WOODS
108 Dean PRIE/Library & Technology .... Dr. Daniel MIRAMONTEZ
35 Dean Student Affairs .... Dr. Cheryl BARNARD
124 Dean Matriculation & Student Dev .... Dr. Tonia TERESH
103 Associate Dean Career Education .... Ms. Claudia ESTRADA-HOWELL
35 Associate Dean Outreach/School Rel .... Mr. Truongson (Sonny) NGUYEN
04 Executive Assistant to President .... Ms. Malia KUNST
26 Public Information Officer .... Mr. Steve QUIS
37 Financial Aid Officer .... Mr. Vincent NGO
07 Admissions & Records Officer .... Ms. Dana STACK

San Diego Global Knowledge University (B)

1095 K Street Suite B, San Diego CA 92101
County: San Diego Identification: 667294
Unit ID: 493512
Telephone: (619) 934-0797 Carnegie Class: Not Classified
FAX Number: N/A Calendar System: Semester
URL: www.sdgku.edu
Established: 2007 Annual Undergrad Tuition & Fees: $6,476
Enrollment: 93 Coed
Affiliation or Control: Proprietary IRS Status: Proprietary
Highest Offering: Master's
Accreditation: ACICS

01 President .... Dr. Miguel A. CARDENAS
05 Chief Academic Officer .... Dr. Miguel A. CARDENAS, JR.
07 Dir of Admissions & Registrar .... Devahn PARKER
32 Director of Student Services .... Beatriz ESCOBEDO
11 Director of Administration .... Ilian ROSALES
08 Librarian .... Alexei ZALDUA
10 Financial/Business Officer .... Farah PALOMAS
13 Chief Information Technology Ofcr .... Dr. Andres MEJIA
15 Chief Compliance Officer .... Tonya PARKER-JONES

San Francisco Art Institute (C)

800 Chestnut Street, San Francisco CA 94133-2206
County: San Francisco FICE Identification: 003948
Unit ID: 122454
Telephone: (415) 771-7020 Carnegie Class: Spec-4-yr-Arts
FAX Number: (415) 749-4590 Calendar System: Semester
URL: www.sfai.edu
Established: 1871 Annual Undergrad Tuition & Fees: $46,064
Enrollment: 41 Coed
Affiliation or Control: Independent Non-Profit IRS Status: 501(c)3
Highest Offering: Master's
Accreditation: WC, ART

00 Chair of the Board .... Pam RORKE LEVY
02 Chief Operating Officer .... Mark KUSHNER
05 Chief Academic Officer .... Jennifer RISSLER
10 Interim Chief Financial Officer .... Mark KUSHNER
11 VP of Operations & Facilities .... Heather HICKMAN HOLLAND
111 VP Institutional Advancement .... Amory SHARPE
08 Librarian .... Jeff GUNDERSON
20 Assistant Dean of Academic Affairs .... Zeina BARAKEH
110 Development & Communications Mgr .... Niki KORTH
20 Director of Academic Affairs .... Diana VASQUEZ
31 Exhibitions/Evnts & Ptnrships Dir .... Kat TRATARIS
37 Director of Financial Aid .... Annita ALLDREDGE
84 Enrollment Operations & System Mgr .... Jeremy SIMMONS
09 Dir Inst Research & Registrar .... Jose DE LOS REYES
110 Campaign Manager .... Natalie TITONE
85 Assoc Dir of Global Programs & PDSO .... Ana SUEK
18 Director of Operations & Facilities .... John SEDEN
90 Academic Technology Manager .... Mark HELLAR
113 Accountant .... Bobbi EVANS
24 Photography Studio Manager .... Alex PETERSON
24 Film Studio Manager & Technical Dir .... Chris PADDOCK
15 Human Resources Manager .... Coree WALLMAN
58 Director of MFA Programs .... Tony LABAT
58 Director of MA Programs .... Claire DAIGLE

† SFAI not accepting students for fall semester 2020

San Francisco Conservatory of Music (D)

50 Oak Street, San Francisco CA 94102-6011
County: San Francisco FICE Identification: 001278
Unit ID: 122506
Telephone: (415) 864-7326 Carnegie Class: Spec-4-yr-Arts
FAX Number: (415) 503-6299 Calendar System: Semester
URL: www.sfcm.edu
Established: 1917 Annual Undergrad Tuition & Fees: $49,050
Enrollment: 410 Coed
Affiliation or Control: Independent Non-Profit IRS Status: 501(c)3
Highest Offering: Beyond Master's But Less Than Doctorate
Accreditation: WC

01 President .... David STULL
05 Provost and Dean .... Jonas WRIGHT
10 Vice Pres Finance & Administration .... Kathryn WITTENMYER
45 Vice Pres Marketing/Admissions/PR .... Beth GINDICESSI
111 Vice Pres Advancement .... Kathleen NICELY
20 Assoc Dean of Academic Affairs .... Ryan BROWN
32 Associate Dean of Student Life .... Jason SMITH
64 Assoc Dean for New Media/Music Tech .... Taurin BARRERA
15 Assoc VP Human Resources .... Michael PATTERSON
07 Director of Admission .... Lisa NICKELS
37 Director of Financial Aid .... Doris HOWARD
56 Director PreCollege/Extension .... Michael ROEST
06 Registrar & VA Certifying Official .... Connor CALLAGHAN
18 Chief Facilities Engineer .... David MITCHELL
35 Asst Director of Student Affairs .... Susannah WHITE
20 Exec Assistant to the Dean .... Ava HARMON
29 Alumni Relations Officer .... Danielle CHEIKEN
04 Executive Assistant to President .... Marina KENNEDY
102 Institutional Gifts Manager .... Rhiannon LEWIS
19 Director Security/Safety .... Stephanie MENDOZA
30 Chief Development/Advancement .... Kathleen NICELY
44 Director of Legacy Giving .... Nic MEREDITH

San Francisco Film School (E)

155 Sansome Street 2nd Floor, San Francisco CA 94104
County: San Francisco FICE Identification: 042340
Unit ID: 486372
Telephone: (415) 824-7000 Carnegie Class: Not Classified
FAX Number: (415) 824-7007 Calendar System: Semester
URL: sanfranciscofilmschool.edu
Established: 2005 Annual Undergrad Tuition & Fees: N/A
Enrollment: 40 Coed
Affiliation or Control: Proprietary IRS Status: Proprietary
Highest Offering: Associate Degree
Accreditation: COE

01 President .... Jeremiah BIRNBAUM

San Joaquin College of Law (F)

901 Fifth Street, Clovis CA 93612-1312
County: Fresno FICE Identification: 025000
Unit ID: 122649
Telephone: (559) 323-2100 Carnegie Class: Spec-4-yr-Law
FAX Number: (559) 323-5566 Calendar System: Semester
URL: www.sjcl.edu
Established: 1969 Annual Graduate Tuition & Fees: N/A
Enrollment: 183 Coed
Affiliation or Control: Independent Non-Profit IRS Status: 501(c)3
Highest Offering: Doctorate; No Undergraduates
Accreditation: WC

01 Dean .... Janice L. PEARSON
18 Facilities Manager .... Richard RODRIGUEZ
10 Chief Financial Officer .... Jill A. RANDLES
32 Director of Student Services .... Joyce K. MORODOMI
37 Financial Aid Administrator .... Melisa NILMEIER
08 Library Director .... Mark MASTERS
26 Public Relations Director .... Missy M. CARTIER
15 Chief of Personnel .... Beth PITCOCK
30 Chief Development .... Janice L. PEARSON
84 Director Enrollment Management .... Diane M. STEEL
61 Law Program Coordinator .... Pat A. SMITH
35 Dean of Students .... Logan TENNERELLI

San Joaquin Delta College (G)

5151 Pacific Avenue, Stockton CA 95207-6370
County: San Joaquin FICE Identification: 001280
Unit ID: 122658
Telephone: (209) 954-5151 Carnegie Class: Assoc/MT-VT-High Trad
FAX Number: (209) 954-7001 Calendar System: Semester
URL: www.deltacollege.edu
Established: 1935 Annual Undergrad Tuition & Fees (In-District): $1,288
Enrollment: 18,224 Coed
Affiliation or Control: State/Local IRS Status: 501(c)3
Highest Offering: Associate Degree
Accreditation: WJ, ADNUR

01 Acting Superintendent/ President .... Dr. Lisa AGUILERA LAWRENSON
05 Asst Supt/VP of Instruction .... Mr. Joseph GONZALES
32 Asst Supt/VP of Student Svcs .... Dr. Lonita CORDOVA
10 Vice Pres of Administrative Svcs .... Dr. Amanda PRESTON-NELSON
15 Vice Pres of Human Resources .... Vacant
38 Dean Counseling & Special Svcs .... Vacant
09 Dean Institutional Effectiveness .... Ms. Tina AKERS
103 Dean Workforce/Economic Development .... Vacant
108 Dean Student Learning & Assessment .... Dr. Ginger HOLDEN
08 Div Dean Library/Learning Res/Lang .... Ms. Sheli AYERS
12 Dean of Tracy Center .... Dr. Jessie GARZA-RODERICK
26 Dir Marketing/Stdnt Outreach .... Mr. Alex BREITLER
18 Director Facilities Management .... Ms. Stacy PINOLA
07 Director of Admissions & Records .... Vacant
37 Director of Financial Aid/Vet Svcs .... Ms. Tina LENT
04 Exec Assistant to the President .... Ms. Robin SADBERRY
19 District Police Chief .... Mr. Robert DI PIERO
13 Director IT & Data Center Services .... Ms. Chelsy PHAM
41 Athletic Director .... Mr. Tony ESPINOZA

San Joaquin Valley College, Inc. - Visalia (H)

8344 West Mineral King Avenue, Visalia CA 93291-9283
County: Tulare FICE Identification: 021207
Unit ID: 122685
Telephone: (559) 651-2500 Carnegie Class: Bac/Assoc-Assoc Dom
FAX Number: (559) 651-0574 Calendar System: Other
URL: www.sjvc.edu/campuses/central-california/visalia
Established: 1977 Annual Undergrad Tuition & Fees: N/A
Enrollment: 1,927 Coed
Affiliation or Control: Proprietary IRS Status: Proprietary
Highest Offering: Baccalaureate
Accreditation: WC, COARC, DH

01 Campus President .... Mr. Nick GOMEZ
05 Provost .... Dr. Sumer AVILA
07 VP Admissions/Grad Services .... Mr. Anthony ROMO
10 VP Administration .... Mr. Scott HAGER

San Joaquin Valley College-Antelope Valley (Lancaster) (I)

42135 10th Street West, Ste 147, Lancaster CA 93534
Telephone: (661) 974-8282 Identification: 770968
Accreditation: &WC

San Joaquin Valley College-Bakersfield (J)

201 New Stine Road, Bakersfield CA 93309-2668
Telephone: (661) 834-0126 FICE Identification: 023135
Accreditation: &WC, COARC, SURGT

† Regional accreditation is carried under the parent institution in Visalia, CA.

San Joaquin Valley College-Fresno (K)

295 East Sierra Avenue, Fresno CA 93710-3616
Telephone: (559) 448-8282 Identification: 666008
Accreditation: &WC, SURGT

† Regional accreditation is carried under the parent institution in Visalia, CA.

San Joaquin Valley College-Fresno Trades Education Center (L)

4985 East Andersen Avenue, Fresno CA 93727
Telephone: (559) 453-0123 Identification: 666009
Accreditation: &WC

† Regional accreditation is carried under the parent institution in Visalia, CA.

San Joaquin Valley College-Modesto (M)

5380 Pirrone Road, Salida CA 95368-9090
Telephone: (209) 543-8800 Identification: 666128
Accreditation: &WC

† Regional accreditation is carried under the parent institution in Visalia, CA.

San Joaquin Valley College-Ontario (A)

4580 Ontario Mills Parkway, Ontario CA 91764
Telephone: (909) 948-7582 Identification: 666096
Accreditation: &WC, COARC

† Regional accreditation is carried under the parent institution in Visalia, CA.

San Joaquin Valley College-Rancho Cordova (B)

11050 Olson Drive, Suite 210,
Rancho Cordova CA 95670-5600
Telephone: (916) 638-7582 Identification: 666133
Accreditation: &WC, COARC, SURGT

† Regional accreditation is carried under the parent institution in Visalia, CA.

San Joaquin Valley College-Santa Maria (C)

303 E Plaza Drive, Santa Maria CA 93454
Telephone: (805) 608-3104 FICE Identification: 025780
Accreditation: &WC

San Joaquin Valley College-Temecula (D)

27270 Madison Avenue, Suite 103, Temecula CA 92590
Telephone: (951) 296-6015 Identification: 770507
Accreditation: &WC, COARC, SURGT

San Joaquin Valley College-Victor Valley (Hesperia) (E)

9331 Mariposa Road, Hesperia CA 92344-8000
Telephone: (760) 948-1947 Identification: 667044
Accreditation: &WC

† Regional accreditation is carried under the parent institution in Visalia, CA.

*San Jose/Evergreen Community College District (F)

40 South Market Street, San Jose CA 95113-2367
County: Santa Clara FICE Identification: 029042
Unit ID: 122737
Telephone: (408) 274-6700 Carnegie Class: N/A
FAX Number: (408) 531-8722
URL: www.sjeccd.edu

01 Chancellor .... Dr. Byron D. CLIFT BRELAND
11 Vice Chanc Administrative Services .... Mr. Jorge L. ESCOBAR
15 Vice Chanc Human Resources .... Ms. Beatriz S. CHAIDEZ
13 Vice Chanc Information Tech Svcs .... Dr. Ben SEABERRY
18 AVC Physical Plant Dev/Operations .... Mr. Terrance DEGRAY
103 Interim Exec Dir of Workforce Inst .... Mr. William WATSON
09 Exec Dir Inst Effect/Stdnt Success .... Ms. Ann MACHAMER
86 Exec Dir Government/External Affs .... Ms. Rosalie LEDESMA
10 Interim Controller .... Ms. Manuela KOPLIN
26 Dir Communications/Community Rels .... Mr. Sam HO
27 Marketing & Public Info Officer .... Mr. Ryan BROWN

*Evergreen Valley College (G)

3095 Yerba Buena Road, San Jose CA 95135-1598
County: Santa Clara FICE Identification: 012452
Unit ID: 114266
Telephone: (408) 274-7900 Carnegie Class: Assoc/MT-VT-Mix Trad/Non
FAX Number: (408) 238-3179 Calendar System: Semester
URL: www.evc.edu
Established: 1975 Annual Undergrad Tuition & Fees (In-District): $1,448
Enrollment: 8,699 Coed
Affiliation or Control: State/Local IRS Status: 501(c)3
Highest Offering: Associate Degree
Accreditation: WJ, ADNUR

02 President .... Dr. Tammeil Y. GILKERSON
05 VP Academic Affairs .... Dr. Matais POUNCIL
32 EVP Student Affairs .... Mr. Howard WILLIS
10 VP Administrative Services .... Ms. Andrea ALEXANDER
50 Div Dean Business & Workforce .... Dr. Maniphone DICKERSON
66 Div Dean Nursing & Allied Health .... Ms. Lynette APEN
81 Div Dean Math/Science/Engineering .... Dr. Antoinette HERRERA
83 Div Dean Soc Sci/PE/Arts/Humanities .... Dr. Brad CAROTHERS
84 Div Dean Enrollment Services .... Vacant
49 Div Dean Language Arts .... Robert GUTIERREZ
08 Div Dean Library/Lrng Res/Adult Ed .... Dr. Roberta KUNKEL
121 Div Dean Student Success/Counseling .... Dr. Victor GARZA, JR.
93 Director Student Svcs & Wellness .... Mr. Michael OSORIO
37 Director Fin Aid & Scholarship Pgm .... Ms. Ebonnie HOPKINS
35 Director Student Dev & Activities .... Ms. Raniyah JOHNSON
88 Director Special Programs .... Ms. Elizabeth TYRRELL
20 Supervisor Academic Services .... Ms. Tina NGUYEN
13 Supervisor Campus Tech Svcs .... Mr. Eugenio CANOY
88 Dir Student Outreach & Recruitment .... Mr. Song-Ho TRAN
26 Dir Marketing/Public Relations .... Mr. Josh RUSSELL

*San Jose City College (H)

2100 Moorpark Avenue, San Jose CA 95128-2799
County: Santa Clara FICE Identification: 001282
Unit ID: 122746
Telephone: (408) 298-2181 Carnegie Class: Assoc/MT-VT-Mix Trad/Non
FAX Number: (408) 298-1935 Calendar System: Semester
URL: www.sjcc.edu
Established: 1921 Annual Undergrad Tuition & Fees (In-District): $1,362
Enrollment: 8,378 Coed
Affiliation or Control: State/Local IRS Status: 501(c)3
Highest Offering: Associate Degree
Accreditation: WJ, DA, NAEYC

02 President .... Dr. Rowena TOMANENG
05 Vice President Academic Affairs .... Dr. Elizabeth PRATT
11 Int VP Admin/Financial Svcs .... Ms. Marilyn MORIKANG
32 Vice President Student Affairs .... Mr. Roland MONTEMAYOR
45 Vice Pres Strategic Partnerships .... Dr. Lena TRAN
10 Chief Financial/Business Officer .... Ms. Marilyn MORIKANG
88 Director Support Programs .... Vacant
37 Financial Aid Director .... Mr. Takeo KUBO
41 Dean of Athletics & Kinesiology .... Mr. Lamel HARRIS
04 Assistant to the President .... Ms. Maria GAETA
50 Assoc Dir Business/Workforce Devel .... Ms. Christine JENSEN
79 Dean Humanities/Social Science .... Ms. Ilder A. BENTANCOURT LOPEZ
38 Dean Counseling/Matriculation .... Dr. Eliazer AYALA-AUSTIN
49 Dean Language Arts .... Dr. Celia CRUZ-JOHNSON
81 Dean Mathematics/Sciences Division .... Mr. Robert GUTIERREZ
09 Director of Institutional Research .... Dr. Joyce LUI
07 Director of Admissions .... Ms. Teresa PAIZ
26 Dir Marketing & Public Relations .... Mr. Daniel GARZA

*San Mateo County Community College District Office (I)

3401 CSM Drive, San Mateo CA 94402-3651
County: San Mateo FICE Identification: 004697
Unit ID: 122782
Telephone: (650) 574-6500 Carnegie Class: N/A
FAX Number: (650) 574-6566
URL: www.smccd.edu

01 Chancellor .... Mr. Michael CLAIRE
15 Director of Human Resources .... Mr. David FEUNE
05 Vice Chanc Educ Svcs/Plng .... Dr. Aaron MCVEAN
18 Vice Chanc Facil Plng/Maint/Oper .... Mr. Jose NUNEZ
109 Vice Chanc Auxiliary Services .... Mr. Tom BAUER
100 Chief of Staff .... Mr. Mitchell A. BAILEY
104 Provost International Education .... Dr. Jing LUAN
10 Chief Financial Officer .... Ms. Bernata SLATER
13 Chief Technology Officer .... Mr. Daman GREWAL

*Cañada College (J)

4200 Farm Hill Boulevard, Redwood City CA 94061-1099
County: San Mateo FICE Identification: 006973
Unit ID: 111434
Telephone: (650) 306-3100 Carnegie Class: Assoc/HT-Mix Trad/Non
FAX Number: (650) 306-3457 Calendar System: Semester
URL: www.canadacollege.edu
Established: 1968 Annual Undergrad Tuition & Fees (In-District): $1,362
Enrollment: 5,231 Coed
Affiliation or Control: State/Local IRS Status: 501(c)3
Highest Offering: Associate Degree
Accreditation: WJ, RAD

02 Interim President .... Ms. Kim LOPEZ
05 VP Instruction .... Dr. Tammy ROBINSON
32 VP Student Services .... Dr. Manuel Alejandro PEREZ
11 VP Administrative Services .... Mr. Graciano MENDOZA
10 College Business Officer .... Ms. Mary Chries CONCHA THIA
38 Dean Counseling .... Mr. C. Max HARTMAN
06 Interim Registrar .... Ms. Maria LARA
26 Dir Cmty Relations & Marketing .... Ms. Megan RODRIGUEZ ANTONE
45 Dean PRIE .... Dr. Karen ENGEL
37 Int Director Financial Aid Services .... Ms. Andrea GARCIA-RITTGERS
18 Facility Manager .... Ms. Karen PINKHAM
103 Dean Business/Design/Workforce .... Ms. Hyla LACEFIELD
79 Dean Humanities & Soc Sci .... Mr. James CARRANZA
81 Dean Science & Tech .... Mr. Ameer THOMPSON
121 Dean Acad Support & Learning Tech .... Mr. David REED
84 Int Dean Enrollment Services .... Mr. Wissem BENNANI

*College of San Mateo (K)

1700 W Hillsdale Boulevard, San Mateo CA 94402-3795
County: San Mateo FICE Identification: 001181
Unit ID: 122791
Telephone: (650) 574-6161 Carnegie Class: Assoc/HT-Mix Trad/Non
FAX Number: (650) 574-6680 Calendar System: Semester
URL: www.collegeofsanmateo.edu
Established: 1922 Annual Undergrad Tuition & Fees (In-District): $1,434
Enrollment: 7,494 Coed
Affiliation or Control: State/Local IRS Status: 501(c)3
Highest Offering: Associate Degree
Accreditation: WJ, DA

02 Acting President .... Ms. Kim LOPEZ
05 Vice President Instruction .... Mr. Mike HOLTZCLAW
10 Vice Pres Administrative Services .... Ms. Eloisa BRIONES
32 Acting Vice Pres Student Services .... Ms. Kristi RIDGWAY
84 Dean Enrollment Svcs/Support Pgms .... Ms. Lizette BRICKER
38 Dean Counsel/Advis/Matriculation .... Ms. Krystal DUNCAN
09 Int Dean Plng/Research/Inst Effect .... Dr. Hilary GOODKIND
20 Dean Academic Support/Learning Tech .... Ms. Tarana CHAPPIE
35 Dean Student Services/Counseling .... Ms. Marsha RAMEZANE
79 Dean Language Arts Division .... Dr. Chris GIBSON
68 Dean Kinesiology/Athletics Division .... Mr. Andreas WOLF
81 Dean Math/Science Division .... Dr. Charlene FRONTIERA
83 Dean Creative Arts/Social Sci Div .... Dr. Laura DEMSETZ
50 Dean Business & Technology Division .... Mr. Francisco GOMEZ
06 Registrar .... Mr. Steven TRINH
37 Director Financial Aid Services .... Ms. Claudia I. MENJIVAR
26 Dir Marketing/Comm/Public Relations .... Ms. Cherie COLIN
18 Dir Maintenance/Operations .... Ms. Michele RUDOVSKY
15 Chief Human Resources Officer .... Ms. Marie BILLIE
96 Purchasing Services Supervisor .... Mr. Bob DOMENICI

*Skyline College (L)

3300 College Drive, San Bruno CA 94066-1698
County: San Mateo FICE Identification: 007713
Unit ID: 123509
Telephone: (650) 738-4100 Carnegie Class: Bac/Assoc-Assoc Dom
FAX Number: (650) 738-4338 Calendar System: Semester
URL: www.skylinecollege.edu
Established: 1969 Annual Undergrad Tuition & Fees (In-District): $1,464
Enrollment: 8,747 Coed
Affiliation or Control: State/Local IRS Status: 501(c)3
Highest Offering: Baccalaureate
Accreditation: WJ, ACBSP, COARC, SURGT

02 President .... Dr. Melissa MORENO
05 Interim Vice President Instruction .... Ms. Danni REDDING LAPUZ
11 Vice Pres Administrative Services .... Ms. Eloisa M. BRIONES
32 Vice President Student Services .... Dr. Newin ORANTE
84 Dean Enrollment Svcs/Financial Aid .... Mr. William MINNICH
09 Dean Plng/Research/Inst Effective .... Ms. Ingrid VARGAS
83 Act Dean Soc Sciences/Creative Arts .... Dr. Nicole D. PORTER
50 Dean Business/Educ/Prof Pgm .... Mr. Michael KANE
60 Dean Language Arts/Learning Res .... Mr. Christopher GIBSON
68 Dean Kinesiology/Athletics/Dance .... Mr. Joseph MORELLO, JR.
81 Dean Science/Math/Technology .... Dr. Carla GRANDY
38 Dean Counsel/Advis/Matric .... Dr. Luis ESCOBAR
103 Dean Strat Partnerships/WF Devel .... Ms. Andrea VIZENOR
85 Dean Global Learning Programs .... Mr. Russell WALDON
121 Dean Acad Support & Learning Tech .... Mr. Rolin MOE
103 Director SparkPoint at Skyline Col .... Mr. Chad THOMPSON
26 Dir Community Rels/Marketing .... Ms. Cherie COLIN
08 Director Learning Commons .... Gabriela NOCITO
22 Exec Dir of the Equity Institute ..... Dr. O'KenZoe SELASSIE-OKPE
06 Registrar .... Ms. Susan LORENZO
04 Executive Asst to President .... Ms. Theresa TENTES
104 Director Study Abroad .... Mr. Zaid GHORI
18 Facilities Operation Manager .... Mr. John DOCTOR
19 Public Safety Captain .... Mr. Jim VANGELE
37 Director Student Financial Aid .... Ms. Regina MORRISON
21 Finance and Operations Manager .... Mr. Paul CASSIDY

Sanford Burnham Prebys Medical Discovery Institute (M)

10901 North Torrey Pines Road, La Jolla CA 92037
County: San Diego Identification: 667069
Unit ID: 481535
Telephone: (858) 646-3100 Carnegie Class: Spec-4-yr-Other Health
FAX Number: (858) 646-3199 Calendar System: Quarter
URL: www.sbpdiscovery.org
Established: 2005 Annual Graduate Tuition & Fees: N/A
Enrollment: 26 Coed
Affiliation or Control: Independent Non-Profit IRS Status: 501(c)3
Highest Offering: Doctorate; No Undergraduates
Accreditation: WC

01 President .... Dr. Kristiina VUORI
10 Chief Financial/Admin Officer .... Mr. Louie COFFMAN
05 Dean Grad Sch Biomedical Sciences .... Dr. Guy SALVESEN
15 Chief Human Resources Officer .... Mr. Doug BATTISTA
88 Sr Vice Pres Drug Discovery/Devel .... Dr. Michael JACKSON
30 Vice Pres Business Development .... Dr. Lee BLUMENFELD
100 Vice Pres/Chief of Staff .... Ms. Tara MARATHE
26 Director of Communications .... Ms. Susan GAMMON

The Santa Barbara and Ventura Colleges of Law (N)

4475 Market Street, Ventura CA 93003
County: Ventura Identification: 667229
Unit ID: 125037
Telephone: (805) 765-9300 Carnegie Class: Spec-4-yr-Law
FAX Number: (805) 658-0529 Calendar System: Semester
URL: www.collegesoflaw.edu
Established: 1969 Annual Graduate Tuition & Fees: N/A
Enrollment: 230 Coed
Affiliation or Control: Independent Non-Profit IRS Status: 501(c)3
Highest Offering: Doctorate; No Undergraduates
Accreditation: WC

01 President .... Dr. Matthew NEHMER
05 Dean .... Ms. Jackie GARDINA
07 Director of Admissions .... Mr. Shawn TAYLOR
06 Asst Dean & Registrar .... Ms. Barbara DOYLE
32 Student Services Coordinator .... Ms. Jennifer MACKIE
10 Business Mgr/Spec Assist to Pres .... Ms. Alexis BURDICK
26 Public Affairs Director .... Mr. Kryztofr KAINE
106 Fac Dir Hybrid & Online Programs .... Ms. Andrea FUNK

Santa Barbara City College (A)

721 Cliff Drive, Santa Barbara CA 93109-2394
County: Santa Barbara FICE Identification: 001285
Unit ID: 122889
Telephone: (805) 965-0581 Carnegie Class: Assoc/HT-Mix Trad/Non
FAX Number: (805) 963-7222 Calendar System: Semester
URL: www.sbcc.edu
Established: 1909 Annual Undergrad Tuition & Fees (In-District): $1,374
Enrollment: 12,525 Coed
Affiliation or Control: State/Local IRS Status: 501(c)3
Highest Offering: Associate Degree
Accreditation: WJ, ADNUR, CAHIIM, RAD

01 Interim Superintendent/President .... Dr. Kindred MURILLO
05 Int Exec VP Educational Programs .... Dr. Kathy SCOTT
10 VP Business Services .... Ms. Lyndsay MAAS
15 VP Human Resources .... Mr. Michael SHANAHAN
13 Exec Dir Information Technology .... Dr. Dean NEVINS
56 VP Sch of Extended Learning .... Dr. Melissa MORENO
72 Dean Educational Programs .... Mr. Arturo RODRIGUEZ
76 Dean Educational Programs .... Dr. Alan PRICE
81 Dean Educational Programs .... Dr. Jens-Uwe KUHN
57 Dean Educational Programs .... Dr. Priscilla MORA
72 Dean Educational Programs .... Mr. Kenley NEUFELD
50 Dean Educational Programs .... Ms. Carola SMITH
32 Dean Student Affairs .... Ms. Paloma ARNOLD
07 Assoc Dean Admissions/Stdnt Support .... Mr. Christopher JOHNSON
08 Librarian .... Ms. Elizabeth BOWMAN
102 Exec Dir Foundation for SBCC .... Mr. Geoff GREEN
09 Dir Institutional Research & Plng .... Dr. Z. REISZ
26 Exec Dir Public Affs/Communications .... Ms. Martha SWANSON
37 Director of Student Financial Aid .... Ms. Maureen GOLDBERG
18 Director of Facilities .... Mr. Robert MORALES
85 Director International Students .... Ms. Carola SMITH
06 Director of Records .... Mr. Michael MEDEL
96 Manager of Purchasing .... Mr. Robert MORALES
04 Executive Asst to President .... Ms. Jasmine TUAZON
19 Director Security/Safety .... Mr. Erik FRICKE
41 Athletic Director .... Mr. Rocco CONSTANTINO
84 Coordinator for Enrollment Services .... Ms. Vanessa PELTON
28 Director of Diversity .... Mr. Luis GIRALDO

Santa Clara University (B)

500 El Camino Real, Santa Clara CA 95053-0001
County: Santa Clara FICE Identification: 001326
Unit ID: 122931
Telephone: (408) 554-4000 Carnegie Class: DU-Mod
FAX Number: (408) 554-2700 Calendar System: Quarter
URL: www.scu.edu
Established: 1851 Annual Undergrad Tuition & Fees: $52,998
Enrollment: 8,616 Coed
Affiliation or Control: Independent Non-Profit IRS Status: 501(c)3
Highest Offering: Doctorate
Accreditation: WC, IPSY, LAW, THEOL

01 Acting President .... Ms. Lisa KLOPPENBERG
05 Interim Provost/VP Academic Affairs .... Ms. Kate MORRIS
10 Vice President Finance/Admin .... Mr. Michael CROWLEY
43 Interim General Counsel .... Ms. Bridget COLBERT
111 Vice President University Relations .... Mr. James LYONS
100 Chief of Staff to the President .... Ms. Molly MCDONALD
49 Dean of Arts & Sciences .... Dr. Daniel PRESS
50 Dean of Business .... Dr. Ed GRIER
53 Dean Educ & Counseling Psych .... Dr. Sabrina ZIRKEL
54 Dean of Engineering .... Dr. Elaine SCOTT
61 Dean of Law .... Mr. Michael KAUFMAN
73 Dean of JST .... Rev. Joseph MUELLER, SJ
20 Vice Provost Academic Affairs .... Ms. Elsa Y. CHEN
32 Vice Provost and Dean Student Life . Ms. Jeanne ROSENBERGER
84 Vice President for Enrollment Mgmt .... Ms. Eva BLANCO
45 Vice Prov Inst Effectiveness .... Dr. Ed RYAN
13 CIO/Vice Provost Info Services .... Dr. Robert OWEN
20 Assoc Provost Undergraduate Studies .... Dr. Katharine HEINTZ
88 Assoc Vice Provost Faculty Devel .... Dr. Eileen R. ELROD
07 Dean Undergraduate Admission .... Ms. Becky KONOWICZ
37 Dean University Financial Aid Svcs .... Ms. Nan MERZ
21 Int Assoc Vice President Finance .... Ms. Ramona SAUTER
15 Associate VP Human Resources .... Vacant
30 Assoc Vice President Development .... Mr. Mike J. WALLACE
109 Asst Vice Pres Auxiliary Services .... Ms. Robin REYNOLDS
35 Assoc Dean for Student Life .... Mr. Matthew DUNCAN
06 University Registrar .... Mr. Duane VOIGT
29 Asst Vice President Alumni Rels .... Ms. Kathy KALE
41 Athletics Director .... Dr. Renee BAUMGARTNER
90 Deputy CIO Academic Technology .... Ms. Nancy CUTLER
36 Director Career Center .... Ms. Rose NAKAMOTO
09 Director Institutional Research .... Ms. Barbara A. STEWART
25 Director Sponsored Projects .... Ms. Mary-Ellen FORTINI
38 Director Health & Counseling Svcs .... Dr. Jill ROVARIS
85 Assoc Provost International Pgm .... Ms. Susan POPKO
115 Chief Investment Officer .... Mr. John E. KERRIGAN
21 Controller .... Ms. Ramona SAUTER
18 Director of Facilities .... Ms. Marissa PIMENTEL
96 Director University Support Service .... Mr. Ed MERRYMAN
19 Director Campus Safety Services .... Mr. Philip BELTRAN
40 General Manager Bookstore .... Vacant
42 Vice President Mission and Ministry .... Dr. Alison BENDERS
22 EEO & Title IX Coordinator .... Ms. Belinda GUTHRIE
88 Director de Saisset Museum .... Ms. Rebecca M. SCHAPP
88 Exec Dir Markkula Ctr Applied Ethic .... Mr. Don HEIDER
110 Assoc Vice President Development .... Ms. Nancy T. CALDERON
28 VP Diversity/Equity & Inclusion .... Dr. Shá DUNCAN SMITH
44 Asst Vice President Advance Svcs .... Mr. Jeff BEACHY
92 Director University Honors Program .... Dr. Naomi LEVY
94 Director Women & Gender Studies .... Dr. Linda GARBER
93 Director Ethnic Studies .... Dr. Anna C. SAMPAIO
04 Exec Assistant to the President .... Mrs. Bonnie SHEIKH
102 Exec Dir Corp & Found Relations .... Mr. Ali HASSAN
104 Director Study Abroad .... Vacant
105 Webmaster .... Mr. Brian WASHBURN
26 AVP Marketing & Communications .... Ms. Celine SCHMIDEK
39 Director of Residence Life .... Ms. Heather DUMAS-DYER

Santa Monica College (C)

1900 Pico Boulevard, Santa Monica CA 90405-1628
County: Los Angeles FICE Identification: 001286
Unit ID: 122977
Telephone: (310) 434-4000 Carnegie Class: Bac/Assoc-Assoc Dom
FAX Number: (310) 434-4386 Calendar System: Semester
URL: www.smc.edu
Established: 1929 Annual Undergrad Tuition & Fees (In-District): $1,148
Enrollment: 25,948 Coed
Affiliation or Control: State/Local IRS Status: 501(c)3
Highest Offering: Associate Degree
Accreditation: WJ, ADNUR, #COARC, NAEYC

01 Superintendent/President .... Dr. Kathryn E. JEFFERY
10 Vice President Business/Admin .... Mr. Christopher BONVENUTO
15 Vice President Human Resources .... Ms. Sherri LEE-LEWIS
05 Vice President Academic Affairs .... Dr. Bradley LANE
84 Vice Pres Enrollment Development .... Dr. Teresita RODRIGUEZ
32 Vice President Student Affairs .... Mr. Michael TUITASI
20 Dean Academic Affairs .... Dr. Dione CARTER
16 Dean Human Resources .... Dr. Tre'Shawn HALL-BAKER
08 Dir Library & Information Services .... Mr. Steve HUNT
85 Dean International Education .... Mr. Pressian NICOLOV
56 Dean Noncredit/External Programs .... Mr. Scott SILVERMAN
38 Interim Dean Counseling .... Ms. Janet ROBINSON
13 Chief Director Info Technology .... Mr. Marc DRESCHER
88 Dean Education Enterprise .... Mr. Mitch HESKEL
43 Campus Counsel .... Mr. Robert MYERS
106 Int Assoc Dean Online Svcs/Support .... Ms. Tammara WHITAKER
35 Associate Dean of Students Life .... Dr. Isaac RODRIGUEZ
76 Associate Dean of Health Sciences .... Mr. Eric WILLIAMS
26 Public Information Officer .... Ms. Grace SMITH
31 Dean Community & Academic Relations .... Ms. Kiersten ELLIOTT
86 Sr Director Government Relations .... Mr. Don GIRARD
84 Dean Enrollment Services .... Dr. Esau TOVAR
37 Assoc Dean Financial Aid/Scholarshp .... Ms. Tracie HUNTER
18 Director Facilities Mgmt/Operations .... Mr. Devin STARNES
114 Budget Manager .... Ms. Veronica DIAZ
09 Dean Institutional Research .... Ms. Hannah LAWLER
104 Assoc Dean International Education .... Ms. Catherine WEIR
41 Asst Director Athletics .... Mr. Reggie ELLIS
25 Director of Grants .... Vacant
88 Director of Classified Personnel .... Ms. Carol LONG
91 Director Network Services .... Mr. Matthew KIAMAN
25 Director of Contracts .... Mr. Charlie YEN
96 Director of Purchasing .... Mr. Greg TATAR
19 Chief of Campus Police .... Mr. Johnnie ADAMS
04 Admin Asst to the President .... Ms. Letty KILIAN
40 Bookstore Manager .... Mr. David DEVER
103 Dean Academic Affairs .... Dr. Patricia RAMOS
101 Coordinator Board of Trustees .... Ms. Lisa ROSE
88 Director Radio Station (KCRW) .... Ms. Jennifer FERRO
88 Assoc Dean Facilities Programming .... Ms. Linda SULLIVAN
88 Dir Sustainability Coordination .... Mr. Ferris KAWAR
88 Dir Instr Services/External Pgms .... Ms. Maral HYELER
88 Dir Supplemental Instruct/Tutoring .... Ms. Wendi DEMORST
88 Int Assoc Dean Career/Technical Ed .... Ms. Sasha KING
29 Dir Student and Alumni Rels .... Ms. Deirdre WEAVER
105 Interim Web/Social Media Manager .... Mr. Paul TRAUTWEIN
102 Dean Foundation/Inst Advancement .... Ms. Lizzy MOORE
23 Associate Dean Health & Well-Being .... Dr. Susan FILA
124 Assoc Dean Outreach/Onboarding .... Mr. Jose HERNANDEZ

Santa Rosa Junior College (D)

1501 Mendocino Avenue, Santa Rosa CA 95401-4395
County: Sonoma FICE Identification: 001287
Unit ID: 123013
Telephone: (707) 527-4011 Carnegie Class: Assoc/HVT-High Trad
FAX Number: (707) 527-4816 Calendar System: Semester
URL: www.santarosa.edu
Established: 1918 Annual Undergrad Tuition & Fees (In-District): $1,324
Enrollment: 16,757 Coed
Affiliation or Control: State/Local IRS Status: 501(c)3
Highest Offering: Associate Degree
Accreditation: WJ, DH, DIETT, EMT, RAD

01 Superintendent/President .... Dr. Frank CHONG
05 VP Academic Affairs .... Dr. Jane SALDANA-TALLEY
10 VP Finance and Admin Services .... Ms. Kate JOLLEY
32 VP Student Svcs/Asst Superintendent .... Mr. Pedro AVILA
15 VP Human Resources .... Mr. Gene DURAND
88 Sr Director Capital Projects .... Mr. Serafin FERNANDEZ
75 Dean Career/Tech Ed/Economic Dev .... Mr. Jerry MILLER
18 Director Facilities Operations .... Vacant
88 Dean Curriculum/Education Support .... Mr. Josh ADAMS
49 Dean Liberal Arts & Sciences .... Vacant
08 Sr Dean Learning Res/Educ Tech .... Ms. Phyllis USINA
19 Dean Public Safety .... Ms. April CHAPMAN
81 Dean Sci/Tech/Engr/Math .... Mr. Victor TAM
17 Dean Health Sciences .... Ms. Deborah CHIGAZOLA
50 Dean Business/Professional Studies .... Mr. Joshua ADAMS
79 Dean Arts & Humanities .... Mr. Kerry LOEWEN
79 Dean Language Arts/Acad Foundation .... Mr. Robert HOLCOMB
41 Dean Kinesiology/Dance/Athletic Dir . Mr. Matthew MARKOVITCH
22 Dean Disabled Students Pgm & Svcs .... Ms. Kim STARKE
84 Dean Instr/Enrollment Svcs Petaluma .... Ms. Catherine WILLIAMS
35 Dean Student Services Petaluma .... Mr. Matthew LONG
88 Mgr Child Development Services .... Ms. Maleese WARNER
121 Sr Dean Counseling & Stdnt Success .... Ms. Li COLLIER
47 Dean Agriculture/Natural Resources .... Mr. Benjamin GOLDSTEIN
19 Chief of Police .... Mr. Robert BROWNLEE
13 Int Sr Dir Information Technology .... Mr. Kevin SNYDER
103 Dean Workforce Development .... Mr. Brad DAVIS
21 Director of Finance .... Ms. Whitney SCHULTZ
37 Int Director Student Financial Svcs .... Ms. Rachael CUTCHER
23 Director Student Health Services .... Ms. Susan QUINN
09 Director Institutional Research .... Dr. KC GREANEY
35 Sr Dean of Students .... Mr. Robert ETHINGTON
96 Dir Purchasing & Risk Mgmt .... Ms. Stephanie JARRETT
40 Director Bookstore .... Vacant
102 Executive Director Foundation .... Ms. J. MULLINEAUX
66 Associate Degree Nursing Program .... Ms. Anna VALDEZ
06 Dean Acad Records/Intl Admissions .... Ms. Freyja PEREIRA
07 Director Admissions/Enrollment Svcs .... Ms. Vayta SMITH
31 Director Community Education .... Mr. Jeffrey RHOADES
16 Director Human Resources .... Ms. Sarah HOPKINS
26 Dir District & Community Relations .... Ms. Erin BRICKER
90 Manager Instructional Computing .... Mr. Michael ROTH
24 Manager Media Services Petaluma .... Mr. Matt PEARSON
04 Exec Assistant to the President .... Ms. Zehra SONKAYNAR

Saybrook University (E)

55 Eureka Street, Pasadena CA 91103
County: Alameda FICE Identification: 021206
Unit ID: 123095
Telephone: (510) 626-5300 Carnegie Class: Spec-4-yr-Other
FAX Number: (510) 455-7046 Calendar System: Semester
URL: www.saybrook.edu
Established: 1971 Annual Graduate Tuition & Fees: N/A
Enrollment: 785 Coed
Affiliation or Control: Independent Non-Profit IRS Status: 501(c)3
Highest Offering: Doctorate; No Undergraduates
Accreditation: WC, CACREP

01 President .... Dr. Nathan LONG
05 VP Academics Affairs .... Dr. Devin BYRD
07 AVP Admissions .... Ms. Karyn LEE
06 Registrar .... Ms. Crystal ISHIHARA
08 Librarian .... Mr. Noah LOWENSTEIN
04 Executive Assistant .... Ms. Val SMITH
26 Dir University Relations .... Ms. Carmen BOWAN
10 Director Business Operations .... Ms. Jolene PRUITT
32 Dean of Students .... Ms. Shaniece MCGILL
15 Human Resources Coordinator .... Ms. Stephany LOLI
09 Director of Institutional Research .... Ms. Laura BREWER
20 Dir Academic Affairs/Admin/Projects .... Ms. Julia SONDEJ

Scripps College (F)

1030 Columbia Avenue, Claremont CA 91711
County: Los Angeles FICE Identification: 001174
Unit ID: 123165
Telephone: (909) 621-8000 Carnegie Class: Bac-A&S
FAX Number: (909) 621-8323 Calendar System: Semester
URL: www.scrippscollege.edu
Established: 1926 Annual Undergrad Tuition & Fees: $57,188
Enrollment: 958 Female
Affiliation or Control: Independent Non-Profit IRS Status: 501(c)3
Highest Offering: Baccalaureate
Accreditation: WC

01 Interim President .... Ms. Amy MARCUS-NEWHALL
05 Actg VP Acad Affs/Dean of Faculty .... Ms. Gretchen EDWARDS-GILBERT
111 VP for External Rels/Advancement .... Ms. Binti HARVEY
10 VP for Business Affairs/Treasurer .... Mr. Dean CALVO
32 Int VP Student Affs/Dean of Stdnts .... Mr. Adriana DI BARTOLO-BECKMAN
84 Vice President for Enrollment .... Ms. Victoria ROMERO
101 VP/Secretary of Board of Trustees .... Ms. Denise NELSON NASH
04 Executive Asst to the President .... Ms. Maria MANCERA
20 Associate Dean of Faculty .... Ms. Jennifer ARMSTRONG
15 AVP of Human Capital & Risk Mgmt .... Ms. Jennifer L. BERKLAS
09 Dir of Assessment/Inst Research .... Ms. Eulena JONSSON
08 Dir of Ella Strong Denison Library .... Ms. Jennifer WORMSER
06 Registrar .... Ms. Kelly HOGENCAMP
37 Director of Financial Aid .... Mr. Patrick MOORE
36 Exec Dir Center for Leadership .... Ms. Vicki P. KLOPSCH
13 Exec Dir of Information Technology .... Mr. Jeff SESSLER
18 Exec Director of Facilities .... Mr. Josh REEDER
104 Director of Off-Campus Study .... Ms. Neva BARKER

The Scripps Research Institute (A)

10550 N Torrey Pines Road, TPC19,
La Jolla CA 92037-1000
County: San Diego FICE Identification: 033213
Unit ID: 435338
Telephone: (858) 784-8469 Carnegie Class: Not Classified
FAX Number: (858) 784-2802 Calendar System: Quarter
URL: www.scripps.edu
Established: 1989 Annual Graduate Tuition & Fees: N/A
Enrollment: N/A Coed
Affiliation or Control: Independent Non-Profit IRS Status: 501(c)3
Highest Offering: Doctorate; No Undergraduates
Accreditation: WC

01 President/CEO ....Dr. Peter G. SCHULTZ
46 EVP/Director Scripps Research ....Dr. Eric TOPOL
05 EVP Research & Academic Affairs ....Dr. James R. WILLIAMSON
26 VP Marketing/Communications ....Ms. Anna-Marie ROONEY
15 VP Human Resources ....Ms. Karen HAGGENMILLER
11 Chief Operating Officer ....Dr. Matthew TREMBLAY
10 Chief Financial Officer/Treasurer ....Ms. Alice FENG

Shasta Bible College and Graduate School (B)

2951 Goodwater Avenue, Redding CA 96002-1544
County: Shasta FICE Identification: 023593
Unit ID: 123280
Telephone: (530) 221-4275 Carnegie Class: Spec-4-yr-Faith
FAX Number: (530) 221-6929 Calendar System: Semester
URL: www.shasta.edu
Established: 1972 Annual Undergrad Tuition & Fees: $12,860
Enrollment: 41 Coed
Affiliation or Control: Independent Non-Profit IRS Status: 501(c)3
Highest Offering: Master's
Accreditation: TRACS

01 President/CEO ....Dr. David R. NICHOLAS
04 Exec Assistant to the President ....Ms. Jane DEANGELO
05 Vice President of Academics ....Dr. Stephen G. BROWN
32 Vice President of Student Services ....Mr. George A. GUNN
10 Chief Finance Officer ....Mr. Eric BROWN
49 Dean Undergraduate Studies ....Mrs. Faith MCCARTHY
34 Dean of Women ....Mrs. Donna R. NICHOLAS
18 Director Maintenance ....Mr. Ted RIVERS
06 Registrar ....Mrs. Faith MCCARTHY
37 Director of Financial Aid ....Ms. Linda ILES
08 Head Librarian ....Mrs. Virginia M. WILLIAMS

Shasta College (C)

PO Box 496006, 11555 Old Oregon Tr,
Redding CA 96049-6006
County: Shasta FICE Identification: 001289
Unit ID: 123299
Telephone: (530) 242-7500 Carnegie Class: Bac/Assoc-Assoc Dom
FAX Number: (530) 225-4990 Calendar System: Semester
URL: www.shastacollege.edu
Established: 1950 Annual Undergrad Tuition & Fees (In-District): $1,187
Enrollment: 8,121 Coed
Affiliation or Control: State/Local IRS Status: Exempt
Highest Offering: Baccalaureate
Accreditation: WJ, CAHIIM, DH, @PTAA

01 Superintendent/President ....Dr. Joe WYSE
04 Asst to Superintendent/President ....Ms. Andree BLANCHIER
102 Executive Director SC Foundation ....Ms. Eva JIMENEZ
10 Asst Supt/Int VP of Admin Svcs ....Mr. Greg SMITH
05 Asst Supt/VP of Instruction ....Dr. Frank NIGRO
32 Asst Supt/VP of Student Services ....Dr. Kevin O'RORKE
103 Asst Supt/VP of EWD ....Ms. Eva JIMENEZ
15 Int AVP of Human Resources ....Dr. Marrianne WILLIAMS
16 Director of Human Resources ....Ms. Amy WESTLUND
84 AVP of SS/Dean Enrollment Services ....Dr. Timothy JOHNSTON
35 Dean Student Services ....Ms. Sandra HAMILTON SLANE
35 Int Assoc Dean of Student Services ....Dr. Zhanjing (John) YU
57 Dean Arts/Communication/Soc Science ....Ms. Stacey BARTLETT
50 Dean Business/Ag/Ind/Tech/Safety ....Mr. Zachary ZWEIGLE
56 Dean Extended Education ....Dr. Andy FIELDS
76 Dean Health Sciences ....Ms. Ioanna IATRIDIS
88 Dir Hlth Sci Operations & Outreach ....Ms. Kim GILES
08 Exec Dean Educ Tech/Lrng Svcs/Rsrch ....Mr. William BREITBACH
68 Dean Phys Education and Athletics ....Mr. Mike MARI
81 Dean Science/Language Arts/Math ....Mr. Carlos REYES
09 Dn Innovation/Strategic Initiative ....Dr. Kate MAHAR
13 AVP of Info Services & Tech ....Ms. Becky MCCALL
21 Comptroller ....Ms. Jill AULT
19 Director of Campus Safety ....Mr. Lonnie SEAY
88 Director of Center of Excellence ....Ms. Sara PHILLIPS
109 Director of Food Services ....Ms. Denise AXTELL
25 Director of Grant Development ....Ms. Amy WEBB
14 Director of Information Technology ....Mr. James CRANDALL
35 Assoc Dean of Student Services ....Ms. Buffy TANNER
26 Director of Marketing & Outreach ....Mr. Peter GRIGGS
18 Director of Physical Plant ....Mr. George ESTRADA
39 Director Residence Life ....Mr. Nick WEBB
88 Int Dir Lrng Svcs & Special Pgms ....Ms. Tina DUENAS
81 Director of TRIO ....Ms. Sue HUIZINGA

Sierra College (D)

5100 Sierra College Blvd., Rocklin CA 95677
County: Placer FICE Identification: 001290
Unit ID: 123341
Telephone: (916) 624-3333 Carnegie Class: Assoc/MT-VT-High Trad
FAX Number: N/A Calendar System: Semester
URL: www.sierracollege.edu
Established: 1914 Annual Undergrad Tuition & Fees (In-District): $1,156
Enrollment: 17,503 Coed
Affiliation or Control: State/Local IRS Status: 501(c)3
Highest Offering: Associate Degree
Accreditation: WJ

01 Superintendent/President ....Mr. William H. DUNCAN
05 Supt/Vice President Instruction ....Dr. Rebecca BOCCHICCHIO
10 Vice Pres Administrative Services ....Mr. Erik SKINNER
32 Vice Pres Student Services ....Dr. James E. TODD
04 Exec Assistant Presidents Office ....Ms. Stacey CARROLL
08 Dean Library/Learning Resource Ctr ....Ms. Sabrina PAPE
50 Dean Business & Technology ....Ms. Amy SCHULZ
81 Dean Science & Mathematics ....Dr. Rancy LEHR
49 Dean Liberal Arts ....Dr. Anne FLEISCHMANN
41 Dean Phys Ed/Athletics Dir ....Ms. Rachel JOHNSON
09 Dean Planning/Research/Res Devel ....Mr. Erik COOPER
66 Dean Nursing & Allied Health ....Ms. Nancy JAMES
13 Chief Information Officer/IIT ....Mr. Tom BENTON
114 Dir of Budget & Financial Planning ....Ms. Judy AHLQUIST
15 Director Human Resources ....Mr. Cameron ABBOTT
18 Dir of Facilities & Construction ....Ms. Laura DOTY
37 Director Financial Aid ....Dr. Linda WILLIAMS
31 Community Education Pgm Manager ....Ms. Jill ALCORN
22 Director EEO/Diversity & Title IX ....Ms. LaToya JACKSON
26 Dir Marketing/Community Relations ....Mr. Joshua D. MORGAN
39 Residence Life Supervisor ....Ms. Cortney MAGORIAN
84 Dir Enrol Svcs/Registrar/Admissions ....Ms. Mariella CRANDALL

Simpson University (E)

2211 College View Drive, Redding CA 96003-8606
County: Shasta FICE Identification: 001291
Unit ID: 123457
Telephone: (530) 224-5600 Carnegie Class: Masters/S
FAX Number: (530) 226-4860 Calendar System: Semester
URL: www.simpsonu.edu
Established: 1921 Annual Undergrad Tuition & Fees: $33,630
Enrollment: 855 Coed
Affiliation or Control: The Christian And Missionary Alliance
IRS Status: 501(c)3
Highest Offering: Master's
Accreditation: WC, NURSE

00 Chair of the Board of Trustees ....Dr. James POSTMA
01 President ....Dr. Norman D. HALL
11 Chief Operating Officer ....Mr. Walter QUIRK
05 Provost ....Dr. Dale H. SIMMONS
10 Chief Financial Officer ....Mr. Timothy N. DIETZ
88 Faculty President ....Dr. Scott BARNETT
111 Executive Director Advancement ....Mr. Roy S. MELENDEZ
26 Director of Marketing ....Mr. Tony SMARRELLA
88 Director of Admissions Data & Comm ....Vacant
73 Executive Dean AW Tozer Seminary ....Dr. Patrick A. BLEWETT
53 Exec Dean of Education/Diversity ....Mrs. Irene T. LOPEZ
66 Dean School of Nursing ....Mrs. Misty D. SMITH
88 Director Degree Completion ....Ms. Wendy J. SMITH
88 Director of Veterans Success Center ....Mr. Andrew TUGGLE
13 Director of Information Services ....Mr. David GUERCIA
41 Director of Athletics ....Mr. Thomas SEITZ
32 Dean of Students/Title IX Coord ....Mr. Mark C. ENDRASKE
38 Director of Wellness Center ....Vacant
15 Director of Human Resources ....Mrs. Melissa TURLEY
109 Director of Campus Operations ....Mr. Paul R. DAVIS
20 Dean/College of Arts & Sciences ....Dr. John AYABE
121 Associate Dean of Student Services ....Mr. Louis E. BURKWHAT
35 Associate Dean of Campus Life ....Ms. Sarah A. JOBSON
08 Director of Library Service ....Ms. Heather MCCULLEY
21 Controller ....Mr. Jared K. GRECO
06 Registrar ....Mrs. Adrienne CURRINGTON
04 Exec Assistant to the President ....Mrs. Elise WILSON
19 Campus Safety Operations Coord ....Mr. Dennis SMITH
40 Bookstore Manager ....Vacant
07 Director of Admissions ....Mr. Tony SMARRELLA
25 Senior Presidential Advisor ....Vacant
26 Communications Specialist ....Vacant
28 Executive Dean of Diversity ....Mrs. Irene T. LOPEZ
29 Director Alumni & Church Relations ....Mr. Raymond VAN GILST
37 Director Student Financial Services ....Ms. Shondra DICKSON
58 Director of M.A. Org Leadership ....Dr. Daniel SLOAN
50 Chair of Business Department ....Mr. Paul WOOD
60 Chair of Communications Dept ....Mrs. Molly RUPERT
81 Chair of Science and Math Dept ....Mr. Berkeley SHORTHILL
64 Chair of Music Department ....Mr. Steve KIM
82 Chair of History & Poli Science ....Mr. Tim ORR

Sofia University (F)

1069 E Meadow Circle, Palo Alto CA 94303-4231
County: Santa Clara FICE Identification: 022676
Unit ID: 110778
Telephone: (888) 820-1484 Carnegie Class: Spec-4-yr-Other Health
FAX Number: (650) 493-6835 Calendar System: Quarter
URL: www.sofia.edu
Established: 1975 Annual Undergrad Tuition & Fees: N/A
Enrollment: 1,514 Coed
Affiliation or Control: Proprietary IRS Status: Proprietary
Highest Offering: Doctorate
Accreditation: WC

01 President & CEO ....Dr. Allan CAHOON
05 Provost & CAO ....Dr. Stuart SIGMAN
10 VP Admin & CFO ....Mr. Chris NGUYEN
32 Dean Student Services ....Ms. Rosalie COOK
04 Chief of Staff ....Ms. Renate KROGDAHL

† Formerly Institute of Transpersonal Psychology.

Soka University of America (G)

1 University Drive, Aliso Viejo CA 92656-8081
County: Orange FICE Identification: 038144
Unit ID: 399911
Telephone: (949) 480-4000 Carnegie Class: Bac-A&S
FAX Number: (949) 480-4001 Calendar System: Semester
URL: www.soka.edu
Established: 2001 Annual Undergrad Tuition & Fees: $33,962
Enrollment: 403 Coed
Affiliation or Control: Independent Non-Profit IRS Status: 501(c)3
Highest Offering: Master's
Accreditation: WC

01 President/Professor of Economics ....Dr. Edward M. FEASEL
101 Exec Asst to President/Board Sec ....Mr. Hiro SAKAI
05 Vice Pres Academic Affairs/CAO ....Dr. Michael WEINER
10 Vice President Finance & Admin/CFO ....Mr. Archibald E. ASAWA
09 VP Inst Rsch/Dean of Graduate Sch ....Dr. Tomoko TAKAHASHI
15 Vice Pres of Human Resources ....Ms. Katherine KING
46 VP Sponsored Research/Ext Acad Rels ....Dr. Bryan E. PENPRASE
88 Vice Pres Mission Integration ....Dr. Kevin MONCRIEF
84 Dean of Enrollment Services ....Mr. Andrew WOOLSEY
32 Dean of Students ....Dr. Hyon J. MOON
11 Chief of Operations ....Mr. Tom HARKENRIDER
43 University Counsel ....Mr. David WELCH
39 Assoc Dean of Students ....Ms. Michelle HOBBY-MEARS
19 Director of Public Safety ....Mr. Don HODGSON
31 Director of Community Relations ....Ms. Wendy WETZEL HARDER
41 Director of Athletics & Recreation ....Mr. Mike MOORE
35 Director of Student Services ....Mr. Brian DURICK
30 Director of Development ....Ms. Linda KENNEDY
13 Director Information Technology ....Mr. John MIN
44 Dir of International Development ....Ms. Toshiko SATO
104 Dir Study Abroad & Intl Internships ....Mr. Alex H. OKUDA
06 Registrar ....Ms. Nancy YOSHIMURA
08 Director of Library ....Mr. Hiroko TONONO
26 Director of Marketing ....Mr. Martin BECK

Solano Community College (H)

4000 Suisun Valley Road, Fairfield CA 94534-3197
County: Solano FICE Identification: 001292
Unit ID: 123563
Telephone: (707) 864-7000 Carnegie Class: Bac/Assoc-Assoc Dom
FAX Number: (707) 864-0361 Calendar System: Semester
URL: www.solano.edu
Established: 1945 Annual Undergrad Tuition & Fees (In-District): $1,168
Enrollment: 9,251 Coed
Affiliation or Control: State/Local IRS Status: 501(c)3
Highest Offering: Baccalaureate
Accreditation: WJ

01 Superintendent/President ....Dr. Celia ESPOSITO-NOY
05 VP Academic Affairs ....Dr. David WILLIAMS
10 Vice President Finance & Admin ....Vacant
13 Interim Chief Technology Officer ....Mr. James (Kimo) CALILAN
32 Vice President Student Services ....Dr. Shannon COOPER
38 Dean Counseling/Special Services ....Dr. Kristin CONNER
37 Director Financial Aid ....Vacant
09 Dean Research and Planning ....Vacant
84 Dean of Enrollment Services ....Ms. Alysa BORELLI
15 Human Resources Director ....Mr. Salavatore ABBATE
18 Director Facilities ....Mr. Lucky LOFTON
88 Director Children's Programs ....Ms. Christie SPECK
103 Assoc Dean Workforce Development ....Vacant
26 Outreach/Public Relations Manager ....Vacant
96 Purchasing Tech/Buyer ....Ms. Laura SCOTT
36 Career & Job Placement Coordinator ....Ms. Patricia YOUNG
49 Dean School of Liberal Arts ....Mr. Neil GLINES
83 Dean Sch of Social/Behav Science ....Mr. Sandy LAMBA
81 Dean School Math/Science ....Mr. Joseph RYAN
72 Dean Sch Applied Tech Education ....Ms. Lisa NEELEY
76 Dean of Health Sciences ....Dr. Sheila HUDSON
20 Dean Academic Support Services ....Dr. Shirley LEWIS
41 Director of Athletics ....Mr. Erik VISSER

South Baylo University (I)

1126 N. Brookhurst Street, Anaheim CA 92801-1702
County: Orange FICE Identification: 025973
Unit ID: 123633
Telephone: (714) 533-1495 Carnegie Class: Spec-4-yr-Other Health
FAX Number: (714) 533-6040 Calendar System: Quarter
URL: www.southbaylo.edu
Established: 1977 Annual Undergrad Tuition & Fees: N/A
Enrollment: 306 Coed
Affiliation or Control: Independent Non-Profit IRS Status: 501(c)3
Highest Offering: Doctorate
Accreditation: ACUP

01 President .... Dr. Edwin FOLLICK
03 University Dean .... Dr. Chris LARSEN
05 Academic Dean .... Dr. Pia MELEN
15 Personnel Director .... Ms. Sohila MOHIYEDDINI
17 Director of Clinics .... Dr. Sandjaya TRI
10 Director of Finance .... Ms. Michelle JANG
06 Registrar .... Dr. Woo Jin HAN
07 Director of Admissions .... Ms. Seon KIM
58 Master Program Director .... Dr. Hyo Jeong KANG
58 Doctoral Program Director .... Dr. Ki Haeng CHO
32 Program Student Advisor .... Dr. Henry CHOI
88 Doctoral Clerkship Coordinator .... Dr. Anne AHN
35 Student/Alumni Coordinator .... Ms. Alyona CARRICO
85 International Student Advisor .... Dr. Woo Jin HAN
13 Director IT Systems .... Mr. James KIM
37 Financial Aid Officer .... Ms. Mimi PARK
38 CCE Coordinator .... Dr. Henry CHOI
08 University Librarian .... Dr. Edwin FOLLICK
18 Chief of Facilities .... Mr. Yong Hee PARK

South Coast College (A)

2011 W Chapman Avenue, Orange CA 92868-2609
County: Orange FICE Identification: 022774
Unit ID: 123642
Telephone: (714) 867-5009 Carnegie Class: Spec 2-yr-Other
FAX Number: (714) 867-5026 Calendar System: Quarter
URL: www.southcoastcollege.com
Established: 1961 Annual Undergrad Tuition & Fees: $13,073
Enrollment: 254 Coed
Affiliation or Control: Proprietary IRS Status: Proprietary
Highest Offering: Associate Degree
Accreditation: ACCSC

01 President .... Ms. Jean GONZALEZ
10 Dean Finance & Admin .... Ms. Jila ANDELIBI
11 Director of Operations .... Mr. Kevin MAGNER
37 Director of Financial Aid .... Mr. Michael LY
06 Registrar .... Ms. Yoshiko IZUMI

*South Orange County Community College District (B)

28000 Marguerite Parkway, Mission Viejo CA 92692-3697
County: Orange FICE Identification: 033433
Unit ID: 432144
Telephone: (949) 582-4850 Carnegie Class: N/A
FAX Number: (949) 364-2726
URL: www.socccd.edu

01 Chancellor .... Dr. Kathleen F. BURKE
05 Vice Chanc Technology/Learning Svcs .. Dr. Robert S. BRAMUCCI
15 Vice Chancellor Human Resources .... Ms. Cindy VYSKOCIL
10 Vice Chancellor Business Svcs .... Ms. Ann-Marie GABEL
26 Dir Public Affairs/Govt Relations .... Ms. Letitia CLARK
12 President Saddleback College .... Dr. Elliot STERN
12 President Irvine Valley College .... Dr. John HERNANDEZ

*Irvine Valley College (C)

5500 Irvine Center Drive, Irvine CA 92618-4399
County: Orange FICE Identification: 025395
Unit ID: 116439
Telephone: (949) 451-5100 Carnegie Class: Assoc/HT-Mix Trad/Non
FAX Number: (949) 451-5270 Calendar System: Semester
URL: www.ivc.edu
Established: 1979 Annual Undergrad Tuition & Fees (In-District): $1,146
Enrollment: 12,199 Coed
Affiliation or Control: State/Local IRS Status: 501(c)3
Highest Offering: Associate Degree
Accreditation: WJ

02 President .... Dr. John C. HERNANDEZ
100 Manager Office of the President .... Ms. Sandy JEFFRIES
05 Vice President Instruction .... Dr. Christopher MCDONALD
32 Vice President Student Services .... Dr. Martha MCDONALD
11 Vice President Admin Services .... Mr. Davit KHACHATRYAN
26 Exec Dir Marketing/Creative Svcs .... Ms. Diane G. OAKS
102 Exec Director College Foundation .... Ms. Elissa ORANSKY
41 Dean Kinesiology/Health/Athletics .... Mr. Keith SHACKLEFORD
83 Dean Social & Behavioral Sciences .... Ms. Traci FAHIMI
38 Dean Counseling Services .... Dr. Elizabeth CIPRES
09 Dir Research/Planning/Accreditation .... Dr. Loris FAGIOLI
19 Chief of Police .... Mr. Scott KENNEDY
79 Dean Liberal Arts .... Dr. Brooke BUI
103 Dean Career & Continuing Educ . Ms. Debbie VANSCHOELANDT
81 Dean Math/Sciences and Engr .... Dr. Lianna ZHAO
57 Dean The Arts .... Mr. Joseph POSHEK
84 Dean of Enrollment Services .... Mr. Corey RODGERS
23 Asst Dean Health/Wellness/Vet Svcs .. Ms. Nancy MONTGOMERY
37 Director of Financial Aid .... Mr. Korey LINDLEY
85 Dir International Student Programs .... Ms. Christina DELGADO
18 Director IVC Facilities .... Mr. Jeffrey HURLBUT
44 Director Annual Giving/Devel Svcs .... Ms. Karen ORLANDO
35 Director Student Life & Equity .... Mr. Amrik JOHAL
88 Manager of Outreach Services .... Mr. Frank RIVERA
93 Interim Mgr of Student Equity .... Ms. Erin POLLARD
121 Director Student Success/Support .... Mr. Deejay SANTIAGO
13 Director Technology Services .... Mr. Nick WILKENING
06 Registrar/Admissions/Records .... Mr. Ruben GUZMAN

*Saddleback College (D)

28000 Marguerite Parkway, Mission Viejo CA 92692-3635
County: Orange FICE Identification: 008918
Unit ID: 122205
Telephone: (949) 582-4500 Carnegie Class: Assoc/HT-Mix Trad/Non
FAX Number: (949) 347-0438 Calendar System: Semester
URL: www.saddleback.edu
Established: 1968 Annual Undergrad Tuition & Fees (In-District): $1,330
Enrollment: 18,984 Coed
Affiliation or Control: State/Local IRS Status: 501(c)3
Highest Offering: Associate Degree
Accreditation: WJ, ADNUR, CAHIIM, EMT, NAEYC

02 President .... Dr. Elliot STERN
05 Vice President of Instruction .... Ms. Tram VO-KUMAMOTO
10 Vice Pres Administrative Svcs .... Mr. Cory WATHEN
32 Vice President of Student Services .... Dr. Juan AVALOS
20 Asst VP Cmty Ed/Emeritus & K-12 .... Dr. Karima FELDHUS
84 Dean of Enrollment Services .... Mr. Christian ALVARADO
100 Manager Office of the President .... Mr. Ryan BROOK
45 Director Planning/Research/Accred .... Ms. Shouka TORABI
06 Registrar .... Dr. James M. FEIGERT
19 Chief Of Police .... Mr. Pat HIGA
26 Dir Marketing/Communications .... Ms. Jennie MCCUE
102 Exec Dir College Foundation .... Ms. Elizabeth MCCANN
35 Director Student Life .... Mr. Christopher HARGRAVES
88 Assistant Dean Emeritus Institute .... Mr. Dan PREDOEHL
44 Director Annual/Planned Giving .... Ms. Erin MCHENRY
66 Director of Nursing .... Ms. Dee OLIVERI
18 Dir Facilities/Maint/Operation .... Mr. Timothy WOOTTON
23 Director Student Health Center .. Dr. Jeanne HARRIS-CALDWELL
13 Director Technology Services .... Dr. Anthony MACIEL
37 Director Financial Assistance .... Ms. Amber GALLAGHER
96 Director of Purchasing .... Mr. Nicholas NEWKIRK
85 Director of Intl Student Program .... Ms. Angela YANG
92 Honors Program .... Ms. Alannah ROSENBERG
38 Dean Counseling Svcs/Special Pgms .... Ms. Penny SKAFF
57 Dean Fine Arts .... Dr. Scott FARTHING
50 Dean Bus Science/Econ/Workforce Dev .... Dr. John JARAMILLO
76 Dean Health Sciences/Human Svcs .... Dr. Sherrie LOEWEN
81 Dean Math/Science & Engineering .... Dr. Akira NITTA
79 Dean Liberal Arts/Learning Res .... Dr. Kevin O'CONNOR
106 Dean Online Education/Learning Res .... Dr. Marina AMINY
72 Dean Advanced Tech Appl Science .... Dr. Anthony TENG
68 Dean Kinesiology/Athletic Director .... Mr. Daniel CLAUSS
83 Dean Social/Behavioral Sciences .... Dr. Christina HINKLE
121 Director Learning Assistance .... Dr. Kim D'ARCY
22 Dean Student Equity & Spec Programs .... Dr. Georgina GUY
103 Dir Economic/Workforce Development .... Mr. Israel DOMINGUEZ
25 Director Fiscal Contract Services .... Ms. Roxanne METZ
41 Athletic Director .... Mr. Randy TOTORP

Southern California Institute of Architecture (E)

960 E 3rd Street, Los Angeles CA 90013-1822
County: Los Angeles FICE Identification: 020758
Unit ID: 123952
Telephone: (213) 613-2200 Carnegie Class: Spec-4-yr-Arts
FAX Number: (213) 613-2260 Calendar System: Semester
URL: www.sciarc.edu
Established: 1972 Annual Undergrad Tuition & Fees: $49,278
Enrollment: 481 Coed
Affiliation or Control: Independent Non-Profit IRS Status: 501(c)3
Highest Offering: Master's
Accreditation: WC

01 Director .... Mr. Herman DIAZ ALONSO
05 Vice Director/Chief Academic Ofcr .... Mr. John ENRIGHT
10 Chief Financial Officer .... Ms. Sue GOSNEY
11 Chief Administration Officer .... Mr. Paul HOLLIDAY
13 Chief Information Officer .... Mr. Vic JABRASSIAN
111 Chief Advancement Officer .... Ms. Kate O'NEAL
30 Assoc Director Development .... Vacant
58 Graduate Program Chair .... Ms. Elena MANFERDINI
48 Undergraduate Program Chair .... Mr. Tom WISCOMBE
04 Executive Assistant to Director .... Ms. Yasil NAVARRO
07 Admissions Director .... Mr. Angel MONTES
26 Communications Director .... Ms. Stephanie ATLAN
15 Human Resources Director .... Ms. Liliana CLOUGH
06 Registrar/International Advisor .... Ms. Lisa RUSSO
37 Financial Aid Manager .... Ms. Marisela DE LA TORRE
08 Library Manager .... Mr. Kevin MCMAHON
88 Wood & Metal Shop Manager .... Mr. Rodney ROJAS
18 Facilities Director .... Mr. Emil TATEVOSIAN
20 Academic Affairs Coordinator .... Ms. Andrea YOUNG
19 Security Manager .... Mr. Reginald BENSON

Southern California Institute of Technology (F)

525 North Muller Street, Anaheim CA 92801-5454
County: Orange FICE Identification: 031136
Unit ID: 399869
Telephone: (714) 300-0300 Carnegie Class: Spec-4-yr-Eng
FAX Number: (714) 300-0311 Calendar System: Quarter
URL: www.scitech.edu
Established: 1987 Annual Undergrad Tuition & Fees: $18,390
Enrollment: 568 Coed
Affiliation or Control: Proprietary IRS Status: Proprietary
Highest Offering: Baccalaureate
Accreditation: ACCSC

01 President .... Dr. Parviz SHAMS
03 Vice President .... Mrs. Nazila SHAMS
11 Director of Operations .... Mr. Arian SHAMS

Southern California Seminary (G)

2075 E Madison Avenue, El Cajon CA 92019-1108
County: San Diego FICE Identification: 033323
Unit ID: 117575
Telephone: (619) 201-8999 Carnegie Class: Spec-4-yr-Faith
FAX Number: (619) 201-8975 Calendar System: Trimester
URL: www.socalsem.edu
Established: 1946 Annual Undergrad Tuition & Fees: $16,884
Enrollment: 174 Coed
Affiliation or Control: Independent Non-Profit IRS Status: 501(c)3
Highest Offering: Doctorate
Accreditation: TRACS

00 Chancellor .... Dr. David JEREMIAH
01 President .... Dr. Gary F. COOMBS
05 Provost & Chief Academic Officer .... Dr. Gino PASQUARIELLO
83 Dean Grad Sch Behavioral Science .... Dr. Elizabeth ELENWO
73 Dean of Biblical Studies/Theology .... Mr. James I. FAZIO
06 Registrar .... Mr. Brian BARGA
32 Director of Student Services .... Ms. Lisa PACHECO
37 Financial Aid Counselor .... Ms. Brianna ANDERSON
08 Library Director .... Miss Jennifer EWING
07 Admissions Officer .... Mr. Leroy HILL
113 Student Accounts .... Ms. Erin NEILL

Southern California State University (H)

3470 Wilshire Blvd, Ste 380, Los Angeles CA 90010
County: Los Angeles Identification: 667374
Telephone: (213) 382-5300 Carnegie Class: Not Classified
FAX Number: (213) 403-5636 Calendar System: Quarter
URL: www.scsu.us
Established: 2012 Annual Undergrad Tuition & Fees: N/A
Enrollment: N/A Coed
Affiliation or Control: Independent Non-Profit IRS Status: 501(c)3
Highest Offering: Master's
Accreditation: TRACS

Southern California University of Health Sciences (I)

16200 E Amber Valley Drive, Whittier CA 90604-4051
County: Los Angeles FICE Identification: 001229
Unit ID: 117672
Telephone: (562) 947-8755 Carnegie Class: Spec-4-yr-Other Health
FAX Number: (562) 947-5724 Calendar System: Trimester
URL: www.scuhs.edu
Established: 1911 Annual Undergrad Tuition & Fees: N/A
Enrollment: 1,225 Coed
Affiliation or Control: Independent Non-Profit IRS Status: 501(c)3
Highest Offering: First Professional Degree
Accreditation: WC, ACUP, #ARCPA, CHIRO

01 President .... Dr. John SCARINGE
100 VP Operations/Chief of Staff .... Mr. Chuck SWEET
05 Provost/Chief Academic Officer .... Dr. Tamara ROZHON
10 VP Finance/CFO .... Mr. Thomas K. ARENDT
17 VP SCU Health Sys/Chief Clin Ofcr .... Dr. Melissa NAGARE
04 Exec Asst to President/BOR .... Ms. Michelle BERNHEIM
07 Asst VP Admissions .... Mr. Erick DE LA ROSA
32 Asst VP Student Services .... Ms. Shelby GUGEL
108 AVP of Institutional Effectiveness .... Dr. Josephine WELSH
88 AVP Health System/Clinical COS .... Mr. Robb RUSSELL
20 Asst Provost Academic Initiatives .... Dr. Michael RAMCHARAN
20 Asst Provost Academic Affairs .... Dr. Jonathon EGAN
88 Dean LACC .... Dr. Ana CAMPOS FACCHINATO
63 Dean College of Eastern Medicine .... Dr. Jenny YU
37 Director of Financial Aid .... Ms. Sybil SMITH
06 Assistant Registrar .... Ms. Raquel CHANG
81 Director Accelerated Sciences .... Dr. Winmar WAY
21 Asst VP for Accounting .... Mrs. Kelly GALLO
109 Asst VP Auxiliary Services .... Mr. Joseph EGGLESTON
08 Exec Dir of Seabury Learning Center .... Ms. Kathleen E. SMITH
15 Human Resources/Payroll Specialist .... Ms. Cindy SCHEIBEL
29 Dir Alumni/Constituent Relations .... Dr. Elizabeth ROBLEDO
18 Director of Physical Plant .... Mr. Bob HARRISON
88 Assistant Controller .... Mrs. Christine HUYNH
121 Director Academic Support Office .... Ms. Samaneh SADRI
26 Executive Director Marketing .... Mr. Jim BRENNER
45 Director Finance Planning/ Analysis .... Ms. Jennifer CHAMBERS-TAUBE
88 Director Faculty/Dev/Curriculum .... Ms. Swati RAMANI

Southern States University (J)

2855 Michelle Drive 380, Irvine CA 92606
Telephone: (949) 833-8868 Identification: 770629
Accreditation: ACICS

Southern States University (K)

1094 Cudahy Place, Suite 120, San Diego CA 92110
County: San Diego Identification: 667108
Unit ID: 490063

Telephone: (619) 298-1829 Carnegie Class: Spec-4-yr-Bus
FAX Number: (619) 704-0175 Calendar System: Quarter
URL: www.ssu.edu
Established: 1985 Annual Undergrad Tuition & Fees: $5,913
Enrollment: 358 Coed
Affiliation or Control: Proprietary IRS Status: Proprietary
Highest Offering: Master's
Accreditation: ACICS

01 Chancellor .... John D. TUCKER
05 Chief Academic Officer .... Charlotte HISLOP
06 Univ Registrar/Compliance Officer .... Wendy DU
08 University Librarian .... Christine WALCZYK
37 Financial Aid/Human Resources Mgr .... Denise MASTRO

Southwestern College (A)

900 Otay Lakes Road, Chula Vista CA 91910-7299
County: San Diego FICE Identification: 001294
Unit ID: 123800
Telephone: (619) 421-6700 Carnegie Class: Assoc/HT-High Trad
FAX Number: (619) 482-6413 Calendar System: Semester
URL: www.swccd.edu
Established: 1961 Annual Undergrad Tuition & Fees (In-District): $1,340
Enrollment: 17,621 Coed
Affiliation or Control: State/Local IRS Status: 501(c)3
Highest Offering: Associate Degree
Accreditation: WJ, ADNUR, DH, EMT, MLTAD, SURGT

01 Superintendent/President .... Dr. Mark SANCHEZ
05 Asst Supt/VP Academic Affairs .... Dr. Minou SPRADLEY
10 Asst Supt/VP Business & Fin Affs .... Dr. Kelly HALL
32 Asst Supt/VP Student Affairs .... Dr. Tina KING
12 Dn High Ed Ctr Otay Mesa/San Ysidro .... Ms. Silvia CORNEJO
12 Dn High Ed Ctr Natl City/Crown Cove .... Ms. Christine PERRI
79 Dean Language & Literature .... Dr. Joel LEVINE
81 Dean Math/Science Engineering .... Dr. Michael ODU
68 Dean Wellness/Ex Sci/Athletics .... Mr. James SPILLERS
50 Dean Business & Technology .... Dr. Mink STAVENGA
57 Dean School of Arts/Comm and SS .... Dr. Cynthia MCGREGOR
09 Dean Inst Research & Planning .... Mr. Guillermo ABASOLO
108 Dean Inst Effect/Dir of Foundation .... Ms. Mia MCCLELLAN
26 Chief Public Info/Govt Relations .... Ms. Lillian LEOPOLD
15 Exec Asst Supt/VP Human Resources .... Ms. Janene MCINTYRE
88 Director Payroll Services .... Ms. Kimberly FROST
88 Dir Center Ops HEC San Ysidro .... Ms. Patricia BARTOW
88 Dir Rest Justice & Off Campus Pgm .... Ms. Patrice MILKOVICH
37 Director Financial Aid/Veterans .... Ms. Adrianne LEE
07 Director Admissions/Records .... Mr. Nicholas MONTEZ
35 Interim Dean Student Services .... Ms. Rachel FISCHER
88 Director Disability Support Svcs .... Ms. Malia FLOOD
124 Director EOPS .... Mr. Omar ORIHUELA
88 Acting Dir Child Development Ctr .... Ms. Isabel CARRASCO
22 Exec Officer of Equity & Engagement .... Ms. Janelle WILLIAMS
04 Special Assistant to Super/Pres .... Ms. Zaneta ENCARNACION
13 Chief Info Technology Officer (CIO) .... Vacant
28 Dir Equity/Inclusion/Diversity .... Dr. Guadalupe CORONA
102 Executive Director Foundation .... Ms. Sofia ROBITAILLE
88 Int Dir Student Development .... Mr. Ronnie HANDS
88 Director of Police Academy .... Mr. David ESPIRITU
103 Dean Cont Educ & Workforce Dev .... Ms. Jennifer LEWIS
88 Director EMT & Paramedic .... Mr. Jason HUMS
52 Interim Director Dental Hygiene .... Ms. Gay TEEL
66 Sr Dir Nursing & Health Occupations .... Ms. Samantha GIRARD
88 Director MEDOPS .... Ms. Deanna REINACHER
16 Director for Human Resources .... Ms. Angela RIGGS
88 Director of ER and Title IX .... Ms. Janene MCINTYRE
51 Dir Cont Education & Spec Projects .... Ms. Myesha JACKSON
109 Int Food Services Ops Supervisor .... Ms. Claudia ACOSTA
18 Int Dir Facilities Ops & Planning .... Ms. Aurora AYALA
21 Director of Finance .... Ms. Alison HUNTER

Southwestern Law School (B)

3050 Wilshire Boulevard, Los Angeles CA 90010-1106
County: Los Angeles FICE Identification: 001295
Unit ID: 123970
Telephone: (213) 738-6700 Carnegie Class: Spec-4-yr-Law
FAX Number: (213) 383-1688 Calendar System: Semester
URL: www.swlaw.edu
Established: 1911 Annual Graduate Tuition & Fees: N/A
Enrollment: 886 Coed
Affiliation or Control: Independent Non-Profit IRS Status: 501(c)3
Highest Offering: Master's; No Undergraduates
Accreditation: LAW

00 Chairman of the Board .... Mr. Charles P. FAIRCHILD
01 President/Dean .... Ms. Darby DICKERSON
03 EVP & Chief Administrative Officer .... Dr. Michael CARTER
10 Chief Financial Officer .... Ms. Linda ROSS
13 Chief Information Officer .... Mr. Sean MURPHY
26 Chief Comm & Marketing Officer .... Ms. Hillary KANE
05 Vice Dean .... Ms. Anahid GHARAKHANIAN
05 Vice Dean/Dir of Externship .... Mr. Dov WAISMAN
04 Exec Assistant to the Dean/Pres .... Ms. Janis K. YOKOYAMA
20 Sr Assoc Dean for Academic Admin .... Ms. Doreen E. HEYER-RANEY
11 Assoc Dean of Operations & Risk .... Ms. Marcie CANAL
32 Assoc Dean of Student Affairs .... Dr. Robert MENA
27 Asst Director Comm & Marketing .... Mr. Steven B. LOPEZ
28 Dean of Students/Diversity Affairs .... Ms. Nydia DUEÑEZ
111 VP for Institutional Advancement .... Mr. Jeff POLTORAK
09 Assoc Dean for Research .... Ms. Hila KEREN
44 Director of Annual Giving .... Ms. Emily CARDINAS
110 Assoc Dean for Institutional Advanc .... Ms. Debra L. LEATHERS
08 Assoc Dean and Law Library Director .... Ms. Margaret HALL
36 Assoc Dean of Career Services .... Ms. Shahrzad POORMOSLEH
88 Assoc Dean for SCALE .... Ms. Harriet M. ROLNICK
88 Assoc Dean Strategic Initiatives .... Mr. Byron G. STIER
88 Assoc Dean Experiential Learning .... Ms. Julie K. WATERSTONE
121 Asst Dean of Academic Success .... Ms. Natalie RODRIGUEZ
07 Assoc Dean of Admissions .... Ms. Lisa L. GEAR
37 Director of Financial Aid .... Ms. Lina BORJORQUEZ
88 Director of Immigration Law Clinic .... Ms. Andrea RAMOS
88 Director of Bar Preparation .... Ms. Tina SCHINDLER
88 Assoc Dean for Learning Outcomes .... Ms. Tracy TURNER
88 Director Biederman EML Institute .... Ms. Orly RAVID
92 Co-Director of Moot Court Honors .... Ms. Catherine CARPENTER
92 Co-Director of Moot Court Honors .... Ms. Alexandra D'ITALIA
92 Co-Director of Trial Ad Honors .... Mr. Bill H. SEKI
92 Co-Director of Trial Ad Honors .... Mr. Joseph P. ESPOSITO
92 Co-Director of Negotiation Honors .... Ms. Cristina C. KNOLTON
06 Registrar/Princ Des Sch Ofcl .... Ms. Monic CLARE
39 Property Manager of Residences .... Ms. Michelle TAFOYA
88 Faculty Director General LL.M. .... Ms. Priya GUPTA
85 Assoc Director International Prog .... Mr. Vik KANWAR
88 Director of Public Service Program .... Ms. Michelle TAKAGISHI-ALMEIDA
61 Tech Law & Entrepreneur Director .... Mr. Michael B. DORFF
88 Director of Entertainment and Media .... Mr. Michael M. EPSTEIN
61 Director of Public Interest Law .... Ms. Julia VAZQUEZ
100 Chief of Staff .... Mr. Timothy CRAVEC

Spartan College of Aeronautics and Technology (C)

8911 Aviation Blvd, Inglewood CA 90301
County: Los Angeles FICE Identification: 025964
Unit ID: 413680
Telephone: (310) 879-0554 Carnegie Class: Spec 2-yr-Tech
FAX Number: N/A Calendar System: Other
URL: www.spartan.edu
Established: 2014 Annual Undergrad Tuition & Fees: N/A
Enrollment: 391 Coed
Affiliation or Control: Proprietary IRS Status: Proprietary
Highest Offering: Associate Degree
Accreditation: COE

01 President .... Mr. Rick MENDOZA

Stanbridge University (D)

2041 Business Center Dr., Suite 107, Irvine CA 92612
County: Orange FICE Identification: 038893
Unit ID: 446561
Telephone: (949) 794-9090 Carnegie Class: Spec-4-yr-Other Health
FAX Number: (949) 794-9098 Calendar System: Other
URL: www.stanbridge.edu
Established: 1996 Annual Undergrad Tuition & Fees: N/A
Enrollment: 1,698 Coed
Affiliation or Control: Proprietary IRS Status: Proprietary
Highest Offering: Master's
Accreditation: ACCSC, NURSE, OT, OTA, PTAA

01 Chief Executive Officer .... Mr. Yasith WEERASURIYA
10 Chief Financial Officer .... Ms. Nazi MASOUM
05 Vice Pres of Instruction .... Dr. Kelly HAMILTON
105 Exec VP Internet & Media Technology .... Mr. Monir BOKTOR
66 Director of VN Program .... Ms. Renee HYPOLITE
66 Director of RN Program .... Ms. Annabelle ANGLO
66 Director of BSN & MSN Program .... Dr. Margaret SANTANDREA
76 Director of OTA Program .... Mr. Satch PURCELL
76 Interim Director of OT Program .... Dr. Mark PETERSEN
76 Director of PTA Program .... Dr. Christie KARLE
32 Dean of Students .... Ms. Elizabeth PEYTON
37 Director of Financial Aid .... Mr. Brian SILVANO
07 Director of Admission Operations .... Mr. Greg LOW
74 Int Director of ASVT .... Ms. Emma CUSACK
88 Asst Program Director ASVT .... Ms. Kristin ILARDI
08 Librarian .... Mr. Fred POLING
36 Director of Career Services .... Mr. John ANDREWS

Stanford University (E)

450 Jane Stanford Way, Stanford CA 94305-2004
County: Santa Clara FICE Identification 001305
Unit ID: 243744
Telephone: (650) 723-2300 Carnegie Class: DU-Highest
FAX Number: (650) 725-6847 Calendar System: Quarter
URL: www.stanford.edu
Established: 1885 Annual Undergrad Tuition & Fees: $56,169
Enrollment: 15,953 Coed
Affiliation or Control: Independent Non-Profit IRS Status: 501(c)3
Highest Offering: Doctorate
Accreditation: WC, ARCPA, CAMPEP, IPSY, LAW, MED, PDPSY

01 President .... Dr. Marc TESSIER-LAVIGNE
43 Vice President & General Counsel .... Ms. Debra L. ZUMWALT
05 Provost .... Dr. Persis DRELL
26 VP/Chief External Relations Ofcr .... Mr. Martin SHELL
10 Vice President Business Affairs/CFO .... Mr. Randy LIVINGSTON
30 Vice Pres for Development .... Mr. Jon DENNEY
86 Sr Assoc VP for Public Affairs .... Mr. Ryan ADESNIK
15 Vice President for Human Resources .... Ms. Elizabeth ZACHARIAS
27 Vice President for Communications .... Ms. Farnaz KHADEM
29 President of Alumni Association .... Vacant
46 Vice Provost/Dean of Research .... Dr. Kathryn A. MOLER
20 Vice Provost Undergrad Education .... Dr. Sarah CHURCH
20 Vice Provost for Academic Affairs .... Dr. Stephanie KALFAYAN
88 Vice Provost Faculty Development .... Ms. Karen COOK
18 Vice President for Land & Buildings .... Mr. Robert C. REIDY
114 Vice Provost Budget & Auxiliaries .... Mr. Timothy R. WARNER
32 Vice Provost Student Affairs .... Ms. Susie BRUBAKER-COLE
100 Chief of Staff .... Ms. Megan PIERSON
106 Vice Prov Teaching & Learning .... Mr. Michael KELLER
63 Dean School of Medicine .... Dr. Lloyd MINOR
50 Dean Graduate School Business .... Dr. Jonathan LEVIN
65 Dean School of Earth Sciences .... Dr. Stephen GRAHAM
53 Dean School of Education .... Dr. Daniel SCHWARTZ
54 Dean School of Engineering .... Dr. Jennifer WIDOM
49 Dean School Humanities & Sciences .... Dr. Debra SATZ
61 Dean School of Law .... Ms. Jenny S. MARTINEZ
87 Dean Summer Session/Cont Stds .... Dr. Charles L. JUNKERMAN
42 Dean for Religious Life .... Dr. Tiffany STEINWERT
88 Director Hoover Institution .... Ms. Condoleezza RICE
88 Director SLAC .... Mr. Chi-Chang KAO
13 Chief Information Officer .... Mr. Steve GALLAGHER
08 Vice Provost/University Librarian .... Mr. Michael A. KELLER
41 Athletic Director .... Mr. Bernard MUIR
07 Dean of Admission and Financial Aid .... Mr. Richard H. SHAW, JR.
88 CEO Stanford Management Company .... Mr. Robert WALLACE
06 Registrar .... Ms. Johanna METZGAR
36 Director Career Development Center .... Mr. Farouk DEY
09 Dir Inst Research/Assessment .... Ms. Corrie POTTER
37 Director of Student Financial Aid .... Ms. Karen S. COOPER
27 AVP Stanford News Service .... Ms. Donna LOVELL
19 Director Public Safety .... Ms. Laura L. WILSON
96 AVP Procurement Services .... Ms. Cindy WILKINSON
35 Dir Prof Dev/Student Activities .... Ms. Ellen OH
38 Director Student Counseling .... Dr. Ronald ALBURCHER
102 Sr Dir Foundation/Corp Relations .... Ms. Kathy VEIT
88 Director Knight-Hennessy Scholars .... Dr. John L. HENNESSY

Stanton University (F)

9618 Garden Grove Blvd., Ste 201,
Garden Grove CA 92844
County: Orange Identification: 667370
Telephone: (714) 539-6561 Carnegie Class: Not Classified
FAX Number: (714) 539-6542 Calendar System: Quarter
URL: www.stantonuniversity.com
Established: 1996 Annual Undergrad Tuition & Fees: N/A
Enrollment: N/A Coed
Affiliation or Control: Independent Non-Profit IRS Status: 501(c)3
Highest Offering: Master's
Accreditation: @WC

01 President .... Dr. David K. KIM
05 Chief Academic Officer .... Dr. James HEIDEMAN
20 Director Academic Affairs .... Mr. Anhtu NGUYEN
10 Director of Business Affairs .... Ms. Han Na KIM
32 Director of Student Affairs .... Mr. Daniel KIM
07 Director of Admissions and Records .... Ms. Jean CHO
06 Registrar .... Ms. Raquel CRUZ

Starr King School for the Ministry (G)

5000 MacArthur Blvd, Oakland CA 94613
County: Oakland FICE Identification: 004080
Unit ID: 123916
Telephone: (510) 845-6232 Carnegie Class: Spec-4-yr-Faith
FAX Number: (510) 845-6273 Calendar System: Semester
URL: www.sksm.edu
Established: 1904 Annual Graduate Tuition & Fees: N/A
Enrollment: 87 Coed
Affiliation or Control: Unitarian Universalist IRS Status: 501(c)3
Highest Offering: Doctorate; No Undergraduates
Accreditation: THEOL

01 President .... Rev. Rosemary Bray MCNATT
111 Vice President Advancement .... Ms. Jessica CLOUD
10 VP for Finance & Admin .... Mr. Kelly GIBBS
32 Vice Pres Student Services .... Ms. Rain JORDAN
05 Dean of the Faculty .... Dr. Gabriella LETTINI
35 Dean of Students .... Dr. Chris SCHELIN
06 Registrar .... Ms. Juliet CHAN
07 Director Admissions/Recruitment .... Mr. Matthew WATERMAN
20 Coordinator of Academic Programs .... Ms. Shannon EIZENGA
106 Director Online Education .... Dr. Hugo CORDOVA QUERO
26 Communications Officer .... Mr. Xander HUFFMAN
18 Facilities Director .... Mr. Fred WILLIAMSON

*State Center Community College District (H)

1171 Fulton Street, Fresno CA 93721
County: Fresno FICE Identification: 001306
Unit ID: 123925
Telephone: (559) 243-7100 Carnegie Class: N/A
FAX Number: N/A
URL: www.scccd.edu

01 Interim Chancellor .... Dr. Douglas HOUSTON
10 Vice Chancellor Finance & Admin .... Ms. Cheryl SULLIVAN
05 VC Educ Svcs/Inst Effectiveness .... Mr. Jerome COUNTEE

15	Vice Chanc Human Resources	Ms. Julianna MOSIER
11	Vice Chancellor Operations & IS	Ms. Christine MIKTARIAN
26	Exec Dir Pub/Legislative Rels	Ms. Lucy RUIZ
102	Executive Director Foundation	Mr. Rico GUERRERO
43	General Counsel	Mr. Matthew BESMER
25	Dir Grants/External Funding	Ms. Oxana AGHAEI
16	Director Human Resources	Ms. Samerah CAMPBELL
96	Director of Purchasing	Mr. Randy VOGT
21	Director of Finance	Mr. William SCHOFIELD
13	Chief Technology Officer	Dr. Ben SEABERRY
16	Director of Classified Personnel	Vacant

*Clovis Community College (A)

10309 N. Willow Avenue, Fresno CA 93730

County: Fresno — Identification: 667125
Unit ID: 489201
Telephone: (559) 325-5200 — Carnegie Class: Assoc/HT-High Trad
FAX Number: (559) 499-6065 — Calendar System: Semester
URL: www.cloviscollege.edu
Established: 2007 — Annual Undergrad Tuition & Fees (In-District): $1,304
Enrollment: 8,868 — Coed
Affiliation or Control: State/Local — IRS Status: 501(c)3
Highest Offering: Associate Degree
Accreditation: WJ

02	President	Dr. Lori BENNETT
05	VP Instruction	Ms. Monica CHAHAL
10	VP Administrative Services	Ms. Lorrie HOPPER
32	VP Student Services	Mr. Marco J. DE LA GARZA
79	Dean of Instruction Humanities	Dr. James ORTEZ
75	Dean of Instruction CTE & Athletics	Ms. Pamm ZIERFUSS-HUBBARD
81	Dean of Instruction STEM	Dr. John FORBES
35	Dean of Students Services	Ms. Kira TIPPINS
13	Director of Technology	Mr. Teng HER
26	Director of Marketing	Ms. Stephanie BABB
27	Director of DSP&S	Dr. Jacquelyn RUBALCABA
35	Dean of Student Services	Ms. Gurdeep HEBERT
09	Director of Institutional Research	Vacant
37	Director of Financial Aid	Mr. Matt LEVINE
38	Director of SBDC	Mr. Rich MOSTERT
07	Admissions & Records Manager	Ms. Reynani HAWKINS
04	Assistant to the President	Ms. Bonnie BOONTHAVONGKHAM
18	Chf Facilities/Physical Plant Ofcr	Mr. Sergio SALINAS

*Fresno City College (B)

1101 E University Avenue, Fresno CA 93741-0002

County: Fresno — FICE Identification: 001307
Unit ID: 114789
Telephone: (559) 442-4200 — Carnegie Class: Assoc/MT-VT-Mix Trad/Non
FAX Number: (559) 499-6045 — Calendar System: Semester
URL: www.fresnocitycollege.edu
Established: 1910 — Annual Undergrad Tuition & Fees (In-District): $1,304
Enrollment: 22,278 — Coed
Affiliation or Control: State/Local — IRS Status: 501(c)3
Highest Offering: Associate Degree
Accreditation: WJ, CAHIIM, COARC, DH, RAD

02	President	Dr. Carole GOLDSMITH
05	Vice President of Instruction	Mr. Don LOPEZ
32	VP of Student Services	Dr. Lataria HALL
10	Vice Pres Administrative Services	Mr. Omar GUTIERREZ
108	VP of Educ Svcs/Inst Effectiveness	Dr. Robert PIMENTEL
07	District Dir Admissions & Records	Ms. Robin TORRES
121	Dean Student Success/Learning	Dr. Donna COOPER
50	Dean Business Division	Dr. Tim WOODS
57	Dean Fine/Performing/Comm Arts	Ms. Cyndie LUNA
79	Dean Humanities Division	Ms. Tabitha VILLALBA
54	Dean Math/Science/Engineering Div	Ms. Shirley MCMANUS
83	Dean Social Sciences Division	Ms. Cherylyn CRILL-HORNSBY
76	Dean Health Sciences Division	Ms. Lorraine SMITH
72	Dean Applied Technology Division	Dr. Becky BARABE
38	Dean Counseling/Guidance	Ms. Monica CUEVAS
35	Dean of Student Services	Mr. Sean HENDERSON
75	Dean Educ Svcs/Pathway Effective	Mr. Gurminder SANGHA
22	Director of Student Equity	Dr. Raymond RAMIREZ
88	Dir Disabled Stdnt Pgms & Svcs	Ms. Susan ARRIOLA
09	Dir Institutional Research	Dr. Alex ADAMS
88	Director Police Academy	Mr. Gary FIEF
35	Director of Student Activities	Dr. Ernie MARTINEZ
26	Director Marketing/Communications	Ms. Cris M. BREMER
37	Director Financial Aid	Ms. Mikki JOHNSON
27	Public Information Officer	Ms. Kathleen BONILLA
41	Assoc Dean Athletics	Mr. Derrick JOHNSON
106	Dir Distance Education/Inst Tech	Dr. Jodie STEELEY
72	Director of Technology	Ms. Jennifer LAVAL
88	Dir College Relations & Outreach	Mr. Nickolas LUCIO
66	Director of Nursing	Ms. Keisha LEWIS
88	Director CalWORKs Program	Ms. Mary Beth MOSSETTE
06	Director Admissions & Records	Ms. Mirna DUARTE
88	Director TRIO Programs	Mr. Bernardo REYNOSO
124	Director EOPS/CARE	Mr. Thomas GAXIOLA-ROWLES
38	Dir Counseling/Special Programs	Dr. George ALVARADO

*Madera Community College (C)

30277 Avenue 12, Madera CA 93638

County: Madera — Identification: 667399
Telephone: (559) 675-4800 — Carnegie Class: Not Classified
FAX Number: N/A — Calendar System: Semester
URL: www.maderacenter.com
Established: 1996 — Annual Undergrad Tuition & Fees (In-District): N/A
Enrollment: N/A — Coed
Affiliation or Control: State/Local — IRS Status: 501(c)3
Highest Offering: Associate Degree
Accreditation: WJ

02	Campus President	Mr. Angel REYNA

*Reedley College (D)

995 N Reed Avenue, Reedley CA 93654-2099

County: Fresno — FICE Identification: 001308
Unit ID: 117052
Telephone: (559) 638-0300 — Carnegie Class: Assoc/HT-Mix Trad/Non
FAX Number: N/A — Calendar System: Semester
URL: www.reedleycollege.edu
Established: 1926 — Annual Undergrad Tuition & Fees (In-District): $1,304
Enrollment: 6,796 — Coed
Affiliation or Control: State/Local — IRS Status: 501(c)3
Highest Offering: Associate Degree
Accreditation: WJ

02	College President	Dr. Jerry L. BUCKLEY
05	Vice President of Instruction	Mr. Dale VAN DAM
11	Vice Pres Administrative Svcs	Ms. Melanie HIGHFILL
32	Vice Pres of Student Services	Ms. Renee CRAIG-MARIUS
35	Dean of Student Services	Ms. Shannon SOLIS
47	Dean of Instruction/Agri/Nat Res	Mr. David CLARK
79	Dean of Instruction/Humanities	Dr. G. Todd DAVIS
81	Dean Instruct/Math/Sci/Tech/PE/Hlth	Mr. Juan BEDOLLA
121	Dean Student Success & Achievement	Ms. Natalie CULVER-DOCKINS
09	Int Dir IR/Effectiveness & Planning	Mr. Darnell HARRIS
26	Dir Marketing/Communications	Mr. George TAKATA
28	Director DSP&S	Dr. Samuel MORGAN
22	Director EOPS	Mr. Mario GONZALES
13	Director of Technology	Mr. Dan DEMMERS
37	Financial Aid Manager	Ms. Chris CORTES
07	Admissions & Records Mgr/Registrar	Ms. Monique GARZA
08	Librarian	Ms. Shivon HESS
41	Director of Athletics	Dr. David SANTESTEBAN
04	Exec Assistant to the President	Ms. Sarina TORRES

Stockton Christian Life College (E)

9023 West Lane, Stockton CA 95210

County: San Joaquin — Identification: 667333
Telephone: (209) 476-7840 — Carnegie Class: Not Classified
FAX Number: (209) 476-7868 — Calendar System: Semester
URL: www.clc.edu
Established: 1949 — Annual Undergrad Tuition & Fees: N/A
Enrollment: N/A — Coed
Affiliation or Control: Independent Non-Profit — IRS Status: 501(c)3
Highest Offering: Baccalaureate
Accreditation: WC

01	President & CEO	Rev. Eli LOPEZ
11	Chief Operations Officer	Rev. Laird G. SILLIMON
05	Chief Academic Officer	Rev. Micah JOHNSON
32	Dean of Students	Richard BISHOP
10	Chief Financial Officer	Dr. William RIDDELL
113	Student Financial Services Asst	Joshua ABREGO
04	Special Asst to the CEO	Andrew PUENTES
06	Registrar	Jennifer C. LLAMAS
124	Recruitment & Retention	Joanne GRESHAM
09	Director of Institutional Research	Kenneth FITZPATRICK
105	Web/Media Services/Creative Design	Josh RIVAS
108	Office of Assessment	Israel RODRIGUEZ
121	Academic Advising	Jasmin JOHNSON
13	Director of Information Technology	Timothy MILLER
15	Director of Human Resources	James LANGSTON
29	Alumni Affairs	Ralph GRESHAM
53	General Education Chair	Tina ROYER
73	Bible & Theology Chair	William RIDDELL
96	Purchasing	Connie SMITH
106	Dir of Online Svcs/Lrng Resources	Regina LOPEZ
22	Title IX Coordinator	Tamara FITZPATRICK

SUM Bible College and Theological Seminary (F)

1101 Investment Blvd, Suite 115, Eldorado Hills CA 95762

County: El Dorado — FICE Identification: 037524
Unit ID: 447953
Telephone: (916) 306-1628 — Carnegie Class: Spec-4-yr-Faith
FAX Number: (510) 568-1024 — Calendar System: Trimester
URL: www.sum.edu
Established: 1999 — Annual Undergrad Tuition & Fees: $10,604
Enrollment: 584 — Coed
Affiliation or Control: Independent Non-Profit — IRS Status: 501(c)3
Highest Offering: Master's
Accreditation: WC, BI

01	President/Chancellor	Rev. George NEAU
05	Chief Academic Officer	Dr. Sanejo LEONARD
20	Vice President Cohort Development	Rev. Melanie FRANCIS
10	Chief Financial Officer	Ms. Lisa GODDARD
11	Chief Operating Officer	Vacant
84	Director of Enrollment Management	Mr. Daniel MULLEN
09	Director Institutional Research	Dr. Andrew ANANE-ASANE
08	Librarian	Mr. Gary AVERILL
32	Director Student Life/Ministries	Ms. Crystal GONZALES
20	Assoc Academic Dean	Dr. Aaron YOM
06	Registrar	Mr. Tyler HUSON
07	Admissions Specialist	Ms. Alex MELLIZA
21	Business Office Coordinator	Ms. Maritza GONZALEZ
26	Marketing Manager	Mr. Matt REVEILE

† Affiliated with School of Urban Missions-New Orleans, Gretna, LA.

Taft College (G)

29 Cougar Court, Taft CA 93268-2329

County: Kern — FICE Identification: 001309
Unit ID: 124113
Telephone: (661) 763-7700 — Carnegie Class: Assoc/MT-VT-High Non
FAX Number: (661) 763-7703 — Calendar System: Semester
URL: www.taftcollege.edu
Established: 1922 — Annual Undergrad Tuition & Fees (In-District): $1,104
Enrollment: 3,566 — Coed
Affiliation or Control: State/Local — IRS Status: 501(c)3
Highest Offering: Associate Degree
Accreditation: WJ, DH

01	Superintendent/President	Dr. Debra DANIELS
10	Exec Vice Pres/Administrative Svcs	Mr. Brock MCMURRAY
05	Vice President of Instruction	Dr. Leslie MINOR
32	Vice Pres of Student Services	Vacant
15	Vice President of Human Resources	Ms. Heather DEL ROSARIO
04	Assistant to the President	Ms. Sarah CRISS
30	Director Foundation & Development	Ms. Sheri HORN BUNK
13	Director Information Services	Ms. Xiaonong LI
08	Research and Instruction Librarian	Ms. Terri SMITH
26	Exec Dir Marketing/Cmty Relations	Ms. Susan GROVEMAN
09	Director Inst Research/Assessment	Ms. Xiaohong LI
41	Director Athletics	Ms. Kanoe BANDY
21	Director of Fiscal Services	Ms. Amanda BAUER
07	Director of Admissions & Records	Ms. Rebecca MUNILLO
18	Supervisor Facilities and Planning	Mr. Richard TREECE
37	Director Student Financial Aid	Ms. Barbara AMERIO
121	Dean of Student Success	Vacant

Taft Law School (H)

3700 South Susan Street, Office 200,
Santa Ana CA 92704-6954

County: Orange — Identification: 666398
Telephone: (714) 850-4800 — Carnegie Class: Not Classified
FAX Number: (714) 708-2082 — Calendar System: Other
URL: www.taftu.edu
Established: 1976 — Annual Undergrad Tuition & Fees: N/A
Enrollment: N/A — Coed
Affiliation or Control: Proprietary — IRS Status: Proprietary
Highest Offering: Doctorate
Accreditation: DEAC

02	Dean	Ms. Melody JOLLY
07	Dean of Admissions	Ms. Joan L. SLAVIN
11	Director of Administration	Ms. Christine A. BALDWIN
37	Director of Financial Aid	Ms. Lucy CORDOVA

Teachers College of San Joaquin (I)

2721 Transworld Dr, Stockton CA 95206

County: San Joaquin — Identification: 667087
Unit ID: 488800
Telephone: (209) 468-4926 — Carnegie Class: Spec-4-yr-Other
FAX Number: (209) 468-9124 — Calendar System: Semester
URL: teacherscollegesj.edu
Established: 2009 — Annual Graduate Tuition & Fees: N/A
Enrollment: 868 — Coed
Affiliation or Control: State — IRS Status: 501(c)3
Highest Offering: Master's; No Undergraduates
Accreditation: WC

01	President	Dr. Diane CARNAHAN
58	Director Graduate Studies	Dr. Crescentia THOMAS
04	Senior Admin Asst to President	Ms. Victoria L. DE PRATER
10	Chief Business Officer	Mr. Scott ANDERSON
88	Director of Credential Programs	Ms. Michele BADOVINAC
09	Director of Institutional Research	Dr. Katherine BURNS

Theatre of Arts (J)

6476 Santa Monica Boulevard, Hollywood CA 90038

County: Los Angeles — Identification: 667098
Unit ID: 486123
Telephone: (323) 463-2500 — Carnegie Class: Spec 2-yr-A&S
FAX Number: (323) 463-2500 — Calendar System: Trimester
URL: www.toa.edu
Established: 1927 — Annual Undergrad Tuition & Fees: $19,800
Enrollment: 22 — Coed
Affiliation or Control: Proprietary — IRS Status: Proprietary
Highest Offering: Associate Degree
Accreditation: THEA

01	Campus Director	David LAW
37	Dir Student Financial Services	Norma CELLS

Thomas Aquinas College (K)

10,000 Ojai Road, Santa Paula CA 93060-9621

County: Ventura — FICE Identification: 023580
Unit ID: 124292
Telephone: (805) 525-4417 — Carnegie Class: Bac-A&S

FAX Number: (805) 525-9342 Calendar System: Semester
URL: www.thomasaquinas.edu
Established: 1971 Annual Undergrad Tuition & Fees: $26,000
Enrollment: 462 Coed
Affiliation or Control: Independent Non-Profit IRS Status: 501(c)3
Highest Offering: Baccalaureate
Accreditation: WC

01 President ... Dr. Michael F. MCLEAN
04 Executive Assistant to President ... Miss Amanda T. O'HARA
88 Director of Special Projects ... Mrs. Anne S. FORSYTH
111 Vice President for Advancement ... Dr. Paul J. O'REILLY
30 Executive Director of Advancement ... Mr. James LINK
43 General Counsel ... Mr. John Q. MASTELLER
10 Vice Pres for Admin & Finance ... Mr. Dennis K. MCCARTHY
05 Academic Dean ... Dr. John GOYETTE
112 Director of Gift Planning ... Mr. Paul F. BLEWETT
29 Director of Alumni/Parent Relations ... Mr. Robert A. BAGDAZIAN
07 Director of Admissions ... Mr. Jonathan P. DALY
44 Director of the Annual Fund ... Mr. Matthew PLAISTED
37 Director of Financial Aid ... Mr. Gregory J. BECHER
15 Director of Human Resources ... Vacant
11 Director of Operations ... Mr. Mark KRETSCHMER
08 Librarian ... Ms. Richena CURPHEY
32 Asst Dean for Student Affairs ... Dr. Jared KUEBLER
42 Chaplain ... Fr. Paul RAFTERY, OP
27 Director of Communications ... Mr. Christopher WEINKOPF
88 Advancement Database Manager ... Mr. Francis DONNELLY
13 Chief Information Technology Office ... Mr. Pat NICHOLS
18 Chief Facilities/Physical Plant Ofc ... Mr. Clark TULBERG
102 Dir Foundation/Corporate Relations ... Mrs. Sharon REISER

Thomas Jefferson School of Law (A)

701 B Street, Ste. 110, San Diego CA 92101
County: San Diego FICE Identification: 010854
Unit ID: 126049
Telephone: (619) 297-9700 Carnegie Class: Spec-4-yr-Law
FAX Number: (619) 961-4370 Calendar System: Semester
URL: www.tjsl.edu
Established: 1969 Annual Graduate Tuition & Fees: N/A
Enrollment: 247 Coed
Affiliation or Control: Independent Non-Profit IRS Status: 501(c)3
Highest Offering: Doctorate; No Undergraduates
Accreditation: @WC, LAW

01 President & General Counsel ... Karin K. SHERR
05 Assoc Dean Acad Affairs & Professor ... Dean Steve SEMERARO
10 VP and Chief Financial Officer ... Nancy VU
32 Assistant Dean for Student Affairs ... Lisa FERREIRA
84 Asst Dean of Enrollment Mgmt .. Michelle SLAUGHTER ALLISON
88 Non-JD Enrol Mgr/Instruct Designer ... Nancy ANZALONE
08 Library Director ... Robert WICKMAN
36 Director of Career Services ... Judybeth TROPP
20 Director of Academic Administration ... Natasha DABNEY
37 Director of Financial Assistance ... Marc BERMAN
06 Registrar ... Carrie KAZYAKA
21 Financial Operations Specialist ... Vacant
88 Externship Director/Pro Bono ... Judybeth TROPP
15 Director of Human Resources ... Lisa CHIGOS
13 Director of IT ... Gil SUSANA

Touro University California (B)

1310 Club Drive, Vallejo CA 94592
County: Solano FICE Identification: 041426
Unit ID: 459736
Telephone: (707) 638-5200 Carnegie Class: Spec-4-yr-Med
FAX Number: (707) 638-5255 Calendar System: Trimester
URL: www.tu.edu
Established: 1997 Annual Undergrad Tuition & Fees: N/A
Enrollment: 1,321 Coed
Affiliation or Control: Independent Non-Profit IRS Status: 501(c)3
Highest Offering: Doctorate
Accreditation: WC, ARCPA, NURSE, &OSTEO, PH, PHAR

00 President & CEO Univ System ... Dr. Alan KADISH
02 CEO/Sr Provost Touro Western Div ... Hon. Shelley BERKLEY
05 Provost & Chief Academic Officer ... Dr. Sarah SWEITZER
32 Dean of Student Affairs ... Dr. Steven JACOBSON
35 Associate Dean of Students ... Dr. James BINKERD
07 Director of Admissions ... Mr. Steven DAVIS
09 AVP Institutional Effectiveness ... Dr. Meiling TANG
10 Dir of Fiscal Affairs & Accounting ... Ms. Amber SHOMO
15 Director Employee Relations ... Ms. Kathy LOWE
11 Associate VP of Administration ... Vacant
08 Director University Library ... Ms. Tamara TRUJILLO
63 Dean College of Osteopathic Med ... Dr. Michael CLEARFIELD
67 Dean College of Pharmacy ... Mr. James SCOTT
53 Dean Col of Education & Health Sci ... Dr. Lisa NORTON
13 Director of Information Technology ... Mr. Scott OLDS
111 AVP Univ Advancement ... Ms. Andrea GARCIA
37 Financial Aid Director ... Ms. Kim KANE
35 Director of Campus Life ... Rabbi Elchonon TENENBAUM
23 Asst Dir of Student Health Center ... Ms. Marcia GREENE
06 Registrar ... Mr. Ron TRAVENICK

Touro University Worldwide (C)

10601 Calle Lee Ste 179, Los Alamitos CA 90720
County: Orange FICE Identification: 041425
Unit ID: 459727
Telephone: (818) 575-6800 Carnegie Class: Masters/S
FAX Number: (818) 707-0316 Calendar System: Semester
URL: www.tuw.edu
Established: 2005 Annual Undergrad Tuition & Fees: N/A
Enrollment: 2,131 Coed
Affiliation or Control: Independent Non-Profit IRS Status: 501(c)3
Highest Offering: Doctorate
Accreditation: WC, MFCD, @SW

01 Interim CEO ... Mr. Roy FINALY
05 Provost & Chief Academic Officer ... Dr. Shelia LEWIS
10 Chief Financial Officer (CFO) ... Mr. Jayson CAPUNO
11 Chief Operating Officer (COO) ... Mr. Roy FINALY
15 Exec Dir Human Resources/Admin ... Mrs. Melody ERBES
06 Registrar/Exec Dir Enrollment Mgmt ... Ms. Wei REN

Touro College Los Angeles (D)

1317 N Crescent Heights Blvd, West Hollywood CA 90046
Telephone: (310) 822-9700 Identification: 770944
Accreditation: &WC

† Branch campus of Touro University Worldwide, Los Alamitos, CA.

Trident University International (E)

5757 Plaza Drive, Suite 100, Cypress CA 90630
County: Orange FICE Identification: 041279
Unit ID: 450979
Telephone: (714) 816-0366 Carnegie Class: DU-Mod
FAX Number: (714) 816-0367 Calendar System: Semester
URL: www.trident.edu
Established: 1998 Annual Undergrad Tuition & Fees: N/A
Enrollment: N/A Coed
Affiliation or Control: Proprietary IRS Status: Proprietary
Highest Offering: Doctorate
Accreditation: WC

01 President/CEO ... Mr. John KLINE
03 Senior Vice President ... Mr. Travis ALLEN
05 Provost/Chief Academic Officer ... Dr. Ruki JAYARAMAN
10 Chief Financial Officer ... Mr. David BARRETT
13 Chief Information Officer ... Mr. Vahid SHARIAT
07 Vice President of Admissions ... Ms. Christina HOANG
53 Dean College of Education ... Dr. Heidi SMITH
50 Dean GJ Col Business/Info Systems ... Dr. Lisa MOHANTY
76 Dean Educ/Health Sciences ... Dr. Mickey SHACHAR
04 Executive Assistant ... Ms. Patricia PARKS
06 Registrar ... Ms. Abby DOLAN
37 Student Finance Manager ... Ms. Brittney DRAKE
09 Director of Institutional Research ... Dr. Heidi SATO
08 Librarian ... Ms. Leslie ANDERSEN
21 Director of Financial Operation ... Vacant
18 Facilities Manager ... Mr. Fred WILSON
101 Board of Trustees Secretary ... Mr. Stanley MENGEL

Trinity Law School (F)

2200 N Grand Avenue, Santa Ana CA 92705
Telephone: (714) 836-7500 Identification: 770098
Accreditation: &HLC

† Branch campus of Trinity International University, Deerfield, IL

Union University of California (G)

14200 Goldenwest Street, Westminster CA 92683
County: Orange Identification: 667269
Telephone: (714) 903-2762 Carnegie Class: Not Classified
FAX Number: N/A Calendar System: Semester
URL: www.uuc.edu
Established: 1986 Annual Graduate Tuition & Fees: N/A
Enrollment: N/A Coed
Affiliation or Control: Independent Non-Profit IRS Status: 501(c)3
Highest Offering: Doctorate; No Undergraduates
Accreditation: DEAC

01 President/CEO ... Dr. Linh DOAN
04 Special Assistant to President ... Dr. Son Xuan NGUYEN
05 Vice President Academic Affairs ... Dr. Michael HUNG TRUONG
32 Vice Pres Student Affairs ... Dr. Kim-Lien THI NGO
10 Vice Pres Finance/CFO ... Mr. Tom DUONG
13 SVP/COO/CIO ... Mr. Philip NGUYEN
07 Director Admissions/Registrar ... Dr. Kim-Lien THI NGO

United States University (H)

7675 Mission Valley Road, San Diego CA 92108
County: San Diego FICE Identification: 040053
Unit ID: 447050
Telephone: (619) 876-4250 Carnegie Class: Masters/M
FAX Number: N/A Calendar System: Semester
URL: www.usuniversity.edu
Established: 1997 Annual Undergrad Tuition & Fees: $6,480
Enrollment: 1,981 Coed
Affiliation or Control: Proprietary IRS Status: Proprietary
Highest Offering: Master's
Accreditation: WC, NURSE

01 President and CEO ... Dr. Steven A. STARGARDTER
05 Provost/Chief Academic Officer ... Vacant
84 VP of Enroll Mgmt/Stdnt Svcs/Mktg ... Vacant
37 VP Student Financial Aid ... Jennifer ROBINSON
10 Chief Financial Officer ... Mr. Ming TAN
20 Assoc Provost Accred/Curriculum ... Dr. Elizabeth ARCHER
07 Director of Enrollment/Admissions ... Mr. Ken COOK
06 Registrar ... David NORIEGA
29 Director Alumni Relations ... Vacant
85 International Student Advisor ... Tina RICAFRENTE

Unitek College (I)

4670 Auto Mall Parkway, Fremont CA 94538
County: Alameda FICE Identification: 041697
Unit ID: 459204
Telephone: (888) 775-1514 Carnegie Class: Spec-4-yr-Other Health
FAX Number: (510) 249-9125 Calendar System: Other
URL: www.unitekcollege.edu
Established: 1992 Annual Undergrad Tuition & Fees: $35,284
Enrollment: 3,618 Coed
Affiliation or Control: Proprietary IRS Status: Proprietary
Highest Offering: Baccalaureate
Accreditation: ACCSC, NURSE

00 CEO ... Ms. Janis PAULSON
02 Fremont Campus Director ... Mr. Frederick HOLLAND

University of Antelope Valley (J)

44055 Sierra Hwy, Lancaster CA 93534
County: Los Angeles FICE Identification: 034275
Unit ID: 442930
Telephone: (661) 726-1911 Carnegie Class: Bac-Diverse
FAX Number: (661) 726-5158 Calendar System: Other
URL: www.uav.edu
Established: 1997 Annual Undergrad Tuition & Fees: N/A
Enrollment: 731 Coed
Affiliation or Control: Proprietary IRS Status: Proprietary
Highest Offering: Master's
Accreditation: WC, EMT

01 President ... Mr. Marco JOHNSON
10 Vice President/CFO ... Ms. Sandra JOHNSON
05 Assoc Dean of Academic Affairs ... Ms. Chonnea HARRIS
32 Dean of Student Affairs ... Mr. Ronald FELTS
37 Financial Aid Director ... Ms. Araceli JIMENEZ
09 Dir Institutional Effectiveness ... Ms. Crystal STEPHENS
13 Director Information Technology ... Mr. Noel SANCHEZ
36 Director Career Services ... Ms. Karyn FRAHM
07 Director of Admissions ... Ms. Mirna TURCIOS

University of Arizona Global Campus (K)

8620 Spectrum Center Blvd, San Diego CA 92123
County: San Diego FICE Identification: 001881
Unit ID: 154022
Telephone: (866) 711-1700 Carnegie Class: Masters/L
FAX Number: (866) 685-4091 Calendar System: Semester
URL: www.ashford.edu
Established: 1918 Annual Undergrad Tuition & Fees: $14,278
Enrollment: 31,115 Coed
Affiliation or Control: Proprietary IRS Status: Proprietary
Highest Offering: Master's
Accreditation: WC, CAHIIM, IACBE, NURSE

01 University President/CEO ... Mr. Paul PASTOREK
05 Int SVP Academic Affairs/CAO ... Dr. Iris OBILLE LAFFERTY
10 SVP Finance/Chief Finance Officer ... Mr. Jim SMITH
11 SVP University Svcs & Strat Plng ... Ms. Sheri JONES
15 VP Human Resources ... Ms. Anna ALLEN
06 VP/University Registrar ... Ms. Katie SCHEIE
21 VP Accounting Controller ... Ms. Heather WEINMANN
35 AVP Student Affairs ... Ms. Poppy FITCH
88 AVP Center for Teaching/Learning ... Ms. Morgan JOHNSON
12 President Clinton Campus ... Dr. Charlie MINNICK
49 Dean College of Arts/Sciences ... Dr. Iris LAFFERTY
69 Dean College of Health/Human Svcs ... Dr. Laura SLIWINSKI
88 Dean Doctoral Studies ... Dr. Iris LAFFERTY
97 Dean Division of General Education ... Dr. Justin HARRISON
50 Dean Forbes School of Business ... Mr. Bob DAUGHERTY
53 Dean College of Education ... Dr. Tony FARRELL
37 Dir Financial Aid & Policy ... Ms. Stephanie COWSERT
09 Director of Institutional Research ... Dr. Stephen NETTLES
101 Secretary of the Institution/Board ... Ms. Patricia OGDEN
29 Director Alumni Affairs ... Ms. Graciela WILLIAMSON
22 Title IX Coordinator ... Dr. Poppy FITCH
04 Executive Administrative Manager ... Ms. Thuy LIEN

*University of California Office of the President (L)

1111 Franklin Street, 12th Floor, Oakland CA 94607-5200
County: Alameda FICE Identification: 001311
Unit ID: 124557
Telephone: (510) 987-0700 Carnegie Class: N/A
FAX Number: (510) 987-0328
URL: www.ucop.edu

01 President ... Michael V. DRAKE
05 Provost/EVP Academic Affairs ... Michael BROWN
10 EVP/Chief Financial Officer ... Nathan E. BROSTROM
11 EVP/Chief Operating Officer ... Rachael NAVA
17 Exec Vice Pres UC Health ... Carrie BYINGTON
26 SVP External Rels/Communications ... Claire HOLMES

27 AVP External Rels/Communications ... Diana HARVEY
108 SVP Compliance/Audit Services ... Alexander BUSTAMANTE
47 VP Agriculture/Natural Resources ... Glenda HUMISTON
115 Vice President of Investments ... Jagdeep S. BACHHER
09 Vice Pres Inst Rsrch/Acad Planning ... Pamela BROWN
88 VP Office of National Laboratories ... Craig LEASURE
15 Int Vice Pres Human Resources ... Cheryl LLOYD
43 General Counsel/VP Legal Affairs ... Charles F. ROBINSON
32 Vice President Student Affairs ... Yvette GULLATT
13 VP/CIO Information Technology Svcs ... Tom ANDRIOLA
28 Vice Prov Equity/Diversity/Inclus ... Yvette GULLATT
20 Vice Provost Academic Personnel ... Susan CARLSON
21 Assoc VP Budget Analysis/Planning ... David ALCOCER
04 Exec Assistant to the President ... Sutton BENNETT

*University of California-Berkeley (A)

Berkeley CA 94720-0001
County: Alameda FICE Identification: 001312
Unit ID: 110635
Telephone: (510) 642-6000 Carnegie Class: DU-Highest
FAX Number: (510) 643-5499 Calendar System: Semester
URL: www.berkeley.edu
Established: 1868 Annual Undergrad Tuition & Fees (In-State): $14,312
Enrollment: 42,327 Coed
Affiliation or Control: State IRS Status: 501(c)3
Highest Offering: Doctorate
Accreditation: WC, CLPSY, DIETD, IPSY, LAW, LSAR, OPT, OPTR, PCSAS, PH, PLNG, SCPSY, SW

02 Chancellor ... Carol CHRIST
05 Exec Vice Chancellor/Provost ... Paul ALIVISATOS
11 Vice Chancellor Administration ... Marc FISHER
10 Chief Financial Officer ... Elena WEN JIANG
46 Vice Chancellor for Research ... Randy KATZ
32 Vice Chancellor Student Affairs ... Steve SUTTON
30 Vice Chanc Univ Dev/Alumni Rels ... Vacant
53 Vice Chanc Undergrad Education ... Cathy KOSHLAND
22 Vice Chanc Equity & Inclusion ... Oscar DUBON
43 Chief Campus Counsel ... David ROBINSON
100 Ast Vice Chanc/Chief of Staff ... Ann JEFFREY
25 Asst VC Research Admin & Compliance ... Patrick SCHLESINGER
13 Asst Vice Chanc Info Technology ... Jen STRINGER
07 AVC/Dir of Admissions ... Amy JARICH
87 AVC/Dean Summer Session/Stdy Abroad ... Richard RUSSO
27 AVP Communications/Public Affairs ... Diana HARVEY
21 Asst Vice Chanc Finance/Controller ... Vacant
35 Assc Vice Chanc/Dean of Students ... Sunny LEE
37 Asst VC/Dir Fin Aid & Scholarship ... Cruz GRIMALDO
08 University Librarian ... Jeffrey MACKIE-MASON
06 Registrar ... Walter WONG
38 Dir Counseling & Psychological Svcs ... Vacant
36 Director Career Center ... Thomas C. DEVLIN
41 Director of Athletics ... James KNOWLTON
58 Vice Prov/Dean of Graduate Division ... Lisa GARCIA BEDOLLA
61 Dean Boalt School of Law ... Erwin CHEMERINSKY
88 Dean School of Optometry ... John FLANAGAN
54 Dean College of Engineering ... Tsu-Jae KING LIU
88 Dean of Environmental Design ... Jennifer WOLCH
65 Dean College of Natural Resources ... David D. ACKERLY
50 Dean Haas School of Business ... Richard K. LYONS
70 Dean School of Social Welfare ... Jeffrey EDELSON
72 Dean School of Information ... AnnaLee SAXENIAN
69 Dean School of Public Health ... Michael C. LU
53 Dean Graduate School of Education ... Prudence CARTER
60 Dean Graduate School of Journalism ... Ed WASSERMAN
81 Dean College of Chemistry ... Douglas S. CLARK
80 Dean Goldman School Public Policy ... Henry E. BRADY
79 Dean of Arts and Humanities ... Anthony CASCARDI
81 Dean of Biological Sciences ... Michael R. BOTCHAN
81 Dean Mathematical/Physical Sciences ... Frances HELLMAN
49 Dean College of Letters & Sciences ... Carla HESSE
97 Dean of the Undergrad Division ... Bob JACOBSON
56 Dean of University Extension ... Diana WU

*University of California-Davis (B)

One Shields Avenue, Davis CA 95616-5270
County: Yolo FICE Identification: 001313
Unit ID: 110644
Telephone: (530) 752-1011 Carnegie Class: DU-Highest
FAX Number: N/A Calendar System: Quarter
URL: www.ucdavis.edu
Established: 1905 Annual Undergrad Tuition & Fees (In-State): $14,597
Enrollment: 39,074 Coed
Affiliation or Control: State IRS Status: 501(c)3
Highest Offering: Doctorate
Accreditation: WC, ARCPA, CAMPEP, DIETD, DIETI, IPSY, LAW, LSAR, MED, MT, NURSE, PAST, PH, VET

02 Chancellor ... Dr. Gary S. MAY
05 Provost & Exec Vice Chancellor ... Dr. May CROUGHAN
100 Associate Chancellor/Chief of Staff ... Mr. Karl M. ENGELBACH
26 Chief Marketing & Comm Officer ... Ms. Dana TOPOUSIS
46 Vice Chancellor Research ... Dr. Prasant MOHAPATRA
30 Vice Chanc Dev/Alumni Relations ... Dr. Shaun B. KEISTER
32 Vice Chancellor Student Affairs ... Dr. Pablo G. REGUERIN
10 VC Finance/Operation & Admin ... Ms. Kelly RATLIFF
28 VC Diversity/Equity/Inclusion ... Ms. Renetta GARRISON
17 VC Human Hlth Sci/CEO UC Davis Hlth ... Dr. David A. LUBARSKY
66 Assoc VC/Dean Sch of Nursing ... Dr. Heather M. YOUNG
31 Assoc Exec VC Campus Cmty Relations ... Mr. Rahim REED
11 Asst VC Office of the COO ... Mr. Blair STEPHENSON
88 Exec Assoc VC Research ... Dr. Cindy M. KIEL
88 Assoc Vice Provost Global Affairs ... Dr. Ermias KEBREAB
88 Assoc Vice Provost Global Affairs ... Dr. Fadi FATHALLAH
88 Assoc VC Research ... Dr. Paul DODD
88 Assoc VC Research ... Dr. Dushyant PATHAK
15 Chief Human Resources Officer ... Ms. Christine LOVELY
110 Assoc VC Development ... Mr. Jason L. WOHLMAN
110 Assoc VC Development ... Mr. Paul PROKOP
88 Assoc VC Development Health Sci ... Ms. Chong U. PORTER
39 Int Assoc VC Student Affs/Aux Svcs ... Mr. Mike SHEEHAN
35 Assoc VC Student Affairs/Stdnt Life ... Dr. Sheri ATKINSON
84 Assoc VC Enrollment Management ... Mr. Donlad E. HUNT
88 Assoc VC Safety Services ... Mr. Eric KVIGNE
88 Assoc VC Design & Construct ... Mr. Jim CARROLL
18 Assoc VC Facilities Management ... Mr. Allen TOLLEFSON
45 AVC Campus Plng/Env Stewardship ... Mr. Robert B. SEGAR
88 Asst VC Student Affairs Div Svcs ... Mr. Cory N. VU
86 Int Lead Govt & Cmty Relations ... Ms. Mabel SALON
21 Asst VC & Campus Controller ... Mr. Matt OKAMOTO
88 Asst Exec Vice Chanc Provost Ofc ... Mr. Karl MOHR
114 Asst VC Budget ... Ms. Sarah MANGUM
88 Asst VC Capital Plng & Real Estate ... Mr. Grant ROCKWELL
88 Asst VC Development Outreach ... Ms. Angela JOENS
88 Asst VC Development ... Ms. Beth BRENNER
112 Asst VC Planned Giving ... Mr. Brian CASEY
102 Asst VC Foundation & Corp Giving ... Vacant
88 Asst VC Student Affs & Chf of Staff ... Ms. Emily PRIETO-TSEREGOUNIS
29 AVC/Exec Director Alumni Relations ... Mr. Richard R. ENGEL
13 CIO & VP Info/Educ Tech ... Ms. Viji MURALI
97 VP & Dean Undergraduate Educ ... Dr. Carolyn THOMAS
58 Interim VP Grad Educ/Dean Grad Stds ... Dr. Jean-Pierre DELPLANQUE
20 Vice Provost Academic Affairs ... Dr. Phil KASS
104 VP & Assoc Chanc Global Affairs ... Dr. Joanna REGULSKA
47 Dean Agricultural/Environ Sci ... Dr. Helene DILLARD
81 Dean Biological Sciences ... Dr. Mark WINEY
54 Dean Engineering ... Dr. Jennifer SINCLAIR CURTIS
49 Int Dean College of Letters/Science ... Mr. Ari KELMAN
61 Dean School of Law ... Dr. Kevin R. JOHNSON
50 Dean Grad School of Management ... Dr. H. Rao UNNAVA
74 Dean Veterinary Medicine ... Dr. Michael D. LAIRMORE
53 Dean School of Education ... Dr. Lauren LINDSTROM
51 Dean Div of Cont/Prof Education ... Dr. Susan D. CATRON
63 Interim Dean School of Medicine ... Dr. Lars BERGLUND
88 Exec Director Mondavi Center ... Dr. Don F. ROTH
109 Exec Dir Campus Rec/Unions ... Mr. Jason LORGAN
36 Exec Dir Internship & Career Center ... Ms. Marcie KIRK-HOLLAND
23 Exec Student Health Services ... Dr. Margaret WALTER
37 Director Financial Aid ... Ms. Deborah G. AGEE
88 Medical Director ... Dr. Cindy M. SCHORZMAN
38 Director Student Health Counseling ... Dr. Sarah HAHN
41 Dir Intercollegiate Athletics ... Mr. Kevin BLUE
116 Dir Audit & Mgmt Advisory Services ... Ms. Leslyn KRAUS
88 Int Director Student Health Admin ... Ms. Julienne DEGEYTER
19 Chief of Police ... Chief Joseph FARROW
43 Chief Campus Counsel ... Mr. Michael SWEENEY
06 Interim University Registrar ... Mr. David R. FLORES
08 University Librarian ... Ms. MacKenzie SMITH

*University of California-Hastings College of the Law (C)

200 McAllister Street, San Francisco CA 94102-4978
County: San Francisco FICE Identification: 003947
Unit ID: 110398
Telephone: (415) 565-4600 Carnegie Class: Spec-4-yr-Law
FAX Number: (415) 565-4865 Calendar System: Semester
URL: www.uchastings.edu
Established: 1878 Annual Graduate Tuition & Fees: N/A
Enrollment: 1,026 Coed
Affiliation or Control: State IRS Status: 501(c)3
Highest Offering: First Professional Degree; No Undergraduates
Accreditation: WC, LAW

02 Chancellor and Dean ... Dean David L. FAIGMAN
05 Academic Dean and Provost ... Mr. Morris RATNER
43 General Counsel ... Mr. John DIPAOLO
10 Chief Financial Officer ... Mr. David SEWARD
11 Chief Operating Officer ... Ms. Rhiannon BAILARD
13 Chief Information Officer ... Ms. Camilla TUBBS
30 Chief Development Officer ... Mr. Eric DUMBLETON
32 Assistant Dean of Students ... Ms. Grace HUM
84 Sr Asst Dean Enrollment Management ... Ms. June SAKAMOTO
15 Chief Human Resources Officer ... Mr. Andrew SCOTT
35 Director of Student Services ... Ms. Emily HAAN
06 Registrar ... Ms. Sarah REED
07 Director of Admissions ... Mr. Bryan ZERBE
36 Asst Dean Career & Professional Dev ... Ms. Amy KIMMEL
26 Chief Communications Officer ... Ms. Sybill WYATT
09 Dir of Accreditation & Assessment ... Ms. Andrea BING
93 Director LEOP ... Ms. Elizabeth MCGRIFF
100 Chief of Staff and Assistant C&D ... Dr. Jenny KWON
21 Controller ... Ms. Sandra PLENSKI
37 Director Financial Aid ... Dr. Yma-Richel NABONG
109 Property Manager ... Mr. Jarda BRYCH
96 Director of Business Services ... Mr. Adrian BROWN
29 Director of Alumni Engagement ... Ms. Meredith JAGGARD
04 Executive Assistant ... Ms. Sonia CHAHAL
19 Director Security/Safety ... Vacant
25 Chief Contract/Grants Administrator ... Mr. Yael NADEL-CADAXA

*University of California-Irvine (D)

Campus Drive, Irvine CA 92697-0001
County: Orange FICE Identification: 001314
Unit ID: 110653
Telephone: (949) 824-5011 Carnegie Class: DU-Highest
FAX Number: N/A Calendar System: Quarter
URL: www.uci.edu
Established: 1965 Annual Undergrad Tuition & Fees (In-State): $13,753
Enrollment: 36,303 Coed
Affiliation or Control: State IRS Status: 501(c)3
Highest Offering: Doctorate
Accreditation: WC, CAMPEP, CEA, IPSY, LAW, MACTE, MED, MT, NURSE, PH, PLNG, RADDOS

02 Chancellor ... Howard A. GILLMAN
05 Int Provost & Exec Vice Chancellor ... Hal S. STERN
10 Vice Chanc Admin/Finance & CFO ... Ronald CORTEZ
46 Vice Chancellor for Research ... Pramod KHARGONEKAR
32 Vice Chanc Student Affairs ... Willie L. BANKS
111 Vice Chanc Univ Advancement ... Brian T. HERVEY
17 Vice Chancellor Health Affairs ... Steve GOLDSTEIN
20 Acting Vice Prov for Acad Planning ... Valerie JENNESS
88 Vice Provost for Academic Personnel ... Diane K. O'DOWD
28 Vice Provost for AED & Inclusion ... Douglas M. HAYNES
100 Associate Chancellor/Chief of Staff ... Lars T. WALTON
20 Int Assoc Prov/Exec Vice Chancellor ... Dave LEINEN
22 Assoc Chancellor ED & Inclusion ... Kirsten K. QUANBECK
88 Assoc Chancellor Sustainability ... Wendell BRASE
15 Assoc Chancellor & Chief HR Exec ... Ramona AGRELA
26 Assoc Chanc Comms & Public Affairs ... Ria M. CARLSON
35 Asst VC Stdnt Affs/Chief of Staff ... Edgar J. DORMITORIO
35 Asst Vice Chanc/Dean of Students ... Rameen A. TALESH
23 Assoc VC/Chief of Staff Health Affs ... Rebecca BRUSUELAS-JAMES
13 Interim Chief Information Officer ... Kian COLESTOCK
84 Asst Vice Chanc Enrollment Services ... Patricia MORALES
21 Assoc Vice Chanc Admin/Business Svc ... Richard COULON
06 University Registrar ... Elizabeth C. BENNETT
43 Chief Campus Counsel ... Andrea GUNN EATON
51 Dean Continuing Educ/Summer Session ... Gary W. MATKIN
08 University Librarian ... Lorelei A. TANJI
36 Assoc Vice Prov Div Career Pathway ... Suzanne C. HELBIG
37 Director Financial Aid ... Rebecca SANCHEZ
41 Director Intercollegiate Athletics ... Paula Y. SMITH
09 Asst Vice Chanc Inst Research ... Ryan M. CHERLAND
97 Dean Undergrad Education & VP ... Michael DENNIN
58 Dean Graduate Division & VP ... Gillian R. HAYES
49 Dean Arts ... Stephen BARKER
50 Dean Paul Merage School of Business ... Eric SPANGENBERG
53 Dean School of Education ... Richard ARUM
81 Dean Biological Sciences ... Frank LAFERLA
54 Interim Dean School of Engineering ... Michael GREEN
79 Dean Humanities ... Tyrus MILLER
77 Dean Bren Sch of Info & Comp Sci ... Marios PAPAEFTHYMIOU
61 Dean of Law School ... L. Song RICHARDSON
63 Dean School of Medicine ... Michael STAMOS
81 Dean Physical Sciences ... James BULLOCK
83 Dean Social Ecology ... Nancy GUERRA
83 Dean School of Social Sciences ... William M. MAURER
66 Dean School of Nursing ... Dr. Adey NYAMATHI
88 Chair Academic Senate ... James STEINTRAGER

*University of California-Los Angeles (E)

405 Hilgard Avenue, Los Angeles CA 90095-1405
County: Los Angeles FICE Identification: 001315
Unit ID: 110662
Telephone: (310) 825-4321 Carnegie Class: DU-Highest
FAX Number: N/A Calendar System: Quarter
URL: www.ucla.edu
Established: 1919 Annual Undergrad Tuition & Fees (In-State): $13,249
Enrollment: 44,589 Coed
Affiliation or Control: State IRS Status: 501(c)3
Highest Offering: Doctorate
Accreditation: WC, CAMPEP, CLPSY, CYTO, DENT, EMT, IPSY, LAW, LIB, MAC, MED, NURSE, PAST, PCSAS, PH, PLNG, RAD, SW, THEA

02 Chancellor ... Gene D. BLOCK
05 Exec Vice Chancellor & Provost ... Emily A. CARTER
11 Administrative Vice Chancellor ... Michael J. BECK
10 Vice Chancellor/CFO ... Gregg GOLDMAN
15 Vice Chancellor Academic Personnel ... Michael LEVINE
28 VC Equity/Diversity & Inclusion ... Anna S. BRADLEY
26 Vice Chancellor External Affairs ... Rhea TURTELTAUB
23 Vice Chancellor Health Sciences ... John MAZZIOTTA
43 Vice Chancellor Legal Affairs ... Louise C. NELSON
46 Vice Chancellor Research ... Roger WAKIMOTO
32 Vice Chancellor Student Affairs ... Monroe GORDEN, JR.
58 Vice Provost & Dean Graduate Educ ... Susan ETTNER
20 Vice Provost & Dean Undergrad Educ ... Adriana GALVAN
13 Vice Provost Information Technology ... James DAVIS
88 Vice Prov Inst of American Cultures ... David K. YOO
88 VProv Interdiscip/Cross-Campus Affs ... Timothy BREWER
104 Vice Prov Intl Studies/Global Engmt ... C. Cindy FAN
13 Assoc VC/Chief Information Officer ... Lucy AVETISYAN
17 President UCLA Health ... Johnese Maria SPISSO
79 Dean of Humanities ... David SCHABERG
88 Dean of Life Sciences ... Victoria SORK
81 Dean of Physical Sciences ... Miguel GARCIA-GARIBAY
83 Dean of Social Sciences ... Darnell HUNT

52 Dean School of Dentistry ... Paul KREBSBACH
48 Dean Sch of the Arts & Arch ... Brett STEELE
53 Dean Grad Sch Educ & Info Studies ... Christina CHRISTIE
54 Dean Sch of Eng & App Sci ... Jayathi Y. MURTHY
61 Dean School of Law ... Jennifer L. MNOOKIN
50 Dean Graduate School of Mgmt ... Antonio BERNARDO
63 Dean School of Medicine ... Kelsey C. MARTIN
64 Dean School of Music ... Eileen STREMPEL
66 Dean School of Nursing ... Linda SARNA
80 Dean School of Public Affairs ... Gary M. SEGURA
69 Dean Sch of Public Health ... Ronald S. BROOKMEYER
88 Dean School of Theater Film & TV ... Brian KITE
51 Dean Continuing Ed and Extension ... Eric BULLARD
88 Assoc VC Academic Planning & Budget ... Jeff ROTH
29 Assoc VC Alumni Affairs/Advancemnt ... Julie SINA
16 Assoc VC Campus Human Resources ... Lubbe LEVIN
21 Assoc Vice Chancellor/Controller ... Allison BAIRD-JAMES
30 Assoc VC Development ... Laura PARKER
84 Vice Provost Enrollment Management ... Youlonda COPELAND-MORGAN
35 Asst VC of Student Development ... Suzanne SEPLOW
35 Asst VC of Campus Life ... Mick DELUCA
27 Exec Dir Comm/Public Outreach ... Steve RITEA
20 Assistant Provost ... Emily ROSE
20 Assistant Provost ... Margaret LEAL-SOTELO
18 Asst VC Facilities Management ... Kelly J. SCHMADER
86 Assoc VC Govt/Community Relations ... Jennifer POULAKIDAS
39 Asst VC Housing & Hospitality Svcs ... Peter ANGELIS
25 Asst VC Research/Compliance ... Ann M. POLLACK
04 Executive Asst to the Chancellor ... Rena TORRES
88 Executive Director ASUCLA ... Pouria ABBASSI
09 Executive Director Inst Research ... Adam SUGANO
88 Director Volunteer Center ... Ashley LOVE-SMITH
96 Dir Campus Purchasing & Payables ... William S. PROPST
36 Int Director Career Center ... Christine WILSON
85 Int Director Ctr for Intl Students ... Sam NAHIDI
37 Exec Director Financial Aid Office ... Marvin SMITH
41 Director Intercollegiate Athletics ... Martin JARMOND
90 Chief Technologist ... Scott FRIEDMAN
38 Exec Dir Couns & Psych Svcs ... Nicole GREEN
07 Director Undergraduate Admission ... Gary A. CLARK
06 Registrar ... Frank Y. WADA
08 University Librarian ... Virginia STEEL
19 Chief of Police ... Tony LEE
100 Chief of Staff ... Yolanda GORMAN
102 Exec Dir Foundation/Corporate Rels ... Stellar KIM

*University of California-Merced (A)

5200 North Lake Road, Merced CA 95343
County: Merced FICE Identification: 041271
Unit ID: 445188
Telephone: (209) 228-4400 Carnegie Class: DU-Higher
FAX Number: (209) 228-4424 Calendar System: Semester
URL: www.ucmerced.edu
Established: 2005 Annual Undergrad Tuition & Fees (In-District): $14,100
Enrollment: 9,018 Coed
Affiliation or Control: State/Local IRS Status: 501(c)3
Highest Offering: Doctorate
Accreditation: WC

02 Interim Chancellor ... Nathan BROSTROM
03 Assoc Chancellor & Senior Advisor ... Luanna PUTNEY
05 Provost/Exec Vice Chancellor ... Dr. Gregg CAMFIELD
10 Interim VC & Chief Fin/Admin Ofcr ... Mike RILEY
30 VC Strat Partnerships/External Affs ... Ed KLOTZBIER
32 Vice Chancellor Student Affairs ... Dr. Charles NIES
114 Vice Chancellor Budget/Planning ... Mike RILEY
46 Vice Chancellor Research ... Dr. Samuel TRAINA
84 Assoc Vice Chanc Enrollment Mgmt ... Jill ORCUTT
26 Asst Vice Chanc Univ Communications ... Ed KLOTZBIER
58 Vice Provost/Dean of Graduate Educ ... Marjorie ZATZ
20 Vice Provost UG Education ... Sarah FREY
86 Exec Director of Govt Relations ... Cori LUCERO
04 Exec Assistant to the Chancellor ... Molly ELAZIER
13 AVC Information Technology ... Ann KOVALCHICK
65 Dean Natural Sciences ... Dr. Betsy DUMONT
79 Interim Dean School of SSHA ... Jeffrey GILGER
54 Dean Engineering ... Dr. Mark MATSUMOTO
07 Director of Admissions ... Vacant
06 University Registrar ... Erin WEBB
37 Director of Financial Aid ... Ron RADNEY
41 Director of Campus Athletics & Rec ... David DUNHAM
23 Assoc Vice Chanc Health & Wellness ... Vacant
85 Director of International Affairs ... Garett GIETZEN
08 University Librarian ... Haipeng LI
39 AVC Housing/Residence/Stdnt Life ... Martin REED
43 Campus Counsel ... Elisabeth GUNTHER
100 Associate Chancellor/Chief of Staff ... Luanna PUTNEY
19 Chief of Police ... Chou HER
09 Director of Inclusive Research ... Andres HERNANDEZ
15 Chief Human Resources Officer ... Nicole POLLACK
18 Chief Facilities/Physical Plant Ofc ... Michael MCLEOD
21 Associate Business Officer ... Connie MCBRIDE
28 Director of Diversity ... Dania MATOS
29 Dir Alumni Affairs/Mktg/Public Rels ... Chris ABRESCY
35 Associate Student Affairs Officer ... Charles NIES
36 Exec Director Student Placement ... Brian O'BRUBA
38 Int Director Student Counseling ... Tania GONZALEZ
96 Director of Purchasing ... Stephanie ZUNIGA

*University of California-Riverside (B)

900 University Avenue, Riverside CA 92521
County: Riverside FICE Identification: 001316
Unit ID: 110671
Telephone: (951) 827-1012 Carnegie Class: DU-Highest
FAX Number: N/A Calendar System: Quarter
URL: www.ucr.edu
Established: 1954 Annual Undergrad Tuition & Fees (In-State): $14,024
Enrollment: 26,434 Coed
Affiliation or Control: State IRS Status: 501(c)3
Highest Offering: Doctorate
Accreditation: WC, IPSY, MED, SCPSY

02 Chancellor ... Dr. Kim A. WILCOX
100 Associate Chancellor ... Dr. Christine VICTORINO
05 Provost/Exec Vice Chanc ... Dr. Elizabeth WATKINS
10 CFO & Vice Chanc Planning & Budget ... Mr. Gerry BOMOTTI
32 Vice Chancellor Student Affairs ... Dr. Brian HAYNES
111 Vice Chanc University Advancement ... Mr. Peter A. HAYASHIDA
46 Vice Chanc Research & Econ Dev ... Dr. Rodolfo H. TORRES
63 Dean School of Med/CEO Clin Affs ... Dr. Deborah DEAS
20 Vice Provost Academic Personnel ... Dr. Daniel R. JESKE
18 Assoc Vice Chanc Facilities Svcs ... Vacant
84 Interim Assoc Vice Chanc Enrollment ... Ms. Emily D. ENGELSCHALL
30 Assoc Vice Chanc Development ... Ms. Marie SCHULTZ
09 Assoc Vice Chanc for Research ... Mr. Charles GREER
28 VC & Chief Diversity Officer ... Dr. Mariam LAM
58 Dean Graduate Division ... Dr. Shaun BOWLER
50 Dean School of Business Admin ... Dr. Yunzeng WANG
53 Interim Dean Grad School of Educ ... Dr. Louie F. RODRIGUEZ
54 Dean Bourns College of Engineering ... Dr. Christopher LYNCH
79 Dean Col of Humanities/Arts/Soc Sci ... Dr. Daryle WILLIAMS
81 Dean Col of Nat and Agr Sciences ... Dr. Kathryn UHRICH
06 Registrar ... Ms. Bracken J. DAILEY
80 Dean School of Public Policy ... Dr. Anil DEOLALIKAR
36 Director Career Center ... Mr. Sean GIL
37 Director Financial Aid ... Mr. Jose A. AGUILAR
38 Director Counseling Center ... Dr. Elizabeth MONDRAGON
07 Director of Admissions ... Ms. Emily D. ENGELSCHALL
21 Assoc VC Business & Financial Svcs ... Ms. Bobbi MCCRACKEN
08 Head Librarian ... Mr. Steven MANDEVILLE-GAMBLE
04 Int Exec Asst to the Chancellor ... Mr. George RUELAS
41 Interim Athletics Director ... Mr. Wesley MALLETTE
13 Interim Assoc Vice Chanc/CIO ... Mr. Josh BRIGHT
15 Interim Assoc VC Human Resources ... Mr. John HENDERSON
26 Asst VC & Chief Communications Ofcr ... Mr. Johnny CRUZ
43 Chief Campus Counsel ... Mr. David BERGQUIST
86 AVC Govt/Community Relations ... Ms. Elizabeth ROMERO
102 Exec Dir Foundation Development ... Mr. Bryan CARLSON
104 Director of Education Abroad ... Dr. Karolyn ANDREWS
108 Asst VC Institutional Research ... Mr. Scott HEIL
109 Assoc Vice Chanc Auxiliary Svcs ... Ms. Heidi M. SCRIBNER
44 Director Gift Administration ... Ms. Lisa M. WILSON

*University of California-San Diego (C)

9500 Gilman Drive, La Jolla CA 92093-0014
County: San Diego FICE Identification: 001317
Unit ID: 110680
Telephone: (858) 534-2230 Carnegie Class: DU-Highest
FAX Number: (858) 534-6523 Calendar System: Quarter
URL: www.ucsd.edu
Established: 1960 Annual Undergrad Tuition & Fees (In-State): $14,648
Enrollment: 39,576 Coed
Affiliation or Control: State IRS Status: 501(c)3
Highest Offering: Doctorate
Accreditation: WC, AUD, CAMPEP, CEA, CLPSY, DIETI, DMS, IPSY, LC, MED, MT, PAST, PDPSY, PHAR

02 Chancellor ... Dr. Pradeep K. KHOSLA
05 EVC Academic Affairs ... Dr. Elizabeth H. SIMMONS
46 Vice Chancellor Research ... Dr. Sandra BROWN
63 VC Health Science/Dean Sch Med ... Dr. David A. BRENNER
65 Vice Chancellor Marine Sciences ... Dr. Margaret LEINEN
32 VC Student Affairs ... Dr. Alysson SATTERLUND
10 VC and Chief Financial Officer ... Mr. Pierre-Yves OUILLET
11 Vice Chanc Resource Mgmt/Planning ... Mr. Gary C. MATTHEWS
28 VC for Equity/Diversity & Inclusion ... Dr. Becky R. PETITT
111 Vice Chancellor Advancement ... Vacant
43 Chief Campus Counsel ... Mr. Daniel W. PARK
100 Assistant Chancellor/Chief of Staff ... Mr. Jeffrey P. GATTAS
22 Chief Ethics and Compliance Officer ... Ms. Judith BRUNER
88 Associate Chancellor ... Ms. Suzi M. STERNER
13 Chief Information Officer ... Mr. Vince KELLEN
88 Assoc VC Public Programs ... Dr. Mary L. WALSHOK
21 AVC Business Fin Svcs/Controller ... Ms. Cheryl ROSS
08 University Librarian ... Dr. Erik T. MITCHELL
88 Director Policy Admin ... Ms. Paula J. JOHNSON
23 Exec Dir Student Health/Wellness ... Vacant
26 Chief Comm and Marketing ... Ms. Anne L. BUCKLEY
20 Sr Assoc VC Academic Affairs ... Dr. Robert E. CONTINETTI
20 AVC Education Innovation ... Dr. Carlos JENSEN
15 Chief Human Resources Officer ... Vacant
46 Sr Assoc Vice Chancellor Research ... Dr. Miroslav KRSTIC
88 AVC Innovation & Commercialization ... Mr. Paul W. ROBEN
84 Assoc Vice Chanc Enrollment Mgmt ... Vacant
06 University Registrar ... Ms. Cindy G. LYONS
23 CEO UCSD Medical Center ... Ms. Patty MAYSENT
35 Asst VC Student Life ... Ms. Patricia MAHAFFEY
96 Assoc Controller/Chief Procurement ... Mr. Ted JOHNSON
35 AVC Student Retention Success ... Dr. Maruth FIGUEROA

54 Dean Jacobs Sch of Engineering ... Dr. Albert P. PISANO
49 Dean Arts & Humanities ... Dr. Cristina DELLA COLETTA
81 Dean Div of Biological Sciences ... Dr. Kit POGLIANO
83 Dean of Social Sciences ... Dr. Carol A. PADDEN
50 Dean Rady School of Management ... Dr. Lisa D. ORDONEZ
81 Dean Div of Physical Science ... Dr. Steven E. BOGGS
82 Dean Global Policy and Strategy ... Dr. Caroline FREUND
58 Dean Graduate Studies ... Dr. Kit POGLIANO
12 Provost John Muir College ... Dr. K. Wayne YANG
12 Prov Thurgood Marshall Coll ... Dr. Leslie CARVER
12 Provost Earl Warren College ... Dr. Marisa A. ABRAJANO
12 Provost Revelle College ... Dr. Paul K. YU
12 Provost Eleanor Roosevelt College ... Dr. Ivan EVANS
12 Provost Sixth College ... Dr. Lakshmi CHILUKURI
12 Provost Seventh College ... Dr. Kate ANTONOVICS
38 Director Stdt Psych/Counseling Svcs ... Dr. Reina JUAREZ
18 AVC EH&S and Facilities Management . Mr. Stephen B. JACKSON
97 Dean of Undergraduate Education ... Dr. John C. MOORE
41 Intercollegiate Athletics Director ... Mr. Earl W. EDWARDS
19 Police Chief Community Safety ... Vacant

*University of California-San Francisco (D)

513 Parnassus Avenue, Box 0402, San Francisco CA 94143
County: San Francisco FICE Identification: 001319
Unit ID: 110699
Telephone: (415) 476-1000 Carnegie Class: Spec-4-yr-Med
FAX Number: N/A Calendar System: Quarter
URL: www.ucsf.edu
Established: 1864 Annual Graduate Tuition & Fees: N/A
Enrollment: 3,201 Coed
Affiliation or Control: State IRS Status: 501(c)3
Highest Offering: Doctorate; No Undergraduates
Accreditation: WC, CAMPEP, DENT, DIETI, IPSY, MED, MIDWF, NURSE, PAST, PHAR, PTA

02 Chancellor ... Dr. Sam HAWGOOD
03 Executive Vice Chancellor & Provost ... Dr. Daniel H. LOWENSTEIN
15 SVP/Assoc VC Human Resources ... Mr. Corey JACKSON
100 Associate Chancellor ... Dr. Theresa O'BRIEN
10 Senior VC Finance & Administration ... Mr. Paul JENNY
21 Sr Assoc VC & CFO ... Mr. Michael CLUNE
05 Vice Provost Academic Affairs ... Dr. Brian ALLDREDGE
32 Vice Chanc Student Academic Affairs ... Dr. Elizabeth WATKINS
30 VC Univ Development/Alumni Rels ... Ms. Jennifer ARNETT
26 Vice Chanc Communications ... Mr. Won HA
86 VC Community & Govt Relations ... Ms. Francesca VEGA
28 VC Diversity & Outreach ... Dr. Renee NAVARRO
13 Assoc VC & Chief Info Officer ... Vacant
109 Assoc VC & Campus Life Services ... Vacant
18 Assoc VC Cap Pgms/Campus Architect ... Mr. Michael BADE
20 Vice Dean Academic Affairs ... Dr. Elena FUENTES-AFFLICK
37 Director Student Financial Aid ... Mr. Jerry LOPEZ
43 Chief Campus Counsel ... Ms. Greta SCHNETZLER
08 University Librarian/Asst VC ... Mr. Chris SHAFFER
63 Dean School of Medicine/VC Med Affs ... Dr. Talmadge E. KING, JR.
19 Chief of Police ... Vacant
66 Dean School of Nursing ... Dr. Catherine GILLISS
52 Dean School of Dentistry ... Dr. Michael REDDY
67 Dean School of Pharmacy ... Dr. B. Joseph GUGLIELMO
58 Dean Graduate Division ... Dr. Elizabeth WATKINS
96 Assoc VC/Chief Procurement Officer ... Mr. James HINE
06 Registrar/Asst VC Student Info ... Mr. Douglas CARLSON
88 Associate Registrar ... Ms. Jina SHAMIM
36 Asst VC Career Advancement ... Mr. William LINDSTAEDT
23 Asst VC Student Health & Counseling ... Dr. Chaitali MUKHERJEE
09 Director Institutional Research ... Dr. Ning WANG

*University of California-Santa Barbara (E)

552 University Road, Santa Barbara CA 93106-0001
County: Santa Barbara FICE Identification: 001320
Unit ID: 110705
Telephone: (805) 893-8000 Carnegie Class: DU-Highest
FAX Number: N/A Calendar System: Quarter
URL: www.ucsb.edu
Established: 1909 Annual Undergrad Tuition & Fees (In-State): $14,406
Enrollment: 26,179 Coed
Affiliation or Control: State IRS Status: 501(c)3
Highest Offering: Doctorate
Accreditation: WC, IPSY, PSPSY

02 Chancellor ... Dr. Henry T. YANG
04 Exec Assistant to the Chancellor ... Ms. Diane O'BRIEN
05 Executive Vice Chancellor Academics ... Dr. David B. MARSHALL
46 Vice Chancellor Research ... Dr. Joe INCANDELA
11 Vice Chancellor Admin Services ... Mr. Garry MAC PHERSON
32 Vice Chancellor Student Affairs ... Ms. Margaret KLAWUNN
10 AVC/Controller Bus & Fin Svc ... Mr. Jim R. CORKILL
15 Int Vice Pres Human Resources ... Ms. Cheryl LLOYD
28 VC Diversity/Equity/Acad Policy ... Ms. Belinda ROBNETT
20 AVC/Dean Undergraduate Education ... Dr. Jeffrey STOPPLE
30 Assoc Vice Chancellor Development ... Ms. Beverly COLGATE
26 AVC Public Affairs & Communications ... Mr. John LONGBRAKE
84 AVC Enrollment Services ... Mr. Mike MILLER
121 Acting AVC Student Acad Support Svc ... Ms. Lupe GARCIA

114 Asst Chanc Fin & Resource Mgmt ..... Mr. Chuck HAINES
29 Assoc Director Alumni Affairs ..... Ms. Samantha PUTNAM
13 AVC IT & Chief Information Officer ..... Mr. Matthew HALL
88 Interim Dean Col Creative Studies ..... Dr. Kathy FOLTZ
54 Dean College of Engineering ..... Dr. Rod ALFERNESS
58 Dean Graduate Division ..... Dr. Carol GENETTI
53 Dean Gevirtz Grad Sch Educ ..... Dr. Jeffrey MILEM
65 Dean Bren School of Env Sci & Mgmt ..... Dr. Steven D. GAINES
51 Dean Professional and Cont Educ ..... Dr. Robert YORK
35 Dean of Student Life ..... Ms. Katya ARMISTEAD
49 Exec Dean College Letters & Sci ..... Dr. Pierre WILTZIUS
79 Dean Humanities & Fine Arts ..... Dr. John MAJEWSKI
87 Director Summer Sessions ..... Dr. James FORD
83 Dean Social Sciences ..... Dr. Charles R. HALE
85 Dir International Students/Scholars ..... Dr. Simran SINGH
06 Registrar ..... Ms. Leesa BECK
16 Director Human Resources ..... Ms. Cynthia SENERIZ
37 Director Financial Aid ..... Dr. Michael MILLER
116 Acting Dir Audit & Advisory Service ..... Ms. Jessie MASEK
07 Director Admissions ..... Ms. Lisa PRZEKOP
09 Director Institutional Research ..... Dr. Steven C. VELASCO
23 Exec Director Student Health Svcs ..... Dr. Mary FERRIS
39 AVC Housing/Dining & Aux Enterprise ..... Mr. Wilfred E. BROWN
40 Director of UCSB Bookstore ..... Mr. Mark BEISECKER
19 Chief of Police ..... James BROCK
41 Director Intercollegiate Athletics ..... Mr. John MCCUTCHEON
86 Dir Governmental Relations ..... Ms. Kirsten DESHLER
21 Director Finance/Administration ..... Vacant
08 University Librarian ..... Ms. Kristin ANTELMAN
89 Director Orientation Programs ..... Ms. Tricia RASCON
88 Acting Director Capital Development ..... Mr. Mark NOCCIOLO
88 Director Campus Planning & Design ..... Ms. Alissa HUMMER
88 Executive Director Arts & Lectures ..... Ms. Celesta BILLECI
22 Director Disabled Students Pgm ..... Mr. Gary R. WHITE
104 Dir Campus Education Abroad Program ..... Dr. Juan E. CAMPO
88 Director Env Health & Safety ..... Mr. John STERRITT
28 Director MultiCultural Center ..... Ms. Zaveeni KHAN-MARCUS
38 Assoc Dir Counseling & Psych Svcs ..... Dr. Brian OLOWUDE
94 Director Women's Center ..... Ms. Kim EQUINOA
88 Campus Ombudsman ..... Ms. Caroline ADAMS
88 Exec Dir Instructional Devel ..... Mr. George H. MICHAELS
36 Director Career Services ..... Mr. Ignacio GALLARDO
43 Chief Campus Counsel ..... Ms. Nancy G. HAMILL
22 Dir EO & Discrimination Prevention ..... Mr. Ricardo ALCAINO
88 Dir Design & Construction ..... Mr. Julie HENDRICKS
88 Director Univ Center/Events Center ..... Mr. Gary LAWRENCE
88 Director of Recreation ..... Mr. Jeff HUSKEY
92 Honors Program Analyst ..... Ms. Summer HOWATT-NAB
108 Institutional Assessment Coord ..... Dr. Amanda BREY
44 Director Annual Giving ..... Mr. Brandon FRIESEN

*University of California-Santa Cruz (A)

1156 High Street, Santa Cruz CA 95064-1077
County: Santa Cruz FICE Identification: 001321
Unit ID: 110714
Telephone: (831) 459-0111 Carnegie Class: DU-Highest
FAX Number: (831) 459-0146 Calendar System: Quarter
URL: www.ucsc.edu
Established: 1965 Annual Undergrad Tuition & Fees (In-State): $14,025
Enrollment: 19,161 Coed
Affiliation or Control: State IRS Status: 501(c)3
Highest Offering: Doctorate
Accreditation: WC, IPSY

02 Chancellor ..... Dr. Cynthia LARIVE
05 Campus Provost/Exec Vice Chancellor ..... Dr. Lori KLETZER
10 Vice Chanc Business/Admin Services ..... Dr. Sarah LATHAM
45 Vice Chancellor Planning/Budget ..... Dr. Peggy DELANEY
46 Int Vice Chancellor Research ..... Mr. John MACMILLAN
30 Vice Chanc Univ Relations ..... Mr. Mark DELOS REYES DAVIS
13 Int VC Information Technology ..... Mr. Byron WALKER
20 Vice Prov/Dean Undergrad Educ ..... Dr. Richard HUGHEY
20 Vice Provost Academic Affairs ..... Dr. Herbert LEE
84 Assoc VC Enrollment Mgmt ..... Ms. Michelle L. WHITTINGHAM
16 Asst VC Academic Personnel ..... Ms. Grace MCCLINTOCK
18 Campus Architect ..... Mr. Felix ANG
15 Assoc VC/Chief HR Officer ..... Mr. Steve STEIN
32 Vice Chanc Student Affairs/Success ..... Ms. Jennifer BASZILE
08 University Librarian ..... Ms. Elizabeth COWELL
79 Dean of Humanities ..... Dr. Tyler STOVALL
81 Dean Physical & Biological Sci ..... Dr. Paul KOCH
49 Interim Dean of the Arts ..... Dr. Ted WARBURTON
83 Dean of Social Sciences ..... Dr. Katharyne MITCHELL
54 Dean of Engineering ..... Dr. Alexander WOLF
58 Vice Prov/Dean of Grad Studies ..... Dr. Peter BIEHL
65 Director Institute Marine Sciences ..... Dr. Daniel COSTA
81 Director Institute Particle Physics ..... Dr. Steven RITZ
88 Director UCO/Lick Observatory ..... Dr. Claire MAX
12 Provost Stevenson College ..... Dr. Alice YANG
12 Provost Cowell College ..... Dr. Alan CHRISTY
12 Provost Crown College ..... Dr. Manel CAMPS
12 Provost Merrill College ..... Dr. Elizabeth ABRAMS
12 Provost Porter College ..... Dr. Sean KEILEN
12 Provost Kresge College ..... Dr. Ben LEEDS CARSON
12 Provost Rachel Carson College ..... Dr. Sue CARTER
12 Provost College Nine & Ten ..... Dr. Flora LU
12 Interim Provost Oakes College ..... Dr. Marcia OCHOA
06 Registrar ..... Mr. Tchad SANGER
09 Director Institutional Research ..... Dr. Julian L. FERNALD
37 Director Financial Aid/Operations ..... Mr. Patrick REGISTER
22 Assoc Dir EEO/Affirmative Action ..... Ms. Sonje DAYRIES
29 Director of Alumni Relations ..... Ms. Shayna KENT

26 Dir Marketing/Communications ..... Ms. Lisa NIELSEN
86 Director Government Relations ..... Ms. Melissa WHATLEY
38 Director Student Counseling ..... Dr. Gary DUNN
07 Director of Admissions ..... Ms. Blia YANG
41 Director Athletics/ Recreation ..... Ms. Susan WITTMANN HARRIMAN
108 Asst Director for Assessment ..... Dr. Anna SHER
102 Dir Foundation/Corporate Relations ..... Ms. Lynne STOOPS

University of East-West Medicine (B)

595 Lawrence Expressway, Sunnyvale CA 94085
County: Santa Clara FICE Identification: 039953
Unit ID: 447801
Telephone: (408) 733-1878 Carnegie Class: Spec-4-yr-Other Health
FAX Number: (408) 636-7705 Calendar System: Trimester
URL: www.uewm.edu
Established: 1997 Annual Undergrad Tuition & Fees: N/A
Enrollment: 119 Coed
Affiliation or Control: Proprietary IRS Status: Proprietary
Highest Offering: Master's
Accreditation: ACUP

01 President ..... Dr. Eric TAO
05 VP Academic Affairs ..... Dr. Bei LIU
30 VP Development ..... Dr. Ying Q. WANG
07 Director of Admissions/Admin ..... Dr. Sharon ZHOU
37 Director of Financial Aid/Govt Rels ..... Ms. Huiping LO

University of La Verne (C)

1950 Third Street, La Verne CA 91750-4443
County: Los Angeles FICE Identification: 001216
Unit ID: 117140
Telephone: (909) 593-3511 Carnegie Class: DU-Mod
FAX Number: (909) 593-0965 Calendar System: Semester
URL: www.laverne.edu
Established: 1891 Annual Undergrad Tuition & Fees: $45,850
Enrollment: 6,983 Coed
Affiliation or Control: Independent Non-Profit IRS Status: 501(c)3
Highest Offering: Doctorate
Accreditation: WC, #ARCPA, #CAATE, CLPSY, LAW, SPAA

01 President ..... Dr. Devorah A. LIEBERMAN
05 Provost & Vice President ..... Dr. Kerop JANOYAN
10 Chief Financial Officer ..... Mr. Avedis (Avo) KECHICHIAN
111 Vice President Univ Advancement ..... Mrs. Sherri MYLOTT
84 Vice Pres Strategic Enrollment Mgmt ..... Mrs. Mary AGUAYO
50 Dean College Business/Public Mgmt ..... Dr. Emmeline DE PILLIS
53 Dean College Educ/Org Ldrship ..... Dr. Kimberly WHITE-SMITH
61 Dean College of Law ..... Mr. Kevin MARSHALL
32 Chief Student Affairs Officer ..... Mr. Juan REGALDO
12 Associate Provost Grad Program/ROC ..... Dr. Kristan VENEGAS
07 Director of Undergraduate Admission ..... Dr. Adam WU
124 AVP Acad Support/Retent Svcs ..... Mr. Carlos CAVANTES
21 Associate Vice President of Finance ..... Ms. Lori K. GORDIEN
18 Sr Dir Physical Plant Ops & Svcs ..... Mr. Garth JONES
29 Sr Dir Advancement Oper & Services ..... Ms. Bianca ROMERO
38 Dir Counseling & Psych Services ..... Dr. Elleni R. KOULOS
113 Exec Director Student Accounts ..... Ms. Xochitl E. MARTINEZ
96 Director Purchasing & Procurement ..... Mrs. Deborah S. DEACY
28 Director Multicultural Affairs ..... Dr. Daniel L. LOERA
23 Director of Health Services ..... Ms. Jamie SOLIS
36 Director Career Center ..... Ms. Denise GIANOUSSOPAULOUS
88 Dir Center for Adv/Teaching & Lrng ..... Mr. Jeremy SCHNEIDER
121 Director Academic Success Center ..... Ms. Savannah GARCIA
41 Athletic Director ..... Mr. Scott WINTERBURN
06 Registrar ..... Mr. Adam EVANS
08 University Librarian ..... Dr. Vinaya L. TRIPURANENI
28 Chief Diversity Officer ..... Dr. Alexandra BURREL
09 Director of Institutional Research ..... Dr. Leeshawn MOORE
42 Chaplain/Dir of Campus Ministry ..... Dr. Zandra L. WAGONER
90 Sr Dir Admission Oper/Tech Svcs ..... Mrs. Loreto D'MONTE
88 Asst Director of Civic Engagement ..... Ms. Julissa ESPINOZA
04 Dir President Office/Board Affairs ..... Dr. Shannon CAPALDI
19 Director Security/Safety ..... Mr. Ruben IBARRA
26 AVP of Strategic Communications ..... Mr. Rod LEVEQUE
37 Director Student Financial Aid ..... Mr. Nicholas NOVELLO

University Massachusetts Global (D)

16355 Laguna Canyon Road, 1st Floor, Irvine CA 92618
County: Orange FICE Identification: 041618
Unit ID: 262086
Telephone: (949) 753-4774 Carnegie Class: DU-Mod
FAX Number: (714) 753-7875 Calendar System: Other
URL: www.umassglobal.edu
Established: 1958 Annual Undergrad Tuition & Fees: $12,480
Enrollment: 10,986 Coed
Affiliation or Control: Independent Non-Profit IRS Status: 501(c)3
Highest Offering: Doctorate
Accreditation: WC, CAEPN, NURSE, SW

01 Chancellor ..... Dr. Gary BRAHM
10 Exec Vice Chancellor/CFO ..... Mr. Phillip DOOLITTLE
32 EVC Enrollment/Student Affairs ..... Ms. Saskia KNIGHT
11 Campus Director ..... Ms. Melissa REYES
05 Exec VC Acad Affs/CAO/Provost ..... Mr. Charles BULLOCK
06 Registrar ..... Vacant

† A member of the Chapman University System.

University of the Pacific (E)

3601 Pacific Avenue, Stockton CA 95211-0197
County: San Joaquin FICE Identification: 001329
Unit ID: 120883
Telephone: (209) 946-2011 Carnegie Class: DU-Mod
FAX Number: (209) 946-2845 Calendar System: Semester
URL: www.pacific.edu
Established: 1851 Annual Undergrad Tuition & Fees: $51,094
Enrollment: 6,263 Coed
Affiliation or Control: Independent Non-Profit IRS Status: 501(c)3
Highest Offering: Doctorate
Accreditation: WC, ACAE, ARCPA, AUD, CAATE, CEA, DENT, DH, @DIETC, IPSY, LAW, MUS, PHAR, PTA, SP, @SW

01 President ..... Christopher CALLAHAN
05 Provost/VP Academic Affairs ..... Dr. Maria PALLAVICINI
10 VP Business & Finance ..... Ken MULLEN
32 VP Student Life ..... Maria Q. BLANDIZZI
30 VP Development & Alumni Relations ..... Scott BIEDERMANN
13 VP Technology/CIO ..... Art SPRECHER
21 Assoc VP Business & Finance ..... Ron ELLISON
84 VP Enrollment Management ..... Dr. Chris FERGUSON
26 Assoc VP Marketing & Communication ..... Marge GREY
119 Assoc VP Info Security/CISO ..... Ken KERRICK
115 Asst VP Treasury/Chf Invest Ofcr ..... Jol MANILAY
04 Exec Asst to the President ..... Ashley WILLIAMS
49 Dean College of the Pacific ..... Rena FRADEN
50 Dean Eberhardt School of Business ..... Tim CARROLL
52 Dean Dugoni School of Dentistry ..... Nader NADERSHAHI
53 Dean Benerd School of Education ..... Patricia CAMPBELL
54 Dean School of Eng/Comp Sci ..... Steven HOWELL
61 Dean McGeorge School of Law ..... Michael H. SCHWARTZ
64 Dean Conservatory of Music ..... Peter WITTE
67 Dean Long School Pharm/Hlth Sci ..... Phillip R. OPPENHEIMER
36 Assoc VP/Exec Dir Career Dev ..... Tom VECCHIONE
08 Int Dean University Library ..... Edie SPARKS
58 Interim Dean Graduate School ..... Cyd JENEFSKY
51 Dean University College ..... Patricia CAMPBELL
25 Sponsored Pgms Administrator ..... Vacant
29 AVP Alumni Relations ..... Kelli PAGE
37 Exec Director Financial Aid ..... Aquila GALGON
07 Interim Exec Director Admissions ..... Jonathan LATTA
06 Assoc University Registrar ..... Michael SNYDER
09 Assoc Prov Inst Research ..... Mike ROGERS
35 Exec Director Campus Life ..... Marc FALKENSTEIN
96 Director Purchasing ..... Ronda MARR
92 Director Honors Program ..... Balint SZATARAY
93 Dir Intercultural Student Success ..... Vacant
94 Director Gender Studies ..... Traci ROBERTS-CAMPS
38 Director Counseling Services ..... Stacie TURKS
39 Exec Director Residential Life ..... Joe BERTHIAUME
41 Director of Athletics ..... Janet LUCAS
42 Director Religious & Spiritual Life ..... Laura STEED
15 Asst VP Human Resources ..... Linda JEFFERS
40 Director Bookstore ..... Nicole CASTILLO
19 Exec Director Public Safety ..... Grant BEDFORD
18 Director Physical Plant ..... Steve GREENWOD
82 Director School Intl Studies ..... Dr. William HERRIN
110 Sr Assoc VP Development ..... Scott BIEDERMANN
88 Asst VP Development ..... Judy NAGAI
100 Chief of Staff to the President ..... Vacant
104 Dir International Programs Services ..... Ryan GRIFFITH
43 General Counsel ..... Kevin MILLS
12 Director Sacramento Campus ..... Dr. Patrick FAVERTY
88 Asst Dean Admissions ..... Tracy SIMMONS
117 Director Enterprise Risk Mgmt ..... Roberta MARTOZA
116 Director Internal Audit ..... Randy SCHWANTES
114 Director University Budget ..... Jonallie PARRA
105 Director Web Services ..... Vacant
108 Vice Prov Strategy/Educ Effective ..... Cyd JENEFSKY
11 Asst Dean Operations ..... Kyle HARKNESS
22 Director Affirmative Action/EEO ..... Deborah FREEMAN
44 Exec Director Annual Giving ..... Michael RICHMOND
90 Asst VP Tech Customer Experience ..... Peggy KAY
91 Asst Dir Integrated Services ..... Raoul VILLALPANDO
88 Asst VP Development ..... Molly BYRNE
101 Exec Director Board of Regents ..... Janine SWANSON
102 Asst Dir Corp/Foundation Relations ..... Emily NOVICK

University of the People (F)

595 East Colorado Blvd Ste 623, Pasadena CA 91101
County: Los Angeles Identification: 667160
Unit ID: 488846
Telephone: (626) 264-8880 Carnegie Class: Bac/Assoc-Mixed
FAX Number: N/A Calendar System: Other
URL: www.uopeople.edu
Established: 2009 Annual Undergrad Tuition & Fees: $1,200
Enrollment: 43,722 Coed
Affiliation or Control: Independent Non-Profit IRS Status: 501(c)3
Highest Offering: Master's
Accreditation: DEAC

01 President & Founder ..... Mr. Shai RESHEF
05 Provost ..... Dr. David HARRIS COHEN
11 Sr Vice Pres Operations ..... Mr. Rami ISH-HURVITZ
45 VP for Strategy & Planning ..... Mr. Yoav VENTURA
84 Sr Vice President Enrollment ..... Mr. Asaf WOLFF
13 Vice Pres Technology ..... Ms. Hadass ADMON
10 Chief Financial Officer ..... Mr. Paul AFFUSO
37 Financial Aid Officer ..... Ms. Hanan EID

University of Phoenix Bay Area Campus (A)

3590 N First Street, San Jose CA 95134-1805
Telephone: (800) 266-2107 Identification: 770193
Accreditation: &HLC, ACBSP

† Branch campus of University of Phoenix, Tempe, AZ. No longer accepting campus-based students.

University of Phoenix Central Valley Campus (B)

45 River Park Place West, Suite 201,
Fresno CA 93720-1552
Telephone: (559) 312-1133 Identification: 770190
Accreditation: &HLC, ACBSP

† Branch campus of University of Phoenix, Tempe, AZ

University of Phoenix Sacramento Valley Campus (C)

2860 Gateway Oaks Drive, Sacramento CA 95833-4334
Telephone: (800) 266-2107 Identification: 770191
Accreditation: &HLC, ACBSP

† Branch campus of University of Phoenix, Tempe, AZ

University of Phoenix San Diego Campus (D)

9645 Granite Ridge Dr, Suite 200,
San Diego CA 92123-2658
Telephone: (800) 473-4346 Identification: 770192
Accreditation: &HLC, ACBSP

† Branch campus of University of Phoenix, Tempe, AZ

University of Phoenix Southern California Campus (E)

3110 E. Guasti Rd, Ontario CA 91761
Telephone: (800) 888-1968 Identification: 770189
Accreditation: &HLC, ACBSP

† Branch campus of University of Phoenix, Tempe, AZ.

University of Redlands (F)

PO Box 3080, Redlands CA 92373-0999
County: San Bernardino FICE Identification: 001322
Unit ID: 121691
Telephone: (909) 793-2121 Carnegie Class: Masters/L
FAX Number: (909) 793-2029 Calendar System: Semester
URL: www.redlands.edu
Established: 1907 Annual Undergrad Tuition & Fees: $52,500
Enrollment: 4,566 Coed
Affiliation or Control: Independent Non-Profit IRS Status: 501(c)3
Highest Offering: Doctorate
Accreditation: WC, ACBSP, MUS, PAST, SP, THEOL

01 President ... Ms. Krista L. NEWKIRK
05 Provost/Chief Academic Officer ... Dr. Kathy OGREN
10 Vice Pres Finance & CFO ... Mr. Kevin M. DYERLY
32 University Dean of Student Affairs ... Dr. Donna EDDLEMAN
84 Vice President for Enrollment ... Vacant
111 Vice Pres for Advancement ... Ms. Tamara M. JOSSERAND
11 Vice President Administration ... Dr. Michelle L. ROGERS
26 Chief Communications Officer ... Ms. Mika ONO
43 General Counsel ... Mr. Brent G. GERATY
100 Chief of Staff ... Ms. Jennifer L. THOMPSON
53 Dean School of Education ... Dr. Mario MARTINEZ
50 Dean School of Business ... Dr. Thomas HORAN
49 Interim Dean Col of Arts & Sciences ... Dr. Steven WUHS
64 Dean School of Music ... Dr. Joseph MODICA
21 Director Financial Ops & Controller ... Ms. Patricia M. CAUDLE
28 Sr Diversity & Inclusion Officer ... Mr. Christopher L. JONES
42 Chaplain ... Vacant
06 Registrar ... Ms. Maria JOHNSON
104 Director Study Abroad ... Mr. Leo ROWLAND
37 Director of Financial Aid ... Ms. Emily BAKER
08 Director of Library Services ... Vacant
15 Director of Human Resources ... Vacant
09 Asst Provost Institutional Research ... Dr. Yan XIE
19 Chief of Public Safety ... Mr. Jeffrey TALBOTT
18 Director of Facilities Management ... Mr. Roger CELLINI
29 Director of Alumni Relations ... Ms. Shelli STOCKTON
20 Asst Dean of Academic/Student Life ... Ms. Amy WILMS
38 Director Student Counseling Ctr ... Dr. Matt GRAGG
41 Director of PE & Athletics ... Mr. Jeffrey MARTINEZ
36 Director Student Employment ... Ms. Kathryn WOOD
07 Director of Admissions ... Ms. Belinda SANDOVAL
13 Chief Information Officer ... Mr. Steve GARCIA
04 Executive Assistant to President ... Vacant
39 Director of Student Housing ... Ms. Cassandra MORTON
88 Dir Military & Veteran Services ... Ms. Monique POPE
44 Director Annual Giving ... Ms. Molly WIDDICOMBE
88 Dir Community Service Learning ... Mr. Tony MUELLER
103 Exec Dir Career & Prof Dev ... Dr. Kelly DRIES

University of St. Augustine for Health Sciences (G)

700 Windy Point Drive, San Marcos CA 92069
County: San Diego FICE Identification: 031713
Unit ID: 367954
Telephone: (800) 241-1027 Carnegie Class: Spec-4-yr-Other Health
FAX Number: N/A Calendar System: Trimester
URL: www.usa.edu
Established: 1979 Annual Graduate Tuition & Fees: N/A
Enrollment: 4,711 Coed
Affiliation or Control: Proprietary IRS Status: Proprietary
Highest Offering: Doctorate; No Undergraduates
Accreditation: WC, NURSE, OT, PTA

01 CEO/Interim President ... Ms. Vivian SANCHEZ
05 Chief Academic Officer/Exec Dean ... Dr. Brian GOLDSTEIN
10 Interim CFO ... Mr. Patrick GRAMLING
15 Exec Director Human Resources ... Ms. Susan WAUGH
13 Exec Director IT ... Mr. Matt MOLINE
09 Director of Institutional Research ... Ms. Nga PHAN
37 Director Student Financial Aid ... Ms. Vanessa FLOWERS
84 Director Enrollment Management ... Ms. Julie GONICK
06 Registrar ... Ms. Diane RONDINELLI
08 Director Library Services ... Ms. Julie EVENER
106 Dean of Online Education ... Dr. Maria PUZZIFERRO
18 Exec Dir Campus Opers & Facilities ... Ms. Sylvia BERENGUER
07 Director of Admissions & Enrollment ... Ms. Minh-Ha HOANG
123 Assoc Dir Graduate Admissions ... Ms. Erika GARWOOD
09 Dir Inst Research & Planning ... Dr. Margaret LEARY
108 Dir Inst Effectiveness/Strat Init ... Dr. Elizabeth GIDDENS
90 Sr Director Customer Support ... Ms. Shahra MESHKATY
91 Sr Dir Enterprise Applications ... Ms. Steffanie HOIE
102 Director Foundation Relations ... Mr. Bruce EDWARDS
112 Director Major & Planned Giving ... Ms. Erin JONES
29 Senior Director Alumni Relations ... Mr. Charles BASS
36 Senior Director Career Dev Center ... Ms. Robin DARMON
37 Director Financial Aid Services ... Ms. Kellie NEHRING
113 Dir Student Financial Services ... Ms. Rosemary STALLBAUMER
92 Director Honors Program ... Dr. Susannah STERN
39 Asst Dean of Students ... Mr. Luke LACROIX
85 Dir International Students/Scholars ... Ms. Chia-Yen LIN
104 Asst Provost International Affairs ... Dr. Kira A. ESPIRITU
93 Director Multicultural Commons ... Dr. Mayte PEREZ-FRANCO
27 Sr Director Media Relations ... Ms. Lissette MARTINEZ
96 Director Procurement Services ... Ms. Theresa L. ROBINSON HARRIS
25 Director Sponsored Programs ... Ms. Traci MERRILL
23 Director Student Health Center ... Ms. Pamela J. SIKES
40 Director Bookstore ... Mr. James THRAILKILL
106 Dir Online Education ... Ms. Roxanne MORRISON
22 Dir Title IX/EEO ... Dr. Nicole A. SCHUESSLER VELOZ
117 Director Risk Management ... Ms. Robin ESKOW
118 Director Benefits ... Ms. Claire WEATHERFORD
88 AVP Student Wellness ... Dr. Chris BURDEN

University of Saint Katherine (H)

1637 Capalina Road, San Marcos CA 92069
County: San Diego Identification: 667263
Telephone: (760) 471-1316 Carnegie Class: Not Classified
FAX Number: (760) 704-1314 Calendar System: Semester
URL: www.usk.edu
Established: Annual Undergrad Tuition & Fees: N/A
Enrollment: N/A Coed
Affiliation or Control: Independent Non-Profit IRS Status: 501(c)3
Highest Offering: Master's
Accreditation: WC

01 President & Founder ... Dr. Frank PAPATHEOFANIS
05 Chief Academic Officer ... Dr. Tina KEATING
10 Chief Financial Officer ... Charlotte FOWLER
09 Dir of Inst Research/Effectiveness ... Hilari TARAZI
07 Dean of Admissions/Registrar ... Marina TRIGONIS
32 Director of Student Affairs ... Dr. Tina KEATING

University of San Diego (I)

5998 Alcala Park, San Diego CA 92110-2492
County: San Diego FICE Identification: 010395
Unit ID: 122436
Telephone: (619) 260-4600 Carnegie Class: DU-Higher
FAX Number: (619) 260-6833 Calendar System: 4/1/4
URL: www.sandiego.edu
Established: 1949 Annual Undergrad Tuition & Fees: $52,864
Enrollment: 8,861 Coed
Affiliation or Control: Roman Catholic IRS Status: 501(c)3
Highest Offering: Doctorate
Accreditation: WC, CACREP, CEA, IPSY, LAW, MFCD, NURSE

01 President ... Dr. James T. HARRIS
04 Special Assistant to the President ... Ms. Elaine ATENCIO
05 Vice President & Provost ... Dr. Gail F. BAKER
10 VP Finance/Chief Financial Officer ... Ms. Katy ROIG
45 VP Inst Effectiveness/Strat Init ... Dr. Andrew ALLEN
42 Vice President Mission Integration ... Dr. Michael LOVETTE-COLYER
32 Vice President Student Affairs ... Ms. Charlotte JOHNSON
111 Vice President Univ Advancement ... Mr. Richard P. VIRGIN
11 Vice President Univ Operations ... Mr. Ky L. SNYDER
49 Dean College of Arts & Sciences ... Dr. Noelle NORTON
50 Dean School of Business ... Dr. Timothy KEANE
54 Dean Shiley-Marcos School of Engr ... Dr. Chell ROBERTS
61 Dean School of Law ... Mr. Robert SCHAPIRO
53 Dean Sch Leadership/Educ Sciences ... Dr. Joi SPENCER
66 Dean Sch Nursing/Health Sci ... Dr. Jane GEORGES
88 Dean School of Peace Studies ... Dr. Patricia MARQUEZ
08 Dean University Library ... Dr. Theresa BYRD
43 General Counsel & Advisor to Pres ... Mr. Thomas SKINNER
20 Int Vice Provost Academic Affairs ... Dr. Roger PACE
13 Chief Information Officer ... Dr. Elazar HAREL
06 University Registrar ... Ms. Elizabeth SILVA
46 Associate Provost Research & Dev ... Dr. Eileen FRY-BOWERS
28 Vice Prov Diversity/Equity/Inclus ... Dr. Regina DIXON-REEVES
88 Assoc Provost International Affairs ... Dr. Denise DIMON
21 Controller ... Vacant
114 Budget Director ... Ms. Marie DAVIS
41 Assoc VP & Exec Dir of Athletics ... Mr. Bill MCGILLIS
84 Asst VP Enrollment Management ... Mr. Stephen F. PULTZ
15 AVP & Chief Human Resources Officer ... Dr. Karen BRIGGS
18 Asst VP Facilities Management ... Mr. Andre HUTCHINSON
30 Assoc Vice President Development ... Ms. Sandra CIALLELLA
26 AVP University Communications ... Mr. Peter MARLOW
44 Asst VP Advancement Operations ... Mr. Philip GARLAND
86 Asst Vice Pres Cmty/Local/Govt Rels ... Vacant
19 Asst VP & Chief Public Safety ... Mr. James MIYASHIRO
35 Asst VP & Dean of Students ... Dr. Donald R. GODWIN
35 Asst VP Student Life ... Dr. Cynthia AVERY
109 Asst VP Auxiliary Services ... Mr. Andre MALLIE

University of San Francisco (J)

2130 Fulton Street, San Francisco CA 94117-1080
County: San Francisco FICE Identification: 001325
Unit ID: 122612
Telephone: (415) 422-5555 Carnegie Class: DU-Mod
FAX Number: (415) 422-2303 Calendar System: 4/1/4
URL: www.usfca.edu
Established: 1855 Annual Undergrad Tuition & Fees: $52,482
Enrollment: 10,068 Coed
Affiliation or Control: Roman Catholic IRS Status: 501(c)3
Highest Offering: Doctorate
Accreditation: WC, CLPSY, IPSY, LAW, NURSE, PH, SPAA

01 President ... Rev. Paul J. FITZGERALD, SJ
05 Provost & VP Acad Affairs ... Dr. Chinyere OPARAH
10 Vice President Business & Finance ... Mr. Charles E. CROSS
26 Vice Pres Marketing/Communications ... Ms. Ellen RYDER
30 Interim Vice President Development .. Ms. Lindsey MCCLENAHAN
43 General Counsel ... Ms. Donna J. DAVIS
13 Vice President IT & CIO ... Mr. Opinder BAWA
20 Senior Vice Provost Acad Affairs ... Dr. Shirley MCGUIRE
32 Vice Provost Student Life ... Ms. Julie J. ORIO
28 Vice Prov Diversity & Cmty Outreach ... Vacant
114 Vice Prov Inst Budget/Plng/Analytic ... Dr. Jeff HAMRICK
84 Vice Provost Strategic Enroll Mgmt ... Mr. Michael BESEDA
61 Dean School of Law ... Ms. Susan FREIWALD
49 Interim Dean College Arts & Science ... Dr. Eileen FUNG
08 Interim Dean of University Library ... Dr. Shawn CALHOUN
53 Dean School of Education ... Dr. Shabnam KOIRALA-AZAD
66 Dean School of Nursing/Health Prof ... Dr. Margaret W. BAKER
50 Dean School of Management ... Dr. Charles MOSES
18 Assoc Vice Pres Facilities Mgmt ... Mr. Michael E. LONDON
21 Assoc Vice Pres Finance & Treasury ... Ms. Stacy LEWIS
15 Assoc Vice Pres Human Resources ... Ms. Diane NELSON
114 AVP Accounting & Business Svcs ... Mr. Desmond DAIR
88 Rector of Jesuit Community ... Rev. Timothy S. GODFREY, SJ
42 Assoc Director University Ministry ... Ms. Angelica QUIONEZ
37 Asst Vice Prov Student Fin Svcs ... Vacant
04 Exec Asst to President/Sec BOT ... Ms. Jaci E. NEESAM
27 Media Relations Specialist ... Ms. Kellie SAMSON
45 Assoc Vice Prov Planning and Budget ... Mr. Michael J. HARRINGTON
110 Sr Assoc VP Development ... Vacant
06 Assoc Dean University Registrar ... Mr. Robert L. BROMFIELD
96 Dir Purchasing & Ancillary Svc ... Ms. Janet L. TEYMOURTASH
38 Senior Dir Counseling & Psych Svcs ... Dr. Barbara J. THOMAS
36 Senior Director Career Svcs ... Mr. Alex HOCHMAN
19 Senior Director of Public Safety ... Dr. Daniel L. LAWSON
123 Asst Vice Prov Graduate Enrollment ... Mr. Michael HUGHES
88 Asst Vice Prov Integ Enrollment Mgt ... Mr. Patrick KAO
104 Director Ctr for Global Education ... Ms. Sharon F. LI
07 Asst Vice Prov Undergrad Admissions ... Ms. April CRABTREE
85 Director Intl Student/Scholar Svcs ... Ms. Marcella PITCHER DEPROTO
41 Director of Athletics ... Ms. Joan MCDERMOTT
29 Assoc VP for Development ... Ms. Leslie WETZEL
44 Assoc VP Giving & Devel Svc & PR&M ... Vacant
102 Dir Corp/Foundation Relations ... Vacant
29 Director University Initiatives ... Mr. Bill CARTWRIGHT
16 Dir of Employee Relations ... Ms. Liliana ROJAS
09 AVP Institutional Research ... Mr. Joe HENSON
39 Sr Dir Student Housing/Resident Ed ... Mr. Torry BROUILLARD-BRUCE
24 Dir Ctr Learning Instruct & Tech ... Dr. John BANSAVICH
105 Sr Dir Web & Digital Communication ... Ms. Marlene K. TOM
108 AVP Educ Effectiveness/Assessment ... Ms. Deborah PANTER
25 Director Contracts/Grants Admin ... Ms. Karina FANTILLO
22 Asst Dean/Director Disability Svcs ... Mr. Tom MERRELL
14 AVP & Dir Educ Technology Services ... Mr. David KIRMSE
88 Asst Vice Prov Enroll Communication ... Ms. Katherine EDWARDS
116 AVP Tax Compliance & Internal Audit ... Mr. Dominic DAHER
101 Secretary of the Board ... Ms. Jaci NEESAM

University of Silicon Andhra (A)

1521 California Circle, Milpitas CA 95035

County: Santa Clara — Identification: 667397
Telephone: (844) 872-8680 — Carnegie Class: Not Classified
FAX Number: N/A — Calendar System: Semester
URL: www.universityofsiliconandhra.org
Established: — Annual Graduate Tuition & Fees: N/A
Enrollment: N/A — Coed
Affiliation or Control: Independent Non-Profit — IRS Status: 501(c)3
Highest Offering: Master's; No Undergraduates
Accreditation: @WC

01 President/CEO .... Anand KUCHIBHOTLA
05 Provost .... Raju CHAMARTHI
10 Vice Pres Finance/Administration .. Deena BABU KONDUBHATLA
32 Manager Student Services .... Mamatha KUCHIBHOTLA
07 Manager Admissions .... Sridevi GANTI

University of Silicon Valley (B)

191 Baypointe Parkway, San Jose CA 95134-1697

County: Santa Clara — FICE Identification: 001177
Unit ID: 112394
Telephone: (408) 498-5100 — Carnegie Class: Bac-Diverse
FAX Number: (408) 877-7373 — Calendar System: Trimester
URL: https://usv.edu/
Established: 1887 — Annual Undergrad Tuition & Fees: $21,784
Enrollment: 524 — Coed
Affiliation or Control: Proprietary — IRS Status: Proprietary
Highest Offering: Master's
Accreditation: WC

01 CEO and President .... Mr. Charles RESTIVO
05 Provost/Chief Academic Officer .... Dr. Brian SHEPARD
10 Chief Financial Officer .... Ms. Ilona KREYNIS
84 VP of Enrollment .... Mr. Eric RAJASALU
13 VP Info Technology/Campus Svcs .... Dr. Audrey FEDIN
09 Vice Pres Inst Research & QA .... Ms. Milla ZLATANOV
07 VP of Admissions .... Ms. Sheri STEIN
88 Chief Compliance Officer .... Dr. Reba SMITH
20 Dean of Education .... Mr. Jerome SOLOMON
32 Dean of Students .... Ms. Carolus BROWN
06 Registrar .... Ms. Angela ACUNA
04 Executive Assistant to President .... Ms. Monique TAYLOR
36 Dir Career Services .... Mr. Jason ARANA
08 Librarian & Resource Center Manager . Ms. Louise PASTERNACK
37 Director of Financial Aid .... Ms. Stacey VALENTINE
15 Director of Human Resources .... Ms. Leslie ANDERSON

University of South Los Angeles (C)

555 W Redondo Beach Blvd, Gardena CA 90248

County: Los Angeles — Identification: 667326
Telephone: (310) 756-0001 — Carnegie Class: Not Classified
FAX Number: (310) 756-0004 — Calendar System: Quarter
URL: www.uosla.org
Established: 1993 — Annual Undergrad Tuition & Fees: N/A
Enrollment: N/A — Coed
Affiliation or Control: Proprietary — IRS Status: Proprietary
Highest Offering: Doctorate
Accreditation: TRACS

01 Chancellor .... Dr. Peter CHOI
11 Vice Chanc Admin & Student Affs .... Dr. Richard KANG
10 CFO & Director of Admin .... Jackie JUNG
05 Chief Academic Officer .... Dr. Guy LANGVARDT
32 Dean of Student Affairs .... Dr. Tania MAYNC
07 Dir of Admiss & Records/Registrar .... Vacant

University of Southern California (D)

University Park, Los Angeles CA 90089-0012

County: Los Angeles — FICE Identification: 001328
Unit ID: 123961
Telephone: (213) 740-2111 — Carnegie Class: DU-Highest
FAX Number: (213) 740-8502 — Calendar System: Semester
URL: www.usc.edu
Established: 1880 — Annual Undergrad Tuition & Fees: $60,275
Enrollment: 46,287 — Coed
Affiliation or Control: Independent Non-Profit — IRS Status: 501(c)3
Highest Offering: Doctorate
Accreditation: WC, ANEST, ARCPA, CAEPN, CLPSY, DENT, DH, DIETC, HSA, IPSY, JOUR, LAW, LIB, LSAR, MED, NURSE, OT, PCSAS, PDPSY, PH, PHAR, PLNG, PTA, @SP, SPAA, SW

01 President .... Dr. Carol L. FOLT
05 Provost & SVP Academic Affairs .... Dr. Charles F. ZUKOSKI
26 Interim SVP University Relations .... Mr. Samuel GARRISON
111 Int Sr VP University Advancement .... Ms. Tracey VRANICH
17 CEO for USC Health .... Mr. Rodney HANNERS
115 Chief Investment Officer .... Ms. Amy DIAMOND
27 SVP/Chief Communication Officer .... Mr. Kyle HENLEY
10 Sr VP Finance & CFO .... Mr. James STATEN
41 Athletic Director .... Mr. Mike BOHN
15 Sr VP Human Resources .... Ms. Felicia WASHINGTON
11 Sr VP Administration .... Mr. David W. WRIGHT
43 Senior VP and General Counsel .... Mr. Beong-Soo KIM
32 VP for Student Affairs .... Mr. Winston B. CRISP
84 VP for Enrollment Management .... Ms. Kedra ISHOP
46 VP for Research .... Dr. Ishwar PURI
88 VP for Athletic Compliance .... Mr. Michael BLANTON
18 Interim VP Capital Construction .... Mr. Christopher TOOMEY
88 VP Health Sciences Advancement .... Ms. Kathryn CARRICO
88 VP of Professionalism/Ethics .... Mr. Michael BLANTON
100 Chief of Staff .... Ms. Rene K. PAK
60 Dean Annenberg School Communication .... Dr. Willow C. BAY
48 Dean School of Architecture .... Mr. Milton S. CURRY
50 Dean Marshall School of Business .... Mr. Geoff GARRETT
88 Dean School of Cinematic Arts .... Dr. Elizabeth M. DALEY
66 Dean Kaufman School of Dance .... Dr. Robert A. CUTIETTA
52 Dean Ostrow School of Dentistry .... Dr. Avishai SADAN
53 Dean Rossier School of Education .... Dr. Pedro NOGUERA
54 Dean Viterbi School of Engineering .... Dr. Yannis C. YORTSOS
57 Dean Roski School of Fine Arts .... Dr. Erica MUHL
88 Dean Davis School of Gerontology .... Dr. Pinchas COHEN
61 Dean Gould School of Law .... Dr. Andrew GUZMAN
63 Dean Keck School of Medicine .... Dr. Laura MOSQUEDA
64 Dean Thornton School of Music .... Dr. Robert A. CUTIETTA
67 Dean School of Pharmacy .... Dr. Vassilios PAPADOPOULOS
70 Dean School of Social Work .... Dr. Sarah GEHLERT
88 Int Dean School of Dramatic Arts .... Ms. Elizabeth DALEY
80 Dean School of Public Policy .... Dr. Dana GOLDMAN
49 Dean Dornsife Col Ltrs/Arts & Sci .... Dr. Amber D. MILLER
42 Dean Religious Life .... Dr. Varun SONI
06 Registrar .... Dr. Frank CHANG
08 Dean University Libraries .... Ms. Catherine QUINLAN
07 Dean of Admission .... Mr. Timothy BRUNOLD
37 Dean of Financial Aid .... Mr. Thomas MCWHORTER
29 Assoc Sr VP and Campaign Director .... Mr. Sam M. LOPEZ
38 Dir Counseling & Psychological Svcs .... Dr. Ilene ROSENSTEIN
88 Vice Provost and Senior Advisor .... Dr. Martin L. LEVINE
58 Vice Prov for Graduate Programs .... Dr. Sally PRATT
20 Vice Prov for Undergraduate Program .... Dr. Andrea HODGE
13 Chief Information Officer .... Dr. Douglas SHOOK
20 Vice Prov Academic Ops .... Dr. Mark TODD
88 Exec Dir USC Stevens Ctr for Innov .... Ms. Jennifer DYER
85 VP of Global Initiatives .... Dr. Anthony BAILEY
20 Vice Prov for Acad/Faculty Affairs .... Dr. Elizabeth GRADDY

University of the West (E)

1409 Walnut Grove Avenue, Rosemead CA 91770-3709

County: Los Angeles — FICE Identification: 036963
Unit ID: 449870
Telephone: (626) 571-8811 — Carnegie Class: Bac-A&S
FAX Number: (626) 571-1413 — Calendar System: Semester
URL: www.uwest.edu
Established: 1991 — Annual Undergrad Tuition & Fees: $13,556
Enrollment: 238 — Coed
Affiliation or Control: Independent Non-Profit — IRS Status: 501(c)3
Highest Offering: Doctorate
Accreditation: WC

01 President .... Dr. Minh-hoa TA
05 Chief Academic Officer .... Dr. Jane IWAMURA
32 Chief Student Services Officer .... Ms. Vanessa KARAM
10 Chief Financial Officer .... Ms. Amy CHONG
13 Director Information Technology .... Mr. Rafael WU
08 Director of Library .... Ms. Ling Ling KUO
06 Registrar .... Ms. Jeanette ANDERSON
07 Enrollment/Admissions Coordinator .... Ms. Nadia SIMONE
35 Student Life Coordinator .... Mr. Eddie ESCALANTE
73 Chair of Religious Studies .... Dr. Miroj SHAKYA
50 Chair of Business Admin .... Dr. Bill CHEN
97 Chair of General Education .... Dr. Kanae OMURA
83 Chair of Psychology .... Dr. Ashley COLEMAN
88 Acting Chair of English .... Ms. Jennifer AVILA
04 Exec Assistant to the President .... Ms. Grace HSIAO
37 Director Financial Aid .... Ms. Lezli FANG
39 Coordinator Housing/Resident Life .. Mr. Eduardo (Eddie) BERNAL
15 Director Human Resources .... Ms. Janice LEE

University of West Los Angeles (F)

9800 La Cienga Blvd., 12th Floor,
Inglewood CA 90301-4423

County: Los Angeles — Identification: 667301
Unit ID: 484862
Telephone: (310) 342-5200 — Carnegie Class: Not Classified
FAX Number: N/A — Calendar System: Semester
URL: www.uwla.edu
Established: 1966 — Annual Undergrad Tuition & Fees: N/A
Enrollment: 229 — Coed
Affiliation or Control: Proprietary — IRS Status: Proprietary
Highest Offering: First Professional Degree
Accreditation: WC

01 President .... Robert BROWN
10 Chief Financial Officer .... Ryan FULLMER
84 VP/Director Recruitment .... Troy BROWN
43 VP/General Counsel .... Tiffany CLINTON
11 VP/Director Business Office .... Johnetta HEGWOOD
61 Dean School of Law .... Jay FRYKBERG
09 Director Institutional Research .... Jesse ALDAVA

Valley College of Medical Careers (G)

8399 Topanga Canyon Blvd Ste 200, West Hills CA 91304

County: Los Angeles — FICE Identification: 041145
Unit ID: 449445
Telephone: (818) 883-9002 — Carnegie Class: Not Classified
FAX Number: (818) 883-9003 — Calendar System: Semester
URL: https://www.valleycollegeofmedicalcareers.info/vcmc.html
Established: — Annual Undergrad Tuition & Fees: N/A
Enrollment: 129 — Coed
Affiliation or Control: Proprietary — IRS Status: Proprietary
Highest Offering: Associate Degree
Accreditation: ABHES, SURTEC

01 President .... Mr. Ronny SUSSMAN

Vanguard University of Southern California (H)

55 Fair Drive, Costa Mesa CA 92626-6597

County: Orange — FICE Identification: 001293
Unit ID: 123651
Telephone: (714) 556-3610 — Carnegie Class: Masters/S
FAX Number: (714) 957-9317 — Calendar System: Semester
URL: www.vanguard.edu
Established: 1920 — Annual Undergrad Tuition & Fees: $36,550
Enrollment: 2,289 — Coed
Affiliation or Control: Assemblies Of God Church — IRS Status: 501(c)3
Highest Offering: Master's
Accreditation: WC, MUS, NURSE, THEA

01 President .... Dr. Michael J. BEALS
100 Dir Org Strategy/Compliance .... Ms. Shree CARTER
04 Exec Assistant to the President .... Mrs. Alexis SCHNOOR
05 Provost/SVP Academic Affairs .... Dr. Pete MENJARES
49 Assoc Provost/Dean Col Arts & Sci .... Dr. Michael D. WILSON
107 Dean Professional Studies .... Vacant
73 Director of Graduate Religion .... Dr. Roger HEUSER
58 Director for Graduate Education .... Dr. Sylvia KANE
83 Director for Graduate Psychology .... Vacant
06 Dean Academic Records/Registrar .... Ms. Julie COWEN
104 Director Global Outreach/Educ .... Ms. Kayli HILLEBRAND
09 VP of Institutional Research .... Mr. John KIM
08 Head Librarian .... Ms. Pamela CRENSHAW
41 Athletic Director .... Mr. Jeff BUSSELL
10 Vice President Finance/CFO .... Mr. Jeremy MOSER
21 Controller .... Ms. Jill ROBINSON
96 Director of Fiscal Management .... Ms. Katy MCINTOSH
19 Dir of Campus Safety Services .... Mr. Kenton FERRIN
13 Director Informational Technology .... Mr. Sean MACLEAN
15 Senior Director of Human Resources .... Mr. Joe BAFFA
18 Director of Facility Operations .... Vacant
40 Bookstore Manager .... Ms. Stephanie BUNT
101 Board Professional .... Ms. Shree CARTER
42 Associate University Pastor .... Rev. Michael WHITFORD
32 VP of Student Affs/Dean of Students .... Dr. Tim YOUNG
39 Student Housing Coordinator .... Ms. Megan SISK
121 Dir Stdnt Success/Acad Res/Fam Rels .... Ms. Amanda LEBRECHT
38 Director of Counseling Services .... Dr. Doug HUTCHINSON
36 Career Planning Coordinator .... Vacant
28 Chief Diversity Officer .... Mr. Pete MENJARES
84 VP for Enrollment Management .... Ms. Kim JOHNSON
07 Director of Admissions Recruitment .... Vacant
123 Dir of Grad/Prof Studies Admissions .... Vacant
37 Assoc Dir of Student Financial Aid .... Ms. Denise PENA
111 VP University Advancement .... Mr. Justin MCINTEE
44 Director of Annual Fund .... Vacant
29 Director of Alumni Engagement .... Mrs. Laura CAPO
26 Chief Communications Officer .... Vacant
86 Director of Veteran/Government Rels .... Ms. Shree CARTER
102 Director of External Relations .... Vacant
108 Director Institutional Assessment .... Ms. Ludmilla PRASLOVA
106 Dean of Teaching and Learning .... Ms. Bonni STACHOWIAK

*Ventura County Community College District (I)

761 East Daily Drive, Suite 200, Camarillo CA 93010

County: Ventura — FICE Identification: 006863
Unit ID: 125019
Telephone: (805) 652-5500 — Carnegie Class: N/A
FAX Number: N/A
URL: www.vcccd.edu

01 Chancellor .... Dr. Greg GILLESPIE
10 Vice Chanc Business Svcs/Fin Mgmt .... Dr. David EL FATTAL
15 Vice Chanc of Human Resources .... Ms. Laura BARROSO
108 Vice Chancellor Inst Effectiveness .... Dr. Cynthia HERRERA
13 Assoc Vice Chanc of IT .... Mr. Dan WATKINS
12 Moorpark College President .... Dr. Julius SOKENU
12 Oxnard College President .... Mr. Luis SANCHEZ
12 Ventura College President .... Dr. Kimberly HOFFMANS
26 Director Public Relations/Marketing .... Ms. Patti BLAIR

*Moorpark College (J)

7075 Campus Road, Moorpark CA 93021-1695

County: Ventura — FICE Identification: 007115
Unit ID: 119137
Telephone: (805) 378-1400 — Carnegie Class: Assoc/HT-High Trad
FAX Number: (805) 378-1499 — Calendar System: Semester
URL: www.moorparkcollege.edu
Established: 1967 — Annual Undergrad Tuition & Fees (In-State): $1,394
Enrollment: 14,361 — Coed
Affiliation or Control: State — IRS Status: 501(c)3
Highest Offering: Associate Degree
Accreditation: WJ, ADNUR, RAD

02 President .... Dr. Julius SOKENU
05 Vice President Academic Affairs .... Ms. Mary REES

10 Vice President Business Services .... Dr. Jennifer CLARK
32 Vice President Student Support .... Dr. Amanuel GEBRU
04 Executive Assistant to President .... Ms. Linda RESENDIZ
20 Dean of Student Learning .... Mr. Howard DAVIS
20 Dean of Student Learning .... Ms. Priscilla MORA
20 Dean of Student Learning .... Mr. Monica GARCIA
20 Dean of Student Learning .... Mr. Robert CABRAL
20 Dean of Student Learning .... Mr. Matthew CALFIN
20 Dean of Student Learning .... Ms. Khushnur DADABHOY
20 Dean of Student Learning .... Mr. Oleg BESPALOV
18 Director Maintenance/Operations .... Mr. John SINUTKO
109 College Fiscal Services Supervisor .... Ms. Michele PERRY
13 Director Information Technology .... Mr. Dan MCMICHAEL
113 Bursar .... Ms. Lindy CHAU
23 Director Student Health Services .... Ms. Allison CASE BARTON
41 Athletic Director .... Mr. Matt CRATER
121 Supervisor Student Success Services .... Ms. Claudia SITLINGTON
37 Student Financial Aid Officer .... Ms. Kim KORINKE
06 Registrar .... Mr. David ANTER
111 Director of Inst Advancement .... Mr. John LOPRIENO
35 Student Activities Specialist .... Ms. Kristen ROBINSON
85 Director Outreach & International .... Ms. Claudia WILROY

*Oxnard College (A)

4000 S Rose Avenue, Oxnard CA 93033-6699

County: Ventura FICE Identification: 012842
Unit ID: 120421
Telephone: (805) 678-5800 Carnegie Class: Assoc/HT-High Trad
FAX Number: (805) 678-5806 Calendar System: Semester
URL: www.oxnardcollege.edu
Established: 1975 Annual Undergrad Tuition & Fees (In-District): $1,394
Enrollment: 6,994 Coed
Affiliation or Control: State/Local IRS Status: 501(c)3
Highest Offering: Associate Degree
Accreditation: WJ, DH, IFSAC

02 President .... Mr. Luis P. SANCHEZ
05 Vice Pres Academic Affairs .... Dr. Art SANDFORD
10 Vice Pres Business Services .... Mr. Christopher RENBARGER
32 Vice Pres Student Development .... Dr. Oscar COBIAN
79 Dean Library & Liberal Studies .... Dr. Luis GONZALEZ
75 Dean Career & Technical Education .... Dr. Armine DERDIARIAN
81 Dean Math/Science/Hlth/PE/Athletics .... Dr. Carolyn INOUYE
09 Dean Inst Effectiveness .... Dr. Keller MAGENAU
121 Dean Student Success .... Ms. Leah ALARCON
18 Director Maintenance/Operations .... Mr. Bob SUBE
41 Director of Athletics .... Mr. Jonas CRAWFORD
06 Registrar .... Mr. Joel DIAZ
88 Director STEM .... Dr. Marcella KLEIN-WILLIAMS
37 Financial Aid Officer .... Ms. Linda FAASUA
109 College Services Supervisor .... Mr. Gilbert DOWNS
04 Exec Assistant to the President .... Ms. Karla BANKS
13 Chief Information Technology Office ...... Mr. Michael ALEXANDER
19 Dean of Public Safety .... Mr. Matthew JEWETT

*Ventura College (B)

4667 Telegraph Road, Ventura CA 93003-3899

County: Ventura FICE Identification: 001334
Unit ID: 125028
Telephone: (805) 289-6000 Carnegie Class: Assoc/HT-High Trad
FAX Number: (805) 289-6466 Calendar System: Semester
URL: www.venturacollege.edu
Established: 1925 Annual Undergrad Tuition & Fees (In-District): $1,394
Enrollment: 11,789 Coed
Affiliation or Control: State/Local IRS Status: 501(c)3
Highest Offering: Associate Degree
Accreditation: WJ, ADNUR, EMT

02 President .... Dr. Kim HOFFMANS
05 Vice President Academic Affairs .... Dr. Jennifer KALFSBEEK-GOETZ
32 Vice Pres Student Affairs .... Dr. Damien A. PEÑA
10 Vice Pres Business/Admin Services .... Ms. Cathy BOJORQUEZ
04 Exec Assistant to the President .... Ms. Andrea RAMBO
108 Dean Institutional Effectiveness .... Mr. Phillip BRIGGS
38 Dean Counseling/Student Engagement .... Leticia CANALES
81 Dean Sciences .... Mr. Dan KUMPF
68 Dean Health/Kines/Ath/Perf Ar .... Mr. Bernard GIBSON
83 Dean Behav & Social Sci/Lang .... Ms. Lisa PUTNAM
103 Dean Career Education .... Ms. Debbie NEWCOMB
103 Dean Career Education .... Ms. Felicia DUEÑAS
81 Dean Eng/Math/Lrng Resources .... Ms. Boglarka KISS
12 Dean East Campus & Stdnt Engage .... Dr. Jesus VEGA
102 Executive Director Foundation .... Ms. Anne KING
06 Registrar .... Ms. Gabriella ASAMSAMA-ACUNA
18 Director Maintenance/Operations .... Mr. Orlando DE LEON
35 Coordinator Student Activities .... Ms. Libby FATTA
37 Financial Aid Officer .... Ms. Alma RODRIGUEZ
09 Institutional Research .... Mr. Michael CALLAHAN
23 Director Student Health Center .... Ms. Mary JONES
19 Campus Police .... Lt. Mike PALLOTO
26 Director Marketing and Outreach .... Ms. Su-Lin RUBALCAVA
41 Athletic Director .... Mr. Jimmy WALKER

Veritas International University (C)

3000 W. MacArthur Blvd, Suite 207, Santa Ana CA 92704

County: Orange Identification: 667103
Telephone: (714) 966-8500 Carnegie Class: Not Classified
FAX Number: (714) 966-8510 Calendar System: Semester
URL: www.ves.edu
Established: 2008 Annual Graduate Tuition & Fees: N/A
Enrollment: N/A Coed
Affiliation or Control: Independent Non-Profit IRS Status: 501(c)3
Highest Offering: Doctorate; No Undergraduates
Accreditation: TRACS

00 Chancellor .... Norman L. GEISLER
01 President .... Joseph M. HOLDEN
07 Director of Admissions .... Peter DIAZ
05 Academic Dean .... Frank CORREA
08 Library Director .... Joe MCELROY
10 Chief Business Officer .... Delia BELTRAN
09 Dir Inst Effectiveness/Assessment .... Frank CORREA
32 Director Student Affairs/Careers .... Deborah DELARGY
15 Business Manager/Human Resources .... Megan YORIMITSU

Victor Valley College (D)

18422 Bear Valley Road, Victorville CA 92395-5850

County: San Bernardino FICE Identification: 001335
Unit ID: 125091
Telephone: (760) 245-4271 Carnegie Class: Assoc/HVT-Mix Trad/Non
FAX Number: (760) 245-9019 Calendar System: Semester
URL: www.vvc.edu
Established: 1961 Annual Undergrad Tuition & Fees (In-District): $1,424
Enrollment: 10,777 Coed
Affiliation or Control: State/Local IRS Status: 501(c)3
Highest Offering: Associate Degree
Accreditation: WJ, COARC, EMT

01 Superintendent/President .... Dr. Daniel W. WALDEN
05 Vice President Instruction .... Dr. Todd SCOTT
10 Deputy Supt/Exec VP Admin Svcs .... Mr. John NAHLEN
32 Vice President Student Development .... Dr. Karen ENGELSEN
15 Vice President Human Resources .... Ms. Monica MARTINEZ
72 Dean Public Safety/Industrial Tech .... Ms. McKenzie TARANGO
79 Dean Humanities/Arts & Social Sci ... Ms. Jacqueline AUGUSTINE
21 Director Fiscal Services .... Ms. Shawntee MILTON
07 Director of Admissions .... Mr. David VAZQUEZ
26 Director Public Info/Marketing .... Mr. Robert SEWELL
41 Director Athletics/Athletic Trainer .... Mr. Arthur LOPEZ
18 Exec Dir Facilities/Operations .... Mr. John NAHLEN
37 Director Financial Aid .... Mr. Jason JUDKINS
109 Director Auxiliary Services/ASB Adv .... Mrs. Deanna SANABRIA
35 Assoc VP Matriculation & Athletics .... Mr. Arthur LOPEZ
19 Chief Campus Police .... Mr. Leonard KNIGHT
13 Chief Information Officer .... Mr. Yogesh MARIMUTHU
88 Dir EOPS/CARE/CALWORKS .... Mr. Carl SMITH
09 Exec Dean Inst Effectiveness .... Ms. Virginia MORAN
04 Executive Asst to President .... Mrs. Michelle PAINTER
08 Head Librarian .... Ms. Leslie HUINER
102 Exec Dir Foundation .... Mrs. Kirsten ACOSTA
104 Facilitator Study Abroad .... Vacant
103 Director Workforce Development .... Ms. Frank CASTANOS

Viridis Graduate Institute (E)

417 Bryant Circle, Ojai CA 93023

County: Ventura Identification: 667375
Telephone: (805) 889-0169 Carnegie Class: Not Classified
FAX Number: N/A Calendar System: Trimester
URL: www.viridis.edu
Established: 2011 Annual Undergrad Tuition & Fees: N/A
Enrollment: N/A Coed
Affiliation or Control: Independent Non-Profit IRS Status: 501(c)3
Highest Offering: Doctorate
Accreditation: DEAC

01 President/CAO .... Dr. Lori PYE
05 Academic Dean .... Dr. Leslie STOUPAS

Virscend University (F)

16490 Bake Parkway Ste 100, Irvine CA 92618

County: Orange Identification: 667414
Telephone: (949) 502-6252 Carnegie Class: Not Classified
FAX Number: N/A Calendar System: Semester
URL: www.virscend.com
Established: Annual Undergrad Tuition & Fees: N/A
Enrollment: N/A Coed
Affiliation or Control: Proprietary IRS Status: Proprietary
Highest Offering: Master's
Accreditation: @WC

01 President .... Dr. Robert CHI

Weimar University (G)

20601 W. Paoli Lane, Weimar CA 95736

County: Placer Identification: 667302
Telephone: (530) 422-7927 Carnegie Class: Not Classified
FAX Number: N/A Calendar System: Semester
URL: www.weimar.edu
Established: 1978 Annual Undergrad Tuition & Fees: N/A
Enrollment: N/A Coed
Affiliation or Control: Independent Non-Profit IRS Status: 501(c)3
Highest Offering: Master's
Accreditation: WC

01 President .... Neil NEDLEY
05 Vice President Academic Affairs .... George ARAYA
10 Chief Financial Officer .... Dale NORTHROP
09 Director of Institutional Research .... Christina HARRIS
32 Director Student Services .... Rodolfo RAMIREZ
84 Director of Enrollment Management .... Wanda SWENSEN
06 Registrar .... Erica KINJO

West Coast Baptist College (H)

4010 E. Lancaster Boulevard, Lancaster CA 93535

County: Los Angeles Identification: 667268
Telephone: (661) 946-2274 Carnegie Class: Not Classified
FAX Number: (661) 946-4510 Calendar System: Semester
URL: www.wcbc.edu
Established: 1995 Annual Undergrad Tuition & Fees: N/A
Enrollment: N/A Coed
Affiliation or Control: Baptist IRS Status: 501(c)3
Highest Offering: Master's
Accreditation: TRACS

01 Founder & President .... Dr. Paul CHAPPELL
11 Exec Vice Pres/Chief Operating Ofcr .... Dr. John GOETSCH
05 Chief Academic Officer .... Dr. Thomas SHEPHERD
11 Dean of Administrative Affairs .... Dr. Jerry GODDARD
32 Vice Pres/Dean of Students .... Dr. Jim SCHETTLER
06 Registrar .... Ms. Kristi LONGHOFER

West Coast Ultrasound Institute (I)

3580 Wilshire Boulevard, 4th Floor,
Los Angeles CA 90010

County: Los Angeles FICE Identification: 036393
Unit ID: 441229
Telephone: (310) 289-5123 Carnegie Class: Spec 2-yr-Health
FAX Number: (310) 289-5136 Calendar System: Quarter
URL: www.wcui.edu
Established: 1998 Annual Undergrad Tuition & Fees: $18,600
Enrollment: 809 Coed
Affiliation or Control: Proprietary IRS Status: Proprietary
Highest Offering: Baccalaureate
Accreditation: ACCSC

01 CEO/Campus Director .... Ms. Myra CHASON
06 Registrar .... Ms. Erika BRIZUELA
07 Director of Admissions .... Ms. Leslie SANTANA
10 Assisant Campus Director .... Ms. Mieke WIBOWO
11 Chief of Operations .... Mr. Andrew HIGH
36 Director Career Development .... Mr. Anthony SHARP
37 Director Student Financial Aid .... Ms. Dora RUIZ
29 Director Alumni Affairs .... Mr. Tommy SHIN
05 Director Education .... Mr. Michael STEWART

West Coast Ultrasound Institute (J)

3700 E. Inland Empire Blvd, Ste 235, Ontario CA 91764

Telephone: (909) 483-3808 Identification: 770942
Accreditation: ACCSC

† Main campus is West Coast Ultrasound Institute in Los Angeles, CA.

West Coast University (K)

151 Innovation Dr., Irvine CA 92617

Telephone: (949) 783-4800 Identification: 770480
Accreditation: &WC, DH

West Coast University (L)

12215 Victory Boulevard, North Hollywood CA 91606-3206

County: Los Angeles FICE Identification: 036983
Unit ID: 443331
Telephone: (818) 299-5500 Carnegie Class: Spec-4-yr-Other Health
FAX Number: (818) 299-5545 Calendar System: Semester
URL: www.westcoastuniversity.edu
Established: 1909 Annual Undergrad Tuition & Fees: $35,110
Enrollment: 2,413 Coed
Affiliation or Control: Proprietary IRS Status: Proprietary
Highest Offering: Doctorate
Accreditation: WC, NURSE, OT, PHAR, PTA

01 Co-President .... Dr. Jeb EGBERT
01 Co-President .... Ms. Sandra PHAM
10 Chief Financial Officer .... Mr. Scott MEHLBERGER
05 Provost .... Mr. Arte LIBUNAO
66 Dean of Nursing Los Angeles Campus .... Dr. Robyn NELSON
20 Academic Dean .... Dr. Miriam KAHAN
07 Director of Admissions .... Ms. Julie WONG
37 Exec Director of Financial Aid .... Ms. Amanda SCHROEDER
32 Director of Student Affairs .... Mr. Anthony STEIN
08 Librarian .... Ms. Angelica LYONS
06 Registrar .... Vacant

West Coast University (M)

2855 E Guasti Road, Suite 100, Ontario CA 91761

Telephone: (909) 467-6100 Identification: 770484
Accreditation: &WC

*West Hills Community College District (N)

275 Phelps Avenue, Coalinga CA 93210

County: Fresno Identification: 667041
Telephone: (559) 934-2180 Carnegie Class: N/A

FAX Number: (559) 934-2810
URL: www.westhillscollege.com

01 Chancellor ... Dr. Kristin CLARK
10 Deputy Chancellor ... Dr. Richard STORTI
05 Vice Chanc Education & Technology ... Dr. Kelly COOPER
102 Exec Director WHCC Foundation ... Mr. Alex PEREZ
09 Dir of Accred/Research/Inst Eff ... Mr. Kyle CRIDER
26 Dir of Marketing/Comm/Public Info ... Ms. Amber MYRICK
15 Director of Human Resources ... Ms. Becky CAZARES
21 Interim Director of Fiscal Services ... Ms. Christine ALCARAZ
13 Dir of Info Technology Systems ... Mr. Shaun VETTER
14 Dir of IT Infrastructure & Security ... Mr. Jeff SEED
25 Director of Grants ... Mr. Brian BOOMER
103 Director of Special Grant Programs ... Mr. David CASTILLO
103 Director of Special Grant Programs ... Mr. Cecilio MORA
103 Director of Special Grant Programs ... Mr. Francisco LOPEZ
88 Dir of Child Development Centers ... Ms. Conne CLEVELAND
04 Executive Assistant to Chancellor ... Ms. Donna ISAAC

*West Hills College Coalinga (A)

300 Cherry Lane, Coalinga CA 93210-1399
County: Fresno FICE Identification: 001176
Unit ID: 125462
Telephone: (559) 934-2000 Carnegie Class: Assoc/HT-Mix Trad/Non
FAX Number: N/A Calendar System: Semester
URL: www.westhillscollege.com/coalinga
Established: 1932 Annual Undergrad Tuition & Fees (In-District): $1,380
Enrollment: 4,229 Coed
Affiliation or Control: State/Local IRS Status: Exempt
Highest Offering: Associate Degree
Accreditation: WJ

02 Interim President ... Mr. Samasoni AUNAI
05 Vice Pres of Educational Services ... Mr. Samasoni AUNAI
32 Vice President of Student Services ... Ms. Angela TOS
20 Dean of Educational Services ... Dr. Justin GARCIA
12 Dean of North District Center ... Ms. Bethany MATOS
35 Dean of Student Services ... Mr. Javier CAZARES
41 Associate Dean of Athletics ... Mr. Joe HASH
28 Director of Title IV Projects ... Ms. April BETTERSON
07 Dir Admissions & Records/Registrar ... Ms. Rosalind TOLIVER
37 Director of Financial Aid ... Vacant
103 Director of Apprenticeship Programs ... Mr. Nickolas TRUJILLO
88 Director of MESA ... Mr. Zack SOTO
25 Director of Special Grants ... Ms. Rebecca FARLEY
47 Director of Farm of the Future ... Mr. Terry BRASE
18 Dir of Maintenance & Operations ... Mr. Shaun BAILEY
04 Administrative Asst to President ... Ms. Amy MARTINEZ

*West Hills College Lemoore (B)

555 College Avenue, Lemoore CA 93245-9248
County: Kings FICE Identification: 041113
Unit ID: 448594
Telephone: (559) 925-3000 Carnegie Class: Assoc/MT-VT-High Trad
FAX Number: (559) 924-1243 Calendar System: Semester
URL: www.westhillscollege.com/lemoore
Established: 2002 Annual Undergrad Tuition & Fees (In-District): $1,380
Enrollment: 3,932 Coed
Affiliation or Control: State/Local IRS Status: Exempt
Highest Offering: Associate Degree
Accreditation: WJ, EMT

02 Interim President ... Mr. James PRESTON
05 Vice President of Educational Svcs ... Mr. James PRESTON
32 Vice President of Student Services ... Mr. Valentin GARCIA
20 Dean of Educational Services ... Dr. Kurt STERLING
35 Dean of Student Services ... Mr. Elmer AGUILAR
75 Dean of Career & Tech Education ... Ms. Kris COSTA
103 Assoc Dean of Categorical Programs ... Ms. Maria De La Luz GONZALEZ
41 Associate Dean of Athletics ... Ms. Andrea PICCHI
06 Director Admiss & Records/Registrar ... Mr. Nestor LOMELI
37 Director of Financial Aid ... Ms. Kathleen SCHOENECKER
88 Director of Upward Bound ... Mr. Oscar VILLARREAL
66 Director of Nursing ... Ms. Kathryn DEFEDE
88 Regnl Dir of Advanced Manufacturing ... Mr. Gary POTTER
18 Dir of Maintenance & Operations ... Mr. Joshua ALLEN
04 Administrative Asst to President ... Ms. Amber AVITIA

*West Valley-Mission Community College District (C)

14000 Fruitvale Avenue, Saratoga CA 95070-5698
County: Santa Clara FICE Identification: 029139
Unit ID: 125222
Telephone: (408) 741-2011 Carnegie Class: N/A
FAX Number: (408) 867-8273
URL: www.wvm.edu

01 Chancellor ... Mr. Bradley J. DAVIS
04 Exec Assistant to Chancellor/BOT ... Ms. Brenda ROGERS
11 Vice Chanc Administrative Services ... Mr. Ed MADULI
15 Vice Chanc Human Resources ... Mr. Albert MOORE
13 Director Information Systems ... Mr. Mike MCDONNELL
18 AVP of Facilities ... Mr. Javier CASTRUITA
19 Chief of Police ... Mr. Dalton Chris ROLEN
10 Assoc Vice Chanc Finance ... Ms. Ngoc CHIM

*Mission College (D)

3000 Mission College Boulevard, Santa Clara CA 95054-1897
County: Santa Clara FICE Identification: 021191
Unit ID: 118930
Telephone: (408) 855-5000 Carnegie Class: Assoc/HT-Mix Trad/Non
FAX Number: N/A Calendar System: Semester
URL: www.missioncollege.edu
Established: 1976 Annual Undergrad Tuition & Fees (In-District): $1,200
Enrollment: 6,504 Coed
Affiliation or Control: State/Local IRS Status: 501(c)3
Highest Offering: Associate Degree
Accreditation: WJ

02 President ... Mr. Daniel A. PECK
05 Vice President of Instruction ... Ms. Lorrie RANCK
32 Vice President Student Services ... Dr. Omar MURILLO
11 Vice Pres Administrative Services ... Mr. Danny NGUYEN
13 Vice Chancellor Info Technology ... Mr. Dan BORGES
15 Vice Chance Human Resources ... Mr. Eric RAMONES
35 Dean of Student Support Services ... Mr. Richard ALFARO
20 Dean of Instruction ... Ms. Valerie JENSEN
26 Director of Marketing/Public Rels ... Mr. Niall ADLER
50 Dean Business/Tech & Kinesiology ... Mr. Jeff PALLIN
19 Chief of Police ... Lt. Chris ROLEN
18 Manager of Facilities ... Mr. Don HOUSTON
07 Director of Admissions ... Ms. Maria ESCOBAR
09 Director of Institutional Research ... Mr. Brian GOO
37 Dir Student Enroll & Financial Aid ... Ms. Maria ESCOBAR
04 Sr Exec Assistant to the President ... Ms. Milani ZEPEDA
76 Dean of Health Occupations ... Ms. Yuko KAWASAKI
81 Dean of Math/Science & Engineering ... Mr. Clement LAM
83 Dean Humanities/Social Sci & Art ... Mr. Brian MILLER
75 Dean of Career Education ... Ms. Jackie ESCAJEDA
101 Exec Asst of the Board of Trustees ... Ms. Rebecca ALVAREZ
88 Assistant to Advancement/Foundation ... Ms. Nicole AGUINALDO
103 Director Workforce Development ... Mr. Rob GAMBLE
104 Director of International Students ... Ms. Chigusa KATOKU
22 Director Student Equity & Success ... Mr. Ken SONGCO
41 Athletic Director ... Mr. John VLAHOS
96 Director of Purchasing ... Mr. Michael ROBINS

*West Valley College (E)

14000 Fruitvale Avenue, Saratoga CA 95070-5698
County: Santa Clara FICE Identification: 001338
Unit ID: 125499
Telephone: (408) 867-2200 Carnegie Class: Assoc/HT-Mix Trad/Non
FAX Number: (408) 867-5033 Calendar System: Semester
URL: www.westvalley.edu
Established: 1963 Annual Undergrad Tuition & Fees (In-District): $1,486
Enrollment: 7,513 Coed
Affiliation or Control: State/Local IRS Status: 501(c)3
Highest Offering: Associate Degree
Accreditation: WJ, ART

02 President ... Ms. Stephanie KASHIMA
05 VP Instruction ... Ms. Stacy GLEIXNER
32 VP Student Services ... Ms. Debra GRIFFITH
10 VP Administrative Services ... Ms. Marilyn MORIKANG
20 Dean Instruction ... Mr. Chris DYER
111 Executive Director of Advancement ... Ms. Melissa JOHNS
36 Dean Career Pgm/Wrkforce Dev ... Mr. Bradley WEISBERG
26 Director Marketing/Communications ... Vacant
121 Dean Academic Counseling ... Mr. Murrell GREEN
100 Assoc Vice Chanc Human Resources ... Mr. Eric RAMONES
57 Dean School of Art & Design ... Ms. Shannon PRICE
22 Dir of Student Equity Experience ... Ms. Stacy NOJIMA
18 Chief Facilities/Physical Plant ... Mr. Bill TAYLOR
37 Dir Student Financial Aid/Admiss ... Vacant
04 Executive Assistant to the Pres ... Vacant
41 Dean of Athletics ... Mr. John VLAHOS

Westcliff University (F)

17877 Von Karan Avenue, #400, Irvine CA 92614
County: Orange Identification: 667203
Unit ID: 490133
Telephone: (888) 491-8686 Carnegie Class: Spec-4-yr-Bus
FAX Number: (888) 409-7306 Calendar System: Trimester
URL: www.westcliff.edu
Established: 1993 Annual Undergrad Tuition & Fees: $13,560
Enrollment: 3,214 Coed
Affiliation or Control: Proprietary IRS Status: Proprietary
Highest Offering: Doctorate
Accreditation: WC, ACBSP

01 CEO/President ... Dr. Anthony LEE
05 CAO/Provost ... Dr. David C. MCKINNEY
10 Chief Financial Officer ... Mr. Sean MURRAY
06 Director of Registrar Office ... Ms. Amanda OLMOS

Western Covenant University (G)

680 Wilshire Place, Ste 310, Los Angeles CA 90005
County: Los Angeles Identification: 667350
Telephone: (213) 293-1771 Carnegie Class: Not Classified
FAX Number: (213) 896-7265 Calendar System: Quarter
URL: www.wcuniversity.edu
Established: 2014 Annual Undergrad Tuition & Fees: N/A
Enrollment: N/A Coed
Affiliation or Control: Independent Non-Profit IRS Status: 501(c)3
Highest Offering: Master's
Accreditation: TRACS

01 President/CEO ... David K. OH
05 Chief Academic Officer ... Sin Ho KIM
10 Chief Financial Officer ... Ireen HONG

Western State University College of Law (H)

16715 Von Karmen Avenue, #100, Irvine CA 92606
Telephone: (714) 459-1101 FICE Identification: 010832
Accreditation: &WC, LAW

Western University of Health Sciences (I)

309 E 2nd Street, Pomona CA 91766-1854
County: Los Angeles FICE Identification: 024827
Unit ID: 112525
Telephone: (909) 623-6116 Carnegie Class: Spec-4-yr-Med
FAX Number: N/A Calendar System: Semester
URL: www.westernu.edu
Established: 1977 Annual Graduate Tuition & Fees: N/A
Enrollment: 3,813 Coed
Affiliation or Control: Independent Non-Profit IRS Status: 501(c)3
Highest Offering: Doctorate; No Undergraduates
Accreditation: WC, ARCPA, DENT, NURSE, OPT, OSTEO, PHAR, POD, PTA, VET

01 Interim President ... Dr. Sylvia MANNING
05 Sr VP & Provost ... Dr. David BARON
10 Interim CFO & Treasurer ... Mr. Joshua MCFARLEN
11 Sr VP & COO ... Dr. Clive HOUSTON-BROWN
46 Sr VP Research ... Dr. Devendra AGRAWAL
32 SVP Univ Student Affs/Enroll Mgmt . Dr. Beverly SANKS GUIDRY
111 Sr VP University Advancement ... Dr. Diane ABRAHAM
15 VP Human Resources Admin ... Ms. Linda EMILIO
25 Asst VP Spons Pgms/Contract Mgmt ... Mr. Matthew KATZ
20 Vice Provost for Academic Dev ... Dr. Elizabeth REGA
106 Asst Provost Online Learning ... Mr. Jonathan DAITCH
88 Asst Provost Ventures ... Dr. Dean SMYLIE
18 Exec Dir Facilities/Physical Plant ... Mr. Todd CLARK
86 Chief of Community & Gov Affairs ... Mr. Jeffery KEATING
07 Interim Director Admissions ... Ms. Marie ANDERSON
17 Exec Dir for Patient Ctr Clinic ... Dr. Robert WARREN
08 Dir University Library ... Ms. Karoline ALMANZAR
37 Co-Director of Financial Aid ... Ms. Theresa POULLARD
37 Co-Director of Financial Aid ... Ms. Linda FRENZA
13 Senior Director IT/Business Process ... Ms. Denise WILCOX
96 Director of Procurement Services ... Mr. Michael BUTLER
26 Chief Communications Officer ... Ms. Barbara O'MALLEY
88 Sr VP/Chief of Mission Integration ... Dr. Stephanie BOWLIN
09 Director of Institutional Research ... Dr. Juan RAMIREZ
40 Bookstore Director ... Ms. Elizabeth GUERRA
63 Dean College of Osteopathic Med ... Dr. Paula CRONE
52 Dean College of Dental Medicine .. Dr. Steven W. FRIEDRICHSEN
67 Dean College of Pharmacy ... Dr. Sunil PRABHU
88 Founding Dean College of Optometry ... Dr. Elizabeth HOPPE
88 Dean College of Podiatry ... Dr. Kathleen SATTERFIELD
76 Dean Col of Health Sciences ... Dr. Dee SCHILLING
66 Dean Col of Graduate Nursing ... Dr. Mary LOPEZ
58 Int Dean Grad Col Biomedical Sci ... Dr. Alissa CRAFT
74 Dean College of Veterinary Medicine ... Dr. Phil NELSON
63 Chr Dept Osteopath Manipulative Med ... Dr. Rebecca GIUSTI
88 Chair Dept of Physical Therapy ... Dr. Dayle ARMSTRONG
88 Chair Dept of Health Sciences ... Dr. Gail EVANS
88 Chair Physician Assistant Program ... Mr. Roy GUIZADO
63 Chair Department Family Medicine ... Dr. Dat Q. TRINH
06 Registrar ... Mr. Ivan NOE
19 Director Security/Safety ... Mr. David SEVESIND
29 Sr Director Alumni Relations ... Ms. Susan TERRAZAS
04 Administrative Asst to President ... Ms. Liz PAWELL
102 Dir Foundation/Corporate Relations ... Mr. Bill BURROWS
44 Sr Director of Annual Giving ... Ms. Susan TERRAZAS
16 Exec Director Human Resources ... Ms. Cynthia FERRINI
88 Director Center for Innovation ... Mr. Miary ANDRIAMIARISOA
43 General Counsel ... Ms. Simone MILLER

Westminster Theological Seminary in California (J)

1725 Bear Valley Parkway, Escondido CA 92027-4128
County: San Diego FICE Identification: 022768
Unit ID: 125718
Telephone: (760) 480-8474 Carnegie Class: Spec-4-yr-Faith
FAX Number: (760) 480-0252 Calendar System: Semester
URL: www.wscal.edu
Established: 1979 Annual Graduate Tuition & Fees: N/A
Enrollment: 134 Coed
Affiliation or Control: Independent Non-Profit IRS Status: 501(c)3
Highest Offering: Master's; No Undergraduates
Accreditation: WC, THEOL

01 President ... Rev. Joel KIM
05 Academic Dean ... Dr. Ryan GLOMSRUD
11 Vice President for Administration ... Dr. Marcus MCARTHUR
111 Vice President for Advancement ... Ms. Dawn DOORN
10 Chief Financial Officer ... Mr. Brett WATSON
84 VP for Enrollment Management ... Mr. Mark MACVEY
08 Library Director ... Mr. James LUND
32 Dean of Students ... Rev. Charles TEDRICK
06 Registrar ... Mr. Ryan THOMAS

Westmont College (A)

955 La Paz Road, Santa Barbara CA 93108-1089
County: Santa Barbara FICE Identification: 001341
Unit ID: 125727
Telephone: (805) 565-6000 Carnegie Class: Bac-A&S
FAX Number: (805) 565-7006 Calendar System: Semester
URL: www.westmont.edu
Established: 1937 Annual Undergrad Tuition & Fees: $48,180
Enrollment: 1,226 Coed
Affiliation or Control: Independent Non-Profit IRS Status: 501(c)3
Highest Offering: Baccalaureate
Accreditation: WC, MUS

01 President .... Dr. Gayle D. BEEBE
05 Interim Provost & Dean of Faculty .... Mr. Rick IFLAND
10 VP Finance .... Mr. Douglas W. JONES
32 VP Student Life/Dean of Students .... Dr. Edee SCHULZE
111 VP for Advancement & IT .... Dr. Reed L. SHEARD
84 VP Enrollment/Mktg/Communications .... Mrs. Irene NELLER
121 Dean of Student Success/Engagement .... Dr. Angela D'AMOUR
39 Dean of Students for Res Life .... Dr. Stu CLEEK
06 Registrar .... Mrs. Michelle M. HARDLEY
20 Vice Provost .... Dr. Patti HUNTER
15 Director of Human Resources .... Ms. Beth CAUWELS
18 Director of Physical Plant .... Mr. Thomas BEVERIDGE
21 Controller .... Mr. Paul V. LARSON
23 Director of Student Health Services .... Dr. David HERNANDEZ
19 Chief of Public Safety .... Mr. William BOYD
26 Director of Public Events .... Mrs. Mary Pat WHITNEY
36 Director of Career/Development .... Mr. Paul BRADFORD
37 Director of Financial Aid .... Mr. Sean SMITH
38 Director Counseling Services .... Dr. Eric NELSON
39 Director of Housing/Parking .... Mr. Jon YOUNG
40 Asst Director Bookstore .... Mrs. Joanne GISH
41 Athletic Director .... Mr. David ODELL
42 Campus Pastor .... Mr. Scott LISEA
45 Director of Campus Planning .... Mr. Randy JONES
96 Assc Dir Procurement/Auxiliary Svcs .... Mr. Bill GROENEVELD
28 Director of Intercultural Programs .... Mr. Blake THOMAS
88 Dean of Curriculum/Educ Effective .... Dr. Tatiana NAZARENKO
07 Director of Admission .... Mr. Mike MCKINNISS
88 Dir of Institutional Resilience .... Mr. Jason TAVAREZ
09 Dir of Institutional Research .... Dr. Tim LOOMER
88 Associate Dean of Faculty .... Dr. Eileen MCQUADE
88 Assistant VP for Advancement .... Mrs. Sarah CAMP
110 Assoc VP for Advancement .... Mr. Steve BAKER
112 Assistant VP for Major Gifts .... Mr. Alex NIZET
27 Director of College Communications .... Mrs. Nancy PHINNEY
88 Dir of Conference Services .... Mrs. Melinda HARRIMAN
08 Dir of Library & Information Svcs .... Mrs. Jana MAYFIEDL MULLEN

Whittier College (B)

13406 E Philadelphia St, PO Box 634,
Whittier CA 90608-4413
County: Los Angeles FICE Identification: 001342
Unit ID: 125763
Telephone: (562) 907-4200 Carnegie Class: Bac-A&S
FAX Number: (562) 907-4242 Calendar System: 4/1/4
URL: www.whittier.edu
Established: 1887 Annual Undergrad Tuition & Fees: $49,514
Enrollment: 1,564 Coed
Affiliation or Control: Independent Non-Profit IRS Status: 501(c)3
Highest Offering: Doctorate
Accreditation: WC, SW

01 President .... Dr. Linda OUBRÉ
10 Vice Pres Finance & Administration .... Mr. James DUNKELMAN
05 VP Acad Affs/Dean of Faculty .... Dr. Sal JOHNSTON
88 VP of Innovation & New Ventures .... Mr. Timothy ANDERSON
84 VP Enrollment Management .... Mr. Falone SERNA
30 VP Development .... Ms. Eva SEVCIKOVA
32 Interim VP & Dean of Students ... Dr. Deanna MERINO CONTINO
37 Director of Student Financial Aid .... Ms. Julie ALDAMA
08 Interim Library Director and System .... Mr. Nick VELKAVRH
20 Dir Whtr Scholar Pgm/Assc Acad Dean .... Ms. Andrea REHN
26 VP Marketing & Communication .... Ms. Ana Lilia BARRAZA
13 Director of Computing Services .... Mr. Troy GREENUP
09 Dir of Institutional Research .... Mr. Gary WHISENAND
41 Director of Athletics .... Mr. Rock CARTER
62 Dir Lib Educ Pgm/Assoc Acad Dean .... Dr. Fritz SMITH
15 VP/Chief Administrative Officer .... Ms. Cynthia JOSEPH
19 Director of Campus Safety .... Mr. Jose PADILLA
06 Registrar .... Ms. Julie T. KHELLA

William Carey International University (C)

1605 East Elizabeth St, Pasadena CA 91104
County: Los Angeles Identification: 667383
Telephone: (626) 398-2222 Carnegie Class: Not Classified
FAX Number: N/A Calendar System: Trimester
URL: www.wciu.edu
Established: 1977 Annual Graduate Tuition & Fees: N/A
Enrollment: N/A Coed
Affiliation or Control: Independent Non-Profit IRS Status: 501(c)3
Highest Offering: Master's; No Undergraduates
Accreditation: DEAC

01 President .... Dr. Kevin HIGGINS
05 Vice President of Academic Affairs .... Dr. Daniel LOW
03 Executive Vice President .... Dr. Peter MCLALLEN
10 Chief Financial Officer .... Mr. Mark HARRIS
06 Registrar .... Mr. Tom RUTHERFORD

William Jessup University (D)

2121 University Avenue, Rocklin CA 95765-3707
County: Placer FICE Identification: 001281
Unit ID: 122728
Telephone: (916) 577-2200 Carnegie Class: Bac-Diverse
FAX Number: (916) 577-2203 Calendar System: Semester
URL: www.jessup.edu
Established: 1939 Annual Undergrad Tuition & Fees: $37,000
Enrollment: 1,840 Coed
Affiliation or Control: Independent Non-Profit IRS Status: 501(c)3
Highest Offering: Master's
Accreditation: WC

01 President .... Dr. John JACKSON
05 Vice Pres Academic Affairs .... Dr. Phil ESCAMILLA
10 Chief Financial Officer .... Mrs. Diane AHN
30 Chief Development Officer .... Vacant
13 Chief Operating Officer .... Mrs. Judy RENTZ
108 Accreditation Liaison Officer .... Dr. Kay LLOVIO
32 Chief Student Life Ofcr/Assoc Prov .... Vacant
15 Human Resources Manager .... Ms. Linda GIUSTI
21 Controller .... Ms. Diane AHN
08 Director of Library Services .... Ms. Belinda SILVA
88 Director of Church Relations .... Mr. Jim JESSUP
35 Dean of Students .... Vacant
06 Registrar .... Mrs. Tina PETERSEN
84 Assoc VP of Enrollment Management .... Mr. Steve JIN
09 Institutional Research Director .... Mrs. Karen LAMBRECHTSEN
42 Campus Pastor .... Mr. PJ GARZA
41 Athletic Director .... Mr. Lance VON VOGT
04 Executive Asst to President .... Mrs. Janice NEWMAN
19 Director of Campus Safety .... Mr. Paul YBARRA
36 Director Student Placement .... Ms. Christy JEWELL
37 Director Student Financial Aid .... Mr. John SWAN

Woodbury University (E)

7500 North Glenoaks Boulevard, Burbank CA 91504-7520
County: Los Angeles FICE Identification: 001343
Unit ID: 125897
Telephone: (818) 767-0888 Carnegie Class: Masters/M
FAX Number: (818) 767-3470 Calendar System: Semester
URL: www.woodbury.edu
Established: 1884 Annual Undergrad Tuition & Fees: $42,596
Enrollment: 1,132 Coed
Affiliation or Control: Independent Non-Profit IRS Status: 501(c)3
Highest Offering: Master's
Accreditation: WC, ACBSP, ART, CIDA

01 President .... David M. STEELE-FIGUEREDO
101 Secretary of the Institution/Board .... Seta JAVOR
05 Senior Vice Pres Academic Affairs .... Randy STAUFFER
10 VP Finance & Accounting .... David LEUNG
11 VP Administration & Human Resources .... Natalie AVALOS
84 Assoc VP Admissions .... Sabrina TAYLOR
30 VP Development & Marketing .... David MASCARINA
13 VP Information Technology .... Eric WANG
32 Dean of Students .... Tracci JOHNSON
50 Dean School of Business .... Joan MARQUES
48 Dean School of Architecture .... Ingalill WAHLROOS-RITTER
07 Director of Admissions .... Ani BONIADI
20 Dean of Faculty .... Christoph KORNER
49 Int Dean College of Liberal Arts .... Reuben ELLIS
09 Director of Institutional Research .... Christie RAINEY
82 Dean of International Affairs .... Mauro DIAZ
08 University Librarian .... Nedra PETERSON
06 Registrar .... Adam BROWN
19 Director Security/Safety .... Natalie AVALOS
04 Admin Assistant to the President .... Andrea BRUNO

World Mission University (F)

500 Shatto Place, Suite 600, Los Angeles CA 90020-1789
County: Los Angeles FICE Identification: 038683
Unit ID: 401223
Telephone: (213) 385-2322 Carnegie Class: Spec-4-yr-Faith
FAX Number: (213) 385-2332 Calendar System: Semester
URL: www.wmu.edu
Established: 1989 Annual Undergrad Tuition & Fees: $6,440
Enrollment: 370 Coed
Affiliation or Control: Independent Non-Profit IRS Status: 501(c)3
Highest Offering: First Professional Degree
Accreditation: BI, THEOL

01 President .... Dr. Paul S. LIM
05 Vice President/Chief Acad Officer .... Dr. Seonmook P. SHIN
32 Dean of Student Affairs .... Dr. Imsang YOON
10 Chief Financial Officer .... Rev. Paul J. LIM
06 Registrar .... Vacant
37 Dir Financial Aid/Admissions Coord .... Ms. KyungHae KIM

The Wright Institute (G)

2728 Durant Avenue, Berkeley CA 94704-1796
County: Alameda FICE Identification: 008846
Unit ID: 126012
Telephone: (510) 841-9230 Carnegie Class: Spec-4-yr-Other Health
FAX Number: (510) 841-0167 Calendar System: Trimester
URL: www.wi.edu
Established: 1969 Annual Graduate Tuition & Fees: N/A
Enrollment: 514 Coed
Affiliation or Control: Independent Non-Profit IRS Status: 501(c)3
Highest Offering: Doctorate; No Undergraduates
Accreditation: WC, CLPSY, IPSY

01 President .... Mr. Peter DYBWAD
05 VP for Academic Affairs .... Dr. Gilbert NEWMAN
10 VP of Finance & Administrative Affs .... Ms. Tricia O'REILLY
32 Dean of Students/Registrar .... Ms. Ginny MORGAN
32 Dir of Admissions/Student Svcs .... Mr. John PITTS
08 Library Director .... Mr. Jason STRAUSS
37 Director of Financial Aid .... Ms. Mindy BERGERON

Yeshiva Ohr Elchonon Chabad/ West Coast Talmudical Seminary (H)

7215 Waring Avenue, Los Angeles CA 90046-7660
County: Los Angeles FICE Identification: 022624
Unit ID: 126076
Telephone: (323) 937-3763 Carnegie Class: Spec-4-yr-Faith
FAX Number: (323) 937-9456 Calendar System: Semester
URL: www.yoec.edu
Established: 1953 Annual Undergrad Tuition & Fees: $15,700
Enrollment: 135 Male
Affiliation or Control: Independent Non-Profit IRS Status: 501(c)3
Highest Offering: Baccalaureate
Accreditation: RABN

01 Chief Executive Officer .... Rabbi Ezra B. SCHOCHET
03 Executive Vice President .... Rabbi Mendel SPALTER
05 Curriculum Super/Education Counsel .... Rabbi Shimon RAICHIK
37 Director Student Financial Aid .... Mrs. Hendy TAUBER
06 Registrar .... Rabbi Chaim CITRON
38 Director Student Counseling .... Rabbi Mendel SCHAPIRO
08 Head Librarian .... Rabbi Ben Zion OSTER

Yo San University of Traditional Chinese Medicine (I)

13315 W Washington Boulevard, Los Angeles CA 90066
County: Los Angeles FICE Identification: 030982
Unit ID: 401250
Telephone: (310) 577-3000 Carnegie Class: Spec-4-yr-Other Health
FAX Number: (310) 577-3033 Calendar System: Trimester
URL: www.yosan.edu
Established: 1989 Annual Undergrad Tuition & Fees: N/A
Enrollment: 136 Coed
Affiliation or Control: Independent Non-Profit IRS Status: 501(c)3
Highest Offering: Doctorate; No Lower Division
Accreditation: ACUP

01 President/CEO .... Dr. Lawrence LAU
10 Chief Financial Officer .... Sum-Yee WANG
06 Director Operations & Registrar .... Tora FLINT
63 Dean MATCM Program .... Dr. Brady CHIN
63 Dean DAOM Program .... Dr. Robert HOFFMAN
84 Director Enrollment Management .... Daouia AMRIR
37 Financial Aid Coordinator .... Edgar TROVADA
32 Library Svcs & Student Affairs Ofcr .... Sean GATES

*Yosemite Community College District (J)

PO Box 4065, Modesto CA 95352-4065
County: Stanislaus FICE Identification: 009146
Unit ID: 126100
Telephone: (209) 575-6509 Carnegie Class: N/A
FAX Number: (209) 575-6565
URL: www.yosemite.edu

01 Chancellor .... Mr. Henry YONG
11 Vice Chancellor Administrative Svcs .... Mr. Trevor STEWART
05 Vice Chancellor Educ Support Svcs .... Mr. G. H JAVAHERIPOUR
13 Sr Dir Information Technology .... Mr. Joshua HASH
04 Executive Assistant to Chancellor .... Ms. Graciela MOLINA
26 District Director Public Affairs .... Vacant
15 Sr Director Human Resources .... Ms. Kathren PRITCHARD
19 Dir District Security/Comp & EP .... Vacant
117 Dir Risk Management/Purch & Rec .... Ms. Dorothy PIMENTEL

*Columbia College (K)

11600 Columbia College Drive, Sonora CA 95370-8580
County: Tuolumne FICE Identification: 007707
Unit ID: 112561
Telephone: (209) 588-5100 Carnegie Class: Assoc/HT-High Trad
FAX Number: (209) 588-5104 Calendar System: Semester
URL: www.gocolumbia.edu
Established: 1968 Annual Undergrad Tuition & Fees (In-District): $1,270
Enrollment: 2,132 Coed
Affiliation or Control: State/Local IRS Status: 501(c)3
Highest Offering: Associate Degree
Accreditation: WJ, ACFEI

02 Interim President .... Dr. G.H JAVAHERIPOUR
05 Vice Pres Instruction .... Dr. Brian SANDERS

11 VP College & Administrative Svcs ....Vacant
32 Vice Pres Student Services ....Dr. Melissa RABY
72 Dean Instruct Svcs/Career Tech Educ ....Mr. Steve AMADOR
49 Dean of Instruction/Arts & Sciences ....Ms. Raelene JUAREZ
41 Athletic Director ....Ms. LaDeane HANSTEN
37 Financial Aid Manager ....Ms. Marnie SHIVELY
10 Fiscal Services Supervisor ....Ms. Amy MCKINNEY
30 Director of Development ....Ms. Amy NILSON
06 Registrar ....Ms. Lesley MICHTAVY
09 Dir of Institutional Rsrch & Plng ....Dr. Benjamin J. MARCUS
40 Bookstore Manager ....Vacant
18 Interim Manager Facilities/Oper ....Ms. Crista NOAKES

*Modesto Junior College (A)

435 College Avenue, Modesto CA 95350-9977
County: Stanislaus FICE Identification: 001240
Unit ID: 118976
Telephone: (209) 575-6550 Carnegie Class: Bac/Assoc-Assoc Dom
FAX Number: (209) 575-6630 Calendar System: Semester
URL: www.mjc.edu
Established: 1921 Annual Undergrad Tuition & Fees (In-District): $1,270
Enrollment: 16,365 Coed
Affiliation or Control: State/Local IRS Status: 501(c)3
Highest Offering: Baccalaureate
Accreditation: WJ, COARC, MAC

02 President ....Dr. Santanu BANDYOPADHYAY
05 Vice President for Instruction ....Dr. Jennifer ZELLET
32 Vice Pres for Student Services ....Vacant
10 VP College & Administrative Svcs ....Dr. Sarah SCHRADER
57 Div Dean Arts/Humanities/Comm ....Mr. Mike SUNDQUIST
83 Div Dean Business/Behav/Social Sci ....Dr. Nancy SILL
76 Div Dean Inst/All Hlth/Fam/Con Sci ....Ms. Martha ROBLES
79 Dean Literature/Language Arts ....Ms. Jillian DALY
54 Div Dean Science/Math/Engineering ....Dr. Laura MAKI
47 Dean Agri/Envir Science/Tech Ed ....Dr. Donald BORGES
88 Dean Public Safety/Tech Ed/Cmty Ed ....Mr. Pedro MENDEZ
09 Dean Institutional Effectiveness ....Mrs. Komal BANDYOPADHYAY
07 Director Admissions & Records ....Vacant
37 Int Director Student Financial Svcs ....Ms. Aurelia GONZALEZ
26 Director of Public Relations ....Ms. Jeanette FONTANA

The Young Americans College of Performing Arts (B)

1132 Olympic Dr, Corona CA 92881
County: Riverside Identification: 667330
Unit ID: 493619
Telephone: (951) 493-6753 Carnegie Class: Not Classified
FAX Number: (951) 493-6793 Calendar System: Semester
URL: yacollege.edu
Established: 2002 Annual Undergrad Tuition & Fees: $14,030
Enrollment: 27 Coed
Affiliation or Control: Independent Non-Profit IRS Status: 501(c)3
Highest Offering: Associate Degree
Accreditation: WJ

01 Chief Executive Officer ....Mr. Leif GREEN
05 Dean of Instruction ....Mr. Mohammad SHAHISAMAN
32 Dean of Students ....Ms. Kisha BASHKIHARATEE
11 Chief Administration Officer ....Mr. Brian DEBRECENI

*Yuba Community College District (C)

425 Plumas Blvd., Yuba City CA 95991
County: Yuba Identification: 666478
Telephone: (530) 741-6700 Carnegie Class: N/A
FAX Number: N/A
URL: www.yccd.edu

01 Chancellor ....Dr. Douglas B. HOUSTON
05 VC Educ Planning & Services ....Dr. Sonja LOLLAND
11 VC Administrative Services ....Ms. Kuldeep KAUR
32 Vice Pres Student Services ....Mr. Dwayne HUNT
13 Chief Technology Officer ....Mr. Devin CROSBY
102 Grants/Research/Development Officer ....Ms. Tonya MACK
15 Chief Human Resources Officer ....Ms. Terri PYER
37 Director of Financial Aid ....Ms. Kimberly REED
10 Director of Fiscal Services ....Ms. Martha SERVIN

*Woodland Community College (D)

2300 East Gibson Road, Woodland CA 95776-5156
County: Yolo FICE Identification: 041438
Unit ID: 455512
Telephone: (530) 661-5700 Carnegie Class: Assoc/HVT-Mix Trad/Non
FAX Number: (530) 666-9028 Calendar System: Semester
URL: www.yccd.edu/woodland/
Established: 2008 Annual Undergrad Tuition & Fees (In-District): $1,124
Enrollment: 4,598 Coed
Affiliation or Control: State/Local IRS Status: 501(c)3
Highest Offering: Associate Degree
Accreditation: WJ

02 President ....Dr. Art PIMENTEL
05 Vice Pres Academic/Student Svcs ....Ms. Kasey GARDNER
04 Executive Asst to President ....Mr. Edwin ORTEGA BELTRAN
04 Executive Asst to Vice President ....Ms. Carid SERVIN
75 Dean Career Technical Education ....Ms. Sandra FOWLER
49 Dean Arts and Sciences ....Ms. Shannon REED
09 Dean Student Succes/Inst Effective ....Dr. Siria MARTINEZ
32 Dean Student Services ....Dr. Genevieve SIWABESSY
37 Director Student Financial Aid ....Ms. Kimberly REED
06 District Registrar ....Ms. Sonya HORN
07 Director of Matriculation ....Ms. Mariella GUZMAN-AGUILAR

*Yuba College (E)

2088 N Beale Road, Marysville CA 95901-7699
County: Yuba FICE Identification: 001344
Unit ID: 126119
Telephone: (530) 741-6700 Carnegie Class: Assoc/HVT-High Trad
FAX Number: (530) 741-3541 Calendar System: Semester
URL: https://yc.yccd.edu/
Established: 1927 Annual Undergrad Tuition & Fees (In-District): $1,128
Enrollment: 5,175 Coed
Affiliation or Control: State/Local IRS Status: 501(c)3
Highest Offering: Associate Degree
Accreditation: WJ, RAD

02 President ....Dr. Tawny M. DOTSON
05 Exec Vice Pres Academic Affairs ....Dr. Carla TWEED
32 Vice President of Student Services ....Dr. Dwayne (Dalexh) HUNT
50 Dean Applied Academics ....Dr. Pete VILLARREAL
09 Dean Inst Research/Student Success ....Mr. Jeremy BROWN
38 Director Counseling ....Ms. Cristina SANCHEZ
88 Dir Child Dev Center/Foster Care ....Ms. Karen STANIS
66 Director Nursing/Allied Health ....Ms. Toni CHRISTOPHERSON
19 Director Public Safety ....Mr. Brian VIZZUSI
57 Dean of Arts & Education ....Mr. Donald SMITH
37 Director Financial Aid ....Mr. Martin GUTIERREZ
68 Director Athletics/Health/PE ....Mr. Erick BURNS
81 Dean STEM & Outreach Centers ....Dr. Michael BAGLEY
121 Director Academic Excellence ....Ms. Kristina VANNUCCI
04 Exec Assistant to the President ....Ms. Zulema ZERMENO
06 Registrar ....Ms. Sonya HORN
07 Director of Admissions ....Vacant
10 Chief Financial/Business Officer ....Ms. Kuldeep KAUR
101 Secretary of the Institution/Board ....Ms. Kathryn WILKINS
102 Director Foundation/Corporate Rels ....Mr. Jay LOWDEN

Zaytuna College (F)

2401 Le Conte Avenue, Berkeley CA 94709
County: Alameda Identification: 667230
Unit ID: 458575
Telephone: (510) 356-4760 Carnegie Class: Not Classified
FAX Number: (510) 327-2688 Calendar System: Semester
URL: www.zaytuna.edu
Established: 2009 Annual Undergrad Tuition & Fees: $19,250
Enrollment: N/A Coed
Affiliation or Control: Independent Non-Profit IRS Status: 501(c)3
Highest Offering: Master's
Accreditation: WC

01 President ....Hamza YUSUF
05 Provost ....Dr. Omar QURESHI
20 Dean of Faculty ....Dr. Mark Damien DELP
32 Director of Student Life ....Dawood YASIN
108 Dir of Assessment & Accreditation ....Sumaira AKHATAR
07 Director of Admissions ....Faisal HAMID
15 Human Reources Manager ....Pepy PRAWIRA
10 Director of Administrative Svcs ....Naima JAMESON

COLORADO

Adams State University (G)

208 Edgemont Boulevard, Alamosa CO 81101-2320
County: Alamosa FICE Identification: 001345
Unit ID: 126182
Telephone: (719) 587-7011 Carnegie Class: Masters/L
FAX Number: N/A Calendar System: Semester
URL: www.adams.edu
Established: 1921 Annual Undergrad Tuition & Fees (In-State): $9,560
Enrollment: 3,164 Coed
Affiliation or Control: State IRS Status: 501(c)3
Highest Offering: Doctorate
Accreditation: HLC, CACREP, MUS, NURSE

01 President ....Dr. Cheryl D. LOVELL
04 Executive Asst to the President ....Ms. Carol OSBORN
05 VP for Academic Affairs ....Dr. Kent BUCHANAN
84 Director Enrollment Management ....Ms. Karla HARDESTY
26 Dir Public Relations & Marketing ....Mr. Chris LOPEZ
18 Director of Facilities Services ....Mr. Wade SMITH
10 Chief Financial Officer ....Ms. Heather HEERSINK
20 Associate VP for Academic Affairs ....Ms. Margaret DOELL
32 VP for Student Services ....Mr. Henry ROBINSON
09 Senior Research Analyst ....Ms. Sarah RHETT
08 Director Library ....Mr. Jeffrey BULLINGTON
37 Director Student Financial Aid ....Ms. Heidi MARKEY
06 Registrar ....Ms. Belen MAESTAS
13 Chief Information Officer ....Mr. Kevin S. DANIEL
41 Co-Athletic Director ....Ms. Katelyn SMITH
41 Co-Athletic Director ....Mr. Justin BOYD
109 Director of Auxiliary Services ....Mr. Bruce DEL TONDO
28 Director of Diversity ....Vacant
38 Director Counseling/Career Svcs ....Ms. Aftin GILLESPIE
25 Chief Contract and Grants Administr ....Ms. Tawney BECKER
15 Director Human Resources ....Ms. Tracy ROGERS
102 Executive Director ASU Foundation ....Ms. Tammy L. LOPEZ
29 Director Alumni and Donor Relations ....Ms. Ashley A. MAESTAS
39 Dir Resident Life/Student Housing ....Mr. Bruce DELTONDO
96 Director of Purchasing ....Ms. Renee VIGIL
19 Dir Adams State Univ Police Dept ....Ms. Erika DEROUIN
103 Director Workforce Development ....Vacant
40 Director Bookstore ....Ms. Amy GOODWIN
60 Chair English/Communication ....Dr. Beth BONNSTETTER
50 Chair Business & Economics ....Dr. Liz HENSLEY
82 Chair HAPPS ....Dr. Rich LOOSBROCK
77 Chair Chemistry/Computer Sci/Math ....Dr. Christina MILLER
81 Chair Biology/Earth Science ....Dr. Benita BRINK
53 Chair Teacher Education ....Dr. Curtis L. GARCIA
57 Chair Art ....Mr. Dana PROVENCE
57 Chair Theatre ....Dr. John TAYLOR
88 Chair Kinesiology ....Dr. Terry DUPLER
88 Chair Counselor Education ....Dr. Mark MANZANARES
83 Chair Sociology ....Dr. Stephanie HILWIG
83 Chair Psychology ....Dr. Colleen SCHAFFNER
66 Chair Nursing ....Dr. Melissa MILNER

Aims Community College (H)

Box 69, Greeley CO 80632-0069
County: Weld FICE Identification: 007582
Unit ID: 126207
Telephone: (970) 330-8008 Carnegie Class: Assoc/HT-High Non
FAX Number: N/A Calendar System: Semester
URL: www.aims.edu
Established: 1967 Annual Undergrad Tuition & Fees (In-District): $2,762
Enrollment: 5,981 Coed
Affiliation or Control: Local IRS Status: 501(c)3
Highest Offering: Associate Degree
Accreditation: HLC, ADNUR, EMT, IFSAC, SURGT

01 President ....Dr. Leah L. BORNSTEIN
05 Executive Vice Pres & Academic Affs ....Dr. Russ ROTHAMER
10 VP Admin Services ....Mr. Chuck JENSEN
32 Vice President Student Affairs ....Dr. Sarah WYSCAVER
26 Vice President Cmty & College Rels ....Mr. Timothy ULLMANN
20 Associate VP Academic Affairs ....Dr. Trish RAND
49 Dean Arts & Sciences ....Mr. Scott REICHEL
50 Dean Business & Technology ....Mr. Jeff SMITH
80 Dean Public Svcs & Transportation ....Mr. Robert ABERNATHY
76 Dean Allied Health & Wellness ....Mr. Terry ANDERSON
35 Dean of Students ....Ms. Shannon MCCASLAND
102 Executive Director Foundation ....Ms. Kelly JACKSON
15 Exec Director Human Resources ....Ms. Dee SHULTZ
09 Int Exec Dir Inst Research/Assess ....Mr. Jeffrey ADCOCK
114 Budget Director/Asst Controller ....Ms. Kailey BLOCK
18 Exec Director Facilities/Operations ....Mr. Michael MILLSAPPS
37 Executive Director Financial Aid ....Mr. Chris PETERSON
06 Registrar ....Vacant
13 Exec Director IT Admin Services ....Ms. Andria BRABO
21 Assistant VP/Controller ....Ms. Kara BERG
27 Exec Dir Comm/Public Info Ofcr ....Mr. Zachary MCFARLANE
35 Exec Dir Student Leadership & Dev ....Dr. Patrick CALL
12 Exec Campus Dir Loveland ....Ms. Heather LELCHOOK
12 Exec Campus Dir Windsor ....Ms. Mary GABRIEL
12 Exec Campus Dir Fort Lupton ....Ms. Julie LUEKENGA
04 Admin Assistant to the President ....Ms. Megan SELF

Arapahoe Community College (I)

5900 S Santa Fe Drive, Littleton CO 80120
County: Arapahoe FICE Identification: 001346
Unit ID: 126289
Telephone: (303) 797-4222 Carnegie Class: Assoc/MT-VT-High Non
FAX Number: (303) 797-5935 Calendar System: Semester
URL: www.arapahoe.edu
Established: 1965 Annual Undergrad Tuition & Fees (In-State): $4,027
Enrollment: 12,001 Coed
Affiliation or Control: State IRS Status: Exempt
Highest Offering: Baccalaureate
Accreditation: HLC, ADNUR, CAHIIM, EMT, FUSER, MLTAD, NAEYC, PTAA

01 President ....Dr. Stephanie FUJII
05 Interim Vice President & Provost ....Dr. Josie MILLS
32 Vice President of Student Affairs ....Dr. Lisa MATYE EDWARDS
10 VP of Finance & Admin Svcs ....Dr. Belinda AARON
103 AVP/Dean Bus/Workforce Partnershp ....Dr. Eric DUNKER
20 Assoc Vice Pres for Instruction ....Dr. Josie MILLS
35 Dean of Students ....Mr. Javon BRAME
124 Exec Dir of Advising & Retention ....Mr. Mark NELSON
84 Assoc Dean of Enrollment Services ....Vacant
37 Dir of Student Financial Services ....Ms. Gail MCKINNEY
79 Dean Comm/Hum/Arts and Design ....Dr. Danielle STAPLES
81 Dean Mathematics & Sciences ....Vacant
69 Dean of Health and Public Services ....Dr. Darius NAVRAN
102 Executive Director Foundation ....Ms. Courtney LOEHFELM
13 Director Information Technology ....Mr. Jeff NESHEIM
21 AVP Fiscal & Admin Svcs ....Ms. Jill BECKER-LUTZ
19 Chief of Police ....Mr. Joseph MORRIS
09 Director Institutional Research ....Mr. Yared BELETE
08 Director Learning Resource Center ....Ms. Lisa CHESTNUT
26 Dir of Marketing/Public Relations ....Ms. Tina GRIESHEIMER
22 Assoc Dean Compliance & Equity ....Ms. Jennifer HUSUM
96 Purchasing Manager ....Mr. Daniel HOHN
15 Director Personnel Services ....Ms. Angela JOHNSON
04 Executive Assistant ....Ms. Carol PATTERSON
108 Exec Dir Institutional Assessment ....Dr. Terry BARMANN
06 Registrar ....Ms. Theresa GROFF
106 Director E-learning ....Ms. Lee C. CHRISTOPHER
28 Chief Inclusive Excellence Officer ....Ms. Quill PHILLIPS

Aspen University (A)

1660 S. Albion Street Suite 525, Denver CO 80222
County: Denver FICE Identification: 040803
Unit ID: 454829
Telephone: (303) 333-4224 Carnegie Class: Masters/L
FAX Number: (303) 200-7428 Calendar System: Semester
URL: www.aspen.edu
Established: 1987 Annual Undergrad Tuition & Fees: $5,110
Enrollment: 9,563 Coed
Affiliation or Control: Proprietary IRS Status: Proprietary
Highest Offering: Doctorate
Accreditation: DEAC, NURSE

00 Chairman & CEO BOT .... Mr. Michael MATHEWS
01 President/Chief Academic Officer .... Dr. Cheri ST. ARNAULD
11 Chief Operating Officer .... Vacant
10 Chief Financial Officer .... Ms. Shannyn STERN
05 Provost .... Dr. Kevin THRASHER
06 Registrar .... Ms. Katie BROWN

Auguste Escoffier School of Culinary Arts (B)

637 South Broadway, Ste H, Boulder CO 80305
County: Boulder FICE Identification: 037763
Unit ID: 454810
Telephone: (303) 494-7988 Carnegie Class: Not Classified
FAX Number: N/A Calendar System: Quarter
URL: www.escoffier.edu
Established: Annual Undergrad Tuition & Fees: N/A
Enrollment: 7,600 Coed
Affiliation or Control: Proprietary IRS Status: Proprietary
Highest Offering: Associate Degree
Accreditation: CNCE, ACFEI

01 President .... Kirk BACHMANN
07 Director of Admissions .... Matt VEARIL
37 Director of Financial Aid .... Pamela TRANDAHL
36 Director of Career Services .... Kate SWEASY
06 Registrar and Compliance Manager .... Meghann SHAFFER

Augustine Institute (C)

6160 S. Syracuse Way #310,
Greenwood Village CO 80111
County: Arapahoe Identification: 667219
Telephone: (303) 937-4420 Carnegie Class: Not Classified
FAX Number: (303) 468-2933 Calendar System: Semester
URL: augustineinstitute.org
Established: 2005 Annual Graduate Tuition & Fees: N/A
Enrollment: N/A Coed
Affiliation or Control: Roman Catholic IRS Status: 501(c)3
Highest Offering: Master's; No Undergraduates
Accreditation: THEOL

01 President .... Mr. Tim GRAY
05 Academic Dean .... Dr. Sean INNERST
10 Chief Financial Officer .... Ms. Angie PARSONS

Bel-Rea Institute of Animal Technology (D)

1681 S Dayton Street, Denver CO 80247-3048
County: Arapahoe FICE Identification: 012670
Unit ID: 126359
Telephone: (303) 751-8700 Carnegie Class: Spec 2-yr-Health
FAX Number: (303) 751-9969 Calendar System: Quarter
URL: www.belrea.edu
Established: 1971 Annual Undergrad Tuition & Fees: $12,338
Enrollment: 306 Coed
Affiliation or Control: Proprietary IRS Status: Proprietary
Highest Offering: Associate Degree
Accreditation: ACCSC

01 President/Dean of Education .... Nolan RUCKER
11 Chief Operating & Compliance Ofcr .... Tracy PETERSON
04 Administrative Assistant .... Mimi PFAFF
32 Director Student Services .... John GANZAR
10 Director of Business and Financial .... Stacey SLOAN
18 Facilities Director .... Walter FRANKEWICZ
07 Admissions Manager .... Natalie ALAMAT
37 Financial Aid Manager .... Stasi BOTTINELLI
06 Registrar .... Jennifer HILLGROVE

College for Financial Planning (E)

9000 E. Nichols Avenue #200, Centennial CO 80112
County: Denver Identification: 666809
Telephone: (303) 220-1200 Carnegie Class: Not Classified
FAX Number: (303) 220-4940 Calendar System: Other
URL: www.cffp.edu
Established: 1972 Annual Graduate Tuition & Fees: N/A
Enrollment: N/A Coed
Affiliation or Control: Proprietary IRS Status: Proprietary
Highest Offering: Master's; No Undergraduates
Accreditation: HLC

01 President .... Mr. Dirk PANTONE
05 Vice Pres Academic Affairs/Provost .... Dr. Amy RELL

CollegeAmerica Colorado Springs (F)

2020 N Academy Boulevard, Ste 100,
Colorado Springs CO 80909
Telephone: (719) 227-0170 Identification: 666293
Accreditation: #ACCSC

† Branch campus of CollegeAmerica Denver, Denver, CO.

Colorado Academy of Veterinary Technology (G)

2766 Janitell Road, Colorado Springs CO 80906
County: El Paso FICE Identification: 041850
Unit ID: 461953
Telephone: (719) 219-9636 Carnegie Class: Spec 2-yr-Health
FAX Number: (719) 302-5577 Calendar System: Quarter
URL: www.cavt.edu
Established: 2007 Annual Undergrad Tuition & Fees: $17,354
Enrollment: 65 Coed
Affiliation or Control: Proprietary IRS Status: Proprietary
Highest Offering: Associate Degree
Accreditation: #COE

01 CEO/Admissions Officer/Registrar .... Dr. Steve RUBIN
05 Program Director .... Ms. Stephanie WINTERS
38 Dir Student Counseling/Fin Aid .... Mrs. Traci THOMPSON

Colorado Christian University (H)

8787 W Alameda Avenue, Lakewood CO 80226-7499
County: Jefferson FICE Identification: 009401
Unit ID: 126669
Telephone: (303) 963-3000 Carnegie Class: Masters/M
FAX Number: (303) 963-3001 Calendar System: Semester
URL: www.ccu.edu
Established: 1914 Annual Undergrad Tuition & Fees: $34,750
Enrollment: 7,839 Coed
Affiliation or Control: Independent Non-Profit IRS Status: 501(c)3
Highest Offering: Doctorate
Accreditation: HLC, CACREP, MUS, NURSE

01 President .... Dr. Donald W. SWEETING
03 Executive Vice President .... Mr. Daniel L. COHRS
05 VP of Academic Affairs CUS .... Dr. Janet M. BLACK
05 VP of Academic Affairs CAGS .... Dr. Sarah SCHERLING
111 VP of University Advancement .... Mr. Eric HOGUE
10 VP Business Affairs/CFO .... Mr. David PUNT
18 VP of Campus Development .... Mr. Shannon DREYFUSS
32 VP of Enrollment & Student Life .... Mr. Jim S. MCCORMICK
35 Asst VP Stdnt Pgm/Dean of Students .... Ms. Sharon M. FELKER
84 VP of Enrollment CAGS .... Ms. Allison SIEVERS
121 VP of Student Success .... Mr. Roger CHANDLER
50 Dean School of Business/Leadership .... Dr. Peter KERR
72 Dean School of Business/Technology .... Dr. Mellani J. DAY
53 Dean School of Education .... Dr. Debora SCHEFFEL
83 Dean of Social Science & Humanities .... Dr. Ryan HARTWIG
53 Dean School of Education Prof .... Dr. Wendy WENDOVER
64 Dean School of Music .... Mr. Steven T. TAYLOR
73 Dean School of Theology .... Dr. David KOTTER
66 Dean of Nursing & Sciences .... Dr. Barbara WHITE
73 Dean of Biblical Studies & Theology .... Dr. Earl WAGGONER
07 Dir of Undergraduate Admissions .... Ms. Jo Leda MARTIN
43 University Counsel .... Mr. Thomas SCHEFFEL
21 Asst VP and Controller .... Mr. David SCHULL
06 University Registrar .... Mr. Jeremy WALLACE
41 Athletic Director .... Mr. Brian WALL
38 Director of Counseling Services .... Ms. Alisa SHANKS
88 Director of Centennial Institute .... Mr. Jeff HUNT
18 Director of Facilities .... Mr. Mathew J. GOTHARD
37 Asst VP of Financial Aid .... Mr. Steve M. WOODBURN
23 Director of Health Services .... Ms. Anita LIEBSCH
15 Asst VP Human Resources .... Mr. Rick GARRIS
13 Assoc VP Information Systems/CIO .... Ms. Renee MARTIN
08 Library Director .... Ms. Gayle C. GUNDERSON
36 Director of Life Directions Center .... Ms. Leah SMITH
39 Director of Residence Life .... Mr. Neal ANDERSON
19 Director of Security .... Mr. John MAXFIELD
26 Director of Communications .... Vacant
29 Director Alumni Relations .... Ms. Kara JOHNSTON
105 Asst VP of Creative Services .... Ms. Chris FRANZ
106 Asst VP of Technical Support .... Mr. Jordan HEERSINK
04 Executive Assistant to President .... Ms. Betsy SIMPSON

Colorado College (I)

14 E Cache La Poudre St.,
Colorado Springs CO 80903-3294
County: El Paso FICE Identification: 001347
Unit ID: 126678
Telephone: (719) 389-6000 Carnegie Class: Bac-A&S
FAX Number: (719) 634-4180 Calendar System: Other
URL: www.coloradocollege.edu
Established: 1874 Annual Undergrad Tuition & Fees: $60,864
Enrollment: 2,050 Coed
Affiliation or Control: Independent Non-Profit IRS Status: 501(c)3
Highest Offering: Master's
Accreditation: HLC

01 President .... Ms. L. Song RICHARDSON
100 SVP/Chief of Staff .... Mr. Mike EDMONDS
05 Acting Provost/Dean of Faculty .... Dr. Claire GARCIA
10 Sr VP/Finance & Administration .... Mr. Robert G. MOORE
111 Vice Pres for Advancement .... Ms. Mary Ann GRAFFEO
100 Chief of Staff/Special Asst of BOT .... Dr. Kim WALDRON
84 Vice Pres Enrollment Management .... Mr. Mark HATCH
32 VP Student Life/Dean of Students .... Ms. Rochelle DICKEY
13 Co-VP for Information Technology .... Mr. Tulio WOLFORD
13 Co-VP for Information Technology .... Ms. Katharina GROVES
45 Asst VP for Inst Planning & Eff .... Ms. Lyrae WILLIAMS
20 Assoc Dean of Academic Programs .... Dr. Emily CHAN
110 Asst VP Advancement Operations .... Ms. Molly BODNAR
35 Sr Assc VP for Student Life .... Mr. John LAUER
35 Sr Associate Dean of Students .... Ms. Rochelle MASON
37 Director of Financial Aid .... Ms. Shannon AMUNDSON
06 Registrar .... Mr. Phillip C. APODACA
26 Vice President for Communications .... Ms. Jane TURNIS
41 Vice Pres/Director of Athletics .... Mrs. Lesley IRVINE
104 Director International Programs .... Mr. Allen BERTSCHE
15 Director Human Resource .... Mrs. Heather KISSACK
07 Director of Admissions .... Mr. Matthew BONSER
18 Assoc VP of Facilities .... Ms. Amber BRANNIGAN
19 Director Campus Safety .... Ms. Maggie SANTOS
08 Library Director .... Ms. JoAnn JACOBY
36 Director Career Center .... Ms. Megan NICKLAUS
28 Asst VP/Director of Butler Ctr .... Vacant
29 Director Alumni Relations .... Mrs. Tiffany KELLY
09 Dir Assessment/Program Review .... Ms. Amanda UDIS-KESSLER
21 Assoc VP of Finance/Controller .... Mrs. Lori SEAGER
105 Director Web & Digital .... Ms. Karen TO
114 Senior Budget Analyst .... Vacant
38 Director of Counseling Center .... Mr. Bill DOVE
22 Director of Accessibility Resources .... Ms. Jan EDWARDS
27 Director of News & Media Relations .... Ms. Leslie WEDDELL
103 Dir Collaborative Cmty Engagement .... Ms. Jordan RADKE
42 Chaplain .... Vacant
04 Executive Asst to the President .... Ms. Lori HAMACHER
39 Assoc Dir Ofc of Housing & Conf .... Vacant

Colorado Mesa University (J)

1100 North Avenue, Grand Junction CO 81501-3122
County: Mesa FICE Identification: 001358
Unit ID: 127556
Telephone: (970) 248-1020 Carnegie Class: Masters/S
FAX Number: (970) 248-1076 Calendar System: Semester
URL: www.coloradomesa.edu
Established: 1925 Annual Undergrad Tuition & Fees (In-State): $8,686
Enrollment: 9,110 Coed
Affiliation or Control: State IRS Status: 501(c)3
Highest Offering: Doctorate
Accreditation: HLC, ADNUR, #ARCPA, CAATE, MLTAD, MUS, NURSE, PNUR, RAD, SURGT, SW

01 President .... Mr. John MARSHALL
05 Vice Pres Academic Affairs .... Dr. Kurt HAAS
10 Vice President Financial/Admin Svcs .... Ms. Laura GLATT
12 Actg Vice Pres Community College .... Ms. Brigitte SUNDERMANN
109 Asst Vice Pres Auxiliary Services .... Mr. Andy RODRIGUEZ
32 VP of Student Services .... Vacant
13 VP of Information Technology/Comm .... Mr. Jeremy BROWN
08 Library Director .... Ms. Sylvia RAEL
30 Director of Development .... Vacant
37 Director Financial Aid .... Mr. Curt MARTIN
26 Director of Media Relations .... Vacant
06 Registrar .... Ms. Holly TEAL
09 Dir of Inst Research/Assessment .... Ms. Heather MCKIM
18 Actg Dir Facilities/Physical Plant .... Mr. David DETWILER
29 Director Alumni Relations .... Mr. Jared MEIER
07 Director of Admissions .... Vacant
15 Director of Human Resources .... Ms. Jill KNUCKLES
28 Director of Diversity .... Mr. Bob LANG
41 Co-Athletic Director .... Ms. Erin HILTNER
41 Co-Athletic Director .... Mr. Bryan ROOKS
96 Purchasing Manager .... Ms. Suzanne ELLINWOOD
108 Director Institutional Assessment .... Dr. Morgan BRIDGE
39 Director Residence Life .... Ms. Jody DIERS
04 Admin Assistant to the President .... Ms. Megan O'NEILL
100 Chief of Staff .... Ms. Liz HOWELL
84 AVP Enrollment Management .... Ms. Kimberly MEDINA

Colorado Mesa University-Montrose Campus (K)

245 South Cascade Avenue, Montrose CO 81401
Telephone: (970) 249-7009 Identification: 770031
Accreditation: &HLC

Colorado Mountain College (L)

802 Grand Avenue, Glenwood Springs CO 81602-3961
County: Garfield FICE Identification: 004506
Unit ID: 126711
Telephone: (970) 945-8691 Carnegie Class: Bac/Assoc-Mixed
FAX Number: (970) 947-8385 Calendar System: Semester
URL: www.coloradomtn.edu
Established: 1965 Annual Undergrad Tuition & Fees (In-District): $4,740
Enrollment: 5,315 Coed
Affiliation or Control: Local IRS Status: 501(c)3
Highest Offering: Baccalaureate
Accreditation: HLC, ADNUR, EMT, NAEYC, NUR

01 President .... Dr. Carrie BESNETTE HAUSER
05 VP Academic Affairs .... Ms. Kathryn REGJO

10 Vice Pres Fiscal Affairs .... Ms. Mary BOYD
32 VP Student Affairs .... Mr. Shane LARSON
15 Director of Human Resources .... Ms. Angela WURTSMITH
26 Public Relations Officer .... Ms. Debbie CRAWFORD
13 Chief Information Officer .... Vacant
37 Director of Financial Aid .... Ms. Janelle COOK
18 Director of College Facilities .... Mr. Sean NESBITT
27 Director of Marketing/Publications .... Mr. Brian BARKER
96 Director of Purchasing .... Ms. Julie HANSON
04 Administrative Asst to President .... Ms. Debbie NOVAK
100 COO/Chief of Staff .... Dr. Matt GIANNESCHI
43 Dir Legal Services/General Counsel .... Mr. Richard GONZALES
06 Registrar .... Ms. Natalie TORRES
09 Director of Institutional Research .... Ms. Veneeya KINION
28 Senior Inclusivity Officer .... Mr. Richard GONZALES

Colorado Mountain College Alpine Campus (A)

1275 Crawford Avenue, Steamboat Springs CO 80487
Telephone: (970) 870-4444 Identification: 770038
Accreditation: &HLC

Colorado Mountain College Aspen (B)

0255 Sage Way, Aspen CO 81611
Telephone: (970) 925-7740 Identification: 770032
Accreditation: &HLC

Colorado Mountain College Leadville (C)

901 South Hwy 24, Leadville CO 80461
Telephone: (719) 486-2105 Identification: 770036
Accreditation: &HLC

Colorado Mountain College Rifle (D)

3695 Airport Road, Rifle CO 81650
Telephone: (970) 625-1871 Identification: 770037
Accreditation: &HLC

Colorado Mountain College Roaring Fork Campus-Spring Valley (E)

690 Colorado Avenue, Carbondale CO 81623
Telephone: (970) 963-2172 Identification: 770035
Accreditation: &HLC

Colorado Mountain College Summit Campus-Breckinridge Center (F)

PO Box 2208/107 Denison Placer Dr, Breckinridge CO 80424
Telephone: (970) 453-6757 Identification: 770033
Accreditation: &HLC

Colorado Mountain College Vail Valley Campus at Edwards (G)

150 Miller Ranch Road, Edwards CO 81632
Telephone: (970) 569-2900 Identification: 770034
Accreditation: &HLC, MAC

Colorado Northwestern Community College (H)

500 Kennedy Drive, Rangely CO 81648-3598
County: Rio Blanco FICE Identification: 001359
Unit ID: 126748
Telephone: (970) 675-2261 Carnegie Class: Assoc/MT-VT-High Non
FAX Number: (970) 675-5046 Calendar System: Semester
URL: www.cncc.edu
Established: 1962 Annual Undergrad Tuition & Fees (In-District): $4,140
Enrollment: 993 Coed
Affiliation or Control: State/Local IRS Status: 170(c)1
Highest Offering: Associate Degree
Accreditation: HLC, ADNUR, DH

01 President .... Mr. Lisa JONES
32 Vice Pres Student Services .... Mr. John ANDERSON
05 Vice Pres Instruction .... Mr. Keith PETERSON
10 Vice Pres Business/Administration .... Mr. James CALDWELL
13 Director of Information Technology .... Mr. Fred BYERS
06 Registrar .... Ms. Grace STEWART
08 Library Director .... Ms. Leana COX
26 Director of Marketing .... Mr. Reuben TALBOT
15 Human Resource Director .... Ms. Angie MILLER
102 CNCC Foundation Director .... Ms. Sue SAMANIEGO
18 Facilities Director .... Ms. Lindsey BLAKE
09 Director of Institutional Research .... Ms. Kelly SCOTT
121 Director of Student Support .... Ms. Caitlan MOORE
37 Financial Aid Director .... Ms. Merrie BYERS
49 Dean of Arts & Science .... Mr. Todd WARD
75 Dean of CTE Craig .... Ms. Martha POWELL-CASE
75 Dean of CTE Rangely .... Ms. Meghan DAVIS
41 Athletics Director .... Ms. Candra ROBIE
113 Bursar .... Ms. Janet MACKAY
103 Exec Dir Workforce Education .... Ms. Sasha NELSON
96 Purchasing Coordinator .... Ms. Kathy KOTTENSTETTE
04 Admin Assistant to the President .... Ms. Keely ELLIS

Colorado Northwestern Community College Craig (I)

2801 W 9th Street, Craig CO 81625
Telephone: (970) 824-1101 Identification: 770039
Accreditation: &HLC

Colorado School of Mines (J)

1500 Illinois Street, Golden CO 80401-1843
County: Jefferson FICE Identification: 001348
Unit ID: 126775
Telephone: (303) 273-3000 Carnegie Class: DU-Higher
FAX Number: (303) 273-3278 Calendar System: Semester
URL: www.mines.edu
Established: 1874 Annual Undergrad Tuition & Fees (In-State): $19,100
Enrollment: 6,744 Coed
Affiliation or Control: State IRS Status: 501(c)3
Highest Offering: Doctorate
Accreditation: HLC

01 President .... Dr. Paul C. JOHNSON
05 Provost .... Dr. Richard HOLZ
11 Executive Vice Pres Admin & Ops .... Ms. Kirsten VOLPI
100 Chief of Staff/VP External Rels .... Mr. Peter HAN
32 Vice Pres Student LIfe .... Dr. Dan FOX
46 Sr VP Research & Tech Transfer .... Dr. Stefanie TOMPKINS
111 Pres for Institutional Advancement .... Mr. Brian WINKELBAUER
65 Dean Earth Resources & Environ Pgms .... Dr. Terri HOGUE
92 Dean Honors/Integrative Programs .... Dr. Kevin MOORE
88 Dean Energy & Materials Pgm .... Dr. John BERGER
43 Vice Pres & General Counsel .... Ms. Anne WALKER
84 Assoc Prov Enrollment Management .... Ms. Lori KESTER
20 Associate Provost .... Dr. Wendy ZHOU
10 Assoc Prov Finance & Admin .... Ms. Victoria NICHOL
20 Assoc Provost .... Dr. John BERGER
35 AVP Student Service & Admin .... Ms. Rebecca FLINTOFT
15 Director of Human Resources .... Ms. Stacie ALTMAN
11 AVP Infrastructure & Operations .... Mr. Gary BOWERSOCK
15 AVP Organizational Strategy .... Vacant
13 Chief Information Officer .... Ms. Monique SENDZE
26 Chief Marketing Officer .... Mr. Jason HUGHES
35 Dean of Students .... Dr. Derek MORGAN
35 Assoc Dean of Students .... Mr. Colin TERRY
88 Exec Dir for Strategic Development .... Ms. Deb LASICH
04 Sr Executive Asst to the President .... Ms. Tammy STRANGE
04 President's Office Executive Asst .... Vacant
41 Athletic Director .... Mr. David HANSBURG
08 University Librarian .... Ms. Carol SMITH
88 Dir of Trefny Innov & Instruction .... Dr. Sam SPIEGEL
37 Director of Financial Aid .... Ms. Jill ROBERTSON
88 Director of WISEM .... Ms. Annette PILKINGTON
09 Director of Institutional Research .... Ms. Tricia DOUTHIT
92 Director Honors Program .... Dr. Tonya LEFTON
06 Registrar .... Mr. Paul MYSKIW
93 Dir Multicultural Engineering Pgm .... Ms. Andrea MORGAN
29 Director Alumni Relations .... Mr. Damian FRIEND
91 Director Enterprise Systems .... Ms. Angie REYES
104 Asst Provost for International Affs .... Dr. David WRIGHT
108 Sr Assessment Associate .... Ms. Megan SANDERS
44 Senior Director Annual Giving .... Ms. Sara POND
102 Dir Foundation/Corporate Relations .... Ms. Emily KELTON
38 Dir of Counseling Center .... Ms. Sandra SIMS
96 Director of Procurement/Contracting .... Mr. Ryan MCGUIRK
27 Director Communication Center .... Ms. Allyce HORAN
21 Controller .... Ms. Noelle SANCHEZ
115 Associate Treasurer .... Mr. Kevin GRAVINA
25 Director Research Admin .... Ms. Johanna EAGAN
109 Dir Student Life Business Admin .... Ms. Lisa GOBERIS
114 Director Budget .... Ms. Danielle LOWRY
113 Bursar .... Ms. Jenny PHOU
16 Assoc Dir Human Resources .... Ms. Jill MURPHY
118 Benefits Manager .... Ms. Ann HIX
28 Director of Diversity .... Dr. Amy LANDIS
19 Director Public Safety .... Mr. Dustin OLSON
18 Director Facilities Mgmt .... Mr. Samuel CRISPIN
14 Deputy Chief Info Officer .... Vacant
119 Chief Information Security Officer .... Mr. Phillip ROMIG
07 Exec Director of Admissions .... Mr. Dale GAUBATZ
123 Director of Graduate Admissions .... Ms. Megan STEELMAN
39 Director Housing/Residence Life .... Ms. Mary ELLIOTT
121 Dir of Acad Services and Advising .... Ms. Jennifer DRUMM
85 Asst Provost International Affairs .... Mr. David WRIGHT
117 Exec Dir of Bus Ops/Risk Mgmt .... Ms. Natalie VEGA
88 Manager Classroom Technology .... Ms. Sara SCHWARZ
89 Dir New Student/Trans Services .... Ms. Jessica KEEFER
88 Dir of Title IX Programs .... Ms. Katryn SCHMALZEL
88 Dir Office Design & Construction .... Mr. Mike BOWKER
88 Dir of Research Compliance .... Mr. Ralph BROWN
88 Dir Infrastructure Solutions .... Mr. Jorge RICARDINO CSAPO
88 Director Business Services .... Ms. Anna WELSCOTT
88 Dir Entrepreneurship/Innovator .... Mr. Werner KUHR
88 Dir Intramural & Club Sports .... Mr. John HOWARD
88 Dir Acad Affairs Operations .... Ms. Jennie KENNEY
88 Dir of Campus Events .... Ms. Brandy BURGESS
88 Dir of Fitness .... Ms. Heather HAMILTON
88 Dir Intramurals .... Mr. Adam HICKLE
88 Dir Administrative Processing Svcs .... Ms. Janice LANDER
88 Dir of Student Activities .... Ms. Kelsi STREICH
88 Dir of Wellness Programs .... Ms. Emma GRIFFIS
88 Dir Outdoor Recreation .... Mr. Nathanael BONDI
88 Dir Research & Technology Transfer .... Mr. William VAUGHAN
88 Dir Research Development .... Ms. Lisa KINZEL
88 Dir Facilities/Aquatics .... Mr. Bradford AVENIA
22 Dir Student Disability Services .... Ms. Marla DRAPER
88 Manager Application Systems .... Mr. Bryan SIEBUHR
88 Exec Dir Envir Health & Safety .... Ms. Barbara O'KANE
88 Exec Dir of Oper Excellence . Ms. Tressa CONSTANTINEAU RIES
88 Museum Curator .... Ms. Renata LAFLER

Colorado School of Trades (K)

1575 Hoyt Street, Lakewood CO 80215-2996
County: Jefferson FICE Identification: 011572
Unit ID: 126784
Telephone: (303) 233-4697 Carnegie Class: Spec 2-yr-Tech
FAX Number: (303) 233-4723 Calendar System: Other
URL: www.schooloftrades.edu
Established: 1947 Annual Undergrad Tuition & Fees: N/A
Enrollment: 96 Coed
Affiliation or Control: Proprietary IRS Status: Proprietary
Highest Offering: Associate Degree
Accreditation: ACCSC

01 President .... Mr. Ryan LISHNER

Colorado School of Traditional Chinese Medicine (L)

1441 York Street, Suite 202, Denver CO 80206-2127
County: Denver FICE Identification: 036863
Unit ID: 381352
Telephone: (303) 329-6355 Carnegie Class: Spec-4-yr-Other Health
FAX Number: (303) 388-8165 Calendar System: Trimester
URL: www.cstcm.edu
Established: 1989 Annual Undergrad Tuition & Fees: N/A
Enrollment: 84 Coed
Affiliation or Control: Proprietary IRS Status: Proprietary
Highest Offering: Master's
Accreditation: ACUP

01 President .... Mark H. MANTON
11 Administrative Director .... William WALLIN
05 Int Academic Dean/Dean of Faculty .... Parago JONES
20 Assistant Academic Dean .... Christopher SHIFLETT
17 Clinic Director .... Zack GUTMAN
88 Assistant Clinic Director .... Carol RIDSDALE
37 Financial Aid Administrator .... Joel SPENCER
10 Finance Administrator .... Yanyun WANG
06 Registrar .... Christine SCHULTZE
07 Recruiting Director .... Timothy FARAD
88 Administrator for the Dean .... Sam MACDONALD

*Colorado State University System Office (M)

555 17th Street, Suite 1000, Denver CO 80202
County: Denver FICE Identification: 033437
Telephone: (303) 534-6290 Carnegie Class: N/A
FAX Number: (303) 534-6298
URL: www.csusystem.edu

01 Chancellor .... Dr. Tony FRANK
10 Chief Financial Officer .... Mr. Henry SOBANET
43 General Counsel .... Mr. Jason JOHNSON
05 Chief Academic Officer .... Dr. Rick MIRANDA
88 Chief Educational Innovation Office ... Dr. Becky TAKEDA-TINKER
13 Chief Information Officer .... Mr. Patrick BURNS
26 AVC for External Relations .... Ms. Tiana NELSON

*Colorado State University (N)

200 W. Lake Street, Fort Collins CO 80523-0015
County: Larimer FICE Identification: 001350
Unit ID: 126818
Telephone: (970) 491-1101 Carnegie Class: DU-Highest
FAX Number: (970) 491-0501 Calendar System: Semester
URL: www.colostate.edu
Established: 1870 Annual Undergrad Tuition & Fees (In-State): $11,814
Enrollment: 32,428 Coed
Affiliation or Control: State IRS Status: 501(c)3
Highest Offering: Doctorate
Accreditation: HLC, ART, CACREP, CAEPT, CEA, CIDA, CONST, COPSY, DIETC, DIETD, IPSY, JOUR, LSAR, MFCD, MUS, OT, PH, SW, VET

02 President .... Ms. Joyce E. MCCONNELL
05 Senior Exec Vice Pres/Provost .... Dr. Mary PEDERSEN
46 Vice President for Research .... Dr. Alan S. RUDOLPH
32 Vice Pres Student Affairs .... Dr. Blanche M. HUGHES
11 VP for University Operations .... Ms. Lynn JOHNSON
111 VP University Advancement .... Ms. Kim TOBIN
84 Vice Pres for Enrollment/Access .... Ms. Leslie TAYLOR
26 VP for University Communications .... Ms. Yolanda BEVILL
56 VP Outreach and Engagement .... Dr. Blake NAUGHTON
13 VP for IT .... Mr. Brandon BERNIER
20 Vice Prov for Undergraduate Affairs .... Dr. Kelly LONG
58 Vice Provost Graduate Affairs .... Dr. Mary STOMBERGER
85 Vice Provost for International Affs .... Ms. Kathleen FAIRFAX
36 Director Career Services .... Mr. Jon CLEVELAND
28 VP for Inclusive Excellence .... Dr. Kauline CIPRIANI
29 Exec Director Alumni Relations .... Ms. Kristi BOHLENDER
41 Athletic Director .... Mr. Joe PARKER
35 Dean of Students .... Dr. Jody DONOVAN
43 Deputy General Counsel .... Ms. Jannine R. MOHR

47 Dean Agriculture Sciences ....Dr. James PRITCHETT
76 Dean Applied Human Sciences ....Dr. Lise YOUNGBLADE
50 Dean of Business ....Dr. Beth WALKER
54 Dean of Engineering ....Dr. David MCLEAN
49 Dean of Liberal Arts ....Dr. Ben WITHERS
65 Dean of Natural Resources ....Dr. John HAYES
81 Dean of Natural Sciences ....Dr. Janice L. NERGER
74 Dean of Veterinary Med & Biomed Sci ....Dr. Mark STETTER
08 Dean of Libraries ....Dr. Karen ESTLUND
06 Registrar ....Ms. D. TOBIASSEN BAITINGER
18 Chief Facilities/Physical Plant ....Mr. Tom SATTERLY
22 VP for Equity/Equal Oppty/Title IX ....Ms. Diana PRIETO
37 Director of Student Financial Aid ....Mr. Joe DONLAY
39 Exec Dir Housing & Dining Services ....Dr. Mari STROMBOM
40 Director of Bookstore ....Mr. John PARRY
96 Director of Procurement Services ....Ms. Linda MESERVE
92 Director University Honors Program ....Dr. Donald MYKLES
94 Director Center for Women's Studies ....Dr. Caridad SOUZA
09 Vice Provost Institutional Research ....Dr. Laura JENSEN
100 Chief of Staff Office of the Pres ....Ms. Ann CLAYCOMB

*Colorado State University Global (A)

585 Salida Way, Aurora CO 80011
County: Arapahoe FICE Identification: 042087
Unit ID: 476975
Telephone: (800) 462-7845 Carnegie Class: Masters/L
FAX Number: N/A Calendar System: Trimester
URL: https://csuglobal.edu
Established: 2008 Annual Undergrad Tuition & Fees (In-State): $8,400
Enrollment: 12,578 Coed
Affiliation or Control: State IRS Status: 170(c)1
Highest Offering: Master's
Accreditation: HLC, ACBSP

02 President ....Pamela TONEY
05 Provost/VP Strategic Development ....Dr. Karen FERGUSON
26 AVP of Marketing & Engagement ....Andrew DIXON
10 Sr Dir Finance & Inst Integrity ....Yvonne HARRIS-LOTT

*Colorado State University-Pueblo (B)

2200 Bonforte Boulevard, Pueblo CO 81001-4901
County: Pueblo FICE Identification: 001365
Unit ID: 128106
Telephone: (719) 549-2100 Carnegie Class: Masters/S
FAX Number: (719) 549-2650 Calendar System: Semester
URL: www.csupueblo.edu
Established: 1933 Annual Undergrad Tuition & Fees (In-State): $8,591
Enrollment: 5,925 Coed
Affiliation or Control: State IRS Status: 501(c)3
Highest Offering: Master's
Accreditation: HLC, MUS, NUR, SW

02 President ....Dr. Timothy MOTTET
05 Provost/EVP for Academic Affs ....Dr. Mohamed ABDELRAHMAN
10 VP Finance & Administration ....Mr. Alejandro ROJAS SOSA
84 VP Enrollment Mgmt/Student Affairs ....Ms. Chrissy HOLLIDAY
18 Asst VP Facilities Management ....Mr. Craig CASON
108 Exec Dir Assessment/Inst Effect ....Dr. Helen CAPRIOGLIO
13 Executive Director of IT ....Mr. Chris MILLIKEN
08 Dean Library Services ....Ms. Rhonda GONZALES
50 Dean Hasan School of Business ....Dr. Bruce RAYMOND
79 Dean Col of Humanities/Arts/Soc Sci ....Dr. William FOLKESTAD
76 Dean Col Health/Education/Nursing ....Dr. Bernard FRANTA
81 Int Dean Col Science/Tech/Engr/Math ....Dr. David LEHMPUHL
102 President/CEO Foundation ....Mr. Todd KELLY
26 Exec Director Marketing ....Mr. Greg HOYE
09 Dir Institutional Research/Analysis ....Mr. Corey SHILLING
21 Director of BFS/Controller ....Ms. Juanita PENA
37 Director Student Financial Services ....Vacant
06 Registrar ....Ms. Amy ROBERTSHAW
36 Director Career Center ....Mrs. Michelle B. GJERDE
41 Director Athletics ....Mr. Paul PLINSKE
15 Director Human Resources ....Ms. Kat ABERNATHY
39 Dir Residence Life & Housing ....Ms. Gwendolyn YOUNG
109 Director Auxiliary Services ....Mr. Chris FENDRICH
23 Dir Student Health/Counseling ....Ms. Carolyn DAUGHERTY
29 Director Alumni Relations ....Ms. Tracy SAMORA
88 Director Center for Acad Enrichment ....Dr. John SANDOVAL
07 Director of Admissions ....Ms. Tiffany KINGREY
32 Dean of Student Affairs ....Dr. Marie HUMPHREY
100 Chief of Staff ....Ms. Niki TOUSSAINT
19 Manager Parking and Safety ....Ms. Laurie KILPATRICK
22 Int Dir Affirm Action/Equal Opp ....Mr. Bobby SMITH
38 Director of Counseling ....Ms. Cori CAMERON
43 Deputy General Counsel ....Ms. Johnna DOYLE
96 Director of Purchasing ....Ms. Geraldine TRUJILLO-MARTINEZ
30 Chief Strategy Officer ....Ms. Donna SOUDER

Colorado Technical University (C)

3151 South Vaughn Way, Suite 150, Aurora CO 80014
Telephone: (303) 632-2300 Identification: 666732
Accreditation: &HLC, ACBSP

† Regional accreditation is carried under the parent institution in Colorado Springs, CO.

Colorado Technical University (D)

4435 N Chestnut Street, Colorado Springs CO 80907-3896
County: El Paso FICE Identification: 010148
Unit ID: 126827
Telephone: (719) 598-0200 Carnegie Class: DU-Mod
FAX Number: (719) 598-3740 Calendar System: Quarter
URL: www.coloradotech.edu
Established: 1965 Annual Undergrad Tuition & Fees: $12,573
Enrollment: 28,244 Coed
Affiliation or Control: Proprietary IRS Status: Proprietary
Highest Offering: Doctorate
Accreditation: HLC, ACBSP, NURSE

01 Campus President ....Mr. Andrew HURST
05 Chief Academic Officer/Provost ....Dr. Connie JOHNSON
10 Vice President Finance ....Ms. Erin KRAFT
07 Vice President of Admissions ....Mr. Keith ARMSTRONG
11 VP Univ Strategy/Operations ....Ms. Elise BASKEL
32 Vice President Student Affairs ....Ms. Terri HINES
20 Vice Provost ....Dr. Douglas STEIN

Community College of Aurora (E)

16000 E Centre Tech Parkway, Aurora CO 80011-9036
County: Arapahoe FICE Identification: 022769
Unit ID: 126863
Telephone: (303) 360-4700 Carnegie Class: Assoc/HT-High Non
FAX Number: (303) 360-4761 Calendar System: Semester
URL: www.ccaurora.edu
Established: 1983 Annual Undergrad Tuition & Fees (In-State): $3,940
Enrollment: 7,835 Coed
Affiliation or Control: State IRS Status: 501(c)3
Highest Offering: Associate Degree
Accreditation: HLC, EMT

01 President ....Dr. Mordecai I. BROWNLEE
05 Vice President of Academic Affairs ....Dr. Bobby PACE
32 Vice President of Student Affairs ....Dr. Angela MARQUEZ
45 VP of Institutional Effectiveness ....Dr. Chris WARD
15 Director of Human Resources ....Ms. Cindy HESSE
10 VP of Administrative Services ....Ms. Lynne WINCHELL
21 Controller ....Ms. Xochil HERRERA
35 Dean of Students ....Dr. Reyna ANAYA
20 Dean Academic Affairs ....Dr. Carmen WADE
20 Dean Academic Affairs ....Mr. Chris TOMBARI
19 Director of Security ....Mr. Travis HOGAN
36 Director of Advising ....Ms. LeeDel COHENOUR
13 Director Information Technology ....Ms. Wendy MUENCH
18 Facilities Director ....Mr. John BOTTELBERGHE
26 Director Marketing/Communications ....Mr. Alex SCHULTZ
37 Director Financial Aid ....Mr. John YOUNG
06 Registrar/Director Admissions ....Ms. Kristen CUSACK
08 Director Library Services ....Mr. Dan LAWRENCE
09 Director of Institutional Research ....Dr. HyeKyung LEE
102 Exec Dir CCA Foundation ....Mr. John WOLFKILL
22 College Equity Officer ....Vacant

Community College of Denver (F)

Campus Box 250, PO Box 173363,
Denver CO 80217-3363
County: Denver FICE Identification: 009542
Unit ID: 126942
Telephone: (303) 556-2400 Carnegie Class: Bac/Assoc-Assoc Dom
FAX Number: (303) 556-8555 Calendar System: Semester
URL: www.ccd.edu
Established: 1967 Annual Undergrad Tuition & Fees (In-State): $4,788
Enrollment: 7,273 Coed
Affiliation or Control: State IRS Status: 501(c)3
Highest Offering: Associate Degree
Accreditation: HLC, CSHSE, DH, RAD, SURGT

01 President ....Dr. Marielena DESANCTIS
05 Provost/Chief Academic Officer ....Ms. Ruthanne ORIHUELA
10 Vice Pres Finance & Admin/CFO ....Ms. Kathryn KAOUDIS
32 Vice Pres Student Affairs ....Vacant
84 VP of Enrollment Administration ....Ms. Gillian MCKNIGHT-TUTEIN
83 Dean Arts/Behavioral & Social Sci ....Dr. Robert STUDINGER
76 Dean Health & Natural Sciences ....Dr. Fida OBEIDI
89 Dean Math/English & FYE ....Mr. Peter LINDSTROM
50 Dean Business/Industry & Tech ....Mr. Thomas WILLIAMS
20 Dean of Instruction ....Dr. Kaylah ZELIG
124 Dean Student Success ....Mrs. Tina GARCIA
35 Director of Student Life ....Ms. Kathryn MAHONEY
37 Director Financial Aid ....Ms. Theresa LAVIN
15 Exec Director Human Resources ....Ms. Patty DAVIES
09 Director Institutional Research ....Ms. Katherine HILL
06 Registrar/Dir Registration & Recs ....Ms. Anastacia RODRIGUEZ
18 Dir Emergency Prep & Facilities ....Mr. Nick GODDARD
102 Foundation Director ....Ms. Leah GOSS
13 IT Services Manager ....Ms. Claudia FORBES

Concorde Career College (G)

111 N Havana Street, Aurora CO 80010-4314
County: Arapahoe FICE Identification: 008871
Unit ID: 126687
Telephone: (303) 861-1151 Carnegie Class: Spec 2-yr-Health
FAX Number: (303) 839-5478 Calendar System: Other
URL: www.concorde.edu
Established: 1969 Annual Undergrad Tuition & Fees: N/A
Enrollment: 329 Coed
Affiliation or Control: Proprietary IRS Status: Proprietary
Highest Offering: Associate Degree
Accreditation: ACCSC, COARC, DH, PNUR, PTAA, RAD, SURGT

01 Campus President ....Mr. Thomas WICKE
05 Academic Dean ....Ms. Sue KUHL
37 Director of Financial Aid ....Ms. Kimberly MARTINEZ
07 Director of Admissions ....Mr. Nick HRUBY

Denver College of Nursing (H)

1401 19th Street, Denver CO 80202
County: Denver FICE Identification: 041483
Unit ID: 454856
Telephone: (303) 292-0015 Carnegie Class: Spec-4-yr-Other Health
FAX Number: (720) 974-0290 Calendar System: Quarter
URL: https://www.denvercollegeofnursing.edu/
Established: 2003 Annual Undergrad Tuition & Fees: N/A
Enrollment: 1,042 Coed
Affiliation or Control: Proprietary IRS Status: Proprietary
Highest Offering: Master's
Accreditation: HLC, ADNUR, NUR, NURSE

01 President ....Dr. Cathy MAXWELL
10 Director of Business Operations ....Mr. Tim HEINTZ
32 Director of Student Services ....Mr. Michael RUSCHIVAL
05 Dean/Dir of Nursing Education Pgms ....Dr. Z. JoAnna HILL
37 Director of Financial Aid ....Ms. Geri REICHMUTH
07 Director of Admissions ....Mr. Jeff JOHNSON
06 Registrar ....Mr. Jacob DENNING

Denver Seminary (I)

6399 S Santa Fe Drive, Littleton CO 80120-2912
County: Arapahoe FICE Identification: 001352
Unit ID: 126979
Telephone: (303) 761-2482 Carnegie Class: Spec-4-yr-Faith
FAX Number: (303) 761-8060 Calendar System: Semester
URL: www.denverseminary.edu
Established: 1950 Annual Graduate Tuition & Fees: N/A
Enrollment: 856 Coed
Affiliation or Control: Interdenominational IRS Status: 501(c)3
Highest Offering: Doctorate; No Undergraduates
Accreditation: HLC, CACREP, PAST, THEOL

01 President ....Dr. Mark S. YOUNG
05 VP Academic Affairs/Dean ....Dr. Don PAYNE
10 Vice President of Finance ....Ms. Deborah KELLAR
111 Vice President of Advancement ....Mr. Chris JOHNSON
32 VP Student Life & Enrollment Mgmt ....Mr. Dusty DI SANTO
06 Registrar ....Ms. Georgia WRIGHT
35 Dean of Students ....Mrs. Kristy MCGARVEY
84 Director of Enrollment Management ....Ms. Amy CARR
109 Director of Auxiliary Services ....Vacant
13 Director of Information Systems ....Mr. Jason ADAMS
26 Sr Director of Communications ....Mrs. Andrea WEYAND
18 Director of Facilities ....Mr. Rob BACHMAN
37 Director of Financial Aid ....Mrs. Gina KELBERT
08 Director of Library Services ....Mr. Matt WASIELEWSKI
73 Director of DMin Program ....Dr. Marshall SHELLEY
21 Controller/Dir Financial Services ....Ms. Diana SMITH
15 Director of Human Resources ....Mrs. Wendi GOWING
28 Assoc Dean for Ethnic Communities ....Mr. Wilmer RAMIREZ
56 Assoc Dean Innovation/Ed Systems ....Mr. Tim KOLLER
04 Executive Asst to the President ....Mrs. Christy GROSVENOR
106 Associate Dean of Educational Tech ....Mr. Aaron JOHNSON
88 Assist Director of DMinistry ....Ms. Angie WARD
09 Dir Office of Innov & Educ System ....Mrs. Nancy BROWN
100 Chief of Staff ....Mr. Josh BLEEKER

Fort Lewis College (J)

1000 Rim Drive, Durango CO 81301-3999
County: La Plata FICE Identification: 001353
Unit ID: 127185
Telephone: (970) 247-7010 Carnegie Class: Bac-A&S
FAX Number: (970) 247-7175 Calendar System: Semester
URL: www.fortlewis.edu
Established: 1911 Annual Undergrad Tuition & Fees (In-State): $8,896
Enrollment: 3,469 Coed
Affiliation or Control: State IRS Status: 170(c)1
Highest Offering: Master's
Accreditation: HLC, CAEPT, MUS

01 President ....Dr. Tom STRITIKUS
05 Provost/Vice Pres Academic Affairs ....Dr. Cheryl NIXON
10 Vice Pres Finance & Administration ....Mr. Steven J. SCHWARTZ
111 Vice President for Advancement ....Ms. Melissa MOUNT
32 Dean Student Engagement ....Mr. Jeffrey DUPONT
21 Assoc Vice Pres Finance & Admin ....Ms. Michele PETERSON
06 Registrar ....Ms. Theresa E. RODRIGUEZ
21 Controller ....Ms. Holly ESTELLE
25 Dir of Sponsored Research ....Mr. Michael BROWN
37 Director Financial Aid ....Ms. Tracey PICCOLI
07 Director of Admission ....Ms. Jess SAVAGE
38 Dir Counseling Center ....Ms. Amie BRYANT
08 Director of the Library ....Ms. Astrid OLIVER
15 Dir Human Res/Equal Opportunity ....Ms. Erin BEEZLEY
41 Athletic Director ....Mr. Brandon LEIMBACH
13 Director Computing & Telecomm ....Mr. Matt MCGLAMERY
29 Director Alumni Engagement ....Mr. Ryan LAZO
96 Director of Purchasing ....Ms. April ZION
26 Public Relations Officer ....Ms. Lauren SAVAGE
49 Dean Arts and Science ....Dr. Jesse PETERS
50 Dean Sch of Business Admin ....Dr. Steven M. ELIAS
20 Assoc VP Academic Affairs ....Vacant

53 Dean of Teacher Education .... Dr. Jennifer TRUJILLO
04 Admin Assistant to the President .... Ms. Vikki AGOVINO
09 Director of Institutional Research .... Ms. Orien S. MCGLAMERY
18 Chief Facilities/Physical Plant Ofc .... Mr. Jeff MILLER
19 Director Security/Safety .... Mr. Brett DEMING
28 Director of Diversity .... Mr. LeManuel BITSOI
39 Dir Resident Life/Student Housing .... Mr. Edgar ANAYA

Front Range Community College (A)

3645 W 112th Avenue, Westminster CO 80031-2105
County: Adams FICE Identification: 007933
Unit ID: 127200
Telephone: (303) 404-5000 Carnegie Class: Assoc/HT-Mix Trad/Non
FAX Number: (303) 466-1623 Calendar System: Semester
URL: www.frontrange.edu
Established: 1968 Annual Undergrad Tuition & Fees (In-State): $4,032
Enrollment: 18,703 Coed
Affiliation or Control: State IRS Status: 501(c)3
Highest Offering: Baccalaureate
Accreditation: HLC, ADNUR, CAHIIM, DA, NAEYC, NURSE, SURGT

02 President .... Mr. Andrew R. DORSEY
04 Asst to the President .... Ms. Denise BUCHER
10 VP Finance/Administration .... Ms. Patti ARROYO
05 VP Acad Affairs & Online Learning .... Dr. Rebecca WOULFE
12 VP Westminster Campus/Brighton Ctr .... Dr. Tricia JOHNSON
12 Vice Pres Larimer Campus .... Dr. Jean RUNYON
12 Vice Pres Boulder County Campus .... Dr. Aparna PALMER
84 VP Enrollment Svs & Student Success .... Dr. Tamara WHITE
15 Exec Director of Human Resources .... Ms. JoAnne WILKINSON
102 Exec Director of Foundation .... Mr. Ryan MCCOY
26 Lead Dir Marketing/Communications .... Ms. Marian MAHARAS
28 Exec Director of Equity & Inclusion .... Mr. Abenicio RAEL
18 Assoc VP Facilities Planning/Mgmt .... Mr. Derek BROWN
20 Dean of Instruction Larimer .... Dr. Shashi UNNITHAN
20 Dean of Instruction Larimer .... Ms. Anne Marie JACOBSON
20 Dean of Instruction Larimer .... Mr. Nicholas SPEZZA
20 Dean of Instruction Boulder County .... Mr. Matt JAMISON
20 Dean of Instruction Westminster .... Dr. Andrea DECOSMO
20 Dean of Instruction Boulder County .... Ms. MaryLee GEARY
20 Dean of Instruction Boulder County .... Ms. Deborah CRAVEN
32 Dean of Student Svcs Boulder County .... Ms. Carla STEIN
106 Dean of Std Affairs,Online Learning .... Mr. Chico GARCIA
32 Dean of Student Svcs Westminster .... Ms. Erica INGALLS
09 Director of Institutional Research .... Ms. Kim WALLACE
114 Director of Budget & Auxiliary Svcs .... Ms. Karen STEINER
06 Registrar .... Ms. Sonia GONZALES
07 Director of Admissions .... Vacant
37 Dir of Financial Aid Larimer .... Ms. Carolee GOLDSMITH
08 Librarian .... Vacant
18 Director of Facilities Westminster .... Vacant
18 Director of Facilities Larimer .... Mr. Dennis DEREMER
35 Director Student Life Westminster .... Ms. Mindy KINNAMAN
35 Director Student Life Larimer ...... Ms. Mary BRANTON-HOUSLEY
35 Dir Student Life Boulder County .... Ms. Amanda CLANCY
27 Public Information Officer .... Ms. Jessica PETERSON
13 Dir of Information Technology Svcs . Ms. Malinda MASCARENAS
19 Dir Campus Security/Preparedness .... Mr. Gordon GOLDSMITH

Front Range Community College-Boulder County Campus (B)

2190 Miller Drive, Longmont CO 80501
Telephone: (303) 678-3722 Identification: 770041
Accreditation: &HLC

Front Range Community College Larimer Campus (C)

4616 S Shields Street, Fort Collins CO 80526
Telephone: (970) 226-2500 Identification: 770040
Accreditation: &HLC, ADNUR, PNUR

Holmes Institute of Consciousness Studies (D)

573 Park Point Drive, Golden CO 80401
County: Jefferson Identification: 666255
Telephone: (720) 496-1370 Carnegie Class: Not Classified
FAX Number: (303) 526-0913 Calendar System: Quarter
URL: www.holmesinstitute.edu
Established: 1972 Annual Graduate Tuition & Fees: N/A
Enrollment: N/A Coed
Affiliation or Control: Other IRS Status: 501(c)3
Highest Offering: Master's; No Undergraduates
Accreditation: DEAC

01 President .... Rev Dr. Kim KAISER
06 Registrar .... Mr. Dan HERFURT
56 Dean of Distance Education .... Rev Dr. Christina TILLOTSON

IBMC College (E)

3842 South Mason Street, Fort Collins CO 80526
County: Larimer FICE Identification: 030063
Unit ID: 372329
Telephone: (970) 223-2669 Carnegie Class: Assoc/HVT-High Non
FAX Number: (970) 223-2796 Calendar System: Quarter
URL: www.ibmc.edu
Established: 1987 Annual Undergrad Tuition & Fees: $14,400
Enrollment: 408 Coed
Affiliation or Control: Proprietary IRS Status: Proprietary
Highest Offering: Associate Degree
Accreditation: ACCSC

01 CEO/Campus Director .... Mr. Steven STEELE
05 Director of Education .... Ms. Katie WILKINSON
06 Registrar .... Ms. Jami ZENNER

IBMC College (F)

2863 35th Avenue, Greeley CO 80634-9421
Telephone: (970) 356-4733 Identification: 770631
Accreditation: ACCSC

Iliff School of Theology (G)

2323 E. Iliff Ave, Denver CO 80210-4798
County: Denver FICE Identification: 001354
Unit ID: 127273
Telephone: (303) 744-1287 Carnegie Class: Spec-4-yr-Faith
FAX Number: (303) 765-1141 Calendar System: Quarter
URL: www.iliff.edu
Established: 1892 Annual Graduate Tuition & Fees: N/A
Enrollment: 215 Coed
Affiliation or Control: United Methodist IRS Status: 501(c)3
Highest Offering: Doctorate; No Undergraduates
Accreditation: HLC, THEOL

01 President and CEO .... Rev Dr. Thomas V. WOLFE
05 Vice Pres/Dean Academic Affairs .... Rev Dr. Boyung LEE
10 VP of Business Affairs/Controller .... Mr. Jason WARR
84 VP of Enrollment Management .... Dr. Stephanie KRUSEMARK
111 VP of Institutional Advancement .... Ms. Kelsey COCHRANE
09 VP of Innovation/Learning and IR .... Dr. Theodore M. VIAL
42 Dean of the Chapel .... Rev Dr. Cathie KELSEY
26 Director of Communications .... Dr. Soon Beng YEAP
06 Registrar .... Ms. Kylie A. PARISH
13 Chief Information Officer .... Mr. Michael HEMENWAY
04 Executive Asst to President .... Mrs. Alisha ENO
18 Dir of Facilities Mgmt .... Mr. Andy RIEDER
15 Director of Human Resources .... Vacant
11 Chief Operating Officer .... Dr. Caran WARE JOSEPH
37 Director Student Financial Aid .... Ms. Goldie ECTOR

Institute of Business and Medical Careers (H)

2315 North Main Street, Longmont CO 80501
Telephone: (303) 651-6819 Identification: 770630
Accreditation: ACCSC

Institute of Taoist Education and Acupuncture (I)

317 West South Boulder Road, Ste 5, Louisville CO 80027
County: Boulder FICE Identification: 041212
Unit ID: 454838
Telephone: (720) 890-8922 Carnegie Class: Spec-4-yr-Other Health
FAX Number: (720) 890-7719 Calendar System: Other
URL: www.itea.edu
Established: 1996 Annual Graduate Tuition & Fees: N/A
Enrollment: 28 Coed
Affiliation or Control: Independent Non-Profit IRS Status: 501(c)3
Highest Offering: Master's; No Undergraduates
Accreditation: ACUP

01 President .... Hilary SKELLON
05 Vice President .... Brittany SANELLI
06 Registrar .... Kale DENNIS
10 Financial Administrator .... Kathy KNAUS

IntelliTec College (J)

2315 E Pikes Peak Avenue, Colorado Springs CO 80909-6096
County: El Paso FICE Identification: 022537
Unit ID: 128179
Telephone: (719) 632-7626 Carnegie Class: Assoc/HVT-High Trad
FAX Number: (719) 632-7451 Calendar System: Quarter
URL: www.intellitec.edu
Established: 1965 Annual Undergrad Tuition & Fees: N/A
Enrollment: 585 Coed
Affiliation or Control: Proprietary IRS Status: Proprietary
Highest Offering: Associate Degree
Accreditation: ACCSC

00 President .... Wayne ZELLNER
02 Campus Director .... David SCOTT
07 Director of Academics .... Catherine LECKMAN

Lamar Community College (K)

2401 S Main, Lamar CO 81052-3999
County: Prowers FICE Identification: 001355
Unit ID: 127389
Telephone: (719) 336-2248 Carnegie Class: Assoc/MT-VT-Mix Trad/Non
FAX Number: (719) 336-2448 Calendar System: Semester
URL: www.lamarcc.edu
Established: 1937 Annual Undergrad Tuition & Fees (In-State): $4,133
Enrollment: 723 Coed
Affiliation or Control: State IRS Status: 501(c)3
Highest Offering: Associate Degree
Accreditation: HLC, ADNUR

01 President .... Dr. Linda LUJAN
05 VP Academic Services/Student Svcs .... Dr. Lisa SCHLOTTERHAUSEN
11 VP Admin Svcs/Inst Effectiveness .... Mr. Chad DE BONO
20 Dean of Academic Services .... Dr. Annessa STAGNER
26 Director of Communication .... Vacant
06 Registrar .... Vacant
08 Library Tech .... Ms. Jennifer GOODLAND
18 Director of Facilities .... Mr. Sean LIRLEY
15 Director Personnel Services .... Ms. Shelly TOMBLESON
39 Director Student Housing .... Vacant
38 Director Student Counseling .... Mrs. Rosalind SMITH
96 Director of Purchasing .... Ms. Ava BAIR
41 Athletic Director .... Mr. Scott CRAMPTON
37 Director Financial Aid .... Ms. Teresa TURNER
07 Director of Admissions .... Vacant
21 Controller .... Mrs. Aubrie CLEAVINGER
111 Dir Inst Advancement/Foundation Dir .... Mrs. Anne-Marie CRAMPTON
09 Coordinator Institutional Research .... Ms. Kim WALLACE
84 Coord for Concurrent Enrollment .... Mr. Del CHASE
04 Admin Assistant to the President .... Ms. Misti FRONTERHOUSE
13 Chief Information Technology Ofcr .... Mr. Robert VAZQUEZ

Lincoln College of Technology (L)

11194 East 45th Avenue, Denver CO 80239
County: Denver FICE Identification: 007547
Unit ID: 126951
Telephone: (303) 722-5724 Carnegie Class: Spec 2-yr-Tech
FAX Number: (303) 778-8264 Calendar System: Semester
URL: www.lincolntech.edu
Established: 1963 Annual Undergrad Tuition & Fees: N/A
Enrollment: 1,529 Coed
Affiliation or Control: Proprietary IRS Status: Proprietary
Highest Offering: Associate Degree
Accreditation: ACCSC

01 Campus President .... Dr. Kelly THUMM MOORE
07 Sr Director of Admissions .... Ms. Jennifer HASH
05 Academic Dean .... Mr. Dwayne ISBELL
04 Administrative Asst to President .... Ms. Beverly SOTELO
06 Registrar .... Ms. Stacy SWINBURN
36 Director of Career Services .... Ms. Joseph OLIVER
11 Director of Admin Services .... Ms. Christine GRAY
37 Director of Financial Aid .... Ms. Loriann WEISS
13 IT Administrator .... Mr. Johnathan CARRIGER
18 Chf Facilities/Physical Plant Ofcr .... Mr. Gary BILLOCK

Metropolitan State University of Denver (M)

PO Box 173362, Campus Box 48, Denver CO 80217-3362
County: Denver FICE Identification: 001360
Unit ID: 127565
Telephone: (303) 556-5740 Carnegie Class: Masters/L
FAX Number: (303) 556-3912 Calendar System: Semester
URL: https://www.msudenver.edu/
Established: 1963 Annual Undergrad Tuition & Fees (In-State): $8,693
Enrollment: 19,086 Coed
Affiliation or Control: State IRS Status: 501(c)3
Highest Offering: Master's
Accreditation: HLC, ART, CAATE, COSMA, CSHSE, DIETD, @DIETT, EXSC, MT, MUS, NUR, @SP, SW, THEA

01 President .... Dr. Janine A. DAVIDSON
05 Provost/EVP Academic Affairs .... Dr. Alfred W. TATUM
10 Vice Pres Admin/Finance & COO .... Mr. Larry SAMPLER
111 VP Advancement/Exec Dir Foundation .... Ms. Christine MARQUEZ-HUDSON
32 VP Student Affairs .... Dr. Will SIMPKINS
28 VP Ofc of Diversity/Inclusion .... Dr. Michael BENITEZ, JR.
45 Interim VP Strategy .... Mr. Eric MASON
43 General Counsel/Secretary to Board .... Mr. David FINE
13 AVP Info Technology Services/CIO .... Mr. Kevin TAYLOR
84 Assoc VP Enrollment Services .... Ms. Mary SAUCEDA
35 AVP Stdnt Engage & Well/Dean Stdnts .... Dr. Braelin PANTEL
29 Asst VP Strategic Engagement .... Ms. Jamie HURST
50 Dean School Business .... Dr. Ann B. MURPHY
107 Int Dean Sch Professional Studies .... Dr. Rebecca TRAMMELL
15 AVP Human Resources .... Ms. Stacy M. DVERGSDAL
06 Registrar .... Ms. Connie SANDERS
37 Interim Director Financial Aid .... Mr. Michael NGUYEN
41 Athletic Director .... Dr. G. Anthony GRANT
36 Assoc VP Classroom 2 Career Hub .... Dr. Adrienne MARTINEZ
07 Director of Admissions .... Mr. Vaughn TOLAND
09 Director of Data & Analytics .... Mr. Sean PETRANOVICH
04 Exec Assistant to the President .... Ms. Summer VALDEZ
106 Director Online Learning .... Dr. Matt GRISWOLD
25 Chief Contract/Grants Administrator .... Ms. Betsy JINKS
53 Dean School of Education .... Dr. Liz HINDE
100 Chief of Staff .... Mr. Edward BROWN

Morgan Community College (N)

920 Barlow Road, Fort Morgan CO 80701-4399
County: Morgan FICE Identification: 009981
Unit ID: 127617
Telephone: (970) 542-3100 Carnegie Class: Assoc/MT-VT-High Non
FAX Number: (970) 542-3115 Calendar System: Semester
URL: www.morgancc.edu
Established: 1967 Annual Undergrad Tuition & Fees (In-State): $3,850

Enrollment: 1,376 Coed
Affiliation or Control: State IRS Status: Exempt
Highest Offering: Baccalaureate
Accreditation: HLC, ADNUR, PTAA

01 President .... Dr. Curt FREED
10 Vice Pres Finance/Admin Services .... Vacant
05 Vice President of Instruction .... Ms. Kathy FRISBIE
32 Vice President of Student Services .... Mr. Scott SCHOLES
04 Assistant to the President .... Ms. Jane FRIES
20 Dean of Gen Ed & Health Sciences .... Dr. Christiane OLIVO
88 Dean of Concurrent Enrollment .... Ms. Kim MAXWELL
103 Dean of Workforce Development .... Mr. John PROUTY
06 Registrar .... Ms. Connie MESE
26 Dir of Comm/Mktg & Recruitment .... Ms. Ariella GONZALES-VONDY
30 Director of Development .... Ms. Roberta BIGALK
37 Director of Financial Aid .... Ms. Sally SHAWCROFT
15 Director of Human Resources .... Ms. Julie BEYDLER
07 Director of Admissions & Advising .... Ms. Maria CARDENAS
08 Director of Learning Resources .... Ms. April AMACK
09 Enrollment Research & Data Support .... Mr. Michael TRANTER
96 Director of Purchasing .... Ms. Chloe HIRSCHFELD
13 Director Information Technology .... Mr. Mark FRASCO
109 Director of Auxiliary Operations .... Ms. Kellie OVERTURF
18 Director of Physical Facilities .... Mr. Gene KIND
40 Coordinator of College Store .... Ms. Debbie CASTENEDA

Naropa University (A)

2130 Arapahoe Avenue, Boulder CO 80302-6697
County: Boulder FICE Identification: 021175
Unit ID: 127653
Telephone: (303) 444-0202 Carnegie Class: Masters/M
FAX Number: (303) 444-0410 Calendar System: Semester
URL: www.naropa.edu
Established: 1974 Annual Undergrad Tuition & Fees: $34,600
Enrollment: 855 Coed
Affiliation or Control: Independent Non-Profit IRS Status: 501(c)3
Highest Offering: Master's
Accreditation: HLC

01 President .... Mr. Charles G. LIEF
100 Special Advisor to the President .... Ms. Joy VALANIA
05 Chief Academic Officer .... Ms. Sue WEST
10 Vice President of Operations/CFO .... Mr. Tyler KELSCH
84 VP Enroll/Marketing/Student Success .... Ms. Ann Marie KLOTZ
30 Int Vice President of Development .... Mr. Jason EMBRY
21 AVP for Budget/Financial Affairs .... Ms. Yvonne GATES
108 Sr Advisor for Inst Effectiveness .... Ms. Cheryl BARBOUR
13 Director of IT .... Mr. David EDMINSTER
28 VP Mission/Culture/Inclusive Cmty .... Ms. Regina SMITH
38 Director Counseling Center .... Ms. Jo-Lynne PARKS
06 Registrar .... Vacant
08 Library Director .... Ms. Amanda RYBIN KOOB
18 Director of Safety/Facilities & Ops .... Mr. Aaron COOK
37 Dir Student Financial Services .... Ms. Jessica BREJC
15 Director of Human Resources .... Mr. Kert HUBIN
106 Director of Online Education .... Mr. Jirka HLADIS

Nazarene Bible College (B)

1465 Kelly Johnson Blvd, Colorado Springs CO 80920
County: El Paso FICE Identification: 013007
Unit ID: 127714
Telephone: (719) 884-5000 Carnegie Class: Spec-4-yr-Faith
FAX Number: (719) 884-5199 Calendar System: Trimester
URL: www.nbc.edu/people/
Established: 1964 Annual Undergrad Tuition & Fees: $10,320
Enrollment: 608 Coed
Affiliation or Control: Church Of The Nazarene IRS Status: 501(c)3
Highest Offering: Baccalaureate
Accreditation: HLC, BI

01 President .... Dr. Scott S. SHERWOOD
05 Vice President for Academic Affairs .... Dr. Alan D. LYKE
10 Vice President for Finance .... Mrs. Shirley A. CADLE
84 VP for Enrollment Management .... Dr. David M. CHURCH
37 Financial Aid Officer .... Mrs. Jan EDWARDS
06 Registrar .... Rev. Duane A. MATHIAS
13 Chief Information Officer .... Mr. Fred R. PHILLIPS
04 Executive Asst to President .... Rev. Susan P. MCKEITHEN
09 Institutional Research .... Mrs. Jan EDWARDS
15 Director Personnel Services .... Mrs. Carol A. CRIPPEN
29 Director Alumni Relations .... Rev. Susan P. MCKEITHEN
90 Director Academic Computing .... Vacant
07 Director of Admissions/Enrollment .... Rev. Will MACKEY
88 Exec Asst to VP Academic Affairs .... Ms. Karen COLSTON
88 Exec Asst to VP Enroll Mgt/Finance .... Ms. Avery SUNNARBORG
08 Librarian .... Mr. Addison LUCCHI
88 Recruiting Representative .... Dr. Gary HAINES
88 Alliance Director .... Mrs. Cheryl GRAVES
88 Admissions Counselor .... Mr. Quinn NORTH
88 Admissions Counselor .... Mr. Stephen EDWARDS
121 Academic Advisor .... Mr. Gabe HAYSE

Northeastern Junior College (C)

100 College Avenue, Sterling CO 80751-2399
County: Logan FICE Identification: 001361
Unit ID: 127732
Telephone: (970) 521-6600 Carnegie Class: Assoc/MT-VT-Mix Trad/Non
FAX Number: (970) 522-4945 Calendar System: Semester
URL: www.njc.edu
Established: 1941 Annual Undergrad Tuition & Fees (In-State): $5,288
Enrollment: 1,293 Coed
Affiliation or Control: State IRS Status: 501(c)3
Highest Offering: Associate Degree
Accreditation: HLC, ADNUR

01 President .... Mr. Jay LEE
05 Vice President Instruction .... Dr. Linda MERKL
10 Vice Pres Finance & Administration .... Ms. Lisa LEFEVRE
32 Vice President Student Services .... Mr. Steven SMITH
29 Alumni Director .... Ms. Heather BRUNGARDT
102 Executive Director NJC Foundation .... Ms. Vivian HADLEY
06 Director Records/Admission Process .... Ms. Lisa SCHAEFER
37 Director of Financial Aid .... Ms. Ashley UNREIN
39 Dir Resident Life/Student Activity .... Mr. Timothy STAHLEY
18 Physical Plant Director .... Mr. Tracey KNOX
15 Human Resources Director .... Ms. Jeri ESTRADA
41 Athletic Director .... Ms. Marci HENRY
96 Director of Purchasing .... Ms. Martha GAREIS
09 Dir of Inst Research/Plng/Devel .... Ms. Leslie WEINSHEIM
26 Director of Communications .... Ms. Jesse QUINLIN
21 Controller .... Ms. Judy MCFADDEN
13 Director Information Technology .... Ms. Cherie BRUNGARDT
40 Bookstore Director .... Ms. Heather BRUNGARDT
04 Executive Asst to President .... Ms. Shawn ROSE
07 Director of Admissions .... Ms. Camille ROSE
106 Dir Online Education/E-learning .... Vacant
108 Director Institutional Assessment .... Ms. Catheryne TRENKLE
25 Chief Contracts/Grants Admin .... Ms. Cyndi HOFMEISTER

Otero Junior College (D)

1802 Colorado Avenue, La Junta CO 81050-3346
County: Otero FICE Identification: 001362
Unit ID: 127778
Telephone: (719) 384-6800 Carnegie Class: Assoc/HT-Mix Trad/Non
FAX Number: (719) 384-6933 Calendar System: Semester
URL: www.ojc.edu
Established: 1941 Annual Undergrad Tuition & Fees (In-State): $4,100
Enrollment: 1,216 Coed
Affiliation or Control: State IRS Status: 501(c)3
Highest Offering: Associate Degree
Accreditation: HLC, ADNUR, MLTAD

01 President .... Dr. Timothy ALVAREZ
10 Vice Pres Administrative Services .... Mr. Pat MALOTT
05 VP Academic & Student Affairs .... Mrs. Rana BROWN
84 Assoc VP Enrollment Management .... Mrs. Angela MOORE
20 Assoc VP Academic Affairs .... Vacant
32 Dean of Student Affairs .... Mr. Gary ADDINGTON
15 Director of Human Resources .... Mrs. Kelsey BARBEE
18 Director of Physical Plant .... Mr. David GIRARD
40 Bookstore Coordinator .... Ms. Taylor DONNELL
37 Director of Financial Aid .... Mrs. Amber ASBURY
109 Director of Auxiliary Services .... Mr. Dillon MARTIN
26 Dir of Communications/Development .... Mrs. Angela MOORE
13 Director of Computer Services .... Mr. Shawn BORTON
09 Director of Institutional Research .... Vacant
04 Admin Assistant to the President .... Ms. Sarah PETRAMALA
41 Athletic Director .... Mr. Chris CARRILLO

Pikes Peak Community College (E)

5675 S Academy Boulevard,
Colorado Springs CO 80906-5498
County: El Paso FICE Identification: 008896
Unit ID: 127820
Telephone: (719) 502-2000 Carnegie Class: Assoc/HT-Mix Trad/Non
FAX Number: (719) 502-2201 Calendar System: Semester
URL: www.ppcc.edu
Established: 1968 Annual Undergrad Tuition & Fees (In-State): $3,967
Enrollment: 12,506 Coed
Affiliation or Control: State IRS Status: 501(c)3
Highest Offering: Baccalaureate
Accreditation: HLC, ACFEI, ADNUR, DA, EMT, NAEYC, SURGT

01 President .... Dr. Lance BOLTON
04 Exec Assistant to the President .... Vacant
05 Vice Pres of Instruction .... Vacant
32 Vice President Student Services .... Mr. Homer WESLEY
10 Vice Pres Administrative Services .... Mr. Duane RISSE
103 Vice Pres of Workforce Development .... Vacant
35 Assoc Vice Pres of Student Services .... Ms. Dawna HAYNES
88 Director of Instructional Support .... Ms. Rose ANGRY
37 Director of Financial Aid .... Mr. Ronald SWARTWOOD
08 Director of Libraries .... Ms. Carole OLDS
15 Exec Dir of Human Resource Services .... Mr. Carlton BROOKS
26 Exec Dir Marketing/Communications .... Mr. Warren EPSTEIN
28 Exec Director of Diversity/Equity .... Mr. Keith BARNES
21 Director of Business Svcs .... Mr. Alberto TEIXEIRA
06 Registrar/Coordinator of Records .... Ms. Twila HUMPHREY
07 Director of Admissions .... Mr. Kevin HUDGENS
102 Exec Director of Foundation .... Ms. Lisa JAMES
18 Director Facilities .... Mr. Roland SCOBEE
13 Chief Technology Officer .... Mr. Cyrille PARENT
19 Dir Public Safety/Emergency Mgmt .... Mr. Jim BARRENTINE
09 Exec Dir of Inst Effectiveness .... Dr. Patrica DIWARA
88 Director of Advising & Testing .... Mr. Lincoln WULF
96 Director of Purchasing .... Ms. Rockie HURRELL
38 Director Counseling Center .... Ms. Yolanda HARRIS
109 Director Auxiliary Services .... Ms. Lorelle DAVIES
09 Director of Institutional Research .... Vacant
88 Project Dir of Stdnt Support Svcs .... Mr. Michael COUILLARD
76 Dean Health and Science .... Ms. Kristen JOHNSON
81 Dean Mathematics & English .... Mr. Joe SOUTHCOTT
50 Dean Business/Public Service/SS .... Mr. Rob HUDSON
60 Dean Comm/Humanities/Tech Studies .... Ms. Fran HETRICK
88 Dean of High School Programs .... Ms. Chelsy HARRIS
20 Dean of Academic Resources .. Ms. Jacquelyn GAITERS-JORDAN

Pima Medical Institute (F)

13750 E. Mississippi Avenue, Aurora CO 80012
County: Arapahoe FICE Identification: 041771
Unit ID: 461689
Telephone: (303) 368-7462 Carnegie Class: Spec 2-yr-Health
FAX Number: N/A Calendar System: Other
URL: pmi.edu
Established: 2012 Annual Undergrad Tuition & Fees: N/A
Enrollment: 362 Coed
Affiliation or Control: Proprietary IRS Status: Proprietary
Highest Offering: Associate Degree
Accreditation: ABHES

01 Campus Director .... Ms. Terri SPENCER

Pima Medical Institute-Colorado Springs (G)

5725 Mark Dabling Blvd, Suite 150,
Colorado Springs CO 80919
Telephone: (719) 482-7462 Identification: 770516
Accreditation: ABHES

† Branch campus of Pima Medical Institute-Tucson, Tucson, AZ

Pima Medical Institute-Denver (H)

7475 Dakin Street, Suite 100, Denver CO 80221
Telephone: (303) 426-1800 Identification: 666171
Accreditation: ABHES, COARC, OTA, PTAA, RAD, SURTEC

† Branch campus of Pima Medical Institute, Tucson, AZ.

Platt College (I)

3100 S Parker Road, Suite 200, Aurora CO 80014-3141
County: Arapahoe FICE Identification: 030149
Unit ID: 260813
Telephone: (303) 369-5151 Carnegie Class: Spec-4-yr-Other Health
FAX Number: (303) 745-1433 Calendar System: Quarter
URL: www.plattcolorado.edu
Established: 1986 Annual Undergrad Tuition & Fees: $20,590
Enrollment: 227 Coed
Affiliation or Control: Proprietary IRS Status: Proprietary
Highest Offering: Baccalaureate
Accreditation: ACCSC, NUR

00 Owner .... Mr. Jerald B. SIRBU
01 President .... Dr. Julie BASLER
10 Chief Financial Officer .... Mr. Robert CRAVER
37 Director of Financial Aid .... Mr. Michael J. VIGIL
08 Head Librarian .... Ms. Laura CULLERTON
66 Dean College of Nursing .... Dr. Frances RICKER
06 Registrar .... Ms. Katie AL-ADAYLEH
07 Admissions Representative .... Mr. Patrick HUDDY
13 Coordinator of IT Services .... Mr. Mark FINKEN

Pueblo Community College (J)

900 W Orman Avenue, Pueblo CO 81004-1499
County: Pueblo FICE Identification: 021163
Unit ID: 127884
Telephone: (719) 549-3200 Carnegie Class: Bac/Assoc-Assoc Dom
FAX Number: (719) 544-1179 Calendar System: Semester
URL: www.pueblocc.edu
Established: 1933 Annual Undergrad Tuition & Fees (In-State): $4,520
Enrollment: 5,551 Coed
Affiliation or Control: State IRS Status: 501(c)3
Highest Offering: Baccalaureate
Accreditation: HLC, ACFEI, ADNUR, CAHIIM, COARC, DH, EMT, OTA, PTAA, SURGT

01 President .... Dr. Patricia ERJAVEC
04 Executive Asst to President .... Ms. Julie JIMENEZ
10 VP of Administration and Finance .... Mr. Robert GONZALES
05 VP of Academic Support .... Dr. Todd ECKLUND
32 VP of Student Success .... Dr. Heather SPEED
15 VP of Human Resources .... Mr. Ken NUFER
12 Executive Dean PCCSW Campus .... Dr. Samuel DOSUMU
12 Executive Dean Fremont Campus .... Dr. Mark PEACOCK
76 Dean Health & Public Safety .... Dr. Andrew MILLER
49 Dean Arts & Sciences .... Dr. Young KIM
50 Dean Business & Advanced Technology ... Dr. Jennifer SHERMAN
26 Director Marketing/Communications .... Ms. Erin HERGERT
09 Director Institutional Research .... Dr. Cory BUTTS
13 Dir Information Technology Services .... Mr. Bryan CRAWFORD
88 Exec Dir Pueblo Corporate College .... Ms. Amanda CORUM
102 Director of PCC Foundation .... Ms. Martha SIMMONS
07 Dir Admissions & Records/Registrar .... Ms. Barbara BENEDICT
21 Controller .... Ms. Robin ARWOOD
37 Director Financial Aid .... Ms. Monica HARDWICK
18 Director Facilities Services .... Mr. Joe WANEKA
88 Director Learning Center .... Vacant
08 Director Library Services .... Ms. Christina MCGRATH

35 Dean of Students ... Mr. Vernon JAMES
96 Director Purchasing ... Mr. Edmond INIGUEZ
121 Dir Student Support & Outreach Svcs ... Mr. Michael GAGE
120 Multimedia Tech Specialist ... Mr. Robin LEACH
06 Registrar ... Ms. Barbara BENEDICT
19 Director Public Safety ... Mr. William BROWN

Pueblo Community College Fremont Campus (A)

51320 W Highway 50, Canon City CO 81212
Telephone: (719) 296-6100 Identification: 770042
Accreditation: &HLC

Pueblo Community College Southwest Campus (B)

33057 Highway 160, Mancos CO 81328
Telephone: (970) 564-6200 Identification: 770044
Accreditation: &HLC

Red Rocks Community College (C)

13300 W Sixth Avenue, Lakewood CO 80228-1255
County: Jefferson FICE Identification: 009543
Unit ID: 127909
Telephone: (303) 914-6600 Carnegie Class: Bac/Assoc-Assoc Dom
FAX Number: (303) 914-6666 Calendar System: Semester
URL: www.rrcc.edu
Established: 1969 Annual Undergrad Tuition & Fees (In-State): $4,379
Enrollment: 6,029 Coed
Affiliation or Control: State IRS Status: 501(c)3
Highest Offering: Master's
Accreditation: HLC, ARCPA, MAC, NAEYC, RAD

01 President ... Dr. Michele HANEY
04 Exec Assistant to the President ... Ms. Kathy SCHISSLER
10 Vice Pres Administrative Services ... Mr. Bryan BRYANT
05 Vice President Academic Affairs ... Dr. Beverly CLARK, III
32 Vice Pres Stdnt Svc/Enrollment Mgt ... Vacant
35 Vice Pres Student Success ... Dr. Lisa FOWLER
103 Vice Pres Workforce/Community Devel ... Ms. Angela KING
20 Dean Academic Services ... Vacant
20 Dean Instructional Services ... Ms. Barbra SOBHANI
20 Dean Instructional Services ... Mr. Mike COSTE
13 Dean Technology CTE ... Ms. Dorothy WELTY
88 Dean of Instruct/Exec Dir RMEC-OSHA ... Ms. Joan SMITH
85 Director International Education ... Ms. Linda YAZDANI
07 Dir Student Recruit/Advising/Admiss ... Vacant
21 Controller ... Ms. Holly GENTRY
37 Director Financial Aid ... Ms. Shannon WEBBER
06 Dean Enrollment Services ... Ms. Jen MACKEN
18 Director Facilities ... Mr. Mark BANA
15 Interim Director Human Resources ... Mr. Arnie OUDENHOVEN
102 Assoc VP of Inst Advancement ... Vacant
26 Director Marketing/Communications ... Ms. Wren BARNES
35 Director Campus Life ... Dr. Steven ZEEH
88 Dir Childhood Ed & Support Svcs ... Ms. Janiece KNEPPE
09 Director Institutional Research ... Mr. Charles DUELL
28 Coordinator of Diversity/Inclusion ... Vacant
96 Coordinator Purchasing ... Ms. Renee MURILLO
36 Director Student Outreach ... Vacant
46 Exec Dir Planning/Rsrch/Inst Effect ... Mr. Derek GRUBB

Red Rocks Community College Arvada Campus (D)

10280 W. 55th Avenue, Arvada CO 80002
Telephone: (303) 914-6010 Identification: 770045
Accreditation: &HLC

Regis University (E)

3333 Regis Boulevard, #B-4, Denver CO 80221-1099
County: Denver FICE Identification: 001363
Unit ID: 127918
Telephone: (303) 458-4100 Carnegie Class: DU-Mod
FAX Number: (303) 964-5449 Calendar System: Semester
URL: www.regis.edu
Established: 1877 Annual Undergrad Tuition & Fees: $38,558
Enrollment: 6,310 Coed
Affiliation or Control: Roman Catholic IRS Status: 501(c)3
Highest Offering: Doctorate
Accreditation: HLC, CACREP, CAHIIM, MFCD, NURSE, PHAR, PTA

01 President ... Rev. John P. FITZGIBBONS, SJ
43 Chief Legal Officer ... Dr. Janelle RAMSEL
05 Provost ... Dr. Janet HOUSER
10 Sr Vice President/CFO ... Dr. Salvador D. ACEVES
111 Vice President Advancement ... Ms. Myrna HALL
100 Chief of Staff to President ... Ms. Terri CAMPBELL
88 Vice President Mission ... Fr. Kevin F. BURKE, SJ
32 Vice President Student Affairs ... Dr. Barbara WILCOTS
50 Dean of Regis College ... Dr. Thomas BOWIE
109 Assoc VP Auxiliary & Business Svcs ... Mr. Josef RILL
15 Assoc VP Human Resources ... Dr. Liz WHITMORE
18 Assoc VP Physical Plant ... Mr. Michael J. REDMOND
26 Assoc VP Marketing/Communication ... Mr. Todd COHEN
110 Asst VP University Advancement ... Ms. Abigail PALSIC
29 Asst VP Alumni Engagement Pgms ... Ms. Margaret LINN-ADDISON
13 Chief Information Officer ... Mr. Jaganmohan GUDUR
77 Dean Anderson College ... Dr. Shari PLANTZ-MASTERS
76 Dean Health Professions ... Dr. Linda OSTERLUND
88 Assoc Dean Health Professions ... Dr. Tristen AMADOR
66 Dean School of Nursing ... Dr. Catherine WITT
08 Dean of Libraries ... Dr. Erin MCCAFFREY
35 Dean of Students ... Mr. Patrick ROMERO-ALDAZ
07 Dean of Admissions ... Ms. Kim FRISCH
37 Director Financial Aid ... Ms. Cindy HEJL
06 Director Registration ... Ms. Cathy GORRELL
06 Director Academic Records ... Ms. Terry GAURMER
38 Dir Counseling/Personal Dev ... Ms. Melissa AURINGER
19 Director of Campus Safety ... Mr. Lance JONES
88 Director of Advancement Services ... Ms. Jean CAMBER
42 Director of University Ministry ... Mr. Kyle TURNER
41 Asst VP/Director Athletics ... Mr. David SPAFFORD
04 Executive Assistant to President ... Ms. Rita CONTRERAS
39 Assoc Dir Resident Life/Housing ... Mr. Eric BARNES
28 Associate Provost Diversity ... Dr. Nicki GONZALES
44 Assistant Director Annual Giving ... Mr. Alec THORNTON

Rocky Mountain College of Art & Design (F)

1600 Pierce Street, Lakewood CO 80214-1433
County: Denver FICE Identification: 007649
Unit ID: 127945
Telephone: (303) 753-6046 Carnegie Class: Spec-4-yr-Arts
FAX Number: (303) 759-4970 Calendar System: Semester
URL: www.rmcad.edu
Established: 1963 Annual Undergrad Tuition & Fees: $20,725
Enrollment: 1,643 Coed
Affiliation or Control: Proprietary IRS Status: Proprietary
Highest Offering: Master's
Accreditation: HLC, ART, CIDA

01 President ... Mr. Brent FITCH
05 Senior Vice Pres Academic Affairs ... Dr. Darcy OROZCO
26 Senior Vice Pres of Marketing ... Mr. Daron RODRIGUEZ
07 Vice President of Admissions ... Mr. Brian BELLIVEAU
32 Dean of Students ... Mr. Robert FLADRY
108 Director Accreditation/Compliance ... Dr. Terence BRENNAN

Rocky Vista University (G)

8401 South Chambers Road, Parker CO 80134
County: Douglas Identification: 667002
Unit ID: 480790
Telephone: (303) 373-2008 Carnegie Class: Spec-4-yr-Med
FAX Number: N/A Calendar System: Other
URL: www.rvu.edu
Established: 2006 Annual Graduate Tuition & Fees: N/A
Enrollment: 1,332 Coed
Affiliation or Control: Proprietary IRS Status: Proprietary
Highest Offering: Doctorate; No Undergraduates
Accreditation: HLC, #ARCPA, OSTEO

01 President ... Dr. David FORSTEIN
04 Executive Administrative Assistant ... Ms. Michele SOBCZYK
05 Provost ... Dr. David FORSTEIN
09 VP for Institutional Effectiveness ... Vacant
84 VP of Enrollment Management ... Ms. Julie ROSENTHAL
88 Compliance Coordinator ... Ms. Laura DEMENT
10 Controller ... Mr. David IRONS
37 Dir Student Financial Svc ... Ms. Fran LATA
32 Assoc Dean Student Affairs ... Dr. David ROOS
06 Registrar ... Mr. David PALTZA
08 Director of Library Services ... Dr. Brian SCHWARTZ
19 Manager Security/Safety ... Mr. Andrew STEVENS
15 VP of Human Resources ... Mr. Jerry ARMSTRONG
101 Secretary of the Institution/Board ... Ms. Michele SOBCZYK
38 Mental Health & Wellness Counselor ... Ms. Karen ROBINSON
39 Director Resident Life/Student Hous ... Ms. Vielane VAN NOY
88 Dean RVUCOM ... Dr. Heather FERRILL
13 Manager Information Services ... Mr. Brad ELLIS

St. John Vianney Theological Seminary (H)

1300 S Steele Street, Denver CO 80210-2526
County: Denver Identification: 666127
Telephone: (303) 282-3427 Carnegie Class: Not Classified
FAX Number: (303) 282-3453 Calendar System: Semester
URL: www.sjvdenver.edu
Established: 1999 Annual Graduate Tuition & Fees: N/A
Enrollment: N/A Male
Affiliation or Control: Roman Catholic IRS Status: 501(c)3
Highest Offering: Master's; No Undergraduates
Accreditation: THEOL

01 Rector ... Rev. Daniel LEONARD
03 Vice Rector ... Rev. Jason WALLACE
05 Academic Dean ... Rev. Luis GRANADOS
10 Director of Finance ... Mr. Paul VILLAMARIA
08 Library Director ... Mr. Stephen SWEENEY
06 Registrar ... Ms. Denise SEERY
04 Administrative Asst to President ... Ms. Val CAREY

Southwest Acupuncture College (I)

6630 Gunpark Drive Suite 200, Boulder CO 80301-3339
Telephone: (303) 581-9955 Identification: 666618
Accreditation: ACUP

† Branch campus of Southwest Acupuncture College, Santa Fe, NM.

Spartan College (J)

10851 W 120th Avenue, Broomfield CO 80021-3401
County: Broomfield FICE Identification: 007297
Unit ID: 126605
Telephone: (303) 466-1714 Carnegie Class: Spec 2-yr-Tech
FAX Number: (303) 496-0211 Calendar System: Other
URL: www.spartan.edu
Established: 1965 Annual Undergrad Tuition & Fees: $14,199
Enrollment: 292 Coed
Affiliation or Control: Proprietary IRS Status: Proprietary
Highest Offering: Associate Degree
Accreditation: ACCSC

01 Campus President ... Mr. Nicholas BROWN
05 Dean of Academic Affairs ... Ms. Karen LENOX
07 Director of Admissions ... Mr. Jeremy COOPER
32 Dean of Student Affairs ... Mr. Corey O'BRIEN
06 Registrar ... Ms. Vicki MIDDEKER
37 Director of Student Finance ... Mr. Nicholas DIMANNA

The Taft University System (K)

3333 South Wadsworth Blvd, Ste D228, Lakewood CO 80227
County: Jefferson FICE Identification: 041004
Unit ID: 454689
Telephone: (303) 867-1155 Carnegie Class: Spec-4-yr-Other
FAX Number: (303) 867-1156 Calendar System: Semester
URL: www.taft.edu
Established: 1976 Annual Undergrad Tuition & Fees: N/A
Enrollment: 614 Coed
Affiliation or Control: Proprietary IRS Status: Proprietary
Highest Offering: Doctorate
Accreditation: DEAC

01 President ... Dr. Neil A. JOHNSON
11 Director Administration/Registrar ... Ms. Christine A. BALDWIN
50 Dean School of Business ... Dr. Anita CASSARD
53 Dean School of Education ... Dr. Barry RESNICK
05 Chief Academic Officer ... Dr. Neil A. JOHNSON
07 Director of Admissions ... Ms. Ni PHAM
26 Director of Digital Marketing ... Ms. Megan MENENDEZ
32 Director of Student Affairs ... Ms. Stephanie ESTLOW
37 Director Student Financial Aid ... Ms. Deanna SANDOVAL
45 Chief Institutional Planning Ofcr ... Dr. Richard BOOROM

† Tuition varies by degree program.

Trinidad State Junior College (L)

600 Prospect, Trinidad CO 81082-2396
County: Las Animas FICE Identification: 001368
Unit ID: 128258
Telephone: (719) 846-5011 Carnegie Class: Assoc/MT-VT-High Non
FAX Number: (719) 846-5667 Calendar System: Semester
URL: www.trinidadstate.edu
Established: 1925 Annual Undergrad Tuition & Fees (In-State): $5,299
Enrollment: 1,404 Coed
Affiliation or Control: State IRS Status: 501(c)3
Highest Offering: Baccalaureate
Accreditation: HLC, ADNUR

01 President ... Dr. Rhonda EPPER
05 Vice President of Academic Affairs ... Ms. Lynette BATES
32 VP Student Services ... Ms. Kerry GABRIELSON
11 Vice Pres Administrative Services ... Ms. Shannon SHIVELEY
10 Controller ... Ms. Amanda VIGIL
20 Dean of Instruction ... Ms. LoriRae HAMILTON
88 Special Initiatives ... Mr. Keith GIPSON
37 Director Financial Aid ... Ms. Wilma ATENCIO
06 Registrar ... Ms. Christy HOLDEN
18 Director of Physical Plant Opers ... Vacant
12 Vice President Valley Campus ... Mr. James KYNOR
106 Dir Online Educ/Dir of Technology ... Mr. Doug BAK
04 Admin Asst to President ... Ms. Linda PERRY
41 Athletic Director ... Mr. Michael SALBATO
09 Director of Institutional Research ... Ms. Annette LUJAN
15 Human Resources Director ... Ms. Yvette ATENCIO
39 Housing Director ... Mr. Seth KRAVIG
84 Director Enrollment Management ... Mr. David HARDMAN

Trinidad State Junior College San Luis Valley Campus (M)

1011 Main Street, Alamosa CO 81101
Telephone: (719) 589-7000 Identification: 770047
Accreditation: &HLC

UCH Memorial Hospital School Of Radiologic Technology (N)

2420 E. Pikes Peak Avenue, Colorado Springs CO 80910
County: El Paso Identification: 667097
Telephone: (719) 365-8291 Carnegie Class: Not Classified
FAX Number: (719) 365-5374 Calendar System: Semester
URL: www.uchealth.org/radschool
Established: 1969 Annual Undergrad Tuition & Fees: N/A
Enrollment: N/A Coed

Affiliation or Control: Independent Non-Profit IRS Status: 501(c)3
Highest Offering: Associate Degree
Accreditation: RAD

01 Director Elaine R. IVAN
05 Dean of Education Jarad MUASAU
11 Administrator Joseph DAILY
06 Registrar/Clinical Coordinator Danielle MASSAGEE
07 Director of Admissions Elaine R. IVAN
08 Librarian Megan MCCREIGHT

*University of Colorado System Office (A)

1800 Grant Street, Suite 800, Denver CO 80203
County: Denver FICE Identification: 007996
Unit ID: 128300
Telephone: (303) 860-5600 Carnegie Class: N/A
FAX Number: (303) 860-5610
URL: www.cu.edu

01 President Mr. Todd SALIMAN
05 Vice Pres Academic Affairs Dr. Michael LIGHTNER
100 Senior VP & Chief of Staff Mr. Leonard DINEGAR
10 VP & Chief Financial Officer Vacant
43 VP/University Counsel/Secy Board Mr. Jeremy HUETH
111 Interim Assoc VP for Advancement Ms. Annie BACCARY
15 Sr AVP/Chief Human Resource Ofcr Vacant
86 VP Government Relations Ms. Tanya KELLY-BOWRY
26 Assoc VP University Relations Mr. Mike SANDLER
21 Asst VP & University Controller Mr. Robert KUEHLER
13 Asst VP & Chief Information Ofcr Mr. Scott MUNSON
27 Sr Asst VP for University Relations Ms. Elizabeth COLLINS
88 Asst VP External Rels & Advocacy Mr. Tony SALAZAR
45 Asst VP Strategic Initiatives Ms. Angelique FOSTER
28 Chief Diversity Officer Ms. Theodosia COOK

*University of Colorado Boulder (B)

Regent Drive At Broadway, Boulder CO 80309-0001
County: Boulder FICE Identification: 001370
Unit ID: 126614
Telephone: (303) 492-1411 Carnegie Class: DU-Highest
FAX Number: N/A Calendar System: Semester
URL: www.colorado.edu
Established: 1876 Annual Undergrad Tuition & Fees (In-State): $12,466
Enrollment: 37,437 Coed
Affiliation or Control: State IRS Status: 501(c)3
Highest Offering: Doctorate
Accreditation: HLC, AUD, CEA, CLPSY, IPSY, JOUR, LAW, MUS, SP

02 Chancellor Dr. Phillip P. DISTEFANO
05 Provost & Exec VC for Acad Affairs Dr. Russell MOORE
10 Chief Financial Officer Ms. Carla HO-A
11 Chief Operating Officer Mr. Patrick O'ROURKE
46 Vice Chancellor for Research Dr. Terri FIEZ
88 VC Infrastructure/Sustainability Mr. David KANG
32 Vice Chanc Student Affairs Dr. Akirah BRADLEY
28 Vice Chanc for Diversity/Equity Dr. Robert BOSWELL
26 Senior Assoc VC Strategic Comm Mr. Jon LESLIE
111 Interim VC for Advancement Mr. Derek C. BELLIN
20 Vice Prov/Assoc VC for UG Education Dr. Mary KRAUS
20 Exec Vice Prov Acad Resource Mgmt Dr. Ann SCHMIESING
20 Assoc Vice Chanc Faculty Affairs Dr. Michele N. MOSES
13 Assoc VC for IT/Chief Info Officer Dr. Lawrence M. LEVINE
29 Asst Vice Chanc Alumni Relations Mr. Ryan CHREIST
18 Asst VC Facilities Operations/Svcs Mr. Brian LINDOERFER
100 Chief of Staff Ms. Catherine SHEA
58 Dean of the Graduate School Dr. E. Scott ADLER
61 Dean of Law Dr. Lolita BUCKNER INNISS
49 Dean of Arts & Sciences Dr. James WHITE
54 Interim Dean of Engineering Dr. Keith MOLENAAR
50 Dean of Business Dr. Sharon MATUSIK
53 Dean of Education Dr. Katherine SCHULTZ
64 Dean of Music Dr. John DAVIS
60 Dean of Media/Communications/Info Dr. Lori BERGEN
51 Dean of Division of Continuing Educ Dr. Sara THOMPSON
08 Dean of Libraries Mr. Robert H. MCDONALD
35 Dean of Students Mr. Austin J. BANKS
37 Director of Financial Aid Ms. Ofelia A. MORALES
07 Exec Director of Admissions Mr. Clark BRIGGER
06 Registrar Dr. Kristi WOLD-MCCORMICK
22 Exec Director Title IX Programs Ms. Valerie SIMONS
09 Asst Vice Chanc Institutional Rsrch Mr. Robert STUBBS
25 Dir of Contracts and Grants Ms. Denitta D. WARD
15 Chief Human Resources Officer Ms. Charlotte Katherine ERWIN
41 Athletic Director Mr. Rick GEORGE
19 Chief of Police Ms. Doreen JOKERST
36 Director of Career Services Ms. Lisa LOVETT
39 Exec Dir Housing & Dining Services Ms. Amy D. BECKSTROM
88 Director of Museum Dr. Patrick KOCIOLEK
104 Director of Education Abroad Ms. Mary DANDO
43 Managing Assoc Univ Counsel Ms. Elvira U. STREHLE-HENSON
38 Dir Counseling & Psychiatric Svcs Dr. Monica NG

*University of Colorado Colorado Springs (C)

1420 Austin Bluffs Parkway, Colorado Springs CO 80918
County: El Paso FICE Identification: 004509
Unit ID: 126580
Telephone: (719) 255-8227 Carnegie Class: DU-Higher
FAX Number: (719) 255-3362 Calendar System: Semester
URL: www.uccs.edu
Established: 1965 Annual Undergrad Tuition & Fees (In-State): $8,580
Enrollment: 12,380 Coed
Affiliation or Control: State IRS Status: 501(c)3
Highest Offering: Doctorate
Accreditation: HLC, CAATE, CACREP, CAEP, CLPSY, DIETD, NURSE, SPAA, @SW

02 Chancellor Dr. Venkat REDDY
05 Interim Provost Dr. Kelli KLEBE
10 Vice Chanc Admin & Finance Charles LITCHFIELD
111 Vice Chanc Univ Advancement Martin WOOD
32 Vice Chanc Student Affairs Carlos GARCIA
20 Assoc VC Academic Affairs Dr. Susan TAYLOR
18 Chief Facilities/Physical Plant Kent MARSH
43 Assistant Legal Counsel Tia LUBER
13 AVC Info Technology/CIO Harper JOHNSON
46 Assoc Vice Chanc Research Dr. Jessi L. SMITH
25 Director of Sponsored Programs Gwen GENNARO
09 Director of Institutional Research Dr. Robyn MARSCHKE
15 Asst Vice Chanc Human Resources Laura ALEXANDER
19 Director Public Safety Marc PINO
37 Director Financial Aid Jevita ROGERS
26 Asst VC Marketing Communications Chris VALENTINE
38 Director Student Counseling Dr. Benek ALTAYLI
41 Director of Athletics Nathan GIBSON
29 Director Alumni Relations Joanna BEAN
35 Dean of Students Amanda ALLEE
49 Dean of Letters/Arts/Science Dr. Lynn VIDLER
50 Dean of Business Dr. Karen MARKEL
53 Dean of Education Dr. Valerie CONLEY
54 Dean of Engineering Dr. Don RABERN
80 Dean of Public Affairs Dr. George REED
66 Dean Nursing/Health Sciences Dr. Kevin LAUDNER
58 Dean of Graduate School Vacant
08 Dean of Library Seth PORTER
39 Director Campus Housing Ralph GIESE
06 Registrar Tracy BARBER
07 Dir of Admissions/Recruitment Chris BEISWANGER
04 Executive Asst to the Chancellor Elizabeth WYATT
105 Director Web Services Craig DECKER
40 Director of Bookstore Paul DENISTON
104 Director Study Abroad Dr. Mandy HANSEN
106 Director of Extended Studies Candida BENNETT
30 Director of Development Melinda HAGEMANN
100 Chief of Staff Andrea CORDOVA
28 Interim Assoc Vice Chanc Diversity Stephany ROSE SPAULDING
84 Sr Exec Dir of Enrollment Mgmt Mathew COX
86 Director of Partnerships & Govt Jenifer FURDA
91 Dir Networks & Infrastructure Greg WILLIAMS

*University of Colorado Denver | Anschutz Medical Campus (D)

P.O. Box 173364, Denver CO 80217
County: Denver FICE Identification: 004508
Unit ID: 126562
Telephone: (303) 556-2400 Carnegie Class: DU-Highest
FAX Number: N/A Calendar System: Semester
URL: www.ucdenver.edu
Established: 1912 Annual Undergrad Tuition & Fees (In-State): $9,401
Enrollment: 24,723 Coed
Affiliation or Control: State IRS Status: 501(c)3
Highest Offering: Doctorate
Accreditation: HLC, AA, ARCPA, CACREP, CAMPEP, CLPSY, DENT, DMS, HSA, IPSY, LSAR, MED, MFCD, MIDWF, NURSE, PAST, PH, PHAR, PLNG, PTA, SCPSY, SPAA

02 Chancellor - CU Denver Dr. Michelle MARKS
02 Chancellor - CU Anschutz Med Campus Mr. Donald M. ELLIMAN, JR.
17 VP Health Affairs/Exec VC AMC Ms. Lilly MARKS
46 Vice Chancellor for Research Dr. Thomas FLAIG
10 Sr Vice Chanc Admin/Finance & CFO Ms. Jennifer SOBANET
63 VC Health Affairs/Dean of Medicine Dr. John REILLY
26 Int Vice Chanc Univ Communications Ms. Karen KLIMCZAK
05 Provost & VC Academic/Student Affs Dr. Roderick NAIRN
111 Vice Chanc of Advancement Anschutz Mr. Scott ARTHUR
111 Vice Chanc of Advancement Denver Ms. Melissa BALDWIN
32 Int VProv/SVC Student Success Ms. Alana JONES
52 Dean School of Dental Medicine Dr. Denise KASSEBAUM
66 Dean College of Nursing Dr. Elias PROVENCIO-VASQUEZ
67 Dean School of Pharmacy Dr. Ralph ALTIERE
69 Dean CO School of Public Health Dr. David GOFF
58 Interim Dean Graduate School Dr. Terry POTTER
64 Dean College of Arts/Media Dr. Laurence KAPTAIN
80 Dean School of Public Affairs Dr. Paul TESKE
49 Dean College Liberal Arts & Sci Dr. Pamela JANSMA
48 Dean College of Arch/Planning Mr. Mark GELERNTER
50 Dean Business School Ms. Sueann AMBRON
53 Dean School of Education Dr. Rebecca KANTOR
54 Dean College of Engineering Dr. Marc INGBER
88 Assoc Vice Chancellor for Research Dr. Robert DAMRAUER
20 Assoc VC Academic Affairs Dr. Laura GOODWIN
28 Assoc VC Diversity/Inclusion Dr. Brenda ALLEN
21 Assoc VC Finance/Controller Ms. E. Kim HUBER
18 Assoc VC Facilities Management Mr. David C. TURNQUIST
20 Assoc VC of Academic Planning Dr. Terry POTTER
15 Assoc VC Human Resources Ms. Carolyn BROWNAWELL
13 Asst VC Information Technology Svcs Mr. Russell POOLE
106 Asst VC Acad Tech/Extended Learning Mr. Robert TOLSMA
84 Asst VC UG Admissions/K-12 Outreach Mr. Chris DOWEN
09 Asst VC Institutional Research Dr. Christine STROUP-BENHAM
121 Asst VC Student Success Ms. Peggy LORE
88 Interim Asst VC University Life Mr. Sam KIM
06 Registrar Ms. Ingrid ESCHHOLZ
08 Director Auraria Library Dr. Mary SOMERVILLE
08 Interim Dir Health Sciences Library Ms. Melissa DESANTIS
27 Director PR/Media Relations Vacant
37 Director Financial Aid Svcs Mr. Justin JARAMILLO
19 Chief of Police Mr. Doug ABRAHAM
29 Director Alumni Relations Ms. Joy FRENCH
43 Assistant University Counsel Mr. Christopher PUCKETT
23 AVC of Health for Student Success Dr. Kristin KUSHMIDER
104 Director International Education Mr. John SUNNYGARD
45 Chief Institutional Planning Vacant

University of Denver (E)

2199 S. University Blvd., Denver CO 80208-0001
County: Denver FICE Identification: 001371
Unit ID: 127060
Telephone: (303) 871-2000 Carnegie Class: DU-Higher
FAX Number: (303) 871-3301 Calendar System: Quarter
URL: www.du.edu
Established: 1864 Annual Undergrad Tuition & Fees: $53,775
Enrollment: 13,856 Coed
Affiliation or Control: Independent Non-Profit IRS Status: 501(c)3
Highest Offering: Doctorate
Accreditation: HLC, ART, CAEP, CEA, CLPSY, COPSY, IPSY, LAW, LIB, MPCAC, MUS, SCPSY, SW

01 Chancellor Dr. Jeremy HAEFNER
05 Provost & Exec Vice Chancellor Dr. Mary CLARK
43 Vice Chanc Legal Affs/Gen Counsel Mr. Paul H. CHAN
32 Vice Chancellor Student Affairs Mr. Todd ADAMS
10 SVC Business/Financial Affairs Ms. Leslie BRUNELLI
100 Chief of Staff/Sr Vice Chancellor Dr. Nancy NICELY
41 Vice Chanc Athletics and Recreation Mr. Karlton CREECH
111 Senior VC University Advancement Ms. Val OTTEN
26 Vice Chancellor Communications Ms. Renea MORRIS
13 Vice Chancellor/Chief Info Officer Mr. Russell KAURLOTO
84 Vice Chancellor for Enrollment Mr. Todd RINEHART
37 Assoc Vice Chanc Financial Aid Mr. John E. GUDVANGEN
88 Director of Chancellor Engagement Ms. Allison RIOLA
20 Vice Provost Academic Program Dr. Jennifer KARAS
07 AVC Enroll/Dir Undergrad Admissions Vacant
35 AVC Student Affs/Inclusive Excel Dr. Niki LATINO
88 Assoc Vice Chanc Inst Effectiveness Dr. Niki LATINO
86 Assoc VC Government/Cmty Relations Ms. Stephanie O'MALLEY
28 VC Diversity/Equity/Inclusion Dr. Chris M. WHITT
58 Senior Vice Prov Research/Grad Ed Dr. Corinne LENGSFELD
08 Dean/Dir University Libraries Mr. Michael LEVINE-CLARK
34 Dean CO Women's College Dr. Ann AYERS
20 Senior Assoc Provost Academic Admin Dr. Linda KOSTEN
88 Assoc Vice Chanc Global Networks Mr. Brandon BUZBEE
30 Asst Vice Chanc Development Ms. Lissy GARRISON
06 Registrar Mr. Dennis M. BECKER
21 Controller Mr. Andrew CULLEN
29 Dir Alumni/Career/Prof Development Ms. Cindy HYMAN
22 Dir Diversity & Equal Opportunity Dr. Kristin DEAL
18 Assoc Vice Chancellor Facilities Mr. James ROSNER
09 Asst Provost Institutional Research Mr. Mike FURNO
15 Int Vice Chanc Human Resources Mr. Jerron LOWE
19 Int Director Campus Safety Mr. Mike HOLT
113 Dir Student Financial Services Ms. Janet BURKHARDT
91 Asst Vice Chanc Enterprise Services Mr. Rohini ANANTHAKRISHNAN
38 Exec Dir Health/Counseling Center Dr. Michael J. LAFARR
54 Dean Engr/Computer Science Mr. J.B HOLSTON
79 Dean Arts/Humanities/Social Science Dr. Daniel MCINTOSH
81 Dean Chemistry/Biochemistry Dr. Andrei KUTATELADZE
50 Dean College of Business Mr. Vivek CHOUDHURY
61 Dean College of Law Dr. Bruce SMITH
82 Dean Graduate Sch of Intl Studies Mr. Fritz MAYER
70 Dean Graduate School of Social Work Dr. Amanda MCBRIDE
55 Dean University College Mr. Michael MCGUIRE
53 Dean College of Education Dr. Karen RILEY
88 Director Newman Center Ms. Andryn ARITHSON
88 Exec Dir Conference Event Services Ms. Amanda FUDALA
57 Director School of Art/Art History Dr. Annabeth HEADRICK
101 Secretary of the Institution/Board Ms. Nancy NICELY
105 Senior Digital Design and Architect Mr. Matt ESCHENBAUM
88 Director University Teaching Ms. Virgina PITTS
108 Director of Assessment Dr. Christina PAGUYO

University of Northern Colorado (F)

501 20th Street, Greeley CO 80639-6900
County: Weld FICE Identification: 001349
Unit ID: 127741
Telephone: (970) 351-1890 Carnegie Class: DU-Mod
FAX Number: (970) 351-1880 Calendar System: Semester
URL: www.unco.edu
Established: 1889 Annual Undergrad Tuition & Fees (In-State): $10,062
Enrollment: 11,460 Coed
Affiliation or Control: State IRS Status: 501(c)3
Highest Offering: Doctorate
Accreditation: HLC, AUD, CAATE, CACREP, CEA, COPSY, DIETD, DIETI, IPSY, MUS, NURSE, PH, SCPSY, SP, THEA

01 President Mr. Andrew FEINSTEIN
05 Provost/Vice Pres Academic Affairs Dr. Mark ANDERSON
10 Sr Vice Pres/Chief Finance Officer Ms. Michelle QUINN

43 Vice President/General Counsel .... Mr. Dan SATRIANA
111 VP for Advancement .... Ms. Allie STEG HASKETT
32 VP Student Affairs/Campus Cmty .... Dr. Katrina RODRIGUEZ
58 Dean Grad School .... Ms. Linda BLACK
29 AVP Alumni Relations .... Ms. Lyndsey CRUM
20 Ast VP Undergrad Stds/Dean Univ Col .... Vacant
114 Asst Vice Pres Budgets/Analysis .... Ms. Susan SIMMERS
13 Asst Vice President Info Technology .... Mr. Bret NABER
110 Asst VP for Development .... Mr. Ben BARNHART
84 Asst Vice Pres for Enrollment Mgmt .... Mr. Tobias GUZMAN
26 AVP Marketing .... Mr. Jason HUGHES
28 AVP for Equity and Inclusion .... Ms. Fleurette KING
79 Dean Humanities/Social Sciences .... Dr. Laura CONNOLLY
50 Dean Business .... Dr. Paul BOBROWSKI
53 Dean Education/Behavioral Sciences .... Dr. Eugene SHEEHAN
76 Dean Natural & Health Sciences .... Dr. Englert BURKHARD
57 Dean Performing Visual Arts .... Dr. Leo WELCH
08 Dean University Libraries .... Ms. Helen REED
35 Dean of Students .... Dr. Gardiner TUCKER
102 President University Foundation .... Mr. Rod ESCH
06 Registrar .... Mr. Charlie COUCH
07 Director of Admissions .... Dr. Sean M. BROGHAMMER
25 AVP Sponsored Pgms/Research .... Dr. Robert HOUSER
37 Dir Student Financial Resources .... Mr. Marty SOMERO
36 Director of Career Services .... Ms. Renee WELCH
15 Director of Human Resources .... Mr. Marshall PARKS
18 Director Facilities Management .... Mr. Kirk LEICHLITER
41 Director of Athletics .... Mr. Darren DUNN
39 Director of Residential Education .... Mr. Montez BUTTS
38 Director Student Counseling .... Ms. Kim WILCOX
19 Chief of University Police .... Mr. Dennis PUMPHREY
44 Director of Annual Giving .... Vacant
27 Dir News & Public Relations .... Mr. Nate HAAS
96 Director of Purchasing .... Ms. Cristal SWAIN
85 Director Ctr for International Educ .... Ms. Maureen ULEVICH
104 Director Study Abroad .... Ms. Teneisha ELLIS
108 Director Institutional Assessment .... Ms. Kim BLACK
04 Exec Assistant to President .... Ms. Lori RILEY
100 Chief of Staff .... Ms. Gloria REYNOLDS
105 Director Web Services .... Mr. Jesse CLARK
106 Dir Online Education/E-learning .... Ms. Nancy RUBIN
22 Dir Affirmative Action/EEO .... Mr. Larry LOFTEN

U.S. Career Institute (A)

2001 Lowe Street, Fort Collins CO 80525
County: Larimer | Identification: 666776
Telephone: (970) 207-4500 | Carnegie Class: Not Classified
FAX Number: (970) 223-1678 | Calendar System: Other
URL: www.uscareerinstitute.edu
Established: 1981 | Annual Undergrad Tuition & Fees: N/A
Enrollment: N/A | Coed
Affiliation or Control: Proprietary | IRS Status: Proprietary
Highest Offering: Associate Degree
Accreditation: DEAC

01 President .... Mr. Earl WESTON
32 Vice Pres Student Affairs/Marketing .... Ms. Holly COOK
05 Vice Pres of Academics/Compliance .... Ms. Janet PERRY
106 Dean of Curriculum .... Ms. Leslie BALLENTINE
07 Director Admissions/Student Rels .... Ms. Jennifer MANNS

Western Colorado Community College-Tilman M. Bishop Campus (B)

2508 Blichmann Avenue, Grand Junction CO 81505
Telephone: (970) 255-2600 | Identification: 770030
Accreditation: &HLC

Western Colorado University (C)

1 Western Way, Gunnison CO 81231-0001
County: Gunnison | FICE Identification: 001372
Unit ID: 128391
Telephone: (970) 943-0120 | Carnegie Class: Masters/S
FAX Number: (970) 943-7069 | Calendar System: Semester
URL: www.western.edu
Established: 1901 | Annual Undergrad Tuition & Fees (In-State): $10,646
Enrollment: 3,203 | Coed
Affiliation or Control: State | IRS Status: 501(c)3
Highest Offering: Master's
Accreditation: HLC, MUS

01 Interim President .... Ms. Nancy CHISHOLM
11 Exec Vice Pres and COO .... Mr. Brad BACA
05 Vice Pres for Academic Affairs .... Dr. Bill NIEMI
111 Vice Pres Advancement .... Mr. Mike LAPLANTE
10 VP Finance & Administration/CFO .... Ms. Julie BACA
121 VP Student Success/Enrollment .... Dr. Abel CHAVEZ
32 VP Student Affairs/Dean of Students .... Mr. Gary PIERSON
20 Assoc Vice Pres Academic Affairs .... Dr. Kevin ALEXANDER
35 AVP Student Affairs/Title IX Admin .... Mr. Chris LUEKENGA
06 Registrar .... Ms. Laurel BECKER
37 Director of Financial Aid .... Ms. Carrie SHAW
104 Dir Intl Student Pgms/Study Abroad .... Ms. Katie WHEATON
41 Athletic Director .... Mr. Miles VAN HEE
15 Director of Human Resources .... Ms. Kim GAILEY
40 Director Retail Operations .... Ms. Teri HAUS
13 Chief Information Ofcr/IT Director .... Mr. Chad ROBINSON
08 Director Library Services .... Mr. Dustin FIFE
39 Director of Residence Life .... Ms. Shelley JANSEN
36 Career Services Coordinator .... Mr. Craig BEEBE
29 Director of Alumni Relations .... Ms. Ann JOHNSTON
44 Director Annual & Special Gifts .... Mr. Tom BURGRAFF
28 Director of Multicultural Center .... Ms. Sally ROMERO
07 Dir Recruitment/Admissions .... Ms. Lauren SHONDECK
96 Business Services Manager .... Ms. Sherry FORD
04 Admin Assistant to the President .... Ms. Joy KEAN
105 Director Web Services .... Mr. RJ TONEY
106 Director Online Education .... Mr. Dustin FIFE
18 Chief Facilities/Physical Plant Ofc .... Mr. Bryce HANNA
19 Director Security/Safety .... Mr. Nathan KUBES
25 Chief Contract Grants Admin .... Ms. Janice WELBORN
50 Dean School of Business .... Mr. Peter SHERMAN

CONNECTICUT

Albertus Magnus College (D)

700 Prospect Street, New Haven CT 06511-1189
County: New Haven | FICE Identification: 001374
Unit ID: 128498
Telephone: (203) 773-8550 | Carnegie Class: Masters/M
FAX Number: (203) 773-9539 | Calendar System: Semester
URL: www.albertus.edu
Established: 1925 | Annual Undergrad Tuition & Fees: $35,410
Enrollment: 1,384 | Coed
Affiliation or Control: Independent Non-Profit | IRS Status: 501(c)3
Highest Offering: Master's
Accreditation: EH, ACATE, IACBE

01 President .... Dr. Marc M. CAMILLE
05 Vice Pres Academic Affairs .... Dr. Sean P. O'CONNELL
10 Int Vice Pres Finance/Treasurer .... Ms. JoAnne WILLIAMS
13 VP Information Technology Services .... Dr. Steven GSTALDER
32 Vice President for Student Services .... Mr. Andrew FOSTER
84 VP Enrollment Mgmt & Marketing .... Ms. Andrea E. KOVACS
111 Vice President for Advancement .... Ms. Mary YOUNG
88 Executive Director College Events .... Ms. Carolyn A. BEHAN KRAUS
35 Asst Dean Campus Act/Orientation .... Ms. Erin MORRELL
21 Controller .... Mr. David LAVALLEY
06 Registrar .... Mrs. Melissa DELUCIA
113 Bursar .... Mr. Terence MCPARTLAND
08 Director Library/Information Svcs .... Vacant
09 Dir Inst Research & Assessment .... Mr. Jeffrey E. LUOMA
37 Director Financial Aid .... Mrs. Michelle COCHRAN
41 Director of Athletics .... Mr. James ABROMAITIS
58 Director MALS Program .... Vacant
121 Director of Academic Advising .... Ms. Heather WOTTON
92 Co-Director of Honors Program .... Mr. Jonathan SOZEK
92 Co-Director of Honors Program .... Vacant
11 Asst VP Operations .... Mr. James A. SCHAFRICK
15 Director Human Resources .... Ms. Renee SULLIVAN
36 Director Career Services .... Mr. Patrick CLIFFORD
42 Coord of Dominican Ministries .... Ms. Hallie DOUGLAS
18 Supervisor of Facilities Services .... Mr. Dan SECORE
04 Administrative Asst to President .... Ms. Lynne M. HENNESSY
07 Director of Admissions .... Mr. Ben AMARONE
107 Dean Prof & Graduate Studies .... Ms. Annette BOSLEY-BOYCE
29 Director Alumni & Parent Engagement .... Ms. Anissa CONNOR
39 Director Resident Life & Community .... Ms. Haley MCCONVILLE
44 Director Annual & Individual Giving .... Ms. Siobhan LIDINGTON
105 Director Web Services .... Mr. Daniel ALVES
108 Director Institutional Assessment .... Mr. Jeffrey LUOMA
19 Director Security/Safety .... Mr. Zachariah MIHALY
50 Dean of Business .... Mr. William ANISKOVICH
96 Director of Purchasing .... Mr. James SCHAFRICK

Charter Oak State College (E)

55 Paul Manafort Drive, New Britain CT 06053-2142
County: Hartford | FICE Identification: 029171
Unit ID: 128780
Telephone: (860) 515-3800 | Carnegie Class: Bac-A&S
FAX Number: (860) 606-9615 | Calendar System: Other
URL: www.charteroak.edu
Established: 1973 | Annual Undergrad Tuition & Fees (In-State): $8,553
Enrollment: 1,634 | Coed
Affiliation or Control: State | IRS Status: 501(c)3
Highest Offering: Master's
Accreditation: EH, CAHIIM, NURSE

01 President .... Mr. Edward KLONOSKI
05 Provost .... Dr. David FERREIRA
10 Chief Financial/Administrative Ofcr .... Mr. Michael J. MORIARTY
13 Chief Information Officer .... Vacant
09 Dir Institutional Effectiveness .... Mr. Michael BRODERICK
06 Registrar .... Ms. Jennifer WASHINGTON
37 Dir Financial Aid/Veterans Benefits .... Mr. Ralph BRASURE, III
20 Director Academic Services .... Ms. Wanda WARSHAUER
07 Director Admissions .... Ms. Lori GAGNE PENDLETON
88 Dir Prior Learning Assessment Pgm .... Ms. Linda WILDER
26 Director Marketing/Public Relations .... Ms. Carolyn HEBERT
04 Administrative Asst to President .... Ms. Carol HALL
30 Assoc Director Development .... Ms. Carol HALL
105 Web Developer .... Mr. Jon ELLIS
15 Director Personnel Services .... Ms. Rowena MCGOLDRICK
29 Director Alumni Relations .... Ms. Carol HALL

*Connecticut Board of Regents for Higher Education (F)

61 Woodland Street, Hartford CT 06105-2345
County: Hartford | Identification: 666655
Telephone: (860) 723-0000 | Carnegie Class: N/A
FAX Number: (860) 723-0009
URL: www.ct.edu

01 President CTCU .... Mr. Mark E. OJAKIAN
05 Provost/SVP Acad & Student Affairs .... Dr. Jane McBride GATES
88 VP for CT State Universities .... Dr. Elsa NUNEZ
88 VP for Cmty Colleges at CT BOR .... Vacant
15 VP for Human Resources .... Mr. Andrew KRIPP
18 VP Facilities/RE/Infrastruct Plng .... Mr. Keith EPSTEIN
10 Chief Financial Officer .... Mr. Benjamin BARNES
13 Chief Information Officer .... Mr. Joseph TOLISANO
101 Assoc Director Board Affairs .... Ms. Erin FITZGERALD
04 Admin Assistant to the President .... Ms. Victoria Lee THOMAS
100 Chief of Staff .... Dr. Alice PRITCHARD
26 Asst Dir Public Relations/Marketing .... Ms. Terri RAIMONDI
09 Director of Institutional Research .... Dr. William GAMMELL
43 Dir Legal Services/General Counsel .... Ms. Ernestine WEAVER
27 Director of Communications .... Ms. Leigh APPLEBY

*Central Connecticut State University (G)

1615 Stanley Street, New Britain CT 06050-4010
County: Hartford | FICE Identification: 001378
Unit ID: 128771
Telephone: (860) 832-3000 | Carnegie Class: Masters/L
FAX Number: (860) 832-3033 | Calendar System: Semester
URL: www.ccsu.edu
Established: 1849 | Annual Undergrad Tuition & Fees (In-State): $11,502
Enrollment: 10,652 | Coed
Affiliation or Control: State | IRS Status: 501(c)3
Highest Offering: Doctorate
Accreditation: EH, ANEST, CAATE, CACREP, CAEPN, CONST, EXSC, MFCD, MUS, NAIT, NURSE, SW

02 President .... Dr. Zulma R. TORO
04 Exec Assistant to the President .... Ms. Susan MATTERAZZO
05 Interim Provost/VPAA .... Dr. Kimberly KOSTELIS
32 Interim VP Student Affairs .... Dr. John TULLY
35 Associate Dean Student Affairs .... Mr. Ramon HERNANDEZ
58 Assoc VP Graduate Studies/Research .... Dr. Christina ROBINSON
43 University Counsel .... Ms. Carolyn MAGNAN
11 Chief Operations Officer .... Mr. Sal CINTORINO
114 Interim Chief Budget Officer .... Ms. Lisa BUCHER
15 Chief Human Resources Officer .... Mrs. Anna SUSKI-LENCZEWSKI
28 VP for Equity & Inclusion .... Dr. Stacey MILLER
49 Dean Liberal Arts/Soc Sciences .... Dr. Robert WOLFF
50 Dean School of Business .... Dr. Joseph FARHAT
53 Int Dean School Educ/Prof Studies .... Dr. James MULROONEY
54 Int Dean School Engr/Science/Tech .... Dr. Jeremiah JARRETT
104 Dir Center International Education .... Dr. Momar NDIAYE
51 Dir Continuing Educ/Cmty Engagement .... Ms. Christa STERLING
07 Director Admissions & Recruitment .... Mr. Lawrence HALL
41 Interim Director Athletics .... Mr. Thomas PINCINCE
39 Director Residence Life .... Ms. Jean ALICANDRO
19 Interim Director Public Safety .... Mr. Christopher CERVONI
37 Director Financial Aid .... Ms. Keri LUPACHINO
26 Int AVP Marketing & Communications .... Ms. Janice PALMER
08 Director Library Services .... Mr. Carl ANTONUCCI
36 Dir Career Success Center .... Mr. Paul ROSSITTO
23 Dir Student Wellness Svcs .... Dr. Michael RUSSO
06 Registrar .... Mr. Patrick TUCKER
38 Coordinator Office Wellness Educ .... Mr. Jonathan POHL
21 University Controller .... Ms. Julie DEFALCO
96 Contract Compliance/Procurement .... Mr. Charles ZSEBIK
09 Dir Inst Research/Assessment .... Ms. Yvonne KIRBY
13 Chief Info Technology Officer .... Dr. George CLAFFEY
84 Assoc VP Enrollment Management .... Ms. Karissa PECKHAM

*Eastern Connecticut State University (H)

83 Windham Street, Willimantic CT 06226-2295
County: Windham | FICE Identification: 001425
Unit ID: 129215
Telephone: (860) 465-5000 | Carnegie Class: Masters/S
FAX Number: (860) 465-4690 | Calendar System: Semester
URL: www.easternct.edu
Established: 1889 | Annual Undergrad Tuition & Fees (In-State): $12,304
Enrollment: 4,644 | Coed
Affiliation or Control: State | IRS Status: 501(c)3
Highest Offering: Master's
Accreditation: EH, CAEPN, SW

02 President .... Dr. Elsa M. NUNEZ
05 Provost .... Dr. William SALKA
10 VP Finance/Administration .... Mr. James R. HOWARTH
32 Vice Pres Student Affairs .... Mr. Walter DIAZ
111 Vice Pres Institutional Advance .... Mr. Kenneth J. DELISA
28 VP Equity & Diversity .... Dr. LaMar COLEMAN
35 Dean of Students .... Ms. Michelle DELANY
13 Chief Information Officer .... Mr. Garry BOZYLINSKY
09 Dean of Academic Analytics .... Dr. Jennifer BROWN
41 Director of Athletics .... Ms. Lori RUNKSMEIER
08 Director of Library Services .... Ms. Janice WILSON

84 Dir of Enrollment Mgmt/Fin Aid ... Mr. Christopher DORSEY
36 Director of Career Services ... Mr. Clifford MARRETT
29 Director of Alumni Affairs ... Mr. Michael STENKO
06 Registrar ... Ms. Jennifer HUOPPI
19 Police Chief & Dir of Public Safety ... Mr. Stephen TAVARES
39 Director Housing/Residence Life ... Ms. Angela BAZIN
40 Director of Bookstore ... Ms. Allyson HALL
42 Director of Campus Ministry ... Rev. Laurence LAPOINTE
18 Dir of Facilities Mgmt/Planning ... Ms. Renee KEECH
26 Director University Relations ... Mr. Edward H. OSBORN
49 Dean of Arts & Sciences ... Dr. Patricia SZCZYS
58 Dean Educ/Prof Studies/Grad Pgm ... Dr. Niti PANDEY
96 Assoc Dir Fiscal Affs/Acquisition ... Ms. Terry O'BRIEN
38 Dir Counseling/Psych Svcs ... Dr. Bryce CRAPSER
07 Director of Admissions ... Mr. Christopher DORSEY
21 University Controller ... Ms. Shirley AUDET
14 Director IT ... Mr. Andrew JOHNSON
110 Director Institutional Advancement ... Mr. Joesph MCGANN
88 Director Energy Institute ... Ms. Lynn STODDARD
15 Chief Human Resources Officer ... Mr. Kenneth DELISA

*Southern Connecticut State University (A)

501 Crescent Street, New Haven CT 06515-0901
County: New Haven — FICE Identification: 001406
Unit ID: 130493
Telephone: (203) 392-7278 — Carnegie Class: Masters/L
FAX Number: N/A — Calendar System: Semester
URL: www.southernct.edu
Established: 1893 — Annual Undergrad Tuition & Fees (In-State): $11,802
Enrollment: 9,331 — Coed
Affiliation or Control: State — IRS Status: 501(c)3
Highest Offering: Doctorate
Accreditation: EH, #CAATE, CACREP, CAEPN, EXSC, LIB, MFCD, MUS, NURSE, PH, SP, SW

02 President ... Dr. Joe BERTOLINO
04 Admin Assistant to the President ... Ms. Charmaine R. LLOYD
05 Provost/Vice Pres Acad Affairs ... Dr. Robert PREVANT
10 EVP for Finance & Administration ... Mr. Mark ROZEWSKI
32 Vice Pres Student Affairs ... Dr. Tracy TYREE
111 Vice President Inst Advancement ... Dr. Michael KINGAN
28 VP of Diversity & Equity Pgm ... Dr. Diane M. ARIZA
84 Assoc VP for Enrollment Management ... Dr. Julie EDSTROM
15 Chief Human Resources Officer ... Dr. Melitha PRZYGODA
18 Assoc VP Capital Budgeting/Fac Ops ... Mr. Eric LESSNE
13 Chief Info Tech Officer ... Dr. Dennis REIMAN
49 Dean School Arts & Sciences ... Dr. Bruce KALK
50 Dean School of Business ... Dr. Jennifer ROBIN
53 Dean School Education ... Dr. Stephen HEGEDUS
58 Dean School Graduate Studies ... Dr. Manohar SINGH
70 Int Dean School Health/Human Svcs ... Dr. Sandra BULMER
41 Director of Athletics ... Mr. Christopher BARKER
26 Director of Public Affairs ... Mr. Patrick DILGER
29 Director Alumni Affairs ... Mr. Gregory BERNARD
07 Director Admissions ... Mr. Alick LETANG
06 Registrar ... Ms. Alicia CARROLL
08 Director of Library Services ... Dr. Clara OGBAA
19 Director of Public Safety ... Mr. Joseph M. DOOLEY
25 Director of Sponsored Research ... Ms. Amy TAYLOR
37 Director of Financial Aid ... Ms. Sage C. STACHOWIAK
23 Director of Health Services ... Dr. Diane S. MORGENTHALER
35 Dean of Student Affairs ... Dr. Jules TETREAULT
88 Assoc VP for Strategic Initiatives ... Dr. Colleen Q. BIELITZ
38 Director of Counseling Services ... Dr. Nick PINKERTON
21 University Controller ... Ms. Loren LOOMIS HUBBELL
92 Director of Honors Program ... Dr. Terese GEMME
94 Director of Women's Studies ... Dr. Yi-Chun Tricia LIN
121 Dir of Academic & Career Advising ... Mr. Harry TWYMAN
39 Director of Residence Life ... Mr. Robert C. DEMEZZO

*Western Connecticut State University (B)

181 White Street, Danbury CT 06810-6885
County: Fairfield — FICE Identification: 001380
Unit ID: 130776
Telephone: (203) 837-8200 — Carnegie Class: Masters/M
FAX Number: (203) 837-8276 — Calendar System: Semester
URL: www.wcsu.edu
Established: 1903 — Annual Undergrad Tuition & Fees (In-State): $11,781
Enrollment: 5,246 — Coed
Affiliation or Control: State — IRS Status: 501(c)3
Highest Offering: Doctorate
Accreditation: EH, ART, CACREP, CAEPN, MUS, NURSE, PH, SW, THEA

02 President ... Dr. John B. CLARK
05 Provost/Vice Pres Academic Affairs ... Dr. Missy ALEXANDER
10 Chief Financial Officer ... Ms. Beatrice FEVRY
32 VP Student Affairs ... Dr. Keith BETTS
111 Int VP of Inst Advancement ... Ms. Lynne LEBARRON
57 Dean of Visual/Performing Arts ... Mr. Brian VERNON
35 Dean of Student Affairs ... Dr. Walter CRAMER
49 Dean Macricostas Sch Arts & Sci ... Dr. Michelle L. BROWN
50 Dean of Ancell Sch of Business ... Dr. David MARTIN
107 Int Dean Sch of Prof Studies ... Dr. Joan PALLADINO
15 Chief Human Resources Officer ... Mr. Frederic W. CRATTY
13 Chief Information Officer ... Mr. John DEROSA
21 Director Fiscal Affairs/Controller ... Mr. Peter ROSA
28 Chief Diversity Officer ... Ms. Jesenia MINIER
06 Registrar ... Mr. Keith R. GAUVIN
08 Director of Library Services ... Ms. Veronica KENAUSIS
09 Director Inst Research/Assessment ... Dr. Jerome WILCOX
25 Director of Grant/Programs ... Ms. Gabrielle E. JAZWIECKI
38 Director of Counseling Svcs ... Dr. Rée GUNTER
37 Director of Financial Aid ... Ms. Melissa STEPHENS
36 Director of Career Services ... Ms. Kathleen LINDENMAYER
88 Special Assistant to the President ... Mr. Paul STEINMETZ
39 Director Housing & Residence Life ... Dr. Ron MASON
35 Dir Center for Student Involvement ... Mr. Dennis LESZKO
41 Director of Athletics ... Ms. Lori MAZZA
29 Director of Alumni Relations ... Mr. Thomas CRUCITTI
07 Director of Admissions ... Mr. Luis SANTIAGO
88 Dir of Planning & Engineering ... Mr. Daniel CASSINELLI
11 Director of Administrative Services ... Ms. Amy LOPEZ
18 Assoc VP Facilities ... Mr. Luigi MARCONE
88 Dir Event & Conf Mgmt ... Mr. John MURPHY
114 Director of Fin Planning & Budgets ... Mr. Mufu WENG
27 Assoc Dir of Public Relations ... Ms. Sherri HILL
19 Chief of Police ... Mr. Roger CONNOR
14 Digital Information Officer ... Ms. Rebecca WOODWARD
04 Exec Asst to President ... Ms. Janet MCKAY
84 Assoc VP Enrollment Services ... Mr. Jay MURRAY
30 Major Gifts Officer ... Ms. Julie PRYOR-BENNETT

*Asnuntuck Community College (C)

170 Elm Street, Enfield CT 06082-3800
County: Hartford — FICE Identification: 011150
Unit ID: 128577
Telephone: (860) 253-3000 — Carnegie Class: Assoc/HVT-High Trad
FAX Number: (860) 253-3014 — Calendar System: Semester
URL: www.asnuntuck.edu
Established: 1972 — Annual Undergrad Tuition & Fees (In-State): $4,556
Enrollment: 1,304 — Coed
Affiliation or Control: State — IRS Status: 501(c)3
Highest Offering: Associate Degree
Accreditation: EH, NAEYC

01 Chief Executive Officer ... Dr. Michelle COACH
04 Exec Asst to Chief Exec Officer ... Ms. Sharntae WILSON
12 Regional President NW Region ... Dr. James P. LOMBELLA
88 Exec Asst to Reg President NW ... Ms. Margaret G. VAN COTT
05 Interim Dean of Academic Affairs ... Dr. Teresa FOLEY
32 Interim Dean of Student Services ... Mr. Tim ST. JAMES
88 Interim Dean of AMTC ... Ms. Mary BIDWELL
15 HR Generalist North Region ... Ms. Erin RANSFORD
11 Associate Dean of Campus Operations ... Mr. Alfredo DIMAURO
10 Assoc Dir Finance/Admin ... Mr. Chad GLABACH
06 Interim Registrar ... Ms. Stacey MUSULIN
88 Interim Assistant Registrar ... Mr. Jeff SHUMAN
37 Interim Director of Financial Aid ... Ms. Beth-Anne EGAN
09 Dir Plng/Rsrch/Inst Effectiveness ... Ms. Caitlin BOGER-HAWKINS
102 Executive Dir of the Foundation ... Mr. Keith MADORE
103 Chief Regional Workforce Dev Ofcr ... Ms. Eileen PELTIER
18 Bldg Superintendent III/Bldg Svcs ... Mr. Joseph MULLER
75 Dir Business/Tech & Industry Trng ... Mr. Gary CARRA
07 Interim Director of Admissions ... Ms. Jennifer MENY
13 Acting Asst Director of IT ... Mr. Charles KNUREK
121 Dir Ctr for Advising/Stdnt Achvmt ... Ms. Jill RUSHBROOK

*Capital Community College (D)

950 Main Street, Hartford CT 06103-1207
County: Hartford — FICE Identification: 007635
Unit ID: 129367
Telephone: (860) 906-5000 — Carnegie Class: Assoc/MT-VT-High Trad
FAX Number: (860) 520-7906 — Calendar System: Semester
URL: www.capitalcc.edu
Established: 1967 — Annual Undergrad Tuition & Fees (In-State): $4,556
Enrollment: 2,715 — Coed
Affiliation or Control: State — IRS Status: 501(c)3
Highest Offering: Associate Degree
Accreditation: EH, ADNUR, EMT, MAC, NAEYC, RAD

02 Chief Executive Officer ... Dr. G. Duncan HARRIS
05 Dean of Academic & Student Affairs ... Dr. Miah LAPIERRE DREGER
32 Associate Dean of Student Affairs ... Mr. Jason SCAPPATICCI
11 Associate Dean of Campus Operations ... Mr. Eduardo MIRANDA
51 Dean Cont Educ/Workforce Dev ... Dr. Linda GUZZO
09 Director of Institutional Research ... Ms. Jenny WANG
10 Director Finance/Administration ... Mr. Ted HALE
06 Registrar ... Mr. Argelio MARRERO
08 Director of Library Services ... Ms. Eileen RHODES
84 Director Student Development Svcs ... Ms. Marsha BALL-DAVIS
37 Director of Financial Aid ... Ms. Margaret MALASPINA
13 Interim Asst Director of IMT ... Ms. Stephanie CALHOUN-WARD
66 Dir Cont Educ Nurse/Allied Health ... Dr. Ruth KREMS
26 Dir of Marketing/Public Relations ... Ms. Vivian NABETA
15 Human Resources Generalist ... Ms. Frances LEON
88 Asst to the Academic Dean ... Mr. Ryan PIERSON
111 Director Institutional Advancement ... Mr. John MCNAMARA
04 Interim Executive Assistant ... Ms. Liza ITURRINO
18 Chief Facilities ... Mr. John BOUDREAU
19 Director Security/Safety ... Mr. James GRIFFIN

*Gateway Community College (E)

20 Church St., New Haven CT 06510-5970
County: New Haven — FICE Identification: 008037
Unit ID: 130396
Telephone: (203) 285-2000 — Carnegie Class: Assoc/MT-VT-High Trad
FAX Number: (203) 285-2018 — Calendar System: Semester
URL: www.gatewayct.edu
Established: 1968 — Annual Undergrad Tuition & Fees (In-State): $4,496
Enrollment: 6,003 — Coed
Affiliation or Control: State — IRS Status: 501(c)3
Highest Offering: Associate Degree
Accreditation: EH, ADNUR, DIETT, DMS, NAEYC, NMT, RAD, RTT, SURGT

02 Chief Executive Officer ... Dr. William T. BROWN
30 Dean of Devel/Community Partnership ... Ms. Mary Ellen CODY
05 Dean of Academics ... Dr. Mark KOSINSKI
51 Dean of Cont Educ/Workforce Develop ... Vacant
15 Regional Human Resources Manager ... Vacant
04 Executive Assistant to President ... Ms. Tanya R. GIBBS
09 Director Institutional Research ... Dr. Vincent P. TONG
26 Assoc Dn Communications/Marketing ... Ms. Evelyn GARD
10 Director Finance & Admin Svcs ... Ms. Jill MCDOWELL
08 Director Library ... Mr. Miguel A. GARCIA, III
36 Director Career Services ... Ms. Leigh ROBERTS
37 Director Financial Aid ... Mr. Raymond ZEEK
124 Int Dir Advising/Retention ... Ms. Kathleen AHERN
32 Director of Student Activities ... Mr. Alfred GUANTE
24 Director of Educational Technology ... Mr. Alfonzo LEWIS
25 Grants Development Specialist ... Ms. Andrea MACNOW
13 Director Information Technology ... Mr. Lawrence SALAY
88 Director Early Learning Center ... Ms. Sarah CHAMBERS
121 Director of Academic Support ... Ms. Clara MENA
50 Chair Business Department ... Vacant
79 Chair Humanities Department ... Ms. Susan CHENARD
83 Chair Social Sciences Department ... Mr. Jonah COHEN
88 Coord Early Childhood Education ... Ms. Carmelita E. VALENCIA-DAYE
88 Coord Drug/Alcohol Rehab Counseling ... Vacant
67 Coordinator Pharmacy Tech Program ... Ms. Louise A. PETROKA
81 Chair Math/Natural Sci Department ... Mr. Rocky TREMBLAY
88 Director Dietetic Technician Pgm ... Ms. Marcia DORAN
76 Director Allied Health ... Ms. Sheila SOLERNOU
54 Dir Engineering/Applied Technology ... Mr. Eric F. FLYNN
18 Chief Facilities/Physical Plant ... Mr. Lucian SIMONE
06 Registrar/Dir Enrollment Mgmt ... Ms. Maribel LOPEZ

*Housatonic Community College (F)

900 Lafayette Boulevard, Bridgeport CT 06604-4704
County: Fairfield — FICE Identification: 004513
Unit ID: 129543
Telephone: (203) 332-5000 — Carnegie Class: Assoc/MT-VT-High Trad
FAX Number: (203) 332-5123 — Calendar System: Semester
URL: www.housatonic.edu
Established: 1967 — Annual Undergrad Tuition & Fees (In-State): $4,496
Enrollment: 3,821 — Coed
Affiliation or Control: State — IRS Status: 501(c)3
Highest Offering: Associate Degree
Accreditation: EH, NAEYC, SURGT

02 Chief Executive Officer ... Dr. Dwayne SMITH
05 Dean of Academic Affairs ... Ms. Robin AVANT
11 Associate Dean of Campus Operations ... Mr. Mario PIERCE
32 Dean of Student Services ... Dr. Kim M. MCGINNIS
20 Dir Academic Advising/Success ... Ms. Jeanine GIBSON
06 Registrar & Director of Enrollment ... Mr. James CONNOLLY
07 Director of Admissions ... Mr. Earl GRAHAM
08 Librarian ... Ms. Shelly STROHM
37 Director of Financial Aid ... Mr. Omar LIVINGSTON
26 Associate Dean Comm & Marketing ... Ms. Evelyn GARD
19 Director of Security ... Mr. Christopher GOUGH
09 Director Institutional Research ... Dr. Vincent TONG
13 Assistant Director of IT ... Mr. Bruce BOMELEY
15 Director of Human Resources ... Ms. Marlene CORDERO
30 Director of Community Campus Rels ... Mr. Richard DUPONT
10 Director of Finance/Admin Svcs ... Ms. Teresa ORAVETZ
18 Coordinator of Facilities ... Vacant
04 Executive Asst to CEO ... Ms. Camilla COSTANTINI
38 Director Counseling/Wellness ... Ms. Lisa SLADE
102 Exec Director of HCC Foundation ... Ms. Kristy JELENIK
121 Director of Academic Support Ctr ... Ms. Marianne TECUN

*Manchester Community College (G)

PO Box 1046, Great Path, Manchester CT 06045-1046
County: Hartford — FICE Identification: 001392
Unit ID: 129695
Telephone: (860) 512-3000 — Carnegie Class: Assoc/MT-VT-High Trad
FAX Number: (860) 512-3631 — Calendar System: Semester
URL: www.manchestercc.edu
Established: 1963 — Annual Undergrad Tuition & Fees (In-State): $4,516
Enrollment: 4,448 — Coed
Affiliation or Control: State — IRS Status: 501(c)3
Highest Offering: Associate Degree
Accreditation: EH, ACFEI, COARC, DA, MUS, NAEYC, OTA, RAD, RTT, SURGT

02 Chief Executive Officer ... Dr. Nicole ESPOSITO
05 Interim Dean Academic Affairs ... Dr. Tuesday COOPER
32 Interim Dean of Student Affairs ... Mr. Peter HARRIS
11 Dean of Administrative Affairs ... Mr. James MCDOWELL
102 Int Executive Dir MCC Foundation ... Ms. Susan ALSTON
51 Dean of Continuing Education ... Vacant
20 Associate Dean of Academic Affairs ... Dr. Pamela MITCHELL
10 Dir Finance & Admin Services ... Ms. Regina FERRANTE
07 Int Assoc Director of Admissions ... Mr. Elijah OLIVER
06 Registrar ... Ms. Anita SPARROW
08 Dir Library Svcs/Educational Tech ... Ms. Deborah HERMAN
13 Director of Information Technology ... Mr. Barry GRANT
09 Director Plng/Research & Assessment ... Mr. David NIELSEN
15 Director of Human Resources ... Ms. Patricia LINDO

18 Dir Facilities Management/ Planning ... Ms. Darlene MANCINI-BROWN
26 Dir Marketing and Public Relations ... Ms. Charlene TAPPAN
37 Director of Financial Aid ... Ms. Anna TORRES
79 Director of Liberal & Creative Arts ... Ms. Samantha GONZALEZ
35 Director of Student Activities ... Mr. Trent J. BARBER
30 Dir of Development & Alumni Affairs ... Ms. Diana REID
38 Dir Counseling and Career Svcs ... Ms. Julie GREENE
84 Dir of Enrollment Management ... Ms. Sara VINCENT
04 Interim Executive Assistant ... Ms. Karyn CASE
103 Assoc Dean Cont Ed/Workforce Dev ... Mr. Miguel PIGOTT
90 Director of Academic Support Ctr ... Mr. Brian CLEARY
28 Chief Diversity Officer ... Ms. Debra FREUND
96 Assoc Director of Purchasing ... Mr. Paul MOUNDS

*Middlesex Community College (A)

100 Training Hill Road, Middletown CT 06457-4889
County: Middlesex FICE Identification: 008038
Unit ID: 129756
Telephone: (860) 343-5800 Carnegie Class: Assoc/MT-VT-Mix Trad/Non
FAX Number: (860) 344-7488 Calendar System: Semester
URL: www.mxcc.edu
Established: 1966 Annual Undergrad Tuition & Fees (In-State): $4,476
Enrollment: 2,106 Coed
Affiliation or Control: State IRS Status: 501(c)3
Highest Offering: Associate Degree
Accreditation: EH, CAHIIM, NAEYC, OPD, RAD

02 Campus CEO ... Dr. Steven MINKLER
05 Dean of Academic & Student Affairs ... Dr. Donna BONTATIBUS
11 Dean of Administration ... Ms. Kimberly HOGAN
32 Assoc Dean of Student Affairs ... Dr. Sara HANSON
04 Executive Assistant to the CEO ... Ms. Corey MARTELL
08 Director of the Learning Commons ... Ms. Melissa BEHNEY
09 Director of Institutional Research ... Dr. Paul CARMICHAEL
13 Director Information Technology ... Ms. Annie SCOTT
84 Director of Enrollment Mgmt ... Dr. Samantha PLOURD
15 Reg Mgr Human Resources ... Ms. Kimberly CAROLINA
37 Director Financial Aid ... Ms. Irene MARTIN
10 Assoc Dir of Finance/Administration ... Ms. Valerie COOPER
124 Retention Specialist ... Ms. Yhara ZELINKA
22 Disability Services Coordinator ... Ms. Hilary PHELPS
06 Registrar ... Ms. Joanne FAUST
18 Chief Facilities/Physical Plant ... Mr. Steven CHESTER

*Naugatuck Valley Community College (B)

750 Chase Parkway, Waterbury CT 06708-3089
County: New Haven FICE Identification: 006982
Unit ID: 129729
Telephone: (203) 575-8044 Carnegie Class: Assoc/MT-VT-High Trad
FAX Number: (203) 575-8096 Calendar System: Semester
URL: www.nv.edu
Established: 1964 Annual Undergrad Tuition & Fees (In-State): $4,516
Enrollment: 5,083 Coed
Affiliation or Control: State IRS Status: 501(c)3
Highest Offering: Associate Degree
Accreditation: EH, ADNUR, COARC, NAEYC, PTAA, RAD

02 Chief Executive Officer ... Dr. Lisa DRESDNER
11 Interim Dean of Administration ... Ms. Dana ELM
05 Dean of Academic Affairs ... Dr. Justin MOORE
30 Associate Dean of Development ... Ms. Angela CHAPMAN
32 Dean of Student Services ... Ms. Sarah GAGER
31 Dean of Community Engagement ... Vacant
13 Assoc Dean Information Technology ... Vacant
06 Registrar ... Ms. Lourdes CRUZ
37 Director of Financial Aid ... Ms. Catherine HARDY
84 Assoc Dean of Enrollment Management ... Ms. Noel ROSAMILIO
22 Affirmative Action Officer ... Vacant
08 Director Learning Resource Ctr ... Ms. Jaime HAMMOND
10 Director of Finance/Admin Services ... Ms. Lisa PALEN
35 Director of Student Activities ... Ms. Karen BLAKE
18 Chief Facilities/Physical Plant ... Vacant
09 Int Dir of Institutional Research ... Ms. Sohair OMAR
121 Dir of Student Development Services ... Ms. Bonnie GOULET
15 Director of Human Resources ... Vacant
26 Director of Marketing ... Ms. Sydney VOGHEL-OCHS

*Northwestern Connecticut Community-Technical College (C)

Park Place E, Winsted CT 06098-1798
County: Litchfield FICE Identification: 001398
Unit ID: 130040
Telephone: (860) 738-6300 Carnegie Class: Assoc/MT-VT-Mix Trad/Non
FAX Number: (860) 738-6488 Calendar System: Semester
URL: www.nwcc.commnet.edu/
Established: 1965 Annual Undergrad Tuition & Fees (In-State): $4,516
Enrollment: 1,228 Coed
Affiliation or Control: State IRS Status: 501(c)3
Highest Offering: Associate Degree
Accreditation: EH, ADNUR, NAEYC

02 President ... Dr. Michael ROOKE
05 Dean of Academic & Student Affairs ... Dr. David FERREIRA
07 Associate Dean of Enrollment ... Ms. Kalia KELLOGG
11 Associate Dean of Campus Operations ... Mr. Brian PLESSINGER
08 Director of Library Services ... Mr. James PATTERSON
06 Registrar ... Ms. Debra ZAVATKAY
15 Director of Human Resources ... Ms. Wendy BOVIA
32 Dir of Student Development ... Ms. Ruth GONZALEZ
09 Director of Institutional Research ... Ms. Caitlin BOGER-HAWKINS
26 Director Marketing/Public Relations ... Mr. Grantley ADAMS
10 Director Financial/Admin Services ... Ms. Kimberly DRAGAN
04 Admin Assistant to the President ... Ms. Susan A. STILLER
13 Chief Information Technology Ofcr ... Mr. Richard COUTANT

*Norwalk Community College (D)

188 Richards Avenue, Norwalk CT 06854-1655
County: Fairfield FICE Identification: 001399
Unit ID: 130004
Telephone: (203) 857-7000 Carnegie Class: Assoc/MT-VT-Mix Trad/Non
FAX Number: (203) 857-7287 Calendar System: Semester
URL: www.norwalk.edu
Established: 1961 Annual Undergrad Tuition & Fees (In-State): $4,546
Enrollment: 4,420 Coed
Affiliation or Control: State IRS Status: 501(c)3
Highest Offering: Associate Degree
Accreditation: EH, ADNUR, COARC, MAC, NAEYC, PTAA

02 Chief Executive Officer ... Ms. Cheryl DEVONISH
32 Dean of Students ... Dr. Kellie BYRD DANSO
05 Interim Dean of Academics ... Dr. Michael BUTCARIS
30 Executive Director of Development ... Ms. Carrie BERNIER
103 Assoc Dean Ext Stds/Workforce Dev ... Vacant
10 Director of Finance/Administration ... Ms. Carrie MCGEE-YUROFF
08 Director of Library Services ... Ms. Linda LERMAN
37 Director Financial Aid ... Ms. Fany STUBBS
66 Int Director of Nursing Education ... Dr. Ezechiel DOMINIQUE
06 Registrar ... Mr. Steve MENDES
15 Assoc Director Human Resources ... Vacant
26 Director of Public Relations ... Vacant
38 Director Student Counseling ... Ms. Catherine MILLER
07 Director of Admissions ... Mr. Curtis ANTRUM
10 Director Finance/Administration ... Vacant
18 Chief Facilities/Physical Plant ... Mr. Craig CARLSON
04 Executive Asst to CEO ... Mrs. Thomasina L. CALISE
09 Director of Institutional Research ... Ms. Rachael DIPIETRO

*Quinebaug Valley Community College (E)

742 Upper Maple Street, Danielson CT 06239-1440
County: Windham FICE Identification: 010530
Unit ID: 130217
Telephone: (860) 932-4000 Carnegie Class: Assoc/HT-High Trad
FAX Number: (860) 932-4306 Calendar System: Semester
URL: www.qvcc.edu
Established: 1971 Annual Undergrad Tuition & Fees (In-State): $4,506
Enrollment: 1,161 Coed
Affiliation or Control: State IRS Status: 501(c)3
Highest Offering: Associate Degree
Accreditation: EH, MLTAB, NAEYC

02 Interim Chief Executive Officer ... Dr. Rose R. ELLIS
05 Dean Academic Affs & Student Svcs ... Dr. Joesph CULLEN
11 Dean of Administrative Services ... Vacant
08 Director of Library Services ... Ms. M'Lyn HINES
37 Director of Student Financial Aid ... Vacant
09 Director of Institutional Research ... Mr. Patrick KELLER
10 Dir Finance/Administrative Svcs ... Ms. Alessandra LUNDBERG
18 Chief Facilities/Physical Plant ... Mr. Martin CHARETTE
26 Chief Public Relations Officer ... Ms. Susan BREAULT
111 Dir of Institutional Advancement ... Ms. Monique WOLANIN
32 Dir of Student Services/Registrar ... Mr. Matt SOUCY
27 Coordinator of Marketing ... Ms. Paige CARITO
07 Associate Director of Admissions ... Ms. Sarah HENDRICK
04 Administrative Asst to President ... Ms. Jennifer GREEN
13 Chief Info Technology Officer (CIO) ... Mr. Jarrod BOREK
15 Director Personnel Services ... Ms. Karla DESJARDINS
29 Director Alumni Relations ... Ms. Elle GOSLIN
06 Registrar ... Ms. Nicole MARCOUX-BOWEN

*Three Rivers Community College (F)

574 New London Turnpike, Norwich CT 06360
County: New London FICE Identification: 009765
Unit ID: 129808
Telephone: (860) 215-9000 Carnegie Class: Assoc/MT-VT-High Trad
FAX Number: (860) 215-9901 Calendar System: Semester
URL: www.threerivers.edu
Established: 1963 Annual Undergrad Tuition & Fees (In-State): $4,556
Enrollment: 3,160 Coed
Affiliation or Control: State IRS Status: 501(c)3
Highest Offering: Associate Degree
Accreditation: EH, ADNUR, NAEYC

02 President ... Dr. Mary Ellen JUKOSKI
05 Interim Dean Academics/Student Svcs ... Dr. Kem BARFIELD
11 Dean of Administration/IT ... Mr. Stephen H. GOETCHIUS
13 Acting Director of IT ... Mr. Skye COHEN
111 Dir Institutional Advancement ... Ms. Betty BAILLARGEON
06 Registrar ... Mr. Kevin KELLY
15 Interim Dean Human Resources Dept ... Mr. Stephen GOETCHIUS
32 Assoc Dean of Student Services ... Ms. Jodi CALVERT
10 Dir of Finance/Admin Svcs ... Ms. Gayle O'NEILL
08 Director Library Services ... Ms. Pamela WILLIAMS
37 Actg Dir Student Financial Aid ... Mr. Kenneth BRIGGS
18 Director of Facilities ... Mr. Arnie DELAROSSA
09 Office of Institutional Research ... Dr. Kem BARFIELD
26 Dir of Marketing/Public Relations ... Ms. Kathryn GAFFNEY
90 Dir of Educational Technology ... Dr. Kem BARFIELD
04 Exec Assistant to President ... Ms. April HODSON
07 Acting Director of Admissions ... Mr. Jonathan LAMIOTTE
35 Director of Student Programs ... Ms. Alycia ZIEGLER
103 Acting Director of Non-Credit Pgms ... Ms. Erin SULLIVAN

*Tunxis Community College (G)

271 Scott Swamp Road, Farmington CT 06032-3187
County: Hartford FICE Identification: 009764
Unit ID: 130606
Telephone: (860) 773-1300 Carnegie Class: Assoc/MT-VT-High Trad
FAX Number: N/A Calendar System: Semester
URL: www.tunxis.edu/
Established: 1969 Annual Undergrad Tuition & Fees (In-State): $4,556
Enrollment: 3,365 Coed
Affiliation or Control: State IRS Status: 501(c)3
Highest Offering: Associate Degree
Accreditation: EH, ACBSP, DA, DH, NAEYC

02 Regional President ... Dr. James P. LOMBELLA
10 Chief Regional Fiscal Officer ... Mr. Gennaro DEANGELIS
11 Campus CEO ... Dr. Darryl REOME
05 Interim Dean of Academic Affairs ... Ms. Amy FEEST
09 Director of Institutional Research ... Dr. Qing Lin MACK
21 Dir Finance/Administrative Services ... Ms. Nancy ESCHENBRENNER
32 Dean of Student Affairs ... Mr. Charles CLEARY
13 Interim Director of Info Technology ... Mr. Peter HAFFNER
15 Regional HR Manager ... Ms. Wendy BOVIA
18 Director of Facilities ... Mr. John LODOVICO
26 Interim Director Marketing & PR ... Ms. Melissa LAMAR
06 Interim Registrar ... Ms. Magaly CORREA
12 Director Tunxis@Bristol ... Mr. Victor MITCHELL
35 Director of Student Activities ... Mr. Christopher LAPORTE
88 Director Early Childhood Center ... Ms. Debra COLLINS
102 Executive Director TXCC Foundation ... Mr. Keith MADORE
90 Director of Education Technology ... Ms. Adrianne DUNHAM
124 Dir College Transition and Outreach ... Mr. Peter MCCLUSKEY
103 Chief Reg Workforce Dev Officer ... Ms. Eileen PELTIER
84 Interim Assoc Dean of Enrollment ... Ms. Jean MAIN
07 Associate Director of Admissions ... Ms. Ashkhen STRACK
07 Associate Director of Admissions ... Ms. Alison MCCARTHY
37 Director Financial Aid Services ... Ms. Sandy VITALE
28 Interim VP Diversity and Equity ... Dr. Kimberly JAMES
72 Director STEAM & Adv Manufacturing ... Mr. Mathew SPINELLI

Connecticut College (H)

270 Mohegan Avenue, New London CT 06320-4125
County: New London FICE Identification: 001379
Unit ID: 128902
Telephone: (860) 447-1911 Carnegie Class: Bac-A&S
FAX Number: (860) 439-2700 Calendar System: Semester
URL: www.conncoll.edu
Established: 1911 Annual Undergrad Tuition & Fees: $59,025
Enrollment: 1,737 Coed
Affiliation or Control: Independent Non-Profit IRS Status: 501(c)3
Highest Offering: Master's
Accreditation: EH

01 President ... Dr. Katherine BERGERON
05 Dean of the Faculty ... Dr. Jeffrey COLE
10 Vice Pres Finance and Admin ... Mr. Richard MADONNA
111 Vice President College Advancement . Ms. Kimberly VERSTANDIG
08 Vice Pres of Info Svcs/Librarian ... Dr. W. Lee HISLE
26 Vice President Communications ... Ms. Pamela DUMAS SERFES
07 VP of Admission & Financial Aid ... Mr. Andrew STRICKLER
15 Asst VP HR/Professional Development ... Vacant
20 Dean of the College ... Dr. Jefferson SINGER
32 Dean of Students ... Dr. Victor J. ARCELUS
28 Dean of Institution Equity and Incl ... Dr. John MCKNIGHT
20 Associate Dean of Faculty ... Dr. Anne BERNHARD
06 Registrar ... Ms. Elisabeth S. LABRIOLA
09 Director of Institutional Research ... Dr. John D. NUGENT
21 Controller ... Ms. Amanda B. MAYFIELD
37 Director of Financial Aid ... Mr. Sean MARTIN
41 Director of Athletics ... Ms. Maureen WHITE
29 Director of Alumni Relations ... Ms. Tori MCKENNA
38 Director Student Counseling Service ... Dr. Janet D. SPOLTORE
96 Director of Purchasing ... Mr. Christopher RUST
04 Executive Asst to the President ... Ms. Lauren MIDDLETON
102 Dir Foundation/Corporate Relations ... Ms. Naima GHERBI
13 Asst VP Enterprise/Tech Systems ... Ms. Jean KILBRIDE
19 Director Security/Safety ... Ms. Mary SAVAGE
22 Dir Affirmative Action/EEO ... Dr. John MCKNIGHT
36 Director Student Placement ... Ms. Persephone HALL
39 Director Student Housing ... Dr. Sara ROTHENBERGER
44 Director Annual or Planned Giving ... Ms. Ellen BREMNER
104 Director Study Abroad ... Ms. Shirley PARSON
18 Chf Facilities/Physical Plant Ofcr ... Ms. Trina LEARNED
105 Director Web Services ... Ms. Christelle LACHAPELLE

Fairfield University (I)

1073 N Benson Road, Fairfield CT 06824-5195
County: Fairfield FICE Identification: 001385
Unit ID: 129242
Telephone: (203) 254-4000 Carnegie Class: Masters/L
FAX Number: (203) 254-4101 Calendar System: Semester
URL: www.fairfield.edu

Established: 1942 Annual Undergrad Tuition & Fees: $51,325
Enrollment: 5,513 Coed
Affiliation or Control: Roman Catholic IRS Status: 501(c)3
Highest Offering: Doctorate
Accreditation: EH, ANEST, CACREP, CAEPN, @DIETC, MFCD, MIDWF, NURSE, @SW

01 University President ..... Dr. Mark R. NEMEC
42 University Chaplain ..... Rev. Keith A. MACZKIEWICZ
42 Chaplain/Dir of Mission ..... Rev. Gerry R. BLASZCZAK, SJ
05 Provost ..... Dr. Christine SIEGEL
10 VP Finance/CFO and Treasurer ..... Mr. Michael TRAFECANTE
111 Vice Pres Univ Advancement ..... Mr. Wally HALAS
15 Vice President of Human Resources ..... Mr. Scott ESPOSITO
88 Vice Pres for Mission and Ministry ..... Rev. Paul ROURKE, SJ
26 VP Marketing and Communications ..... Ms. Jennifer ANDERSON
84 VP Strategic Enrollment Management ..... Mr. Corry D. UNIS
32 Vice President for Student Life ..... Ms. Karen A. DONOGHUE
88 Vice Provost Undergrad Excellence ..... Dr. Mark LIGAS
58 Vice Prov Grad/Cont & Prof Stds ..... Dr. Walter RANKIN
18 Vice President Facilities Mgmt ..... Mr. David W. FRASSINELLI
38 Assoc VP Health & Wellness ..... Dr. Susan N. BIRGE
109 Asst Vice Pres Auxiliary Services ..... Mr. James D. FITZPATRICK
88 Assoc VP SC & Cmty Engagement ..... Dr. Jocelyn BORYCZKA
09 Dir Institutional Research ..... Ms. Amy BOCZER
06 University Registrar ..... Ms. Lynn M. KOHRN
13 Chief Information Officer ..... Mr. Jonathan CARROLL
37 Director of Financial Aid ..... Ms. Diana M. DRAPER
36 Dir Career & Professional Dev ..... Ms. Cathleen M. BORGMAN
29 Asst Vice Pres of Alumni Relations ..... Ms. Janet A. CANEPA
19 Director of Public Safety ..... Mr. Todd A. PELAZZA
41 Director of Athletics ..... Mr. Paul SCHLICKMANN
49 Dean College Arts & Science ..... Dr. Richard GREENWALD
50 Dean Dolan Sch of Business ..... Dr. Zhan LI
54 Dean School of Engineering ..... Dr. Andres CARRANO
66 Dean School of Nursing/Health Stds ..... Dr. Meredith W. KAZER
53 Dean Grad Sch of Educ & Human Dev ..... Dr. Laurie GRUPP
88 Asst VP Ofc of Conference & Events ..... Mr. Matthew A. DINNAN
35 Dean of Students ..... Mr. William H. JOHNSON
39 Sr Assoc Dir Residence Life ..... Mr. Charles SOUSA
104 Assoc Vice Provost Global Strategy ..... Ms. Jennifer EWALD
92 Co-Director of Honors Program ..... Dr. Laura NASH
08 Dean of Library/Univ Librarian ..... Ms. Christina MCGOWAN
23 Director of the Health Center ..... Ms. Julia A. DUFFY
16 Asst VP HR Operations ..... Ms. Faith HUNT
96 Director of Purchasing ..... Mr. Peter PEREZ

Goodwin University (A)

One Riverside Drive, East Hartford CT 06118-2777
County: Hartford FICE Identification: 022449
Unit ID: 129154
Telephone: (860) 528-4111 Carnegie Class: Spec-4-yr-Other Health
FAX Number: (860) 291-9550 Calendar System: Semester
URL: www.goodwin.edu
Established: 1999 Annual Undergrad Tuition & Fees: $20,998
Enrollment: 3,312 Coed
Affiliation or Control: Independent Non-Profit IRS Status: 501(c)3
Highest Offering: Master's
Accreditation: EH, ADNUR, COARC, DH, FUSER, HT, MAC, NAEYC, NURSE, OPD, OTA

01 President ..... Mr. Mark E. SCHEINBERG
05 VP Academic Affs/Dean Faculty ..... Vacant
10 Vice President for Finance/CFO ..... Mr. Eddie MEYER
45 Sr Vice Pres Economic/Strategic Dev ..... Mr. Todd J. ANDREWS
18 Vice Pres Facilities/Technology ..... Mr. Bryant L. HARRELL
84 Vice Pres Enrollment/Mrktg/Comm ..... Vacant
111 Vice President for Advancement ..... Mr. Rich MCCARTY
15 VP Human Resources ..... Ms. Jean MCGILL
32 VP Stdnt Affs/Dean of Students ..... Mr. Tyrone BLACK
108 VP Inst Effectiveness ..... Dr. Melissa QUINLAN
88 Asst VP Strategy/Business Devel ..... Dr. Clifford THERMER
84 Asst VP Enrollment Services ..... Mr. Nicholas LENTINO
08 Director of Library Services ..... Ms. Susan HANSEN
36 Director of Career Services ..... Ms. Stephanie HERTZ
26 Dir Marketing/Communications ..... Mr. Phil MOORE
21 Sr Director of Finance/Controller ..... Mr. Bryan SOLTIS
13 Director Information Technology ..... Mr. John RUGGIRELLO
37 Sr Director of Financial Aid ..... Ms. Bonnie SOLTZ-KNOWLTON
07 Director of Admissions ..... Mr. Dan WILLIAMSON
09 Asst Director of Inst Research ..... Ms. Grace LIBBY
106 Director of Online Learning ..... Dr. Lisa MANLEY
06 Registrar ..... Ms. Allison MISKY
29 Alumni Rels/Stdnt Engagement Coord .. Ms. Vanessa PERGOLIZZI
04 Executive Assistant to President ..... Ms. Alyse MARION
66 Director of Nursing ..... Ms. Christina NIEVES
19 Dir of Campus Safety & Security ..... Mr. Richard VIBBERTS

Hartford Seminary (B)

77 Sherman Street, Hartford CT 06105-2260
County: Hartford FICE Identification: 001387
Unit ID: 129491
Telephone: (860) 509-9500 Carnegie Class: Spec-4-yr-Faith
FAX Number: (860) 509-9509 Calendar System: Semester
URL: www.hartsem.edu
Established: 1834 Annual Graduate Tuition & Fees: N/A
Enrollment: 120 Coed
Affiliation or Control: Independent Non-Profit IRS Status: 501(c)3
Highest Offering: Doctorate; No Undergraduates
Accreditation: EH, THEOL

01 President ..... Dr. Joel LOHR
05 Chief Academic Officer ..... Dr. David GRAFTON
07 Director of Recruitment/Admissions ..... Ms. Tina DEMO
08 Director Library Services/COO ..... Ms. Ann CRAWFORD
10 Chief Business Officer ..... Mr. Michael SANDNER
06 Registrar/Financial Aid Coord ..... Ms. Danielle LAVINE
04 Exec Assistant to the President ..... Ms. Lorraine BROWNE
26 Director of Communications ..... Ms. Susan SCHOENBERGER
15 Acting Director Human Resources ..... Mr. Michael SANDNER

Holy Apostles College and Seminary (C)

33 Prospect Hill Road, Cromwell CT 06416-2027
County: Middlesex FICE Identification: 001389
Unit ID: 129534
Telephone: (860) 632-3010 Carnegie Class: Spec-4-yr-Faith
FAX Number: (860) 632-3030 Calendar System: Semester
URL: www.holyapostles.edu
Established: 1956 Annual Undergrad Tuition & Fees: $8,720
Enrollment: 648 Coed
Affiliation or Control: Roman Catholic IRS Status: 501(c)3
Highest Offering: Beyond Master's But Less Than Doctorate
Accreditation: EH, THEOL

01 President & Rector ..... VRev. Peter S. KUCER, MSA
30 VP External Affs/Govt Compliance ..... Dr. Sebastian P. MAHFOOD, OP
05 Chief Acad Ofcr/Acad Dean ..... Dr. Andrew BLASKI
10 Chief Financial Officer ..... Mr. William RUSSELL
08 Director of Library Services ..... Ms. Clare ADAMO
07 Director of Admissions ..... Dr. Elizabeth REX
04 Admin Assistant to the President ..... Mrs. Alicia FLECK
06 Registrar ..... Mrs. Alicia SHUKIS
09 Director of Institutional Research ..... Dr. Cynthia TOOLIN
105 Director Web Services ..... Mrs. Jennifer MURPHY
106 Director Online Learning ..... Mrs. Jennifer AREL
13 Chief Information Technology Office ..... Mr. Manish BHARDWAJ
18 Chf Facilities/Physical Plant Ofcr ..... Mr. Kurt O'BRIEN
19 Director Security/Safety ..... Mr. Matthew GONZALEZ
37 Director Student Financial Aid ..... Mr. Jason GILL

Mitchell College (D)

437 Pequot Avenue, New London CT 06320-4498
County: New London FICE Identification: 001393
Unit ID: 129774
Telephone: (860) 701-5000 Carnegie Class: Bac-Diverse
FAX Number: (860) 701-5090 Calendar System: Semester
URL: www.mitchell.edu
Established: 1938 Annual Undergrad Tuition & Fees: $35,072
Enrollment: 599 Coed
Affiliation or Control: Independent Non-Profit IRS Status: 501(c)3
Highest Offering: Baccalaureate
Accreditation: EH

01 President ..... Dr. Tracy ESPY
05 VP Academic Affs/Dean of College ..... Dr. Elizabeth BEAULIEU
84 VP for Enrollment Mgmt/Athletics ..... Mr. Jamie ROMEO
07 Director of Admission/Financial Aid ..... Mr. Kelby CHAPPELLE
41 Director of Athletics ..... Mr. Matthew FINLAYSON
111 Chief Advancement/Alumni Affair ..... Ms. Nancy COWSER
06 Registrar ..... Ms. Amy VAN OOT
88 Director of Thames @ Mitchell ..... Ms. Beverly SCULLY
10 Chief Financial/Business Officer ..... Mr. Robert PERUZZOTTI
20 Assoc Dn Acad Affs/First Year Exp ..... Ms. Jennifer R. WELSH
18 Director of Facilities ..... Mr. Joseph PARDEE
113 Bursar ..... Ms. Amanda CARTER
04 Executive Asst to the President ..... Ms. Kristen PISANI
32 Dean Student Experience/Belonging ..... Dr. Alicia MARTINEZ
121 Asst Dean of Advising/Stdnt Support .. Ms. Christina CHAPPELLE
38 Director Health & Wellness ..... Ms. Kerry PHELON
19 Director Security/Safety ..... Mr. Erik COSTA
26 Director of Marketing ..... Ms. Lisa STINSON
36 Director Career Services ..... Mr. Paul DUNN
15 Human Resource Manager ..... Ms. Aruna IYER
39 Director of Residence Life ..... Mr. Matthew BRANCACCIO

Paier College of Art (E)

20 Gorham Avenue, Hamden CT 06514-3902
County: New Haven FICE Identification: 007459
Unit ID: 130110
Telephone: (203) 287-3031 Carnegie Class: Spec-4-yr-Arts
FAX Number: (203) 287-3021 Calendar System: Semester
URL: www.paiercollegeofart.edu
Established: 1946 Annual Undergrad Tuition & Fees: $19,670
Enrollment: 128 Coed
Affiliation or Control: Proprietary IRS Status: Proprietary
Highest Offering: Baccalaureate
Accreditation: ACCSC

01 President ..... Mr. Joseph BIERBAUM
03 Provost ..... Dr. Summer CERRUTO AMOROSINO
05 Dean of the College ..... Ms. Tammy VAZ
57 Director Design/Graphics ..... Mr. Peter MISERENDINO
102 Director Foundation/Arts ..... Mr. Robert E. ZAPPALORTI
08 Librarian ..... Ms. Beth HARRIS
37 Director Student Financial Aid ..... Mr. John DE ROSE
32 Director of Student Services ..... Mrs. Angela DEROSE
88 Director Interior Design ..... Mr. Pierre STRAUCH

88 Director Photography ..... Mr. Peter BENSON
07 Director of Admissions ..... Ms. Lynn PASCALE

Post University (F)

800 Country Club Road, Waterbury CT 06723-2540
County: New Haven FICE Identification: 001401
Unit ID: 130183
Telephone: (203) 596-4500 Carnegie Class: Masters/L
FAX Number: (203) 841-1163 Calendar System: Semester
URL: www.post.edu
Established: 1890 Annual Undergrad Tuition & Fees: $16,610
Enrollment: 13,844 Coed
Affiliation or Control: Proprietary IRS Status: Proprietary
Highest Offering: Doctorate
Accreditation: EH, ACBSP, NAEYC, NUR, NURSE

01 Chief Executive Officer & President ..... Mr. John L. HOPKINS
03 Vice President ..... Mr. Mark CHESNEY
05 Provost/CAO ..... Dr. Elizabeth JOHNSON
11 Chief Operations Officer ..... Mr. Bobby REESE
10 Chief Financial Officer ..... Mr. Scott T. ALLEN
13 Chief Information Officer ..... Mr. Greg THEISEN
15 Chief Assoc Experience Officer ..... Ms. Vicki WHISENHANT
86 Chief Regulatory Officer ..... Ms. Elaine NEELY
41 Director of Athletics ..... Mr. Ronnie PALMER
50 Dean of School of Business ..... Dr. Jeremy BAUER
80 Dean John P Burke Sch Pub Svcs & Ed ..... Dr. James WHITLEY
49 Dean of School of Arts & Sciences ..... Dr. Dylan CLYNE

Quinnipiac University (G)

275 Mount Carmel Avenue, Hamden CT 06518-1908
County: New Haven FICE Identification: 001402
Unit ID: 130226
Telephone: (203) 582-8200 Carnegie Class: DU-Mod
FAX Number: (203) 582-4703 Calendar System: Semester
URL: www.quinnipiac.edu
Established: 1929 Annual Undergrad Tuition & Fees: $50,760
Enrollment: 9,746 Coed
Affiliation or Control: Independent Non-Profit IRS Status: 501(c)3
Highest Offering: First Professional Degree
Accreditation: EH, AA, ANEST, ARCPA, CAATE, CAEPN, LAW, MED, NURSE, OT, PA, PERF, PTA, RAD, SW

01 President ..... Dr. Judy D. OLIAN
05 Provost ..... Dr. Debra J. LIEBOWITZ
100 Vice President/Chief of Staff ..... Dr. Bethany C. ZEMBA
10 VP Finance/Chief Financial Ofcr ..... Mr. Mark VARHOLAK
26 Vice Pres Marketing/Communications ..... Mr. Daryl RICHARD
18 Vice Pres Facilities & Capital Plng ..... Mr. Salvatore FILARDI
15 Gen Counsel/VP for Human Resources ..... Ms. Elicia SPEARMAN
84 VP for Enrollment Management ..... Mr. Eric SYKES
114 Assoc VP Budget & Fin Planning ..... Mr. Sandip PATEL
30 Vice Pres Devel & Alumni Affairs ..... Mr. Todd SLOAN
32 Vice President & Dean of Students ..... Dr. Monique DRUCKER
13 VP/Chief Info & Tech Officer ..... Vacant
20 VP for Acad Innovation & Effective ..... Dr. Annalisa ZINN
27 AVP Integrated Mktg Communications ..... Mr. James P. RYAN
27 Assoc VP for Public Relations ..... Mr. John MORGAN
06 Registrar ..... Mr. Joshua BERRY
106 Interim Asst VP for QU Online ..... Vacant
28 VP for Equity & Inclusion ..... Mr. Donald C. SAWYER
35 Assoc Dean Student Affairs ..... Ms. Lynn Nicole HENDRICKS
39 Director of Resident Life ..... Mr. Mark DEVILBISS
23 Dir of Student Health Services ..... Ms. Christy CHASE
38 Exec Director of Health & Wellness ..... Ms. Kerry PATTON
19 Chief of Public Safety ..... Chief Otoniel REYES
08 Director of Arnold Bernhard Library ..... Mr. Robert JOVEN
41 Director of Athletics & Recreation ..... Mr. Greg AMODIO
40 Campus Store Manager ..... Ms. Cheryl CARTIER
104 Director of International Svcs ..... Ms. Erin SABATO
21 Assoc VP for Finance/Controller ..... Mr. Stephen A. ALLEGRETTO
96 Manager of Strategic Sourcing ..... Ms. Daniella VIZZIELLO
109 Assoc VP for Auxiliary Services ..... Mr. John MERIANO
29 Sr Dir Parent/Family Development ..... Ms. Melinda FORMICA
37 Director of Financial Aid ..... Ms. Victoria HAMPTON
108 Dir Institutional Assess/Research ..... Ms. Sungah KIM
90 Director of Academic Technology ..... Ms. Lauren ERARDI
66 Dean School of Nursing ..... Dr. Lisa G. O'CONNOR
50 Dean School of Business ..... Dr. Holly RAIDER
49 Dean College of Arts & Sciences ..... Dr. Adam ROTH
76 Dean School of Health Sciences ..... Dr. Janelle CHIASERA
61 Dean School of Law ..... Dr. Jennifer G. BROWN
60 Dean School of Communications ..... Mr. Chris G. ROUSH
53 Dean School of Education ..... Dr. Anne M. DICHELE
63 Dean School of Medicine ..... Dr. Philip BOISELLE
54 Dean School of Engineering ..... Vacant
94 Director of Women's Studies ..... Dr. Jennifer SACCO
04 Admin Assistant to the President ..... Ms. Gina FALCIGNO
44 Director Annual Giving ..... Ms. Andy BERNSTEIN

Rensselaer at Hartford (H)

275 Windsor Street, Hartford CT 06120-2991
Telephone: (860) 548-2400 FICE Identification: 002804
Accreditation: &M

† Regional accreditation is carried under the parent institution, Rensselaer Polytechnic Institute, NY.

Sacred Heart University (A)

5151 Park Avenue, Fairfield CT 06825-1000
County: Fairfield | FICE Identification: 001403
Unit ID: 130253
Telephone: (203) 371-7999 | Carnegie Class: DU-Mod
FAX Number: (203) 365-7652 | Calendar System: Semester
URL: www.sacredheart.edu
Established: 1963 | Annual Undergrad Tuition & Fees: $44,350
Enrollment: 9,313 | Coed
Affiliation or Control: Independent Non-Profit | IRS Status: 501(c)3
Highest Offering: Doctorate
Accreditation: **EH**, ADNUR, ARCPA, CAATE, CAEP, CEA, NURSE, OT, PTA, RAD, SP, SW

01 President & CEO ... Dr. John J. PETILLO
05 Acting Provost/VP Academic Affairs ... Dr. Robin CAUTIN
32 Sr VP Student Affairs & Athletics ... Mr. James M. BARQUINERO
11 Sr VP Administration & Planning ... Dr. David COPPOLA
15 VP Human Resources ... Mr. Robert M. HARDY
26 Chief of Staff/VP Mktg/Comm ... Mr. Michael L. IANNAZZI
88 VP Mission/Catholic Identity ... Fr. Anthony CIORRA
10 Sr VP Finance ... Mr. Philip J. MCCABE
13 VP Information Technology ... Ms. Shirley CANAAN
111 Interim VP University Advancement ... Ms. Marie MUHVIC
43 University General Counsel ... Mr. Michael D. LAROBINA
49 Acting Dean of Arts & Sciences ... Dr. Mark BEEKEY
50 Dean College of Business ... Dr. Martha J. CRAWFORD
76 Dean Col Health Professions ... Dr. Maura IVERSEN
53 Dean College of Education ... Dr. Michael ALFANO
66 Dean College of Nursing ... Dr. Karen DALEY
58 Dean Graduate Studies ... Dr. Brian V. CAROLAN
12 Dean St. Vincent's College ... Ms. Maryanne DAVIDSON
108 President University Acad Assembly ... Mr. Dom PINTO
07 Exec Director Undergrad Admissions ... Ms. Pam PILLO
06 Registrar ... Ms. Angela PITCHER

Trinity College (B)

300 Summit Street, Hartford CT 06106-3100
County: Hartford | FICE Identification: 001414
Unit ID: 130590
Telephone: (860) 297-2000 | Carnegie Class: Bac-A&S
FAX Number: (860) 297-5359 | Calendar System: Semester
URL: www.trincoll.edu
Established: 1823 | Annual Undergrad Tuition & Fees: $59,050
Enrollment: 2,241 | Coed
Affiliation or Control: Independent Non-Profit | IRS Status: 501(c)3
Highest Offering: Master's
Accreditation: **EH**

01 President ... Dr. Joanne BERGER-SWEENEY
10 Vice Pres Finance/CFO ... Mr. Dan HITCHELL
05 Dean of Faculty/VP Academic Affairs ... Dr. Sonia CARDENAS
13 Vice Pres Information Svcs/CIO ... Ms. Kristen ESHLEMAN
111 Vice Pres College Advancement ... Mr. Michael CASEY
32 Vice Pres Student Affairs ... Mr. Joseph DICHRISTINA
84 Vice Pres Enrollment/Stdnt Success ... Mr. Joseph DICHRISTINA
26 VP of Marketing/Communications ... Ms. Caroline DEVEAU
28 VP Diversity/Equity and Inclusion ... Ms. Anita DAVIS
43 General Counsel & Secretary ... Mr. Dickens MATHIEU
100 Chief of Staff/AVP External Affairs ... Mr. Jason ROJAS
15 AVP Human Resources ... Ms. Michelle CABRAL
07 Director of Admissions ... Mr. Anthony T. BERRY
37 Director of Financial Aid ... Ms. Ashley DUTTON
27 Director of Media Relations ... Ms. Stacy SNEED
06 Registrar ... Ms. Alexis YUSOV-BALDONI
21 Director of Business Operations ... Mr. Michael ELLIOTT
114 Budget Director ... Ms. Marcia PHELAN JOHNSON
19 Director of Campus Safety ... Mr. Robert LUKASKIEWICZ
30 Director of Development ... Mr. Christopher FRENCH
21 Comptroller ... Mr. Guy DRAPEAU
41 Director of Athletics ... Mr. Drew GALBRAITH
09 Dir Analytics/Strategic Initiatives ... Mr. David ANDRES
39 Director of Residential Life ... Ms. Susan SALISBURY
42 College Chaplain ... Rev. Marcus HALLEY
38 Director Student Counseling ... Dr. Randolph LEE
96 Director of Purchasing ... Mr. Michael S. ELLIOTT
82 Dean of Urban and Global Studies ... Dr. Xiangming CHEN
29 Director of Alumni Relations ... Mr. Steve DONOVAN
08 Head Librarian ... Ms. Janine S. KINEL
101 Special Assistant to the President ... Ms. Karolina KWIECINSKA
04 Executive Asst to President ... Ms. Patrice A. LEMOINE
108 Director Institutional Assessment ... Mr. Mark HUGHES
22 Director Affirm Action/Equal Opp ... Ms. Tapiwanashe NHUNDU
86 Director Government Relations ... Mr. Jason ROJAS

University of Bridgeport (C)

126 Park Avenue, Bridgeport CT 06604-5620
County: Fairfield | FICE Identification: 001416
Unit ID: 128744
Telephone: (203) 576-4000 | Carnegie Class: DU-Mod
FAX Number: (203) 576-4653 | Calendar System: Semester
URL: www.bridgeport.edu
Established: 1927 | Annual Undergrad Tuition & Fees: $35,760
Enrollment: 4,155 | Coed
Affiliation or Control: Independent Non-Profit | IRS Status: 501(c)3
Highest Offering: Doctorate
Accreditation: **EH**, ACBSP, ACUP, ARCPA, ART, CACREP, CAEP, CHIRO, DH, MT, NATUR, NURSE

01 President ... Dr. Danielle E. WILKEN
04 Executive Assistant to President ... Ms. Brenda PIOLI
05 Provost & VP for Academic Affairs ... Dr. Manyul E. IM
11 VP & Chief Admin Officer ... Mr. Daniel NOONAN
10 Chief Financial Officer ... Mr. David TAYLOR
111 VP Advancement & College Initiative ... Mr. Rich M. MCCARTY
41 VP Athletics ... Mr. James MORAN
88 Chief Operating Officer for Admin ... Mr. Robert SCHMIDT
32 Dean of Students ... Mr. Craig LENNON
08 Director of Library ... Mr. Scott HUGHES
15 Director Human Resources ... Ms. Cheryl M. NYARADY
21 Controller ... Mr. Malhar SHARMA
37 Director Financial Aid & Compliance ... Ms. Jamie GRIEFF
19 Exec Director of Campus Security ... Mrs. April J. VOURNELIS
121 Dir of Student & Academic Success ... Ms. Jill JEMMOTT
38 Director of Counseling Services ... Vacant
06 University Registrar ... Ms. Carmen ROSA
85 Director of Intl Student Affairs ... Ms. Yumin WANG
76 Dean College of Health Sciences ... Dr. Michael CIOLFI
39 Director of Residential Life ... Mrs. Cindy SANDERS
35 Dir Student Involvement ... Ms. Kelli A. MEYER
30 Dir of Devel & Alumni Relations ... Ms. Jhanay ABRAMS
23 Director of Health Center ... Vacant
88 Director of Acupuncture Institute ... Dr. Jennifer BRETT
40 Manager of the Bookstore ... Mr. Richard HEBERT
36 Director of Career Services ... Vacant
54 Dean Engr/Business/Education ... Dr. Khaled M. ELLEITHY
49 Dean Arts & Sciences ... Dr. Kathleen ENGELMANN
53 Dir School of Education ... Dr. Nancy DEJARNETTE
88 Dir School of Chiropractic ... Dr. Michael A. CIOLFI
50 Dir School of Business ... Mr. Timonthy RAYNOR
52 Dir School of Dental Hygiene ... Dr. Marion MANSKI
106 Associate Provost ... Dr. Jaria ALJOE
88 Dir Physician Assistant Institute ... Ms. Lauren WEINDLLING
91 Dir Acad & Campus Tech Services ... Vacant
07 Dean of Admissions ... Mr. Jeff MON
105 Web Master ... Ms. Brittany LADD

University of Connecticut (D)

352 Mansfield Road, Storrs CT 06269-1048
County: Tolland | FICE Identification: 001417
Unit ID: 129020
Telephone: (860) 486-2337 | Carnegie Class: DU-Highest
FAX Number: (860) 486-2627 | Calendar System: Semester
URL: www.uconn.edu
Established: 1881 | Annual Undergrad Tuition & Fees (In-State): $17,834
Enrollment: 27,215 | Coed
Affiliation or Control: State | IRS Status: 501(c)3
Highest Offering: Doctorate
Accreditation: **EH**, ART, AUD, CAATE, CACREP, CAEPN, CEA, CGTECH, CLPSY, DIETC, DIETD, DIETI, DMOLS, IPSY, JOUR, LAW, LSAR, MT, MUS, NURSE, PHAR, PTA, SCPSY, SP, SPAA, SW

01 Interim President ... Andrew AGWUNOBI
100 Chief of Staff/General Counsel ... Nicole GELSTON
05 Provost/Exec VP Academic Affs ... Carl W. LEJUEZ
111 President & CEO UConn Fdtn ... Vacant
17 Exec VP for Health Affairs and CEO ... Andrew AGWUNOBI
10 Interim VP for Finance and CFO ... Lloyd BLANCHARD
32 Vice President for Student Affairs ... Michael GILBERT
46 VP for Research/Innovation & Entr ... Radenka MARIC
101 Exec Sec to Board/Dep Dir Athletics ... Rachel RUBIN
26 Vice Pres for Communications ... P. Tysen KENDIG
41 Director of Athletics ... David BENEDICT
13 Vice President & Chief Info Officer ... Michael MUNDRANE
114 Assoc VP for Budget & Planning ... Lloyd BLANCHARD
19 Assoc VP for Public Safety ... Hans RHYNHART
28 Vice Pres/Chief Diversity Officer ... Franklin A. TUITT
22 Assoc VP for Institutional Equity ... Letissa REID
09 AVP Inst Research & Effectiveness ... Lloyd BLANCHARD
20 Sr Vice Prov for Academic Affairs ... Jeffrey SHOULSON
20 Vice Prov Faculty/Staff/Stdnt Dev ... Michael BRADFORD
84 VP Enrollment Planning & Mgmt ... Nathan FUERST
08 Dean of Univ Library ... Anne LANGLEY
12 Director Stamford Campus ... David SOUDER
12 Director Avery Point Campus ... Annemarie SEIFERT
12 Director Waterbury Campus ... William J. PIZZUTO
12 Director Hartford Campus ... Mark OVERMYER-VELAZQUEZ
92 AVProv Enrich Pgms/Dir Honors Pgms ... Jennifer LEASE BUTTS
25 AVP Research/Sponsored Pgm Svcs ... Michael GLASGOW
86 Sr Director Government Relations ... Joann LOMBARDO
86 Dir Govt Relations/Health Affairs ... Vacant
06 Registrar ... Gregory BOUQUOT
07 Director Undergrad Admissions ... Vern GRANGER
37 Director Student Financial Aid ... Suzanne PETERS
29 Asst Vice Pres Alumni Relations ... Montique COTTON KELLY
23 Exec Dir Student Health/Wellness ... Suzanne ONORATO
15 Exec Director of Human Resources ... Aliza WILDER
96 Interim AVP Univ Business Svcs ... Gregory DANIELS
47 Dean Col of Agric/Natural Resources ... Indrajeet CHAUBEY
50 Dean School of Business ... John ELLIOTT
53 Dean Neag School of Education ... Jason IRIZARRY
54 Dean of Engineering ... Kazem KAZEROUNIAN
88 Assoc Vice Prov Excell Teach/Lrng ... Peter DIPLOCK
57 Dean of Fine Arts ... Anne D'ALLEVA
58 Vice Prov Grad Ed/Dean Grad Sch ... Kent HOLSINGER
61 Dean School of Law ... Eboni S. NELSON
49 Dean Col of Lib Arts/Sciences ... Juli WADE
66 Dean School of Nursing ... Deborah A. CHYUN
67 Dean School of Pharmacy ... Philip HRITCKO
70 Dean School of Social Work ... Nina ROVINELLI HELLER
52 Dean of Dental Medicine ... Steven LEPOWSKY
63 Dean School of Medicine ... Bruce LIANG
38 Director of Mental Health ... Kristina STEVENS
39 Executive Director Residential Life ... Pamela SCHIPANI
27 AVP Communications/Sr Adv to Pres ... Michael KIRK
88 AVP Plng/Design/Const/Chf Architect ... Laura CRUICKSHANK
85 Vice President for Global Affairs ... Daniel WEINER
36 Asst VProv/Exec Dir Career Services ... James R. LOWE
121 Assoc Vice Prov for Student Success ... Tadarrayl STARKE
27 AVP Marketing Communications ... Vacant
88 Ombuds ... James WOHL
88 Dir Institute for Materials Science ... Steven L. SUIB
04 Executive Asst to President ... Jennifer BURCKARDT
104 Director Education Abroad ... Vacant
18 Assoc VP Facilities Ops & Bldg Svcs ... P. Michael JEDNAK
112 VP of Principal and Planned Gifts ... Brian OTIS
30 Senior VP for Development ... Jake LEMON
106 Dir Online Education/E-learning ... Peter DIPLOCK
88 Dir Vet Affs & Military Programs ... Alyssa KELLEHER

University of Connecticut Health Center (E)

263 Farmington Avenue, Farmington CT 06030-1827
Telephone: (860) 679-2000 | FICE Identification: 009867
Accreditation: **&EH**, DENT, MED, PH

† Regional accreditation is carried under the parent institution in Storrs, CT.

University of Connecticut School of Law (F)

55 Elizabeth Street, Hartford CT 06105-2290
Telephone: (860) 570-5000 | Identification: 770108
Accreditation: **&EH**, LAW

University of Hartford (G)

200 Bloomfield Avenue, West Hartford CT 06117-1599
County: Hartford | FICE Identification: 001422
Unit ID: 129525
Telephone: (860) 768-4100 | Carnegie Class: DU-Mod
FAX Number: (860) 768-4070 | Calendar System: Semester
URL: www.hartford.edu
Established: 1877 | Annual Undergrad Tuition & Fees: $43,560
Enrollment: 6,493 | Coed
Affiliation or Control: Independent Non-Profit | IRS Status: 501(c)3
Highest Offering: Doctorate
Accreditation: **EH**, ART, CAEPN, CLPSY, COARC, DANCE, MUS, NURSE, OPE, PTA, RAD, THEA

01 President ... Dr. Gregory S. WOODWARD
05 Provost/VP Academic Affairs ... Dr. H. Frederick SWEITZER
10 Vice Pres Finance & Administration ... Ms. Laura WHITNEY
30 Vice Pres Development/Alumni Affs ... Ms. Kate PENDERGAST
32 Vice Pres Student Affs/Dean Stdnts ... Dr. Aaron ISAACS
26 Vice Pres Marketing/Enrollment ... Ms. Molly POLK
21 Controller ... Mr. Darryl LONGLEY
04 Senior Advisor to the President ... Ms. Susan FITZGERALD
35 Assoc Vice Pres for Student Life ... Dr. Jessica NICKLIN
21 Assoc Vice Pres/Treasurer ... Vacant
43 Vice Pres/Gen Counsel & Secretary ... Ms. Maria FEELEY
84 Sr Assoc Provost/Dean Enroll Mgmt ... Vacant
58 Int Assoc Prov/Dean of Grad Studies ... Dr. Clark SAUNDERS
07 Dean of Admission ... Mr. Richard A. ZEISER
04 Exec Assistant to the President ... Ms. Ilena ROSENSTEIN
08 Director University Libraries ... Ms. Randi L. ASHTON-PRITTING
06 Registrar ... Ms. Natalie DURANT
38 Dir Counsel & Personal Development ... Dr. Jeffrey BURDA
36 Exec Director of Career Services ... Ms. Brooke PENDERS
13 Asst VP Ops/Info Tech Svcs ... Mr. Sebby SORRENTINO
19 Director Public Safety ... Mr. Michael KASELOUSKAS
23 Director Health Services ... Ms. Amy WISNIEWSKI
24 Director User Services ... Mr. Sebastian SORRENTINO
25 Dir Inst Prtnrshp/Sponsored Rsrch ... Mr. Christopher STANDISH
18 Assoc Vice Pres for Facilities/Mgmt ... Mr. Norman YOUNG
104 Director International Studies ... Ms. Nicole KURKER-STEWART
108 Dir Institutional Effectiveness ... Ms. Kathleen NEAL
94 Director of Women's Center ... Ms. Kenna GRANT
88 Director of Student Conduct & Admin ... Mr. David STENDER
96 Director of Purchasing ... Ms. Lisa CONDON
92 Director of University Honors ... Dr. Donald JONES
106 Asst Prov Online Lrng/Dean Univ Pgm ... Dr. R. J. MCGIVNEY
57 Dean Hartford Art School ... Dr. Nancy M. STUART
72 Dean College Engineer/Tech/Arch ... Dr. Hisham ALNAJJAR
49 Dean College Arts & Science ... Dr. Katherine BLACK
53 Int Dean Col of Educ/Nurs/Hlth Prof ... Dr. Cesarina THOMPSON
64 Dean Hartt School ... Dr. Larry Alan SMITH
12 Dean Hillyer College ... Dr. David H. GOLDENBERG
27 Dir of Marketing/Communications ... Mr. Jonathan EASTERBROOK
102 Dir Foundation/Corporate Relations ... Ms. Lynn BARONAS
15 Manager Human Resources Svcs/Pgms ... Ms. Lindsay MCKEEGAN
28 Exec Dir Diversity/Cmty Engagement ... Ms. Christine GRANT

University of New Haven (H)

300 Boston Post Road, West Haven CT 06516-1916
County: New Haven | FICE Identification: 001397
Unit ID: 12994-
Telephone: (203) 932-7000 | Carnegie Class: Masters/L
FAX Number: (203) 931-6060 | Calendar System: Semester
URL: www.newhaven.edu
Established: 1920 | Annual Undergrad Tuition & Fees: $41,654
Enrollment: 6,961 | Coed
Affiliation or Control: Independent Non-Profit | IRS Status: 501(c)3
Highest Offering: Doctorate

Accreditation: **EH**, ART, DH, DIETC, DIETD, DIETI, FEPAC, HSA

01 President ... Dr. Steven H. KAPLAN
05 Interim Provost/SVP of Acad Affairs ... Dr. Mario GABOURY
10 VP of Finance & Administration ... Mr. George S. SYNODI
84 VP of Enrollment & Student Success ... Mr. Gregory EICHHORN
111 VP of Advancement ... Mr. Stephen J. MORIN
15 Assoc VP of HR and Org Dev ... Ms. Jennifer CINQUE
100 VP and Chief of Staff ... Ms. Jean HUSTED
41 Director of Athletics & Recreation ... Dr. Sheahon ZENGER
28 VP for Diversity & Inclusion ... Dr. Lorenzo BOYD
54 Dean Tagliatela Col Engineering ... Dr. Ronald HARICHANDRAN
50 Dean College Business ... Dr. Brian KENCH
76 Dean School of Health Sciences ... Dr. Summer J. MCGEE
49 Dean of Arts & Sciences ... Dr. Shaily MENON
83 Actg Dean Crim Justice/Forensic Sci ... Dr. David SCHROEDER
20 Deputy Provost ... Dr. Glenn MCGEE
32 Dean Stdnts/Chief Student Affs Ofcr ... Dr. Ophelie ROWE-ALLEN
21 Associate VP for Finance ... Mr. Patrick TORRE
18 Associate VP for Facilities ... Mr. Lou ANNINO
19 Assoc VP for Public Safety/Admin ... Mr. Ron QUAGLIANI
13 Assoc VP for Information Technology ... Mr. Vincent P. MANGIACAPRA
113 Assoc VP Financial/Registrar Svcs ... Mr. Marc MANIATIS
26 AVP of Marketing & Public Relations ... Mr. Doug WHITING
16 Exec Director of Human Resources ... Ms. Iris CALOVINE
09 Director Institutional Research ... Ms. Susan TURNER
08 University Librarian ... Ms. Hanko H. DOBI
37 Director of Financial Aid ... Mr. Erin CHIARO
110 Assoc VP for Advancement Operations ... Ms. Lisa HONAN
30 Associate VP for Development ... Ms. Roslyn REABACK
06 University Registrar ... Ms. Elizabeth REZENDES
19 Chief of University Police ... Chief James T. GILMAN
35 Senior Associate Dean of Students ... Mr. Ric BAKER
35 Exec Dir of Student Activities ... Mr. Gregory OVEREND
39 Associate Dean of Residential Life ... Ms. Nicole MCGRATH
07 Executive Director of UG Admissions ... Mr. Jason RIENDEAU
123 Sr Exec Dir Graduate Admissions ... Ms. Selina O'TOOLE
04 President's Office Coordinator ... Ms. Jennifer FAZEKAS
91 Dir Enterprise Applications ... Mr. Todd MCINERNEY
96 Director of Purchasing ... Mr. Robert STEVENS
103 Exec Director of Career Development ... Mr. Matthew CAPORALE
85 Exec Dir of International Services ... Ms. Kathy KAUTZ
29 Director of Alumni Relations ... Ms. Jennifer PJATAK

University of Saint Joseph (A)

1678 Asylum Avenue, West Hartford CT 06117-2791
County: Hartford — FICE Identification: 001409
Unit ID: 130314
Telephone: (860) 232-4571 — Carnegie Class: DU-Mod
FAX Number: (860) 232-6927 — Calendar System: Semester
URL: www.usj.edu
Established: 1932 — Annual Undergrad Tuition & Fees: $41,736
Enrollment: 2,305 — Coed
Affiliation or Control: Roman Catholic — IRS Status: 501(c)3
Highest Offering: Doctorate
Accreditation: **EH**, ARCPA, CACREP, CAEP, CAEPN, DIETD, DIETI, MFCD, NURSE, PHAR, SW

01 President ... Dr. Rhona C. FREE
05 Provost ... Dr. Michelle KALIS
10 VP Finance and Administration ... Ms. Lucy LUCKER
111 VP Inst Advancement ... Ms. Maggie PINNEY
84 VP Enrollment Management ... Ms. Kimberly CRONE
32 Dean of Student Affairs ... Mr. Brandon DAWSON
26 Dir Marketing & Communications ... Ms. Stacy ROUTHIER
67 Dean Sch Pharmacy/PA Studies ... Dr. Ahmed ABDELMAGEED
49 Dean Sch Arts/Sci/Business/Ed ... Dr. Raouf BOULES
76 Dean Sch Interdisc Health & Science ... Dr. Elizabeth FRANCIS-CONNOLLY
08 Librarian ... Ms. Roseanne KRZANOWSKI
06 Registrar ... Ms. Angela ANDERSON
41 Director of Athletics ... Ms. Amanda DEVITT
15 Director of Human Resources ... Ms. Deborah SPENCER
13 Director of Info Tech (CIO) ... Mr. Jason LAWRENCE
18 Director of Facilities ... Mr. Andrew LEVESQUE
19 Director of Public Safety ... Mr. Derrick MCBRIDE
07 Director of Admissions ... Dr. Molly MINER
114 Director Budget & Planning ... Ms. Mary HUNT
37 Director of Student Financial Svcs ... Ms. Stacey DOWNING
36 Dir Career Dev/Women's Ldrship Ctr ... Ms. Melanie SINCHE
28 Director of Diversity/Title IX ... Ms. Rayna DYTON-WHITE
23 Director of Health Services ... Ms. Janet FLINK
38 Director of Counseling & Wellness ... Dr. Meredith YUHAS
29 Dir of Alumni Rels/Annual Giving ... Ms. Katie BURKE
09 Research Analyst ... Mr. Chris LOSO
04 Exec Asst to President ... Ms. Ruth FOXMAN

Wesleyan University (B)

45 Wyllys Avenue, Middletown CT 06459
County: Middlesex — FICE Identification: 001424
Unit ID: 130697
Telephone: (860) 685-2000 — Carnegie Class: Bac-A&S
FAX Number: (860) 685-2001 — Calendar System: Semester
URL: www.wesleyan.edu
Established: 1831 — Annual Undergrad Tuition & Fees: $59,686
Enrollment: 3,053 — Coed
Affiliation or Control: Independent Non-Profit — IRS Status: 501(c)3
Highest Offering: Doctorate
Accreditation: **EH**

01 President ... Dr. Michael S. ROTH
05 Provost/Vice Pres Academic Affairs ... Dr. Nicole STANTON
10 SVP/Chief Admin Ofcr/Treasurer ... Mr. Andrew Y. TANAKA
100 Chief of Staff ... Ms. Anne LASKOWSKI
26 Vice President University Relations ... Mr. Frantz WILLIAMS, JR.
28 Int VP Equity/Inclusion/Title IX ... Dr. Alison WILLIAMS
32 Vice Pres of Student Affairs ... Mr. Michael J. WHALEY
13 VP Information Technology/CIO ... Dr. David BAIRD
30 Senior Development Officer ... Vacant
20 Associate Provost ... Dr. Mark HOVEY
20 Associate Provost ... Ms. Sheryl CULOTTA
18 Asst Vice President for Facilities ... Ms. Joyce TOPSHE
35 Asst Vice Pres/Dean of Students ... Mr. Richard CULLITON
58 Dir Cont Stds/Graduate Liberal Stds ... Ms. Jennifer CURRAN
07 Vice Pres/Dean Admissions/Fin Aid ... Mr. Amin Abdul-Malik GONZALEZ
06 Registrar ... Ms. Anna VAN DER BURG
08 University Librarian ... Mr. Andrew WHITE
09 Director of Institutional Research ... Mr. Michael E. WHITCOMB
37 Director Financial Aid ... Mr. Robert D. COUGHLIN
36 Director Career Development ... Ms. Sharon CASTONGUAY
15 Chief Human Resources Officer ... Ms. Lisa BROMMER
19 Director Public Safety ... Mr. Scott ROHDE
41 Director of Athletics ... Mr. Michael WHALEN
04 Admin Assistant to the President ... Ms. Heather BROOKE
104 Director Study Abroad ... Ms. Emily GORLEWSKI
108 Director Institutional Assessment ... Ms. Rachael BARLOW
38 Director Student Counseling ... Ms. Jennifer D'ANDREA
39 Dir Resident Life/Student Housing ... Ms. Frances KOERTING
90 Director Academic Computing ... Ms. Rachel SCHNEPPER
91 Director Administrative Computing ... Mr. Steve MACHUGA
96 Director of Purchasing ... Ms. Olga BOOKAS

Yale University (C)

3 Prospect Street, New Haven CT 06520
County: New Haven — FICE Identification: 001426
Unit ID: 130794
Telephone: (203) 432-2550 — Carnegie Class: DU-Highest
FAX Number: (203) 432-7105 — Calendar System: Semester
URL: www.yale.edu
Established: 1701 — Annual Undergrad Tuition & Fees: $57,700
Enrollment: 12,060 — Coed
Affiliation or Control: Independent Non-Profit — IRS Status: 501(c)3
Highest Offering: Doctorate
Accreditation: **EH**, ARCPA, CAMPEP, CLPSY, IPSY, LAW, MED, MIDWF, NURSE, PAST, PCSAS, PH, THEOL

01 President ... Peter SALOVEY
05 Provost ... Scott A. STROBEL
11 Senior Vice President Operations ... Jack F. CALLAHAN, JR.
32 Secretary & VP Student Affairs ... Kimberly GOFF-CREWS
10 Vice Pres Finance & CFO ... Stephen MURPHY
30 VP Development/Alumni Affairs ... Joan E. O'NEILL
43 Sr Vice President & General Counsel ... Alexander DREIER
15 Vice Pres Human Resources ... Janet LINDNER
46 Vice Provost of Research ... Peter SCHIFFER
88 Vice President Global Strategy ... Pericles LEWIS
20 Vice Prov Health Affairs and Acad ... Stephanie SPANGLER
20 Vice Provost Academic Resources ... J. Lloyd SUTTLE
18 VP Facilities & Campus Development ... John H. BOLLIER
20 Vice Provost ... Emily P. BAKEMEIER
26 Vice President for Communications ... Nathaniel NICKERSON
102 Assoc VP/Dir Corp & Found Rels ... Patricia E. PEDERSEN
08 Univ Librarian & Deputy Provost ... Susan GIBBONS
09 AVP Academic Business Ops/Strategy ... Tim PAVLIS
13 Assoc VP & Chief Information Ofcr ... John BARDEN
96 Assoc VP Administration Operations ... John A. MAYES
19 Dir Public Safety/Chief Univ Police ... Ronnell A. HIGGINS
06 University Registrar ... Emily SHANDLEY
07 Dean Undergraduate Admissions ... Jeremiah QUINLAN
29 Exec Director Assoc of Yale Alumni ... Weili CHENG
35 Sr Assoc Dean & Dean Student Affs ... Mark SCHENKER
22 Sr Dir Ofc Equal Opportunities ... Valarie J. STANLEY
23 Director University Health Services ... Dr. Paul GENECIN
25 Exec Dir Sponsored Projects ... Lisa MOSLEY
36 Assoc Dean/Director Career Services ... Jeanine DAMES
37 University Director Financial Aid ... Caesar T. STORLAZZI
112 Univ Director Planned Giving ... Marybeth CONGDON
39 Dir Grad & Prof Student Housing ... George E. LONGYEAR, JR.
41 Director Athletics ... Victoria CHUN
42 University Chaplain ... Sharon KUGLER
48 Dean of the School of Architecture ... Deborah BERKE
49 Dean of Yale College ... Marvin CHUN
50 Dean School of Management ... Kerwin CHARLES
85 Director Intl Students & Scholars ... Ann KUHLMAN
54 Dean School of Engineering ... Jeffrey BROCK
57 Dean of the School of Art ... Marta KUZMA
58 Dean of Grad Sch Arts & Science ... Lynn COOLEY
57 Dean of the School of Drama ... James A. BUNDY
61 Dean of the Law School ... Heather GERKEN
64 Dean of the School of Music ... Robert L. BLOCKER
65 Dean Sch of Forestry & Environ Stds ... Indy BURKE
73 Dean of the Divinity School ... Gregory E. STERLING
88 Director Inst of Sacred Music ... Martin D. JEAN
63 Dean of the School of Medicine ... Dr. Robert J. ALPERN
66 Dean of the School of Nursing ... Ann KURTH
69 Dean of Public Health ... Sten VERMUND
28 AVP Emp Engage/Chief Diversity Ofcr ... Deborah STANLEY-MCAULAY
104 Sr Assoc Dean Intl/Prof Experience ... Jane EDWARDS
88 Assoc VP New Haven Aff & Univ Prop ... Lauren ZUCKER
100 Chief of Staff/YSM Dean's Office ... Cynthia DWYER

DELAWARE

Delaware College of Art and Design (D)

600 N Market Street, Wilmington DE 19801-3007
County: New Castle — FICE Identification: 041398
Unit ID: 432524
Telephone: (302) 622-8000 — Carnegie Class: Spec 2-yr-A&S
FAX Number: (302) 622-8870 — Calendar System: Semester
URL: www.dcad.edu
Established: 1997 — Annual Undergrad Tuition & Fees: $25,770
Enrollment: 107 — Coed
Affiliation or Control: Independent Non-Profit — IRS Status: 501(c)3
Highest Offering: Associate Degree
Accreditation: **M**, ART

01 President ... Ms. Jean DAHLGREN
05 Academic Dean ... Ms. Katy RO
20 Assistant Dean ... Vacant
10 Director of Finance ... Vacant
08 Library Director ... Vacant
30 Director of Development ... Ms. Meg CLIFTON NORTH
37 Director of Financial Aid ... Mr. Avery THOMAS
32 Director of Student Services ... Mr. Marcus FREEMAN
07 Director of Admissions ... Mr. Randle REED
06 Registrar ... Vacant
04 Admin Assistant to the President ... Ms. Kristen A. BLANCHARD

Delaware State University (E)

1200 N DuPont Highway, Dover DE 19901-2275
County: Kent — FICE Identification: 001428
Unit ID: 130934
Telephone: (302) 857-6000 — Carnegie Class: DU-Higher
FAX Number: (302) 857-6069 — Calendar System: Semester
URL: www.desu.edu
Established: 1891 — Annual Undergrad Tuition & Fees (In-State): $8,358
Enrollment: 4,739 — Coed
Affiliation or Control: State — IRS Status: 501(c)3
Highest Offering: Doctorate
Accreditation: **M**, CAEP, DIETC, NUR, SW

01 President ... Dr. Tony ALLEN
05 Provost/Exec Vice President ... Dr. Saundra DELAUDER
10 Vice President Finance ... Mr. Robert SCHROF
111 Vice Pres Inst Advancement ... Dr. Vita C. PICKRUM
32 Vice Pres Student Affairs ... Dr. Stacy L. DOWNING
84 Vice Pres Strategic Enrollment ... Mr. Antonio BOYLE
46 Vice President for Research ... Vacant
13 CIO ... Mr. Darrell MCMILLON
09 Exec Dir Research/Planning/Analysis ... Mr. Vaughn K. HOPKINS
15 Vice Pres Human Resources ... Ms. Irene HAWKINS
20 Associate Provost ... Dr. Bradley SKELCHER
43 General Counsel ... Mr. Cleon CAULEY
18 AVP of Facilities ... Vacant
06 Registrar/AVP ... Mr. Terrell HOLMES
07 Exec Director of Admissions ... Mr. Kareem MCLEMORE
08 Dean University Libraries ... Ms. Rebecca BATSON
37 Exec Director of Financial Aid ... Mr. Al DORSETT
29 Executive Director Alumni Relations ... Dr. Marcia TAYLOR
36 AVP Career Services ... Ms. Jasmine BUXTON
19 Director of Public Safety ... Mr. Harry W. DOWNES
38 Director of Student Counseling ... Mr. Ralph ROBINSON
27 Director News Services ... Mr. Carlos HOLMES
41 Director of Athletics ... Dr. D. Scott GINES
44 Director Annual Giving ... Ms. Dawn HOPKINS
86 Dir Government/Cmty Relations ... Mrs. Jackie GRIFFITH
100 Chief of Staff ... Ms. Tamara L. STONER
104 Director Study Abroad ... Dr. Fengshan LIU
105 Director Web Services ... Mr. Stuart GROOBY
58 Dean Grad & Extended Studies ... Dr. Patrice GILLIAM JOHNSON
26 AVP Marketing & Communications ... Dr. Dawn MOSLEY
39 Director of Housing ... Mr. Phillip HOLMES
50 Dean Business ... Mrs. Francine EDWARDS
47 Dean Agricult/Science & Technology ... Dr. Dyremple MARSH

Delaware Technical Community College, Orlando J. George Campus (F)

300 N. Orange Street, Wilmington DE 19801
Telephone: (302) 571-5300 — Identification: 770855
Accreditation: **&M**, CAHIIM, COARC, DH, DMS, MAC, OTA, PTAA, RAD

Delaware Technical Community College, Owens Campus (G)

21179 College Drive, Georgetown DE 19947-0610
Telephone: (302) 259-6000 — FICE Identification: 007053
Accreditation: **&M**, ADNUR, COARC, CSHSE, DMS, MLTAD, OTA, PNUR, PTAA, RAD

Delaware Technical Community College, Stanton Campus (H)

400 Stanton-Christiana Road, Newark DE 19713-2197
Telephone: (302) 454-3900 — FICE Identification: 021449
Accreditation: **&M**, ACFEI, ADNUR, CSHSE, HT, NMT

Delaware Technical Community College, Terry Campus (A)

100 Campus Drive, Dover DE 19904-1383
County: Kent FICE Identification: 011727
Unit ID: 130907
Telephone: (302) 857-1000 Carnegie Class: Bac/Assoc-Assoc Dom
FAX Number: (302) 857-1096 Calendar System: Semester
URL: www.dtcc.edu/terry
Established: 1972 Annual Undergrad Tuition & Fees (In-State): $4,945
Enrollment: 12,955 Coed
Affiliation or Control: State IRS Status: 501(c)3
Highest Offering: Baccalaureate
Accreditation: M, ACFEI, ADNUR, CSHSE, EMT, NUR, PNUR, SURGT

01 Vice President & Campus Director .... Ms. Cornelia JOHNSON
05 Dean Instruction .... Mr. John M. BUCKLEY
32 Dean Student Affairs .... Ms. Kerri HARMON
26 Director Communication and Planning .... Dr. Lisa STRUSOWSKI
103 Director Workforce Development .... Ms. Kristen YENCER
15 Director of Human Resources .... Ms. Marybeth ROACH
18 Director of Facilities .... Mr. Ray PARSONS
10 Director Business Services .... Ms. Noelle SUGALSKI
88 Asst Director of Facilities .... Mr. Allan NELSON
20 Assistant Dean of Instruction .... Mr. Bill J. MORROW

Goldey-Beacom College (B)

4701 Limestone Road, Wilmington DE 19808-0551
County: New Castle FICE Identification: 001429
Unit ID: 130989
Telephone: (302) 998-8814 Carnegie Class: Spec-4-yr-Bus
FAX Number: (302) 998-8631 Calendar System: Semester
URL: www.gbc.edu
Established: 1886 Annual Undergrad Tuition & Fees: $25,500
Enrollment: 1,184 Coed
Affiliation or Control: Independent Non-Profit IRS Status: 501(c)3
Highest Offering: Doctorate
Accreditation: M, ACBSP

01 President .... Dr. Colleen PERRY KEITH
10 Exec Vice President Admin/ Finance .... Ms. Kristine M. SANTOMAURO
05 Vice President for Academic Affairs .... Ms. Alison Boord WHITE
32 VP of Student Affairs & Athletics .... Mr. Charles A. HAMMOND
84 Dean Enrollment Mgmt .... Vacant
06 Registrar .... Mr. Ryan QUANN
13 Chief Informaton Officer .... Mr. Peter RYSAVY
15 Asst VP Finance/HR .... Ms. Susan M. MANNERING
111 Exec Director of Advancement .... Vacant
88 Director of the DBA Program .... Dr. William D. YOUNG
39 Director of Residence/Student Life .... Ms. Jocelyn MOSES
41 Director of Athletics .... Mr. Jeremy BENOIT
30 Director of External Affairs .... Ms. Janine SORBELLO
18 Director of Facilities/Operations .... Mr. Meezie FOSTER
08 Director of Library/Learning Center .... Mr. Russell MICHALAK
09 Dir Institutional Research/Training .... Dr. Monica RYSAVY
36 Career Services Coordinator .... Ms. Elizabeth KIRKER

University of Delaware (C)

104 Hullihen Hall, Newark DE 19716
County: New Castle FICE Identification: 001431
Unit ID: 130943
Telephone: (302) 831-2000 Carnegie Class: DU-Highest
FAX Number: (302) 831-8000 Calendar System: 4/1/4
URL: www.udel.edu
Established: 1743 Annual Undergrad Tuition & Fees (In-State): $14,660
Enrollment: 23,613 Coed
Affiliation or Control: State Related IRS Status: 501(c)3
Highest Offering: Doctorate
Accreditation: M, CAATE, CAEP, CEA, CLPSY, CSHSE, DIETD, DIETI, IPSY, LSAR, MT, MUS, NURSE, PCSAS, PTA, SP, SPAA

01 President .... Dr. Dennis ASSANIS
05 Provost .... Dr. Robin W. MORGAN
03 Exec VP & Chief Operating Officer .... Mr. John LONG
15 Interim VP Human Resources .... Mr. Jared AUPPERLE
101 Vice Pres & University Secretary .... Ms. Beth G. BRAND
26 VP Comm & Marketing .... Mr. Glenn CARTER
08 Vice Prov Libraries & Museums .... Mr. Trevor A. DAWES
30 VP Development & Alumni Relations .... Mr. James DICKER
43 Vice Pres and General Counsel .... Ms. Laure ERGIN
20 Vice Provost for Faculty Affairs .... Dr. Matt KINSERVIK
18 VP Facilities/Real Est/Aux Svcs .... Mr. Peter KRAWCHYK
84 Vice Pres Enrollment Management .... Mr. Rodney MORRISON
20 Deputy Provost Academic Affairs .... Dr. Lynn OKAGAKI
10 Vice Pres Finance/Dept Treasurer .... Mr. Gregory S. OLER
13 VP Information Technologies .... Ms. Sharon PITT
41 Dir Intercol Athletics & Rec Svcs .... Ms. Christine RAWAK
45 VP Strategic Planning & Analysis .... Ms. Mary M. REMMLER
32 Vice President for Student Life .... Dr. José-Luis RIERA
46 VP Research/Scholarship/Innovation .... Dr. Charles RIORDAN
28 Interim Vice Provost for Diversity .... Dr. Michael VAUGHAN
47 Interim Dean Ag & Natural Resources .... Dr. Calvin KEELER
49 Dean Arts & Sciences .... Dr. John A. PELESKO
50 Dean Lerner Col Business & Econ .... Dr. Bruce WEBER
65 Dean Earth Ocean & Environment .... Dr. Estella ATEKWANA
53 Dean Educ & Human Development .... Dr. Gary HENRY
54 Dean Engineering .... Dr. Levi T. THOMPSON
58 Dean Graduate College .... Dr. Louis ROSSI
76 Dean Health Sciences .... Dr. Kathleen MATT
92 Dean Honors College .... Dr. Michael J. CHAJES
80 Dean Biden Sch Pub Policy & Admin .... Dr. Maria P. ARISTIGUETA
28 Interim Chief Diversity Officer .... Ms. Fatimah R. CONLEY
51 AVP Professional/Cont Studies .... Dr. George IRVINE
09 AVP Inst Research & Effectiveness .... Mr. Richard J. REEVES
09 Director Institutional Research .... Dr. Heather A. KELLY
108 Dir Ctr Teach/Assessment/Lrng .... Dr. Matthew TREVETT-SMITH
29 AVP Alumni Engagement/Annual Giving .... Ms. Lauren E. SIMIONE
85 Assoc Deputy Prov Global Pgms & Svs .... Mr. Ravi AMMIGAN
104 Interim Assoc Dir Study Abroad .... Mr. Matthew DREXLER
37 Exec Dir Student Financial Svcs .... Ms. Mary BOOKER
36 Director Career Center .... Mr. Nathan ELTON
19 Assoc VP & Chief of Police .... Chief Patrick OGDEN
07 Exec Director Undergrad Admissions .... Dr. William D. ZANDER
123 Director of Graduate Admissions .... Mr. Michael ALEXO
16 Assoc VP HR Strategic Operations .... Ms. Darcell GRIFFITH
96 Manager Purchasing Services .... Mr. George WALUEFF
06 University Registrar .... Ms. Amanda STEELE-MIDDLETON
114 Assoc VP & Chief Budget Officer .... Ms. Mandy MINNER
22 Interim Title IX Coordinator .... Ms. Danica A. MYERS
35 Dean of Students .... Mr. Adam D. CANTLEY
38 Dir Ctr for Counseling/Student Dev .... Dr. Brad WOLGAST
35 Assoc VP Student Life .... Dr. Kathleen G. KERR
23 Director Student Health Services .... Dr. Timothy F. DOWLING
04 Exec Assistant to the President .... Ms. Susan L. WILLIAMS

Widener University Delaware Law School (D)

4601 Concord Pike, Wilmington DE 19803-0406
Telephone: (302) 477-2100 FICE Identification: 012962
Accreditation: &M, LAW

† Branch campus of Widener University in Pennsylvania. This listing reflects the administrators for the school of law for the Harrisburg (PA) and Delaware campuses.

Wilmington University (E)

320 N Dupont Highway, New Castle DE 19720-6491
County: New Castle FICE Identification: 007948
Unit ID: 131113
Telephone: (302) 356-4636 Carnegie Class: DU-Mod
FAX Number: (302) 328-5902 Calendar System: Trimester
URL: www.wilmu.edu
Established: 1967 Annual Undergrad Tuition & Fees: $11,480
Enrollment: 14,769 Coed
Affiliation or Control: Independent Non-Profit IRS Status: 501(c)3
Highest Offering: Doctorate
Accreditation: M, CACREP, CAEP, IACBE, NURSE

00 Chairman of the Board .... Hon. Joseph J. FARNAN, JR.
01 President .... Dr. LaVerne T. HARMON
100 Executive Director .... Ms. Donna M. QUINN
11 Senior Vice President/COO .... Dr. Erin DIMARCO
10 Senior VP/CFO Financial Affairs .... Ms. Heather A. O'CONNELL
88 VP Administrative Services .... Ms. Carole D. PITCHER
86 VP External Affairs .... Dr. Peter A. BAILEY
05 VP Academic Affairs .... Dr. James D. WILSON, JR.
43 VP Admin & Legal Affairs .... Dr. Christian A. TROWBRIDGE
84 VP Enrollment Management .... Dr. Eileen G. DONNELLY
32 VP Student Affairs/Alumni Rel .... Dr. Tina M. BARKSDALE
111 VP Institutional Advancement .... Dr. Jacque R. VARSALONA
35 AVP Student Affairs .... Dr. Regina C. ALLEN-SHARPE
19 AVP Admin & Legal Affairs .... Dr. Joseph P. AVIOLA
35 AVP Student Services .... Dr. Bonnie L. KIRKPATRICK
21 Asst Vice President/Controller .... Mr. David R. LEWIS
88 AVP Admin Affs & Dean of Location .... Mr. Robert P. MILLER
88 AVP Academic Support Services .... Ms. Peg P. MITCHELL
106 AVP Admin Affs/Dean Online .... Dr. Sallie A. REISSMAN
20 AVP Academic Affairs .... Dr. Robert W. RESCIGNO
15 Asst Vice President/CHRO .... Dr. Nicole ROMANO
20 AVP Academic Affairs .... Dr. Sheila M. SHARBAUGH
108 Assistant Vice President .... Dr. Angela C. SUCHANIC
26 AVP University Relations .... Mr. Bill F. SWAIN
13 Asst Vice President/CIO .... Mr. Peter E. LUTUS
101 Liaison to the Board of Trustees .... Ms. Ashley R. MUNDY
125 President Emeritus .... Dr. Jack P. VARSALONA
88 Exec Director Admin & Legal Affairs .... Ms. Linda M. ANDRZJEWSKI
41 AVP & Athletics Director .... Dr. Stefanie A. WHITBY
06 Registrar .... Ms. Misty B. WILLIAMS
88 Senior Dir External Affairs .... Ms. Melanie C. BALDWIN
105 Sr Dir of Web/System Communications .... Mr. Kevin G. BARRY
14 Senior Dir Information Technology .... Mr. Brian C. BEARD
120 Sr Dir Online Learning Ed Tech .... Dr. Matthew H. DAVIS
88 Sr Dir Academic Support Services .... Dr. Elizabeth P. JORDAN
07 Sr Director of Admissions .... Dr. Laura M. MORRIS
09 Sr Dir of Institutional Research .... Dr. Dana S. CHAPMAN
53 Dean College of Education .... Dr. John C. GRAY
83 Dean College of Soc & Beh .... Dr. Edward L. GUTHRIE
50 Dean College of Business .... Dr. Kathy S. KENNEDY-RATAJACK
49 Dean College of Arts and Sciences .... Dr. Mary Ann K. WESTERFIELD
76 Dean College of Health Professions .... Dr. Denise Z. WELLS
72 Dean College of Technology .... Dr. Antony J. CARCILLO
88 Dir Center for Teaching Excellence .... Dr. Adrienne M. BEY
85 Director International Affairs .... Ms. Angelina L. BURNS
78 Director Cooperative Learning .... Dr. David C. CAFFO
29 Director Alumni Relations .... Mr. Stuart J. HANF
121 Dir Student Success Center .... Ms. Sally J. HEALY
08 Director Library .... Mr. James M. MCCLOSKEY
37 Director Financial Aid .... Ms. Nicole L. MCDANIEL-SMITH
30 Director of Development .... Ms. Felicia K. QUINN
16 Sr Dir Human Resources .... Ms. Karen A. SHEATS
40 Bookstore Manager .... Ms. Carmen L. CASANOVA
89 Chair First Year Experience .... Dr. Matthew J. WILSON
118 Benefits Coordinator .... Ms. Jennifer L. WORKMAN

DISTRICT OF COLUMBIA

American University (F)

4400 Massachusetts Avenue, NW, Washington DC 20016
FICE Identification: 001434
Unit ID: 131159
Telephone: (202) 885-1000 Carnegie Class: DU-Higher
FAX Number: N/A Calendar System: Semester
URL: www.american.edu
Established: 1893 Annual Undergrad Tuition & Fees: $51,361
Enrollment: 14,001 Coed
Affiliation or Control: United Methodist IRS Status: 501(c)3
Highest Offering: Doctorate
Accreditation: M, CAEPN, CLPSY, IPSY, JOUR, LAW, MUS, PH, SPAA

01 President .... Sylvia M. BURWELL
05 Acting Provost/Chief Academic Ofcr .... Dr. Peter STARR
30 Vice President Development & Alumni .... Courtney SURLS
10 Vice President Finance & Treasurer .... Vacant
32 VP Campus Life/Inclusive Excellence .... Dr. Fanta AW
43 Vice President & General Counsel .... Traevena BYRD
20 Vice Provost for Academic Admin .... Prita PATEL
106 Vice Provost/Chief Online Officer .... Joseph RIQUELME
18 Asst VP Facilities Management .... Vincent HARKINS
35 Asst VP Campus Life .... Dr. Traci CALLANDRILLO
35 Dean of Students .... Jeffery BROWN
108 Asst Provost Inst Rsrch/Assessment .... Karen L. FROSLID JONES
30 AVP Development & Alumni Relations .... Raina LENNEY
21 Assoc VP of Finance/Asst Treasurer .... Laura MCANDREW
28 Asst VP Diversity/Equity/Inclusiv .... Dr. Amanda TAYLOR
84 Vice Provost Undergrad Enrollment .... Dr. Sharon ALSTON
13 Vice President & CIO .... Steve MUNSON
100 VP & Chief of Staff .... Seth GROSSMAN
20 Int Deputy Provost/Dean of Faculty .... Dr. Monica JACKSON
58 Dean Graduate Studies .... Dr. Wendy BOLAND
20 Dean UG Ed & VP Acad Student Svcs .... Dr. Jessica WATERS
49 Int Dean College Arts & Sciences .... Dr. Max Paul FRIEDMAN
60 Dean School of Communication .... Mr. Sam FULWOOD, III
50 Dean Kogod Sch of Business .... Dr. John T. DELANEY
61 Actg Dean Washington College of Law .... Dr. Robert DINERSTEIN
82 Dean School of Intl Service .... Dr. Christine CHIN
80 Dean School of Public Affairs .... Dr. Vicky WILKINS
15 Asst VP of Human Resources .... Beth MUHA
36 Exec Director Career Center .... Gihan FERNANDO
88 Assoc Vice Provost/Acad Admin .... Vacant
26 Vice President of Communication .... Matthew BENNETT
27 Asst Vice Pres Communications/Media .... Lisa STARK
06 Assistant University Registrar .... Dr. Michael GIESE
08 University Librarian .... Jeehyun DAVIS
21 AVP & University Controller .... Nicole BRESNAHAN
113 Dir Student Account Operations .... Darrell COOK
114 Asst VP Budget & Finance Res Ctr .... Nana AN
42 University Chaplain .... Rev. Bryant OSKVIG
19 AVP Risk/Safety/Transportation .... Daniel NICHOLS
37 Asst Vice Provost Financial Aid .... Brian LEE SANG
38 Exec Director Counseling Center .... Dr. Jeff VOLKMANN
102 Sr Dir Corp Relations/Foundation .... Amy BUTLER
96 Sr Dir Procurement and Contracts .... Brian BLAIR
07 Asst Vice Provost UG Adm .... Dr. Andrea FELDER
85 Director Intl Student/Scholar Svcs .... Senem BAKAR
92 Faculty Dir Univ Honors Program .... Dr. Patrick T. JACKSON
41 Director Athletics & Recreation .... Dr. William (Billy) WALKER
104 Executive Director AU Abroad .... Sara E. DUMONT
45 AVP Planning & Project Mgmt .... David DOWER
88 AVP Lifetime/Special Campaigns .... Lee HOLSOPPLE
88 Asst Vice Provost Ops/Enrollment .... Robert LINSON
04 Senior Assistant to the President .... Stephanie LEIGH
22 Sr Dir Employee Relations/Recruit .... Deadre JOHNSON
25 Dir Office of Sponsored Programs .... Dr. Vibeke SVENSSON
09 Asst Provost Inst Res & Assessment .... Karen L. FROSLID JONES
88 Sr Dir Talent Development .... Michelle FREDERICK
53 Dean School of Education .... Dr. Cheryl HOLCOMB-MCCOY
86 AVP Community/Government Relations .... Ed FISHER
101 Asst Secretary to the Board .... Leslie WONG
46 Vice Provost for Research .... Dr. Diana BURLEY
31 Dir Cmty Rels President's Office .... Maria BARRY
88 Exec Dir Strategic Implementation .... Geralynn FRANCESCHINI
88 Dir Speech Writing/Ofc of President .... Margaret HENDERSON
39 Director of Residence Life .... Lisa FREEMAN
119 Chief Information Security Officer .... Cathy HUBBS
14 AVP IT Customer Services .... Terry FERNANDEZ
93 Dir Ctr for Diversity & Inclusion .... Robin ADAMS

Bay Atlantic University (G)

1510 H Street NW, Washington DC 20005
Identification: 667329
Telephone: (844) 922-8228 Carnegie Class: Not Classified
FAX Number: N/A Calendar System: Semester
URL: www.bau.edu
Established: 2014 Annual Undergrad Tuition & Fees: N/A
Enrollment: N/A Coed
Affiliation or Control: Independent Non-Profit IRS Status: 501(c)3
Highest Offering: Master's

Accreditation: ACICS

01 President/CEO Dr. Sinem VATANARTIRAN
05 Dean of Academic Affairs Dr. Billur COHEN
10 CFO/Human Resources Dir Ms. Melek EDIB
06 Registrar Ms. Izel UGUR
08 Librarian Ms. Taylor NICKELS
07 Director of Admissions Ms. Mayte TARAZON
28 Director of Diversity/Inclusion Mr. Tyler CARGILL
32 Student Relations Supervisor Ms. Linh TRUONG

The Catholic University of America (A)

620 Michigan Avenue, NE, Washington DC 20064-0002
FICE Identification: 001437
Unit ID: 131283
Telephone: (202) 319-5100 Carnegie Class: DU-Higher
FAX Number: (202) 319-4441 Calendar System: Semester
URL: www.cua.edu
Established: 1887 Annual Undergrad Tuition & Fees: $49,416
Enrollment: 5,366 Coed
Affiliation or Control: Roman Catholic IRS Status: 501(c)3
Highest Offering: Doctorate
Accreditation: M, CAEPN, CLPSY, IPSY, LAW, LIB, MUS, NURSE, SW, THEOL

01 President Mr. John H. GARVEY
100 Chief of Staff/Counselor to Pres Mr. Lawrence J. MORRIS
05 Provost Dr. Aaron DOMINGUEZ
10 Vice Pres Finance & Treasurer Mr. Robert M. SPECTER
32 Vice President Student Affairs Dr. Judi BIGGS GARBUIO
84 Vice Pres Enrollment Mgmt Mr. Christopher P. LYDON
85 Vice Provost for Global Strategies Dr. Duilia DE MELLO
11 Vice Provost for Administration Vacant
35 Assoc VP Student Life/Dean Students Mr. Jonathan C. SAWYER
43 General Counsel Mr. Matthew DOLAN
15 Sr Assoc VP for Admin/CHRO Mr. Matthew MCNALLY
18 Assoc VP Facilities Operations Ms. Debra NAUTA-RODRIGUEZ
41 Assoc VP & Director Athletics Dr. Sean M. SULLIVAN
39 Executive Director for Housing Mr. Timothy CARNEY
111 Vice Pres for Univ Advancement Mr. Scott REMBOLD
26 VP for University Communications Ms. Karna LOZOYA
110 Assoc VP Univ Advancement Ms. Deborah BROWN
110 Assoc VP University Advancement Mr. William WARREN
25 Assoc Prov Sponsored Research Mr. Ralph ALBANO
58 Dean Graduate Studies Dr. J. Steven BROWN
48 Dean of Architecture Mr. Mark FERGUSON
49 Dean of Arts & Sciences Dr. Thomas SMITH
50 Dean School of Business Dr. Andrew V. ABELA
54 Dean of Engineering Dr. John JUDGE
61 Dean of Law Mr. Stephen C. PAYNE
64 Dean of Music/Drama and Art Dr. Jacqueline LEARY-WARSAW
70 Dean Natl Cath Sch Social Svcs Dr. Jo Ann R. COE REGAN
66 Dean of Nursing Dr. Patricia MCMULLEN
73 Dean Theology/Religious Studies VRev. Mark MOROZOWICH
107 Dean Metro Sch Professional Studies Dr. Vincent KIERNAN
79 Dean of Philosophy Dr. John C. MCCARTHY
88 Dean of Canon Law Msgr. Ronny JENKINS
07 Dean of Undergrad Admissions Vacant
13 Chief Information Officer Mr. Matthew MCNALLY
08 Director of Libraries Mr. Stephen CONNAGHAN
06 Registrar Ms. Danielle SPINATO
36 Director of Career Services Mr. Anthony CHIAPPETTA
19 Assoc VP Public Safety & Emergency Mr. Kirk MCLEAN
38 Director of Counseling Center Dr. T. Monroe RAYBURN
23 Medical Director of Health Center Dr. Loretta STAUDT
37 Dir Student Financial Assistance Ms. Mindy SCHAEFFER
35 Assoc Dean of Students Ms. Heidi E. ZEICH
44 Director of Regional Engagement Mr. Patrick DAVEY
42 Director University Campus Ministry Rev. Jude DEANGELO, OFM CONV
09 Assoc VP Fin Plng/Inst Res/Assess Dr. Brian A. JOHNSTON
20 Vice Provost & Assoc Dean Undergrad Dr. Lynn MAYER
96 Director of Procurement Ms. Yssa RESURRECCION
22 Title IX Coordinator/EOO Mr. Frank VINIK
40 Manager Bookstore Mr. Brett MCMICHAEL
04 Exec Assistant to the President Ms. Ruth BARWICK
101 Secretary of the Board Mr. Lawrence J. MORRIS
102 Director Institutional Partnership Ms. Jo Anna NORRIS
105 Director Digital Strategy Mr. Bart POLLOCK
29 Director of Alumni Engagement Mr. Chris JOHNSON

Chicago School of Professional Psychology-Washington DC (B)

901 15th Street NW, Washington DC 20005
Telephone: (202) 706-5000 Identification: 770493
Accreditation: &WC, CACREP, CLPSY

† Branch campus of Chicago School of Professional Psychology Los Angeles Campus, Los Angeles, CA

Gallaudet University (C)

800 Florida Avenue, NE, Washington DC 20002-3695
FICE Identification: 001443
Unit ID: 131450
Telephone: (202) 651-5005 Carnegie Class: DU-Higher
FAX Number: (202) 651-5508 Calendar System: Semester
URL: www.gallaudet.edu
Established: 1864 Annual Undergrad Tuition & Fees: $17,038
Enrollment: 1,451 Coed
Affiliation or Control: Independent Non-Profit IRS Status: 501(c)3
Highest Offering: Doctorate
Accreditation: M, ACBSP, AUD, CACREP, CAEP, CEA, CLPSY, SP, SW

01 President Ms. Roberta (Bobbi) CORDANO
11 Chief Operating Officer Mr. Dominic LACY
05 Interim Provost Dr. Jeffrey LEWIS
88 Interim Chief Bilingual Officer Dr. Laurene SIMMS
10 Chief Finance Officer Mr. Brad HERMES
30 Exec Dir Advance & Alumni Relations Mr. Nicholas GOULD
43 General Counsel Ms. Natalie SINICROPE
28 Chief Diversity Officer Dr. Elizabeth MOORE
12 Chief Admin Ofcr L. Clerc Natl Ctr Ms. Nicole SUTLIFFE
20 Chief Academic Officer Ms. Marianne BELSKY
101 Board Liaison/Presidential Support Vacant
100 Chief of Staff to President Ms. Heather HARKER
45 Exec Dir Strategic Planning Ms. Susan JACOBY
20 Interim Dean of Faculty Dr. Khadijat RASHID
58 Dean Grad School & Cont Studies Dr. Guarav MATHUR
32 Dean Student Affs/Acad Support Mr. Travis IMEL
07 Int Dean of Undergrad Admiss Dr. Genie GERTZ
121 Assoc Prov Stdnt Succ/Acad Quality Dr. Thomas HOREJES
96 Exec Dir Business Support Services Ms. Davina KWONG
18 Director Facilities Vacant
112 Dir Major Gifts Vacant
26 Chief Marketing/Undergrad Admiss Ms. Brandi RARUS
09 Director Institutional Research Ms. Lindsay BUCHKO
29 Exec Director Alumni Relations Mr. Samuel SONNENSTRAHL
15 Exec Director Human Resources Svcs Ms. Christina SHEN-AUSTIN
13 Exec Director Technology Services Mr. Earl PARKS
14 Dir Enterprise Info Systems Mr. Daryl FRELICH
88 University Ombuds Ms. Elizabeth STONE
08 Dir Library Deaf Collection/Archive Vacant
22 Director Equal Opportunity Programs Ms. Sharrell MCCASKILL
06 Registrar Ms. Elice PATTERSON
88 Director of Admissions Ms. Young Hae PARK

George Washington University (D)

1918 F Street, NW, Washington DC 20052-0002
FICE Identification: 001444
Unit ID: 131469
Telephone: (202) 994-1000 Carnegie Class: DU-Highest
FAX Number: (202) 994-0458 Calendar System: Semester
URL: www.gwu.edu
Established: 1821 Annual Undergrad Tuition & Fees: $58,640
Enrollment: 27,017 Coed
Affiliation or Control: Independent Non-Profit IRS Status: 501(c)3
Highest Offering: Doctorate
Accreditation: M, ACATE, ARCPA, ART, CACREP, CAEPN, CIDA, CLPSY, FEPAC, HSA, IPSY, LAW, MED, MT, NURSE, PH, PLNG, PTA, SP, SPAA

01 President Dr. Thomas J. LEBLANC
100 Chief of Staff President's Office Mr. Aristide J. COLLINS
05 Int Prov & Exec VP Academic Affairs Dr. Christopher A. BRACEY
84 Vice Provost of Enrollment Mgmt Mr. Jay GOFF
30 Vice Pres for Dev/Alumni Relations Ms. Donna ARBIDE
10 Exec Vice President & Treasurer Mr. Mark DIAZ
43 Interim Senior VP & General Counsel Mr. Charles BARBER
26 Vice President External Relations Vacant
45 VP Financial Planning & Ops Mr. Jared ABRAMSON
114 Vice Provost of Budget and Finance Vacant
28 Vice Provost Diversity & Inclusion Ms. Caroline LAGUERRE-BROWN
15 VP & Chief People Officer Ms. Dana BRADLEY
13 Interim Chief Technology Officer Mr. Jared W. JOHNSON
20 Vice Provost Faculty Affairs Dr. Christopher A. BRACEY
18 Assoc VP Facil Plng/Const & Mgmt Mr. David D. DENT
32 Dean of Student Experience Dr. Marcia L. PETTY
88 Assoc Provost Diversity & Inclusion Ms. Helen CANNADAY SAULNY
90 Deputy Chief Academic Tech Officer Vacant
108 Assoc VP of Acad Plng & Assessment Dr. Cheryl BEIL
46 Vice President for Research Dr. Pamela NORRIS
88 AVP Budget & Financial Analysis Ms. Cynthia VILLAVERDE
21 Assoc VP & University Controller Ms. Neena ALI
09 Director Inst Research & Planning Mr. Joachim W. KNOP
86 Asst VP Government Relations Ms. Renee MCPHATTER
104 Associate VP for International Pgms Vacant
08 University Librarian Ms. Geneva HENRY
27 Asst VP for Communications Ms. Sarah GEGENHEIMER BALDASSARO
27 Exec Dir of Media Relations Ms. Maralee B. CSELLAR
111 Associate VP Advancement Services Mr. Gail FERRIS
06 Registrar Ms. Elizabeth A. AMUNDSON
07 Dean of Undergrad Admissions Mr. Benjamin A. TOLL
38 Director Counseling Center Vacant
37 Executive Director Financial Aid Ms. Michelle C. ARCIERI
36 Asst Provost Career Center Ms. Rachel A. BROWN
85 Director International Services Ms. Jennifer H. DONAGHUE
19 VP Safety & Facilities Mr. Scott G. BURNOTES
22 Dir EEO & Affirmative Action Ms. Vickie FAIR
23 Director Student Health Services Dr. Isabel GOLDENBERG
40 Director GW Bookstore Ms. Janet F. UZZELL
107 Dean Col Professional Studies Dr. Melissa FEUER
49 Dean Columbian Col Arts/Sci Dr. Paul J. WAHLBECK
63 Dean Medicine & Health Sciences Dr. Barbara BASS
69 Dean School of Public Health Dr. Lynn R. GOLDMAN
61 Dean Law School Dr. Dayna B. MATTHEW
54 Dean Engineering/Applied Science Dr. John LACH
53 Dean Education/Human Development Dr. Michael J. FEUER
50 Dean School of Business Dr. Anuj MEHROTRA
82 Int Dean Elliott Sch Intl Affairs Dr. Ilana FELDMAN
66 Interim Dean School of Nursing Dr. Pamela SLAVEN-LEE
41 Director Athletics/Recreation Ms. Tanya VOGEL
92 Director University Honors Program Dr. Bethany E. KUNG
93 Director Multicultural Student Svc Mr. Michael R. TAPSCOTT
39 Director Student Housing Mr. Seth D. WEINSHEL

Georgetown University (E)

37th & O Streets, NW, Washington DC 20057-1947
FICE Identification: 001445
Unit ID: 131496
Telephone: (202) 687-0100 Carnegie Class: DU-Highest
FAX Number: N/A Calendar System: Semester
URL: www.georgetown.edu
Established: 1789 Annual Undergrad Tuition & Fees: $57,928
Enrollment: 19,371 Coed
Affiliation or Control: Roman Catholic IRS Status: 501(c)3
Highest Offering: Doctorate
Accreditation: M, ANEST, CAMPEP, CEA, HSA, LAW, MED, MIDWF, NURSE, PAST

01 President Dr. John (Jack) J. DEGIOIA
46 SVP Research/Chief Technology Ofcr Dr. Spiros DIMOLITSAS
05 Provost Dr. Robert M. GROVES
17 Exec Vice Pres Health Sciences Dr. Edward B. HEALTON
61 Exec Vice Pres/Dean of Law School Dr. William M. TREANOR
111 Vice Pres for Advancement Mr. R. Bartley MOORE
42 Vice Pres for Mission and Ministry Rev. Mark BOSCO, SJ
13 Vice Pres/CIO Mr. Judd NICHOLSON
26 VP Public Affairs & Strategic Dev Mr. Erik SMULSON
32 VP Student Affairs Dr. Todd OLSON
28 VP for Inst Diversity & Equity Ms. Rosemary KILKENNY
19 Chief of Police Dept Public Safety Mr. Jay GRUBER
43 VP & General Counsel Ms. Lisa M. BROWN
85 VP for Global Engagement Dr. Thomas BANCHOFF
11 VP & COO Main Campus Mr. Darryl E. CHRISTMON
10 Sr AVP Budget/Financial Planning Ms. Stella APEKEY
109 Assoc VP for Auxiliary Services Ms. Joelle D. WIESE
118 AVP Benefits/Chief Benefits Officer Mr. Charles E. DESANTIS
20 Vice Provost Education Dr. Randall BASS
88 Vice Provost Research Dr. Janet MANN
20 Vice Provost Faculty Dr. Reena AGGARWAL
21 Assoc Vice President for Operations Ms. Christina ROBERTS
114 Asst VP Finance Planning & Budget Mr. Matthew C. GREAVES
06 Assoc VP & University Registrar Ms. Annamarie BIANCO
35 Assoc VP Student Affairs Dr. Jeanne F. LORD
23 Asst VP for Student Health Dr. Vince C. WINKLERPRINS
08 University Librarian Ms. Artemis G. KIRK
88 Ex Dir Ctr New Designs Lrng/Schlrs Dr. Edward J. MALONEY
25 Senior Research Compliance Officer Ms. Mary E. SCHMIEDEL
49 Dean Georgetown College Dr. Christopher CELENZA
82 Dean School Foreign Service Dr. Joel HELLMAN
50 Dean School of Business Dr. Paul A. ALMEIDA
63 Dean Medical School Dr. Edward B. HEALTON
66 Dean Sch of Nursing/Health Stds Dr. Patricia CLOONAN
51 Dean Continuing Studies Dr. Kelly OTTER
58 Dean of Graduate School Vacant
80 Dean McCourt School Public Policy Dr. Michael A. BAILEY
31 Dir Partnerships & Cmty Engagement Ms. Brenda ATKINSON-WILLOUGHBY
96 Asst VP Procurement Mr. O.T WELLS
104 Director of Global Education Mr. Craig RINKER
22 Director Affirmative Action Pgm Mr. Michael W. SMITH
24 Exec Dir Classroom Educ/Tech Svcs Mr. Mark J. COHEN
38 Director Counseling Center Dr. Philip W. MEILMAN
39 Director of Residence Life Ms. Stephanie J. LYNCH
108 Asst Dir CNDLS/Assessment Ms. Mindy MCWILLIAMS
112 Exec Director Gift Planning Mr. Stephen LINK
15 Director Human Resources Ms. Eileen FENRICH

Howard University (F)

2400 Sixth Street, NW, Washington DC 20059-0001
FICE Identification: 001448
Unit ID: 131520
Telephone: (202) 806-6100 Carnegie Class: DU-Higher
FAX Number: (202) 806-5934 Calendar System: Semester
URL: https://home.howard.edu/
Established: 1867 Annual Undergrad Tuition & Fees: $28,440
Enrollment: 10,859 Coed
Affiliation or Control: Independent Non-Profit IRS Status: 501(c)3
Highest Offering: Doctorate
Accreditation: M, ART, CAEP, CLPSY, COPSY, DENT, DH, DIETC, IPSY, JOUR, LAW, MED, MT, MUS, NURSE, OT, PHAR, #PTA, #RTT, SP, SW, THEA, THEOL

01 President Dr. Wayne FREDERICK
05 Provost/Chief Academic Officer Dr. Anthony K. WUTOH
11 EVP/Chief Operating Officer Dr. Tashni-Ann DUBROY
43 VP/General Counsel/Bd Secretary Ms. Florence PRIOLEAU
10 Int Chief Financial Ofcr/Treasurer Ms. Annemieke MARTINEZ
26 VP/Chief Communications Ofcr Mr. Frank TRAMBLE
15 AVP/Chief Human Resources Ofcr Mr. Larry A. CALLAHAN
30 SVP Development & Alumni Relations Mr. David P. BENNETT
17 CEO University Hospital Mr. James DIEGEL
46 Assoc Provost Research/Grad Studies Dr. Gary L. HARRIS
20 Associate Provost Dr. Joseph P. REIDY
20 Assoc Provost Undergraduate Studies Dr. Melanie CARTER
32 Vice President Student Affairs Dr. Cynthia EVERS
88 AVP Regulatory/Research Compliance Dr. Thomas O. OBISESAN
88 AVP for Research and Faculty Dr. Kristy F. WOODS
13 Chief Information Officer Mr. Jonathan PIERSOL
88 CIO Howard Univ Hospital Mr. Kevin DAWSON
100 Chief of Staff Mr. D. Paul MONTEIRO, JR.
58 Interim Dean Graduate School Dr. Dana WILLIAMS

49 Int Dean College Arts/Sciences .... Dr. Edna MEDFORD
50 Dean School of Business .... Dr. Barron H. HARVEY
61 Dean School of Law .... Ms. Danielle R. HOLLEY-WALKER
63 Dean Medicine/VP Clinical Affairs .... Dr. Hugh E. MIGHTY
52 Dean College of Dentistry .... Dr. Dexter A. WOODS
54 Dean Col Engineering/Architecture .... Dr. Achille MESSAC
53 Dean School of Education .... Dr. Dawn WILLIAMS
60 Dean School of Communications .... Dr. Gracie LAWSON-BORDERS
66 Int Dean Nursing/Allied Hlth Sc .... Dr. Mary HILL
70 Dean School of Social Work .... Dr. Sandra CREWE
73 Dean School of Divinity .... Dr. Yolanda PIERCE
67 Dean School of Pharmacy .... Dr. Toyin TOFADE
48 Director School of Architecture .... Prof. Hazel EDWARDS
76 Assoc Dean/Div Allied Health Sci .... Dr. Shirley J. JACKSON
66 Assoc Dean/Div of Nursing .... Ms. Tammi L. DAMAS
57 Assoc Dean Division of Fine Arts .... Dr. Lisa E. FARRINGTON
81 Assoc Dean/Div Natural Sciences .... Dr. Robert CATCHINGS
83 Interim Assoc Dean/Social Sciences .... Dr. Terri ADAMS
79 Associate Dean Humanities .... Dr. James J. DAVIS
06 Registrar/Director of Admissions .... Ms. Latrice BYAM
37 Director Financial Aid .... Vacant
42 Dean Andrew Rankin Chapel .... Dr. Bernard L. RICHARDSON
35 Dean Student Life & Activities .... Vacant
39 Int Dir Residence Life/Univ Housing .... Mr. Joe UTER
36 Director Career Services Office .... Dr. Joan M. BROWNE
08 Executive Director Libraries .... Ms. Rhea BALLARD-THROWER
08 Interim Director Law Library .... Ms. Eileen SANTOS
24 Dir Teaching/Learning/Assessmnt Ctr .... Dr. Helen BOND
16 Senior Director Human Resources .... Mr. Michael MCFADDEN
22 Dir Equal Employment Opportunity .... Mr. Antwan LOFTON
29 Director Alumni Relations .... Ms. Sharon STRANGE LEWIS
44 Principal Gift Officer .... Mr. Ken ASHWORTH
27 AVP of External Affairs .... Mr. Paul MONTEIRO
18 AVP Facilities .... Vacant
19 Chief of Campus Police .... Mr. Alonzo F. JOY
31 Director HU Community Association .... Ms. Maybelle T. BENNETT
109 Director Auxiliary Enterprises .... Mr. Antwan D. CLINTON
41 Athletics Director .... Mr. Kery DAVIS
23 Exec Director Student Health Center .... Dr. Michelle R. CARTER
40 Gen Manager Barnes & Noble at HU .... Mr. Alex BAMFO
94 Director of Women's Studies .... Vacant
18 Director Physical Facilities .... Mr. Victor MCNAUGHTON
108 Director Institutional Assessment .... Dr. Gerunda B. HUGHES
88 Director Events & Protocol .... Mr. Andrew RIVERS

The Institute of World Politics (A)

1521 16th Street, NW, Washington DC 20036-1464

FICE Identification: 041144
Unit ID: 455804
Telephone: (202) 462-2101 — Carnegie Class: Spec-4-yr-Other
FAX Number: (202) 464-0335 — Calendar System: Semester
URL: www.iwp.edu
Established: 1990 — Annual Graduate Tuition & Fees: N/A
Enrollment: 120 — Coed
Affiliation or Control: Independent Non-Profit — IRS Status: 501(c)3
Highest Offering: Doctorate; No Undergraduates
Accreditation: M

01 President .... Dr. James ANDERSON
03 Executive Vice President .... Lawrence COSGRIFF
32 SVP/Dean of Students .... Jason JOHNSRUD
05 Academic Dean .... Dr. Francis (Frank) MARLO
120 Senior Advisor Cyber Intelligence .... Dean LANE
88 SVP Professional Affiliations .... CAPT. Chris GLASS
111 VP Institutional Advancement .... John BERGHOLZ
06 Registrar .... Iman RIDDICK
123 VP Graduate Recruitment .... Tim STEBBINS
29 VP Alumni Affs/Communications .... Katie BRIDGES
36 Director of Career Services .... Derrick DORTCH
37 Director of Financial Aid .... Thelbert SNOWDEN
08 Director of Library Services .... Dmitry KULIK

Inter-American Defense College (B)

210 B Street SW, Bldg 52, Ft McNair,
Washington DC 20319-5008

County: USA — Identification: 667275
Telephone: (202) 646-1337 — Carnegie Class: Spec-4-yr-Other
FAX Number: N/A — Calendar System: Semester
URL: iadc.edu
Established: 1962 — Annual Graduate Tuition & Fees: N/A
Enrollment: N/A — Coed
Affiliation or Control: Independent Non-Profit — IRS Status: 501(c)3
Highest Offering: Master's; No Undergraduates
Accreditation: M, ACICS

01 Director .... MGen. James E. TAYLOR
05 Chief of Studies .... BGen. Ruben Dario DIAZ ESPARZA
03 Vice Director .... RAdm. Silvio LUIS

Moreland University (C)

1701 K Street NW, Ste 250, Washington DC 20006

Identification: 667305
Telephone: (844) 283-2246 — Carnegie Class: Not Classified
FAX Number: N/A — Calendar System: Other
URL: https://www.moreland.edu/
Established: 2012 — Annual Graduate Tuition & Fees: N/A
Enrollment: N/A — Coed
Affiliation or Control: Proprietary — IRS Status: Proprietary
Highest Offering: Master's; No Undergraduates
Accreditation: DEAC, CAEP

00 Founder/CEO .... Dr. Emily FEISTRITZER
01 President .... Dr. Kevin J. RUTH
05 Chief Learning Officer .... Ms. Kunali SANGHVI
10 Chief Financial Officer .... Mr. Richard FEISTRITZER
26 Vice Pres Marketing .... Vacant
11 Director of Operations .... Vacant
07 Admissions Officer .... Mr. Andre BARNES
06 Registrar .... Ms. Bernadette GORMALLY
08 Chief Library Officer .... Ms. Courtney STOLL
13 Chief Information Technology Ofcr . Mr. Manish BHATTACHARYA

Pontifical Faculty of the Immaculate Conception at the Dominican House of Studies (D)

487 Michigan Avenue, NE, Washington DC 20017-1585

FICE Identification: 012803
Unit ID: 131405
Telephone: (202) 495-3820 — Carnegie Class: Spec-4-yr-Faith
FAX Number: (202) 495-3873 — Calendar System: Semester
URL: www.dhs.edu
Established: 1902 — Annual Graduate Tuition & Fees: N/A
Enrollment: 83 — Coed
Affiliation or Control: Roman Catholic — IRS Status: 501(c)3
Highest Offering: Master's; No Undergraduates
Accreditation: M, THEOL

00 Chancellor .... VRev. Gerard TIMONER, OP
01 President .... VRev. Thomas PETRI, OP
05 Vice President/Academic Dean ..... VRev. Dominic LANGEVIN, OP
20 Secretary of Studies .... Fr. Brian CHRZASTEK, OP
08 Librarian .... Fr. John Martin RUIZ, OP
18 Acting Director of Facilities .... Ms. Shauna ROYE
42 Chaplain to Commuter Students .... Fr. James BRENT, OP
06 Registrar/Accred Liaison .... Ms. Audrey QUADE
10 Treasurer/Director of Financial Aid .... Ms. Shauna ROYE
111 Executive Assistant for Advancement .... Ms. Theresa RYLAND
13 IT Director .... Mr. Carlos MOLINA
04 Chief of Staff .... Mrs. Patricia WORK
88 Administrative Secretary .... Ms. Katie PARKER

Pontifical John Paul II Institute for Studies on Marriage and Family (E)

620 Michigan Ave, NE, McGivney Hall,
Washington DC 20064

FICE Identification: 041427
Unit ID: 455813
Telephone: (202) 526-3799 — Carnegie Class: Spec-4-yr-Faith
FAX Number: (202) 269-6090 — Calendar System: Other
URL: www.johnpaulii.edu
Established: 1988 — Annual Graduate Tuition & Fees: N/A
Enrollment: 74 — Coed
Affiliation or Control: Roman Catholic — IRS Status: 501(c)3
Highest Offering: Doctorate; No Undergraduates
Accreditation: M

01 President .... RevMsg. Philippe BORDEYNE
03 Vice President .... Carl A. ANDERSON
05 Provost .... Fr. Antonio LOPEZ
20 Dean for Academic Affairs .... David S. CRAWFORD
11 Assoc Dean Programs/Administration .... Nick J. BAGILEO
07 Director of Admissions .... Sara L. TRUDEAU

† Affiliated with The Catholic University of America, DC.

Quantic School of Business and Technology (F)

712 H Street NE, Suite 1802, Washington DC 20002

Identification: 667384
Telephone: (571) 483-8002 — Carnegie Class: Not Classified
FAX Number: N/A — Calendar System: Other
URL: https://quantic.edu
Established: 2016 — Annual Graduate Tuition & Fees: N/A
Enrollment: N/A — Coed
Affiliation or Control: Proprietary — IRS Status: Proprietary
Highest Offering: Master's; No Undergraduates
Accreditation: DEAC

01 President/CEO .... Bill FISHER
05 Chief Academic Officer .... Alexie HARPER

Saint Michael College of Allied Health (G)

1106 Bladensburg Road, NE, Washington DC 20002

Identification: 667226
Unit ID: 486424
Telephone: (202) 388-5500 — Carnegie Class: Spec 2-yr-Health
FAX Number: (202) 388-9588 — Calendar System: Other
URL: www.stmichaelcollegeva.us
Established: 2007 — Annual Undergrad Tuition & Fees: $16,325
Enrollment: 124 — Coed
Affiliation or Control: Proprietary — IRS Status: Proprietary
Highest Offering: Associate Degree
Accreditation: COE, PNUR

01 EVP/Campus Director .... Catherine ADEDOKUN

Strayer University (H)

1133 15th Street, NW, Suite 200,
Washington DC 20005-2710

FICE Identification: 001459
Unit ID: 131803
Telephone: (202) 379-7808 — Carnegie Class: Masters/M
FAX Number: (202) 419-1423 — Calendar System: Quarter
URL: www.strayer.edu
Established: 1892 — Annual Undergrad Tuition & Fees: $13,515
Enrollment: 745 — Coed
Affiliation or Control: Proprietary — IRS Status: Proprietary
Highest Offering: Master's
Accreditation: M, ACBSP

01 President .... Dr. Andrea BACKMAN
05 Provost/Chief Academic Ofcr .... Mr. Cale HOLMAN
20 Vice Provost of Academics .... Ms. Jennifer NEWELL
32 Dean of Students .... Dr. Christy KARNES
08 University Librarian .... Ms. Mary SNYDER
06 University Registrar .... Ms. Alison MORRISON
07 Vice President Admissions .... Dr. Amy DUNN
106 Global Online Campus Dean .... Ms. Elizabeth CARDOSO
20 Chamblee GA Campus Dean .... Ms. Tonya MOORE
12 Chamblee GA Campus Director .... Ms. Miriam SANCHEZ
20 Chesterfield VA Campus Dean .... Dr. Carol WILLIAMS
12 Research Triangle Pk NC Campus Dir .... Mr. Patrick DIXON
20 Morrow GA Campus Dean .... Dr. Shadrack KOROS
12 Takoma Park DC Campus Director .... Mr. Cristen JONES
12 Morrow GA Campus Director .... Ms. Allisha OUSLEY
12 North Charlotte NC Campus Director ..... Ms. Stephanie JOHNSON
20 Nashville TN Campus Dean .... Dr. Kimberly MALONE-HADDOX
12 Nashville TN Campus Director .... Ms. Kelley BUCKLEY
20 Owings Mills MD Campus Dean .... Ms. LaToya HALE
12 Owings Mills MD Campus Director .... Ms. Shawne SCOTT
20 Arlington VA Campus Dean .... Dr. Mimi GETACHEW
12 Center City PA Campus Director .... Mr. Isaac WALTERS
20 Shelby TN Campus Dean .... Dr. Clinton MILLER
20 Rockville MD Campus Dean .... Dr. Angel CLAY
20 Takoma Park DC Campus Dean .... Mr. Vishnu DZIDZIENYO
12 Shelby TN Campus Director .... Mr. Sam THOMAS
20 Maitland FL Campus Dean .... Ms. Judith ZAYAS
20 Prince Georges MD Campus Dean .... Dr. Camilla CRAIG
20 Decatur AL Campus Dean .... Dr. Andrain YELDELL JONES
12 Decatur AL Campus Director .... Ms. Julie PRYOR
20 Mobile AL Campus Dean .... Dr. Mark PANTALEO
12 Mobile AL Campus Director .... Mr. Justin SULLIVAN
12 Miramar FL Campus Director .... Ms. Esmerelda AVILA
20 Montgomery AL Campus Dean .... Mr. Kenneth MACON
12 Montgomery AL Campus Director .... Mr. Eric WALKER
12 Arlington VA Campus Director .... Ms. Patrice JONES
20 Wilmington DE Campus Dean .... Ms. Sharmina ELLIS
12 Wilmington DE Campus Director .... Mr. Michael GRANT
20 Tallahassee FL Campus Dean .... Ms. Gabrielle NAVAS
12 Tallahassee FL Campus Director .... Ms. Kristy KEGLEY
20 Chattanooga TN Campus Dean .... Dr. Clinton MILLER
12 Chattanooga TN Campus Director .... Ms. Jeanne POINDEXTER
20 El Paso TX Campus Dean ... Ms. Nicole FRANCISCO-CAMPBELL
20 Anne Arundel MD Campus Dean .... Ms. Aerin GILBERT
12 El Paso TX Campus Director .... Mr. Donald WHITE
12 Rockville MD Assoc Campus Director .... Ms. Asija PRITCHETT
20 Fort Worth TX Campus Dean .... Dr. Dennis CARLSON
12 Fort Worth TX Campus Director .... Ms. Latrissa JACOBS
20 Killeen TX Campus Dean .... Dr. David WELLS
12 Killeen TX Campus Director .... Mr. Nicholas PEREZ
20 South Charlotte NC Campus Dean .... Dr. Jeffrey ROMANCZUK
20 Tampa FL East Campus Dean .... Ms. DeNeen ATTORD
12 South Charlotte NC Campus Director .... Ms. Christine VITO
20 Virginia Beach VA Campus Dean .... Dr. JoeAnn PACE
12 Anne Arundel MD Campus Director .... Ms. Cherone VALLEY
12 Orlando FL East Campus Director .... Mr. Jason MARTINE
12 Tampa FL East Campus Director .... Mr. Jeffrey KEITH
20 Alexandria VA Campus Dean .... Dr. Peter DEDOMINICI
20 Woodbridge VA Campus Dean .... Dr. Ras ACOLASTE
20 Lithonia GA Campus Dean .... Ms. Tariva SMITH
12 Woodbridge VA Campus Director .... Ms. Toni THORTON
12 Thousand Oaks TN Campus Director .... Ms. Mara JEFFERSON
20 Thousand Oaks TN Campus Dean .... Mr. Stanley WOOTEN
20 Miramar FL Campus Dean .... Dr. Joann RAPHAEL
20 Washington DC Campus Dean .... Ms. Timera WILLIAMS
12 Savannah GA Campus Director .... Ms. Dora JENKINS
12 Washington DC Campus Director .... Ms. Diane CLARK-FAGGS
20 Palm Beach Gardens FL Campus Dean .... Dr. Joann RAPHAEL
20 White Marsh MD Campus Dean .... Ms. Tafadzwa NHIRA
12 Alexandria VA Assoc Campus Director .... Ms. Natalie THOMAS
20 Macon GA Assoc Campus Dean .... Mr. Akinola DARE
12 Macon GA Campus Director .... Ms. Clairesse QUADIR
12 Lithonia GA Campus Director .... Mr. Etuwe OTUYA
20 Center City PA Campus Dean .... Ms. Saadia OULAMINE
20 South Raleigh NC Campus Dean .... Ms. Kimberly WILLIAMS
12 Birmingham AL Campus Director .... Ms. Irina ROGERS
20 Birmingham AL Campus Dean .... Mr. Keith JOHNSON
20 Chesapeake VA Campus Dean .... Ms. Amber EAKIN
12 Chesapeake VA Campus Director .... Mr. Tom LOTITO
20 Northwest Houston TX Campus Dean .... Dr. Johnny JONES
20 Savannah GA Campus Dean .... Dr. Denise OGDEN
20 Huntsville AL Campus Dean .... Mr. Dustin VICK
12 Huntsville AL Campus Director .... Ms. Julie PRYOR
20 Little Rock AR Campus Dean .... Dr. Stephanie COX
12 Little Rock AR Campus Director .... Mr. Charles BLOCKETT
12 Palm Beach Gardens FL Campus Dir .... Ms. Cathy HUCKABY
20 Orlando FL East Campus Dean .... Ms. Judith ZAYAS
20 Baymeadows FL Campus Dean .... Ms. Sarah FRADEN

12 South Raleigh NC Campus Director .... Mr. Matthew KOCH
12 Baymeadows FL Campus Director .... Mr. Joshua NOVATON
12 Northwest Houston TX Campus Dir .... Ms. Tracey MARTIN
20 Fort Lauderdale FL Campus Dean ....Dr. Joann RAPHAEL
12 Fort Lauderdale FL Campus Director .... Mr. Geoffrey RAMGOLAM
20 Augusta GA Campus Dean ....Dr. Isaac MOONZWE
12 Augusta GA Campus Director ....Mr. Louis DAVIS
12 Chesterfield VA Campus Director .... Mr. Thomas BERNHARDT
20 Allentown PA Campus Dean ....Ms. Holli QUINN
20 Columbus GA Campus Dean ....Dr. Kanidrus PRATHER
12 Columbus GA Campus Director ....Mr. Jonathan MURRAY
20 Douglasville GA Campus Dean ....Dr. A. Fitzgerald JONES
12 Douglasville GA Campus Director .... Ms. Monica POINTER
12 Charleston SC Campus Director .... Mr. Scott ANDERSON
20 Jackson MS Campus Dean .... Dr. Dana EVANS
12 Allentown PA Campus Director ....Mr. Michael GRANT
12 Jackson MS Campus Director ....Ms. Angela MILLER
20 Cherry Hill NJ Campus Dean ....Dr. R. Renee THOMPSON
12 Cherry Hill NJ Campus Director ....Ms. Allegra GLIEM
20 San Antonio TX Campus Dean .... Mr. Kendall JOHNSON
20 Henrico VA Campus Dean .... Mr. Marcus RALPH
20 Piscataway NJ Campus Dean .... Mr. Jared ELLISON
12 Piscataway NJ Campus Director .... Mr. Khioverny DUARTE
12 Warrendale PA Campus Director .... Ms. Molly MAZZARINI
20 Teays Valley WV Campus Dean ....Dr. Joel GOLDSTEIN
20 Warrendale PA Campus Dean ....Mr. Timothy GRIFFIN
20 Willingboro NJ Campus Dean ....Dr. A. Renee THOMPSON
12 Willingboro NJ Campus Director ....Ms. Allegra GLIEM
20 Knoxville TN Campus Dean ....Dr. Chelsie SWEPSON
20 Huntersville NC Campus Dean ....Dr. Jonita HENRY POWELL
12 Huntersville NC Campus Director .... Ms. Krystal MOREHEAD
12 San Antonio TX Campus Director .... Mr. Coner GILL
12 Henrico VA Campus Director .... Ms. Sarah HOYT
12 Knoxville TN Campus Director .... Mr. Jason ADKINS
20 Cedar Hill TX Campus Dean ....Dr. LeAllen HAWKINS
12 Lower Bucks PA Campus Director ....Ms. Lauren PLINER
12 Cedar Hill TX Campus Director ....Ms. Marisol GREENWOOD
20 Charleston SC Campus Dean ....Mr. Elliot DILLIHAY
20 Newport News VA Campus Dean ....Dr. Mavis CARR
20 North Austin TX Campus Dean .... Mr. Kendall JOHNSON
12 North Austin TX Campus Director .... Mr. Coner GILL
20 North Dallas TX Campus Dean ....Dr. T.A ESSEX
20 Lower Bucks PA Campus Dean ....Dr. Byron WESS
12 North Dallas TX Campus Director ....Ms. Kedecia RITCHIE-MITCHELL
12 Teays Valley WV Campus Director ....Ms. Christine VITO
20 Cobb County GA Campus Dean ....Dr. Timothy SHERMAN
12 Cobb County GA Campus Director .... Mr. Richard WYLIE
12 Virginia Beach VA Campus Director .... Mr. Patrick DIXON
12 Prince Georges MD Campus Director .... Ms. Candy COLLINS
20 Columbia SC Campus Dean .... Ms. Piper LORICK
12 Columbia SC Campus Director ....Mr. Ryan BUCKSON
12 Newport News VA Campus Director ....Ms. Colette REID
20 Delaware County PA Campus Dean ...... Ms. Cornelia ZAVADSKY
12 Delaware Cty PA Assoc Campus Dir ....Mr. Charles MCCARTHY
20 Fredericksburg VA Campus Dean ....Mr. Terrell MASON
12 Fredericksburg VA Campus Director .... Mr. Duan BUTLER
20 North Charlotte NC Campus Dean .... Ms. Shawna MAGBIE-CARR
20 Greensboro NC Campus Dean ....Ms. Melissa REID ALSTON
12 Greensboro NC Campus Director ....Ms. Dorende CRAIGG
20 Research Triangle Park NC Campus Dn ....Dr. JoeAnn PARKER
12 Maitland FL Campus Director .... Mr. Jason MARTINE
20 Greenville SC Campus Dean ....Dr. William DUERR
12 Greenville SC Campus Director .... Ms. Jeanne POINDEXTER
20 Loudoun VA Campus Dean ....Dr. Richelle RESTO
12 Loudoun VA Campus Director ....Ms. Ashley COLLINS
20 Manassas VA Campus Dean .... Ms. Leila STEGLICH
12 White Marsh MD Campus Director .... Mr. Leator KNUCKLES
12 Manassas VA Campus Director ....Mr. Debra SANFORD
20 North Raleigh NC Campus Dean ....Ms. Ashley CASTLE
12 North Raleigh NC Campus Director .... Mr. Jason HARRIS

Trinity Washington University (A)

125 Michigan Avenue, NE, Washington DC 20017-1090

FICE Identification: 001460
Unit ID: 131876
Telephone: (202) 884-9000 Carnegie Class: Masters/M
FAX Number: (202) 884-9229 Calendar System: Semester
URL: www.trinitydc.edu
Established: 1897 Annual Undergrad Tuition & Fees: $25,110
Enrollment: 1,846 Female
Affiliation or Control: Roman Catholic IRS Status: 501(c)3
Highest Offering: Master's
Accreditation: M, CACREP, CAEP, NURSE, OT, #OTA

01 President .... Ms. Patricia A. MCGUIRE
05 Provost ....Dr. Carlota OCAMPO
10 Vice President Fiscal Affairs/CFO .... Mr. Walter BROOKS
111 Vice Pres Institutional Advancement ....Ms. Ann PAULEY
84 Vice Pres Enrollment Services ....Ms. Cathy GEIER
26 Vice Pres Media Relations ....Ms. Ann PAULEY
32 Vice President for Student Affairs ....Dr. Karen GERLACH
13 Chief Info Technology Officer (CIO) .... Mr. Michael BURBACK
30 Chief Development Officer ....Mr. Patrick KELLOGG
49 Dean College of Arts & Science ....Dr. Sita RAMAMURTI
53 Dean School of Education .... Dr. Nicole STRANGE-MARTIN
107 Dean School of Professional Studies ....Dr. Peggy LEWIS
66 Dean Sch Nursing/Health Professions ....Dr. Mary ROMANELLO
35 Dean of Student Services ....Ms. Michelle BOWIE
15 Exec Director of Human Resources ..... Ms. Tracey PRINCE ROSS
41 Athletic Director ....Ms. Monique MCLEAN
42 Director of Campus Ministry ....Sr. Ann HOWARD
18 Director Facilities Services .... Mr. William (Bill) SHAFFER
29 Director Alumnae Affairs .... Ms. Stephanie MELVIN
07 Executive Director of Admissions .... Ms. Sarah PRINCE
08 University Librarian .... Ms. Trisha SMITH
21 Assoc Controller/Business Officer .... Ms. Danielle MADDEN
51 Director Continuing Education .... Ms. Katie OMENITSCH

University of the District of Columbia (B)

4200 Connecticut Avenue, NW,
Washington DC 20008-1174

FICE Identification: 001441
Unit ID: 131399
Telephone: (202) 274-5000 Carnegie Class: Masters/M
FAX Number: (202) 274-5304 Calendar System: Semester
URL: www.udc.edu
Established: 1976 Annual Undergrad Tuition & Fees (In-District): $6,152
Enrollment: 3,725 Coed
Affiliation or Control: Local IRS Status: 501(c)3
Highest Offering: First Professional Degree
Accreditation: M, ACBSP, ADNUR, CACREP, CAEP, COARC, DIETD, FUSER, LAW, NUR, SP, SW

01 President ....Mr. Ronald MASON, JR.
05 Chief Academic Officer .... Dr. Lawrence POTTER
32 Chief Student Devel & Success Ofcr .... Dr. William LATHAM
11 Chief Operating Officer .... Mr. David FRANKLIN
43 General Counsel .... Ms. Avis RUSSELL
100 Chief of Staff/Senior Vice Pres .... Ms. Monique GUILLORY
15 Vice President Human Resources .... Ms. Deborah SULLIVAN
18 VP Real Estate & Facility Mgmt .... Mr. Erik THOMPSON
111 Vice President for Advancement ....Mr. Rodney TRAPP
13 Vice President Information Tech .... Mr. Suresh MURUGAN
26 Vice President Marketing and Comm .... Vacant
10 Chief Financial Officer ....Mr. Munetsi MUSARA
49 Dean Arts & Sciences .... Dr. April MASSEY
50 Dean Sch Business & Public Admin ....Dr. Mohamad SEPEHRI
61 Dean School of Law .... Ms. Renee MCDONALD HUTCHINS
54 Dean Engineering/Applied Scis ....Dr. Devdas SHETTY
56 Dean CAUSES ....Dr. Dwane JONES
46 VP Research & Sponsored Programs .... Dr. Victor MCCRARY
84 Interim AVP Enrollment Services .... Ms. Nailah WILLIAMS
06 University Registrar ....Ms. Tiffany COOPER
37 Director Student Financial Aid ....Mr. Wayne MONTGOMERY
08 Director of Learning Resources .... Ms. Melba BROOME
25 Capital Program Officer ....Ms. Cassandra PARKER
41 Athletic Director ....Ms. Patricia A. THOMAS
88 General Manager UDC Cable TV ....Mr. Edward JONES, JR.
09 Dir of Institutional Effectiveness ....Mrs. Maria BYRD
38 Director Student Counseling .... Ms. Serena BUTLER-JOHNSON
121 Dean Student Achievement UDC-CC ....Ms. Hermina P. PETERS
103 Dean Workforce Development ....Ms. Mashonda SMITH
19 Interim Dir Public Safety .... Mr. Orlando TREADWELL
36 Exec Director Career Services ....Mr. Jared E. MOFFETT
86 Exec Director State & Local Affairs .... Vacant
21 Deputy Chief Operating Officer .... Vacant
81 Director STEM .... Ms. Barbara J. HOLMES
29 Director Alumni Affairs ....Ms. Phomika PALMER
97 Assistant Director of General Educ ....Ms. Kimberly CREWS
102 Director Sponsored Programs ....Ms. Laura-Lee DAVIDSON
13 Dir Information Technology ....Mr. Michael ROGERS
07 Director Admissions/TRIO Programs .... Ms. Saundra CARTER
101 Exec Secretary Office the Board ....Ms. Frenika RIVERS
16 Director of Labor & Employee Rels .... Vacant
35 Asst Director of Student Success .... Ms. Latosha BALDWIN
39 Director of Residence Life ....Mr. Quintin VEASLEY
96 Chief Contracting Officer .... Ms. Mary Ann HARRIS

University of the Potomac (C)

1401 H Street NW, Suite 100, Washington DC 20005

FICE Identification: 032183
Unit ID: 384412
Telephone: (202) 274-2303 Carnegie Class: Spec-4-yr-Bus
FAX Number: N/A Calendar System: Semester
URL: www.potomac.edu
Established: 1991 Annual Undergrad Tuition & Fees: $6,660
Enrollment: 232 Coed
Affiliation or Control: Proprietary IRS Status: Proprietary
Highest Offering: Doctorate
Accreditation: M

01 President/Chief Executive Officer ....Dr. Clinton GARDNER
05 Dean of Academics .... Dr. Sergei ANDRONIKOV
10 Chief Financial Officer ....Stewart BROWN
11 Chief Operating Officer ....Andrea FORD
08 Director of Learning Resource Ctr .... Edward ROBINSON

Wesley Theological Seminary (D)

4500 Massachusetts Avenue, NW,
Washington DC 20016-5690

FICE Identification: 001464
Unit ID: 131973
Telephone: (202) 885-8600 Carnegie Class: Spec-4-yr-Faith
FAX Number: (202) 885-8605 Calendar System: Semester
URL: www.wesleyseminary.edu
Established: 1882 Annual Graduate Tuition & Fees: N/A
Enrollment: 530 Coed
Affiliation or Control: United Methodist IRS Status: 501(c)3
Highest Offering: Doctorate; No Undergraduates
Accreditation: M, THEOL

01 President ....Dr. David MCALLISTER-WILSON
04 Executive Assistant to President ....Mr. Andrew C. DENHAM
10 Vice Pres Finance/CFO ....Mr. Jeffrey STRAITS
05 Dean .... Dr. Philip WINGEIER-RAYO
20 Associate Dean Academic Affairs .... Dr. Michael KOPPEL
32 Assoc Dean for Campus Life .... Dr. Asa LEE
88 Vice President of Intl Relations .... Dr. Kyunglim SHIN LEE
84 VP Strategic Initiative Enrollment ....Rev. Beth LUDLUM
30 Vice Pres Development .... Rev. Brian MCCOLLUM
21 Controller .... Mr. William WALKER
06 Registrar ....Mr. Joseph E. ARNOLD
88 Dir Luce Ctr for Arts & Religion ....Dr. Aaron ROSEN
31 Director Community Engagement Inst ....Dr. Lorena PARRISH
88 Director Ctr for Public Theology .... Mr. Michael MCCURRY
88 Faculty Dir Ctr Public Theology ....Mr. Rick ELGENDY
26 Director Communications/Marketing .... Ms. Sheila GEORGE
88 Director Doctor of Ministry Program .... Dr. Douglas TZAN
24 Director of Educational Technology ....Ms. Berkeley COLLINS
88 Director of Enrollment .... Ms. JaNice PARKS
88 Director Heal the Sick Initiative .... Thomas PRUSKI
15 Director Human Resources ....Dr. Josie HOOVER
39 Director of Housing ....Ms. Monica PETTY
85 Dir International Student Services .... Ms. Karen SANTIAGO
88 Dir Lewis Ctr Church Leadership ....Dr. F. Douglas POWE
08 Director of Library .... Mr. Andy KLENKLEN
88 Dir Practice Ministry in Mission ....Dr. Joseph BUSH
37 Director Student Financial Aid ....Mr. Dane SMITH
88 Director Writing Center .... Ms. Raedorah STEWART
18 Chief Facilities/Physical Plant .... Mr. Oscar PALENCIA
28 Diversity Officer .... Mr. Matt LYONS

FLORIDA

Academy for Five Element Acupuncture (E)

305 SE Second Avenue, Gainesville FL 32601-6811

County: Alachua FICE Identification: 035243
Unit ID: 451079
Telephone: (352) 335-2332 Carnegie Class: Spec-4-yr-Other Health
FAX Number: (352) 337-2535 Calendar System: Trimester
URL: www.acupuncturist.edu
Established: 1998 Annual Graduate Tuition & Fees: N/A
Enrollment: 91 Coed
Affiliation or Control: Independent Non-Profit IRS Status: 501(c)3
Highest Offering: Master's; No Undergraduates
Accreditation: ACUP

01 President .... Ms. Misti OXFORD-PICKERAL
10 Vice President Administration .... Ms. Joanne EPSTEIN
05 Academic Dean .... Mr. Chuck GRAHAM
32 Student Dean .... Ms. Patty GETFORD
10 Finance Director .... Ms. Odalis CRUZ
06 Registrar .... Ms. Jessica BABAKER
07 Admissions .... Ms. Isabelle WINZELER

Academy for Nursing and Health Occupations (F)

5154 Okeechobee Blvd #201, West Palm Beach FL 33417

County: Palm Beach FICE Identification: 033463
Unit ID: 412173
Telephone: (561) 683-1400 Carnegie Class: Spec 2-yr-Health
FAX Number: (561) 683-6773 Calendar System: Other
URL: www.anho.edu
Established: 1978 Annual Undergrad Tuition & Fees: N/A
Enrollment: 703 Coed
Affiliation or Control: Independent Non-Profit IRS Status: 501(c)3
Highest Offering: Associate Degree
Accreditation: COE, ADNUR

01 Executive Director .... Dr. Lois M. GACKENHEIMER
05 Academic Dean .... Neala ASSER
32 Dean of Student Svcs .... Sherri ADDUCI
10 Assistant Director .... Renee WERNER
06 Registrar ....Elizabeth RODRIGUEZ
37 Financial Aid Director .... Sherri ADDUCI
07 Admissions Specialist .... Angela STILES

Acupuncture & Massage College (G)

10506 N Kendall Drive, Miami FL 33176-1509

County: Miami-Dade FICE Identification: 034145
Unit ID: 439969
Telephone: (305) 595-9500 Carnegie Class: Spec-4-yr-Other Health
FAX Number: (305) 595-2622 Calendar System: Semester
URL: www.amcollege.edu
Established: 1983 Annual Undergrad Tuition & Fees: $10,943
Enrollment: 171 Coed
Affiliation or Control: Proprietary IRS Status: Proprietary
Highest Offering: Master's
Accreditation: ACCSC, ACUP

01 President .... Ms. Christy WOOD
05 Academic Dean .... Dr. Yaly FLORES-SOTO
17 Clinic Director .... Dr. Jean Pierre CHACON
37 Financial Aid Director .... Mr. Guy JACKMAN
07 Admissions Director .... Mr. Joe CALARESO
06 Registrar/Student Services .... Ms. Maria GARCIA

Advance Science International College (A)

5190 North West 167 Street, Ste 200,
Miami Lakes FL 33014

County: Miami-Dade FICE Identification: 037573
Unit ID: 444334
Telephone: (305) 626-6007 Carnegie Class: Not Classified
FAX Number: N/A Calendar System: Semester
URL: asicollege.edu
Established: 1998 Annual Undergrad Tuition & Fees: N/A
Enrollment: 53 Coed
Affiliation or Control: Proprietary IRS Status: Proprietary
Highest Offering: Associate Degree
Accreditation: ACCSC

01 President/Director of School .... Pablo PEREZ

AdventHealth University (B)

671 Winyah Drive, Orlando FL 32803-1204

County: Orange FICE Identification: 031155
Unit ID: 133872
Telephone: (407) 303-9798 Carnegie Class: Spec-4-yr-Other Health
FAX Number: (407) 303-5671 Calendar System: Trimester
URL: www.ahu.edu
Established: 1992 Annual Undergrad Tuition & Fees: $19,800
Enrollment: 1,802 Coed
Affiliation or Control: Seventh-day Adventist IRS Status: 501(c)3
Highest Offering: Doctorate
Accreditation: SC, ANEST, ARCPA, DMS, HSA, NMT, NURSE, OT, OTA, PTA, RAD

01 President .... Dr. Edwin I. HERNANDEZ
05 Provost .... Dr. Sandra DUNBAR-SMALLEY
11 SVP Operational Strategy .... Dr. Deena SLOCKETT
10 Sr VP for Finance/CFO .... Mr. Ruben O. MARTINEZ
32 Sr VP for Student Services .... Dr. Stephen H. ROCHE
26 VP Marketing & Public Relations .... Mr. Lonnie MIXON
106 Director AHU Online .... Ms. Leanna NEUBRANDER
09 Dir of Inst Effectiveness/Accred .... Mr. Joe HAWKINS
37 Director of Financial Aid .... Ms. Daisy TABACHOW
06 Registrar .... Dr. Janet CALDERON
88 Dir Ctr for Academic Achievement .... Dr. Ndala BOOKER
08 Library Director .... Mr. Neal SMITH
07 Director of Enrollment Services .... Ms. Lillian GARRIDO
21 Chief Accountant .... Mr. Grayson GOODMAN
39 Director of Residence Hall .... Ms. Cassandra PHILOGENE
30 Director of Philanthropy .... Dr. Carol BRADFIELD
15 Director of Human Resources .... Ms. Jennifer CARPENTER
13 Director of Information Technology .... Mr. Travis WOOLEY
04 Executive Asst to the President .... Ms. Viviana CALANDRA
88 Chief Compliance Officer .... Ms. Starr S. BENDER
29 Director Alumni Relations .... Ms. Dawn H. CREFT
19 Director Security/Safety .... Mr. Eric GOEBELBECKER

American Medical Academy (C)

12215 SW 112th Street, Miami FL 33186

County: Miami-Dade FICE Identification: 041921
Unit ID: 475714
Telephone: (305) 271-6555 Carnegie Class: Spec 2-yr-Health
FAX Number: (305) 271-6556 Calendar System: Semester
URL: www.ama.edu
Established: 2006 Annual Undergrad Tuition & Fees: N/A
Enrollment: 527 Coed
Affiliation or Control: Proprietary IRS Status: Proprietary
Highest Offering: Baccalaureate
Accreditation: ABHES

01 Chief Executive Officer .... Dr. Eduardo GUTIERREZ

Ana G. Mendez University Metro Orlando Campus (D)

5601 S Semoran Boulevard, #55, Orlando FL 32822
Telephone: (407) 207-3363 Identification: 770921
Accreditation: &M

† Branch campus of Universidad Ana G. Mendez, Rio Piedras, PR

Ana G. Mendez University South Florida Campus (E)

15201 NW 79th Court, Miami Lakes FL 33016
Telephone: (954) 885-5595 Identification: 770922
Accreditation: &M

† Branch campus of Universidad Ana G. Mendez, Rio Piedras, PR

Ana G. Mendez University Tampa Bay Campus (F)

3655 West Waters Avenue, Tampa FL 33614
Telephone: (813) 932-7500 Identification: 770923
Accreditation: &M

† Branch campus of Universidad Ana G. Mendez, Rio Piedras, PR

Antigua College International (G)

14505 Commerce Way, Suite 522,
Miami Lakes FL 33016-1573

County: Miami-Dade Identification: 667344
Telephone: (786) 391-1167 Carnegie Class: Not Classified
FAX Number: (786) 452-9265 Calendar System: Semester
URL: www.antigua.edu
Established: 2012 Annual Undergrad Tuition & Fees: N/A
Enrollment: N/A Coed
Affiliation or Control: Proprietary IRS Status: Proprietary
Highest Offering: Baccalaureate
Accreditation: ABHES

00 CEO .... Diony ANTIGUA
01 President .... Jose ANTIGUA
10 Chief Financial Officer .... Justin GARCIA
11 Vice President of Operations .... Taima GONZALEZ
07 Director of Admissions .... Debbie VALDES
08 Chief Library Officer .... Julian PEREZ

The Art Institute of Tampa, a branch of Miami International University of Art & Design (H)

4401 North Himes Avenue, Suite 150, Tampa FL 33614
Telephone: (813) 393-5321 Identification: 770935
Accreditation: &SC

† Branch campus of Miami International University of Art & Design, Miami, FL.

ATA Career Education-Spring Hill (I)

7351 Spring Hill Drive, Suite 11, Spring Hill FL 34606
Telephone: (866) 438-2432 Identification: 770521
Accreditation: ABHES

† Branch campus of ATA College, Louisville, KY

Atlantic Institute of Oriental Medicine (J)

100 E Broward Boulevard, Suite 100,
Fort Lauderdale FL 33301-3510

County: Broward FICE Identification: 034296
Unit ID: 439446
Telephone: (954) 763-9840 Carnegie Class: Spec-4-yr-Other Health
FAX Number: (954) 763-9844 Calendar System: Trimester
URL: www.atom.edu
Established: 1994 Annual Graduate Tuition & Fees: N/A
Enrollment: 174 Coed
Affiliation or Control: Independent Non-Profit IRS Status: 501(c)3
Highest Offering: Doctorate; No Undergraduates
Accreditation: ACUP

01 President .... Dr. Johanna C. YEN
03 Exec Vice Pres/DAOM Director .... Dr. Di FU
05 Academic Dean .... Allyson WILSON
11 Exec Director Administration .... Dort BIGG
10 Financial Officer .... Celia MUNOZ
06 Registrar .... Milagros FERREIRA
08 Head Librarian .... Jeanne THOMAS
37 Financial Aid Manager .... Michelle WELDY

† Granted candidacy at the Doctorate level.

Atlantis University (K)

1442 Biscayne Boulevard, Miami FL 33132

County: Miami-Dade FICE Identification: 042339
Unit ID: 485768
Telephone: (305) 377-8817 Carnegie Class: Bac-Diverse
FAX Number: (305) 377-9557 Calendar System: Semester
URL: www.atlantisuniversity.edu
Established: 1975 Annual Undergrad Tuition & Fees: $10,800
Enrollment: 550 Coed
Affiliation or Control: Proprietary IRS Status: Proprietary
Highest Offering: Master's
Accreditation: ACCSC, CEA

01 Chancellor/President .... Mr. Omar PALACIOS
11 Executive Director/Dir Compliance .... Ms. Carol PALACIOS

Ave Maria School of Law (L)

1025 Commons Circle, Naples FL 34119

County: Collier FICE Identification: 036914
Unit ID: 442295
Telephone: (239) 687-5300 Carnegie Class: Spec-4-yr-Law
FAX Number: (239) 353-3173 Calendar System: Semester
URL: www.avemarialaw.edu
Established: 2000 Annual Graduate Tuition & Fees: N/A
Enrollment: 286 Coed
Affiliation or Control: Roman Catholic IRS Status: 501(c)3
Highest Offering: First Professional Degree; No Undergraduates
Accreditation: LAW

01 President and Dean .... Mr. Kevin CIEPLY
04 Executive Assistant to the Dean .... Ms. Pamela KRAMER
05 Assoc Dean Academic Affairs .... Ms. Maureen MILLIRON
32 Assoc Dean Student Engagement .... Ms. Claire O'KEEFE
10 Assoc Dean Finance/Student Admin .... Ms. Kaye CASTRO
08 Director of the Law Library .... Mr. Ulysses JAEN
42 Chaplain .... Msgr. Frank MCGRATH
06 Registrar .... Mr. Anthony COLE
37 Director of Financial Aid .... Mr. Kevin MCGOWAN
111 Chief Advancement Officer .... Ms. Donna HEISER
36 Director of Career Services .... Ms. Jennifer LUCAS-ROSS
13 Chief Information Officer .... Ms. Monica RENGIFO
07 Assoc Director of Admissions .... Ms. Tabitha CANALDA
15 Director of Human Resources .... Ms. Kathleen SHELMERDINE

Ave Maria University (M)

5050 Ave Maria Boulevard, Ave Maria FL 34142-9505

County: Collier FICE Identification: 039413
Unit ID: 446048
Telephone: (239) 280-2500 Carnegie Class: Bac-A&S
FAX Number: (239) 352-2392 Calendar System: Semester
URL: www.avemaria.edu
Established: 2003 Annual Undergrad Tuition & Fees: $23,188
Enrollment: 1,108 Coed
Affiliation or Control: Independent Non-Profit IRS Status: 501(c)3
Highest Offering: Doctorate
Accreditation: SC, NUR

00 Chancellor .... Mr. Thomas S. MONAGHAN
01 Interim President .... Dr. Roger P. NUTT
05 VP Academic Affairs & Provost .... Dr. Roger NUTT
10 VP Finance/Administration .... Mr. Eugene MUNIN
30 VP Institutional Advancement .... Mr. Tim DOCKERY
32 VP Student Affairs .... Ms. Kimberly KING
26 VP Marketing/Communications .... Mr. Kevin MURPHY
13 Chief Information Officer .... Mr. Eddie DEJTHAI
07 AVP of Admissions .... Ms. Dee GIPSON
06 Registrar .... Ms. Kathryn DIONNE
41 Athletic Director .... Mr. Joseph PATTERSON
42 Director of Campus Ministry .... Fr. Rick MARTIGNETTI
44 Sr Director of Principal Gifts .... Mr. Patrick O'CONNELL
35 Director of Student Life .... Ms. Rachel FLOWERS
88 Director of Mission/Outreach .... Mr. Kerry ESTES
08 Director of Library Services .... Ms. Jennifer NODES
15 Director of Human Resources .... Ms. Kathy PHELPS
18 Director Physical Plant .... Mr. Brent JOHNSON
38 Director Counseling Services .... Ms. AnaMaria LI-ROSI
39 Director Resident Life .... Mr. Ryan WELCH
19 Director Security/Safety .... Mr. Michael MILLER
37 Director Financial Aid .... Ms. Sandra SHIMP
04 Admin Assistant to the President .... Ms. Cristine BUZZANCA
29 Program Manager Alumni Relations .... Ms. Paula SHUTE

Aviator College of Aeronautical Science & Technology (N)

3800 St. Lucie Boulevard, Fort Pierce FL 34946

County: Saint Lucie FICE Identification: 039863
Unit ID: 447847
Telephone: (772) 466-4822 Carnegie Class: Spec 2-yr-Tech
FAX Number: (772) 462-4886 Calendar System: Semester
URL: www.aviator.edu
Established: 1984 Annual Undergrad Tuition & Fees: $31,211
Enrollment: 305 Coed
Affiliation or Control: Proprietary IRS Status: Proprietary
Highest Offering: Associate Degree
Accreditation: ACCSC, CEA

01 President .... Mr. Michael E. COHEN
10 Sr Vice Pres/Chief Financial Ofcr .... Ms. T.J METE
05 Vice Pres Academic Affairs .... Mr. Pierre LAVIAL
06 Registrar/Director Student Services .... Mrs. Calandria YEE-BULLOCK
37 Financial Aid Officer .... Ms. Jacqueline ORTIZ
43 Legal Counsel/Compliance .... Mr. Kendall PHILLIPS

Azure College (O)

3201 W Commercial Blvd, Suite 127,
Fort Lauderdale FL 33309

County: Highlands Identification: 667116
Unit ID: 483762
Telephone: (954) 500-2987 Carnegie Class: Spec 2-yr-Health
FAX Number: N/A Calendar System: Quarter
URL: www.azure.edu
Established: 2004 Annual Undergrad Tuition & Fees: N/A
Enrollment: N/A Coed
Affiliation or Control: Proprietary IRS Status: Proprietary
Highest Offering: Baccalaureate
Accreditation: ABHES

01 Campus Director .... Mr. Jose NAPOLEON

The Baptist College of Florida (P)

5400 College Drive, Graceville FL 32440-3306

County: Jackson FICE Identification: 021596
Unit ID: 132408
Telephone: (850) 263-3261 Carnegie Class: Spec-4-yr-Faith
FAX Number: (850) 263-9026 Calendar System: Semester
URL: www.baptistcollege.edu
Established: 1943 Annual Undergrad Tuition & Fees: $12,150
Enrollment: 418 Coed

Affiliation or Control: Southern Baptist — IRS Status: 501(c)3
Highest Offering: Master's
Accreditation: SC, MUS

01 President ... Dr. Thomas A. KINCHEN
30 Vice President for Development ... Vacant
05 Academic Dean ... Dr. G. Robin JUMPER
06 Registrar ... Ms. Stephanie W. ORR
13 Chief Information Technology Ofcr ... Vacant
32 Director of Student Life/Marketing ... Mrs. Sandra K. RICHARDS
09 Director of Institutional Research ... Dr. Ed SCOTT
37 Director of Financial Aid & VA ... Mrs. Stephanie E. POWELL
18 Maintenance Director ... Mr. Olan C. STRICKLAND
10 Associate Business Officer ... Ms. Polly K. FLOYD
04 Administrative Asst to President ... Ms. Laura L. TICE
08 Head Librarian ... Mrs. Della M. JUSTICE
39 Housing Manager ... Mrs. Rose A. STRICKLAND
41 Athletic Coordinator ... Mr. Edward C. BOOTH
19 Director of Campus Safety ... Mr. Olan C. STRICKLAND

Barry University (A)

11300 NE Second Avenue, Miami Shores FL 33161-6695
County: Dade — FICE Identification: 001466
Unit ID: 132471
Telephone: (305) 899-3000 — Carnegie Class: DU-Mod
FAX Number: (305) 899-3054 — Calendar System: Semester
URL: www.barry.edu
Established: 1940 — Annual Undergrad Tuition & Fees: $30,940
Enrollment: 7,515 — Coed
Affiliation or Control: Roman Catholic — IRS Status: 501(c)3
Highest Offering: Doctorate
Accreditation: SC, ANEST, ARCPA, CAATE, CACREP, EXSC, HT, LAW, MACTE, MT, NURSE, OT, PERF, POD, SW, THEOL

01 President ... Dr. Michael ALLEN
04 Administrative Coordinator ... Mr. Miguel A. CALVO, JR.
125 President Emerita ... Sr. Linda BEVILACQUA
05 Provost ... Dr. John D. MURRAY
20 Associate Provost ... Dr. Victor ROMANO
20 Associate Provost Extended Learning ... Dr. David KOPP
08 Director Library Services ... Dr. Jan FIGA
49 Dean College of Arts/Sciences ... Dr. Karen A. CALLAGHAN
10 Vice Pres Business & Finance ... Mrs. Susan ROSENTHAL
11 Vice Pres University Administration ... Mrs. Jennifer N. BOYD-PUGH
111 VP for Institutional Advancement ... Ms. Bernadine DOUGLAS
110 Assoc VP for Development ... Mr. Pietro BONACOSSA
32 VP Mission & Student Engagement ... Dr. Scott F. SMITH
13 VP Strategic Initiatives & CIO ... Ms. Yvette KOOTTUNGAL
43 General Counsel ... Mr. David DUDGEON
50 Dean School of Business ... Dr. Joan M. PHILLIPS
53 Dean School of Education ... Dr. Jill FARRELL
76 Dean College of Health Sciences ... Dr. John MCFADDEN
61 Dean School of Law ... Dr. Leticia M. DIAZ
63 Dean School of Podiatric Medicine ... Dr. Bryan CALDWELL
20 Associate Vice Provost ... Dr. Victor ROMANO
70 Dean School of Social Work ... Dr. Phyllis SCOTT
35 Associate VP & Dean of Students ... Dr. Maria L. ALVAREZ
29 Assoc VP Alum Rels & Annual Giving ... Vacant
84 Assoc Vice Pres Recruit & Admission ... Ms. Roxanna CRUZ
26 Associate VP Marketing ... Mr. Michel SILY
19 Director Public Safety & Emerg Mgt ... Mr. John BUHRMASTER
42 Chaplain ... Fr. Cristobal TORRES
06 University Registrar ... Ms. Viviana CARABANNA
39 Director Housing and Residence Life ... Mr. Matthew R. CAMERON
36 Director Career Services ... Mr. John MORIARTY
37 Director Financial Aid ... Mrs. Aida CLARO
92 Director Honors Program ... Dr. Pawena SIRIMANGKALA
38 Director Student Counseling Center ... Dr. Hossiella LONGORIA
123 Director of Graduate Admission ... Ms. Betsy THOMAS
09 Director Institutional Research ... Ms. Shaunette GRANT
14 AVP & Chief Technology Officer ... Mr. Hernan LONDONO
41 Director of Athletics ... Mr. Michael COVONE
102 Dir Foundation Rels & Major Gifts ... Mr. Frank SAAVEDRA
27 Dir Marketing Product Dev & Design ... Mr. Miguel RAMIREZ
109 Dir Student Union & Food Services ... Mr. Mickie VOUTSINAS
25 Director Grant & Sponsored Programs ... Ms. Michelle GOODING
40 Manager Bookstore ... Mr. Jean REYES
96 Dir Procurement & Accounts Payable ... Ms. Brooke PALLOT
18 Director Facilities Management ... Mr. Raul GONZALEZ
44 Director Annual Giving ... Mr. Anthony DICKEY

Beacon College (B)

105 E Main Street, Leesburg FL 34748-5162
County: Lake — FICE Identification: 033733
Unit ID: 384254
Telephone: (352) 787-7660 — Carnegie Class: Bac-Diverse
FAX Number: (352) 787-0721 — Calendar System: Semester
URL: www.beaconcollege.edu
Established: 1989 — Annual Undergrad Tuition & Fees: $42,900
Enrollment: 427 — Coed
Affiliation or Control: Independent Non-Profit — IRS Status: 501(c)3
Highest Offering: Baccalaureate
Accreditation: SC

01 President ... Dr. George J. HAGERTY
05 Provost ... Dr. Shelly CHANDLER
32 AVP Student Engagement & Success ... Ms. Sheryl NICHOLS
111 VP for Institutional Advancement ... Mr. Richard KILLION
10 VP of Finance/CFO ... Ms. Sandi RYSELL
84 VP of Enrollment Management ... Ms. Dale HEROLD
06 Registrar ... Ms. Carrie SANTAW
18 Director of Facilities ... Mr. Ken RAMELLA
37 Dir Enroll Svcs & Financial Aid ... Ms. Stephanie KNIGHT
08 Director of Library Resources ... Ms. Tiffany REITZ
13 Director of Information Technology ... Mr. Tim PAIGE
04 Exec Assistant to the President ... Ms. Tamara SYNDER
15 Acting Director of Human Resources ... Ms. Linda ALLISON
101 Admin Asst to the Board ... Ms. Tamara SNYDER
36 Director of Career Development ... Ms. Theresa ELLIOTT
23 Executive Director Student Health ... Ms. Monika SMITH
19 Interim Director of Campus Safety ... Mr. James BORDEN
39 Dir Student Housing/Judicial Affs ... Mr. Matthew HARDING
38 Director Student Counseling ... Ms. Dana MANZO
44 Director Annual Giving ... Ms. Keri Jo PANNELLA

Bethesda College of Health Sciences (C)

3800 S Congress Avenue, Suite 9,
Boynton Beach FL 33426
County: Palm Beach — Identification: 667258
Telephone: (561) 364-3064 — Carnegie Class: Not Classified
FAX Number: (561) 364-3059 — Calendar System: Semester
URL: www.bethesdacollege.net
Established: 2011 — Annual Undergrad Tuition & Fees: N/A
Enrollment: N/A — Coed
Affiliation or Control: Independent Non-Profit — IRS Status: 501(c)3
Highest Offering: Associate Degree
Accreditation: ACICS, ADNUR, RAD

01 Dean ... Amanda MURPHY

Bethune Cookman University (D)

640 Dr. Mary McLeod Bethune Blvd,
Daytona Beach FL 32114-3099
County: Volusia — FICE Identification: 001467
Unit ID: 132602
Telephone: (386) 481-2000 — Carnegie Class: Bac-A&S
FAX Number: (386) 481-2010 — Calendar System: Semester
URL: www.cookman.edu
Established: 1904 — Annual Undergrad Tuition & Fees: $14,794
Enrollment: 2,845 — Coed
Affiliation or Control: United Methodist — IRS Status: 501(c)3
Highest Offering: Master's
Accreditation: SC, ACBSP, CAATE, CAEP, MUS, NUR, PH

01 President ... Dr. E. LaBrent CHRITE
00 Chair Board of Trustees ... Mr. Belvin PERRY
125 President Emerita ... Dr. Trudie KIBBE REED
03 Sr Advisor to the President for IE ... Dr. Narendra H. PATEL
10 CFO/VP for Fiscal Affairs ... Mr. John PITTMAN
05 SVP for Academic Affairs/Provost ... Dr. Helena MARIELLA-WALROND
32 VP for Student Affairs ... Vacant
84 VP for Enrollment Management ... Vacant
111 VP for Institutional Advancement ... Vacant
13 CIO/VP for Information Technology ... Dr. Franklin E. PATTERSON
41 VP for Intercollegiate Athletics ... Mr. Lynn W. THOMPSON
43 VP for Legal Affairs ... Vacant
21 AVP for Fiscal Affairs ... Vacant
20 Assoc Prov/Chief Research Officer ... Vacant
20 Associate Provost for Faculty ... Dr. Herbert THOMPSON
25 AVP Title III & Spons Research ... Ms. Chelsea WASHINGTON
35 AVP/Dean of Students ... Vacant
39 Assoc Dean Res Life & Housing ... Dr. Janice WADE
102 AVP Foundations & Corp Relations ... Ms. Chipella JORDAN
23 Asst VP for Health & Wellness ... Mrs. Nadine HEUSNER
50 Dean College of Business ... Mrs. Ida WRIGHT
53 Dean College of Education ... Dr. Stephanie PASLEY-HENRY
58 Dean School of Graduate Studies ... Dr. Deanna WATHINGTON
76 Exec Dean College of Health Sci ... Dr. Deanna WATHINGTON
88 Dean Hospitality Management ... Dr. Deanne WILLIAMS-BRYANT
49 Dean College of Liberal Arts ... Dr. Janice ALLEN-KELSEY
66 Dean School of Nursing ... Dr. Sandra TUCKER
104 Dean Global Online ... Dr. Arletha MCSWAIN
60 Dean Perf Arts & Communication ... Dr. Hiram POWELL
73 Dean School of Religion ... Dr. Randolph BRACY, JR.
81 Dean Science/Engineering and Math ... Dr. Herbert THOMPSON
08 Dean of the Library/Chief Librarian ... Dr. Tasha LUCAS-YOUMANS
19 Exec Director Campus Safety ... Mr. Gary PRICE
07 Int Dir of Undergrad Admissions ... Mr. Billy (Malik) DAJUSTE
04 Executive Asst to the President ... Ms. Fanita KIRKLAND LEWIS
37 Director of Financial Aid ... Ms. Salina HAMILTON
91 Director of Administrative Systems ... Ms. Anna HEIN
06 Registrar ... Mr. Hubert L. JAMES, II
15 Exec Director of Human Resources ... Dr. Arlesia WELCH
42 Chaplain ... Rev. Kenya LOVELL
101 Board Liaison ... Vacant
36 Director of Career Development ... Ms. Davita BONNER
26 Director of Communications ... Ms. Joy JONES
30 Director of Development ... Mrs. Ashley STOEKEL
88 Director of Testing ... Ms. Annette YEARBY
105 Director Web Services ... Mr. Julian WALKER
29 Director Alumni Affairs ... Ms. Marah BELTZ
33 Dir Male Development Initiatives ... Mr. Jermaine MCKINNEY
121 Director New Student Services ... Ms. LaToya SHANNON
113 Director Student Accounts ... Ms. Sandra BROWN
108 Assessment Coordinator ... Mrs. Jennifer DASH

Braxton College (E)

27975 Old 41 Road, Suite 201, Bonita Springs FL 34135
County: Lee — Identification: 667266
Telephone: (239) 992-4624 — Carnegie Class: Not Classified
FAX Number: (239) 405-8024 — Calendar System: Semester
URL: www.braxton.edu
Established: 2008 — Annual Undergrad Tuition & Fees: N/A
Enrollment: N/A — Coed
Affiliation or Control: Proprietary — IRS Status: Proprietary
Highest Offering: Baccalaureate
Accreditation: ABHES

01 Medical Director/Founder ... Dr. Antonio GANDIA
05 Vice President of Academics ... Mr. Bill MCGRATH
07 VP Admissions & Compliance ... Mr. Richard GONZALEZ
13 Director of Information Technology ... Mr. Freddie BATISTA

Broward College (F)

111 E Las Olas Boulevard,
Fort Lauderdale FL 33301-2298
County: Broward — FICE Identification: 001500
Unit ID: 132709
Telephone: (954) 201-7350 — Carnegie Class: Bac/Assoc-Assoc Dom
FAX Number: (954) 201-7576 — Calendar System: Trimester
URL: www.broward.edu
Established: 1959 — Annual Undergrad Tuition & Fees (In-State): $2,830
Enrollment: 33,243 — Coed
Affiliation or Control: State — IRS Status: 501(c)3
Highest Offering: Baccalaureate
Accreditation: SC, ADNUR, ART, CAHIIM, COARC, DA, DH, DMS, EMT, MUS, NMT, NURSE, OPD, PTAA, RAD, RTT, THEA

01 President ... Mr. Gregory Adam HAILE
05 Provost/SVP Academic Affs ... Dr. Jeffrey NASSE
11 Sr Vice Pres Finance/Operations ... Mr. John DUNNUCK
32 Vice Provost Student Services ... Ms. Janice STUBBS
26 VP Communications & Cmty Relations ... Ms. Isabel GONZALEZ
10 Vice President Finance ... Mr. Caleb CORNELIUS
111 VP Advancement/Exec Dir Foundation ... Ms. Nancy O'DONNELL-WILSON
13 VP Information Technology ... Mr. Tony CASCIOTTA
86 VP Policy/Govt Affairs/Gen Counsel ... Ms. Lacey HOFMEYER
103 Sr VP Workforce Development ... Dr. Mildred COYNE
100 Chief of Staff ... Ms. Isabel GONZALEZ
12 Campus President North Campus ... Dr. Sunem BEATON-GARCIA
12 Campus President Central Campus ... Dr. Stephen DUNNIVANT
12 Interim Campus Pres South Campus ... Dr. Sunem BEATON-GARCIA
18 Interim AVP Facilities ... Mr. Marcus WILSON
09 Chief Data Officer ... Vacant
45 AVP Inst Planning/Effectiveness ... Ms. Renee LAW
08 Dean of Libraries/ASCs ... Dr. Monique BLAKE
37 Asst Director Financial Aid ... Ms. Celestine HUNTLEY
15 Vice President Talent/Culture ... Sophia GALVIN
06 Registrar/AVP Academic Affairs ... Ms. Karen LEE MURPHY
29 Alumni Engagement/Maj Gifts Officer ... Ms. Jill HOROWITZ
04 Sr Exec Asst to the President ... Ms. Marisol CORTEZ-DIAZ
19 AVP Security/Safety ... Mr. Grant GUNDLE
25 Chief Contracts/Grants Admin ... Ms. Kareen TORRES
96 Director of Purchasing ... Dr. Judy SCHMELZER

Cambridge College (G)

5150 Linton Boulevard, Suite 340, Delray Beach FL 33484
County: Palm Beach — FICE Identification: 040834
Unit ID: 454865
Telephone: (561) 381-4990 — Carnegie Class: Spec 2-yr-Health
FAX Number: (561) 381-4992 — Calendar System: Other
URL: www.cambridgehealth.edu
Established: — Annual Undergrad Tuition & Fees: $14,908
Enrollment: 654 — Coed
Affiliation or Control: Proprietary — IRS Status: Proprietary
Highest Offering: Associate Degree
Accreditation: ABHES, DMS

01 Chancellor and CEO ... Dr. Terrence LAPIER

Cambridge Institute of Allied Health & Technology-Altamonte Springs (H)

460 E. Altamonte Drive, Third Floor,
Altamonte Springs FL 32701
County: Seminole — FICE Identification: 038425
Unit ID: 446109
Telephone: (407) 265-8383 — Carnegie Class: Not Classified
FAX Number: (407) 265-8384 — Calendar System: Other
URL: www.cambridgehealth.edu
Established: — Annual Undergrad Tuition & Fees: $15,330
Enrollment: 377 — Coed
Affiliation or Control: Proprietary — IRS Status: Proprietary
Highest Offering: Associate Degree
Accreditation: ABHES, DMS

00 President ... Dr. Terrance LAPIER
01 Campus Dean ... Gabriel GARCES
06 Registrar ... Kristie MORALES
08 Librarian Online ... Stacey CRAIN

37 Financial Aid Manager .... Monica ROBLES
36 Careers Services Director .... Theresa MANTOVANI

Center of Cinematography, Art & Television (A)

1637 NW 27th Avenue, Miami FL 33125
Telephone: (305) 634-0550 Identification: 770562
Accreditation: ACCSC

† Branch campus of Colegio de Cinematografia, Artes y Television, Bayamon, PR

Chamberlain University-Jacksonville (B)

5200 Belfort Road, Suite 100, Jacksonville FL 32256
Telephone: (904) 251-8100 Identification: 770501
Accreditation: &HLC, NURSE

† Branch campus of Chamberlain University-Addison, Addison, IL

Chamberlain University-Miramar (C)

2300 SW 145th Avenue, Miramar FL 33027
Telephone: (954) 885-3510 Identification: 770498
Accreditation: &HLC, NURSE

† Branch campus of Chamberlain University-Addison, Addison, IL

Chi University (D)

9650 West Highway 318, Reddick FL 32686
County: Marion Identification: 667354
Telephone: (352) 591-5385 Carnegie Class: Not Classified
FAX Number: (844) 873-2868 Calendar System: Other
URL: www.chiu.edu
Established: 1998 Annual Graduate Tuition & Fees: N/A
Enrollment: N/A Coed
Affiliation or Control: Proprietary IRS Status: Proprietary
Highest Offering: Master's; No Undergraduates
Accreditation: DEAC

01 President .... Dr. Huisheng XIE
03 Executive VP/Campus Director .... Mr. Zhen ZHAO
10 VP Finance .... Ms. Yanru ZHAO
05 Provost .... Dr. Lisa TREVISANELLO

Chipola College (E)

3094 Indian Circle, Marianna FL 32446-3065
County: Jackson FICE Identification: 001472
Unit ID: 133021
Telephone: (850) 526-2761 Carnegie Class: Bac/Assoc-Mixed
FAX Number: (850) 718-2388 Calendar System: Semester
URL: www.chipola.edu
Established: 1947 Annual Undergrad Tuition & Fees (In-District): $3,120
Enrollment: 1,943 Coed
Affiliation or Control: State/Local IRS Status: 501(c)3
Highest Offering: Baccalaureate
Accreditation: SC, ADNUR, EMT, NUR

01 President .... Dr. Sarah CLEMMONS
05 VP of Instructional Affairs .... Dr. Pam RENTZ
10 Vice Pres of Admin & Business Svcs .... Mr. Steve YOUNG
15 Assoc VP of HR/Equity/Title IX .... Mrs. Wendy PIPPEN
13 Associate VP Information Systems .... Mr. Dennis F. EVERETT
32 Assoc VP of Student Affairs .... Ms. Bonnie SMITH
108 Dean Assessment/Compliance & Grant .... Dr. Matthew HUGHES
18 Dir Facilities & Campus Operations .... Mr. Dennis KOSCIW
26 Director Public Relations .... Dr. Bryan C. CRAVEN
07 Dir of Enrollment Services .... Mr. Shannon MERCER
37 Director of Financial Aid .... Ms. Beverly HAMBRIGHT
41 Director of Athletics .... Mr. Jeff JOHNSON
06 Registrar .... Ms. Ashley HARVEY
04 Executive Assistant .... Ms. Jan CUMMINGS
103 Dean Workforce/Economic Development .... Mr. Darwin GILMORE
08 Dir of Learning Resources .... Ms. Vikki MILTON
102 Dir Found/Corporate Relations .... Ms. Julie FUQUA
50 Dean School of Business/Tech .... Dr. David BOUVIN
53 Dean School of Education .... Dr. Gina MCALLISTER
101 Secretary of the Institution/Board .... Dr. Sarah CLEMMONS
91 AVP Administrative Computing .... Mr. Dennis EVERETT

City College (F)

177 Montgomery Road, Altamonte Springs FL 32714
County: Seminole FICE Identification: 030799
Unit ID: 417327
Telephone: (407) 831-9816 Carnegie Class: Assoc/HVT-High Trad
FAX Number: (407) 831-1147 Calendar System: Quarter
URL: https://www.citycollege.edu/locations/altamonte-springs-orla
Established: 1997 Annual Undergrad Tuition & Fees: $15,056
Enrollment: 242 Coed
Affiliation or Control: Independent Non-Profit IRS Status: 501(c)3
Highest Offering: Associate Degree
Accreditation: ABHES, ADNUR, EMT, SURTEC

01 President .... Mrs. Esther FIKE-CURRY
05 Executive Director .... Mrs. Heidi K. POLLPETER

City College (G)

2000 W Commercial Boulevard,
Fort Lauderdale FL 33309-1916
County: Broward FICE Identification: 025154
Unit ID: 244233
Telephone: (954) 492-5353 Carnegie Class: Bac/Assoc-Mixed
FAX Number: (954) 958-9257 Calendar System: Quarter
URL: www.citycollege.edu
Established: 1983 Annual Undergrad Tuition & Fees: $14,876
Enrollment: 297 Coed
Affiliation or Control: Independent Non-Profit IRS Status: 501(c)3
Highest Offering: Baccalaureate
Accreditation: ABHES, EMT, SURTEC

01 President .... R. Esther CURRY
05 Director of Education .... Dr. Anie BONILLA
36 Director of Career Development .... Anide HARRIGAN-CRUZ
07 Director of Admissions .... Stacey KRAHE
13 Director Information Technology .... Alan BUSHKIN
08 Director of Library .... Cathy DIETERLY
06 Registrar .... Jennifer TOSUN
15 Director Human Resources .... Natasga GROYSMAN
37 Asst Director Student Financial Aid .... Patty PATTERSON
106 Dir Online Education/E-learning .... Dr. Suzanne MORRISON-WILLAIMS
108 Dir Institutional Effectiveness .... Heather PAYNE
18 Director of Facilities .... Donna VARELA

City College (H)

7001 NW Fourth Boulevard, Gainesville FL 32607
Telephone: (352) 415-4497 Identification: 666413
Accreditation: ABHES, EMT

† Branch campus of City College, Fort Lauderdale, FL.

City College (I)

6565 Taft Street, Hollywood FL 33024
Telephone: (954) 744-1777 Identification: 770674
Accreditation: ABHES, EMT

City College (J)

9300 S Dadeland Blvd, Suite 200, Miami FL 33156
Telephone: (305) 925-0934 Identification: 666414
Accreditation: ABHES, AT, EMT, SURTEC

† Branch campus of City College, Fort Lauderdale, FL.

College of Business and Technology (K)

8230 W. Flagler Street, Miami FL 33144
County: Miami-Dade FICE Identification: 030716
Unit ID: 417318
Telephone: (305) 273-4499 Carnegie Class: Bac/Assoc-Mixed
FAX Number: (305) 270-0779 Calendar System: Semester
URL: www.cbt.edu
Established: 1988 Annual Undergrad Tuition & Fees: N/A
Enrollment: N/A Coed
Affiliation or Control: Proprietary IRS Status: Proprietary
Highest Offering: Associate Degree
Accreditation: ACICS

00 CEO/President .... Mr. Luis LLERENA
01 Campus Director .... Mr. Peter BASTIONY
10 Finance Director/COO .... Ms. Maricel SPEZZACATENA
37 Financial Aid Director .... Mrs. Yazmin PALMA
13 Information Systems Manager .... Mr. Jorge CUBILLO
12 Campus Director Hialeah .... Ms. Alexandra RAMIREZ
05 Director of Academic Operations .... Mr. Hector DUENAS

College of Business and Technology - Cutler Bay (L)

19151 South Dixie Highway, Ste 205, Cutler Bay FL 33157
Telephone: (786) 693-8801 Identification: 770677
Accreditation: ACICS, CAHIIM

College of Business and Technology - Hialeah Campus (M)

935 West 49th Street, Suite 203, Hialeah FL 33012
Telephone: (305) 273-4499 Identification: 770675
Accreditation: ACICS

College of Central Florida (N)

3001 S.W. College Road, Ocala FL 34474
County: Marion FICE Identification: 001471
Unit ID: 132851
Telephone: (352) 237-2111 Carnegie Class: Bac/Assoc-Mixed
FAX Number: (352) 291-4450 Calendar System: Semester
URL: www.cf.edu
Established: 1957 Annual Undergrad Tuition & Fees (In-District): $2,710
Enrollment: 6,150 Coed
Affiliation or Control: Local IRS Status: 501(c)3
Highest Offering: Baccalaureate
Accreditation: SC, ADNUR, CAHIIM, DA, EMT, NUR, PTAA, RAD, SURGT

01 President .... Dr. James D. HENNINGSEN
10 Vice Pres Administration & Finance .... Mr. Charles PRINCE
05 Vice President Academic Affairs .... Dr. Mark PAUGH
32 Vice President Student Affairs .... Dr. Saul REYES
12 Vice President Regional Campuses .... Dr. Vernon LAWTER, JR.
86 Director Government Relations .... Ms. Jessica MCCLAIN
09 VP Inst Effectiveness/College Rels .... Dr. Jillian RAMSAMMY
26 Director Marketing/Public Relations .. Ms. Lois BRAUCKMULLER
102 VP Development/CEO Foundation .... Mr. Christopher KNIFE
21 Assistant VP for Finance .... Mr. Steven ASH
12 Provost Jack Wilkinson Levy Campus . Ms. Holland MCGLASHAN
80 Dean Public Service/Criminal Just .... Mr. Charles MCINTOSH
75 Dean Bus Tech Careers & Tech Educ .... Dr. Rob WOLF
35 Dean Student Services .... Dr. Henri BENLOLO
49 Associate Vice Pres Arts & Sciences .... Dr. Allan DANUFF
121 Director Advising & Stdnt Success .... Ms. Chenita HART
103 Assoc Vice Pres Career & Prof Pgms .... Dr. Jennifer FRYNS
76 Dean Health Sciences .... Dr. Stephanie CORTES
106 Dean E-learning & Learning Resource .... Dr. Tamara VIVIANO-BRODERICK
37 Director Financial Aid .... Ms. Jean IMES
09 Dir Inst Research & Effectiveness .... Ms. Judy MENADIER
07 Dir Admissions/Stdnt Recruitment .... Dr. Raphel ROBINSON
18 Manager of Plant Operations .... Ms. Katerine HUNT
15 Director Human Resources .... Ms. Jennifer KLEPFER
35 Director Student Life .... Ms. Marjorie MCGEE
88 Director Student Support Services .... Dr. Lisa SMITH
41 Director Athletics/Wellness .... Mr. Bob ZELINSKI
22 Director Access and Counsel Service .... Vacant
88 Dir Stdnt Success & Educ Outreach .... Dr. Leonard EVERETT
88 Director Appleton Museum of Art .... Mr. Jason STEUBER
25 Director of Resource Dev/Accred .... Mr. Matt MATTHEWS
96 Dir Purchasing & Risk Mgmt .... Mr. Stewart TRAUTMAN
08 Library Director .... Ms. Teresa FAUST
19 Manager Public Safety .... Mr. Mickey GUERIN
109 Manager Printing & Postal Service .... Mr. Tony DENIS
109 Manager Conference & Food Service .... Ms. Cheryl CROSBY
13 Associate VP Information Technology .... Mr. Ron KIELTY
06 Director Enroll Services/Registrar .... Dr. Alton AUSTIN
30 Director of Development .... Ms. Traci MASON
28 Director of Diversity & Inclusion .... Dr. Mary Ann BEGLEY

The College of the Florida Keys (O)

5901 College Road, Key West FL 33040-4397
County: Monroe FICE Identification: 001485
Unit ID: 133960
Telephone: (305) 296-9081 Carnegie Class: Bac/Assoc-Assoc Dom
FAX Number: (305) 292-5155 Calendar System: Trimester
URL: www.cfk.edu
Established: 1963 Annual Undergrad Tuition & Fees (In-District): $3,276
Enrollment: 856 Coed
Affiliation or Control: State/Local IRS Status: 501(c)3
Highest Offering: Baccalaureate
Accreditation: SC, ADNUR

01 President .... Dr. Jonathan GUEVERRA
05 Vice President Academic Affairs .... Mrs. Brittany SYNDER
10 Vice Pres Business & Admin Svcs .... Vacant
111 Vice President Advancement .... Dr. Frank WOOD
84 Assoc Dean Enrollment Mgmt .... Mrs. Kathleen CLARK
19 Dir Institute for Public Safety .... Mrs. Cathy TORRES
04 Director President's Office .... Ms. Rachel OROPEZA
26 Dir Marketing and Public Relations .... Mrs. Amber ERNST-LEONARD
06 Registrar .... Mrs. Kathleen CLARK
08 Director Learning Resources .... Ms. Kristina NEIHOUSE
37 Director Financial Aid .... Mr. Jeffrey SMITH
18 Dir Purchasing & Plant Operations .... Mr. Greg O'FLYNN
13 Director of IT .... Vacant
15 Director Human Resources .... Mrs. Beren LINDENBERG
21 Controller .... Ms. Heather GARCIA
09 Director Institutional Research .... Vacant
81 Dean of Science & Nursing .... Mr. Mark ROBY
50 Dean Business and Marine Science .... Mr. Jack SUEBERT
49 Dean Arts & Sciences .... Mr. Michael MCPHERSON

Concorde Career Institute (P)

7259 Salisbury Road, Jacksonville FL 32256
County: Duval FICE Identification: 020896
Unit ID: 133845
Telephone: (904) 725-0525 Carnegie Class: Spec 2-yr-Health
FAX Number: (904) 721-9944 Calendar System: Semester
URL: https://www.concorde.edu/campus/jacksonville-florida
Established: 1988 Annual Undergrad Tuition & Fees: N/A
Enrollment: 555 Coed
Affiliation or Control: Proprietary IRS Status: Proprietary
Highest Offering: Associate Degree
Accreditation: ACCSC, COARC, PTAA, SURGT

01 Campus President .... Ray RILEY
07 Director of Admissions .... Lee KELLY

Concorde Career Institute (Q)

10933 Marks Way, Miramar FL 33025
County: Broward FICE Identification: 022751
Unit ID: 133854
Telephone: (954) 731-8880 Carnegie Class: Spec 2-yr-Health
FAX Number: (954) 484-2961 Calendar System: Other
URL: https://www.concorde.edu/campus/miramar-florida
Established: 1989 Annual Undergrad Tuition & Fees: N/A
Enrollment: 434 Coed

Affiliation or Control: Proprietary IRS Status: Proprietary
Highest Offering: Associate Degree
Accreditation: ACCSC, COARC, OTA, PTAA, SURGT

01 Campus President .... Robert BURNFIELD
07 Director of Admissions .... Brandon PAUL

Concorde Career Institute (A)

3444 McCrory Place, Orlando FL 32803
Telephone: (407) 812-3060 Identification: 770563
Accreditation: ACCSC, DH, SURGT

Concorde Career Institute (B)

4202 West Spruce Street, Tampa FL 33607-4127
County: Hillsborough FICE Identification: 021727
Unit ID: 133863
Telephone: (813) 874-0094 Carnegie Class: Spec 2-yr-Health
FAX Number: (813) 872-6884 Calendar System: Other
URL: https://www.concorde.edu/campus/tampa-florida
Established: 1978 Annual Undergrad Tuition & Fees: N/A
Enrollment: 405 Coed
Affiliation or Control: Proprietary IRS Status: Proprietary
Highest Offering: Associate Degree
Accreditation: ACCSC, COARC, DH, SURGT

01 Campus President .... Ms. Debra WENINGER

Daytona College (C)

425 South Nova Road, Ormond Beach FL 32174-8449
County: Volusia FICE Identification: 039396
Unit ID: 447014
Telephone: (386) 267-0565 Carnegie Class: Spec 2-yr-Health
FAX Number: (386) 267-0567 Calendar System: Semester
URL: www.daytonacollege.edu
Established: 1996 Annual Undergrad Tuition & Fees: N/A
Enrollment: 236 Coed
Affiliation or Control: Proprietary IRS Status: Proprietary
Highest Offering: Baccalaureate
Accreditation: ACCSC, ADNUR

01 President/CEO .... Mr. Roger BRADLEY
05 Director of Education .... Dr. Khaliff ALI

Daytona State College (D)

PO Box 2811, Daytona Beach FL 32120-2811
County: Volusia FICE Identification: 001475
Unit ID: 133386
Telephone: (386) 506-3000 Carnegie Class: Bac/Assoc-Mixed
FAX Number: N/A Calendar System: Semester
URL: www.DaytonaState.edu
Established: 1957 Annual Undergrad Tuition & Fees (In-District): $3,106
Enrollment: 12,728 Coed
Affiliation or Control: State/Local IRS Status: 501(c)3
Highest Offering: Baccalaureate
Accreditation: SC, ADNUR, CAHIIM, COARC, DA, DH, EMT, MAC, NUR, OTA, PTAA, SURGT

01 President .... Dr. Thomas LOBASSO
03 Executive Vice President .... Mr. Brian T. BABB
05 Provost .... Dr. Amy LOCKLEAR
10 VP Finance/Chief Business Officer .... Mr. Martin CASS
13 SVP Information Technology .... Mr. Roberto LOMBARDO
84 VP Enrollment Services .... Dr. Erik D'AQUINO
32 VP Student Development .... Mr. Keith KENNEDY
111 VP Advancement/Exec Dir Foundation .... Mr. Timothy NORTON
15 AVP Human Resources .... Ms. Robin BARR
103 AVP Workforce & Cont Educ .... Dr. Sherryl WEEMS
08 Head Librarian .... Ms. Mercedes CLEMENT
49 AVP Arts & Science .... Dr. Alycia EHLERT
76 AVP College of Health .... Dr. Colin CHESLEY
18 AVP Facilities Planning .... Mr. Christopher WAINWRIGHT
21 AVP Finance/Controller .... Ms. Tina MYERS
50 AVP Business/Engr & Tech .... Mr. Dante LEON
106 Director Instructional Resources .... Mr. Hector VALLE
09 Dir Institutional Research .... Dr. Andrea GIBSON
37 Director Financial Aid .... Ms. Heidi PINNEY
69 Int Dean School Health & Wellness .... Ms. Robin BARR
19 Director Campus Safety .... Mr. Louie MERCER
12 Dean DeLand & Deltona Campuses .... Mr. Neil CLEMONS
12 Dean New Smyrna Beach Campus .... Mr. Clarence MCCLOUD
43 General Counsel .... Mr. Brian BABB
51 Director Ctr for Business/Industry .... Mr. Frank MERCER
35 Asst Dean Student Life .... Mr. Bruce COOK
121 Director Academic Advising .... Ms. Michelle GOLDYS
07 Director Admissions/Recruitment .... Ms. Karen SANDERS
22 Director of Equity & Inclusion .... Mr. Lonnie THOMPSON
06 Director of Records/Registrar .... Ms. Carri BLACK HUDGINS
113 Director Student Accounts .... Ms. Cerese RAMOS
26 Director of Marketing .... Mr. Chris THOMES
09 Dean Institutional Effectiveness .... Dr. Karla MOORE
29 Director Alumni Relations .... Ms. Kristen HANSON
96 Exec Director of Business Services .... Ms. Elaine THIEL

Dolphin Research Center Training Institute (E)

58901 Overseas Hwy, Grassy Key FL 33050
County: Monroe Identification: 667338
Telephone: (305) 289-1121 Carnegie Class: Not Classified
FAX Number: (305) 289-8902 Calendar System: Other
URL: https://dolphins.org/drcti
Established: 2012 Annual Undergrad Tuition & Fees: N/A
Enrollment: N/A Coed
Affiliation or Control: Independent Non-Profit IRS Status: 501(c)3
Highest Offering: Associate Degree
Accreditation: ACCSC

01 President & CEO .... Rita IRWIN
05 Director .... Linda ERB
06 Registrar .... Kristen R. TROTT
04 Admin Assistant to the President .... Amy BAYER
10 VP Finance/Chief Financial Officer .... Peggy MCGILL

Doral College (F)

2525 NW 112th Ave, Doral FL 33172
County: Miami-Dade Identification: 667335
Telephone: (305) 463-7210 Carnegie Class: Not Classified
FAX Number: (305) 477-3525 Calendar System: Semester
URL: www.doral.edu
Established: 2011 Annual Undergrad Tuition & Fees: N/A
Enrollment: N/A Coed
Affiliation or Control: Independent Non-Profit IRS Status: 501(c)3
Highest Offering: Baccalaureate
Accreditation: DEAC

01 President .... Judith MARTY
05 VP for Academic Affairs .... Guillermo RIVERA
32 VP for Student Affairs .... Cristina GUERRA ROMERO
10 VP for Financial Affairs .... Manny DIAZ

Dragon Rises College of Oriental Medicine (G)

1000 NE 16th Ave., Building F, Gainesville FL 32601-4557
County: Alachua FICE Identification: 038883
Unit ID: 449481
Telephone: (352) 371-2833 Carnegie Class: Spec-4-yr-Other Health
FAX Number: (352) 244-0003 Calendar System: Semester
URL: www.dragonrises.edu
Established: 2001 Annual Undergrad Tuition & Fees: N/A
Enrollment: 42 Coed
Affiliation or Control: Independent Non-Profit IRS Status: 501(c)3
Highest Offering: Master's
Accreditation: ACUP

01 Director/CEO .... Ms. Karen MARTIN-BROWN
05 Academic Dean .... Dr. Eduardo ALVAREZ
07 Director of Admissions .... Ms. Christina MCNIEL
08 Chief Library Officer .... Mr. Daniel HORAK
13 Chief Information Technology Office .... Mr. Brandon WEINTRAUB

East West College of Natural Medicine (H)

3808 N Tamiami Trail, Sarasota FL 34234-5362
County: Sarasota FICE Identification: 034297
Unit ID: 439394
Telephone: (941) 355-9080 Carnegie Class: Spec-4-yr-Other Health
FAX Number: (941) 355-3243 Calendar System: Trimester
URL: www.ewcollege.edu
Established: 1994 Annual Undergrad Tuition & Fees: N/A
Enrollment: 79 Coed
Affiliation or Control: Proprietary IRS Status: Proprietary
Highest Offering: Master's
Accreditation: ACCSC, ACUP

01 President .... Dr. Yoseph FELEKE
05 VP/Academic Dean .... Dr. Hailin WU
07 Director of Admissions/Career Svcs .... Ms. Sherry INGBRITSEN

Eastern Florida State College (I)

3865 N. Wickham Road, Melbourne FL 32935
County: Brevard FICE Identification: 001470
Unit ID: 132693
Telephone: (321) 632-1111 Carnegie Class: Bac/Assoc-Assoc Dom
FAX Number: (321) 633-4565 Calendar System: Semester
URL: www.easternflorida.edu
Established: 1960 Annual Undergrad Tuition & Fees (In-District): $2,496
Enrollment: 13,937 Coed
Affiliation or Control: Local IRS Status: 501(c)3
Highest Offering: Baccalaureate
Accreditation: SC, ADNUR, #COARC, DA, DH, DMS, EMT, MLTAD, NURSE, PTAA, RAD, SURGT

01 President .... Dr. James H. RICHEY
10 VP Operations/Chief Financial Ofcr .... Mr. Mark CHERRY
05 VP Academic & Student Affairs/CLO .... Dr. Randy FLETCHER
41 Assoc Vice Pres of Athletics .... Mr. Jeffrey CARR
18 AVP Facilities & Special Projects .... Mr. Stockton WHITTEN
15 AVP Human Resources .... Ms. Darla FERGUSON
20 AVP Academic Affairs .... Dr. Sandy HANDFIELD
35 AVP Student Affairs .... Dr. Laura VERRY SIDORAN
86 VP External Affairs .... Mr. Jack PARKER
26 AVP Communications .... Mr. John GLISCH
12 Provost Palm Bay Campus .... Dr. Wayne STEIN
12 Provost Cocoa Campus .... Dr. Dedra SIBLEY
12 Provost Titusville Campus/eLearning .... Dr. Philip SIMPSON
103 Executive Director Workforce Pgms .... Mr. Stephen TAYLOR
37 Director Collegewide Financial Aid .... Ms. Eileen BRZOZOWSKI
84 Dean Enrollment Mgmt .... Ms. Michelle LOUFEK
04 Executive Asst to the President .... Ms. Gina TAYLOR
06 Registrar .... Vacant
09 Exe Dir Plng/Assessment/CIRO .... Dr. Mark QUATHAMER
102 Director EFSC Foundation .... Vacant
36 Exec Dir Career Plng/Development .... Dr. Cathy CADY
13 Chief Information Technology Office .... Mr. Bill WHITE
19 Director Security/Safety .... Mr. Joe AMBROSE
29 Director Alumni Affairs .... Ms. Tonya CHERRY
39 Dir Resident Life/Student Housing .... Ms. Lena COPELAND

Eckerd College (J)

4200 54th Avenue S, Saint Petersburg FL 33711-4700
County: Pinellas FICE Identification: 001487
Unit ID: 133492
Telephone: (727) 867-1166 Carnegie Class: Bac-A&S
FAX Number: (727) 864-1877 Calendar System: 4/1/4
URL: www.eckerd.edu
Established: 1958 Annual Undergrad Tuition & Fees: $47,704
Enrollment: 1,822 Coed
Affiliation or Control: Presbyterian Church (U.S.A.) IRS Status: 501(c)3
Highest Offering: Baccalaureate
Accreditation: SC

01 President .... Dr. Damian J. FERNANDEZ
05 VP Academic Affs/Dean of Faculty .... Dr. Suzan HARRISON
10 VP Business and Finance .... Mr. Christopher P. BRENNAN
03 VP and Secretary of the College .... Dr. Lisa A. METS
111 Vice President Advancement .... Mr. Matthew S. BISSET
107 VP/Dean for Executive Education .... Mr. Kelly KIRSCHNER
32 VP Student Life/Dean of Students .... Dr. James J. ANNARELLI
84 VP Enrollment Management .... Mr. John SULLIVAN
20 Assoc Dean Faculty Development .... Dr. Kathryn J. WATSON
26 VP Marketing and Communications .... Ms. Valerie GLIEM
15 Asst VP Human Resources .... Ms. Liana HEMINGWAY
09 Exec Director Inst Effectiveness .... Ms. Jacqueline MACNEIL
21 AVP/Controller .... Ms. Robin REMLEY
20 Assoc Dean/Exec Dir Acad Excellence .... Dr. Marjorie SANFILIPPO
110 Assoc VP Advancement .... Mr. Tom SCHNEIDER
11 Assistant VP Operations .... Mr. Adam COLBY
105 Dir Web/Marketing/Communication .... Mr. Michel FOUGERES
88 Director of ASPEC .... Mr. Ken WOLFE
104 Director of International Education .... Vacant
85 Dir International Student Programs .... Mr. Olivier DEBURE
13 Director of Information Technology .... Mr. Ashley BURT
06 Registrar .... Vacant
08 Director of Library .... Ms. Lisa JOHNSTON
38 Exec Director Counseling & Outreach .... Ms. Linda ABBOTT
29 Director Alumni Engagement .... Ms. Kyla SMITH
19 Director Campus Safety .... Ms. Tonya WOMACK
37 Director Financial Aid .... Dr. Pat E. WATKINS
41 Athletics Director .... Mr. Tom RYAN
07 Director of Admission .... Mr. Jacob BROWNE
42 Chaplain .... Rev. Doug MCMAHON
25 Director of Grant Development .... Ms. Anna RUTH
124 Asst Dean Students for Engagement .... Mr. Fred SABOTA
51 Associate Dean Cont Education .... Ms. Amy APICERNO
04 Exec Asst to President .... Ms. Jolene QATATO

ECPI University College of Nursing (K)

660 Century Point, Ste 1050,
Orlando (Lake Mary) FL 32746
Telephone: (407) 562-9100 Identification: 770566
Accreditation: &SC, NURSE, PTAA

† Branch campus of ECPI University, Virginia Beach, VA

Edward Waters College (L)

1658 Kings Road, Jacksonville FL 32209-6199
County: Duval FICE Identification: 001478
Unit ID: 133526
Telephone: (904) 470-8000 Carnegie Class: Bac-Diverse
FAX Number: (904) 470-8039 Calendar System: Semester
URL: www.ewc.edu
Established: 1866 Annual Undergrad Tuition & Fees: $14,878
Enrollment: 2,273 Coed
Affiliation or Control: African Methodist Episcopal IRS Status: 501(c)3
Highest Offering: Master's
Accreditation: SC, IACBE

01 President .... Dr. A. Zachary FAISON, JR.
11 Executive Vice President/COO .... Dr. Donna H. OLIVER
100 Chief of Staff .... Dr. Pamela RICHARDSON-WILKS
05 Provost/Sr VP Academic Affairs .... Dr. Donna H. OLIVER
10 VP Finance Admin/Bus Innovation .... Mr. Randolph MITCHELL, JR.
111 VP Inst Advance/Dev/Mktg/Comm .... Dr. Veronica COHEN
84 VP Enroll Mgt/Strat Matriculant Svc .... Dr. Jennifer PRICE
121 VP Student Success/Engagement .... Mr. Jame'l R. HODGES
21 Assoc VP Business and Finance .... Vacant
15 Director Human Resources .... Ms. Carla GRAVES
09 Director Institutional Research .... Mr. Brian SEYMORE
25 Dir Title III & Sponsored Pgms .... Vacant
06 Registrar .... Ms. Detrenyona CHESTER
20 Assoc Provost Acad Stdnt Success/Rl .... Dr. Stephanie CAMPBELL
37 Director Financial Aid .... Ms. Janice NOWAK
88 Director Upward Bound .... Dr. Delacy SANFORD
36 Dir Career Development/Placement .... Ms. Ofori QUEEN

30 Director Development .... Vacant
07 Exec Dir Admissions/Enrollment Mgmt ..... Mr. Kendrick DUNKLIN
88 Director of Support Services .... Ms. Andrea M. CUMMINGS
31 Dir Community Resource Center .... Ms. Marie HEATH
88 Director of CTL .... Vacant
13 Director IT .... Mr. David SIMFUKWE
08 Library Director .... Ms. Brenda HARRELL
101 Secy of the College/Clerk of Board .... Ms. Felicia GROVER
26 Marketing/Communication Manager .... Vacant
29 Director of Alumni Affairs .... Vacant
38 Director Counseling Center .... Ms. Ragan SUMMERS
32 AVP/Dean of Students .... Dr. Lanita HOLSEY
96 Purchasing Clerk .... Ms. Valerie CRIMES

Embry-Riddle Aeronautical University-Daytona Beach (A)

1 Aerospace Boulevard, Daytona Beach FL 32114-3900

County: Volusia | FICE Identification: 001479
Unit ID: 133553
Telephone: (386) 226-6000 | Carnegie Class: Masters/M
FAX Number: N/A | Calendar System: Semester
URL: www.erau.edu
Established: 1926 | Annual Undergrad Tuition & Fees: $37,964
Enrollment: 8,797 | Coed
Affiliation or Control: Independent Non-Profit | IRS Status: 501(c)3
Highest Offering: Doctorate
Accreditation: SC, AAB, ACBSP, CEA, IFSAC

01 President .... Dr. Barry BUTLER
05 SVP Academic Affairs & Provost .... Mr. Lon D. MOELLER
10 SVP for Finance and CFO .... Dr. Randy B. HOWARD
30 SVP Philanthropy/Alumni Engagement .... Vacant
15 VP/Chief Human Resources Officer .... Mr. Brandon L. YOUNG
43 Vice President & General Counsel ...... Mr. Charlie W. SEVASTOS
26 VP Marketing & Communications .... Vacant
27 AVP News & Research .... Ms. Ginger PINHOLSTER
84 VP Enrollment Management .... Dr. Jason RUCKERT
13 Chief Information Officer .... Ms. Becky L. VASQUEZ
09 Exec Dir of Institutional Research .... Ms. Maria FRANCO
29 Exec Director Engagement Initiative ... Mr. William G. THOMPSON
39 Dir of Housing & Res Life .... Mr. Edward j. WALICKI
41 Director of Athletics .... Mr. John M. PHILLIPS
04 Senior Executive Asst to President ...... Ms. Chantal C. CRISWELL
104 Dir Office of Global Engagement .... Mrs. Sue A. MACCHIARELLA
108 Exec Dir of Academic Assessment .... Ms. Tiffany D. PHAGAN
32 Assoc Provost and Dean of Students .... Ms. Lisa S. KOLLAR
36 Executive Director of Career Svcs .... Ms. Alicia SMYTH
37 Director Student Financial Aid .... Ms. Barbara DRYDEN
49 Dean College of Arts & Sciences .... Dr. Karen GAINES
88 Dean College of Aviation .... Dr. Alan STOLZER
50 Dean O'Maley College of Business .... Dr. Shanan GIBSON
54 Dean College of Engineering .... Dr. James W. GREGORY
08 Hunt Library Director .... Ms. Anne M. CASEY
25 Chief Contract/Grants Administrator .... Dr. Nanette GUZMAN

Embry-Riddle Aeronautical University-Worldwide (B)

1 Aerospace Boulevard, Daytona Beach FL 32114-3900
Telephone: (800) 522-6787 | Identification: 666089
Accreditation: &SC, AAB, ACBSP

† Regional accreditation is carried under the parent institution in Daytona Beach, FL.

Emergency Educational Institute (C)

3111 N. University Dr., Ste 300, Coral Springs FL 33065
County: Broward | Identification: 667310
Telephone: (954) 753-6869 | Carnegie Class: Not Classified
FAX Number: (954) 755-9050 | Calendar System: Other
URL: www.eei.edu
Established: 2002 | Annual Undergrad Tuition & Fees: N/A
Enrollment: N/A | Coed
Affiliation or Control: Proprietary | IRS Status: Proprietary
Highest Offering: Associate Degree
Accreditation: ABHES

01 CEO/Owner .... Michelle UGALDE
05 EMS Medical Director .... Antonio GANDIA

Everglades University (D)

5002 T-Rex Avenue, Suite 100,
Boca Raton FL 33431-4493
County: Palm Beach | FICE Identification: 031085
Unit ID: 385619
Telephone: (888) 772-6077 | Carnegie Class: Masters/M
FAX Number: (561) 912-1191 | Calendar System: Semester
URL: www.evergladesuniversity.edu
Established: 1990 | Annual Undergrad Tuition & Fees: $18,320
Enrollment: 2,247 | Coed
Affiliation or Control: Independent Non-Profit | IRS Status: 501(c)3
Highest Offering: Master's
Accreditation: SC

01 President/CEO .... Ms. Kristi L. MOLLIS
20 Curriculum and Faculty Developer .... Dr. Kimberly PAVLIK
12 Vice President Boca Raton Campus .... Mr. Joseph DALTO
12 Vice President Miami Campus .... Ms. Debra COHEN
12 Vice President Orlando Campus .... Mr. Timothy DAUBER
12 Vice President Sarasota Campus .... Ms. Caroline KING
12 Vice President Tampa Campus .... Ms. Dina SIGANOS
12 Vice President Online Division .... Mr. Jeffrey DAY
05 Vice President of Academic Affairs .... Mr. Jared BEZET
37 Regional Director of Financial Aid .... Mrs. Seeta SINGH MOONILALL
10 Chief Financial Officer .... Mr. Joseph BERARDINELLI
26 Director of Marketing .... Ms. Kristi L. MOLLIS
84 Regional Dir Enrollment Management .... Mr. Ryan HEINTZ
09 Director of Inst Effectiveness .... Ms. Grace DESSA
08 Director of Library .... Mr. Adam BRODY
04 Executive Asst to the President .... Ms. Amy MOUTENOT

Flagler College (E)

74 King Street, Saint Augustine FL 32084-4342
County: Saint Johns | FICE Identification: 007893
Unit ID: 133711
Telephone: (904) 819-6200 | Carnegie Class: Bac-Diverse
FAX Number: (904) 824-6017 | Calendar System: Semester
URL: www.flagler.edu
Established: 1968 | Annual Undergrad Tuition & Fees: $20,040
Enrollment: 2,687 | Coed
Affiliation or Control: Independent Non-Profit | IRS Status: 501(c)3
Highest Offering: Master's
Accreditation: SC

01 President .... Mr. John A. DELANEY
10 Vice President Business Services .... Mr. David L. CARSON
111 VP of Institutional Advancement .... Ms. Kristina MYERS
05 Vice President Academic Affairs .... Dr. Art VANDEN HOUTEN
26 Vice Pres Marketing/Communications .... Ms. Carol BRANSON
09 Dir Inst Research & Effectiveness .... Ms. Jessica STOWELL
27 Director of News and Information .... Mr. Brian L. THOMPSON
84 Vice Pres for Enrollment Mgmt .... Ms. Deborah L. THOMPSON
32 Vice President of Student Affairs .... Dr. Sandra MILES
20 Dean of Academic Life .... Dr. Craig WOELFEL
35 Dean of Student Affairs .... Dr. Dirk HIBLER
38 Director of Counseling .... Dr. Kathy O. PAYNE
06 Registrar .... Ms. Sarah DEAGLE
37 Director of Financial Aid .... Ms. Sheia I. PLEASANT-DOINE
124 Dean of Student Engagement/Careers .... Ms. Tara STEVENSON
08 Director of Library Services .... Mr. Brian NESSELRODE
41 Director Intercollegiate Athletics .... Mr. Jud DAMON
19 Int Director of Safety & Security .... Dr. Dirk HIBLER
40 Bookstore Manager .... Mr. Pete PREVITE
24 Director Educational Media Services .... Mr. William JACKSON
13 Chief Information Officer .... Ms. Gwen PECHAN
39 Director of Residence Life .... Dr. Dirk HIBLER
35 Director of Student Activities .... Ms. Kristina LOMBARDO
12 Dean Flagler College - Tallahassee .... Dr. Wayne RIGGS
22 Dir of Disability Services .... Mr. Phillip POWNALL
18 Superintendent of Plant & Grounds .... Mr. Victor CHENEY
04 Assistant to the President .... Ms. Laura STEVENSON DUMAS
21 Director of Business Services .... Ms. Sarah PRODROMOU
29 Sr Dir Alumni & College Relations .... Ms. Margo THOMAS
30 Sr Director of Development .... Mr. Jeffrey DAVITT
15 Chief Human Resources Officer .... Mr. Kelly TOASTON
88 Senior Woman Admin Athletic Dept .... Ms. Karen HUDGINS
07 Dean of Admissions .... Ms. Rachel U. BRANCH
104 Director Study Abroad .... Ms. Lisa FIALA
105 Director Web Services .... Ms. Holly L. HILL
106 Dir Online Education & Inst Design .... Ms. Amy COOK
50 Dean Sch Business/Educ/Math .... Dr. Kurt SEBASTIAN
86 Director Government Relations .... Ms. Beth SWEENY
96 Director of Purchasing .... Ms. Sarah PRODROMOU

Florida Academy of Nursing (F)

12002 Miramar Parkway, Miramar FL 33025
County: Broward | Identification: 667382
Telephone: (954) 322-1612 | Carnegie Class: Not Classified
FAX Number: (954) 241-6842 | Calendar System: Quarter
URL: www.fanstudent.com
Established: 2013 | Annual Undergrad Tuition & Fees: N/A
Enrollment: N/A | Coed
Affiliation or Control: Proprietary | IRS Status: Proprietary
Highest Offering: Baccalaureate
Accreditation: ACCSC

01 Chief Executive Officer .... Ms. Lisa TELFER
66 Director of Nursing .... Ms. Irene ROMAN
10 Director of Finance .... Ms. Annette AGLIETTI
07 Director of Admissions .... Ms. Lisa-Anne SHAW

Florida Career College (G)

1743 N Congress Avenue, Boynton Beach FL 33426
Telephone: (561) 810-1810 | Identification: 770678
Accreditation: COE

Florida Career College (H)

3750 West 18th Avenue, Hialeah FL 33012-7028
Telephone: (786) 534-0940 | Identification: 666624
Accreditation: COE

Florida Career College (I)

6600-10 Youngerman Circle, Jacksonville FL 32244
Telephone: (904) 990-8500 | Identification: 770679
Accreditation: COE

Florida Career College (J)

3383 North State Road 7,
Lauderdale Lakes FL 33319-5617
Telephone: (954) 908-4700 | Identification: 666622
Accreditation: COE

Florida Career College - Margate Campus (K)

3271 North State Road 7, Margate FL 33063
Telephone: (954) 935-7921 | Identification: 770681
Accreditation: COE

Florida Career College (L)

1321 SW 107th Avenue, Suite 201B,
Miami FL 33174-2521
County: Miami-Dade | FICE Identification: 023058
Unit ID: 133997
Telephone: (786) 534-0500 | Carnegie Class: Assoc/HVT-Mix Trad/Non
FAX Number: (786) 534-0558 | Calendar System: Quarter
URL: www.floridacareercollege.edu
Established: 1982 | Annual Undergrad Tuition & Fees: N/A
Enrollment: 504 | Coed
Affiliation or Control: Proprietary | IRS Status: Proprietary
Highest Offering: Associate Degree
Accreditation: COE

01 President/CEO .... Dr. Fardad FATERI
06 Registrar .... Ms. Cheyla DAVILA
11 Campus Director .... Ms. Marcela MUNERA

Florida Career College (M)

989 N Semoran Boulevard, Orlando FL 32807
Telephone: (321) 430-8300 | Identification: 770613
Accreditation: COE

Florida Career College (N)

7891 Pines Boulevard, Pembroke Pines FL 33024-6916
Telephone: (954) 399-4801 | Identification: 666025
Accreditation: COE

Florida Career College (O)

9950 Princess Palm Avenue, Tampa FL 33619
Telephone: (813) 906-5900 | Identification: 770682
Accreditation: COE

Florida Career College (P)

6058 Okeechobee Boulevard, West Palm Beach FL 33417
Telephone: (561) 408-9910 | Identification: 770683
Accreditation: COE

Florida Coastal School of Law (Q)

8787 Baypine, Jacksonville FL 32256-8528
County: Duval | FICE Identification: 033743
Unit ID: 434715
Telephone: (904) 680-7700 | Carnegie Class: Spec-4-yr-Law
FAX Number: N/A | Calendar System: Semester
URL: www.fcsl.edu
Established: 1995 | Annual Graduate Tuition & Fees: N/A
Enrollment: 194 | Coed
Affiliation or Control: Proprietary | IRS Status: Proprietary
Highest Offering: First Professional Degree; No Undergraduates
Accreditation: LAW

01 Dean/President .... Mr. Peter GOPLERUD
07 Director of Admissions .... Ms. Megan SCHADE
32 Assistant Dean of Student Affairs .... Mr. James ARTLEY
09 Mgr of Institutional Effectiveness .... Ms. Karen EUBANKS
10 Comptroller .... Mr. Ron BAMBACUS

Florida College (R)

119 N Glen Arven Avenue,
Temple Terrace FL 33617-5578
County: Hillsborough | FICE Identification: 001482
Unit ID: 133809
Telephone: (813) 988-5131 | Carnegie Class: Bac/Assoc-Mixed
FAX Number: (813) 899-6772 | Calendar System: Semester
URL: www.floridacollege.edu
Established: 1944 | Annual Undergrad Tuition & Fees: $18,060
Enrollment: 488 | Coed
Affiliation or Control: Independent Non-Profit | IRS Status: 501(c)3
Highest Offering: Baccalaureate
Accreditation: SC, MUS

01 President .... Dr. Harry E. PAYNE, JR.
05 Academic Dean .... Dr. John WEAVER
32 Dean of Student Services .... Mr. Mike BENSON
10 Chief Business Officer .... Mr. Jamie LEWIS
37 Director Student Financial Aid .... Mr. Stephen BLAYLOCK
07 Dir of Admissions & Retention Svcs .... Miss Virginia MANESS
09 Director of Institutional Research .... Mr. Ryan BARCLAY
121 Director of Advising .... Mr. Todd CHANDLER

06 Registrar .... Mr. Ryan BARCLAY
08 Director of Library .... Ms. Jennifer KEARNEY
13 Director of Information Technology .... Mr. Jon RAE
30 Director of Development .... Mr. Jeff MATHIS
29 Director of Alumni Relations .... Mrs. Deborah BREWER
40 Manager of Bookstore .... Mrs. Carrie BLACK
88 Events Coordinator .... Mrs. Sierra SCHMIDT
41 Athletic Director .... Mr. Chase TEICHMANN
18 Chief Facilities/Physical Plant .... Mr. Tom GARLAND

Florida College of Integrative Medicine (A)

7100 Lake Ellenor Drive, Orlando FL 32809-5721
County: Orange FICE Identification: 032383
Unit ID: 434441
Telephone: (407) 888-8689 Carnegie Class: Spec-4-yr-Other Health
FAX Number: (407) 888-8211 Calendar System: Semester
URL: www.fcim.edu
Established: 1990 Annual Undergrad Tuition & Fees: N/A
Enrollment: 71 Coed
Affiliation or Control: Proprietary IRS Status: Proprietary
Highest Offering: Master's; No Lower Division
Accreditation: ACUP

01 President .... Mr. Lincoln Z. ZHAO
03 Vice President .... Ms. Jenjen HAN
108 Vice Pres/Chief Quality Officer .... Ms. Yuan-Yuan HAN
05 Dean of Academic Affairs .... Dr. Lin CHAI
10 Director of Finance .... Ms. Susan HOEH
07 Admissions Representative .... Ms. Michelle COLON
37 Director of Financial Aid .... Ms. Mary SIMMONS

Florida Gateway College (B)

149 SE College Place, Lake City FL 32025-2007
County: Columbia FICE Identification: 001501
Unit ID: 135160
Telephone: (386) 752-1822 Carnegie Class: Bac/Assoc-Assoc Dom
FAX Number: (386) 755-1521 Calendar System: Semester
URL: www.fgc.edu
Established: 1947 Annual Undergrad Tuition & Fees (In-State): $3,100
Enrollment: 3,018 Coed
Affiliation or Control: State IRS Status: 501(c)3
Highest Offering: Baccalaureate
Accreditation: SC, ADNUR, CAHIIM, EMT, NAEYC, NURSE, PTAA

01 President .... Dr. Lawrence BARRETT
10 Vice President Business Services .... Ms. Michelle HOLLOWAY
04 Assistant to the President .... Ms. Katy MCCRARY
05 Vice President for Academic Affairs .... Dr. Brian DOPSON
84 VP Enroll Mgmt & Student Affairs .... Mr. Anthony CARDENAS
20 Dean of Academic Pgm & Bacc Liaison .... Dr. Paula GAVIN
20 Associate Dean Academic Programs .... Dr. Matthew PEACE
13 Exec Dir Info Technology/CIO .... Mr. Travis GREEN
15 Executive Director Human Resources .... Ms. Cassie BUCKLES
72 Exec Dir of Tech Pgm & Public Svcs .... Mr. John JEWETT
53 Exec Dir Teacher Prep Programs .... Ms. Pamela CARSWELL
121 Director of Student Success .... Ms. Elizabeth MCCARDLE
37 Director Financial Aid .... Mr. Travis GEORGE
07 Assoc Dean Enrollment Management .... Ms. Kacey SCHRADER
32 Associate Dean Student Affairs .... Ms. Sandra TOMLINSON
06 Registrar & Dir of Enrollment Svcs .... Ms. Gayle HUNTER
21 Director Business Services .... Mr. Joseph HOLMES
09 Director of Inst Effect & Assess .... Dr. Natalie WRIGHT
66 Exec Director Nursing .... Dr. Shane NEELY-SMITH
18 Director Facilities .... Mr. Lance JONES
96 Director Procurement & Contracts .... Ms. Misty TAYLOR
27 Director Marketing .... Mr. Rob CHAPMAN
88 Director Dual Enrollment .... Ms. Julie CANNON
41 Athletic Director .... Ms. Rebecca GOLDEN
08 Director Library .... Ms. Christine BOATRIGHT
35 Director of Student Life .... Ms. Amy DEKLE
26 Exec Dir Public Info & Govt Rels .... Mr. Mike MCKEE
30 Exec Director Resource Development .... Mr. Lee PINCHOUCK
88 Dir ASDN & Certificate Program .... Ms. Patricia ORENDER

Florida Institute of Technology (C)

150 W University Boulevard, Melbourne FL 32901-6975
County: Brevard FICE Identification: 001469
Unit ID: 133881
Telephone: (321) 674-8000 Carnegie Class: DU-Higher
FAX Number: (321) 984-8461 Calendar System: Semester
URL: www.fit.edu
Established: 1958 Annual Undergrad Tuition & Fees: $43,246
Enrollment: 6,775 Coed
Affiliation or Control: Independent Non-Profit IRS Status: 501(c)3
Highest Offering: Doctorate
Accreditation: SC, AAB, ABAI, CLPSY, CONST, IACBE

01 President .... Dr. T. Dwayne MCCAY
04 Exec Asst to Pres .... Ms. Rebecca CROOK
05 Exec VP & Provost .... Dr. Marco CARVALHO
10 Chief Financial Officer .... Michael JONES
88 Sr Advisor to the President .... Capt. Winston SCOTT
100 Chief of Staff .... Vacant
88 Dean College of Aeronautics .... Dr. Ulreen MCKINNEY
50 Dean College of Business .... Dr. Theodore RICHARDSON
54 Int Dean Col of Engineering/Science .... Dr. Daniel KIRK
83 Int Dean Col of Psych/Lib Arts .... Dr. Robert TAYLOR
08 Dean of Libraries .... Dr. Holly MILLER
29 Sr VP Alumni & Student Affairs .... Mr. Albino P. CAMPANINI
30 Sr VP of Development .... Mr. Gary GRANT
84 Vice Pres Enrollment Mgmt .... Mr. Brian EHRLICH
13 Chief Information Officer .... Mr. Mark LUMSDEN
18 Vice Pres Facilities Operations .... Mr. Brian LESLIE
26 VP Communication .... Dr. Wesley D. SUMNER
106 VP Online Learning/Off Campus .... Ms. Julie SHANKLE
15 Vice President Human Resources .... Ms. Dondi KUENNEN
25 Director of Sponsored Programs .... Ms. Carolyn LOCKYER
37 AVP Enrollment Mgmt/Financial Aid .... Mr. Jay LALLY
09 AVP Inst Research & Effectiveness .... Ms. Jessica ICKES
20 Assistant Provost .... Dr. Munevver SUBASI
86 Federal Government Programs Manager .... Dr. Tristan FIEDLER
21 Controller .... Vacant
32 AVP Student Affs/Dean of Students .... Mr. Rodney BOWERS
39 AVP Housing and Campus Services .... Mr. Gregory CONNELL
06 Registrar .... Ms. Caroline JOHNSTON
121 Director Academic Support Services .... Mr. Rodd NEWCOMBE
41 Director Athletics .... Mr. Jamie JOSS
19 Director Campus Security .... Mr. Frank IANNONE
36 Director Career Services .... Ms. Dona E. GAYNOR
38 Dir Counseling/Psychological Svcs .... Dr. Robyn TAPLEY
88 Director Creative Services .... Ms. Christena CALLAHAN
88 Dir Environ/Regulatory Compliance .... Mr. Selvin MCLEAN
85 Director Intl Student Services .... Ms. Jackie LINGNER
104 Director Study Abroad .... Ms. Heather WAUTLET
07 Exec Dir of Admissions .... Mr. Michael PERRY
90 Executive Director Ellucian .... Ms. Rebecca ARCHER
28 Exec Dir Comp & Risk/Title IX .... Ms. Fanak BAARMAND
96 Director of Purchasing .... Vacant
89 Dir of First Year Experience .... Dr. Jessica HA BITTNER

Florida Memorial University (D)

15800 NW 42nd Avenue, Miami Gardens FL 33054-6199
County: Miami-Dade FICE Identification: 001486
Unit ID: 133979
Telephone: (305) 626-3600 Carnegie Class: Bac-Diverse
FAX Number: N/A Calendar System: Semester
URL: www.fmuniv.edu
Established: 1879 Annual Undergrad Tuition & Fees: $16,176
Enrollment: 928 Coed
Affiliation or Control: Independent Non-Profit IRS Status: 501(c)3
Highest Offering: Beyond Master's But Less Than Doctorate
Accreditation: SC, AAB, ACBSP, MUS, SW

01 President .... Dr. Jaffus HARDRICK
05 Provost & Executive VP .... Dr. Adrienne T. COOPER
32 AVP Student Aff/Dean of Students .... Dr. Kelley C. KIMPLE
20 Associate Provost .... Dr. Tameka B. HOBBS
04 Executive Assistant to President .... Ms. Amanda EDUN
49 Interim Dean of Arts and Sciences .... Dr. William E. HOPPER
10 Controller/AVP Finance & Admin. .... Mr. Rodney SOBELSON
07 Director of Admissions .... Vacant
111 Vice Pres University Advancement .... Mr. Cory WITHERSPOON
45 Assc VP Institutional Effectiveness ... Dr. William E. HOPPER, JR.
88 Chair Aviation and Safety .... Dr. Jorge GUERRA
50 Dean School of Business .... Dr. J. Preston JONES
53 Dean School of Education .... Dr. Jacqueline HILL
81 Chair Health and Natural Sciences .... Dr. Rose Mary STIFFIN
83 Interim Chair Social Sciences .... Vacant
64 Chair Visual/Perf Arts .... Vacant
77 Chair Comp Science/Math & Tech .... Dr. Ben WONGSAROJ
79 Chair Humanities .... Dr. William HOBBS, III
124 Dir Ctr Acad Resources & Support .... Dr. Rebecca DEVEREAUX
08 Interim Director Library Services .... Ms. Cheryl WILCHER
37 Dir Financial Aid & Scholarships .... Mrs. Kimberly W. JONES
06 Registrar .... Dr. Prudence LEWIS-BHOLA
09 Director of Institutional Research .... Dr. Carlos CANAS
15 Director Human Resources .... Ms. Youseline POTEAU
41 Director Intercollegiate Athletics .... Mr. Jason HORN
36 Director Career Development Ctr .... Ms. Megan D. ADERELE
39 Director Housing & Residence Life .... Ms. Myra M. MCPHEE
19 Dir Campus Safety & Emergency Mgt .... Dr. Gregory A. SALTERS
18 Dir Facility Mgmt/Plant Operations .... Mr. David JACCARINO
42 Dean of Campus Ministry .... Dr. Jeffrey D. SWAIN
29 Director Alumni Affairs .... Vacant
35 Director Student Engagement .... Ms. Sharhonda L. FORD
85 International Student Advisor .... Mr. Trevor LEWIS
13 CIO/Director of IMT .... Mr. Greg NICHOLS
07 Assistant Director of Admissions .... Vacant
105 IT Solutions Engineer .... Mr. Joslin "Joe" ATHIS
26 VP Public Relations/Marketing .... Vacant
38 Dir. Univ. Counseling/Support Serv .... Dr. Jason-Anthony K. PRENDERGAST
30 Exec Dir Advancement/Alumni Affairs .... Mrs. Shelia P. COHEN
43 Legal Counsel .... Sonya A. MILLER, ESQ
84 Asst. VP Enrollment Management .... Dr. Heather MUNNS

Florida National University Hialeah Campus (E)

4425 W. Jose Regueiro (20th) Ave,
Hialeah FL 33012-4108
County: Dade FICE Identification: 025476
Unit ID: 408844
Telephone: (305) 821-3333 Carnegie Class: Bac/Assoc-Mixed
FAX Number: (305) 362-0595 Calendar System: Semester
URL: www.fnu.edu
Established: 1982 Annual Undergrad Tuition & Fees: $13,688
Enrollment: 4,173 Coed
Affiliation or Control: Proprietary IRS Status: Proprietary
Highest Offering: Master's
Accreditation: SC, COARC, NURSE, PTAA

01 President/CEO .... Dr. Maria C. REGUEIRO
09 VP of Assessment & Research/FA Dir .... Mr. Omar SANCHEZ
11 Vice President of Operations .... Mr. Frank ANDREU
05 Vice President of Academic Affairs .... Dr. Anthony BERRIOS
12 Campus Dean .... Mrs. Yedi CEPERO
10 Controller .... Dr. Lourdes ANDREU
88 Director of Accreditation .... Dr. Kelly KRENKEL
07 University Admissions Director .... Mr. Robert LOPEZ
88 Distance Learning Admissions Dir .... Mr. Giancarlo LIGNAROLO
06 University Registrar .... Mr. Jose L. VALDES
106 Director of Distance Learning .... Dr. Emry SOMNARAIN
32 Student Services Officer .... Mr. Seilyn SANTOS
50 Business & Economics Division Head .... Dr. Ernesto GONZALEZ
76 Allied Health Division Head .... Dr. Loreto ALMONTE
79 Humanities & Liberal Arts Div Head .... Vacant
88 ESL Division Head .... Mr. Reynaldo ALES
66 Nursing Division Head .... Dr. Penelope PATTALITAN
83 Psychology Division Head .... Dr. Jose PEREZ
15 Human Resources Generalist .... Mrs. Andrea WYBRANSKI
32 Student Services Officer .... Ms. Seilyn SANTOS
41 Athletic Director .... Mr. Ryan RAPOSO
88 Military Admissions Advisor .... Mrs. Yolanda NAVARRO
31 Director Community Relations .... Vacant
36 Career Services Officer .... Mrs. Ariadne LOPEZ
88 Social Media Director .... Mrs. Lucia SERGE
26 Digital Marketing Director .... Mrs. Maria ZEGARRA
108 Director Assessment & Research .... Mr. Rodrigo LOAIZA
08 Library Director .... Mrs. Ida TOMSHINSKY
121 Academic Advisor .... Dr. Rosa HERNANDEZ
13 Systems Administrator .... Mr. Michael ANDREU
16 Human Resources Generalist .... Mrs. Isel CASALES
88 Assistant Campus Dean .... Mr. Harold FLORES
88 Assistant Campus Dean .... Dr. Juan TAPIA
85 International Student Advisor .... Mrs. Julia SANCHEZ
88 Director of Military Affairs .... Mr. Edward LEWIS
36 Career Services Director .... Mr. Angel URQUIOLA

Florida National University South Campus (F)

11865 SW 26th Street Unit H-3, Miami FL 33175
Telephone: (305) 821-3333 Identification: 666691
Accreditation: &SC, NURSE

† Regional accreditation is carried under the parent institution Florida National College, Hialeah, FL.

Florida National University Training Center (G)

4206 West 12th Avenue, Hialeah FL 33012
Telephone: (305) 821-3333 Identification: 666690
Accreditation: &SC

† Regional accreditation is carried under the parent institution Florida National College, Hialeah, FL.

Florida Southern College (H)

111 Lake Hollingsworth Drive, Lakeland FL 33801-5698
County: Polk FICE Identification: 001488
Unit ID: 134079
Telephone: (863) 680-4111 Carnegie Class: Masters/M
FAX Number: (863) 680-4112 Calendar System: Semester
URL: www.flsouthern.edu
Established: 1883 Annual Undergrad Tuition & Fees: $38,980
Enrollment: 3,413 Coed
Affiliation or Control: United Methodist IRS Status: 501(c)3
Highest Offering: Doctorate
Accreditation: SC, MT, MUS, NURSE, @PTA

01 President .... Dr. Anne B. KERR
05 Provost .... Dr. Brad HOLLINGSHEAD
111 Vice President Advancement .... Vacant
10 Vice President Finance & Admin .... Mr. Terry DENNIS
84 VP Enrollment Management .... Mr. John GRUNDIG
20 Assoc Provost Experiential Educ .... Dr. Tracey TEDDER
30 VP Development .... Ms. Heather PHARRIS
32 VP of Student Life .... Dr. Susan FREEMAN
102 Asst VP Foundation/Corp Relations .... Ms. Kathy ELLIS
15 AVP Operations/HR Director .... Ms. Katherine PAWLAK
42 Chaplain Director Campus Ministry .... Rev. Timothy S. WRIGHT
13 Chief Information Officer .... Ms. Francine NEILING
21 Controller .... Ms. Judy ROBINSON
104 Coordinator Student Travel .... Ms. Bridgette MCARTHUR
49 Dean Art and Sciences .... Dr. Sara HARDING
50 Dean Business and Free Enterprise .... Dr. Michael WEBER
53 Dean Education .... Dr. Victoria GIORDANO
66 Dean Nursing and Health Science .... Dr. Linda S. COMER
121 Dean of Student Success .... Ms. Shari SZABO
35 Asst Dean of Student Development .... Ms. Amanda BLOUNT
07 Director of Admissions .... Ms. Arden MITCHELL
123 Director of Adult & Graduate Admiss .... Ms. Kristen PINNER
44 Director Annual Giving .... Vacant
41 Director of Athletics .... Mr. Drew HOWARD
36 Executive Director Career Services .... Dr. Lauren ALBAUM
39 Director of Community Living .... Mr. Casey YODER
23 Director of Health Services .... Ms. Katherine PAWLAK
112 Director of Major Gifts .... Ms. Sara OLSON
92 Director of Honors Program .... Mr. Brian HAMILTON
09 Dir Inst Research/Effectiveness .... Ms. Jazmine EVERHEART
119 Director of IT Services .... Vacant
08 Director of the Library .... Mr. Randall M. MACDONALD
28 Director Multicultural Appreciation .... Ms. Vanessa BECKHAM

26 VP of Marketing ... Ms. Kelly SEMRAU
18 Director of Operations ... Mr. Jon CAMP
06 Registrar ... Ms. Lindsay THIBODAUX
19 Director of Security/Safety ... Mr. Eric RAUCH
38 Director of Student Counseling ... Mr. David ARANDA
37 Director of Student Financial Aid ... Mr. William L. HEALY
105 Sr Web Developer ... Mr. James JARRETT
106 Director Teaching/Learning Ctr ... Ms. Autumn GRUBB
27 Director Communication/Marketing ... Ms. Tara JOHNSON
04 Executive Asst to President ... Ms. LeeAnna CATULLO
40 Manager Bookstore ... Mr. James BAUER

Florida SouthWestern State College (A)

8099 College Parkway, SW, Fort Myers FL 33919-5566
County: Lee FICE Identification: 001477
Unit ID: 133508
Telephone: (239) 489-9300 Carnegie Class: Bac/Assoc-Mixed
FAX Number: N/A Calendar System: Semester
URL: www.fsw.edu
Established: 1961 Annual Undergrad Tuition & Fees (In-State): $3,401
Enrollment: 15,141 Coed
Affiliation or Control: State IRS Status: 501(c)3
Highest Offering: Baccalaureate
Accreditation: SC, ADNUR, CAHIIM, COARC, CVT, DH, EMT, NUR, RAD

01 President ... Dr. Jeffery ALLBRITTEN
100 Chief of Staff ... Dr. Henry PEEL
05 Provost ... Dr. Eileen DELUCA
32 Vice Provost Student Affairs ... Dr. Michele YOVANOVICH
11 VP Administrative Services ... Dr. Gina DOEBLE
26 VP Economic Dev/External Affairs ... Vacant
111 VP Inst Advancement/Found Exec Dir ... Vacant
43 General Counsel ... Mr. Joe COLEMAN
50 Dean Business & Technology ... Vacant
76 Dean Health Professions ... Vacant
53 Dean Education and Charter Schools ... Dr. April FLEMING
79 Dean Arts/Hum & Social Sci ... Dr. Deborah TEED
81 Dean Pure & Applied Sci ... Dr. Martin MCCLINTON
41 Director Intercollegiate Athletics ... Mr. George SANDERS
45 Asst VP Office of Planning ... Mr. Tobias DISCENZA
84 Asst VP Enrollment/Student Success ... Dr. Christy GILFERT
12 Campus Director ... Ms. Gail MURPHY
32 Dean of Students ... Vacant
06 Registrar ... Mrs. Brenda KNIGHT
13 Chief Information Officer ... Mr. Jason DUDLEY
08 Director Library Services ... Dr. Richard HODGES
110 Sr Director Devel & Major Gifts ... Ms. Susan DESANTIS
27 Exec Director Marketing & Media ... Mr. Greg TURCHETTA
108 AVP Inst Research/Assessment ... Dr. Joseph VAN GAALEN
12 Director Hendry/Glades Center ... Ms. Amanda LEHRIAN
113 Bursar ... Ms. Amber REDFERN
19 Director Public Safety ... Dr. Jerry CONNOLLY
109 Director Auxiliary Services ... Vacant
37 Director Student Financial Aid ... Ms. Jodi WALKER
15 Chief HR & Organizational Dev Ofc ... Ms. Susan BRONSTEIN
07 Director Admissions ... Ms. Amber MCCOWN
18 Dir Facilities Plng & Space Mgmt ... Mr. JR SHERMAN
121 Director Academic Support Programs ... Ms. Monica MOORE
39 Dir Housing & Res Life ... Mr. Justin LONG
88 Director Adaptive Services ... Ms. Angela HARTSELL
96 Director of Procurement Services ... Ms. Lisa TUDOR
88 Director Testing Services ... Vacant
22 Title IX Coord Equity Officer ... Ms. Jana SABO
10 Director Finance and Accounting ... Ms. Kathleen PORTER
88 Chief Operations Officer ... Mr. Kevin ANDERSON
30 Chief Development Officer ... Dr. Joseph KRAMP
88 Director Exhibitions & Collections ... Mr. Jade DELLINGER
88 Director Strategic Initiatives ... Ms. Whitney RHYNE
88 Director Corp Training & Services ... Mr. Adrian KERR
88 Director Simulation Education ... Mr. Tommy MANN
104 Director International Education ... Mr. Michael MESSINA

Florida State College at Jacksonville (B)

501 W State Street, Jacksonville FL 32202-4097
County: Duval FICE Identification: 001484
Unit ID: 133702
Telephone: (904) 646-2300 Carnegie Class: Bac/Assoc-Mixed
FAX Number: N/A Calendar System: Semester
URL: www.fscj.edu
Established: 1965 Annual Undergrad Tuition & Fees (In-District): $2,878
Enrollment: 22,344 Coed
Affiliation or Control: Local IRS Status: Exempt
Highest Offering: Baccalaureate
Accreditation: SC, ACBSP, ACFEI, ADNUR, CAHIIM, COARC, CVT, DA, DH, EMT, FUSER, HT, MLTAD, NUR, OTA, PTAA, SURGT

01 College President ... Dr. John AVENDANO
05 Provost/Vice President Academics ... Dr. John WALL
10 Vice Pres of Business Services ... Vacant
43 Assistant General Counsel ... Mr. Romualdo MARQUINEZ
32 Vice President Student Services ... Dr. Linda HERLOCKER
108 VP Institutional Effectiveness ... Dr. Jerrett DUMOUCHEL
18 Assoc Vice Pres Facilities ... Mr. Morris A. BELLICK, II
88 AVP Academic Operations ... Dr. Rich TURNER
88 AVP Strategic Priorities ... Dr. Deborah FONTAINE
35 AVP Student Support Services ... Ms. Pamela WALKER
49 Assoc Provost Liberal Arts/Sciences ... Dr. Ian NEUHARD
56 Executive Dir Outreach & Extension ... Dr. Heather KENNEY
20 Assoc Prov Curriculum/Instruction ... Dr. Kathleen CIEZ-VOLZ
21 AVP Finance ... Mr. Stephen STANFORD
121 AVP Student Success ... Dr. Erin RICHMAN
103 AVP Workforce Dev/Entrepreneurship ... Dr. Cedrick GIBSON
84 AVP Enrollment Management ... Ms. Jacquelyn THOMPSON
15 Chief Human Resource Officer ... Mr. Mark LACEY
13 Chief Information Tech Officer ... Mr. Ronald SMITH
28 Chief Ofcr Diversity/Equity/Inclsn ... Ms. Lisa J. MOORE
88 Exec Director Artist Series ... Dr. Milton A. RUSSOS
16 Exec Director Talent Acquisition ... Ms. Lisa MOORE
91 Executive Director Enterprise App ... Mr. Chris MARTIN
08 Executive Dean of Library Services ... Dr. Tom MESSNER
14 Exec Dir Computer Infrastructure ... Mr. Ron SMITH
88 Exec Dir Military Affs/Veteran Svcs ... Mr. James W. STEVENSON
12 Executive Director of Nassau Center ... Ms. Donna MARTIN
102 Executive Director Foundation ... Mr. Cleve WARREN
96 Executive Director Purchasing ... Ms. Randi BROKVIST
19 Director of Security ... Mr. Gordon BASS
37 Director Financial Aid ... Ms. Christine HIBBARD
41 Director of Athletics ... Ms. Ginny ALEXANDER
25 Director of Resource Development ... Ms. Jennifer PETERSON
06 Registrar ... Ms. Jacqueline SCHMIDT
09 Director Student Analytics/Research ... Mr. Gregory MICHALSKI
26 Chief Communications Officer ... Ms. Jill K. JOHNSON
04 Administration Support Mgr OCP ... Mr. Calvin LEAVELL
07 Director of Admissions ... Ms. Megan DROSS
101 Administration Support Mgr OCP ... Ms. Kimberli SODEK
92 Director Honors Program ... Ms. Maria DONAIRE-CIRSOVIUS
105 Web Communications Manager ... Mr. Michael AHMED
29 Development Officer ... Ms. Danielle THOMPSON
30 Development Officer ... Mr. Socrates RIVERS
44 Director Annual Giving ... Ms. Danielle THOMPSON
50 Dean of Career Education ... Ms. Annette BARRINEAU
53 Dean of Education & Human Svcs ... Dr. Tara HALEY
54 Dean Engr Technology & Industry ... Dr. Douglas BRAUER

Florida Technical College (C)

1199 S Woodland Boulevard, Deland FL 32720-7415
Telephone: (386) 734-3303 Identification: 666419
Accreditation: &M

Florida Technical College (D)

3831 West Vine Street, Suite 50, Kissimmee FL 34741
Telephone: (844) 402-3337 Identification: 770684
Accreditation: &M, ACFEI

Florida Technical College (E)

4715 South Florida Avenue, Suite 4,
Lakeland FL 33813-2101
Telephone: (866) 967-8822 FICE Identification: 025981
Accreditation: &M

Florida Technical College (F)

12900 Challenger Parkway, Orlando FL 32826
Telephone: (407) 447-7300 FICE Identification: 022187
Accreditation: &M

Florida Technical College (G)

12520 Pines Boulevard, Pembroke Pines FL 33027
Telephone: (844) 332-3409 Identification: 770685
Accreditation: &M

Fortis College (H)

19600 South Dixie Highway, Ste B, Cutler Bay FL 33157
Telephone: (786) 345-5300 Identification: 770565
Accreditation: ACCSC, ADNUR

† Branch campus of Fortis College, Centerville, OH.

Fortis College (I)

700 Blanding Boulevard, Suite 16, Orange Park FL 32065
County: Clay FICE Identification: 034343
Unit ID: 439792
Telephone: (904) 269-7086 Carnegie Class: Spec 2-yr-Health
FAX Number: (904) 269-6664 Calendar System: Semester
URL: www.fortis.edu
Established: 1985 Annual Undergrad Tuition & Fees: $15,060
Enrollment: 489 Coed
Affiliation or Control: Proprietary IRS Status: Proprietary
Highest Offering: Associate Degree
Accreditation: ACCSC, ADNUR, SURGT

01 Campus President ... Mr. Ben SEDRINE
05 Academic Dean ... Dr. Evelyn E. PRESLEY

Fortis Institute-Port St. Lucie (J)

9022 South US Highway 1, Port St. Lucie FL 34952
Telephone: (772) 221-9799 Identification: 770527
Accreditation: ABHES, ADNUR

† Branch campus of Fortis Institute, Baton Rouge, LA.

Full Sail University (K)

3300 University Boulevard, Winter Park FL 32792
County: Orange FICE Identification: 023621
Unit ID: 134237
Telephone: (407) 679-0100 Carnegie Class: Masters/L
FAX Number: (407) 679-9685 Calendar System: Other
URL: www.fullsail.edu
Established: 1979 Annual Undergrad Tuition & Fees: $25,820
Enrollment: 24,627 Coed
Affiliation or Control: Proprietary IRS Status: Proprietary
Highest Offering: Master's
Accreditation: ACCSC, CEA

01 President ... Mr. Garry JONES
07 Sr Vice President of Admissions ... Mr. Matt PENGRA

Future-Tech Institute (L)

3446 8th St, Ste 213, Miami FL 33135
County: Miami-Dade FICE Identification: 041164
Unit ID: 459310
Telephone: (305) 774-0227 Carnegie Class: Not Classified
FAX Number: (305) 445-2217 Calendar System: Semester
URL: www.futuretechinstitute.com
Established: 2000 Annual Undergrad Tuition & Fees: $17,863
Enrollment: 105 Coed
Affiliation or Control: Proprietary IRS Status: Proprietary
Highest Offering: Associate Degree
Accreditation: ACCSC

01 School Director ... Ana MONCADA
10 Financial Director ... Miriam HODGES
07 Admissions Director ... David NEWCOMB
15 Human Resources Director ... Ivania MONCADA

Galen College of Nursing (M)

10200 Dr Martin Luther King Jr St N,
St. Petersburg FL 33716
Telephone: (727) 577-1497 Identification: 770539
Accreditation: &SC, ADNUR, NURSE

† Branch campus of Galen College of Nursing, Louisville, KY

Gulf Coast State College (N)

5230 W Highway 98, Panama City FL 32401-1058
County: Bay FICE Identification: 001490
Unit ID: 134343
Telephone: (850) 769-1551 Carnegie Class: Bac/Assoc-Assoc Dom
FAX Number: (850) 913-3319 Calendar System: Semester
URL: www.gulfcoast.edu
Established: 1957 Annual Undergrad Tuition & Fees (In-State): $2,370
Enrollment: 4,410 Coed
Affiliation or Control: State Related IRS Status: 501(c)3
Highest Offering: Baccalaureate
Accreditation: SC, ACFEI, ADNUR, COARC, DA, DH, EMT, NURSE, PTAA, RAD, SURGA, SURGT

01 President ... Dr. John R. HOLDNAK
10 Vice Pres Administration & Finance ... Mr. John D. MERCER
05 VP Academic Affairs ... Dr. Holly KUEHNER
32 VP Inst Effect & Student Affairs ... Dr. Cheryl L. FLAX-HYMAN
45 VP Economic Dev & Strategic Init ... Mr. Glen MCDONALD
13 Chief Information Officer ... Mr. Greg ELLER
08 Exec Director E-Learning & Library ... Ms. Lori DRISCOLL
84 Dean of Enrollment Services ... Ms. Sharon O. TODD
15 Exec Director of Human Resources ... Mr. Lee WOOD
26 Exec Director Community Engagement ... Ms. Katie MCCURDY
103 Dean Workforce Education ... Mr. Al MCCAMBRY
96 Exec Dir Procurement & Auxil Svcs ... Ms. Tonia LAWSON
37 Exec Director Student Financial Svc ... Mr. Christopher J. WESTLAKE
09 Institutional Research Analyst ... Ms. Amber COKER
04 Executive Asst to President ... Ms. Dottie TERRYN
19 Director Security/Safety ... Mr. Damian SOUTH
41 Athletic Director ... Mr. Mike KANDLER
06 Registrar ... Ms. Merissa HUDSON
21 Dean Business Affairs ... Ms. Leslie HAPNER
35 Dean Student Life ... Dr. Kelli WALSINGHAM
121 Dean Student Engagement ... Mr. J. Loyd HARRIS

HCI College (O)

1764 North Congress Avenue,
West Palm Beach FL 33409
County: Palm Beach Identification: 667104
Unit ID: 490054
Telephone: (561) 586-0121 Carnegie Class: Spec 2-yr-Health
FAX Number: (561) 471-4010 Calendar System: Semester
URL: www.hci.edu
Established: 1993 Annual Undergrad Tuition & Fees: $17,670
Enrollment: 709 Coed
Affiliation or Control: Proprietary IRS Status: Proprietary
Highest Offering: Associate Degree
Accreditation: ACCSC

01 President/CEO ... Pedro DE GUZMAN
10 Vice President Finance ... Ryan MILLER
05 VP Academic/Regulatory Affairs ... Dr. Arlette PETERSSON

11 Vice President Administration ... Caren STEWART
12 Campus President WPB ... David SHELPMAN, JR.

Herzing University (A)

1865 SR 436, Winter Park FL 32792
Telephone: (407) 641-5227 Identification: 666422
Accreditation: &HLC, ADNUR, NURSE, PTAA

† Regional accreditation is carried under the parent institution in Madison, WI.

Hillsborough Community College (B)

39 Columbia Drive, Tampa FL 33606
County: Hillsborough FICE Identification: 007870
Unit ID: 134495
Telephone: (813) 253-7000 Carnegie Class: Assoc/HT-High Trad
FAX Number: N/A Calendar System: Semester
URL: www.hccfl.edu
Established: 1968 Annual Undergrad Tuition & Fees (In-State): $2,506
Enrollment: 19,532 Coed
Affiliation or Control: State IRS Status: 501(c)3
Highest Offering: Associate Degree
Accreditation: SC, ACFEI, ADNUR, COARC, CSHSE, DA, DH, DIETT, DMS, EMT, MT, MUS, NMT, OPD, RAD, RTT

01 President ... Dr. Ken ATWATER
10 VP Administration/CFO ... Mr. Al ERDMAN
05 VP for Academic Affairs ... Mr. Richard SENKER
13 VP IT/Chief Information Officer ... Mr. Daya PENDHARKAR
32 VP Student Services/Enrollment Mgt ... Dr. Ken RAY
12 Campus President Dale Mabry ... Dr. Paige NIEHAUS
12 Campus President Ybor City Campus ... Dr. Ginger CLARK
12 Campus President Plant City Campus ... Dr. Martyn CLAY
12 Campus President Brandon ... Dr. Deb KISH-JOHANSEN
12 Campus President South Shore Campus ... Dr. Jennifer CHINA
28 CDO for Equity & Diversity ... Vacant
26 Exec Dir Marketing/Public Relations ... Ms. Ashley CARL
45 VP Strategic Planning & Analysis ... Dr. Paul NAGY
102 Exec Director HCC Foundation ... Mr. Stephen SHEAR
43 College Attorney ... Ms. Martha Kaye KOEHLER
15 Exec Dir Human Resources ... Ms. Kristin SMUDER
21 Controller ... Ms. Kimberly MCMILLON
75 Associate VP AS Programs ... Dr. Brian MANN
88 Director Assoc in Arts Programs ... Dr. Karen GRIFFIN
90 Dir of Instructional Technology ... Dr. Mark LEWIS
20 Dean of Academic Affairs ... Dr. Keith BERRY
20 Dean of Acad Affairs - Plant City ... Dr. Anthony BORRELL
20 Dean of Academic Affairs - Brandon ... Dr. Patricia RAND
49 Dean of AS Programs - Brandon ... Dr. Randall ROCKEFELLER
35 Associate Dean Arts/Human/Comm DM ... Ms. Aimee BUSQUET
49 Dean of AS Programs - Dale Mabry ... Dr. Barry HUBBARD
81 Dean AA Math/Science Dale Mabry ... Dr. Dustin LEMKE
76 Dean of Health Sciences ... Dr. Leif PENROSE
37 Financial Aid Director ... Ms. Tierra SMITH
06 Registrar ... Ms. Nevaler DAVIS
18 Director Facilities/Physical Plant ... Mr. Ben MARSHALL
96 Director of Purchasing ... Ms. Vonda MELCHIOR
19 Director Security/Safety ... Mr. John "Sam" COX
04 ESA to the President ... Ms. Suzy HOLLEY
29 Director Alumni Affairs ... Vacant
30 Director of Development ... Ms. Lee LOWRY
101 Secretary of the Institution/Board ... Ms. Christina HESKETT
103 Associate VP PSAV Programs ... Mr. John MEEKS
104 Director Study Abroad ... Dr. Michael BRENNAN
108 Director of Information Management ... Ms. Nicole JAGUSZTYN
39 Dir Resident Life/Student Housing ... Mr. Joseph BENTROVATO
41 Athletic Director ... Ms. Sarah SUMMERFIELD
09 Director of Institutional Research ... Dr. Aiisa ZUJOVICH
86 Director Government Relations ... Mr. Eric JOHNSON
121 Dean Student Services Brandon ... Dr. Julie WHITE
121 Dean Student Services Plant City ... Ms. Christine LEGNER
20 Dean Academic Affairs South Shore ... Ms. Nadia KOTULA
120 Dir Online Education/E-learning ... Ms. Laurie SAYLOR

Hobe Sound Bible College (C)

PO Box 1065, Hobe Sound FL 33475
County: Martin FICE Identification: 021889
Unit ID: 134510
Telephone: (772) 546-5534 Carnegie Class: Spec-4-yr-Faith
FAX Number: (772) 545-1422 Calendar System: Semester
URL: www.hsbc.edu
Established: 1960 Annual Undergrad Tuition & Fees: $7,048
Enrollment: 159 Coed
Affiliation or Control: Independent Non-Profit IRS Status: 501(c)3
Highest Offering: Master's
Accreditation: BI

01 President ... Dr. Daniel STETLER
05 Academic Dean ... Dr. Clifford W. CHURCHILL
10 Director of Finance ... Mr. Aaron HAMILTON
11 Director of Administrative Services ... Mr. Wesley HOLDEN
32 Director of Student Life ... Mr. John S. JONES
08 Librarian ... Mr. Phil JONES
106 Dean of HOBE Online ... Dr. Brent JONES
06 Registrar ... Mr. Tim COLE
07 Admissions Director ... Ms. Elizabeth MCMILLAN
111 Dir Institutional Advancement/PR ... Mr. Paul STETLER
37 Director of Financial Aid ... Ms. Molly SPRUILL

Hodges University (D)

2647 Professional Circle, Naples FL 34119
County: Collier FICE Identification: 030375
Unit ID: 367884
Telephone: (239) 513-1122 Carnegie Class: Masters/S
FAX Number: (239) 598-6251 Calendar System: Trimester
URL: www.hodges.edu
Established: 1990 Annual Undergrad Tuition & Fees: $14,660
Enrollment: 700 Coed
Affiliation or Control: Independent Non-Profit IRS Status: 501(c)3
Highest Offering: Master's
Accreditation: SC, CACREP, IACBE, NUR, PTAA

01 President ... Dr. John D. MEYER
10 Exec Vice Pres Admin Operations/CFO ... Ms. Erica VOGT
05 Sr Vice Pres Academic Affairs ... Vacant
26 Asst VP Marketing/Public Info Ofcr ... Ms. Teresa M. ARAQUE
32 Asst Vice Pres Student Experience ... Mr. Joshua CARCOPA
84 Asst Vice Pres Enrollment Mgmt ... Vacant
37 Director of Financial Aid ... Ms. Sheri MORAN
28 Chief Diversity Officer ... Ms. Gail B. WILLIAMS
50 Dean Johnson School of Business ... Dr. Todd KATZ
107 Dean Nichols School of Prof Studies ... Dr. Mary NUOSCE
97 Dean School of Liberal Studies ... Dr. Elsa P. ROGERS
72 Assoc Dean Fisher School of Tech ... Ms. Tracey M. LANHAM
76 Dir School of Health Sciences ... Dr. Diana C. SCHULTZ
108 Dir Institutional Effectiveness ... Mr. Christopher PARFITT
08 Director of the Library ... Vacant
13 Director of Information Technology ... Vacant
15 Director of Human Resources ... Ms. Gloria WRENN
18 Dir Facilities Mgmt/Campus Security ... Mr. Skip L. CAMP
07 Director or Admissions ... Ms. Carol AMES
04 Executive Asst to President ... Ms. Victoria WALKER

Hope College of Arts & Sciences (E)

1200 SW 3rd Street, Pompano Beach FL 33069
County: Broward FICE Identification: 042517
Unit ID: 488332
Telephone: (954) 532-9614 Carnegie Class: Spec-4-yr-Other Health
FAX Number: N/A Calendar System: Other
URL: www.hcas.edu
Established: 2011 Annual Undergrad Tuition & Fees: N/A
Enrollment: 122 Coed
Affiliation or Control: Proprietary IRS Status: Proprietary
Highest Offering: Baccalaureate
Accreditation: ACICS

05 Dean of Nursing ... Ms. Andre DERBY
13 Distance Learning/IT Director ... Mr. Felipe LOPEZ
37 Director of Financial Aid ... Ms. Carmen TIRADO
07 Director of Admissions ... Vacant
06 Registrar ... Mr. Joseph GARVER

Indian River State College (F)

3209 Virginia Avenue, Fort Pierce FL 34981-5596
County: Saint Lucie FICE Identification: 001493
Unit ID: 134608
Telephone: (772) 462-4772 Carnegie Class: Bac/Assoc-Mixed
FAX Number: (772) 462-4796 Calendar System: Semester
URL: www.irsc.edu
Established: 1960 Annual Undergrad Tuition & Fees (In-District): $2,764
Enrollment: 15,236 Coed
Affiliation or Control: Local IRS Status: 501(c)3
Highest Offering: Baccalaureate
Accreditation: SC, ADNUR, CAHIIM, COARC, DA, DH, EMT, MAC, MLTAD, NUR, PTAA, RAD, SURGT

01 President ... Dr. Timothy MOORE
84 Vice President Student Success ... Ms. Elizabeth GASKIN
03 Exec VP Strategic Initiatives ... Mr. Michael HAGELOH
45 VP Institutional Effectiveness ... Dr. Angela BROWNING
05 Vice President Academic Affairs ... Dr. Heather BELMONT
10 Vice President Financial Services ... Dr. Marvin PYLES
32 Vice President Student Affairs ... Mr. Frank WATKINS
13 Vice President Institutional Tech ... Dr. Timothy MARSHALL
17 Dean Health Science ... Dr. Ann HUBBARD
12 Dean Northwest Center ... Ms. Adriene JEFFERSON
08 Interim Admin Dir Library Services ... Ms. Mia TIGNOR
75 Interim Dean Industrial Education ... Mr. William SOLOMON
12 Provost Pt St Lucie/St Lucie W ... Vacant
12 Campus President Okeechobee County ... Mr. Russ BROWN
12 Campus President Martin County ... Dr. Alessandro ANZALONE
12 Campus Pres Indian River County ... Mr. Casey LUNCEFORD
102 Executive Director Foundation ... Ms. Ann DECKER
83 Dean Liberal Arts & Social Science ... Dr. Scott STEIN
66 Dean Nursing ... Dr. Patricia GAGLIANO
80 Dean Public Service Education ... Mr. Raimundo SOCORRO
50 Dean Business ... Dr. Prashanth PILLY
72 Dean Advanced Technology ... Mr. Kevin COOPER
53 Dean School of Education ... Dr. Kelly AMATUCCI
15 Vice President Human Resources ... Ms. Melissa PROCHASKA
18 Dean Facilities & Sustainability ... Mr. Sean DONAHUE
81 Dean Science ... Dr. Anthony DRIBBEN
21 Dean Finance ... Ms. Edith PACACHA
14 Dean Enterprise Systems ... Dr. Meredith COUGHLIN
41 Director Athletics ... Mr. Scott KIMMELMAN
106 Vice President Global ... Ms. Kendall ST. HILAIRE
88 Title IX Coordinator ... Mrs. Adriene JEFFERSON
100 Chief of Staff ... Mr. Andrew TREADWELL
26 Director Mktg/Media/Brand Strategy ... Ms. Suzanne SELDES
121 Admin Dir Advising Services ... Ms. Dale HAYES
36 Director Career & Transfer Services ... Dr. Calvin WILLIAMS
37 Director Financial Aid ... Ms. Mary LEWIS
35 Director Student Development ... Ms. Rochelle POPP-FINCH
22 Equity Officer ... Ms. Adriene JEFFERSON
96 Purchasing Agent ... Mr. Don WINDHAM
19 Director Safety/Security ... Mr. Alan MONTGOMERY
07 Admin Dir Recruitment & Admissions ... Ms. Emily MASS
102 Exec Director IRSC Foundation ... Ms. Ann DECKER

International College of Health Sciences (G)

2300 S. Congress Avenue #105, Boynton Beach FL 33426
County: Palm Beach Identification: 667238
Telephone: (561) 202-6333 Carnegie Class: Not Classified
FAX Number: (561) 296-9647 Calendar System: Semester
URL: https://www.ichs.edu/
Established: Annual Undergrad Tuition & Fees: N/A
Enrollment: N/A Coed
Affiliation or Control: Proprietary IRS Status: Proprietary
Highest Offering: Master's
Accreditation: ACCSC, ADNUR, CVT, NUR

01 Campus President ... Karyn J. VIDAL
05 Director of Education ... Vacant

Jacksonville University (H)

2800 University Boulevard N, Jacksonville FL 32211-3394
County: Duval FICE Identification: 001495
Unit ID: 134945
Telephone: (904) 256-8000 Carnegie Class: Masters/L
FAX Number: N/A Calendar System: Semester
URL: www.ju.edu
Established: 1934 Annual Undergrad Tuition & Fees: $39,900
Enrollment: 4,053 Coed
Affiliation or Control: Independent Non-Profit IRS Status: 501(c)3
Highest Offering: Doctorate
Accreditation: SC, AAB, CACREP, DANCE, DENT, MUS, NURSE, OT, SP

00 Chairman Board of Trustees ... Mr. Jamie SHELTON
01 President ... Mr. Timothy P. COST
05 Provost/SVPAA ... Dr. Christine SAPIENZA
10 SVP/CFO ... Mr. Randal FREEBOURN
32 SVP/Dean of Students ... Dr. Kristie GOVER
43 SVP/Chief Compliance/Legal/HR ... Ms. Allana FORTE
111 SVP Strategic Operations ... Mr. Scott BACON
41 SVP Athletic Director ... Mr. Alexander RICKER-GILBERT
86 SVP EDEE ... Ms. Margaret DEES
21 Assoc VP for Financial Management ... Mr. Matthew SWANSON
09 Exec Dir Institutional AESP ... Dr. William MILLER
06 Asst Vice President/Registrar ... Mr. Robert BERWICK
124 Assoc VP Student Experience ... Mr. Thomas TAGGART
20 Vice Provost ... Dr. Sherri JACKSON
13 Director/CIO ... Mr. Dominic VENETO
76 Dean BRCHS ... Dr. Mark TILLMAN
50 Dean College of Business ... Dr. Barbara RITTER
57 Dean of Fine Arts ... Dr. Timothy SNYDER
49 Dean College of Arts & Sciences ... Dr. Matthew CORRIGAN
19 Director of Campus Security ... Mr. Kevin BENNETT
38 Director Counseling Center ... Dr. Kristin ALBERTS
39 Director of Residential Life ... Ms. Jenny BOYER
22 Director of Equity & Inclusion ... Ms. Patrice ABNER
35 Associate Dean of Students ... Ms. DaVina HAMILTON
35 Assistant Dean of Students ... Ms. Jamie BURKET
46 Dir Research & Sponsored Pgms ... Ms. Renee ROSSI
08 Director of the Library ... Ms. Casanna JACKSON
25 Grant & Contract Administrator ... Mr. Stuart MEYER
113 Bursar ... Ms. Marcia GIBAJA
37 Director of Financial Aid ... Mr. Charles MOORE
109 Exec Director of Campus Services ... Mr. Michael BOBBIN
18 Sr Director of Facilities Services ... Mr. Brendan MCCARTHY
110 Assoc Vice President of Development ... Ms. Leslie REDD
29 Sr Dir of Engage/Annual Philanth ... Ms. Lauren GRIFFITH
102 Dir Corporate/Foundation Relations ... Ms. Annie TUTT
112 Director Major Gifts ... Mr. Chipper HOFFMAN
26 Chief Public Relations Officer ... Ms. Laura PHELPS
105 Director Web Svc & Mkt Data ... Ms. Amanda BILLY
04 Exec Assistant to the President ... Ms. Debra HODGINS
42 Campus Minister ... Mr. Lance BEAUCHAMP

Johnson University Florida (I)

1011 Bill Beck Boulevard, Kissimmee FL 34744-5301
Telephone: (407) 847-8966 FICE Identification: 021567
Accreditation: &SC, &BI

† Branch campus of Johnson University, Knoxville, TN

Jose Maria Vargas University (J)

10131 Pines Boulevard, Pembroke Pines FL 33026
County: Broward FICE Identification: 041620
Unit ID: 461281
Telephone: (954) 322-4460 Carnegie Class: Spec-4-yr-Other
FAX Number: (954) 322-4131 Calendar System: Semester
URL: www.jmvu.edu
Established: 2003 Annual Undergrad Tuition & Fees: $10,480
Enrollment: 111 Coed
Affiliation or Control: Proprietary IRS Status: Proprietary
Highest Offering: Master's

Accreditation: ACICS

01 President .... Dr. Alicia F. PARRA
05 Vice President Academic Affairs .... Ms. Lelis ORTIZ PARRA

Keiser University **(A)**
1800 Business Park Blvd, Daytona Beach FL 32114
Telephone: (386) 274-5060 Identification: 770900
Accreditation: &SC, ACBSP, DMS, MAC, OTA, RAD

Keiser University (B)
1900 West Commercial Blvd, Fort Lauderdale FL 33309
County: Broward FICE Identification: 021519
Unit ID: 135081
Telephone: (954) 776-4476 Carnegie Class: DU-Mod
FAX Number: N/A Calendar System: Semester
URL: www.keiseruniversity.edu
Established: 1977 Annual Undergrad Tuition & Fees: $21,008
Enrollment: 20,330 Coed
Affiliation or Control: Independent Non-Profit IRS Status: 501(c)3
Highest Offering: Doctorate
Accreditation: SC, ACBSP, ADNUR, #ARCPA, CAHIIM, COARC, DIETI, DMS, MLTAD, NURSE, OT, OTA, PTAA, RAD

01 Chancellor/CEO .... Dr. Arthur KEISER
11 Executive Vice Chancellor/COO .... Mr. Peter CROCITTO
05 Vice Chancellor of Academic Affairs .... Dr. John SITES
31 Vice Chancellor of Community Rels .... Mrs. Belinda KEISER
84 Vice Chancellor of Enrollment Mgmt .... Ms. Teri DEL VECCHIO
10 Sr Vice Chancellor of Finance .... Mr. Joseph BERARDINELLI
85 Vice Chancellor International Affs .... Mr. Xun LI
26 Coord Multimedia/Public Relations .... Ms. Marianly HERNANDEZ PRIMMER
06 Registrar .... Ms. Jazmine FERNANDEZ
09 Asst Vice Chanc Institutional Rsrch .... Dr. Syeda QADRI
29 Director Alumni Relations .... Ms. Kerri PERCY
32 AVP Student Affairs/Student Life .... Ms. Jacqueline BONERI

Keiser University **(C)**
9100 Forum Corporate Pkwy, Fort Myers FL 33905
Telephone: (239) 277-1336 Identification: 770901
Accreditation: &SC, ACBSP, DMS, OTA, @PTAA, RAD

Keiser University-Jacksonville Campus **(D)**
6430 Southpoint Pkwy, Jacksonville FL 33216
Telephone: (904) 296-3440 Identification: 770902
Accreditation: &SC, ACBSP, ADNUR, OTA, PTAA, RAD

Keiser University **(E)**
2400 Interstate Drive, Lakeland FL 33805
Telephone: (863) 682-6020 Identification: 770903
Accreditation: &SC, ACBSP, ADNUR, DIETC, NMT, #PTAA, RAD

Keiser University **(F)**
900 South Babcock Street, Melbourne FL 32901
Telephone: (321) 409-4800 Identification: 770904
Accreditation: &SC, ACBSP, ACFEI, ADNUR, DIETC, DMS, OTA, #PTAA, RAD

Keiser University **(G)**
2101 NW 117th Avenue, Miami FL 33172
Telephone: (305) 596-2226 Identification: 770905
Accreditation: &SC, ACBSP, ADNUR, OTA, PTAA, RAD

Keiser University **(H)**
3909 Tamiami Trail East, Naples FL 34112
Telephone: (239) 513-1135 FICE Identification: 039393
Accreditation: &SC, ANEST

Keiser University **(I)**
6014 US Hwy 19 North, Ste 250,
New Port Richey FL 34652
Telephone: (727) 484-3110 Identification: 770854
Accreditation: &SC, DMS

Keiser University **(J)**
5600 Lake Underhill Road, Orlando FL 32807
Telephone: (407) 273-5800 Identification: 770906
Accreditation: &SC, ACBSP, ADNUR, HT, MLTAD, OTA

Keiser University **(K)**
1640 SW 145th Avenue, Pembroke Pines FL 33027
Telephone: (954) 431-4300 Identification: 770907
Accreditation: &SC, ACBSP, DIETC, OTA

Keiser University **(L)**
9400 Discovery Way, Port Saint Lucie FL 34987
Telephone: (772) 398-9990 Identification: 666289
Accreditation: &SC, ACBSP, ADNUR, DIETC

† Regional accreditation is carried under the parent institution Keiser University, Fort Lauderdale, FL.

Keiser University **(M)**
6151 Lake Osprey Drive, Sarasota FL 34240
Telephone: (941) 907-3900 Identification: 770908
Accreditation: &SC, ACBSP, ACFEI, ADNUR, #PTAA, RAD

Keiser University **(N)**
1700 Halstead Blvd, Bldg 2, Tallahassee FL 32309
Telephone: (850) 906-9494 Identification: 770909
Accreditation: &SC, ACBSP, ACFEI, ADNUR, OTA

Keiser University **(O)**
5002 West Waters Avenue, Tampa FL 33634
Telephone: (813) 885-4900 Identification: 770910
Accreditation: &SC, ACBSP, ADNUR, OTA

Keiser University **(P)**
2085 Vista Parkway, West Palm Beach FL 33411-2719
Telephone: (561) 471-6000 Identification: 667032
Accreditation: &SC, ACBSP, ADNUR, CHIRO, OTA, PTAA, RAD

† Regional accreditation is carried under the parent institution Keiser University, Fort Lauderdale, FL.

Keiser University at Clearwater **(Q)**
16120 US Hwy 19 N, Clearwater FL 33764
Telephone: (727) 576-6500 Identification: 666758
Accreditation: &SC, ADNUR, SURGT

Key College (R)
1040 Bayview Drive, Suite 200, Fort Lauderdale FL 33304
County: Broward FICE Identification: 023251
Unit ID: 134422
Telephone: (754) 312-2898 Carnegie Class: Spec-4-yr-Law
FAX Number: (954) 900-3446 Calendar System: Quarter
URL: www.keycollege.edu
Established: 1982 Annual Undergrad Tuition & Fees: $11,085
Enrollment: 29 Coed
Affiliation or Control: Proprietary IRS Status: Proprietary
Highest Offering: Associate Degree
Accreditation: ACCSC

01 President .... Mr. Ronald H. DOOLEY
05 EVP/Director of Academic Affairs .... Ms. Marella DOOLEY
07 Director of Admissions .... Mr. Ron DOOLEY
37 Director of Financial Services .... Ms. Linda GOLAN
06 Registrar .... Mr. Guy ETIENNE
08 Librarian .... Ms. Barbara HIJEK
20 Academic Coordinator .... Vacant
106 Information Technology Technician .... Mr. Mark ROSE

Knox Theological Seminary (S)
5555 N Federal Highway, Fort Lauderdale FL 33308-3209
County: Broward FICE Identification: 039923
Unit ID: 484288
Telephone: (954) 771-0376 Carnegie Class: Spec-4-yr-Faith
FAX Number: (954) 351-3343 Calendar System: Semester
URL: www.knoxseminary.edu
Established: 1989 Annual Undergrad Tuition & Fees: N/A
Enrollment: N/A Coed
Affiliation or Control: Independent Non-Profit IRS Status: 501(c)3
Highest Offering: Doctorate
Accreditation: THEOL

01 President & CEO .... Dr. Scott MANOR
05 Provost .... Dr. Timothy SANSBURY
32 Dean of Students .... Mr. Josh BRUCE
106 Director of Distance Education .... Dr. Tim FOX
30 Director of Development .... Ms. Janet COPLAND
06 Registrar .... Ms. Lori GOTTSHALL
10 Director of Finance .... Ms. Janet CUNNINGHAM
04 Administrative Asst to President .... Ms. Stephanie ZAMORA
07 Senior Admissions Advisor .... Mr. Derek FREDERICKSON
13 Director Information Technology .... Mr. Chris ZAMORA
15 Director of Human Resources .... Ms. Markita DUNCOMBE

Lake Erie College of Osteopathic Medicine Bradenton **(T)**
5000 Lakewood Ranch Boulevard, Bradenton FL 34211
Telephone: (941) 756-0690 Identification: 770160
Accreditation: &M, DENT, &OSTEO, PHAR

† Branch campus of Lake Erie College of Osteopathic Medicine, Erie, PA

Lake-Sumter State College (U)
9501 US Highway 441, Leesburg FL 34788-8751
County: Lake FICE Identification: 001502
Unit ID: 135188
Telephone: (352) 787-3747 Carnegie Class: Bac/Assoc-Assoc Dom
FAX Number: (352) 365-3548 Calendar System: Semester
URL: www.lssc.edu
Established: 1962 Annual Undergrad Tuition & Fees (In-District): $3,292
Enrollment: 4,760 Coed
Affiliation or Control: State/Local IRS Status: 501(c)3
Highest Offering: Baccalaureate
Accreditation: SC, ADNUR, NUR

01 President .... Dr. Stanley SIDOR
10 Prov & Exec VP Admin/Business Svcs .... Dr. Heather BIGARD
05 Senior VP Academic Affairs .... Dr. Michael VITALE
21 Assoc VP Fin Svcs & Controller .... Ms. Melinda BARBER
12 Assoc VP South Lake Expansion .... Mr. Thom KIEFT
15 Dir Human Resources Operations .... Ms. Beisy HERNANDEZ
13 Chief Information Officer .... Mr. Nicholas KEMP
111 Sr VP Inst Advancement/Foundation .... Dr. Laura BYRD
18 Director Facilities .... Vacant
08 Dean of Library & Learning Center .... Ms. Katie SACCO
35 Dean of Students .... Ms. Carolyn SCOTT
97 Dean of General Studies .... Ms. Karen HOGANS
66 Dean of Nursing .... Vacant
26 Exec Dir Strategic Communication .... Mr. Kevin YURASEK
37 Director Financial Aid .... Ms. Arminta JOHNSON
06 Registrar .... Ms. Caitlin MOORE
41 Exec Director Athletics .... Mr. Michael K. MATULIA
106 Exec Dir Strategic Inn/Dig Educ .... Mr. Mike NATHANSON
84 Exec Director Enrollment Mgmt .... Vacant
96 Purchasing and Accounts Payable Mgr .... Ms. Tammy SPENCER
04 Executive Asst to the President .... Ms. Claudia MORRIS
103 Dean Workforce Development .... Dr. Amy ALBEE

Larkin University (V)
18301 North Miami Avenue, Suite 1, Miami FL 33169
County: Miami-Dade Identification: 667288
Telephone: (305) 760-7500 Carnegie Class: Not Classified
FAX Number: N/A Calendar System: Semester
URL: ularkin.org
Established: Annual Graduate Tuition & Fees: N/A
Enrollment: N/A Coed
Affiliation or Control: Independent Non-Profit IRS Status: 501(c)3
Highest Offering: Doctorate; No Undergraduates
Accreditation: @PHAR

01 Chief Executive Officer/President .... Dr. Rudi H. ETTRICH
05 Director of Clinical Programs .... Dr. Alexis ARANGO
67 Vice President/Dean of Pharmacy .... Dr. Gary M. LEVIN
81 Vice Pres/Dean Biomedical Sci .... Dr. Marti ECHOLS
10 Vice Pres of Finance/CFO .... Alan FESSENDEN
13 Director of Technology .... Dr. Jorge E. MACHADO
08 Director of the Library .... Dr. Sharon ARGOV
15 Director of Human Resources .... Ms. Frida MUSILA

Lynn University (W)
3601 N Military Trail, Boca Raton FL 33431-5598
County: Palm Beach FICE Identification: 001505
Unit ID: 132657
Telephone: (561) 237-7000 Carnegie Class: Masters/L
FAX Number: (561) 237-7100 Calendar System: Semester
URL: www.lynn.edu
Established: 1962 Annual Undergrad Tuition & Fees: $39,350
Enrollment: 3,232 Coed
Affiliation or Control: Independent Non-Profit IRS Status: 501(c)3
Highest Offering: Doctorate
Accreditation: SC, CACREP, IACBE, MUS

01 President .... Dr. Kevin M. ROSS
00 President Emeritus .... Dr. Donald E. ROSS
11 Sr Vice President Administration .... Mr. Gregory J. MALFITANO
05 Vice President Academic Affairs .... Dr. Katrina CARTER-TELLISON
84 Vice Pres Enrollment Management .... Dr. Gareth FOWLES
32 Vice President for Student Life .... Dr. Anthony ALTIERI
30 Vice Pres Development/Alumni Affs .... Mr. Gregory J. MALFITANO
13 Chief Strategy & Technology Officer .... Mr. Chris G. BONIFORTI
10 Chief Financial Officer/Treasurer .... Mr. Thomas ROONEY
26 Chief Marketing Officer .... Mrs. Sherrie WELDON
35 Dean of Students .... Mr. Gary MARTIN
43 General Counsel .... Mr. Michael ANTONELLO
20 Academic Dean .... Mr. Mike PETROSKI
113 Exec Dir Stdnt Administrative Svcs .... Ms. Evelyn C. NELSON
39 Director Housing & Residence Life .... Ms. Meagan ELSBERRY
36 Executive Director Career Develop .... Ms. Barbara CAMBIA
41 Director of Athletics .... Mr. Devin CROSBY
109 Director Auxiliary Services .... Mr. Matthew P. CHALOUX
23 Director Health Center .... Ms. Rita ALBERT
27 Director of Marketing and Comm .... Ms. Stephanie BROWN
07 Dir Undergraduate Admissions .... Mr. Stefano PAPALEO
37 Dir of Financial Aid .... Mr. John CHAMBERS
38 Director of the Counseling Center .... Ms. Nicole R. OVEDIA
96 Director of Purchasing .... Ms. Maria BIMONTE
06 Registrar .... Ms. Jenifer SCHOLL
21 Director of Accounting .... Mr. Michael C. BOLDUC
123 Dir Graduate & Online Admission .... Mr. Steven PRUITT
09 Director of Institutional Research .... Mrs. Lara MARTIN
15 Director of Employee Services .... Mr. Aaron GREENBERG
40 Campus Store Manager .... Ms. Monaco CASTRO
50 Dean College Business & Management .... Mr. RT GOOD
49 Dean College of Arts & Sciences .... Dr. Gary VILLA
88 Dean College of Aeronautics .... Dr. Jeffrey C. JOHNSON
53 Dean Ross College of Education .... Dr. Kathleen WEIGEL
60 Dean College Comm and Design .... Dr. David L. JAFFE
64 Dean Conservatory of Music .... Dr. Jon H. ROBERTSON
88 Exe Dir Inst Achievement Learning .... Mr. Shaun EXSTEEN
08 Director of the Library .... Ms. Amy FILIATREAU
104 Director of International Programs .... Mrs. Erin GARCIA
19 Campus Safety Chief .... Mr. John MCAVOY
44 Director Annual Programs .... Ms. Lisa MILLER

Marconi International University (A)

141 NE 3rd Ave., 7th Floor, Miami FL 33132
County: Miami-Dade Identification: 667377
Telephone: (305) 266-7678 Carnegie Class: Not Classified
FAX Number: (786) 866-2106 Calendar System: Semester
URL: www.miuniversity.edu
Established: 2018 Annual Undergrad Tuition & Fees: N/A
Enrollment: N/A Coed
Affiliation or Control: Proprietary IRS Status: Proprietary
Highest Offering: Master's
Accreditation: **ACICS**

01 President .... Pablo CARDONA
03 Executive Vice President .... Rafael GARCIA
07 Director of Admissions .... Vacant
37 Director Student Financial Aid .... Elba CASTANOS
06 Registrar .... Heydi DAVILA
38 Director Student Counseling .... Alfredo VILLALOBOS

Med-Life Institute-Naples (B)

4995 Tamiami Trail E, Naples FL 34113
County: Collier Identification: 667220
Unit ID: 487834
Telephone: (239) 732-1300 Carnegie Class: Spec 2-yr-Health
FAX Number: (239) 417-5110 Calendar System: Semester
URL: www.medlifeinstitute.com
Established: 2003 Annual Undergrad Tuition & Fees: N/A
Enrollment: N/A Coed
Affiliation or Control: Proprietary IRS Status: Proprietary
Highest Offering: Associate Degree
Accreditation: **#ABHES**

01 President .... Mr. Cleophat TANIS

† School will close December 2020.

Mercy Hospital College of Nursing (C)

3663 South Miami Ave Ste 1500, Miami FL 33133
County: Miami-Dade Identification: 667222
Unit ID: 419217
Telephone: (305) 285-2777 Carnegie Class: Not Classified
FAX Number: (305) 285-2671 Calendar System: Semester
URL: www.mercymiami.com/professionals/college-of-nursing
Established: 2008 Annual Undergrad Tuition & Fees: N/A
Enrollment: 91 Coed
Affiliation or Control: Proprietary IRS Status: Proprietary
Highest Offering: Associate Degree
Accreditation: **ABHES**, ADNUR, PNUR

66 Dean .... Ms. Elizabeth HERNANDEZ

Meridian College (D)

7020 Professional Pkwy E, Sarasota FL 34240
County: Sarasota FICE Identification: 023268
Unit ID: 244279
Telephone: (941) 377-4880 Carnegie Class: Spec 2-yr-Health
FAX Number: (941) 378-2842 Calendar System: Other
URL: www.meridian.edu
Established: 1982 Annual Undergrad Tuition & Fees: N/A
Enrollment: 194 Coed
Affiliation or Control: Proprietary IRS Status: Proprietary
Highest Offering: Associate Degree
Accreditation: **ACCSC**

01 Campus Director/Student Svcs .... Mr. Patrick MCDERMOTT
07 Director of Admissions .... Ms. Kim MILES
36 Director Career Services .... Ms. Tracy FORDHAM

Miami Dade College (E)

300 NE Second Avenue, Miami FL 33132-2204
County: Miami-Dade County FICE Identification: 001506
Unit ID: 135717
Telephone: (305) 237-8888 Carnegie Class: Bac/Assoc-Mixed
FAX Number: (305) 237-7913 Calendar System: Semester
URL: www.mdc.edu
Established: 1960 Annual Undergrad Tuition & Fees (In-State): $2,838
Enrollment: 46,523 Coed
Affiliation or Control: State IRS Status: 501(c)3
Highest Offering: Baccalaureate
Accreditation: **SC**, ADNUR, ARCPA, ART, CAHIIM, COARC, DANCE, DH, DMS, EMT, FUSER, HT, MLTAD, MUS, NMT, NUR, NURSE, OPD, PTAA, RAD, THEA

01 President .... Ms. Madeline PUMARIEGA
05 Executive Vice President & Provost .... Dr. Malou HARRISON
10 Sr Vice Provost/CFO/IT .... Mr. Jayson IROFF
11 Vice Provost Business Affairs .... Mr. Christopher STARLING
13 Vice Provost Information Tech/CIO .... Ms. Tanya ACEVEDO
18 Vice Provost Facilities .... Mr. Leobardo BOBADILLA
15 Vice Provost Human Resources .... Ms. Iliana CASTILLO-FRICK
108 VP Strategy & Inst Effectiveness .... Ms. Wanda SMITH
12 Campus President Hialeah .... Dr. Anthony CRUZ
12 Campus President Wolfson .... Ms. Beatriz GONZALEZ
12 Campus President Kendall .... Dr. Pascale CHARLOT
12 Campus President Medical .... Dr. Bryan STEWART
12 Campus President North .... Mr. Fermin VAZQUEZ
12 Campus President EPC .... Dr. Alanka BROWN
12 Campus President Homestead .... Dr. Oscar LOYNAZ
12 Campus President West .... Dr. Beverly MOORE-GARCIA
21 Assoc Vice Prov Business Affs .... Ms. Delilah ALMEDA
32 Vice Prov Stdnt Affs/Chief Enroll .... Dr. Jaime ANZALOTTA
102 Executive Dir MDC Foundation .... Ms. Shannon RODDY
37 Assoc VP Student Financial Services .... Ms. Mercedes AMAYA
06 Collegewide Registrar .... Dr. Elisabet VIZOSO
26 Chief Public Rels Officer/Dir Comm .... Mr. Juan MENDIETA
29 Director Alumni Relations .... Mr. Adlar GARCIA
35 Director Student Life .... Ms. Annielys SOSA
88 Dir Testing Admin/Pgm Evaluation .... Mr. Silvio RODRIGUEZ
22 Dir Equal Opportunity Pgm/ADA Coord .... Dr. Joy C. RUFF
121 Director Student Advisement .... Ms. Veronica GONZALES
84 Exc Dir Enrollment Management .... Mr. Miguel MURPHY
96 Director of Purchasing .... Mr. Roman MARTINEZ
41 Director Intercollegiate Athletics .... Ms. Alysia DYER
09 Director Research & Data Analysis .... Dr. Ivana FREDOTOVIC
43 Legal Counsel .... Mr. Javier LEY-SOTO
86 Director Governmental Affairs .... Ms. Maggie PEREZ
100 Chief of Staff .... Ms. Maryam LAGUNA BORREGO
103 Vice Provost Workforce Pgm .... Dr. Loretta OVUERAYE
104 Director Global Student Pgm .... Ms. Gabriela ESTEVES
105 College Webmaster .... Mr. Andrew SEAGA
08 Head Librarian/Dir Lrng Resources .... Mr. Erick DOMINICIS
85 Dir International Student Services .... Ms. Adriana MENKE

Miami International University of Art & Design (F)

1501 Biscayne Boulevard, Suite 100,
Miami FL 33132-1418
County: Miami-Dade FICE Identification: 008878
Unit ID: 134811
Telephone: (305) 428-5700 Carnegie Class: Spec-4-yr-Arts
FAX Number: (305) 374-7946 Calendar System: Quarter
URL: www.artinstitutes.edu/miami
Established: 1965 Annual Undergrad Tuition & Fees: $19,354
Enrollment: 934 Coed
Affiliation or Control: Independent Non-Profit IRS Status: 501(c)3
Highest Offering: Master's
Accreditation: **SC**, CIDA

01 President .... Ms. Leslie BAUGHMAN
05 Dean of Academic Affairs .... Mr. Alfonso GUTIERREZ
10 Dir Admin & Financial Services .... Ms. Leslie THEROULDE
32 Dean of Student Affairs .... Mr. John OSBORNE
08 Librarian .... Ms. Catherine DIETERLYL

Miami Regional University (G)

700 S. Royal Poinciana Blvd #100,
Miami Springs FL 33166
County: Miami-Dade FICE Identification: 041284
Unit ID: 451103
Telephone: (305) 442-9223 Carnegie Class: Spec-4-yr-Other Health
FAX Number: (305) 442-8723 Calendar System: Other
URL: www.mru.edu
Established: 1996 Annual Undergrad Tuition & Fees: N/A
Enrollment: 818 Coed
Affiliation or Control: Proprietary IRS Status: Proprietary
Highest Offering: Master's
Accreditation: **ACCSC**, ADNUR, NUR

01 President & CEO .... Ophelia SANCHEZ
43 Exec Vice President/General Counsel .... Richard GRILLO
05 Provost/SVP Academic Affairs .... Dr. Dario A. CORTES
32 Senior Director Student Services .... Vacant
07 Assist VP Admissions .... Vacant
08 Librarian .... Katia NUNEZ
10 VP Finance/Enrollment .... Henry BABANI
15 VP Employee Affs/Public Relation .... Mitsy SOUSA
36 Lead Career Services Rep .... Mirizza MENENDEZ
37 Assoc VP Student Financial Aid .... Vacant

Millennia Atlantic University (MAU) (H)

3801 NW 97th Avenue, Suite 100, Doral FL 33178
County: Miami-Dade FICE Identification: 041825
Unit ID: 461883
Telephone: (786) 331-1000 Carnegie Class: Spec-4-yr-Bus
FAX Number: (305) 503-9680 Calendar System: Semester
URL: www.maufl.edu
Established: 2007 Annual Undergrad Tuition & Fees: $9,876
Enrollment: 196 Coed
Affiliation or Control: Proprietary IRS Status: Proprietary
Highest Offering: Master's
Accreditation: **ACCSC**, ACICS

01 President .... Dr. Aristides MAZA-DUERTO
05 Director of Academic Programs .... Dr. Octavio MAZA
00 Chancellor .... Mr. Luis E. MARTINEZ
10 CFO/VP Admin & Finance .... Mrs. Orianna M. MOSS
20 Vice Director of Academic Programs .... Mrs. Teresa L. FITZGERALD
06 Registrar .... Ms. Natasha ALEONG
37 Financial Aid Manager .... Ms. Latia JONES
26 Dir of Marketing & Admissions .... Ms. Alma I. UBILLA
36 Student Services and Placement Mgr .... Ms. Angela D. PENAS
08 Librarian .... Ms. Natasa HOGUE
113 Bursar .... Mrs. Jenice C. MAZA-DUERTO

Naaleh College (I)

16375 NE 18th Avenue Ste 304,
North Miami Beach FL 33162
County: Miami-Dade Identification: 667347
Telephone: (305) 944-0035 Carnegie Class: Not Classified
FAX Number: (305) 944-0335 Calendar System: Semester
URL: www.naalehcollege.edu
Established: 2011 Annual Undergrad Tuition & Fees: N/A
Enrollment: N/A Coed
Affiliation or Control: Independent Non-Profit IRS Status: 501(c)3
Highest Offering: Baccalaureate
Accreditation: **DEAC**

01 President .... Rabbi Harold REICHMAN
03 Dean .... Chana PRERO
05 Educational Director .... Rabbi Hillel RUDOLPH
20 Assistant Academic Director .... Rabbi Ari ACKERMAN
11 Director & VP of Operations .... Tzipora KLAVER
07 Admissions Director .... Chaya OCHS
06 Registrar/Student Services Director .... Elisheva STEINHART

New York Film Academy, South Beach (J)

420 Lincoln Rd #200, Miami Beach FL 33139
Telephone: (305) 534-6009 Identification: 770984
Accreditation: **&WC**, ART

† Regional accreditation is carried under the parent institution in Burbank, CA.

North Broward Technical Center (K)

1871 West Hillsboro Blvd, Deerfield Beach FL 33442
County: Broward Identification: 667357
Telephone: (954) 427-8830 Carnegie Class: Not Classified
FAX Number: (954) 427-8836 Calendar System: Other
URL: nbtechcenter.com/
Established: Annual Undergrad Tuition & Fees: N/A
Enrollment: N/A Coed
Affiliation or Control: Proprietary IRS Status: Proprietary
Highest Offering: Associate Degree
Accreditation: **ABHES**

01 Program Manager .... Dr. Herard LAFRANCE

North Florida College (L)

325 NW Turner Davis Drive, Madison FL 32340-1610
County: Madison FICE Identification: 001508
Unit ID: 136145
Telephone: (850) 973-2288 Carnegie Class: Bac/Assoc-Assoc Dom
FAX Number: (850) 973-1696 Calendar System: Semester
URL: www.nfc.edu
Established: 1958 Annual Undergrad Tuition & Fees (In-State): $3,054
Enrollment: 1,181 Coed
Affiliation or Control: State IRS Status: 501(c)3
Highest Offering: Baccalaureate
Accreditation: **SC**, ADNUR, EMT, NUR

01 President .... Mr. John GROSSKOPF
05 Dean of Academic Affairs/CAO .... Ms. Jennifer PAGE
10 Chief Business Officer .... Mr. Micah RODGERS
84 Dean of Enrollment/Student Services .... Ms. Kay HOGAN
13 Dir Info Technology/CIO .... Mr. Nick SKIPPER
15 Director of Employee Services .... Mr. Tyler COODY
08 Director of Learning Resources .... Ms. Lynn WYCHE
103 Assoc Dean Econ Dev/Workforce Educ .... Mr. Rick DAVIS
06 Registrar .... Ms. Lori PLEASANT
18 Chief Facilities/Physical Plant .... Mr. Glenn STRICKLAND
111 Dir College Advancement .... Ms. Kim SCARBORO
102 Dir Foundation/Alumni Relations .... Ms. Judy LUNDELL
37 Director Student Financial Aid .... Ms. Brooke TURNER
28 Director of Diversity/Equity .... Ms. Denise BELL
04 Executive Asst to President .... Ms. Michelle WHEELER
19 Director Security/Safety .... Mr. Larry AKERS

Northwest Florida State College (M)

100 College Boulevard, Niceville FL 32578-1295
County: Okaloosa FICE Identification: 001510
Unit ID: 136233
Telephone: (850) 678-5111 Carnegie Class: Bac/Assoc-Mixed
FAX Number: (850) 729-5215 Calendar System: Semester
URL: www.nwfsc.edu
Established: 1963 Annual Undergrad Tuition & Fees (In-State): $3,133
Enrollment: 5,004 Coed
Affiliation or Control: State IRS Status: 501(c)3
Highest Offering: Baccalaureate
Accreditation: **SC**, ADNUR, DA, EMT, NURSE, @PTAA, RAD

01 President .... Dr. Devin STEPHENSON
03 Senior Vice President .... Ms. Cristie KEDROSKI
05 Vice Pres of Academic Affairs .... Dr. Deidre PRICE
10 Vice Pres of Business Operations .... Mr. Randy WHITE
13 Chief Information Officer .... Mr. Cole ALLEN
09 AVP of Research & Assessment .... Ms. Pauline ANDERSON
43 General Counsel .... Ms. Whitney RUTHERFORD
04 Executive Assistant to President .... Ms. Melissa WOLF-BATES
49 Dean of Art and Sciences .... Dr. Dana BIGHAM-STEPHENS
88 Dean/CHS Principal .... Mr. Anthony BOYER

75 Dean Career & Technical Education .... Dr. Michael ERNY
66 Dean Health Science & Public Safety .... Dr. Charlotte KUSS
121 Exec Dir Student Success Navigation .... Ms. Heather DIETZOLD
06 Exec Dir Acad Records/Enrollment .... Ms. Stephanie LINARD
37 Exec Dir Fin Planning/Scholarships .... Dr. Aimee WATTS
103 Exec Dir Workforce & Cont Educ .... Mr. Paul JOHNSON
15 Exec Dir Human Resources/Diversity .... Ms. Roberta MACKEY
25 Exec Dir of Grant Development .... Mr. Sam RENFROE
21 Exec Dir of Accounting/Finance .... Mr. Edward ROSENTEL
26 Exec Dir Strategic Communications .... Ms. Julie SCHRODT
106 Exec Dir of Academic Strategies .... Dr. KC WILLIAMS
08 Learning Commons Director .... Ms. Lisa HADDORFF
18 Facilities Director .... Mr. John MCKEON
19 Director of College Safety/Security .... Mr. Aaron MURRAY
30 Director of Development .... Ms. Carla REINLIE
57 Director Mattie Kelly Arts Center .... Ms. Jeanette SHIRES
41 Athletic Director .... Mr. Ramsey ROSS
96 Director of Purchasing .... Ms. Katherine ST. ONGE
113 Student Accounts & Billing Mgr .... Ms. Kaycee ARTHUR

Nova Southeastern University (A)

3301 College Avenue, Fort Lauderdale FL 33314-7796
County: Broward FICE Identification: 001509
Unit ID: 136215
Telephone: (800) 541-6682 Carnegie Class: DU-Higher
FAX Number: (954) 262-3800 Calendar System: Trimester
URL: www.nova.edu
Established: 1964 Annual Undergrad Tuition & Fees: $33,430
Enrollment: 20,888 Coed
Affiliation or Control: Independent Non-Profit IRS Status: 501(c)3
Highest Offering: Doctorate
Accreditation: SC, AA, ACAE, #ARCPA, AUD, CACREP, CAEP, CAEPN, CAHIIM, CLPSY, #COARC, CVT, DENT, DIETC, @DIETD, #DMS, IACBE, IPSY, LAW, #MED, MFCD, NURSE, OPT, OPTR, OSTEO, OT, PH, PHAR, PTA, SCPSY, SP, SPAA

01 President & CEO .... Dr. George L. HANBURY, II
05 Provost & EVP Academic Affairs .... Dr. Ronald J. CHENAIL
10 VP Finance/CFO .... Ms. Alyson SILVA
00 Chancellor Nova Southeastern Univ .... Mr. Ray FERRERO, JR.
17 Chancellor Health Professions Div .... Dr. Fred LIPPMAN
11 EVP/Chief Operating Officer .... Dr. Harry K. MOON
88 Sr VP for Trans Rsrch & Econ Dev ... Dr. Ken DAWSON-SCULLY
100 Deputy Chief of Staff .... Ms. Jennifer RAMOS
08 Interim VP Info Svcs/Univ Librarian .... Mr. James HUTCHENS
43 VP Legal Affairs .... Mr. Joel BERMAN
46 VP Research Tech Transfer .... Dr. Gary S. MARGULES
32 VP Student Affairs/Dean UG Studies .... Dr. Brad WILLIAMS
111 VP Univ Advancement/Chief of Staff .... Mr. Terry J. MULARKEY
13 VP Info Tech/Chief Info Ofcr .... Mr. Tom WEST
15 VP Human Resources .... Mr. Robert J. PIETRYKOWSKI
84 VP Enrollment and Stdnt Svcs .... Dr. Stephanie BROWN
21 VP Business Services .... Mr. Marc CROCQUET
106 VP Reg Campus & Online Educ .... Dr. Ricardo BELMAR
18 VP Facilities Mgmt .... Mr. Daniel ALFONSO
23 Vice Pres Clinical Operations .... Mr. Leonard POUNDS
26 VP University Relations .... Ms. Kyle FISHER
19 Director Public Safety .... Mr. James EWING
09 VP Institutional Effectiveness .... Dr. Donald J. RUDAWSKY
108 Dir Accreditation/Acad Pgm Rev .... Mr. Adam ROSENTHAL
24 Exec Dir Ed Tech/Digital Media Prod .... Ms. Diane LIPPE
25 Director Sponsored Programs .... Ms. Cathy HARLAN
86 Exec Dir Licensure/State Relations .... Dr. Greg F. STIBER
12 Headmaster University School .... Dr. William KOPAS
27 Exec Dir University Publications .... Ms. Bernadette BRUCE
36 Asst Dean Academic & Prof Succes .. Ms. Mignon BISSONNETTE
29 Exec Dir Alumni Relations/Advance .... Ms. Barbara SAGEMAN
06 Dir University Registrar's Office .... Ms. G. Elaine N. POFF
41 Asst VP UA/Director Athletics .... Mr. Michael MOMINEY
88 Director Campus Recreation .... Mr. Tom VITUCCI
116 Executive Dir Internal Auditing .... Mr. Ron MIDEI
88 VP Compliance/Chief Integrity Ofcr .... Ms. Robin SUPLER
88 Dir Museum of Art .... Ms. Bonnie CLEARWATER
63 Dean College Osteopathic Medicine .... Dr. Elaine WALLACE
67 Dean College Pharmacy .... Dr. Michelle CLARK
88 Dean College Optometry .... Dr. Linda ROUSE
76 Interim Dean College of HC Sciences .... Dr. Guy NEHRENZ
54 Dean College Engineering/Computing ...... Dr. Meline KEVORKIAN
61 Dean Shepard Broad Law
Center .... Mr. José (Beto) R. JUÁREZ, JR.
49 Halmos College of Arts and Sciences . Dr. Holly BAUMGARTNER
66 Dean College of Nursing .... Dr. Marcella M. RUTHERFORD
50 Dean Huizenga Col of Bus/Entrepren .... Dr. Andrew ROSMAN
92 Dean Farquhar Honors College .... Dr. Andrea SHAW-NEVINS
83 Dean College of Psychology .... Dr. Karen GROSBY
52 Dean of Dental Medicine .... Dr. Steven KALTMAN
53 Dean Fischler College of Education .... Dr. Kimberly DURHAM
88 Dean College Allopathic Med .... Dr. Johannes VIEWEG
117 Exec Director NSUBIC .... Dr. John WENSVEEN
118 VP Operations of HPD .... Dr. Irving ROSENBAUM

NRI Institute of Health Sciences (B)

503 Royal Palm Blvd, Royal Palm Beach FL 33411
County: Palm Beach FICE Identification: 042108
Unit ID: 481252
Telephone: (561) 688-5112 Carnegie Class: Spec 2-yr-Health
FAX Number: (561) 688-5113 Calendar System: Semester
URL: www.nriinstitute.edu
Established: 2006 Annual Undergrad Tuition & Fees: N/A
Enrollment: 126 Coed
Affiliation or Control: Proprietary IRS Status: Proprietary
Highest Offering: Associate Degree
Accreditation: COE

01 President & Director .... Elizabeth STOLKOWSKI

Palm Beach Atlantic University (C)

901 S. Flagler Drive, West Palm Beach FL 33401
County: Palm Beach FICE Identification: 008849
Unit ID: 136330
Telephone: (561) 803-2000 Carnegie Class: DU-Mod
FAX Number: (561) 803-2186 Calendar System: Semester
URL: www.pba.edu
Established: 1968 Annual Undergrad Tuition & Fees: $33,475
Enrollment: 3,704 Coed
Affiliation or Control: Interdenominational IRS Status: 501(c)3
Highest Offering: Doctorate
Accreditation: SC, CAATE, IACBE, MUS, NURSE, PHAR, THEOL

01 President .... Dr. Debra A. SCHWINN
05 Provost/CAO .... Dr. E. Randolph RICHARDS
10 Sr VP for Finance/Admin & CFO .... Mr. John KAUTZ, III
30 Vice President Development .... Mrs. Laura BISHOP
84 Vice President Enrollment Mgmt .... Dr. Nancy BRAINARD
15 VP of Human Resources .... Ms. Mona L. HICKS
32 Vice President Student Development .... Dr. Bob LUTZ
88 VP for Spiritual Development .... Dr. Bernard CUETO
13 VP Information Tech Svcs/CIO .... Mr. Scott BARNES
09 Asst Provost Rsrch/Effectiveness .... Mrs. Carolanne BROWN
96 AVP Auxiliary Svcs/Procurement .... Ms. AnnMarie TAYLOR
26 Assoc VP Univ Relations & Marketing ...... Mrs. Rebecca PEELING
51 Dean MacArthur School of Leadership .... Dr. Craig DOMECK
49 Dean School of Arts & Sciences .... Dr. Robert LLOYD
50 Dean School of Business .... Dr. Brian STROW
53 Dean School of Education .... Ms. Chelneca TEMPLETON
57 Dean School of Music/Fine Arts .... Mr. Jason LESTER
66 Dean School of Nursing .... Ms. Phyllis KING
67 Dean Gregory School of Pharmacy .... Vacant
60 Dean School Communication/Media .... Vacant
73 Dean School of Ministry .... Dr. Jonathan GRENZ
06 Registrar .... Ms. Kathy MAJZNER
08 Director of the Warren Library .... Mr. John DONCEVIC
20 Associate Provost for Instruction .... Dr. Nathan LANE
18 Director of Physical Plant .... Mr. Martin SHUTTERLY
29 Director of Alumni Relations .... Mr. Steve ESHELMAN
31 Dir of Campus and Community Events .... Mrs. Mary WARD
35 Assistant Dean of Students .... Ms. Kate MAGRO
37 Director of Financial Aid .... Vacant
41 Director of Athletics .... Ms. Courtney LOVELY
42 Director of Campus Ministries .... Mr. Mark KAPRIVE

Palm Beach State College (D)

4200 Congress Avenue, Lake Worth FL 33461-4796
County: Palm Beach FICE Identification: 001512
Unit ID: 136358
Telephone: (561) 967-7222 Carnegie Class: Bac/Assoc-Assoc Dom
FAX Number: (561) 868-3504 Calendar System: Semester
URL: www.palmbeachstate.edu
Established: 1933 Annual Undergrad Tuition & Fees (In-State): $2,444
Enrollment: 26,666 Coed
Affiliation or Control: State IRS Status: 501(c)3
Highest Offering: Baccalaureate
Accreditation: SC, ACBSP, ADNUR, CAHIIM, COARC, DA, DH, DMS, EMT, MAC, NUR, RAD, SURGT

01 President .... Ms. Ava L. PARKER
05 Int VP of Academic Affairs .... Dr. Tunjarnika COLEMAN-FERRELL
88 VP of Academic Innovation/Strategy .... Dr. Roger YOHE
10 VP Administration/Business Services .... Mr. James DUFFIE
32 Vice President Student Services .... Dr. Peter BARBATIS
13 Vice President Information Svcs .... Dr. Ginger L. PEDERSEN
31 Exec Director Community
Engagement .... Ms. Rachael E. BONLARRON
43 General Counsel .... Mr. Kevin A. FERNANDER
111 Vice President Advancement .... Mr. David RUTHERFORD
20 Int Assoc VP Academic Affairs .... Dr. Holly L. BENNETT
75 Int Dean Business/Trade/Industry .... Ms. Barbara M. CIPRIANO
20 Provost Boca Raton .... Mr. Van P. WILLAIMS
20 Dean Academic Affairs Loxahatchee .. Ms. Kimberley LANCASTER
20 Int Prov Academic Affs Lake Worth .... Dr. Peter BARBATIS
20 Dean Academic Affairs Boca Raton .... Dr. Roy M. VARGAS
97 Int Dean Bachelor Degree Programs .... Dr. Don GLADNEY
20 Dean Curriculum .... Dr. Velmarie ALBERTINI
20 Exec Dean Belle Glade Campus .... Ms. Latanya L. MCNEAL
84 Dean Enrollment Management .... Dr. Stephen JOYNER
37 Director Financial Aid .... Mr. Eddie VIERA
09 Exec Dir Inst Rsrch/Effectiveness .... Mr. David WEBER
18 Facilities Director .... Mr. Bob PRIOLO
15 Exec Director Human Resources .... Mr. Michael PUSTIZZI
26 Dir College Relations & Mktg .... Mr. Diego MEEROFF
21 Controller .... Mr. James E. DUFFIE
06 College Registrar .... Mr. Peter BIEGEL
96 Procurement Director .... Mr. David CHOJNACKI
13 Chief Information Officer .... Mr. Ken LIBUTTI
25 Dir Resource & Grant Development .... Ms. Maureen CAPP
106 E-Learning Director .... Mr. Sidney BEITLER
108 Assessment Director .... Dr. Karen D. PAIN
19 Security & Risk Management Director .... Ms. Delsa BUSH
76 Dean Health Services .... Dr. Edward WILLEY

Palmer College of Chiropractic, Florida Campus (E)

4777 City Center Parkway, Port Orange FL 32129-4153
Telephone: (386) 763-2709 Identification: 666330
Accreditation: &HLC, &CHIRO

† Regional accreditation is carried under the parent institution in Davenport, IA.

Pasco-Hernando State College (F)

10230 Ridge Road, New Port Richey FL 34654-5112
County: Pasco FICE Identification: 010652
Unit ID: 136400
Telephone: (727) 847-2727 Carnegie Class: Bac/Assoc-Assoc Dom
FAX Number: (727) 816-1815 Calendar System: Semester
URL: www.phsc.edu
Established: 1972 Annual Undergrad Tuition & Fees (In-District): $3,155
Enrollment: 9,886 Coed
Affiliation or Control: State/Local IRS Status: 501(c)3
Highest Offering: Baccalaureate
Accreditation: SC, ADNUR, DH, EMT, NURSE, SURGT

01 President .... Dr. Timothy L. BEARD
05 Exec VP & Chief Academic Officer .... Dr. Stanley M. GIANNET
32 Sr VP & Chief Student Affs/Enroll .... Dr. Robert E. BADE
10 Sr VP of Financal Opers & CFO .... Mr. Brian S. HORN
12 Provost of the East Campus .... Dr. Edwin G. GOOLSBY
12 Interim Provost North Campus .... Mr. Reggie L. WILSON
12 Provost Spring Hill Campus .... Dr. Amy E. ANDERSON
12 Provost Porter Campus at Wiregrass .... Dr. Kevin F. O'FARRELL
103 Dean of Workforce Dev/Career/Tech .... Dr. Marcia M. AUSTIN
120 SVP & Chief Tech/Distance Ed Ofcr .... Dr. Melissa L. HARTS
84 Dean Stdnt Affairs & Enroll Mgmt .. Ms. Chiquita A. HENDERSON
20 Asst VP Academic Affairs .... Ms. Sonia B. THORN
49 Dean Arts and Sciences .... Dr. Gerene M. THOMPSON
18 Asst VP Facilities Mgmt .... Mr. Tony A. RIVAS
09 Assoc Dean Inst Effectiveness .... Ms. Carla M. ROSSITER-SMITH
13 Assoc Dean of Enterprise Systems .... Ms. Janice L. SCOTT
111 Assoc VP Alum/Col Rels/Exec Dir
Fdn .... Dr. Lisa A. RICHARDSON
66 Associate Dean of Nursing .... Ms. Tennille I. O'CONNOR
07 Dean of Admissions & Enroll Mgmt .... Mr. Chris J. BIBBO
37 Dean Financial Aid .... Ms. Rebecca SHANAFELT
43 Asst VP of Policy/General Counsel .... Vacant
08 Director of Libraries .... Ms. Ingrid L. PURRENHAGE
26 Assoc Dean Marketing/Comm & Media ...... Ms. Melanie WAXLER
18 Director of Facilities .... Mr. Keith V. BRAUN
15 Exec Director of Human Resources .... Mr. Darrell L. CLARK
109 Director of Auxiliary Services .... Mr. John D. COLLINS
22 Dir of Global & Multi Aware & Spec .... Mr. Imani D. ASUKILE
96 Procurement & Contract Admin Mgr ...... Ms. Christy L. AULICINO
04 Executive Asst to President & DBOT .... Ms. Rhonda M. DODGE
29 Director Alumni & Donor
Relations .... Ms. Michelle L. BULLWINKEL
41 Athletics Director/Instructor .... Mr. Stephen A. WINTERLING

Pensacola Christian College (G)

250 Brent Lane, Pensacola FL 32503
County: Escambia Identification: 667101
Telephone: (850) 478-8496 Carnegie Class: Not Classified
FAX Number: (850) 479-6552 Calendar System: Semester
URL: www.pcci.edu
Established: 1974 Annual Undergrad Tuition & Fees: N/A
Enrollment: N/A Coed
Affiliation or Control: Independent Non-Profit IRS Status: 501(c)3
Highest Offering: Doctorate
Accreditation: TRACS, NURSE

01 President .... Dr. Troy SHOEMAKER
03 Executive Vice President .... Dr. Jon LANDS
05 Academic Vice President .... Dr. Raylene COCHRAN
32 Vice President for Student Affairs .... Mr. Tim MCLAUGHLIN
10 Chief Financial Officer .... Mr. Jim THOMPSON
06 Registrar .... Mr. Adam SCHRODER
09 Dir Institutional Effectiveness .... Dr. Mark SMITH
41 Athletic Director .... Mr. Addison CALLEY
08 Chief Librarian .... Mr. Kelly GRANDSTAFF
07 Director of Admissions .... Mrs. Amy ABBOTT
106 Director of Online Learning .... Mr. Steve MARTIN
19 Chief of Safety and Security .... Mr. Reggie BARTKOWSKI
13 Chief Information Officer .... Mr. Troy ARWINE

Pensacola State College (H)

1000 College Boulevard, Pensacola FL 32504-8998
County: Escambia FICE Identification: 001513
Unit ID: 136473
Telephone: (850) 484-1000 Carnegie Class: Bac/Assoc-Assoc Dom
FAX Number: (850) 484-1826 Calendar System: Semester
URL: www.pensacolastate.edu
Established: 1948 Annual Undergrad Tuition & Fees (In-District): $2,364
Enrollment: 9,226 Coed
Affiliation or Control: Local IRS Status: 501(c)3
Highest Offering: Baccalaureate
Accreditation: SC, ACFEI, ADNUR, CAHIIM, DH, EMT, MAC, NUR, NURSE, PNUR, PTAA, RAD, SURGT

01 President .... Dr. Ed MEADOWS
05 VP Academic and Student Affairs .... Dr. Erin SPICER

11 VP Administrative Services Mr. Tom GILLIAM
10 VP Business Affairs Mrs. Anita KOVACS
20 Dean Bacc Studies/Academic Sup Dr. Kirk BRADLEY
20 Senior Dean Academic Affairs Dr. Brenda KELLY
12 Dean Milton Campus Ms. Jennifer HILL-FARON
76 Dean Health Sciences Dr. Dusti SLUDER
102 Exec Director College Foundation Ms. Andrea KRIEGER
13 Assoc VP Information Systems Mr. Michael JOHNSTON
14 Exec Director ITS Mr. Steve WHITING
86 Associate VP Govt Relations Ms. Sandy RAY
26 Exec Dir Marketing/College Info Ms. Sheila NICHOLS
105 Coordinator Internet Systems Mr. Jason KING
28 Ex Dir Inst Diversity/Stdnt Conduct Dr. Lynsey LISTAU
06 Registrar Ms. Stephanie DENMARK
25 Dean Grants and Federal Programs Dr. Debbie DOUMA
18 Director Facilities and Planning Ms. Diane BRACKEN
88 Director Technology Support Ms. Liz GOMEZ
15 Director Human Resources Ms. Tammy HENDERSON
37 Dir Fin Aid/Veterans/Scholarships Ms. Joanne ROZBORSKI
75 Director Career & Technical Educ Ms. Deborah HOOKS
38 Director Student Support Services Ms. Rachelle BURNS
19 Director Public Safety Mr. Robert GOLEY
43 General Counsel Mr. Thomas J. GILLIAM
08 District Dept Head Libraries Ms. LisaMarie BARTUSIK
96 Director Purchasing Ms. Ted YOUNG
91 Director MIS Support Mr. Beau MCHENRY
21 Comptroller Ms. Nan JACKSON
29 Exec Director Alumni Affairs Ms. Hailey LOTZ
07 Director Admissions Ms. Samantha HILL
36 Asst Dean Advising & Career Svcs Dr. Monique COLLINS
41 Director Athletics Mr. Bryan LEWALLYN
32 Dean Student Affairs Ms. Kathy DUTREMBLE
12 Director South Santa Rosa Center Ms. Karen MCCABE
12 Director Century Center Mr. Alex ANDREWS
51 Coordinator Continuing Education Ms. Deven WALTHER-THEAD
04 Exec Assistant to the President Ms. Patricia S. CREWS

Polk State College (A)

999 Avenue H, NE, Winter Haven FL 33881-4299
County: Polk FICE Identification: 001514
Unit ID: 136516
Telephone: (863) 297-1000 Carnegie Class: Bac/Assoc-Mixed
FAX Number: (863) 297-1065 Calendar System: Semester
URL: www.polk.edu
Established: 1964 Annual Undergrad Tuition & Fees (In-District): $3,366
Enrollment: 9,961 Coed
Affiliation or Control: Local IRS Status: 501(c)3
Highest Offering: Baccalaureate
Accreditation: SC, ADNUR, COARC, CVT, DMS, EMT, NUR, OTA, #PTAA

01 President Dr. Angela FALCONETTI
05 Vice Pres Academic Affairs Dr. Thomas LEE
10 VP Business Admin/Finance Dr. Allen BOTTORFF
32 Vice Pres Student Services Mr. Reginald WEBB
111 Vice Pres Inst Advanc/Exec Dir PSCF Ms. Tracy PORTER
09 VP Inst Effectiveness/Accred/Rsrch Dr. Mary CLARK
103 Vice Pres Workforce Educ/Econ Dev Dr. Orathai NORTHERN
13 Chief Information Officer Mr. Robert STACK
28 Chief Diversity Officer Ms. Valparisa BAKER
26 AVP Communications & Public Affs Ms. Tamara SAKAGAWA
20 Dean Academic Affairs-WH Ms. April ROBINSON
15 Int Asst Director Human Resources Ms. Kristen SYKES
35 Exec Dean Student Services-WH Mr. Lawrence PAKOWSKI
35 Dean Student Services-LK Mr. Sylvester LITTLE
20 Dean of Academic Success Mr. Donald PAINTER
21 Controller Ms. Erin MONTGOMERY
84 Director Stdnt Enrollment/Registrar Ms. Susan MORGAN
37 Director Student Financial Svcs Ms. Ronshetta HOWELL
66 Director Nursing Dr. Joan CONNORS
102 Int Dir Financial Affs/PSC Fndn Ms. Cindy BAKER
18 Director Facilities Mr. George URBANO
103 Director Corporate College Mr. Howard DRAKE
88 Principal Chain of Lakes CHS Mr. Keith BONNEY
88 Principal Lakeland Col HS Mr. Rick JEFFRIES
88 Center Director JDA Mr. Andy OGUNTOLA
41 Athletic Director Mr. Stanley CROMARTIE
96 Director Purchasing Mr. Mark LILLQUIST
04 Administrative Asst to President Mrs. Christine LEE
104 Director Study Abroad Ms. Kim SIMPSON
106 Dir Instructional Tech/e-learning Mr. Christopher AMATO
19 Director Security/Safety Ms. Denise ANDREU
25 Chief Contracts/Grants Admin Ms. Jennifer FIORENZA
29 Director Alumni Relations Mrs. Marianne GEORGE
38 Dir Disability/Counseling Services Ms. Kim PEARSALL
43 Dir Legal Services/General Counsel Mr. Don WILSON
50 Program Director Business Ms. Maria LOHOCZKY
53 Program Director Education Dr. Patty LINDER
54 Program Director Engineering Tech Dr. Mori TOOSI

Polytechnic University of Puerto Rico (B)

8180 NW 36th Street, Suite 401, Miami FL 33166-6674
Telephone: (305) 418-8000 Identification: 666238
Accreditation: &M

† Regional accreditation is carried under the parent institution, Universidad Politecnica de Puerto Rico, San Juan, PR.

Polytechnic University of Puerto Rico-Orlando Campus (C)

550 N Econlockhatchee Trail, Orlando FL 32825
Telephone: (407) 677-7000 Identification: 770172
Accreditation: &M

† Branch campus of Universidad Politecnica De Puerto Rico, San Juan, PR

The Praxis Institute (D)

1850 SW 8th Street, 4th Floor, Miami FL 33135
County: Miami-Dade FICE Identification: 031147
Unit ID: 430582
Telephone: (305) 642-4104 Carnegie Class: Not Classified
FAX Number: (305) 642-6063 Calendar System: Semester
URL: www.praxis.edu
Established: 1988 Annual Undergrad Tuition & Fees: N/A
Enrollment: 405 Coed
Affiliation or Control: Proprietary IRS Status: Proprietary
Highest Offering: Associate Degree
Accreditation: COE, OTA, PTAA

01 Executive Director Rebeca ALFIE
05 VP Acad Affs & Campus Director Dario ALFIE
06 Campus Registrar Zoila ESPINOSA

Premiere International College (E)

2055 Central Avenue, Fort Myers FL 33901
County: Lee Identification: 667295
Telephone: (239) 454-5000 Carnegie Class: Not Classified
FAX Number: (239) 454-0456 Calendar System: Quarter
URL: www.picollege.edu
Established: 2009 Annual Undergrad Tuition & Fees: N/A
Enrollment: N/A Coed
Affiliation or Control: Proprietary IRS Status: Proprietary
Highest Offering: Associate Degree
Accreditation: ACICS, ADNUR

01 CEO/Owner Cynthia RUE
05 Director of Education Dr. Lori BARNES

Rasmussen University - Fort Myers (F)

9160 Forum Corporate Parkway, Fort Myers FL 33905
Telephone: (239) 477-2100 Identification: 667062
Accreditation: &HLC, ADNUR, MAAB, RAD

† Regional accreditation is carried under the parent institution in Saint Cloud, MN. The tuition figure is an average, actual tuition may vary.

Rasmussen University - Ocala (G)

4755 SW 46th Court, Ocala FL 34474
Telephone: (352) 629-1941 FICE Identification: 008501
Accreditation: &HLC, ADNUR, MAAB, @PTAA, RAD

† Regional accreditation carried under the parent institution in Saint Cloud, MN. The tuition figure is an average, actual tuition may vary.

Rasmussen University - Tampa/Brandon (H)

330 Brandon Town Center Dr, Brandon FL 33511
Telephone: (813) 246-7600 Identification: 667067
Accreditation: &HLC, ADNUR, MAAB

† Regional accreditation is carried under the parent institution in Saint Cloud, MN. The tuition figure is an average, actual tuition may vary.

Reformed Theological Seminary (I)

1231 Reformation Drive, Oviedo FL 32765-7197
Telephone: (407) 366-9493 Identification: 666628
Accreditation: &SC, THEOL

† Regional accreditation is carried under the parent institution in Jackson, MS.

Ringling College of Art and Design (J)

2700 N Tamiami Trail, Sarasota FL 34234-5895
County: Sarasota FICE Identification: 012574
Unit ID: 136774
Telephone: (941) 351-5100 Carnegie Class: Spec-4-yr-Arts
FAX Number: (941) 359-7517 Calendar System: Semester
URL: www.ringling.edu
Established: 1931 Annual Undergrad Tuition & Fees: $49,540
Enrollment: 1,624 Coed
Affiliation or Control: Independent Non-Profit IRS Status: 501(c)3
Highest Offering: Baccalaureate
Accreditation: SC, ART, CIDA

01 President Dr. Larry R. THOMPSON
03 Executive Vice President Dr. Tracy A. WAGNER
04 Executive Assistant to the Pres Ms. Kerry SCHAFFER
100 Special Assistant to the Pres Vacant
05 VP for Academic Affairs Dr. Peter MCALLISTER
84 VP for Enrollment Mgmt/Mktg Dr. Jason GOOD
20 Assoc VP for AA/Dean of Faculty Mr. David H. JACKSON
20 Assoc VP for AA/Dean of UG Studies Mr. Jeff SCHWARTZ
51 Asst VP/Dir Cont Stds/Special Pgms Dr. Mona CALLIES
06 Registrar Mr. Justin SELPH
36 Director Career Services Mr. Charles KOVACS
08 Dir of Library Services Dr. Kristina KEOGH
26 Int Dir Marketin/Digital Strategies Vacant
27 Editorial & PR Manager Ms. Chelsea GARNER-FERRIS
108 Director of Assessment Ms. Kelly BEACHLER
111 VP for Advancement Ms. Stacey CORLEY
110 Sr Director Constituent Engagement Ms. Jeney SLUSSER
112 Asst VP for Strategic Philanthropy Ms. Lora WEY
29 Dir Alumni Relations/Annual Giving Ms. Susan BOROZAN
10 VP for Finance & Administration Vacant
21 Asst VP for Fin & Admn/Controller Ms. Monica K. WAID
18 Asst VP/Dir Facilities Operations Mr. Viron LYNCH
19 Director of Public Safety Vacant
37 Dir of Financial Aid Mr. Lee HARRELL
09 Asst VP for Planning & IE Dr. Pat MIZAK
16 Dir of Human Resources Mr. Darren MATHEWS
32 VP for Student Life/Dean Stdnts Dr. Tammy S. WALSH
39 Assoc Dean of Students/Res Life Vacant
35 Assoc Dean of Students/Student Dev Mr. Jekeyma ROBINSON
23 Assoc Dean/Dir Student Health Svcs Dr. Erin ROBINSON
07 Director of Admissions Mr. Gregg PRIGERSON
13 Dir of Institutional Technology Ms. Mahmoud PEGAH
90 Dir of Academic Computing Ms. Karissa MILLER
91 Dir of Administrative Computing Ms. Kris PEGAH
28 Assoc Dean Diversity & Inclusion Yoleidy ROSARIO
30 Director of Fundraising Events Ms. Stacy QUAID

The Robert E. Webber Institute for Worship Studies (K)

4001 Hendricks Ave, Jacksonville FL 32207
County: Duval Identification: 666616
Telephone: (904) 264-2172 Carnegie Class: Not Classified
FAX Number: (904) 379-5534 Calendar System: Semester
URL: www.iws.edu
Established: 1998 Annual Graduate Tuition & Fees: N/A
Enrollment: N/A Coed
Affiliation or Control: Independent Non-Profit IRS Status: 501(c)3
Highest Offering: Doctorate; No Undergraduates
Accreditation: BI, THEOL

01 Chief Executive Officer/President Dr. James R. HART
05 Academic Dean Dr. Dinelle FRANKLAND
10 VP of Finance & Administration Ms. Christi G. MATTESON
42 VP of Spiritual Life Dr. Darrell A. HARRIS
84 VP Enrollment Management Mr. Mark J. MURRAY
08 Library Director Ms. Susan A. MASSEY
29 Director Alumni Relations Dr. Kent L. WALTERS
24 Dir of Technical Services Dr. Samuel L. HOROWITZ
04 Asst to the President Vacant
32 Dir Student Services/Office Admin Ms. Sandy E. DINKINS
45 Dir of Institutional Effectiveness Dr. Steve E. HUNTLEY
13 Information Technology Coordinator Dr. James Kenneth RUSHING
26 Dir of Missional Relations Dr. Frank FORTUNATO
30 Development Coordinator Ms. Carol HART
88 Director of Recruitment Mr. Joseph JAMERSON
07 Director of Admissions Mr. Juan LOPEZ

Rollins College (L)

1000 Holt Avenue, Winter Park FL 32789-4499
County: Orange FICE Identification: 001515
Unit ID: 136950
Telephone: (407) 646-2000 Carnegie Class: Masters/L
FAX Number: (407) 646-2600 Calendar System: Semester
URL: www.rollins.edu
Established: 1885 Annual Undergrad Tuition & Fees: $53,716
Enrollment: 3,104 Coed
Affiliation or Control: Independent Non-Profit IRS Status: 501(c)3
Highest Offering: Doctorate
Accreditation: SC, ABAI, CACREP, MUS

01 President Dr. Grant H. CORNWELL
05 VP Acad Affairs/Provost Dr. Susan R. SINGER
32 Vice President Student Affairs Ms. Donna LEE
10 Vice President Business/Finance Mr. Ed KANIA
13 Chief Information Officer Mr. Troy THOMASON
20 Dean of the Faculty Dr. Jennifer CAVENAUGH
35 Asst VP Stdnt Affs/Int Dn of Stdnts Mr. Leon HAYNER
84 VP of Enrollment Mgmt and Marketing Dr. Faye F. TYDLASKA
50 Dean Crummer Grad Sch of Business Dr. Deborah F. CROWN
55 Dean Holt School Dr. Robert SANDERS
42 Dean of Religious Life Rev. Katrina JENKINS
21 Assoc VP Finance/Asst Treasurer Mr. William SHORT
26 VP Communications & External Rels Mr. Sam STARK
15 Assoc VP Human Res/Risk Management Mr. Matt HAWKS
108 Asst Provost Inst Effectiveness Dr. Toni STROLLO HOLBROOK
41 Athletic Director Ms. Pennie PARKER
37 Director of Financial Aid Mr. Steve BOOKER
104 Director of International Programs Ms. Giselda BEAUDIN
07 Dean of Admission Ms. Zaire MCCOY
36 Asst VP of Career & Life Planning Dr. Lisa JOHNSON
18 Asst VP of Facilities Management Mr. Jeremy WILLIAMSON
19 Assistant VP Public Safety Mr. Ken MILLER
29 Sr Director Alumni Engagement Ms. Andria SILVA
111 VP for Institutional Advancement Ms. Laurie HOUCK
102 Director of Foundation Relations Mr. Joseph MONTI
06 Registrar Ms. Stephanie HENNING
40 Manager of Bookstore Ms. Mary VITELLI
04 Exec Assistant to the President Ms. Jillian SCHUMM
23 Director of Wellness Ms. Connie BRISCOE
25 Director Contracts/Grants Admin Ms. Devon MASSOT
35 Asst VP Student Affairs/Community Ms. Michele MEYER
08 Director of Olin Library Dr. Deborah PROSSER

88 Director of Institutional Analytics .... Mr. Meghal PARIKH
113 Director of Student Accounts/Bursar .... Mr. Cory BADEN

Saber College (A)

3990 West Flagler Street, Ste 103, Miami FL 33134
County: Miami-Dade FICE Identification: 036964
Unit ID: 449506
Telephone: (305) 443-9170 Carnegie Class: Spec 2-yr-Health
FAX Number: (305) 443-8441 Calendar System: Other
URL: www.sabercollege.edu
Established: 1972 Annual Undergrad Tuition & Fees: N/A
Enrollment: 41 Coed
Affiliation or Control: Independent Non-Profit IRS Status: 501(c)3
Highest Offering: Associate Degree
Accreditation: COE, PTAA

01 Chief Administrator .... Ms. Josefina HABIF
05 Dean of Academic Affairs .... Ms. Amarilis SOMOZA
66 Director Nursing Program .... Ms. Ronda MIMS
76 Dir Physical Therapist Asst Program .... Ms. Karen AROCHA

St. John Vianney College Seminary (B)

2900 SW 87th Avenue, Miami FL 33165-3244
County: Miami-Dade FICE Identification: 008075
Unit ID: 137272
Telephone: (305) 223-4561 Carnegie Class: Spec-4-yr-Faith
FAX Number: (305) 223-0650 Calendar System: Semester
URL: www.sjvcs.edu
Established: 1959 Annual Undergrad Tuition & Fees: $23,100
Enrollment: 77 Male
Affiliation or Control: Roman Catholic IRS Status: 501(c)3
Highest Offering: Master's
Accreditation: SC

01 Rector & President .... Rev. Pablo A. NAVARRO
32 Vice Rector/Dean of Students .... Rev. Bryan GARCIA
42 Head Spiritual Director .... Rev. Daniel MARTIN
05 Chief Academic Officer .... Dr. Paola BERNARDINI
06 Registrar .... Dr. Pablo MARTINEZ
07 Director of Admissions .... Rev. Pablo A. NAVARRO
09 Director of Institutional Research .... Dr. Jose ORTA
10 Chief Financial/Business Officer .... Deacon Edgar KELLY
15 Chief Human Resources Officer .... Deacon Edgar KELLY
18 Chief Facilities/Physical Plant .... Rev. Pablo A. NAVARRO
26 Chief Public Relations Officer .... Mr. Iancarlo ARISPE

St. Johns River State College (C)

5001 St. Johns Avenue, Palatka FL 32177-3897
County: Putnam FICE Identification: 001523
Unit ID: 137281
Telephone: (386) 312-4200 Carnegie Class: Bac/Assoc-Assoc Dom
FAX Number: (386) 312-4229 Calendar System: Semester
URL: www.sjrstate.edu
Established: 1958 Annual Undergrad Tuition & Fees (In-District): $2,830
Enrollment: 6,828 Coed
Affiliation or Control: State/Local IRS Status: 501(c)3
Highest Offering: Baccalaureate
Accreditation: SC, ADNUR, ART, CAHIIM, COARC, EMT, NUR, RAD

01 President .... Mr. Joe PICKENS
43 Senior VP/General Counsel .... Dr. Melissa C. MILLER
32 Vice President Student Affairs .... Dr. Gilbert L. EVANS, JR.
05 VP & CAO/Exec Dir St Augustine .... Dr. Melanie A. BROWN
10 Vice President Finance & Admin/CFO .... Dr. Lynn POWERS
30 Vice Pres Develop/External Affairs .... Mrs. Caroline D. TINGLE
108 VP Assessment/Research & Tech .... Dr. Rosalind M. HUMERICK
103 VP Workforce/CTE .... Dr. David CAMPBELL
20 Associate VP Academic Affairs .... Dr. Edward K. JORDAN
13 Chief Information Officer .... Mr. Richard C. ANDERSON
15 Director of Human Resources .... Ms. Edie BRUCE
09 Assistant VP Ass/Research & Grants .... Dr. Ellen BURNS
21 Assistant VP for Finance .... Mr. Randall PETERSON
49 Dean of Arts & Sciences .... Mr. Mike KELLER
19 Dean of Crim Justice/Public Safety .... Dr. Jeffrey C. LEE
53 Dean of Teacher Education .... Dr. Myrna L. ALLEN
57 Dean of Florida School of the Arts .... Mr. Alain R. HENTSCHEL
08 Dean of Library Services .... Dr. Christina WILL
66 Dean of Nursing .... Dr. Diane P. PAGANO
55 Dean of Adult Education .... Dr. Melissa PERRY
76 Dean of Allied Health .... Dr. Holly COULLIETTE
75 Dean of Technical Education .... Dr. John W. PATERSON
88 Exec Dir Thrasher-Horne Center .... Mr. Bob OLSON
37 Director of Financial Aid .... Ms. Suzanne M. EVANS
77 Director of Computer Education .... Dr. John ETIENNE
50 Director of Business Education .... Mr. Joel C. ABO
102 Dir of Foundation/Alumni Engagement .... Mr. Brian BERGEN
51 Dir of Dual Enroll & College Access .... Mrs. Meghan DEPUTY
26 Director of Public Relations .... Mrs. Susan B. KESSLER
121 Director of Academic Advising .... Ms. Karen THOMAS
88 Director of Testing/Student Support .... Ms. Sarah TAYLOR
106 Director of eLearning .... Mr. Jack C. HALL
06 Registrar .... Mrs. Susanne B. LINEBERGER

Saint Leo University (D)

33701 State Road 52 W, Saint Leo FL 33574-6665
County: Pasco FICE Identification: 001526
Unit ID: 137032
Telephone: (352) 588-8200 Carnegie Class: Masters/L
FAX Number: (352) 588-8654 Calendar System: Semester
URL: www.saintleo.edu
Established: 1889 Annual Undergrad Tuition & Fees: $24,640
Enrollment: 9,832 Coed
Affiliation or Control: Roman Catholic IRS Status: 501(c)3
Highest Offering: Doctorate
Accreditation: SC, ACBSP, CEA, COSMA, SW

01 President .... Dr. Jeffrey SENESE
05 VP Academic Affairs .... Dr. Mary SPOTO
84 VP University Enrollment Management .... Dr. Senthil KUMAR
10 VP Business Affairs/CFO .... Mr. John NISBET
111 VP University Advancement .... Ms. Carla WILLIS
32 VP Student Affairs .... Dr. Jen SHAW
03 Senior Vice President .... Ms. Melanie STORMS
04 Assistant to the President .... Ms. Abigail APPLETON
13 Chief Technology Officer .... Mr. Daron MCNAB
88 Associate VP Regional Accreditation .... Dr. Diane BALL
43 Associate VP/General Counsel .... Ms. Staci SHELLEY
15 AVP Human Resources .... Ms. Susan MARTIN
42 Chaplain for University Ministries .... Fr. Randall MEISSEN
35 Associate VP Student Affairs .... Mr. Kenneth POSNER
85 AVP Worldwide Student Services .... Mr. Shadel HAMILTON
38 Director Counseling Services .... Mr. Lawson JOLLY
49 Dean School of Arts & Sciences .... Dr. Heather PARKER
53 Dean School of Educ/Social Svcs .... Dr. Susan KINSELLA
50 Dean School of Business .... Vacant
58 Dir Grad Studies Criminal Justice .... Dr. Phillip NEELEY
58 Dir Grad Studies in Education .... Dr. Fern AEFSKY
70 Dir Grad Studies in Social Work .... Ms. Courtney WIEST
73 Dir Graduate Studies in Theology .... Dr. Randall WOODARD
88 Director Graduate Creative Writing .... Dr. Steven KISTULENTZ
06 Registrar .... Mrs. Karen HATFIELD
08 Director Library Services .... Dr. Doris VAN KAMPEN-BREIT
88 Asst VP of Learning Design .... Dr. Karen HAHN
88 Director Student Learning .... Vacant
39 Dir Residence Life & Leadership .... Vacant
88 Exec Dir Academic Administration .... Mr. Joseph TADEO
41 Director Intercollegiate Athletics .... Mr. Francis REIDY
18 AVP Facilities Management .... Mr. Jose CABAN
19 Director Campus Security & Safety .... Mr. Vincent D'AMBROSIO
22 Director Accessibility Services .... Mr. Michael BAILEY
29 Director Alumni Engagement .... Vacant
110 Director Advancement Services .... Vacant
85 Exec Director PDSO Global Affairs .... Ms. Paige RAMSEY-HAMACHER
16 Director Human Resources .... Ms. Jennifer ALEXANDER
21 Senior Assoc VP Finance .... Mr. James DETUCCIO
96 Mgr Accts Payable/Sponsor Billing .... Ms. Laura SOLBERG
114 Director of Budgets .... Vacant
116 Director Internal Audit Services .... Ms. Monica KESSEL
12 Asst VP Military Center Operations .... Vacant
12 Asst VP Tampa Region .... Mr. Tyler UPSHAW
12 Asst VP Florida Region .... Ms. Katie DEGNER
103 Learning & Development Manager .... Mr. Joe ARNER
109 Director Dining Services .... Mr. Justin BUSH
88 Executive Officer .... Ms. Marcia MALIA
37 Associate VP of Financial Aid .... Ms. Melinda CLARK
26 AVP University Communications .... Ms. Marie THORNSBERRY
108 Dir of Institutional Effectiveness .... Vacant
89 Director First Year Experience .... Ms. Dawn MCELVEEN
119 Director Information Security .... Mr. Darius LEWIS
121 Chief Ofcr World Wide Stdnt Success .... Ms. Zaheda HERMAN
09 Chief Institutional Officer .... Dr. William HAMILTON

St. Petersburg College (E)

PO Box 13489, Saint Petersburg FL 33733-3489
County: Pinellas FICE Identification: 001528
Unit ID: 137078
Telephone: (727) 341-4772 Carnegie Class: Bac/Assoc-Mixed
FAX Number: (727) 341-3318 Calendar System: Semester
URL: www.spcollege.edu
Established: 1927 Annual Undergrad Tuition & Fees (In-District): $2,682
Enrollment: 26,430 Coed
Affiliation or Control: Local IRS Status: 501(c)3
Highest Offering: Baccalaureate
Accreditation: SC, ADNUR, CAHIIM, CEA, COARC, DH, EMT, FUSER, NURSE, PTAA, RAD

01 President .... Dr. Tonjua L. WILLIAMS
05 VP Academic Affairs .... Dr. Matthew LIAO-TROTH
32 VP Student Affairs .... Dr. Jamelle CONNER
10 VP Finance and Business Operations .... Janette HUNT
18 Associate VP Facilities/Inst .... Rodney WHEATON
15 Chief Human Resources/Talent Ofcr .... Darryl WRIGHT-GREENE
111 VP Inst Advance/Exec Dir Foundation .... Jesse TURTLE
114 Associate VP Budgeting .... Dr. Hector LORA
84 Assoc Student Exp & Strat Innov .... Dr. Patrick RINARD
37 Assoc VP Financial Asst Svcs .... Michael J. BENNETT
20 Assoc VP Academic Affs/Partnership .... Catherine C. KENNEDY
21 AVP Business & Financial Svcs .... Mike MEIGS
108 AVP Institutional Effect/Acad Svcs .... Dr. Sabrina CRAWFORD
103 Career Connections Director .... Dr. Jason KRUPP
43 General Counsel .... Suzanne GARDNER
12 Provost Clearwater Campus .... Dr. Stanley VITTETOE
12 Provost/Health Ed Ctr and Allstate .... Dr. Eric CARVER
12 Provost St Petersburg Campus .... Dr. Leslie HAFER
12 Provost Seminole Campus/eCampus .... Dr. Mark STRICKLAND
12 Provost Tarpon Springs Campus .... Dr. Rodrigo DAVIS
12 Provost Downtown/Midtown .... Dr. Tashika GRIFFITH
22 Dir Equal Access/Equal Opp/Title IX .... Pam SMITH
96 Director of Procurement .... Vacant
38 Student Support Manager .... Vacant
61 Dean Col of Policy/Ethics/Leg Stds .... Dr. Susan S. DEMERS
83 Dean Social & Behavioral Sciences .... Dr. Joseph SMILEY
88 Associate VP Collegiate High School .... Starla METZ
88 President Faculty Senate .... Dr. Robin BOWER
50 Dean College of Business .... Vacant
81 Dean Mathematics .... Jimmy CHANG
65 Dean Natural Science .... Dr. Natavia MIDDLETON
79 Dean Humanities/Fine Arts .... Dr. Barbara HUBBARD
53 Dean College of Education .... Dr. Kimberly HARTMAN
60 Dean Communications .... Joseph LEOPOLD
76 Dean College of Health Sciences .... Dr. Deanna STENTIFORD
74 Assoc Dean Veterinary Technology .... Dr. Cynthia GREY
72 Dean College of Comp & Info Tech .... Dr. John DUFF
66 Dean College of Nursing .... Dr. Louisana LOUIS
90 Exec Director Academic Technology .... Christopher HARVEY
110 Exec Director Advancement Svcs .... Theresa MCFARLAND
08 Exec Director Learning Resources .... Matthew BODIE
07 Director of Admissions and Records .... Eva CHRISTENSEN
09 Director of Institutional Research .... Djuan FOX
100 Chief of Staff .... Jackie SKRYD
104 Director International Programs .... Frank JURKOVIC
108 Dir Institutional Effectiveness .... Magaly TYMMS
13 Chief Information Officer .... Zoran STANISIC
19 Director College Security Services .... Daniel BARTO
25 Exec Dir of Grants Development .... Dr. Katie SHULTZ
86 Director Government Relations .... Eired EDDY
41 Athletic Director .... Davie GILL
26 Exec Dir Marketing & Strategic Comm .... Rita FARLOW
30 Executive Director of Development .... Vacant
28 Equity Diversity and Incl Director .... Dr. Devona PIERRE
88 Exec Dir Institutional Eff/Acad Svc .... Dr. Kellie ZIEMAK
101 Secretary of the Institution/Board .... Rebecca TURNER

St. Thomas University (F)

16401 NW 37th Avenue, Miami Gardens FL 33054-6498
County: Miami-Dade FICE Identification: 001468
Unit ID: 137476
Telephone: (305) 625-6000 Carnegie Class: Masters/L
FAX Number: (305) 628-6510 Calendar System: Semester
URL: www.stu.edu
Established: 1961 Annual Undergrad Tuition & Fees: $32,940
Enrollment: 5,601 Coed
Affiliation or Control: Roman Catholic IRS Status: 501(c)3
Highest Offering: Doctorate
Accreditation: SC, LAW, NURSE, @THEOL

01 President .... Mr. David A. ARMSTRONG
05 Provost/Chief Academic Officer .... Dr. Jeremy L. MORELAND
10 VP Admin/Chief Financial Officer .... Ms. Linda WAGNER
111 Vice Pres Philanthropy .... Ms. Robyn S. HOFFMAN
106 Vice Provost Online/Adult Education .... Vacant
20 VP Acad Affs/Dean of Academic Pgms .... Dr. Luis C. FERNANDEZ-TORRES
26 VP of Marketing/Communications .... Mr. Carlos A. DE YARZA
42 VP for Mission & Ministry .... Rev. Rafael CAPÓ
06 Registrar .... Mrs. Maria ABDEL
37 Director Financial Aid .... Ms. Margherite POWELL
08 Associate Library Director .... Ms. Jessica OROZCO
21 Assoc VP Finance & Controller .... Mrs. Maribel SMITH
18 Facilities Supervisor .... Mr. Christopher TARRANT
15 Director of Human Resources .... Ms. Monica CRUZ
09 Director of Institutional Research .... Dr. Eric GODIN
41 Director of Athletics .... Mr. William E. RYCHEL
32 AVP of Student Affairs/Compliance .... Mr. Matthew ROCHE
121 Director of Student Success Center .... Ms. Gretell GARCIA
88 SACSCOC Liaison .... Dr. Pamela CINGEL
07 Director of Admissions .... Ms. Whitney E. BATTOE
04 Exec Admin Assistant to the Pres .... Ms. Marina UGALDE
100 Chief of Staff/VP of Enrollment .... Ms. Jameka A. WINDHAM
61 Law School Dean .... Ms. Tamara F. LAWSON

St. Vincent De Paul Regional Seminary (G)

10701 S Military Trail, Boynton Beach FL 33436-4899
County: Palm Beach FICE Identification: 008223
Unit ID: 136701
Telephone: (561) 732-4424 Carnegie Class: Spec-4-yr-Faith
FAX Number: (561) 737-2205 Calendar System: Semester
URL: www.svdp.edu
Established: 1963 Annual Graduate Tuition & Fees: N/A
Enrollment: 142 Coed
Affiliation or Control: Roman Catholic IRS Status: 501(c)3
Highest Offering: Master's; No Undergraduates
Accreditation: THEOL

01 Rector/President .... Rev. Alfredo I. HERNANDEZ
03 Vice Rector/Dean Human Formation .... Rev. Gregg CAGGIANELLI
05 Academic Dean .... Rev. Timothy CUSICK
10 Treasurer .... Mr. Keith PARKER
08 Director of the Library .... Mr. Arthur QUINN
04 Administrative Asst to President .... Mrs. Herminia C. GARCIA
09 Dir Inst Research/Assessment .... Dr. S. Mary KRYSIAK BITTAR
111 Chief Development/Advancement .... Ms. Deb LINDSAY
06 Registrar .... Mrs. Alicia RUEFF

San Ignacio University (H)

3905 NW 107th Ave, Suite 301, Doral FL 33178
County: Miami-Dade Identification: 667130
Unit ID: 486239
Telephone: (305) 629-2929 Carnegie Class: Spec-4-yr-Bus

FAX Number: N/A Calendar System: Semester
URL: www.sanignaciouniversity.edu
Established: 2007 Annual Undergrad Tuition & Fees: $10,400
Enrollment: 232 Coed
Affiliation or Control: Proprietary IRS Status: Proprietary
Highest Offering: Master's
Accreditation: ACICS

01 President Dr. Federico MARTINEZ
11 VP Operations/Corporate Affairs Ezer TOSSAS
05 Dean of Academic Affairs Dr. Althia ELLIS
08 Head Librarian Silvia LOPEZ
15 Human Resources Senior Coordinator Ivette BAJANDAS
37 Financial Aid Coordinator Fabiola LAGARDERE
10 Director of Administration/Finance Carmen RODRIGUEZ
06 Registrar Jennifer GONZALEZ
07 Director of Admissions Carolina LANDAETA
09 Director of Institutional Research Vacant
54 Dean of Engineering Vacant

Santa Fe College (A)

3000 NW 83rd Street, Gainesville FL 32606-6200
County: Alachua FICE Identification: 001519
Unit ID: 137096
Telephone: (352) 395-5000 Carnegie Class: Bac/Assoc-Assoc Dom
FAX Number: (352) 395-5581 Calendar System: Semester
URL: www.sfcollege.edu
Established: 1965 Annual Undergrad Tuition & Fees (In-District): $2,563
Enrollment: 12,607 Coed
Affiliation or Control: Local IRS Status: 501(c)3
Highest Offering: Baccalaureate
Accreditation: SC, ADNUR, CAHIIM, COARC, CONST, CVT, DA, DH, DMS, EMT, MT, NMT, NURSE, POLYT, PTAA, RAD, SURGT

01 President Dr. Paul BROADIE, II
05 Interim Provost/VP Academic Affairs Dr. Lisa ARMOUR
10 Chief Financial Ofcr/VP Admin Affs Mr. Andy BARNES
32 Vice President Student Affairs Dr. Naima BROWN
111 Vice President Ofc for Advancement Mr. Chuck CLEMONS
04 Assistant to the President Ms. Cathy KEEN
20 Assoc Vice Pres Academic Affairs Dr. Jodi LONG
20 Assoc Vice Pres Academic Affairs Dr. Stefanie WASCHULL
104 Asst VP Academic Affairs Dr. Vilma FUENTES
13 Assoc VP Information Tech Services Mr. Bill PENNEY
18 Assoc VP Gov Affs & Facilities Svcs Mr. Liam MCCLAY
35 Assoc VP Student Affairs Dr. Dan RODKIN
22 Dean Access and Inclusion Dr. Cheryl CALHOUN
25 Director Sponsored Projects Ms. Claudia GRANT
35 Asst Vice Pres Student Affairs Dr. Beatrice AWONIYI
43 Legal Counsel Ms. Patti P. LOCASCIO
06 College Registrar Mr. Mike HUTLEY
88 Dir High Sch Dual Enrollment Pgm Ms. Jennifer HOMARD
121 Dir Advising & Career Exploration Ms. Andrea EVANGELIST
41 Athletic Director Mr. Greg MCVEY
08 Interim Director Library Service Ms. Nance LEMPINEN-LEEDY
19 Director Institute of Public Safety Mr. Tom ACKERMAN
35 Director of Student Life Dr. Tracey REEVES
96 Director of Purchasing Mr. David SHLAFER
28 Coordinator Col Achievement Pgm Ms. Dana LINDSEY
37 Director Student Financial Aid Ms. Kamia MWANGO
15 Director Human Resources Ms. Lela FRYE
09 Director of Institutional Research Mr. Gary HARTGE
07 Coordinator Admissions & Advising Ms. Carolyn DAS
26 Chief Public Relations/Marketing Ms. Teri MCCLELLAN
110 Assoc VP Advancement Mr. John HOOKER
106 Asst VP Academic Technologies Ms. Page JERZAK

Sarasota University (B)

5104 N Lockwood Ridge Road, Ste 102,
Sarasota FL 34234
County: Sarasota Identification: 667337
Telephone: (866) 582-8448 Carnegie Class: Not Classified
FAX Number: N/A Calendar System: Trimester
URL: www.sarasotauniversity.edu
Established: 2013 Annual Graduate Tuition & Fees: N/A
Enrollment: N/A Coed
Affiliation or Control: Independent Non-Profit IRS Status: 501(c)3
Highest Offering: Master's; No Undergraduates
Accreditation: DEAC

01 Founder & President Dr. Ronald OGRODNIK
05 Vice Pres Academic Affairs Dr. Chuck MLYNARCZYK
11 Dir of Operations/Regulatory Affs Dr. Doug RIEDMILLER

Schiller International University (C)

400 N. Tampa St., Suite 1700, Tampa FL 33602
County: Pinellas FICE Identification: 023141
Unit ID: 404338
Telephone: (727) 736-5082 Carnegie Class: Spec-4-yr-Bus
FAX Number: (727) 738-8405 Calendar System: Semester
URL: www.schiller.edu
Established: 1964 Annual Undergrad Tuition & Fees: $14,360
Enrollment: 30 Coed
Affiliation or Control: Proprietary IRS Status: Proprietary
Highest Offering: Master's
Accreditation: ACICS

05 Provost Dr. Victoria BAMOND
32 Dean of Students Ms. Jeanette ESPINAL

Seminole State College of Florida (D)

100 Weldon Boulevard, Sanford FL 32773-6199
County: Seminole FICE Identification: 001520
Unit ID: 137209
Telephone: (407) 708-4722 Carnegie Class: Bac/Assoc-Assoc Dom
FAX Number: (407) 708-2139 Calendar System: Semester
URL: www.seminolestate.edu
Established: 1965 Annual Undergrad Tuition & Fees (In-District): $3,131
Enrollment: 16,298 Coed
Affiliation or Control: Local IRS Status: 501(c)3
Highest Offering: Baccalaureate
Accreditation: SC, ACBSP, ADNUR, CAHIIM, CIDA, COARC, EMT, NUR, PTAA

01 President Dr. Georgia LORENZ
10 Vice Pres Business Operations/CFO Mr. Joe MAZUR
05 VP Academic Affairs/CAO Dr. Laura ROSS
32 VP Student Affairs Dr. Johnny CRAIG
13 VP Information Resources/CIO Dr. Dick HAMANN
30 VP Resource Develop & Economic Dev Dr. John GYLLIN
21 AVP Finance & Budget Ms. Judi COOPER
35 AVP Student Development Dr. Jan LLOYD-LESLEY
07 AVP Admissions Mrs. Pamela MENNECHEY
12 Dean of Students Altamonte Springs Ms. Lynn GARRETT
12 Dean of Students Oviedo Campus Mr. Jeffery GIBBS
08 Dean Learning Resources Vacant
107 AVP School of Career & Profession Dr. Cheryl CICOTTI
54 AVP Engineering/Design & IT Mr. Basim KHARTABIL
26 Dir College & Community Relations Ms. Deborah RICHARD
91 Director Networks Mr. Julio VALENTIN
38 Director Counseling and Advising Ms. Deborah LYNCH
20 Director Curriculum Ms. Carlene MCNEIL
15 AVP Human Resources Ms. Mae ASHBY
06 Director Enrollment Svcs/ Registrar Ms. Barbara RODRIGUEZ-LAMAS
37 Interim Director Financial Aid Ms. Melina ABREU
09 Director Inst Effectiveness Dr. Thomas HOKE
41 Director Intercollegiate Athletics Mr. Kurt ESSER
36 Asst Director Career Development Ms. Lisette GUILLEN-DOLBY
14 AVP Information Technology Ms. Pilar ACOSTA
106 Dir Online Education/E-learning Mr. Brian CROSE
28 AVP Equity & Diversity/Title IX Ms. Janet BALANOFF
102 Dir Foundation Finance & Operations Mr. Sean BARTH
110 Assistant Director of Development Ms. Laura SCHUMACHER
04 Admin Assistant to the President Ms. Cheryl R. DALEY
19 Director Security/Safety Mr. Miguel SIERRA
43 Director Legal Svcs/General Counsel Mr. J. Paul CARLAND
103 Dean Workforce Development Mr. Joseph HUSTON
18 Director Facilities Mr. Douglas BENTLEY
96 Director of Purchasing Mr. Gregory LONG

South Florida Bible College (E)

2200 SW 10th Street, Deerfield Beach FL 33442
County: Broward FICE Identification: 032643
Unit ID: 366003
Telephone: (954) 637-2268 Carnegie Class: Spec-4-yr-Faith
FAX Number: (954) 719-3780 Calendar System: Semester
URL: www.sfbc.edu
Established: 1985 Annual Undergrad Tuition & Fees: $7,140
Enrollment: 313 Coed
Affiliation or Control: Interdenominational IRS Status: 501(c)3
Highest Offering: Doctorate
Accreditation: BI

01 President Dr. Mary A. DRABIK
03 Vice President Josiah STEPHAN
05 Chief Academic Officer Dr. Jodyann REID
10 Chief Financial Officer David SAYERS
06 Registrar Dr. Michael RACKLEY
08 Librarian Paula STEVENSON
20 Dean of Faculty Dr. Esa AUTERO
32 Dean of Students Vacant
29 Director Alumni Relations Casey PALACIOUS
84 Director Enrollment Management Germil AGENOR
13 Chief Info Technology Officer (CIO) Vacant
04 Administrative Asst to President Neeta PRAKASH
09 Director of Institutional Research Davi BAKTHAKUMAR
15 Chief Human Resources Officer Crystal BERTLING
19 Director Security/Safety Hector PEREZ
37 Director Student Financial Aid Dr. Thomas DRABIK
07 Director of Admissions Jeremy SCOTT

South Florida State College (F)

600 W College Drive, Avon Park FL 33825-9399
County: Highlands FICE Identification: 001522
Unit ID: 137315
Telephone: (863) 453-6661 Carnegie Class: Bac/Assoc-Assoc Dom
FAX Number: (863) 453-0165 Calendar System: Trimester
URL: www.southflorida.edu
Established: 1965 Annual Undergrad Tuition & Fees (In-District): $3,165
Enrollment: 2,710 Coed
Affiliation or Control: Local IRS Status: 501(c)3
Highest Offering: Baccalaureate
Accreditation: SC, ADNUR, DA, DH, EMT, NUR, RAD

01 President Dr. Thomas C. LEITZEL
05 Vice Pres Educational/Stdnt Svcs Dr. Sidney VALENTINE
10 Controller Mrs. Theresa VOROUS
11 Vice Pres Administrative Services Mr. Peter ELLIOTT
75 Dean Applied Science & Tech Mr. Erik CHRISTENSEN
49 Dean Arts & Sciences Dr. James HAWKER
28 Director Cultural Programs Ms. Cynthia GARREN
111 Exec Dir Institutional Advancement Mrs. Jamie BATEMAN
32 Dean Student Services Mr. Mark BUKOWSKI
12 Director DeSoto Campus Mrs. Asena MOTT
12 Director Hardee Campus Ms. Teresa CRAWFORD
12 Director Lake Placid Center Mr. Randall K. PAEPLOW
26 Director Community Relations Mrs. Melissa KUEHNLE
106 Director eLearning Vacant
15 Director Human Res/EA-EO & ADA Ofcr Mr. Donald KESTERSON
18 Dir Remodeling/Reno & Maint Dr. Robert E. FLORES
06 Registrar Mr. Jonathan STERN
41 Athletic Director Mr. Richard J. HITT
36 Director Career Development Center Mr. Robert HAMPTON
37 Director Financial Aid Mrs. Tina STETSON
13 Chief Information Officer Dr. Christopher VAN DER KAAY
38 Chair Counseling Mrs. Charla ELLERKER
08 Library Services Ms. Lena PHELPS
96 Coordinator Purchasing Mrs. Deborah OLSON
07 Director of Admissions Vacant
76 Dean Division of Health Services Dr. Michele HESTON

South University (G)

9801 Belevedere Road, Royal Palm Beach FL 33411
Telephone: (561) 273-6500 Identification: 666117
Accreditation: &SC, ACBSP, #ARCPA, CACREP, NURSE, PTAA

† Regional accreditation is carried under the parent institution in Savannah, GA.

South University (H)

4401 North Himes Ave Ste 175, Tampa FL 33614-7095
Telephone: (813) 393-3800 Identification: 770913
Accreditation: &SC, ACBSP, ARCPA, NURSE, OTA, PTAA

† Branch campus of South University, Savannah, GA

Southeastern College (I)

5875 NW 163rd Street, Ste 101, Miami Lakes FL 33014
Telephone: (305) 820-5003 Identification: 666290
Accreditation: ACCSC, ADNUR, DMS, SURGT

† Branch campus of Southeastern College, West Palm Beach, FL.

Southeastern College (J)

1756 North Congress Avenue,
West Palm Beach FL 33409
County: Palm Beach FICE Identification: 031239
Unit ID: 428170
Telephone: (561) 433-2330 Carnegie Class: Spec 2-yr-Health
FAX Number: (561) 433-9025 Calendar System: Other
URL: www.sec.edu
Established: 1988 Annual Undergrad Tuition & Fees: $20,246
Enrollment: 690 Coed
Affiliation or Control: Proprietary IRS Status: Proprietary
Highest Offering: Associate Degree
Accreditation: ACCSC, DMS, SURGT

01 President Ms. Dana HUTTON
05 Dean Academic Affairs Ms. Doris COMBS
37 Director of Financial Aid Mr. Travis SMITH
06 Registrar Ms. Cindy GALT
32 Director Student Services Ms. Latoya JAMES

Southeastern University (K)

1000 Longfellow Boulevard, Lakeland FL 33801-6099
County: Polk FICE Identification: 001521
Unit ID: 137564
Telephone: (863) 667-5000 Carnegie Class: Masters/M
FAX Number: (863) 667-5200 Calendar System: Semester
URL: www.seu.edu
Established: 1935 Annual Undergrad Tuition & Fees: $27,520
Enrollment: 9,546 Coed
Affiliation or Control: Assemblies Of God Church IRS Status: 501(c)3
Highest Offering: Doctorate
Accreditation: SC, ACBSP, NURSE, SW, THEOL

01 President Dr. Kent INGLE
03 Executive Vice President Dr. James (Chris) OWEN
05 Provost Dr. Meghan GRIFFIN
32 VP for Student Development Mrs. Bethany THOMAS
84 VP for Enrollment Management Mr. Roy ROWLAND, IV
09 VP Inst Research/Effectiveness Dr. Cody LLOYD
10 VP for Finance Mr. Jeff SPEAR
31 VP of Strategic Partnerships Mr. Justin LATHROP
88 VP for Unrestricted Education Mr. Nicholas WALLSTEADT
08 Director of Library Services Mrs. Amy BEATTY
06 Registrar Mrs. Melissa MAISENBACHER
37 Exec Dir Student Financial Services Mr. Michael YOHE
88 Director of Hispanic Learning Ctr Ms. Betania TORRES
07 Exec Director of Admissions Trad Mrs. Sarah E. CLARK
15 Director Human Resources Mr. Geoffrey OTT
29 Director Alumni Relations Mr. Joel JOHNSON
18 Exec Dir Facilities/Physical Plant Mr. Norman (Mike) M. ALDERMAN
20 Director Academic Auxiliary Svcs Mrs. Laura C. BROWN
36 Director of Career Services Mrs. Emilee HILL

121 Dir Academic Center for Enrichment .... Mr. Paul CARTER
28 Dir of Multicultural Affairs .... Mr. Ray ALLEN
21 Senior Director Finance & Treasury .... Vacant
84 Director Enrollment Marketing .... Vacant
38 Dir Counseling/Health & Wellness .... Ms. Megan WAGNER
13 Chief Info Technology Officer (CIO) .... Dr. Cody LLOYD
19 Director Security/Safety .... Mr. David BRIGHT
20 Associate Provost .... Mrs. Amy BRATTEN
35 Exec Dir of Student Services .... Mrs. Sarahi S. FLEMING
100 Chief of Staff .... Mr. Michael STEINER
13 Sr Dir Info Mgmt & Digital Learning .... Mr. Justin E. ROSE
41 Athletic Director .... Mr. Drew WATSON
26 Chief Communications Officer .... Mrs. Dana DAVIS
39 Dir Resident Life/Student Housing .... Mr. Charlie MCNULTY

Southern Technical College (A)

1685 Medical Lane, Fort Myers FL 33907-1158

County: Lee FICE Identification: 022788
Unit ID: 366553
Telephone: (239) 939-4766 Carnegie Class: Bac/Assoc-Mixed
FAX Number: (239) 790-2118 Calendar System: Quarter
URL: www.southerntech.edu
Established: 1974 Annual Undergrad Tuition & Fees: $13,895
Enrollment: 1,125 Coed
Affiliation or Control: Proprietary IRS Status: Proprietary
Highest Offering: Baccalaureate
Accreditation: **ACICS**, ADNUR, SURTEC

01 Executive Director .... Mr. Mark GUTMANN
05 Director Education .... Mr. Esmail DARIAROW

Southern Technical College-Auburndale (B)

450 Havendale Boulevard, Auburndale FL 33823
Telephone: (863) 551-1112 Identification: 770705
Accreditation: **ACCSC**

Southern Technical College (C)

1485 Florida Mall Avenue, Orlando FL 32809

County: Orange FICE Identification: 039035
Unit ID: 446552
Telephone: (407) 438-6000 Carnegie Class: Assoc/HVT-High Trad
FAX Number: (407) 438-6005 Calendar System: Quarter
URL: www.southerntech.edu
Established: Annual Undergrad Tuition & Fees: N/A
Enrollment: 1,712 Coed
Affiliation or Control: Proprietary IRS Status: Proprietary
Highest Offering: Associate Degree
Accreditation: **ACCSC**

01 Executive Director .... Sandra MUSKOPF
05 Director of Education .... Rachel KINSER

Southern Technical College-Port Charlotte (D)

950 Tamiami Trail, Unit 109, Port Charlotte FL 33953
Telephone: (941) 391-8888 Identification: 770709
Accreditation: **ACICS**, SURTEC

Southern Technical College-Sanford (E)

2910 South Orlando Drive, Sanford FL 32773
Telephone: (407) 917-7658 Identification: 770704
Accreditation: **ACCSC**

Southern Technical College-Tampa (F)

3910 Riga Boulevard, Tampa FL 33619-1269
Telephone: (813) 630-4401 Identification: 770708
Accreditation: **ACICS**, DMS, SURTEC

State College of Florida, Manatee-Sarasota (G)

PO Box 1849, Bradenton FL 34206-7046

County: Manatee FICE Identification: 001504
Unit ID: 135391
Telephone: (941) 752-5000 Carnegie Class: Bac/Assoc-Mixed
FAX Number: (941) 727-6230 Calendar System: Semester
URL: www.scf.edu
Established: 1957 Annual Undergrad Tuition & Fees (In-District): $3,074
Enrollment: 9,242 Coed
Affiliation or Control: Local IRS Status: 501(c)3
Highest Offering: Baccalaureate
Accreditation: **SC**, ADNUR, DH, NUR, OTA, PTAA, RAD

01 President .... Dr. Carol F. PROBSTFELD
04 Exec Assistant to President .... Ms. Susan MARROCCO
10 VP Finance/Admin Services .... Ms. Julie JAKWAY
05 Executive Vice President & Provost .... Dr. Todd FRITCH
32 Dean Student Services .... Ms. Jaquelyn MCNEIL
108 Actg VP Inst Research/Effectiveness .... Mr. Ryan HALE
06 College Registrar .... Mr. Billy C. BENTON
20 Assoc Prov Academic/Faculty Affairs .... Mr. Mike KIEFER
102 Executive Director SCF Foundation .... Ms. Cassandra HOLMES
12 Dean Lakewood Ranch .... Vacant
84 AVP Student/Enrollment Services .... Ms. Stacey SHARPLES
26 AVP Communications & Marketing .... Ms. Jamie M. SMITH
18 AVP Facilities .... Mr. Chris WELLMAN
103 Director Workforce Services .... Ms. Lee KOTWICKI
08 Director Library Services .... Ms. Margaret E. HAWKINS
09 Director Institutional Research .... Mr. Bryce PRIDE
13 Director IT Operations .... Ms. Karla LAUER
43 General Counsel .... Mr. Steve PROUTY
88 Head of SCF Collegiate School .... Ms. Kelly MONOD
106 Director Online Learning .... Mr. Gary BAKER
19 Director Public Safety .... Mr. Shawn PATTEN
15 Director Human Resources .... Mr. Paul BERKLE

*State University System of Florida, Board of Governors (H)

325 W Gaines Street, Suite 1614,
Tallahassee FL 32399-0400

County: Leon FICE Identification: 008068
Unit ID: 137449
Telephone: (850) 245-0466 Carnegie Class: N/A
FAX Number: (850) 245-9685
URL: www.flbog.edu

01 Chancellor .... Mr. Marshall M. CRISER, III
05 Vice Chanc Academic/Student Affairs .... Dr. Christy ENGLAND
10 Vice Chanc Budget & Finance .... Mr. Tim JONES
43 General Counsel .... Mrs. Vikki SHIRLEY
22 Inspector General & Compliance .... Mrs. Julie LEFTHERIS
101 Corporate Secretary .... Mrs. Vikki SHIRLEY
86 Assoc Vice Chanc Govt Relations .... Mrs. Kristin WHITAKER
04 Assistant to the Chancellor .... Mrs. Shannon M. TRUE
26 Director of Communications .... Mrs. Renee FARGASON
13 Chief Info Technology Officer (CIO) .... Mr. Gene KOVACS
15 Director Personnel Services .... Mrs. Abigail MARTIN
18 Chief Facilities/Physical Plant .... Mr. Kevin PICHARD
09 Chief Data Officer .... Mr. Jason JONES
106 Assoc VC Innovation & Online Educ .... Dr. Nancy C. MCKEE
28 Chief Diversity/Equity & Inclusion .... Dr. Traki L. TAYLOR

*Florida Agricultural and Mechanical University (I)

1601 S. Martin Luther King Jr. Blvd, Tallahassee FL 32307

County: Leon FICE Identification: 001480
Unit ID: 133650
Telephone: (850) 599-3000 Carnegie Class: DU-Higher
FAX Number: (850) 599-3952 Calendar System: Semester
URL: www.famu.edu
Established: 1887 Annual Undergrad Tuition & Fees (In-State): $5,785
Enrollment: 9,184 Coed
Affiliation or Control: State IRS Status: 501(c)3
Highest Offering: Doctorate
Accreditation: **SC**, ACBSP, CAEP, CAHIIM, COARC, HSA, JOUR, LAW, NUR, OT, PH, PHAR, PTA, SW

00 Chair Board of Trustees .... Mr. Kelvin LAWSON
02 President .... Dr. Larry ROBINSON
05 Provost/VP Academic Affairs .... Dr. Maurice EDINGTON
10 VP Finance & Administration/CFO .... Dr. Alan D. ROBERTSON
32 Vice President Student Affairs .... Dr. William HUDSON, JR.
46 VP Research .... Dr. Charles WEATHERFORD
111 VP Univ Advancement/Exec Dir Fndn .... Dr. Shawnta FRIDAY-STROUD
116 VP Audit .... Mr. Joseph MALESZEWSKI
45 VP Strategic Planning/Analysis/IE .... Ms. Beverly BARRINGTON
43 VP Legal Affairs/Gen Counsel .... Ms. Denise WALLACE
100 Chief of Staff/BOT Liaison .... Ms. Linda BARGE-MILES
41 VP and Director Athletics .... Mr. Kortne GOSHA
26 Interim Director Communications .... Mr. Keith MILES
86 Director Governmental Relations .... Ms. Danielle MCBETH
04 Executive Asst to the President .... Ms. Cynthia HENRY
117 Chief Ethics and Compliance Officer .... Ms. Rica CALHOUN
53 Dean Education .... Dr. Allyson WATSON
67 Dean Pharmacy .... Dr. Johnnie EARLY
72 Dean Science & Technology .... Dr. Richard ALO
47 Dean Agriculture & Food Sciences .... Dr. Robert TAYLOR
83 Dean Social Sci/Arts & Humanities ... Dr. Valencia E. MATTHEWS
54 Dean FAMU-FSU Engineering .... Dr. J. Murray GIBSON
61 Dean College of Law .... Dr. Deidre KELLER
48 Dean Architecture & Engr Tech .... Mr. Rodner WRIGHT
76 Dean Allied Health Sciences .... Dr. Cynthia HUGHES HARRIS
50 Dean Business and Industry .... Dr. Shawnta FRIDAY-STROUD
60 Int Dean Journalism/Graphic Comm .... Dr. Bettye GRABLE
65 Dean School of the Environment .... Dr. Victor IBEANUSI
66 Dean Nursing .... Dr. Shelley JOHNSON
58 Assoc Provost & Dean Grad Studies ...... Dr. David JACKSON, JR.
08 Dean University Libraries .... Ms. Faye WATKINS
20 Assoc Provost for Undergrad Educ .... Dr. Lewis JOHNSON
20 Assoc Provost Faculty Affairs & Dev .... Dr. Genyne BOSTON
06 University Registrar .... Dr. Agatha ONWUNLI
89 Asst VP Freshman Studies .... Dr. Jennifer COLLINS
84 Assoc VP Enrollment Management .... Ms. Terri LITTLE-BERRY
37 Director Financial Aid .... Ms. Lisa STEWART
07 Interim Director Admissions .... Mr. Chester HOOD
19 Chief of Police/Dir Public Safety .... Mr. Terence CALLOWAY
35 Assoc VP Student Affairs .... Mr. Bomani SPELL
88 University Ombuds & Student Life .... Mr. Bryan F. SMITH
84 Assoc VP Student Affairs .... Mr. Nigel EDWARDS
13 Associate VP/CIO Info Tech Svcs .... Mr. Ronald HENRY
18 Assoc VP Facilities/Construction .... Mr. Chris HESSEL
15 Associate VP Human Resources .... Ms. Joyce INGRAM
28 Assoc VP HR/Director of Diversity .... Ms. Joyce INGRAM
09 Asst VP/Dir Institutional Research .... Dr. Khoi TO
21 Asst VP/Univ Controller .... Ms. Tonya JACKSON
104 Asst VP International Educ & Dev .... Dr. William HYNDMAN, III
88 Exec Dir Title III Programs .... Dr. Erick AKINS
105 Director ITS Services & Telecomm .... Mr. Ronald HENRY
36 Director Career Center .... Ms. Shereada HARRELL
25 Director Contracts & Grants .... Ms. Pamela BLOUNT
39 Director Student Housing .... Dr. Jennifer WILDER
38 Director Counseling Services .... Ms. Anika FIELDS
96 Director Procurement Services .... Ms. Mattie HOOD
23 Director Student Health Services .... Ms. Tanya TATUM
108 Director University Assessment .... Dr. Melanie WICINSKI
112 Asst VP Major/Principal Gifts .... Ms. Kimberly HANKERSON
30 Asst VP Fin Mgmt/Donor Relations .... Ms. Juanita JOHNSON
29 Asst VP Alumni Affairs .... Ms. Carmen CUMMINGS
22 Director EEO .... Ms. Carrie GAVIN
51 Director Continuing Education .... Ms. Phyllis WATSON
120 Director Instr Tech & Distance Ed .... Ms. Franzetta FITZ
109 Asst VP Administrative Services .... Ms. Rebecca BROWN
119 Chief Information Security Officer .... Mr. Clifford STOKES
114 Director University Budgets .... Ms. Nichole MURRY
122 Director of Student Activities .... Mr. Andre GREEN

*Florida Atlantic University (J)

PO Box 3091, 777 Glades Road,
Boca Raton FL 33431-0991

County: Palm Beach FICE Identification: 001481
Unit ID: 133669
Telephone: (561) 297-3000 Carnegie Class: DU-Higher
FAX Number: (561) 297-3942 Calendar System: Semester
URL: www.fau.edu
Established: 1961 Annual Undergrad Tuition & Fees (In-State): $4,879
Enrollment: 30,805 Coed
Affiliation or Control: State IRS Status: 501(c)3
Highest Offering: Doctorate
Accreditation: **SC**, CACREP, CAEP, CAMPEP, IPSY, MED, MUS, NURSE, PLNG, SP, SPAA, SW

02 President .... Dr. John KELLY
05 Provost/VP Academic Affairs .... Dr. Bret DANILOWICZ
10 VP Strategic Initiatives & CFO .... Vacant
32 VP Student Affairs/Enrollment .... Dr. Larry FAERMAN
46 Vice President Research .... Dr. Daniel FLYNN
11 Vice Pres Administrative Affairs .... Ms. Stacy VOLNICK
41 VP of Intercollegiate Athletics .... Mr. Brian WHITE
111 Vice President for Advancement .... Vacant
26 Vice President Public Affairs .... Mr. Peter HULL
43 General Counsel .... Mr. David KIAN
20 Vice Provost Academic Affairs .... Dr. Michele HAWKINS
20 Senior Associate Provost .... Dr. Russ IVY
13 Assoc Provost IT/CIO .... Mr. Jason BALL
12 Associate VP Jupiter Campus .... Dr. Rodney MURPHEY
12 Interim Assoc VP Broward Campus .... Ms. Linda JOHNSON
106 Exec Dir Online & Cont Educ .... Dr. Julie GOLDEN-BOTTI
88 Asst Vice Pres Acad Finance .... Ms. Christa EITEL
88 Asst Provost Acad Opers & Planning .... Dr. James CAPP
108 Asst Provost IEA .... Dr. Ying LIU
35 Assoc VP Student Affairs/Dean .... Ms. Audrey PUSEY
22 Exec Dir Equity/Inclusion/Compl .... Vacant
37 Asst VP Financial Aid/New Student .... Ms. Tracy BOULUKOS
80 Interim Dean of Design/Inquiry .... Dr. Naelys LUNA
49 Dean of Arts & Letters .... Dr. Michael HORSWELL
50 Dean of Business .... Dr. Daniel GROPPER
53 Dean of Education .... Dr. Stephen SILVERMAN
54 Dean of Engineering/Comp Sci .... Dr. Stella BATALAMA
92 Interim Dean of Honors College .... Dr. Timothy STEIGENGA
63 Dean of Medicine .... Vacant
66 Dean of Nursing .... Dr. Safiya GEORGE
81 Dean of Science .... Dr. Ata SARAJEDINI
97 Dean Undergraduate Studies .... Dr. Edward E. PRATT
58 Dean of Graduate Studies .... Dr. Robert STACKMAN
62 University Libraries Dean .... Vacant
88 Asst Dean/PK-12 Sch/Educational Pgm .... Mr. Joel HERBST
90 Director Enterprise Computing Svcs . Mr. Mehran BASIRATMAND
15 Asst Vice Pres Human Resources .... Ms. Chitra IYER
85 Exec Dir Center Global Engagement .... Dr. Mihaela METIANU

*Florida Gulf Coast University (K)

10501 FGCU Boulevard S, Fort Myers FL 33965-6565

County: Lee FICE Identification: 032553
Unit ID: 433660
Telephone: (239) 590-1000 Carnegie Class: Masters/L
FAX Number: (239) 590-1166 Calendar System: Semester
URL: www.fgcu.edu
Established: 1991 Annual Undergrad Tuition & Fees (In-State): $6,118
Enrollment: 15,358 Coed
Affiliation or Control: State IRS Status: 501(c)3
Highest Offering: Doctorate
Accreditation: **SC**, ANEST, #ARCPA, CAATE, CACREP, CAEP, IPSY, MT, MUS, NURSE, OT, PTA, SPAA, SW

02 President .... Dr. Michael V. MARTIN
05 EVP & Provost .... Dr. Mark RIEGER
10 Vice Pres Admin Services/Finance .... Mr. David VAZQUEZ
111 VP Univ Advance/Exec Dir Foundation .... Ms. Katherine GREEN
88 VP/VProv Strategy/Pgm Innovation .... Dr. Aysegul TIMUR
43 Vice President & General Counsel .... Ms. Vee LEONARD
32 Vice Pres Stdnt Success/Enrol Mgmt .... Dr. Mitch CORDOVA
20 AVP Academic Pgms/Curriculum Devel .... Dr. Dawn KIRBY
45 Sr Asc Prov/AVP Plng & Inst Perform .... Vacant
46 Interim VP Research Admin .... Mr. James CASEY

26 AVP Communications & Marketing ... Ms. Deborah WILTROUT
18 Asst VP Physical Plant ... Mr. Jim HEHL
04 Asst to Pres/University Ombuds ... Ms. Monique MCKAY
21 Assoc VP Admin Svcs & Finance ... Mr. Joseph MCDONALD
13 Asst VP information Technology Svcs ... Ms. Mary BANKS
15 Sr Assoc VP Admin Svcs ... Ms. Sara STENSRUD
20 Assoc Provost/VP Academic Affs ... Dr. Tony BARRINGER
21 Controller ... Ms. June GUTKNECHT
35 Int Asst VP/Dean of Students ... Dr. Christopher BLAKELY
49 Dean College Arts & Sciences ... Dr. Chuck LINDSEY
50 Dean Lutgert Col of Business ... Dr. Chris WESTLEY
53 Interim Dean College of Education ... Dr. Tom ROBERTS
76 Int Dean Col of Health/Human Svcs ... Dr. Shawn FELTON
54 Interim Dean U.A. Whitaker Col Engr ... Dr. Huzefa KAGDI
62 Dean Library Services ... Dr. Tracy ELLIOTT
38 Sr Dir Counseling/Wellness Svcs ... Dr. Jon L. BRUNNER
84 Assoc VP Enrollment Management ... Dr. Lisa JOHNSON
96 Director of Procurement Services ... Ms. Maryan EGAN
19 Chief University Police Dept ... Chief Kelli SMITH
18 Director Facilities Planning ... Mr. Greg LARSON
37 Asst VP Student Enroll & Fin Svc ... Mr. Jorge LOPEZ
06 University Registrar ... Mr. Christopher SAXBY
23 Medical Director ... Dr. Brian BOZZA
41 Director of Athletics ... Mr. Kenneth KAVANAGH
28 Dir EEC & Title IX Coord ... Ms. Precious GUNTER
85 Asst VP Acad Affairs Intl Programs ... Dr. Michael MCDONALD
106 Director Instructional Technology ... Mr. David JAEGER
13 Deputy CIO/Chief Info Security Ofcr ... Mr. Sven HAHUES
36 Director Career Development Svcs ... Ms. Rose FULLER
29 Director Alumni Relations ... Ms. Kimberly WALLACE
92 Dean Honors College ... Dr. Clay MOTLEY
09 Director Inst Research/Analysis ... Dr. Robert VINES
114 Director University Budgets ... Ms. Megan CLIPSE
39 Assoc VP Student Engagement ... Dr. Brian FISHER
86 Director Government Relations ... Ms. Jennifer GOEN
88 Dir Environmental Health/Safety ... Ms. Rhonda HOLTZCLAW
51 Asst VP Innovative Educ/Partnership ... Ms. Kristen VANSELOW
88 General Manager/WGCU ... Mr. Corey LEWIS
40 Manager Barnes & Noble at FGCU ... Mr. Larry DAVIS
121 Dir Ctr Academic Achievement ... Ms. Lindsay SINGH
04 Dir of Operations/President's Ofc ... Ms. Beverly D. BROWN
07 Asst VP University Admissions ... Mr. Derrell PUSTIZZI
101 Director Board Relations ... Ms. Tiffany REYNOLDS
104 Asst Director Study Abroad ... Mr. Matt RYAN
105 Director Web Services/AVP Marketing ... Mr. Jeffrey GARNER
108 Director Assessment/Accreditation ... Ms. Lenore BENEFIELD
25 Director Research/Sponsored Pgms ... Ms. Donna GILMORE
30 Sr Director of Development ... Ms. Dolly FARRELL

*Florida International University (A)

University Park, 11200 SW 8 Street, Miami FL 33199-0001
County: Miami-Dade FICE Identification: 009635
Unit ID: 133951
Telephone: (305) 348-2000 Carnegie Class: DU-Highest
FAX Number: N/A Calendar System: Semester
URL: www.fiu.edu
Established: 1965 Annual Undergrad Tuition & Fees (In-State): $6,565
Enrollment: 58,836 Coed
Affiliation or Control: State IRS Status: 501(c)3
Highest Offering: Doctorate
Accreditation: SC, ANEST, #ARCPA, ART, CAATE, CACREP, CAEP, CAEPN, CAHIIM, CIDA, CLPSY, CONST, DIETD, DIETI, FEPAC, HSA, IPSY, JOUR, LAW, LSAR, MED, MUS, NURSE, OPE, OT, PH, PTA, SP, SPAA, SW, THEA

01 President ... Dr. Mark ROSENBERG
100 Chief of Staff ... Vacant
05 Provost/EVP Academic Affairs ... Dr. Kenneth FURTON
20 SVP Student/Academic Affairs ... Dr. Elizabeth BEJAR
88 VP for Engagement ... Mr. Saif ISHOOF
10 CFO & Sr VP for Administration ... Dr. Kenneth JESSELL
111 Sr Vice President for Advancement ... Mr. Howard LIPMAN
09 AVP Analysis/Info Mgmt ... Dr. Hiselgis PEREZ
32 Dean of Students ... Dr. Bares PELAEZ
46 Vice President of Research ... Dr. Andres GIL
13 Vice President/CIO ... Mr. Robert GRILLO
12 Vice Provost BBC ... Mr. Michael HEARON
84 VP Enrollment Mgmt Services ... Dr. Kevin COUGHLIN
88 Ombudsperson ... Dr. Sofia TRELLES
15 Sr Vice President Human Resources ... Ms. El Pagnier HUDSON
18 Assoc VP Facilities Operations ... Mr. John CAL
07 Dir Undergraduate Admissions ... Ms. Jody GLASSMAN
49 Dean Col Arts/Sciences/Educ ... Dr. Michael HEITHAUS
50 Dean College Business Admin ... Dr. Joanne LI
54 Dean Col Engineering/Computing ... Dr. John VOLAKIS
53 Director College of Education ... Dr. Laura DINEHART
88 Dean Sch Hospitality Mgmt ... Dr. Michael CHENG
82 Dean School Intl/Pub Affairs ... Dr. John STACK
66 Dean Col Nursing/Health Science ... Dr. Ora STRICKLAND
69 Dean College of Public Health ... Dr. Tomas GUILARTE
61 Dean College of Law ... Dr. Antony PAGE
63 Dean Col Medicine/SVP Health Affs ... Dr. Robert SACKSTEIN
92 Dean Honors College ... Dr. Juan Carlos ESPINOSA
48 Dean Col Comm/Architecture/Arts ... Dr. Brian SCHRINER
77 Dir Sch Computing/Info Sciences ... Dr. Sundararaj IYENGAR
38 Dir Stdnt Hlth & Counseling ... Dr. Todd LENGNICK
22 Director Equal Opportunity Program ... Ms. Shirlyon J. MCWHORTER
62 Dean of Libraries ... Dr. Anne PRESTAMO
41 Athletics Director ... Mr. Pete GARCIA
86 VP for Government Relations ... Ms. Michelle PALACIO
06 University Registrar ... Ms. Dulce BELTRAN
26 Sr Vice President Ext Relations ... Ms. Sandra GONZALEZ-LEVY
37 Director Student Financial Aid ... Mr. Francisco VALINES
36 Director Career Services ... Ms. Ivette DUARTE
23 Medical Director Stdnt Hlth Svcs ... Dr. Saara SCHWARTZ
39 Dir of Housing/Residential Life ... Mr. Joe PAULICK
22 Director Disability Student Svcs ... Dr. Amanda NIGUIDULA
116 Chief Audit Executive ... Mr. Trevor WILLIAMS
24 Dir University IT/Media Support ... Mr. Matthew HAGOOD
21 Associate VP and Univ Controller ... Ms. Katharine BROPHY
88 Dir Environmental Health/Safety ... Ms. Tamece KNOWLES
19 Chief of Police ... Chief Alexander CASAS
27 Asst VP Media Relations ... Ms. Maydel SANTANA-BRAVO
43 General Counsel ... Mr. Carlos CASTILLO
85 Sr Dir International Stdnt Svcs ... Ms. Alejandra PARRA
25 Assistant VP for Research ... Mr. Roberto GUTIERREZ
04 Assistant Chief of Staff ... Ms. Claudia GONZALEZ
102 Sr Dir Corporate/Found Relations ... Ms. Karla HERNANDEZ

*Florida Polytechnic University (B)

4700 Research Way, Lakeland FL 33805-8531
County: Polk Identification: 667279
Unit ID: 482936
Telephone: (863) 583-9050 Carnegie Class: Bac-Diverse
FAX Number: N/A Calendar System: Semester
URL: www.floridapoly.edu
Established: 2012 Annual Undergrad Tuition & Fees (In-State): $4,940
Enrollment: 1,422 Coed
Affiliation or Control: State IRS Status: 501(c)3
Highest Offering: Master's
Accreditation: SC

02 President ... Dr. Randy K. AVENT
05 Provost ... Dr. Terry PARKER
43 Vice President & General Counsel ... Miss Gina DEIULIO
111 Vice President Advancement ... Ms. Kathy BOWMAN
10 Vice President/CFO ... Mr. Mark MROCZKOWSKI
07 Vice Provost Admissions/Fin Aid ... Mr. Ben MATTHEW CORPUS
32 Vice Provost Student Affairs ... Ms. Kathryn MILLER
37 Director Financial Aid ... Ms. Carola MANN
15 Assoc Director Human Resources ... Ms. DeAnn DOLL
04 Admin Assistant to the President ... Ms. Michele RUSH
06 Registrar ... Mr. Andrew KONAPELSKY
09 Director of Institutional Research ... Mr. Kevin CALKINS
13 Chief Information Technology Office ... Mr. Mike DIECKMANN
18 Chief Facilities/Physical Plant Ofc ... Mr. David CALHOUN
19 Director Security/Safety ... Chief Richard HOLLAND

*Florida State University (C)

222 S. Copeland Street, Tallahassee FL 32306
County: Leon FICE Identification: 001489
Unit ID: 134097
Telephone: (850) 644-2525 Carnegie Class: DU-Highest
FAX Number: (850) 644-9936 Calendar System: Semester
URL: www.fsu.edu
Established: 1851 Annual Undergrad Tuition & Fees (In-State): $5,656
Enrollment: 43,569 Coed
Affiliation or Control: State IRS Status: 501(c)3
Highest Offering: Doctorate
Accreditation: SC, ACATE, ANEST, #ARCPA, ART, CACREP, CEA, CIDA, CLPSY, DANCE, DIETD, DIETI, IPSY, LAW, LIB, MED, MFCD, MUS, NURSE, PH, PLNG, PSPSY, SP, SPAA, SW, THEA

02 President ... Dr. Richard MCCULLOUGH
05 Prov/Exec VP Academic Affairs ... Dr. Sally E. MCRORIE
10 Vice Pres Finance & Admin ... Mr. Kyle CLARK
32 Vice President Student Affairs ... Dr. Amy HECHT
46 Vice President Research ... Dr. Gary K. OSTRANDER
26 Assoc VP University Relations ... Vacant
45 VP Planning and Programs ... Vacant
111 VP University Advancement ... Vacant
102 Exec VP FSU Foundation ... Mr. Andy A. JHANJI
20 Vice Pres Faculty Development ... Dr. Janet KISTNER
100 Chief of Staff to President ... Ms. Liz HIRST
88 Assoc Vice President for Research ... Dr. Laurel FULKERSON
18 Associate VP for Facilities ... Mr. Dennis A. BAILEY
21 Assoc VP Finance & Admin ... Mr. Michael WILLIAMS
13 AVP Info Tech Svcs/CIO ... Ms. Jane LIVINGSTON
20 Asst VP for Academic Affairs ... Mr. Paul HARLACHER
15 Director of Human Resources ... Ms. Phaedra HARRIS
11 Asst VP for Administrative Services ... Mr. Steven CONNER
07 AVP Admissions ... Mr. John BARNHILL
27 Asst VP of University Communication ... Ms. Browning BROOKS
88 Dir Academic Pgm Professional Svcs ... Mr. Bill LINDNER
49 Dean Arts & Sciences ... Dr. Sam HUCKABA
50 Dean Business ... Dr. Michael HARTLINE
53 Dean Education ... Dr. Damon ANDREW
59 Dean Human Sciences ... Dr. Michael DELP
60 Dean Communication & Information ... Dr. Larry DENNIS
66 Dean Nursing ... Dr. Laurie GRUBBS
88 Dean Criminology ... Dr. Thomas BLOMBERG
61 Dean Law ... Dr. Erin O'HARA O'CONNOR
83 Dean Social Sciences ... Dr. Timothy CHAPIN
70 Dean Social Work ... Dr. James J. CLARK
88 Dean Motion Picture Arts ... Mr. Reb BRADDOCK
64 Dean Music ... Dr. Patricia J. FLOWERS
57 Dean Fine Arts ... Mr. James FRAZIER
54 Dean Engineering ... Dr. Murray GIBSON
63 Dean Medicine ... Dr. John FOGARTY
58 Dean Graduate School ... Dr. Mark RILEY
97 Dean Undergraduate Studies ... Dr. Karen L. LAUGHLIN
12 Dean Panama City Branch Campus ... Dr. Randy HANNA
06 University Registrar ... Dr. Kimberly BARBER
92 Dir University Honors Program ... Ms. Annette SCHWABE
37 Director Student Financial Aid ... Mr. Somnath CHATTERJEE
08 Director Libraries ... Ms. Gale ETSCHMAIER
90 Sr Director Enterprise Applications ... Mr. Byron MENCHION
43 General Counsel ... Ms. Carolyn EGAN
104 Director International Programs ... Dr. James E. PITTS
114 Chief Budget Officer ... Mr. Michael P. LAKE
09 Director Institutional Research ... Dr. James HUNT
86 Director Governmental Relations ... Ms. Kathy MEARS
41 Athletic Director ... Dr. David COBURN
38 Director Student Counseling ... Dr. Carlos J. GOMEZ
19 Director Public Safety ... Mr. David L. PERRY
23 Director University Health Services ... Dr. Amy MAGNUSON
36 Director Career Center ... Ms. Myrna HOOVER
116 Chief Audit Officer ... Dr. Sam MCCALL
28 Dir Diversity/Equal Opportunity ... Ms. Michelle DOUGLAS
39 Director Student Housing ... Ms. Shannon STATEN
109 Director Business Services ... Mr. Charles FRIEDRICH, II
25 Director Sponsored Research ... Ms. Pamela RAY
14 Director Information Technology ... Mr. Kenneth JOHNSON

*New College of Florida (D)

5800 Bay Shore Road, Sarasota FL 34243-2109
County: Sarasota FICE Identification: 001507
Unit ID: 262129
Telephone: (941) 487-4100 Carnegie Class: Bac-A&S
FAX Number: (941) 487-4101 Calendar System: 4/1/4
URL: www.ncf.edu
Established: 1960 Annual Undergrad Tuition & Fees (In-State): $6,916
Enrollment: 675 Coed
Affiliation or Control: State IRS Status: 501(c)3
Highest Offering: Master's
Accreditation: SC

02 President ... Dr. Patricia OKKER
05 Provost ... Dr. Suzanne SHERMAN
10 Vice Pres Finance & Administration ... Mr. Chris KINSLEY
79 Chair of Humanities ... Dr. Miriam WALLACE
81 Chair of Natural Sciences ... Dr. Sandra GILCHRIST
83 Chair of Social Sciences ... Dr. Barbara HICKS
08 Interim Dean Cook Library ... Ms. Tammera RACE
84 Vice President of Enrollment ... Dr. Damon WADE
32 Vice President of Student Affairs ... Ms. S. Marjorie THOMAS
28 Dean Outreach/Engage/Inclusion ... Dr. William WOODSON
07 Associate Dean of Admissions ... Ms. Sonia WU
20 Associate Academic Officer ... Dr. Emily HEFFERNAN
21 Associate Business Officer ... Ms. Melissa SHIPPEE
13 Dir of Information Technology ... Mr. Ben FOSS
14 Director of Technology Support ... Mr. Jeff SMITH
29 Asst Director Alumnae/i Association ... Ms. Kathleen MCCOY
06 Registrar ... Mr. Brian SCHOLTEN
26 Director Marketing/Communications ... Ms. Ann COMER-WOODS
38 Director Counseling ... Dr. Anne E. FISHER
09 Director of Institutional Research ... Ms. Hui-Men WEN
100 Chief of Staff President's Office ... Dr. Bradley THIESSEN
15 Interim Assoc VP of Human Resources ... Ms. Kristie HARRIS
18 Chief Facilities/Physical Plant ... Mr. Alan BURR
96 Director of Purchasing ... Ms. Jean HARRIS
37 Director Student Financial Aid ... Ms. Tara KARAS
43 General Counsel ... Mr. David FUGETT
25 Contract Administrator ... Mr. Justin MILLER
30 Chief Development ... Ms. MaryAnne YOUNG
19 Chief of Police ... Sgt. Michael KESSIE
39 Director Student Housing ... Dr. Mark STIER
41 Athletic Director ... Mr. Colin JORDAN
04 Administrative Asst to President ... Ms. Shelley WILBUR
104 Director Study Abroad ... Ms. Florence ZAMSKY
36 Director Student Placement ... Vacant

*University of Central Florida (E)

PO Box 160000, Orlando FL 32816-0001
County: Orange FICE Identification: 003954
Unit ID: 132903
Telephone: (407) 823-2000 Carnegie Class: DU-Highest
FAX Number: N/A Calendar System: Semester
URL: www.ucf.edu
Established: 1963 Annual Undergrad Tuition & Fees (In-State): $6,368
Enrollment: 71,881 Coed
Affiliation or Control: State IRS Status: 501(c)3
Highest Offering: Doctorate
Accreditation: SC, CAATE, CACREP, CAHIIM, CEA, CLPSY, FEPAC, HSA, IPSY, MED, MT, MUS, NURSE, PLNG, PTA, SP, SPAA, SW, THEA

02 President ... Dr. Alexander N. CARTWRIGHT
05 Int Provost/Vice Pres for Acad Affs ... Dr. Michael D. JOHNSON
11 Int VP & Chief Operating Officer ... Ms. Misty SHEPHERD
10 Senior VP for Admin and Finance ... Mr. Gerald HECTOR
43 Int Vice President/General Counsel ... Ms. Youndy C. COOK
32 Int VP Student Dev/Enrollment Svcs ... Dr. Adrienne O. FRAME
102 Interim CEO Foundation ... Ms. Karen COCHRAN
31 Vice President Community Relations ... Ms. Helen DONEGAN
63 VP Health Affairs/Dean Med College ... Dr. Deborah GERMAN
41 Vice Pres & Dir of Athletics ... Mr. Terry MOHAJIR
49 Dean College of Arts & Humanities ... Mr. Jeffrey MOORE
50 Dean College of Business Admin ... Dr. Paul JARLEY
53 Dean Col of Comm Innovation & Educ ... Dr. Pamela S. CARROLL
54 Dean College of Engr/Comp Sci ... Dr. Michael GEORGIOPOULOS
76 Dean Col Health Prof/Sciences ... Dr. Christopher INGERSOLL
88 Dean Rosen College Hospitality Mgt ... Dr. Youcheng WANG

66 Dean College of Nursing ... Dr. Mary L. SOLE
88 Dean Col of Optics/Photonics ... Dr. David HAGAN
81 Interim Dean College of Sciences ... Dr. Tosha DUPRAS
92 Dean Burnett Honors Col ... Dr. Sheila PINERES
13 VP Info Tech & Chief Info Officer ... Mr. Matthew J. HALL
100 Chief of Staff ... Mr. Mike KILBRIDE
35 Asst VP UCF Downtown Student Svcs ... Dr. Chanda TORRES
46 Assoc VP Research Administration ... Ms. Dorothy YATES
58 Vice Pres Res/Dean Grad Studies ... Dr. Elizabeth KLONOFF
09 AVP/Chief Analytics Officer ... Dr. M. Paige BORDEN
18 Assoc VP Facilities & Safety ... Mr. Duane SIEMEN
97 VProv/Dean Col Undergrad Studies ... Dr. Theodorea BERRY
111 Assoc VP for Advancement ... Mr. Jeff COATES
84 Assoc VP Enrollment Services ... Dr. Gordon CHAVIS
20 Vice Prov Faculty Excellence ... Dr. Jana JASINSKI
26 AVP Communications & Marketing ... Mr. Patrick BURT
37 Dir Student Financial Aid ... Ms. Alicia KEATON
06 University Registrar ... Mr. Brian BOYD
08 Interim Director Libraries ... Mr. Frank ALLEN
15 Assoc VP HR/Chief HR Officer ... Ms. Maureen BINDER
19 Assoc VP Safety & Chief of Police ... Mr. Carl METZGER
93 Dir Multicultural Acad Support Svcs ... Mr. Wayne JACKSON
14 AVP/COO UCF IT ... Mr. Michael SINK
38 Director Counseling Center ... Dr. Karen HOFMANN
22 Dir Office of Institutional Equity ... Ms. Nancy F. MYERS
23 Assoc VP Student Health Services ... Dr. Michael G. DEICHEN
39 Exec Dir Housing and Residence Life ... Dr. April HICKS KONVALINKA
28 Int Chief Equity/Inclus/Div Ofcr ... Dr. S. Kent BUTLER
96 Associate Director Procurement ... Ms. Nellie NIDO
36 Exec Director Career Services ... Ms. Lynn HANSEN

*University of Florida (A)

235 Tigert Hall, Gainesville FL 32611-9500
County: Alachua FICE Identification: 001535
Unit ID: 134130
Telephone: (352) 392-3261 Carnegie Class: DU-Highest
FAX Number: (352) 392-8735 Calendar System: Semester
URL: www.ufl.edu
Established: 1853 Annual Undergrad Tuition & Fees (In-State): $6,381
Enrollment: 53,372 Coed
Affiliation or Control: State IRS Status: 501(c)3
Highest Offering: Doctorate
Accreditation: SC, ARCPA, ART, AUD, CACREP, CAEP, CAMPEP, CEA, CIDA, CLPSY, CONST, COPSY, DANCE, DENT, DIETD, DIETI, HSA, IFSAC, IPSY, JOUR, LAW, LSAR, MED, MUS, NURSE, OT, PH, PHAR, PLNG, PTA, SCPSY, SP, THEA, VET

02 President ... Dr. W. Kent FUCHS
05 Provost & Senior Vice President ... Dr. Joseph GLOVER
47 Vice Pres Agric/Natural Res ... Dr. Jay Scott ANGLE
17 Sr Vice Pres Health Affairs ... Dr. David NELSON
10 VP/Chief Financial Ofcr ... Dr. Christopher COWEN
11 Sr Vice Pres/Chief Operating Ofcr ... Dr. Charles E. LANE
111 Vice President Advancement ... Mr. Thomas J. MITCHELL
21 Vice President Business Affairs ... Mr. Curtis REYNOLDS
32 Vice President Student Affairs ... Dr. D'Andra MULL
86 Vice President Govt & Cmty Relation ... Mr. Mark KAPLAN
26 VP Strategic Comm & Marketing ... Ms. Nancy PATON
15 Vice Pres Human Resources ... Ms. Jodi D. GENTRY
46 Vice President Research ... Dr. David P. NORTON
43 Vice President and General Counsel ... Ms. Amy M. HASS
13 Vice President & CIO ... Mr. Elias G. ELDAYRIE
84 Vice Pres Enroll Mgmt/Assoc Provost ... Dr. Mary PARKER
100 Exec Chief of Staff ... Dr. Winfred PHILLIPS
28 Chief Diversity Officer ... Vacant
86 Assoc VP Government Relations ... Vacant
88 Assoc Provost Teaching/ Technology ... Dr. William A. MCCOLLOUGH
27 Asst VP Communications ... Mr. Stephen F. ORLANDO
21 AVP Business Affs/Finance/Admin ... Mr. Craig R. HILL
18 Asst VP Fac/Plng/Construction ... Mr. Carlos DOUGNAC
20 Associate Provost Academic Affairs ... Dr. Chris J. HASS
20 Assoc Provost Undergrad Affairs ... Dr. Angela LINDNER
09 Asst Provost/Dir Inst Research/Plng ... Dr. Cathy LEBO
35 Assoc Vice Pres/Dean of Students ... Ms. Heather WHITE
08 Dean University Libraries ... Ms. Judith RUSSELL
50 Dean of Business Administration ... Dr. Sabyasachi MITRA
49 Dean of Liberal Arts & Science ... Mr. David E. RICHARDSON
68 Dean of Health/Human Performance ... Dr. Michael B. REID
61 Dean of Law ... Ms. Laura A. ROSENBURY
66 Dean of Nursing ... Dr. Anna M. MCDANIEL
67 Dean of Pharmacy ... Dr. Julie A. JOHNSON
54 Dean of Engineering ... Dr. Cammy ABERNATHY
47 Dean Agricultural/Life Sciences ... Dr. R. Elaine TURNER
60 Dean of Journalism/Comm ... Dr. Hubert BROWN
76 Dean Pub Health/Health Professions ... Dr. Michael PERRI
53 Dean of Education ... Dr. Glenn GOOD
47 Interim Dean IFAS Extension ... Dr. Thomas OBREZA
74 Dean of Veterinary Medicine ... Dr. Dana ZIMMEL
57 Dean of the Arts ... Dr. Onye OZUZU
48 Dean Design Construction Planning ... Dr. Chimay ANUMBA
63 Dean of Medicine ... Dr. Colleen KOCH
46 Dean of IFAS Research ... Dr. Robert GILBERT
52 Dean of Dentistry ... Dr. Isabel GARCIA
58 Dean Graduate School/Assoc Provost ... Dr. Nicole STEDMAN
65 Dir School Natural Res/Envir ... Dr. Thomas K. FRAZER
06 University Registrar ... Mr. Stephen J. PRITZ
23 Director of Student Health ... Dr. Ronald BERRY
38 Assoc Dir of Counseling & Well Ctr ... Dr. Alvin LAWRENCE
37 Director Student Financial Aid ... Ms. Donna KOLB
36 Sr Dir of Career Connections Ctr ... Ms. Ja'Net GLOVER
14 Director of Computer Center ... Mr. Timothy J. FITZPATRICK
19 Director of University Police ... Ms. Linda J. STUMP-KURNICK
24 Director of Academic Technology ... Dr. Mark MCCALLISTER
65 Director of Forestry ... Dr. Timothy L. WHITE
39 Director of Housing ... Ms. Tina KUHLENGEL HORVATH
41 Athletic Director ... Mr. Scott STRICKLIN
29 Int Exec Dir FL Alumni Affairs ... Mr. Brian DANFORTH
96 Director of Purchasing ... Ms. Lisa DEAL
07 Director of Admissions ... Mr. Rick BRYANT
04 Executive Asst to President ... Ms. Beth BOONE
106 Dir Online Education/E-learning ... Ms. Evangeline CUMMINGS
108 Director Institutional Assessment ... Dr. Timothy S. BROPHY
101 Secretary of the Institution/Board ... Mr. Mark KAPLAN

*University of North Florida (B)

1 UNF Drive, Jacksonville FL 32224-7699
County: Duval FICE Identification: 009841
Unit ID: 136172
Telephone: (904) 620-1000 Carnegie Class: DU-Mod
FAX Number: (904) 620-2414 Calendar System: Semester
URL: www.unf.edu
Established: 1965 Annual Undergrad Tuition & Fees (In-State): $6,389
Enrollment: 16,926 Coed
Affiliation or Control: State IRS Status: 501(c)3
Highest Offering: Doctorate
Accreditation: SC, ANEST, ART, CAATE, CACREP, CAEP, CAEPN, CONST, COSMA, DIETD, DIETI, EXSC, HSA, IPSY, JOUR, MUS, NURSE, PH, PTA, SPAA, SW

02 President ... Dr. David SZYMANKSI
05 Provost ... Dr. Karen PATTERSON
86 VP Government & Community Relations ... Ms. Heather DUNCAN
43 VP/General Counsel ... Ms. Karen J. STONE
30 VP Development/Alumni Affairs ... Ms. Ann S. MCCULLEN
88 VP Data Analytics ... Dr. Bob J. COLEMAN
36 VP of Jobs ... Ms. Karen E. BOWLING
26 VP Marketing Communications ... Mr. Eric BRUDER
28 VP Chief Diversity Officer ... Ms. Whitney MEYER
84 Assoc VP Enrollment Services ... Dr. Terrence CURRAN
116 Assoc VP & Compliance Officer ... Dr. Joann N. CAMPBELL
10 VP Admin & Finance ... Mr. Scott BENNETT
45 Asst VP Research ... Dr. John KANTNER
35 Asst VP Student Affairs ... Ms. Ruth LOPEZ
35 Asst VP Student Affairs ... Ms. Christine S. MALEK RICHARD
58 Dean of the Graduate School ... Dr. John KANTNER
08 Dean of the Library ... Dr. Brent MAI
97 Int AVP Undergraduate Studies ... Dr. Susan PEREZ
50 Dean Coggin College of Business ... Dr. Richard J. BUTTIMER
49 Dean Arts & Sciences ... Dr. George RAINBOLT
53 Dean College of Education ... Dr. Diane YENDOL-HOPPEY
76 Dean Brooks College of Health ... Dr. Curt LOX
77 Dean Computing/Engr/Constr ... Dr. William KLOSTERMEYER
07 Director of Admissions ... Ms. Terry R. EVANS
22 Dir Equal Opportunity Programs ... Ms. Marlynn JONES
103 Dir Professional Dev Training ... Mr. Kelly G. HARRISON
114 Chief Budget Officer ... Mrs. Devany GROVES
21 Controller ... Ms. Valerie O. STEVENSON
88 Senior Associate Athletic Director ... Ms. Donna R. KIRK
88 Dir Environment Health/Safety ... Mr. Daniel D. ENDICOTT
22 Dir ADA Compliance ... Ms. Rocelia T. GONZALEZ
14 Dir IT Networking ... Mr. Jeffrey A. DURFEE
21 Treasurer ... Mr. Michael S. NEGLIA
18 Dir Campus Planning ... Mr. Paul STEWART
88 Dir University Center ... Mr. George ANDROUIN
19 Dir Safety Security ... Mr. Francis J. MACKESY
88 Dir Child Development Center ... Ms. Mahreen N. MIAN
23 Dir Student Health Services ... Dr. Valerie A. MORRISON
38 Dir Univ Counseling Center ... Dr. Richmond D. WYNN
39 Dir Housing Residence Life ... Mr. Robert J. BOYLE
41 Athletic Director ... Mr. Nick MORROW
88 Int Assoc VP Faculty Enhancement ... Dr. Gordon RAKITA
108 Director of Assessment ... Dr. Amanda KULP
37 Dir Student Financial Aid ... Ms. Anissa AGNE
06 Registrar ... Mr. Charles N. LEARCH
09 Dir Institutional Research ... Dr. Abby WILLCOX
88 Exec Dir FL Inst of Education ... Dr. Cheryl A. FOUNTAIN
88 Dir Small Business Dev Ctr ... Mr. Huston PULLEN
96 Dir Purchasing ... Ms. Shawn ASMUTH
51 Dean Continuing Education ... Ms. Abdullah E. EDYTHE
106 Asst VP Digital Learning/Innovation ... Dr. Deb MILLER
04 Admin Assistant to the President ... Ms. Melonie HANDERSON
101 Secretary of the Institution/ Board ... Ms. Andrea HOLCOMBE
104 Director Study Abroad ... Dr. Luisa MARTINEZ
105 Director Web Services ... Ms. Katherine THOMPSON
15 Chief Human Resources Officer ... Ms. Carrie GUTH
29 Director Alumni Affairs ... Ms. Michelle MCGRIFF
44 Director Annual Giving ... Ms. Kristine HERRINGTON

*University of South Florida (C)

4202 E Fowler Avenue, SVC 2172, Tampa FL 33620-6100
County: Hillsborough FICE Identification: 001537
Unit ID: 137351
Telephone: (813) 974-2011 Carnegie Class: DU-Highest
FAX Number: N/A Calendar System: Semester
URL: www.usf.edu
Established: 1956 Annual Undergrad Tuition & Fees (In-State): $6,410
Enrollment: 50,626 Coed
Affiliation or Control: State IRS Status: 501(c)3
Highest Offering: Doctorate
Accreditation: SC, ABAI, ANEST, ARCPA, ART, AUD, CAATE, CACREP, CAEP, CAMPEP, CEA, CLPSY, DANCE, DIETI, HSA, IPSY, LIB, MED, MUS, NURSE, PCSAS, PH, PHAR, PLNG, PTA, SCPSY, SP, SPAA, SW, THEA

02 President ... Dr. Steven C. CURRALL
45 Sr VP Business/Financial Strategy ... Mr. David LECHNER
100 Chief of Staff President's Office ... Dr. Cynthia S. VISOT
43 General Counsel ... Mr. Gerard SOLIS
05 Prov/Exec Vice Pres Academic Affs ... Dr. Ralph WILCOX
15 Vice Provost for HR and Space Plng ... Vacant
20 Vice Provost for Plng/Perf & Acct ... Dr. Theresa H. CHISOLM
20 Vice Provost and VP USF World ... Vacant
104 Director Education Abroad ... Dr. Amanda C. MAURER
46 Sr Vice Pres Research & Innovation ... Dr. Paul SANBERG
111 SVP Advance/Alumni Affs/CEO Found ... Mr. Jay STROMAN
17 Sr Vice Pres USF Health ... Dr. Charles LOCKWOOD
58 Sr Vice Provost/Dean Grad School ... Dr. Dwayne SMITH
10 Vice Pres Business & Finance ... Mr. Nick TRIVUNOVICH
88 Assistant Treasurer ... Ms. Dawn M. RODRIGUEZ
11 Vice Pres Administrative Services ... Mr. Calvin WILLIAMS
18 Asst VP Physical Plant ... Mr. Chris DUFFY
32 Asst VP and Dean of Students ... Ms. Danielle MCDONALD
13 Vice Pres Information Technology ... Mr. Sidney FERNANDES
14 AVP Information Technology ... Ms. Jenny PAULSEN
14 AVP Information Technology ... Mr. Swapna CHACKRAVARTHY
105 Director Information Technology ... Mr. Christopher L. AKIN
29 Assoc Vice Pres Alumni Affairs ... Mr. Bill MCCAUSLAND
22 Chief Diversity Officer ... Dr. Haywood BROWN
121 Vice Provost for Student Success ... Dr. Paul J. DOSAL
16 Vice Pres Human Resources ... Ms. Angela SKLENKA
86 Asst Vice Pres Government Rels ... Mr. Mark WALSH
88 University Ombudsman ... Mr. Steven D. PREVAUX
39 Asst VP Housing/Residential Educ ... Ms. Ana HERNANDEZ
83 Dean Behavioral/Community Sci ... Dr. Julianne SEROVICH
50 Dean Business Administration ... Dr. Moez LIMAYEM
53 Dean College of Education ... Dr. Robert C. KNOEPPEL
54 Dean Engineering ... Dr. Robert H. BISHOP
57 Dean College of the Arts ... Dr. James S. MOY
67 Dean College of Pharmacy ... Dr. Kevin B. SNEED
49 Dean Arts & Sciences ... Dr. Eric EISENBERG
92 Dean Honors College ... Dr. Charles H. ADAMS
88 Dean Marine Science ... Dr. Jacqueline DIXON
69 Dean Public Health ... Dr. Donna PETERSEN
88 Int Dean Global Sustainability ... Dr. Govindan PARAYIL
89 Dean Undergraduate Studies ... Dr. Paul ATCHLEY
106 Asst Vice Provost Innovative Educ ... Dr. Cynthia A. DELUCA
48 Dir Sch of Architecture/Cmty Design ... Mr. Robert MACLEOD
12 Regional Chanc Sarasota-Manatee ... Dr. Karen HOLBROOK
12 Reg Chanc USF St Petersburg ... Dr. Martin TADLOCK
21 Controller ... Ms. Jennifer CONDON
26 Director of Media Relations ... Mr. Adam FREEMAN
06 Registrar ... Vacant
114 University Budget Officer ... Ms. Nell PETERSON
37 Assoc VP Financial Aid ... Ms. Billie Jo HAMILTON
38 Director Counseling Center ... Dr. Scott STRADER
36 Asst Vice President Career Services ... Ms. Ruth Ann ATCHLEY
19 Chief of Police ... Mr. Chris DANIEL
08 USF Libraries Dean ... Dr. Todd CHAVEZ
41 Director of Athletics ... Mr. Michael KELLY
28 Director of Diversity & Inclusion ... Ms. Patsy FELICIANO
96 Int Director Purchasing & Property ... Mr. George COTTER
09 Asst VP Office of Decision Support ... Dr. Valeria GARCIA

*University of South Florida St. Petersburg (D)

140 7th Avenue S, Saint Petersburg FL 33701-5016
Telephone: (727) 873-4873 FICE Identification: 009016
Accreditation: &SC, CAEPN, JOUR

*University of South Florida Sarasota-Manatee (E)

8350 North Tamiami Trail, Sarasota FL 34243
Telephone: (941) 359-4200 Identification: 667058
Accreditation: &SC, CAEPN

*University of West Florida (F)

11000 University Parkway, Pensacola FL 32514-5750
County: Escambia FICE Identification: 003955
Unit ID: 138354
Telephone: (850) 474-2000 Carnegie Class: Masters/L
FAX Number: (850) 474-3131 Calendar System: Semester
URL: uwf.edu
Established: 1963 Annual Undergrad Tuition & Fees (In-State): $6,360
Enrollment: 13,061 Coed
Affiliation or Control: State IRS Status: 501(c)3
Highest Offering: Doctorate
Accreditation: SC, #CAATE, CAEP, EXSC, MPCAC, MT, MUS, NURSE, PH, SW

02 President ... Dr. Martha D. SAUNDERS
05 Provost & Senior Vice President ... Dr. George B. ELLENBERG
20 Vice Provost ... Dr. Kimberly MCCORKLE
111 Vice Pres for Univ Advancement ... Dr. Howard J. REDDY
10 VP Finance & Administration ... Ms. Betsy BOWERS
32 VP Acad Engagement & Student Affs ... Dr. Kim LEDUFF
15 AVP Human Resources ... Ms. Jamie SPRAGUE
18 AVP Facilities/Operations ... Dr. Melinda BOWERS
21 AVP Finance/Controller ... Mr. Jeffrey DJERLEK
30 AVP for Development ... Mr. Brett BERG
119 AVP Cybersecurity ... Dr. Eman EL-SHEIKH
46 AVP of Research Administration ... Dr. Matthew SCHWARTZ
35 AVP/Dean of Students ... Dr. Vannee C. NGUYEN

110 AVP of Advancement .... Mr. Daniel LUCAS
88 Chief Compliance Officer .... Mr. Matthew W. PACKARD
43 General Counsel .... Vacant
116 Chief Audit Executive .... Mrs. Cynthia TALBERT
19 Chief of University Police .... Mr. Marc COSSICH
49 Dean Arts/Social Sci/Humanities .... Dr. Steven BROWN
50 Dean College of Business .... Dr. Richard FOUNTAIN
107 Dean Education & Prof Studies .... Dr. William CRAWLEY
81 Dean Science/Engineering/Health .... Dr. Jaromy KUHL
08 Dean University Libraries .... Ms. Stephanie CLARK
58 Dean Graduate Programs .... Dr. Kuiyuan LI
13 Exec Dir/Chief Tech Officer ITS .... Mrs. Melanie J. HAVEARD
76 Interim Dean College of Health .... Dr. Steve BROWN
07 Executive Director of Admissions .... Ms. Katherine CONDON
09 Dir Institutional Research .... Mr. Keith KING
108 Dir Institutional Effectiveness .... Dr. Angela BRYAN
96 Director Procurement & Contracts .... Ms. Angela JONES
109 Director Business/Auxiliary Svcs .... Mr. James ADAMS
124 Dir Student Involvement .... Dr. Ben STUBBS
38 Exec Dir Counseling Services .... Ms. Michele MANASSAH
37 Director of Financial Aid .... Ms. Kelly MCGAUGHEY
84 Exec Dir of Enrollment Mgmt & Svcs .... Vacant
06 Registrar .... Dr. Leana WILSON
39 Interim Dir of Housing/Res Life .... Mrs. Jennifer NAGIM
22 Interim Dir Equity & Diversity .... Ms. Aurora OSBORN
92 Dir of Kugelman Honors Pgm .... Dr. Gregory TOMSO
104 Asst Dir of International Programs .... Mr. Randolph SCOTT
26 Exec Dir Institutional Comm .... Vacant
29 Director of Alumni Relations .... Mrs. Melissa H. GRACE
41 Athletic Director .... Mr. David SCOTT
86 Sr Exec Spc Governmental Relations .... Mr. Andrew ROMER
101 Executive Specialist to BOT .... Ms. Becky LUNTSFORD

Stetson University (A)

421 N Woodland Boulevard, DeLand FL 32723-0001
County: Volusia FICE Identification: 001531
Unit ID: 137546
Telephone: (386) 822-7000 Carnegie Class: Masters/L
FAX Number: (386) 822-8832 Calendar System: Semester
URL: www.stetson.edu
Established: 1883 Annual Undergrad Tuition & Fees: $49,500
Enrollment: 4,462 Coed
Affiliation or Control: Independent Non-Profit IRS Status: 501(c)3
Highest Offering: Doctorate
Accreditation: **SC**, CACREP, CAEP, LAW, MUS

01 President .... Dr. Christopher ROELLKE
05 Exec VP & Provost .... Dr. Noel PAINTER
10 Exec Vice Pres & CFO .... Mr. F. Robert HUTH
111 VP for Devel & Alumni Engagement .... Vacant
84 VP Enrollment Management .... Mr. Ray NAULT
26 VP for University Marketing .... Mr. Bruce CHONG
32 Vice Pres for Student Affairs .... Dr. Lua HANCOCK
61 Dean College of Law .... Ms. Michele ALEXANDRE
49 Dean Col Arts & Sciences .... Dr. Elizabeth SKOMP
50 Interim Dean School of Business .... Dr. Yiorgos BAKAMITSOS
64 Dean of School of Music .... Dr. Washington GARCIA
08 Dean of duPont-Ball Library .... Ms. Susan RYAN
20 Assoc Provost for Faculty Develop .... Dr. Rosalie RICHARDS
06 Registrar .... Ms. Terri RICHARDS
41 Director of Athletics .... Mr. Jeffrey P. ALTIER
13 Assoc VP & CIO .... Dr. Jose BERNIER
15 Assoc VP for Human Resources .... Ms. Drew MACAN
18 Assoc Vice Pres Facilities Mgmt .... Ms. Bonita DUKES
21 Assoc Vice Pres for Finance .... Mr. Jeffrey MARGHEIM
114 Assoc VP Budget .... Mr. Jeremy DIGORIO
35 Dean of Students .... Ms. Lynn SCHOENBERG
36 Exec Dir Career Dev & Advising .... Mr. Timothy STILES
09 Dir Institutional Research .... Vacant
104 Director of International Learning .... Ms. Paula HENTZ
112 Asst VP for Devel/Alumni Engagement .... Ms. Rina ARROYO
30 Assoc VP Dev & Communications .... Ms. Amy GIPSON
07 Director of Admissions .... Ms. Dana DOLBOW
37 Dir Student Financial Aid .... Ms. Heidi GOLDSWORTHY
39 Dir of Res Educ & Housing .... Dr. Larry CORRELL-HUGHES
16 Director Human Resources .... Ms. Betty WHITEMAN
96 Director of Purchasing .... Ms. Valinda WIMER
19 Chief Public Safety .... Mr. Francisco ORTIZ
04 Executive Asst to President .... Ms. Joan BEASLEY
102 Dir Ofc of Grants/Sponsored Rsrch .... Ms. Carol BUCKELS
38 Director Counseling Ctr .... Dr. Leigh BAKER
105 Director Web Services .... Mr. Gary SIPE
44 Director Donor Relations .... Mr. Don BURRHUS

Suncoast College of Health (B)

6513 14th Street West #103, Bradenton FL 34207
County: Manatee Identification: 667296
Telephone: (941) 727-2273 Carnegie Class: Not Classified
FAX Number: (941) 727-2274 Calendar System: Quarter
URL: www.suncoastcollege.edu
Established: Annual Undergrad Tuition & Fees: N/A
Enrollment: N/A Coed
Affiliation or Control: Proprietary IRS Status: Proprietary
Highest Offering: Baccalaureate
Accreditation: **ACICS**

01 President .... Reynoso SEIDE
05 Chief Academic Officer .... Joyce LAING

Tallahassee Community College (C)

444 Appleyard Drive, Tallahassee FL 32304-2895
County: Leon FICE Identification: 001533
Unit ID: 137759
Telephone: (850) 201-6200 Carnegie Class: Bac/Assoc-Assoc Dom
FAX Number: (850) 201-8682 Calendar System: Semester
URL: www.tcc.fl.edu
Established: 1966 Annual Undergrad Tuition & Fees (In-District): $2,026
Enrollment: 11,245 Coed
Affiliation or Control: Local IRS Status: 501(c)3
Highest Offering: Baccalaureate
Accreditation: **SC**, ADNUR, COARC, DA, DH, EMT, NUR, SURGT

01 President .... Dr. Jim MURDAUGH
05 Provost/VP Academic Affairs .... Dr. Calandra STRINGER
10 Vice Pres Administrative Svcs/CFO .... Dr. Barbara WILLS
13 VP Information Technology .... Mr. Bret INGERMAN
32 Vice President for Student Affs .... Dr. Sheri ROWLAND
103 Vice Pres Workforce Development .... Ms. Kimberly MOORE
26 VP Communications and Marketing .... Mr. Al MORAN
108 VP Institutional Effectiveness .... Dr. Lei WANG
12 Exec Dir Florida Public Safety Inst .... Mr. Steve OUTLAW
12 Exec Dir Wakulla Environmental Inst .... Mr. Bob BALLARD
100 Chief of Staff .... Ms. Candice GRAUSE
88 Dir of Business Process Improvement .... Ms. Renae TOLSON
21 Asst Vice President Admin Services .... Mr. Bobby JONES
20 Associate VP of Academic Affairs .... Dr. Anthony JONES
79 Dean Communications & Humanities .... Dr. Donmetrie CLARK
83 Dean Behavioral/Social Science/Educ .... Dr. Bryan HOOPER
50 Dean Business Industry & Technology .... Dr. Joey WALTER
97 Dean Transitional Studies .... Ms. Sharisse TURNER
08 Director of Library Services .... Mr. Stephen BANISTER
76 Dean Health Care Professions .... Ms. Stephanie SOLOMON
37 Director of Financial Aid .... Mr. William SPIERS
84 Dean of Enrollment Services .... Ms. Melinda RODGERS
36 Dean of Career & Academic Planning .... Ms. Pamela JOHNSTON
35 Associate VP of Student Affairs .... Dr. Gerald JONES
15 Director of Human Resources .... Ms. Nyla DAVIS
102 Director of TCC Foundation .... Ms. Heather MITCHELL
41 Director of Athletics .... Mr. Rob CHANEY
18 Dir Facilities/Construction/Plng .... Mr. Don HERR
09 Director of Institutional Research .... Ms. Margaret THOMPSON
106 Dir of TCC Online .... Dr. Lemond HALL
85 Coordinator Intl Student Services .... Vacant
14 Director of User Services .... Mr. Chip SINGLETARY
14 Director of Enterprise Systems .... Mr. Mike ROBECK
14 Director of IT Infrastructure .... Mr. Jason FOWLER
114 Dir of Financial Svcs/Spons Mgmt .... Ms. Amy BRADBURY
25 Director Grants & Special Projects .... Mr. Steven SOLOMON
96 Dir of Purchasing and General Svcs .... Mr. Bobby HINSON
19 Chief of Police .... Vacant
36 Director of Career Services .... Vacant
43 Dir Legal Services/General Counsel .... Mr. Craig KNOX
27 Director of Integrated Marketing .... Ms. Lauren SCHOENBERGER
04 Executive Coordinator .... Ms. Lenda KLING

Talmudic College of Florida (D)

4000 Alton Road, Miami Beach FL 33140
County: Dade FICE Identification: 025089
Unit ID: 137777
Telephone: (305) 534-7050 Carnegie Class: Spec-4-yr-Faith
FAX Number: (305) 534-8444 Calendar System: Semester
URL: www.talmudicu.edu
Established: 1974 Annual Undergrad Tuition & Fees: $13,250
Enrollment: 30 Male
Affiliation or Control: Independent Non-Profit IRS Status: 501(c)3
Highest Offering: Master's
Accreditation: **RABN**

01 President .... Rabbi Yitzchak ZWEIG
05 Dean/Vice President .... Rabbi Yochanan ZWEIG
06 Registrar .... Rabbi Yitzchak WINKLER
37 Director Student Financial Aid .... Ms. Sharon BRECHER
20 Director Educational Programs .... Rabbi Akiva ZWEIG
07 Director of Admissions .... Rabbi Yaakov BURSTYN

Taylor College (E)

5190 SE 125th Street, Belleview FL 34420
County: Marion FICE Identification: 041166
Unit ID: 449524
Telephone: (352) 245-4119 Carnegie Class: Spec 2-yr-Health
FAX Number: (352) 245-0276 Calendar System: Other
URL: www.taylorcollege.edu
Established: 1999 Annual Undergrad Tuition & Fees: $12,039
Enrollment: 228 Coed
Affiliation or Control: Proprietary IRS Status: Proprietary
Highest Offering: Associate Degree
Accreditation: **ABHES**, ADNUR, PNUR, PTAA

01 President .... Jeff GEORGESON
10 Sr Director Finance/Operations .... Amy DINELLA
66 Director Nursing .... Arlene SALIBA EL HABRE
76 Director Physical Therapy .... Stacy CAMPBELL
53 Director General Education .... Elizabeth THOMPSON
37 Director Financial Aid .... Brandy BAUDOUX
36 Director Career Svcs/Compliance .... Ingrid ZEKAN
06 Registrar .... Susie BRADLEY

Trinity Baptist College (F)

800 Hammond Boulevard, Jacksonville FL 32221-1398
County: Duval FICE Identification: 031019
Unit ID: 137953
Telephone: (904) 596-2451 Carnegie Class: Bac-Diverse
FAX Number: (904) 596-2532 Calendar System: Semester
URL: www.tbc.edu
Established: 1974 Annual Undergrad Tuition & Fees: $13,130
Enrollment: 362 Coed
Affiliation or Control: Baptist IRS Status: 501(c)3
Highest Offering: Master's
Accreditation: **TRACS**

00 Chancellor .... Dr. Thomas C. MESSER
01 President/CEO .... Mr. Mac HEAVENER
05 Senior Vice President .... Dr. Matthew BEEMER
32 Vice President of Student Affairs .... Mr. Jeremiah STANLEY
84 VP Enrollment Mgmt & Development .... Mr. Matthew HEAVENER
37 Director of Financial Aid .... Mr. Mark ELKINS
06 Registrar .... Mrs. Shelby DOWNING
08 Head Librarian .... Dr. John LUCY
10 Chief Business Officer .... Mr. Mike AKINS
41 Athletic Director .... Mr. John JONES
18 Chief Facilities/Physical Plant .... Mr. Dennis RIFFLE
19 Director Security/Safety .... Mr. John CASH, JR.
29 Director Alumni Relations .... Vacant
07 Director of Admissions .... Mrs. Jenny STANLEY
106 Dean or Director Online Education/E .... Mrs. Teresa DUSTMAN
30 Director of Development .... Mr. Michael HEAVENER

Trinity College of Florida (G)

2430 Welbilt Boulevard, Trinity FL 34655-4401
County: Pasco FICE Identification: 030282
Unit ID: 137962
Telephone: (727) 376-6911 Carnegie Class: Spec-4-yr-Faith
FAX Number: (727) 376-0781 Calendar System: Semester
URL: www.trinitycollege.edu
Established: 1932 Annual Undergrad Tuition & Fees: $16,300
Enrollment: 214 Coed
Affiliation or Control: Independent Non-Profit IRS Status: 501(c)3
Highest Offering: Baccalaureate
Accreditation: **BI**

01 President .... Dr. Mark T. O'FARRELL
32 Vice President Student Development .... Rev. Al DEPOUTOT
05 Vice President Academic Affairs .... Dr. Eric BARGERHUFF
111 Vice President for Advancement .... Dr. Charlie MARTIN
10 VP Business and Finance .... Vacant
06 Registrar .... Mrs. Sheila M. JOHNSON
26 Asst VP Marketing/Communications .... Vacant
07 Director of Admissions .... Mr. Kenyata HAYES
04 Administrative Asst to President .... Mrs. Billie O'FARRELL
08 Head Librarian .... Dr. Krista MALLO
13 Chief Info Technology Ofcr/CIO .... Mr. Cory JOY
84 Director Enrollment Management .... Mr. Anthony ABELL
37 Director Student Financial Aid .... Mrs. Karly DOOLEY

Ultimate Medical Academy-Clearwater (H)

1255 Cleveland Street, Clearwater FL 33755
County: Pinellas FICE Identification: 035493
Unit ID: 441371
Telephone: (727) 298-8685 Carnegie Class: Spec 2-yr-Health
FAX Number: (727) 446-2489 Calendar System: Semester
URL: www.ultimatemedical.edu
Established: 1998 Annual Undergrad Tuition & Fees: N/A
Enrollment: 7,124 Coed
Affiliation or Control: Independent Non-Profit IRS Status: 501(c)3
Highest Offering: Associate Degree
Accreditation: **ABHES**

01 Campus Director .... Ms. Rebecca SARLO

Ultimate Medical Academy Online-Tampa (I)

3101 W Dr. Martin Luther King Blvd, Tampa FL 33607
Telephone: (888) 205-2456 Identification: 770528
Accreditation: **ABHES**, CAHIIM

United International College (J)

3130 Commerce Pkwy, Miramar FL 33025
County: Broward Identification: 667155
Unit ID: 486354
Telephone: (954) 607-4344 Carnegie Class: Spec-4-yr-Bus
FAX Number: (954) 357-1766 Calendar System: Semester
URL: www.unilatina.edu
Established: 2001 Annual Undergrad Tuition & Fees: $8,907
Enrollment: 56 Coed
Affiliation or Control: Proprietary IRS Status: Proprietary
Highest Offering: Baccalaureate
Accreditation: **ACICS**

01 President .... Angelica B. MOYANO

Universal Career School (A)

10720 W. Flagler Street Ste 21, Sweetwater FL 33174

County: Miami-Dade FICE Identification: 038563
Unit ID: 446589
Telephone: (305) 485-7700 Carnegie Class: Not Classified
FAX Number: (305) 485-8515 Calendar System: Semester
URL: www.ucs.edu
Established: Annual Undergrad Tuition & Fees: N/A
Enrollment: 596 Coed
Affiliation or Control: Proprietary IRS Status: Proprietary
Highest Offering: Associate Degree
Accreditation: **COE**

01 Director .... Blanca BURGOS

University of Fort Lauderdale (B)

4131 NW 16th Street, Lauderhill FL 33313

County: Broward FICE Identification: 041563
Unit ID: 457402
Telephone: (954) 486-7728 Carnegie Class: Spec-4-yr-Other
FAX Number: (954) 486-7667 Calendar System: Other
URL: www.uftl.edu
Established: 1995 Annual Undergrad Tuition & Fees: $7,410
Enrollment: 57 Coed
Affiliation or Control: Non-denominational IRS Status: 501(c)3
Highest Offering: Doctorate
Accreditation: **TRACS**

00 Chancellor/CEO .... Dr. Henry B. FERNANDEZ
01 President .... Vacant
05 VP of Academics/Provost .... Dr. Kaira CARTER
10 Chief Financial Officer .... Vacant
20 Chief Academic Officer .... Dr. Dawn PIPER
06 Registrar .... Ms. Lenice BARNETT
07 Director Admissions/Student Svcs .... Dr. Debra WHITE
37 Director Financial Aid .... Mr. Larry MOORE
21 Comptroller .... Ms. Daneida BENJAMIN
100 Executive Assistant to President .... Ms. Tiffany BACON
41 Athletic Director .... Mr. Fernando VALENZUELA
09 Dir Inst Compliance/Effectiveness .... Ms. Cloris UNDERWOOD

University of Miami (C)

1252 Memorial Drive, Coral Gables FL 33124

County: Miami-Dade FICE Identification: 001536
Unit ID: 135726
Telephone: (305) 284-2211 Carnegie Class: DU-Highest
FAX Number: N/A Calendar System: Semester
URL: www.miami.edu
Established: 1925 Annual Undergrad Tuition & Fees: $53,682
Enrollment: 17,809 Coed
Affiliation or Control: Independent Non-Profit IRS Status: 501(c)3
Highest Offering: Doctorate
Accreditation: **SC**, ANEST, CAATE, CAMPEP, CEA, CLPSY, COPSY, DENT, HSA, IPSY, LAW, MED, MUS, NURSE, PH, PTA

01 President .... Dr. Julio FRENK
05 Executive Vice President & Provost .... Dr. Jeffrey DUERK
10 Exec VP Business/Finance & COO .... Dr. Jacqueline TRAVISANO
21 Vice President & CFO .... Mr. Brandon GILLILAND
17 Interim CEO UHealth .... Mr. Joseph ECHEVARRIA
111 SVP Development & Alumni Relations .... Mr. Joshua FRIEDMAN
84 VP Enrollment Management .... Mr. John G. HALLER
115 Treasurer/Chief Investment Ofcr .... Mr. Charmel MAYNARD
18 VP Facilities Operations & Planning .... Ms. Jessica BRUMLEY
26 VP University Communications .... Ms. Jacqueline R. MENENDEZ
15 VP Human Resources .... Mrs. Mary HARPER HAGAN
43 VP/General Counsel .... Ms. Aileen M. UGALDE
32 Sr VP Student Affairs .... Dr. Patricia A. WHITELY
00 Chairman Board of Trustees .... Ms. Laurie SILVERS
100 President's Chief of Staff .... Mr. Rodolfo J. FERNANDEZ
20 Sr Vice Provost/Dean Undergrad Educ .... Dr. William S. GREEN
46 Vice Provost Research .... Dr. Erin KOBETZ
20 Vice Provost Faculty Affairs .... Dr. Guillermo PRADO
41 Director Athletics .... Mr. Blake JAMES
16 Interim AVP Med Human Resources .... Ms. Brianne C. NEUBURGER
27 Executive Director Comm & PR .... Ms. Megan M. ONDRIZEK
19 Chief of Police .... Chief David A. RIVERO
63 Dean School of Medicine .... Dr. Henri FORD
49 Dean College of Arts & Sciences .... Dr. Leonidas G. BACHAS
48 Dean School of Architecture .... Dr. Rodolphe EL-KHOURY
50 Dean Miami Business School .... Dr. John A. QUELCH
60 Dean School Communication .... Dr. Karin J. WILKINS
53 Dean Education/Human Development .... Dr. Laura KOHN-WOOD
54 Int Dean College of Engineering .... Dr. Daniel BERG
61 Dean School of Law .... Ms. Nell J. NEWTON
64 Dean School of Music .... Dr. Shelton G. BERG
65 Dean Marine & Atmospheric Science .... Dr. Roni AVISSAR
66 Dean Nursing & Health Studies .... Dr. Cindy L. MUNRO
58 Dean Graduate School .... Dr. Guillermo PRADO
35 AVP Stdnt Affs & Dean of Students .... Dr. Ryan C. HOLMES
07 Asst VP Undergrad Admissions & Mktg .... Mr. Nate CROZIER
38 Director Student Counseling .... Dr. Rene MONTEAGUDO
85 Executive Director Intl Services .... Ms. Teresa S. DE LA GUARDIA
39 AVP Student Affs/Housing/Strat Init .... Mr. James G. SMART
96 Executive Director Purchasing .... Ms. Susan R. MONTES
91 AVP Enterprise Business Solutions .... Mr. Anurag SARIN
119 Assoc VP and CISO .... Mr. Thomas MURPHY
90 AVP Chief Academic Tech Officer .... Mr. Allan GYORKE
14 Assoc VP Information Technology .... Mr. Brad ROHRER
109 Executive Director Auxiliary Svcs .... Ms. Ana ALVAREZ
51 Dean Continuing & Intl Education .... Dr. Rebecca MACMILLAN FOX
40 Director Bookstore .... Ms. Wendy SMITH
06 Registrar .... Ms. Karen J. BECKETT
08 Dean Libraries .... Dr. Charles ECKMAN
101 University Secretary .... Ms. Leslie DELLINGER ACEITUNO
102 Exec Director Foundation Relations .... Ms. Joanna DE VELASCO
36 Assoc Dean Career Services .... Mr. Christian GARCIA
104 Asst Dean & Director Study Abroad .... Ms. Devika M. MILNER
22 AVP Workplace Equity .... Ms. Beverly PRUITT
88 Asst VP Business Services .... Mr. Humberto M. SPEZIANI
37 Exec Director Financial Assistance .... Ms. Carrie GLASS
13 VP Information Technology & CIO .... Mr. Ernie FERNANDEZ
44 Assoc VP Engagement .... Ms. Erica ARROYO
114 AVP Financial Planning & Analysis .... Ms. Aintzane CELAYA
04 Administrative Manager to President .... Ms. Alicia BLATCHFORD
86 Sr VP for Pub Affairs & Comm .... Mr. Rodolfo J. FERNANDEZ
116 VP/Chief Audit/Compliance Officer .... Ms. Blanca MALAGON
117 Executive Director Risk Management .... Mr. Craig MCALLISTER
09 Assc Provost Institutional Research .... Dr. Dave BECHER
106 Exec Director Online Education .... Dr. Rebecca MACMILLAN FOX
108 Assoc Prov Institutional Assessment .... Ms. Patty MURPHY
30 Assoc VP Development & Alum Rels .... Ms. Cynthia BEAMISH
28 Title IX Coord/AVP Equity & Inclus .... Ms. Beverly PRUITT
29 Director Alumni Affairs .... Ms. Heather KOPEC

University of Phoenix Central Florida Main Campus (D)

8325 South Park Circle Ste 100, Orlando FL 32819

Telephone: (407) 345-8868 Identification: 770932
Accreditation: **&HLC**, ACBSP

† No longer accepting campus-based students.

University of Phoenix North Florida Campus (E)

4500 Salisbury Road, Jacksonville FL 32216-0959

Telephone: (904) 636-6645 Identification: 770197
Accreditation: **&HLC**, ACBSP

† No longer accepting campus-based students.

University of Phoenix South Florida Main Campus (F)

2400 SW 145th Avenue, Miramar FL 33027-4145

Telephone: (954) 628-1605 Identification: 770237
Accreditation: **&HLC**

† No longer accepting campus-based students.

University of St. Augustine for Health Sciences (G)

One University Boulevard, St. Augustine FL 32086

Telephone: (904) 826-0084 Identification: 770939
Accreditation: **&WC**, OT, PTA

† Branch campus of University of St. Augustine for Health Sciences, San Marcos, CA.

University of Tampa (H)

401 W Kennedy Boulevard, Tampa FL 33606-1490

County: Hillsborough FICE Identification: 001538
Unit ID: 137847
Telephone: (813) 253-3333 Carnegie Class: Masters/L
FAX Number: (813) 258-7207 Calendar System: Other
URL: www.ut.edu
Established: 1931 Annual Undergrad Tuition & Fees: $30,884
Enrollment: 9,605 Coed
Affiliation or Control: Independent Non-Profit IRS Status: 501(c)3
Highest Offering: Doctorate
Accreditation: **SC**, #ARCPA, ART, CAATE, CAEP, COSMA, FEPAC, MUS, NURSE

01 President .... Dr. Ronald L. VAUGHN
05 Provost/Vice Pres Academic Affairs .... Dr. David STERN
10 Vice Pres Administration/Finance .... Mr. Kevin LAFFERTY
84 Vice President Enrollment .... Mr. Dennis L. NOSTRAND
30 Vice Pres Development/Univ Rels .... Mr. L. Keith TODD
45 Vice Pres Operations & Planning .... Dr. Linda W. DEVINE
13 Chief Information Security Officer .... Ms. Tammy L. CLARK
32 Dean of Students .... Ms. Stephanie R. KREBS
20 Assoc Provost & Dean of Acad Svcs .... Mr. C. Jay PENDELTON
06 Registrar .... Ms. Michelle PELAEZ
08 Director of the Library .... Ms. Marlyn PETHE-COOK
29 Director of Alumni Relations .... Vacant
37 Director of Financial Aid .... Ms. Jacqueline LATORELLA
26 Director of Public Information .... Mr. Eric D. CARDENAS
18 Director of Facilities Management .... Vacant
15 Exec Director of Human Resources .... Ms. Donna B. POPOVICH
07 Dir Enrollment Mgmt/Admissions .... Mr. Brent W. BENNER
41 Athletic Director .... Mr. Larry J. MARFISE
40 Manager Campus Store .... Mr. Nick FAGNONI
39 Director of Residence Life .... Vacant
22 Affirmative Action Officer .... Ms. Donna B. POPOVICH
19 Director Safety & Security .... Mr. Kevin A. HOWELL
23 Dir Health Center/Stdnt Counseling .... Ms. Sharon P. SCHAEFER
38 Director Student Counseling .... Ms. Sharon P. SCHAEFER
96 Director of Procurement .... Ms. Cyn D. EZELL
09 Dir Institutional Effectiveness .... Mr. Drew KELLY
92 Director of Honors Program .... Dr. Gary S. LUTER
50 Dean College of Business .... Dr. F. Frank GHANNADIAN
83 Dean Social Science/Math Education .... Dr. Jack M. GELLER
81 Dean College Natural/Health Sci .... Dr. Paul GREENWOOD
57 Dean College of Arts/Letters .... Dr. David GUDELUNAS
51 Assoc Dean Graduate/Continuing Stds .... Dr. Donald D. MORRILL
89 Dir First Year/Baccalaureate Exp .... Ms. Edesa SCARBOROUGH
36 Assoc Dean Career Dev & Engagement .... Mr. Timothy HARDING
104 Assoc Dean International Programs .... Dr. Anne Liese BUSCH
04 Executive Asst to President .... Vacant

Valencia College (I)

PO Box 3028, Orlando FL 32802-3028

County: Orange FICE Identification: 006750
Unit ID: 138187
Telephone: (407) 299-5000 Carnegie Class: Bac/Assoc-Assoc Dom
FAX Number: (407) 426-8970 Calendar System: Semester
URL: www.valenciacollege.edu
Established: 1967 Annual Undergrad Tuition & Fees (In-State): $2,474
Enrollment: 45,949 Coed
Affiliation or Control: State IRS Status: 501(c)3
Highest Offering: Baccalaureate
Accreditation: **SC**, ADNUR, CAHIIM, CEA, COARC, CVT, DH, DMS, EMT, NURSE, RAD

01 President .... Dr. Kathleen A. PLINSKE
45 VP Analytics & Planning .... Dr. Brandon MCKELVEY
05 VP Academic Affairs .... Dr. Isis ARTZE VEGA
10 VP Business Ops & Finance .... Mr. Loren J. BENDER
107 VP Global/Prof & Cont Education .... Mr. Joe N. BATTISTA
15 VP Org Dev & Human Resources .... Dr. Amy N. BOSLEY
43 VP Policy & General Counsel .... Dr. Bill J. MULLOWNEY
26 VP Public Affairs & Marketing .... Mr. Jay R. GALBRAITH, II
32 VP Student Affairs .... Dr. Joe C. RICHARDSON
84 Associate VP Enrollment Management .... Dr. Sonya F. JOSEPH
88 Assoc General Counsel .... Dr. Leslie B. GOLDEN
07 Asst VP Admiss/Records & Grad .... Mr. Edwin SANCHEZ VELEZ
13 Chief Information Officer .... Ms. Patti T. SMITH
114 Asst VP Budgets & Analysis .... Mr. Oscar J. CRISTANCHO MERCADO
103 Asst VP Career & Workforce Educ .... Dr. Nasser HEDAYAT
90 Managing Dir Campus Tech Svcs .... Dr. Jamie D. ROST
84 Asst VP Recruit/Enroll/Retention .... Dr. Amy E. PARKER
18 Asst VP Facilities & Maint Ops .... Mr. Shaun D. ANDREWS
37 Asst VP Fin Aid/Vet Affairs .... Mr. Daniel T. BARKOWITZ
88 Asst VP Analytics & Reporting .... Mr. Daryl J. DAVIS
21 Asst VP Financial Services .... Ms. Jackie D. LASCH
51 Asst VP Global & Cont Educ .... Ms. Lisa G. ELI
27 Asst VP Marketing .... Ms. Traci A. BJELLA
11 Asst VP Operations .... Mr. Paul ROONEY
28 Asst VP Equity & Access .... Mr. Ryan D. KANE
16 Asst VP Org Development .... Ms. Carla L. MCKNIGHT
51 Asst VP Prof & Continuing Education .... Dr. Carolyn R. MCMORRAN
25 Asst VP Resource Development .... Ms. Kristeen R. GAMMON
88 Asst VP Educ Equity Partnership .... Ms. Eda DAVIS-LOWE
88 Asst VP Teaching & Learning .... Dr. Wendi M. DEW
12 Campus President East/Winter Park .... Vacant
12 Interim Campus President EC/WP .... Dr. Wendy L. GIVOGLU
12 Campus President Osceola/LNC/PNC .... Vacant
12 Interim Campus President LNC/PNC .... Mr. Stanton G. REED
12 Interim Campus President OSC .... Dr. Melissa D. PEDONE
12 Campus President West/Downtown .... Vacant
12 Interim Campus President WC/DT .... Dr. Terri A. GRAHAM
20 Executive Dean Downtown .... Dr. Eugene G. JONES, II
20 Executive Dean Lake Nona .... Dr. Mike BOSLEY
20 Executive Dean Poinciana .... Dr. Jennifer ROBERTSON
88 Executive Dean School Public Safety .... Dr. Jeff W. GOLTZ
20 Interim Executive Dean Winter Park .... Mr. John C. NISS
57 Int Dean Sch of Arts/Entertainment .... Mr. Rob MCCAFFREY
102 Foundation President and CEO .... Dr. Geraldine M P. GALLAGHER
20 Dean Academic Affairs East .... Ms. Michelle R. FOSTER
20 Int Dean Academic Affairs Osceola .... Ms. Marlene M. TEMES
20 Dean Academic Affairs West .... Dr. Molly MCINTIRE
115 Foundation VP & CFO .... Vacant
97 Dean Learning Support East .... Dr. Leonard C. BASS
97 Dean Learning Support Osceola .... Dr. Landon P. SHEPHARD
97 Int Dean Learning Support West .... Ms. Jennifer TOMLINSON
35 Dean of Students East/WP .... Mr. Joe M. SARRUBBO, JR.
35 Dean of Students Osceola .... Dr. Jill M. SZENTMIKLOSI
35 Dean of Students West .... Dr. Andel P. FILS AIME
35 Dean of Students DTC .... Dr. Edna D. JONES MILLER
76 Dean School of Allied Health .... Ms. Marie E. VASQUEZ-BROOKS
49 Dean Arts & Humanities West .... Ms. Ana J. CALDERO FIGUEROA
83 Dean Behav/Soc Science West .... Dr. Susan C. DUNN
50 Dean Bus/Info Tech/Pub Svcs .... Ms. Shara K. TSCHEULIN
50 Interim Dean Business West .... Dr. Cheri L. CUTTER
75 Int Dean Career & Technical Pgm .... Dr. Sonia P. CASABLANCA
60 Dean Communications East .... Ms. Linda R. NEAL
60 Dean Comm/Languages Osceola .... Ms. Jenni L. CAMPBELL
60 Dean Communications West .... Dr. Wesley T. JOHNSON
54 Dean Engr/Computer Pgm & Tech .... Dr. Paul J. WILDER
79 Int Dean Human/Foreign Lang East .... Mr. Eric WALLMAN
79 Dean Humanities/Social Science .... Dr. Scott F. CREAMER
81 Dean Math East .... Ms. Keri S. SILER
81 Dean Math Osceola .... Dr. Nichole A. SEGARRA
81 Dean Math West .... Dr. Paul D. BLANKENSHIP
66 Interim Dean School of Nursing .... Dr. Ruby ALVAREZ
49 Dean Science East .... Dr. Jennifer L. SNYDER
81 Dean Science Osceola .... Dr. Anitza M. SAN MIGUEL

49 Dean Science West ... Dr. Bob F. GESSNER
83 Dean Social Science East ... Dr. Mark G. COLLINS
88 Dean School of Hospitality/Culinary ... Mr. Alex ERDMANN
08 Campus Director Library W ... Ms. Ruth S. SMITH
29 Director Alum Engage/Annual Giving ... Ms. Erin C. OHLSEN
109 Director Auxiliary Services ... Mr. Jeffrey D. FILKO
109 Director Auxiliary Services ... Ms. Mona Liza COLON
116 Director Compliance & Audit .. Ms. Cynthia SANTIAGO-GUZMAN
102 Dir Corporate/Foundation Relations ... Vacant
88 Dir Strategic Lrng Initiatives ... Dr. Robyn M. BRIGHTON
88 Dir Curriculum & Articulation ... Dr. Cheryl ROBINSON
16 Director HR Policy & Compliance ... Ms. Michelle T. SEVER
22 Director Equal Opportunity ... Ms. Lauren E. KELLY
119 Managing Dir Network & Security ... Mr. John E. KNIGHTS
108 Director Institutional Evaluation ... Dr. Laura N. BLASI
09 Dir Institutional Effectiveness ... Mr. Darren A. SMITH
120 Faculty Director Teaching & Lrng ... Dr. Claudine BENTHAM
19 Managing Director Safety & Security ... Mr. Mike D. FAVORIT
96 Managing Director Procurement ... Ms. Yaremis P. FULLANA
44 Chief Philanthropy Officer ... Ms. Angela J. MENDOLARO
04 Senior Executive Assistant ... Ms. Barbara E. HALSTEAD

Warner University (A)

13895 Highway 27, Lake Wales FL 33859-2549
County: Polk FICE Identification: 008848
Unit ID: 138275
Telephone: (863) 638-1426 Carnegie Class: Bac-Diverse
FAX Number: (863) 638-1472 Calendar System: Semester
URL: www.warner.edu
Established: 1968 Annual Undergrad Tuition & Fees: $24,200
Enrollment: 978 Coed
Affiliation or Control: Church Of God IRS Status: 501(c)3
Highest Offering: Master's
Accreditation: SC, SW

01 President ... Dr. David A. HOAG
05 VP for Academic Affairs ... Dr. Gentry SUTTON
10 SVP Opers/Administraton/CFO ... Mr. Mike PICHA
111 Vice President for Advancement ... Mrs. Andrea THIES
84 VP for Enrollment Mgmt ... Mrs. Andrea THIES
32 VP of Student Life ... Ms. Anne TOHME
06 AVP Student Success/Registrar ... Mrs. Sara F. KANE
37 Director Student Financial Aid ... Ms. Elease COX
29 Alumni & Annual Fund Coord ... Ms. Abby CRAWFORD
18 Chief Facilities/Physical Plant ... Mr. Mark THOMAS
97 Director of General Studies ... Dr. Daniel JULICH
13 VP for Information Tech/Facilities ... Mr. Mark THOMAS
19 Director Campus Security ... Mrs. Janet CRAIGMILES
88 Director Academic Skills Ctr ... Mrs. Lisa WEATHERS
106 Assoc Dean Online Education ... Mr. Shawn TAYLOR
04 Executive Asst to President ... Mrs. Jera LAUREL
15 VP for Human Resources ... Mrs. Janet CRAIGMILES
21 Director of Accounting ... Mrs. Mandy RAMOS
07 Director of Admissions ... Mrs. Scarlett JACKSON
41 Athletic Director ... Mrs. Chrissy MOSKOVITS

Webber International University (B)

1201 Scenic Highway N/P.O. Box 96,
Babson Park FL 33827-0096
County: Polk FICE Identification: 001540
Unit ID: 138293
Telephone: (863) 638-1431 Carnegie Class: Bac-Diverse
FAX Number: (863) 638-2823 Calendar System: Semester
URL: www.webber.edu
Established: 1927 Annual Undergrad Tuition & Fees: $28,268
Enrollment: 812 Coed
Affiliation or Control: Independent Non-Profit IRS Status: 501(c)3
Highest Offering: Master's
Accreditation: SC, @OTA

01 President/CEO ... Dr. H. Keith WADE
05 Academic Dean/CAO ... Dr. Charles SHIEH
10 Vice President Finance ... Ms. Christina JORDON
09 VP of Inst Effectiveness/Research ... Dr. Nelson MARQUEZ
32 Campus VP of Student Life ... Mr. Jay CULVER
06 Vice Pres of Student Record Svcs ... Vacant
36 Dir Career Service & Cmty Outreach ... Mrs. Devyn MONTALVO
08 Director Library Services ... Ms. Sue DUNNING
41 Athletic Director ... Mr. Darren RICHIE
13 Director Information Technology ... Mr. Davius ROSIUS
18 Director of Campus Svcs/Maintenance ... Mr. Matt YENTES
40 Director of Bookstore ... Mr. Matt SALIBA
07 Director of Admissions ... Ms. Bobbi ANDREWS
20 Director of Academic Planning ... Ms. Lacy EDWARDS
50 Chair of Business Education ... Dr. Jeanette EBERLE
53 Chair of General Education Division ... Dr. Charles WUNKER
04 Executive Asst to President ... Ms. Gerlinde DANCY
19 Director Security/Safety ... Mr. Michael RITTER
29 Dir Annual Fund/Alumni Relations ... Ms. Jeanne LAWRIE
22 Assoc Dean Title IX Compliance ... Dr. Eileen FARCHMIN

West Coast University - Miami (C)

9250 NW 36th Street, Doral FL 33178
Telephone: (786) 501-7070 Identification: 770936
Accreditation: &WC

† Branch campus of West Coast University, North Hollywood, CA.

WMU - Cooley Law School Tampa Bay Campus (D)

9445 Camden Field Parkway, Riverview FL 33578
Telephone: (813) 419-5100 Identification: 770290
Accreditation: &HLC

† Branch campus of Western Michigan University Cooley Law School, Lansing, MI

Yeshiva Gedolah Rabbinical College (E)

1140 Alton Road, Miami Beach FL 33139-4708
County: Dade FICE Identification: 032563
Unit ID: 363712
Telephone: (305) 653-8770 Carnegie Class: Spec-4-yr-Faith
FAX Number: (305) 653-6790 Calendar System: Semester
URL: www.YGMiami.com
Established: 1973 Annual Undergrad Tuition & Fees: $8,300
Enrollment: 48 Male
Affiliation or Control: Independent Non-Profit IRS Status: 501(c)3
Highest Offering: Master's
Accreditation: RABN

01 Executive Vice President ... Rabbi Benzion KORF
05 Dean ... Rabbi Abraham KORF
06 Registrar ... Ayelet BORTUNK
07 Director of Admissions ... Rabbi Chaim STERN
11 Administration ... Colaiv FREEDMAN

GEORGIA

Abraham Baldwin Agricultural College (F)

ABAC 1 - 2802 Moore Highway, Tifton GA 31793-2601
County: Tift FICE Identification: 001541
Unit ID: 138558
Telephone: (229) 391-5001 Carnegie Class: Bac/Assoc-Mixed
FAX Number: (229) 391-5002 Calendar System: Semester
URL: www.abac.edu
Established: 1908 Annual Undergrad Tuition & Fees (In-State): $3,565
Enrollment: 3,990 Coed
Affiliation or Control: State IRS Status: 501(c)3
Highest Offering: Baccalaureate
Accreditation: SC, ADNUR, NUR

01 President ... Dr. David BRIDGES
05 Provost and VP for Academic Affairs ... Dr. Jerry BAKER
10 VP for Finance and Operations ... Ms. Deidra A. JACKSON
111 Int VP External Affairs/Advancement ... Mr. Paul WILLIAMS
13 AVP of Info Tech/CTO ... Mr. Allen C. SAYLOR, JR.
12 Exec Dir ABAC at Bainbridge ... Dr. Michael KIRKLAND
08 Director of Library Services ... Mr. David EDENS
32 Dean of Students ... Ms. Bernice HUGHES
41 Athletic Director ... Dr. Alan KRAMER
06 Registrar ... Dr. Amy WILLIS
37 Director of Financial Aid ... Ms. Brenda TAYLOR-HICKEY
15 Director of Human Resources ... Mr. Richard SPANCAKE
26 Dir of Marketing/Communications ... Ms. Lindsey CARNEY
108 Director of Assessment ... Vacant
84 Dir Enrollment Mgmt/Admissions ... Ms. Donna WEBB
96 Director of Procurement ... Ms. Teri MATHIS
19 Chief of Police ... Mr. Frank STRICKLAND
04 Admin Associate to President ... Ms. Jordan BEARD
39 Director of Student Housing ... Dr. Chris S. KINSEY
30 Chief Development Officer ... Ms. Deidre MARTIN

† Part of the University System of Georgia.

Agnes Scott College (G)

141 E. College Avenue, Decatur GA 30030-3770
County: DeKalb FICE Identification: 001542
Unit ID: 138600
Telephone: (404) 471-6000 Carnegie Class: Bac-A&S
FAX Number: (404) 471-6067 Calendar System: Semester
URL: www.agnesscott.edu
Established: 1889 Annual Undergrad Tuition & Fees: $44,250
Enrollment: 1,080 Female
Affiliation or Control: Presbyterian Church (U.S.A.) IRS Status: 501(c)3
Highest Offering: Master's
Accreditation: SC

01 President ... Ms. Leocadia (Lee) I. ZAK
05 VP Academic Affairs/Dean of College ... Dr. Christine COZZENS
32 Int VP Student Affs/Dean Students ... Ms. Marti FESSENDEN
10 Int VP Business & Finance ... Mr. Scott RANDAZZA
111 VP for College Advancement ... Dr. Robiaun R. CHARLES
84 VP for Enrollment/Dean of Admission ... Ms. Alexa GAETA
26 VP Communications/Marketing ... Ms. Danita KNIGHT
22 VP for Equity & Inclusion ... Dr. Yves-Rose PORCENA
101 Associate VP & Board Secretary ... Ms. Lea Ann HUDSON
13 Assoc VP Technology ... Ms. LaNeta COUNTS
15 Associate VP for Human Resources ... Ms. Karen GILBERT
06 Registrar ... Ms. Gail N. MEIS
08 Director of Library Services ... Ms. Elizabeth BAGLEY
29 Senior Director Alumnae Relations ... Ms. Mary Frances KERR
18 Director of Facilities ... Mr. Dave MARDER

42 Chaplain ... Rev. Whitney B. LOCKARD
37 Director of Financial Aid ... Mr. Patrick BONONES
09 Director of Institutional Research ... Dr. Corey DUNN
07 Sr Director of Admissions ... Ms. Aimee S. KAHN-FOSS
23 Wellness Center Director ... Dr. Michelle HAMM
19 Director of Public Safety ... Mr. Henry HOPE
36 Director of Career Development ... Ms. Dawn KILLENBERG

Albany State University (H)

504 College Drive, Albany GA 31705-2796
County: Dougherty FICE Identification: 001544
Unit ID: 138716
Telephone: (229) 500-2000 Carnegie Class: Masters/M
FAX Number: N/A Calendar System: Semester
URL: https://www.asurams.edu
Established: 1903 Annual Undergrad Tuition & Fees (In-State): $5,934
Enrollment: 6,509 Coed
Affiliation or Control: State IRS Status: 501(c)3
Highest Offering: Beyond Master's But Less Than Doctorate
Accreditation: SC, ACBSP, ADNUR, CACREP, CAHIIM, COARC, DH, DMS, EMT, FEPAC, HT, MLTAD, NUR, OTA, PTAA, RAD, SPAA, SW

01 President ... Mrs. Marion FEDRICK
100 VP Univ Relations/Chief of Staff ... Dr. Wendy WILSON
05 Provost/VP Academic Affairs ... Dr. Angela PETERS
10 VP Admin & Fiscal Affairs ... Mr. Shawn MCGEE
13 VP Information Technology Svcs/CIO ... Mr. William MOORE
84 VP Enrollment Mgmt/Student Success ... Mrs. Kenyatta JOHNSON
111 VP Institutional Advancement ... Mr. A.L FLEMING
32 VP Student Affairs ... Dr. Terry LINDSAY
108 VP Institutional Effectiveness ... Vacant
43 Chief Legal Affairs Officer ... Mr. Joel WRIGHT
116 Exec Dir Internal Audits ... Ms. Katherine KIKIVARAKIS
41 Director of Athletics ... Mr. Anthony DUCKWORTH
49 Dean College of Arts and Sciences ... Dr. Melanie HATCH
107 Dean Professional Studies ... Dr. Alicia JACKSON
76 Dean Health Professions ... Dr. Sarah BRINSON
19 Chief of Police ... Mr. Gregory ELDER
06 Registrar ... Mr. Frank MALINOWSKI
21 Controller ... Mr. Jeffrey HALL
53 Chair Teacher Education ... Dr. Rhonda PORTER
88 Chair Counseling Ed Leadership ... Dr. Deborah BEMBRY
57 Chair Visual & Performing Arts ... Dr. Marcia HOOD
65 Chair Biological Sciences ... Dr. Olabisi OJO
66 Chair Nursing ... Dr. Cathy WILLIAMS
68 Chair Health & Human Performance ... Dr. Timothy HUGHLEY
82 Chair History/Political Sci ... Dr. Babafemi ELUFIEDE
83 Chair Sociology & Psychology ... Dr. Hema DAVIS
70 Chair Social Work ... Dr. Barbara NOWAK
80 Chair Public Administration ... Dr. Peter NGWAFU
79 Chair English Modern Lang Mass Comm ... Dr. Henry MACK
60 Chair English/Mod Lang/Mass Comm ... Dr. Jeffrey MACK
81 Chair Math & Computer Sciences ... Dr. Robert OWOR
114 Chief Budget Officer ... Mrs. Marion RYANT
113 Bursar ... Ms. Jan ROGERS
18 Dir Facilities Management ... Mr. Oren HOWELL
15 Int Chief Human Resources Officer ... Mr. Larry JOHNSON
91 Director Application Services ... Mr. Sekar PONNAR
120 Director Online/Distance Learning ... Ms. Dominique HINES
92 Director Honors Program ... Dr. Florence LYONS
104 Director International Programs ... Dr. Nneka-Nora OSAKWE
36 Director Career Services ... Ms. Tracy WILLIAMS
38 Director Counseling/Disability Svcs ... Dr. Stephanie HARRIS-JOLLY
23 Director Student Health Services ... Dr. Vicki PHILLIPS
07 Interim Director of Admissions ... Ms. Michele APPLING
37 Interim Director of Financial Aid ... Mr. John BODIFORD
08 Director Library Services ... Dr. LaVerne MCLAUGHLIN
30 Director of Development ... Mr. Andrew FLOYD
40 Director Bookstore ... Ms. Tara JOHNSON
44 Director of Annual Giving ... Mrs. Ossie POLITE-WILLIAMS
119 Chief Information Security Officer ... Mr. Travis BARRON
96 Director of Purchasing ... Mrs. Joy CAUSEY
121 Dir Academic Advising/Retention ... Ms. Carolyn BROWN
39 Director Housing & Residence Life ... Ms. Keigan EVANS
123 Director Graduate Programs ... Dr. Charles OCHIE
109 Interim Dir Auxiliary Svcs ... Mrs. Martha SNOW

† Part of the University System of Georgia.

Albany Technical College (I)

1704 S Slappey Boulevard, Albany GA 31701-3587
County: Dougherty FICE Identification: 005601
Unit ID: 138682
Telephone: (229) 430-3500 Carnegie Class: Assoc/HVT-Mix Trad/Non
FAX Number: (229) 430-3594 Calendar System: Semester
URL: www.albanytech.edu
Established: 1961 Annual Undergrad Tuition & Fees (In-State): $2,996
Enrollment: 3,022 Coed
Affiliation or Control: State IRS Status: 501(c)3
Highest Offering: Associate Degree
Accreditation: SC, ADNUR, DA, EMT, MAC, #RAD, SURGT

01 President ... Dr. Anthony O. PARKER
100 Special Assistant to the President ... Mrs. Lorraine ALEXANDER
05 Vice Pres Academic Affairs ... Dr. Emmett GRISWOLD
10 Vice Pres Administrative Services ... Mrs. Kathy SKATES
26 Dir Public Relations/Marketing ... Mr. Bobby ELLIS
32 VP Student Affairs/Enrollment Mgmt ... Mrs. Barbara BROWN
36 Assoc Vice Pres of Career Svcs ... Mrs. Judy JIMMERSON
46 Vice President Economic Development ... Mr. Matt TRICE

55 Vice Pres of Adult Education .... Mrs. Linda COSTON
15 Executive Director Human Resources .... Mrs. Lola EDWARDS
09 Vice Pres Inst Effectiveness .... Dr. Steve EIDSON
51 Dean of Cont Educ & Off-Campus Pgm ...... Mrs. Tracy WALLACE
55 Dean of Evening Administration .... Mr. Don LAYE
37 Director of Financial Aid .... Mrs. Helen CATT
20 Dean of Academic Affairs .... Ms. Lisa STEPHENS
20 Dean of Academic Affairs .... Ms. Tomekia COOPER
20 Dean of Academic Affairs .... Mrs. Lisa HARRELL
88 Assoc Dean Early Childhood .... Mrs. Angela ROBINSON
56 Academic Dean Instructional Tech .... Mrs. Troycia WEBB
18 Director of Facilities .... Mr. Mike ALLIGOOD
84 Director of Enrollment .... Mr. Kenneth WILLIAMS
21 Director of Accounting Services .... Ms. Janet HAYES
06 Registrar .... Ms. Kennosha HAWKINS
35 Director Student Activities .... Dr. Mary RICHARDSON
13 Director of Computer/Info Systems .... Mr. Dennis SLEDGE
04 Executive Asst to the President .... Mrs. Natasha PRICE
08 Chief Library Officer .... Mr. Roy CALHOUN

American InterContinental University - Atlanta (A)

6600 Peachtree Dunwoody Road, Atlanta GA 30328
Telephone: (404) 965-6500 Identification: 666723
Accreditation: &HLC, ACBSP

† Regional accreditation is carried under the parent institution in Schaumburg, IL.

Andrew College (B)

501 College Street, Cuthbert GA 39840-5550
County: Randolph FICE Identification: 001545
Unit ID: 138761
Telephone: (229) 732-2171 Carnegie Class: Bac/Assoc-Assoc Dom
FAX Number: (229) 732-2176 Calendar System: Semester
URL: www.andrewcollege.edu
Established: 1854 Annual Undergrad Tuition & Fees: $19,172
Enrollment: 301 Coed
Affiliation or Control: United Methodist IRS Status: 501(c)3
Highest Offering: Baccalaureate
Accreditation: SC, #COARC

01 President .... Dr. Linda R. BUCHANAN
05 Dean of Academic Affairs .... Mrs. Karan B. PITTMAN
10 Vice President for Finance .... Mrs. Julie CADLE
111 Vice President for Advancement .... Mr. Spencer SEALY
84 Vice President for Enrollment .... Mr. Andy GEETER
21 Controller .... Ms. Beth STRICKLAND
32 Dean of Student Affairs .... Mr. James MCCOY
41 Athletic Director .... Mr. Blake WILLIAMS
42 Chaplain .... Ms. Ivelisse QUINONES
08 Director of Library Services .... Ms. Mckenzie RAGAN
40 Director of Bookstore .... Ms. McKenzie RAGAN
26 Dir of Communications & Marketing .... Ms. Heather BRADLEY
06 Registrar .... Ms. Carol DOLBERRY
18 Director of Maintenance .... Mr. Charles CORSON
19 Campus Security/Synergy .... Mr. Leon PARAMORE
39 Director of Residence Life .... Vacant
105 Web Services .... Mr. Brice HERRIN
22 ADA Director .... Mrs. Carol DOLBERRY
09 Director of Student Success Ctr/IR .... Ms. Julia WILLIAMS
37 Director of Financial Aid .... Ms. Daphne HARDEN
15 Director of Human Resources .... Mrs. Jennifer MITCHELL

The Art Institute of Atlanta (C)

6600 Peachtree Dunwoody Road, Atlanta GA 30328-1635
County: Fulton FICE Identification: 009270
Unit ID: 138813
Telephone: (770) 394-8300 Carnegie Class: Spec-4-yr-Arts
FAX Number: (770) 394-0008 Calendar System: Quarter
URL: www.artinstitutes.edu/atlanta/
Established: 1949 Annual Undergrad Tuition & Fees: $19,354
Enrollment: 814 Coed
Affiliation or Control: Independent Non-Profit IRS Status: 501(c)3
Highest Offering: Baccalaureate
Accreditation: SC, ACFEI, CIDA

01 Interim President .... Mr. Elden MONDAY
05 Dean of Academic Affairs .... Mr. Max SHANGLE
84 Director of Enrollment .... Quinisha STORY
37 Director of Student Financial Svcs ... Ms. Angela DAVIS-HAYNES
09 Dir of Inst Effectiveness/ Research .... Dr. Christopher S. BJORNSTAD
06 Registrar .... Mr. Willis PONDER
36 Director of Career Services .... Ms. Vicky BOLLING
15 Human Resources Manager .... Mr. Daniel KLAAS

Ashworth College (D)

5051 Peachtree Corner Circle, Ste 2, Norcross GA 30092
County: Gwinnett Identification: 666106
Telephone: (770) 729-8400 Carnegie Class: Not Classified
FAX Number: (770) 729-9296 Calendar System: Semester
URL: www.ashworthcollege.edu
Established: 2000 Annual Undergrad Tuition & Fees: N/A
Enrollment: N/A Coed
Affiliation or Control: Proprietary IRS Status: Proprietary
Highest Offering: Master's
Accreditation: DEAC

01 President .... Mr. Frank F. BRITT
05 Chief Academic Officer .... Mr. William KAKISH

Athens College of Ministry (E)

PO Box 7593, Athens GA 30604
County: Clarke Identification: 667306
Telephone: (706) 769-1472 Carnegie Class: Not Classified
FAX Number: (706) 769-1479 Calendar System: Semester
URL: www.acmin.org
Established: 2012 Annual Undergrad Tuition & Fees: N/A
Enrollment: N/A Coed
Affiliation or Control: Interdenominational IRS Status: 501(c)3
Highest Offering: Master's
Accreditation: TRACS

01 President .... Dr. Marcia WILBUR
05 Chief Academic Officer .... Dr. Jesse COYNE
32 Director of Student Affairs .... Mr. Alex FIELDS
58 Graduate Program Chair .... Dr. Suresh THOMAS
20 Undergraduate Program Chair .... Mr. Kurt GENTEMAN

Athens Technical College (F)

800 US Highway 29 N, Athens GA 30601-1500
County: Clarke FICE Identification: 005600
Unit ID: 246813
Telephone: (706) 355-5000 Carnegie Class: Assoc/HVT-High Trad
FAX Number: (706) 369-5753 Calendar System: Semester
URL: www.athenstech.edu
Established: 1958 Annual Undergrad Tuition & Fees (In-State): $3,062
Enrollment: 4,294 Coed
Affiliation or Control: State IRS Status: 501(c)3
Highest Offering: Associate Degree
Accreditation: SC, ACBSP, ADNUR, CAHIIM, DA, DH, EMT, PTAA, RAD, SURGT

01 President .... Dr. Andrea D. DANIEL
05 Vice President Academic Affairs .... Mr. Glenn HENRY
32 Vice President Student Affairs .... Mr. Lenzy REID, III
10 Vice Pres Administrative Services .... Ms. Kathryn S. THOMAS
45 Vice President Economic Development .... Mr. Al MCCALL
55 Vice President Adult Education .... Ms. Stephanie G. BENSON
106 Dean General Educ & Online Learning .... Dr. Jennifer PALMER
72 Dean TEM/Business & Educ .... Mr. Nick CHAPMAN
76 Int Dean Life Sci/Public Safety .... Mr. Stuart FREW
88 Exec Director Economic Development .... Mr. Andrew PALMER
108 Exec Dir Inst Effectiveness .... Dr. Laurie MCDOWELL
37 Int Exec Dir Fin Aid/Stdnt Accounts .... Mr. Octavius DAVIS
18 Executive Director Facilities .... Mr. Jim WALTER
26 Executive Director PR/Foundation .... Mr. Josh PAINE
19 Chief of Police .... Mr. John GAISSERT
06 Director Registration & Records .... Vacant
07 Director Admissions .... Ms. Lauren WILLIAMS
08 Director Library Services .... Ms. Carol STANLEY
35 Director Student Activities .... Mr. James SAUCEDA
121 Director Student Support .... Ms. Jessica FELTS
15 Director Human Resources .... Ms. Sherri HEATH
111 Director Institutional Advancement .... Ms. Jen WELBORN
13 Interim Dir Information Technology .... Mr. Geoff BARROW
21 Director of Accounting .... Mr. Ryan STANLEY

Atlanta Metropolitan State College (G)

1630 Metropolitan Parkway, SW, Atlanta GA 30310-4498
County: Fulton FICE Identification: 012165
Unit ID: 138901
Telephone: (404) 756-4000 Carnegie Class: Bac/Assoc-Mixed
FAX Number: (404) 756-4460 Calendar System: Semester
URL: www.atlm.edu
Established: 1974 Annual Undergrad Tuition & Fees (In-State): $3,505
Enrollment: 1,704 Coed
Affiliation or Control: State IRS Status: 501(c)3
Highest Offering: Baccalaureate
Accreditation: #SC, ACBSP

01 President .... Dr. Georj LEWIS
05 Provost/VP Student Success .... Dr. James MCGEE
10 Int Vice President Fiscal Affairs .... Mr. Nick HENRY
32 Exec Dir Student Svcs/Admissions .... Dr. J.L WYATT
111 VP Strategic Marketing/Advancement .... Ms. Lauretta HANNON
21 Director of Business Services .... Ms. Dakiesha PICKETT
50 Dean Div Business/Information Tech .... Dr. Vincent MANGUM
79 Int Dean Div Humanities/Fine Arts .... Ms. Lisa MALLORY
81 Dean Div of Sci/Math/Health Profess .... Dr. Bryan MITCHELL
83 Int Dean Div of Social Sciences .... Mr. Harry AKOH
06 Registrar/Dir Enrollment Svcs .... Mr. Edward ROSSER
15 Chief Human Resources Officer .... Mrs. Mitzi WILLIAMS
08 Director of the Library .... Mr. Robert QUARLES
35 Dir of Student Life and Leadership .... Ms. Iris SHANKLIN
37 Int Director of Financial Aid .... Ms. Carol JONES
38 Dir of Counseling/Disability Svcs .... Dr. Dorothy WILLIAMS
13 Chief Information/Tech Officer .... Mr. Antonio TRAVIS
108 VP Institutional Effectiveness .... Dr. Mark CUNNINGHAM
19 Chief of Police .... Chief Willey GAMMON, JR.
35 Dir of Student Outreach & Access .... Mr. Stephen WOODALL
18 Dir Plant Operations/Facilities .... Mr. Keith WILLIAMS
40 Bookstore Manager .... Ms. Natasha LAVINE
26 Director of Communications .... Ms. Sonja ROBERTS
41 Athletic Director .... Vacant

† Part of the University System of Georgia.

Atlanta Technical College (H)

1560 Metropolitan Parkway, SW, Atlanta GA 30310-4446
County: Fulton FICE Identification: 008543
Unit ID: 138840
Telephone: (404) 225-4400 Carnegie Class: Assoc/HVT-High Trad
FAX Number: N/A Calendar System: Semester
URL: www.atlantatech.edu
Established: 1967 Annual Undergrad Tuition & Fees (In-State): $3,084
Enrollment: 3,030 Coed
Affiliation or Control: State IRS Status: 501(c)3
Highest Offering: Associate Degree
Accreditation: SC, ACFEI, CAHIIM, DA, DH, EMT, MAC, PTAA, RAD

01 President .... Dr. Victoria SEALS
05 Exec VP Academic & Student Affairs .... Ms. Caroline ANGELO
11 Vice Pres Administrative Services .... Ms. Melanie SEWELL
30 Vice President Economic Development .... Ms. Yulonda DARDEN-BEAUFORD
04 Assistant to the President .... Dr. Joni WILLIAMS
26 Director Communications & Marketing .... Ms. Dorna WERDELIN
37 Director of Financial Aid .... Mr. LaMario PRIMAS
84 Dean Enrollment Services .... Ms. Niya EADY
88 Dean Industrial and Transportation .... Dr. Ian TOPPIN
51 Director of Continuing Education .... Mr. Curtis HALTON
36 Director Career Placement .... Mr. Michael BURNSIDE
50 Dean Business and Public Services .... Mr. Robert LEACH
69 Dean Health and Public Safety .... Dr. Katrina WALKER
06 Registrar .... Ms. Kenya DANIEL
15 Director Human Resources .... Mr. Travis SALLEY
18 VP Operations and IT .... Ms. Gail EDWARDS
09 Director of Institutional Research .... Mr. Britt PITRE
49 Dean Arts and Sciences .... Ms. Sonya MCCOY-WILSON
08 Director of Library Services .... Ms. Tosha BUSSEY
106 Dean Student Success .... Dr. Shawn ADAMS
13 Director of Information Technology .... Mr. Jeffrey SMITH
25 Director of Sponsored Programs .... Mr. Lance WISE
96 Procurement Officer .... Ms. Meinya LESLIE
102 Dir Foundation/Corporate Relations .... Dr. Jamar JEFFERS
19 Chief Security/Safety .... Mr. Charles SPANN

Atlanta's John Marshall Law School (I)

245 Peachtree Center Ave Ste 1900, Atlanta GA 30303
County: Fulton FICE Identification: 031733
Unit ID: 138929
Telephone: (678) 916-2600 Carnegie Class: Spec-4-yr-Law
FAX Number: (404) 873-3802 Calendar System: Semester
URL: www.johnmarshall.edu
Established: 1933 Annual Graduate Tuition & Fees: N/A
Enrollment: 299 Coed
Affiliation or Control: Proprietary IRS Status: Proprietary
Highest Offering: First Professional Degree; No Undergraduates
Accreditation: LAW

01 Dean/CEO .... Mr. Jace C. GATEWOOD
32 Assoc Dean of Students .... Ms. Sheryl E. HARRISON-MERCER
10 CFO .... Mr. Duane WRIGHT
06 Registrar .... Ms. Cheryl FEREBEE
26 Asst Dir Marketing & Communications .... Ms. Hilary WALDO
07 Exec Director of Admissions .... Mrs. Rebecca MILTER
37 Director of Financial Aid .... Ms. Michelle COOPER
29 Alumni Director .... Mr. AJ DOCETT
36 Associate Dean of Career Svcs .... Dr. Bridgett ORTEGA
05 Assoc Dean for Academic Program .... Mr. Scott BOONE
20 Assoc Dean of Academic Admin .... Ms. Judith BARGER
35 Asst Dean of Student Svs .... Ms. Hope JAMISON
08 Director of Law Library .... Mr. Michael LYNCH
15 Director of Human Resources .... Ms. Cynthia DAVENPORTE
04 Executive Assistant to the Dean/CEO .... Mrs. Erika S. MURRAY
84 Director of Recruitment .... Mr. Marc REECE
09 Director of Institutional Research .... Ms. Phylicia THOMPSON
13 Chief Information Technology Office .... Mr. Harold BIEBER
30 Chief Development Officer .... Mrs. Wendy AINA
88 Director of Academic Achievement .... Mr. Scot GOINS

Augusta Technical College (J)

3200 Augusta Tech Drive, Augusta GA 30906-3399
County: Richmond FICE Identification: 005599
Unit ID: 138956
Telephone: (706) 771-4000 Carnegie Class: Assoc/HVT-High Trad
FAX Number: (706) 771-4016 Calendar System: Semester
URL: www.augustatech.edu
Established: 1961 Annual Undergrad Tuition & Fees (In-District): $3,232
Enrollment: 3,863 Coed
Affiliation or Control: State/Local IRS Status: 501(c)3
Highest Offering: Associate Degree
Accreditation: SC, ADNUR, CAHIIM, COARC, CVT, DA, DMS, MAC, OTA, PNUR, RAD, #SURGT

01 President .... Dr. Germaine WHIRL
05 Exec Vice President Academic Affs .. Dr. Melissa FRANK-ALSTON
10 Vice Pres Administrative Services .... Ms. Sheila M. HILL
32 Vice Pres Student Affairs .... Dr. Nichole SPENCER
88 Vice President Economic Development .... Dr. Lisa PALMER
12 Dean of Operations Off Site Campus .... Ms. Julie LANGHAM
108 Dir Inst Effectiveness/Research .... Mrs. Beverly PELTIER
13 Dir Information Technology .... Mr. Pete WILKINSON
37 Director Financial Aid .... Ms. Cicely HARPE

84 Director Enrollment Services ... Ms. Christine BALL
06 Registrar ... Vacant
21 Director Accounting ... Ms. Sherrick L. JOHNSON
26 Dir Cmty Engagements/Public Rels ... Ms. Kimberly HOLDEN
15 Director Human Resources ... Ms. Shannon PATTERSON
36 Director Career Services ... Ms. Donna WENDT
08 Head Librarian ... Ms. Katrina COOKS
18 Facilities Director ... Mr. Garry STEPHENS
19 Director Security/Safety ... Mr. Mike ANCHOR
04 Administrative Asst to President ... Mrs. Charlene LEWIS
12 Coordinator Waynesboro Campus ... Mr. Greg COURSEY
12 Coordinator Thomson Campus ... Ms. Jeanette LOWE
88 High School Coordinator ... Mrs. Jan BLACKBURN
76 Dean Allied Health Science ... Dr. Gwen TAYLOR
50 Dean Business/Public Safety ... Ms. Elizabeth A. JULIAN
49 Dean Arts/Science/Learning Support ... Mr. John RICHARDSON
54 Dean Industrial & Engineering Tech ... Mr. Quentin COOKS
106 Dean of Info Tech/Dist Educ/Lib ... Mrs. Tammy O'BRIEN

Augusta University (A)

1120 Fifteenth Street, Augusta GA 30912-0004
County: Richmond FICE Identification: 001579
Unit ID: 482149
Telephone: (706) 721-0211 Carnegie Class: DU-Mod
FAX Number: N/A Calendar System: Semester
URL: www.augusta.edu
Established: 1828 Annual Undergrad Tuition & Fees (In-State): $9,022
Enrollment: 8,920 Coed
Affiliation or Control: State IRS Status: 501(c)3
Highest Offering: Doctorate
Accreditation: SC, ANEST, ARCPA, ART, CACREP, CAHIIM, CAMPEP, COARC, DENT, DH, DIETI, EMT, IPSY, MED, MIL, MPCAC, MT, MUS, NMT, NURSE, OT, PH, PTA, RTT, SPAA, SW

01 President ... Dr. Brooks A. KEEL
05 Exec VP for Acad Affairs/Provost ... Dr. Neil J. MACKINNON
10 EVP Finance/CBO ... Ms. Yvonne TURNER
26 EVP Operations ... Ms. Karla LEEPER
31 Exec VP External Rel/Chief of Staff ... Mr. Russell KEEN
43 General Counsel/VP Legal Affairs ... Mr. Chris MELCHER
17 EVP Medical Affairs/Dean Medicine ... Dr. David HESS
86 EVP Strategic Partnerships/Econ Dev ... Mr. W. Michael SHAFFER
46 Senior Vice President for Research ... Dr. Michael DIAMOND
30 VP of Development ... Ms. Debra VAUGHN
15 Enterprise VP Human Resources ... Ms. Susan A. NORTON
20 Assoc Provost Faculty Affairs ... Dr. Kathy BROWDER
84 VP Enrollment/Student Affairs ... Dr. Susan B. DAVIES
09 VP Institutional Effectiveness ... Ms. Mickey WILLIFORD
109 AVP Campus Services/Chief Aux Ofcr ... Mr. Dale HARTENBURG
18 VP Facilities Service ... Mr. Ronald BOOTH
27 VP Communications & Marketing ... Ms. Christen ENGEL
20 Vice Prov Instruction/Innovation ... Dr. Zach KELEHEAR
21 Interim Vice Pres for Finance ... Ms. Corrina WARNER
102 Interim VP University Foundations ... Mr. Stephen R. LAMB
88 VP & CMO for Health System ... Dr. Phillip L. COULE
58 Interim Dean The Graduate School ... Dr. Jennifer SULLIVAN
76 Dean Col of Allied Health Sciences ... Dr. Lester PRETLOW
52 Dean Dental College of GA ... Dr. Carol LEFEBVRE
66 Dean College of Nursing ... Dr. Tanya SUDIA
77 Dean Sch of Computer/Cyber Science ... Dr. Alex SCHWARZMANN
50 Dean Hull College of Business ... Dr. Richard M. FRANZA
49 Dean College Arts/Hum/Soc Sci ... Dr. Kim DAVIES
53 Dean College of Education ... Dr. Judi WILSON
81 Dean College of Science & Math ... Dr. John SUTHERLAND
116 VP Audit/Compl/Ethics/Risk Mgmt ... Mr. Barry GROSSE
28 Chief Diversity Officer ... Dr. Tiffany TOWNSEND
13 VP Information Technology/CIO ... Dr. Michael CASDORPH
88 Director Georgia Cancer Center ... Dr. Jorge CORTES
06 Registrar ... Ms. Heather B. METRESS
113 Bursar ... Ms. Beth WELSH
41 Director of Athletics ... Mr. Clint BRYANT
19 Assistant VP Public Safety & Police ... Chief James LYON
08 Interim Director of Libraries ... Ms. Kathy DAVIES
96 Director Supply Management ... Mr. Greg WOODLIEF
88 Asst Chief Aux Services Officer ... Mr. Karl MUNSCHY
32 Asst VP and Dean of Students ... Dr. Scott WALLACE
37 Director of Financial Aid ... Ms. Debra TURNER
07 Director of Admissions ... Ms. Jacqueline DUCA
04 Exec Admin Asst to President ... Mrs. Jacqueline B. STEPHENS
104 Director Study Abroad ... Vacant
22 Affirmative Action/EEO Officer ... Mr. Steven GOLDBERG
29 Director Alumni Engagement ... Ms. Kim KOSS
36 Director Career Services ... Ms. Julie GOLEY
38 Director Student Counseling ... Ms. Elena PETROVA
39 Director Student Housing ... Dr. Heather SCHNELLER
105 Director Web and Digital Services ... Mr. Davin MILLER

† Part of the University System of Georgia.

Berry College (B)

2277 Martha Berry Highway, NW, Mount Berry GA 30149
County: Floyd FICE Identification: 001554
Unit ID: 139144
Telephone: (706) 232-5374 Carnegie Class: Masters/S
FAX Number: (706) 236-2238 Calendar System: Semester
URL: www.berry.edu
Established: 1902 Annual Undergrad Tuition & Fees: $37,946
Enrollment: 2,125 Coed
Affiliation or Control: Independent Non-Profit IRS Status: 501(c)3
Highest Offering: Beyond Master's But Less Than Doctorate
Accreditation: SC, MUS, NURSE

01 President ... Dr. Stephen R. BRIGGS
05 Provost ... Dr. Mary K. BOYD
10 Vice President Finance ... Mr. Brian I. ERB
32 VP Student Affairs/Dean of Students ... Ms. Lindsey TAYLOR
111 Vice Pres Institutional Advancement ... Ms. Cynthia COURT
84 VP of Enrollment Management ... Dr. Andrew BRESSETTE
26 VP Marketing & Communications ... Ms. Nancy REWIS
100 Chief of Staff ... Ms. Debbie HEIDA
42 Chaplain ... Rev. Jonathan HUGGINS
19 Asst VP Campus Police/Emergency Mgt ... Mr. Gary WILL
50 Dean Campbell School of Business ... Dr. Joyce HEAMES
53 Interim Dean Charter School of Educ ... Dr. Alan HUGHES
79 Dean School Humanities/Arts/Soc Sci ... Dr. Gabriel BARRENECHE
66 Director of Nursing ... Dr. Pam DUNAGAN
81 Dean School of Math/Nat Sci ... Dr. Alice SUROVIEC
88 Dean of Personal & Professional Dev ... Dr. Marc HUNSAKER
20 Associate Provost ... Dr. David SLADE
39 Assoc Dean Students/Residence Life ... Mrs. Lindsay NORMAN
07 Dir of Admission/Enroll Management ... Mr. Glenn GETCHELL
30 Asst VP Campaign/Leadership Giving ... Mr. Scott BREITHAUPT
08 Director of the Library ... Ms. Sherre L. HARRINGTON
29 Director of Alumni Affairs ... Ms. Jennifer SCHAKNOWSKI
13 Chief Information Officer ... Ms. Penny EVANS-PLANTS
38 Director of Counseling Center ... Ms. Rebecca SMITH
37 Director Financial Aid ... Ms. Noemi SARRION-CORTES
09 Dir Institutional Research ... Dr. Bryce DURBIN
46 Dir Research & Sponsored Programs ... Ms. Laura TAYLOR
18 Director Physical Plant ... Mr. Todd BRADFORD
92 Director Honors Program ... Dr. Lauren HELLER
94 Director Women's Studies ... Dr. Susan CONRADSEN
96 Director Purchasing ... Mr. Brad BARRIS
85 Director International Experiences ... Dr. Elizabeth DAVIS
15 Director Human Resources ... Mr. Wayne PHIPPS
43 Director of Legal Services ... Mr. Danny PRICE
06 Registrar ... Dr. Bryce DURBIN
41 Director of Athletics ... Dr. Angel MASON
121 Associate Dean for Student Success ... Ms. Anna SHARPE
44 Director of Annual Giving ... Ms. Anne WILSON
35 Director Student Activities ... Ms. Cecily CROW
23 Director Health & Wellness Center ... Ms. Emma CORDLE
88 Associate Dir Academic Transitions ... Ms. Sarah KAUFMAN

Beulah Heights University (C)

892 Berne Street, SE, PO Box 18145,
Atlanta GA 30316-1873
County: Fulton FICE Identification: 030763
Unit ID: 139153
Telephone: (404) 627-2681 Carnegie Class: Spec-4-yr-Faith
FAX Number: (404) 627-0702 Calendar System: Semester
URL: www.beulah.edu
Established: 1918 Annual Undergrad Tuition & Fees: $8,492
Enrollment: 565 Coed
Affiliation or Control: Other Protestant IRS Status: 501(c)3
Highest Offering: Doctorate
Accreditation: BI, TRACS

01 President ... Dr. Benson M. KARANJA
04 Administrative Asst to President ... Ms. Anissa BLAIR
11 Vice Pres Administration/Tech ... Mr. Peter KARANJA
05 Vice Pres/Dean Academic Affairs ... Dr. Rodney JACKSON
88 Vice Pres Asian Affairs ... Dr. Kyung Soo JHO
32 Vice Pres Student Life ... Dr. Wes WILSON
106 Dean of Distance Education ... Dr. Alicia PLANT
42 Dean of Chapel ... Vacant
06 University Registrar ... Ms. Georgia SKINNER
10 Director of Finance/Comptroller ... Mr. Julian IVEY
37 Director of Financial Aid ... Ms. Ukemah D. CODY
07 Director of Admissions ... Ms. Jasmine DOUGLAS
73 Chair Religious Studies ... Dr. Brian K. HODGES
08 Director of Library Services ... Mr. Michael JOHNSON
15 Director of Human Resources ... Ms. Trish STATON
26 Director of Marketing ... Vacant
09 Director of Institutional Research ... Dr. Josiane CAROLINO
39 Dir Resident Life/Student Housing ... Dr. Wes C. WILSON

Brenau University (D)

500 Washington Street, SE, Gainesville GA 30501-3668
County: Hall FICE Identification: 001556
Unit ID: 139199
Telephone: (770) 534-6299 Carnegie Class: Masters/L
FAX Number: (770) 534-6114 Calendar System: Semester
URL: www.brenau.edu
Established: 1878 Annual Undergrad Tuition & Fees: $31,720
Enrollment: 2,813 Coed
Affiliation or Control: Independent Non-Profit IRS Status: 501(c)3
Highest Offering: Doctorate
Accreditation: SC, ACBSP, ARCPA, CIDA, MPCAC, NURSE, OT, PTA

01 President ... Dr. Anne A. SKLEDER
03 Executive VP/CFO ... Dr. David L. BARNETT
05 Provost & VP For Academic Affairs ... Dr. James C. ECK
100 Chief of Staff ... Ms. Jody Y. WALL
10 Vice President Financial Services ... Mr. Toby R. HINTON
84 Vice Pres Enrollment Management ... Vacant
111 Vice Pres External Relations ... Mr. J. Matthew THOMAS
13 Vice Pres Information Technology ... Mr. Chip L. ANDREWS
32 VP for Student Services ... Dr. Amanda LAMMERS
09 Director of Research & Planning ... Ms. Claudia GEORGE
37 Assoc VP & Dir Financial Aid ... Ms. Pam J. BARRETT
21 Director of Accounting Operations ... Ms. Jennifer KELLEY
15 Asst VP Director of Human Resources ... Ms. Kelley L. MADDOX
36 Director of Career Services ... Vacant
121 Director of Learning Center ... Ms. Jennifer WILSON-LOGGINS
41 Vice President of Athletics ... Mr. Mike LOCHSTAMPFOR
53 Dean College of Education ... Dr. Eugene WILLIAMS
76 Dean College of Health Sciences ... Dr. Gale H. STARICH
50 Dean College Business & Comm ... Vacant
79 Dean Coll of Fine Arts & Humanities ... Dr. Andrea C. BIRCH
08 Dean of Library Services ... Ms. Linda KERN
07 Executive Director for Admissions ... Mr. Nathan R. GOSS
06 Registrar & Dir of Student Records ... Ms. Barbara WILSON
29 Exec Director Alumni ... Ms. Ashley CARTER
19 Director Campus Safety & Security ... Ms. Paula DAMPIER
104 Director Study Abroad ... Ms. Jordan ANDERSON

Brewton-Parker College (E)

201 David-Eliza Fountain Circle,
Mount Vernon GA 30445-0197
County: Montgomery FICE Identification: 001557
Unit ID: 139205
Telephone: (912) 583-2241 Carnegie Class: Bac-A&S
FAX Number: (912) 583-4498 Calendar System: Semester
URL: www.bpc.edu
Established: 1904 Annual Undergrad Tuition & Fees: $18,900
Enrollment: 835 Coed
Affiliation or Control: Baptist IRS Status: 501(c)3
Highest Offering: Baccalaureate
Accreditation: SC

01 President ... Dr. Steven F. ECHOLS
04 Executive Asst to President ... Ms. Laura HAY
43 General Counsel ... Mr. Thomas EVERETT
10 Chief Financial Officer ... Dr. Nicole SHEPARD
05 Provost & Senior Vice President ... Dr. Robert M. BRIAN
32 VP for Student Success & Diversity ... Dr. Beverly ROBINSON
35 Assoc VP for Student Development ... Mr. Madison HERRIN
88 Assoc Prov External Programs ... Ms. Lynn ADDISON
84 VP of Enrollment Svcs & Athletics ... Mr. Chris DOOLEY
11 Director of Operations ... Mr. Ted TOWNS
15 Director Human Resources ... Ms. Keri NESTER
37 Director of Financial Aid ... Ms. Loretta WATSON
07 Director of Admissions ... Ms. Michelle HARTER
38 Dir Counseling Services ... Mr. Thadeus HOLLOWAY
06 Registrar ... Dr. Deokhyo KIM
09 Dir of Inst Effectiveness/Research ... Ms. Toni BANKS
26 Dir Public Relations & Marketing ... Mrs. Miranda SIMMONS
111 Director of Advancement ... Mr. Chad RITCHIE
22 Dir Affirmative Action/EEO ... Mr. Forrest RICH
50 Chair Business ... Dr. Sherida HABERSHAM
53 Chair Education/Behavioral Sci ... Dr. Justin RUSSELL
79 Chair Christian Studies/Humanities ... Dr. Grant LILFORD
81 Chair Math & Natural Sciences ... Dr. Helene PETERS
42 Campus Pastor ... Mr. Steve EDWARDS
13 Chief Information Technology Office ... Mr. Michael STEINMETZ

Cambridge Institute of Allied Health & Technology (F)

5669 Peachtree Dunwoody Rd, Ste 100, Atlanta GA 30342
Telephone: (404) 255-4500 Identification: 770938
Accreditation: ABHES, DMS

† Branch campus of Cambridge Institute of Allied Health and Technology, Delray Beach, FL.

Central Georgia Technical College (G)

80 Cohen Walker Drive, Warner Robins GA 31088
County: Houston FICE Identification: 005763
Unit ID: 483045
Telephone: (478) 988-6800 Carnegie Class: Assoc/HVT-Mix Trad/Non
FAX Number: (478) 757-3454 Calendar System: Semester
URL: www.centralgatech.edu
Established: 1966 Annual Undergrad Tuition & Fees (In-State): $3,042
Enrollment: 8,140 Coed
Affiliation or Control: State IRS Status: 501(c)3
Highest Offering: Associate Degree
Accreditation: SC, ADNUR, CVT, DH, EMT, MLTAD, PNUR, POLYT, PTAA, RAD, SURGT

01 President ... Dr. Ivan ALLEN
03 Executive Vice President ... Mr. Jeff SCRUGGS
05 Vice President Academic Affairs ... Dr. Amy HOLLOWAY
10 Vice President Admin/Fin Svcs ... Dr. Michelle SINIARD
32 Vice President Student Affairs ... Dr. Craig JACKSON
31 Vice President Economic Development ... Ms. Andrea GRINER
13 Chief Information Officer ... Dr. Brian SNELGROVE
06 Registrar ... Ms. Sonja JENKINS
111 Asst VP for Advancement ... Ms. Tonya MCCLURE
08 Director Library & Media Services ... Ms. Allison REPZYNSKI
15 Executive Director Human Resources ... Ms. Carol DOMINY
18 Facilities Director ... Mr. Robert DOMINY
51 Director of Continuing Education ... Ms. Ann LEAR
04 Admin Assistant to the President ... Ms. Danielle STEELE
09 Director of Institutional Research ... Ms. Bonnie QUINN
104 Director Study Abroad ... Mr. Rick HUTTO
22 Dir Affirmative Action/Equal Opp ... Ms. Cathy JOHNSON
26 Dir Marketing & Public Relations ... Dr. Janet KELLY
38 Exec Dir for Counseling Svcs ... Ms. Tonja SIMMONS
84 Director Enrollment Management ... Ms. Brandi MITCHEM

Chamberlain University-Atlanta (A)

5775 Peachtree-Dunwoody Rd NE,A100,
Atlanta GA 30342
Telephone: (404) 250-8500 Identification: 770504
Accreditation: &HLC, NURSE

† Branch campus of Chamberlain University-Addison, Addison, IL

Chattahoochee Technical College (B)

980 South Cobb Drive, Marietta GA 30060
County: Cobb FICE Identification: 030290
Unit ID: 140331
Telephone: (770) 528-4545 Carnegie Class: Assoc/HVT-Mix Trad/Non
FAX Number: (770) 975-4126 Calendar System: Quarter
URL: www.chattahoocheetech.edu
Established: 1981 Annual Undergrad Tuition & Fees (In-State): $3,120
Enrollment: 9,432 Coed
Affiliation or Control: State IRS Status: 501(c)3
Highest Offering: Associate Degree
Accreditation: SC, ADNUR, EMT, MAC, MLTAD, NAEYC, OTA, PTAA, RAD, SURGT

01 President .... Dr. Ron NEWCOMB
04 Exec Asst to President .... Ms. Tammy COLLUM
05 Vice President for Academics .... Dr. Jason TANNER
11 Vice Pres for Administrative Svcs .... Ms. Heather PENCE
32 Vice President Student Affairs .... Ms. Missy CUSSACK
18 Vice President for Facilities .... Mr. David SIMMONS
15 Vice President Human Resources .... Mr. Ron PRICE
26 Vice President Advancement .... Ms. Jennifer NELSON

Clark Atlanta University (C)

223 James P. Brawley Drive, SW, Atlanta GA 30314-4391
County: Fulton FICE Identification: 001559
Unit ID: 138947
Telephone: (404) 880-8000 Carnegie Class: DU-Higher
FAX Number: N/A Calendar System: Semester
URL: www.cau.edu
Established: 1988 Annual Undergrad Tuition & Fees: $21,695
Enrollment: 3,776 Coed
Affiliation or Control: United Methodist IRS Status: 501(c)3
Highest Offering: Doctorate
Accreditation: SC, CACREP, CAEP, SPAA, SW

01 President .... Dr. George T. FRENCH, JR.
05 Provost & SVP for Academic Affairs .... Dr. G. Dale WESSON
111 Vice President Institutional Advanc .... Dr. Richard LUCAS
10 CFO & Sr VP Business/Fin Svcs .... Dr. Lanze THOMPSON
07 Assoc VP & Dean UG Admissions .... Ms. Lorri SADDLER-RICE
46 Asst VP Research & Sponsored Pgms .... Ms. De Lisa WILSON
20 Assoc Provost .... Dr. Calvin BROWN
13 Assoc VP/Chief Info Ofcr .... Mr. Charles COOPER
21 Assoc VP & Controller .... Vacant
09 VP Planning/Assess/Inst Rsrch .... Dr. Lauren LOPEZ
43 General Counsel .... Ms. Jennifer ERVIN
06 University Registrar .... Ms. Susan GIBSON
26 Dir of News & Media Relations .... Ms. Jolene BUTTS-FREEMAN
29 Director Alumni Relations .... Ms. Gay-linn JASHO
15 AVP/Chief People Officer .... Ms. Debra HOYT
123 AVP & Dean for Graduate Admissions .... Ms. Cherise Y. PETERS
38 Director University Counseling Ctr .... Dr. Vicki JESTER
32 Dean of Student Svcs/Campus Life .... Dr. Omar TORRES
37 Director Student Financial Aid .... Mr. James STOTTS
96 Director of Purchasing .... Ms. Donna BYRD
41 Director of Athletics .... Mr. J. Lin DAWSON
49 Interim Dean Arts & Sciences .... Dr. Jaideep CHAUDHARY
50 Dean School of Business .... Dr. Silvanus UDOKA
53 Dean School of Education .... Dr. J. Fidel TURNER
70 Dean School of Social Work .... Dr. Jenny L. JONES
19 Chief of Public Safety .... Chief Debra A. WILLIAMS
23 Director Health Services .... Ms. Caroline B. RICHARDS
25 Director Grants & Contracts/Account .... Ms. Rotesha HARRIS
39 Director of Residence Life .... Mr. Larance CARTER
24 Director Instructional Media .... Mr. Frank EDWARDS
101 Coordinator for Board Relations .... Ms. Natalie BAKER
104 Coordinator Multicultural Affairs .... Ms. Gwen WADE
22 University Compliance Officer .... Mr. Robert CLARK
18 Director of Facilities .... Mr. Shelton ANDERSON
108 Exec Dir Institutional Assessment .... Mr. Christopher SEAVEY
04 Executive Asst to President .... Ms. Rita HARDY
100 Chief of Staff .... Dr. Charles GIBBS
102 Asst VP IAUR .... Ms. Quisa FOSTER
106 Assoc Provost Online Lrng/Cont Educ .... Dr. Mary A. HOOPER

Clayton State University (D)

2000 Clayton State Boulevard, Morrow GA 30260-0285
County: Clayton FICE Identification: 008976
Unit ID: 139311
Telephone: (678) 466-4000 Carnegie Class: Masters/M
FAX Number: (770) 961-3700 Calendar System: Semester
URL: www.clayton.edu
Established: 1969 Annual Undergrad Tuition & Fees (In-State): $5,568
Enrollment: 7,052 Coed
Affiliation or Control: State IRS Status: 501(c)3
Highest Offering: Master's
Accreditation: SC, DH, EXSC, MPCAC, MUS, NURSE

01 President .... Dr. T. Ramon STUART
05 Interim Provost/VP Academic Affairs .... Dr. Jill LANE
10 VP for Operations/Planning/Budget .... Ms. Corlis CUMMINGS
32 Vice President for Student Affairs .... Dr. Shakeer ABDULLAH
111 Vice President Univ Advancement .... Mr. Chase MOORE
13 Vice Pres Information Tech & Svcs .... Mr. Bill GRUSZKA
20 Associate Provost .... Vacant
35 Assistant Vice Pres Student Affairs .... Dr. Allen WARD
84 VP for Enrollment Management .... Dr. Stephen SCHULTHEIS
41 Director of Athletics .... Mr. Ryan ERLACHER
88 Executive Director of Spivey Hall .... Mr. Samuel DIXON
15 Director Human Resources & Services .... Mr. Rodney BYRD
49 Dean of Arts & Sciences .... Dr. Nasser MOMAYEZI
50 Dean of Business .... Dr. Jacob CHACKO
76 Dean of Health Sciences .... Dr. W. Michael SCOTT
81 Dean Information/Mathematical Sci .... Dr. Ebrahim KHOSRAVI
08 Dean of Library Services .... Dr. Sonya GAITHER
124 Director Advising & Retention .... Mr. Eric TACK
88 Dir Center for Instructional Dev .... Mr. Justin MAYS
51 Exec Director Continuing Education .... Mr. Reginald TURNER
06 University Registrar .... Ms. Rebecca GMEINER
07 Director of Admissions .... Mr. Will BROWN
109 Asst VP of Auxiliary Services .... Ms. Julie COILE
26 Asst VP Marketing/Communications .... Ms. Asia HAUTER
18 AVP of Facilities Management .... Mr. Harun BISWAS
19 Director of Public Safety .... Chief Antonio LONG
09 Director of Institutional Research .... Dr. Narem REDDY
24 Director Media Services .... Mr. Todd BIRCHFIELD
38 Director of Counseling Services .... Dr. Christine SMITH
37 Director Student Financial Aid .... Mr. Dolapo OGUNMAKIN
96 Procurement Manager .... Ms. Wanda POLITE
29 Director of Alumni Engagement .... Mr. Michael LITTLE
21 AVP Budget & Finance/Comptroller .... Ms. Akwai AGOONS
36 Director of Career Services .... Ms. Bridgette MCDONALD
121 Dir Center for Academic Success .... Ms. Jada MITCHELL
04 Exec Assistant to the President .... Ms. Brenda CARR
104 Director of International Programs .... Mr. Ryan PACKARD
39 Director of Housing/Residence Life .... Ms. Mya RICHARDSON-ECHOLS
44 Dir Annual Giving/Alumni Relations .... Mr. Michael LITTLE
86 Director Government Relations .... Mr. Jim FLOWERS

† Part of the University System of Georgia.

Coastal Pines Technical College (E)

1701 Carswell Avenue, Waycross GA 31503-4016
County: Ware FICE Identification: 005511
Unit ID: 485458
Telephone: (912) 287-6584 Carnegie Class: Assoc/HVT-High Non
FAX Number: N/A Calendar System: Semester
URL: www.coastalpines.edu
Established: 1965 Annual Undergrad Tuition & Fees (In-State): $2,759
Enrollment: 3,606 Coed
Affiliation or Control: State IRS Status: 501(c)3
Highest Offering: Associate Degree
Accreditation: SC, COARC, EMT, MAC, RAD, SURGT

01 President .... Mr. Lonnie ROBERTS
03 Provost .... Vacant
05 Vice Pres for Academic Affairs .... Ms. Amanda MORRIS
11 VP of Administrative Services .... Ms. Melissa LAMB
46 Vice Pres for Economic Development .... Dr. Pete SNELL
32 Vice President for Student Affairs .... Ms. Karla EUBANKS
06 Registrar .... Ms. Janet CARTER
111 Director Institutional Advancement .... Ms. Stephanie ROBERTS
18 Facilities Director .... Mr. Chad BOYETT
36 Career Placement & Develop Coord .... Mr. Buck THIGPEN
37 Director Student Financial Aid .... Ms. Tina MANNING
108 VP for Institutional Effectiveness .... Mr. Vince E. JACKSON
07 Director of Admissions .... Mr. Chris JEANCAKE
15 Human Resources Director .... Ms. Katrina HOWARD
04 Administrative Asst to President .... Ms. Natasha KING
08 Director of Library Services .... Ms. Cassie CLEMONS
13 Chief Info Technology Officer (CIO) .... Mr. Derrell HARRIS
38 Director Student Counseling .... Ms. Cathy MONTGOMERY
19 Campus Police Chief .... Mr. Ethan JOHNSON

College of Coastal Georgia (F)

One College Drive, Brunswick GA 31520-3632
County: Glynn FICE Identification: 001558
Unit ID: 139250
Telephone: (912) 279-5700 Carnegie Class: Bac/Assoc-Mixed
FAX Number: (912) 262-3072 Calendar System: Semester
URL: www.ccga.edu
Established: 1961 Annual Undergrad Tuition & Fees (In-State): $3,933
Enrollment: 3,457 Coed
Affiliation or Control: State IRS Status: 501(c)3
Highest Offering: Baccalaureate
Accreditation: SC, ACFEI, ADNUR, NUR, RAD

01 President .... Dr. Michelle JOHNSTON
05 Provost/VPAA .... Dr. Johnny EVANS
111 VP Advancement .... Mr. James BESSETTE
10 Vice President Business Affairs .... Ms. Michelle HAM
32 VP Student Affairs & Enrollment .... Dr. Jason W. UMFRESS
20 Asst VP Academic Affairs .... Dr. German VARGAS
20 Asst VP Academic Affairs .... Dr. Laura LYNCH
21 Fiscal Dir Budgets and Foundation .... Ms. Lorraine MOYER
84 Asst VP Recruitment & Admissions .... Mr. Scott ARGO
13 Chief Information Officer .... Mr. Alan OURS
19 Chief of Police .... Mr. Bryan SIPE
08 Dean of Library Services .... Ms. Debra HOLMES
35 Dean of Students .... Dr. Michael BUTCHER
49 Dean Sch of Arts & Sciences .... Dr. Andrea WALLACE
50 Dean Sch of Business & Public Mgmt .... Dr. William MOUNTS
66 Dean Sch of Nursing & Health Sci .... Dr. Lydia WATKINS
41 Director of Athletics .... Dr. William CARLTON
12 Director of Camden Center .... Mr. Joseph LODMELL
106 Director of E-Learning .... Dr. Lisa MCNEAL
09 Dir Institutional Effectiveness .... Dr. James LYNCH
15 AVP Human Resources & Auxiliary Svc .... Ms. Phyllis BROADWELL
18 Director of Facilities and Plant Op .... Mr. Paul MELCHOR
37 Director Student Financial Aid .... Ms. Terral HARRIS
06 Registrar .... Ms. Lisa LESSEIG
07 Asst Dir of Admissions Operations .... Ms. Kimberly BURGESS
04 Executive Asst President's Office .... Ms. Judy JOHNSTON
96 Purchasing Officer .... Ms. Deborah MILES
36 Director Career & Academic Advising .... Mr. Brian WEESE
38 Dir Counseling & Disability Svcs .... Ms. Jennifer ZAK
108 Assessment Specialist .... Vacant
29 Asst Dir Development & Alumni Engag .... Ms. Casey HANAK
28 Director of Diversity Initiatives .... Mr. J. Quinton STAPLES

† Part of the University System of Georgia.

Columbia Theological Seminary (G)

P.O. Box 520, 701 S Columbia Drive,
Decatur GA 30031-0520
County: DeKalb FICE Identification: 001560
Unit ID: 139348
Telephone: (404) 378-8821 Carnegie Class: Spec-4-yr-Faith
FAX Number: (404) 377-9696 Calendar System: 4/1/4
URL: www.ctsnet.edu
Established: 1828 Annual Graduate Tuition & Fees: N/A
Enrollment: 201 Coed
Affiliation or Control: Presbyterian Church (U.S.A.) IRS Status: 501(c)3
Highest Offering: Doctorate; No Undergraduates
Accreditation: SC, THEOL

01 President .... Dr. Leanne VAN DYK
05 VP Academic Affairs .... Dr. Love L. SECHREST
10 VP Business and Finance .... Mr. Martin SADLER
32 VP Student Affs/Dean of Students .... Rev. Brandon T. MAXWELL
111 VP Advancement .... Mr. David M. HUFFINE
20 Assoc Dean Academic Administration .... RevDr. Ann Clay ADAMS
13 Assoc Dean Info Svcs/Dir of Library .... Dr. Kelly D. CAMPBELL
107 Assoc Dean Advanced Prof Studies .... Dr. Jeffery L. TRIBBLE, SR.
06 Registrar .... Mr. Mike MEDFORD
84 Enrollment/Student Affairs Coord .... Ms. Felicia R. THIMES
26 Assist Director of Communications .... Ms. Corrie COX
04 Executive Assistant to President .... Ms. Lucy BAUM
29 Director Alumni/Church Relations .... Rev. Julie BAILEY

Columbus State University (H)

4225 University Avenue, Columbus GA 31907-5645
County: Muscogee FICE Identification: 001561
Unit ID: 139366
Telephone: (706) 507-8800 Carnegie Class: Masters/L
FAX Number: (706) 568-2123 Calendar System: Semester
URL: www.columbusstate.edu
Established: 1958 Annual Undergrad Tuition & Fees (In-State): $6,241
Enrollment: 8,372 Coed
Affiliation or Control: State IRS Status: 501(c)3
Highest Offering: Doctorate
Accreditation: SC, ART, CACREP, MUS, NURSE, THEA

01 President .... Dr. Chris MARKWOOD
05 Provost/VP Academic Affairs .... Dr. Deborah BORDELON
10 VP Business & Finance .... Mr. Richard SEARS
32 VP Student Affairs & Enrollment Mgt .... Dr. Gina SHEEKS
111 VP University Advancement .... Dr. Rocky KETTERING
13 Chief Information Officer .... Vacant
43 General Counsel .... Mr. Craig BURGESS
84 Asst VP for Enrollment Mgmt .... Mrs. Sallie MCMULLIN
100 Chief of Staff .... Dr. Ron WILLIAMS
50 Dean Turner College of Business .... Dr. Linda HADLEY
08 Dean of Libraries .... Dr. Alan KARASS
15 Director Human Resources .... Ms. Tamara WADE
09 Director Institutional Research .... Dr. Sri SITHARAMAN
41 Director Intercollegiate Athletics .... Mr. Todd REESER
07 Director of Admissions .... Ms. Kristin WILLIAMS

† Part of the University System of Georgia.

Columbus Technical College (I)

928 Manchester Expressway, Columbus GA 31904-6572
County: Muscogee FICE Identification: 005624
Unit ID: 139357
Telephone: (706) 649-1800 Carnegie Class: Assoc/HVT-High Trad
FAX Number: (706) 649-1885 Calendar System: Semester
URL: www.columbustech.edu
Established: 1961 Annual Undergrad Tuition & Fees (In-State): $3,042
Enrollment: 2,999 Coed
Affiliation or Control: State IRS Status: Exempt
Highest Offering: Associate Degree
Accreditation: SC, ADNUR, COARC, DA, DH, DMS, FUSER, MAC, RAD, SURGT

01 President .... Ms. Martha Ann TODD
11 VP Administrative Services .... Ms. Karen THOMAS
05 Vice President Academic Affairs .... Dr. Kermelle HENSLEY

32 Vice President Student Affairs ... Dr. Tara ASKEW
18 Vice President Operations ... Mr. Tommy WILSON
88 Vice President Economic Development ... Mr. James LOYD
51 Vice President of Adult Education ... Ms. April HOPSON
15 Director of Human Resources ... Mr. Henry GROSS
26 Exec Dir Community/College Rels ... Ms. Cheryl MYERS
37 Exec Director of Financial Aid ... Ms. Carrie WILDER
09 Exec Dir of Inst Effect & Research ... Mr. Kevin PEOPLES
13 Director Information Technology ... Mr. Jonathan NORRED
111 Director Institutional Advancement ... Ms. Susan SEALY
06 Registrar ... Ms. Sylvia DANSBY
07 Director of Admissions ... Mr. Joseph WILSON
08 Chief Library Officer ... Mr. Troy COOK
50 Dean of Business ... Ms. Nicole JACKSON

Covenant College (A)

14049 Scenic Highway, Lookout Mountain TN 30750-4164
County: Dade FICE Identification: 003484
Unit ID: 139393
Telephone: (706) 820-1560 Carnegie Class: Bac-A&S
FAX Number: (706) 820-2165 Calendar System: Semester
URL: www.covenant.edu
Established: 1955 Annual Undergrad Tuition & Fees: $36,710
Enrollment: 911 Coed
Affiliation or Control: Presbyterian Church In America IRS Status: 501(c)3
Highest Offering: Master's
Accreditation: SC

01 President ... Dr. J. Derek HALVORSON
05 Vice Pres of Academic Affairs ... Dr. Jeffrey B. HALL
10 Vice Pres of Finance & Operations ... Mr. Fred VERWOERD
30 Vice President of Development ... Mr. Marc ERICKSON
32 Vice Pres of Student Development ... Mr. Brad VOYLES
84 Asst VP of Enrollment Management ... Mr. Brad TOMAS
09 AVP for Institutional Effectiveness ... Dr. Karen NELSON
08 Director of Library Services ... Mr. John HOLBERG
06 Dean of Records and Registrar ... Mr. Rodney E. MILLER
42 Chaplain ... Mr. Grant LOWE
58 Dean Master of Education Pgm ... Dr. Jim DREXLER
21 Controller ... Mrs. Jennifer BLACK-PATEL
88 Campus Architect ... Mr. David NORTHCUTT
37 Director of Financial Aid ... Mr. Matthew BAZZEL
15 Director of Human Resources ... Mr. Tom DEWEY
41 Director of Athletics ... Mr. Tim SCEGGEL
13 Director of Technology Services ... Ms. Marjorie CROCKER
29 Director of Alumni Relations ... Ms. Sara Kaitlin VAN PUFFELEN
23 Director of Health Services ... Ms. Tina HOLT
26 Dir of Marketing & Communications ... Mr. John HORTON
121 Coordinator of Student Success ... Ms. Becca MOORE
36 Dir of Center for Calling & Career ... Mr. John PLATING
04 Admin Asst to Office of President ... Mrs. Cassandra JONES
19 Director of Safety & Security ... Mr. Keith MCCLEARN
109 Director of Business Operations ... Mr. Caleb MASK
104 Coordinator of Global Education ... Ms. Lindsay SAUNDS

Dalton State College (B)

650 College Drive, Dalton GA 30720-3797
County: Whitfield FICE Identification: 003956
Unit ID: 139463
Telephone: (706) 272-4436 Carnegie Class: Bac-Diverse
FAX Number: (706) 272-4588 Calendar System: Semester
URL: www.daltonstate.edu
Established: 1963 Annual Undergrad Tuition & Fees (In-State): $3,683
Enrollment: 4,794 Coed
Affiliation or Control: State IRS Status: 501(c)3
Highest Offering: Baccalaureate
Accreditation: SC, ADNUR, COARC, MLTAD, NUR, RAD, SW

01 President ... Dr. Margaret VENABLE
05 VP for Academic Affairs ... Dr. Bruno HICKS
10 Vice President Fiscal Affairs ... Mr. Nick HENRY
84 VP Student Affairs & Enroll Mgmt ... Dr. Jodi JOHNSON
20 Associate Provost ... Dr. Mary NIELSEN
37 Director of Financial Aid/Vet Svcs ... Ms. Carol JONES
08 Director Library Services ... Ms. Melissa WHITESELL
18 Director Plant Opers ... Mr. George BREWER
26 Director of Marketing ... Mr. Philip SCHLESINGER
111 Director Institutional Advancement ... Mr. David ELROD
32 Dean of Students ... Dr. Jami HALL
15 Director Human Resources ... Ms. Lori MCCARTY
96 Procurement Director ... Ms. Cynthia PARKER
13 Chief Information Officer ... Mr. Jeff MARSHALL
19 Director Public Safety ... Mr. Michael MASTERS
30 Development Coordinator ... Mr. Josh WILSON
39 Director Student Housing ... Mr. Tim REILLY
50 Dean School of Business ... Dr. Marilyn HELMS
53 Dean School of Education ... Dr. Sharon HIXON
49 Dean School of Arts & Sciences ... Dr. Randall GRIFFUS
76 Dean School of Health Professions ... Dr. Gina KERTULIS-TARTAR
06 Registrar ... Vacant
04 Executive Asst to President ... Ms. Mary Ellen GURLEY
07 Director of Admissions ... Mrs. Katherine LOGAN
41 Exec Dir Athletics & External Rels ... Mr. Jon JAUDON
104 Director Study Abroad ... Dr. Fernando GARCIA
38 Director Student Counseling ... Ms. Cheryl OWENS
86 Dir Government & Alumni Relations ... Ms. Vallarie PRATT
108 Director Institutional Assessment ... Dr. Henry CODJOE
121 Exec Dir Advising & Student Success ... Ms. Elizabeth HUTCHINS

† Part of the University System of Georgia.

East Georgia State College (C)

131 College Circle, Swainsboro GA 30401-3643
County: Emanuel FICE Identification: 010997
Unit ID: 139621
Telephone: (478) 289-2000 Carnegie Class: Bac/Assoc-Assoc Dom
FAX Number: (478) 289-2038 Calendar System: Semester
URL: www.ega.edu
Established: 1973 Annual Undergrad Tuition & Fees (In-State): $3,136
Enrollment: 2,415 Coed
Affiliation or Control: State IRS Status: 501(c)3
Highest Offering: Baccalaureate
Accreditation: SC, NUR

01 Interim President ... Dr. Dawn H. CARTEE
05 VP for Academic & Student Affairs ... Dr. Sandra SHARMAN
10 Vice President for Business Affairs ... Mr. Cliff GAY
13 Vice Pres Information Technology ... Mr. Mike ROUNTREE
100 Chief of Staff/Legal Counsel ... Mrs. Mary C. SMITH
11 Assoc VP for Executive Affairs ... Ms. Norma KENNEDY
08 Interim Library Director ... Ms. Meghan CREWS
06 Registrar ... Ms. Lynette M. SAULSBERRY
09 Dir of Strategic Plng/Inst Research ... Mr. David GRIBBIN
32 Assoc Vice Pres for Student Affairs ... Vacant
15 Director of Human Resources ... Mrs. Tracy WOODS
111 Interim Assoc VP Inst Advancement ... Ms. Norma KENNEDY
12 Assoc VP External Campuses ... Mr. Nick KELCH
19 Dir Public Safety/Chief of Police ... Mr. Deryl M. SECKINGER
07 Director of Admissions ... Mr. Mike MORAN
38 Dir Counseling/Disability Services ... Ms. Lori BURNS
39 Director of Housing ... Ms. Angela STORCK
41 Director of Athletics ... Mr. Chuck WIMBERLY
18 Director of Plant Operations ... Mr. David STEPTOE
12 Director of EGSC Statesboro ... Ms. Jessica WILLIAMSON
106 Associate Director of eLearning ... Mrs. Terri BROWN
121 Dir of Academic Support Services ... Ms. Deborah KITTRELL-MIKELL
97 Director of the Learning Commons ... Ms. Karen MURPHREE
109 Director of Dining Operations ... Ms. Ruth UNDERWOOD
88 Director of Student Conduct ... Ms. Sherrie HELMS
81 Interim Dean of Math & Sciences ... Dr. David CHEVALIER
83 Dean Humanities & Social Sciences ... Dr. Carlos CUNHA
88 Interim Chair of Biology Dept ... Mr. John CADLE
88 Director of FESA ... Ms. Beverley WALKER
66 Director of Nursing ... Dr. Linda UPCHURCH
88 Asst Dir Lrng Commons for Military ... Ms. Denise DANIELS
88 Director Financial Accounting ... Ms. Sheila D. WENTZ
113 Director of Student Accts & Payroll ... Ms. Vera M. WILLIAMS
20 Assoc VP for Academics & Enrollment ... Mr. James BEALL
124 Director of Student Retention ... Mrs. Georgia M. BEASLEY
104 Director Study Abroad ... Mr. Carmine PALUMBO
37 Director Student Financial Aid ... Mr. Michael WERNON

† Part of the University System of Georgia.

Emmanuel College (D)

181 Spring Street, Franklin Springs GA 30639
County: Franklin FICE Identification: 001563
Unit ID: 139630
Telephone: (706) 245-7226 Carnegie Class: Bac-Diverse
FAX Number: (706) 245-4424 Calendar System: Semester
URL: www.ec.edu
Established: 1919 Annual Undergrad Tuition & Fees: $21,220
Enrollment: 883 Coed
Affiliation or Control: Pentecostal Holiness Church IRS Status: 501(c)3
Highest Offering: Baccalaureate
Accreditation: SC

01 President ... Dr. Ronald WHITE
32 Vice President for Student Life ... Vacant
05 Vice President for Academic Affairs ... Vacant
10 Vice President for Finance ... Mr. Greg K. HEARN
30 Vice President for Development ... Mr. W. Brian JAMES
84 Vice Pres Enrollment Mgmt/Marketing ... Ms. Donna QUICK
08 Director of Library Services ... Ms. Deborah MILLIER
06 Registrar ... Mrs. Debra F. GRIZZLE
37 Director of Financial Aid ... Mrs. Lisa WILLIAMSON
13 Director of Information Technology ... Mr. Glenn TONEY
11 Assoc VP of Campus Operations ... Mr. Matt MCREE
41 Athletics Director ... Mr. Nate MOORMAN
42 Dir Spiritual Life/Campus Pastor ... Mr. Chris MAXWELL
15 Director of Human Resources ... Mrs. Joann HARPER
26 Chief Public Relations Officer ... Mrs. Ashley WESTBROOK
96 Director of Accounting Services ... Mrs. Anita RAY
18 Physical Plant Director ... Mr. Wayne CRIDER
09 Director of Institutional Research ... Ms. Sharon SYNAN
29 Director Alumni Relations ... Mr. Brian JAMES
36 Director of Career Services ... Mrs. April JAMES
04 Administrative Asst to President ... Mrs. Mary BEADLES
19 Campus Safety Coordinator ... Mr. T J HAMIL
39 Director Student Housing ... Mrs. Sherri CAREY
07 Director of Admissions ... Ms. Kelley CHAPPA
106 Dir Online Education/E-learning ... Ms. Sharon SYNAN
50 Dean of Business ... Ms. Jennifer BENSON
53 Dean of Education ... Dr. Vicki HOLLINSHEAD
38 Director Student Counseling ... Mrs. Jessica MIDDLEBROOKS

Emory University (E)

201 Dowman Drive, Atlanta GA 30322-0001
County: DeKalb FICE Identification: 001564
Unit ID: 139658
Telephone: (404) 727-6123 Carnegie Class: DU-Highest
FAX Number: (404) 727-5997 Calendar System: Semester
URL: www.emory.edu
Established: 1836 Annual Undergrad Tuition & Fees: $53,868
Enrollment: 13,997 Coed
Affiliation or Control: United Methodist IRS Status: 501(c)3
Highest Offering: Doctorate
Accreditation: SC, AA, ANEST, ARCPA, CAATE, #CAMPEP, CLPSY, DENT, IPSY, LAW, MED, MIDWF, NURSE, PAST, PCSAS, PH, PTA, RAD, THEOL

01 President ... Dr. Gregory L. FENVES
05 Provost/EVP Academic Affairs ... Dr. Ravi V. BELLAMKONDA
10 EVP Business & Admin/CFO ... Mr. Christopher AUGOSTINI
17 Exec Vice Pres Health Affairs ... Dr. Jonathan S. LEWIN
88 Univ Ombuds Ofcr/Sr Advisor to Pres ... Ms. Lynell CADRAY
101 VP/Secretary of the University ... Ms. Alllison K. DYKES
84 VP Enrollment Mgmt ... Dr. Paul P. MARTHERS
100 Chief of Staff ... Ms. Emily FISHER
32 VP/Dean Campus Life ... Ms. Enku GELAYE
26 Sr VP Comm & Public Affairs ... Mr. David B. SANDOR
46 Sr Vice Pres for Research ... Dr. Deborah W. BRUNER
111 SVP Advancement/Alumni Engagement ... Mr. Joshua NEWTON
88 Senior Advisor to the Pres ... Dr. Robert M. FRANKLIN, JR.
43 Sr Vice Pres & General Counsel ... Mr. Stephen D. SENCER
114 Deputy Prov Admin/Plng ... Ms. Susan BONIFIELD
20 Deputy Provost for Academic Affairs ... Dr. Christa D. ACAMPORA
13 Enterprise CIO/Sr VP Lib Svcs ... Mr. Richard A. MENDOLA
117 AVP Enterprise Risk Mgmt/COS ... Ms. Diana CARTER
116 Chief Audit Officer ... Mr. Scott J. STEVENSON
88 VP Research Admin ... Dr. Robert NOBLES
88 Chief Business Officer Research ... Ms. Melanie LAWRENCE
110 Sr AVP Engage/Comm/Mktg/Advance ... Mr. Cutler ANDREWS
112 Sr Assoc VP Principal Gifts ... Mr. Alex BROWN
27 VP Ent Comm & Reput Mgmt ... Mr. Doug BUSK
27 VP Academic Comm & Rep Leadership ... Ms. Nancy SEIDEMAN
15 VP Human Resources ... Ms. Theresa MILAZZO
15 VP Human Resources ... Mr. Del KING
20 Vice Prov Academic Planning ... Dr. Nancy BLIWISE
28 Vice Provost Equity/Inclusion ... Ms. Carol E. HENDERSON
88 VP Strategic Research Initiatives ... Dr. Lanny S. LIEBESKIND
20 VP Faculty Affairs ... Mr. Tim HOLBROOK
20 Vice Prov Undergrad Education ... Dr. Pamela SCULLY
86 VP Governmental Affairs ... Ms. Cameron P. TAYLOR
88 Assoc VP Creative Shared Svc/Co ... Mr. Dave HOLSTON
58 Vice Provost/Dean Graduate Sch ... Dr. Kimberly R. JACOB ARRIOLA
82 Vice Provost International Affairs ... Dr. Philip WAINWRIGHT
88 Advisor ... Dr. Qiang XU
11 VP Business Operations ... Ms. Debby MOREY
45 VP Campus Services/Chief Plng Ofcr ... Mr. Robin MOREY
115 VP Investments ... Mr. Srinivas PULAVARTI
21 VP for Finance & Treasury ... Ms. Belva WHITE
21 Assoc VP Finance & Controller ... Ms. Allison S. BERG
25 Assoc Vice President Research ... Dr. Todd SHERER
07 AVP Undergrad Enroll/Dean of Admiss ... Dr. John LATTING
97 Assoc Vice Prov Undergrad Education ... Ms. Heather MUGG
88 Chief Compliance Officer ... Mr. John LAWLEY
20 Assoc Vice Prov Acad Innovation ... Dr. Paul WELTY
06 Asst Vice Prov/University Registrar ... Ms. JoAnn MCKENZIE
19 Associate VP/Chief of Police ... Ms. Cheryl ELLIOTT
88 Asst Vice Prov Faculty Affairs ... Dr. Carol A. FLOWERS
37 Asst Vice Prov/Dir Student Fin Aid ... Mr. John LEACH
38 Assistant VP Counseling/Psych Svcs ... Dr. Wanda COLLINS
108 Asst Vice Prov Academic Pgm/Plng ... Dr. David M. JORDAN
88 Assoc VP/Exec Dir COVID-19 ... Mr. Amir ST. CLAIR
49 Dean of Emory College ... Dr. Michael A. ELLIOTT
12 Dean & CEO Oxford College ... Dr. Douglas A. HICKS
63 Dean of Medicine ... Dr. Vikas P. SUKHATME
66 Dean of Nursing ... Dr. Linda MCCAULEY
73 Dean of Theology ... Dr. Jan LOVE
61 Dean of Law ... Ms. Mary Anne BOBINSKI
50 Int Dean of Business School ... Ms. Karen SEDATOLE
69 Dean of Public Health ... Dr. James W. CURRAN
42 Univ Chaplain/Dean Spiritual Life ... Rev. Gregory MCGONIGLE
80 Pres & CEO of the Carter Center ... Ms. Paige E. ALEXANDER
36 Exec Director Career Service ... Mr. Paul FOWLER
44 Executive Director of Gift Planning ... Mr. Olen EARL
39 Sr Director Residence Life ... Dr. Scott K. RAUSCH
39 Sr Director Housing Operations ... Ms. Elaine TURNER
40 Director Bookstore ... Mr. Bruce COVEY
88 Dir Communications/Outreach ... Ms. Caroline DRIEBE
96 Asst VP Rsrch Admin/Dir OSP ... Ms. Holly SOMMERS
12 Director Yerkes Research Ctrs ... Dr. Paul JOHNSON
85 Dir Intl Student Scholar Program ... Ms. Shinsaeng KO
09 Asst VP Inst Rsrch/Decision Support ... Dr. Justin SHEPHERD
88 Interim Director M C Carlos Museum ... Ms. Bonna WESCOAT
88 Director Center for Ethics ... Mr. Paul R. WOLPE
41 Asst VP Athletics/Recreation ... Ms. Keiko PRICE
08 Dean & University Librarian ... Ms. Yolanda COOPER

Fort Valley State University (F)

1005 State University Drive, Fort Valley GA 31030-4313
County: Peach FICE Identification: 001566
Unit ID: 139719
Telephone: (478) 825-6211 Carnegie Class: Masters/M
FAX Number: (478) 825-6394 Calendar System: Semester
URL: www.fvsu.edu
Established: 1895 Annual Undergrad Tuition & Fees (In-State): $5,832
Enrollment: 3,079 Coed
Affiliation or Control: State IRS Status: 501(c)3
Highest Offering: Beyond Master's But Less Than Doctorate
Accreditation: SC, AAFCS, CACREP, SW

01 President ... Dr. Paul JONES

05	Int Provost/VP for Academic Affairs	Dr. Olufunke FONTENOT
10	CBO/VP for Business & Finance	Ms. Michelle MARTIN
111	VP for Advancement	Mr. Anthony HOLLOMAN
32	Int VP Student Affairs & Enrollment	Mrs. Maria LUMPKIN
20	AVP Academic Affairs/Dean	Dr. Robert DIBIE, III
56	Extension Administrator	Dr. Mark LATTIMORE
35	Dean of Students	Mr. Wallace KEESE
49	Dean Arts & Sciences	Dr. Berlethia PITTS
21	Assistant Vice President/Controller	Vacant
06	Registrar	Ms. Sharee LAWRENCE
43	Dir of Legal/Government Affairs	Ms. Emma WILLIAMS
13	Chief Information Officer	Mr. Charlie WEAVER
08	Director Hunt Memorial Library	Mr. Frank MAHITAB
07	Executive Director Admissions	Ms. Karyn NOOKS
84	AVP for Enrollment Management	Vacant
29	Director Alumni Affairs	Vacant
15	Chief Human Resources Officer	Ms. Tineke BATTLE
19	Director of Campus Police/Safety	Ms. Anita ALLEN
47	Dean Agriculture	Dr. Ralph NOBLE
23	Dir of Student Health/ Counseling	Ms. Jacqueline CASKEY-JAMES
18	Director of Facilities Management	Mr. Edwidge DUFRESNE
36	Dir Civic Engage/Ldrshp/Prof Dev	Ms. LuWanna WILLIAMS
26	Chief Communications Officer	Vacant
41	Director of Athletics	Mr. Anthony HOLLOMAN
124	Dean of University College	Dr. Kimberly ANDREWS
53	Dean College of Education	Dr. Beth DAY-HAIRSTON
22	Director of Contracts/Compliance	Ms. Patrice TERRELL
25	Director of Sponsored Programs	Ms. Joyce Y. JOHNSON
39	Director Student Housing	Mr. Shawn MODENA
96	Director of Procurement	Ms. Rebecca HORTON
88	Title III Director	Ms. Danyell BARRY
04	Asst to Pres/Dir of Special Events	Mr. RJ MATHIS
100	Interim Chief of Staff	Dr. Olufunke FONTENOT
106	Director Online Learning Office	Dr. Darryl HANCOCK
30	Director of Development	Ms. Nadia RAHAMAN
88	VP Economic Dev/Land Grant Affairs	Dr. Govind KANNAN

† Part of the University System of Georgia.

Georgia Central University (A)

6789 Peachtree Industrial Boulevard, Atlanta GA 30360

County: DeKalb — FICE Identification: 041565 — Unit ID: 461236

Telephone: (770) 279-0507 — Carnegie Class: Bac-Diverse
FAX Number: (770) 279-0308 — Calendar System: Semester
URL: www.gcuniv.edu
Established: 1993 — Annual Undergrad Tuition & Fees: N/A
Enrollment: N/A — Coed
Affiliation or Control: Independent Non-Profit — IRS Status: 501(c)3
Highest Offering: Doctorate
Accreditation: THEOL, CEA

01	President	Dr. Paul C. KIM
05	Vice President/Chief Acad Officer	Dr. Hee Sook SONG
10	Chief Financial Officer	Ms. Eunice KIM
07	Director of Admissions	Ms. Young Sil HWANG
20	Associate Dir of Academic Affairs	Dr. Mia KANG
45	Director of Planning	Mr. Alain GALLIE
12	Dir of New Jersey Extension Site	Dr. Sun Hee CHOI
13	Senior Director of IT	Dr. Byungchil KIM
106	Director of Distance Education	Dr. Kyueil KWAK
24	Director Literature & Information	Dr. Hyun Sung CHO
18	Director of Maintenance	Rev. Min Soo KIM
19	Director Security/Safety	Mr. Samuel KIM
21	Director of Business Affairs	Ms. Kyung KIM
108	Dir of Institutional Effectiveness	Dr. Yong Hwan KIM
29	President of Alumni Relations	Dr. Eunjo LEE
26	Chief Public Relations Officer	Vacant
06	Registrar	Ms. In Sook KIM
37	Director Student Financial Aid	Dr. Hee Sook SONG
50	Dean School of Business	Dr. William STAUFF
73	Dean School of Christianity	Dr. Kyung Hun LEE
73	Dean School of Divinity	Dr. Sung Shik JANG
64	Dean School of Music	Dr. Hee Churl KIM
88	Director of Doctoral Programs	Dr. Eun Moo LEE
88	International Student Advisor	Mr. Rafael MIGUEL
42	Chaplain	Dr. Hyun Sung CHO
08	Director of the Library	Mr. Jarian R. JONES
32	Director of Student Affairs	Dr. Young Jun KIM

Georgia College & State University (B)

231 West Hancock Street, Milledgeville GA 31061-0490

County: Baldwin — FICE Identification: 001602 — Unit ID: 139861

Telephone: (478) 445-5004 — Carnegie Class: Masters/L
FAX Number: (478) 445-1191 — Calendar System: Semester
URL: www.gcsu.edu
Established: 1889 — Annual Undergrad Tuition & Fees (In-State): $9,524
Enrollment: 6,873 — Coed
Affiliation or Control: State — IRS Status: 501(c)3
Highest Offering: Doctorate
Accreditation: SC, CAATE, CAEPN, @MIDWF, MUS, NURSE, SPAA

01	President	Dr. Steve M. DORMAN
04	Special Assistant to the President	Ms. Monica STARLEY
05	Provost/VP for Academic Affairs	Dr. Costas SPIROU
10	Interim VP Finance/Administration	Mr. Lee FRUITTICHER
32	Vice President for Student Affairs	Dr. Shawn BROOKS
111	Int VP for University Advancement	Mr. Lee FRUITTICHER
20	Interim Assoc Provost	Dr. Holley ROBERTS
45	Assoc VP for Strategic Initiatives	Dr. Mark PELTON
26	Assoc VP Strategic Communications	Mr. Omar ODEH
84	Assoc VP for Enrollment Management	Mr. Joel ROBINSON
109	Asst VP for Auxiliary Services	Mr. Kyle CULLARS
114	Sr Dir for Budget Planning & Admin	Mr. Russ WILLIAMS
49	Dean College of Arts & Sciences	Dr. Eric TENBUS
50	Dean College of Business	Dr. Micheal T. STRATTON
53	Dean College of Education	Dr. Joseph PETERS
76	Dean College of Health Sciences	Dr. Sheri NOVIELLO
39	Exec Director of University Housing	Mr. Larry CHRISTENSON
88	Project Manager	Mr. Mark BOWEN
19	Dir Public Safety & Chief of Police	Mr. Brett STANELLE
09	Assoc VP of Institutional Research	Dr. Chris FERLAND
13	Chief Information Officer	Ms. Susan KERR
08	Interim Director of Libraries	Dr. Shaundra WALKER
36	Director Career Center	Ms. Lauren EASOM
15	Chief Human Resources Officer	Mr. Neil JONES
07	Executive Director of Admissions	Mr. Javier FRANCISCO
06	Registrar	Ms. Kay ANDERSON
41	Director of Athletics	Mr. Wendell STATON
29	Asst Dir of Alumni Engagement	Vacant
43	General Counsel	Ms. Qiana WILSON
38	Director of Counseling Services	Dr. Stephen WILSON
37	Director of Financial Aid	Ms. Shannon SIMMONS
88	Sr Dir Materials Mgmt/Central Svcs	Mr. Mark MEEKS
116	Dir of Internal Audit	Ms. Stacy MULVANEY
35	Dean of Students	Dr. Tom MILES
104	Asst VP for International Educ	Dr. James CALLAGHAN
56	Exec Director of Rural Studies	Dr. Veronica WOMACK
28	Assoc VP/Chief Diversity Officer	Dr. Carolyn DENARD

Georgia Gwinnett College (C)

1000 University Center Lane, Lawrenceville GA 30043

County: Gwinnett — FICE Identification: 041429 — Unit ID: 447689

Telephone: (678) 407-5000 — Carnegie Class: Bac-Diverse
FAX Number: N/A — Calendar System: Semester
URL: www.ggc.edu
Established: 2005 — Annual Undergrad Tuition & Fees (In-District): $4,948
Enrollment: 11,627 — Coed
Affiliation or Control: State/Local — IRS Status: 501(c)3
Highest Offering: Baccalaureate
Accreditation: SC, CAEPN, NURSE

01	President	Dr. Jann L. JOSEPH
05	SVP Academic/Stdnt Affairs/Provost	Dr. George S. LOW
84	Vice Pres Enrollment Management	Mr. Michael POLL
13	Vice Pres Information Technology	Dr. Christine MILLER DIVINE
10	Vice Pres Business & Finanance	Mr. Frank HARDYMON
121	Vice Pres Student Engagement & Succ	Dr. Michelle ROSEMOND
04	Executive Asst to President	Mrs. Luann CAUSLAND
15	Assoc Vice Pres Human Resources	Ms. Katherine KYLE
11	Assoc Vice Pres Operations	Mr. Terrance SCHNEIDER
26	Assoc Vice Pres Communications	Ms. Sloan JONES
111	Assoc Vice Pres Advancement	Ms. Jennifer HENDRICKSON
50	Dean School of Business	Dr. Tyler YU
53	Dean School of Education	Dr. Bernard OLIVER
49	Dean School of Liberal Arts	Dr. Teresa WINTERHALTER
81	Dean School Science/Technology	Dr. Chavonda J. MILLS
76	Dean School of Health Sciences	Dr. Diane WHITE
121	Dean Library Services	Ms. Barbara MANN

Georgia Highlands College (D)

3175 Cedartown Highway, Rome GA 30161-3897

County: Floyd — FICE Identification: 009507 — Unit ID: 139700

Telephone: (706) 802-5000 — Carnegie Class: Bac/Assoc-Assoc Dom
FAX Number: (706) 295-6341 — Calendar System: Semester
URL: www.highlands.edu
Established: 1970 — Annual Undergrad Tuition & Fees (In-State): $3,344
Enrollment: 5,680 — Coed
Affiliation or Control: State — IRS Status: 501(c)3
Highest Offering: Baccalaureate
Accreditation: SC, ADNUR, DH, NUR

01	Interim President	Dr. Dana J. NICHOLS
05	Interim CAO & Provost	Dr. Sarah COAKLEY
10	VP Finance & Administration	Mr. Jamie PETTY
13	Chief Information Officer	Mr. Rob LALTRELLO
15	Interim Chief HR Officer	Ms. Tammi WALSH
09	Dean Plng/Assess/Accred/Research	Dr. Jesse BISHOP
12	Campus Dean Cartersville	Ms. Leslie JOHNSON
12	Campus Dean Marietta	Mr. Ken REAVES
119	Chief Information Security Officer	Mr. Ian FLEMING
21	Director of Procurement & Budgets	Ms. Stephanie LOVELESS
20	Asst VP Academic Retention/Resource	Ms. Michelle LOCKETT
84	Executive Dir Enrollment Management	Ms. Jennifer HICKS
04	Executive Asst to the President	Ms. Tammy NICHOLSON
08	Dean Libraries & College Testing	Mr. Julius FLESCHNER
19	Police Chief/Dir of Campus Safety	Mr. David HORACE
41	Director of Athletics	Mr. Brandan HARRELL
18	Director of Facilities	Mr. David VAN HOOK
26	Sr Dir Marketing & Communications	Ms. Sheila JONES
12	Manager Floyd Campus/HR Adm Progrms	Mr. Bradley GILMORE
12	Manager Paulding Site	Ms. Christina HENGGELER
12	Manager Douglasville Site	Ms. Nivenitie MCDANIEL
102	Director Foundation & Annual Fund	Ms. Liz JONES
38	Dir Student Support & Counseling	Ms. Angela WHEELUS
06	Registrar	Vacant
37	Director Financial Aid	Ms. Donna CHILDRES
89	Coord Cocurricular/Transition Pgm	Mr. Clifton PUCKETT
28	Director of Diversity	Dr. Sean CALLAHAN
25	Grants Administrator	Ms. Kristina SHANAHAN
104	Director Study Abroad	Dr. Bronson LONG

† Part of the University System of Georgia.

Georgia Institute of Technology (E)

225 North Avenue, NW, Atlanta GA 30332-0002

County: Fulton — FICE Identification: 001569 — Unit ID: 139755

Telephone: (404) 894-2000 — Carnegie Class: DU-Highest
FAX Number: (404) 894-1277 — Calendar System: Semester
URL: www.gatech.edu
Established: 1885 — Annual Undergrad Tuition & Fees (In-State): $12,852
Enrollment: 39,771 — Coed
Affiliation or Control: State — IRS Status: 501(c)3
Highest Offering: Doctorate
Accreditation: SC, ART, CAMPEP, CEA, IPSY, PLNG

01	President	Dr. Ángel CABRERA
05	Provost/Exec VP Academic Affairs	Dr. Steven W. MCLAUGHLIN
11	Exec VP Administration/Finance	Ms. Kelly FOX
46	Executive Vice President Research	Dr. Chaouki ABDALLAH
100	Senior VP/Chief of Staff	Mr. Frank NEVILLE
30	Vice President Development	Mr. Barrett H. CARSON
26	Vice Pres Institute Communications	Ms. Renee KOPKOWSKI
32	VP Student Engagement & Well-Being	Dr. Luoluo HONG
88	SVP Georgia Tech Rsrch Inst	Dr. James HUDGENS
88	Interim Vice President Research	Ms. Rebecca CARAVATI
86	Vice President Institute Relations	Mr. Bert REEVES
88	Int VP Enterprise Innovation Inst	Mr. David BRIDGES
10	Vice President Finance & Planning	Mr. James FORTNER
29	President GT Alumni Assoc	Mr. Dene SHEHEANE
58	Vice Prov Grad Educ/Faculty Affairs	Dr. Bonnie FERRI
84	Vice Prov Enrollment Services	Dr. Paul KOHN
20	Interim VP Undergraduate Education	Dr. Steven GIRARDOT
35	Dean of Students/AVP Student Life	Mr. John STEIN
43	Chief Legal Counsel	Ms. Ling-Ling NIE
28	VP Diversity/Equity & Inclusion	Dr. Archie ERVIN
15	Assoc VP Human Resources	Dr. Kim HARRINGTON
18	Int VP Infrastruc & Sustainability	Dr. Nazia ZAKIR
88	Assoc Vice Pres Campus Services	Ms. Kasey HELTON
13	VP Information Tech/CIO	Mr. Daren HUBBARD
41	Director of Athletics	Mr. Todd STANSBURY
22	Exec Dir Staff Diversity/Inclusion	Ms. Pearl ALEXANDER
49	Dean College of Liberal Arts	Dr. Kaye HUSBANDS FEALING
48	Int Dean College of Design	Dr. Michelle RINEHART
77	Dean College of Computing	Dr. Charles ISBELL
54	Dean College of Engineering	Dr. Raheem BEYAH
08	Dean Libraries	Dr. Leslie SHARP
50	Dean Scheller College of Business	Dr. Maryam ALAVI
81	Dean College of Sciences	Dr. Susan LOZIER
06	Registrar	Ms. Reta PIKOWSKY
40	Director Georgia Tech Bookstore	Ms. Reshma PATEL
19	Director of Security & Police	Mr. Robert CONNOLLY
107	Dean Professional Education	Dr. Nelson BAKER
36	Assoc Vice Provost for UG Education	Dr. Steven GIRARDOT
37	Director Student Financial Aid	Ms. Marie MONS
23	Sr Director Student Health Svcs	Dr. Benjamin HOLTON
85	Vice Prov International Initiatives	Dr. Yves BERTHELOT
104	Exec Dir International Education	Ms. Amy HENRY
38	Director Counseling Center	Dr. Carla BRADLEY
109	Senior Director Auxiliary Services	Ms. Carolina AMERO
07	Director Undergraduate Admission	Mr. Richard CLARK
96	Director of Procurement Services	Mr. Frans BARENDS
114	Exec Dir Inst Budget Plng & Admin	Ms. Jamie FERNANDES
88	Int Dir Capital Planning/Space Mgmt	Ms. Linda DANIELS
88	Exec Director Strategic Consulting	Dr. Sonia ALVAREZ-ROBINSON
113	Bursar	Ms. Gloria KOBUS

† Part of the University System of Georgia.

Georgia Military College (F)

201 E Greene Street, Milledgeville GA 31061-3398

County: Baldwin — FICE Identification: 001571 — Unit ID: 485111

Telephone: (478) 387-4900 — Carnegie Class: Bac/Assoc-Assoc Dom
FAX Number: N/A — Calendar System: Quarter
URL: www.gmc.edu
Established: 1879 — Annual Undergrad Tuition & Fees: $6,615
Enrollment: 7,501 — Coed
Affiliation or Control: Independent Non-Profit — IRS Status: 501(c)3
Highest Offering: Baccalaureate
Accreditation: SC

01	President	LtGen. William B. CALDWELL, IV
05	Chief Academic Ofcr/Dn of Faculty	Dr. Phillip M. HOLMES
10	Chief Financial Officer	COL. James WATKINS
13	VP Info Technology/Online College	Mr. Jody YEARWOOD
84	Senior VP of Enrollment Management	Mr. Jody YEARWOOD
15	VP Human Resources	Ms. Jill ROBBINS
21	Assoc Vice Pres Resource Management	Ms. Susan MEEKS
06	Associate VP Academic Records	Mr. David FULMER
32	Commandant	COL. Steve PITT
30	Chief Institutional Devel Officer	Mr. Mark STROM
09	Director Institutional Research	Dr. Susan ISAAC
41	Athletic Director	Mr. Rob MANCHESTER
18	Director Facilities/Engineer	Mr. Jeff GRAY
08	Director of Library Services	Ms. Erin NEWTON
19	Chief Security/Safety/Campus Police	Mr. James HODNETT

Code	Title	Name
26	Dir Communication/Public Relations	Ms. Jobie SHIELDS
20	Academic Dean	Ms. Laura BOOTH
04	Executive Asst to President	Ms. Joelle TRUMBO
37	Director Student Financial Aid	Ms. Alisa STEPHENS
100	Director of Staff/Dean of Students	Ms. Jeannie ZIPPERER
29	Director Alumni Affairs	Mr. Craig PORTWOOD
96	Director of Purchasing	Mr. Mark ALAN

Georgia Northwestern Technical College (A)

One Maurice Culberson Drive, Rome GA 30161

County: Floyd FICE Identification: 005257
Unit ID: 139384
Telephone: (706) 295-6963 Carnegie Class: Assoc/HVT-Mix Trad/Non
FAX Number: (706) 295-6944 Calendar System: Semester
URL: www.gntc.edu
Established: 1966 Annual Undergrad Tuition & Fees (In-State): $3,062
Enrollment: 6,608 Coed
Affiliation or Control: State IRS Status: 501(c)3
Highest Offering: Associate Degree
Accreditation: SC, ADNUR, CAHIIM, COARC, DA, DMS, EMT, LC, MAC, PNUR, RAD, SURGT

Code	Title	Name
01	President	Dr. Heidi POPHAM
05	Vice President Academic Affairs	Dr. Elizabeth ANDERSON
11	Vice Pres Administrative Services	Ms. Kelly BARNES
30	Vice Pres Econ Development	Ms. Stephanie SCEARCE
09	Vice President IE & Student Success	Ms. Selena MAGNUSSON
51	Vice President Adult Education	Ms. Melissa SHAW
32	Vice Pres Student Affairs	Mr. Stuart PHILLIPS
20	Assoc Vice Pres Academic Affairs	Ms. Jennifer LOUDERMILK
06	Registrar	Ms. Dana WALKER
08	Director of Library Services	Mr. John LASSITER
19	Director Safety & Security	Mr. Chad CARDIN
37	Exec Director of Financial Aid	Ms. Amber SUMNER
18	Director Facilities Management	Mr. Jeffrey AGAN
26	Dir Marketing/Public Relations	Ms. Amber JORDAN
15	Director of Human Resources	Ms. Elizabeth BARKSDALE
04	Admin Assistant to the President	Ms. Lisa ODOM
13	Director of IT	Mr. Dennis THOMAS
102	Dir Foundation/Corporate Relations	Ms. Lauretta HANNON

Georgia Piedmont Technical College (B)

495 N Indian Creek Drive, Clarkston GA 30021-2397

County: DeKalb FICE Identification: 005622
Unit ID: 244446
Telephone: (404) 297-9522 Carnegie Class: Assoc/HVT-Mix Trad/Non
FAX Number: (404) 297-4234 Calendar System: Semester
URL: www.gptc.edu
Established: 1961 Annual Undergrad Tuition & Fees (In-State): $3,178
Enrollment: 2,615 Coed
Affiliation or Control: State IRS Status: 501(c)3
Highest Offering: Associate Degree
Accreditation: SC, CAHIIM, EMT, #MAC, MLTAD

Code	Title	Name
01	President	Dr. Tavarez HOLSTON
04	Exec Dir & Spec Asst to President	Ms. Kaitlin DUDLEY
05	EVP/VP Academic Affairs	Mr. Cheree WILLIAMS
10	Vice Pres Finance/Administration	Ms. Teresa BROWN
103	VP Economic Development	Mr. Irvin CLARK
32	Vice Pres Student Affairs	Vacant
108	VP Institutional Effectiveness	Ms. Britnee SHANDOR
111	Dir Inst Advancement/Foundation	Mr. Cory THOMPSON
37	Director of Financial Aid	Ms. Felicia AILSTER
35	Dean of Student Affairs	Dr. Candice BUCKLEY
08	Director of Library Services	Ms. Wendy WILMOTH
15	Director of Human Resources	Ms. Sadie WASHINGTON
26	Exec Dir Marketing/Public Relations	Mr. Cory THOMPSON
06	Registrar	Ms. Matilda PEEPLES
07	Director Admissions/Recruiting	Mr. Corey PARKER
18	Director Facilities Services	Mr. Gary WILKINS
13	Director of Information Technology	Mr. Samuel LOCKETT

Georgia Southern University (C)

PO Box 8033, Statesboro GA 30460-8033

County: Bulloch FICE Identification: 001572
Unit ID: 139931
Telephone: (912) 478-4636 Carnegie Class: DU-Higher
FAX Number: N/A Calendar System: Semester
URL: www.georgiasouthern.edu
Established: 1906 Annual Undergrad Tuition & Fees (In-State): $6,485
Enrollment: 26,949 Coed
Affiliation or Control: State IRS Status: 501(c)3
Highest Offering: Doctorate
Accreditation: SC, ART, CAATE, CACREP, CAEPN, CAPRT, CIDA, CLPSY, COARC, CONST, CVT, DIETD, DIETI, DMS, HSA, IPSY, MT, MUS, NMT, NURSE, PH, PTA, RAD, RTT, SP, SPAA, THEA

Code	Title	Name
01	President	Dr. Kyle MARRERO
05	Provost/VPAA	Dr. Carl REIBER
10	Interim VP Business & Finance	Mr. Ron STALNAKER
84	VP Enrollment Management	Dr. Scot LINGRELL
32	VP Student Affairs	Dr. Shay LITTLE
111	VP Univ Advancement	Mr. Trip ADDISON
13	Interim Chief Information Officer	Ms. Ashlea ANDERSON
09	Director of Institutional Research	Mr. Chris OLSON
20	Vice Provost	Dr. Diana CONE
35	AVP & Dean of Students	Dr. Aileen DOWELL
35	Assoc VP Student Engagement	Dr. Ken GASSIOT
28	AVP Inclusive Exc/CDO	Dr. TaJuan WILSON
43	Executive Counsel	Ms. Maura COPELAND
04	Exec Associate to the President	Ms. Leigh PRICE
07	Director of Admissions	Dr. Amy CLINES
58	Dean College of Graduate Studies	Dr. Ashley WALKER
50	Dean Parker College of Business	Dr. Allen AMASON
53	Dean College of Education	Dr. Sharon SUBREENDUTH
76	Dean Waters College of Health Prof	Dr. Barry JOYNER
49	Dean Col of Behavioral/Social Sci	Dr. Ryan SCHROEDER
49	Int Dean College Arts/Humanities	Dr. John KRAFT
81	Dean College Science & Mathematics	Dr. Delana NIVENS
54	Dean AEP College of Engineering	Dr. Mohammad DAVOUD
51	Director Continuing Education	Dr. Diane BADAKHSH
69	Dean JPH College of Public Health	Dr. Stuart TEDDERS
08	Dean University Libraries	Dr. Lisandra CARMICHAEL
88	Dir NCAA Compliance	Mr. Keith ROUGHTON
116	Chief Auditor	Ms. Katrina MCNAIR
26	VP Univ Communications & Marketing	Dr. John LESTER
121	Director Academic Success Center	Ms. Fiona BRANTLEY
37	Director Financial Aid	Ms. Tracey MINGO
06	Registrar	Ms. Cassie MORGAN
109	Assoc VP Auxiliary Services	Mr. Edward D. MILLS
21	Assoc VP Finance	Mr. Justin JANNEY
15	Assoc VP Human Resources	Ms. Rebecca CARROLL
41	Athletic Director	Mr. Jared BENKO
18	Assoc VP Facilities	Ms. Katie TWINING
19	Director Public Safety	Ms. Laura MCCULLOUGH
36	Director Career Services	Mr. Glenn GIBNEY
38	Director Counseling Services	Dr. Jodi K. CALDWELL
23	Interim Director Health Services	Dr. Brian DELOACH
39	Exec Director University Housing	Mr. Peter BLUTREICH
93	Dir Multicultural Student Center	Ms. Takeshia BROWN
88	Dir Leadership/Outreach	Ms. Jodi KENNEDY
88	Director Advancement IT	Ms. Jill GERIG
29	Director Alumni Relations	Ms. Ava EDWARDS
88	Director Botanic Garden	Ms. Carolyn ALTMAN
14	Director Technical Services	Mr. Joey REEVES
88	Director Museum	Dr. Brent THARP
88	Director Wildlife Educ/Raptor Ctr	Mr. Steven M. HEIN
96	Director Procurement & Logistical	Ms. Daphne BURCH
22	Director Equal Opp/Title IX	Ms. Amber CULPEPPER
89	Asst Director First-Year Experience	Ms. Brenda RICHARDSON
92	Dean Honors College	Dr. Steven ENGEL
119	Chief Information Tech Security Ofc	Vacant
88	Int Dir Centers Teaching/Technology	Dr. Debbie WALKER
88	Dir Stdnt Affs/Disability Res Ctr	Ms. Kelly WOODRUFF
102	Director Foundation Acct	Ms. Tina ADAMS
100	Chief of Staff & External Affairs	Ms. Annalee ASHLEY
104	Int Dir Global Engage/Study Abroad	Ms. Kristin KASTING KARAM
108	Int AVP Institutional Effectiveness	Dr. Delana GATCH
25	Dir Research Svcs/Sponsored Program	Ms. Bruxanne HEIN
44	Director Annual Giving	Vacant
86	Director Government Relations	Ms. Annalee ASHLEY

† Part of the University System of Georgia.

Georgia Southwestern State University (D)

800 GA Southwestern State Univ Dr, Americus GA 31709-4693

County: Sumter FICE Identification: 001573
Unit ID: 139764
Telephone: (877) 871-4594 Carnegie Class: Masters/M
FAX Number: N/A Calendar System: Semester
URL: www.gsw.edu
Established: 1906 Annual Undergrad Tuition & Fees (In-State): $5,464
Enrollment: 3,162 Coed
Affiliation or Control: State IRS Status: 501(c)3
Highest Offering: Beyond Master's But Less Than Doctorate
Accreditation: SC, NURSE

Code	Title	Name
01	President	Dr. Neal R. WEAVER
10	Vice Pres Business & Finance	Mr. Jeff HALL
05	Provost/VP for Academic Affairs	Dr. Suzanne F. SMITH
32	Exec VP Student Engagement/Success	Dr. Laura D. BOREN
13	Dir Information Technology/CIO	Mr. Royce HACKETT
41	Athletic Director	Mr. Mike LEEDER
84	Asst VP for Enrollment Management	Dr. Gaye HAYES
102	Asst VP Advance/Exec Dir GSW Found	Mr. Stephen SNYDER
26	Director Marketing & Communications	Ms. Chelsea COLLINS
20	Associate VP of Academic Affairs	Dr. Bryan P. DAVIS
08	Dean of the Library	Ms. Ru STORY-HUFFMAN
49	Dean Arts & Sciences	Dr. Kelly MCCOY
50	Dean Business & Computing	Dr. Gaynor CHEOKAS
53	Dean of Education	Dr. Rachel ABBOTT
66	Dean Nursing & Health Sciences	Dr. Sandra DANIEL
09	Director Institutional Research	Dr. Lisa A. COOPER
06	Registrar	Ms. Krista SMITH
89	Director of First Year Experience	Dr. David JENKINS
07	Dir of Recruitment & Admissions	Mr. Jonathan H. SCOTT
37	Director of Financial Aid	Mr. Michael WRIGHT
39	Director Residential & Campus Life	Ms. LaToya STACKHOUSE
21	Comptroller	Vacant
15	Director of Human Resources	Ms. Gena WILSON
96	Purchasing Director	Ms. Michelle W. UNDERWOOD
18	Physical Plant Director	Mr. Jim POSEY
19	Director of Public Safety	Chf. Michael LEWIS
113	Director of Student Accounts	Ms. Christy BARRY
24	Technology Services Director	Mr. Robert SLENKER
91	Director Enterprise Services	Ms. Beverly CARROLL
105	Network Administrator	Mr. Dean CRUMBLEY
119	Information Security Officer	Mr. Andrew JERNIGAN
38	Asst Director of Counseling	Ms. Alma G. KEITA
29	Alumni Engagement Specialist	Ms. Angela SMITH
44	Annual Giving Specialist	Ms. Kim COMER
04	Exec Assistant to the President	Ms. Terry THORPE

† Part of the University System of Georgia.

Georgia State University (E)

PO Box 3999, Atlanta GA 30302-3999

County: Fulton FICE Identification: 001574
Unit ID: 139940
Telephone: (404) 413-2000 Carnegie Class: DU-Highest
FAX Number: (404) 413-1380 Calendar System: Semester
URL: www.gsu.edu
Established: 1913 Annual Undergrad Tuition & Fees (In-State): $9,286
Enrollment: 36,360 Coed
Affiliation or Control: State IRS Status: 501(c)3
Highest Offering: Doctorate
Accreditation: SC, ADNUR, ART, CACREP, CEA, CLPSY, COARC, COPSY, DH, DIETC, EXSC, HSA, IPSY, LAW, MUS, NURSE, OT, PH, PTA, SCPSY, SP, SPAA, SW

Code	Title	Name
01	President	Dr. Mark P. BECKER
05	Provost & VP Academic Affairs	Dr. Lisa ARMISTEAD
10	Sr VP Finance & Administration	Dr. Jerry J. RACKLIFFE
12	Dean Perimeter College	Dr. Nancy P. KROPF
46	VP Research/Economic Dev	Dr. Timothy DENNING
32	SVP Student Engagement Success	Dr. Allison CALHOUN-BROWN
30	Vice President Development	Vacant
26	VP PR & Mktg Communications	Mr. Don HALE
43	University Attorney	Dr. Kerry L. HEYWARD
49	Dean Arts & Sciences	Dr. Sara ROSEN
50	Dean Business	Dr. Richard D. PHILLIPS
53	Dean Education & Human Development	Dr. Paul A. ALBERTO
66	Int Dean Nursing/Health Professions	Dr. Huanbiao MO
69	Interim Dean Public Health	Dr. Rodney LYN
61	Interim Dean Law	Dr. Leslie WOLF
80	Dean Policy Studies	Dr. Sally WALLACE
92	Dean Honors College	Dr. Larry S. BERMAN
08	Dean Libraries	Mr. Jeff STEELY
58	Assoc Provost Grad Programs	Vacant
09	Assoc Provost Inst Effectiveness	Dr. Michael GALCHINSKY
82	Assc Prov International Initiatives	Dr. Wolfgang SCHLOER
20	Assoc Provost Faculty Affairs	Dr. Kavita PANDIT
88	Assistant Provost Admin Operations	Mr. Christopher D. HILL
45	Assoc VP Research Integrity	Dr. Brenda J. CHAPMAN
13	Chief Innovation Officer for IT	Mr. Phil VENTIMIGLIA
18	Assoc VP Facilities	Mr. Ramesh VAKAMUDI
21	Assoc VP Finance & Comptroller	Mr. Bruce R. SPRATT
88	Assoc VP Central Development	Ms. Tabatha MICHEL
110	Assoc VP Constituent Programs Dev	Vacant
102	Assoc VP GSU Foundation	Mr. Dale J. PALMER
35	Dean of Students	Ms. Lanette BROWN
27	Assoc VP Public Relations/Marketing	Ms. Andrea JONES
07	Asst VP Undergraduate Admissions	Mr. Scott M. BURKE
124	Asst VP Student Retention	Dr. Allison CALHOUN-BROWN
29	Asst VP Alumni Relations	Ms. Christina C. MILLION
15	Asst VP Human Resources	Vacant
22	Asst VP Opp Dev/Diversity Educ	Vacant
19	Asst VP/Chief University Police	Mr. Joseph SPILLANE
06	Registrar	Ms. Tarrah N. MIRUS
121	Exec Director Student Success	Dr. Timothy M. RENICK
85	Dir Intl Students/Scholars Svcs	Ms. Heather L. HOUSLEY
39	Interim Director University Housing	Ms. Shannon COREY
38	Director Psychological & Health Svc	Dr. Jill LEE-BARBER
28	Director Diversity Programs	Mr. John R. DAY
88	Director Application Engineering	Mr. John M. BANDY, JR.
36	Director University Career Svcs	Ms. Catherine NEINER
37	Director Financial Aid	Vacant
96	Dir of Business Services/Purchasing	Mr. Michael E. DAVIDSON
116	Dir Univ Auditing & Advisory Svcs	Ms. Wanda L. RILEY
117	Director Emergency Management	Mr. Keith P. SUMAS
31	Sr Director Govt/Community Affairs	Ms. Julie M. KERLIN
41	Athletic Director	Mr. Charles G. COBB
04	Assistant to the President	Ms. Ethel B. WRIGHT

† Part of the University System of Georgia.

Gordon State College (F)

419 College Dr., Barnesville GA 30204-1746

County: Lamar FICE Identification: 001575
Unit ID: 139968
Telephone: (678) 359-5555 Carnegie Class: Bac/Assoc-Mixed
FAX Number: (678) 359-5080 Calendar System: Semester
URL: www.gordonstate.edu
Established: 1852 Annual Undergrad Tuition & Fees (In-State): $3,789
Enrollment: 3,231 Coed
Affiliation or Control: State IRS Status: 501(c)3
Highest Offering: Baccalaureate
Accreditation: SC, ADNUR, NUR

Code	Title	Name
01	President	Dr. Kirk NOOKS
05	Provost & VP Academic Affairs	Dr. Jeffery KNIGHTON
10	VP Finance and Administration	Vacant
32	VP Enrollment Mgmt/Student Affairs	Vacant
111	VP Institutional Advancement	Ms. Montrese ADGER FULLER
20	Asst VP Innovative Education and SI	Dr. Ric CALHOUN

08 Library Director .... Ms. Angiah DAVIS
09 Director of Institutional Research .... Mr. Britt LIFSEY
49 Dean School of Arts & Sciences .... Dr. Barry KICKLIGHTER
53 Dean School of Education .... Dr. Joseph JONES
66 Dean School of Nursing .... Dr. Victor VILCHIZ
121 Assistant VP Academic Excellence .... Vacant
21 Controller .... Ms. Felicia JESTER
15 Director of Human Resources .... Ms. Madelyn BROWN
113 Bursar .... Ms. Candice BROWN
114 Dir of Budgets & Aux Operations .... Vacant
18 Director of Facilities .... Mr. Reggie HAMM
37 Senior Director of Financial Aid .... Mrs. Jody DEFORE
13 Director of Information Technology .... Vacant
19 Director of Public Safety .... Vacant
41 Athletic Director .... Dr. Tonya MOORE
38 Director of Counseling Services .... Ms. Alicia DORTON
39 Director of Residence Life .... Ms. Tonya R. COLEMAN
35 Director of Student Activities .... Ms. Brienne MCDANIEL
06 Registrar .... Mrs. Kristi HAYES
30 Development Officer .... Vacant
26 Chief Public Information Officer .... Vacant
40 Bookstore Manager .... Ms. Teresa THOMPSON
04 Special Assistant to the President .... Ms. LaSha SANDERS
07 Director of Admissions .... Vacant
103 Director of Career Services .... Dr. Tonya MOORE
29 Alumni & Annual Fund Administrator .... Vacant

† Part of the University System of Georgia.

Gupton Jones College of Funeral Service (A)

5141 Snapfinger Woods Drive, Decatur GA 30035-4022
County: DeKalb FICE Identification: 010771
Unit ID: 139995
Telephone: (770) 593-2257 Carnegie Class: Spec 2-yr-A&S
FAX Number: (770) 593-1891 Calendar System: Quarter
URL: www.gupton-jones.edu
Established: 1920 Annual Undergrad Tuition & Fees: $11,970
Enrollment: 266 Coed
Affiliation or Control: Independent Non-Profit IRS Status: 501(c)3
Highest Offering: Associate Degree
Accreditation: FUSER

01 President .... Ms. Hope INGLEHART
05 Campus Dean .... Mr. Mark PALUMBO

Gwinnett College (B)

4230 Highway 29, Suite 11, Lilburn GA 30047-3447
County: Gwinnett FICE Identification: 025830
Unit ID: 140003
Telephone: (770) 381-7200 Carnegie Class: Assoc/HVT-Mix Trad/Non
FAX Number: (770) 381-0454 Calendar System: Other
URL: www.gwinnettcollege.com
Established: 1976 Annual Undergrad Tuition & Fees: $9,925
Enrollment: 225 Coed
Affiliation or Control: Proprietary IRS Status: Proprietary
Highest Offering: Associate Degree
Accreditation: ACICS

01 President .... Mr. Michael DAVIS
05 Dir Education/Campus Director .... Ms. Lisa MCLARIO

Gwinnett College-Marietta (C)

1130 North Chase Parkway, Suite 100, Marietta GA 30067
County: Cobb FICE Identification: 038044
Unit ID: 444714
Telephone: (770) 859-9779 Carnegie Class: Spec 2-yr-Health
FAX Number: (770) 859-9778 Calendar System: Quarter
URL: https://www.gwinnettcollege.edu/
Established: Annual Undergrad Tuition & Fees: N/A
Enrollment: 274 Coed
Affiliation or Control: Proprietary IRS Status: Proprietary
Highest Offering: Associate Degree
Accreditation: COE

01 President .... Mr. Lenny DAVIS
11 Campus Director .... Mr. Keith CRAVENS

Gwinnett College-Sandy Springs (D)

6690 Roswell Rd, NE, Ste 2200, Sandy Springs GA 30328
County: Fulton FICE Identification: 034183
Unit ID: 425250
Telephone: (770) 457-2021 Carnegie Class: Spec 2-yr-Health
FAX Number: (404) 574-2234 Calendar System: Other
URL: www.risingspirit.edu
Established: 1994 Annual Undergrad Tuition & Fees: N/A
Enrollment: 114 Coed
Affiliation or Control: Proprietary IRS Status: Proprietary
Highest Offering: Associate Degree
Accreditation: ACCSC

01 Campus Director .... Mr. Ty DAVIS

Gwinnett Technical College (E)

5150 Sugarloaf Parkway, Lawrenceville GA 30043-5702
County: Gwinnett FICE Identification: 022884
Unit ID: 140012
Telephone: (770) 962-7580 Carnegie Class: Assoc/HVT-Mix Trad/Non
FAX Number: (770) 962-7985 Calendar System: Semester
URL: www.gwinnetttech.edu
Established: 1984 Annual Undergrad Tuition & Fees (In-State): $3,236
Enrollment: 8,576 Coed
Affiliation or Control: State IRS Status: 501(c)3
Highest Offering: Associate Degree
Accreditation: SC, ACFEI, ADNUR, CAHIIM, COARC, CONST, CVT, DA, DMS, EMT, MAC, NAEYC, RAD, SURGT

01 President .... Dr. D. Glen CANNON
05 VP of Academic Affairs .... Ms. Rebecca ALEXANDER
111 VP of Inst Advancement .... Mr. Charles MCKINNON
32 VP of Student Affairs .... Dr. Kohle PAUL
103 VP Economic Development .... Mr. Melvin EVERSON
13 VP Technology & Operations .... Mr. Galen MARTIN
15 VP of Human Resources .... Ms. LaShanta' COX
53 VP of Adult Education .... Ms. Stephanie ROOKS
11 VP Administrative Services .... Ms. Sonya MCDANIEL
19 Chief of Campus Police & Security .... Mr. Mike BLOUIN
84 Exec Dir Enrollment Processing ... Ms. Betsy HARRIS-BRACKETT
07 Exec Dir Enrollment Support .... Ms. Janelle PIERCE
08 Director of Library Services .... Ms. Deborah GEORGE
09 Dir Inst Research & Effectiveness .... Vacant
36 Director of Career Services .... Ms. Ave MILLER
37 Director of Financial Aid .... Ms. Andra PETERSON
06 Registrar .... Mr. Brad THOMAS
04 Exec Assistant to the President .... Ms. Melissa FLANAGAN

Helms College (F)

5171 Eisenhower Pkwy, Macon GA 31206-5309
County: Bibb FICE Identification: 042064
Unit ID: 481155
Telephone: (478) 471-4394 Carnegie Class: Spec 2-yr-A&S
FAX Number: N/A Calendar System: Quarter
URL: helms.edu
Established: 2007 Annual Undergrad Tuition & Fees: $13,460
Enrollment: 280 Coed
Affiliation or Control: Independent Non-Profit IRS Status: 501(c)3
Highest Offering: Associate Degree
Accreditation: CNCE

01 President .... Mr. James STIFF
05 Director of Education .... Mr. Bill DINDY
84 Vice Pres Enrollment Management .... Mr. Andrew ROBINSON
06 Registrar .... Ms. Freda GAINES
07 Sr Admissions Manager .... Ms. Ariel SMITH
36 Vice Pres Career Services .... Ms. Leah PONTANI
88 VP Hospitality Education .... Mr. Bruce OZGA

Herzing University (G)

50 Hurt Plaza SE, Suite 400, Atlanta GA 30303
Telephone: (404) 816-4533 FICE Identification: 020897
Accreditation: &HLC, NURSE

† Regional accreditation is carried under the parent institution in Madison, WI.

Hudson Taylor University (H)

2855 Rolling Pin Lane, Suwanee GA 30024
County: Gwinnett Identification: 667416
Telephone: (770) 831-8882 Carnegie Class: Not Classified
FAX Number: N/A Calendar System: Semester
URL: hudsontayloruniversity.org
Established: 2013 Annual Undergrad Tuition & Fees: N/A
Enrollment: N/A Coed
Affiliation or Control: Independent Non-Profit IRS Status: 501(c)3
Highest Offering: Doctorate
Accreditation: @BI

01 President .... Dr. David J. BREWER

Interactive College of Technology (I)

5303 New Peachtree Road, Chamblee GA 30341-2818
County: DeKalb FICE Identification: 022843
Unit ID: 138655
Telephone: (770) 216-2960 Carnegie Class: Spec 2-yr-Other
FAX Number: (678) 287-3474 Calendar System: Semester
URL: www.ict.edu
Established: 1986 Annual Undergrad Tuition & Fees: $10,250
Enrollment: 730 Coed
Affiliation or Control: Proprietary IRS Status: Proprietary
Highest Offering: Associate Degree
Accreditation: COE

00 Chief Executive Officer .... Mr. Elmer R. SMITH
01 President .... Mr. Thomas A. BLAIR
10 Vice President/CFO .... Mr. J. Andrew BOU
12 Vice President/Campus Dir Chamblee .... Ms. Jo Ann KOCH
12 Campus Director Pasadena Texas .... Mr. Greg WEAVER
12 Campus Dir SW Houston Texas .... Ms. Diane NGUYEN
12 Campus Dir North Houston Texas .... Ms. Alyssa MAYHEW
12 Campus Director Newport KY .... Ms. Hope Michelle TOUEY
12 Campus Director Morrow GA .... Mr. Jonathon LEWIS
12 Campus Administrator Gainesville GA .... Ms. Sofia LUKAS
88 Senior Administrative Assistant .... Ms. Liesa PEAVY
26 Director of Marketing .... Mr. Drew CARL
88 Director of Compliance .... Ms. Christina JONES
04 Administrative Asst to President .... Ms. Karen A. MILLER
06 Registrar .... Ms. Rosalind HOLT
07 Director of Admissions .... Ms. Nicole CARUSO
37 Director Student Financial Aid .... Ms. Nataliya CHORNIY

Interactive College of Technology (J)

2323-C Browns Bridge Road, Gainesville GA 30504
Telephone: (678) 456-0550 Identification: 770533
Accreditation: COE

Interactive College of Technology (K)

1580 Southdale Parkway, Morrow GA 30260
Telephone: (770) 960-1298 Identification: 770534
Accreditation: COE

Interdenominational Theological Center (L)

700 Martin L. King, Jr. Drive, SW, Atlanta GA 30314-4143
County: Fulton FICE Identification: 001568
Unit ID: 140146
Telephone: (404) 527-7700 Carnegie Class: Spec-4-yr-Faith
FAX Number: (404) 527-0901 Calendar System: Semester
URL: www.itc.edu
Established: 1958 Annual Graduate Tuition & Fees: N/A
Enrollment: 285 Coed
Affiliation or Control: Interdenominational IRS Status: 501(c)3
Highest Offering: Doctorate; No Undergraduates
Accreditation: SC, THEOL

01 President .... Rev. Matthew W. WILLIAMS
05 VP for Academic Services/Provost .... Dr. Maisha HANDY
10 Interim Chief Financial Officer .... Rev Dr. Sydney WILLIAMS
111 VP Institutional Advancement .... Ms. Nancy L. JONES
06 Registrar .... Ms. Arlene V. CLARKE
32 AVP Student Affairs .... Dr. Catherine BINUYA
37 Financial Aid Director .... Mr. Johnny NIMES
11 Interim Chief Operations Officer .... Mr. Carl PATTEN, II
07 Director of Admissions/Recruitment .... Ms. Natasha JORDAN
42 Chaplain .... Dr. Willie F. GOODMAN
108 Director Institutional Assessment .... Dr. Itihari TOURE
04 Executive Admin Asst to President .... Ms. Yolanda DOWERY
39 Resident Life & Student Experience .... Ms. Angelicia HEATH-MCKENZIE

Kennesaw State University (M)

1000 Chastain Road, NW, Kennesaw GA 30144
County: Cobb FICE Identification: 001577
Unit ID: 486840
Telephone: (470) 578-6000 Carnegie Class: DU-Higher
FAX Number: (470) 578-9117 Calendar System: Semester
URL: www.kennesaw.edu
Established: 1963 Annual Undergrad Tuition & Fees (In-State): $6,436
Enrollment: 41,181 Coed
Affiliation or Control: State IRS Status: 501(c)3
Highest Offering: Doctorate
Accreditation: SC, ART, CGTECH, CONST, CSHSE, MUS, NURSE, OPE, SPAA, SW, THEA

01 President .... Dr. Pamela WHITTEN
10 Chief Business Officer .... Mr. Aaron HOWELL
108 EVP Institutional Effectiveness .... Ms. Danielle BUEHRER
05 Provost/VP Academic Affairs .... Dr. Kathy S. SCHWAIG
111 VP Advancement/CEO Univ Foundation .... Mr. Lance BURCHETT
32 Vice Pres Student Affairs .... Mr. Eric ARNESON
11 Chief Administrative Officer .... Dr. Tricia CHASTAIN
26 VP for External Affairs and COS .... Mr. Alex MCGEE
27 AVP Marketing/Communications .... Ms. Alice WHEELWRIGHT
103 VP Economic Dev/Cmty Engagement .... Vacant
20 Senior Vice Provost Academic Affs .... Vacant
20 Assoc Vice Pres for Curriculum .... Dr. Pamela COLE
97 Dean University College .... Dr. Lynn DISBROW
15 AVP Human Resources .... Ms. Karen MCDONNELL
13 Chief Information Officer .... Mr. Jeff DELANEY
84 Vice Pres Enrollment Svcs .... Ms. Brenda STOPHER
106 AVP Technology Enhanced Learning .... Vacant
88 AVP Strategic Comm/Issues Mgmt .... Ms. Tammy DEMEL
08 Asst Vice Pres for Library Services .... Dr. J. David EVANS
18 Asst Vice Pres Facilities Services .... Mr. Andrew YAKIMOVICH
09 Asst VP Institutional Research .... Dr. Phaedra CORSO
79 Dean Humanities/Social Science .... Dr. Shawn LONG
81 Dean College Science & Mathematics . Dr. Kojo MENSA-WILMOT
53 Dean Bagwell College of Education .... Dr. Cynthia REED
50 Dean Coles College of Business .... Dr. Robin CHERAMIE
76 Int Dean College Health/Human Svcs .... Dr. Scott GORDON
57 Dean College of the Arts .... Dr. Ivan PULINKALA
48 Int Dean Architecture/Constr Mgmt .... Dr. Kathryn BEDETTE
77 Dean Col Computing/Software Eng .... Dr. Jon PRESTON
58 Dean Graduate College .... Dr. Mike DISHMAN
92 Dean Honors College .... Dr. Rita BAILEY
51 Assoc Dean Continuing/Prof Educ ..... Dr. Timothy BLUMENTRITT
54 Assoc Dean of Engineering/Eng Tech .... Dr. Renee BUTLER
80 Dir Sch Government/Intl Affairs .... Dr. Kerwin SWINT
35 Dean of Students .... Vacant
121 Assoc VP/Dir Student Success Svcs .... Vacant
28 Chief Diversity Officer .... Ms. Sylvia CAREY-BUTLER
06 Registrar .... Ms. Ana EDWARDS
91 Exec Dir Enterprise Systems & Svcs .... Vacant
37 Director Student Financial Aid .... Mr. Rondall H. DAY

07 Exec Dir Undergraduate Programs .... Vacant
25 Director Procurement & Contracting .... Vacant
88 Exec Dir Internships & Coops .... Ms. Ana BAIDA
41 Director of Athletics .... Mr. Milton OVERTON
29 Director Alumni Relations .... Ms. Jyll KAFER
19 AVP Public Safety/Chief of Police .... Mr. Edward STEPHENS
100 Exec Admin to Pres/Chf of Protocol .... Mr. James TAYLOR
104 Education Abroad Program Coord .... Ms. Nicole MEANOR
105 Dir Web Services/Mobile Development .... Mr. Chris WARD
39 Director University Housing .... Mr. Christopher BRUNO
86 Assoc VP of Government Relations .... Ms. Julia AYERS
116 Chief Internal Auditor .... Vacant
88 Director of Financial Compliance .... Mr. Robert BRIDGES

† Part of the University System of Georgia.

LaGrange College (A)

601 Broad Street, La Grange GA 30240-2999
County: Troup FICE Identification: 001578
Unit ID: 140234
Telephone: (706) 880-8000 Carnegie Class: Bac-Diverse
FAX Number: (706) 880-8358 Calendar System: 4/1/4
URL: www.lagrange.edu
Established: 1831 Annual Undergrad Tuition & Fees: $32,370
Enrollment: 854 Coed
Affiliation or Control: United Methodist IRS Status: 501(c)3
Highest Offering: Master's
Accreditation: SC, ACBSP, CACREP, NUR

01 President .... Dr. Susanna BAXTER
04 Executive Assistant to President .... Mrs. Carla RHODES
41 VP of Athletics .... Ms. Terlynn OLDS
05 VP Academic Affairs .... Dr. Karen AUBREY
32 VP of Student Engagement .... Dr. Brian A. CARLISLE
06 Registrar .... Mrs. Amber BALDRIDGE
08 Director of Library Services .... Ms. Kelly ANSLEY
09 Director Inst Effectiveness .... Dr. Carol YIN
36 Director Career Development Center .... Dr. Karen PRUETT
38 Director Counseling Center .... Mrs. Pamela TREMBLAY
20 Associate Provost .... Dr. Maranah SAUTER
39 Director Res Educ & Housing .... Vacant
30 VP of External Relations .... Mrs. Rebecca ROTH NICKS
26 Sr Director Communications/Mktg .... Mr. Dean A. HARTMAN
37 Director Student Financial Aid .... Mrs. Michelle REEVES
110 Director of Development .... Mr. Mark E. DAVIS
29 Director Alumni & Cmty Relations .... Mrs. Martha W. PIRKLE
84 VP of Enrollment .... Mr. Joseph C. MILLER
112 Major Gift Officer .... Vacant
07 Director of Admission .... Ms. Nicole MADDOX
105 Asst Director Communications & Mktg .... Vacant
10 VP of Finance & Operations .... Ms. Deborah P. HALL
21 Director of Finance .... Mrs. Patti D. HOXSIE
18 Manager Facilities/Physical Plant .... Mr. Michael CONIGLIO
19 Director of Security .... Mr. Wayne MICHAUX
13 Sr Director Information Technology .... Mr. James BLACKWOOD
42 Director Spiritual Life & Chaplain .... Dr. Adam ROBERTS
106 Director Online Instruction .... Dr. Jon ERNSTBERGER
91 Database Administrator .... Vacant
88 Events Coordinator .... Ms. Tammy ROGERS

Lanier Technical College (B)

2535 Lanier Tech Drive, Gainesville GA 30507
County: Hall FICE Identification: 005254
Unit ID: 140243
Telephone: (770) 533-7000 Carnegie Class: Assoc/HVT-High Trad
FAX Number: (678) 989-3107 Calendar System: Semester
URL: www.laniertech.edu
Established: 1964 Annual Undergrad Tuition & Fees (In-State): $3,666
Enrollment: 5,045 Coed
Affiliation or Control: State IRS Status: 501(c)3
Highest Offering: Associate Degree
Accreditation: SC, CAHIIM, DA, DH, EMT, MAC, PTAA, RAD, SURGT

01 President .... Mr. Tim MCDONALD
103 Vice President Economic Development .... Mr. Carl ROGERS
05 Vice President Academic Affairs .... Mrs. Donna BRINSON
45 Vice President IE .... Dr. Joanne P. TOLLESON
32 Vice President Student Affairs .... Ms. Nancy BEAVER
10 Vice Pres Administrative Services .... Mr. Les SALTER
13 Vice Pres Information Technology .... Mr. Anthony HARDY
04 Executive Assistant to President .... Ms. Karen MINOR
75 Dean Business/Public Safety/Profess .... Ms. Beth HEFNER
54 Dean Advanced Tech/Engr .... Dr. John DUNBAR
72 Dean of Applied Technology .... Mr. Christian TETZLAFF
97 Dean of General Education .... Ms. Kathy ALDEN
76 Dean of Allied Health .... Dr. Deanne COLLINS
12 Dean of Barrow Campus .... Mr. Chip REYNOLDS
12 Dean of Dawson Campus .... Mr. Troy LINSEY
12 Dean of Jackson Campus .... Mr. Chip REYNOLDS
09 Dir of Institutional Effectiveness .... Mr. Brad GADBERRY
111 Vice Pres Institutional Advancement .... Ms. Lauren TALLEY
07 Director of Admissions .... Ms. Holly BATES
06 Registrar .... Ms. Mandy ORR
37 Director Student Financial Aid .... Ms. Courtney RAY
21 Director Administrative Services .... Ms. Teri AURORA
15 Director of Human Resources .... Ms. Jill CANTRELL
18 Director of Facilities .... Mr. Mike SCHMIDT
36 Career Services Coordinator .... Ms. Sarah CROWE
22 Disability Services Coordinator .... Ms. Allison HAYNES
08 Library Services Director .... Ms. Kathryn S. THOMPSON
19 College Police Chief .... Mr. Jeff STRICKLAND
96 Purchasing Agent .... Ms. Kathy PHAGAN

Life University (C)

1269 Barclay Circle, Marietta GA 30060-2996
County: Cobb FICE Identification: 020748
Unit ID: 140252
Telephone: (770) 426-2600 Carnegie Class: Spec-4-yr-Other Health
FAX Number: (770) 429-4819 Calendar System: Quarter
URL: www.life.edu
Established: 1974 Annual Undergrad Tuition & Fees: $13,596
Enrollment: 2,761 Coed
Affiliation or Control: Independent Non-Profit IRS Status: 501(c)3
Highest Offering: Doctorate
Accreditation: SC, CHIRO, DIETD, DIETI

01 President .... Dr. Rob SCOTT
125 Chancellor Emeritus .... Dr. Guy F. RIEKEMAN
05 VP Academic Affairs .... Dr. Tim GROSS
10 Exec VP of Finance .... Mr. William JARR
18 Director of Facilities .... Mr. Ignacio MANZANERA
41 Director of Athletics .... Ms. Jayme PENDERGAST
13 Chief Information Officer .... Mr. John ALTIKULAC
88 Dean College of Chiropractic .... Dr. Leslie KING
20 Dean College of Grad and Undergrad .... Dr. Jana W. HOLWICK
104 VP Global Initiatives .... Dr. John DOWNES
14 Director Information Technology .... Mr. Thorton MUIR
29 Director Alumni Relations .... Ms. Darcie WALLACE
58 Assoc Dean Grad & Undergrad Studies .... Dr. Michael D. SMITH
88 Assoc Dean College of Chiropractic .... Dr. Michael CLUSSERATH
32 Dean of Students .... Dr. Janna BREDESON
106 Dean Online Education .... Dr. Richard BELCASTRO
23 Associate Dean of Clinics .... Dr. Bernadette LAVENDER
88 Associate Dean .... Dr. Mary Catherine FAUST
81 Chair Basic Sciences .... Dr. Mamie WARE
21 Controller .... Ms. Jo Ann MILLER
101 Board Secretary .... Ms. Nita LOONEY
114 Budget Director .... Ms. Amy MCILVANE
88 Director Student Advocacy .... Ms. Sandra TERRY
15 Director Human Resources .... Ms. Lisa REED
27 Director of Marketing .... Ms. Shelly BATCHER
88 Dir of Student Administrative Svcs .... Ms. Melissa WATERS
08 Director of Library .... Ms. Kathleen WILLIAMS
37 Director Student Financial Aid .... Ms. Jessica MAGAZU
44 Director of Advancement Services .... Ms. Lauren NIELSON
108 Director of Inst Effectiveness .... Dr. Vince ERARIO
09 Director of Institutional Research .... Dr. Howard WRIGHT
06 Registrar .... Ms. Heather HOFFMAN
17 Executive Director Clinic Ops .... Dr. Shayan SHEYBANI
88 Director of Peak .... Dr. John MARKMAN
88 Assistant Dean Liberal Studies .... Dr. Christopher WELLS
121 Director of University Advising .... Ms. Tameka GLASS
121 Director Student Success .... Dr. Lisa RUBIN
88 Director Chiropractic Research .... Dr. Stephanie SULLIVAN
30 Director of Development .... Ms. Erin DANCER
88 Director Academic Support .... Dr. Nicoly MYLES
88 Director Clinics .... Dr. Steven MIRTSCHINK
88 Director CETL .... Mr. William WATSON
88 Director of the Harris Center .... Dr. Krista BOLINE
89 Assistant Dean Student Engagement .... Ms. Jennifer STROBLE
88 Division Chair Clinical Sciences .... Dr. Mark FERDARKO
36 Director of Career Services .... Ms. Susan DUDT
32 VP for Student Services .... Dr. Marc SCHNEIDER
113 Director Student Accounts .... Ms. Phyllis SHROPSHIRE
16 Employee Relations Officer .... Ms. Monica WARD
96 Interim Director of Purchasing .... Mr. Mel BURTON
39 Asst Dean Community Living .... Mr. Andre CLANTON
88 Director Special Events .... Ms. Brenda BOONE
22 Director Disability Services .... Dr. Genelle HANEY
88 Director Sports Information .... Mr. William HUDSPETH
11 VP of Operations .... Mr. John MCGEE
88 Director Clinical Education .... Dr. Melissa LOSCHIAVO
84 VP of Enrollment & Mktg .... Dr. Cynthia BOYD
26 VP of Professional Relations .... Dr. Gilles LAMARCHE
88 Presidential Liaison for Ext Rels .... Dr. Gerald CLUM
88 Chair Chiropractic Sciences .... Dr. Lydia DEVER
88 Asst Dean Natural Sciences .... Dr. Saphronia JOHNSON
88 Director of Post Graduate Educ .... Ms. Kathleen BANNISTER
88 Director Athletics Health Care .... Mr. Christopher MARKIE
88 Asst Dean Sports Health Science .... Dr. Richard WILLIAMS
88 Director Clinical Assessment .... Dr. Stephen PATERNO
88 Director of Training-CCISE .... Ms. Jennifer VALTOS
88 Director of Clinics .... Dr. Joseph FORESE
88 Director GR & UG Enrollment .... Mr. Keith JORDAN
88 Director Clinic Advising .... Dr. Frank SCHWITZ
88 Director Sports Information .... Mr. William MANGUM
84 Director Enrollment Operations .... Ms. Khrystal STANLEY
88 Dir Student Athletic Performance .... Mr. Tommy STUCKY

Luther Rice College and Seminary (D)

3038 Evans Mill Road, Lithonia GA 30038-2454
County: DeKalb FICE Identification: 031009
Unit ID: 135364
Telephone: (770) 484-1204 Carnegie Class: Spec-4-yr-Faith
FAX Number: (770) 484-1155 Calendar System: Semester
URL: www.lutherrice.edu
Established: 1962 Annual Undergrad Tuition & Fees: $8,448
Enrollment: 693 Coed
Affiliation or Control: Independent Non-Profit IRS Status: 501(c)3
Highest Offering: Doctorate
Accreditation: SC, BI, TRACS

01 President .... Dr. Steven STEINHILBER
10 Vice President Financial Affairs .... Mr. Casey KUFFREY
05 Vice President for Academic Affairs .... Dr. Evan POSEY
58 Director Doctor of Ministry Program .... Dr. Ron K. COBB
13 Chief Info Technology Officer (CIO) .... Mr. Ken STOKES

Mercer University (E)

1501 Mercer University Drive, Macon GA 31207-0003
County: Bibb FICE Identification: 001580
Unit ID: 140447
Telephone: (478) 301-2700 Carnegie Class: DU-Higher
FAX Number: (478) 301-2108 Calendar System: Semester
URL: www.mercer.edu
Established: 1833 Annual Undergrad Tuition & Fees: $37,808
Enrollment: 9,006 Coed
Affiliation or Control: Independent Non-Profit IRS Status: 501(c)3
Highest Offering: Doctorate
Accreditation: SC, ARCPA, CAATE, CACREP, CEA, CLPSY, LAW, MED, MFCD, MUS, NURSE, PH, PHAR, PTA, THEOL

01 President and CEO .... Mr. William D. UNDERWOOD
125 Chancellor .... Dr. R. Kirby GODSEY
10 Executive VP for Admin & Finance .... Dr. James S. NETHERTON
26 Sr VP for Mktg Comm/Chief of Staff .... Mr. Larry D. BRUMLEY
05 Provost .... Dr. D. Scott DAVIS
45 Sr VP for Strategic Initiatives .... Ms. Kellie APPEL
111 Sr VP for University Advancement .... Mr. John A. PATTERSON
110 Senior Assoc VP for Advancement .... Mr. Allen S. LONDON
84 Sr VP for Enrollment Management .... Dr. Penny L. ELKINS
43 Sr Vice President & General Counsel .... Mr. William G. SOLOMON
13 Assoc VP & Chief Technology Officer .... Vacant
41 Director of Athletics .... Mr. Jim COLE
46 Assoc Dean & Sr Vice Prov for Rsrch .... Dr. Wayne C. GLASGOW
108 Vice Provost for Inst Effectiveness .... Dr. Susan C. MALONE
21 Assoc VP for Finance & Treasurer .... Ms. Julia T. DAVIS
18 Assoc Vice President for Facilities .... Mr. Russell VULLO
15 Assoc Vice Pres for Human Resources .... Ms. Candace WHALEY
27 Sr Asst VP for Mktg Communications .... Mr. Richard L. CAMERON
37 Assoc VP for Student Financial Plng .... Ms. Maria A. HAMMETT
32 VP Stdnt Affairs & Dean of Students .... Dr. Doug R. PEARSON
35 Assoc Dean of Student Services .... Dr. Stephen R. BROWN
39 Director of Residence Life .... Mr. Jeff TAKAC
49 Dean College of Liberal Arts & Sci .... Dr. Anita O. GUSTAFSON
61 Dean School of Law .... Ms. Cathy COX
67 Dean School of Pharmacy .... Dr. Brian CRABTREE
63 Dean School of Medicine .... Dr. Jean R. SUMNER
54 Dean School of Engineering .... Dr. Laura W. LACKEY
50 Dean School of Business .... Dr. Julie PETHERBRIDGE
73 Dean Sch of Theology/Dir of Dev .... Dr. C. Gregory DELOACH
53 Dean College of Education .... Dr. Thomas R. KOBALLA, JR.
66 Dean College of Nursing .... Dr. Linda A. STREIT
107 Dean Col of Prof Advancement .... Dr. Priscilla R. DANHEISER
64 Dean School of Music .... Dr. C. David KEITH
76 Dean Col of Health Professions .... Dr. Lisa M. LUNDQUIST
08 Dean of The Univ Library .... Dr. Jeffrey A. WALDROP
42 Univ Minister & Dean of Chapel .... Dr. Craig T. MCMAHAN
06 University Registrar .... Ms. Alba RODRIGUEZ
19 Director of Mercer Police .... Mr. Gary COLLINS
09 Director of Institutional Research .... Ms. Sarah E. MAY
36 Exec Dir Ctr for Career & Prof Dev .... Ms. Kim MEREDITH
38 Dir Counseling & Psychological Svcs .... Dr. Emily PIASSICK
96 Director of Purchasing .... Ms. Lisa J. BUTLER
04 Admin Asst to the President .... Ms. Vonne SHEFFIELD
29 Assoc VP & Exec Dir Alumni Assn .... Ms. Jill H. KINSELLA
86 VP for Government Relations .... Mr. Hugh D. SOSEBEE, JR.
07 Asst VP for Enrollment Mgmt .... Dr. Kelly L. HOLLOWAY
25 Director of Grants & Contracts .... Ms. DeLaine SAMPLES
105 Dir of Digital Communications .... Mr. Matthew R. SMITH
28 Dir of Div/Inclusion Initiatives .... Dr. Ansley A. BOOKER

Middle Georgia State University (F)

100 University Parkway, Macon GA 31206-5145
County: Bibb FICE Identification: 007728
Unit ID: 482158
Telephone: (478) 471-2700 Carnegie Class: Bac-Diverse
FAX Number: (478) 471-2846 Calendar System: Semester
URL: www.mga.edu
Established: 1884 Annual Undergrad Tuition & Fees (In-State): $4,060
Enrollment: 8,404 Coed
Affiliation or Control: State IRS Status: 501(c)3
Highest Offering: Doctorate
Accreditation: SC, AAB, ADNUR, COARC, NUR, OTA, @SW

01 President .... Dr. Christopher BLAKE
05 Provost/Vice Pres Academic Affairs .... Dr. David JENKS
10 Exec VP Finance & Operations .... Ms. Nancy STROUD
32 VP Student Affairs .... Dr. Jennifer BRANNON
111 VP Univ Advancement/Exec Dir Fdn .... Ms. Mary MCDONALD
20 Associate Provost .... Dr. Michael GIBBONS
20 Associate Provost .... Dr. Deepa ARORA
79 Dean School of Arts and Letters .... Dr. Mary WEARN
100 Chief of Staff/Govt Relations Ofcr .... Ms. Ember BISHOP BENTLEY
13 Chief Information Officer .... Mr. Geoffrey DYER
43 Dir Legal Services/General Counsel .... Ms. Renee RAINEY
26 VP Recruit/Mktg & Chief Mktg Ofcr .... Ms. Cheryl CARTY
15 Exec Dir Human Resources .... Ms. Pamela BOOKER
112 Exec Dir Major and Planning Giving .... Ms. Julie DAVIS
35 Asst VP Student Affairs .... Dr. Michael STEWART
18 Asst VP Facilities .... Mr. David SIMS
19 Asst VP Risk Mgmt and Police Svcs .... Mr. Shane ROLAND
21 Controller .... Mr. Brian STANLEY
06 Registrar .... Ms. Dian MITCHELL

07 Director of Admissions .... Ms. Margo WOODHAM
29 Director Alumni Relations .... Ms. Natalie RISCHBIETER
41 Director Athletics/Rec/Wellness .... Mr. Chip SMITH
109 Director Auxiliary Services .... Mr. Ryan GREENE
40 Director Campus Stores .... Ms. Jessica HALL
38 Director Counseling .... Ms. Predita HOWARD
37 Director Financial Aid .... Ms. LeeAnn KIRKLAND
25 Director Grants and Contracts .... Ms. Barbara RATZLAFF
09 Assoc Dir Institutional Research .... Ms. Samantha BOSWELL
08 Director Library Services .... Ms. Tamatha LAMBERT
96 Director Purchasing .... Ms. Barbara BURNS
39 Director of Residence Life .... Mr. Brian HARRELL
12 Director Cochran/Eastman Campuses .... Mr. Henry WHITFIELD
20 Associate Provost .... Dr. Kevin CANTWELL
88 Dean Aviation .... Mr. Adon CLARK
50 Dean of Business .... Dr. Stephen MORSE
53 Dean of Education & Behavioral Sci .... Dr. David BIEK
81 Dean Health & Natural Sciences .... Dr. Tara UNDERWOOD
77 Dean Computing .... Dr. Alex KOOHANG
88 Special Assistant to the President .... Dr. Kevin CANTWELL
04 Admin Assistant to the President .... Ms. Carey WIMBERLY
28 Dir Diversity/Inclusion & Equity .... Ms. Jenia BACOTE

† Part of the University System of Georgia.

Miller-Motte Technical College (A)

621 Frontage Road NW, Augusta GA 30907
Telephone: (706) 619-2090 Identification: 770710
Accreditation: ACCSC

† Branch campus of Platt College, Tulsa, OK.

Miller-Motte Technical College (B)

1800 Box Road, Columbus GA 31907
Telephone: (706) 225-5637 Identification: 770711
Accreditation: ACCSC

† Branch campus of Platt College, Tulsa, OK.

Miller-Motte Technical College (C)

175 Tom Hill Sr Boulevard, Macon GA 31210
Telephone: (478) 257-3912 Identification: 770844
Accreditation: ACCSC

† Branch campus of Platt College, Tulsa, OK.

Morehouse College (D)

830 Westview Drive SW, Atlanta GA 30314-3773
County: Fulton FICE Identification: 001582
Unit ID: 140553
Telephone: (404) 639-0999 Carnegie Class: Bac-A&S
FAX Number: (404) 681-2650 Calendar System: Semester
URL: www.morehouse.edu
Established: 1867 Annual Undergrad Tuition & Fees: $29,468
Enrollment: 2,152 Male
Affiliation or Control: Independent Non-Profit IRS Status: 501(c)3
Highest Offering: Baccalaureate
Accreditation: SC, MUS

01 President .... Dr. David A. THOMAS
05 Sr VP of Academic Affairs/Provost .... Dr. Kendrick T. BROWN
04 Sr Exec Assistant to the President .... Vacant
04 Exec Assistant to the President .... Ms. Nakia WASHINGTON
116 Chief Audit Officer .... Ms. Undria STALLING
10 SVP Business/Finance & CFO .... Ms. Undria STALLING
11 Sr VP & Chief Administrative Ofcr .... Ms. Karen MILLER
111 VP for Institutional Advancement .... Ms. Monique DOZIER
13 VP of Information Technology & CIO .... Mrs. Kimberley MARSHALL
26 VP Strategic Comm/Chief Mktg Ofcr .... Mr. Jose MALLABO
29 VP Ext Relations/Alumni Engagement .... Mr. Henry GOODGAME
43 VP Legal Affs/GC/Chief Compl Ofcr .... Mrs. Joy WHITE
32 VP Student Svcs/Dean of College .... Mr. Kevin BOOKER
19 Chief of Campus Police .... Chief Valerie DALTON
15 AVP for HR/Chief Compliance Officer .... Mrs. Cassandra TARVER-ROSS
84 VP of Enrollment Management .... Mr. Terrance DIXON
21 AVP & Controller .... Mr. Haskell RUFF
42 Dean Martin Luther King Jr Chapel .... Dr. Lawrence E. CARTER
06 Dean/Registrar .... Ms. Marie BROWN
35 Assoc Dean for Student Services .... Mr. Kevin BOOKER
07 Director Admissions & Recruitment .... Mr. Darryl ISOM
37 Director of Financial Aid .... Mr. Tarik BOYD
09 Dir Inst Research/Effectiveness .... Ms. Sharmyne EVANS
41 Athletic Director .... Mr. Curtis CAMPBELL
85 AVP Advancement/Ldrshp Initiatives .... Dr. Jann ADAMS
38 Director for Student Counseling .... Mr. Steven ALLWOOD
105 Director Web Services .... Ms. Kara WALKER
22 Dir Title IX/Ethics/Compliance .... Ms. Cassandra TARVER-ROSS
39 Sr Assoc Dean Residential Educ .... Mr. DeMarcus CREWS

Morehouse School of Medicine (E)

720 Westview Drive, SW, Atlanta GA 30310-1495
County: Fulton FICE Identification: 024821
Unit ID: 140562
Telephone: (404) 752-1500 Carnegie Class: Spec-4-yr-Med
FAX Number: (404) 752-1027 Calendar System: Semester
URL: www.msm.edu
Established: 1975 Annual Graduate Tuition & Fees: N/A
Enrollment: 665 Coed
Affiliation or Control: Independent Non-Profit IRS Status: 501(c)3
Highest Offering: Doctorate; No Undergraduates
Accreditation: SC, #ARCPA, MED, PH

01 President/Dean .... Dr. Valerie MONTGOMERY RICE
10 Sr Vice Pres Finance/CFO .... Dr. John CASE
43 Sr Vice President/General Counsel .... Mr. Michael RAMBERT
111 Sr Vice Pres of Inst Advancement .... Dr. Bennie L. HARRIS
43 Sr Vice Pres/General Counsel .... Mr. Michael RAMBERT
46 VP/Ex Vice Dean Research/Acad Admin .... Ms. Sandra HARRIS-HOOKER
88 VP Operation at Morehouse Hlthcare .... Dr. Stewart WITHERELL
21 VP Finance/Strategic Financial Plng .... Ms. Katherine NAPIER
100 Chief of Staff/Chief Admin Ofcr .... Dr. Monique GUILLORY
26 Chief Marketing Officer .... Ms. Goldie TAYLOR
15 Chief Human Resources Officer .... Ms. Denise BRITT
102 Assoc VP Development/Advance .... Mr. John WHITE
20 Sr Assoc Dean Educational Affairs .... Dr. Martha ELKS
20 Assoc Dean Faculty Affairs .... Dr. Erika BROWN
86 Exec Director of Government Affairs .... Mr. Daniel DAWES
37 Director Student Fiscal Affairs .... Ms. Cynthia H. HANDY
08 Library Manager .... Mr. Joe SWANSON, JR.
29 Dir Alumni Constituent Engagement .... Ms. Rochelle LINDSEY
07 Assoc Dn Admissions/Student Affairs .... Dr. Ngozi F. ANACHEBE
116 Internal Audit Director .... Mr. Curt MENCER
22 Interim Chief Compliance Officer .... Ms. Alecia BELL
13 Chief Information Officer .... Mr. Reginald BRINSON
06 Registrar .... Ms. Angela FREEMAN
19 Dir Public Safety/Chief of Police .... Mr. Joseph CHEVALIER, JR.
09 Director of Institutional Research .... Ms. Grace SUN
18 Director of Facilities .... Mr. Michael FLOOD

Morris Brown College (F)

643 Martin Luther King Jr Drive, Atlanta GA 30314
County: Fulton Identification: 667423
Telephone: (404) 458-6085 Carnegie Class: Not Classified
FAX Number: N/A Calendar System: Semester
URL: morrisbrown.edu
Established: 1881 Annual Undergrad Tuition & Fees: N/A
Enrollment: N/A Coed
Affiliation or Control: Independent Non-Profit IRS Status: 501(c)3
Highest Offering: Baccalaureate
Accreditation: @TRACS

01 President .... Dr. Kevin E. JAMES

North Georgia Technical College (G)

PO Box 65, Clarkesville GA 30523-0065
County: Habersham FICE Identification: 005619
Unit ID: 140678
Telephone: (706) 754-7700 Carnegie Class: Assoc/HVT-High Trad
FAX Number: (706) 754-7777 Calendar System: Semester
URL: www.northgatech.edu
Established: 1943 Annual Undergrad Tuition & Fees (In-State): $3,022
Enrollment: 2,548 Coed
Affiliation or Control: State IRS Status: 501(c)3
Highest Offering: Associate Degree
Accreditation: SC, ACFEI, ADNUR, EMT, MAC, MLTAD

01 President .... John WILKINSON
05 Vice President for Academic Affairs .... Mindy GLANDER
32 Vice President for Student Affairs .... Dr. Michael KING
11 VP for Administrative Services .... Dr. Michele SHIRLEY
30 VP of Economic Development .... Leslie MCFARLIN
26 VP College & Community Relations .... Amy HULSEY
15 Human Resources Coordinator .... Lorna CHAPMAN
18 Chief Facilities/Physical Plant .... Michael BOYD
19 Chief of Campus Police .... David SAVAGE
29 Dir Alumni Relations/Inst Advance .... Cynthia BROWN
35 Campus Life Director .... Sherry SEAL
07 Director of Admissions .... Kallan WILLIAMS
37 Financial Aid Director .... Audra JIMENEZ
20 Dean for Academic Affairs .... Michelle LIKINS
108 Institutional Effectiveness Dir .... Janet LOVELL
20 Dean for Academic Affairs .... Michelle OGLESBY
20 Dean for Academic Affairs .... Christy BIVINS
106 Education Technology Specialist .... Samantha MARCHANT
06 Registrar .... Kelsey MCINTIRE
13 Information Technology Director .... Savonda TURNER
96 Procurement Officer .... Rebekah FRANKLIN

Oconee Fall Line Technical College-North Campus (H)

1189 Deepstep Road, Sandersville GA 31082-9337
County: Washington FICE Identification: 031555
Unit ID: 420431
Telephone: (478) 553-2050 Carnegie Class: Assoc/HVT-Mix Trad/Non
FAX Number: (478) 553-2118 Calendar System: Semester
URL: www.oftc.edu
Established: 1996 Annual Undergrad Tuition & Fees (In-State): $3,072
Enrollment: 1,835 Coed
Affiliation or Control: State IRS Status: 501(c)3
Highest Offering: Associate Degree
Accreditation: SC

01 President .... Ms. Erica HARDEN
05 Vice Pres Academic Affairs .... Ms. Michelle STRICKLAND
10 Vice Pres Administrative Services .... Ms. Rosemary SELBY
30 Vice Pres Economic Development .... Ms. Kim DAVID
32 Vice Pres Student Affairs .... Dr. Saketha ADAMS
49 Dean Arts & Sciences/Business Svcs .... Ms. Michele STRICKLAND
06 Registrar .... Ms. Jennifer THIGPEN
07 Director of Admissions .... Ms. Raydor CONEWAY
15 Director Human Resources .... Ms. Lynn MCDONALD
21 Director of Administrative Services .... Ms. Penny KITCHENS
18 Director Facilities/Physical Plant .... Mr. Jim HARRISON
37 Director Financial Aid .... Ms. Rebecca ETHREDGE
28 Dir of Spec Populations/Stdnt Life .... Ms. Susan HAMMOCK

Oconee Fall Line Technical College-South Campus (I)

560 Pinehill Road, Dublin GA 31021-1599
County: Laurens FICE Identification: 022795
Telephone: (478) 275-6589 Carnegie Class: Not Classified
FAX Number: (478) 275-6642 Calendar System: Semester
URL: www.oftc.edu
Established: 1984 Annual Undergrad Tuition & Fees (In-State): N/A
Enrollment: N/A Coed
Affiliation or Control: State IRS Status: 501(c)3
Highest Offering: Associate Degree
Accreditation: SC, COARC, MAC, RAD

01 President .... Ms. Erica I. HARDEN
05 Vice President of Academic Affairs .... Ms. Michelle STRICKLAND
09 VP Inst Effectiveness/Plng/Research .... Dr. Katie DAVIS
32 Dean Student Affairs .... Mr. Jay MULLIS
06 Registrar .... Ms. Jennifer THIGPEN
18 Director Facilities .... Mr. Ragan GREEN
111 Exec Dir Institutional Advancement .... Ms. Kathy AARON
76 Dean Allied Health/Prof Svcs .... Ms. Tammy BAYTO
37 Asst Director Financial Aid .... Ms. Teresa CRAFTON
08 Director Library Services .... Mr. Ben MULLIS
07 Director of Admissions .... Mr. Raydor CONEWAY
36 Coord Career Services .... Ms. Saketta BROWN
19 Coord Safety/Security .... Mr. Mark ROGERS

Ogeechee Technical College (J)

One Joseph E. Kennedy Boulevard,
Statesboro GA 30458-8049
County: Bulloch FICE Identification: 030300
Unit ID: 366465
Telephone: (912) 681-5500 Carnegie Class: Assoc/HVT-Mix Trad/Non
FAX Number: (912) 486-7704 Calendar System: Semester
URL: www.ogeecheetech.edu
Established: 1986 Annual Undergrad Tuition & Fees (In-State): $3,140
Enrollment: 2,153 Coed
Affiliation or Control: State IRS Status: 170(c)1
Highest Offering: Associate Degree
Accreditation: SC, CAHIIM, DA, DMS, FUSER, MAC, OPD, RAD, SURGT

01 President .... Ms. Lori S. DURDEN
04 Exec Assistant to the President .... Ms. Karen MOBLEY
05 Exec VP Academic & Student Affairs .... Dr. Ryan FOLEY
103 Vice President Economic Development .... Ms. Jan MOORE
108 VP Institutional Effectiveness .... Ms. Brandy TAYLOR
10 Vice President for Administration .... Ms. Eyvonne HART
13 VP Technology & Institutional Supp .... Mr. Jeff DAVIS
111 VP for College Advancement .... Mrs. Michelle DAVIS
09 Director for Inst Research & Plng .... Mrs. Kathryn FINCH
08 Director for Library Services .... Ms. Lisa LANIER
51 Dir Continuing Educ & Ind Training .... Ms. Kathleen KOSMOSKI
07 Director for Admissions .... Ms. Molly BICKERTON
06 Registrar .... Vacant
37 Director for Financial Aid .... Ms. Kristie SANDERS
15 Director for Human Resources .... Mr. Steve MILLER
109 Exec Director Auxiliary Services .... Mr. J.J ALTMAN
18 Director for Plant Operations .... Mr. Charlie COLLINS
19 Director Campus Safety & Security .... Mr. Ryan MCNEAL
20 Dean for Academic Affairs .... Ms. Leanne ROBINSON
97 Senior Academic Dean .... Ms. Jennifer WITHERINGTON
20 Dean for Academic Affairs .... Mr. Neal OWENS
21 Asst VP for Administration .... Ms. Tonya VICKERS
55 Dean of Adult Education .... Ms. Samantha SMITH
35 Assistant VP for Student Affairs .... Mrs. Christy RIKARD
36 Career Placement/Stdnt Supp Svc Dir .... Ms. Cindy PHILLIPS

Oglethorpe University (K)

4484 Peachtree Road, NE, Atlanta GA 30319-2797
County: DeKalb FICE Identification: 001586
Unit ID: 140696
Telephone: (404) 261-1441 Carnegie Class: Bac-A&S
FAX Number: N/A Calendar System: Semester
URL: www.oglethorpe.edu
Established: 1835 Annual Undergrad Tuition & Fees: $41,160
Enrollment: 1,452 Coed
Affiliation or Control: Independent Non-Profit IRS Status: 501(c)3
Highest Offering: Baccalaureate
Accreditation: SC

01 President .... Dr. Nicholas LADANY
05 Interim Provost .... Dr. Kendra KING MOMON
10 Vice Pres for Business & Finance .... Mr. Pete STOBIE
30 Vice Pres Devel & Alumni Relations .... Vacant
84 VP Enrollment/Fin Aid/Admissions .... Ms. Whitney LEWIS
26 VP Marketing/Communications .... Vacant
32 Dean of Students/VP Campus Life .... Ms. Michelle HALL
20 Assistant Provost .... Mr. Brian COLDREN

04 Exec Assistant to the President ... Ms. Colleen DONALDSON
08 Int Univ Librarian/Library Director ... Mr. Eli ARNOLD
06 Registrar ... Mr. Brian COLDREN
09 Director of Institutional Research ... Ms. Carolyn MATA
41 Athletic Director ... Mr. Todd BROOKS
37 Director of Financial Aid ... Mr. Chris SUMMERS
39 Asst Director of Residence Life ... Mr. Blake PETTY
21 Director of Finance/Controller ... Mr. Mark BERGER
13 Chief Information Officer ... Ms. Tanya THOMPSON
27 Dir University Communications ... Ms. Renee VARY KEELE
29 Director of Alumni/Donor Relations ... Ms. Mary RINALDI WINN
36 Director of Career Development ... Ms. Erin SHERRILL
44 Director of Donor Relations ... Ms. Barb HENRY
15 Director Human Resources ... Vacant
31 Director A_LAB for Civic Engagement ... Ms. Beth CONCEPCION
18 Director Facilities/Physical Plant ... Mr. Lance KNIGHT
40 Bookstore Manager ... Ms. Kathleen GUY

Pacific College of Technology (A)

3510 DeKalb Technology Parkway, Atlanta GA 30340

County: DeKalb Identification: 667239
Telephone: (770) 559-0580 Carnegie Class: Not Classified
FAX Number: (770) 609-6850 Calendar System: Quarter
URL: www.pacifictech.edu
Established: 1999 Annual Undergrad Tuition & Fees: N/A
Enrollment: N/A Coed
Affiliation or Control: Proprietary IRS Status: Proprietary
Highest Offering: Associate Degree
Accreditation: ACICS

01 President ... Mr. Alain GALLIE
05 Chief Academic Officer ... Dr. Jilou KODJO

Paine College (B)

1235 Fifteenth Street, Augusta GA 30901-3182

County: Richmond FICE Identification: 001587
Unit ID: 140720
Telephone: (706) 821-8200 Carnegie Class: Bac-Diverse
FAX Number: (706) 821-8373 Calendar System: Semester
URL: www.paine.edu
Established: 1882 Annual Undergrad Tuition & Fees: $14,595
Enrollment: 189 Coed
Affiliation or Control: Multiple Protestant Denominations
IRS Status: 501(c)3
Highest Offering: Baccalaureate
Accreditation: TRACS

01 President ... Dr. Cheryl EVANS JONES
04 Office Manager/President's Office ... Ms. Henrietta HAYES
05 Provost/VP Academic Affairs ... Dr. Curtis E. MARTIN
10 VP Administrative & Fiscal Affairs ... Mr. Norman JONES
111 VP Institutional Advancement ... Ms. Helene T. CARTER
32 Vice President of Student Affairs ... Vacant
42 Campus Pastor ... Dr. Luther FELDER
41 Director of Athletics ... Mrs. Selina KOHN
88 Exec Asst to Provost/VP AA ... Ms. Frances WIMBERLY
50 Chair Business Dept ... Dr. Okoroafor NZEH
53 Chair Education Dept ... Vacant
79 Chair Humanities Dept ... Ms. Nancy BOOKHART
81 Chair Math Sci Tech Dept ... Dr. Raul PETERS
60 Chair Media Studies Dept ... Ms. Teri BURNETTE
83 Interim Chair Social Sciences Dept ... Dr. Elias E. ETINGE
09 Dir Inst Research/Qual Enhance Plan ... Mrs. Alice M. SIMPKINS
08 Director Library/LRC ... Mrs. Alana LEWIS
06 Registrar ... Mrs. Symphoni WIGGINS
36 Director Career Services ... Mrs. April EWING
38 Dir Counseling & Wellness Ctr ... Ms. Jenease HORSTEAD
39 Residence Life Coordinator ... Mrs. Shelia PAIGE
19 Chief of Police ... Chief Leroy MORGAN, JR.
13 Interim Dir Information Technology ... Mr. Jeffrey OWENS
37 Director of Financial Aid ... Ms. Consuelo QUINN
15 Coordinator Human Resources ... Mrs. Troyline GRIFFIN
29 Director Alumni Relations ... Vacant
26 Dir Communications & Marketing ... Vacant
25 Dir Sponsored Prog/Title III ... Mr. Chester WHEELER
108 Dir of Assessment/Evaluation ... Vacant
24 Info Tech Mgr Learning Resources ... Mrs. Rosa L. MARTIN
07 Admissions Coordinator ... Mrs. Felicia FENNER
88 Sr Women's Athletics Administrator ... Ms. Kisha LUCETTE
21 Chief Fiscal Officer ... Mr. Norman JONES

Philadelphia College of Osteopathic Medicine Georgia Campus (C)

625 Old Peachtree Road NW, Suwanee GA 30024

Telephone: (678) 225-7500 Identification: 770165
Accreditation: &M, &OSTEO, PHAR, PTA

† Branch campus of Philadelphia College of Osteopathic Medicine, Philadelphia, PA

Piedmont University (D)

PO Box 10, Demorest GA 30535-0010

County: Habersham FICE Identification: 001588
Unit ID: 140818
Telephone: (706) 778-3000 Carnegie Class: Masters/L
FAX Number: (706) 776-0701 Calendar System: Semester
URL: www.piedmont.edu
Established: 1897 Annual Undergrad Tuition & Fees: $27,520
Enrollment: 2,350 Coed
Affiliation or Control: United Church Of Christ IRS Status: 501(c)3
Highest Offering: Doctorate
Accreditation: SC, ACBSP, #CAATE, CVT, NUR

01 President ... Dr. James F. MELLICHAMP
05 Vice Pres Academic Affairs/Provost ... Dr. Daniel SILBER
10 Vice Pres Administration & Finance ... Mr. Brant WRIGHT
84 Vice Pres Enrollment Management ... Vacant
111 Vice President for Advancement ... Mr. Craig ROGERS
13 AVP of Information Technology ... Dr. Shahryar HEYDARI
04 Exec Assistant to the President ... Ms. Erin FORESTER
32 Dir Transition/Student Success ... Ms. Ineke DYER
07 AVP of Admiss/Undergrad Enrol Mgmt ... Ms. Cynthia L. PETERSON
08 Dean of Libraries/College Librarian ... Mr. Robert GLASS, JR.
06 Registrar ... Ms. Courtney THOMAS
09 Director of Institutional Research ... Mr. Jody ANDERSON
123 AVP Graduate Enrollment ... Ms. Kathleen CARTER
07 Director Undergraduate Admissions ... Ms. Brenda BOONSTRA
37 Director of Financial Aid ... Ms. Cathy NIX
42 Campus Minister ... Rev. Timothy GARVIN-LEIGHTON
15 AVP Human Resources ... Ms. Rose Mariee ALLISON
26 Dir Marketing/Communications ... Ms. Rachel PLEASANT
41 Dir of Intercollegiate Athletics ... Mr. Jim PEEPLES
21 AVP Finance/Controller/Human Res ... Ms. Kristi WILLIAMS
19 AVP Facilities Mgmt/Safety ... Mr. Fred BUCHER
66 Dean School of Nursing/Health Sci ... Dr. Julie BEHR
50 Dean School of Business Admin ... Dr. J. Kerry WALLER
49 Dean School of Arts & Sciences ... Dr. Steven NIMMO
53 Dean School of Education ... Dr. Kelly LAND

Point University (E)

507 West 10th St, West Point GA 31833

County: Troup FICE Identification: 001547
Unit ID: 138868
Telephone: (706) 385-1000 Carnegie Class: Bac-Diverse
FAX Number: (706) 645-9473 Calendar System: Semester
URL: www.point.edu
Established: 1937 Annual Undergrad Tuition & Fees: $21,850
Enrollment: 1,946 Coed
Affiliation or Control: Christian Churches And Churches of Christ
IRS Status: 501(c)3
Highest Offering: Master's
Accreditation: SC, @SW

01 President ... Mr. Dean C. COLLINS
05 Chief Academic Officer ... Dr. Stephen WAERS
111 Chief Advancement & Enrollment Ofcr ... Dr. Stacy BARTLETT
124 Chief Student Dev & Retention Ofcr ... Bernard HILL
10 Chief Financial Officer ... Nadeena POWER
19 Chief of Security ... Eric FLOURNOY
15 Director of Human Resources ... Margaret HODGE
20 Vice Pres for Academic Initiative ... Dr. Chris DAVIS
13 Vice Pres for Info Technology ... Bill DORMINY
84 Dean of Enrollment Management ... Rusty HASSELL
121 Dean of Point Academic Support Svcs ... Valarie WILLIAMS
06 Registrar ... Cassidy WITT
37 Director of Financial Aid ... Rachal WORTHAM
113 Director of Student Accounts ... Amanda SCHMIDT
120 Director of Online Learning and Ins ... Kyle MALMBERG
32 Dean of Students ... Laura SCHAAF
26 Director of Communications ... Vacant
29 Director of Alumni and Church Rels ... Tavaris TAYLOR
41 Athletic Director ... Alan WILSON
08 Director of Library Resources ... Adam SOLOMON
09 Institutional Research Manager ... Amanda YANCEY
28 Chief Diversity Officer ... Leonard PHILLIPS

† Formerly Atlanta Christian College

Reformed University (F)

1724 Atkinson Road, Lawrenceville GA 30043

County: Gwinnett Identification: 667247
Unit ID: 490230
Telephone: (770) 232-2717 Carnegie Class: Not Classified
FAX Number: N/A Calendar System: Semester
URL: www.runiv.edu
Established: 1992 Annual Undergrad Tuition & Fees: $5,360
Enrollment: 168 Coed
Affiliation or Control: Presbyterian Church In America IRS Status: Exempt
Highest Offering: Master's
Accreditation: TRACS

01 President ... Dr. Jae-sig PARK
03 Executive Vice President ... Dr. Won W. MOON
05 Deanr of Academic Affairs ... Dr. Mark HARDGROVE
07 Director of Admissions ... Dr. Charlie KIM
08 Chief Library Officer ... Ms. Na Ryung KIM
10 Director of Business Affairs ... Ms. Jae Rye KIM
104 Director Study Abroad ... Dr. Hyang-joo KIM
106 Director of Distance Education ... Dr. Peter SHIROKOV
108 Director Institutional Assessment ... Dr. Heung-sung NHO
37 Director of Financial Aid ... Mr. YeJoon KANG

Reinhardt University (G)

7300 Reinhardt Circle, Waleska GA 30183-2981

County: Cherokee FICE Identification: 001589
Unit ID: 140872
Telephone: (770) 720-5600 Carnegie Class: Masters/S
FAX Number: (770) 720-5602 Calendar System: Semester
URL: www.reinhardt.edu
Established: 1883 Annual Undergrad Tuition & Fees: $25,228
Enrollment: 1,399 Coed
Affiliation or Control: United Methodist IRS Status: 501(c)3
Highest Offering: Master's
Accreditation: SC, MUS, NURSE

01 President ... Dr. Mark A. ROBERTS
04 Sr Executive Assistant to President ... Mrs. Angela D. PHARR
05 VPAA ... Dr. John D. MILES
10 Chief Financial Officer ... Mrs. Stephanie R. OWENS
32 Dean of Students ... Dr. Walter P. MAY
84 VP Enrollment Mgt/External Affairs ... Mrs. Tish SZYMURSKI
41 VP for Athletics & Athletic Dir ... Mr. William C. POPP
101 Asst Secretary Board of Trustees ... Mrs. Angela D. PHARR
18 Director of Facilities Management ... Mr. Jeffrey DALE
26 Dir of Marketing & Communications ... Ms. Laura LONG
13 Director of IT ... Mr. Bernard GALLOF
88 Director of Funk Heritage Ctr ... Mr. Jeff BISHOP
07 Director of Admissions ... Ms. Jennifer M. PRINE
06 Registrar ... Ms. Janet M. RODNING
09 Dir Inst Research/Effectiveness ... Vacant
08 Director of Library Services ... Mr. Joel C. LANGFORD
19 Director of Public Safety ... Mr. Jay R. DUNCAN
42 Coordinator of Spiritual Life ... Mr. Josh GARNER
21 Controller ... Ms. Beverly SMITH
37 Director Student Financial Aid ... Mr. Joseph STEELMAN
15 Director Human Resources ... Ms. Kristy L. DEBORD
39 Director of Residence Life ... Vacant
23 University Nurse ... Vacant
35 Asst Dean of Students ... Mrs. Jamie M. JOHNSTON
38 Director of Counseling Svcs ... Mr. Adam C. POWELL
121 Dir Center for Student Success ... Dr. Catherine B. EMANUEL
36 Dir Vocation & Career Services ... Vacant
40 Bookstore Manager ... Vacant
49 Int Dean School Arts & Humanities ... Dr. Peggy M. MORLIER
81 Int Dean School of Math & Sciences ... Dr. Irma M. SANTORO
50 Dean McCamish Sch Bus & Sport Stdy ... Dr. Joseph W. MULLINS
53 Dean Price School of Education ... Ms. Tamara J. SMITH
64 Dean School of Performing Arts ... Dr. Fredrick A. TARRANT
107 Int Dean Sch Professional Studies ... Mr. Lester W. DRAWDY
66 Dean School Nursing/Health Sciences ... Dr. D. LeAnne WILHITE

SAE Institute Atlanta (H)

215 Peachtree Street NE, Suite 300,
Atlanta GA 30303-1739

Telephone: (404) 526-9366 FICE Identification: 042066
Accreditation: ACCSC

Savannah College of Art and Design (I)

342 Bull Street, PO Box 3146, Savannah GA 31402-6263

County: Chatham FICE Identification: 021415
Unit ID: 140951
Telephone: (912) 525-5000 Carnegie Class: Spec-4-yr-Arts
FAX Number: (912) 525-6263 Calendar System: Quarter
URL: www.scad.edu
Established: 1978 Annual Undergrad Tuition & Fees: $38,075
Enrollment: 14,265 Coed
Affiliation or Control: Independent Non-Profit IRS Status: 501(c)3
Highest Offering: Master's
Accreditation: SC, CIDA

01 President ... Mrs. Paula WALLACE
11 Chief Operating Officer ... Mr. Glenn WALLACE
10 Chief Financial Officer ... Mr. J.J WALLER
113 VP for Student Financial Services ... Mr. Scott LINZEY
05 Chief Academic Officer ... Dr. Gokhan OZAYSIN
43 VP International & Legal Services ... Ms. Hannah FLOWER
12 VP SCAD Atlanta ... Ms. Audra PRICE PITTMAN
88 VP for Industry Relations ... Mr. Khoi VO
84 Sr VP Admission/Student Success ... Dr. Philip ALLETTO
13 Sr VP for Technology/Development ... Mr. Brad GRANT
106 VP for SCAD Savannah ... Mr. John BUCKOVICH
15 Chief Human Resources Officer ... Ms. Lesley HANAK
09 VP for Institutional Effectiveness ... Ms. Erin O'LEARY
07 VP for Admission ... Mr. Steve MINEO
20 Dean of Academic Svcs Atlanta ... Mr. Dale CLIFFORD
18 Exec Dir of Physical Resources ... Ms. Helen MORGAN
08 Senior Director of Library Services ... Mr. Darrell NAYLOR-JOHNSON
37 Director of Financial Aid ... Ms. Kim BEVERIDGE
07 AVP for Admissions ... Ms. Jenny JAQUILLARD
19 VP for University Safety ... Mr. John BUCKOVICH
41 Athletics Director ... Mr. Doug WOLLENBURG
38 Dir Counseling/Student Support Svc ... Dr. Latoya MOSS
06 Sr Dir of Registrar Services ... Ms. Sarah MCCARN
88 Dean of School of Building Arts ... Dr. Geoffrey TAYLOR
88 Dean of School Communication Arts ... Mr. Anthony FISHER
106 Dean Sch of Design/Exec Dir eLrng ... Mr. Victor ERMOLI
88 Dean of School of Digital Media ... Ms. Marilynn ALMY
57 Dean of School of Fine Arts ... Ms. Maureen GARVIN
49 Dean Sch Liberal Arts/Library Svcs ... Ms. Kate NEWELL
88 Dean School of Fashion ... Mr. Michael FINK
97 Dean School of Foundation Studies ... Ms. Maureen GARVIN
88 Dean of Entertainment Arts ... Mr. Andra REEVE-RABB
36 AVP for Career & Alumni Success ... Ms. Kimberly LOPEZ
20 AVP of Academic Services ... Mr. Jesus ROJAS
121 Dean of Student Success ... Mr. Lucas BUCKOVICH
35 Dean of Students Savannah ... Mr. David BLAKE
104 Director SCAD Study Abroad ... Ms. Stephanie JACKSON
39 Assoc Dean/Dir of Residence Life ... Mr. Jason RIGSBEE

Savannah State University (A)

3219 College Street, Savannah GA 31404-5308
County: Chatham FICE Identification: 001590
Unit ID: 140960
Telephone: (912) 358-3004 Carnegie Class: Masters/S
FAX Number: N/A Calendar System: Semester
URL: www.savannahstate.edu
Established: 1890 Annual Undergrad Tuition & Fees (In-State): $5,902
Enrollment: 3,488 Coed
Affiliation or Control: State IRS Status: 501(c)3
Highest Offering: Master's
Accreditation: SC, JOUR, SPAA, SW

01 University President ....Dr. Kimberly BALLARD-WASHINGTON
05 Interim Provost/VP Academic Affairs ....Dr. Sametria R. MCFALL
10 VP Business & Financial Affairs ....Ms. Megan DAVIDSON
111 VP Advancement/Exec Dir Foundation ....Vacant
32 VP Enrollment Mgmt/Student Affairs .... Mr. Raymond CLARKE
26 Vice Pres Marketing & Communication ....Ms. Annette OGLETREE-MCDOUGAL
13 Exec Dir Info Technology Svcs ....Ms. Patricia OGDEN
50 Interim Dean College Business Admin ..Dr. Shalonda MULLGRAV
81 Dean Col Science & Tech ....Dr. Mohamad MUSTAFA
49 Dean Col Liberal Arts/Social Sci .... Dr. Shannon MATHEWS
53 Interim Dean College of Education .... Dr. Cora THOMPSON
07 Director of Admissions for Recruit .... Mr. Brian DAWSEY
15 Chief Human Resources Officer ..... Ms. Jacqueline STEPHERSON
08 Interim Librarian ....Mr. Patrick MORGAN
19 Interim Chief of Police ....Mr. Frederick DENSON
18 Director Facilities/Physical Plant ....Mr. Randall LOWERY
43 Dir Legal Services/General Counsel ....Ms. Flora DEVINE
09 Int AVP Inst Rsrch/Plng/Assessment ....Dr. Jonathan LAMBRIGHT
29 Director Alumni Relations .... Ms. Barbara S. MYERS
37 Director Financial Aid ....Vacant
41 Director Athletics ....Mr. Opio MASHARIKI
35 Director of Student Development .... Ms. Jacqueline AWE
06 Registrar .... Ms. Kathleen PLATT
04 Exec Asst to President .... Ms. Lisa SCIPIO
39 Housing Coordinator .... Mr. Michael SHARPE
100 Chief of Staff .... Ms. Cynthia HOKE
106 Dir Online Education/E-learning ....Vacant
104 Asst Dir International Education .... Ms. Joline KEEVY
84 Asst VP Enrollment Management .... Dr. Dedra ANDREWS
38 Director Student Counseling ..... Dr. Shawntell PHOENIX-MARTIN
96 Director of Purchasing .... Ms. Alicia WILLIAMS
30 Director of Development ....Mr. Phil COLE
35 AVP Student Affs/Dean of Students ....Ms. Bonita BRADLEY

† Part of the University System of Georgia.

Savannah Technical College (B)

5717 White Bluff Road, Savannah GA 31405-5521
County: Chatham FICE Identification: 005618
Unit ID: 140942
Telephone: (912) 443-5700 Carnegie Class: Assoc/HVT-Mix Trad/Non
FAX Number: (912) 443-5705 Calendar System: Semester
URL: www.savannahtech.edu
Established: 1967 Annual Undergrad Tuition & Fees (In-State): $3,042
Enrollment: 3,649 Coed
Affiliation or Control: State IRS Status: 501(c)3
Highest Offering: Associate Degree
Accreditation: SC, DA, DH, EMT, MAC, SURGT

01 President ....Dr. Kathy S. LOVE
11 Vice Pres Administrative Services ....Ms. Connie CLARK
32 Vice President for Student Affairs .... Ms. Ashley MORRIS
51 Vice Pres Adult Education .... Dr. Brent STUBBS
108 VP Institutional Effectiveness ....Mr. Paul SCOTT
111 Exec Dir Inst Advancement & Comm .... Ms. Gail EUBANKS
13 Exec Director Information Tech .... Mr. Jamie DAVIS
07 Director of Admissions .... Ms. Tiffany WALTER
37 Director Financial Aid ....Ms. Faith ANDERSON
06 Registrar ....Ms. Regina THOMAS-WILLIAMS
18 Director Facilities ....Mr. Gary STRICKLAND
15 Director Human Resources .... Ms. Melissa BANKS
08 Library Services Director ....Ms. Kaitlin DOTSON
26 Director of Communications ....Ms. Amy SHAFFER
12 Campus Dean Liberty Campus ....Ms. Terrie SELLERS
12 Campus Dean Effingham Campus ....Dr. Tristam ALDRIDGE
96 Purchasing Manager .... Mr. Kevin CHIEVES
76 Dean Health Science .... Ms. Kathleen BOMBERY
50 Dean Business and Professional Svcs .... Ms. Debra GEIGER
97 Dean General Studies .... Dr. Lonnie GRIFFIN
88 Dean Industrial Technology .... Mr. Daniel KRAUTHEIMER
88 Dean Aviation Technology ....Mr. Tal LOOS
56 Dean of Adult Education ....Dr. Thomas BULLOCK
88 Military Outreach Coordinator .... Mr. Steven CISNEROS
91 Dir of Enterprise Technology Svcs ....Ms. Tammy BRANNEN
19 Chief of Police .... Mr. Wayne WILLCOX
36 Coordinator of Career Services .... Ms. Kelly MORRIS
88 Student Navigator ....Ms. Kelley RIFFE
88 High School Initiatives Coordinator ....Ms. Shatealy JOHNSON
22 Special Population Disability Svcs ....Ms. Melanie WILDER

Shorter University (C)

315 Shorter Avenue, Rome GA 30165-4298
County: Floyd FICE Identification: 001591
Unit ID: 140988
Telephone: (706) 291-2121 Carnegie Class: Masters/S
FAX Number: (706) 236-1515 Calendar System: Semester
URL: www.shorter.edu
Established: 1873 Annual Undergrad Tuition & Fees: $22,810
Enrollment: 1,410 Coed
Affiliation or Control: Baptist IRS Status: 501(c)3
Highest Offering: Master's
Accreditation: SC, COSMA, MUS, NURSE

01 President ....Dr. Donald V. DOWLESS
05 Interim Provost ....Dr. John D. REAMS
11 VP for Administrative Affairs ....Vacant
10 VP for Finance & CFO ....Ms. Michelle STRICKLIN
84 Vice Pres Enrollment Management ....Mr. Karl HATTON
30 Vice President for Advancement ....Dr. Ben BRUCE
32 VP Student Affairs/Dean of Students .... Mr. Ken WHITLOW
26 Assoc VP University Communications ....Dr. Dawn C. TOLBERT
06 Registrar ....Mrs. Gina FLOYD
35 Director of Student Life ....Ms. Julia BOLTON
08 Director of Libraries ....Mr. John SHAFFETT
09 Director of Inst Planning/Research ....Dr. Earl KELLETT
37 Director of Financial Aid ....Ms. Colleen LASSITER
15 Human Resources Manager ....Mrs. Brenda LONG
56 Director Special Programs ....Vacant
13 Director of Information Technology ....Mr. Jeff BRAMLETTE
109 VP of Auxiliary Services ....Mr. Lance MOORE
38 Director of Student Support Svcs ....Ms. Moriah PENDER
23 Director of Health Services ....Ms. Loretta WILLIAMS
41 Athletic Director ....Mr. Richard HENDRICKS
44 Director of Annual Giving ....Vacant
07 Director of Admissions ....Mr. Patrick MCELHANEY
39 Dir Resident Life/Student Conduct ....Ms. Liz BARNES
40 Bookstore Manager ....Ms. Jan PEARSON
57 Interim Dean School of the Arts .... Dr. Tara WARFIELD
50 Dean College of Business ....Dr. Heath HOOPER
53 Dean School of Education ....Dr. Dana KING
66 Dean School of Nursing ....Dr. Roxanne JOHNSTON
81 Dean Col of Natural Sci/Mathematics ....Dr. Clint HELMS
79 Dean Col of Humanities/Soc Sciences ....Dr. Earl KELLETT
73 Chair Dept of Christian Studies .... Dr. Brent BASKIN
77 Chair Dept of Mathematics ....Dr. Diana SWANAGAN
60 Chair Dept of Communication Arts ....Dr. Bill MULLEN
83 Chair Dept of Social Sciences .... Dr. Jared LINEBACH
42 Campus Minister ....Rev. David E. ROLAND

South Georgia State College (D)

100 W College Park Drive, Douglas GA 31533-5098
County: Coffee FICE Identification: 001592
Unit ID: 482699
Telephone: (912) 260-4200 Carnegie Class: Bac/Assoc-Mixed
FAX Number: (912) 260-4441 Calendar System: Semester
URL: www.sgsc.edu
Established: 1906 Annual Undergrad Tuition & Fees (In-State): $3,310
Enrollment: 2,028 Coed
Affiliation or Control: State IRS Status: 501(c)3
Highest Offering: Baccalaureate
Accreditation: SC, ADNUR, NUR

01 President .... Dr. Ingrid THOMPSON-SELLERS
05 Vice Pres Academic/Student Affs ....Dr. Robert PAGE
84 Vice Pres Enrollment Mgmt/Info Tech ....Mr. Jimmy HARPER
10 Vice Pres Fiscal Affs/Admin ....Ms. Suzie BROWN
111 VP Advancement/Govt Rels/Athletics ....Dr. Greg TANNER
12 Dir of Waycross Campus/Devel ....Mr. Taylor HEREFORD
37 Director of Financial Aid .... Mr. Doug TANNER
08 Director of Libraries ....Ms. Lynn KELLY
06 Registrar ....Ms. Ame WILKERSON
15 Director of Human Resources .... Ms. Maria KING
07 Director of Admissions .... Ms. Arlena STANLEY
39 Dean of Students & Housing ....Ms. Sandra ADAMS
09 Dir of Inst Effectiveness & Rsrch .... Ms. Dani SUTLIFF
19 Director of Public Safety ....Ms. Sonja MCCULLOCH
121 Director of Academic Success ....Ms. Brandi ELLIOTT
66 Dean School of Nursing .... Dr. Jaime CARTER
107 Dean School Arts & Prof Studies .... Dr. Jodi FISSEL
81 Dean School of Sciences .... Dr. Charles JOHNSON
26 Asst Dir Marketing/Comm/Grants .... Ms. Amy HANCOCK
89 Asst Director of Entry Programs .... Ms. Joanne JONES
18 Director of Facilities .... Mr. Daniel WARREN
124 Director Recruitment/Special Proj .... Ms. Jaleen WASHINGTON
40 Bookstore Manager ....Ms. Daphne FRENCH

† Part of the University System of Georgia.

South Georgia Technical College (E)

900 South Georgia Tech Parkway,
Americus GA 31709-8167
County: Sumter FICE Identification: 005617
Unit ID: 141006
Telephone: (229) 931-2394 Carnegie Class: Assoc/HVT-Mix Trad/Non
FAX Number: (229) 931-2924 Calendar System: Semester
URL: www.southgatech.edu
Established: 1948 Annual Undergrad Tuition & Fees (In-State): $3,662
Enrollment: 1,814 Coed
Affiliation or Control: State IRS Status: 501(c)3
Highest Offering: Associate Degree
Accreditation: SC

01 President .... Dr. John WATFORD
05 Vice President for Academic Affairs .... David KUIPERS
10 Vice Pres Administrative Services ....Lea COE
32 Vice President of Student Affairs ....Eulish KINCHENS
111 Vice Pres Institutional Advancement ....Su Ann BIRD
18 Vice President of Operations .... Karen WERLING
13 Technology Director ....Dianne TRUEBLOOD
84 Dean Enrollment Management ....Julie PARTAIN
37 Director of Financial Aid ....Kelly EVERETT
20 Dean of Academic Affairs ....Dr. David FINLEY
15 Director Personnel Services ....Vacant
21 Director of Accounting ....Robin BELL
11 Director of Administrative Services .... Mark BROOKS
06 Registrar ....Kari BODREY
07 Director of Admissions ....Candie WALTERS
41 Athletic Director .... James FREY
38 Director Student Counseling .... Jennifer ROBINSON
32 Asst Vice Pres of Student Affairs .... Vanessa WALL
08 Librarian ....Jerry STOVALL
96 Purchasing Agent .... Gail CLARY
19 Director Security/Safety ....Sammy STONE
04 Admin Assistant to the President ....Teresa O'BRYANT
51 Continuing Education Director .... Paul FARR
21 Director of Business & Industry Svc ....Michelle MCGOWAN

South University (F)

709 Mall Boulevard, Savannah GA 31406-4881
County: Chatham FICE Identification: 013039
Unit ID: 139579
Telephone: (912) 201-8000 Carnegie Class: Spec-4-yr-Other Health
FAX Number: (912) 201-8070 Calendar System: Quarter
URL: www.southuniversity.edu
Established: 1899 Annual Undergrad Tuition & Fees: $17,014
Enrollment: 818 Coed
Affiliation or Control: Independent Non-Profit IRS Status: 501(c)3
Highest Offering: Doctorate
Accreditation: SC, AA, ACBSP, ARCPA, CACREP, MAC, NURSE, PHAR, PTAA

01 Chancellor ....Dr. Steven YOHO
12 Campus Director Montgomery Campus .... Dr. Kandis STEELE
12 President West Palm Beach Campus .... Dr. Mark EVERETT
12 Int President Columbia Campus .... Dr. April TAYLOR
12 Campus Director Richmond Campus ....Dr. Jason CRITTENDEN
12 President Tampa Campus .... Mr. James F. MCCOY, JR.
12 Campus Dir Virginia Beach Campus .... Dr. Donald JOHNSON
12 President Austin Campus ....Dr. Jeffery MUSGROVE
12 Campus Coord High Point Campus .... Ms. Sandy BARKER
12 President Savannah Campus .... Dr. Valarie TRIMARCHI
13 Assoc Vice Chancellor Technology .... Mr. Dustin BARRETT
88 Vice Chancellor Compliance ....Ms. Deanna ECHOLS
10 Vice Chancellor for Finance .... Mr. John PAPP
05 Vice Chancellor Academic Affairs ....Dr. Brian MCAULAY
20 Assoc Vice Chan Academic Ops .... Dr. Frances W. OBLANDER
04 Executive Assistant to Chancellor ....Ms. Jocelyn PICCOLO
08 Asst Vice Chanc Univ Library .... Ms. Nancy SPEISSER
06 University Registrar ....Ms. Toni Lynn DEBORD
86 Director of State Licensing .... Ms. Misty BLACKSTON
49 Dean College of Arts & Sciences .... Dr. April TAYLOR
50 Dean College of Business ....Dr. Cheryl NOLL
76 Dean College of Health Professions .... Ms. Gina SCARBORO
66 Dean College of Nursing & PH ....Dr. Mable H. SMITH
67 Dean School of Pharmacy .... Dr. Dean ARNESON
07 Asst Vice Chancellor of Admissions ....Ms. Ashley WEEKS
15 Vice Chancellor of Human Resources .... Ms. Lynne HAINES
16 Director of Human Resources .... Ms. Cathy GIRARDEAU
32 Vice Chancellor for Student Success .... Ms. Alisa KROUSE
18 Director of Facilities .... Mr. John BIALOWAS
26 VP Marketing ....Mr. Ken BAKER
27 Dir Campus Marketing/Communications ....Ms. Jennifer FLATT

Southeastern Technical College (G)

3001 E First Street, Vidalia GA 30474-8817
County: Toombs FICE Identification: 030665
Unit ID: 368911
Telephone: (912) 538-3100 Carnegie Class: Assoc/HVT-Mix Trad/Non
FAX Number: (912) 538-3156 Calendar System: Semester
URL: www.southeasterntech.edu
Established: 1989 Annual Undergrad Tuition & Fees (In-State): $3,127
Enrollment: 1,792 Coed
Affiliation or Control: State IRS Status: 501(c)3
Highest Offering: Associate Degree
Accreditation: SC, ADNUR, DH, EMT, MAC, MLTAD, RAD

01 President ....Mr. Larry CALHOUN
05 Vice Pres Academic Affairs ....Ms. Teresa COLEMAN
11 Vice Pres Administrative Services ....Ms. Denise POWELL
32 Vice President Student Affairs ....Dr. Barry DOTSON
84 Director Enrollment Services ....Mr. Brad HART
06 Registrar ....Ms. Amanda LIVELY
37 Director Financial Aid .... Ms. Rebecca ETHRIDGE
36 Director Job Placement ....Mr. Lance HELMS
103 Special Populations Coordinator .... Ms. Helen THOMAS
40 Bookstore Manager .... Ms. Stacy FREEMAN
26 Dir Marketing & Public Relations .... Ms. Natalie OSBORNE
08 Head Librarian .... Mrs. Leah DASHER
19 Director Security/Safety ....Mr. Travis AKRIDGE

Southern Crescent Technical College (H)

501 Varsity Road, Griffin GA 30223-2042
County: Spalding FICE Identification: 005621
Unit ID: 139986
Telephone: (770) 228-7348 Carnegie Class: Assoc/HVT-High Trad
FAX Number: (770) 229-3227 Calendar System: Semester
URL: www.sctech.edu
Established: 1963 Annual Undergrad Tuition & Fees (In-State): $3,126

Enrollment: 5,232 Coed
Affiliation or Control: State IRS Status: 501(c)3
Highest Offering: Associate Degree
Accreditation: SC, ACFEI, COARC, CVT, DA, EMT, MAC, SURGT

01 President ... Dr. Alvetta P. THOMAS
03 Executive Vice President ... Dr. Mark ANDREWS
05 Vice Pres for Academic Affairs ... Dr. Steve PEARCE
04 Exec Admin Asst to President ... Ms. Kim SANTERRE
32 Vice Pres for Student Affairs ... Dr. Xenia JOHNS
10 Vice Pres Administrative Svcs ... Ms. Stacy ACEY
111 Vice President Advancement ... Ms. Barbara Jo COOK
09 Vice Pres Inst Effectiveness ... Dr. Chris DANIEL
18 AVP Facilities & Operations ... Dr. Alan STANFIELD
06 Registrar ... Ms. Kathlyn STROZIER
26 Dir Marketing & Public Relations ... Ms. Anna TAYLOR
37 Director of Financial Aid ... Dr. Michelle BEDFORD
49 Dean Arts & Sciences ... Dr. Sean BRUMFIELD
76 Dean Allied Health & ParaMedicine ... Ms. Kimberly REGISTER
75 Dean Film/Public Safety/Ind Tech ... Mr. Lemuel MERCADO
50 Dean Business/CIS/Prof Services ... Dr. Roslyn MCCURRY
84 Assoc Vice Pres of Enrollment Mgt ... Dr. Drew TODD
15 Director of Human Resources ... Ms. Sharon HILL
35 Director of Student Support Svcs ... Ms. Cherryl BURKS
21 Director of Administrative Services ... Vacant
36 Director of Career Placement & Acad ... Ms. Annita WHITE
19 Campus Police Chief ... Mr. Antonio FLETCHER
13 Chief Information Officer ... Mr. Michael SHIVER
08 Director of Library Services ... Ms. Denise BARBOUR
106 Dir of Online Education/E-learning ... Dr. Jennifer EDWARDS

Southern Regional Technical College (A)

15689 US Highway 19 N, Thomasville GA 31792-2622
County: Thomas FICE Identification: 005615
Unit ID: 487162
Telephone: (229) 225-4096 Carnegie Class: Assoc/HVT-High Non
FAX Number: (229) 225-4330 Calendar System: Semester
URL: www.southernregional.edu
Established: 2015 Annual Undergrad Tuition & Fees (In-State): $3,002
Enrollment: 4,154 Coed
Affiliation or Control: State IRS Status: 501(c)3
Highest Offering: Associate Degree
Accreditation: SC, ADNUR, #COARC, EMT, MAC, MLTAD, RAD, SURGT

01 President ... Mr. Jim GLASS
11 Vice Pres Administrative Services ... Mr. Ross COX
05 Vice Pres Academic Affairs ... Dr. Ron O'MEARA
32 Exec Vice President Student Affairs ... Ms. Leigh WALLACE
103 Vice President Economic Development ... Mr. Dennis LEE
09 VP Institutional Effectiveness ... Dr. Vic BURKE
76 Dean School of Health Sciences ... Ms. Carla BARROW
50 Dean School of Bus/Industrial Tech ... Ms. Abby CARTER
107 Dean School of Professional Svcs ... Ms. Tara RAKESTRAW
49 Dean School of Art and Sciences ... Ms. Kathryn KENT
37 Director Financial Aid ... Ms. Amy SCOGGINS
26 VP Marketing/Inst Devel/Public Rels ... Dr. Amy MAISON
55 Director Adult Education ... Mr. Andy SEMONES
07 Director of Admissions ... Ms. Wanda HANCOCK
35 Director Student Affairs/Admissions ... Ms. Lisa GRIFFIN
06 Registrar ... Ms. Lora Beth SHORT
08 Executive Director Library Services ... Ms. Polly SWILLEY
36 Dir Career Services & Counseling ... Dr. Jeanine LONG
15 Coordinator Human Resources ... Mrs. Jennifer SIMPSON
18 Executive Director Facilities ... Mr. George GRIFFIN

Spelman College (B)

350 Spelman Lane, SW, Atlanta GA 30314-4399
County: Fulton FICE Identification: 001594
Unit ID: 141060
Telephone: (404) 681-3643 Carnegie Class: Bac-A&S
FAX Number: N/A Calendar System: Semester
URL: www.spelman.edu
Established: 1881 Annual Undergrad Tuition & Fees: $29,972
Enrollment: 2,207 Female
Affiliation or Control: Independent Non-Profit IRS Status: 501(c)3
Highest Offering: Baccalaureate
Accreditation: SC, CAEPN, MUS

01 President ... Dr. Mary SCHMIDT CAMPBELL
100 Chief of Staff/Govt Relations Dir ... Ms. Helga GREENFIELD
05 Provost & Sr VP of Academic Affairs ... Prof. Sharon DAVIES
10 CFO & VP Business & Financial Affs ... Ms. Dawn ALSTON
32 VP of Student Affairs ... Dr. Darryl HOLLOMAN
84 Sr VP of Enrollment Management ... Ms. Ingrid HAYES
111 Sr VP of Institutional Advancement ... Mr. Jessie BROOKS
45 VP of IR/Planning & Effectiveness ... Dr. Myra BURNETT
101 Sr VP/Secretary of College ... Dr. Terri REED
13 VP & Chief Info Officer ... Mr. John WILSON
88 Executive Dir of Endowment Mgmt ... Ms. Rhonda HONEGAN
114 Director of Budgets & Contracts ... Ms. Asella BRAXTON
21 Controller ... Ms. April AUSTIN
26 Interim Director of Communications ... Ms. Jazmyn BURTON
04 Special Assistant to the President ... Ms. Jarvis RIDGES
88 Dir Office of Civic Engagement ... Ms. Jilo TISDALE
20 Dean of Undergraduate Studies ... Dr. Desiree PEDESCLEAUX
42 Dean of Sisters Chapel ... Dr. Neichelle GUIDRY
06 Registrar ... Mr. John BROWN
07 Director of Admissions ... Ms. Chelsea HOLLEY
29 Director of Alumnae Operations ... Ms. Linda PATTON
37 Director of Financial Aid ... Ms. Lenora JACKSON
36 Director Career Planning/Devel ... Mr. Harold BELL
78 Director of Cooperative Education ... Vacant
15 Director of Human Resources ... Ms. Bernadette COHEN
38 Director of Counseling Services ... Dr. Ave MARSHALL
09 Director of Institutional Research ... Mr. James SANDERS
88 Director of Women's Resource Center ... Dr. Beverly GUY-SHEFTAL
18 Director Facilities Mgmt & Svcs ... Mr. Arthur E. FRAZIER, III
19 Director of Public Safety ... Mr. Steve BOWSER
24 Technology Services Coordinator ... Ms. Belinda GRIFFITH
88 Dir of Corporate Rels/Partnerships ... Ms. Cassandra JOSEPH
102 Director of Foundation Relations ... Ms. Eda GARCIA
88 Director of Special Events ... Ms. Heather HAWES
39 Dir of Housing & Residence Life ... Ms. Alison CUMMINGS
28 Coord Diversity & Inclusion Pgms ... Ms. Letitia J. DENARD
08 Library Director/CEO ... Ms. Loretta PARHAM
23 Director of Health Services ... Ms. Dana LLOYD
46 Assoc Provost of Research ... Dr. Tasha INNISS
35 Dean of Students ... Dr. Bonnie TAYLOR
40 Bookstore Manager ... Mr. Andrew HALL
96 Dir Administrative Support Svcs ... Ms. Jacqueline JAMES
21 AVP Business & Financial Affairs ... Ms. Marissa PACE
105 Asst Dir of Web Communications ... Ms. Ingrid LASSITER
44 Director Annual Giving ... Vacant

Thomas University (C)

1501 Millpond Road, Thomasville GA 31792-7499
County: Thomas FICE Identification: 001555
Unit ID: 141167
Telephone: (229) 226-1621 Carnegie Class: Masters/M
FAX Number: (229) 226-1653 Calendar System: Semester
URL: www.thomasu.edu
Established: 1950 Annual Undergrad Tuition & Fees: $16,970
Enrollment: 1,303 Coed
Affiliation or Control: Independent Non-Profit IRS Status: 501(c)3
Highest Offering: Master's
Accreditation: SC, CACREP, MT, NUR, SW

01 President ... Dr. Andy SHEPPARD
05 Vice President of Academic Affairs ... Dr. John MEIS
111 Vice Pres Institutional Advancement ... Mr. Kurt STRINGFELLOW
32 Vice President Student Life ... Dr. Robert BOHMAN
84 VP Enrollment Management ... Dr. Susan BACKOFEN
08 Director of Library Services ... Ms. Tara HAGAN
06 Registrar ... Mrs. Michelle WENDEL
09 Director of Institutional Research ... Dr. Dañae JOHNSON
37 Director of Financial Aid ... Mr. Clifton MITCHELL
41 Director of Athletics ... Mr. Rick PEARCE
10 Controller ... Ms. Sue STONE
44 Director of Annual Fund ... Vacant
26 Director of Communications ... Mrs. Cindy MONTGOMERY
04 Assistant to the President ... Mrs. Linda M. HERNDON

Toccoa Falls College (D)

107 Kincaid Drive, Toccoa Falls GA 30598-0068
County: Stephens FICE Identification: 001596
Unit ID: 141185
Telephone: (706) 886-6831 Carnegie Class: Bac-Diverse
FAX Number: (706) 282-6005 Calendar System: Semester
URL: www.tfc.edu
Established: 1907 Annual Undergrad Tuition & Fees: $21,120
Enrollment: 1,698 Coed
Affiliation or Control: The Christian And Missionary Alliance
IRS Status: 501(c)3
Highest Offering: Master's
Accreditation: SC, MUS, NURSE

01 President ... Dr. Robert M. MYERS
00 Chairman of the Board ... Mr. John W. ALLEN
04 Sr Exec Administrative Assistant ... Mrs. Paula S. ELKINS
32 VP Student Affairs ... Miss Abigail H. DAVIS
10 Vice President for Finance ... Dr. Dewanna MOONEY
05 VP for Academic Affairs ... Dr. Kieran CLEMENTS
84 VP for Enrollment Services ... Mrs. Emily C. KERR
42 Director Spiritual Formation ... Mr. Jordan BROWN
09 Director Institutional Research ... Ms. Allison BRADY
39 Director Residence/Community Life ... Mrs. Katie THORNE
29 Director Alumni Assoc/Col Relations ... Mrs. Deborah WILKES
106 Dean of Online & Dual Enrollment Ed ... Mr. Andrew THORNE
37 Director Student Financial Aid ... Mrs. Wanda PICKENS
06 Registrar ... Mr. Kelly G. VICKERS
41 Athletic Director ... Mr. Caleb BARNES
18 Chief Facilities/Physical Plant ... Mr. Merlin SCHENCK
19 Director of Security/Safety ... Mr. Stephen JOHANNES
15 Director Human Resources ... Ms. Mary Kaye RITCHEY
40 Director of Business Services ... Mrs. Allison HOTALEN
66 Dean of Nursing ... Dr. Kristi HENDRIX
11 Associate VP for Operations ... Mr. Merlin SCHENCK
88 Assistant VP Enrollment ... Mr. Ronnie STEWART
08 Head Librarian ... Mrs. Selina SLATE
13 Information Technology Director ... Mr. Zachary HIGHTOWER
30 Development Officer ... Vacant
121 Director of Academic Success ... Mrs. Nancy HYNDMAN
38 Dir Counseling/Career Svcs ... Mrs. Amy MARSHALL

Truett McConnell University (E)

100 Alumni Drive, Cleveland GA 30528-1264
County: White FICE Identification: 001597
Unit ID: 141237
Telephone: (706) 865-2134 Carnegie Class: Bac-Diverse
FAX Number: (706) 243-4968 Calendar System: Semester
URL: www.truett.edu
Established: 1946 Annual Undergrad Tuition & Fees: $21,938
Enrollment: 2,923 Coed
Affiliation or Control: Baptist IRS Status: 501(c)3
Highest Offering: Master's
Accreditation: SC, MUS, NURSE

01 President ... Dr. Emir CANER
05 Vice Pres Academic Services ... Dr. Brad REYNOLDS
32 Vice President of Student Services ... Mr. Chris EPPLING
10 VP Finance/Operations/CFO ... Dr. Jason GRAFFAGNINO
21 Assoc Vice President of Finance ... Mr. Paul WILLARD
88 Assoc VP Enterprise Data Mgmt ... Mr. Truitt FRANKLIN
04 Executive Assistant to President ... Ms. Cindy ERBELE
41 Athletic Director ... Mrs. Jenni SHEPARD
06 Registrar ... Mrs. Kamille GAUNTT
37 Director of Financial Aid ... Mrs. Karli GREENFIELD
08 Director of Library Resources ... Dr. Phillip NOTT
86 Director of Public Policy ... Dr. John YARBROUGH
07 Director of Admissions ... Vacant
42 Director of Alumni/Church Relations ... Dr. David DRAKE
40 Campus Store Director ... Mr. Eddie O'BRIEN
18 Director of Facilities ... Mr. Justin COALLEY
09 Director Institutional Research ... Mrs. Melissa FORTNER
121 Director of Student Success ... Mr. Andrew GAILEY
19 Director of Campus Safety ... Mr. Kerry SEABOLT
120 Director of Online Learning ... Mrs. Amy HAYES
35 Director of Student Development ... Mr. Bryan WISDOM

Underwood University (F)

2855 Rolling Pin Lane, Suite 200, Suwanee GA 30024
County: Gwinnett Identification: 667361
Telephone: (770) 831-9500 Carnegie Class: Not Classified
FAX Number: (770) 831-8858 Calendar System: Semester
URL: underwooduniversity.com
Established: 2011 Annual Undergrad Tuition & Fees: N/A
Enrollment: N/A Coed
Affiliation or Control: Independent Non-Profit IRS Status: 501(c)3
Highest Offering: Doctorate
Accreditation: TRACS

01 President ... Richard S. YOON
05 VP/Chief Academic Officer ... Rev. Howoo LEE
07 Director of Admissions ... Rita WONG

University of Georgia (G)

Athens GA 30602-0001
County: Clarke FICE Identification: 001598
Unit ID: 139959
Telephone: (706) 542-3000 Carnegie Class: DU-Highest
FAX Number: N/A Calendar System: Semester
URL: www.uga.edu
Established: 1785 Annual Undergrad Tuition & Fees (In-State): $12,080
Enrollment: 39,147 Coed
Affiliation or Control: State IRS Status: 501(c)3
Highest Offering: Doctorate
Accreditation: SC, AAFCS, ART, CAATE, CACREP, CEA, CIDA, CLPSY, COPSY, DANCE, DIETD, DIETI, JOUR, LAW, LSAR, MFCD, MPCAC, MUS, PCSAS, PH, PHAR, PLNG, SCPSY, SP, SPAA, SW, THEA, VET

01 President ... Mr. Jere W. MOREHEAD
100 Chief of Staff ... Dr. Kathy R. PHARR
04 Assistant to the President ... Dr. Kyle TSCHEPIKOW
04 Assistant to the President ... Ms. Sheila J. DAVIS
04 Assistant to the President ... Mr. Alton M. STANDIFER
05 Sr VP Academic Affs/Provost ... Dr. Jack HU
10 Sr Assoc VP Finance & Admin ... Mr. James SHORE
20 Vice Provost Academic Affairs ... Dr. Marisa A. PAGNATTARO
11 Vice Pres for Finance & Admin ... Mr. Ryan A. NESBIT
30 Vice Pres for Devel & Alumni Rels ... Mr. Kelly K. KERNER
20 Vice President for Instruction ... Dr. Rahul SHRIVASTAV
46 Vice President for Research ... Dr. David C. LEE
88 Vice Pres Public Svc/Outreach ... Dr. Jennifer L. FRUM
32 Vice President Student Affairs ... Dr. Victor K. WILSON
86 Vice President for Govt Relations ... Mr. Tobin R. CARR
26 Vice President for Marketing & Comm ... Dr. Kathy R. PHARR
13 VP for Information Technology ... Dr. Timothy M. CHESTER
92 Assoc Prov/Dir of Honors Program ... Dr. David S. WILLIAMS
104 Assoc Provost of International Educ ... Dr. Noel FALLOWS
28 Vice Prov Diversity & Inclusion ... Dr. Michelle G. COOK
20 Assoc Provost Academic Programs ... Dr. Margaret AMSTUTZ
08 Assoc Provost/University Librarian ... Dr. Toby GRAHAM
88 Assoc Provost Faculty Affairs ... Ms. Elizabeth WEEKS
07 Assoc VP Admissions/Enroll Mgmt ... Mr. Barkley BARTON II
21 Assoc VP Univ Business & Acct Svcs ... Mr. Chad CLEVELAND
18 Assoc VP Facilities Management ... Mr. Ralph F. JOHNSON
15 Associate VP Human Resources ... Mr. Juan JARRETT
43 Executive Director Legal Affairs ... Mr. Michael RAEBER
49 Dean of Arts & Sciences ... Dr. Alan T. DORSEY
47 Dean of Agricultural & Environ Sci ... Dr. Nick T. PLACE
61 Dean of Law ... Mr. Peter RUTLEDGE
67 Dean of Pharmacy ... Dr. Kelly M. SMITH
65 Dean Forestry & Natural Resources ... Dr. Dale GREENE
53 Dean of Education ... Dr. Denise SPANGLER
58 Dean of the Graduate School ... Dr. Rom WALCOTT
50 Dean of Business ... Dr. Benjamin C. AYERS
60 Dean Journalism & Mass Comm ... Dr. Charles N. DAVIS
59 Dean of Family & Consumer Sci ... Dr. Linda K. FOX
74 Dean of Veterinary Medicine ... Dr. Lisa K. NOLAN
70 Dean of Social Work ... Dr. Anna M. SCHEYETT

48 Dean of Environment & Design ... Dr. Sonia A. HIRT
80 Dean Public/International Affs ... Dr. Matthew R. AUER
69 Dean of Public Health ... Dr. Marsha DAVIS
88 Dean School of Ecology ... Dr. John L. GITTLEMAN
63 Dean GRU/UGA Medical ... Dr. Shelley NUSS
54 Dean of Engineering ... Dr. Donald LEO
41 Athletic Director ... Mr. Josh BROOKS
22 Director of Equal Opportunity ... Ms. Qiana N. WILSON
06 Registrar ... Ms. Fiona B. LIKEN
19 Chief of Police ... Chief Dan SILK
37 Director of Student Financial Aid ... Ms. Nancy FERGUSON
36 Director of Career Services Center ... Mr. Scott T. WILLIAMS
39 Executive Director of Housing ... Ms. Linda KASPER
23 Exec Director of Health Services ... Dr. Garth S. RUSSO
35 Dean of Students ... Dr. William M. MCDONALD
38 Dir Counseling/Psychological Svcs ... Dr. Ash THOMPSON
88 Director Georgia Center ... Dr. Dawn H. CARTEE
29 Exec Dir of Alumni Relations ... Ms. Meredith G. JOHNSON
110 Sr AVP for Dev & Alumni Relations ... Mr. Jay STROMAN
09 Director of Institutional Research ... Mr. Paul KLUTE
121 Director of Academic Enhancement ... Dr. Naomi NORMAN
94 Director Inst of Women's Studies . Dr. Juanita JOHNSON-BAILEY
96 Director of Purchasing ... Ms. Annette EVANS
106 Dir Online Education/E-learning ... Dr. Stephen P. BALFOUR
88 Sr Director for Accreditation ... Mr. Allan AYCOCK
44 Exec Dir Annual or Planned Giving ... Vacant
103 Director Office of Economic Dev ... Mr. Sean MCMILLAN

† Part of the University System of Georgia.

University of North Georgia (A)

82 College Circle, Dahlonega GA 30597-1001
County: Lumpkin FICE Identification: 001585
Unit ID: 482680
Telephone: (706) 864-1800 Carnegie Class: Masters/M
FAX Number: (706) 864-1478 Calendar System: Semester
URL: ung.edu
Established: 1873 Annual Undergrad Tuition & Fees (In-State): $4,976
Enrollment: 19,793 Coed
Affiliation or Control: State IRS Status: 501(c)3
Highest Offering: Doctorate
Accreditation: SC, ART, CAATE, CACREP, CAEPN, CSHSE, NUR, PTA

01 President ... Dr. Bonita JACOBS
05 Provost & Senior VP Acad Affairs ... Dr. Chaudron GILLE
10 Sr VP Business & Finance ... Dr. Frank J. MCCONNELL
88 Sr VP Leadership & Global Engage ... Dr. Billy WELLS
32 VP Student Affairs ... Dr. James CONNEELY
12 VP of Gainesville Campus ... Dr. Richard OATES
111 VP of University Advancement ... Mr. Jeff TARNOWSKI
20 Vice Provost ... Dr. Steve LLOYD
108 Assoc Provost Inst Effectiveness ... Dr. Holly VERHASSELT
46 Assoc Prov & Chief Research Officer ... Vacant
20 Assoc VP & Dean Univ College ... Dr. Carol ADAMS
21 AVP Financial Svcs & Comptroller ... Dr. Donna CALDWELL
109 Assoc VP Aux Services & Real Estate ... Mr. Gerald SULLIVAN
13 Chief Information Officer ... Mr. Steve MCLEOD
84 Assoc VP Enrollment Management ... Dr. Brett E. MORRIS
35 Asst VP Stdnt Affs & Dean of Stdnts ... Dr. Michelle BROWN
35 Assoc VPSA & Dean of Students ... Dr. Alyson PAUL
29 Director Alumni Relations & Annual ... Ms. Wendy HUGULEY ROTHIER
106 Dir Distance Educ/Tech Integration ... Dr. Irene KOKKALA
07 Director of Undergrad Admissions ... Ms. Molly POTTS
07 Director of Cadet Admissions ... Mr. Mike IVY
92 Director of Honors Program ... Dr. Royce DANSBY-SPARKS
41 Director of Athletics ... Ms. Mary Rob PLUNKETT
116 Director of Internal Audit ... Ms. Jill HOLMAN
06 Interim University Registrar ... Mr. Brett MERRITT
25 Director of Grants & Contracts ... Dr. Yolanda CARR
37 Director of Financial Aid ... Ms. Jill RAYNER
09 Director Institutional Research ... Ms. Linda ROWLAND
08 Dean of Libraries ... Dr. Joy BOLT
49 Dean College of Arts & Letters ... Dr. Christopher JESPERSEN
50 Dean M C College of Business ... Dr. Mary A. GOWAN
53 Dean of College of Education ... Dr. Sheri HARDEE
81 Dean College of Science & Math ... Dr. John LEYBA
76 Dean College of Health Sciences ... Dr. Carolynn DESANDRE
104 Assoc VP International Programs ... Ms. Sheila SCHULTE
15 Assoc VP Human Resources ... Ms. Beth ARBUTHNOT
18 Asst VP of Facilities ... Mr. Ken CROWE
19 Director of Public Safety ... Vacant
100 VP Univ Relations & Chief of Staff ... Dr. Kate MAINE
35 Commandant Corp of Cadets ... Col. Joseph MATTHEWS
36 Director of Career Services ... Ms. Diane FARRELL
38 Director Counseling Services ... Dr. Simon CORDERY
39 Director of Residence Life ... Ms. Treva SMITH
23 Director of Student Health Services ... Ms. Karen TOMLINSON
12 Exec Dir Cumming Campus ... Mr. Jason PRUITT
12 Exec Director Oconee Campus ... Dr. Cyndee MOORE
108 Dir Accreditation & Assessment ... Ms. Betsy CANTRELL
51 Director Continuing Education ... Dr. Wendy ESTES
86 Exec Dir Gov Relations & Econ Dev ... Mr. Ben JARRAD
43 General Counsel ... Mr. Reggie LAMPKIN
96 Director Procurement ... Mr. Milton HANSEN
85 Dir Multicultural Student Affairs ... Mr. Wade MANORA, JR.
04 Admin Asst to the President ... Ms. Ellen CORMACK
28 Director of Diversity & Inclusion ... Dr. Pablo MENDOZA
105 Director Web Services ... Ms. Joanie CHEMBARS
91 Asst CIO ... Mr. Rick CRAIN
26 Exec Director for Communications ... Ms. Sylvia CARSON

† Part of the University System of Georgia.

University of Phoenix Atlanta Campus (B)

859 Mount Vernon Hwy NE, Atlanta GA 30328
Telephone: (678) 731-0555 Identification: 770200
Accreditation: &HLC, ACBSP

† No longer accepting campus-based students.

University of West Georgia (C)

1601 Maple Street, Carrollton GA 30118-0001
County: Carroll FICE Identification: 001601
Unit ID: 141334
Telephone: (678) 839-5000 Carnegie Class: DU-Mod
FAX Number: N/A Calendar System: Semester
URL: www.westga.edu
Established: 1906 Annual Undergrad Tuition & Fees (In-State): $6,521
Enrollment: 13,419 Coed
Affiliation or Control: State IRS Status: 501(c)3
Highest Offering: Doctorate
Accreditation: SC, ART, CACREP, JOUR, MUS, NURSE, SP, SPAA, THEA

01 President ... Dr. Brendan KELLY
05 Provost/VP for Academic Affairs ... Dr. Jon PRESTON
10 VP Business & Financial Services ... Mr. John HAVEN
32 VP Student Affairs/Enrollment Mgt ... Dr. André FORTUNE
111 VP for University Advancement ... Dr. Meredith BRUNEN
11 VP of Administrative Services ... Ms. Annemarie EADES
30 Exec Dir of Development ... Ms. Nichole FANNIN
84 AVP for Enrollment Management ... Dr. Jennifer JORDAN
35 AVP and Dean of Students ... Dr. Lakiesa RAWLINSON
20 Assoc VP for Academic Affairs ... Dr. Jill DRAKE
20 Assoc VP for Academic Affairs ... Vacant
20 Assoc VP Academic Affairs ... Vacant
21 Assoc VP Finance/Univ Controller ... Mr. Richard SEARS
13 Asst VP of IT/CIO ... Mr. Dale DRIVER
50 Dean Richards College of Business ... Dr. Faye S. MCINTYRE
53 Interim Dean Education ... Dr. Laura SMITH
81 Dn Arts/Culture/Scientific Inquiry ... Dr. Pauline GAGNON
92 Dean Honors College ... Dr. Janet DONOHOE
06 Registrar ... Ms. Donna HALEY
07 Assoc VP of Admissions ... Mr. Justin BARLOW
08 Dean of Libraries ... Ms. Andrea STANFIELD
37 Director Financial Aid ... Ms. Leigh Ann HUSSEY
36 Director Career Services ... Ms. Ginny Rae TURNER
51 Director Continuing Education ... Mr. Marty DAVIS
15 Asst VP/Chief HR Officer ... Ms. Terri WALTHOUR
18 Asst VP Campus Planning/Facilities ... Mr. Brendan BOWEN
19 Police Chief ... Dr. George E. WATSON
23 Interim Dir of Health Services ... Dr. Michael POSS
39 Director Housing & Residence Life ... Mr. Stephen WHITLOCK
41 Director of Athletics ... Mr. Jason CARMICHAEL
38 Director Counseling Center ... Dr. Lisa ADAMS SOMERLOT
109 Sr Assoc VP Auxiliary Services ... Mr. Mark REEVES
108 AVP Inst Effectiveness & Assessment ... Dr. Catherine JENKS
29 Exec Dir of Alumni Relations ... Ms. Allyson BRETCH
26 Assoc VP Constituent Rels/Engage ... Ms. Jami BOWER
58 Dean of the Graduate School ... Dr. Toby ZIGLAR
106 Dean USG eCore/Exec Dir Ext Lrng ... Dr. Melanie N. CLAY
43 University General Counsel ... Ms. Kristi CARMAN
102 Dir of Advancement Services ... Mr. Bart GILLESPIE
66 Dean Tanner School of Nursing ... Dr. Jennifer SCHUESSLER
96 Director of Purchasing ... Ms. Lisa ELLIOTT LITTLE
22 Interim Dir Equal Op/Title IX Coord ... Ms. Erin WILLIAMS
100 Assoc VP/Chief of Staff to the Pres ... Mr. Russell CRUTCHFIELD
12 Sr Dir/Ch Admin Ofcr Off-Camp Pgms ... Dr. Robert HEABERLIN
40 Bookstore Manager ... Ms. Wanda WALKER
85 Dir Intl Student Admiss & Pgms ... Mr. Brett REICHERT
28 Dir Diversity Educ & Community Init ... Ms. Deirdre HAYWOOD-ROUSE
04 Exec Assistant to the President ... Ms. Tina BENNETT
104 Director Study Abroad ... Dr. Maria DOYLE
105 Director Web Services ... Ms. Ewa ZENNERMANN

† Part of the University System of Georgia.

*University System of Georgia Office (D)

270 Washington Street, SW, Atlanta GA 30334-9007
County: Fulton FICE Identification: 008290
Telephone: (404) 962-3000 Carnegie Class: N/A
FAX Number: (404) 962-3013
URL: www.usg.edu

01 Acting Chancellor ... Ms. Teresa MACCARTNEY
04 Executive Assistant to Chancellor ... Ms. Shelia ELDER
11 Exec Vice Chanc Administration ... Ms. Teresa MACCARTNEY
05 Exec Vice Chanc/Chief Academic Ofcr ... Dr. Tristan DENLEY
45 Exec VC Strategy/Fiscal Affairs ... Ms. Tracey COOK
116 VC for Internal Audit & Compliance ... Ms. Claire ARNOLD
20 Vice Chancellor Academic Affairs ... Dr. Martha VENN
18 Vice Chancellor Facilities ... Ms. Sandra NEUSE
43 Vice Chancellor Legal Affairs ... Mr. Edward TATE
26 Vice Chancellor for Communications ... Mr. Aaron DIAMANT
13 Vice Chanc/Chief Information Ofcr ... Mr. Jonathan PIERSOL
10 Vice Chancellor for Fiscal Affairs ... Mr. Jeff DAVIS
32 Vice Chancellor for Student Affairs ... Dr. Joyce JONES
30 Vice Chancellor for Development ... Ms. Karen MCCAULEY
88 Vice Chancellor Org Effectiveness ... Mr. John FUCHKO
15 Vice Chancellor for Human Resources ... Dr. Juanita HICKS
09 Vice Chanc of Research & Policy ... Dr. Angela BELL
100 Vice Chancellor for Leadership ... Dr. Stuart RAYFIELD
86 VC for External Affairs & COS ... Ms. Ashley JONES

Valdosta State University (E)

1500 N Patterson Street, Valdosta GA 31698-0010
County: Lowndes FICE Identification: 001599
Unit ID: 141264
Telephone: (229) 333-5800 Carnegie Class: DU-Mod
FAX Number: (229) 333-7400 Calendar System: Semester
URL: www.valdosta.edu
Established: 1906 Annual Undergrad Tuition & Fees (In-State): $6,583
Enrollment: 12,304 Coed
Affiliation or Control: State IRS Status: 501(c)3
Highest Offering: Doctorate
Accreditation: SC, ART, CAATE, CACREP, CAEP, EXSC, LIB, MFCD, MUS, NURSE, SP, SPAA, SW, THEA

01 President ... Dr. Richard CARVAJAL
05 Provost & VPAA ... Dr. Robert T. SMITH
10 Vice President for Finance & Admin ... Ms. Traycee F. MARTIN
111 Vice President for Univ Advancement ... Mr. John D. CRAWFORD
32 VP for Student Affairs ... Dr. Vince MILLER
58 Assoc Prov Grad Studies & Research ... Dr. Becky DACRUZ
20 Assoc Provost Academic Affairs ... Dr. Sharon L. GRAVETT
30 AVP Development/Alumni Relations ... Mrs. Hilary H. GIBBS
79 Dean Col of Humanities & Social Sci ... Dr. James T. LAPLANT
81 Int Dean College of Science & Math ... Dr. Theresa GROVE
50 Dean College of Business Admin ... Dr. Wayne L. PLUMLY
57 Dean College of the Arts ... Mr. Arthur B. PEARCE
53 Int Dean Col of Educ & Human Svc ... Dr. Karla HULL
66 Dean Col of Nursing/Health Sci ... Dr. James PACE
92 Dean of Honors College ... Dr. Michael P. SAVOIE
08 Univ Librarian & Dean of Faculty ... Dr. Alan BERNSTEIN
06 Registrar ... Mr. Stanley JONES
106 Assoc Dir of Ofc of Extended Lrng ... Ms. Marsha B. DUKES
13 Chief Information Officer ... Mr. Kevin OVERLAUR
14 Chief Technology Officer ... Mr. Joseph A. NEWTON
124 VP Div of Student Success ... Dr. Rodney CARR
39 Dir Housing & Residence Life ... Dr. Zduy CHU
41 Director of Athletics ... Mr. Herb REINHARD
37 Director of Financial Aid ... Mr. Douglas R. TANNER
36 Int Dir of Career Opportunities ... Ms. Carla JORDAN
29 Exec Dir of External Affairs ... Ms. Merritt WALL
15 Director of Human Resources ... Ms. Jeanine BODDIE-LAVAN
88 Director Division Aerospace Studies ... LtCol. Adam LEE
22 Director of Social Equity ... Dr. Maggie J. VIVERETTE
43 University Attorney ... Mr. Lee DAVIS
18 Dir Phys Plant & Facilities Plng ... Mr. Ray SABLE
26 Exec Dir of Communications & Mktg ... Dr. Keith WARBURG
38 Director of Counseling Center ... Dr. Tricia A. HALE
121 Exec Director of Advising ... Mr. Rob FREIDHOFF
40 Manager of Bookstore ... Mr. Keith KUPETS
23 Director of Student Health Services ... Dr. Richard RICKMAN
19 Dir Public Safety/Police Chief ... Mr. Alan ROWE
108 Director of Inst Effectiveness ... Dr. Michael M. BLACK
88 Dir of Info Tech Svcs for Adv Svcs ... Ms. Amelia REAMS
100 Sr Dir of Presidential Initiatives ... Ms. Melinda CUTCHENS
96 Dir of Procurement & Accounting ... Ms. Antolina PILGRIM
09 Director Inst Research ... Mr. Barrie D. FITZGERALD
07 Director of Admissions ... Mr. Ryan HOGAN
104 Director of Intl Programs ... Dr. Ivan NIKOLOV
105 Director of Creative Services ... Mr. Jeff GRANT
28 Dir of Stdnt Diversity & Inclusion ... Ms. Sandra JONES
25 Dir Spons Pgm & Research Admin ... Ms. Elizabeth OLPHIE

† Part of the University System of Georgia.

Wesleyan College (F)

4760 Forsyth Road, Macon GA 31210-4462
County: Bibb FICE Identification: 001600
Unit ID: 141325
Telephone: (478) 477-1110 Carnegie Class: Bac-A&S
FAX Number: (478) 757-4030 Calendar System: Semester
URL: www.wesleyancollege.edu
Established: 1836 Annual Undergrad Tuition & Fees: $25,190
Enrollment: 779 Female
Affiliation or Control: United Methodist IRS Status: 501(c)3
Highest Offering: Master's
Accreditation: SC, NURSE

01 President ... Dr. Vivia L. FOWLER
05 Provost/VP for Academic Affairs ... Dr. Melody A. BLAKE
111 VP Institutional Advancement ... Ms. Andrea G. WILLIFORD
10 Vice Pres Finance/Treasurer ... Mr. Robert L. MOYE
32 Dean of Students ... Ms. Christy S. HENRY
84 VP for Strategic Enrollment ... Mr. Clinton G. HOBBS
06 Assistant Dean/Registrar ... Ms. Angie WRIGHT
04 Assistant to the President ... Mrs. Denise W. HOLLOWAY
08 Library Director ... Ms. Kristi PEAVY
13 Director of Information Services ... Mr. Kevin L. ULSHAFER
29 Director of Alumnae Affairs ... Ms. Cathy C. SNOW
26 Director of Communications ... Ms. Mary Ann HOWARD
44 Director of Annual Fund ... Ms. Whitney DAVIS
37 Director of Financial Aid ... Mr. Daniel MILLER
39 Director of Residence Life ... Ms. Dionne GEORGE
18 Director of Physical Plant ... Mr. James FLEENOR
41 Athletic Director ... Ms. Penny SIQUEIROS
42 Chaplain ... Rev. Tyler SCHWALLER
19 Director Security/Safety ... Mr. Emory KENDRICK
15 Director Human Resources ... Ms. Meagon DAVIS
07 Director of Admissions ... Mr. Clinton G. HOBBS
09 Director of Institutional Research ... Ms. Glenda FERGUSON
35 Chief Student Life Officer ... Ms. Melissa RODRIGUEZ
36 Director Career Development ... Ms. Stephanie BAUGH

38 Director Student Counseling .... Ms. Myrana CRAIG
109 Director of Auxiliary Services .... Mrs. Alycia WARD
20 Associate Academic Officer .... Vacant
21 Associate Business Officer .... Ms. Quintress HOLLIS
22 Director of Disability and Advocacy .... Ms. Jill AMOS
28 Director of Diversity & Inclusion .... Ms. LaTonya PARKER
30 Chief Development Officer .... Mrs. Susan B. ALLEN

West Georgia Technical College (A)

176 Murphy Campus Boulevard, Waco GA 30182-2407
County: Haralson FICE Identification: 010487
Unit ID: 139278
Telephone: (770) 537-6000 Carnegie Class: Assoc/HVT-Mix Trad/Non
FAX Number: (770) 537-7976 Calendar System: Semester
URL: www.westgatech.edu
Established: 1968 Annual Undergrad Tuition & Fees (In-State): $3,052
Enrollment: 6,437 Coed
Affiliation or Control: State IRS Status: 501(c)3
Highest Offering: Associate Degree
Accreditation: SC, ACBSP, ADNUR, CAHIIM, DH, MAC, MLTAD, SURGT

01 President .... Dr. Juli POST
11 VP Admin Services .... Ms. Carol REID
05 Vice President Academic Affairs .... Dr. Kristen DOUGLAS
32 Vice President Student Affairs .... Dr. Tonya F. WHITLOCK
09 VP Institutional Effectiveness .... Mr. John PARTON
103 VP Economic Development .... Ms. Angela BERCH
51 VP of Adult Education .... Mrs. Kerri HOSMER
08 Exec Director Library Services .... Ms. Michelle BARSOM
06 Registrar .... Mrs. Laura THORNTON
13 Dir Information Technology .... Mr. Ryan DAHLBERG
07 Director of Admissions .... Mrs. Lori BASHAM
18 Director Facilities .... Mr. Michael JILES
04 Executive Asst to President .... Mrs. Julia WATSON
36 Manager Career Services .... Ms. Dawne WHITE
37 Director Student Financial Aid .... Mrs. Kim KELLEY
15 Exec Director of Human Resources .... Mr. Rodd RUSSOW
19 Chief of Police .... Mr. James PERRY
50 Dean Sch of Business & Public Svcs .... Ms. Babs RUSSELL
49 Dean Sch of Arts & Sciences .... Mr. Brian BARKLEY
54 Dean Sch of Trade & Technology .... Mr. Gary WELBORN
106 Director Online Learning .... Ms. Myranda STEPHENS
108 Director Institutional Assessment .... Mr. AJ THOMAS
26 Dir of Public Relations & Info .... Mr. Ben CHAMBERS
111 Exec Dir of Institutional Advance .... Ms. Brittney HENDERSON

Wiregrass Georgia Technical College (B)

4089 Val Tech Road, Valdosta GA 31602
County: Lowndes FICE Identification: 005256
Unit ID: 141255
Telephone: (229) 333-2100 Carnegie Class: Assoc/HVT-High Non
FAX Number: (229) 333-2129 Calendar System: Semester
URL: www.wiregrass.edu
Established: 1963 Annual Undergrad Tuition & Fees (In-State): $3,152
Enrollment: 3,709 Coed
Affiliation or Control: State IRS Status: 501(c)3
Highest Offering: Associate Degree
Accreditation: SC, ADNUR, CAHIIM, DA, DH, EMT, MAC, RAD, SURGT

01 Interim President .... Ms. DeAnnia CLEMENTS
05 Interim VP Academic Affairs .... Ms. April MCDUFFIE
18 Vice President Facilities .... Ms. Lidell GREENWAY
11 VP for Administrative Services .... Ms. Keren WYNN
84 VP for Enrollment Management .... Ms. Shannon MCCONICO
108 Assoc VP for Inst Effectiveness .... Mrs. April MCDUFFIE
28 VP Community Affs/Minority Recruit .... Vacant
103 Assoc VP Economic Development .... Ms. Brandy WILKES
13 Chief Info Technology Officer (CIO) .... Mr. Jarrod BROGDON
88 Dir Administrative Services .... Ms. Chymeka GIBBS
32 Dean of Student Affairs .... Ms. Shannon MCCONICO
26 Dir for Cmty/College Relations .... Ms. Lydia HUBERT
07 Executive Dir High School Services .... Ms. Brooke JARAMILLO
04 Executive Asst to President .... Ms. Cheryl ACREE
06 Registrar .... Ms. Julie DREXLER
08 Head Librarian .... Ms. Kathryn TOMLINSON
105 Director Web Services .... Mr. Steve SAULS
106 Exec Director Online Education .... Ms. Sabrina COX
15 Assoc VP of Human Resources .... Ms. Shalonda SANDERS
19 Chief of Police .... Mr. Tim ALLMOND
37 Financial Aid Coordinator .... Ms. Paula HERRING
96 Director of Purchasing .... Ms. Ronshekua SIMS
20 Dean of Academic Affairs .... Ms. Holly GREENE
49 Dean of Arts and Science .... Mr. Michael WILLIAMS
76 Dean of Allied Health .... Mr. Stevan VAN HOOK

Young Harris College (C)

1 College Street, Young Harris GA 30582-0098
County: Towns FICE Identification: 001604
Unit ID: 141361
Telephone: (706) 379-3111 Carnegie Class: Bac-A&S
FAX Number: (706) 379-4319 Calendar System: Semester
URL: www.yhc.edu
Established: 1886 Annual Undergrad Tuition & Fees: $29,667
Enrollment: 1,417 Coed
Affiliation or Control: United Methodist IRS Status: 501(c)3
Highest Offering: Master's
Accreditation: SC, MUS

01 President .... Dr. Drew L. VAN HORN
05 Provost .... Dr. Jason PIERCE
10 CFO .... Mr. Wade M. BENSON
32 Vice Preside of Student Development .. Dr. Laura WHITAKER-LEA
111 Vice President of Advancement .... Mr. Mark DOTSON
09 Asst VP for Institutional Research ..... Ms. Rosemary R. ROYSTON
13 Chief Technology Officer .... Mr. Ken FANEUFF
29 Director of Alumni Engagement .... Ms. Dana ENSLEY
20 Assoc VP for Academic Affairs .... Dr. Keith DEFOOR
08 Dean of Library Services .... Ms. Debra MARCH
38 Director of Student Counseling .... Ms. Susan MURPHY
06 Registrar .... Ms. Tammy GIBSON
37 Director of Financial Aid .... Ms. Michelle BERNARD
26 Dir of Communication & Marketing .... Ms. Jaime LEVINS
18 Facilities General Manager .... Mr. Mark WILLIAMS
41 Director of Athletics .... Ms. Jennifer RUSHTON
42 Chaplain & Dean of the Chapel .... Rev. Ryan SNIDER
04 Executive Asst to the President .... Ms. Teresa KELLEY
44 Director of Annual Giving .... Ms. Mackenzie HARKINS
11 Chief Operations Officer .... Mr. Bo WRIGHT
39 Director of Residence Life .... Mr. Mark JESTEL
07 Director of Admissions .... Mr. Andra BRANTLEY
19 Campus Police Chief .... Mr. Robbie RICH

HAWAII

Brigham Young University Hawaii (D)

55-220 Kulanui Street, Laie, Oahu HI 96762-1294
County: Honolulu FICE Identification: 001606
Unit ID: 230047
Telephone: (808) 675-3211 Carnegie Class: Bac-Diverse
FAX Number: (808) 675-3329 Calendar System: Semester
URL: www.byuh.edu
Established: 1955 Annual Undergrad Tuition & Fees: $5,890
Enrollment: 3,180 Coed
Affiliation or Control: Latter-day Saints IRS Status: 501(c)3
Highest Offering: Baccalaureate
Accreditation: WC, AAQEP, SW

01 President .... Dr. John S. KAUWE, III
05 Academic Vice President .... Dr. Isaiah H. WALKER
10 Administrative Vice President .... Mr. Steve W. TUELLER
32 Student Life Vice President .... Mr. Jonathan K. KAU
11 Operations Vice President .... Mr. Cory HIGGINS
26 Assistant to Pres Communications .... Mrs. Laura TEVAGA
100 Chief of Staff .... Mr. Keni REID
108 Assoc Acad VP Curriculum/Assessment .... Dr. Rosalind RAM
73 Assoc Acad VP Religious Education .... Mr. Aaron SHUMWAY
20 Assoc Academic VP for Faculty .... Dr. Yifen BEUS
81 Dean Faculty of Sciences .... Dr. Jess KOHLERT
77 Dean Faculty of Math/Computing .... Dr. James D. LEE
79 Dean Fac of Culture/Lang/Perf Arts .... Dr. Tevita KAILI
49 Dean Faculty of Arts & Letters .... Dr. Patricia PATRICK
50 Dean Faculty of Business/Government .... Dr. Brian HOUGHTON
53 Dean Faculty of Educ & Social Work .... Dr. Mark WOLFERSBERGER
13 Chief Information Officer .... Mr. Kevin SCHLAG
35 Dean of Students .... Mr. James FAUSTINO
08 Director Library & Academic Success .... Mr. Michael ALDRICH
114 Budget Director .... Mr. Michael TEJADA
21 Director of Financial Services .... Mr. Eric MARLER
19 Director Campus Safety/Security .... Mr. Anthony PICKARD
15 Director of Human Resources .... Mr. Reid MILLERBERG
18 Director Facilities Management .... Mr. Randy SHARP
23 Director of Health Services .... Mrs. Laurie ABREGANO
116 Chief Compliance Officer .... Mr. David GALLOWAY
88 Title IX Deputy Coordinator .... Mr. Leland SIKAHEMA
38 Dir Counseling/Disability Services .... Mrs. Rachel KEKAULA
39 Director of Campus Life .... Ms. Alison WHITING
109 Director Food Services .... Mr. David KEALA
88 Manager of Univ Testing/Evaluation .... Mrs. Candace TUPOU
06 Registrar .... Mrs. Daryl WHITFORD
88 Event Services & Outreach Manager .... Ms. Diedra ULII
40 Camp Store/Aux Services Manager .... Mr. David FONOIMOANA

† Affiliated with Brigham Young University, Provo, UT.

Chaminade University of Honolulu (E)

3140 Waialae Avenue, Honolulu HI 96816-1578
County: Honolulu FICE Identification: 001605
Unit ID: 141486
Telephone: (808) 735-4711 Carnegie Class: Masters/L
FAX Number: N/A Calendar System: Semester
URL: www.chaminade.edu
Established: 1955 Annual Undergrad Tuition & Fees: $26,914
Enrollment: 2,208 Coed
Affiliation or Control: Independent Non-Profit IRS Status: 501(c)3
Highest Offering: Doctorate
Accreditation: WC, CAEPT, CIDA, CLPSY, IACBE, MACTE, NURSE

01 President .... Dr. Lynn BABINGTON
05 Provost .... Dr. Lance ASKILDSON
111 VP for Institutional Advancement .... Mr. Gary CORDOVA
10 Vice President Finance/Facilities .... Ms. Aulani KAANOI
84 Dean of Enrollment Management .... Ms. Lisa TRUMBULL
32 VP of Student Affairs .... Ms. Allison JEROME
15 VP of HR & Legal Affairs .... Ms. Christine DENTON
26 VP Communications & Marketing .... Ms. Lisa FURUTA
90 Sr Dir Network/Desktop Services .... Mr. Jules SUKHABUT
29 Director of Alumni Relations .... Ms. Jeannie LUM

41 Director of Athletics .... Mr. Tom BUNING
42 Director of Campus Ministry .... Mr. Jeremiah CARTER
36 Dir Advising & Career Development .... Ms. Danielle MASUDA
18 Asst Dir of Facilities Operations .... Ms. Lori AUKAI-PAIA
21 Director of Finance .... Mr. Choong LIM
08 Director of Library .... Ms. Sharon LEPAGE
19 Director of Security .... Mr. Damien BARR
38 Director of Counseling Services .... Dr. Sharolyn TANI
06 Asst VP Student Success & Registrar .... Ms. Jennifer CREECH
37 Dean of Financial Aid .... Mr. Jeff SCOFIELD
09 Dir of Institutional Research .... Mr. Hieu NGUYEN

Hawaii Medical Institute Inc. DBA Hawaii Medical College (F)

1221 Kapiolani Blvd Suite 102, Honolulu HI 96814
County: Honolulu FICE Identification: 041822
Unit ID: 460756
Telephone: (808) 237-5140 Carnegie Class: Spec 2-yr-Health
FAX Number: (808) 237-5805 Calendar System: Other
URL: www.hmi.edu
Established: 2007 Annual Undergrad Tuition & Fees: $26,037
Enrollment: 150 Coed
Affiliation or Control: Proprietary IRS Status: Proprietary
Highest Offering: Associate Degree
Accreditation: CNCE

01 President/CEO .... Ashton CUDJOE
05 Director of Education .... Kevin AWAYA
06 Registrar .... Ashley WANG
07 Assoc Director of Admissions .... Julie BANNISTER
10 Chief Financial Officer .... Renz BELTRAN
106 Dean Online Education/E-learning .... Rodney A. WEST
13 Chief Information Technology Ofcr .... Kevin BORRAS
15 Human Resources Administrator .... Josephine BUSANO
18 Chief Facilities/Phys Plant Ofcr .... Justin MERRILL
36 Director Career Services .... Jared NAMUMNART
37 Director Student Financial Aid .... Bradley TAGUINOD
38 Director Student Counseling .... Cheryl CHAR

Hawaii Pacific University (G)

1164 Bishop Street, Suite 800, Honolulu HI 96813-2882
County: Honolulu FICE Identification: 007279
Unit ID: 141644
Telephone: (808) 544-0200 Carnegie Class: Masters/L
FAX Number: (808) 544-1136 Calendar System: Semester
URL: www.hpu.edu
Established: 1965 Annual Undergrad Tuition & Fees: $29,300
Enrollment: 4,243 Coed
Affiliation or Control: Independent Non-Profit IRS Status: 501(c)3
Highest Offering: Doctorate
Accreditation: WC, AAQEP, NURSE, SW

01 President .... Mr. John GOTANDA
00 President Emeritus .... Mr. Chatt G. WRIGHT
05 Sr VP and Provost .... Dr. Jennifer WALSH
11 Sr Vice Pres Admin/Gen Counsel .... Ms. Janet BOIVIN
10 Sr VP/Chief Financial Officer .... Mr. David KOSTECKI
84 Vice Pres Enrollment Management .... Mr. Greg GRAUMAN
26 VP Communication/Marketing .... Mr. Stephen WARD
111 VP of Advancement .... Ms. Brooke CARROLL
15 Int AVP of Human Resources .... Vacant
13 Assoc VP/Chief Information Officer .... Mr. Cody DOWN
35 AVP/Dean of Students .... Ms. Marites MCKEE
21 Associate VP/Controller .... Mr. James BRESE
06 AVP of Enrollment Management .... Ms. Sara SATO
18 AVP of Facilities Safety/Security .... Mr. Kevin G. MATSUKADO
50 Interim Dean College Business .... Mr. Mani SEHGAL
76 Dean College Health Society .... Dr. Halaevalu VAKALAHI
81 Dean Col Natural/Computational Sci .... Dr. Brenda JENSEN
49 Dean College of Liberal Arts .... Dr. Allison GOUGH
56 Dean College of Prof Studies .... Mr. Mani SEHGAL
07 Assoc Dir International Admissions .... Vacant
97 Asst Dean College of Prof Studies .. Dr. Valentina ABORDONADO
07 Director of Admissions .... Ms. Marissa BRATTON
104 Director Intl Exchange/Study Abroad ... Ms. Melissa MATSUBARA
37 Assoc Director Financial Aid .... Ms. Alyson MACHADO
41 Exec Director of Athletics .... Dr. Debbie SNELL
08 Actg Dir Libraries/Learning Commons .... Dr. Valentina ABORDONADO
29 Sr Dir Development/Alumni Relations .... Ms. Tara K. WILSON

Hawaii Tokai International College (H)

91-971 Farrington Hwy, Kapolei HI 96707
County: Honolulu FICE Identification: 037603
Telephone: (808) 983-4000 Carnegie Class: Not Classified
FAX Number: (808) 983-4107 Calendar System: Quarter
URL: www.htic.edu
Established: 1992 Annual Undergrad Tuition & Fees: N/A
Enrollment: N/A Coed
Affiliation or Control: Independent Non-Profit IRS Status: 501(c)3
Highest Offering: Associate Degree
Accreditation: WJ

01 Chancellor .... Dr. Gene AWAKUNI
05 Vice Chanc for Academic Affairs .... Dr. Jon MATSUOKA
11 Vice Chanc Administrative Affairs .... Mr. Lloyd UNEBASAMI
05 Dean of Instruction .... Dr. Sandra WU-BOTT
07 Director of Admissions .... Mr. Darrell KICKER

Institute of Clinical Acupuncture and Oriental Medicine (A)

100 N Beretania Street, Suite 203 B,
Honolulu HI 96817-4709
County: Honolulu FICE Identification: 037353
Unit ID: 444699
Telephone: (808) 521-2288 Carnegie Class: Spec-4-yr-Other Health
FAX Number: (808) 521-2271 Calendar System: Semester
URL: www.orientalmedicine.edu
Established: 1996 Annual Graduate Tuition & Fees: N/A
Enrollment: 54 Coed
Affiliation or Control: Proprietary IRS Status: Proprietary
Highest Offering: Master's; No Undergraduates
Accreditation: ACUP

01 President ... Dr. Wai Hoa LOW
05 Chancellor Academic Affairs ... Dr. Edmund BERNAUER
32 Director of Student Affairs ... Dr. Craig TWENTYMAN
10 Director of Finance ... Dr. Catherine Yu-Ling LOW
06 Registrar ... Ms. Jeanne BERNAUER

Pacific Rim Christian University (B)

2223 Ho'one'e Place, Honolulu HI 96819
County: Honolulu Identification: 667010
Unit ID: 457484
Telephone: (808) 518-4791 Carnegie Class: Bac-A&S
FAX Number: (808) 670-3957 Calendar System: Semester
URL: www.pacrim.edu
Established: 1998 Annual Undergrad Tuition & Fees: $11,900
Enrollment: 147 Coed
Affiliation or Control: Independent Non-Profit IRS Status: 501(c)3
Highest Offering: Master's
Accreditation: BI

01 Interim President ... Craig PANKOW
05 Vice Pres Academics/Student Life ... Dr. Jennifer KELLY
84 Vice Pres Enrollment ... Craig PANKOW
07 Director of Admissions ... Jade RANESES
20 Dean of Academics/Student Life ... Vicki LEPICK
08 Library Director ... Karen CLARKE
37 Director of Financial Aid ... Eli JENNINGS
13 Director IT & Facilities ... James MCELMURRY
06 Registrar/Career Svcs Director ... Melodie GARCIA
35 Director of Student Life ... Garret CHANG
10 Director of Business Operations ... Erica JANSEN

*University of Hawaii System (C)

2444 Dole Street, Honolulu HI 96822
County: Honolulu FICE Identification: 007885
Unit ID: 141963
Telephone: (808) 956-8207 Carnegie Class: N/A
FAX Number: (808) 956-5286
URL: www.hawaii.edu

01 President ... Dr. David K. LASSNER
05 VP for Academic Strategy ... Vacant
46 VP for Research and Innovation ... Dr. Vassilis L. SYRMOS
43 VP for Legal Affs/Univ Gen Counsel ... Ms. Carrie K. OKINAGA
10 VP for Budget and Finance/CFO ... Mr. Kalbert K. YOUNG
88 VP for Community Colleges ... Dr. Erika L. LACRO
11 VP for Administration ... Ms. Jan N. GOUVEIA
13 VP for Information Tech/CIO ... Mr. Garret T. YOSHIMI
111 VP for Advancement/CEO UH Found ... Mr. Timothy DOLAN
32 Assoc VP Student Affairs ... Ms. Hae K. OKIMOTO
21 Director of Budget ... Mr. Michael M. NG
15 Interim Sys Dir Human Resources ... Ms. Kimberly M. HASHIRO
14 Director Management Info Systems ... Ms. Susan K. INOUYE
45 Interim Dir Ofc of Research Svcs ... Dr. Vassilis L. SYRMOS
21 AVP Budget & Finance/Controller ... Ms. Amy S. KUNZ
09 Director Data Govt & Operations ... Ms. Sandra K. FURUTO
22 Interim Director EEO/AA ... Dr. Dee E. UWONO
26 Director of Communications ... Mr. Dan T. MEISENZAHL
101 Exec Administrator/Sec to the BOR ... Ms. Kendra T. OISHI
86 Director Government Relations ... Ms. Stephanie C. KIM
100 Executive Asst to President ... Ms. Lynne K. MONACO
100 Executive Asst to President ... Ms. Amy M. LUKE
04 Admin & Fiscal Support Specialist ... Ms. Courtney N. DOMINGO

*University of Hawaii at Hilo (D)

200 W Kawili Street, Hilo HI 96720-4091
County: Hawaii FICE Identification: 001611
Unit ID: 141565
Telephone: (808) 932-7348 Carnegie Class: DU-Mod
FAX Number: (808) 932-7338 Calendar System: Semester
URL: www.hilo.hawaii.edu
Established: 1947 Annual Undergrad Tuition & Fees (In-State): $7,838
Enrollment: 3,165 Coed
Affiliation or Control: State IRS Status: 501(c)3
Highest Offering: Doctorate
Accreditation: WC, AAQEP, MPCAC, NUR, NURSE, PHAR

02 Chancellor ... Dr. Bonnie D. IRWIN
05 Vice Chancellor Academic Affairs ... Dr. Kristen RONEY
10 Int Vice Chanc Admin Affairs ... Mr. Kalei RAPOZA
46 Vice Chancellor for Research ... Vacant
32 Vice Chancellor Student Affairs ... Ms. Farrah-Marie GOMES
35 Int Asst VC for Student Affairs ... Ms. Kainoa ARIOLA-SUKISAKI
114 Exec Budget Director & Business Mgt ... Ms. Lois M. FUJIYOSHI
88 Director University Disability Svcs ... Ms. Susan SHIRACHI
15 Acting Director Human Resources ... Ms. Annette SUGIMOTO
18 Director Facilities Planning ... Mr. Jerry WATANABE
26 Int Director University Relations ... Ms. Alyson KAKUGAWA-LEONG
08 University Librarian ... Mr. Joseph SANCHEZ
24 Director Media Relations ... Ms. Alyson Y. KAKUGAWA-LEONG
07 Director Admissions ... Vacant
38 Clinical Team Leader ... Mr. Andrew POLLOI
39 Director of Housing ... Ms. Sherri AKAU
35 Acting Director of Campus Center ... Ms. Lai Sha BUGADO
37 Director Financial Aid ... Ms. Sherrie PADILLA
06 University Registrar ... Ms. Chelsea KAY-WONG
49 Int Dean College of Arts & Sciences ... Dr. Michael BITTER
50 Int Dean Col of Business/Economics ... Dr. Emmeline DE PILLIS
67 Dean College of Pharmacy ... Dr. Carolyn MA
47 Dean Col Agri/For/Nat Res Mgmt ... Dr. Bruce MATHEWS
51 Actg Dir Ctr for Community Engage ... Dr. Julie MOWRER
41 Director of Athletics ... Mr. Patrick J. GUILLEN
40 Bookstore Manager ... Ms. Margaret STANLEY
85 Exec Dir Intl Student Services ... Mr. James P. MELLON
36 Director Career Services ... Ms. Kainoa ARIOLA-SUKISAKI
09 Institutional Research Analyst ... Dr. Bradley THIESSEN
27 Dir Marketing Imiloa Astronomy Ctr ... Ms. Yu Yok PEARRING
23 Director Medical Services ... Ms. Heather HIRATA
88 Dir College of Hawaiian Language ... Ms. Keiki KAWAI`AE`A
19 Director Security/Safety ... Mr. Richard MURRAY

*University of Hawaii at Manoa (E)

2500 Campus Road, Honolulu HI 96822-2217
County: Honolulu FICE Identification: 001610
Unit ID: 141574
Telephone: (808) 956-8111 Carnegie Class: DU-Highest
FAX Number: N/A Calendar System: Semester
URL: www.manoa.hawaii.edu
Established: 1907 Annual Undergrad Tuition & Fees (In-State): $12,186
Enrollment: 18,025 Coed
Affiliation or Control: State IRS Status: 501(c)3
Highest Offering: Doctorate
Accreditation: WC, AAQEP, #CAATE, CEA, CLPSY, DH, DIETD, IPSY, LAW, LIB, MED, MT, MUS, NURSE, PH, PLNG, SP, SPAA, SW

00 Chair Board of Regents ... Mr. Randolph G. MOORE
02 President ... Dr. David LASSNER
05 Provost ... Dr. Michael BRUNO
22 Dir & Title IX Coord ... Dr. Dee UWONO
88 Native Hawaiian Affairs Pgm Officer ... Dr. Kaiwipuni LIPE
10 Vice Chanc Admin/Finance/Ops ... Ms. Alexandra S. FRENCH
113 Bursar ... Ms. Denise L. DEARMENT
92 Asst VC Undergrad Edu ... Dr. Ronald CAMBRA
96 Dir Procure/Real Prop Mgmt UH Sys ... Mr. Duff ZWALD
116 Director Internal Audit ... Mr. Glenn Y. SHIZUMURA
21 Dir Finance & Accounting ... Ms. Alexandra FRENCH
20 Interim Assoc VC Academic Affairs ... Dr. Laura LYONS
46 Interim VC Research ... Dr. Velma KAMEOKA
15 Asst VC Academic Personnel ... Dr. Beverly MCCREARY
32 Int Vice Chancellor Students ... Dr. Lori IDETA
13 VP Info Technology/CIO UH System ... Mr. Garret YOSHIMI
06 Interim University Registrar ... Ms. Sherise TIOGANGCO
08 Interim University Librarian ... Dr. Monica GHOSH
37 Director Financial Aid Services ... Ms. Jodie M. KUBA
38 Dir Counseling/Student Devel Ctr ... Dr. Allyson M. TANOUYE
23 Director University Health Center ... Dr. Andrew W. NICHOLS
39 Int Dir Student Affairs/Housing ... Ms. Laurie FURUTANI
40 Director University Bookstore ... Ms. Tricia R. EJIMA
41 Athletics Director ... Mr. David MATLIN
86 Director of Cmty/Govt Affairs ... Mr. Elmer KAAI
28 Dir Student Affs/Equity/Excl/Div ... Dr. Christine QUEMUEL
36 Director of the Manoa Career Center ... Ms. Wendy SORA
15 Interim Director Human Resources ... Ms. Donna KIYOSAKI
88 Director Cancer Center ... Dr. Randall HOLCOMBE
88 Interim Dir Institute for Astronomy ... Dr. Robert MCLAREN
88 Director Waikiki Aquarium ... Dr. Andrew ROSSITER
88 Dir Pacific Bioscience Research Ctr ... Dr. Margaret MCFALL-NGAI
51 Int Dean Outreach College ... Dr. William G. CHISMAR
50 Dean Shidler College of Business ... Dr. V. Vance ROLEY
58 Dean Graduate Education ... Dr. Krystyna AUNE
88 Int Dean Sch of Travel Industry Mgt ... Mr. Tom BINGHAM
53 Dean College of Education ... Dr. Nathan MURATA
54 Dean College of Engineering ... Dr. Brennon MORIOKA
47 Dean Col Trop Agric & Human Res ... Dr. Nicholas COMERFORD
63 Dean John A Burns Sch of Med ... Dr. Jerris R. HEDGES
66 Dean Sch Nursing & Dental Hygiene ... Dr. Mary G. BOLAND
70 Dean M P Thompson Sch of Soc Work ... Dr. Noreen K. MOKUAU
61 Dean Wm S Richardson Sch of Law ... Ms. Camille NELSON
48 Interim Dean School of Architecture ... Dr. William CHAPMAN
49 Dean College Arts & Humanities ... Dr. Peter ARNADE
81 Dean College Natural Sciences ... Dr. Aloysius HELMINCK
83 Dean College Social Sciences ... Dr. Denise E. KONAN
88 Dean Sch Ocean & Earth Sci & Tech ... Dr. Brian TAYLOR
88 Dean Pacific and Asian Studies ... Dr. R. Anderson SUTTON
88 Dean Sch of Hawaiian Knowledge ... Dr. Jonhathan OSORIO
09 Director Institutional Research ... Dr. Yang ZHANG
04 Executive Assistant to President ... Ms. Debra ISHII
04 Executive Assistant to President ... Ms. Amy LUKE
07 Assoc Director of Admissions ... Mr. Ryan YAMAGUCHI
101 Exec Administrator & Secy to BOR ... Ms. Kendra OISHI
104 Director Study Abroad ... Dr. Sarita RAI
11 VP Administration UH System ... Ms. Jan GOUVEIA
19 Chief Public Safety ... Mr. Andrew BLACK
22 Dir Affirm Action/Equal Opp UH Sys ... Mr. Mark AU
25 Director Research Services UH Sys ... Mr. Leonard R. GOUVEIA, JR.
26 Director Communications UH System ... Mr. Dan MEISENZAHL
43 VP Legal Affairs UH System ... Ms. Carrie OKINAGA
84 Asst VC Enroll Mgmt & Dir of Admiss ... Ms. Roxie SHABAZZ
90 Asc VP Stdnt Aff/Dir Acad Tech UHS ... Ms. Hae OKIMOTO
102 VP Advance & CEO UH Foundation ... Mr. Tim DOLAN
109 Director Campus Services ... Mr. Kevin H. ISHIDA

*University of Hawaii - West Oahu (F)

91-1001 Farrington Highway, Kapolei HI 96707
County: Honolulu FICE Identification: 021078
Unit ID: 141981
Telephone: (808) 689-2770 Carnegie Class: Bac-Diverse
FAX Number: (808) 689-2771 Calendar System: Semester
URL: www.uhwo.hawaii.edu
Established: 1976 Annual Undergrad Tuition & Fees (In-State): $7,584
Enrollment: 3,168 Coed
Affiliation or Control: State IRS Status: 501(c)3
Highest Offering: Baccalaureate
Accreditation: WC, ACBSP, CAEP

02 Chancellor ... Dr. Maenette BENHAM
05 Vice Chanc Academic Affairs ... Dr. Jeffrey MONIZ
32 Int Vice Chanc for Student Affairs ... Dr. Jan JAVINAR
11 Vice Chanc for Administration ... Mr. Kevin ISHIDA
84 Director for Enrollment Services ... Ms. Ellen KENOLIO
09 Director of Institutional Research ... Mr. John STANLEY
26 Director of Communications ... Ms. Leila SHIMOKAWA
08 Library Director ... Ms. Michiko JOSEPH
06 Registrar ... Ms. Vicky DEL PRADO
37 Director of Financial Aid ... Mr. James OSHIRO
15 Director of Human Resources ... Ms. Nancy K. NAKASONE
10 Fiscal Manager ... Ms. Sheri CHING
07 Director of Admissions ... Ms. Michelle COHEN
13 Chief Info Technology Officer ... Ms. Therese NAKADOMARI
18 Dir Facilities/Physical Plant Ofc ... Ms. Bonnie ARAKAWA

*University of Hawaii Community Colleges (G)

2444 Dole Street, Honolulu HI 96822-2411
County: Honolulu FICE Identification: 006751
Unit ID: 420592
Telephone: (808) 956-7038 Carnegie Class: N/A
FAX Number: (808) 956-9219
URL: www.hawaii.edu

01 Vice Pres for Community Colleges ... Dr. Erika L. LACRO
05 Assoc Vice Pres Academic Affairs ... Ms. Tammi CHUN-OYADOMARI
11 Assoc Vice Pres Admin/Cmty Col Oper ... Mr. Michael T. UNEBASAMI
04 Executive Assistant to the VP & Dir ... Ms. Deborah NAKAGAWA
10 Director Budget & Planning ... Mr. Lance YAMAMOTO
15 Director Human Resources ... Ms. Sandra UYENO
18 Director Facilities/Physical Plant ... Ms. Denise YOSHIMORI-YAMAMOTO
22 Director Affirmative Action/EEO ... Ms. Mary PERREIRA

*Kapiolani Community College (H)

4303 Diamond Head Road, Honolulu HI 96816-4221
County: Honolulu FICE Identification: 001613
Unit ID: 141796
Telephone: (808) 734-9000 Carnegie Class: Assoc/MT-VT-Mix Trad/Non
FAX Number: N/A Calendar System: Semester
URL: www.kapiolani.hawaii.edu
Established: 1957 Annual Undergrad Tuition & Fees (In-State): $3,284
Enrollment: 6,369 Coed
Affiliation or Control: State IRS Status: 501(c)3
Highest Offering: Associate Degree
Accreditation: WJ, ACBSP, ACFEI, ADNUR, COARC, DA, EMT, MAC, MLTAD, OTA, PTAA, RAD, SURGT

02 Chancellor ... Dr. Louise PAGOTTO
05 Interim VC Academic Affairs ... Dr. Maria BAUTISTA
10 Vice Chancellor for Admin Services ... Mr. Brian FURUTO
32 Vice Chancellor Student Affairs ... Mr. Thomas KEOPUHIWA
49 Dean Arts and Sciences ... Mr. Nawa'a NAPOLEON
50 Dean Hospitality/Business/Legal ... Mr. John RICHARDS
76 Dean Health Programs ... Ms. Lisa RADAK
51 Dir Continuing Educ & Training ... Vacant
04 Exec Asst to the Chancellor ... Ms. Joanne WHITAKER
09 Dir Institutional Effectiveness ... Dr. Robert FRANCO
08 Interim Head Librarian ... Ms. Annie THOMAS
06 Registrar ... Ms. Jerilyn ENOKAWA
37 Financial Aid Officer ... Ms. Jennifer BRADLEY
109 Auxiliary Services Officer ... Mr. Sean NATHAN
51 Dean Community & Continuing Educ ... Dr. Carol HOSHIKO
30 Development Officer ... Ms. Linh HOANG POE
15 Int Manager Human Resources ... Ms. Linda RENIO
21 Fiscal Officer ... Mr. Justin KASHIWAEDA

*University of Hawaii - Hawaii Community College (I)

1175 Manono Street, Hilo HI 96720-5096
County: Hawaii FICE Identification: 005258
Unit ID: 383190
Telephone: (808) 934-2800 Carnegie Class: Assoc/MT-VT-High Trad

FAX Number: (808) 934-2501 Calendar System: Semester
URL: www.hawaii.hawaii.edu
Established: 1941 Annual Undergrad Tuition & Fees (In-State): $3,204
Enrollment: 2,430 Coed
Affiliation or Control: State IRS Status: 501(c)3
Highest Offering: Associate Degree
Accreditation: WJ, ACFEI, ADNUR

02 Chancellor ..... Dr. Rachel H. SOLEMSAAS
05 Vice Chanc Academic Affairs ..... Ms. Joni Y. ONISHI
10 Interim Vice Chanc Admin Affairs ... Mr. Kenneth K. KALEIWAHEA
32 Vice Chanc Student Affairs ..... Ms. Dorinna CORTEZ
51 Director Continuing Educ/Training ..... Ms. Jessica YAMAMOTO
37 Financial Aid Manager ..... Vacant
12 Interim Director Palamanui ..... Ms. Raynette (Kalei) HALEAMAU-KAM
15 Human Resource Manager ..... Ms. Mari CHANG
06 Registrar/A&R Mgr ..... Ms. Sherise TIOGANGCO
114 Budget Analyst ..... Ms. Jodi MINE
04 Private Secretary to the Chancellor ..... Ms. Callie MARTIN
19 Campus Safety and Security Chief ..... Vacant
49 Dean for Liberal Arts & Public Svcs ..... Dr. Melanie WILSON
88 Director of KoEC ..... Dr. Kei-Lin CERF

*University of Hawaii Honolulu Community College (A)

874 Dillingham Boulevard, Honolulu HI 96817-4598
County: Honolulu FICE Identification: 001612
Unit ID: 141680
Telephone: (808) 845-9211 Carnegie Class: Assoc/HVT-Mix Trad/Non
FAX Number: (808) 845-9173 Calendar System: Semester
URL: www.honolulu.hawaii.edu
Established: 1920 Annual Undergrad Tuition & Fees (In-State): $3,174
Enrollment: 3,378 Coed
Affiliation or Control: State IRS Status: 501(c)3
Highest Offering: Associate Degree
Accreditation: WJ

02 Interim Chancellor ..... Ms. Karen LEE
11 Vice Chancellor of Admin Svcs ..... Mr. Derek INAFUKU
05 Int Vice Chancellor of Acad Affairs ..... Ms. Susan NISHIDA
88 Int Dean Transport & Trades ..... Ms. Preshess WILLETS-VAQUILAR
27 Dean Communications & Services ..... Mr. Wayne SUNAHARA
08 Librarian in Charge ..... Ms. Stefanie SASAKI
37 Financial Aid Officer ..... Ms. Heather FLORENDO
15 Human Resources Mgr/EEO/AA Coord ... Ms. Monique TINGKANG
32 Director Student Affairs ..... Ms. Emily Ann KUKULIES
06 Registrar ..... Ms. Jennifer NAGUWA
09 Director Management Info & Research .... Mr. Steven SHIGEMOTO
36 Dir Student Placement/Counselor ..... Ms. Silvan CHUNG
20 Dean University College ..... Ms. Jennifer HIGA-KING
10 Chief Business Officer ..... Ms. Myrna PATTERSON
26 Chief Public Relations Officer ..... Vacant
121 Interim Dean of Academic Support ..... Ms. Silvan CHUNG
96 Acting Director of Purchasing ..... Ms. Myrna PATTERSON
88 Director Secondary Education Pgms ..... Ms. Lara SUGIMOTO
13 Chief Info Technology Officer (CIO) ..... Mr. Michael MEYER
35 Dean of Student Services ..... Ms. Lara SUGIMOTO

*University of Hawaii Kauai Community College (B)

3-1901 Kaumualii Highway, Lihue HI 96766-9500
County: Kauai FICE Identification: 001614
Unit ID: 141802
Telephone: (808) 245-8311 Carnegie Class: Assoc/HVT-High Trad
FAX Number: (808) 245-8220 Calendar System: Semester
URL: kauai.hawaii.edu/
Established: 1964 Annual Undergrad Tuition & Fees (In-State): $3,252
Enrollment: 1,461 Coed
Affiliation or Control: State IRS Status: 501(c)3
Highest Offering: Associate Degree
Accreditation: WJ, ACFEI, ADNUR, MAC

02 Chancellor ..... Dr. Joseph DAISY
05 Vice Chanc Academic Affairs ..... Dr. Frankie HARRISS
32 Vice Chanc Student Affairs ..... Ms. Margaret SANCHEZ
11 Vice Chanc Administrative Services ..... Mr. Calvin SHIRAI
10 Chief Financial Officer ..... Ms. Deanne KOSHI
51 Director Continuing Educ/Training ..... Mr. Calvin SHIRAI
08 Head Librarian ..... Mr. Robert KAJIWARA
37 Financial Aid Officer ..... Mr. Jeff ANDERSON
15 Human Resource Manager ..... Ms. JoRae BAPTISTE
35 Counselor/Student Life Coordinator ..... Mr. John CONSTANTINO
09 Dir Institutional Effect/Univ Ctr ..... Dr. Valerie BARKO

*University of Hawaii - Leeward Community College (C)

96-045 Ala Ike, Pearl City HI 96782-3393
County: Honolulu FICE Identification: 004549
Unit ID: 141811
Telephone: (808) 455-0011 Carnegie Class: Assoc/HT-Mix Trad/Non
FAX Number: (808) 455-0471 Calendar System: Semester
URL: www.leeward.hawaii.edu
Established: 1968 Annual Undergrad Tuition & Fees (In-State): $3,209
Enrollment: 6,363 Coed
Affiliation or Control: State IRS Status: 501(c)3
Highest Offering: Associate Degree
Accreditation: WJ, AAQEP, ACFEI, CAHIIM

02 Chancellor ..... Dr. Carlos PEÑALOZA
05 Interim Vice Chanc Academic Affairs ..... Ms. Kay ONO
11 Interim Vice Chanc Admin Services ..... Ms. Lori Lei HAYASHI
10 Fiscal Manager ..... Ms. Cecilia LUCAS
49 Dean Arts & Sciences ..... Mr. James GOODMAN
72 Dean Career & Tech Education ..... Mr. Ron UMEHIRA
32 Interim Dean Student Services ..... Ms. Kami KATO
20 Interim Dean of Academic Services ..... Ms. Leanne RISELEY
08 Librarian ..... Mr. Wayde OSHIRO
06 Registrar ..... Mr. Grant HELGESON
37 Financial Aid Officer ..... Mr. Gregg YOSHIMURA
18 Aux & Facilities Services Mgr ..... Mr. Grant OKAMURA
09 Interim Policy/Plng/Assess Coord ..... Ms. Jayne BOPP
26 Marketing Speciallist ..... Mr. Tad SAIKI
15 Human Resources Mgr/EEO/AA Coord ..... Ms. Lori Lei HAYASHI
13 Information Technology Coord ..... Mr. Byron WATANABE
12 Coord Waianae Education Center ..... Mr. Danny WYATT
24 Interim Media Coordinator ..... Ms. Rachael INAKE
35 Student Activities Coordinator ..... Ms. Lexer CHOU

*University of Hawaii Maui College (D)

310 Kaahumanu Avenue, Kahului HI 96732-1644
County: Maui FICE Identification: 001615
Unit ID: 141839
Telephone: (808) 984-3500 Carnegie Class: Bac/Assoc-Assoc Dom
FAX Number: (808) 984-3546 Calendar System: Semester
URL: maui.hawaii.edu
Established: 1931 Annual Undergrad Tuition & Fees (In-State): $3,278
Enrollment: 2,936 Coed
Affiliation or Control: State IRS Status: 501(c)3
Highest Offering: Baccalaureate
Accreditation: WC, ACFEI, ADNUR, DH, NAEYC

02 Chancellor ..... Dr. Lui HOKOANA
05 Vice Chanc Academic Affairs ..... Vacant
32 Vice Chancellor of Student Affs ..... Ms. Debra NAKAMA
10 Vice Chanc of Administrative Affs ..... Mr. David TAMANAHA
51 Director Continuing Educ/Training ..... Ms. Karen HANADA
08 Librarian ..... Ms. Ellen PETERSON
88 Director University Center Maui ..... Ms. Tomone Karen HANADA
07 Director of Admissions ..... Ms. Flora MORA
09 Director of Institutional Research ..... Vacant
15 Director Human Resources ..... Ms. Susan TOKUNAGA
18 Chief Facilities/Physical Plant ..... Mr. Melvin HIPOLITO
21 Fiscal Administrator ..... Ms. Cindy YAMAMOTO
30 Director of Development ..... Ms. Jocelyn Romero DEMIRBAG
36 Director Student Placement ..... Ms. Debra NAKAMA
37 Financial Aid Director ..... Ms. Davileigh NAE`OLE
38 Director Student Counseling ..... Mr. Shane PAYBA
06 Registrar ..... Ms. Flora MORA
19 Director Security/Safety ..... Ms. Angela GANNON

*University of Hawaii Windward Community College (E)

45-720 Keaahala Road, Kaneohe HI 96744-3598
County: Honolulu FICE Identification: 011220
Unit ID: 141990
Telephone: (808) 235-7400 Carnegie Class: Assoc/HT-High Non
FAX Number: (808) 247-5362 Calendar System: Semester
URL: www.windward.hawaii.edu
Established: 1972 Annual Undergrad Tuition & Fees (In-State): $3,194
Enrollment: 2,299 Coed
Affiliation or Control: State IRS Status: 501(c)3
Highest Offering: Associate Degree
Accreditation: WJ

02 Chancellor ..... Dr. Ardis ESCHENBERG
05 Vice Chancellor Academic Affairs ..... Mr. Charles S. SASAKI
32 Int Vice Chancellor Student Affairs ..... Dr. Judy OLIVEIRA
11 Int Vice Chanc Administrative Svcs ..... Ms. Kelli BRANDVOLD
20 Dean of Academic Affairs Div I ..... Ms. Colette HIGGINS
20 Int Dean of Academic Affairs Div II ..... Dr. David KRUPP
78 Int Dir Vocational/Cmty Education ..... Dr. Maria-Elena DIAZ
08 Head Librarian ..... Ms. Sarah Gilman SUR
06 Registrar ..... Vacant
09 Director of Institutional Research ..... Vacant
37 Director Student Financial Aid ..... Ms. Dayna ISA
15 Personnel Officer ..... Ms. Karen CHO
26 Marketing/Public Relations Dir ..... Ms. Bonnie BEATSON
19 Director Security/Safety ..... Vacant

University of Phoenix Hawaii Campus (F)

949 Kamokila Blvd. Suite 101, Kapolei HI 96707
Telephone: (808) 536-2686 Identification: 770202
Accreditation: &HLC, ACBSP, CAEPN

† Branch campus of University of Phoenix, Phoenix, AZ

IDAHO

Boise Bible College (G)

8695 W Marigold Street, Boise ID 83714-1220
County: Ada FICE Identification: 022345
Unit ID: 142090
Telephone: (208) 376-7731 Carnegie Class: Spec-4-yr-Faith
FAX Number: (208) 376-7743 Calendar System: Semester
URL: www.boisebible.edu
Established: 1945 Annual Undergrad Tuition & Fees: $13,100
Enrollment: 101 Coed
Affiliation or Control: Christian Churches And Churches of Christ
IRS Status: 501(c)3
Highest Offering: Baccalaureate
Accreditation: BI

01 President ..... Dr. Derek VOORHEES
05 VP of Academic Affairs ..... Mr. Charles FABER
32 VP of Institutional Operations ..... Dr. Cody CHRISTENSEN
10 Director of Finance/Administration ..... Mr. Steven MARSHALL
111 VP of Institutional Advancement ..... Mr. David DAVOLT
06 Registrar ..... Mr. Ross KNUDSEN
84 VP of Enrollment Management ..... Mr. Russell GROVE
08 Librarian ..... Mrs. Amber GROVE
37 Financial Aid Director ..... Mr. Ben BISHOP
18 Director of Physical Plant ..... Mr. Mike MORRIS
04 Executive Assistant to President ..... Mrs. Rhonda HETHERINGTON

Boise State University (H)

1910 University Drive, Boise ID 83725-1000
County: Ada FICE Identification: 001616
Unit ID: 142115
Telephone: (208) 426-1000 Carnegie Class: DU-Higher
FAX Number: (208) 426-3765 Calendar System: Semester
URL: www.boisestate.edu
Established: 1932 Annual Undergrad Tuition & Fees (In-State): $8,068
Enrollment: 24,069 Coed
Affiliation or Control: State IRS Status: 501(c)3
Highest Offering: Doctorate
Accreditation: NW, ART, CAATE, CACREP, CAEP, COARC, CONST, DMS, MUS, NURSE, RAD, SW, THEA

01 President ..... Dr. Marlene TROMP
05 Provost/VP of Academic Affairs ..... Dr. John BUCKWALTER
10 VP/Chief Financial Officer ..... Mr. Mark HEIL
32 VP Student Affairs/Enrollment Mgmt ..... Vacant
111 VP University Advancement ..... Mr. Matthew EWING
11 AVP Campus Operations ..... Ms. Randi MCDERMOTT
20 Vice Provost Academic Planning ..... Dr. Zeynep HANSEN
97 Vice Provost Undergrad Studies ..... Ms. Susan SHADLE
21 Assoc VP Finance & Administration ..... Ms. Jo Ellen DINUCCI
110 AVP Advancement Services ..... Mr. Joseph BOEKE
35 Assoc VP for Student Affairs ..... Dr. Eric SCOTT
46 Interim VP Research & Economic Dev ..... Dr. Nancy GLENN
13 Assoc VP/Chief Info Tech ..... Mr. Max DAVIS-JOHNSON
08 Dean of University Library ..... Dr. Tracy BICKNELL-HOLMES
35 Dean of Students ..... Dr. Chris WUTHRICH
84 Assoc VP Enrollment Service ..... Ms. Kris COLLINS
15 Assoc VP Human Resources ..... Mr. Shawn MILLER
29 Executive Director Alumni Relations ..... Ms. Lisa GARDNER
17 Exec Dir of Health Services ..... Dr. Julia BEARD
06 Registrar ..... Ms. Mandy NELSON
19 Int Assoc VP Public Safety ..... Mr. Jon UDA
09 Director Institutional Research ..... Dr. Shari ELLERTSON
07 Director of Admissions ..... Dr. Kelly TALBERT
26 Assoc VP for Comm/Mktg/Creative Str ..... Ms. Lauren GRISWOLD
41 Exec Director Athletics ..... Mr. Jeramiah DICKEY
22 Exec Director of Compliance ..... Mr. John MCDONALD
38 Director Counseling Services ..... Dr. Matthew NIECE
37 Director of Financial Aid ..... Ms. Kelley CHRISTIANSON
51 Dean Extended Studies ..... Mr. Mark WHEELER
49 Interim Dean of Arts & Sciences ..... Dr. Leslie DURHAM
50 Dean Business & Economics ..... Dr. Mark BANNISTER
53 Interim Dean of Education ..... Dr. Jennifer SNOW
58 Acting Dean of the Graduate College ..... Dr. Scott LOWE
76 Dean of Health Sciences ..... Dr. Tim DUNNAGAN
54 Dean of Engineering ..... Dr. JoAnn LIGHTY
88 Dean of Innovation & Design ..... Mr. Gordon JONES
104 Asst Prov for Global Educ ..... Dr. Gonzalo BRUCE
80 Interim Dean School Public Svcs ..... Dr. Andrew GIACOMAZZI
104 Dir Intl Learning/Student Success ..... Ms. Corrine HENKE
39 Exec Dir Housing/VP Asst ..... Dr. Luke JONES
23 Director of Wellness Services ..... Ms. Holly LEVIN
36 Director Career Center ..... Ms. Debbie KAYLOR
106 Exec Director e-Campus Center ..... Ms. Christine BAUER
28 Dir of Student Diversity/Inclusion ..... Mr. Francisco SALINAS
102 Dir of Corp & Foundation Rels ..... Ms. Virginia PELLEGRINI
30 Sr Exec Development Director ..... Ms. Jennifer NEIL
100 Chief of Staff/VP Univ Affairs ..... Ms. Alicia ESTEY

Brigham Young University-Idaho (I)

525 South Center Street, Rexburg ID 83460
County: Madison FICE Identification: 001625
Unit ID: 142522
Telephone: (208) 496-1411 Carnegie Class: Bac-Diverse
FAX Number: (208) 496-1103 Calendar System: Semester
URL: www.byui.edu
Established: 1888 Annual Undergrad Tuition & Fees: $4,300
Enrollment: 44,481 Coed
Affiliation or Control: Latter-day Saints IRS Status: 501(c)3
Highest Offering: Baccalaureate
Accreditation: NW, MUS, NURSE, PTAA, SW

01 President ..... Dr. Henry J. EYRING
05 Academic Vice President ..... Dr. Jon F. LINFORD
11 University Resources Vice President ..... Mr. Brett COOK
32 Student Life Vice President ..... Mrs. Amy R. LABAUGH
106 Online Vice President ..... Mr. Kendall D. PECK
45 Exec Strategy & Planning VP ..... Mr. Robert J. GARRETT

20 Assoc Academic VP Instruction ....Mr. Sid L. PALMER
20 Assoc Acad VP Curriculum ....Dr. Van D. CHRISTMAN
121 Assoc Acad VP Student Success ....Dr. Scott W. GALER
35 Dean of Students ....Mr. Wynn N. HILL
88 Student Well-Being Mng Director ....Ms. Kristie LORDS
13 Chief Information Officer ....Mr. Joe MCWILLIAMS
09 Inst Research Managing Director ....Dr. Ben FRYAR
45 Institutional Planning Managing Dir ....Mr. Aaron SANNS
06 Registrar ....Mrs. Lauri D. ARENSMEYER
37 Financial Aid Director ....Mr. Ken L. JACKSON
08 University Librarian ....Mr. Chris OLSEN
10 Univ Operations Managing Director ....Mr. Kyle R. WILLIAMS
15 Human Resources Director ....Mr. Kevin L. PRICE
23 Student Health Services Director ....Mr. Shaun ORR
38 Student Counseling Center Director ....Mr. Reed J. STODDARD
19 University Public Safety Director ....Mr. Stephen P. BUNNELL
07 Admissions Director ....Mr. Riley HALL
29 Alumni Engagement Director ....Mr. Steven J. DAVIS
36 BYU-I Career Center Mng Director ....Mr. Derek R. FAY
26 University Relations Mng Director ....Mr. Merv R. BROWN
30 Philanthropies Director ....Ms. Tanise CHUNG-HOON
39 Housing & Student Living Director ....Dr. Troy J. DOUGHERTY
43 Associate University Counsel ....Mr. Josh FIGUEIRA
21 Financial Services Mng Director ....Mr. Shane WEBSTER
88 Student Development Mng Director ....Mrs. Jill EVANS
96 Purchasing & Travel Director ....Mr. Mike B. THUESON
35 Student Svcs Managing Director ....Mr. Kyle R. MARTIN
40 University Store Director ....Mr. Brent G. ASHCRAFT
104 International Services Director ....Mr. Bryan H. JUSTESEN
36 Career and Academic Advising Dir ....Mr. Sam R. BRUBAKER
109 Auxiliary Services Mng Director ....Mr. Ryan J. BUTTARS
04 Assistant to the President ....Mrs. Kathy L. WEBB
50 Dean of Business/Communications ....Mr. Kirk GIFFORD
53 Dean of Education & Hum Dev ....Mr. David R. PECK
54 Dean of Physical Sciences & Engr ....Mr. Greg ROACH
88 Dean of Faculty Development ....Mrs. Susan WARD
81 Dean of Agriculture & Life Sciences ....Mr. John ZENGER
79 Dean of Language & Letters ....Mr. Jason R. WILLIAMS
57 Dean of Performing & Visual Arts ....Mr. Brian MEMMOTT
88 Dean of Interdisciplinary Studies ....Ms. Danae ROMRELL
88 Dean of Teacher Preparation ....Mr. Scott GARDNER
106 Dean of Online Programs ....Mr. Jake ROMNEY

Carrington College - Boise (A)

1122 N Liberty Street, Boise ID 83704-8741
Telephone: (208) 377-8080 FICE Identification: 022180
Accreditation: &WJ, ADNUR, DH, MAAB, PNUR, PTAA

† Regional accreditation is carried under the parent institution in Sacramento, CA.

College of Eastern Idaho (B)

1600 S 25th E, Idaho Falls ID 83404-5788
County: Bonneville FICE Identification: 011133
Unit ID: 142179
Telephone: (208) 524-3000 Carnegie Class: Assoc/HVT-High Trad
FAX Number: (208) 524-3007 Calendar System: Semester
URL: www.cei.edu
Established: 1969 Annual Undergrad Tuition & Fees (In-State): $4,126
Enrollment: 1,803 Coed
Affiliation or Control: State IRS Status: 501(c)3
Highest Offering: Associate Degree
Accreditation: NW, MAC, SURGT

01 President ....Dr. Rick AMAN
10 Vice President of Finance and Admin ....Mr. Byron MILES
05 VP Instruction/Student Affairs ....Ms. Lori BARBER
06 Registrar ....Mrs. Raquel CUEVAS
21 Controller ....Mr. Don E. BOURNE
103 Mgr Workforce Trng/Cmty Education ....Mr. Jeff SNEDDONN
37 Financial Aid Director ....Mrs. Tiffany CLEVERLY
04 President Administrative Assistant ....Mrs. Amanda LOGAN
26 Director of College Relations ....Mr. Todd WIGHTMAN
102 Foundation Director ....Mr. David FACER
50 Business/Office/Technology Div Mgr ....Mr. Leslie JERNBERG
76 Health Care Technology Div Manager ....Ms. Jodene TRIMBLE
88 Trades/Industry Division Manager ....Mr. Kent E. BERGGREN
51 Adult Basic Education Div Manager ....Mrs. Sandra TAKAHASHI
09 Dir of Institutional Effectiveness ....Mr. Lee STIMPSON
13 Chief Info Technology Officer ....Mr. Ray FOX
15 Chief Human Resources Officer ....Ms. Mary TAYLOR
96 Director of Purchasing ....Ms. Heidi MOORE
00 Chairman of the Board ....Mr. Park PRICE
97 Dean of General Education ....Mr. Jacob HAEBERLE
75 Dean of Career and Technical Ed ....Mr. Chuck BOHLEKE
76 Dean of Healthcare ....Dr. Angela SACKETT
32 Dean of Student Affairs ....Mr. Michael WALKER
08 Chief Library Officer ....Mr. Nathan BROWN
106 Director Online Learning Svcs ....Mr. Ryan FAULKNER
18 Director of Facilities ....Mr. Greg HORTON
38 Director Student Counseling ....Mrs. Hailey HOLLAND

The College of Idaho (C)

2112 Cleveland Boulevard, Caldwell ID 83605-4432
County: Canyon FICE Identification: 001617
Unit ID: 142294
Telephone: (208) 459-5011 Carnegie Class: Bac-A&S
FAX Number: (208) 454-2077 Calendar System: Other
URL: www.collegeofidaho.edu
Established: 1891 Annual Undergrad Tuition & Fees: $32,855
Enrollment: 1,114 Coed
Affiliation or Control: Independent Non-Profit IRS Status: 501(c)3
Highest Offering: Master's
Accreditation: NW

01 Co-President ....Mr. Doug BRIGHAM
01 Co-President ....Mr. Jim EVERETT
05 Provost/Dean of Faculty ....Dr. David DOUGLASS
10 Vice Pres Finance/Administration ....Mr. Richard ERNE
32 Vice President Student Affairs ....Dr. Paul BENNION
84 Vice President for Enrollment Mgmt ....Mr. Brian BAVA
111 VP for College Relations ....Mr. Jack CAFFERTY
20 Associate Dean of Faculty ....Dr. Andrew GADES
20 Associate Dean of Faculty ....Dr. Lynda DANIELSON
06 Registrar ....Ms. Cassandra HEATH
41 Vice President of Athletics ....Ms. Reagan ROSSI
26 Dir of Marketing & Communications ....Mr. Joe HUGHES
29 Dir of Alumni & Parent Relations ....Ms. Danielle DOUGHERTY DURHAM
44 Director of Boone Fund ....Vacant
08 Director of Library ....Ms. Christine SCHUTZ
21 Controller ....Ms. Kim NAPOLI
37 Director of Financial Services ....Ms. Terri SCOTT
15 Human Resources Director ....Ms. Nancy JOHNSON-CASSULO
36 Director Student Placement ....Ms. Nicole CAMMANN
92 Director of Honors Program ....Dr. Rochelle JOHNSON
39 Director of Residential Life ....Mr. Matt GIER
93 Asst Dean of Students/Dir of Inclus ....Mr. Arnold HERNANDEZ
42 Campus Minister/Asc Dean Students ....Dr. Phil ROGERS
19 Director of Campus Safety ....Mr. Ben MOSLEY
09 Assc VP Institutional Effectiveness ....Mr. Mark HEIDRICH
07 Director of Admissions ....Mr. Mike BURDINE
40 College Store Manager ....Ms. Liza SAFFORD
23 Director of Health/Wellness Center ....Ms. Natalie DAVISON
04 Exec Asst to Co-Pres External Rels ....Ms. Adrianne BARBER
18 Chief Facilities/Physical Plant ....Mr. Richard ERNE
27 Director External Affairs & Events ....Ms. Deidre FRIEDLI
103 VP of High Impact Practices ....Ms. Latonia HANEY KEITH

College of Southern Idaho (D)

PO Box 1238, 315 Falls Avenue,
Twin Falls ID 83303-1238
County: Twin Falls FICE Identification: 001619
Unit ID: 142559
Telephone: (208) 733-9554 Carnegie Class: Assoc/MT-VT-High Non
FAX Number: (208) 736-3015 Calendar System: Semester
URL: www.csi.edu
Established: 1965 Annual Undergrad Tuition & Fees (In-District): $4,560
Enrollment: 7,321 Coed
Affiliation or Control: Local IRS Status: 501(c)3
Highest Offering: Baccalaureate
Accreditation: NW, ADNUR, DH, EMT, MAC, PTAA, RAD, SURGT

01 President ....Dr. L. Dean FISHER
00 Chairman of the Board ....Mr. Laird STONE
05 Provost ....Dr. Todd SCHWARZ
10 VP Finance & Administration ....Mr. Jeff HARMON
13 Chief Information Officer ....Mr. Kevin MARK
32 VP Learner & Community Services ....Dr. Michelle SCHUTT
09 Dean of IE/ALO & Communication ....Mr. Chris BRAGG
121 Dean of Student Success ....Mr. John HUGHES
04 Exec Admin Asst to President ....Ms. Ginger NUKAYA
21 Controller ....Ms. Kristy CARPENTER
20 Instructional Dean ....Ms. Tiffany SEELEY-CASE
20 Instructional Dean ....Dr. Barry PATE
20 Instructional Dean ....Dr. Jayson LLOYD
35 Dean of Students ....Mr. Jason OSTROWSKI
15 Director Human Resources ....Mr. Eric NIELSON
06 Registrar ....Dr. Jonathan LORD
37 Director of Student Financial Aid ....Ms. Jennifer J. ZIMMERS
08 Director of Library ....Vacant
102 Executive Director Foundation ....Vacant
103 Sr Director Workforce Development ....Ms. Janet PRETTI
14 Dir Application/Data Architecture ....Mr. Ed DITLEFSEN
14 Dir Systems/Network Architecture ....Mr. Bruce NUKAYA
41 Athletic Director ....Mr. Joel C. BATE
18 Director Physical Plant ....Mr. Spencer CUTLER
19 Director Security & Safety ....Mr. Jim MUNN
26 Public Information Officer ....Ms. Kim LAPRAY
40 Bookstore Manager ....Ms. Jayme KETTERLING
92 Coordinator Honors Program ....Mr. Brian DOBBS

College of Western Idaho (E)

6056 Birch Lane, Nampa ID 83687
County: Canyon FICE Identification: 042118
Unit ID: 455114
Telephone: (208) 562-3000 Carnegie Class: Assoc/HT-High Non
FAX Number: (888) 562-3216 Calendar System: Semester
URL: cwi.edu
Established: 2007 Annual Undergrad Tuition & Fees (In-District): $4,336
Enrollment: 10,200 Coed
Affiliation or Control: Local IRS Status: 501(c)3
Highest Offering: Associate Degree
Accreditation: NW, ACBSP, ADNUR, DA, MAC, PTAA, SURGT

01 Interim President ....Ms. Denise ABERLE-CANNATA
05 Provost ....Ms. Denise ABERLE-CANNATA
11 Executive VP Operations ....Mr. Craig BROWN
86 VP College Relations ....Mr. Mark BROWNING
15 VP Human Resources ....Mr. Ryan HERRING
10 Vice Pres Finance & Administration ....Mr. Karl SPIECKER
04 Executive Asst President's Office ....Ms. Janice MCGEHEE
13 Chief Information Officer ....Mr. Michael CHACON
84 AVP Enrollment & Student Services ....Mr. Patrick TANNER
103 AVP Economic Development ....Ms. Christi GILCHRIST
09 Exec Dir Inst Effectiveness ....Ms. Alexis MALEPEAI-RHODES
102 Director CWI Foundation ....Mr. Michael JENSEN
18 Exec Dir Facilities/Plng & Mgmt ....Mr. Jeff FLYNN
32 Dean of Students ....Mr. Chad TRISLER
57 Dean Arts & Humanities ....Mr. Justin VANCE
50 Dean Business/Comm & Technology ....Ms. Kelly STEELY
76 Dean Health ....Ms. Cathleen CURRIE
54 Dean Industry/Engr & Trades ....Mr. Pat NEAL
81 Dean Math & Science ....Ms. Kae JENSEN
83 Dean Social Sciences & Public Affs ....Ms. Courtney SANTILLAN
07 Dean Admissions & One Stop ....Mr. Luis CALOCA
121 Director Advising ....Ms. Allison MOLITOR
37 Director Financial Aid ....Ms. Jenee SNYDER
06 Registrar ....Ms. Connie BLACK
55 Director Basic Skills ....Mr. Jac WEBB
88 Director Business & Manufacturing ....Mr. Marc SWINNEY
88 Dean Center for Teaching & Learning ....Ms. Courtney COLBY BOND
88 Exec Dir Dual Credit ....Mr. Stephen CRUMRINE
08 Director Learning Commons ....Ms. Kim REED
26 Exec Dir Comm & Marketing ....Ms. Audrey ELDRIDGE
21 Comptroller ....Ms. Mary Jo HAYES
43 In-House General Counsel ....Ms. Andrea FONTAINE

Idaho College of Osteopathic Medicine (F)

1401 E. Central Drive, Meridian ID 83642
County: Ada Identification: 667328
Telephone: (208) 795-4266 Carnegie Class: Not Classified
FAX Number: N/A Calendar System: Semester
URL: www.idahocom.org
Established: 2016 Annual Graduate Tuition & Fees: N/A
Enrollment: N/A Coed
Affiliation or Control: Proprietary IRS Status: Proprietary
Highest Offering: First Professional Degree; No Undergraduates
Accreditation: @OSTEO

01 President ....Dr. Tracy FARNSWORTH
05 Dean & Chief Academic Ofcr ....Dr. Thomas MOHR
07 Director of Admissions ....Janette MARTIN
37 Director of Financial Aid ....Nicole MCMILLIN
10 Chief Financial Officer ....Dale CASSIDY
43 Chief Legal Officer ....John FULLERTON

Idaho State University (G)

921 S 8th Ave, Pocatello ID 83209-0009
County: Bannock FICE Identification: 001620
Unit ID: 142276
Telephone: (208) 282-0211 Carnegie Class: DU-Higher
FAX Number: (208) 282-4000 Calendar System: Semester
URL: www.isu.edu
Established: 1901 Annual Undergrad Tuition & Fees (In-State): $7,872
Enrollment: 11,766 Coed
Affiliation or Control: State IRS Status: 501(c)3
Highest Offering: Doctorate
Accreditation: NW, ADNUR, ARCPA, AUD, CAATE, CACREP, CAEPN, CAHIIM, CLPSY, COARC, COMTA, DENT, DH, DIETD, DIETI, EMT, MAC, MT, MUS, NAEYC, NAIT, NURSE, OT, OTA, PH, PHAR, PTA, PTAA, RAD, SP, SW, THEA

01 President ....Dr. Kevin SATTERLEE
04 Executive Assistant to President ....Ms. Jennifer FORSHEE
05 Interim Provost ....Dr. Karen APPLEBY
10 VP Finance & Business Affairs ....Mr. Glen NELSON
111 Vice Pres of University Advancement ....Mr. Kyle MCGOWAN
32 Vice Pres Student Affairs ....Ms. Lyn REDINGTON
46 Vice President for Research ....Ms. Donna LYBECKER
17 VP Kasiska Division Health Sciences ....Dr. Rex FORCE
43 General Counsel/Chief Comp Officer ....Mr. Blake CHRISTENSEN
41 Athletic Director ....Ms. Pauline THIROS
20 Vice Provost Academic Affairs ....Ms. Joanne TOKLE
84 AVP for Enrollment Management ....Vacant
18 AVP for Facilities Services ....Ms. Cheryl HANSON
58 Dean of Graduate School ....Dr. Adam BRADFORD
54 Dean College Science & Engineering ....Dr. Scott SNYDER
67 Dean College of Pharmacy ....Dr. Walter L. FITZGERALD, JR.
50 Dean College of Business ....Mr. Shane HUNT
49 Dean College of Arts & Letters ....Dr. Kandi TURLEY-AMES
53 Dean College of Education ....Dr. Jean MCGIVNEY-BURELLE
72 Interim Dean College of Technology ....Ms. Debra RONNEBURG
12 Dean of Academic Pgm ISU-Meridian ....Vacant
12 Vice Provost/Dean for IF AA ....Dr. Lyle CASTLE
08 Dean & University Librarian ....Dr. Sandra SHROPSHIRE
06 Registrar & Dir of Undergrad Admiss ....Ms. Laura MCKENZIE
13 Chief Information Officer ....Ms. Renae SCOTT
29 Director Alumni Relations ....Mr. Ryan SARGENT
09 Director Institutional Research ....Mr. Vince MILLER
37 Dir Student Fin Aid/Scholarships ....Mr. James R. MARTIN
15 Director Human Resources ....Mr. Brian SAGENDORF
23 Director Student Health Center ....Vacant
22 Dir EEO/Affirm Action & Diversity ....Ms. Stacey GIBSON
19 Director Public Safety ....Mr. Lewis EAKINS
26 Assoc VP Marketing & Communication ....Mr. Stuart SUMMERS
86 Director Government Relations ....Vacant
88 Director Events Management ....Mr. George CASPER
35 Dean of Students ....Mr. Craig CHATRIAND
38 Director of Counseling & Testing ....Dr. Richard PONGRATZ
85 Assoc Dir Admiss/Intl Svcs ....Mr. Shawn BASCOM
07 Director Admissions & Recruitment ....Ms. Nicole JOSEPH

39 Director University Housing .... Mr. Craig THOMPSON
96 Interim Dir Purchasing Services .... Ms. Lisa LEYSHON
44 Director Annual Giving .... Vacant
100 Chief of Staff .... Ms. Dani DUNSTAN
25 Director Contract/Grants Accounting .... Ms. Lisa WOOD

Lewis-Clark State College (A)

500 8th Avenue, Lewiston ID 83501-2698
County: Nez Perce FICE Identification: 001621
Unit ID: 142328
Telephone: (208) 792-5272 Carnegie Class: Bac-Diverse
FAX Number: (208) 792-2831 Calendar System: Semester
URL: www.lcsc.edu
Established: 1893 Annual Undergrad Tuition & Fees (In-State): $6,982
Enrollment: 3,856 Coed
Affiliation or Control: State IRS Status: 501(c)3
Highest Offering: Baccalaureate
Accreditation: **NW**, CAEPN, EMT, IACBE, MAC, NURSE, PTAA, RAD, SW

01 President .... Dr. Cynthia L. PEMBERTON
05 Interim VP Academic Affairs .... Dr. Fredrick CHILSON
10 VP Finance and Administration .... Dr. Julie CREA
32 Sr Vice President Student Affairs .... Dr. Andrew HANSON
75 Dean Career & Technical Education .... Mr. Jeffrey OBER
107 Int Dean Professional Studies .... Dr. Luther MADDY
49 Dean Liberal Arts & Sciences .... Mr. Martin GIBBS
08 Director of Library Services .... Ms. Johanna BJORK
103 Director of Workforce Training .... Vacant
07 Director of Admissions/Recruitment .Ms. Soo Lee BRUCE-SMITH
06 Registrar .... Mr. Ted UNZICKER
09 Dir Inst Research & Effectiveness .... Dr. Grace ANDERSON
13 Chief Technology Officer .... Mr. Marty GANG
41 Athletic Director .... Ms. Brooke HENZE
15 Director of Human Resources .... Ms. Vikki SWIFT-RAYMOND
26 Director Communications & Marketing .... Mr. Logan FOWLER
37 Director of Student Financial Aid .... Ms. Laura HUGHES
111 Director of College Advancement .... Ms. Erika ALLEN
18 Director of Physical Plant .... Mr. Tom GARRISON
121 Director of Advising Center .... Ms. Debra LYBYER
96 Director of Purchasing .... Ms. Sheila KOM
19 Director Security/Safety .... Vacant
04 Exec Assistant to the President .... Ms. Lori RUDDELL
106 Dir E-learning/Testing Ctr/Acces .... Ms. Dawn LESPERANCE
25 Assoc Dir Grants & Contracts .... Dr. Chris BELCHER
38 Dir Student Counseling/Health Svcs .... Mr. Doug STEELE
39 Director Resident Life .... Ms. Debbie KOLSTAD

Mercy In Action College of Midwifery (B)

3018 West Overland Rd, Boise ID 83705
County: Ada Identification: 667393
Telephone: (208) 258-9334 Carnegie Class: Not Classified
FAX Number: N/A Calendar System: Semester
URL: mercycollegeofmidwifery.edu
Established: 1991 Annual Undergrad Tuition & Fees: N/A
Enrollment: N/A Coed
Affiliation or Control: Independent Non-Profit IRS Status: 501(c)3
Highest Offering: Baccalaureate
Accreditation: **MEAC**

01 Executive Director .... Vicki PENWELL
05 Academic Director .... Kristen BENOIT

New Saint Andrews College (C)

PO Box 9025, Moscow ID 83843-1525
County: Latah Identification: 666166
Unit ID: 440396
Telephone: (208) 882-1566 Carnegie Class: Bac-A&S
FAX Number: (208) 882-4293 Calendar System: Other
URL: www.nsa.edu
Established: 1994 Annual Undergrad Tuition & Fees: $13,550
Enrollment: 221 Coed
Affiliation or Control: Independent Non-Profit IRS Status: 501(c)3
Highest Offering: Master's
Accreditation: **TRACS**

01 President .... Dr. Ben MERKLE
05 Academic Dean .... Dr. Timothy EDWARDS
73 Director Theology MA Program .... Dr. Timothy EDWARDS
53 Dir Classical Christian Studies Pgm .... Mr. Christopher SCHLECT
58 Director MFA Program .... Mr. Nate WILSON
06 Registrar .... Ms. Grace BURNETT
07 Director of Admissions .... Mrs. Brenda SCHLECT
08 Head Librarian .... Mr. Caleb HARRIS
30 Director of Development .... Mr. Derek MONJURE
84 Director of Recruiting .... Ms. Grace HENDRIX

North Idaho College (D)

1000 W Garden Avenue, Coeur d'Alene ID 83814-2199
County: Kootenai FICE Identification: 001623
Unit ID: 142443
Telephone: (208) 769-3300 Carnegie Class: Assoc/HT-Mix Trad/Non
FAX Number: (208) 765-2761 Calendar System: Semester
URL: www.nic.edu
Established: 1933 Annual Undergrad Tuition & Fees (In-District): $4,960
Enrollment: 4,737 Coed
Affiliation or Control: Local IRS Status: 501(c)3
Highest Offering: Associate Degree
Accreditation: **NW**, ADNUR, DH, MAC, MLTAD, PTAA, RAD, SURGT

01 Interim President .... Dr. Michael SEBAALY
05 Vice President for Instruction .... Dr. Lita BURNS
10 VP for Finance & Business Affairs .... Mr. Christopher MARTIN
32 Vice President for Student Services .... Dr. Graydon STANLEY
86 Chief Communications/Govt Rels Ofcr .... Ms. Laura RUMPLER
103 Dean of Career Tech/Workforce Educ .... Vacant
97 Dean of General Studies .... Vacant
76 Dean of Health Prof & Nursing .... Ms. Christy DOYLE
07 Director of Admissions/Registrar .... Ms. Tami HAFT
88 Accreditation Liaison Officer .... Dr. Steve KURTZ
08 Library Director .... Mr. George MCALISTER
13 Chief Information Officer .... Mr. Ken WARDINSKY
15 Chief Human Resources Officer .... Ms. Karen HUBBARD
37 Director of Financial Aid .... Ms. Stephanie HOUSE
121 Dir of Advising/Student Success .... Ms. Ellen CRABTREE
18 Director of Facilities .... Mr. Garry STARK
30 Director of Development .... Ms. Rayelle ANDERSON
35 Director Student Involvement .... Ms. Dodi STILKEY
21 Controller .... Ms. Sarah GARCIA
72 Technology Coordinator .... Mr. Andy FINNEY
29 Alumni Relations Coordinator .... Ms. Pam NOAH
04 Sr Executive Assistant .... Ms. Shannon GOODRICH
106 Director of E-learning .... Dr. Thomas SCOTT
25 Grants Development Manager .... Vacant
41 Athletic Director .... Mr. Bobby LEE
19 Supervisor Security .... Vacant

Northwest Nazarene University (E)

623 S. University Boulevard, Nampa ID 83686-5897
County: Canyon FICE Identification: 001624
Unit ID: 142461
Telephone: (208) 467-8011 Carnegie Class: Masters/L
FAX Number: (208) 467-8099 Calendar System: Semester
URL: www.nnu.edu
Established: 1913 Annual Undergrad Tuition & Fees: $32,780
Enrollment: 2,109 Coed
Affiliation or Control: Church Of The Nazarene IRS Status: 501(c)3
Highest Offering: Doctorate
Accreditation: **NW**, ACBSP, CACREP, CAEPN, NURSE, SW, THEOL

01 President .... Mr. Joel K. PEARSALL
05 Vice Pres Academic Affairs/Dean .... Dr. Brad KURTZ-SHAW
10 Vice Pres Finance & Operations .... Mr. Steve EMERSON
32 Vice President Student Life .... Dr. Carey W. COOK
88 Exec Dir Univ Mission/Ministry .... Dr. Fred C. FULLERTON
111 Vice Pres for External Relations .... Mr. Mark WHEELER
84 Chief Admissions Officer .... Mrs. Stacey BERGGREN
26 Assoc Vice Pres for Marketing .... Mr. Mark CORK
41 Athletic Director .... Ms. Kelli LINDLEY
06 Registrar .... Ms. Ann CRABB
07 Director of Admissions .... Mr. Richard R. VASQUEZ
123 Director of Graduate Admissions .... Ms. Lynette KINGSMORE
124 Chief Retention Officer .... Mr. Dave COVINGTON
121 Dir of Student Success/Advising .... Mrs. Heidi TRACHT
08 Director of the Library .... Ms. Amy RICE
29 Director of Alumni Relations .... Mr. Darl L. BRUNER
51 Dir Center for Professional Devel .... Ms. Christa SANDIDGE
120 Dir of Instructional Design/Tech .... Mrs. Bethany SCHULTZ
42 Dean of the Chapel .... Rev. Dustin METCALF
40 Campus Store Manager .... Ms. Gail D. WALKER
35 Assoc Vice Pres Student Engagement .... Mrs. Karen L. PEARSON
38 Director of Wellness Center .... Dr. Bryon HEMPHILL
21 Controller .... Vacant
35 Director of Community Life .... Mr. Grant T. MILLER
36 Director of Career Center .... Ms. Amanda F. MARBLE
13 Exec Director of Info Technology .... Mr. Todd BAKER
119 IT Security Officer .... Mr. Terrance PATERNOSTER
37 Director of Financial Aid .... Mrs. Ann CRABB
15 Director of Human Resources .... Mrs. Larissa BUNKER
91 Dir of Administrative Computing .... Mr. Brian C. STILLMAN
18 Chief Facilities/Physical Plant .... Mr. Eric JACKSON
04 Administrative Asst to President .... Mrs. Michelle KUYKENDALL
09 Director of Institutional Research .... Dr. Duane SLEMMER
19 Director Security/Safety .... Mr. Scott CHANDLER

University of Idaho (F)

875 Perimeter Drive, Moscow ID 83844
County: Latah FICE Identification: 001626
Unit ID: 142285
Telephone: (208) 885-6111 Carnegie Class: DU-Higher
FAX Number: N/A Calendar System: Semester
URL: www.uidaho.edu
Established: 1889 Annual Undergrad Tuition & Fees (In-State): $8,304
Enrollment: 10,791 Coed
Affiliation or Control: State IRS Status: 501(c)3
Highest Offering: Doctorate
Accreditation: **NW**, ART, CAATE, CAEP, CAEPN, CAPRT, CEA, CIDA, DIETC, IPSY, #JOUR, LAW, LSAR, MUS, NAIT

01 President .... Mr. C. Scott GREEN
05 Provost & Executive VP .... Dr. Torrey LAWRENCE
10 VP Finance and Administration .... Mr. Brian R. FOISY
111 VP University Advancement .... Ms. Mary Kay MCFADDEN
13 VP Information Technology/CIO .... Mr. Dan EWART
46 VP Research & Econ Dev .... Dr. Christopher NOMURA
32 VP Stdnt Affs/Dean of Students .... Dr. Blaine ECKLES
84 Vice Provost Strategic Enroll Mgmt .... Mr. Dean KAHLER
124 Int Vice Prov Academic Initiatives .... Dr. Dean PANTTAJA
20 Vice Provost for Faculty .... Dr. Diane KELLY-RILEY
26 Alumni Relations & AVP Comm .... Ms. Kathy BARNARD
41 Athletic Director .... Ms. Terry GAWLIK
43 General Counsel .... Mr. Jim CRAIG
103 CEO Boise Ctr/Sr Assoc to Pres .... Ms. Chandra ZENNER FORD
88 Special Asst Strategy .... Ms. Toni BROYLES
86 Special Asst State Govt Relations .... Mr. Joe STEGNER
28 Chf Div Ofcr/Exec Dir Tribal Rels .... Dr. Yolanda BISBEE
08 Dean Library Services .... Mr. Ben HUNTER
49 Dean Col of Ltrs/Arts/Social Sci .... Dr. Sean QUINLAN
47 Dean College of Agric/Life Sci .... Dr. Michael PARRELLA
50 Dean College of Business & Econ .... Dr. Marc CHOPIN
53 Int Dean Col of Educ/Hlth/Human Sci .... Dr. Philip SCRUGGS
54 Dean College of Engineering .... Vacant
58 Dean Graduate Studies .... Dr. Jerry MCMURTY
65 Dean College of Natural Resources .... Dr. Michael PARRELLA
61 Dean College of Law .... Ms. Johanna KALB
48 Dean College of Art & Arch .... Dr. Shauna CORRY
81 Dean College of Science .... Dr. Ginger CARNEY
109 Asst VP Auxiliary Services .... Ms. Cami MCCLURE
15 Director of Human Resources .... Ms. Brandi TERWILLIGER
114 AVP Budget/Planning .... Ms. Trina MAHONEY
12 Executive Officer Coeur d'Alene Ctr .... Dr. Charles BUCK
12 Int Exec Officer Idaho Falls Ctr .... Dr. Lee OSTROM
18 Director Facilities .... Mr. Rusty VINEYARD
19 Exec Dir Environment Health/ Safety .... Mr. Samir Shahat ABD EL-FATAH
117 Dir Emergency Mgmt & Security Sys .... Mr. Todd PERRY
108 IR Dir Inst Effectiveness & Accred .... Mr. Wes MCCLINTICK
37 Director Student Financial Aid .... Ms. Randi CROYLE
07 Assistant Vice Provost SEM .... Ms. Bobbi J. GERRY
38 Director Counseling & Testing Ctr .... Dr. Gregory LAMBETH
39 Director University Residences .... Ms. Dee Dee KANIKKEBERG
44 Director Annual Giving .... Ms. Stacy RAUCH
92 Director Honors Program .... Ms. Sandra REINEKE
93 Dir Multicultural Affairs .... Mr. Jesse MARTINEZ
94 Director Women's Center .... Ms. Lysa SALSBURY
40 Mgr VandalStore/Trademark .... Ms. Tricia DURGIN
96 Director Purchasing Services .... Ms. Julia MCILROY
36 Director Career Services .... Mr. Christopher COOK
25 Director Research Admin .... Ms. Deborah SHAVER
121 Exec Dir Student Success Initiative .... Ms. Cynthia CASTRO
06 Registrar .... Ms. Lindsey BROWN
102 Exec Director UI Foundation .... Ms. Joy FISHER
88 Dir Admissions Operations .... Ms. Melissa GOODWIN
22 Dir Civil Rights & Investigation .... Ms. Erin AGIDIUS
104 Director International Services .... Ms. Dana BROLLEY
100 Chief of Staff President's Office .... Ms. Brenda HELBLING

ILLINOIS

Adler University (G)

17 North Dearborn Street, Chicago IL 60602
County: Cook FICE Identification: 020681
Unit ID: 142832
Telephone: (312) 662-4000 Carnegie Class: Spec-4-yr-Other Health
FAX Number: (312) 662-4099 Calendar System: Semester
URL: www.adler.edu
Established: 1952 Annual Graduate Tuition & Fees: N/A
Enrollment: 1,726 Coed
Affiliation or Control: Independent Non-Profit IRS Status: 501(c)3
Highest Offering: Doctorate; No Undergraduates
Accreditation: **HLC**, CACREP, CLPSY, IPSY, MFCD

01 President .... Dr. Raymond E. CROSSMAN
101 Board Secy/Dir Ofc of the Pres .... Ms. Mitzi NORTON
11 Vice President Administration .... Mrs. Jo Beth CUP
05 Vice President Academic Affairs .... Dr. Wendy PASZKIEWICZ
10 Vice President Finance & IT .... Vacant
07 Vice President Admissions .... Mr. Craig HINES
28 VP Diversity & Inclusion .... Ms. Tamara JOHNSON
26 Vice President Communications .... Mr. Mark BRANSON
111 AVP Institutional Advancement .... Ms. Heather SCHUSTER
06 Registrar .... Ms. Sheba JONES
32 Assoc Vice President Student Affs .... Dr. Quincy PADEN
19 Ex Dir Inst Pub Safety/Soc Justice .... Dr. Elena QUINTANA
37 Director Student Financial Aid .... Mr. David NELSON
13 AVP Technology .... Mr. Jomar MCDONALD
12 Exec Dean Vancouver Campus .... Mr. Bradley O'HARA
106 Executive Dean Online Campus .... Dr. Michelle DENNIS
15 Vice Pres People/Culture .... Ms. Dona MCCULLOUGH
29 Director Alumni Relations .... Vacant
04 Administrative Asst to President .... Ms. Elizabeth BLONDEL
18 Chief Facilities/Physical Plant .... Mr. Tom ROHNER
43 Dir Legal Services/General Counsel .... Ms. Julie PROSCIA
08 Director Library Services .... Ms. Ariel ORLOV
102 Dir Foundation/Corporate Relations .... Ms. Ingrid PARKER
108 Dir Institutional Effectivenes .... Ms. Katy SELINKO

Ambria College of Nursing (H)

5210 Trillium Boulevard, Hoffman Estates IL 60192
County: Cook FICE Identification: 041247
Unit ID: 457527
Telephone: (847) 397-0300 Carnegie Class: Spec-4-yr-Other Health
FAX Number: (847) 397-0313 Calendar System: Other
URL: www.ambria.edu
Established: 2006 Annual Undergrad Tuition & Fees: N/A
Enrollment: 229 Coed
Affiliation or Control: Proprietary IRS Status: Proprietary
Highest Offering: Baccalaureate
Accreditation: **ABHES**, ADNUR

01 President .... Jon OLIVEROS
66 Director of Nursing Education .... Sharon ORTEGA

American Academy of Art College (A)

332 S Michigan Avenue, Chicago IL 60604-4302
County: Cook   FICE Identification: 001628
Unit ID: 142887
Telephone: (312) 461-0600   Carnegie Class: Spec-4-yr-Arts
FAX Number: (312) 294-9570   Calendar System: Semester
URL: www.aaart.edu
Established: 1923   Annual Undergrad Tuition & Fees: $35,270
Enrollment: 169   Coed
Affiliation or Control: Independent Non-Profit   IRS Status: 501(c)3
Highest Offering: Baccalaureate
Accreditation: HLC

01 President .... Mr. Richard H. OTTO
05 Academic Dean .... Mr. Duncan WEBB
06 Registrar .... Ms. Marcia R. THOMAS
36 Career Services Coordinator .... Ms. Lindsay SANDBOTHE
37 Financial Aid Director .... Ms. Ione FITZGERALD
07 Director of Admissions .... Mr. Stuart ROSENBLOOM

American Islamic College (B)

640 W. Irving Park Rd, Chicago IL 60613
County: Cook   Identification: 667378
Unit ID: 142957
Telephone: (773) 281-4700   Carnegie Class: Not Classified
FAX Number: N/A   Calendar System: Semester
URL: www.aicusa.edu
Established: 1981   Annual Undergrad Tuition & Fees: $7,600
Enrollment: 16   Coed
Affiliation or Control: Independent Non-Profit   IRS Status: 501(c)3
Highest Offering: Master's
Accreditation: @HLC

01 President .... Daoud CASEWIT

Augustana College (C)

639 38th Street, Rock Island IL 61201-2296
County: Rock Island   FICE Identification: 001633
Unit ID: 143084
Telephone: (309) 794-7000   Carnegie Class: Bac-A&S
FAX Number: (309) 794-7422   Calendar System: 4/1/4
URL: www.augustana.edu
Established: 1860   Annual Undergrad Tuition & Fees: $45,136
Enrollment: 2,389   Coed
Affiliation or Control: Evangelical Lutheran Church In America
IRS Status: 501(c)3
Highest Offering: Baccalaureate
Accreditation: HLC, MUS, @SP

01 President .... Mr. Steven C. BAHLS
05 Provost and Dean of the College .. Dr. Wendy HILTON-MORROW
10 Vice Pres of Finance and Admin .... Mr. Kirk D. ANDERSON
30 Executive VP External Relations .... Mr. W. Kent BARNDS
32 VP/Dean of Student Life .... Dr. Wesley BROOKS
28 VP Diversity/Equity and Inclusion .... Dr. Monica SMITH
20 Associate Dean of the College .... Dr. Michael EGAN
20 Associate Dean of the College .... Dr. Kristin DOUGLAS
20 Associate Dean of the College .... Dr. Jessica SCHULTZ
42 Chaplain .... Rev. Melinda PUPILLO
06 College Registrar .... Ms. Liesl A. FOWLER
09 Asst Dean/Director Inst Research .... Dr. Tsooane MOLAPO
08 Director of the Library .... Dr. Chris SCHAFER
36 Associate VP Careers & Prof Devel .... Ms. Laura KESTNER-RICKETTS
13 Director of ITS .... Mr. Chris VAUGHAN
37 Director of Student Financial Aid .... Mr. John CAGE
96 Dir Financial Plng & Procurement .... Mr. Malhar SAHEED
19 Chief of Public Safety .... Mr. Thomas M. PHILLIS
41 Director of Athletics .... Mr. Mike ZAPOLSKI
15 Director Human Resources .... Mr. Brandon TIDWELL
18 Director Facilities Services .... Mr. Robert LANZEROTTI
38 Director Student Counseling .... Mr. William IAVARONE
35 Assistant Dean of Student Life .... Ms. Laura L. SCHNACK
26 Assistant VP of Comm & Marketing .... Ms. Keri RURSCH
29 Director Alumni/Parent Relations .... Ms. Kelly NOACK
07 Executive Director of Admissions .... Ms. Emma ADEBAYO
04 Executive Assistant to President .... Ms. Mary KOSKI
104 Dir Intl Student & Scholar Svcs .... Ms. Xong Sony YANG
43 Dir Legal Services/General Counsel .... Ms. Sheri L. CURRAN
100 Chief of Staff .... Mr. Kai SWANSON
102 Dir Foundation/Corporate Relations .... Ms. Lori RODERICK
39 Director of Residential Life .... Mr. Christopher BEYER
105 Director Web Services & News Media .... Ms. Leslie M. DUPREE
50 Dean of Business .... Dr. Amanda BAUGOUS
53 Dean of Education .... Dr. Michael SCARLETT
54 Dean of Engineering .... Dr. Nathan FRANK
86 Director Government Relations .... Mr. Kai SWANSON
44 Director Annual Giving .... Ms. Erin WILLIAMS

Aurora University (D)

347 S Gladstone Avenue, Aurora IL 60506-4892
County: Kane   FICE Identification: 001634
Unit ID: 143118
Telephone: (630) 892-6431   Carnegie Class: DU-Mod
FAX Number: (630) 844-5463   Calendar System: Semester
URL: www.aurora.edu
Established: 1893   Annual Undergrad Tuition & Fees: $25,600
Enrollment: 6,265   Coed
Affiliation or Control: Independent Non-Profit   IRS Status: 501(c)3
Highest Offering: Doctorate
Accreditation: HLC, CAATE, NURSE, SW

01 President .... Dr. Rebecca L. SHERRICK
03 Executive Vice President .... Dr. Lora DE LACEY
05 Vice President for Academic Affairs .... Vacant
10 Vice President for Finance .... Ms. Sharon MAXWELL
18 Chief Operating Officer .... Mr. Jeff KING
121 Vice President for Student Success .... Dr. Jennifer BUCKLEY
84 Vice President for Enrollment .... Mr. James LANCASTER
30 Vice President for Development .... Ms. Meg HOWES
26 VP for Marketing and Communications .... Ms. Deb MAUE
31 Vice President Community Relations .... Ms. Sarah R. RUSSE
29 VP for Alumni Relations .... Ms. Teri TOMASZKIEWICZ
15 Vice President of Human Resources .... Vacant
32 Vice President for Student Life .... Dr. Amy GRAY
41 Vice President for Athletics .... Mr. James HAMAD
37 Dean of Student Financial Services .... Ms. Heather L. GRANART
123 Assistant VP for Adult and Graduate .... Mr. Jason HARMON
07 Associate VP for Enrollment .... Ms. Emily MORALES
21 Assistant VP for Finance .... Mr. William SANDERS
06 Registrar .... Ms. Melody NABORS
08 Director University Library .... Ms. Kathy CLARK
19 Chief of Police .... Mr. John MCIVOR
38 Director of Counseling Center .... Dr. Marcie WISEMAN
66 Dean of Sch of Nursing/Allied Hlth .... Dr. Pamela TAYLOR
70 Dean School of Social Work .... Ms. Brenda BARNWELL
88 Faculty Development Liaison .... Dr. Julie HIPP
49 Dean College of Art and Sciences .... Dr. Karol DEAN
53 Dean School of Educ/Human Perf .... Dr. Jennifer BUCKLEY
50 Dean Dunham Sch Bus/Public Policy .... Dr. Toby ARQUETTE
106 Dean of Online Enroll/Cont Educ .... Dr. Donna LILJEGREN
20 Dean Academic Administration .... Dr. Mary TARLING
04 Executive Assistant to President .... Ms. Becca FLAMINIO
09 Director of University Analytics .... Ms. Katie THARP
39 Dean of Student Life .... Ms. Ann ALMASI-BUSH

Benedictine University (E)

5700 College Road, Lisle IL 60532-0900
County: DuPage   FICE Identification: 001767
Unit ID: 145619
Telephone: (630) 829-6000   Carnegie Class: DU-Mod
FAX Number: N/A   Calendar System: Semester
URL: www.ben.edu
Established: 1887   Annual Undergrad Tuition & Fees: $34,290
Enrollment: 3,779   Coed
Affiliation or Control: Roman Catholic   IRS Status: 501(c)3
Highest Offering: Doctorate
Accreditation: HLC, DIETD, DIETI, NURSE, PH

01 President .... Mr. Charles GREGORY
05 Provost/Chief Academic Officer .... Dr. Kenneth F. NEWBOLD, JR.
10 Int Chief Financial Officer .... Mr. John SCHADE
32 Dean of Students .... Mr. Marco MASINI
20 Assoc Provost .... Dr. Cheryl HEINZ
42 Director University Ministry .... Ms. Carrie ANKENY
06 Registrar .... Mr. Jason HEIDENFELDER
08 Int Director Library Services .... Ms. Lou Ann DEGREVE
37 Director Financial Aid .... Mr. Adrian GONZALEZ
09 Director of Institutional Research .... Dr. Amy SHIN
36 Director Career Development .... Dr. Julie COSIMO
23 Director Health Services .... Ms. Pamela DEELY
50 Dean College of Business .... Dr. Darrell RADSON
81 Dean College of Science/Health .... Dr. Elizabeth RITT
49 Dean College of Lib Arts .... Dr. Joseph INCANDELA
51 Pgm Dir Adult/Profess Bus Pgms .... Ms. Larissa ADAMIEC
88 Chief Mission Officer .... Dr. Peter HUFF
124 Chief Enroll/Retention Officer .... Ms. Karen CAMPANA
100 Chief of Staff .... Ms. Patricia ARIANO
11 Chief Operations Officer .... Mr. Chad TREISCH
35 Dir Student Activities/Recreation .... Mr. Harold WATSON
13 Chief Information Officer .... Mr. Timothy HOPKINS
07 Director of Admissions .... Mr. Matthew JONES
04 Executive Asst to the President .... Ms. Deborah A. SUTLIFF
29 Director Alumni Relations .... Mr. Jon-Pierre BRADLEY
41 Director of Athletics .... Mr. Paul NELSON
43 Chief Compliance Ofcr/Legal Counsel .... Ms. Nancy STOECKER
18 Dir Facilities Mgmt/Planning .... Mr. Bryan GOODWIN
86 Assoc Compliance Officer .... Mr. Kevin RAPPEL

Bexley Seabury (F)

1407 E 60th St, Chicago IL 60637
County: Cook   FICE Identification: 037473
Unit ID: 443702
Telephone: (773) 380-6780   Carnegie Class: Spec-4-yr-Faith
FAX Number: (773) 380-6788   Calendar System: Semester
URL: www.bexleyseabury.edu
Established: 1824   Annual Graduate Tuition & Fees: N/A
Enrollment: 68   Coed
Affiliation or Control: Protestant Episcopal   IRS Status: 501(c)3
Highest Offering: Doctorate; No Undergraduates
Accreditation: THEOL

01 President .... RevDr. Micah JACKSON
05 Academic Dean .... Mr. Jason FOUT
10 Chief Financial Officer .... Mr. Curt SHORT
07 Director of Admissions .... Mr. Jaime BRICENO

Black Hawk College (G)

6600 34th Avenue, Moline IL 61265-5899
County: Rock Island   FICE Identification: 001638
Unit ID: 143279
Telephone: (309) 796-5000   Carnegie Class: Assoc/MT-VT-High Non
FAX Number: (309) 792-5976   Calendar System: Semester
URL: www.bhc.edu
Established: 1946   Annual Undergrad Tuition & Fees (In-District): $7,500
Enrollment: 3,743   Coed
Affiliation or Control: Local   IRS Status: 501(c)3
Highest Offering: Associate Degree
Accreditation: HLC, ADNUR, EMT, PTAA, SURGT

01 President .... Mr. Tim WYNES
05 VP of Instruction .... Dr. Amy MAXEINER
10 VP Finance/Admin & Board Treasurer .... Mr. Steve FROMMELT
20 Executive Dean of East Campus .... Dr. Jeffry HAWES
15 Director of Human Resources .... Ms. Stacey CARY
19 Chief of Police .... Mr. Shawn CISNA
09 Director Plng & Inst Effectiveness .... Ms. Kathy MALCOLM
26 Director Marketing/Public Relations .... Mr. John MEINEKE
13 Co-CIO/IT Systems Manager .... Mr. Ryan WHITE
13 Co-CIO/Manager of Admin Systems .... Ms. Sandy COX
102 Exec Dir BHC Foundation QC Campus .Ms. Maureen DICKINSON
51 Dean Adult/Continuing Educ .... Ms. Glenda NICKE
81 Academic Dean .... Mr. Ken NICKELS
04 Executive Asst to the President .... Ms. Heather BENNETT
36 Director Career Services Center .... Dr. Bruce STOREY
37 Director of Financial Aid .... Vacant
08 Librarian .... Ms. Ashtin TRIMBLE
55 Director Adult Education .... Ms. Bianca PERKINS
06 Registrar/Dean Enrollment Mgmt .... Ms. Heather BJORGAN
40 Bookstore Manager Quad Cities .... Ms. Aimee MUHLEMAN
96 Purchasing Manager .... Mr. Mike MELEG
50 Dept Chair Business & Technology .... Ms. Carrie DELCOURT
79 Dept Chair Human/Languages/Journal .... Mr. Bill DESMOND
81 Dept Chair Mathematics/Comp Science .... Ms. Connie MCLEAN
54 Dept Chair Natural Science/Engrng .... Mr. Brian GLASER
83 Dept Chair Social Sciences .... Mr. Mark ESPOSITO
47 Department Chair Agriculture .... Dr. Jeffrey HAWES
66 Dept Chair Nursing .... Ms. Trudy STARR
76 Dept Chair Allied Health/HPE .... Ms. Dianne ABELS
38 Dept Chair Counseling .... Ms. Wendy BOCK
62 Dept Chair Lrg Resource Center .... Vacant
53 Dept Chair Psych/Sociology/Educ .... Dr. Traci DAVIS
72 Dept Chair Career Technologies .... Ms. Jamie HILL
18 Chief Facilities/Physical Plant .... Mr. Bob MCCHURCH

Black Hawk College East Campus (H)

26230 Black Hawk Road, Galva IL 61434
Telephone: (309) 854-1700   Identification: 770069
Accreditation: &HLC

Blackburn College (I)

700 College Avenue, Carlinville IL 62626-1498
County: Macoupin   FICE Identification: 001639
Unit ID: 143288
Telephone: (217) 854-3231   Carnegie Class: Bac-A&S
FAX Number: (217) 854-5700   Calendar System: Semester
URL: www.blackburn.edu
Established: 1837   Annual Undergrad Tuition & Fees: $24,950
Enrollment: 516   Coed
Affiliation or Control: Presbyterian Church (U.S.A.)   IRS Status: 501(c)3
Highest Offering: Baccalaureate
Accreditation: HLC

01 President .... Dr. Mark L. BIERMANN
05 Provost .... Dr. Carla MCCAIN
10 Vice Pres Administration & Finance .... Vacant
111 VP for Institutional Advancement .... Ms. Lauren DODGE
32 VP/Dean of Student Affairs .... Vacant
101 Exec Asst to Pres/Sec Bd Trustees .... Mrs. Shawna POE
102 Sr Dir of Devel/Foundation Rels .... Ms. Sarah KOPLINSKI
29 Exec Dir Advance/Alumni Relations .... Ms. Alisha KAPP
37 Director of Financial Aid .... Mrs. Alisha KAPP
38 Director Counseling Services .... Mr. Tim MORENZ
06 College Registrar .... Mrs. Dianna RUYLE
41 Interim Athletic Director .... Mr. Rob STEINKUEHLER
26 Dir of Marketing/Public Relations .... Mr. Kyle LOWDEN
09 Director of Institutional Research .... Dr. Kristi NELMS
21 Controller .... Ms. Deana ROGERS
44 Exec Dir for Annual Giving .... Ms. Teresa KIRK
84 Enrollment Services Administrator .... Mrs. Kathy RUITER
13 Chief Info Technology Officer (CIO) .... Mr. Jason CLONINGER
88 Dean of Work .... Mrs. Angie MORENZ

Blessing-Rieman College of Nursing & Health Sciences (J)

3609 North Marx Drive, Quincy IL 62305-7005
County: Adams   FICE Identification: 006214
Unit ID: 143297
Telephone: (217) 228-5520   Carnegie Class: Spec-4-yr-Other Health
FAX Number: (217) 223-4661   Calendar System: Semester
URL: www.brcn.edu
Established: 1891   Annual Undergrad Tuition & Fees: N/A
Enrollment: 177   Coed
Affiliation or Control: Independent Non-Profit   IRS Status: 501(c)3
Highest Offering: Master's

Accreditation: HLC, CAHIIM, COARC, MLTAD, NURSE, RAD

01 President/CEO .... Dr. Brenda BESHEARS
05 Academic Dean .... Dr. Jan AKRIGHT
84 Dean of Enroll Mgmt/Business Mgr .... Ms. Jenna CRABTREE
06 Registrar .... Ms. Rachel CRAMSEY

Bradley University (A)

1501 W Bradley Avenue, Peoria IL 61625-0001
County: Peoria FICE Identification: 001641
Unit ID: 143358
Telephone: (309) 676-7611 Carnegie Class: Masters/L
FAX Number: N/A Calendar System: Semester
URL: www.bradley.edu
Established: 1897 Annual Undergrad Tuition & Fees: $35,480
Enrollment: 5,855 Coed
Affiliation or Control: Independent Non-Profit IRS Status: 501(c)3
Highest Offering: Doctorate
Accreditation: HLC, ART, CACREP, CONST, DIETC, DIETD, DIETI, MUS, NURSE, PTA, SW, THEA

01 President .... Mr. Stephen STANDIFIRD
05 Provost/Vice Pres Academic Affs .... Dr. Walter R. ZAKAHI
32 Vice President Student Affairs .... Mr. Nathan THOMAS
84 VP Enrollment Management .... Mr. Justin BALL
111 Vice President Advancement .... Ms. Erin GENOVESE
43 Vice Pres Legal Affairs/Gen Counsel .... Ms. Erin KASTBERG
41 VP for Intercollegiate Athletics .... Dr. Chris REYNOLDS
10 Chief Financial Officer .... Ms. Sheryl COX
19 Chief of Campus Police .... Mr. Brian JOSCHKO
20 Interim Associate Provost .... Dr. Jobie SKAGGS
58 Assoc Provost/Dean Res/Grad School .... Dr. Jeffrey BAKKEN
20 Assistant to the Provost .... Mrs. Tracy ZUERCHER
114 Assistant VP Budgeting and Planning .... Mr. Demetrius L. CARMICHAEL
50 Interim Dean Foster Col Business .... Dr. Matt O'BRIEN
57 Dean Slane Col Commun/Fine Arts .... Dr. Jeffrey H. HUBERMAN
53 Dean Educ & Health Sciences .... Dr. Jessica CLARK
54 Int Dean Engineering & Technology .... Dr. Julie REYER
49 Interim Dean Liberal Arts/Sciences ... Dr. Kelly MCCONNAUGHAY
106 Associate Dean Distance Education .... Dr. Molly CLUSKEY
08 Interim Exec Director of Library .... Mr. Todd SPIRES
39 Dir Ctr Residential Living/Ldrshp .... Mr. Ryan BAIR
36 Exec Dir Smith Career Center .... Mr. Jon NEIDY
29 Director of Alumni Relations .... Ms. Tory JENNETTEN
51 Executive Director Continuing Educ .... Ms. Janet LANGE
26 Exec Dir Public Relations .... Ms. Renee CHARLES
06 Registrar .... Mr. Andreas KINDLER
37 Director Financial Aid .... Ms. Debra JACKSON
15 Director of Human Resources .... Ms. Crystal ELLIOTT
18 Director Facilities Management .... Mr. Larry MCGUIRE
23 Medical Director Health Services .... Dr. Jessica HIGGS
13 Chief Information Officer .... Mr. Zach GORMAN
27 Public Relations Specialist .... Ms. Haley KRUS
78 Director Springer Center .... Mrs. Dawn KOELTZOW
87 Dir Summer/Interim Sessions .... Ms. Janet LANGE
28 Exec Dir Diversity/Inclusion .... Mr. Norris CHASE
92 Director of Honors Program .... Dr. Kyle DZAPO
94 Dir of Women's Studies & Gender .... Dr. Amy SCOTT
108 Dir of Institutional Effectiveness .... Ms. Jennifer G. BURGE
40 Manager Bookstore .... Mr. Paul KROENKE
88 Dir of Health Prof Advising Ctr .... Dr. Valerie BENNETT
61 Dir Center for Legal Studies .... Ms. Jerelyn MAHER
07 Asst Dir Admissions .... Mr. Joshua JONES
104 Director Study Abroad .... Dr. Christine BLOUCH

Carl Sandburg College (B)

2400 Tom L. Wilson Boulevard, Galesburg IL 61401-9576
County: Knox FICE Identification: 007265
Unit ID: 143613
Telephone: (309) 344-2518 Carnegie Class: Assoc/MT-VT-High Non
FAX Number: (309) 344-1395 Calendar System: Semester
URL: www.sandburg.edu
Established: 1966 Annual Undergrad Tuition & Fees: $7,190
Enrollment: 1,755 Coed
Affiliation or Control: Independent Non-Profit IRS Status: 501(c)3
Highest Offering: Associate Degree
Accreditation: HLC, ADNUR, DH, EMT, FUSER, MAC, PNUR

01 President .... Dr. Seamus REILLY
37 Director Financial Aid .... Ms. Lisa HANSON
07 Director of Recruitment .... Ms. Zoe KUDLA-POLAY
41 Athletic Director .... Mr. Jerry THOR
06 Director of Admissions & Records .... Mr. Rick EDDY
19 Director of Public Safety .... Mr. Kipton CANFIELD
16 Director of Human Resources .... Ms. Gina KRUPPS
45 Dean of Institutional Planning .... Ms. Michelle JOHNSON
103 Dean Career/Technical Education .... Ms. Ellen BURNS
88 Director of Corporate & Leisure .... Vacant
12 Director of Branch Campus .... Dr. Ellen HENDERSON-GASSER
81 Assoc Dean Math/Natural Sciences ..... Ms. Marjorie SMOLENSKY
05 VP of Academic Services .... Ms. Carrie HAWKINSON
20 Assoc VP Academic/Student Svcs/Plng .... Vacant
79 Assoc Dean Humanities/Fine Arts .... Mr. James HUTCHINGS
50 Assoc Dean Social & Business Sci .... Ms. Lara ROEMER
75 Assoc Dean CTHE .... Vacant
76 Dean of Health Professions .... Ms. Kristina GRAY
04 Assistant to President & Board .... Ms. Lindsey HUBER
32 VP of Student Services .... Mr. Steve NORTON
10 Chief Financial Officer/Treasurer .... Mr. Cory GALL
15 Dean HR/Institutional Effectiveness .... Vacant

26 Director Marketing/Public Relations .... Ms. Brittany GRIMES
111 Director of Advancement .... Ms. Emily WEBEL
13 Director of Technology Services .... Mr. Rob STEVENS
84 Dean of Student Success .... Ms. Autumn SCOTT
121 Director of TRIO SSS .... Ms. Amy BURFORD
121 Director TRIO Upward Bound .... Vacant
121 Director TRIO UB Math Science .... Ms. Stephanie WOODARD

Carl Sandburg College The Branch Campus (C)

305 Sandburg Drive, Carthage IL 62321
Telephone: (217) 357-3129 Identification: 770071
Accreditation: &HLC

Catholic Theological Union (D)

5416 S Cornell Avenue, Chicago IL 60615-5698
County: Cook FICE Identification: 009232
Unit ID: 143659
Telephone: (773) 371-5400 Carnegie Class: Spec-4-yr-Faith
FAX Number: (773) 324-8490 Calendar System: Semester
URL: www.ctu.edu
Established: 1968 Annual Graduate Tuition & Fees: N/A
Enrollment: 227 Coed
Affiliation or Control: Roman Catholic IRS Status: 501(c)3
Highest Offering: Doctorate; No Undergraduates
Accreditation: THEOL

01 President .... Sr. Barbara E. REID, OP
05 Int Vice President/Academic Dean .... Rev. Roger SCHROEDER, SVD
10 Vice Pres Administration & Finance .... Mr. Kevin DOHERTY
111 Vice Pres Institutional Advancement .... Ms. Colleen KENNEDY
30 Director of Development .... Ms. Rachel KUHN
08 Director of the Library .... Ms. Kristine VELDHEER
06 Registrar .... Mrs. Maria De Jesus LEMUS
07 Asst Director Admissions .... Ms. Sarai MARTINEZ
13 Director of Information Technology .... Ms. Latisha AIKONS
04 Assistant to the President .... Sr. Pam PAULOSKI, SP
84 Director Enrollment Management ..... Mrs. Ellen ROMER-NIEMIEC
104 Director Study Abroad .... Rev. Ferdinand OKORIE
106 Director Online Educ/E-learning .... Mr. Richard MAUNEY
18 Director Facilities .... Mr. Marty FITZGERALD
26 Communications Manager .... Ms. Kellene URBANIAK
29 Director Alumni Affairs .... Vacant
32 Manager of Events/Student Services .... Vacant
15 Chief Human Resources Officer .... Ms. Carmen SALAS
36 Director Student Placement .... Ms. Christine HENDERSON

*Chamberlain University-Administrative Office (E)

500 Monroe Street, Suite 28, Chicago IL 60661
County: DuPage Identification: 667149
Telephone: (703) 416-7300 Carnegie Class: N/A
FAX Number: (703) 416-7490
URL: www.chamberlain.edu

01 President .... Dr. Karen COX
11 VP Campus Operations .... Dr. Patrick ROMBALSKI
05 Provost .... Dr. Carla SANDERSON
84 VP Enrollment Management .... Scott MURPHY
32 VP Student Services .... June MARLOWE
06 University Registrar .... Abbey MCELLIGOTT
09 Assoc Prov Inst Effect/Accred/Rsrch .... Dr. Linda HOLLINGER-SMITH

*Chamberlain University-Addison (F)

1221 N. Swift Road, Addison IL 60101
County: DuPage FICE Identification: 006385
Unit ID: 454227
Telephone: (630) 953-3660 Carnegie Class: Spec-4-yr-Other Health
FAX Number: (630) 628-1154 Calendar System: Semester
URL: www.chamberlain.edu/addison
Established: 1889 Annual Undergrad Tuition & Fees: $20,381
Enrollment: 29,481 Coed
Affiliation or Control: Proprietary IRS Status: Proprietary
Highest Offering: Doctorate
Accreditation: HLC, NURSE, @SW

02 Campus President .... Dr. Jan SNOW
05 Dean Academic Affairs .... Crystal PAUNAN
32 Director Student Services .... Lisa PETSCHENKO
07 Director Admissions .... Roz CASTRO

† Master's and Doctorate programs are only offered online.

**Chamberlain University-Chicago* (G)

3300 North Campbell Avenue, Chicago IL 60618
Telephone: (773) 961-3000 Identification: 770495
Accreditation: &HLC, NURSE

**Chamberlain University-Tinley Park* (H)

18624 West Creek Drive, Tinley Park IL 60477
Telephone: (708) 560-2000 Identification: 770496
Accreditation: &HLC, NURSE

Chicago College of Oriental Medicine (I)

180 N. Michigan Ave, Ste 1919, Chicago IL 60601
County: Cook Identification: 667406
Telephone: (312) 368-0900 Carnegie Class: Not Classified
FAX Number: (312) 368-1080 Calendar System: Trimester
URL: www.ccoom.org
Established: Annual Graduate Tuition & Fees: N/A
Enrollment: N/A Coed
Affiliation or Control: Proprietary IRS Status: Proprietary
Highest Offering: Master's; No Undergraduates
Accreditation: @ACUP

01 Chancellor .... Dr. Yong Gao WONG

Chicago School of Professional Psychology-Chicago (J)

325 N Wells Street, Chicago IL 60654-8158
Telephone: (312) 329-6600 Identification: 770349
Accreditation: &WC, ABAI, CACREP, CLPSY, MPCAC, SCPSY

† Branch campus of Chicago School of Professional Psychology Los Angeles Campus, Los Angeles, CA

Chicago State University (K)

9501 S King Drive, Chicago IL 60628-1598
County: Cook FICE Identification: 001694
Unit ID: 144005
Telephone: (773) 995-2000 Carnegie Class: Masters/L
FAX Number: (773) 995-2563 Calendar System: Semester
URL: www.csu.edu
Established: 1867 Annual Undergrad Tuition & Fees (In-State): $11,204
Enrollment: 2,644 Coed
Affiliation or Control: State IRS Status: 501(c)3
Highest Offering: Doctorate
Accreditation: HLC, ACBSP, ART, CACREP, CAHIIM, CAPRT, LIB, MUS, NUR, OT, #PHAR, SW

01 President .... Ms. Zaldwaynaka (Z) SCOTT
05 Int Provost/SVP Academic Affairs .... Dr. Leslie A. ROUNDTREE
10 Vice President/CFO .... Mr. Craig DUETSCH
114 Executive Director Budget/Resource ... Mrs. Arrileen PATAWARAN
13 Interim Chief Information Officer .... Mr. Magdi ODEH
84 Vice Pres of Enrollment Management .... Dr. Andrea WELCH
11 Int VP Administrative Services .... Mr. Michael HOLMES
09 Dir Inst Effectiveness & Research .... Dr. Jane STOUT
32 Dean of Student Affairs & FYE .... Vacant
49 Dean Col of Arts & Sciences .... Dr. LeRoy JONES, II
53 Dean Col of Education .... Dr. Carolyn THEARD-GRIGGS
67 Dean College of Pharmacy .... Dr. Matthew FETE
76 Interim Dean Col of Health Sciences .... Dr. Gregory PAVEZA
50 Dean College of Business .... Mr. Derrick K. COLLINS
08 Dean of Library/Instruct Services .... Dr. Richard DARGA
51 Int Dean Cont Educ Nontrad Pgms .... Ms. Nelly MAYNARD
92 Dean Honors College .... Dr. Steven ROWE
06 Registrar .... Mr. Caleb WESTBERG
37 Director of Financial Aid .... Ms. Rhonda SMITH
07 Director of Admissions/Recruitment .... Dr. Carlos GOODEN
26 VP of External Affairs .... Ms. Erin STEVA
15 Asst Director Talent Relation .... Mrs. Abbie MILES
36 Director of Career Development ...... Mrs. LaCael PALMER-PRATT
18 Director Facilities/Physical Plant .... Mr. Joseph SIMONETTI
20 Assoc Provost Academic Affairs .... Dr. Bernard ROWAN
38 Director Counseling Center .... Dr. Shenay BRIDGES-CARTER
20 Assoc Provost Academic Innov Strat .... Dr. Mary DANIELS
25 Int Assoc VP of Sponsored Programs .... Dr. David KANIS
43 Assoc VP Gen Counsel/Ethics Officer .... Ms. Robin HAWKINS
19 Chief of Police .... Mr. Eddie WELCH
39 Director Student Housing .... Mr. Robert KING
41 Athletic Director .... Mr. Elliot CHARLES
43 Interim General Counsel .... Mr. Walter PRYOR
100 Chief of Staff .... Mr. Kim H. TRAN
88 Deputy Chief of Staff .... Ms. Aspen CLEMONS
04 Special Asst to the President .... Mrs. Jimell BYRD-RENO

Chicago Theological Seminary (L)

1407 East 60th Street, Chicago IL 60637-1284
County: Cook FICE Identification: 001661
Unit ID: 144014
Telephone: (773) 896-2400 Carnegie Class: Spec-4-yr-Faith
FAX Number: (773) 643-1284 Calendar System: Semester
URL: www.ctschicago.edu
Established: 1855 Annual Graduate Tuition & Fees: N/A
Enrollment: 294 Coed
Affiliation or Control: United Church Of Christ IRS Status: 501(c)3
Highest Offering: Doctorate; No Undergraduates
Accreditation: HLC, THEOL

01 President .... Rev. Stephen G. RAY, JR.
05 VP Academic Affairs/Academic Dean . Dr. Stephanie B. CROWDER
10 Vice President for Finance & Admin .... Ms. Karen WALKER
111 Int Vice Pres for Advancement .... Mr. Chad R. SCHWICKERATH
32 VP Student Svcs/Dean of Students .... Mr. Jason FREY
06 Registrar .... Ms. Tina SHELTON
08 Director of the Lapp Learning Ctr .. Ms. Jasmine ABOU-EL-KHEIR
07 Director Recruitment/Admission .... Mr. Jason FREY
04 Assistant to the President .... Ms. Kim M. JOHNSON

26 Director of Communications Mr. Steven MCFARLAND
18 Director of Facilities Ms. Shauna WARREN

*City Colleges of Chicago (A)

180 N. Wabash, Suite 200, Chicago IL 60601

County: Cook FICE Identification: 001647
Unit ID: 144500
Telephone: (312) 553-2500 Carnegie Class: N/A
FAX Number: (312) 553-2699
URL: www.ccc.edu

01 Chancellor Mr. Juan SALGADO
05 Provost Dr. Mark POTTER
10 Chief Financial Officer Ms. Maribel RODRIGUEZ
13 Chief Information Officer Mr. Jerrold MARTIN
43 General Counsel Mr. Karla GOWEN
15 Chief Talent Officer Ms. Carol DUNNING
100 Chief of Staff and Strategy Ms. Veronica HERRERO

*City Colleges of Chicago Harold Washington College (B)

30 E Lake Street, Chicago IL 60601-2449

County: Cook FICE Identification: 001652
Unit ID: 144209
Telephone: (312) 553-5600 Carnegie Class: Assoc/HT-Mix Trad/Non
FAX Number: (312) 553-5964 Calendar System: Semester
URL: www.ccc.edu/hwc
Established: 1962 Annual Undergrad Tuition & Fees (In-District): $11,520
Enrollment: 6,479 Coed
Affiliation or Control: State/Local IRS Status: 501(c)3
Highest Offering: Associate Degree
Accreditation: HLC, ACBSP, NAEYC

02 President Dr. Daniel LOPEZ
05 Vice Pres Academic/Student Affairs Dr. Shiang-Kwei WANG
10 Vice Pres Finance/Operations Mr. Kent LUSK
37 Director of Financial Aid Ms. Tenika BURNS
18 Chief Engineer Mr. Jeremy GONZALEZ
36 Executive Director COEB Ms. Dawn FUENTES-ALANIS
08 Librarian Mr. John KIERALDO
15 HR Business Partner Mr. Thomas LINDSAY
20 Dean of Instruction Mr. Asif WILSON
13 Director Information Technology Mr. Brandon HOPKINS
32 Dean of Student Services Ms. Jackie WERNER
35 Assoc Dean of Student Services Ms. Patricia CUEVAS
46 Asst Director Research/Planning Ms. Sandy VUE
06 Registrar Mr. Nicholas AMBROSE
19 Director of Security Ms. Bernessa TATE
09 Director Strategy/Initiatives Vacant
84 Dean of Enrollment Vacant

*City Colleges of Chicago Harry S Truman College (C)

1145 W Wilson Avenue, Chicago IL 60640-5691

County: Cook FICE Identification: 001648
Unit ID: 144184
Telephone: (773) 907-4700 Carnegie Class: Assoc/MT-VT-High Non
FAX Number: (773) 907-4464 Calendar System: Semester
URL: www.trumancollege.edu
Established: 1956 Annual Undergrad Tuition & Fees (In-District): $11,520
Enrollment: 5,186 Coed
Affiliation or Control: State/Local IRS Status: 501(c)3
Highest Offering: Associate Degree
Accreditation: HLC, NAEYC

02 President Dr. Shawn L. JACKSON
05 VP Academic & Student Affairs Dr. Kate CONNOR
20 Dean of Instruction Dr. Susan MARCUS
06 Registrar Ms. My Linh TRAN
32 Dean of Student Services Ms. Mary Ann SOLEY
35 Associate Dean of Student Services Ms. Chanel BISHOP
56 Dean of Adult Education Dr. Lee M. JACKSON
20 Associate Dean of Instruction Ms. Gail GORDON-ALLEN
20 Associate Dean of Instruction Ms. Laura CHEATHAM
10 VP of Finance & Operations Mr. Thomas DUNHAM
19 Director of Security Mr. Andres DURBAK
37 Director of Financial Aid Ms. Maria PINTO
15 Human Resource Business Partner Mr. Michael ROBERTS
13 Interim Director of Info Technology Mr. David YEH
21 Business Manager Ms. Nina CAO
53 Dean of Education & Teacher Pgms Ms. Hollie WAREJAYE
88 Dir of Student Development Projects Ms. Aubrey SCHEFFEY
103 Director of Workforce Development Ms. Danielle WALLINGTON-HARRIS
18 Manager of Operations & Purchasing Mr. Charles TALBERT
35 Associate Dean of Student Services Ms. Allison ZURES
88 Associate Dean of Adult Education Mr. Steven TEREF
36 Dir of Career Planning & Placement Ms. Meredith GALLO-MURPHY
41 Director Intercollegiate Athletics Ms. Jasmine GREEN
22 Director of Disability Access Ctr Ms. Lauren DALEY
88 Director Teaching & Learning Pgms Ms. Leslie LAYMAN
04 Assistant to the President Ms. Zsa POPIELARCZYK
121 Director Student Support Svcs TRIO Mr. Anthony KWIATKOWSKI
84 Director of Enrollment Management Mr. Kisalan GLOVER
51 Dean of Career & Cont Educ Programs Dr. Vincent D. WIGGINS
09 Director of Research & Planning Mr. Sean HUDSON

*City Colleges of Chicago Kennedy-King College (D)

6301 South Halsted Street, Chicago IL 60621-3798

County: Cook FICE Identification: 001654
Unit ID: 144157
Telephone: (773) 602-5000 Carnegie Class: Assoc/MT-VT-High Non
FAX Number: N/A Calendar System: Semester
URL: www.ccc.edu/colleges/kennedy
Established: 1934 Annual Undergrad Tuition & Fees (In-District): $11,520
Enrollment: 1,878 Coed
Affiliation or Control: State/Local IRS Status: 501(c)3
Highest Offering: Associate Degree
Accreditation: HLC

02 President Dr. Gregory THOMAS
05 Vice Pres Academic/Student Affairs Mr. Eddie PHILLIPS
32 Dean Student Services Vacant
72 Dean Dawson Tech Inst/Col to Career Ms. Lucretzia JAMISON
84 Dean Enrollment Management Ms. Tonishea TERRY-JACKSON
51 Dean Adult/Continuing Education Mr. Henry HORACE
20 Dean of Instruction Ms. Darby JOHNSEN
35 Assoc Dean Student Services Dr. Zalika LANDRUM
88 Exec Dean Washburne Culinary Inst Dr. Jason LAFFERTY
37 Director Financial Aid Ms. Ashley BALLARD
13 Director Information Technology Mr. Lonnie WASHINGTON
121 Director Academic Support Services Ms. Shandria HOLMES
10 Exec Dir Business/Operations Mr. Baha AWADALLAH
06 Registrar Mr. Eric HAYES
04 Executive Office Manager Ms. Cris SAYRE
109 Director of Auxiliary Services Mr. Robert GRAHAM
45 Director Strategic Initiatives Mr. Patrick GIPSON
19 Director Security/Safety Mr. Hershey NORISE
41 Athletic Director Mr. Maurice CULPEPPER

*City Colleges of Chicago Olive-Harvey College (E)

10001 S Woodlawn Avenue, Chicago IL 60628-1645

County: Cook FICE Identification: 009767
Unit ID: 144175
Telephone: (773) 291-6100 Carnegie Class: Assoc/HT-High Non
FAX Number: (773) 291-6304 Calendar System: Semester
URL: www.ccc.edu/colleges/olive-harvey/pages/default.aspx
Established: 1970 Annual Undergrad Tuition & Fees (In-District): $11,520
Enrollment: 1,955 Coed
Affiliation or Control: State/Local IRS Status: 501(c)3
Highest Offering: Associate Degree
Accreditation: HLC, NAEYC

02 President Ms. Kimberly HOLLINGSWORTH
04 Executive Office Manager Ms. Maria PIOTROWSKI
05 Dean of Instruction Dr. Stephanie DECICCO
81 Dean STEM/Ctr Teaching & Lrng Ms. Adamma LOTSU
32 Dean Student Services Ms. Michelle ADAMS
51 Dean Adult & Continuing Education Ms. Lautauscha DAVIS
72 Dean of College to Career Ms. LaTonya ARMSTRONG
35 Assoc Dean of Student Services Ms. Inesha B. KELLY
10 Exec Dir Bus/Admin/Auxiliary Svcs Mr. Richard SLATER
13 Director Information Technology Mr. Jason CAMPBELL
36 Director Career Planning/Placement Ms. Charlene HAYMOND-BUSSELL
37 Director Financial Aid Mr. Richard HAYES
06 Registrar Ms. Nailah WATSON
19 Director Security & Safety Mr. Regynold JOHNSON
88 Director Child Development Center Ms. Carol PURNELL
41 Director of Athletics Mr. Rob FLETCHER
15 Director Human Resources Ms. Latasha LARRY
38 Manager Wellness Center Ms. LaTia LANE
18 Chief Engineer Mr. Robert LUMPKIN

*City Colleges of Chicago Richard J. Daley College (F)

7500 S Pulaski Road, Chicago IL 60652-1299

County: Cook FICE Identification: 001649
Unit ID: 144193
Telephone: (773) 838-7500 Carnegie Class: Assoc/MT-VT-High Non
FAX Number: (773) 838-7524 Calendar System: Semester
URL: daley.ccc.edu
Established: 1960 Annual Undergrad Tuition & Fees (In-District): $11,520
Enrollment: 4,929 Coed
Affiliation or Control: State/Local IRS Status: 501(c)3
Highest Offering: Associate Degree
Accreditation: HLC, NAEYC

02 President Dr. Janine E. JANOSKY
05 Vice Pres Academic/Student Affs Ms. Anne PANOMITROS
20 Dean of Instruction Mr. George KINLAW
55 Dean Adult Education Ms. Dena GIACOMETTI
32 Dean of Student Development Mr. Douglas GEIGER
31 Dir Community Education Programs Mr. Luis BERMUDEZ
10 Exec Director Business Operations Ms. Crystal WASHINGTON
18 Chief Engineer/Physical Plant Mr. Kevin NOLAN
19 Director Security Mr. Ronald MARTIN
06 Registrar Mr. Victor SANCHEZ
84 Director Enrollment Management Mr. Rafael GODINA
15 Human Resources Business Partner Ms. Ericka WILLIAMS
13 Director of Information Technology Ms. Karen ALLEN
37 Director Student Financial Aid Mr. Tom PANAS

*City Colleges of Chicago Wilbur Wright College (G)

4300 N Narragansett Avenue, Chicago IL 60634-1591

County: Cook FICE Identification: 001655
Unit ID: 144218
Telephone: (773) 777-7900 Carnegie Class: Assoc/HT-High Non
FAX Number: (773) 481-8185 Calendar System: Semester
URL: www.ccc.edu/wright
Established: 1934 Annual Undergrad Tuition & Fees (In-District): $11,520
Enrollment: 7,946 Coed
Affiliation or Control: State/Local IRS Status: 501(c)3
Highest Offering: Associate Degree
Accreditation: HLC, OTA

00 Chancellor Mr. Juan SALGADO
02 President Dr. David POTASH
05 VP Academic/Student Affairs Ms. Pamela MONACO
10 VP Finance/Operations Ms. Phoebe WOOD
20 Interim Dean of Instruction Mr. Gabe ESTILL
32 Dean of Student Services Ms. Romell MURDEN
121 Assoc Dean Student Svcs Advising Ms. Maria LLOPIZ
07 Assoc Dean Student Svcs Admissions Ms. Linda HUERTAS
37 Interim Financial Aid Director Mr. Noberto VALENTIN
09 Dir Institutional Research/Plng Mr. Brian TRZEBIATOWSKI
13 Director Information Technology Mr. Anthony GAMBOA
109 Director of Auxiliary Services Ms. Dina LEILER
15 Human Resources Director Ms. Alison GUENGERICH
38 Director of Wellness Center Ms. Kathryn CHAPMAN
19 Director of Security Mr. Jack MURPHY
06 Assistant Registrar Ms. Sherrea WASHINGTON
41 Athletic Director Mr. John MCDONNELL
55 Dean of Adult Education Ms. Emily ANDERSON
51 Dean of Continuing Education Ms. Alba PEZZAROSSI
78 Dean of HPVEC Mr. Kenneth SANTIAGO
31 Community Affairs Liaison Ms. Iris MILLAN
36 Dean of College to Careers (C2C) Vacant
101 Chief Advisor to the Board Ms. Tracey FLEMING

*Malcolm X College, One of the City Colleges of Chicago (H)

1900 W. Jackson Boulevard, Chicago IL 60612-3197

County: Cook FICE Identification: 001650
Unit ID: 144166
Telephone: (312) 850-7000 Carnegie Class: Assoc/HVT-High Non
FAX Number: (312) 850-7039 Calendar System: Semester
URL: www.ccc.edu/malcolmx
Established: 1911 Annual Undergrad Tuition & Fees (In-District): $11,520
Enrollment: 7,273 Coed
Affiliation or Control: State/Local IRS Status: 501(c)3
Highest Offering: Associate Degree
Accreditation: HLC, ADNUR, CAHIIM, COARC, DH, EMT, FUSER, MAC, NAEYC, PTAA, RAD

01 President Mr. David SANDERS
05 Vice President of Academic Affairs Mrs. Katonja WEBB-WALKER
108 VP Institutional Effectiveness Mrs. Annie ZALEWSKI
10 VP of Finance & Operations Ms. Tiffany DIXON
32 Dean Student Services Ms. Lisa WILLIS
15 HR Business Partner Mr. Seth BAKER
20 Dean Instruction Dr. Shawna BUSHELL
20 Associate Dean Instruction Ms. Glasetta BARKSDALE
20 Associate Dean Instruction Mr. Byron JAVIER
13 Director Information Technology Mr. Ben ROOHANI
06 Registrar Ms. Patrice JARRETT
35 Associate Dean of Student Services Mr. Brian HALL
37 Director Financial Aid Ms. Tiffany MORRISON
88 Director Child Care Center Ms. Saundra PARKER
19 Director Security/Public Safety Ms. Gissella LIMON
18 Chief Engineer Mr. John MORLEY
21 Business Manager Ms. Jennifer WILLIAMS
76 Dean Health Sciences Programs Mr. Roy WALKER, III
56 Dean Adult Education Programs Ms. Inesha KELLY
56 Dean of West Side Learning Center Ms. Barbara MESCHINO
51 Dean Continuing Education Ms. Lizz GARDNER
66 Dean of Nursing Ms. Tammy SCOTT-BRAND
121 Assoc Dean Student Development Vacant
88 Assoc Dean Health Careers Vacant
36 Dir Career Planning/Placement Mrs. Toya JOHNSON
103 Director Workforce Partnerships Ms. Rhonda HARDEMON
26 Director of Media Relations Vacant
46 Director Strategic Initiatives Ms. Pamela PERRY
109 Director of Auxiliary Services Ms. Jessica HOLLOWAY
09 Director of Research and Planning Mr. Steve DAMARJIAN
84 Director of Enrollment Management Mr. Rolando MARTINEZ
11 Exec Dir of Projects & Initiatives Ms. Elizabeth GMITTER
04 Executive Office Mgr Pres Office Mrs. Alanna S. WITHERSPOON

College of DuPage (I)

425 Fawell Boulevard, Glen Ellyn IL 60137-6599

County: DuPage FICE Identification: 006656
Unit ID: 144865
Telephone: (630) 942-2800 Carnegie Class: Assoc/MT-VT-High Non
FAX Number: (630) 858-9399 Calendar System: Semester
URL: www.cod.edu
Established: 1965 Annual Undergrad Tuition & Fees (In-District): $9,732
Enrollment: 21,010 Coed
Affiliation or Control: State/Local IRS Status: 501(c)3
Highest Offering: Associate Degree

Accreditation: HLC, ACFEI, ADNUR, ART, #AT, CAHIIM, COARC, CSHSE, DH, DMS, MAC, NMT, PTAA, RAD, SURGA, SURGT

01 President ... Dr. Brian CAPUTO
05 Provost ... Dr. Mark CURTIS-CHAVEZ
10 Int Chief Financial Ofcr/Treasurer ... Mr. Scott BRADY
45 VP Planning & Inst Effectiveness ... Mr. James BENTE
11 Vice Pres Administrative Affairs ... Ms. Ellen ROBERTS
15 Vice Pres Human Resources ... Ms. Maritza RUANO
111 VP Institutional Advancement ... Mr. Walter JOHNSON
26 VP Public Rels/Comm/Marketing ... Ms. Wendy E. PARKS
49 Dean Liberal Arts ... Dr. Robyn SCHIFFMAN
83 Dean Social & Behavioral Sci/Lib ... Mr. Mark RUDISILL
51 Dean Cont Ed/Extended Learning ... Dr. Joseph CASSIDY
81 Dean Science/Tech/Engineering/Math ... Ms. Jennifer CUMPSTSON
32 Dean Student Affairs ... Dr. Nathania MONTES
21 Controller ... Mr. Scott BRADY
13 Dir Information Technology Services ... Ms. Donna BERLINER
18 Dir Facilities Planning and Dev ... Mr. Don INMAN
121 Dir Pathways for Student Success ... Mr. Roberto VALADEZ
09 Director Research & Analytics ... Mr. James KOSTECKI
116 Dir Compliance/Internal Auditor ... Mr. James E. MARTNER
57 Director McAninch Arts Center ... Mrs. Diana MARTINEZ
41 Asst Athletic Director ... Mr. Matt FOSTER
19 Chief of Police ... Mr. Joseph MULLIN
79 Associate Dean Humanities ... Dr. Sandra MARTINS
86 Director Legislative Relations ... Ms. Wendy MCCAMBRIDGE
07 Director Admissions & Outreach ... Ms. Tamara MCCLAIN

College of Lake County (A)

19351 W Washington Street, Grayslake IL 60030-1198
County: Lake FICE Identification: 007694
Unit ID: 146472
Telephone: (847) 543-2000 Carnegie Class: Assoc/MT-VT-High Non
FAX Number: N/A Calendar System: Semester
URL: www.clcillinois.edu
Established: 1969 Annual Undergrad Tuition & Fees (In-District): $9,632
Enrollment: 11,854 Coed
Affiliation or Control: Local IRS Status: 501(c)3
Highest Offering: Associate Degree
Accreditation: HLC, ADNUR, CAHIIM, DH, MAC, RAD, SURGT

01 President ... Dr. Lori SUDDICK
10 Vice Pres Business Svcs/Finance/CFO ... Vacant
32 Vice President Student Development ... Ms. Karen HLAVIN
05 Vice Pres Education/Chief Acad Ofcr ... Dr. Sonya WILLIAMS
103 VP Cmty & Workforce Partnership ... Dr. Ali O'BRIEN
12 Dean Southlake Campus ... Dr. Viki CVITKOVIC
12 Dean Lakeshore Campus ... Mr. Jesus RUIZ
08 Dean Library/Testing & Acad Success ... Ms. Tanya WOLTMANN
21 Controller ... Ms. Connie KRAVITZ
50 Dean of Business/Social Science Div ... Dr. Jeffrey STOMPER
76 Dean Biological/Health Sciences ... Mr. Jeet SAINI
79 Dean Comm Arts/Humanities/Fine Arts ... Mr. Sheldon WALCHER
54 Dean Engr/Math/Physical Science ... Mr. Richard AMMON
51 Dean Adult Basic Education/GED/ ESL ... Dr. Arlene SANTOS-GEORGE
103 Exec Director Community Programming ... Ms. Roneida MARTIN
26 Director Public Relations & Mktg ... Ms. Anne O'CONNELL
35 Dean Student Life ... Mr. Gabriel LARA
102 Executive Director CLC Foundation ... Mr. Kurt PETERSON
15 Exec Director Human Resources ... Ms. Sue FAY
88 Exec Dir James Lumber Ctr Perf Arts ... Ms. Gwethalyn BRONNER
09 Dir Inst Effect/Plng/Research ... Ms. Sandra VILLANUEVA
41 Director of Athletics ... Mr. Bradley UNGER
86 Dir Resource Dev/Legislative Affs ... Mr. Nick C. KALLIERIS
13 Chief Information Officer ... Mr. Greg KOZAK
14 Director User Services/User Support ... Mr. David AYKROID
88 Dir Application Svcs/Development ... Mr. Jay MEYER
35 Director Student Services Lakeshore ... Mr. David WEATHERSPOON
18 Director of Facilities ... Mr. Mike WELCH
88 Dir Children's Learning Center ... Ms. Carlotta CONLEY
22 Dir Ofc Students with Disabilities ... Mr. Thomas CROWE
19 Chief of Police ... Mr. Brian HENRY
36 Exec Dir Career/Placement Services ... Ms. Sylvia M. JOHNSON JONES
66 Director Nursing Education ... Vacant
23 Director Health Services ... Ms. Michelle M. GRACE
37 Director Financial Aid ... Mr. Vatistas VATISTAS
88 Director Educational Technology ... Mr. Scott RIAL
107 Director Professional Development ... Vacant
88 Director Technical Services ... Mr. James SENFT
07 Dir Student Recruiting/ Onboarding ... Ms. Sharon SANDERS-FUNNYE
04 Exec Assistant to President ... Ms. Laura LABA
106 Director Online Student Success ... Ms. Meredith TUMILTY
121 Dir Student Success Strategy ... Mr. Nick BRANSON
109 Director Business Operations ... Ms. Patricia ARGOUDELIS

College of Lake County Lakeshore Campus (B)

33 North Genesee Street, Waukegan IL 60085
Telephone: (847) 543-2191 Identification: 770073
Accreditation: &HLC

College of Lake County Southlake Campus (C)

1120 South Milwaukee Avenue, Vernon Hills IL 60061
Telephone: (847) 543-6501 Identification: 770072
Accreditation: &HLC

Columbia College Chicago (D)

600 S Michigan Avenue, Chicago IL 60605-1996
County: Cook FICE Identification: 001665
Unit ID: 144281
Telephone: (312) 369-1000 Carnegie Class: Masters/M
FAX Number: (312) 369-8069 Calendar System: Semester
URL: www.colum.edu
Established: 1890 Annual Undergrad Tuition & Fees: $27,786
Enrollment: 6,769 Coed
Affiliation or Control: Independent Non-Profit IRS Status: 501(c)3
Highest Offering: Master's
Accreditation: HLC, CIDA

01 President and CEO ... Dr. Kwang-Wu KIM
05 Provost/SVP Academic Affairs ... Ms. Marcella DAVID
10 Sr VP Business Affairs/CFO ... Mr. Jerry TARRER
43 VP Legal Affairs/General Counsel ... Ms. Patricia BERGESON
30 VP Development/Alumni Relations ... Mr. Shawn WAX
84 VP Enrollment Management ... Mr. Michael JOSEPH
32 VP Student Affairs ... Dr. Sharon WILSON-TAYLOR
13 Chief Information Officer ... Ms. Kathie KOCH
20 Asst Provost Acad Services ... Mr. Brian MARTH
06 Registrar ... Ms. Keri WALTERS
108 Assoc Provost AASL ... Mr. Neil PAGANO
15 AVP of Human Resources ... Ms. Norma DE JESUS
18 AVP Fac & Construction ... Ms. Ann KALAYIL
37 AVP Student Financial Svcs ... Ms. Cynthia GRUNDEN
100 Chief of Staff ... Mr. Laurent PERNOT
04 Exec Assistant to the President ... Ms. Yvonne SODE
19 AVP Safety & Security ... Mr. Ronald SODINI
35 Dean of Students ... Mr. John PELRINE
57 Dean Sch Fine/Performing Arts ... Ms. Rosita SANDS
49 Dean School Liberal Arts/Sciences ... Dr. Steven COREY
60 Dean School of Media Arts ... Mr. Eric FREEDMAN
35 Assistant Dean of Student Life ... Ms. Sheila CARTER
36 Assoc Dean Career Development ... Mr. Erik FRIEDMAN
07 Asst VP Undergrad Admissions ... Mr. Derek BRINKLEY
29 Sr Director Alumni Relations ... Mr. Dirk MATTHEWS
09 Dir Inst Research & Reporting ... Mr. Brian CHAMBERLIN
121 Director of Academic Advising ... Mr. Keith LUSSON
39 Director of Residential Operations ... Ms. Mary OAKES
88 Asst Provost Global Education ... Mr. David COMP
08 Director of the Library ... Ms. Jo CATES
25 Grants & Contract Manager ... Mr. David WEINER

Concordia University Chicago (E)

7400 Augusta Street, River Forest IL 60305-1499
County: Cook FICE Identification: 001666
Unit ID: 144351
Telephone: (708) 771-8300 Carnegie Class: Masters/L
FAX Number: (708) 209-3176 Calendar System: Semester
URL: www.cuchicago.edu
Established: 1864 Annual Undergrad Tuition & Fees: $33,636
Enrollment: 6,491 Coed
Affiliation or Control: Lutheran Church - Missouri Synod
IRS Status: 501(c)3
Highest Offering: Doctorate
Accreditation: HLC, #ACBSP, CACREP, CAEP, CAEPN, MUS

01 President ... Dr. Russell DAWN
05 Provost ... Dr. Erik ANKERBERG
10 Sr Vice Pres of Finance/CFO ... Ms. Lisa M. KRALINA
111 CEO Foundation/VP for Advancement ... Mr. Jeff HYNES
88 Asst Vice President for Enrollment ... Ms. Gwen E. KANELOS
26 AVP Univ Communications & Marketing ... Mr. Eric MATANYI
49 Asst Dean Col Theol/Arts/Humanities ... Ms. Kristin R. WASSILAK
50 Dean College of Business ... Dr. Claudia SANTIN
09 Dir Inst Planning & Effectiveness ... Dr. Elizabeth OWOLABI
37 Exec Director of Financial Aid ... Ms. Aida ASENCIO-PINTO
08 Director of Library Services ... Ms. Liesl COTTRILL
36 Director Career Services ... Mr. Gerald PINOTTI
11 Assoc Vice Pres for Administration ... Mr. Glen D. STEINER
29 Sr Dir Alumni Rels/Annual Giving ... Ms. Paige CRAIG
38 Director Schmieding Counseling Ctr ... Dr. Carol A. JABS
109 Dir Contract Mgmt/Auxiliary Svcs ... Mr. Pete D. BECKER
41 Director of Athletics ... Mr. Peter D. GNAN
21 Controller ... Mr. Andrew WINKELMAN
114 Director of Budget Services ... Ms. Tina NEPOMUCENO
42 University Pastor ... Rev. Jeffrey LEININGER
24 Director of Video Production Svcs ... Mr. James A. KOSINSKY
19 Director of Public Safety ... Mr. David WITKEN
121 Dir Academic Advising/Study Abroad ... Vacant
96 Director of Purchasing ... Ms. Denise JAMES
91 Dir of Admin Information System ... Ms. Linda C. BERRY
123 Asst VP Grad Admission/Student Svcs ... Ms. Deborah NESS
04 Exec Assistant to the President ... Ms. Kimberly CASEY
06 Registrar ... Ms. Brooke JOHNSON
15 Director Human Resources ... Ms. Margaret K. O'BRIEN

Coyne College (F)

1 N. State Street, Suite 400, Chicago IL 60602
County: Cook FICE Identification: 007549
Unit ID: 144485
Telephone: (773) 577-8100 Carnegie Class: Assoc/HVT-High Trad
FAX Number: (312) 226-3818 Calendar System: Other
URL: www.coynecollege.edu
Established: 1899 Annual Undergrad Tuition & Fees: N/A
Enrollment: 531 Coed
Affiliation or Control: Proprietary IRS Status: Proprietary
Highest Offering: Associate Degree
Accreditation: ACCSC

01 President ... Michelle K. FREEMAN
05 Director of Education ... Virginia HANSON
06 Registrar ... Tina FANUCCHI
08 Librarian ... Diana BARTHELEMY
36 Director of Career Services ... Jenny GONZALEZ
37 Director of Financial Aid ... Amelia KING
04 Admin Assistant to the President ... Maria R. CORTES
10 Chief Financial/Business Officer ... Steven A. STRIEN

Danville Area Community College (G)

2000 E Main Street, Danville IL 61832-5199
County: Vermilion FICE Identification: 001669
Unit ID: 144564
Telephone: (217) 443-3222 Carnegie Class: Assoc/MT-VT-High Non
FAX Number: (217) 443-8560 Calendar System: Semester
URL: www.dacc.edu
Established: 1949 Annual Undergrad Tuition & Fees (In-District): $8,325
Enrollment: 2,171 Coed
Affiliation or Control: State/Local IRS Status: 501(c)3
Highest Offering: Associate Degree
Accreditation: HLC, ADNUR, CAHIIM, RAD

01 President ... Dr. Stephen D. NACCO
11 VP Operations/Board Secretary ... Ms. Kerri L. THURMAN
05 VP Academic Affairs ... Dr. Carl BRIDGES
15 VP Human Resource/AA Ofcr/Labor Rel ... Ms. Jill A. CRANMORE
10 VP Finance/Chief Financial Officer ... Ms. Tammy L. BETANCOURT
32 VP Student Services ... Ms. Stacy L. EHMEN
28 Asst VP Student Services/CDO ... Ms. Carla M. BOYD
35 Asst VP Student Services ... Mr. Brian C. HENSGEN
102 Foundation Executive Director ... Ms. Tonya L. HILL
26 Exec Director College Relations ... Ms. Lara L. CONKLIN
18 Exec Dir Maintenance & Facilities ... Mr. Doug ADAMS
81 Dean Math/Sciences & Health Prof ... Ms. Kathy R. STURGEON
49 Dean Liberal Arts & Library Service ... Dr. Penny J. MCCONNELL
50 Dean Business & Technology ... Ms. Terri CUMMINGS
55 Dean Adult Ed/Literacy/CE & MC ... Ms. Laura M. WILLIAMS
09 Director Institutional Research ... Mr. Tom CAREY
88 Director Student Support Svcs/TRIO ... Ms. Shanay M. WRIGHT
21 Asst VP Finance ... Mr. Carl LEWIS
37 Director Financial Aid ... Ms. Janet M. INGARGIOLA
91 Programmer/Systems Administrator ... Ms. Jessica MILES
13 Director Information Technology ... Mr. Mark BARNES
41 Director Athletics ... Mr. Tim M. BUNTON
88 Director Small Business Development ... Mr. Earle STEINER
07 Director Admissions & Registrar ... Mr. Timothy MORGAN
36 Dir Career Services/Veterans Center ... Mr. Nick CATLETT
31 Coord Campus & Community Resources ... Ms. Dawn S. NASSER
19 Supervisor Safety & Security ... Vacant
12 Director Hoopeston Extension Site ... Ms. Karla J. COON
51 Director Community Educ/Video Prod ... Ms. Laura M. HENSGEN
88 Exec Director Corporate Education ... Ms. Stephanie L. YATES
88 Sr Director Corporate Education ... Ms. Brittany WOODWORTH
88 Director Medical Imagery Programs ... Ms. Tammy L. HOWARD
88 Director Health Info Technology ... Ms. Kelly JOHNSON
66 Director Nursing ... Ms. Susan KOSS
121 Dir Acad Advis/Couns/Transf Articu ... Ms. Stephane POTTS
88 Coord Recruitment/Social Media ... Mr. David GROVES, JR.

DePaul University (H)

1 E Jackson Boulevard, Chicago IL 60604-2287
County: Cook FICE Identification: 001671
Unit ID: 144740
Telephone: (312) 362-8610 Carnegie Class: DU-Higher
FAX Number: (312) 362-5322 Calendar System: Quarter
URL: www.depaul.edu
Established: 1898 Annual Undergrad Tuition & Fees: $41,202
Enrollment: 21,922 Coed
Affiliation or Control: Roman Catholic IRS Status: 501(c)3
Highest Offering: Doctorate
Accreditation: HLC, ANEST, CACREP, CLPSY, LAW, MUS, NURSE, PH, @SP, SPAA, SW

01 President ... Dr. A. Gabriel ESTEBAN
00 Chancellor ... Rev. Dennis H. HOLTSCHNEIDER, CM
05 Provost ... Dr. Salma GHANEM
10 Executive Vice President ... Mrs. Sherri SIDLER
32 VP Student Affairs ... Dr. Gene ZDZIARSKI
84 Vice Pres Enroll Mgmt/Marketing ... Dr. Soumitra GHOSH
111 Vice Pres for Advancement ... Dr. Daniel ALLEN
15 Vice President Human Resources ... Ms. Stephanie SMITH
18 Vice President Facilities Operation ... Mr. Robert J. JANIS
43 VP/General Counsel & Secretary ... Ms. Kathryn STIEBER
29 Assoc VP Communication & Engagement ... Ms. Tracy KRAHL
28 VP Inst Diversity & Equity ... Dr. Elizabeth F. ORTIZ
26 VP Public Relations & Communication ... Ms. Linda BLAKLEY
121 Assoc Prov Student Success/Accred ... Dr. Caryn CHADEN
106 Assoc Prov Global Eng and Online ... Dr. GianMario BESANA
100 Chief of Staff ... Mr. Steve STOUTE
13 VP Information Services ... Mr. Robert MCCORMICK
35 Assoc Vice Pres Student Affairs ... Dr. Ashley KNIGHT
35 Assoc Vice Pres Student Affairs ... Mr. Rico TYLER
09 AVP Inst Research/Market Analytics ... Dr. Liz SANDERS
36 AVP Div Planning & Mgmt/Career Ctr ... Ms. Jane MCGRATH
42 Assoc VP University Ministry ... Mr. Mark LABOE
108 AVP & COS Student Affairs ... Dr. Ellen MEENTS-DECAIGNY
27 Exec Dir News & Integrated Content ... Ms. Carol HUGHES
21 VP for Finance & Controller ... Ms. Sherri SIDLER
90 Dir Faculty Instructional Tech Svcs ... Dr. Sharon GUAN

37 Int Assoc Vice Pres Financial Aid .... Ms. Karen LEVEQUE
25 Assoc Provost for Research ....Dr. Daniela STAN RAICU
19 Director Public Safety .... Mr. Robert WACHOWSKI
38 Director Student Counseling .... Dr. Jeffery LANFEAR
39 Director of Housing & Student Ctrs .... Mr. Rick MORECI
41 Athletics Director .... Mr. DeWayne PEEVY
06 Director of Registration/Records .... Ms. Patricia HUERTA
104 Director Study Abroad .... Ms. Martha MCGIVERN
123 AVP Graduate & Adult Admission ....Ms. Suzanne DEPEDER
07 Dean of Undergraduate Admission ....Vacant
77 Dean Computing & Digital Media .... Dr. David MILLER
49 Dean Liberal Arts & Social Sciences ....Dr. Guillermo VASQUEZ DE VELASCO
50 Int Dean Bus Coll/Grad Sch Bus .... Mr. Thomas DONLEY
60 Int Dean Col of Communication .... Dr. Alexandra MURPHY
64 Dean School of Music ....Dr. Ronald CALTABIANO
61 Dean College of Law ....Ms. Jennifer R. PEREA
57 Dean Theatre School .... Mr. John CULBERT
53 Dean School of Education .... Dr. Paul ZIONTS
51 Int Dean School for New Learning .... Dr. Don OPITZ
76 Dean Col of Science & Health ....Dr. Dorothy KOZLOWSKI
08 Head Librarian ....Vacant
04 Sr Executive Asst to President ....Ms. Phyllis GREGG
100 Deputy Chief of Staff ....Ms. Annette WILSON
86 Assoc VP Community & Govt Relations .... Mr. Peter COFFEY

*DeVry University - Home Office (A)

3005 Highland Parkway, Suite 100,
Downers Grove IL 60515

County: DuPage | FICE Identification: 001672 | Unit ID: 144777
Telephone: (630) 515-3000 | Carnegie Class: N/A
FAX Number: (630) 571-0317
URL: www.devry.edu

01 President/CEO .... Mr. Thomas L. MONAHAN, III
26 Chief Marketing Officer ....Mr. Remberto DEL REAL
84 VP Enrollment Management ....Ms. Elise AWWAD
05 Provost/VP Academic Affairs .... Mr. Shantanu BOSE
13 VP Information Technology .... Mr. Chris CAMPBELL
15 VP Human Resources & Univ Relations ....Mr. David BARNETT
10 Chief Financial Officer .... Mr. John LORENZ

*DeVry University - Chicago Campus (B)

3300 N Campbell Avenue, Chicago IL 60618

County: Cook | FICE Identification: 010727 | Unit ID: 482477
Telephone: (773) 929-8500 | Carnegie Class: Masters/L
FAX Number: (773) 348-1780 | Calendar System: Semester
URL: www.devry.edu
Established: 1931 | Annual Undergrad Tuition & Fees: $17,680
Enrollment: 20,832 | Coed
Affiliation or Control: Proprietary | IRS Status: Proprietary
Highest Offering: Master's
Accreditation: HLC, ACBSP, CAHIIM

02 Center Dean .... Ms. Ruth PINEDA

† Regional accreditation is carried under the parent institution in Downers Grove, IL.

Dominican University (C)

7900 W Division Street, River Forest IL 60305-1099

County: Cook | FICE Identification: 001750 | Unit ID: 148496
Telephone: (708) 366-2490 | Carnegie Class: Masters/L
FAX Number: (708) 524-5990 | Calendar System: Semester
URL: www.dom.edu
Established: 1901 | Annual Undergrad Tuition & Fees: $35,420
Enrollment: 3,189 | Coed
Affiliation or Control: Roman Catholic | IRS Status: 501(c)3
Highest Offering: Doctorate
Accreditation: HLC, ARCPA, DIETC, DIETD, LIB, NURSE, SW

01 President ....Dr. Glena G. TEMPLE
05 Provost .... Dr. Jeffrey CARLSON
20 Assoc Provost Strategic Initiatives ....Dr. Roberto CURCI
10 VP Finance/Business Affairs .... Mr. Mark TITZER
42 VP Mission & Planning .... Dr. Claire NOONAN
111 VP University Advancement .... Ms. Sara ACOSTA
121 VP Student Success & Engagement ....Dr. Barrington PRICE
84 VP Enrollment Management/Marketing ......Mr. Genaro BALCAZAR
13 Interim CIO .... Mr. Todd KLEINE
15 Exec Director Human Resources ....Ms. Roberta MCMAHON
28 Chief Diversity Officer .... Dr. Precious PORRAS
07 AVP Enroll Mgt/Dir Undergrad Admiss ....Mr. Glenn HAMILTON
20 Assistant Provost ....Mr. Matthew J. HLINAK
27 Exec Dir of External Engagement ....Ms. Leslie RODRIGUEZ
26 Director of Public Relations ....Ms. Jessica MACKINNON
32 Dean of Students ....Ms. Norah COLLINS PIENTA
76 Dean Borra College Health Sciences ....Dr. Kavita DHANWADA
83 Dean Applied/Social Sciences ....Dr. Jacob BUCHER
50 Dean Brennan School of Business ....Dr. Roberto CURCI
62 Director School Information Stds .... Ms. Kate MAREK
53 Director Teacher Educ Programs .... Ms. Josephine SARVIS
88 Assoc Dean/Licensure Pgm Coord .... Dr. Ben FREVILLE
51 Asst Dean Student Svcs Cont Stds .... Ms. Monica HALLORAN
70 Director School of Social Work ....Ms. Joyce SHIM
49 Dean Rosary College ....Mr. Chad ROHMAN
08 University Librarian ....Mr. Estevan MONTAÑO
06 Registrar .... Ms. Kelly M. SIMMONS
36 Director Career Development ....Ms. Keli WOJCIECHOWSKI
29 Director Alumnae/i Relations .... Ms. Vimla HOMAN
09 Dir Institutional Rsrch/Assessment .... Ms. Elizabeth SILK
07 Director Transfer/Adult Admission ...... Mr. Michael MORSOVILLO
88 AVP Student Enrollment Services ....Ms. Victoria SPIVAK
23 Director Wellness Center .... Ms. Elizabeth RITZMAN
41 Director Athletics ....Mr. Erick BAUMANN
104 Director International Studies ....Dr. Sue PONREMY
04 Assistant to the President .... Ms. Kathleen REDMOND
102 Director Foundation/Corporate Rels ....Ms. Sharon RYAN
44 Director Annual Giving ....Ms. Sarah SULLIVAN

East-West University (D)

816 S Michigan Avenue, Chicago IL 60605-2185

County: Cook | FICE Identification: 021686 | Unit ID: 144883
Telephone: (312) 939-0111 | Carnegie Class: Bac-A&S
FAX Number: (312) 939-0083 | Calendar System: Quarter
URL: www.eastwest.edu
Established: 1980 | Annual Undergrad Tuition & Fees: $22,650
Enrollment: 419 | Coed
Affiliation or Control: Independent Non-Profit | IRS Status: 501(c)3
Highest Offering: Baccalaureate
Accreditation: HLC

01 Chancellor .... Dr. M. Wasiullah KHAN
05 Provost .... Dr. Madhu JAIN
20 Academic Dean .... Vacant
30 Dean Development/Univ Relations ....Mr. Zafar A. MALIK
32 Director Counseling/Student Affairs ....Dr. Nadia HALLAK
37 Director of Financial Aid ....Mr. Cesar CAMPOS
06 Registrar .... Mr. Daniel DIAZ
04 Assistant to the Chancellor ....Vacant
19 Director of Security .... Mr. Tasleem RAJA
10 Director of Business .... Dr. Madhu JAIN
44 Dir Devel/Univ Rels/Publications .... Ms. Barbara ABRAJANO
26 Manager Public Relations ....Vacant
18 Facilities Manager .... Mr. Tasleem RAJA
85 International Student Advisor .... Ms. Kate PETEK
21 Associate Business Officer ....Vacant
84 Director Enrollment Management .... Ms. Claudia SILVERMAN

Eastern Illinois University (E)

600 Lincoln Avenue, Charleston IL 61920-3099

County: Coles | FICE Identification: 001674 | Unit ID: 144892
Telephone: (217) 581-5000 | Carnegie Class: Masters/L
FAX Number: (217) 581-2722 | Calendar System: Semester
URL: www.eiu.edu
Established: 1895 | Annual Undergrad Tuition & Fees (In-State): $12,136
Enrollment: 8,626 | Coed
Affiliation or Control: State | IRS Status: 501(c)3
Highest Offering: Beyond Master's But Less Than Doctorate
Accreditation: HLC, AAFCS, ART, #CAATE, CACREP, CAEP, CAEPN, CAPRT, DIETD, DIETI, JOUR, MUS, NURSE, SP, THEA

01 President ....Dr. David M. GLASSMAN
05 Provost/Vice Pres Academic Affairs ....Dr. Jay D. GATRELL
10 Vice Pres Business Affairs .... Mr. Sean D. REEDER
32 Vice Pres Student Affairs ....Dr. Anne G. FLAHERTY
111 Vice Pres University Advancement ....Dr. Ken A. WETSTEIN
35 Special Asst to VP Student Affairs ....Dr. Jennifer L. SIPES
26 Int Dir Marketing/Communications .... Ms. Christy E. KILGORE
08 Dean of Library Services .... Mr. Zach NEWELL
92 Dean Honors College ....Dr. Richard ENGLAND
15 Int Director Human Resources .... Ms. Linda C. HOLLOWAY
22 Director Civil Rights/Diversity .... Dr. Shawn PEOPLES
45 Int Dir Planning/Budget/IR .... Mr. Lakshmikara PADMARAJU
07 Director of Admissions .... Ms. Kelly MILLER
37 Director of Financial Aid ....Ms. Amanda STARWALT
06 Registrar .... Mr. Brad BENNINGTON
29 Asst VP for Univ Advancement ....Mr. Steve W. RICH
18 Dir Facilities/Planning Management .... Mr. Timothy P. ZIMMER
96 Dir Procure/Disburse/Contract Svcs .... Ms. Danielle M. GREEN
38 Int Asst Dir of Counseling Center .... Ms. Lindsay WILSON
25 Director of Research & Grants .... Dr. Robert W. CHESNUT
41 Director of Athletics ....Mr. Thomas R. MICHAEL
93 Exec Dir Inclusion/Acad Engagement ....Dr. Mona DAVENPORT
39 Director of Housing/Dining Service .... Mr. Mark A. HUDSON
21 Dir Business Services/Treasurer .... Mr. Paul A. MCCANN
36 Director of Career Services ....Ms. Bobbi KINGERY
58 Dean Graduate School .... Dr. Ryan C. HENDRICKSON
76 Int Dean College Health/Human Svcs .... Dr. Ryan C. HENDRICKSON
50 Dean Lumpkin Col Bus and Tech ....Dr. Austin C. CHENEY
49 Dean College Liberal Arts/ Sciences .... Dr. Barbara E. BONNEKESSEN
53 Dean College of Education ....Dr. Laretta HENDERSON
43 General Counsel .... Ms. Laura L. MCLAUGHLIN
84 Assoc VP Enrollment Management .... Mr. Josh L. NORMAN
13 Exec Director for ITS ....Mr. Ryan W. GIBSON

Elgin Community College (F)

1700 Spartan Drive, Elgin IL 60123-7193

County: Kane | FICE Identification: 001675 | Unit ID: 144944
Telephone: (847) 697-1000 | Carnegie Class: Assoc/MT-VT-Mix Trad/Non
FAX Number: (847) 214-7995 | Calendar System: Semester
URL: www.elgin.edu
Established: 1949 | Annual Undergrad Tuition & Fees (In-District): $7,140
Enrollment: 7,882 | Coed
Affiliation or Control: Local | IRS Status: 501(c)3
Highest Offering: Associate Degree
Accreditation: HLC, ADNUR, COMTA, CSHSE, DA, HT, MLTAD, PTAA, RAD, RADMAG, SURGT

01 President .... Dr. David SAM
10 VP Business & Finance ....Dr. Kimberly WAGNER
05 VP Teaching/Learning/Student Dev ....Dr. Peggy HEINRICH
20 Dean Academic Dev/Learning Resource ....Dr. Mi HU
50 Dean Sustain/Business/Career Tech .... Ms. Cathy TAYLOR
83 Dean Comm/Behavioral Sciences .... Dr. Ruixuan MAO
57 Dean Liberal/Visual/Performing Arts ....Ms. Mary HATCH
32 Asst VP/Dean Student Svcs & Dev .... Dr. Gregory ROBINSON
88 Dean of Col Transitions/Partnership .... Dr. Mary PERKINS
51 Dean Adult Basic Education ....Ms. Elizabeth HOBSON
76 Dean Health Prof/Math/Science/Eng ....Dr. Wendy MILLER
88 Assoc Dean Comm/Behavioral Sciences .... Dr. Kristina GARCIA
106 Assoc Dean Inst Improve/Dist Lrng .... Mr. Timothy MOORE
124 Asc Dean TRIO/Reten/Stdnt Outreach .... Dr. L. Bruce AUSTIN
07 Sr Director of Admissions/Registrar ....Ms. Ann KALAS
18 Managing Director Facilities .... Mr. Cal BYRD
13 Chief Information Officer ....Dr. Michael CHAHINO
26 Chief Marketing/Communications Ofcr .... Dr. Toya WEBB
15 Chief Human Resources Officer .... Mr. Anthony RAY
30 Exec Dir Inst Advance/ECC Found .... Mr. David DAVIN
20 Asst VP Teaching/Lrng/Student Dev ......Ms. Annamarie SCHOPEN
45 VP Planning/Inst Effect/Tech ....Dr. Philip GARBER
09 Managing Dir Institutional Research ....Mr. David RUDDEN
37 Managing Dir Student Financial Svcs .... Ms. Amy PERRIN
21 Asst VP Business and Finance .... Ms. Heather SCHOLL
84 Managing Director Enrollment Svcs ....Dr. Jennifer MCCLURE
22 Paralegal/EEO/AA Title IX/FOIA Ofcr ....Ms. Marilyn PRENTICE
41 Director Athletics & Wellness ....Mr. Kent PAYNE
96 Managing Director Business Services ....Ms. Melissa TAIT
121 Assoc Dean of Student Success ....Ms. Peggy GUNDRUM
35 Director Orientation/Student Life .... Ms. Amybeth MAURER
86 Mng Dir Cmty Eng/Legislative Affs ..... Dr. Lourdes BLACKSMITH
04 Sr Exec Asst to Pres/Board Recorder ....Ms. Diane KERRUISH
08 Assoc Dean of Library .... Ms. Shannon POHRTE
51 Assoc Dean of Adult Educ ....Ms. Marcia LUPTAK
43 General Counsel ....Mr. Respicio VAZQUEZ
19 Chief of Police ....Mr. David KINTZ
28 Exec Dir Equity/Diversity/Inclusion ....Mr. Anthony RAMOS

Elmhurst University (G)

190 Prospect Avenue, Elmhurst IL 60126-3296

County: DuPage | FICE Identification: 001676 | Unit ID: 144962
Telephone: (630) 279-4100 | Carnegie Class: Masters/L
FAX Number: (630) 617-3282 | Calendar System: 4/1/4
URL: www.elmhurst.edu
Established: 1871 | Annual Undergrad Tuition & Fees: $38,654
Enrollment: 3,421 | Coed
Affiliation or Control: United Church Of Christ | IRS Status: 501(c)3
Highest Offering: Master's
Accreditation: HLC, NURSE, OT, SP

01 President ....Dr. Troy VANAKEN
10 Interim VP for Business & Finance ....Ms. Yvonne BERRY
05 VP Academic Affs/Dean of Faculty ....Dr. Dean PRIBBENOW
13 VP for Operations & Technology ....Mr. Kurt ASHLEY
111 Interim VP of Advancement ....Mr. Andrew KNAP
32 VP for Student Affairs .... Dr. Phil RIORDAN
07 VP for Admission .... Dr. Timothy RICORDATI
20 Associate Dean of Faculty ....Dr. Brian WILHITE
88 Exec Dir Center for Pro Excellence .... Mr. Martin GAHBAUER
18 Exec Director Facilities Management .... Mr. Michael EMERSON
26 Exec Dir of Mktg & Communication ....Mr. Jonathan SHEARER
42 Chaplain ....Rev. H. Scott MATHENEY
06 Registrar ....Ms. Linda DUFORT
27 Sr Dir Communications/Public Affs ....Ms. Desiree CHEN-MENICHINI
08 Interim Director of the Library .... Ms. Peg COOK
36 Director of Career Education .... Ms. Julie NOSAL
38 Director of Counseling Services .... Dr. Amy SWARR
29 Director of Alumni Engagement ....Mr. Scottie WILLIAMS
15 Exec Director of Human Resources .... Mr. David CRONAN
19 Exec Dir of Campus Security .... Mr. Marc MOLINA
37 Director of Financial Services ....Mr. Nathan HANCOCK
07 Assistant Director of Admissions .... Mr. Tim AHLBERG
123 Sr Dir Grad Admission & Enrollment ....Mr. Tim PANFIL
39 Dir of Housing & Res Life ....Ms. Sarah MEANEY
41 Director Intercollegiate Athletics ....Ms. Wendy MCMANUS
04 Executive Asst to President ....Ms. Molly NIESPO
101 Asst to President Office & Trustees .... Ms. Britney HEALD
89 Sr Dir 1st Year & Intl Admission .... Ms. Christine GRENIER
53 Dept Chair Education ....Dr. Lisa BURKE
108 Asst Dean for Assessment & Accred ....Dr. A. Andrew DAS
88 Asst Dean For Faculty Development .... Dr. Kimberly LAWLER-SAGARIN
09 Inst Research/Assessment Specialist ....Dr. Yanli MA
22 Director of Diversity & Inclusion .... Ms. Jasmin ROBINSON
104 Director of Intl Education ....Ms. Kathleen HEAD
25 Grants Coordinator ....Vacant

Erikson Institute (H)

451 N. Lasalle Street, Chicago IL 60654

County: Cook | FICE Identification: 035103 | Unit ID: 409254
Telephone: (312) 755-2250 | Carnegie Class: Spec-4-yr-Other

FAX Number: (312) 755-0928 Calendar System: Semester
URL: www.erikson.edu
Established: 1966 Annual Graduate Tuition & Fees: N/A
Enrollment: 457 Coed
Affiliation or Control: Independent Non-Profit IRS Status: 501(c)3
Highest Offering: Master's; No Undergraduates
Accreditation: HLC, SW

01 Interim President Patricia LAWSON
05 Int SVP Acad Affs/Dean of Faculty Pamela EPLEY
10 Vice President Finance/CFO Patricia LAWSON
45 Vice Pres Inst Effectiveness & Plng Charles CHANG
111 Vice Pres Institutional Advancement Maura DALY
84 Sr Assoc VP Enrollment Management David BEHRS
06 Sr Dir Enrollment/Student Records David SAENZ
32 Interim Director of Student Affairs Margaret BRETT
26 Dir of Communications and Marketing Sheila HAENNICKE
13 Chief Information Officer Charles CHANG
30 Dir Development/Alumni Relations Patricia OFFER

Eureka College (A)

300 E College Avenue, Eureka IL 61530-1500
County: Woodford FICE Identification: 001678
Unit ID: 144971
Telephone: (309) 467-3721 Carnegie Class: Bac-Diverse
FAX Number: (309) 467-6386 Calendar System: Semester
URL: www.eureka.edu
Established: 1855 Annual Undergrad Tuition & Fees: $28,360
Enrollment: 511 Coed
Affiliation or Control: Christian Church (Disciples Of Christ)
IRS Status: 501(c)3
Highest Offering: Baccalaureate
Accreditation: HLC

01 President Dr. Jamel WRIGHT
04 Administrative Asst to President Mrs. Jyl ZUBIATE
05 Provost & Dean of the College Dr. Ann FULOP
10 VP of Finance/Facilities/CFO Mr. Craig MAYNARD
32 Int Dean of Students Dr. Deb GARRETT
06 Registrar Ms. Kendi ONNEN
18 Director of Physical Plant Mr. Jeremy MISCHLER
42 Chaplain Rev. Bruce M. FOWLKES
36 Director of Career Development Ms. Kelly BAY
13 Director of Computer Services Dr. Kanaka VIJITHA-KUMARA
37 Director of Financial Aid Mrs. Tammy CROTHERS
41 Athletic Director Mr. Bryan MOORE
29 Director Alumni Relations Mrs. Shellie SCHWANKE
39 Director Student Housing Mrs. Lisa ALLEN
28 Chief Diversity Officer Dr. Jamel WRIGHT
26 Director of Communications Ms. Brttany PARKER
84 Int VP of Enrollment Management Ms. Cindy SISSON
108 Director Institutional Assessment Dr. Ann FULOP
104 Director Study Abroad Dr. Emily EATON
19 Director of Campus Security Mr. Loren MARION

Flashpoint Chicago, a Campus of Columbia College Hollywood (B)

28 North Clark Street, Suite 500, Chicago IL 60602
Telephone: (312) 506-0600 Identification: 667083
Accreditation: &WC

Fox College (C)

18020 Oak Park Avenue, Tinley Park IL 60477
County: Cook FICE Identification: 025228
Unit ID: 145239
Telephone: (708) 444-4500 Carnegie Class: Spec 2-yr-Health
FAX Number: (708) 444-4520 Calendar System: Semester
URL: www.foxcollege.edu
Established: 1932 Annual Undergrad Tuition & Fees: $15,340
Enrollment: 404 Coed
Affiliation or Control: Proprietary IRS Status: Proprietary
Highest Offering: Associate Degree
Accreditation: HLC, MAAB, OTA, PTAA

01 President Ms. Jackie FLYNN
05 hief Academic Officer Ms. Rachel KREFT
08 Head Librarian Mr. Matthew JOHNSON
37 Director Student Financial Aid Ms. Kerry DEMARS

Garrett-Evangelical Theological Seminary (D)

2121 Sheridan Road, Evanston IL 60201-3298
County: Cook FICE Identification: 001682
Unit ID: 145275
Telephone: (847) 866-3900 Carnegie Class: Spec-4-yr-Faith
FAX Number: (847) 866-3884 Calendar System: Semester
URL: www.garrett.edu
Established: 1853 Annual Graduate Tuition & Fees: N/A
Enrollment: 283 Coed
Affiliation or Control: United Methodist IRS Status: 501(c)3
Highest Offering: Doctorate; No Undergraduates
Accreditation: HLC, THEOL

01 President Dr. Lallene J. RECTOR
05 Vice Pres Academic Affairs/Dean Dr. Mai-Anh L. TRAN
112 Senior VP for Planned Giving Dr. David L. HEETLAND
30 Vice President of Development Mr. Joe EMMICK
84 Vice Pres Student Svcs/Enrollment Rev. Becky J. EBERHART
10 Vice President Business Affairs/CFO Mr. Kevin MILLER
45 Asst VP of Strategic Initiatives Ms. Erin B. MOORE
06 Registrar/Dir of Academic Studies Ms. Krista MCNEIL
08 Director of United Library Dr. Lucy CHUNG
18 Senior Director of B&G Mr. Josten BERCZY
37 Director of Financial Aid Mr. Jason GILL
26 Exec Director of Communications Mr. Shane NICHOLS
32 Asst VP/Dean of Students Rev. Benjamin REYNOLDS
04 Exec Assistant to the President Ms. April LONDON
07 Director of Admissions Rev. Katie FAHEY

Governors State University (E)

1 University Parkway, University Park IL 60484-0975
County: Will FICE Identification: 009145
Unit ID: 145336
Telephone: (708) 534-5000 Carnegie Class: Masters/L
FAX Number: (708) 534-4107 Calendar System: Semester
URL: www.govst.edu
Established: 1969 Annual Undergrad Tuition & Fees (In-State): $10,108
Enrollment: 4,650 Coed
Affiliation or Control: State IRS Status: 501(c)3
Highest Offering: Doctorate
Accreditation: HLC, CACREP, CAEP, HSA, NUR, OT, PTA, SP, SPAA, SW

01 President Dr. Cheryl F. GREEN
05 Provost/VP Academic Affairs Dr. Beth CADA
111 VP Advancement/CEO Foundation Mr. William DAVIS
13 Assoc VP/CIO Information Tech Svcs Mr. Chuck PUSTZ
43 Legal Counsel/VP Ms. Therese KING NOHOS
45 Director Budget Planning/Inst Rsrch Ms. Sandra ZURAWSKI
09 Assoc Dir of Institutional Research Mr. Marco KRCATOVICH, II
29 Director of Alumni Assoc Vacant
50 Dean College of Business Dr. Jun ZHAO
49 Dean College Arts Sciences Dr. Andrae MARAK
76 Dean Col Health Professions Dr. Elizabeth BALTHAZAR
53 Dean College Education Dr. Shannon DERMER
32 AVP Dean of Students/Int CDO Mr. Corey WILLIAMS
08 Dean University Library Vacant
06 Registrar Mr. Timothy CARROLL
37 Director Financial Aid Mr. John PERRY
20 Associate Provost/AVP Academic Affs Dr. Colleen SEXTON
15 Director Human Resources Vacant
18 Director Physical Plant Mr. John POTEMPA
19 Director Dept Public Safety Mr. James MCGEE
38 Dir Student Devel/Counseling Center Vacant
36 Director of Career Services Ms. Darcie R. CAMPOS
96 Dir of Procurement/Auxiliary Svcs Ms. Tracy SULLIVAN
11 Chief of Administrative Operations Ms. Penny PERDUE
39 Director Student Housing Mr. Mujahid CHOUDHARY
41 Athletic Director Mr. Anthony BATES
86 Director Government Relations Ms. Maureen KELLY

Greenville University (F)

315 E College, Greenville IL 62246
County: Bond FICE Identification: 001684
Unit ID: 145372
Telephone: (618) 664-7100 Carnegie Class: Masters/S
FAX Number: (618) 664-6841 Calendar System: 4/1/4
URL: www.greenville.edu
Established: 1892 Annual Undergrad Tuition & Fees: $28,956
Enrollment: 994 Coed
Affiliation or Control: Free Methodist IRS Status: 501(c)3
Highest Offering: Master's
Accreditation: HLC, CAEPT, IACBE, SW

01 President Mrs. Suzanne DAVIS
05 Chief Academic Officer Dr. Brian HARTLEY
15 Chief Culture & Diversity Officer Mrs. Katrina LISS
30 Chief Development Officer Mr. Scott GIFFEN
10 Chief Financial Officer Mr. Mark BIDDINGER
26 Chief Marketing & Comm Officer Mrs. Terri SUNDERLAND
11 Strategies and Operations Officer Mr. Mike ADEN
58 Dean of Adult and Graduate Studies Dr. Dave HOLDEN
110 Campaign Director Mr. Breck NELSON
13 Chief Information Officer Mr. Patrick FARMER
84 Chief Enrollment Officer Mrs. Victoria CLARK
20 Associate Chief Academic Officer Dr. Kathryn TAYLOR
88 Faculty Moderator Dr. Eugene DUNKLEY
88 Associate Faculty Moderator Dr. Doug FAULKNER
32 Dean of Student Development Mr. Ross BAKER
19 Dir of Comm Standards & Safety Mr. Shawn FOLES
07 Director of Undergrad Admissions Mrs. Elizabeth KIRBY
08 Director of Library Ms. Gail HEIDEMAN
06 Registrar Mrs. Michelle SUSSENBACH
37 Director of Financial Aid Mr. David KESSINGER
112 Director of Major & Planned Gifts Mr. Brett BRANNON
42 Dean Chapel & Dir Spiritual Form Vacant
18 Director of Facilities Mr. Mark OWENS
04 Executive Assistant to President Mrs. Regina ROBART
29 Director Alumni Affairs Mr. Dewayne NEELEY

Harper College (G)

1200 W Algonquin Road, Palatine IL 60067-7398
County: Cook FICE Identification: 003961
Unit ID: 149842
Telephone: (847) 925-6000 Carnegie Class: Assoc/HT-High Non
FAX Number: (847) 925-6034 Calendar System: Semester
URL: www.harpercollege.edu
Established: 1965 Annual Undergrad Tuition & Fees (In-District): $9,942
Enrollment: 12,199 Coed
Affiliation or Control: State/Local IRS Status: 501(c)3
Highest Offering: Associate Degree
Accreditation: HLC, ACBSP, ADNUR, CAHIIM, COMTA, DH, @DIETI, DMS, MAC, MUS, NAEYC, PNUR, PTAA, RAD, SURGT

01 President Dr. Avis PROCTOR
100 Chief of Staff Mr. Jeff JULIAN
05 Provost Dr. MaryAnn JANOSIK
10 Exec VP Finance & Admin Services Mr. Rob GALICK
11 VP Strat All & Innov/Brd Liaison Dr. Maria COONS
111 VP & Chief Advancement Officer Ms. Laura BROWN
103 VP Workforce Solutions Dr. Michele' SMITH
45 VP Planning/Research/Inst Eff Ms. Darlene SCHLENBECKER
28 VP Diversity/Equity/Inclusion Dr. Tamara JOHNSON
20 Interim Assoc Provost Academics Dr. Travaris HARRIS
15 Chief Human Resources Officer Mr. Roger SPAYER
13 Interim Chief Information Officer Ms. Sue CONTARINO
21 Controller Mr. Robert GRAPENTHIEN
18 Exec Dir of Facilities Management Mr. Darryl KNIGHT
84 Assoc Provost Enrollment Svcs Mr. Robert PARZY
32 Assoc Provost Student Affairs Dr. Claudia MERCADO
75 Dean Career & Technical Programs Dr. Joanne IVORY
76 Dean Health Careers Dr. Kimberly CHAVIS
08 Dean Resources for Learning Ms. Njambi KAMOCHE
35 Dean of Students Ms. Mary Kay HARTON
121 Dean Student Development Dr. Vicki ATKINSON
50 Interim Dean Business & Soc Science Ms. Darice TROUT
81 Interim Dean Mathematics & Sciences Ms. Kimberley POLLY
106 Dean Teaching/Learning/Distance Edu Dr. Michael BATES
49 Dean Liberal Arts Ms. Jaime RIEWERTS
124 Assoc Dean Advising Svcs Dr. Kristin HOFFHINES
102 Assoc Exec Dir Fndn/Dir Major Gifts Ms. Heather ZOLDAK
19 Chief of Police Mr. John LAWSON
27 Director Marketing Services Mr. Mike BARZACCHINI
36 Director Job Placement Resource Ctr Ms. Kathleen CANFIELD
91 Director IT Client Services Ms. Sue CONTARINO
09 Director Institutional Research Dr. Katherine COY
51 Director Adult Educational Dev Ms. Andrea FIEBIG
37 Dir Student Financial Assistance Ms. Laura MCGEE
66 Director Nursing Ms. Jennifer SMITH
06 Registrar/Int Sr Dir Enroll Svcs Ms. Sue SKORA
07 Dir Admissions Outreach Vacant
41 Director of Athletics & Fitness Mr. Doug SPIWAK
88 Campus Architect Mr. Steve PETERSEN

Heartland Community College (H)

1500 W Raab Road, Normal IL 61761-9446
County: McLean FICE Identification: 030838
Unit ID: 384342
Telephone: (309) 268-8000 Carnegie Class: Assoc/HT-High Non
FAX Number: (309) 268-7999 Calendar System: Semester
URL: www.heartland.edu
Established: 1990 Annual Undergrad Tuition & Fees (In-District): $9,540
Enrollment: 4,485 Coed
Affiliation or Control: State/Local IRS Status: 501(c)3
Highest Offering: Associate Degree
Accreditation: HLC, ADNUR, MAC, PTAA, RAD

01 President Dr. Keith CORNILLE
05 Provost/Vice Pres Academic Affairs Dr. Rick PEARCE
10 Vice Pres Finance/Administration Ms. Letisha TREPAC
86 Vice Pres External Relations Ms. Kelli HILL
84 Vice Pres Enrollment/Student Svcs Dr. Sarah DIEL-HUNT
32 Assoc VP Enrollment/Student Service Dr. Amy PAWLIK
20 Assoc VP Academic Affairs Dr. Traci VAN PROOYEN
15 Exec Director Human Resources Mrs. Barb LEATHERS
18 Executive Director of Facilities Mr. James HUBBARD
13 Chief Information Officer Mr. Scott BROSS
26 Exec Director of Marketing Mr. Tim BILL
30 Exec Dir Development/Foundation Mr. Chris DOWNING
106 Exec Dir Online Educ/E-learning Dr. Anna CATTERSON
21 Controller Ms. Sharon MCDONALD
07 Dean Enrollment Services Ms. Lindsay EICKHORST
37 Director of Financial Aid Mr. Todd BURNS
41 Director of Athletics Mr. Ryan KNOX
121 Dean of Student Success Ms. Kimberly KELLEY
06 Registrar Ms. Cindy ALFANO
35 Director of Student Engagement Mr. Skylar GUIMOND
04 Executive Assistant Ms. Laura MAI
22 Assoc Dir Equity/Complianc/Title IX Mr. Terrance BOND
96 Associate Director Business Office Ms. Jd DAVIS
09 Director of Institutional Research Mr. Dan HAGBERG

Hebrew Theological College (I)

7135 N Carpenter Road, Skokie IL 60077-3263
County: Cook FICE Identification: 001685
Unit ID: 145497
Telephone: (847) 982-2500 Carnegie Class: Spec-4-yr-Faith
FAX Number: (847) 674-6381 Calendar System: Semester
URL: www.htc.edu
Established: 1922 Annual Undergrad Tuition & Fees: $13,760
Enrollment: 181 Coordinate
Affiliation or Control: Independent Non-Profit IRS Status: 501(c)3
Highest Offering: Master's
Accreditation: HLC

01 Chief Executive Officer Rabbi Shmuel SCHUMAN
05 Chief Academic Officer Dr. Zev ELEFF
20 Rosh Hayeshiva Rabbi Avraham FRIEDMAN
11 Vice President for Administration Rabbi Sender KUTNER

33 Mashgiach Ruchani-Dean .... Rabbi Zvi ZIMMERMAN
20 Dean Blitstein Institute .... Dr. Chani TESSLER
34 Menahel Ruchani-Dean .... Rabbi Binyamin OLSTEIN
06 Registrar .... Rabbi Gavriel BACHRACH
07 Director of Admissions .... Rabbi Joshua ZISOOK
30 Director of Development .... Vacant
44 Development Coordinator .... Rabbi Yaakov FRIEDMAN
33 Assistant Dean of Men's Division .... Dr. Michael VERDERAME
125 Chancellor Emeritus .... Dr. Jerold ISENBERG

† Separate campuses for male and female students. Part of the Touro College and University System.

Highland Community College (A)

2998 W Pearl City Road, Freeport IL 61032-9341
County: Stephenson FICE Identification: 001681
Unit ID: 145521
Telephone: (815) 235-6121 Carnegie Class: Assoc/MT-VT-High Non
FAX Number: (815) 235-6130 Calendar System: Semester
URL: www.highland.edu
Established: 1962 Annual Undergrad Tuition & Fees (In-District): $6,846
Enrollment: 1,276 Coed
Affiliation or Control: State/Local IRS Status: 501(c)3
Highest Offering: Associate Degree
Accreditation: HLC, ADNUR, MAC

01 President .... Mrs. Christina KUBERSKI
05 Vice Pres Academic Services/CAO .... Dr. David NAZE
10 Vice Pres Administrative Services .... Ms. Jill M. JANSSEN
50 VP Business/Tech & Community Pgms . Mr. Scott R. ANDERSON
32 Vice Pres Student Dev & Support Svc ... Ms. Elizabeth L. GERBER
79 Dean Humanities/Social Sci & FA .... Mr. Jim PHILLIPS
81 Dean Natural Science & Math .... Dr. Brendan C. DUTMER
66 Dean Nursing & Allied Health .... Vacant
51 Director Adult Education Programs .... Ms. Rachel FELDHAUS
41 Director Athletics .... Mr. Peter E. NORMAN
84 Director Enrollment & Records .... Mr. Jeremy BRADT
18 Director Facilities & Safety .... Mr. Kurt SIMPSON
37 Director Financial Aid .... Ms. Kathy BANGASSER
15 Director Human Resources .... Ms. Karen BROWN
09 Director Institutional Research .... Dr. Michelle THRUMAN
13 Director Information Technology .... Mr. Pete FINK
124 Director Retention & Learning Svcs .... Ms. Carolyn PETSCHE
26 Director Marketing & Community Rel .... Ms. Leslie SCHMIDT
88 Dir Retired & Senior Volunteer Pgm .... Ms. Cindi MIELKE
22 Director TRIO Services .... Mr. Anthony SAGO
88 Coordinator Upward Bound Program .... Vacant
21 Manager Accounting .... Ms. Mary J. LLOYD
40 Manager Bookstore .... Ms. Madonna KEENEY
101 Exec Asst to President/Board Sec .... Ms. Terri A. GRIMES
102 Foundation Executive Director .... Mr. Jeff REINKE
112 Foundation Major Gift Officer .... Mr. Dan DICK
88 Foundation Director of Operations .... Ms. Patricia A. DUNN

Illinois Central College (B)

1 College Drive, East Peoria IL 61635-0001
County: Tazewell FICE Identification: 006753
Unit ID: 145682
Telephone: (309) 694-5422 Carnegie Class: Assoc/HT-Mix Trad/Non
FAX Number: (309) 694-5450 Calendar System: Semester
URL: www.icc.edu
Established: 1966 Annual Undergrad Tuition & Fees (In-District): $9,900
Enrollment: 7,813 Coed
Affiliation or Control: State/Local IRS Status: 501(c)3
Highest Offering: Associate Degree
Accreditation: HLC, ACFEI, ADNUR, COARC, DH, EMT, MAC, MLTAD, MUS, OTA, PNUR, PTAA, RAD, SURGT

01 President .... Dr. Sheila QUIRK-BAILEY
10 Exec VP Administration/Finance .... Mr. Bruce BUDDE
26 VP of Marketing/Advancement .... Ms. Kim ARMSTRONG
05 Interim VP of Academic Affairs .... Dr. Charles SWAIM
28 VP of Workforce & Diversity .... Dr. Rita ALI
32 VP of Student Success .... Mr. Bill HEBERT
15 AVP of Human Resources .... Ms. Michelle BUGOS
108 AVP of Assess/Accred & Acad Svcs .... Dr. Jill WRIGHT
102 Exec Dir Education Foundation .... Ms. Stephanie HOLMES
09 Exec Dir Inst Research & Planning .... Mr. David COOK
103 Exec Dir Workforce Operations .... Ms. Paula NACHTRIEB
35 Dean of Students .... Dr. Emily POINTS
84 Dean of Enrollment Management .... Ms. Kris BINARD
51 Dean of Corp/Cont Education .... Ms. Julie HOWAR
36 Dean of College/Career Readiness .... Ms. Arnitria SHAW
79 Dean of Humanities .... Dr. Lonetta OLIVER
81 Dean of Math/Science/Engineering .... Mr. Joe BERGMAN
50 Dean of Business/Legal/Info Systems ... Ms. Michelle WEGHORST
57 Dean of Arts & Communications .... Ms. Kari SCHIMMEL
47 Dean of Agriculture/Industrial Tech .... Dr. Robert SHAW
76 Dean of Health Careers .... Ms. Wendee GUTH
18 Sr Director Facilities Services .... Mr. Jeff LAGROW
16 Director Human Resources .... Ms. Kim MALCOLM
08 Director Library Services .... Ms. Cathryne KAUFMAN
41 Interim Director Athletics & PE .... Ms. Heather DOTY
13 Director Network & Desktop Svc .... Mr. William NEWPORT
14 Director Enterprise Systems .... Mr. Brad FINLEY
104 Director Intl Educ Program .... Ms. Tia VAN HESTER
121 Director Advisement .... Ms. Karmen FEURTADO
19 Campus Police Chief .... Mr. Thomas LARSON
21 Controller .... Mr. Ed BABCOCK
22 Coordinator Access Services .... Ms. Terri INGLES
06 Registrar .... Ms. Nikisha WRIGHT ANDERSON
04 Administrative Asst to President .... Ms. Lori SUTTON
101 Admin Asst to EVP/Sec to the Board .... Ms. Sue BULITTA

Illinois College (C)

1101 W College Avenue, Jacksonville IL 62650-2299
County: Morgan FICE Identification: 001688
Unit ID: 145691
Telephone: (217) 245-3000 Carnegie Class: Bac-A&S
FAX Number: (217) 245-3034 Calendar System: Semester
URL: www.ic.edu
Established: 1829 Annual Undergrad Tuition & Fees: $34,620
Enrollment: 1,154 Coed
Affiliation or Control: Independent Non-Profit IRS Status: 501(c)3
Highest Offering: Master's
Accreditation: HLC, NURSE

01 President .... Dr. Barbara A. FARLEY
05 Provost and Dean of the College .... Dr. Catharine E. O'CONNELL
10 Vice President of Business Affairs .... Mr. Kent SILTMAN
111 Vice President External Relations .... Ms. Stephanie CHIPMAN
20 Dean of the Faculty .... Dr. Laura COREY
32 Assoc Dean Students/Title IX Coord .... Dr. Jennie HEMINGWAY
07 Dean of Admiss & Stdnt Fin Svcs .... Mr. Evan WILSON
39 Exec Dir of Residential Life .... Mr. Denny SCHUMACHER
09 Exec Dir for Inst Research .... Dr. Robert A. SWEATMAN
06 Registrar .... Ms. Helen KUHN
13 Chief Info Technology Officer (CIO) .... Mr. Patrick BROWN
37 Assoc Director of Financial Aid .... Ms. Rebecca BIRDSELL
30 Exec Dir of Development & Alumni .... Ms. Kris HOUSER
26 Director Marketing/Communications .... Mr. Bryan LEONARD
08 Library Director .... Mr. Luke BEATTY
18 Director of Facilities Operations .... Mr. Al DILLOW
36 Exec Dir of Career Readiness & EXL .... Ms. Kelly POOL
21 Controller .... Ms. Melissa J. DYSON
35 Dir Center for Student Involvement .... Ms. Karen K. HOMOLKA
42 Chaplain .... Mr. Tim MCGEE
15 Director of Human Resources .... Ms. Lauren HAYS
38 Lead Mental Health Counselor .... Ms. Leah HAMILTON
28 Dir of Diversity/Equity/Inclusion .... Ms. Valeria CUETO
41 Athletic Director .... Mr. Mike SNYDER

Illinois College of Optometry (D)

3241 S Michigan Avenue, Chicago IL 60616-3878
County: Cook FICE Identification: 001689
Unit ID: 145628
Telephone: (312) 225-1700 Carnegie Class: Spec-4-yr-Other Health
FAX Number: (312) 225-1724 Calendar System: Quarter
URL: www.ico.edu
Established: 1872 Annual Undergrad Tuition & Fees: N/A
Enrollment: 531 Coed
Affiliation or Control: Independent Non-Profit IRS Status: 501(c)3
Highest Offering: First Professional Degree
Accreditation: HLC, OPT, OPTR

01 President .... Dr. Mark C. COLIP
05 Vice Pres for Academic Affairs/Dean .... Dr. Stephanie MESSNER
10 VP for Finance & Business/CFO .... Ms. Christina OJEDA
11 Vice President for Administration .... Vacant
111 VP for Strategy/Inst Advancement .... Dr. Leonard V. MESSNER
32 Dean of Student Affairs .... Dr. Erik MOTHERSBAUGH
06 Assoc Dean for Academic/Registrar ... Dr. Geoffrey GOODFELLOW
07 Director of Admissions .... Ms. Teisha JOHNSON
35 Assistant Dean for Student Success .... Ms. Beth KARMIS
84 Sr Dir of Enrollment Mgmt Tech .... Ms. Milissa J. BARTOLD
29 Director Alumni Relations .... Ms. Connie M. SCAVUZZO
18 Chief Facilities/Physical Plant .... Mr. Gary YOUNG
08 Chief Library Officer .... Ms. Christine WEBER
13 Chief Info Technology Officer .... Mr. Amit CHOKSI
04 Chief Exec Asst to the President .... Ms. Maggie LOPEZ
19 Director Security/Safety .... Mr. Tim CAPPARELLI
36 Director of Career Development .... Ms. Daphne ANDERSON

*Illinois Eastern Community Colleges System Office (E)

233 E Chestnut Street, Olney IL 62450-2298
County: Richland FICE Identification: 009135
Unit ID: 443368
Telephone: (618) 393-2982 Carnegie Class: N/A
FAX Number: (618) 392-4816
URL: www.iecc.edu

01 Chancellor .... Dr. Ryan GOWER
05 Assistant Dean of Academic Services .... Mrs. Alyssa MAGLONE
10 Chief Finance Officer/Treasurer .... Mr. Ryan HAWKINS
103 Dean Workforce Education .... Mr. Michael THOMAS
25 Pgm Dir of Grants and Compliance .... Mrs. Libby MCVICKER
85 Pgm Dir of International Stdnt Pgm .... Ms. Cassandra GOLDMAN
15 Director of Human Resources .... Mrs. Andrea MCDOWELL
88 Director TRIO Upward Bound .... Ms. Tiffany COWGER
88 Pgm Dir Student Learning Assessment .... Mr. Brandon WEGER
121 Director TRIO Student Support Svcs .... Mr. Wain DAVIS
06 Registrar .... Mr. Steve PATBERG
07 Assoc Dean of Admissions & Records .... Mrs. Amber MALONE
37 Director of Financial Aid .... Mrs. Andrea PUCKETT
84 Director Enrollment Management .... Mrs. Andrea LOLL

*Illinois Eastern Community Colleges Frontier Community College (F)

Frontier Drive, Fairfield IL 62837-9801
County: Wayne FICE Identification: 020744
Unit ID: 403469
Telephone: (618) 842-3711 Carnegie Class: Assoc/MT-VT-High Non
FAX Number: (618) 842-4425 Calendar System: Semester
URL: www.iecc.edu/fcc
Established: 1976 Annual Undergrad Tuition & Fees (In-District): $9,992
Enrollment: 1,262 Coed
Affiliation or Control: State/Local IRS Status: 501(c)3
Highest Offering: Associate Degree
Accreditation: &HLC, ADNUR

02 President .... Dr. Gerald EDGREN, JR.
05 Dean of Instruction .... Dr. Paul BRUINSMA
51 Director of Adult Education .... Ms. Angelique MAGUIRE
10 Director of Business .... Mrs. Mary JOHNSTON
08 Director of Learning Resource Ctr .... Ms. Lori NOE
41 Interim Athletic Director .... Ms. Amanda KOTCH
37 Coordinator of Financial Aid .... Ms. Justn YOUNG
50 Dir of Business & Industry .... Ms. Sharmila KAKAC

† Regional accreditation is carried under the parent institution Illinois Eastern Community Colleges System Office in Olney, IL.

*Illinois Eastern Community Colleges Lincoln Trail College (G)

11220 State Highway 1, Robinson IL 62454-5707
County: Crawford FICE Identification: 009786
Unit ID: 403478
Telephone: (618) 544-8657 Carnegie Class: Assoc/HT-High Non
FAX Number: (618) 544-7423 Calendar System: Semester
URL: www.iecc.edu/ltc
Established: 1969 Annual Undergrad Tuition & Fees (In-District): $9,435
Enrollment: 723 Coed
Affiliation or Control: State/Local IRS Status: 501(c)3
Highest Offering: Associate Degree
Accreditation: &HLC, ADNUR

02 President .... Dr. Zahi ATALLAH
05 Dean of the College .... Mr. Brent TODD
37 Coordinator of Financial Aid .... Ms. Krystle RIGGLE
08 Dir of Instructional Support Svcs .... Ms. Rena GOWER
10 Director of Business .... Ms. Jamie HENRY
41 Athletic Director .... Mr. Kevin BOWERS
26 Coord Public Information/Marketing .... Mr. Christopher FORDE

† Regional accreditation is carried under the parent institution Illinois Eastern Community Colleges System Office in Olney, IL.

*Illinois Eastern Community Colleges Olney Central College (H)

305 North West Street, Olney IL 62450-1099
County: Richland FICE Identification: 001742
Unit ID: 145707
Telephone: (618) 395-7777 Carnegie Class: Assoc/MT-VT-High Non
FAX Number: (618) 392-3293 Calendar System: Semester
URL: www.iecc.edu/occ
Established: 1962 Annual Undergrad Tuition & Fees (In-District): $9,435
Enrollment: 906 Coed
Affiliation or Control: State/Local IRS Status: 501(c)3
Highest Offering: Associate Degree
Accreditation: &HLC, ADNUR, RAD

02 President .... Mr. Rodney RANES
05 Dean of Instruction .... Dr. Michael CONN
76 Interim Assoc Dean of Allied Health .... Dr. Anne HUSTAD
08 Director Learning Skills Center/LRC .... Vacant
88 Director Cosmetology .... Ms. Courtney MEADOWS
10 Director Business .... Mr. Doug SHIPMAN
41 Athletic Director/Coach .... Mr. Dennis CONLEY
37 Financial Aid Coordinator .... Ms. Taryn BUNTING

† Regional accreditation is carried under the parent institution Illinois Eastern Community Colleges System Office in Olney, IL.

*Illinois Eastern Community Colleges Wabash Valley College (I)

2200 College Drive, Mount Carmel IL 62863-2657
County: Wabash FICE Identification: 001779
Unit ID: 403487
Telephone: (618) 262-8641 Carnegie Class: Assoc/HVT-High Non
FAX Number: (618) 262-5347 Calendar System: Semester
URL: www.iecc.edu/wvc
Established: 1960 Annual Undergrad Tuition & Fees (In-District): $9,435
Enrollment: 2,222 Coed
Affiliation or Control: State/Local IRS Status: 501(c)3
Highest Offering: Associate Degree
Accreditation: &HLC, ADNUR

02 President .... Mr. Matt FOWLER
05 Dean of Instruction .... Mr. Robert CONN
121 Director of Academic Advising .... Mr. Tim ZIMMER
08 Director of LRC .... Ms. Sandy CRAIG

60 Director of Broadcasting ... Mr. Kyle PEACH
41 Athletic Director ... Mr. Mike CARPENTER
10 Director of Business ... Mrs. Reilly BAUMGART
37 Financial Aid Coordinator ... Ms. Jane OWEN
18 Groundskeeper ... Mr. Adam ROESCH

† Regional accreditation is carried under the parent institution Illinois Eastern Community Colleges System Office in Olney, IL.

Illinois Institute of Technology (A)

10 West 35th Street, Chicago IL 60616-3793
County: Cook
FICE Identification: 001691
Unit ID: 145725
Telephone: (312) 567-3000
Carnegie Class: DU-Higher
FAX Number: (312) 567-3004
Calendar System: Semester
URL: www.iit.edu
Established: 1890
Annual Undergrad Tuition & Fees: $50,490
Enrollment: 6,325
Coed
Affiliation or Control: Independent Non-Profit
IRS Status: 501(c)3
Highest Offering: Doctorate
Accreditation: HLC, CACREP, CEA, CLPSY, LSAR

01 President ... Dr. Alan CRAMB
05 Provost ... Dr. Peter KILPATRICK
84 Vice Pres Enrollment/Vice Provost ... Dr. Mike GOSZ
10 VP Finance/CFO & Treasurer ... Dr. Michael D. HORAN
18 VP Admin/Facilities/Pub Safety ... Mr. Bruce WATTS
111 Vice Pres Institutional Advancement ... Vacant
88 Vice Pres International Affairs ... Dr. Darsh T. WASAN
86 Vice President External Affairs ... Mr. Jess GOODE
43 Vice President General Counsel ... Mr. Anthony D'AMATO
88 Sr VP & Dir IIT Research Inst ... Dr. David MCCORMICK
88 VP & Dir Inst Food Safety & Health ... Dr. Robert BRACKETT
13 CIO & Vice Provost ... Mr. Ophir TRIGALO
28 Vice Provost Student Diversity ... Vacant
58 Vice Provost Grad Academic Affairs ... Dr. Jamshid MOHAMMADI
46 Vice Provost for Research ... Dr. Fred HICKERNELL
32 Vice Provost Student Affairs ... Ms. Katherine MURPHY-STETZ
61 Dean Chicago-Kent College of Law ... Dr. Anita K. KRUG
49 Interim Dean Col of Sci & Letters ... Dr. Xiaofan LI
54 Dean Armour Col of Engineering ... Dr. Natacha DEPAOLA
50 Dean Stuart School of Business ... Vacant
48 Dean College of Architecture ... Mr. Reed KROLOFF
83 Dean Lewis Col of Human Sciences ... Dr. Christine HIMES
12 Dean Institute of Design ... Mr. Denis WEIL
72 Dean School of Applied Technology ... Dr. Bob CARLSON
08 Interim Dean of Libraries ... Mr. Devin SAVAGE
88 Associate General Counsel ... Ms. Candida MIRANDA
21 Assoc VP Finance & Controller ... Mr. Ken JOHNSTON
15 Associate VP Human Resources ... Ms. Hilary HUDSON HOSEK
88 Assoc Vice Prov Grad Acad Affs ... Ms. Holli PRYOR HARRIS
41 AVP Director of Athletics ... Mr. Joseph HAKES
07 Assoc Vice Pres Enrollment Svcs ... Ms. Abigail MCGRATH
07 Asst Vice Pres UG Admissions ... Ms. Toni RILEY
123 Asst VP Grad/Prof Admissions ... Mr. Rishab MALHOTRA
39 AVP Residence & Greek Life ... Vacant
14 Assoc CIO Enterprise Systems ... Mr. Vince BATTISTA
14 Assoc CIO Technology Infrastructure ... Mr. Ibukun OYEWOLE
14 Assoc CIO User & Technical Svcs ... Mr. Eric BREESE
23 Assoc VP Student Health & Wellness ... Ms. Anita OPDYCKE
29 Assoc VP Alumni & Donor Rels ... Vacant
96 Director of Purchasing ... Ms. Snow RUTKOWSKE
06 Interim Registrar ... Vacant
37 Director of Financial Aid ... Ms. Elizabeth WAHLSTROM HELGREN
22 Director Diversity/Inclusions/EE ... Ms. Lisa MONTGOMERY
25 Director Sponsored Research ... Mr. Robert LAPOINTE
88 Dir Environmental Health & Safety ... Ms. Cynthia CHAFFEE
108 Director of Assessment ... Dr. Carol-Ann EMMONS
105 Director Web Development/Services ... Mr. Brian BAILEY
106 Dir IIT Online Tech Svcs ... Ms. Lauren WOODS
04 Director President's Office ... Ms. Sandra LAPORTE
90 Manager Academic Computing ... Vacant

Illinois Institute of Technology Downtown Campus (B)

565 W Adams Street, Chicago IL 60661
Telephone: (312) 906-5000
Identification: 770075
Accreditation: &HLC, LAW

Illinois Institute of Technology Rice Campus (C)

201 East Loop Road, Wheaton IL 60189
Telephone: (630) 682-6000
Identification: 770077
Accreditation: &HLC

Illinois State University (D)

201 S. School St., Campus Box 3490, Normal IL 61761-2521
County: McLean
FICE Identification: 001692
Unit ID: 145813
Telephone: (309) 438-2111
Carnegie Class: DU-Higher
FAX Number: N/A
Calendar System: Semester
URL: https://illinoisstate.edu/
Established: 1857
Annual Undergrad Tuition & Fees (In-State): $15,319
Enrollment: 20,720
Coed
Affiliation or Control: State
IRS Status: 501(c)3
Highest Offering: Doctorate
Accreditation: HLC, AAFCS, ART, AUD, CAATE, CAEP, CAEPN, CAHIIM, CAPRT, CIDA, CONST, DIETD, DIETI, IPSY, MT, MUS, NAIT, NURSE, PH, SCPSY, SP, SW, THEA

01 President ... Dr. Terri KINZY
100 Interim Assistant to President ... Ms. Kathleen KILLIAN
04 Administrative Asst to President ... Mr. Dave BENTLIN
05 VP Academic Affairs & Provost ... Dr. Aondover TARHULE
10 VP Finance & Planning ... Mr. Daniel STEPHENS
32 VP Student Affairs ... Dr. Levester JOHNSON
35 Assistant VP Student Affairs ... Dr. Adam PECK
111 VP University Advancement ... Mr. Pat VICKERMAN
13 Assoc VP & Chief Info Officer ... Mr. Charles EDAMALA
41 Director Intercollegiate Athletics ... Mr. Kyle BRENNAN
86 Director State Government Relations ... Dr. Jonathan LACKLAND
28 Int Asst to Pres for Diversity/Incl ... Dr. Doris HOUSTON
43 General Counsel ... Ms. Lisa HUSON
22 Interim Dir Equal Opp & Access ... Mr. Jeff LANGE
20 Associate Provost ... Dr. Ani YAZEDJIAN
58 Assoc VP Grad Studies/Research ... Dr. Craig MCLAUGHLAN
88 Assoc VP Undergrad Education ... Dr. Amy HURD
88 Int Assoc VP Global Education ... Dr. Perry SCHOON
88 Asst VP Academic Planning ... Dr. J. Cooper CUTTING
121 Interim Asst VP Student Success ... Dr. Amelia NOEL-ELKINS
88 Interim Assoc VP Academic Admin ... Dr. Roberta TRITES
88 Assoc VP Acad Fiscal Mgmt ... Dr. Dan ELKINS
84 Assoc VP Enrollment Management ... Dr. Jana ALBRECHT
15 Interim Assoc VP Human Resources ... Ms. Janice BONNEVILLE
21 Assoc VP Fin Info & Comptroller ... Mr. Doug SCHNITTKER
18 Assoc VP Fac Mgmt/Planning & Opers ... Mr. Mike GEBEKE
114 Assistant VP Budget & Planning ... Ms. Sandra CAVI
35 Assistant VP Student Affairs ... Dr. Danielle MILLER-SCHUSTER
08 Dean University Libraries ... Dr. Dallas LONG
06 University Registrar ... Mr. Jess RAY
07 Director Admissions ... Mr. Jeff MAVROS
88 Interim Director University College ... Ms. Wendy WHITMAN
30 Executive Director of Development ... Ms. Joy HUTCHCRAFT
37 Director Financial Aid ... Ms. Bridget CURL
29 Exec Director Alumni Engagement ... Ms. Kristin HARDING
85 Director International Studies ... Dr. Luis CANALES
92 Acting Director Honors Program ... Dr. Katina THOMPSON
94 Director Women's Studies ... Dr. Alison BAILEY
96 Director of Purchasing Office ... Mr. Ernest OLSON
49 Int Dean College Arts & Sciences ... Dr. Diane ZOSKY
50 Dean College Business ... Dr. Ajay SAMANT
53 Dean College Education ... Dr. Jim WOLFINGER
72 Dean College Applied Sci/Tech ... Dr. Todd MCLODA
57 Dean Wonsook Kim College Fine Arts ... Ms. Jean MILLER
66 Dean Mennonite College ... Dr. Judy NEUBRANDER
35 Assistant VP & Dean of Students ... Dr. John DAVENPORT
38 Director Student Counseling ... Dr. Sandy COLBS
39 Director University Housing ... Ms. Stacey MWILAMBWE
23 Director Student Health Services ... Dr. Christina NULTY
19 Chief University Police ... Mr. Aaron WOODRUFF
44 Director Annual Giving ... Ms. Jillian NELSON
27 Exec Dir University Marketing/Comm ... Mr. Brian BEAM
45 Dir Planning/Rsch/Policy Analysis ... Ms. Angela ENGEL
108 Director University Assessment ... Dr. Ryan SMITH
105 Director Web & Interactive Comm ... Mr. Arturo RAMIREZ

Illinois Valley Community College (E)

815 N Orlando Smith Road, Oglesby IL 61348-9692
County: La Salle
FICE Identification: 001705
Unit ID: 145831
Telephone: (815) 224-2720
Carnegie Class: Assoc/HVT-High Non
FAX Number: (815) 224-3033
Calendar System: Semester
URL: www.ivcc.edu
Established: 1966
Annual Undergrad Tuition & Fees (In-District): $13,232
Enrollment: 2,413
Coed
Affiliation or Control: Local
IRS Status: 501(c)3
Highest Offering: Associate Degree
Accreditation: HLC, ADNUR, DA, EMT, NAEYC

01 President ... Dr. Jerry M. CORCORAN
05 Vice Pres for Academic Affairs ... Dr. Deborah L. ANDERSON
10 Vice Pres Business Svcs/Finance ... Dr. Matthew SEATON
20 Assoc Vice Pres Academic Affairs ... Ms. Bonnie L. CAMPBELL
32 Vice President Student Services ... Mr. Mark J. GRZYBOWSKI
24 Director of Learning Resources ... Dr. Patrice HESS
31 Exec Dir Cmty Relations/Marketing ... Mr. Francis R. BROLLEY
13 Dir of Information Technology Svcs ... Mr. Christopher DUNLAP
51 Dir Cont Educ/Business Svcs ... Ms. Jennifer C. SCHERI
15 Director Human Resources ... Ms. Leslie A. HOFER
37 Director of Financial Aid ... Mr. Eric JOHNSON
07 Director of Admissions/Records ... Vacant
08 Public Services Librarian ... Ms. Stephanie REEDER
30 Director of Development ... Mr. Francis R. BROLLEY
96 Director of Purchasing ... Ms. Michelle L. CARBONI
18 Director of Facilities ... Mr. Scott CURLEY
09 Director of Institutional Research ... Mr. Matthew P. SUERTH
81 Dean Natural Science/Business ... Mr. Ron W. GROLEAU
66 Dean of Nursing ... Vacant
79 Dean Humanities/Fine Arts/Soc Sci ... Vacant
103 Dean Workforce Development ... Mr. Shane LANGE

Illinois Wesleyan University (F)

PO Box 2900, 1312 Park Street, Bloomington IL 61702-2900
County: McLean
FICE Identification: 001696
Unit ID: 145646
Telephone: (309) 556-1000
Carnegie Class: Bac-A&S
FAX Number: (309) 556-3411
Calendar System: Other
URL: www.iwu.edu
Established: 1850
Annual Undergrad Tuition & Fees: $51,336
Enrollment: 1,636
Coed
Affiliation or Control: Independent Non-Profit
IRS Status: 501(c)3
Highest Offering: Baccalaureate
Accreditation: HLC, MUS, NURSE

01 President ... Dr. S. Georgia NUGENT
05 Provost & Dean of Faculty ... Dr. Mark BRODL
10 Vice President Business & Finance ... Mr. Matt BIERMAN
30 Vice President for Advancement ... Mr. Steve SEIBRING
27 Director for Communications ... Ms. Ann AUBRY
32 VP Student Affairs/Dean Students ... Dr. Karla CARNEY-HALL
84 VP of Enrollment & Marketing ... Ms. LeAnn HUGHES
07 Dean Admissions/AVP Enrollment Mgmt ... Mr. Greg KING
09 AVP for Institutional Effectiveness ... Dr. Michael THOMPSON
86 Dir Government/Community Relations ... Mr. Carl F. TEICHMAN
04 Exec Assistant to the President ... Ms. Julie ANDERSON
20 Assoc Provost ... Prof. Rebecca ROESNER
20 Assoc Dean Curricular/Faculty Dev ... Vacant
15 Dir Human Resources/Title IX Coord ... Ms. Cindy LOTZ
13 Chief Technology Officer ... Mr. Leon LEWIS
110 Asst Vice Pres for Advancement ... Mr. Bob GERATY
29 Asst VP of Alumni Engagement ... Vacant
38 Exec Director Counseling/Health ... Dr. Vickie FOLSE
35 Asst VP Stdnt Affs/Dir Campus Life ... Dr. Kevin CAREY
08 University Librarian/Copyright Ofcr ... Ms. Stephanie DAVIS-KAHL
06 Registrar ... Dr. Leslie BETZ
42 Univ Chaplain/Assoc Dean Students ... Vacant
21 Controller ... Mr. John BRYANT
37 Director of Financial Aid ... Mr. Scott SEIBRING
64 Director of School of Music ... Dr. Franklin LAREY
57 Director of School of Art ... Prof. Julie JOHNSON
57 Director of School of Theatre Arts ... Dr. Jean KERR
66 Director of School of Nursing ... Dr. Vickie FOLSE
41 Director of Athletics ... Prof. Mike WAGNER
29 Director of Alumni Engagement ... Vacant
102 Dir Grants/Foundation Relations ... Mr. Dick FOLSE
44 Director of Wesleyan Annual Fund ... Ms. Elizabeth CHAMBERS-KLATT
36 Director of Career Center ... Mr. Warren KISTNER
18 Director of Physical Plant ... Mr. James J. BLUMBERG
88 Dir of Athletic Communications ... Ms. Katie GONZALES
93 Dean for Inclusion & Advocacy ... Mr. Prince ROBERTSON
35 Director of Student Involvement ... Vacant
94 Dir of Women's & Gender Studies ... Dr. Carole MYSCOFSKI
104 Director of International Office ... Ms. Stacey SHIMIZU
40 Bookstore Manager ... Ms. Sarah HASTINGS
26 Director of Marketing ... Mr. Andrew KREISS

Institute for Clinical Social Work (G)

1345 W. Argyle St, Chicago IL 60640
County: Cook
FICE Identification: 025737
Unit ID: 145886
Telephone: (312) 935-4232
Carnegie Class: Spec-4-yr-Other Health
FAX Number: (312) 935-4255
Calendar System: Semester
URL: www.icsw.edu
Established: 1981
Annual Graduate Tuition & Fees: N/A
Enrollment: 128
Coed
Affiliation or Control: Independent Non-Profit
IRS Status: 501(c)3
Highest Offering: Doctorate; No Undergraduates
Accreditation: HLC

01 President ... Dr. Michelle C. STEWART
10 Vice Pres Finance/Operations ... Mr. Michael BAUMAN
05 Academic Dean ... Dr. Joan SERVATIUS
37 Director of Student Financial Svcs ... Vacant
07 Dir of Admissions/Enrollment Mgmt ... Mr. Kenneth FRIERSON
32 Chief Student Affairs Officer ... Ms. Andrea DUNBAR

John A. Logan College (H)

700 Logan College Road, Carterville IL 62918-2500
County: Williamson
FICE Identification: 008076
Unit ID: 146205
Telephone: (618) 985-2828
Carnegie Class: Assoc/HVT-High Non
FAX Number: (618) 985-2248
Calendar System: Semester
URL: www.jalc.edu
Established: 1967
Annual Undergrad Tuition & Fees (In-District): $5,506
Enrollment: 3,328
Coed
Affiliation or Control: State/Local
IRS Status: 501(c)3
Highest Offering: Associate Degree
Accreditation: HLC, ADNUR, DA, DMS, MLTAD, OTA, SURGT

01 President ... Dr. Kirk OVERSTREET
05 Provost ... Ms. Melanie PECORD
10 Interim VP Business Services ... Ms. Stacy BUCKINGHAM
11 Interim VP for Administration ... Dr. Clay BREWER
32 Dean Student Services ... Mr. Tim WILLIAMS
07 Assoc Dean of Admissions ... Ms. Christy STEWART
21 Dean Financial Operations ... Ms. Stacy BUCKINGHAM
20 Dean Academic Affairs ... Dr. Stephanie HARTFORD
75 Assoc Dean of Career/Technical Educ ... Mr. Scott WERNSMAN
20 Assoc Dean of Academic Affairs ... Mr. Nathan ARNETT
103 Dir of Academic & Workforce Pgms ... Ms. Michelle HAMILTON
37 Director of Student Financial Asst ... Ms. Pat JACKSON
26 Director of Public Relations ... Dr. Steve O'KEEFE
35 Assoc Dean of Student Activities ... Ms. Adrienne BARKLEY-GIFFIN
36 Dir of Career Services and Intl Ed ... Ms. Beth STEPHENS
102 Executive Director of Foundation ... Ms. Staci SHAFER
66 Director of Nursing ... Ms. Kristin YOSANOVICH
88 Director of Testing Services ... Ms. Christy MCBRIDE
15 Director of Human Resources ... Ms. Johnna HERREN

18 Dir Buildings and Grounds ....Mr. Jeremy MUELLER
09 Director Institutional Research ....Mr. Eric PULLEY
25 Grant Writer ....Dr. Tammy GWALTNEY
04 Senior Exec Asst to President .... Ms. Carmen CUTSINGER
101 Assistant to Pres/Board of Trustees .... Ms. Susan MAY
28 Director of Diversity & Inclusion ....Ms. Toyin FOX
41 Athletic Director .... Mr. Greg STARRICK
117 Dir of Emergency Plng & Risk Mgmt ....Vacant
88 Business Analyst ....Mr. Jason SNIDER
38 Director of Student Success ....Ms. Nikki BROOKS
121 Director Academic Advisement .... Ms. Stacy HOLLOWAY
96 Dir of Purchasing/Auxiliary Svcs .... Ms. Sue ZAMORA
88 Dir Child Care Resources/Referral ....Ms. Missy BROWN
88 Director of ASE ....Ms. Crystal HOSSELTON
56 Director of Adult Education .... Ms. Karla TABING
50 Dir of Business & Industry Training ....Mr. Dennis WHITE
88 Exec Dir of Integrated Technology ....Mr. Scott ELLIOTT
51 Director of Continuing Education ....Vacant
18 Director of Facility Services .... Mr. Chris NAEGELE
104 Coord of International Educ ....Vacant
105 WebMaster ....Mr. Phillip LANE
106 Assoc Dean of Education Technology .... Ms. Krystal REAGAN
08 Director of Library Services ....Mr. Adam RUBIN

John Wood Community College (A)

1301 S 48th Street, Quincy IL 62305-8736
County: Adams FICE Identification: 012813
Unit ID: 146278
Telephone: (217) 224-6500 Carnegie Class: Assoc/HVT-Mix Trad/Non
FAX Number: (217) 224-4208 Calendar System: Semester
URL: www.jwcc.edu
Established: 1974 Annual Undergrad Tuition & Fees (In-District): $8,190
Enrollment: 1,881 Coed
Affiliation or Control: State/Local IRS Status: 501(c)3
Highest Offering: Associate Degree
Accreditation: HLC, SURGT

01 President .... Mr. Michael ELBE
05 Vice President for Instruction .... Dr. Laurel KLINKENBERG
10 Dean Business Svcs/Inst Effective ....Mr. Joshua WELKER
49 Dean Arts and Sciences ....Ms. Stephanie PHILLIPS
75 Dean Careers/Tech/Health Education .... Mr. David HETZLER
06 Registrar/Dean Records/Fin Aid ....Ms. Melanie LECHTENBERG
07 Director Admissions ....Ms. Kristen RITTERBUSCH
32 Dean Students/Enrollment Management ....Ms. Tracy ORNE
21 Director Fiscal Services ....Ms. Nora KLINGELE
121 Director Support Services ....Mr. Robert HODGSON
13 Director Information Technology .... Mr. Joshua BRUECK
08 Director Learning Resource Center .... Ms. Barbara LIEBER
26 Director Public Relations/Marketing .... Ms. Tracy HAGMAN
111 Director Advancement ....Ms. Barbara HOLTHAUS
15 Director Human Resources .... Ms. Dana KEPPNER
18 Director Physical Plant ....Mr. Lou BARTA
37 Director Financial Aid ....Ms. Melanie LECHTENBERG
19 Dean of Ops/Chief of Campus Police ....Mr. Bill LATOUR
41 Director Athletics ....Mr. Brad HOYT
40 Manager Campus Services ....Ms. Darla SNYDER
47 Dept Chair Ag Sciences ....Mr. Mike TENHOUSE
50 Dept Chair Business/Computer Sci .... Mr. Devron STERNKE
81 Department Chair Mathematics ....Ms. Brenda GRAFF
65 Dept Chair Natural Sci/Engineering ....Dr. Christopher KAELKE
79 Dept Chair Communications/Lang/Lit ....Mr. Todd SAXTON
83 Dept Chair Social/Behavior Science .... Ms. Beth REINHARDT
57 Dept Chair Fine Arts/Hum/Educ .... Mr. Steven SOEBBING
04 Executive Asst to President ....Ms. Leah BENZ

Joliet Junior College (B)

1215 Houbolt Road, Joliet IL 60431-8938
County: Will FICE Identification: 001699
Unit ID: 146296
Telephone: (815) 729-9020 Carnegie Class: Assoc/MT-VT-Mix Trad/Non
FAX Number: N/A Calendar System: Semester
URL: www.jjc.edu
Established: 1901 Annual Undergrad Tuition & Fees (In-District): $4,440
Enrollment: 10,267 Coed
Affiliation or Control: State/Local IRS Status: 501(c)3
Highest Offering: Associate Degree
Accreditation: HLC, ACBSP, ACFEI, ADNUR, CAHIIM, DMS, MUS

01 President .... Dr. Judy MITCHELL
10 VP Finance & Admin Services ....Dr. Cecil LUCY
05 VP Academic Affairs .... Dr. Amy GRAY
13 Chief Information Officer ....Mr. Jim SERR
32 VP Student Development .... Dr. Yolanda FARMER
07 Director Admissions & Recruitment ....Ms. Jennifer KLOBERDANZ
37 Director Financial Aid ....Ms. Deanna FISK
15 Chief HR Officer .... Dr. Nicole WHITEHEAD
16 Director Human Resources ....Ms. Judy CONNELLY
18 Sr Director Facility Services ....Mr. Patrick VAN DUYNE
109 Sr Director Business/Auxiliary Svcs .... Ms. Janice REEDUS
26 Exec Dir Commun/External Rels ..... Ms. Kelly ROHDER-TONELLI
36 Director Career Services ....Vacant
41 Director Athletics .... Mr. Gregory BRAUN
21 Director Financial Svcs/Controller .... Mr. Jeffrey HEAP
19 Dir Campus Safety & Police Chief .... Mr. Brandon CAMPBELL
111 Ex Dir Inst Adv Exec Dir JJC Found .... Ms. Kristin MULVEY
09 Director of Institutional Research .... Mr. Joseph OFFERMANN
29 Mgr Annual Giving & Alumni Rels .... Ms. Jennifer DAVIS
49 Dean Arts & Sciences ....Vacant
103 Dean Applied Arts/Wrkforce Ed/Trng ....Ms. Amy MURPHY
75 Dean CTE ....Ms. Patty ZUCCARELLO

108 Sr Director Inst Effectiveness ....Ms. Kristin CIESEMIER
121 Dean of Student Success ....Dr. Angie KAYSEN-LUZBETAK
04 Executive Asst to President ....Mrs. Kelly ROGERS
101 Secretary of the Institution/Board ....Ms. Joan TIERNEY
104 International Education Coord ....Vacant
106 Dir Online Education/E-learning .... Mr. Chris OSTWINKLE
84 Dean of Enrollment Mgmt & Registrar .... Mr. Robert MORRIS
110 Asst Dir Inst Advancement ....Ms. Amanda QUINN

Judson University (C)

1151 N State Street, Elgin IL 60123-1498
County: Kane FICE Identification: 001700
Unit ID: 146339
Telephone: (847) 628-2500 Carnegie Class: Masters/S
FAX Number: (847) 628-1027 Calendar System: Semester
URL: www.judsonu.edu
Established: 1913 Annual Undergrad Tuition & Fees: $29,870
Enrollment: 1,173 Coed
Affiliation or Control: American Baptist IRS Status: 501(c)3
Highest Offering: Doctorate
Accreditation: HLC

01 President ....Dr. Gene CRUME
03 Executive Vice President .... Dr. Nikki FENNERN
05 Provost/Chief Academic Officer . Dr. A. Gillian STEWART-WELLS
10 VP for Business Affairs .... Ms. Sarah TAYLOR
06 VP for Student Success & Registrar ....Ms. Virginia GUTH
20 Assoc Provost/Academic Curriculum ....Dr. Lanette POTEETE-YOUNG
08 Library Director ....Mr. Larry WILD
37 Director of Financial Aid .... Ms. Diana WINTON
26 Director of Comm & Marketing .... Ms. Mary DULABAUM
36 Director of Career Services .... Ms. Colleen JONES
38 Dir of Counseling & Wellness .... Ms. Belinda ADAME
18 Asst VP for Campus Operations .... Mr. Nick SALZMANN
41 Athletic Director .... Mr. Joel POPENFOOSE
89 Dir of 1st Year Exp & Persistence .... Ms. Jaimee BARTHA
85 International Advisor ....Ms. Andrea SINNAEVE
92 Honors Director ....Dr. James HALVERSON
101 Asst Sec to Board of Trustees .... Ms. Tena ROBOTHAM
09 Director of Institutional Research .... Mr. Chad BRIGGS
39 Coordinator Student Housing .... Ms. McKenna HAAS
88 RISE Program Director .... Ms. Gineen VARGAS
111 VP for Advancement and Alumni .... Ms. Kristen EGAN
32 Dean of Student Life & Leadership ....Ms. Aubree FLICKEMA
121 Dean Student Academic Support Svcs ...... Ms. Heather JOHNSON
42 Dean of University Ministries ....Mr. Chris LASH
15 Human Resources Generalist .... Ms. Jennifer CHICAS

Kankakee Community College (D)

100 College Drive, Kankakee IL 60901-6505
County: Kankakee FICE Identification: 007690
Unit ID: 146348
Telephone: (815) 802-8100 Carnegie Class: Assoc/HVT-High Non
FAX Number: (815) 802-8101 Calendar System: Semester
URL: www.kcc.edu
Established: 1966 Annual Undergrad Tuition & Fees (In-District): $13,200
Enrollment: 2,245 Coed
Affiliation or Control: State/Local IRS Status: 501(c)3
Highest Offering: Associate Degree
Accreditation: HLC, ADNUR, COARC, MLTAD, PNUR, PTAA

01 President ....Dr. Michael BOYD
04 Exec Asst to Pres & BOT .... Ms. Karen SLAGER
05 Vice President Academic Affairs ....Dr. Kiana BATTLE
10 Vice President Business Affairs .... Ms. Beth NUNLEY
06 Dir Enrollment Services/Registrar .... Ms. Kate WACHTOR
32 Vice President Student Affairs ....Vacant
09 Dir Inst Effectiveness/Assessment ....Ms. Lesley COOPER
31 Director Adult & Community Educ ....Ms. Margaret WOLF
103 Director of Workforce Development .... Ms. Dana WASHINGTON
37 Director Financial Aid .... Ms. Michelle HASIK
41 Director Athletics ....Mr. Todd POST
15 Director Human Resources ....Mr. David CAGLE
50 Dean Business & Technology ....Mr. Paul CARLSON
51 Dean Cont Educ & Career Svcs .... Ms. Mary POSING
18 Director Facilities ....Mr. Rob KENNEY
76 Dean Health Careers Div .... Ms. Sheri CAGLE
121 Director Student Success .... Ms. Meredith PURCELL
76 Director Respiratory Therapist Pgm .... Ms. Jaclyn CRUZ
76 Director Medical Lab Technology .... Ms. Glenda FORNERIS
66 Director Nursing .... Ms. Kellee HAYES
88 Dir Physical Therapy Asst Pgm ....Ms. Jennifer BLANCHETTE
49 Dean Liberal Arts & Sciences .... Ms. Jennifer HUGGINS
76 Director Radiology Technology Pgm .... Ms. Darla JEPSON
13 Director Information Tech Svcs .... Mr. Michael O'CONNOR
102 Exec Director of KCC Foundation ....Dr. Phillip THOMPSON
88 Director Institutional Tech/Fac Dev .... Mr. Craig KEIGHER
08 Director of Library .... Ms. Tracy CONNER
26 Dir Marketing/Public Relations ....Ms. Kari NUGENT
101 Exec Asst to Pres & BOT .... Ms. Karen SLAGER
88 Director Support Services .... Ms. Kimberlee HARPIN
19 Chief Police & Dir Public Safety .... Mr. Eric SPRINGER

Kaskaskia College (E)

27210 College Road, Centralia IL 62801-7878
County: Clinton FICE Identification: 001701
Unit ID: 146366
Telephone: (618) 545-3000 Carnegie Class: Assoc/MT-VT-High Non
FAX Number: (618) 532-1990 Calendar System: Semester
URL: www.kaskaskia.edu
Established: 1940 Annual Undergrad Tuition & Fees (In-District): $7,530
Enrollment: 2,785 Coed
Affiliation or Control: State/Local IRS Status: 501(c)3
Highest Offering: Associate Degree
Accreditation: HLC, ADNUR, COARC, DA, EMT, PTAA, RAD

01 President .... Mr. George EVANS
11 Vice Pres Administrative Services ....Mrs. Judy HEMKER
05 Vice Pres Instructional Services .... Mrs. Julie OBERMARK
32 Vice President of Student Services .... Dr. Susan BATCHELOR
75 Dean Career & Technical Education ....Ms. Traci MASAU
49 Dean of Arts & Sciences .... Mrs. Kellie HENEGAR
66 Dean Nursing & Health Sciences ....Vacant
09 Dir Institutional Effectiveness .... Mr. Bruce FISCHER
108 Associate Dean of Inst Assessment .... Mr. Alan BOERNGEN
15 Director of Human Resources .... Mrs. Jill HERCULES
18 Director Facilities/Physical Plant ....Mr. Jennings CARTER
96 Director Purchasing/Auxiliary Svcs ....Mr. Craig ROPER
37 Director of Financial Aid ....Mrs. Jill KLOSTERMANN
76 Director of Radiologic Technology .... Mrs. Mimi POLCZYNSKI
13 Chief Information Officer .... Mr. George KRISS
26 Director of Marketing ....Mr. Travis HENSON
07 Dean of Enrollment Services ....Ms. Amy TROUTT
88 Regional Director of Educ Centers ....Mrs. Cheryl BOEHNE
111 Dir Inst Advancement Programs .... Mrs. Suzanne CHRIST
19 Director of Public Safety .... Mr. Todd WAGNER
04 Admin Assistant to the President .... Mrs. Cathy QUICK
06 Registrar ....Mrs. Jenna LAMMERS
08 Chief Library Officer ....Ms. Laura VAHLKAMP

Kishwaukee College (F)

21193 Malta Road, Malta IL 60150-9600
County: De Kalb FICE Identification: 007684
Unit ID: 146418
Telephone: (815) 825-2086 Carnegie Class: Assoc/HVT-Mix Trad/Non
FAX Number: (815) 825-2072 Calendar System: Semester
URL: www.kish.edu
Established: 1968 Annual Undergrad Tuition & Fees (In-District): $9,390
Enrollment: 2,626 Coed
Affiliation or Control: State/Local IRS Status: 501(c)3
Highest Offering: Associate Degree
Accreditation: HLC, ADNUR, EMT, RAD

01 President .... Dr. Laurie BOROWICZ
05 Vice President Instruction ....Dr. Joanne KANTNER
32 Vice President Student Services .... Ms. Michelle ROTHMEYER
20 Asst Vice President of Instruction .... Mr. Judson CURRY
11 Exec Director of Campus Operations .... Mr. Dave DAMMON
20 Director of Curriculum & Programs ....Ms. Terry Lyn FUNSTON
06 Enrollment Services & Registrar ....Ms. Tina SWIGER
49 Dean Liberal Arts/Science/Business ....Mr. Chase BUDZIAK
10 CFO ....Ms. Jill HANSEN
102 Exec Director College Relations ....Ms. Kayte HAMEL
13 Director Information Technology .... Mr. Robert MCGARRY
30 Director Development & Compliance ....Mr. Nick PIAZZA
15 Exec Dir Human Resources ....Ms. Cindy MCCLUSKEY
35 Director Student Involvement .... Mr. Scott KAWALL
04 Executive Assistant to President ....Ms. Carolyn CHRUSCIEL
66 Director of Nursing ....Ms. Angie DELMONT
09 Director of Institutional Research .... Mr. Matthew CRULL
103 Director of Business Partnerships .... Ms. LaCretia KONAN
25 Chief Contract/Grants Administrator .... Ms. Barbara LEACH
37 Manager of Financial Aid .... Mr. Adam GISSELER
96 Purchasing Accountant ....Ms. Brittney ZICK

Knox College (G)

2 E South Street, Galesburg IL 61401-4999
County: Knox FICE Identification: 001704
Unit ID: 146427
Telephone: (309) 341-7000 Carnegie Class: Bac-A&S
FAX Number: (309) 341-7090 Calendar System: Trimester
URL: www.knox.edu
Established: 1837 Annual Undergrad Tuition & Fees: $49,974
Enrollment: 1,154 Coed
Affiliation or Control: Independent Non-Profit IRS Status: 501(c)3
Highest Offering: Baccalaureate
Accreditation: HLC

01 President .... Dr. Andrew MCGADNEY
101 Secretary of the College .... Ms. Peggy J. WARE
05 Provost/Dean of College ....Dr. Michael A. SCHNEIDER
10 Vice Pres for Finance & Admin Svcs ....Mr. Paul W. EISENMENGER
111 Vice President for Advancement ....Ms. Beverly HOLMES
07 Vice Pres Enrollment/Dean of Admiss ....Mr. Paul R. STEENIS
32 VP for Student Development ....Vacant
45 VP for Strategic Initiatives ....Ms. Heather BUMPS
26 Executive Director of Communication ....Ms. Lisa K. VAN RIPER
06 Acting Registrar .... Dr. Jerry MINER
35 Dean of Students ....Ms. Debbie SOUTHERN
20 Associate Dean of College .... Dr. Timothy J. FOSTER
37 Director Financial Aid ....Ms. Leigh T. BRINSON
08 Librarian ....Ms. Anne THOMASON
36 Exec Dir Career Development ....Mr. Scott CRAWFORD
13 VP/CIO Information Technology Svcs ....Mr. Steven HALL
15 AVP Director Human Resources .... Ms. Amy CHAMBERS
18 Director Facilities Services ....Mr. Scott MAUST
21 Controller ....Ms. Sara A. KING
86 Dir Government & Community Relation ....Vacant
29 Dir Alumni Engagement/Annual Giving ....Ms. Sarah E. BYRD
38 Director of Counseling Services ....Ms. Janell J. MCGRUDER

19 Director Campus Safety .... Mr. Nathan R. KEMP
09 Dir Institutional Research/Assess .... Ms. Anna J. CLARK
102 Dir Corporate/Foundation Relations .... Ms. Jan K. WOLBERS
39 Assistant Dean for Campus Life .... Mr. Jake MCLEAN
41 Director of Athletics .... Ms. Daniella J. IRLE
28 Executive Director of DIE .... Ms. Tianna N. CERVANTEZ

Lake Forest College (A)

555 N Sheridan Road, Lake Forest IL 60045-2338
County: Lake FICE Identification: 001706
Unit ID: 146481
Telephone: (847) 234-3100 Carnegie Class: Bac-A&S
FAX Number: N/A Calendar System: Semester
URL: www.lakeforest.edu
Established: 1857 Annual Undergrad Tuition & Fees: $49,822
Enrollment: 1,583 Coed
Affiliation or Control: Independent Non-Profit IRS Status: 501(c)3
Highest Offering: Master's
Accreditation: HLC, IPSY

01 President .... Mr. Stephen D. SCHUTT
05 VP Student Affairs/Dean of Students .... Ms. Andrea CONNOR
04 Admin Assistant to the President .... Ms. Dominique ALLION
06 Registrar .... Mr. BJ WHITE
84 Vice President of Enrollment .... Mr. Chris ELLERTSON
08 Director of the Library .... Ms. Cathy MAYER
09 Institutional Research Analyst .... Mr. Kyle DIEP
10 VP for Finance & Planning .... Ms. Lori SUNDBERG
104 Coordinator of Global Engagement .... Ms. Alexandra OLSON
13 Chief Information Officer .... Mr. Martin RIEDEL
15 Director of Human Resources .... Ms. Agnes STEPEK
18 Director of Facilities Management .... Mr. Dave SIEBERT
19 Director of Public Safety .... Mr. Richard COHEN
37 AVP for Financial Aid .... Mr. Jerry CEBRZYNSKI
39 Director of Residence Life .... Mr. Karl TURNLUND
41 Athletic Director .... Mr. Jim CATANZARO

Lake Forest Graduate School of Management (B)

1905 W Field Court, Lake Forest IL 60045-4824
County: Lake FICE Identification: 023192
Unit ID: 146490
Telephone: (847) 234-5005 Carnegie Class: Spec-4-yr-Bus
FAX Number: (847) 295-3656 Calendar System: Semester
URL: www.lfgsm.edu
Established: 1946 Annual Graduate Tuition & Fees: N/A
Enrollment: 395 Coed
Affiliation or Control: Independent Non-Profit IRS Status: 501(c)3
Highest Offering: Master's; No Undergraduates
Accreditation: HLC

01 President .... Mr. Jeffrey J. ANDERSON
10 VP Finance & CFO .... Mr. Thomas PEROZZI
20 Chief Academic Officer .... Dr. Neil HOLMAN
06 Registrar .... Ms. Diana BOOTH
07 Senior Director of Admissions .... Ms. Carolyn BRUNE
32 Director of Student Experience .... Ms. Currie GASCHE
09 Sr Manager Institutional Research .... Ms. Catherine KISSLING
37 Director of Financial Aid .... Ms. Connie ELDRIDGE
88 VP Corporate Learning .... Ms. Carrie BUCHWALD
04 Executive Assistant to President .... Ms. Dana KAECHELE

Lake Land College (C)

5001 Lake Land Boulevard, Mattoon IL 61938-9366
County: Coles FICE Identification: 007644
Unit ID: 146506
Telephone: (217) 234-5253 Carnegie Class: Assoc/HVT-High Non
FAX Number: (217) 234-5400 Calendar System: Semester
URL: https://www.lakelandcollege.edu
Established: 1966 Annual Undergrad Tuition & Fees (In-District): $8,104
Enrollment: 3,862 Coed
Affiliation or Control: State/Local IRS Status: 501(c)3
Highest Offering: Associate Degree
Accreditation: HLC, ADNUR, DH, EMT, MAC, PNUR, PTAA

01 President .... Dr. Josh BULLOCK
100 Chief of Staff .... Ms. Jean Anne GRUNLOH
10 VP for Business Services .... Mr. Greg NUXOLL
05 VP for Academic Services .... Mr. Jon ALTHAUS
32 Vice President for Student Services .... Vacant
88 Dean of Correctional Pgms South .... Mr. Brandon YOUNG
88 Dean of Correctional Pgms North .... Ms. Jennifer BILLINGSLEY
07 Dean of Admissions Services .... Mr. Jon VAN DYKE
88 Assoc Dean Corrections Taylorville .... Mr. Robert EIFERT
88 Assoc Dean Corrections Graham .... Ms. Justy ROTHE
88 Assoc Dean Corrections Western .... Ms. Amber ALEXANDER
88 Assoc Dean Correction IL River .... Ms. Deborah COLLINS
88 Assoc Dean Corrections Southwestern .... Mr. Harvey GROENNERT
88 Assoc Dean Kewanee .... Mr. Aaron SHERBEYN
88 Assoc Dean Correction Lincoln .... Mr. Randall INGMIRE
88 Assoc Dean DOC Logan .... Mr. Dustin KNOLLENBERG
88 Assoc Dean DOC Ill River .... Mr. BJ MCCULLUM
88 Assoc Dean Corrections Vandalia .... Ms. Tabitha WELCH
88 Assoc Dean Corrections Hill .... Mr. Chris WILLIAMS
88 Site Dir Corrections Vienna/Shawnee .... Mr. Rich PATERA
21 Comptroller .... Ms. Madge SHOOT
50 Dir Center for Business & Industry .... Ms. Bonnie MOORE
08 Director of Library Services .... Ms. Sarah HILL
26 Dir of Marketing/Public Relations .... Mrs. Kelly ALLEE
13 Chief Information Officer .... Mr. David STEWART
37 Dir of Financial Aid/Veteran Svcs .... Ms. Jennifer HEDGES
15 Director of Human Resources .... Ms. Dustha WAHLS
25 Dir Grants & Academic Operations .... Ms. Emily RAMAGE
35 Director Student Life .... Vacant
103 Director Workforce Investment .... Ms. Jamie CORDA HADJAOUI
19 Chief of Police .... Mr. Jeff BRANSON
40 Manager of Bookstore .... Ms. Amanda ARENA
111 Exec Dir for College Advancement .... Ms. Christie DONSBACH
36 Director of Career Services .... Ms. Tina MOORE
18 Dir of Physical Plant Operations .... Mr. Scott RAWLINGS
41 Director of Athletics .... Mr. William JACKSON
09 Director of Institutional Research .... Dr. Mary BREER
88 Dir of Data Analytics .... Ms. Lisa COLE
88 Director for Guided Pathways .... Ms. Darci CATHER
88 Assoc Dean Harrisburg IYC .... Ms. Toni PARKS-PARTON
88 Assoc Dean Corrections St Charles .... Mr. Scott HORSCH
88 Assoc Dean Corrections Murphysboro .... Ms. Tomi GRAVATT
88 Assoc Dean Corrections Pickneyville .... Mr. Doug LAUMBATTUS
88 Associate Dean Corrections Sherida .... Mr. Alan MORTENSEN
88 Associate Dean Big Muddy .... Ms. Penny MURPHY
88 Assoc Dean Corrections East Moline .... Ms. Ginger MURRAY
88 Assoc Dean Corrections Southwest .... Ms. Serenna ARNDT
88 Assoc Dean Corrections Robinson .... Mr. Mike PATILLA
88 Associate Dean Joliet .... Mr. Garry SCOTT
88 Assoc Dean Corrections Dixon .... Mr. Keith STEVENSON
88 Assoc Dean Corrections Decatur .... Ms. Lora TAIRA
88 Assoc Dean Corrections Vienna .... Mr. Brian WATSON

Lakeview College of Nursing (D)

903 N Logan Avenue, Danville IL 61832-3788
County: Vermilion FICE Identification: 010501
Unit ID: 146533
Telephone: (217) 709-0920 Carnegie Class: Spec-4-yr-Other Health
FAX Number: (217) 709-0954 Calendar System: Semester
URL: www.lakeviewcol.edu
Established: 1987 Annual Undergrad Tuition & Fees: N/A
Enrollment: 162 Coed
Affiliation or Control: Independent Non-Profit IRS Status: 501(c)3
Highest Offering: Baccalaureate
Accreditation: HLC, NURSE

01 President .... Ms. Sheila MINGEE
05 Dean .... Ms. Lanette STUCKEY
06 Registrar/Director of Enrollment .... Ms. Connie YOUNG
37 Director of Financial Aid .... Ms. Janet INGARGIOLA
08 Library Director/IT Coordinator .... Ms. Miranda SHAKE
04 Administrative Asst to President .... Ms. Karlee THOMEN

Lewis and Clark Community College (E)

5800 Godfrey Road, Godfrey IL 62035-2466
County: Madison FICE Identification: 010020
Unit ID: 146603
Telephone: (618) 468-7000 Carnegie Class: Assoc/HVT-High Non
FAX Number: (618) 466-2798 Calendar System: Semester
URL: www.lc.edu
Established: 1970 Annual Undergrad Tuition & Fees (In-District): $9,552
Enrollment: 4,683 Coed
Affiliation or Control: State/Local IRS Status: 501(c)3
Highest Offering: Associate Degree
Accreditation: HLC, ADNUR, DA, DH, EMT, MAAB, OTA

01 President .... Dr. Ken TRZASKA
05 Vice President Academic Affairs .... Dr. Jill LANE
84 Vice President Enrollment Services .... Vacant
32 Vice Pres Student Engagement .... Dr. Sean HILL
11 Vice President Administration .... Ms. Lori ARTIS
10 Vice President Finance .... Mrs. Mary SCHULTE
114 Chief Budget Officer .... Vacant
88 Director Corp & Comm Learning .... Mrs. Kathy WILLIS
13 Chief Information Officer .... Mr. Jeff WATSON
09 Dir Institutional Res/Library Svcs .... Mr. Dennis KRIEB
06 Registrar .... Ms. Heidi PLUNKETT
41 Director Athletics .... Mr. Doug STOTLER
07 Director of Enrollment Center .... Vacant
15 Director Human Resources .... Mr. Gabe SPRINGER
18 Facilities Manager .... Mr. Mike RANDALL
19 Director Security .... Mr. Brad RAISH
26 Manager Media Services .... Ms. Laura INLOW
28 Coordinator Diversity & Inclusion .... Vacant
30 Director of Development .... Ms. Debbie EDELMAN
37 Director Financial Aid .... Ms. Angela WEAVER

Lewis University (F)

One University Parkway, Romeoville IL 60446-2200
County: Will FICE Identification: 001707
Unit ID: 146612
Telephone: (815) 838-0500 Carnegie Class: Masters/L
FAX Number: (815) 838-9456 Calendar System: Semester
URL: www.lewisu.edu
Established: 1932 Annual Undergrad Tuition & Fees: $34,478
Enrollment: 6,437 Coed
Affiliation or Control: Roman Catholic IRS Status: 501(c)3
Highest Offering: Doctorate
Accreditation: HLC, ACBSP, NURSE, OT, @SP, SW

01 President .... Dr. David J. LIVINGSTON
05 Provost .... Dr. Christopher SINDT
84 Sr VP Enrollment Mgmt & CSO .... Mr. Raymond KENNELLY
111 VP University Advancement .... Mr. Luigi AMENDOLA
10 Vice Pres for Finance & CFO .... Ms. Teresa KREJCI
07 Dean of Undergraduate Admission .... Mrs. Ashley SKIDMORE
32 Dean Student Services .... Ms. Katheryn SLATTERY
124 Associate Provost/Dean of Retention .... Ms. Mary DEGRAW
121 VP Mission/Assoc Prov Stdnt Success .... Dr. Kurt SCHACKMUTH
72 Dean Aviation/Science/Technology .... Dr. Christopher WHITE
50 Dean College Business .... Mr. Ryan BUTT
53 Int Dean Education/Social Sciences .... Dr. Christopher KLINE
79 Dean Humanities/Fine Arts/Comm .... Dr. Laura FRANKLIN
66 Dean Nursing & Health Sciences .... Dr. Susan MULLER
15 Assoc Vice Pres Human Resources .... Ms. Graciela DUFOUR
09 Assoc VP Inst Research/Planning .... Dr. Kang BAI
08 Director of Library .... Mr. Andrew LENAGHAN
06 Registrar .... Mr. Gilbert MARTINEZ
37 Director of Financial Aid .... Ms. Janeen DECHARINTE
26 Director Marketing/Communications .... Dr. Ramona LAMONTAGNE
41 Director of Athletics .... Dr. John PLANEK
38 Director of Counseling Services .... Ms. Jill WHITAKER
19 Chief of Police .... Mr. Michael ZEGADLO
42 Director of University Ministry .... Vacant
88 Dir of Meetings/Events/Conferences .... Ms. Julie PENNER
85 Director International Student Svcs .... Mr. Michael FEKETE
91 Director of Administrative Systems .... Ms. Johanna REBMAN
13 Chief Information Officer .... Dr. LeRoy BUTLER
29 Executive Dir of Alumni Engagement .... Ms. Mary Colleen AHEARN
96 Director of Opers and Purchasing .... Ms. Jennifer SKVARLA
36 Exec Director of Career Services .... Ms. Mary MYERS
04 Executive Asst to President .... Ms. Dawn PECKLER
102 Dir Foundation & Corp Relations .... Ms. Jennifer DOHERTY
104 Director of Intl Study Abroad .... Mr. Christopher SWANSON
105 Director of Web Development .... Mr. Sylvain GOYETTE
18 Assoc VP for Facilities .... Mr. Keith KAMERON
25 Director of Sponsored Programs .... Vacant
23 Director Health Services .... Ms. Lori FORBEAR
39 Director of Residence Life .... Mr. Adam KUBIAK
30 Senior Development Officer .... Ms. Javonda PELMAN
28 VP for Diversity/Assoc Provost .... Dr. Kristi KELLY

Lincoln Christian University (G)

100 Campus View Drive, Lincoln IL 62656-2167
County: Logan FICE Identification: 001708
Unit ID: 146667
Telephone: (217) 732-3168 Carnegie Class: Spec-4-yr-Faith
FAX Number: (217) 732-5914 Calendar System: Semester
URL: www.lincolnchristian.edu
Established: 1944 Annual Undergrad Tuition & Fees: $13,980
Enrollment: 581 Coed
Affiliation or Control: Christian Churches And Churches of Christ
IRS Status: 501(c)3
Highest Offering: Doctorate
Accreditation: HLC, BI, CACREP, THEOL

01 President .... Dr. Silas MCCORMICK
10 Vice President of Finance .... Ms. Danielle FIELDS
32 VP of Student Development .... Mrs. Jill DICKEN
05 Int Vice President Academic Officer .... Dr. Peter VERKRUYSE
84 Vice Pres of Enrollment Management .... Mr. Mac INGMIRE
111 VP of Advancement/Alumni .... Mr. Brady CREMEENS
29 Director of Alumni Services .... Mr. Tracy THOMAS
08 Director of Library Services .... Vacant
101 Admin Asst to Pres/Secy Bd of Gov .... Mrs. Cindy POPEJOY
13 Director of Campus Technology .... Mr. Jeremiah PROCTOR
06 Registrar .... Mr. Shawn SMITH
07 Director of Enrollment .... Ms. Lindsay CLARK
15 Director of Human Resources .... Ms. Taylor PAYNE
18 Director of Facilities .... Mr. Dave RIGGS
20 Director of Academic Services .... Ms. Susan FARWELL
37 Director of Student Financial Aid .... Ms. Nancy SIDDENS

Lincoln College (H)

300 Keokuk Street, Lincoln IL 62656-1699
County: Logan FICE Identification: 001709
Unit ID: 146676
Telephone: (217) 732-3155 Carnegie Class: Bac/Assoc-Mixed
FAX Number: (217) 732-8859 Calendar System: Semester
URL: www.lincolncollege.edu
Established: 1865 Annual Undergrad Tuition & Fees: $19,400
Enrollment: 994 Coed
Affiliation or Control: Independent Non-Profit IRS Status: 501(c)3
Highest Offering: Master's
Accreditation: HLC, IACBE

01 President .... Dr. David M. GERLACH
05 Vice President of Academic Affairs .... Ms. Donna BRADLEY
111 Vice President for Advancement .... Ms. Debbie ACKERMAN
84 VP for Enroll Mgmt & Student Svcs .... Ms. Susan BOEHLER
10 Vice Pres Finance & Administration .... Mr. Greg A. EIMER
07 Executive Director of Admission .... Mr. Jason GARBER
32 Dean of Students .... Mrs. Bridgett THOMAS
107 Exec Dir Center for Adult Learning .... Mr. Vance LAINE
121 Director of Academic Advising .... Mr. Jacob HARNACKE
06 Dir of Inst Records & Research .... Mr. Nathaniel MCCOY
08 Library Director .... Mr. Derrick CASEY
13 Director of Information Technology .... Mr. Kyle LAVERY
21 Controller .... Ms. Tiffany WORTH
15 Director of Human Resources .... Mrs. Kristen ROBINSON

18 Director of Building & Grounds ... Mrs. Ronda PIATT
37 Director of Financial Aid ... Mrs. Sherry SCHONAUER
41 Athletic Director ... Mr. Mark PERDUE
40 Bookstore Manager ... Mrs. Amy RODRIGUEZ
04 Admin Assistant to the President ... Mrs. Amy GALLAGHER
19 Director Security/Safety ... Mr. Jermaine WALLACE
26 Chief Public Relations Officer ... Mrs. Lauren GRENLUND
39 Dir Resident Life/Student Housing .. Mr. Quentin BRACKENRIDGE

Lincoln College of Technology (A)

8317 West North Avenue, Melrose Park IL 60160-1605
County: Cook FICE Identification: 010316
Unit ID: 146700
Telephone: (708) 344-4700 Carnegie Class: Spec 2-yr-Tech
FAX Number: (708) 345-4065 Calendar System: Semester
URL: www.lincolntech.edu
Established: 1950 Annual Undergrad Tuition & Fees: N/A
Enrollment: 944 Coed
Affiliation or Control: Proprietary IRS Status: Proprietary
Highest Offering: Associate Degree
Accreditation: ACCSC

01 Campus President ... Karen M. CLARK
05 Academic Dean ... Leon KELLEY
11 Director Administrative Services ... Karen STEPINA
36 Director of Career Services ... Nancy JOURNET
37 Director of Financial Aid ... Heather MACDONALD
04 Executive Assistant ... Mindy GUARINO
07 Director of Admissions ... Lushanda BYRD
08 Head Librarian ... Karen MCELWAIN

Lincoln Land Community College (B)

5250 Shepherd Road, PO Box 19256,
Springfield IL 62794-9256
County: Sangamon FICE Identification: 007170
Unit ID: 146685
Telephone: (217) 786-2200 Carnegie Class: Assoc/MT-VT-High Non
FAX Number: (217) 786-2468 Calendar System: Semester
URL: www.llcc.edu
Established: 1967 Annual Undergrad Tuition & Fees (In-District): $6,648
Enrollment: 4,977 Coed
Affiliation or Control: Local IRS Status: 501(c)3
Highest Offering: Associate Degree
Accreditation: HLC, ADNUR, COARC, NDT, OTA, PNUR, RAD, SURGT

01 President ... Dr. Charlotte J. WARREN
05 Vice President Academic Services ... Dr. Vern L. LINDQUIST
11 Vice President Administrative Svcs ... Mr. Bryan GLECKLER
32 Vice President Student Services ... Dr. Lesley J. FREDERICK
26 Chief Communications Officer ... Ms. Lynn WHALEN
13 Chief Information Officer ... Mr. Esteban CRUZ
111 VP Advancement/Exec Dir Foundation ... Ms. Karen A. SANDERS
15 AVP Human Resources ... Ms. Nicole RALPH
10 AVP Finance ... Ms. Karie L. LONGHTA
121 Exec Director Academic Success ... Ms. Julie CLEVENGER
09 AVP IR and Effectiveness ... Dr. Tricia A. KUJAWA
57 Dean Arts & Communication ... Mr. Adam WATKINS
76 Dean Health Professions ... Dr. Cynthia L. MASKEY
20 AVP Academic Services ... Dr. Jason DOCKTER
81 Dean Mathematics/Computer Sciences ... Dr. Scott SEARCY
83 Dean Social Science & Business ... Dr. Victor K. BRODERICK
79 Dean English & Humanities ... Dr. Joel DYKSTRA
47 Dean Natural & Agriculture Science ... Dr. Kimberly VOGT
103 Dean Workforce Institute ... Ms. Nancy SWEET
84 AVP Enrollment Services ... Ms. Shanda BYER
86 AVP Corp/Govt Trng & Econ Devel ... Ms. Paula J. LUEBBERT
08 Dean Library ... Ms. Tamara KUHN-SCHNELL
106 Dean Academic Innov/eLearning ... Ms. Becky PARTON
41 Director Athletics ... Mr. Ron RIGGLE
14 Director IT Systems ... Mr. Ben ROTH
14 Director IT Service and Support ... Vacant
18 Director Facilities ... Mr. David BRETSCHER
91 Director IT Development ... Vacant
66 Assoc Dean Nursing ... Ms. Sonja K. HARVEY
120 Dir Instructional Technology ... Mr. Barry P. LAMB
37 Director Financial Aid ... Ms. Allison MILLS
124 Director Student Transitions ... Mr. Chris BARRY
93 Dir Student Support Services ... Dr. Anne ARMBRUSTER
114 Dir Budget & Fiscal Services ... Mr. Jeremy BLISS
117 Dir Construction and EHS ... Mr. Timothy R. ERVIN
109 Director Campus Services ... Mr. Andrew BLAYLOCK
35 AVP Student Success ... Ms. Leslie R. JOHNSON
121 Director Student Success ... Mr. Alex BERRY
118 Director Employment & Benefits ... Ms. Kirsten TAYLOR
07 Director Admissions & Records ... Vacant
12 Director LLCC Litchfield ... Ms. Jessamine BLACKBURN
12 Director LLCC Jacksonville ... Ms. Keri MASON
12 Director LLCC Taylorville ... Ms. Dee KRUEGER
06 Registrar ... Ms. Robin ACKMAN

Loyola University Chicago (C)

1032 W. Sheridan Road, Chicago IL 60660
County: Cook FICE Identification: 001710
Unit ID: 146719
Telephone: (773) 274-3000 Carnegie Class: DU-Higher
FAX Number: (312) 915-7003 Calendar System: Semester
URL: www.luc.edu
Established: 1870 Annual Undergrad Tuition & Fees: $46,060
Enrollment: 16,893 Coed
Affiliation or Control: Roman Catholic IRS Status: 501(c)3
Highest Offering: Doctorate
Accreditation: HLC, CAEP, CAEPN, CAMPEP, CLPSY, COPSY, DENT, DIETI, EMT, FEPAC, LAW, MED, MT, NURSE, PH, SCPSY, SW, THEA, THEOL

01 President ... Dr. Jo Ann ROONEY
05 Provost/Chief Academic Officer ... Dr. Margaret F. CALLAHAN
11 Sr VP Admin Services ... Mr. Thomas M. KELLY
10 Sr Vice Pres/CFO ... Mr. Wayne MAGDZIARZ
84 VP Enrollment Management ... Mr. Paul G. ROBERTS
32 VP Student Development ... Ms. Jane NEUFELD
13 VP Information Services/CIO ... Ms. Susan M. MALISCH
26 Vice Pres Marketing/Communications . Mr. Jeremy W. LANGFORD
15 Vice Pres HR/Chief Diversity Ofcr ... Ms. Winifred WILLIAMS
111 Vice Pres Advancement ... Ms. Karen P. PACIERO
43 VP & General Counsel ... Ms. Pamela G. COSTAS
21 Vice Provost Finance & Operations ... Ms. Joanna PAPPAS
20 Assoc Provost Programs/Planning ... Dr. Robyn MALLETT
46 Vice Provost Research Services ... Dr. Meharvan SINGH
08 Assoc Provost & Dir HSD Library ... Ms. Gail HENDLER
88 Asst Prov Provost Office ... Ms. Anne C. REULAND
20 Vice Provost Faculty Affairs ... Dr. Badia S. AHAD
108 Interim Dir Inst Effectiveness ... Dr. Brian J. ERDMAN
121 Asst VP Student Academic Svcs ... Dr. Lester J. MANZANO
31 Assoc VP Campus/Community Planning ... Ms. Jennifer R. CLARK
18 Assoc VP Capital Projects ... Ms. Kana HENNING
45 Assoc VP Capital Planning ... Mr. David BEALL
91 Assoc VP Informatics/System Dev ... Mr. Ronald N. PRICE
14 Assoc VP Information Services ... Mr. Jim SIBENALLER
16 Assoc VP Human Resources ... Ms. Joan C. STASIAK
14 Assoc VP Information Services ... Mr. Dan VONDER HEIDE
18 Asst VP Facilities ... Mr. Michael LOFTSGAARDEN
35 Asst VP & Dean of Students ... Dr. William RODRIGUEZ
39 Asst VP/Director Residence Life ... Ms. Deborah SCHMIDT-ROGERS
41 Athletic Director ... Mr. Steve WATSON
65 Dean School Environmental Sustain ... Dr. Nancy TUCHMAN
08 Dean Libraries ... Dr. Marianne P. RYAN
58 Dean Grad Sch/Vice Prov Grad Educ ... Dr. Emily BARMAN
49 Dean Arts & Sciences ... Dr. Peter J. SCHRAEDER
63 Dean School of Medicine ... Dr. Sam J. MARZO
66 Dean School of Nursing ... Dr. Lorna FINNEGAN
104 Exec Dir Intl Programs ... Vacant
118 Dir Compensation & Benefits ... Vacant
19 Dir Campus Safety ... Mr. Thomas MURRAY
88 Dir of Student Complex ... Ms. Dawn M. COLLINS
12 Dir Lurec Operations ... Mr. Kevin GINTY
28 Asst Provost Acad Diversity ... Vacant
42 Dir Campus Ministry ... Ms. Ginny MCCARTHY
23 Dir of Wellness Center ... Ms. Joan HOLDEN
37 Dir of Financial Aid ... Mr. Tobyn L. FRIAR
42 Dir Campus Ministry ... Dr. Lisa REITER
85 Dir Global Initiatives ... Fraser S. TURNER
102 Dir of Corporate & Foundation Rels ... Ms. Stephanie KIMMEL
09 Asst Dir Institutional Research ... Dr. Ping TSUI
07 Interim Dean Undergrad Admissions ... Mr. Todd M. MALONE
36 Dir Career Development Center ... Ms. Megan K. TISDALE
106 Dir Online Learning ... Mr. John GURNAK
88 Dir Vietnam Center ... Mr. Richard C. ALBRIGHT
04 Admin Assistant to the President ... Ms. Kate PETERSON
06 Registrar ... Ms. Rita VAZQUEZ
100 Chief of Staff ... Rev. James PREHN
105 Director Web Services ... Mr. John M. DREVS
29 Assoc Alumni Relations Dir ... Mr. Jeremiah MARTIN
38 Director Student Counseling ... Mr. David S. DE BOER
50 Dean of Business ... Dr. Kevin T. STEVENS
53 Interim Dean of Education ... Dr. Markeda L. NEWELL
86 Director Government Relations ... Mr. Philip D. HALE
96 Director of Purchasing ... Ms. Geraldine LECHANTRE
25 Sr Dir Sponsored Pgm Accounting ... Mr. Brian R. SLAVINSKAS
110 Sr Dir of Advancement Svcs ... Dr. Michael S. HALVERSON
44 Assoc Director Annual Giving ... Ms. Carol FLANIGAN

Loyola University Health Sciences Campus (D)

2160 S First Avenue, Maywood IL 60153
Telephone: (708) 216-9000 Identification: 770080
Accreditation: &HLC, PAST

Loyola University Water Tower Campus (E)

820 N Michigan Avenue, Chicago IL 60611
Telephone: (312) 915-6000 Identification: 770079
Accreditation: &HLC

Lutheran School of Theology at Chicago (F)

1100 E 55th Street, Chicago IL 60615-5199
County: Cook FICE Identification: 001712
Unit ID: 146728
Telephone: (773) 256-0700 Carnegie Class: Spec-4-yr-Faith
FAX Number: (773) 256-0782 Calendar System: Semester
URL: www.lstc.edu
Established: 1860 Annual Graduate Tuition & Fees: N/A
Enrollment: 145 Coed
Affiliation or Control: Evangelical Lutheran Church In America
IRS Status: 501(c)3
Highest Offering: Doctorate; No Undergraduates
Accreditation: HLC, THEOL

01 President ... Dr. James NIEMAN
04 Assistant to the President ... Ms. Patti DEBIAS
108 Director Inst Effectiveness ... Mr. Chris HUANG
05 Dean for Academic Affairs ... Dr. Esther MENN
58 Director of Advanced Studies ... Dr. Mark SWANSON
42 Pastor to the Community ... Rev. Erik CHRISTENSEN
111 Vice President for Advancement ... Ms. Sandra H. NELSON
10 Vice President for Finance & Opers ... Mr. Richard VIVIAN
32 Dean of Student Services ... Dr. Scott CHALMERS
06 Registrar ... Mr. Chris HUANG
26 Dir of Strategic Mktg & Comm ... Ms. Elizabeth CHENTLAND
08 Interim Director of Library ... Mr. Barry HOPKINS
13 Director of Information Technology ... Ms. Martha STOCKER
15 Chief Human Resources Officer ... Mr. Aaron COPLEY-SPIVEY
28 Director of Diversity ... Ms. Vimary COUVERTIER-CRUZ

MacCormac College (G)

29 E Madison Street 2nd Floor, Chicago IL 60602-4405
County: Cook FICE Identification: 001716
Unit ID: 146816
Telephone: (312) 922-1884 Carnegie Class: Spec 2-yr-Other
FAX Number: (312) 922-4286 Calendar System: Semester
URL: www.maccormac.edu
Established: 1904 Annual Undergrad Tuition & Fees: $12,700
Enrollment: 276 Coed
Affiliation or Control: Independent Non-Profit IRS Status: 501(c)3
Highest Offering: Associate Degree
Accreditation: HLC

00 Chancellor ... Dr. Grace ALEXIS STEPHENS
01 President/Dean of Finance ... Mr. Matt GAWENDA
10 Dean of Finance/Operations ... Mr. Matt GAWENDA
05 Dean Acad/Dean Student Affairs ... Dr. Kenya GROOMS
06 Registrar ... Ms. Mariza SILVA
37 Director of Financial Aid ... Ms. Jamieta HOSKINS
07 Director of Admission ... Mr. Wentreal HOLLAND
26 Dir Communications/Public Relations ... Mr. Adam HITZEMAN

McCormick Theological Seminary (H)

5460 S University Avenue, Chicago IL 60615-5108
County: Cook FICE Identification: 001721
Unit ID: 146977
Telephone: (773) 947-6300 Carnegie Class: Spec-4-yr-Faith
FAX Number: (773) 288-2612 Calendar System: 4/1/4
URL: www.mccormick.edu
Established: 1829 Annual Graduate Tuition & Fees: N/A
Enrollment: 221 Coed
Affiliation or Control: Presbyterian Church (U.S.A.) IRS Status: 501(c)3
Highest Offering: Doctorate; No Undergraduates
Accreditation: HLC, THEOL

01 President ... Mr. David CRAWFORD
00 Chair of the Board ... Ms. Connie LINDSEY
05 Vice Pres Acad Affs/Dean Faculty ... Dr. Steed DAVIDSON
30 Vice Pres Seminary Rels/Development ... Ms. Lisa M. DAGHER
06 Registrar ... Ms. Chandra WADE
29 Vice Pres Alumni/ae & Church Rels ... Rev. Nannette BANKS
08 Interim Director JKM Library ... Mr. Barry HOPKINS
15 Director Human Resources ... Ms. Ashley WOODFAULK
37 Dir Student Financial Aid/Planning ... Mr. Nate RAMSEY
07 Sr Director Admissions/Enrollment ... Ms. Veronica JOHNSON
88 Assistant to the Dean ... Ms. Jennifer OULD
04 Assistant to the President ... Ms. Joyce LEACHMAN

McHenry County College (I)

8900 US Highway 14, Crystal Lake IL 60012-2796
County: McHenry FICE Identification: 007691
Unit ID: 147004
Telephone: (815) 455-3700 Carnegie Class: Assoc/HVT-High Non
FAX Number: (815) 455-3999 Calendar System: Semester
URL: www.mchenry.edu
Established: 1967 Annual Undergrad Tuition & Fees (In-District): $11,862
Enrollment: 7,814 Coed
Affiliation or Control: State/Local IRS Status: 501(c)3
Highest Offering: Associate Degree
Accreditation: HLC, ADNUR, CAHIIM, EMT, OTA, PTAA

01 President ... Dr. Clinton E. GABBARD
101 Board Liaison ... Ms. Mary CORNETT
05 VP Academic Affairs & Workforce Dev ... Dr. Chris GRAY
32 VP Student Affairs ... Dr. Talia KORONKIEWICZ
103 Assoc VP of Workforce Development ... Ms. Catherine JONES
20 Assoc VP for Academic Affairs ... Dr. Gina MCCONOUGHEY
26 VP Marketing/Comm & Development ... Ms. Christina HAGGERTY
27 Exec Dir Mktg & Creative Services ... Mr. Ryan KLOS
102 Exec Director MCC Foundation ... Mr. Brian DIBONA
25 Director of Grants ... Ms. Wendy LAUEN
88 Manager Conference & Event Services ... Ms. Katherine BELLEN
10 CFO/Treasurer ... Mr. Bob TENUTA
21 Asst VP of Finance ... Ms. Lynn COWLIN
19 Chief of Police ... Mr. J.C PAEZ
18 Asst VP of Facilities ... Mr. Rickey SPARKS
88 Director of Sustainability ... Ms. Kim HANKINS
40 Director of the MCC Store ... Ms. Alma WILHELM
109 Director Food Services ... Ms. Sandra JOHNSTON
96 Director of Business Services ... Ms. Jennifer JONES
13 Chief Information Officer ... Vacant
119 Director Infrastructure & Security ... Mr. Rob RASMUSSEN
14 Director of DevOps Services ... Vacant
09 Director of Institutional Research ... Dr. Amy HUMKE
15 VP of Human Resources ... Ms. Michelle SKINDER

88 Director Talent Management .... Ms. Sandra HESS MOLL
16 Exec Director of Human Resources .... Ms. Carolyn WALSH
16 Director of HR Operations .... Ms. Anita ROEWER
35 Asst VP Student Affairs .... Ms. Sonia REISING
06 Director of Registration & Records .... Ms. Amy HALLER
41 Director Athletics/Intramural & Rec .... Ms. Karen WILEY
88 Director Crisis Intervention .... Ms. Rachael BOLDMAN
88 Director of Upward Bound Program .... Mr. Rene GOVEA
124 Dir of Student Retention & Conduct .... Ms. Lisa BRNCICH
22 Dir Access & Disability Services .... Ms. Lili O'CONNELL
37 Director of Financial Aid .... Mr. Chris HEFTKA
08 Interim Executive Dir of Library .... Vacant
89 Dir College & Career Readiness .... Mr. Mike KENNEDY
20 Director of Teaching & Learning .... Dr. Holly REY
121 Director Academic Advising .... Dr. Jim DISRUDE
84 Director of Enrollment Services .... Ms. Amy CARZOLI
88 Director Pathways to Success .... Ms. Christina SWANSON
81 Dean of Math & Sciences .... Mr. O'Neil WRIGHT
85 Dean of Humanities & Social Science .... Ms. Daniela BRODERICK
69 Dean Social Science/Public Service .... Dr. Dawn KATZ
55 Exec Director of Adult Education .. Mr. Julio CAPELES-DELGADO
88 Manager Nursing Labs .... Ms. Ann STAUCHE
75 Mgr PTA Clinical Education .... Ms. Angela WALLACE
72 Mgr Applied Technology Labs .... Mr. Casey JUSZCZYK
31 Director of Community Education .... Ms. Dori SULLINS
76 Assoc Dean Allied Health & HIT .. Ms. Chris COCLANIS-LODING
66 Director of Nursing Program .... Ms. Betsy SCHNOWSKE
48 Director of Ctr Agrarian Learning .... Ms. Sheri DOYEL
47 Farm Practicum Director CAL .... Ms. Emily ZACK
76 Dir OT Assistant Program .... Ms. Marlene VOGT
88 Mgr IL Small Business Development .... Mr. Mark PIEKOS
75 Dean Career & Technical Educ .... Mr. Tom MCGEE

McKendree University (A)

701 College Road, Lebanon IL 62254-9990
County: Saint Clair FICE Identification: 001722
Unit ID: 147013
Telephone: (618) 537-4481 Carnegie Class: Masters/L
FAX Number: (618) 537-6259 Calendar System: Semester
URL: www.mckendree.edu
Established: 1828 Annual Undergrad Tuition & Fees: $32,200
Enrollment: 2,200 Coed
Affiliation or Control: United Methodist IRS Status: 501(c)3
Highest Offering: Doctorate
Accreditation: **HLC**, CAATE, IACBE, NURSE

01 President .... Mr. Daniel C. DOBBINS
03 Senior Vice President .... Vacant
04 Exec Assistant to the President .... Ms. Yvonne STRODER
05 Provost/Dean of the University .... Dr. Tami EGGLESTON
10 Vice Pres Finance/Administration .... Dr. Marilee K. MONTANARO
07 Vice Pres Admission & Financial Aid .... Mr. Chris HALL
32 Vice President Student Affairs .... Dr. Joni BASTIAN
108 Associate Provost Inst Effective .... Dr. Tami EGGLESTON
20 Associate Provost for Curriculum .... Dr. J. Alan ALEWINE
100 VP of Operations/Chief of Staff .... Mr. Daryl R. HANCOCK
13 CIO/Director Information Technology .... Ms. Christine TWEEDY
06 Registrar/Asst Dean .... Ms. Debra LARSON
08 Director of Holman Library .... Ms. Paula MARTIN
21 Comptroller .... Mrs. Hilary B. SMITH
26 Exec Dir Marketing/Communications .... Mrs. Krysti H. CONNELLY
29 Director Alumni Relations .... Ms. Brandi BROWN-HARRIS
37 Director Financial Aid .... Ms. Ashley BYERS
36 Director Career Services .... Ms. Jennifer K. PICKERELL
15 Director of Human Resources .... Mr. Ricardo ORTEGA
27 Director Media Relations .... Ms. Lisa K. SANDERS
39 Director of Residence Life .... Mrs. Samantha ENGLAR
35 Director of Campus Activities .... Mr. Craig L. ROBERTSON
41 Athletic Director .... Mr. Anthony FRANCIS
42 Chaplain/Director Church Relations .... Rev Dr. B. Timothy HARRISON
40 Bookstore Director .... Ms. Amy BLASDEL
111 Director of Advancement Services .... Mr. Scott L. BILLHARTZ
19 Director Safety & Security .... Mr. Ranodore M. FOGGS
112 Director of Major Gifts .... Mrs. Whitney STRONG
113 Director of Student Accounts .... Ms. Kiara HARMON
28 Director of Diversity .... Mr. Brent W. REEVES
106 Dean of Online .... Dr. Melissa MEEKER
104 Director of Study Abroad .... Ms. Sandee POWERS
09 Director of Institutional Research .... Mrs. Jessica HOPKINS
44 Director Annual Giving .... Mrs. Holly E. SALLEE

Meadville Lombard Theological School (B)

610 South Michigan Avenue, Chicago IL 60605
County: Cook FICE Identification: 001723
Unit ID: 147031
Telephone: (773) 256-3000 Carnegie Class: Spec-4-yr-Faith
FAX Number: (312) 327-7002 Calendar System: Semester
URL: www.meadville.edu
Established: 1844 Annual Graduate Tuition & Fees: N/A
Enrollment: 83 Coed
Affiliation or Control: Unitarian Universalist IRS Status: 501(c)3
Highest Offering: Doctorate; No Undergraduates
Accreditation: **THEOL**

01 President .... Dr. Elias ORTEGA
05 VP Academic/Student Affairs .... RevDr. Pamela LIGHTSEY
10 Vice Pres Finance & Administration .... Ms. Cynthia REDMAN
06 Registrar .... Ms. Elena JIMENEZ
30 Director of Development .... Ms. Evy LIPECKA

Methodist College (C)

7600 N. Academic Drive, Peoria IL 61615
County: Peoria FICE Identification: 006228
Unit ID: 147129
Telephone: (309) 672-5513 Carnegie Class: Spec-4-yr-Other Health
FAX Number: (309) 671-8303 Calendar System: Semester
URL: www.methodistcol.edu
Established: 2000 Annual Undergrad Tuition & Fees: $17,988
Enrollment: 595 Coed
Affiliation or Control: Independent Non-Profit IRS Status: 501(c)3
Highest Offering: Master's
Accreditation: **HLC**, MAC, NURSE, SW

01 Chancellor/President .... Dr. Laurie SHANDERSON
05 CAO and Dean of Arts & Sciences .... Dr. Eileen SETTI
10 Director of Business Services .... Ms. Justina KIRCHGESSNER
66 Dean of Nursing .... Dr. Pam FERGUSON
07 Dean of Student Experience .... Ms. Bobbi BIRINGER
09 Dean Inst Research & Priorities .... Dr. Leah ADAMS-CURTIS
06 Registrar .... Ms. Melissa EARNEST
37 Director Financial Aid .... Ms. Angela ROBINSON
26 Director Mktg/External Affairs .... Ms. Anna BUEHRER
04 Admin Assistant to the President .... Ms. Michelle MARTIN
08 Chief Library Officer .... Ms. Michelle NIELSON OTT
19 Director Security/Safety .... Mr. Ryan SCHUBERT
38 Director Student Counseling .... Ms. Danielle MCCOY
39 Dir Resident Life/Student Housing .... Mr. Andre ALLEN

Midwest College of Oriental Medicine (D)

1601 Sherman Avenue, 3rd Floor, Evanston IL 60201
Telephone: (773) 975-1295 Identification: 666090
Accreditation: **ACUP**

† Branch campus of Midwest College of Oriental Medicine, Racine, WI

Midwestern Career College (E)

100 South Wacker Dr, LL1-50, Chicago IL 60606
County: Cook FICE Identification: 041390
Unit ID: 457536
Telephone: (312) 236-9000 Carnegie Class: Spec 2-yr-Health
FAX Number: (312) 277-1007 Calendar System: Other
URL: mccollege.edu
Established: 2004 Annual Undergrad Tuition & Fees: N/A
Enrollment: 655 Coed
Affiliation or Control: Proprietary IRS Status: Proprietary
Highest Offering: Associate Degree
Accreditation: **COE**, CEA, SURGT

01 President & CEO .... Mr. Jeremy OBERFELD

Midwestern University (F)

555 31st Street, Downers Grove IL 60515-1200
County: DuPage FICE Identification: 001657
Unit ID: 143853
Telephone: (630) 971-6080 Carnegie Class: Spec-4-yr-Med
FAX Number: N/A Calendar System: Quarter
URL: www.midwestern.edu
Established: 1900 Annual Undergrad Tuition & Fees: N/A
Enrollment: 2,980 Coed
Affiliation or Control: Independent Non-Profit IRS Status: 501(c)3
Highest Offering: Doctorate
Accreditation: **HLC**, ARCPA, CLPSY, DENT, OPT, OSTEO, OT, PHAR, PTA, SP

01 President/CEO .... Dr. Kathleen H. GOEPPINGER
10 Sr VP/Chief Financial Officer .... Mr. Gregory J. GAUS
21 VP/Special Asst Finance .... Mr. Dean P. MALONE
88 VP/Special Assistant to President .... Dr. Mary W L. LEE
05 VP/CAO Med & Health Sciences Educ .... Dr. Kathleen N. PLAYER
05 VP/CAO Optometry/Pharm/Vet Educ .... Dr. Joshua C. BAKER
05 VP/CAO Dental/Grad Studies Educ .... Dr. Kyle H. RAMSEY
15 VP Human Resources & Administration .... Ms. Angela L. MARTY
43 VP & General Counsel .... Ms. Barbara L. MCCLOUD
63 Dean Chicago Col of Osteo Medicine .... Dr. Thomas A. BOYLE
67 Dean Col Pharmacy Glendale/DG .... Dr. Mitchell R. EMERSON
76 Dean Col Health Sci Downers Grove .... Dr. Fred D. ROMANO
88 Dean Chicago College of Optometry .... Dr. Melissa A. SUCKOW
52 Dean College of Dental Medicine IL .... Dr. Harold J. HAERING
32 Dean of Students DG and Glendale .... Dr. Ross J. KOSINSKI
07 Director of Admissions .... Mr. Michael J. LAKEN
111 Director Institutional Advancement .... Ms. Stacy GLASS
16 Asst VP Human Resources .... Ms. Amy B. GIBSON
18 Director of Operations DG Campus .... Mr. Kevin M. MCCORMICK
18 Director of Operations Glendale .... Mr. James CIWAY
13 Director Information Technology Svc .... Mr. Erik P. CARROLL
08 Director Library .... Ms. Rebecca A. CATON
09 Director of Institutional Research .... Ms. Donna M. WEGLARZ
06 Registrar .... Ms. Elizabeth N. MORRISON
24 Director of Media Resources .... Ms. Kathleen A M. DOOLEY
46 Asst VP Research & Sponsored Pgms .... Dr. James M. WOODS
19 Director of Safety & Security .... Mr. Paul R. CREEKMORE
27 Director of Communications .... Ms. Dana FAY
37 Director Stdnt Fin Svcs & Registrar .... Mr. Nathan ERNST
14 Dir IT Applications/Clinic Svcs .... Mr. James RUBINSTEIN
88 Asst VP Proj Mgmt DG/Glendale .... Mr. Daniel TAPIA
88 Dean AZ College of Optometry .... Dr. Alicia E. FEIS
74 Dean College of Veterinary Med .... Dr. Thomas K. GRAVES
63 Dean AZ Col of Osteo Medicine .... Dr. Lori A. KEMPER
88 Dean AZ College of Podiatric Med .... Dr. Jeffrey L. JENSEN, DPM
52 Dean College of Dental Medicine AZ .... Dr. P. Bradford SMITH
76 Dean College of Health Sciences DG .... Dr. Jacquelyn M. SMITH
58 Dean College Grad Studies IL & AZ .... Dr. Yir Gloria YUEH
04 Exec Assistant to the President .... Ms. Victoria FRANKS
100 Chief of Staff .... Ms. Monica KRAMER

† Tuition varies by degree program.

Millikin University (G)

1184 W Main Street, Decatur IL 62522-2084
County: Macon FICE Identification: 001724
Unit ID: 147244
Telephone: (217) 424-6211 Carnegie Class: Bac-Diverse
FAX Number: (217) 424-3993 Calendar System: Semester
URL: www.millikin.edu
Established: 1901 Annual Undergrad Tuition & Fees: $39,592
Enrollment: 1,982 Coed
Affiliation or Control: Presbyterian Church (U.S.A.) IRS Status: 501(c)3
Highest Offering: Doctorate
Accreditation: **HLC**, ACBSP, ANEST, #CAATE, MUS, NURSE

01 President .... Dr. James REYNOLDS
05 Interim Provost .... Mrs. Mary BLACK
10 Vice Pres Finance/Business Affs .... Ms. Ruby F. JAMES
111 Vice Pres University Development .... Ms. Gina L. BIANCHI
84 Vice President Enrollment/Marketing .... Ms. Sarah SHUPENUS
32 Vice Pres Student Affairs .... Mrs. Raphaella PRANGE
100 Chief of Staff/Board Secretary .... Ms. Marilyn S. DAVIS
49 Dean of Arts & Sciences .... Dr. Randy M. BROOKS
57 Dean of Fine Arts .... Ms. Laura LEDFORD
107 Dean Col of Professional Stds .... Dr. Pam LINDSEY
50 Dean Tabor School Business .... Dr. Najiba BENABESS
06 Registrar .... Mr. Jason WICKLINE
29 Sr Dir Alumni Engage/Annual Giving .... Mrs. Alyse KNUST
112 Sr Director Major Gifts .... Mr. Dan BAKER
102 Asst Dir Corp/Foundation Relations .... Ms. Megan CAREY
13 Director of Technology .... Mrs. Amy BRILLEY
08 Interim Director of the Library .... Ms. Amanda PIPPITT
30 Sr Director of Operations .... Mrs. Amanda PODESCHI
41 Director of Athletics .... Dr. Craig WHITE
53 Int Director of School of Education .... Dr. Chris CUNNINGS
88 Director Kirkland Fine Arts Center .... Mr. Bryan DIVER
104 Dir Center for Intl Education .... Ms. Briana QUINTENZ
15 Director Human Resources .... Ms. Diane L. LANE
21 Director Financial Services .... Mrs. Vicki A. WRIGLEY
38 Dir Stdnt Mental/Behav Health Svcs .... Mr. Christopher MORRELL
92 Director of Honors Program .... Dr. Michael HARTSOCK
37 Director of Financial Aid .... Mrs. Stacey HUBBARD
58 Director of MBA Program .... Dr. Najibu BENABESS
64 Director School of Music .... Dr. Brian K. JUSTISON
87 Director of Summer School .... Dr. Randy M. BROOKS
19 Dir Dept Public Safety/Chief Police .... Mr. Chris BALLARD
66 Director School of Nursing .... Dr. Wendy KOOKEN
07 Director of Admission .... Mr. Kyle TAYLOR
39 Dean of Campus Life .... Mr. Paul LIDY
18 Director of Facilities Services .... Mr. James FRALEY
26 Director of Marketing .... Mrs. Kylee RONEY
09 Coord of Institutional Research .... Mrs. Laura A. BIRCH
105 Web Developer .... Vacant
88 Dir Ctr for Acad/Prof Perf (CAPP) .... Mrs. Carrie PIERSON
43 Director Legal Services .... Mrs. Caroline BRUDER

Monmouth College (H)

700 E Broadway, Monmouth IL 61462-1963
County: Warren FICE Identification: 001725
Unit ID: 147341
Telephone: (800) 747-2687 Carnegie Class: Bac-A&S
FAX Number: (309) 457-2141 Calendar System: Semester
URL: www.monmouthcollege.edu
Established: 1853 Annual Undergrad Tuition & Fees: $41,330
Enrollment: 860 Coed
Affiliation or Control: Presbyterian Church (U.S.A.) IRS Status: 501(c)3
Highest Offering: Baccalaureate
Accreditation: **HLC**

01 President .... Dr. Clarence R. WYATT
05 Dean/Vice Pres Academic Affairs .... Dr. Mark WILLHARDT
10 Vice President Finance & Business .... Ms. Melony SACOPULOS
32 Vice Pres Student Life/Dn Students .... Ms. Karen OGORZALEK
84 Vice President for Enrollment Mgmt .... Ms. Kristen ENGLISH
30 Vice Pres Development/College Rels .... Ms. Hannah MAHER
26 Assoc VP Communications/Marketing .... Mr. Duane BONIFER
07 Director of Admission .... Vacant
13 Chief Information Officer .... Mr. Nicholas CARLSON
06 Registrar .... Ms. Kristi HIPPEN
08 Director Hewes Library .... Ms. Sarah HENDERSON
15 Director of Personnel Services .... Mr. Mike MCNALL
18 Director Facilities Management .... Ms. Sarah YOUNG
20 Associate Dean of the Faculty .... Dr. Joan WERTZ
21 Controller .... Ms. Jessica R. JOHNSTON
09 Director Institutional Research .... Ms. Christine D. JOHNSTON
32 Vice Pres Student Life/Dn Students .... Ms. Michelle MERRITT
04 Admin Assistant to the President .... Ms. Amy WARRINGTON
29 Director Alumni Affairs .... Ms. Jennifer ARMSTRONG
36 Director Student Placement .... Ms. Marnei DUGAN
37 Director Student Financial Aid .... Ms. Jayne SCHRECK
38 Director Student Counseling .... Ms. Cindy BEADLES

Moody Bible Institute (I)

820 N LaSalle Boulevard, Chicago IL 60610-3263
County: Cook FICE Identification: 001727
Unit ID: 147369

Telephone: (312) 329-4000 | Carnegie Class: Spec-4-yr-Faith
FAX Number: (312) 329-4109 | Calendar System: Semester
URL: www.moody.edu
Established: 1886 | Annual Undergrad Tuition & Fees: $13,970
Enrollment: 2,870 | Coed
Affiliation or Control: Independent Non-Profit | IRS Status: 501(c)3
Highest Offering: Master's
Accreditation: HLC, BI, MUS, THEOL

Code	Title	Name
01	President	Dr. Mark JOBE
05	Provost & Dean of Education	Dr. Dwight A. PERRY
11	Chief Operating Officer	Mr. Mark WAGNER
10	Chief Financial Officer	Mr. Ken HEULITT
43	VP & General Counsel	Mrs. Janet A. STIVEN
20	VP & Dean of UG School	Dr. Bryan O'NEAL
13	Chief Information Officer	Mr. John SAUCEDA
15	VP of Human Resources	Mrs. Debbie ZELINSKI
26	Chief Marketing Officer	Mr. Sam CHOY
32	VP & Dean of Student Life	Dr. Timothy E. ARENS
84	VP/Dean of Student/Enrollment Svcs	Dr. Heather SHALLEY
08	Department Manager Library	Mr. James PRESTON
06	Registrar/Director of Acad Records	Mr. George MOSHER
29	Exec Director Alumni Association	Mrs. Nancy HASTINGS
39	Associate Dean Residence Life	Mr. Bruce R. NORQUIST
35	Associate Dean of Students	Mrs. Rachel PUENTE
36	Assoc Dean of Career Development	Mr. Patrick FRIEDLINE
38	Associate Dean Counseling Services	Mr. Steve BRASEL
35	Associate Dean for Student Programs	Mr. Joseph M. GONZALES, JR.
88	Director of Moody Aviation	Mr. James A. CONRAD
108	Dir Center Teach/Lrng/Assessment	Dr. Andrew BEATY
88	Director Instruct Design and Dev	Mr. Kevin MAHAFFY
88	Director of Student Experience MDL	Mr. John ENGELKEMIER
44	VP of Donor Dev & Channel Strategy	Mr. Bruce EVERHART
30	VP of Stewardship	Mr. James ELLIOTT
96	Manager of Procurement Services	Mr. Stephen RICHARDSON
102	Dir Foundation/Corporate Relations	Mr. Nathan MEDINA
21	Controller	Ms. Linda WAHR
37	Dean of Admissions & Financial Aid	Mrs. Heather SHALLEY
14	Technology Services Director	Mr. Michael JANCHENKO
18	Division Manager of Facilities	Mr. Bill BIELAWSKI
19	Deputy Chief of Public Safety	Mr. Brian M. STOFFER
41	Athletic Director	Mr. Daniel DUNN
23	Admin of Health Service	Ms. Ann MEYER
04	Executive Assistant to President	Ms. Mary OLIVA
28	Asst Dean of Multicultural Stdnts	Mr. Edward JONES
20	Dean of Faculty	Dr. Timothy SISK
12	VP & Dean of MTS	Dr. Winfred NEELY
88	Dean of Ops and Strategic Educ Init	Mr. Doug MURPHY

† Tuition is paid through donor contributions. Fees are $1,950.00 per year.

Moraine Valley Community College (A)

9000 W College Parkway, Palos Hills IL 60465-0937
County: Cook | FICE Identification: 007692
Unit ID: 147378
Telephone: (708) 974-4300 | Carnegie Class: Assoc/HVT-High Non
FAX Number: (708) 974-1184 | Calendar System: Semester
URL: www.morainevalley.edu
Established: 1967 | Annual Undergrad Tuition & Fees (In-District): $8,095
Enrollment: 11,026 | Coed
Affiliation or Control: State/Local | IRS Status: 501(c)3
Highest Offering: Associate Degree
Accreditation: HLC, ACFEI, ADNUR, CAHIIM, COARC, MAC, POLYT, RAD

Code	Title	Name
01	President	Dr. Sylvia JENKINS
05	Vice President Academic Affairs	Dr. Pamela HANEY
32	Vice President Student Devel	Dr. Normah SALLEH-BARONE
11	Vice Pres Administrative Services	Mr. Richard J. HENDRICKS
10	Vice Pres Financial & Business Svcs	Ms. Theresa O'CARROLL
13	Vice Pres Information Technology	Mr. Kamlesh SANGHVI
50	Dean Science/Business/Comp Tech	Dr. Ryen NAGLE
49	Dean Liberal Arts	Dr. Walter FRONCZEK
124	Dean Student Engagement	Dr. Scott FRIEDMAN
84	Dean Enrollment Services	Vacant
51	Exec Dir Corporate/Cmty & Cont Educ	Mr. Steven PAPPAGEORGE
36	Dean Career Programs	Vacant
35	Dean Student Services	Mr. Chester SHAW
88	Dean Learn Enrich & Col Readiness	Mr. Michael MORSCHES
35	Dean of Students/Compliance Officer	Mr. Kent MARSHALL
37	Director Financial Aid	Vacant
09	Dir Institutional Research/Planning	Dr. Sadya KHAN
19	Chief of Police	Vacant
15	Director Human Resources	Ms. Lynn HARRINGTON
07	Director of Admissions/Recruitment	Mr. Andrew SARATA
18	Director Campus Operations	Vacant
109	Director Auxiliary Services	Mr. Kashif SHAH
23	Director Health Education Well Ctr	Mr. William FINN
26	Director Marketing & Communications	Ms. Clare BRINER
25	Dir Res Devel/Extended Programs	Dr. Sharon KATTERMAN
21	Controller	Mr. Michael CIPOLLA
22	Director of Disability Services	Mr. Nathan PAYOVICH
96	Director of Purchasing	Ms. Jane BENTLEY
102	Executive Director Foundation	Ms. Kristy MCGREAL
20	Dean Academic Development/Outreach	Dr. Cynthia ANDERSON
20	Dean Academic Services	Dr. Cherie MEADOR
08	Dean Learning Resource Center	Ms. Terra JACOBSON
121	Dean Student Success	Dr. Jo Ann JENKINS
88	Asst Dean of Enrollment Services	Mr. Emmanuel ESPERANZA, JR.

Code	Title	Name
101	Secretary of the Institution/Board	Ms. Dawn FREDRIKSON
108	Director Curriculum/Assessment	Ms. Carrie BLIXT-DIAZ
29	Director Alumni & Annual Programs	Ms. Patricia FRIEND

Morrison Institute of Technology (B)

701 Portland Avenue, Morrison IL 61270-2959
County: Whiteside | FICE Identification: 008880
Unit ID: 147396
Telephone: (815) 772-7218 | Carnegie Class: Spec 2-yr-Tech
FAX Number: (815) 772-7584 | Calendar System: Semester
URL: www.morrisontech.edu
Established: 1973 | Annual Undergrad Tuition & Fees: $17,400
Enrollment: 79 | Coed
Affiliation or Control: Independent Non-Profit | IRS Status: 501(c)3
Highest Offering: Associate Degree
Accreditation: COE

Code	Title	Name
01	President/Chief Executive Officer	Mr. Christopher D. SCOTT
05	Vice President Academic Affairs	Mr. Scott CONNELLY
10	Vice President for Finance	Mr. Richard PARKINSON
07	Vice President Admissions	Ms. Jodie EAKER
111	Dean Institutional Advancement	Mr. Greg J. TULLY
37	Financial Aid Director	Ms. Lisa KRAMER

Morton College (C)

3801 S Central Avenue, Cicero IL 60804-4398
County: Cook | FICE Identification: 001728
Unit ID: 147411
Telephone: (708) 656-8000 | Carnegie Class: Assoc/MT-VT-Mix Trad/Non
FAX Number: (708) 656-3297 | Calendar System: Semester
URL: www.morton.edu
Established: 1924 | Annual Undergrad Tuition & Fees (In-District): $8,852
Enrollment: 3,618 | Coed
Affiliation or Control: State/Local | IRS Status: 501(c)3
Highest Offering: Associate Degree
Accreditation: HLC, ADNUR, PTAA

Code	Title	Name
01	President	Dr. Stanley FIELDS
05	Provost	Dr. Keith MCLAUGHLIN
11	VP of Administrative Services	Mr. Frank MARZULLO
51	Dean Adult & Continuing Education	Ms. Laurie CASHMAN
32	Dean of Student Services	Ms. Marisol VELAZQUEZ
08	Assoc Dn Library/Instructional Tech	Mr. Micheal KOTT
111	Exec Dir of Inst Advancement	Ms. Blanca JARA
15	Director of Human Resources	Mr. Ronald LULLO
31	Dir of Community & Continuing Educ	Ms. Irina CLINE
09	Director Institutional Research	Ms. Magda BANDA
18	Director of Facilities & Operations	Mr. Joseph FLORIO
37	Director of Financial Aid	Ms. Carissa DAVIS
06	Assoc Dean of Stdnt Svcs/Registrar	Mr. Michael BROWN
10	CFO/Treasurer	Ms. Mireya PEREZ
04	Admin Assistant to the President	Ms. Maria ANDERSON
13	Chief Information Officer	Mr. Ruben RUIZ
41	Athletic Director	Mr. John TREIBER

National Louis University (D)

122 S Michigan Avenue, Chicago IL 60603
County: Cook | FICE Identification: 001733
Unit ID: 147536
Telephone: (888) 658-8632 | Carnegie Class: DU-Mod
FAX Number: N/A | Calendar System: Quarter
URL: www.nl.edu
Established: 1886 | Annual Undergrad Tuition & Fees: $11,505
Enrollment: 7,402 | Coed
Affiliation or Control: Independent Non-Profit | IRS Status: 501(c)3
Highest Offering: Doctorate
Accreditation: HLC, ACFEI, CACREP, CAEP, CLPSY, IACBE

Code	Title	Name
01	President	Dr. Nivine MEGAHED
05	Provost	Dr. Saib OTHMAN
111	VP Inst Advance & Communications	Vacant
15	Vice President Human Resources	Mr. Tom BERGMANN
10	Vice Pres Finance & Administration	Mr. Marty MICKEY
84	Vice Pres Enrollment & Marketing	Mr. Richard YACONIS
32	VP of Student Affairs & Dean	Dr. Aurelio VALENTE
13	VP of Operations & Technology	Mr. Michael GRAHAM
20	Vice Prov Acad Pgm & Fac Dev	Vacant
06	Vice Prov Advising & Univ Registrar	Mr. Stephen NEER
50	Dean CPSA	Dr. Ignacio LOPEZ
53	Dean NCE	Dr. Robert MULLER
08	Dean University Library	Dr. Robert MORRISON
97	Dean Undergraduate College	Ms. Aarti DHUPELIA
28	Director of Employment/Diversity	Vacant
37	Exec Dir Student Financial Services	Ms. Brigid CALLAHAN
108	Exec Dir Institutional Assessment	Dr. Joseph LEVY
07	Director of Admissions	Ms. Lori MARKUSON
51	Director Outreach Academic Pgm	Vacant
35	Director of Student Experience	Dr. Danielle LABAN
04	Administrative Asst to President	Ms. Diane M. TRAUSCH
108	Director Institutional Assessment	Ms. Mital PATEL
18	Chief Facilities/Physical Plant	Mr. Richard SORENSON
25	Director of Grant Development	Vacant
29	Director Alumni & Outreach Programs	Ms. Nagieh OMER
91	Technical Director	Mr. John MAZARIEGOS
96	Purchasing Coordinator	Ms. Caryn SMITH
102	Exec Dir of IA	Ms. Leslie VILLASENOR
12	Florida Exec Director	Mr. Anthony SPANO
45	Exec Dir Strategic Initiatives	Mr. Andi KORITARI
44	Assoc Director Annual Giving	Mr. Patrick BELICS

Code	Title	Name
30	Dir External Funding & Grant Devel	Ms. Arlene STRONG
36	Exec Dir Career Svcs & Placement	Dr. Abiodun DUROJAYE
09	Director of Institutional Research	Ms. Stacy VLAHAKIS
106	Dean Online Education	Dr. BettyJo BOUCHEY
39	Director Residence Life	Ms. Victoria MULLALY

National University of Health Sciences (E)

200 E Roosevelt Road, Lombard IL 60148-4583
County: DuPage | FICE Identification: 001732
Unit ID: 147590
Telephone: (630) 629-2000 | Carnegie Class: Spec-4-yr-Other Health
FAX Number: (630) 889-6600 | Calendar System: Trimester
URL: www.nuhs.edu
Established: 1906 | Annual Undergrad Tuition & Fees: N/A
Enrollment: 529 | Coed
Affiliation or Control: Independent Non-Profit | IRS Status: 501(c)3
Highest Offering: First Professional Degree
Accreditation: HLC, ACUP, CHIRO, COMTA, NATUR

Code	Title	Name
01	President	Dr. Joseph P D. STIEFEL
05	Vice President Academic Services	Dr. Randy L. SWENSON
10	Vice President Business Services	Mr. Ron MENSCHING
11	Vice Pres Administrative Services	Ms. Tracy MCHUGH
76	Dean College Allied Health Sciences	Dr. Jerrilyn CAMBRON
51	Dean College Postprofessional Educ	Dr. Jenna GLENN
23	Dean of Clinics	Dr. Theodore JOHNSON
107	Dean Col Professional Studies FL	Dr. Daniel STRAUSS
107	Dean Col Professional Studies IL	Dr. Sandra ROGERS
46	Dean of Research	Dr. Gregory D. CRAMER
32	Dean of Students	Ms. Yesenia MALDONADO
09	Dean of Institutional Effectiveness	Vacant
88	Dean Accreditation	Vacant
08	Director Learning Resource Center	Ms. Patricia GENARDO
06	University Registrar	Ms. Izabela DUBAK
07	Dir Communication/Enrollment Svcs	Ms. Victoria SWEENEY
21	Director of Financial Services	Ms. Sue UNGER
37	Director of Financial Aid	Mr. Marc YAMBO
18	Director Maintenance & Facilities	Mr. Mark GALVANONI
15	Director of Human Resources	Mr. Andrew WOZNIAK
26	Dir Communications/Enrollment Svcs	Ms. Victoria SWEENEY
30	Dir Alumni Relations & Development	Ms. Tracy MCHUGH
13	Dir Management Information Services	Mr. Ron MENSCHING
40	Bookstore Manager	Ms. Sue ROBERTSON
39	Coordinator of Housing	Ms. Marilyn FREAD
88	Dean of Institutional Compliance	Mr. Daniel DRISCOLL

North Central College (F)

30 N Brainard Street, Naperville IL 60540-4607
County: DuPage | FICE Identification: 001734
Unit ID: 147660
Telephone: (630) 637-5100 | Carnegie Class: Masters/M
FAX Number: (630) 637-5121 | Calendar System: Trimester
URL: www.northcentralcollege.edu
Established: 1861 | Annual Undergrad Tuition & Fees: $41,180
Enrollment: 2,832 | Coed
Affiliation or Control: United Methodist | IRS Status: 501(c)3
Highest Offering: Doctorate
Accreditation: HLC, CAATE, @DIETD, OT

Code	Title	Name
01	President	Dr. Troy D. HAMMOND
04	Exec Assistant to the President	Ms. Kimberly SALZBRUNN
05	Provost/VP Academic Affairs	Dr. Abiodun GOKE-PARIOLA
10	VP of Finance/CFO	Ms. Maryellen SKERIK
111	VP Institutional Advancement	Mr. Rick E. SPENCER
84	VP Enrollment Management/Athletics	Mr. Marty R. SAUER
32	VP Student Affs/Dean of Strat Init	Ms. Kimberly SLUIS
11	VP for Operations	Mr. Michael J. HUDSON
13	VP Information and Technology/CIO	Mr. Matthew BURDEN
15	Asst Vice Pres Human Resources	Ms. Mary SPREITZER
26	Asst VP External Affs/Sp Asst Pres	Mr. James GODO
28	Chief Diversity Officer	Dr. Rebecca GORDON
07	Dean of Admissions	Ms. Martha A. STOLZE
123	Assoc Dean Graduate Enrollment/Svcs	Ms. Wendy E. POCHOCKI
06	Registrar	Ms. Katherine NORRIS
08	Director of the Library	Vacant
36	Director of Career Development Ctr	Ms. Haydee NUNEZ
37	Director of Financial Aid	Mr. Kevin TOWNS
23	Director of the Dyson Wellness Ctr	Ms. Tatiana SIFRI
41	Athletic Director	Mr. James MILLER
39	Director of Residence Life	Mr. Andrew W. ZOBAC
42	Campus Chaplain	Rev. Eric DOOLITTLE
09	Asst Provost/Dir Inst Effect/Plng	Mr. Peter S. BARGER
29	Exec Dir of Development/Alumni Affs	Mr. Adrian M. ALDRICH
28	Asst Dean of Students/Dir MC Affs	Ms. Dorothy J. PLEAS

North Park University (G)

3225 W Foster Avenue, Chicago IL 60625-4895
County: Cook | FICE Identification: 001735
Unit ID: 147679
Telephone: (773) 244-6200 | Carnegie Class: Masters/L
FAX Number: N/A | Calendar System: Semester
URL: www.northpark.edu
Established: 1891 | Annual Undergrad Tuition & Fees: $32,100
Enrollment: 2,831 | Coed
Affiliation or Control: Evangelical Covenant Church Of America
IRS Status: 501(c)3
Highest Offering: Doctorate
Accreditation: HLC, CAATE, IACBE, MUS, NURSE, THEOL

01 President ... Mrs. Mary K. SURRIDGE
05 Provost ... Dr. Michael CARR
84 Vice Pres for Enrollment/Marketing ... Mr. Anthony L. SCOLA
111 Vice President for Advancement ... Vacant
32 VP for Student Engagement ... Ms. Andrea MILLER NEVELS
10 Vice Pres Finance & Admin/CFO ... Mr. Scott STENMARK
73 Seminary Dean ... Dr. David W. KERSTEN
35 AVP and Dean of Students ... Ms. Elizabeth FREDEC
49 Dean of College of Arts & Sciences ... Vacant
107 Dean School of Professional Studies ... Dr. Lori SCREMENTI
50 Dean School of Business & NFP Mgmt ... Dr. Ann HICKS
53 Dean School of Education ... Dr. Rebecca NELSON
64 Dean School of Music ... Dr. Rebecca RYAN
66 Dean School of Nursing ... Dr. Cindy HUDSON
28 Dir Diversity & Intercultural Life ... Ms. Sharee MYRICKS
08 Dean Library & Academic Technology ... Ms. Kathryn MAIER-O'SHEA
07 Director Undergraduate Enrollment ... Mr. Brady MARTINSON
123 Dir of Graduate & Adult Admissions ... Ms. Judy DONOR
23 Director Health & Wellness ... Ms. Laura EBNER
37 Director Financial Aid Services ... Ms. Carolyn LACH
13 Director of Information Technology ... Mr. Jeffrey K. LUNDBLAD
15 Asst VP of Human Resources ... Ms. Ingrid K. TENGLIN
18 Director of Physical Plant ... Mr. Carl H. WISTROM
19 Director of Security ... Mr. Elman MCCLAIN
21 Director of Finance/Comptroller ... Ms. Debbie WILLBURN
26 Dir Univ Marketing & Communications ... Mr. Joseph MILLER
41 Asst VP for Athletics & Sports Mgmt ... Mr. John BORN
42 Director University Ministries ... Mr. Anthony ZAMBLE
36 Asst Dir Career Svcs/Internships ... Ms. Tyra OWENS
06 Registrar ... Mr. Aaron D. SCHOOF
29 Alumni Relations Assoc Dir ... Ms. Kristin ENGLUND
100 Chief of Staff Pres Office ... Ms. Melissa VELEZ-LUCE
104 Director of International Office ... Dr. Sumie SONG
39 Director Student Housing ... Mr. Aidan HOWORTH
108 Assoc Prov Institutional Assessment ... Ms. Lisa NCUBE
106 Assoc Dean Center for Online Educ ... Vacant
44 Director Annual Giving ... Mr. Justin PREVOST-SHULTZ

Northeastern Illinois University (A)

5500 N Saint Louis Avenue, Chicago IL 60625-4699
County: Cook FICE Identification: 001693
Unit ID: 147776
Telephone: (773) 583-4050 Carnegie Class: Masters/L
FAX Number: (773) 442-4900 Calendar System: Semester
URL: www.neiu.edu
Established: 1867 Annual Undergrad Tuition & Fees (In-State): $11,827
Enrollment: 7,119 Coed
Affiliation or Control: State IRS Status: 501(c)3
Highest Offering: Master's
Accreditation: HLC, ART, CACREP, CAEP, MUS, SW

01 President ... Dr. Gloria J. GIBSON
05 Provost & VP Academic Affairs ... Dr. Dennis ROME
07 Exec Director of Admissions ... Mr. Lamont VAUGHN
100 Chief of Staff ... Vacant
32 VP for Student Affs/Dean Students ... Dr. Terry MENA
111 Vice President Inst Advancement ... Ms. Liesl V. DOWNEY
10 Vice Pres Finance & Admin ... Mr. Manish KUMAR
26 Chief of Staff/CMO ... Vacant
20 Associate Academic Officer ... Dr. Shayne COFER
84 Assoc VP Enrollment Services ... Vacant
13 Interim Chief Information Officer ... Ms. Marsha HENFER
114 Executive Director Univ Budgets ... Dr. Michael WENZ
08 Dean Libraries ... Mr. Steven HARRIS
09 Exec Dir Inst Rsrch & Assessment ... Mr. Blase E. MASINI
15 Int Exec Director Human Resources ... Ms. Abby MURRAY
25 Director Sponsored Programs ... Ms. Sharon K. TODD
37 Director Financial Aid ... Dr. Maureen T. AMOS
50 Dean College Bus/Management ... Dr. Michael D. BEDELL
58 Dean College Graduate Studies & Res ... Dr. Michael J. STERN
88 Special Assistant to Provost ... Dr. Sandra BEYDA-LORIE
49 Dean College of Arts & Sciences ... Dr. Katrina BELL-JORDAN
18 Assoc Vice Pres Facilities Mgmt ... Ms. Nancy MEDINA
19 Director University Police Dept ... Mr. John ESCALANTE
21 Director Controller's Office ... Ms. Beni ORTIZ
22 Dir Equal Opportunity/AA & Ethics ... Ms. Natalie POTTS
86 Sr Exec Dir Government Relations ... Dr. Suleyma PEREZ
06 University Registrar ... Mr. Daniel R. WEBER
29 Director of Alumni Relations ... Ms. Damaris TAPIA
110 Director Institutional Advancement ... Mr. John L. BUTLER
96 Director Purchasing ... Ms. Victoria SANTIAGO
23 Director of Student Health Services ... Ms. Sharon HEIMBAUGH
38 Director Student Counseling ... Dr. Nancy EASTON

Northern Illinois University (B)

1425 W. Lincoln Way, De Kalb IL 60115-2828
County: De Kalb FICE Identification: 001737
Unit ID: 147703
Telephone: (815) 753-1000 Carnegie Class: DU-Higher
FAX Number: (815) 753-0198 Calendar System: Semester
URL: www.niu.edu
Established: 1895 Annual Undergrad Tuition & Fees (In-State): $12,352
Enrollment: 16,769 Coed
Affiliation or Control: State IRS Status: 501(c)3
Highest Offering: Doctorate
Accreditation: HLC, ART, AUD, CACREP, CAEP, CAEPN, CLPSY, DIETD, DIETI, IPSY, LAW, MFCD, MT, MUS, NAIT, NURSE, PH, PTA, SCPSY, SP, SPAA, THEA

01 President ... Lisa C. FREEMAN
05 Executive Vice Pres & Provost ... Beth INGRAM
10 VP Administration & Finance/CFO ... Sarah CHINNIAH
51 SAVP University Outreach ... Rena COTSONES
46 VP Research/Innovative Partnership ... Jerry BLAZEY
26 VP Enroll Mgmt/Mktg/Communications ... Sol JENSEN
43 General Counsel ... Bryan PERRY
111 Vice Pres University Advancement ... Catherine SQUIRES
13 Chief Information Officer ... Matt PARKS
09 Exec Dir Inst Research/Analytics ... Greg BARKER
18 AVP Facilities Mgmt/Campus Services ... John HECKMANN
15 Sr AVP for Human Resources ... William HODSON
32 Int VP Student Affairs ... Charlie FEY
23 Director Health Services ... Andrew DIGATE
28 VP Diversity/Equity/Inclusion ... Vernese EDGHILL-WALDEN
20 Vice Provost ... Omar GHRAYEB
50 Dean of Business ... Balaji RAJAGOPALAN
53 Dean of Education ... Laurie ELISH-PIPER
54 Dean of Engineering/Engr Tech ... Donald PETERSON
61 Dean of Law ... Cassandra HILL
49 Dean Liberal Arts & Sciences ... Robert BRINKMANN
76 Dean Health & Human Sciences ... Lynda RANSDALL
57 Dean Visual & Performing Arts ... Paul KASSEL
58 Int Dean Graduate School ... Purush DAMODARAN
85 Interim Sr International Affairs ... Bradley BOND
12 Director Lorado Taft Field Campus ... Diana DENNIS
12 Director NIU Naperville ... Gina KENYON
06 Director/Registrar ... Cody SCHMITZ
37 Director of Student Financial Aid ... Rebecca BABEL
38 Exec Dir Counseling/Consultation ... Vacant
19 Police Chief/Public Safety ... Thomas R. PHILLIPS, SR.
41 AVP/Athletic Director ... Sean FRAZIER
39 Int Sr Dir Housing/Residential Svcs ... Jennifer MANNING
22 Dir Disability Resources Center ... Debra MILLER
29 Dir Alumni Relations/Univ Advance ... Reggie BUSTINZA
96 Dir Procurement/Strategic Sourcing ... Antoinette BRIDGES
07 Director of Admissions ... Quinton CLAY

Northern Seminary (C)

410 Warrenville Road, Suite 300, Lisle IL 60532
County: DuPage FICE Identification: 001736
Unit ID: 147697
Telephone: (630) 620-2180 Carnegie Class: Spec-4-yr-Faith
FAX Number: (630) 620-2190 Calendar System: Quarter
URL: www.seminary.edu
Established: 1913 Annual Graduate Tuition & Fees: N/A
Enrollment: 285 Coed
Affiliation or Control: American Baptist IRS Status: 501(c)3
Highest Offering: Doctorate; No Undergraduates
Accreditation: THEOL

01 President ... Dr. William D. SHIELL
04 Executive Assistant to President ... Ms. Amy S. DISANTO
05 Provost/Dean of Academic Affairs ... Dr. Lynn COHICK
07 Director of Enrollment ... Rev. Greg ARMSTRONG
06 Registrar ... Rev. Linda OWENS
32 Sr Exec Director Student Services ... Rev. Linda OWENS
09 Dean of Program Dev and Innovation ... Dr. Jason GILE
11 Director of Operations ... Ms. Pamela SHELDON

Northwestern College (D)

7725 S. Harlem Avenue, Bridgeview IL 60455
County: Cook FICE Identification: 012362
Unit ID: 147749
Telephone: (708) 237-5050 Carnegie Class: Assoc/HVT-High Trad
FAX Number: (708) 237-5005 Calendar System: Quarter
URL: www.nc.edu
Established: 1902 Annual Undergrad Tuition & Fees: N/A
Enrollment: N/A Coed
Affiliation or Control: Proprietary IRS Status: Proprietary
Highest Offering: Baccalaureate
Accreditation: HLC, ACBSP, CAHIIM, RAD

01 President ... Mr. Lawrence SCHUMACHER
11 Executive VP of Operations ... Mrs. Gail SCHUMACHER
10 Controller ... Ms. Cynthia BERRYMAN
05 Chief Academic Officer ... Ms. Tonya TROKA
13 Exec Dir of Information Technology ... Mr. Omar BERNAL
86 Government and Public Relations Dir ... Ms. Laura POLLASTRINI
08 Director of Library Services ... Ms. Sarah DULAY
37 Exec Dir of Student Financial Svcs ... Mrs. Teresa VALDEZ
18 Exec Dir of Project Management ... Ms. Lauren SCHUMACHER
66 Dean of Nursing ... Ms. Lauren SPRAGGINS
06 Registrar ... Ms. Tina MARFOE

Northwestern University (E)

633 Clark Street, Evanston IL 60208-3854
County: Cook FICE Identification: 001739
Unit ID: 147767
Telephone: (847) 491-8400 Carnegie Class: DU-Highest
FAX Number: (847) 467-3104 Calendar System: Quarter
URL: www.northwestern.edu
Established: 1851 Annual Undergrad Tuition & Fees: $58,701
Enrollment: 22,603 Coed
Affiliation or Control: Independent Non-Profit IRS Status: 501(c)3
Highest Offering: Doctorate
Accreditation: HLC, ARCPA, AUD, CACREP, CLPSY, IPSY, LAW, MED, MFCD, OPE, PCSAS, PH, PTA, SP

01 President ... Dr. Morton O. SCHAPIRO
05 Provost ... Dr. Kathleen M. HAGERTY
10 Sr Vice President Business/Finance ... Mr. Craig JOHNSON
32 Vice President Student Affairs ... Ms. Julie A. PAYNE-KIRCHMEIER
26 VP Global Marketing & Comm ... Vacant
45 Vice Pres Administration & Planning ... Ms. Marilyn MCCOY
13 Vice Pres Information Technology ... Mr. Sean B. REYNOLDS
30 Vice Pres for Alumni Rel & Devel ... Mr. Robert MCQUINN
85 VP of Intl Relations ... Dr. Dévora GRYNSPAN
46 Vice President Research ... Dr. Milan T. MRKSICH
115 Vice Pres/Chief Investment Officer ... Vacant
43 Vice President/General Counsel ... Ms. Stephanie M. GRAHAM
18 Vice Pres of Facilities Management ... Mr. Alex DARRAGH
41 Vice Pres Athletics and Recreation ... Dr. Derrick GRAGG
15 Vice Pres for Human Resources ... Vacant
114 Vice Pres Budget Planning ... Vacant
84 Dean Enrollment/AVP Stdnt Outreach ... Mr. Christopher WATSON
20 Associate Provost Faculty Affairs ... Dr. Lindsay CHASE-LANSDALE
20 Assoc VP & Assoc Provost Academic ... Mr. Jake JULIA
21 Assoc Prov Operations/Facilities ... Mr. Mark J. FRANCIS
86 Spec Asst to Pres for Govt Rels ... Mr. Bruce LAYTON
04 Assistant to the President ... Mr. Eugene Y. LOWE, JR.
100 Chief of Staff/Sr Dir President Ofc ... Ms. Judith V. REMINGTON
54 Dean Sch Engr/Applied Science ... Dr. Julio M. OTTINO
50 Dean Graduate School of Management ... Dr. Francesca CORNELLI
60 Dean School of Journalism ... Dr. Charles WHITAKER
64 Dean School of Music ... Dr. Toni-Marie MONTGOMERY
63 Dean School of Medicine ... Dr. Eric G. NEILSON
107 Dean School of Professional Studies ... Dr. Thomas F. GIBBONS
58 Dean Graduate School ... Dr. Kelly MAYO
60 Dean School of Communication ... Dr. E. Patrick JOHNSON
53 Dean School of Educ & Social Policy ... Dr. David N. FIGLIO
49 Dean College Arts & Science ... Mr. Adrian RANDOLPH
61 Dean School of Law ... Dr. Hari OSOFSKY
08 University Librarian ... Ms. Sarah M. PRITCHARD
36 Exec Dir of University Career Svcs ... Dr. Mark PRESNELL
35 Assistant VP of Student Engagement ... Dr. Kelly SCHAEFER
29 AVP Alumni Relations/Development ... Mr. David LIVELY
88 Assoc Vice President for Research ... Dr. Fruma YHEIELY
88 Assoc Vice President for Research ... Dr. Jian CAO
88 AVP for Rsrch/Innov & New Ventures ... Ms. Alicia LOFFLER
88 Assoc Vice President for Research ... Ms. Ann ADAMS
88 Assoc Vice President for Research ... Dr. Rex CHISHOLM
88 Assoc Vice President for Research ... Dr. Richard D'AQUILA
21 Vice Pres Finance/Treasurer ... Vacant
23 Exec Director Health Services ... Dr. Robert PALINKAS
39 Asst Dean of Students ... Ms. Mary GOLDENBERG
38 Director of Counseling/Psych Svcs ... Dr. John H. DUNKLE
42 University Chaplain ... Rev. Kristen GLASS PEREZ
88 Asst VP for Information ... Mr. Amit PRACHAND
88 AVP Program Review/Spec Project ... Ms. Megan BLACKWELDER
06 University Registrar ... Ms. Jacqualyn CASAZZA
37 Director Financial Aid ... Mr. Phil ASBURY
16 Dir HR Consulting & Policy ... Ms. Stephanie GRIFFIN
19 AVP/Chief of Police & Safety ... Mr. Bruce LEWIS
116 Assoc VP of Audit & Compliance ... Mr. Luke FIGORA
22 Dir Equal Oppty & Access ... Ms. Karen TAMBURRO
96 Exec Director of Procurement ... Mr. Jim KONRAD
28 Assoc Provost Diversity & Inclusion ... Dr. Sekile NZINGA

Oak Point University (F)

1431 N. Claremont Street, 6th Floor, Chicago IL 60622
County: Cook FICE Identification: 006250
Unit ID: 149763
Telephone: (773) 252-6464 Carnegie Class: Spec-4-yr-Other Health
FAX Number: (773) 227-5134 Calendar System: Semester
URL: www.oakpoint.edu
Established: 1982 Annual Undergrad Tuition & Fees: N/A
Enrollment: 753 Coed
Affiliation or Control: Independent Non-Profit IRS Status: 501(c)3
Highest Offering: Doctorate
Accreditation: HLC, CAHIIM, NURSE, RAD

01 President ... Dr. Therese A. SCANLAN
03 Executive Vice President & CFO ... Mr. Matthew HUGHES
05 Dir Student Academic Success ... Ms. Marlena AVALOS
32 VP Student & Employee Affairs ... Vacant
35 Director of Student Life ... Mr. Eric HERNANDEZ
90 Asst Director Student System ... Ms. Valarie LINDSEY
37 Director Financial Aid ... Ms. Dominique COLYER
06 University Registrar ... Ms. Alicia FLEMING
84 Director of Enrollment Management ... Dr. Rochelle KERRIGAN
08 Director of Library Services ... Ms. Liesl COTTRELL
66 Dean of Nursing ... Ms. Connie ZAK
04 Administrative Asst to President ... Ms. Barbara BAILEY
13 Asst Vice Pres of Technology/CIO ... Mr. Matthew HERTZOG
29 Director Alumni Affairs ... Ms. Vickie THORNLEY
09 Director of Institutional Research ... Ms. Watasha HALL
10 Director of Finance ... Mr. Larry KEMNETZ
30 Director of Development ... Ms. Vickie THORNLEY

Oakton Community College (G)

1600 E Golf Road, Des Plaines IL 60016-1256
County: Cook FICE Identification: 009896
Unit ID: 147800
Telephone: (847) 635-1600 Carnegie Class: Assoc/HT-Mix Trad/Non
FAX Number: (847) 635-1992 Calendar System: Semester
URL: www.oakton.edu
Established: 1969 Annual Undergrad Tuition & Fees (In-District): $10,446
Enrollment: 7,313 Coed
Affiliation or Control: Local IRS Status: 501(c)3
Highest Offering: Associate Degree

Accreditation: HLC, ADNUR, CAHIIM, MLTAD, PTAA

01 President ... Dr. Joanne L. SMITH
05 VP Academic Affairs ... Dr. Ileo LOTT
32 VP Student Affairs ... Dr. Karl BROOKS
10 VP Admininstrative Affairs ... Mr. Edwin CHANDRASEKAR
20 Asst VP Academic Affairs ... Ms. Anne BRENNAN
103 AVP Workforce Education ... Mr. Marc BATTISTA
35 Asst VP Student Affairs ... Ms. Juletta PATRICK
13 Chief Information Officer ... Mr. Prashant SHINDE
76 Asst Dean Health Careers ... Ms. Maribel ALIMBOYOGUEN
81 Dean STEM & Health Careers ... Dr. Robert SOMPOLSKI
49 Dean Liberal Arts ... Ms. Linda KORBEL
51 Dean Adult & Cont Education ... Dr. Jesse IVORY
09 AVP Institutional Effectiveness ... Dr. Kelly IWANAGA-BECKER
26 AVP Mktg & Comm/CAO ... Ms. Katherine SAWYER
08 Assistant Dean Library ... Mr. Jacob JEREMIAH
07 Dir of Admissions & Enrollment ... Ms. Michele BROWN
35 Director of Student Life/Inclusion ... Mr. Shedrick DANIELS
121 Dean of Student Success ... Mr. Sebastian CONTRERAS, JR.
124 Dir of Student Learning/Engagement ... Ms. Leana CUELLAR
41 Senior Manager of Athletics ... Ms. Christine PACIERO
78 Dir Workforce & Strat Partnerships ... Dr. Ruben HOWARD, II
21 Controller ... Mr. Andy WILLIAMS
15 Chief Human Resources Officer ... Dr. Colette HANDS
18 Director of Facilities ... Mr. Joseph SCIFO
14 Director Systems & Network Svcs ... Mr. John WADE
14 Dir of Software & User Svcs ... Ms. Renee KOZIMOR
06 Dir Financial Aid/Registrar ... Dr. Cheryl WARMANN
25 Dir of Grant Strategy/Development ... Mr. Al GRIPPE
11 Dir of Operations & Admin ... Ms. Robyn BAILEY
38 Dean of Wellness Services ... Dr. Mark KIEL
19 Chief of Police ... Mr. Jeffrey HOFFMANN
20 Dean Curriculum & Instruction ... Ms. Ruth WILLIAMS
106 Dean Online Learning ... Dr. Raymond LAWSON
27 Director of Marketing ... Dr. Andrea LEHMACHER
84 Dean of Enrollment Management ... Mr. Matthew HUBER

Olivet Nazarene University (A)

One University Avenue, Bourbonnais IL 60914-2345
County: Kankakee　FICE Identification: 001741
Unit ID: 147828
Telephone: (815) 939-5011　Carnegie Class: Masters/L
FAX Number: (815) 935-4998　Calendar System: Semester
URL: www.olivet.edu
Established: 1907　Annual Undergrad Tuition & Fees: $36,950
Enrollment: 3,764　Coed
Affiliation or Control: Church Of The Nazarene　IRS Status: 501(c)3
Highest Offering: Doctorate
Accreditation: HLC, #CAATE, DIETD, MUS, NURSE, SW

01 President ... Dr. Gregg A. CHENOWETH
10 EVP/Chief Financial Officer ... Dr. David J. PICKERING
05 Vice President Academic Affairs ... Dr. Stephen R. LOWE
32 Vice President Student Development ... Dr. Walter W. WEBB
111 Vice Pres Institutional Advancement ... Dr. Brian D. ALLEN
88 Vice Pres for ONU Global ... Mr. Ryan D. SPITTAL
29 Dir Alumni & University Relations ... Mr. Erinn M. PROEHL
06 University Registrar ... Dr. Mark C. MOUNTAIN
08 Dean of Library Services ... Mrs. Pam S. GREENLEE
26 Exec Director of Univ Relations ... Mrs. Susan M. WOLFF
113 Director of Undergraduate Revenue ... Mr. Greg S. BRUNER
13 Chief Information Officer ... Mr. Dennis E. SEYMOUR
41 Athletic Director ... Mr. Mike C. CONWAY
42 Chaplain ... RevDr. Mark E. HOLCOMB
30 Exec Director of Development ... Mr. Brian ALLEN
35 Director Student Activities ... Mrs. Kathy STEINACKER
38 Director Student Counseling ... Mrs. Lisa VANDER VEER
18 Chief Facilities/Physical Plant ... Mr. Rob LALUMENDRE
40 Bookstore Manager ... Mrs. Rachel PIAZZA
36 Director of Career Services ... Vacant
85 International Student Advisor ... Mrs. Darlene SWANSON
26 Director of Marketing ... Mr. Adam ASHER
19 Director Security/Safety ... Mr. Darren BLAIR
49 Dean College of Arts & Sciences ... Dr. Kent OLNEY
73 Dn Sch Theology/Christian Ministry ... Dr. David WINE
53 Chair Education Dept ... Dr. Lance KILPATRICK
107 Dean College Professional Studies ... Dr. Amber RESIDORI
64 Assoc Dean School of Music ... Dr. Don REDDICK
50 Assoc Dean School of Business ... Dr. Glen REWERTS
54 Chair Engineering Dept ... Dr. Joe SCHROEDER
04 Admin Assistant to the President ... Mrs. Amy ZABEL
15 Director of Human Resources ... Mr. Tom ASCHER

Pacific College of Health and Science (B)

65 East Wacker Place 21st Floor, Chicago IL 60601
Telephone: (888) 729-4811　Identification: 666615
Accreditation: &WC, ACUP

† Branch campus of Pacific College of Health and Science, San Diego CA.

Parkland College (C)

2400 W Bradley Avenue, Champaign IL 61821-1899
County: Champaign　FICE Identification: 007118
Unit ID: 147916
Telephone: (217) 351-2200　Carnegie Class: Assoc/HVT-Mix Trad/Non
FAX Number: (217) 351-2581　Calendar System: Semester
URL: www.parkland.edu
Established: 1966　Annual Undergrad Tuition & Fees (In-District): $11,580
Enrollment: 5,758　Coed
Affiliation or Control: State/Local　IRS Status: 501(c)3
Highest Offering: Associate Degree
Accreditation: HLC, ADNUR, COARC, DH, EMT, OTA, RAD, SURGT

01 President ... Dr. Thomas R. RAMAGE
04 Asst to President/Board of Trustees ... Ms. Krystal GARRETT
03 Exec Vice President ... Dr. Pam LAU
05 Vice Pres Academic Services ... Dr. Nancy SUTTON
32 Vice President Student Services ... Dr. Mike TRAME
10 Vice Pres Administrative Svcs/ CFO ... Mr. Christopher M. RANDLES
26 VP Communications/External Affairs ... Ms. Stephanie STUART
35 Dean of Students ... Ms. Marietta TURNER
35 Director Student Life ... Ms. Tracy KLEPARSKI
09 Dean Institutional Effectiveness ... Mr. Kevin KNOTT
49 Dean Arts & Sciences ... Dr. Joseph WALWIK
75 Dean Career & Technical Education ... Mr. Derrick BAKER
66 Dean Health Professions ... Ms. Caroyln RAGSDALE
103 Asst Dean Adult Educ/Workforce Dev ... Ms. Tawanna NICKENS
102 Exec Dir Foundation/Alumni Affairs ... Ms. Tracy WAHFELDT
08 Assoc Dean Learning Commons ... Ms. Morgann QUILTY
31 Director Community Education ... Ms. Triss HENDERSON
27 Director Marketing/Public Rels ... Ms. Erin SHANNON
84 Dean Enrollment Mgmt ... Ms. Kristin SMIGIELSKI
41 Director Athletics ... Mr. Brendan MCHALE
38 Dean Counseling Services ... Ms. Stephanie DAVINGMAN
121 Director Advising Services ... Ms. Julia HAWTHORNE
07 Director Enrollment Services ... Mr. Tim WENDT
19 Director Public Safety ... Mr. Matthew KOPMANN
18 Director Physical Plant ... Mr. James BUSTARD
15 Assoc VP/Chief Human Resources ... Ms. Kathleen MCANDREW
21 Controller ... Mr. Dave DONSBACH
40 Manager of Bookstore ... Ms. Hayden SEIDEL
108 Director Assessment Center ... Mr. Michael BEHRENS
13 Chief Information Tech Officer ... Mr. Amin KASSEM

Prairie State College (D)

202 S Halsted Street, Chicago Heights IL 60411-8226
County: Cook　FICE Identification: 001640
Unit ID: 148007
Telephone: (708) 709-3500　Carnegie Class: Assoc/MT-VT-High Non
FAX Number: (708) 709-3774　Calendar System: Semester
URL: www.prairiestate.edu
Established: 1957　Annual Undergrad Tuition & Fees (In-District): $9,342
Enrollment: 2,716　Coed
Affiliation or Control: State/Local　IRS Status: 501(c)3
Highest Offering: Associate Degree
Accreditation: HLC, ADNUR, DH, PTAA, SURGT

01 Interim President ... Dr. Thomas D. SABAN
10 Vice Pres Finance & Administration ... Dr. Thomas D. SABAN
05 Vice Pres Academic Affairs ... Mr. Elighie WILSON
32 VP Student Affs/Inst Effectiveness ... Dr. Michael D. ANTHONY
49 Dean Liberal Arts & Soc Sciences ... Vacant
81 Dean Math/Nat Scienc/Acad Standards ... Ms. Annette DOLPH
76 Dean Allied Health/Emerg Services ... Dr. Megan HUGHES
75 Dean Career and Tech Education ... Dr. Janice KAUSHAL
15 Exec Dir Human Resources ... Dr. Charmaine SEVIER
13 Exec Dir Info Technology Resources ... Mr. Gregory KAIN
56 Dean Adult Education ... Ms. Kim M. KUNCE
21 Controller/Dir of Business Svcs ... Ms. Cheri TAYLOR-LAWTON
08 Dean Learning Resources/Assess ... Vacant
28 Dean Equity/Inclusion ... Dr. Tiffany BREWER
35 Dean Student Dev/Campus Life ... Mr. Felix SIMPKINS
103 Exec Dir Workforce Dev/Cmty Educ ... Ms. Alisha CLARK
18 Exec Dir Facilities and Operations ... Mr. Timothy J. KOSIEK
111 Exec Dir Inst Advance & Foundation ... Ms. Deborah S. HAVIGHORST
84 Dean Enrollment Management ... Ms. Jaime M. MILLER
19 Chief of Police ... Mr. Anthony MARTIN, SR.
37 Director Financial Aid ... Ms. Grace MCGINNIS
09 Director Inst Research/Planning ... Dr. Adane G. KASSA
41 Director of Athletics ... Mr. Christopher J. KUCHTA
100 Chief of Staff ... Ms. Patricia G. TROST
108 Dir Inst Effect/Plng/Accreditation ... Ms. Jan BONAVIA

Principia College (E)

1 Maybeck Place, Elsah IL 62028-9799
County: Jersey　FICE Identification: 001744
Unit ID: 148016
Telephone: (618) 374-2131　Carnegie Class: Bac-A&S
FAX Number: (618) 374-5500　Calendar System: Semester
URL: www.principiacollege.edu
Established: 1898　Annual Undergrad Tuition & Fees: $30,720
Enrollment: 340　Coed
Affiliation or Control: Independent Non-Profit　IRS Status: 501(c)3
Highest Offering: Baccalaureate
Accreditation: HLC

01 President ... Mr. John W. WILLIAMS
05 Dean of Academics ... Dr. Meggan MADDEN
115 Chief Investment Officer ... Mr. Howard E. BERNER, JR.
10 Chief Financial/Business Officer ... Mr. David WALTERS
111 Chief Advancement Officer ... Mrs. Barbara BLACKWELL
43 Legal Counsel ... Mr. Lee BARRON
06 Registrar ... Ms. Helen WILLS
32 Dean of Students ... Mrs. Maya DIETZ
08 Library Director ... Dr. Edith LIST
104 Director of Principia Abroad ... Mrs. Stephanie LOVSETH
41 Director of Athletics ... Mrs. Ann PIERSON
18 Director of Facilities ... Mr. Lee EUBANK
21 Controller ... Mr. Don MILLER
37 Director of Financial Aid ... Ms. Rachael STOCK
96 Purchasing Agent ... Mrs. Susan CURRY
09 Institutional Research Officer ... Ms. Roz HIBBS
27 Dir Marketing & Communications ... Mrs. Laurel WALTERS
07 Director of Admissions ... Mr. Brett GRIMMER
15 Director of Human Resources ... Mrs. Beth TREVINO
04 Exec Assistant to the President ... Ms. Christina WILSON

Quincy University (F)

1800 College Avenue, Quincy IL 62301-2699
County: Adams　FICE Identification: 001745
Unit ID: 148131
Telephone: (217) 222-8020　Carnegie Class: Bac-Diverse
FAX Number: (217) 228-5257　Calendar System: Semester
URL: www.quincy.edu
Established: 1860　Annual Undergrad Tuition & Fees: $31,160
Enrollment: 1,273　Coed
Affiliation or Control: Roman Catholic　IRS Status: 501(c)3
Highest Offering: Master's
Accreditation: HLC, CACREP

00 Chair Board of Trustees ... Mr. Delmer MITCHELL
01 President ... Dr. Brian R. MCGEE
125 President Emeritus ... Mr. Phillip CONOVER
05 VP for Academic Affairs ... Dr. Teresa REED
42 VP for Mission & Ministry ... Fr. John DOCTOR, OFM
10 VP for Business/Finance ... Mr. Mark STRIEKER
84 VP Student Enrollment & Engagement ... Mr. Tom OLIVER
32 VP for Student Development ... Dr. Christine TRACY
41 Athletic Director ... Mr. Josh RABE
111 VP for University Advancement ... Dr. Robert WYATT
04 Exec Assistant to the President ... Mrs. Julie BUDINE
101 Corporate Secretary ... Fr. John DOCTOR, OFM
21 Controller ... Mrs. Randi KINDHART
20 Associate VP for Academic Affairs ... Dr. Megan BOCCARDI
06 Registrar ... Ms. Nancy GEISSLER
50 Dean School of Business ... Dr. Cynthia HALIEMUN
08 Dean Library/Info Resources ... Ms. Patricia TOMCZAK
79 Dean School of Humanities ... Dr. Robert MANNING
81 Dean School of Science & Technology ... Dr. Kimberly HALE
57 Dean School Fine Arts/Communication ... Dr. Christine DAMM
53 Dean School of Education/Human Svcs ... Dr. Kenneth OLIVER
13 Director of IT Services ... Mr. Michael MCCABE
108 Director of Academic Assessment ... Dr. Barbara ROWLAND
92 Director Honors Program ... Dr. Daniel STRUDWICK
42 Director Campus Ministry ... Ms. Jessica HOWELL
110 Sr Director for Univ Advancement ... Mr. Matthew BERGMAN
37 Director Financial Aid ... Mr. Tom OLIVER
18 Director Facilities Management ... Mr. Troy PETER
121 Director Student Success ... Mrs. Donna HOLTMEYER
39 Director Residence Life ... Mr. Joshua JACOBS
19 Director Safety & Security ... Mr. Sam LATHROP
15 Director Human Resources ... Vacant
07 Director of Admissions ... Mr. Brittany WEISE
36 Director of Experiential Learning ... Mrs. Kristen LIESEN
96 Purchasing ... Ms. Jennifer TRUITT
25 Grant Writer ... Vacant
40 Manager Bookstore ... Mr. Ben MEANS
88 Director of Student Teaching ... Vacant
09 Director of Institutional Research ... Vacant

Rasmussen University - Rockford (G)

6000 E. State Street, 4th Floor, Rockford IL 61108
Telephone: (815) 316-4800　Identification: 667065
Accreditation: &HLC, CAHIIM, MAAB, SURGT

† Regional accreditation carried under the parent institution in Saint Cloud, MN. The tuition figure is an average, actual tuition may vary.

Rasmussen University - Romeoville/Joliet (H)

1400 West Normantown Road, Romeoville IL 60446
Telephone: (815) 306-2600　Identification: 667066
Accreditation: &HLC, MAAB, SURGT

† Regional accreditation carried under the parent institution in Saint Cloud, MN. The tuition figure is an average, actual tuition may vary.

Rend Lake College (I)

468 N Ken Gray Parkway, Ina IL 62846-9801
County: Jefferson　FICE Identification: 007119
Unit ID: 148256
Telephone: (618) 437-5321　Carnegie Class: Assoc/HVT-High Non
FAX Number: (618) 437-5677　Calendar System: Semester
URL: www.rlc.edu
Established: 1967　Annual Undergrad Tuition & Fees (In-District): $6,000
Enrollment: 1,802　Coed
Affiliation or Control: State/Local　IRS Status: 501(c)3
Highest Offering: Associate Degree
Accreditation: HLC, ADNUR, EMT, MAC, RAD

01 President ... Mr. Terry WILKERSON
05 VP of Instruction & Student Affairs ... Mrs. Lori RAGLAND
10 VP of Finance & Administration ... Mrs. Angie KISTNER
32 Assoc VP of Academic & Student Svcs ... Mr. Henry LEECK
26 Assoc VP of Institutional Outreach ... Mr. Chad COPPLE
121 Assoc VP of CTE & Student Support ... Mrs. Kim WILKERSON
37 Director of Financial Aid ... Ms. Cheri RUSHING
41 Athletic Director ... Mr. Tim WILLS
18 Director Physical Plant ... Mr. Donnie MILLENBINE
102 CEO of RLC Foundation ... Mrs. Kathleen ZIBBY-DAMRON

06 Director of Student Records ....Mrs. Kelly DOWNES
84 Dean of Enrollment Services ....Mrs. Vickie SCHULTE

Richland Community College (A)

One College Park, Decatur IL 62521-8513
County: Macon FICE Identification: 010879
Unit ID: 148292
Telephone: (217) 875-7200 Carnegie Class: Assoc/HVT-High Non
FAX Number: (217) 875-6961 Calendar System: Semester
URL: www.richland.edu
Established: 1971 Annual Undergrad Tuition & Fees (In-District): $6,180
Enrollment: 2,235 Coed
Affiliation or Control: State/Local IRS Status: 501(c)3
Highest Offering: Associate Degree
Accreditation: HLC, ACFEI, ADNUR, CAHIIM, RAD, SURGT

01 President ....Dr. Cristobal (Cris) VALDEZ
10 Vice President of Finance & Admin ....Mr. Greg E. FLORIAN
05 Vice Pres Academic Services ....Dr. Denise CREWS
106 Director Online Learning ....Mrs. Kona JONES
111 AVP Inst Advance/Exec Dir Found ....Ms. Julie MELTON
29 Dir Scholarships/Alumni Development ...Mrs. Tricia CORDULACK
15 Director Human Resources ....Ms. Robin BOLLHORST
37 Asst Dir Financial Aid/Veteran Affs ....Ms. Jody BURTNETT
81 Dean Math & Sciences/Business Div ....Dr. Andy HYNDS
76 Dean of Health Professions ....Ms. Ellen COLBECK

Rock Valley College (B)

3301 N Mulford Road, Rockford IL 61114-5699
County: Winnebago FICE Identification: 001747
Unit ID: 148380
Telephone: (815) 921-7821 Carnegie Class: Assoc/MT-VT-High Trad
FAX Number: N/A Calendar System: Semester
URL: www.rockvalleycollege.edu
Established: 1964 Annual Undergrad Tuition & Fees (In-District): $9,314
Enrollment: 5,762 Coed
Affiliation or Control: Local IRS Status: 501(c)3
Highest Offering: Associate Degree
Accreditation: HLC, ADNUR, COARC, DH, SURGT

01 President ....Dr. Howard J. SPEARMAN
11 VP Operations ....Vacant
05 VP Academic Affairs & CAO ....Mr. Ronald GEARY
22 VP Equity & Inclusion ....Mr. Keith R. BARNES
15 VP Human Resources ....Mr. Jim HANDLEY
32 VP Student Affairs ....Dr. Patrick PEYER
81 AVP Science/Tech/Engr/Math ....Ms. Gina CARONNA
103 VP Workforce Development ....Mr. Christopher LEWIS
20 Exec Dir Outcomes Assessment ....Dr. Lisa MEHLIG
16 Executive Director Human Resources ....Mr. Joe SIMPSON
09 VP Inst Effectiveness/Communication ....Ms. Heather SNIDER
30 Chief Development Officer ....Ms. Brittany FREIBERG
18 Exec Dir Facilities Planning & POM ....Ms. Janet TAYLOR
26 Exec Dir Col Comm/Marketing ....Vacant
88 Director Theatre & Arts Park ....Mr. Christopher D. BRADY
19 Chief of Police ....Mr. Rick JENKS
06 Registrar/Director Financial Aid ....Ms. Stacey KOLDER
04 Assistant to the President ....Ms. Ann KERWITZ
04 Assistant to the President ....Ms. Kris FUCHS
41 Athletic Director ....Mr. Darin MONROE
10 VP Finance ....Vacant
106 Exec Dir Online Dev/Innovation ....Ms. Kym BLANCHARD
13 Exec Dir Information Technology ... Ms. Danielle BAUMGARTNER
49 AVP Liberal Arts/Adult Education ....Dr. Amanda SMITH

Rockford Career College (C)

1130 S. Alpine Road, Suite 100, Rockford IL 61108
County: Winnebago FICE Identification: 008545
Unit ID: 148399
Telephone: (815) 965-8616 Carnegie Class: Assoc/HVT-Mix Trad/Non
FAX Number: (815) 965-0360 Calendar System: Quarter
URL: www.rockfordcareercollege.edu
Established: 1862 Annual Undergrad Tuition & Fees: N/A
Enrollment: N/A Coed
Affiliation or Control: Proprietary IRS Status: Proprietary
Highest Offering: Associate Degree
Accreditation: ACCSC, MAAB, MLTAB, SURTEC

00 President/CEO ....Mr. Stephen TAVE
01 Campus President ....Mr. Mike O'HERRON
05 Academic Dean ....Ms. Rochelle REGENAUER
32 Dean of Students/Student Services ....Ms. Danielle HARRIOTT
06 Registrar/Director of Compliance ....Ms. Erin EGGEBRECHT
07 Director of Admissions ....Ms. Doreen STEWART
36 Director Career Services ....Ms. Phyllis LEE
37 Director of Financial Aid ....Ms. Denise ACKLEY
08 Library/Bookstore Coordinator ....Vacant

Rockford University (D)

5050 E State Street, Rockford IL 61108-2393
County: Winnebago FICE Identification: 001748
Unit ID: 148405
Telephone: (815) 226-4000 Carnegie Class: Masters/S
FAX Number: (815) 226-4119 Calendar System: Semester
URL: www.rockford.edu
Established: 1847 Annual Undergrad Tuition & Fees: $33,050
Enrollment: 1,272 Coed
Affiliation or Control: Independent Non-Profit IRS Status: 501(c)3
Highest Offering: Master's
Accreditation: HLC, IACBE, NUR

01 President ....Dr. Eric W. FULCOMER
05 VP of Academic Affairs/Provost ....Dr. Michael PERRY
111 VP for Institutional Advancement ....Mr. Stephen KULL
10 VP for Finance/CFO ....Ms. Lisa CUSTARDO
21 Business Office Accounting Manager ......Mr. John DIRAIMONDO
84 VP Enrollment Management ....Dr. Michael QUINN
32 VP for Student Affairs ....Dr. Randy WORDEN
37 Assistant VP for SAS ....Mr. Todd FISCHER-FREE
11 Director of Operations ....Mr. Ed TOMASZKIEWICZ
13 Director of Information Technology ....Mr. Ryan CUSHING
123 Director of Adult & Grad Admissions ....Ms. Anissa KUHAR
06 Registrar ....Ms. Anna J. JATTKOWSKI-HUDSON
04 Exec Assistant to the President ....Ms. Tara VANDEN BRANDEN
41 Director of Athletics ....Mr. Jason MULLIGAN
15 Director of Human Resources ....Ms. Monique DIVENTI
36 Director Career Services ....Ms. Logan GLENDENNING
26 Director of Communications ....Ms. Bridget JENNISON
09 Coordinator of IR ....Dr. Stephen KIM
85 Director of Global Affairs ....Ms. Maria DIEMER
23 Director Health Services ....Ms. Kristen CLARKE
18 Facilities Director ....Mr. Danny VOLBRECHT
08 Head Librarian ....Ms. Kelly JAMES
19 Director Security/Safety ....Mr. Tim TREVIER
29 Director Alumni Affairs ....Ms. Nicole RILEY
39 Dir Resident Life/Student Housing ....Mr. Scott MITCHELL

Roosevelt University (E)

430 S Michigan Avenue, Chicago IL 60605-1394
County: Cook FICE Identification: 001749
Unit ID: 148487
Telephone: (312) 341-3500 Carnegie Class: DU-Mod
FAX Number: (312) 341-3655 Calendar System: Semester
URL: www.roosevelt.edu
Established: 1945 Annual Undergrad Tuition & Fees: $31,493
Enrollment: 4,680 Coed
Affiliation or Control: Independent Non-Profit IRS Status: 501(c)3
Highest Offering: Doctorate
Accreditation: HLC, ACBSP, CACREP, CLPSY, MUS, NURSE, PHAR

01 President ....Dr. Ali MALEKZADEH
05 Exec Vice President/Univ Provost ....Dr. Lois BECKER
10 Vice Pres of Finance/Admin & CFO ....Mr. Andrew HARRIS
84 Vice Pres Enrollment Mgmt ....Mr. Michael CASSIDY
100 Vice Pres/Chief of Staff/Sec of BOT ....Dr. Michael FORD
111 VP University Advancement ....Ms. Nicole BARRON
32 VP Student Affairs/Dean Students ....Mr. Jamar ORR
13 Chief Information Officer/VP Tech ....Mr. Neeraj KUMAR
15 Vice Pres Human Resources ....Ms. Toyia K. STEWART
09 Assoc VP Inst Research ....Mr. Joseph P. REGAN
105 Assist Vice Pres Web Development ....Mr. Aaron RESTER
43 Interim Assistant Legal Counseling ....Ms. Latoya LAING
21 Associate AVP Finance/Controller ....Mr. Patrick ALFORQUE
19 Shift Director of Campus Safety ....Mr. Paul HUERTA
85 Asst Dir of International Programs ....Ms. Dawn HOUGLAND
46 Assoc Provost Research ....Dr. Mike MALY
121 Assoc Provost Student Success ....Ms. Katrina COAKLEY
49 Int Dean College Arts & Sciences ....Dr. Cami MCBRIDE
50 Dean College of Business ....Dr. Ryan PETTY
57 Dean College of Performing Arts ....Dr. Rudy MARCOZZI
53 Dean College of Education ....Dr. Thomas PHILION
67 Dean College of Pharmacy ....Dr. Melissa HOGAN
88 Int CEO Auditorium Theatre ....Mr. Rich REGAN
37 Director Financial Aid ....Ms. Michelle STIPP
39 Asst Dean Student Life & Housing .....Ms. Hilda ROJAS-DUARTE
41 Director of Athletics ....Mr. John JARAMILLO
08 Director of Libraries ....Mr. Estavan MONTANO
36 Director Career & Prof Development .....Ms. Jennifer WONDERLY
04 Exec Asst to President ....Ms. Kathy BLISS
07 Executive Director of Admissions ....Mr. Kyree WHITEHEAD
96 Mgr Purchasing & Business Affairs ....Ms. Veleicia DIVINITY

Rosalind Franklin University of Medicine & Science (F)

3333 Green Bay Road, North Chicago IL 60064-3095
County: Lake FICE Identification: 001659
Unit ID: 145558
Telephone: (847) 578-3000 Carnegie Class: Spec-4-yr-Med
FAX Number: (847) 578-3401 Calendar System: Quarter
URL: www.rosalindfranklin.edu
Established: 1912 Annual Undergrad Tuition & Fees: N/A
Enrollment: 2,099 Coed
Affiliation or Control: Independent Non-Profit IRS Status: 501(c)3
Highest Offering: Doctorate; No Lower Division
Accreditation: HLC, ANEST, ARCPA, CLPSY, MED, PA, PHAR, POD, PTA

01 President/CEO ....Dr. Wendy RHEAULT
05 Provost ....Dr. Nancy PARSLEY
67 Dean College of Pharmacy ....Dr. Marc ABEL
107 Dean College Health Professions ....Dr. John VITALE
58 Dean Sch Grad PostDoc Stds ....Dr. Joseph X. DIMARIO
63 Dean Scholl Col Podiatric Med ....Dr. Stephanie WU
63 Dean Chicago Medical Sch/VP Med Aff ....Dr. Archana CHATTERJEE
46 Exec VP Research ....Dr. Ronald S. KAPLAN
26 Senior VP University Enhancement ....Ms. Lee CONCHA
32 VP Student Success and Inclusion ....Ms. Rebecca DURKIN
88 VP Partnerships ....Dr. Sandra LARSON
20 VP Academic and Faculty Affairs ....Dr. Moreen CARVAN
111 VP Institutional Advancement ....Mr. Chad RUBACK
10 Exec VP Finance & Admin ....Mr. Gavin FARRY
100 Chief of Staff ....Ms. Lee CONCHA
20 AVP Academic and Faculty Affairs ....Dr. Robert INTINE
13 AVP Technology & Learning Resources ....Mr. Richard LOESCH
114 AVP Financial Plng & Analysis ....Ms. Christie TIPTON
35 AVP Student Affairs ....Ms. Shelly BRZYCKI
07 AVP Admissions/Recruitment ....Dr. Bryan MOODY
06 AVP Student Records/Registrar ....Mr. Jason CELIZ
37 AVP Student Financial Services ....Ms. Maryann DECAIRE
15 AVP Human Resources ....Ms. Sally J. MADDEN
21 Controller ....Ms. Emily NYBLAD
30 Exec Dir of Development ....Mr. George RATTIN
30 Exec Dir of Development ....Ms. Pamela LOWE
29 Exec Dir Alumni Relations ....Ms. Martha KELLY BATES
102 Dir Foundation & Grant Relations ....Ms. Shella BLUE
44 Dir Annual Giving ....Vacant
09 Director of Institutional Research ....Mr. Omer MINHAS
28 Exec Dir Diversity & Inclusion ....Dr. Heather M. KIND-KEPPEL
96 Dir Materials Management ....Mr. Vince BUTERA
19 Dir Campus Security ....Mr. Gordon BLANCHARD
121 Dir Academic Support ....Ms. Nydia STEWART
18 Dir Facilities Management ....Mr. Robert D. JACKSON
25 Dir Sponsored Research ....Ms. Dora ESPINOSA
08 Library Director ....Ms. Charlotte BEYER
16 Dir of Human Resources ....Ms. Mary TELL
118 Benefits Administrator ....Ms. Melissa HALEY
39 Coordinator for Residence Life ....Ms. Amber WOYAK
04 Executive Administrative Assistant ....Ms. Jean MINA
86 Director Government Relations ....Mr. Joseph PIASECKI

Rush University (G)

600 S Paulina, Chicago IL 60612-3832
County: Cook FICE Identification: 009800
Unit ID: 148511
Telephone: (312) 942-7100 Carnegie Class: Spec-4-yr-Med
FAX Number: (312) 942-2219 Calendar System: Semester
URL: www.rushu.rush.edu
Established: 1971 Annual Undergrad Tuition & Fees: N/A
Enrollment: 2,816 Coed
Affiliation or Control: Independent Non-Profit IRS Status: 501(c)3
Highest Offering: Doctorate
Accreditation: HLC, ANEST, ARCPA, AUD, BBT, CAMPEP, COARC, DIETI, DMS, HSA, IPSY, MED, MT, NURSE, OT, PAST, PERF, SP

01 President Rush University ....Dr. Sherine E. GABRIEL
05 Provost/SVP Univ System for Health ....Dr. Susan L. FREEMAN
26 VP Corp/External Affairs ....Vacant
10 Sr VP/CFO/Treasurer ....Ms. Patricia S. O'NEIL
30 Senior Vice President Philanthropy ......Ms. Diane M. MCKEEVER
43 SVP Legal Affairs/Gen Counsel ....Mr. Carl BERGETZ
15 Chief Human Resources Ofcr/Sr VP ....Mr. Marcos B. DELEON
25 VP/Chief Compliance Office ....Dr. Cynthia E. BOYD
21 Chief Finance Business Officer ....Mr. Vince GATTUSO
28 Sr Dir Stdnt Diversity/Cmty Engage ....Dr. Sharon GATES
20 Vice Provost Academic Affairs ....Dr. David KATZ
20 Vice Provost Faculty Affairs ....Dr. Susanna CHUBINSKAYA
32 Vice Provost Student Affairs ....Ms. Gayle B. WARD
76 Dean Col of Health Sciences ....Dr. Charlotte ROYEEN
58 Dean Graduate College ....Dr. Andrew J. BEAN
66 Dean College of Nursing ....Dr. Chrisitne KENNEDY
63 Dean Rush Medical College ....Dr. Badrinath R. KONETY
88 Sr Assoc Dean Medical College ....Dr. Elizabeth A. BAKER
27 Assoc VP Marketing & Comm ....Mr. Ryan NAGDEMAN
08 Director Library ....Mr. Scott THOMPSON
35 Director Student Affairs ....Ms. Kapula PATALINGHUG
37 Dir Student Financial Aid ....Ms. Jill GABLE
38 Interim VP of Wellness ....Ms. Evelyn POCZATEK
29 Director Alumni Relations ....Ms. Krista GIUFFI
18 Director University Facilities ....Mr. Chris KANAKIS
21 Manager of Financial Affairs ....Mr. Patrick MCNULTY
102 Dir Foundation/Corporate Relations ....Ms. Sophia WOROBEC
19 Director Security Services ....Mr. Peter C. ARDNT
46 Interim Vice Provost Research ....Dr. Andrew J. BEAN
04 Exec Asst to the President ....Ms. Sheila M. GREENE
06 Registrar/Sr Dir Enroll Mgmt ....Ms. Brenda L. WEDDINGTON

SAE Institute Chicago (H)

820 N. Orleans St., Ste 125, Chicago IL 60610
Telephone: (312) 300-5685 Identification: 770970
Accreditation: ACCSC

† Branch campus of SAE Institute Nashville, Nashville, TN

Saint Anthony College of Nursing (I)

3301 N. Mulford Rd, Rockford IL 61114
County: Winnebago FICE Identification: 009987
Unit ID: 149028
Telephone: (815) 282-7900 Carnegie Class: Spec-4-yr-Other Health
FAX Number: (815) 282-7901 Calendar System: Semester
URL: https://www.osfhealthcare.org/sacn/
Established: 1915 Annual Undergrad Tuition & Fees: $27,460
Enrollment: 291 Coed
Affiliation or Control: Roman Catholic IRS Status: 501(c)3
Highest Offering: Doctorate
Accreditation: HLC, NURSE

01 President ....Dr. Sandie S. SOLDWISCH
66 Dean Undergraduate Affairs ....Dr. Elizabeth M. CARSON
58 Dean Graduate Affairs & Research ....Dr. Shannon K. LIZER

32 Associate Dean Support Services ... Ms. Nancy A. SANDERS
08 Library Supervisor ... Ms. Heather A. KLEPITSCH
37 Financial Aid Coordinator ... Ms. Serrita WOODS
04 Administrative Asst to President ... Ms. Teresa M. DAUGHERTY
09 Inst Effectiveness/Assessment Spec ... Ms. Elizabeth R. HARP
90 Educational Technology Coordinator ... Ms. Susan K. STAAB

St. Augustine College (A)

1333-45 W Argyle Street, Chicago IL 60640-3501
County: Cook | FICE Identification: 021854
Unit ID: 148876
Telephone: (773) 878-8756 | Carnegie Class: Bac/Assoc-Mixed
FAX Number: (773) 878-0937 | Calendar System: Semester
URL: www.staugustine.edu
Established: 1980 | Annual Undergrad Tuition & Fees: $12,120
Enrollment: 901 | Coed
Affiliation or Control: Independent Non-Profit | IRS Status: 501(c)3
Highest Offering: Baccalaureate
Accreditation: HLC, COARC, SW

01 President ... Dr. Reyes GONZALEZ
05 Acting Provost ... Dr. Carmen ARELLANO
20 Dean Academic Affairs ... Dr. Carmen ARRELLANO
10 COO/CFO ... Mr. Daniel ROMAN
26 VP Marketing & Enrollment Mgmt ... Mr. Cesar MENDOZA
103 VP Institute Workforce Development ... Mr. Norman RUANO
121 Dean of Student Success ... Dr. Juan OJEDA
108 Assoc Dean Academic Effectiveness ... Dr. Ana GIL GARCIA
13 Director of IT ... Ms. Elba GONZALEZ
37 Director of Financial Aid ... Ms. Maria ZAMBONINO
15 Director Human Resources ... Ms. Nancy BOURQUE
07 Director of Admission ... Mr. Dave MARCIAL
08 Dir of Information Commons/Library ... Ms. Kathryn WEBB
06 Registrar ... Ms. Margarita VACA
09 Director of Institutional Research ... Mr. Robert MYERS

Saint Francis Medical Center College of Nursing (B)

511 NE Greenleaf Street, Peoria IL 61603-3783
County: Peoria | FICE Identification: 006240
Unit ID: 148575
Telephone: (309) 655-2201 | Carnegie Class: Spec-4-yr-Other Health
FAX Number: (309) 624-8973 | Calendar System: Semester
URL: https://www.osfhealthcare.org/sfmccon/
Established: 1985 | Annual Undergrad Tuition & Fees: N/A
Enrollment: 466 | Coed
Affiliation or Control: Roman Catholic | IRS Status: 501(c)3
Highest Offering: Doctorate
Accreditation: HLC, NURSE

01 President of the College ... Dr. Sandie S. SOLDWISCH
05 Interim Provost ... Dr. Shannon LIZER
58 Dean Graduate Program ... Dr. Kimberly A. MITCHELL
20 Dean Undergraduate Program ... Dr. Sue C. BROWN
32 Asst Dean of Support Services ... Mr. Kevin N. STEPHENS
07 Director of Admissions/Registrar ... Mr. Austin BLAIR
08 Librarian ... Mr. William KOMANECKI
38 College Counselor ... Mrs. Victoria KAMHI
37 Coord Student Fin/Financial Assist ... Mrs. Nancy S. PERRYMAN
113 Coord Student Finance/Accts Rec ... Ms. Alice C. EVANS
04 Executive Assistant ... Ms. Luann MORELOCK
108 Inst Effectiveness/Assessment Spec ... Mr. Ryan A. WILLIAMS

St. John's College (C)

729 E. Carpenter Street, Springfield IL 62702-5317
County: Sangamon | FICE Identification: 030980
Unit ID: 148593
Telephone: (217) 525-5628 | Carnegie Class: Spec-4-yr-Other Health
FAX Number: (217) 757-6870 | Calendar System: Semester
URL: www.sjcs.edu
Established: 1991 | Annual Undergrad Tuition & Fees: N/A
Enrollment: 118 | Coed
Affiliation or Control: Independent Non-Profit | IRS Status: 501(c)3
Highest Offering: Doctorate
Accreditation: HLC, NUR

01 Chancellor ... Dr. Charlene S. AARON
05 Dean of Academic Affairs ... Dr. Judy SHACKELFORD
07 Admissions Officer/Registrar ... Ms. Britni CARUSO
37 Financial Aid/Compliance Officer ... Mr. Timothy MARTEN

Saint Xavier University (D)

3700 W 103rd Street, Chicago IL 60655-3105
County: Cook | FICE Identification: 001768
Unit ID: 148627
Telephone: (773) 298-3000 | Carnegie Class: Masters/L
FAX Number: (773) 779-9061 | Calendar System: Semester
URL: www.sxu.edu
Established: 1846 | Annual Undergrad Tuition & Fees: $34,730
Enrollment: 3,764 | Coed
Affiliation or Control: Roman Catholic | IRS Status: 501(c)3
Highest Offering: Master's
Accreditation: HLC, CAEPN, MUS, NURSE, SP

01 President ... Dr. Laurie M. JOYNER
05 Int Provost ... Ms. Angela DURANTE
10 Vice Pres Finance/Admin & CFO ... Mr. Daniel P. KLOTZBACH
32 VP Student/Enrollment Services ... Ms. Maureen WOGAN
09 Exec Dir Institutional Research ... Dr. Kathleen CARLSON
26 AVP Marketing/Communications ... Ms. Deb RAPACZ
111 AVP University Advancement ... Ms. Erin R. MUELLER
18 Director of Facilities Management ... Mr. Peter SKACH
20 Int Associate Provost ... Mr. Michael MARSDEN
13 Chief Information Officer ... Ms. Molly GAIK
109 Director Auxiliary Services ... Ms. Linda MORENO
37 Exec Director Financial Aid ... Ms. Susan SWISHER
21 Controller ... Ms. Diane STALLMANN
24 Director CIDAT ... Ms. Yue MA
08 Director Library ... Mr. David STERN
06 Director Records/Registration Svcs ... Ms. Elena CARRILLO
19 Dir Public Safety/Chief of Police ... Mr. Melvin CORNELIUS
85 Dir Center International Education ... Ms. Kelly REIDY-FOX
49 Int Dean Arts & Sciences ... Dr. Bindhu ALAPPAT
53 Dean School of Education ... Vacant
50 Dean Graham School of Management ... Dr. Mark ROSENBAUM
66 Dean School of Nursing ... Dr. Peg GALLAGHER
100 Chief of Staff ... Ms. Maggie EAHEART
15 Director of Human Resources ... Mr. Gerry HORAN
29 Dir Alumni Relations/Advancement ... Ms. Jeanmarie GAINER
84 AVP Enrollment Management ... Mr. Brian HOTZFIELD

Sauk Valley Community College (E)

173 Illinois Route 2, Dixon IL 61021-9188
County: Lee | FICE Identification: 001752
Unit ID: 148672
Telephone: (815) 288-5511 | Carnegie Class: Assoc/HVT-High Non
FAX Number: (815) 288-1880 | Calendar System: Semester
URL: www.svcc.edu
Established: 1965 | Annual Undergrad Tuition & Fees (In-District): $11,588
Enrollment: 1,386 | Coed
Affiliation or Control: State/Local | IRS Status: 501(c)3
Highest Offering: Associate Degree
Accreditation: HLC, ADNUR, PNUR, RAD

01 President ... Dr. David M. HELLMICH
05 Vice Pres Academics/Student Svcs ... Mr. Jon D. MANDRELL
76 Dean of Health Professions ... Ms. Christine L. VINCENT
10 VP of Business Services ... Mr. Kent A. SORENSON
18 Director Facilities ... Mr. David L. BOEHME
15 Director of Human Resources ... Ms. Kathryn C. SNOW
84 Director Enrollment Mgmt/Registrar ... Ms. Pamela S. MEDEMA
111 Dean of Institutional Advancement ... Ms. Lori A. CORTEZ
13 Dir Information Services/Security ... Mr. Eric L. EPPS
41 Director of Athletics ... Mr. Michael P. STEVENSON
37 Director of Financial Assistance ... Ms. Jennifer A. SCHULTZ
91 Learning Technology Supp Specialist ... Ms. Kathleen M. DIRKS

School of the Art Institute of Chicago (F)

37 S Wabash, Chicago IL 60603-3103
County: Cook | FICE Identification: 001753
Unit ID: 143048
Telephone: (312) 899-5100 | Carnegie Class: Spec-4-yr-Arts
FAX Number: (312) 263-0141 | Calendar System: Semester
URL: www.saic.edu
Established: 1866 | Annual Undergrad Tuition & Fees: $53,160
Enrollment: 3,132 | Coed
Affiliation or Control: Independent Non-Profit | IRS Status: 501(c)3
Highest Offering: Master's
Accreditation: HLC

01 President ... Dr. Elissa TENNY
43 Exec Vice Pres/General Counsel ... Ms. Leslie DARLING
05 Provost & SVP of Academic Affairs ... Mr. Martin BERGER
84 Vice Pres Enrollment Management ... Ms. Rose MILKOWSKI
111 VP for Institutional Advancement ... Ms. Stephanie OBERHAUSEN
10 Vice President Finance ... Mr. Brian ESKER
15 Vice President for Human Resources ... Mr. Michael NICOLAI
32 Vice Pres/Dean of Student Affairs ... Dr. Felice DUBLON
20 Vice Provost/Dean Cmty Engagement ... Mr. Paul COFFEY
18 Vice Pres Campus Operations ... Mr. Thomas BUECHELE
20 Int Dean of Faculty/VP Acad Affs ... Ms. Shawn Michelle SMITH
35 Dean of Student Life ... Ms. Deborah MARTIN
21 Exec Dir Academic Accounting ... Vacant
26 Exec Dir Enroll Mktg & Operations ... Ms. Maryann SCHAEFER
29 Exec Director Alumni Relations ... Ms. Ashley SPELL
38 Exec Director Wellness Center ... Dr. Joseph BEHEN
88 Exec Director Enrollment Services ... Ms. Jane BRUMITT
06 Director Registration & Records ... Ms. Christy MICELI
08 Exec Director of School Library ... Ms. Claire EIKE
24 Exec Dir Media/Instruct Resources ... Mr. Craig DOWNS
36 Dean Career & Prof Experience ... Ms. Rosalie SHEMMER
07 Assoc Dir of Undergrad Admissions ... Vacant
123 Director of Graduate Admissions ... Ms. Nicole HALL
37 Director of Student Financial Svcs ... Mr. Patrick JAMES
28 Director of Multicultural Affairs ... Ms. Rashayla BROWN
88 Director of Learning Center ... Ms. Valerie ST. GERMAIN
49 Dean of Undergraduate Studies ... Ms. Tiffany HOLMES
58 Dean of Graduate Studies ... Mr. Arnold KEMP
28 Dir of Acad Affairs/Diversity/Incl ... Dr. Christina GOMEZ

Shawnee Community College (G)

8364 Shawnee College Road, Ullin IL 62992-2206
County: Pulaski | FICE Identification: 007693
Unit ID: 148821
Telephone: (618) 634-3200 | Carnegie Class: Assoc/MT-VT-High Non
FAX Number: (618) 634-3300 | Calendar System: Semester
URL: www.shawneecc.edu
Established: 1967 | Annual Undergrad Tuition & Fees (In-District): $6,090
Enrollment: 1,176 | Coed
Affiliation or Control: Local | IRS Status: 501(c)3
Highest Offering: Associate Degree
Accreditation: HLC, MLTAD, OTA, SURGT

01 President ... Dr. Tim TAYLOR
05 Vice President Academic Affairs ... Dr. Kathleen CURPHY
32 Vice President Student Services ... Dr. Lisa PRICE
21 Int VP Financial/Business Services ... Ms. Brandy WOODS
04 Administrative Asst to President ... Ms. Beth CROWE
20 Dean Academic Affairs ... Dr. Kristin SHELBY
51 Dean Adult Educ/Alternative Instruc ... Dr. Gregory MASON
10 Vice President Financial Services ... Ms. Brandy WOODS
38 Student Support Services Director ... Ms. Amber SUGGS
35 Dean of Student Services ... Vacant
37 Dir Fin Aid/Coord Vet & Mil Personl ... Dr. Tammy CAPPS
41 Athletic Director ... Mr. John SPARKS
13 Director of Information Technology ... Mr. Chris CLARK
12 Director Metropolis Ext Center ... Ms. Jipaum ASKEW-ROBINSON
66 Director of Nursing ... Ms. Connie DRURY
08 Head Librarian ... Ms. Tracey JOHNSON
06 Registrar ... Ms. Danielle BOYD
18 Facilities Director ... Mr. Don KOCH
09 Director of Institutional Research ... Vacant
40 Bookstore Manager ... Ms. Stacy SIMPSON
22 Accessibility & Resource Coord ... Ms. Mindy ASHBY
103 Director Economic Development ... Vacant
26 Director of Public Relations ... Mr. Rob BETTS
36 Career Services Coordinator ... Ms. Leslie WELDON
50 Div Chair Business/Occup/Tech Dp ... Ms. Ruth SMITH
81 Division Chair Math/Science ... Ms. Lori ARMSTRONG
79 Div Chr Social Stds/Humanities/Comm ... Ms. Joella BASLER
76 Div Chair Allied Health ... Ms. Tracy LOHSTROH
15 Human Resources Director ... Ms. Emily FORTHMAN
24 Director of Learning Resources ... Mr. Russ STOUP
56 Director Anna Extension Center ... Ms. Lindsay JOHNSON
88 Education Talent Search Director ... Ms. Deborah JOHNSON

South Suburban College (H)

15800 S State Street, South Holland IL 60473-1270
County: Cook | FICE Identification: 001769
Unit ID: 149365
Telephone: (708) 596-2000 | Carnegie Class: Assoc/MT-VT-High Non
FAX Number: (708) 210-5710 | Calendar System: Semester
URL: www.ssc.edu
Established: 1927 | Annual Undergrad Tuition & Fees (In-District): $11,033
Enrollment: 3,366 | Coed
Affiliation or Control: State/Local | IRS Status: 501(c)3
Highest Offering: Associate Degree
Accreditation: HLC, CVT, OTA

01 President ... Dr. Lynette D. STOKES
05 Vice President Academic Services ... Dr. Tasha WILLIAMS
11 Vice Pres Administration ... Mr. Martin LAREAU
32 VP Student/Enrollment Services ... Dr. Deborah BANESS KING
35 Dean Student Services ... Ms. Devon POWELL
09 AVP Accreditation/Inst Effective ... Dr. Ronald KAWANNA, JR.
49 Dean Liberal Arts/Sciences ... Dr. Anna HELWIG
76 Dean Allied Health/Career Programs ... Dr. Omar SHERIFF
66 Dean Nursing ... Dr. Linda BROWN-ALDRIDGE
56 Dean Adult/Continuing Education ... Dr. Matthew BEASLAND
51 Director Continuing Education ... Ms. Shirley DREWENSKI
10 Treasurer/Controller ... Mr. Tim POLLERT
26 Exec Dir Public Rels/Resource Dev ... Mr. Patrick RUSH
13 Exec Dir Information Technology ... Mr. John MCCORMACK
89 Director Recruitment/Retention Svcs ... Ms. Tiffane JONES
37 Director of Financial Aid ... Ms. Kendra PERDUE-SMITH
18 Director Physical Plant Services ... Mr. Justin PAPP
27 Dir Communication Svcs/Media Design ... Mrs. Lisa MILLER
41 Athletic Director ... Mr. Steve RUZICH
09 Director of Institutional Research ... Dr. Kevin RIORDAN
15 Director Human Resources ... Ms. Kimberly PIGATTI
06 Director Registration/Records ... Ms. Tenial WHITTED
07 Director of Recruitment ... Ms. Tiffane JONES

Southeastern Illinois College (I)

3575 College Road, Harrisburg IL 62946-4925
County: Saline | FICE Identification: 001757
Unit ID: 148937
Telephone: (618) 252-5400 | Carnegie Class: Assoc/HVT-High Non
FAX Number: (618) 252-3156 | Calendar System: Semester
URL: www.sic.edu
Established: 1960 | Annual Undergrad Tuition & Fees (In-District): $6,060
Enrollment: 1,263 | Coed
Affiliation or Control: State/Local | IRS Status: 501(c)3
Highest Offering: Associate Degree
Accreditation: HLC

01 President ... Dr. Jonah RICE
05 Vice President Instruction ... Dr. Karen WEISS
10 Exec Dean Administration/Bus Affs ... Ms. Lisa HITE
20 Exec Dean of Academic Services ... Dr. Tyler BILLMAN
32 Exec Dean Student Services ... Dr. Chad FLANNERY
103 Assoc Dean Workforce & Cmty Educ ... Mrs. Lori COX
08 Assoc Dean of Learning Commons ... Ms. Karla LEWIS
84 Director Enrollment Services ... Ms. Kyla BURFORD
26 Exec Dir Marketing/Public Relations ... Ms. Angela WILSON
37 Financial Aid Director ... Ms. Michelle METTEN
13 Chief Information Officer ... Mr. Greg MCCULLOCH
76 Director Allied Health & Nursing ... Ms. Amy MURPHY

04 Exec Asst to President .... Mrs. Lisa DYE
18 Director of Environmental Services .... Mr. Ed FITZGERALD
15 Director of Human Resources .... Mrs. Sky FOWLER
09 Exec Dir of Institutional Research .... Mr. Chris BARR
28 Dir Bus Svcs/Coord of Diversity .... Ms. Erica GRIFFIN
41 Athletic Director .... Mr. Jeremy IRLBECK

*Southern Illinois University System (A)

Stone Center - 1400 Douglas Drive, Carbondale IL 62901
County: Jackson FICE Identification: 008237
Unit ID: 149240
Telephone: (618) 536-3331 Carnegie Class: N/A
FAX Number: (618) 536-3404
URL: www.siusystem.edu

01 President .... Dr. Daniel F. MAHONY
05 VP Academic Innov/Planning/Partshp .... Dr. Gireesh GUPCHUP
10 SVP Fin/Admin Affs/Bd Treasurer .... Dr. Duane STUCKY
86 Exec Dir Governmental/Public Affs .... Mr. John CHARLES
116 Exec Dir of Internal Audits .... Ms. Kim LABONTE
43 General Counsel .... Mr. Lucas CRATER
04 Assistant to the President .... Ms. Paula S. KEITH

*Southern Illinois University Carbondale (B)

1265 Lincoln Drive, Carbondale IL 62901-6899
County: Jackson FICE Identification: 001758
Unit ID: 149222
Telephone: (618) 453-2121 Carnegie Class: DU-Higher
FAX Number: (618) 453-3250 Calendar System: Semester
URL: siu.edu
Established: 1869 Annual Undergrad Tuition & Fees (In-State): $15,104
Enrollment: 11,366 Coed
Affiliation or Control: State IRS Status: 501(c)3
Highest Offering: Doctorate
Accreditation: HLC, AAB, ABAI, ARCPA, ART, CAEP, CEA, CIDA, CLPSY, #COARC, COPSY, DH, DIETD, DIETI, DMS, FUSER, IFSAC, IPSY, LAW, MED, MUS, NAIT, PH, PTAA, RAD, RADDOS, RADMAG, RTT, SP, SPAA, SW, THEA

02 Chancellor .... Dr. Austin A. LANE
05 Provost/Vice Chanc Acad Affs .... Dr. Meera KOMARRAJU
32 Dean of Students .... Ms. Jennifer L. JONES-HALL
30 Assoc VC Development/Alumni Rels .... Mr. Jeffrey GLEIM
46 Interim VC for Research .... Dr. Gary KINSEL
10 Int Vice Chanc Admin & Finance .... Ms. Julie MCREYNOLDS
28 VC for Diversity/Equity/Inclusion .... Dr. Paul FRAZIER
102 CFO SIU Foundation .... Ms. Cynthia CIGANOVICH
13 Interim Chief Info Officer .... Mr. Scott D. BRIDGES
84 Assoc Chancellor for Enrollment Mgt .... Mr. Wendell WILLIAMS
20 Assoc Provost for Academic Programs .... Dr. Lizette CHEVALIER
100 Chief of Staff .... Mr. Matthew BAUGHMAN
49 Interim Dean Liberal Arts .... Dr. Andrew BALKANSKY
50 Dean College of Business .... Dr. Terry CLARK
53 Dean School of Education .... Mr. M. Cecil SMITH
54 Dean Engineering .... Dr. Xiaoqing LIU
58 Assoc Dean/Dir of Grad School .... Dr. Stephen C. SHIH
61 Dean School of Law .... Ms. Camille DAVIDSON
63 Dean School of Medicine/Provost .... Dr. Jerry E. KRUSE
47 Dean Col Agricultural/Life/Phys Sci .... Mr. Eric BREVIK
76 Dean Health & Human Sciences .... Dr. Robert MORGAN
60 Interim Dean Arts and Media .... Mr. Olusegun OJEWUYI
08 Dean Library Affairs .... Mr. John H. POLLITZ
37 Interim Dir Student Financial Aid .... Ms. Dee ROTOLO
09 Director Institutional Research .... Mr. Scott BRIDGES
26 Chief Marketing & Comm Officer .... Ms. Kim RENDFELD
15 Int Dir Human Resources/Payroll .... Ms. Renee COLOMBO
39 Director University Housing .... Mr. Jon L. SHAFFER
85 Director International Education .... Dr. Andrew CARVER
18 Int Dir Facilities and Energy Mgmt .... Ms. Loann SIMMONS
19 Director of Public Safety .... Mr. Benjamin NEWMAN
23 Director Student Health Services .... Dr. Jamie CLARK
41 Intercollegiate Athletic Director .... Ms. Elizabeth JARNIGAN
106 Int Exec Director Extended Campus .... Dr. Julie DUNSTON
06 Director Registrar's Office .... Ms. Tamora WORKMAN
38 Dir Student Counseling Center .... Dr. Jaime CLARK
96 Director Procurement Services .... Ms. Debbie ABELL

*Southern Illinois University Edwardsville (C)

State Route 157, Edwardsville IL 62026
County: Madison FICE Identification: 001759
Unit ID: 149231
Telephone: (618) 650-2000 Carnegie Class: DU-Mod
FAX Number: (618) 650-2270 Calendar System: Semester
URL: www.siue.edu
Established: 1957 Annual Undergrad Tuition & Fees (In-State): $12,219
Enrollment: 12,860 Coed
Affiliation or Control: State IRS Status: 501(c)3
Highest Offering: Doctorate
Accreditation: HLC, ACATE, ANEST, ART, CAEPN, CAHIIM, CONST, DENT, @DIETC, EXSC, JOUR, MUS, NURSE, PH, PHAR, SP, SPAA, SW, THEA

02 Chancellor .... Dr. Randall G. PEMBROOK
05 Provost/VC for Academic Affairs .... Dr. P. Denise COBB
10 Vice Chancellor for Admin .... Dr. Morris TAYLOR
111 VC Univ Adv & CEO SIUE Foundation .... Ms. Rachel C. STACK
32 Vice Chanc for Student Affairs .... Dr. Jeffrey N. WAPLE
100 Chief of Staff .... Ms. Kimberly H. DURR
22 Equal Opp/Access & Title IX .... Ms. Jamie BALL
20 Assoc Prov Rsch/Dean Grad Sch .... Dr. Jerry B. WEINBERG
35 Dean of Students .... Ms. Kara SHUSTRIN
13 Assoc VC for IT & CIO .... Mr. Steven HUFFSTUTLER
28 VC Equity/Diversity & Inclusion .... Dr. Jessica HARRIS
41 Director of Athletics .... Mr. Tim HALL
84 Assoc VC for Enrollment Management .... Dr. Scott BELOBRAJDIC
49 Dean College of Arts & Sciences .... Dr. Kevin LEONARD
50 Dean School of Business .... Dr. Timothy SCHOENECKER
52 Dean School of Dental Medicine .... Dr. Bruce E. ROTTER
53 Dean Sch of Educ/Hlth & Hum Behav .... Dr. Robin HUGHES
54 Dean School of Engineering .... Dr. Cem KARACAL
66 Dean School of Nursing .... Vacant
67 Dean School of Pharmacy .... Dr. Mark S. LUER
08 Dean Library & Info Services .... Dr. Lis PANKL
114 Budget Director .... Mr. William F. WINTER, JR.
26 Exec Dir Univ Marketing & Comm .... Mr. Doug MCILHAGGA
88 Dir Grant Funded Pgm East StL Ctr .... Dr. Tim STAPLES
124 Dir Retention & Student Success .... Vacant
07 Director Undergraduate Admissions .... Mr. Todd C. BURRELL
29 Dir Constituent Rel & Special Proj .... Ms. Cathy N. TAYLOR
36 Director Career Development Center .... Ms. Susan SEIBERT
38 Director Counseling Services .... Vacant
18 Director Facilities Management .... Mr. Craig HOLAN
23 Director Health Service .... Ms. Riane B. GREENWALT
15 Director Human Resources .... Mr. Robert B. THUMITH
09 Dir Institutional Research/Studies .... Mr. Phillip M. BROWN
85 Exec Director International Affairs .... Dr. Mary WEISHAAR
96 Director of Purchasing .... Mr. Matthew BROWN
37 Int Director Student Financial Aid .... Mr. Jeremy BAKER
39 Director University Housing .... Ms. Mallory SIDAROUS
19 Director University Police .... Mr. Kevin SCHMOLL
06 Registrar .... Ms. Laura A. STROM

*Southern Illinois University Carbondale School of Medicine (D)

PO Box 19620, Springfield IL 62794-9620
Telephone: (217) 545-8000 Identification: 770181
Accreditation: &HLC

Southwestern Illinois College (E)

2500 Carlyle Avenue, Belleville IL 62221-5899
County: Saint Clair FICE Identification: 001636
Unit ID: 143215
Telephone: (618) 235-2700 Carnegie Class: Assoc/HVT-High Non
FAX Number: (618) 277-0631 Calendar System: Semester
URL: www.swic.edu
Established: 1946 Annual Undergrad Tuition & Fees (In-District): $6,390
Enrollment: 6,906 Coed
Affiliation or Control: State/Local IRS Status: 501(c)3
Highest Offering: Associate Degree
Accreditation: HLC, ADNUR, CAHIIM, COARC, EMT, MAC, MLTAD, PTAA, RAD

01 President - District .... Mr. Nick J. MANCE
11 Chief Administrative Svcs Officer .... Mr. Bernie J. YSURSA, JR.
05 Chief Academic Officer .... Dr. Gina L. SEGOBIANO
15 Chief HR & Operations Officer .... Ms. Anna MOYER
10 CFO/Board Treasurer .... Ms. Missy ROCHE
32 Int Chief Student Services Officer .... Ms. Danielle CHAMBERS
84 Exec Dir Enrollment Dev/Planning .... Mr. Robert TEBBE
13 Executive Director of IT .... Ms. Linda ANDRES
96 Director of Purchasing .... Mr. Mike R. THOMAS
49 Dean Liberal Arts .... Dr. Mary RUETTGERS
81 Acting Dean Math & Sciences .... Mr. Stan HATFIELD
76 Dean Health Sci/Homeland Security .... Ms. Julie A. MUERTZ
50 Acting Dean Business/Arts & Sci .... Mr. Brad SPARKS
72 Dean Technical Education .... Mr. Brad SPARKS
51 Director Adult/Continued Education .... Ms. Lisa ATKINS
35 Dean Student Services .... Mr. Robert TEBBE
08 Chief Library Officer .... Ms. Jennifer BONE
100 Chief of Staff/Board Secretary .... Ms. Beverly J. FISS
102 Executive Director Foundation .... Ms. Rena THOELE
26 Communications Specialist/Assoc Dir .... Mr. Jim HAVERSTICK
37 Director Student Financial Aid .... Ms. Jessica EVANS
41 Athletic Director .... Mr. Mike JUENGER

Spertus Institute for Jewish Learning and Leadership (F)

610 S Michigan Avenue, Chicago IL 60605-1994
County: Cook FICE Identification: 001663
Unit ID: 148982
Telephone: (312) 322-1700 Carnegie Class: Spec-4-yr-Faith
FAX Number: (312) 922-6406 Calendar System: Quarter
URL: www.spertus.edu
Established: 1924 Annual Graduate Tuition & Fees: N/A
Enrollment: 117 Coed
Affiliation or Control: Independent Non-Profit IRS Status: 501(c)3
Highest Offering: Doctorate; No Undergraduates
Accreditation: HLC

01 President and CEO .... Dr. Dean P. BELL
05 Dean and Chief Academic Officer .... Dr. Keren FRAIMAN
10 Controller .... Mr. Doug PETERSON
37 Financial Aid Manager .... Ms. Judith WOOD
26 Dir Marketing & Communications .... Ms. Betsy GOMBERG
06 Registrar .... Ms. Victoria BLUM
18 Facilities Manager .... Mr. Phil THOMPSON

Spoon River College (G)

23235 N County Road 22, Canton IL 61520-9801
County: Fulton FICE Identification: 001643
Unit ID: 148991
Telephone: (309) 647-4645 Carnegie Class: Assoc/HT-High Non
FAX Number: (309) 649-6235 Calendar System: Semester
URL: www.src.edu
Established: 1959 Annual Undergrad Tuition & Fees (In-District): $10,590
Enrollment: 1,239 Coed
Affiliation or Control: Local IRS Status: 501(c)3
Highest Offering: Associate Degree
Accreditation: HLC, ADNUR

01 President .... Mr. Curt OLDFIELD
05 Dean Instruction .... Ms. Holly NORTON
11 Vice President .... Mr. Brett STOLLER
04 Executive Asst to the President .... Ms. Julie HAMPTON
75 Dean Career & Technical Education .... Mr. Brad O'BRIEN
32 Dean Student Services .... Ms. Missy WILKINSON
66 Director Nursing .... Ms. Tamatha SCHLEICH
06 Dir of Records & Admissions .... Ms. Melissa WILKINSON
18 Director Facilities .... Mr. Bob A. HAILE
55 Dir Adult and Outreach Education .... Mr. Chad MURPHY
08 Librarian .... Ms. Jeannette GLOVER
13 Chief Information Officer .... Mr. Raj SIDDARAJU
41 Director Athletics/Student Life .... Mr. John BASSETT
109 Director Business & Auxil Services .... Ms. Sarah GRAY
37 Director Financial Aid .... Ms. Salinda Jo BRANSON
15 Director Human Resources .... Ms. Andrea THOMSON
14 Director Technology Services .... Mr. Dean CLARY
84 Director Enrollment Services .... Ms. Janet MUNSON
09 Coord Institutional Reporting .... Mr. Lucas BUCHEN
26 Director Marketing .... Ms. Sherri RADER
27 Coordinator Public Information .... Ms. Sally SHIELDS
102 Director Foundation .... Mr. Colin DAVIS

Spoon River College-Macomb Campus (H)

208 S Johnson Street, Macomb IL 61455
Telephone: (309) 837-5727 Identification: 770097
Accreditation: &HLC

Taylor Business Institute (I)

180 N. Wabash Avenue, Ste. 500, Chicago IL 60601
County: Cook FICE Identification: 011810
Unit ID: 149310
Telephone: (312) 658-5100 Carnegie Class: Assoc/HVT-High Trad
FAX Number: (312) 658-0867 Calendar System: Quarter
URL: www.tbiil.edu
Established: 1962 Annual Undergrad Tuition & Fees: $10,650
Enrollment: 100 Coed
Affiliation or Control: Proprietary IRS Status: Proprietary
Highest Offering: Associate Degree
Accreditation: HLC

01 President/CEO .... Mrs. Janice C. PARKER
05 Dean/Chief Academic Officer .... Mr. Malik IQBAL

Telshe Yeshiva-Chicago (J)

3535 W Foster Avenue, Chicago IL 60625-5598
County: Cook FICE Identification: 020732
Unit ID: 149329
Telephone: (773) 463-7738 Carnegie Class: Spec-4-yr-Faith
FAX Number: (773) 463-2849 Calendar System: Semester
URL: https://telsheyeshivachicago.com/
Established: 1960 Annual Undergrad Tuition & Fees: $14,500
Enrollment: 94 Male
Affiliation or Control: Independent Non-Profit IRS Status: 501(c)3
Highest Offering: Second Talmudic Degree
Accreditation: RABN

01 President .... Rabbi Shmuel Y. LEVIN
03 Executive Vice President .... Rabbi Yitzchok LEVIN
05 Vice President .... Rabbi Chaim D. KELLER
05 Vice President .... Rabbi Moshe SCHMELCZER
11 Administrative Director/Secretary .... Rabbi Shmuel ADLER

Toyota Technological Institute at Chicago (K)

6045 South Kenwood Avenue, Chicago IL 60637
County: Cook Identification: 666367
Unit ID: 445054
Telephone: (773) 834-2500 Carnegie Class: Spec-4-yr-Other Tech
FAX Number: (773) 834-9881 Calendar System: Quarter
URL: www.ttic.edu
Established: 2003 Annual Graduate Tuition & Fees: N/A
Enrollment: 43 Coed
Affiliation or Control: Independent Non-Profit IRS Status: 501(c)3
Highest Offering: Doctorate; No Undergraduates
Accreditation: HLC

01 President .... Dr. Matthew TURK
10 Chief Financial Officer .... Ms. Jessica JOHNSTON
58 Admin Director of Graduate Studies .... Ms. Chrissy COLEMAN
15 Director of Human Resources .... Ms. Amy MINICK

Trinity Christian College (A)

6601 W College Drive, Palos Heights IL 60463-0929
County: Cook   FICE Identification: 001771
Unit ID: 149505
Telephone: (708) 597-3000   Carnegie Class: Bac-Diverse
FAX Number: (708) 239-4826   Calendar System: Semester
URL: www.trnty.edu
Established: 1959   Annual Undergrad Tuition & Fees: $32,075
Enrollment: 1,086   Coed
Affiliation or Control: Independent Non-Profit   IRS Status: 501(c)3
Highest Offering: Master's
Accreditation: HLC, ACBSP, NURSE, SW

01 President ... Mr. Kurt D. DYKSTRA
05 Provost ... Dr. Aaron KUECKER
10 Vice Pres for Finance ... Mr. Michael S. TROCHUCK
32 Vice Pres for Student Life ... Mrs. Rebekah L. STARKENBURG
26 Vice Pres for Comm & Strategic Init ... Mr. Paul BOICE
111 Vice Pres for Advancement ... Vacant
110 Assoc VP for Advancement ... Mr. Dennis HARMS
42 Chaplain ... Vacant
08 Director of Library Services ... Mr. Kyle MCCARRELL
15 Director of Human Resources ... Ms. Julia FOUST
06 Registrar ... Ms. Jaynn TOBIAS-JOHNSON
09 Asst Registrar for Inst Research ... Ms. Kimberly WILLIAMS
21 Controller ... Mrs. Ashleigh VELASQUEZ
36 Director of Career Development ... Mr. Jeff TIMMER
29 Director of Alumni Relations ... Mr. Jeremy KLYN
19 Director Security/Safety ... Mr. Tom KAZEN
13 Director of Technology Systems ... Mr. Kevin JACOBS
14 Director of Technology Support ... Mr. Doug VAN WYNGARDEN
41 AVP Student Life/Dir of Athletics ... Mr. Mark HANNA
28 Dir of Multicultural Engagement ... Mrs. Nicole SAINT-VICTOR
85 Director of Off-Campus Programs ... Ms. Maria HODAPP
37 Director Financial Aid ... Mr. Michael SHIELDS
18 Director of Building/Grounds ... Mr. Tim TIMMONS
112 Director of Planned Giving ... Mr. Jeff ENFIELD
92 Director of Honors Program ... Dr. Craig MATTSON
38 Director of Counseling Services ... Dr. Stephanie GRISWOLD
04 Executive Assistant to President ... Ms. Deborah S. VINCENT
88 Senior Graphic Designer ... Ms. Jyne KING
105 Web Developer ... Ms. Diane BRUNSTING
50 Department Chair of Business ... Dr. Deborah L. WINDES
07 Assoc Dir Admissions Adult & Grad ... Mrs. Alexis HENDERSON

Trinity College of Nursing & Health Sciences (B)

2122 25th Avenue, Rock Island IL 61201-5317
County: Rock Island   FICE Identification: 006225
Unit ID: 146755
Telephone: (309) 779-7700   Carnegie Class: Spec-4-yr-Other Health
FAX Number: (309) 779-7748   Calendar System: Semester
URL: www.trinitycollegeqc.edu
Established: 1994   Annual Undergrad Tuition & Fees: $28,244
Enrollment: 206   Coed
Affiliation or Control: Independent Non-Profit   IRS Status: 501(c)3
Highest Offering: Master's
Accreditation: HLC, NURSE, RAD

01 Chancellor ... Dr. Tracy L. POELVOORDE
05 Dean of Nursing & Health Sciences ... Dr. Teresa WISCHMANN
10 Director of Business Services ... Ms. Rosemary BROWER
32 Director of Student Services ... Ms. Hilary HENKE
06 Registrar ... Ms. Cara BANKS

Trinity International University (C)

2065 Half Day Road, Deerfield IL 60015-1284
County: Lake   FICE Identification: 001772
Unit ID: 149514
Telephone: (847) 945-8800   Carnegie Class: DU-Mod
FAX Number: (847) 317-8090   Calendar System: Semester
URL: www.tiu.edu
Established: 1897   Annual Undergrad Tuition & Fees: $33,298
Enrollment: 1,454   Coed
Affiliation or Control: Evangelical Free Church Of America
IRS Status: 501(c)3
Highest Offering: Doctorate
Accreditation: HLC, CACREP, THEOL

01 President ... Dr. Nicholas PERRIN
73 VP Education/Dean TEDS ... Dr. David PAO
05 Provost ... Dr. Wayne JOHNSON
32 VP Student Life & Univ Services ... Ms. Amanda ONAPITO
11 Sr VP for Administration ... Vacant
10 Chief Financial Officer ... Dr. Jonathan DOCKERY
07 VP for Admissions ... Ms. Shawn WYNNE
18 AVP Facility & Event Services ... Ms. Julie WONG
30 AVP Advancement/University Rels ... Mr. Garrett LUCK
111 Int VP University Advancement ... Mr. Dwight GIBSON
26 VP University Communication ... Mrs. Kimberly MEDAGLIA
27 Director of Marketing/Communication ... Mr. Chris DONATO
13 Chief Information Officer ... Mr. Mike PETERSON
51 Director Adult Academic Programs ... Vacant
20 Dean Trinity Col/Trinity Grad Sch ... Dr. Karen WROBBEL
90 Director of Acad/Desktop Computing ... Mr. Chris MILLER
91 Director Administrative Computing ... Ms. Katie KEMP
61 Dean of Law School ... Mr. Myron STEEVES
19 Director of Security Services ... Mr. Aron FORCH
15 Director of Human Resources ... Mrs. Linda BRUNDIDGE
06 University Registrar ... Vacant
36 Director of Placement ... Dr. Phil SELL
08 Director University Library Svcs ... Ms. Rebecca DONALD
92 Director of Honors Program ... Dr. Joshua HELD
35 Assoc Dean of Students ... Ms. Heather LOGUE
38 Director Student Care & Engagement ... Ms. Mary GUTHRIE
04 Exec Assistant to the President ... Mrs. Jean D. MYERS
22 Dir Affirm Action/Equal Opportunity ... Ms. Linda BRUNDIDGE
41 Athletic Director ... Ms. Heather LOGUE
09 Director of Institutional Research ... Mr. Jonathan DOCKERY

Triton College (D)

2000 Fifth Avenue, River Grove IL 60171-1995
County: Cook   FICE Identification: 001773
Unit ID: 149532
Telephone: (708) 456-0300   Carnegie Class: Assoc/MT-VT-High Non
FAX Number: (708) 583-3112   Calendar System: Semester
URL: www.triton.edu
Established: 1964   Annual Undergrad Tuition & Fees (In-District): $10,890
Enrollment: 8,819   Coed
Affiliation or Control: Local   IRS Status: 501(c)3
Highest Offering: Associate Degree
Accreditation: HLC, ACBSP, ADNUR, DMS, MAC, RAD, SURGT

01 President ... Ms. Mary-Rita MOORE
05 Vice President Academic Affairs ... Dr. Susan CAMPOS
84 Vice Pres Enroll Mgmt/Student Affs ... Dr. Jodi KOSLOW MARTIN
10 Vice President Business Services ... Mr. Sean SULLIVAN
26 Assoc VP Comm & Inst Advancement ... Vacant
101 Secretary for Brd of Trustees ... Ms. Susan PAGE
13 Assoc VP Information Systems ... Mr. Michael GARRITY
41 AVP Athletics/Athletic Activities ... Mr. Garrick ABEZETIAN
18 Assoc VP of Facilities ... Mr. John LAMBRECHT
15 Assoc VP Human Resources ... Mr. Joe KLINGER
20 Assoc VP Academic Innov Workforce ... Mr. Paul JENSEN
32 Dean of Students ... Vacant
124 Dean of Retention/Stdnt Engagement ... Ms. Denise JONES
49 Dean of Arts & Sciences ... Vacant
72 Dean of Business & Technology ... Dr. Jennifer DAVIDSON
51 Dean of Continuing Education ... Dr. Bianca SOLA-PERKINS
121 Dean of Academic Success ... Ms. Hilary MEYER
55 Dean of Adult Education ... Ms. Jacqueline LYNCH
07 Assoc Dean of Enrollment Services ... Ms. Patricia ZINGA
21 Executive Director of Finance ... Mr. James REYNOLDS
27 Executive Director of Marketing ... Mr. Sam TOLIA
09 Executive Director of Research ... Dr. Kurian THARAKUNNEL
25 Exec Dir Grants Development ... Vacant
86 Director Public Affairs ... Vacant
88 Special Assistant to the President ... Ms. Brenda WATKINS
04 Admin Assistant to the President ... Vacant
19 Police Chief ... Mr. Austin WEINSTOCK
45 Exec Dir Strategic Plng & Accred ... Dr. Purva RUSHI

University of Chicago (E)

5801 S Ellis Avenue, Chicago IL 60637-1496
County: Cook   FICE Identification: 001774
Unit ID: 144050
Telephone: (773) 702-1234   Carnegie Class: DU-Highest
FAX Number: N/A   Calendar System: Quarter
URL: www.uchicago.edu
Established: 1890   Annual Undergrad Tuition & Fees: $60,552
Enrollment: 17,834   Coed
Affiliation or Control: Independent Non-Profit   IRS Status: 501(c)3
Highest Offering: Doctorate
Accreditation: HLC, CAMPEP, IPSY, LAW, MED, SW, THEOL

01 President ... Paul ALIVISATOS
100 Executive VP & Chief of Staff ... Katie CALLOW-WRIGHT
05 Provost ... Ka Yee C. LEE
17 EVP for Medical Affairs/Dean of BSD ... Kenneth S. POLONSKY
88 EVP Science/Innovation/Strategy ... Balaji SRINIVASAN
10 Int VP/Chief Financial Officer ... Brett PADGETT
43 Vice President & General Counsel ... Kim TAYLOR
88 VP for National Laboratories ... Juan DE PABLO
26 Vice Pres for Communications ... Paul M. RAND
84 VP Enrollment/Stdnt Advancement ... James G. NONDORF
45 VP for Strategic Initiatives ... Darren REISBERG
29 VP for Alumni Rels & Development ... Sharon MARINE
86 VP for Civic Engagement/Ext Affairs ... Derek DOUGLAS
115 Int Vice Pres/Chief Investment Ofcr ... Patrick O'HARA
20 Vice Provost for Acad Affairs ... Jason MERCHANT
20 Vice Provost ... Daniel ABEBE
20 Vice Provost ... Michael HOPKINS
20 Vice Provost ... Melina HALE
46 Vice Provost for Research ... Vacant
28 Vice Provost ... Melissa GILLIAM
13 AVP/Chief Information Officer ... Kevin BOYD
22 Assoc Prov Equal Opportunity Pgms ... Bridget COLLIER
54 Dean of Molecular Engineering ... Matthew TIRRELL
83 Dean Division of Social Sciences ... Amanda WOODWARD
73 Int Dean of Divinity School ... David NIRENBERG
80 Dean Harris Sch of Public Policy ... Katherine BAICKER
51 Dean of Graham School Cont Educ ... Emily Lynn OSBORN
63 Dean Medicine ... Kenneth POLONSKY
79 Dean of Humanities Division ... Anne ROBERTSON
70 Dean Sch of Social Svcs Admin ... Deborah GORMAN-SMITH
61 Dean of the Law School ... Thomas MILES
50 Dean of Booth School of Business ... Madhav V. RAJAN
49 Dean of the College ... John W. BOYER
65 Dean Physical Sciences Division ... Angela V. OLINTO
42 Dean Rockefeller Memorial Chapel ... Maurice CHARLES
32 Dean of Students in University ... Michele RASMUSSEN
37 Senior Exec Director University Aid ... Amanda FIJAL
06 AVP/Registrar ... Scott CAMPBELL
57 Executive Director of UChicago Arts ... Bill MICHEL
88 Director of Oriental Institute ... Christopher WOODS

*University of Illinois System (F)

506 S Wright Street, 364 HAB, Urbana IL 61801
County: Champaign   FICE Identification: 008001
Unit ID: 149587
Telephone: (217) 333-3070   Carnegie Class: N/A
FAX Number: N/A
URL: www.uillinois.edu

01 President ... Dr. Timothy L. KILLEEN
12 Chancellor/Vice President (Chicago) ... Dr. Michael AMIRIDIS
12 Chancellor/Vice President (Sprgfld) ... Dr. Karen WHITNEY
12 Chancellor/Vice President (Urbana) ... Dr. Robert J. JONES
10 VP & Chief Financial Officer ... Mr. Avijit GHOSH
05 Int Exec Vice Pres and VPAA ... Mr. Avijit GHOSH
45 VP Economic Development/Innovation ... Dr. Jay WALSH
43 University Counsel ... Mr. Thomas R. BEARROWS
26 Int Dir for Univ Relations ... Ms. Kirsten A. RUBY
13 CIO & Sr Assoc VP ... Mr. Kelly J. BLOCK
15 Assoc VP Human Resources ... Ms. Jami PAINTER
101 Secretary Board of Trustees/Univ ... Mr. Greg KNOTT
102 President/CEO Univ Foundation ... Mr. James H. MOORE, JR.
29 Pres UIAA/Assoc VC for Alumni Rel ... Ms. Jennifer NEUBAUER
04 Admin Assistant to the President ... Ms. Kathy J. FOGERSON

*University of Illinois at Chicago (G)

601 S Morgan, M/C 102, Chicago IL 60607-7128
County: Cook   FICE Identification: 001776
Unit ID: 145600
Telephone: (312) 996-7000   Carnegie Class: DU-Highest
FAX Number: (312) 413-3393   Calendar System: Semester
URL: www.uic.edu
Established: 1896   Annual Undergrad Tuition & Fees (In-State): $14,098
Enrollment: 33,518   Coed
Affiliation or Control: State   IRS Status: 501(c)3
Highest Offering: Doctorate
Accreditation: HLC, ATECH, CAHIIM, CEA, CLPSY, DENT, DIETC, DIETD, FEPAC, HSA, IPSY, MED, MIDWF, MIL, NURSE, OT, PH, PHAR, PLNG, PTA, SPAA, SW

02 Chancellor ... Dr. Michael AMIRIDIS
05 Provost/Vice Chanc Academic Affairs ... Dr. Javier REYES
32 Vice Chancellor Student Affairs ... Mr. Rex TOLLIVER
11 Vice Chanc for Admin Svcs ... Mr. John CORONADO
46 Vice Chancellor for Research ... Dr. Joanna GRODEN
26 Int Assoc Chanc Govt & Public Affs ... Ms. Theresa MINTLE
17 CEO Hospital Administration ... Dr. Michael ZENN
29 Exec Director Alumni Engagement ... Ms. Caryn KORMAN
111 Vice Chanc for Advancement ... Mr. Thomas WAMSLEY
84 Vice Prov Acad/Enrollment Svcs ... Mr. Kevin BROWNE
20 Vice Provost for Faculty Affairs ... Dr. Nancy FREITAG
20 Vice Prov Undergrad Affairs ... Dr. Nikos VARELAS
88 Vice Provost for Global Engagement ... Dr. Neal R. MCCRILLIS
114 Assoc Chanc for Resource Plng/Mgmt ... Ms. Janet PARKER
35 Assoc Vice Chanc/Dean Student Affs ... Dr. Linda DEANNA
27 Senior Exec Director Public Affairs ... Ms. Sherri MCGINNIS GONZALEZ
23 Vice Chancellor Health Affairs ... Dr. Robert BARISH
10 Asst VP Business Svcs ... Ms. Gloria KEELEY
48 Dean Col of Arch/Design/Arts ... Dr. Rebecca RUGG
50 Dean College of Business Admin ... Dr. Michael B. MIKHAIL
52 Dean College of Dentistry ... Dr. Clark STANFORD
53 Dean College of Education ... Vacant
54 Dean College of Engineering ... Dr. Peter C. NELSON
76 Dean Col Applied Health Sciences ... Dr. Bo FERNHALL
58 Dean Graduate College ... Dr. Karen COLLEY
92 Dean Honors College ... Dr. Ralph KEEN
49 Dean College Liberal Arts/Sciences ... Dr. Astrida O. TANTILLO
63 Exec Dean College of Medicine ... Dr. Mark ROSENBLATT
66 Dean College of Nursing ... Dr. Terri E. WEAVER
67 Dean College of Pharmacy ... Dr. Glen SCHUMOCK
70 Dean College of Social Work ... Dr. Creasie HAIRSTON
69 Dean School of Public Health ... Dr. Wayne GILES
80 Dean Urban Planning/Public Affairs ... Dr. Michael A. PAGANO
43 University Counsel ... Mr. Thomas R. BEARROWS
08 University Librarian ... Ms. Mary CASE
88 Asst Univ Librarian Health Sciences ... Ms. Kathryn H. CARPENTER
07 Executive Director Admissions ... Ms. Malinda LORKOVICH
41 Director Athletics ... Mr. Michael LIPITZ
38 Director Counseling Services ... Dr. Joseph HERMES
39 Director of Campus Housing ... Ms. Susan TEGGATZ
37 Director Financial Aid ... Ms. Kiely FLETCHER
09 Director of Institutional Research ... Mr. William C. HAYWARD
16 Assoc Vice Provost Faculty Affairs ... Ms. Angela L. YUDT
22 Director Access/Equity ... Ms. Caryn A. BILLS-WINDT
36 Director Career Services ... Vacant
13 CIO/Exec Dir Acad Computing ... Ms. Cynthia E. HERRERA LINDSTROM
56 Asst Vice Chanc Extended Campus ... Ms. Dara CROWFOOT
06 Registrar ... Mr. Robert DIXON
96 Director of Purchasing ... Ms. Debra MATLOCK
18 Exec Dir Operations/Maintenance ... Mr. Clarence F. BRIDGES
28 Assoc Chanc & VP for Diversity ... Dr. Amalia PALLARES
100 Associate Provost/Chief of Staff ... Dr. Aisha EL-AMIN
104 Executive Director of Study Abroad ... Vacant
88 Vice Chancellor for Innovation ... Dr. TJ AUGUSTINE

*University of Illinois Springfield (A)

One University Plaza, Springfield IL 62703-5407
County: Sangamon FICE Identification: 009333
Unit ID: 148654
Telephone: (217) 206-6600 Carnegie Class: Masters/L
FAX Number: (217) 206-6511 Calendar System: Semester
URL: www.uis.edu
Established: 1969 Annual Undergrad Tuition & Fees (In-State): $11,911
Enrollment: 4,146 Coed
Affiliation or Control: State IRS Status: 501(c)3
Highest Offering: Doctorate
Accreditation: HLC, CAATE, CACREP, MT, SPAA, SW

02 Interim Chancellor ... Dr. Karen WHITNEY
05 Vice Chancellor Acad Affs/Provost ... Dr. Dennis PAPINI
32 Int Vice Chancellor Student Affairs ... Ms. Ann COMERFORD
10 Interim Vice Chanc Finance/Admin ... Mr. Arnold HENNING
20 Int Assoc Vice Chanc Undergrad Educ ... Dr. Kathy NOVAK
58 Assoc Vice Chanc for Graduate Educ ... Dr. Cecilia CORNELL
88 Exec Dir Ctr State Policy & Ldrship ... Ms. Molly LAMB
110 Assoc Vice Chanc for Development ... Ms. Lisa WHELPLEY
29 Assoc Vice Chanc for Alumni Rels ... Mr. Charles SCHRAGE
30 Vice Chanc Dev/Sr VP UL Found ... Dr. Jeffrey D. LORBER
18 Assoc Chanc Admin Affs/Facilities ... Mr. Charles CODERKO
26 Assoc Chancellor for Public Affairs ... Ms. Kelsea GURSKI
21 Sr Business & Financial Coordinator ... Mr. Jason BANE
49 Int Dean Col Liberal Arts/Science ... Dr. Lan DONG
50 Dean College Business/Mgmt ... Dr. Somnath BHATTACHARYA
80 Dean Col Public Affs/Admin ... Dr. Robert SMITH
53 Int Dean College Educ/Human Svcs ... Dr. James ERMATINGER
15 Sr Director HR ... Ms. Melissa MLYNSKI
43 Legal Counsel ... Ms. Rhonda PERRY
08 Dean of Library ... Dr. Pattie PIOTROWSKI
27 Director Public Information ... Mr. Derek SCHNAPP
27 Director Marketing ... Ms. Jessie BURRELL
19 Interim Chief Campus Police ... Mr. Ross OWENS
06 Registrar ... Mr. Brian CLEVENGER
35 Director of Student Life ... Ms. Cynthia THOMPSON
41 Interim Director of Athletics ... Mr. Roy BROWN
09 Director Institutional Research ... Ms. Laura DORMAN
96 Director of Purchasing ... Ms. Jill MENEZES
37 Interim Dir Financial Assistance ... Ms. Laurie BUCK
38 Exec Director Counseling Center ... Dr. Bethany BILYEU
85 Director Intl Student Services ... Mr. Rick LANE
13 Assoc Provost for IT/CIO ... Mr. Tulio LLOSA
39 Director Campus Housing ... Mr. Brian KELLEY
07 Director of Admissions ... Ms. Kathryn KLEEMAN
28 Director of Diversity & Inclusion ... Mr. Justin ROSE
36 Director Career Development Center ... Ms. Katherine BATTEE-FREEMAN
84 Director Enrollment Management ... Ms. Natalie HERRING
86 Director Government Relations ... Ms. Joan SESTAK
104 Director Study Abroad ... Dr. Jonathan GOLDBERGBELLE
105 Director Web Services ... Ms. Jessica BAUMBERGER
106 Exec Dir Online/Prof & Engaged Lrng ... Dr. Vickie S. COOK

*University of Illinois Urbana-Champaign (B)

601 E John Street, Champaign IL 61820-5711
County: Champaign FICE Identification: 001775
Unit ID: 145637
Telephone: (217) 333-6677 Carnegie Class: DU-Highest
FAX Number: (217) 244-5352 Calendar System: Semester
URL: www.illinois.edu
Established: 1867 Annual Undergrad Tuition & Fees (In-State): $15,150
Enrollment: 52,679 Coed
Affiliation or Control: State IRS Status: 501(c)3
Highest Offering: Doctorate
Accreditation: HLC, ART, AUD, CEA, CLPSY, COPSY, DANCE, DIETD, DIETI, IPSY, JOUR, LAW, LIB, LSAR, #MED, MUS, PCSAS, PH, PLNG, SP, SW, VET

00 Chief Executive Officer (President) ... Dr. Timothy L. KILLEEN
02 Chancellor ... Dr. Robert J. JONES
05 Prov/Vice Chanc Academic Affs ... Dr. Andreas C. CANGELLARIS
46 Vice Chanc Research & Innovation ... Dr. Susan MARTINIS
32 Vice Chancellor Student Affairs ... Dr. Danita BROWN YOUNG
111 VC Inst Advancement/Found Admin ... Mr. Barry BENSON
88 Associate Chanc Corp/Intl Relations ... Dr. Pradeep KHANNA
20 Exec Vice Provost Academic Affairs ... Dr. William BERNHARD
26 Exec Assoc Chanc for Public Engage ... Dr. Wanda E. WARD
11 Vice Chanc for Admin and Operations ... Mr. Michael DELORENZO
28 VC for Diversity/Equity/Inclusion ... Dr. Sean C. GARRICK
88 Assoc Prov Faculty Development ... Dr. Rosa Milagros SANTOS
100 Chief of Staff/Assoc Chanc ... Dr. Christopher SPAN
27 Associate Chanc Public Affairs ... Ms. Robin KALER
15 Senior Assoc Chancellor for HR ... Vacant
84 Assoc Prov Enrollment Mgmt ... Mr. Daniel MANN
88 Assoc Prov Capital Planning ... Vacant
114 Actg Assoc Chanc/Vice Prov Budget ... Ms. Vicky GRESS
104 Vice Prov Intl Pgms/Global Studies ... Ms. Reitumetse MABOKELA
20 Int Vice Prov for Undergrad Educ ... Dr. Lisa MONDA-AMAYA
21 Exec Assoc Provost Budget Planning ... Ms. Vicky GRESS
88 Exec Assoc Prov Acad Pgms/Policy ... Ms. Kristi KUNTZ
09 Asst Provost Management Info ... Dr. Amy EDWARDS
49 Dean Liberal Arts & Sciences ... Dr. Venetria PATTON
61 Dean Law ... Dr. Vikram AMAR
74 Dean Veterinary Medicine ... Dr. Peter CONSTABLE
54 Dean Engineering ... Dr. Rashid BASHIR
47 Dean Agric/Consumer/Environ Sci ... Dr. Kim KIDWELL
50 Dean Business ... Dr. Jeffrey BROWN
57 Dean Fine & Applied Arts ... Dr. Kevin HAMILTON
63 Dean CI College of Medicine ... Dr. King LI
70 Dean School of Social Work ... Dr. Steven ANDERSON
68 Dean Col Applied Health Sciences ... Dr. Cheryl HANLEY-MAXWELL
60 Dean College of Media ... Dr. Tracy SULKIN
58 Dean Graduate College ... Dr. Wojciech CHODZKO-ZAJKO
62 Dean School of Info Sciences ... Dr. Eunice SANTOS
53 Dean Education ... Dr. James D. ANDERSON
63 Actg Reg Dean Col Med/Urbana-Champ ... Dr. Janet JOKELA
48 Dir School of Architecture ... Mr. Francisco RODRIGUEZ-SUAREZ
16 Dean Labor & Employment Rels ... Dr. Fritz DRASGOW
08 University Librarian & Dean ... Dr. John P. WILKIN
13 Interim Chief Information Officer ... Mr. Scott GENUNG
35 Acting Dean of Students ... Dr. Stephen BRYAN
56 Assoc Dean Extension & Outreach ... Dr. Sharon NICKOLS
41 Director Athletics ... Mr. Josh WHITMAN
10 Asst Vice Pres Bus/Fin Affairs ... Ms. Ginger VELAZQUEZ
43 Deputy Campus Legal Counsel ... Mr. Scott RICE
22 Dir Equal Opportunity & Access ... Ms. Heidi JOHNSON
19 Exec Director Public Safety ... Ms. Alice CARY
18 Interim Exec Director Facilities ... Dr. Ehab KAMARAH
23 Director McKinley Health Center ... Dr. Robert D. PARKER, JR.
36 Director Career Services Center ... Ms. Jennifer NEEF
37 Director Student Financial Aid ... Ms. Michelle TRAME
38 Director Counseling Center ... Dr. Carla MCCOWAN
39 Exec Director Housing Division ... Ms. Alma SEALINE
88 Dir Ctr Innovative Teaching/Lrng ... Dr. Michel BELLINI
06 Registrar ... Ms. Meghan HAZEN
07 Director of Admissions ... Mr. Andy BORST
101 Secretary of the Institution/Board ... Mr. Gregory KNOTT
108 Assoc Prov for Acad Effectiveness ... Dr. Staci J. PROVEZIS
86 Dir Community/Govt Relations ... Mr. Robert FLIDER

*University of Illinois at Chicago College of Medicine at Peoria (C)

One Illini Drive, Peoria IL 61605
Telephone: (309) 671-8402 Identification: 770182
Accreditation: &HLC

*University of Illinois at Chicago College of Medicine at Urbana (D)

Carle Forum LL, 611 West Park St, Urbana IL 61801
Telephone: (217) 333-5465 Identification: 770184
Accreditation: &HLC

*University of Illinois College of Medicine Rockford (E)

1601 Parkview Avenue, Rockford IL 61107
Telephone: (815) 395-0600 Identification: 770183
Accreditation: &HLC, PHAR

*UIC John Marshall Law School (F)

300 S. State Street, Chicago IL 60604-3968
Telephone: (312) 427-2737 FICE Identification: 001698
Accreditation: &HLC, LAW

University of Phoenix Chicago Campus (G)

203 North LaSalle Street, Ste 1300,
Chicago IL 60601-1210
Telephone: (312) 223-1101 Identification: 770205
Accreditation: &HLC, ACBSP

† No longer accepting campus-based students.

University of St. Francis (H)

500 N Wilcox Street, Joliet IL 60435-6188
County: Will FICE Identification: 001664
Unit ID: 148584
Telephone: (815) 740-3400 Carnegie Class: DU-Mod
FAX Number: (815) 740-4285 Calendar System: Semester
URL: www.stfrancis.edu
Established: 1920 Annual Undergrad Tuition & Fees: $35,000
Enrollment: 3,529 Coed
Affiliation or Control: Roman Catholic IRS Status: 501(c)3
Highest Offering: Doctorate
Accreditation: HLC, ACBSP, CAEPN, CAPRT, NURSE, RTT, SW

01 President ... Dr. Arvid C. JOHNSON
05 Provost/VP Academic Affairs ... Dr. Beth ROTH
10 VP Administration & Finance ... Ms. Julee A. GARD
84 VP Admissions/Mktg/Enrollment Svcs ... Mr. Eric WIGNALL
88 VP Mission Int & Univ Ministry ... Sr. Mary Elizabeth IMLER
13 VP Operations/Planning & Technology ... Mr. Terrance L. COTTRELL
111 VP for University Advancement ... Vacant
49 Dean Col Arts & Sciences ... Dr. Elizabeth DAVIES
50 Dean Col Business/Health ... Dr. Orlando GRIEGO
53 Dean Col Education ... Dr. John S. GAMBRO
66 Dean Leach Col Nursing ... Dr. Ebere UME
32 Dean Student Life ... Ms. Mollie ROCKAFELLOW
37 Exec Dir Financial Aid ... Mr. Bruce FOOTE
29 Dir Alumni Relations ... Ms. Aubrey L. KNIGHT
41 Dir Athletics ... Mr. Dave LAKETA
36 Dir Career Success Center ... Ms. Maribeth HEARN
38 Dir Counseling & Wellness ... Dr. Maryann ANDRADE BEKKER
28 Dir Institutional Diversity ... Ms. Allison HEARD
07 Dir Undergrad Admissions ... Mr. Eric RUIZ
123 Dir Grad/Degree Completion Admiss ... Ms. Sandra L. SLOKA
27 Dir Marketing Services ... Ms. Julie FUTTERER
14 Dir Network Support Services ... Mr. Mark T. SNODGRASS
19 Dir Safety/Security ... Mr. Jason WILLIAMS
42 Dir University Ministry ... Vacant
06 Registrar ... Ms. Jennifer ETHRIDGE
08 Head Librarian ... Ms. Brigitte BELL
23 Coordinator of Health Services ... Ms. Phyllis M. PETERSON
09 Dir Enterprise Data & Analytics ... Ms. Rebecca R. GARLAND
44 Director Annual Giving ... Vacant

University of Saint Mary of the Lake-Mundelein Seminary (I)

1000 E Maple Avenue, Mundelein IL 60060-1174
County: Lake FICE Identification: 001765
Unit ID: 148885
Telephone: (847) 566-6401 Carnegie Class: Spec-4-yr-Faith
FAX Number: (847) 566-7330 Calendar System: Semester
URL: www.usml.edu
Established: 1844 Annual Graduate Tuition & Fees: N/A
Enrollment: 186 Male
Affiliation or Control: Roman Catholic IRS Status: 501(c)3
Highest Offering: Doctorate; No Undergraduates
Accreditation: THEOL

00 Chancellor ... Card. Blase CUPICH
01 Rector/President ... V.Rev. John KARTJE
11 Chief Operating Officer ... Mr. James HEINEN
03 Vice Rector ... Rev. Jake BELTRAN
05 Provost ... V.Rev. Thomas A. BAIMA
73 Pres/Pontifical Faculty of Theology ... Rev. Brendan LUPTON
10 Vice President for Finance ... Mr. John F. LEHOCKY
30 Vice President of Development ... Ms. Holly GIBOUT
20 Director of Intellectual Formation ... Ms. Marie PITT-PAYNE
88 Dean of Formation ... Rev. Maina WAITHAKA
73 Director Pre-Theology Program ... Rev. Dennis SPIES
08 Library Director ... Dr. Christopher ROGERS
06 Director of Registration & Records ... Ms. Devona SEWELL
42 Director of Spiritual Life ... Dcn. Pat QUAGLIANA
85 Director of International Students ... Rev. Maina WAITHAKA
07 Director of Admissions ... Vacant
04 Admin Assistant to the President ... Ms. Mary BERTRAM
13 Chief Information Technology Ofcr ... Mr. Brian BICKETT
15 Chief Human Resources Officer ... Mr. Tad GEIGER
19 Director Security/Safety ... Mr. John HUINKER
38 Director Student Counseling ... Rev. Carlos RODRIGUEZ
26 Dir Marketing & Communications ... Mr. Matt PAOLELLI

VanderCook College of Music (J)

3140 S Federal Street, Chicago IL 60616-3731
County: Cook FICE Identification: 001778
Unit ID: 149639
Telephone: (312) 225-6288 Carnegie Class: Spec-4-yr-Other
FAX Number: (312) 225-5211 Calendar System: Semester
URL: www.vandercook.edu
Established: 1909 Annual Undergrad Tuition & Fees: $29,800
Enrollment: 313 Coed
Affiliation or Control: Independent Non-Profit IRS Status: 501(c)3
Highest Offering: Master's
Accreditation: HLC, MUS

01 President ... Dr. Roseanne K. ROSENTHAL
08 Head Librarian ... Mr. Robert DELAND
05 Dean of Undergraduate Studies ... Ms. Stacey L. DOLAN
58 Dean of Graduate Studies ... Dr. Robert L. SINCLAIR
07 Director of Admissions & Alumni ... Ms. Cindy TOVAR
10 Chief Financial Officer ... Ms. Shunita RHODES
37 Director of Financial Aid ... Ms. Sirena COVINGTON
13 Director Information Technologies ... Mr. Rick MALIK
04 President's Assistant ... Ms. Sarah PENG
106 Dir of Continuing Education/COO ... Mr. Patrick BENSON
09 Director of Institutional Reports ... Mr. Gregor MEYER
06 Registrar/Educational Placement Dir ... Mrs. Carolyn BERGHOFF
26 Director Communications ... Vacant
29 Director Alumni Relations ... Ms. Cindy TOVAR

Waubonsee Community College (K)

Route 47 at Waubonsee Drive,
Sugar Grove IL 60554-9799
County: Kane FICE Identification: 006931
Unit ID: 149727
Telephone: (630) 466-7900 Carnegie Class: Assoc/HVT-High Non
FAX Number: (630) 466-7550 Calendar System: Semester
URL: www.waubonsee.edu
Established: 1966 Annual Undergrad Tuition & Fees (In-District): $9,271
Enrollment: 7,564 Coed
Affiliation or Control: Local IRS Status: 501(c)3
Highest Offering: Associate Degree
Accreditation: HLC, ADNUR, ART, CAHIIM, EMT, MAC

01 President ... Dr. Christine J. SOBEK
05 VP Educational Affairs ... Dr. Diane NYHAMMER
10 VP Finance & Administration ... Mr. Douglas MINTER
45 VP Strategy/Community Development ... Dr. Jamal SCOTT
32 VP Student Dev & Exec Dir Found ... Dr. Melinda L. TEJADA

21 Asst Vice President of Finance ... Ms. Darla S. CARDINE
103 Asst VP Education/Workforce Devel ... Ms. Suzette MURRAY
13 Chief Information Officer ... Mr. Terence FELTON
35 Asst VP Student Svc/Alumni Rels ... Dr. Scott PESKA
15 Exec Director Human Resources ... Ms. Michele NEEDHAM
26 Exec Dir Marketing/Communications ... Ms. Amanda GEIST
76 Dean Health Professions/Public Svc ... Mr. Jeffrey GREGOR
88 Dean Faculty Devel/Engagement ... Dr. Laura ORTIZ
49 Exec Dean Liberal Arts/Sciences ... Ms. Sharon GARCIA
83 Dean Soc Sciences/Educ/World Lang ... Vacant
124 Exec Dean Student Success/Retention ... Ms. Kelli SINCLAIR
56 Dean Adult Education ... Mr. Adam SCHAUER
50 Exec Dean Bus/Technology/Wrkfrc Ed ... Ms. Ne'Keisha STEPNEY
07 Dean for Admissions ... Ms. Faith LASHURE
04 Dir Pres Communications/Operations ... Ms. Kimberly CAPONI
37 Dir Student Financial Aid Services ... Dr. Charles BOUDREAU
09 Dean Inst Effective/Title V Proj ... Dr. Stacey RANDALL
35 Chief Diversity Ofcr/Dean of Stdnts ... Mr. Bernard LITTLE
19 Exec Dir Campus Safety/Operations ... Mr. Daniel LARSEN
06 Dir Registration/Records/Registrar ... Mr. Marc DALE
88 Dean Lrng Outcomes/Curric/Pgm Dev ... Dr. Kathleen GORSKI
121 Exec Dean for Academic Support ... Ms. Anita MOORE-BOHANNON
109 Dir Financial/Auxiliary Services ... Mr. Lei XIE
16 Dir Employee Development ... Mr. Tim BIZOUKAS

Western Illinois University (A)

1 University Circle, Macomb IL 61455-1390
County: McDonough FICE Identification: 001780
Unit ID: 149772
Telephone: (309) 298-1414 Carnegie Class: Masters/L
FAX Number: (309) 298-2400 Calendar System: Semester
URL: www.wiu.edu
Established: 1899 Annual Undergrad Tuition & Fees (In-State): $13,314
Enrollment: 7,490 Coed
Affiliation or Control: State IRS Status: 501(c)3
Highest Offering: Doctorate
Accreditation: **HLC**, ART, CACREP, CAPRT, CEA, DIETD, MPCAC, MUS, NURSE, SP, SW, THEA

01 President ... Dr. Guiyou HUANG
05 Provost/Academic VP ... Dr. Martin ABRAHAM
20 Assoc Prov & Assoc VP Academic Affs ... Dr. Mark MOSSMAN
10 Interim VP for Finance & Admin ... Ms. Shannon SUTTON
32 VP Student Services ... Dr. David BAVERMAN
111 Vice Pres Advancement/Public Svcs ... Vacant
29 Director Alumni Programs ... Ms. Amy SPELMAN
43 General Counsel ... Mrs. Elizabeth DUVALL
39 AVP Student Services/Housing ... Mr. John BIERNBAUM
86 Asst to Pres Government Relations ... Ms. Jeanette MALAFA
49 Dean College Arts/ Sciences ... Dr. Susan MARTINELLI-FERNANDEZ
50 Interim Dean College Business/Tech ... Dr. Craig CONRAD
53 Dean Col Educ & Human Svcs ... Dr. Francis GODWYLL
57 Dean Fine Arts & Communication ... Mr. William CLOW
08 Dean University Libraries ... Ms. Jeanne STIERMAN
92 Dean Centennial Honors Col ... Dr. Lorette ODEN
64 Director School of Music ... Dr. Jefrey BROWN
06 Interim Registrar ... Ms. Joani WILSON
13 Int Exec Dir Univ Technology/CIO ... Ms. Rebecca SLATER
26 Exec Director Univ Communication ... Ms. Darcie R. SHINBERGER
09 Director Inst Research & Planning ... Ms. Angela BONIFAS
22 Dir Equal Opportunity & Access ... Ms. Stephanie KINKAID
37 Director Financial Aid ... Ms. Roberta J. SMITH
121 Dir Student Development/Success Ctr ... Ms. Samantha KLINGLER
15 Director Human Resources ... Mrs. Amelia HARTNET
18 Exec Director Physical Plant ... Mr. Troy RHOADS
19 Director Public Safety ... Mr. Derek WATTS
23 Director Health Center ... Ms. John W. SMITH
85 Exec Dir International Affairs ... Dr. Randy GLEAN
40 Retail Manager University Bookstore ... Mr. Jeff MOORE
41 Director Athletics ... Ms. Danielle SURPRENANT
102 Exec Director WIU Foundation ... Mr. Bradley BAINTER
07 Director Undergraduate Admissions ... Mr. Doug FREED
38 Director Student Counseling ... Ms. Amy BUWICK
04 Sr Exec Assistant to the President ... Ms. Athena BROOKS
96 Director of Purchasing ... Vacant
28 Asst to Pres Diversity/Inclusion ... Dr. Sterling SADDLER
30 Exec Director of Development ... Mr. Paul BUBB
84 Interim Dir Enrollment Management ... Mr. Gary SWEGAN

Western Illinois University Quad Cities (B)

3300 River Drive, Moline IL 61265
Telephone: (309) 762-9481 Identification: 770100
Accreditation: **&HLC**

Wheaton College (C)

501 College Avenue, Wheaton IL 60187-5593
County: DuPage FICE Identification: 001781
Unit ID: 149781
Telephone: (630) 752-5000 Carnegie Class: Bac-A&S
FAX Number: (630) 752-5555 Calendar System: Semester
URL: www.wheaton.edu
Established: 1860 Annual Undergrad Tuition & Fees: $39,100
Enrollment: 2,908 Coed
Affiliation or Control: Independent Non-Profit IRS Status: 501(c)3
Highest Offering: Doctorate
Accreditation: **HLC**, CACREP, CLPSY, MFCD, MUS

01 President ... Dr. Philip G. RYKEN
05 Provost ... Dr. Karen LEE
10 VP for Finance ... Mr. Chad RYNBRANDT
32 Vice President Student Development ... Mr. Paul O. CHELSEN
111 VP Advancement/Alumni Rels ... Mr. Kirk FARNEY
84 Chief Enrollment Management Officer ... Mr. Silvio E. VAZQUEZ
93 Chief Intercultural Engagement Ofcr ... Vacant
13 Chief Info & Campus Svc Officer ... Vacant
29 Sr Dir Vocation & Alum Engagement ... Ms. Cindra STACKHOUSE TAETZSCH
04 Special Asst to the President ... Miss Marilee A. MELVIN
58 Dean of the Graduate School ... Dr. Scott MOREAU
79 Dean Biblical/Theol Studies ... Dr. David LAUBER
64 Dean Conservatory/Arts & Comm ... Dr. Michael WILDER
81 Dean Natural Sciences ... Dr. Becky EGGIMANN
83 Dean of Social Sciences & Education ... Dr. Bryan MCGRAW
104 Dean Global Programs & Studies ... Dr. Laura M. MONTGOMERY
83 Dean Psych/Counsel & Fam Therapy ... Dr. Terri WATSON
79 Dean Humanities ... Dr. Jeffry DAVIS
35 Dean of Student Engagement ... Dr. Steve IVESTER
08 Dean Library & Archives ... Mr. Brent ETZEL
88 Dean of Core Studies & Advising ... Dr. Sarah MIGLIO
21 Controller ... Mr. Carlos GARCIA
88 Exec Dir Billy Graham Ctr/Dean MML ... Dr. Ed STETZER
09 Dir Inst Research & Acad Operations ... Dr. Gary LARSON
06 Registrar ... Dr. Diane KRUSEMARK
18 Director of Facilities ... Vacant
36 Dir Ctr Vocation & Career ... Ms. Dee PIERCE
15 Director of Human Resources ... Mrs. Karen TUCKER
07 Dir Undergraduate Admissions ... Mr. Jason KIRCHER
123 Dir Graduate Admissions ... Mr. Terrance CAMPBELL
37 Director Student Financial Svcs ... Ms. Karen BELLING
41 Director of Athletics ... Ms. Julie DAVIS
39 Dean of Residence Life ... Dr. Justin HETH
35 Dean of Student Wellness ... Dr. Toussaint WHETSTONE
38 Director of Student Care ... Ms. Carrie WILLIAMS
42 Interim Chaplain ... Dr. Greg WAYBRIGHT
23 Dir Student Health Services ... Ms. Beth WALSH
26 Director Marketing Communications ... Mr. Joseph MOORE
27 Media Relations Specialist ... Ms. Emily BRATCHER
19 Chief of Public Safety ... Mr. Robert F. NORRIS
117 Director Risk Management ... Ms. Amanda FRANKLIN
105 Director Web Communications ... Mrs. Rebecca LARSON
25 Academic Grants Officer ... Mrs. Virginia SHAFFER

Worsham College of Mortuary Science (D)

495 Northgate Parkway, Wheeling IL 60090-2646
County: Cook FICE Identification: 001783
Unit ID: 369455
Telephone: (847) 808-8444 Carnegie Class: Spec 2-yr-A&S
FAX Number: (847) 808-8493 Calendar System: Quarter
URL: www.worsham.edu
Established: 1911 Annual Undergrad Tuition & Fees: $23,800
Enrollment: 171 Coed
Affiliation or Control: Proprietary IRS Status: Proprietary
Highest Offering: Associate Degree
Accreditation: **FUSER**

01 Director ... Ms. Leili MCMURROUGH

INDIANA

American College of Education (E)

101 West Ohio Street, Suite 1200, Indianapolis IN 46204
County: Marion Identification: 666242
Unit ID: 449889
Telephone: (800) 280-0307 Carnegie Class: Spec-4-yr-Other
FAX Number: N/A Calendar System: Other
URL: www.ace.edu
Established: 2005 Annual Undergrad Tuition & Fees: N/A
Enrollment: 8,112 Coed
Affiliation or Control: Proprietary IRS Status: Proprietary
Highest Offering: Doctorate
Accreditation: **HLC**, CAEP, NURSE

01 President ... Dr. Shawntel D. LANDRY
05 Chief Academic Officer & Provost ... Ms. Stephanie HINSHAW
09 Vice Pres Institutional Analytics ... Dr. George MAKIYA
88 Dir Regulatory Affairs & Compliance ... Mr. Tom BROUWER
07 Director of Admissions ... Ms. Jeannie TAYLOR
04 Executive Asst to President ... Ms. Jill ALGATE
08 Director Library ... Dr. Sandra QUIATKOWSKI
10 Chief Financial Officer ... Mr. Bryce PETERSON
26 Chief Marketing Officer ... Vacant
13 VP Information Technology ... Mr. Swapnal SHAH
15 VP Human Resources ... Ms. KK BYLAND
108 VP Continuous Improvement ... Ms. Alison WITHERSPOON
06 Registrar ... Mr. David GASTON
28 Diversity & Inclusion Advisor ... Ms. Fawzia REZA
29 Alumni Engagement Officer ... Ms. Courtney SHELTON

Anabaptist Mennonite Biblical Seminary (F)

3003 Benham Avenue, Elkhart IN 46517-1999
County: Elkhart FICE Identification: 001823
Unit ID: 151865
Telephone: (574) 295-3726 Carnegie Class: Spec-4-yr-Faith
FAX Number: (574) 295-0092 Calendar System: Semester
URL: www.ambs.edu
Established: 1946 Annual Graduate Tuition & Fees: N/A
Enrollment: 107 Coed
Affiliation or Control: Mennonite Church IRS Status: 501(c)3
Highest Offering: Master's; No Undergraduates
Accreditation: **THEOL**

01 President ... Dr. David BOSHART
05 VP & Academic Dean ... Dr. Beverly K. LAPP
10 Vice President and CFO ... Ms. Deanna A. RISSER
30 Director of Development ... Dr. Bob YODER
06 Assistant Dean & Registrar ... Mr. Scott JANZEN
08 Director of Library Services ... Mr. Karl STUTZMAN
84 VP for Advancement & Enrollment ... Mr. Daniel GRIMES
73 Director of Inst Mennonite Studies ... Dr. Jamie PITTS
04 Exec Asst to Pres & Academic Dean ... Ms. Karen S. STOLTZFUS
13 Director of Information Technology ... Mr. Brent GRABER
26 Dir of Communications/Marketing ... Ms. Melissa TROYER

Anderson University (G)

1100 E Fifth Street, Anderson IN 46012-3495
County: Madison FICE Identification: 001785
Unit ID: 150066
Telephone: (765) 649-9071 Carnegie Class: Masters/M
FAX Number: (765) 641-3851 Calendar System: Semester
URL: www.anderson.edu
Established: 1917 Annual Undergrad Tuition & Fees: $32,100
Enrollment: 1,406 Coed
Affiliation or Control: Church Of God IRS Status: 501(c)3
Highest Offering: Doctorate
Accreditation: **HLC**, ACBSP, #CAATE, CAEP, MUS, NURSE, SW, THEOL

01 President ... Mr. John PISTOLE
05 Provost ... Dr. Joel SHROCK
10 Interim Vice President Finance ... Mr. Daniel COURTNEY
111 Vice President for Advancement ... Ms. Jennifer HUNT
84 VP Enrollment & Marketing ... Ms. Heather KIM
73 Dean Sch of Theology/Christian Min ... Dr. Nathan WILLOWBY
50 Dean Falls School of Business ... Dr. Michael COLLETTE
79 Assoc Prov/Dn Humanities/Behav Sci ... Dr. Elizabeth IMAFUJI
64 Dean School Music/Theatre & Dance ... Dr. Jeffrey WRIGHT
66 Dean Sch Nursing & Kinesiology ... Dr. Lynn SCHMIDT
54 School of Science & Engineering ... Dr. Chad WALLACE
42 Campus Pastor ... Rev. Joshua TANDY
32 Asst Provost/Dean of Students ... Mr. Scott CAGNET
06 University Registrar ... Mr. Arthur LEAK
08 Director of Libraries ... Dr. Janet BREWER
07 Director of Admissions ... Ms. Sarah ROWE
21 Assistant Treasurer/Controller ... Mrs. Suahil HOUSHOLDER
36 Center for Career & Calling ... Ms. Leanne TORRES
13 Director of Info Technology Svcs ... Mr. Michael TUCKER
37 Student Financial Services ... Mrs. Christina MAGGART
15 Director of Work Life Engagement ... Mr. Tim STATES
19 Director Police & Security Services ... Mr. Rick GARRETT
40 Bookstore Manager ... Mr. Dustin MARTIN
41 Athletic Director ... Ms. Marcie TAYLOR
38 Director Counseling Services ... Ms. Christal HELVERING
29 Director of Alumni Relations ... Mr. Trent PALMER
109 Manager Business & Auxiliary Svcs ... Mrs. Whitney JIMENEZ
04 Executive Asst to the President ... Mrs. Ronda REEMER
104 Director Study Abroad ... Vacant
108 Director Institutional Assessment ... Dr. Jaye ROGERS
39 Student Housing Coordinator ... Ms. Stacey CARPENTER
09 Director of Institutional Research ... Ms. Kim WOLFE
100 Special Assistant to the President ... Mr. Dan COURTNEY
105 Web Editor & Content Writer ... Mr. Michael BAKER
106 Asst Dir ITS/Instr Resource Center ... Ms. Jodie REMINDER
26 Director of Marketing ... Ms. Mischon HART
28 Director Cultural Resource Center ... Mr. Brian MARTIN
30 Executive Director of Development ... Mr. Brent BAKER
44 Associate Director Annual Giving ... Mrs. Elyse CROMER
53 Director Teacher Education ... Dr. Katy SAMPLE

Ball State University (H)

2000 W. University Avenue, Muncie IN 47306-1099
County: Delaware FICE Identification: 001786
Unit ID: 150136
Telephone: (765) 285-5555 Carnegie Class: DU-Higher
FAX Number: (765) 285-1461 Calendar System: Semester
URL: www.bsu.edu
Established: 1918 Annual Undergrad Tuition & Fees (In-State): $10,144
Enrollment: 21,597 Coed
Affiliation or Control: State IRS Status: 501(c)3
Highest Offering: Doctorate
Accreditation: **HLC**, ART, #AUD, CAATE, CACREP, CAEP, CEA, CIDA, COARC, CONST, COPSY, DANCE, DIETD, DIETI, IPSY, JOUR, LSAR, MUS, NURSE, PLNG, RAD, SCPSY, SP, SW, THEA

01 President ... Mr. Geoffrey S. MEARNS
05 Provost/EVP Academic Affairs ... Dr. Susana RIVERA-MILLS
10 VP Business Affairs & Treasurer ... Mr. Alan FINN
84 VP Enrollment Mgmt & Planning ... Ms. Paula LUFF
43 VP & General Counsel ... Ms. Sali K. FALLING
13 VP for IT & Chief Information Ofcr ... Mr. Loren MALM
26 VP for Marketing and Comm ... Ms. Kathy M. WOLF
86 VP Government Relations ... Ms. Becca RICE
102 President and CEO BSU Foundation ... Ms. Jean K. CROSBY
41 Director Intercollegiate Athletics ... Ms. Beth GOETZ
20 Vice Provost for AA/Univ College ... Dr. Kecia MCBRIDE
28 AVP for Inclusive Excellence ... Dr. Marsha MCGRIFF

50 Assoc Prov Entrepreneurial Learning ... Ms. Jennifer BLACKMER
09 AVP Inst Research & Decision Sppt ... Dr. Rob SMITH
39 AVP Student Affairs/Dir of Housing ... Dr. Alan HARGRAVE
18 Assoc VP Facilities Planning/Mgmt ... Mr. James LOWE
109 Assoc VP Business/Auxiliary Svcs ... Ms. Julie HOPWOOD
07 AVP Enrollment/Exec Dir of Admiss ... Mr. Christopher T. MUNCHEL
08 Dean University Libraries ... Mr. Matthew SHAW
48 Dean Architecture/Planning ... Mr. David FERGUSON
79 Dean Col of Science/Humanities ... Dr. Maureen MCCARTHY
50 Dean Miller College of Business ... Dr. Steve FERRIS
53 Dean of Teachers College ... Dr. Anand MARRI
57 Dean College of Fine Arts ... Dr. Seth BECKMAN
58 Dean of Graduate School ... Dr. Adam R. BEACH
60 Dean Col of Comm/Info/Media ... Dr. Paaige K. TURNER
76 Dean College of Health ... Dr. Scott RUTLEDGE
92 Dean of Honors College ... Dr. John EMERT
88 Chief Entrepreneurship Officer ... Dr. Michael GOLDSBY
06 Interim Registrar ... Ms. Erin MASON
37 Director Scholarships/Financial Aid ... Dr. John MCPHERSON
15 Director of Human Resources Svcs ... Ms. Kate STOSS
19 Director Public Safety ... Mr. James DUCKHAM
25 Director of Sponsored Projects Admn ... Ms. Liz HANEY
44 Senior Director Annual Giving ... Ms. Amanda HOLMQUIST
30 VP of Development ... Mr. Ray ALLEN
22 Assoc Dean of Students/Title IX ... Ms. Katie SLABAUGH
106 Asst Provost for Online Learning ... Ms. Trudi WEYERMANN
38 Director Counseling/Health Services ... Dr. Bill BETTS
88 Dir Unified Technology Support ... Vacant
36 AVP & Exec Dir Career Center ... Mr. Jim MCATEE
96 Director of Purchasing Services ... Mr. Roger HASSENZAHL
24 Dir of University Media Services ... Mr. Allen GORDON
88 Dir of Economic Development Policy ... Mr. David R. TERRELL
31 AVP for Community Engagement ... Ms. Delaina BOYD
104 Exec Dir International Programs ... Ms. Laurie COX
04 Exec Dir of Presidential Operations ... Ms. Stephanie K. ARRINGTON
101 Exec Asst to the Board of Trustees ... Ms. Mindy KEAR
45 Chief Strategy Officer ... Ms. Sue HODGES MOORE

Bethany Theological Seminary (A)

615 National Road W, Richmond IN 47374-4019

County: Wayne FICE Identification: 001637
Unit ID: 143233
Telephone: (800) 287-8822 Carnegie Class: Spec-4-yr-Faith
FAX Number: (765) 983-1840 Calendar System: Semester
URL: www.bethanyseminary.edu
Established: 1905 Annual Graduate Tuition & Fees: N/A
Enrollment: 71 Coed
Affiliation or Control: Church Of The Brethren IRS Status: 501(c)3
Highest Offering: Master's; No Undergraduates
Accreditation: HLC, THEOL

01 President ... RevDr. Jeffrey W. CARTER
05 Academic Dean ... Dr. Steven J. SCHWEITZER
10 Exec Dir of Finance/Administration ... Mrs. Tammy S. GLENN
30 Exec Dir Institutional Advancement ... Vacant
20 Director of Academic Services ... Ms. April VANLONDEN
26 Director Marketing/Communications ... Mr. Jonathan GRAHAM
32 Director Student Development ... Ms. Karen DUHAI
12 Director Brethren Academy ... Mrs. Janet L. OBER LAMBERT
88 Dir Peace/Cross Cultural Studies ... Mr. Scott HOLLAND
88 Director of the MA Program ... Mrs. Denise KETTERING-LANE
07 Exec Dir of Admissions/Student Svcs ... Mrs. Lori M. CURRENT

Bethel University (B)

1001 Bethel Circle, Mishawaka IN 46545-5509

County: Saint Joseph FICE Identification: 001787
Unit ID: 150145
Telephone: (574) 807-7000 Carnegie Class: Masters/S
FAX Number: (574) 807-7484 Calendar System: Semester
URL: www.betheluniversity.edu
Established: 1947 Annual Undergrad Tuition & Fees: $29,790
Enrollment: 1,362 Coed
Affiliation or Control: Missionary Church IRS Status: 501(c)3
Highest Offering: Master's
Accreditation: HLC, ADNUR, CAEPN, MUS, NUR

01 President ... Dr. Barbara K. BELLEFEUILLE
05 VP for Academic Services ... Dr. Bradley D. SMITH
111 VP for Advancement ... Mr. Brent LAVIGNE
10 VP for Finance & Administration ... Mr. Jerry WHITE
32 VP for Student Development ... Dr. Shawn M. HOLTGREN
84 VP for Enrollment Management ... Dr. Terry ELAM
13 Senior Director of IT ... Ms. Patti J. FISHER
66 Dean of Nursing ... Dr. Deborah GILLUM
49 Dean of Arts & Sciences ... Dr. Janna MCLEAN
83 Dean of Humanities/Social Sciences ... Dr. Robby PRENKERT
35 Dean of Students ... Mrs. Julie BEAM
06 Registrar ... Mrs. Jeanne E. FOX
121 Director of Student Success ... Mrs. Rachel A. KENNEDY
36 Dir Career Devel/Global Engagement ... Mr. Tyler GRANT
37 Director Financial Aid ... Mrs. Cindi M. PEDERSEN
26 Director Marketing & Communication ... Mrs. Lissa DIAZ
41 Director Athletics ... Mr. Tony NATALI
08 Director Library Services ... Mr. Mark J. ROOT
88 Director Teacher Certification ... Mrs. Kimberly J. MEYER
09 Director Institutional Research ... Dr. Raymond E. WHITEMAN
19 Director Campus Safety ... Mr. Paul E. NEEL
85 Director International Students ... Mrs. Susan A. MATTESON
91 Director Administrative Computing ... Mrs. Donna FAUDREE
29 Director Alumni Services ... Mrs. Emily S. SHERWOOD
07 Director of Admission ... Mrs. Stephanie HOCHSTETLER
15 Director Human Resources ... Mrs. Angela PIAZZA
04 Administrative Asst to President ... Mrs. Miriam WERTZ
104 Director Global & Comm Engagement ... Mr. Tyler C. GRANT
108 Director Institutional Assessment ... Dr. Raymond E. WHITEMAN
18 Chief Facilities/Phys Plant Ofcr ... Mr. Joe ZAPPIA

Butler University (C)

4600 Sunset Avenue, Indianapolis IN 46208-3443

County: Marion FICE Identification: 001788
Unit ID: 150163
Telephone: (317) 940-8000 Carnegie Class: Masters/L
FAX Number: (317) 940-9930 Calendar System: Semester
URL: www.butler.edu
Established: 1855 Annual Undergrad Tuition & Fees: $43,400
Enrollment: 5,544 Coed
Affiliation or Control: Independent Non-Profit IRS Status: 501(c)3
Highest Offering: Doctorate
Accreditation: HLC, ARCPA, CACREP, CAEP, DANCE, IPSY, MUS, PHAR, THEA

01 President ... Mr. James M. DANKO
05 Provost/VP Academic Affairs ... Dr. Kathryn MORRIS
10 Vice Pres of Finance/Administration ... Mr. Bruce E. ARICK
111 VP University Advancement ... Mr. Jonathan PURVIS
32 Vice President of Student Affairs ... Dr. Frank E. ROSS, III
41 VP & Director of Athletics ... Mr. Barry S. COLLIER
84 VP of Enrollment Management ... Ms. Lori GREENE
45 VP of Strategy and Innovation ... Ms. Melissa BECKWITH
43 General Counsel ... Ms. Claire AIGOTTI
57 Dean Jordan College Fine Arts ... Dr. Michelle JARVIS
50 Interim Dean School of Business ... Ms. Hilary BUTTRICK
49 Dean Liberal Arts & Science ... Dr. Jay R. HOWARD
53 Dean College of Education ... Dr. Brooke KANDEL-CISCO
67 Dean Pharmacy & Health Sciences ... Dr. Robert P. SOLTIS
60 Dean College of Communication ... Dr. Jay R. HOWARD
08 Dean of Libraries ... Dr. Julie L. MILLER
35 Int Dean Student Services ... Ms. Martha DZIWLIK
38 Asst Dean & Director Counseling Ctr ... Dr. Keith B. MAGNUS
18 AVP of Facilities ... Mr. Doug MORRIS
112 Exec Dir Major Gifts/Planned Giving ... Mr. Michael EIKENBERRY
15 Int Dir of Human Resources ... Mr. Mark OSHIER
26 AVP Marketing & Communication ... Ms. Stephanie JUDGE CRIPE
88 Interim Director Butler Arts Center ... Mr. Aaron HURT
114 Executive Budget Director ... Mr. Robert J. MARCUS
37 Director Financial Aid ... Ms. Melissa J. SMURDON
88 Dir University Events ... Ms. Beth A. ALEXANDER
39 Director Residence Life ... Ms. Karla K. CUNNINGHAM
09 Director Institutional Research ... Ms. Amia FOSTON
85 Director Global Education ... Ms. Jill MCKINNEY
36 Sr Director Career Services ... Mr. Gary R. BEAULIEU
27 Director of Creative Services ... Ms. Nancy LYZUN
28 Exec Dir Equity/Diversity/Inclusion ... Mr. Danny KIBBLE
86 Director of External Relations ... Mr. Michael KALTENMARK
07 Director of Admission ... Mr. Jerome DUEWEKE
06 Registrar ... Ms. Michele NEARY
13 AVP IT/Chief Information Officer ... Mr. Peter WILLIAMS
21 Controller ... Ms. Susan M. WESTERMEYER
40 Manager Bookstore ... Ms. Janine L. FRAINIER
96 Manager of Purchasing ... Ms. Shelly S. RABIDEAU

Calumet College of Saint Joseph (D)

2400 New York Avenue, Whiting IN 46394-2195

County: Lake FICE Identification: 001834
Unit ID: 150172
Telephone: (219) 473-7770 Carnegie Class: Masters/S
FAX Number: (219) 473-4259 Calendar System: Semester
URL: www.ccsj.edu
Established: 1951 Annual Undergrad Tuition & Fees: $20,470
Enrollment: 694 Coed
Affiliation or Control: Roman Catholic IRS Status: 501(c)3
Highest Offering: Master's
Accreditation: HLC

01 President ... Dr. Amy MCCORMACK
84 Sr Vice President for Enrollment ... Mr. Johnny CRAIG
05 Vice President Academic Affairs ... Dr. Derek SHOUBA
111 Dir of Institutional Advancement ... Ms. Ester DIAZ
10 VP Business & Finance ... Ms. Lynn MISKUS
32 VP Student Engagement & Retention ... Dr. Dionne JONES-MALONE
06 Registrar ... Ms. Diana FRANCIS
08 Director Instructional Support Svcs ... Dr. Keith WEROSH
09 Institutional Researcher ... Mr. Darren HENDERSON
26 Dir of Communications & PR ... Ms. Linda GAJEWSKI
41 Athletic Director ... Mr. Michael AVERY
37 Dir Financial Aid/Business Ofc Ops ... Mr. Chris ARTIM
13 Director of Computer Services ... Mr. Kevin KRIEPS
121 Director of Academic Advising ... Mrs. Sally LOBO-TORRES
07 Director of Enrollment Management ... Mr. Andy MARKS

Caris College (E)

2780 Jefferson Centre Way, Ste 103, Jeffersonville IN 47130

County: Clark Identification: 667314
Telephone: (812) 258-9510 Carnegie Class: Not Classified
FAX Number: N/A Calendar System: Quarter
URL: www.cariscollege.edu
Established: 2015 Annual Undergrad Tuition & Fees: N/A
Enrollment: N/A Coed
Affiliation or Control: Proprietary IRS Status: Proprietary
Highest Offering: Associate Degree
Accreditation: ABHES, DMS

01 President & CEO ... Mr. Bruce KEPLEY
11 Campus Director ... Ms. Brittany COTTONER
05 Director of Education ... Ms. Mandy HICKS
06 Registrar/Office Manager ... Ms. Brittany COFFEY
37 Director Financial Aid ... Ms. Heather LISCO
07 Director of Admissions ... Vacant

Chamberlain University-Indianapolis Campus (F)

9100 Keystone Crossing, Suite 300, Indianapolis IN 46240

Telephone: (317) 816-7335 Identification: 770503
Accreditation: &HLC, NURSE

Christian Theological Seminary (G)

1000 W. 42nd Street, Indianapolis IN 46208-3301

County: Marion FICE Identification: 001789
Unit ID: 150215
Telephone: (317) 924-1331 Carnegie Class: Spec-4-yr-Faith
FAX Number: (317) 923-1961 Calendar System: Semester
URL: www.cts.edu
Established: 1925 Annual Graduate Tuition & Fees: N/A
Enrollment: 156 Coed
Affiliation or Control: Christian Church (Disciples Of Christ) IRS Status: 501(c)3
Highest Offering: Doctorate; No Undergraduates
Accreditation: HLC, MFCD, THEOL

01 President ... Dr. David M. MELLOTT
05 Vice Pres of Academics ... Dr. Leah GUNNING-FRANCIS
10 Vice President Finance and Business ... Mr. Mitchell LANNERT
30 Vice President Development ... Ms. Kristin CHAMPA
32 Dean of Students ... Rev. Mary HARRIS
04 Executive Administrator ... Ms. Sarah EVANS
21 Director of Business Affairs ... Mr. Scott SIMS
08 Director of Library ... Dr. Scott SEAY
06 Registrar ... Mr. Matt SCHLIMGEN
75 Director of Field Education ... Rev. Martin WRIGHT
37 Director of Student Financial Aid ... Mr. Robert FISHER
26 Director of Communications ... Rev. Nathan WILSON
13 Chief Information Tech Officer ... Mr. Jesse JOHNSON

College of Court Reporting, Inc. (H)

455 West Lincolnway, Valparaiso IN 46385

County: Lake FICE Identification: 026158
Unit ID: 150251
Telephone: (866) 294-3974 Carnegie Class: Spec 2-yr-Other
FAX Number: (219) 942-1631 Calendar System: Semester
URL: www.ccr.edu
Established: 1984 Annual Undergrad Tuition & Fees: $9,950
Enrollment: 123 Coed
Affiliation or Control: Proprietary IRS Status: Proprietary
Highest Offering: Associate Degree
Accreditation: DEAC

01 President ... Mr. Jeff T. MOODY
03 Executive Director ... Mr. Jay VETTICKAL
05 Director of Education ... Ms. Kay MOODY
07 Director of Admissions ... Ms. Nicky M. RODRIQUEZ
37 Director of Financial Aid ... Ms. Alice LEONARD
32 Director of Student Services ... Ms. Mindi BILLINGS

Concordia Theological Seminary (I)

6600 N Clinton Street, Fort Wayne IN 46825-4996

County: Allen FICE Identification: 020876
Unit ID: 150288
Telephone: (260) 452-2100 Carnegie Class: Spec-4-yr-Faith
FAX Number: (260) 452-2121 Calendar System: Quarter
URL: www.ctsfw.edu
Established: 1846 Annual Graduate Tuition & Fees: N/A
Enrollment: 295 Male
Affiliation or Control: Lutheran Church - Missouri Synod IRS Status: 501(c)3
Highest Offering: Doctorate; No Undergraduates
Accreditation: HLC, THEOL

01 President ... Dr. Lawrence R. RAST
05 Academic Dean ... Dr. Charles A. GIESCHEN
36 Chairman Pastoral Ministry/ Missions ... Dr. Carl C. FICKENSCHER, II
32 Dean of Students ... Rev. Gary ZIEROTH
11 Vice President of Operations ... Mr. Lance HOFFMAN
06 Registrar ... Mrs. Barbara A. WEGMAN
07 Director of Admissions ... Rev. Matthew WIETFELDT
08 Head Librarian ... Prof. Robert V. ROETHEMEYER

DePauw University (J)

313 S Locust Street, Greencastle IN 46135-1772

County: Putnam FICE Identification: 001792
Unit ID: 150400
Telephone: (765) 658-4800 Carnegie Class: Bac-A&S
FAX Number: (765) 658-4177 Calendar System: Semester
URL: www.depauw.edu
Established: 1837 Annual Undergrad Tuition & Fees: $52,710
Enrollment: 1,752 Coed
Affiliation or Control: United Methodist IRS Status: 501(c)3
Highest Offering: Baccalaureate

Accreditation: HLC, MUS

01 President .... Dr. Lori WHITE
04 Executive Assistant to President .... Ms. Elizabeth DEMMINGS
05 VP for Academic Affairs .... Dr. David BERQUE
32 VP Student Affs/Dean of Students .... Mr. Alan P. HILL
10 VP for Finance/Administration .... Mr. Bob LEONARD
84 VP for Enrollment Management .... Ms. Mary Beth PETRIE
30 VP Development/Alumni Engagement .... Ms. Annie S. CUNNINGHAM
28 Exec Dir Ctr Diversity/Inclusion .... Dr. Holbrook HANKINSON
20 Dean of the Faculty .... Dr. Bridget L. GOURLEY
78 Interim Dean Experiential Learning .... Dr. Holbrook HANKINSON
64 Dean of the School of Music .... Ms. Kay HOKE
13 Chief Information Officer .... Ms. Carol L. SMITH
35 Dean of Campus Life .... Mr. Dorian SHAGER
06 Registrar .... Dr. LaTonya BRANHAM
15 Int Exec Dir of Human Resources .... Ms. Angela D. NALLY
37 Director of Financial Aid .... Ms. Jennie S. COY
41 Director of Athletics .... Ms. Stevie BAKER-WATSON
21 Assoc VP for Finance .... Mr. Travis W. LINNEWEBER
08 Director of Libraries .... Mr. Rick E. PROVINE
44 Director of Annual Giving .... Ms. Rosalie BLANKENSHIP
19 Director of Public Safety .... Ms. Charlene P. SHREWSBURY
07 Int Director of Admission .... Mr. Orlando RAMIREZ
18 Assoc VP for Facilities .... Mr. Warren WHITESELL
27 Director of Media Relations .... Ms. Mary DIETER
09 Director of Institutional Research .... Dr. William M. TOBIN
38 Director of Student Counseling .... Dr. Trevor YUHAS
39 Assistant Director of Housing .... Ms. Nicci COLLISI
36 Director Student Placement .... Ms. Erin A. MAHONEY
26 VP of Communications and Marketing .... Ms. Deedie DOWDLE
105 Director Web Services .... Ms. Andrea ADAMCHAK
14 Associate CIO .... Mr. Adam HUGHES
100 Chief of Staff .... Ms. Sarah STEINKAMP
104 Director Study Abroad .... Ms. Amanda M. BROOKINS
29 Exec Director Alumni Engagement .... Ms. Leslie SMITH

Earlham College and Earlham School of Religion (A)

801 National Road W, Richmond IN 47374-4095

County: Wayne | FICE Identification: 001793 | Unit ID: 150455

Telephone: (765) 983-1200 | Carnegie Class: Bac-A&S

FAX Number: (765) 983-1304 | Calendar System: Semester

URL: www.earlham.edu

Established: 1847 | Annual Undergrad Tuition & Fees: $48,091

Enrollment: 815 | Coed

Affiliation or Control: Friends | IRS Status: 501(c)3

Highest Offering: Master's

Accreditation: HLC, THEOL

01 President .... Anne HOUTMAN
05 Vice President Academic Affairs .... Mike DEIBEL
10 Vice President Business Affairs .... Stacy L. DAVIDSON
73 Interim Dean School of Religion .... Len CLARK
84 VP of Enrollment .... David HAWSEY
32 Interim VP/Dean of Student Life .... Bonita WASHINGTON-LACY
20 Associate VP Academic Affairs .... Vacant
20 Associate Academic Dean .... James LOGAN
111 Assoc VP for Institutional Advance .... Vacant
29 Director of Alumni Relations .... Alyssa TEGELER
21 Controller .... Carrie ERVIN
06 Interim Registrar .... Robert HENSLEY
121 Director Academic Enrichment Svcs .... Penny YAN
88 Admissions School of Religion .... Julie DISHMAM
41 Interim Athletic Director .... Steve SAKOSITS
13 Director of Computing Services .... Vacant
37 Director of Financial Aid .... Katherine GOTTSCHALK
15 Director of Human Resources/Ops .... Vacant
85 Director of International Programs .... Roger ADKINS
26 Director Marketing & Communications .... Kristen LAINSBURY
27 Director of Media Relations .... Brian ZIMMERMAN
19 Director of Public Safety .... Christopher LITTLE
08 Interim Director of Library .... Amy BRYANT
28 Director of Diversity & Inclusion .... Vacant
04 Executive Assistant .... Alisha TRIANA
39 Director Residence Life .... Shane PETERS
09 Director of Institutional Research .... Vacant
38 Director Student Counseling .... Jessica SANFORD
102 Dir Foundation/Corporate Relations .... Sara PAULE
104 Director Study Abroad .... Vacant
105 Director Web Services .... Ryan WOOLEY
44 Director Annual Giving .... Vacant
07 Director of Admissions .... Yuliya CORMIER

Faith Bible Seminary (B)

2000 Elmwood Ave, Lafayette IN 47904

County: Tippecanoe | Identification: 667250

Telephone: (765) 448-1986 | Carnegie Class: Not Classified

FAX Number: (765) 448-2985 | Calendar System: Semester

URL: www.faithlafayette.org/seminary

Established: 2005 | Annual Graduate Tuition & Fees: N/A

Enrollment: N/A | Coed

Affiliation or Control: Independent Non-Profit | IRS Status: 501(c)3

Highest Offering: Master's; No Undergraduates

Accreditation: BI

01 President .... Dr. Brent AUCOIN
05 Academic Dean .... Dr. Rob GREEN
84 Dean of Enrollment Management .... Mr. Kirk FATOOL

Fortis College (C)

9001 N Wesleyan Road Suite 101, Indianapolis IN 46268

Telephone: (317) 808-4800 | Identification: 770574

Accreditation: ACCSC, MAAB

† Branch campus of Fortis College, Centreville, OH.

Franklin College of Indiana (D)

101 Branigin Boulevard, Franklin IN 46131-2623

County: Johnson | FICE Identification: 001798 | Unit ID: 150604

Telephone: (317) 738-8000 | Carnegie Class: Bac-A&S

FAX Number: (317) 738-8013 | Calendar System: 4/1/4

URL: www.franklincollege.edu

Established: 1834 | Annual Undergrad Tuition & Fees: $33,954

Enrollment: 994 | Coed

Affiliation or Control: American Baptist | IRS Status: 501(c)3

Highest Offering: Master's

Accreditation: HLC, #ARCPA, CAATE

01 President .... Mr. Kerry N. PRATHER
04 Assistant to the President .... Ms. Janet D. SCHANTZ
10 Vice President and CFO .... Vacant
05 Acting VP Acad Affs/Dean of College .... Dr. Kristin C. FLORA
84 VP for Enrollment & Marketing .... Mr. Thandabantu B. MACEO
30 VP for Development/Alumni Engage .... Mrs. Dana CUMMINGS
20 Acting AVP for Academic Affairs .... Vacant
32 VP for Student Dev/Dean of Students .... Dr. Andrew B. JONES
29 Dir Alumni Engage/Campus Prtnrshps .... Ms. Emily S. WOOD
06 Registrar .... Ms. Lisa MAHAN
18 AVP of Physical Facilities .... Mr. Thomas PATZ
38 Director of Counseling Center .... Mrs. Sara KINDER
121 Dean Student Success/Retention .... Dr. Andrew B. JONES
46 Director of Academic Partnerships .... Ms. Betsy SCHMIDT
110 Sr Dir Development/Planned Giving .... Mrs. Nora BREMS
37 Director of Financial Aid .... Mr. James VINCENT-DUNN
42 Director of Religious Life/ Chaplain .... Rev. Hannah ADAMS INGRAM
41 Director of Athletics .... Mr. Andrew HENDRICKS
13 Acting Dir of Info Tech Svcs .... Mr. Jason MCHENRY
36 Director Career Development .... Mr. Kirk J. BIXLER
88 Dir Professional Dev/Employer Rels .... Dr. Jeremy VAN ANDEL
104 Dir Office of Global Education .... Ms. Jennifer CATALDI
109 General Manager Parkhurst Dining .... Mr. Rob COYNE
44 AVP for Alumni Engage/Annual Giving .... Ms. Lee Ann JOURDAN
07 Director of Admissions .... Mr. Ryan MCCLARNON
27 Director of Communications .... Ms. Deidra BAUMGARDNER
26 Director of Marketing .... Ms. Ann SMITH
08 Director of Library Services .... Ms. Denise SHOREY
19 Dir of Security/Title IX Coord .... Mr. Steve LEONARD
105 Website Administrator .... Ms. Ann SMITH
15 Director of Human Resources .... Ms. June HENDERSON
22 Asst Vice Pres Physical Facilities .... Mr. Thomas PATZ
40 Bookstore Manager .... Mr. Matthew NEAU
21 Business Office Manager .... Mr. Bradley JONES
23 Coordinator Student Health Center .... Ms. Tracey LUNSFORD
28 Director of Diversity & Inclusion .... Ms. Maegan POLLONAIS
50 Head Business/Computing/Math Div .... Dr. Justin GASH
53 Head Education Division .... Dr. Amy SCHULZ
79 Head Humanities Division .... Dr. Susan CRISAFULLI
60 Head Journalism Division .... Mr. Joel CRAMER
65 Head Natural Sciences Division .... Dr. Benjamin O'NEAL
83 Head Social Sciences Division .... Dr. Jason JIMERSON
57 Head Fine Arts Division .... Dr. Svetlana RAKIC

Goshen College (E)

1700 S Main Street, Goshen IN 46526-4794

County: Elkhart | FICE Identification: 001799 | Unit ID: 150668

Telephone: (574) 535-7000 | Carnegie Class: Bac-Diverse

FAX Number: (574) 535-7060 | Calendar System: Semester

URL: www.goshen.edu

Established: 1894 | Annual Undergrad Tuition & Fees: $35,230

Enrollment: 899 | Coed

Affiliation or Control: Mennonite Church | IRS Status: 501(c)3

Highest Offering: Doctorate

Accreditation: HLC, CAEP, NURSE, SW

01 President .... Dr. Rebecca J. STOLTZFUS
05 VP Academic Affairs/Academic Dean .... Dr. Ann VENDRELY
10 Vice President for Finance .... Mr. Thomas STUCKEY
111 VP for Advancement .... Mr. Todd A. YODER
84 VP for Enroll Management/ Marketing .... Ms. Dominique BURGUNDER-JOHNSON
26 VP Communications & People Strategy .... Ms. Jodi BEYELER
32 VP for Student Life .... Mr. Gilberto PEREZ, JR.
66 Director of Undergraduate Nursing .... Ms. Jewel YODER
66 Director of Graduate Nursing .... Dr. Ruth STOLTZFUS
70 Director of Social Work .... Dr. Jeanne M. LIECHTY
53 Director of Elementary Teacher Educ .... Dr. Kathryn MEYER REIMER
08 Library Director .... Mr. Fritz HARTMAN
82 Director of International Education ...... Dr. Jan BENDER SHETLER
53 Director of Secondary Education .... Ms. Suzanne EHST
13 Director of Information Tech Svcs .... Ms. Patricia GOODMAN
09 Director of Institutional Research .... Mr. Justin HEINZEKEHR
06 Registrar .... Ms. Jan KAUFFMAN
37 Director Student Financial Aid .... Mr. Stephen WOLMA
29 Director of Alumni/Parent Relations .... Mr. Dan LIECHTY
28 Dir Diversity/Equity & Inclusion .... Rev. LaKendra HARDWARE
42 Campus Minister .... Ms. Joanne GALLARDO
36 Director of Career Services .... Mr. David KENDALL
18 Director of Facilities .... Ms. Cynthia GOOD KAUFMANN
15 Director of Human Resources .... Ms. Delores JOHNSON
58 Director Adult & Graduate Studies .... Dr. Duane STOLTZFUS
19 Director Campus Safety & Housing .... Mr. Chad COLEMAN
04 Exec Assistant to the President .... Ms. Kathleen YODER
108 Director Institutional Assessment .... Mr. Justin HEINZEKEHR
41 Athletic Director .... Ms. Erica ALBERTIN
38 Director Student Counseling .... Vacant
07 Director of Undergraduate Admission .... Mr. Steve WOLMA

Grace College and Seminary (F)

200 Seminary Drive, Winona Lake IN 46590-1294

County: Kosciusko | FICE Identification: 001800 | Unit ID: 150677

Telephone: (574) 372-5100 | Carnegie Class: Masters/M

FAX Number: (574) 372-5139 | Calendar System: Semester

URL: www.grace.edu

Established: 1937 | Annual Undergrad Tuition & Fees: $27,432

Enrollment: 1,901 | Coed

Affiliation or Control: | IRS Status: 501(c)3

Highest Offering: Doctorate

Accreditation: HLC, CACREP, CAEPN, THEOL

01 President .... Dr. William J. KATIP
04 Exec Assistant to the President .... Mrs. Sarah E. PRATER
73 VP & Dean Seminary & School of Min .... Dr. Frederick CARDOZA, II
111 VP Advancement and Marketing .... Dr. Andrew R. FLAMM
10 VP of Financial Affairs/CFO .... Mr. Doug BAUMGARDNER
11 VP Administration & Compliance .... Dr. Carrie A. YOCUM
84 Associate VP Enrollment Management .... Dr. Mark A. POHL
11 Chief Operations Officer .... Mr. Paul G. BLAIR
32 Associate VP Student Affairs .... Mr. Aaron T. CRABTREE
49 Dean of School of Arts & Sciences .... Dr. Mark M. NORRIS
83 Dean of Sch of Behavioral Science .... Dr. Thomas J. EDGINGTON
50 Dean of School of Business .... Dr. Jeffrey K. FAWCETT
53 Dean of School of Education .... Dr. Laurinda A. OWEN
106 Dean School of Prof/Online Ed .... Dr. Timothy J. ZIEBARTH
121 Dean of Academic Engagement/ Success .... Mrs. Jacqueline S. SCHRAM
42 Dean of Chapel .... Mr. Brent T. MENCARELLI
06 Registrar .... Mr. Timothy J. ZIEBARTH
08 Dir Library Services .... Mrs. Tonya L. FAWCETT
13 Dir Information Technology .... Mr. Donald W. FLUKE
23 Dir Student Health & Counseling .... Dr. Debra S. MUSSER
37 Dir Student Financial Aid .... Mrs. Charlette R. SAUDERS
15 Chief Human Resource Officer .... Mr. Norman BAKHIT
26 Dir of Marketing .... Mr. Matthew R. METZGER
18 Director Physical Plant .... Mr. Randy KLEINHANS
19 Director Security/Safety .... Mr. Glenn A. GOLDSMITH
29 Director Alumni Engagement .... Mr. Dennis L. DUNCAN
41 Director of Athletics .... Mr. Chad C. BRISCOE
36 Director Career Connections .... Mrs. Denise A. TERRY
100 Chief of Staff .... Dr. Carrie A. YOCUM
07 Director of Admissions .... Dr. Mark POHL
30 Director of Development .... Mr. Stephen D. GERBER
39 Director Residence Life .... Mrs. Emily J. BRENNEMAN

Hanover College (G)

517 Ball Drive, Hanover IN 47243

County: Jefferson | FICE Identification: 001801 | Unit ID: 150756

Telephone: (812) 866-7000 | Carnegie Class: Bac-A&S

FAX Number: (812) 866-2164 | Calendar System: Other

URL: www.hanover.edu

Established: 1827 | Annual Undergrad Tuition & Fees: $39,650

Enrollment: 1,028 | Coed

Affiliation or Control: Presbyterian Church (U.S.A.) | IRS Status: 501(c)3

Highest Offering: Doctorate

Accreditation: HLC, CAEPN, @PTA

01 President .... Dr. Lake LAMBERT, III
100 Chief of Staff/Exec Asst to Pres .... Shelley PREOCANIN
05 Provost/VP Academic Affairs .... Dr. Carey ADAMS
10 Vice President Business Affairs .... Morris VINCE
41 Vice President of Athletics .... Lynn HALL
111 Vice President College Advancement .... Melba RODRIGUEZ
84 Vice Pres Marketing/Enrollment .... Peter ASHLEY
32 Vice President/Dean Student Life .... Dr. Dewain LEE
35 Associate Dean of Student Outcomes ..... Katy LOWE-SCHNEIDER
39 Assoc Dean Students Residence Life .... Lindsay FAULSTICK
06 Registrar .... Dr. Ken PRINCE
07 Exec Director of Admissions .... Rachel SCHMIDTKE
36 Exec Director Levett Career Center .... Jenny MOSS
13 Chief Technology Officer .... Kevin STORMER
42 Chaplain .... Catherine KNOTT
29 Director of Alumni Engagement .... Christy HUGHES
19 Director of Campus Safety .... Jim HICKERSON
08 Director of Duggan Library .... Kelly JOYCE
37 Assoc Director of Financial Aid .... Jennifer SHELLEY
23 Director of Health Services .... Christy OWNBEY
15 Director of Human Resources .... Heather BUHR
18 Director of Physical Plant .... Kevin BROWN
104 Director of Study Abroad .... Uschi APPELT
38 Director of Student Counseling .... Catherine LE SAUX
21 Controller .... Heather CHISM
88 Special Asst to the President .... Kay STOKES

Holy Cross College (A)

PO Box 308, Notre Dame IN 46556-0308
County: Saint Joseph FICE Identification: 007263
Unit ID: 150774
Telephone: (574) 239-8400 Carnegie Class: Bac-Diverse
FAX Number: (574) 239-8323 Calendar System: Semester
URL: www.hcc-nd.edu
Established: 1966 Annual Undergrad Tuition & Fees: $33,250
Enrollment: 455 Coed
Affiliation or Control: Roman Catholic IRS Status: 501(c)3
Highest Offering: Baccalaureate
Accreditation: HLC

01 President .... Rev. David TYSON, CSC
05 Interim Provost .... Dr. Michael GRIFFIN
10 Vice President of Finance .... Ms. Monica MARKOVICH
32 Dean & VP for Student Life .... Mr. Andrew POLANIECKI
26 AVP Communications & Development .. Ms. JudeAnne HASTINGS
20 Dean of the College .... Dr. Anthony MONTA
06 Registrar .... Ms. Hiroko HARRISON
07 Director of Admissions .... Ms. Marisa SIMON
38 Director of Student Counseling Svcs .... Mr. Thomas DEHORN
13 Director of Information Technology .... Mr. Douglas BLAIR
08 Director of Library Services .... Ms. Sarah KOLDA
42 Director of Campus Ministry .... Mr. Andrew OUELLETTE
15 Director of Human Resources .... Ms. Gwen DEMAEGD
19 Chief Security Officer .... Mr. Greg RUNNELS
29 Director of Career Development .... Mr. Adam DEBECK
96 Director of Purchasing .... Mr. John PAJAKOWSKI
26 Assoc Dir for Special Events .... Ms. Jodie BADMAN
04 Admin Assistant to the President .... Mrs. Diane WELIHAN
37 Director Student Financial Aid .... Mr. Rick GONSIOREK
41 Athletic Director .... Mr. Tom ROBBINS

Horizon University (B)

7700 Indian Lake Road, Indianapolis IN 46236
County: Marion FICE Identification: 041405
Unit ID: 457226
Telephone: (800) 553-4674 Carnegie Class: Spec-4-yr-Faith
FAX Number: N/A Calendar System: Semester
URL: www.horizonuniversity.edu
Established: 1993 Annual Undergrad Tuition & Fees: $9,300
Enrollment: 42 Coed
Affiliation or Control: Independent Non-Profit IRS Status: 501(c)3
Highest Offering: Master's
Accreditation: BI

01 President .... Dr. Randall DODGE
05 Academic Dean .... Mr. Dave KOSOBUCKI
11 Dean of Administration .... Vacant
10 Chief Financial Officer .... Ms. Debbie MARSHALL
32 Dean of Students .... Mr. Tracy GRAY
26 Dir Marketing/Communications .... Mr. Andrew LOCKERBIE
06 Registrar/Dir Student Financial Aid .... Mrs. Judy SLACK
07 Director of Admissions .... Miss Jacki CURTIS
13 Chief Information Tech Officer .... Mr. Dave LOVELL
19 Director Security/Safety .... Mr. Paul LANGE

Huntington University (C)

2303 College Avenue, Huntington IN 46750-9986
County: Huntington FICE Identification: 001803
Unit ID: 150941
Telephone: (260) 356-6000 Carnegie Class: Masters/S
FAX Number: (260) 359-4086 Calendar System: 4/1/4
URL: www.huntington.edu
Established: 1897 Annual Undergrad Tuition & Fees: $26,846
Enrollment: 1,391 Coed
Affiliation or Control: United Brethren Church IRS Status: 501(c)3
Highest Offering: Doctorate
Accreditation: HLC, CAEP, NURSE, OT, OTA, SW

01 President .... Dr. Sherilyn R. EMBERTON
05 VP Academic Affairs/Dean Faculty .... Dr. Luke S. FETTERS
11 VP/Chief Operating Officer .... Dr. Russ J. DEGITZ
10 Vice Pres Finance & Treasurer .... Mrs. Connie C. BONNER
84 VP Enrollment Mgmt & Marketing .... Mr. Daniel F. SOLMS
111 VP for Advancement .... Dr. Stephen T. WEINGART
32 VP for Student Life .... Dr. Ron L. COFFEY
04 Executive Asst to President .... Ms. Peg DEBOLT
42 VP Spiritual Formation .... Rev. Arthur L. WILSON
58 Dir of Grad & Professional Programs . Ms. Wendy S. SPEAKMAN
36 Dean Student Life/Career Dev .... Ms. Martha J. SMITH
35 Dean of Students .... Mr. Brian R. JAWORSKI
37 Director of Financial Aid .... Ms. Lisa M. MONTANY
06 Registrar .... Ms. Sarah J. HARVEY
08 Director of Library Services .... Ms. Noelle C. KELLER
13 Dir Information/Technology Services .... Mr. Adam L. SKILES
88 Dir Academic Center for Excellence .... Ms. Erica A. MARSHALL
41 Athletic Director .... Ms. Lori L. CULLER
18 Director of Facilities .... Ms. Marcie NOFZIGER
29 Dir Alumni & Foundation Relations .... Ms. Janelle L. TAYLOR
19 Chief of Campus Police/Safety .... Mr. Keirsh A. COCHRAN
15 Human Resources Manager .... Ms. Jean M. COLE
93 Dir of Intercultural Enrichment .... Ms. Chynna M. PRESLEY
13 Chief Information Technology Office .... Mr. Adam L. SKILES
121 Director of Student Success .... Mr. Isaac C. BARBER
21 Sr Staff Accountant/Budget Analyst .... Mr. Joseph A. PRETORIUS
26 Chief Public Relations Officer .... Ms. Lynette D. FAGER

Indiana State University (D)

200 N 7th Street, Terre Haute IN 47809-1902
County: Vigo FICE Identification: 001807
Unit ID: 151324
Telephone: (812) 237-6311 Carnegie Class: DU-Mod
FAX Number: N/A Calendar System: Semester
URL: indstate.edu
Established: 1865 Annual Undergrad Tuition & Fees (In-State): $9,466
Enrollment: 10,829 Coed
Affiliation or Control: State IRS Status: 501(c)3
Highest Offering: Doctorate
Accreditation: HLC, ARCPA, ART, CAATE, CACREP, CAEP, CIDA, CLPSY, CONST, DIETC, MUS, NAIT, NUR, OT, PTA, SCPSY, SP, SW

01 President .... Dr. Deborah CURTIS
100 Chief of Staff .... Ms. Teresa D. EXLINE
86 Exec Dir of Govt Rel/Univ Comm .... Mr. Greg J. GOODE
05 Provost/Vice Pres Academic Affs .... Dr. Christopher OLSEN
10 Sr VP Finance & Admin/Univ Treas .... Ms. Diann E. MCKEE
32 VP Student Affairs .... Dr. Michele SOLIZ
88 Vice Pres Univ Engagement .... Dr. Nancy B. ROGERS
111 Vice Pres Univ Advancement/CEO Fndn .... Ms. Andrea L. ANGEL
43 General Counsel Legal Affairs .... Ms. Bridget K. BUTWIN
20 Assoc VP Academic Affairs .... Dr. Susan POWERS
13 Int Assoc VP/Chief Info Officer .... Mr. Robert BARLEY
26 Int AVP Marketing .... Ms. Carrie LUTZ
07 Int Exec Dir Admissions/HS Rels .... Ms. Regina ATKINS
29 Exec Director of Alumni Engagement .... Mr. Rex KENDALL
15 Exec Director Human Resources . Ms. Tami WEINZAPFEL-SMITH
14 Exec Dir Information Technology .... Mr. Yancy PHILLIPS
21 Assoc VP/Univ Controller .... Mr. Jeff JACSO
06 Registrar .... Dr. April HAY
22 AVP for Inclusive Excellence .... Dr. Rana JOHNSON
28 Exec Dir Multicultural Svcs & Pgms .... Dr. Elonda ERVIN
41 Director of Athletics .... Mr. Sherard CLINKSCALES
36 Executive Director Career Svcs .... Mr. Alex ALLEN
25 Director Sponsored Programs .... Ms. Liz METZGER
09 Director of Institutional Research .... Ms. Patty MCCLINTOCK
19 Director of Public Safety .... Ms. Michele BARRETT
96 Dir Purchasing/Central Receiving .... Mr. Kevin BARR
39 Executive Dir of Residential Life .... Dr. Amanda KNERR
38 Director of Student Counseling .... Dr. Kenneth CHEW
37 Director Student Financial Aid .... Ms. Donna SIMMONDS
49 Int Dean of Arts & Sciences .... Dr. Bassam YOUSIF
50 Dean of Business .... Dr. Terry DAUGHERTY
53 Dean of Education .... Dr. Janet BUCKENMEYER
68 Dean Health & Human Svcs .... Dr. Caroline MALLORY
72 Dean of Technology .... Dr. Nesli ALP
58 Dean of Grad/Professional Studies .... Dr. Denise COLLINS
08 Dean of Library Services .... Dr. Robin CRUMRIN
56 Director of Extended Learning .... Ms. Samantha PENNEY
35 Assoc VP Student Affairs .... Mr. Brooks MOORE
04 Admin Assistant to the President .... Ms. Kay PONSOT
105 Web Director .... Mr. TJ (Garrett) ROOD
106 Exec Director of Online Education .... Dr. Tim LONDON
108 Director Institutional Assessment ... Dr. Kelley WOODS-JOHNSON
44 Director Annual Giving .... Ms. Hilary DUNCAN

Indiana Tech (E)

1600 E Washington Boulevard, Fort Wayne IN 46803-1297
County: Allen FICE Identification: 001805
Unit ID: 151290
Telephone: (260) 422-5561 Carnegie Class: Masters/M
FAX Number: (260) 420-1453 Calendar System: Semester
URL: www.IndianaTech.edu
Established: 1930 Annual Undergrad Tuition & Fees: $28,000
Enrollment: 2,370 Coed
Affiliation or Control: Independent Non-Profit IRS Status: 501(c)3
Highest Offering: Doctorate
Accreditation: HLC, CAHIIM, IACBE

01 President .... Dr. Karl W. EINOLF
10 Exec VP Finance & Administration .... Ms. Judy K. ROY
05 VP for Academic Affairs .... Dr. Kathleen WATLAND
26 VP for Marketing & Communications ... Mr. Brian W. ENGELHART
84 VP for Enrollment Management .... Mr. Steve A. HERENDEEN
32 VP for Student Affairs .... Dr. Daniel J. STOKER
111 VP for Institutional Advancement .... Mr. Dan G. GRIGG
28 VP of Diversity & Inclusion .... Ms. Lisa D. GIVAN
11 Associate VP for Operations .... Ms. Sharon LOKUTA
50 Dean of Business .... Dr. Angie L. FINCANNON
97 Dean of General Studies .... Dr. Anne M. GULL
54 Dean of Engineering/Computer Sci .... Dr. Ying SHANG
58 Director Global Leadership Program .... Vacant
15 Human Resources Director .... Ms. Julie A. HENDRYX
21 Controller .... Ms. Shelly R. MUSOLF
13 VP Information Technology Svc .... Mr. Jeff S. LEICHTY
06 Registrar .... Ms. Heidi L. KANTENWEIN
08 Director of McMillen Library .... Mr. Brian A. HICKMAN
41 Athletic Director .... Ms. Jessie N. BIGGS
18 Dir Security & Facilities Mgmt .... Mr. R. Michael TOWNSLEY
37 Student Financial Services Director .... Mr. Scott W. THUM
07 Director of Admissions .... Mr. Robert N. CONFER
36 Dir Career Ctr/Regional Services .... Ms. Cynthia P. VERDUCE
39 Assoc VP Student Services .... Mr. Chris M. DICKSON
07 Director of Admissions Indianapolis .... Mr. Robert A. STASH
19 Director of Security .... Mr. Devin K. BLACKFORD
09 Director of Institutional Research ...... Mr. Stephen VANCHHAWNG
100 Dir of Advancement & Exec Opers .... Ms. Jennifer A. ROSS
25 Asst Dir of Advancement & Grants .... Ms. Erin E. JOHNSON
96 Director of Procurement .... Mr. Mark A. HUNSBERGER

04 Admin Assistant to the President .... Ms. Shayla D. RIVERA
105 Web Developer .... Mr. Joel A. KUHN
112 Sr Dir of Institutional Advance .... Ms. Mary LASITS
29 Director of Alumni Relations .... Mrs. Kristi JARMUS
27 Dir of Marketing/Communications .... Mr. Matthew S. BAIR
119 Information Security Officer .... Mr. Michael C. MULLEN

*Indiana University (F)

107 S. Indiana Ave., Bryan Hall 200,
Bloomington IN 47405-7000
County: Monroe FICE Identification: 008002
Unit ID: 151351
Telephone: (812) 855-4613 Carnegie Class: N/A
FAX Number: (812) 855-9586
URL: www.indiana.edu

01 President .... Dr. Pamela S. WHITTEN
05 Interim EVP/Provost IUB .... Mr. John S. APPLEGATE
03 Exec VP IU/Chancellor IUPUI .... Dr. Nasser H. PAYDAR
20 Interim EVP Univ Academic Affairs ... Dr. Sue SCIAME-GIESECKE
46 Vice Pres for Research .... Dr. Fred H. CATE
28 VP Diversity/Equity/Multicult Aff .... Dr. James C. WIMBUSH
18 Vice Pres Capital Planning & Facil ..... Dr. Thomas A. MORRISON
10 Vice President/CFO .... Mr. John SEJDINAJ
100 Chief of Staff .... Dr. Karen H. ADAMS
13 Vice President Info Tech/CIO .... Mr. Rob LOWDEN
43 Vice Pres/General Counsel .... Ms. Jacqueline A. SIMMONS
104 Vice Pres for International Affairs .... Ms. Hannah BUXBAUM
86 VP Gov Relations/Econ Engagement .... Mr. William B. STEPHAN
41 VP/Dir Intercollegiate Athletics .... Mr. Scott M. DOLSON
63 EVP Univ Clinical Affs/Dean Sch Med .... Dr. Jay L. HESS
15 VP Human Resources .... Mr. John WHELAN
84 Vice Provost Enrollment Management .... Dr. David B. JOHNSON
21 University Treasurer .... Mr. Donald S. LUKES
22 Dir Univ Ofc Institutional Equity .... Ms. Jennifer KINCAID
29 CEO/Exec Dir IU Alumni Assoc .... Mr. J. Thomas FORBES
102 Interim President/CEO IU Foundation .... Mr. J. Thomas FORBES
21 AVP/University Controller .... Ms. Anna K. JENSEN
116 AVP/Chief Audit Officer .... Mr. Stewart T. COBINE
04 Executive Asst to President .... Ms. Brittany F. SANTA
25 Exec Dir Grant Services .... Mr. Jim BECKER
32 Dean Students/V Prov Student Affair .... Mr. M. Dave O'GUINN
37 Univ Director of Financial Aid .... Ms. Jenny STEPHENS
19 AVP Public Safety/Inst Assurance .... Mr. Ben HUNTER
06 Associate Vice Provost & Registrar .... Mr. Mark MCCONAHAY
07 AV Prov/Exec Director of Admissions .... Ms. Sacha THIEME ARTERBERRY
08 Interim Dean University Libraries .... Ms. Diane M. DALLIS-COMENTALE
09 AVP Univ Inst Research/Reporting .... Mr. Todd J. SCHMITZ
101 Secretary of the Board .... Ms. Deborah A. LEMON
106 AVP/Director Office of Online Educ .... Dr. Chris J. FOLEY
39 Exec Dir Residential Pgms & Svcs .... Mr. Lukas D. LEFTWICH
44 IUF Exec Dir Mktg/Annual Giving .... Ms. Lindsey K. PEARSEY
50 Dean of Business .... Dr. Idalene F. KESNER
53 Interim Dean of Education .... Dr. Anastasia (Stacy) MORRONE
54 Interim Dean Info/Comp/Engineering .... Dr. Dennis GROTH
103 Exec Dir for Career Development .... Mr. Pat DONAHUE
96 Assoc VP for Procurement .... Mr. Baris KIYAR
26 Interim VP Comm & Marketing .... Ms. Rebecca CARL
27 Director of Media Relations .... Mr. Chuck CARNEY
38 Dir Student Counseling/Psych Svcs .... Dr. Denise HAYES

*Indiana University Bloomington (G)

107 S. Indiana Avenue, Bloomington IN 47405-7000
County: Monroe FICE Identification: 001809
Unit ID: 151351
Telephone: (812) 855-4848 Carnegie Class: DU-Highest
FAX Number: (812) 855-5678 Calendar System: Semester
URL: www.iub.edu
Established: 1820 Annual Undergrad Tuition & Fees (In-State): N/A
Enrollment: N/A Coed
Affiliation or Control: State IRS Status: 501(c)3
Highest Offering: Doctorate
Accreditation: HLC, ART, AUD, CAATE, CAEP, CAPRT, CEA, CIDA, CLPSY, COPSY, DIETD, IPSY, JOUR, LAW, LIB, MPCAC, MUS, OPT, OPTR, PCSAS, PH, SCPSY, SP, SPAA, THEA

02 President .... Dr. Michael A. MCROBBIE
05 Exec VP & Provost .... Ms. Lauren ROBEL
03 Exec VP & Chancellor IUPUI .... Mr. Nasser PAYDAR
20 Exec VP Univ Academic Affairs .... Mr. John S. APPLEGATE
10 VP & CFO .... Mr. John SEJDINAJ
17 Exec VP University Clinical Affairs .... Dr. Jay L. HESS
18 VP Capital Planning & Facilities .... Mr. Thomas A. MORRISON
22 VP Diversity/Equity/Multicult Affs .... Mr. James C. WIMBUSH
46 VP for Research .... Mr. Fred H. CATE
86 VP for Govt Rels/Econ Engagement .... Mr. Bill STEPHAN
32 VProv Stdnt Affairs/Dean of Stdnts .... Mr. Dave O'GUINN
13 VP of IT/Comms/Mktg & CIO .... Mr. Rob LOWDEN
20 Vice Prov for Undergraduate Educ .... Mr. Kurt ZORN
20 Vice Prov Faculty & Academic Affs .... Ms. Eliza PAVALKO
84 Vice Prov Enrollment Mgmt .... Mr. David JOHNSON
58 Vice Prov Grad Educ & Health Sci .... Mr. David DALEKE
21 Vice Prov Finance and Strategy .... Mr. Munirpallam A. VENKATARAMANAN
28 Vice Prov for Diversity/Inclusion .... Mr. John NIETO-PHILLIPS
21 Assoc VP & Univ Controller .... Ms. Anna JENSEN
15 VP Human Resources .... Mr. John WHELAN
104 Assoc VP for International Svcs .... Dr. Christopher VIERS
116 Assoc VP & Chief Audit Officer .... Mr. Stewart COBINE

49 Executive Dean Col Arts & Sciences ... Mr. Rick VAN KOOTEN
08 Ruth Lilly Dean Univ Libraries ... Ms. Carolyn WALTERS
50 Dean Kelley School of Business ... Ms. Idalene F. KESNER
53 Int Dean School of Education ... Ms. Anastasia MORRONE
69 Dean School of Public Health ... Mr. David ALLISON
88 Dean School of Optometry ... Dr. Joseph A. BONANNO
61 Dean School of Law ... Mr. Austen L. PARRISH
64 Dean Jacobs School of Music ... Mr. Gwyn RICHARDS
60 Dean Media School ... Mr. James SHANAHAN
57 Dean School of Art/Arch & Design ... Ms. Peg FAIMON
77 Dean Sch Informatics/Comp/Eng ... Mr. Raj ACHARYA
82 Dean School of Global and Intl Stds ... Mr. Lee FEINSTEIN
80 Dean School of Public/Env Affairs ... Dr. SiGn MOONEY
88 Assoc Dean School of Nursing ... Ms. Mary Lynn DAVIS-AJAMI
85 VP International Affairs ... Ms. Hannah BUXBAUM
92 Dean Hutton Honors College ... Mr. Andrea CICCARELLI
70 Dean of Social Work ... Dr. Tamara DAVIS
29 CEO Alumni Association ... Mr. J.T FORBES
39 Exec Dir Residential Pgm & Svcs ... Mr. Pat CONNOR
06 Assoc Vice Provost/Registrar ... Mr. Mark MCCONAHAY
43 VP & General Counsel ... Ms. Jacqueline SIMMONS
19 Chief of Police ... Ms. Jill LEES
41 Vice President & Dir of Athletics ... Mr. Scott DOLSON
88 Dir Eskenazi Museum of Art ... Mr. David BRENNEMAN
07 Vice Prov & Exec Dir Admissions ... Ms. Sacha THIEME
100 Chief of Staff ... Ms. Karen ADAMS
101 Secretary of the Institution/Board ... Ms. Deborah A. LEMON
106 Assoc VP & Dir Online Education ... Mr. Chris FOLEY
21 University Treasurer ... Mr. Don LUKES
88 Dir Office of Sustainability ... Mr. Andrew PREDMORE
37 Dir Student Financial Assistance ... Ms. Jackie KENNEDY-FLETCHER
04 Exec Assistant to the President ... Ms. Nicole TODD
88 Vice Provost for Research ... Dr. Jeff ZALESKI
26 Int Vice Provost Comm & Mkt ... Ms. Rebecca CARL
66 Dean School of Nursing ... Dr. Robin NEWHOUSE
88 Dir Strategic Comm & Marketing ... Ms. Jessica PARRY

*Indiana University East (A)

2325 Chester Boulevard, Richmond IN 47374-1289

County: Wayne
FICE Identification: 001811
Unit ID: 151388
Telephone: (765) 973-8200
Carnegie Class: Masters/S
FAX Number: N/A
Calendar System: Semester
URL: www.iue.edu
Established: 1946
Annual Undergrad Tuition & Fees (In-State): $7,715
Enrollment: 3,434
Coed
Affiliation or Control: State
IRS Status: 501(c)3
Highest Offering: Master's
Accreditation: HLC, ACBSP, CAEP, NUR

02 Chancellor ... Dr. Kathryn GIRTEN
05 Deputy Chancellor ... Dr. Michelle MALOTT
26 Vice Chanc External Affs/Marketing ... Mr. Jason TROUTWINE
10 Vice Chancellor Admin & Finance ... Ms. Leisa JULIAN
32 Dean of Students ... Ms. Amy JARECKI
13 Director Information Technology ... Mr. Todd DUKE
30 Director of Gift Development ... Ms. Paula Kay KING
06 Registrar ... Mr. Dennis HICKS
08 Director Library/Media Services ... Dr. Frances YATES
15 Director Human Resources ... Ms. Evelyn GORDON
36 Director Career Services ... Vacant
07 Executive Director of Admissions ... Ms. Molly VANDERPOOL
37 Exec Dir Fin Aid & Scholarships ... Ms. Sarah SOPER
121 Director Student Success ... Ms. Cherie DOLEHANTY
40 Manager of Barnes & Noble Bookstore ... Vacant
35 Director of Campus Life ... Ms. Rebeckah HESTER
113 Assistant Bursar ... Ms. Shelley DODSON
70 Director Social Work/Human Services ... Mr. Ed FITZGERALD
27 Director Communications & Marketing ... Mr. John DALTON
29 Director Alumni Relations ... Ms. Terry WIESEHAN
50 Dean Business/Economics ... Dr. Denise SMITH
83 Dean Humanities/Social Sciences ... Dr. Daren SNIDER
81 Dean Natural Science & Math ... Dr. Markus POMPER
66 Dean Nursing/Ctr Health Promotion ... Dr. Karen CLARK
53 Dean of Education ... Dr. Jerry WILDE
09 Director of Institutional Research ... Dr. Mengie PARKER
18 Director of Physical Facilities ... Mr. Gail SMOKER
41 Director of Athletics ... Mr. Joe GRIFFIN
38 Director of Behavioral Health ... Ms. Jennifer CLAYPOOLE
19 Division Chief of Police ... Mr. Scott DUNNING
22 Dir Affirmative Action/EEOC/TitleIX ... Ms. Tracy AMYX
28 Chief Diversity Ofcr/Special Asst ... Ms. Yemi MAHONEY

*Indiana University Kokomo (B)

2300 S Washington, Box 9003, Kokomo IN 46904-9003

County: Howard
FICE Identification: 001814
Unit ID: 151333
Telephone: (765) 453-2000
Carnegie Class: Bac-Diverse
FAX Number: (765) 455-9444
Calendar System: Semester
URL: www.iuk.edu
Established: 1945
Annual Undergrad Tuition & Fees (In-State): $7,715
Enrollment: 3,227
Coed
Affiliation or Control: State
IRS Status: 501(c)3
Highest Offering: Master's
Accreditation: HLC, CAEP, NUR, NURSE, RAD

02 Chancellor ... Dr. Susan SCIAME-GIESECKE
05 Int Deputy Chanc/Exec VC Acad Affs ... Dr. Mark CANADA
10 Vice Chancellor for Finance ... Mr. Jared HAYMAN
20 Assoc Vice Chanc Academic Affairs ... Dr. Christina DOWNEY
20 Assoc VC for Academic Affairs ... Dr. Julie SAAM
32 Vice Chanc Student Affs/Enroll Mgmt ... Ms. Tess BARKER
111 Vice Chancellor for Advancement ... Ms. Crystal JONES
26 Asst VC Media & Marketing ... Ms. Marie LINDSKOOG
07 Asst VC for Admissions ... Ms. Angie SIDERS
08 Dean of the Library ... Vacant
37 Director Financial Aid ... Ms. Dara JOHNSON
27 Dir External Rels/Public Affairs ... Ms. Catherine VALCKE
06 Asst VC for Academic Affs/Registrar ... Ms. Stacey THOMAS
100 Chief of Staff ... Ms. Sarah SARBER
36 Manager Career/Accessibility Center ... Ms. Tracy SPRINGER
28 Coord Stdnt Life & Campus Diversity ... Vacant
35 Dean of Students ... Ms. Audra DOWLING
18 Director Facilities/Physical Plant ... Mr. John SARBER
50 Dean School of Business ... Dr. Chitti GOVINDARAJULU
79 Dean Sch Humanities/Social Sciences ... Dr. Eric BAIN-SELBO
66 Dean School of Nursing ... Dr. Susan HENDRICKS
53 Dean School of Education ... Dr. Leah NELLIS
81 Dean School of Sciences ... Dr. Christian CHAURET
13 Chief Info Technology Officer (CIO) ... Mr. Nick RAY
15 Director Human Resources ... Ms. April EVANS
41 Athletic Director ... Mr. Greg COOPER
29 Director Alumni Affairs ... Mr. Benjamin A. LIECHTY
30 Director of Development ... Ms. Catherine CLEARWATERS

*Indiana University Northwest (C)

3400 Broadway, Gary IN 46408-1197

County: Lake
FICE Identification: 001815
Unit ID: 151360
Telephone: (219) 980-6500
Carnegie Class: Masters/S
FAX Number: (219) 980-6670
Calendar System: Semester
URL: www.iun.edu
Established: 1921
Annual Undergrad Tuition & Fees (In-State): $7,715
Enrollment: 3,801
Coed
Affiliation or Control: State
IRS Status: 501(c)3
Highest Offering: Master's
Accreditation: HLC, CAEP, CAHIIM, DA, DH, DMS, NUR, RAD, RTT, SPAA

02 Chancellor ... Mr. Ken IWAMA
100 Chief of Staff ... Vacant
05 Exec VC Academic Affairs ... Dr. Victoria ROMAN-LAGUNAS
32 Vice Chanc Student Svcs/Enroll Mgmt ... Vacant
10 Vice Chancellor for Finance ... Ms. Michelle DICKERSON
111 Vice Chanc Advancement & Ext Affs ... Ms. Jeri Pat GABBERT
13 Chief Information Officer ... Mr. Nick RAY
20 Assoc Vice Chanc Academic Affs ... Dr. Cynthia O'DELL
09 Asst VC Inst Effectiveness & Rsrch ... Mr. John NOVAK
49 Dean College of Arts & Sciences ... Dr. Mark HOYERT
69 Interim Dean Health & Human Svcs ... Dr. Linda DELUNAS
50 Dean School of Business & Economics ... Dr. Cynthia ROBERTS
53 Interim Dean School of Education ... Dr. Mark SPERLING
80 Interim Dir Public & Environ Affs ... Dr. Christopher YOUNG
70 Director Social Work ... Dr. Darlene LYNCH
06 Registrar ... Mr. Peter ZACHOCKI
88 Director Pre-Professional Pgm ... Dr. Michael LAPOINTE
07 Director of Admissions ... Ms. Dorothy FRINK
37 Director Financial Aid ... Ms. Gina PIRTLE
36 Director Career & Placement ... Ms. Sharese DUDLEY
35 Director Student Activities ... Mr. Scott FULK
18 Interim Dir Facilities/Operations ... Mr. Gary GREINER
19 Director Security ... Mr. Monte DAVIS
29 Director Alumni Relations ... Vacant
66 Director Division of Nursing ... Dr. Linda DELUNAS
24 Director Instr Media ... Mr. Aaron PIGORS
08 Dean of the Library ... Ms. Latrice BOOKER
21 Director of Accounting Services ... Ms. Terri CHANCE
25 Grant Coord/Senior Grant Writer ... Ms. Sandra MCMULLEN
15 Director Human Resources ... Ms. Mianta' DIMING
28 Director Diversity Programming ... Mr. James WALLACE, JR.
38 Director of Counseling Services ... Ms. Barbara A. DAHL
22 Interim Director Affirmative Action ... Ms. Carolyn HARTLEY
88 Dir Schlrshp in Teaching & Learning ... Dr. Christopher YOUNG
88 Dir Urban & Regional Excellence ... Dr. Ellen SZARLETA
105 Web Tech Services Manager ... Ms. Nicolle KRAUSE
106 Dir Online Education/E-learning ... Mr. Christopher YOUNG
41 Athletic Director ... Mr. Ryan SHELTON

*Indiana University-Purdue University Indianapolis (D)

420 University Blvd., Indianapolis IN 46202

County: Marion
FICE Identification: 001813
Unit ID: 151111
Telephone: (317) 274-5555
Carnegie Class: DU-Higher
FAX Number: N/A
Calendar System: Semester
URL: www.iupui.edu
Established: 1969
Annual Undergrad Tuition & Fees (In-State): $9,944
Enrollment: 29,390
Coed
Affiliation or Control: State
IRS Status: 501(c)3
Highest Offering: Doctorate
Accreditation: HLC, AA, ACATE, ARCPA, ART, CAEP, CAHIIM, CAMPEP, CIDA, CLPSY, COARC, CONST, CYTO, DA, DENT, DH, @DIETC, DIETI, DT, EMT, FEPAC, HSA, HT, IPSY, LAW, LIB, MED, MT, MUS, NMT, NURSE, OT, PA, PAST, PH, PTA, RAD, RADDOS, RTT, SPAA, SW

02 Chancellor IUPUI/Exec Vice Pres IU ... Dr. Nasser H. PAYDAR
100 Chief of Staff ... Ms. Margie SMITH-SIMMONS
28 Vice Chanc Diversity/Equity/Inclus ... Dr. Karen L. DACE
05 Exec Vice Chanc/Chief Acad Ofcr ... Dr. Kathy E. JOHNSON
10 Vice Chanc Finance & Admin ... Ms. Camy BROEKER
30 VP for Development/Foundation ... Ms. Dee METAJ
86 Vice Chanc Community Engagement ... Ms. Amy C. WARNER
32 Vice Chancellor Student Affairs ... Dr. Eric A. WELDY
46 Vice Chancellor Research ... Dr. Janice BLUM
13 Dean Information Technology ... Dr. Garland C. ELMORE
08 Dean University Library ... Ms. Kristi L. PALMER
84 Assoc Vice Chanc Enrollment Mgmt ... Mr. Boyd A. BRADSHAW
06 Registrar ... Vacant
113 Bursar ... Ms. Kelly SMITH-WELLER
26 Director of Communications ... Dr. Becky WOOD
22 Director Equal Opportunity ... Ms. Anne L. MITCHELL
38 Director Student Counseling ... Dr. Julie LASH
39 Director Housing/Residence Life ... Mr. Josh SKILLMAN
36 Director Career Services ... Mr. Joshua D. KILLEY
41 Director of Athletics ... Dr. Roderick D. PERRY
29 Asst VC Alumni Engagement ... Ms. Andrea SIMPSON
27 Asst Dir Strategic Communications ... Ms. Amber DENNEY
09 Asst Vice Chanc Inst Research ... Dr. Michele J. HANSEN
07 Dir of Undergraduate Admissions ... Mr. Errol L. WINT
37 Director Student Financial Aid ... Mr. Marvin L. SMITH
15 Senior HR Dir/Dir Fin Services ... Ms. Juletta TOLIVER
23 Director Student Health Svcs ... Dr. Stephen F. WINTERMEYER
18 Assoc Vice Chan Campus Facility Svc ... Mr. Jeffrey PLAWECKI
19 Chief of Police ... Mr. Doug JOHNSON
92 Exec Assoc Dean Honors College ... Dr. Kristina H. SHEELER
45 Sr Advisor to the Chancellor Plng ... Dr. Stephen P. HUNDLEY
12 Vice Chanc & Dean IUPU Columbus ... Dr. Reinhold R. HILL
57 Dean Herron School of Art & Design ... Ms. Nan GOGGIN
52 Dean School of Dentistry ... Dr. Carol A. MURDOCH-KINCH
54 Dean School of Engr/Technology ... Dr. David J. RUSSOMANNO
77 Sr Exec Asc Dn of Informatics/Comp ... Dr. Mathew J. PALAKAL
61 Dean McKinney Sch of Law ... Dr. Karen E. BRAVO
49 Interim Dean School of Liberal Arts ... Dr. Robert REBEIN
63 Dean School of Medicine ... Dr. Jay L. HESS
66 Dean School of Nursing ... Dr. Robin P. NEWHOUSE
68 Dean Sch of Health & Human Science ... Dr. Rafael E. BAHAMONDE
81 Interim Dean School of Science ... Dr. John F. DITUSA
70 Dean School of Social Work ... Dr. Tamara S. DAVIS
69 Dean Fairbanks Sch of Public Health ... Dr. Paul K. HALVERSON
88 Dean Lilly Fam Sch of Philanthropy ... Dr. Amir PASIC
53 Interim Dean School of Education ... Ms. Tambra JACKSON
80 Exec Assoc Dean Public/Environ Affs ... Dr. Thomas D. STUCKY
85 Assoc VC International Affairs ... Dr. Hilary E. KAHN
50 Exec Assoc Dean School of Business ... Dr. Ken A. CAROW
58 Vice Chanc Graduate Education ... Dr. Janice S. BLUM
89 Dean University College ... Dr. James M. GLADDEN

*Indiana University South Bend (E)

1700 Mishawaka Avenue, South Bend IN 46634-7111

County: Saint Joseph
FICE Identification: 001816
Unit ID: 151342
Telephone: (574) 520-4872
Carnegie Class: Masters/M
FAX Number: (574) 520-4834
Calendar System: Semester
URL: www.iusb.edu
Established: 1940
Annual Undergrad Tuition & Fees (In-State): $7,715
Enrollment: 4,942
Coed
Affiliation or Control: State
IRS Status: 501(c)3
Highest Offering: Master's
Accreditation: HLC, CACREP, CAEP, DH, MT, MUS, NURSE, @OT, RAD, @SP, SPAA

02 Chancellor ... Dr. Susan ELROD
05 Int Exec Vice Chanc Acad Affairs ... Dr. Linda CHEN
10 Actg Vice Chanc Admin & Finance ... Mr. Philemon YEBEI
26 Int Vice Chanc University Relations ... Mr. Thomas STEVICK
32 VC Stdnt Engage/Dean of Students ... Ms. Monica PORTER
100 Chief of Staff ... Ms. Elizabeth PAICE
13 Regional Chief Information Officer ... Mr. Nick RAY
20 Assoc Vice Chanc Academic Affs ... Dr. Doug MCMILLEN
84 Assoc Vice Chanc Enrollment Mgt ... Vacant
06 Registrar ... Mr. Keith DAWSON
41 Executive Director of Athletics ... Mr. Steve BRUCE
18 Director Facilities Management ... Mr. Michael PRATER
19 Director of Safety & Security ... Mr. Kurt M. MATZ
15 Director of Human Resources ... Ms. Deborah SCHMITT
29 Dir Alumni Affs/Campus Ceremonies ... Ms. Moira DYCZKO
27 Dir Comm/Marketing/Chief of Staff ... Ms. Paige RISSER
52 Director of Dental Auxiliary Educ ... Ms. Mallory EDMONDSON
51 Director of Extended Learning ... Mr. Mike MANCINI
38 Director Student Counseling Ctr ... Mr. Kevin GRIFFITH
07 Director of Admissions ... Ms. Connie PETERSON-MILLER
28 Director of Institutional Equity ... Ms. Laura HARLOW
30 Director of Development ... Ms. Dina HARRIS
39 Director of Student Housing ... Mr. Scott STRITTMATTER
21 Director of Accounting ... Ms. Kathleen PIZANA
37 Director of Financial Aid ... Ms. Lorie WILLIAMS
08 Dean of Library Services ... Ms. Vicki BLOOM
50 Int Dean of Business & Economics ... Dr. Tracey ANDERSON
53 Dean School of Education ... Dr. Hope DAVIS
57 Interim Dean of the Arts ... Dr. Jorge MUNIZ
76 Dean Col of Health Sciences ... Dr. Thomas FISHER
49 Dean of Liberal Arts & Sciences ... Dr. Brenda PHILLIPS

*Indiana University Southeast (F)

4201 Grant Line Road, New Albany IN 47150-2158

County: Floyd
FICE Identification: 001817
Unit ID: 151379
Telephone: (812) 941-2333
Carnegie Class: Masters/M
FAX Number: (812) 941-2475
Calendar System: Semester
URL: www.ius.edu
Established: 1941
Annual Undergrad Tuition & Fees (In-State): $7,715
Enrollment: 4,678
Coed

Affiliation or Control: State IRS Status: 501(c)3
Highest Offering: Master's
Accreditation: **HLC**, CAEP, CAHIIM, NURSE

02 Chancellor ... Dr. Ray WALLACE
05 Executive VC Academic Affairs ... Dr. Kelly A. RYAN
10 VC Administration/Finance ... Mr. Dana C. WAVLE
84 VC Enrollment/Mktg/Student Affairs ... Ms. Amanda G. STONECIPHER
111 VC Advancement/Alumni/External Affs ... Ms. Betty S. RUSSO
20 Assoc VC Academic Affairs ... Dr. Donna J. DAHLGREN
13 Chief Information Officer ... Mr. Nicholas T. RAY
07 Director Admissions ... Mr. Chris CREWS
04 Exec Secretary to the Chancellor ... Ms. Donna J. HARVEY
35 Dean for Student Life ... Dr. Seuth CHALEUNPHONH
06 Registrar ... Mr. James (Jay) MCTYIER
37 Director Student Financial Aid ... Ms. Jennifer A. SHELLEY
08 Director Library Services ... Ms. Kate B. MOORE
36 Director Career Development ... Ms. Donna REED
18 Exec Dir of Facility Operations ... Mr. Robert C. POFF
14 Dir IT Communications & Support ... Mr. Steve BENNISON
41 Director Athletics ... Mr. Joseph M. GLOVER
15 Director Human Resources ... Mr. Ray KLEIN
09 Dir Institutional Effectiveness ... Mr. Ronald E. SEVERTIS, JR.
19 Chief Safety & Security ... Mr. Stephen MILLER
38 Dir Personal Counseling ... Dr. Michael DAY
26 Dir Marketing & Communications ... Ms. Nancy J. TRAFTON
79 Dean School Arts & Letters ... Mr. James HESSELMAN
81 Dean School Natural Sciences ... Dr. Elaine HAUB
83 Interim Dean School Social Sciences ... Dr. Gregory T. KORDSMEIER
50 Dean School Business ... Dr. David EPLION
53 Dean School Education ... Dr. Faye M. CAMAHALAN
66 Dean School Nursing ... Dr. Donna J. BOWLES
46 Dean for Research & Grad Studies ... Dr. Diane E. WILLE
28 Director Staff Equity & Diversity ... Mr. James J. WILKERSON
121 Director of Advising ... Ms. Rebecca TURNER
88 Exec Dir Academic Acct Services ... Ms. Melissa D. HILL
113 Exec Dir Student Acct Services ... Ms. Ashley M. MCKAY
88 Academic Information Officer ... Mr. Steven KROLAK
30 Director Development ... Mr. David C. DEWITT
39 Dir Residence Life & Housing ... Ms. Abbie DUPAY

* *Indiana University-Purdue University Columbus* (A)

4601 Central Avenue, Columbus IN 47203
Telephone: (812) 348-7390 Identification: 770185
Accreditation: **&HLC**, CAEP, NURSE

Indiana Wesleyan University (B)

4201 S Washington Street, Marion IN 46953-4999
County: Grant FICE Identification: 001822
Unit ID: 151801
Telephone: (765) 674-6901 Carnegie Class: Masters/S
FAX Number: (765) 677-2499 Calendar System: 4/1/4
URL: www.indwes.edu
Established: 1920 Annual Undergrad Tuition & Fees: $28,184
Enrollment: 3,108 Coed
Affiliation or Control: Wesleyan Church IRS Status: 501(c)3
Highest Offering: Doctorate
Accreditation: **HLC**, ACBSP, CAATE, CACREP, CAEP, CAEPN, EXSC, MFCD, MUS, NURSE, OT, OTA, PTA, SW, THEOL

01 President ... Dr. David WRIGHT
05 Chief Academic Officer/Provost ... Dr. Stacy HAMMONS
12 Chancellor IWU-Marion ... Dr. Rod REED
12 Chancellor IWU-National & Global ... Dr. Matt LUCAS
28 VP for Diversity & Inclusion ... Ms. Diane MCDANIEL
10 Executive VP & CFO ... Mrs. Nancy SCHOONMAKER
11 President Wesley Seminary ... Dr. Colleen DERR
20 VP for Academic Affairs/CAPS ... Dr. Mike MANNING
20 VP for Academic Affairs/SON ... Dr. Barbara IHRKE
111 VP for Advancement ... Dr. Scott TURCOTT
20 Associate Provost ... Dr. Don SPROWL
26 VP Univ Communications ... Mr. Jerry SHEPHERD
27 VP Mktg/IWU-N&G ... Ms. Erica ELLIOTT
107 VP Life Calling & Integrative Lrng ... Dr. Brandon HILL
11 VP of Operations/Residential Campus ... Mr. John JONES
58 Dean Graduate School ... Dr. Joanne BARNES
73 Dean of the Seminary ... Dr. Abson JOSEPH
76 Dean School of Health Sciences ... Dr. Martin RICE
50 Dean Devoe School of Business ... Dr. Christopher DAVIS
37 Executive Director Financial Svcs ... Ms. Emily MATTISON
88 Dean of Developmental Learning ... Mr. Andrew PARKER
08 Director Library Resources ... Mrs. Shelia CARLBLOM
08 Director Off-campus Library Svcs ... Mrs. Jule KIND
29 Director of Alumni ... Vacant
07 Dir Admissions/Residential Educ ... Mr. Ian SLATER
15 Exec Director Human Resources ... Mr. Mark PEDERSON
06 University Registrar ... Mrs. Kim NICHOLSON
43 University Counsel ... Mr. Shawn MATTER
21 Controller ... Mrs. Tiffany LEWIS
41 VP for Student Dev & Athletics ... Mr. Mark DEMICHAEL
42 Dean of the Chapel ... Dr. John BRAY
92 Dean Honors College ... Mr. David RIGGS
09 Director Institutional Research ... Mr. Tony PARANDI
18 AVP Facilities Services ... Mr. Don ROWLEY
19 Director Campus Police ... Mr. Kyle BEAL
25 Director of Research Support ... Vacant
13 VP for Digital Transformation & CIO ... Mr. Scott GILREATH
121 Dean Center for Student Success ... Mr. Nathan HERRING
102 Dir Foundation/Corporate Relations ... Dr. Michael MOFFITT
04 Exec Assistant to the President ... Ms. Lynn MUNDAY
30 Director of Development ... Mr. Kenneth GRIFFIN
44 Director Annual Giving ... Vacant

International Business College (C)

7205 Shadeland Station, Indianapolis IN 46256-3997
County: Marion FICE Identification: 004579
Unit ID: 151457
Telephone: (317) 813-2300 Carnegie Class: Bac/Assoc-Mixed
FAX Number: (317) 841-6419 Calendar System: Semester
URL: www.intlbusinesscollege.com
Established: 1889 Annual Undergrad Tuition & Fees: N/A
Enrollment: N/A Coed
Affiliation or Control: Proprietary IRS Status: Proprietary
Highest Offering: Associate Degree
Accreditation: **ACCSC**, DA, MAC

01 Campus Director ... Ms. Amee AUGENSTEIN
05 Director of Education ... Ms. Judith THAMES
32 Director of Student Services ... Ms. Sarah LAWSON
36 Director of Career Services ... Ms. Diane DALTON

* Ivy Tech Community College of Indiana-Systems Office (D)

50 W Fall Creek Parkway N Drive,
Indianapolis IN 46208-5752
County: Marion FICE Identification: 008546
Unit ID: 363563
Telephone: (317) 921-4882 Carnegie Class: N/A
FAX Number: (317) 921-4753
URL: www.ivytech.edu

01 President ... Dr. Sue J. ELLSPERMANN
43 College Counsel ... James CLARK
43 College Counsel ... J.D LUX
04 Sr Administrative Asst to President ... Angelina GONZALEZ
116 Asst VP Internal Audit ... Mike DAVIS
05 Provost/Sr Vice President ... Dr. Kara MONROE
20 Vice Pres Academic Affairs ... Dr. Russell D. BAKER
108 Asst VP Academic Qlty/Assessment ... Dr. Marcus KOLB
124 Asst VP Acad Transitions/Support ... Gwenn ELDRIDGE
106 Asst VP Ed Tech and Ivy OnLine ... Matthew PITTMAN
20 Asst VP Curriculum ... Dr. Nichole STITT
20 Asst VP Curriculum ... Vearl TURNPAUGH
20 Asst VP Curriculum ... Glenn ROBERSON
102 SVP/Pres Ivy Tech Foundation ... John MURPHY
112 Asst VP Philanthropy ... Becky MILLER
30 Asst VP Development Operations ... Annette FLICKINGER
88 Chief Financial Officer Foundation ... Kevin HONIGFORD
10 Sr Vice President/CFO ... Matt HAWKINS
45 Asst VP Strategy & Innovation ... Lakshmi HASANADKA
88 Asst VP Continuous Improvement ... Jeff KRAFT
15 Sr Vice President Human Resources ... Julie LORTON-ROWLAND
16 VP Human Resources ... Michaels MCNICHOLS
118 Asst VP Employee Benefits ... Jen FISHER
88 Asst VP Talent Development ... Kirsten BIEL
103 Sr VP Workforce & Career ... Chris LOWERY
88 VP Information Technology ... Linda CALVIN
109 VP Business Logistics/Supply Chain ... Aaron BAUTE
66 VP Healthcare ... Mary Anne SLOAN
72 VP Technology ... Sue SMITH
36 VP Career Coaching/Employer Connect ... Caroline DOWD-HIGGINS
88 Asst VP Workforce Operations ... Dr. Stacy TOWNSLEY
26 Vice Pres Marketing & Communication ... Jeff FANTER
27 Asst VP Marketing & Communications ... Kelsey BATTEN
18 Vice Pres Cap Plng & Facilities ... Amanda WILSON
86 VP Government Relations ... Mary Jane MICHALAK
88 VP K-14 Initiatives ... Dr. Rebecca RAHSCHULTE
28 VP Diversity/Equity & Belonging ... Doneisha POSEY
88 Sr VP & Chief Strategy Offiicer ... Kristen MORELAND
88 VP Strategic Operations ... Michelle SIMMONS
88 VP Strategic Operations ... Chad BOLSER
32 Vice President Student Success ... Dr. Corey CLASEMANN-RYAN
35 Asst VP Student Life ... Kat STREMIECKI
121 Asst VP Academic Advising ... Susan HAWKINS-WILDING
114 VP Financial Planning & Mgmt ... William BOGARD
113 Asst VP Cash/Debt Mgmt ... Tom SKIDMORE
21 VP Finance/Sourcing/Asst Treasurer ... Dominick CHASE
14 Chief Technology Officer ... Thomas RIEBE
88 Asst VP Student Advocacy ... Dr. Carey TREAGER-HUBER
13 Sr VP & Chief Information Officer ... Matt ETCHISON
06 College Registrar ... Ann YATER
21 Asst VP Accounting & Fin Reporting ... Christy GELBACK-DIAZ
37 Asst VP Financial Aid ... Vacant
19 VP Public Safety/Emer Preparedness ... Jon BAREFOOT
84 Asst VP Enrollment Management ... Sarah CLEVELAND

* Ivy Tech Community College of Indiana-Indianapolis (E)

50 W Fall Creek Parkway North Drive,
Indianapolis IN 46208-5752
County: Marion FICE Identification: 009917
Unit ID: 150987
Telephone: (317) 921-4882 Carnegie Class: Assoc/MT-VT-High Non
FAX Number: (317) 921-4753 Calendar System: Semester
URL: www.ivytech.edu/indianapolis/
Established: 1966 Annual Undergrad Tuition & Fees (In-State): $4,637
Enrollment: 63,809 Coed
Affiliation or Control: State IRS Status: 501(c)3
Highest Offering: Associate Degree
Accreditation: **HLC**, ACBSP, ACFEI, ART, CAHIIM, COARC, CSHSE, FUSER, MAC, NAEYC, NAIT, RAD, SURGT

02 Chancellor ... Dr. Lorenzo ESTERS
05 VC of Academic Affairs ... Dr. Rod BROWN
32 VC of Student Affairs/Success ... Dr. LaWanda JOBE
84 VC of Enrollment Services ... Dr. Tracy BERENS-FUNK
10 Executive Director of Finance ... Vacant
15 Exec Director of Human Resources ... Ms. Sara HAUGER
11 Exec Dir of Administrative Services ... Mr. Aaron ROBERTS
103 Exec Dir of CCEC ... Mr. Ben CARTER
30 Exec Director of Development ... Mrs. Danielle STILES-POLK
35 Asst Vice Chanc Student Success ... Mrs. Amy GRIFFIN
37 Director of Financial Aid ... Vacant
06 Registrar ... Mr. Andrew PENALVA
09 Institutional Research Analyst ... Mr. Christopher G. SLEPPPY
36 Director of Career Services ... Ms. Rebecca PATTEN-LEMONS
96 Director of Purchasing ... Ms. Carissa CARTWRIGHT-COLLINS
20 Asst Vice Chanc Academic Support ... Ms. Rhonda ANGSMAN
26 Exec Dir Marketing/Communications ... Mrs. Tracey ALLEN

* *Ivy Tech Community College of Indiana-Anderson* (F)

104 West 53rd Street, Anderson IN 46013-1502
Telephone: (800) 644-4882 Identification: 770239
Accreditation: **&HLC**, DA, DH, MAC, NAIT

* *Ivy Tech Community College of Indiana-Bloomington* (G)

200 N Daniels Way, Bloomington IN 47404-9772
Telephone: (812) 332-1559 FICE Identification: 035213
Accreditation: **&HLC**, ACBSP, ACFEI, COARC, CSHSE, EMT, NAEYC, NAIT, RTT

* *Ivy Tech Community College of Indiana-Columbus* (H)

4475 Central Avenue, Columbus IN 47203-1868
Telephone: (812) 372-9925 FICE Identification: 010038
Accreditation: **&HLC**, ACBSP, CSHSE, DA, MAC, NAEYC, NAIT, SURGT

* *Ivy Tech Community College of Indiana-Evansville* (I)

3501 N First Avenue, Evansville IN 47710-1881
Telephone: (812) 426-2865 FICE Identification: 009925
Accreditation: **&HLC**, ACBSP, CSHSE, EMT, MAC, NAEYC, NAIT, SURGT

* *Ivy Tech Community College of Indiana-Fort Wayne* (J)

3800 N Anthony Boulevard, Fort Wayne IN 46805-1489
Telephone: (260) 482-9171 FICE Identification: 009926
Accreditation: **&HLC**, ACBSP, ACFEI, CAHIIM, COARC, COMTA, CSHSE, EMT, MAC, NAEYC, NAIT

* *Ivy Tech Community College of Indiana-Kokomo* (K)

1815 E Morgan Street, Box 1373, Kokomo IN 46903-1373
Telephone: (765) 459-0561 FICE Identification: 010041
Accreditation: **&HLC**, ACBSP, CSHSE, DA, EMT, MAC, NAEYC, NAIT, SURGT

* *Ivy Tech Community College of Indiana-Lafayette* (L)

3101 S Creasy Lane, Box 6299, Lafayette IN 47903-6299
Telephone: (765) 269-5000 FICE Identification: 010039
Accreditation: **&HLC**, ACBSP, COARC, CSHSE, DA, MAC, NAEYC, NAIT, SURGT

* *Ivy Tech Community College of Indiana-Lake County* (M)

1440 E 35th Avenue, Gary IN 46409-1499
Telephone: (219) 981-1111 FICE Identification: 010040
Accreditation: **&HLC**, ACBSP, ACFEI, COARC, CSHSE, NAEYC, NAIT, PTAA

* *Ivy Tech Community College of Indiana-Lawrenceburg-Riverfront* (N)

50 Walnut Street, Lawrenceburg IN 47025
Telephone: (812) 537-4010 Identification: 770242
Accreditation: **&HLC**, MAC, NAIT

* *Ivy Tech Community College Madison* (O)

590 Ivy Tech Drive, Madison IN 47250-1883
Telephone: (812) 265-2580 FICE Identification: 009923
Accreditation: **&HLC**, ACBSP, CSHSE, EMT, MAC, NAIT

* *Ivy Tech Community College of Indiana-Marion* (P)

261 S Commerce Drive, Marion IN 46953
Telephone: (765) 651-3100 Identification: 770244
Accreditation: **&HLC**, NAIT

* Ivy Tech Community College of Indiana-Michigan City (A)

3714 Franklin Drive, Michigan City IN 46360
Telephone: (219) 879-9137 Identification: 770245
Accreditation: &HLC, MAC, NAIT

* Ivy Tech Community College of Indiana-Muncie (B)

345 South High Street, Muncie IN 47305
Telephone: (765) 289-2291 FICE Identification: 009924
Accreditation: &HLC, ACBSP, ACFEI, CSHSE, MAC, NAEYC, NAIT, PTAA, RAD, SURGT

* Ivy Tech Community College of Indiana-Richmond (C)

2357 Chester Boulevard, Richmond IN 47374-1298
Telephone: (765) 966-2656 FICE Identification: 010037
Accreditation: &HLC, ACBSP, CSHSE, MAC, NAEYC, NAIT

* Ivy Tech Community College of Indiana-Sellersburg (D)

8204 Highway 311, Sellersburg IN 47172-1897
Telephone: (812) 246-3301 FICE Identification: 010109
Accreditation: &HLC, ACBSP, COARC, CSHSE, DA, MAC, MLTAD, NAEYC, NAIT, PTAA

* Ivy Tech Community College of Indiana-South Bend/Elkhart (E)

220 Dean Johnson Boulevard, South Bend IN 46601-3415
Telephone: (574) 289-7001 FICE Identification: 008423
Accreditation: &HLC, ACBSP, ACFEI, COARC, CSHSE, DA, DH, EMT, MAC, MLTAD, NAEYC, NAIT

* Ivy Tech Community College of Indiana-Terre Haute (F)

8000 S. Education Drive, Terre Haute IN 47802-4833
Telephone: (812) 299-1121 FICE Identification: 008547
Accreditation: &HLC, ACBSP, COARC, CSHSE, DMS, EMT, MAC, MLTAD, NAEYC, NAIT, RAD, SURGT

* Ivy Tech Community College of Indiana-Valparaiso Campus (G)

3100 Ivy Tech Drive, Valparaiso IN 46383
Telephone: (219) 464-8514 Identification: 770246
Accreditation: &HLC, EMT, NAIT, SURGT

John Patrick University of Health and Applied Sciences (H)

100 E. Wayne Street, Suite 140, South Bend IN 46601
County: St. Joseph Identification: 667156
Unit ID: 488776
Telephone: (574) 232-2408 Carnegie Class: Spec-4-yr-Other Health
FAX Number: (574) 232-2200 Calendar System: Semester
URL: www.jpu.edu
Established: 2009 Annual Undergrad Tuition & Fees: $16,100
Enrollment: 133 Coed
Affiliation or Control: Proprietary IRS Status: Proprietary
Highest Offering: Master's
Accreditation: ACCSC, RADDOS

01 President/Dean .... Brent D. MURPHY
11 Dir of Administrative Services .... Betsy DATEMA
26 Dir of Marketing/Recruiting .... Linda MURPHY

Lincoln College of Technology (I)

7225 Winton Drive, Building 128,
Indianapolis IN 46268-4198
County: Marion FICE Identification: 007938
Unit ID: 151661
Telephone: (317) 632-5553 Carnegie Class: Spec 2-yr-Tech
FAX Number: (317) 851-3273 Calendar System: Semester
URL: www.lincolntech.edu
Established: 1962 Annual Undergrad Tuition & Fees: N/A
Enrollment: 999 Coed
Affiliation or Control: Proprietary IRS Status: Proprietary
Highest Offering: Associate Degree
Accreditation: ACCSC

01 Campus President .... Brent JENKINS
05 Academic Dean .... Rodney ALLEE
11 Director of Administrative Services .... Andy RAHIMI
37 Director Student Financial Aid .... Alison JONES
07 Director of Admissions .... Shannon BIGELOW
88 Co-Dir of High School Admissions .... Charles LIVORNO
88 Co-Dir of High School Admissions .... David RITZ
36 Director of Career Services .... Christine JOYCE
13 IT Administrator .... Blake BROOKS
18 Facilities Manager .... Roger PARK
10 Business Office Coordinator .... Dawn KEMP

Manchester University (J)

604 E College Avenue, North Manchester IN 46962-1225
County: Wabash FICE Identification: 001820
Unit ID: 151777
Telephone: (260) 982-5000 Carnegie Class: Bac-Diverse
FAX Number: (260) 982-5043 Calendar System: 4/1/4
URL: www.manchester.edu
Established: 1889 Annual Undergrad Tuition & Fees: $34,436
Enrollment: 1,449 Coed
Affiliation or Control: Church Of The Brethren IRS Status: 501(c)3
Highest Offering: Doctorate
Accreditation: HLC, CAATE, CAEP, PHAR, SW

01 President .... Dr. David F. MCFADDEN
05 VP Academic Affairs .... Dr. Celia B. COOK-HUFFMAN
32 VP for Student Affairs/Student Exp .... Dr. Abby L. VAN VLERAH
10 Chief Business Officer/VP Finance .... Mr. Clair W. KNAPP, IV
17 VP Health Sciences/Dean Health Prof .... Dr. Lea A. JOHNSON
111 Vice President Advancement .... Mrs. Melanie B. HARMON
84 VP for Enrollment/Marketing .... Mr. Ryon KAOPUIKI
09 Dir of Institutional Research .... Mr. Adam HOHMAN
13 Senior Director of ITS .... Mr. Travis STEELE
20 Associate Dean Academic Affairs .... Dr. Stacy L. ERICKSON-PESETSKI
20 Associate Dean of Academic Programs .... Ms. Jennifer CAMPBELL
108 Director of Assessment .... Ms. Michelle J. CORDOVA-KIBIGER
107 Dir of Executive Education .... Mr. Shane L. THOMSON
07 Director of Admissions .... Ms. Brandi C. CHAUNCEY
29 Director of Alumni Relations .... Ms. Kylee B. MOSS
08 Interim Director of the Library .... Ms. Darla V. HAINES
06 Registrar .... Ms. Audrey N. HAMPSHIRE
24 Instructional Designer .... Mr. Justin P. LUNSFORD
24 Director of Educational Media .... Ms. Melissa RASMUSSEN
104 Dir of Study Abroad .... Ms. Thelma ROHRER
38 Asst Director of Counseling .... Ms. April D. WHITE
36 Dir Career/Professional Development .... Ms. Tish KALITA
121 Dir Student Success/Acad Advising .... Ms. Mara YOUNGBAUER
39 Asst Dir of Residence Life .... Ms. Jane WEBB
42 University Pastor .... Mrs. Bekah HOUFF
41 Athletic Director .... Mr. Rick ESPESET
19 Director of Security .... Ms. Tina L. EDWARDS
18 Asst VP for Facilities .... Ms. Alexis D. YOUNG
44 Director of the Manchester Fund .... Ms. Janeen W. KOOI
37 Director of Student Financial Aid .... Ms. Sherri L. SHOCKEY
28 Dir Student Diversity/Inclusion .... Ms. Maegan D. POLLONAIS
26 Asst Director Media Relations .... Ms. Anne GREGORY
23 Director of Health Services .... Ms. Erin FOREMAN
21 Controller .... Ms. Cindy L. SEITZ
35 Director Student Activities .... Ms. Samantha A. ALLEY
96 Director of Purchasing .... Ms. Heather K. GOCHENAUR
40 Campus Bookstore Manager .... Ms. Heather K. GOCHENAUR
04 Administrative Asst to President .... Ms. Jill R. MANNS
100 Executive Assistant to President .... Ms. Julie J. KNUTH
25 Director of Grants .... Ms. Elena M. BOHLANDER
50 Dean of College of Business .... Mr. Timothy A. OGDEN
67 Dean Pharmacy & Grad Life Sciences .... Dr. Walter (Tommy) T. SMITH
49 Dean of Arts & Sciences .... Dr. Judd CASE

Marian University (K)

3200 Cold Spring Road, Indianapolis IN 46222-1997
County: Marion FICE Identification: 001821
Unit ID: 151786
Telephone: (317) 955-6000 Carnegie Class: Masters/M
FAX Number: (317) 955-6448 Calendar System: Semester
URL: www.marian.edu
Established: 1851 Annual Undergrad Tuition & Fees: $36,000
Enrollment: 3,706 Coed
Affiliation or Control: Roman Catholic IRS Status: 501(c)3
Highest Offering: Doctorate
Accreditation: HLC, ANEST, CAEP, IACBE, NURSE, OSTEO, @SW

01 President .... Mr. Daniel J. ELSENER
05 EVP & Provost .... Dr. Alan SILVA
10 SVP Finance & Operations .... Mr. Greg GINDER
45 SVP Strategic Growth & Innovation .... Dr. Kenith BRITT
17 SVP for Health Professions .... Ms. Marsha CASEY
26 VP Enrollment/Mktg/Communication .... Mr. Brad R. WUCHER
42 VP Mission & Ministry .... Mr. Adam SETMEYER
32 VP Student Success & Engagement .... Ms. Ruth RODGERS
13 VP and Chief Information Officer .... Mr. Ray STANLEY
43 SVP Strat Ptnrshps/General Counsel .... Ms. Deborah LAWRENCE
111 VP Institutional Advancement .... Mr. John FINKE
88 VP for Mission Effectiveness .... Sr. Mary Beth GIANOLI
20 Assistant Provost .... Dr. Elizabeth OSIKA
20 Assistant Provost .... Mr. William HARTING
37 Director of Financial Aid .... Ms. Monique WARE
18 Director Campus Operations .... Mr. Mike MILLER
41 Director of Athletics .... Mr. Steve DOWNING
29 Dir Alumni/Parent Engagement .... Ms. Cathy SILER
06 Registrar .... Ms. Jennifer SCHWARTZ
08 Library Director .... Ms. Jessica TRINOSKEY
35 Dean of Students .... Ms. Karen CANDLISH
88 Director Student Activities .... Ms. Sarah BALANA MOLTER
19 Chief of Police Services .... Mr. Robert RICHARDSON
27 Exec Dir Marketing Communications .... Ms. Maggie KUCIK
121 Director Academic Support Services .... Mrs. Marjorie BATIC
55 Exec Director Adult Programs .... Ms. Amy BENNETT
38 Director of Counseling Services .... Dr. Marla SMITH
09 Director of Institutional Research .... Ms. Brooke KILE
15 Director of Human Resources .... Ms. Amy KOCH

21 Director of Business Services .... Ms. Alice SHELTON
40 Bookstore Manager .... Ms. Margaret CIHLAR
04 Executive Asst to President .... Ms. Cyndi KAMP
104 Director Study Abroad .... Dr. Wendy WESTPHAL
39 Dir Residential & Commuter Life .... Ms. Kate DOTY

Martin University (L)

2186 North Sherman Drive, Indianapolis IN 46218
County: Marion FICE Identification: 021408
Unit ID: 151810
Telephone: (317) 543-3235 Carnegie Class: Bac-Diverse
FAX Number: (317) 543-3257 Calendar System: Semester
URL: www.martin.edu
Established: 1977 Annual Undergrad Tuition & Fees: $13,200
Enrollment: 220 Coed
Affiliation or Control: Independent Non-Profit IRS Status: 501(c)3
Highest Offering: Master's
Accreditation: HLC

01 President .... Dr. Sean L. HUDDLESTON
05 Vice Pres Academic Affairs/Provost .... Dr. Lashun ARON-SMITH
09 VP of Institutional Effectiveness .... Dr. Brian STEUERWALD
10 VP Fiscal Affairs .... Mr. Michael MOOS
84 VP of Enrollment Management .... Mr. Ezell MARRS
37 Director Financial Aid .... Ms. Kristie LAW
32 Director Student Success .... Ms. Angela ADAMS
111 Dir of Institutional Advancement .... Ms. Gail SPICER
13 Dir Information Tech/Communications .... Ms. Carol BRANSON

Mid-America College of Funeral Service (M)

3111 Hamburg Pike, Jeffersonville IN 47130-9630
County: Clark FICE Identification: 010618
Unit ID: 151962
Telephone: (812) 288-8878 Carnegie Class: Spec-4-yr-Other
FAX Number: (812) 288-5942 Calendar System: Quarter
URL: www.mid-america.edu
Established: 1980 Annual Undergrad Tuition & Fees: $12,700
Enrollment: 92 Coed
Affiliation or Control: Independent Non-Profit IRS Status: 501(c)3
Highest Offering: Baccalaureate
Accreditation: FUSER

01 President .... Dr. Mitch MITCHELL
37 Dir of Financial Aid/Office Mgr .... Mr. Jason KESSINGER
08 Librarian .... Ms. Sonja PIERCE
07 Director of Admissions .... Ms. Victoria THOMAS

Mid-America Reformed Seminary (N)

229 Seminary Drive, Dyer IN 46311-1069
County: Lake FICE Identification: 039893
Unit ID: 373030
Telephone: (219) 864-2400 Carnegie Class: Not Classified
FAX Number: (219) 864-2410 Calendar System: Semester
URL: www.midamerica.edu
Established: 1981 Annual Graduate Tuition & Fees: N/A
Enrollment: N/A Coed
Affiliation or Control: Independent Non-Profit IRS Status: 501(c)3
Highest Offering: Master's; No Undergraduates
Accreditation: THEOL

01 President .... Dr. Cornelius VENEMA
32 Dean of Students .... Rev. Mark D. VANDER HART
111 Vice President of Advancement .... Mr. Mike DECKINGA
11 Vice President of Operations .... Mr. Keith LEMAHIEU
36 Director of Apprenticeship Program .... Rev. Mark VANDERHART
06 Registrar .... Rev. Alan STRANGE
84 Director of Enrollment Management .... Mr. Brian BLUMMER
108 Director Institutional Assessment .... Rev. Marcus MININGER
08 Theological Librarian .... Rev. Alan STRANGE
26 Manager Marketing/Digital/Pubs .... Mr. Jared LUTTJEBOER

Oakland City University (O)

138 N Lucretia Street, Oakland City IN 47660-1099
County: Gibson FICE Identification: 001824
Unit ID: 152099
Telephone: (812) 749-4781 Carnegie Class: Bac-Diverse
FAX Number: (812) 749-1233 Calendar System: Semester
URL: www.oak.edu
Established: 1885 Annual Undergrad Tuition & Fees: $24,990
Enrollment: 1,241 Coed
Affiliation or Control: Baptist IRS Status: 501(c)3
Highest Offering: Doctorate
Accreditation: HLC, CAEPN, IACBE, THEOL

01 President .... Dr. Ron DEMPSEY
11 Vice President for Administration .... Mr. Clint WOOLSEY
05 VP for Academic Affairs & Provost .... Vacant
10 Chief Financial Officer .... Mr. Todd WAHL
111 VP for University Advancement .... Mr. Brian BAKER
32 AVP for Student Life .... Mr. Brad KNOTTS
20 Asst Prov for Non-Trad Enterprise .... Vacant
50 Dean School of Business .... Dr. Cathy ROBB
53 Dean School of Education .... Dr. Rachel YARBROUGH
73 Dean Religious Studies .... Dr. Douglas LOW
49 Dean of Arts and Science .... Dr. Justin MURPHY
108 Asst Provost for Assessment .... Dr. Paul BOWDRE

37 Director of Financial Aid .... Mrs. Nicole SHARP
22 Compliance Officer .... Ms. Patricia ENDICOTT
06 Registrar .... Mrs. Linda TIPTON
08 Director of Library .... Mrs. Denise PINNICK
42 Campus Minister .... Rev. Jeffrey BRALLEY
18 Director of Facilities .... Mr. Greg BURKE
15 Director of Human Resource .... Mrs. Stephanie KIRBY
19 Chief of Security .... Mr. Mike MCGREGOR
29 Director of Alumni Affairs .... Ms. Susan SULLIVAN
35 Director of Student Activities .... Mr. Kelso ROWLAND
88 Director of Directions Program .... Mrs. Charity JULIAN
36 Dir Center for Calling & Career ...... Ms. Jennifer STROUGHMATT
88 Interim Upward Bound Director .... Mrs. Charity JULIAN
21 Director of Business Office .... Mrs. Elizabeth CARLISLE
113 Students Account Manager .... Mrs. Anita MISKELL
88 Director of Housekeeping .... Ms. Angie WELLS
04 Exec Assistant to President .... Mrs. Mary NOSSETT
07 Senior Director of Admissions .... Mr. Brent MAGRUDER
105 Director Web Services .... Mrs. Andrea TURNER
28 Director of Diversity .... Vacant
39 Dir Resident Life/Student Housing .... Vacant
41 Athletic Director .... Mr. T-Ray FLETCHER
13 Director of Information Technology .... Mr. Eric MURPHY
96 Director of Purchasing .... Ms. Candy PANCAKE

Purdue University Global (A)

9000 Keystone Crossing, Ste 800, Indianapolis IN 46240
County: Marion FICE Identification: 004586
Unit ID: 260901
Telephone: (317) 208-5311 Carnegie Class: DU-Mod
FAX Number: N/A Calendar System: Quarter
URL: www.purdueglobal.edu
Established: 1937 Annual Undergrad Tuition & Fees (In-State): N/A
Enrollment: N/A Coed
Affiliation or Control: State IRS Status: 501(c)3
Highest Offering: Doctorate
Accreditation: HLC, ACBSP, CAHIIM, IFSAC, MAC, NURSE

01 Chancellor .... Dr. Frank DOOLEY
00 President .... Mr. Mitchell DANIELS, JR.
05 Provost .... Dr. John HARBOR
10 Chief Financial Officer .... Mr. Chris RUHL
20 VP Faculty & Academic Resources .... Dr. Carolyn NORSTROM
06 Registrar .... Mr. Michael LORENZ

Purdue University Main Campus (B)

610 Purdue Mall, West Lafayette IN 47907-2040
County: Tippecanoe FICE Identification: 001825
Unit ID: 243780
Telephone: (765) 494-4600 Carnegie Class: DU-Highest
FAX Number: N/A Calendar System: Semester
URL: www.purdue.edu
Established: 1869 Annual Undergrad Tuition & Fees (In-State): $9,992
Enrollment: 46,655 Coed
Affiliation or Control: State IRS Status: 501(c)3
Highest Offering: Doctorate
Accreditation: HLC, AAB, ART, AUD, CAATE, CAEP, CAEPN, CAMPEP, CIDA, CLPSY, CONST, COPSY, DIETC, DIETD, IPSY, LSAR, NAIT, NURSE, PCSAS, PHAR, SP, THEA, #VET

01 President .... Mr. Mitchell E. DANIELS, JR.
10 Chief Financial Officer & Treasurer .... Mr. Christopher A. RUHL
05 Provost/Exec VP for Acad Affairs .... Dr. Jay AKRIDGE
21 Sr VP Business Svcs/Asst Treasurer .... Mr. James S. ALMOND
26 Exec Vice Pres Communications .... Mr. Dan HASLER
13 EVP Information Tech/Purdue Online .... Dr. William G. MCCARTNEY
15 Vice President Human Resources ... Ms. Hannah M. AUSTERMAN
20 Int Vice Prov Teaching/Learning .... Dr. Jenna RICKUS
28 Vice Chanc Diversity/Inclusion .... Dr. John GATES
20 Vice Pres Faculty Affairs .... Dr. Peter HOLLENBECK
32 Vice Provost Student Life .... Dr. Beth MCCUSKEY
08 Dean of Libraries .... Ms. Beth MCNEIL
29 President & CEO Alumni Association .... Vacant
07 Dean Admiss/VP Enrollment Mgmt .... Dr. Kris WONG-DAVIS
37 Exe Director Financial Aid .... Ms. Heidi A. CARL

Purdue University Fort Wayne (C)

2101 E Coliseum Boulevard, Fort Wayne IN 46805-1499
County: Allen FICE Identification: 001828
Unit ID: 151102
Telephone: (260) 481-6100 Carnegie Class: Masters/L
FAX Number: (260) 481-6880 Calendar System: Semester
URL: www.pfw.edu
Established: 1964 Annual Undergrad Tuition & Fees (In-State): $8,730
Enrollment: 8,093 Coed
Affiliation or Control: State IRS Status: 501(c)3
Highest Offering: Doctorate
Accreditation: HLC, ART, CACREP, CAEP, MUS, PH, RAD, @SP, THEA

02 Chancellor .... Dr. Ronald ELSENBAUMER
05 Vice Chanc Academic Affairs .... Dr. Carl DRUMMOND
10 Vice Chanc Financial/Admin Affairs .... Mr. Glen NAKATA
84 Vice Chanc Enroll/Stdnt Experience .... Dr. Krissy CREAGER
30 Vice Chancellor for Development .... Vacant
26 Vice Chanc Marketing/Comm .... Jerry LEWIS
06 Assoc Vice Chanc/Registrar .... Dr. Cheryl HINE
49 Dean College of Liberal Arts .... Janet BADIA
20 Assoc Vice Chanc Academic Programs .... Dr. Terri SWIM
100 Chief of Staff .... Kimberly WAGNER
13 Chief Information Ofcr/Dir IT Svcs .... Mitch DAVIDSON
18 Associate Vice Chance of Facilities .... Greg JUSTICE
29 Director of Alumni Relations .... Emily VENDERLEY
08 Dean of Library .... Vacant
15 Associate VC HR/OIE .... Cynthia SPRINGER
41 Director of Athletics & Recreation .... Kelley HARTLEY-HUTTON
96 Director of Purchasing .... Pam THOMPSON
19 Chief of Police .... Tim POTTS
16 Associate Director of HR .... Christine M. MARCUCCILLI
85 Director International Programs .... Brian MYLREA
37 Director Financial Aid .... Douglas HESS
09 Director of Institutional Research .... Irah MODRY-CARON
51 Exec Director Continuing Studies .... Karen VANGORDER
81 Dean College of Science .... Dr. Ronald FRIEDMAN
72 Dean Engr Tech/Computer Sci .... Dr. Manoochehr ZOGHI
53 Director School of Education .... Dr. Isabel NUNEZ
50 Dean Business .... Dr. Melissa GRUYS
57 Dean Visual/Performing Arts .... John O'CONNELL
04 Admin Assistant to the Chancellor .... Gayle BELLAM
39 Dir Housing/Residential Education .... Jordyn HOGAN

Purdue University Northwest (D)

2200 169th Street, Hammond IN 46323-2094
County: Lake FICE Identification: 001827
Unit ID: 490805
Telephone: (219) 989-2204 Carnegie Class: Masters/L
FAX Number: (219) 989-2581 Calendar System: Semester
URL: www.pnw.edu
Established: 1946 Annual Undergrad Tuition & Fees (In-State): $7,942
Enrollment: 9,363 Coed
Affiliation or Control: State IRS Status: 501(c)3
Highest Offering: Doctorate
Accreditation: HLC, CACREP, CAEP, CEA, MFCD, NAIT, NUR, SW

01 Chancellor .... Dr. Thomas L. KEON
05 Vice Chanc Acad Affs & Provost .... Dr. Kenneth HOLFORD
10 Vice Chanc Finance & Admin .... Mr. Stephen TURNER
111 Vice Chanc for Inst Advancement .... Dr. Lisa GOODNIGHT
13 Vice Chanc Info Services .... Mr. Tim WINDERS
84 VC Enroll Mgmt & Student Affairs ...... Ms. Yohlunda M. MOSLEY
26 Assoc Vice Chanc Marketing .... Ms. Kris FALZONE
09 Assoc VCAA Inst Effectiveness .... Dr. Rebecca STANKOWSKI
21 Asst VC Finance & Business Svcs .... Ms. Kimberly THOMAS
32 Assoc Vice Chanc Stdnt Affs/EOP .... Mr. Colin FEWER
15 Asst Vice Chanc Human Resources .... Ms. Susan MILLLER
83 Dean College of Hum Educ & Soc Sci .... Ms. Elaine CAREY
54 Int Dean College of Engr & Science .... Dr. Niaz LATIF
72 Dean College of Technology .... Dr. Niaz LATIF
50 Dean College of Business .... Dr. Lawrence HAMER
66 Dean College of Nursing .... Dr. Lisa HOPP
53 Dir School of Education .... Ms. Anne GREGORY
58 Director of Graduate Studies .... Ms. Joy COLWELL
06 Registrar .... Ms. Cheryl ARROYO
37 Exec Dir of Financial Aid .... Mr. Michael J. BIEL
41 Director of Athletics .... Mr. Richard J. COSTELLO
38 Director Counseling Center .... Dr. Kenneth JACKSON
46 Dir Research & Sponsored Programs ...... Ms. Maja MARJANOVIC
07 Exec Dir Undergrad Admiss & EM .... Mr. George F. KACENGA
96 Dir of Procurement/Auxiliary Svcs .... Ms. Jennifer HUPKE
39 Director Housing Residential Educ .... Ms. Scott IVERSON
92 Dean Honors College/Undergrad Study ...... Dr. Jonathan SWARTS
20 Interim Assc VC Academic Affairs .... Dr. Rachel CLAPP-SMITH
04 Sr Exec Asst Strat Initiatives .... Ms. Julie WIEJAK
90 Asst Vice Chanc Student Succes Tech ..... Ms. Heather ZAMOJSKI
25 Exec Director CVIS .... Dr. Chenn ZHOU
28 Director of Equity & Diversity .... Ms. Linda B. KNOX
36 Director Career Dev & Services .... Ms. Natalie CONNORS
88 AVC Campus Plng/Proj & Space Mgmt ...... Mr. Jacob G. LENSON
29 Exec Dir PNW Alumni Community .... Ms. Ashley GERODIMOS
18 Senior Dir of Facilities & Grounds .... Mr. Scott PARSONS
124 Exec Dir Student Success/Retention .... Ms. Karen L. STACHYRA
100 Interim Chief of Staff .... Dr. Lisa GOODNIGHT
19 Director of Public Safety .... Mr. Brian E. MILLER
30 Executive Director of Development .... Ms. Jamie MANAHAN

Purdue University Northwest, Westville Campus (E)

1401 S US 421, Westville IN 46391
Telephone: (219) 785-5200 FICE Identification: 001826
Accreditation: &HLC

† Branch Campus of Purdue University Northwest, Hammond, IN.

Rose-Hulman Institute of Technology (F)

5500 Wabash Avenue, Terre Haute IN 47803-3920
County: Vigo FICE Identification: 001830
Unit ID: 152318
Telephone: (812) 877-1511 Carnegie Class: Spec-4-yr-Eng
FAX Number: (812) 877-9925 Calendar System: Quarter
URL: www.rose-hulman.edu
Established: 1874 Annual Undergrad Tuition & Fees: $52,914
Enrollment: 1,990 Coed
Affiliation or Control: Independent Non-Profit IRS Status: 501(c)3
Highest Offering: Master's
Accreditation: HLC

01 President .... Mr. Robert A. COONS
10 Vice President for Finance .... Mr. Matthew D. DAVIS
05 Provost & Vice Pres Academic Affs .... Dr. Richard E. STAMPER
111 VP Inst Advancement .... Mr. Steven P. BRADY
32 VP Student Affs & Dean of Students .... Mr. Erik Z. HAYES
26 VP Communications/Marketing .... Mr. Santhana NAIDU
15 Vice Pres Human/Environmental Svcs ...... Ms. Megan C. ELLIOTT
84 Vice President Enrollment Mgmt .... Dr. Thomas BEAR
88 Sr Director Venture .... Mr. Brian C. DOUGHERTY
88 Associate Dean of Innovation .... Vacant
20 Dean of Faculty .... Dr. Russell L. WARLEY
88 Dir for Micronano Devices & Sys .... Dr. Azad SIAHMAKOUN
88 Associate Dean of Learning & Tech .... Dr. Kay C. DEE
13 Vice Pres Info Tech and CIO .... Dr. Wayne DENNISON
18 Director Facilities Operations .... Mr. Chad T. WEBER
36 Dir Career Services/Employee Rels .... Mr. Scott K. TIEKEN
07 Dean of Admissions .... Ms. Lisa M. NORTON
29 Interim Director Alumni Relations .... Mr. Charlie RICKER
37 Director of Financial Aid .... Ms. Melinda L. MIDDLETON
41 Director of Athletics .... Mr. Jeffrey L. JENKINS
28 Associate Dir Center for Diversity .... Mr. Nick DAVIS
30 Executive Director of Development .... Mr. Chris AIMONE
110 Exec Director Advancement Service .... Ms. Jennifer KENZOR
06 Registrar .... Ms. Jan PINK
08 Sr Director Logan Library & Info .... Ms. Bernadette EWEN
19 Director of Public Safety .... Vacant
40 Bookstore Manager .... Ms. Sheryl E. FULK
85 Dir of Intl Student Services .... Ms. Karen A. DEGRANGE
04 Exec Asst to the President/BOT .... Ms. Amy TIMBERMAN
21 Director of Business Operations .... Ms. Linda L. PRICE
11 Director Administrative Services .... Mr. Bryan T. BROMSTRUP
09 Director of Institutional Research .... Dr. Timothy CHOW
35 Assoc Dean of Student Affairs .... Mr. Ryan BRIMBERRY
35 Director of Student Services .... Ms. Kristen J. LOYD
24 Instructional Technology Manager .... Ms. Cheryl DAVIDSON
24 Emerging Digital Technologies Mgr .... Mr. Alan WARD
108 Sr Dir of Institutional Research .... Dr. Matthew D. LOVELL
38 Director Student Counseling Center .... Mr. Michael LATTA
39 Director Residence Life .... Mr. Cory PARDIECK

St. Anthony School of Echocardiography (G)

1201 S. Main Street, Crown Point IN 46307
County: Lake Identification: 667119
Telephone: (219) 757-6132 Carnegie Class: Not Classified
FAX Number: (219) 681-6725 Calendar System: Semester
URL: https://www.franciscanhealth.org/EchoSchoolNWI
Established: 2004 Annual Undergrad Tuition & Fees: N/A
Enrollment: N/A Coed
Affiliation or Control: Independent Non-Profit IRS Status: 501(c)3
Highest Offering: Associate Degree
Accreditation: DMS

01 Co-Program Director .... Lori HULT
05 Co-Program Director .... Karin KOLISZ

Saint Mary-of-the-Woods College (H)

1 St Mary of Woods College,
St Mary of the Woods IN 47876-1099
County: Vigo FICE Identification: 001835
Unit ID: 152381
Telephone: (812) 535-5151 Carnegie Class: Masters/S
FAX Number: (812) 535-5231 Calendar System: Semester
URL: www.smwc.edu
Established: 1840 Annual Undergrad Tuition & Fees: $31,150
Enrollment: 1,099 Coed
Affiliation or Control: Roman Catholic IRS Status: 501(c)3
Highest Offering: Doctorate
Accreditation: HLC, ACATE, MUS, NURSE

01 President .... Dr. Dottie KING
05 VP for Academic & Student Affairs .... Dr. Janet CLARK
10 VP for Finance & Administration .... Ms. Jaclyn WALTERS
111 VP for Advancement & Strategic Init .... Ms. Karen DYER
84 VP for Enrollment Management .... Mr. Brennan RANDOLPH
06 Registrar .... Ms. Deanna SMITHEE
32 Associate VP for Student Affairs .... Dr. Aimee JANSSEN-ROBINSON
37 AVP for Financial Aid & Admissions .... Ms. Darla HOPPER
21 Associate VP/Controller .... Ms. Kari WOLFE
110 Associate VP for Advancement .... Ms. Catherine SAUNDERS
28 VP for Diversity/Equity/Inclusion .... Ms. Dee REED
15 Associate VP of Human Resources .... Mr. Terry BOWE
29 Director of Alumni Relations .... Ms. Sarah MAHADY
08 Director of the Library .... Dr. Rusty TRYON
07 Executive Director of Admissions .... Mr. Chris LOZIER
20 Executive Director Academic Affairs .... Ms. Sara BOYER
18 Director of Facilities .... Mr. Josh WOOD
09 Director of Institutional Research .... Mr. Mike KING
19 Director of Campus Security .... Mr. Greg EWING
04 Exec Assistant for the President .... Ms. Peggy NASH
108 Director of Assessment .... Ms. Kimberli ZORNES
38 Campus Counselor .... Ms. Kalista LAWRENCE

Saint Mary's College (I)

Notre Dame IN 46556
County: Saint Joseph FICE Identification: 001836
Unit ID: 152390
Telephone: (574) 284-4000 Carnegie Class: Bac-A&S
FAX Number: (574) 284-4716 Calendar System: Semester
URL: www.saintmarys.edu

Established: 1844 Annual Undergrad Tuition & Fees: $45,720
Enrollment: 1,581 Female
Affiliation or Control: Roman Catholic IRS Status: 501(c)3
Highest Offering: Doctorate
Accreditation: HLC, CAEP, MUS, NURSE, SP, SW

01 President Dr. Katie CONBOY
04 Special Asst to the President Ms. Michelle EGAN
05 Provost/Sr VP Academic Affairs Dr. Titilayo UFOMATA
26 Int Vice Pres College Relations Ms. Libby KOULTOURIDES
32 Int Vice Pres for Student Affairs Ms. Gloria JENKINS
10 Vice President Strategy & Finance Dr. Dana STRAIT
84 Vice Pres for Enrollment Management Ms. Mona BOWE
88 Interim Vice President for Mission Ms. Molly GOWER
43 General Counsel Vacant
28 Exec Dir of Inclusion & Equity Dr. Redgina HILL
121 Dean of Student Academic Services Dr. Karen CHAMBERS
06 Dir of Academic Advising/Registrar Ms. Nadia EWING
07 Director of Admission Ms. Sarah DVORAK
08 Director of Library Mr. Joseph THOMAS
09 Director of Institutional Research Ms. Julie SISCO
29 Director of Alumnae Relations Ms. Kara O'LEARY
37 Director of Financial Aid Ms. Kathleen M. BROWN
27 Director of Public Relations Ms. Lisa KNOX
38 Int Director of Health & Counseling Ms. Cynthia HORTON-CAVANAUGH
13 Chief Information Officer Mr. Todd NORRIS
15 Director of Human Resources Ms. Kris URSCHEL
19 Director of Safety & Security Mr. James BAMBENEK
40 Manager Bookstore Ms. Judith MCKEE
41 Director of Athletics Ms. Julie SCHROEDER-BIEK
42 Director of Campus Ministry Vacant
18 Director of Facilities Mr. Benjamin BOWMAN
96 Director of Purchasing Ms. Kathleen CARLSON
88 Director of Student Involvement Vacant
85 Director of Multicultural Program Vacant
04 Senior Exec Asst to the President Ms. Vicki WICKIZER

Saint Meinrad School of Theology (A)

200 Hill Drive, St. Meinrad IN 47577-1030
County: Spencer FICE Identification: 007276
Unit ID: 152451
Telephone: (812) 357-6611 Carnegie Class: Spec-4-yr-Faith
FAX Number: (812) 357-6964 Calendar System: Semester
URL: www.saintmeinrad.edu
Established: 1861 Annual Graduate Tuition & Fees: N/A
Enrollment: 176 Coed
Affiliation or Control: Roman Catholic IRS Status: 501(c)3
Highest Offering: Master's; No Undergraduates
Accreditation: HLC, THEOL

01 President & Rector Rev. Denis ROBINSON, OSB
03 Vice Rector Rev. Tobias COLGAN, OSB
05 Academic Dean Dr. Robert ALVIS
42 Director of Spiritual Formation Rev. Guerric DEBONA, OSB
20 Dir of Graduate Theology Programs Sr. Jeana VISEL, OSB
30 Vice President of Development Mr. Duane SCHAEFER
10 Business Manager & Treasurer Mrs. Lisa CASTLEBURY
08 Library Director Dr. Daniel KOLB
06 Registrar Mrs. Donna BALBACH
88 Dir of Clergy Formation Pgm Dcn. Rick WAGNER
114 Director of Budget Mrs. Pam DOWLAND
37 Director of Student Financial Aid Mrs. Ruth KRESS
26 Director of Communications Mrs. Mary Jeanne SCHUMACHER
29 Director of Alumni Relations Mr. Tim FLORIAN
38 Director of Student Counseling Ctr Sr. Diane PHARO, SCN
23 Director of Health Services Ms. Kristin BREE
04 Executive Secretary Mrs. Karen SCHERZER
13 Chief Info Technology Officer (CIO) Mr. Dave GRAMELSPACHER
105 Director Web Services Mrs. Mary Jeanne SCHUMACHER
106 Dir Online Education/E-learning Sr. Jeana VISEL, OSB
15 Director Human Resources Ms. Jackie SCHERLE
07 Director of Admissions Dr. John SCHLACHTER
44 Director of Annual Giving Vacant
108 Director Institutional Assessment Dr. John SCHLACHTER
18 Chief Facilities/Physical Plant Ofc Mr. Mark HOFFMAN
101 Secretary of the Institution/ Board Br. Francis DeSales WAGNER, OSB
19 Director Security/Safety Mr. Darren SROUFE

St. Vincent College of Health Professions (B)

2001 West 86th Street, Indianapolis IN 46260
County: Marion Identification: 667315
Telephone: (317) 338-3879 Carnegie Class: Not Classified
FAX Number: (317) 338-3720 Calendar System: Semester
URL: www.stvincent.org
Established: 2015 Annual Undergrad Tuition & Fees: N/A
Enrollment: N/A Coed
Affiliation or Control: Independent Non-Profit IRS Status: 501(c)3
Highest Offering: Associate Degree
Accreditation: ABHES, DMS, EMT, RAD

01 President/Exec Dir Medical Educ Dr. Jeffrey ROTHENBERG
05 Dean/Program Director Mr. Mark ADKINS

Taylor University (C)

West 236 Reade Avenue, Upland IN 46989-1001
County: Grant FICE Identification: 001838
Unit ID: 152530
Telephone: (765) 998-2751 Carnegie Class: Bac-Diverse
FAX Number: (765) 998-4910 Calendar System: 4/1/4
URL: www.taylor.edu
Established: 1846 Annual Undergrad Tuition & Fees: $36,800
Enrollment: 2,110 Coed
Affiliation or Control: Independent Non-Profit IRS Status: 501(c)3
Highest Offering: Master's
Accreditation: HLC, ACBSP, CAEPN, CEA, MUS, SW

01 President Dr. Michael LINDSAY
04 Admin Assistant to the President Ms. Shelly GRAMLING
100 VP for Strategy and Chief of Staff Mr. Will HAGEN
45 Special Assistant to the President Mr. Ron SUTHERLAND
88 Admin Asst to Special Asst to Pres Ms. Janis RIVERA
05 Interim Provost Dr. Tom JONES
88 Admin Assistant to the Provost Ms. Deb CARPENTER
111 VP for University Advancement Mr. Rex BENNETT
10 VP Business/Finance/CFO Mr. Stephen OLSON
32 VP Student Development Dr. Skip TRUDEAU
28 VP Intercult Ldrship/Church Rels Mr. Greg DYSON
13 Chief Information Officer Mr. Rob LINEHAN
84 VP for Enrollment & Marketing Vacant
81 Dean of Sciences Dr. Grace JU MILLER
49 Int Dean Arts/Humanities/Bus & HE Dr. Nancy DAYTON
104 Dean International Programs Dr. Charles BRAINER
20 Dean Faculty Development/Dir BCTLE Dr. Barb BIRD
37 Assoc VP of Financial Aid Mr. Timothy NACE
07 Exec Director Admissions Mr. Andy GAMMONS
35 Dean of Students Mr. Jesse BROWN
39 Assc Dean Res Life & Discipleship Ms. Julia HURLOW
06 Registrar Ms. Janet ROGERS
08 Interim Director of Library Ms. Lana WILSON
108 Dir Assessment/Quality Improvements Dr. Kim CASE
09 Director IR/Assoc Registrar Dr. Edwin WELCH
88 Exec Director for Campaigns Mr. David RITCHIE
112 Assoc VP Advancement/Major Gifts Mr. Mike FALDER
30 Exec Director of Development Ms. Kristie JACOBSON
29 Exec Dir Alumni & Parent Relations Mr. Brad YORDY
124 Dean of Student Engagement Dr. Drew MOSER
41 Director of Athletics Mr. Kyle GOULD
36 Director Calling and Career Office Mr. Jeff AUPPERLE
42 Campus Pastor Mr. Jon CAVANAGH
15 Director of Human Resources Ms. Nicole MURPHY
106 Director of Online Learning Ms. Carrie MEYER
25 Dir of Sponsored Programs Dr. Kris JOHNSON
18 Director of Facility Services Mr. Gregg HOLLOWAY
38 Director of Counseling Ctr Ms. Kathy CHAMBERLAIN
19 Chief of Police/Taylor Police Mr. Jeff WALLACE
21 Dir of Acctng/Financial Reporting Mr. David LLOYD
21 Director Financial Operations Ms. Michele BRAGG
26 Sr Dir Parent & Community Rels Ms. Joyce WOOD
118 Dir of Payroll & Benefits Ms. Toni NEWLIN
114 Bursar/Student Accounts Ms. Jill THURMAN
90 Director Academic Computing Mr. TR KNIGHT

TCM International Institute (D)

6337 Hollister Drive, Indianapolis IN 46224
County: Marion Identification: 666333
Telephone: (317) 299-0333 Carnegie Class: Not Classified
FAX Number: (317) 290-8607 Calendar System: Semester
URL: www.tcmi.edu
Established: 1991 Annual Graduate Tuition & Fees: N/A
Enrollment: N/A Coed
Affiliation or Control: Independent Non-Profit IRS Status: 501(c)3
Highest Offering: Master's; No Undergraduates
Accreditation: HLC

01 President Dr. Tony TWIST
05 VP Educational Advancement Dr. Richard JUSTICE
11 U.S. Director of Operations Ms. Carol FIELDS
10 Director of Finance Ms. Julie RICE

Trine University (E)

1 University Avenue, Angola IN 46703-1764
County: Steuben FICE Identification: 001839
Unit ID: 152567
Telephone: (260) 665-4100 Carnegie Class: Masters/M
FAX Number: (260) 665-4292 Calendar System: Semester
URL: www.trine.edu
Established: 1884 Annual Undergrad Tuition & Fees: $33,490
Enrollment: 3,573 Coed
Affiliation or Control: Independent Non-Profit IRS Status: 501(c)3
Highest Offering: Doctorate
Accreditation: HLC, ACBSP, #ARCPA, CAEP, PTA, SURGT

01 President Dr. Earl D. BROOKS, II
05 Vice President for Academic Affairs Dr. John SHANNON
10 Vice President Finance Ms. Kayla WARREN
84 Vice Pres Enrollment Management Ms. Kim BENNETT
100 VP Administration/Chief of Staff Ms. Gretchen MILLER
32 Dean of Students Mr. Francisco ORTIZ
26 VP Univ Marketing/Communications Mr. Dave JARZYNA
29 VP Alumni/Development Mr. David FRABONI
41 Athletic Director/Asst VP Athletics Mr. Matt LAND
49 Dean Jannen School of Arts & Sci Ms. Sarah FRANZEN
107 Asst VP Prof Studies/Trine Online Ms. Keirsten EBERTS
15 Human Resources Ms. Jamie NORTON
06 Registrar Ms. Debra F. HELMSING
08 Director of the Library Ms. Michelle BLANK
36 Director of Placement/Coop Educ Ms. Linda COOPER
09 Director Inst Planning/Analysis Ms. Christina ZUMBRUN

Union Bible College (F)

PO Box 900, Westfield IN 46074
County: Hamilton Identification: 667253
Telephone: (317) 896-9324 Carnegie Class: Not Classified
FAX Number: (317) 867-0784 Calendar System: Semester
URL: www.ubca.org
Established: 1911 Annual Undergrad Tuition & Fees: N/A
Enrollment: N/A Coed
Affiliation or Control: Interdenominational IRS Status: 501(c)3
Highest Offering: Baccalaureate
Accreditation: BI

01 President C. Adam BUCKLER
05 Vice Pres Academic Affairs John WHITAKER
10 Director of Finance Lanae WHITAKER
11 Director of Operations Vacant
32 Dean of Student Life Joe CAREY
09 Director of Institutional Research Isabel RUNDELL
06 Registrar Elizabeth DAVIS
07 Director of Admissions Phil HOARD

University of Evansville (G)

1800 Lincoln Avenue, Evansville IN 47722-1586
County: Vanderburgh FICE Identification: 001795
Unit ID: 150534
Telephone: (812) 488-2000 Carnegie Class: Masters/S
FAX Number: (812) 488-2320 Calendar System: Semester
URL: www.evansville.edu
Established: 1854 Annual Undergrad Tuition & Fees: $38,686
Enrollment: 2,323 Coed
Affiliation or Control: United Methodist IRS Status: 501(c)3
Highest Offering: Doctorate
Accreditation: HLC, ANEST, ARCPA, CAATE, CAEP, MUS, NUR, PTA

01 President Mr. Christopher M. PIETRUSZKIEWICZ
05 Exec VP Academic Affairs Dr. Michael AUSTIN
111 VP Advancement Ms. Abigail WERLING
10 VP Fiscal Affairs & Admin Ms. Donna TEAGUE
32 VP Student Affairs Dr. Dana CLAYTON
108 Assoc Provost for Academic Affairs Dr. Dave DWYER
84 VP Enrollment/Marketing Dr. Jill G. GRIFFIN
35 Asst VP Student Affs/Dir Res Life Mr. Michael A. TESSIER
13 Chief Information Officer/OTS Mr. Michael SMITH
49 Dean of Arts & Sciences Dr. Ray LUTGRING
50 Dean College Business/Engineering Dr. Beverly BROCKMAN
53 Dean of Educ/Health Science Ms. Mary KESSLER
51 Sr Dir Ctr Advancement of Learning Ms. Cynthia FELTS
85 Director International Programs Dr. Patricia Lorena ANDUEZA
41 Director of Athletics Mr. Mark SPENCER
26 Sr Dir Marketing/Communication Ms. Holly SMITH
06 University Registrar Ms. Keely CUTTS
08 University Librarian Mr. Robb WALTNER
42 University Chaplain Rev. Andy PAYTON
96 Manager of Admin Service/Purchasing Ms. Kim WINSETT
29 Sr Director of Alumni/Engagement Ms. Jennifer CALDERONE
36 Sr Dir Ctr Career Development Mr. Gene WELLS
38 Director of Counseling/Health Educ Ms. Karen STENSTROM
37 Director of Student Financial Svcs Ms. Becky HAMILTON
15 Dir of HR/Institutional Equity Mr. Keith GEHLHAUSEN
18 Exec Dir Facilities Mgmt & Plng Mr. Chad MILLER
19 Chief of Safety & Security Mr. Jason CULLUM
104 Principal Harlaxton College Dr. Holly CARTER
40 Director of Bookstore Ms. Becky LAMONT
28 Chief Diversity Officer Dr. Robert SHELBY
112 Sr Dir of Major Gifts/Campaigns Ms. Jennifer WHITAKER
121 Director of Academic Advising Vacant
07 Director of Admissions Mr. Kenton HARGIS
04 Exec Assistant to the President Ms. Patricia A. LIPPERT

University of Indianapolis (H)

1400 E Hanna Avenue, Indianapolis IN 46227-3697
County: Marion FICE Identification: 001804
Unit ID: 151263
Telephone: (317) 788-3368 Carnegie Class: DU-Mod
FAX Number: (317) 788-3300 Calendar System: Semester
URL: www.uindy.edu
Established: 1902 Annual Undergrad Tuition & Fees: $32,268
Enrollment: 5,638 Coed
Affiliation or Control: United Methodist IRS Status: 501(c)3
Highest Offering: Doctorate
Accreditation: HLC, ACBSP, ART, CAATE, CAEP, CAEPN, CLPSY, COARC, COSMA, @DIETI, EXSC, MPCAC, MUS, NURSE, OT, PTA, PTAA, SW

01 President Dr. Robert L. MANUEL
45 Exec VP for Innovation & Planning Dr. Neil PERDUE
05 Interim VP & Provost Dr. Mary Beth BAGG
84 VP for Enrollment Services Ms. Lara G. MANN
10 VP & Chief Financial Officer Mr. Jason DUDICH
111 Vice President for Univ Advancement Vacant
41 VP for Intercollegiate Athletics Mr. Scott YOUNG
42 VP for Mission Dr. Michael G. CARTWRIGHT
43 Vice President & General Counsel Ms. Andrea NEWSOM
32 VP Stdnt/Campus Affs/Dean of Stdnts Ms. Kory M. VITANGELI
13 VP/Chief Technology Officer Mr. Steven R. HERRIFORD
22 VP/Chief Incl & Equity Officer Dr. Amber SMITH
29 VP of Alumni/Univ Events/Ext Rel Mr. Andrew KOCHER
26 Assoc VP for Marketing Ms. Stacey LEE
26 Assoc VP for Communications Ms. Sara GALER
06 Registrar Ms. Josh HAYES

49 Dean College of Arts & Sciences .... Dr. Patrick VAN FLEET
50 Dean School of Business .... Dr. Lawrence BELCHER
53 Dean School of Education .... Dr. John KUYKENDALL
66 Dean School of Nursing .... Ms. Norma HALL
76 Dean College of Health Sciences .... Dr. Stephanie KELLY
83 Dean Psychological Sciences .... Dr. Torrey WILSON
20 Int Assoc Prov Rsrch/Grad/Acad Ptnr .... Ms. Ellen MILLER
108 Assoc VP for Accreditation .... Dr. Mary C. MOORE
84 Director of Admissions Recruitment .... Ms. Katie ASHCRAFT
08 Library Director .... Ms. Marisa ALBRECHT
15 Director Human Resources .... Mrs. Erin P. FARRELL
37 Director of Financial Aid .... Mr. Nathan LOHR
58 Director Graduate Business Pgms .... Mr. Stephen A. TOKAR
18 Executive Director Facilities Mgmt .... Mr. Dave STATLER
19 Director Safety & Police Services .... Mr. David K. SELBY
31 Director of Service Learning .... Dr. Marianna K. FOULKROD
42 Chaplain/Dir Lantz Center .... Rev. Jeremiah GIBBS
85 Director International Division .... Ms. Marilyn O. CHASE
38 Director Counseling Center .... Dr. Kelly M. MILLER
40 Bookstore Manager .... Ms. Kimberly MILLION
07 Director of Admissions Operations .... Ms. Jennifer OUTLAW

University of Notre Dame (A)

400 Main Building, Notre Dame IN 46556
County: Saint Joseph
FICE Identification: 001840
Unit ID: 152080
Telephone: (574) 631-5000
Carnegie Class: DU-Highest
FAX Number: (574) 631-6700
Calendar System: Semester
URL: www.nd.edu
Established: 1842
Annual Undergrad Tuition & Fees: $57,699
Enrollment: 12,809
Coed
Affiliation or Control: Roman Catholic
IRS Status: 501(c)3
Highest Offering: Doctorate
Accreditation: HLC, ART, CLPSY, IPSY, LAW, THEOL

01 President .... Rev. John I. JENKINS, CSC
05 Provost .... Dr. Marie Lynn MIRANDA
03 Executive Vice President .... Mr. Shannon B. CULLINAN
20 Vice Pres/Sr Associate Provost .... Dr. Christine M. MAZIAR
20 Vice Pres/Associate Provost .... Dr. Maura A. RYAN
89 Vice Pres/Associate Provost .... Dr. Hugh R. PAGE, JR.
82 VP/Provost Internationalization .... Dr. Michael PIPPENGER
32 Vice President for Student Affairs .... Rev. Gerard J. OLINGER
10 Vice President for Finance .... Mr. Trent A. GROCOCK
46 Vice President for Research .... Dr. Robert J. BERNHARD
43 Vice President & General Counsel .... Ms. Marianne CORR
115 Vice Pres/Chief Investment Ofcr .... Mr. Mike DONOVAN
41 Vice Pres & Director of Athletics .. Mr. John B. SWARBRICK, JR.
15 Vice Pres Human Resources .... Mr. Robert K. MCQUADE
26 Vice President University Relations .... Mr. Louis M. NANNI
27 VP Public Affairs/Communications .... Vacant
13 VP & Chief Information Officer .... Ms. Jane LIVINGSTON
88 VP Mission Engagmnt/Church Affairs .... Rev. Austin COLLLINS, CSC
58 VP/Assoc Prov/Dean Graduate Sch .... Dr. Laura CARLSON
45 VP Strategic Planning .... Mr. David C. BAILEY
100 Vice President/Chief of Staff .... Ms. Ann M. FIRTH
19 Vice Pres Campus Safety/Univ Ops .... Mr. Mike SEAMON
28 Chief Diversity Officer .... Mr. Eric LOVE
84 Assoc VP Undergraduate Enrollment .... Mr. Donald C. BISHOP
18 VP Facilities & Design .... Mr. Douglas K. MARSH
109 Vice Pres Univ Enterprises/Events .... Ms. Micki KIDDER
06 Registrar .... Mr. Charles T. HURLEY
96 Director Procurement .... Mr. Gilberto CARLES
50 Dean College of Business .... Dr. Martijn CREMERS
61 Dean of Law School .... Fr. Marcus G. COLE
54 Interim Dean College of Engineering .... Dr. Thomas E. FUJA
49 Dean of Arts & Letters .... Dr. Sarah A. MUSTILLO
81 Dean of Science .... Dr. Mary E. GALVIN
48 Dean of Architecture .... Dr. Stefanos POLYZOIDES
82 Dean School of Global Affairs .... Dr. Scott APPLEBY
29 Exec Director Alumni Assoc .... Ms. Dolly DUFFY
08 Dir of University Libraries .... Ms. Diane PARR WALKER
42 Director of Campus Ministry .... Rev. Peter M. MCCORMICK, CSC
37 Dir of Student Financial Aid .... Ms. Mary B. NUCCIARONE
36 Director of Undergrad Career Svcs .. Ms. LoriAnn EDINBOROUGH
38 Director of Counseling Center .... Dr. Christine G. CONWAY
19 Director of Security/Police .... Ms. Keri Kei SHIBATA
07 Director of Admissions .... Ms. Christy PRATT
101 Secretary of the Institution/Board .... Ms. Anne GRIFFITH
09 Director of Institutional Research .... Ms. Eva NANCE
102 Dir Foundation/Corporate Relations .... Mr. Rudy REYES
104 Director Study Abroad .... Ms. Hong ZHU
39 Director Student Housing .... Ms. Karen M. KENNEDY
04 Administrative Asst to President .... Ms. Sarah A. GOTSCH
86 Director Government Relations .... Mr. Timothy D. SEXTON
25 Chief Contract/Grants Administrator .... Ms. Michelle JOYCE
30 Director of Development .... Ms. Jill CALDERONE
44 Director Annual Giving .... Mr. Brian DISS

University of Saint Francis (B)

2701 Spring Street, Fort Wayne IN 46808-3994
County: Allen
FICE Identification: 001832
Unit ID: 152336
Telephone: (260) 399-7700
Carnegie Class: Masters/L
FAX Number: N/A
Calendar System: Semester
URL: www.sf.edu
Established: 1890
Annual Undergrad Tuition & Fees: $32,420
Enrollment: 2,271
Coed
Affiliation or Control: Roman Catholic
IRS Status: 501(c)3
Highest Offering: Doctorate
Accreditation: HLC, ACBSP, ADNUR, ANEST, #ARCPA, ART, CAEP, DIETC, MLTAD, NURSE, PTAA, RAD, SURGT, SW

01 President .... RevDr. Eric A. ZIMMER
05 VP Academic Affairs .... Dr. Lance B. RICHEY
11 VP Administration .... Vacant
111 VP Institutional Advancement .... Ms. Ellen PAXTON
10 VP of Operations .... Mr. Richard A. BIENZ
32 VP Student Affairs .... Mr. Robert PASTOOR
84 VP Enrollment Management .... Ms. Beth M. TERRELL
20 Assoc VP Academic Affairs .... Mrs. Trish J. BUGAJSKI, OFS
88 Assistant VP Mission Integration ..... Sr. M. Anita HOLZMER, OSF
50 Dean Keith Busse School of Business .... Vacant
57 Dean School of Creative Arts .... Vacant
17 Dean School of Health Sciences .... Dr. Angela HARRELL
49 Dean Business/Arts & Sciences .... Dr. Andrea GEYER
12 Dean Crown Point Site .... Dr. Marsha M. KING
36 Exec Dir Acad & Career Devel Ctr .... Vacant
106 Exec Dir Enrollment Management .. Mrs. Michelle L. KUHLHORST
13 Exec Dir Univ Technology Svcs .... Vacant
21 VP for Finance .... Mr. Craig M. TEETSEL
06 Registrar .... Vacant
42 Chaplain .... Mr. John SHEEHAN
121 Director Academic Advising .... Ms. Melissa J. REESMAN
29 Director Alumni Relations .... Mr. Tony S. DIDIER
41 Director Athletics .... Mr. Michael H. MCCAFFREY
42 Director Campus Ministry .... Vacant
28 Dir Diversity & Inclusion .... Dr. Paul PORTER
102 Dir Found Relations/Grant Writer .... Ms. Jessica H. EGGERS-BUTTES
15 Dir Human Resources & Org Develop .... Mrs. Carol L. COFFEE
92 Dir John Duns Scotus Honors Program .... Dr. Kenneth A. BUGAJSKI
105 Director Marketing .... Mrs. Carla S. PYLE
88 Director Sports Information .... Mr. William J. SCOTT
88 Dir Student Service Learning/Engage .. Mrs. Katrina P. BOEDEKER
08 Assoc Dir Information/Instruc Svcs .. Mrs. Maureen E. MCMAHAN
37 Assistant Director Financial Aid .... Mr. Michael L. CARPENTER
15 Assistant Dir Human Resources .... Mr. Andy MCKEE
53 Chair Department of Education .... Dr. Mary E. REIPENHOFF
19 Supervisor Campus Safety/Security ..... Mr. Edward A. LAROCQUE
18 Supervisor Maintenance/Grounds .... Mr. Ramon S. DEMOND
44 Senior Gift Officer .... Vacant
09 Research/Assessment Analyst .... Mrs. Kim E. DIETRICH
04 Executive Assistant to President .... Mrs. Melissa STUDEBAKER
109 Mgr Creative Dining Food Service .... Ms. Scott KAMMERER
40 Mgr Barnes & Noble Campus Shoppe .... Mrs. Robin HUFFMAN

University of Southern Indiana (C)

8600 University Boulevard, Evansville IN 47712-3596
County: Vanderburgh
FICE Identification: 001808
Unit ID: 151306
Telephone: (812) 464-8600
Carnegie Class: Masters/L
FAX Number: (812) 464-1960
Calendar System: Semester
URL: www.usi.edu
Established: 1965
Annual Undergrad Tuition & Fees (In-State): $9,285
Enrollment: 10,203
Coed
Affiliation or Control: State
IRS Status: 501(c)3
Highest Offering: Doctorate
Accreditation: HLC, ART, CAEP, CAEPN, CEA, COARC, COSMA, DA, DH, DIETD, DMS, EXSC, NURSE, OT, OTA, RAD, SW

01 President .... Dr. Ronald S. ROCHON
100 Exec Assistant to the President .... Mrs. Nita R. MUSICH
100 Sr Exec Assistant to the President .... Mrs. Carey BEURY
05 Provost .... Dr. Mohammed KHAYUM
10 Vice President for Finance & Admin .... Mr. Steven J. BRIDGES
32 VP for Student Affairs .... Dr. Khalilah DOSS
26 VP Marketing & Communications .... Mrs. Kindra L. STRUPP
20 Assoc Provost for Academic Affairs .... Dr. Shelly B. BLUNT
38 Int Director of Counseling Center .... Dr. Robin SANABRIA
21 Assoc VP Finance & Administration .... Ms. Mary A. HUPFER
86 Chief Government/Legal Affairs Ofcr .... Mr. Aaron C. TRUMP
09 Chief Data Officer .... Dr. Katherine A. DRAUGHON
58 Director of Graduate Studies .... Dr. Michael D. DIXON
06 Registrar .... Mrs. Sandy K. FRANK
84 Executive Director of Enrollment .... Mr. Rashad E. SMITH
08 Director of Library .... Ms. Marna M. HOSTETLER
30 VP for Dev/Pres USI Foundation .... Mr. David A. BOWER
92 Director Honors Program .... Dr. Sarah E. STEVENS
29 Dir Alumni Relations/Volunteer USI .... Mrs. Janet L. JOHNSON
37 Dir Student Financial Assistance .... Mrs. Mary J. HARPER
15 Exec Director of Human Resources ..... Mr. Andrew R. LENHARDT
35 Dean of Students .... Dr. Jennifer R. HAMMAT
85 Int Dir Center for Int'l Programs .... Ms. Emilija ZLATKOVSKA
28 Director Multicultural Center .... Mrs. Pamela F. HOPSON
13 Chief Information Officer .... Mr. Richard J. TOENISKOETTER
90 Academic Services Coordinator .... Mr. Juzar AHMED
18 Dir of Facility Operations & Plng .... Mr. James E. WOLFE
96 Director of Procurement .... Mr. Jeffrey M. SPONN
27 Director of Univ Communications .... Mr. John A. FARLESS
19 Director of Public Safety .... Mr. Stephen L. BEQUETTE
39 Director of Housing/Residence Life .... Ms. Amy S. PRICE
41 Athletic Director .... Mr. Jon Mark HALL
50 Dean Romain College of Business .... Dr. Catherine CAREY
49 Int Dean College of Liberal Arts .... Dr. Melinda R. ROBERTS
66 Dean College Nursing/Health Prof .... Dr. Ann H. WHITE
81 Dean College of Sci/Engr/Educ .... Dr. Zane W. MITCHELL, JR.
51 Exec Dir of Outreach & Engagement ... Ms. Dawn M. STONEKING
120 Exec Dir of Online Learning .... Dr. Belle COWDEN
105 Director of Web Services .... Mrs. Brandi S. HESS

Valparaiso University (D)

Valparaiso IN 46383-6493
County: Porter
FICE Identification: 001842
Unit ID: 152600
Telephone: (219) 464-5000
Carnegie Class: DU-Mod
FAX Number: (219) 464-5381
Calendar System: Semester
URL: valpo.edu
Established: 1859
Annual Undergrad Tuition & Fees: $43,286
Enrollment: 3,122
Coed
Affiliation or Control: Lutheran
IRS Status: 501(c)3
Highest Offering: Doctorate
Accreditation: HLC, #ARCPA, CACREP, CAEP, MUS, NURSE, SW

01 President .... Mr. Jose D. PADILLA
05 Provost/Exec VP for Academic Affs .... Mr. Eric W. JOHNSON
32 VP for Student Affairs .... Mr. Steve JANOWIAK
84 VP for Enroll/Mktg/Communications .... Mr. Brian O'ROURKE
58 Acting Dean Grad School/Cont Educ .... Ms. Trisha MILEHAM
111 VP for Advancement .... Ms. Lisa HOLLANDER
110 AVP for Advancement .... Mr. Jason PETROVICH
26 Chief Communication Officer .... Ms. Nicole NIEMI
43 VP/General Counsel .... Mr. Darron C. FARHA
10 Senior VP for Finance .... Ms. Susan SCROGGINS
100 VP Cmty & Govt Rels/Chief of Staff .... Mr. Rick AMRHEIN
92 Dean of Christ College .... Dr. Susan VANZANTEN
49 Dean College Arts & Sciences .... Dr. Jon T. KILPINEN
61 Dean School of Law .... Mr. David CLEVELAND
54 Dean College of Engineering .... Dr. Eric JOHNSON
50 Dean College of Business Admin .... Dr. James BRODZINSKI
66 Dean College of Nursing .... Dr. Karen ALLEN
08 Dean Library Services .... Ms. Trisha MILEHAM
35 Dean of Students .... Dr. Timothy S. JENKINS
88 AVP Enrollment Management .... Mr. David FEVIG
42 AVP for Mission & Ministry .... Dr. Susan VANZANTEN
06 Interim Registrar .... Ms. Allison URBANCZYK
19 Chief University Police .... Ms. Rebecca A. WALKOWIAK
39 Asst Dean Students/Residential Life .... Mr. Ryan BLEVINS
104 Assoc Dir of Study Abroad .... Ms. Erin KUNERT
85 Assoc Dir of International Program .... Ms. Janice LIN
29 Exec Director Alumni Relations .... Ms. Linda ROETTGER
15 Exec Dir Human Resource Services .... Mr. Scott HARRISON
18 Exec Dir of Facilities .... Mr. Jason KUTCH
36 Director Career Center .... Mr. Tom CATH
38 Director of Counseling Services .... Dr. Stewart E. COOPER
41 Director Athletics .... Mr. Mark LABARBERA
20 Asst Provost for Faculty Affairs .... Dr. Lissa YOGAN
21 Controller .... Ms. Tamara GINGERICH
28 Int Asst Prov Inclusion/Stdnt Succ .... Mr. Byron MARTIN
09 Exec Dir Inst Effectiveness .... Mr. Greg STINSON
42 Interim University Pastor .... Dcs. Kristin LEWIS
42 University Pastor .... Rev. James WETZSTEIN
37 Director of Financial Aid .... Ms. Karen KLIMCZYK
04 Administrative Asst to President .... Ms. Gwen GRAHAM
07 Director of Admission Programs .... Ms. Barb LIESKE
102 Dir Foundation/Corporate Relations .... Ms. Kathy GROTH
13 Chief Info Technology Officer (CIO) .... Mr. Dave SIERKOWSKI

Veritas Baptist College (E)

181 U.S. 50 East, Suite 204, Greendale IN 47025
County: Dearborn
FICE Identification: 038626
Unit ID: 482228
Telephone: (812) 221-1714
Carnegie Class: Spec-4-yr-Faith
FAX Number: (540) 785-5441
Calendar System: Semester
URL: www.vbc.edu
Established: 1984
Annual Undergrad Tuition & Fees: $6,716
Enrollment: 216
Coed
Affiliation or Control: Baptist
IRS Status: 501(c)3
Highest Offering: Master's
Accreditation: TRACS

01 President .... John EDMONDS
00 Chancellor .... Dr. Don FORRESTER
05 Academic Dean .... Ann RILL
10 Chief Financial Officer .... Sherry DAVIS
37 Director Student Financial Aid .... Delaney JOHNSTON
07 Director of Admissions .... Michele E. CATLIN

Vincennes University (F)

1002 N First Street, Vincennes IN 47591-1504
County: Knox
FICE Identification: 001843
Unit ID: 152637
Telephone: (812) 888-8888
Carnegie Class: Bac/Assoc-Assoc Dom
FAX Number: (812) 888-5868
Calendar System: Semester
URL: www.vinu.edu
Established: 1801
Annual Undergrad Tuition & Fees (In-State): $6,251
Enrollment: 16,048
Coed
Affiliation or Control: State
IRS Status: 501(c)3
Highest Offering: Baccalaureate
Accreditation: HLC, ACBSP, ADNUR, ART, CAEP, CAHIIM, FUSER, NUR, PNUR, PTAA, SURGT

01 President .... Dr. Charles R. JOHNSON
05 Provost/VP Instructional Services .... Dr. Laura TREANOR
86 Vice Pres Government Relations .... Mr. Tony HAHN
10 Vice Pres Financial Services .... Ms. Linda WALDROUP
103 VP Workforce Dev/Comm Services .... Mr. David A. TUCKER
12 Asst Vice Pres/Dean Jasper Campus .... Mr. Christian BLOME
21 Controller .... Ms. Conya R. WAMPLER
32 Asst Provost Student Affairs .... Ms. Whitney N. DAUGHERTY

20 Asst Provost Curriculum & Inst .... Mr. Rick A. KRIBS
26 Sr Director External Relations ....Ms. Sarah E. FORTUNE
07 Director of Admissions ....Mr. Ryan J. BARBAULD
09 Sr Dir Inst Effectiveness/Research ....Mr. Dale R. PIETRZAK
13 Director of Mgmt Information Center ....Mr. Bob G. WISLER
88 Director of University Events ....Vacant
36 Director Career Center ....Ms. Donna TAYLOR-BOUCHIE
37 Director of Student Financial Aid ....Mr. Stanley J. WERNE
22 Dir Diverse Abilities/Accommodation ....Ms. Sarah Jill STEELE
40 Manager of Bookstore ....Ms. Karen R. FAULKNER
102 Executive Director VU Foundation ....Ms. Kristi R. DEETZ
41 Athletic Director ....Mr. Harry L. MEEKS
88 Sr Dir Dual Credit Partnerships ....Ms. Heather MARCHINO
29 Int Director of Alumni Programs .... Ms. Savannah C. LINENBURG
28 Director Multicultural Affairs ....Vacant
18 Director of Physical Plant ....Mr. William KROEGER
19 Int Director of Campus Police ....Mr. Adam DAUGHERTY
113 Bursar ....Ms. Terri PERRY
06 Registrar ....Ms. Rebecca K. LITTLE
35 Dean of Students ....Mr. Robert L. DOTSON
39 Assoc Dean Housing/Residence Life .... Mr. Adam D. BOOHER
27 Director of Multimedia & Analytics ....Mr. Ryan EVANCOE
96 Director of Procurement ....Mr. Michael L. MORRISON
121 Director Student Success Center .... Ms. Gaye WALTHALL
88 Dir Architectural Svcs/Facilities ....Mr. Andrew YOUNG
15 Director Human Resources/ AAO ....Ms. Regina L. MCCORD-FITHIAN
76 Dean College Health Sci/Human Perf ...... Ms. Michelle CUMMINS
50 Dean College of Business/Public Svc .. Ms. Susan BROCKSMITH
72 Dean College of Technology ....Mr. Ty FREED
81 Dean College of Sc/Engr/Math .... Mr. Curt COFFMAN
83 Dean Soc Sci/Perf Arts/Comm .... Dr. Cynthia RAGLE
114 AVP Finance Svcs/Budget Director ....Mr. Tim EATON
79 Dean College of Humanities .... Ms. Joan PUCKETT
88 Dir Avia Tech Ctr Indianapolis ....Mr. Michael D. GEHRICH
88 Dean of Academic Early College ....Ms. Nicole SHANKLE
88 Dir Out of State Military Educ Pgm ... Mr. Matthew J. SCHWARTZ
88 Director Military Education Pgms .... Mr. Alex SIEVERS
88 Dir Plainfield Logistics Center .... Mr. Scott A. BACON
04 Administrative Asst to President .... Ms. Nancy A. IRWIN
88 Director International Recruitment .... Mr. Ze (Wade) CHEN
23 Dir University Primary Care Clinic ....Ms. Deborah A. BEDWELL
85 Director International Affairs ....Vacant
51 Asst VP Lifelong Learning .... Ms. Shanni E. SIMMONS

Vincennes University-Jasper Center (A)

850 College Avenue, Jasper IN 47546
Telephone: (812) 482-3030 Identification: 770107
Accreditation: &HLC

Wabash College (B)

301 W Wabash Avenue, PO Box 352,
Crawfordsville IN 47933-0352
County: Montgomery FICE Identification: 001844
Unit ID: 152673
Telephone: (765) 361-6100 Carnegie Class: Bac-A&S
FAX Number: (765) 361-6461 Calendar System: Semester
URL: www.wabash.edu
Established: 1832 Annual Undergrad Tuition & Fees: $45,850
Enrollment: 868 Male
Affiliation or Control: Independent Non-Profit IRS Status: 501(c)3
Highest Offering: Baccalaureate
Accreditation: HLC

01 President ....Dr. Scott E. FELLER
05 Acting Dean of the College .... Dr. Todd F. MCDORMAN
10 Chief Financial Officer & Treasurer .... Ms. Kendra COOKS
32 Dean of Students ....Dr. Gregory REDDING
111 Dean for Advancement/Development .... Ms. Michelle L. JANSSEN
84 Dean for Enrollment Management ... Mr. Charles (Chip) TIMMONS
07 Assoc Director of Admissions ....Mr. Matt BOWERS
28 Dean Prof Dev & Malcolm X Institute ....Mr. Steven L. JONES
100 Chief of Staff ....Mr. James L. AMIDON
20 Sr Associate Dean of the College ....Dr. Ann TAYLOR
08 Head Librarian & Dir Lilly Library ....Mr. Jeffery BECK
06 Registrar & Assoc Dean ....Dr. Jonathon D. JUMP
13 Director of IT Services ....Mr. Bradley K. WEAVER
37 Director of Financial Aid ....Mr. Alex DELONIS
35 Associate Dean of Students ....Mr. Marc WELCH
36 Director of Career Development ....Mr. Roland MORIN
29 Dir of Alumni & Parent Relations .... Mr. Steve HOFFMAN
109 Director of Business Auxiliaries ....Mr. Thomas E. KEEDY
41 Dir of Athletics & Campus Wellness .... Mr. Matt TANNEY
110 Associate Dean for Advancement .... Mr. Joseph R. KLEN
15 Director of Human Resources ....Ms. Catherine A. METZ
18 Director of Campus Services .... Mr. David MORGAN
21 Controller ....Mr. Douglas SMITH
38 Director of Counseling Services ....Ms. Jamie DOUGLAS
88 Director of Inquiries CILA ....Dr. Charles F. BLAICH
88 Dir Wabash Ctr Teaching/Learning .Ms. Nancy Lynne WESTFIELD
19 Director of Safety and Security ....Mr. Nicholas GRAY
09 Director of Institutional Research .... Mr. David DALENBERG
101 Secretary of the Institution/Board ....Mr. James L. AMIDON, JR.
102 Dir Foundation/Corporate Relations ....Ms. Deborah WOODS
104 Director International Programs ....Ms. Amy WEIR
26 Chief Public Relations/Marketing .... Ms. Kimberly JOHNSON
96 Director of Purchasing ....Mr. Thomas E. KEEDY
04 Admin Assistant to the President ....Ms. Beverly CUNNINGHAM
44 Director Annual Giving ....Mr. Aaron SHELBY
28 Diversity/Equity and Inclusion .... Dr. Jill LAMBERTON

IOWA

Allen College (C)

1825 Logan Avenue, Waterloo IA 50703-1999
County: Black Hawk FICE Identification: 030691
Unit ID: 152798
Telephone: (319) 226-2000 Carnegie Class: Spec-4-yr-Other Health
FAX Number: (319) 226-2010 Calendar System: Semester
URL: www.allencollege.edu
Established: 1989 Annual Undergrad Tuition & Fees: $19,512
Enrollment: 678 Coed
Affiliation or Control: Independent Non-Profit IRS Status: 501(c)3
Highest Offering: Doctorate
Accreditation: HLC, DMS, MT, NURSE, OT, @PTA, RAD

01 President ....Dr. Jared SELIGER
05 Provost ....Dr. Bob LOCH
10 Exec Director Business/Admin Svcs ....Ms. Denise HANSON
66 Dean School of Nursing ....Dr. Kendra WILLIAMS-PEREZ
76 Dean School of Health Sciences .... Dr. Peggy FORTSCH
84 Dean Enrollment Management .... Dr. Joanna RAMSDEN-MEIER
37 Director of Financial Aid ....Ms. Renae CARRILLO
24 Media Specialist ....Ms. Robin NICHOLSON
06 Registrar ....Ms. Michelle KOEHN
08 Director of Library Services ....Dr. Ruth YAN
07 Director of Admissions ....Ms. Molly QUINN
09 Coord Inst Research/Effectiveness ....Dr. Lisa BRODERSEN
04 Administrative Asst to President ....Ms. Rhonda GILBERT
28 Director of Diversity ....Vacant

Antioch School of Church Planting and Leadership Development (D)

2400 Oakwood Road, Ames IA 50014
County: Story Identification: 667026
Telephone: (515) 292-9694 Carnegie Class: Not Classified
FAX Number: (515) 292-1933 Calendar System: Other
URL: www.antiochschool.edu
Established: 2006 Annual Undergrad Tuition & Fees: N/A
Enrollment: N/A Coed
Affiliation or Control: Independent Non-Profit IRS Status: 501(c)3
Highest Offering: Doctorate
Accreditation: DEAC

01 President ....Jeff REED
05 Academic Dean ....Stephen KEMP

The Art of Education University (E)

518 Main Street, Ste A, Osage IA 50461
County: Mitchell Identification: 667385
Telephone: (515) 650-3198 Carnegie Class: Not Classified
FAX Number: N/A Calendar System: Other
URL: theartofeducation.edu
Established: 2011 Annual Graduate Tuition & Fees: N/A
Enrollment: N/A Coed
Affiliation or Control: Proprietary IRS Status: Proprietary
Highest Offering: Master's; No Undergraduates
Accreditation: DEAC

01 President ....Jessica BALSLEY
05 Chief Academic Officer ....Cheryl HAYEK
07 Director of Admissions .... Shannon LAUFFER
10 Chief Financial/Business Officer ....Gwen JASS
15 Chief Human Resources Officer ....Maria THOMAS

*Board of Regents, State of Iowa (F)

11260 Aurora Avenue, Urbandale IA 50322-7905
County: Polk FICE Identification: 033443
Telephone: (515) 281-3934 Carnegie Class: N/A
FAX Number: (515) 281-6420
URL: www.iowaregents.edu

01 President ....Dr. Michael J. RICHARDS
00 Executive Director & COO ....Mr. Mark J. BRAUN
05 Chief Academic Officer ....Dr. Rachel L. BOON
43 Board Counsel ....Mrs. Aimee K. CLAEYS
04 Executive Assistant ....Mrs. Laura M. DICKSON

*Iowa State University (G)

1750 Beardshear Hall, 515 Morrill R, Ames IA 50011
County: Story FICE Identification: 001869
Unit ID: 153603
Telephone: (515) 294-4111 Carnegie Class: DU-Highest
FAX Number: (515) 294-2592 Calendar System: Semester
URL: www.iastate.edu
Established: 1858 Annual Undergrad Tuition & Fees (In-State): $9,316
Enrollment: 31,822 Coed
Affiliation or Control: State IRS Status: 501(c)3
Highest Offering: Doctorate
Accreditation: HLC, ART, CAATE, CEA, CIDA, COPSY, DIETC, DIETD, IPSY, JOUR, LSAR, MUS, NAIT, PLNG, VET

02 President ....Dr. Wendy WINTERSTEEN
04 Assistant to the President ....Ms. Shirley J. KNIPFEL
43 University Counsel ....Mr. Michael E. NORTON
05 Sr Vice President and Provost ....Dr. Jonathan A. WICKERT
10 Sr VP for Operations & Finance ....Ms. Pam CAIN
32 Sr Vice Pres for Student Affairs ....Dr. Toyia YOUNGER
88 Int VP for Econ Dev/Business Engag ...... Mr. David P. SPALDING
46 Vice Pres Research ....Dr. Sarah M. NUSSER
56 Vice Pres Extension/Outreach ....Dr. John D. LAWRENCE
13 Vice Pres/Chief Info Officer ....Dr. Kristin P. CONSTANT
28 Vice Pres for Diversity & Inclusion ....Vacant
20 Associate Provost Academic Programs .... Dr. Ann Marie VANDERZANDEN
20 Assoc Prov Faculty ....Dr. Dawn BRATSCH-PRINCE
18 Assoc Vice Pres Facilities Planning .... Mr. Paul FULIGNI
15 Vice President Human Resources ....Ms. Kristi DARR
35 Assoc Vice Pres & Dean of Students ....Dr. Vernon J. HURTE
84 Assoc VP Stdnt Affs for Enroll Mgmt .... Ms. Laura J. DOERING
88 Assoc VP Strategic Relations/Comm ....Ms. Jacy R. JOHNSON
22 Asst Vice Pres Equal Opportunity ....Ms. Margo FOREMAN
19 Asst VP and Chief of Police .... Mr. Michael R. NEWTON
39 Asst VP for St Aff/Dir of Residence ....Dr. Peter D. ENGLIN
38 Asst VP Stdnt Health/Wellness ....Ms. Erin BALDWIN
30 President of ISU Foundation ...... Ms. Larissa HOLTMYER-JONES
29 President of Alumni Association ....Dr. Jeffrey W. JOHNSON
41 Director of Athletics .... Mr. Jamie B. POLLARD
06 Registrar .... Dr. Jennifer SUCHAN
37 Director of Financial Aid ....Ms. Roberta L. JOHNSON
07 Director of Admissions ....Ms. Katharine JOHNSON SUSKI
09 Exec Director of Inst Research .... Dr. Karen A. ZUNKEL
104 Director Study Abroad .... Dr. Frank PETERS
91 Associate CIO ....Mr. David M. POPELKA
25 Assoc Director/Sponsored Pgm Admin ... Ms. Tamara R. POLASKI
88 Director Ames Laboratory .... Dr. Adam SCHWARTZ
96 Director of Procurement ....Mr. Cory L. HARMS
40 Director University Bookstore ....Ms. Rita M. PHILLIPS
102 Sr Dir Dev/Corporate Relations ....Mr. Mark BOECK
102 Sr Dir Dev/Foundation Relations ....Ms. Donna VAN PELT
44 Exec Dir of Annual & Special Giving .... Ms. Mary EVANSON
26 Director of University Marketing ....Ms. Carole A. CUSTER
27 Director of Communications .... Mr. Rob SCHWEERS
58 Dean Graduate College ....Dr. William R. GRAVES
08 Dean of Library Services ....Ms. Hillary SEO
47 Dean College of Agriculture .... Dr. Daniel J. ROBISON
50 Dean College of Business .... Mr. David P. SPALDING
48 Dean College of Design .... Mr. Luis C. RICO-GUTIERREZ
53 Dean College of Human Sciences .... Dr. Laura JOLLY
54 Dean College of Engineering ....Dr. W. Samuel EASTERLING
49 Dean Col of Lib Arts & Sciences ....Dr. Beate SCHMITTMANN
74 Dean College of Veterinary Medicine .... Dr. Daniel L. GROOMS

*University of Iowa (H)

5 W. Jefferson St, Iowa City IA 52242
County: Johnson FICE Identification: 001892
Unit ID: 153658
Telephone: (319) 335-3565 Carnegie Class: DU-Highest
FAX Number: (319) 335-3560 Calendar System: Semester
URL: www.uiowa.edu
Established: 1847 Annual Undergrad Tuition & Fees (In-State): $9,606
Enrollment: 30,318 Coed
Affiliation or Control: State IRS Status: 501(c)3
Highest Offering: Doctorate
Accreditation: HLC, ANEST, ARCPA, AUD, CAATE, CACREP, CAMPEP, CEA, CLPSY, COPSY, DANCE, DENT, @DIETC, DMS, EMT, HSA, IPSY, JOUR, LAW, LIB, MED, MFCD, MUS, NMT, NURSE, PAST, PCSAS, PERF, PH, PHAR, PLNG, PTA, RAD, RTT, SCPSY, SP, SW, THEA

02 President .... Dr. Barbara J. WILSON
05 Exec Vice Pres & Provost .... Dr. Kevin KREGEL
46 VP for Research .... Dr. Martin SCHOLTZ
10 SVP Fin & Ops/Chief Financial Ofcr .... Mr. Rod LEHNERTZ
32 Vice Pres Student Life ....Ms. Sarah HANSEN
17 VP Med Affairs/Dean College of Med ......Dr. J. Brooks JACKSON
30 Vice Pres External Relations .... Mr. Peter R. MATTHES
26 Asst VP External Relations .... Ms. Laura MCLERAN
88 Chief Innovation Officer .... Mr. Jon DARSEE
27 Senior Director Marketing Comm ....Mr. Ben HILL
20 Associate Provost Faculty .... Dr. Kevin KREGEL
28 AVP Diversity/Equity/Inclusion ....Dr. Liz TOVAR
97 Assoc Provost/Dean Univ College ....Dr. Tanya UDEN-HOLMAN
45 Sr Assoc Vice President Research .... Dr. Richard D. HICHWA
11 Assoc VP/Dir of Admin and Planning ..Mr. Donald J. SZESZYCKI
15 Assoc VP Human Resources ....Ms. Cheryl REARDON
18 Assoc VP/Dir Facilities Management ....Mr. Donald J. GUCKERT
13 Assoc Vice President & CIO ....Mr. Steven R. FLEAGLE
17 Assoc VP/CEO Univ Hosp & Clinics ....Mr. Suresh GUNASEKARAN
25 Exec Director Sponsored Programs .... Ms. Jennifer LASSNER
19 Asst VP & Director Public Safety .... Mr. Scott BECKNER
85 Provost/Dean International Programs ....Mr. Russell GANIM
43 VP Legal Affairs & General Counsel ....Ms. Carroll REASONER
08 University Librarian ....Mr. John P. CULSHAW
102 Pres/CEO Univ Ctr for Advancement ...Ms. Lynette L. MARSHALL
44 Asst VP Annual Giving .... Ms. Erin ALLEN
07 Director Admissions/Enrollment ....Mr. Kirk R. KLUVER
37 Director Student Financial Aid ....Ms. Cindy SEYFER
06 Interim Registrar/Assistant Provost .... Ms. Julie FELL
36 Director Career Center ....Ms. Angi MCKIE
38 Director Univ Counseling Services .... Dr. Barry SCHREIER
39 Asst VP Stdnt Life/Sr Dir Hous/Din ....Mr. Von STANGE
41 Director Athletics Administration .... Mr. Gary BARTA
49 Dean Col of Lib Arts & Sci ....Ms. Sara SANDERS
50 Dean College of Business .... Ms. Amy KRISTOF-BROWN
52 Interim Dean College of Dentistry ....Dr. Galen SCHNEIDER
53 Dean College of Education ....Dr. Daniel CLAY
54 Dean College of Engineering ....Ms. Harriet NEMBHARD

58 Assoc Provost/Dean Graduate College ....Ms. Amanda THEIN
61 Dean College of Law ....Dr. Kevin WASHBURN
66 Dean College of Nursing ....Dr. Julie ZERWIC
67 Dean College of Pharmacy ....Dr. Donald E. LETENDRE
69 Dean College of Public Health ....Dr. Edith PARKER
22 Dir Equal Opportunity/Diversity ....Ms. Jennifer A. MODESTOU
86 Director State Relations ....Mr. Keith SAUNDERS
40 Director University Bookstore ....Mr. George E. HERBERT
96 Assoc VP & Director Purchasing ....Ms. Deborah J. ZUMBACH
92 Interim Director Honors Program ....Ms. Emily HILL
87 Director Summer Session ....Dr. Marlys BOOTE
35 AVP/Dean of Students ....Dr. Angie REAMS
84 Assoc VP/Enrollment Management ....Dr. Brent GAGE
100 Chief of Staff ....Mr. Peter MATTHES
104 Director Study Abroad ....Mr. Douglas LEE

*University of Northern Iowa (A)

1227 W 27th Street, Cedar Falls IA 50614-0001

County: Black Hawk FICE Identification: 001890
Unit ID: 154095
Telephone: (319) 273-2311 Carnegie Class: Masters/L
FAX Number: (319) 273-2885 Calendar System: Semester
URL: https://uni.edu/
Established: 1876 Annual Undergrad Tuition & Fees (In-State): $8,938
Enrollment: 9,507 Coed
Affiliation or Control: State IRS Status: 501(c)3
Highest Offering: Doctorate
Accreditation: HLC, CAATE, CACREP, CAPRT, CEA, CIDA, MUS, SP, SW, THEA

02 President ....Dr. Mark A. NOOK
05 Exec VP & Provost ....Dr. José HERRERA
10 Sr VP Finance & Operations ....Dr. Michael A. HAGER
32 Vice President for Student Affairs ....Vacant
111 Vice President for Univ Advancement ....Mr. Jim JERMIER
84 Sr Assoc VP Enroll Mgmt/Stdt Suc ....Dr. Kristin L. WOODS
18 Asst VP & Director Facilities Mgmt ....Mr. Michael W. ZWANZIGER
39 Exec Dir of Housing/Dining Admin ...... Mr. Nicholas RAFANELLO
20 Assoc Provost Acad Affairs ....Dr. Patrick P. PEASE
20 Assoc Provost for Faculty ....Dr. John F. VALLENTINE
13 Chief Information Officer ....Ms. Marty L. MARK
09 Dir Inst Research & Effectiveness ....Dr. Kristin M. MOSER
06 University Registrar ....Vacant
29 Director Alumni Relations ....Ms. Leslie J. PRIDEAUX
37 Director of Financial Aid ....Mr. Timothy L. BAKULA
15 Dir Human Resource Services ....Ms. Michelle C. BYERS
83 Dean Col Soc/Behav Sciences ....Dr. Brenda L. BASS
53 Dean College of Education .... Dr. Colleen S. MULHOLLAND
49 Dean Col Hum/Arts & Science ....Dr. John E. FRITCH
51 Dean Cont Educ/Special Programs ....Dr. Kent M. JOHNSON
58 Dean Graduate College ....Dr. Jennifer WALDRON
50 Dean Col Business Admin ....Dr. Leslie K. WILSON
35 Dean of Students ....Ms. Allyson RAFANELLO
38 Exec Dir Health & Rec Svcs ....Ms. Shelley M. O'CONNELL
22 Asst to Pres Compliance/Equity Mgmt ..Ms. Leah K. GUTKNECHT
41 Athletic Director ....Mr. David W. HARRIS
21 Controller/Treasurer ....Ms. Tonya GERBRACHT
86 State Relations Officer ....Ms. Mary C. BRAUN
104 Exec Director Intl Programs ....Vacant
97 Director Undergraduate Studies ....Dr. Deirdre A. HEISTAD
19 Chief of Police/Dir Public Safety ....Ms. Helen M. HAIRE
25 Dir Research & Sponsored Programs ....Mr. Tolif R. HUNT
43 University Counsel ....Mr. Timothy J. MCKENNA
109 Dir Business Operations ....Ms. Christina GEWEKE
28 Asst to Pres/Chief Div Officer ....Ms. Gwennette C. BERRY
112 VP for Principal Gifts ....Ms. Noreen M. HERMANSEN
36 Director Career Services ....Mr. Robert J. FREDERICK
101 Asst to Pres for Board & Govt Rels ....Dr. Andrew MORSE
26 Director of University Relations ....Ms. Cassie MATHES
08 Dean of the Library ....Ms. Theresa WESTBROCK

Briar Cliff University (B)

3303 Rebecca Street, Sioux City IA 51104-2324

County: Woodbury FICE Identification: 001846
Unit ID: 152992
Telephone: (712) 279-5321 Carnegie Class: Bac-Diverse
FAX Number: (712) 279-5410 Calendar System: Semester
URL: www.briarcliff.edu
Established: 1929 Annual Undergrad Tuition & Fees: $33,308
Enrollment: 1,076 Coed
Affiliation or Control: Roman Catholic IRS Status: 501(c)3
Highest Offering: Doctorate
Accreditation: HLC, NURSE, PTA, SW

01 President ....Ms. Rachelle L. KARSTENS
05 VP Academic Affairs ....Dr. Todd KNEALING
10 VP Finance & Treasurer ....Mr. Patrick JACOBSON-SCHULTE
111 VP University Relations ....Mrs. Tina STROUD
84 VP Enrollment Management ....Mr. Matt THOMSEN
06 Registrar ....Mrs. Deidre ENGEL
08 Librarian/Dir Information Services ....Ms. Breanne KIRSCH
13 Director Computer Center ....Ms. Leah WARD
36 Director Career Development ....Ms. Nicole MCGLAUFLIN
37 Director Financial Aid ....Ms. Laurie OSWALD
40 Director Bookstore ....Ms. Nancy WATSON
41 VP Athletics & Operations ....Mr. Nic SCANDRETT
42 Director Campus Ministry ....Mr. Jason SALISBURY
18 Director Physical Plant ....Mr. Greg PRANKE
26 AVP for Marketing & Communications ....Mrs. Suzie FISCHER
15 Director Human Resources ....Ms. Cheryl HANSEN
39 Director of Campus Life & Security ....Mr. Dave ARENS
38 Director Student Counseling ....Ms. Therese COPPLE
09 Director of Institutional Research ....Ms. Deidre ENGEL
30 Director of Philanthropy ....Mrs. Carolyn ELLWANGER
19 Director Security/Safety ....Mr. Marty POTTEBAUM
04 Admin Assistant to the President ....Ms. Bernice METZ

Buena Vista University (C)

610 W Fourth Street, Storm Lake IA 50588-1798

County: Buena Vista FICE Identification: 001847
Unit ID: 153001
Telephone: (712) 749-2351 Carnegie Class: Masters/M
FAX Number: (712) 749-2037 Calendar System: 4/1/4
URL: www.bvu.edu
Established: 1891 Annual Undergrad Tuition & Fees: $36,426
Enrollment: 1,863 Coed
Affiliation or Control: Presbyterian Church (U.S.A.) IRS Status: 501(c)3
Highest Offering: Master's
Accreditation: HLC, SW

01 President ....Dr. Brian A. LENZMEIER
04 Assistant to the President ....Ms. Angie DYE
05 Int Provost/VP Academic Affairs ....Dr. Kim LINDUSKA
10 Vice Pres Finance & Administration ....Ms. Suzette RADKE
84 Vice Pres for Enrollment Management ...Mr. Kevin M. MCINTYRE
32 Int VP Student Success ....Dr. Nicholas PICCOLO
111 Vice Pres for Inst Advancement ....Ms. Joan CANTY
30 Assistant VP of Development ....Vacant
81 Dean School of Science ....Dr. Thom BONAGURA
50 Dean HWS School of Business ....Ms. Lisa BEST
53 Dean School of Education ....Dr. Brittany GARLING
49 Dean School of Liberal Arts ...... Dr. Dixee BARTHOLOMEW-FEIS
56 VP for Extended University Programs ....Ms. Jean BRAL
06 Registrar ....Ms. Stephanie WILHELM
07 Exec Director of Admissions .... Mr. Conner ELLINGHUYSEN
15 Human Resources Manager ....Ms. Melissa BUTCHER
08 Actg Dir of Library/Ref Librarian ....Ms. Jodie MORIN
26 Chief Marketing Officer ....Vacant
29 Director of Alumni Engagement ....Ms. Kristie SPOTTS
44 Director of Annual Campaigns ....Ms. Barbara AIONA
13 Chief Information Officer ....Vacant
18 Interim Director Facilities Mgmt ....Mr. Andy TAYLOR
36 Dir Career & Personal Development ....Ms. Mandi MOLLRING
37 Director of Financial Assistance ....Vacant
28 Sr Dir of Diversity & Inclusion ....Mr. Joel BERRIEN
41 Athletic Director ....Mr. Scott BROWN
42 Chaplain ....Dr. Melanie HAUSER
19 Director of Campus Security ....Ms. Jessica GARLING
09 Institutional Researcher ....Mr. James E. HEWETT
96 Purchasing Administrator ....Ms. Tanya LANDGRAF

Central College (D)

812 University, Pella IA 50219-1999

County: Marion FICE Identification: 001850
Unit ID: 153108
Telephone: (641) 628-9000 Carnegie Class: Bac-A&S
FAX Number: (641) 628-5316 Calendar System: Semester
URL: www.central.edu
Established: 1853 Annual Undergrad Tuition & Fees: $18,600
Enrollment: 1,120 Coed
Affiliation or Control: Reformed Church In America IRS Status: 501(c)3
Highest Offering: Baccalaureate
Accreditation: HLC, CAATE, MUS

01 President ....Dr. Mark L. PUTNAM
05 VP Academic Affairs/Dean of Faculty ....Dr. Mary M. STREY
111 Vice President Advancement ....Mrs. Sunny EIGHMY
10 Vice Pres for Finance & Admin ....Mr. Thomas JOHNSON
32 VP Student Development ....Mrs. Carol WILLIAMSON
84 Dean of Enrollment Management ....Mr. Chevy FREIBURGER
20 Assoc Dean Curriculum/Faculty Dev ....Mr. Brian PETERSON
20 Director of Academic Resources ....Mr. Eric JONES
21 Controller/Assistant Treasurer ....Mr. Jeff SANGER
110 Director of Advancement Services ....Mrs. Peggy VAN DEN BERG
26 Dir of Integrated Mktg/Comm/Media ....Mrs. Denise LAMPHIER
13 Director of Information Technology ....Mr. Lee WEERS
36 Dir of Career & Prof Development ....Mrs. Jessica KLYN DE NOVELO
44 Dir Annual Giving & Alumni Engage ....Mr. Corey FALTER
37 Director Financial Aid ....Mr. Wayne DILLE
42 Chaplain ....Rev. Joe BRUMMEL
15 Director of Human Resources ....Ms. Paula RYAN
41 Athletics Director ....Mr. Eric VAN KLEY
18 Dir of Facilities Management ....Mr. Craig ROOSE
06 Registrar ....Ms. Leslie DUININK
04 Administrative Asst to President ....Ms. Carma STURTZ
09 Institutional Research Director ....Vacant
96 Dir of Purchasing & Facility Svcs ....Mrs. Janine FONTANA
112 Major Gifts Officer ....Mrs. Michelle WILKIE
27 Director of External Engagement ....Ms. Jenae JENISON
109 Director of Dining Services ....Mr. Iwan WILLIAMS
88 Director of Conferences/Events ....Mrs. Susan CANFIELD

Clarke University (E)

1550 Clarke Drive, Dubuque IA 52001-3198

County: Dubuque FICE Identification: 001852
Unit ID: 153126
Telephone: (563) 588-6300 Carnegie Class: DU-Mod
FAX Number: (563) 588-6789 Calendar System: Semester
URL: www.clarke.edu
Established: 1843 Annual Undergrad Tuition & Fees: $35,750
Enrollment: 855 Coed
Affiliation or Control: Roman Catholic IRS Status: 501(c)3
Highest Offering: Doctorate
Accreditation: HLC, CAATE, MUS, NURSE, PTA, SW

01 President ....Dr. Thom D. CHESNEY
04 Exec Admin Assistant to President ....Ms. Kathy TEIG
05 Vice Pres Academic Affairs ....Ms. Eden WALES FREEDMAN
111 Vice Pres Institutional Advancement ....Mr. Bill BIEBUYCK
32 Vice President Student Life ....Ms. Kate ZANGER
10 Vice President Business & Finance .... Ms. Elizabeth MCGRATH
84 Vice President Enrollment Mgmt ....Dr. Charles COTTON, III
06 Registrar ....Ms. Kristi BAGSTAD
08 Director of Library ....Ms. Susanne LEIBOLD
58 Dean College of Prof & Grad Studies ....Dr. Paula SCHMIDT
49 Dean College of Arts & Sciences ....Dr. David DIMATTIO
37 Director of Financial Aid ....Mr. Robert HOOVER
26 Director of Marketing ....Ms. Amy ERRTHUM
13 Chief Technology Officer ....Mr. Andy BELLINGS
18 Exec Dir of Facilities Management ....Mr. Steven KIRSCHBAUM
36 Asst Dir of Counseling/Career Svcs ....Ms. Becky HERRIG
15 Director of Human Resources ....Ms. Jody PFOHL
41 Director of Athletics ....Mr. Curt LONG
42 Director of Campus Ministry ....Mr. Hunter DARROUZET
40 Director of the Bookstore ....Ms. Sarah HAAS
23 Director of Health Services ....Ms. Tammy MOORE
90 Asst Dean Acad Affairs/Inst Supp ....Mr. Pat MADDUX
88 Dir Institute for Prof Excellence ....Ms. Liz KRUSE
07 Director of Admissions ....Ms. Ali BOYD
30 Exec Director of Development ....Ms. Courtney LEONARD
29 Director of Alumni Relations ....Ms. Kaley RIGDON
85 International Students Advisor ....Ms. Evelyn NADEAU
09 Dir Institutional Rsrch/Assessment ....Mr. James UHLENKAMP

Coe College (F)

1220 1st Avenue, NE, Cedar Rapids IA 52402-5092

County: Linn FICE Identification: 001854
Unit ID: 153144
Telephone: (319) 399-8000 Carnegie Class: Bac-A&S
FAX Number: (319) 399-8830 Calendar System: Semester
URL: www.coe.edu
Established: 1851 Annual Undergrad Tuition & Fees: $47,220
Enrollment: 1,394 Coed
Affiliation or Control: Independent Non-Profit IRS Status: 501(c)3
Highest Offering: Baccalaureate
Accreditation: HLC, MUS, NURSE

01 President ....Mr. David HAYES
05 Provost/Dean of Faculty ....Dr. Paula O'LOUGHLIN
111 Assoc Vice Pres for Advancement ....Ms. Barb TUPPER
84 VP for Enroll/Marketing/Inst Effect ....Ms. Julie STAKER
15 AVP for Human Resources ....Ms. Kristina BRIDGES
06 Registrar ....Mr. Jesse UPAH
08 Director Library Services ....Ms. Jill JACK
29 Director Alumni Programs ....Ms. Emily EHRHARDT
09 Director of Institutional Research ....Vacant
37 Director of Financial Aid ....Ms. Julie STAKER
20 Associate Dean ....Dr. Angela ZISKOWSKI
35 Assoc Dean of Students ....Mr. Ron BINDER
85 International Student Advisor ....Mr. John CHAIMOV
42 Chaplain ....Ms. Melea WHITE
41 Director of Athletics ....Mr. Steve COOK
18 Director of Physical Plant ....Ms. Lisa CIHA
36 Dir of Career Services ....Ms. Nanci YOUNG
04 Administrative Asst to President ....Ms. Kim PRIBYL
13 Chief Info Technology Officer ....Ms. Deb BAHR
19 Director Security/Safety ....Mr. Carlos VELEZ
44 Director Annual/Planned Giving ....Ms. Mary SPRINGER

Cornell College (G)

600 First Street SW, Mount Vernon IA 52314-1098

County: Linn FICE Identification: 001856
Unit ID: 153162
Telephone: (319) 895-4000 Carnegie Class: Bac-A&S
FAX Number: (319) 895-4492 Calendar System: Other
URL: www.cornellcollege.edu
Established: 1853 Annual Undergrad Tuition & Fees: $45,914
Enrollment: 1,002 Coed
Affiliation or Control: United Methodist IRS Status: 501(c)3
Highest Offering: Master's
Accreditation: HLC

01 President ....Mr. Jonathan BRAND
05 Provost/VP Acad & Student Affairs .... Dr. Ilene CRAWFORD
10 VP/COO and CFO ....Mr. Dan LAYZELL
84 Vice Pres Enrollment Management ...... Ms. Wendy BECKEMEYER
88 Special Assistant to the President ....Mr. John W. HARP
111 Assoc VP Alumni/College Advancement .....Ms. Kristi COLUMBUS
32 Assoc VP/Dean of Students ....Dr. Gwendolyn SCHIMEK
20 Associate Dean ....Dr. Kate KAUPER
20 Associate Dean ....Dr. Craig TEAGUE
09 Dir Institutional Effectiveness ....Ms. Angie BAUMAN POWER
37 Director of Student Financial Asst ....Ms. Pamela PERRY
06 Registrar ....Ms. Megan HICKS
08 College Librarian ....Mr. Gregory COTTON
30 Director of Development ....Mr. AJ PLUMMER
26 Senior Dir Marketing/Communications ....Ms. Jen VISSER
42 Chaplain ....Rev Dr. Catherine M. QUEHL-ENGEL
41 Athletics Director ....Mr. Seth WING
18 Facilities Operations Manager ....Mr. Luke FISCHER
36 Senior Dir Berry Career Institute ....Ms. Jodi SCHAFER
38 Director Student Counseling ....Dr. Brenda C. LOVSTUEN

15 Director of Human Resources ....Ms. Stefanie BRAY
07 Director of Admission Operations ....Ms. Sharon GRICE
13 Director of Information Technology ....Mr. Jeff GIBSON
40 Manager Bookstore ....Ms. Vicki MOORE
04 Executive Asst to President ....Ms. RuthAnn SCHEER
19 Campus Safety Director ....Mr. Mark WINDER
28 Director of Diversity ....Mr. Hemie COLLIER

Des Moines Area Community College (A)

2006 S Ankeny Boulevard, Ankeny IA 50023-3993
County: Polk FICE Identification: 007120
Unit ID: 153214
Telephone: (515) 964-6200 Carnegie Class: Assoc/HT-High Non
FAX Number: N/A Calendar System: Semester
URL: www.dmacc.edu
Established: 1966 Annual Undergrad Tuition & Fees (In-District): $5,100
Enrollment: 23,051 Coed
Affiliation or Control: State/Local IRS Status: 501(c)3
Highest Offering: Associate Degree
Accreditation: HLC, ACFEI, ADNUR, COARC, DA, DH, EMT, FUSER, IFSAC, MAC, MLTAD, SURGT

01 President/CEO ....Dr. Rob DENSON
11 Exec Vice Pres College Operations ....Vacant
05 Vice President Academic Affairs ....Mr. M.D ISLEY
06 Dir. of Innovation & Special Projec ....Ms. Karen STILES
84 VP Enrollment Svcs/Student Success ....Ms. Shelli ALLEN
13 Exec Dir Information Solutions ....Mr. Mark CLARK
12 Provost Urban Campus ....Dr. Anne HOWSARE
12 Provost Boone Campus ....Mr. Andrew NELSON
12 Provost Carroll Campus ....Mr. Joel LUNDSTROM
12 Provost Newton Campus ....Dr. Joe DEHART
12 Provost West Campus ....Dr. Tony PAUSTIAN
15 Executive Director Human Resources ....Dr. Jenifer OWENSON
18 Executive Director Physical Plant ....Mr. Greg MARTIN
102 Executive Director Foundation ....Ms. Tara CONNOLLY
51 Exec Dir Continuing Education ....Mr. Michael HOFFMAN
36 Director Student Development ....Mr. Wade ROBINSON
37 Director Financial Aid ....Vacant
26 Director Marketing/Public Relations ....Mr. Todd JONES
25 Director Grants/Contracts ....Ms. Deb KOUA
19 Dir Energy Mgt/Safety/Security ....Mr. Jay TIEFENTHALER
06 Registrar ....Mr. Steve PANKEY
27 Media Liaison ....Mr. Dan IVIS
81 Dean Sciences & Humanities ....Mr. Jim STICK
72 Dean Industrial & Technology ....Dr. Jennifer FOSTER
76 Dean Health/Public Service ....Mr. Art BROWN
50 Dean Business/Mgmt/Information Tech .. Dr. Jeanie MCCARVILLE
55 Dean SEMSS ....Mr. Scott SCHULTZ
106 Dean Online Learning ....Vacant
55 Dean Evening & Weekend College ....Ms. Andrea ISEMINGER
08 Head Librarian ....Ms. Rebecca FUNKE
45 Sourcing Specialist ....Ms. Julie KLOCKE
41 Athletic Director ....Mr. BJ MCGINN
101 Secretary of the Board ....Ms. Carolyn FARLOW
04 Admin Assistant to the President ....Vacant
09 Director of Institutional Research ....Vacant

Des Moines Area Community College Boone Campus (B)

1125 Hancock Drive, Boone IA 50036
Telephone: (515) 432-7203 Identification: 770048
Accreditation: &HLC

Des Moines Area Community College Carroll Campus (C)

906 North Grant Road, Carroll IA 51401-2525
Telephone: (712) 792-1755 Identification: 770049
Accreditation: &HLC

Des Moines Area Community College Newton Campus (D)

600 N 2nd Avenue West, Newton IA 50208
Telephone: (641) 791-3622 Identification: 770051
Accreditation: &HLC

Des Moines Area Community College Urban Campus (E)

1100 7th Street, Des Moines IA 50314
Telephone: (515) 244-4226 Identification: 770050
Accreditation: &HLC

Des Moines Area Community College West Des Moines Campus (F)

5959 Grand Avenue, West Des Moines IA 50266
Telephone: (515) 633-2407 Identification: 770052
Accreditation: &HLC

Des Moines University (G)

3200 Grand Avenue, Des Moines IA 50312-4198
County: Polk FICE Identification: 001855
Unit ID: 154156
Telephone: (515) 271-1400 Carnegie Class: Spec-4-yr-Med
FAX Number: (515) 271-1532 Calendar System: Other
URL: www.dmu.edu
Established: 1898 Annual Graduate Tuition & Fees: N/A
Enrollment: 1,559 Coed
Affiliation or Control: Independent Non-Profit IRS Status: 501(c)3
Highest Offering: First Professional Degree; No Undergraduates
Accreditation: HLC, ARCPA, HSA, OSTEO, PH, POD, PTA

01 President/CEO ....Dr. Angela L. WALKER FRANKLIN
05 Provost ....Dr. Ralitsa AKINS
10 Senior Vice President & CFO ....Mr. Mark PEIFFER
84 VP Enrollment Mgmt/Student Svcs ....Ms. Kimberly BROWN
86 Chief External & Govt Affs Officer ....Ms. Susan HUPPERT
46 Vice President for Research ....Vacant
06 Registrar ....Ms. Melinda SHERZER
08 Director of Library ....Vacant
15 Chief Human Resources Officer ....Dr. Marc WACHTFOGEL
13 Chief Information Officer ....Ms. Carolyn WEAVER
37 Director of Financial Aid ....Ms. Mary PAYNE
18 Director of Facilities Management ....Mr. John HARRIS
19 Building Services Manager ....Mr. Philip BAUGHMAN
108 Chief Compliance Officer ....Ms. Erika LINDEN
69 Director Public Health Program ....Dr. Rachel REIMER
26 Chief Strategic Comm Officer ....Mr. Mark DANES
76 Dean College Health Sciences ....Dr. Wallace BOEVE
63 Dean Col Podiatric Medicine/Surg ....Dr. Kevin SMITH
63 Dean Col Osteopathic Medicine ....Dr. Steven HALM
04 Executive Asst to President ....Ms. Christina HENDERSON
07 Director of Admissions/Recruitment ....Ms. Molly MOELLER
32 Director of Student Services ....Ms. Alicia LYNCH
28 Dir Multicult Affs/Chief Div Ofcr ....Dr. Richard SALAS
29 Director Alumni Relations ....Ms. Krystal KRUSE
30 Chief Development Officer ....Ms. Stephanie GREINER
101 Secretary of the Institution/Board ....Ms. Linda KADING
38 Director Student Counseling ....Dr. Ciara LEWIS
44 Director Annual Giving ....Ms. Melanie WEIBEL
25 Grants and Contract Manager ....Ms. Mollie LYON

† Tuition varies by degree program.

Divine Word College (H)

102 Jacoby Drive, SW, PO Box 380,
Epworth IA 52045-0380
County: Dubuque FICE Identification: 001858
Unit ID: 153241
Telephone: (563) 876-3353 Carnegie Class: Spec-4-yr-Faith
FAX Number: (563) 876-3407 Calendar System: Semester
URL: www.dwci.edu
Established: 1918 Annual Undergrad Tuition & Fees: $13,780
Enrollment: 69 Coed
Affiliation or Control: Roman Catholic IRS Status: 501(c)3
Highest Offering: Baccalaureate
Accreditation: HLC

01 President ....Rev. Thomas ASCHEMAN, SVD
05 Vice President Academic Affairs ..Rev. John A. SZUKALSKI, SVD
32 VP Formation/Dean of Students ......Rev. Long Phi NGUYEN, SVD
07 Vice President Admissions ....Mr. Len UHAL
11 Vice President Operations ....Mr. Steven WINGER
30 Director Development ....Rev. Linh PHAM, SVD
26 Director Public Relations ....Ms. Sandy WILGENBUSCH
29 Director Alumni ....Rev. Thang HOANG, SVD
04 Executive Sec to the President ....Ms. Donna PUCCIO
108 Director Inst Effectiveness ....Dr. Yasmin RIOUX
08 Director Library ....Mr. Daniel C. WILLIAMS
06 Registrar ....Ms. Kimberly BURNETT-HACKBARTH
104 Coordinator Study Abroad ....Rev. Kenneth ANICH, SVD
38 Counselor ....Sr. Aprilia UNTARTO, SSPS
42 Chaplain ....Rev. Sonny DECLASS, SVD
23 Coordinator Health Services ....Bro. Mike DECKER, SVD
37 Coordinator Financial Aid ....Ms. Carolyn WAECHTER
10 Director Business Office ....Ms. Marlene DECKER
13 Director Information Systems ....Mr. Brad FLORENCE
18 Director Maintenance ....Bro. Vinh TRINH, SVD

Dordt University (I)

700 7th St. NE, Sioux Center IA 51250-1697
County: Sioux FICE Identification: 001859
Unit ID: 153250
Telephone: (712) 722-6000 Carnegie Class: Bac-Diverse
FAX Number: (712) 722-6035 Calendar System: Semester
URL: www.dordt.edu
Established: 1955 Annual Undergrad Tuition & Fees: $32,820
Enrollment: 1,662 Coed
Affiliation or Control: Christian Reformed Church IRS Status: 501(c)3
Highest Offering: Master's
Accreditation: HLC, NURSE, SW

01 President ....Dr. Erik HOEKSTRA
111 Vice President Advancement ....Mr. John BAAS
84 VP for Enrollment & Marketing ....Mr. Brandon HUISMAN
05 VP for Academic Affairs ....Dr. Leah ZUIDEMA
11 Vice President for Univ Operations ....Mr. Howard WILSON
85 Director of Global Education ....Mr. Adam ADAMS
10 Vice President for Finance & Risk ....Mrs. Stephanie BACCAM
37 Director Financial Aid ....Mr. Harlan HARMELINK
06 Registrar ....Mr. James BOS
88 Asst Dir for Research & Scholarship ....Vacant
58 Director Graduate Studies ....Dr. Steve HOLTROP
36 Career Services Coordinator ....Ms. Amy WESTRA
26 Marketing and Public Relations ....Ms. Sarah MOSS
18 Director Physical Plant ....Mr. Nate VAN NIEJENHUIS
32 Vice Pres for Student Success ....Mr. Robert TAYLOR
42 Chief of Staff/Dean of Chapel ....Rev. Aaron BAART
41 Director of Athletics ....Mr. Ross DOUMA
112 Director of Planned Giving ....Mr. Dave VANDER WERF
15 Director Human Resources ....Mrs. Sue DROOG
91 Director of Computer Services ....Mr. Brian VAN DONSELAAR
08 Director of Library Services ....Ms. Jennifer BREEMS
23 Director of Health Services ....Ms. Beth BAAS
88 Director Academic Skills Center ....Ms. Sharon ROSENBOOM
04 Exec Admin Asst to President ....Mrs. LeeAnn MOERMAN
07 Director of Admissions ....Mr. Greg VAN DYKE
29 Director Alumni Affairs ....Mrs. Alicia BOWAR
30 Director of Development ....Mr. Lyle HUISMAN
39 Dir Resident Life/Student Housing ....Mr. Derek BUTEYN

Drake University (J)

2507 University Avenue, Des Moines IA 50311-4505
County: Polk FICE Identification: 001860
Unit ID: 153269
Telephone: (515) 271-2011 Carnegie Class: DU-Mod
FAX Number: (515) 271-3016 Calendar System: Semester
URL: www.drake.edu
Established: 1881 Annual Undergrad Tuition & Fees: $44,376
Enrollment: 4,774 Coed
Affiliation or Control: Independent Non-Profit IRS Status: 501(c)3
Highest Offering: Doctorate
Accreditation: HLC, ART, CAATE, CACREP, JOUR, LAW, MUS, OT, PHAR

01 President ....Mr. Earl F. MARTIN
05 Provost ....Dr. Sue MATTISON
10 Chief Financial Officer ....Mr. Adam VOIGTS
11 Chief Administrative Officer ....Ms. Venessa MACRO
111 Vice Pres University Advancement ....Mr. John SMITH
20 Deputy Provost for Academic Affairs ....Dr. Renee CRAMER
28 Assoc Prov for Equity & Inclusion ....Dr. Jennifer HARVEY
07 Dean of Admission ....Ms. Anne KREMER
32 Chief Student Affairs Officer ....Dr. Jerry PARKER
35 Assoc Provost Student Affairs ....Ms. Melissa STURM-SMITH
15 Human Resources Director ....Ms. Maureen DE ARMOND
13 Chief Tech Information Officer ....Ms. Keren FIORENZA
09 Dir of Inst Research & Assessment ....Mr. Kevin SAUNDERS
88 Director of Student Records ....Mr. Kevin P. MOENKHAUS
08 Dean Cowles Library ....Ms. Gillian GREMMELS
85 Exec Dir Global Eng & Intl Pgm ....Dr. Annique KIEL
19 Director Public Safety ....Mr. Scott LAW
26 Director University Communications ....Ms. Leslie MAYNES
29 Alumni/Parent Programs ....Mr. Andrew VERLENGIA
49 Dean Arts & Sciences ....Dr. Gesine GERHARD
53 Dean School Education ....Dr. Ryan WISE
61 Dean Law School ....Mr. Jerry ANDERSON
50 Dean Business/Public Administration .Mr. Alejandro HERNANDEZ
67 Dean Pharmacy/Health Science ....Dr. Renae CHESNUT
60 Dean Journalism/Mass Communications ....Ms. Kathleen RICHARDSON
41 Director Intercollegiate Athletics ....Mr. Brian HARDIN
37 Director Financial Aid ....Mr. Ryan ZANTINGH
38 Director University Counseling Ctr ....Dr. Mark KLOBERDANZ
92 Assistant Director Honors Program ....Ms. Charlene SKIDMORE
94 Director Women's Studies ....Dr. Nancy REINCKE
39 Director Office of Residence Life ....Ms. Lorissa SOWDEN
04 Asst to President ....Ms. Cheryle ANANIA
100 Chief of Staff ....Mr. Nate REAGEN
30 Director of Development ....Mr. John AMATO
06 Registrar ....Ms. Jenny TRAN-JOHNSON

*Eastern Iowa Community College District (K)

101 West Third Street, Davenport IA 52801-1221
County: Scott FICE Identification: 004075
Unit ID: 153311
Telephone: (563) 336-3300 Carnegie Class: N/A
FAX Number: (563) 322-0129
URL: www.eicc.edu

01 Chancellor ....Dr. Donald S. DOUCETTE
30 Exec Dir Resource Development ....Dr. Ellen BLUTH
26 Associate Director Communications ....Ms. Johnna KERRES
10 Chief Business Officer ....Mr. Suteesh TANDON
101 Secretary of the Institution/Board ....Ms. Honey BEDELL
15 Director Personnel Services ....Ms. Deb SULLIVAN
18 Chief Facilities/Physical Plant ....Mr. Matt SCHMIT
84 Director Enrollment Management ....Ms. Erin SNYDER

*Clinton Community College (L)

1000 Lincoln Boulevard, Clinton IA 52732-6299
County: Clinton FICE Identification: 001853
Telephone: (563) 244-7001 Carnegie Class: Not Classified
FAX Number: (563) 244-7107 Calendar System: Semester
URL: www.eicc.edu
Established: 1966 Annual Undergrad Tuition & Fees (In-District): N/A
Enrollment: N/A Coed
Affiliation or Control: State/Local IRS Status: 501(c)3
Highest Offering: Associate Degree
Accreditation: &HLC, EMT

02 President ....Mr. Brian KELLY
05 Dean of the College ....Mr. Gabe KNIGHT
32 Dean of Student Development ....Dr. Michelle ALLMENDINGER

102 Asst to Pres/Exec Dir Sharar Found .... Ms. Ann EISENMAN

† Regional accreditation is carried under the parent institution Eastern Iowa Community College District in Davenport, IA.

*Muscatine Community College (A)

152 Colorado Street, Muscatine IA 52761-5396
County: Muscatine — FICE Identification: 001882
Telephone: (563) 288-6001 — Carnegie Class: Not Classified
FAX Number: (563) 288-6074 — Calendar System: Semester
URL: www.eicc.edu
Established: 1929 — Annual Undergrad Tuition & Fees (In-District): N/A
Enrollment: N/A — Coed
Affiliation or Control: State/Local — IRS Status: 501(c)3
Highest Offering: Associate Degree
Accreditation: &HLC, EMT

02 President .... Dr. Naomi DEWINTER
04 Assistant to the President .... Ms. Lisa WIEGEL
05 Dean of the College .... Dr. Jeremy PICKARD
32 Dean of Student Development .... Ms. Shelly CRAM-RAHLF
06 Registrar .... Ms. Robin MITCHELL
08 Library Specialist .... Ms. Nancy LUIKART

† Regional accreditation is carried under the parent institution Eastern Iowa Community College District in Davenport, IA.

*Scott Community College (B)

500 Belmont Road, Bettendorf IA 52722-6804
County: Scott — FICE Identification: 001885
Telephone: (563) 441-4001 — Carnegie Class: Not Classified
FAX Number: (563) 441-4154 — Calendar System: Semester
URL: www.eicc.edu
Established: 1966 — Annual Undergrad Tuition & Fees (In-District): N/A
Enrollment: N/A — Coed
Affiliation or Control: State/Local — IRS Status: 501(c)3
Highest Offering: Associate Degree
Accreditation: &HLC, CAHIIM, DA, EMT, RAD, SURGT

02 President .... Dr. Ann LAWLER
32 Dean of Student Development/Affs .... Dr. Michael BEANE
103 Dean Career Assistance Center .... Dr. Scott SCHNEIDER
11 Dean of Operations .... Dr. Matt SCHMIT
37 Director Student Financial Aid .... Ms. Katy RUSH
36 Job Placement Specialist .... Mr. Wayne COLE

† Regional accreditation is carried under the parent institution Eastern Iowa Community College District in Davenport, IA.

Emmaus Bible College (C)

2570 Asbury Road, Dubuque IA 52001-3096
County: Dubuque — FICE Identification: 023289
Unit ID: 153302
Telephone: (563) 588-8000 — Carnegie Class: Spec-4-yr-Faith
FAX Number: (563) 588-1216 — Calendar System: Semester
URL: www.emmaus.edu
Established: 1941 — Annual Undergrad Tuition & Fees: $19,250
Enrollment: 194 — Coed
Affiliation or Control: Independent Non-Profit — IRS Status: 501(c)3
Highest Offering: Baccalaureate
Accreditation: HLC, BI

01 President .... Mr. Philip BOOM
10 VP for Administration and Finance .... Mr. Joseph ABDY
05 Vice President for Academic Affairs .... Mr. Raju KUNJUMMEN
111 Vice President for Advancement .... Mr. Chad CUNNINGHAM
32 VP for Student Development .... Mr. Israel CHAVEZ
84 Vice President Enrollment & Mktg .... Mr. Tom KOOK
73 Chair Bible & Theology .... Dr. Mark STEVENSON
08 Librarian .... Mr. John H. RUSH
37 Financial Aid Officer .... Mr. Steve C. SEEMAN
21 Controller .... Mr. Steve M. JENSEN
06 Registrar .... Mrs. Janice G. BENNETT
106 Dir Online Education/E-learning .... Mr. Ray GUERRA
108 Director Institutional Assessment .... Vacant
29 Director Alumni Relations .... Vacant
41 Athletic Director .... Mr. Chris MCHUGH
07 Director Enrollment Management .... Ms. Laurel R. RASMUSSEN
18 Chief Facilities/Physical Plant .... Mr. Jeremy MAU
04 Administrative Asst to President .... Ms. Becky PERKINS
50 Chair Business Department .... Mr. Kim PARCHER
39 Dir Resident Life/Student Housing .... Ms. Anna HENNING
13 Director of Technology .... Mr. Mark NEWLAND

Faith Baptist Bible College and Seminary (D)

1900 NW 4th Street, Ankeny IA 50023-2152
County: Polk — FICE Identification: 007121
Unit ID: 153320
Telephone: (515) 964-0601 — Carnegie Class: Spec-4-yr-Faith
FAX Number: (515) 964-1638 — Calendar System: Semester
URL: www.faith.edu
Established: 1921 — Annual Undergrad Tuition & Fees: $17,650
Enrollment: 504 — Coed
Affiliation or Control: Independent Non-Profit — IRS Status: 501(c)3
Highest Offering: Doctorate
Accreditation: HLC, BI

01 President .... Dr. James R. TILLOTSON
03 Executive Vice President .... Dr. Martin T. HERRON
05 VP for Academic Services .... Dr. Kenneth D. RATHBUN
73 Dean of Seminary .... Dr. Douglas E. BROWN
10 VP for Business/CFO .... Mr. Paul BRAY
111 VP for Advancement/Church Rels .... Mr. Daniel H. BJOKNE
34 Dean of Women .... Mrs. Sandy CAPON
32 Dean of Students .... Mr. Noah KEPHART
26 Director of Communications .... Mr. Andrew GOGERTY
06 Registrar .... Mr. Jeff BUNJER
37 Director Student Financial Aid .... Ms. Alice BUNJER
08 Head Librarian .... Dr. Paul A. HARTOG
04 Administrative Asst to President .... Miss Briana K. HARRIER
84 VP for Enrollment and Student Life .... Mr. Mark L. DAVIS
106 Dir Online Education/E-learning .... Dr. Christopher E. ELLIS
41 Athletic Director .... Mr. Brian S. FINCHAM

Graceland University (E)

1 University Place, Lamoni IA 50140-1699
County: Decatur — FICE Identification: 001866
Unit ID: 153366
Telephone: (641) 784-5000 — Carnegie Class: Masters/L
FAX Number: (641) 784-5480 — Calendar System: Trimester
URL: www.graceland.edu
Established: 1895 — Annual Undergrad Tuition & Fees: $31,320
Enrollment: 1,517 — Coed
Affiliation or Control: Other — IRS Status: 501(c)3
Highest Offering: Doctorate
Accreditation: HLC

01 President .... Dr. Patricia H. DRAVES
05 Interim VP for Academic Affairs .... Dr. Peter VISCUSI
10 Vice Pres Business/Finance .... Mr. David SIDDALL
32 VP Student Life/Dean of Students .... Mr. Dave SCHAAL
111 Vice President for Institutional Ad .... Ms. Kristi HETTRICK
108 Exec Dir Planning & Effectiveness .... Ms. Beth HIGDON
51 Director Graduate/Continuing Educ .... Mr. Paul BINNICKER
39 Director of Residence Life .... Ms. Morgan BRADFORD DIAZ
07 Dean of Undergraduate Admissions .... Ms. Deborah SKINNER
06 Registrar .... Mrs. Peggy MOTHERSHEAD
29 Director of Alumni Relations .... Mr. Paul J. DAVIS
15 Director Human Resources .... Mrs. Ondrea GREENE
04 Executive Asst to President .... Mrs. Jodi SEYMOUR
44 Director of Annual Fund/Stewardship .... Ms. Paula ANDERSON
85 Director Intercultural Office .... Ms. Diana JONES
50 Dean School of Business .... Mr. Jeff MCELROY
53 Dean Sch of Education & Social Sci .... Dr. Michele DICKEY-KOTZ
66 Dean School of Nursing .... Dr. Jolene LYNN
13 Chief Information Officer .... Ms. Talia BROWN
26 Director Marketing & Communications .... Mr. Shane ADAMS
37 Director Student Financial Services .... Ms. Sherri BRENIZER

Grand View University (F)

1200 Grandview Avenue, Des Moines IA 50316-1599
County: Polk — FICE Identification: 001867
Unit ID: 153375
Telephone: (515) 263-2800 — Carnegie Class: Bac-Diverse
FAX Number: (515) 263-6095 — Calendar System: Semester
URL: www.grandview.edu
Established: 1896 — Annual Undergrad Tuition & Fees: $29,792
Enrollment: 1,874 — Coed
Affiliation or Control: Evangelical Lutheran Church In America
IRS Status: 501(c)3
Highest Offering: Master's
Accreditation: HLC, CAATE, NURSE, SW

01 President .... Mr. Kent L. HENNING
04 Exec Admin Asst to the President .... Ms. Corinna KING
05 Provost/Vice Pres Academic Affairs .... Dr. Carl MOSES
79 Dean College of Humanities & Educ .... Vacant
83 Dean College of Social/Nat Science .... Dr. Paul RIDER
10 Vice Pres Administration & Finance .... Mr. Christopher LEE
111 Vice President Advancement .... Mr. William H. BURMA
84 Vice Pres Enrollment Management .... Ms. Debbie M. BARGER
26 Vice Pres Marketing/Communications .... Ms. Kendall DILLON
32 Vice President Student Affairs .... Dr. Jay B. PRESCOTT
13 Vice President Information Svcs/CIO .... Mr. Tim T. WHEELDON
37 Director Financial Aid .... Vacant
20 Special Assistant to the Provost .... Ms. Pamela M. CHRISTOFFERS
51 Dean Graduate/Adult Programs .... Dr. Patricia A. WILLIAMS
35 Associate VP for Student Affairs .... Mr. Jason K. BAUER
06 Registrar .... Ms. Debbie K. GANNON
42 Senior Campus Pastor .... Rev. Russell L. LACKEY
09 Director Inst Planning/Research .... Ms. Debbie M. BARGER
36 Director Career Center .... Ms. Susan M. STEARNS
08 Director of the Library .... Ms. Pamela D. REES
40 Director Bookstore & Campus Svcs .... Mr. Tim REGER
07 Director of Admissions .... Mr. Ryan THOMPSON
18 Director Buildings & Grounds .... Ms. Kim I. BUTLER
38 Director Leadership & Counseling .... Mr. Kent A. SCHORNACK
28 Dir Multicultural & Cmty Outreach .... Mr. Alex H. PIEDRAS
41 Athletic Director .... Mr. Troy A. PLUMMER
15 Human Resources Manager .... Ms. Erica L. KLUVER

Grinnell College (G)

1121 Park Street, Grinnell IA 50112-1690
County: Poweshiek — FICE Identification: 001868
Unit ID: 153384
Telephone: (641) 269-4000 — Carnegie Class: Bac-A&S
FAX Number: (641) 269-3408 — Calendar System: Semester
URL: www.grinnell.edu
Established: 1846 — Annual Undergrad Tuition & Fees: $56,680
Enrollment: 1,493 — Coed
Affiliation or Control: Independent Non-Profit — IRS Status: 501(c)3
Highest Offering: Baccalaureate
Accreditation: HLC

01 President .... Anne HARRIS
100 Chief of Staff/VP Planning .... Angela VOOS
05 Int VP Academic Affs/Dean of Col .... Elaine MARZLUFF
30 Vice Pres Development/Alumni Rels .... Jaci A. THIEDE
115 Chief Investment Officer .... Jainen THAYER
10 VP for Finance/Treasurer of College .... Keith A. ARCHER
20 Associate Dean of College .... Cynthia HANSEN
20 Associate Dean of College .... Jin FENG
20 Associate Dean of College .... Timothy ARNER
07 VP Enroll/Dean Admission & Fin Aid .... Joseph P. BAGNOLI
30 Director of Development Operations .... Adam LAUG
37 Dir Student Fin Aid & Asst VP Enrol .... Brad LINDBERG
15 VP of Human Resources .... Jana L. GRIMES
26 Vice President for Communications .... Debra LUKEHART
06 Interim Registrar .... Mark LEVANDOSKI
08 Librarian .... Mark CHRISTEL
29 Director of Alumni Relations .... Jayn CHANEY
13 Chief Information Tech Officer .... Dave ROBINSON
09 Assoc VP Analytics/Inst Research .... Catherine RENNER
85 Director Intl Student Services .... Karen K. EDWARDS
40 Manager Bookstore .... Cassandra J. WHERRY
41 Athletic Director .... Andrew HAMILTON
23 Dir Stdnt Health/Counseling Svcs .... Deb SHILL
121 Dean Student Success/Acad Advising .... Joyce STERN
38 Dean for Health & Counseling .... Terry MASON
18 Asst Vice Pres Facilities Mgmt .... Richard WHITNEY
19 Dir of Campus Safety .... James SHROPSHIRE
42 Chaplain/Dean of Rel Life .... Deanna SHORB
102 Director Corp/Found/Govt Rels .... Susan FERRARI
32 VP Student Affairs .... Sarah MOSCHENROSS
35 AVP Student Affs/Dean of Students .... Ben NEWHOUSE
31 VP Community Engagement/Strat Plng .... Monica CHAVEZ-SILVA
36 Dean & Dir Career Life & Service .... Mark PELTZ
04 Executive Asst to President .... Karen DILLON
101 Secretary of the College .... Meg JONES BAIR
104 Director of Off-Campus Study .... Alicia STANLEY
28 Chief Diversity Ofcr/VP Diversity .... Schvalla RIVERA
39 Director Residence Life .... Dennis PERKINS
44 Director Annual Giving .... Mae PARKER
96 Procurement Manager .... Amanda JONES

Hawkeye Community College (H)

Box 8015, Waterloo IA 50704-8015
County: Black Hawk — FICE Identification: 004595
Unit ID: 153445
Telephone: (319) 296-2320 — Carnegie Class: Assoc/HVT-High Non
FAX Number: (319) 296-2874 — Calendar System: Semester
URL: www.hawkeyecollege.edu
Established: 1966 — Annual Undergrad Tuition & Fees (In-District): $5,790
Enrollment: 5,042 — Coed
Affiliation or Control: State/Local — IRS Status: 501(c)3
Highest Offering: Associate Degree
Accreditation: HLC, COARC, DA, DH, EMT, MAC, MLTAD, OTA, PTAA

01 President .... Dr. Todd HOLCOMB
05 Provost & VP Academic Affairs .... Ms. Lynn LAGRONE
10 Vice Pres Administration & Finance .... Mr. Dan GILLEN
32 Vice Pres Student Affairs .... Ms. Nina GRANT
111 Exec Dir Institutional Advancement .... Ms. Holly JOHNSON
15 Exec Dir Human Resource Services .... Ms. Susan C. HAUBER
51 Exec Director Business & Cmty Educ .... Mr. Aaron SAUERBREI
106 Dean School of Online Learning .... Mr. Robin GALLOWAY
49 Dean Arts & Sciences .... Ms. Catharine FREEMAN
75 Dean Applied Science/Eng Technology .... Mr. David GRUNKLEE
76 Dean Interprof Health & Safety Svcs .... Mr. Eugene LEUTZINGER
35 Dean of Students .... Ms. Nancy HENDERSON
88 Dean of Transitional Programs .... Vacant
41 Director of Athletics .... Mr. Ethan CRAWFORD
21 Director Business Services .... Ms. Julie THOMAS
13 Chief Information Officer .... Mr. Brian MCCORMICK
08 Director Library Services .... Ms. Candace HAVELY
18 Director Plant & Facilities .... Mr. Terence FLYNN
06 Registrar/Records & Registration .... Mr. Anthony SMOTHERS
19 Dir Public Safety/Emergency Mgr .... Mr. John KRAMER
09 Director Institutional Research .... Ms. Connie BUHR
26 Exec Dir Public Relations/Marketing .... Ms. Mary Pat MOORE
28 Director of Inclusion & Diversity .... Ms. Rhonda MCRINA
12 Director Adult Learning Center .... Ms. Laura HIDLEBAUGH
103 Dir Workforce/Career Development .... Mr. Christopher HANNAN
37 Director Student Financial Aid .... Ms. Gisella BAKER
25 Director of Grants & Resource Dev .... Ms. Constance GRIMM
35 Assoc Dir of Student Life .... Vacant
04 Assistant to President .... Ms. Annette STAPLES

Indian Hills Community College (I)

525 Grandview Avenue, Ottumwa IA 52501-1398
County: Wapello — FICE Identification: 008403
Unit ID: 153472
Telephone: (641) 683-5111 — Carnegie Class: Assoc/MT-VT-High Non
FAX Number: (641) 683-5184 — Calendar System: Quarter
URL: www.indianhills.edu
Established: 1966 — Annual Undergrad Tuition & Fees (In-District): $4,440
Enrollment: 3,279 — Coed
Affiliation or Control: State/Local — IRS Status: 501(c)3
Highest Offering: Associate Degree

Accreditation: HLC, ACFEI, CAHIIM, DA, DH, EMT, MLTAD, OTA, PTAA, RAD

01 President ... Dr. Matt THOMPSON
10 Chief Financial Officer ... Mr. Michael LEE
05 VP Learning/Engagement ... Dr. Jill BUDDE
32 VP Student Development/Operations ... Dr. Brett MONAGHAN
103 Exec Dean Career/Workforce Educ ... Dr. Jennifer WILSON
49 Assoc Dean Arts & Sciences ... Dr. Don WALTENBERGER
06 Exec Dean Enrollment Srvs/Registrar ... Ms. Joni KELLEY
12 Dean Centerville Campus/Lrng Svcs ... Ms. Noel GORDEN
102 Exec Dir Foundation/Development ... Ms. Blaire SIEMS
13 Chief Information Officer ... Mr. Cory LAMB
15 Director Human Resources ... Mr. Zeke FLICK
18 Director Physical Facilities ... Mr. Rick FOSDYCK
41 Associate Athletic Director ... Mr. Ricky WEBSTER
88 Asst Chief Flight/Aviation Programs ... Mr. Brian HAMMACK
07 Director of Admissions ... Ms. Ranae MOLKENTHIN
09 Director of Institutional Research ... Dr. Stephanie HOLLIMAN-GINKENS
26 Dir Marketing & Comm Relations ... Dr. Bianca MYERS
35 Success Center ... Ms. Rhonda CONRAD

Iowa Central Community College (A)

One Triton Circle, Fort Dodge IA 50501

County: Webster FICE Identification: 001865
Unit ID: 153524
Telephone: (515) 576-7201 Carnegie Class: Assoc/MT-VT-High Non
FAX Number: (515) 576-7207 Calendar System: Semester
URL: www.iowacentral.edu
Established: 1966 Annual Undergrad Tuition & Fees (In-District): $5,700
Enrollment: 4,704 Coed
Affiliation or Control: Local IRS Status: 501(c)3
Highest Offering: Associate Degree
Accreditation: HLC, DH, EMT, MAC, MLTAD, RAD

01 President ... Dr. Jesse ULRICH
04 Assistant to the President ... Mrs. Ally P. WALTER
05 Vice President of Instruction ... Dr. Stacy METZER
32 Vice Pres Enroll Mgmt/Student Devel ... Mr. Thomas J. BENEKE
10 Vice President of Business Affairs ... Mrs. Angela A. MARTIN
86 VP External Affairs/Govt Rels ... Mr. James B. KERSTEN
50 Business & Ind Technology Dean ... Mr. Neale J. ADAMS
76 Health Sciences Dean ... Mr. John HANSEN
49 Liberal Arts & Sciences Dean ... Mrs. Jennifer M. CONDON
106 Distance Learning Dean ... Mr. Timothy J. MARTIN
09 Inst Effectiveness Coord ... Mrs. Randi GRUVER
30 Development/Alumni Rels Exec Dir ... Mrs. Mary LUDWIG
103 Econ Wrkfc Dev/Cont Educ Exec Dir ... Mrs. Shelly R. BLUNK
06 Registrar ... Ms. Courtney A. KOPP
07 Enrollment Management Director ... Mrs. Sara A. SCHARF
37 Financial Aid Director ... Mrs. Lindsey M. CHRISTIE
21 Business Office Director ... Mr. Luke J. GROVE
15 Human Resources Director ... Ms. Stacy IHRIG
16 Human Resources Coordinator ... Ms. Sandi J. PIEPER
41 Athletic Director ... Mr. Kevin TWAIT
39 Housing Director ... Mr. Jeremy D. CONLEY
38 Mental Health Counselor ... Ms. Linnea NEWELL
35 Student Life & Activities Director ... Mr. David L. PEARSON
88 Academic Resource Services Director ... Mrs. Lori L. WALTON
18 Physical Facilities Director ... Mr. Shan L. BEECHER
12 Storm Lake Center Director ... Mr. Chris CLEVELAND
12 Webster City Center Director ... Ms. Colette BERTRAN
26 Public Information Director ... Mr. Paul A. DECOURSEY
13 Institutional Technology Director ... Mr. Jeff A. NELSEN
13 Institutional Technology Director ... Mr. Troy D. CRAMPTON
14 Sr Computer System Analyst ... Mr. Warren K. BAUER
40 Bookstore Manager ... Mrs. Samantha E. MCCLAIN

Iowa Lakes Community College (B)

19 S Seventh Street, Estherville IA 51334-2234

County: Emmet FICE Identification: 001864
Unit ID: 153533
Telephone: (712) 362-2604 Carnegie Class: Assoc/MT-VT-High Non
FAX Number: (712) 362-8363 Calendar System: Semester
URL: www.iowalakes.edu
Established: 1967 Annual Undergrad Tuition & Fees (In-District): $6,748
Enrollment: 2,288 Coed
Affiliation or Control: State/Local IRS Status: 501(c)3
Highest Offering: Associate Degree
Accreditation: HLC, MAC, SURGT

01 President ... Ms. Valerie K. NEWHOUSE
11 Vice President of Administration ... Mr. Robert A. LEIFELD
12 Exec Dean Emmetsburg Campus ... Mr. Thomas S. BROTHERTON
26 Exec Director of Marketing ... Ms. Beth ELMAN
18 Exec Dir of Facilities Management ... Ms. Delaine S. HINEY
15 Exec Director Human Resources ... Ms. Kathy A. MULLER
31 Exec Dir Cmty & Business Relations ... Ms. Jolene R. ROGERS
10 Chief Financial Officer ... Mr. Jeff D. SOPER
12 Exec Dean Estherville Campus ... Mr. Scott STOKES
32 Executive Dean of Students ... Ms. Julie R. WILLIAMS
111 Exec Dir Foundation/Govt Affairs ... Mr. Daniel LUTAT

Iowa Lakes Community College Emmetsburg Campus (C)

3200 College Drive, Emmetsburg IA 50536

Telephone: (712) 852-3554 Identification: 770055
Accreditation: &HLC

Iowa Lakes Community College Spencer Campus (D)

Gateway N 1900 Grand Ave, Ste B-1, Spencer IA 51301

Telephone: (712) 262-7141 Identification: 770056
Accreditation: &HLC

*Iowa Valley Community College District (E)

3702 S Center Street, Marshalltown IA 50158-4760

County: Marshall FICE Identification: 033436
Telephone: (641) 752-4643 Carnegie Class: N/A
FAX Number: (641) 754-1336
URL: www.iavalley.edu

01 Chancellor ... Dr. Kristie FISHER
51 Vice Chanc Continuing Educ/Training ... Ms. Jacque GOODMAN
10 Vice Chanc Finance/Admin Svcs/CFO ... Ms. Gena GARBER
13 Chief Information Officer ... Mr. Mike MOSHER
12 Provost Ellsworth Community College ... Dr. Martin REIMER
12 Provost Marshalltown Community Col ... Dr. Robin SHAFFER LILIENTHAL
12 Dean of Iowa Valley Grinnell ... Ms. Mary Anne NICKLE
26 Director of Marketing ... Ms. Julie EASTRIDGE
09 Institutional Researcher ... Dr. Lisa BREJA
04 Asst to Chancellor/Board Secretary ... Ms. Barbara JENNINGS
86 Director of Government Affairs ... Ms. Cynthia SCHULTE
15 Director of Human Resources ... Ms. Gena GARBER

*Ellsworth Community College (F)

1100 College Avenue, Iowa Falls IA 50126-1199

County: Hardin FICE Identification: 001862
Unit ID: 153296
Telephone: (641) 648-4611 Carnegie Class: Assoc/HT-High Trad
FAX Number: (641) 648-3128 Calendar System: Semester
URL: https://www.iavalley.edu/
Established: 1890 Annual Undergrad Tuition & Fees (In-District): $4,968
Enrollment: 731 Coed
Affiliation or Control: State/Local IRS Status: 501(c)3
Highest Offering: Associate Degree
Accreditation: &HLC, MAC

02 Provost ... Dr. Martin REIMER
05 Dean of Academic Affairs ... Dr. Amanda ESTEY
32 Dean of Student Affairs ... Dr. Barb KLEIN
08 Library Service Manager ... Ms. Sandra GREUFE
32 Director of Athletics/Student Life ... Mr. Nate FORSYTH
37 Director Financial Aid ... Ms. Tara MILLER
44 Dir Annual Plan Giving/Dir Alum Rel ... Ms. Gwen GROEN
07 Director of Admissions ... Ms. Adriane SIETSEMA

† Regional accreditation is carried under the parent institution Iowa Valley Community College District in Marshalltown, IA.

*Marshalltown Community College (G)

3700 S Center Street, Marshalltown IA 50158

County: Marshall FICE Identification: 001875
Unit ID: 153922
Telephone: (641) 752-4643 Carnegie Class: Assoc/MT-VT-High Non
FAX Number: (641) 752-8149 Calendar System: Semester
URL: www.mcc.iavalley.edu
Established: 1927 Annual Undergrad Tuition & Fees (In-District): $4,968
Enrollment: 1,836 Coed
Affiliation or Control: State/Local IRS Status: 501(c)3
Highest Offering: Associate Degree
Accreditation: &HLC, DA

02 Chancellor ... Dr. Kristie FISHER
05 Provost ... Dr. Robin SHAFFER LILIENTHAL
10 Chief Financial Officer/Director HR ... Ms. Gena GARBER
20 Dean of Academic Affairs ... Mr. Vincent BOYD
84 Dean Enrollment/Student Life ... Ms. Angie REDMOND
32 Dean of Students/Learning Svcs/TRIO ... Mr. Nate CHUA
06 Dir of Student Success/Registrar ... Ms. Ashtyn BEEK
76 Assoc Dean of Health Occupations ... Ms. Beth JOHANNS
102 Executive Director MCC Foundation ... Ms. Carol GEIL
37 Financial Aid Administrator ... Ms. Rachael KOEHLER
26 Director of Marketing ... Ms. Julie EASTRIDGE
41 Director of Athletics ... Mr. John KRIEBS
39 Dir Student Engagement/Res Life ... Mr. Chris BREES
121 Sr Academic Advising Specialist ... Mr. Dan KEY
08 Library Services Manager ... Ms. Emily HORNER
40 MCC Bookstore Manager ... Ms. Paulla HARTMAN
07 Admissions Office Associate ... Ms. Amy GOOD

† Regional accreditation is carried under the parent institution Iowa Valley Community College District in Marshalltown, IA.

Iowa Wesleyan University (H)

601 N Main, Mount Pleasant IA 52641-1398

County: Henry FICE Identification: 001871
Unit ID: 153621
Telephone: (319) 385-8021 Carnegie Class: Bac-Diverse
FAX Number: (319) 385-6296 Calendar System: Semester
URL: www.iw.edu
Established: 1842 Annual Undergrad Tuition & Fees: $25,280
Enrollment: 704 Coed
Affiliation or Control: United Methodist IRS Status: 501(c)3
Highest Offering: Master's
Accreditation: HLC, NUR

01 President ... Ms. Chris PLUNKETT
05 Provost ... Dr. DeWayne FRAZIER
84 VP for Enrollment & Marketing ... Ms. Meg RICHTMAN
111 VP for Advancement & Athletics ... Mr. Derek ZANDER
32 Dean of Students ... Mr. Matthew KLUNDT
13 Director of IT ... Mr. Jim COLLINS
06 Registrar ... Ms. Megan HILLS
37 Senior Financial Aid Counselor ... Ms. LaShawnda ROBERTS
10 Controller & Director of Finance ... Ms. Deb LILLIE
15 Director of Human Resources ... Ms. Kathy MOOTHART
44 Director of Advancement Operations ... Ms. Amy FRANTZ
41 Associate Athletics Director ... Ms. Courtney CARL
18 Director of Physical Plant ... Mr. Sean GRAY
36 Director of Career Development ... Ms. Nikki GERLING
40 Bookstore Director ... Ms. Amy MABEUS
04 Asst to the President ... Ms. Mary NOTESTEIN
105 Webmaster ... Ms. Cindee VANDIJK
30 Development Director ... Mr. Jim PEDRICK
30 Development Director ... Mr. Adam MCLAUGHLIN
58 Director of Graduate Studies ... Ms. Valerie HENESSEE
39 Dir Resident Life/Student Housing ... Vacant
28 Director of Title IX & Diversity ... Ms. Tina YOUNG
29 Director for Alumni Engagement ... Ms. Diane DAVIS

Iowa Western Community College (I)

2700 College Road, Council Bluffs IA 51503-0567

County: Pottawattamie FICE Identification: 004598
Unit ID: 153630
Telephone: (712) 325-3200 Carnegie Class: Assoc/MT-VT-High Non
FAX Number: (712) 325-3424 Calendar System: Semester
URL: www.iwcc.edu
Established: 1966 Annual Undergrad Tuition & Fees (In-District): $6,120
Enrollment: 5,791 Coed
Affiliation or Control: State/Local IRS Status: 501(c)3
Highest Offering: Associate Degree
Accreditation: HLC, ACFEI, DA, DH, EMT, MAC, SURGT

01 President ... Dr. Daniel KINNEY
04 Assistant to the President ... Mrs. Erin MCKEE
05 Vice President for Academic Affairs ... Vacant
10 Vice President of Finance ... Mr. Edwin HOLTZ
32 Vice President for Student Services ... Ms. Kim HENRY
26 Vice Pres of Marketing/Public Rels ... Mr. Donald KOHLER
30 Vice Pres Institutional Advancement ... Mrs. Molly NOON
103 VP Economic/Workforce Devel ... Vacant
09 Dean Institutional Research/Accred ... Mrs. Tina KNAUSS
84 Dean Enrollment Services ... Mr. Thomas GILMORE
121 Dean of Academic Support ... Mrs. Samantha LARSON
35 Dean Student Life/Student Success ... Ms. Reanna HEIM
106 Dean Distance Educ/Pathway Dev ... Mr. Matthew MANCUSO
81 Dean Science/Tech/Engineering/Math ... Mrs. Barb GODDEN
79 Dean of Comm/Education/Fine Arts ... Mrs. Jenny KRUGER
76 Dean of Health & Sports Sciences ... Mrs. Barb GODDEN
51 Director of Continuing Education ... Vacant
50 Dean Ag/Bus/Computer Info/Soc Sci ... Mrs. Ambe DOWDELL-WHITE
06 Registrar ... Mrs. Jill CLARK
07 Director of Admissions ... Mrs. Nyssa GREER
15 Director of Human Resources ... Mrs. Robyn PORTER
29 Director of Alumni Relations ... Mrs. Stacy SHOCKEY
37 Director of Student Financial Aid ... Ms. Lisa MORRISON
21 Director Accounting ... Ms. Randi BISSEN
13 Director Information Technology ... Mrs. Victoria HOSKOVEC
41 Athletic Director ... Mr. Shane LARSON
39 Director of Residence Life ... Mr. Griffen FARRAR
18 Director Physical Plant ... Mr. Brian SUTTER
96 Director of Purchasing ... Mrs. Diane OSBAHR
40 College Store Manager ... Mrs. Maggie SOBCZYK-BARRON
88 Food Service Manager ... Mr. Stephan BRYANT

Kirkwood Community College (J)

6301 Kirkwood Blvd. SW, Cedar Rapids IA 52404

County: Linn FICE Identification: 004076
Unit ID: 153737
Telephone: (319) 398-5411 Carnegie Class: Assoc/MT-VT-High Non
FAX Number: (319) 398-1037 Calendar System: Semester
URL: www.kirkwood.edu
Established: 1966 Annual Undergrad Tuition & Fees (In-District): $5,140
Enrollment: 12,277 Coed
Affiliation or Control: Local IRS Status: 501(c)3
Highest Offering: Associate Degree
Accreditation: HLC, ACFEI, COARC, DA, DH, DT, EMT, MAC, MLTAD, MUS, NDT, OTA, PTAA, SURGT

01 President ... Dr. Lori SUNDBERG
51 VP Cont Education/Training Svcs ... Ms. Jasmine ALMOAYYED
10 Vice President/Chief Fin/Oper Ofcr ... Mr. Jim CHOATE
111 Vice President Advancement ... Ms. Jody PELLERIN
05 Vice President Academic Affairs ... Dr. Jennifer BRADLEY
32 Vice President Student Services ... Mr. Jon BUSE
20 Assoc Vice President Acad Affairs ... Ms. Colette ATKINS
12 Dean Iowa City Campus ... Vacant
35 Executive Dean of Students ... Ms. Melissa PAYNE
15 Vice President Human Resources ... Mr. Wes FOWLER
13 Vice President Technology Services ... Mr. Jon NEFF
106 Dean Distance Learning ... Mr. Dave HUNT
07 Director Admissions ... Mr. Mike ESPINOZA
18 VP Facilities & Public Safety ... Mr. Troy MCQUILLEN
25 Director Grants & Fed Programs ... Ms. Doris NYAGA

41 Athletic Director .... Mr. Doug WAGEMESTER
06 Registrar .... Ms. Dena RAUCH
110 Director of Advancement .... Ms. Jody DONALDSON
37 Financial Aid Director .... Mr. Matt FALDUTO
47 Dean Agriculture Science .... Mr. Scott ERMER
72 Dean Industrial Technology .... Dr. Emily LOGAN
79 Assoc Vice Pres Liberal Arts .... Dr. Brooke STRAHN-KOLLER
76 Dean Allied Health .... Ms. Nicky CLINE
83 Interim Dean Social Sciences .... Ms. Amanda HUMPHREY
81 Dean Math/Science .... Ms. Wendy JAMISON
66 Dean Nursing .... Dr. Kathryn DOLTER
76 Dean Health Occupations .... Ms. Katie LYMAN
50 Dean Business & Information Tech .... Ms. Tamara ALT
08 Dean Learning Services/Dir Library .... Mr. Arron WINGS
04 Asst to President .... Ms. Peg SPRENGELER
104 Dean Global Learning .... Ms. Dawn WOOD
19 Assoc Vice President Public Safety ... Mr. Andrew MACPHERSON
26 Exec Dir Communications/Marketing .... Mr. Kevin HANSEN
112 Director Planned & Endowed Giving .... Vacant
14 Exec Dir IT Infrastructure .... Mr. Darren ZABLOUDIL
21 Exec Director Finance .... Vacant
88 Dean Secondary Programs .... Ms. Carla ANDORF
09 Director Institutional Research .... Mr. Cort IVERSON
86 Government Relations .... Mr. Justin HOEHN
108 VP of Institutional Effectiveness .... Dr. Connie THURMAN
44 Director Annual Giving .... Mr. Eric WEILER

Loras College (A)

1450 Alta Vista, Dubuque IA 52004-0178
County: Dubuque FICE Identification: 001873
Unit ID: 153825
Telephone: (563) 588-7100 Carnegie Class: Bac-Diverse
FAX Number: (563) 588-7964 Calendar System: Semester
URL: www.loras.edu
Established: 1839 Annual Undergrad Tuition & Fees: $35,218
Enrollment: 1,404 Coed
Affiliation or Control: Roman Catholic IRS Status: 501(c)3
Highest Offering: Master's
Accreditation: HLC, CAATE, SW

01 President .... Mr. James E. COLLINS
05 VP Academic Affairs .... Dr. Donna N. HEALD
10 Treasurer .... Mr. Michael H. DOYLE
03 Senior Vice President .... Dr. Mary Ellen CARROLL
111 VP Institutional Advancement .... Mr. Michael H. DOYLE
32 VP Student Development .... Dr. Arthur W. SUNLEAF
04 Executive Assistant to President .... Ms. Heather L. JUNGBLUT
42 Chaplain .... Rev. Dustin L. VU
91 Sr Dir Technology Services .... Mr. Thomas D. KRUSE
26 VP of Marketing .... Ms. Demeri C. MULLIKIN
15 Dir Human Resources .... Mr. Troy M. WRIGHT
09 Director of Institutional Research .... Mr. Christopher R. FEIT
38 Director Center for Counseling .... Ms. Tricia S. BORELLI
07 Director of Admissions-UG .... Mr. Kyle J. KLAPATAUSKAS
08 Library Director .... Ms. Kristen L. SMITH
35 Assistant Dean of Students .... Ms. Molly A. BURROWS-SCHUMACHER
41 Dir Intercollegiate Athletics .... Ms. Denise A. UDELHOFEN
18 Asst VP Physical Resources .... Mr. John R. MCDERMOTT
40 Director of Bookstore .... Ms. Angel M. BELL
23 Director of Health Center .... Ms. Tammy S. MARTI
42 Campus Ministry/P&J Coordinator .... Ms. Anastacia M. MCDERMOTT
06 Registrar .... Mr. Christopher R. FEIT
19 Dir Res Life & Campus Safety .... Ms. Molly A. BURROWS-SCHUMACHER
35 Assoc Dean of Students .... Ms. Kimberly A. WALSH
37 Director of Financial Planning .... Mr. Zachery W. GRIES
96 Controller for Business Office .... Ms. Rennie A. ROOT
36 Academic Internship Coordinator .... Ms. Jennifer L. WEBER

Luther College (B)

700 College Drive, Decorah IA 52101-1045
County: Winneshiek FICE Identification: 001874
Unit ID: 153834
Telephone: (563) 387-2000 Carnegie Class: Bac-A&S
FAX Number: (563) 387-2158 Calendar System: Other
URL: www.luther.edu
Established: 1861 Annual Undergrad Tuition & Fees: $45,610
Enrollment: 1,802 Coed
Affiliation or Control: Evangelical Lutheran Church In America
IRS Status: 501(c)3
Highest Offering: Baccalaureate
Accreditation: HLC, #CAATE, MUS, NURSE, SW

01 President .... Dr. Jenifer K. WARD
05 Provost .... Dr. Lynda SZYMANSKI
88 Assistant to the Provost .... Ms. Arleen ORVIS
30 Vice President for Development .... Mr. Stephen K. SPORER
10 Vice President for Finance & Admin .... Mr. Andrew BAILEY
26 Vice Pres Communications/Marketing ... Mr. Brad CHAMBERLAIN
13 Exec Dir Library & Information Svcs .... Mr. Mark FRANZ
84 VP for Enrollment Management .... Mr. Derek HARTL
21 Controller .... Ms. Peggy LENSING
18 Director of Facilities Services .... Mr. Jay L. UTHOFF
91 Exec Director Information Systems .... Mr. Mark FRANZ
110 Senior Development Officer .... Mr. Doug NELSON
06 Registrar .... Dr. Richard BERNATZ
20 Associate Dean/Dir Faculty Devel .... Dr. Sean BURKE
15 Director Human Resources .... Ms. Marsha WENTHOLD

41 Director Intercollegiate Athletics .... Ms. Renae HARTL
29 Exec Director of Alumni Relations .... Ms. Sherry B. ALCOCK
27 Director of Publications & Design .... Mr. Michael BARTELS
04 Exec Assistant to the President .... Ms. Tara QUASS
35 Assistant Dean Student Life .... Mr. Jake DYER
36 Director Career Center .... Ms. Sarah CROSE
38 Director Counseling Service .... Ms. Meg HAMMES
37 Director Student Financial Planning .... Mr. Aaron STEFFENS
42 Dir Campus Ministry & Cong Rels .... Rev. Marsha BILLS
40 Director Book Shop/Union Services ...... Ms. Deanna CASTERTON
39 Assistant Dean & Dir Res Life .... Ms. Kristine FRANZEN
85 Exec Dir Ctr Global Learn & Int Adm .... Mr. Jon LUND
23 Director Health Services .... Ms. Diane TAPPE
19 Director Security/Safety .... Mr. Robert HARRI
88 Director Campus Programming .... Ms. Kristen UNDERWOOD
09 Director Assessment/Inst Research .... Ms. Ashlesha PAWAR
124 Dean of Student Engagement .... Ms. Ashley BENSON
28 Director of Diversity Center .... Ms. Wintlett TAYLOR-BROWNE
08 Library Director .... Mr. Ryan GJERDE

Maharishi International University (C)

1000 N 4th Street, Fairfield IA 52557-0001
County: Jefferson FICE Identification: 011113
Unit ID: 153861
Telephone: (641) 472-7000 Carnegie Class: Masters/L
FAX Number: (641) 472-1179 Calendar System: Semester
URL: www.miu.edu
Established: 1971 Annual Undergrad Tuition & Fees: $16,530
Enrollment: 2,015 Coed
Affiliation or Control: Independent Non-Profit IRS Status: 501(c)3
Highest Offering: Doctorate
Accreditation: HLC, IACBE

01 President .... Dr. John HAGELIN
05 VP Academic Affairs .... Dr. Craig PEARSON
11 Vice President of Operations .... Mr. Thomas BROOKS
30 VP Development & Alumni Relations .... Mr. Brad MYLETT
84 VP Enrollment & Student Affairs .... Mr. Rod EASON
05 Dean of Faculty .... Dr. Vicki ALEXANDER-HERRIOTT
10 Treasurer .... Mr. Michael SPIVAK
88 International Vice President .... Dr. Michael DILLBECK
88 International Vice President .... Dr. Susan DILLBECK
11 Chief Administrative Officer .... Mr. David TODT
43 Legal Counsel/Dean Global Develop .... Mr. Bill GOLDSTEIN
07 Dean of Admissions .... Mr. Ron BARNETT
32 Associate Dean of Students .... Mr. Manyu HESSE
35 Assoc Dean Enrollment/Student Affs .... Ms. Selin OZBUDAK
06 Registrar .... Ms. Taniya HALLMAN
26 Media Relations .... Mr. Jim KARPEN
106 Dir Distance Educ/Intl Programs .... Mr. Dennis HEATON
27 Director of Press .... Mr. Harry BRIGHT
39 Director of Housing .... Mr. Mahmood ALI
37 Director of Student Financial Aid .... Mr. Dan WASIELEWSKI
13 Manager of Information Services .... Mr. Gilberto RODRIGUEZ
20 Dean Academic Programs .... Dr. Chris JONES
15 Director Human Resources .... Ms. Carol PASSOS
29 Director Alumni .... Mr. Paul STOKSTAD
36 Career Development Services .... Ms. Ayesha SENGUPTA
18 Chief Facilities/Physical Plant .... Mr. Nathan GERDES
49 Dean College of Arts & Sciences .... Dr. Chris JONES
77 Dean College of Computer Sci & Math ...... Mr. Gregory GUTHRIE
58 Dean of Graduate School .... Dr. Frederick TRAVIS
04 Administrative Asst to President .... Ms. Jane AIKENS
08 Director of Library .... Ms. Rouzanna VARDANYAN
41 Athletic Director .... Mr. Dustin MATTHEWS
101 Secretary of the Board of Trustees .... Ms. Susan TRACY
19 Director of Security and Safety .... Ms. Beata NACSA
106 Dir Online Education/E-learning .... Mr. Eric LIU
38 Assoc Dir Student Support Services .... Ms. Leslie DOYLE
104 Director Study Abroad .... Dr. Cathy GORINI
105 Director Web Services .... Mr. Michael MATZKIN
35 Director Student Activities .... Mr. Chris GRACE

Mercy College of Health Sciences (D)

928 Sixth Avenue, Des Moines IA 50309-1239
County: Polk FICE Identification: 006273
Unit ID: 153977
Telephone: (515) 643-3180 Carnegie Class: Spec-4-yr-Other Health
FAX Number: (515) 643-6698 Calendar System: Semester
URL: www.mchs.edu
Established: 1995 Annual Undergrad Tuition & Fees: $18,332
Enrollment: 869 Coed
Affiliation or Control: Roman Catholic IRS Status: 501(c)3
Highest Offering: Baccalaureate
Accreditation: HLC, ADNUR, DMS, EMT, MT, NURSE, PTAA, RAD, SURGT

01 President .... Dr. Douglas J. FIORE
05 Provost & VP Academic Affairs .... Dr. Nancy K. KERTZ
10 VP of Business & Regulatory Affairs .... Dr. Thomas LEAHY
106 Exec VP & Chancellor Mercy Col Plus ...... Mr. Matthew ROMKEY
15 VP of Employee Engagement & HR .... Ms. Anne DENNIS
20 Academic Dean .... Dr. Ryan "Bud" MARR
08 Dir of Library and Media Services .... Ms. Jennie E. VER STEEG
06 Registrar .... Ms. Carolyn BUCKLIN
37 Senior Director Financial Aid .... Mr. Joe BROOKOVER
32 Dean of Student Affairs .... Ms. Lyneene RICHARDSON
13 Director of Information Technology .... Mr. David VON ARB
84 Director Enrollment Management .... Mr. Andrew GRESS
101 Board Liaison/Communications Spec .... Ms. Mackenzie KELLOGG

Morningside College (E)

1501 Morningside Avenue, Sioux City IA 51106-1751
County: Woodbury FICE Identification: 001879
Unit ID: 154004
Telephone: (712) 274-5000 Carnegie Class: Masters/L
FAX Number: (712) 274-5101 Calendar System: Semester
URL: www.morningside.edu
Established: 1894 Annual Undergrad Tuition & Fees: $33,970
Enrollment: 2,411 Coed
Affiliation or Control: United Methodist IRS Status: 501(c)3
Highest Offering: Doctorate
Accreditation: HLC, MUS, NURSE

01 President .... Mr. John C. REYNDERS
05 Vice President for Academic Affairs ...... Dr. Christopher L. SPICER
10 Vice President Business & Finance .... Mr. Ronald A. JORGENSEN
32 Vice Pres Student Life & Enrollment .... Mrs. Terri A. CURRY
111 Vice Pres Institutional Advancement .. Mrs. Kari L. WINKLEPLECK
26 Vice Pres External Relations .... Mrs. Erin M. EDLUND
35 Dean of Students .... Dr. Karmen TEN NAPEL
20 Associate Dean for Acad Affairs .... Dr. Alden STOUT
06 Registrar .... Mrs. Jen DOLPHIN
37 Director Student Financial Planning .... Ms. Karen WIESE
13 Exec Dir of Information Services .... Mr. Mike HUSMANN
29 Director of Alumni Relations .... Mr. Shiran NATHANIEL
07 Director of Admissions .... Ms. Steph PETERS
18 Director of Physical Plant .... Mr. Tim PAUL
19 Director of Security .... Mr. Brett LYON
23 Director of Student Health .... Ms. Judi NESWICK
36 Director of Career Services .... Ms. Stacie HAYS
40 Director of Bookstore .... Ms. Jodi STROHBEEN
41 Athletic Director .... Mr. Tim JAGER
42 Campus Ministry .... Rev. Andy NELSON
112 Director of Gift Planning .... Mr. Jonathan BLUM
15 Director Human Resources .... Ms. Cindy WELP
21 Controller .... Mr. Paul TREFT
04 Administrative Asst to President .... Mrs. Lisa KROHN
105 Digital Communications Mgr .... Ms. Kim SANGWIN
39 Director Residence Life .... Ms. Sheri HINEMAN
08 Library Director .... Mr. Adam FULLERTON
38 Personal Counselor .... Ms. Bobbi MEISTER
101 Secretary of the Institution/Board .... Mrs. Lisa KROHN
91 Director Administrative Computing .... Ms. Carla GREGG
84 Director Enrollment Management .... Mrs. Terri A. CURRY
30 Director of Development .... Mr. Mike FREEMAN
44 Director Annual Giving .... Ms. J.J MARLOW
53 Dean of Education .... Dr. LuAnn M. HAASE
96 Director of Purchasing .... Mr. Ronald A. JORGENSEN
22 Dir Affirmative Action/Equal Opp .... Ms. Cindy WELP
28 Director of Diversity .... Mr. Andre MCWELL

Mount Mercy University (F)

1330 Elmhurst Drive NE, Cedar Rapids IA 52402-4797
County: Linn FICE Identification: 001880
Unit ID: 154013
Telephone: (319) 363-8213 Carnegie Class: Masters/M
FAX Number: (319) 363-5270 Calendar System: 4/1/4
URL: www.mtmercy.edu
Established: 1928 Annual Undergrad Tuition & Fees: $35,506
Enrollment: 1,705 Coed
Affiliation or Control: Roman Catholic IRS Status: 501(c)3
Highest Offering: Doctorate
Accreditation: HLC, MFCD, NURSE, SW

01 President .... Dr. Robert BEATTY
05 Provost/Vice President Academic .... Dr. Timothy LAURENT
10 VP for Business & Finance .... Ms. Anne GILLESPIE
84 VP Enrollment & Marketing .... Vacant
30 VP of Development/Alumni Relations .... Ms. Brenda HAEFNER
42 VP of Mission and Ministry .... Sr. Linda BECHEN
32 Vice Pres for Student Success .... Dr. Nate KLEIN
20 Assoc Prov/Exec Dir Acad Innovation .... Dr. Tom CASTLE
06 Registrar .... Mr. Chance MCWORTHY
08 Director of Library Services .... Ms. Kristy RAINE
36 Director of Career Services .... Ms. Kalindi GARVIN
110 Asst VP for Development/Alumni Rel ...... Ms. Lonna DREWELOW
37 Director of Financial Aid .... Ms. Bethany DAVENPORT
26 Director of Marketing .... Ms. Jamie JONES
41 Director of Athletics .... Mr. Paul GAVIN
38 Director of Counseling .... Ms. Karol WHITE
19 Director of Public Safety .... Mr. Joe CERRUTO
24 Academic Technology Librarian .... Mr. Greg ENNIS
15 Director of Human Resources .... Mr. Thomas DOERMANN
18 Director of Facilities .... Mr. Dennis GEHRING
92 Director of Honors Program .... Dr. Richard BARRETT
04 Assistant to the President .... Ms. Kim BLANKENHEIM
09 Exec Dir of Institutional Research .... Ms. Lori HEYING

North Iowa Area Community College (G)

500 College Drive, Mason City IA 50401-7299
County: Cerro Gordo FICE Identification: 001877
Unit ID: 154059
Telephone: (641) 423-1264 Carnegie Class: Assoc/MT-VT-High Non
FAX Number: (641) 423-1711 Calendar System: Semester
URL: www.niacc.edu
Established: 1917 Annual Undergrad Tuition & Fees (In-District): $5,791
Enrollment: 2,681 Coed
Affiliation or Control: State/Local IRS Status: 501(c)3
Highest Offering: Associate Degree

Accreditation: HLC, ADNUR, MAC, PTAA

01 President ... Dr. Steven D. SCHULZ
05 Vice President Academic Affairs ... Dr. Charlene K. WIDENER
10 Vice Pres Administrative Services ... Ms. Noele M. BEAVER
32 Vice President of Student Services ... Ms. Bridgett E. GOLMAN
111 Director Institutional Advancement ... Mrs. Molly H. KNOLL
88 Director of JPEC ... Mr. Timothy J. PUTNAM
15 VP Organizational Development/HR ... Dr. Shelly M. SCHMIT
06 Registrar ... Mrs. Michelle L. PETZNICK
83 Chair Hum/Human & Public Svcs/Bus ... Mr. Joe D. DAVIS
76 Chair Health Sciences & STEM ... Ms. Heather M. RISSLER
50 Chair Agriculture/Skilled Trades ... Ms. Laura L. WOOD
51 Dean of Continuing Education ... Mrs. Patti L. HANSON
37 Director of Financial Aid ... Vacant
20 Director Learning Services ... Ms. Dalila A. SAJADIAN
13 Chief Information Officer ... Mr. Josh C. MACK
103 WIOA Title I Director Region 2 ... Vacant
121 Director of TRIO ... Ms. Jennifer L. PATTERSON
41 Director of Athletics ... Mr. Camron M. OLSON
18 Director of Facilities Management ... Mr. Tony A. PAPPAS
21 Comptroller ... Ms. Mindy R. EASTMAN
39 Director Student Housing ... Mr. Jeremy G. WINTERS
08 Librarian/Media Specialist ... Ms. Rhonda K. NESHEIM-KAUFFMAN
26 Dir Marketing/Community Relations ... Mrs. Valerie F. ZAHORSKI-SCHMIDT
88 Director Accelerator/Incubator ... Vacant
88 Director SBDC ... Mr. Brook S. BOEHMLER
88 Director of School Partnerships ... Mr. Brian M. WOGEN
88 Dir of Operations/Continuing Educ .. Mrs. Constance J. GLANDON
88 Director of Sales & Programming ... Ms. Amy MARKHAM
09 Director of Institutional Research ... Dr. Shelly M. SCHMIT
102 Grant Writer/Inst Fund Develop Spec ... Ms. Jana T. GRZENDA
106 Educational Software Administrator ... Ms. Erica S. MCBRIDE
29 Director Alumni Relations ... Ms. Andrea J. MUJICA
07 Director of Admissions ... Dr. Rachel L. MCGUIRE
28 Director of Diversity ... Dr. Shelly M. SCHMIT
04 Administrative Asst to President ... Ms. Taylor Ann HENDRICKS
22 Director Affirmative Action/EEO ... Dr. Shelly M. SCHMIT

Northeast Iowa Community College (A)

Box 400, Calmar IA 52132-0400
County: Winneshiek FICE Identification: 004587
Unit ID: 154110
Telephone: (844) 642-2338 Carnegie Class: Assoc/HVT-High Non
FAX Number: (563) 562-3983 Calendar System: Semester
URL: www.nicc.edu
Established: 1966 Annual Undergrad Tuition & Fees (In-District): $6,000
Enrollment: 4,162 Coed
Affiliation or Control: Local IRS Status: 501(c)3
Highest Offering: Associate Degree
Accreditation: HLC, CAHIIM, COARC, DA

01 President ... Dr. Liang C. WEE
10 Vice Pres Finance & Administration ... Mr. David W. DAHMS
05 Chief Acad Ofcr/VP Academic Affairs ... Dr. Kathy J. NACOS-BURDS
46 Vice Pres Bus & Community Solutions ... Dr. Wendy A. MIHM-HEROLD
11 Assoc Vice President for Operations ... Ms. Rhonda K. SEIBERT
108 VP of Institutional Effectiveness ... Ms. Wendy S. KNIGHT
15 Exec Director of Human Resources ... Ms. Connie KUENNEN
106 Dean of Instructional Innovation ... Mr. Kyle T. COLLINS
13 Director Computer Information Sys ... Mr. Craig R. MEIRICK
09 Director of Institutional Research ... Ms. Lor M. MILLER
103 Director Economic Development ... Mr. Gregory A. WILLGING
37 Director of Financial Aid ... Mr. Randy D. MASHEK
06 District Registrar ... Ms. Karla R. WINTER
84 Director of Enrollment/Retention ... Ms. Sheila R. BECKER
36 Career Services Manager ... Mr. Chris E. ENTRINGER
07 Director of Admissions ... Ms. Kristi L. STRIEF
26 Dir Marketing/News/Publications ... Ms. Shea A. HERBST

Northeast Iowa Community College Peosta Campus (B)

8342 NICC Drive, Peosta IA 52068
Telephone: (844) 642-2338 Identification: 770063
Accreditation: &HLC, EMT, MAC, RAD

Northwest Iowa Community College (C)

603 W Park Street, Sheldon IA 51201-1046
County: Sioux FICE Identification: 004600
Unit ID: 154129
Telephone: (712) 324-5061 Carnegie Class: Assoc/HVT-High Non
FAX Number: (712) 324-4136 Calendar System: Semester
URL: www.nwicc.edu
Established: 1966 Annual Undergrad Tuition & Fees (In-District): $6,390
Enrollment: 1,666 Coed
Affiliation or Control: State/Local IRS Status: 501(c)3
Highest Offering: Associate Degree
Accreditation: HLC, CAHIIM, RAD

01 President ... Dr. John HARTOG, III
05 Exec Dir Student & Academic Svcs ... Ms. Erin LATONA
111 Director College Advancement ... Ms. Kristi LANDIS
10 Exec Dir Operations & Finance ... Mr. Brian NASH
72 Dean Applied Technology ... Mr. Steve WALDSTEIN
49 Dean Arts & Sci/Business/Health ... Ms. Leah MURPHY
21 Director of Business Services ... Ms. Jessica WILLIAMS
37 Director Financial Aid ... Ms. Karna HOFMEYER
84 Director Enrollment Management ... Ms. Lisa L. STORY
08 Coordinator of Library Services ... Ms. Renee FRANKLIN
13 Director of Technology & Info Svcs ... Mr. Mike OLDENKAMP
88 Coordinator of TRIO ... Ms. Tracy GORTER
06 Registrar/Assoc Dean of Students ... Ms. Beth SIBENALLER-WOODALL
15 Director of Human Resources ... Ms. Renee CARLSON
26 Director Community Relations ... Ms. Kristin E. KOLLBAUM
18 Director Physical Facilities ... Mr. Randy BAARTMAN

Northwestern College (D)

101 Seventh Street, SW, Orange City IA 51041-1996
County: Sioux FICE Identification: 001883
Unit ID: 154101
Telephone: (712) 707-7000 Carnegie Class: Bac-Diverse
FAX Number: (712) 707-7247 Calendar System: Semester
URL: www.nwciowa.edu
Established: 1882 Annual Undergrad Tuition & Fees: $32,920
Enrollment: 1,496 Coed
Affiliation or Control: Reformed Church In America IRS Status: 501(c)3
Highest Offering: Master's
Accreditation: HLC, #ARCPA, IACBE, NURSE, SW

01 President ... Mr. Gregory E. CHRISTY
32 Dean of Student Life ... Dr. Julie VERMEER ELLIOTT
05 Vice President for Academic Affairs ... Dr. D. Nathan PHINNEY
10 Vice President for Finance & Opers ... Mr. Kent WIERSEMA
111 Vice President Advancement ... Mr. Jay WIELENGA
84 Vice President Enrollment & Mktg ... Ms. Tamara FYNAARDT
41 Vice President for Athletics ... Dr. Micah PARKER
08 Director of the Library ... Ms. Greta GROND
06 Registrar ... Ms. Sandy VAN KLEY
37 Director of Financial Aid ... Mr. Eric ANDERSON
13 Director of Computing Services ... Mr. Harlan R. JORGENSEN
26 Director of Public Relations ... Mr. Duane L. BEESON
36 Director of Career and Calling ... Dr. Elizabeth PITTS
38 Dir Student Counseling Services ... Dr. Sally EDMAN
18 Director of Maintenance/Operations ... Vacant
29 Director Alumni Relations ... Mr. Corky KOERSELMAN
15 Director of Human Resources ... Mrs. Deb SANDBULTE
09 Director of Institutional Research ... Mr. Michael WALLINGA
04 Administrative Asst to President ... Ms. Jill HAARSMA
19 Director Security/Safety ... Mr. Andrew VAN OMMEREN
07 Dean of Admissions ... Ms. Jackie DAVIS
106 Dean of Graduate & Adult Learning ... Dr. Rebecca HOEY
39 Dean of Residence Life ... Mr. Marlon HAVERDINK

Orion Technical College (E)

1011 E 53rd Street, Davenport IA 52807-2616
County: Scott FICE Identification: 012064
Unit ID: 153427
Telephone: (563) 386-3570 Carnegie Class: Spec-4-yr-Other Tech
FAX Number: (563) 386-6756 Calendar System: Semester
URL: https://orion.edu/
Established: 1969 Annual Undergrad Tuition & Fees: $14,275
Enrollment: 120 Coed
Affiliation or Control: Proprietary IRS Status: Proprietary
Highest Offering: Baccalaureate
Accreditation: ACCSC, MAC

01 President/CEO ... Mrs. Susan SPIVEY
32 Dir Students/Career Services ... Mrs. Michelle PETERSON
07 Director Student Admissions ... Mrs. Michelle LOPEZ

Palmer College of Chiropractic (F)

1000 Brady Street, Davenport IA 52803-5287
County: Scott FICE Identification: 012300
Unit ID: 154174
Telephone: (563) 884-5000 Carnegie Class: Spec-4-yr-Other Health
FAX Number: (563) 884-5409 Calendar System: Trimester
URL: www.palmer.edu
Established: 1897 Annual Undergrad Tuition & Fees: N/A
Enrollment: 2,178 Coed
Affiliation or Control: Independent Non-Profit IRS Status: 501(c)3
Highest Offering: First Professional Degree
Accreditation: HLC, CHIRO

01 Chancellor ... Dr. Dennis M. MARCHIORI
05 College Provost ... Dr. Daniel J. WEINERT
88 Vice Chanc Inst Effectiveness ... Dr. Robert E. PERCUOCO
32 Vice Chancellor Student Affairs ... Dr. Kevin A. CUNNINGHAM
07 Vice Chancellor for Admissions ... Mr. Michael C. NORRIS
10 Vice Chancellor for Finance ... Ms. Jennifer RANDAZZO
46 Dean of Research ... Dr. Cynthia LONG
26 Vice Chancellor for Mktg & Comm ... Mr. James O'CONNOR
111 VC for Institutional Advancement ... Ms. Barbara MELBOURNE
20 Dean of Academic Affairs ... Vacant
17 Exec Dean of Clinic Affairs ... Dr. Ron BOESCH
20 Assoc Dean of Academic Affairs ... Dr. Michael TUNNING
20 Assoc Dean of Academic Affairs ... Dr. Michelle DROVER
110 Exec Dir Advancement ... Ms. Clare THOMPSON
06 Senior Director/Registrar ... Ms. Mindy S. LEAHY
09 Sr Dir Inst Research/Effectiveness ... Dr. Dustin C. DERBY
88 Sr Dir Accreditation & Licensure ... Ms. Beth BARCLAY
21 Senior Dir for Financial Affairs ... Ms. Kathleen GRAVES
13 Senior Dir Information Technology ... Mr. Mark WISELEY
15 Senior Dir of Human Resources ... Mr. Barry PENCE
18 Senior Director of Facilities ... Mr. Michael ERNSTER
51 Sr Dir Continuing Education ... Dr. Mary FROST
07 Director of Campus Enrollment ... Mr. Erik SELLAS
37 Senior Dir of Financial Planning ... Ms. Abbey NAGLE-KUCH
108 Senior Director for Assessment ... Dr. Troy STARK
121 Dir of Academic Support Services ... Ms. Holly FISCHER
08 Senior Director of Library ... Ms. Christine DEINES
88 Sr Dir Quality Assurance/System Org ... Ms. Earlye A. JULIEN
19 Sr Dir Campus Safety and Security ... Mr. Brian SHARKEY
88 Sr Dir Clinic Operations ... Ms. Tara SCHULZ
27 Sr Dir Marketing ... Ms. Kimberly KENT
27 Sr Dir of Communication ... Ms. Jillian MCCLEARY
101 Exec Director Board Affairs ... Ms. Lynne LINDSTROM
88 Assoc Dean of Clinic Research ... Dr. Robert VINING
43 Exec Dir Legal Affairs ... Ms. Amber WELLS

St. Ambrose University (G)

518 W Locust Street, Davenport IA 52803-2898
County: Scott FICE Identification: 001889
Unit ID: 154235
Telephone: (563) 333-6000 Carnegie Class: Masters/L
FAX Number: (563) 333-6243 Calendar System: Semester
URL: www.sau.edu
Established: 1882 Annual Undergrad Tuition & Fees: $32,758
Enrollment: 3,003 Coed
Affiliation or Control: Roman Catholic IRS Status: 501(c)3
Highest Offering: Doctorate
Accreditation: HLC, ACBSP, ARCPA, NURSE, OT, PTA, SP, SW

01 President ... Sr. Joan LESCINSKI, CSJ
05 Provost & VP Academic/Student Affs ... Dr. Paul KOCH
10 Vice President Finance ... Mr. Michael C. POSTER
42 Chaplain ... Rev. Thomas J. HENNEN
111 Vice President Advancement ... Mr. James R. STANGLE
84 Vice Pres Enrollment Management ... Mr. James P. LOFTUS
46 Assoc Vice Pres Assess/Research ... Dr. Tracy SCHUSTER-MATLOCK
11 Director Administrative Services ... Ms. Carol A. GLINES
26 Director of Communications ... Mr. Craig J. DEVRIEZE
32 Dean of Students ... Mr. Christopher A. WAUGH
15 Director Human Resources ... Ms. Audrey D. BLAIR
13 Exec Dir of Information Resources ... Ms. Mary B. HEINZMAN
29 Director Alumni Rels & Spec Project ... Ms. Anne A. GANNAWAY
37 Director Financial Aid ... Ms. Julie A. HAACK
38 Director Counseling ... Dr. Sarah E. OLIVER
18 Director Physical Plant ... Mr. Jim M. HANNON
06 Registrar ... Mr. Dan L. ZEIMET
23 Director of Health Services ... Ms. Nancy A. HINES
19 Director of Security ... Mr. Robert CHRISTOPHER
39 Director of Residence Life ... Mr. Matt HANSEN
08 Interim Director Library ... Ms. Julia B. SALTING
36 Director Career Development ... Ms. Kimberly MATTESON
41 Athletic Director ... Mr. Michael S. HOLMES
40 Manager of Bookstore ... Mr. Cory W. SAMBDMAN
104 Coordinator Education Abroad ... Ms. Paige ECHELE
73 Director Masters Pastoral Theology ... Dr. Micah D. KIEL
88 Director Masters Criminal Justice ... Dr. Chrisopher C. BARNUM
49 Dean College Arts & Sciences ... Dr. Paula M. MCNUTT
50 Dean College Business ... Dr. Maritza ESPINA
76 Dean Health & Human Services ... Dr. Sandra L. CASSADY
55 Dean Academic Adult & Graduate Pgm ... Dr. Regina M. MATHESON
54 Chair Engineering & Physical Sci ... Dr. Andrew J. LUTZ
57 Chair Fine Arts ... Ms. Kristin QUINN
75 Director Occupational Therapy ... Dr. Lynn J. KILBURG
88 Director Masters of Accounting ... Dr. Allison S. AMBROSE
58 Director MBA Pgm ... Dr. Russell W. WRIGHT
28 Director of Diversity ... Mr. Ryan C. SADDLER
04 Senior Asst to President ... Ms. Jana M. SEUTTER
44 Assoc VP Legacy Giving/Campaign Dir ... Ms. Sally E. CRINO
53 Interim Dir School of Education ... Dr. Gene F. BECHEN
86 Dir Corporate & Community Relations ... Mr. Ty J. GRUNDER
101 Secretary of the Institution/Board ... Sr. Joan LESCINSKI, CSJ
106 Director Online Learning ... Mr. Donnie L. INGRAM
108 Director Institutional Assessment ... Dr. Tracy SCHUSTER-MATLOCK
96 Director of Purchasing ... Ms. Carol A. GLINES
22 Dir Compliance & Title IX Coord ... Mr. Kevin R. CARLSON

St. Luke's College (H)

2720 Stone Park Boulevard, Sioux City IA 51104-0010
County: Woodbury FICE Identification: 007291
Unit ID: 154262
Telephone: (712) 279-3149 Carnegie Class: Spec-4-yr-Other Health
FAX Number: (712) 233-8017 Calendar System: Semester
URL: www.stlukescollege.edu
Established: 1995 Annual Undergrad Tuition & Fees: $20,940
Enrollment: 211 Coed
Affiliation or Control: Independent Non-Profit IRS Status: 501(c)3
Highest Offering: Baccalaureate
Accreditation: HLC, ADNUR, COARC, MT, NURSE, PAST, RAD

01 President ... Dr. Kendra ERICSON
05 Chief Academic Office/Provost ... Dr. Robert LOCH
32 Dean Student Services ... Ms. Danelle D. JOHANNSEN
20 Dean of Academics ... Dr. Lorraine SACINO MURPHY
66 Associate Dean Nursing ... Dr. Shannon MERK
06 Registrar ... Ms. Michelle FITCH

113 Bursar ... Ms. Lori MEIER
84 Enrollment Mgmt/Marketing Coord ... Ms. Sherry MCCARTHY
08 Dept Chair/Library ... Ms. Nancy ZUBROD
29 Alumni/Events Coordinator ... Vacant

Shiloh University (A)

416 D Avenue, Kalona IA 52247
County: Washington Identification: 667095
Unit ID: 480499
Telephone: (319) 656-2447 Carnegie Class: Spec-4-yr-Faith
FAX Number: (319) 656-2448 Calendar System: Trimester
URL: www.shilohuniversity.edu
Established: 2006 Annual Undergrad Tuition & Fees: $5,250
Enrollment: 49 Coed
Affiliation or Control: Independent Non-Profit IRS Status: 501(c)3
Highest Offering: Doctorate
Accreditation: DEAC

00 Chancellor ... Vacant
01 President ... Mr. Christopher REEVES
05 Vice President of Academics ... Dr. Mark GLENN
13 Vice President of Technology ... Mr. James WIRTHLIN
73 Dean BA New Testament/Biblical Pgm ... Dr. Steven TODD
58 Dean Doctoral Studies ... Dr. Mark GLENN
58 Dean Graduate Programs ... Dr. Ana I. WOOD
06 Registrar ... Mr. Joshua WHEELER
07 Admissions Coordinator ... Mr. Vania GOMEZ
08 Library Director ... Mrs. Julie MCPHAIL
11 Chief of Operations/Administration ... Vacant

Simpson College (B)

701 North C Street, Indianola IA 50125-1297
County: Warren FICE Identification: 001887
Unit ID: 154350
Telephone: (515) 961-6251 Carnegie Class: Bac-A&S
FAX Number: (515) 961-1623 Calendar System: Other
URL: www.simpson.edu
Established: 1860 Annual Undergrad Tuition & Fees: $42,246
Enrollment: 1,267 Coed
Affiliation or Control: United Methodist IRS Status: 501(c)3
Highest Offering: Master's
Accreditation: HLC, MUS

01 President ... Ms. Marsha KELLIHER
05 Sr Vice Pres/Dean Academic Affairs ... Mr. John WOELL
10 Vice President Business/Finance ... Mr. Philip PENA
111 Vice President College Advancement ... Mr. Robert J. LANE
32 Vice President Student Development ... Dr. Heidi LEVINE
84 Vice President Enrollment ... Mr. Leigh MLODZIK
13 VP Info Svcs/Chief Info Officer ... Vacant
37 Asst VP Enrollment/Financial Aid ... Ms. Tracie PAVON
06 Registrar ... Ms. Jody RAGAN
35 Dean of Students ... Mr. Luke BEHAUNEK
26 Vice President Marketing and PR ... Vacant
08 Director of Library ... Ms. Cynthia M. DYER
15 Director of Human Resources ... Ms. Mary E. BARTLEY
36 Director of Career Services ... Ms. Bobbi SULLIVAN
41 Athletic Director ... Mr. Marty BELL
96 Director of Procurement ... Vacant
35 Assistant Dean of Students ... Mr. Richard O. RAMOS
42 Chaplain ... Rev. Mara BAILEY
18 Director Campus Services ... Vacant
21 Controller/Assistant VP ... Vacant
19 Coordinator of Campus Security ... Mr. Chris FRERICHS
51 Dean Adult Learning/Online Programs ... Ms. Amy GIESEKE
104 Director of International Education ... Mr. Jay WILKINSON
04 Director Presidential Initiatives ... Ms. Megan SHULTZ
29 Director Alumni Relations ... Mr. Andy ENGLISH

Simpson College West Des Moines (C)

1415 28th Street, #250, West Des Moines IA 50266
Telephone: (515) 309-3099 Identification: 770064
Accreditation: &HLC

Southeastern Community College (D)

1500 W Agency Road, PO Box 180,
West Burlington IA 52655-0180
County: Des Moines FICE Identification: 001848
Unit ID: 154378
Telephone: (319) 752-2731 Carnegie Class: Assoc/MT-VT-High Non
FAX Number: (319) 752-4957 Calendar System: Semester
URL: www.scciowa.edu
Established: 1966 Annual Undergrad Tuition & Fees (In-District): $5,910
Enrollment: 2,260 Coed
Affiliation or Control: State/Local IRS Status: 501(c)3
Highest Offering: Associate Degree
Accreditation: HLC, COARC, EMT, MAC

01 President ... Dr. Michael ASH
05 Vice Pres of Academic Affairs ... Dr. Janet SHEPHERD
32 Vice President of Student Services ... Ms. Joan WILLIAMS
11 Vice Pres Administrative Services ... Mr. Kevin CARR
111 Exec Director for Inst Advancement ... Ms. Val GIANNETTINO
37 Financial Aid Officer ... Ms. Stacey ABELL
84 Enrollment Coordinator ... Ms. Dana CHRISMAN
06 Registrar ... Mr. Dennis MARINO
15 Director Human Resources ... Ms. Laurie HEMPEN
49 Dean Arts and Sciences ... Dr. Chris SEDLACK
76 Dean oi Health ... Ms. Kristi SCHROEDER
75 Dean Career/Technical Education ... Dr. Ashlee SPANNAGEL
26 Dir Marketing/Communications ... Mr. Jeff EBBING
04 Admin Assistant to the President ... Ms. Darcy BURDETTE
09 Director of Institutional Research ... Dr. Hope CLARK

Southeastern Community College Keokuk Campus (E)

335 Messenger Road, Keokuk IA 52632
Telephone: (319) 313-1928 Identification: 770065
Accreditation: &HLC

Southwestern Community College (F)

1501 W Townline Street, Creston IA 50801-1098
County: Union FICE Identification: 001857
Unit ID: 154396
Telephone: (641) 782-7081 Carnegie Class: Assoc/MT-VT-High Non
FAX Number: (641) 782-3312 Calendar System: Semester
URL: www.swcciowa.edu
Established: 1966 Annual Undergrad Tuition & Fees (In-State): $6,336
Enrollment: 1,503 Coed
Affiliation or Control: State IRS Status: 501(c)3
Highest Offering: Associate Degree
Accreditation: HLC

01 President/CEO ... Dr. Majorie MCGUIRE-WELCH
03 Vice President Economic Development ... Mr. Thomas L. LESAN
05 Vice President Instruction ... Ms. Lindsay STOAKS
10 Chief Financial Officer ... Mrs. Tia SAMO
32 Dean of Student Services ... Ms. Kim BISHOP
20 Asst Vice Pres of Instruction ... Mr. John FRANKLIN
106 Director of Distance Education ... Mr. Doug GREENE
15 Director of Human Resources ... Mrs. Jolene GRIFFITH
26 Director Marketing/Enrollment Mgmt ... Mrs. Terri HIGGINS
08 Director Learning Resource Center ... Mrs. Ann COULTER
13 Director of Information Technology ... Mr. Scott HELM
37 Director of Financial Aid ... Ms. Kylee KLOMMHAUS
06 Registrar ... Ms. Alyssa RILEY
04 Administrative Asst to President ... Ms. Carmalee WOODS
07 Director of Admissions ... Ms. Caitlyn MAITLEN
39 Dir Resident Life/Student Housing ... Ms. Lindsay STUMPFF
41 Athletic Director ... Mr. Nick WEINMEISTER

University of Dubuque (G)

2000 University Avenue, Dubuque IA 52001-5099
County: Dubuque FICE Identification: 001891
Unit ID: 153278
Telephone: (563) 589-3115 Carnegie Class: Masters/M
FAX Number: (563) 589-3110 Calendar System: 4/1/4
URL: www.dbq.edu
Established: 1852 Annual Undergrad Tuition & Fees: $36,610
Enrollment: 2,180 Coed
Affiliation or Control: Presbyterian Church (U.S.A.) IRS Status: 501(c)3
Highest Offering: Doctorate
Accreditation: HLC, AAB, #ARCPA, NURSE, THEOL

01 President ... Rev Dr. Jeffrey F. BULLOCK
04 Exec Admin to President/BOT ... Mrs. Sandra M. LUDESCHER
05 VP Academic Affairs/Dean of Faculty ... Dr. Mark WARD
84 VP Enroll Mgmt/Dean Admissions ... Mr. Robert BROSHOUS
10 Vice Pres Finance/Auxiliary Svcs ... Mr. James D. STEINER
84 Vice Pres Enrollment/Univ Rels ... Vacant
32 Dean of Student Formation ... Mr. Mike J. DURNIN
20 Dean of the Seminary ... Dr. Annette BOURLAND HUIZENGA
07 Sr Director of Admission ... Mr. Shane BESLER
13 Dir of Technology/Communications ... Ms. Sherry CUSICK
06 Registrar ... Ms. Kim WULFEKUHLE-ISAAC
08 Director of the Library ... Mr. Christopher DOLL
15 Director of Human Resources ... Ms. Julie MACTAGGART
37 AVP/Dean Student Financial Planning ... Ms. Teresa BRAHM
58 Dean for Acad Affs Grad/Adult Pgms ... Dr. Richardo CUNNINGHAM
36 Director Vocation/Civic Engagement ... Ms. Marie MAGUINA HELLER
29 Director for Alumni Engagement ... Ms. Katie KRAUS
40 Director of Campus Stores ... Ms. Margo KETELS
41 Director of Athletics ... Mr. Dan RUNKLE
18 Director of Facilities ... Mr. Craig KLOFT
88 Executive Director Heritage Center ... Mr. Thomas J. ROBBINS

Upper Iowa University (H)

605 Washington, Box 1857, Fayette IA 52142-1857
County: Fayette FICE Identification: 001893
Unit ID: 154493
Telephone: (563) 425-5200 Carnegie Class: Masters/L
FAX Number: (563) 425-5271 Calendar System: Semester
URL: www.uiu.edu
Established: 1857 Annual Undergrad Tuition & Fees: $32,945
Enrollment: 3,610 Coed
Affiliation or Control: Independent Non-Profit IRS Status: 501(c)3
Highest Offering: Master's
Accreditation: HLC, NURSE

01 President ... Dr. William R. DUFFY, II
05 VP Academic Affairs ... Dr. Doug BINSFELD
10 VP Finance ... Ms. Kathy FRANKEN
84 VP Enrollment Management ... Ms. Kathy FRANKEN
30 VP of External Affairs ... Mr. Andrew WENTHE
41 VP Athletics ... Mr. Rick HARTZELL
32 Dean Students ... Ms. Danielle CUSHION
12 South Central Region Director ... Ms. Cynthia BENTLEY
12 Director North Central ... Ms. Jen WEBB
07 Exec Director of Admissions ... Mrs. Kathy WENTHOLD
06 Registrar ... Mrs. Holly STREETER
08 Director Library Services ... Mr. Kelly DONOVAN
04 Exec Assistant to the President ... Mrs. Holly D. WOLFF
105 Director Internet Development ... Mr. Tony PHAN
21 Controller ... Mrs. Stacie BURINGTON
36 Director of Career Development ... Ms. Anne PUFFETT
35 Director Student Activities ... Vacant
26 Exec Dir Communications & Marketing ... Vacant
29 Director of Alumni Relations ... Mr. Andrew WENTHE
13 Director Information Technology ... Mr. Terry SMID
15 VP Human Resources ... Mr. Beau SUDTELGTE
88 Director Sports Info Services ... Mr. Howard THOMPSON
18 Exec Director of Facilities ... Mr. Jesse PLEGGENKUHLE
40 Bookstore Manager ... Ms. Janelle SOPPE
37 Director Student Financial Aid ... Ms. Kelli BELL
38 Director Student Counseling ... Ms. Crystal COLE
109 Campus Store Manager ... Mrs. Holly WOLFF

Waldorf University (I)

106 S 6th Street, Forest City IA 50436-1713
County: Winnebago FICE Identification: 001895
Unit ID: 154518
Telephone: (641) 585-2450 Carnegie Class: Masters/M
FAX Number: (641) 585-8194 Calendar System: Semester
URL: www.waldorf.edu
Established: 1903 Annual Undergrad Tuition & Fees: $23,088
Enrollment: 3,025 Coed
Affiliation or Control: Proprietary IRS Status: Proprietary
Highest Offering: Master's
Accreditation: HLC

01 President ... Dr. Robert ALSOP
05 Dean of Col/Vice Pres Acad Affs ... Dr. Vincent BEACH
10 Vice President Business Affairs ... Ms. Bev RETLAND
84 Vice President Enrollment ... Mr. Mike HEITKAMP
11 Vice President Plant/Ancillary Svcs ... Mr. Brian KEELY
04 Assistant to the President ... Ms. Cindy CARTER
32 Dean of Students ... Mr. Jason RAMAKER
92 Dean of Honors Program ... Dr. Suzanne FALCK-YI
07 Director Admissions ... Mr. Scott PITCHER
08 Library Director ... Ms. Sarah BEITING
29 Director of Alumni Affairs ... Ms. Jaclyn SIFERT
06 Registrar ... Mr. Darrell BARBOUR
37 Director of Financial Aid ... Mr. Duane POLSDOFER
18 Director of Facilities Services ... Mr. Tim SEVERSON
26 Marketing Director ... Ms. Audrey SPARKS
44 Director of Annual Fund ... Ms. Teresa NICHOLSON
38 Counselor ... Mr. Nic DETERMANN
41 Athletic Director ... Mr. Chad GASSMAN
36 Director Student Placement ... Ms. Kathy ROLLEFSON
40 Bookstore Manager ... Ms. Karla SCHAEFER
15 Director Human Resources ... Ms. Dawn RAMAKER

Wartburg College (J)

PO Box 1003, 100 Wartburg Boulevard,
Waverly IA 50677-0903
County: Bremer FICE Identification: 001896
Unit ID: 154527
Telephone: (319) 352-8200 Carnegie Class: Bac-A&S
FAX Number: (319) 352-8247 Calendar System: Other
URL: www.wartburg.edu
Established: 1852 Annual Undergrad Tuition & Fees: $45,680
Enrollment: 1,563 Coed
Affiliation or Control: Evangelical Lutheran Church In America
IRS Status: 501(c)3
Highest Offering: Master's
Accreditation: HLC, MUS, SW

01 President ... Dr. Darrel D. COLSON
05 VP Acad Affairs/Dean Faculty ... Dr. Debora JOHNSON-ROSS
32 VP Student Life/Dean Students ... Dr. Daniel KITTLE
10 VP for Finance and Administration ... Mr. Richard SEGGERMAN
111 Vice Pres Institutional Advancement ... Mr. Scott C. LEISINGER
84 Vice Pres Enrollment Management ... Dr. Edith J. WALDSTEIN
07 Executive Director of Admissions ... Ms. Tara WINTER
06 Registrar ... Ms. Sheree S. COVERT
26 Dir of Marketing & Communication ... Mr. Chris KNUDSON
13 Asst VP for Information Tech/CIO ... Ms. Loni ABBAS
08 Director of Library ... Ms. Susan MEYERAAN
29 Dir Alumni & Parent Engagement ... Ms. Ellen ENGH
37 Director of Financial Aid ... Ms. Jen L. SASSMAN
41 Exec Dir of Athletics and Wellness ... Mr. Eric R. WILLIS
42 Dean of Spiritual Life/Campus Life ... Rev.Dr. Brian BECKSTROM
18 Director of Plant Operations ... Mr. Scott SHARAR
39 Dir Res Life/Chief Student Conduct ... Ms. Cassie HALES
36 Dir of Pathways/Career Services ... Mr. Derek N. SOLHEIM
43 Chief Compliance Officer ... Ms. Karen THALACKER
38 Director of Counseling Svcs ... Ms. Stephanie R. NEWSOM
40 Store Mgr & Textbook Services Dir ... Ms. Janet HUEBNER
85 Dir of International Student Svcs ... Mr. Zafrul AMIN
35 Director of Student Engagement ... Ms. Lindsey LEONARD
09 Director of Institutional Research ... Vacant
15 Director of HR ... Ms. Jamie HOLLAWAY

112 Senior Gift Planner ... Mr. Donald J. MEYER
92 Director Honors Program ... Dr. Leilani ZART
101 Exec Admin President Office/Sec BOR ... Ms. Janeen K. STEWART
20 Asst Dean of the Faculty ... Mr. Douglas D. KOSCHMEDER
28 Dir Multicultural Student Services ... Ms. Krystal MADLOCK
19 Int Dir Campus Security & Safety ... Mr. Dean COCKERHAM
21 Executive Director of Business & HR ... Ms. Lisa ARNOLD
88 Director of Financial Reporting ... Ms. Carolyn HUGHES

Wartburg Theological Seminary (A)

333 Wartburg Place, Dubuque IA 52003
County: Dubuque — FICE Identification: 001897
Unit ID: 154536
Telephone: (563) 589-0200 — Carnegie Class: Spec-4-yr-Faith
FAX Number: (563) 589-0333 — Calendar System: 4/1/4
URL: www.wartburgseminary.edu
Established: 1854 — Annual Graduate Tuition & Fees: N/A
Enrollment: 203 — Coed
Affiliation or Control: Evangelical Lutheran Church In America
IRS Status: 501(c)3
Highest Offering: Master's; No Undergraduates
Accreditation: HLC, THEOL

01 President ... RevDr. Kristin K. LARGEN
05 Academic Dean of the Seminary ... RevDr. Craig L. NESSAN
10 Vice Pres for Finance & Operations ... Mr. Andy B. WILLENBORG
30 Vice President for Development ... Mr. Paul K. ERBES
07 Vice Pres for Admiss & Student Svcs ... Rev. Elizabeth ALBERTSON
08 Library Director ... Ms. Susan J S. EBERTZ
06 Registrar/Admin Assistant to Dean ... Dr. Kevin L. ANDERSON
04 Executive Assistant ... Ms. Lynne BAUMHOVER
37 Director Student Financial Aid ... Ms. Barbara ROLING

Western Iowa Tech Community College (B)

PO Box 5199, 4647 Stone Avenue,
Sioux City IA 51102-5199
County: Woodbury — FICE Identification: 007316
Unit ID: 154572
Telephone: (712) 274-6400 — Carnegie Class: Assoc/HVT-High Non
FAX Number: (712) 274-6412 — Calendar System: Semester
URL: www.witcc.edu
Established: 1966 — Annual Undergrad Tuition & Fees (In-District): $4,488
Enrollment: 5,360 — Coed
Affiliation or Control: State/Local — IRS Status: 501(c)3
Highest Offering: Associate Degree
Accreditation: HLC, ADNUR, DA, EMT, MAC, PNUR, PTAA, SURGT

01 President ... Dr. Terry MURRELL
05 VP Learning ... Ms. Juline ALBERT
10 VP Finance/Administrative Svcs ... Mr. Troy JASMAN
15 Dean Human Resources ... Ms. Jackie PLENDL
13 Dean of Information Technologies ... Mr. Mike LOGAN
32 Dean of Students ... Vacant
20 Executive Dean of Instruction ... Mr. Darin MOELLER
35 Director Student Support Services ... Ms. Sara KLATT
30 Exec Director College Development ... Mr. Jim BRAUNSCHWEIG
08 Library Manager ... Ms. Kendra BERGENSKE
88 Director Small Business Devel Ctr ... Mr. Todd RAUSCH
18 Director Physical Plant ... Mr. Kyle HUESER
06 Registrar ... Ms. Lora VANDER ZWAAG
26 Director Marketing/Publications ... Ms. Andrea ROHLENA
37 Director of Financial Aid ... Mr. Merlyn KATHOL
04 Admin Assistant to the President ... Ms. Theresa PETTY
102 Director Foundation/Corporate Rels ... Mr. Jim BRAUNSCHWEIG

William Penn University (C)

201 Trueblood Avenue, Oskaloosa IA 52577-1799
County: Mahaska — FICE Identification: 001900
Unit ID: 154590
Telephone: (641) 673-1001 — Carnegie Class: Bac-Diverse
FAX Number: (641) 673-1396 — Calendar System: Semester
URL: www.wmpenn.edu
Established: 1873 — Annual Undergrad Tuition & Fees: $26,600
Enrollment: 1,350 — Coed
Affiliation or Control: Friends — IRS Status: 501(c)3
Highest Offering: Master's
Accreditation: HLC, NURSE

01 President ... Mr. John OTTOSSON
05 Vice Pres for Academic Affairs ... Dr. Noel STAHLE
111 Vice Pres for Advancement ... Ms. Marsha RIORDAN
10 VP for Financial Operations ... Ms. Bonnie JOHNSON
84 VP for Retention & Evening Enroll ... Ms. Kerra STRONG
32 Dean of Students ... Ms. Heidi SCHOLES
108 Director of Assessment ... Dr. Jared PEARCE
06 Registrar ... Ms. DeAnne DOLL
37 Director of Financial Aid ... Ms. Cyndi PEIFFER
36 Career Services Coordinator ... Ms. Debbie STEVENS
08 Head Librarian ... Ms. Jennifer STERLING
15 Human Resource Coordinator ... Ms. Angella DURIAN-GAMBELL
35 Director of Student Activities ... Mr. Jon HAUGEN
09 Director of Institutional Research ... Mr. Michael EDWARDS
40 Bookstore Manager ... Vacant
83 Chair Div of Social/Behavioral Sci ... Dr. Michael COLLINS
72 Co-Chair Div of Applied Technology ... Dr. Ted MCCOY
72 Co-Chair Div of Applied Technology ... Mr. Jim HOEKSEMA
53 Chair Division of Education ... Ms. Cathy WILLIAMSON
50 Chair Div of Business Admin ... Mr. David MEINERT
79 Chair Division of Humanities ... Dr. Anita MEINERT
76 Chair Div of Health & Life Sciences ... Dr. Gary CHRISTOPHER
66 Chair Div of Nursing ... Dr. Kimberley BROWN
04 Executive Asst to President ... Ms. Angella DURIAN-GAMBELL
13 Director of Information Services ... Mr. William HUGHES
19 Director of Campus Safety ... Mr. Troy BOSTON
38 Campus Counselor ... Ms. Tyne SMITH
39 Director of Residence Life ... Ms. Tanya MAMMEN
41 Athletic Director ... Mr. Nik RULE
07 Director of Admissions ... Ms. Madison STEINKE
101 Secretary of the Institution/Board ... Ms. Angella M. DURIAN-GAMBELL
29 Director Alumni Affairs ... Mr. James KOBUS

KANSAS

Allen County Community College (D)

1801 N Cottonwood, Iola KS 66749-1698
County: Allen — FICE Identification: 001901
Unit ID: 154642
Telephone: (620) 901-6400 — Carnegie Class: Assoc/HT-Mix Trad/Non
FAX Number: (620) 365-7406 — Calendar System: Semester
URL: www.allencc.edu
Established: 1923 — Annual Undergrad Tuition & Fees (In-District): $3,080
Enrollment: 2,113 — Coed
Affiliation or Control: State/Local — IRS Status: 501(c)3
Highest Offering: Associate Degree
Accreditation: HLC

01 President ... Mr. John A. MASTERSON
05 Vice President for Academic Affairs ... Mr. Jon MARSHALL
10 Chief Financial Officer ... Mrs. Roberta NICKELL
32 Vice Pres Student Affairs ... Ms. Cynthia JACOBSON
20 Dean for Academic Affairs Onsite ... Mrs. Tosca HARRIS
106 Dean for Academic Affairs Online ... Vacant
08 Director of Library ... Mrs. Virginia SHAFFER
13 Director of MIS ... Mr. Doug DUNLAP
37 Director of Financial Aid ... Mrs. Kim MURRY
18 Director of Physical Plant Opers ... Vacant
84 Director of Advising & Enrollment ... Vacant
41 Director of Athletics ... Mr. Doug DESMARTEAU
40 Director of Bookstore ... Mrs. Reine LOFLIN
85 Foreign Student Advisor ... Mr. Nate RODRIGUEZ
09 Director Inst Research/Reporting ... Mrs. Deanna CARPENTER
35 Director Student Life ... Mr. Josiah D'ALBINI
06 Registrar ... Mrs. Bobbie HAVILAND
15 Human Resources Specialist ... Mrs. Shellie REGEHR
30 Director of Development ... Vacant
121 Director of Advisement ... Mrs. Nikki PETERS

Allen County Community College Burlingame Campus (E)

100 Bloomquist, Burlingame KS 66413
Telephone: (785) 654-2416 — Identification: 770249
Accreditation: &HLC

Baker University (F)

618 Eighth Street/PO Box 65,
Baldwin City KS 66006-0065
County: Douglas — FICE Identification: 001903
Unit ID: 154688
Telephone: (785) 594-6451 — Carnegie Class: DU-Mod
FAX Number: (785) 594-2522 — Calendar System: 4/1/4
URL: www.bakeru.edu
Established: 1858 — Annual Undergrad Tuition & Fees: $30,770
Enrollment: 2,279 — Coed
Affiliation or Control: United Methodist — IRS Status: 501(c)3
Highest Offering: Doctorate
Accreditation: HLC, ACBSP, CAEP, EXSC, MUS, NURSE

01 President ... Dr. Lynne MURRAY
05 Vice Pres for Academic Affairs ... Dr. Marcus CHILDRESS
111 VP of Advancement/Enrollment Mgt ... Ms. Danielle JONES REASE
10 VP of Finance & Administration ... Dr. Shelley KNEUVEAN
53 Interim Dean School of Education ... Dr. Verneda EDWARDS
66 Dean of School of Nursing ... Dr. Mary HOBUS
49 Dean College of Arts & Sciences ... Dr. Darcy RUSSELL
107 Dean SPGS ... Dr. Kirk HASKINS
41 Director Of Athletics ... Mr. Nate HOUSER
07 Director of Admissions ... Vacant
26 Exec Dir Marketing & Communications ... Mr. Jason HANNAH
06 University Registrar ... Ms. Ramie NATION
21 Chief Accounting Officer/Controller ... Ms. Melissa VAN LEIDEN
18 Dir of Physical Plant/Facility Ops ... Mr. Tommy WOOD
42 Minister to the University ... Rev. Kevin HOPKINS
37 Senior Director of Financial Aid ... Ms. Jana PARKS
15 Chief Human Resources Officer ... Ms. Dawn TOMEY
32 Dean of Students ... Dr. Cassy BAILEY
09 Director of Institutional Research ... Mr. Eric HAYS
29 Director of Alumni Relations ... Mr. Doug BARTH
36 Director of Career Services ... Mr. Gary HARDY
38 Dir of Health & Counseling Center ... Dr. Tim HODGES
08 Director of Library Services ... Mr. Ray WALLING

Baker University School of Professional and Graduate Studies (G)

PO Box 65, 615 Dearborn Street, Baldwin City KS 66006
Telephone: (785) 594-6451 — Identification: 770250
Accreditation: &HLC

Barclay College (H)

607 N Kingman, Haviland KS 67059-0288
County: Kiowa — FICE Identification: 001917
Unit ID: 155070
Telephone: (620) 862-5252 — Carnegie Class: Spec-4-yr-Faith
FAX Number: (620) 862-5242 — Calendar System: Semester
URL: www.barclaycollege.edu
Established: 1917 — Annual Undergrad Tuition & Fees: $21,780
Enrollment: 215 — Coed
Affiliation or Control: Independent Non-Profit — IRS Status: 501(c)3
Highest Offering: Master's
Accreditation: HLC, BI

01 President ... Dr. Royce FRAZIER
00 Chancellor ... Dr. Adrian HALVERSTADT
05 VP Academic Services ... Dr. Derek BROWN
10 VP Business Services ... Mr. Lee ANDERS
32 VP Student Services ... Mr. Ryan HAASE
111 VP Institutional Advancement ... Mr. Mark MILLER
06 Registrar ... Mr. Aaron STOKES
37 Director Student Financial Aid ... Ms. Ginger MAGGARD
84 Director Enrollment Services ... Mr. Justin KENDALL
08 Director of Library ... Mrs. Jeannie ROSS
106 Dir Online Education/E-learning ... Mr. Aaron STOKES
13 Chief Info Technology Officer (CIO) ... Mr. Trent MAGGARD
15 Director Personnel Services ... Mrs. Gayle MORTIMER
18 Chief Facilities/Physical Plant ... Mr. CD FITCH
41 Athletic Director ... Mr. Shane SHETLEY

Barton County Community College (I)

245 NE 30th Road, Great Bend KS 67530-9107
County: Barton — FICE Identification: 004608
Unit ID: 154697
Telephone: (620) 792-2701 — Carnegie Class: Assoc/HT-High Non
FAX Number: (620) 792-5624 — Calendar System: Semester
URL: www.bartonccc.edu
Established: 1965 — Annual Undergrad Tuition & Fees (In-District): $3,776
Enrollment: 4,094 — Coed
Affiliation or Control: State/Local — IRS Status: 501(c)3
Highest Offering: Associate Degree
Accreditation: HLC, ADNUR, EMT, MLTAD

01 President ... Dr. Carl R. HEILMAN
11 VP of Administration ... Mr. Mark DEAN
05 VP of Instruction ... Mrs. Elaine SIMMONS
32 VP of Student Services ... Mrs. Angela MADDY
13 Chief Information Officer ... Mrs. Michelle KAISER
20 Dean of Academics ... Mr. Brian HOWE
88 Dean Military Acad/Tech Ed/Outrch ... Mr. Kurtis TEAL
37 Chief Accreditation/Dir Fin Aid ... Mrs. Myrna PERKINS
20 Assoc Dean of Instruction ... Mrs. Claudia MATHER
111 Exec Dir Institutional Advancement ... Mrs. Coleen CAPE
75 Exec Dir Workforce Trng & Econ Dev ... Ms. Mary FOLEY
76 Exec Dir Healthcare/Public Service ... Vacant
41 Director of Athletics ... Mr. Trevor ROLFS
25 Director of Grants ... Ms. Cathie OSHIRO
26 Dir of Public Relations & Marketing ... Mr. Brandon STEINERT
09 Director of Institutional Research ... Mr. Todd MOBRAY
04 Assistant to the President ... Ms. Amye SCHNEIDER
08 Director of Library & Archives ... Mrs. ReGina REYNOLDS-CASPER
21 Comptroller & Budget Manager ... Mr. Terry BARROW
15 Director of Human Resources ... Mrs. Julie KNOBLICH
07 Director of Admissions ... Ms. Tana COOPER
06 Registrar ... Mrs. Lori CROWTHER
40 Bookstore Manager ... Mrs. Connie KERNS
39 Director of Student Life ... Mr. Jonathan DIETZ
23 Nurse ... Vacant
121 Dir Testing/Advisement/Career Svc ... Mrs. Judy JACOBS
19 Coordinator of Facility Management ... Mr. Jim IRELAND
103 Dean of Workforce Training/Cmty Ed ... Dr. Kathy KOTTAS

Benedictine College (J)

1020 N 2nd Street, Atchison KS 66002-1499
County: Atchison — FICE Identification: 010256
Unit ID: 154712
Telephone: (913) 367-5340 — Carnegie Class: Bac-Diverse
FAX Number: (913) 367-6566 — Calendar System: Semester
URL: www.benedictine.edu
Established: 1858 — Annual Undergrad Tuition & Fees: $31,630
Enrollment: 2,217 — Coed
Affiliation or Control: Roman Catholic — IRS Status: 501(c)3
Highest Offering: Master's
Accreditation: HLC, MUS, NURSE

01 President ... Mr. Stephen D. MINNIS
05 Dean of the College ... Dr. Kimberly C. SHANKMAN
10 Chief Financial Officer ... Mr. Ronald J. OLINGER
111 Vice President Advancement ... Ms. Kelly J. VOWELS
84 Dean of Enrollment Management ... Mr. Pete HELGESEN
32 Vice President of Student Life ... Dr. Linda HENRY

35 Dean of Students .... Dr. Joseph WURTZ
41 Athletic Director .... Mr. Charles GARTENMAYER
26 Vice President for College Rels .... Mr. Tom HOOPES
20 Assoc Dean & Registrar .... Sr. Linda HERNDON, OSB
09 Director of Institutional Research .... Vacant
58 Exec Dir of Grad Business Programs .... Mr. Michael KING
58 Director of MASL/Asst Prof Educ .... Vacant
37 Director of Student Financial Aid .... Mr. Tony TANKING
27 Dir of Marketing & Communications .... Mr. Steve JOHNSON
38 Director of Counseling Center .... Vacant
23 Director of Student Health Services .... Ms. Janet ADRIAN
18 Director of Operations .... Mr. Matt FASSERO
13 Dir of Tech & Information Sys .... Mr. Chuck WELTE
88 Director of International Program .... Mr. Daniele MUSSO
08 Library Director .... Mr. Steven GROMATZKY
39 Director of Residence Life .... Mr. Eli PRUNEDA
113 Bursar .... Ms. Becky MILLER
36 Director of Career Services .... Ms. Megan KLEBBA
29 Director of Planned Giving & Alumni .... Mr. Tim ANDREWS
04 Exec Assistant to the President .... Mrs. Abby BARTLETT
15 Int Director of Human Resources .... Ms. Charo KELLEY
19 Security Account Manager .... Mr. Danny FAIRLEY
53 Chair Education Department .... Dr. Matthew RAMSEY
54 Chair Engineering Department .... Dr. Darrin MUGGLI

Bethany College (A)

335 E Swensson Street, Lindsborg KS 67456-1895
County: McPherson FICE Identification: 001904
Unit ID: 154721
Telephone: (785) 227-3380 Carnegie Class: Bac-Diverse
FAX Number: (785) 227-2004 Calendar System: 4/1/4
URL: www.bethanylb.edu
Established: 1881 Annual Undergrad Tuition & Fees: $30,820
Enrollment: 790 Coed
Affiliation or Control: Evangelical Lutheran Church In America
IRS Status: 501(c)3
Highest Offering: Baccalaureate
Accreditation: HLC, MUS

01 President .... Dr. Elizabeth K. MAUCH
05 VP of Academic and Student Affairs .... Dr. Adam PRYOR
10 Chief Financial Officer .... Ms. Krista HARRIS
06 Registrar .... Mr. Mark BANDRE
84 VP of Enrollment Management .... Mr. Matt PFANNENSTIEL
11 VP of Administration/Gen Counsel .... Ms. Amie BAUER
41 Dean of Athletics and AD .... Ms. Laura MORENO
111 Executive Director for Advancement .... Mrs. Karissa HOFFMAN
09 Director of Institutional Research .... Vacant
21 Interim Controller .... Mr. Christoffer LARSEN
07 Director of Admissions & Operations .... Ms. Vicki CORNETT
37 Interim Director of Financial Aid .... Mr. Jeffrey ROUSH
08 Dir of Wallerstedt Learning Center .... Ms. Denise K. CARSON
32 Director of Student Affairs .... Ms. Tessa PETERS
13 Director of Technology Services .... Mr. Joshua BIEBER
15 Director Human Resources .... Mrs. Jeanne LUCAS
29 Director of Alumni Development .... Ms. Ashtyn SNIDER
27 Sports Information Director .... Mr. Bradlee YODER
30 Director of Development .... Mr. Bill NELSON
35 Director Campus Activities .... Vacant
38 Director of Clinical Counseling .... Ms. Ginny REYES
39 Director of Residential Education .... Vacant
88 Dir of Information Services .... Ms. Vicki CORNETT
27 Director of Publications .... Mr. Frank BALLEW
36 Director Career Services .... Vacant
121 Dir of Student Success Center .... Ms. Christi WICKS
20 Asst Dean of Acad Affairs .... Vacant
108 Spec Asst to Dean Assessment .... Dr. Duke ROGERS
97 Director of Core Education .... Dr. Mary Beth HARRIS
89 Dir of Ministry & 1st Yr Experience .... Vacant
18 Director of Campus Facilities .... Mr. Dean ALLMAN
40 Bookstore Manager .... Ms. Angie SHOGREN
42 Campus Pastor .... Ms. Amy TRUHE
04 Exec Assistant to President .... Ms. Taylor DEUTSCHER
57 Director of Digital & Media Arts .... Mr. Ed POGUE
53 Program Director Teacher Education .... Dr. Gretchen NORLAND
57 Chair of Theatre Department .... Mr. Greg LEGAULT
61 Chair of Criminal Justice Dept .... Mr. Randy REPP
64 Dir of Oratorio & Choral Activities .... Dr. Mark LUCAS
64 Chair of the Music Department .... Dr. Dan MASTERSON
73 Chair of Religion & Philosophy Dept .... Dr. John MULLEN
76 Athletic Training Program Director .... Ms. Laura JACKSON-STENLUND
81 Dir of Math/Science Depts .... Dr. Lucas MCCORMICK
83 Dir of Psychology Department .... Ms. Andrea RING
106 Director of Program Innovation .... Vacant
88 Director of Food Services .... Mr. Kevin MCCOY
92 Honors Program Coordinator .... Dr. Kristin VAN TASSEL
105 Dir Web Services & Social Media .... Ms. Molly CARVER
28 Director of Multicultural Programs .... Vacant
50 Director Business Department .... Mr. Robert CARLSON
19 Director of Campus Safety .... Mr. Joshua SNIDER
96 Purchasing Specialist .... Ms. Melanie SCHALLOCK

Bethel College (B)

300 E 27th Street, North Newton KS 67117-0531
County: Harvey FICE Identification: 001905
Unit ID: 154749
Telephone: (316) 283-2500 Carnegie Class: Bac-Diverse
FAX Number: (316) 284-5286 Calendar System: 4/1/4
URL: www.bethelks.edu
Established: 1887 Annual Undergrad Tuition & Fees: $30,264
Enrollment: 484 Coed
Affiliation or Control: Mennonite Church IRS Status: 501(c)3
Highest Offering: Baccalaureate
Accreditation: HLC, CAEP, NURSE, SW

01 President .... Dr. Jonathan C. GERING
04 Assistant to the President .... Ms. Rosa M. BARRERA
05 Vice President Academic Affairs .... Dr. Robert W. MILLIMAN
32 Vice President Student Life .... Mr. Samuel C. HAYNES
41 Athletic Director .... Mr. Tony HOOPS
111 Vice President Advancement .... Mr. Bradley A. KOHLMAN
10 VP for Business and Finance .... Vacant
84 VP for Enrollment Management .... Ms. Heidi HOSKINSON
06 Registrar .... Ms. Marcia K. MILLER
26 Dir Marketing and Communications .... Ms. Tricia CLARK
29 Director of Alumni Engagement .... Mr. Bradley SCHMIDT
37 Director of Financial Aid .... Mr. Clark OSWALD
30 Director of Development .... Mr. Garrett WHORTON
08 Co-Director of Libraries .... Mrs. Barbara THIESEN
08 Co-Director of Libraries .... Mr. John THIESEN
42 Coordinator of Church Relations .... Mr. Benjamin LICHTI
18 Director of Facilities .... Mr. Adam AKERS
13 Chief Info Technology Officer (CIO) .... Mr. Adam HAAG
38 Director of Student Wellness .... Mrs. Jill HOOPES
15 Director of HR .... Mrs. Janet FULMER
28 Dir Diversity/Equity & Inclusion .... Vacant

Butler Community College (C)

712 Rose Hill Road, Rose Hill KS 67133
Telephone: (316) 776-9429 Identification: 770256
Accreditation: &HLC

Butler County Community College (D)

901 S. Haverhill Road, El Dorado KS 67042-3225
County: Butler FICE Identification: 001906
Unit ID: 154800
Telephone: (316) 321-2222 Carnegie Class: Assoc/HT-High Trad
FAX Number: (316) 322-3109 Calendar System: Semester
URL: www.bc3.edu
Established: 1927 Annual Undergrad Tuition & Fees (In-District): $3,706
Enrollment: 7,175 Coed
Affiliation or Control: Local IRS Status: 501(c)3
Highest Offering: Associate Degree
Accreditation: HLC, ADNUR

01 President .... Dr. Kimberly KRULL
05 Vice President of Academics .... Dr. Tom NEVILL
10 Vice President of Finance .... Mr. Kent WILLIAMS
32 Vice President of Student Services .... Mr. Bill RINKENBAUGH
102 Exec Director of the Foundation .... Mr. Tom BORREGO
08 Director of Library Services .... Ms. Judy BASTIN
06 Registrar .... Ms. Willow DEAN
09 AVP of Research/Inst Effectiveness .... Dr. Esam MOHAMMAD
15 Assoc VP of Human Resources .... Ms. Shelley STULTZ
21 Associate Business Officer .... Ms. Kim SHERWOOD
29 Director Alumni Relations .... Vacant
36 Director Student Placement .... Vacant
37 Director Student Financial Aid .... Ms. Heather WARD
35 Associate VP of Student Services .... Ms. Jessica OHMAN
26 Director of Institutional Marketing .... Ms. Kelly SNEDDEN
18 Director Facilities .... Mr. Lynn UMHOLTZ
96 Director of Purchasing .... Ms. Yolanda HACKLER
07 Director of Admissions .... Ms. Kirsten ALLEN
38 Director Student Counseling .... Vacant
13 VP of Digital Transformation .... Mr. Bill YOUNG
19 Director Security/Safety .... Mr. Jason KENNEY
39 Director Residence Life .... Mr. David NEWELL
41 Athletic Director .... Mr. Todd CARTER
04 Admin Assistant to the President .... Ms. Lora JARVIS
106 Dean Online Learning .... Dr. Heather RINKENBAUGH

Butler of Andover (E)

1810 N Andover Road, Andover KS 67002
Telephone: (316) 733-0071 Identification: 770253
Accreditation: &HLC

Butler of Council Grove (F)

131 West Main, Council Grove KS 66846
Telephone: (620) 382-2183 Identification: 770254
Accreditation: &HLC

Butler of Marion (G)

701 E. Main, Hill Building, Marion KS 66861
Telephone: (620) 382-2183 Identification: 770255
Accreditation: &HLC

Butler of McConnell (H)

Ed Ctr, Bldg 412, 53474 Lawrence Ct, McConnell AFB KS 67221
Telephone: (316) 681-3522 Identification: 770257
Accreditation: &HLC

Central Baptist Theological Seminary (I)

6601 Monticello Road, Shawnee KS 66226-3513
County: Johnson FICE Identification: 001907
Unit ID: 154837
Telephone: (913) 667-5700 Carnegie Class: Spec-4-yr-Faith
FAX Number: (913) 371-8110 Calendar System: Semester
URL: cbts.edu
Established: 1901 Annual Graduate Tuition & Fees: N/A
Enrollment: N/A Coed
Affiliation or Control: Baptist IRS Status: 501(c)3
Highest Offering: Doctorate; No Undergraduates
Accreditation: HLC, THEOL

01 President .... Dr. Molly T. MARSHALL
05 Provost/Dean of the Seminary .... Dr. Robert E. JOHNSON
03 Executive Vice President .... Mr. George TOWNSEND
06 Registrar .... Ms. Jessica C. WILLIAMS
26 Director of Seminary Relations .... Ms. Robin SANDBOTHE
85 International Student Officer .... Ms. Jessica C. WILLIAMS

Central Christian College of Kansas (J)

1200 S Main, PO Box 1403, McPherson KS 67460
County: McPherson FICE Identification: 001908
Unit ID: 154855
Telephone: (620) 241-0723 Carnegie Class: Bac-Diverse
FAX Number: (620) 241-6032 Calendar System: Semester
URL: www.centralchristian.edu
Established: 1884 Annual Undergrad Tuition & Fees: $20,100
Enrollment: 629 Coed
Affiliation or Control: Free Methodist IRS Status: 501(c)3
Highest Offering: Master's
Accreditation: HLC

01 President .... Dr. Leonard FAVARA, JR.
05 Chief Academic Officer .... Dr. Jacob KAUFMAN
111 VP of Advancement .... Dr. Dean KROEKER
32 Chief Student Engagement Officer .... Mrs. Cathy BROWN
10 Chief Financial Officer .... Mrs. LeAnn MOORE
41 Athletic Director .... Mr. Kyle MOODY
07 Director of Admissions/Marketing .... Ms. Elizabeth CARON
06 Registrar .... Mrs. Michele AUGUST
08 Library Director .... Mrs. Bev KELLEY
18 Director of Physical Plant .... Mr. Kelly PAULS
04 Executive Administrator .... Mrs. Hannah LITWILLER
13 Chief Info Technology Officer (CIO) .... Col. Doug VANDERHOOF
104 Dir International Student Programs .... Vacant
09 Institution Effectiveness Analyst .... Mr. Matt MALONE
102 Exec Director CCC Foundation .... Dr. David FERRELL
37 Director Student Financial Aid .... Vacant
29 Director Alumni Affairs .... Mrs. Adriane CARR
15 Accounts Payable/HR Officer .... Mrs. Katy POTTER

Cleveland University - Kansas City (K)

10850 Lowell Avenue, Overland Park KS 66210
County: Johnson FICE Identification: 020907
Unit ID: 177038
Telephone: (913) 234-0600 Carnegie Class: Spec-4-yr-Other Health
FAX Number: (913) 234-0904 Calendar System: Trimester
URL: www.cleveland.edu
Established: 1922 Annual Undergrad Tuition & Fees: $14,400
Enrollment: 608 Coed
Affiliation or Control: Independent Non-Profit IRS Status: 501(c)3
Highest Offering: First Professional Degree
Accreditation: HLC, CHIRO, OTA

01 President .... Dr. Carl S. CLEVELAND, III
05 VP Academic Affairs .... Dr. Cheryl CARPENTER-DAVIS
10 Chief Operating Officer .... Mr. Jeff KARP
84 VP Enrollment Management .... Mr. Alex BACH
26 VP of Campus and Alumni Relations .... Dr. Clark BECKLEY
15 Vice Pres HR/Organizational Devel .... Mr. Dale MARRANT
63 Dean of Chiropractic Education .... Dr. Jon WILSON
32 Dean of Student Affairs .... Mr. David FOOSE
06 Registrar .... Ms. Kathy HALE
21 Controller .... Ms. Marla COPE
37 Director of Financial Aid .... Ms. Caprice CALAMAIO
09 Director of Research .... Dr. Mark T. PFEFER
29 Director of Campus/Alumni Relations .... Ms. Jalonna BOWIE
07 Director of Admissions .... Ms. Melissa DENTON
08 Library Director .... Ms. Simone BRIAND
18 Director of Facilities Management .... Mr. Frank HANEY

Cloud County Community College (L)

2221 Campus Drive, Concordia KS 66901-1002
County: Cloud FICE Identification: 001909
Unit ID: 154907
Telephone: (785) 243-1435 Carnegie Class: Assoc/HT-High Non
FAX Number: (785) 243-1459 Calendar System: Semester
URL: www.cloud.edu
Established: 1965 Annual Undergrad Tuition & Fees (In-District): $3,390
Enrollment: 1,589 Coed
Affiliation or Control: State/Local IRS Status: 501(c)3
Highest Offering: Associate Degree
Accreditation: #HLC, ADNUR

01 President .... Ms. Amber KNOETTGEN
05 Vice Pres for Academic Affairs .... Ms. Kimberly ZANT
11 Vice Pres for Administrative Svcs .... Vacant
13 Director of Information Technology .... Mr. Thomas ROBERTS
111 Director Institutional Advancement .... Vacant
84 Director of Enrollment Management .... Ms. Britni TREMBLAY

08 Director of Library Services ....Ms. Jennifer SCHROEDER
41 Athletic Director ....Mr. Matthew BECHARD
06 Registrar ....Ms. Cassie WURTZ
18 Chief Facilities/Physical Plant ....Mr. Rex E. SICARD
26 Coordinator of Marketing ....Ms. Jessica LEDUC
102 Dir Cloud County Cmty College Fndn .....Ms. Heather GENNETTE
37 Director Student Financial Aid ....Ms. Suzi KNOETTGEN
124 Director Advising & Retention ....Ms. Kris FARMER
15 Director of Human Resources ....Ms. Christine WILSON
09 Director Institutional Research ....Vacant

Coffeyville Community College (A)

400 W 11th Street, Coffeyville KS 67337-5064
County: Montgomery FICE Identification: 001910
Unit ID: 154925
Telephone: (620) 251-7700 Carnegie Class: Assoc/HT-High Non
FAX Number: (620) 252-7098 Calendar System: Semester
URL: www.coffeyville.edu
Established: 1923 Annual Undergrad Tuition & Fees (In-District): $3,040
Enrollment: 1,368 Coed
Affiliation or Control: State/Local IRS Status: 501(c)3
Highest Offering: Associate Degree
Accreditation: HLC, EMT, MAC, MLTAD

01 President .... Dr. Marlon THORNBURG
05 Vice President Academic Services ....Ms. Aron POTTER
10 Vice Pres for Operations & Finance ....Mr. Jeff MORRIS
88 VP for Innovation/Bus Initiatives .... Dr. Marlon THORNBURG
12 Columbus Campus Coordinator ....Ms. Kari SOPER
102 Exec Director College Foundation ....Mr. Dickie ROLLS
32 Student Life Manager ....Mr. Garrett FRANCIS
09 Dir Institutional Research/Records ....Mr. Chuck REED
26 Sr Director College Relations ....Ms. Yvonne HULL
121 Sr Director Academic Advising ....Ms. Pam FEERER
45 Dir Institutional Effectiveness .... Mr. Marty EVENSVOLD
37 Director of Financial Aid ....Ms. Robin ADAMSON
15 Director of Human Resources ....Mrs. Kelli BAUER
41 Athletics Director ....Mr. Jeff LEIKER
18 Director of Maintenance ....Ms. Kris WECH
106 Director of Distance Learning ....Mr. Brad WEBER
40 Bookstore Manager ....Mrs. Karen STRIMPLE
06 Interim Registrar ....Ms. Kristin HORNER

Colby Community College (B)

1255 S Range, Colby KS 67701-4099
County: Thomas FICE Identification: 001911
Unit ID: 154934
Telephone: (785) 462-3984 Carnegie Class: Assoc/MT-VT-High Non
FAX Number: (785) 460-4699 Calendar System: Semester
URL: www.colbycc.edu
Established: 1964 Annual Undergrad Tuition & Fees (In-District): $3,934
Enrollment: 1,327 Coed
Affiliation or Control: State/Local IRS Status: 501(c)3
Highest Offering: Associate Degree
Accreditation: HLC, ADNUR, PTAA

01 President ....Mr. Seth M. CARTER
05 Vice Pres of Academic Affairs ....Dr. Tiffany EVANS
32 Vice President of Student Affairs ....Ms. Nikol NOLAN
10 Vice President of Business Affairs .... Ms. Carolyn KASDORF
08 Librarian ....Mrs. Tara SCHROER
26 Director of Public Information ....Mr. Doug JOHNSON
37 Director of Financial Aid ....Ms. Kathy RAMSEY
111 Dir of Inst Advancement/Foundation ... Ms. Jennifer SCHOENFELD
41 Athletic Director ....Mr. Mike SADDLER
13 IT Director ....Mr. Douglass MCDOWALL
06 Registrar ....Ms. Brette HANKIN

Cowley College (C)

125 S Second, PO Box 1147,
Arkansas City KS 67005-1147
County: Cowley FICE Identification: 001902
Unit ID: 154952
Telephone: (620) 442-0430 Carnegie Class: Assoc/HT-High Trad
FAX Number: (620) 441-5350 Calendar System: Semester
URL: www.cowley.edu
Established: 1922 Annual Undergrad Tuition & Fees (In-District): $3,750
Enrollment: 2,475 Coed
Affiliation or Control: Local IRS Status: 501(c)3
Highest Offering: Associate Degree
Accreditation: HLC, EMT

01 President ....Dr. Dennis C. RITTLE
05 Vice President of Academic Affairs .... Dr. Michelle SCHOON
10 Vice Pres of Finance/Administration ....Ms. Holly HARPER
13 Vice Pres Information Technology ....Mr. Paul ERDMANN
30 Vice Pres Institutional Development ....Dr. Kori GREGG
20 AVP Secondary Partnerships/Acad .... Ms. Janice STOVER
84 Exec Director Enrollment Management ....Ms. Kristi SHAW
32 Exec Director of Student Affairs ....Mr. Jason O'TOOLE
41 Athletic Director ....Mr. Shane LARSON
35 Director of Student Life ....Vacant
103 AVP Business/Industry Advancement ....Vacant
106 AVP Distance Learning & Site Mgmt ....Mr. Eddie ANDREO
26 Dir Inst Comm/Public Relations ....Mr. Rama PEROO
06 Registrar ....Mr. Devin GRAVES
15 Director of Human Resources .... Ms. Jenette HANNA
11 Campus Operations Officer ....Ms. Janet GRACE
04 Admin Assistant to the President ....Ms. Tiffany VOLLMER
09 Director of Institutional Research .... Ms. Deborah PHELPS

Dodge City Community College (D)

2501 N 14th Avenue, Dodge City KS 67801-2399
County: Ford FICE Identification: 001913
Unit ID: 154998
Telephone: (620) 225-1321 Carnegie Class: Assoc/MT-VT-High Non
FAX Number: (620) 227-9366 Calendar System: Semester
URL: www.dc3.edu
Established: 1935 Annual Undergrad Tuition & Fees (In-District): $3,990
Enrollment: 1,459 Coed
Affiliation or Control: State/Local IRS Status: 501(c)3
Highest Offering: Associate Degree
Accreditation: HLC, ADNUR

01 President ....Dr. Harold E. NOLTE, JR.
05 Provost Flight Program ....Dr. Adam JOHN
10 VP of Administration/Finance & CFO ....Mr. Jeff CERMIN
32 VP of Student Affairs ....Dr. Jay KINZER
20 Vice President of Academic Affairs ....Dr. Jane HOLWERDA
102 Dir DCCC Foundation/Cmty Relations ....Mrs. Christina HASELHORST
55 Director Adult Learning Center ....Ms. Maria ROJAS
15 AVP of Admin & Human Resources ...Ms. Kristi OHLSCHWAGER
06 Registrar ....Mrs. Susan GIBBS
08 Director Learning Resource Center ....Mrs. Holly MERCER
66 Dean Nursing/Allied Health ....Dr. Mechele HAILEY
41 Athletic Director ....Mr. Jacob RIPPLE
37 Director of Financial Aid ....Miss Haley LINDSEY
18 Director of Facilities & Operations ....Mr. Russ MCBEE
04 Exec Assistant to the President ....Ms. Renee A. ALLEN
103 Dir Workforce Development/Title V ....Dr. Clayton TATRO
09 Dir of Inst Research/Accreditation ....Vacant
21 Financial Accountant ....Mrs. Marinita ARAGON
19 Director Security/Safety ....Mr. Joshua THOMPSON
84 Director of Enrollment Management ....Mrs. Brittany PENNO
13 Chief Information Technology Office .... Mr. Michael WEBSTER
38 Dir Dual Credit/Student Counseling .... Ms. Gayla RODENBUR
106 Dean of Online Education/E-learning ....Dr. Jodi RUST
28 Dir of Student Support & Diversity .... Dr. Gregory ROBERTS

Donnelly College (E)

608 N 18th Street, Kansas City KS 66102-4298
County: Wyandotte FICE Identification: 001914
Unit ID: 155007
Telephone: (913) 621-8700 Carnegie Class: Bac/Assoc-Mixed
FAX Number: (913) 621-8719 Calendar System: Semester
URL: www.donnelly.edu
Established: 1949 Annual Undergrad Tuition & Fees: $8,100
Enrollment: 336 Coed
Affiliation or Control: Roman Catholic IRS Status: 501(c)3
Highest Offering: Baccalaureate
Accreditation: HLC

01 President ....Msgr. Stuart SWETLAND
05 VP of Academic & Student Affairs ....Mrs. Lisa STOOTHOFF
111 Vice President of Advancement .... Ms. Emily BUCKLEY
10 CFO ....Mr. Bernard BARRY
09 Institutional Effectiveness Coord ....Ms. Jennifer BALES
32 Director of Student Success .... Dr. Mary PFLANZ
06 Registrar ....Ms. Megan JORDAN
07 Director of Admissions ....Ms. Katy SIEBERT

Emporia State University (F)

1 Kellogg Circle, Emporia KS 66801-5415
County: Lyon FICE Identification: 001927
Unit ID: 155025
Telephone: (620) 341-1200 Carnegie Class: Masters/L
FAX Number: (620) 341-5553 Calendar System: Semester
URL: www.emporia.edu
Established: 1863 Annual Undergrad Tuition & Fees (In-State): $6,971
Enrollment: 5,828 Coed
Affiliation or Control: State IRS Status: 501(c)3
Highest Offering: Doctorate
Accreditation: HLC, ACATE, ART, CAATE, CACREP, CAEP, CAEPN, CEA, LIB, MUS, NUR

01 President ....Dr. Allison GARRETT
05 Provost/VP for Academic Affairs ....Dr. George ARASIMOWICZ
11 VP Admin/Fiscal Affairs ....Ms. Diana E. KUHLMANN
32 Vice President Student Affairs ....Dr. James E. WILLIAMS
13 Assoc Vice Pres Info Technology ....Mr. Cory FALLDINE
09 Asst Provost Inst Effectiveness ....Dr. JoLanna KORD
85 Dean of International Education ....Mr. Mark DALY
35 Dean of Students ....Ms. Lynn M. HOBSON
102 President ESU Foundation ....Mr. Shane SHIVLEY
84 Asst VP for Enrollment Management ....Dr. Shelly GEHRKE
29 Director of Alumni ....Mr. Jose FELICIANO, JR.
88 Director Natl Teachers Hall of Fame ....Ms. Carol STRICKLAND
22 Affirmative Action Officer ....Mr. Ray LAUBER
53 Dean of The Teachers College ....Dr. Joan BREWER
49 Dean College of Liberal Arts/Sci ....Dr. R. Brent THOMAS
50 Dean School of Business ....Dr. Ed BASHAW
62 Dean School of Library/Info Mgmt ....Dr. Wooseob JEONG
58 Dean Graduate Studies ....Dr. James SPOTSWOOD
88 Exec Dir Jones Inst Educ Excel ....Vacant
06 Registrar ....Ms. Sheila MARKOWITZ
08 Dean University Libraries/Archives ....Dr. Michelle HAMMOND
106 Director Distance Education ....Dr. James SPOTSWOOD
37 Director Student Financial Aid ....Ms. Jaime MORRIS
36 Director Career Services ....Mr. Ryan HORSCH

38 Director Stdnt Wellness/Counseling ....Ms. Lindsay BAYS
26 Chief Marketing Officer ....Ms. Kelly HEINE
41 Director Athletics ....Mr. Kent L. WEISER
18 Dir Facilities/Phys Plant ....Mr. Bill MCKERNON
15 Director Human Resources ....Mr. Ray LAUBER
23 Director Health Services ....Ms. Mary MCDANIEL
39 Dir Residential Life/Orientation ....Ms. Cass COUGHLIN
40 Manager Bookstore ....Mr. Michael MCRELL
19 Chief Police & Safety ....Capt. Jerry COOK
43 General Counsel ....Mr. Kevin JOHNSON
21 Controller ....Ms. Pamela NORTON
92 Associate Provost Honors College ....Dr. Gary WYATT
28 Director Diversity & Inclusion ....Vacant
04 Administrative Asst to President ....Ms. Sarah MCKERNAN
91 Assoc CIO Academic & User Support ....Dr. Rob GIBSON

Flint Hills Technical College (G)

3301 W 18th Avenue, Emporia KS 66801-5957
County: Lyon FICE Identification: 005264
Unit ID: 155052
Telephone: (620) 343-4600 Carnegie Class: Assoc/HVT-High Non
FAX Number: (620) 343-4610 Calendar System: Semester
URL: www.fhtc.edu
Established: 1965 Annual Undergrad Tuition & Fees (In-District): $6,200
Enrollment: 1,222 Coed
Affiliation or Control: State/Local IRS Status: 501(c)3
Highest Offering: Associate Degree
Accreditation: HLC, DA, DH

01 President ....Dr. Caron DAUGHERTY
05 Vice Pres Instructional Services ....Mr. Steve LOEWEN
32 Vice Pres Student Services ....Ms. Lisa KIRMER
10 Vice Pres Business Services ....Mrs. Nancy THOMPSON
15 Director Personnel Services ....Mrs. Sandy WEEKS
37 Director Student Financial Aid ....Ms. Erica CLARK
84 Director Enrollment Management ....Ms. Brenda CARMICHAEL
04 Administrative Asst to President ....Ms. Jacqui ANDERSON
30 Chief Development/Advancement ....Mr. Mike CROUCH

Fort Hays State University (H)

600 Park Street, Hays KS 67601-4099
County: Ellis FICE Identification: 001915
Unit ID: 155061
Telephone: (785) 628-4000 Carnegie Class: Masters/L
FAX Number: (785) 628-4096 Calendar System: Semester
URL: www.fhsu.edu
Established: 1902 Annual Undergrad Tuition & Fees (In-State): $5,430
Enrollment: 15,033 Coed
Affiliation or Control: State IRS Status: 501(c)3
Highest Offering: Doctorate
Accreditation: HLC, CAATE, CACREP, CAEP, MUS, NAIT, NURSE, RAD, SP, SW

01 President ....Dr. Tisa MASON
05 Provost ....Dr. Jill ARENSDORF
10 Vice Pres Administration & Finance ....Mr. Mike BARNETT
32 Vice Pres Student Affairs ....Dr. Joseph LINN
35 Asst VP Student Affairs/Compliance .... Dr. Teresa CLOUNCH
20 Associate Provost ....Dr. Tim CROWLEY
88 Asst Provost/Learning Tech ....Dr. Andrew FELDSTEIN
09 Asst VP Institutional Effectiveness ....Dr. Sangki MIN
58 Dean Graduate Studies ....Dr. Angela POOL-FUNAI
84 Assoc VP Student Affairs/Enrollment ....Dr. Dennis KING
06 Registrar ....Mr. Craig KARLIN
07 Director of Admissions ....Mr. Jon ARMSTRONG
29 Exec Director Alumni ....Vacant
114 Director Budget & Planning ....Mr. Robert MANRY
36 Director Career Services ....Ms. Karen MCCULLOUGH
37 Dir Student Financial Aid ....Ms. Vanessa FLIPSE
26 Chief Communications Officer ....Mr. Scott CASON
08 Interim Dean Forsyth Library .... Ms. MaryAlice WADE
15 Director Personnel Services .... Ms. Shannon LINDSEY
106 Interim Director FHSU Online .... Ms. Kayla HICKEL
53 Dean College Education ....Dr. Paul ADAMS
49 Int Dean Col Arts/Hum/Soc Sci .... Dr. Daniel BLANKENSHIP
50 Dean Col Bus/Entrepreneurship .... Dr. Muhammad CHISHTY
76 Dean Col Health/Behavior Sciences ....Dr. Jeff BRIGGS
18 Dir Building & Maint Operations ....Mr. Terry PFEIFER
121 Dir Acad Advise/Career Exploration ....Dr. Patricia L. GRIFFIN
28 Asst VP/Student Engagement ....Ms. Taylor KRILEY
19 Director University Police ....Mr. Ed HOWELL
22 Univ Compliance Officer ....Ms. Amy SCHAFFER
102 President/CEO Foundation ....Mr. Jason WILLIBY
25 Interim Chief Contract/Grants Admin ....Dr. Whitney WHITAKER
41 Athletic Director ....Mr. Curtis HAMMEKE
104 Director Intl Student Services ....Ms. Carol SOLKO-OLLIFF
43 General Counsel ....Dr. Joe BAIN
81 Dean College Science/Tech/Math ....Dr. P. Grady DIXON
13 Director Information Technology ....Mr. Mark GRIFFIN
96 Director of Purchasing ....Ms. Kathy HERRMAN
39 Director Residential Life ....Mr. David BOLLIG
04 Exec Assistant to the President ....Ms. Tara GARCIA
45 Chief Institutional Planning Office ....Mr. Dana CUNNINGHAM

Fort Scott Community College (I)

2108 S Horton, Fort Scott KS 66701-3140
County: Bourbon FICE Identification: 001916
Unit ID: 155098
Telephone: (620) 223-2700 Carnegie Class: Assoc/MT-VT-High Non
FAX Number: (620) 223-4927 Calendar System: Semester
URL: www.fortscott.edu
Established: 1919 Annual Undergrad Tuition & Fees (In-District): $3,510

Enrollment: 1,617 Coed
Affiliation or Control: State/Local IRS Status: 501(c)3
Highest Offering: Associate Degree
Accreditation: HLC, ADNUR

01 President Alysia JOHNSTON
05 VP of Academic Affairs Adam BORTH
10 Vice Pres of Finance and Operations Julie EICHENBERGER
32 Vice President of Student Affairs Tom HAVRON
13 Director of Research & Technology Jacob REICHARD
07 Director Admissions Brian LANCASTER
08 Director of Library Susie ARVIDSON
06 Registrar Courtney METCALF
26 Director of Strategic Communication Kassie FUGATE-CATE
66 Director Nursing Jordan HOWARD
14 Information Technology Director Jason SIMON
12 Dean Crawford County Santos MANRIQUE
12 Dean of Miami County Campus Buddy Jo TANCK
121 VP of Student Support Services Janet FANCHER
15 Human Resource Director Juley MCDANIEL
30 Director of Development/Alumni Jeff TADTMAN
37 Director Student Financial Aid Lillie GRUBB
88 Director of Gordon Parks Museum Kirk SHARP
21 Director Business Operations Marianne CULBERTSON
04 Administrative Asst to President Darlene WOOD
39 Director Student Housing Marci MYERS
25 Director Grants & Special Projects Ralph BEACHAM

Friends University (A)

2100 W University Avenue, Wichita KS 67213-3397
County: Sedgwick FICE Identification: 001918
Unit ID: 155089
Telephone: (316) 295-5000 Carnegie Class: Masters/L
FAX Number: (316) 295-5060 Calendar System: Semester
URL: www.friends.edu
Established: 1898 Annual Undergrad Tuition & Fees: $30,120
Enrollment: 1,671 Coed
Affiliation or Control: Independent Non-Profit IRS Status: 501(c)3
Highest Offering: Master's
Accreditation: HLC, CAEP, MFCD, MUS

01 President Dr. Amy BRAGG CAREY
04 Executive Asst to the President Ms. Natasha PEREZ
05 VP Academic Affairs/Dean Faculty Dr. Kenneth STOLTZFUS
10 VP of Finance Mr. Vernon DOLEZAL
32 VP of Student Affairs Dr. Guy CHMIELESKI
111 Assoc VP of University Advancement Ms. Brie BOULANGER
11 VP of Administration Ms. Kelley WILLIAMS
84 VP of Enrollment Management Ms. Deb STOCKMAN
06 University Registrar Mr. Eric SANFORD
49 Academic Dean Dr. Ken STOLTZFUS
50 Chair Business & IT Dr. James LONG
57 Chair Fine Arts Dr. Joan GRIFFING
81 Chair Natural Science/Math Dr. Nora STRASSER
73 Chair Religion/Humanities Dr. Jeremy GALLEGOS
53 Chair Teacher Education Ms. Janet EUBANK
83 Chair Social/Behavioral Science Dr. Tor WYNN
08 Director Library Ms. Anne CRANE
18 Chief Facilities/Physical Plant Mr. Roger DANLEY
07 Director Recruiting/CBASE Admiss Ms. Jordan AUDETTE
37 Director Financial Aid Ms. Crystal ROACH
42 Dean Campus Ministries Dr. Guy CHMIELESKI
39 Director of Residence Life Ms. Lacey LANDENBERGER
27 Director of Marketing Ms. Rachel MILLARD
29 Director of Alumni Relations Mr. Michael WALZ
12 Site Manager - Kansas City Ms. Christy CARTER
09 Director of Institutional Research Mr. Aidan DUNLEAVY
19 Director Security/Safety Mr. Richard VINROE
106 Dir Online Education/E-learning Ms. Nancy ARTAZ
41 AVP Athletics Dr. Rob RAMSEYER
91 Director Administrative Computing Mr. Roger SCALES
13 Director Infrastructure Technology Mr. Gil OLIVA

Garden City Community College (B)

801 Campus Drive, Garden City KS 67846-6398
County: Finney FICE Identification: 001919
Unit ID: 155104
Telephone: (620) 276-7611 Carnegie Class: Assoc/MT-VT-High Non
FAX Number: (620) 276-9573 Calendar System: Semester
URL: www.gcccks.edu
Established: 1919 Annual Undergrad Tuition & Fees (In-District): $3,360
Enrollment: 1,868 Coed
Affiliation or Control: Local IRS Status: 501(c)3
Highest Offering: Associate Degree
Accreditation: HLC, ADNUR, EMT

01 President/CEO Dr. Ryan RUDA
05 VP for Instructional Services Mr. Marc MALONE
32 VP Student Services/Asst AD Mr. Colin LAMB
10 Vice President Admin Services/CFO Ms. Karla ARMSTRONG
35 Exec Director of Student Services Ms. Tammy TABOR
06 Registrar Ms. Nancy UNRUH
103 Dean Technical Educ/Workforce Dev Mr. Chuck PFEIFER
15 Director of Human Resources Ms. Kellee MUNOZ
18 Dean Physical Plng/Facilities Mgmt Mr. Derek RAMOS
26 Director of Media Relations Ms. Melody BROOKS
37 Director Student Financial Aid Ms. Melinda HARRINGTON
39 Director Residential Life Vacant
20 Dean of Academics Mr. Phil TERPSTRA
04 Executive Assistant to President Ms. Jodie TEWELL
09 Director of Institutional Research Ms. Brenda BARRETT

21 Comptroller Ms. Debra NICHOLSON
19 Campus Police Chief Mr. Rodney DOZIER
08 Director Library Services Mr. Trent SMITH
44 Executive Director Endowment Mr. Jeremy GIGOT
41 Athletic Director Mr. Jeff TATUM
121 Director of Advising Ms. Leslie WENZEL
22 Coord Disability Svcs & Compliance Ms. Kari ADAMS
106 Director Online Services Ms. Jamie DURLER
07 Director of Admissions Ms. Sydnee SASSAMAN
13 Chief Information Technology Office Mr. Lance MILLER

Grantham University (C)

16025 W 113th Street, Lenexa KS 66219
County: Johnson FICE Identification: 004283
Unit ID: 442569
Telephone: (888) 947-2684 Carnegie Class: Masters/L
FAX Number: (913) 309-4949 Calendar System: Other
URL: www.grantham.edu
Established: 1951 Annual Undergrad Tuition & Fees: $8,280
Enrollment: 6,465 Coed
Affiliation or Control: Proprietary IRS Status: Proprietary
Highest Offering: Master's
Accreditation: DEAC, IACBE, NUR, NURSE

01 Interim President Dr. Lindsey BRIDGEMAN
15 Vice President Human Resources Tracy GALLERY
13 Chief Information Officer Baz ABOUELENEIN
37 Director Student Financial Service Lindsay BRIDGEMAN
26 AVP of Marketing Operations Stephen RENTSCHLER

Haskell Indian Nations University (D)

155 Indian Avenue, #5030, Lawrence KS 66046-4800
County: Douglas FICE Identification: 010438
Unit ID: 155140
Telephone: (785) 749-8404 Carnegie Class: Tribal
FAX Number: N/A Calendar System: Semester
URL: www.haskell.edu
Established: 1884 Annual Undergrad Tuition & Fees: $480
Enrollment: 731 Coed
Affiliation or Control: Federal IRS Status: Exempt
Highest Offering: Baccalaureate
Accreditation: HLC, CAEP

01 Acting President Ms. Tamarah PFEIFFER
05 Acting Vice Pres Academic Affairs Ms. Cheryl CHUCKLUCK
11 Vice President University Services Ms. Tonia SALVINI
10 Chief Finance Officer Ms. Marie THORNE
13 Chief Information Officer Mr. David FIRE
111 Acting Dir Academic Support Ctr Ms. Carrie CORNELIUS
39 Acting Dir Resident Housing Ms. Barbara STUMBLINGBEAR
37 Financial Aid Officer Ms. Carlene MORRIS
06 Registrar Ms. Lou HARA
07 Director of Admissions Ms. Dorothy D. STITES
09 Dir Instl Research/Sponsored Pgms Ms. Cynthia GROUNDS
36 Career Development Specialist Vacant
38 Director Student Counseling Vacant
15 Human Resources Liaison Vacant
96 Acquisitions Ms. Janice BEGAY
26 Special Asst to the President Ms. Mona GONZALES
18 Acting Facilities Manager Ms. Karla VAN NOY

Hesston College (E)

301 S. Main Street, Hesston KS 67062-8901
County: Harvey FICE Identification: 001920
Unit ID: 155177
Telephone: (620) 327-4221 Carnegie Class: Bac/Assoc-Mixed
FAX Number: (620) 327-8300 Calendar System: Semester
URL: www.hesston.edu
Established: 1909 Annual Undergrad Tuition & Fees: $28,440
Enrollment: 359 Coed
Affiliation or Control: Mennonite Church IRS Status: 501(c)3
Highest Offering: Baccalaureate
Accreditation: HLC, NURSE

01 President Dr. Joseph MANICKAM
05 Vice Pres of Academics Dr. Carren MOHAM
07 Vice President of Admissions Mr. Del HERSHBERGER
10 Vice Pres Finance & Auxiliary Svcs Mrs. Lisa GEORGE
32 Vice Pres Student Life Mrs. Deb ROTH
111 Vice Pres Advancement Mrs. Rachel SWARTZENDRUBER MILLER
29 Coordinator of Advancement Services Ms. Sheri ESAU
06 Registrar/Dean of Assessment Mrs. Sandra HIEBERT
21 Business Manager Mr. Karl BRUBAKER

Highland Community College (F)

606 W Main, Highland KS 66035
County: Doniphan FICE Identification: 001921
Unit ID: 155186
Telephone: (785) 442-6000 Carnegie Class: Assoc/HT-High Non
FAX Number: (785) 442-6100 Calendar System: Semester
URL: www.highlandcc.edu
Established: 1858 Annual Undergrad Tuition & Fees (In-District): $3,600
Enrollment: 2,700 Coed
Affiliation or Control: Local IRS Status: 501(c)3
Highest Offering: Associate Degree
Accreditation: HLC, ADNUR

01 President Ms. Deborah FOX
05 Vice President for Academic Affairs Dr. Erin SHAW
32 Vice President for Student Services Dr. Eric INGMIRE
10 Vice Pres for Finance/Operations Mr. Randy WILLY
72 Director of Technical Education Mr. Lucas HUNZIGER
06 Registrar Ms. Alice HAMILTON
37 Financial Aid Director Ms. Sarah WINDMEYER
13 Director of IT Mr. Marc JEAN
09 Director of Institutional Research Mr. Jeffrey HURN
38 Campus Counselor Ms. Vanessa CHAVEZ
41 Athletic Director Dr. Bryan DORREL
08 Library Director Ms. Cindy DAVIS
18 Supervisor of Buildings & Grounds Mr. Barry SIMMONS
29 Director Alumni Relations Ms. Kelly TWOMBLY
39 Coord of Student Life Mr. Jacob DAVIS
15 Director of Human Resources Ms. Eileen C. GRONNIGER
40 Bookstore Coordinator Ms. Shannon WIEDMER
07 Director of Admissions Ms. Stephanie PETERSON
106 Assoc Dean Online Educ/E-learning Ms. Denise PETERS
35 Director of Student Life Mr. Joshua CLARY
04 Admin Assistant to the President Ms. Heather FUHRMAN

Hutchinson Community College (G)

1300 N Plum Street, Hutchinson KS 67501-5894
County: Reno FICE Identification: 001923
Unit ID: 155195
Telephone: (620) 665-3500 Carnegie Class: Assoc/MT-VT-High Non
FAX Number: (620) 665-3310 Calendar System: Semester
URL: www.hutchcc.edu
Established: 1928 Annual Undergrad Tuition & Fees (In-District): $3,480
Enrollment: 4,907 Coed
Affiliation or Control: State/Local IRS Status: 501(c)3
Highest Offering: Associate Degree
Accreditation: HLC, ADNUR, CAHIIM, COARC, EMT, PNUR, PTAA, RAD, SURGT

01 President Dr. Carter FILE
05 Vice President of Academic Affairs Dr. Cindy HOSS
10 Vice President Finance/Operations Ms. Julie BLANTON
103 VP Workforce Development/Outreach Mr. Bryce MCFARLAND
32 Vice President of Students Mr. Brett BRIGHT
26 Director of Marketing & Info Mr. Denny STOECKLEIN
13 Chief Information Officer Mr. Loren L. MORRIS
06 Registrar Mrs. Christina LONG
41 Athletic Director Mr. Josh GOOCH
15 Director of Personnel Mr. Brooks E. MANTOOTH
37 Financial Aid Officer Mr. Nathan BUCHE
07 Director of Admissions Mr. Corbin STROBEL
18 Director of Plant Facilities Mr. Don ROSE
39 Director of Residence Life Ms. Dana HINSHAW
29 Director Alumni Relations Mrs. Cindy KEAST
08 Coordinator of Library Services Mr. Brad FENWICK
09 Coord of Institutional Research Mr. Rex CHEEVER
106 Director Online Education Dr. Rhonda CORWIN

Independence Community College (H)

1057 West College Avenue,
Independence KS 67301-0708
County: Montgomery FICE Identification: 001924
Unit ID: 155201
Telephone: (620) 331-4100 Carnegie Class: Assoc/HT-High Non
FAX Number: (620) 331-5344 Calendar System: Semester
URL: www.indycc.edu
Established: 1925 Annual Undergrad Tuition & Fees (In-District): $4,650
Enrollment: 798 Coed
Affiliation or Control: State/Local IRS Status: 501(c)3
Highest Offering: Associate Degree
Accreditation: HLC

01 President Dr. Vincent BOWHAY
05 VP for Academic Affairs Ms. Taylor CRAWSHAW
10 VP for Administration/Finance Mr. Jonathan SADHOO
32 VP for Student Affairs Mr. David ADAMS
13 Interim Chief Information Officer Mr. Brett BERTIE
26 Marketing Coordinator Ms. Kris ADAMS
15 VP for Human Resources Ms. Lori BOOTS
102 Foundation Director Ms. Mandy MONROY
06 Registrar Ms. Wendy NIEMEYER
08 Director Library Services Ms. Sarah OWEN
18 Director of Maintenance/Facilities Mr. Benny BEURSKENS
37 Financial Aid Director Ms. Laura ALLISON
09 Dir of Institutional Research Ms. Anita CHAPPUIE
04 Executive Asst to President Mrs. Cherie STOCKTON
40 Bookstore Manager Ms. Toni BRUINGTON
88 Upward Bound Program Director Ms. Angela HOUSTON
106 Director of Online Education Vacant
121 Assoc Dean Tutoring/Accessibility Vacant
39 Student Housing General Manager Ms. Mary BAILEY
84 Director Enrollment/Retention Mgmt Ms. Brittany THORNTON
41 Athletic Director Mr. Eric FIGURSKI

Johnson County Community College (I)

12345 College Boulevard, Overland Park KS 66210-1299
County: Johnson FICE Identification: 008244
Unit ID: 155210
Telephone: (913) 469-8500 Carnegie Class: Assoc/HT-High Non
FAX Number: (913) 469-2559 Calendar System: Semester
URL: www.jccc.edu
Established: 1969 Annual Undergrad Tuition & Fees (In-District): $3,360
Enrollment: 13,891 Coed

Affiliation or Control: State/Local IRS Status: 501(c)3
Highest Offering: Associate Degree
Accreditation: **HLC**, ACBSP, ACFEI, ADNUR, COARC, DH, EMT, IFSAC, NDT

01 President .... Dr. Andrew BOWNE
05 Exec Vice Pres Academic Affs/CAO .... Dr. Mickey MCCLOUD
32 Vice Pres Student Success/CSO .... Dr. Randy WEBER
11 Exec VP Admin & Finance/COO .... Mr. Mike NEAL
04 Exec Asst to the President & Board .... Ms. Terri SCHLICHT
15 Vice President Human Resources .... Dr. Leslie HARDIN
51 Interim Vice Pres Continuing Educ .... Ms. Elisa WALDMAN
26 VP Strategic Comm & Mktg .... Mr. Chris GRAY
13 Interim CIO .... Ms. Del LOVITT
111 VP Inst Advancement/Govt Affairs .... Ms. Kate ALLEN
108 Exec Dir Institutional Assessment .... Mr. John CLAYTON
43 Senior Legal Counsel .... Ms. Kelsey NAZAR
10 AVP Financial Services/CFO .... Ms. Rachel LIERZ
116 Director Audit/Advisory Svcs .... Mr. Justin MCDAID
18 AVP Campus Services .... Mr. Tom HALL
20 AVP Instruction .... Dr. Gurbhushan SINGH
35 Dean Learner Engagement .... Ms. Pam VASSAR
07 Dean Enrollment Services .... Ms. MargE SHELLEY
96 AVP Business Services .... Ms. Janelle VOGLER
117 Exec Dir Mission Cont/Risk Mgmt .... Dr. Sandra WARNER
06 Registrar .... Ms. Leslie QUINN
88 Director Testing and Assessment .... Ms. Mary Ann DICKERSON
37 Director Student Financial Aid .... Ms. Christal WILLIAMS
07 Director of Admissions .... Mr. Peter BELK
41 Director of Athletics .... Mr. Randy STANGE
08 Director Library Services .... Mr. Mark DAGANAAR
09 Director of Institutional Research .... Ms. Natalie ALLEMAN-BEYERS
92 Director Honors Program .... Ms. Anne DOTTER

Kansas Christian College (A)

7401 Metcalf, Overland Park KS 66204-1995
County: Johnson Identification: 667134
Unit ID: 155308
Telephone: (913) 722-0272 Carnegie Class: Spec-4-yr-Faith
FAX Number: (913) 601-3826 Calendar System: Semester
URL: www.kansaschristian.edu
Established: 1938 Annual Undergrad Tuition & Fees: $9,340
Enrollment: 152 Coed
Affiliation or Control: Independent Non-Profit IRS Status: 501(c)3
Highest Offering: Baccalaureate
Accreditation: **BI**

01 President .... Mr. Chad POLLARD
00 Chairman of the Board .... Rev. Rodney L. DAVIS
101 Secretary of the Board .... Mr. Dwight PURTLE
05 Vice Pres Academic Affairs .... Dr. Dennis CROCKER
03 Executive Vice President .... Rev. Matthew LEE
41 Vice Pres of Athletic Development .... Dr. Jim POTEET
32 Dean of Student Services .... Mr. David CARPENTER
18 Director of Facilities .... Mr. Tony ASKEW
08 Head Librarian .... Mrs. Dorie SCOFIELD
06 Registrar .... Rev. Christopher W. SUMPTER
09 Director of Institutional Research .... Mrs. Dorothy PURTLE
37 Director Student Financial Aid .... Mrs. Marcia KELLEY
04 Admin Assistant to the President .... Ms. Kim LEONARD
106 Dir Online Education/E-learning .. Dr. Kenneth L. MERSCHBROCK
39 Dir Resident Life/Student Housing .... Mrs. Leandra MARTIN

Kansas City Kansas Community College (B)

7250 State Avenue, Kansas City KS 66112-3003
County: Wyandotte FICE Identification: 001925
Unit ID: 155292
Telephone: (913) 334-1100 Carnegie Class: Assoc/MT-VT-Mix Trad/Non
FAX Number: (913) 288-7609 Calendar System: Semester
URL: www.kckcc.edu
Established: 1923 Annual Undergrad Tuition & Fees (In-District): $3,300
Enrollment: 5,148 Coed
Affiliation or Control: State/Local IRS Status: 501(c)3
Highest Offering: Associate Degree
Accreditation: **#HLC**, ACBSP, ADNUR, COARC, EMT, FUSER, MAC, PTAA

01 President .... Dr. Greg MOSIER
10 Chief Financial Officer .... Mr. Michael BEACH
05 Interim Vice Pres Academic Affairs .... Mr. Jerry POPE
32 VP Student Affairs .... Dr. Delfina WILSON
26 VP Strategic Initiative & Outreach .... Ms. Tami BARTUNEK
81 Dean Math/Science/Business .... Dr. Ed KREMER
84 Dean Enrollment Management .... Dr. Stephen TERRY
51 Director Continuing Education .... Mr. David BEACH
103 Exec Dir Entrep & Workforce Dev .... Vacant
79 Interim Dean Arts/Humanities .... Dr. Aaron MARGOLIS
13 Chief Information Officer .... Mr. Peter GABRIEL
09 Dir of Institutional Effectiveness .... Dr. Mihir CHAND
76 Dean of Health Professions .... Dr. Tiffany BOHM
36 Director Pioneer Career Ctr .... Ms. Marcia IRVINE
88 Director of Academic Resource Ctr .... Ms. Amanda WILLIAMS
41 Director of Athletics .... Mr. Anthony (Tony) TOMPKINS
40 Director of Bookstore .... Mr. Kasey MAYER
18 Director of Buildings/Grounds .... Mr. Jeff SIXTA
19 Director of Campus Police .... Chief Robert PUTZKE
14 Director of Computing .... Mr. James BENNETT
121 Dean of Student Svcs/Success Ctr .... Mr. Shawn DERRITT
38 Director Counseling-Advocacy Ctr .... Ms. Linda WARNER
37 Director of Financial Aid .... Ms. Mary I. DORR
21 Controller .... Ms. Lesley STROHSCHEIN
92 Director of Honors/Phi Theta Kappa .... Dr. Stacy TUCKER
28 Director of Intercultural Center .... Ms. Barbara CLARK-EVANS
08 Director of Learning Commons .... Ms. Amanda WILLIAMS
24 Director Media Services Technology .... Mr. Randy ROYER
106 Director of Online Services .... Ms. Susan STUART
35 Director of Student Activities .... Ms. Andrica WILCOXEN
07 Director Admissions/First Year Exp .... Ms. Tina CHURCH LEWANDOWSKI
06 Registrar .... Ms. Theresa HOLLIDAY
15 Chief Human Resources Officer .... Ms. Christina MCGEE
88 Director Wellness Center .... Mr. Rob M. CRANE
28 Director of Cultural Outreach .... Mr. Brian PATRICK
66 Director Nursing .... Ms. Susan ANDERSEN
66 Director Practical Nursing .... Ms. Susan K. WHITE
72 Director Technical Programs .... Mr. Richard PIPER
72 Director Technical Programs Perkins .... Ms. Donna S. SHAWN
88 Director Performing Arts Center .... Mr. Gary MOSBY
04 Executive Admin Partner .... Ms. Risala ALLEN
105 Web Services .... Mr. Omar BRENES
22 Dir Affirmative Action/EEO .... Vacant
39 Student Housing Supervisor .... Mr. Ronnie MOORE
102 Exec Dir Foundation .... Ms. Mary SPANGLER
25 Chief Contract/Grants Administrator .... Ms. Connie NORTHUP
96 Director of Purchasing .... Ms. Linda BURGESS
108 Dean Academic Support/Assessment .... Ms. Cecelia BREWER

Kansas State University (C)

919 Mid-Campus Drive North, Manhattan KS 66506
County: Riley FICE Identification: 001928
Unit ID: 155399
Telephone: (785) 532-6250 Carnegie Class: DU-Highest
FAX Number: (785) 532-2120 Calendar System: Semester
URL: www.k-state.edu
Established: 1863 Annual Undergrad Tuition & Fees (In-State): $10,466
Enrollment: 20,854 Coed
Affiliation or Control: State IRS Status: 501(c)3
Highest Offering: Doctorate
Accreditation: **HLC**, ART, CACREP, CAEPN, CEA, CIDA, CONST, DIETC, DIETD, IPSY, JOUR, LSAR, MFCD, MUS, PH, PLNG, SP, SPAA, SW, THEA, VET

01 President .... Mr. Richard B. MYERS
04 Exec Asst to the President .... Ms. Dana M. HASTINGS
05 Provost & Executive Vice President .... Dr. Charles S. TABER
10 CFO & Dir Budget Planning .... Mr. Ethan E. ERICKSON
11 Vice President & COO .... Ms. Cindy A. BONTRAGER
46 VP for Research .... Dr. David V. ROSOWSKY
32 VP Student Life/Dean of Students .... Dr. Thomas A. LANE
26 VP for Communications & Marketing .... Mr. Jeffery B. MORRIS
15 VP Human Capital .... Mr. Jay W. STEPHENS
13 Chief Information Officer .... Dr. Gary L. PRATT
28 Int Chief Diversity/Inclusion Ofcr .... Dr. BeEtta L. STONEY
102 President/CEO of Foundation .... Mr. Greg WILLEMS
29 Alumni Association President .... Ms. Amy Button RENZ
41 Athletics Director .... Mr. Gene TAYLOR
43 General Counsel .... Ms. Shari F. CRITTENDON
100 Chief of Staff/Dir Community Rels .... Ms. Linda J. COOK
86 Chief Governmental Rels Officer .... Dr. Susan K. PETERSON
88 Exec Dir Military/Veterans Affairs .... Dr. Arthur S. DE GROAT, II
84 Vice Provost Enrollment Mgmt .... Dr. Karen D. GOOS
121 Vice Provost Student Success .... Dr. Jeannie B. LEONARD
108 Int Assoc Prov Inst Effectiveness .... Dr. Tanya GONZALEZ
09 Assoc Prov Institutional Research .... Dr. Bin NING
22 Director Institutional Equity .... Ms. Stephanie LOTT
08 Acting Dean of Libraries .... Dr. Michael HADDOCK
47 Dean of Agriculture .... Dr. J. Ernest MINTON
48 Dean Architecture/Planning/Design .... Mr. Timothy DE NOBLE
49 Dean of Arts & Sciences .... Dr. Amitabha CHAKRABARTI
50 Dean of Business Admin .... Dr. Kevin P. GWINNER
106 Dean Global Campus .... Dr. Karen L. PEDERSEN
53 Dean of Education .... Dr. Debbie K. MERCER
54 Dean of Engineering .... Dr. Matt J. O'KEEFE
58 Vice Prov Grad Ed/Dean Grad School .. Dr. Claudia A. PETRESCU
59 Int Dean of Health & Human Science .... Dr. Craig A. HARMS
72 CEO/Dean Technology/Aviation .... Dr. Alysia H. STARKEY
74 Dean of Veterinary Medicine .... Dr. Bonnie R. RUSH
12 Int Dean & CEO K-State Olathe .... Dr. Jacqueline D. SPEARS
117 Univ Risk & Compliance Officer .... Mr. Elliot C. YOUNG
18 Asst VP Engr/Utilities/Maintenance .... Mr. Casey S. LAUER
19 Asst VP Univ Police & Public Safety .... Mr. Ronnie D. GRICE
96 Purchasing Manager .... Ms. Cathy OEHM
07 Exec Dir Recruitment/Admissions .... Ms. Tammy BYLAND
06 Registrar .... Ms. Kelley L. BRUNDAGE
37 Dir Student Fin Assistance .... Mr. Robert GAMEZ
39 Assoc VP Housing & Dining Svcs .... Mr. Derek A. JACKSON
36 Exec Director Career Center .... Ms. Kerri D. KELLER

Kansas State University Polytechnic, College of Technology and Aviation (D)

2310 Centennial Road, Salina KS 67401-8196
Telephone: (785) 826-2601 FICE Identification: 004611
Accreditation: **&HLC**, AAB

† Regional accreditation is carried under the parent institution in Manhattan, KS.

Kansas Wesleyan University (E)

100 E Claflin Avenue, Salina KS 67401-6196
County: Saline FICE Identification: 001929
Unit ID: 155414
Telephone: (785) 827-5541 Carnegie Class: Bac-Diverse
FAX Number: (785) 827-0927 Calendar System: Semester
URL: www.kwu.edu
Established: 1886 Annual Undergrad Tuition & Fees: $30,570
Enrollment: 803 Coed
Affiliation or Control: United Methodist IRS Status: 501(c)3
Highest Offering: Master's
Accreditation: **HLC**, CAEPN, NURSE, @SW

01 President and CEO .... Dr. Matthew R. THOMPSON
04 Executive Assistant to President .... Ms. Jan M. SHIRK
05 Provost .... Dr. Damon KRAFT
32 Vice President Student Development .... Ms. Bridget R. WEISER
10 Chief Finance Officer .... Ms. Rhonda BETHE
06 Registrar .... Mrs. Jasmin DAUNER
111 VP Advancement & Mktg/Admiss .... Mr. Kenneth OLIVER
37 Assoc Dir Student Financial Plng .... Ms. Michelle JENSEN
07 Director of Admissions .... Ms. Claire HOUK
88 Admin Assistant to EVP/Provost .... Ms. Jill KOSTER
121 Director of Student Success Center .... Mr. Bryan L. MCCULLAR
26 Director Marketing & Communications .... Mr. Brad SALOIS
08 Director of Library Services .... Ms. Kelley WEBER
24 Production Manager .... Mr. Paul GREEN
13 Director of Information Systems .... Mr. Justin TAYLOR
19 Director of Emergency Management .... Dr. Lonnie BOOKER
18 Director of Plant Operations .... Mr. John SWAGERTY
40 Manager of Yotee's .... Ms. Jennifer RYAN
42 Campus Minister .... Mr. Scott JAGODZINSKE
41 Athletic Director .... Mr. Steve WILSON
53 Director of Teacher Education .... Dr. Eileen ST. JOHN
79 Div Chair Humanities/Teach Educ .... Dr. Phil MECKLEY
76 Div Chair Nursing Educ & Health Sci .... Ms. Janeane HOUCHIN
83 Division Chair Social Sciences .... Dr. Steve HOEKSTRA
57 Division Chair Fine Arts .... Prof. Barbara J. NICKELL
81 Div Chair Natural Sciences/Math .... Dr. Dorothy HANNA
15 Human Resources Asst Director .... Ms. Becky MATHEWS
106 Academic Dean .... Dr. William BACKLIN
39 Resident Hall Director .... Mr. Charles STENNETT
29 Director Alumni Relations .... Vacant
25 Chief Contract & Grants Admin .... Ms. Melissa ANDERSON
38 Director Student Counseling .... Ms. Patsy STOCKHAM
28 Dir of Diversity & Student Success .... Dr. Allen D. SMITH

Labette Community College (F)

200 S 14th, Parsons KS 67357-4299
County: Labette FICE Identification: 001930
Unit ID: 155450
Telephone: (620) 421-6700 Carnegie Class: Assoc/HVT-Mix Trad/Non
FAX Number: (620) 421-0921 Calendar System: Semester
URL: www.labette.edu
Established: 1923 Annual Undergrad Tuition & Fees (In-District): $3,488
Enrollment: 1,464 Coed
Affiliation or Control: Local IRS Status: 501(c)3
Highest Offering: Associate Degree
Accreditation: **HLC**, ADNUR, COARC, DA, DMS, #PTAA, RAD

01 President .... Dr. Mark WATKINS
04 Executive Assistant to President .... Mrs. Jennifer G. THOMPSON
05 Vice President Academic Affairs .... Mr. Jason SHARP
10 Vice President Finance & Operations .... Ms. Leanna J. DOHERTY
32 Vice President Student Affairs .... Ms. Tammy FUENTEZ
84 Dean of Enrollment Management .... Mrs. Theresa HUNDLEY
20 Dean of Instruction .... Ms. Kara WHEELER
13 Director of Information Technology .... Mrs. Jody BURZINSKI
30 Dir Resource Devel/Alumni Rels .... Mrs. Lindi D. FORBES
08 Director of Library Services .... Mr. Scott M. ZOLLARS
18 Director of Physical Plant .... Mr. Kevin DOHERTY
66 Director of Nursing .... Mrs. Delyna BOHNENBLUST
41 Athletic Director .... Mr. Aaron J. KEAL
26 Director of Public Relations .... Mrs. Bethany KENDRICK
06 Assistant Registrar .... Ms. Cindy DYSON
15 Director of Human Relations .... Ms. Janice S. EVERY
37 Director Student Financial Aid .... Ms. Megan FUGATE
35 Student Life Coordinator .... Mrs. Terri LEROY
40 Bookstore Specialist .... Ms. Elizabeth KITTERMAN
101 Secretary of the Institution/Board .... Mrs. Jennifer THOMPSON
103 Director Workforce Development .... Mr. Ross HARPER
29 Director Alumni Affairs .... Mrs. Lindi FORBES
07 Director of Admissions .... Ms. Kylie LUCAS

Manhattan Area Technical College (G)

3136 Dickens Avenue, Manhattan KS 66503-2499
County: Riley FICE Identification: 005500
Unit ID: 155487
Telephone: (785) 587-2800 Carnegie Class: Assoc/HVT-High Non
FAX Number: (785) 587-2804 Calendar System: Semester
URL: www.manhattantech.edu
Established: 1965 Annual Undergrad Tuition & Fees (In-District): $7,440
Enrollment: 842 Coed
Affiliation or Control: State/Local IRS Status: 501(c)3
Highest Offering: Associate Degree
Accreditation: **HLC**, ADNUR, MLTAD

01 President/CEO .... Dr. James GENANDT
05 Vice Pres Student Success/CAO/CSSO .... Ms. Sarah PHILLIPS
11 Vice Pres Operations/CFO/CHRO .... Ms. Carmela JACOBS
13 Chief Information Security Officer .... Mr. Josh GFELLER
32 Dean Student Services .... Mr. Neil ROSS
75 Dean Career & Technical Education .... Mr. Nathan ROBERTS
06 Registrar .... Ms. Morgen STOECKLEIN
09 Dir Inst Reporting/Instruct Tech .... Ms. Kim WITHRODER
16 Human Resources Coordinator .... Ms. Jasmyn GRIFFIN
37 Director Financial Aid .... Ms. Laura WEISS-COOK

Manhattan Christian College (A)

1415 Anderson Avenue, Manhattan KS 66502-4081
County: Riley FICE Identification: 001931
Unit ID: 155496
Telephone: (785) 539-3571 Carnegie Class: Spec-4-yr-Faith
FAX Number: (785) 539-0832 Calendar System: Semester
URL: www.mccks.edu
Established: 1927 Annual Undergrad Tuition & Fees: $17,250
Enrollment: 170 Coed
Affiliation or Control: Christian Churches And Churches of Christ
IRS Status: 501(c)3
Highest Offering: Baccalaureate
Accreditation: HLC, BI

01 President ... Mr. J. Kevin INGRAM
05 Vice President for Academics ... Dr. Greg DELORT
10 VP for Financial & Admin Services ... Mr. Rob BERARD
32 Vice President for Student Life ... Dr. Rick L. WRIGHT
06 Registrar ... Ms. Jennifer ANDERSON
111 Director Institutional Advancement ... Mrs. Jolene K. RUPE
08 Director of Library Services ... Mr. Caleb MAY
41 Athletic Director ... Mr. Jordan STROM
29 Alumni Relations Director ... Mrs. Genae DENVER
04 Admin Asst to President ... Mrs. April WENDT
37 Director Student Financial Services ... Mrs. Trish RUNION
07 Director of Admissions ... Mr. Ben FIELD
13 Director of Information Technology ... Mr. JT VANGILDER
39 Director of Student Development ... Mr. Ben GROGG

McPherson College (B)

1600 E Euclid, PO Box 1402, McPherson KS 67460-1402
County: McPherson FICE Identification: 001933
Unit ID: 155511
Telephone: (620) 242-0400 Carnegie Class: Bac-Diverse
FAX Number: (620) 241-8443 Calendar System: 4/1/4
URL: www.mcpherson.edu
Established: 1887 Annual Undergrad Tuition & Fees: $31,154
Enrollment: 868 Coed
Affiliation or Control: Church Of The Brethren IRS Status: 501(c)3
Highest Offering: Master's
Accreditation: HLC, CAEPN

01 President ... Mr. Michael P. SCHNEIDER
05 Provost/VP Academic Affairs ... Dr. Bruce CLARY
111 Vice President Advancement ... Mr. Roger BRIMMERMAN
10 Vice President for Finance ... Mr. Rick TUXHORN
84 VP Enrollment Management ... Ms. Christi HOPKINS
100 Chief of Staff ... Ms. Abby ARCHER-RIERSON
32 Director of Student Life ... Ms. Gabrielle WILLIAMS
36 Exec Director Career Services ... Ms. Amy BECKMAN
41 Athletic Director ... Mr. Andrew EHLING
06 Registrar ... Ms. Tricia HARTSHORN
37 Dir Financial Aid/Admissions Opers ... Ms. Sara BRUBAKER
08 Library Director ... Ms. Jaime MAKATCHE
26 Director of Public Relations ... Ms. Tina GOODWIN
15 Director Human Resources ... Mr. Marty SIGWING
29 Director Alumni Relations ... Ms. Monica RICE
18 Director of Facilities ... Mr. Marty SIGWING
07 Director of Admissions ... Mr. Josh HUBIN
09 Assoc Dean Inst Research/Assessment ... Ms. Cari LOTT
35 Operations Specialist Student Affs ... Mr. Justin WILTFONG

MidAmerica Nazarene University (C)

2030 E College Way, Olathe KS 66062-1899
County: Johnson FICE Identification: 007032
Unit ID: 155520
Telephone: (913) 782-3750 Carnegie Class: Masters/M
FAX Number: (913) 971-3290 Calendar System: Semester
URL: www.mnu.edu
Established: 1966 Annual Undergrad Tuition & Fees: $32,872
Enrollment: 1,636 Coed
Affiliation or Control: Church Of The Nazarene IRS Status: 501(c)3
Highest Offering: Master's
Accreditation: HLC, ACBSP, CACREP, CAEP, MUS, NURSE

01 President ... Dr. David J. SPITTAL
05 Vice Pres/Chief Academic Officer ... Dr. Nancy DAMRON
10 Vice President Finance ... Mr. Darrel ANDERSON
111 Vice Pres University Advancement ... Mr. Jon D. NORTH
32 Vice President Student Development ... Mr. Daniel RINCONES
46 Vice President Strategic Expansion ... Dr. Mark C. FORD
110 Assoc VP University Advancement ... Mr. Tim KEETON
42 University Chaplain ... Mr. Brady J. BRAATZ
13 Associate VP for Instructional Tech ... Dr. Martin CROSSLAND
09 Dir Institutional Effectiveness ... Dr. Jordan MANTHA
66 Dean School of Nursing ... Dr. Sarah MILLER
49 Dean College of Arts & Sciences ... Mr. Jamie MYRTLE
06 Registrar ... Mrs. Rhonda RILEY
08 Director Mabee Learning Commons ... Mr. Mark HAYSE
29 Director of Alumni Relations ... Mr. Pete S. BRUMBAUGH
37 Director of Student Financial Svcs ... Mr. Cathy L. COLAPIETRO
41 Athletic Director ... Mr. Todd L. GARRETT
15 Director of Human Resources ... Mr. Rich CLIFFE
18 Director of Facility Services ... Mr. Jon N. SPENCE
40 Director MERC/Postmaster ... Mr. Nikos KELLEPOURIS
19 Director of Campus Safety ... Mr. Richard M. PACHECO
121 Director Academic Success Center ... Ms. Giselle TAYLOR
04 Administrative Asst to President ... Mrs. Kelly GIBSON
103 Dir Workforce/Career Development ... Mrs. Linda ALEXANDER
104 Director Study Abroad ... Mr. James GARRISON
28 Coord Diversity/Cultural Competency ... Dr. Victoria HAYNES

Neosho County Community College (D)

800 W 14th Street, Chanute KS 66720-2699
County: Neosho FICE Identification: 001936
Unit ID: 155566
Telephone: (620) 431-2820 Carnegie Class: Assoc/HVT-High Non
FAX Number: N/A Calendar System: Semester
URL: www.neosho.edu
Established: 1935 Annual Undergrad Tuition & Fees (In-District): $5,032
Enrollment: 1,727 Coed
Affiliation or Control: Local IRS Status: 501(c)3
Highest Offering: Associate Degree
Accreditation: HLC, ACBSP, ADNUR, CAHIIM, OTA, SURGT

01 President ... Dr. Brian L. INBODY
05 Vice President Student Learning ... Ms. Sarah ROBB
11 Vice President for Operations ... Mr. Kerry RANABARGAR
10 Chief Financial Officer ... Ms. Sondra K. SOLANDER
103 Dean Outreach/Workforce Development ... Ms. Brenda L. KRUMM
32 Dean of Student Services ... Ms. Kerrie COOMES
15 Director of Human Resources ... Ms. Karin JACOBSON
106 Dean for Ottawa & Online Campuses ... Ms. Marie GARDNER
13 Dean for Operations/CIO ... Vacant
30 Director of Development/Alumni Rels ... Ms. Kelly COLTER
08 Coordinator of Library Services ... Mr. Todd KNISPEL
37 Director Student Financial Aid ... Ms. Jennifer DAISY
66 Director of Nursing ... Ms. Pamela COVAULT
105 Dir of Tech Services/Webmaster ... Vacant
41 Athletic Director ... Ms. Riann MULLIS
85 Dir International Student Services ... Ms. Sarah CADWALLADER
06 Registrar ... Mr. Ryan ROSE
09 Coordinator/Institutional Research ... Ms. LuAnn HAUSER
40 Chanute Asst Bookstore Coordinator ... Ms. Pamela EHMKE
40 Ottawa Bookstore Coordinator ... Ms. Sheri WOOLMAN
26 Advertising/Media Coordinator ... Vacant
39 Director of Residence/Student Life ... Ms. Khiera ALMANZA
04 AA to the President/Board Clerk ... Ms. Naomi REESE
18 Director of Facilities ... Mr. Kyle SEUFERT
07 Director of Admissions ... Ms. Amy MORRIS

Newman University (E)

3100 McCormick, Wichita KS 67213-2097
County: Sedgwick FICE Identification: 001939
Unit ID: 155335
Telephone: (316) 942-4291 Carnegie Class: Masters/L
FAX Number: (316) 942-4483 Calendar System: Semester
URL: www.newmanu.edu
Established: 1933 Annual Undergrad Tuition & Fees: $33,000
Enrollment: 2,053 Coed
Affiliation or Control: Roman Catholic IRS Status: 501(c)3
Highest Offering: Doctorate
Accreditation: HLC, ANEST, CAEP, COARC, NURSE, OTA, RAD, SW

01 President ... Dr. Kathleen S. JAGGER
05 Provost & Vice Pres Acad Affairs ... Dr. Kimberly MCDOWALL LONG
10 VP Finance & Administration ... Mr. Anthony BEATA
84 Interim VP Enrollment Management ... Dr. Paul CARNEY
32 Vice Pres Student Affairs ... Vacant
20 Assoc VP Academic Affairs ... Ms. Rosemary NIEDENS
42 Director of Campus Ministry ... Fr. Adam GRELINGER
29 Director of Alumni Relations ... Ms. Laura HARTLEY
41 Director of Athletics ... Ms. Joanna PRYOR
08 Library Director ... Mr. Steve HAMERSKY
06 Registrar ... Ms. Lori GIBBON
37 Director of Financial Aid ... Ms. Myra PFANNENSTIEL
40 Director of Bookstore ... Mr. Larry WILLIAMS
13 Chief Information Officer ... Mr. Icer VAUGHAN
19 Director of Security ... Mr. Morris FLOYD
15 Director of Human Resources ... Mr. Jason POOL
21 Controller ... Ms. Diana GRIBLIN
39 Director Residence Life ... Mr. Scott MUDLOFF
35 Dean of Students ... Ms. Christine SCHNEIKERT-LUEBBE
49 Dean of Arts & Sciences ... Dr. Lori STEINER
58 Dean School of Catholic Studies ... Fr. Joseph GILE
50 Dean School of Business ... Dr. Jill FORT
53 Dean of Education & Social Work ... Dr. Cameron CARLSON
104 Director Study Abroad ... Dr. Cheryl GOLDEN
26 Chief Public Relations/Marketing ... Mr. Clark SCHAFER
18 Chief Facilities/Plant ... Mr. Paco GONZALEZ
09 Director of Institutional Research ... Mr. William GRAVES
30 Director of Development ... Ms. Beth FATKIN
04 Executive Asst/Sec of the Corp ... Ms. Gabrielle DODOSH

North Central Kansas Technical College (F)

PO Box 507, Beloit KS 67420-0507
County: Mitchell FICE Identification: 005265
Unit ID: 155593
Telephone: (785) 738-2276 Carnegie Class: Assoc/HVT-Mix Trad/Non
FAX Number: (785) 738-2903 Calendar System: Semester
URL: www.ncktc.edu
Established: 1964 Annual Undergrad Tuition & Fees (In-District): $7,324
Enrollment: 843 Coed
Affiliation or Control: State/Local IRS Status: 501(c)3
Highest Offering: Associate Degree
Accreditation: HLC, ADNUR

01 President ... Mr. Eric BURKS
10 VP of Finance & Hays Operations ... Ms. Diana BAUMANN
05 VP Student & Instructional Services ... Mr. Corey ISBELL
20 Dean of Instruction ... Ms. Jennifer BROWN
06 Registrar ... Ms. Judy HEIDRICK
32 Dean of Student Experience ... Mr. Shane BRITT
37 Financial Aid Director ... Ms. Leah BERGMANN
04 Administrative Asst to President ... Ms. Liz FIXSEN
102 Director of Advancement ... Ms. Mendi ANSCHUTZ
101 Clerk of the Institution/Board ... Ms. Liz FIXSEN
13 Chief Info Technology Officer (CIO) ... Mr. Robert MCCREIGHT
121 Dean of Student Success ... Ms. Jayme FILE
26 Marketing Director ... Ms. Chandra FELDMAN
84 Dean of Enrollment Mgmt ... Ms. Tricia CLINE

North Central Kansas Technical College (G)

2205 Wheatland Avenue, Hays KS 67601
Telephone: (785) 625-2437 Identification: 770259
Accreditation: &HLC

Northwest Kansas Technical College (H)

1209 Harrison Street, PO Box 668,
Goodland KS 67735-3441
County: Sherman FICE Identification: 005267
Unit ID: 155618
Telephone: (785) 890-3641 Carnegie Class: Assoc/HVT-High Non
FAX Number: (785) 899-5711 Calendar System: Semester
URL: www.nwktc.edu
Established: 1964 Annual Undergrad Tuition & Fees (In-District): N/A
Enrollment: 676 Coed
Affiliation or Control: State/Local IRS Status: 501(c)3
Highest Offering: Associate Degree
Accreditation: HLC, COARC, MAC

01 President ... Mr. Ben SCHEARS
05 Dean of Academic Advancement ... Mr. Matt POUNDS
11 Vice President of Operations ... Mrs. Sherri KNITIG
13 Vice Pres for Information Tech ... Mr. Brad BERGSMA
07 Director of Admissions ... Mrs. Kayla LUERA
41 Athletic Director ... Mr. Rory KLING
30 Director of Endowment/Career Svcs ... Mrs. Kelly JAMES

Ottawa University (I)

1001 S Cedar Street, Ottawa KS 66067-3399
County: Franklin FICE Identification: 001937
Unit ID: 155627
Telephone: (785) 242-5200 Carnegie Class: Bac-Diverse
FAX Number: (785) 229-1020 Calendar System: Semester
URL: www.ottawa.edu
Established: 1865 Annual Undergrad Tuition & Fees: $32,180
Enrollment: 797 Coed
Affiliation or Control: American Baptist IRS Status: 501(c)3
Highest Offering: Master's
Accreditation: HLC, ACBSP, CAEP, CAEPN, NURSE

00 University President & CEO ... Dr. Bill TSUTSUI
02 President ... Dr. Reggies WENYIKA
05 University Provost & CAO ... Dr. Terry HAINES
10 Exec VP & Chief Financial Officer ... Mr. J. Clark RIBORDY
106 EVP Online Unit ... Ms. Nancy WINGERT
111 Vice President Advancement ... Ms. Janet PETERS
06 University Registrar ... Mrs. Margaret HERRON
26 Public Rels & Social Media Manager ... Mr. Scott ALBRIGHT
21 Controller & Dir Fiscal Operations ... Mr. Thomas CORLEY
15 Director Human Resources ... Ms. Joanna WALTERS
29 Director Alumni Programs ... Ms. Courtney KLAUS
08 Director Library Services ... Ms. Gloria CREED-DIKEOGU
41 Director Athletics ... Ms. Arabie CONNER
18 Director of Facilities ... Mr. David BIRD
04 Exec Asst to University President ... Ms. Courtney STEPHENS
20 Acting Academic Dean ... Dr. Kevin MARET
53 Dean School of Education ... Dr. Amy HOGAN
84 Director of Admissions & Enrollment ... Mr. Andy OTTO
50 Dean School of Business ... Dr. Marylou DEWALD
49 Dean School of Arts & Sciences ... Dr. Karen OHNESORGE
88 Associate VP University Compliance ... Ms. Carrie STEVENS
13 Director Software Solutions ... Ms. Brandi SERVAES
35 Dean of Student Life & Services ... Mr. Donald ANDERSON
44 Director Annual Giving ... Ms. Nori HALE
104 Dean Study Abroad Program ... Dr. Marylou DEWALD
106 Director Instr Design/Academic Tech ... Dr. Carine ULLOM
19 Safety/Security Supervisor ... Mr. Kevin MOORE
36 Career Services Coordinator ... Dr. Christine CURRIER
101 Secretary of the Institution/Board ... Ms. Courtney STEPHENS
38 Director Student Counseling ... Ms. Angela SPRUILL
90 Director Academic Computing ... Mr. Adam CAYLOR

† The Online division is included in the institution's enrollment count.

Ottawa University Overland Park, KS (J)

4370 W. 109th Street, Suite 200,
Overland Park KS 66211-1302
Telephone: (913) 266-8600 Identification: 666083
Accreditation: &HLC

† Regional accreditation is carried under the parent institution in Ottawa, KS.

Pittsburg State University (A)

1701 S Broadway, Pittsburg KS 66762-7500
County: Crawford FICE Identification: 001926
Unit ID: 155681
Telephone: (620) 231-7000 Carnegie Class: Masters/L
FAX Number: (620) 235-4080 Calendar System: Semester
URL: www.pittstate.edu
Established: 1903 Annual Undergrad Tuition & Fees (In-State): $7,504
Enrollment: 6,398 Coed
Affiliation or Control: State IRS Status: 501(c)3
Highest Offering: Doctorate
Accreditation: **HLC**, CAEP, CAEPN, CAPRT, CEA, MUS, NURSE, SW

01 President .... Dr. Steven A. SCOTT
05 Provost & VP for Academic Affairs .... Dr. Howard SMITH
11 CFO & VP Administration .... Mr. Doug BALL
111 VP University Advancement .... Ms. Kathleen FLANNERY
06 Registrar .... Ms. Melinda ROELFS
32 VP Student Life .... Dr. Steve ERWIN
26 Chief Marketing & Comm Officer .... Ms. Abigail FERN
49 Dean of Arts & Sciences .... Dr. Mary Carol POMATTO
50 Dean of Business .... Dr. Paul GRIMES
53 Dean of Education .... Dr. James TRUELOVE
72 Dean of Technology .... Dr. Bob FRISBEE
08 Dean of Library Services .... Mr. Randy ROBERTS
108 Director of Assessment .... Ms. Nora HATTON
27 Director of Media Relations .... Ms. Andra STEFANONI
29 Dir Alumni Rels/Constituent Svcs .... Dr. Jon A. BARTLOW
13 Chief Information Officer .... Ms. Angela NERIA
15 Director Human Resource Services .... Ms. Lori DREILING
85 Director of International Programs .... Mr. Aaron HURT
45 Chief Strategy Officer .... Dr. Shawn NACCARATO
88 Director of Building Trades .... Mr. Tom AMERSHEK
18 Director of Services & Grounds .... Mr. Tim SENECAUT
19 Director of University Police .... Mr. Stu HITE
22 Director of Institutional Equity .... Ms. Lori DREILING
37 Director of Financial Aid .... Mr. Scott DONALDSON
41 Director Intercollegiate Athletics .... Mr. Jim JOHNSON
07 Director of Admissions .... Mr. Scott DONALDSON
36 Director Career Services .... Ms. Mindy E. CLONINGER
09 Director of Institutional Research .... Mr. Bill HOYT
96 Director of Purchasing .... Mr. Jim HUGHES
28 Senior Diversity Officer .... Ms. Deatrea ROSE
10 Controller .... Ms. Barbara J. WINTER
39 Director of University Housing .... Mr. Tom WESTHOFF
100 Chief of Staff .... Ms. Jaime DALTON
43 General Counsel .... Dr. Jamie BROOKSHER
30 Exec Director of Univ Development .... Ms. Becky MCDANIEL
114 Director of Budget .... Ms. Lauren WERNER
25 Chief Grants Administrator .... Ms. Cindy JOHNSON

Pratt Community College (B)

348 NE SR 61, Pratt KS 67124-8432
County: Pratt FICE Identification: 001938
Unit ID: 155715
Telephone: (620) 672-2700 Carnegie Class: Assoc/MT-VT-High Non
FAX Number: (620) 450-2283 Calendar System: Semester
URL: www.prattcc.edu
Established: 1938 Annual Undergrad Tuition & Fees (In-District): $3,780
Enrollment: 1,164 Coed
Affiliation or Control: State/Local IRS Status: 501(c)3
Highest Offering: Associate Degree
Accreditation: **HLC**, ACBSP

01 President .... Dr. Mike CALVERT
05 Vice President Instruction .... Ms. Monette DEPEW
10 Vice President Finance/Operations .... Mr. Kent ADAMS
84 Vice Pres Student Enroll Management .... Ms. Lisa MILLER
30 Exec Director of Inst Advancement .... Mr. Barry FISHER
41 Director of Athletics .... Mr. Tim SWARTZENDRUBER
07 Director of Admissions .... Ms. Sarah BINFORD
06 Registrar .... Ms. Caitlin MILLER
13 Chief Information Officer .... Mr. Jerry SANKO
37 Director of Financial Aid .... Ms. Rose FRAME
08 Dir Linda Hunt Memorial Library .... Mr. Frank STAHL
15 Director of Personnel .... Ms. Rita PINKALL
21 Controller .... Ms. Christy WRIGHT
18 Director of Buildings & Grounds .... Mr. Al WIESE
39 Director of Residence Life .... Mr. Charles KEEFER
04 Administrative Asst to President .... Ms. Donna MEIER PFEIFER
29 Director Alumni Relations .... Mr. Barry FISHER
108 Director of Planning & Assessment .... Ms. Monette DEPEW
09 Director of Institutional Research .... Ms. Amanda CORDES
26 Chief Public Relations/Marketing .... Ms. Audra ROGERS
36 Director Student Placement .... Ms. Amy JACKSON

Rasmussen University-Kansas City/Overland Park (C)

11600 College Boulevard, Suite 100,
Overland Park KS 66210
Telephone: (913) 491-7870 Identification: 770489
Accreditation: &**HLC**, ADNUR

† Regional accreditation carried under the parent institution in Saint Cloud, MN. The tuition figure is an average, actual tuition may vary.

Saint Paul School of Theology (D)

13720 Roe Avenue, Building C, Leawood KS 66224
County: Johnson FICE Identification: 002509
Unit ID: 179317
Telephone: (913) 253-5000 Carnegie Class: Spec-4-yr-Faith
FAX Number: (913) 253-5075 Calendar System: Semester
URL: www.spst.edu
Established: 1958 Annual Graduate Tuition & Fees: N/A
Enrollment: 101 Coed
Affiliation or Control: United Methodist IRS Status: 501(c)3
Highest Offering: Doctorate; No Undergraduates
Accreditation: **HLC**, THEOL

01 President .... Rev. Neil B. BLAIR
05 VP Academic Affairs/Dean .... Dr. Jeanne HOEFT
111 Vice President for Inst Advancement .... Mr. Jay SIMMONS
32 Associate Dean of Students .... Rev. Margaretta S. NARCISSE
15 Director of Human Resources .... Mr. Matthew MILLS
06 Registrar .... Ms. Michelle HATCHER
37 Dir of Financial Aid .... Ms. Michelle HATCHER
07 Director of Admissions .... Ms. Shannon HANCOCK
26 Director of Communications .... Mrs. Heather SNODGRASS
08 Librarian .... Mr. Richard LIANTONIO
10 CFO/COO .... Mr. Matthew MILLS

Salina Area Technical College (E)

2562 Centennial Road, Salina KS 67401
County: Saline FICE Identification: 005499
Unit ID: 155830
Telephone: (785) 309-3100 Carnegie Class: Assoc/HVT-High Non
FAX Number: (785) 309-3101 Calendar System: Semester
URL: www.salinatech.edu
Established: 1965 Annual Undergrad Tuition & Fees (In-District): $8,127
Enrollment: 697 Coed
Affiliation or Control: State/Local IRS Status: 501(c)3
Highest Offering: Associate Degree
Accreditation: **HLC**, DA

01 President .... Mr. Gregory A. NICHOLS
05 Vice Pres of Instruction .... Mr. Stanton GARTIN
11 Vice Pres of Administrative Service .... Mrs. Jamie PALENSKE
32 Vice Pres of Student Services .... Mrs. Jennifer CALLIS
09 Director of Inst Research/Registrar .... Mrs. Denise R. HOEFFNER
15 Human Resources Coordinator .... Mrs. Tamera WILCOX
18 Director of Maintenance .... Mr. Dale CASTILLO
102 Exec Dir of SATC Foundation .... Vacant
84 Director Enrollment Management .... Vacant
37 Student Financial Aid Specialist .... Mrs. Racheal GALVAN
06 Registrar .... Mrs. Paige AYLWARD

Seward County Community College (F)

1801 N Kansas Avenue, Liberal KS 67901-2054
County: Seward FICE Identification: 008228
Unit ID: 155858
Telephone: (620) 624-1951 Carnegie Class: Assoc/HVT-High Trad
FAX Number: (620) 417-1169 Calendar System: Semester
URL: www.sccc.edu
Established: 1967 Annual Undergrad Tuition & Fees (In-District): $3,648
Enrollment: 1,580 Coed
Affiliation or Control: State/Local IRS Status: 501(c)3
Highest Offering: Associate Degree
Accreditation: **HLC**, ADNUR, COARC, MLTAD, SURGT

01 Interim President .... Mr. Dennis SANDER
10 VP of Finance & Operations .... Mr. Dennis M. SANDER
05 Vice President of Academic Affairs .... Mr. Luke DOWELL
32 Vice President of Student Services .... Ms. Celeste DONOVAN
13 Chief Information Officer .... Mr. Louie S. LEMERT
06 Registrar .... Ms. Alaina M. RICE
26 Exec Dir of Marketing & PR .... Ms. Rachel C. COLEMAN
25 Exec Director of Grant Development .... Ms. Charity HORINEK
30 Chief Development Officer .... Mr. Kyle WOODROW
41 Director of Athletics .... Mr. Dan ARTAMENKO
04 Executive Assistant .... Ms. Karla MORALES
76 Dean of Allied Health .... Dr. Suzanne CAMPBELL
51 Dean Industrial Tech/Cont Educ .... Vacant
35 Dean of Students .... Ms. Annette HACKBARTH-ONSON
15 Director of Human Resources .... Vacant
09 Institutional Research/Data Analyst .... Ms. Teresa WEHMEIER
19 Security Supervisor/Asst DOF .... Mr. Wendall WEHMEIER
18 Director of Facilities .... Mr. Roger SCHEIB
39 Director of Student Living Center .... Ms. Jennifer L. MALIN
78 Director of Outreach .... Mr. Mike BAILEY
35 Dir of Student Life & Leadership .... Mr. Wade LYON
37 Director of Financial Aid .... Ms. Amy BRIDENSTINE
66 Director of Nursing .... Ms. Susan INGLAND
84 Director of Admissions .... Mr. Eric D. VOLDEN
50 Director of Business & Industry .... Mrs. Norma Jean DODGE
08 Director of Library Services .... Ms. Casandra NORIN
14 Network Administrator .... Mr. Doug BROWNE
40 Director of Bookstore .... Ms. Laci FURR
91 Systems Administrator .... Mr. Cecil STOLL
105 Website Specialist .... Mr. Craig DUSEK
07 Director of Admissions .... Mr. Eric VOLDEN
44 Assoc Director Annual Giving .... Ms. Sara THOMPSON

Southwestern College (G)

100 College Street, Winfield KS 67156-2499
County: Cowley FICE Identification: 001940
Unit ID: 155900
Telephone: (620) 229-6000 Carnegie Class: Masters/M
FAX Number: (620) 229-6224 Calendar System: Semester
URL: www.sckans.edu
Established: 1885 Annual Undergrad Tuition & Fees: $33,250
Enrollment: 1,413 Coed
Affiliation or Control: United Methodist IRS Status: 501(c)3
Highest Offering: Doctorate
Accreditation: **HLC**, CAEP, CAEPN, MUS

01 President .... Dr. Bradley J. ANDREWS
03 Executive Vice President .... Mr. Dean CLARK
05 VP Acad Affairs/Dean of the College .... Dr. Ross PETERSON-VEATCH
10 Vice President Finance .... Mr. Tony CROUCH
124 VP Student Retention & Success .... Dr. Dawn E. PLEAS
84 VP Enroll Mgmt Main Campus .... Mr. Adam JENKINS
45 Exec Dir Institute for Discipleship .... Dr. Stephen K. WILKE
111 Vice Pres Institutional Advancement .... Mr. Patrick WAGNER
26 Vice President Communications .... Ms. Kaydee RIGGS-JOHNSON
32 VP Student Life/Dean Students .... Mr. Dan FALK
29 Director Alumni Programs .... Ms. Jessica DIBBLE
08 Library Director .... Ms. Marjorie SNYDER
37 Director Financial Aid .... Ms. Brenda D. HICKS
06 Registrar .... Ms. Linda WEIPPERT
41 Director of Athletics .... Mr. Mike MCCOY
15 Director Human Resources .... Ms. Lonnie BOYD
04 Exec Asst to President .... Ms. Doreen FAST
42 Campus Minister .... Rev. Benjamin C. HANNE

Sterling College (H)

125 W Cooper Street, Sterling KS 67579-1533
County: Rice FICE Identification: 001945
Unit ID: 155937
Telephone: (620) 278-2173 Carnegie Class: Bac-Diverse
FAX Number: N/A Calendar System: 4/1/4
URL: www.sterling.edu
Established: 1887 Annual Undergrad Tuition & Fees: $27,300
Enrollment: 678 Coed
Affiliation or Control: Presbyterian IRS Status: 501(c)3
Highest Offering: Master's
Accreditation: **HLC**, CAATE

01 President .... Dr. Scott RICH
05 Vice President Academic Affairs .... Dr. Ken BROWN
111 Vice President for Inst Advancement .... Mr. David EARLE
32 Vice President Student Life .... Mr. Jason BRIAR
11 Vice Pres Admin/Inst Initiatives .... Mr. David LANDIS
07 Vice President Enrollment .... Ms. Mitzi SUHLER
41 Vice President of Athletics .... Mr. Scott DOWNING
10 CFO/Financial Services .... Ms. Michelle HALL
20 Assoc Vice Pres Academic Affairs .... Dr. Erin LAUDERMILK
04 Exec Assistant to the President .... Ms. Renee DODSON
41 Assoc VP Athletics/Facility Mgmt .... Mr. Justin MORRIS
26 Dir Marketing/Pres Communications .... Mr. Brad EVENSON
37 Asst Director of Financial Aid .... Ms. Sara HIATT
06 Registrar .... Ms. Kendra GRIZZLE
29 Director of Alumni .... Ms. Susie CARNEY
42 Chaplain/AVP Student Life .... Mr. Paul BRANDES
08 Library Director .... Ms. Laurel WATNEY
36 Director of Career Services .... Mr. Terry EHRESMAN
15 Director Human Resources/Title IX .... Ms. Angie PLETT
04 Administrative Asst to President .... Vacant
30 Director of Development .... Mr. Aaron WEBER

Tabor College (I)

400 S Jefferson Street, Hillsboro KS 67063-1753
County: Marion FICE Identification: 001946
Unit ID: 155973
Telephone: (620) 947-3121 Carnegie Class: Bac-Diverse
FAX Number: (620) 947-2607 Calendar System: 4/1/4
URL: www.tabor.edu
Established: 1908 Annual Undergrad Tuition & Fees: $32,100
Enrollment: 642 Coed
Affiliation or Control: Mennonite Brethren Church IRS Status: 501(c)3
Highest Offering: Master's
Accreditation: **HLC**, MUS, NURSE, SW

01 President .... Dr. David JANZEN
05 Exec VP of Academics & Compliance .... Dr. Frank JOHNSON
10 Vice President Business/CFO .... Dr. Michael JAMES
111 Vice President Advancement .... Mr. Ronald BRAUN
11 Exec VP of Operations .... Mr. Rusty ALLEN
32 Dean of Student Life .... Mr. Emir RUIZ-ESPARZA
06 Registrar .... Mr. Scott FRANZ
08 Director of Library Services .... Ms. Janet WILLIAMS
37 Assoc Director of Financial Aid .... Ms. Cathy CASTLE
29 Director Alumni Relations .... Mr. Rod HAMM
26 Director of Communications .... Vacant
18 Director Facilities/Physical Plant .... Mr. Terry ENS
121 Director Student Success .... Mrs. Erica KRUCKENBERG
09 Institutional Research .... Mr. David FABER
13 Director IT Infrastructure .... Mr. Chris GLANZER
14 Director of IT Operations .... Mr. Wayne KLIEWER
15 Personnel/Benefits Manager .... Ms. Misty SMITHSON
04 Admin Assistant to the President .... Mrs. Miriam KLIEWER
07 Dean of Enrollment Mgmt .... Mr. Grant MYERS
36 Director Student Placement .... Mrs. Sydney FOUNTAIN

University of Kansas Main Campus (J)

1450 Jayhawk Boulevard, Room 230,
Lawrence KS 66045-7518
County: Douglas FICE Identification: 001948
Unit ID: 155317
Telephone: (785) 864-3131 Carnegie Class: DU-Highest

FAX Number: (785) 864-4120 Calendar System: Semester
URL: www.ku.edu
Established: 1866 Annual Undergrad Tuition & Fees (In-State): $11,166
Enrollment: 26,744 Coed
Affiliation or Control: State IRS Status: 501(c)3
Highest Offering: Doctorate
Accreditation: HLC, ABAI, ART, CAEPN, CEA, CLPSY, COPSY, HSA, IPSY, JOUR, LAW, MPCAC, MUS, PH, PHAR, PLNG, SCPSY, SP, SPAA, SW

01 Chancellor ....Dr. Douglas A. GIROD
05 Provost/Exec Vice Chancellor ....Dr. Barbara BICHELMEYER
12 Exec Vice Chancellor - KUMC ....Dr. Robert SIMARI
26 Vice Chanc Pub Affairs/Econ Dev ....Dr. David COOK
46 Vice Chancellor Research ....Dr. Simon ATKINSON
100 Chief of Staff to Chancellor ....Ms. Julie N. MURRAY
43 General Counsel ....Mr. Brian WHITE
20 Vice Provost Faculty Development ....Dr. Christopher BROWN
10 CFO ....Mr. Jeffrey DEWITT
32 Vice Provost for Student Affairs ....Dr. Tammara DURHAM
15 Vice Provost for Administration ....Mr. Michael ROUNDS
28 Int Vice Prov Div/Equity/Inclusion ....Dr. D.A GRAHAM
84 Vice Provost Enrollment Management ....Dr. Matt MELVIN
13 Chief Information Officer ....Dr. Mary WALSH
104 Assoc VP International Affairs ....Dr. Charles BANKART
30 President Endowment Association ....Mr. Dale SEUFERLING
29 President Alumni Association ....Mr. Heath J. PETERSON
07 Director Admissions ....Ms. Lisa P. KRESS
21 Sr Dir Financial Analysis/Reporting ....Ms. Katrina M. YOAKUM
21 Vice Provost for Finance ....Mr. Jason HORNBERGER
06 University Registrar/Asst VP ....Ms. Tiffany ROBINSON
09 Chief Data Ofcr Analytics/Research ....Mr. Nick STEVENS
85 Director International Student Svcs ....Dr. Chuck OLCESE
38 Director Counseling/Psych Services ....Dr. Michael MAESTAS
88 Director Design & Construction Mgmt ....Mr. James E. MODIG
37 Director Financial Aid/Scholarships ....Ms. Angela KARLIN
36 Exec Director Career Center ....Mr. David GASTON
41 Director Intercollegiate Athletics ....Mr. Travis GOFF
18 Director Facilities Service ....Mr. Shawn HARDING
22 Director Inst Opportunity & Access ....Mr. Josh JONES
93 Interim Dir Multicultural Affairs ....Dr. Kevin JOSEPH
23 Medical Director Watkins Health ....Dr. Graig NICKEL
14 Dir Info Tech Business Operations ....Mr. Chris CROOK
39 Director Student Housing ....Ms. Sarah WATERS
86 Director State Relations ....Ms. Kelly WHITTEN
92 Director Honors Program ....Dr. Sarah CRAWFORD-PARKER
86 Assoc VC Federal Relations ....Mr. Jack CLINE
40 Director KU Bookstore ....Ms. Jen O'CONNOR
51 Exec Dir Continuing Education ....Ms. Sharon D. GRAHAM
25 Assoc Dir Contract Negotiations ....Ms. Lucille MARINO
63 Exec Dean School of Medicine ....Dr. Akinlolu OJO
12 Dean of Edwards Campus ....Dr. Stuart DAY
49 Interim Dean Liberal Arts/Science ....Dr. John COLOMBO
61 Dean of Law ....Mr. Stephen W. MAZZA
54 Dean of Engineering ....Dr. Arvin AGAH
48 Int Dean Architecture & Design ....Dr. Mahbub RASHID
50 Dean of Business ....Dr. L. Paige FIELDS
67 Dean of Pharmacy ....Dr. Ron E. RAGAN
60 Dean of Journalism ....Dr. Ann M. BRILL
53 Dean of Education ....Dr. Rick GINSBERG
64 Dean of Music ....Dr. Robert L. WALZEL, JR.
70 Dean of Social Welfare ....Dr. Michelle CARNEY
08 Dean Libraries ....Mr. Kevin L. SMITH
19 Director Security/Safety ....Vacant

† Medical Center and Main campus enrollments should be combined for the total institution enrollment.

University of Kansas Medical Center (A)

3901 Rainbow Boulevard, Kansas City KS 66160-0001
Telephone: (913) 588-5000 FICE Identification: 024579
Accreditation: &HLC, ANEST, AUD, CAHIIM, CAMPEP, COARC, DIETI, DMOLS, DMS, IPSY, MED, MIDWF, MT, NMT, NURSE, OT, PDPSY, PTA

† Enrollment at the Medical Center is included within the published enrollment for the University of Kansas Main Campus. Regional accreditation is carried under the parent institution in Lawrence, KS.

University of Saint Mary (B)

4100 S 4th Street, Leavenworth KS 66048-5082
County: Leavenworth FICE Identification: 001943
Unit ID: 155812
Telephone: (913) 682-5151 Carnegie Class: Masters/M
FAX Number: (913) 758-6140 Calendar System: Semester
URL: www.stmary.edu
Established: 1923 Annual Undergrad Tuition & Fees: $30,800
Enrollment: 1,229 Coed
Affiliation or Control: Roman Catholic IRS Status: 501(c)3
Highest Offering: Doctorate
Accreditation: HLC, CAATE, CAEP, CAEPN, CAHIIM, IACBE, NURSE, PTA

01 President ....Sr. Diane STEELE
05 Provost & Academic Vice President ....Dr. Michelle METZINGER
10 VP Finance & Administrative Svcs ....Ms. Nancy BRAMLETT
07 VP Admissions & Marketing ....Mr. John SHULTZ
111 VP for Advancement ....Mr. Matt ASTLEFORD
41 VP of Athletics ....Mr. Rob MILLER
32 VP for Student Life ....Mr. Bob SCHUCHARDT
20 Academic Dean ....Dr. Gwen LANDEVER
06 Registrar ....Ms. Maureen SCHUCHARDT
09 Institutional Research & Assessment ....Ms. Christine HAMILTON
26 Director of Marketing Operations ....Ms. Sara BELL
37 Director of Financial Aid ....Ms. Heidi REID
42 Campus Minister ....Vacant
112 Development Officer Planned Giving ....Ms. Jane LIEBERT
15 Director Human Resources ....Ms. Michelle CARMITCHEL
121 Director Keleher Learning Commons ....Ms. Ashley CREEK
21 Controller ....Ms. Nicole BIBLER
38 Campus Counselor ....Dr. Christina DUNN CARPENTER
18 Director of Plant Operations ....Vacant
40 Bookstore Manager ....Ms. Cynthia FORRESTER
13 Director of Information Services ....Mr. Marvin SOMMERFELD
04 Executive Administrative Assistant ....Ms. Sharron LUCAS
19 Public Safety Coordinator ....Ms. Adriana HABR
106 Educational Technologist ....Ms. Debra OLBERDING
88 Director of Partnership Dev and OPC ....Dr. Charlie MACKIE
29 Alumni Relations Manager ....Ms. Dannie HARRIS
44 Development Manager/Annual Giving ....Ms. Madeleine BRYCE

Washburn University (C)

1700 SW College Avenue, Topeka KS 66621-0001
County: Shawnee FICE Identification: 001949
Unit ID: 156082
Telephone: (785) 670-1010 Carnegie Class: DU-Mod
FAX Number: (785) 670-1089 Calendar System: Semester
URL: www.washburn.edu
Established: 1865 Annual Undergrad Tuition & Fees (In-District): $8,762
Enrollment: 5,880 Coed
Affiliation or Control: Local IRS Status: 501(c)3
Highest Offering: Doctorate
Accreditation: HLC, ART, CAEP, CAEPN, CAHIIM, CEA, COARC, DMS, LAW, MUS, NURSE, OTA, PTAA, RAD, RTT, SURGT, SW

01 President ....Dr. Jerry B. FARLEY
05 Vice Pres Academic Affairs ....Dr. JuliAnn MAZACHEK
10 Vice Pres Admin & Treasurer ....Mr. Chris KUWITZKY
32 Vice President for Student Life ....Dr. Eric GROSPITCH
04 Special Assistant to the President ....Ms. Cynthia HOLTHAUS
84 Exec Director Enrollment Management ....Dr. Richard W. LIEDTKE
43 University Legal Counsel ....Mr. Marc FRIED
35 Assoc Vice Pres of Student Life ....Mr. Joel BLUML
20 Assoc Vice Pres Acad Affairs ....Vacant
102 President WU Foundation ....Mr. Marshall MEEK
06 Registrar ....Ms. Stephanie LANNING
08 Dean of Libraries ....Dr. Alan BEARMAN
37 Director Student Financial Aid ....Mr. Andy FOGEL
07 Director of Admissions ....Mr. Joseph TINSLEY
15 Director of Human Resources ....Ms. Teresa LEE
13 CIO/Int Dir Info Systems & Services ....Mr. John HAVERTY
09 Director Strategic Analysis & Rep ....Ms. Christa SMITH
49 Dean College Arts/Sciences ....Dr. Laura STEPHENSON
88 Dean School Applied Studies ....Dr. Zach FRANK
61 Dean School of Law ....Dr. Carla PRATT
50 Dean School of Business ....Dr. David SOLLARS
66 Dean School of Nursing ....Dr. Jane CARPENTER
41 Director of Athletics ....Mr. Loren FERRE
22 Director Equal Opportunity ....Dr. Pam FOSTER
18 Director of Facility Services ....Mr. Eric JUST
23 Director Health Services ....Ms. Tiffany MCMANUS
29 Alumni Association Director ....Ms. Susie HOFFMANN
92 Dean Honors Program ....Dr. Kerry WYNN
39 Director Student Housing ....Ms. Molly PIERSON
40 Director Ichabod Shop ....Ms. Brielle BARRETT
35 Dir Student Involvement/Development ....Mr. Isaiah COLLIER
38 Director Student Counseling ....Ms. Crystal LEMING
26 Director of University Relations ....Mr. Patrick EARLY
36 Director Career Services ....Mr. Kent MCANALLY
19 Director of Police ....Mr. Chris ENOS
28 Dir of Diversity & Inclusion ....Ms. Danielle DEMPSEY-SWOPES
96 Director of Purchasing ....Ms. Sherry DRAPER

Wichita State University (D)

1845 N Fairmount, Wichita KS 67260-0001
County: Sedgwick FICE Identification: 001950
Unit ID: 156125
Telephone: (316) 978-3456 Carnegie Class: DU-Higher
FAX Number: (316) 978-3770 Calendar System: Semester
URL: www.wichita.edu
Established: 1895 Annual Undergrad Tuition & Fees (In-State): $8,433
Enrollment: 14,999 Coed
Affiliation or Control: State IRS Status: 501(c)3
Highest Offering: Doctorate
Accreditation: HLC, #ARCPA, ART, AUD, CAATE, CACREP, CAEP, CLPSY, COSMA, DANCE, DENT, DH, MT, MUS, NURSE, PTA, SP, SPAA, SW

01 President ....Dr. Richard D. MUMA
05 Provost ....Dr. Richard D. MUMA
10 VP Administration & Finance ....Mr. Werner M. GOLLING
32 VP Student Affairs ....Dr. Teri HALL
43 General Counsel ....Ms. Stacia BODEN
26 VP Strategic Communications ....Ms. Shelly COLEMAN-MARTINS
09 Chief Data Officer ....Dr. David WRIGHT
84 VP Enrollment Management ....Dr. Carolyn SHAW
20 Assoc VP Academic Affairs ....Dr. Linnea GLENMAYE
46 VP Research & Technology Transfer ....Dr. John S. TOMBLIN
88 Vice President for Diversity ....Dr. Marche FLEMING-RANDLE
49 Dean Liberal Arts & Sciences ....Dr. Andrew HIPPISLEY
50 Dean Barton School of Business ....Dr. Larisa GENIN
53 Dean Education ....Dr. Shirley LEFEVER-DAVIS
54 Dean Engineering ....Dr. Dennis LIVESAY
57 Dean Fine Arts ....Dr. Rodney E. MILLER
76 Interim Dean Health Professions ....Dr. Stephen ARNOLD
58 Dean Graduate School ....Dr. Coleen PUGH
08 Dean Libraries ....Ms. Kathy DOWNES
86 Exec Director Government Relations ....Mr. Andrew SCHLAPP
24 Dir Media Resources Center ....Mr. John JONES
102 CEO & President WSU Foundation ....Ms. Elizabeth H. KING
41 Director of Athletics ....Mr. Darron BOATRIGHT
15 Director Human Resources ....Ms. Judy ESPINOZA
114 Director Budgets ....Mr. David MILLER
06 Registrar ....Ms. Gina D. CRABTREE
07 Director Admissions ....Mr. Bobby GANDU
37 Director Financial Aid ....Ms. Sheelu M. SURENDER
38 Director Counseling & Testing ....Dr. Jessica PROVINES
18 Director Physical Plant ....Mr. Bob SMITH, JR.
45 Director of Facilities Planning ....Ms. Emily A. PATTERSON
19 Chief of University Police ....Mr. Rodney E. CLARK
23 Director Student Health Services ....Ms. Camille CHILDERS
39 Director Stdnt Housing & Resid Life ....Mr. Scott JENSEN
28 Director Diversity & Inclusion ....Ms. Alicia SANCHEZ
40 Manager Bookstore ....Mr. Kevin J. KONDA
21 Assoc VP Financial Operations ....Ms. Lois TATRO
96 Director of Purchasing ....Mr. Steven WHITE
29 Executive Director Alumni Assoc ....Ms. Courtney MARSHALL
106 Dir Online Education/E-learning ....Mr. Mark D. PORCARO
22 Title IX Coordinator ....Ms. Sara ZAFAR
105 Director Web Services ....Mr. Tim HART
111 Chief Devel/Advancement Officer ....Dr. Keith PICKUS
44 Director Annual/Planned Giving ....Mr. Michael LAMB
108 Director Institutional Assessment ....Ms. Kaye MONK-MORGAN

Wichita State University Campus of Applied Sciences and Technology (E)

4004 N Webb Road, Wichita KS 67226-8101
County: Sedgwick FICE Identification: 005498
Unit ID: 156107
Telephone: (316) 677-9400 Carnegie Class: Assoc/HVT-High Non
FAX Number: (316) 677-9510 Calendar System: Semester
URL: https://wsutech.edu/
Established: 1965 Annual Undergrad Tuition & Fees (In-District): $6,602
Enrollment: 4,606 Coed
Affiliation or Control: State/Local IRS Status: 501(c)3
Highest Offering: Associate Degree
Accreditation: HLC, DA, SURGT

01 President ....Dr. Sheree UTASH
05 Chief of Academic Affairs ....Mr. Scott LUCAS
10 Vice Pres Finance/Administration ....Ms. Marlo DOLEZAL
20 VP General Educ/Health Sciences ....Dr. Jennifer SEYMOUR
32 Vice President Student Services ....Mr. Justin PFEIFER
26 Exec Dir Strategic Communications ....Mr. Andy MCFAYDEN
13 Exec Dir Information Tech ....Mr. Randy ROEBUCK
15 Exec Director Human Resources ....Ms. Judy MOUNT
09 Exec Dir Institutional Research ....Ms. Kristen JOHNSTON

Wichita Technical Institute (F)

2051 South Meridian Avenue, Wichita KS 67213-1927
County: Sedgwick FICE Identification: 010503
Unit ID: 156134
Telephone: (316) 943-2241 Carnegie Class: Spec 2-yr-Tech
FAX Number: (316) 943-5438 Calendar System: Quarter
URL: www.wti.edu
Established: Annual Undergrad Tuition & Fees: N/A
Enrollment: 1,157 Coed
Affiliation or Control: Proprietary IRS Status: Proprietary
Highest Offering: Associate Degree
Accreditation: ACCSC

01 Campus Director ....Mr. Rod MOORE

KENTUCKY

Alice Lloyd College (G)

Purpose Road, Pippa Passes KY 41844-9703
County: Knott FICE Identification: 001951
Unit ID: 156189
Telephone: (606) 368-2101 Carnegie Class: Bac-Diverse
FAX Number: (606) 368-6212 Calendar System: Semester
URL: www.alc.edu
Established: 1923 Annual Undergrad Tuition & Fees: $14,230
Enrollment: 569 Coed
Affiliation or Control: Independent Non-Profit IRS Status: 501(c)3
Highest Offering: Baccalaureate
Accreditation: SC

01 President ....Dr. Joe A. STEPP
03 Executive Vice President ....Dr. Jim STEPP
05 Vice President Academic Affairs ....Dr. Claude CRUM
10 Vice President of Business Affairs ....Mr. David JOHNSON
32 Dean of Students & Community Life ....Mr. Scott CORNETT
07 Director of Admissions ....Mrs. Tori NAIRN
06 Registrar ....Ms. Dana DOTSON
08 Director of Library ....Ms. Jeannie GALLOWAY
37 Director of Financial Aid ....Mr. Joseph LITTLE
88 Director of Student Work Program ....Mr. Kerry RATLIFF
53 Director of Teacher Education ....Mrs. Katrina SLONE
18 Director of Physical Plant ....Mr. Ryan GIBSON
39 Director of Student Housing ....Mr. John MILLS

29 Director of Alumni Relations ....Mrs. Teresa GRENDER
35 Director of Student Activities ....Ms. Christine STUMBO
26 Dir of Marketing & Communications ....Ms. Jennifer HALL
09 Director of Institutional Research ....Mrs. Katrina SLONE
30 Director of Development ....Mrs. Allison SOUTHARD
102 Dir Foundation/Corporate Relations ....Ms. Priscilla FRALEY
41 Athletic Director ....Mr. David HATFIELD
15 Chief Human Resources Officer ....Mr. Larry ADAMS

† Cost of tuition is guaranteed for students from 108 county territories.

American National University (A)

50 National College Boulevard, Pikeville KY 41502
County: Pike FICE Identification: 010489
Unit ID: 157021
Telephone: (606) 478-7200 Carnegie Class: Bac/Assoc-Assoc Dom
FAX Number: (606) 437-4952 Calendar System: Quarter
URL: www.an.edu
Established: 1941 Annual Undergrad Tuition & Fees: $11,136
Enrollment: 210 Coed
Affiliation or Control: Proprietary IRS Status: Proprietary
Highest Offering: Associate Degree
Accreditation: ABHES

01 Campus Director ....Mr. James C. HESS

American National University (B)

4205 Dixie Highway, Louisville KY 40216
Telephone: (502) 447-7634 Identification: 666443
Accreditation: ABHES, CAHIIM

† Branch campus of American National University, Pikeville, KY.

Asbury Theological Seminary (C)

204 N Lexington Avenue, Wilmore KY 40390-1199
County: Jessamine FICE Identification: 001953
Unit ID: 156222
Telephone: (859) 858-3581 Carnegie Class: Spec-4-yr-Faith
FAX Number: N/A Calendar System: 4/1/4
URL: www.asburyseminary.edu
Established: 1923 Annual Graduate Tuition & Fees: N/A
Enrollment: 1,755 Coed
Affiliation or Control: Independent Non-Profit IRS Status: 501(c)3
Highest Offering: Doctorate; No Undergraduates
Accreditation: SC, CACREP, THEOL

01 President ....Dr. Timothy C. TENNENT
05 Provost/SVP of Academic Affairs ....Dr. Gregg OKESSON
10 Vice Pres Finance/Admin/CFO ....Mr. Bryan P. BLANKENSHIP
111 Vice President of Advancement ....Mr. Jay MANSUR
88 Vice President Formation ....Ms. Donna COVINGTON
84 Vice Pres Enrollment Management ....Mr. Kevin BISH
20 Associate Provost ....Dr. Christine L. JOHNSON
12 Assoc VP of Florida Campus ....Mr. Steve GOBER
06 Registrar ....Vacant
07 Director of Admissions ....Mr. Randy OZAN
37 Director of Student Financial Aid ....Ms. Rachael TUBB
18 Director of Facilities & Security ....Mr. Brian U'REN
09 Dir Inst Effectiveness/Assessment ....Dr. Alexandra H. ANDERSON
15 Director of Human Resources ....Mrs. Barbara ANTROBUS
29 Director Alumni/Church Relations ....Ms. Tammy CESSNA
73 Dean School of Theology & Formation ......Dr. James THOBABEN
88 Dean ESJ School World of Missions ....Dr. Gregg OKESSON
88 Dean School Biblical Interpretation ....Dr. David BAUER
73 Dean Beeson Sch Practical Theology ....Dr. Tom TUMBLIN
46 Dean Advanced Research Programs ....Dr. Lalsangkima PACHUAU
04 Executive Asst to President ....Ms. Angela CLOYD
08 Dean Library Info & Tech Services ....Dr. Paul A. TIPPEY

Asbury University (D)

1 Macklem Drive, Wilmore KY 40390-1198
County: Jessamine FICE Identification: 001952
Unit ID: 156213
Telephone: (859) 858-3511 Carnegie Class: Masters/S
FAX Number: (859) 858-3921 Calendar System: Semester
URL: www.asbury.edu
Established: 1890 Annual Undergrad Tuition & Fees: $32,028
Enrollment: 1,741 Coed
Affiliation or Control: Independent Non-Profit IRS Status: 501(c)3
Highest Offering: Beyond Master's But Less Than Doctorate
Accreditation: SC, CAEPN, MUS, SW

01 President ....Dr. Kevin J. BROWN
05 Provost ....Dr. Timothy T. WOOSTER
10 VP Business Affairs & Treasurer ....Mr. Glenn R. HAMILTON
32 VP Student Life & Dean of Students ....Dr. Sarah T. BALDWIN
111 VP Inst Advance/Strat Partnerships ....Dr. Mark J. TROYER
41 VP Athletics & Strategic Comms ....Mr. Mark H. WHITWORTH
20 Vice Provost ....Dr. Timothy G. CAMPBELL
50 Dean Howard Dayton Sch Business ....Dr. Michael J. KANE
60 Dean of School of Comm Arts ....Dr. James R. OWENS
53 Dean School of Education ....Dr. Sharon G. BIXLER
81 Dean School Science/Health & Math ....Dr. Vins H. SUTLIVE
49 Dean College of Arts & Sciences ....Dr. Stephen K. CLEMENTS
07 Director of Admissions ....Mr. Brandon J. COMBS
08 Director of Library Services ....Mr. Jared L. PORTER
09 AVP Inst Research & Effectiveness ....Dr. Paul STEPHENS
21 AVP Business Affairs ....Mr. Gary E. HOWARD
13 AVP Information Tech Svcs/CIO ....Mr. Paul J. DUPREE
15 Director of HR/Risk Mgt ....Mr. Gregory R. MCGEE
19 Director of Safety & Security ....Mr. David P. HAY
18 Director of Physical Plant ....Mr. Eric C. MCMILLION
37 Director of Financial Aid ....Mr. Ron M. ANDERSON
42 Assoc Dean for Spiritual Life ....Rev. Greg K. HASELOFF
85 AVP Intercultural Affairs ....Rev. Esther D. JADHAV
39 Assoc Dean for Community Life ....Mr. Joe W. BRUNER
36 Assoc Dean of Career & Calling ....Ms. Michelle B. KRATZER
38 Assoc Dean of Wholeness & Wellness ......Mr. Kevin M. BELLEW
112 Senior Planned Giving Officer ....Rev. Stuart A. SMITH
29 Director of Alumni Relations ....Ms. Lisa D. HARPER
26 Director Strategic Communications ....Mrs. Jennifer J. MCCHORD
06 Registrar ....Mrs. Sheryl VOIGTS
40 Manager of Bookstore ....Mr. C. David TRAMMELL
23 Director Student Health Services ....Mrs. Heidi L. SUNNY
04 Exec Assistant to the President ....Ms. Michelle C. BUTCHER

ATA College (E)

10200 Linn Station Road, Suite 125, Louisville KY 40223
County: Jefferson FICE Identification: 040383
Unit ID: 447935
Telephone: (502) 371-8383 Carnegie Class: Spec 2-yr-Health
FAX Number: (502) 371-8598 Calendar System: Quarter
URL: www.ata.edu
Established: 1994 Annual Undergrad Tuition & Fees: $13,120
Enrollment: 298 Coed
Affiliation or Control: Proprietary IRS Status: Proprietary
Highest Offering: Associate Degree
Accreditation: ABHES

01 President/CEO ....Mr. Donald A. JONES

Baptist Seminary of Kentucky (F)

400 E. College Street, Box 358, Georgetown KY 40324
County: Scott Identification: 667211
Telephone: (502) 863-8300 Carnegie Class: Not Classified
FAX Number: (502) 863-8300 Calendar System: Semester
URL: www.bsk.edu
Established: 2002 Annual Graduate Tuition & Fees: N/A
Enrollment: N/A Coed
Affiliation or Control: Independent Non-Profit IRS Status: 501(c)3
Highest Offering: Master's; No Undergraduates
Accreditation: THEOL

01 President ....Dr. David CASSADY
05 Academic Dean ....Dr. Dalen C. JACKSON
07 Director of Admissions ....Ms. Abby SIZEMORE
06 Registrar/Academic Coordinator ....Ms. Jessalynn CORNETT

Beckfield College (G)

16 Spiral Drive, Florence KY 41042-4866
County: Boone FICE Identification: 024911
Unit ID: 247065
Telephone: (859) 371-9393 Carnegie Class: Bac/Assoc-Mixed
FAX Number: (859) 371-5096 Calendar System: Quarter
URL: www.beckfield.edu
Established: 1984 Annual Undergrad Tuition & Fees: $13,295
Enrollment: 748 Coed
Affiliation or Control: Proprietary IRS Status: Proprietary
Highest Offering: Baccalaureate
Accreditation: ABHES, NURSE

01 Chief Executive Officer/CFO ....Ms. Diane G. WOLFER
05 Vice Pres Education & Accreditation ....Mr. Lee FOLEY
37 Director Student Financial Services ....Mr. Jeff HUBER
13 Vice Pres Information Technology ....Mr. Charles WILSON
07 Director Admissions ....Mr. Jeff BAKER
36 Director Career Services ....Ms. Karen SHELDON
22 Director of Compliance ....Mr. Lee FOLEY
06 Registrar ....Ms. Jocelyn ROY
08 Director of Library Services ....Ms. Gayle ECABERT
50 Dean of Business/Technology ....Dr. Erica OKERE
66 Dean of Nursing ....Dr. Deborah SMITH-CLAY
76 Dean of Allied Health ....Ms. Kate BEHAN
97 Dean of General Education ....Ms. Mindy HODGES
88 Dean of Criminal Justice ....Ms. Brandy EXELER

Bellarmine University (H)

2001 Newburg Road, Louisville KY 40205-0671
County: Jefferson FICE Identification: 001954
Unit ID: 156286
Telephone: (502) 272-8000 Carnegie Class: DU-Mod
FAX Number: (502) 272-8033 Calendar System: Semester
URL: www.bellarmine.edu
Established: 1950 Annual Undergrad Tuition & Fees: $43,470
Enrollment: 3,293 Coed
Affiliation or Control: Independent Non-Profit IRS Status: 501(c)3
Highest Offering: Doctorate
Accreditation: SC, CAATE, CAEP, COARC, MT, NURSE, PTA, RTT

01 President ....Dr. Susan M. DONOVAN
03 Senior Vice President ....Dr. Sean J. RYAN
05 Provost/Vice Pres Academic Affairs ....Dr. Paul GORE
20 Vice Provost ....Dr. Mark WIEGAND
20 Vice Provost Faculty Development ....Dr. Anne BUCALOS
10 Vice President for Admin & Finance ....Vacant
32 Vice President for Student Affairs ....Dr. Helen G. RYAN
30 VP for Dev & Alumni Relations ....Mr. Glenn F. KOSSE
84 VP for Enrollment/Marketing & Comm ....Dr. Mike MARSHALL
04 Administrative Asst to President ....Ms. Lucy BURNS
50 Dean School of Business ....Dr. Natasha VIJAY MUNSHI
53 Dean Annsley Frazier Thornton Educ ....Dr. Elizabeth DINKINS
49 Dean Bellarmine College ....Dr. Mary HUFF
66 Dean Nursing & Clinical Sciences ....Dr. Nancy YORK
75 Dean Movement & Rehabilitation Sci ....Dr. Tony BROSKY
15 Chief Human Resources Officer ....Ms. Lynn M. BYNUM
21 Asst VP Business Affairs ....Ms. Denise BROWN-CORNELIUS
110 Associate VP Development ....Ms. Tina KAUFFMAN
35 Associate VP Student Affairs ....Mr. Patrick ENGLERT
85 Exec Dir Stdy Abroad & Intl Learn ....Dr. Gabriele W. BOSLEY
35 Dean of Students ....Dr. Sean MCGREEVEY
92 Director Honors Program ....Dr. Jonathan W. BLANDFORD
41 Athletic Director ....Mr. Scott P. WIEGANDT
18 Asst VP Facilities Management ....Mr. Jeffrey DEAN
07 Dean of Admission ....Mr. Timothy A. STURGEON
123 Dean of Graduate Admission ....Dr. Sara Y. PETTINGILL
08 Director of the Library ....Dr. John K. STEMMER
19 Director of Safety & Security ....Ms. Debbie FOX
06 Registrar ....Ms. Ann E. OLSEN
96 Purchasing Manager ....Mr. Patrick COONS
42 Director Campus Ministry ....Ms. Laura KLINE
39 Assoc Dean Stdnt/Dir Residence Life ....Dr. Leslie MAXIE
76 Vice Prov Col of Health Professions ....Dr. Mark WIEGAND
13 Chief Information Officer ....Mr. Eric SATTERLY
28 Chief Div/Equity/Inclusion Ofcr ...Dr. Donald (DJ) MITCHELL, JR.
37 Director Student Financial Aid ....Ms. April TRETTER
36 Director of Career Development ....Dr. Lilly MASSA-MCKINLEY
29 Assistant VP for Alumni Relations ....Mr. Peter W. KREMER
26 Director of Media Relations ....Mr. Jason A. CISSELL
38 Director of Counseling Center ....Dr. Gary PETIPRIN
09 Director of Institutional Research ....Mr. Drew THIEMANN
45 Vice Provost for Inst Effectiveness ....Dr. James BRESLIN

Berea College (I)

101 Chestnut Street, Berea KY 40404-0003
County: Madison FICE Identification: 001955
Unit ID: 156295
Telephone: (859) 985-3000 Carnegie Class: Bac-A&S
FAX Number: N/A Calendar System: Semester
URL: www.berea.edu
Established: 1855 Annual Undergrad Tuition & Fees: $45,092
Enrollment: 1,432 Coed
Affiliation or Control: Independent Non-Profit IRS Status: 501(c)3
Highest Offering: Baccalaureate
Accreditation: SC, CAEP, NURSE

01 President ....Dr. Lyle D. ROELOFS
10 Vice President Finance ....Mr. Jeff S. AMBURGEY
29 VP Alumni & College Relations ....Mr. Chad BERRY
32 VP Labor and Student Life ....Dr. Channell BARBOUR
11 VP Operations and Sustainability ....Mr. Derrick SINGLETON
05 Provost ....Dr. Scott STEELE
45 VP Strategic Initiatives ....Ms. Teri THOMPSON
20 Dean of the Faculty ....Dr. Matthew SADERHOLM
26 Assoc VP of Int Marketing/Comm ....Ms. Kim BROWN
30 AVP Development Operations ....Ms. Candis ARTHUR
35 Asst Vice Pres for Student Life ....Mr. Gus GERASSIMIDES
37 Dir of Student Financial Aid Svcs ....Ms. Theresa LOWDER
38 Dir Counseling/Psychological Svcs ....Ms. Sue REIMONDO
110 Dir Campaign/Strategic Initiatives ....Ms. Joanne SINGH
112 Executive Dir Major & Planned Gifts ......Ms. Teresa KASH DAVIS
108 Director of Academic Assessment ....Dr. Robert SMITH
13 Chief Information Officer ....Mr. Phillip LOGSDON
07 AVP of Admissions Operations ....Mr. Luke HODSON
88 Associate VP of Alumni Relations ....Ms. Jackie COLLIER
15 Associate VP of Human Resources ....Mr. Steve LAWSON
18 Assoc Director of Facilities Mgmt ....Mr. Jeff REED
88 Director of Appalachian Center ....Dr. Chris GREEN
09 Director of Inst Rsrch/Assessment ....Ms. Judith WECKMAN
27 Dir Publications/Media Relations ....Ms. Abbie DARST
08 Director of Library Services ....Mr. Calvin GROSS
41 Director of Athletics ....Mr. Ryan HESS
42 Director Campus Christian Center .... Rev. Loretta REYNOLDS
43 General Counsel ....Mr. Judge WILSON
19 Director of Public Safety ....Mr. V. Lavoyed HUDGINS
28 Director Black Cultural Center ....Vacant
88 Dean of Labor ....Ms. Sylvia ASANTE
85 Director International Center ....Dr. Richard CAHILL
40 Retail Manager College Store ....Ms. Sarah CAUDILL
96 Purchasing Manager ....Ms. Aurelia BRANDENBURG
88 Director Ctr Teaching/Learning ...Ms. Leslie ORTQUIST-AHRENS
88 Director Woodson Center ....Dr. Jessica KLANDERUD
88 Director of CELTS ....Ms. Ashley COCHRANE
23 Director of Health and Wellness ....Ms. Jill GURTATOWSKI
88 Director of Internships ....Ms. Esther LIVINGSTON
103 Director of Career Development ....Ms. Amanda TUDOR
104 Education Abroad Advisor ....Ms. Ann BUTWELL
06 Registrar ....Ms. Judy GINTER
100 Executive Assistant to President ....Ms. Judy MOTT
105 Director Web Design/Development ....Mr. Charlie CAMPBELL
04 Executive Assistant to President ....Ms. Sherry THIELE

Brescia University (J)

717 Frederica Street, Owensboro KY 42301-3023
County: Daviess FICE Identification: 001958
Unit ID: 156356
Telephone: (270) 685-3131 Carnegie Class: Bac-Diverse
FAX Number: (270) 686-6422 Calendar System: Semester
URL: www.brescia.edu

Established: 1950 Annual Undergrad Tuition & Fees: $25,100
Enrollment: 986 Coed
Affiliation or Control: Roman Catholic IRS Status: 501(c)3
Highest Offering: Master's
Accreditation: SC, @SP, SW

01 President Rev. Larry HOSTETTER
05 Vice President & Academic Dean Mr. Jeffrey BARNETTE
10 Sr Vice President Business/Finance Mr. Dale CECIL
84 Vice President of Enrollment Mr. Christopher HOUK
111 Int VP Institutional Advancement Ms. Sydney WARREN
32 Vice Pres Stdnt Affs/Dean Students Mr. Joshua R. CLARY
39 Director Residence Life Mr. Issac DUNCAN
35 Director Stdnts Act/Leadership Dev Ms. Patricia LOVETT
06 Registrar Sr. Helena FISCHER, OSU
106 Director of Operations BU Online Ms. Shanda LARUE
38 Director of Counseling Center Ms. Eva G. ATKINSON
08 Director of Library Services Sr. Judith N. RINEY, OSU
88 Director of UCTL Dr. Anna KUTHY
15 Director of Human Resources Ms. Tammy S. KELLER
13 Director of Information Technology Mr. Chris FORD
18 Director of Physical Plant Mr. Mike WARD
37 Director of Financial Aid Ms. Kristi EIDSON
41 Director of Athletics Mr. Brian SKORTZ
26 Director of Public Relations Ms. Rachel WHELAN
29 Director of Alumni & Donor Rels Mr. Jake DAVIS
44 Director of Annual Giving Ms. Lauren OSOWICZ
112 Director of Major Gifts Ms. Sydney WARREN
09 Director of Institutional Research Ms. Stephanie CLARY
58 Director of Graduate Program-MBA Dr. Sandra O. OBILADE
42 Director of Campus Ministry Sr. Pam MUELLER, OSU
07 Director of Admissions Ms. Christy ROHNER
21 Asst Director Business & Finance Ms. Nancy W. REYNOLDS
36 Director of Career Services Ms. Morgan RUSSELBURG
20 Associate Academic Dean Ms. Amanda MORRIS
40 Bookstore Manager Ms. Megan MCCARTHY
100 Chief of Staff Dr. Lauren MCCRARY

Campbellsville University (A)

1 Universty Drive, Campbellsville KY 42718-2799
County: Taylor FICE Identification: 001959
Unit ID: 156365
Telephone: (270) 789-5000 Carnegie Class: Masters/L
FAX Number: (270) 789-5050 Calendar System: Semester
URL: www.campbellsville.edu
Established: 1906 Annual Undergrad Tuition & Fees: $25,400
Enrollment: 12,771 Coed
Affiliation or Control: Baptist IRS Status: 501(c)3
Highest Offering: Doctorate
Accreditation: SC, CAEP, IACBE, MFCD, MUS, NUR, SW

01 Interim President Dr. H. Keith SPEARS
11 SVP for Operations/Administration Mr. Otto TENNANT
05 Provost and VP for Academic Affairs Dr. Donna HEDGEPATH
30 Vice President for Development Dr. Benji KELLY
84 VP for Enrollment Dr. Shane GARRISON
32 VP for Student Svcs/Athletics Mr. Rusty HOLLINGSWORTH
20 Associate Academic Officer Dr. Jeanette PARKER
10 Vice President for Finance Mr. Tim JUDD
09 Director of Institutional Research Mrs. Anna PAVY
38 Director of Student Counseling Ms. Erin JARRETT
92 Director of Honors Program Dr. Craig L. ROGERS
40 Director of Bookstore Vacant
42 Director of Campus Ministries Mr. Jamie LAWRENCE
13 Director of Computing/Communication Mr. Eric SMITH
37 Director of Financial Aid Mrs. Robyn SOLLBERGER
29 Director of Alumni Relations Mrs. Ashley FOX
08 Director of Library Services Mrs. Kay ALSTON
15 Director of Personnel Services Mr. Jason LAWSON
18 Director of Maintenance Mr. Steve MORRIS
26 Director of News Information Mrs. Joan C. MCKINNEY
06 Registrar Mrs. Rita A. CREASON
04 Director for Presidential Operation Mrs. Kellie VAUGHN
96 Director of Purchasing Mrs. Lisa FERGUSON
88 Director of Custodial Services Mr. Bob STOTTS
19 Director Security/Safety Mr. Kyle DAVIS
35 Dean of Students Mr. Rusty WATKINS
39 Director of Residence Life Mr. Elijah COFFEY
86 Director Government Relations Dr. John CHOWNING
28 Director of Diversity Dr. Carey RUIZ
41 Athletic Director Mr. Jim HARDY

Centre College (B)

600 W Walnut Street, Danville KY 40422-1394
County: Boyle FICE Identification: 001961
Unit ID: 156408
Telephone: (859) 238-5200 Carnegie Class: Bac-A&S
FAX Number: (859) 238-6977 Calendar System: Other
URL: www.centre.edu
Established: 1819 Annual Undergrad Tuition & Fees: $44,300
Enrollment: 1,333 Coed
Affiliation or Control: Independent Non-Profit IRS Status: 501(c)3
Highest Offering: Baccalaureate
Accreditation: SC

01 President Dr. Milton C. MORELAND
05 Vice Pres Acad Affs/Dean of College Dr. Ellen S. GOLDEY
10 Vice Pres/CFO & Treasurer Mr. Brian G. HUTZLEY
32 Vice Pres for Student Life Ms. Barbara LOMONACO
30 VP Devel/Alumni Engagement Ms. Kelly KNETSCHE
43 VP for Legal Affairs/Gift Planning Mr. James P. LEAHEY
15 VP for Human Resources/Admin Svcs Mrs. Kay L. DRAKE
53 Assoc Professor/Chair Education Dr. Sarah A. MURRAY
28 Assoc VP Diversity/Sp Asst to Pres Dr. Andrea C. ABRAMS
07 Dean of Admissions & Financial Aid Mr. Robert M. NESMITH
20 Associate Dean of the College Dr. Alex M. MCALLISTER
38 Director of Counseling Services Ms. Ann E. GOODWIN
104 Director of Global Citizenship Dr. Lori L. HARTMANN
08 Director of Library Services Ms. Carolyn A. FREY
04 Exec Assistant to the President Ms. Yvonne Y. MORLEY
37 Assoc Dean/Dir of Financial Aid Mr. Kevin D. LAMB
06 Registrar Mr. Thomas E. MANUEL
26 Chief Communications Officer Dr. Michael P. STRYSICK
36 Dir Ctr for Career/Professional Dev Ms. Joy ASHER
39 Director Student Life & Housing Ms. Ann S. YOUNG
41 Director of Athletics & Recreation Mr. W. Bradley FIELDS
19 Co-Director of Public Safety Mr. Kevin S. MILBY
19 Co-Director of Public Safety Mr. Gary D. BUGG
09 Director of Institutional Research Dr. Brian CUSATO
13 Chief Information Officer Mr. Andrew J. RYAN
24 Int Dir Ctr for Teaching/Learning Dr. Robyn E. CUTRIGHT
18 Director of Facilities Management Mr. D. Wayne KING
21 Controller Mr. R. Scott OWENS
42 College Chaplain Dr. Richard D. AXTELL
96 Asst Dir Procurement/Capital Proj Ms. Ann T. SMITH
29 Dir of Alumni & Family Engagement Ms. Megan H. MILBY
57 Director Norton Center for Arts Mr. Steven A. HOFFMAN
102 Dir Foundation/Corporate Relations Ms. Elizabeth E. GRAVES

Clear Creek Baptist Bible College (C)

300 Clear Creek Road, Pineville KY 40977-9754
County: Bell FICE Identification: 025356
Unit ID: 156417
Telephone: (606) 337-3196 Carnegie Class: Spec-4-yr-Faith
FAX Number: (606) 337-2372 Calendar System: Semester
URL: www.ccbbc.edu
Established: 1926 Annual Undergrad Tuition & Fees: $9,870
Enrollment: 131 Coed
Affiliation or Control: Southern Baptist IRS Status: 501(c)3
Highest Offering: Master's
Accreditation: SC, BI

01 President Dr. Donnie S. FOX
05 Academic Dean Dr. Jay SULFRIDGE
10 Director of Business Affairs Ms. Monique BAILEY
11 Administrative Dean Mr. Jeremy ANDERSON
111 Dean of Institutional Advancement Mr. Matthew BLACK
08 Director of Library Svcs Ms. Andrea SCHMIDT
42 Director Christian Service Rev. Joshua SMITH
18 Director of Physical Plant Mr. Allen SANDERS
37 Director Financial Aid Mr. Eddie BARKER
06 Registrar Mr. Jacob YATES
07 Director of Admissions Mr. Douglas SAUNDERS
26 Director of College Relations Mr. Michael DELAND
13 Dir of Information Technologies Mr. Eric GREENE
56 Coord of Distance Education Mr. David DOWELL

Daymar College-Bowling Green (D)

2421 Fitzgerald Industrial Drive,
Bowling Green KY 42101-4071
Telephone: (270) 843-6750 Identification: 666439
Accreditation: ACCSC

† Branch campus of Daymar College, Nashville, TN.

Eastern Kentucky University (E)

521 Lancaster Avenue, Richmond KY 40475-3102
County: Madison FICE Identification: 001963
Unit ID: 156620
Telephone: (859) 622-1000 Carnegie Class: Masters/L
FAX Number: (859) 622-1020 Calendar System: Semester
URL: www.eku.edu
Established: 1906 Annual Undergrad Tuition & Fees (In-State): $9,876
Enrollment: 14,465 Coed
Affiliation or Control: State IRS Status: 501(c)3
Highest Offering: Doctorate
Accreditation: SC, ADNUR, CAATE, CACREP, CAEP, CAEPN, CAHIIM, CAPRT, CLPSY, CONST, DIETD, EMT, FEPAC, IFSAC, MT, MUS, NAIT, NURSE, OT, PH, SP, SPAA, SW

01 President Dr. David MCFADDIN
05 Provost/Exec VP Acad Affairs Dr. Jerry POGATSHNIK
10 Senior VP of Finance & Admin Mr. Barry POYNTER
121 SVP Student Success/Engagement/Opp Dr. Tanlee WASSON
30 VP Development Ms. Betina GARDNER
32 VP Student Life/Chief Diversity Dr. Dannie MOORE
84 Asst VP Enrollment Mgmt Ms. Elizabeth BALLOU
124 Asst VP Retention & Graduation Dr. Gill HUNTER
21 AVP for Finance & Controller Mr. Brad COMPTON
86 AVP Govt & Cmty Relations Mr. Ethan WITT
32 Dean of Students Dr. Lara VANCE
26 Asst VP Communications & Brand Mgmt Mr. Doug CORNETT
26 Chief External Affairs Officer Ms. Kristi MIDDLETON
114 Exec Dir Budget/Fin Plng & Effect Mr. Ryan GREEN
49 Dean Letters/Arts/Social Sciences Dr. Sara ZEIGLER
76 Interim Dean Health Sciences Dr. Colleen SCHNECK
81 Dean Science Dr. Tom OTIENO
50 Dean Business Vacant
53 Dean Education Dr. Sherry POWERS
88 Interim Dean Justice & Safety Dr. Derek PAULSEN
43 University Counsel Ms. Dana FOHL
19 Chief of Police Mr. Brian MULLINS
08 Dean of Libraries Ms. Julie GEORGE
06 Registrar Ms. Shannon TIPTON
88 Dir Corporate Educ Partnerships Mr. Benton SHIREY
07 Senior Director of Admissions Dr. Jill PAGE
25 Director Sponsored Programs Mr. Gus BENSON
92 Exec Director Honors Program Dr. David COLEMAN
108 Sr Dir Inst Effectiveness/Research Dr. Bethany MILLER
46 AVP Research & Econ Development Dr. Tom MARTIN
85 Director International Student Svcs Vacant
38 Director Counseling Center Dr. Melissa BARTSCH
88 Int Sr Director Student Conduct Ms. Emily DAVIS
39 Exec Dir Housing/Residence Life Mr. Robert BROWN
37 Dir Student Financial Assistance Vacant
23 Health Services Manager Dr. Brenda CAUDILL
15 Chief Human Resources Officer Mr. John DIXON
13 Chief Information Officer Mr. Jeff WHITAKER
41 VP for Athletics & Campus Rec Mr. Matt ROAN
96 Director University Procurement Ms. Andrea CASHELL
04 Admin Asst to the President Ms. Cassie MALICK
100 Exec Dir Office of the President Dr. Ryan WILSON
58 Dean Graduate Studies Dr. Ryan BAGGETT
20 Associate Provost Dr. Jennifer WIES
29 Assoc VP Dev & Alum Engagement Mr. Dan MCBRIDE
19 AVP Facilities & Safety Mr. Bryan MAKINEN
116 Director of Internal Audit Ms. Beth BALLARD
103 Dir Workforce Dev & Cmty Engage Ms. Susan CORNELIUS
22 Director Inst Equity/Title IX Coord Ms. Lindsey CARTER
106 Exec Dir e-Campus Learning Mr. Tim MATTHEWS

Frontier Nursing University (F)

2050, Lexington Road KY 40383
County: Woodford FICE Identification: 030070
Unit ID: 156727
Telephone: (859) 251-4700 Carnegie Class: Spec-4-yr-Other Health
FAX Number: N/A Calendar System: Quarter
URL: www.frontier.edu
Established: 1939 Annual Graduate Tuition & Fees: N/A
Enrollment: 2,436 Coed
Affiliation or Control: Independent Non-Profit IRS Status: 501(c)3
Highest Offering: Doctorate; No Undergraduates
Accreditation: SC, MIDWF, NUR

01 President Dr. Susan STONE
05 Associate Dean of Academic Affairs Dr. Rachel MACK
66 Dean of Nursing Dr. Joan SLAGER
37 Associate Director of Financial Aid Mr. Andrew DEZARN
07 Director of Admissions Ms. Rainie BOGGS

Galen College of Nursing (G)

3050 Terra Crossing Boulevard, Louisville KY 40245
County: Jefferson FICE Identification: 030837
Unit ID: 156471
Telephone: (502) 410-6200 Carnegie Class: Spec-4-yr-Other Health
FAX Number: N/A Calendar System: Quarter
URL: www.galencollege.edu
Established: 1989 Annual Undergrad Tuition & Fees: N/A
Enrollment: 2,986 Coed
Affiliation or Control: Proprietary IRS Status: Proprietary
Highest Offering: Master's
Accreditation: SC, ADNUR, NUR, NURSE

02 Director of Campus Operations Mr. Marshall MOORE
106 Dean of Online Programs Dr. Kathy BURLINGAME
66 Dean Dr. Lisa PEAK

Georgetown College (H)

400 E College Street, Georgetown KY 40324-1696
County: Scott FICE Identification: 001964
Unit ID: 156745
Telephone: (502) 863-8000 Carnegie Class: Bac-A&S
FAX Number: (502) 868-8891 Calendar System: Semester
URL: www.georgetowncollege.edu
Established: 1829 Annual Undergrad Tuition & Fees: $40,800
Enrollment: 1,565 Coed
Affiliation or Control: Non-denominational IRS Status: 501(c)3
Highest Offering: Master's
Accreditation: SC, #CAATE, CAEP

01 Acting President Dr. Rosemary ALLEN
05 Provost/Dean of the College Dr. Rosemary ALLEN
10 CFO/Treasurer Mr. David WILHITE
04 Exec Asst to President/Bd Secretary Ms. Leah STUBBS
111 Vice President of Advancement Mr. John DAVIS
32 VP Student Life/Dean of Students Dr. Curtis SANDBERG
84 Vice President Enrollment Dr. Jonathan SANDS WISE
13 Assoc VP for Info Tech Services Mr. Donald L. BLAKEMAN
11 Vice President Business Operations Ms. Sally WIATROWSKI
41 Vice President of Athletics Mr. Brian EVANS
110 Asst VP Advancement/Community Rel Ms. Christy MAI
21 Controller Mr. Brad KAUFMAN
121 Assoc Dean Student Success Ms. Alexandra LOPEZ
42 Assoc Dean Student Life/Campus Min Mr. Bryan LANGLANDS
35 Assistant Dean of Students Mr. Terry EVANS
06 Assoc Dean Academic Svc & Registrar Mr. Jason SNIDER
15 Director of Human Resources Ms. Debbie CLARK
113 Bursar Ms. Christy DOLAN
53 Interim Dean of Education Ms. Kim WALTERS-PARKER

07 Director of Admissions ....Mr. Ticha CHIKUNI
37 Dir of Student Financial Planning ....Mr. Bob FULTZ
30 Director of Development ....Ms. Hanna KROSKIE
09 Director of Institutional Research ....Ms. Amber AUSTIN
08 Director of Library Services ....Mr. Andrew ADLER
29 Director of Alumni Relations ....Ms. Olivia COLEMAN-DUNN
26 Exec Dir Mktg/Community Relations ....Ms. Abigail MALIK
36 Dir Graves Ctr for Calling & Career ....Ms. Faith CRACRAFT
19 Director Campus Safety/Title IX ....Mr. Joshua MASTERSON
38 Director of Counseling/Health Svcs ....Vacant
18 Dir Facilities and Grounds ....Mr. Tyler LAWS
28 Director of Diversity ....Ms. Robbi BARBER
112 Director of Donor Relations ....Ms. Tammy OWENS
88 Director Faithways Academy ....Ms. Hollis DUDGEON
88 Coord Academic Success Initiatives ....Ms. Devin HARRIS-DAVIS
88 Assoc Athletic Director Compliance ....Ms. Kimberly CHANDLER

Interactive College of Technology (A)

76 Caruthers Road, Newport KY 41071
Telephone: (859) 282-8989 Identification: 770535
Accreditation: COE

† Branch campus of Interactive College of Technology, Chamblee, GA

Kentucky Christian University (B)

100 Academic Parkway, Grayson KY 41143-2205
County: Carter FICE Identification: 001965
Unit ID: 157100
Telephone: (606) 474-3000 Carnegie Class: Bac-Diverse
FAX Number: (606) 474-3189 Calendar System: Semester
URL: www.kcu.edu
Established: 1919 Annual Undergrad Tuition & Fees: $21,200
Enrollment: 689 Coed
Affiliation or Control: Christian Churches And Churches of Christ
IRS Status: 501(c)3
Highest Offering: Master's
Accreditation: SC, NURSE, SW

01 President/CEO ....Dr. Terry L. ALLCORN
10 VP of Business Operations ....Mr. Daniel R. WHITE
05 VP of Academic Affairs ....Mr. Calvin O. LINDELL
32 VP of Student Services ....Mr. Donald M. DAMRON
84 VP of Enrollment Mgmt & Athletics ....Mr. Corey C. FIPPS
30 Director of Development ....Mrs. Megan B. RAWLINGS
06 Registrar ....Mrs. Emily A. MILLER
13 Director of Campus Technology ....Mr. Greg C. RICHARDSON
08 Library Director ....Mrs. Naulayne R. ENDERS
108 Director Institutional Assessment ....Vacant
42 Campus Minister ....Mr. Jacob F. SHOCKEY
37 Director Financial Aid ....Mrs. Jennie M. BENDER
15 Human Resource Officer ....Mr. Terry L. YANKEY
38 Student Counseling Coordinator ....Mrs. Lori A. SMITH-WARD
39 Director of Residence Services ....Vacant
18 Director of Facilities ....Mr. Paul C. PEPPARD
29 Alumni Relations Officer ....Ms. Vicky L. MADDEN
58 Dean of the Graduate School ....Mr. Robert G. O'LYNN
07 Director of Enrollment Services ....Mrs. Sheree GREER
40 Manager of Retail Operations ....Mrs. Kyleigh M. PERRY-MCCLURE
105 Website Manager ....Mr. David A. BENNETT

*Kentucky Community and Technical College System (C)

300 N Main Street, Versailles KY 40383-1245
County: Woodford FICE Identification: 006724
Unit ID: 157854
Telephone: (859) 256-3100 Carnegie Class: N/A
FAX Number: (859) 256-3119
URL: www.kctcs.edu

01 President ....Dr. Jay BOX
00 Chancellor ....Dr. Kristin WILLIAMS
10 Vice President Finance ....Mr. Wendell FOLLOWELL
13 Vice President Information Tech ....Dr. Paul CZARAPATA
111 VP Institutional Advancement ....Mr. Benjamin MOHLER
32 Vice President Student Affairs ....Dr. Gloria MCCALL
103 VC Econ Dev/Workforce Solutions ....Mr. Shannon GILKEY
09 VC Research and Analysis ....Dr. Alicia CROUCH
100 Chief of Staff ....Ms. Hannah RIVERA

*Ashland Community and Technical College (D)

1400 College Drive, Ashland KY 41101-3617
County: Boyd FICE Identification: 001990
Unit ID: 156231
Telephone: (606) 326-2000 Carnegie Class: Assoc/HVT-High Trad
FAX Number: (606) 326-2185 Calendar System: Semester
URL: www.ashland.kctcs.edu
Established: 1938 Annual Undergrad Tuition & Fees (In-State): $4,488
Enrollment: 2,400 Coed
Affiliation or Control: State IRS Status: 501(c)3
Highest Offering: Associate Degree
Accreditation: SC, ADNUR, COARC, IFSAC, NAEYC, SURGT

02 President ....Dr. Larry FERGUSON
32 Dean Student Success/Enroll Svcs ....Mr. Steven WOODBURN
10 Dean of Business Affairs ....Ms. Karen BLEVINS
09 Dean Inst Plng/Research/Effective ....Mr. Steve FLOUHOUSE
05 Dean of Academic Affairs ....Dr. Todd BRAND
26 Director Marketing/Communications ....Ms. Taylor ALEXANDER
30 Director of Resource Development ....Ms. Brooke SEASOR
08 Director of Library Services ....Ms. Pamela KLINEPETER
07 Director of Admissions/Registrar ....Ms. Robin LEWIS
28 Director of Cultural Diversity ....Mr. Alvin BAKER
15 Director of Human Resources ....Ms. Kellie ALLEN
37 Director of Financial Aid ....Mr. Adam CHAPMAN
121 Director of Student Support Svcs ....Ms. Megan HORNE

*Big Sandy Community and Technical College (E)

1 Bert T. Combs Drive, Prestonburg KY 41653-9502
County: Floyd FICE Identification: 001996
Unit ID: 157553
Telephone: (606) 886-3863 Carnegie Class: Assoc/MT-VT-Mix Trad/Non
FAX Number: (606) 886-2677 Calendar System: Semester
URL: www.bigsandy.kctcs.edu
Established: 1964 Annual Undergrad Tuition & Fees (In-State): $4,488
Enrollment: 2,426 Coed
Affiliation or Control: State IRS Status: 501(c)3
Highest Offering: Associate Degree
Accreditation: SC, COARC, DA, DH

02 President/CEO ....Dr. Sherry ZYLKA
32 Chief Student Affs Ofcr/Registrar ....Mr. Jimmy WRIGHT
05 Provost/Chief Academic Officer ....Dr. Denise KING
10 Chief Business Affairs Officer ....Ms. Michelle MEEK
18 Director of Facilities Management ....Mr. Randy HANEY
08 Director of Library Services ....Ms. Judy HOWELL
15 Coordinator of Human Resources ....Ms. Bryen-Lynn GOBLE
06 Registrar ....Ms. Carla BRANHAM
37 Director of Financial Aid ....Ms. Cathy HURD-CRANK
09 Director of Inst Effectiveness ....Ms. Denese ATKINSON
14 Director of Information Technology ....Mr. Casey MUSIC
40 Bookstore Manager ....Ms. Stephanie JENKINS
26 Dir of Strategic Communications ....Ms. Greta SLONE
28 Director of Cultural Diversity ....Vacant
103 Director of Workforce/Economic Dev ....Ms. Rachelle BURCHETT
04 Exec Admin Asst to President ....Ms. Velissa MURPHY

*Bluegrass Community and Technical College (F)

470 Cooper Dr, Lexington KY 40506
County: Fayette FICE Identification: 009707
Unit ID: 156392
Telephone: (859) 246-6200 Carnegie Class: Assoc/MT-VT-High Trad
FAX Number: (859) 246-4664 Calendar System: Semester
URL: www.bluegrass.kctcs.edu
Established: 1965 Annual Undergrad Tuition & Fees (In-State): $4,568
Enrollment: 10,180 Coed
Affiliation or Control: State IRS Status: 501(c)3
Highest Offering: Associate Degree
Accreditation: SC, ADNUR, COARC, DH, DMS, IFSAC, MAC, RAD, SURGT

02 President ....Dr. Koffi C. AKAKPO
05 VP of Academics/WFD/Provost ....Dr. Gregory FEENEY
32 AVP Dean of Students ....Ms. Tania CRAWFORD GROSS
10 VP Finance & Administration ....Ms. Lisa G. BELL
111 VP Advancement & Org Development ....Mr. Mark MANUEL
28 Assoc VP Diversity/Equity/Inclusion ....Mr. Taran MCZEE
20 Assoc Vice President Academics ....Dr. Karen MAYO
20 Dean Academics ....Ms. Tammy LILES
103 Dean of Academics/Workforce Devel ....Ms. Pam HATCHER
121 Dean of Academic Support ....Dr. Rebecca SIMMS
06 Assoc Dean of Student Records ....Ms. Becky HARP-STEPHENS
37 Financial Aid Director ....Ms. Runan EVANS
07 Admissions Director ....Ms. Shelbie HUGLE
110 Associate VP Institutional Develop ....Ms. Deborrah L. CATLETT
26 Assoc VP Strategic Communications ....Ms. Michelle SJOGREN
79 Assistant Dean Humanities ....Ms. Angella KING
76 Asst Dean Allied Health/Nat Science ....Dr. Yasemin CONGLETON
66 Assistant Dean Nursing ....Dr. Melinda BAKER
81 Asst Dean Mathematics/Statistics ....Ms. Kausha MILLER
77 Asst Dean Business/CIS ....Ms. Lauren CAMPBELL
72 Asst Dean Advanced Mfg and Trade ....Mr. Ralph POTTER
83 Asst Dean Comm/Hist/Lang/Social Sci ....Dr. Jenny JONES
08 Director Library/Tutoring Services ....Ms. Terry BUCKNER
51 Director Adult Education ....Mr. David STURGILL
106 Assistant Dean Distance Learning ....Dr. Kevin DUNN
18 Director of Maintenance/Operations ....Mr. Michael BALL
09 Director of Institutional Research ....Mr. Aaron GAY
96 Director of Purchasing ....Ms. Kimberly CAMERON

*Elizabethtown Community and Technical College (G)

600 College Street Road, Elizabethtown KY 42701
County: Hardin FICE Identification: 001991
Unit ID: 156648
Telephone: (270) 769-2371 Carnegie Class: Assoc/MT-VT-High Non
FAX Number: (270) 769-0736 Calendar System: Semester
URL: www.elizabethtown.kctcs.edu
Established: 1963 Annual Undergrad Tuition & Fees (In-State): $4,488
Enrollment: 5,850 Coed
Affiliation or Control: State IRS Status: 501(c)3
Highest Offering: Associate Degree
Accreditation: SC, ADNUR, COARC, DMS, IFSAC, RAD

02 President/CEO ....Dr. Juston PATE
05 Interim Provost/CAO ....Mr. Darrin POWELL
32 Chief Student Affairs Officer ....Dr. Dale BUCKLES
12 Campus Education Center Director ....Vacant
103 Workforce Solutions/Tech Div Chair ....Mr. Michael HAZZARD
10 Dean of Business Affairs ....Mr. Brent HOLSCLAW
20 Dean of Instruction/Prof Develop ....Vacant
15 Director of Human Resources ....Ms. Whitney TAYLOR
06 Registrar ....Mr. Bryan SMITH
13 Interim Director of IT ....Mr. Michael MEANOR
37 Director of Financial Aid ....Mr. Michael BARLOW
30 Chief Development ....Ms. Megan STITH
26 Director of Public Relations ....Ms. Sarah BERKSHIRE
24 Learning Center Coordinator ....Ms. Pam HARPER
36 Counselor ....Vacant
38 Counselor ....Vacant
40 Bookstore Manager ....Ms. Melissa WILSON
108 Director Inst Effectiveness ....Ms. Sarah EDWARDS
18 Maintenance/Operations Supervisor ....Mr. Charles COBB
57 Chair Div of Arts/Humanities ....Ms. Jacqueline HAWKINS
81 Chair Div of Biological Science ....Ms. Anna HAMILTON
81 Chair Div of Physical Science ....Dr. Shawn KELLIE
75 Chair Div Occupational Technology ....Mr. Mike HAZZARD
83 Chair Div Social & Behavioral Sci ....Mr. John WALDRON
28 Director of Diversity ....Ms. Jerisia LAMONS
04 Exec Admin Assistant to President ....Ms. Emily ALLEN
105 Director Web Services ....Ms. Deanna YATES
08 Director of Library Services ....Ms. Katie MEYER
25 Dir of Grants & Sponsored Projects ....Ms. Susan COOPER

*Gateway Community and Technical College (H)

500 Technology Way, Florence KY 41042
County: Boone FICE Identification: 005273
Unit ID: 157438
Telephone: (859) 441-4500 Carnegie Class: Assoc/MT-VT-Mix Trad/Non
FAX Number: (859) 341-6859 Calendar System: Semester
URL: www.gateway.kctcs.edu
Established: 1961 Annual Undergrad Tuition & Fees (In-State): $4,568
Enrollment: 4,299 Coed
Affiliation or Control: State IRS Status: 501(c)3
Highest Offering: Associate Degree
Accreditation: SC, CAHIIM, EMT, IFSAC

02 President/CEO ....Dr. Fernando FIGUEROA
05 Provost and VP Academic Affairs ....Dr. Teri VONHANDORF
49 Dean of Arts and Sciences ....Dr. Susan SANTOS
50 Dean of Business/IT/Prof Services ....Dr. Amy CARRINO
76 Dean of Health Professions ....Ms. Amber CARTER
72 Dean of Manufacturing & Trans Tech ....Mr. Sam COLLIER
35 AVP for Student Development ....Ms. Mallis GRAVES
20 Associate VP Academic Services ....Mr. Doug PENIX
38 Director of Counseling Services ....Dr. Tiffany MINARD
84 Associate VP Enrollment ....Mr. Andre WASHINGTON
06 Registrar ....Ms. Ann SCHULTZ
18 Director Maintenance & Operations ....Mr. Mike BAKER
19 Director Security/Safety ....Mr. Matt BUNNING
37 Director of Financial Aid ....Ms. Ellen TEEGARDEN
13 Director of Information Technology ....Ms. Melissa SEARS
08 Director of Library ....Ms. Elizabeth HARTLAUB
66 Director of Nursing ....Ms. Michele SIMMS
89 Director Early College Initiatives ....Ms. Shelby KRENTZ
108 Dean Institutional Effectiveness ....Dr. Denise FRITSCH
26 Asst Dir Mktg & Communications ....Mr. Patrick LAMPING
27 Asst Dir Mktg & Communications ....Ms. Erica MARYE
30 VP Devel & External Relations ....Ms. Adrijana KOWATSCH
10 VP Admin & Business Affairs ....Mr. James YOUNGER
32 VP Student Development ....Ms. Ingrid WASHINGTON
103 Associate VP Workforce Solutions ....Ms. Christi GODMAN
15 VP of Human Resources ....Ms. Amy HATFIELD
110 Director of Development ....Vacant
04 Exec Admin Asst to President ....Ms. Jane FRANTZ
28 AVP Inclusion Intervention Services ....Dr. Tiffany MINARD

*Hazard Community and Technical College (I)

One Community College Drive, Hazard KY 41701-2402
County: Perry FICE Identification: 006962
Unit ID: 156790
Telephone: (606) 436-5721 Carnegie Class: Assoc/MT-VT-High Non
FAX Number: (606) 487-3604 Calendar System: Semester
URL: www.hazard.kctcs.edu
Established: 1968 Annual Undergrad Tuition & Fees (In-State): $4,488
Enrollment: 2,630 Coed
Affiliation or Control: State IRS Status: 501(c)3
Highest Offering: Associate Degree
Accreditation: SC, DMS, IFSAC, PTAA, RAD, SURGT

02 President/CEO ....Dr. Jennifer LINDON
05 Chief Academic Officer ....Dr. Ella STRONG
32 Chief Student Affairs Officer ....Dr. Deronda MOBELINI
10 Chief Financial Officer ....Ms. Connie WATTS
103 Dean of Workforce Solutions ....Mrs. Keila MILLER
13 Chief Information Officer ....Ms. Donna ROARK
15 Senior Director of Human Resources ....Ms. Vickie COMBS
18 Dean of Operations ....Mr. Stu FUGATE
26 Dir of Marketing & Communications ....Mrs. Delcie COMBS
21 Dean of Business Services ....Ms. Jackie HALL
08 Director Library Services ....Mrs. Cathy BRANSON
97 Academic Dean General Education ....Ms. Leila SMITH

75 Acad Dean Occupational Technologies ... Mr. Tony BACK
76 Acad Dean Allied Health Sci ... Ms. Mavis CLEMONS
06 Registrar ... Ms. Libby PETERS
07 Director of Admissions ... Mr. Scott GROSS
09 Coord of Inst Effectiveness ... Ms. Lois PUFFER

*Henderson Community College (A)

2660 S Green Street, Henderson KY 42420-4699
County: Henderson FICE Identification: 001993
Unit ID: 156851
Telephone: (270) 827-1867 Carnegie Class: Assoc/MT-VT-Mix Trad/Non
FAX Number: (270) 831-9600 Calendar System: Semester
URL: www.henderson.kctcs.edu
Established: 1960 Annual Undergrad Tuition & Fees (In-State): $4,488
Enrollment: 1,331 Coed
Affiliation or Control: State IRS Status: 501(c)3
Highest Offering: Associate Degree
Accreditation: SC, ADNUR, MAC, MLTAD, NAEYC

02 President ... Dr. Jason D. WARREN
05 Provost ... Dr. Reneau WAGGONER
10 Chief Business Officer ... Vacant
111 Director of Advancement ... Ms. Jennifer PRESTON
09 Director of Knowledge Management ... Mr. Brian MCMURTRY
15 Director of Human Resources ... Ms. Kim JONES
84 Dean of Enrollment Mgmt/Registrar ... Dr. Chad PHILLIPS
08 Library Director ... Mr. Mike W. KNECHT
66 Director of Nursing ... Ms. Chardae KELLY
28 Coordinator of Diversity ... Dr. Michelle CHAPPELL
57 Coordinator of Preston Arts Center ... Mr. Steve MCCARTY
13 Director of Technology Solutions ... Mr. Joe HEERDINK
18 Maintenance/Oper Supervisor ... Mr. Drew MARX
36 Career Services Coordinator ... Ms. Angela WATSON
37 Director Financial Aid ... Ms. Whitney LAIRD
49 Div Chair Liberal Arts/Prof Studies ... Ms. Lilia JOY
76 Div Chair Allied Health ... Dr. Carole MATTINGLY
81 Div Chair STEM ... Mr. Barry PHELPS
04 Administrative Asst to President ... Ms. Karen GUESS
103 Coordinator Workforce Solutions ... Ms. Amanda BLOHM-THOMPSON

*Hopkinsville Community College (B)

720 North Drive, PO Box 2100,
Hopkinsville KY 42241-2100
County: Christian FICE Identification: 001994
Unit ID: 156860
Telephone: (270) 707-3700 Carnegie Class: Assoc/HT-Mix Trad/Non
FAX Number: (270) 886-0237 Calendar System: Semester
URL: www.hopkinsville.kctcs.edu
Established: 1965 Annual Undergrad Tuition & Fees (In-State): $4,488
Enrollment: 2,076 Coed
Affiliation or Control: State IRS Status: 501(c)3
Highest Offering: Associate Degree
Accreditation: SC, ADNUR, SURGT

02 President ... Dr. Alissa YOUNG
04 Exec Admin Asst to President ... Ms. Janice JONES
05 Chief Academic Affairs Officer ... Dr. Chris BOYETT
10 Chief Business Affairs Officer ... Dr. Dale LEATHERMAN
32 Chief Student Affairs Officer ... Ms. Angel PRESCOTT
103 Chief Cmty/Workforce/Economic Dev ... Ms. Carol KIRVES
06 Registrar ... Ms. Tiffanie WITT
08 Director Library Services ... Ms. Elysa PARKS
09 Dir Institutional Effectiveness ... Mr. James HUNTER
12 Director Fort Campbell Campus ... Ms. Allisha LEE
13 Director Information Technology ... Mr. Tony NELSON
15 Director Human Resources ... Vacant
18 Director Maintenance/Operations ... Mr. Dan HAMBY
26 Director Marketing & Communication ... Ms. Rena YOUNG
28 Cultural Diversity Coordinator ... Ms. Deloria SCOTT
30 Chief Institutional Advancement Ofc ... Ms. Yvette EASTHAM
37 Director Financial Aid ... Ms. Janet GUNTHER
38 Advising Center Director ... Ms. Deloria SCOTT
40 Bookstore Director ... Ms. Sheena KOCH
36 Coordinator Career Services ... Ms. Kanya ALLEN
19 Safety Specialist ... Mr. James KAUFFMAN
49 Chair Liberal Arts and Sciences Div ... Ms. Julia LAFFOON-JACKSON
72 Chr Professional/Technical Studies ... Mr. Robert SMITH
66 Chair Nursing Division ... Ms. Joyce LAMBRUNO
81 Chair Mathematics & Sciences Div ... Mr. Ted H. WILSON
76 Chair Allied Health Division ... Dr. Beth BEVERLY

*Jefferson Community and Technical College (C)

109 E Broadway, Louisville KY 40202-2000
County: Jefferson FICE Identification: 006961
Unit ID: 156921
Telephone: (502) 213-5333 Carnegie Class: Assoc/HT-Mix Trad/Non
FAX Number: (502) 213-2115 Calendar System: Semester
URL: www.jefferson.kctcs.edu
Established: 1967 Annual Undergrad Tuition & Fees (In-State): $4,568
Enrollment: 12,196 Coed
Affiliation or Control: State IRS Status: 501(c)3
Highest Offering: Associate Degree
Accreditation: SC, ADNUR, CAHIIM, COARC, EMT, IFSAC, MAC, MLTAD, OTA, PTAA, RAD, SURGT

02 President ... Dr. Ty J. HANDY
05 VP of Academic & Student Affairs . Dr. Diane CALHOUN-FRENCH
10 VP of Administration and CFO ... Mr. Gary DRYDEN, JR.
45 VP of College Advancement/Planning ... Mr. Don SCHIEMAN
21 Controller ... Vacant
20 Dean Academic Affs Tech Pgms ... Dr. Telly SELLARS
97 Dean of General Education/Transfer ... Dr. Randy DAVIS
12 Coordinator Shelby Campus ... Ms. Maia LANGLEY
32 Dean Student Affs/Enrollment Mgmt ... Dr. Laura SMITH
08 Library Services Director ... Ms. Sheree WILLIAMS
13 Chief Information Technology Office ... Mr. Thomas ROGERS
09 Dir Inst Research/Effectiveness ... Dr. Brittany INGE
07 Director of Admissions ... Mr. Jimmy KIDD
28 Dir Diversity/Inclusion/Cmty Engage ... Ms. Danielle R. SIMS
06 Registrar ... Ms. Amanda TINDALL
26 Public Relations/Marketing ... Ms. Nikolette LANGDON
15 Human Resources Director ... Ms. Toni WHALEN
18 Facilities Director ... Ms. Pamela TURNER
37 Director of Financial Aid ... Ms. Lindsay DRISKELL
30 Inst Advance/Development Coord ... Ms. Karla HALL
38 Student Counseling ... Ms. Diane CALHOUN-FRENCH
96 Director of Purchasing ... Ms. Tineke SANTOS
12 Director of Carrollton Campus ... Ms. Heather YOCUM
12 Dean of Extended Campuses/Academic ... Vacant
04 Administrative Asst to President ... Ms. Teresa B. HARPER
106 Dir Online Education/E-learning ... Mr. Aaron NUSZ
25 Chief Contracts/Grants Admin ... Ms. Joanna LYNCH
19 Int Chief Campus Safety/Security ... Mr. Gary DRYDEN
103 Director Workforce Development ... Ms. Nickie COBB
105 Director Web Services ... Vacant

*Madisonville Community College (D)

2000 College Drive, Madisonville KY 42431-9199
County: Hopkins FICE Identification: 009010
Unit ID: 157304
Telephone: (270) 821-2250 Carnegie Class: Assoc/MT-VT-High Non
FAX Number: (270) 824-1866 Calendar System: Semester
URL: www.madisonville.kctcs.edu
Established: 1968 Annual Undergrad Tuition & Fees (In-State): $4,488
Enrollment: 3,104 Coed
Affiliation or Control: State IRS Status: 501(c)3
Highest Offering: Associate Degree
Accreditation: SC, ADNUR, COARC, EMT, IFSAC, MLTAD, OTA, PTAA, RAD, SURGA, SURGT

02 President ... Dr. Cynthia S. KELLEY
05 Provost ... Dr. Scott COOK
10 Chief Business Affairs Officer ... Mr. Ray GILLASPIE
11 Vice Pres Quality Assurance & Admin ... Dr. Jay PARRENT
103 Director Workforce Solutions ... Mr. Mike DAVENPORT
25 Dir Grants/Planning & Effectiveness ... Mr. David A. SCHUERMER
19 Director of Public Protection ... Mr. Joe BLUE
21 Dean of Business Affairs ... Mr. Michael L. JOHNSON
20 Dean of Academic Affairs ... Ms. Lisa A. HOWERTON
32 Dean of Student Affairs ... Dr. Cathy A. VAUGHAN
84 Dean of Enrollment Management ... Ms. Aimee J. WILKERSON
13 Director of Information Technology ... Mr. Joe HEERDINK
111 Director of Advancement ... Ms. Raegina SCOTT
15 Director of Human Resources ... Ms. Kim JONES
04 Sr Admin Assistant to the President . Mr. Grayson P. HAGERMAN
72 Division Chair Applied Technology ... Mr. Matt LUCKETT
66 Div Chr Nursing/Related Tech ... Dr. Marsha WOODALL
79 Div Chr Humanities/Related Tech ... Ms. Christy ADKINS
83 Div Chr Social Science/Related Tech ... Ms. Natalie F. COOPER
81 Div Chr Mathematics and Sciences ... Ms. Dawn TILLEN
76 Div Chr Allied Health/Related Tech ... Ms. Tonia R. GIBSON
56 Extended Campus Director ... Ms. Britney HERNANDEZ-STEVENSON
06 Registrar ... Ms. Casie RICHARDSON
37 Director of Financial Aid ... Ms. Karen MILLER
26 Public Relations Coordinator ... Ms. Emily RAY
36 Director of Counseling Services ... Dr. Cathy A. VAUGHAN
08 Director of Library Services ... Mr. Colin MAGEE
28 Director of Cultural Diversity ... Mr. James H. BOWLES
40 Bookstore Manager ... Ms. Sonya L. PARKER

*Maysville Community and Technical College (E)

1755 US Highway 68, Maysville KY 41056-8910
County: Mason FICE Identification: 006960
Unit ID: 157331
Telephone: (606) 759-7141 Carnegie Class: Assoc/HVT-Mix Trad/Non
FAX Number: (606) 759-7176 Calendar System: Semester
URL: www.maysville.kctcs.edu
Established: 1968 Annual Undergrad Tuition & Fees (In-State): $4,488
Enrollment: 3,446 Coed
Affiliation or Control: State IRS Status: 501(c)3
Highest Offering: Associate Degree
Accreditation: SC, COARC, EMT, IFSAC, MAC, MLTAD, PTAA

02 Interim President ... Mr. Russ WARD
05 Provost ... Dr. Thomas WARE
10 Chief Finance Officer ... Ms. Barbara CAMPBELL
84 Chief Ofcr Enrollment/Student Svc ... Ms. Jessica KERN
20 Assoc Dean Academic Support Svc ... Dr. Dana CALLAND
09 Assoc Dean Institutional Rsrch/Plng ... Ms. Pam STAFFORD
08 Director Library Services ... Ms. Sonja EADS
13 Director Information Technology ... Mr. Brett CABLE
111 Director Advancement/Foundation ... Ms. Cara CLARKE
37 Director Financial Aid ... Ms. Sandy POWER
06 Registrar ... Ms. Lori GAUNCE
28 Director of Diversity ... Ms. Millicent HARDING
15 Int Director of Human Resources ... Ms. Amanda K. CONLEY
106 Coordinator Distance Learning ... Vacant
50 Div Chr Business/Info Technologies ... Ms. Natasha MADDOX
49 Div Chair Liberal Arts/Education ... Ms. Melinda WALKER
81 Div Chair Math/Science/Agriculture ... Dr. Angela FULTZ
76 Associate Dean Health Sciences ... Ms. Ginger CLARKE
72 Associate Dean Industrial Tech ... Vacant

*Owensboro Community and Technical College (F)

4800 New Hartford Road, Owensboro KY 42303-1899
County: Daviess FICE Identification: 030345
Unit ID: 247940
Telephone: (270) 686-4400 Carnegie Class: Assoc/MT-VT-High Non
FAX Number: (270) 686-4496 Calendar System: Semester
URL: https://owensboro.kctcs.edu/
Established: 1986 Annual Undergrad Tuition & Fees (In-State): $4,488
Enrollment: 3,901 Coed
Affiliation or Control: State IRS Status: 501(c)3
Highest Offering: Associate Degree
Accreditation: SC, EMT, IFSAC, MAC, RAD, SURGT

02 President/CEO ... Dr. Scott WILLIAMS
04 Assistant to the President ... Ms. Kittridge MIDKIFF
05 VP of Academic Affairs ... Dr. Veena SALLAN
32 VP of Student Affairs ... Mr. Kevin BEARDMORE
10 VP of Business Affairs ... Ms. Sarah PRICE
13 VP Information Technology ... Mr. James HARTZ
103 VP Workforce Solutions ... Ms. Cynthia FIORELLA
08 Library Services Director ... Ms. Donna ABELL
06 Registrar ... Ms. Christy ELLIS
15 Director of Human Resources ... Ms. Shanna BALLARD
37 Dean of Student Affairs ... Dr. Andrea BORREGARD
111 Dir Institutional Advancement ... Mr. Michael RODGERS
26 Director of Public Relations ... Ms. Bernadette TOYE-HALE
28 Director of Diversity ... Dr. Ade OREDEIN
96 Director of Purchasing ... Ms. Sarah PRICE
40 Bookstore Manager ... Ms. Sonya SOUTHARD
88 TV Production Manager ... Mr. John BRYENTON
07 Senior Admissions Advisor ... Ms. Linda CALHOUN
36 Career Resource/Placemnt Ctr Coord ... Ms. Katie BALLARD
79 Assoc Dean Humanities/Fine Arts ... Dr. Julia LEDFORD
49 Academic Dean Arts & Sciences ... Dr. Marc MALTBY
75 Assoc Dean Prof/Tech Studies ... Mr. Dean AUTRY
66 Associate Dean Nursing ... Ms. Terri LANHAM
20 Dean Acad Affs Prof/Tech ... Dr. Stacy EDDS-ELLIS
09 Coord Institutional Effectiveness ... Vacant
19 Director Security/Safety ... Mr. Jeff HENDRICKS

*Somerset Community College (G)

808 Monticello Street, Somerset KY 42501-2973
County: Pulaski FICE Identification: 001997
Unit ID: 157711
Telephone: (877) 629-9722 Carnegie Class: Assoc/HVT-High Trad
FAX Number: N/A Calendar System: Semester
URL: somerset.kctcs.edu
Established: 1965 Annual Undergrad Tuition & Fees (In-State): $4,488
Enrollment: 4,837 Coed
Affiliation or Control: State IRS Status: 501(c)3
Highest Offering: Associate Degree
Accreditation: SC, ADNUR, COARC, EMT, IFSAC, MLTAD, PTAA, RAD, SURGT

02 President/CEO ... Dr. Carey CASTLE
05 Senior VP of Academic Affairs ... Dr. Clint HAYES
10 Vice President of Administration ... Ms. Jill MEECE
11 Vice President of Operations ... Mr. Larry ABBOTT
76 Dean for Health Sciences ... Ms. Nancy L. POWELL
09 VP of Institutional Effectiveness ... Mr. Bruce GOVER
32 Vice President of Student Affairs ... Ms. Tracy L. CASADA
103 VP of Workforce Solutions ... Ms. Alesa JOHNSON
111 VP of Institutional Advancement ... Ms. Cindy D. CLOUSE
49 Dean Arts and Sciences ... Mr. Jon BURLEW
81 Dean Math/Natural Science ... Dr. Michael GOLEMAN
50 Dean Business/Applied Tech ... Mr. Kevin BRADFORD
37 Director of Financial Aid ... Mr. Patrick MAYER
06 Registrar ... Ms. Jami EVANS
15 Director of Human Resources ... Ms. Kathy PATSCHECK
28 Director of Equity/Inclusion ... Ms. Elaine WILSON
12 Director McCreary & Clinton Centers ... Ms. Jill LAWSON
12 Director Casey & Russell Centers ... Ms. Regina HAUGEN

*Southcentral Kentucky Community and Technical College (H)

1845 Loop Drive, Bowling Green KY 42101-9202
County: Warren FICE Identification: 005271
Unit ID: 156338
Telephone: (270) 901-1000 Carnegie Class: Assoc/MT-VT-Mix Trad/Non
FAX Number: (270) 901-1145 Calendar System: Semester
URL: www.bowlinggreen.kctcs.edu
Established: 1939 Annual Undergrad Tuition & Fees (In-State): $4,488
Enrollment: 4,137 Coed
Affiliation or Control: State IRS Status: 501(c)3
Highest Offering: Associate Degree
Accreditation: SC, COARC, IFSAC, RAD, SURGT

02 President & CEO ... Dr. Phillip W. NEAL

05 Provost ... Dr. James MCCASLIN
32 VP Student Services ... Ms. Brooke JUSTICE
10 Vice President Business Services ... Mr. Chris CUMENS
06 Registrar ... Ms. Amy CANNON
15 VP Administrative Services ... Ms. Sherri L. FORESTER
26 Director of Public Relations ... Ms. Rebecca LEE
111 Director of Inst Advancement ... Ms. Heather ROGERS
37 Director of Financial Aid ... Ms. Jennifer WELLS
09 Director Institution Effectiveness ... Mr. Mark GARRETT

*Southeast Kentucky Community and Technical College (A)

700 College Road, Cumberland KY 40823-1099
County: Harlan FICE Identification: 001998
Unit ID: 157739
Telephone: (606) 589-2145 Carnegie Class: Assoc/HT-Mix Trad/Non
FAX Number: (606) 589-3175 Calendar System: Semester
URL: www.southeast.kctcs.edu
Established: 1960 Annual Undergrad Tuition & Fees (In-State): $4,488
Enrollment: 2,505 Coed
Affiliation or Control: State IRS Status: 501(c)3
Highest Offering: Associate Degree
Accreditation: SC, ADNUR, COARC, EMT, PTAA, RAD, SURGT

02 President ... Dr. Vic ADAMS
05 Int Chief Academic Officer ... Dr. Kevin LAMBERT
111 Vice Pres Inst Advancement ... Dr. Michele DYKES-ANDERSON
15 Director Human Resources ... Ms. Billie FRANKS
08 Head Librarian ... Ms. Lynn COX
13 Director of Information Technology ... Mr. Merrill GALLOWAY
28 Vice Pres Diversity & Inclusion ... Dr. Carolyn SUNDY
32 Chief Student Affairs Officer ... Dr. Rebecca PARROTT
07 Director of Admissions ... Ms. Felicia CARROLL
37 Director Financial Aid ... Ms. Barbara GENT
06 Registrar ... Ms. Anita BARNHILL
09 Dean of Institutional Effectiveness ... Dr. Rick MASON
103 Dir Workforce/Career Development ... Ms. Sherri CLARK
18 Chief Facilities/Physical Plant ... Mr. Lige BUELL

*West Kentucky Community and Technical College (B)

4810 Alben Barkley Drive, Paducah KY 42002-7380
County: McCracken FICE Identification: 001979
Unit ID: 157483
Telephone: (270) 554-9200 Carnegie Class: Assoc/MT-VT-High Non
FAX Number: (270) 554-6217 Calendar System: Semester
URL: www.westkentucky.kctcs.edu
Established: 1909 Annual Undergrad Tuition & Fees (In-State): $4,488
Enrollment: 4,893 Coed
Affiliation or Control: State IRS Status: 501(c)3
Highest Offering: Associate Degree
Accreditation: SC, ACBSP, ACFEI, ADNUR, DA, DMS, IFSAC, MLTAD, NAEYC, PNUR, PTAA, RAD, SURGT

02 President/CEO ... Dr. Anton REECE
103 VP of Workforce Solutions ... Mr. Kevin O'NEILL
05 VP of Academic Affairs ... Dr. Uppinder MEHAN
32 VP of Student Services ... Ms. Emily PECK
11 VP of Administrative Services ... Mr. Shay NOLAN
10 Int VP Business Affairs ... Ms. Bridget CANTER
111 VP Institutional Advancement ... Ms. Lee EMMONS
20 Associate VP Academic Affairs ... Dr. Kate SENN
08 Library Services Director ... Ms. Amy SULLIVAN
37 Financial Aid Director ... Mr. Mark SMITH
26 Public Relations Director ... Ms. Janett BLYTHE
13 Director Information Technology ... Ms. Ruby RODGERS
15 Director Human Resources ... Ms. Bridget CANTER
06 Registrar/Dir of Admissions ... Ms. Jess PUFFENBARGER
35 Student Activities Coordinator ... Ms. Amy ELMORE
79 Dean Humanities/Fine Arts/Soc Sci ... Mr. Britton SHURLEY
66 Dean Nursing Division ... Ms. Shari GHOLSON
76 Dean Allied Health Division ... Ms. Carrie HOPPER
75 Dean Applied Tech Division ... Ms. Stephanie MILLIKEN
81 Dean Math/Science & Computer ... Mr. Corey WADLINGTON
09 Associate VP of IE ... Dr. Renea AKIN
04 Administrative Asst to President ... Ms. Melissa ALLCOCK
19 Interim Director Security/Safety ... Mr. David WALLACE
28 Director of Diversity ... Vacant
29 Director Alumni Affairs ... Mr. Kyle FISHER
07 Director of Admissions ... Mr. Trent JOHNSON
106 Director Online Learning ... Dr. Kate SENN

Kentucky Mountain Bible College (C)

855 Highway 541, Jackson KY 41339
County: Breathitt FICE Identification: 030021
Unit ID: 157030
Telephone: (606) 693-5000 Carnegie Class: Spec-4-yr-Faith
FAX Number: (888) 742-1124 Calendar System: Semester
URL: www.kmbc.edu
Established: 1931 Annual Undergrad Tuition & Fees: $9,760
Enrollment: 87 Coed
Affiliation or Control: Interdenominational IRS Status: 501(c)3
Highest Offering: Baccalaureate
Accreditation: BI

01 President ... Dr. Philip E. SPEAS
03 Executive Vice President ... Rev. Thomas LORIMER
05 Academic Dean ... Mr. Zane DARLAND
10 Chief Business Manager/CIO ... Mr. Steve A. LORIMER
08 Head Librarian ... Ms. Patricia A. BOWEN
06 Registrar ... Dr. Richard E. ENGLEHARDT
07 Chief Admissions Counselor ... Mr. David W. LORIMER
37 Director Student Financial Aid ... Mr. Joe RITTER
32 Dean of Students ... Rev. James H. NELSON
18 Chief Facilities/Physical Plant ... Rev. Doug DUNN
20 Associate Academic Officer ... Mrs. Sara BAGBY
29 Director of Alumni Relations ... Mrs. Hannah AVERY
106 Dir Online Education/E-learning ... Rev. Jason GOBEN
88 Title 9 Coordinator ... Miss Elizabeth DIETZ
108 Director Institutional Assessment ... Mr. Zane E. DARLAND
13 Chief Info Technology Officer ... Mr. Steve E. LORIMER
38 Director Student Counseling ... Mrs. Ruth E. DARLAND

Kentucky State University (D)

400 E Main Street, Frankfort KY 40601-2355
County: Franklin FICE Identification: 001968
Unit ID: 157058
Telephone: (502) 597-6000 Carnegie Class: Bac-Diverse
FAX Number: (502) 597-6490 Calendar System: Semester
URL: www.kysu.edu
Established: 1886 Annual Undergrad Tuition & Fees (In-State): $8,800
Enrollment: 2,290 Coed
Affiliation or Control: State IRS Status: 501(c)3
Highest Offering: Doctorate
Accreditation: SC, ACBSP, ADNUR, CAEP, MUS, NUR, SPAA, SW

01 Acting President ... Ms. Clara ROSS STAMPS
100 Chief of Staff ... Vacant
10 VP Finance & Administration/CFO ... Mr. Gregory M. RUSH
05 Provost & VP Academic Affairs ... Dr. Leroy HAMILTON, JR.
26 VP Brand Identity & University Rels ... Ms. Clara ROSS STAMPS
32 Int VP Student Engage & Campus Life ... Dr. Pernella DEAMS
111 VP Institutional Advancement ... Vacant
43 General Counsel ... Ms. Lisa K. LANG
20 Vice Prov of Acad Qual/Rsrch/Innov ... Dr. Beverly SCHNELLER
13 Chief Information Officer ... Ms. Wendy D. DIXIE
121 Vice Provost for Student Success ... Dr. Charles HOLLOWAY
106 Vice Prov/Dir Online Programs ... Dr. Stashia EMANUEL
117 Safety and Compliance Officer ... Mr. Eric ROBINSON
65 Dean and Director of Land Grant ... Dr. Kirk W. POMPER
88 Chair Sch Aquaculture & Aquatic Sci ... Dr. James H. TIDWELL
47 Chair School of Agric/Cmty & Envir ... Dr. John SEDLACEK
50 Int Dean Col Hum/Business/ Society ... Dr. Margery COULSON-CLARK
81 Chair Math & Science ... Dr. Fariba BIGDELI JAHED
77 Chair Computer Science ... Dr. Chi SHEN
107 Chair Professional Studies ... Dr. Jo Anne RAINEY
83 Chair Psychology ... Dr. Tierra FREEMAN-TAYLOR
58 Assoc Dean & Interim Dir Grad Stds ... Dr. Kenneth ANDRIES
41 Interim Director Athletics ... Mr. Ramon JOHNSON
15 Director Human Resource Svcs ... Ms. Candace RAGLIN
04 Sr Exec Assistant to President ... Ms. Amy GAMBERG
21 Controller ... Vacant
06 Registrar ... Ms. Yolanda S. BENSON
113 Bursar ... Ms. Natalie T. TURNER
114 Director Budget ... Vacant
08 Director Library ... Ms. Sheila A. STUCKEY
121 Academic Advisor/Success Coach ... Vacant
09 Dir Inst Research & Effectiveness ... Ms. Yuliana SUSANTO-ONG
07 Dir BREDS/Admissions ... Ms. Jennifer WILLIAMS
37 Director Financial Aid ... Ms. Russelle KEESE
96 Director of Purchasing ... Ms. Jessica BURTON
29 Director Alumni Relations ... Vacant
19 Chief of Police ... Vacant
44 Director Annual Fund and Analytics ... Mr. Michael DECOURCY
108 Dir Institutional Effectiveness ... Ms. Lauren GRAVES
88 Chair STEM ... Dr. Scott WICKER
53 Chair Sch of Educ/Hum Dev/Con Sci ... Dr. Timothy FORDE
66 Chair & Program Director of Nursing ... Dr. Betty OLINGER
50 Chair School of Business ... Dr. Stevie WATSON
79 Chair Sch of Humanities/Perf Arts ... Dr. Lori HICKS
70 Chair Sch of Social Work ... Dr. Mindy BROOKS-EAVES
80 Chair Sch of Public Administration ... Dr. Elgie C. MCFAYDEN, JR.
82 Chair Sch of Criminal Jus/Pol Sci ... Dr. Frederick WILLIAMS

Kentucky Wesleyan College (E)

3000 Frederica Street, Owensboro KY 42301
County: Daviess FICE Identification: 001969
Unit ID: 157076
Telephone: (270) 926-3111 Carnegie Class: Bac-Diverse
FAX Number: (270) 926-3112 Calendar System: Semester
URL: www.kwc.edu
Established: 1858 Annual Undergrad Tuition & Fees: $28,540
Enrollment: 887 Coed
Affiliation or Control: United Methodist IRS Status: 501(c)3
Highest Offering: Baccalaureate
Accreditation: SC, IACBE

01 President ... Dr. Thomas M. MITZEL
05 VP Acad Affairs/Dean of the College ... Dr. James P. COUSINS
10 Vice President of Finance ... Mr. Dan FRAZIER
124 VP of Exec Initiatives & Retention ... Mr. Scott E. KRAMER
32 VP of Student Services ... Ms. Rebecca MCQUEEN
13 Dir of Information Services ... Mr. Jeff ARNOLD
111 Vice President for Advancement ... Mr. Eddie KENNY
07 VP of Admissions and Financial Aid ... Mr. Matthew RUARK
06 Registrar ... Ms. Lindsey CROWE
09 Dir of Inst Effectiveness/Research ... Ms. Jenna BRASHEAR
15 Director of Human Resources ... Mrs. Linda B. KELLER
37 Director of Financial Aid ... Ms. Crystal HAMILTON
08 Director of Library Learning Center ... Vacant
41 Interim Director of Athletics ... Mr. Mark SHOOK
30 Dir of Development/Campus Relations ... Ms. Kathy RUTHERMAN
42 Director of Campus Ministries ... Mr. Shawn TOMES
110 Dir Development/Donor Rels ... Mr. M. Blake HARRISON
04 Assistant to President ... Ms. Chanda F. PRATER
106 Assoc Dean/Dir Online Education ... Mrs. Rebecca FRANCIS
36 Dir of Career Services ... Ms. Deborah JONES
39 Director of Residence Life ... Ms. Lori ETHERIDGE
29 Director Alumni Affairs ... Ms. Summer CRICK
38 Director Student Counseling ... Ms. Terri PETZOLD

Lexington Theological Seminary (F)

230 Lexington Green Circle, Ste 300, Lexington KY 40503
County: Fayette FICE Identification: 001971
Unit ID: 157207
Telephone: (859) 252-0361 Carnegie Class: Spec-4-yr-Faith
FAX Number: (859) 281-6042 Calendar System: Other
URL: www.lextheo.edu
Established: 1865 Annual Graduate Tuition & Fees: N/A
Enrollment: 88 Coed
Affiliation or Control: Christian Church (Disciples Of Christ)
IRS Status: 501(c)3
Highest Offering: Doctorate; No Undergraduates
Accreditation: THEOL

01 President ... Dr. Charisse L. GILLETT
05 VP Academic Affairs/Dean ... RevDr. Loida MARTELL
111 Vice President for Advancement ... Mr. Mark V. BLANKENSHIP
10 Chief Financial Officer ... Mrs. Karen C. WAGERS
06 Registrar ... Ms. Windy KIDD
08 Librarian ... Ms. Dolores YILIBUW
13 Director Information Services ... Mr. Ben WYATT
07 Director Admission ... Rev. Erin CASH
15 Director Personnel Services ... Ms. Karen C. WAGERS
18 Chief Facilities/Physical Plant ... Ms. Karen C. WAGERS
29 Director Alumni Relations ... Mr. Mark V. BLANKENSHIP
37 Director Student Financial Aid ... Ms. Windy KIDD
96 Director of Purchasing ... Ms. Robin VARNER

Lindsey Wilson College (G)

210 Lindsey Wilson Street, Columbia KY 42728-1298
County: Adair FICE Identification: 001972
Unit ID: 157216
Telephone: (270) 384-2126 Carnegie Class: Masters/L
FAX Number: (270) 384-8200 Calendar System: Semester
URL: www.lindsey.edu
Established: 1903 Annual Undergrad Tuition & Fees: $25,718
Enrollment: 2,764 Coed
Affiliation or Control: United Methodist IRS Status: 501(c)3
Highest Offering: Doctorate
Accreditation: SC, CACREP, CAEP, IACBE, NURSE

01 President ... Dr. William T. LUCKEY, JR.
00 Chancellor ... Dr. John B. BEGLEY
05 Vice President Academic Affairs ... Dr. Patricia PARRISH
10 Vice President Administration ... Mr. Mark COLEMAN
111 Vice President Advancement ... Mr. Kevin A. THOMPSON
04 Executive Assistant ... Mrs. Amy THOMPSON-WELLS
32 Vice Pres Student Svcs/Enroll Mgmt ... Dr. Dean ADAMS
37 Vice Pres Student Financial Svcs ... Vacant
35 Dean of Students ... Mr. Christopher SCHMIDT
88 Dean of Chapel ... Dr. Terry W. SWAN
07 Dean of Admissions ... Mrs. Traci M. POOLER
07 Director of Admissions ... Mrs. Charity F. FERGUSON
41 Athletic Director ... Mr. Willis POOLER, III
06 Registrar ... Mrs. Claudia FROEDGE
15 Director of Human Resources ... Mrs. Karen F. WRIGHT
88 Dir Civic Engagement & Stdnt Ldrshp ... Ms. Natalie VICKOUS
36 Director Career Services ... Mrs. Laura BURWASH
08 Librarian ... Ms. Ashley OREHEK
18 Director of Physical Plant ... Mr. Robert KARAM
109 Director of Auxiliary Services ... Mr. Jeff WILLIS
40 Bookstore Manager ... Mrs. Amy M. COOPER
35 Director of Student Activities ... Mrs. Anna BUCKMAN
85 Dir International Student Programs ... Ms. Sabine EASTHAM
13 Director of Information Systems ... Mrs. Harriet B. GOLD
26 Public Relations Officer ... Mrs. Venus POPPLEWELL
29 Director of Alumni Affairs ... Ms. Lafawn NETTLES
19 Director Safety/Security ... Mr. Michael STATEN
42 Chaplain ... Mr. Benjamin MARTIN
37 Director Student Financial Services ... Ms. Marilyn RADFORD
38 Director Student Counseling ... Dr. Jeff CRANE
66 Director of Nursing ... Mrs. Emiley BUTTON

Louisville Presbyterian Theological Seminary (H)

1044 Alta Vista Road, Louisville KY 40205-1798
County: Jefferson FICE Identification: 001974
Unit ID: 157298
Telephone: (502) 895-3411 Carnegie Class: Spec-4-yr-Faith
FAX Number: (502) 895-1096 Calendar System: 4/1/4
URL: www.lpts.edu
Established: 1853 Annual Graduate Tuition & Fees: N/A
Enrollment: 151 Coed
Affiliation or Control: Presbyterian Church (U.S.A.) IRS Status: 501(c)3
Highest Offering: Doctorate; No Undergraduates
Accreditation: SC, MFCD, THEOL

01 President .... Dr. Alton POLLARD, III
111 VP Institutional Advancement .... Ms. Anne MONELL
10 Vice President for Finance & Admin .... Ms. Angela TRAYLOR
05 Dean of Seminary .... Dr. Debra MUMFORD
32 Dean of Community Life .... Dr. Kilen GRAY
20 Assoc Dean BCS/DMin Studies .... Dr. Angela COWSER
06 Registrar/Assoc Dean IR&E .... Dr. Steve COOK
29 Dir of Annual Giving/Alum Relations .... Ms. Andrea STEVENS
111 Dir of Institutional Advancement .... Ms. Erin HAMILTON
14 Director of Data Management .... Ms. Heather GRIFFIN
26 Director of Communications .... Mr. Chris WOOTON
08 Director of Library Services .... Dr. Anita COLEMAN
21 Controller .... Ms. Peggy MEREDITH
78 Director of Field Education .... Mr. Marcus HONG
07 Director of Admissions .... Rev. Sandra MOON
18 Director of Facilities .... Mr. Tim WILLIAMS
04 Administrative Asst to President .... Ms. Susan A. DILUCA

MedQuest College (A)

10400 Linn Station Rd, Ste 120, Louisville KY 40223
County: Jefferson FICE Identification: 042293
Unit ID: 484066
Telephone: (502) 245-6177 Carnegie Class: Not Classified
FAX Number: (502) 245-4438 Calendar System: Other
URL: www.medquestcollege.edu
Established: 2010 Annual Undergrad Tuition & Fees: N/A
Enrollment: 337 Coed
Affiliation or Control: Proprietary IRS Status: Proprietary
Highest Offering: Associate Degree
Accreditation: ABHES

01 Executive Director .... Ms. Robin BOUGHEY

Midway University (B)

512 E Stephens Street, Midway KY 40347-1112
County: Woodford FICE Identification: 001975
Unit ID: 157377
Telephone: (859) 846-4421 Carnegie Class: Masters/S
FAX Number: (859) 846-5349 Calendar System: Semester
URL: www.midway.edu
Established: 1847 Annual Undergrad Tuition & Fees: $24,850
Enrollment: 1,381 Coed
Affiliation or Control: Christian Church (Disciples Of Christ)
IRS Status: 501(c)3
Highest Offering: Master's
Accreditation: SC, ADNUR, NUR

01 President .... Dr. John P. MARSDEN
05 Interim VP of Academic Affairs .... Dr. Carrie J. CHRISTENSEN
04 Exec Assistant to the President .... Ms. Elisabet BORDT
10 Vice Pres of Finance/Administration .... Mrs. Leah B. RICE
111 Vice President of Advancement .... Mr. Timothy CULVER
26 Vice Pres of Marketing & Comm .... Mrs. Ellen D. GREGORY
07 VP of Admissions & Athletics .. Mr. William "Rusty" KENNEDY, II
88 Director Undergraduate Admissions .... Ms. Ashley DUDGEON
13 Dean of Online Admissions & CIO .... Dr. Salah SHAKIR
06 Registrar .... Ms. Susie POWERS
08 Director of Library Services .... Mr. Michael GARNER
14 Technical Support Specialist .... Mr. Jimmy ROWE
15 Exec Director of Human Resources .... Ms. Trish JONES
37 Director of Financial Aid .... Ms. Erin TEVES
18 Director of Facilities .... Mr. Russell FISHER
50 Dean Business/Equine/Sport Stds .... Dr. Mark A. GILL
49 Dean School of Arts & Sciences .... Vacant
76 Dean School of Health Sciences .... Dr. Diane CHLEBOWY
19 Director Security/Safety .... Mr. Ric JACOB
36 Director Office of Student Success .... Ms. Mackenzie HANES
32 Dean of Students .... Mr. Joseph RYAN
09 Director of Institutional Research .... Mr. Jeffrey SUMMERS
39 Asst Director Residence Life .... Ms. Katie MORGAN
29 Dir Alumni Affairs/Annual Giving .... Mrs. Michelle PETERSON

Morehead State University (C)

150 University Boulevard, Morehead KY 40351-1689
County: Rowan FICE Identification: 001976
Unit ID: 157386
Telephone: (800) 585-6781 Carnegie Class: Masters/L
FAX Number: N/A Calendar System: Semester
URL: www.moreheadstate.edu
Established: 1887 Annual Undergrad Tuition & Fees (In-State): $9,290
Enrollment: 9,304 Coed
Affiliation or Control: State IRS Status: 501(c)3
Highest Offering: Doctorate
Accreditation: SC, ADNUR, ART, CAEP, COARC, DMS, MPCAC, MUS, NAIT, NURSE, RAD, RADMAG, SPAA, SW, THEA

01 President .... Dr. Joseph A. MORGAN
05 Provost/VP for Academic Affairs .... Dr. Antony NORMAN
10 VP Fiscal Svcs/Chief Financial Ofcr .. Mrs. Mary FISTER-TUCKER
32 Vice Pres for Student Affairs .... Mr. Russell F. MAST
111 Int Vice Pres for Univ Advancement .... Mr. Richard HESTERBERG
20 Assoc Provost UG Educ/Stdnt Success .... Dr. Laurie L. COUCH
88 Director of Testing Center .... Ms. Sharon S. REYNOLDS
06 Registrar .... Mr. Keith MOORE
51 Asst VP Regional Educ & Outreach .... Dr. Dan J. CONNELL
84 Asst Vice Pres Enrollment Services .... Mr. Tim RHODES
18 AVP Facilities Management .... Mr. Kim H. OATMAN
109 Exec Director Auxiliary Services .... Mr. Charles GANCIO
29 Asst VP Alumni Relations & Develop .... Ms. Melinda C. HIGHLEY
13 Chief Information Officer .... Dr. Chris HOWES
35 AVP Student Life/Dean of Students .... Mr. Maxwell J. AMMONS
08 Dean of Library Services .... Dr. David L. GREGORY
07 Dir of Undergraduate Admissions .... Ms. Holly L. POLLOCK
09 Dir Inst Research & Analysis .... Mrs. Courtney ANDREWS
15 Interim Director of Human Resources .... Dr. Caroline ATKINS
19 Chief of Police .... Mr. Merrell J. HARRISON
21 Director Accounting/Financial Svcs .... Ms. Kelli D. OWEN
37 Director Financial Aid .... Ms. Denise M. TRUSTY
36 Director Career Services .... Ms. Megan BOONE
39 Director of Housing/Residence Educ .... Dr. Alan M. RUCKER
41 Director of Athletics .... Dr. James D. GORDON
43 General Counsel .... Ms. Jane FITZPATRICK
96 Director Procurement Services .... Ms. Andrea STONE
38 Director of Counseling/Health Svcs .... Ms. Goldie C. WILLIAMS
50 Dean Smith Col Business/Tech .... Dr. Johnathan K. NELSON
53 Interim Dean College of Education .... Dr. April D. MILLER
81 Dean College of Science .... Dr. Wayne C. MILLER
79 Dean Arts/Hum/Soc Sciences .... Dr. Scott A. DAVISON
106 Director Distance Educ/Instr Design .... Mr. David FLORA
108 Director University Assessment .... Dr. Shannon L. HARR
88 Director of Military Initiatives .... Dr. Silas SESSION
114 Exec Dir Budgets/Financial Planning .... Ms. Teresa LINDGREN
101 Secretary of the Board of Regents .... Ms. Jacqueline N. GRAVES
58 Director of Graduate School .... Dr. Susan MAXEY
46 Director Research & Sponsored Pgms .... Ms. Darlene ALLEN

Murray State University (D)

102 Curris Center, Murray, KY 42071,
Murray KY 42071-3318
County: Calloway FICE Identification: 001977
Unit ID: 157401
Telephone: (270) 809-3011 Carnegie Class: Masters/L
FAX Number: (270) 809-3413 Calendar System: Semester
URL: www.murraystate.edu
Established: 1922 Annual Undergrad Tuition & Fees (In-State): $9,168
Enrollment: 9,449 Coed
Affiliation or Control: State IRS Status: 501(c)3
Highest Offering: Doctorate
Accreditation: SC, ANEST, ART, CACREP, CAEP, DIETD, DIETI, EXSC, JOUR, MPCAC, MUS, NURSE, OT, SP, SW, THEA

01 President .... Dr. Robert JACKSON
05 Provost and VP Academic Affairs .... Dr. Tim TODD
10 VP Finance and Administratve Svcs .... Jacklyn DUDLEY
32 VP Student Affairs/Enrollment Mgmt .... Dr. Don ROBERTSON
58 Assoc Provost .... Dr. Robert PERVINE
13 Chief Information Officer .... Brian VERKAMP
19 Chief of Police .... Jeffrey GENTRY
43 General Counsel .... Robert MILLER
102 President MSU Foundation .... Dr. David W. DURR
30 Executive Director of Development .... Dr. C. Tina BERNOT
29 Director of Alumni Relations .... Carrie MCGINNIS
15 Interim Director of Human Resources .... Courtney HIXON
09 Exec Dir Strategic Enrollment Mgmt .... Dr. K. Renee FISTER
86 Exec Dir Government/Inst Relations .... Jordan SMITH
18 Director of Facilities Management .... Jason YOUNGBLOOD
41 Director of Athletics .... Kevin SAAL
26 Exec Dir of Marketing/Communication .... Shawn TOUNEY
28 Exec Dir IDEA & Title IX Coord .... Camisha DUFFY
06 Registrar .... Tracy ROBERTS
113 Bursar/Dir Student Fin Services .... Wendy CAIN
101 Sr Exec Coord for Pres/Board Rels .... T. Jill HUNT
07 Dir Undergrad Admiss/Transfer Ctr .... Maria ROSA
123 Coord Graduate Admissions/Records .... Kaitlyn BURZYNSKI
36 Director of Career Services .... Matt PURDY
38 Dir University Counseling Services .... Angie TRZEPACZ
96 Director of Procurement Services .... Beth WARD

Northern Kentucky University (E)

Nunn Drive, Highland Heights KY 41099-0000
County: Campbell FICE Identification: 009275
Unit ID: 157447
Telephone: (859) 572-5100 Carnegie Class: DU-Mod
FAX Number: (859) 572-5566 Calendar System: Semester
URL: www.nku.edu
Established: 1968 Annual Undergrad Tuition & Fees (In-State): $10,296
Enrollment: 16,211 Coed
Affiliation or Control: State IRS Status: 501(c)3
Highest Offering: Doctorate
Accreditation: SC, ANEST, #CAATE, CACREP, CAEP, CAEPN, COARC, CONST, LAW, MUS, NURSE, RAD, SPAA, SW

01 President .... Dr. Ashish VAIDYA
05 Provost/Exec VP Academic Affairs .... Dr. Matt CECIL
32 Vice Pres Student Affairs .... Dr. Eddie J. HOWARD, JR.
111 Vice Pres University Advancement .... Mr. Eric C. GENTRY
43 VP Legal Affairs & General Counsel .... Ms. Joan GATES
20 Vice Prov Undergrad Academic Affs .... Vacant
84 VP Enrollment/Degree Management .... Ms. Kimberly SCRANAGE
58 Vice Prov Grad Educ/Rsrch/
Outreach .... Ms. Samantha LANGLEY-TURNBAUGH
46 Vice Pres/Chief Strategy Officer .... Dr. Bonita BROWN
20 Assoc Provost Academic Admin .... Mr. Chad OGLE
13 Chief Information Officer .... Mr. Timothy FERGUSON
10 Chief Financial Officer .... Mr. Mike HALES
28 Chief Div/Equity/Incl Ofcr/TI IX .... Mr. Darryl A. PEAL
08 Dean of the Library .... Ms. Andrea FALCONE
35 AVP Student Affairs .... Mr. Arnie SLAUGHTER
86 Director of Economic Engagement .... Ms. Jenny SAND
49 Dean College of Arts & Sciences .... Dr. Diana MCGILL
50 Dean College of Business .... Dr. Hassan HASSABELNABY
88 Dean College of Informatics .... Dr. Kevin KIRBY
53 Dean College of Education .... Dr. Ginni FAIR
61 Dean Chase College of Law .... Ms. Judith DAAR
66 Dean College of Health Professions .... Dr. Dale STEPHENSON
18 Asst VP Facilities Management .... Mr. Syed ZAIDI
18 Director Operations & Maintenance .... Mr. Jon PRABELL
26 Asst VP Marketing & Communications .... Dr. Roy GIFFORD
21 Dir Fin & Operational Auditing .... Mr. Larry MEYER
109 Dir Business Ops/Auxiliary Services .... Mr. Andy MEEKS
88 Sr Director Planning/Design/Const .... Ms. Mary Paula SCHUH
15 Senior Director Human Resources .... Ms. Lori SOUTHWOOD
21 Comptroller .... Mr. Russell A. KERDOLFF
19 Chief of Police .... Mr. John GAFFIN
96 Int Director Procurement Services .... Mr. Blaine GILMORE
92 Dean of Honors College .... Mr. James BUSS
07 Director Undergraduate Admissions .... Ms. Melissa GORBANDT
104 Exec Dir Intl Education Center .... Dr. Francois LEROY
06 Registrar .... Mr. W. Allen COLE, III
37 AVP Enrollment & Financial Aid .... Ms. Leah STEWART
78 Exec Dir Ctr for Civic Engagement .... Mr. Mark NEIKIRK
25 Director Research/Grants/Contracts .... Ms. Mary UCCI
89 Int Director First Year Programs .... Ms. Tracy HART
09 Exec Dir Planning/Inst Research .... Mr. Shawn RAINEY
88 Director Campus Recreation .... Mr. Shomari KEE
38 Director Health/Counseling/Prev .... Ms. Amy CLARK
124 Director of Student Engagement .... Ms. Tiffany MAYSE
36 Director Career Services .... Mr. Bill FROUDE
41 Dir of Intercollegiate Athletics .... Mr. Ken BOTHOF

Simmons College of Kentucky (F)

1018 South 7th Street, Louisville KY 40203-3322
County: Jefferson FICE Identification: 041780
Unit ID: 461759
Telephone: (502) 776-1443 Carnegie Class: Spec-4-yr-Faith
FAX Number: (502) 776-2227 Calendar System: Semester
URL: www.simmonscollegeky.edu
Established: 1879 Annual Undergrad Tuition & Fees: $6,990
Enrollment: 140 Coed
Affiliation or Control: Baptist IRS Status: 501(c)3
Highest Offering: Baccalaureate
Accreditation: BI

01 President .... Dr. Kevin W. COSBY
05 Provost .... Dr. Barbara YOUNG
03 Executive VP for Faith & Cmty Rels .... Dr. Frank M. SMITH, JR.
111 Executive VP Inst Advancement .... Dr. Ken B. JOBST
05 Vice Pres Academic Affairs .... Dr. Chris CALDWELL
32 Vice Pres Student Affs/Dir
Admiss .... Dr. Christine COSBY-GAITHER
22 Title III Director .... Dr. Barbara YOUNG
06 Registrar .... Ms. Deborah THOMAS
08 Library Director .... Mr. Andrew CHALK
30 Director of Development .... Mr. Von PURDY

The Southern Baptist Theological Seminary (G)

2825 Lexington Road, Louisville KY 40280-2899
County: Jefferson FICE Identification: 001982
Unit ID: 157748
Telephone: (502) 897-4011 Carnegie Class: Spec-4-yr-Faith
FAX Number: (502) 899-1770 Calendar System: Other
URL: www.sbts.edu
Established: 1859 Annual Undergrad Tuition & Fees: $11,896
Enrollment: 4,337 Coed
Affiliation or Control: Southern Baptist IRS Status: 501(c)3
Highest Offering: Doctorate
Accreditation: SC, MUS, THEOL

01 President .... Dr. R. Albert MOHLER, JR.
100 Chief of Staff/SVP Administration .... Mr. Jonathan AUSTIN
04 Exec Admin Asst Office of President .... Ms. Anna ARRASTIA
05 Sr VP Academic Admin/Provost .... Dr. Matthew HALL
111 Sr VP Institutional Advancement .... Mr. Craig PARKER
11 Vice President of Operations .... Mr. Andrew VINCENT
110 VP of Advancement/Communications .... Mr. Edward HEINZE
13 VP Campus Technology .... Mr. Jason HEATH
58 Vice President for Doctoral Studies .... Dr. Timothy Paul JONES
108 Assoc VP Institutional Assessment .... Dr. Joseph HARROD
84 Assoc VP Enrollment Management .... Mr. Matt MINIER
15 Assoc VP of Human Resources .... Mr. Brent SMALL
18 Chief Facilities/Physical Plant .... Mr. Henry LACHER
41 Director of Health & Recreation .... Mr. Michael MCCARTY
07 Director of Admissions .... Mr. Jeremy PELTON
08 Librarian .... Dr. Berry DRIVER
37 Manager of Financial Aid .... Mrs. Ana WILLIAMS
73 Dean of School of Theology .... Dr. Hershael YORK
88 Dean Missions Evangel Chrch Growth .... Dr. Paul AKIN
12 Dean Boyce College .... Dr. Dustin BRUCE
06 Registrar .... Mr. Norm CHUNG
39 Director of Campus Housing & Legacy .... Mr. Caleb DYE
106 Assoc VP for the Global Campus .... Mr. Brian RENSHAW

Spalding University (H)

845 S Third Street, Louisville KY 40203-2213
County: Jefferson FICE Identification: 001960
Unit ID: 157757
Telephone: (502) 585-9911 Carnegie Class: DU-Mod
FAX Number: (502) 585-7158 Calendar System: Other
URL: www.spalding.edu

Established: 1814 Annual Undergrad Tuition & Fees: $25,975
Enrollment: 1,596 Coed
Affiliation or Control: Independent Non-Profit IRS Status: 501(c)3
Highest Offering: Doctorate
Accreditation: SC, #CAATE, CAEP, CAEPN, CLPSY, IACBE, NURSE, OT, SW

01 President ... Ms. Tori MURDEN MCCLURE
05 Provost ... Dr. John BURDEN
111 Chief Advancement Officer ... Ms. Caroline HEINE
11 Chief of Staff/Dean of Operations ... Mr. Chris HART
58 Dean of Graduate Studies ... Dr. Kurt JEFFERSON
20 Dean of Undergraduate Education ... Dr. Tomarra ADAMS
32 Dean of Students ... Ms. Janelle RAE
10 Chief Financial Officer ... Mr. Rush SHERMAN
43 General Counsel ... Ms. Emily NORRIS
84 Dean of Enrollment Management ... Dr. Melissa CHASTAIN
121 Director Academic Advising Center ... Ms. Nikki SHEDLETSKY
06 Registrar ... Ms. Jennifer GOHMANN
13 Chief Information Officer ... Mr. Ezra KRUMHANSL
37 Director Financial Aid ... Ms. Michelle STANDRIDGE
15 Exec Dir of Human Resources ... Ms. Jennifer BROCKHOFF
09 Director of Inst Effectiveness ... Ms. Elizabeth DYER
41 Director of Athletics ... Mr. Roger BURKMAN
21 Controller ... Ms. Katherine WEYHING
18 JLL Facilities Manager ... Mr. Kevin WEBER
07 Director of Admissions ... Ms. Jill GAINES

Sullivan University (A)

3101 Bardstown Road, Louisville KY 40205-3000
County: Jefferson FICE Identification: 004619
Unit ID: 157793
Telephone: (502) 456-6504 Carnegie Class: Masters/L
FAX Number: (502) 456-0040 Calendar System: Quarter
URL: www.sullivan.edu
Established: 1962 Annual Undergrad Tuition & Fees: $13,860
Enrollment: 3,165 Coed
Affiliation or Control: Proprietary IRS Status: Proprietary
Highest Offering: Doctorate
Accreditation: SC, ARCPA, CAHIIM, CIDA, MAC, NURSE, PHAR, RAD, SURGT

00 Chancellor Sullivan Univ System ... Mr. Glenn D. SULLIVAN
02 President ... Dr. Jay D. MARR
05 Sr VP for Academic Affairs/Provost ... Dr. Diana LAWRENCE
11 Sr Vice Pres for Administration ... Mr. Chris ERNST
10 Vice President Finance ... Mr. Patrick MCMURRAY
84 VP of Enrollment Mgmt ... Ms. Nina MARTINEZ
86 Vice Pres of Community Partnerships ... Mr. David KEENE
12 VP Lexington Campus ... Dr. David TUDOR
15 Vice Pres of Human Resources ... Ms. Melissa LOWE
58 Assoc Provost/Dean Graduate School ... Dr. Tim SWENSON
88 Exec Dir College of Hosp Studies ... Mr. David HENDRICKSEN
06 Registrar ... Ms. Kim MITCHELL
08 Director of University Libraries ... Dr. Jackie YOUNG
13 Dir of IT Services ... Mr. Drew ARNETTE
36 Sr Dir of Career Svcs & Alumni Affs ... Mr. Sam MANNINO
37 Sr Dir Student Financial Planning ... Ms. Angela MILLER
40 Bookstore Manager ... Mr. Bryan NEEDY
96 Director of Purchasing ... Ms. Ann VEST
56 Dir of Ft Knox Extension Campus ... Ms. Barbara DEAN
88 University Ombudsman ... Mr. Jim KLEIN
18 Manager Campus Facilities ... Mr. Mike FOWLER

Thomas More University (B)

333 Thomas More Parkway,
Crestview Hills KY 41017-3495
County: Kenton FICE Identification: 002001
Unit ID: 157809
Telephone: (859) 341-5800 Carnegie Class: Masters/M
FAX Number: (859) 344-3345 Calendar System: Semester
URL: www.thomasmore.edu
Established: 1921 Annual Undergrad Tuition & Fees: $33,420
Enrollment: 2,037 Coed
Affiliation or Control: Roman Catholic IRS Status: 501(c)3
Highest Offering: Master's
Accreditation: SC, ACBSP, CAEP, NUR

01 President ... Dr. Joseph L. CHILLO
04 Exec Assistant to the President ... Ms. Charlene BARLOW
10 Chief Financial/Business Officer ... Mr. Mark A. GOSHORN
05 Provost ... Dr. Molly SMITH
100 Chief of Staff/VP ... Ms. Kelly FRENCH
32 Chief of Student Affairs/Life ... Ms. Annabelle BAUISTA
111 Vice Pres Institutional Advancement ... Mr. Kevin REYNOLDS
84 Vice Pres Enrollment Management ... Vacant
07 Dean of Admissions ... Mr. Justin VOGEL
21 Controller ... Ms. Penny MCCRELESS
37 Director of Financial Aid ... Mr. Mark MESSINGSCHLAGER
13 Director of IT ... Mr. Sean KAPSAL
26 Dir Communications/Media Relations ... Ms. Rebecca STRATTON
41 Athletic Director ... Mr. Terry D. CONNOR
42 Chaplain ... Rev. Gerald E. TWADDELL
11 Chief of Operations/Administration ... Mr. Noah WELTE
19 Director of Campus Safety ... Mr. Dennis LEHMKUHL
15 Director of Human Resources ... Ms. Laura CUSTER
18 Director of Facilities ... Mr. Joey ETHERIDGE
29 Director of Alumni ... Mrs. Bailey BUNDY
36 Dir of Career Planning/Coop Educ ... Ms. Robin NORTON
73 Director of Campus Ministry ... Mr. Andrew COLE
08 Director of Library ... Mr. Mike WELLS
06 Registrar ... Ms. Michelle VEZINA

92 Director of Honors Program ... Dr. Catherine SHERRON
44 Director Annual Giving ... Ms. Beth MALEY
113 Bursar ... Mr. Robert FISHER
50 Dean of Business ... Dr. Bruce ROSENTHAL
39 Coordinator of Residence Life ... Vacant
30 Director of Development ... Ms. Denise CARL
09 Dir of Inst Planning/Effectiveness ... Vacant

Transylvania University (C)

300 N Broadway, Lexington KY 40508-1797
County: Fayette FICE Identification: 001987
Unit ID: 157818
Telephone: (859) 233-8300 Carnegie Class: Bac-A&S
FAX Number: (859) 233-8797 Calendar System: Other
URL: www.transy.edu
Established: 1780 Annual Undergrad Tuition & Fees: $41,610
Enrollment: 963 Coed
Affiliation or Control: Christian Church (Disciples Of Christ)
IRS Status: 501(c)3
Highest Offering: Baccalaureate
Accreditation: SC

01 President ... Mr. Brien LEWIS
05 VP Acad Affs/Dean of the University ... Dr. Rebecca THOMAS
10 Vice President Finance & Business ... Mr. Marc MATHEWS
84 Interim VP for Enrollment ... Mr. Johnnie JOHNSON
111 VP for Advancement ... Mr. Shawn LYONS
32 VP for Student Affairs ... Dr. Michael COVERT
13 VP for Information Technology ... Ms. Deepa DUBAL
26 VP for Marketing & Communications ... Ms. Megan MOLONEY
09 VP for Institutional Effectiveness ... Dr. Rhyan M. CONYERS
41 VP for Athletics ... Dr. Holly SHEILLEY
28 VP for Diversity and Inclusion ... Dr. Deidra DENNIE
06 Registrar ... Ms. Michelle RAWLINGS
08 Director of Library ... Ms. Susan M. BROWN
104 Dir Global & Intercult Engagement ... Ms. Courtney SMITH
20 Assistant Dean for Academic Affairs ... Ms. Tracy DUNN
15 Director Human Resources ... Ms. Alison BEGOR
18 Director of Facilities ... Mr. Danny KNOX
19 Director Security/Safety ... Mr. Joe MCCLURE
96 Director of Purchasing ... Ms. Shawn T. SINGLETON
39 Director Residence Life ... Mr. Keith JONES
37 Director of Financial Aid ... Ms. Jennifer PRIEST
29 Director Alumni Relations ... Ms. Natasa PAJIC MONGIARDO
04 Executive Assistant to President ... Ms. Amanda TURCOTTE
88 Assist Athletic Dir for Compliance ... Mr. Jeff CHANEY

Union College (D)

310 College Street, Barbourville KY 40906-1499
County: Knox FICE Identification: 001988
Unit ID: 157863
Telephone: (606) 546-4151 Carnegie Class: Masters/S
FAX Number: (606) 546-1217 Calendar System: Other
URL: www.unionky.edu
Established: 1879 Annual Undergrad Tuition & Fees: $28,000
Enrollment: 1,179 Coed
Affiliation or Control: United Methodist IRS Status: 501(c)3
Highest Offering: Master's
Accreditation: SC, CAEP, CAEPN, NURSE

01 President ... Dr. Marcia HAWKINS
04 Executive Assistant to President ... Ms. Sherry JENKINS
31 Exec Dir Cmty Rels & Events ... Ms. Meghann CHESNUT
42 College Minister ... Rev. David MILLER
05 VP for Academic Affairs ... Dr. Marisa GREER
79 Dean School of Humanities ... Dr. Karl WALLHAUSSER
58 Dean Professional and Grad Studies ... Dr. David WILLIAMS
111 VP of Advancement/Communications ... Mr. Brian STRUNK
26 Senior Director of Communications ... Mrs. Maisie NELSON
29 Director of Alumni Relations ... Mrs. Courtney OLIVER
84 VP for Enrollment Management ... Vacant
32 Dean of Students ... Mr. James BECKNELL
39 Director of Housing ... Mr. Jason ELS
35 Assistant Director of Campus Life ... Vacant
10 Chief Business Officer ... Mr. Steve MORRIS
114 Asst VP Business/Financial Svcs ... Mr. Randle TEAGUE
15 Exec Director of Human Resources ... Ms. Lynn SMITH
118 Coordinator of Payroll/Benefits ... Ms. Samantha NANTZ
21 Controller ... Ms. Jessica JUSTICE
06 Registrar ... Ms. Kathy INKSTER
18 Director of Physical Plant (NMRC) ... Mr. Shain SIZEMORE
41 Athletic Director ... Mr. Tim CURRY
09 Director of Institutional Research ... Ms. Anisa JAMES
121 Associate Dean for Student Success ... Ms. Stephanie SMITH
08 Head Librarian ... Ms. Tara L. COOPER
37 Director of Financial Aid ... Ms. Andra BUTLER
19 Safety Team Leader ... Mr. Mike GRAY
13 Director of IT ... Mr. Eric EVANS
105 Director Web Services ... Mr. Phillip HORN
44 Director Annual Giving ... Mr. Derrick REYNOLDS

University of the Cumberlands (E)

6191 College Station Drive, Williamsburg KY 40769-1372
County: Whitley FICE Identification: 001962
Unit ID: 156541
Telephone: (606) 549-2200 Carnegie Class: DU-Mod
FAX Number: (606) 539-4280 Calendar System: Semester
URL: www.ucumberlands.edu
Established: 1888 Annual Undergrad Tuition & Fees: $9,875
Enrollment: 19,110 Coed
Affiliation or Control: Baptist IRS Status: 501(c)3
Highest Offering: Doctorate
Accreditation: SC, ARCPA, CACREP, CAEP, IACBE, NURSE

01 President ... Dr. Larry L. COCKRUM
05 EVP Academic/Student Affs/Provost ... Dr. Emily COLEMAN
10 EVP Finance/Chief Financial Officer ... Dr. Quentin YOUNG
11 EVP of Operations/COO ... Mr. Travis WILSON
37 Director of Financial Aid ... Mr. Ian FREYBERG
41 Athletic Director ... Mr. Chris KRAFTICK
13 EVP for Information Technology/CIO ... Dr. Donnie GRIMES
84 EVP for Enrollment & Communication ... Dr. Jerry JACKSON
06 Registrar ... Ms. Kathryn MCCUNE
38 Director of School Counseling ... Dr. Susan ROSE
111 EVP Inst Advance/Chief of Staff ... Mrs. Leslie C. RYSER
35 Dean Student Life ... Vacant
15 Director of Human Resources ... Mr. Steve ALLEN
42 Director of Church Relations ... Dr. Rick FLEENOR
36 Exec Dir Extended Services ... Dr. Jamirae HOLBROOK
08 Director of Library ... Ms. Jan WREN
58 Director of Graduate Advising ... Mrs. Shonda POWERS
18 Director of Physical Plant ... Mr. David ROOT
21 Bursar ... Ms. Jo DUPIER
29 Exec Director of Alumni Relations ... Mrs. Erica HARRIS
30 VP of Development ... Mr. Bill STOHLMAN

University of Kentucky (F)

101 Main Building, Lexington KY 40506-0003
County: Fayette FICE Identification: 001989
Unit ID: 157085
Telephone: (859) 257-2000 Carnegie Class: DU-Highest
FAX Number: (859) 257-4000 Calendar System: Semester
URL: www.uky.edu
Established: 1865 Annual Undergrad Tuition & Fees (In-State): $12,484
Enrollment: 29,986 Coed
Affiliation or Control: State IRS Status: 501(c)3
Highest Offering: Doctorate
Accreditation: SC, ARCPA, CACREP, CAEPN, CAMPEP, CIDA, CLPSY, COPSY, DENT, DIETC, DIETD, DIETI, HSA, IPSY, JOUR, LAW, LIB, LSAR, MED, MFCD, MT, MUS, NURSE, PAST, PCSAS, PH, PHAR, PTA, SCPSY, SP, SPAA, SW, THEA

01 President ... Dr. Eli I. CAPILOUTO
46 Vice President Research ... Dr. Lisa A. CASSIS
05 Acting Provost ... Dr. Robert DIPAOLA
11 Exec VP Finance/Administration ... Dr. Eric N. MONDAY
17 Executive VP for Health Affairs ... Dr. Mark NEWMAN
32 VP for Student Success ... Dr. Kirsten TURNER
13 Chief Information Officer ... Mr. Brian NICHOLS
35 Stdnt Affs/Dean of Students ... Dr. Trisha CLEMENT MONTGOMERY
22 Actg Assoc VP Institutional Equity ... Ms. Thalethia ROUTT
30 Vice President for Philanthropy ... Dr. D. Michael RICHEY
10 VP Health Affs/Chief Financial Ofcr ... Mr. Craig COLLINS
45 VP Financial Planning & CBO ... Ms. Angela S. MARTIN
18 VP Facilities Mgmt & Chief Facil ... Ms. Mary S. VOSEVICH
28 Interim VP Inst Diversity/Sr Adv ... Dr. George WRIGHT
26 VP University Relations ... Mr. Thomas W. HARRIS
15 VP Human Resources Admin & CHRO ... Ms. Kimberly P. WILSON
19 Asst Vice Pres Public Safety ... Mr. Anthony BEATTY
109 Exec Director Auxiliary Services ... Ms. Sarah F. NIKIRK
21 Assoc VP Res Admin & Fiscal Affs ... Mr. Jack SUPPLEE, JR.
25 Exec Director Sponsored Projects ... Ms. Kim C. CARTER
88 Assoc VP UKHC/EVPHA ... Mr. Joe CLAYPOOL
58 Acting Assoc Provost Graduate Sch ... Dr. Martha PETERSON
88 Assoc Provost Faculty Advancement ... Dr. Gene T. LINEBERRY
84 Chief Enrollment Officer ... Ms. Christine HARPER
08 Interim Dean of Libraries ... Dr. Deirdre SCAGGS
27 Chief Communications Officer ... Mr. Jay D. BLANTON
43 General Counsel ... Mr. William E. THRO
41 Director Athletics ... Mr. Mitch S. BARNHART
37 Exec Director Student Financial Aid ... Ms. Kathy BIALK
09 Interim Director of Inst Research ... Dr. Chris THURINGER
36 Asst Dean for Career & Academic Exp ... Mr. Ray R. CLERE
38 Director Counseling & Testing ... Dr. Mary C. BOLIN
29 Associate Vice President for Alumni ... Ms. Jill SMITH
21 Controller ... Ms. Shanhong WANG
47 Dean of Agriculture/Food & Envir ... Dr. Nancy M. COX
19 Chief of Police ... Mr. Joseph W. MONROE
88 Dean of Design ... Ms. Mitzi VERNON
88 Int Exec Director Gatton Stdnt Ctr ... Mr. Scott HENRY
49 Int Dean of Arts & Sciences ... Dr. Christian BRADY
50 Dean of Business & Economics ... Dr. Simon J. SHEATHER
53 Dean of Education ... Dr. Julian VASQUEZ HEILIG
54 Dean of Engineering ... Dr. Rudolph BUCHHEIT
57 Dean of Fine Arts ... Mr. Mark SHANDA
60 Dean of Communication & Information ... Dr. Jennifer GREER
61 Dean of Law ... Dr. Mary DAVIS
70 Dean of Social Work ... Dr. Justin (Jay) MLLER
76 Dean of Health Sciences ... Dr. Scott M. LEPHART
52 Dean of Dentistry ... Dr. Jeff OKESON
63 Acting Dean of Medicine ... Dr. Charles GRIFFITH, III
66 Dean of Nursing ... Dr. Janie H. HEATH
67 Dean of Pharmacy ... Dr. Kip GUY
69 Dean Public Health ... Dr. Donna ARNETT
92 Acting Dean Lewis Honors College ... Dr. Laura BRYAN
96 Exec Director Purchasing & CPO ... Mr. Barry SWANSON
108 Director of Inst Effectiveness ... Dr. Michael RUDOLPH
44 Director Annual Giving ... Mr. Andrew PALMER
116 Chief Accountability Officer Audit ... Mr. Joe REED
04 Admin Assistant to the President ... Ms. Renee SMITH
06 Registrar ... Ms. Kimberly TAYLOR
39 Dir Resident Life/Student Housing ... Dr. Justin BLEVINS

University of Louisville (A)

2301 S Third Street, Louisville KY 40292-0001
County: Jefferson FICE Identification: 001999
Unit ID: 157289
Telephone: (502) 852-5555 Carnegie Class: DU-Highest
FAX Number: (502) 852-7013 Calendar System: Semester
URL: www.louisville.edu
Established: 1798 Annual Undergrad Tuition & Fees (In-State): $12,162
Enrollment: 22,211 Coed
Affiliation or Control: State IRS Status: 501(c)3
Highest Offering: Doctorate
Accreditation: SC, AUD, CACREP, CAEP, CAMPEP, CIDA, CLPSY, COPSY, COSMA, DENT, DH, EXSC, HSA, IPSY, LAW, MED, MFCD, MUS, NURSE, PH, PLNG, SP, SPAA, SW, THEA

01 President ....Dr. Neeli BENDAPUDI
05 Provost/EVP Academic Affairs ....Dr. Lori STEWART GONZALEZ
17 Exec Vice Pres for Health Affairs ....Vacant
46 Executive VP for Research ....Dr. Kevin GARDNER
10 Vice Pres & Chief Financial Officer ....Mr. Daniel DURBIN
11 Sr Assoc VP for Operations ....Mr. Mark WATKINS
111 Vice Pres Univ Advancement ....Dr. Jasmine FARRIER
13 Vice President & CIO ....Mr. M. Rehan KHAN
31 Vice President Community Engagement ....Dr. Ralph FITZPATRICK
15 Vice President Human Resources ....Ms. Mary Elizabeth MILES
41 Vice President for Athletics ....Mr. Vince TYRA
18 Assoc VP Facilities/Physical Plant ....Mr. Mark WATKINS
29 Asst VP for Alumni Relations ....Mr. Josh HAWKINS
100 Chief of Staff for the President ....Mr. Michael W. SMITH
43 General Counsel/VP Legal Affs ....Ms. Angela CURRY
58 Vice Prov/Dean Grad Affs ....Dr. Beth BOEHM
28 Sr Assoc VP Diversity/Equity ....Dr. V. Faye JONES
09 Vice Prov Assmnt Decision Supp/Anl ....Mr. Robert S. GOLDSTEIN
84 Vice Provost Enrollment Management ....Mr. James BEGANY
106 Int Co Vice Prov Online Learn ....Ms. Kristen BROWN
88 Dir Accreditation & Acad Planning ....Ms. Kay VETTER
21 Controller/Treasurer ....Ms. Beverly SANTAMOURIS
07 Executive Director Admissions ....Ms. Jenny L. SAWYER
06 University Registrar ....Mr. Scott A. BURKS
37 Dir Financial Aid Svcs ....Mr. Joseph DABLOW
26 Sr AVP Communications/Marketing ....Mr. John DREES
16 Asst Dir Employee Relations ....Ms. Donna ERNST
19 Dir Public Safety/Chief of Police ....Mr. Gary D. LEWIS, JR.
09 Exec Dir Inst Research & Planning ....Ms. Becky PATTERSON
45 Director Inst Effectiveness ....Dr. Katie PARTIN
39 Director Residence Admin ....Dr. Thomas HARDY
105 Director of Brand Design ....Mr. Brian A. FAUST
27 Director Media Relations ....Mr. John KARMAN
116 Director Audit Services ....Ms. Cheri JONES
92 Exec Director of Honors Program ....Dr. Joy HART
96 Chief Procurement Officer ....Ms. Sally MOLSBERGER
36 Director Career Development ....Mr. Bill FLETCHER
38 Director Counseling Center ....Ms. Aesha UQDAH
08 Dean of University Libraries ....Mr. Robert FOX
49 Int Dean College Arts & Sciences ....Dr. David OWEN
50 Dean College of Business ....Dr. Todd MOORADIAN
52 Dean School of Dentistry ....Dr. Thomas G. BRADLEY
53 Int Dean Col of Educ/Human Devel ....Dr. Amy LINGO
70 Dean Kent School Social Work ....Dr. David A. JENKINS
64 Dean School of Music ....Dr. Teresa REED
61 Int Dean Brandeis School of Law ....Mr. Lars SMITH
66 Dean School of Nursing ....Dr. Sonya HARDING
54 Dean Speed School Engineering ....Dr. Emmanuel COLLINS
63 Dean School of Medicine ....Dr. Toni GANZEL
69 Dean Public Health/Information Sci ....Dr. Craig H. BLAKELY
35 Dean of Students/Vice Provost ....Dr. Michael MARDIS
104 Director Study Abroad ....Dr. Virginia HOSONO

University of Pikeville (B)

147 Sycamore Street, Pikeville KY 41501-1194
County: Pike FICE Identification: 001980
Unit ID: 157535
Telephone: (606) 218-5250 Carnegie Class: Bac-A&S
FAX Number: (606) 218-5269 Calendar System: Semester
URL: www.upike.edu
Established: 1889 Annual Undergrad Tuition & Fees: $22,050
Enrollment: 2,240 Coed
Affiliation or Control: Presbyterian Church (U.S.A.) IRS Status: 501(c)3
Highest Offering: Doctorate
Accreditation: SC, NUR, OPT, OSTEO, SW

00 Chancellor ....Mr. Paul E. PATTON
01 President ....Dr. Burton J. WEBB
05 Provost ....Dr. Lori WERTH
49 Dean College Arts/Sciences ....Dr. Jennifer DUGAN
88 Dean College of Optometry ....Dr. Michael BACIGALUPI
50 Dean College of Business ....Dr. Howard V. ROBERTS
53 Dean College of Education ....Vacant
10 Vice Pres Finance/Business Affairs ....Mr. Barry BENTLEY
111 Vice President for Advancement ....Mr. David HUTCHENS
26 Dir of Public Affairs/Advancement ....Mrs. Kelly ROWE-JONES
63 Dean KYCOM ....Dr. Joe KINGERY
32 Dean of Students ....Dr. Justin OWENS
07 Director of Admissions ....Mr. Gary JUSTICE
08 Director of Library Services ....Ms. Edna FUGATE
06 University Registrar ....Mrs. Gia POTTER
09 Director of Institutional Research ....Dr. Meg SIDLE
13 Senior Info Services Administrator ....Mr. Jonathan WILLIAMSON
18 Director for Facilities ....Mr. Charles ATKINSON
37 Director of Student Financial Svcs ....Mr. Daniel DONNER

15 AVP Operations/Human Resources ....Mr. Michael PACHECO
04 Executive Asst to President ....Mrs. Sherrie MARRS
19 Director Security/Safety ....Mr. Allen ABSHIRE
41 Athletic Director ....Mr. Kelly WELLS
105 Coordinator of New Media ....Mr. Larry EPLING
25 Chief Contracts/Grants Admin ....Mrs. Tiffany THACKER
29 Director Alumni Relations ....Ms. Lisa BLACKBURN
121 Director Student Success ....Dr. Mathys MEYER
39 Housing Operations Supervisor ....Mr. Chris ROBINSON
44 Director Annual or Planned Giving ....Vacant
104 Director Study Abroad ....Dr. Timothy WHITTIER
28 Director of Diversity ....Dr. Katrina RUGLESS

Western Kentucky University (C)

1906 College Heights Blvd, Bowling Green KY 42101-3576
County: Warren FICE Identification: 002002
Unit ID: 157951
Telephone: (270) 745-0111 Carnegie Class: DU-Mod
FAX Number: (270) 745-5387 Calendar System: Semester
URL: www.wku.edu
Established: 1906 Annual Undergrad Tuition & Fees (In-State): $10,802
Enrollment: 17,517 Coed
Affiliation or Control: State IRS Status: 501(c)3
Highest Offering: Doctorate
Accreditation: SC, ADNUR, ART, CACREP, CAEP, CAHIIM, CAPRT, DANCE, DH, DIETD, DIETI, JOUR, MUS, NAEYC, NAIT, NURSE, PH, PTA, SP, SPAA, SW, THEA

01 President ....Dr. Timothy C. CABONI
04 Assistant to the President ....Ms. Kim LANCASTER
05 Provost/VP Academic Affairs ....Dr. Robert FISCHER
46 Assoc Provost for Research ....Dr. Ranjit KOODALI
26 Assoc VP Marketing & Brand Strategy ....Mr. John-Mark FRANCIS
30 Assoc VP Philanthropy & Alumni ....Mr. John Paul BLAIR
29 Exec Director Alumni Engagement ....Mr. Anthony MCADOO
84 VP Enrollment & Student Experience ....Dr. Ethan LOGAN
10 Exec VP Strategy Operations/Finance ....Ms. Susan HOWARTH
07 Director Recruitment & Admissions ....Dr. Jace T. LUX
106 Assoc VP Ext Learning & Outreach ....Dr. Beth LAVES
79 Dean Arts & Letters ....Dr. Terrance BROWN
50 Dean Business ....Dr. Christopher SHOOK
53 Dean Education/Behavioral Sci ....Dr. Corinne MURPHY
76 Dean Health & Human Services ....Dr. Tania BASTA
54 Dean Science & Engineering ....Dr. David BROWN
62 Dean Libraries ....Ms. Susann DEVRIES
21 Interim Chief Financial Officer ....Ms. Kristi SMITH
06 University Registrar ....Ms. Jennifer HAMMONDS
13 Interim Assistant VP IT ....Mr. Jeppie SUMPTER
15 Interim Director Human Resources ....Ms. Andrea SHERRILL
27 Director of Media Relations ....Mr. Jace LUX
86 Director Govt & Community Relations ....Ms. Jennifer B. SMITH
121 Assistant VP Advising & Career Dev ....Mr. Christopher JENSEN
39 Assistant VP Housing/Residence Life ....Dr. Mike REAGLE
19 Chief of Police ....Mr. Mitch WALKER
102 Pres College Heights Foundation ....Dr. Donald L. SMITH
37 Dir Student Financial Assistance ....Mr. Bryson DAVIS
51 Dir Continuing & Professional Dev ....Mr. Derek OLIVE
09 Director Institutional Research ....Dr. Tuesdi HELBIG
22 Director EEO/Title IX/ADA ....Mr. Joshua HAYES
24 Dir Educational Telecommunications ....Mr. David BRINKLEY
41 Director Intercollegiate Athletics ....Mr. Todd M. STEWART
85 Assoc Provost Global Learning ....Mr. John SUNNYGARD
92 Exec Dir Honors College ....Dr. Craig COBANE
18 Chief Facilities Officer ....Mr. Bryan RUSSELL
28 Dir Student Conduct/Chief Diversity ....Mr. Michael CROWE
28 Asst Provost/Chief Diversity Ofcr ....Dr. Molly KERBY
38 Director Counseling & Testing Ctr ....Dr. Peggy CROWE
43 General Counsel ....Ms. Andrea ANDERSON

LOUISIANA

Baton Rouge School of Computers (D)

9352 Interline Avenue, Baton Rouge LA 70809-1909
County: East Baton Rouge FICE Identification: 021975
Unit ID: 158343
Telephone: (225) 923-2524 Carnegie Class: Spec 2-yr-Tech
FAX Number: (225) 923-2979 Calendar System: Other
URL: www.brsc.edu
Established: 1979 Annual Undergrad Tuition & Fees: N/A
Enrollment: 48 Coed
Affiliation or Control: Proprietary IRS Status: Proprietary
Highest Offering: Associate Degree
Accreditation: ACCSC

01 President/Director ....Mrs. Betty D. TRUXILLO

Bridges Christian College (E)

PO Box 15138, New Orleans LA 70175
County: Orleans Identification: 667417
Telephone: (855) 702-7434 Carnegie Class: Not Classified
FAX Number: N/A Calendar System: Trimester
URL: bridgeschristiancollege.com
Established: 2011 Annual Undergrad Tuition & Fees: N/A
Enrollment: N/A Coed
Affiliation or Control: Assemblies Of God Church IRS Status: 501(c)3
Highest Offering: Baccalaureate
Accreditation: @BI

01 President ....Dr. Richard MILLER

Centenary College of Louisiana (F)

PO Box 41188, Shreveport LA 71134-1188
County: Caddo FICE Identification: 002003
Unit ID: 158477
Telephone: (318) 869-5011 Carnegie Class: Bac-A&S
FAX Number: N/A Calendar System: Semester
URL: www.centenary.edu
Established: 1825 Annual Undergrad Tuition & Fees: $38,060
Enrollment: 563 Coed
Affiliation or Control: United Methodist IRS Status: 501(c)3
Highest Offering: Master's
Accreditation: SC, MUS

01 President ....Dr. Christopher HOLOMAN
04 Exec Assistant to the President ....Mrs. Connie WHITTINGTON
05 Provost & Dean of the College ....Dr. Karen SOUL
10 Vice President for Finance/Admin ....Mr. Bob BLUE
50 Dean of the School of Business ....Vacant
64 Dean of the School of Music ....Dr. Cory WIKAN
30 Vice Pres for Development ....Mr. Fred LANDRY
84 Vice President Enrollment & Mktg ....Mr. Calhoun ALLEN
20 Vice Provost for Academic Affairs ....Dr. Jeanne HAMMING
09 Assoc Prov Inst Rsrch & Planning ....Dr. Katherine BEARDEN
13 Director of Information Technology ....Mr. Scott MERRITT
21 Business Manager ....Mrs. Monica POWELL
41 Director of Athletics & Recreation ....Mr. David ORR
32 Dean of Students ....Mr. Mark MILLER
38 Director of Counseling ....Ms. Tina FELDT
37 Director of Financial Aid ....Mrs. Lynette VISKOZKI
08 Librarian ....Ms. Christy WRENN
26 Dir of Strategic Communications ....Mrs. Kate PEDROTTY
29 Director Alumni/Family Relations ....Ms. Katie CHOPIN
18 Director of Facilities ....Mr. Chris SAMPITE
25 Director Sponsored Research ....Ms. Patty J. ROBERTS
07 Director Admissions/Recruitment ....Ms. Lauren HAWKINS
15 Human Resources Director ....Ms. Edie CUMMINGS
19 Director of Public Safety ....Mr. Eddie WALKER
104 Director Study Abroad ....Mrs. Anne-Marie BRUNER-TRACEY
39 Director Res Life & Student Conduct ....Ms. Katherine SHAMBURGER
06 Registrar ....Mrs. Deborah SCARLATO

Chamberlain University-New Orleans (G)

400 Lebarre Road, Jefferson LA 70121
Telephone: (504) 565-7995 Identification: 770983
Accreditation: &HLC, NURSE

† Branch campus of Chamberlain University-Addison, Addison, IL

Delta College of Arts & Technology (H)

7380 Exchange Place, Baton Rouge LA 70806-3851
County: East Baton Rouge FICE Identification: 025383
Unit ID: 366270
Telephone: (225) 407-4562 Carnegie Class: Spec 2-yr-A&S
FAX Number: N/A Calendar System: Other
URL: www.deltacollege.com
Established: 1983 Annual Undergrad Tuition & Fees: N/A
Enrollment: N/A Coed
Affiliation or Control: Proprietary IRS Status: Proprietary
Highest Offering: Associate Degree
Accreditation: COE

Dillard University (I)

2601 Gentilly Boulevard, New Orleans LA 70122-3097
County: Orleans FICE Identification: 002004
Unit ID: 158802
Telephone: (504) 283-8822 Carnegie Class: Bac-A&S
FAX Number: N/A Calendar System: Semester
URL: www.dillard.edu
Established: 1869 Annual Undergrad Tuition & Fees: $19,281
Enrollment: 1,215 Coed
Affiliation or Control: United Methodist IRS Status: 501(c)3
Highest Offering: Baccalaureate
Accreditation: SC, ACBSP, NUR

01 President ....Dr. Walter M. KIMBROUGH
111 Vice Pres Inst Advancement ....Mr. Marc BARNES
05 Provost/Sr VP for Academic Affairs ....Dr. Yolanda PAGE
32 Vice President for Student Success ....Dr. Roland BULLARD
43 VP for Legal Affairs ....Mr. Brendan GREENE
10 VP for Finance/CFO ....Mr. R. JOHNSON
84 Vice Pres Enrollment Management ....Mr. David PAGE
07 Dir of Recruitment & Admissions ....Ms. Monica WHITE
18 Dir of Facilities Mgmt ....Mr. Shaun LEWIS
36 Director of Career/Prof Services ....Mr. Jonathan WRIGHT
06 Dir of Records & Registration ....Mr. Robert MITCHELL, JR.
37 Dir Financial Aid/Scholarships ....Ms. Denise SPELLMAN
46 Assoc VP Research & Spons Programs ....Mr. Theodore CALLIER
30 Director of Development ....Mrs. Adrian GUY-ANDERSON
04 Exec Assistant to the President ....Ms. Kathy TAYLOR
31 Director Community Development ....Mr. Nick L. HARRIS
19 Chief of Police ....Ms. Angela HONORA
15 Director of Human Resources ....Mrs. Brittany RICHARDSON
26 Dir of Marketing/Communications ....Mr. Eddie FRANCIS
08 Director of Library/Learning ....Ms. Jennifer COLLINS
49 Dean of College of Arts & Sciences ....Dr. Eartha JOHNSON

96 Purchasing Officer .... Vacant
103 Dir Workforce/Career Development .... Vacant
13 Chief Info Technology Officer (CIO) .... Mr. Cederic KONYAOLE
22 Dir Affirmative Action/EEO .... Ms. Sheila JUDGE
39 Director Student Housing .... Mr. Jamar SIMMONS
41 Athletic Director .... Dr. Kiki BAKER-BARNES
50 Interim Dean of Business .... Dr. Richard IGWIKE
29 Director Alumni Relations .. Mrs. Rebecca ARMSTONG-ENGLISH
44 Annual Fund Officer .... Mr. Braxton MCSHAN
09 Director of Institutional Research .... Mr. Jacques J. DETIEGE

Fortis College (A)

14111 Airline Highway, Suite 101, Baton Rouge LA 70817
County: East Baton Rouge FICE Identification: 034803
Unit ID: 439738
Telephone: (225) 248-1015 Carnegie Class: Spec 2-yr-Health
FAX Number: (225) 248-9517 Calendar System: Other
URL: www.fortis.edu
Established: 1991 Annual Undergrad Tuition & Fees: $15,030
Enrollment: 408 Coed
Affiliation or Control: Proprietary IRS Status: Proprietary
Highest Offering: Associate Degree
Accreditation: **ABHES**, MLTAD, SURTEC

01 Campus President .... John ESTORAGE

Franciscan Missionaries of Our Lady University (B)

5414 Brittany Drive, Baton Rouge LA 70808
County: East Baton Rouge FICE Identification: 031062
Unit ID: 160074
Telephone: (225) 768-1700 Carnegie Class: Spec-4-yr-Other Health
FAX Number: (225) 768-0811 Calendar System: Semester
URL: www.franu.edu
Established: 1923 Annual Undergrad Tuition & Fees: $14,535
Enrollment: 1,366 Coed
Affiliation or Control: Roman Catholic IRS Status: 501(c)3
Highest Offering: Doctorate
Accreditation: **SC**, ANEST, ARCPA, COARC, DIETI, MT, NUR, PTA, PTAA, RAD

01 President .... Dr. Tina HOLLAND
05 Provost/VP for Academic Affairs .... Br. Edward VIOLETT
111 VP for Institutional Advancement .... Ms. Judith ROBERSON
10 VP for Operations & Finance .... Ms. Angelia BERCEGEAY
84 VP Enrollment Mgmt/Student Affairs .... Ms. Rebecca CANNON
88 VP for Mission Identity .... Sr. Martha Ann ABSHIRE
66 Dean School of Nursing .... Dr. Amy HALL
76 Dean School of Health Professions .... Dr. Susan STEELE-MOSES
32 Dean of Students .... Dr. Alison WELLS
49 Dean School of Arts & Sciences .... Dr. Brian RASH
37 Director Financial Aid .... Vacant
06 Registrar .... Ms. Kimberly JONES-JAMES
76 Director Physician Asst Program .... Ms. Sarah DEYO
76 Director Nurse Anesthesia Program .... Dr. Mandy BROUSSARD
76 Director Radiologic Technology .... Ms. Nicole ST. GERMAIN
76 Director Medical Lab Science .... Dr. Debbie FOX
76 Director Physical Therapist Asst .... Dr. Marty AIME
88 Dir Master of Health Administration .... Dr. Elaine PURDY
76 Director Respiratory Therapy .... Ms. Sue DAVIS
88 Dir Doctor of Physical Therapy Pgm .... Dr. Kirk NELSON
88 Director FNP Program .... Dr. Alicia BATES
88 Director Nutritional Sciences Prog .... Dr. Rachel FOURNET
88 Dir Simulated Clinical Educ .... Ms. Tabitha JONES-THOMAS
24 Director Learning Resource Center .... Ms. Jalan WOODWARD
13 Director of Information Systems .... Mr. Craig WHITE
07 Director of Admissions .... Ms. Christy SEVIER
09 Asst Provost Inst Effectiveness .... Dr. Candi MCELHENY
04 Executive Asst to President .... Ms. Kimberly MELANCON
44 Director Annual Giving/Alumni Rels .... Mr. Corey WILLIAMS
113 Bursar .... Ms. Erin ELLIS
42 Director Campus Ministry .... Ms. Tammy VIDRINE
90 Director Educational Technology .... Ms. Liza MAYEUX
112 Director Donor Relations .... Ms. Aimee GREENE
88 Director Service Learning .... Dr. Rhoda REDDIX
08 Co-Director Library .... Mr. Lucas HUNTINGTON
08 Co-Director Library .... Ms. Maggie MCCANN
18 Director of Operations .... Ms. Denice DORSEY
19 Director Health and Safety .... Ms. Denise GILLESPIE
38 Director Counseling .... Dr. Lynn BROWNING
30 Director of Development .... Ms. Laura ST. BLANC
88 Director Quality Enhancement Plan .... Dr. Valerie SCHLUTER
15 Human Resources Business Partner .... Ms. Jennifer STRICKLAND
25 Contract and Grants Manager .... Mr. Mark OURSO
36 Director Career & Leadership .... Ms. Tinicia TURNER

Herzing University (C)

3900 North Causeway Blvd, Suite 800, Metarie LA 70002
Telephone: (504) 613-4295 Identification: 666450
Accreditation: **&HLC**, SURTEC

† Regional accreditation is carried under the parent institution in Madison, WI.

ITI Technical College (D)

13944 Airline Highway, Baton Rouge LA 70817-5998
County: East Baton Rouge FICE Identification: 021662
Unit ID: 159197
Telephone: (225) 752-4230 Carnegie Class: Spec 2-yr-Tech
FAX Number: (225) 756-0903 Calendar System: Quarter
URL: www.iticollege.edu
Established: 1973 Annual Undergrad Tuition & Fees: $11,156
Enrollment: 603 Coed
Affiliation or Control: Proprietary IRS Status: Proprietary
Highest Offering: Associate Degree
Accreditation: **ACCSC**

01 President .... Mr. Earl Joe MARTIN, III
03 Vice President .... Mr. Mark WORTHY
05 Dean of Education .... Ms. Carol BOUDREAUX
11 Administrative Director .... Mr. Michael CHAMPAGNE
07 Director of Admissions .... Mr. Shawn NORRIS

Louisiana College (E)

1140 College Drive, Pineville LA 71359-0001
County: Rapides FICE Identification: 002007
Unit ID: 159568
Telephone: (318) 487-7000 Carnegie Class: Masters/S
FAX Number: (318) 487-7800 Calendar System: Semester
URL: www.lacollege.edu
Established: 1906 Annual Undergrad Tuition & Fees: $17,500
Enrollment: 1,153 Coed
Affiliation or Control: Southern Baptist IRS Status: 501(c)3
Highest Offering: Master's
Accreditation: **SC**, ACBSP, MUS, NURSE, PTAA, SW

01 President .... Dr. Rick BREWER
03 Executive Vice President .... Vacant
05 Provost/Vice Pres Academic Affairs .... Dr. Cheryl CLARK
10 Exec Dir or Finance/CFO .... Mrs. Evelyn DEAN
111 VP Advancement .... Vacant
32 AVP Stdnt Engagement/Enrichment .... Dr. Joshua DARA
06 Registrar .... Ms. Eileen DEBOER
07 Exec Director of Admissions .... Mrs. Renee MELDER
37 Director of Financial Aid .... Ms. Brandie BASS
08 Director of the Library .... Dr. Lillian PURDY
26 Coordinator of College Relations .... Dr. Elizabeth CHRISTIAN
13 Exec Dir of Information Technology .... Mr. Bryce SANDERS
18 Maintenance Facility Supervisor .... Mr. Walt GOODMAN
21 Director of Business Office .... Ms. Beverly INGRAM
39 Director of Residence Life .... Mr. Gage DOWLING
41 Athletic Director .... Mr. Reni MASON
42 Baptist Student Union Director .... Mr. Thomas WORSHAM
85 Director International Student Affs .... Mrs. Casey DOWLING
36 Exec Dir of Calling and Career .... Mrs. Meredith RENNIER
38 Director of Mental Health .... Ms. Taylor DAUZAT
15 Executive Director Human Resources .... Ms. Christelle CARLEY
40 Bookstore Manager .... Ms. Linda BILLINGSLEY
29 Exec Dir of Development/Alumni Affs .... Mrs. Beth PALMER
19 Chief of Safety & Security .... Mr. Clifford GATLIN
23 Coordinator of Health Services .... Ms. Janet SANDERS
04 Executive Asst President's Office .... Mrs. Lori SCOTT
26 Director of Marketing .... Ms. Jennifer DYKES

*Louisiana Community & Technical College System (F)

265 S Foster Drive, Baton Rouge LA 70806-4104
County: East Baton Rouge Identification: 666188
Telephone: (225) 922-2800 Carnegie Class: N/A
FAX Number: (225) 922-2786
URL: www.lctcs.edu

01 President .... Dr. Monty SULLIVAN
05 Chief Academic Affairs Officer .... Dr. Rene CINTRON
10 Chief Financial Officer/COO .... Mr. Joseph F. MARIN
26 Chief Public Affairs Officer .... Mr. Quintin TAYLOR
84 Chief Enrollment Management Officer .... Dr. Emily CAMPBELL

*Baton Rouge Community College (G)

201 Community College Drive,
Baton Rouge LA 70806-4156
County: East Baton Rouge FICE Identification: 037303
Unit ID: 437103
Telephone: (866) 217-9823 Carnegie Class: Assoc/MT-VT-High Trad
FAX Number: (225) 216-8100 Calendar System: Semester
URL: www.mybrcc.edu
Established: 1998 Annual Undergrad Tuition & Fees (In-District): $4,221
Enrollment: 7,376 Coed
Affiliation or Control: State/Local IRS Status: 501(c)3
Highest Offering: Associate Degree
Accreditation: **SC**, ACBSP, ACFEI, ADNUR, CONST, DMS, NAIT, SURGT

02 Chancellor .... Dr. Willie E. SMITH
04 Asst to the Chancellor .... Ms. Tuesday A. GRAY
26 Chief PR & Marketing Officer .... Ms. Kizzy PAYTON
05 VC Academic & Student Affairs .... Dr. Sarah BARLOW
103 Vice Chanc for Workforce Solutions .... Dr. Girard MELANCON
111 Vice Chanc for Inst Advance/Found .... Mr. Philip L. SMITH, JR.
10 Vice Chanc for Finance & Admin .... Mr. Corlin LEBLANC
21 Asst VC for Finance .... Ms. Lyndra SMITH
114 Director of Budgets .... Vacant
13 Chief Information Officer .... Mr. Ronald SOLOMON
15 Chief HR Officer .... Ms. Annette ARBONEAUX
19 Chief of Police .... Ms. Genoria TILLEY
25 Dir Grants Resource Center .... Ms. Ann ZANDERS
46 Dir of Business Process Improv .... Ms. Dionne ANDRUS
18 Chief Facilities Officer .... Mr. Anthony BROWN
29 Alumni Relations Manager .... Ms. Georgia SCOBEE
35 Assoc Dean of Students .... Ms. Stacia HARDY
36 Director of Career Services .... Ms. Lisa HIBNER
37 Director of Financial Aid .... Ms. Miracle DAVIS
41 Interim Athletic Director .... Ms. Paula LEE
121 Dir of Academic Learning Center .... Ms. Jeanne STACY
88 Upward Bound Program Director .... Ms. Darica SIMON
96 Director of Purchasing .... Ms. Hilary STEPHENSON
06 Registrar .... Ms. Taylor DAVID

*Bossier Parish Community College (H)

6220 East Texas Street, Bossier City LA 71111-6922
County: Bossier FICE Identification: 020554
Unit ID: 158431
Telephone: (318) 678-6000 Carnegie Class: Assoc/MT-VT-High Trad
FAX Number: (318) 678-6389 Calendar System: Semester
URL: www.bpcc.edu
Established: 1966 Annual Undergrad Tuition & Fees (In-District): $4,284
Enrollment: 6,090 Coed
Affiliation or Control: State/Local IRS Status: 501(c)3
Highest Offering: Associate Degree
Accreditation: **SC**, ACFEI, ADNUR, COARC, EMT, MAC, NAIT, OTA, PTAA, SURGT

02 Chancellor .... Dr. Douglas R. BATEMAN
05 VC Academic Affairs .... Ms. Lesa TAYLOR DUPREE
32 VC of Student Services .... Ms. Karen RECCHIA
10 Assoc VC Finance .... Mr. Raymond ABRAHAM
45 Assoc VC Inst Planning & Assessment .. Dr. Holly FRENCH-HART
103 Assoc VC Workforce Solutions .... Ms. Sandra HARVEY
08 Dean of Learning Resources .... Mr. Adrian CRAWFORD
37 Director Student Financial Aid .... Ms. Vicki TEMPLE
06 Registrar .... Mr. Richard COCKERHAM
15 Director of Human Resources .... Ms. Teri BASHARA
35 Director of Student Life .... Ms. Marjoree HARPER
13 Chief Information Officer .... Mr. Wesley BANGE
22 Diversity/Multicultural Affairs .... Ms. Marjoree HARPER
72 Dean of Educational Technology .... Mr. Charley CAMERON
18 Dir Physical Plant & Maintenance .... Mr. Chad JOHNSTON
111 Dir Institutional Advance/Grants .... Dr. Jennifer LAWRENCE
96 Director of Purchasing .... Ms. Gayle DOUCET
04 Exec Assistant to Chancellor .... Ms. Christy MOORE
84 Dean of Enrollment Management .... Ms. Kathy VERCHER
108 Dir Institutional Effectiveness .... Ms. Allison MARTIN
19 Chief of Campus Police .... Mr. Jimmy STEWART
60 Dean of Comm & Performing Arts .... Dr. Ray Scott CRAWFORD
50 Dean of Business .... Ms. Peggy FULLER
54 Dean of TEM .... Ms. Megan BANGE
66 Dean of Sci/Nursing/Allied Health .... Ms. Carolyn BURROUGHS
49 Dean of Liberal Arts .... Ms. Vicki DENNIS
83 Dean of Behavioral Social Sciences .... Ms. Kay BOSTON
121 Dean of Student Success .... Ms. Peggy FULLER
41 Athletic Director .... Ms. Karen RECCHIA
100 Chief of Staff .... Dr. Jennifer LAWRENCE

*Central Louisiana Technical College Avoyelles Campus (I)

508 Choupique Street, Cottonport LA 71327-3743
County: Avoyelles FICE Identification: 008317
Unit ID: 158237
Telephone: (318) 876-2401 Carnegie Class: Not Classified
FAX Number: (318) 876-2634 Calendar System: Semester
URL: https://www.cltcc.edu/campuses/ward-h-nash-avoyelles-campus
Established: 1938 Annual Undergrad Tuition & Fees (In-District): N/A
Enrollment: N/A Coed
Affiliation or Control: State/Local IRS Status: 501(c)3
Highest Offering: Associate Degree
Accreditation: **COE**

02 Interim Campus Dean .... Ms. Tiffany HOWARD

*Central Louisiana Technical Community College (J)

516 Murray St., Alexandria LA 71301
County: Rapides FICE Identification: 005489
Unit ID: 158088
Telephone: (318) 487-5443 Carnegie Class: Spec 2-yr-Other
FAX Number: (318) 487-5970 Calendar System: Semester
URL: www.cltcc.edu
Established: 1965 Annual Undergrad Tuition & Fees (In-State): $4,098
Enrollment: 2,192 Coed
Affiliation or Control: State IRS Status: 501(c)3
Highest Offering: Associate Degree
Accreditation: **COE**

02 Chancellor .... Dr. James (Jimmy) R. SAWTELLE, III
05 Vice Chanc Academic Affairs .... Mr. William TULAK
10 Vice Chanc of Finance/Admin .... Mr. Joseph BORNE
32 Exec VC Stdnt Affs/Enroll Mgmt .... Ms. Heather POOLE
103 Vice Chanc Workforce .... Ms. Misty SLAYTER
04 Admin Assistant to the President .... Vacant
06 Registrar .... Ms. Lynda GARVIN
08 Chief Library Officer .... Ms. Daenel VAUGHAN-TUCKER
09 Director of Institutional Research .... Dr. Stephen COX
13 Chief Information Technology Ofcr .... Dr. Sharon LAYCOCK
15 Chief Human Resources Officer .... Ms. Angel MCGEE
37 Director Student Financial Aid .... Ms. Kelly CARUSO

*Central Louisiana Technical & Community College-Huey P. Long Campus (A)

5960 Highway 167 N, PO Box 871, Winnfield LA 71483
County: Winn FICE Identification: 005480
Unit ID: 159090
Telephone: (318) 628-4342 Carnegie Class: Not Classified
FAX Number: (318) 628-7768 Calendar System: Semester
URL: www.cltcc.edu
Established: 1939 Annual Undergrad Tuition & Fees (In-District): N/A
Enrollment: N/A Coed
Affiliation or Control: State/Local IRS Status: 501(c)3
Highest Offering: Associate Degree
Accreditation: COE

05 Campus Dean & Director .... Mr. Jeff JOHNSON

*Delgado Community College (B)

615 City Park Avenue, New Orleans LA 70119-4399
County: Orleans FICE Identification: 004625
Unit ID: 158662
Telephone: (504) 671-5000 Carnegie Class: Assoc/MT-VT-High Trad
FAX Number: (504) 361-6699 Calendar System: Semester
URL: www.dcc.edu
Established: 1921 Annual Undergrad Tuition & Fees (In-District): $4,079
Enrollment: 13,251 Coed
Affiliation or Control: State/Local IRS Status: 501(c)3
Highest Offering: Associate Degree
Accreditation: SC, ACBSP, ACFEI, ADNUR, CAHIIM, COARC, DMS, EMT, FUSER, MLTAD, NAIT, NMT, OTA, POLYT, PTAA, RAD, RTT, SURGT

02 Chancellor .... Dr. Larissa LITTLETON STEIB
10 VC Business/Admin Affairs .... Mr. Ronald RUSSO
05 VC Academic & Stdnt Affs/Provost .... Dr. Cheryl MYERS
103 VC Wkfrc Dev/Tech Educ/Inst Advance .... Ms. Arlanda WILLIAMS
32 AVC Stdnt Affairs/Exec Dean SC .... Dr. Tamika DUPLESSIS
66 Int Exec Dean Charity Sch/Nursing .... Dr. Deborah SKEVINGTON
76 AVC Acad Affs/Dean Allied Health .... Mr. Harold GASPARD
60 Dean Communication Division .... Ms. Emily COSPER
81 Dean Science & Math .... Dr. Mostofa SARWAR
79 Dean Arts and Humanities .... Ms. Patrice MOORE
106 Dean Distance Lrng/Instruct Tech .... Vacant
12 Exec Dean West Bank/Dean Bus & Tech .... Dr. Peter CHO
12 Exec Dean Sidney Collier .... Dr. Tamika DUPLESSIS
15 Asst Vice Chanc for Human Resources .... Ms. Carla MAJOR
13 Chief Information Officer .... Mr. James P. HOBBS, III
21 Exec Dir Fin Svcs/Assoc Controller .... Ms. Amy LASZCZ
18 Asst VC Facilities & Planning .... Mr. James ROYER
04 Executive Asst to the Chancellor .... Ms. Traci SMOTHERS
72 Asst Dean Business & Technology .... Ms. Karen MUHSIN
09 Director Planning & Research .... Dr. Patricia ROSS
88 Exec Dir Curriculum & Pgm Devel .... Mr. Timothy STAMM
08 Dean Library .... Mr. Timothy STAMM
41 Athletic Director .... Mr. Joe SCHEUERMANN
06 College Registrar .... Ms. Maria CISNEROS
07 Director Admissions/Enrollment Svcs .... Ms. Michelle GRECO
44 Director Restricted Funds .... Ms. Sarah CAMANIA VINNETT
84 Director Enrollment Management .... Mrs. Michelle GRECO
121 Director Advising & Testing .... Vacant
96 Director Purchasing .... Ms. Tracey SHEFFIELD
19 Director Campus Police .... Mr. Warren RILEY

*L.E. Fletcher Technical Community College (C)

1407 Highway 311, Schriever LA 70395
County: Terrebonne FICE Identification: 005761
Unit ID: 160481
Telephone: (985) 448-7900 Carnegie Class: Assoc/HVT-Mix Trad/Non
FAX Number: (985) 446-3308 Calendar System: Semester
URL: www.fletcher.edu
Established: 1948 Annual Undergrad Tuition & Fees (In-State): $3,981
Enrollment: 2,105 Coed
Affiliation or Control: State IRS Status: Exempt
Highest Offering: Associate Degree
Accreditation: SC, ACBSP, ADNUR, COARC, MLTAD, NAIT, PNUR, SURGT

02 Chancellor .... Dr. Kristine STRICKLAND
05 Vice Chanc Academic Affairs .... Dr. Regina VERDIN
10 Vice Chanc Finance/Administration .... Dr. Mark MCLEAN
06 Registrar .... Ms. Alexis KNIGHT
09 Dir Inst Research & Effectiveness .... Dr. Carrie CORTEZ
32 Dean of Student Services .... Ms. Angie PELLEGRIN
66 Dean of Nursing and Allied Health .... Ms. Danielle VAUCLIN
84 Executive Director of Enrollment .... Ms. Ana NANNEY
15 Director of Human Resources .... Ms. Gina MARCEL
100 Special Assistant to the Chancellor .... Mrs. Crystal GIENGER
08 Director of Library Services .... Mrs. Jodi DUET
26 VC Ext Rels/Workforce Innovation .... Mr. W. Chandler LEBOEUF
49 Dean of Liberal Arts/CDYC/Business .... Mr. William LOPEZ
30 Development Coordinator .... Ms. Logan BORNE
96 Manager of Purchasing & Travel .... Ms. Jill SEVIER

*Louisiana Delta Community College (D)

7500 Millhaven Road, Monroe LA 71203
County: Ouachita Parish FICE Identification: 041301
Unit ID: 483212
Telephone: (318) 345-9000 Carnegie Class: Assoc/HVT-Mix Trad/Non
FAX Number: N/A Calendar System: Semester
URL: www.ladelta.edu
Established: 2001 Annual Undergrad Tuition & Fees (In-District): $4,076
Enrollment: 3,874 Coed
Affiliation or Control: State/Local IRS Status: 501(c)3
Highest Offering: Associate Degree
Accreditation: SC, ADNUR, EMT, NAIT

02 Chancellor .... Dr. Randy E. ESTERS
05 Vice Chanc of Academic Affairs .... Vacant
10 CFO .... Ms. Naomi MITCHELL
103 Exec Dir of Workforce Development .... Dr. Wendi TOSTENSON
84 Exec Dir of Enrollment Management .... Vacant
30 Dir Inst Advancement/Development .... Ms. Missy AMY
13 Chief Information Officer .... Mr. Bradley MASTERS
26 Director of Public Relations .... Ms. Darian ATKINS
04 Admin Assistant to the President .... Mrs. Connie L. CARR
09 Dir of IR & Effectiveness .... Ms. Stacy LYNCH
106 Director Online Education/E-learnin .... Mrs. Sharon BOWMAN
15 Exec Director of Human Resources .... Ms. Kendra HOUGH
18 Director of Facilities .... Mr. Randy WILKERSON
38 Director Student Counseling .... Mrs. Traci CLARK
06 Registrar .... Mrs. Gwenn HALL
07 Director of Recruitment/Admissions .... Mr. Michael ANDERSON
19 Director Security/Safety .... Mr. Downey BLACK
37 Director Student Financial Aid .... Mrs. Kimberly BRUCE
08 Chief Library Officer .... Ms. Amelia BRISTER

*Northshore Technical Community College (E)

65556 Centerpoint Blvd, Lacombe LA 70437
County: St. Tammany FICE Identification: 006756
Unit ID: 160667
Telephone: (985) 545-1500 Carnegie Class: Assoc/HVT-High Non
FAX Number: N/A Calendar System: Semester
URL: www.northshorecollege.edu
Established: 1930 Annual Undergrad Tuition & Fees (In-District): $4,103
Enrollment: 3,552 Coed
Affiliation or Control: State/Local IRS Status: 501(c)3
Highest Offering: Associate Degree
Accreditation: SC

02 Chancellor .... Dr. William S. WAINWRIGHT
05 Provost/Vice Chancellor of Academic .... Dr. Daniel ROBERTS
10 Vice Chancellor Finance & Admin .... Mr. Marc CHAUVIN
45 Vice Chanc Strategic Initiative .... Dr. Jim CARLSON
108 Assist Provost Programs/Assessment .... Dr. Paul DONALDSON
09 Director of Accreditation/Reporting .... Dr. Melandie MCGEE
32 Vice Chancellor of Student Affairs .... Dr. Christy MONTGOMERY
06 Registrar .... Ms. Darriona LEE
76 Assoc Provost Health Sci/Nursing .... Ms. Christi MARCEAUX
75 Associate Provost Technical Studies .... Mr. Dewayne LAMBERT
12 Dean of Campus Administration FL .... Ms. Kim FINCH
12 Dean of Campus Admin Hammond .... Ms. Sandy YAEGER
15 Human Resources Director .... Ms. Christi BROWN
18 Director of Facilities .... Mr. Rocky BORK
08 Director of Library Services .... Ms. Cynthia KNIGHT
37 Financial Aid Director .... Ms. Nichole LABAT
13 Director Information Tech/Elearning .... Vacant
12 Dean Campus Administration (LF) .... Ms. Owen SMITH
12 Dean Campus Administration (LE/LI) .... Dr. Lizette LEADER
111 Director Institutional Advancement .... Ms. Mary SLAZER
103 Director of Workforce Training .... Ms. Bridget LABORDE
21 Director of Accounting .... Ms. Kim SHOWERS
113 Bursar .... Ms. Lisa KILLENS
96 Purchasing Manager .... Ms. Sharon JONES
07 Director of Admissions .... Ms. Alverneece JOHNSON

*Northwest Louisiana Technical Community College (F)

9500 Industrial Drive, Minden LA 71055
County: Webster FICE Identification: 009975
Unit ID: 160010
Telephone: (318) 371-3035 Carnegie Class: Spec 2-yr-Tech
FAX Number: (318) 371-3325 Calendar System: Trimester
URL: www.nltcc.edu
Established: 1952 Annual Undergrad Tuition & Fees (In-District): $4,109
Enrollment: 935 Coed
Affiliation or Control: State/Local IRS Status: 501(c)3
Highest Offering: Associate Degree
Accreditation: COE, NAIT

02 Chancellor .... Dr. Earl MEADOR
103 Vice Chancellor of Workforce .... Dr. Jayda SPILLERS
05 Vice Chancellor of Academics .... Ms. Treva ASKEY
32 Vice Chancellor of Student Affairs .... Ms. Treva ASKEY
10 Vice Chancellor of Finance .... Ms. Melanie SOTAK
15 Director of Human Resources .... Ms. Amber SAUNDERS
06 Registrar .... Ms. Stacy SHEPHERD
37 Director of Financial Aid .... Ms. Mary Helen SIMMS

*Nunez Community College (G)

3710 Paris Road, Chalmette LA 70043-1297
County: Saint Bernard FICE Identification: 021661
Unit ID: 158884
Telephone: (504) 278-6200 Carnegie Class: Assoc/HVT-High Non
FAX Number: (504) 278-6480 Calendar System: Semester
URL: www.nunez.edu
Established: 1992 Annual Undergrad Tuition & Fees (In-District): $4,255
Enrollment: 2,166 Coed
Affiliation or Control: State/Local IRS Status: 501(c)3
Highest Offering: Associate Degree
Accreditation: SC, EMT, NAIT

02 Chancellor .... Dr. Tina M. TINNEY
05 VC Educ Training/Student Success .... Dr. Cherie K. LAROCCA
10 Int Vice Chanc Finance/Operations .... Mr. Tai NGUYEN
15 Director Human Resources .... Vacant
20 Dean of Academic Affairs .... Vacant
51 Int Exec Dean Continuing Education .... Mr. Leonard UNBEHAGEN
103 Director Workforce Development .... Mr. Brian GIBSON
06 Registrar .... Ms. Meg GREENFIELD
07 Director of Admissions .... Mrs. Brittney BARRAS
37 Director Financial Aid .... Ms. Treasure BURTCHAELL
26 Director of Communications .... Mr. Jason BROWNE
18 Coordinator of Facilities .... Ms. Dawn HART-THORE
30 Director of Development .... Ms. Katherine LEMOINE
13 IT Manager .... Mr. Jason HOSCH

*River Parishes Community College (H)

PO Box 2367, Gonzales LA 70707
County: Ascension FICE Identification: 037894
Unit ID: 436304
Telephone: (225) 743-8500 Carnegie Class: Assoc/MT-VT-High Non
FAX Number: (225) 644-8210 Calendar System: Semester
URL: www.rpcc.edu
Established: 1999 Annual Undergrad Tuition & Fees (In-District): $4,079
Enrollment: 2,755 Coed
Affiliation or Control: State/Local IRS Status: 501(c)3
Highest Offering: Associate Degree
Accreditation: SC, NAIT

02 Interim Chancellor .... Dr. Jim CARLSON
10 VC Business/Finance/Administration .... Charles CAMBRE
05 VC of Acad Affairs/Enroll & Effect .... Dr. Emily CAMPBELL
103 VC Workforce Development .... Dr. Bruce WAGUESPACK
111 Director Institutional Advancement .... Lillie MURPHY
32 Assoc VC of Student Services & DEI .... Monica MORRISON
37 Director Financial Aid .... Lisa JACKSON
38 Director of Student Advising .... Natasha JOHNSON
08 Director of Library Services .... Wendy JOHNSON
15 Human Resource Manager .... Aarika DORSEY
09 Director of Institutional Research .... Melba KENNEDY
06 Registrar .... Arthur GILLIS

*South Louisiana Community College (I)

1101 Bertrand Drive, Lafayette LA 70506-4124
County: Lafayette FICE Identification: 039563
Unit ID: 434061
Telephone: (337) 521-9000 Carnegie Class: Assoc/HVT-Mix Trad/Non
FAX Number: (337) 521-9061 Calendar System: Semester
URL: www.solacc.edu
Established: 1998 Annual Undergrad Tuition & Fees (In-District): $4,205
Enrollment: 5,855 Coed
Affiliation or Control: State/Local IRS Status: 501(c)3
Highest Offering: Associate Degree
Accreditation: #SC, ACFEI, ADNUR, EMT, MLTAD, NAIT

02 Chancellor .... Dr. Vincent JUNE
04 Exec Assistant to the Chancellor .... Ms. Kelly GREENE
10 Vice Chanc Finance & Administration .... Mr. Bryan GLATTER
103 Vice Chanc Econ & Workforce Devel .... Dr. Jermaine FORD
108 Assoc Vice Chanc Inst Effectiveness .... Dr. Charles MILLER
05 Int Vice Chanc Acad & Student Affs .... Dr. Darcee BEX
37 Director of Financial Aid .... Mrs. Tiffany WILLIAMS
08 Director of Library Services .... Ms. Katherine ROLFES
113 Director of Student Accounts .... Ms. Wendi ROBICHEAUX
21 Director of Accounting .... Ms. Carla ORTEGO
18 Director of Facilities .... Mr. Edwin LOPEZ
15 Exec Dir Strategic Engr/Employ Svcs .... Ms. Alicia HULIN
06 Registrar .... Ms. Connie CHOPIN
19 Director Security/Safety .... Mr. Stephen NORTH
26 Communications & Marketing Director .... Ms. Christine PAYTON
84 Director Enrollment Management .... Ms. Debbie TABCHOURI
111 Vice Chanc Inst Advancement .... Ms. Lana FONTENOT
106 Director Distance Education .... Dr. Stasia HERBERT-MCZEAL
13 Chief Information Technology Office .... Mr. Brad BREAUX
28 Director Student Engagement .... Ms. Erica PRECHT
79 Interim Dean Lib Arts & Humanities .... Dr. Stasia HERBERT-MCZEAL
81 Dean STEM/Transportation & Energy .... Dr. Darcee BEX
66 Dean Nursing & Allied Health .... Dr. Carry DEATLEY
50 Dean Business/Info Tech & Tech Stds .... Mr. Sam HARB
25 Director of Grants Administrator .... Dr. Jessica BAUDOIN
32 Assoc Vice Chanc Student Affairs .... Vacant
38 Dir Counseling & Disability Svcs .... Dr. Cheryl FRUGE
96 Purchasing Manager .... Ms. Nicole MANUEL

*SOWELA Technical Community College (J)

PO Box 16950, Lake Charles LA 70616-6950
County: Calcasieu FICE Identification: 005467
Unit ID: 160579
Telephone: (337) 421-6565 Carnegie Class: Spec 2-yr-Tech
FAX Number: (337) 491-2135 Calendar System: Semester
URL: www.sowela.edu
Established: 1938 Annual Undergrad Tuition & Fees (In-District): $4,265
Enrollment: 2,914 Coed

Affiliation or Control: State/Local IRS Status: 501(c)3
Highest Offering: Associate Degree
Accreditation: SC, ACFEI, ADNUR, NAIT, SURGT

02 Chancellor ... Dr. Neil ASPINWALL
04 Assistant to the Chancellor ... Ms. Mary REEDER
05 Vice Chancellor Academic Affairs ... Dr. Paula HELLUMS
10 Vice Chancellor Finance ... Ms. Jeanine NEWMAN
103 Exec Dir of Workforce Solutions ... Mr. David HAYES
13 Chief Info Res & Tech Officer ... Dr. Martha J. SCHEXNEIDER
84 Exec Dir Enroll Mgmt/Stdnt Affs ... Ms. Pam BOERSIG
21 Controller ... Ms. Lindsey REPPOND
37 Director of Financial Aid ... Ms. Allison DERING
08 Director of Library Services ... Ms. Mary Frances SHERWOOD
15 Director of Human Resources ... Vacant
35 Director of Student Support Svcs ... Ms. Christine COLLINS
18 Director Facilities Planning & Mgmt ... Mr. Davidson DARBONE
09 Exec Director Planning & Analysis ... Dr. Fitzpatrick U. ANYANWU
111 Exec Dir Institutional Advancement ... Ms. Kelly PEPPER
06 Registrar ... Ms. Laura LAFLEUR
36 Director Student Placement ... Mr. Joseph LAVERGNE
53 Dean of Education ... Ms. Stephanie SMITH

* *Central Louisiana Technical Community College Natchitoches Campus* (A)

6587 Highway 1 Bypass, P.O. Box 657,
Natchitoches LA 71457
Telephone: (318) 357-3162 FICE Identification: 021602
Accreditation: COE

† Branch campus of Northwest Louisiana Technical College Northwest Campus, Minden, LA.

* *Northwest Louisiana Technical College Shreveport Campus* (B)

Box 78527, 2010 N Market Street,
Shreveport LA 71137-8527
Telephone: (318) 676-7811 FICE Identification: 005469
Accreditation: COE

† Branch campus of Northwest Louisiana Technical College Northwest Campus, Minden, LA.

Louisiana Culinary Institute (C)

10550 Airline Highway, Baton Rouge LA 70816-4109
County: East Baton Rouge FICE Identification: 041123
Unit ID: 449612
Telephone: (225) 769-8820 Carnegie Class: Spec 2-yr-A&S
FAX Number: (225) 769-8792 Calendar System: Semester
URL: www.lci.edu
Established: 2002 Annual Undergrad Tuition & Fees: $14,575
Enrollment: 114 Coed
Affiliation or Control: Proprietary IRS Status: Proprietary
Highest Offering: Associate Degree
Accreditation: COE

01 Chief Executive Officer ... Keith RUSH

*Louisiana State University Administration (D)

3810 W Lakeshore Drive, Baton Rouge LA 70808-4600
County: East Baton Rouge FICE Identification: 002009
Telephone: (225) 578-2111 Carnegie Class: N/A
FAX Number: (225) 578-5524
URL: www.lsu.edu

01 President ... Mr. William F. TATE, IV
05 Int Exec VP/Provost ... Dr. Matt LEE
10 Int Exec VP Finance & Admin/CFO ... Ms. Donna K. TORRES
84 VP Enrollment Management ... Mr. Jose AVILES
18 AVP Facilities/Property Oversight ... Mr. Tony LOMBARDO
32 VP Student Affairs ... Mr. Jeremiah SHINN
43 Vice Pres Legal Affairs/Gen Counsel ... Mr. Winston G. DECUIR, JR.
28 Vice Provost Diversity ... Mr. Dereck ROVARIS, SR.
116 System Director Internal Audit ... Mr. Chad BRACKIN

*Louisiana State University and Agricultural and Mechanical College (E)

Baton Rouge LA 70803-0100
County: East Baton Rouge FICE Identification: 002010
Unit ID: 159391
Telephone: (225) 578-3202 Carnegie Class: DU-Highest
FAX Number: (225) 578-6400 Calendar System: Semester
URL: www.lsu.edu
Established: 1860 Annual Undergrad Tuition & Fees (In-State): $11,962
Enrollment: 34,285 Coed
Affiliation or Control: State IRS Status: 501(c)3
Highest Offering: Doctorate
Accreditation: SC, ART, CAATE, CACREP, CAEP, CAMPEP, CIDA, CLPSY, CONST, COSMA, DIETD, IPSY, JOUR, LAW, LIB, LSAR, MUS, SCPSY, SP, SPAA, SW, THEA, VET

02 President ... Dr. William F. TATE, IV
05 Exec Vice Pres/Provost ... Dr. Stacia HAYNIE
43 VP Legal Affairs/General Counsel ... Mr. Winston G. DECUIR, JR.
10 Exec Vice Pres Finance & Admin/CFO ... Mr. Daniel LAYZELL
100 Chief of Staff ... Ms. Ashley ARCENEAUX
46 Vice Pres Research & Econ Dev ... Mr. Sam BENTLEY
45 Vice Pres Strategic Initiatives ... Dr. Isiah M. WARNER
32 Vice Pres Student Affairs ... Dr. Jeremiah SHINN
26 VP Strategic Communications ... Mr. Jim SABOURIN
102 President/CEO LSU Foundation ... Mr. Robert M. STUART, JR.
28 Vice Prov Office of Diversity ... Dr. Dereck ROVARIS
20 Sr Vice Prov Academic Affairs ... Dr. Jane CASSIDY
20 Vice Prov Academic Programs ... Dr. Matt LEE
106 Vice Prov Digital & Continuing Educ ... Dr. Sasha THACKABERRY
15 Assoc VP/Chief Human Resources Ofcr ... Mr. Clayton JONES
84 VP for Enrollment Management ... Mr. Jose AVILES
85 Assoc VP International Programs ... Dr. Hector ZAPATA
37 Director Student Aid ... Ms. Amy MARIX
08 Dean LSU Libraries ... Mr. Stanley WILDER
79 Dean of Col Hum & Soc Sciences ... Dr. Troy BLANCHARD
54 Dean College of Engineering ... Dr. Judy WORNAT
47 Dean College of Agriculture ... Dr. William RICHARDSON
50 Dean Ourso College of Business ... Dr. Jared LLORENS
64 Int Dean Col Music & Dramatic Arts ... Ms. Kristin SOSNOWSKY
81 Dean College of Science ... Dr. Cynthia PETERSON
62 Dir Sch of Library & Info Science ... Dr. Carol BARRY
53 Dean Col Human Science/Education ... Dr. Roland MITCHELL
57 Dean College of Art & Design ... Mr. Alkis TSOLAKIS
74 Dean Veterinary Medicine ... Dr. Oliver GARDEN
60 Int Dean Manship Sch of Mass Comm ... Dr. Josh GRIMM
92 Dean Honors College ... Dr. Jonathan H. EARLE
65 Dean Sch of Coast & Environ ... Dr. Christopher D'ELIA
88 Exec Dir University College ... Ms. Andrea JONES
35 Assoc Dean of Student Affairs ... Ms. Angela GUILLORY
88 Sr Ex Dir SN Ctr Security Rsch Trng ... Mr. Jeff MOULTON
88 Exec Director Center Energy Stds ... Mr. David DISMUKES
29 President LSU Alumni Association ... Mr. Gordon MONK
88 Exec Director LSU Museum of Art ... Dr. Daniel STETSON
18 Assoc VP for Fac & Prop Oversight ... Mr. Tony LOMBARDO
13 Assoc VP & Chief Technology Officer ... Mr. John BORNE
75 Int Dir Sch Human Res Ed & Wk Dev ... Dr. Reid BATES
80 Director Public Admin Institute ... Dr. Jared LLORENS
27 Director LSU Press ... Ms. Alisa PLANT
41 Athletic Director ... Mr. Scott WOODWARD
06 University Registrar ... Mr. Clayton BENTON
36 Director Olinde Career Center ... Mr. Jesse G. DOWNS
09 Director of Institutional Research ... Mr. Bernie BRAUN
93 Director Multicultural Affairs ... Ms. Michelle CARTER
65 Director Museum of Natural Science ... Dr. Christopher AUSTIN
88 Director Rural Life Museum ... Mr. Bill STARK
96 Asst VP Procurement & Property Mgt ... Ms. Sally MCKECHNIE
07 Director of Admissions ... Mr. Danny BARROW
19 Chief of LSU Police Dept ... Mr. Bart THOMPSON
39 Exec Director of Residential Life ... Mr. Peter TRENTACOSTE
101 Assoc Vice President for the Board ... Dr. Jason DRODDY
104 Director Study Abroad ... Mr. Harald LEDER
105 Director Info/PR/Publication/Prod ... Ms. Lori MARTIN

*Louisiana State University at Alexandria (F)

8100 Highway 71 S, Alexandria LA 71302-9121
County: Rapides FICE Identification: 002011
Unit ID: 159382
Telephone: (318) 445-3672 Carnegie Class: Bac-A&S
FAX Number: (318) 473-6418 Calendar System: Semester
URL: www.lsua.edu
Established: 1959 Annual Undergrad Tuition & Fees (In-State): $6,669
Enrollment: 3,706 Coed
Affiliation or Control: State IRS Status: 501(c)3
Highest Offering: Baccalaureate
Accreditation: SC, ACBSP, ADNUR, CAEP, MLTAD, MT, NUR, RAD

02 Chancellor ... Dr. Paul COREIL
05 Provost/VC Academic Affairs ... Dr. John ROWAN
10 Vice Chanc Finance/Admin Svcs ... Mr. Deron THAXTON
84 VC Enrollment & Student Engagement ... Dr. Abbey BAIN
111 Asst Vice Chanc Univ Advancement ... Ms. Melinda F. ANDERSON
50 Dept Chair Business Admin ... Dr. Randall DUPONT
49 Dept Chair Arts/English/Humanities ... Dr. Holly WILSON
83 Dept Chair Behavioral & Social Sci ... Dr. Jerry SANSON
81 Dept Chair Math & Physical Sciences ... Dr. Nathan PONDER
53 Department Chair Education ... Vacant
76 Department Chair Allied Health ... Dr. Haywood JOINER
66 Department Chair Nursing ... Dr. Cathy CORMIER
49 Dept Chair Biological Sciences ... Dr. Nathan PONDER
83 Dept Chair Psychology ... Dr. Mary TREUTING
88 Dept Chair Criminal Justice ... Ms. Beth WHITTINGTON
18 Director of Facility Services ... Mr. Kevin VERCHER
08 Director Library Services ... Ms. Michelle WALLER
37 Director of Financial Aid ... Mr. Jeff MASSEY
13 Exec Dir Info Educational Tech Svcs ... Mr. Jason NORMAND
15 Director Human Resource Management ... Ms. Lynette BURLEW
51 Director Continuing Education ... Ms. Lakeshia WILLIAMS
09 Dir Inst Research/Effectiveness ... Mr. Scott COLLEY
96 Dir Procurement Svcs/Property Mgmt ... Ms. Mary LEMOINE
41 Director Athletics ... Mr. Bob AUSTIN
06 Registrar ... Ms. Jerri WESTON
19 Chief of Police ... Mr. Donald COLLINS
04 Senior Exec Asst to Chancellor ... Ms. Chancey SLIDER
07 Director of Admissions ... Ms. Shelly GILL
106 Director Distance Learning ... Ms. Teresa SEYMOUR
26 Dir of Marketing & Communications ... Ms. Elizabeth JONSON

*Louisiana State University at Eunice (G)

2048 Johnson Highway, Eunice LA 70535-6726
County: Acadia FICE Identification: 002012
Unit ID: 159407
Telephone: (337) 457-7311 Carnegie Class: Assoc/MT-VT-High Trad
FAX Number: (337) 546-6620 Calendar System: Semester
URL: www.lsue.edu
Established: 1964 Annual Undergrad Tuition & Fees (In-State): $4,730
Enrollment: 3,142 Coed
Affiliation or Control: State IRS Status: 501(c)3
Highest Offering: Associate Degree
Accreditation: SC, ACBSP, ADNUR, COARC, DMS, RAD, SURGT

02 Chancellor ... Dr. Nancee SORENSON
05 Vice Chancellor Academic Affairs ... Dr. John HAMLIN
84 Dean of Enrollment Management ... Vacant
10 Interim VC Business Affairs ... Ms. Amy GREAGOFF
32 Int Dean Student Affs/Enrollment ... Dr. Kyle D. SMITH
26 Interim Dir of Public Relations ... Mr. Travis WEBB
06 Registrar/Director of Admissions ... Mr. Donnie THIBODEAUX
37 Director of Financial Aid ... Ms. Jacqueline LA CHAPELLE
30 Dir Foundation & Inst Development ... Ms. Carey LAWSON
09 Dir Inst Effectiveness/Devel Educ ... Dr. Paul FOWLER
51 Dir Cont Educ/Workforce Innovation ... Vacant
18 Director Physical Plant ... Mr. Michael BROUSSARD
15 Director Personnel Services ... Vacant
81 Interim Dean Div of Sciences/Math ... Dr. Brandon BORILL
50 Dean Div Bus/Nursing/Allied Health ... Ms. Dotty MCDONALD
49 Interim Dean Div of Liberal Arts ... Dr. Michael ALLEMAN
13 Director Information Technology ... Mr. Stephen HEYWARD
41 Athletic Director ... Mr. Jeff WILLIS
08 Director of the Library ... Ms. Cassie JOBE-GANUCHEAU
19 Director Security/Safety ... Mr. Joseph C. LALONDE
39 Dir Resident Life/Student Housing ... Ms. Victoria THROOP
04 Executiv Assistant to the President ... Ms. Courtney FRUGE
28 Dir Diversity/Equal Opp/Affirm Act ... Ms. Katie TUCKER

*Louisiana State University Health Sciences Center-New Orleans (H)

433 Bolivar Street, New Orleans LA 70112-2223
County: Orleans FICE Identification: 002014
Unit ID: 159373
Telephone: (504) 568-4808 Carnegie Class: Spec-4-yr-Med
FAX Number: N/A Calendar System: Semester
URL: www.lsuhsc.edu
Established: 1931 Annual Undergrad Tuition & Fees (In-State): N/A
Enrollment: 2,827 Coed
Affiliation or Control: State IRS Status: 501(c)3
Highest Offering: Doctorate
Accreditation: SC, ANEST, ARCPA, AUD, CACREP, COARC, CVT, DENT, DH, DT, IPSY, MED, MT, NURSE, OT, PH, PTA, SP

02 Chancellor ... Dr. Larry H. HOLLIER
10 Vice Chancellor Finance/Admin ... Mr. Keith SCHROTH
05 Vice Chanc Acad Aff/Dean Grad Stds ... Dr. Joseph M. MOERSCHBAECHER
31 Vice Chanc Community Affairs ... Mr. Edwin MURRAY
17 Vice Chanc Clinic Affairs ... Dr. J. Chris WINTERS
28 Vice Chanc Diversity & Inclusion ... Dr. Timothy FAIR
102 President & CEO Foundation ... Mr. Matthew ALTIER
100 Chief of Staff ... Mr. Louis COLLETTA
43 Interim General Counsel ... Ms. Tammy SIMIEN
63 Dean Medicine NO ... Dr. Steve NELSON
52 Dean School of Dentistry ... Dr. Robert LAUGHLIN
66 Dean of Nursing ... Dr. Demetrius PORCHE
76 Dean Allied Health Professions ... Dr. Jimmy R. CAIRO
69 Dean of Public Health ... Dr. Dean SMITH
21 Assoc Vice Chanc Admin & Finance ... Ms. Wendy SIMONEAUX
103 Asst VC Econ Dev & Strat Initiative ... Mrs. Nicole HONOREE
13 Director Information Services ... Ms. Leslie L. CAPO
18 Assoc VC Properties & Facilities ... Mr. John BALL
13 Asst VC Information Technology ... Mr. Ken BOE
88 Exec Dir for Accounting Services ... Mrs. Arlean WEHLE
109 Dir Supply Chain & Aux Enterprise ... Mr. Rob PARKER
06 Registrar ... Ms. Alicia EDWARDS
08 Director of Libraries ... Mr. J. Dale PRINCE
37 Dir Student Financial Aid ... Mr. Patrick GORMAN
85 Director of International Services ... Ms. Remy E. ALLEN
108 Director Institutional Effectivenes ... Ms. Christine MANALLA
04 Administrative Officer ... Ms. Jennifer CRISP
45 Financial Planning Officer ... Mrs. Vy APOSTOLAKIS
116 Compliance Officer ... Ms. Lori FERRO

*Louisiana State University Health Sciences Center at Shreveport (I)

1501 Kings Highway, Shreveport LA 71103
County: Caddo FICE Identification: 008067
Unit ID: 435000
Telephone: (318) 675-5240 Carnegie Class: Spec-4-yr-Med
FAX Number: (318) 675-5244 Calendar System: Semester
URL: www.lsuhs.edu
Established: 1969 Annual Undergrad Tuition & Fees (In-State): N/A
Enrollment: 982 Coed
Affiliation or Control: State IRS Status: Exempt
Highest Offering: Doctorate
Accreditation: SC, ARCPA, COARC, DENT, MED, MT, OT, PH, PTA, SP

02 Chancellor ... Dr. Ghali E. GHALI
11 Vice Chancellor Administration ... Ms. Cindy RIVES
46 Vice Chancellor Research Affairs ... Dr. Chris KEVIL
05 Vice Chancellor Academic Affairs ... Dr. Alan KAYE
10 Chief Financial Officer ... Ms. Sheila FAOUR
43 Senior Legal Counsel ... Mr. Carranza PRYOR
76 Dean Sch Allied Health Prof ... Dr. Sharon DUNN
58 Dean School of Graduate Studies ... Dr. Chris KEVIL
17 Vice Chancellor Clinical Affairs ... Dr. Charles FOX
86 Vice Chancellor Government Affairs ... Dr. Markey PIERRE
26 Exec Dir Comm/Public Relations ... Ms. Lisa BABIN
13 Chief Info Technology Officer (CIO) ... Mr. Kenneth BROWN
07 Assoc Dean for Admissions SOM ... Dr. Wanda S. THOMAS
32 Asst Dean for Student Affairs SOM ... Dr. Debbie CHANDLER
15 Exec Director of Human Resources ... Ms. Lisa EBARB
23 Executive Director Medical Services ... Ms. Leisa OGLESBY
18 Chief Facilities/Physical Plant ... Mr. Marc GIBSON
19 Director of Public Safety ... Mr. Philip BURRIS
09 Exec Dir Planning & Effectiveness ... Mr. Jeffrey D. HOWELLS
25 Asst Vice Chancellor for Research ... Ms. Annella NELSON
06 Registrar ... Ms. Kim CARMEN
08 Executive Director of Library ... Mr. William OLMSTADT
37 Director Student Financial Aid ... Ms. Katraya WILLIAMS
28 Asst Vice Chancellor for Diversity ... Dr. Toni THIBEAUX
29 Director Alumni Relations ... Ms. Mary COBB
96 Director of Purchasing ... Ms. Mary A. TEMPLETON
63 Dean School of Medicine ... Dr. David F. LEWIS

† Tuition varies by degree program.

*Louisiana State University Shreveport (A)

One University Place, Shreveport LA 71115-2399
County: Caddo FICE Identification: 002013
Unit ID: 159416
Telephone: (318) 797-5000 Carnegie Class: Masters/L
FAX Number: (318) 797-5180 Calendar System: Semester
URL: www.lsus.edu
Established: 1967 Annual Undergrad Tuition & Fees (In-State): $7,160
Enrollment: 9,955 Coed
Affiliation or Control: State IRS Status: 501(c)3
Highest Offering: Doctorate
Accreditation: SC, CACREP, CAEP, PH

02 Chancellor ... Mr. Lawrence S. CLARK
05 Provost/VC Academic Affairs ... Dr. Helen TAYLOR
10 Vice Chancellor Business Affairs ... Ms. Barbie CANNON
32 Assoc VC Dean of Students ... Dr. Paula ATKINS
102 Executive Director LSUS Foundation ... Ms. Laura PERDUE
29 Director Alumni Affairs ... Vacant
88 Vice Chanc Strategic Initiatives ... Dr. Julie LESSITER
06 Registrar ... Ms. Darlenna M. ATKINS
15 Director of Human Resource Mgmt ... Mr. Bill WOLFE
08 Dean Noel Memorial Library ... Mr. Brian SHERMAN
37 Director of Student Financial Aid ... Ms. Chelsey CHANCE
07 Director of Admissions ... Ms. Jennie BYNOG
38 Director Counseling Services ... Ms. Angela PELLERIN
13 Assoc VC & CIO/IT ... Mr. Shelby C. KEITH
40 Director of Bookstore ... Ms. Renee MARTIN
96 Director of Purchasing ... Mr. Bill WOLFE
26 Dir of Media/External Relations ... Mr. Wendell RILEY
04 Assistant to the Chancellor ... Ms. Shelley MOORE
19 Dir of University Police ... Mr. Donald W. WRAY
41 Athletic Director ... Mr. Lucas MORGAN
49 Dean of Arts and Sciences ... Dr. Tibor SZARVAS
58 Dean of Graduate Studies ... Dr. Sanjay T. MENON
50 Dean of Business ... Vacant
106 Director Online Learning ... Ms. Rhonda FAILEY
18 Dir Physical Plant/Facility Svcs ... Mr. Art SHILLING
53 Dean of Education/Human Development ... Dr. Dennis R. WISSING
28 Director of Diversity ... Dr. Kenna FRANKLIN

*University of New Orleans (B)

2000 Lakeshore Drive, New Orleans LA 70148-2000
County: Orleans FICE Identification: 002015
Unit ID: 159939
Telephone: (504) 280-6000 Carnegie Class: DU-Higher
FAX Number: (504) 280-5522 Calendar System: Semester
URL: www.uno.edu
Established: 1958 Annual Undergrad Tuition & Fees (In-State): $9,072
Enrollment: 8,375 Coed
Affiliation or Control: State IRS Status: 501(c)3
Highest Offering: Doctorate
Accreditation: SC, ART, CACREP, CAEPN, MUS, PLNG, SPAA, THEA

02 President ... Dr. John W. NICKLOW
05 Provost/VP Academic Affairs ... Dr. Mahyar AMOUZEGAR
10 VP Business Affairs/CFO ... Dr. Gloria WALKER
32 Associate VP and Dean of Students ... Dr. Carolyn GOLZ
13 Chief Information Officer ... Dr. Ray WANG
85 Asst Prov International Education ... Ms. Alea COT
19 Chief of Police ... Mr. Thomas HARRINGTON
50 Int Dean of Business Administration ... Dr. Pamela KENNETT-HENSEL
54 Dean of Engineering ... Dr. Taskin KOCAK
49 Dean Liberal Arts & Education ... Dr. Kim MARTIN LONG
08 Dean Library/Information Services ... Dr. Ray WANG
81 Dean of Sciences ... Dr. Steve JOHNSON
06 University Registrar ... Ms. Kara BISCEGLIE
29 Director Alumni Affairs ... Ms. Rachel MASSEY
26 Chief Communications Officer ... Mr. Adam NORRIS
96 Director of Purchasing ... Ms. Susan VARBLE
41 VP/Director Athletics ... Mr. Tim DUNCAN
39 Director Student Housing ... Ms. Amanda ROBBINS
121 Director Learning Resource Center ... Ms. Margaret WILLIAMSON
04 Exec Asst to the President ... Ms. Elizabeth LAND
09 Dir Inst Effectiveness & Research ... Dr. Colby STOEVER
15 Assoc VP Human Resource Management ... Ms. Karen PAISANT
18 Assoc VP for Facility Services ... Ms. Deborah HADAWAY
30 Exec Director of Univ Advancement ... Mr. Anthony GREGORIO
36 Director Career Services ... Ms. Celyn BOYKIN
37 Dir Student Financial Aid & Scholar ... Ms. Ann LOCKRIDGE
38 Director Student Counseling ... Ms. Portia GORDON
84 Assoc VP Admissions & Enrollment ... Ms. Mary Beth MARKS

Loyola University New Orleans (C)

6363 Saint Charles Avenue, New Orleans LA 70118-6195
County: Orleans FICE Identification: 002016
Unit ID: 159656
Telephone: (504) 865-2011 Carnegie Class: DU-Mod
FAX Number: (504) 865-3851 Calendar System: Semester
URL: www.loyno.edu
Established: 1912 Annual Undergrad Tuition & Fees: $42,278
Enrollment: 4,497 Coed
Affiliation or Control: Roman Catholic IRS Status: 501(c)3
Highest Offering: Doctorate
Accreditation: SC, CACREP, JOUR, LAW, MUS, NURSE

01 President ... Ms. Tania TETLOW
04 Senior Exec Asst to the President ... Ms. Desiree RODRIGUEZ
05 Prov/Sr Vice Pres Academic Affairs ... Dr. Tanuja SINGH
10 Vice Pres COO/Finance/Admin ... Ms. Carol MARKOWITZ
111 VP University Advancement ... Mr. Chris WISEMAN
42 Vice Pres for Mission & Ministry ... Fr. Justin DAFFRON
28 VP Equity and Inclusion Officer ... Mr. Kedrick PERRY
13 Chief Information Officer ... Mr. Alan SCHOMAKER
43 General Counsel ... Ms. Sharonda WILLIAMS
29 Asst Vice Pres Alumni Engagement ... Ms. Laura E. LEIVA
14 Senior Director of IT ... Mr. Joe LOCASCIO
26 Chief Communications Officer ... Ms. Rachel HOORMAN
11 Asst Vice Pres Administration ... Mr. Thomas J. RAYMOND
20 Vice Provost ... Dr. Carol Ann MACGREGOR
108 Coord Internal Reporting/Assessment ... Ms. Donna BOURGEOIS
27 Assoc Dir Public Affs/External Rels ... Ms. Patricia MURRET
06 Dir Stdnt Records/Registration Svcs ... Ms. Kathy R. GROS
15 Director of Human Resources ... Ms. Rachel DIRMANN
40 Bookstore Manager ... Mr. Maris HAZNERS
41 Director Athletics & Wellness ... Mr. Brett SIMPSON
36 Director Career Development Center ... Mr. Jill BOATRIGHT
32 Chief Student Affairs Officer ... Dr. Alicia BOURQUE
19 Director University Police ... Mr. Todd W. WARREN
37 Director Scholarships/Financial Aid ... Ms. Anna DAIGLE
08 Director of the Law Library ... Mr. Brian BARNES
104 Dir Center for International Educ ... Ms. Mariette THOMAS
38 Director Counseling & Health Svcs ... Dr. Asia WONG
96 Director of Purchasing ... Ms. Lynn DAVIS
06 Dir Admin Services/Student Records ... Mr. Michael RACHAL
49 Dean Arts and Sciences ... Dr. Maria CALZADA
61 Dean of Law ... Dr. Madeleine LANDRIEU
64 Dean of Music and Media ... Mr. Kern MAASS
50 Dean of Business ... Dr. Michael CAPELLA
66 Dean Nursing/Health ... Dr. Shelli COLLINS
08 Dean of Libraries ... Ms. Laurie PHILLIPS
88 Director of Service Learning ... Ms. Typhanie JASPER-BUTLER
88 Director of Women's Resource Ctr ... Ms. Patricia BOYETT
92 Dir of University Honors Program ... Dr. Jonathan PETERSON
121 Director of Student Success Center ... Ms. Liz RAINEY
07 Director of Admissions ... Mr. Nathan AMENT
18 Senior Director of Facilities ... Mr. Bryan HAYDEN
25 Grants and Research Officer ... Ms. Anne WEAVER
117 Director of Risk Management ... Mr. John CAIN
39 Director of Residence Life ... Mr. Chris RICE

McCann School of Business and Technology (D)

2319 Louisville Avenue, Monroe LA 71201-6126
Telephone: (318) 323-2889 FICE Identification: 026068
Accreditation: ACCSC

NationsUniversity (E)

650 Poydras St., Ste 1400, PMB 133,
New Orleans LA 70130
County: Orleans Identification: 667257
Telephone: (866) 617-6446 Carnegie Class: Not Classified
FAX Number: N/A Calendar System: Other
URL: www.nationsu.edu
Established: 1996 Annual Undergrad Tuition & Fees: N/A
Enrollment: N/A Coed
Affiliation or Control: Independent Non-Profit IRS Status: 501(c)3
Highest Offering: Master's
Accreditation: DEAC

00 Chair of the Board ... Mr. Ernie CLEVENGER
01 Chancellor/CEO ... Dr. Mac LYNN
88 Vice Chancellor ... Dr. Herman ALEXANDER
05 Chief Academic Officer ... Dr. David B. SRYGLEY
06 Registrar ... Mrs. Mary V. MABERY
10 Chief Financial/Business Officer ... Mr. Joe SLOAN
11 Chief of Operations/Administration ... Vacant
20 Dean of Faculty ... Dr. Richard YOUNGBLOOD
32 Director of Student Services ... Mrs. Marty LYNN
38 Director of Student Advising ... Mrs. Gail HEIDERICH
26 Director of Communications ... Mr. Jon R. SLOAN
91 IT Director ... Mr. Mike BUSH
90 IT Administrator ... Mr. Glenn BEVILLE

New Orleans Baptist Theological Seminary (F)

3939 Gentilly Boulevard, New Orleans LA 70126
County: Orleans FICE Identification: 002019
Unit ID: 159948
Telephone: (504) 282-4455 Carnegie Class: Spec-4-yr-Faith
FAX Number: (504) 283-3631 Calendar System: Semester
URL: www.nobts.edu
Established: 1917 Annual Undergrad Tuition & Fees: $9,320
Enrollment: 2,293 Coed
Affiliation or Control: Southern Baptist IRS Status: 501(c)3
Highest Offering: Doctorate
Accreditation: SC, MUS, THEOL

01 President ... Dr. James Kenneth DEW, JR.
05 Provost ... Dr. Norris C. GRUBBS
111 Vice Pres Institutional Advancement ... Dr. Mike WETZEL
10 Vice President for Business Admin ... Dr. Larry LYON
84 Assoc Vice President Enrollment ... Mr. Matthew JAMES
12 Dean Leavell College ... Dr. L. Thomas STRONG, III
32 AVP Student Affs/Dean of Students ... Dr. Craig GARRETT
06 Registrar ... Dr. Paul E. GREGOIRE, JR.
08 Dean of Libraries ... Dr. Jeff D. GRIFFIN
13 Assoc VP Information Technology ... Dr. Laurie S. WATTS
73 Assoc Dean Prof Doctoral Pgms ... Dr. Reggie R. OGEA
58 Assoc Dean Research Doctoral Pgms ... Dr. Charles A. RAY, JR.
35 Director of Student Services ... Mr. Conner HINTON
30 Director of Development ... Ms. Betty Lynn CAMPBELL
15 Director of Human Resources ... Ms. Shelly COOPER
26 Dir Office of Communications ... Mr. Gary D. MYERS
29 Director of Alumni Relations ... Mr. Robert SMITH
36 Director of Student Enlistment ... Mr. Michael REED
37 Director of Financial Aid ... Mr. Michael WANG
38 Director of Testing & Counseling ... Dr. Jeffery W. NAVE
88 Director of Innovative Learning ... Dr. Donna B. PEAVEY
41 Athletic Director ... Mr. Tim DUNCAN

Notre Dame Seminary, Graduate School of Theology (G)

2901 S Carrollton Avenue, New Orleans LA 70118-4391
County: Orleans FICE Identification: 002022
Unit ID: 160029
Telephone: (504) 866-7426 Carnegie Class: Spec-4-yr-Faith
FAX Number: (504) 866-3119 Calendar System: Semester
URL: www.nds.edu
Established: 1923 Annual Undergrad Tuition & Fees: N/A
Enrollment: N/A Coed
Affiliation or Control: Roman Catholic IRS Status: 501(c)3
Highest Offering: Master's
Accreditation: SC, THEOL

01 President - Rector ... V.Rev. James A. WEHNER, STD
05 Academic Dean ... Dr. Rebecca S. MALONEY
08 Director of Library ... Mr. Thomas B. BENDER, IV
09 Dir IE/Planning/Faculty Development ... Dr. Rebecca S. MALONEY
10 Business Manager ... Ms. Michelle W. KLEIN
06 Registrar ... Ms. Debora PANEPINTO

Remington College-Baton Rouge Campus (H)

4520 S Sherwood Forest Blvd, Baton Rouge LA 70816
Telephone: (225) 236-3200 Identification: 666449
Accreditation: ACCSC

† Branch campus of Remington College, Cleveland, OH.

Remington College-Lafayette Campus (I)

4021-A Ambassador Caffery Pkwy #100,
Lafayette LA 70503
Telephone: (337) 981-4010 FICE Identification: 005203
Accreditation: ACCSC

† Branch campus of Remington College, Cleveland, OH.

Remington College-Shreveport (J)

2106 Bert Kouns Industrial Loop, Shreveport LA 71118
Telephone: (318) 671-4000 Identification: 666302
Accreditation: ACCSC

† Branch campus of Remington College, Cleveland, OH.

Saint Joseph Seminary College (K)

75376 River Road, Saint Benedict LA 70457-9999
County: Saint Tammany FICE Identification: 002027
Unit ID: 160409
Telephone: (985) 867-2232 Carnegie Class: Spec-4-yr-Faith
FAX Number: (985) 867-2270 Calendar System: Semester
URL: www.sjasc.edu
Established: 1891 Annual Undergrad Tuition & Fees: $21,550
Enrollment: 107 Male
Affiliation or Control: Roman Catholic IRS Status: 501(c)3

Highest Offering: Baccalaureate
Accreditation: SC

01 President & Rector ... V.Rev. Gregory M. BOQUET, OSB
05 Academic Dean ... Dr. Daniel P. BURNS
03 Vice-Rector ... Rev. Matthew CLARK, OSB
08 Librarian ... Ms. JoAnn MONTALBANO
10 Business Officer ... Mrs. Jennifer WHITEHOUSE
37 Director Financial Aid/Registrar ... Mrs. Wendy VAN DALEN
29 Director of Alumni Affairs ... Rev. Matthew CLARK, OSB
30 Director of Development ... Mr. Scott WALLACE
26 Director of Communications ... Mr. James SHIELDS
32 Dean of Students ... Rev. Jonathan WALLIS, OSB
108 Director Institutional Assessment ... Dr. Dianna LAURENT
13 Chief Info Technology Officer ... Mr. Todd RUSSELL
18 Chief Facilities/Physical Plant ... Mr. Jim ROBEAU
04 Admin Assistant to the President ... Mrs. Cindy MARKHAM
15 Chief Human Resources Officer ... Mrs. Carla GRAVES
41 Athletic Director ... Mr. Brenton ADDISON

*Southern University and Agricultural & Mechanical College System (A)

JS Clark Admin Building, 4th Floor,
Baton Rouge LA 70813-0001
County: East Baton Rouge Parish — FICE Identification: 009637
Unit ID: 160533
Telephone: (225) 771-4680 — Carnegie Class: N/A
FAX Number: (225) 771-5522
URL: www.sus.edu

01 President-Chancellor ... Dr. Ray L. BELTON
05 Executive VCAA/Provost ... Dr. Bijoy K. SAHOO
10 System VP Finance/Business Affairs ... Mr. Flandus MCCLINTON
84 VC Enroll Mgmt & Student Success ... Dr. Jacqueline PREASTLY
13 Assoc VP Information Technology ... Dr. Gabriel FAGBEYIRO
106 Director Office of E-Learning ... Ms. Tracy BARLEY
30 CEO SU System Foundation ... Mr. Alfred E. HARRELL, III
43 General Counsel to the System/Board ... Ms. Corinne BLACHE
26 VP of External Affairs ... Dr. Robyn M. MERRICK
27 System Director of Communications ... Ms. Janene TATE
45 VP Strategic Planning ... Dr. V. Alexander APPEANING
06 Registrar ... Ms. Dianna GILBERT-DEPRON
07 Executive Director of Admissions ... Ms. Heather FREEMAN
104 Dean of International Education ... Dr. Barbara CARPENTER
29 Exec Dir Alumni Federation ... Ms. LaQuitta THOMAS
36 Director of Career Services ... Ms. Tamara F. MONTGOMERY
37 Director Student Financial Aid ... Ms. Taishieka DAVIS
38 Director Student Counseling ... Dr. ValaRay IRVIN
39 Director Student Housing ... Ms. Tracie A. ABRAHAM
41 Athletic Director ... Mr. Roman BANKS, JR.
50 Dean College of Business ... Dr. Donald ANDREWS
53 Director of Education ... Dr. VerJanis PEOPLES
54 Dean College of Sci/Engineering ... Dr. Patrick CARRIERE
96 Director of Purchasing ... Ms. Linda ANTOINE

*Southern University and A&M College (B)

Harding Boulevard, Baton Rouge LA 70813-0001
County: East Baton Rouge — FICE Identification: 002025
Unit ID: 160621
Telephone: (225) 771-4500 — Carnegie Class: Masters/L
FAX Number: (225) 771-2018 — Calendar System: Semester
URL: www.subr.edu
Established: 1880 — Annual Undergrad Tuition & Fees (In-State): $9,340
Enrollment: 6,917 — Coed
Affiliation or Control: State — IRS Status: 501(c)3
Highest Offering: Doctorate
Accreditation: SC, CACREP, CAEP, DIETI, JOUR, MUS, NURSE, SP, SPAA, SW

02 President/Chancellor ... Dr. Ray BELTON
05 EVC Academic Affairs ... Dr. Bijoy K. SAHOO
100 Chief of Staff ... Dr. Katara A. WILLIAMS
10 Sys VP Finance and Admin ... Mr. Flandus MCCLINTON
45 System VP SPPIE ... Dr. Vladimir A. APPEANING
26 System VP External Affairs ... Dr. Robyn M. MERRICK
43 General Counsel ... Ms. Corinne BLACHE
15 AVP Human Resources ... Ms. Tracie J. WOODS
13 AVP for IT/Chief Information Ofcr ... Dr. Gabriel FAGBEYIRO
115 AVP of Finance & Treasury ... Ms. Catherine MILES
106 AVP Online Learning Services ... Ms. Tracy BARLEY
108 AVP SPPIE ... Dr. Toni L. MANOGIN
116 Exec Director Internal Audit ... Mr. Brian ADAMS
102 CEO SU System Foundation ... Mr. Alfred E. HARRELL
18 Exec Director Facilities ... Mr. Eli G. GUILLORY, III
29 Exec Dir SU Alumni Federation ... Mr. Derrick WARREN
114 VC Finance & Administration ... Mr. Benjamin PUGH
84 VC Enroll Management/Stdnt Success ... Dr. Jacqueline G. PREASTLY
32 VC Student Affairs ... Dr. Frederick WALTON
46 VC Research & Strategic Initiatives ... Dr. Michael A. STUBBLEFIELD
41 Athletic Director ... Mr. Roman BANKS
124 AVC for Student Affairs ... Mr. Anthony JACKSON
21 AVC Finance and Administration ... Mrs. Monica MEALIE
121 Exec Dir Center Student Success ... Ms. Latrina COLLINS
35 Dean of Students ... Ms. Montrice O'NEAL
50 Dean College of Business ... Dr. Donald R. ANDREWS
54 Dean Col of Sciences/Engineering ... Dr. Patrick CARRIERE
80 Dean College of Government/Soc Sci ... Dr. Damien EJIGIRI
79 Dean College of Humanities and IDS ... Dr. Cynthia D. BRYANT
51 Asst Dean Continuing Education ... Dr. Nadia GADSON
92 Dean of Honors College ... Dr. Karen CROSBY
47 Chancellor/Dean Agr Rsrch & Ext Ctr ... Dr. Orlando F. MCMEANS
66 Dean Nursing/Allied Health ... Dr. Sandra BROWN
58 Dean of the Graduate School ... Dr. Ashagre A. YIGLETU
53 Director School of Education ... Dr. Verjanis PEOPLES
16 Director Human Resources ... Ms. Dawn HARRIS
27 Director of Communications ... Ms. Janene TATE
120 Director Online Education/E-learnin ... Ms. Tracy BARLEY
96 Director of Purchasing ... Mrs. Linda B. ANTOINE
06 Registrar ... Mrs. Dianna DEPRON
37 Director of Financial Aid ... Mrs. Taisheika DAVIS
39 Director Residential Housing ... Mrs. Tracie A. ABRAHAM
07 Exec Dir Admissions/Recruitment ... Ms. Heather FREEMAN
19 Chief of Police ... Ms. Joycelyn JOHNSON
36 Director Career Services ... Mrs. Tamara F. MONTGOMERY
09 Dir of Inst Research & Assessment ... Mr. Srinivas R. GAVINI
25 Assoc Controller for Sponsored Pgm ... Ms. Famika SARGENT
88 Assoc Controller for Financial Op ... Mrs. Cary HOLLINS
08 Dean of Libraries ... Mrs. Dawn KIGHT
104 Dean Intl Affairs & Univ Outreach ... Dr. Barbara W. CARPENTER
105 Director Web Services ... Ms. Rachel CARRIERE
38 Director Student Counseling ... Dr. ValaRay J. IRVIN
04 Admin Assistant to the President ... Ms. Patricia HANDY
101 Secretary of the Institution/Board ... Mrs. Tracey TAYLOR JARELL
90 Director Academic Computing ... Mr. Maurice PITTS
91 Director Administrative Computing ... Ms. Willie FRANCOIS

*Southern University at New Orleans (C)

6400 Press Drive, New Orleans LA 70126-1009
County: Orleans — FICE Identification: 002026
Unit ID: 160630
Telephone: (504) 286-5000 — Carnegie Class: Masters/M
FAX Number: (504) 286-5131 — Calendar System: Semester
URL: www.suno.edu
Established: 1956 — Annual Undergrad Tuition & Fees (In-State): $7,059
Enrollment: 2,264 — Coed
Affiliation or Control: State — IRS Status: 501(c)3
Highest Offering: Master's
Accreditation: SC, AAFCS, CAEPN, CAHIIM, SW

02 Chancellor ... Dr. James H. AMMONS, JR.
04 Exec Assoc to the Chancellor ... Mr. Harry DOUGHTY
05 EVC for Academic Affairs & SACS ... Dr. Gregory FORD
10 VC for Admin & Finance ... Dr. Teresa HARDEE
32 VC Student Affs/Enroll Mgmt ... Dr. Adriel HILTON
46 VC for Research/Title III Programs ... Dr. Brenda W. JACKSON
111 VC Advance/Community Outreach ... Dr. Kim RUGON
09 Dir IR/IE & Strategic Planning ... Mrs. Ada KWANBUNBUMPEN
108 Lrng Outcomes/Assessment Coord ... Ms. Safia JENKINS
25 Dir Grants & Sponsored Programs ... Dr. William R. BELISLE
06 Registrar ... Ms. Gilda DAVIS
21 Comptroller ... Ms. Shawn M. CHARLES
08 Director of Library ... Mrs. Shatiqua A. MOSBY-WILSON
36 Dir Career Counseling & Vet Liaison ... Vacant
13 Int Dir of Information Technology ... Mr. Peter BONNEE
15 Director of Human Resources ... Ms. Dana DOUGLAS
19 Police Chief Campus Police ... Mr. Bruce ADAMS
41 Director of Athletics ... Vacant
26 Dir of Comm and Public Relations ... Ms. Regine WILLIAMS
96 Director of Purchasing ... Mrs. Marilyn G. MANUEL
106 Director of E-Learning ... Ms. Shelia WOOD
70 Dean School of Social Work ... Dr. Rebecca CHAISSON
50 Dean College of Business/Pub Admin ... Dr. Igwe E. UDEH
88 Director of Museum Studies ... Dr. Haitham EID
58 Director of Graduate Studies ... Ms. Deidrea JONES-HAZURE
49 Dean College of Arts & Sciences ... Dr. Evelyn HARRELL
53 Dean College of Education ... Dr. Willie JONES
22 Dir Svcs for Stdnts w/Disabilities ... Vacant
35 Dir of Student Activities/Orgs ... Dr. Mary JACKSON
38 Dir of Student Development Center ... Dr. Josephine OKORONKWO
121 Dir Student Support Services Pgm ... Ms. Linda D. FREDERICK
88 Dir Ctr for African & American Stds ... Dr. Clyde ROBERTSON
18 Director of Facilities Management ... Mr. Derrick JAMES
37 Director Student Financial Aid ... Ms. LaCharlotte GARRETT
07 Director of Admissions ... Mr. Cornelius WILLIAMS

*Southern University at Shreveport-Louisiana (D)

3050 Martin Luther King Jr. Drive,
Shreveport LA 71107-4795
County: Caddo — FICE Identification: 007686
Unit ID: 160649
Telephone: (318) 670-6000 — Carnegie Class: Assoc/HVT-Mix Trad/Non
FAX Number: (318) 670-6374 — Calendar System: Semester
URL: www.susla.edu
Established: 1964 — Annual Undergrad Tuition & Fees (In-State): $4,789
Enrollment: 3,013 — Coed
Affiliation or Control: State — IRS Status: 501(c)3
Highest Offering: Associate Degree
Accreditation: SC, ADNUR, CAHIIM, COARC, DH, MLTAD, RAD, SURGT

02 Chancellor ... Dr. Rodney A. ELLIS
05 Vice Chanc Acad Affs/Workforce Dev ... Dr. Terry KID
32 Vice Chanc Student Affairs ... Ms. Melva WILLIAMS
10 Vice Chanc Finance/Administration ... Mr. Antonius PEGUES
103 Assoc VC Cmty Outreach/WFD ... Mrs. Janice B. SNEED
11 Chief Admin/Operations Officer ... Ms. Leslie R. MCCLELLON
35 Asst Vice Chanc Student Affairs ... Dr. Fatina ELLIOTT
09 Vice Chanc for RSPIE ... Dr. Regina ROBINSON
21 Chief Financial Officer ... Mrs. Brandy JACOBSEN
111 Chief Advancement Officer ... Ms. Stephanie ROGERS
113 Director of Student Accounts ... Ms. Katrina HEARD
06 Registrar ... Dr. Lalita ROGERS
08 Library Director ... Mrs. Jane O'RILEY
35 Director of Student Activities ... Mrs. Rebecca GILLIAM
41 Athletics Director ... Mr. Stephen LATSON
07 Director of Admission & Recruitment ... Mr. Jorge SOUSA, III
37 Director of Financial Aid ... Ms. Katraya WILLIAMS
102 Exec Director SUSLA Foundation ... Mr. Frank WILLIAMS, JR.
26 Dir University Relations/Marketing ... Ms. Rasheeda SIMMONS
19 Chief University Police ... Mr. Edward REYNOLDS
13 Dir Information Tech Center/CIO ... Ms. Carolyn MILLER
121 Director Student Support Services ... Ms. Karen COCO
38 University Counselor ... Ms. Kaye L. WASHINGTON
15 Director Human Resources ... Mr. Wayne H. BRYANT
18 Director Facilities & Risk ... Vacant
114 University Budget Officer ... Ms. Regina WINN
72 Director Radiologic Technology ... Ms. Sheila SWIFT
88 Exec Dir TRIO Community Outreach ... Ms. Betty C. FAGBEYIRO
52 Int Director Dental Hygiene ... Ms. Lynne EATMAN
66 Director of Nursing ... Dr. Tiffany VARNER

*Southern University Law Center (E)

PO Box 9294, Baton Rouge LA 70813
County: East Baton Rouge — Identification: 667233
Unit ID: 440916
Telephone: (225) 771-2552 — Carnegie Class: Spec-4-yr-Law
FAX Number: N/A — Calendar System: Semester
URL: www.sulc.edu
Established: 1947 — Annual Graduate Tuition & Fees: N/A
Enrollment: 843 — Coed
Affiliation or Control: State — IRS Status: 501(c)3
Highest Offering: First Professional Degree; No Undergraduates
Accreditation: SC, LAW

02 Chancellor ... Mr. John K. PIERRE
05 Vice Chanc Academic Affairs ... Mr. Shawn VANCE
06 Director of Records & Registration ... Mrs. D'Andrea J. LEE
07 Director of Admissions/Recruitment ... Ms. Andrea LOVE
09 VC Inst Accountability/Accred ... Ms. Regina JAMES
10 Vice Chanc Finance & Administration ... Mr. Terry HALL
20 AVC Academic Support/Bar Prep ... Ms. Cynthia REED
18 Director of Facilities ... Ms. Angela GAINES
26 Director of External Affairs ... Ms. Jasmine HUNTER
29 Director of Alumni Affairs ... Ms. Robbin THOMAS
30 Director of Development ... Vacant
32 Vice Chanc Student Affairs ... Mr. Donald NORTH
36 Director of Career Services ... Ms. Koshaneke GILBERT
37 Director of Financial Aid ... Ms. Calaundra CLARKE
21 Assoc Vice Chanc Finance/Admin ... Ms. Demetria GEORGE
35 Assoc Vice Chanc Student Affairs ... Ms. Shenequa GREY
28 AVC Diversity/Equity/Inclusion ... Ms. Kerii LANDRY-THOMAS
96 Director of Purchasing ... Ms. Terry STEWARD

Tulane University (F)

6823 St. Charles Avenue, New Orleans LA 70118-5698
County: Orleans — FICE Identification: 002029
Unit ID: 160755
Telephone: (504) 865-5000 — Carnegie Class: DU-Highest
FAX Number: (504) 865-5202 — Calendar System: Semester
URL: www.tulane.edu
Established: 1834 — Annual Undergrad Tuition & Fees: $58,852
Enrollment: 13,927 — Coed
Affiliation or Control: Independent Non-Profit — IRS Status: 501(c)3
Highest Offering: Doctorate
Accreditation: SC, CAEPT, DIETI, HSA, IPSY, LAW, MED, PH, SCPSY, SW

01 President ... Mr. Michael A. FITTS
05 Sr Vice Pres Acad Affairs/Provost ... Dr. Robin FORMAN
111 Sr Vice Pres for Advancement ... Ms. Ginny WISE
108 Sr VP Strategic Init/Inst Effect ... Mr. Richard MATASAR
11 SVP/Chief Operations Officer ... Mr. Patrick NORTON
63 Sr Vice Pres/Dn School of Medicine ... Dr. Lee L. HAMM
43 General Counsel ... Ms. Victoria D. JOHNSON
13 VP Information Technology/CIO ... Mr. Noel WONG
10 Vice President Finance & Controller ... Mr. James WANDLING
115 Chief Investment Officer ... Mr. Richard CHAU
32 VP Student Affairs ... Dr. J. Davison PORTER
58 Assoc Provost Graduate Studies ... Dr. Michael CUNNINGHAM
84 Sr Vice Pres Enrollment Management ... Mr. Satya DATTAGUPTA
18 VP Facilities Management ... Mr. Randolph PHILIPSON
26 Vice Pres University Communications ... Ms. Libby ECKHARDT
46 Vice President for Research ... Dr. Giovanni PIEDIMONTE
110 Vice President Advancement ... Ms. Luann D. DOZIER
15 AVP Human Resources/Inst Equity ... Mr. Jonathan SMALL
117 Vice Pres Insurance & Risk Mgmt ... Ms. Joyce K. FRED
86 Assoc VP Government Relations ... Ms. Sharon P. COURTNEY
109 Assoc VP Auxiliary Svcs/Student Ctr ... Mr. Robert C. HAILEY
37 Assoc Vice President Financial Aid ... Mr. Michael GOODMAN
114 Director Budgets & Planning ... Ms. Judy VITRANO
29 VP for Alumni Affairs ... Mr. James STOFAN
08 Dean Library & Academic Information ... Mr. David BANUSH
38 Exec Dir Educ Resources/Couns ... Dr. Donna BENDER
36 Exec Dir Career Services Center ... Dr. Amjad AYOUBI
12 Dir Tulane Natl Primate Res Ctr ... Mr. Jay RAPPAPORT
27 Executive Director Public Relations ... Mr. Michael J. STRECKER
39 Assoc VP Housing Services/Residence ... Dr. Brian JOHNSON

96 Director Central Procurement Svcs ....Mr. William VAN CLEAVE
41 Director Athletics ....Mr. Troy DANNEN
51 Dean Professional Advancement ....Dr. Suri DUITCH
49 Dean School of Liberal Arts ....Dr. Brian EDWARDS
49 Dean Newcomb-Tulane College ....Dr. Lee SKINNER
61 Dean School of Law ....Mr. David D. MEYER
69 Dean Sch Public Health/Trop Med ....Dr. Thomas LAVEIST
54 Dean School Science & Engineering ....Dr. Kimberly FOSTER
48 Dean School of Architecture ....Dr. Inaki ALDAY
50 Dean AB Freeman School of Business ....Dr. Ira SOLOMON
70 Dean School of Social Work ....Dr. Patrick BORDNICK
09 Director of Institutional Research ....Mr. Shawn POTTER
88 Exec Dir of CELT ....Dr. Toni WEISS
85 Assoc Dean Ctr for Global Education ....Dr. Casey LOVE
88 CPS Executive Director ....Dr. Agnieszka NANCE
04 Senior Aide to the President ....Ms. Jennifer JUMONVILLE
07 Director of Admissions ....Mr. Jeffrey SCHIFFMAN
06 Registrar ....Ms. Colette RAPHEL
101 Secretary to the Board ....Ms. Cyndy ENGLISH
100 Chief of Staff ....Mrs. Elizabeth BROWN

University of Holy Cross (A)

4123 Woodland Drive, New Orleans LA 70131-7399

County: Orleans FICE Identification: 002023
Unit ID: 160065
Telephone: (504) 394-7744 Carnegie Class: Masters/S
FAX Number: (504) 391-2421 Calendar System: Semester
URL: www.uhcno.edu
Established: 1916 Annual Undergrad Tuition & Fees: $15,280
Enrollment: 1,137 Coed
Affiliation or Control: Roman Catholic IRS Status: 501(c)3
Highest Offering: Doctorate
Accreditation: SC, CACREP, CAEP, IACBE, NDT, NUR, RAD

01 President ....Dr. Stanton F. MCNEELY
05 Int Provost/VP Academic Affairs ....Dr. Lisa M. SULLIVAN
10 Vice Pres for Finance & CFO ....Mr. Chris BUNDICK
30 Vice Pres for Philanthropy/Planning ....Vacant
84 Vice Pres Enrollment Management ....Dr. Rosaria GUASTELLA
32 Assoc Vice Pres of Student Affairs ....Ms. Meredith REED
88 Vice Pres for Mission Integration ....Ms. Angela RUIZ
08 Director of Library Services ....Ms. Diana SCHAUBHUT
83 Dean Couns/Educ/Business ....Dr. Carolyn WHITE
66 Dean Nursing/Allied Health ....Dr. Patricia PRECHTER
49 Dean Liberal Arts and Science ....Dr. Michael LABRANCHE
32 Director Student Life ....Ms. Mallory OTTAWAY
06 Registrar ....Ms. Leslie M. JONES
42 Campus Minister ....Ms. Angela RUIZ
15 Director Human Resources ....Ms. Christine WATTS
44 Director of Annual Fund ....Vacant
13 Int Director of Info Tech Services ....Ms. Audrey B. CLEMENTS
37 Director of Financial Aid ....Mr. Jason CALLICO
04 Administrative Asst to President ....Vacant
19 Asst Director Campus Public Safety ....Mr. Garry FLOT
26 Director Marketing/Communications ....Ms. Jessica A. PIERCE
29 Director Alumni/Parent Relations ....Mr. Matthew PICARD

*University of Louisiana System Office (B)

1201 N Third Street, Suite 7-300,
Baton Rouge LA 70802-5243

County: East Baton Rouge FICE Identification: 033444
Unit ID: 247083
Telephone: (225) 342-6950 Carnegie Class: N/A
FAX Number: (225) 342-6473
URL: www.ulsystem.net

01 President & CEO ....Dr. James B. HENDERSON
11 Exec VP/Chief Operating Officer ....Dr. Marcus JONES
05 Provost and VP for Academic Affairs ....Dr. Jeannine KAHN
10 VP of Business and Finance ....Mr. Eddie MECHE
32 VP for Student Affairs & Governance ....Ms. Erica CALAIS
26 VP for External Affairs ....Ms. Cami GEISMAN
04 Exec Asst to President & CEO ....Ms. Sandra GREEN

*Grambling State University (C)

403 Main Street, Grambling LA 71245

County: Lincoln FICE Identification: 002006
Unit ID: 159009
Telephone: (318) 274-3811 Carnegie Class: Masters/L
FAX Number: (318) 274-6172 Calendar System: Semester
URL: www.gram.edu
Established: 1901 Annual Undergrad Tuition & Fees (In-State): $7,635
Enrollment: 5,438 Coed
Affiliation or Control: State IRS Status: 501(c)3
Highest Offering: Doctorate
Accreditation: SC, CAEPN, CAPRT, MUS, NUR, SPAA, SW, THEA

02 President ....Mr. Richard GALLOT, JR.
05 Provost/VP Academic Affairs ....Dr. Connie WALTON
10 Exec VP Finance & Admin/COO ....Mr. Martin LEMELLE, JR.
32 Vice Pres Student Affairs ....Vacant
111 VP Institutional Advancement ....Vacant
13 AVP of Info Technology ....Mrs. Peggy HANLEY
15 AVP of Operations/CHRO ....Vacant
19 University Police Chief ....Mr. Jerry MELTON
50 Dean College of Business ....Dr. Donald WHITE
53 Dean College of Education ....Vacant
49 Dean College of Arts & Sci ....Dr. Stacey D. DUHON

92 Dean Honors College ....Dr. Ellen SMILEY
18 Director Facilities Management ....Mr. Fredrick CARR
09 Director of Institutional Research ....Vacant
41 Athletic Director ....Vacant
07 Int Director of Admissions ....Vacant
06 University Registrar ....Mrs. Patricia J. HUTCHERSON
37 Dir Student Financial Aid ....Dr. Gavin HAMMS
29 Exec Director of Alumni Affairs ....Mr. Shanon REEVES
23 Director of Health Services ....Mrs. Patrice OUTLEY
38 Director Counseling Center ....Dr. Coleen SPEED
39 Director of Residential Life ....Ms. Carnelia BARFIELD
96 Director of Purchasing ....Mr. Timothy GRAHAM
40 Manager University Bookstore ....Mr. Alfredo MORELOS
106 Director of Distance Learning ....Mr. Eldrie HAMILTON
88 Special Assistant to Provost and VP ....Mrs. JoAnn BROWN
36 Director of Career Services ....Mrs. Kellye BLACKBURN

*Louisiana Tech University (D)

PO Box 3168, Ruston LA 71272-0001

County: Lincoln FICE Identification: 002008
Unit ID: 159647
Telephone: (318) 257-0211 Carnegie Class: DU-Higher
FAX Number: (318) 257-2928 Calendar System: Quarter
URL: www.latech.edu
Established: 1894 Annual Undergrad Tuition & Fees (In-State): $10,065
Enrollment: 11,126 Coed
Affiliation or Control: State IRS Status: 501(c)3
Highest Offering: Doctorate
Accreditation: SC, AAB, AAFCS, ADNUR, ART, AUD, CACREP, CAEP, CAEPN, CAHIIM, CIDA, COPSY, DIETD, DIETI, MT, MUS, SP

02 President ....Dr. Leslie K. GUICE
05 Provost ....Dr. Terry M. MCCONATHY
111 Vice President for Univ Advancement ....Mr. Brooks HULL
46 Chief Research & Innovation Officer ....Dr. Davy NORRIS, JR.
10 Vice President of Finance ....Mrs. Lisa L. COLE
11 AVP of Administration & Facilities ....Mr. Sam G. WALLACE
09 AVP Inst Effect/Research & Planning . Dr. Sheryl S. SHOEMAKER
88 AVP Acad Advancement & Partnerships ....Dr. Donna JOHNSON
58 AVP Research & Dean Grad School ....Dr. Ramu RAMACHANDRAN
88 AVP Research & Partnerships ....Dr. Sumeet DUA
32 AVP Student Advancement ....Dr. Dickie CRAWFORD
115 CFO & Exec Dir University Services ....Ms. Pam GILLEY
04 EA to Pres Compliance/Title IX ....Mrs. Carrie FLOURNOY
50 Dean of Business ....Dr. Chris MARTIN
53 Dean of Education ....Dr. Don N. SCHILLINGER
54 Dean of Engineering & Science ....Dr. Hisham HEGAB
65 Dean of Applied & Natural Sciences ....Dr. Gary KENNEDY
49 Dean of Liberal Arts ....Dr. Don KACZVINSKY
121 Dean Student Svcs & Acad Support ....Mrs. Stacy GILBERT
84 Dean Stdnt Engage/Undergrad Recruit ....Mr. Sam SPEED
116 Internal Auditor ....Mr. Robert GRAFTON
43 Legal Counsel ....Mr. Justin KAVALIR
26 Exec Dir University Communications ......Ms. Tonya OAKS SMITH
15 Director Human Resources ....Ms. Sheila TRAMMEL
113 Comptroller ....Vacant
07 Director of Admissions ....Mr. Tree GEORGE
13 Chief Info Technology Officer ....Mr. Tom HOOVER
91 Director of Computer Center ....Mr. Mike COLYAR
90 Interim Dir Infrastructure & IT ....Mr. Danny SCHALES
37 Director Student Financial Aid ....Ms. Aimee F. BAXTER
06 Registrar ....Vacant
08 Executive Director Libraries Svcs ....Vacant
38 Dir Career Ctr/Student Counseling ....Mr. Ron CATHEY
89 Director of Freshmen Studies ....Ms. Jennifer CARTER
92 Director of Honors Program ....Dr. Ernest RUFLETH
93 Director of Multicultural Affairs .... Ms. Devonia LOVE-VAUGHN
96 Director of Procurement ....Ms. Melissa HUGHES
18 Director Physical Plant ....Mr. Joe PEEL
41 Athletics Director ....Vacant
117 Director Envir Health & Safety ....Mr. Don BRASWELL
39 Dir Resident Life & Summer Camps ....Ms. Casey INGRAM
85 Director Intl Students/Scholars ....Mr. Jay LIGON
19 Chief University Police ....Mr. Randal HERMES
40 Director Bookstore ....Mr. Elliot JONES
118 HR Coordinator Benefits ....Ms. Taryn SOIGNIER
25 Director Sponsored Programs ....Ms. Courtney JARRELL
100 Coordinator of Planning & Advance ....Mr. Ryan W. RICHARD

*McNeese State University (E)

4205 Ryan Street, Lake Charles LA 70605

County: Calcasieu FICE Identification: 002017
Unit ID: 159717
Telephone: (337) 475-5000 Carnegie Class: Masters/L
FAX Number: (337) 475-5012 Calendar System: Semester
URL: www.mcneese.edu
Established: 1939 Annual Undergrad Tuition & Fees (In-State): $8,382
Enrollment: 7,284 Coed
Affiliation or Control: State IRS Status: 501(c)3
Highest Offering: Beyond Master's But Less Than Doctorate
Accreditation: SC, ABAI, ART, CACREP, CAEP, CAEPN, DIETD, DIETI, MT, MUS, NURSE, RAD

02 President ....Dr. Daryl BURCKEL
05 Interim Provost/VP Acad Affairs/EM ....Dr. Frederick LEMIEUX
10 Interim VP Business Affairs ....Ms. Mona WHITE
111 VP University Advancement ....Dr. Wade ROUSSE
32 VP Student Affairs ....Dr. Christopher THOMAS
84 Assoc VP Enrollment Management ....Dr. Toby OSBURN

20 Asst VP Academic Affairs ....Ms. Jessica HUTCHINGS
47 Dean College of Agriculture ....Dr. Frederick LEMIEUX
50 Dean College of Business ....Dr. Shuming BAI
53 Dean College of Education ....Dr. Angelique OGEA
49 Dean College of Liberal Arts ....Dr. Michael BUCKLES
54 Dean Col of Science/Engr/Math ....Dr. Tim HALL
66 Int Dean Col of Nursing/Health Prof ....Dr. Ann WARNER
35 Dean Student Affairs ....Dr. Kedrick NICHOLAS
13 Chief Information Technology ....Mr. Chad THIBODEAUX
19 University Police Chief ....Mr. William SCHEUFENS
28 Director of Diversity ....Ms. Krisshunn YOUNGBLOOD
41 Director of Athletics ....Mr. Heath SCHROYER
18 Director Facilities & Plant Opers ....Mr. Richard R. RHODEN
15 Dir Human Res/Student Employment ......Ms. Charlene R. ABBOTT
37 Director Student Financial Aid ....Ms. Taina J. SAVOIT
88 Director of Scholarships ....Ms. Ralynn F. CASTETE
07 Dir of Admissions and Recruiting ....Ms. Kourtney ISTRE
96 Director Purchasing/Property Cntrl ....Ms. Roxane FONTENOT
29 Director Alumni Affairs ....Vacant
92 Director of Honors College ....Dr. Scott E. GOINS
14 Director of Univ Computing Services ....Mr. Alfred FRUGE
08 Director of Library ....Ms. Debbie L. JOHNSON-HOUSTON
85 Director of International Programs ....Ms. Preble GIRARD
26 Director Public Relations ....Ms. Candace V. TOWNSEND
38 Director Student Counseling/Health ....Dr. Troy HIDALGO
106 Director of Electronic Learning ....Ms. Wendi PRATER
110 Director University Advancement ....Ms. Melissa NORTHCUTT
40 Bookstore Manager ....Ms. Donna MARTIN
06 Registrar ....Ms. Catrina BOENIG
04 Administrative Asst to President ....Ms. Deb KINGREY

*Nicholls State University (F)

906 East First Street, Thibodaux LA 70310-0001

County: Lafourche FICE Identification: 002005
Unit ID: 159966
Telephone: (985) 448-4003 Carnegie Class: Masters/L
FAX Number: (985) 448-4920 Calendar System: Semester
URL: www.nicholls.edu
Established: 1948 Annual Undergrad Tuition & Fees (In-State): $7,946
Enrollment: 6,769 Coed
Affiliation or Control: State IRS Status: 501(c)3
Highest Offering: Beyond Master's But Less Than Doctorate
Accreditation: SC, ART, CACREP, CAEPN, DIETD, DIETI, JOUR, MUS, NAIT, NURSE

02 President ....Dr. Jay CLUNE
03 Executive Vice President ....Vacant
05 Provost/VP Academic & Student Affs . Dr. Velma S. WESTBROOK
20 Vice Provost ....Dr. Todd KELLER
32 VP Stdnt Affairs/Dean of Students ....Dr. Michele E. CARUSO
18 Superint Facility/Proj Manager .... Mr. Owen Scott WILLIAMS
10 VP for Finance & Administration ....Mr. Terry BRAUD
45 Exec Dir of Planning/Effectiveness ....Mrs. Renee G. HICKS
81 Dean of Sciences & Technology ....Dr. John DOUCET
66 Dean of Nursing ....Dr. Velma S. WESTBROOK
50 Dean Business Administration ....Dr. Marilyn MACIK-FREY
53 Dean Educ/Behavioral Sciences ....Dr. Scot RADEMAKER
121 Director of Academic Services ....Ms. Cambria BOUZIGARD
09 Dir Assess/Institutional Research ....Ms. Melanie COLLINS
08 Director of Library ....Ms. Elizabeth BATTE
19 Director of University Police ....Mr. Alexander BARNES
36 Director of Career Services ....Ms. Kristie R. TAUZIN
37 Director of Student Financial Aid ....Ms. Casie TRICHE
13 Director of Computing Center ....Mr. Sam CAGLE
15 AVP of Human Resources/CDIO ....Mr. Steven H. KENNEY
26 Director of University Relations ....Mr. Jerad DAVID
51 Dir of Continuing Education ....Mrs. Elizabeth MCCURRY
41 Athletic Director ....Mr. Jonathan TERRELL
29 Exec Dir Alumni & External Affairs ....Ms. Monique CROCHET
88 Exec Dir Leadership & Master's Pgm ....Dr. Eugene A. DIAL
06 Director Records & Registration ....Mr. Kelly J. RODRIGUE
07 Director of Admissions ....Mrs. Becky L. DUROCHER
39 Director Residence Life ....Mr. Alex COAD
84 Director of Enrollment Services ....Mrs. Courtney CASSARD
96 Director of Purchasing ....Mr. Terry G. DUPRE
46 Director Research & Sponsored Pgms ....Mrs. Debra BENOIT
58 Director of Graduate Programs ....Dr. Anthony KUNKEL
88 Director of Printing & Design ....Mr. Bruno RUGGIERO
109 Director of Auxiliary Services ....Ms. Margo BADEAUX
88 Coordinator of Veterans Services ....Mr. Gilberto BURBANTE
106 Dir Online Education/E-learning ....Dr. Andrew SIMONCELLI
49 Dean of Liberal Arts ....Mrs. Jean DONEGAN
04 Admin Assistant to the President ....Mrs. Allison FORD
108 Director Institutional Assessment ....Ms. Melanie COLLINS
28 Chief Diversity & Inclusion Officer .... Mr. Steven H. KENNEY, JR.
35 Dean of Students ....Dr. Janice LYN
38 Director of Student Counseling ....Ms. Adrienne BOLTON
90 Director Academic Computing ....Mr. Perry LAWLESS

*Northwestern State University (G)

310 Sam Sibley Drive, Suite 223,
Natchitoches LA 71497-0002

County: Natchitoches FICE Identification: 002021
Unit ID: 160038
Telephone: (318) 357-6441 Carnegie Class: Masters/L
FAX Number: (318) 357-4223 Calendar System: Semester
URL: www.nsula.edu
Established: 1884 Annual Undergrad Tuition & Fees (In-State): $8,672
Enrollment: 11,447 Coed
Affiliation or Control: State IRS Status: 501(c)3
Highest Offering: Doctorate

Accreditation: SC, ADNUR, ANEST, ART, CACREP, CAEP, CAEPN, MUS, NURSE, RAD, SW, THEA

02 President ... Dr. Chris MAGGIO
05 Provost/VP Academic Affairs ... Dr. Greg HANDEL
26 Vice President for External Affairs ... Mr. Jerry D. PIERCE
46 VP for Tech/Innovation/Econ Dev ... Dr. Darlene WILLIAMS
10 Chief Financial Officer ... Mr. Pat JONES
32 Dean of Students ... Mrs. Frances CONINE
53 Dean Col of Education/Human Dev ... Dr. Kimberly MCALISTER
49 Dean Col of Arts & Sciences ... Dr. Francene LEMOINE
66 Dean Col of Nursing & Allied Health ... Dr. Joel HICKS
50 Dean Col of Business & Tech ... Vacant
13 Chief Information Officer ... Mr. Ron WRIGHT
92 Interim Director Scholars College ... Dr. Thomas REYNOLDS
12 Exec Director CENLA Campus ... Mr. Jason PARKS
09 Director Institutional Research ... Ms. Dawn MITCHELL
84 Director of Enrollment Management ... Mrs. Jana LUCKY
11 Director University Affairs ... Ms. Jennifer KELLY
06 Registrar ... Mrs. Barbara PRESCOTT
08 Director of Libraries ... Ms. Abbie LANDRY
111 Asst VP External Affs/Univ Advance ... Mr. Drake OWENS
37 Director Student Financial Aid ... Ms. Lauren JACKSON
88 Asst Dir Creative & Performing Arts ... Mr. Scott BURRELL
27 Director NSU Press ... Mrs. Leah JACKSON
36 Director Counseling & Career Svcs ... Mrs. Rebecca BOONE
41 Athletic Director ... Mr. Greg BURKE
23 Director of Health Services ... Ms. Carla WALKER
07 Director of University Recruiting ... Vacant
15 Director Human Resources ... Ms. Lisa HARRIS
18 Physical Plant Director ... Mr. Dale WOHLETZ
96 Director of Purchasing ... Mr. Dale MARTIN

*Southeastern Louisiana University (A)

500 West University Avenue, Hammond LA 70402
County: Tangipahoa — FICE Identification: 002024
Unit ID: 160612
Telephone: (985) 549-2000 — Carnegie Class: Masters/L
FAX Number: (985) 549-2061 — Calendar System: Semester
URL: www.southeastern.edu
Established: 1925 — Annual Undergrad Tuition & Fees (In-State): $8,289
Enrollment: 14,426 — Coed
Affiliation or Control: State — IRS Status: 501(c)3
Highest Offering: Doctorate
Accreditation: SC, AAFCS, ART, CAATE, CACREP, CAEPN, COSMA, MUS, NAIT, NURSE, SP, SW

02 President ... Dr. John L. CRAIN
05 Provost/VP Academic Affairs ... Dr. Tena GOLDING
10 VP Administration/Finance ... Mr. Sam DOMIANO
111 Vice Pres University Advancement ... Ms. Wendy LAUDERDALE
32 Vice President Student Affairs ... Dr. Eric SUMMERS
84 Chief Enrollment Management Officer ... Dr. Kay MAURIN
13 Chief Information Officer ... Dr. Mike M. ASOODEH
21 Controller ... Ms. Khalli s. HAGAN
06 Registrar ... Ms. Aime ANDERSON
08 Int Director of Library ... Ms. Janie BRANHAM
36 Director Career Development Svcs ... Mr. Ken W. RIDGEDELL
109 Director Auxiliary Services ... Ms. Connie DAVIS
29 Director of Alumni Services ... Ms. Michelle BIGGS
39 Dir Student Housing & Resident Svcs ... Mr. Chris ASPRION
15 Director Human Resources ... Ms. Tara DUPRE
19 Director University Police ... Vacant
46 Dir Sponsored Research/Programs ... Ms. Cheryl HALL
41 Athletic Director ... Mr. Jay ARTIGUES
18 Director Facility Planning ... Mr. Ken D. HOWE
92 Director Honors Program ... Dr. Claire PROCOPIO
23 Director Health Services ... Ms. Andrea PEEVY
38 Director of the Counseling Center ... Dr. Peter EMERSON
37 Director Financial Aid ... Ms. Mandy HOFFMAN
09 Director Inst Research/Assessment ... Dr. Michelle HALL
26 Sr Dir Public Information/Marketing ... Dr. Mike RIVAULT
96 Dir Purchasing/Property Control ... Mr. Richard HIMBER
35 Dean of Students ... Mr. Gabe WILLIS
22 Coordinator EEO/ADA ... Mr. Gene E. PREGEANT
49 Int Dn Col Arts/Human/Soc Sciences ... Dr. Karen FONTENOT
50 Int Dean of College of Business ... Dr. Antoinette PHILLIPS
53 Dean College of Education ... Dr. Paula CALDERON
66 Dean Col of Nursing & Health Sci ... Dr. Ann CARRUTH
72 Dean Col of Science & Technology ... Dr. Daniel MCCARTHY

*University of Louisiana at Lafayette (B)

104 University Circle, Lafayette LA 70503-0001
County: Lafayette — FICE Identification: 002031
Unit ID: 160658
Telephone: (337) 482-1000 — Carnegie Class: DU-Higher
FAX Number: (337) 482-6195 — Calendar System: Semester
URL: www.louisiana.edu
Established: 1898 — Annual Undergrad Tuition & Fees (In-State): $10,358
Enrollment: 16,450 — Coed
Affiliation or Control: State — IRS Status: 501(c)3
Highest Offering: Doctorate
Accreditation: SC, ART, CACREP, CAEP, CAHIIM, CIDA, JOUR, MUS, NAIT, NURSE, SP, THEA

02 President ... Dr. E. Joseph SAVOIE
05 Provost/VP for Academic Affairs ... Dr. Jaimie HEBERT
10 VP Administration & Finance ... Mr. Jerry L. LEBLANC
32 Vice President for Student Affairs ... Ms. Patricia COTTONHAM
111 VP University Advancement ... Mr. John BLOHM
46 Vice President for Research ... Dr. Ramesh KOLLURU
84 VP for Enrollment Management ... Dr. DeWayne BOWIE
13 Chief Information Officer ... Mr. Gene FIELDS
26 AVP Communications/Marketing ... Dr. Jennifer STEPHENS
11 Director of Administrative Services ... Ms. Lisa C. LANDRY
21 Asst Vice Pres Financial Services ... Ms. Debra CALAIS
45 Asst VP Inst Effectiveness ... Dr. Blanca BAUER
20 Asst VP Academic Affairs ... Dr. Robert MCKINNEY
35 Dean of Students ... Dr. Margarita PEREZ
35 Assoc Dean Students/Dir Stdnt Life ... Ms. Heidie LINDSEY
25 Director of Research/Sponsored Pgms ... Vacant
91 Director of Information Systems ... Ms. Paula BREAUX
14 Director Computing Support Services ... Mr. Patrick LANDRY
08 Dean University Libraries ... Ms. Susan RICHARD
07 Director of UG Admissions ... Ms. Amy DESORMEAUX
09 Director of Institutional Research ... Ms. Lisa LORD
55 Director University Connection ... Ms. Amanda DOYLE
37 Director of Financial Aid ... Ms. Cindy SHOWS-PEREZ
96 AVP Finance and Director Purchasing ... Ms. Marie FRANK
27 Interim Editorial Director ... Mr. James SAVAGE
36 Director Career Services ... Ms. Kim A. BILLEAUDEAU
19 Chief of Police ... Mr. Timothy HANKS
23 Chief Administrator Officer SHS ... Ms. Madeline HUSBAND-ARDOIN
49 Dean Liberal Arts ... Dr. Jordan KELLMAN
54 Dean of Engineering ... Dr. Ahmed KHATTAB
53 Dean of Education ... Dr. Nathan ROBERTS
66 Dean of Nursing ... Dr. Melinda OBERLEITNER
58 Dean of Graduate School ... Dr. Mary FARMER-KAISER
50 Dean of Business Admin ... Dr. Linda NICHOLS
81 Dean of Sciences ... Dr. Azmy ACKLEH
97 Dean of University College ... Dr. Bobbie DECUIR
57 Interim Dean College of the Arts ... Mr. Michael MCCLURE
77 Director Ctr Adv Computer Studies ... Dr. Magdy A. BAYOUMI
18 Director Physical Plant ... Mr. William J. CRIST
43 Director of Operational Review ... Ms. Megan BREAUX
39 Director Housing ... Ms. Dawn MILLER
40 Manager Bookstore ... Mr. Robert RICHARD
24 Director Univ Media/Printing Svcs ... Vacant
41 Vice President for Athletics ... Dr. Bryan MAGGARD
85 Exec Dir Global Engagement ... Dr. Gabriel CARRANZA
51 Director of Continuing Education ... Dr. Martha BRYANT
31 Dean of Community Service ... Mr. David YARBROUGH
29 Exec Director Alumni Affairs ... Mr. John Claude ARCENEAUX
112 Planned Giving Officer ... Vacant
38 Director Counseling and Testing ... Mr. Brian FREDERICK
15 Chief Human Resources Officer ... Mr. Paul THOMAS
06 Interim Registrar ... Ms. Lori FREDERICK
120 Director of Distance Learning ... Dr. Claire ARABIE
92 Director of Honors Program ... Dr. Julia FREDERICK
121 Exec Director of Student Success ... Dr. Elizabeth GIROIR
89 Director of First-Year Experience ... Vacant
28 Director of Diversity ... Dr. Taniecea MALLERY
108 Director Institutional Assessment ... Dr. Alise HAGAN
30 Exec Director of Development ... Ms. Lisa CAPONE
44 Director Annual Giving ... Ms. Claire ST. ROMAIN
113 Bursar ... Mr. Kyle CALAIS
119 Director of IT Security ... Mr. Charles BROOME
39 Director of Residence Life ... Ms. Maylen ALDANA
105 Director of Digital Communications ... Ms. Aimee ABSHIRE
22 Director Equal Opportunity Programs ... Ms. Lelanya DOUET

*University of Louisiana at Monroe (C)

700 University Avenue, Monroe LA 71209-0001
County: Ouachita — FICE Identification: 002020
Unit ID: 159993
Telephone: (318) 342-1000 — Carnegie Class: DU-Mod
FAX Number: (318) 342-5161 — Calendar System: Semester
URL: www.ulm.edu
Established: 1931 — Annual Undergrad Tuition & Fees (In-State): $9,070
Enrollment: 8,888 — Coed
Affiliation or Control: State — IRS Status: 501(c)3
Highest Offering: Doctorate
Accreditation: SC, CACREP, CAEP, CAEPN, CONST, DH, EXSC, MFCD, MT, MUS, NURSE, OT, OTA, PHAR, RAD, SP, SW

02 President ... Dr. Ronald L. BERRY
10 Vice President for Business Affairs ... Dr. William T. GRAVES
32 Vice President for Student Affairs ... Dr. Valerie FIELDS
05 Vice President for Academic Affairs ... Vacant
13 VP for Info Svcs/Student Success ... Dr. Michael CAMILLE
84 Int VP Enrollment Svcs & Univ Rels ... Ms. Lisa MILLER
43 Legal/Compliance Counsel ... Ms. Sherrye CARRADINE
45 Chief Strategy Officer ... Mr. Seth HALL
46 Chief Innovation & Research Officer ... Dr. John SUTHERLIN
88 Director Enrollment & Scholarship ... Dr. Robyn JORDAN
41 Director of Athletics ... Mr. Scott MCDONALD
26 Exec Director of Communications ... Dr. Kelsey BOHL
96 Director of Purchasing ... Ms. Cheri PERKINS
116 Internal Audit ... Mr. Ferando CORDOVA
49 Dean Arts/Education & Sciences ... Dr. John PRATTE
50 Dean Business & Social Sciences ... Dr. Michelle MCEACHARN
67 Dean Pharmacy ... Dr. Glenn ANDERSON
76 Dean College Health Science ... Dr. Donald SIMPSON
58 Dean Graduate School ... Dr. Sushma KRISHNAMURTHY
108 Director Assessment and Evaluation ... Mrs. Allison L. THOMPSON
09 Dir Univ Planning/Analysis ... Mr. Jason CONSTANT
08 Director Library ... Ms. Megan LOWE
120 Int Director of Online Education ... Ms. Jessica GRIGGS
06 Registrar ... Mr. Anthony MALTA
37 Director Financial Aid Services ... Ms. Marla HERRINGTON
85 Dir Intl Student Program and Svcs ... Ms. Gina WHITE
124 Director of University Retention ... Mrs. Barbara MICHAELIDES
102 Executive Director Foundation ... Mrs. Susan CHAPPELL
39 Director Residential Life ... Ms. Tresea L. BUCKHAULTS
114 Budget Officer ... Ms. Nicole WALKER
21 Controller ... Mr. Mark LABUDE
15 Director Human Resources ... Ms. Melissa DUCOTE
14 Director Computer Center ... Mr. Chance W. EPPINETTE
109 Exec Dir Auxiliary Enterprises ... Mr. Tommy WALPOLE
40 Manager University Bookstore ... Ms. Stacey CORDELL
18 Director Physical Plant Admin ... Mr. Chris RINGO
88 Facilities Planning Officer ... Mr. Michael DAVIS
22 Spec Projects Ofcr/Title IX Coord ... Ms. Treina KIMBLE
38 Director Counseling Center ... Ms. Karen FOSTER
19 Director of University Police ... Mr. Tom TORREGROSSA
36 Director Career Center ... Ms. Kristin CHANDLER
88 Dir Recreational Svcs/Facilities ... Mr. Brandon BRUSCATO
88 Technology and Comm Liaison ... Mr. Lindsey S. WILKERSON
29 Director of Alumni Affairs ... Ms. Sarah SIEREVELD
04 Assistant to the President ... Ms. Kathy MASTERS
25 Dir Sponsored Programs & Research ... Ms. Lawanna GILBERT-BELL
53 Director School of Education ... Dr. Myra LOVETT
07 Exec Dir Recruitment/Admissions ... Ms. Sami OWENS
28 Dir of Diversity/Equity & Inclusion ... Dr. Pamela SAULSBERRY

WorldQuant University (D)

201 S. Charles Ave, Ste 2500, New Orleans LA 70170
County: Orleans — Identification: 667408
Telephone: (504) 662-1946 — Carnegie Class: Not Classified
FAX Number: N/A — Calendar System: Other
URL: wqu.org
Established: 2015 — Annual Graduate Tuition & Fees: N/A
Enrollment: N/A — Coed
Affiliation or Control: Independent Non-Profit — IRS Status: 501(c)3
Highest Offering: Master's; No Undergraduates
Accreditation: DEAC

01 CEO ... Daphne KIS

Xavier University of Louisiana (E)

One Drexel Drive, New Orleans LA 70125-1098
County: Orleans — FICE Identification: 002032
Unit ID: 160904
Telephone: (504) 486-7411 — Carnegie Class: Masters/S
FAX Number: (504) 520-7904 — Calendar System: Semester
URL: www.xula.edu
Established: 1925 — Annual Undergrad Tuition & Fees: $25,822
Enrollment: 3,383 — Coed
Affiliation or Control: Roman Catholic — IRS Status: 501(c)3
Highest Offering: Doctorate
Accreditation: SC, ACBSP, #ARCPA, CACREP, CAEP, MUS, PHAR, @SP

01 President ... Dr. C. Reynold VERRET
05 Provost and Sr VP Academic Affairs ... Dr. Anne MCCALL
100 VP Administration & Chief of Staff ... Ms. Patrice BELL
116 Dir Office of Internal Audits ... Mr. William BOSTICK
88 Deputy Chief of Staff ... Dr. Rae BORDEN
20 Sr Assoc Provost & Chief IR Officer ... Dr. Marguerite GIGUETTE
88 Int Dir Ctr Eq Just/Human Spirit ... Ms. Shellond CHESTER
20 Asst Provost & COO Acad Affairs ... Ms. Shellond CHESTER
121 Asst Provost for Student Success ... Dr. Nathaniel HOLMES
84 VP Enrollment Management ... Ms. Keyana SCALES
111 Vice President Inst Advancement ... Mr. Phillip D. ADAMS
32 Vice President Student Affairs ... Mr. Curits WRIGHT
10 CFO and VP Fiscal Services ... Mr. Edward J. PHILLIPS
13 VP Technology Administration ... Dr. Mable J. MOORE
18 VP Facility Planning & Mgmt ... Mr. Marion BRACY
15 Assoc VP Human Resources ... Mr. Kevin WOLF
110 Assoc VP Inst Advancement ... Ms. Kimberly REESE
46 Assoc VP Research/Sponsored Pgms ... Ms. Kaneisha B. AKINPELUMI
88 Asst VP & Director Title III ... Dr. Rachel THOMAS
14 Asst VP Tech/Deputy CIO ... Ms. Melva D. WILLIAMS
41 Asst VP Stdnt Affairs/Dir Athletics ... Vacant
07 Sr Assoc Dir of Admissions ... Ms. Kendra LAWRENCE
19 Asst VP/Chief of Police ... Ms. Changamire DURALL
22 Asst VP Stdnt Affs/Dep Chf Inc Ofcr ... Ms. Kerri ALEXANDER
07 Asst VP Enrollment Mgmt ... Vacant
88 Assoc Dean Health & Wellness ... Ms. Virginia PELLERIN
49 Int Dean Col of Arts & Sciences ... Dr. Anderson SUNDA-MEYA
35 Asst Dean Student Life ... Mr. Darryl KELLER
88 Exec Dir Advancement Services ... Mrs. Kendra TIRCUIT
39 Exec Director Residential Education ... Ms. Chermele CHRISTY
101 Dir Board Relations Pres Office ... Ms. Kris POTTHARST
35 Dir Opers/Sp Asst to VP Stdnt Affs ... Ms. Anitra CALVIN
06 University Registrar ... Mrs. Avis STUARD
67 Dean College of Pharmacy ... Dr. Kathleen KENNEDY
116 Controller/Dir Fin Rep/Exec Audit ... Ms. Ingenue S. SCHEXNIDER-FIELDS
88 Director Payroll ... Ms. Joyce SANDIFER
23 Med Dir Student Health Services ... Dr. Robert MERCADEL
21 Director Operations ... Ms. Lori GIE
36 Director Career Services ... Ms. Tracey JACKSON
37 Director Financial Aid ... Vacant
38 Dir Counsel Wellness/Disability Svc ... Dr. Angela GRAHAM-WILLIAMS
08 Director University Library ... Ms. Tamera HANKEN
09 Dir Inst Rsrch & Effectiveness ... Dr. Clair WILKINS-GREEN
37 Interim Dir Financial Aid ... Mrs. Sandy LIVINGS-VEALS
88 Dir Inst Compliance/Extern Report ... Dr. Treva A. LEE

29 Dir Alum Rels & Annual Giving .... Ms. Lacretia JONES
88 Dir Apps Pgm/Banner Proj Mgr .... Mrs. L'Tanya C. SETTLE
104 Dir Div of Global Engagement .... Dr. Yu JIANG
88 Dir Violence Prevention Educ .... Ms. Jennifer BODNAR
113 Bursar .... Ms. Patrica VAULTZ
88 Dir Inst of Blk Catholic Studies ....Dr. Kathleen D. BELLOW
42 Dir Campus Ministry ....Mrs. Lisa L. MCCLAIN
91 Manager Datacenter Operations ....Vacant
88 Dir Environmental Health & Safety ....Mr. Raymond BROWN
25 Director Grants and Contracts ....Ms. Shirley B. MASSENBURG
88 Dir Xavier Exponential ....Dr. Shearon ROBERTS
102 Dir Foundation/Corp Relations ....Dr. Jeff A. HALE
88 Dir Ctr Adv of Teaching & Fac Dev .... Dr. Elizabeth HAMMER
88 Dir Data Science & Analytics .... Ms. Rebecca OSAKWE
88 Sr Conduct Officer/Parent Programs .... Ms. Judy BRACY
106 Distance Education Coordinator .... Dr. Karen NICHOLS
119 IT Security Officer .... Mr. Gregory JONES
26 Dir Marketing/Communication ....Ms. Ashley IRVIN
105 Sr Mgr Website Dev/Innov/Analytics ....Ms. Ashley DANIELS
42 University Chaplain ....Fr. Etido S. JEROME
40 Manager Bookstore ....Ms. Rose NAQUIN

MAINE

Bates College (A)

2 Andrews Road, Lewiston ME 04240-6047
County: Androscoggin FICE Identification: 002036
Unit ID: 160977
Telephone: (207) 786-6255 Carnegie Class: Bac-A&S
FAX Number: (207) 786-6123 Calendar System: Other
URL: www.bates.edu
Established: 1855 Annual Undergrad Tuition & Fees: $57,353
Enrollment: 1,876 Coed
Affiliation or Control: Independent Non-Profit IRS Status: 501(c)3
Highest Offering: Baccalaureate
Accreditation: EH

01 President ....Dr. A. Clayton SPENCER
05 VP Academic Affairs/Dean of Faculty ....Dr. Malcolm HILL
10 VP Finance & Admin/Treasurer .... Mr. Geoffrey SWIFT
08 VP for ILS & College Librarian .... Ms. Patricia SCHOKNECHT
100 VP for Institutional Affairs .... Mr. Michael HUSSEY
111 VP Advancement ....Ms. Sarah R. PEARSON
26 VP Communications & Public Affairs ....Mr. Sean T. FINDLEN
32 VP for Campus Life & DOS .... Mr. Joshua MCINTOSH
84 VP Enrollment/Dean of Admission .... Ms. Leigh WEISENBURGER
21 Asst Vice Pres Financial Planning ....Mr. Douglas W. GINEVAN
20 Assoc Dean of Faculty .... Ms. Aslaug ASGEIRSDOTTIR
20 Assoc Dean of Faculty .... Ms. Krista M. ARONSON
31 Director of Community Partnerships ....Ms. Darby K. RAY
06 Registrar .... Ms. Mary MESERVE
09 Dir Inst Rsch/Analysis and Planning .... Mr. Tom MCGUINNESS
15 Asst VP Human Resources ....Ms. Hope BURNELL
29 Assistant VP of Alumni Engagement .... Ms. Heather CORBETT
18 Dir of Facilities Svcs Operations .... Mr. Jay PHILLIPS
88 Dir Capital Planning/Construction ......Ms. Pamela J. WICHROSKI
19 Director Campus Safety ....Mr. Paul MENICE
23 Director Student Health Support ....Vacant
37 Dir Student Financial Services .... Ms. Wendy G. GLASS
40 Dir Bookstore/Contract Officer .... Ms. Gail S. ST. PIERRE
36 Sr Assoc Dean of PW & Career Dev ....Mr. Allen DELONG
91 Dir Sys Development & Integration ... Ms. Eileen P. ZIMMERMAN
88 Director of Client Services ....Mr. Scott TINER
41 Director of Athletics ....Mr. Jason FEIN
42 Multifaith Chaplain .... Ms. Brittany LONGSDORF
39 Senior Assoc Dean of Students ....Ms. Erin FOSTER ZSIGA
102 Dir Corporate/Foundation Relations ....Ms. Rachel WRAY
104 Assoc Dean/Dir for Global Education .... Mr. Darren GALLANT
28 AVP and Chief Diversity Officer .... Ms. Noelle CHADDOCK
07 Sr Assoc Dean Admiss/Dir Intl Enrol .... Mr. Scott ALEXANDER
04 Exec Assistant to the President ....Ms. Claire B. SCHMOLL
45 Chief Institutional Planning Office .... Mr. Tom MCGUINNESS

† Tuition figure is a comprehensive fees figure.

Beal University (B)

99 Farm Road, Bangor ME 04401-6831
County: Penobscot FICE Identification: 005204
Unit ID: 160995
Telephone: (207) 947-4591 Carnegie Class: Assoc/HVT-High Trad
FAX Number: (207) 947-0208 Calendar System: Other
URL: www.beal.edu
Established: 1891 Annual Undergrad Tuition & Fees: N/A
Enrollment: 493 Coed
Affiliation or Control: Proprietary IRS Status: Proprietary
Highest Offering: Baccalaureate
Accreditation: ACCSC, CAHIIM, MAC

01 President ....Ms. Sheryl DEWALT
11 Chief Operations Officer .... Mr. Steve VILLETT
10 Director of Finance ....Ms. Renee DUNTON
09 Compliance Officer ....Mr. Jeffrey BODIMER
05 Dean of Education ....Ms. Susan HAWES
07 Admissions Representative .... Ms. Sarah OSBOURNE
37 Director Student Financial Aid .... Mr. Steve VILLETT
06 Registrar .... Ms. Miriam THOMPSON
08 Chief Librarian .... Ms. Donna BANCROFT
18 Superintendent Physical Plant ....Mr. Kevin HARDY
36 Director Career Services ....Ms. Robin TARDIFF
50 Director Business Studies .... Mr. Steve VILLETT
75 Director Welding Technology ....Mr. Jesse CROSBY
66 Director Nursing ....Ms. Colleen KOOB

Bowdoin College (C)

255 Maine Street, Brunswick ME 04011
County: Cumberland FICE Identification: 002038
Unit ID: 161004
Telephone: (207) 725-3000 Carnegie Class: Bac-A&S
FAX Number: (207) 725-3123 Calendar System: Semester
URL: www.bowdoin.edu
Established: 1794 Annual Undergrad Tuition & Fees: $56,350
Enrollment: 1,777 Coed
Affiliation or Control: Independent Non-Profit IRS Status: 501(c)3
Highest Offering: Master's
Accreditation: EH

01 President ....Dr. Clayton ROSE
10 Sr VP Finance/Admin/Treasurer .... Mr. Matthew ORLANDO
30 Sr VP Devel & Alumni Relations ....Mr. Scott MEIKLEJOHN
26 Sr VP Communications/Public Affairs .... Mr. Scott W. HOOD
13 SVP/Chief Information Officer ....Mr. Michael CATO
28 SVP Inclusion & Diversity ....Mr. Michael E. REED
15 Vice President of Human Resources ....Vacant
32 SVP & Dean of Student Affairs ....Ms. Janet LOHMANN
05 SVP/Dean for Academic Affairs ....Ms. Jennifer SCANLON
07 Dean of Admissions/Financial Aid ....Vacant
09 SVP Inst Rsrch/Analytics Consulting ..Dr. Christina M. FINNERAN
29 Director Alumni Relations ....Ms. Rodie F. LLOYD
08 College Librarian ....Ms. Marjorie HASSEN
37 Director of Student Financial Aid ....Mr. Mike ALBANO
06 Registrar .... Ms. Martina DUNCAN
19 Executive Director of Security .... Mr. Randall NICHOLS
36 Exec Dir Career Exploration & Dev ....Ms. Kristin BRENNAN
38 Director of Counseling Service .... Dr. Bernie HERSHBERGER
41 Director of Athletics ....Mr. Timothy M. RYAN
23 Director of Health Services ....Dr. Jeffrey MAHER
18 Int Dir Facilities Ops/Maintenance ....Mr. Jeff TUTTLE
24 Instructional Media Librarian ....Ms. Carmen M. GREENLEE
39 Director of Residential Life .... Ms. Whitney HOGAN
109 Dir Dining & Bookstore Services ....Ms. Mary M. KENNEDY
35 Director of Student Activities ....Mr. Nate HINTZE
35 Dean of Students ....Ms. Kristina Bethea ODEJIMI
88 Co-Director of the Museum of Art .... Ms. Anne GOODYEAR
88 Co-Director of the Museum of Art .... Mr. Frank GOODYEAR
18 Director of Capital Projects ....Mr. Donald V. BORKOWSKI

Colby College (D)

4000 Mayflower Hill, Waterville ME 04901-8840
County: Kennebec FICE Identification: 002039
Unit ID: 161086
Telephone: (207) 859-4000 Carnegie Class: Bac-A&S
FAX Number: (207) 859-4603 Calendar System: 4/1/4
URL: www.colby.edu
Established: 1813 Annual Undergrad Tuition & Fees: $59,430
Enrollment: 2,155 Coed
Affiliation or Control: Independent Non-Profit IRS Status: 501(c)3
Highest Offering: Baccalaureate
Accreditation: EH

01 President ....Dr. David A. GREENE
05 Provost and Dean of Faculty .... Dr. Margaret T. MCFADDEN
10 Vice President Admin & CFO .... Mr. Douglas C. TERP
111 VP/Chief Advancement Ofcr ....Mr. Matt PROTO
32 Dean of the College ....Dr. Karlene A. BURRELL-MCRAE
100 Vice President & Chief of Staff ....Ms. Ruth JACKSON
07 AVP/Dean Admission & Financial Aid ...... Mr. Randi ARSENAULT
121 VP and Dean of Student Advancement .... Dr. C. Andrew MCGADNEY
45 Vice President of Planning ....Mr. Brian J. CLARK
43 VP/Gen Counsel/Sec of the Col ....Mr. Richard Y. UCHIDA
41 VP/Director of Athletics ....Mr. Mike WISECUP
20 Assoc Provost & Dean of Faculty .... Dr. Russell R. JOHNSON
18 Asst VP Facilities and Campus Plng ....Ms. Minakshi M. AMUNDSEN
35 Dean of Students ....Ms. Barbara E. MOORE
15 Assoc Vice Pres Human Resources .... Mr. Mark CROSBY
37 Asst Dean/Director Financial Aid ....Ms. Jill A. PIERCE
06 Registrar ....Ms. Lindsey C. NELSON
08 Director of the Colby Libraries ....Ms. Lareese M. HALL
88 Director of Special Programs ....Mr. Brian BRAY
19 Director of Safety ....Mr. Wade P. BEHNKE
13 Int Chief Information Officer ....Mr. Jason PARKHILL
23 Medical Director ....Dr. Paul D. BERKNER
38 Director of Counseling Services ....Dr. Eric S. JOHNSON
09 Dir Inst Research & Assessment .... Ms. Rebecca H. BRODIGAN
21 AVP Finance/Controller ....Ms. Alicia J. GARDINER
40 Director of the Bookstore ....Ms. Barbara C. SHUTT
104 Director of Off-Campus Study .... Dr. Nancy DOWNEY
102 Director of Grants/Sponsored Pgms ...Mr. William C. LAYTON, III

College of the Atlantic (E)

105 Eden Street, Bar Harbor ME 04609-1198
County: Hancock FICE Identification: 011385
Unit ID: 160959
Telephone: (207) 288-5015 Carnegie Class: Bac-A&S
FAX Number: (207) 288-3780 Calendar System: Trimester
URL: www.coa.edu
Established: 1969 Annual Undergrad Tuition & Fees: $43,542
Enrollment: 370 Coed
Affiliation or Control: Independent Non-Profit IRS Status: 501(c)3
Highest Offering: Master's
Accreditation: EH

01 President ....Dr. Darron COLLINS
05 Academic Dean .... Dr. Ken HILL
10 Director Administrative Svcs .... Ms. Marie STIVERS
32 Dean of Student Life ....Ms. Sarah LUKE
111 Dean Institutional Advancement ....Ms. Lynn BOULGER
07 Dean of Admission .... Ms. Heather ALBERT-KNOPP
06 Registrar ....Ms. Judy ALLEN
08 Director of Thorndike Library ....Ms. Jane HULTBERG
21 Comptroller .... Mrs. Melissa COOK
37 Int Director of Financial Aid ....Ms. Linda BLACK
36 Director of Internship/Career Svcs ....Ms. Jill BARLOW-KELLEY
26 Public Relations Mgr/Dir Comm ....Mr. Rob LEVIN

Husson University (F)

1 College Circle, Bangor ME 04401-2929
County: Penobscot FICE Identification: 002043
Unit ID: 487524
Telephone: (207) 941-7000 Carnegie Class: DU-Mod
FAX Number: (207) 941-7139 Calendar System: Semester
URL: www.husson.edu
Established: 1898 Annual Undergrad Tuition & Fees: $19,772
Enrollment: 3,473 Coed
Affiliation or Control: Independent Non-Profit IRS Status: 501(c)3
Highest Offering: Doctorate
Accreditation: EH, CACREP, IACBE, NURSE, OT, PHAR, PTA

01 President .... Dr. Robert A. CLARK
05 Sr VP for Academic Affairs/Provost .... Dr. Lynne COY-OGAN
10 VP Finance & Admin/Treasurer .... Craig HADLEY
111 Vice President for Advancement ....Sara C. ROBINSON
84 VP Enrollment Management ....Michael J. FOX
13 AVP Information Technology ....Garth CORMIER
50 Dean College of Business ....Dr. Marie HANSEN
67 Dean College of Health and Pharmacy . Dr. Rhonda WASKIEWICZ
49 Dean College of Science/Humanities .... Dr. Patricia BIXEL
26 Exec Director of Communications .... Eric GORDON
32 Dean of Student Life ....Pamela KROPP-ANDERSON
53 Director School of Education ....Vacant
07 Director of Admissions ....Melissa ROSENBURGI
37 Director of Financial Aid ....Anne TABOR
06 Registrar ....Nancy FENDERS
09 Director of Institutional Research ....Dr. Cristi CARSON
108 Director Institutional Assessment ....Travis E. ALLEN
106 Dir Online and Extended Learning .... Dr. David HAUS
36 Director Career Services ....James WESTHOFF
41 Director of Athletics ....Francis PERGOLIZZI
35 Int Assoc Dean Student Life ....Troy MOREHOUSE
15 Exec Director Human Resources ....Janet KELLE
29 Director of Alumni Relations ....Keith PIEHLER
18 Director of Maintenance .... Gary GEROW
08 Head Librarian ....Susanna PATHAK
30 Director of Advancement Services ....Sarah ROBINSON
04 Executive Assistant to President ....Kandi HALE
100 Chief of Staff ....Kandi HALE
19 Director Safety and Security ....Chris GROTTON
38 Director of Counseling Services ....Vacant
105 Director Digital Communications ....Matthew GREEN-HAMANN
109 Assoc Vice Pres Auxiliary Services ....Thomas WARREN

Institute for Doctoral Studies in the Visual Arts (G)

795 Congress Street, Portland ME 04102
County: Cumberland FICE Identification: 041888
Unit ID: 462044
Telephone: (207) 879-8757 Carnegie Class: Spec-4-yr-Other
FAX Number: N/A Calendar System: Semester
URL: www.idsva.edu
Established: 2007 Annual Graduate Tuition & Fees: N/A
Enrollment: 88 Coed
Affiliation or Control: Independent Non-Profit IRS Status: 501(c)3
Highest Offering: Doctorate; No Undergraduates
Accreditation: EH

01 President ....George SMITH
10 Exec Vice President/CFO ....Amy CURTIS
05 Vice Pres Acad Affs/Dir of School .... Dr. Simonetta MORO

The Landing School (H)

286 River Road, Arundel ME 04046
County: York FICE Identification: 023613
Unit ID: 161208
Telephone: (207) 985-7976 Carnegie Class: Spec 2-yr-Tech
FAX Number: (207) 985-7942 Calendar System: Semester
URL: www.landingschool.edu
Established: 1978 Annual Undergrad Tuition & Fees: $25,012
Enrollment: 48 Coed
Affiliation or Control: Independent Non-Profit IRS Status: 501(c)3
Highest Offering: Associate Degree
Accreditation: ACCSC

01 President/Chief Executive Officer ... Mr. Frederick J. FAWCETT, III
10 Vice President of Finance ....Ms. Kate BALDWIN
05 Dean of Education .... Mr. Ken RUSINEK
18 Operations & Industry Relations ....Vacant
07 Director of Admissions/Recruitment .... Ms. Kaitlin ST. PETER
08 Librarian ....Mr. James CUMISKEY
15 Human Resources Officer ....Ms. Kate BALDWIN

37 Financial Aid & VA Administrator .... Mrs. Jeanne BOUCHER
96 Director of Purchasing .... Mr. Michael CROSBY

Maine College of Art (A)

522 Congress St, Portland ME 04101
County: Cumberland FICE Identification: 011673
Unit ID: 161509
Telephone: (207) 699-5521 Carnegie Class: Spec-4-yr-Arts
FAX Number: (207) 775-5087 Calendar System: Semester
URL: www.meca.edu
Established: 1882 Annual Undergrad Tuition & Fees: $38,310
Enrollment: 435 Coed
Affiliation or Control: Independent Non-Profit IRS Status: 501(c)3
Highest Offering: Master's
Accreditation: EH, ART

01 President .... Ms. Laura FREID
03 Executive Vice President .... Ms. Beth ELICKER
05 VP Academic Affairs/Dean of College .... Mr. Ian ANDERSON
111 Assoc VP Institutional Advancement .... Ms. Lauren GLENNON
06 Registrar .... Ms. Anne DENNISON
32 Director of Student Life .... Ms. Jennifer DOEBLER
07 Director of Admissions .... Ms. Jennifer CAMPANARO
13 Director Technology .... Mr. Seth CLAYTER
26 Dir of Marketing & Communications .... Mr. Steve BOWDEN
10 Director of Business Services .... Ms. Holly HIGGINS
37 Director of Financial Aid .... Ms. Carri FRECHETTE
51 Director Continuing Studies .... Ms. Nik BSULLAK
18 Director of Facilities .... Mr. Douglas DOERING
08 Library Director .... Ms. Shiva DARBANDI
04 Executive Assistant .... Ms. Melissa SULLIVAN
29 Director Alumni Relations .... Vacant
36 Director of Artists at Work .... Ms. Jessica TOMLINSON
101 Secretary of the Institution/Board .... Ms. Heather YORK
15 Chief Human Resources Officer .... Ms. Tanya GUAY

Maine College of Health Professions (B)

70 Middle Street, Lewiston ME 04240-7027
County: Androscoggin FICE Identification: 006305
Unit ID: 161022
Telephone: (207) 795-2840 Carnegie Class: Spec 2-yr-Health
FAX Number: (207) 795-2849 Calendar System: Semester
URL: www.mchp.edu
Established: 1891 Annual Undergrad Tuition & Fees: $13,905
Enrollment: 216 Coed
Affiliation or Control: Independent Non-Profit IRS Status: 501(c)3
Highest Offering: Baccalaureate
Accreditation: EH, ADNUR, NURSE, PNUR, RAD

01 President .... Dr. Monika BISSELL
10 Vice President of Finance .... Ms. Lesa ROSE
05 VP of Academic/Student Affairs .... Dr. Alexander CLIFFORD
88 Dean of Medical Imaging .... Mrs. Judith RIPLEY
07 Director of Admissions .... Ms. Erica WATSON
06 Registrar/Stdnt Financial Aid Couns .... Mrs. Nicole DEBLOIS
66 Dean of Nursing .... Dr. Lynne GOTJEN
22 Title IX Coordinator .... Dr. Alexander CLIFFORD

*Maine Community College System (C)

323 State Street, Augusta ME 04330-7131
County: Kennebec Identification: 666092
Unit ID: 409713
Telephone: (207) 629-4000 Carnegie Class: N/A
FAX Number: (207) 629-4048
URL: www.mccs.me.edu

01 President .... Mr. David DAIGLER
05 VP & Chief Academic Officer .... Ms. Janet SORTOR
10 Chief Financial Officer .... Mrs. Pamela REMIERES-MORIN
15 Chief Counsel Labor & Employment .... Mr. Robert NADEAU
13 Chief Info/Technology Officer .... Mr. Martin GANG

*Central Maine Community College (D)

1250 Turner Street, Auburn ME 04210-6498
County: Androscoggin FICE Identification: 005276
Unit ID: 161077
Telephone: (207) 755-5100 Carnegie Class: Assoc/MT-VT-High Trad
FAX Number: (207) 755-5491 Calendar System: Semester
URL: www.cmcc.edu
Established: 1964 Annual Undergrad Tuition & Fees (In-State): $3,844
Enrollment: 3,115 Coed
Affiliation or Control: State IRS Status: 501(c)3
Highest Offering: Associate Degree
Accreditation: EH, ADNUR

02 Interim President .... Ms. Betsy LIBBY
32 Dean of Student Services .... Mr. Nicholas HAMEL
05 Interim Dean Academic Affairs .... Ms. Margaret BREWER
13 Dean Info Tech/Chief Info Security .... Mr. Robert BOUCHER
10 Dean of Finance & General Services .... Ms. Maureen AUBE
103 Dean Workforce & Professional Dev .... Ms. Michelle HAWLEY
04 Executive Asst to the President .... Ms. Alyson DANIELS
06 Registrar .... Ms. Sonya SAMPSON
84 Associate Dean of Enrollment Mgmt .... Mr. Andrew MORONG
37 Director of Financial Aid .... Mr. John BOWIE
35 Assoc Dean of Student Services .... Mr. Grimes WILLIAMS
18 Manager Facilities/Central Svcs .... Ms. Kellie MORRIS
07 Interim Director of Admissions .... Mr. Connor SHEEHY
39 Director of Housing/Athletic Dir .... Mr. David GONYEA
15 Director of Human Resources .... Ms. Suzanna GALLANT
27 Director of Communications .... Ms. Heather B. SEYMOUR
121 Director of Learning & Advising .... Mr. Eric MEADER
21 Assoc Dean of Finance & Gen Svcs .... Ms. Allie JOHNSON
09 Director of Institutional Research .... Ms. Brianna DOYLE
08 Director of Learning Commons .... Ms. Judith MORENO

*Eastern Maine Community College (E)

354 Hogan Road, Bangor ME 04401-4280
County: Penobscot FICE Identification: 005277
Unit ID: 161138
Telephone: (207) 974-4600 Carnegie Class: Assoc/HVT-Mix Trad/Non
FAX Number: (207) 974-4608 Calendar System: Semester
URL: www.emcc.edu
Established: 1966 Annual Undergrad Tuition & Fees (In-State): $3,877
Enrollment: 2,042 Coed
Affiliation or Control: State IRS Status: 501(c)3
Highest Offering: Associate Degree
Accreditation: EH, ADNUR, EMT, MAC, RAD, SURGT

02 President .... Dr. Lisa LARSON
05 VP of Academic & Student Affairs .... Dr. Brian DOORE
10 Dir Finance & Auxiliary Services .... Mrs. Cynthia KASPRZAK
09 Director of Institutional Research .... Ms. Kelsey GILBERT
88 Professional Services Coordinator .... Vacant
07 Director of Admissions .... Ms. Stacy GREEN
15 Director of Human Resources .... Ms. Jody MACDONALD
08 Librarian .... Mr. William COOK
37 Director of Financial Aid .... Ms. Candace WARD
13 Dean of Communication/Info Tech .... Mr. Bert AUDETTE
18 Dir Facilities Mgmt/Student Life .... Vacant
111 Dir of Inst Advancement/Development .... Ms. Erica HUTCHINSON
04 Admin Asst to the President .... Ms. Terri ADAM
19 Director of Safety & Security .... Mr. David WILSON
38 Director of Student Advising .... Ms. Sarah SAWYER
39 Director of Residential Life .... Ms. Kris KELLEY
103 Director Workforce Development .... Mr. Christopher WINSTEAD
26 Dir Marketing & Public Relations .... Ms. Mariah HUGHES

*Kennebec Valley Community College (F)

92 Western Avenue, Fairfield ME 04937-1367
County: Somerset FICE Identification: 009826
Unit ID: 161192
Telephone: (207) 453-5000 Carnegie Class: Assoc/HVT-Mix Trad/Non
FAX Number: (207) 453-5010 Calendar System: Semester
URL: www.kvcc.me.edu
Established: 1970 Annual Undergrad Tuition & Fees (In-State): $3,882
Enrollment: 2,297 Coed
Affiliation or Control: State IRS Status: 501(c)3
Highest Offering: Associate Degree
Accreditation: EH, ACBSP, ADNUR, CAHIIM, COARC, EMT, MAC, OTA, PTAA, RAD

02 Interim President .... Ms. Karen NORMANDIN
05 Academic Dean .... Ms. Kathy ENGLEHART
13 Dean of Tech/Chief Security Officer .... Mr. Kevin CASEY
32 Interim Dean Student Affairs .... Mr. Crichton MCKENNA
10 Dean of Finance & Administration .... Mr. Russell BEGIN
84 Asst Dean of Enrollment Management .... Ms. Teresa SMITH
06 Registrar .... Mr. Christian HANSEN
30 Director of Development .... Ms. Michelle WEBB
37 Director of Financial Aid .... Ms. Kathryn BLAIR
09 Director of Institutional Research .... Ms. Karen GLEW
100 Chief of Staff to the President .... Ms. Monica BRENNAN
103 Dean of Workforce Training .... Ms. Elizabeth FORTIN
18 Director of Operations & Compliance .... Ms. Brianne PUSHOR
19 Campus Safety & Security Manager .... Mr. Timothy MCDONALD

*Northern Maine Community College (G)

33 Edgemont Drive, Presque Isle ME 04769-2099
County: Aroostook FICE Identification: 005760
Unit ID: 161484
Telephone: (207) 768-2810 Carnegie Class: Assoc/HVT-Mix Trad/Non
FAX Number: (207) 768-2831 Calendar System: Semester
URL: www.nmcc.edu
Established: 1961 Annual Undergrad Tuition & Fees (In-State): $3,830
Enrollment: 775 Coed
Affiliation or Control: State IRS Status: 501(c)3
Highest Offering: Associate Degree
Accreditation: EH, ACBSP, ADNUR, EMT, MAC

02 President .... Mr. Timothy D. CROWLEY
05 Academic Dean .... Ms. Angela BUCK
32 Dean of Students .... Mr. Matthew GRILLO
10 Dean of Finance .... Mr. Michael WILLIAMS
51 Asst Dean Continuing Education .... Ms. Leah BUCK
30 Dean of Development/College Rels .... Dr. Dorothy MARTIN
07 Director of Admissions .... Ms. Wendy BRADSTREET
06 Registrar .... Ms. Shannon COOK
37 Director for Financial Aid .... Mr. Brian HALL
39 Director of Housing & Resident Life .... Mr. Jon A. BLANCHARD
38 Director of Counseling .... Ms. Tammy NELSON
18 Dean of Tech and Facilities .... Mr. Barry INGRAHAM
21 Business Manager .... Ms. Wendy CAVERHILL
40 College Store Manager .... Mr. Kenneth J. KELMER, JR.
08 Head Librarian .... Dr. Ann SPINNEY
19 College Safety/Security Officer .... Mr. Peter GOHEEN
15 Human Resource Coordinator .... Ms. Lindsy LEBLANC

*Southern Maine Community College (H)

2 Fort Road, South Portland ME 04106-1698
County: Cumberland FICE Identification: 005525
Unit ID: 161545
Telephone: (207) 741-5500 Carnegie Class: Assoc/MT-VT-Mix Trad/Non
FAX Number: (207) 741-5751 Calendar System: Semester
URL: www.smccme.edu
Established: 1946 Annual Undergrad Tuition & Fees (In-State): $3,880
Enrollment: 5,789 Coed
Affiliation or Control: State IRS Status: 501(c)3
Highest Offering: Associate Degree
Accreditation: EH, ACFEI, ADNUR, COARC, CVT, EMT, MAAB, RAD

02 President/CEO .... Joseph L. CASSIDY
05 Vice President & Academic Dean .... Dr. Paul CHARPENTIER
11 Dean of Administration .... Tiffanie L. BENTLEY
32 Dean of Student Success/Enrollment .... Barbara CONNER
103 Dean of Workforce Development .... James WHITTEN
10 Dean of Finance .... Robert COOMBS
13 Dean of Data/Tech & Info Security .... Timothy DUNNE
88 Dean of Academic Excellence .... Dr. Matthew GOODMAN
88 Int Dean Bus & Cmty Partnerships .... Julie CHASE
04 Exec Assistant to the President .... Lori HALL
06 Assoc Dean of Registration/Registrr .... Jeremy DILL
121 Associate Dean of Student Success .... Kathleen DOAN
20 Assoc Dean Academics/Learning .... Holly GURNEY
39 Acting Assoc Dean of Students .... Jason SAUCIER
41 Assoc Dean Stdnt Life/Dir Athletics .... Matthew RICHARDS
114 Director of Budget & Financial Rpt .... Shaun GRAY
37 Director of Financial Aid Systems .... Michel LUSSIER
84 Assistant Dean of Enrollment Mgmt .... Amy LEE
19 Director Campus Security .... Joseph MANHARDT
18 Plant Maintenance Engineer III .... Vacant
40 Manager Campus Store .... Katharine DUCHETTE
113 Business Mgr Student Billing/Bursar .... Coleen LAPRISE
15 Director of Human Resources .... Diane ABRAMSON
38 Dir Counseling & Disability Svcs .... Sandra LYNHAM
27 Director of Communications .... Clarke CANFIELD
105 Director Web Services .... Ken POOLEY
106 Dir Online Education/E-learning .... Michael HART
36 Director Career & Transfer .... Adrienne LAROCHE

*Washington County Community College (I)

One College Drive, Calais ME 04619-9704
County: Washington FICE Identification: 009231
Unit ID: 161581
Telephone: (207) 454-1000 Carnegie Class: Assoc/HVT-High Trad
FAX Number: (207) 454-1092 Calendar System: Semester
URL: www.wccc.me.edu
Established: 1969 Annual Undergrad Tuition & Fees (In-State): $3,850
Enrollment: 354 Coed
Affiliation or Control: State IRS Status: 501(c)3
Highest Offering: Associate Degree
Accreditation: EH, MAC

02 President .... Mrs. Susan MINGO
05 Dean of Academic Affairs .... Mr. Darin MCGAW
10 Dean of Finance .... Ms. Desiree THOMPSON
15 Dir of HR/Devel/Communications .... Mrs. Tina ERSKINE
84 Dean Enrollment Mgmt/Student Svcs .... Mr. Tyler STOLDT
103 Dean of Workforce & Prof Dev .... Ms. Nichole SAWYER
37 Financial Aid Director .... Mrs. Linda FITZSIMMONS
39 Director of Res Life .... Ms. Karen GOOKIN
04 Exec Asst to the Pres/HR Coord .... Mrs. Robyn LEIGHTON
21 Business Manager .... Mrs. Ashley MACDONALD
18 Manager Facilities .... Mr. Richard RAMSEY
13 Information Systems Specialist .... Mr. Robert FINN
06 Registrar/Asst to Academic Dean .... Mrs. Donna GEEL
113 Student Accounts .... Mrs. Heather SMALE
08 Dir of Library & Learning Resources .... Mrs. Elizabeth PHILLIPS
22 Instructional Technologist/AAO .... Ms. Tatiana OSMOND

*York County Community College (J)

112 College Drive, Wells ME 04090-0529
County: York FICE Identification: 031229
Unit ID: 420440
Telephone: (207) 646-9282 Carnegie Class: Assoc/MT-VT-Mix Trad/Non
FAX Number: (207) 646-9675 Calendar System: Semester
URL: www.yccc.edu
Established: 1994 Annual Undergrad Tuition & Fees (In-State): $3,720
Enrollment: 1,575 Coed
Affiliation or Control: State IRS Status: 501(c)3
Highest Offering: Associate Degree
Accreditation: EH

02 President .... Mr. Michael FISCHER
05 Academic Dean .... Dr. Doreen ROGAN
10 Dean of Finance & Administration .... Mr. Samuel ELLIS
32 Dean of Students .... Mr. Jason AREY
09 Assoc Dean of Inst Research .... Vacant

84 Director of Enrollment Management .... Ms. Caitlin GRANT
20 Assoc Academic Dean .... Ms. Amber TATNALL
30 Special Asst to the Pres & Dev Dir .... Vacant
84 Director of Enrollment Services .... Ms. Jessica MASI
26 Dir of Marketing & Communications .... Ms. Stacy CHILICKI
37 Director Financial Aid .... Mr. David DAIGLE
103 Dean Workforce Dev/Community Educ .... Vacant
13 Director of Technology .... Vacant
19 Safety & Security Manager .... Mr. Mark PARADIS
21 Manager of Financial Services .... Mrs. Tracy SLATER
15 Int Director of Human Resources .... Mr. Jason AREY
18 Manager of Facilities .... Vacant
100 Chief of Staff .... Ms. Barbara OWEN

Maine Maritime Academy (A)

1 Pleasant Street, Castine ME 04420-0001
County: Hancock FICE Identification: 002044
Unit ID: 161299
Telephone: (207) 326-4311 Carnegie Class: Bac-Diverse
FAX Number: (207) 326-2218 Calendar System: Semester
URL: www.mainemaritime.edu
Established: 1941 Annual Undergrad Tuition & Fees (In-State): $14,058
Enrollment: 941 Coed
Affiliation or Control: State IRS Status: 501(c)3
Highest Offering: Master's
Accreditation: EH

01 President .... Dr. William J. BRENNAN
05 VP Academic Affairs .... Mr. Keith WILLIAMSON
10 VP Financial & Institutional Svcs .... Mr. Richard ROSEN
84 VP Stdnt Svcs/Enrollment Mgmt .... Dr. Elizabeth TRUE
111 Vice President for Advancement .... Mr. Christopher HALEY
15 Human Resource Officer .... Ms. Heidi PUGLIESE
32 Dean of Student Svcs/Enroll Mgmt .... Ms. Deidra DAVIS
36 Director of Career Services .... Mr. Bryce POTTER
07 Director of Admissions .... Ms. Kelly GUALTIERI
06 Registrar .... Ms. Amy GUTOW
29 Director Alumni Relations .... Mr. Jeff WRIGHT
37 Director Student Financial Aid .... Ms. Kathy HEATH
38 Director Student Counseling .... Mr. Paul FERREIRA
08 Director of Library Services .... Ms. Lauren STARBIRD
21 Director of Fiscal Operations .... Ms. Alice HERRICK
18 Director of Facilities Mgmt/Safety .... Mr. Peter STEWART
20 Dean of Faculty .... Dr. Susan LOOMIS
26 Director of College Relations .... Vacant
39 Director of Residential Life .... Ms. Janice FOLK
09 Director of Institutional Research .... Mr. Ryan KING
04 Exec Asst to Pres/Chief of Staff .... Ms. Janet ACKER
13 AVP/Chief Technology Officer .... Ms. Lisa ROY
19 Director of Safety & Compliance .... Mr. Peter STEWART
41 Director of Athletics .... Mr. Stephen PEED

Maine Media College (B)

70 Camden St., PO Box 200, Rockport ME 04856
County: Knox Identification: 667339
Telephone: (207) 236-8581 Carnegie Class: Not Classified
FAX Number: (207) 236-2558 Calendar System: Other
URL: www.mainemedia.edu
Established: 1973 Annual Graduate Tuition & Fees: N/A
Enrollment: N/A Coed
Affiliation or Control: Independent Non-Profit IRS Status: 501(c)3
Highest Offering: Master's; No Undergraduates
Accreditation: @EH

01 President .... Michael P. MANSFIELD
05 Provost .... Elizabeth GREENBERG
10 Dir of Finance & Administration .... Cathi FINNEMORE
06 Registrar .... Kerry CURREN

Saint Joseph's College of Maine (C)

278 Whites Bridge Road, Standish ME 04084-5236
County: Cumberland FICE Identification: 002051
Unit ID: 161518
Telephone: (207) 892-6766 Carnegie Class: Masters/L
FAX Number: (207) 893-7861 Calendar System: Semester
URL: www.sjcme.edu
Established: 1912 Annual Undergrad Tuition & Fees: $38,820
Enrollment: 1,967 Coed
Affiliation or Control: Roman Catholic IRS Status: 501(c)3
Highest Offering: Master's
Accreditation: EH, CAHIIM, NURSE, SW

01 President .... Dr. James S. DLUGOS
06 Director Academic Records/Registrar .... Mr. Kevin PAQUETTE
08 Director Library .... Ms. Shelly DAVIS
23 Director of Student Health Center .... Ms. Sheri PIERS
05 VP & Chief Officer of Learning .... Dr. Michael PARDALES
10 Chief Business & Finance Ofcr/VP .... Mr. Robert WILSON
111 VP & Chief Advancement Officer .... Ms. Joanne BEAN
88 VP for Sponsorship & Mission .... Dr. Christopher FULLER
84 AVP & Chief Enrollment Officer .... Ms. Lynne ROBINSON
32 AVP/CSAO/Dean of Campus Life .... Dr. Liz WIESEN
15 AVP/Chief Human Resources Officer .... Ms. Kristine AVERY
13 AVP Chief Information Officer .... Mr. Chip STILES
26 AVP & Chief Brand/Marketing Ofcr .... Mr. Oliver GRISWOLD
35 Director of Student Engagement .... Mr. Matthew GAWEL

Thomas College (D)

180 W River Road, Waterville ME 04901-5097
County: Kennebec FICE Identification: 002052
Unit ID: 161563
Telephone: (207) 859-1111 Carnegie Class: Masters/S
FAX Number: (207) 859-1114 Calendar System: Semester
URL: www.thomas.edu
Established: 1894 Annual Undergrad Tuition & Fees: $28,430
Enrollment: 1,705 Coed
Affiliation or Control: Independent Non-Profit IRS Status: 501(c)3
Highest Offering: Master's
Accreditation: EH

01 President .... Ms. Laurie G. LACHANCE
03 Executive Vice President .... Mr. Bernie OUELLETTE
05 Provost .... Dr. Thomas EDWARDS
10 Vice Pres Financial Affairs .... Ms. Joan PARKER-LOW
32 Vice President Student Affairs .. Ms. Lisa DESAUTELS-POLIQUIN
13 Vice Pres Information Services/CIO .... Mr. Christopher RHODA
111 Associate Vice Pres Advancement .... Ms. Erin BALTES
07 Asst Vice Pres Admissions .... Ms. Wendy MARTIN
26 Asst VP Marketing/Communications .... Mr. Robert FIELD
35 Dean of Students .... Ms. Hannah GLADSTONE
15 Chief Human Resources Officer .... Ms. Michelle JOLER-LABBE
37 Director Student Financial Services .... Ms. Jeannine ROSS
36 Sr Director Career Services .... Mr. Corey PELLETIER
18 Director Physical Plant .... Mr. Matt BRESLIN
06 Associate Registrar .... Ms. Michelle YATES
04 Executive Asst to President .... Ms. Leta BILODEAU
41 Director of Athletics .... Mr. Christopher PARSONS
19 Director Security/Safety .... Vacant

Unity College (E)

90 Quaker Hill Road, Unity ME 04988-9502
County: Waldo FICE Identification: 006858
Unit ID: 161572
Telephone: (207) 509-7100 Carnegie Class: Bac-Diverse
FAX Number: (207) 512-1192 Calendar System: Other
URL: www.unity.edu
Established: 1965 Annual Undergrad Tuition & Fees: $12,640
Enrollment: 1,429 Coed
Affiliation or Control: Independent Non-Profit IRS Status: 501(c)3
Highest Offering: Master's
Accreditation: EH

01 President .... Dr. Melik Peter KHOURY
88 VP of Hybrid Learning .... Mr. Zachary FALCON
106 VP of Distance Education .... Vacant
05 President of the Enterprise/CAO .... Dr. Erika LATTY
111 Chief Advancement Officer .... Vacant
100 Chief of Staff .... Vacant
101 Secretary to Board .... Ms. Christine MELANSON
04 Special Assistant to the President .... Ms. Maren MCGILLICUDDY
10 Director of Business Office .... Mr. Thomas DRESSLER
13 Director of IT .... Mr. Charles BELLANTONI
06 Registrar .... Ms. Kerry HAFFORD
30 Director of Development & Grants .... Vacant
32 Dean of Student Success .... Ms. Doreen ROGAN
09 Dir of Institutional Effectiveness .... Vacant
26 Executive Director Brand Strategy .... Ms. Alecia SUDMEYER
41 Director of Athletics & Wellness .... Vacant
109 Director of Dining Services .... Vacant
36 Director of Career Services .... Vacant
88 Director Unity College Sky Lodge .... Mr. Casey MOREY
18 Dir of Facilities Management .... Mr. Christopher BOND
37 Dir Student Finance/Enrollment Svcs .... Ms. Sherry WATSON
23 Director of Wellness .... Vacant
15 Director Human Resources .... Ms. Gabrielle NIEWADOMSKI
08 Director Library & Info Services .... Vacant
39 Asst Dean of Students .... Mr. Stephen S. NASON
22 ADA Coord/Learning Specialist .... Vacant
88 Dean of Curricular Innovation .... Dr. Jennifer CARTIER
27 Assoc Dir of Media Relations .... Mr. Joseph HEGARTY
19 Director of Public Safety .... Mr. Dennis PICARD
40 Manager Bookstore .... Ms. Leigh JUSKEVICE

*University of Maine System (F)

15 Estabrooke Drive, Orono ME 04469
County: Penobscot FICE Identification: 008012
Unit ID: 161280
Telephone: N/A Carnegie Class: N/A
FAX Number: N/A
URL: www.maine.edu

01 Chancellor .... Mr. Dannel P. MALLOY
05 Vice Chancellor Academic Affairs .... Dr. Robert PLACIDO
10 Vice Chanc for Finance & Treasurer .... Mr. Ryan LOW
43 Deputy General Counsel .... Ms. Laurel HYLE
86 Dir of Comm/Governmental Rels .... Ms. Samantha C. WARREN
101 Clerk of the Board .... Ms. Ellen DOUGHTY
32 AVC Stdnt Success/Credential Attain .... Ms. Rosa REDONNETT
13 Chief Information Officer .... Dr. David DEMERS
18 Chief General Services Officer .... Mr. M. F. Chip GAVIN
15 Chief Human Resources Officer .... Ms. Loretta SHIELDS
26 Exec Director of Public Affairs .... Mr. Daniel DEMERITT

*University of Maine (G)

168 College Avenue, Orono ME 04469-0001
County: Penobscot FICE Identification: 002053
Unit ID: 161253
Telephone: (207) 581-1865 Carnegie Class: DU-Higher
FAX Number: (207) 581-1604 Calendar System: Semester
URL: www.umaine.edu
Established: 1865 Annual Undergrad Tuition & Fees (In-State): $11,744
Enrollment: 11,741 Coed
Affiliation or Control: State IRS Status: 501(c)3
Highest Offering: Doctorate
Accreditation: EH, ART, CAATE, CAEP, CLPSY, DIETD, DIETI, IPSY, MUS, NURSE, SP, SW

02 President .... Dr. Joan FERRINI-MUNDY
05 EVP Academic Affairs/Provost .... Dr. John VOLIN
10 Int VP/Chief Business Officer .... Ms. Joanne YESTRAMSKI
102 Pres Univ of Maine Foundation .... Vacant
32 VP Student Life & Dean of Students .... Dr. Robert Q. DANA
46 Vice President for Research .... Dr. Kody VARAHRAMYAN
84 VP Enrollment Management .... Mr. Chris RICHARDS
88 VP Innovation/Economic Development .... Mr. James WARD, IV
15 Vice President of Human Resources .... Mr. Chris LINDSTROM
21 Chief Business Officer .... Mrs. Claire I. STRICKLAND
20 Sr Assoc Prov/Dean Undergrad Educ .... Dr. Jeffrey E. ST. JOHN
100 Chief of Staff .... Ms. Kimberly WHITEHEAD
08 Dean of Libraries .... Ms. Joyce V. RUMERY
13 Dir Project Mgt Ofc/Campus IT Ofcr .... Ms. Robin SHERMAN
18 Exec Dir Facilities/Capital Mgt Svc .... Mr. Stewart A. HARVEY
26 Sr Exec Dir Marketing/Communication .... Mr. Dan DEMERITT
109 Exec Director of Auxiliary Services .... Mr. Daniel H. STURRUP
25 Director Research Administration ..... Mr. Christopher E. BOYNTON
06 Registrar .... Mr. W. Sam CARRELL
07 Director of Transfer Admissions .... Ms. Sharon M. OLIVER
37 Director of Financial Aid .... Ms. Connie SMITH
36 Director of Career Center .... Ms. Crisanne BLACKIE
09 Director Institutional Studies .... Dr. Debra ALLEN
85 Sr Director International Programs .... Ms. Sarah JOUGHIN
41 Athletic Director .... Mr. Ken RALPH
28 Director Equal Employment Diversity .... Vacant
19 Chief Police Dept .... Chief Roland J. LACROIX
29 Vice President Alumni Association .... Mr. John N. DIAMOND
40 Assoc Director of Retail Operations .... Mr. Dean GRAHAM
96 Director of Procurement Services .... Mr. Kevin CARR
38 Director Student Counseling .... Mr. Douglas P. JOHNSON
49 Dean Liberal Arts & Sciences .... Dr. Emily A. HADDAD
50 Dean Undergrad School of Business .... Ms. Faye GILBERT
50 Dean Graduate School of Business .... Dr. Michael WEBER
53 Dean Educ/Human Development .... Dr. Penny BISHOP
54 Dean Engineering .... Dr. Dana N. HUMPHREY
65 Dean Natural Science/Forestry/Agric .... Dr. Diane ROWLAND
51 Dean Lifelong Learning .... Dr. Monique M. LAROCQUE
58 Dean Graduate School .... Dr. Kody VARAHRAMYAN
04 Exec Assistant to the President .... Ms. Josette A. MCWILLIAMS
86 Director Government Relations .... Ms. Samantha WARREN

*University of Maine at Augusta (H)

46 University Drive, Augusta ME 04330-9410
County: Kennebec FICE Identification: 006760
Unit ID: 161217
Telephone: (207) 621-3000 Carnegie Class: Bac-Diverse
FAX Number: (207) 621-3116 Calendar System: Semester
URL: www.uma.edu
Established: 1965 Annual Undergrad Tuition & Fees (In-State): $8,378
Enrollment: 4,202 Coed
Affiliation or Control: State IRS Status: 501(c)3
Highest Offering: Master's
Accreditation: EH, CSHSE, DA, DH, NUR

02 President .... Dr. Rebecca M. WYKE
05 Vice President/Provost .... Dr. Joseph S. SZAKAS
10 Interim Chief Business Officer .... Mr. Buster NEEL
111 Exec Dir of Advance & Strat Proj .... Ms. Joyce BLANCHARD
84 VP Enrollment Mgmt & Marketing .... Mr. Jonathan HENRY
08 Director of UMA Library Svcs .... Vacant
32 Dean of Students .... Ms. Sheri FRASER
107 Dean College of Prof Studies .... Ms. Brenda MCALEER
07 AVP Admission/Stdnt Financial Svcs .... Ms. Brandy FINCK
06 Registrar .... Ms. Ann CORBETT
15 Director of Human Resources .... Ms. Amie PARKER
18 Director of Facilities Management .... Mr. James W. KAUPPILA
38 Director of Counseling .... Ms. Jennifer MASCARO
121 Director of Advising .... Ms. Tricia DYER
26 Exec Dir Planning & Communications .... Ms. Domna GIATAS
49 Dean College of Arts & Sciences .... Dr. Pamela MACRAE
04 Exec Assistant to the President .... Ms. Renee SHERMAN
35 Director of Student Life/Athletics .... Vacant
09 Director of Institutional Research .... Dr. Hirosuke HONDA
19 Director Campus Safety & Security .... Mr. Robert MARDEN

*University of Maine at Farmington (I)

224 Main Street, Farmington ME 04938-1911
County: Franklin FICE Identification: 002040
Unit ID: 161226
Telephone: (207) 778-7000 Carnegie Class: Bac-Diverse
FAX Number: (207) 778-7247 Calendar System: Semester
URL: www.umf.maine.edu
Established: 1864 Annual Undergrad Tuition & Fees (In-State): $9,572
Enrollment: 1,862 Coed
Affiliation or Control: State IRS Status: 501(c)3
Highest Offering: Master's
Accreditation: EH, CAEP

02 President .... Dr. Edward SERNA

05 Provost/VP Academic Affairs Dr. Eric BROWN
10 Chief Business Officer Ms. Laurie A. GARDNER
32 VP Student Affs/Enrollment Mgmt Ms. Christine WILSON
04 Admin Assistant to the President Ms. Amy PERREAULT
20 Assoc Provost Dr. Steven QUACKENBUSH
92 Director of Honors Program Dr. John D. MESSIER
121 Dir Student Development Center Ms. Katie FOURNIER
37 Financial Aid Director Mr. Ronald P. MILLIKEN
21 Director of Finance Ms. Kathleen P. FALCO
27 Assoc Director of Media Relations Ms. April C. MULHERIN
13 IT Operations Manager Ms. Nicole WOODHOUSE
41 Dir Athletics/Fitness & Recreation Ms. Julie A. DAVIS
35 Director Student Life Mr. Brian K. UFFORD
18 Director of Facilities Management Mr. Keenan FARWELL
19 Director of Public Safety Mr. Brock E. CATON
26 Dir of Marketing and Communications Ms. Ryan MASTRANGELO
07 Director of Admissions Ms. Lisa ELLRICH
09 Director of Institutional Research Mr. Nathan GRANT
111 Director for Advancement Ms. Lauren SERNA
29 Dir Alumni Relations/Annual Fund Ms. Kathleen O'DONNELL
88 Sustainability Coordinator Mr. Mark PIRES

*University of Maine at Fort Kent (A)

23 University Drive, Fort Kent ME 04743-1292

County: Aroostook　FICE Identification: 002041
Unit ID: 161235
Telephone: (207) 834-7500　Carnegie Class: Bac-Diverse
FAX Number: (207) 834-7503　Calendar System: Semester
URL: www.umfk.edu
Established: 1878　Annual Undergrad Tuition & Fees (In-State): $8,475
Enrollment: 1,624　Coed
Affiliation or Control: State　IRS Status: 501(c)3
Highest Offering: Baccalaureate
Accreditation: EH, IACBE, NURSE

02 President/Provost Ms. Deborah HEDEEN
10 Chief Business Officer Ms. Pamela ASHBY
32 Dean of Students Mr. Matthew MORRIN
84 Exec Dir of Enrollment Management Vacant
26 Dir Marketing & Communications Ms. Kerri WATSON-BLAISDELL
15 HR Business Partner Ms. Debra PELLETIER
31 Dean of Community Education Mr. Scott A. VOISINE
08 Dean of Information Svcs/Library Ms. Leslie E. KELLY
66 Dean of Nursing/Int Assoc Prov AA Ms. Erin SOUCY
49 Int Dean Arts & Sciences/Prof Stds Dr. Nicole BOUDREAU
37 Director of Financial Aid Ms. Lisa MICHAUD
18 Director of Facilities Management Vacant
07 Director of Admissions Ms. Sarah BRAUN
09 Assoc Dir of Institutional Research Vacant
30 Development Officer Ms. Shannon LUGDON
06 Registrar Mr. Alexander MYHRE
04 Admin Assistant to the President Ms. Janna GREGORY
39 Dir Resident Life/Student Housing Vacant
41 Athletic Director Ms. Carly FLOWERS

*University of Maine at Machias (B)

116 O'Brien Avenue, Machias ME 04654-1397
Telephone: (207) 255-1200　FICE Identification: 002055
Accreditation: &EH

*University of Maine at Presque Isle (C)

181 Main Street, Presque Isle ME 04769-2888

County: Aroostook　FICE Identification: 002033
Unit ID: 161341
Telephone: (207) 768-9400　Carnegie Class: Bac-Diverse
FAX Number: (207) 768-9608　Calendar System: Semester
URL: www.umpi.edu
Established: 1903　Annual Undergrad Tuition & Fees (In-State): $8,585
Enrollment: 1,467　Coed
Affiliation or Control: State　IRS Status: 501(c)3
Highest Offering: Baccalaureate
Accreditation: EH, MLTAD, PTAA, SW

02 President & Provost Dr. Raymond J. RICE
05 Director of Education Dr. Alana MARGESON
10 Chief Business Officer Mr. Benjamin SHAW
49 Dean of Arts and Sciences Dr. Jason JOHNSTON
107 Dean of Professional Programs Ms. Barbara BLACKSTONE
111 Exec Dir for University Advancement Dr. Debbie ROARK
84 Executive Director of Enroll Mgmt Vacant
32 Dean of Students Mr. Matthew MORRIN
35 Associate Dean of Students Ms. Mary Kate BARBOSA
07 Director of Admissions Ms. Susan ARMSTRONG
06 Registrar Mr. Alexander MYHRE
15 Labor Relations Mgr UMPI HR Leader Ms. Dorianna PRATT
08 Director of Library Services Mr. Roger GETZ
36 Director of Career Preparation Ms. Nicole FOURNIER
39 Associate Director Residence Life Mr. Donald GIBSON
41 Director of Athletics Mr. Daniel C. KANE
26 Director Marketing & Communications Ms. Rachel RICE
37 Director Financial Services Mr. Christopher BELL
18 Director of Facilities Management Mr. Joe MOIR
19 Director Security/Safety Mr. Frederick A. THOMAS
04 Special Assistant to the President Ms. Lisa M. SMITH
29 Director Alumni Affairs Mr. Craig C. CORMIER

*University of Southern Maine (D)

96 Falmouth Street, PO Box 9300,
Portland ME 04101-9300

County: Cumberland　FICE Identification: 002054
Unit ID: 161554
Telephone: (207) 780-4141　Carnegie Class: Masters/L
FAX Number: (207) 780-4933　Calendar System: Semester
URL: www.usm.maine.edu
Established: 1878　Annual Undergrad Tuition & Fees (In-State): $9,528
Enrollment: 8,022　Coed
Affiliation or Control: State　IRS Status: 501(c)3
Highest Offering: Doctorate
Accreditation: EH, ART, CAATE, CACREP, CAEPT, EXSC, LAW, MUS, NAIT, NURSE, OT, PH, SW

02 President Dr. Glenn T. CUMMINGS
05 Provost/EVP for ASA Dr. Jeannine UZZI
102 President USM Foundation Ms. Ainsely WALLACE
110 VP USM Foundation Ms. Corey HASCALL
15 VP Human Resources Ms. Natalie JONES
84 VP Enrollment Mgmt & Marketing Mr. Jared CASH
109 VP Corp Engagement/Auxiliary Svcs Ms. Jeanne PAQUETTE
10 COO & CBO Mr. Alexander PORTEOUS
20 Asst Provost Academic Affairs Dr. Susan MCWILLIAMS
09 Sr Assoc Institutional Research Ms. Patricia DAVIS
18 Exec Director Facilities Management Mr. John SOUTHER
08 University Librarian Mr. David NUTTY
108 Director Academic Assessment Ctr Ms. Susan L. KING
23 Director of Health Services Ms. Lisa BELANGER
26 Director Public Affairs Mr. Marc GLASS
37 Director Financial Aid Ms. Jami JANDREAU
121 Director Academic Advising Ms. Elizabeth HIGGINS
58 Director Graduate Studies Mr. Andrew KING
07 Director of Admissions Ms. Rachel MORALES
06 Registrar/Director of Registration Ms. Karin PIRES
106 Director Online Teaching/Learning Mr. Paul COCHRANE
41 Director of Athletics Mr. Al BEAN
39 Director of Residential Life Ms. Christina LOWERY
40 General Manager of USM Bookstore Ms. Catherine JOHNSON
61 Dean School of Law Ms. Leigh INGALLS SAUFLEY
50 Dean College of Mgmt/Human Svcs Dr. Joanne WILLIAMS
72 Dean College of Sci/Tech & Health Dr. Jeremy QUALLS
49 Dean Arts/Humanities/Soc Sci Dr. Adam TUCHINSKY
12 Int Dean Lewiston-Auburn College Dr. Brian TOY
94 Director of Women & Gender Studies Dr. Rose CLEARY
27 Director of Marketing Ms. Traci ST. PIERRE
46 Director of Research Ms. Kris SAHONCHIK

University of New England (E)

11 Hills Beach Road, Biddeford ME 04005-9988

County: York　FICE Identification: 002050
Unit ID: 161457
Telephone: (207) 283-0171　Carnegie Class: DU-Higher
FAX Number: (207) 282-6379　Calendar System: Semester
URL: www.une.edu
Established: 1831　Annual Undergrad Tuition & Fees: $38,750
Enrollment: 7,208　Coed
Affiliation or Control: Independent Non-Profit　IRS Status: 501(c)3
Highest Offering: Doctorate
Accreditation: EH, ACBSP, ANEST, ARCPA, CAATE, DENT, DH, @DIETC, EXSC, NUR, OSTEO, OT, PH, PHAR, PTA, SW

01 President Dr. James HERBERT
04 Executive Asst to the President Ms. Holly HAMMOND NASS
05 Provost/Sr VP Academic Affairs Dr. Karen PARDUE
06 Registrar Ms. Kathy DAVIS
07 VP of University Admissions Mr. Scott STEINBERG
26 VP for Strategy & Communications Dr. Ellen BEAULIEU
18 Vice President for Operations Mr. Alan THIBEAULT
10 Senior Vice Pres Finance and Admin Ms. Nicole TRUFANT
111 Vice Pres Institutional Advancement Mr. Bill CHANCE
32 Asst VP of Student Affairs Ms. Jennifer DEBURRO
15 Associate VP Human Resources Ms. Annmarie ALLEN
82 VP Global Affairs Dr. Anouar MAJID
121 Associate Provost Student Success Dr. Jeanne HEY
20 Associate Provost Academic Affairs Dr. Michael SHELDON
106 Dean College of Grad/Prof Studies Dr. Martha WILSON
49 Dean College Arts & Sciences Dr. Jonathan MILLEN
76 Dean Health Professions Dr. Karen PARDUE
63 Dean College Osteopathic Medicine Dr. Jane CARREIRO
67 Dean College of Pharmacy Dr. Robert MCCARTHY
52 Dean of College Dental Medicine Dr. Jon RYDER
62 Dean Library Services Mr. Andrew GOLUB
46 Associate Provost Research/Scholars Dr. Karen HOUSEKNECHT
110 Assistant VP Inst Advancement Ms. Amy HAILE
09 Director for Institutional Research Ms. Kelly DUARTE
19 Director Campus Safety & Security Mr. Jeffrey GREENE
45 Associate Director for Planning Mr. Gregory HOGAN
08 Director Reference Services Ms. Barbara SWARTZLANDER
28 Dir Multicultural Student Affairs Ms. Erica ROUSSEAU
25 Director Sponsored Programs Mr. Nicholas GERE
38 Assistant Provost Student Support Mr. Hahna PATTERSON
113 Asst VP Student Financial Services Mr. Paul HENDERSON
100 Senior Advisor to President Mr. John TUMIEL
104 Director Study Abroad/Global Educ Ms. Emily DRAGON
13 Chief Info Technology Officer (CIO) Mr. Craig LOFTUS
36 Director Career Services Mr. Jeff NEVERS
102 Sr Dir Foundation/Corp Relations Ms. Ellen RIDLEY
41 Athletic Director Ms. Heather DAVIS
22 Title IX Coordinator Ms. Angela SHAMBARGER

39 Assoc Dir for Housing/Resident Life Mr. Anthony MONTALBANO
44 Director Annual Giving Ms. Anne WASHBURNE
108 Assoc Director of Assessment Ms. Jennifer MANDEL
21 Assistant VP of Financial Planning Mr. Matthew KOGUT
88 Assistant VP Compl/Finance & Admin Mr. Jeffery CROCKER

MARYLAND

Allegany College of Maryland (F)

12401 Willowbrook Road, SE,
Cumberland MD 21502-2596

County: Allegany　FICE Identification: 002057
Unit ID: 161688
Telephone: (301) 784-5000　Carnegie Class: Assoc/HVT-High Trad
FAX Number: (301) 784-5050　Calendar System: Semester
URL: www.allegany.edu
Established: 1961　Annual Undergrad Tuition & Fees (In-District): $8,270
Enrollment: 2,523　Coed
Affiliation or Control: Local　IRS Status: 501(c)3
Highest Offering: Associate Degree
Accreditation: M, ADNUR, COARC, CSHSE, DH, MAC, MLTAD, OTA, PTAA

01 President Dr. Cynthia S. BAMBARA
05 Sr Vice Pres Instructional Affairs Dr. Kurt HOFFMAN
10 Vice President Finance/Admin Ms. Christina KILDUFF
111 VP Advancement/Community Rels Mr. David R. JONES

Anne Arundel Community College (G)

101 College Parkway, Arnold MD 21012-1895

County: Anne Arundel　FICE Identification: 002058
Unit ID: 161767
Telephone: (410) 777-2222　Carnegie Class: Assoc/HT-High Trad
FAX Number: (410) 777-2489　Calendar System: Semester
URL: www.aacc.edu
Established: 1961　Annual Undergrad Tuition & Fees (In-District): $8,540
Enrollment: 11,948　Coed
Affiliation or Control: State/Local　IRS Status: 501(c)3
Highest Offering: Associate Degree
Accreditation: M, ACFEI, ADNUR, CSHSE, EMT, MAC, MLTAD, PTAA, RAD, SURGT

01 President Dr. Dawn S. LINDSAY
05 VP for Learning Dr. Tanya C. MILLNER
10 VP Learning Resources Management Ms. Melissa A. BEARDMORE
84 VP for Learner Support Services Ms. Felicia L. PATTERSON
106 Dean of Virtual Campus Dr. Colleen EISENBEISER
20 Associate VP for Learning Dr. Alycia MARSHALL
30 Director of Development Mr. Vollie D. MELSON
89 Dean of College Transitions Ms. Deneen DANGERFIELD
76 Dean School Health/Wellness/Phys Ed Dr. Elizabeth H. APPEL
66 Director of Nursing Ms. Beth Anne BATTURS
49 Dean School of Liberal Arts Dr. Alicia MORSE
50 Dean School of Business & Law Ms. Karen COOK
81 Dean School of Science & Technology Dr. Lance BOWEN
51 Dean Sch Cont Educ & Workforce Dev Dr. Kip KUNSMAN
22 Controller Ms. Martha D. ROTHSCHILD
21 Executive Director of Finance Mr. Andrew P. LITTLE
13 Chief Technology Officer/Info Svcs Mr. Richard C. KRALEVICH
08 Director of Library Ms. Cynthia K. STEINHOFF
06 Registrar Ms. Nancy A. BEIER
09 Assoc Vice Pres Planning/Research Dr. Shuang LIU
15 Exec Director of Human Resources Ms. Suzanne L. BOYER
26 Exec Dir Strategic Communications Mr. Dan B. BAUM
37 Director of Financial Aid Ms. Tara CAREW
07 Dir Admissions/Enroll Development Ms. Cassandra S. MOORE
11 Exec Dir of Administrative Services Mr. Maury L. CHAPUT, JR.
32 Dean of Student Engagement Vacant
07 Dean Enrollment Services Dr. John F. GRABOWSKI
124 Dean of Student Success Ms. Bonnie J. GARRETT
35 Director of Student Engagement Ms. Amberdawn CHEATHAM
22 Federal Compliance Officer Dr. Tiffany F. BOYKIN
40 College Bookstore Manager Mr. Steven M. PEGG
19 Director Public Safety Mr. Sean KAPFHAMMER
96 Director Purchasing/Contracting Ms. Melanie L. HENRICKSON
30 Director of Development Ms. Wendy THOMAS
23 Coordinator Health Services Ms. Beth A. MAYS
41 Athletic Director Mr. Duane HERR
07 Assistant Director Admissions Mr. Brian O'NEIL
94 Coordinator of Women's Studies Dr. Suzanne J. SPOOR
88 Director of Environmental Center Dr. M. Stephen AILSTOCK
88 Director Center Study Local Issues Dr. Daniel D. NATAF
88 Dir Homeland Sec/Crim Justice Inst Dr. Tyrone POWERS
53 Director TEACH Institute Ms. Stacie BURCH
88 Director Hosp/Cul Arts/Tourism Inst Mr. Matthew HERRON
38 Coord Institute for the Future Mr. Steven T. HENICK
88 Dir Sarbanes Center/Pub & Cmty Svc Ms. Cathleen H. DOYLE
28 Chief Diversity Officer Vacant
04 Special Asst to President Ms. Monica RAUSA WILLIAMS
18 Dir Facilities Plng & Construction Mr. James TAYLOR
25 Director Sponsored Programs Ms. Susan GALLAGHER
101 Secretary of the Institution/Board Vacant
103 Director Workforce Development Ms. Sonja GLADWIN
105 Director Web Services Ms. Amanda SACHS

Bais HaMedrash & Mesivta of Baltimore (A)

6823 Old Pimlico Road, Baltimore MD 21209
County: Baltimore FICE Identification: 041884
Unit ID: 476601
Telephone: (410) 486-0006 Carnegie Class: Spec-4-yr-Faith
FAX Number: (410) 602-9738 Calendar System: Semester
Established: 1997 Annual Undergrad Tuition & Fees: $13,100
Enrollment: 60 Male
Affiliation or Control: Independent Non-Profit IRS Status: 501(c)3
Highest Offering: First Talmudic Degree
Accreditation: RABN

01 Rosh Yeshiva .... Rabbi Chaim COHEN

Baltimore City Community College (B)

2901 Liberty Heights Avenue, Baltimore MD 21215-7893
County: Baltimore City FICE Identification: 002061
Unit ID: 161864
Telephone: (410) 462-8300 Carnegie Class: Assoc/MT-VT-High Trad
FAX Number: (410) 462-7795 Calendar System: Semester
URL: www.bccc.edu
Established: 1947 Annual Undergrad Tuition & Fees (In-State): $3,314
Enrollment: 4,181 Coed
Affiliation or Control: State IRS Status: 501(c)3
Highest Offering: Associate Degree
Accreditation: M, ACBSP, ADNUR, CAHIIM, COARC, DH, EMT, PTAA, SURGT

01 President .... Dr. Debra L. MCCURDY
32 VP for Student Affairs .... Ms. Rose REINHART
05 VP Academic Affairs .... Dr. Liesl B. JONES
103 VP Workforce Dev/Cont Education .... Mr. Michael THOMAS
46 VP Institutional Rsrch/Effect/Plng .... Ms. Becky BURRELL
111 VP Advance/Strategic Partnership .... Ms. Dawn KIRSTAETTER
18 Vice Pres Facilities .... Ms. Katherine DIXON
10 VP Administration/Finance/CFO .... Ms. Channa WILLIAMS
13 Chief Information Tech Officer .... Mr. Stephan A. BYAM
43 General Counsel/Chief of Staff .... Ms. Maria E. RODRIGUEZ
84 Dean of Enrollment Management .... Ms. Sylvia ROCHESTER
21 Controller/Chief of Accounting .... Ms. Eileen WAITSMAN
37 Director Financial Aid .... Ms. Dawn LANGDON
08 Director Library/Media Services .... Mr. David-Xudong JIN
15 Exec Director of Human Resources .... Ms. Danielle PORTER
09 Director of Institutional Research .... Ms. Eileen HAWKINS
26 Director of Marketing .... Ms. Daviedra SAULDSBERRY
96 Director of Procurement .... Mr. Daniel D. SCHUSTER
04 Executive Asst to the President .... Vacant
07 Director of Admissions .... Mr. Jason MORGAN
06 Associate Registrar .... Ms. Wendy HARRIS
106 Director of E-Learning .... Mr. Brian TERRILL
19 Director of Public Safety .... Mr. Leonard WILLIS
41 Director of Athletics .... Dr. Darryl POPE
86 Director Government Relations .... Mr. Kevin LARGE
29 Director Alumni Relations .... Ms. Marie HINTON
30 Director of Development .... Ms. Jennifer LAFLEUR
20 Dean of Academic Operations .... Vacant

Capitol Technology University (C)

11301 Springfield Road, Laurel MD 20708-9759
County: Prince Georges FICE Identification: 001436
Unit ID: 162061
Telephone: (800) 950-1992 Carnegie Class: Spec-4-yr-Other Tech
FAX Number: (301) 369-2310 Calendar System: Semester
URL: www.captechu.edu
Established: 1927 Annual Undergrad Tuition & Fees: $26,874
Enrollment: 754 Coed
Affiliation or Control: Independent Non-Profit IRS Status: 501(c)3
Highest Offering: Doctorate
Accreditation: M

01 President .... Dr. Bradford L. SIMS
05 Vice President for Academic Affairs .... Dr. Richard BAKER
10 VP Finance .... Ms. Kathleen WERNER
84 Sr VP for Enrollment Mgmt & Mktg .... Ms. Dianne M. O'NEILL
20 AVP Academic Assessment .... Dr. Natasha MILLER
32 VP Student Engagement & Univ Devel .... Ms. Melinda BUNNELL-RHYNE
54 Chair Electrical Engineering .... Dr. Richard BAKER
06 Director of Registration & Records .... Mr. Greg HUGHES
08 Dir Library/Information Literacy .... Mr. Allen EXNER
15 Director Human Resources .... Ms. Shirley WASHINGTON
26 Director Communications .... Ms. Olivia BATHERSFIELD
30 AVP Development/Fundraising .... Vacant
07 Director Admissions .... Mr. Cameron NEWSOME
37 Director of Financial Aid .... Vacant
51 Director of Continuing Education .... Vacant
18 VP Facilities Management .... Mr. Gary BURKE
04 Executive Admin Asst to President .... Ms. Brielle O'BRIEN
103 Director of Career Services .... Ms. Constance HARRINGTON
106 Dir Online Education/E-learning .... Mr. William DRAYTON
13 Director Information Services .... Mr. Terrell MOORE
35 Dean of Students .... Mr. Jason KILMER

Carroll Community College (D)

1601 Washington Road, Westminster MD 21157-6913
County: Carroll FICE Identification: 031007
Unit ID: 405872
Telephone: (410) 386-8000 Carnegie Class: Assoc/HT-High Trad
FAX Number: (410) 386-8181 Calendar System: Semester
URL: www.carrollcc.edu
Established: 1993 Annual Undergrad Tuition & Fees (In-District): $6,588
Enrollment: 3,060 Coed
Affiliation or Control: Local IRS Status: 501(c)3
Highest Offering: Associate Degree
Accreditation: M, EMT, PTAA

01 President .... Dr. James D. BALL
11 Exec Vice Pres Administration .... Mr. Alan M. SCHUMAN
05 Provost .... Dr. Rosalie MINCE
45 Vice Pres of Plng/Mktg & Assessment .... Vacant
51 Vice Pres of Cont Educ/Training .... Ms. Libby TROSTLE
111 Exec Dir Inst Advance/College Fndn .... Mr. Steven WANTZ
26 Chief Communications Officer .... Ms. Patricia CARROLL
50 Div Chair Business & Technology .... Mr. Robert BROWN
60 Div Chair Communication Arts .... Ms. Siobhan WRIGHT
76 Div Chair Allied Health/Nursing .... Dr. Nancy PERRY
83 Div Chair Social Sciences/Health .... Ms. Sharon BRUNNER
54 Div Chair Mathematics/Engineer .... Ms. Brianna MCGINNIS
81 Div Chair Sciences .... Dr. Raza KHAN
53 Div Chair Educ & Trans Studies .... Ms. Susan SIES
79 Div Chair Humanities/Art/Music .... Dr. Robert YOUNG
57 Div Chair Applied & Theater Arts .... Mr. Scott GORE
32 Assoc Prov Student Affs/Marketing .... Dr. Kristie CRUMLEY
06 Sr Dir of Records/Stdnt Data Analy .... Ms. Laurie SHIELDS
121 Sr Dir Advising/Ret/Student Place .... Dr. April HERRING
84 Sr Director Enrollment Development .... Ms. Candace EDWARDS
28 Compliance/Integrity Judge Advocate .... Mr. Jonathan FOWE
37 Director of Financial Aid .... Mr. John GAY
36 Director Career Development .... Ms. Barb GREGORY
35 Director of Student Life .... Ms. Jennifer MILAM
08 Dir Library/Media Services .... Mr. Jeremy GREEN
106 Director Online Learning .... Ms. Andrea GRAVELLE
27 Sr Director Marketing .... Dr. Maya DEMISHKEVICH
09 Director Institutional Research .... Dr. Natalie CRESPO
103 Sr Dir Corporate Svcs/Workforce Dev .... Ms. Janet LADD
45 Dir CET Research/Strategic Analysis .... Ms. Jean MARRIOTT
88 Sr Dir Career & Continuing Educ .... Mr. Steven BERRY
55 Director Lifelong Learning .... Ms. Kathy MAYAN
105 Director of Network & Tech Services .... Ms. Patti DAVIS
10 Director Fiscal Affairs .... Mr. Timothy LEAGUE
15 Director Human Resources .... Ms. Lisa KUHN
18 Director Facilities Plng Management .... Ms. Lisa AUGHENBAUGH
19 Chief of Public Safety & Security .... Mr. Brian LINTZ
88 Assoc VP Program Dev/Partnerships .... Dr. Melody MOORE
22 Director Disability Support Svcs .... Mr. Joseph TATELA
108 Assoc Provost Assess/Inst Rsrch .... Dr. Michelle KLOSS
04 Executive Associate to President .... Ms. Marianne ANDERSON
41 Athletic Director .... Mr. Bill KELVEY

Cecil College (E)

One Seahawk Drive, North East MD 21901-1999
County: Cecil FICE Identification: 008308
Unit ID: 162104
Telephone: (410) 287-6060 Carnegie Class: Assoc/HT-High Trad
FAX Number: (410) 287-1026 Calendar System: Semester
URL: www.cecil.edu
Established: 1968 Annual Undergrad Tuition & Fees (In-District): $8,040
Enrollment: 2,090 Coed
Affiliation or Control: State/Local IRS Status: 501(c)3
Highest Offering: Associate Degree
Accreditation: M, ADNUR, EMT, MAC, PTAA

01 President .... Dr. Mary WAY BOLT
05 Vice President Academic Programs .... Dr. Christy DRYER
10 Vice President Finance .... Mr. Christopher MILLS
32 VP Students/Enrollment Management .... Dr. Kimberly JOYCE
13 Sr Director of IT Services .... Mr. Ian COOPER
111 VP Cmty/Govt Rels & College Advance .... Ms. Chris Ann SZEP
15 Executive Director Human Resources .... Ms. Lauren FLECK
20 Dean of Academic Programs .... Vacant
66 Dean Nursing/Allied Hlth/Hlth Sci .... Ms. Nancy NORMAN-MARZELLA
49 Acting Dean Arts & Sciences .... Dr. Veronica DOUGHERTY
18 Director of Facilities .... Mr. Keith BROWN
37 Director of Financial Aid Services .... Ms. Amanda SOLECKI
26 Director of Marketing .... Ms. Amy HENDERSON
93 Director Minority Student Services .... Ms. Mayra CASTILLO
09 Director of Institutional Research .... Ms. Tracy BAKOWSKI
06 Director of Records & Registration .... Ms. S. Tomeka SWAN
08 Director of Library Services .... Ms. Amanda DEMERS
41 Director Athletics .... Mr. Ed DURHAM
29 Coordinator Alumni Relations .... Ms. Mary MOORE
04 Exec Assistant to the President .... Ms. Sherry HARTMAN
21 Controller .... Mr. Craig WHITEFORD
19 Director Security/Safety .... Mr. Walt BEAUPRE
103 Director Workforce Development .... Mr. Miles DEAN
101 Secretary of the Institution/Board .... Dr. Mary W. BOLT
86 Director Government Relations .... Ms. Chris Ann SZEP

Chesapeake College (F)

PO Box 8, 1000 College Circle, Wye Mills MD 21679-0008
County: Queen Annes FICE Identification: 004650
Unit ID: 162168
Telephone: (410) 822-5400 Carnegie Class: Assoc/MT-VT-High Trad
FAX Number: (410) 827-5800 Calendar System: Semester
URL: www.chesapeake.edu
Established: 1965 Annual Undergrad Tuition & Fees (In-District): $5,552
Enrollment: 1,904 Coed
Affiliation or Control: State/Local IRS Status: 501(c)3
Highest Offering: Associate Degree
Accreditation: M, ADNUR, EMT, PTAA, RAD, SURGT

01 President .... Dr. Clifford COPPERSMITH
05 Vice President for Academics .... Mr. David HARPER
11 VP for Administrative Services .... Ms. Karen SMITH
32 VP for Student Success & Enrollment .... Mr. Kamari COLLINS
106 Dean for Teaching and Learning .... Dr. Chandra M. GIGLIOTTI
20 Dean for Faculty .... Dr. Juliet SMITH
103 Dean for Workforce Programs .... Ms. Elaine WILSON
18 Director of Facilities .... Mr. Paul RENSHAW
15 Director of Human Resources .... Ms. Susan A. CIANCHETTA
37 Director of Financial Aid .... Ms. Princess WILLIAMS
09 Dir Inst Plng/Research/Assessment .... Mr. Chris HALL
26 Dir College Relations & Marketing .... Ms. Danielle DARLING
06 Registrar .... Mr. James A. DAVIDSON
84 Dean for Enrollment & Advising .... Ms. Joan M. SEITZER
101 Exec Assoc to President/Board .... Ms. Kate MAXWELL
13 Chief Information Technology Office .... Mr. Greg WANNER
30 Director of Constituent Engagement .... Vacant

College of Southern Maryland (G)

PO Box 910, La Plata MD 20646-0910
County: Charles FICE Identification: 002064
Unit ID: 162122
Telephone: (301) 934-2251 Carnegie Class: Assoc/HT-High Trad
FAX Number: (301) 934-7698 Calendar System: Semester
URL: www.csmd.edu
Established: 1958 Annual Undergrad Tuition & Fees (In-District): $6,870
Enrollment: 6,164 Coed
Affiliation or Control: Local IRS Status: 501(c)3
Highest Offering: Associate Degree
Accreditation: M, ACBSP, ADNUR, EMT, MLTAD, PNUR, PTAA

01 President .... Dr. Maureen MURPHY
05 Provost and VP Academic Affairs .... Dr. Rodney REDMOND
84 VP Student Equity and Success .... Dr. Tracy HARRIS
103 AVP Continuing Educ & Workforce Dev .... Ms. Ellen FLOWERS-FIELDS
10 VP Financial & Admin Services .... Vacant
11 VP Operations and Planning .... Dr. William COMEY
43 Vice President/General Counsel .... Mr. Craig PATENAUDE
100 Chief of Staff .... Ms. Larisa PFEIFFER
09 AVP Plng/Inst Effective/Rsrch .... Dr. Erin EBERSOLE
15 AVP of Human Resources .... Mr. Ivan SMITH
26 AVP Marketing/Communication .... Ms. Avis MCMILLON
37 Director Financial Assistance .... Mr. Christian ZIMMERMANN
06 Dean Enrollment Services .... Ms. Carol HARRISON
18 Exec Director of Facilities .... Mr. Ron TOWARD
76 Dean Health Sciences .... Dr. Laura POLK
32 Dean Student Development .... Ms. Michelle RUBLE
109 Exec Dir Auxiliary Services .... Ms. Marcy GANNON
07 Director Admissions Department .... Mr. David JONES
96 Exec Dir of Procurement/Contracts .... Mr. Joe PICCOLO
28 Exec Dir Diversity and Inclusion .... Vacant
19 Exec Director Security/Safety .... Mr. Bill BESSETTE
25 Grants Development Coordinator .... Ms. Lesley QUATTLEBAUM
30 Exec Director Development .... Ms. Chelsea BROWN
108 Director Institutional Assessment .... Mr. Roland KEECH
86 Director Government Relations .... Ms. Karen SMITH-HUPP

The Community College of Baltimore County (H)

7201 Rossville Blvd., Baltimore MD 21237-3899
County: Baltimore FICE Identification: 002063
Unit ID: 434672
Telephone: (443) 840-2222 Carnegie Class: Assoc/MT-VT-High Trad
FAX Number: (443) 840-1100 Calendar System: Semester
URL: www.ccbcmd.edu
Established: 1957 Annual Undergrad Tuition & Fees (In-District): $7,474
Enrollment: 17,573 Coed
Affiliation or Control: Local IRS Status: 501(c)3
Highest Offering: Associate Degree
Accreditation: M, ACBSP, ADNUR, ART, CAHIIM, COARC, COMTA, DANCE, DH, EMT, FUSER, HT, MAC, MLTAD, MUS, OTA, POLYT, RAD, RTT, SURGT, THEA

01 President .... Dr. Sandra L. KURTINITIS
111 Vice Pres Institutional Advancement .... Mr. Kenneth WESTARY
10 Vice Pres Finance/Administration .... Ms. Melissa HOPP
05 Chancellor/VP Instruction .... Dr. Joaquin MARTINEZ
51 VP External Outreach Initiative .... Mr. Michael NETZER
26 Sr Director for Public Relations .... Ms. Amy FILARDO
15 Senior Director Human Resources .... Ms. Penny MILSOM

Frederick Community College (I)

7932 Opossumtown Pike, Frederick MD 21702-2097
County: Frederick FICE Identification: 002071
Unit ID: 162557
Telephone: (301) 846-2400 Carnegie Class: Assoc/HT-Mix Trad/Non
FAX Number: (301) 846-2498 Calendar System: Semester
URL: www.frederick.edu
Established: 1957 Annual Undergrad Tuition & Fees (In-District): $7,396
Enrollment: 5,756 Coed
Affiliation or Control: State/Local IRS Status: 501(c)3
Highest Offering: Associate Degree
Accreditation: M, ACFEI, ADNUR, COARC, SURGT

01 Interim President .... Dr. Thomas POWELL
11 Chief of Operations .... Mr. Lewis GODWIN

05 Provost/EVP Academic Affairs & CEWD ... Dr. Tony HAWKINS
10 VP for Finance ... Dr. Cathy JONES
32 VP for Learning Support ... Dr. Nora CLARK
121 AVP for Student Success ... Dr. Candice BALDWIN
25 Director of Grants Management ... Ms. Pamela DUBITSKY
111 Exec Dir Institutional Advancement ... Ms. Deborah POWELL
13 Chief Information Officer ... Mr. Joseph MCCORMICK
76 AVP for AA/Dean of Health ... Dr. Sandy MCCOMBE WALLER
84 AVP for Admissions/Enrollment Svcs ... Ms. Laura MEARS
15 VP for Human Resources ... Vacant
21 AVP for Finance ... Ms. Amy STAKE
06 Exec Dir of Registration & Records ... Ms. Deirdre WEILMINSTER
49 AVP for AA/Dean of Liberal Arts ... Dr. Brian STIPELMAN
35 AVP/Dean of Students ... Mr. Jerry HAYNES
124 Exec Director of Student Engagement ... Ms. Jeanni WINSTON-MUIR
09 Spec Asst to President Inst Effect ... Mr. Gerald BOYD
18 Director of Capital Planning ... Mr. John ANZINGER
08 Director of Library Services ... Ms. Colleen MCKNIGHT
108 Exec Dir Assessment and Research ... Dr. Gohar FARAHANI
26 Exec Director of Marketing and Web ... Mr. Michael BAISEY
04 Exec Assoc to the President & BOT ... Ms. Kari MELVIN
103 AVP for CEWD ... Ms. Patricia MEYER
117 Exec Director MACEM & Public Safety ... Ms. Kathy FRANCIS
14 Associate Chief Information Officer ... Mr. Adam RENO
41 Director of Athletics ... Vacant
66 Director of Clinical Education ... Ms. Ashley DICKS
106 Director Online Learning ... Dr. Yazdan RODD
36 Exec Dir Career & Academic Planning ... Dr. Chad ADERO
88 Director Office of Adult Services ... Ms. Janice BROWN
22 Dir of Disability Access Services . Dr. Kate KRAMER-JEFFERSON
88 Dir Veterans &d Military Services ... Ms. Amy COLDREN
40 Director of Bookstore ... Mr. Frederick HOCKENBERRY
88 Foundation Scholarship Manager ... Mr. Michael THORNTON
19 Director College Safety & Security ... Ms. Robin SHUSKO
28 Exec Dir Diversity/Equity/Inclusion ... Dr. Beth DOUTHIRT COHEN
88 Director Arts Center ... Mr. Wendell POINDEXTER
88 Exec Dir Open Campus & Dual Enroll ... Ms. Elizabeth DUFFY
88 Director for Testing Center ... Dr. Alesha ROSEN
18 Director of Plant Operations ... Mr. Greg SOLBERG
93 Director Multicultural Student Svcs ... Ms. Chianti BLACKMON
113 Exec Dir Student Finance/Bursar ... Ms. Jane BEATTY
91 Exec Dir Network Infrastructure ... Mr. Scott REECE
24 Director Audio-Visual Tech ... Mr. Bryan VALKO

Garrett College (A)

687 Mosser Road, McHenry MD 21541

County: Garrett FICE Identification: 010014
Unit ID: 162609
Telephone: (301) 387-3000 Carnegie Class: Assoc/HT-Mix Trad/Non
FAX Number: N/A Calendar System: Semester
URL: www.garrettcollege.edu
Established: 1967 Annual Undergrad Tuition & Fees (In-District): $8,848
Enrollment: 624 Coed
Affiliation or Control: State/Local IRS Status: 501(c)3
Highest Offering: Associate Degree
Accreditation: M, EMT

01 President ... Dr. Richard MIDCAP
04 Executive Assistant to President ... Ms. Marcia KNEPP
10 Dean of Business & Finance ... Ms. Dallas OUELLETTE
32 Chief Student Affairs Officer ... Mr. Robert KERNS
05 Dean of Academic Affairs ... Dr. Ryan HARROD
51 Dean of Cont Educ/Workforce Devel ... Ms. Julie YODER
13 Director of IT ... Mr. Andrew DURST
30 Dir Develop/Exec Dir Foundation ... Ms. Cherie KRUG
06 Assoc Dean Student Affs/Registrar ... Ms. Kim DEGIOVANNI
37 Director of Financial Aid ... Mr. Andrew HARVEY
08 Dir of Library/Learning Commons ... Ms. Jennifer MESLENER
15 Director of Human Resources ... Ms. Janis BUSH
35 Director of Student Development ... Mr. Rich SCHOFIELD
65 Dir of Natural Res/Wildlife Tech ... Mr. Kevin DODGE
41 Director of Athletics ... Vacant
18 Director of Facilities ... Ms. Kathy MEAGHER
121 Coord of Student Advis & Acad Supp ... Ms. Ashley RUBY
96 Purchasing/Accounts Payable ... Ms. Bonnie BROADWATER
40 Bookstore Manager ... Ms. Lois ANDERSON
105 Web Developer ... Mr. David LANTZ
106 Coord of DL & Inst Design ... Vacant
19 Coord of Safety & Security ... Mr. Steven BAKER
26 Coordinator of Marketing and PR ... Ms. Stacy HOLLER
07 Director of Admissions ... Ms. Melissa WASS
25 Chief Contract/Grants Administrator ... Ms. Kearstin HINEBAUGH
22 Director of Equity & Compliance ... Ms. Shelley MENEAR
09 Director of Institutional Research ... Ms. Kelli SISLER

Goucher College (B)

1021 Dulaney Valley Road, Baltimore MD 21204-2780

County: Baltimore FICE Identification: 002073
Unit ID: 162654
Telephone: (410) 337-6000 Carnegie Class: Bac-A&S
FAX Number: N/A Calendar System: Semester
URL: www.goucher.edu
Established: 1885 Annual Undergrad Tuition & Fees: $47,200
Enrollment: 2,015 Coed
Affiliation or Control: Independent Non-Profit IRS Status: 501(c)3
Highest Offering: Master's
Accreditation: M

01 President ... Mr. Kent DEVEREAUX
05 Provost/Sr VP Academic Affairs ... Dr. Elaine MEYER-LEE
111 Vice Pres Advancement ... Ms. Michele Y. EWING
26 VP Marketing & External Relations ... Ms. Stephanie COLDREN
13 Vice Pres for Technology & Planning ... Mr. Bill LEIMBACH
43 General Counsel ... Vacant
41 Assoc Dean Students/Dir Athletics ... Dr. Andrew WU
07 Director of Admissions ... Ms. Lisa HILL
08 Librarian ... Vacant
29 Exec Dir for Alumnae/i Engagement ... Ms. Jennifer PAWLO - JOHNSTONE
36 Director of Career Development ... Ms. Traci MARTIN
58 Director Grad Program in Education ... Dr. Annalisa CZEZULIN
06 Registrar ... Ms. Genevieve COLE
37 Director Student Financial Services ... Ms. Stephanie ALFORD
105 Webmaster ... Mr. John PERRELLI
39 Director Residential Life ... Ms. Lindy BOBBIT
38 Director Student Counseling Center ... Ms. Monica NEEL
04 Admin Assistant to the President ... Ms. Christine STEWART
09 Director Institutional Effectivenes ... Ms. Shama AKHTAR
102 Asst Dir Foundation/Corporate Rels ... Ms. Janeisa LASHLEY
104 Director Study Abroad ... Dr. Luchen LI
11 Chief of Operations/Administration ... Mr. David VALENTINE
15 AVP Human Resources ... Ms. Kristi YOWELL
18 VP Campus Operations ... Mr. Erik THOMPSON
28 Assoc Dean Diversity/Equity/Inclus ... Mr. Juan HERNANDEZ
32 VP Student Affairs ... Dr. Aarika CAMP
44 Director Annual Giving ... Ms. Ali SCHILLER-SMITH
84 VP Enrollment Management ... Mr. Jonathan LINDSAY
91 Director Administrative Computing ... Mr. Robert SMITH

Hagerstown Community College (C)

11400 Robinwood Drive, Hagerstown MD 21742-6590

County: Washington FICE Identification: 002074
Unit ID: 162690
Telephone: (240) 500-2000 Carnegie Class: Assoc/MT-VT-Mix Trad/Non
FAX Number: (301) 393-3682 Calendar System: Semester
URL: www.hagerstowncc.edu
Established: 1946 Annual Undergrad Tuition & Fees (In-District): $6,360
Enrollment: 3,433 Coed
Affiliation or Control: State/Local IRS Status: 501(c)3
Highest Offering: Associate Degree
Accreditation: M, ADNUR, DA, DH, EMT, PNUR, RAD

01 President ... Dr. James S. KLAUBER, SR.
05 VP of Academic Affs & Student Svcs ... Dr. David WARNER
10 Vice Pres Administration/ Finance ... Dr. Heike I. SOEFFKER-CULICERTO
32 Dean of Students ... Dr. Christine A. OHL-GIGLIOTTI
09 Dean Plng/Inst Effectiveness ... Ms. Carlee K. RANALLI
103 Dean Workforce Solutions & Cont Ed ... Ms. Theresa M. SHANK
18 Dir Facilities Management & Plng ... Mr. Vincent T. IPPOLITO
07 Dir of Admissions & Enrollment Mgmt . Mr. Kevin L. CRAWFORD
111 Senior Director College Advancement ... Dr. Ashley N. WHALEY
26 Sr Dir Public Relations & Marketing ... Ms. Elizabeth L. KIRKPATRICK
37 Director of Financial Aid ... Dr. Charles M. SCHEETZ
106 Dean of Distance Education ... Ms. Vidda P. BEACHE
21 Director of Finance ... Mr. David C. BITTORF
21 Director of Business Services ... Ms. Lita J. ORNER
66 Director of Nursing ... Ms. Karen S. HAMMOND
15 Exec Director of Human Resources ... Ms. Jennifer A. CHILDS
41 Dir Athletics/Phys Ed/Leisure Stds ... Mr. Robert C. ROHAN
13 Sr Dir Information Technology ... Mr. Craig M. FENTRESS
04 Exec Assistant to the President ... Ms. Barbara W. ROULETTE
06 Registrar ... Mr. Christopher BAER
19 Director Security/Safety ... Mr. Eric C. BYERS

Harford Community College (D)

401 Thomas Run Road, Bel Air MD 21015-1698

County: Harford FICE Identification: 002075
Unit ID: 162706
Telephone: (443) 412-2000 Carnegie Class: Assoc/HT-Mix Trad/Non
FAX Number: (443) 412-2120 Calendar System: Semester
URL: www.harford.edu
Established: 1957 Annual Undergrad Tuition & Fees (In-District): $6,065
Enrollment: 5,256 Coed
Affiliation or Control: Local IRS Status: 501(c)3
Highest Offering: Associate Degree
Accreditation: M, ADNUR, EMT, HT, MAC

01 President ... Dr. Theresa FELDER
05 Vice President Academic Affairs ... Dr. Timothy SHERWOOD
10 VP Finance & Administration ... Mr. Trevor JACKSON
32 VP Student Affairs ... Dr. Jacqueline JACKSON
13 Chief Information Officer ... Mr. Tom ALCIDE
84 Assoc VP Enrollment Services ... Mr. Patrick ELLIOTT
35 Assoc VP Student Development ... Ms. Jennie TOWNER
21 Director for Finance & Accounting ... Ms. Karina JACKSON
106 Dean Teaching/Learning/Innovation ... Dr. Karen M. REGE
18 Director for Campus Operations ... Mr. Lou CLAYPOOLE
37 Director Financial Aid ... Ms. Amy R. SPINNATO
06 Registrar ... Ms. Courtney MITCHELL
26 Director for Communications ... Ms. Nancy J. DYSARD
15 AVP Human Resources/Employee Dev ... Ms. Donna SHOPULSKI
30 Director College/Alumni Development ... Ms. Denise M. DREGIER
08 Dean of Information & Innovation ... Ms. Karen REGE
09 Director for Inst Effectiveness ... Vacant
38 Dir Advising/Career/Transfer Svcs ... Ms. J. Bonnie SULZBACH
40 Coordinator College Store ... Mr. Joseph BUSKIRK
07 Dir for Admissions ... Ms. Katie REYNOLDS
110 Event Coordinator & Gift Officer ... Ms. Jordan WILLIAMS
81 Dean Science/Tech/Engr/Math ... Ms. Pamela PAPE-LINDSTROM
83 Dean Behavioral & Social Sciences ... Mr. Tony WOHLERS
79 Dean of Arts & Humanities ... Mr. Todd ABRAMOVITZ
50 Dean of CEBAT ... Ms. Kelly KOERMER
66 Interim Dean of NAHP ... Ms. Sonia GALVAN
19 Director Security/Safety ... Vacant
41 Athletic Director ... Vacant

Hood College (E)

401 Rosemont Avenue, Frederick MD 21701-8575

County: Frederick FICE Identification: 002076
Unit ID: 162760
Telephone: (301) 663-3131 Carnegie Class: Masters/L
FAX Number: (301) 694-7653 Calendar System: Semester
URL: www.hood.edu
Established: 1893 Annual Undergrad Tuition & Fees: $42,300
Enrollment: 2,042 Coed
Affiliation or Control: Independent Non-Profit IRS Status: 501(c)3
Highest Offering: Doctorate
Accreditation: M, ACBSP, CACREP, NURSE, SW

01 President ... Dr. Andrea E. CHAPDELAINE
05 Provost/VP Academic Affairs ... Dr. Deborah RICKER
10 Vice Pres Finance ... Mr. Charles G. MANN
111 VP for Institutional Advancement ... Ms. Nancy E. GILLECE
32 Dean of Students ... Dr. Ron WIAFE
84 VP Undergrad/Grad Enrollment ... Mr. William BROWN
26 VP Marketing/Communications Officer ... Ms. Laurie WARD
07 Director of Admissions ... Ms. Nikki BAMONTI
58 Dean of Graduate School ... Dr. April BOULTON
08 Director of Library Service ... Mr. Toby PETERSON
15 Director of Human Resources ... Vacant
13 Chief Technology Officer ... Mr. Bill HOBBS
04 Executive Asst to President ... Ms. Diane K. WISE
104 Director Study Abroad ... Mr. Scott PINCIKOWSKI
19 Director Security/Safety ... Mr. Thurmond MAYNARD
39 Director Student Housing ... Mr. Matthew TROUTMAN
102 Dir Foundation/Corporate Relations ... Ms. Jaime CACCIOLA
06 Registrar ... Ms. Ashley ANDERSON
09 Director of Institutional Research ... Dr. Shaowei WU
108 Asst Dir Institutional Assessment ... Vacant
29 Director Alumni Affairs ... Ms. Kellye GREENWALD
37 Director Student Financial Aid ... Ms. Melena VERITY
41 Athletic Director ... Dr. Susan KOLB
44 Director Annual Giving ... Ms. Niccole ROLLS
28 VP for Community & Inclusivity ... Ms. Tammi SIMPSON

Howard Community College (F)

10901 Little Patuxent Parkway, Columbia MD 21044-3197

County: Howard FICE Identification: 008175
Unit ID: 162779
Telephone: (443) 518-1000 Carnegie Class: Assoc/HT-High Trad
FAX Number: N/A Calendar System: Semester
URL: www.howardcc.edu
Established: 1966 Annual Undergrad Tuition & Fees (In-District): $6,408
Enrollment: 9,566 Coed
Affiliation or Control: State/Local IRS Status: 501(c)3
Highest Offering: Associate Degree
Accreditation: M, ACFEI, ADNUR, ART, CVT, DH, DMS, EMT, MLTAD, MUS, PNUR, PTAA, RAD

01 President ... Dr. Kathleen B. HETHERINGTON
32 Vice President of Student Services ... Dr. Cynthia J. PETERKA
05 Vice Pres of Academic Affairs ... Dr. Jean M. SVACINA
10 Vice Pres of Administration/Finance ... Ms. Lynn C. COLEMAN
13 Vice Pres Information Technology ... Ms. Linda WU
51 Associate VP Cont Ed/Workforce Dev ... Ms. Minah C. WOO
84 Acting Assoc VP Enrollment Services ... Ms. Zakia JOHNSON
35 AVP for Student Development ... Ms. Debra GREENE
15 Associate Vice Pres Human Resources ... Mr. Joseph B. PETTIFORD
21 Associate Vice Pres of Finance ... Mr. Chris W. HESTON
18 Exec Dir Capital Proj/Facilities ... Mr. Charles W. NIGHTINGALE
101 Executive Associate to President ... Ms. Cheryl CUDZILO
114 Director of Budget and Finance ... Ms. Verna A. BERNOI
30 Dir of Dev/Exec Dir Educ Foundation ... Ms. Melissa L. MATTEY
109 Director Auxiliary Services ... Mr. L. Dewey GRIM
19 Director of Public Safety ... Mr. G. William DAVIS
35 Acting Director Student Life ... Mr. Clinton NEILL
04 Exec Assistant to the President ... Ms. Mary F. HONG
96 Director of Procurement ... Mr. Domonic A. CUSIMANO
06 Acting Registrar ... Ms. Katelyn PIPER
07 Director of Admissions & Advising ... Mrs. Mary C. O'ROURKE
104 Director of International Education ... Ms. Mary L. ALLEN
105 Web Enterprise Services Manager ... Mr. Roger F. STOTT
37 Director of Financial Aid Services ... Ms. Tamika BYBEE
41 Interim Director of Athletics ... Mr. Michael SMELKINSON
26 Exec Dir Public Relations/Mktg ... Ms. Elizabeth S. HOMAN
09 Exec Dir Plng/Research & Org Dev ... Ms. Zoe A. IRVIN
38 Director Counseling & Career Svcs ... Dr. Jay J. COUGHLIN, III
20 Assoc Vice Pres Academic Affairs ... Dr. Laura J. CRIPPS

Johns Hopkins University (G)

3400 N. Charles Street, Baltimore MD 21218-2680

County: Independent City FICE Identification: 002077
Unit ID: 162928
Telephone: (410) 516-8000 Carnegie Class: DU-Highest
FAX Number: N/A Calendar System: Semester
URL: www.jhu.edu
Established: 1876 Annual Undergrad Tuition & Fees: $54,160
Enrollment: 28,890 Coed
Affiliation or Control: Independent Non-Profit IRS Status: 501(c)3

Highest Offering: Doctorate
Accreditation: M, ANEST, CACREP, CAMPEP, DIETC, DMS, HSA, IPSY, MED, MIL, NMT, NURSE, PH

01 President ... Mr. Ronald J. DANIELS
100 Vice President/Chief of Staff ... Ms. Kerry A. ATES
05 Provost & Sr VP Acad Affs ... Dr. Sunil KUMAR
17 CEO Johns Hopkins Medicine ... Dr. Paul D. ROTHMAN
10 Sr VP Finance & Administration ... Mr. Laurent HELLER
11 Vice Pres & Chief Admin Officer ... Vacant
29 VP for Development & Alum Relations ... Mr. Fritz SCHROEDER
26 Vice Pres for Communications ... Mr. Andrew GREEN
43 Vice Pres/General Counsel ... Mr. Paul PINEAU
86 Vice Pres Govt/Community Affairs ... Vacant
18 Vice Pres Facilities/Real Estate ... Mr. Robert MCLEAN
15 Vice Pres Human Resources ... Vacant
21 Vice Pres/CFO & Treasurer ... Ms. Helene GRADY
115 Vice Pres Chief Investment Officer ... Mr. Jason PERLIONI
117 Vice Provost and Chief Risk Officer ... Dr. Jonathan LINKS
32 Interim Vice Prov Student Affairs ... Mr. Kevin SHOLLENBERGER
50 Vice Provost Career Services ... Dr. Farouk DEY
20 Vice Provost Faculty Affairs ... Dr. Andrew DOUGLAS
07 Vice Provost Admiss & Fin Aid ... Mr. David PHILLIPS
23 Vice Prov Student Health ... Mr. Kevin SHOLLENBERGER
28 Chief Diversity Officer ... Dr. Katrina CALDWELL
58 Vice Prov Grad and Prof Education ... Dr. Nancy KASS
13 Vice Pres/Chief Technology Officer ... Vacant
22 Vice Provost Institutional Equity ... Ms. Shanon SHUMPERT
46 Vice Provost Research ... Dr. Denis WIRTZ
09 Vice Provost Institutional Research ... Dr. Ratna SARKAR
88 Assoc Vice Prov International Svcs ... Mr. James BRAILER
06 University Registrar ... Ms. Amynah MITHANI
82 Int Dean School Adv Intl Studies ... Dr. Kent CALDER
49 Dean Krieger Sch Arts/Sciences ... Dr. Christopher CELENZA
50 Dean Carey Business School ... Dr. Alexander TRIANTIS
53 Dean School of Education ... Dr. Christopher MORPHEW
54 Dean Whiting Sch Engineering ... Dr. Ed SCHLESINGER
63 Dean School of Medicine ... Dr. Paul ROTHMAN
66 Dean School of Nursing ... Dr. Sarah SZANTON
69 Dean Bloomberg School Public Health ... Dr. Ellen MACKENZIE
08 Dean Sheridan Libraries and Museums ... Mr. Winston G. TABB
64 Dean Peabody Institute ... Dr. Fred BRONSTEIN
88 Director Applied Physics Lab ... Mr. Ralph SEMMEL
96 Chief Procurement Officer ... Mr. Brian SMITH
21 Controller ... Mr. Scott JONAS
19 Vice President for Public Safety ... Dr. Branville BARD, JR.
116 Exec Director Internal Audits ... Mr. James JARRELL
27 Asst Vice Pres Strategic Comms ... Ms. Marianne VON NORDECK
104 Director Study Abroad ... Dr. Lori A. CITTI
28 Chair Diversity Leadership Council ... Vacant
41 Athletic Director ... Ms. Jennifer BAKER
101 Secretary of the Institution/Board ... Ms. Maureen MARSH
04 Admin Assistant to the President ... Ms. Jodi MILLER
37 Assistant Vice Prov Financial Aid ... Mr. Tom MCDERMOTT

Lincoln College of Technology (A)

9325 Snowden River Parkway, Columbia MD 21046
County: Howard FICE Identification: 007936
Unit ID: 163028
Telephone: (410) 290-7100 Carnegie Class: Assoc/HVT-High Trad
FAX Number: (410) 290-7880 Calendar System: Quarter
URL: www.lincolntech.com
Established: 1978 Annual Undergrad Tuition & Fees: N/A
Enrollment: 870 Coed
Affiliation or Control: Proprietary IRS Status: Proprietary
Highest Offering: Associate Degree
Accreditation: ACCSC

01 Campus President ... Mr. Cory HUGHES

Loyola University Maryland (B)

4501 N Charles Street, Baltimore MD 21210-2694
County: Independent City FICE Identification: 002078
Unit ID: 163046
Telephone: (410) 617-2000 Carnegie Class: Masters/L
FAX Number: (410) 322-2768 Calendar System: Semester
URL: www.loyola.edu
Established: 1852 Annual Undergrad Tuition & Fees: $51,100
Enrollment: 5,282 Coed
Affiliation or Control: Roman Catholic IRS Status: 501(c)3
Highest Offering: Doctorate
Accreditation: M, CACREP, CLPSY, SP

01 President ... Rev. Brian F. LINNANE, SJ
03 Senior Vice President ... Dr. Terrence SAWYER
88 VP/Special Asst to the President ... Dr. Rob KELLY
05 Vice Pres Academic Affairs/Provost ... Dr. Amanda THOMAS
10 VP for Finance/Admin & Treasurer ... Mr. John COPPOLA
111 Sr Vice Pres Advancement ... Mr. Terrence SAWYER
32 VP Student Development ... Vacant
84 Vice Pres Enrollment Management ... Mr. Eric NICHOLS
09 Director of Institutional Research ... Ms. Nicole JACOBS
18 Assoc VP Facilities/Campus Services ... Ms. Helen SCHNEIDER
15 Assoc Vice Pres for Human Resources ... Ms. Kathleen PARNELL
110 Asst Vice Pres for External Affairs ... Ms. Joan FLYNN
114 AVP Budget/Business Planning ... Mr. Sean FRANCIS
35 Asst Vice Pres Student Development ... Ms. Michelle CHEATEM
26 Assoc VP Marketing/Communications ... Vacant
41 Asst VP/Director of Athletics ... Ms. Donna WOODRUFF
07 Dean Undergraduate Admissions ... Ms. Jennifer LOUDEN
123 Exec Dir of Graduate Admissions ... Ms. Maureen BUSH
27 Dir Marketing and Communications ... Ms. Rita BUETTNER
06 Director of Records ... Ms. Deborah MILLER
85 Dean of International Programs ... Dr. Andre COLOMBAT
08 Director of Library ... Vacant
42 Director of Campus Ministry ... Mr. Sean BRAY
88 Dir CCSJ/York Road Initiative ... Ms. Erin O'KEEFE
88 PM Women's Ctr/Sex Assault Prev ... Ms. Melissa LEES
28 Director ALANA Services ... Ms. Raven WILLIAMS
21 Asst Dir Accounting/Controller ... Ms. Cecelia JACKSON-GOODE
109 Director Event Svcs/Auxiliary Mgmt ... Mr. Joseph BRADLEY
88 Director Environment Health/Safety ... Mr. Thomas HETTLEMAN
19 Dir of Public Safety/Campus Police ... Mr. Adrian BLACK
29 Director Alumni Engagement ... Ms. Colleen RIOPKO
49 Dean College of Arts & Sciences ... Dr. Steve FOWL
53 Dean School of Education ... Dr. Joshua SMITH
50 Dean Sellinger Sch Business & Mgmt ... Vacant
83 Assoc Dean Social Sciences/Graduate ... Dr. Jeffrey BARNETT
50 Asst Dean for Business Programs ... Ms. Susan HASLER
18 Sr Assoc Director Facilities ... Mr. Joseph GRIFFIN
105 Dir Web Development/Design ... Mr. David BLOHM

Maple Springs Baptist Bible College & Seminary (C)

4130 Belt Road, Capitol Heights MD 20743-5712
County: Prince Georges FICE Identification: 038224
Unit ID: 446394
Telephone: (301) 736-3631 Carnegie Class: Spec-4-yr-Faith
FAX Number: (301) 735-6507 Calendar System: Semester
URL: www.msbbcs.edu
Established: 1986 Annual Undergrad Tuition & Fees: $5,400
Enrollment: N/A Coed
Affiliation or Control: Baptist IRS Status: 501(c)3
Highest Offering: Doctorate
Accreditation: TRACS

01 Acting President ... Dr. Carl KEELS
05 Vice President Academic Affairs ... Dr. Luther S. BUCK
10 Vice Pres Finance & Administration ... Mr. Keith DUKES
73 Academic Dean Seminary Division ... Dr. Dana A. VAN BRAKLE
73 Academic Dean Bible College Div ... Dr. Carl E. KEELS
30 Chief Development/Advancement Ofcr ... Dr. George HOLMES
06 Director Admissions & Records ... Rev. Alonzo K. JACKSON, SR.
09 Dir Institutional Plng/Assessment ... Dr. Marquez BALL
32 Director Student Affairs ... Dr. Catherine BORGES-JOHNSON
08 Dir Library/Instruc Resource Center ... Mr. Darren JONES
37 Director Financial Aid ... Rev. Himie PICKETT
07 Asst Dir of Admissions/Records ... Mr. Timothy L. WASHINGTON
21 Associate Business Officer ... Mrs. Diane JENKINS

Maryland Institute College of Art (D)

1300 W. Mount Royal Avenue, Baltimore MD 21217-4191
County: Independent City FICE Identification: 002080
Unit ID: 163295
Telephone: (410) 669-9200 Carnegie Class: Spec-4-yr-Arts
FAX Number: (410) 669-9206 Calendar System: Semester
URL: www.mica.edu
Established: 1826 Annual Undergrad Tuition & Fees: $49,190
Enrollment: 1,892 Coed
Affiliation or Control: Independent Non-Profit IRS Status: 501(c)3
Highest Offering: Master's
Accreditation: M, ART

01 President ... Mr. Samuel HOI
05 Vice Pres Academic Affairs/Provost ... Ms. Tiffany HOLMES
10 Vice Pres Finance & Business Svcs ... Mr. Martin LEMELLE
32 Vice Pres Student Affairs ... Mr. Michael PATTERSON
07 VP Admissions/Financial Aid ... Dr. Audrey TANNER
13 Vice Pres Technology Systems & Svcs ... Ms. Alexa KIM
111 Vice Pres for Advancement ... Mr. Don JONES
26 VP for Strategic Communications ... Mr. Christian LALLO
97 Vice Provost Open Studies ... Mr. David GRACYALNY
46 Vice Provost Research/Grad Studies ... Ms. Stacey SALAZAR
04 Executive Assistant to President ... Ms. Lisa SHEPPLEY
37 Assoc VP Financial Aid ... Mr. DeRodrick JONKINS
15 VP People Belonging Culture ... Ms. Shanna HINES
20 Assoc VP Academic Services ... Ms. Wendy PRICE
123 Director of Graduate Admissions ... Mr. Christopher HARRING
51 Assoc Dean Continuing/Open Studies ... Ms. Crystal SHAMBLEE
06 Assoc Dean Enrol Svcs/Registrar ... Ms. Christine PETERSON
114 Director Budget ... Ms. Brigitte SULLIVAN
39 Director Residence Life ... Mr. Scott STONE
36 Director Career Development ... Ms. Jennine STANKIEWICZ
23 AVP Health Services ... Ms. Judith KINNEY
35 Director Student Activities ... Ms. Karol MARTINEZ-DOANE
88 Director Admissions Operations ... Vacant
08 Director & Head Librarian ... Ms. Heather SLANIA
44 Director Annual Fund ... Mr. Mansoor ALI
88 Director Exhibitions ... Mr. Gerald ROSS
88 Dir Data Mgmt/Registration Cont Std ... Ms. Sarah MARAVETZ
84 Dir Enroll Svcs/Stdnt Records/Rsrch ... Mr. Hadley GARBART
19 Director of Campus Safety ... Mr. Marlon BYRD
88 Director Events ... Mr. Jon LIPITZ
88 Director Operation Services ... Mr. Chris BOHASKA
102 Director Corp/Found/Govt Relations ... Ms. Sara WARREN
24 Director Technical Support Services ... Mr. John RHODES
91 Director Administrative Systems ... Vacant
105 Director Network Services ... Mr. David APAW
40 Manager College Store ... Ms. Kerri LITZ

Maryland University of Integrative Health (E)

7750 Montpelier Road, Laurel MD 20723-6010
County: Howard FICE Identification: 025784
Unit ID: 164085
Telephone: (410) 888-9048 Carnegie Class: Spec-4-yr-Other Health
FAX Number: (410) 888-9004 Calendar System: Trimester
URL: www.muih.edu
Established: 1981 Annual Graduate Tuition & Fees: N/A
Enrollment: 815 Coed
Affiliation or Control: Independent Non-Profit IRS Status: 501(c)3
Highest Offering: Doctorate; No Undergraduates
Accreditation: M, ACUP

01 President/CFO/COO ... Mr. Marc LEVIN
05 Provost/VP Academic Affairs ... Dr. Christina SAX
26 VP Marketing/Enrollment Management ... Mr. Nigel LONG
20 Assoc Provost Academic Operations ... Ms. Mary Ellen HRUTKA
108 Asst Provost Acad Assessment/Accred ... Ms. Deneb FALABELLA
20 Dean of Academic Affairs ... Mr. James SNOW
32 Dean of Student Affairs ... Ms. Michelle COLEMAN
76 Asst Dean of Academic Affairs ... Dr. Kathleen WARNER
07 Director of Admissions ... Mr. Kevin GORE
37 Director Student Financial Aid ... Ms. Kristina DEAN
06 Registrar ... Ms. Rhonda STOKES
13 Director IT ... Mr. Lesly ELVARD
15 Director Human Enrichment ... Ms. Melissa L. CAHILL
04 Exec Asst to the President ... Ms. Elizabeth BOSTIC
08 Head Librarian ... Ms. Carissa HERNANDEZ
09 Director of Institutional Research ... Mr. Lawrence MCGILL

McDaniel College (F)

2 College Hill, Westminster MD 21157-4390
County: Carroll FICE Identification: 002109
Unit ID: 164270
Telephone: (410) 848-7000 Carnegie Class: Masters/L
FAX Number: (410) 857-2279 Calendar System: Semester
URL: www.mcdaniel.edu
Established: 1867 Annual Undergrad Tuition & Fees: $45,876
Enrollment: 2,931 Coed
Affiliation or Control: Independent Non-Profit IRS Status: 501(c)3
Highest Offering: Master's
Accreditation: M, CAEPN, SW

01 President ... Dr. Julia JASKEN
100 Chief of Staff ... Ms. Marissa LANDER
05 Provost ... Dr. Rosa RIVERA-HAINAJ
10 Vice Pres Administration & Finance ... Mr. Eric SIMON
84 VP of Enrollment Management ... Ms. Janelle HOLMBOE
30 Interim VP for Development ... Mr. Bill TORREY
32 Dean of Students ... Ms. Elizabeth TOWLE
41 Director Athletics ... Mr. Adam HERTZ
15 Assoc VP for Administration ... Ms. Jennifer GLENNON
29 Assoc VP Alumni and Admissions ... Ms. Heidi REIGEL
111 Sr AVP of Institutional Advancement ... Mr. Chip JUNKIN
20 Dean of Faculty ... Ms. Wendy MORRIS
58 Dean Graduate/Prof Studies ... Dr. Vickie MAZER
10 Controller ... Ms. Julie FISHER
07 Dir Admissions & Financial Aid ... Ms. Kemia HIMON
28 Director of Diversity and Inclusion ... Mr. Jose MORENO
89 Dir of First Year Experience ... Ms. Erin BENEVENTO
39 Director of Residence Life ... Mr. Michael ROBBINS
38 Director of Wellness Center ... Ms. Heidi HUBER
19 Director of Campus Safety ... Mr. Eric IMMLER
08 Director of Hoover Library ... Mr. David BRENNAN
92 Director of Honors Program ... Dr. Corey WRONSKI-MAYERSAK
06 Assoc Registrar ... Ms. Marylin BELL
09 Director Institutional Research ... Ms. Robin DEWEY
106 Director Online Educ/E-learning ... Mr. Steve KERBY
15 Director Human Resources ... Ms. Rose MERCIER
22 Title IX Coordinator ... Ms. Jennifer KENT
13 Chief Information Officer ... Mr. Courtney CARPENTER
18 Director Physical Plant ... Ms. Keri ZEIGLER
96 Director of Purchasing/Receiving ... Ms. Ellen RUGEMER
109 Dir Conferences/Auxiliary Services ... Ms. Mary J. COLBERT
40 Manager Bookstore ... Mr. Kyle MELOCHE
26 Director of Public Relations ... Ms. Cheryl KNAUER
105 Website Manager ... Ms. Tara DUNSMORE
36 Assoc Dir Career Development ... Mr. Rich GOODMAN
104 Assoc Dir International Programs ... Ms. Brooke HAIN

Montgomery College (G)

9221 Corporate Boulevard, Rockville MD 20850
County: Montgomery FICE Identification: 006911
Unit ID: 163426
Telephone: (240) 567-5267 Carnegie Class: Assoc/HT-High Trad
FAX Number: (240) 567-9129 Calendar System: Semester
URL: www.montgomerycollege.edu
Established: 1946 Annual Undergrad Tuition & Fees (In-District): $10,254
Enrollment: 20,037 Coed
Affiliation or Control: Local IRS Status: 501(c)3
Highest Offering: Associate Degree
Accreditation: M, ADNUR, ART, CAHIIM, DMS, MUS, NAEYC, POLYT, PTAA, RAD, SURGT

01 Interim President ... Dr. Charlene M. DUKES
05 Sr VP for Academic Affairs ... Dr. Sanjay RAI
32 Sr VP for Student Affairs ... Dr. Monica R. BROWN

11 SVP Fiscal/Administrative Svcs .... Mr. Sherwin COLLETTE
111 SVP Advancement/Cmty Engagement .... Mr. David SEARS
100 Chief of Staff/Chief Strategy Ofcr .... Dr. Stephen D. CAIN
88 Deputy COS Pres Pub/Ops .... Dr. Meghan GIBBONS
88 Deputy COS Planning & Policy ....Dr. Kevin LONG
35 Assoc SVP for Student Affairs .... Dr. Melissa GREGORY
10 Assoc SVP for Admin & Fiscal Svcs .... Ms. Nadine PORTER
20 Assoc SVP for Academic Affairs .... Dr. Carolyn TERRY
20 Assoc SVP for Academic Affairs .... Dr. Elena SAENZ
86 Chief Government Relations Officer .... Ms. Susan MADDEN
43 General Counsel ....Mr. Timothy D. DIETZ
04 Assistant to the President ....Ms. Lisannie MONTILLA
101 BOT/Spec Asst to the President ....Dr. Michelle T. SCOTT
101 Mgr of Bd of Trustees Svcs & Ops .... Ms. Lily LEE
12 VP & Provost Rockville Campus ....Dr. Kimberly KELLEY
12 VP & Provost Germantown Campus ....Ms. Margaret LATIMER
12 VP & Prov Takoma Pk/Silver Spring C ....Dr. Brad J. STEWART
103 VP/Prov App Tech/Tech Ed/WD&CE ....Mr. George M. PAYNE
119 Int Chief Info Security Officer .... Ms. Nell FELDMAN
13 Chief Technology Officer ....Mr. Anwar KARIM
15 VP Human Res & Strat Talent Mgmt .... Ms. Krista WALKER
18 VP Facilities & Security .... Mr. Marvin J. MILLS
26 Assoc SVP Advance & Cmty Engagement ....Mr. Ray GILMER
25 Assoc SVP Advance/Cmty Engagement ....Ms. Rose GARVIN AQUILINO
106 VP E-Learning/Innov/Teaching Exc .... Dr. Michael MILLS
50 Dean Acct/Bus Admin/Econ/Paralegal .... Dr. Kathryn DAVIS
88 Acting Dean Eng/Dev Eng/Reading ....Dr. Elizabeth BENTON
83 Int Dean Anth/Cr Just/Ed/Psych/Soc ....Dr. Eric M. BENJAMIN
81 Dean Biology/Biotech/Chemistry .... Dr. James SNIEZEK
54 Dean Eng/Comp Sci/Netwk/Cyber Sec ....Dr. Muhammad KEHNEMOUYI
88 Chief Analytics & Insight Officer ....Mr. John HAMMAN
76 Int Dean Health Sci/Health/PE/Nurs .... Dr. Monique DAVIS
88 Dean ELAP Linguistics/Comm Studies ....Dr. Fiona GLADE
79 Dean Hist/PolSci/World Lang/Am Sign ....Dr. Sharon FECHTER
75 Dean Applied Tech & Gudelsky Inst .... Mr. Ed ROBERTS
50 Dean Bus Info/Tech/Safety .... Mr. Steve GREENFIELD
51 Dean Cmty Educ & Extended Learning ....Ms. Dorothy UMANS
51 Dean Adult Eng Lang & GED Programs ...... Dr. Donna KINERNEY
81 Dean Mathematics/Dev Math/Stats .... Dr. Milton NASH
57 Dean Visual/Perform & Media Arts ....Dr. Frank TREZZA
35 Dean Stdnt Affairs Gtown Campus ....Dr. Jamin BARTOLOMEO
35 Dean Stdnt Affairs Rockville Campus .... Dr. Tonya MASON
35 Int Dean Stdnt Affairs TP/SS Campus .... Ms. Janee MCFADDEN
53 Dir School of Education ....Ms. Debra POESE
41 Athletic Director ....Ms. Tarlough GASQUE
30 Exec MC Foundation/VP Dev ....Ms. Joyce MATTHEWS
112 Major and Planned Gifts Director .... Ms. Francene WALKER
88 Exec Dir H. Pinkney Life Sci Park ... Ms. Martha SCHOONMAKER
09 Dir Inst Research & Effectiveness ....Dr. Arlene BLAYLOCK
96 Dir of Procurement ....Mr. Patrick JOHNSON
37 Collegewide Dir of Financial Aid ....Ms. Judith M. TAYLOR
84 Dir Enroll Svcs & College Registrar ....Mr. Ernest CARTLEDGE
19 Int Dir Pub Safety/Emergency Mgmt ....Mr. Adam REID
28 Chief Equity & Diversity Officer ....Ms. Sharon BLAND
108 Dir of Assessment ....Dr. Cassandra JONES
102 Dir Corp and Foundation Relations .... Mr. Stuart TART
29 Dir Alumni Relations .... Mr. Greg ENLOE
08 Dir College Libraries & Info Svcs ....Ms. Suzette SPENCER
16 Dir Employee & Labor Relations .... Mr. Santo A. SCRIMENTI
104 Coord of Travel & Study Abroad .... Dr. Gregory MALVEAUX

Morgan State University (A)

1700 East Cold Spring Lane, Baltimore MD 21251-0001

County: Independent City | FICE Identification: 002083
Unit ID: 163453
Telephone: (443) 885-3333 | Carnegie Class: DU-Higher
FAX Number: (443) 885-3698 | Calendar System: Semester
URL: www.morgan.edu
Established: 1867 | Annual Undergrad Tuition & Fees (In-State): $7,628
Enrollment: 7,634 | Coed
Affiliation or Control: State | IRS Status: 501(c)3
Highest Offering: Doctorate
Accreditation: M, AAFCS, CAEPN, #DIETD, JOUR, LSAR, MT, MUS, NURSE, PH, PLNG, SW

01 President .... Dr. David WILSON
05 Provost/Sr VP Academic Affairs .... Dr. Hongtao YU
10 Vice Pres Finance & Management ....Mr. Sidney EVANS
13 Vice Pres for Technology & CIO ....Dr. Adebisi OLADIPUPO
32 Vice Pres Student Affairs .... Dr. Kevin BANKS
30 Vice Pres Institutional Advancement .... Ms. Donna HOWARD
84 VP for Enroll Mgmt/Student Success .... Dr. Kara TURNER
21 Assoc Vice Pres Finance/Deputy CFO .... Mr. David LACHINA
20 Assoc Vice Pres for Academic Affs ....Ms. Patricia WILLIAMS-LESSANE
35 Associate VP Student Affairs ....Vacant
100 Chief of Staff .... Dr. Don-Terry VEAL
49 Dean College of Liberal Arts ....Dr. Mbare NGOM
50 Dean School Business & Management ....Dr. Fikru BOGHOSSIAN
53 Dean School of Education ....Dr. Glenda PRIME
54 Dean School of Engineering .... Dr. Oscar BARTON
58 Dean of the Graduate School ....Dr. Mark GARRISON
48 Dean School of Architecture ....Dr. Mary Anne AKERS
70 Dean School of Social Work .... Dr. Anna MCPHATTER
69 Dean School of Community Health .... Dr. Kim SYDNOR
37 Director of Financial Aid .... Ms. Tanya WILKERSON
38 Director of Counseling Services ....Vacant
08 Director of Library .... Dr. Richard BRADBERRY
06 Director of Records/Registration ....Ms. Keisha CAMPBELL
07 Interim Director of Admissions ....Ms. Keisha CAMPBELL

36 Director of Placement .... Ms. Seana COULTER
15 Int Assoc Vice Pres Human Resources .... Mrs. Nicole CREDLE
29 Director Alumni Association ....Mrs. Joyce BROWN
14 Director Computer Center .... Mr. Gilbert MORGAN
86 Director Government Relations ...... Mrs. Joan CARTER-CONWAY
09 Director of Institutional Research ....Ms. Cheryl ROLLINS
18 Director Physical Plant .... Mr. Robert RIESNER
26 Asst Vice Pres Public Relations ....Mr. Larry JONES
84 Director Enrollment Management ....Vacant
96 Director of Procurement .... Mr. David LACHINA
28 Asst VP for Diversity/EEO/Title IX .... Ms. Tara BERRIEN
45 Asst Vice Pres Planning/Inst Effect .... Dr. Linda MEHLINGER
104 Director Study Abroad ....Mrs. Marisa GRAY
106 Director Online Education/E-learnin ....Ms. Cynthia BROWN-LAVEIST
108 Asst VP Institutional Assessment ....Dr. Solomon ALAO
19 Chief of Police ....Mr. Lance HATCHER
39 Director Residence Life & Housing ....Dr. Douglas GWYNN
41 Athletic Director ....Dr. Edward SCOTT
43 General Counsel ....Ms. Julie GOODWIN

Mount St. Mary's University (B)

16300 Old Emmitsburg Road, Emmitsburg MD 21727-7799

County: Frederick | FICE Identification: 002086
Unit ID: 163462
Telephone: (301) 447-6122 | Carnegie Class: Masters/M
FAX Number: (301) 447-5634 | Calendar System: Semester
URL: msmary.edu
Established: 1808 | Annual Undergrad Tuition & Fees: $43,650
Enrollment: 2,560 | Coed
Affiliation or Control: Roman Catholic | IRS Status: 501(c)3
Highest Offering: Master's
Accreditation: M, CAEPN, CEA, IACBE, THEOL

01 President ....Dr. Timothy E. TRAINOR
05 Provost .... Dr. Boyd CREASMAN
03 Vice President/Rector .... Msgr. Andrew R. BAKER
100 Chief of Staff ....Vacant
10 Vice Pres for Business & Finance ....Mr. William E. DAVIES
26 VP Marketing and Communications .... Mr. Jack J. CHIELLI
32 Vice President for Student Life ....Dr. Bernard FRANKLIN
28 Vice President for Equity & Success ....Dr. Paula M. WHETSEL-RIBEAU
84 Vice President of Enrollment Mgmt .... Mr. Jack J. CHIELLI
111 Vice President for Advancement .... Mr. Robert J. BRENNAN
11 Vice President University Affairs . Ms. Pauline A. ENGLESTATTER
20 Assoc Provost ....Dr. David M. MCCARTHY
58 Assoc Provost Grad/Continuing Ed ....Dr. Jennifer L. STAIGER
49 Dean College of Liberal Arts ....Dr. Peter A. DORSEY
50 Dean Richard J Bolte Sr Sch of Bus .....Dr. Michael J. DRISCOLL
81 Dean School Natural Science & Math ....Dr. Kraig E. SHEETZ
53 Dean of the Education Division .... Dr. Barbara A. MARINAK
04 Sr Exec Assistant to the President ....Ms. June B. MILLER
41 Director of Athletics .... Ms. Lynne P. ROBINSON
35 Dean of Students ....Mr. Levi ESSES
42 Chaplain/Dir of Campus Ministry ....Fr. Martin O. MORAN
36 Director Career Center ....Ms. Claire M. TAURIELLO
108 Director Institutional Assessment ....Dr. Jeffrey SIMMONS
37 Director of Financial Aid ....Ms. Brenda K. DAYHOFF
06 Registrar ....Mr. Christopher WEBER
07 Director of Admissions ....Mr. Eric M. DANIELSON
08 Director of the Library ....Ms. Jessica J. WHITMORE
27 Director of PR & Communications ....Ms. Donna J. KLINGER
105 Assoc Director Web Services .... Mr. Joseph F. PACIELLA
30 Director of Development ....Ms. Kimberly T. JOHNSON
29 Director of Alumni Engagement ....Ms. Emily A. MYERS
112 Major Gifts Officer ....Mr. Kevin J. KALIS
88 Director of University Operations .... Ms. Maureen PLANT
15 Director of Human Resources .... Ms. Kristin M. HURLEY
38 Director Student Counseling .... Mr. Gerald T. ROOTH
19 Director of Public Safety ....Mr. Rodney F. GRAYS
24 Director of Media Systems ....Mr. John B. BREWER, JR.
21 Controller .... Ms. Christine SNEERINGER
114 Director of Budget ....Ms. Tina RYDER
39 Assoc Director of Residence Life ....Ms. Jamie C. BROWN
88 Director Office of Social Justice ....Mr. Ian C. VANANDEN
92 Director of the Honors Program .... Dr. Sarah SCOTT
18 Director of Physical Plant ....Ms. Kimberly S. KLABE
96 Purchasing Agent ....Ms. Maria L. TOPPER
40 Manager of College Store .... Ms. Margaret A. PEREGORD

Ner Israel Rabbinical College (C)

400 Mount Wilson Lane, Baltimore MD 21208-1198

County: Baltimore | FICE Identification: 002087
Unit ID: 163532
Telephone: (410) 484-7200 | Carnegie Class: Spec-4-yr-Faith
FAX Number: (410) 484-3060 | Calendar System: Semester
URL: www.nirc.edu
Established: 1933 | Annual Undergrad Tuition & Fees: $12,400
Enrollment: 471 | Male
Affiliation or Control: Independent Non-Profit | IRS Status: 501(c)3
Highest Offering: Doctorate
Accreditation: RABN

01 President ....Rabbi Boruch Y. NEUBERGER
05 Chief Academic Officer .... Rabbi Aharon FELDMAN
88 Executive Director .... Mr. Jerome H. KADDEN
07 Director of Admissions ....Rabbi Beryl WEISBORD
11 Director of Administrative Services ....Mr. Larry RIBAKOW
06 Registrar ....Rabbi Chaim D. LAPIDUS
06 Registrar ....Rabbi Joseph IFRAH
85 Foreign Student Advisor .... Rabbi Eliyahu HAKKAKIAN
30 Director of Development ....Rabbi Louis HOFFMAN
45 Director of Planning .... Rabbi Leonard OBERSTEIN
37 Director Student Financial Aid ....Rabbi Shmuel SCHACHTER
18 Chief Physical Plant .... Mr. David FRIEDMAN
08 Head Librarian .... Rabbi Avrohom SHNIDMAN
39 Director of Student Housing ....Rabbi Emanuel GOLDFEIZ
29 Associate Director Alumni Relations ....Rabbi Eli GREENGART

Notre Dame of Maryland University (D)

4701 N Charles Street, Baltimore MD 21210-2404

County: Independent City | FICE Identification: 002065
Unit ID: 163578
Telephone: (410) 435-0100 | Carnegie Class: Masters/L
FAX Number: (410) 532-5791 | Calendar System: Semester
URL: www.ndm.edu
Established: 1873 | Annual Undergrad Tuition & Fees: $39,675
Enrollment: 2,233 | Female
Affiliation or Control: Roman Catholic | IRS Status: 501(c)3
Highest Offering: Doctorate
Accreditation: M, ACBSP, CAEPN, CEA, NURSE, PHAR

01 President .... Dr. Marylou YAM
05 Vice President Academic Affairs .... Dr. Sharon SLEAR
111 Vice Pres Institutional Advancement ....Ms. Kelley KILDUFF
84 Vice Pres Enrollment Management ....Mr. Scott BRIELL
10 Vice Pres for Finance & Admin ....Mr. Sean DELANEY
32 Assoc Vice President Student Life ....Dr. Brandy GARLIC
20 Associate VP Academic Affairs ....Dr. Suzan HARKNESS
37 Director of Financial Aid ....Mr. Christopher HANLON
100 Chief of Staff .... Mr. Gregory FITZGERALD
06 Registrar ....Ms. Susanna PRICE
36 Director Career Center ....Mr. Alan JONES
13 Director Information Technology ....Mr. Warren SZELISTOWSKI
29 Director of Alumnae Relations ....Ms. Alexandra DEJOHN
08 Librarian ....Ms. Barbara PREECE
49 Assoc Dean School Arts/Sciences/Bus ....Dr. Jennifer ERDMAN
07 Interim Director of Admissions ....Ms. Marci LEADBETER
09 Dir Inst Research/Effectiveness ....Ms. Luz CACEDA
15 Director of Human Resources ....Ms. Theresa SHRADER
18 Director of Facility Management ....Vacant
21 Controller .... Ms. Victoria WASHINGTON
38 Director Counseling Center ....Ms. Amy PROVAN
19 Director of Public Safety ....Mr. Gene TAYLOR
40 Bookstore Manager ....Vacant
41 Athletic Director ....Ms. Ashley HODGES
42 Director Mission & Campus Ministry .... Ms. Julia CAMPAGNA
67 Dean School of Pharmacy ....Dr. Anne LIN
07 Director Pharmacy Admissions ....Mr. Larry SHATTUCK
25 Chief Contracts/Grants Admin ....Mr. Carroll GALVIN
26 Sr Dir University Communications ....Ms. Damita MCDONALD

Prince George's Community College (E)

301 Largo Road, Largo MD 20774-2199

County: Prince Georges | FICE Identification: 002089
Unit ID: 163657
Telephone: (301) 546-7422 | Carnegie Class: Assoc/MT-VT-High Trad
FAX Number: N/A | Calendar System: Semester
URL: www.pgcc.edu
Established: 1958 | Annual Undergrad Tuition & Fees (In-District): $6,026
Enrollment: 11,357 | Coed
Affiliation or Control: Local | IRS Status: 501(c)3
Highest Offering: Associate Degree
Accreditation: M, ADNUR, CAHIIM, COARC, EMT, MAC, NMT, RAD, SURGT

01 President .... Dr. Falecia D. WILLIAMS
05 Exec Vice Pres and Provost for TLSS ....Dr. Clayton A. RAILEY
32 Interim Vice Pres Student Affairs ....Cathryn L. CAMP
10 Vice Pres Admin/Financial Svcs ....Terri K. BACOTE-CHARLES
13 Vice Pres Enterprise Technology .... Dr. Rhonda SPELLS
26 AVP of Strategy/Planning/Effect ....Vacant
103 AVP Workforce Development/Cont Educ ..Dr. Yvette J. SNOWDEN
15 AVP Human Resources (HROD) .... Dr. Lynne I. ADAMS
20 Assistant VP Curr/Programs and Regs ....Aundrea WHEELER
88 AVP Administrative Support ....Dr. Mara R. DOSS
121 Dean Student Success/Engagement ....Dr. Scheherazade W. FORMAN
76 Dean Health Sci/Business/Public Svc .... Angela D. ANDERSON
79 Dean Humanities/English/Social Sci .... Nicole A. CURRIER
84 Dean of Student Enrollment Services ....Vacant
54 Interim Dean Science/Tech/Engr .... Calvin E. STANSBURY
81 Interim Associate Dean STEM ....Regina R. BENTLEY
78 Dean of Adult & Community Education .... Barbara DENMAN
88 Associate Dean of HES .... Mirian TORAIN
23 Associate Dean Health and Wellness .... Natalie WEBB
09 Exec Dir Research/Assessment/Effect ....Dr. Laura ARIOVICH
88 Executive Director Adjunct Fac Dev .... Dr. Beverly REED
86 Senior Director of Compliance ....Susan V. WATSON
88 Associate Dean Health/PSCE ....Laura R. ELLSWORTH
27 Senior Director Comm/Marketing .... Angie D. CREWS
19 Acting Chief of Police/DPS .... Dr. Meloyde R. BATTEN-MICKENS
88 Controller Admin and Financial Svcs ....Dwight WASHINGTON
12 Program Director Laurel College Ctr .... Nancy GRINBERG
55 Director of Adult Education ....Sara MCDONOUGH
109 Director of Auxiliary Services .... LaNiece TYREE
88 Interim Director Prof and Org Dev .... Dr. Audrey DAVIS

12 Program Director UTC ... Dr. Rosa SMITH
88 Director Entrepreneurial Dev ... June EVANS
88 Director HR Compensation/Benefits ... Dr. Keith E. MURVIN
18 Executive Director of Facilities ... Vacant
111 Executive Director Inst Advancement ... Brenda MITCHELL
14 Executive Director ERP Applications ... William ANDERSON
21 Director Admin/Financial Support ... Toni E. HILL
96 Director of Procurement ... Beth V. KIRK
08 Director Library/Learning Resources ... Priscilla C. THOMPSON
117 Director Emergency Management ... Dr. Meloyde R. BATTEN-MICKENS
88 Program Director Const/Energy/Trans ... Marra ANTHONY
88 Director Facilities Operations ... Clarence V. BRYANT
88 Director College/Career Transition ... Cecilia KNOX
36 Dir of Student Acad/Career Adv ... Crystal M. SMITH
37 Director Student Financial Aid ... Thelma ROSS
88 Program Director Disability Support ... Thomas MAYS
41 Director Intercollegiate Athl/Intr ... JoAnn TODARO
88 Program Director Student Engagement ... Paulett MCINTOSH
93 Director Student Support and Trio ... Dr. Roosevelt CHARLES
07 Director Recruitment/Admissions ... Ronald D. WEIST
06 Registrar ... Rachel A. POLETO
88 Principal Director Nat Cyberwatch ... Michael W. SMITH
119 Director Network Infrastructure/Adm ... Manuel A. ARRINGTON
88 Senior Director Tech Client Support .. Paulette R. FOXX-DAWODU
88 Director of ERP Solution Services ... Doris M. HARRIS
88 Director of Testing Center ... William GARDNER
28 Director Governance and Diversity ... Andristine M. ROBINSON
25 Director Grants/Resource Dev ... Anne SHEPARD
04 Exec Associate to the President ... Greta R. MARTIN
30 Assistant Director of Development ... Dena L. WILSON

St. John's College (A)

60 College Avenue, Annapolis MD 21401

County: Anne Arundel FICE Identification: 002092
Unit ID: 163976
Telephone: (410) 263-2371 Carnegie Class: Bac-A&S
FAX Number: (410) 626-2886 Calendar System: Semester
URL: www.sjc.edu
Established: 1784 Annual Undergrad Tuition & Fees: $35,935
Enrollment: 446 Coed
Affiliation or Control: Independent Non-Profit IRS Status: 501(c)3
Highest Offering: Master's
Accreditation: M

01 President ... Vacant
05 Dean of College ... Mr. Joseph MACFARLAND
30 VP Development/Alumni Relations ... Ms. Kelly BROWN
84 Vice President of Enrollment ... Mr. Benjamin BAUM
58 Assoc Dean for Graduate Program ... Ms. Emily LANGSTON
10 Treasurer/Financial Officer ... Ms. Ally GONTANG-HIGHFIELD
06 Registrar ... Mr. Mason DAVENPORT
102 Director Corporate/Foundation Rels ... Ms. Susan BORDEN
37 Director of Financial Aid ... Mr. Steven BELL
08 Library Director ... Ms. Catherine DIXON
15 Director of Human Resources ... Ms. Lynn HOBBS
18 Director of Buildings and Grounds ... Mr. J.R PAPPAS
19 Director of Public Safety ... Mr. Robert MUECK
23 Director of Student Health ... Ms. Nancy CALABRESE
26 Director of Communications ... Ms. Carol CARPENTER
32 Director of Student Services ... Ms. Taylor WATERS
36 Director of Career Services ... Ms. Jaime DUNN
21 Controller ... Ms. Sarah MACDONALD
29 Director of Alumni Relations ... Mr. Chris AAMOT
20 Assistant to the Dean ... Ms. Heather LATHAM
04 Executive Asst to President ... Ms. Amy WEBB
40 Bookstore Manager ... Mr. Robin DUNN
41 Athletic Director ... Mr. Christopher KRUEGER

† See Affiliate: St. John's College at Santa Fe, NM.

St. Mary's College of Maryland (B)

47645 College Drive, Saint Mary's City MD 20686-3001

County: Saint Mary's FICE Identification: 002095
Unit ID: 163912
Telephone: (240) 895-2000 Carnegie Class: Bac-A&S
FAX Number: (240) 895-4462 Calendar System: Semester
URL: www.smcm.edu
Established: 1840 Annual Undergrad Tuition & Fees (In-State): $15,124
Enrollment: 1,508 Coed
Affiliation or Control: State IRS Status: 501(c)3
Highest Offering: Master's
Accreditation: M

01 President ... Dr. Tuajuanda C. JORDAN
05 Interim VP for Academic Affairs ... Dr. Jeffrey J. BYRD
05 Interim Dean of Faculty ... Dr. Katherine L. GANTZ
10 VP Business & Finance ... Mr. Paul A. PUSECKER
111 VP for Institutional Advancement ... Ms. Carolyn S. CURRY
84 VP Enrollment Management ... Mr. David L. HAUTANEN, JR.
32 VP for Student Affairs ... Dr. Jerri D. HOWLAND
21 Asst Vice President for Finance ... Mr. Christopher J. TRUE
101 Exec Assistant to President ... Ms. Betsy BARRETO
28 Interim Chief Diversity Officer ... Mr. Kelsey R. BUSH
22 Asst VP of Equity and Inclusion ... Mr. Michael K. DUNN
88 Director of Equity Programming ... Dr. Jose R. BALLESTEROS
26 Asst VP of Marketing/Communication . Mr. Michael L. BRUCKLER
29 Director Alumni Relations ... Mr. David M. SUSHINSKY
06 Registrar ... Mr. Nickolas B. TULLEY
37 Director of Financial Aid ... Mr. Rob W. MADDOX
88 Director Enrollment Operations ... Ms. Bhargavi BANDI

07 Director of Admission ... Ms. Sara S. RAMIREZ
38 Dir of the Wellness Center ... Ms. Laurie L. SCHERER
41 Director of Athletics/Recreation ... Ms. Crystal L. GIBSON
20 Assoc Dean of Curriculum ... Dr. Christine A. WOOLEY
18 Director of Physical Plant ... Mr. Bradley D. NEWKIRK
19 Director of Public Safety ... Ms. Tressa A. SETLAK
40 Director of the Campus Store ... Mr. Richard T. WAGNER
15 Asst VP of Human Resources ... Ms. Shannon K. JARBOE
23 Director of Health Services ... Vacant
124 Assoc Dean Retention/Stdnt Success ... Ms. Joanne A. GOLDWATER
13 Asst VP of Information Technology ... Ms. Jenell SARGENT
44 Sr Devel Ofcr Annual Giving ... Mr. Richard J. EDGAR
08 Interim Dir of Library/Media Svcs ... Ms. Katherine H. RYNER
102 Dir Corporate/Foundation Relations ... Ms. Lauren K. SAMPSON
21 Comptroller/Director of Accounting ... Mr. Gabriel A. MBOMEH
43 Assistant Attorney General ... Ms. Allison J. BOYLE
16 Assoc Dir Human Resources ... Mr. Melvin A. MCCLINTOCK
25 Director of Sponsored Research ... Dr. Sabine DILLINGHAM
109 Procurement Ofcr/Dir of Auxiliary ... Mr. Patrick G. HUNT
92 Director DeSousa Brent Scholars Pgm ... Dr. Frederico J. TALLEY
88 Director Events and Conferences ... Ms. Peggy R. AUD
30 Asst VP Development ... Ms. Karen C. RALEY
104 Director of International Education ... Ms. Aurora MARGARITA-GOLDKAMP
36 Dir of Career Development ... Vacant
04 Executive Asst to President ... Ms. Jennifer L. SIVAK
91 Director Administrative Computing ... Vacant
39 Exec Dir of Student Life ... Mr. Derek M. YOUNG
09 Director of Institutional Research ... Dr. Anne Marie BRADY
105 Director Web Services ... Ms. Jeannette L. MODIC
108 Coordinator of Assessment ... Dr. Katy E. ARNETT

Saint Mary's Seminary and University (C)

5400 Roland Avenue, Baltimore MD 21210-1994

County: Baltimore City FICE Identification: 002096
Unit ID: 163842
Telephone: (410) 864-4000 Carnegie Class: Not Classified
FAX Number: (410) 864-4278 Calendar System: Semester
URL: www.stmarys.edu
Established: 1791 Annual Undergrad Tuition & Fees: N/A
Enrollment: N/A Coed
Affiliation or Control: Roman Catholic IRS Status: 501(c)3
Highest Offering: First Professional Degree
Accreditation: M, THEOL

01 President/Rector ... Rev. Phillip J. BROWN
10 Vice President for Finance ... Ms. Victoria V. SEMANIE
111 Vice Pres Advancement/Human Res ... Mrs. Elizabeth L. VISCONAGE
05 Dean School Theology ... Rev. Gladstone STEVENS
73 Dean St Mary's Ecumenical Institute ... Dr. D. Brent LAYTHAM
73 Dean Ecclesiastical Fac/Sch Theol ... Rev. Thomas BURKE
06 University Registrar ... Ms. Paula M. THIGPEN
113 Ecumenical Inst Billing Officer ... Ms. Marcia HANCOCK
08 Director of Knott Library ... Mr. Thomas RASZEWSKI
13 Director Information Services ... Mr. Arryn MILNE
84 Director of Recruitment ... Ms. Kaye GUIDUGLI

The SANS Technology Institute (D)

11200 Rockville Pike, Suite 200,
North Bethesda MD 20852

County: Montgomery Identification: 667006
Telephone: (301) 654-7267 Carnegie Class: Not Classified
FAX Number: (301) 951-0140 Calendar System: Other
URL: www.sans.org
Established: 2006 Annual Graduate Tuition & Fees: N/A
Enrollment: N/A Coed
Affiliation or Control: Proprietary IRS Status: Proprietary
Highest Offering: Master's; No Undergraduates
Accreditation: M

01 President ... Mr. Alan PALLER
03 Executive Director ... Mr. Eric PATTERSON

Stevenson University (E)

1525 Greenspring Valley Road,
Stevenson MD 21153-0641

County: Baltimore FICE Identification: 002107
Unit ID: 164173
Telephone: (410) 486-7000 Carnegie Class: Masters/L
FAX Number: (410) 486-3552 Calendar System: Semester
URL: www.stevenson.edu
Established: 1947 Annual Undergrad Tuition & Fees: $37,868
Enrollment: 3,492 Coed
Affiliation or Control: Independent Non-Profit IRS Status: 501(c)3
Highest Offering: Doctorate
Accreditation: M, CSHSE, IACBE, MT, NURSE

01 President ... Dr. Elliot HIRSHMAN
04 Assistant to President ... Ms. Lauree WOODRING
05 Exec VP Academic Affairs/Provost ... Dr. Susan T. GORMAN
10 Vice Pres Administration & Finance ... Ms. Melanie EDMONDSON
111 Vice Pres University Advancement ... Mr. Chris VAUGHAN
84 Vice Pres Enrollment Management ... Mr. Mark J. HERGAN
32 Vice President Student Affairs ... Ms. Tiffany SANCHEZ
26 VP Marketing/Digital Communications ... Mr. John BUETTNER

15 Vice Pres for Human Resources ... Mr. Dave JORDAN
100 Vice President & Chief of Staff ... Ms. Sue B. KENNEY
36 Vice President Career Services ... Ms. Sue B. GORDON
81 Dean Sch of Sciences/Int Dean SOHNP ... Dr. Meredith DURMOWICZ
53 Dean School of Education ... Dr. Christine MORAN
106 Dean Stevenson Univ Online ... Dr. Lee K. KRAHENBUHL
79 Dean Sch of Humanities/Social Sci ... Dr. Cheryl WILSON
88 Dean School of Design ... Ms. Amanda HOSTALKA
13 Interim CIO ... Ms. P.B GARRETT
23 Assoc Dean/Dir of Wellness Center ... Ms. Linda REYMANN
66 Associate Dean GPS Nursing ... Dr. Judith FEUSTLE
18 Asst VP Facilities & Campus Svcs ... Mr. Leland R. BEITEL
37 Director Financial Aid ... Ms. Melanie MASON
35 Assoc VP/Dean of Students ... Dr. Jeffrey M. KELLY
09 Dir Inst Research/Assessment ... Vacant
08 Int Director of Library Services ... Ms. Sara GODBEE
06 Registrar ... Ms. Tracy L. BOLT
19 Director of Security ... Mr. Steve GOSSAGE
41 Director Athletics ... Mr. Brett C. ADAMS
109 Director Auxiliary Services ... Mr. Robert REED
29 Director Alumni Relations ... Ms. Allison HUMPHRIES
22 Dir of Disability Services ... Ms. Mary FORTHUBER

Stratford University Baltimore Campus (F)

210 S. Central Avenue, Baltimore MD 21202

Telephone: (410) 762-4031 Identification: 770616
Accreditation: ACICS, ACFEI

† Branch campus of Stratford University, Falls Church, VA

*The University System of Maryland Office (G)

701 E. Pratt St., Baltimore MD 21202

County: Independent City FICE Identification: 007959
Unit ID: 164146
Telephone: (301) 445-2740 Carnegie Class: N/A
FAX Number: (301) 445-1931
URL: www.usmd.edu

01 Chancellor ... Dr. Jay A. PERMAN
05 Sr VC Academic Affairs ... Dr. Joann BOUGHMAN
10 Vice Chanc Admin & Finance ... Ms. Ellen HERBST
111 VC Advancement & CEO USM Foundation ... Mr. Leonard R. RALEY
86 VC Governmental Relations ... Mr. Patrick N. HOGAN
26 VC for Communications ... Mr. Timothy J. MCDONOUGH
20 Assoc Vice Chanc Academic Affairs ... Dr. Antoinette COLEMAN
13 Assistant VC for IT & Interim CIO ... Mr. Michael EISMEIER
100 Chief of Staff to Chancellor ... Ms. Denise WILKERSON
116 Director Internal Audit ... Mr. David MOSCA
114 Director Budget Analysis ... Ms. Monica WEST

*University of Maryland College Park (H)

1101 Miller Administration Building,
College Park MD 20742

County: Prince Georges FICE Identification: 002103
Unit ID: 163286
Telephone: (301) 405-1000 Carnegie Class: DU-Highest
FAX Number: (301) 314-9560 Calendar System: Semester
URL: www.umd.edu
Established: 1856 Annual Undergrad Tuition & Fees (In-State): $10,779
Enrollment: 40,709 Coed
Affiliation or Control: State IRS Status: 501(c)3
Highest Offering: Doctorate
Accreditation: M, AAQEP, AUD, CEA, CLPSY, COPSY, DANCE, DIETD, DIETI, IPSY, JOUR, LIB, LSAR, MFCD, MUS, PCSAS, PH, PLNG, SCPSY, SP, SPAA

02 President ... Dr. Darryll J. PINES
05 Senior Vice President & Provost ... Dr. Jennifer K. RICE
100 Asst to President & Chief of Staff ... Ms. Michele A. EASTMAN
11 Vice President & Chief Admin Ofcr ... Mr. Carlo COLELLA
32 Vice President for Student Affairs ... Dr. Patty PERILLO
111 Vice President University Relations ... Mr. Brodie REMINGTON
46 Vice President for Research ... Dr. Laurie LOCASCIO
13 Vice President and CIO ... Dr. Jeffrey K. HOLLINGSWORTH
10 VP & Chief Financial Officer ... Mr. Greg OLER
43 Vice President and General Counsel ... Mr. Michael R. POTERALA
28 Vice Pres for Diversity & Inclusion ... Dr. Georgina DODGE
26 VP Marketing & Communications ... Mr. Brian ULLMANN
47 Dean Col Agriculture/Natl Resources ... Dr. Craig BEYROUTY
48 Dean School of Architecture ... Dr. Dawn JOURDAN
79 Dean College Arts & Humanities ... Dr. Bonnie T. DILL
83 Dean Col Behavioral/Social Sciences ... Dr. Gregory F. BALL
50 Dean Smith School of Business ... Dr. Prabhudev KONANA
81 Dean Col of Comp/Math/Natural Sci ... Dr. Amitabh VARSHNEY
53 Acting Dean College of Education ... Dr. Laura STAPLETON
54 Int Dean Clark Sch of Engineering ... Mr. Robert BRIBER
69 Dean School of Public Health ... Dr. Boris D. LUSHNIAK
60 Dean Merrill College of Journalism ... Ms. Lucy A. DALGLISH
62 Dean College of Information Studies ... Dr. Keith MARZULLO
80 Dean School of Public Policy ... Dr. Robert C. ORR
20 Dean Undergraduate Studies ... Dr. William A. COHEN
58 Dean Graduate School ... Dr. Steve FETTER
08 Dean of the Libraries ... Dr. Adriene LIM
20 SVP Innovation & Entrepreneurship ... Dr. Dean CHANG
85 Assoc VP International Affairs ... Dr. Ross D. LEWIN
20 AVP Acad Affairs/Finance Personnel ... Mr. Dylan BAKER

09 Asst VP Inst Research & Planning ....Ms. Sharon A. LA VOY
84 Assoc VP Enrollment Management .... Ms. Barbara A. GILL
20 Assoc Provost Faculty Affairs ....Dr. John BERTOT
108 Assoc Provost Acad Planning & Pgms ....Dr. Elizabeth J. BEISE
20 Assoc Provost Planning/Special Proj ....Mr. David CRONRATH
20 Assoc Prov Enterprise Resource Plng ....Dr. Jack BLANCHARD
20 Exec Dir Teach/Learn Transform Ctr .... Mr. Marcio OLIVEIRA
07 Exec Dir Undergraduate Admissions ....Ms. Shannon GUNDY
06 University Registrar ....Dr. Adrian R. CORNELIUS
92 Executive Director Honors College ....Dr. Peter MALLIOS
37 Director Student Financial Aid .... Mr. Dawit LEMMA
104 Dir Intl Student & Scholar Services ....Ms. Susan-Ellis DOUGHERTY
18 Assoc VP & Chief Facilities Officer ....Mr. Charles R. REUNING
96 Asst VP Procurement Str Sourcing ....Ms. Kimberly WATSON
15 Int Asst VP Human Resources .... Ms. Rythee LAMBERT-JONES
88 Asst VP for Real Estate ....Mr. Edward MAGINNIS, JR.
88 Asst VP Administration Finance ....Ms. Anne MARTENS
19 Dir Pub Safety/Chief Campus Police .... Mr. David B. MITCHELL
117 Exec Dir Env Safety/Sustain/Risk ....Ms. Maureen KOTLAS
21 Controller ....Ms. Lillian NASH
113 Bursar/Assoc Comptroller ....Ms. Alisa ABADINSKY
35 Asst VP for Student Affairs ....Dr. Mary HUMMEL
35 Asst VP for Student Affairs .... Dr. Warren KELLEY
35 Asst VP for Student Affairs ....Mr. Terry ZACKER
35 Asst VP for Student Affairs ....Dr. Brooke SUPPLE
36 Director University Career Center ....Mr. Kelley BISHOP
109 Director Stamp Student Union ....Dr. Marsha A. GUENZLER-STEVENS
23 Director University Health Center . Dr. Spyridon MARINOPOULOS
38 Director Counseling Center ....Dr. Chetan JOSHI
122 Director Fraternity Sorority Life ....Dr. Matthew SUPPLE
39 Director Resident Life ....Ms. Valronica SCALES
30 AVP University Development ....Mr. Jim HARRIS
112 Asst VP University Relations ....Vacant
110 Asst VP University Relations .... Ms. Bernadette MALDONADO
29 Exec Director Alumni Association ....Ms. Amy EICHHORST
88 Assoc VP for Research ....Ms. Denise CLARK
88 Assoc VP Research Development ....Mr. Eric CHAPMAN
103 AVP Innovation/Econ Development ....Ms. Julie LENZER
25 Director Research Administration ....Ms. Wendy MONTGOMERY
14 Asst VP Chief Technology Officer ....Ms. Tripti SINHA
14 Asst VP Academic Tech & Innovation ......Dr. Marcio A. OLIVEIRA
91 Exec Dir Enterprise Engineering ....Mr. Axel PERSAUD
119 Director Chief IT Security Officer ....Mr. Gerry SNEERINGER
90 Director Enterprise Planning ....Mr. Joseph DRASIN
86 Exec Director Government Relations ....Mr. Ross STERN
41 Director Intercollegiate Athletics ....Mr. Damon EVANS

*University of Maryland, Baltimore (A)

220 Arch Street, 14th Floor, Baltimore MD 21201-1508
County: Independent City FICE Identification: 002104
Unit ID: 163259
Telephone: (410) 706-7002 Carnegie Class: Spec-4-yr-Med
FAX Number: (410) 706-0500 Calendar System: Semester
URL: www.umaryland.edu
Established: 1807 Annual Undergrad Tuition & Fees (In-State): N/A
Enrollment: 7,137 Coed
Affiliation or Control: State IRS Status: 501(c)3
Highest Offering: Doctorate
Accreditation: M, ANEST, ARCPA, CAMPEP, DENT, DH, DIETI, IPSY, LAW, MED, MT, NURSE, PA, PH, PHAR, PTA, RADDOS, SW

02 President ....Dr. Bruce E. JARRELL
05 Vice Dean & Vice Provost Grad Sch ....Dr. Flavius LILLY
17 Exec VP Medical Affairs/Dean ....Dr. E. Albert REECE
10 Chief Admin & Finance Officer/VP ....Ms. Dawn M. RHODES
25 VP/Chf Enterprise/Econ Dev Ofcr ....Mr. James L. HUGHES
13 VP/Chief Information Officer ....Dr. Peter J. MURRAY
46 VP of Research ....Dr. Laurie LOCASCIO
32 Vice Prov Academic/Student Affs ....Dr. Flavius LILLY
26 Sr VP External Relations ....Ms. Jennifer B. LITCHMAN
28 VP & Chief Diversity/Equity & Incl ....Dr. Diane FORBES BERTHOUND
30 Int Chief Philanthropy Officer/VP ....Mr. James L. HUGHES
86 Chief Govt Affairs Officer/AVP ....Mr. Kevin P. KELLY
43 Chief University Counsel ....Ms. Susan GILLETTE
19 Interim Police Chief ....Dep. Thomas A. LEONE
108 VP & Chief Accountability Officer ....Dr. Susan BUSKIRK
18 Assoc VP Facilities & Operations ....Mr. Terry MORSE
15 Int Assoc VP Human Resources ....Ms. Juliet DICKERSON
37 Assoc VP Student Financial Asst ....Ms. Patricia A. SCOTT
113 Assoc VP Budget & Finance ....Mr. Scott BITNER
27 Assoc VP Communications/Public Affs ....Ms. Laura A. KOZAK
14 Asst VP Information Technology ....Mr. Fred SMITH
09 Asst VP Inst Rsrch & Accountability .. Mr. Gregory C. SPENGLER
96 AVP Strategic Sourcing & Acquis ....Mr. John JENSEN
88 AVP Sponsored Projects Accounting .... Ms. Laura SCARANTINO
88 AVP ORD Marketing & Operations .... Ms. Linda KENDERDINE
88 AVP ORD Sponsored Programs Admin ......Mr. Dennis PAFFRATH
88 AVP ORD Technology Transfer ....Mr. Philip ROBILOTTO
88 AVP ORD Center for Clinical Trials ....Mr. Michael ROLLOR
88 AVP ORD Economic Development ....Ms. Jane SHAAB
102 Treasurer & Dir of Operations UMBF ....Ms. Pamela HECKLER
08 Exec Dir Health Sci/Human Svc Libr ....Ms. Mary J. TOOEY
90 Exec Dir Enterprise Applications ....Mr. Michael SMITH
31 Exec Dir Cmty Initiatives/Engage ....Ms. Ashley R. VALIS
06 Director Records & Registration ....Mr. Ryan HOLTZ
16 Director Benefits & Compensation ....Ms. Patricia HOFFMANN
22 Director EEO/Affirmative Action .... Ms. Sheila GREENWOOD-BLACKSHEAR
28 Director Diversity and Inclusion ....Ms. Mikhel A. KUSHNER

85 Director International Services .... Ms. Amy RAMIREZ
38 Director Counseling ....Ms. Emilia K. PETRILLO
41 Director Univ Recreation & Fitness ......Mr. William P. CROCKETT
23 Director Student Health Center .... Dr. James BARONAS
35 Director Student Services .... Ms. Cynthia E. RICE
39 Director of UM Housing ....Ms. Margaret SCHOTTO
21 Director of Financial Services ....Mr. Larry MILLER
105 Dir Web Dev Interactive Media ....Mr. Amir CHAMSAZ
58 Dean Graduate School ....Dr. Roger J. WARD
52 Dean School of Dentistry ....Dr. Mark A. REYNOLDS
61 Dean School of Law ....Mr. Donald TOBIN
63 Dean School of Medicine ....Dr. E. Albert REECE
66 Dean School of Nursing .... Dr. Jane M. KIRSCHLING
67 Dean School of Pharmacy ....Dr. Natalie D. EDDINGTON
58 Dean Graduate School ....Dr. Roger J. WARD
70 Dean School of Social Work ....Dr. Judy L. POSTMUS
04 Admin Assistant to the President .... Ms. Clara WOODLY

*University of Maryland Baltimore County (B)

1000 Hilltop Circle, Baltimore MD 21250-0001
County: Baltimore FICE Identification: 002105
Unit ID: 163268
Telephone: (410) 455-1000 Carnegie Class: DU-Higher
FAX Number: (410) 455-1210 Calendar System: 4/1/4
URL: www.umbc.edu
Established: 1966 Annual Undergrad Tuition & Fees (In-State): $9,420
Enrollment: 13,497 Coed
Affiliation or Control: State IRS Status: 501(c)3
Highest Offering: Doctorate
Accreditation: M, ABAI, CAEP, CLPSY, DANCE, DMS, EMT, IPSY, MUS, SW

02 President ....Dr. Freeman A. HRABOWSKI
05 Provost/Sr Vice Pres Academic Affs ....Dr. Philip ROUS
10 Vice Pres Finance/Administration .... Ms. Lynne SCHAEFER
32 Vice President Student Affairs .... Dr. Nancy YOUNG
111 Vice Pres Institutional Advancement ....Mr. Gregory SIMMONS
13 Vice Pres Information Technology .... Mr. Jack J. SUESS
46 Vice President of Research ....Dr. Karl V. STEINER
49 Dean Col of Arts/Humanities/Soc Sci ....Dr. Kimberly MOFFITT
81 Dean Col Natural/Math Sciences .... Dr. William LACOURSE
54 Dean College of Engr/Info Tech ....Dr. Keith BOWMAN
84 Asst Dean Graduate Enrollment Mgmt ....Ms. K. Jill BARR
20 Vice Provost/Dean Undergrad Educ ....Dr. Katharine COLE
107 Vice Provost Professional Studies .... Dr. Christopher STEELE
20 Vice Provost Academic Affairs ....Dr. Antonio R. MOREIRA
58 Dean/Vice Provost for Graduate Educ .... Dr. Janet RUTLEDGE
15 Vice Provost Faculty Affairs .... Dr. Patrice MCDERMOTT
84 Vice Provost Enrollment Management ..... Dr. Yvette MOZIE-ROSS
21 Assoc VP Financial Services .... Ms. Kathy DETTLOFF
26 Assistant to Pres/Assoc VP Mktg/PR ....Ms. Lisa G. AKCHIN
11 Assoc VP Administrative Services ....Ms. Terry COOK
16 Chief HR Officer/Assoc VP ....Ms. Valerie A. THOMAS
29 Director Alumni Relations .... Ms. Stanyell ODOM
88 Asst VP New Media/Instruction Tech ....Mr. John FRITZ
18 Asst VP Facilities Management ....Mr. Lenn CARON
04 Senior Advisor to the President .... Dr. Peter HENDERSON
96 Director of Procurement ....Dr. Elizabeth MOSS
92 Director Honors College ....Dr. Simon STACEY
41 Dir Athletics/Physical Educ/Rec ....Dr. Brian BARRIO
19 Chief of University Police ....Mr. Paul DILLON
36 Asst VP Career & Corp Partnership ....Ms. Caroline BAKER
23 Director Health Services ....Dr. Bruce HERMAN
37 Director Financial Aid ....Ms. Andrea CIPOLLA
25 Asst Director Sponsored Programs ....Mr. Stanley JACKSON
40 Director of the Bookstore ....Ms. Erin MCGONIGLE
85 Assoc Vice Prov International Educ ....Dr. David DIMARIA
08 Director Library ....Mr. Patrick DAWSON
06 Registrar ....Ms. Pamela HAWLEY
43 General Counsel ....Mr. David GLEASON
07 Asst Vice Prov Admiss/Orientation ....Mr. Dale BITTINGER
39 Director Residential Life ....Mr. John FOX
09 Director of Institutional Research ....Dr. Connie PIERSON
38 Director Student Counseling ....Dr. Bruce HERMAN
100 Chief of Staff President's Office ...... Ms. Candace DODSON-REED
108 Director Institutional Assessment .... Mr. Robert CARPENTER
22 Dir Affirm Action/Equal Opportunity ....Mr. Bobbie HOYE
28 Director of Diversity ....Ms. Lisa GRAY
30 Director of Development ....Mr. Mike BUCCINO
44 Director Annual Giving ....Mr. Carl FOWLKES
90 Director Academic Computing ....Mr. Damian DOYLE
91 Director Administrative Computing ....Mr. Joseph KIRBY
88 Dean Erickson Sch of Aging Studies .... Dr. Dana BRADLEY
102 Director Foundation Relations ....Mr. Bruce LYONS
104 Assoc Dir Education Abroad .... Ms. Caylie MIDDLETON

*University of Maryland Center for Environmental Science (C)

PO Box 775, Cambridge MD 21613
County: Dorchester Identification: 667159
Telephone: (410) 228-9250 Carnegie Class: Not Classified
FAX Number: (410) 228-3843 Calendar System: Semester
URL: www.umces.edu
Established: 1925 Annual Graduate Tuition & Fees: N/A
Enrollment: N/A Coed
Affiliation or Control: State IRS Status: 501(c)3
Highest Offering: Doctorate; No Undergraduates
Accreditation: M

02 President ....Dr. Peter GOODWIN

05 Vice Pres for Education ....Dr. Larry SANFORD
10 Vice President for Finance .... Ms. Lynn REHN

*University of Maryland Eastern Shore (D)

11868 Academic Oval, Princess Anne MD 21853-1299
County: Somerset FICE Identification: 002106
Unit ID: 163338
Telephone: (410) 651-2200 Carnegie Class: DU-Higher
FAX Number: (410) 651-6105 Calendar System: Semester
URL: www.umes.edu
Established: 1886 Annual Undergrad Tuition & Fees (In-State): $8,558
Enrollment: 2,646 Coed
Affiliation or Control: State IRS Status: 501(c)3
Highest Offering: Doctorate
Accreditation: M, AAFCS, #ARCPA, CACREP, CONST, DIETD, DIETI, PHAR, PTA

02 President ....Dr. Heidi M. ANDERSON
100 Chief of Staff .... Dr. Robert C. MOCK
05 Provost/VP Academic Affairs .... Dr. Nancy S. NIEMI
10 VP Administration and Finance ....Mr. Lester S. PRIMUS
84 Vice President Enrollment Mgmt ....Mr. Hans S. COOPER
111 VP Institutional Advancement .... Mr. David A. BALCOM
13 Chief Information Officer ....Mr. Jerry WALDRON
20 Vice Provost Academic Affairs ....Dr. Latasha WADE
114 Budget Director ....Ms. Beatrice V. WRIGHT
15 Director of Human Resources .... Ms. Gertrude J. HAIRSTON
35 Asst VP Student Affairs ....Vacant
29 Director Alumni Affairs .... Mr. James G. LUNNERMON, II
08 Interim Dean Library Services ....Ms. Sharon D. BROOKS
37 Interim Director Financial Aid ....Mr. Marcel E. JAGNE-SHAW
23 Director Student Health Services ....Ms. Sharone V. GRANT
96 Director Procurement ....Ms. Jacqueline M. COLLINS
07 Director of Admissions & Enrollment ....Mr. Alphonso GARRETT, JR.
06 Registrar ....Ms. Cheryl HOLDEN-DUFFY
12 Int Gen Mgr Richard A Henson Center ....Ms. Ciera E. NIMMONS
36 Director Career Services ....Dr. Theresa QUEENAN
09 Director Inst Research/Plng/Assess ......Dr. Stanley M. NYIRENDA
19 Interim Director Public Safety ....Mr. Mark TYLER
18 Interim Director Physical Plant . Ms. Jicola R. JOYNES-STURGIS
39 Interim Director Residence Life ....Ms. Shannon N. WARREN
41 Athletic Director ....Mr. Keith S. DAVIDSON
21 Comptroller ....Ms. Bonita E. BYRD
46 Director Sponsored Research ....Ms. Catherine BOLEK
124 Director Student Retention ....Ms. Kimberly CLARK-SHAW
88 Director Upward Bound ....Dr. Nicole L. GALE
35 Coord Student Activities ....Mr. Dewayne J. GILLIARD
88 Director Title III Program ....Dr. LaTashia H. SWAIN-GILLIARD
26 Director Public Relations ....Mr. William ROBINSON
30 Director Development ....Vacant
111 Director Advancement Services ....Ms. Chenita R. REDDICK
51 Coordinator Continuing Education ....Ms. Gretchen M. BOGGS
38 Coordinator Counseling Services ....Dr. Patricia E. TILGHMAN
58 Dean Graduate Studies & Research ....Dr. Lakeisha L. HARRIS
47 Dean School Agric/Natural Sciences ....Dr. Moses T. KAIRO
57 Dean Sch Educ/Soc Sci/The Arts .... Dr. Marshall STEVENSON
50 Dean School Business & Tech ....Dr. Derrek B. DUNN
67 Dean Sch Pharmacy/Health Prof ....Dr. Rondall E. ALLEN
28 Director of Diversity ....Mr. Jason A. CASARES
04 Exec Admin Asst to the President ....Ms. Crystal SANKAR
104 Int Director Center for Intl Educ ....Dr. Lombuso S. KHOZA
105 Webmaster ....Mr. Jeremy W. TOWNSEND
106 Int Dir Online Education/E-learning ....Ms. Catherine HANSENS-PASSERI
43 General Counsel ....Mr. Matthew A. TAYLOR
86 Director Government Relations ....Mr. Jim N. MATHIAS
90 Int Director Information Technology ....Mr. Joseph R. SMITH

*University of Maryland Global Campus (E)

3501 University Boulevard East, Adelphi MD 20783-7998
County: Prince Georges FICE Identification: 011644
Unit ID: 163204
Telephone: (301) 985-7000 Carnegie Class: Masters/L
FAX Number: N/A Calendar System: Semester
URL: www.umuc.edu
Established: 1947 Annual Undergrad Tuition & Fees (In-State): $7,560
Enrollment: 58,526 Coed
Affiliation or Control: State IRS Status: 501(c)3
Highest Offering: Doctorate
Accreditation: M, CAEPN, CAHIIM, IACBE, NURSE

02 President .... Dr. Gregory FOWLER
05 Sr Vice Pres/Chief Academic Officer ....Ms. Blakely POMIETTO
84 VP Enrollment Mgmt ....Mr. Brian CHRISTIE
26 Sr Vice President Communications ....Mr. Michael FREEDMAN
88 Sr VP Global Military Operations ....Mr. Lloyd MILES
45 Sr VP Institutional Effectiveness ....Vacant
100 Chief of Staff/Sr VP Strategy .... Mr. Nicholas EREMITA
88 Special Advisor to the President ...... Mr. George SHOENBERGER
10 Vice Pres Financial Operations .... Mr. Eugene D. LOCKETT, JR.
43 Vice President & General Counsel .... Ms. Sherri SAMPSON
15 Vice President Human Resources .... Ms. JulieAnn GARCIA
86 Vice Pres Govt Affs/Strat Prtnrshp .....Mr. Frank J. PRINCIPE, JR.
111 Vice Pres Inst Advancement ....Ms. Cathy SWEET
28 VP/Chief Diversity Ofcr/Ombudsman ....Dr. Blair HAYES
07 Vice Pres Admissions ....Ms. Jamie JAYNES
18 Associate Vice President Facilities .... Mr. George TRUJILLO

86 Director of State Govt Relations .... Ms. Erin FAVAZZA
37 AVP Student Financial Aid .... Ms. Cheryl STORIE
58 Vice Provost/Dean Graduate School .... Ms. Kathryn KLOSE
08 Assoc Provost of Library Services .... Mr. Stephen MILLER
06 Acting Registrar .... Mr. Kristophyre MCCALL
49 Actg VP/Dean Sch of Arts & Sciences .... Dr. Randy HANSEN
09 Sr Director Institutional Research .... Mr. Wei ZHOU
04 Exec Assistant to the President .... Ms. Lisa JACKSON
19 Director Security .... Mr. William BROGAN
29 Assoc VP Alumni Programs .... Ms. Nikki SANDOVAL

*Bowie State University (A)

14000 Jericho Park Road, Bowie MD 20715-3318

County: Prince Georges FICE Identification: 002062
Unit ID: 162007
Telephone: (301) 860-4000 Carnegie Class: Masters/L
FAX Number: (301) 860-3510 Calendar System: Semester
URL: www.bowiestate.edu
Established: 1865 Annual Undergrad Tuition & Fees (In-State): $8,444
Enrollment: 6,250 Coed
Affiliation or Control: State IRS Status: 501(c)3
Highest Offering: Doctorate
Accreditation: M, ACBSP, CACREP, CAEP, NUR, SPAA, SW

02 President .... Dr. Aminta BREAUX
05 Provost/Vice Pres Academic Affs .... Dr. Carl GOODMAN
10 VP Finance & Administration .... Mr. Anthony SAVIA
109 Assoc VP Auxiliary Services .... Mr. Wade HENLEY
21 Asst VP Finance & Administration .... Mr. Michael ATKINS
111 Vice Pres Institutional Advancement .... Mr. Brent SWINTON
32 VP Student Affairs/Campus Life .... Dr. Demetrius JOHNSON
35 Asst VP Student Affairs/Campus Life .... Vacant
43 Vice Pres & General Counsel .... Ms. Karen JOHNSON SHAHEED
13 VP Office of Information Technology .... Mr. Maurice A. TYLER
84 VP for Enrollment Management .... Dr. Brian CLEMMONS
88 Asst to Prov Institutional Effect .... Ms. Gayle M. FINK
06 University Registrar .... Ms. Shari CHRISTIE
08 Assoc Library Director/Interim Dean .... Ms. Marian RUCKER-SHAMU
36 Acting Director Career Services .... Ms. Rosetta PRICE
15 Sr Director of Human Resources .... Ms. Sheila HOBSON
19 Chief of Campus Police .... Mr. James W. BOOKER
58 Int Dean Sch of Grad Stds/Research .... Dr. Cosmos NWOKEAFOR
49 Dean College of Arts & Sciences .... Dr. George ACQUAAH
50 Dean College of Business .... Dr. Lawrence R. MCNEIL, JR.
53 Dean College of Education .... Dr. Rhonda JETER-TWILLEY
107 Dean College Professional Studies .... Dr. Cheryl H. BLACKMAN
92 Director UCE Honors Program .... Dr. Monika GROSS
23 Director University Wellness Center .... Dr. Rita WUTOH
41 Director Athletics .... Mr. Clyde DOUGHTY, JR.
26 Dir University Relations/ Marketing .... Ms. Cassandra M. ROBINSON
37 Director Financial Aid .... Ms. Deborah STANLEY
18 Director Facilities .... Mr. Darryl WILLIFORD
29 Director of Alumni Relations .... Ms. Carla HOPKINS
96 Director of Purchasing .... Mr. Steve A. JOST
09 Director of Institutional Research .... Ms. Shaunette GRANT
04 Administrative Asst to President .... Ms. Tanya P. JONES
108 Director Institutional Assessment .... Dr. Becky VERZINSKI
38 Director Student Counseling .... Dr. Tonya SWANSON
39 Asst Dir of Student Housing .... Ms. Tammy TIMBERS
44 Director Annual Giving .... Ms. Rosalind MUCHIRI
90 Director Academic Computing .... Dr. Fabio CHACON
100 Chief of Staff .... Mrs. Karen JOHNSON-SHAHEED
104 Director Study Abroad .... Mr. Patrick FRAZIER
105 Sr Graphic Designer .... Mr. Michael FLEISHMAN
86 Director Government Relations .... Mr. Derrick COLEY

*Coppin State University (B)

2500 W North Avenue, Baltimore MD 21216-3698

County: Baltimore City FICE Identification: 002068
Unit ID: 162283
Telephone: (410) 951-3000 Carnegie Class: Masters/S
FAX Number: (410) 333-5369 Calendar System: Semester
URL: www.coppin.edu
Established: 1900 Annual Undergrad Tuition & Fees (In-State): $6,716
Enrollment: 2,348 Coed
Affiliation or Control: State IRS Status: 501(c)3
Highest Offering: Doctorate
Accreditation: M, ACBSP, CACREP, CAEPN, CAHIIM, NURSE, SW

02 President .... Dr. Anthony L. JENKINS
05 Provost/VP Academic Affairs .... Dr. Leontye LEWIS
111 VP Institutional Advancement .... Mr. Joshua HUMBERT
10 VP Administration & Finance .... Mr. Steve DANIK
32 VP Student Affairs/Enrollment Mgmt .... Dr. Michael FREEMAN
13 VP Information Systems/CIO .... Dr. Ahmed EL-HAGGAN
45 Asst VP Planning/Assessment .... Mr. Michael BOWDEN
20 Asst VP Academic Operations .... Dr. Rolande MURRAY
18 Asst VP Facilities Management .... Mr. Roy THOMAS
15 Assoc VP of Human Resources .... Dr. Lisa EARLY
07 Director of Admissions .... Ms. Jinawa MCNEIL
06 Registrar .... Ms. Karen BARLAND
21 Controller .... Mrs. Crystal MOSLEY
08 Director of the Library .... Dr. Mary WANZA
37 Director of Financial Aid .... Mr. Marcus BYRD
36 Director of Career Services Center .... Vacant
19 Chief of Public Safety .... Mr. Dameon R. CARTER, SR.
39 Director of Housing/Residence Life .... Ms. Jacquelyn WONSEY
41 Director of Athletics .... Mr. Derek CARTER
112 Donor Relations & Stewardship Coord .... Ms. Deidre JOHNSON
96 Asst Vice President of Procurement .... Mr. Thomas E. DAWSON, JR.
26 Director of Communications .... Vacant
88 Director Client Computing Services .... Mr. Emmanuel OWUSU-SEKYERE
105 Senior Web Developer .... Ms. Melissa C. RIGBY
49 Interim Dean CASE .... Dr. Mary OWENS-SOUTHALL
92 Dean Honors College & McNair Pgms .... Ms. DeChelle FORBES
58 Dean Graduate School .... Dr. Mary E. OWENS-SOUTHHALL
66 Dean of Nursing .... Dr. Tracey L. MURRAY
83 Dean Col of Behavioral/Social Sci .... Dr. Beverly O'BRYANT
50 Interim Dean Col Of Business .... Dr. Sadie GREGORY
04 Executive Assistant to President .... Ms. Daphine M. THOMAS
09 Director of Institutional Research .... Mr. Beryl HARRIS
29 Director Alumni Engagement .... Ms. Kimberly NELSON
38 Director Student Counseling .... Ms. Michelle REYNOLDS
100 Chief of Staff .... Ms. Angela GALEANO
25 Chief Contract/Grants Administrator .... Dr. Dianna J. VASS
43 Legal Counsel & Govt Rels Officer .... Mr. Matthew FRALING, III
44 Annual Fund Manager .... Mr. Brandon BROWN

*Frostburg State University (C)

101 Braddock Road, Frostburg MD 21532-2303

County: Allegany FICE Identification: 002072
Unit ID: 162584
Telephone: (301) 687-4000 Carnegie Class: Masters/L
FAX Number: (301) 687-7070 Calendar System: Semester
URL: www.frostburg.edu
Established: 1898 Annual Undergrad Tuition & Fees (In-State): $9,410
Enrollment: 4,857 Coed
Affiliation or Control: State IRS Status: 501(c)3
Highest Offering: Doctorate
Accreditation: M, #ARCPA, CAATE, CAEPN, CAPRT, EXSC, MPCAC, NURSE, SW

02 President .... Dr. Ronald NOWACZYK
05 Interim Provost .... Dr. Michael MATHIAS
32 VP Student/Education Svcs .... Dr. Artie TRAVIS
10 Interim VP for Admin & Finance .... Mr. Troy DONOWAY
111 Vice Pres University Advancement .... Mr. John SHORT
15 Chief Human Resources Officer .... Ms. Lisa HERSCH
43 University Counsel .... Mr. Bradford NIXON
20 Associate Provost .... Vacant
35 Sr Assoc VP Student Affairs .... Dr. Jeff GRAHAM
26 Asst VP Marketing/Communications .... Mr. Gregg SEKSCIENSKI
114 Asst VP Budget & Planning .... Ms. Denise MURPHY
49 Dean Col Liberal Arts/Sciences .... Dr. Kim HIXSON
50 Dean College of Business .... Dr. Sudhir SINGH
53 Dean College of Education .... Dr. Boyce WILLIAMS
08 Director of the Library .... Ms. Lea MESSMAN-MANDICOTT
37 Director of Financial Aid .... Mrs. Angela L. HOVATTER
108 Interim Assistant VP Analytics .... Dr. Sara Beth BITTINGER
58 Interim Dir of Graduate Services .... Dr. Sara Beth BITTINGER
18 Interim Director Physical Plant .... Mr. John BREWER
36 Director Career & Prof Dev Ctr .... Ms. Amy SHIMKO
38 Director Counseling & Psych Svcs .... Vacant
40 Asst Mgr Bookstore & ID Services .... Mr. Kenneth EMERICK
41 Athletic Director .... Mr. Troy DELL
19 Chief University Police .... Col. Cynthia SMITH
13 Interim Chief Information Officer .... Mr. Timothy PELESKY
91 Director of Technology Services .... Vacant
29 Director of Alumni .... Ms. Shannon L. GRIBBLE
07 Director of Admissions .... Ms. Natalie WAGONER
28 Director of Diversity .... Ms. Robin WYNDER
44 Major Gifts Officer .... Vacant
14 Dir Networking/Telecommunications .... Mr. Gary TRENUM
96 Coord Procurement/Material Handling .... Mr. Alan R. SNYDER
23 Director Health Services .... Ms. Christina BURKE
39 Director Residence Life .... Ms. Kimberly HINDS-BRUSH
06 Registrar .... Dr. Jay HEGEMAN
90 Director Academic Computing .... Vacant
102 Dir Foundation/Corporate Relations .... Ms. Janelle MOFFETT
104 Director Study Abroad .... Ms. Victoria GEARHART
105 Director Web Services .... Mr. Wade BLUEBAUGH
30 Director of Development .... Ms. Lynn KETTERMAN
86 VP Regional Dev & Engagement .... Mr. Al DELIA
09 Interim Dir Institutional Research .... Ms. Selina SMITH
04 Exec Admin Asst III to Pres .... Mrs. Donnell VANSKIVER

*Salisbury University (D)

1101 Camden Avenue, Salisbury MD 21801-6860

County: Wicomico FICE Identification: 002091
Unit ID: 163851
Telephone: (410) 543-6000 Carnegie Class: Masters/L
FAX Number: (410) 548-2587 Calendar System: Semester
URL: www.salisbury.edu
Established: 1925 Annual Undergrad Tuition & Fees (In-State): $10,044
Enrollment: 8,124 Coed
Affiliation or Control: State IRS Status: 501(c)3
Highest Offering: Doctorate
Accreditation: M, CAATE, CAEPN, COARC, EXSC, MT, MUS, NURSE, PH, SW

02 President .... Dr. Charles A. WIGHT
05 Provost/SVP of Academic Affairs .... Dr. Karen L. OLMSTEAD
100 Chief of Staff .... Mr. Eli J. MODLIN
10 VP Admin and Finance .... Dr. Janet WORMACK
32 Vice Pres of Student Affairs .... Dr. Dane R. FOUST
111 Vice Pres Advancement/External Affs .... Mr. Jason E. CURTIN
84 Asst VP of Enrollment Management .... Vacant
22 Assoc VP Institutional Equity .... Mr. Humberto X. ARISTIZABAL
28 Assoc VP of Diversity & Inclusion .... Ms. Joan J. WILLIAMS
35 Associate VP of Student Affairs .. Dr. Wallace SOUTHERLAND, III
20 Asst Provost for Faculty Success .... Dr. Jessica CLARK
85 Asst Provost for International Ed .... Dr. Brian N. STIEGLER
20 Assoc Vice Pres Academic Affairs .... Dr. Melissa M. BOOG
18 Assoc VP Facilities & Cap Mgmt .... Mr. Eric J. BERKHEIMER
35 Asst VP Student Affs/Dean Students .... Ms. Valerie J. RANDALL-LEE
13 Chief Information Officer .... Mr. Ken F. KUNDELL
26 Director of Public Relations .... Mr. Jason F. RHODES
27 Director of Marketing Strategy .... Ms. Katie M. CURTIN
41 Director of Athletics .... Dr. Gerard R. DIBARTOLO
92 Dean of Honors Program .... Dr. Andrew P. MARTINO
06 Registrar .... Mr. Martin J. HUNTER
07 Director of Admissions .... Ms. Elizabeth A. SKOGLUND
09 Special Asst to Pres for UARA .... Dr. Kara M. OWENS
08 Dn of Libraries/Instruct Resources .... Dr. Beatriz B. HARDY
38 Acting Dir of Counseling Center .... Ms. Nikki DYER
36 Director of Career Services .... Dr. Kevin C. FALLON
37 Director of Financial Aid .... Mr. Mason M. WHITE
15 Assoc VP for HR .... Mr. Kevin A. VEDDER
29 Dir Alumni Relations & Gift Develop .... Mr. Jayme E. BLOCK
23 Director of Student Health Services .... Ms. Victoria A. LENTZ
35 Director Ct For Student Inv & Lead .... Ms. Tricia G. SMITH
86 Dir of Govt & Community Relations .... Mr. Eli J. MODLIN
43 General Counsel .... Ms. Karen A. TREBER
39 Director Housing/Residence Life .... Mr. David P. GUTOSKEY
19 Director of Public Safety .... Mr. Edwin L. LASHLEY
40 Director of Bookstore .... Ms. Lisa G. GRAY
18 Director of Physical Plant .... Mr. Kevin J. MANN
96 Director of Purchasing .... Mr. Jeff H. CANADA
81 Dean Henson Sch Science/Tech .... Dr. Michael S. SCOTT
50 Dean Perdue School of Business .... Dr. Christy H. WEER
49 Dean Fulton School of Liberal Arts .... Dr. Maarten L. PEREBOOM
53 Dean Seidel School of Education .... Dr. Laurie A. HENRY
76 Dean College of Health & Human Svcs .... Dr. Kelly A. FIALA
58 Dean Graduate Studies/Research .... Dr. Clifton P. GRIFFIN
88 Dir Ctr for Student Achievement .... Dr. Heather W. HOLMES
04 Asst to the President .... Ms. Tracy F. HAJIR

*Towson University (E)

8000 York Road, Baltimore MD 21252-0001

County: Baltimore FICE Identification: 002099
Unit ID: 164076
Telephone: (410) 704-2000 Carnegie Class: DU-Mod
FAX Number: N/A Calendar System: 4/1/4
URL: www.towson.edu
Established: 1866 Annual Undergrad Tuition & Fees (In-State): $10,198
Enrollment: 21,917 Coed
Affiliation or Control: State IRS Status: 501(c)3
Highest Offering: Doctorate
Accreditation: M, ARCPA, AUD, CAATE, CAEPN, DANCE, FEPAC, IPSY, MPCAC, MUS, NURSE, OT, SP, THEA

02 President .... Dr. Kim SCHATZEL
05 Provost/Exec VP Academic Affs .... Dr. Melanie PERREAULT
10 Vice Pres Administration & Finance ... Mr. Benjamin LOWENTHAL
111 Vice Pres University Advancement .... Mr. Brian J. DEFILIPPIS
46 VP Strategic Prtship/Applied Rsrch .... Dr. Daraius IRANI
26 Assoc VP Comm/Media Relations .... Mr. Sean WELSH
22 Asst VP of Inclusion & Equity .... Ms. Patricia BRADLEY
32 VP for Student Affairs .... Dr. Vernon HURTE
84 Assoc VP Enrollment Mgmt/Registrar .... Mr. Robert GIORDANI
30 Assoc Vice President Development .... Mr. Todd LANGENBERG
29 Assoc Vice Pres Alumni Relations .... Ms. Lori B. ARMSTRONG
13 Assoc Vice President/CIO .... Mr. Jeffrey SCHMIDT
18 Assoc VP Facilities Management .... Mr. Kevin PETERSEN
109 AVP Financial Affs/Auxiliary Svcs .... Mr. Robert CAMPBELL
15 Assoc Vice Pres Human Resources .... Mr. C. Stephen JONES
35 Assoc Vice Pres Student Affairs .... Dr. Anthony SKEVAKIS
35 Asst Vice President Campus Life .... Mr. Matthew LENNO
39 Asst VP Housing & Residence Life .... Ms. Kelly HOOVER
37 Director for Financial Aid .... Mr. David HORNE
25 Asst VP Sponsored Programs/Research .... Ms. Nancy DUFAU
07 Asst VP University Admissions .... Ms. Amy MOFFATT
19 Dir Public Safety/Chief of Police .... Chief Charles HERRING
53 Dean College of Education .... Dr. Laurie MULLEN
50 Dean College of Business/Economics .. Dr. Shohreh A. KAYNAMA
49 Dean College of Liberal Arts .... Dr. Chris CHULOS
81 Dean J&M Fisher Col of Science/Math .... Dr. David VANKO
57 Dean Col of Fine Arts/Comm .... Dr. Regina CARLOW
76 Dean College of Health Professions .... Dr. Lisa PLOWFIELD
58 Assoc Dean Graduate Studies .... Dr. Karen ESKOW
92 Rector Honors College .... Dr. Terry COONEY
43 VP of Legal Affairs/Gen Counsel .... Ms. Sara SLAFF
08 Dean of University Libraries .... Dr. Suzanna CONRAD
104 Director Study Abroad .... Ms. Liz SHEARER
94 Chair Women's & Gender Studies .Dr. Cindy H. GISSENDANNER
09 Director Institutional Research .... Mr. Tim BIBO, JR.
41 Director of Athletics .... Mr. Timothy LEONARD
23 Director of Health Services .... Mr. Yu-Ling SHAO
40 Director of University Store .... Ms. Stacy ELOFIR
96 Director of Procurement .... Ms. Sandi CLIFFORD
38 Clinical Director Counseling Center .... Dr. Maria WYDRA
36 Asst VP Career Center .... Ms. Lorie LOGAN-BENNETT
06 Assoc Director Records/Registration .... Ms. Sheena LYONS

*University of Baltimore (F)

1420 N Charles Street, Baltimore MD 21201-5779

County: Independent City FICE Identification: 002102
Unit ID: 161873
Telephone: (410) 837-4200 Carnegie Class: Masters/L
FAX Number: N/A Calendar System: Semester

URL: www.ubalt.edu
Established: 1925 Annual Undergrad Tuition & Fees (In-State): $9,096
Enrollment: 4,169 Coed
Affiliation or Control: State IRS Status: 501(c)3
Highest Offering: Doctorate
Accreditation: M, LAW, SPAA

02 President .... Mr. Kurt L. SCHMOKE
05 Interim Provost .... Ms. Catherine ANDERSEN
20 Associate Provost .... Dr. Candace CARACO
10 CFO/VP Administration & Finance .... Ms. Beth AMYOT
84 VP Enrollment Management .... Ms. Roxie SHABAZZ
111 Vice Pres Institutional Advancement .... Ms. Theresa SILANSKIS
86 VP Government & Public Affairs .... Ms. Anita HAREWOOD
18 VP Facil Mgmt/Campus Safety .... Mr. Neb SERTSU
13 Vice Pres Technology/CIO .... Mr. David BOBART
32 AssocVP Student Success & Services .... Ms. Nicole MARANO
31 Dir Office of Community Life .... Dr. Llatetra ESTERS
15 Assoc Vice Pres Human Resources .... Ms. Sally REED
09 Asst Vice Pres Institutional Rsrch .... Mr. Paul MONIODIS
28 Dir Diversity & Culture Center .... Vacant
08 Dean of Bogomolny Library .... Mr. Jeffrey HUTSON
19 Acting Captain UB Police .... Mr. Jason KUNZ
07 AVP Enrollment Services .... Mr. Mark JACQUE
96 Director of Procurement & Supply .... Ms. Joselyn JOHNSON
44 AVP Alumni & Donor Services .... Ms. Kate CRIMMINS
36 Director Career & Internship Center .... Ms. Lakeisha MATHEWS
06 Assistant Registrar .... Ms. Brenda DER
26 Manager Public Information .... Mr. Chris HART
80 Dean College of Public Affairs .... Dr. Roger HARTLEY
49 Dean College of Arts & Sci .... Dr. Christine SPENCER
61 Dean of the School of Law .... Dr. Ronald WEICH
50 Dean School of Business .... Mr. Murray DALZIEL
88 Dir Center for Education Access .... Dr. Karyn SCHULZ
21 AVP Admin & Finance .... Ms. Barbara AUGHENBAUGH
29 Director Alumni Relations .... Ms. Kelley CHASE
37 Executive Director Financial Aid .... Mr. Terry RICHARDS
25 Asst Provost Sponsored Research .... Ms. Margarita CARDONA

Washington Adventist University (A)

7600 Flower Avenue, Takoma Park MD 20912-7794
County: Montgomery FICE Identification: 002067
Unit ID: 162210
Telephone: (301) 891-4000 Carnegie Class: Masters/S
FAX Number: (301) 270-1618 Calendar System: Semester
URL: www.wau.edu
Established: 1904 Annual Undergrad Tuition & Fees: $25,200
Enrollment: 968 Coed
Affiliation or Control: Seventh-day Adventist IRS Status: 501(c)3
Highest Offering: Master's
Accreditation: M, MUS, NURSE, RAD

01 President .... Dr. Weymouth SPENCE
05 Provost .... Dr. Cheryl HARRIS KISUNZU
10 Exec Vice Pres Finance .... Mr. Patrick FARLEY
11 Chief of Operations & Compliance .... Ms. Janette NEUFVILLE
32 Vice Pres Student Life .... Dr. Ralph JOHNSON
84 VP Marketing & Enrollment .... Mr. William JACKSON
13 Director Information Technology .... Mr. Ricardo FLORES
15 Assoc VP of Human Resources .... Ms. Jeannie WRIGHT
58 Dean Sch Grad/Professional Studies .... Ms. Brenda CHASE
121 Dean of Student Success .... Vacant
06 Registrar .... Dr. Reginald GARCON
33 Dean of Men .... Mr. Tim NELSON
34 Dean of Women .... Ms. Renee PHILLIPS
08 Library Director .... Mr. Don ESSEX
30 Exec Dir Development/Alumni Rels .... Ms. Jennifer ALBURY
19 Director Safety & Security .... Mr. John CAKE
41 Athletic Director .... Mr. Patrick CRAREY, II
07 Director of Admissions/ Recruitment .... Ms. Wanda COLON-CANALES
26 VP for Communications .... Mr. Richard CASTILLO
78 Dir Coop Educ/Acad Support & Test .... Mr. Fitzroy THOMAS
18 Chief Facilities/Physical Plant .... Mr. Steve LAPHAM
37 Director Student Financial Aid ... Ms. Lana GREAVES-BENJAMIN
38 Campus Counseling .... Mr. Kean BAXTER
40 Manager the College Bookstore .... Mr. Lloyd YUTUC
85 Director of International Students .... Dr. Beulah MANUEL
04 Executive Asst to President .... Ms. Lydée BATTLE
09 Chief Institutional Research .... Ms. Janette NEUFVILLE

Washington College (B)

300 Washington Avenue, Chestertown MD 21620-1197
County: Kent FICE Identification: 002108
Unit ID: 164216
Telephone: (410) 778-2800 Carnegie Class: Bac-A&S
FAX Number: (410) 778-7850 Calendar System: Semester
URL: www.washcoll.edu
Established: 1782 Annual Undergrad Tuition & Fees: $48,214
Enrollment: 1,089 Coed
Affiliation or Control: Independent Non-Profit IRS Status: 501(c)3
Highest Offering: Master's
Accreditation: M

01 President .... Dr. Michael SOSULSKI
05 Provost/Dean of College .... Dr. Michael HARVEY
45 VP Planning & Policy/Chief of Staff .... Dr. Victor SENSENIG
10 Vice Pres Finance .... Dr. Teresa SMITH
111 Vice Pres College Advancement .... Ms. Susie CHASE
84 Vice Pres Enrollment Mgmt/Marketing .... Dr. Lorna HUNTER
32 VP Student Affairs/Dean of Students .... Dr. Sarah FEYERHERM
20 Asst Dn First Yr Exp/Stdnt Success .... Vacant
31 Director of Campus Special Events .... Ms. Gina RALSTON
41 Director of Athletics .... Mr. Thad MOORE
06 Registrar .... Ms. Rachelle MARKS
08 Director of Miller Library .... Ms. Mary Alice BALL
21 Controller .... Vacant
18 Associate VP for Facilities .... Mr. Vic COSTA
15 Director of Human Resources .... Ms. Carolyn BURTON
19 Director of Public Safety .... Ms. Pamela HOFFMAN
07 Director of Recruitment .... Mrs. Kelsey MILLER
37 Director of Financial Aid .... Ms. Jennifer GALLAGHER
39 Dir Res Life/Assoc Dean of Students .... Mr. Greg KRIKORIAN
23 Clinical Director Health Services .... Mrs. Lisa M. MARX
38 Director of Counseling Center .... Ms. Miranda ALTMAN
36 Director of Career Development .... Mrs. Nanette COOLEY
28 Asst Dean Stdnts/Dir Intercult Affs .... Ms. Carese BATES
40 Bookstore Manager .... Ms. Shannon WYBLE

Women's Institute of Torah Seminary (C)

6602 Park Heights Avenue, Baltimore MD 21215
County: Baltimore Identification: 667271
Telephone: (410) 358-3144 Carnegie Class: Not Classified
FAX Number: (866) 990-1983 Calendar System: Semester
URL: www.wits.edu
Established: 1998 Annual Undergrad Tuition & Fees: N/A
Enrollment: N/A Female
Affiliation or Control: Jewish IRS Status: 501(c)3
Highest Offering: Baccalaureate
Accreditation: AIJS

01 President .... Dr. Aviva WEISBORD
05 Academic Dean .... Dr. Leslie G. KLEIN

Wor-Wic Community College (D)

32000 Campus Drive, Salisbury MD 21804-1486
County: Wicomico FICE Identification: 020739
Unit ID: 164313
Telephone: (410) 334-2800 Carnegie Class: Assoc/HVT-High Trad
FAX Number: (410) 334-2951 Calendar System: Semester
URL: www.worwic.edu
Established: 1975 Annual Undergrad Tuition & Fees (In-District): $6,480
Enrollment: 2,705 Coed
Affiliation or Control: Local IRS Status: 501(c)3
Highest Offering: Associate Degree
Accreditation: M, ACFEI, EMT, OTA, #PTAA, RAD

01 President .... Dr. Murray K. HOY
05 Vice Pres Academic Affairs .... Dr. Kristin L. MALLORY
84 Vice Pres Enroll Mgmt & Student Svc .... Dr. Bryan NEWTON
10 Vice Pres Administrative Services .... Ms. Jennifer A. SANDT
26 Vice Pres Institutional Affairs .... Dr. Reenie MCCORMICK
51 Dean Continuing Education .... Ms. Ruth E. BAKER
97 Dean General Education .... Dr. Patricia L. RILEY
76 Dean Health Professions .... Dr. Karie SOLEMBRINO
88 Dean Occupational & Emerging Tech .... Mr. Paul SILBERQUIT
07 Director Admissions & Records .... Ms. Angie N. HAYDEN
13 Chief Information Officer .... Ms. Ruth F. GILL
36 Director Career & Testing Services .... Ms. Lori SMOOT
37 Director Financial Aid .... Ms. Katie ABREU
21 Director Finance .... Ms. Megan H. SMITH
15 Executive Director Human Resources .... Ms. Karen BERKHEIMER
121 Director of Student Success .... Mr. Aaron PREBENDA
27 Director Marketing .... Ms. Janet S. KENNINGTON
09 Director Inst Research .... Ms. Carol A. MENZEL
30 Director Development .... Ms. Jessica HALES
06 Registrar .... Ms. Amanda MESSATZZIA
32 Sr Director of Student Development .... Dr. Deirdra G. JOHNSON
07 Sr Director Enrollment Services .... Vacant
08 Director of Library Services .... Ms. Diana MILLS
18 Sr Director Facilities Management .... Mr. Gregory D. GREY
96 Director Purchasing & Auxiliary Svc .... Ms. Allison M. CANADA
105 Web Developer .... Mr. Joshua W. TOWNSEND
19 Director Public Safety .... Mr. Linnie VANN, JR.
108 Dir Inst Assessment & Effectiveness .... Dr. Julio BIRMAN
88 Director Early College Initiatives .... Mr. Richard C. WEBSTER
25 Director Grants .... Ms. Jo Ellen BYNUM

Yeshiva College of the Nation's Capital (E)

1216 Arcola Avenue, Silver Spring MD 20902-3408
County: Montgomery FICE Identification: 039373
Unit ID: 434937
Telephone: (301) 649-7077 Carnegie Class: Spec-4-yr-Faith
FAX Number: (301) 649-7053 Calendar System: Semester
URL: https://www.yeshiva.college/
Established: 1995 Annual Undergrad Tuition & Fees: $10,600
Enrollment: 31 Male
Affiliation or Control: Independent Non-Profit IRS Status: 501(c)3
Highest Offering: Second Talmudic Degree
Accreditation: RABN

01 President .... Rabbi Yitzchok MERKIN
05 Rosh Yeshiva .... Rabbi Aaron LOPIANSKY
37 Financial Aid Director .... Ms. Maryanna WALLS
11 Administrator .... Rabbi Yitzi LABELL

MASSACHUSETTS

American International College (F)

1000 State Street, Springfield MA 01109-3155
County: Hampden FICE Identification: 002114
Unit ID: 164447
Telephone: (413) 737-7000 Carnegie Class: Masters/L
FAX Number: (413) 205-3084 Calendar System: Semester
URL: www.aic.edu
Established: 1885 Annual Undergrad Tuition & Fees: $38,220
Enrollment: 2,612 Coed
Affiliation or Control: Independent Non-Profit IRS Status: 501(c)3
Highest Offering: Doctorate
Accreditation: EH, IACBE, NURSE, OT, PTA

01 President .... Dr. Vincent M. MANIACI
05 Exec Vice Pres Academic Affairs .... Dr. Velmer BURTON
11 COO/Chief of Staff .... Ms. Nicolle M. CESTERO
13 Chief Information Officer .... Ms. Mimi ROYSTON
35 VP Student Affairs/Dean of Students .... Mr. Matthew SCOTT
10 Vice President for Finance .... Mr. Christopher GARRITY
111 Exec Dir of Institutional Advance .... Ms. Jennifer MCDONOUGH
26 Int Dir Marketing & Communications .... Mr. Michael ERIQUEZZO
123 Director of Graduate Admissions .... Ms. Hannah HARTZSCH
07 Vice Pres of UG Admissions .... Mr. Kerry COLE
41 Athletic Director .... Ms. Jessica CHAPIN
76 Dean Health Sciences .... Dr. Karen ROUSSEAU
49 Dean Business/Arts/Sciences .... Dr. Susanne SWANKER
53 Dean of Education .... Vacant
109 Associate VP for Auxiliary Services .... Mr. Jeffrey BEDNARZ
06 Registrar .... Ms. Pamela ROBINSON
08 Director of Library .... Ms. Estelle H. SPENCER
38 Director Counseling Center .... Dr. Renee ROSADO
36 Dir of Career Services .... Mr. J. A. MARSHALL
66 Interim Dir of Division of Nursing .... Dr. Ellen FURMAN
50 Int Director of Business Programs .... Dr. Robyn POOLE
37 Director for Financial Aid .... Mr. Stephen PODESZWA
04 Exec Admin Asst to President .... Ms. Lani KRETSCHMAR
108 Dir of Institutional Effectiveness .... Dr. Kristy HUNTLEY

Amherst College (G)

PO Box 5000, Amherst MA 01002-5000
County: Hampshire FICE Identification: 002115
Unit ID: 164465
Telephone: (413) 542-2000 Carnegie Class: Bac-A&S
FAX Number: (413) 542-2621 Calendar System: Semester
URL: www.amherst.edu
Established: 1821 Annual Undergrad Tuition & Fees: $60,890
Enrollment: 1,745 Coed
Affiliation or Control: Independent Non-Profit IRS Status: 501(c)3
Highest Offering: Baccalaureate
Accreditation: EH

01 President .... Dr. Carolyn (Biddy) A. MARTIN
05 Provost/Dean of the Faculty .... Dr. Catherine A. EPSTEIN
10 Chief Financial/Admin Officer .... Mr. Kevin C. WEINMAN
32 Chief Student Affairs Officer .... Vacant
18 Chief of Campus Operations .... Mr. James D. BRASSORD
07 Dean Admission/Financial Aid .... Dr. Matthew MCGANN
111 Chief Advancement Officer .... Ms. Betsy CANNON SMITH
43 Chief Policy Ofcr/General Counsel .... Ms. Lisa H. RUTHERFORD
28 Chief Diversity Officer .... Vacant
13 Chief Information Officer .... Mr. David L. HAMILTON
100 Chief of Staff/Sec of the Board .... Ms. Bett K. SCHUMACHTER
26 Chief Communications Officer .... Ms. Sandy GENELIUS
20 Associate Dean of the Faculty .... Dr. John CHENEY
20 Associate Dean of the Faculty .... Dr. Austin D. SARAT
37 Dean of Financial Aid .... Ms. Gail W. HOLT
09 Director of Institutional Research .... Mr. Jesse D. BARBA
21 Controller .... Mr. Stephen M. NIGRO
06 Registrar .... Vacant
08 Director of the Library .... Mr. Martin L. GARNAR
23 Director of Student Health Services .... Dr. Emily M. JONES
15 Director of Human Resources .... Vacant
38 Director of Counseling Center .... Dr. Jacqueline ALVAREZ
41 Director of Athletics .... Mr. Donald R. FAULSTICK
36 Director of the Career Center .... Ms. Emily GRIFFEN
109 Director of Dining Services .... Mr. Joseph T. FLUECKIGER
19 Chief of Campus Police .... Mr. John B. CARTER

Anna Maria College (H)

50 Sunset Lane, Paxton MA 01612-1198
County: Worcester FICE Identification: 002117
Unit ID: 164492
Telephone: (508) 849-3333 Carnegie Class: Masters/M
FAX Number: (508) 849-3311 Calendar System: Semester
URL: www.annamaria.edu
Established: 1946 Annual Undergrad Tuition & Fees: $39,470
Enrollment: 1,492 Coed
Affiliation or Control: Roman Catholic IRS Status: 501(c)3
Highest Offering: Beyond Master's But Less Than Doctorate
Accreditation: EH, EMT, MUS, NUR, SW

01 President .... Ms. Mary Lou RETELLE
05 VP for Academic Affairs .... Dr. Christine L. HOLMES
10 Vice President/Chief Financial Ofcr .... Mr. Alex MOWATT
11 Exec VP/Chief Operations Officer .... Mr. Michael MIERS
32 VP for Student Affairs .... Mr. Andrew O. KLEIN

84 Vice Pres for Enrollment ... Mr. John HAMEL
31 VP for External Relations/CCO ... Mr. Hugh DRUMMOND
09 Asst VP Institutional Research ... Ms. Irene IRUDAYAM
35 Assoc VP for Student Affairs ... Ms. Jessica ECKSTROM
111 Exec Director Advancement ... Ms. Bridget LEUNG-ROGALA
26 Director Marketing/Communications ... Ms. Maureen HALLEY
06 Registrar ... Mr. William PURNELL
88 Director of the Learning Center ... Mr. Dennis VANASSE
23 Director of Health Services ... Ms. Sherri GRANDE-DIREDA
08 Director of Library Services ... Mr. Wilfredo RIVERA-SCOTTI
29 Director of Alumni Engagement ... Ms. Patricia SCHAFFER
36 Director Career Counsel/Placement ... Ms. Brooke BRIGHAM
37 Director Financial Aid ... Mr. Emir MORAIS
13 Chief Information Officer ... Mr. Michael MIERS
04 Executive Asst to the President ... Ms. Kay FLICK
18 Director Physical Plant ... Mr. Matthew SIMPSON
41 Athletic Director ... Mr. Joseph BRADY
42 Director Campus Ministry ... Ms. Melissa LANEVE
15 Director of Human Resources ... Ms. Joellen ANDREWS
88 Dean of Mission Effectiveness ... Sr. Rollande QUINTAL
51 Director Grad/Continuing Educ ... Mr. Paul VACCARO
19 Director Security/Safety ... Vacant
102 Corporate & Foundation Rels Ofcr ... Mr. Richard RICARDI
28 Dir of Diversity/Equity/Inclusion ... Mr. Sherman COWAN
39 Director of Residence Life ... Ms. Marissa CARPINETTI

Assumption University (A)

500 Salisbury Street, Worcester MA 01609-1296
County: Worcester FICE Identification: 002118
Unit ID: 164562
Telephone: (508) 767-7000 Carnegie Class: Masters/M
FAX Number: (508) 767-7169 Calendar System: Semester
URL: www.assumption.edu
Established: 1904 Annual Undergrad Tuition & Fees: $43,978
Enrollment: 2,448 Coed
Affiliation or Control: Roman Catholic IRS Status: 501(c)3
Highest Offering: Beyond Master's But Less Than Doctorate
Accreditation: EH, CACREP, MPCAC

01 President ... Dr. Francesco C. CESAREO
10 VP for Finance and Administration ... Mr. Peter D. WELLS
05 Provost/Academic Vice Pres ... Dr. Gregory WEINER
32 Vice President for Student Affairs ... Dr. Deborah CADY MELZER
121 Vice President for Student Success ... Dr. Conway C. CAMPBELL
111 Vice Pres Institutional Advancement ... Vacant
42 Vice President Mission ... Rev. Richard E. LAMOUREUX, AA
84 Vice Pres for Enrollment Management ... Vacant
43 General Counsel ... Dr. Michael H. RUBINO
58 Dean School of Graduate Studies ... Dr. Kimberly A. SCHANDEL
50 Dean School of Business ... Mr. Joseph FOLEY
66 Dean School of Nursing ... Ms. Caitlin M. STOVER
49 Dean Col of Liberal Arts & Sciences . Ms. Paula A. FITZPATRICK
107 Dir of Professional Studies ... Vacant
76 Dean School of Health Professions ... Vacant
07 Dir of Admission/Recruitment ... Ms. Shannell CARTAGENA
20 Assoc VP Academic Affairs/Grant Dev ... Dr. Eloise KNOWLTON
20 Asst VP of Academic Affairs ... Dr. Jennifer K. MORRISON
13 Chief Information Technology Office ... Mr. Wayne ROBIN
42 Director of Campus Ministry ... Mr. Paul F. COVINO
38 Director of Counseling Services ... Vacant
08 Director of Library Services ... Ms. Robin MADDALENA
10 Director of Finance ... Ms. Cathleen R. CULLEN
09 Director Inst Research and Ac Asst ... Mr. Stuart J. MUNRO
06 Registrar ... Ms. Heather PECORARO
15 Director of Human Resources ... Ms. Robin PELLEGRINO
26 Executive Director of Communication . Mr. Michael K. GUILFOYLE
88 Assistant VP for Student Success ... Ms. Mary BRESNAHAN
30 Asst VP Development/Alumni ... Ms. Linda ROSENLUND
110 Asst VP for Leadership Giving ... Ms. Melanie DEMARAIS
44 Director of Assumption Fund ... Mr. Timothy R. MARTIN
121 Director of Academic Support Center ... Dr. Allen A. BRUEHL
35 Assoc Dean of Students ... Mr. Joseph ZITO
41 Director of Athletics ... Ms. Christine LOWTHERT
19 Director of Public Safety ... Mr. Steven B. CARL
23 Director of Health Services ... Ms. Sarah K. SHERWOOD
24 Director of Media Services ... Mr. Ted HALEY
37 Director of Financial Aid ... Ms. Monica M. BLONDIN
21 Director of Business Services ... Mr. Todd DERDERIAN
86 Exec Asst for Govt/Cmty Relations ... Mr. Daniel F. DITULLIO
36 Director of Career Services ... Ms. Shannon CURTIS
04 Exec Admin Asst to President ... Ms. Sharon A. MAHONEY
39 Director of Residential Life ... Mr. Benjamin A. KADAMUS

Babson College (B)

231 Forest Street, Babson Park MA 02457-0310
County: Norfolk FICE Identification: 002121
Unit ID: 164580
Telephone: (781) 235-1200 Carnegie Class: Spec-4-yr-Bus
FAX Number: (781) 239-5231 Calendar System: Semester
URL: www.babson.edu
Established: 1919 Annual Undergrad Tuition & Fees: $54,144
Enrollment: 3,340 Coed
Affiliation or Control: Independent Non-Profit IRS Status: 501(c)3
Highest Offering: Master's
Accreditation: EH

01 President ... Dr. Stephen SPINELLI
05 VP AA/Dean of the College ... Dr. Kenichi MATSUNO
111 Senior VP for Advancement ... Mr. Edward CHIU
10 Chief Administrative Officer ... Ms. Katherine CRAVEN
11 Chief Operating Officer ... Ms. Kelly LYNCH
26 VP/Chief Marketing Officer ... Mr. Kerry SALERNO
15 VP Human Resources ... Ms. Donna BONAPARTE
84 VP Enrollment Management ... Ms. Courtney MINDEN
43 VP and General Counsel ... Mr. Michael D. LAYISH
32 VP Learner Success/Dean of Campus ... Dr. Lawrence P. WARD
12 CEO Babson Global ... Mr. David ABDOW
04 Exec Assistant to the President ... Ms. Leila LAMOUREUX
12 CEO Babson Executive Education ... Ms. Karen HEBERT-MACCARO
13 VP & Chief Information Officer ... Mr. Phillip KNUTEL
31 VP Programming/Community Outreach ... Ms. Jane EDMONDS
28 Chief Diversity & Inclusion Officer ... Dr. Sadie BURTON-GOSS
18 AVP Facilities Mgmt & Construction ... Ms. Tricia LYONS
36 Dir Center for Career Development ... Ms. Cheri PAULSON
06 Registrar ... Ms. Linda KEAN
37 Dir Student Financial Aid ... Ms. Meredith A. STOVER
94 Exec Dir Ctr for Wms Entrep Ldrshp ... Dr. Susan DUFFY
19 ExDir Campus Safety/Chief of Police ... Ms. Erin CARCIA
41 Director of Athletics ... Mr. Michael LYNCH

Bard College at Simon's Rock (C)

84 Alford Road, Great Barrington MA 01230-9702
Telephone: (413) 644-4400 FICE Identification: 009645
Accreditation: &M

Bay Path University (D)

588 Longmeadow Street, Longmeadow MA 01106-2292
County: Hampden FICE Identification: 002122
Unit ID: 164632
Telephone: (413) 565-1000 Carnegie Class: Masters/L
FAX Number: (413) 565-1105 Calendar System: Semester
URL: www.baypath.edu
Established: 1897 Annual Undergrad Tuition & Fees: $35,781
Enrollment: 3,224 Female
Affiliation or Control: Independent Non-Profit IRS Status: 501(c)3
Highest Offering: Doctorate
Accreditation: EH, ARCPA, NURSE, OT

01 President ... Ms. Sandra J. DORAN
05 Int VP Academic Affairs/Provost ... Dr. Stacy SWEENEY
10 VP Finance/Administrative Services ... Mr. Michael GIAMPIETRO
111 VP Development/Planned Giving ... Ms. Allison GEARING-KALILL
26 VP Univ Relations & Board Liaison ... Ms. Kathleen BOURQUE
45 Chief Strategy Officer Springfield ... Ms. Caron T. HOBIN
07 Vice Prov Admissions/Mktg/Analytics ... Vacant
04 Assistant to the President ... Vacant
88 Deputy Chief Ops Effectiveness/TAWC ... Ms. Amanda GOULD
21 Controller ... Mr. John O'ROURKE
25 Asst Dean Research/Acad Resource ... Mr. Peter TESTORI
12 Director of the Concord Campus ... Ms. Karen CARLSON
27 Director of Univ Communications ... Ms. Kathleen WROBLEWSKI
37 Exec Dir of Student Financial Svcs ... Ms. Stephanie KING
36 Exec Dir Career & Life Planning ... Ms. Laureen CIRILLO
08 Director of the Library ... Vacant
06 Registrar ... Mr. Marshall BRADWAY
44 Associate Director of Annual Giving ... Ms. Amanda GENO
23 Director of Health Services ... Ms. Deborah BAKER
15 Asst VP & Dir of Human Resources ... Ms. Kathleen HALPIN-ROBBINS
18 Dir Facilities/Campus Services ... Mr. Paul E. STANTON
13 Exec Dir Information Technology ... Mr. Douglas SLAVAS
14 Director of IT Infrastructure ... Mr. Christopher KNERR
41 Director of Athletics ... Mr. Steven J. SMITH
88 Executive Director Brand Strategy ... Ms. Karen WOODS
32 Dean of Students ... Vacant
94 Deputy Chief Learning Officer ... Ms. Maura DEVLIN
88 Dir Business Programs TAWC ... Ms. Piccus MEGAN
88 Dir MBA Entrepr Thnkg/Innov Practic ... Mr. Mo SATTAR
88 Dir Grad Pgms Nonprofit Mgmt/Philan ... Ms. Sylvia DE HAAS PHILLIPS
49 Vice Provost/Dean Liberal Studies ... Ms. Kristine BARNETT
96 Exec Dir of Purchasing/Office Svcs ... Mr. Ted LETH-STEENSEN
102 Dir Foundation/Corporate Relations ... Ms. Janine MCVAY
53 Dean School Educ/Human/Hlth Sci ... Dr. Elizabeth FLEMING
81 Dean School of Science & Management ... Dr. Thomas LOPER
76 Dir Occupational Therapy Program ... Dr. Beverly ST. PIERRE
123 Dean Graduate Admissions ... Ms. Sheryl KOSAKOWSKI
57 Director MFA Program ... Ms. Leanna JAMES BLACKWELL
88 Director ABA Program ... Dr. Susan AINSLEIGH
88 Director PA Program ... Ms. Theresa RIETHLE
77 Dir Computer Sci & Cyber Security ... Mr. Matthew SMITH
88 Dir Higher Education Administration ... Ms. Lauren WAY
88 Dir Finance & Accounting Program ... Ms. Kara STEVENS
88 Program Director Genetic Counseling ... Ms. Janice BELINER
88 Program Director Healthcare Mgmt ... Ms. Theresa DEVITO
88 Director MS Leadership/Negotiation ... Mr. Joshua WEISS
88 Dir Ctr Excellence Women in Science ... Ms. Gina SEMPREBON
83 Director Graduate Psychology Pgm ... Mr. Mark BENANDER
88 Director MS Applied Data Science ... Ms. Ning JIA
88 Director Neuroscience Program ... Vacant
09 Director of Institutional Research ... Ms. Ashley MURACZEWSKI
39 Dir Resident Life/Student Housing ... Ms. Lindsie LAVIN

Bay State College (E)

31 St. James Avenue, Boston MA 02116-2975
County: Suffolk FICE Identification: 003965
Unit ID: 164641
Telephone: (617) 217-9000 Carnegie Class: Bac-Diverse
FAX Number: (617) 249-0400 Calendar System: Semester
URL: www.baystate.edu
Established: 1946 Annual Undergrad Tuition & Fees: $29,200
Enrollment: 691 Coed
Affiliation or Control: Proprietary IRS Status: Proprietary
Highest Offering: Baccalaureate
Accreditation: EH, ADNUR, NURSE, PTAA

01 President ... Dr. Steven COMBS
05 Dean of Col/Chief Academic Officer ... Dr. Jeff MASON
32 Dean of Students ... Jeremy SHEPARD
10 Chief Financial Officer ... Kevin DERRIVAN
07 Dean of Admissions ... Justin SCHWARZ
09 Director of Institutional Research ... Dr. Jerome DEAN
06 Registrar ... Shannon GOO
08 Librarian ... Sherry COWAN
113 Student Account Admin/Bursar ... Vacant
36 Director Career Services ... Linh NGUYEN
38 Director Student Counseling ... Vacant
15 Director Human Resources ... Ethel DANIEL
13 Chief Info Technology Officer ... Jeffrey MYERS

Benjamin Franklin Institute of Technology (F)

41 Berkeley Street, Boston MA 02116-6296
County: Suffolk FICE Identification: 002151
Unit ID: 165884
Telephone: (617) 588-1368 Carnegie Class: Spec-4-yr-Other Tech
FAX Number: (617) 482-3706 Calendar System: Semester
URL: www.bfit.edu
Established: 1908 Annual Undergrad Tuition & Fees: $17,550
Enrollment: 463 Coed
Affiliation or Control: Independent Non-Profit IRS Status: 501(c)3
Highest Offering: Baccalaureate
Accreditation: EH, OPD

01 Chief Executive Officer ... Aisha FRANCIS
125 President Emeritus ... Anthony BENOIT
05 Dean of Academic Affairs ... Marvin LOISEAU
10 Dean of Finance/Operations & CFO ... Kevin HEPNER
32 Dean of Students/Title IX Coord ... Jackie CORNOG
06 Registrar ... James KLASEN
08 Librarian ... Sharon B. BONK
07 Assoc Dean Admissions/Recruitment ... Calvin CONYERS
111 Chief Advancement Officer ... Angela JOHNSON
121 Director of Student Success ... Shawn AYALA
09 Director of Institutional Research ... James KLASEN
15 Director Human Resources ... Diane DANIELS
19 Director of Facilities ... Myftar MYRTAJ
36 Director of Career Services ... Emily LEOPOLD
37 Director Financial Aid ... Shani WILKERSON
04 Administrative Asst to President ... Vacant
13 Dean of Information Technology ... Larson ROGERS

Bentley University (G)

175 Forest Street, Waltham MA 02452-4705
County: Middlesex FICE Identification: 002124
Unit ID: 164739
Telephone: (781) 891-2000 Carnegie Class: Masters/L
FAX Number: (781) 891-2569 Calendar System: Semester
URL: www.bentley.edu
Established: 1917 Annual Undergrad Tuition & Fees: $53,790
Enrollment: 5,177 Coed
Affiliation or Control: Independent Non-Profit IRS Status: 501(c)3
Highest Offering: Doctorate
Accreditation: EH

01 President ... Dr. E. LaBrent CHRITE
43 VP General Counsel/Sec to Corp ... Ms. Judith MALONE
05 Provost/VP Academic Affairs ... Dr. Donna Maria BLANCERO
10 VP and Chief Financial Officer ... Ms. Maureen FORRESTER
111 VP University Advancement ... Ms. Maureen E. FLORES
32 VP Student Affairs ... Dr. J. Andrew SHEPARDSON
84 VP Enrollment Management ... Ms. Carolina FIGUEROA
49 Dean of Arts and Sciences ... Dr. Eric OCHES
50 Dean of Business/Grad School ... Dr. William READ
20 Associate Provost ... Dr. Patrick SCHOLTEN
26 VP Marketing & Communications ... Mr. Christopher J. JOYCE
20 Assoc Provost Undergrad Education ... Ms. Catherina CARLSON
121 Director Grad Acad Advising ... Ms. Colleen K. MURPHY
15 VP of Human Resources & CHRO ... Mr. George CANGIANO
21 Associate VP Finance & Operations ... Ms. Nancy ANTUNES
06 Registrar ... Ms. Kathy POSEY
88 Ombudsperson ... Ms. Eliane MARKOFF
38 Director of Counseling Center ... Dr. Peter FORKNER
09 Director of Business Intelligence ... Ms. Kelly GIARDULLO
39 Assoc Dean Student Affairs/Res Ctr ... Mr. John PIGA
08 Director of Library ... Ms. Hope HOUSTON
90 Director Academic Tech Center ... Mr. Gaurav SHAH
25 Director of Sponsored Programs ... Ms. Susan RICHMAN
124 Assoc VP Enrollment Management ... Ms. Donna KENDALL
28 Chief Diversity & Inclusion Officer ... Ms. Katherine LAMPLEY
123 AVP Enrollment/Dir Grad Admissions ... Ms. Jennifer FLAGEL
18 Exec Director Facilities Management ... Mr. Thomas KANE
35 Dir of Student Pgm & Engagement ... Ms. Nicole CHABOT-WIEFERICH
04 Exec Asst to President ... Ms. Susan HAYES
104 Director of International Education ... Ms. Natalie SCHLEGEL

Berklee College of Music (H)

1140 Boylston Street, Boston MA 02215-3693
County: Suffolk FICE Identification: 002126
Unit ID: 164748
Telephone: (617) 266-1400 Carnegie Class: Spec-4-yr-Arts

FAX Number: (617) 247-5878 Calendar System: Semester
URL: www.berklee.edu
Established: 1945 Annual Undergrad Tuition & Fees: $45,660
Enrollment: 6,631 Coed
Affiliation or Control: Independent Non-Profit IRS Status: 501(c)3
Highest Offering: Master's
Accreditation: EH

01 President Erica MUHL
100 Chief of Staff Melissa HOWE
12 SVP/Exec Dir Boston Conservatory Cathy YOUNG
05 Sr VP Academic Affairs/Provost Lawrence J. SIMPSON
32 Sr VP Student Enrollment/Engagement Betsy NEWMAN
106 Sr VP Online Learning/Continuing Ed Deborah CAVALIER
84 VP Enrollment Marketing/Management Mike KING
111 Sr VP Institutional Advancement Cindy ALBERT LINK
10 SVP Fin/Admin/Chief Financial Ofcr Richard M. HISEY
45 Sr VP Innovation/Strategy Panos A. PANAY
13 VP Technology Resources David GREGORY
15 VP Human Resources Eileen ALVITI
103 VP Educ Outreach/Social Entrepren Krystal BANFIELD
28 VP Diversity and Inclusion Lacretia FLASH
21 VP Finance Alison DONNELLY
20 VP Acad Affs Boston Conservatory Andy VORES
86 VP Community/Govt & Auxiliary Rels Robert CHAMBERS
88 VP for Real Estate Maureen HICKEY
85 Asst Vice Pres Global Initiative Jason CAMELIO
20 VP Academic Affairs/Vice Provost Jay KENNEDY
26 VP for External Affairs Tom RILEY
88 Vice Pres Academic Strategy Carin NUERNBERG
88 Dean of Prof Performance Div Ron SAVAGE
107 Dean of Prof Education Division Darla S. HANLEY
06 Registrar Jeffrey KINNAMON
39 Director of Campus Life Rosemary DOWLING
37 Director of Student Aid Services Kevin FIGUEIREDO
07 Dean of Admissions Damien S. BRACKEN
36 Assoc VP Career & Digital Strategy Stefanie HENNING
18 Assistant VP for Facilities Kevin ANDERSON
08 Dean of Learning Resources Heather REID
09 Dean Inst Rsrch/Assessment/Accred Sharon KRAMER
19 Sr Director Public Safety Services Mark LOUNEY
28 VP Student Affs/Diversity/ Inclusion Christopher KANDUS-FISHER
29 Sr Director of Alumni Affairs Fritz KUHNLENZ
104 Assoc Director Study Abroad Tracey MELLOR
27 Sr Dir Marketing/Communications Janelle BROWNING

Boston Architectural College (A)

320 Newbury Street, Boston MA 02115-2795
County: Suffolk FICE Identification: 003966
Unit ID: 164872
Telephone: (617) 262-5000 Carnegie Class: Spec-4-yr-Arts
FAX Number: (617) 585-0111 Calendar System: Semester
URL: www.the-bac.edu
Established: 1889 Annual Undergrad Tuition & Fees: $21,924
Enrollment: 742 Coed
Affiliation or Control: Independent Non-Profit IRS Status: 501(c)3
Highest Offering: Master's
Accreditation: EH, CIDA, LSAR

01 President Mr. Mahesh DAAS
05 Vice President Academic Affairs Ms. Victoria LIPTAK
10 Vice President for Finance/Admin Mr. Sydney LEO
111 VP Institutional Advancement Ms. Heather SULLIVAN
84 VP of Enrollment Management Mr. James RYAN
18 Director of Facilities Ms. Ellen YEE
32 Assoc Vice Pres/Dean of Students Mr. Richard M. GRISWOLD
48 Dean Interior Architecture Ms. Denise RUSH
88 Dean Sch Landscape Architecture Ms. Maria BELLALTA
88 Dean School of Design Studies Mr. Donald HUNSICKER
48 Dean School of Architecture Ms. Karen L. NELSON
88 Dean & Faculty of Practice Mr. Len CHARNEY
13 Director of Information Technology Mr. Jason O'BRIEN
88 Dir of Master's Thesis Arch Mr. Ian TABERNER
88 Director of Digital Media Mr. Peter ATWOOD
78 Dir of Applied Learning in Practice Ms. Beth GARVER
88 Director of Media Arts Mr. Luis MONTALVO
08 Director of the Library Mr. Robert ADAMS
07 Director of Admissions Ms. Meredith SPINNATO
37 Director of Financial Aid Mr. Janice WILKOS-GREENBERG
06 Registrar Ms. Katherine KWOLEK
11 Dir of Administrative Operations Ms. Patti VAUGHN
88 Director of Foundation Studios Mr. Lee PETERS
15 Director of Human Resources Vacant
29 Dir of Special Events & Alumni Vacant
21 Assoc VP for Finance & Admin Ms. Diane MERCIER
121 Director Foundation Student Support Mr. Michael DANIELS
04 Executive Asst to President Ms. Shannon THORIN
26 Dir of Marketing & Communications Ms. Nancy FINN
39 Coordinator of Student Life Mr. Zachary TRIPSAS
90 Manager of IT Operations & Projects Ms. Janet MCCLAIN

Boston Baptist College (B)

950 Metropolitan Avenue, Hyde Park MA 02136
County: Suffolk FICE Identification: 032483
Unit ID: 164614
Telephone: (617) 364-3510 Carnegie Class: Spec-4-yr-Faith
FAX Number: (775) 245-1498 Calendar System: Semester
URL: www.boston.edu
Established: 1976 Annual Undergrad Tuition & Fees: $12,600
Enrollment: 60 Coed
Affiliation or Control: Baptist IRS Status: 501(c)3
Highest Offering: Baccalaureate
Accreditation: TRACS

01 President Rev. David V. MELTON
05 Vice President/Chief Academic Ofcr Rev. Randall WARD
11 Vice President for Operations Rev. Randall WARD
10 Chief Financial Officer Vacant
08 Head Librarian Mr. Fred TATRO

Boston College (C)

140 Commonwealth Avenue, Chestnut Hill MA 02467-3934
County: Middlesex FICE Identification: 002128
Unit ID: 164924
Telephone: (617) 552-3000 Carnegie Class: DU-Highest
FAX Number: (617) 552-8828 Calendar System: Semester
URL: www.bc.edu
Established: 1863 Annual Undergrad Tuition & Fees: $60,202
Enrollment: 14,934 Coed
Affiliation or Control: Roman Catholic IRS Status: 501(c)3
Highest Offering: Doctorate
Accreditation: EH, ANEST, CAEP, COPSY, LAW, MPCAC, NURSE, SW, THEOL

01 President Rev. William P. LEAHY, S.J.
05 Provost & Dean of Faculties Dr. David QUIGLEY
03 Executive Vice President Mr. Michael J. LOCHHEAD
111 Senior VP University Advancement Mr. James J. HUSSON
04 Vice Pres/Exec Asst to President Mr. Kevin J. SHEA
10 Financial Vice President/Treasurer Mr. John D. BURKE
32 Vice Pres Student Affairs Ms. Shawna COOPER-GIBSON
15 Vice President for Human Resources Mr. David P. TRAINOR
13 Vice Pres Information Technology Mr. Michael J. BOURQUE
88 Vice Pres Univ Mission & Ministry Rev. John T. BUTLER, S.J.
86 Vice Pres Govt/Community Affairs Mr. Thomas J. KEADY
18 Vice Pres Facilities Management Mr. Daniel F. BOURQUE
09 Vice Pres Inst Research & Planning Ms. Mara HERMANO
20 Vice Provost Undergrad Acad Affairs Dr. Akua SARR
84 Vice Prov for Enrollment Management Mr. John MAHONEY, JR.
20 Vice Provost for Faculties Dr. Billy SOO
30 Vice President for Development Ms. Amy YANCEY
20 AV Provost Undergrad Acad Affairs Dr. J. Joseph BURNS
18 Assoc VP Capital Projects Ms. Mary S. NARDONE
29 Associate VP Alumni Relations Ms. Leah DECOSTA
16 Assoc VP Human Resources Mr. William MURPHY
109 Assoc VP Auxiliary Services Ms. Patricia A. BANDO
49 Dean Morrissey Col Arts & Sciences Rev. Gregory KALSCHEUR, S.J.
88 Assoc Dean of Strategic Initiatives Mr. David M. GOODMAN
53 Dean Lynch Sch Education/Human Dev Dr. Stanton WORTHAM
61 Dean Law School Vacant
50 Dean Carroll School of Management Dr. Andrew C. BOYNTON
66 Dean Connell School of Nursing Dr. Katherine GREGORY
70 Dean School of Social Work Dr. Gautam N. YADAMA
73 Dean School of Theology & Ministry Rev. Thomas STEGMAN, SJ
20 Dean Woods Col of Advancing Studies Ms. Karen MUNCASTER
35 Assoc VP Student Affairs Dr. Melinda STOOPS
08 University Librarian Dr. Thomas WALL
28 Exec Dir Institutional Diversity Ms. Patricia LOWE
06 Int Exec Director Student Services Mr. Adam KRUEKEBERG
07 Director Undergraduate Admissions Mr. Grant M. GOSSELIN
27 AVP Office of Univ Communications Mr. John B. DUNN
102 Assoc VP Schools & Org Giving Ms. Renee DECESARE
41 Director Athletics Mr. Patrick KRAFT
36 Assoc VP Student Affairs Mr. Joseph DUPONT
42 Assoc VP Campus Ministry Rev. Anthony PENNA
31 Director of Community Affairs Mr. William R. MILLS
38 Director of Univ Counseling Svcs Mr. Craig D. BURNS
37 Director Financial Aid Ms. Ebony MARSALA
23 Director Health Services Dr. Douglas COMEAU
39 Assoc VP Residential Life Mr. George A. AREY
25 Director Sponsored Programs Ms. Jennifer LOPEZ
19 Dir Public Safety/Chief of Police Mr. William B. EVANS
40 Director Bookstore Mr. Robert STEWART
43 General Counsel Ms. Nora FIELD
24 Director Media Technology Services Mr. David CORKUM
85 Dir Office of International Pgms Dr. Nick GOZIK
88 Dir Jesuit Inst/VProv Global Engage Rev. James F. KEENAN, SJ
93 Director AHANA/Intercultural Center Rev. Michael DAVIDSON
86 Director Governmental Relations Ms. Jeanne LEVESQUE
96 Director Procurement Services Mr. Paul MCGOWAN
108 AV Provost Assessment/Accreditation Dr. Jessica A. GREENE

Boston Graduate School of Psychoanalysis (D)

1581 Beacon Street, Brookline MA 02446-4602
County: Norfolk FICE Identification: 031943
Unit ID: 164915
Telephone: (617) 277-3915 Carnegie Class: Spec-4-yr-Other Health
FAX Number: (617) 277-0312 Calendar System: Semester
URL: www.bgsp.edu
Established: 1973 Annual Graduate Tuition & Fees: N/A
Enrollment: 142 Coed
Affiliation or Control: Independent Non-Profit IRS Status: 501(c)3
Highest Offering: Doctorate; No Undergraduates
Accreditation: EH

01 President Dr. Jane SNYDER
10 Vice President Finance Dr. Carol PANETTA
58 Dean of Graduate Studies Dr. Lynn PERLMAN
07 Director of Admissions Dr. Paula BERMAN
06 Registrar Ms. Dianne KAELI
37 Director of Financial Aid Ms. Stephanie WOOLBERT
21 Controller Ms. Gayle DOLAN
08 Head Librarian Ms. Amy COHEN-ROSE
88 Director of the Center for Research Dr. Stephen SOLDZ

Boston University (E)

One Silber Way, Boston MA 02215-1700
County: Suffolk FICE Identification: 002130
Unit ID: 164988
Telephone: (617) 353-2000 Carnegie Class: DU-Highest
FAX Number: N/A Calendar System: Semester
URL: www.bu.edu
Established: 1839 Annual Undergrad Tuition & Fees: $58,072
Enrollment: 32,718 Coed
Affiliation or Control: Independent Non-Profit IRS Status: 501(c)3
Highest Offering: Doctorate
Accreditation: EH, ARCPA, ART, CAATE, CACREP, CAHIIM, CEA, CLPSY, COPSY, DENT, DIETD, DIETI, FEPAC, HSA, IPSY, LAW, MED, MUS, OT, PCSAS, PH, PTA, SP, SW, THEOL

01 President Robert A. BROWN
05 University Provost Jean MORRISON
17 Provost Med Campus/Dean Sch of Med Karen H. ANTMAN
100 VP & Chief of Staff to President Douglas A. SEARS
04 Exec Asst to President's Office Megan S. COHEN
49 Dean Col/Grad Sch Arts & Sciences Stan SCLAROFF
60 Dean College of Communication Mariette DICHRISTINA
53 Dean Wheelock Col of Educ & HD David CHARD
54 Dean College of Engineering Kenneth R. LUTCHEN
57 Dean College of Fine Arts Harvey YOUNG
97 Dean College General Studies Natalie MCKNIGHT
88 Dean School of Hospitality Admin Arun UPNEJA
61 Dean of School of Law Angela ONWUACHI-WILLIG
50 Dean Questrom School of Business Susan FOURNIER
42 Dean of Marsh Chapel Robert A. HILL
51 Dean Metropolitan College/Ext Ed Tanya ZLATEVA
76 Dean SAR Health & Rehab Sciences Christopher A. MOORE
70 Dean School of Social Work Jorge DELVA
73 Dean School of Theology Sujin PAK
82 Dean Pardee Sch of Global Studies Adil NAJAM
52 Int Dean Goldman Sch Dental Med Cataldo LEONE
69 Dean School of Public Health Sandro GALEA
32 Associate Provost/Dean of Students Kenneth ELMORE
46 VP & Assoc Provost Research Gloria WATERS
28 Vice Pres & Assoc Provost Cmty/Incl Crystal A. WILLIAMS
58 Assoc Provost Graduate Affairs Daniel L. KLEINMAN
58 Assoc Provost Graduate Affairs Neena VERMA
114 Assoc Provost Budget & Planning Patricia O'BRIEN
88 Chief of Staff Provost's Office Laura JENKS
20 Assoc Provost Undergraduate Affairs Vacant
106 Assoc Prov Digital Lrng/Innovation Chris DELLAROCAS
101 Sr VP/Sr Counsel & Board Secy Todd L C. KLIPP
11 Senior Vice President Operations Gary W. NICKSA
26 Senior VP External Relations Stephen P. BURGAY
30 Senior VP Devel/Alumni Relations Scott G. NICHOLS
10 Senior Vice Pres/CFO & Treasurer Martin J. HOWARD
109 Vice President Auxiliary Services Peter SMOKOWSKI
43 VP & General Counsel Erika GEETTER
86 Vice President Federal Relations Jennifer GRODSKY
18 VP Campus Planning & Operations Michael DONOVAN
45 VP Budget Planning & Business Affs Derek HOWE
110 Vice President Development Karen ENGELBOURG
85 VP/Assoc Provost Global Programs Willis G. WANG
13 VP Info Svcs & Tech/Chief Data Ofcr Tracy SCHROEDER
84 VP/Assoc Prov Enroll & Stdnt Admin Christine W. MCGUIRE
86 VP Government/Community Rels Jake SULLIVAN
29 VP Alumni Relations Steven A. HALL
27 VP Marketing & Creative Services Amy HOOK
115 Chief Investment Officer Lila HUNNEWELL
19 Exec Dir Pub Safety/Chief of Police Kelly A. NEE
103 Exec Dir Career Development Vacant
15 VP Operations/Chief HR Officer Patricia SHEEHAN
07 Assoc VP Enrol & Dean of Admissions Kelly A. WALTER
35 Assoc VP Enroll & Student Affairs Denise MOONEY
88 AVP Student Info Systems/Comm & PM Marylou O'DONNELL-RUNDLETT
25 Assoc VP Sponsored Programs Diane BALDWIN
114 AVP Budget/Plng & Business Affairs Ines GARRANT
21 VP of Financial Operations Nicole TIRELLA
09 Asst VP Analytical Svcs & Inst Rsch Linette A. DECARIE
88 Asst VP PostAward Financial Opers Gretchen HARTIGAN
87 Assistant Dean Summer Term Vacant
35 Asst Dean Stdnts/Ex Dir Stdnt Activ John BATTAGLINO, JR.
108 Interim Asst Prov Acad Assessment Megan M. SULLIVAN
21 Asst VP Business Affairs Melanie MADAIO-O'BRIEN
41 Asst VP & Director of Athletics Drew MARROCHELLO
06 Asst VP & University Registrar Christine S. PAAL
96 Asst VP/Chief Procurement Officer Randall MOORE
104 Exec Director Study Abroad Gareth MCFEELY
37 Exec Dir Financial Assistance Julie WICKSTROM
39 Director of Housing/Dining Vacant
85 Mng Dir Intl Student/Scholars Ofc Jeanne KELLEY
28 Director Howard Thurman Center Katherine J. KENNEDY
88 Director Center for Anti-Racism Ibram X. KENDI
09 Director Institutional Research Elizabeth CAMPBELL
22 Exec Dir Equal Opportunity Kim RANDALL
36 Director Student Employment Mary Ann FRENCH
08 University Librarian Vacant
88 Dir Ugrad Rsrch Opportunities Pgm John CELENZA
88 General Manager Agganis Arena Kristoffer W. BRASSIL
88 Exec Director Physical Ed Rec/Dance Timothy MOORE

23 Director Student Health Services .... Judy T. PLATT
35 Senior Assoc Dir Student Activities .... Bryan ADAMS
102 Assoc VP Industry Engagement .... Marc SCATAMACCHIA
105 Assoc Director Web Services .... Ron YEANY
38 Director Student Counseling .... Carrie LANDA
90 Director of Research Computing .... Wayne GILMORE
91 SVP Applications & Enterprise Svcs .... Janet O'BRIEN

Brandeis University (A)

415 South Street, Waltham MA 02453
County: Middlesex FICE Identification: 002133
Unit ID: 165015
Telephone: (781) 736-2000 Carnegie Class: DU-Highest
FAX Number: (781) 736-8699 Calendar System: Semester
URL: www.brandeis.edu
Established: 1948 Annual Undergrad Tuition & Fees: $57,615
Enrollment: 5,440 Coed
Affiliation or Control: Independent Non-Profit IRS Status: 501(c)3
Highest Offering: Doctorate
Accreditation: EH

01 President .... Dr. Ronald D. LIEBOWITZ
05 Provost .... Dr. Carol A. FIERKE
10 Exec VP for Finance/Administration .... Mr. Stewart URETSKY
111 Sr Vice Pres Inst Advancement .... Ms. Zamira KORFF
43 Sr VP and General Counsel .... Mr. Steven S. LOCKE
26 Sr VP of Communications/Marketing .... Mr. Dan KIM
21 Chief Financial Officer & Treasurer .... Mr. Samuel SOLOMON
28 Chief Diversity Officer .... Dr. Mark BRIMHALL-VARGAS
100 Chief of Staff/Sr Advisor to Pres ....Mr. William R. O'REILLY, JR.
18 Vice Pres for Campus Operations .... Ms. Lois A. STANLEY
29 VP of Alumni Relations .... Ms. Patsy FISCHER
13 Chief Information Officer .... Mr. James LACRETA
15 Vice Pres Human Resources .... Mr. Robin SWITZER
32 Vice Pres of Student Affairs .... Mr. Raymond LU-MING OU
45 VP Planning/Institutional Research .... Mr. Dan FELDMAN
102 Asst VP Corp & Foundation Relations .... Mr. Michael DETTELBACH
35 Asst Vice Pres Student Affairs .... Ms. Andrea B. DINE
37 Asst VP Student Financial Services .... Ms. Sherri M. AVERY
49 Dean of Arts & Sciences .... Dr. Dorothy L. HODGSON
70 Dn Heller Sch Social Pol & Mgt .... Dr. David WEIL
50 Dean International Business Sch .... Dr. Kathryn GRADDY
06 University Registrar .... Dr. Mark S. HEWITT
08 University Librarian .... Mr. Matthew SHEEHY
07 Dean of Admissions/Financial Aid .... Ms. Jennifer WALKER
41 Athletic Director .... Ms. Lauren HAYNIE

Cambridge College (B)

500 Rutherford Avenue, Boston MA 02129
County: Suffolk FICE Identification: 021829
Unit ID: 165167
Telephone: (800) 877-4723 Carnegie Class: Masters/L
FAX Number: (617) 349-3545 Calendar System: Trimester
URL: www.cambridgecollege.edu
Established: 1971 Annual Undergrad Tuition & Fees: $16,266
Enrollment: 2,764 Coed
Affiliation or Control: Independent Non-Profit IRS Status: 501(c)3
Highest Offering: Doctorate
Accreditation: EH, CAEPT

01 President .... Deborah C. JACKSON
05 Interim Provost & VP of AA .... Dr. Jerry ICE
10 CFO/VP of Finance & Administration .... John SPINARD
15 VP of Human Resources .... Lauretta SIGGERS
86 VP of Strategic Partnerships .... Phillip PAGE
45 VP of Innovation/Strat Initiatives .... Mark ROTONDO
111 VP of Institutional Advancement .... Vacant
26 VP Marketing/Communications and PR .... Jacqueline CONRAD
43 General Counsel .... Judith SIZER
20 Assoc Provost Student Learning .... Dr. Tracy MCLAUGHLIN-VOLPE
13 Director of Information Technology .... Achal KHATRI
113 Dir of Student Financial Services .... Christina GRIECCI
37 Director of Financial Aid .... Frank LAUDER
21 Controller .... Dorothy WHALEN
88 Assistant Controller .... Sharon DELESKEY
06 Registrar .... Amy CAVELIER
09 Director of Institutional Research .... Stephanie FUNDERBURG
12 Director of Puerto Rico .... Dr. Santiago MENDEZ-HERNANDEZ
12 Director of Southern California .... Rita CLEMONS
12 Director of Lawrence MA .... Dr. Melissa Sue PADILLA
12 Executive Director Springfield MA .... Teresa (Terrie) FORTE
88 Senior Director SIS .... Robyn SHAHID-BELLOT
110 Managing Dir Advancement Services .... John A. BEAHM
112 Dir Strategic Partnerships .... Alex MORR
29 Dir Annual Fund/Alumni Engagement .... Erik RYAN
27 Dir of Marketing & Digital Strategy .... Maria VASALLO
97 Dean Undergraduate Studies .... Dr. James LEE
83 Dean School of Psychology .... Dr. Niti SETH
32 Dean Student Affairs/Student Life .... Regina ROBINSON
53 Interim Dean School of Education .... Dr. Mary GARRITY
50 Dean School of Management .... Vacant
88 Dir Center for Learning/Teaching .... Brooks WINCHELL
108 Director of Academic Compliance .... Dr. Joseph MIGLIO
121 Dir Undergrad Academic Advising .... Michael DICKINSON
04 Sr Exec Assistant to President .... Robyn CARROLL
106 Dean of Online Programming .... Dr. Michael E. MARRAPODI

Clark University (C)

950 Main Street, Worcester MA 01610-1477
County: Worcester FICE Identification: 002139
Unit ID: 165334
Telephone: (508) 793-7711 Carnegie Class: DU-Higher
FAX Number: (508) 793-7780 Calendar System: Semester
URL: www.clarku.edu
Established: 1887 Annual Undergrad Tuition & Fees: $48,602
Enrollment: 3,405 Coed
Affiliation or Control: Independent Non-Profit IRS Status: 501(c)3
Highest Offering: Doctorate
Accreditation: EH, CLPSY

01 President .... Dr. David B. FITHIAN
10 Executive VP/CFO & Treasurer .... Ms. Danielle MANNING
05 Provost & Vice Pres Academic Affs .... Dr. Sebastian ROYO
111 Vice Pres University Advancement .... Mr. Jeffrey GILLOOLY
26 Vice Pres Marketing & Communication .... Ms. Jill FRIEDMAN
13 Vice Pres for Information Tech/CIO .... Mr. Joseph KALINOWSKI
86 VP Government/Cmty Affs/Campus Svcs .... Vacant
45 VP Planning & Strategic Initiatives .... Mr. David CHEARO
32 Dean of Students .... Vacant
46 Dean of Research/Dean Grad Studies .... Dr. Yuko AOYAMA
49 Assoc Provost/Dean of College .... Dr. Betsy HUANG
20 Assoc Provost/Dean of the Faculty .... Dr. Esther JONES
58 Dean School of Management .... Dr. Alan EISNER
07 Dean of Admissions & Financial Aid .... Ms. Meredith TWOMBLY
37 Director of Financial Aid .... Vacant
08 University Librarian .... Ms. Laura ROBINSON
10 Controller .... Ms. Anne RANDALL
36 Director Career Development .... Ms. Michelle FLINT
06 Registrar .... Mr. John OHOTNICKY
15 Dir of HR/Affirm Act .... Mr. David EVERITT
18 Director of Facilities Management .... Mr. Daniel RODERICK
41 Director of Athletics .... Ms. Trish CRONIN
114 Chief University Budget Officer .... Mr. Paul WYKES
19 Chief of Campus Police .... Mr. Stephen P. GOULET
23 Director of Health Services .... Ms. Robin MCNALLY
28 Chief Officer Diversity/Inclusion .... Ms. Sheree OHEN
04 Assistant to the President .... Ms. Katrina BANKS-BINICI
88 Senior Advisor to the President .... Mr. James COLLINS
109 Business & Auxiliary Services Mgr .... Mr. Anthony PENNY
09 Dir Strat Analytics/Inst Research .... Ms. Elissa LU
104 Director Study Abroad .... Ms. Alissa KRAMER
39 Interim Dir Res Life & Housing .... Mr. Woodrow FREESE
22 Title IX Coord/Asst Dean Wellness .... Ms. Lynn LEVEY
102 Dir Foundation/Corporate Relations .... Ms. Jennifer HITT
105 Dir of Digital Content Strategy .... Ms. Meredith KING

College of the Holy Cross (D)

1 College Street, Worcester MA 01610-2395
County: Worcester FICE Identification: 002141
Unit ID: 166124
Telephone: (508) 793-2011 Carnegie Class: Bac-A&S
FAX Number: (508) 793-3030 Calendar System: Semester
URL: www.holycross.edu
Established: 1843 Annual Undergrad Tuition & Fees: $54,770
Enrollment: 2,970 Coed
Affiliation or Control: Roman Catholic IRS Status: 501(c)3
Highest Offering: Baccalaureate
Accreditation: EH, THEA

01 President .... Mr. Vincent D. ROUGEAU
04 Sr Exec Assistant to the President .... Ms. Melanie MITCHELL
10 VP Admin & Finance/Treasurer .... Ms. Dottie HAUVER
42 Vice President for Mission .... Vacant
84 Vice Provost for Enrollment Mgmt .... Mr. Cornell B. LESANE, II
05 Provost/Dean of the College .... Dr. Margaret FREIJE
26 VP for Communications .... Ms. Marisa GREGG
111 VP for Advancement .... Ms. Tracy BARLOK
32 VP Student Affairs/Dean of Students .... Ms. Michelle MURRAY
115 Chief Investment Officer .... Vacant
28 Assoc Provost for Diversity/Equity .... Mr. Amit TANEJA
20 Dean of the Faculty .... Dr. Ann Marie LESHKOWICH
20 Dean of the Faculty .... Dr. Mary EBBOTT
21 Director of Finance/Asst Treasurer .... Mr. Charles ESTAPHAN
22 Director of Title IX and EO .... Mr. Derek DEBOBES
06 Registrar .... Ms. Patricia RING
07 Int Director of Admissions .... Ms. Lynn VERRECCHIA
08 Director of Library Services .... Mr. Mark SHELTON
37 Director of Financial Aid .... Ms. Nicole CUNNINGHAM
25 Director of Sponsored Research .... Ms. Stacy RISEMAN
42 Director Ofc of College Chaplains .... Ms. Marybeth KEARNS-BARRETT
88 Director Ctr Interdisc Studies .... Dr. Lorelle SEMLEY
36 Director of Career Planning .... Ms. Amy MURPHY
13 Director Information Tech Services .... Dr. Ellen J. KEOHANE
29 Director of Alumni Relations .... Ms. Kristyn M. DYER
19 Director of Public Safety .... Ms. Shawn DE JONG
35 Director of Campus Center .... Mr. Jeremiah O'CONNOR
18 Director of Physical Plant .... Mr. Scott M. MERRILL
41 Int Co-Dir Intercol Athletics .... Mr. Nick SMITH
41 Int Co-Dir Intercol Athletics .... Ms. Rose SHEA
21 Controller .... Ms. Charlene BELLOWS
38 Director Counseling Center .... Dr. Paul GALVINHILL
23 Health Services Director .... Ms. Kelsey R. DEVOE
15 Chief Human Resources Ofcr .... Ms. Marymichele DELANEY
96 Assistant Director Purchasing .... Mr. Scott SLABODEN
09 Ofc of Assessment/Research .... Dr. Denise BELL
86 Dir of Govt/Community Rels .... Mr. Jamie D. HOAG
43 General Counsel .... Ms. Elizabeth SMALL
104 Director Study Abroad .... Dr. Brittain SMITH

College of Our Lady of the Elms (E)

291 Springfield Street, Chicopee MA 01013-2839
County: Hampden FICE Identification: 002140
Unit ID: 167394
Telephone: (413) 594-2761 Carnegie Class: Masters/M
FAX Number: (413) 592-4871 Calendar System: Semester
URL: www.elms.edu
Established: 1928 Annual Undergrad Tuition & Fees: $38,391
Enrollment: 1,355 Coed
Affiliation or Control: Roman Catholic IRS Status: 501(c)3
Highest Offering: Doctorate
Accreditation: EH, IACBE, NURSE, SW

01 President .... Dr. Harry E. DUMAY
05 Vice President of Academic Affairs .... Dr. Walter C. BREAU
10 Vice Pres Finance/Administration .... Katie LONGLEY
84 VP Enrollment Mgmt & Marketing .... Jonathan SCULLY
111 VP Institutional Advancement .... Bernadette NOWAKOWSKI
32 VP Stdnt Affs/Chf Diversity Officer .... Dr. Antoinette CANDIA-BAILEY
35 Dean of Students .... Teresa WINTERS
13 Chief Information Officer .... Vacant
07 Director of Admissions .... Jenna STOLARIK
20 AVP Academic Affs/Strat Initiatives .... Dr. Joyce HAMPTON
121 Asst Acad Dean for Student Support .... Vacant
15 Director Human Resources/Personnel .... Deborah METHE
06 Registrar .... Brooke BEDARD
113 Bursar .... Kathleen CURRY
21 Controller .... Gary RUSSETT
08 Director of Library .... Anthony FONSECA
26 Director of Communications .... Vacant
37 Director of Financial Aid .... Richard O'CONNOR
36 Dir of Career Development .... Vacant
04 Executive Assistant to President .... Kimberly HANNAH
09 Dir of Inst Assessment & Research .... Karalee YVON
44 Dir of Annual Giving .... Vacant
18 Dir of Campus Operations & Planning .... Ron RICKEY
39 Dir of Residence Life .... Vacant
19 Director of Public Safety .... Pablo MADERA
29 Dir of Alumni Relations .... Andrea HOLDEN
41 Director of Athletics .... Michael THEULEN
66 Dean School of Nursing .... Dr. Kathleen SCOBLE
58 Dean School of Grad & Prof Studies .... Dr. Elizabeth HUKOWICZ
28 Dir of Diversity & Inclusion .... Vacant
38 Director of Counseling Center .... Dr. Nicole HADDAD
23 Director of Health Center .... Jessie CHENIER
42 Director of Campus Ministry .... Eileen KIRK
120 Academic Technology Specialist .... Sara FLINK
119 Mgr of Ntwk/Infrastructure Security .... Alexander ZMACZYNSKI
105 Web Manager .... Eugene DEYKIN
104 Director of International Programs .... Vacant

Conway School of Landscape Design (F)

88 Village Hill Road, Northampton MA 01060
County: Hampshire FICE Identification: 022743
Unit ID: 165495
Telephone: (413) 369-4044 Carnegie Class: Spec-4-yr-Arts
FAX Number: (413) 203-6914 Calendar System: Trimester
URL: www.csld.edu
Established: 1972 Annual Graduate Tuition & Fees: N/A
Enrollment: 13 Coed
Affiliation or Control: Independent Non-Profit IRS Status: 501(c)3
Highest Offering: Master's; No Undergraduates
Accreditation: EH

01 Executive Director .... Mr. Bruce STEDMAN
05 Academic Director .... Mr. Ken BYRNE
10 Finance Manager .... Ms. Paulina KISLYUK
11 Administrative Director .... Ms. Priscilla NOVITT
06 Registrar .... Ms. Elaine WILLIAMSON
07 Admissions Manager .... Ms. Kate CHOLAKIS
29 Director of Alumni Relations .... Ms. Elaine WILLIAMSON

Curry College (G)

1071 Blue Hill Avenue, Milton MA 02186-2395
County: Norfolk FICE Identification: 002143
Unit ID: 165529
Telephone: (617) 333-0500 Carnegie Class: Masters/M
FAX Number: (617) 979-3540 Calendar System: Semester
URL: www.curry.edu
Established: 1879 Annual Undergrad Tuition & Fees: $42,425
Enrollment: 2,410 Coed
Affiliation or Control: Independent Non-Profit IRS Status: 501(c)3
Highest Offering: Master's
Accreditation: EH, IACBE, NURSE

01 President .... Mr. Kenneth K. QUIGLEY, JR.
05 EVP Academic Affairs/Provost .... Dr. David SZCZERBACKI
111 VP Institutional Advancement .... Ms. Sally MURRAY
84 VP Enrollment Management .... Mr. Edmond CABELLON
10 EVP/Chief Financial Officer .... Mr. David M. ROSATI
15 VP of Human Resources .... Ms. Mirlen MAL
07 Associate VP and Dean of Admission .... Mr. Keith ROBICHAUD
32 VP of Student Affairs .... Ms. Maryellen M. KILEY
45 Special Advisor to the President .... Dr. Susan W. PENNINI
04 Exec Assistant to the President .... Ms. Amy M. BIANCHI
08 Director Library .... Ms. Katharine G. EASTMAN

13 Chief Information Officer .... Vacant
06 Registrar .... Ms. June KOUKOL
18 Director of Buildings & Grounds .... Mr. Robert G. O'CONNELL
110 Assoc VP of Institutional Advance .... Ms. Michelle O'REGAN
36 Director of Student Placement .... Ms. Kerrie ABORN
37 Assoc VP of Finance for SFS .... Ms. Stephanny J. ELIAS
38 Director of Student Counseling .... Dr. Alison W. MARKSON
09 Director of Institutional Research .... Ms. Jennifer DUNNE
105 Director Web Services .... Mr. John EAGAN
41 Athletic Director .... Mr. Vincent ERUZIONE
39 Director Student Housing .... Ms. Jennifer MAITINO

Dean College (A)

99 Main Street, Franklin MA 02038-1994
County: Norfolk FICE Identification: 002144
Unit ID: 165574
Telephone: (508) 541-1508 Carnegie Class: Bac/Assoc-Mixed
FAX Number: (508) 541-8726 Calendar System: Semester
URL: www.dean.edu
Established: 1865 Annual Undergrad Tuition & Fees: $41,318
Enrollment: 1,180 Coed
Affiliation or Control: Independent Non-Profit IRS Status: 501(c)3
Highest Offering: Baccalaureate
Accreditation: EH, IACBE

01 President .... Dr. Paula M. ROONEY
100 Chief of Staff .... Ms. Sandra CAIN
05 VP Academic Affairs .... Dr. Kathleen VRANOS
10 Vice Pres Financial Svcs/Treasurer .... Mr. Dan MODELANE
84 VP Enrollment & Retention .... Ms. Cindy T. KOZIL
111 Vice Pres Institutional Advancement .... Ms. Coleen RESNICK
13 VP/Chief Information Officer .... Mr. Darrell KULESZA
44 Asst VP Individual & Corporate Gift .... Mr. J.J ALBERTS
21 Assoc VP/Controller/Asst Treasurer .... Ms. Kathleen MCGUIRE
07 Assoc VP Enrollment/Dean Admission .... Ms. Iris GODES
121 Assc VP Student Success/Career Plng .... Ms. Wendy ADLER
20 Asst VP Academic Affairs .... Ms. Melissa READ
18 Assoc VP Capital Plng/Facilities .... Mr. Brian KELLY
26 VP Marketing & Business Development .... Mr. Gregg CHALK
32 Dean of Students .... Mr. David DRUCKER
51 Dean School of Continuing Studies .... Mr. Paul RESTEN
50 Dean School of Business .... Dr. P. Gerard SHAW
49 Dean School of Liberal Arts .... Dr. Brad HASTINGS
57 Dean Palladino School of Dance/Arts .... Mr. Marc ARENTSEN
06 Registrar .... Ms. Louise MONAST
19 Dir Law Enforcement Services .... Mr. Ken CORKRAN
08 Director of the Library .... Mr. Stan SKRABUT
41 Athletic Director .... Mr. George MARTIN
39 Assistant Dean of Students .... Ms. Shannon OVERCASH
35 Dir Orientation/Community Service .... Ms. Jennifer POLIMER
40 Director of Bookstore .... Ms. Jackie CALDERONE
37 Dean Student & Financial Plng/Svcs .... Mr. Frank MULLEN
07 Director Enrollment Operations .... Ms. Kathleen RYAN
36 Dir Career Planning/Internships .... Ms. Thea CERIO
38 Director of Counseling Services .... Ms. Mary Ann SILVESTRI
29 Director Alumni Relations .... Ms. Jennifer SHEYTANIAN

Eastern Nazarene College (B)

23 E Elm Avenue, Quincy MA 02170-2999
County: Norfolk FICE Identification: 002145
Unit ID: 165644
Telephone: (617) 745-3000 Carnegie Class: Bac-Diverse
FAX Number: (617) 745-3907 Calendar System: 4/1/4
URL: www.enc.edu
Established: 1918 Annual Undergrad Tuition & Fees: $26,952
Enrollment: 699 Coed
Affiliation or Control: Church Of The Nazarene IRS Status: 501(c)3
Highest Offering: Master's
Accreditation: EH, SW

01 President .... Dr. Jack CONNELL
05 VP Academic Affairs/Academic Dean .... Dr. William MCCOY
10 Vice President for Finance/CFO .... Mr. Robert CORNELL
32 Vice Pres Student Devel/Title IX .... Mr. Ian SLATER
111 Vice President Inst Advancement .... Vacant
84 Vice President of Enrollment .... Mr. Dave BURKE
93 VP of Multicultural Affairs .... Mr. Robert BENJAMIN
07 Asst Director of Admissions .... Ms. Madison FLOWERS
123 Dir Grad/Online/Adult Admissions .... Mr. James SHEETS
39 Dir of Residential Life .... Mr. Matthew GALIANO-WILLIAMS
06 Registrar .... Mr. Timothy MCDONALD
37 Director of Financial Aid .... Mr. Troy MARTIN
08 Director of Library Services .... Ms. Amy HWANG
19 Director Safety and Security .... Mr. Floyd BARTROM
38 Dir Counseling & Career Services .... Mr. Bradford THORNE
88 Curriculum Director .... Ms. Melinda SMITH
41 AVP of Athletics .... Dr. Bradford ZARGES
18 Asst Director of Facilities .... Mr. Joseph FERNANDES
21 Controller .... Ms. Patricia CONSTANTINO
15 Director Human Resources .... Ms. Nadine PFAUTZ
40 Director Bookstore .... Ms. Keri LEWIS
13 Chief Information Officer .... Mr. Charles BURT
04 Executive Asst to the President .... Ms. Sharim SHOMAN
09 Director of Institutional Research .... Mr. Ryan PIESCO
29 Assoc Dir Inst Adv/Alum Rels Coord .... Vacant
36 Director Student Placement .... Vacant
20 Associate Dean for Academic Affairs .... Vacant
30 Development Associate .... Ms. Laura NASE
88 Instructional Resource Ctr Coord .... Ms. Patricia VAZQUEZ

Emerson College (C)

120 Boylston Street, Boston MA 02116-4624
County: Suffolk FICE Identification: 002146
Unit ID: 165662
Telephone: (617) 824-8500 Carnegie Class: Masters/L
FAX Number: (617) 824-8511 Calendar System: Semester
URL: www.emerson.edu
Established: 1880 Annual Undergrad Tuition & Fees: $51,148
Enrollment: 5,115 Coed
Affiliation or Control: Independent Non-Profit IRS Status: 501(c)3
Highest Offering: Master's
Accreditation: EH, SP

01 Interim President .... Dr. William GILLIGAN
43 Vice President & General Counsel .... Ms. Meredith AINBINDER
10 Vice President for Admin & Finance .... Mr. Paul DWORKIS
05 Provost & VP of Academic Affairs .... Dr. Michaele WHELAN
13 VP for Information Technology .... Mr. Brian BASGEN
26 AVP Communications/Marketing .... Ms. Sofiya CABALQUINTO
28 VP Social Justice Center .... Dr. Sylvia SPEARS
84 Vice Pres Enrollment Management .... Dr. Ruthanne MADSEN
21 Assoc Vice Pres for Finance .... Mr. Robert BUTLER
15 Sr AVP for Human Resources .... Ms. Shari STIER
29 AVP Alumni Engagement .... Ms. Leigh GASPAR
86 VP Government/Community Relations .... Ms. Margaret Ann INGS
09 AVP Institutional Research .... Mr. Michael DUGGAN
58 Dean Grad Studies/AVP Acad Affairs .... Ms. Jan ROBERTS-BRESLIN
32 Vice Pres/Dean of Students .... Mr. James HOPPE
107 Exec Director Professional Studies .... Ms. Lesley NICHOLS
08 Exec Director of Library & Learning .... Ms. Cheryl MCGRATH
123 Director of Graduate Admission .... Ms. Leanda MIRANDA
36 Director of Career Services .... Ms. Carol SPECTOR
38 Director Counseling/Health Center .... Mr. Brandin DEAR
41 Director Athletics .... Ms. Patricia NICOL
39 Assoc Dean Campus Life .... Mr. Erik MUURISEPP
21 Controller .... Mr. Jonathan PEARSALL
06 Registrar .... Mr. JP PESTANA
42 Campus Chaplain .... Ms. Julie AVIS ROGERS
101 VP President's Office & BOT .... Ms. Anne SHAUGHNESSY
18 Director of Facilities .... Mr. Joseph KNOLL
37 Director Financial Aid .... Ms. Angela GRANT
04 Sr Executive Assistant to President .... Ms. Mary Beth PESSIA
104 Director Study Abroad .... Mr. David GRIFFIN
19 Chief of Police .... Mr. Robert SMITH
25 Exec Director Research/Scholarship .... Mr. Eric ASETTA
111 VP Institutional Advancement .... Mr. John MALCOLM

Emmanuel College (D)

400 The Fenway, Boston MA 02115-5798
County: Suffolk FICE Identification: 002147
Unit ID: 165671
Telephone: (617) 277-9340 Carnegie Class: Bac-A&S
FAX Number: (617) 735-9877 Calendar System: Semester
URL: https://www.emmanuel.edu/
Established: 1919 Annual Undergrad Tuition & Fees: $42,516
Enrollment: 1,946 Coed
Affiliation or Control: Roman Catholic IRS Status: 501(c)3
Highest Offering: Master's
Accreditation: EH, NURSE

01 President .... Sr. Janet EISNER, SND
100 Exec Asst to the President .... Ms. Michelle ERICKSON
04 Sr Asst to the Pres/Dir Spec Events .... Ms. Lori SIMMONS
10 VP of Finance/Treasurer (CFO) .... Sr. Anne DONOVAN, SND
05 VP Academic Affairs & Dean .... Dr. Josef KURTZ
15 Vice President of Human Resources . Ms. Erin FARMER NOONAN
30 VP of Development .... Ms. Danielle KELLERMANN
37 Assoc VP for Student Financial Svcs .... Ms. Jennifer PORTER
26 VP of College Relations .... Ms. Molly DILORENZO
45 VP Alumni Rels/Strategic Engagement .... Ms. Kristen CONROY
42 VP of Mission and Ministry .... Fr. Terrence DEVINO
84 Dean of Enrollment .... Ms. Sandra ROBBINS
35 Dean of Students .... Ms. Jennifer FORRY
09 Dean Inst Effect/Chief Data Ofcr .... Dr. Beth ROSS
20 Dean Academic Admin/Grad & Prof Pgm .... Ms. Cindy O'CALLAGHAN
88 Asst Dean Cmty Stdrds & Family Pgms . Ms. Mary Beth THOMAS
121 Assoc Dean of Academic Advising ....Sr. Susan THORNELL, SND
79 Assoc Dean Humanities/Soc Science .... Dr. Lisa STEPANSKI
66 Assoc Dean Nursing/Clinical Science .... Dr. Diane SHEA
81 Assoc Dean of Sciences/Health .... Dr. Paul MARCH
53 Associate Dean of Education .... Sr. Karen HOKANSON, SND
50 Associate Dean of Business and Mgmt .... Ms. Anne Marie PASQUALE
08 Assoc Dn of Library/Lrng Resources ... Ms. Karen STORIN LINITZ
36 Executive Director Career Ctr .... Ms. Maureen ASHBURN
41 Director of Athletics & Recreation .... Mr. Brendan MCWILLIAMS
90 Director of Academic Resource Ctr .... Ms. Wendy LABRON
09 Director of Institutional Research .... Dr. Alison VALLEREUX
13 VP Information Resources/Planning .... Mr. Sean PHILPOTT
19 Director Security/Safety .... Mr. John KELLY
06 Registrar .... Ms. Kimberly CAMASSO
28 AVP Diversity & Incl/Chief Div Ofcr .... Mr. Jeffrey SMITH, JR.
39 Asst Dean Residence Life/Housing .... Ms. Susan BENZIE

Endicott College (E)

376 Hale Street, Beverly MA 01915-2098
County: Essex FICE Identification: 002148
Unit ID: 165699
Telephone: (978) 927-0585 Carnegie Class: Masters/L
FAX Number: (978) 927-0084 Calendar System: 4/1/4
URL: www.endicott.edu
Established: 1939 Annual Undergrad Tuition & Fees: $35,320
Enrollment: 4,287 Coed
Affiliation or Control: Independent Non-Profit IRS Status: 501(c)3
Highest Offering: Doctorate
Accreditation: EH, ART, CAATE, CIDA, COSMA, NUR, NURSE

01 President .... Dr. Steven DISALVO
100 Chief of Staff .... Ms. Jillian DUBMAN
10 Vice President of Finance/CFO .... Mr. Tony FERULLO
05 Provost .... Dr. Beth SCHWARTZ
111 Vice Pres Institutional Advancement .... Mr. Patrick HEWETT
84 VP Admissions/Financial Aid .... Mr. Evan E. LIPP
26 VP Communications/Marketing .... Mr. Bryan CAIN
41 Asst Vice President/Dir Athletics .... Dr. Brian WYLIE
32 VP Student Affs/Chief Divers Ofcr .... Ms. Brandi JOHNSON
04 Executive Administrative Assistant .... Ms. Frances POISSON
04 Executive Admin Asst to the Provost .... Ms. Amy ASTOLFI
15 Vice President Human Resources .... Mr. Aaron MORRISON
35 AVP & Dean of Students .... Mr. Marlin NABORS
21 Assoc Vice Pres Business Office .... Ms. Renee CRAWFORD
88 Exec Director Misselwood Events .... Ms. Eileen GEYER
90 Assoc Dean of Academic Technology .... Mr. Kent BARCLAY
07 AVP/Dean of Admission .... Ms. Meghan MONACO
06 Registrar .... Ms. Rosa CADENA
08 Director Library .... Mr. Brian COURTEMANCHE
37 Dean of Financial Aid .... Ms. Marcia D. TOOMEY
13 Chief Information Officer .... Ms. Amy DONOVAN
38 Director Counseling Center .... Ms. Maureen GEBHARDT
36 Dean Internship and Career Center .... Ms. Dale MCLENNAN
09 Director Endicott Research Center .... Mr. Donny FEMINO
96 Director of Purchasing .... Ms. Susan AYERS
85 Dean International Education .... Dr. Warren JAFERIAN
49 Dean School of Arts & Sciences .... Dr. Gene WONG
53 Dean of Education/Scholars Program .... Dr. Sara QUAY
57 Dean Visual & Performing Arts .... Mr. Mark TOWNER
59 Dean School of Hospitality Mgmt .... Dr. Todd COMEN
68 Dean Sports Science/Fitness Studies .... Dr. Deborah SWANTON
66 Director of PhD Nursing .... Dr. Nancy MEEDZAN
50 Dean School of Business .... Dr. Michael PAIGE
60 Dean School of Communication .... Dr. Laurel HELLERSTEIN
19 Director Public Safety & Police .... Ms. Kerry RAMSDELL
104 Study Abroad Advisor .... Ms. Alicia VINAL
29 Director of Alumni Relations .... Ms. Tory PILBIN
44 Director of Annual Giving .... Ms. Sarah EARNEST
39 Assoc Dir Res Life & Housing Opers .... Ms. Corie QUILL
121 Director Stdnt Success & Retention .... Ms. Teresa MCGRATH
107 Dean of Professional Studies .... Ms. Laura DOUGLASS
58 Dir of Grad Education/Fellowships .... Dr. Aubry THRELKELD
58 Dir Grad Pgm in Autism/ABA Studies .... Dr. Mary Jane WEISS

FINE Mortuary College (F)

150 Kerry Place, Norwood MA 02062
County: Norfolk FICE Identification: 033164
Unit ID: 436599
Telephone: (781) 762-1211 Carnegie Class: Spec 2-yr-A&S
FAX Number: (781) 762-7177 Calendar System: Quarter
URL: www.fmc.edu
Established: 1996 Annual Undergrad Tuition & Fees: $20,520
Enrollment: 100 Coed
Affiliation or Control: Proprietary IRS Status: Proprietary
Highest Offering: Associate Degree
Accreditation: FUSER

01 President .... Mr. Kevin KOCH
05 Program Director .... Ms. Melissa CYFERS
11 Campus Manager .... Ms. Laura HEWEY

Fisher College (G)

118 Beacon Street, Boston MA 02116-1500
County: Suffolk FICE Identification: 002150
Unit ID: 165802
Telephone: (617) 236-8800 Carnegie Class: Bac-Diverse
FAX Number: (617) 236-8858 Calendar System: Semester
URL: www.fisher.edu
Established: 1903 Annual Undergrad Tuition & Fees: $32,700
Enrollment: 1,419 Coed
Affiliation or Control: Independent Non-Profit IRS Status: 501(c)3
Highest Offering: Master's
Accreditation: EH, CAHIIM, IACBE, NURSE

01 President .... Mr. Steven RICH
03 Executive Vice President .... Ms. Ana DA CUNHA
05 Vice President Academic Affairs .... Dr. Janet KUSER
10 VP for Finance and Administration .... Vacant
84 VP of Enrollment Management .... Mr. Robert MELARAGNI
107 VP Online/Graduate/Prof Studies .... Ms. Kathleen EHLERS
111 VP Advancement & Alumni Engagement .... Ms. Brenda SANCHEZ
32 Dean of Students .... Ms. Shiela LALLY
88 Dean Intl Acad Oper/Curriculum Dev .... Ms. Nancy PITHIS
49 Asst Dean School of Liberal Arts .... Mr. Willem WALLINGA
06 College Registrar .... Mr. Jesse AVALOS
41 Director of Athletics .... Mr. Scott DULIN
15 Director of HR/Title IX Coord .... Mr. William OPAVA
26 Dir Marketing & Communications .... Vacant
07 Director of Admissions .... Mr. Zacchary SONGER
113 Director of Student Accounts .... Mr. Kevin KELLY
13 Director Systems/Client Services .... Mr. Michael CUTILLO
18 Director of Facilities .... Mr. Paul MCBRINE

37 Director of Financial Aid .... Ms. Jennifer WILHELM
20 Dir Academic Advising/Support Ctr .... Mr. Arthur ASBURY
19 Dir Public Safety/Chief of Police .... Mr. Brian PERRIN
36 Director of Career Services .... Ms. Ally BALDWIN
22 Director of Accessibility Service .... Ms. Ferna PHILLIPS
113 College Bursar .... Ms. Kristen MARTINEZ
08 College Librarian .... Mr. Joshua MCKAIN
09 Director of Institutional Research .... Mr. Roland PEARSALL
58 Assistant Dean Grad/MBA Programs .... Dr. Neil TROTTA
39 Interim Director Student Housing .... Ms. Shiela LALLY
124 Dir Student Engagement & Retention .... Mr. Jesse FORD
105 Webmaster & Digital Content Coord .... Ms. Elissa SPINNER
104 Director Study Abroad .... Mr. Jesse FORD

Franklin W. Olin College of Engineering (A)

Olin Way, Needham MA 02492-1200
County: Norfolk FICE Identification: 039463
Unit ID: 441982
Telephone: (781) 292-2300 Carnegie Class: Spec-4-yr-Eng
FAX Number: (781) 292-2210 Calendar System: Semester
URL: www.olin.edu
Established: 1997 Annual Undergrad Tuition & Fees: $57,356
Enrollment: 310 Coed
Affiliation or Control: Independent Non-Profit IRS Status: 501(c)3
Highest Offering: Baccalaureate
Accreditation: EH

01 President .... Dr. Gilda A. BARABINO
04 Exec Asst to President .... Ms. Kelly SUTHERLAND
05 Provost/Dean of Faculty .... Mr. Mark SOMERVILLE
32 Dean of Student Affairs & Resources .... Ms. Rae-Anne BUTERA
06 Assoc Dean for Acad Pgms/Registrar .... Ms. Linda T. CANAVAN
07 Dean of Admission and Financial Aid . Ms. Emily ROPER-DOTEN
37 Director of Financial Aid .... Ms. Jean RICKER
08 Library Director .... Vacant
10 VP for Financial Affairs & CFO .... Ms. Patricia GALLAGHER
13 Chief Information Officer .... Mr. Rick OSTERBERG
26 Assoc VP for Marketing & Comm .... Ms. Anne-Marie DORNING
09 Director of Inst Research .... Vacant
111 Vice President of Advancement .... Ms. Beth KRAMER
11 VP for Admin Services & Innovation .... Mr. Jeremy GOODMAN

† All admitted students who enroll at Olin College receive an Olin Scholarship covering half tuition during the eight semesters of the baccalaureate program.

Gordon College (B)

255 Grapevine Road, Wenham MA 01984-1899
County: Essex FICE Identification: 002153
Unit ID: 165936
Telephone: (978) 927-2300 Carnegie Class: Bac-A&S
FAX Number: (978) 867-4659 Calendar System: Semester
URL: www.gordon.edu
Established: 1889 Annual Undergrad Tuition & Fees: $39,230
Enrollment: 1,816 Coed
Affiliation or Control: Independent Non-Profit IRS Status: 501(c)3
Highest Offering: Master's
Accreditation: EH, MUS, SW

01 President .... Dr. Michael HAMOND
05 EVP for Academic Affairs .... Dr. Sandy DONESKI
84 VP for Enrollment .... Dr. Larry HOEZEE
10 VP for Finance/Business Development .... Mr. John J. TRUSCHEL
07 AVP Enrollment .... Ms. June BODONI
32 Vice President for Student Life .... Mr. Daniel TYMANN
26 VP of Marketing and Communications .... Mr. Rick SWEENEY
111 Acting VP of Advancement .... Mr. Mark DILLON
08 Director of Library Services .... Mr. Myron SCHIRER-SUTER
06 Registrar .... Mrs. Alice A. FALCONE
13 Chief Information Officer .... Mr. Christopher HANSEN
37 Sr Dir of Student Financial Svcs .... Mr. Daniel O'CONNELL
15 AVP for Human Resources .... Mr. Christopher JONES
18 Director of Facilities .... Mr. Dima BORISYUK
21 Dir of Finance and Controller .... Mr. Stephen LACORAZZA
110 AVP for Advancement .... Mrs. Britt CARLSON
36 Exec Director of Career Services .... Mr. Alexander LOWRY
96 Dir of Purchasing and Distribution .... Mr. Michael NAWOICHIK
09 AVP of Strategy & Decision Support .... Vacant
19 Chief of Police .... Mr. Glenn DECKERT
88 Dir of Advancement Service .... Mr. Rick HOUSTON
41 Director of Athletics .... Mr. Jon TYMANN
105 Creative Dir and Web Team Lead .... Mr. Stephen DAGLEY
35 Dean of Student Life .... Mr. Terry CHAREK
124 Dean of Student Engagement .... Dr. Nicholas ROWE
121 Dean of Student Success .... Mr. Christopher CARLSON
100 Deputy Chief of Staff .... Mr. William HAGEN
104 Dean Acad Init & Global Education .... Dr. Jewerl MAXWELL

Gordon-Conwell Theological Seminary (C)

130 Essex Street, South Hamilton MA 01982-2317
County: Essex FICE Identification: 009747
Unit ID: 165945
Telephone: (978) 468-7111 Carnegie Class: Spec-4-yr-Faith
FAX Number: (978) 468-6691 Calendar System: Semester
URL: www.gordonconwell.edu
Established: 1884 Annual Graduate Tuition & Fees: N/A
Enrollment: 1,489 Coed
Affiliation or Control: Independent Non-Profit IRS Status: 501(c)3
Highest Offering: Doctorate; No Undergraduates
Accreditation: EH, CACREP, THEOL

01 President .... Dr. Scott W. SUNQUIST
10 Vice Pres Finance & Operations/CFO .... Mr. Gregg HANSEN
111 Vice President of Advancement .... Mr. Brian GARDNER
112 Director Planned Giving .... Vacant
12 Dean of Boston Campus .... Dr. Virginia WARD
12 Dean of Charlotte Campus .... Dr. Gerald WHEATON
12 Dean of Hamilton Campus .... Dr. Mateus DE CAMPOS
12 Dean of Jacksonville Campus .... Dr. Bradley HOWELL
32 Dean of Students .... Ms. Jana HOLIDAY
15 Director of Human Resources .... Dr. Steven GREISDORF
13 Chief Information Officer .... Dr. Alex KOH
18 Director of Physical Plant .... Mr. Timothy INGRAHAM
08 Director of Libraries .... Mr. Brad HOWELL
58 Dean of Doctor of Ministry .... Dr. David CURRIE
37 Director of Financial Aid .... Mr. Stacey T. GLIDDEN
40 Director of Support Services .... Mr. David SHOREY
07 Director of Admissions .... Mr. Chris ANDERSON
21 Controller & Dir Financial Svcs .... Mrs. Heidi O'CONNOR
29 Director Alumni Relations .... Ms. Laura CARMER
39 Director Student Housing .... Mr. Jason STRZEPEK
06 Institutional Registrar .... Ms. Natalie CROWSON
100 Chief of Staff .... Mrs. Mia ERTEL
101 Secretary of the Institution/Board .... Mrs. Mia ERTEL
84 Director Enrollment Management .... Mr. Chris ANDERSON

Hampshire College (D)

893 West Street, Amherst MA 01002-3372
County: Hampshire FICE Identification: 004661
Unit ID: 166018
Telephone: (413) 549-4600 Carnegie Class: Bac-A&S
FAX Number: (413) 559-5584 Calendar System: 4/1/4
URL: www.hampshire.edu
Established: 1965 Annual Undergrad Tuition & Fees: $51,768
Enrollment: 522 Coed
Affiliation or Control: Independent Non-Profit IRS Status: 501(c)3
Highest Offering: Baccalaureate
Accreditation: EH

01 President .... Mr. Edward WINGENBACH
125 President Emeritus .... Dr. Jonathan LASH
101 Secretary of the College .... Ms. Carol SALZMAN
05 Vice Pres Acad Affs/Dean of Faculty .... Mr. Christoph COX
32 VP Student Affairs/Dean of Students .... Ms. Zauyah WAITE
10 VP Finance & Admin/Treasurer .... Mr. Carl RIES
15 Director HR/Title IX Coord .... Mr. Greg NARLESKI
111 Chief Advancement Officer .... Ms. Jennifer CHRISLER
20 AVP of Academic Affairs .... Ms. Yaniris FERNANDEZ
37 Dean of Financial Aid .... Mr. Fumio SUGIHARA
08 Director of Library .... Ms. Rachel BECKWITH
06 Director of Central Records .... Ms. Rachael GRAHAM
29 Director Alumni & Family Relations .... Ms. Melissa MILLS-DICK
36 Director Student Placement .... Ms. Carin RANK
38 Director Student Counseling .... Dr. Eliza MCARDLE
04 Admin Assistant to the President .... Ms. Cathy HEWS
11 Chief of Operations/Administration .... Ms. Elizabeth CRAUN
07 Dean of Admissions .... Mr. Fumio SUGIHARA
28 Co-Dean of Institutional Diversity .... Ms. Amy JORDAN
28 Co-Dean of Institutional Diversity .... Ms. Roosbelinda CARDENAS

Harvard University (E)

1350 Massachusetts Ave, Cambridge MA 02138-3800
County: Middlesex FICE Identification: 002155
Unit ID: 166027
Telephone: (617) 495-1000 Carnegie Class: DU-Highest
FAX Number: (617) 495-0500 Calendar System: Semester
URL: www.harvard.edu
Established: 1636 Annual Undergrad Tuition & Fees: $54,002
Enrollment: 30,391 Coed
Affiliation or Control: Independent Non-Profit IRS Status: 501(c)3
Highest Offering: Doctorate
Accreditation: EH, CAMPEP, CLPSY, DENT, IPSY, LAW, LSAR, MED, PCSAS, PH, PLNG, THEOL

01 President .... Lawrence S. BACOW
05 Provost .... Alan GARBER
49 Dean Arts and Sciences .... Claudine GAY
58 Dean Graduate School of A&S .... Emma DENCH
50 Dean Harvard Business School .... Srikant DATAR
49 Dean Harvard College .... Rakesh KHURANA
51 Dean Continuing Educ/Extension .... Nancy COLEMAN
52 Dean School of Dental Medicine .... William V. GIANNOBILE
48 Dean Graduate School of Design .... Sarah M. WHITING
73 Dean Harvard Divinity School .... David N. HEMPTON
53 Dean Graduate School of Education .... Bridget T. LONG
54 Dean Engineering/Applied Sciences .... Francis J. DOYLE
80 Dean Kennedy School of Government .... Douglas ELMENDORF
61 Dean Harvard Law School .... John F. MANNING
63 Dean Harvard Medical School .... George Q. DALEY
69 Dean School of Public Health .... Michelle A. WILLIAMS
88 Dean Inst for Advanced Studies .... Tomiko BROWN-NAGIN
21 Treasurer .... Paul J. FINNEGAN
03 Executive Vice President .... Katherine N. LAPP
43 VP and General Counsel .... Diane E. LOPEZ
29 VP Alumni Affairs/Development .... Brian K. LEE
10 VP for Finance & CFO .... Thomas HOLLISTER
101 VP and Secretary of the University .... Marc GOODHEART
100 Chief of Staff & Strategic Advisor .... Patricia BELLINGER
26 VP Public Affairs and Communication .... Paul ANDREW
15 VP for Human Resources .... Manuel CUEVAS-TRISAN
45 VP Planning & Project Management .... Vacant
08 VP for the Harvard Library .... Martha J. WHITEHEAD
13 VP Info Technology/CIO .... Klara JELINKOVA
18 VP for Campus Services .... Meredith WEENICK

Hebrew College (F)

160 Herrick Road, Newton Centre MA 02459-2237
County: Middlesex FICE Identification: 002157
Unit ID: 166045
Telephone: (617) 559-8600 Carnegie Class: Spec-4-yr-Faith
FAX Number: (617) 559-8601 Calendar System: Semester
URL: www.hebrewcollege.edu
Established: 1921 Annual Undergrad Tuition & Fees: N/A
Enrollment: 137 Coed
Affiliation or Control: Independent Non-Profit IRS Status: 501(c)3
Highest Offering: Beyond Master's But Less Than Doctorate
Accreditation: EH

01 President .... Rabbi Sharon C. ANISFELD
03 Vice President .... Dr. Susie TANCHEL
05 Dean and Chief Academic Officer .... Rabbi Dan JUDSON
10 Chief Financial and Admin Officer .... Mr. Keith DROPKIN
32 Director of Student Services .... Mr. Bob GIELOW
35 Dean of Student Life .... Rabbi Daniel KLEIN
06 Registrar .... Ms. Marcia SPELLMAN
15 Director Human Resources .... Ms. Steffi BOBBIN
04 Executive Asst to the President .... Ms. Shana BURSTYN
13 Manager Information Technology .... Mr. Jim KENN
08 Chief Library Officer .... Mr. Harvey SUKENIC
37 Director Student Financial Aid .... Mr. Bob GIELOW

Hellenic College-Holy Cross Greek Orthodox School of Theology (G)

50 Goddard Avenue, Brookline MA 02445-7496
County: Norfolk FICE Identification: 002154
Unit ID: 166054
Telephone: (617) 731-3500 Carnegie Class: Spec-4-yr-Faith
FAX Number: (617) 850-1460 Calendar System: Semester
URL: www.hchc.edu
Established: 1937 Annual Undergrad Tuition & Fees: $22,490
Enrollment: 126 Coed
Affiliation or Control: Greek Orthodox IRS Status: 501(c)3
Highest Offering: Master's
Accreditation: EH, THEOL

01 President .... Mr. George M. CANTONIS
73 Dean School of Theology .... Fr. Thomas FITZGERALD
05 VP for Academic Affairs .... Dr. Diana DEMETRULIAS
111 VP Institutional Advancement .... Vacant
32 Dean of Students .... Fr. Michael KOUREMETIS
10 VP Admin Affs/Operations/Finance .... RevDcn. Gary ALEXANDER
07 Director of Enrollment Mgmt .... Dr. Bruce BECK
08 Library Director .... Bishop Joachim COTSONIS
37 Financial Aid Director .... Mr. Michael KIRCHMAIER
06 Registrar .... Mr. Jay OSTROSKY
13 Technology/Digital Media Mgr .... Mr. Emanuel SABAU
29 Director of Alumni Office .... Vacant
113 Bursar .... Vacant
40 Bookstore Manager .... Ms. Nikoleta MAIDOU
39 Director of Housing/Security .... Vacant
15 Director of Human Resources .... Mr. David VOLZ
30 Director of Development .... Ms. Frances LEVAS
45 Director Strategic Initiatives .... Mr. Gary ALEXANDER
03 Executive Vice President .... Vacant

Hult International Business School (H)

One Education Street, Cambridge MA 02141-1805
County: Middlesex FICE Identification: 041432
Unit ID: 164368
Telephone: (617) 746-1990 Carnegie Class: Spec-4-yr-Bus
FAX Number: (617) 746-1991 Calendar System: Other
URL: www.hult.edu
Established: 1964 Annual Undergrad Tuition & Fees: $49,950
Enrollment: 1,814 Coed
Affiliation or Control: Proprietary IRS Status: Proprietary
Highest Offering: Doctorate
Accreditation: EH

01 President .... Dr. Stephen J. HODGES
05 Chief Academic Officer .... Dr. Johan ROOS
11 Chief Operating Officer .... Mr. David ARTHUR
10 Chief Financial Officer .... Mr. Martin ASP
13 Chief Technology Officer .... Mr. John PROKOS
36 Vice President Career Development .... Ms. Katharine BOSHKOFF
03 Executive Vice President UG .... Dr. Jannicke ROOS
03 Executive Vice President PG .... Ms. Melissa FREDETTE
88 Chief Innovation Officer .... Dr. Mukul KUMAR
20 Director of Central Academics .... Ms. Caroline HAYES
20 Dean of Central Academics .... Dr. Ian DOUGAL
12 Senior Associate Dean Boston Campus ... Ms. Mary DUTKIEWICZ
12 Dean San Francisco Campus .... Dr. Mona DHILLON
84 Regional Director Enrollment .... Mr. Steve WYNN
36 Dir of Career Services Boston .... Ms. Maggie DALEY
32 Dir Student Services Boston .... Ms. Nayeli VIVANCO
06 Registrar Boston Campus .... Vacant
06 Registrar San Francisco Campus .... Vacant
37 Director Student Financial Aid .... Ms. Karen VAN DYNE

Laboure College (A)

303 Adams Street, Milton MA 02186-4253
County: Suffolk | FICE Identification: 006324
Unit ID: 165264
Telephone: (617) 322-3500 | Carnegie Class: Spec-4-yr-Other Health
FAX Number: (617) 296-7947 | Calendar System: Trimester
URL: www.laboure.edu
Established: 1892 | Annual Undergrad Tuition & Fees: $32,813
Enrollment: 1,188 | Coed
Affiliation or Control: Roman Catholic | IRS Status: 501(c)3
Highest Offering: Baccalaureate
Accreditation: EH, ADNUR, NDT, NURSE, RTT

01 President .... Lily HSU
10 VP of Administration and Finance .... William MCDONALD
05 Vice Pres Academic Affairs .... Marilyn GARDNER
84 VP of Enrollment Management .... Justin ROY
32 Asst VP Student Affairs .... Matthew GREGORY
04 Executive Asst to President .... Megan D. CURRIVAN
06 Registrar .... John SACCO
08 Director of Library .... Anicia KUCHESKY
29 Director Alumni Affairs .... Katelyn DWYER
37 Director Student Financial Aid .... Erin HANLON

Lasell University (B)

1844 Commonwealth Avenue, Newton MA 02466-2716
County: Middlesex | FICE Identification: 002158
Unit ID: 166391
Telephone: (617) 243-2000 | Carnegie Class: Masters/M
FAX Number: (617) 243-2389 | Calendar System: Semester
URL: www.lasell.edu
Established: 1851 | Annual Undergrad Tuition & Fees: $39,000
Enrollment: 1,951 | Coed
Affiliation or Control: Independent Non-Profit | IRS Status: 501(c)3
Highest Offering: Master's
Accreditation: EH, ACBSP, CAATE, COSMA, EXSC

01 President .... Michael B. ALEXANDER
05 Provost .... Eric M. TURNER
10 VP Admin & Finance .... Vacant
84 VP Enrollment & Marketing .... Chrystal PORTER
88 President Lasell Village .... Anne DOYLE
111 VP University Advancement .... Chelsea GWYTHER
21 Assoc VP Admin & Operations .... Diane PARKER
28 Asst VP/Chief Diversity Officer .... Jesse TAURIAC
32 Asst VP/Dean of Student Affairs .... David HENNESSEY
76 Dean Health Sciences .... Cris HAVERTY
57 Interim Dean Comms & The Arts .... Meryl PERLSON
88 Dean Fashion .... Kathleen POTTER
79 Dean Human/Educ/Just & Soc Sc .... Lori ROSENTHAL
50 Dean Business .... Matthew REILLY
110 Asst VP University Advancement .... Caroline WEATHERBEE
07 Director of Admission .... Yavuz KIREMIT
37 Dir Student Financial Planning .... Jennifer MULDOWNEY
09 Dir Institutional Research .... Eric LANTHIER
06 Registrar .... Linda ARCE
26 Dir Communications .... Ian MEROPOL
29 Dir Alumni Relations/Annual Giving .... Thomas WILLIAMS
89 Dir Student Act & Orientation .... Jennifer GRANGER SULLIVAN
23 Dir Health Services .... Richard ARNOLD
08 Dir Library .... Anna SARNESO
41 Dir Athletics .... Kristy WALTER
15 Dir Human Resources .... Vacant
38 Dir Counseling Center .... Sharon HARRINGTON-HOPE
107 Asst VP Graduate & Prof Studies .... Adrienne FRANCIOSI
13 Chief Information Officer .... Jonathan GORHAM
19 Director of Public Safety .... Robert SHEA
43 Asst VP Legal Affairs .... Jennifer OKEEFFE
04 Executive Asst to the President .... Henry PUGH
85 Dir International Student Services .... Maria ADKINS
105 Dir Marketing .... Christopher LYNETT
36 Dir Career Readiness & Intern Pgm .... Donnell TURNER
39 Dir Resident Life/Student Housing .... Scott LAMPHERE

Lesley University (C)

29 Everett Street, Cambridge MA 02138-2790
County: Middlesex | FICE Identification: 002160
Unit ID: 166452
Telephone: (617) 868-9600 | Carnegie Class: DU-Mod
FAX Number: (617) 349-8717 | Calendar System: Semester
URL: www.lesley.edu
Established: 1909 | Annual Undergrad Tuition & Fees: $29,550
Enrollment: 4,200 | Coed
Affiliation or Control: Independent Non-Profit | IRS Status: 501(c)3
Highest Offering: Doctorate
Accreditation: EH, ACBSP, ART, CAEPT, @SW

01 President .... Dr. Janet L. STEINMAYER
05 Provost/CAO .... Dr. Jonathan JEFFERSON
11 Vice President for Administration .... Ms. Marylou BATT
10 Vice President of Finance/CFO .... Ms. Diane KIMBALL
111 VP of Advancement .... Ms. Veronica JORGE-CURTIS
84 VP of Enrollment Initiatives .... Mr. Thomas ENGLEHARDT
114 VP for Budgeting & Fin Planning .... Vacant
43 Vic Pres & General Counsel .... Ms. Shirin PHILIPP
45 VP Strategy & Implementation .... Dr. MaryPat LOHSE
20 Asst Provost Academic Success .... Mr. Randi KORN
58 Int Dean Grad Sch Arts & Social Sci .... Dr. Sandra WALKER
53 Interim Dean School of Education .... Dr. Amy RUTSTEIN-RILEY

32 Dean of Student Life & Academic Dev .... Dr. Nathaniel MAYS
49 Dean College of Liberal Arts & Sci .... Dr. Steven SHAPIRO
57 Dean of College of Art and Design .... Dr. Amy DEINES
13 Assoc VP Info Technology .... Mr. Charles COOPER
123 AVP of Graduate Admissions .... Ms. Barbara SELMO
15 Director of Human Resources .... Ms. Samantha CARPINELLA
37 Director of Financial Aid .... Ms. Michelle HEYDE
08 Head of Libraries .... Ms. Abigail MANCINI
07 Asst Dir Undergrad Admissions .... Mr. Shawn KITHCART
108 Assoc Dir Assessment/Accreditation .... Ms. Se-Ah SIEGEL
09 Dir of Institutional Research .... Mr. Alexander WAGNER
04 Assistant to the President .... Vacant
06 Registrar .... Ms. Adrianne ZONDERMAN
28 Cmty Standards/EO/Title IX Admin .... Ms. Sana AMINI

Longy School of Music of Bard College (D)

27 Garden Street, Cambridge MA 02138
Telephone: (617) 876-0956 | Identification: 770137
Accreditation: &M

† Branch campus of Bard College, Annandale-On-Hudson, NY

*Massachusetts Board of Higher Education (E)

One Ashburton Place, Room 1401,
Boston MA 02108-1696
County: Suffolk | FICE Identification: 029283
Telephone: (617) 994-6950 | Carnegie Class: N/A
FAX Number: (617) 727-6397
URL: www.mass.edu

01 Commissioner .... Dr. Carlos SANTIAGO
103 Assoc Comm Workforce Development .... Mr. David CEDRONE
45 Senior Assoc Comm Strategic Plng .... Dr. Winifred M. HAGAN
09 Sr Comm Research/Planning .... Dr. Jonathan KELLER
43 General Counsel .... Ms. Constantia PAPANIKOLAOU
10 Deputy Commissioner Admin/Finance .... Mr. Tom SIMARD
37 Sr Dep Comm Student Financial Aid .... Dr. Clantha MCCURDY

*University of Massachusetts System Office (F)

One Beacon Street, 31st Floor, Boston MA 02108
County: Suffolk | FICE Identification: 008017
Unit ID: 166665
Telephone: (617) 287-7050 | Carnegie Class: N/A
FAX Number: (617) 287-7167
URL: www.umassp.edu

01 President .... Mr. Martin T. MEEHAN
03 Executive Vice President .... Mr. James JULIAN, JR.
05 SVP Acad/Student Affs & Econ Dev .... Dr. Katherine NEWMAN
10 Sr VP Admin/Finance & Treasurer .... Ms. Lisa CALISE
26 Executive Director Communications .... Mr. John HOEY
11 Deputy Chief Operating Officer .... Ms. Susan KELLY
86 Associate VP of Govt Affairs .... Mr. David MCDERMOTT
43 General Counsel .... Mr. Gerard LEONE
13 Chief Information Officer .... Vacant
101 Secretary to Board of Trustees .... Ms. Zunilka BARRETT
116 Director for University Auditing .... Mr. Kyle DAVID
15 Chief Human Resources Officer .... Mr. John DUNLAP
106 CEO UMassOnline .... Mr. Donald KILBURN

*University of Massachusetts (G)

Amherst MA 01003
County: Hampshire | FICE Identification: 002221
Unit ID: 166629
Telephone: (413) 545-0111 | Carnegie Class: DU-Highest
FAX Number: N/A | Calendar System: Semester
URL: www.umass.edu
Established: 1863 | Annual Undergrad Tuition & Fees (In-State): $16,439
Enrollment: 31,642 | Coed
Affiliation or Control: State | IRS Status: 501(c)3
Highest Offering: Doctorate
Accreditation: EH, ART, AUD, CLPSY, DIETD, DIETI, IPSY, LSAR, MUS, NURSE, PH, PLNG, SCPSY, SP

02 Chancellor .... Dr. Kumble R. SUBBASWAMY
05 Sr VC/Provost Academic Affairs .... Dr. John J. MCCARTHY
03 Deputy Chancellor/Chf Planning Ofcr .... Dr. Steven D. GOODWIN
88 Assoc Chancellor for Compliance .... Ms. Christine M. WILDA
28 VC Diversity/Equity/Inclusion .... Ms. Nefertiti A. WALKER
100 Chief of Staff .... Dr. Rolanda C. BURNEY
10 Vice Chancellor Admin/Finance .... Mr. Andrew P. MANGELS
111 Int VC Advancement .... Ms. Theresa CURRY
46 VC Research & Engagement .... Dr. Michael F. MALONE
32 VC Student Affairs/Campus Life .... Dr. Brandi HEPHNER LABANC
26 VC University Relations .... Mr. John KENNEDY
13 VC Information Services & CIO .... Mr. Christopher P. MISRA
15 VC & Chief Human Resources Officer .... Mr. William D. BRADY
41 Director of Athletics .... Mr. Ryan BAMFORD
43 Senior Counsel .... Mr. Brian W. BURKE
22 Interim Dir Equal Opportunity .... Mr. Ryan K. MORSE
20 Sr Vice Provost for Acad Affairs .... Dr. Tilman WOLF
20 Sr Vice Provost for Acad Affairs .... Dr. Farshid HAJIR
20 Sr Vice Prov/Dean Undergrad Educ .... Dr. Carol A. BARR
88 Assoc Prov Interdisciplinary Stds .... Joseph BARTOLOMEO
58 Vice Provost/Dean of Grad School .... Dr. Jacqueline URLA

106 Sr Vice Provost Lifelong Learning .... Dr. John WELLS
84 Vice Provost Enrollment Management .... Dr. James ROCHE
20 Vice Provost Faculty Development .... Michelle BUDIG
09 Exec Dir Strategic Analytics .... Dr. Barb CHALFONTE
88 Assoc Provost Academic Personnel .... Mr. Michael J. EAGEN
11 Assoc Prov Admin & Finance .... Ms. Deborah M. GOULD
108 Assoc Prov Assessment/Educ Effect .... Dr. Martha L. STASSEN
88 Assoc Provost Equity & Inclusion .... Amel AHMED
85 Assoc Provost International Pgms .... Dr. Kalpen TRIVEDI
121 Assoc Provost Student Success .... Dr. Carolyn S. BASSETT
07 Director of Admissions .... Mr. Michael DRISH
87 Director of Summer Programs .... Ms. Sarah CRAIG
06 Sr Assoc Graduate Registrar .... Ms. Kate C. WOODMANSEE
37 Int Dir Financial Aid Services .... Ms. Lauren LAMICA
06 University Registrar .... Dr. Patrick SULLIVAN
92 Dean Commonwealth Honors College .... Dr. Mari CASTEÑEDA
79 Dean Col Humanities & Fine Arts .... Dr. Barbara KRAUTHAMER
77 Dean Col Computer & Info Sci .... Dr. Laura M. HAAS
81 Dean Col Natural Science .... Dr. Tricia R. SERIO
83 Dean Col Social & Behavioral Sci .... Dr. R. Karl RETHEMEYER
53 Dean School of Education .... Dr. Cynthia GERSTL-PEPIN
54 Dean College of Engineering .... Dr. Sanjay RAMAN
50 Dean School of Management .... Dr. Anne MASSEY
66 Dean College of Nursing .... Dr. Allison VORDERSTRASSE
69 Dean Sch Public Health/Hlth Sci .... Dr. Anna Maria SIEGA-RIZ
08 Director of Libraries .... Vacant
56 Director of Extension .... Ms. Jody L. JELLISON
47 Dir Stockbridge School Agriculture .... Dr. Wesley AUTIO
57 Director Fine Arts Center .... Ms. Jamilla DERIA
114 Budget Director .... Ms. Lynn C. MCKENNA
109 Executive Dir Auxiliary Enterprises .... Mr. Kenneth K. TOONG
113 Bursar .... Ms. Erin SCHADEL
18 Assoc VC Facilities & Campus Svcs .... Mr. Shane R. CONKLIN
19 Asst Vice Chancellor/Chief Police .... Mr. Tyrone PARHAM
40 Director Univ Store .... Ms. Melissa PETERSON
35 Dean of Students .... Dr. Evelyn ASHLEY
39 Dir Residential Life/Student Svcs .... Ms. Dawn BOND
89 Dir Assessment/Student Affairs .... Dr. Marcy R. CLARK
104 Dir Education Abroad .... Mr. Mark ECKMAN
122 Coord Fraternities & Sororities .... Mr. Thomas J. MARTIN
23 Exec Dir University Health Services .... Dr. George A. COREY
38 Dir Ctr Counseling & Psych Hlth .... Dr. Melissa S. ROTKIEWICZ
36 Director Career Services .... Ms. Candice J. SERAFINO
29 Asst VC Alumni Relations .... Ms. Deborah GOODHIND
44 Exec Dir Annual Giving .... Mr. Nathan ADAMS
27 Assoc VC University Relations .... Dr. Nancy BUFFONE
88 Exec Dir News & Media Relations .... Mr. Edward F. BLAGUSZEWSKI
88 Sr Dir Executive Communications .... Ms. Amy C. GLYNN
86 Exec Dir Government Relations .... Mr. Christopher DUNN
102 Dir Foundation/Corporate Relations .... Ms. Liz M. SMITH
112 Assoc Director Planned Gifts .... Mr. Joe JAYNE
25 Dir Grants & Contracts (Post-Award) .... Ms. Carol SPRAGUE
90 Int Dir Instructional Innovation .... Mr. Matthew DALTON
119 Chief Information Security Officer .... Mr. Matthew DALTON
105 Director of Infrastructure Ops .... Mr. Randy SAILER
30 Assoc VC Development .... Vacant

*University of Massachusetts Boston (H)

100 Morrissey Boulevard, Boston MA 02125-3393
County: Suffolk | FICE Identification: 002222
Unit ID: 166638
Telephone: (617) 287-5000 | Carnegie Class: DU-Higher
FAX Number: (617) 265-7173 | Calendar System: Semester
URL: www.umb.edu
Established: 1964 | Annual Undergrad Tuition & Fees (In-State): $14,677
Enrollment: 16,259 | Coed
Affiliation or Control: State | IRS Status: 501(c)3
Highest Offering: Doctorate
Accreditation: EH, CACREP, CLPSY, COPSY, MPCAC, NURSE, SCPSY, SPAA

02 Chancellor .... Dr. Marcelo M. SUAREZ-OROZCO
05 Provost/VC Academic Affairs .... Dr. Joseph BERGER
03 Deputy Chancellor .... Dr. Hannah SEVIAN
20 Associate Provost .... Mr. Brian WHITE
10 Vice Chanc for Admin & Finance .... Ms. Kathleen KIRLEIS
111 VC for University Advancement .... Mr. Adam WISE
32 Int Vice Chancellor Student Affs .... Ms. Shawn DEVEAU
84 Vice Chanc for Enrollment Managemen .... Dr. John DREW
26 VC for Marketing & Engagement .... Ms. Megan DELAGE SULLIVAN
15 Vice Chanc for Human Resources .... Ms. Marie BOWEN
13 Vice Chanc Information Svcs/CIO .... Mr. Ray LEFEBVRE
20 Assoc VP for Academic Affairs .... Ms. Anita MILLER
45 AVP/Exec Dir Strategic Initiatives .... Ms. Mya M. MANAGAWANG
41 Director of Athletics .... Ms. Jacqueline SCHUMAN
86 Asst Chanc Govt Rels & Public Affs .... Mr. Matt FENLON
22 Asst Chancellor/Equity & Inclusion .... Ms. Georgianna MELENDEZ
53 Int Dean Col of Educ & Human Dev .... Dr. Laura HAYDEN
66 Interim Dean College of Nursing .... Dr. Rosanna DEMARCO
79 Dean of Liberal Arts .... Dr. Tyson D. KING-MEADOWS
81 Dean of Math & Science .... Dr. Robin COTE
50 Interim Dean College of Management .... Dr. Arindam BANDOPADHYAYA
08 Interim Dean of Univ Libraries .... Ms. Joanne RILEY
09 Assoc Prov Institutional Research .... Mr. James J. HUGHES
92 Dean of Honors College .... Vacant
82 Dean Sch Global Incl & Social Dev .... Vacant
80 Int Dn Grad Sch Policy/Global Stds .... Dr. Rita Kiki EDOZIE
58 VP Research & Dean of Grad Studies .... Mr. Bala SUNDARAM
121 Vice Prov for Academic Support Svcs .... Ms. Liya ESCALERA

100 Chief of Staff ... Ms. Anne RILEY
27 Director of Communications ... Mr. DeWayne LEHMAN
88 Dean of Faculty ... Dr. Rajini SRIKANTH

*University of Massachusetts Dartmouth (A)

285 Old Westport Road, North Dartmouth MA 02747-2300
County: Bristol — FICE Identification: 002210 — Unit ID: 167987
Telephone: (508) 999-8000 — Carnegie Class: DU-Higher
FAX Number: (508) 999-8901 — Calendar System: Semester
URL: www.umassd.edu
Established: 1895 — Annual Undergrad Tuition & Fees (In-State): $14,408
Enrollment: 7,869 — Coed
Affiliation or Control: State — IRS Status: 501(c)3
Highest Offering: Doctorate
Accreditation: EH, ART, CIDA, LAW, MT, NURSE

01 Chancellor ... Dr. Mark FULLER
03 Deputy Chancellor ... Dr. Mark PREBLE
100 Chief of Staff ... Ms. Robyn PIGGOT
05 Acting Provost/VC Academic Affairs ... Dr. Michael GOODMAN
10 VC Administration & Finance ... Mr. David GINGERELLA
111 VC University Advancement ... Mr. Dean HICKEY
28 Chief Diversity Officer ... Mr. David GOMES
110 Asst VC Advancement Services ... Ms. Valerie AU
15 Asst VC HR Operations ... Ms. Kimberly PENNOCK
04 Executive Office Director ... Ms. Lori NICKERSON
26 Assoc VC for Public Affairs ... Vacant
20 Assoc Provost UGRD/Faculty Affairs ... Dr. Robert JONES
58 Assoc Provost Grad Studies ... Dr. Tesfay MERESSI
46 Vice Provost Research & Acad Affs ... Dr. Ramprasad BALASUBRAMANIAN
84 Interim VC Enrollment Management ... Mr. James ANDERSON
21 Assoc VC Admin & Finance ... Ms. Susan AMATRUDO
18 Associate VC Facilities Management ... Mr. James JERUE, JR.
88 Asst VC for Org Behavior ... Ms. Deborah MAJEWSKI
32 Vice Chancellor Student Affairs ... Vacant
13 Assoc VC IT/CIO ... Mr. Holger DIPPEL
35 Assistant VC Student Success ... Ms. Carol SPENCER-MONTEIRO
49 Dean College Arts & Science ... Dr. Pauline ENTIN
50 Dean Charlton College Business ... Dr. John WILLIAMS
54 Dean College of Engineering ... Dr. Jean VANDERGHEYNST
66 Dean College of Nurse & Health Sci ... Dr. Kimberly CHRISTOPHER
57 Dean College Visual Perf Arts ... Dr. A. Lawrence JENKENS
88 Interim Dean School Marine Sci/Tech ... Dr. Jean VANDERGHEYNST
61 Dean School of Law ... Dr. Eric MITNICK
08 Interim Dean Library Services ... Ms. Dawn GROSS
51 Asst VC Online & Continuing Educ ... Mr. David PEDRO
58 Dir Graduate Studies/Admissions ... Mr. Scott WEBSTER
96 Assoc VC for Admin Operations ... Mr. Michael LAGRASSA
21 Controller ... Ms. Suzanne AUDET
88 Director Faculty Development ... Mr. Jay ZYSK
94 Dir Center Women/Gender/Sexuality ... Dr. Juli PARKER
121 Dir Advising/Support & Planning ... Vacant
06 University Registrar ... Ms. Audra CALLAHAN
07 Director of Admissions ... Ms. Hanan KHAMIS
37 Director Financial Aid ... Ms. Korinne PETERSON
09 Dir Inst Research/Assessment ... Ms. Tammy A. SILVA
19 Dir Public Safety/Chief of Police ... Ms. Haydee MARTINEZ
36 Director Career Development Center ... Mr. Un Yeong PARK
38 Dir Counseling/Student Devel Ctr ... Dr. Catherine PERRY
90 Exec Dir IT Service Assurance ... Ms. Margaret S. DIAS
29 Director of Alumni Relations ... Mr. Joshua SYLVESTER
18 Director Facilities/Physical Plant ... Mr. Jeffrey LOURO
41 Interim Director of Athletics ... Ms. Linda MOULTON
23 Director of Health Services ... Ms. Marianne SULLIVAN
39 Dir Housing/Residential Education ... Ms. Lucinda POUDRIER-AARONSON
44 Asst VC for Annual Giving ... Ms. Ellen CACCIA
27 Asst VC for Univ Marketing ... Ms. Hillary SYLVIA
113 Bursar ... Ms. Michelle PEZZULLI
35 Asst VC Student Affairs ... Vacant
35 Associate Dean of Students ... Ms. Shelly METIVIER SCOTT
104 Asst Director Study Abroad Pgms ... Ms. Gina REIS
85 Exec Dir International Education ... Mr. Daniel PIRBUDAGOV
93 Assoc Dir Fred Douglas Unity House ... Mr. Lasella HALL
88 Director Academic Resource Center ... Mr. Sokratis KOUMAS
105 Webmaster ... Vacant
103 Dir Experiential Learning & Intern ... Ms. Amelia ALBURN
106 Dir Center for Access & Success ... Ms. Wendi CHAKA
25 Dir Research Administration ... Ms. Megan HENNESSEY-GREENE
28 Director Diversity & Inclusion ... Vacant
45 Assoc VC Capital Planning & Ops Mgt ... Mr. Jeffrey MARTIN
103 Exec Dir Economic Development ... Vacant
88 Acting Director of Media Relations ... Mr. Ryan MERRILL
88 Asst VC Civic Engagement ... Mr. Matthew ROY
88 Director of Academic Budget ... Mr. Christopher VALADAO
44 Director of Annual Giving ... Vacant
88 Dir Frederick Unity House ... Ms. Moise SAINT-LOUIS

*University of Massachusetts Lowell (B)

1 University Avenue, Lowell MA 01854-2881
County: Middlesex — FICE Identification: 002161 — Unit ID: 166513
Telephone: (978) 934-4000 — Carnegie Class: DU-Higher
FAX Number: (978) 934-3000 — Calendar System: Semester
URL: www.uml.edu
Established: 1894 — Annual Undergrad Tuition & Fees (In-State): $15,698
Enrollment: 18,150 — Coed
Affiliation or Control: State — IRS Status: 501(c)3
Highest Offering: Doctorate
Accreditation: EH, ART, CAMPEP, DIETC, @DIETD, MT, MUS, NURSE, PTA

02 Chancellor ... Dr. Jacqueline F. MOLONEY
05 Provost ... Dr. Joseph HARTMAN
10 Sr VC Financial Opers & Stat Plng ... Mr. Steven O'RIORDAN
26 VC University Relations ... Ms. Patricia MCCAFFERTY
46 VC of Research & Innovation ... Dr. Julie CHEN
111 Vice Chancellor for Advancement ... Mr. John FEUDO
32 VC Student Affs/Univ Events ... Dr. Joseph HARTMAN
15 Sr Assoc VC Human Resources & EOO ... Dr. Lauren TURNER
58 Vice Provost Grad & Prof Studies ... Dr. Steven TELLO
18 Assoc VC Facilities Management ... Ms. Jean ROBINSON
27 Assoc VC Marketing ... Mr. Bryce HOFFMAN
20 Vice Provost Academic Affairs ... Dr. Julie NASH
84 Dean Enrollment Management ... Ms. Kerri JOHNSTON
41 Director of Athletics ... Mr. Peter CASEY
49 Dean Col Fine Arts/Hum/Soc Sci ... Dr. Luis FALCON
81 Dean Kennedy College of Sciences ... Dr. Noureddine MELIKECHI
54 Dean College of Engineering ... Dr. Jim SHERWOOD
76 Dean College of Health Sciences ... Dr. Shortie MCKINNEY
50 Dean Manning School of Business ... Dr. Sandra RICHTERMEYER
20 Dean Academic Services ... Ms. Kerry DONOHOE
06 Registrar ... Ms. Mai NGUYEN
37 Assoc Dean Enrollment/Dir Fin Aid ... Ms. Joyce MCLAUGHLIN
38 Director of Counseling Svcs ... Dr. Deborah EDELMAN-BLANK
29 Exec Dir Alumni & Donor Relations ... Ms. Heather MAKREZ ALLEN
19 Chief Univ Police Dir Public Safety ... Mr. Randolph BRASHEARS
123 Asst Dean Graduate Recruitment ... Dr. Shahram HAYDARI
96 Chief Procurement Officer ... Mr. Thomas HOOLE
07 Asst Dean Undergrad Admissions ... Ms. Christine BRYAN
119 Dir Security Tech & UCAPS ... Mr. Jon VICTORINE
22 Assoc VC Equal Opportunity/Outreach ... Ms. Clara REYNOLDS
36 Assoc Dean Student Affs/Career Dev ... Mr. Gregory DENON
35 Dean Student Affairs & Enrichment ... Mr. James KOHL
23 Dir Student Health Svcs ... Ms. Diana WALKER MOYER
35 Dean Student Affairs & Event Svcs ... Ms. Brenda EVANS
13 Assoc VC Info Tech & CIO ... Mr. Michael CIPRIANO
104 Director Intl Exper/Study Abroad ... Ms. Fern MACKINNON
92 Dean Honors College ... Dr. Jenifer WHITTEN-WOODRING
100 Chief of Staff ... Mr. Chris MULLIN
44 Director Annual Giving ... Ms. Deidra MILES
86 Exec Director Government Relations ... Mr. D.J CORCORAN

*UMass Chan Medical School (C)

55 Lake Avenue N, Worcester MA 01655-0001
County: Worcester — FICE Identification: 009756 — Unit ID: 166708
Telephone: (508) 856-8989 — Carnegie Class: Spec-4-yr-Med
FAX Number: (508) 856-8181 — Calendar System: Semester
URL: www.umassmed.edu
Established: 1962 — Annual Graduate Tuition & Fees: N/A
Enrollment: 1,292 — Coed
Affiliation or Control: State — IRS Status: 501(c)3
Highest Offering: Doctorate; No Undergraduates
Accreditation: EH, IPSY, MED, NURSE

02 Chancellor & SVP Health Sciences ... Dr. Michael F. COLLINS
05 Provost/Dean/Exec Deputy Chancellor ... Dr. Terence R. FLOTTE
10 Exec VC Administration & Finance ... Mr. John LINDSTEDT
88 Exec VC Innovation and Business Dev ... Mr. Parth CHAKRABARTI
111 VC for Advancement ... Mr. John J. HAYES
28 VC Diversity & Inclusion ... Dr. Marlina DUNCAN
88 Exec Vice Chancellor MassBiologics ... Ms. Mireli W. FINO
11 Exec VC Commonwealth Medicine ... Ms. Lisa COLOMBO
86 VC for Government Relations ... Mr. John ERWIN
26 Vice Chancellor of Communications ... Ms. Jennifer BERRYMAN
20 Vice Provost Faculty Affairs ... Dr. Mary AHN
88 Vice Prov/Sr Assoc Dean Educ Affs ... Dr. Anne LARKIN
63 Sr Assc Dean Clin Aff/Assc Dean GME ... Dr. Deborah DEMARCO
66 Dean Graduate School of Nursing ... Dr. Joan VITELLO
32 Interim Assoc Dean Student Affs ... Dr. Anne GARRISON
58 Dean Grad School Biomedical Science ... Dr. Mary Ellen LANE
18 Assoc VC Facilities Mgmt ... Mr. John T. BAKER
06 Registrar ... Mr. Michael F. BAKER
13 Chief Information Officer ... Mr. Greg WOLF
07 Assoc Dean for Admissions ... Dr. Mariann M. MANNO
37 Director Financial Aid ... Mr. Shawn MORRISSEY
08 Director of Library ... Dr. Mary PIORUN
100 Assoc VC for Mgmt/Chief of Staff ... Mr. Brendan H. CHISHOLM
04 Spec Assistant to the Chancellor ... Mr. Luke GLYNN
46 Vice Prov Rsrch/Strat Initiatives ... Dr. Michael GREEN
88 Vice Provost for Clin/Trans Science ... Dr. Katherine LUZURIAGA
88 Chief of Staff to Dean/Provost ... Ms. Kristen MAKI
88 Exec Asst to Dean/Prov/Exec Deputy ... Ms. Kimberly LAPERLE
04 Exec Assistant to the Chancellor ... Ms. Lisa BARRY
11 Dep EVC of Management ... Mr. James HEALY
15 Dep EVC People Strategy ... Ms. Deborah HARNOIS

*Bridgewater State University (D)

131 Summer Street, Bridgewater MA 02325-0001
County: Plymouth — FICE Identification: 002183 — Unit ID: 165024
Telephone: (508) 531-1000 — Carnegie Class: Masters/L
FAX Number: N/A — Calendar System: Semester
URL: www.bridgew.edu
Established: 1840 — Annual Undergrad Tuition & Fees (In-State): $10,732
Enrollment: 10,651 — Coed
Affiliation or Control: State — IRS Status: 501(c)3
Highest Offering: Master's
Accreditation: EH, AAB, ART, CAATE, CACREP, MPCAC, MUS, SP, SPAA, SW

02 President ... Mr. Frederick CLARK
05 Provost & VP Academic Affairs ... Dr. Karim ISMAILI
10 Vice President and CFO ... Mr. Doug SHROPSHIRE
32 VP Student Affs/Enrollment Mgmt ... Dr. Joseph ORAVECZ
36 VP Outreach and Engagement ... Dr. Brenda MOLIFE
15 VP Human Resources & Talent Mgmt ... Ms. Keri POWERS
26 VP Marketing & Communication ... Mr. Paul JEAN
28 VP of Student Success & Diversity ... Dr. Sabrina GENTLEWARRIOR
11 Vice President Operations ... Ms. Karen W. JASON
88 Int Vice President External Affairs ... Dr. Deniz LEUENBERGER
100 Chief of Staff/VP Plng & Strategy ... Dr. Deniz ZEYNEP LEUENBERGER
22 Director EOO/Title IX ... Ms. Jocelyn FRAWLEY
35 Assoc VP & Dean of Students ... Ms. Denine ROCCO
84 Assoc Dean for Enrollment Services ... Mr. Todd AUDYATIS
20 Assoc Provost Faculty Affairs ... Dr. Pamela RUSSELL
45 Sr Assoc Provost/Chief Data Officer ... Dr. Michael YOUNG
79 Dean Col Humanities/Social Sci ... Dr. Arnaa ALCON
53 Dean Col Education/Allied Studies ... Dr. Tom TONG-CHING WU
51 Dean Col of Continuing Studies ... Dr. David CRANE
50 Dean Ricciardi Col of Business ... Dr. Jeanean DAVIS-STREET
07 Dean of University Admissions ... Mr. Gregg A. MEYER
13 VP & Chief Information Officer ... Mr. Steve ZUROMSKI
06 Registrar ... Mr. Joseph WOLK
121 Exec Director Academic Achievement ... Ms. Laura FOLLONI
29 Exec Director Alumni Relations ... Ms. Ellen CUTTLE-OLIVER
30 Director Development ... Ms. Betsy DUBUQUE
41 Director Athletics/Recreation ... Dr. Marybeth LAMB
21 Director University Services ... Dr. Margarida BAGANHA
19 Chief of Police ... Mr. David TILLINGHAST
36 Director Career Services ... Mr. John PAGANELLI
37 Director of Financial Aid ... Ms. Laura BIECHLER
23 Executive Director Wellness Center ... Dr. Christopher FRAZER
08 Director Library Administration ... Vacant
93 Director Multicultural Affairs ... Vacant
27 Asst Dir Creative Svcs/Publications ... Ms. Jaime KNIGHT
25 Director Grants/Sponsored Projects ... Ms. Mia ZOINO
96 Director of Procurement Services ... Dr. Jennifer SIPIORA
28 Director of Institutional Diversity ... Dr. Luis F. PAREDES
81 Dean Bartlett Col Science & Math ... Dr. Kristen PORTER-UTLEY
58 Dean College of Graduate Studies ... Dr. Lisa KRISSOFF BOEHM
09 Director of Institutional Research ... Dr. Kate MCLAREN-POOLE
88 Director Teaching and Learning ... Dr. Roben TOROSYAN
46 Asst Prov High Impact Ed Practices ... Dr. Jenny SHANAHAN
85 Assoc Dir Intl Students/Scholars ... Ms. Jennifer CURRIE
104 Director Study Abroad ... Mr. Michael SANDY
14 AVP Information Technology ... Ms. Kelley BARAN
105 Director of Web Development ... Ms. Eileen O'SULLIVAN
27 Asst VP & Chief Marketing Officer ... Ms. Eva GAFFNEY
88 AVP University News and Video ... Mr. David ROBICHAUD
38 Clinical Dir Counseling Center ... Ms. Donna SHIAVO
39 Dir Residence Life and Housing ... Mr. Justin MCCAULEY
108 Director of Assessment ... Dr. Ruth SLOTNICK
88 Sr Admin Fellow Civics/Social Just ... Vacant
88 Asst Provost for Global Engagement ... Dr. Wing-Kai TO
04 Dir Presidential Initiatives & Oper ... Ms. Kelly HESS SALISBURY
88 Special Advisor to the President ... Mr. Vinny DE MACEDO
97 Dean of Undergraduate Studies ... Dr. Rita MILLER

*Fitchburg State University (E)

160 Pearl Street, Fitchburg MA 01420-2697
County: Worcester — FICE Identification: 002184 — Unit ID: 165820
Telephone: (978) 345-2151 — Carnegie Class: Masters/L
FAX Number: (978) 665-3693 — Calendar System: Semester
URL: www.fitchburgstate.edu
Established: 1894 — Annual Undergrad Tuition & Fees (In-State): $10,830
Enrollment: 6,728 — Coed
Affiliation or Control: State — IRS Status: 501(c)3
Highest Offering: Master's
Accreditation: EH, CAEPN, CSHSE, IACBE, NURSE

02 President ... Dr. Richard S. LAPIDUS
05 Provost/VP Academic Affairs ... Dr. Alberto CARDELLE
10 Vice Pres Finance & Administration ... Mr. Jay BRY
20 Associate VP Academic Affairs ... Dr. Catherine CANNEY
32 Vice President Student Affairs ... Dr. Laura BAYLESS
111 Vice President of Inst Advancement ... Mr. Jeffrey WOLFMAN
21 AVP Finance & Administration ... Ms. Mary Beth MCKENZIE
09 Asst VP Institutional Research ... Ms. Pamela MCCAFFERTY
15 Asst VP of Human Resources/Payroll ... Ms. Jessica MURDOCH
18 Asst VP Capital Planning ... Mr. Joseph LOBUONO
35 Asst Dean for Student Development ... Dr. Henry C. PARKINSON, III
06 Registrar ... Ms. Barbara CORMIER
41 Director Athletics ... Mr. Matthew BURKE
07 Director of Admissions ... Ms. Jinawa MCNEIL
36 Director Career Counseling ... Ms. Melisa ALVES
38 Director Counseling ... Dr. Robert HYNES
29 Director of Alumni Relations ... Vacant
19 Director of Campus Police ... Chief Michael CLOUTIER
44 Director of Annual Giving ... Ms. Tanya CROWLEY
18 Dir Capital Planning & Construction ... Vacant
25 Director Grants & Sponsored Pgm ... Ms. Jeanette ROBICHAUD
37 Director Financial Aid ... Ms. Denise BRINDLE
106 Dir of Digital Learning ... Ms. Nicole CHELONIS
13 Chief Info Technology Officer (CIO) ... Mr. Stephen E. SWARTZ
39 Dean of the Library ... Ms. Jacalyn KREMER
04 Special Asst to President ... Ms. Gail M. DOIRON

53 Dean of Education ... Dr. Nancy MURRAY
81 Dean of Health & Natural Sciences ... Dr. Margaret HOEY
58 Dean of Graduate & Cont Educ ... Dr. Becky COPPER GLENZ
49 Dean of Arts & Sciences ... Dr. Franca BARRICELLI

*Framingham State University (A)

100 State Street, PO Box 9101,
Framingham MA 01701-9101
County: Middlesex | FICE Identification: 002185
Unit ID: 165866
Telephone: (508) 620-1220 | Carnegie Class: Masters/L
FAX Number: (508) 626-4592 | Calendar System: Semester
URL: www.framingham.edu
Established: 1839 | Annual Undergrad Tuition & Fees (In-State): $11,380
Enrollment: 4,876 | Coed
Affiliation or Control: State | IRS Status: 501(c)3
Highest Offering: Master's
Accreditation: EH, ART, CAEPN, DIETC, DIETD, IACBE, NURSE

02 President ... Dr. F. Javier CEVALLOS
03 Executive Vice President ... Dr. Dale M. HAMEL
05 Vice President Academic Affairs ... Dr. Ellen ZIMMERMAN
32 Vice Pres Enrollment & Student Dev ... Dr. Lorretta HOLLOWAY
43 Vice President/General Counsel ... Ms. Ann MCDONALD
20 Associate Vice President ... Vacant
13 Associate Vice President ... Mr. Patrick LAUGHRAN
18 Assistant Vice President ... Ms. Patricia WHITNEY
84 Dean of Enrollment Management ... Mr. Jeremy SPENCER
35 Dean of Students ... Dr. Meg NOWAK
39 Associate Dean Student Affairs ... Mr. Glenn COCHRAN
07 Associate Dean Undergrad Admissions ... Ms. Shayna EDDY
88 Assistant Dean Student Affairs ... Mr. David N. BALDWIN
88 Assistant Dean Student Affairs ... Dr. Christopher GREGORY
06 Executive Director/Registrar ... Mr. Mark R. POWERS
15 Asst Vice Pres Human Resources ... Ms. Kimberly DEXTER
19 Interim Chief Public Safety ... Mr. John SANTORO
121 Director Academic Support ... Ms. LaDonna BRIDGES
108 Director Assessment ... Dr. Mark NICHOLAS
41 Director Athletics ... Mr. Thomas KELLEY
36 Director Career Services ... Mr. Rich DAVINO
37 Director Financial Aid ... Ms. Carla MINCHELLO
10 Director Financial Services ... Ms. Rachel TRANT
89 Director First Year Programs ... Mr. Benjamin J. TRAPANICK
23 Director Health Services ... Ms. Ilene HOFRENNING
104 Director International Education ... Ms. Jane DECATUR
08 Director Library Services ... Mrs. Millie GONZALEZ
38 Director Counseling Center ... Dr. Andrew LIPSKY
88 Director Student Involvement ... Ms. Rachel LUCKING
113 Director Student Accounts ... Mr. Gregory JACKSON
30 Director Development ... Mr. Eric GUSTAFSON
25 Director Grants/Sponsored Programs ... Ms. Patricia BOSSANGE
09 Director Institutional Research ... Ms. Ann CASO
04 Executive Assistant ... Ms. Katie HEBERT
22 Director of Equal Opportunity ... Ms. Kimberly DEXTER
58 Dean of Graduate Studies ... Dr. Yasar NAJJAR
26 Chief Public Relations Officer ... Mr. Daniel MAGAZU
28 Chief Diversity & Inclusion Officer ... Ms. Connie CABELLO
29 Director of Alumni Relations ... Ms. Jennier DEFRONZO

*Massachusetts College of Art and Design (B)

621 Huntington Avenue, Boston MA 02115-5882
County: Suffolk | FICE Identification: 002180
Unit ID: 166674
Telephone: (617) 879-7000 | Carnegie Class: Spec-4-yr-Arts
FAX Number: (617) 566-4034 | Calendar System: Semester
URL: www.massart.edu
Established: 1873 | Annual Undergrad Tuition & Fees (In-State): $14,200
Enrollment: 1,894 | Coed
Affiliation or Control: State | IRS Status: 501(c)3
Highest Offering: Master's
Accreditation: EH

02 President ... Dr. Mary K. GRANT
10 VP of Administration & Finance ... Mr. Robert PERRY
05 Interim Provost ... Mr. James MASON
32 Vice President Student Development ... Dr. Maureen KEEFE
111 Vice Pres Institutional Advancement ... Ms. Marjorie O'MALLEY
09 Exec Dir IR/Effectiveness/Planning ... Ms. Karalynn GAU
21 Asst VP Fiscal Affairs ... Ms. Gina SPAZIANI
100 Chief of Staff President's Office ... Mr. Robert CHAMBERS
07 Dean of Admissions/Enrollment ... Ms. Lauren WILSHUSEN
35 Assoc VP/Dean of Students ... Dr. Jamie COSTELLO
06 Registrar ... Mr. Jonathan RAND
37 Director of Financial Aid ... Mr. Aurelio RAMIREZ
88 Director MassArt Art Museum ... Ms. Lisa TUNG
08 Librarian ... Mr. Greg WALLACE
15 Exec Director Human Resources ... Ms. Justine CARON
28 Dean of Diversity ... Ms. Lyssa PALU-AY
22 Exec Director of Compliance ... Ms. Alisa CHAPMAN
18 Asst VP Facilities & Planning ... Mr. Howie LAROSEE
11 Exec Dir of Administrative Services ... Mr. James MCDAID
26 Exec Dir Marketing/Communications ... Ms. Ellen CARR
13 Chief Information Officer ... Mr. Patrick O'CONNOR
19 Chief of Police ... Mr. Dwayne FARLEY
104 Dir International Education Center ... Ms. Erica PUCCIO O'BRIEN
38 Director Counseling & Wellness ... Dr. Shauna SUMMERS
29 Director Alumni Relations ... Ms. Darlene GILLAN
39 Director Student Housing ... Vacant

*Massachusetts College of Liberal Arts (C)

375 Church Street, North Adams MA 01247-4100
County: Berkshire | FICE Identification: 002187
Unit ID: 167288
Telephone: (413) 662-5000 | Carnegie Class: Bac-A&S
FAX Number: (413) 662-5010 | Calendar System: Semester
URL: www.mcla.edu
Established: 1894 | Annual Undergrad Tuition & Fees (In-State): $11,306
Enrollment: 1,202 | Coed
Affiliation or Control: State | IRS Status: 501(c)3
Highest Offering: Master's
Accreditation: EH, #CAATE, RAD

02 President ... Dr. James BIRGE
05 Interim VP Academic Affairs ... Dr. Adrienne WOOTTERS
45 VP Strategic Initiatives ... Ms. Gina PUC
32 VP Student Affairs ... Dr. Catherine HOLBROOK
111 VP Institutional Advancement ... Mr. Robert ZIOMEK
10 VP Administration & Finance ... Mr. Joseph DASILVA
28 Chief Diversity Officer ... Dr. Christopher MACDONALD-DENNIS
15 Executive Director Human Resources ... Ms. Barbara CHAPUT
04 Executive Assistant to President ... Ms. Lisa LESCARBEAU
26 Director Marketing & Communications ... Ms. Bernadette ALDEN
13 Chief Information Officer ... Mr. Ian BERGERON
20 Interim Dean Academic Affairs ... Dr. Ely JANIS
35 Dean of Students ... Ms. Heather QUIRE
121 Dean Student Success ... Ms. Theresa O'BRYANT
21 Director of Fiscal Affairs ... Mr. Curt CELLANA
08 Associate Dean Library Services ... Ms. Emily ALLING
51 Associate Dean DGCE ... Mr. Paul PETRITIS
30 Senior Director of Development ... Mr. Marc MORANDI
07 Director Admissions ... Ms. Kayla HOLLINS
41 Director Athletics ... Ms. Laura MOONEY
37 Director Student Financial Services ... Ms. Bonnie HOWLAND
38 Director Counseling Services ... Ms. Heidi RIELLO
19 Director Public Safety ... Mr. Daniel COLONNO
23 Director Health Services ... Dr. Jacki KRZANIK
29 Senior Dir Constituent Engagement ... Ms. Kate GIGLIOTTI
39 Director Residential Programs ... Ms. Dianne MANNING
06 Interim Registrar ... Ms. Deborah CURRIE
09 Assistant Dir Effectiveness ... Mr. Jason CANALES
22 Dir Equal Opportunity & Title IX ... Ms. Nicole COMSTOCK
120 Director Academic Technology ... Dr. Gerol PETRUZELLA
18 Assistant Dir Facilities ... Mr. Robert FORTINI
25 Director of Development for Grants ... Ms. Lynette BOND
108 Director Assessment ... Ms. Erin MILNE
105 Web and Applications Manager ... Mr. Steven PESOLA
114 Budget Manager ... Ms. Jennifer DIX
96 Purchasing Manager ... Mr. William NORCROSS

*Massachusetts Maritime Academy (D)

101 Academy Drive, Buzzards Bay MA 02532-3400
County: Barnstable | FICE Identification: 002181
Unit ID: 166692
Telephone: (508) 830-5000 | Carnegie Class: Bac-Diverse
FAX Number: (508) 830-5004 | Calendar System: Semester
URL: www.maritime.edu
Established: 1891 | Annual Undergrad Tuition & Fees (In-State): $11,687
Enrollment: 1,637 | Coed
Affiliation or Control: State | IRS Status: 501(c)3
Highest Offering: Master's
Accreditation: EH, IACBE

02 President ... RADM. Francis X. MCDONALD
05 Vice President ... CAPT. Brigid PAVILONIS
10 Vice Pres Finance ... Ms. Rose CASS
32 Vice Pres Student Services ... CAPT. Edward ROZAK
84 Vice Pres External Relations ... CAPT. Elizabeth SIMMONS
13 Vice President/CIO ... Ms. Anne Marie FALLON
18 Vice President Operations ... Mr. Allen METCALFE
36 Director Career/Professional Svcs ... CDR. Maryanne RICHARDS
07 Director of Admissions ... CDR. Joshua TEFFT
06 Director Student Records/Registrar ... Ms. Danielle BUMPUS
08 Director Library ... Ms. Susan BERTEAUX
111 Assistant Dean of Advancement ... Ms. Kelley LESSARD
108 Dir of Institutional Effectiveness ... Dr. Marlene CLAPP
15 Dean Human Resources ... Mrs. Elizabeth BENWAY
29 Director Alumni Relations ... Ms. Michelle BADGER
37 Director Student Financial Aid ... Mrs. Cathy KEDSKI
96 Director of Purchasing ... Mr. Paul AIROZO
41 Athletic Director ... Mr. Michael KELLEY
20 Dean of Undergraduate Studies ... Dr. James MCKENNA
58 Dean of Graduate & Continuing Educ ... CAPT. James MCDONALD
28 Director of Diversity ... Mr. Michael ORTIZ

*Salem State University (E)

352 Lafayette Street, Salem MA 01970-5353
County: Essex | FICE Identification: 002188
Unit ID: 167729
Telephone: (978) 542-6000 | Carnegie Class: Masters/L
FAX Number: (978) 542-6970 | Calendar System: Semester
URL: www.salemstate.edu
Established: 1854 | Annual Undergrad Tuition & Fees (In-State): $11,675
Enrollment: 7,242 | Coed
Affiliation or Control: State | IRS Status: 501(c)3
Highest Offering: Master's
Accreditation: EH, ART, CAATE, MUS, NMT, NURSE, OT, SW, THEA

02 President ... Mr. John KEENAN
05 Provost & Academic VP ... Dr. David J. SILVA
03 Executive Vice President ... Vacant
111 VP Institutional Advancement ... Ms. Cheryl CROUNSE
10 VP Finance and Facilities ... Ms. Karen HOUSE
43 VP & General Counsel ... Ms. Rita COLUCCI
26 Asst VP Marketing/Creative Svcs ... Mr. Corey CRONIN
13 CIO-CISO ... Mr. Curt KING
121 Vice President of Student Success ... Dr. Nate BRYANT
21 Assoc VP Financial Svcs ... Vacant
15 Assistant VP for HR & EEO ... Mr. Mark R. QUIGLEY
20 Assoc Provost ... Vacant
86 Senior Director External Relations ... Ms. Adria DUIJVESTEIJN
08 Director Library ... Ms. Elizabeth MCKEIGUE
50 Dean School of Business ... Dr. Raminder LUTHER
53 Dean of Education ... Dr. Joseph CAMBONE
58 Assoc Dean Sch Grad & Prof Studies ... Dr. Barbara LAYNE
49 Dean School of Arts & Sciences ... Dr. Gail GASPARICH
32 Dean of Students ... Dr. Carla PANZELLA
110 AVP Institutional Advancement ... Ms. Mandy RAY
04 Asst to Pres/Asst Secy to BOT ... Vacant
19 Director Public Safety ... Mr. Gene R. LABONTE
41 Director Athletics ... Ms. Nicolle WOOD
06 Registrar ... Ms. Megan M. MILLER
84 Int VP for Enroll Mgmt/Marketing ... Ms. Bonnie GALINSKI
18 AVP Capital Plng/Business Affairs ... Vacant
28 Director of Diversity ... Mr. Thomas ALEXANDER
37 Director of Financial Aid ... Mr. Scott JEWELL
38 Asst Dean of Students/Wellness ... Ms. Elisa CASTILLO
96 Sr Director Purchasing/Vendor Rels ... Mr. Reynaldo RAMOS
25 Asst Dir Sponsored Pgms & Research ... Ms. Elaine MILO
07 Director of Admissions ... Ms. Jackie HAAS
45 Exec Dir Strategic Planning ... Dr. Chunju CHEN
39 Director Residence Life ... Ms. Joy SCHMELZER
76 Int Dean Col of Health & Human Svcs ... Dr. Sami ANSARI
04 Special Asst to President ... Ms. Lynne MONTAGUE
44 Director of Annual Giving ... Ms. Lori BOUDO

*Westfield State University (F)

577 Western Avenue, Westfield MA 01086-1630
County: Hampden | FICE Identification: 002189
Unit ID: 168263
Telephone: (413) 572-5300 | Carnegie Class: Masters/M
FAX Number: (413) 572-8147 | Calendar System: Semester
URL: www.westfield.ma.edu
Established: 1839 | Annual Undergrad Tuition & Fees (In-State): $11,139
Enrollment: 5,395 | Coed
Affiliation or Control: State | IRS Status: 501(c)3
Highest Offering: Beyond Master's But Less Than Doctorate
Accreditation: EH, AAQEP, #ARCPA, #CAATE, EXSC, MUS, NURSE, SW

02 President ... Dr. Linda THOMPSON
100 Chief of Staff ... Ms. Tricia OLIVER
05 Int Provost/VP Academic Affairs ... Dr. Juline MILLS
32 Vice Pres Student Affairs ... Dr. Gloria LOPEZ
84 VP Enrollment Management ... Mr. Dan FORSTER
10 VP Administration & Finance ... Mr. Stephen TAKSAR
111 VP Institutional Advancement ... Dr. Erica BROMAN
21 Assoc VP Administration/Finance ... Ms. Lisa FREEMAN
15 Asst VP Human Resources ... Dr. Jalisa D. WILLIAMS
124 Interim Dean of Faculty ... Dr. Enrique MORALES-DIAZ
49 Dean of Undergrad Studies ... Vacant
58 Dean Graduate/Continuing Educ ... Vacant
81 Int Dean College of Math & Sciences .. Dr. Jennifer HANSELMAN
53 Dean College Educ/Health/Human Svcs ... Dr. Juline MILLS
79 Int Dean Coll Arts/Human/Soc Sc ... Dr. Emily TODD
35 Assoc Dean of Students ... Ms. Shannon BRODERICK
06 Registrar ... Dr. Monique LOPEZ
09 Assoc Dean Inst Research/Assess ... Dr. Lisa PLANTEFABER
08 Dean Acad Info Svcs/Dir Library . Mr. Thomas RAFFENSPERGER
39 Assoc Director Residential Life ... Dr. Joshua HETTRICK
19 Director Public Safety ... Mr. Tony CASCIANO
36 Director Career Services ... Mr. Junior DELGADO
90 Exec Director Acad Tech Services ... Mr. Christopher HIRTLE
13 Chief Information Officer ... Mr. Alan BLAIR
91 Director Admin Systems ... Vacant
18 Exec Dir Facilities/Capital Plan ... Ms. Maureen SOCHA
41 Director Athletics ... Mr. Richard LENFEST
38 Assoc Director Counseling Center ... Ms. Suzanna ADAMS
23 Interim Director Health Services ... Ms. Lisa BROSNAN
37 Director of Financial Aid ... Mr. Michael MAZEIKA
07 Director of Admissions ... Vacant
88 Assoc Dir of Admissions ... Ms. Emily GIBBINGS
96 Director of Procurement ... Mr. Gary DUGGAN
25 Director Grants Sponsored Programs ... Ms. Louann D'ANGELO
102 Dir Budget & Financial Planning ... Ms. Maria FEUERSTEIN
04 Executive Assistant to President ... Ms. Michelle LEDOUX
101 Admin Asst to Board of Trustees ... Ms. Jean BEAL
104 Director of International Program ... Vacant
88 Veteran & Military Svcs Coord ... Ms. Lisa DUCHARME
106 Dir Center for Instructional Tech ... Ms. Lynn ZAYAC
22 Dir Non-Discrimination Compliance ... Dr. Jalisa D. WILLIAMS
26 Acting Dir of Campus Communications ... Ms. Lorraine MARTINELLE
29 Director Alumni Relations ... Vacant

*Worcester State University (G)

486 Chandler Street, Worcester MA 01602-2597
County: Worcester | FICE Identification: 002190
Unit ID: 168430
Telephone: (508) 929-8000 | Carnegie Class: Masters/L
FAX Number: (508) 929-8191 | Calendar System: Semester
URL: www.worcester.edu

Established: 1874 Annual Undergrad Tuition & Fees (In-State): $10,586
Enrollment: 5,724 Coed
Affiliation or Control: State IRS Status: Exempt
Highest Offering: Master's
Accreditation: EH, CAEPT, NURSE, OT, SP

02 President ... Mr. Barry M. MALONEY
05 Provost/VP of Academic Affairs ... Dr. Lois A. WIMS
10 Vice Pres Administration & Finance ... Ms. Kathleen EICHELROTH
32 Vice President of Student Affairs ... Ms. Julie KAZARIAN
111 Vice Pres University Advancement ... Mr. Thomas MCNAMARA
84 Vice Pres for Enrollment Management ... Dr. Ryan FORSYTHE
20 Assoc VP for Academic Affairs ... Dr. Henry THERIAULT
21 Assoc VP Administration & Finance ... Ms. Robin QUILL
13 Assoc VP/CIO Univ Technology Svcs ... Dr. Anthony ADADE
58 Assoc VP CE & Dean Grad Stds ... Dr. Roberta KYLE
108 Asst VP for Assessment & Planning ... Dr. Sarah STROUT
81 Dean Sch of Health/Natural Sci ... Dr. Linda LARRIVEE
79 Dean Sch of Human & Social Sciences ... Dr. Russ POTTLE
53 Dean of Education ... Dr. Raynold LEWIS
51 Assoc Dean of Grad/Cont Educ ... Ms. Sara GRADY
88 Dir Alternatives Ind Devel Pgm ... Ms. Laxmi BISSOONDIAL
19 Chief of Campus Police ... Mr. Jason KAPURCH
100 Chief of Staff ... Mr. Carl HERRIN
26 AVP Communications/Marketing ... Ms. Maureen O. STOKES
08 Executive Director of the Library ... Mr. Matthew BEJUNE
43 Gen Counsel/Asst to the Pres ... Ms. Stacey LUSTER
18 Staff Associate of Facilities ... Mr. Stephen M. BANDARRA
37 Interim Dir of Financial Aid ... Ms. Jennifer ENGLISH
84 Dean of Enrollment ... Mr. Joseph DICARLO
39 Asst Dean & Dir Res Life/Housing ... Mr. Adrian GAGE
15 Exec Dir of HR & Benefits ... Ms. Susan MOORE
113 Dir of Student Accounts/One Card ... Ms. Julie CARMEL
96 Dir Procurement/Business Manager ... Ms. Brenda BUSSEY
09 Director of Institutional Research ... Mr. Kenneth SMITH
38 Assoc Dean for Heath & Wellness ... Ms. Laura MURPHY
85 Director of International Programs ... Ms. Katey PALUMBO
36 Director of Career Services ... Ms. Jillian ANDERSON
41 Director of Athletics ... Mr. Michael A. MUDD
109 Director of Admin Support Services ... Ms. Nancy M. RAMSDELL
29 Executive Director Alumni ... Ms. Tara A. HANCOCK
30 Exec Dir of University Advancement ... Ms. Jodi M. BRIGGS-PICKETT
114 Dir of Budget/Planning/Policy Dev ... Ms. Anisa HOXHA
06 Registrar ... Ms. Julie A. CHAFFEE
04 Admin Assistant to the President ... Ms. Catherine E. SWEENEY
28 Director of Diversity ... Ms. Maria GARIEPY

*Berkshire Community College (A)

1350 West Street, Pittsfield MA 01201-5786
County: Berkshire FICE Identification: 002167
Unit ID: 164775
Telephone: (413) 499-4660 Carnegie Class: Assoc/MT-VT-High Trad
FAX Number: N/A Calendar System: Semester
URL: www.berkshirecc.edu
Established: 1960 Annual Undergrad Tuition & Fees (In-State): $5,492
Enrollment: 1,465 Coed
Affiliation or Control: State IRS Status: 501(c)3
Highest Offering: Associate Degree
Accreditation: EH, ADNUR, COARC, PTAA

02 President ... Dr. Ellen KENNEDY
10 VP Admininstration & Finance/CFO ... Ms. Andrea WADSWORTH
05 VP Academic Affairs ... Dr. Kierstyn HUNTER
84 VP Student Affairs & Enrollment Mgm ... Mr. Adam KLEPETAR
15 Exec Dir HR/Affirm Action Officer ... Ms. Melissa LOIODICE
32 Dean of Students ... Ms. Celia NORCROSS
06 Registrar ... Mr. Adam EMERSON
102 Exec Dir BCC Foundation ... Vacant
13 Director Information Technology ... Mr. Stephen VIEIRA
84 Dean of Enrollment Management ... Vacant
37 Director Student Financial Aid ... Ms. Kelly OSORIO
08 Dean of Library & Learning Commons ... Mr. Richard FELVER
09 Dir Institutional Effectiveness ... Dr. Margaret STEPHENSON
18 Dir Facilities/Physical Plant ... Vacant
19 Director of Safety & Security ... Mr. Ellis RICHARDSON
38 Senior Academic Counselor ... Ms. Lisa MATTILA
04 Assistant to the President ... Ms. Heather SEELY
105 Director Web Services ... Mr. Justin OBER
26 Chief Public Rels/Mktg/Commun Ofcr ... Mr. Jonah SYKES
29 Director Alumni Affairs ... Ms. Toni BUCKLEY
30 Director of Development ... Ms. Shela LEVANTE
96 Director of Purchasing ... Vacant
108 Director Institutional Assessment ... Ms. Margaret STEPHENSON
25 Grants Administrator ... Ms. Gina STEC
41 Athletic Director ... Mr. Daryl SHREVE
50 Interim Dean of Business ... Ms. Christina WYNN

*Bristol Community College (B)

777 Elsbree Street, Fall River MA 02720-7395
County: Bristol FICE Identification: 002176
Unit ID: 165033
Telephone: (508) 678-2811 Carnegie Class: Assoc/HT-High Trad
FAX Number: (508) 730-3270 Calendar System: Semester
URL: www.bristolcc.edu
Established: 1965 Annual Undergrad Tuition & Fees (In-State): $5,136
Enrollment: 6,256 Coed
Affiliation or Control: State IRS Status: 501(c)3
Highest Offering: Associate Degree
Accreditation: EH, ADNUR, CAHIIM, DH, MAC, MLTAD, OTA

02 President ... Dr. Laura L. DOUGLAS
05 Vice President of Academic Affairs ... Dr. Suzanne BUGLIONE
50 Dean of Business & Exp Education ... Mr. Vidyanidhi REGE
79 Interim Dean of Arts & Humanities ... Ms. Jennifer PUNIELLO
83 Dean of Behavioral & Soc Sciences ... Dr. Kathleen PEARLE
76 Dean of Health Sciences ... Vacant
81 Dean of Math/Science & Engineering ... Dr. Sarmad SAMAN
10 VP of Administration & Finance ... Mr. Steven KENYON
32 VP of Student Svcs/Enrollment Mgmt ... Ms. Kate O'HARA
13 Chief Information & Data Officer ... Ms. Jo-Ann M. PELLETIER
26 VP Marketing and Communications ... Ms. Joyce BRENNAN
103 Acting VP of Economic/Business Dev ... Ms. Jennifer MENARD
32 Director Student/Family Engagement ... Ms. Emma MONTAGUE
84 Dean of Enrollment Mgmt ... Vacant
12 Dean of New Bedford Campus ... Ms. Shanna HOWELL
12 Dean of Attleboro Campus ... Vacant
06 Registrar ... Ms. Jennifer VINCENT
12 Dean of Taunton Center ... Mr. Robert REZENDES
25 Dean of Grant Development ... Ms. Jennifer MENARD
37 Director Financial Aid ... Ms. Kate O'HARA
38 Dean of Counseling ... Mr. Michael BENSINK
15 Executive Director of HR ... Mr. Gary CONVERTINO
30 Executive Director of Development ... Vacant
18 Director of Facilities Management ... Ms. Karen PARKER
19 Director Public Safety Preparedness ... Mr. Mark NATALY
21 Comptroller ... Mr. Keith TONI
11 Assoc VP Administration/Facilities ... Ms. Jo Ann BENTLEY
22 Dir of Disability Services ... Ms. Julie JODOIN-KRAUZYK
78 Director Coop Education ... Ms. Nicole HEANEY
106 Dean of Online Learning ... Mr. Michael MURPHY
92 Commonwealth Honors Coordinator ... Ms. Denise DIMARZIO
96 Director of Purchasing ... Ms. Philicia PACHECO
41 Athletic Director ... Mr. Derek VIVEIROS
04 Sr Executive Assistant to President ... Ms. Kathleen A. WORDELL

*Bunker Hill Community College (C)

250 New Rutherford Avenue, Boston MA 02129-2925
County: Suffolk FICE Identification: 011210
Unit ID: 165112
Telephone: (617) 228-2400 Carnegie Class: Assoc/HT-High Trad
FAX Number: (617) 228-2050 Calendar System: Semester
URL: www.bhcc.edu
Established: 1973 Annual Undergrad Tuition & Fees (In-State): $5,160
Enrollment: 9,924 Coed
Affiliation or Control: State IRS Status: 501(c)3
Highest Offering: Associate Degree
Accreditation: EH, ADNUR, CEA, DMS, EMT, MLTAD, RAD, SURGT

02 President ... Dr. Pam Y. EDDINGER
10 VP of Administration and Finance ... Mr. John PITCHER
05 VP Academic Affairs/Student Service ... Dr. James F. CANNIFF
15 AVP Human Resources/Labor Relations ... Ms. Molly AMBROSE
32 Dean of Students ... Ms. Julie B. ELKINS
26 Exec Director of Communications ... Ms. Karen NORTON
18 Facilities Manager ... Mr. John CHIRICHIELLO
79 Dean of Humanities ... Ms. Lori A. CATALLOZZI
54 Dean of Science/Engineering/Math ... Dr. Laurie K. MCCORRY
83 Dean Behavioral/Social Sciences ... Ms. Liya ESCALERA
107 Dean of Professional Studies ... Ms. Austin A. GILLILAND
66 Director Nurse Education ... Ms. Elizabeth TOBIN
12 Associate Provost Chelsea Campus ... Dr. Alice MURILLO
21 Comptroller ... Ms. Champa NAGAGE
25 Exec Director of Grants Development ... Mr. Steven A. ROLLER
35 Director of Student Services ... Vacant
06 Registrar ... Mr. Miguel SAHAGUN
08 Director Library and Learning Comm ... Vacant
13 Chief Information Officer ... Mr. Tim OGAWA
27 Executive Director of Marketing ... Ms. Karen M. NORTON
19 Executive Dir and Chief of Police ... Mr. Robert BARROWS
37 Exec Dir Student Financial Svcs ... Ms. Melissa HOLSTER
96 Director of Purchasing ... Mr. Mukti RAUT
84 Dean Enrollment Management ... Ms. Grace Y. YOUNG
30 Executive Director of Development ... Ms. Marilyn KUHAR
100 Exec Asst to the President ... Mr. George HALLSMITH
09 Interim Dean Institutional Research ... Ms. Arlene VALLIE
04 Staff Assistant to President ... Ms. Frances H. JARVIS
102 Dir Foundation/Corporate Relations ... Ms. Marilyn KUHAR
103 Director Workforce Development ... Ms. Kristen P. MCKENNA
105 Director of Digital Communications ... Ms. Nicole MORO
41 Athletic Director ... Ms. Loreto JACKSON
07 Director of Admissions ... Ms. Francine KUPFERMAN
106 Dean of Online Learning ... Ms. Danielle LEEK

*Cape Cod Community College (D)

2240 Iyannough Road, West Barnstable MA 02668-1599
County: Barnstable FICE Identification: 002168
Unit ID: 165194
Telephone: (508) 362-2131 Carnegie Class: Assoc/HT-Mix Trad/Non
FAX Number: (508) 362-3988 Calendar System: Semester
URL: www.capecod.edu
Established: 1960 Annual Undergrad Tuition & Fees (In-State): $5,352
Enrollment: 2,710 Coed
Affiliation or Control: State IRS Status: 501(c)3
Highest Offering: Associate Degree
Accreditation: EH, ADNUR, DH, FUSER, MAC, NAEYC

02 President ... Dr. John L. COX
05 Vice Pres Academic/Student Affairs ... Dr. Arlene RODRIGUEZ
10 Vice President Finance & Operations ... Mr. Christopher CLARK
18 Director Facilities ... Mr. Joseph MACKINNON
49 Dean Arts & Humanities ... Dr. Cathy MCCARRON
81 Dean Science/Tech/Math/Business ... Dr. Donald CRAMPTON
121 Dean Learning Res & Student Success ... Mr. David ZIEMBA
84 Dean Enroll Mgmt/Advising Services ... Ms. Christine MCCAREY
83 Dean Health/Social Sci/Human Svcs ... Mr. Patrick PRESTON
15 Associate VP Human Resources ... Mr. Paul ALEXANDER
13 Chief Info/Technology Officer ... Mr. Richard WIXSOM
07 Director Admissions ... Ms. Sheila VAUGHN
37 Director of Financial Aid ... Vacant
26 Director Communications/Marketing ... Mr. Patrick STONE
06 Registrar ... Ms. Lucina HOLMES
19 Chief Public Safety ... Ms. Maria PADILLA
04 Exec Assistant to President ... Ms. Mia HAZLETT
09 Dir Inst Research & Effectiveness ... Ms. Maureen O'SHEA

*Greenfield Community College (E)

1 College Drive, Greenfield MA 01301-9739
County: Franklin FICE Identification: 002169
Unit ID: 165981
Telephone: (413) 775-1000 Carnegie Class: Assoc/MT-VT-High Trad
FAX Number: (413) 774-4676 Calendar System: Semester
URL: www.gcc.mass.edu
Established: 1962 Annual Undergrad Tuition & Fees (In-State): $5,570
Enrollment: 1,620 Coed
Affiliation or Control: State IRS Status: 501(c)3
Highest Offering: Associate Degree
Accreditation: EH, ADNUR, EMT, MAC, NAEYC

02 President ... Dr. Rick HOPPER
05 Chief Academic/Stdnt Affs Ofcr ... Ms. Mary Ellen FYDENKEVEZ
10 Chief Financial Officer ... Ms. Karen PHILLIPS
84 Dean of Enrollment Services ... Vacant
32 Dean of Students ... Ms. Anna BERRY
79 Int Dean Humanities ... Mr. Matthew BARLOW
81 Dean Engr/Math/Nurs & Sciences ... Ms. Mary Ellen FYDENKEVEZ
30 Exec Director Resource Development ... Ms. Regina CURTIS
18 Director Physical Plant ... Mr. Jeffrey MARQUES
37 Director Financial Aid ... Ms. Linda DESJARDINS
19 Director Public Safety ... Mr. Alex WILTZ
96 Director of Purchasing ... Mr. Ryan AIKEN
08 Head of Library Services ... Ms. Laura GARCIA
21 Comptroller ... Mr. Mark BOUDREAU
06 Registrar ... Ms. Holly FITZPATRICK
38 Co-Coord Learning Asst Programs ... Ms. Cynthia SNOW
38 Co-Coord Learning Asst Programs ... Mr. Norman BEEBE
88 Coordinator of Student Assessment ... Ms. Catherine DEVLIN
35 Coordinator of Student Activities ... Ms. Mary MCENTEE
04 Staff Assistant to President ... Ms. Shannon LARANGE
108 Director Institutional Assessment ... Ms. Marie BREHENY

*Holyoke Community College (F)

303 Homestead Avenue, Holyoke MA 01040-1099
County: Hampden FICE Identification: 002170
Unit ID: 166133
Telephone: (413) 538-7000 Carnegie Class: Assoc/HT-High Trad
FAX Number: (413) 534-8927 Calendar System: Semester
URL: www.hcc.edu
Established: 1946 Annual Undergrad Tuition & Fees (In-State): $5,378
Enrollment: 4,209 Coed
Affiliation or Control: State IRS Status: 501(c)3
Highest Offering: Associate Degree
Accreditation: EH, ADNUR, MUS, PNUR, RAD

02 President ... Dr. Christina ROYAL
11 Vice Pres Administration & Finance ... Mr. Narayan SAMPATH
05 Int VP Academic/Student Affairs ... Dr. Sharale MATHIS
111 Vice Pres Institutional Advancement ... Ms. Amanda SBRISCIA
103 Vice Pres for Business & Community ... Mr. Jeffrey HAYDEN
20 Assistant VP of Academic Admin ... Ms. Idelia SMITH
08 Dean Library ... Ms. Mary DIXEY
84 Dean of Enrollment Management ... Ms. Renee TASTAD
15 Dean Human Resources ... Vacant
36 Dean Coop Education & Career Svcs ... Vacant
06 Registrar ... Ms. Allison WROBEL
37 Director of Financial Aid ... Ms. Patricia BILLINGS
91 Director Administrative Computing ... Vacant
18 Dir Facilities & Engineering Svcs ... Mr. Dan CAMPBELL
10 Comptroller ... Mr. Curt FOSTER
13 Interim Chief Information Officer ... Mr. Walter KERCE
96 Asst Comptroller/Purchasing ... Ms. Maria BRUNELLE
09 Director Institutional Research ... Ms. Veena DHANKHER
26 Dir of Marketing/Public Relations ... Ms. JoAnne ROME
111 Dir of Institutional Advancement ... Mr. Patrick CARPENTER
35 Dean of Student Services ... Vacant
19 Interim Director Security/Safety ... Mr. Dale BROWN
07 Director Admissions & Onboarding ... Mr. Mark HUDGIK
100 Chief of Staff ... Vacant
22 Dir Affirm Action/Equal Opportunity ... Ms. Olivia L. KYNARD
41 Athletic Director ... Mr. Thomas STEWART
04 Admin Assistant to the President ... Ms. Karen DESJEANS

*Massachusetts Bay Community College (G)

50 Oakland Street, Wellesley Hills MA 02481-5357
County: Norfolk FICE Identification: 002171
Unit ID: 166647
Telephone: (781) 239-3000 Carnegie Class: Assoc/HT-Mix Trad/Non
FAX Number: (781) 237-1061 Calendar System: Semester
URL: www.massbay.edu
Established: 1961 Annual Undergrad Tuition & Fees (In-State): $5,376
Enrollment: 3,762 Coed

Affiliation or Control: State IRS Status: 501(c)3
Highest Offering: Associate Degree
Accreditation: EH, ADNUR, EMT, NAEYC, PNUR, RAD, SURGT

02 President .... Dr. David PODELL
04 Executive Director Ofc of the Pres .... Ms. Karen BRITTON
05 VP for Academic Affairs and Provost .... Dr. Lynn HUNTER
10 VP for Finance & Administration .... Mr. Neil BUCKLEY
15 Exec Director of Human Resources .... Ms. Samaria STALLINGS
84 Asst VP Enrollment Management .... Ms. Lisa SLAVIN
32 VP for Student Development .... Dr. Elizabeth BLUMBERG
45 VP Institutional Effectiveness .... Dr. Courtney JACKSON
13 Chief Information Officer .... Mr. Curtis CORMIER
50 Dean Business & Prof Studies .... Dr. Susan MAGGIONI
102 Director of Corp Partnerships .... Ms. Phara BOYER
76 Dean Health Sciences Division .... Dr. Lynne DAVIS
20 Assistant Provost .... Dr. Christopher LA BARBERA
81 Dean STEM Division .... Dr. Chitra JAVDEKAR
06 Registrar .... Ms. Jennifer MCANDREW
21 AVP Finance & Admin .... Mr. Marcus EDWARD
88 Dir Academic Achievement Center .... Ms. Barbara BERNARD
121 Director of Academic Advising .... Ms. Sarah SALERNO
91 Director Administrative Computing .... Mr. Terry KRAMER
07 Assoc Dean of Admissions .... Ms. Alison MCCARTY
36 Director of Career & Internship Svc .... Ms. Julie GINN
38 Director of Counseling .... Mr. Jon EDWARDS
37 Director of Financial Aid .... Ms. Robyn BUTTERFIELD
18 Director of Facilities .... Mr. Joseph DELISLE
08 Director of Learning Services .... Mr. Timothy RIVARD
25 Director of Grants Development .... Ms. Sunny STICH
26 Asst VP Inst Advance/Mktg/Comms .... Mr. Jeremy SOLOMON
19 Director of Public Safety .... Mr. Vincent O'CONNELL
124 Associate Dean for Student Success .... Mr. Richard WILLIAMS
35 Coordinator Student Engagement .... Ms. Julie SCHLEICHER
28 Chief Diversity Officer .... Dr. Lynn MOORE
79 Dean Humanities/Social Sciences .... Ms. Nina KEERY
88 Int Dean of Automotive Technology .... Mr. Howie FERRIS
22 Director of Equity Compliance .... Ms. Lisa MACDONALD
41 Director of Athletics .... Mr. Adam NELSON
106 Assistant Director Online Education .... Ms. Bernadette SIBUMA
96 Dir Procurement & Business Opers .... Ms. Lauren CURLEY

*Massasoit Community College (A)

1 Massasoit Boulevard, Brockton MA 02302-3996
County: Plymouth FICE Identification: 002177
Unit ID: 166823
Telephone: (508) 588-9100 Carnegie Class: Assoc/HVT-High Trad
FAX Number: (508) 427-1202 Calendar System: Semester
URL: www.massasoit.mass.edu
Established: 1966 Annual Undergrad Tuition & Fees (In-State): $5,160
Enrollment: 5,665 Coed
Affiliation or Control: State IRS Status: 501(c)3
Highest Offering: Associate Degree
Accreditation: EH, ADNUR, COARC, DA, EMT, MAC, NAEYC, RAD

02 President .... Dr. Gena GLICKMAN
05 Provost Academic/Student Services .... Dr. Deanna YAMEEN
10 VP Administration/CFO .... Mr. William MITCHELL
20 Assoc Vice Provost Academic Affairs .... Ms. Pamela WITCHER
111 Chief Advancement Officer .... Mr. Paul GRAND PRÉ
28 Chief Diversity Officer .... Ms. Yolanda DENNIS
13 CIO/Dir Enterprise Systems .... Mr. William MORRISON
09 Assoc Dean Institutional Research .... Ms. Mary GOODHUE LYNCH
26 Director of Communications/PR .... Ms. Sarah YUNITS
26 Director of Marketing & Creative .... Mr. James LYNCH
84 Dean of Enrollment Management .... Ms. Shilo HENRIQUES
35 Dean of Students .... Ms. Slandie DIEUJUSTE
07 Director of Admissions .... Ms. Michelle HUGHES
37 Director Student Financial Aid .... Mr. Todd HUGHES
06 Registrar .... Ms. Jannie GILSON
121 Director of Advisement & Counseling .... Ms. Alessandra MONTEIRO
41 Director of Athletics .... Mr. Benjamin WARNICK
21 Comptroller .... Ms. Patricia MARCELLA
18 Director Facilities/Physical Plant .... Mr. Gregory HABEREK
96 Director of Purchasing .... Mr. John CAFFELLE
29 Director Alumni Relations .... Vacant
50 Dean Business & Technology .... Dr. Michael ROGGOW
79 Dean Humanities/Communication Arts .... Dr. Harriette SCOTT
76 Interim Dean Allied Health .... Ms. Susan CLOVER
83 Dean Public Svc/Social Science .... Ms. Karyn BOUTIN
81 Dean Science & Math .... Mr. Douglas BROWN
72 Exec Dean Canton/Emergent Tech .... Ms. Carine SAUVIGNON
15 VP of Human Resources .... Ms. Margaret GAZZARA HESS
103 VP of Corporate & Community Educ .... Ms. Melanie HABER
100 Chief of Staff .... Ms. Lydia CAMARA
19 Chief of Police .... Mr. Christopher CUMMINGS

*Middlesex Community College (B)

591 Springs Road, Bedford MA 01730-1197
County: Middlesex FICE Identification: 009936
Unit ID: 166887
Telephone: (781) 280-3200 Carnegie Class: Assoc/HT-High Trad
FAX Number: (781) 275-0741 Calendar System: Semester
URL: www.middlesex.mass.edu
Established: 1969 Annual Undergrad Tuition & Fees (In-State): $6,048
Enrollment: 6,885 Coed
Affiliation or Control: State IRS Status: 501(c)3
Highest Offering: Associate Degree
Accreditation: EH, ADNUR, CEA, DA, DH, DMS, DT, MAC, MLTAD, NAEYC, RAD

02 President .... Mr. Philip J. SISSON
05 Int Provost & VP Acad/Student Affs .... Ms. Arlene RODRIGUEZ
15 VP Human Resources .... Ms. Mary EMERICK
10 VP of Finance/CFO .... Mr. Frank NOCELLA
04 Exec Assistant Ofc of the President .... Ms. Donna CORBIN
32 AVP Student Affs/Dean of Students .... Ms. Pamela B. FLAHERTY
46 Dean Research & Planning .... Ms. Jennifer LUDDY
79 Dean Humanities and Social Sciences .... Mr. Matthew OLSON
72 Dean Bus/Educ & Public Service .... Ms. Judith HOGAN
17 Dean of Health and STEM .... Ms. Kathleen J. SWEENEY
107 Dean Professional/Instructional Dev .... Ms. Susan ANDERSON
22 Asst Dir HR/Affirm Action Officer .... Mr. Reginald NICHOLS
11 Chief Administrative Officer .... Ms. Colleen COX
96 Director of Procurement .... Mrs. Christina KELLEY
84 Dean of Enrollment Services .... Ms. Audrey NAHABEDIAN
111 Exec Dir Inst Advancement .... Ms. Judith M. BURKE
07 Dean of Admissions .... Ms. Camille BROWN
09 Dean Institutional Research .... Ms. Linda HEINEMAN
27 Exec Director Public Affairs .... Mr. Patrick COOK
26 Dir Marketing/Communication .... Ms. Elizabeth J. NOEL
29 Director of Alumni Affairs .... Ms. Amy LEE
37 Assoc Director of Financial Aid .... Ms. Mary MULLENS
21 Comptroller .... Ms. Kathy RICH
08 Director Library Services .... Ms. Donna MATURI
06 Registrar .... Ms. Kayla BOYD

*Mount Wachusett Community College (C)

444 Green Street, Gardner MA 01440-1000
County: Worcester FICE Identification: 002172
Unit ID: 166957
Telephone: (978) 632-6600 Carnegie Class: Assoc/MT-VT-High Trad
FAX Number: (978) 630-9559 Calendar System: Semester
URL: www.mwcc.edu
Established: 1963 Annual Undergrad Tuition & Fees (In-State): $5,668
Enrollment: 3,187 Coed
Affiliation or Control: State IRS Status: 501(c)3
Highest Offering: Associate Degree
Accreditation: EH, ADNUR, DA, DH, MLTAD, PNUR, PTAA

02 President .... Dr. James L. VANDER HOOVEN
05 VP Academic/Student Affairs .... Dr. Paul HERNANDEZ
103 VP Lifelong Learning/Wkfc Dev .... Dr. Rachel FRICK CARDELLE
10 VP Finance & Administration .... Mr. Robert LABONTE
26 VP Marketing/Communications .... Ms. Lea Ann SCALES
111 VP Planning/Development/Inst Rsrch .... Mr. Joseph STISO
15 VP Human Resources/Payroll .... Mr. Peter SENNETT
20 Assistant VP of Academic Affairs .... Vacant
32 Sr Dean Student Affairs .... Mr. Jason ZELESKY
08 Asst Dean Library Services .... Vacant
09 Asst Dean of Records/Inst Research .... Ms. Rebecca FOREST
13 Executive Director IT .... Mr. Daniel HORLANDER
18 Director Maintenance/Mechanical Sys .... Mr. William SWIFT
68 Director Mount Fitness .... Mr. Jason SNOONIAN
19 Chief Public Safety & Security .... Ms. Karen KOLIMAGA
27 Director of Media Services .... Mr. Arthur COLLINS
04 Sr Staff Assoc to the President .... Ms. Jo-Ann MEAGHER
07 Dean of Admissions/Strat Enrollment .... Ms. Marcia ROSBURY-HENNE
37 Director Student Financial Aid .... Ms. Heather RULAND
41 Athletic Director .... Mr. Jason SNOONIAN
44 Director Annual Giving .... Ms. Carla ZOTTOLI

*North Shore Community College (D)

1 Ferncroft Road, PO Box 3340, Danvers MA 01923-0840
County: Essex FICE Identification: 002173
Unit ID: 167312
Telephone: (978) 762-4000 Carnegie Class: Assoc/MT-VT-High Trad
FAX Number: (978) 762-4020 Calendar System: Semester
URL: www.northshore.edu
Established: 1965 Annual Undergrad Tuition & Fees (In-State): $5,352
Enrollment: 4,783 Coed
Affiliation or Control: State IRS Status: 501(c)3
Highest Offering: Associate Degree
Accreditation: EH, ADNUR, COARC, MAC, NAEYC, OTA, PNUR, PTAA, RAD, SURGT

02 President .... Dr. William HEINEMAN
05 Interim Vice Pres Academic Affairs .... Ms. Andrea DEFUSCO-SULLIVAN
10 Vice Pres Administration/Finance .... Ms. Janice M. FORSSTROM
32 Interim VP Student Affairs .... Mr. Stephen CREAMER
15 Int VP Human Resource/Affirm Action .... Ms. Thanh GIDDARIE
103 Dean Workforce Dev/Corp Educ .... Ms. Dianne PALTER-GILL
07 Exec Dir Admissions & Enrollment .... Ms. Kim ODUSAMI
08 Director Library/Tutoring .... Mr. Rex KRAJEWSKI
13 Dir of Networking/Info Services .... Mr. Gary HAM
37 Director of Financial Aid .... Ms. Susan SULLIVAN
09 Asst Vice Pres Planning & Research .... Ms. Laurie LACHAPELLE
18 Asst Vice Pres Facilities Mgmt .... Mr. Richard RENEY
19 Campus Police Chief .... Mr. David COOK
21 Comptroller .... Ms. Eileen GERENZ
26 Director Public Relations/New Media .... Ms. Linda BRANTLEY
36 Director Student Placement .... Ms. Lynn MARCUS
121 Director Student Support & Advising .... Mr. Daniel O'NEILL
27 Director Marketing Communications .... Ms. Samantha MCGILLOWAY
40 Bookstore Manager .... Mr. Shawn CRONIN
06 Registrar .... Ms. Mary DULATRE
04 Staff Assistant to the President .... Ms. Susan MULVEY

*Northern Essex Community College (E)

100 Elliott Street, Haverhill MA 01830-2399
County: Essex FICE Identification: 002174
Unit ID: 167376
Telephone: (978) 556-3700 Carnegie Class: Assoc/MT-VT-High Trad
FAX Number: (978) 556-3729 Calendar System: Semester
URL: www.necc.mass.edu
Established: 1960 Annual Undergrad Tuition & Fees (In-State): $5,544
Enrollment: 4,715 Coed
Affiliation or Control: State IRS Status: 501(c)3
Highest Offering: Associate Degree
Accreditation: EH, ADNUR, COARC, CSHSE, DA, EMT, MAC, NAEYC, PNUR, POLYT, RAD

02 President .... Dr. Lane A. GLENN
05 Vice President of Academic Affairs .... Vacant
111 Vice Pres Institutional Advancement .... Ms. Allison DOLAN-WILSON
10 VP of Administration & Finance/ CFO .... Mr. Michael R. MCCARTHY
32 Vice President Student Affairs .... Ms. Jennifer MEZQUITA
12 VP of Lawrence Campus .... Dr. Noemi CUSTODIA-LORA
09 Dean of Institutional Research .... Ms. Audrey ELLIS
30 Dean of Development .... Vacant
35 Dean of Students .... Mr. Jonathan L. MILLER
103 Dir of Workforce Devel/Cont Educ .... Mr. Alexander RODRIGUEZ
13 Chief Information Officer .... Mr. David MCASKILL
06 Registrar .... Ms. Sue SHAIN
37 Director of Financial Aid .... Ms. Despina LAMBROPOULOUS
26 Director of Public Relations .... Ms. Ernestine GREENSLADE
29 Director Alumni Relations .... Ms. Lindsey GRAHAM
18 Chief Facilities/Physical Plant .... Mr. Paul MIEDZIONOSKI
96 Director of Purchasing .... Ms. Elizabeth DONOVAN
100 Chief of Staff to President .... Ms. Cheryl GOODWIN
08 Chief Library Officer .... Mr. Michael HEARN
19 Director Security/Safety .... Ms. Deborah CRAFTS
41 Athletic Director .... Mr. Daniel BLAIR
04 Admin Assistant to the President .... Ms. Linda J. BUCKLEY
15 Chief Human Resources Officer .... Ms. Patricia M. GAURON

*Quinsigamond Community College (F)

670 W Boylston Street, Worcester MA 01606-2092
County: Worcester FICE Identification: 002175
Unit ID: 167534
Telephone: (508) 853-2300 Carnegie Class: Assoc/MT-VT-High Trad
FAX Number: (508) 852-6943 Calendar System: Semester
URL: www.qcc.edu
Established: 1963 Annual Undergrad Tuition & Fees (In-State): $5,830
Enrollment: 6,942 Coed
Affiliation or Control: State IRS Status: 501(c)3
Highest Offering: Associate Degree
Accreditation: EH, ADNUR, COARC, CSHSE, DA, DH, EMT, MAC, NAEYC, OTA, PNUR, RAD, SURGT

02 President .... Dr. Luis PEDRAJA
05 VP of Academic Affairs .... Dr. James KEANE
10 VP of Administration .... Mr. Stephen T. MARINI
32 VP of Student Enrollment/Develop .... Dr. Lillian M. ORTIZ
20 Associate VP Academic Affairs .... Ms. Kathy RENTSCH
30 VP for External Relations .... Dr. Viviana ABREU-HERNANDEZ
04 Executive Assistant to President .... Ms. Selina M. BORIA
21 Asst VP for Finance/Comptroller .... Ms. Debra A. LAFLASH
79 Dean Humanities & Education .... Mr. Brady HAMMOND
76 Dean Health Care .... Mr. C. Pat SCHMOHL
50 Dean Business/Engineer/Technology .... Ms. Betty LAUER
81 Dean Science & Mathematics .... Mr. Benjamin BENTON
06 Registrar .... Ms. Barbara ZAWALICH
62 Dean of Library Services .... Ms. Cary MORSE
09 Dean of Inst Research/Planning .... Dr. Ingrid SKADBERG
121 Associate VP of Student Success .... Ms. Michelle TUFAU-AFRIYIE
106 Dean of Digital Learning .... Mr. Ken DWYER
35 Director Student Life & Leadership .... Ms. Ashlee GIVINS
18 Executive Director of Facilities .... Mr. James RACKI
37 Director Student Financial Aid .... Ms. Karen GRANT
96 Purchasing Manager .... Ms. Juliana ESPOSITO
19 Chief of Campus Police .... Mr. Kevin RITACCO
26 Dir Institutional Communications .... Mr. Joshua MARTIN
38 Social Worker/Mental Health Couns .... Ms. Tina WELLS
28 Director Disability Services .... Ms. Kristen PROCTOR
35 Dean of Students .... Ms. Terry VECCHIO
07 Director of Admissions .... Ms. Ai Co ABERCROMBIE

*Roxbury Community College (G)

1234 Columbus Avenue,
Roxbury Crossing MA 02120-3423
County: Suffolk FICE Identification: 011930
Unit ID: 167631
Telephone: (617) 427-0060 Carnegie Class: Assoc/HT-High Trad
FAX Number: N/A Calendar System: Semester
URL: rcc.mass.edu
Established: 1973 Annual Undergrad Tuition & Fees (In-State): $5,784
Enrollment: 1,200 Coed
Affiliation or Control: State IRS Status: 501(c)3
Highest Offering: Associate Degree
Accreditation: EH, RAD

02 President .... Dr. Valerie R. ROBERSON

04	Executive Asst to the President	Ms. Judy M. PUGH
05	Int VP Academic/Student Affairs	Ms. Cecile REGNER
108	Exec VP Institutional Effectiveness	Ms. Cecile REGNER
10	Vice President of Admin & Finance	Vacant
32	Dean of Students	Ms. Robyn SHAHID-BELLOT
103	Assoc VP Workforce Development	Dr. Hillel SIMS
13	Chief Information Tech Officer	Mr. Patrick KANGETHE
15	Exec Director Human Resources	Ms. Sandra KNIGHT
08	Director of Library	Mr. William HOAG
23	Director of Health Services	Ms. Ruth HINES
30	Exec Dir Dev/Alumni/Foundation	Ms. Mishawn DAVIS-EYENE
06	Registrar	Mr. Bryan D. JONES
26	Director Marketing/Communications	Ms. Jordan SMOCK
57	Dir of Visual/Performing/Media Arts	Vacant
37	Assoc Director Financial Aid	Mr. Christopher LEWIS
25	Grants Research Specialist	Ms. Cecile REGNER
09	Director of Institutional Research	Vacant
19	Director Public Safety	Mr. David ALBENESE
81	Dean of STEM	Dr. Hillel SIMS
90	Director Academic Computing	Vacant
41	Manager of RLTAC	Mr. Jelani TOWNSELL

*Springfield Technical Community College (A)

Armory Square, Springfield MA 01105-1296

County: Hampden FICE Identification: 008078
Unit ID: 167905

Telephone: (413) 781-7822 Carnegie Class: Assoc/HVT-High Trad
FAX Number: (413) 755-6309 Calendar System: Semester
URL: www.stcc.edu
Established: 1967 Annual Undergrad Tuition & Fees (In-State): $5,560
Enrollment: 4,327 Coed
Affiliation or Control: State IRS Status: 501(c)3
Highest Offering: Associate Degree
Accreditation: EH, ADNUR, CAHIIM, COARC, DA, DH, DMS, MAC, MLTAD, OTA, PTAA, RAD, SURGT

02	President	Dr. John B. COOK
05	VP of Academic Affairs	Dr. Geraldine DE BERLY
10	VP of Administration/CFO	Ms. Andrea NATHANSON
111	Int VP Advancement/External Affairs	Dr. Shai BUTLER
32	VP Student Affairs	Ms. Darcy KEMP
103	Int Asst VP Workforce Development	Ms. Gladys N. FRANCO
15	Int AVP of Human Resources	Ms. Kathryn SENIE
13	AVP/CIO	Ms. Mary KASELOUSKAS
20	Dean of Academic Initiatives	Mr. Matthew GRAVEL
04	Executive Asst to the President	Ms. Nanette FLORES
66	Director of Nursing	Ms. Lisa FUGIEL
76	Dean Health and Patient Simulation	Mr. Christopher D. SCOTT
81	Dean STEM	Ms. Lara SHARP
107	Dean Liberal/Professional Studies	Mr. Richard GRECO
51	Senior Director of Business Service	Dr. Debbie BELLUCCI
07	Dean of Admissions	Ms. Louisa M. DAVIS FREEMAN
06	Registrar	Mr. Anthony (Tony) SBALBI
41	Director of Athletics	Mr. Jenkin GOULD
121	Director of Advising	Vacant
26	Dir Marketing/Communications	Mr. Keith PAUL
36	Director of Coop/Career Placement	Ms. Pamela WHITE
37	Dean of Student Financial Services	Mr. Jeremy GREENHOUSE
88	Fiscal/Financial Project Manager	Vacant
35	Coord Student Activities/Devel	Ms. Andrea TARPEY
27	Coordinator of Media Relations	Mr. James DANKO
114	Senior Director Finance/Budgets	Mr. Jason COHEN
14	Sr Director of IT Applications	Mr. Douglas SLAVAS
08	Dean Library Services	Ms. Erica EYNOUF
21	Controller	Mr. Jonathan TUDRYN
09	Dean of Institutional Research	Ms. Suzanne SMITH
108	Director of Assessment	Dr. Tracey TROTTIER
22	Director of Access/Student Success	Mr. Jose LOPES-FIGUEROA
88	Director of Gateway to College	Ms. Katara ROBINSON
18	Dir of Facilities Quality and Svcs	Ms. Kerri KANE
25	Dir Grants Development & Admin	Ms. Kimberley BRODERICK
88	Senior Director of Accounting	Ms. Dorothy UNGERER
101	Liaison to the Board of Trustees	Ms. Nanette FLORES
19	Sr Director Public Safety	Mr. Jose RIVERA

Massachusetts Institute of Technology (B)

77 Massachusetts Avenue, Cambridge MA 02139-4307

County: Middlesex FICE Identification: 002178
Unit ID: 166683

Telephone: (617) 253-1000 Carnegie Class: DU-Highest
FAX Number: N/A Calendar System: 4/1/4
URL: web.mit.edu
Established: 1861 Annual Undergrad Tuition & Fees: $53,450
Enrollment: 11,254 Coed
Affiliation or Control: Independent Non-Profit IRS Status: 501(c)3
Highest Offering: Doctorate
Accreditation: EH, PLNG

01	President	Dr. L. Rafael REIF
88	Chair of the Corporation	Ms. Diane GREENE
05	Provost	Prof. Martin A. SCHMIDT
00	Chancellor	Prof. Melissa NOBLES
46	Vice President for Research	Prof. Maria T. ZUBER
106	Vice President for Open Learning	Prof. Sanjay SARMA
106	Acting VP for Open Learning	Prof. Krishna RAJAGOPAL
10	Exec Vice President & Treasurer	Mr. Glen SHOR
101	VP & Secretary of the Corporation	Ms. Suzanne GLASSBURN
20	Chancellor for Academic Advancement	Prof. W. Eric L. GRIMSON
43	Vice President & General Counsel	Mr. Mark DIVINCENZO
26	VP for Communications	Mr. Alfred IRONSIDE
30	VP for Resource Development	Ms. Julie LUCAS
29	CEO MIT Alumni Association	Ms. Whitney T. ESPICH
115	President MIT Investment Mgmt Co	Mr. Seth ALEXANDER
15	VP for Human Resources	Ms. Ramona ALLLEN
18	VP Campus Services & Stewardship	Mr. Joe HIGGINS
13	VP for IS&T	Mr. Mark SILIS
21	Vice President for Finance	Ms. Katie HAMMER
48	Dean Sch of Architecture & Planning	Prof. Hashim SARKIS
54	Dean School of Engineering	Prof. Anantha CHANDRAKASAN
79	Dean Sch Hum/Arts/Soc Sciences	Prof. Agustín RAYO
81	Dean School of Science	Prof. Nergis MAVALVALA
50	Dean Sloan School of Management	Prof. David C. SCHMITTLEIN
77	Dean Schwarzman Col of Computing	Dr. Daniel HUTTENLOCHER
20	Associate Provost	Prof. Timothy JAMISON
20	Associate Provost	Prof. Philip S. KHOURY
20	Associate Provost	Prof. Richard K. LESTER
20	Associate Provost/Assoc VP Research	Prof. Krystyn VAN VLIET
08	Director of Libraries	Ms. Chris BOURG
28	Institute Community & Equity Ofcr	Mr. John DOZIER
58	Vice Chancellor UG & Grad Education	Prof. Ian A. WAITZ
32	Vice Chancellor/Dean Student Life	Dr. Suzy NELSON
88	Director Lincoln Laboratory	Dr. Eric D. EVANS
86	Director MIT Washington Office	Mr. David GOLDSTON
07	Dean of Admissions/Student Fin Svcs	Mr. Stuart SCHMILL
23	Medical Dir & Head MIT Medical	Dr. Cecilia Warpinski STUOPIS
45	Director of Campus Planning	Mr. Jon ALVAREZ
102	Exec Dir Foundation Relations	Ms. Alicia SANCHEZ
25	Asst Provost for Research Admin	Ms. Colleen M. LESLIE
96	Dir of Strategic Sourcing/Contracts	Ms. Christina T. LO
41	Director of Athletics	Dr. G. Anthony GRANT
09	Director of Institutional Research	Mrs. Lydia S. SNOVER
88	Director Teaching & Learning Lab	Dr. Janet RANKIN
85	Assoc Dean & Dir Intl Students Ofc	Mr. David ELWELL
36	Exec Dir Career Advising & Prof Dev	Ms. Deborah L. LIVERMAN
93	Associate Dean and Director OME	Ms. DiOnetta CRAYTON
06	Registrar	Mr. Brian CANAVAN
27	Director & Publisher MIT Press	Ms. Amy BRAND
39	Sr Assoc Dean Housing & Res Svs	Mr. David FRIEDRICH
42	Interim Chaplain to Institute	Rev. Thea KEITH-LUCAS
38	Sr Assoc Dean Support & Wellbeing	Mr. David RANDALL
94	Director Women's and Gender Studies	Prof. Helen Elaine LEE
104	Executive Director MISTI	Ms. April JULICH PEREZ
24	Director MIT Audio Visual Services	Mr. Christopher WAY
90	Associate Vice President Technology	Mr. Olu BROWN
04	Exec Assistant to the President	Ms. Karla CASEY

Massachusetts School of Law at Andover (C)

500 Federal Street, Andover MA 01810-1094

County: Essex FICE Identification: 032353
Unit ID: 369002

Telephone: (978) 681-0800 Carnegie Class: Spec-4-yr-Law
FAX Number: (978) 681-6330 Calendar System: Semester
URL: www.mslaw.edu
Established: 1988 Annual Graduate Tuition & Fees: N/A
Enrollment: 295 Coed
Affiliation or Control: Independent Non-Profit IRS Status: 501(c)3
Highest Offering: Doctorate; No Undergraduates
Accreditation: EH

00	Dean Emeritus	Mr. Lawrence R. VELVEL
01	Dean	Prof. Michael COYNE
10	Chief Financial Officer	Mr. Clifford ABELSON
37	Director of Financial Aid	Ms. Lynn BOWAB
06	Registrar	Ms. Rosa FIGUEIREDO
07	Director of Admissions	Mr. Rohit BHASIN
26	Director of Media	Ms. Kathryn VILLARE
05	Dir Academic Svcs/Career Devel	Ms. Paula COLBY-CLEMENTS
13	Director of Technology	Mr. Michael COYNE
08	Director of Library	Mr. Daniel HARAYDA

MCPHS University (D)

179 Longwood Avenue, Boston MA 02115-5896

County: Suffolk FICE Identification: 002165
Unit ID: 166656

Telephone: (617) 732-2800 Carnegie Class: Spec-4-yr-Other Health
FAX Number: (617) 732-2801 Calendar System: Semester
URL: www.mcphs.edu
Established: 1823 Annual Undergrad Tuition & Fees: $34,650
Enrollment: 7,501 Coed
Affiliation or Control: Independent Non-Profit IRS Status: 501(c)3
Highest Offering: Doctorate
Accreditation: EH, ARCPA, CVT, DH, DMS, NMT, NURSE, OPT, PH, PHAR, PTA, RAD, RTT

01	President	Richard LESSARD
05	VP for Acad Affairs/Provost	Dr. Caroline ZEIND
10	Chief Financial Officer	Keith BELLUCCI
111	VP for Advancement & Chief of Staff	Sue GORMAN
20	Assoc Provost Acad & Prof Affairs	Dr. Jeanine MOUNT
09	Assoc Prov Inst Research/Effective	Dr. Henriette PRANGER
106	Assoc Provost Academic Innovation	Dr. Barbara MACAULAY
43	Assoc General Counsel/Legal Affs	Mary TANONA
32	Assoc Provost for Student Success	Dr. Craig MACK
67	Interim Dean of Pharmacy Boston	Dr. Stephen KERR
67	Interim CAO WM/Dean of Pharmacy WM	Dr. Anna MORIN
08	Dean Library & Learning Resources	Richard KAPLAN
49	Dean School of Arts and Sciences	Dr. Delia C. ANDERSON
88	Dean School of Healthcare Bus	Michael SPOONER
66	Interim Dean of Nursing	Tammy GRAVEL
107	Dean Sch of Prof Studies	Carol STUCKEY
52	Int Dean Forsyth Sch of Dental Hyg	Dr. Dianne SMALLIDGE
88	Director of Physical Therapy	Dr. Frances KISTNER
88	Director of PA Studies Boston	Christopher COOPER
88	Director of PA Studies Wor/Man	Kristy ALTONGY-MAGEE
69	Director Master of Public Health	Carly LEVY
88	Dean of Optometry	Dr. Maryke NEIBERG
88	Dean of Acupuncture & Oriental Med	Dennis MOSEMAN
75	Director of Occupational Therapy	Dr. Douglas SIMMONS
15	Chief Human Resources Officer	Kevin DOLAN
06	Admin Dean/University Registrar	Stacey TAYLOR
13	Director of Information Svcs/CIO	Tom SCANLON
12	Exec Director Wor/Man Campuses	Dr. Seth P. WALL
88	Title IX Coordinator	Dawn BALLOU
84	Chief Enrollment Officer	Kathleen RYAN
96	Director of Purchasing	Peg CRAWFORD
38	Exec Dir Counseling Services	Molly PAYNE
26	Director of Communications	Michael RATTY
18	Director of Facilities Boston	Jeff WARD
18	Director of Facilities Worcester	Glen WARD
19	Chief of Public Safety	Kevin NOLAN
105	Manager of Web Services	Charlene ROBERTSON
108	Exec Dir Inst Research & Assessment	Laura UERLING
04	Special Assistant to the President	Sheryl CHEAL
25	Program Director Regulatory Affairs	Frederick FRANKHAUSER
28	Asst Dean Diversity & Inclusion	Julia GOLDEN-BATTLE
29	Exec Dir Prof Career Dev/Alum Svcs	Karen SINGLE
36	Dir Center for Prof Career Develop	Melissa HAWKINS
36	Dir Center for Prof Career Devel WM	Jeanette DOYLE
37	Director Student Financial Services	Elizabeth GORHAM
104	Director Study Abroad	Sara SANFORD
22	Director Affirm Action/Equal Opp	Vacant
91	Director Administrative Computing	Kevin MCGOVERN
13	Chief Academic Technology Officer	Dr. Daniel JAMOUS
07	Director of Admission	Alex COLE
39	Director of Residence Life	Irene STEFANAKOS

MCPHS-Worcester Campus (E)

19 Foster Street, Worcester MA 01608-1715

Telephone: (508) 890-8855 Identification: 770112
Accreditation: &EH, ACUP, CVT, DMS

Merrimack College (F)

315 Turnpike Street, North Andover MA 01845-5800

County: Essex FICE Identification: 002120
Unit ID: 166850

Telephone: (978) 837-5000 Carnegie Class: Masters/L
FAX Number: (978) 837-5222 Calendar System: Semester
URL: www.merrimack.edu
Established: 1947 Annual Undergrad Tuition & Fees: $45,074
Enrollment: 5,418 Coed
Affiliation or Control: Roman Catholic IRS Status: 501(c)3
Highest Offering: Master's
Accreditation: EH, CAATE, @DIETC

01	President	Dr. Christopher E. HOPEY
03	Executive Vice President	Mr. Jeffrey DOGGETT
04	Director Office of the President	Ms. Lisa JEBALI
05	Provost	Dr. John (Sean) CONDON
45	VP Institutional Effectiveness	Dr. Jonathan LYON
10	VP Finance & Chief Business Officer	Mr. Andrew MAYLOR
84	VP Enrollment/Dean of Admissions	Mr. Darren CONINE
42	Vice Pres Mission & Ministry	Rev. Raymond DLUGOS, OSA
30	VP Development/Alumni Relations	Ms. Leila RICE
43	Vice President & General Counsel	Mr. Nicholas MCDONALD
15	Interim VP Human Resources	Vacant
58	AVP Graduate/Continuing Studies	Mr. Mark GOULD
86	AVP Campus Planning & Development	Mr. Felipe SCHWARZ
26	VP Communications/Chief of Staff	Ms. Bethany LOMONACO
27	Vice Pres Marketing	Ms. Courtney JOHANSON
21	Interim Controller	Ms. Joanne FORAN
29	Assoc VP Develop & Alumni Relations	Ms. Joanne MERMELSTEIN
32	VP Student Affairs/Dean Students	Ms. Allison GILL
13	AVP Information Technology/CIO	Mr. Peter HASTINGS
50	Dean Girard School of Business	Vacant
54	Dean Sch of Science & Engineering	Dr. Naira CAMPBELL-KYUREGHYAN
49	Interim Dean of Liberal Arts	Dr. John (Sean) CONDON
53	Dean School of Education	Vacant
76	Dean School Health Sciences	Vacant
37	Director Financial Aid	Vacant
41	Director of Athletics	Mr. Jeremy GIBSON
09	Dir Institutional Research & Plng	Vacant
08	Director of the Library	Vacant
42	Director of Campus Ministry	Vacant
23	Director Hamel Health	Vacant
19	Director of Police Services	Mr. Michael DELGRECO
24	Dir of Media Instructional Services	Mr. Kevin SALEMME
96	Director of Purchasing	Mr. Michael MAGNER
105	Director of Web Services	Vacant
28	Director Diversity Education	Vacant
06	Registrar	Mr. Kevin GATELY

MGH Institute of Health Professions (A)

36 1st Avenue, Boston MA 02129-4557
County: Suffolk FICE Identification: 022316
Unit ID: 166869
Telephone: (617) 726-2947 Carnegie Class: Spec-4-yr-Other Health
FAX Number: (617) 726-3716 Calendar System: Semester
URL: www.mghihp.edu
Established: 1977 Annual Undergrad Tuition & Fees: N/A
Enrollment: 1,269 Coed
Affiliation or Control: Independent Non-Profit IRS Status: 501(c)3
Highest Offering: Doctorate
Accreditation: EH, ARCPA, NURSE, OT, PTA, SP

01 President .....Dr. Paula MILONE-NUZZO
05 Provost/VP Academic Affairs .....Dr. Alex JOHNSON
10 VP Finance/Administration .....Mr. Atlas EVANS
11 Chief Operating Officer .....Mr. Denis STRATFORD
100 Chief of Staff .....Ms. Elizabeth PIPES
26 Chief Communications Officer .....Mr. Paul MURPHY
30 Chief Development Officer .....Ms. Clare MCCULLY

† Tuition varies by degree program.

Montserrat College of Art (B)

23 Essex Street, Beverly MA 01915-4508
County: Essex FICE Identification: 020630
Unit ID: 166911
Telephone: (978) 921-4242 Carnegie Class: Spec-4-yr-Arts
FAX Number: (978) 922-4268 Calendar System: Semester
URL: www.montserrat.edu
Established: 1970 Annual Undergrad Tuition & Fees: $35,300
Enrollment: 362 Coed
Affiliation or Control: Independent Non-Profit IRS Status: 501(c)3
Highest Offering: Baccalaureate
Accreditation: EH, ART

01 President .....Dr. Kurt T. STEINBERG
05 Dean of Academic Affairs .....Mr. Brian PELLINEN
32 Dean of Students .....Ms. Maureen WARK
30 Director of Development .....Mr. Paul KOTAKIS
26 Dean College Rels/Spec Asst to Pres .....Ms. Jo BRODERICK
10 Chief Financial Officer .....Ms. Cara CALLANAN
13 Director of Information Technology .....Ms. Ari GROSVENOR
08 Librarian .....Ms. Cheri COE
06 Registrar .....Mrs. Theresa SKELLY
15 Human Resources Generalist .....Ms. Christin BOURANIS
07 Director of Admissions .....Mr. Jeffrey NEWELL
04 Executive Asst to the President .....Ms. Olivia LEJEUNE
37 Director of Financial Aid .....Mrs. Joanne RACOK
18 Facilities Manager .....Mr. James MCCARTHY
88 Dir Academic Access Studio .....Ms. Meagan GRANT
39 Director of Campus Life .....Ms. Haley MCCONVILLE

Mount Holyoke College (C)

50 College Street, South Hadley MA 01075-1424
County: Hampshire FICE Identification: 002192
Unit ID: 166939
Telephone: (413) 538-2000 Carnegie Class: Bac-A&S
FAX Number: (413) 538-2391 Calendar System: Semester
URL: www.mtholyoke.edu
Established: 1837 Annual Undergrad Tuition & Fees: $54,618
Enrollment: 2,040 Female
Affiliation or Control: Independent Non-Profit IRS Status: 501(c)3
Highest Offering: Master's
Accreditation: EH

01 President .....Sonya C. STEPHENS
05 VP Acad Affairs/Dean of Faculty .....Dorothy E. MOSBY
10 VP Finance and Administration .....Shannon GUREK
84 VP Enrollment/Dean of Admissions .....Robin RANDALL
111 VP College Relations .....Kassandra JOLLEY
32 VP Student Life/Dean of Students .....Marcella RUNELL HALL
28 VP for Equity and Inclusion/CDO ..Kijua SANDERS-MCMURTRY
101 Secretary of the College .....Lenore REILLY
06 Registrar .....Elizabeth PYLE
13 Chief Information Officer .....Alex WIRTH-CAUCHON
29 Exec Director Alumnae Association .....Nancy PEREZ

New England College of Optometry (D)

424 Beacon Street, Boston MA 02115-1129
County: Suffolk FICE Identification: 002164
Unit ID: 167093
Telephone: (617) 266-2030 Carnegie Class: Spec-4-yr-Other Health
FAX Number: (617) 424-9202 Calendar System: Semester
URL: www.neco.edu
Established: 1894 Annual Undergrad Tuition & Fees: N/A
Enrollment: 528 Coed
Affiliation or Control: Independent Non-Profit IRS Status: 501(c)3
Highest Offering: Doctorate
Accreditation: EH, OPT, OPTR

01 President .....Dr. Howard B. PURCELL
125 President Emeritus .....Dr. Clifford SCOTT
05 VP & Dean of Academic Affairs .....Dr. Erik WEISSBERG
10 EVP Finance/Admin/CFO .....Ms. Traci LOGAN
86 VP Professional Affairs .....Dr. Gary CHU
20 Dean Academic Resources & Admin .....Dr. Sandra MOHR
17 Assoc Dean of Clinical Affairs .....Dr. Kristen BROWN
15 Exec Dir of Human Resources .....Ms. Joanna HURIER
07 Director of Admissions .....Ms. Kristen TOBIN
37 Director Student Financial Aid .....Ms. Esther BANDOO-GOMES
06 Registrar .....Mr. Craig KELLER
08 Director of Library Services .....Ms. Heather EDMONDS
04 Executive Asst to the President .....Ms. Donna Marie FERRI
09 Director of Institutional Research .....Ms. Jane GWIAZDA
18 Chief Facilities/Physical Plant .....Ms. Shawne GILLIES
26 Chief Public Relations Officer .....Ms. Julie CORWIN
28 Diversity & Inclusion Liaison .....Dr. Angela ABRAHAM
30 Chief Development Officer .....Ms. Kimberly CARVALHO

New England Conservatory of Music (E)

290 Huntington Avenue, Boston MA 02115-5018
County: Suffolk FICE Identification: 002194
Unit ID: 167057
Telephone: (617) 585-1100 Carnegie Class: Spec-4-yr-Arts
FAX Number: (617) 262-0500 Calendar System: Semester
URL: www.necmusic.edu
Established: 1867 Annual Undergrad Tuition & Fees: $52,440
Enrollment: 701 Coed
Affiliation or Control: Independent Non-Profit IRS Status: 501(c)3
Highest Offering: Doctorate
Accreditation: EH

01 President .....Ms. Andrea KALYN
05 Provost and Dean of Faculty .....Mr. Benjamin SOSLAND
10 Chief Financial Officer .....Ms. Breean FORTIER
111 SVP Institutional Advancement .....Ms. Kathleen KELLY
26 Dir Marketing/Brand Strategy .....Ms. Valerie SZEPIWDYCZ
32 Dean of Students/Campus Life .....Ms. Christina DAVIS
07 Asst Director of Admissions .....Mr. Zach SCHWARTZ
21 AVP for Finance/Controller .....Ms. Kristina MARTIN
18 Dir Facilities/Campus Security .....Mr. Chris HAYDEN
06 Registrar/Dir of Inst Research .....Mr. Robert WINKLEY
08 Director of Libraries .....Vacant
37 Associate Dean for Fin Aid .....Ms. Lauren URBANEK
39 Director Residence Life/Activities .....Ms. Josie REED
110 Sr Dir Institutional Advancement .....Ms. Hilary WIRTZ
15 Director of Human Resources .....Mr. Nick MACKE
13 Chief Information Officer .....Ms. Heather WOODS
35 Sr Associate Dean of Students .....Ms. Rebecca TEETERS
38 Director of Counseling Services .....Mr. Squire PAIGE
23 Director of Health Services .....Ms. Leah MCKINNON-HOWE
04 Admin Assistant to the President .....Ms. Amy GIANNINI
20 Dean of Academic Affairs/Admin .....Ms. Alison GARNER

New England Law | Boston (F)

154 Stuart Street, Boston MA 02116-5687
County: Suffolk FICE Identification: 008916
Unit ID: 167215
Telephone: (617) 451-0010 Carnegie Class: Spec-4-yr-Law
FAX Number: (617) 422-7333 Calendar System: Semester
URL: www.nesl.edu
Established: 1908 Annual Undergrad Tuition & Fees: N/A
Enrollment: 904 Coed
Affiliation or Control: Independent Non-Profit IRS Status: 501(c)3
Highest Offering: First Professional Degree
Accreditation: LAW

01 President/CEO/Dean .....Mr. Scott BROWN
05 Associate Dean .....Ms. Allison M. DUSSIAS
05 Associate Dean .....Ms. Lisa FREUDENHEIM
07 Assoc Director of Admission .....Ms. Angela SMITH ROWE
10 Chief Financial Officer .....Ms. Anne Marie MARTORANA
13 Director of Information Technology .....Mr. Gareth FLANAGAN
26 Chief Marketing/Communications Ofcr .....Ms. Jennifer KELLY
08 Director of the Law Library .....Ms. Kristin C. MCCARTHY
36 Asst Director of Career Services .....Ms. Larissa BREWSTER
07 Dean of Admissions .....Mr. John CHALMERS
37 Director of Financial Aid .....Mr. Eric A. KRUPSKI
06 Registrar .....Ms. Lexi OBERACKER
18 Director of Facilities/Security .....Mr. Miguel ALVARADO
32 Director of Student Services .....Ms. Jacqui PILGRIM
30 Dir of Development/Alumni Rels .....Ms. Jocelyn J. COLETTI
88 Director of the Clinical Law Office .....Mr. Russell ENGLER

New England School of Acupuncture (G)

19 Foster Street, Worcester MA 01608-1715
County: Middlesex FICE Identification: 025798
Telephone: (508) 890-8855 Carnegie Class: Spec-4-yr-Other Health
FAX Number: (508) 890-8515 Calendar System: Trimester
URL: https://www.mcphs.edu/academics/school-of-acupuncture
Established: 1975 Annual Undergrad Tuition & Fees: N/A
Enrollment: N/A Coed
Affiliation or Control: Independent Non-Profit IRS Status: 501(c)3
Highest Offering: Master's; No Lower Division
Accreditation: ACUP

01 Executive Director .....Susan L. GORMAN
05 Interim Academic Dean .....Amy HULL

† Affiliate of MCPHS University.

Nichols College (H)

Center Road, PO Box 5000, Dudley MA 01571-5000
County: Worcester FICE Identification: 002197
Unit ID: 167260
Telephone: (508) 213-1560 Carnegie Class: Spec-4-yr-Bus
FAX Number: N/A Calendar System: Semester
URL: www.nichols.edu
Established: 1815 Annual Undergrad Tuition & Fees: $36,540
Enrollment: 1,518 Coed
Affiliation or Control: Independent Non-Profit IRS Status: 501(c)3
Highest Offering: Master's
Accreditation: EH, COSMA, IACBE

01 President .....Glenn M. SULMASY
05 Vice President for Academic Affairs .....Mauri S. PELTO
111 Vice President for Advancement .....William C. PIECZYNSKI
84 Vice President for Enrollment .....William BOFFI
32 Vice President for Student Affairs .....Pamela J. BOGGIO
10 VP for Business & Finance/CFO .....Jamie SKOWYRA
18 Vice President for Operations .....Robert W. LAVIGNE
26 AVP Advancement/Col Communications .....Susan VESHI
124 Assoc Dir of Enroll & Retention .....Katie MOULTON
13 Chief Technology Officer .....Jared HAMILTON
58 Associate Director GPS .....Thomas STEWART
04 Assistant to the President .....Lynn S. LOOBY
41 Director of Athletics .....Eric GOBIEL
07 Director of Admissions .....Katelynn MOCHUN
06 Assistant Dean for Registration .....Betin ROBICHAUD
08 Director of Library .....Carrie GRIMSHAW
15 Director of Human Resources .....Darcy VANGEL
29 Director of Alumni Relations .....Molly THIENEL
35 Dir Student Activities/Orientation .....Elizabeth GIONFRIDDO
36 Director of Career Services .....Elizabeth HORGAN
37 Director of Financial Aid .....Lindsay LOUIS
38 Director Mental Health Services .....Kate LOGAN
09 Dir of Inst Research & Reporting .....Emily REARDON
19 Director Public Safety .....Eric STREICH
23 Director Health Services .....Katherine NICOLETTI
35 Assistant Dean of Students .....Marney BUSS
39 Director of Residence Life & PDSO .....Amanda DESAI
105 Webmaster .....Dave LEARY
28 Director CDEI .....Alicia MCKENZIE

Northeastern University (I)

360 Huntington Avenue, Boston MA 02115-0195
County: Suffolk FICE Identification: 002199
Unit ID: 167358
Telephone: (617) 373-2000 Carnegie Class: DU-Highest
FAX Number: N/A Calendar System: Semester
URL: www.northeastern.edu
Established: 1898 Annual Undergrad Tuition & Fees: $55,452
Enrollment: 22,905 Coed
Affiliation or Control: Independent Non-Profit IRS Status: 501(c)3
Highest Offering: Doctorate
Accreditation: EH, ANEST, ARCPA, COPSY, COSMA, LAW, NURSE, PH, PHAR, PTA, SCPSY, SP, SPAA

01 President .....Dr. Joseph E. AOUN
03 Chancellor and SVP for Learning .....Mr. Ken HENDERSON
04 Exec Assistant to the President .....Ms. Susan CROMWELL
05 Sr VP Academic Affairs and Provost .....Dr. David MADIGAN
100 Chief of Staff .....Vacant
111 Sr VP University Advancement .....Ms. Diane N. MACGILLIVRAY
43 Sr VP and General Counsel .....Mr. Ralph C. MARTIN, II
26 Sr VP External Affairs .....Mr. Michael A. ARMINI
12 Seattle Campus Dean & CEO .....Mr. David THURMAN
12 Regional Dean & CEO Silicon Valley .....Ms. Hillary MICKELL
12 Interim Charlotte Campus Dean & CEO .Dr. Margaret BERNHARD
08 Vice Provost for Info Collaboration .....Dr. Dan COHEN
46 Sr Vice Prov Research .....Dr. David LUZZI
20 Sr Vice Prov Educ Innovation .....Dr. Susan AMBROSE
124 Int Vice Chanc Learner Engagement .....Dr. Laura A. WANKEL
13 VP & CIO .....Mr. Cole CAMPLESE
88 VP Enrollment Management .....Mr. Sundar KUMARASAMY
20 Sr Vice Prov & Sr Vice Chancellor .....Dr. Mary LUDDEN
32 Sr Vice Chancellor Student Affairs .....Ms. Madeleine A. ESTABROOK
30 VP Development .....Ms. Luanne KIRWIN
15 VP & Chief Human Resources Officer .....Ms. Michele GRAZULIS
18 VP Facilities .....Ms. Maria CIMILLUCA
86 VP Government Relations .....Vacant
31 VP City & Community Affairs .....Mr. John M. TOBIN
117 Director of Risk Services .....Ms. Sonya ROSS
45 VP & Chief Campus Planning and Dev .Ms. Kathy SPIEGELMAN
20 Sr Vice Provost Academic Affairs .....Ms. Debra FRANKO
114 Sr Vice Prov Budget/Planning/Admin .....Ms. Breean FORTIER
28 Sr Vice Prov Chief Inclusion Ofcr .....Dr. Karl REID
76 Dean Health Sciences .....Dr. Carmen SCEPPA
37 Dean Student Financial Svcs .....Mr. Robert REDDY
36 Sr Assoc VP Employer Engagement .....Mr. Manny CONTOMANOLIS
88 V Provost & Deputy General Counsel .....Ms. Lisa SINCLAIR
88 Vice Provost Faculty Diversity .....Dr. Phil HE
21 VP of Admin & Financial Planning .....Dr. Anthony RINI
88 AVP Research Administration .....Ms. Dana CARROLL
35 Vice Chancellor Dean of Students .....Dr. Chong KIM-WONG
09 AVP Inst Rsrch & Data Admin .....Ms. Rana GLASGAL
06 Assoc VP & University Registrar .....Ms. Siham DOUGHMAN
27 VP Communications .....Ms. Renata NYUL
27 VP Marketing .....Ms. Rebecca ANZUONI
88 AVP International Advancement .....Mr. Robert DIETRICH

44 VP & Asst Treasurer .... Ms. Alysa GERLACH
92 Director University Honors Program .... Ms. Laurie KRAMER
42 Exec Dir Spirituality & Dialogue .... Mr. Alexander KERN
19 Director of Public Safety .... Mr. Michael DAVIS
41 Director of Athletics .... Mr. James MADIGAN
10 Sr VP Finance & Treasurer .... Mr. Thomas NEDELL
77 Int Dean Khoury Col Comp Science .... Dr. Alan MISLOVE
54 Dean College of Engineering .... Dr. Gregory ABOWD
81 Dean College of Science .... Dr. Hazel SIVE
50 Dean D'Amore-McKim School of Bus .... Dr. Raj ECHAMBADI
57 Dean College of Arts/Media/Design .... Dr. Elizabeth HUDSON
61 Dean School of Law .... Dr. James HACKNEY
83 Dean Col of Soc Sci & Humanities .... Dr. Uta POIGER
107 Interim Dean Col Prof Studies .... Dr. David FIELDS
12 Dean Toronto Campus .... Ms. Aliza LAKHANI
106 Chief Admin Officer Roux Institute .... Mr. Chris MALLETT
29 VP Alumni Relations .... Mr. Rick DAVIS
39 Dean Cultural/Resident/Spirit Life .... Mr. Robert JOSE
101 Secretary of the Institution/Board .... Ms. Camille KLUTZ-LEACH

Northpoint Bible College (A)

320 South Main Street, Haverhill MA 01835
County: Essex FICE Identification: 035705
Unit ID: 217606
Telephone: (978) 478-3400 Carnegie Class: Spec-4-yr-Faith
FAX Number: (978) 478-3406 Calendar System: Semester
URL: www.northpoint.edu
Established: 1924 Annual Undergrad Tuition & Fees: $13,493
Enrollment: 294 Coed
Affiliation or Control: Assemblies Of God Church IRS Status: 501(c)3
Highest Offering: Master's
Accreditation: BI

01 President .... Rev Dr. David J. ARNETT
05 Academic Dean .... Rev Dr. Daniel HOWELL
32 Dean of Student Development .... Rev. Karen JACOB
10 Financial Services Manager .... Mrs. Pam PERRON
84 Dean of Enrollment .... Rev Dr. David MUNLEY
37 Director of Financial Aid .... Miss Patricia STAUFFER
06 Registrar .... Mrs. Amy MARANVILLE
13 Chief Info Technology Officer (CIO) .... Vacant

Pope St. John XXIII National Seminary (B)

558 South Avenue, Weston MA 02493-2699
County: Middlesex FICE Identification: 002202
Unit ID: 167464
Telephone: (781) 899-5500 Carnegie Class: Spec-4-yr-Faith
FAX Number: (781) 899-9057 Calendar System: Semester
URL: www.psjs.edu
Established: 1964 Annual Graduate Tuition & Fees: N/A
Enrollment: 54 Male
Affiliation or Control: Roman Catholic IRS Status: 501(c)3
Highest Offering: Master's; No Undergraduates
Accreditation: THEOL

01 Rector and President .... Rev. Brian R. KIELY
03 Vice Rector .... Rev. Paul E. MICELI
05 Academic Dean .... Dr. Anthony KEATY
08 Librarian .... Mrs. Barbara NEEM
10 Business Manager .... Mrs. Kyle RYAN
06 Registrar .... Dr. Paul MICELI
30 Chief Development Officer .... Mrs. Kate FOLAN
32 Chief Student Life Officer .... Rev. Stephen LINEHAN

Quincy College (C)

1250 Hancock Street, Quincy MA 02169-4324
County: Norfolk FICE Identification: 002205
Unit ID: 167525
Telephone: (617) 984-1700 Carnegie Class: Assoc/MT-VT-Mix Trad/Non
FAX Number: (617) 984-1779 Calendar System: Semester
URL: www.quincycollege.edu
Established: 1958 Annual Undergrad Tuition & Fees (In-District): $6,960
Enrollment: 3,154 Coed
Affiliation or Control: Local IRS Status: 501(c)3
Highest Offering: Associate Degree
Accreditation: EH, MLTAD, PTAA, SURGT

01 President .... Dr. Richard DECRISTOFARO
100 Chief of Staff/VP of Operations .... Mr. Christopher BELL
05 Chief Academic Officer .... Dr. Servet YATIN
84 SVP Enroll Mgmt & Strategic Mgmt .... Ms. Jennifer LUDDY
13 VP Technology & Mission Support .... Mr. Tom C. PHAM
43 General Counsel .... Ms. Jessica CHERRY
10 VP of Finance .... Mr. Martin AHERN
04 Exec Asst to President .... Ms. Meaghan SHEEHAN
108 Director Institutional Assessment .... Ms. Amanda COLLIGAN
12 Dean of Operations Plymouth Campus .... Ms. Catherine MALONEY
66 Dean of Nursing .... Dr. Diane GILLIS
49 Dean of Liberal Arts & Prof Program .... Dr. William CARROLL
81 Dean of Natural & Health Sciences .... Ms. Andrea MCLAIN
37 Assoc VP for Financial Aid .... Ms. Rose M. DEVITO
18 Dir of Admin Services & Facilities .... Mr. William C. HALL
15 Human Resources Analyst .... Ms. Yveline EXANTUS
26 Exec Dir of Comm & Marketing .... Mr. Matthew MCGOWAN
84 AVP of Enrollment Management .... Mr. Joshua TEFFT
106 Assoc Dean & Dir Online Learning .... Ms. Lisa DESRUISSEAUX
35 Student Development Specialist .... Mr. Matthew MESSIER
08 Librarian .... Ms. Sarah DOLAN
103 AVP Workforce Dev & Cmty Engagement .... Ms. Kate LOPCI
41 Athletic Director .... Mr. John RAYMER

Regis College (D)

235 Wellesley Street, Weston MA 02493-1571
County: Middlesex FICE Identification: 002206
Unit ID: 167598
Telephone: (781) 768-7000 Carnegie Class: Spec-4-yr-Other Health
FAX Number: (781) 768-8339 Calendar System: Semester
URL: www.regiscollege.edu
Established: 1927 Annual Undergrad Tuition & Fees: $43,715
Enrollment: 3,460 Coed
Affiliation or Control: Independent Non-Profit IRS Status: 501(c)3
Highest Offering: Doctorate
Accreditation: EH, ACBSP, ADNUR, DH, DMS, NMT, NUR, OT, RAD, SP, SW

01 President .... Dr. Antoinette M. HAYS
11 SVP/Chief Operating Officer .... Ms. Kara KOLOMITZ
10 VP Finance/Business & CFO .... Mr. Richard KELLEY
05 Vice President Academic Affairs .... Dr. Mary Erina DRISCOLL
26 Vice President of Marketing & Comm .... Vacant
123 Vice President Grad Enrollment .... Ms. Kate SUTHERLAND
111 Vice Pres Inst Advancement .... Ms. Staci SHEA
109 AVP Auxiliary and Business Svcs .... Mr. Michael O'KEEFE
28 AVP Inclusive Excellence/CDO .... Ms. Audrey GRACE
07 Dean of Undergraduate Admission .... Dr. Laura BERTONAZZI
37 Director of Financial Aid .... Ms. Tanya JEAN-FRANCOIS
06 Registrar .... Ms. Esther A. GHAZARIAN
09 Dean of Institutional Research .... Vacant
15 AVP of Human Resources .... Ms. Joan D. SULLIVAN
18 Director of Physical Plant .... Mr. Joseph SHAUGHNESSY
21 Director Finance & Business .... Mr. Jonathan AMARI
29 Director of Alumni Relations .... Ms. Molly ZUCCARINI
32 VP Student Affairs & UG Enrollment .... Dr. Kara KOLOMITZ
23 Director of Health Services .... Ms. Tammi MAGAZZU
08 Director of Library .... Ms. Jane PECK
13 Chief Information Officer .... Ms. Kate KORZENDORFER
41 Dean of Athletics .... Ms. Pamela ROECKER
42 Director Campus Ministry .... Mr. Daniel LEAHY
31 Director of Housing .... Ms. Bridget BUONICONTI
35 Director of Student Engagement .... Ms. Erica DEVINE
104 Director Study Abroad .... Dr. Megan GIBBONS
19 Director of Campus Safety .... Vacant

Saint John's Seminary (E)

127 Lake Street, Brighton MA 02135-3898
County: Suffolk FICE Identification: 002214
Unit ID: 167677
Telephone: (617) 254-2610 Carnegie Class: Spec-4-yr-Faith
FAX Number: (617) 787-2336 Calendar System: Semester
URL: www.sjs.edu
Established: 1884 Annual Undergrad Tuition & Fees: N/A
Enrollment: 105 Coed
Affiliation or Control: Roman Catholic IRS Status: 501(c)3
Highest Offering: Master's
Accreditation: EH, THEOL

01 Rector .... Rev. Stephen SALOCKS
03 Vice Rector .... Rev. Thomas MACDONALD
10 Vice Pres Finance/Administration .... Ms. Patricia FRASER
05 Academic Dean .... Dr. Paul METILLY
32 Dean of Students .... Rev. Edward RILEY
07 Director of Admissions & Records .... Mrs. Maureen DEBERNARDI
08 Librarian .... Rev. Raymond VAN DE MOORTELL
108 Executive Institutional Assessment .... Mr. Tomasz KIERUL
04 Admin Assistant to the President .... Ms. Susan EDWARDS
06 Registrar .... Ms. Maureen DEBERNARDI

Sattler College (F)

100 Cambridge Street, Ste 1701, Boston MA 02114
County: Suffolk Identification: 667410
Telephone: (617) 420-1820 Carnegie Class: Not Classified
FAX Number: N/A Calendar System: Semester
URL: www.sattlercollege.org
Established: 2018 Annual Undergrad Tuition & Fees: N/A
Enrollment: N/A Coed
Affiliation or Control: Non-denominational IRS Status: 501(c)3
Highest Offering: Baccalaureate
Accreditation: @TRACS

01 President .... Mr. Dean TAYLOR
05 Dean Academic Affairs .... Mr. Michael MILLER

Simmons University (G)

300 The Fenway, Boston MA 02115-5898
County: Suffolk FICE Identification: 002208
Unit ID: 167783
Telephone: (617) 521-2000 Carnegie Class: DU-Mod
FAX Number: (617) 521-3065 Calendar System: Semester
URL: www.simmons.edu
Established: 1899 Annual Undergrad Tuition & Fees: $41,917
Enrollment: 6,263 Coordinate
Affiliation or Control: Independent Non-Profit IRS Status: 501(c)3
Highest Offering: Doctorate
Accreditation: EH, ABAI, DIETD, DIETI, LIB, NURSE, PH, PTA, SW

01 President .... Lynn PERRY WOOTEN
04 Assistant to the President .... Alva CEDENO
05 Provost .... Russell PINIZZOTTO
111 Int VP Advancement .... Cate MCLAUGHLIN
10 VP/Chief Financial Ofcr/Treasurer .... Meghan KASS
20 Vice Provost .... Stephanie COSNER BERZIN
76 Dean Sch Nursing & Health Sciences .... Lepaine SHARP-MCHENRY
50 Dean School of Management .... Patricia H. DEYTON
32 Dean of Student Experience .... Rae-Anne BUTERA
06 Registrar/Dir Academic Records .... Shirley ALEXANDER-HUNT
08 Library Director .... Vivienne B. PIROLI
25 Director Sponsored Programs .... Elena GLATMAN
09 Director Institutional Research .... Lan GAO
36 Director Career Education Center .... Barbara ZERILLO
13 VP Technology/Chief Info Ofcr .... David BRUCE
18 VP Real Estate/Facilities Mgmt .... Laura BRINK
38 Clinical Director Counseling Svcs .... Sherri ETTINGER
41 Director Athletics .... Ali KANTOR
35 Assoc Dir Campus Rec/Stdnt Wellnes .... Ryan BRADSHAW
43 SVP/General Counsel/Chief of Staff .... Kathleen R. ROGERS
15 Assistant VP Human Resources .... Elizabeth HURLEY
28 Asst VP for Inclusion/Diversity .... Rachel DELEVEAUX

Smith College (H)

10 Elm Street, Northampton MA 01063-0001
County: Hampshire FICE Identification: 002209
Unit ID: 167835
Telephone: (413) 584-2700 Carnegie Class: Bac-A&S
FAX Number: (413) 585-2123 Calendar System: Semester
URL: www.smith.edu
Established: 1871 Annual Undergrad Tuition & Fees: $54,224
Enrollment: 2,504 Female
Affiliation or Control: Independent Non-Profit IRS Status: 501(c)3
Highest Offering: Doctorate
Accreditation: EH, SW

01 President .... Kathleen MCCARTNEY
05 Provost/Dean of the Faculty .... Michael THURSTON
10 VP for Finance & Administration .... David DESWERT
28 Vice President for Inclusion/Equity .... Floyd CHEUNG
30 SVP Alumnae Relations/Development .... Beth RAFFELD
32 VP Campus Life/Dean of the College .... Baishakhi TAYLOR
84 VP for Enrollment .... Joanna MAY
13 VP Information Technology .... Samantha EARP
45 VP for Strategic Initiatives .... Laurie FENLASON
26 VP College Relations/Communications .... Julia YAGER
100 Chief of Staff .... Joanna OLIN
101 Secretary Board of Trustees/College .... Elena PALLADINO
20 Associate Provost .... Bill PETERSON
20 Assoc Dean of Faculty/Academic Dev .... Héline VISENTIN
70 Dean School for Social Work .... Marianne YOSHIOKA
08 Dean of Libraries .... Vacant
09 AVP Analytics & Inst Research .... Cate ROWEN
15 Assoc VP for Human Resources .... Anne-Marie SZMYT
88 ED Sustainability/Campus Planning .... Dano J. WEISBORD
114 Dir of Budgets/Financial Planning .... Kate GOLA
18 AVP for Facilities & Operations .... Jim GRAY
21 Controller .... Matthew D. MOTYKA
22 Dir Equal Opportunity/Title IX .... Amy HUNTER
88 Dean of Multicultural Affairs .... LÆTanya B. RICHMOND
42 Dir of Religious/Spiritual Life .... Matilda CANTWELL
29 VP for Alumnae Relations .... Denise W. MATERRE
111 AVP for Advancement .... Sandra L. DOUCETT
110 AVP for Development .... Betsy CARPENTER
35 Dean of Students/Assoc Dean College .... Julianne OHOTNICKY
35 Associate Dean of Students .... Becky SHAW
39 Director of Residence Life .... Hannah L. DURRANT
38 Interim Dir of Health and Wellness .... Kris EVANS
88 Dean of Senior Class .... Danielle D. CARR RAMDATH
41 Director of Athletics .... Kristin HUGHES
104 Dean for International Study .... Rebecca HOVEY
85 Assoc Dean International Students .... Caitlin B. SZYMKOWICZ
88 Assoc Dean Integrative Learning .... Borjana MIKIC
36 Director Career Development Office .... Stacie HAGENBAUGH
88 Disability Services Director .... Laura M. RAUSCHER
07 Dean of Admission .... Deanna DIXON
06 Registrar .... Gretchen B. HERRINGER
37 Dir Student Financial Services .... David J. BELANGER
04 Executive Asst to the President .... Beth BERG

Springfield College (I)

263 Alden Street, Springfield MA 01109-3797
County: Hampden FICE Identification: 002211
Unit ID: 167899
Telephone: (413) 748-3000 Carnegie Class: Masters/L
FAX Number: N/A Calendar System: Semester
URL: www.springfieldcollege.edu
Established: 1885 Annual Undergrad Tuition & Fees: $40,480
Enrollment: 3,068 Coed
Affiliation or Control: Independent Non-Profit IRS Status: 501(c)3
Highest Offering: Doctorate
Accreditation: EH, ACATE, ARCPA, CAATE, CACREP, CAPRT, COPSY, EMT, EXSC, IACBE, OT, PTA, SW

01 President .... Dr. Mary-Beth A. COOPER
05 Provost & VP Academic Affairs .... Dr. Martha POTVIN
111 VP Institutional Advancement .... Ms. Beth ZAPATKA
10 VP for Finance & Admin .... Mr. William GUERRERO
32 VP for Student Affairs .... Dr. Slandie DIEUJUSTE

43 VP & General Counsel .... Ms. Elle MORGAN
28 VP for Inclusion & Com Engagement .... Dr. Calvin R. HILL
26 Vice President of Communications .... Mr. Stephen ROULIER
20 Assoc VP Academic Affairs .... Dr. Mary Ann COUGHLIN
25 Assoc Director Grants/Spons Rsrch .... Mr. Anthony MOTYL
15 Director of Human Resources .... Mr. Jonathan HOWELL
30 Director of Development .... Vacant
84 VP of Enrollment Management .... Dr. Stuart JONES
06 Registrar .... Mr. Marshall BRADWAY
08 Director of Library .... Ms. Andrea S. TAUPIER
29 Director of Alumni Relations .... Ms. Tamie KIDESS LUCEY
37 Director of Financial Aid .... Mr. Troy DAVIS
36 Director of Career Center .... Mr. Scott DRANKA
13 Chief Information Officer .... Mr. Anthony MUTTI
90 Director of Network Systems .... Mr. Nadim EL-KHOURY
38 Director of Counseling Center .... Mr. Brian KRYLOWICZ
19 Exec Dir Public Safety/Chief .... Ms. Karen LEARY
85 Director of International Center .... Dr. Deborah ALM
42 Director Campus Ministry .... Mr. David MCMAHON
18 Director of Facilities/Campus Svcs .... Mr. Kevin ROY
41 Executive Director of Athletics .... Dr. Craig POISSON
96 Director of Purchasing .... Ms. Lita ADAMS
09 Director of Institutional Research .... Dr. Raldy LAGUILLES
102 Exec Dir Corporate Partnerships .... Mr. John WHITE
39 Director Housing & Residence Life .... Mr. Robert YANEZ
44 Director Annual Giving .... Ms. Kylie MARTIN
100 Chief of Staff .... Dr. Kathleen MARTIN

Stonehill College (A)

320 Washington Street, Easton MA 02357-6110
County: Bristol FICE Identification: 002217
Unit ID: 167996
Telephone: (508) 565-1000 Carnegie Class: Bac-A&S
FAX Number: (508) 565-1500 Calendar System: Semester
URL: www.stonehill.edu
Established: 1948 Annual Undergrad Tuition & Fees: $46,642
Enrollment: 2,504 Coed
Affiliation or Control: Roman Catholic IRS Status: 501(c)3
Highest Offering: Master's
Accreditation: EH

01 President .... Rev. John F. DENNING, CSC
100 Chief of Staff .... Mrs. Heather L. HEERMAN
05 Provost/VP for Academic Affairs .. Dr. DeBrenna LaFa AGBENYIGA
10 Vice Pres for Finance & Treasurer .... Ms. Jeanne FINLAYSON
111 Vice President for Advancement .... Mr. Doug SMITH
32 Vice President of Student Affairs .... Ms. Pauline DOBROWSKI
21 AVP for Finance & Operations .... Mr. Craig BINNEY
35 Assoc VP for Student Affairs .... Mr. Kevin PISKADLO
37 Asst VP of Student Fin Assistance .... Mr. William C. SMITH
04 Sr Executive Asst to the President .... Mrs. Jessica L. GRACIA
121 Assoc Prov for Academic Achievement .... Dr. Craig KELLEY
43 Vice President and General Counsel .... Mr. Thomas V. FLYNN
21 Controller .... Ms. Jennifer MATHEWS
84 Vice Pres for Enrollment Management .... Mr. Joe DACEY
06 Registrar .... Rev. Jeffrey L. ALLISON, CSC
09 Dir of Inst Research/Assessment .... Mr. Brian M. OLES
08 Interim Director of College Library ... Ms. Jennifer M. MACAULAY
26 Dir of Media Rels & Communications .... Mr. Martin P. MCGOVERN
29 Director of Alumni Affairs .... Ms. Anne M. SANT
15 Director of Human Resources .... Mrs. Lily A. KRENTZMAN
38 Dir of Counseling & Testing Center ... Ms. Maria A. KAVANAUGH
13 Chief Information Officer .... Ms. Tamara ANDERSON
19 Chief of Police .... Mr. David G. WORDELL
42 Director Campus Ministry .... Rev. Anthony SZAKALY, CSC
90 Assoc Dir of Instructional Tech .... Ms. Janice HARRISON
88 Director of Academic Development .... Ms. Bonnie L. TROUPE
91 Dir of Enterprise Infrastructure .... Mr. Thomas MCGRATH
23 Director of Health Services .... Ms. Maria SULLIVAN
36 Director of Career Services .... Mrs. Christina M. BURNEY
41 Dir of Intercollegiate Athletics .... Mr. Dean R. O'KEEFE
92 Director of Honors Program .... Prof. Allyson SHECKLER
20 Dir Academic Services/Advising .... Mr. Zachariah D. BROWN
96 Director of Purchasing .... Mr. Gregory WOLFE
45 Asst VP for Planning & Budgeting .... Mr. Stephen BEAUREGARD
39 Director of Residence Life .... Ms. Kristen PIERCE
24 Dir of Media/Videography Services ...... Mr. Michael PIETROWSKI
40 Manager of College Bookstore .... Mrs. Mary DUNCKLEE
18 Director of Facilities Management .... Mr. Bruce BOYER
104 Director International Programs .... Ms. Aliki E. KARAGIANNIS
28 Director of Intercultural Affairs .... Ms. Kristine DIN
49 Dean School of Arts and Sciences .... Fr. Kevin SPICER
123 Dean of Graduate Admissions .... Ms. Melissa RATLIFF
102 Dir of Corp/Foundation & Donor Rels .... Mrs. Marie C. KELLY
07 Dean of Undergraduate Admissions .... Mr. Scott SESESKE
27 Director of Marketing .... Mr. Shane LAPRADE
108 Dir of Inst Research & Assessment .... Mr. Brian OLES
44 Director the Annual Fund .... Ms. Lisa RICHARDS

Suffolk University (B)

8 Ashburton Place, Boston MA 02108-2770
County: Suffolk FICE Identification: 002218
Unit ID: 168005
Telephone: (617) 573-8000 Carnegie Class: Masters/L
FAX Number: (617) 573-8353 Calendar System: Semester
URL: www.suffolk.edu
Established: 1906 Annual Undergrad Tuition & Fees: $41,648
Enrollment: 6,830 Coed
Affiliation or Control: Independent Non-Profit IRS Status: 501(c)3
Highest Offering: Doctorate
Accreditation: EH, ART, CIDA, CLPSY, HSA, IPSY, LAW, RADDOS, RTT, SPAA

01 President .... Dr. Marisa KELLY
05 Provost .... Dr. Julie SANDELL
10 Sr VP Finance/Admin/Treasurer .... Ms. Laura SANDER
111 Sr Vice Pres for Advancement .... Mr. Colm RENEHAN
09 AVP Inst Research & Assessment .... Dr. Gary FIREMAN
84 Dean of Admissions & Financial Aid ...... Ms. Donna GRAND PRE
26 VP Communications .... Mr. Greg GATLIN
86 Sr VP External Affairs .... Mr. John A. NUCCI
37 AVP/Dir of Financial Aid .... Ms. Jennifer H. RICCIARDI
32 AVP/Dean of Students .... Dr. Ann C. COYNE
06 AVP/University Registrar .... Ms. Mary LALLY
15 Chief HR Officer .... Mr. Boris LAZIC
28 VP Diversity/Access & Inclusion .... Ms. Joyya SMITH
13 Chief Information Officer .... Dr. Thomas LYNCH, III
43 General Counsel .... Mr. Thomas DORER
49 Dean College Arts & Science .... Dr. Maria TOYODA
61 Dean of the Law School .... Mr. Andrew PERLMAN
50 Dean Sawyer Business School .... Ms. Amy ZENG
88 Asst Dean for Acad Svcs Law School .... Ms. Lorraine D. COVE
19 Chief University Police .... Mr. Kenneth WALSH
04 Admin Assistant to the President .... Ms. Valerie VENTURA
25 Chief Contract/Grants Administrator .... Mr. Michael MULLAHY
44 Director Annual Giving .... Mr. John IRVIN
07 Director Undergraduate Admission .... Ms. Lark KRAJESKI
123 Director Graduate Admission .... Ms. Heather O'LEARY
29 Director Alumni Affairs/Law School .... Ms. Caitlin HAUGHEY
08 Director Law Library .... Mr. Richard BUCKINGHAM
08 Acting Director of Sawyer Library .... Ms. Sarah GRIFFIS
36 Exec Dir Career Development Center .... Mr. Dave MERRY
41 Director of Athletics .... Mr. Cary MCCONNELL
39 Director Residence Life .... Mr. Shigeo IWAMIYA
38 Director of Health and Wellness .... Mr. Nicholas SCULL
35 Dir Student Ldrship & Involvement .... Mr. Dave DEANGELIS
96 Business Manager .... Mr. John KINEAVY
18 Director Construction Services .... Mr. Andre VEGA
104 Director Study Abroad .... Mr. Gregory JABAUT
106 Dean Online Education/E-learning .... Ms. Tracey RILEY

Tufts University (C)

419 Boston Avenue, Medford MA 02155
County: Middlesex FICE Identification: 002219
Unit ID: 168148
Telephone: (617) 628-5000 Carnegie Class: DU-Highest
FAX Number: N/A Calendar System: Semester
URL: www.tufts.edu
Established: 1852 Annual Undergrad Tuition & Fees: $60,862
Enrollment: 12,219 Coed
Affiliation or Control: Independent Non-Profit IRS Status: 501(c)3
Highest Offering: Doctorate
Accreditation: EH, ARCPA, DENT, MED, OT, PH, PLNG, @PTA, VET

01 President .... Dr. Anthony P. MONACO
100 Chief of Staff .... Mr. Marty RAY
03 Executive Vice President .... Mr. Michael HOWARD
05 Provost & Senior VP .... Ms. Nadine AUBRY
43 SVP Univ Relations & Gen Counsel .... Ms. Mary R. JEKA
111 SVP University Advancement .... Mr. Eric C. JOHNSON
11 Vice President for Operations .... Ms. Barbara STEIN
10 VP Finance/Treasurer .... Mr. James HURLEY
15 VP for Human Resources .... Vacant
26 VP Communications/Marketing .... Mr. Michael RODMAN
13 VP & CIO .... Mr. Chris SEDORE
20 Vice Provost .... Mr. Kevin DUNN
46 Associate Provost & Sr Intl Officer .... Ms. Diana CHIGAS
09 Associate Provost .... Dr. Dawn G. TERKLA
21 Administrative Associate Provost .... Ms. Celia CAMPBELL
110 Exec Dir University Advancement .... Ms. Margot BIGGIN
28 Assoc Prov/Chief Diversity Officer .... Dr. Joyce A. SACKEY
28 Assoc Prov/Chief Diversity Officer .... Mr. Rob MACK
23 Exec Director Health & Wellness .... Ms. Michelle D. BOWDLER
37 Director of Financial Aid .... Ms. Patricia REILLY
27 Executive Director Public Relations .... Mr. Patrick COLLINS
36 Interim Exec Director Career Center .... Ms. Donna ESPOSITO
08 Director Tisch Library .... Ms. Dorothy MEANEY
22 Exec Director Equal Opportunity .... Ms. Jill A. ZELLMER
38 Director Mental Health Services .... Dr. Julie S. ROSS
19 Interim Exec Director Public Safety .... Mr. Chip COLETTA
49 Dean Arts & Sciences .... Mr. James GLASER
54 Dean of Engineering .... Dr. Jianmin QU
60 Dean of SMFA at Tufts .... Dr. Nancy BAUER
58 Dean Grad School of A&S .... Mr. Robert G. COOK
61 Dean Fletcher Sch of Law/Diplomacy .... Ms. Rachel KYTE
52 Dean of Dental Medicine .... Dr. Nadeem KARIMBUX
74 Dean Cummings School Vet Med .... Dr. Alastair CRIBB
63 Interim Dean Medical School .... Dr. Helen BOUCHER
81 Dean Grad Sch Biomedical Sciences .... Dr. Daniel JAY
76 Dean Friedman School .... Dr. Dariush MOZAFFARIAN
80 Dean Tisch College of Civic Life .... Mr. Alan SOLOMONT
121 Dean Academic Adv & Undergrad Study .... Dr. Carmen LOWE
32 Dean of Student Affairs .... Ms. Camille LIZARRIBAR
07 Dean of Admissions/Enroll Mgmt .... Mr. Joseph T. DUCK
96 Sr Dir Purchasing & Strat Sourcing .... Mr. John HOMICH
41 Director Athletics .... Mr. John MORRIS
42 University Chaplain .... Vacant
102 Sr Dir Corp & Foundation Relations .... Ms. Ippolita A. CANTUTI-CASTELVETRI
104 Sr Dir Study Abroad/Global Educ .... Ms. Melanie Mala GHOSH
39 Director Res Life & Learning .... Mr. Joshua HARTMAN
112 Senior Director Gift Planning .... Ms. Brooke ANDERSON
31 Director Community Relations .... Mr. Rocco DIRICO
18 Senior Facilities Director .... Mr. Cory POULIOT

Urban College of Boston (D)

2 Boylston St, Boston MA 02116
County: Suffolk FICE Identification: 031305
Unit ID: 429128
Telephone: (617) 449-7070 Carnegie Class: Spec 2-yr-Other
FAX Number: (617) 830-3137 Calendar System: Semester
URL: www.urbancollege.edu
Established: 1993 Annual Undergrad Tuition & Fees: $7,124
Enrollment: 554 Coed
Affiliation or Control: Independent Non-Profit IRS Status: 501(c)3
Highest Offering: Associate Degree
Accreditation: EH

01 President .... Mr. Michael TAYLOR
05 Chief Academic Officer .... Ms. Clea ANDREADIS
06 Registrar .... Mr. Alexander WOLNIAK
84 Chief Student Services Officer .... Dr. Keiko BROOMHEAD
37 Director of Financial Aid .... Mr. David VERA
11 Director Operations and Finance .... Ms. Karen LUCAS
30 Chief Advancement Officer .... Ms. Caitlin CALLAHAN
10 Chief Financial/Business Officer .... Ms. Mimoza VREKA

Wellesley College (E)

106 Central Street, Wellesley MA 02481-8203
County: Norfolk FICE Identification: 002224
Unit ID: 168218
Telephone: (781) 283-1000 Carnegie Class: Bac-A&S
FAX Number: (781) 283-3639 Calendar System: Semester
URL: www.wellesley.edu
Established: 1875 Annual Undergrad Tuition & Fees: $58,448
Enrollment: 2,280 Female
Affiliation or Control: Independent Non-Profit IRS Status: 501(c)3
Highest Offering: Baccalaureate
Accreditation: EH

01 President .... Paula A. JOHNSON
05 Provost & Dean of the College .... Andrew SHENNAN
10 VP Finance Administration/Treasurer .... Piper ORTON
32 Vice Pres/Dean of Students .... Sheilah SHAW HORTON
07 Dean of Admission/Financial Aid .... Joy ST. JOHN
30 VP Development .... Mary CASEY
26 Chief Communications Officer .... Tara MURPHY
43 General Counsel .... Karen PETRULAKIS
115 Chief Investment Officer .... Debby KUENSTNER
15 Asst VP/Director Human Resources/EO .... Carolyn SLABODEN
20 Dean of Academic Affairs .... Michael JEFFRIES
20 Dean of Faculty Affairs .... Megan NUÑEZ
09 Assc Provost Institutional Planning .... Pamela L. TAYLOR
28 Assc Prov Acad/Dir Dvrsty/Inclusion .... Vacant
29 Executive Director Alumnae Assn .... Kathryn MACKINTOSH
18 Asst VP Facilities Management/Plng .... David CHAKRABORTY
13 Chief Information Officer .... Ravi RAVISHANKER
36 Assoc Prov/Dir Exec Ctr Work/Svc .... Jennifer POLLARD
101 Clerk Board of Trustees .... Marianne B. COOLEY
06 Registrar .... Carol SHANMUGARATNAM
37 Director of Student Financial Svcs .... Kari DIFONZO
38 Administrative Counseling Svcs .... Robin COOK-NOBLES
96 Purchasing Manager .... Tina M. DOLAN
42 Dean Religious/Spiritual Life .... Jacqueline MARQUEZ
35 Dir Student Involvement/Leadership .... Jessica GRADY
04 Admin Assistant to the President .... Teresa GARCIA
08 Director Library Collections .... Karen BOHRER
104 Director Study Abroad .... Jennifer THOMAS-STARCK
39 Dir Resident Life/Student Housing .... Helen Y. WANG
41 Athletic Director .... Bethany ELLIS

Wentworth Institute of Technology (F)

550 Huntington Avenue, Boston MA 02115-5998
County: Suffolk FICE Identification: 002225
Unit ID: 168227
Telephone: (617) 989-4590 Carnegie Class: Masters/M
FAX Number: (617) 989-4591 Calendar System: Semester
URL: www.wit.edu
Established: 1904 Annual Undergrad Tuition & Fees: $35,970
Enrollment: 4,389 Coed
Affiliation or Control: Independent Non-Profit IRS Status: 501(c)3
Highest Offering: Master's
Accreditation: EH, ART, CIDA, CONST, IACBE

01 President .... Dr. Mark A. THOMPSON
100 Chief of Staff .... Mr. Erik COTE
04 Executive Coordinator .... Mr. Edward CULLINANE
101 VP and University Secretary .... Ms. Amy INTILLE
88 AVP Organizational Development .... Ms. Courtney MCKENNA
86 Director of Cmty & Govt Relations .... Ms. Johanna SENA
05 SVP of Academic Affairs/Provost .... Dr. Ian LAPP
15 VP Employee Relations/Engagement .... Ms. Melanie DESANTIS
111 VP Inst Advancement & Ext Rels .... Ms. Crate HERBERT
43 VP and General Counsel .... Ms. Lynn MCCORMICK
13 Vice Pres Technology Svcs/CIO .... Mr. Vish PARADKAR
84 VP Enrollment Management .... Ms. Kristin TICHENOR
28 VP Diversity/Equity/Inclusion .... Ms. Nicole PRICE
19 AVP Public Safety/Chief of Police .... Mr. Edgar RODRIGUEZ
10 Vice President Finance .... Mr. Robert TOTINO
32 VP Student Affairs/Dean of Stdnts .... Ms. Annamaria WENNER
11 Vice President Business .... Mr. David A. WAHLSTROM
50 Dean for Management .... Dr. Abigail CHAREST
48 Dean for Architecture & Design .... Dr. Sedef DONAGER
81 Interim Dean Sciences & Humanities .... Dr. Lizzie FALVEY

54 Dean for Engineering .... Dr. Jose SANCHEZ
77 Dean for Computing and Data Science .... Dr. Durga SURESH-MENON
20 Associate Provost .... Mr. Joseph MARTEL-FOLEY
14 Assoc VP Information Technology .... Mr. Jim MCFARLAND
21 Assoc Vice President Finance .... Mr. David GILMORE
26 AVP Marketing & Communications .... Mr. Ted REED
35 Assoc Vice President of Students .... Mr. Peter FOWLER
102 Exec Dir Corp/Foundation Rels .... Ms. Lori FRIEDMAN
08 Director of Library .... Mr. Kevin KIDD
06 Registrar .... Ms. Joan ROMANO
36 Dir Of Cooperative Educ/Career Svcs .... Ms. Robbin BEAUCHAMP
37 Director Financial Aid .... Ms. Anne-Marie CARUSO
38 Director of Counseling .... Ms. Maura MULLIGAN
39 Director Housing & Residential Life .... Ms. Kara CUCIO
88 Associate Athletic Director .... Mr. William P. GORMAN
41 Director of Athletics .... Ms. Cheryl AARON
18 Director of Physical Plant .... Mr. John MARUJO
35 Director Office of Campus Life .... Ms. Carissa DURFEE

Western New England University (A)

1215 Wilbraham Road, Springfield MA 01119-2684
County: Hampden — FICE Identification: 002226
Unit ID: 168254
Telephone: (413) 782-3111 — Carnegie Class: DU-Mod
FAX Number: (413) 782-1746 — Calendar System: Semester
URL: www.wne.edu
Established: 1919 — Annual Undergrad Tuition & Fees: $39,216
Enrollment: 3,673 — Coed
Affiliation or Control: Independent Non-Profit — IRS Status: 501(c)3
Highest Offering: Doctorate
Accreditation: EH, COSMA, LAW, OT, PHAR, SW

01 President .... Dr. Robert E. JOHNSON
04 Executive Asst to President .... Ms. Robin SAVITT-KING
05 Int Provost/VP Academic Affairs .... Mr. Curt HAMAKAWA
26 AVP for Marketing/External Affairs .... Ms. Barbara A. MOFFAT
10 Vice Pres Finance & Administration .... Dr. Richard WAGNER
84 VP Enrollment Mgmt/Marketing .... Mr. Bryan J. GROSS
32 VP Student Affairs/Dean of Students .... Dr. Jeanne S. HART-STEFFES
111 Vice President Advancement .... Ms. Beverly J. DWIGHT
13 Chief Information Officer .... Mr. Scott J. COOPEE
15 Chief Human Resources Officer .... Ms. Joanne OLLSON
61 Dean of the School of Law .... Prof. Sudha SETTY
67 Dean of the College of Pharmacy .... Dr. John PEZZUTO
49 Interim Dean College of A&S .... Dr. Josie BROWN
50 Dean of the College of Business .... Dr. Sharianne WALKER
54 Dean of the College of Engineering .... Dr. S. Hossein CHERAGHI
08 Assoc Dean Law Library/Info Res .... Ms. Patricia NEWCOMBE
39 Interim Dir Residence Life .... Ms. Caitlin DALEY
28 Asst Dean of Diversity Programs .... Mrs. Yvonne BOGLE
06 Exec Dir Enroll Svcs/Univ Registrar .... Ms. Julie RICHARDSON
37 Director of Financial Aid .... Ms. Kathleen CHAMBERS
41 Director of Athletics .... Mr. Matthew LABRANCHE
36 Director Career Development Center .... Ms. Andrea ST. JAMES
38 Director of Counseling Services .... Dr. Wayne D. CARPENTER
08 Director of D'Amour Library .... Mrs. Priscilla L. PERKINS
23 Director of Health Services .... Vacant
18 Director of Facilities Management .... Vacant
90 Dir Educational Technology Center .... Mr. Steven NARMONTAS
91 Dir of Administrative Info Systems .... Vacant
29 Director of Alumni Engagement .... Ms. Katie DEBEER
25 Corporate/Foundation Relations Ofc .... Vacant
42 Spiritual Life Coordinator .... Ms. Sheila HANIFIN
19 Director of Public Safety .... Mr. Adam WOODROW
11 Director Administrative Services .... Ms. Arlene M. ROCK
07 Dir of Undergraduate Admissions .... Mr. Christopher WYSTEPEK
123 Exec Dir of Graduate Admissions .... Mr. Matthew FOX
20 Academic Scheduling Controller .... Dr. Linda M. CHOJNICKI
09 Director Inst Research & Planning .... Mrs. Mary GREY
43 General Counsel .... Ms. Cheryl SMITH

Wheaton College (B)

26 E Main Street, Norton MA 02766-2322
County: Bristol — FICE Identification: 002227
Unit ID: 168281
Telephone: (508) 286-8200 — Carnegie Class: Bac-A&S
FAX Number: N/A — Calendar System: Semester
URL: www.wheatoncollege.edu
Established: 1834 — Annual Undergrad Tuition & Fees: $56,366
Enrollment: 1,670 — Coed
Affiliation or Control: Independent Non-Profit — IRS Status: 501(c)3
Highest Offering: Baccalaureate
Accreditation: EH

01 President .... Dr. Dennis M. HANNO
05 Interim Provost .... Dr. Touba GHADESSI
10 Int VP Finance & Administration .... Mr. Philip SHAPIRO
111 Vice President College Advancement .... Ms. Merritt CROWLEY
84 VP of Enrollment .... Mr. Walter CAFFEY
32 VP Stdnt Affairs/Dean Stdnts .... Mr. Darnell PARKER
26 VP Marketing and Communications .... Mr. Gene P. BEGIN
37 Dean of Stdnt Aid/Admissions .... Mr. Walter CAFFEY
15 Assoc VP Human Resources .... Ms. Omaira ROY
18 Asst VP Business Svcs/Phys Plant .... Mr. John M. SULLIVAN
26 Director of Communications .... Ms. Sandy COLEMAN
13 Assistant VP Info Tech Services .... Mr. Joe LACASCIO
121 Executive Dean of Student Success .... Vacant
06 Registrar/Dean Academic Systems .... Ms. Sally BUCKLEY
104 Dean Center for Global Education .... Ms. Gretchen YOUNG

29 Director Alumni Relations .... Ms. Courtney SHURTLEFF
44 Director Annual Fund .... Vacant
102 Dir Corporate & Foundation Rels .... Ms. Patricia DEMARCO
38 Director Counseling Center .... Ms. Valerie TOBIA
07 Acting Director of Admission .... Mr. Jeff CUTTING
09 Director of Institutional Research .... Dr. Kimberly PUHALA
39 Director Stdnt Life/Housing .... Mr. Edward T. BURNETT
19 Director Public Safety .... Chief Robert WINSOR
41 Director of Athletics & Recreation .... Mr. Gavin VIANO
14 Dir Information Tech Services .... Ms. Regina CARVELL
36 Director of Career Services .... Ms. Lisa GAVIGAN
101 Asst to President/Sec Brd Trustees .... Ms. Kelsey ANDRADE
04 Executive Asst to President .... Ms. Pam VAZ

William James College (C)

1 Wells Avenue, Newton MA 02459-3211
County: Middlesex — FICE Identification: 021636
Unit ID: 166717
Telephone: (617) 327-6777 — Carnegie Class: Spec-4-yr-Other Health
FAX Number: (617) 327-4447 — Calendar System: Semester
URL: www.williamjames.edu
Established: 1974 — Annual Graduate Tuition & Fees: N/A
Enrollment: 805 — Coed
Affiliation or Control: Independent Non-Profit — IRS Status: 501(c)3
Highest Offering: Doctorate; No Undergraduates
Accreditation: EH, CLPSY, IPSY, SCPSY

01 President .... Dr. Nicholas COVINO
04 Executive Asst to the President .... Ms. Lilly MANOLIS
05 Vice Pres Academic Affairs .... Dr. Stacey LAMBERT
10 VP Finance & Operations .... Mr. Daniel BRENT
37 Director Financial Aid .... Ms. Hilary BAXTER
06 Registrar .... Ms. Sonji PAIGE
32 Dean of Students .... Mr. Josh COOPER
07 Director of Admissions .... Mr. Mario MURGA
51 Director Continuing Prof Education .... Mr. Dean ABBY
26 Director of Marketing/Communication .... Mrs. Katie O'HARE
13 Dir Information Technology .... Mr. Jeff CHOO
08 Head Librarian .... Ms. Julia CLEMENT
15 Human Resource Director .... Mrs. Ellen COLLINS
18 Facilities Manager .... Mr. Kevin COSTELLO
29 Director Alumni Relations .... Vacant
09 Director Institutional Research .... Dr. Yashu KAUFFMAN
28 Director of Diversity .... Ms. Gloria NORONHA
102 Director Foundation/Corporate Relat .... Mr. Adrian SANTIAGO

† Formerly Massachusetts School of Professional Psychology

Williams College (D)

880 Main Street, Williamstown MA 01267
County: Berkshire — FICE Identification: 002229
Unit ID: 168342
Telephone: (413) 597-3131 — Carnegie Class: Bac-A&S
FAX Number: N/A — Calendar System: 4/1/4
URL: www.williams.edu
Established: 1793 — Annual Undergrad Tuition & Fees: $50,450
Enrollment: 1,987 — Coed
Affiliation or Control: Independent Non-Profit — IRS Status: 501(c)3
Highest Offering: Master's
Accreditation: EH

01 President .... Maud S. MANDEL
05 Provost .... David LOVE
20 Dean of the Faculty .... Safa ZAKI
10 VP for Fin & Admin and Treasurer .... Frederick W. PUDDESTER
28 VP for Inst Diversity & Equity .... Leticia HAYNES
111 VP for College Relations .... Megan MOREY
26 Chief Communications Officer .... Jim REISCHE
04 Asst to Pres/Secretary of the Col .... Keli A. GAIL
20 Dean of the College .... Marlene J. SANDSTROM
18 Exec Director Facilities Operations .... Christina V. SANBORN
06 Registrar .... Kath DUNLOP
07 Director of Admission .... Sulgi LIM
37 Director of Financial Aid .... Ashley BIANCHI
08 Director of Libraries .... Jonathan MILLER
21 Controller .... Susan S. HOGAN
29 Director Alumni Relations .... Brooks L. FOEHL
15 Director of Human Resources .... Danielle GONZALEZ
36 Director of Career Center .... Donald J. KJELLEREN
109 Director of Dining Services .... Temesgen ARAYA
13 Chief Technology Officer .... Barron KORALESKY
09 Director of Institutional Research .... Jason E. RIVERA
23 Director Integrative Wellbeing Svc .... Wendy ADAM
35 Director Office of Student Life .... Douglas J. SCHIAZZA
41 Director of Athletics/PE .... Lisa M. MELENDY
42 Chaplain .... Valerie BAILEY FISCHER

Woods Hole Oceanographic Institution (E)

266 Woods Hole Road, Woods Hole MA 02543-1535
County: Barnstable — FICE Identification: 002230
Telephone: (508) 548-1400 — Carnegie Class: Not Classified
FAX Number: N/A — Calendar System: 4/1/4
URL: www.whoi.edu
Established: 1930 — Annual Graduate Tuition & Fees: N/A
Enrollment: N/A — Coed
Affiliation or Control: Independent Non-Profit — IRS Status: 501(c)3
Highest Offering: Doctorate; No Undergraduates
Accreditation: EH

01 President and Director .... Dr. Peter DE MENOCAL
04 Exec Assistant to the President .... Ms. Diane MCCARTHY
09 Deputy Dir/VP for Research .... Dr. Rick MURRAY
05 VP of Academic Programs and Dean .... Dr. Margaret K. TIVEY
10 VP of Operations/CFO .... Mr. Jeffrey FERNANDEZ
18 VP Marine Facilities/Operations .... Mr. Robert MUNIER
43 VP Bus & Legal Affs/Gen Counsel .... Mr. Christopher LAND
111 VP Advancement & CMO .... Mr. Samuel HARP
20 Associate Dean of Academic Programs .... Dr. Delia W. OPPO
06 Registrar .... Ms. Julia WESTWATER
08 Library Director .... Ms. Lisa RAYMOND
100 Sr Advisor to the President .... Mr. Colin REED
13 Sr Dir Information Services .... Mr. Keith GLAVIN
15 Chief Human Resources Officer .... Ms. Kathi BENJAMIN
25 Dir Grants and Contracts .... Mr. David STEPHENS
26 Chief Communications Officer .... Ms. Danielle FINO
86 Director Government Relations .... Mr. Peter HILL

Worcester Polytechnic Institute (F)

100 Institute Road, Worcester MA 01609-2280
County: Worcester — FICE Identification: 002233
Unit ID: 168421
Telephone: (508) 831-5000 — Carnegie Class: DU-Higher
FAX Number: (508) 831-5753 — Calendar System: Semester
URL: www.wpi.edu
Established: 1865 — Annual Undergrad Tuition & Fees: $54,416
Enrollment: 6,920 — Coed
Affiliation or Control: Independent Non-Profit — IRS Status: 501(c)3
Highest Offering: Doctorate
Accreditation: EH

01 President .... Dr. Laurie LESHIN
05 Provost/SVP .... Dr. Winston SOBOYEJO
10 Executive Vice President & CFO .... Mr. Jeffrey S. SOLOMON
84 Senior Vice President Enrollment .... Ms. Kristin R. TICHENOR
111 VP for University Advancement .... Ms. Donna K. STOCK
26 VP/Chief Marketing Officer .... Ms. Maureen DEIANA
13 VP Information Technology/CIO .... Ms. Patricia L. PATRIA
18 Asst Vice President for Facilities .... Mr. Eric L. BEATTIE
15 VP Talent/Chief Diversity Ofcr .... Ms. Alicia MILLS
20 AVP Academic Affairs .... Mr. Kristopher SULLIVAN
32 Sr VP of Student Affairs .... Mr. Philip N. CLAY
43 SVP/General Counsel .... Mr. David BUNIS
36 Exec Director Career Devel Center .... Mr. Stefan KOPPI
100 Vice President/Chief of Staff .... Ms. Amy MORTON
35 Asst VP & Dean of Students .... Mr. Greg SNODDY
07 Exec Director of Admissions .... Ms. Jennifer A. CLUETT
06 University Registrar .... Ms. Sarah L. MILES
27 AVP Public Relations .... Ms. Eileen BRANGAN MELL
96 Director of Procurement Services .... Ms. Laurie COLELLA
21 University Controller .... Mr. Patrick HITCHCOCK
21 Assoc VP of Finance .... Ms. Mary CALARESE
38 Assoc Dean/Dir Counseling/SDCC .... Mr. Charles C. MORSE
88 Associate Director LSBC .... Mr. Andrew BUTLER
37 Dir Student Aid/Financial Literacy .... Ms. Jessica SABOURIN
19 Dir Public Safety/Chief WPI Police .... Chief Cheryl A. MARTUNAS
28 Dir Diversity/Inclusive Excellence .... Mr. Rame HANNA
29 Asst VP Lifetime Engagement .... Ms. Monica ELLIS

MICHIGAN

Adrian College (G)

110 S Madison Street, Adrian MI 49221-2575
County: Lenawee — FICE Identification: 002234
Unit ID: 168528
Telephone: (517) 265-5161 — Carnegie Class: Bac-Diverse
FAX Number: (517) 264-3331 — Calendar System: Semester
URL: www.adrian.edu
Established: 1859 — Annual Undergrad Tuition & Fees: $38,730
Enrollment: 1,865 — Coed
Affiliation or Control: United Methodist — IRS Status: 501(c)3
Highest Offering: Master's
Accreditation: HLC, CAATE, CAEP, SW

01 President .... Dr. Jeffrey R. DOCKING
05 Vice Pres/Dean for Academic Affairs .... Dr. Andrea MILNER
111 Vice Pres Institutional Advancement .... Mr. James MAHONY
84 Vice President of Enrollment .... Mr. Frank J. HRIBAR
10 Vice Pres Business Affairs/CFO .... Mr. Jerry WRIGHT
32 Dean of Student Affairs .... Mrs. Melinda SCHWYN
20 Asst Dean of Academic Affairs .... Dr. Katie RASMUSSEN
30 Director of Development .... Vacant
42 Chaplain/Director Church Relations .... Vacant
06 Registrar .... Ms. Kristina SCHWEIKERT
86 Dir of Govt & Foundation Relations .... Vacant
15 Director of Human Resources .... Ms. Christina CORSON
40 Bookstore Manager .... Ms. Rachelle M. DUFFY
93 The Inst of Cross Cultural Studies .... Dr. David GOLDBERG
29 Director Alumni Relations .... Ms. Jennifer CARLSON
41 Director of Athletics .... Mr. Michael DUFFY
19 Director of Campus Safety .... Mr. Wade BIETELCHIES
36 Director of Career Planning .... Mrs. Janna D'AMICO
88 Director of Conferences .... Ms. DeAnne LEWIN
38 Director of Counseling .... Ms. Kellie BERGER
08 Head Librarian .... Mr. David CRUSE
23 Director of Health Center .... Dr. Emily KIST
96 Director of Purchasing .... Ms. Donna WARD
37 Director of Financial Aid .... Ms. Lori KOSARUE
18 Director of Facilities .... Mr. Chris STIVER
09 Director of Institutional Research .... Ms. Beth L. HEISS

88 Director of Academic Services .... Mr. Stephen MITCHELL
100 Chief of Staff President's Office .... Mrs. Andrea SAYLOR

Albion College (A)

611 E Porter Street, Albion MI 49224-1831
County: Calhoun FICE Identification: 002235
Unit ID: 168546
Telephone: (517) 629-1000 Carnegie Class: Bac-A&S
FAX Number: (517) 629-0509 Calendar System: Semester
URL: www.albion.edu
Established: 1835 Annual Undergrad Tuition & Fees: $50,775
Enrollment: 1,506 Coed
Affiliation or Control: United Methodist IRS Status: 501(c)3
Highest Offering: Baccalaureate
Accreditation: HLC, CAEPT, MUS

01 President .... Dr. Mathew JOHNSON
05 Provost .... Vacant
32 Vice Pres & Dean Student Affairs .... Mr. Leroy WRIGHT
13 Assoc Vice Pres Info Svcs/CIO .... Mr. Michael DEVER
07 Director of Admissions .... Ms. Mandy DUBIEL
39 Director Residential Life .... Mr. Marcus DAWSON
08 Director of Libraries .... Dr. Michael VAN HOUTEN
38 Director of Counseling .... Dr. Frank KELEMEN
37 Director of Financial Aid .... Mr. Trevor L. MARKOVICH
06 Registrar .... Dr. Andrew M. DUNHAM
109 Director Dining & Hospitality Svcs .... Mrs. Pat MILLER
18 Director of Facilities Operations .... Mr. Doug LADITKA
19 Director of Campus Safety .... Mr. Kenneth SNYDER
41 Athletic Director .... Mr. Matthew AREND
42 College Chaplain .... Rev. Donald PHILLIPS
15 Director of Human Resources .... Mrs. Lisa LOCKE
09 Director of Institutional Research .... Dr. Andrew DUNHAM
96 Director of Purchasing .... Mrs. Susan CLARK
20 Associate Academic Officer .... Vacant
28 Assoc Director Multicultural Affs .... Ms. Keena WILLIAMS
40 Manager of Bookstore .... Mr. Todd SHAYLER

Alma College (B)

614 W Superior Street, Alma MI 48801-1599
County: Gratiot FICE Identification: 002236
Unit ID: 168591
Telephone: (989) 463-7111 Carnegie Class: Bac-Diverse
FAX Number: (989) 463-7277 Calendar System: Other
URL: www.alma.edu
Established: 1886 Annual Undergrad Tuition & Fees: $42,622
Enrollment: 1,435 Coed
Affiliation or Control: Independent Non-Profit IRS Status: 501(c)3
Highest Offering: Master's
Accreditation: HLC, CAEP, MUS, NURSE

01 President .... Dr. Jeff ABERNATHY
05 Provost & SVP for Academic Affairs .... Dr. Kathleen DOUGHERTY
11 SVP Admin/Chief Operating Officer .... Mr. Alan GATLIN
111 Vice President for Advancement .... Vacant
07 Vice President for Admissions .... Ms. Amanda ZIELINSKI SLENSKI
32 Vice President for Student Affairs .... Mr. Damon BROWN
10 VP/Chief Financial Officer .... Mr. James CARMAN
04 Executive Asst to the President .... Mrs. Kelly MASLEY
06 Registrar .... Ms. Mariah ORZOLEK
20 Assistant Provost .... Ms. Susan M. DEEL
42 Chaplain .... Rev Dr. Andrew POMERVILLE
37 Director of Financial Assistance .... Ms. Michelle MCNIER
08 Director of Library .... Mr. Matthew COLLINS
26 Associate VP for Marketing .... Ms. Melinda BOOTH
13 Dir Information Technology Services .... Mr. Kyle WARNER
18 Director Facilities & Service Mgmt .... Mr. Ryan STOUDT
15 Associate VP for Human Resources .... Ms. Amanda DUVAL
21 Controller/Director of Auxil Svcs .... Ms. Cassie TENNANT
36 Director of Career/Personal Dev .... Ms. Carla JENSEN
35 Director of Student Engagement .... Mr. David K. BLANDFORD
38 Assoc VP for Counseling & Wellness .... Ms. Anne K. LAMBRECHT
09 Director for Institutional Research .... Mr. John MACARTHUR
28 Director of Diversity & Inclusion .... Dr. Donnesha BLAKE
41 Athletic Director .... Ms. Sarah DEHRING
29 Sr Dir Alumni & Family Engagement .... Mr. Bill ARNOLD
39 Director Resident Life .... Ms. Alice KRAMER

Alpena Community College (C)

665 Johnson Street, Alpena MI 49707-1495
County: Alpena FICE Identification: 002237
Unit ID: 168607
Telephone: (989) 356-9021 Carnegie Class: Bac/Assoc-Assoc Dom
FAX Number: (989) 358-7553 Calendar System: Semester
URL: www.alpenacc.edu
Established: 1952 Annual Undergrad Tuition & Fees (In-District): $7,110
Enrollment: 1,436 Coed
Affiliation or Control: Local IRS Status: 501(c)3
Highest Offering: Baccalaureate
Accreditation: HLC, ADNUR, PNUR

01 President .... Dr. Donald MACMASTER
05 Vice Pres of Instruction .... Ms. Deborah BAYER
10 Vice President Admin & Finance .... Mr. Richard SUTHERLAND
32 Dean of Students .... Ms. Nancy SEGUIN
21 Controller .... Ms. Lyn KOWALEWSKY
20 Dean Learning Resource Center .... Ms. Wendy BROOKS
25 Director of TAACCT Grants .... Ms. Dawn STONE
13 Co-Director Mgmt Info Systems .... Mr. Jeff BLUMENTHAL
13 Co-Director Mgmt Info Systems .... Mr. Mark GRUNDER
26 Dir Public Information/Marketing .... Mr. Jay WALTERREIT
40 Director of ACC Bookstore .... Mr. William MATZKE
102 Dir Dev/Exec Dir ACC Foundation .... Ms. Brenda HERMAN
18 Director of Facilities Management .... Mr. Nicholas BREGE
06 Registrar .... Ms. Sheila RUPP
15 Director Human Resources .... Ms. Carolyn DAOUST
07 Director of Admissions .... Mr. Mike KOLLIEN
37 Director Financial Aid .... Mr. Robert ROOSE
35 Director Student Life Activities .... Ms. Cynthia DEROCHER

Andrews University (D)

8975 U.S. 31, Berrien Springs MI 49104-0001
County: Berrien FICE Identification: 002238
Unit ID: 168740
Telephone: (269) 471-7771 Carnegie Class: DU-Mod
FAX Number: (269) 471-6900 Calendar System: Semester
URL: www.andrews.edu
Established: 1874 Annual Undergrad Tuition & Fees: $31,008
Enrollment: 3,162 Coed
Affiliation or Control: Seventh-day Adventist IRS Status: 501(c)3
Highest Offering: Doctorate
Accreditation: HLC, CACREP, CAEP, COPSY, DIETD, DIETI, IACBE, MT, MUS, NUR, PH, PTA, SP, SW, THEOL

01 President .... Dr. Andrea T. LUXTON
04 Senior Executive Asst to President .... Ms. Dalry B. PAYNE
05 Provost .... Dr. Christon ARTHUR
108 Assistant Provost Inst Assessment .... Dr. Lynn MERKLIN
10 Vice Pres Financial Admin .... Mr. Glenn MEEKMA
21 Asst VP Financial Admin .... Ms. Valencia MAWUNTU
37 Asst Vice Pres Stdt Financial Svcs .... Ms. Elynda A. BEDNEY
32 Vice Pres Student & Campus Life .... Dr. Frances M. FAEHNER
88 Spec Asst to Pres Univ/Public Affs .... Mr. Stephen D. PAYNE
26 Vice Pres Strategy/Mktg & Enroll .... Mr. Tony YANG
111 Vice President for Advancement .... Dr. David A. FAEHNER
30 Assoc Vice Pres Development .... Ms. Audrey CASTELBUONO
28 Vice Pres for Diversity & Inclusion .... Mr. Michael T. NIXON
43 General Counsel .... Ms. Gwendolyn POWELL BRASWELL
06 Registrar .... Ms. Aimee VITANGCOL REGOSO
49 Dean Col of Arts/Sciences/UG Educ .... Dr. Amy ROSENTHAL
76 Dean College of Health & Human Svcs .... Dr. Emmanuel RUDATSIKIRA
50 Dean College of Professions .... Dr. Ralph TRECARTIN
73 Dean of Theological Seminary .... Dr. Jiri MOSKALA
58 Dean Graduate Studies .... Dr. Alayne THORPE
106 Dean Col of Education/Intl Svcs .... Dr. Alayne THORPE
08 Dean of Libraries .... Ms. Paulette M. JOHNSON
46 Dean of Research .... Dr. Gary BURDICK
13 Chief Information Officer .... Dr. Chris THOMAS
15 Director of Human Resources .... Mr. Darcy L. DE LEON
39 Dir of University Apartment Life .... Mr. Alfredo RUIZ
39 Dir of Residence Life .... Ms. Jennifer R. BURRILL
42 University Chaplain .... Mr. Jose BOURGET
85 Exec Dir Intl Student Services .... Dr. Christian STUART
92 Director of Honors Program .... Dr. L. Monique PITTMAN
38 Dir of Counseling/Testing Center .... Dr. Judith FISHER
123 Director of Graduate Admissions .... Ms. Jillian PANIGOT
07 Exec Dir UG Recruitment/Admissions .... Ms. Wendy KEOUGH
88 Dir of Bridge to Success Program .... Mr. Randy K. GRAVES
29 Director of Alumni Services .... Mr. Andriy KHARKOVYY
19 Director of Campus Safety .... Mr. Benjamin PANIGOT
23 Director of Medical Services .... Dr. Lowell HAMEL
44 Director of Planned Giving .... Ms. Tari POPP
09 Director Institutional Research .... Dr. Sally NORTON
18 Director of Facilities Management .... Mr. Steve NASH
105 Manager of Web Communications .... Mr. Jason STRACK
88 Chair Intl Lang & Global Studies .... Dr. Pedro NAVIA
41 Director of Athletics .... Mr. Rob GETTYS
40 Manager of Bookstore .... Ms. Cynthia SWANSON

Aquinas College (E)

1700 Fulton St. E, Grand Rapids MI 49506-1799
County: Kent FICE Identification: 002239
Unit ID: 168786
Telephone: (616) 632-8900 Carnegie Class: Bac-A&S
FAX Number: (616) 732-4469 Calendar System: Semester
URL: www.aquinas.edu
Established: 1886 Annual Undergrad Tuition & Fees: $35,086
Enrollment: 1,517 Coed
Affiliation or Control: Roman Catholic IRS Status: 501(c)3
Highest Offering: Master's
Accreditation: HLC, CAEP

01 President .... Dr. Kevin G. QUINN
05 Provost/Dean of Faculty .... Dr. Stephen GERMIC
102 Vice Pres Foundation .... Ms. Gina COVERT
10 Vice Pres/Chief Financial Officer .... Ms. Lisa VANDEWEERT
84 Vice President Enrollment .... Ms. Erin CRAIG
04 Chief Exec Assistant to President .... Ms. Mary VARGAS
26 Assoc VP Marketing & Communication .... Ms. Marissa SURA
32 Assoc VP for Student Success .... Mr. Brian MATZKE
21 Controller .... Ms. Melisssa SNYDER
09 Dean of Institutional Effectiveness .... Vacant
53 Dean of School of Education .... Dr. Susan ENGLISH
06 Registrar .... Ms. Elizabeth FLORES
38 Dir of Career & Counseling Services .... Ms. Sharon E. SMITH
51 Director of Continuing Education .... Vacant
104 Assoc Dir International Educ Pgms .... Mr. Tim RAMSAY
94 Director of Women's Studies .... Ms. Amy DUNHAM STRAND
92 Director of Honors Program .... Dr. Michelle DEROSE
58 Int Director of Graduate Management .... Dr. Linda HAGAN
18 Director of Maintenance .... Mr. Dale HAISMA
39 Dir Housing/Residence Life Exp .... Mr. David DURKEE
07 Director of Admissions .... Vacant
37 Director of Financial Aid .... Ms. Darcy KAMPFSCHULTE
35 Assoc VP for Student Affairs .... Mr. Nick DAVIDSON
42 Director Campus Ministry .... Vacant
13 Dir Information Technology & Svcs .... Vacant
29 Director of Alumni Engagement .... Ms. Alexa CAREY
35 Dir Student Leadership & Engagement .... Vacant
112 Senior Director of Philanthropy .... Ms. Mary SLAFKOSKY
36 Director of Career Services .... Dr. Dana HEBREARD
28 Director of Diversity & Inclusion .... Ms. Alicia LLOYD
40 Director Bookstore .... Ms. Heather THOMPSON
08 Library Director .... Ms. Shellie JEFFRIE
42 Campus Chaplain .... Rev. Stanley DRONGOWSKI, OP

*Baker Professional Services, Inc. (F)

1020 S. Washington St, Owosso MI 48867
County: Shiawassee Identification: 666923
Unit ID: 419572
Telephone: (989) 729-3350 Carnegie Class: N/A
FAX Number: (810) 766-2102
URL: www.baker.edu

01 Chief Executive Officer .... Bart DAIG
05 Chief Academic Officer .... Jill LANGEN
11 Chief Operating Officer .... Jacqueline SPICER
15 Chief Human Resources Officer .... Dana CLARK

*Baker College of Auburn Hills (G)

1500 University Drive, Auburn Hills MI 48326-2642
Telephone: (248) 276-8240 Identification: 666940
Accreditation: &HLC, CSHSE, IACBE, PTAA

*Baker College of Cadillac (H)

9600 E 13th Street, Cadillac MI 49601-9169
Telephone: (231) 876-3107 Identification: 666941
Accreditation: &HLC, CSHSE, IACBE, MAC, SURGT

*Baker College of Jackson (I)

2800 Springport Road, Jackson MI 49202-1299
Telephone: (517) 841-4528 FICE Identification: 004680
Accreditation: &HLC, CSHSE, IACBE, RTT

*Baker College of Muskegon (J)

1903 Marquette Avenue, Muskegon MI 49442-3404
Telephone: (231) 777-5248 FICE Identification: 002296
Accreditation: &HLC, ACFEI, CSHSE, IACBE, OTA, PTAA, RAD, SURGT

*Baker College of Owosso (K)

1020 South Washington, Owosso MI 48867-4400
County: Shiawassee FICE Identification: 004673
Unit ID: 168838
Telephone: (989) 729-3431 Carnegie Class: Bac/Assoc-Mixed
FAX Number: (989) 729-3441 Calendar System: Semester
URL: www.baker.edu
Established: 1983 Annual Undergrad Tuition & Fees: N/A
Enrollment: N/A Coed
Affiliation or Control: Independent Non-Profit IRS Status: 501(c)3
Highest Offering: Baccalaureate
Accreditation: HLC, ACFEI, CAEP, CSHSE, DMS, IACBE, MAC, NAEYC, NURSE, OTA, PTAA, RAD

12 Campus Director .... Stavroula ERFOURTH
11 Chief Operating Officer .... Jacqueline SPICER

Bay College West Campus (L)

2801 N US 2, Iron Mountain MI 49801
Telephone: (906) 302-3000 Identification: 770262
Accreditation: &HLC

Bay Mills Community College (M)

12214 W Lakeshore Drive, Brimley MI 49715-9750
County: Chippewa FICE Identification: 030666
Unit ID: 380359
Telephone: (906) 248-3354 Carnegie Class: Tribal
FAX Number: (906) 248-3351 Calendar System: Semester
URL: www.bmcc.edu
Established: 1984 Annual Undergrad Tuition & Fees: $3,320
Enrollment: 438 Coed
Affiliation or Control: Tribal Control IRS Status: 501(c)3
Highest Offering: Baccalaureate
Accreditation: HLC

01 President .... Duane BEDELL
05 Vice President of Academic Affairs .... Samantha CAMERON
10 Vice Pres Business & Finance .... Laura POSTMA
32 Dean of Student Services .... Debra J. WILSON
13 Director Technology/Title III .... Chet KASPER
06 Registrar/Inst Info Systems Mgr .... Sherri SCHOFIELD
37 Director Student Financial Aid .... Tina MILLER

07 Director of Admissions .... Elaine LEHRE
25 Land Grant Director .... Stephen YANNI
30 Director of Development .... Kathy ADAIR
08 Library Director .... Megan CLARKE
15 Human Resources Director .... Stacey WALDEN

Bay de Noc Community College (A)

2001 N Lincoln Road, Escanaba MI 49829-2510
County: Delta FICE Identification: 002240
Unit ID: 168883
Telephone: (906) 786-5802 Carnegie Class: Assoc/MT-VT-High Trad
FAX Number: (906) 789-6952 Calendar System: Semester
URL: www.baycollege.edu
Established: 1962 Annual Undergrad Tuition & Fees (In-District): $8,520
Enrollment: 1,898 Coed
Affiliation or Control: Local IRS Status: 501(c)3
Highest Offering: Associate Degree
Accreditation: HLC, ADNUR, EMT, NAEYC

01 President .... Dr. Laura COLEMAN
11 VP of Operations .... Ms. Eileen SPARPANA
10 VP of Finance .... Ms. Eileen SPARPANA
05 VP of Academic Affairs .... Dr. Matthew BARRON
111 VP of College Advancement .... Ms. Kim CARNE
32 VP of Student Services .... Mr. Travis BLUME
50 Dean Business/Tech/Workforce Dev .... Ms. Cindy CARTER
37 Director of Financial Aid .... Ms. Ruth CARLSON
07 Director of Admissions .... Ms. Jessica LAMARCH
15 Director of Human Resources .... Ms. Beth BERUBE
18 Facilities Manager .... Mr. Steve CARLSON
76 Dean of Allied Health .... Mr. Mitchell CAMPBELL
49 Dean of Arts & Sciences .... Dr. Amy REDDINGER
32 Director of Student Life .... Mr. Dave LAUR
04 Exec Admin Asst to President .... Mrs. Laura JOHNSON
06 Registrar .... Ms. Rebecca LANDENBERGER
106 Exec Director of Online Learning .... Mr. Joseph MOLD
19 Campus Security Clery Officer .... Mr. Cody KUMPALA
41 Athletic Director .... Mr. Matt JOHNSON
09 Director of Institutional Research .... Ms. Penny PAVLAT

Calvin Theological Seminary (B)

3233 Burton Street, SE, Grand Rapids MI 49546-4387
County: Kent FICE Identification: 002242
Unit ID: 169099
Telephone: (616) 957-6036 Carnegie Class: Spec-4-yr-Faith
FAX Number: (616) 957-8621 Calendar System: Semester
URL: www.calvinseminary.edu
Established: 1876 Annual Graduate Tuition & Fees: N/A
Enrollment: 245 Coed
Affiliation or Control: Christian Reformed Church IRS Status: 501(c)3
Highest Offering: Doctorate; No Undergraduates
Accreditation: THEOL

01 President .... Rev. Julius T. MEDENBLIK
05 Dean of Faculty .... Dr. Gary BURGE
20 Assoc Dean of Academic Programs .... Ms. Joan BEELEN
11 Chief of Operations/Administration .... Dr. Margaret MWENDA
06 Registrar .... Ms. Joan BEELEN
32 Dean of Students .... Rev. Jeff SAJDAK
08 Theological Librarian .... Vacant
10 Controller .... Mr. Chris DINH
30 Director of Development .... Mr. Robert KNOOR
36 Director of Vocational Ministry .... Rev. Geoff VANDERMOLEN
07 Dir of Admissions/Enrollment Mgmt .... Mr. Aaron EINFELD
37 Director of Financial Aid .... Mrs. Jennifer SETTERGREN

Calvin University (C)

3201 Burton Street, SE, Grand Rapids MI 49546-4388
County: Kent FICE Identification: 002241
Unit ID: 169080
Telephone: (616) 526-6000 Carnegie Class: Masters/S
FAX Number: (616) 526-8551 Calendar System: 4/1/4
URL: www.calvin.edu
Established: 1876 Annual Undergrad Tuition & Fees: $37,806
Enrollment: 3,307 Coed
Affiliation or Control: Christian Reformed Church IRS Status: 501(c)3
Highest Offering: Master's
Accreditation: HLC, CAEP, CAEPT, NURSE, SP, SW

01 President .... Dr. Michael K. LE ROY
05 Provost .... Dr. Noah TOLY
10 Vice President for Finance .... Vacant
111 Vice President for Advancement .... Mr. Kenneth ERFFMEYER
84 Vice Pres Enrollment Strategy .... Mrs. Lauren J. JENSEN
32 Vice President Student Life .... Dr. Sarah VISSER
15 Vice President People/Strategy/Tech .... Mr. Todd K. HUBERS
13 Assoc Vice President for IT & CIO .... Mr. Brian PAIGE
20 Associate Provost .... Dr. Kevin DEN DULK
28 Exec Assoc for Diversity/Inclusion .... Dr. Michelle LOYD-PAIGE
42 College Chaplain .... Dr. Mary HULST
15 Director of Finance & HR .... Mr. Andrew L. GEORGE
08 Dean of the Library .... Mr. David MALONE
29 Dir of Alumni and Cmty Relations .... Mr. Jeff HAVERDINK
06 Director Academic Svcs/Registrar .... Mr. Thomas L. STEENWYK
35 Dean of Students .... Mr. John WITTE
88 Assoc Dean Campus Involve/Ldrshp .... Mr. JB BRITTON
22 Dir of Safer Spaces/Title IX Coord .... Ms. Jane E. HENDRIKSMA
20 Dean of Faculty Development .... Dr. David WUNDER
20 Dean of Academic Administration .... Dr. Laura DEHAAN
83 Acad Dean Lang/Soc Sci/Context Disc .... Dr. Bernita WOLTERS-FREDLUND
81 Acad Dean Educ/Kinesio/Nat Sci/Math .... Dr. Arlene HOOGEWERF
36 Director of Career Development .... Ms. TaRita JOHNSON
108 Mgr Inst Effectiveness & Analytics .... Mrs. Lauren AMICK
89 Dir Retention/1st Year Initiatives .... Mr. Todd DORNBOS
26 Dir Communications & Brand Steward .... Mr. Timothy L. ELLENS
88 Director Center for Social Research .... Dr. Neil CARLSON
19 Director of Campus Safety .... Mr. William T. CORNER
18 Director of Facilities .... Mr. Russell BRAY
24 Dir Instructional Resources Ctr .... Vacant
38 Director Counseling and Well Center .... Dr. Irene KRAEGEL
23 Director Health Services .... Dr. Laura CHAMPION
92 Director Honors Program .... Dr. Amy WILSTERMANN
41 Athletic Director .... Dr. James TIMMER, JR.
30 Director of Development .... Ms. Jodi COLE
104 Director Study Abroad .... Dr. Cynthia SLAGTER
105 Director Web Services .... Mr. Luke ROBINSON
37 Director of Financial Aid .... Mr. Paul WITTE
44 Director Annual Fund .... Ms. Melanie N. LYONS
53 Dean of Education .... Dr. James ROOKS
07 Director of Undergraduate Admission .... Ms. Melissa ROUSSEAU
101 Exec Asst to Pres/Sec to BOT .... Ms. Sharolyn J. CHRISTIANS

Career Quest Learning Center (D)

3215 S. Pennsylvania Avenue, Lansing MI 48910
County: Ingham FICE Identification: 039153
Unit ID: 446136
Telephone: (517) 318-3330 Carnegie Class: Assoc/HVT-High Non
FAX Number: (517) 318-3331 Calendar System: Other
URL: www.careerquest.edu
Established: 1995 Annual Undergrad Tuition & Fees: N/A
Enrollment: 288 Coed
Affiliation or Control: Proprietary IRS Status: Proprietary
Highest Offering: Associate Degree
Accreditation: COE

00 President & CEO .... Dr. Jim HUTTON
01 Campus President/VP .... Mollie WOODWORTH
07 Director of Admissions .... Chris YOUNG

Central Michigan University (E)

1200 S. Franklin Street, Mount Pleasant MI 48859
County: Isabella FICE Identification: 002243
Unit ID: 169248
Telephone: (989) 774-4000 Carnegie Class: DU-Higher
FAX Number: N/A Calendar System: Semester
URL: www.cmich.edu
Established: 1892 Annual Undergrad Tuition & Fees (In-State): $12,960
Enrollment: 17,311 Coed
Affiliation or Control: State IRS Status: 501(c)3
Highest Offering: Doctorate
Accreditation: HLC, ART, ARCPA, AUD, CAATE, CACREP, CAEP, CAPRT, CEA, CIDA, CLPSY, COSMA, DIETD, DIETI, EXSC, JOUR, MED, MUS, NAEYC, NURSE, PTA, SCPSY, SP, SPAA, SW

01 President .... Dr. Robert O. DAVIES
05 Executive VP/Provost .... Dr. Mary C. SCHUTTEN
20 Sr Vice Provost Academic Affairs .... Dr. Julia R. JOHNSON
10 Vice Pres Finance/Admin Svcs .... Mr. Nicholas K. LONG
86 Assoc Vice Pres Govt/Ext Relations .... Mr. Toby ROTH, JR.
84 VP Student Recruitment & Retention .... Ms. Jennifer E. DEHAEMERS
111 Vice Pres Advancement .... Ms. Heidi L. TRACY
13 Vice President Info Technology/CIO .... Mr. Jim BUJAKI
21 AVP Fin Svcs & Reporting/Controller .... Ms. Mary M. HILL
26 VP Univ Comm & Chief Mktg Officer .... Mr. John M. VEILLEUX
18 Assoc VP Facilities Management .... Mr. Jonathan D. WEBB
109 Exec Dir Auxiliary Services .... Mr. Calvin H. SEELYE, II
39 Exec Dir Res Life/Ldrshp & Pub Svcs .... Ms. Kathleen GARDNER
28 Interim VP/Chief Diversity Officer .... Mr. Stan L. SHINGLES
15 Assoc VP Human Resources .... Ms. Lori L. HELLA
20 Sr Vice Provost Academic Admin .... Dr. Ray L. CHRISTIE
46 VP Research & Innovation/Grad Stds .... Dr. David C. WEINDORF
30 Dir Stewardship & Donor Rels/Advan .... Ms. Kelly M. BERRYHILL
08 Dean of Libraries .... Dr. Kathy M. IRWIN
32 Assoc VP Student Affairs .... Vacant
35 Interim Assoc VP Student Affairs .... Mr. Shaun HOLTGREIVE
29 Exec Dir Alumni Rels & Adv Engage .... Ms. Marcie M. OTTEMAN
09 Exec Dir Academic Planning/Analysis .... Dr. Robert M. ROE
22 Int Ex Dir Civil Rights/Inst Equity .... Ms. Mary A. MARTINEZ
07 Exec Director Admissions .... Ms. Lee F. FURBECK
43 Sr Assoc Dean Legal Affairs/CMED .... Dr. Manuel R. RUPE
06 Registrar .... Mr. Keith J. MALKOWSKI
37 Director Scholarships/Financial Aid .... Mr. Kirk M. YATS
36 Director Career Development Center .... Ms. Julia B. SHERLOCK
38 Exec Dir of Counseling Services .... Ms. Melissa M. HUTCHINSON
114 Exec Dir Financial Plng & Budgets .... Mr. Joseph L. GARRISON
27 Exec Director Communications .... Ms. Heather L. SMITH
19 Chief of Police .... Mr. Larry S. KLAUS
40 Director CMU Bookstore .... Mr. Barry D. WATERS
81 Interim Dean College Sci & Engr .... Dr. Jane M. DAVISON
76 Dean College of Health Professions .... Dr. Thomas J. MASTERSON, JR.
63 VP Health Aff/Dean College Medicine .... Dr. George E. KIKANO
49 Dean Liberal Arts & Soc Sciences .... Dr. Richard M. ROTHAUS
57 Interim Dean College Arts & Media .... Dr. Elizabeth A. KIRBY
50 Dean Business Admin .... Dr. Christopher R. MOBERG
53 Dean Education & Human Svcs .... Dr. Paula E. LANCASTER
04 Executive Assistant to President .... Ms. Mary Jane FLANAGAN
96 Dir Contract & Purchasing Svcs .... Ms. Anne R. THRUSH
92 Director Honors Program .... Ms. Nicole S. BARCO
104 Director Study Abroad .... Ms. Dianne S. DESALVO
116 Director Internal Audit .... Ms. Beth J. TIMMERMAN
44 Director of Annual Giving .... Mr. Bryan L. GRIFFIN
115 Asst Controller Financial Services .... Ms. Kimberly A. WAGESTER
88 Asst Controller Financial Reporting .... Ms. Julia H. MONTROSS
117 Dir/Risk Mgmt Env Health & Safety .... Mr. Benjamin S. COFFMAN
121 Exec Director Student Success .... Dr. Evan L. MONTAGUE
41 Assoc VP/Dir Athletics .... Ms. Amy G. FOLAN

Chamberlain University-Troy (F)

200 Kirts Boulevard, Suite C, Troy MI 48084
Telephone: (248) 817-4140 Identification: 770851
Accreditation: &HLC, NURSE

† Branch campus of Chamberlain University-Addison, Addison, IL

Cleary University (G)

3750 Cleary Drive, Howell MI 48843
County: Livingston FICE Identification: 002246
Unit ID: 169327
Telephone: (800) 686-1883 Carnegie Class: Spec-4-yr-Bus
FAX Number: N/A Calendar System: Semester
URL: www.cleary.edu
Established: 1883 Annual Undergrad Tuition & Fees: $22,230
Enrollment: 658 Coed
Affiliation or Control: Independent Non-Profit IRS Status: 501(c)3
Highest Offering: Master's
Accreditation: HLC

01 President .... Dr. Alan DRIMMER
05 Provost & Chief Acad Officer .... Ms. Emily BARNES
10 VP of Finance .... Ms. Shelly HOLANDA
111 SVP Institutional Advancement .... Dr. Matt BENNETT
109 VP Auxiliary Services .... Mr. Jeffrey BANE
04 Exec Director Ofc of the President .... Ms. Grace R. FARLAY
21 Controller .... Ms. Megan TEMBY
09 Institutional Research Analyst .... Mr. Omar HABAYEB
37 Sr Financial Aid Coord .... Ms. Brandy AKERS
84 VP Enrollment Management .... Vacant
88 Academic Support Assoc .... Ms. Deb SOUTHERLAND
36 Director of Career Development .... Ms. Amy DENTON
41 Athletic Director .... Ms. Heather BATEMAN
15 Human Resources Manager .... Ms. Sandra HAYES
08 Instructional Librarian .... Ms. Jane SCALES
18 Facilities Manager .... Mr. George HORN
32 VP/Dean of Student Affairs .... Ms. Heather BATEMAN
06 Registrar .... Vacant
13 Executive Director of Technology .... Mr. Max GROMAKOV
35 Associate Dean of Students .... Mr. Matthew OLIVER
106 Instructional Design Manager .... Ms. Kirsten SHEPARD
20 Dean of Academic Operations .... Dr. Sara BARNWELL
97 Dean of Undergraduate Studies .... Mr. David HAYES
58 Dean of Graduate Studies .... Dr. Regina BANKS-HALL

College for Creative Studies (H)

201 East Kirby Street, Detroit MI 48202-4034
County: Wayne FICE Identification: 006771
Unit ID: 169442
Telephone: (313) 664-7400 Carnegie Class: Spec-4-yr-Arts
FAX Number: (313) 872-8377 Calendar System: Semester
URL: www.collegeforcreativestudies.edu
Established: 1906 Annual Undergrad Tuition & Fees: $47,585
Enrollment: 1,512 Coed
Affiliation or Control: Independent Non-Profit IRS Status: 501(c)3
Highest Offering: Master's
Accreditation: HLC, ART, CIDA

01 President .... Dr. Donald L. TUSKI
04 Exec Asst to Pres/Asst Sec to Board .... Ms. Sandra WILSON
10 Vice Pres Administration & Finance .... Ms. Anne D. BECK
84 Vice Pres Enrollment & Student Svcs .... Ms. Julie HINGELBERG
111 Vice Pres Institutional Advancement .... Ms. Tracy MUSCAT
26 Vice Pres Strategy & Communication .... Ms. Olga STELLA
28 Chief Diversity Officer/Asst Dean .... Dr. Deirdre YOUNG
58 Dean Graduate Studies .... Mr. Ian LAMBERT
97 Dean Undergraduate Studies .... Mr. Tim FLATTERY
05 Dean of Academic Affairs .... Ms. Nadine ASHTON
106 Exec Dir of Educational Technology .... Mr. Ryan ANSEL
32 Dean of Students .... Mr. Daniel LONG
123 Director Graduate Admissions .... Mr. Anthony MICELI
07 Director Undergraduate Admissions .... Ms. Carla GONZALEZ
37 Director Financial Aid .... Mr. Matthew CATANESE
104 Director Study Abroad .... Ms. Katherine CAMPBELL
06 Registrar .... Ms. Karen LADUCER
51 Dir Continuing/Pre-College Studies .... Ms. Jane STEWART
31 Dir of Community Arts Partnerships .... Mr. Mikel BRESEE
08 Director Library .... Ms. Rebecca PAD
18 Dir of Facilities & Campus Safety .... Mr. Michael BRUGGEMAN
13 Director Information Technology .... Mr. Greg FRASER
21 Director Business Services .... Ms. Kerri MCKAY
15 Director Human Resources .... Ms. Raquel DIROFF
30 Sr Director Development Operations .... Ms. Katie RUSAK
36 Director Career Services .... Vacant
29 Asst Dir Alumni Giv/Alumni Rels .... Mr. Anthony SPANGLER
38 Director Wellness & Counseling .... Ms. Valerie WEISS
40 Manager Bookstore .... Ms. Glen MORREN
39 Director of Residence Life .... Mr. Ryan HARRISON
102 Sr Dir Strategic Ptnrshps/Pgms .... Ms. Shannon MCPARTLON

27 Director of Marketing .... Ms. Megan MESACK
44 Director of Campaigns & Major Gifts .... Ms. Denise THOMAS
102 Assoc Dir of Foundation Relations .... Ms. Alecia HANEY
96 Purchasing & Fixed Assets .... Ms. Mary ROMEO TARTE

Compass College of Cinematic Arts (A)

41 Sheldon Boulevard, SE, Grand Rapids MI 49503
County: Kent FICE Identification: 041633
Unit ID: 459417
Telephone: (616) 988-1000 Carnegie Class: Spec-4-yr-Arts
FAX Number: (616) 458-4676 Calendar System: Other
URL: www.compass.edu
Established: 2003 Annual Undergrad Tuition & Fees: $16,800
Enrollment: 72 Coed
Affiliation or Control: Independent Non-Profit IRS Status: 501(c)3
Highest Offering: Baccalaureate
Accreditation: ACCSC

01 President .... Jay GREER
05 Dean of Education .... William KAVAN
10 Director Finance & Administration .... Fred KOOISTRA
26 Manager of Marketing & Enrollment .... Chuck KUHN
32 Director of Student Affairs .... Ken BOERSMA
07 Admissions Manager .... Chuck KUHN

Concordia University Ann Arbor (B)

4090 Geddes Road, Ann Arbor MI 48105-2797
Telephone: (734) 995-7300 FICE Identification: 002247
Accreditation: &HLC, #ARCPA, CAATE, CAEPN

Cornerstone University (C)

1001 E Beltline Avenue, NE, Grand Rapids MI 49525-5897
County: Kent FICE Identification: 002266
Unit ID: 170037
Telephone: (616) 949-5300 Carnegie Class: Masters/M
FAX Number: (616) 222-1540 Calendar System: Semester
URL: www.cornerstone.edu
Established: 1941 Annual Undergrad Tuition & Fees: $26,250
Enrollment: 1,917 Coed
Affiliation or Control: Independent Non-Profit IRS Status: 501(c)3
Highest Offering: Doctorate
Accreditation: HLC, ACBSP, CAEP, SW, THEOL

01 President .... Dr. Gerson MORENO-RIAÑO
03 Executive Vice President .... Dr. Peter OSBORN
05 VP Traditional Undergrad Academics .... Dr. Shawn NEWHOUSE
10 Chief Financial Officer .... Mr. Scott STEWART
88 Vice President of Broadcasting .... Vacant
32 VP of Student Development .... Mr. Gerald LONGJOHN
111 VP of Advancement .... Mr. Bob SACK
108 Dean of Assessment/Curriculum .... Dr. Ryan ROBERTS
73 EVP Academic/Dean Grad Theol Stdnts .... Dr. John VER BERKMOES
121 Assoc Dean Accr/Stdnt Success .... Mrs. Emily GRATSON
35 Director of Student Services .... Mr. Keith DEBOER
08 Director of Miller Library .... Mrs. Laura WALTON
37 Director Financial Services .... Mrs. Carol CARPENTER
21 Director of Finance and Accounting .... Mr. Stephen POPP
41 Athletic Director .... Mr. Aaron SAGRAVES
15 Dir Human Resources/Title IX Coord .... Mrs. Emilie AZKOUL
19 Director of Campus Safety .... Mr. Brandan BISHOP
29 Director of Alumni .... Mr. Dennis GRAHAM
06 Registrar .... Mrs. Gail DUHON
13 Dir Opers/New Media Tech .... Mr. Dodd MORRIS
38 Director of the Counseling Center .... Mr. Scott COUREY
92 Director of Honors Program .... Mr. Don PERINI
84 Executive Director of Enrollment .... Mrs. Lisa LINK
04 Administrative Asst to President .... Ms. Samantha KENDRICK
28 Dir Diversity/Multicultural Affairs .... Mr. Kenneth RUSSELL
18 Chf Facilities/Physical Plant Ofcr .... Mr. Chris BYNUM
39 Dir Resident Life/Student Housing .... Mr. Mark MUHA

Cranbrook Academy of Art (D)

39221 Woodward Avenue, Bloomfield Hills MI 48304
County: Oakland FICE Identification: 002248
Unit ID: 169424
Telephone: (248) 645-3300 Carnegie Class: Spec-4-yr-Arts
FAX Number: (248) 645-3591 Calendar System: Semester
URL: www.cranbrookart.edu
Established: 1932 Annual Graduate Tuition & Fees: N/A
Enrollment: 126 Coed
Affiliation or Control: Independent Non-Profit IRS Status: 501(c)3
Highest Offering: Master's; No Undergraduates
Accreditation: HLC, ART

01 Interim Director .... Rod SPEARIN
05 Interim Dean .... Gretchen WILKINS
20 Dir Academic Programs & Library .... Judy DYKI
30 Senior Director of Development .... Autumn PARROTT
26 Director of Communications .... Julie FRACKER
84 Mgr Enrollment & Financial Services .... Vacant
29 Alumni Relations & Recruitment Mgr .... Elizabeth DIZIK
32 Student Services Manager .... Vanessa LUCERO-MAZEI
44 Director of Annual Giving .... Kelly LEWIS-GUMP

Davenport University (E)

6191 Kraft Avenue, S.E., Grand Rapids MI 49512
County: Kent FICE Identification: 002249
Unit ID: 169479
Telephone: (616) 698-7111 Carnegie Class: Masters/L
FAX Number: N/A Calendar System: Semester
URL: www.davenport.edu
Established: 1866 Annual Undergrad Tuition & Fees: $20,260
Enrollment: 6,127 Coed
Affiliation or Control: Independent Non-Profit IRS Status: 501(c)3
Highest Offering: Master's
Accreditation: HLC, CAHIIM, COSMA, IACBE, MAC, NURSE, OT, PNUR

01 President .... Dr. Richard J. PAPPAS
111 Exec VP Advancement .... Ms. Rachel RENDER
46 Exec VP of Quality & Effectiveness .... Dr. Scott EPSTEIN
15 Exec VP Human/Organizational Devel .... Mr. Dave VENEKLASE
32 Exec VP Enrollment & Student Svcs .... Dr. Walter O'NEILL
10 Exec Vice President for Finance/CFO .... Mr. Michael S. VOLK
05 Exec VP Academics/Provost .... Dr. Gilda GELY
26 EVP for Marketing/Communications .... Ms. Deb COOPER
07 VP Admissions/Strategic Partnership .... Mr. David LAWRENCE
09 VP for Institutional Research .... Dr. Kathy ABOUFADEL
13 VP Information Technology/CIO .... Mr. Ben WILLIAMS
18 VP Facilities Management .... Mr. Damon P. GONZALES
50 Dean College of Business & Tech .... Dr. Amy MANSFIELD
76 Dean College of Health Professions .... Dr. Karen DALEY
49 Int Dean College of Arts/Sciences .... Dr. Gerald G. NYAMBANE
106 Dean Global Campus .... Mr. Brian MILLER
107 Dean College of Urban Education .... Dr. Susan GUNN
37 Exec Dir Student Financial Services .... Ms. Leah AALDERINK
29 Dir of Alumni & Donor Engagement .... Ms. Whitney ENGE
21 Controller .... Mr. Michael SLEVA
06 University Registrar .... Mr. Christopher MARX
41 Director of Athletics .... Mr. Paul LOWDEN
04 Administrative Asst to President .... Ms. Lisa AMEND-TOMAS
28 Exec Dir Diversity/Equity/Inclusion .... Ms. Latoya BOOKER
39 Exec Dir Campus Life .... Mr. Joseph BISHOP
27 Exec Dir Communications & PR .... Ms. Amy MILLER
105 Dir Web & Media Services .... Mr. Josh ISAAK
25 Exec Dir Sponsored Pgms/AOR/CGO .... Ms. Michele DAVIS
30 Exec Director of Development .... Ms. Ana DOONAN
36 Exec Dir Career Services .... Ms. Shelley LOWE
44 Assistant Director Annual Giving .... Ms. Megan SJOLANDER
96 Dir Procurement & Retail Sales .... Ms. Paula GLEASON-ZEEFF

Davenport University Great Lakes Bay Campus - Midland (F)

3555 E Patrick Road, Midland MI 48642
Telephone: (989) 835-5588 Identification: 770270
Accreditation: &HLC

Davenport University Holland (G)

643 S Waverly Road, Holland MI 49423
Telephone: (616) 395-4600 Identification: 770266
Accreditation: &HLC

Davenport University Lansing (H)

200 S. Grand Avenue, Lansing MI 48933
Telephone: (517) 484-2600 Identification: 770268
Accreditation: &HLC

Davenport University Warren (I)

27650 Dequindre Road, Warren MI 48092
Telephone: (586) 558-8700 Identification: 770272
Accreditation: &HLC

Delta College (J)

1961 Delta Rd., University Center MI 48710-0001
County: Bay FICE Identification: 002251
Unit ID: 169521
Telephone: (989) 686-9000 Carnegie Class: Assoc/MT-VT-High Trad
FAX Number: (989) 667-0620 Calendar System: Semester
URL: www.delta.edu
Established: 1961 Annual Undergrad Tuition & Fees (In-District): $6,680
Enrollment: 6,954 Coed
Affiliation or Control: Local IRS Status: 501(c)3
Highest Offering: Associate Degree
Accreditation: HLC, ADNUR, COARC, DA, DH, DMS, NAEYC, PTAA, RAD, SURGA, SURGT

01 President .... Dr. Michael H. GAVIN
10 Vice President Business/Finance .... Ms. Sarah DUFRESNE
32 Vice President Student & Educ Svcs .... Dr. Karl RISHE
05 VP Instruction/Learning Svcs .... Dr. Reva CURRY
111 Ex Dir Inst Advancement .... Ms. Pam CLARK
20 Dean of Teaching & Learning .... Dr. Martha CRAWMER
35 Dean of Students .... Vacant
36 Dean Career Educ/Learning Part .... Ms. Stephanie HARRISON
84 Dean of Enrollment Management .... Dr. Russell CURLEY
26 Marketing & Public Info Director .... Ms. Leanne GOVITZ
108 Ex Dir Admin Svcs & Inst Effective .... Ms. Andrea L. URSUY
101 Assistant to Pres/Board Secretary .... Ms. Andrea URSUY
25 Director of Corporate Services .... Ms. Jennifer CARROLL
37 Director of Student Financial Aid .... Ms. Lisa BAKER

15 Director of Human Resources .... Mr. Scott LEWLESS
18 Director of Facilities Management .... Mr. Nicholas BOVID
07 Dir Admissions/Career Development .... Mr. Jason PREMO
19 Director of Public Safety .... Mr. Robert BATTINKOFF
88 Director of Learning Centers .... Ms. Kristy NELSON
121 Dean of Student Success .... Ms. Shelly RAUBE
49 Associate Dean Arts & Letters Div .... Mr. Jonathan GARN
50 Associate Dean Business & Tech Div .... Ms. Susan ROCHE
88 Associate Dean Health/Wellness Div .... Dr. Pete FOX
81 Associate Dean Science & Math Div .... Ms. Colleen THOMAS
83 Associate Dean Social Sciences Div .... Dr. Daniel ALLEN
21 Business Services Director .... Mr. Jonathan FOCO
09 Director of Institutional Research .... Dr. Jason YOUNG
06 Registrar .... Ms. Terri GOULD
13 Chief Information Officer .... Vacant
40 Assistant Bookstore Manager .... Mr. Daniel FRANCKE
08 Mgr of Library Programs & Services .... Ms. Michele PRATT

Eastern Michigan University (K)

900 Oakwood St, Ypsilanti MI 48197-2207
County: Washtenaw FICE Identification: 002259
Unit ID: 169798
Telephone: (734) 487-1849 Carnegie Class: DU-Higher
FAX Number: (734) 481-1095 Calendar System: Semester
URL: www.emich.edu
Established: 1849 Annual Undergrad Tuition & Fees (In-State): $13,810
Enrollment: 16,294 Coed
Affiliation or Control: State IRS Status: 501(c)3
Highest Offering: Doctorate
Accreditation: HLC, ARCPA, ART, CAATE, CACREP, CAEP, CAEPN, CEA, CIDA, CLPSY, CONST, DIETC, MT, MUS, NURSE, OPE, OT, SP, SPAA, SW

01 President .... Dr. James M. SMITH
05 Provost and Executive VP .... Dr. Rhonda LONGWORTH
10 Chief Financial Officer .... Mr. Michael VALDES
26 Vice President Communications .... Mr. Walter KRAFT
111 VP Advance/Exec Dir Foundation .... Mr. William SHEPARD
101 VP & Sec to the Board of Regents .... Ms. Vicki REAUME
41 Vice President/Dir Athletics .... Mr. Scott WETHERBEE
84 Vice Pres/Chief Enrollment Officer .... Mr. Kevin KUCERA
86 Int VP Govt/Cmty Relations .... Ms. Vicki REAUME
18 Exec Dir Facilities/Construct Plng .... Mr. Scott STORRAR
15 Assoc VP & Chief HR Officer .... Mr. Brett LAST
43 General Counsel .... Ms. Lauren LONDON
88 Assoc General Counsel .... Mr. Jeffrey AMMONS
13 Chief Information Officer .... Mr. Ron WOODY
19 Exec Dir Public Safety .... Mr. Robert HEIGHES
100 Chief of Staff .... Mr. Leigh GREDEN
11 Assoc Prov/Assoc VP Administration . Dr. James J. CARROLL, III
20 Assoc Prov/Assoc VP Acad Pgm Svcs .... Mr. Michael TEW
49 Dean Col of Art & Sciences .... Dr. Dana HELLER
50 Dean Col of Business .... Dr. Kenneth LORD
53 Dean Col of Education .... Dr. Micheal SAYLER
69 Dean Col Health & Human Svcs .... Dr. Murali NAIR
72 Dean Col Engineering & Technology .... Dr. Mohamad QATU
58 Int Assc Prov/AVP Grad Studies/Rsrc .... Dr. Wade TORNQUIST
08 University Librarian .... Ms. Rhonda FOWLER
32 Sr AVP Student Affs/Dean Students .... Ms. Ellen GOLD
09 Dir Inst Research/Info Mgmt .... Mr. Xunhang (Hank) ZHOU
20 Asst VP Academic Affairs/AHR .... Dr. Brian PAPPAS
88 Exec Dir Foundation Operations/CFO .... Ms. Laura WILBANKS
88 Assoc Director Ombuds .... Ms. Julia HECK
27 Executive Director Media Relations .... Vacant
88 Dir Charter Schools Program .... Dr. Malverne WINBORNE
92 Dean Honors College .... Dr. Ann EISENBERG
39 Dir Housing & Residence Life .... Ms. Jeanette ZALBA
114 Exec Dir Financial Plng & Budget .... Mr. Todd OHMER
112 Dir Planned Giving/Foundation .... Mr. Sam JENSEN
102 Assoc VP Advancement/Foundation .... Ms. Jill HUNSBERGER
88 Exec Dir Integrated Content .... Ms. Darcy GIFFORD
88 Gen Mgr WEMU-FM Public Radio .... Ms. Mary MOTHERWELL
06 Registrar .... Ms. Christina SHELL
88 Director of Engagement @ EMU .... Ms. Jessica ALEXANDER
37 Director Financial Aid .... Ms. Donna HOLUBIK
28 Dir Diversity & Cmty Involvement .... Mr. Steven P. BRYANT
96 Director Purchasing .... Mr. Travis TEMEYER
22 Title IX Coordinator .... Ms. Anika AWAI-WILLIAMS
88 Senior Assoc to CFO .... Mr. Daniel KELLY
21 Controller .... Ms. Doris M. CELIAN
88 Asst Controller/Student Bus Svcs .... Ms. Beth HARDCASTLE
88 Asst Dir Business Systems Support .... Mr. Kenneth R. ADKINS
97 Dir Undergrad Studies/Prov Office .... Dr. Doris FIELDS
88 Dir Disability Resource Ctr .... Dr. LaMarcus HOWARD
85 Dir Office of Intl Stdnt & Scholars .... Ms. Esther GUNEL
04 Admin Associate to the President .... Ms. Casey WOOSTER
29 Interim Exec Dir Alumni Affairs .... Ms. Mia MILTON
38 Director Student Counseling .... Dr. Lisa LAUTERBACH

Ecumenical Theological Seminary (L)

2930 Woodward Avenue, Detroit MI 48201-3035
County: Wayne FICE Identification: 040024
Unit ID: 247162
Telephone: (313) 831-5200 Carnegie Class: Spec-4-yr-Faith
FAX Number: (313) 831-1353 Calendar System: Quarter
URL: www.etseminary.edu
Established: 1980 Annual Undergrad Tuition & Fees: N/A
Enrollment: 76 Coed
Affiliation or Control: Independent Non-Profit IRS Status: 501(c)3
Highest Offering: Doctorate
Accreditation: THEOL

01 President Dr. Kenneth E. HARRIS
05 Asst to President-Academics Dr. Brandon GRAFIUS
11 Asst to President-Operations Mrs. Barbara PYE
10 Finance Officer/Business Mgmt Ms. Jacquelyn HINES
06 Registrar Mrs. Barbara PYE
07 Manager of Enrollment/Recruitment Vacant
73 Director Doctor of Ministry Program Dr. Constance SIMON
58 Director of Masters Program Dr. James WADDELL
73 Director of Urban Ministry Program Dr. Brandon GRAFIUS

Ferris State University (A)

1201 S. State Street, Big Rapids MI 49307-2295
County: Mecosta FICE Identification: 002260
Unit ID: 169910
Telephone: (231) 591-2000 Carnegie Class: DU-Mod
FAX Number: (231) 591-3592 Calendar System: Semester
URL: www.ferris.edu
Established: 1884 Annual Undergrad Tuition & Fees (In-State): $12,376
Enrollment: 11,165 Coed
Affiliation or Control: State IRS Status: 501(c)3
Highest Offering: First Professional Degree
Accreditation: **HLC**, ACBSP, CAEP, CAHIIM, COARC, CONST, DH, DMS, HSA, MLTAD, MT, NMT, NURSE, OPT, OPTR, PHAR, RAD, SW

01 President Dr. David L. EISLER
05 Provost & VPAA Dr. Robert FLEISCHMAN
43 Vice President & General Counsel Mr. Miles J. POSTEMA
10 VP Administration & Finance Mr. Jim BACHMEIER
111 VP of Advancement & Mktg Ms. Shelly PEARCY
32 Vice President Student Affairs Dr. Jeanine WARD-ROOF
12 President KCAD Ms. Tara MCCRACKIN
56 Dean Extended and Intl Operations Dr. Steve REIFERT
28 VP for Diversity and Inclusion Dr. David PILGRIM
108 Int Assoc Provost Accreditation Ms. Mandy SEIFERLEIN
109 Assoc VP of Auxiliary Enterprises Ms. Gheretta HARRIS
21 Assistant VP of Finance Mr. Mike GRANDY
110 Assoc VP for Advancement Mr. Bob MURRAY
15 Assoc VP Human Resources Ms. Fredericka HAYES
18 Assoc VP Physical Plant Mr. Chad STIRRETT
84 Associate Dean Enrollment Services Ms. Kathy LAKE
07 Dean Enroll Svcs/Dir Admissions Dr. Kristen SALOMONSON
114 Director Budget Planning/Analysis Ms. Amy WINKER
13 Chief Technology Officer Ms. Bhavani KONERU
19 Director of Public Safety Mr. John ALLEN
88 Mgr Stdnt Empl & Financial Aid Adv Vacant
88 Director of University Center Mr. Mark SCHUELKE
38 Director Counseling & Health Center Ms. Lindsay BARBER
35 Dean of Student Life Ms. Joy PULSIFER
93 Interim Dir Multicult Student Svcs Mr. Darnell LEWIS
88 Director for CLACS Ms. Angela ROMAN
88 Director University Recreation Mr. Justin HARDEN
29 Assoc VP for External Relations Mr. Jeremy MISHLER
09 Dir of Inst Research & Testing Ms. Mitzi DAY
39 Director Residential Life Mr. Brian MARQUARDT
40 Manager Bookstore Ms. Sheree SCHROT
41 Director of Athletics Mr. Perk WEISENBURGER
44 Dir Annual Giving & Advance Svcs Ms. Jennifer YONTZ
49 Dean of Arts/Sciences & Education Dr. Randy CAGLE
50 Interim Dean of Business Dr. Jimmie JOSEPH
67 Dean of Pharmacy Dr. Steve DURST
76 Dean of Health Professions Dr. Lincoln GIBBS
63 Dean Michigan College Optometry Dr. David DAMARI
72 Dean of Engineering Technology Mr. Michael STALEY
08 Interim Dean of FLITE Dr. Jason BENTLEY
04 Executive Asst to the President Ms. Terri COOK
101 Secretary to the Board of Trustees Ms. Karen HUISMAN
37 Asst Director Financial Aid Ms. Rebecca VOKES
06 Interim Registrar Mr. Eric HANER
104 Executive Dir Office of Intl Educ Dr. Piram PRAKASAM
105 Web Developer Mr. Paul HOBART
22 Director of Equal Opportunity Ms. Kylie PIETTE
106 Exec Director Online Education Dr. Amy L. GREENE
96 Procurement Manager Ms. Cindee WILCOX

Finlandia University (B)

601 Quincy Street, Hancock MI 49930-1882
County: Houghton FICE Identification: 002322
Unit ID: 172440
Telephone: (906) 487-7201 Carnegie Class: Bac-Diverse
FAX Number: (906) 487-7366 Calendar System: Semester
URL: www.finlandia.edu
Established: 1896 Annual Undergrad Tuition & Fees: $23,990
Enrollment: 402 Coed
Affiliation or Control: Evangelical Lutheran Church In America
IRS Status: 501(c)3
Highest Offering: Baccalaureate
Accreditation: **HLC**, MAC, NURSE, PTAA

01 President Dr. Philip JOHNSON
10 Int Chief Financial Officer Ms. Laura SIEDERS
05 VP Academic Affairs Dr. Fredi DE YAMPERT
111 VP External Relations & Advancement Vacant
04 Executive Administrative Assistant Ms. Doreen KORPELA
26 Director Marketing/Communications Mr. Jordan SHAWHAN
08 Head Librarian Ms. Rebecca DALY
32 Dean of Students & Enrollment Ms. Erin BARNETT
42 Campus Pastor Ms. Sarah SEMMLERSMITH
06 Registrar Mr. Darren BAUSANO
13 Director Information Technology Mr. Scott BLAKE
41 Athletic Director Mr. Curtis WITTENBERG
18 Director of Plant and Facilities Mr. Curt HAHKA
37 Director Financial Services Ms. Sandra TURNQUIST
40 Bookstore Manager Ms. April STEVENS
96 Purchaser Ms. Janine NOTTKE
15 Human Resources Manager Mr. Joe KOEPEL
07 Director of Admissions/Enrollment Mr. Anthony SCHWASS
19 Director of Campus Safety/Security Mr. Scott HENDRICKSON
39 Asst Dean of Stdnts Residence Life Ms. Annette SAWADOGO
49 Dean College of Arts & Sciences Dr. Jason OYADOMARI
57 Dean Intl School of Art & Design Ms. Denise VANDEVILLE
76 Dean College of Health Science Dr. Fredi DEYAMPERT
50 Dean Intl School of Business Mr. Kevin MANNINEN
22 Title IX Coordinator Vacant
09 Director of Institutional Research Mr. David BERTHOLF
106 Dir of Innovative & Online Lrng Dr. Michelle RAUCH
108 Director Institutional Assessment Mr. Neil KROMER

Glen Oaks Community College (C)

62249 Shimmel Road, Centreville MI 49032-9719
County: Saint Joseph FICE Identification: 002263
Unit ID: 169974
Telephone: (269) 467-9945 Carnegie Class: Assoc/MT-VT-High Non
FAX Number: (269) 467-4114 Calendar System: Semester
URL: www.glenoaks.edu
Established: 1965 Annual Undergrad Tuition & Fees (In-District): $5,328
Enrollment: 950 Coed
Affiliation or Control: Local IRS Status: 501(c)3
Highest Offering: Associate Degree
Accreditation: **HLC**, MAC

01 President Dr. David DEVIER
05 Vice President of Academics Dr. Michael GOLDIN
10 Vice President of Finance & Admin Mr. Bruce ZAKRZEWSKI
32 Vice President of Student Services Ms. Tonya HOWDEN
66 Dean of Nursing Ms. Sara BIRCH
08 Director Learning Resources Center Ms. Trista NELSON
21 Accountant Ms. Jennifer DODSON
18 Director of Buildings/Grounds Mr. Larry DIEKMAN
07 Director of Admissions Ms. Adrienne SKINNER
37 Dir of Financial Aid/Scholarships Ms. Jean ZIMMERMAN
41 Director of Athletics Mr. Matt BRAWLEY
09 Inst Effectiveness/Research Analyst Dr. Tammy RUSSELL
15 Personnel Coordinator Ms. Candy BOHACZ
26 Public Relations/Marketing Ms. Valorie JUERGENS
04 Exec Assoc Asst to the President Ms. Diane ZINSMASTER
06 Registrar Ms. Amy YOUNG
103 Director Workforce Development Mr. Paul AIVARS
39 Dir Resident Life/Student Housing Ms. April YOST
13 Chief Information Technology Office Mr. Evan DEMBSKEY
22 Dir Affirmative Action/Equal Opp Ms. Jamie YESH

Gogebic Community College (D)

E4946 Jackson Road, Ironwood MI 49938-1366
County: Gogebic FICE Identification: 002264
Unit ID: 169992
Telephone: (906) 932-4231 Carnegie Class: Assoc/HVT-High Trad
FAX Number: (906) 932-5541 Calendar System: Semester
URL: www.gogebic.edu
Established: 1931 Annual Undergrad Tuition & Fees (In-District): $6,808
Enrollment: 896 Coed
Affiliation or Control: Local IRS Status: 501(c)3
Highest Offering: Associate Degree
Accreditation: **HLC**

01 President Dr. George MCNULTY
05 Vice Pres of Academic Affairs Mr. David DARROW
10 Vice Pres of Business Services Mr. Erik M. GUENARD
32 Vice Pres of Student Services Vacant
37 Director Financial Aid Mr. Marc MADIGAN
76 Director of Allied Health Program Ms. Nicole ROWE
88 Director of Ski Area Management Mr. James VANDERSPOEL
08 Dir Learning Resource Center Vacant
13 Director of Computer Services Mr. Steve SPETS
07 Dir of Admission/Public Information Ms. Kim ZECKOVICH
30 Dir of Institutional Development Ms. Kelly MARZCAK
15 Director of Human Resources Ms. Ashley PAQUETTE
88 Transfer Coord/Veterans Services Ms. Tara TREGEMBO
09 Institutional Researcher Ms. Miranda LAWVER
04 Executive Admin Asst to President Ms. Roberta ANDERS
103 Director Workforce Development Mr. Glen ACKERMAN-BEHR
39 Resident Community Manager Mr. Aaron FROELICH
41 Athletic Director Mr. Mike BOERMAN

Grace Christian University (E)

1011 Aldon Street, SW, Grand Rapids MI 49509-1998
County: Kent FICE Identification: 002265
Unit ID: 170000
Telephone: (616) 538-2330 Carnegie Class: Spec-4-yr-Faith
FAX Number: (616) 538-0599 Calendar System: Semester
URL: www.gracechristian.edu
Established: 1939 Annual Undergrad Tuition & Fees: $14,160
Enrollment: 1,052 Coed
Affiliation or Control: Independent Non-Profit IRS Status: 501(c)3
Highest Offering: Master's
Accreditation: **HLC**, BI

01 President Dr. Kenneth B. KEMPER
03 Exec Vice President Mr. Brian P. SHERSTAD
05 Provost Dr. Kim PILIECI
20 Assistant Provost Dr. Timothy RUMLEY
10 Vice Pres Finance/Business Opers Mr. Douglas VRIESMAN
32 Assoc Vice Pres Student Affairs Mr. Kyle BOHL
06 Registrar Ms. Victoria CUMINGS
111 Vice Pres Institutional Advancement Mr. Stephen GOWDY
08 Director Library Services Mrs. Erinn HUEBNER
37 Director of Financial Aid Mr. Kurt POSTMA
13 Director of Information Technology Mr. Robert ELUSKIE
18 Director of Maintenance Mr. Nathan JOHNSON
41 Athletic Director Mr. Gary BAILEY
35 Dean of Students Mr. Jim GAMBLE
26 Assoc Vice President of Marketing Mr. Zak SORENSEN
15 Assoc Vice Pres of Human Resources Mrs. Sherea LACY
07 Director of Admissions on Campus Mr. Aaron COPE
07 Director of Admissions Online Mr. Joshua WILLIAMS

† Name changed from Grace Bible College on July 1, 2018.

Grand Rapids Community College (F)

143 Bostwick Avenue NE, Grand Rapids MI 49503-3295
County: Kent FICE Identification: 002267
Unit ID: 170055
Telephone: (616) 234-4000 Carnegie Class: Assoc/MT-VT-High Trad
FAX Number: (616) 234-4005 Calendar System: Semester
URL: www.grcc.edu
Established: 1914 Annual Undergrad Tuition & Fees (In-District): $7,869
Enrollment: 12,107 Coed
Affiliation or Control: Local IRS Status: 501(c)3
Highest Offering: Associate Degree
Accreditation: **HLC**, ACFEI, ADNUR, ART, DA, DH, MAC, MUS, NAEYC, OTA, PNUR, RAD

01 President Dr. Bill PINK
05 Prov/Exec VP Academic Affairs Dr. Brian KNETL
10 Exec VP Business/Financial Services Ms. Lisa FREIBURGER
13 VP & CIO Lrng Res/Tech Solutions Mr. David ANDERSON
111 AVP Advancement/Exec Dir Foundation Dr. Kathryn MULLINS
28 Chief Equity & Inclusion Officer Dr. Afeni MCNEELY COBHAM
124 Dean of Student Success & Retention Mr. Eric MULLEN
32 Assoc Provost/Dean Student Affairs Dr. Tina HOXIE
49 Dean School of Arts & Sciences Dr. Michael VARGO
103 Dean Workforce Development Dr. Amy MANSFIELD
26 Director of Communications Mr. David MURRAY
37 Director of Financial Aid Ms. Ann ISACKSON
15 Executive Director Human Resources Ms. Cathy KUBIAK
06 Registrar Ms. Valerie BUTTERFIELD
35 Director Student Activities Ms. Caroline BLAIR
88 Assoc Director Student Employment Ms. Luann WEDGE
08 Director of Library Services Mr. Brian BEECHER
18 Executive Director of Facilities Mr. Thomas J. SMITH
19 Chief of Campus Police Ms. Rebecca R. WHITMAN
43 General Counsel Ms. Kathy KEATING
96 Director Purchasing Mr. Mansfield MATTHEWSON
12 Dean of Lakeshore Campus & Outreach Mr. Daniel CLARK

Grand Valley State University (G)

1 Campus Drive, Allendale MI 49401-9403
County: Ottawa FICE Identification: 002268
Unit ID: 170082
Telephone: (616) 331-5000 Carnegie Class: Masters/L
FAX Number: (616) 331-3503 Calendar System: Semester
URL: www.gvsu.edu
Established: 1960 Annual Undergrad Tuition & Fees (In-State): $13,244
Enrollment: 23,350 Coed
Affiliation or Control: State IRS Status: 501(c)3
Highest Offering: Doctorate
Accreditation: **HLC**, ARCPA, ART, @AUD, CAATE, CAEP, CAHIIM, CARTE, CVT, DIETC, DIETD, DMS, HSA, IPSY, MT, MUS, NURSE, OT, PH, PTA, RADDOS, RTT, SP, SPAA, SW

01 President Dr. Philomena V. MANTELLA
05 Int Provost/EVP Acad & Stdnt Affs Dr. Chris PLOUFF
28 Chief of Staff/VP Inclus & Equity Dr. Jesse M. BERNAL
26 VP for Univ Relations/Sec to BOT Mr. Matthew E. MCLOGAN
10 Vice President for Finance & Admin Dr. Greg SANIAL
84 Vice President Enrollment Develop Dr. Brencleveton D. TRUSS
30 VP for Development/Exec Dir Fndn Ms. Laura M. AIKENS
43 General Counsel Ms. Pat SMITH
13 Vice President for IT/CDO Dr. Miloš TOPIC
32 Acting Vice Prov & Dean of Students Dr. Aaron HAIGHT
51 Vice Prov Grad & Lifetime Learning Dr. Kara VAN DAM
46 Vice Prov for Research Admin Dr. Robert SMART
20 Vice Prov Instruct Dev & Innovation Dr. Christine RENER
20 Assoc VP Academic Affairs Dr. Edward ABOUFADEL
20 Assoc VP Academic Affairs Dr. Ellen SCHENDEL
20 Assoc VP Academic Affairs Dr. Suzeanne BENET
20 Assoc VP Academic Affairs Ms. Bonnie BOWEN
21 Assoc VP Business/Finance Mr. Craig WIESCHHORSTER
114 Director of University Budgets Ms. Jennifer SCHICK
15 Chief Human Resources Officer Mr. Mychal COLEMAN
88 Assoc VP Institutional Marketing Ms. Rhonda LUBBERTS
27 Assoc VP for Univ Communications Ms. Mary Eilleen LYON
18 Asst VP Facilities Services Mr. Rence MEREDITH
88 Assoc VP for Facilities Planning Ms. Karen INGLE
12 Assoc VP Fac Svcs GR & Reg Ctrs Ms. Lisa HAYNES
22 Assoc VP for Equity & Compliance Ms. Kathleen VANDERVEEN
35 Assoc VP Inclusion & Student Affs Dr. Marlene KOWALSKI-BRAUN
04 Assoc VP & Exec Assoc to President Dr. Robert KIMBALL
49 Dean Col of Liberal Arts & Sciences Dr. Jennifer DRAKE
50 Dean Seidman Col of Business Dr. Diana LAWSON

53 Dean Col of Educ & Comm Innovation .... Dr. Sherril SOMAN
54 Dean Padnos Col Engr & Computing .... Dr. Paul PLOTKOWSKI
76 Acting Dean Col Health Professions .... Dr. Teresa BECK
88 Dean College Interdisc Studies .... Dr. Mark SCHAUB
66 Acting Dean College of Nursing .... Dr. Lola COKE
58 Assoc Vice Provost Graduate School .... Dr. Jeffrey POTTEIGER
08 Dean University Libraries .... Dr. Annie BELANGER
07 Assoc VP for Admissions .... Ms. Jodi CHYCINSKI
29 Director of Alumni Relations .... Vacant
36 Director of Career Center .... Mr. Troy FARLEY
37 Assoc VP for Financial Aid .... Ms. Michelle RHODES
39 Director of Housing & Res Life .... Mr. Kyle BOONE
14 Assoc VP Information Technology .... Mr. Emil DELGADO
09 Assoc VP Institutional Analysis .... Dr. Philip BATTY
96 Director of Procurement Services .... Mr. Aaron CACCAMO
19 Director Public Safety/Police Chief .... Mr. Brandon DEHAAN
38 Director Univ Counseling Center .... Dr. Amber ROBERTS
41 Athletic Director .... Ms. Keri BECKER
21 Controller .... Ms. Karen MUSHONG
88 General Manager WGVU .... Mr. Jim RADEMAKER II
06 Assoc VP & Registrar .... Ms. Pam WELLS
22 Title IX Coordinator .... Vacant

Great Lakes Christian College (A)

6211 Willow Highway, Lansing MI 48917-1299
County: Eaton FICE Identification: 002269
Unit ID: 170091
Telephone: (517) 321-0242 Carnegie Class: Spec-4-yr-Faith
FAX Number: (517) 321-5902 Calendar System: Semester
URL: www.glcc.edu
Established: 1949 Annual Undergrad Tuition & Fees: $17,220
Enrollment: 169 Coed
Affiliation or Control: Christian Churches And Churches of Christ
IRS Status: 501(c)3
Highest Offering: Baccalaureate
Accreditation: HLC

01 President .... Mr. Lawrence L. CARTER
10 Vice President Finance/Operations .... Mr. Timothy J. WYNSMA
05 Vice President of Academic Affairs .... Dr. Samuel C. LONG
111 Vice Pres Institutional Advancement .... Mr. Philip E. BEAVERS
84 Vice Pres Enrollment Mgmt .... Mr. Gregory STAUFFER
06 Registrar .... Dr. Esther A. HETRICK
08 Director of Library Services .... Mrs. Heather BUNCE
37 Financial Aid Director .... Prof. Ryan APPLE
32 Dean of Students/Dir Student Life .... Mr. Ryan BUSHNELL
41 Athletic Director .... Mr. Richard WESTERLUND
88 Director of Outreach Ministries .... Mrs. Judy BEAVERS
18 Maintenance Supervisor .... Mr. Elijah KOTT
04 Administrative Secretary .... Ms. Marie A. RIGGS

Henry Ford College (B)

5101 Evergreen Road, Dearborn MI 48128-1495
County: Wayne FICE Identification: 002270
Unit ID: 170240
Telephone: (313) 845-9615 Carnegie Class: Bac/Assoc-Assoc Dom
FAX Number: (313) 845-9658 Calendar System: Semester
URL: www.hfcc.edu
Established: 1938 Annual Undergrad Tuition & Fees (In-District): $5,020
Enrollment: 11,345 Coed
Affiliation or Control: Local IRS Status: 501(c)3
Highest Offering: Baccalaureate
Accreditation: HLC, ACFEI, ADNUR, COARC, EMT, LC, MAC, NAEYC, PTAA, RAD, SURGT

01 President .... Dr. Russell A. KAVALHUNA
10 Vice President Financial Services .... Dr. John SATKOWSKI
32 Interim VP of Student Affairs .... Ms. Holly DIAMOND
05 VP of Academic Affairs .... Dr. Michael NEALON
111 Vice Pres of Inst Advancement .... Mr. A. Reginald BEST, JR.
15 VP Strategy and HR .... Dr. Lori GONKO
06 Exec Director Registration/Enroll .... Ms. Holly DIAMOND
38 Assoc Dean Counseling .... Mr. Ibrahim ATALLAH
50 Dean Business/Entrepreneurship/PD .... Ms. Patricia CHATMAN
08 Director Library .... Ms. Kate HARGER
13 Dir Network and Infrastructure .... Mr. Joseph ZITNIK
26 VP of Marketing/Communications .... Ms. Rhonda DELONG
37 Exec Director Student Financial Aid .... Mr. Kevin J. CULLER
92 Director Honors Program .... Vacant
96 Director Purchasing .... Mr. Fred STEINER
40 Manager of College Store .... Ms. Pamela HALL
04 Administrative Asst to President .... Ms. Kathy DIMITRIOU
09 Director of Institutional Research .... Mr. Jacob KROGOL
15 Director Personnel Services .... Vacant
19 Director Security/Safety .... Ms. Karen SCHOEN
41 Athletic Director .... Ms. Rochelle TAYLOR
43 VP Legal Services/General Counsel .... Ms. Amy CLARK
07 Director of Admissions .... Vacant
18 Chief Facilities/Physical Plant Ofc .... Mr. Reuben BRUKLEY

Hillsdale College (C)

33 East College Street, Hillsdale MI 49242-1298
County: Hillsdale FICE Identification: 002272
Unit ID: 170286
Telephone: (517) 437-7341 Carnegie Class: Bac-A&S
FAX Number: (517) 437-3923 Calendar System: Semester
URL: www.hillsdale.edu
Established: 1844 Annual Undergrad Tuition & Fees: $29,482
Enrollment: 1,543 Coed
Affiliation or Control: Independent Non-Profit IRS Status: 501(c)3
Highest Offering: Doctorate
Accreditation: HLC

01 President .... Dr. Larry ARNN
05 Provost .... Dr. Chris VANORMAN
11 VP & Chief Administrative Officer .... Mr. Rich PEWE
43 VP & General Counsel .... Mr. Robert NORTON
07 VP Admissions/Business Development .... Mr. Doug BANBURY
26 VP External Affairs .... Mr. Douglas JEFFREY
10 VP Finance .... Mr. Patrick FLANNERY
111 VP Institutional Advancement .... Mr. John CERVINI
88 VP Marketing .... Mr. Matt SCHLIENTZ
32 VP Student Affairs .... Ms. Diane PHILIPP
27 Associate VP External Affairs .... Mr. Timothy CASPAR
100 Chief Staff Officer .... Mr. Mike HARNER
36 Executive Director Career Services .... Mr. Ken KOOPMANS
15 Associate VP of HR .... Ms. Janet MARSH
13 Associate VP for ITS .... Mr. Jason SHERRILL
29 Executive Director Alumni Affairs .... Ms. Colleen MCGINNESS
41 Director Athletics .... Mr. Don BRUBACHER
19 Director Campus Security .... Mr. William WHORLEY
40 Director College Bookstore .... Ms. Cindy WILLING
37 Director Financial Aid .... Mr. Rich MOEGGENBERG
23 Director Health Services .... Mr. Brock LUTZ
08 Director Library .... Ms. Maurine MCCOURRY
09 Director Institutional Research .... Mr. Joshua TROJNIAK
18 Director Facilities .... Mr. Dave BILLINGTON
35 Director Student Programs .... Ms. Ashlyn NEVEAU
42 Chaplain .... Rev. Adam RICK
21 Controller .... Ms. LeAnn CREGER
33 Dean of Men .... Mr. Aaron PETERSEN
34 Dean of Women .... Ms. Rebekah DELL
06 Registrar .... Mr. Douglas MCARTHUR
04 Exec Assistant to the President .... Ms. Madison MOORE
88 Senior Advisor to the Provost .... Mr. Mark MAIER

Hope College (D)

141 E 12th Street, Holland MI 49423-3607
County: Ottawa FICE Identification: 002273
Unit ID: 170301
Telephone: (616) 395-7000 Carnegie Class: Bac-A&S
FAX Number: (616) 395-7922 Calendar System: Semester
URL: www.hope.edu
Established: 1866 Annual Undergrad Tuition & Fees: $36,650
Enrollment: 3,061 Coed
Affiliation or Control: Reformed Church In America IRS Status: 501(c)3
Highest Offering: Baccalaureate
Accreditation: HLC, ART, CAEP, DANCE, MUS, NURSE, SW, THEA

01 President .... Mr. Matthew A. SCOGIN
05 Interim Provost .... Dr. Gerald GRIFFIN
10 Vice Pres & Chief Financial Officer .... Mr. Thomas W. BYLSMA
07 Vice President for Admissions .... Mr. William VANDERBILT
111 VP of Philanthropy & Engagement .... Mr. Jeffrey PUCKETT
32 VP Student Devel/Dean of Students .... Dr. Richard A. FROST
26 VP for Public Affairs & Marketing .... Mrs. Jennifer FELLINGER
08 Dean of Libraries .... Ms. Kelly G. JACOBSMA
39 Assoc Dean of Students/Housing .... Dr. John E. JOBSON
22 Assc Dn Stdnts/Dir Ctr Div & Incl .... Vacant
94 Director of Women's/Gender Studies .... Dr. Virginia BEARD
81 Dean for Natural & Applied Sciences ... Dr. David G. VAN WYLEN
79 Dean for the Arts & Humanities .... Dr. Sandra L. VISSER
83 Dean for Social Sciences .... Dr. Scott D. VANDER STOEP
88 Dean of the Chapel .... Rev Dr. Trygve D. JOHNSON
37 Director of Financial Aid .... Ms. Jill NUTT
36 Assoc Dean for the Career Dev Ctr .... Mr. Dale F. AUSTIN
21 Director of Finance & Business Svcs .... Mr. Douglas VAN DYKEN
11 Director of Operations .... Ms. Kara SLATER
88 Director of Process and Innovation .... Mr. Carl E. HEIDEMAN
15 Director of Human Resources .... Mrs. Lori MULDER
40 Manager of Hope-Geneva Bookstore .... Mr. Craig THELEN
29 Exec Director of Alumni Engagement .... Mr. Scott TRAVIS
41 Director of Athletics .... Mr. Tim SCHOONVELD
42 Senior Chaplain .... Rev. Paul H. BOERSMA
38 Asst Dean/Director Counseling Ctr .... Dr. Kristen GRAY
04 Executive Asst to the President .... Mrs. Mary HOUSEHOLDER
19 Director Security/Safety .... Mr. Jeffrey HERTEL
13 Dir Computing/Info Technology .... Mr. Jeff PESTUN
30 Assoc VP & Campaign Director .. Mrs. Mary REMENSCHNEIDER
06 Registrar .... Mrs. Carol DE JONG
105 Director Web Communications .... Mr. Jason CASH
28 Chief Officer for Culture & Inclus .... Dr. Sonja TRENT-BROWN
44 Dir of Leadership & Annual Giving .... Ms. Dana GILL

Jackson College (E)

2111 Emmons Road, Jackson MI 49201-8399
County: Jackson FICE Identification: 002274
Unit ID: 170444
Telephone: (517) 787-0800 Carnegie Class: Bac/Assoc-Assoc Dom
FAX Number: (517) 796-8630 Calendar System: Semester
URL: www.jccmi.edu
Established: 1928 Annual Undergrad Tuition & Fees (In-District): $9,318
Enrollment: 4,140 Coed
Affiliation or Control: Local IRS Status: 501(c)3
Highest Offering: Baccalaureate
Accreditation: HLC, COARC, DH, DMS, EMT, RAD

01 President/CEO .... Dr. Daniel J. PHELAN
11 Sr VP/COO .... Ms. Cindy ALLEN
10 Vice President of Finance/CFO .... Mr. Darrell NORRIS
05 Vice Pres Instruction & Stdnt Svcs .... Mr. Jeremy FREW
102 President of JC Foundation .... Mr. Jason VALENTE
06 Registrar .... Mr. Zakary MCNITT
84 Assoc Dean Enrollment Mgmt .... Ms. Julie HAND
08 Library Director .... Ms. Jennifer ADAMS
100 Chief of Staff .... Vacant
103 Dir Workforce/Career Development .... Ms. Tina MATZ
18 Vice President Facilities & IT .... Mr. Jim JONES
19 Director Safety & Security .... Mr. Jeffrey WHIPPLE
28 Chief Diversity Officer .... Mr. Lee HAMPTON
29 Director Alumni Relations .... Ms. Brigette ROBINSON
37 Director Student Financial Aid .... Ms. Andrew SPOHN
39 Director of Housing .... Mr. Glenn RICHARDS
41 Exec Dir Athletics/Stdnt Devel .... Ms. Courtney IVAN

Kalamazoo College (F)

1200 Academy Street, Kalamazoo MI 49006-3295
County: Kalamazoo FICE Identification: 002275
Unit ID: 170532
Telephone: (269) 337-7000 Carnegie Class: Bac-A&S
FAX Number: (269) 337-7251 Calendar System: Quarter
URL: www.kzoo.edu
Established: 1833 Annual Undergrad Tuition & Fees: $52,530
Enrollment: 1,451 Coed
Affiliation or Control: Independent Non-Profit IRS Status: 501(c)3
Highest Offering: Baccalaureate
Accreditation: HLC

01 President .... Dr. Jorge G. GONZALEZ
05 Provost .... Dr. Danette IFERT JOHNSON
10 VP for Business and Finance .... Ms. Karen SISSON
111 VP for College Advancement .... Ms. Karen ISBLE
32 VP Student Devel & Dean of Students .... Dr. Sarah B. WESTFALL
84 VP for Admission & Financial Aid .... Ms. Mj HUEBNER
85 Associate Provost for Intl Pgms .... Dr. Margaret WIEDENHOEFT
13 Chief Information Officer .... Mr. Gregory S. DIMENT
21 Director of Finance .... Ms. Catherine BONNES
09 Director of Inst Support/Research .... Dr. Tara WEBB
35 Assoc Dean of Stdnts/1st Yr Exper .... Ms. Dana JANSMA
06 Registrar .... Ms. Nicole KRAGT
15 Human Resources Manager .... Ms. Renee E. BOELCKE
07 Director of Admission .... Ms. Suzanne LEPLEY
37 Director of Financial Aid .... Ms. Becca MURPHY
18 Director of Facilities Management ...... Ms. Susan K. LINDEMANN
40 Director Bookstore .... Ms. Deborah L. THOMPSON
29 Director of Alumni Relations .... Ms. Kimberly J. ALDRICH
38 Director of Student Counseling .... Dr. Kenlanna FERGUSON
121 Director of Advising .... Ms. Lesley J. CLINARD
36 Dir Center Career/Prof Development ...... Dr. Tricia ZELAYA-LEON
04 Administrative Asst to President .... Ms. Melanie K. WILLIAMS
08 Head Librarian .... Dr. Stacy A. NOWICKI
102 Dir Foundation/Corporate Relations .... Ms. Ann M. JENKS
19 Director Security/Safety .... Mr. Timothy YOUNG
41 Athletic Director .... Ms. Rebecca S. HALL
88 Enrollment Data Specialist .... Ms. Linda WIRGAU
30 Director of Development .... Mr. Andrew M. MILLER
44 Director Annual Giving .... Ms. Laurel S. PALMER

Kalamazoo Valley Community College (G)

6767 West O Avenue, PO Box 4070,
Kalamazoo MI 49003-4070
County: Kalamazoo FICE Identification: 006949
Unit ID: 170541
Telephone: (269) 488-4400 Carnegie Class: Assoc/HT-High Trad
FAX Number: (269) 488-4220 Calendar System: Semester
URL: www.kvcc.edu
Established: 1966 Annual Undergrad Tuition & Fees (In-District): $6,100
Enrollment: 6,656 Coed
Affiliation or Control: Local IRS Status: 501(c)3
Highest Offering: Associate Degree
Accreditation: HLC, ACFEI, ADNUR, COARC, DH, EMT, MAC

01 President .... Dr. L. Marshall WASHINGTON
05 Provost & VP Instr/Student Success .... Dr. Paige EAGAN
11 VP Campus Plng & Operations .... Mr. Dannie ALEXANDER
10 Vice President Finance & Business .... Mr. Brian LUETH
15 Vice President for Human Resources .... Mr. Aaron HILLIARD
13 Vice Pres for Admin Svc/Info Tech .... Mr. Tim WELSH
31 VP for Strategic Business/Cmty Dev .... Mr. Craig JBARA
121 Dean of Student Success .... Vacant
108 AVP for Collab/Compliance/Analytics .... Dr. Tracy LABADIE
19 Director of Public Safety .... Mr. Donald BENTHIN
08 Director of Libraries .... Mr. Mark WALTERS
07 Dir Admissions/Registration/Records .... Ms. Sarah HUBBELL
09 Dir Planning/Research/Accred/Compl .... Mr. Dan MONDOUX
102 Exec Dir Foundation & Development .... Ms. Linda DEPTA
37 Director Financial Aid .... Ms. Alisha CEDERBERG
26 Director of Marketing .... Ms. Linda DEPTA
18 Dir Facilities/Construction Mgmt .... Mr. Dannie ALEXANDER
21 Director of Business Services .... Ms. Muriel HICE
28 Director of Diversity & Inclusion .... Mr. Trice BATSON
41 Athletic Director .... Mr. Russ PANICO
84 Director Enrollment Management .... Ms. Megan PAUKEN
124 Dir of Student Retention Completion .... Mr. Evan PAUKEN
04 Admin Assistant to the President .... Ms. Sherry WEBER
38 Dir Advising & Counseling .... Ms. Angela MARSH-PEEK

Kellogg Community College (H)

450 North Avenue, Battle Creek MI 49017-3397
County: Calhoun FICE Identification: 002276
Unit ID: 170550

Telephone: (269) 965-3931 Carnegie Class: Assoc/MT-VT-High Trad
FAX Number: (269) 962-4290 Calendar System: Semester
URL: www.kellogg.edu
Established: 1956 Annual Undergrad Tuition & Fees (In-District): $6,967
Enrollment: 3,469 Coed
Affiliation or Control: Local IRS Status: 501(c)3
Highest Offering: Associate Degree
Accreditation: HLC, ADNUR, DH, EMT, MAC, NAEYC, NDT, PTAA, RAD

01 President Dr. Adrien BENNINGS
05 Vice President Instruction Dr. Paul WATSON
32 Vice Pres Student & Community Svcs Dr. Kay KECK
10 Chief Financial Officer Mr. Richard SCOTT
57 Chair Arts & Communication Dept Ms. Barbara SUDEIKIS
81 Chair Math & Science Dept Ms. Carole DAVIS
49 Dean Arts and Sciences Ms. Tonya FORBES
102 Executive Director KCC Foundation Ms. Teresa DURHAM
96 Director Purchasing Ms. Angela CLEVELAND
06 Registrar Ms. Colleen WRIGHT
08 Dn Inst Effectiveness/Library Svcs Dr. Michele REID
41 Director Athletics & PE Mr. Tom SHAW
12 Director of Grahl Center Ms. Shari DEEVERS
84 Dean Enrollment Mgmt Ms. Nikki JEWELL
15 Director Human Resources Ms. Vicki RIVERA
18 Dir Inst Facilities Mr. Brad FULLER
51 Director Lifelong Learning Ms. Mary GREEN
09 Director Inst Compliance Reporting Mr. John JONES
21 Director of Finance Ms. Tracy BEATTY
12 Director Regional Mfg Tech Center Ms. Kimberlee ANDREWS-BINGHAM
35 Dean Student & Community Services Ms. Terah ZAREMBA
26 VP Strategy/Relations/Comm Mr. Eric GREENE
07 Director of Fin Aid & Admissions Ms. Nikki JEWELL
40 Bookstore Manager Ms. Catherine JAMES
04 Manager President's Office Vacant
103 Dean Workforce Development Dr. Dennis BASKIN
36 Director Career & Emp Services Mr. Patrick CASEY
37 Director Financial Aid Ms. Nicole COOK
121 Manager Academic Advising Ms. Donna MALASKI
19 Chief of Public Safety Mr. Austin SIMONS

Kendall College of Art and Design of Ferris State University (A)

17 Fountain Street, NW, Grand Rapids MI 49503
Telephone: (800) 676-2787 Identification: 770273
Accreditation: &HLC, ART, CIDA

Kettering University (B)

1700 University Avenue, Flint MI 48504-6214
County: Genesee FICE Identification: 002262
Unit ID: 169983
Telephone: (810) 762-9500 Carnegie Class: Masters/M
FAX Number: (810) 762-9837 Calendar System: Semester
URL: www.kettering.edu
Established: 1919 Annual Undergrad Tuition & Fees: $44,380
Enrollment: 2,030 Coed
Affiliation or Control: Independent Non-Profit IRS Status: 501(c)3
Highest Offering: Master's
Accreditation: HLC, ACBSP

01 President Dr. Robert K. MCMAHAN
04 Executive Assistant to President Ms. Evelyn YAEGER
04 Assistant to President Ms. Megan HANSON
05 Sr VP for Academic Affairs/Provost Dr. James ZHANG
10 VP Administration & Finance Mr. Tom AYERS
84 VP Enrollment Services Mr. Kip DARCY
32 VP Student Life & Dean of Students Mr. LB MCCUNE
111 VP Univ Advancement/Ext Relations Ms. Susan DAVIES
13 VP Instruct/Admin & Info Technology Ms. Viola SPRAGUE
106 VP Kettering Global Ms. Christine WALLACE
20 Associate Provost Dr. Kathryn SVINARICH
15 Director of Human Resources Ms. Camilla KEMP
102 Dir of Philanthropy Corp/Found Mr. Dale PILGER
29 Dir of Alumni Engagement Ms. Starr CORNELL
44 Dir of Philanthropy Indiv Giving Mr. David TINDALL
19 Director of Campus Safety Mr. Paul CRANE
37 Director Student Financial Aid Mr. Bob COVEY-ROBBINS
21 Controller Ms. Nancy FIKE
09 Director of Institutional Research Dr. Mark WOODS
58 Dean Grad Studies & Research Dr. Scott REEVE
18 Director Physical Plant Mr. Joseph ASPERGER
08 Director Library Services Ms. Dina MEIN
07 Director of Enrollment Ms. Tracie JONES
41 Director Athletics/Rec Service Mr. Michael L. SCHAAL
93 Director Minority Student Affairs Mr. Ricky BROWN
104 Director International Office Ms. Laura ALLEN
109 Director Auxiliary Services Ms. Nadine L. THOR
06 Registrar Ms. Judi LANGOLF
23 Director Wellness Center Ms. Cristina REED
39 Director Residence Life Ms. Sybil JACOB
78 Director Coop Educ & Career Svcs Ms. Tracie JONES
88 MI SBDC Regional Director Ms. Janis MUELLER
96 Purchasing Manager Ms. Kathleen A. REMENDER
14 Director of IT Operations Mr. Daniel GARCIA
25 Contract/Grant Specialist Ms. Jodi L. DORR
105 Webmaster Ms. Donna WICKS
88 Dir Enrollment Events/Visitor Rels Ms. Kristin LUKOWSKI
88 Director University Events Ms. Chelsea HERLEIN
121 Asst Dir Academic Success Center Ms. Sam KLASKOW
54 Dean Engineering Dr. Craig HOFF
49 Int Dean Sciences/Liberal Arts Dr. Kathryn SVINARICH
50 Int Dean School of Management Dr. Haseeb AHMED
43 University Counsel Mr. Don ROCKWELL

Keweenaw Bay Ojibwa Community College (C)

111 Beartown Rd, PO Box 519, Baraga MI 49908
County: Baraga FICE Identification: 041647
Unit ID: 461315
Telephone: (906) 353-8400 Carnegie Class: Tribal
FAX Number: (906) 353-8107 Calendar System: Semester
URL: www.kbocc.edu
Established: 1975 Annual Undergrad Tuition & Fees (In-District): $4,400
Enrollment: 79 Coed
Affiliation or Control: Local IRS Status: 501(c)3
Highest Offering: Associate Degree
Accreditation: HLC

01 President Ms. Lori Ann SHERMAN
05 Dean of Instruction Dr. B. Louise VIRTANEN
32 Dean of Students Ms. Amanda NORDSTROM
07 Admissions Officer Ms. Betti SZAROLETTA
06 Registrar Ms. Michelle BIANCO
10 Chief Financial/ Business Officer Mr. Ryan PERRIGO
15 Chief Human Resources Officer Ms. Jody JOKI
37 Director Student Financial Aid Ms. Dalene CHOSA

Kirtland Community College (D)

4800 W. 4 Mile Road, Grayling MI 49738
County: Crawford FICE Identification: 007171
Unit ID: 170587
Telephone: (989) 275-5000 Carnegie Class: Assoc/HVT-Mix Trad/Non
FAX Number: (989) 563-5915 Calendar System: Semester
URL: www.kirtland.edu
Established: 1966 Annual Undergrad Tuition & Fees (In-District): $6,090
Enrollment: 1,330 Coed
Affiliation or Control: Local IRS Status: 501(c)3
Highest Offering: Associate Degree
Accreditation: HLC, CVT, SURGT

01 President Dr. Thomas QUINN
05 Vice Pres of Academic Services Dr. Amy FUGATE
32 Vice Pres of Student Svcs/Registrar Ms. Michelle VYSKOCIL
10 Vice Pres of Business Services Mr. Chris BOWMAN
119 Director of IT Mr. Matt BIERMANN
75 Dean Occupational Programs Vacant
08 Director of Library & Tutoring Svcs Ms. Deb SHUMAKER
37 Director of Financial Aid Ms. Kemmoree DUNCOMBE
18 Director of Facilities Mr. Ron SHARPE
15 Director of Human Resources Mr. Nathan SUTTON
09 Director of Institutional Research Mr. Nick BAKER
102 Foundation Director Mr. David LEPPER
26 Director of Public Information Mr. Tim CHILCOTE
07 Admissions Coordinator Ms. Cesalee KUFFEL
19 Director Security/Safety Mr. Glenn GUTIERREZ
21 Director of Finance Ms. Kristin BARNHART
00 Chair Board of Trustees Ms. MaryAnn FERRIGAN
103 Director Workforce Development Ms. Kathleen FOX
105 Director Web Services Ms. Marj ESCH

Kuyper College (E)

3333 East Beltline Avenue, NE,
Grand Rapids MI 49525-9749
County: Kent FICE Identification: 002311
Unit ID: 171881
Telephone: (616) 222-3000 Carnegie Class: Bac-Diverse
FAX Number: (616) 988-3608 Calendar System: Semester
URL: www.kuyper.edu
Established: 1939 Annual Undergrad Tuition & Fees: $23,970
Enrollment: 152 Coed
Affiliation or Control: Independent Non-Profit IRS Status: 501(c)3
Highest Offering: Master's
Accreditation: HLC, BI, SW

01 President Dr. Patricia HARRIS
05 Academic Dean Dr. Tim DETWILER
06 Registrar Dr. Andrea FRYLING
10 Controller/CFO Ms. Christine MULKA
111 Vice Pres for College Advancement Mr. Ken CAPISCIOLTO
07 Director of Admissions Mr. Kevin GILLIAM
37 Financial Aid Director Ms. Agnes M. RUSSELL
44 Manager of the Annual Fund Ms. Lisa RUSTICUS
04 Assistant to the President Ms. Alyssa BLOM
08 Director of Library Services Ms. Michelle NORQUIST
32 Dean of Students and Work Mr. Curt ESSENBURG
18 Maintenance Supervisor Mr. Tim CHUPP
29 Manager of Alumni Relations Ms. Lisa RUSTICUS
15 Director of Human Resources Ms. Annie FIELDS
13 Director Computing/Info Management Mr. Keith TORNO
20 Dir Academic Support/Academics Mr. Andrew ZWART
70 Program Director Social Work Ms. Jennifer COLIN
85 International Student Services Ms. Jana POSTMA
50 Director of Business Leadership Mr. Marc ANDREAS
106 Director of Online Learning Mr. Darwin GLASSFORD
19 Director of Campus Operations Mr. Ray THOMAS

Lake Michigan College (F)

2755 E Napier, Benton Harbor MI 49022-1899
County: Berrien FICE Identification: 002277
Unit ID: 170620
Telephone: (269) 927-1000 Carnegie Class: Bac/Assoc-Assoc Dom
FAX Number: N/A Calendar System: Semester
URL: www.lakemichigancollege.edu
Established: 1946 Annual Undergrad Tuition & Fees (In-District): $6,743
Enrollment: 2,499 Coed
Affiliation or Control: Local IRS Status: 501(c)3
Highest Offering: Baccalaureate
Accreditation: HLC, ADNUR, DA, DMS, MAC, RAD

01 President Dr. Trevor A. KUBATZKE
10 Chief Financial Officer Ms. Kelli HAHN
04 Senior Exec Asst to President Ms. Rebecca STEFFEN
05 VP Academics Dr. Leslie KELLOGG
32 VP Student Affairs Mr. Nygil LIKELY
103 Dean Career Education Workforce Dr. Ken FLOWERS
49 Dean Arts & Sciences Dr. Gary ROBERTS
76 Dean Health Sciences Ms. Marla CLARK
102 Executive Director Foundation Mr. Doug SCHAFFER
31 Dir Community Outreach & Relations Ms. Barbara CRAIG
88 Manager Mainstage Services Mr. Mike NADOLSKI
18 Director Facilities Management Ms. Sara VANDERVEEN
26 Director Marketing & Communications Ms. Candice ELDERS
06 Registrar Ms. Sara SKINNER
96 Purchasing Manager Mr. Nathan MAIN
90 Director Teaching/Learning Center Mr. Mark KELLY
08 Head Librarian Ms. Diane BAKER
09 Director of Institutional Research Vacant
19 Director Security/Safety Mr. Steve SILCOX
39 Dir Residence Life & Stdnt Conduct Mr. Nicholas HOOPER
41 Athletic Director Ms. Melissa GRAU
37 Director Financial Aid Vacant
07 Director Admission & Recruitment Mr. Jeremy SCHAEFFER
108 Dean of Accreditation/Plng/Quality Ms. Melissa EMERY
15 Executive Director Human Resources Ms. Denise EBERTH
28 Dean Diversity/Equity/Inclusion Mr. Major COOPER

Lake Superior State University (G)

650 W Easterday Avenue,
Sault Sainte Marie MI 49783-1699
County: Chippewa FICE Identification: 002293
Unit ID: 170639
Telephone: (906) 632-6841 Carnegie Class: Bac-Diverse
FAX Number: (906) 635-2111 Calendar System: Semester
URL: www.lssu.edu
Established: 1946 Annual Undergrad Tuition & Fees (In-State): $12,744
Enrollment: 1,909 Coed
Affiliation or Control: State IRS Status: 501(c)3
Highest Offering: Baccalaureate
Accreditation: HLC, ACBSP, #CAEP, EMT, MT, NURSE

01 President Dr. Rodney S. HANLEY
05 Provost/VP Academic Affairs Dr. Lynn GILLETTE
32 Vice Pres Student Affairs Dr. Michael BEAZLEY
10 Vice President Finance Mr. Morrie WALWORTH
111 Vice Pres Advancment Mr. Scott SMITH
26 Dean of Admissions and Marketing Mr. Fred PIERCE
81 Dean Science & Environment Dr. Steven JOHNSON
49 Dean of Educ & Liberal Arts Dr. Barb LIGHT
83 Dean Health and Behavior Dr. Kathy BERCHEM
50 Dean Innovations & Solutions Dr. Kimberly MULLER
18 Director Physical Plant Mr. Jim BECSEY
06 Registrar Ms. Nancy NEVE
07 Interim Director of Admissions Ms. Stacy POST
15 Director of Human Resources Ms. Wendy BEACH
36 Director of Academic Services Ms. Geralyn NARKIEWICZ
37 Interim Director of Financial Aid Ms. Katelynn COON
38 Director of Counseling Ms. Kristin LARSON
28 Diversity Ofcr/Asst Dir Housing Mr. Derric KNIGHT
96 Purchasing Manager Ms. Stacy CHARLES
23 Director Health Services Ms. Karen STOREY
41 Director of Athletics Dr. David PAITSON
35 Director Student Life Ms. Sharmay WOOD
40 Bookstore Manager Ms. Amber MCLEAN

Lansing Community College (H)

610 N Capitol Avenue, Lansing MI 48933
County: Ingham FICE Identification: 002278
Unit ID: 170657
Telephone: (517) 483-1200 Carnegie Class: Assoc/MT-VT-High Trad
FAX Number: (517) 483-1845 Calendar System: Semester
URL: www.lcc.edu
Established: 1957 Annual Undergrad Tuition & Fees (In-District): $7,160
Enrollment: 10,306 Coed
Affiliation or Control: Local IRS Status: 501(c)3
Highest Offering: Associate Degree
Accreditation: HLC, ADNUR, COMTA, CONST, DH, DMS, EMT, NAEYC, NDT, RAD, SURGT

01 President Dr. Steve ROBINSON
05 Provost Dr. Sally WELCH
10 SVP Business Operations Dr. Seleana SAMUEL
21 Chief Financial Officer Mr. Don WILSKE
13 Chief Information Officer Mr. Bill GARLICK
11 Exec Dir Administrative Svcs Mr. Chris MACKERSIE
20 Associate VP Academic Affairs Vacant

30 Assoc VP External Affs/Development .... Dr. Toni GLASSCOE
76 Dean Health & Human Services .... Dr. Jan KARAZIM
103 Dean Community Educ/Workforce Dev .... Mr. Bo GARCIA
49 Dean Arts & Sciences .... Ms. Andrea HOAGLAND
32 Dean Student Affairs .... Ms. Ronda MILLER
72 Dean Technical Careers .... Ms. Cathy WILHM
15 Exec Director Human Resources .... Mr. James MITCHELL
28 Chief Diversity Officer .... Dr. Tonya BAILEY
26 Director Public Affairs .... Ms. Marilyn TWINE
09 Exec Dir Center for Data Science .... Dr. Matt FALL

Lawrence Technological University (A)

21000 W Ten Mile Road, Southfield MI 48075-1058

County: Oakland | FICE Identification: 002279
Unit ID: 170675
Telephone: (248) 204-4000 | Carnegie Class: Masters/L
FAX Number: (248) 204-3727 | Calendar System: Semester
URL: www.ltu.edu
Established: 1932 | Annual Undergrad Tuition & Fees: $36,630
Enrollment: 2,812 | Coed
Affiliation or Control: Independent Non-Profit | IRS Status: 501(c)3
Highest Offering: Doctorate
Accreditation: **HLC**, ART, CIDA, NURSE

01 President and CEO .... Dr. Virinder K. MOUDGIL
04 Exec Assistant to the President .... Ms. Karen MCARDLE
05 Provost .... Dr. Tarek M. SOBH
88 Exec Dir Marburger STEM Center ... Dr. Sibrina Nichelle COLLINS
10 Vice Pres Finance/Admin .... Ms. Linda L. HEIGHT
88 Spec Asst to Pres for Development .... Dr. Greg CASCIONE
26 Vice Pres Mktg & Public Affairs .... Mr. Bruce J. ANNETT, JR.
20 Assistant Provost .... Mr. Jim JOLLY
84 Asst Provost Enrollment Management .... Ms. Lisa R. KUJAWA
48 Dean of Architecture & Design .... Mr. Karl DAUBMANN
49 Dean of Arts & Sciences .... Mr. Srini KAMBHAMPATI
54 Dean of Engineering .... Dr. Nabil F. GRACE
50 Dean of Management .... Dr. Bahman MIRSHAB
32 Dean of Students .... Mr. Kevin FINN
13 Interim Director IT Services .... Dr. Lynn MILLER-WIETECHA
07 Director of Admissions .... Ms. Jane T. ROHRBACK
06 University Registrar .... Ms. Noreen FERGUSON
08 Director Library .... Mr. Gary R. COCOZZOLI
18 Director of Campus Facilities .... Mr. Carey G. VALENTINE
14 Director Help Desk/Services .... Ms. Charlene RAMOS
37 Director of Financial Aid .... Ms. Susie POLI-SMITH
41 Dir of Rec/Athletics & Wellness .... Mr. Scott TRUDEAU
36 Asst Director of Career Services .... Ms. Kerri SEACH
35 Assistant Dean of Students .... Ms. Cyndi SPOTTS
39 Director of Residence Life .... Ms. Kimberly JERDINE
86 Exec Director Business Outreach .... Mr. Mark J. BRUCKI
102 Dir of Corp & Foundations Relations .... Vacant
30 Exec Dir Development Operations .... Ms. Shannon TRANSIT
15 Assoc VP/Chief HR Officer .... Ms. Deshawn JOHNSON
40 Manager Campus Bookstore .... Ms. Adria RAHN
109 Director of Dining Services .... Mr. Leo TYKOSKI
27 Dir of Univ Comm & Academic Editor .... Ms. Renee TAMBEAU
88 Managing Editor Univ News Bureau .... Mr. Matt ROUSH
19 Director of Campus Safety .... Mr. Steven J. BOGDALEK
31 Exec Dir of Outreach & Spec Events .... Ms. Robin LECLERC
110 Coordinator of Advancement Services .... Ms. Brande' OLIVER
88 University Architect .... Mr. Joseph C. VERYSER
121 Dir of Academic Achievement Center .... Dr. Gladys M. AVILES
09 Dir of Inst Research/Academic Plng .... Ms. Noreen FERGUSON
96 Purchasing Supervisor .... Ms. Michelle BUTKOVICH
105 Director of Web Services .... Mr. Christian FORREST
106 eLearning Architect & Pgm Producer .... Dr. Lynn MILLER-WIETECHA
29 Alumni Relations .... Mr. Jay REDMAN
28 Director of Diversity .... Dr. Caryn REED-HENDON

Macomb Community College (B)

14500 Twelve Mile Road, Warren MI 48088-3896

County: Macomb | FICE Identification: 008906
Unit ID: 170790
Telephone: (586) 445-7241 | Carnegie Class: Assoc/MT-VT-Mix Trad/Non
FAX Number: (586) 445-7886 | Calendar System: Semester
URL: www.macomb.edu
Established: 1954 | Annual Undergrad Tuition & Fees (In-District): $5,975
Enrollment: 16,736 | Coed
Affiliation or Control: Local | IRS Status: 501(c)3
Highest Offering: Associate Degree
Accreditation: **HLC**, ACFEI, ADNUR, CAHIIM, COARC, EMT, IFSAC, MAC, NAEYC, OTA, PTAA, SURGT

01 President .... Dr. James SAWYER
05 Interim VP/Provost Learning Unit .... Dr. Donald RITZENHEIN
10 Vice President for Business .... Ms. Elizabeth ARGIRI
15 Vice President for Human Resources .... Ms. Denise WILLIAMS
111 VP College Adv/Community Relations .... Dr. Kevin CHANDLER
26 Dean University Relations .... Vacant
32 Vice President for Student Services .Ms. Jill M. THOMAS-LITTLE
49 Dean Arts & Sciences .... Dr. Marie PRITCHETT
76 Dean Health/Public Services .... Dr. Nara MIRIJANIAN
54 Dean Engineering & Adv Tech .... Mr. Donald HUTCHISON
50 Dean Business & Info Technology .... Dr. Michael BALSAMO
35 Dean of Student Success .... Dr. Susan BOYD
115 Director Finance & Investments .... Ms. Kathi POINDEXTER
88 Director Public Service Institute .... Mr. Michael LOPEZ
27 Director Marketing & Recruitment .... Ms. Audrey TAKACS
09 Director Institutional Research .... Ms. Deirdre SYMS
88 Director Special Research Projects .... Dr. Randall HICKMAN
06 Registrar/Dir Enrollment Services .... Dr. Carrie JEFFERS
102 Director MCC Foundation .... Ms. Christina AYAR
38 Dir Counseling & Academic Advising .... Ms. Michelle KOSS
96 Purchasing Administrator .... Mr. Dennis COSTELLO
41 Director of Athletics .... Mr. Bryan RIZZO
18 Director Facilities Management .... Mr. William SIMONSON
37 Director of Financial Aid .... Mr. Douglas LEVY
36 Director Career Employment Services .... Mr. Robert PENKALA
51 Dir Workforce Continuing Education .... Ms. Elise JOHNSON
13 CIO .... Mr. Michael ZIMMERMAN
08 Dean Libraries/Learning Resources .... Mr. Michael BALSAMO
43 General Counsel .... Mr. Jeffrey STEELE

Madonna University (C)

36600 Schoolcraft Road, Livonia MI 48150-1176

County: Wayne | FICE Identification: 002282
Unit ID: 170806
Telephone: (734) 432-5300 | Carnegie Class: Masters/L
FAX Number: N/A | Calendar System: Semester
URL: www.madonna.edu
Established: 1937 | Annual Undergrad Tuition & Fees: $24,000
Enrollment: 2,792 | Coed
Affiliation or Control: Roman Catholic | IRS Status: 501(c)3
Highest Offering: Doctorate
Accreditation: **HLC**, ACBSP, CAEP, DIETD, FEPAC, NURSE, SW

01 President .... Dr. Michael GRANDILLO
11 Vice President & COO .... Mr. Ian DAY
05 Provost and VP for Academic Admin .... Dr. James O'NEILL
32 Vice President for Student Affairs ... Dr. Connie TINGSON-GATUZ
111 Vice President for Advancement .... Dr. Matthew RHEINECKER
31 Asst to President Community Rels .... Mr. Kellen WINSLOW, SR.
35 Asst VP & Dean of Students .... Dr. Christine BENSON
06 Asst VP Enrollment Svc & Registrar .... Ms. Dina DUBUIS
104 Asst VP Academic Plng/Study Abroad .... Mr. John MAGEE
13 Chief Info Technology Officer .... Mr. John MONTGOMERY
10 Controller .... Mr. Matthew BEATTIE
58 Dean Graduate School .... Dr. Deborah DUNN
49 Dean College of Arts and Sciences .... Dr. Kevin EYSTER
50 Dean School of Business .... Dr. Tara KANE
66 Dean Nursing & Health .... Dr. Judith MCKENNA
53 Dean College of Education .... Dr. Karen OBSNIUK
108 Assoc Dean of Assessment .... Dr. Stewart WOOD
88 Assoc Dean of Inst Effectiveness .... Dr. Anne MORRIS
106 Associate Dean of Online Education .... Dr. Elena QURESHI
88 Asst Dean of Students & 504 Coord .... Dr. Clifford CAMP
07 Executive Director of Admissions .... Mrs. Patricia EVERETT
112 Exec Director Development Maj Gifts .... Mr. John DOYLE
41 Director of Athletics .... Mr. Scott KENNELL
35 Director of Campus Life .... Ms. Annaliese CORACE-LANGBEEN
42 Director of Campus Ministry .... Mr. Jesse COX
36 Director of Career Development .... Mrs. Lenore KOWALSKI
88 Director Center Personalized Instr .... Ms. Dalie RIPLEY
38 Dir Counseling/Disability Res .... Mrs. Cora GARTH
28 Director of Diversity and Inclusion .... Mrs. Claire OFIARA
18 Director of Facilities Management .... Mr. Michael MATICH
89 Director of First-Year Experience .... Mrs. Alyssa WATSON
123 Director Grad & Online Admissions .... Mrs. Sarah HERMANN
85 Director International Students .... Ms. Grace PHILSON
08 Director of Library Services .... Ms. Cynthia SIMPSON
26 Director of Marketing .... Ms. Jennifer KENNEDY
88 Director Nursing Simulation Lab .... Ms. Laura VAN HORN
39 Director of Residence Life .... Mr. Evan OWEN
88 Dir Svcs Learning & Civic Engage .... Ms. Colleen MCLELLAN
88 Director of Special Events .... Ms. Katie ALEXANDER
113 Director Student Financial Services .... Mr. Mark SCHROEDER
07 Director Undergraduate Admissions .... Mrs. Lauren NOBLES
124 Director UG Stdnt Success/Retention .... Ms. Katherine SARTORI
27 Director Univ Communications .... Ms. Karen SANBORN
29 Alumni and Annual Fund Officer .... Ms. Kaitlyn DOUGHERTY
100 Chief of Staff .... Mr. Neil NEIDHARDT
04 Executive Asst to President .... Ms. Stephanie COLEMAN
88 Housing Coordinator .... Ms. Sarah BOLAND
09 Institutional Research Specialist .... Mr. David PIASECKI
15 Asst VP/Chief Human Resources Ofcr .... Ms. Tracey DURDEN

MIAT College of Technology (D)

2955 South Haggerty Road, Canton MI 48188

County: Wayne | FICE Identification: 020603
Unit ID: 169655
Telephone: (734) 423-2139 | Carnegie Class: Spec 2-yr-Tech
FAX Number: (734) 858-5000 | Calendar System: Other
URL: www.miat.edu
Established: | Annual Undergrad Tuition & Fees: $12,838
Enrollment: 1,53? | Coed
Affiliation or Control: Proprietary | IRS Status: Proprietary
Highest Offering: Associate Degree
Accreditation: ACCSC

01 Campus President .... Ms. Jennifer PAUGH

Michigan School of Psychology (E)

26811 Orchard Lake Road, Farmington Hills MI 48334-4512

County: Oakland | FICE Identification: 021989
Unit ID: 169220
Telephone: (248) 476-1122 | Carnegie Class: Spec-4-yr-Other Health
FAX Number: (248) 476-1125 | Calendar System: Semester
URL: www.msp.edu
Established: 1981 | Annual Graduate Tuition & Fees: N/A
Enrollment: 209 | Coed
Affiliation or Control: Independent Non-Profit | IRS Status: 501(c)3
Highest Offering: Doctorate; No Undergraduates
Accreditation: **HLC**, CLPSY

01 President/Chief Executive Officer .... Dr. Fran BROWN
03 Vice President/Chief Operating Ofcr .... Ms. Diane ZALAPI
05 Dean of Academic Programs/ CAO .... Dr. Shannon CHÁVEZ-KORELL
13 Dir of Info Tech & Campus Security .... Mr. Jeffrey CROSS
32 Dean of Student Services/Registrar .... Ms. Amanda MING
07 Admissions/Recruitment Coordinator .... Ms. Carrie HAUSER
11 Dir of Administrative Operations .... Ms. Laura LANE
23 Director of Clinical Training .... Dr. Heidi MARTIN

Michigan State University (F)

426 Auditorium Road, Room 450, East Lansing MI 48824-1046

County: Ingham | FICE Identification: 002290
Unit ID: 171100
Telephone: (517) 355-1855 | Carnegie Class: DU-Highest
FAX Number: N/A | Calendar System: Semester
URL: www.msu.edu
Established: 1855 | Annual Undergrad Tuition & Fees (In-State): $14,460
Enrollment: 49,695 | Coed
Affiliation or Control: State | IRS Status: 501(c)3
Highest Offering: Doctorate
Accreditation: **HLC**, ANEST, CAATE, CACREP, CAEPT, CEA, CIDA, CLPSY, CONST, DIETD, DIETI, FEPAC, IPSY, JOUR, LAW, LSAR, MED, MFCD, MT, MUS, NURSE, OSTEO, PCSAS, PLNG, SCPSY, SP, SW, VET

01 President .... Dr. Samuel L. STANLEY
05 Provost/EVP Academic Affairs .... Dr. Teresa K. WOODRUFF
11 Exec Vice Pres for Administration .... Dr. Melissa WOO
101 Int Secretary to Board .... Mr. Brian QUINN
46 Vice Pres Research/Graduate Studies .... Dr. Doug GAGE
32 VP Student Affairs & Services .... Vacant
86 Vice Pres Governmental Relations .... Dr. Kathleen WILBUR
10 VP Finance/Treasurer .... Ms. Lisa FRACE
111 Vice Pres Univ Advancement .... Ms. Marti HEIL
43 VP Legal Affairs/General Counsel .... Mr. Brian T. QUINN
18 VP Infrastructure Plng & Facilities .... Mr. Dan J. BOLLMAN
109 Vice President Auxiliary Services .... Mr. Vennie GORE
26 VP Communication & Brand Strategy .... Ms. Heather C. SWAIN
27 Vice Pres & Univ Spokesperson . Ms. Emily GERKIN GUERRANT
88 Assistant VP Research & Innovation .... Dr. J.R HAYWOOD
58 Assoc Prov and Dean Grad School .... Dr. Thomas JEITSCHKO
20 Assoc Prov/Dean Undergrad Educ .... Dr. Mark A. LARGENT
31 Int Assoc Prov Univ Outreach/ Engage .... Dr. Laurie A. VAN EGEREN
84 Assoc Provost Acad Svcs/Enroll Mgt .... Dr. John D. GABOURY
16 Assoc Prov/VP Academic Human Res .... Ms. Suzanne LANG
45 Asst VP & Director of Plng/Budgets .... Vacant
15 Int Assoc Vice Pres Human Resources .... Mr. Rick FANNING
13 SVP Info Tech/Chief Info Ofcr .... Ms. Melissa WOO
88 Asst VP Ofc of Sponsored Programs .... Dr. Twila REIGHLEY
21 Controller .... Mr. Greg J. DEPPONG
07 Director of Admissions .... Mr. John AMBROSE
22 Dir Ofc of Institutional Diversity .... Ms. Debra MARTINEZ
28 VP and Chief Diversity Officer .... Dr. Jabbar R. BENNETT
29 Assoc VP for Alumni Relations .... Mr. Bob THOMAS
25 Director Contract & Grant Admin .... Ms. Evonne PEDAWI
36 Exec Dir Career Services/Placement .... Mr. Jeff BEAVERS
38 Director Counseling Center .... Dr. Mark F. PATISHNOCK
88 Dir MI AgBioResearch .... Dr. Doug D. BUHLER
56 Assoc Dir MSU Extension .... Mr. Patrick CUDNEY
37 Director of Financial Aid .... Mr. Richard SHIPMAN
06 Registrar .... Mr. Steve SHABLIN
85 Director Intl Students/Scholars ... Dr. Krista MCCALLUM BEATTY
23 Director MSU Student Health Ctr .... Dr. David P. WEISMANTEL
92 Dean Honors College .... Dr. Cynthia JACKSON-ELMOORE
41 VP & Dir Intercollegiate Athletics .... Mr. Alan HALLER
08 Director of Libraries .... Mr. Joseph SALEM
88 Dir Natl Supercond Cyclotron Lab .... Dr. Thomas GLASMACHER
19 VP Public Safety/Chief of Police .... Mr. Marlon C. LYNCH
47 Dean Col Agricul/Natural Resources .... Dr. Kelly F. MILLENBAH
79 Dean College Arts & Letters .... Dr. Christopher P. LONG
49 Dean Res Col Arts/Humanities .... Dr. Dylan AT MINER
50 Dean Eli Broad Col of Business .... Dr. Sanjay GUPTA
60 Dean Col Communications/Arts & Sci .... Dr. Prabu DAVID
53 Dean College of Education .... Dr. Ann E. AUSTIN
54 Dean College of Engineering .... Dr. Leo C. KEMPEL
63 Dean College Human Medicine .... Dr. Aron SOUSA
82 Dean James Madison College .... Dr. Cameron G. THIES
61 Dean College of Law .... Linda S. GREENE
81 Int Dean Lyman Briggs College .... Dr. Kendra S. CHERUVELIL
64 Dean College of Music .... Mr. James B. FORGER
65 Dean College Natural Science .... Dr. Phillip M. DUXBURY
66 Dean College of Nursing .... Dr. Randolph RASCH
63 Dean Col Osteopathic Medicine .... Dr. Andrea AMALFITANO
83 Dean College of Social Sciences .... Dr. Mary A. FINN
74 Dean College Veterinary Medicine .... Dr. Birgit PUSCHNER
82 Dean Intl Studies & Programs .... Dr. Steven D. HANSON
04 Executive Asst to President .... Ms. Jesselyn NELSON
100 Chief of Staff .... Mr. Michael ZEIG
09 Director of Institutional Research .... Ms. Bethan CANTWELL
102 Dir Foundation/Corporate Relations .... Ms. Deepa SRIKANTA
105 Director Web Services .... Mr. Randy BROWN
30 Chief Development Officer .... Vacant
39 Dir Resident Life/Student Housing .... Mr. Ray Frederick GASSER
44 Director Annual Giving .... Ms. Kathleen DENEAU

96 Director University Services .... Ms. Kristin DEMIR
104 Director Study Abroad .... Dr. Opal LEEMAN BARTZIS

Michigan Technological University (A)

1400 Townsend Drive, Houghton MI 49931-1295

County: Houghton FICE Identification: 002292

Unit ID: 171128

Telephone: (906) 487-1885 Carnegie Class: DU-Higher

FAX Number: (906) 487-2935 Calendar System: Semester

URL: www.mtu.edu

Established: 1885 Annual Undergrad Tuition & Fees (In-State): $16,436

Enrollment: 6,873 Coed

Affiliation or Control: State IRS Status: 501(c)3

Highest Offering: Doctorate

Accreditation: HLC, CONST, MT

01 President .... Dr. Richard J. KOUBEK
05 Provost/Sr Vice Pres Acad Affairs ..... Dr. Jacqueline E. HUNTOON
86 Vice Pres Governmental Relations .... Mr. William R. KORDENBROCK
46 Vice President for Research .... Dr. David D. REED
84 Vice Pres Univ Relations/Enrollment .... Dr. John B. LEHMAN
111 VP Advancement & Alumni Engagement .... Dr. Bill ROBERTS
32 Dean of Students/Assoc Provost .... Dr. Bonnie B. GORMAN
10 CFO/Senior VP for Administration .... Ms. Susan E. KERRY
92 Dean Pavlis Honors College .... Dr. Lorelle MEADOWS
26 Asst VP Univ Mktg/Communications .... Mr. Ian REPP
08 Director of the Library .... Mr. Joshua OLSON
09 Institutional Analysis .... Mr. Richard ELENICH
29 Asst VP of Alumni Engagement .... Ms. Brenda RUDIGER
06 Registrar .... Ms. Theresa K. JACQUES
07 Director Undergraduate Recruitment .... Ms. Allison A. CARTER
15 Director Human Resources .... Ms. Renee HILLER
37 Director of Financial Aid .... Mr. Joe J. COOPER
36 Director Career Services .... Ms. Beth WILLIAMS
18 Exec Director Facilities Management .... Vacant
114 Exec Director Budget and Planning .... Ms. Debbie L. SHELDON
38 Director Counseling Services .... Ms. Amber BENNETT
19 Director and Chief Public Safety .... Mr. Brian J. CADWELL
22 Exec Director Affirmative Programs .... Ms. Beth LUNDE-STOCKERO
96 Director of Purchasing .... Ms. Danielle CYRUS
58 Assoc Provost/Dean Graduate School .... Dr. Will CANTRELL
50 Dean School of Business & Economics ..... Dr. Dean L. JOHNSON
54 Dean College of Engineering .... Dr. Janet CALLAHAN
65 Dean School of Forestry .... Dr. Andrew J. STORER
49 Dean College of Sciences/Arts .... Dr. David HEMMER
77 Dean College of Computing .... Dr. Adrienne MINERICK
13 Chief Information Officer .... Mr. Joshua OLSON
41 Athletic Director .... Dr. Suzanne SANREGRET
25 Chief Contracts/Grants Admin .... Ms. Julie SEPPALA
39 Chief Housing Officer/Director .... Mr. Travis L. PIERCE
04 Dir Presidential Communications .... Ms. Heather L. HERMAN
28 Director of Diversity/Asst Dean .... Ms. Kellie RAFFAELLI
43 General Counsel .... Ms. Sarah H. SCHULTE

Mid Michigan College (B)

1375 S Clare Avenue, Harrison MI 48625-9447

County: Clare FICE Identification: 006768

Unit ID: 171155

Telephone: (989) 386-6622 Carnegie Class: Assoc/MT-VT-Mix Trad/Non

FAX Number: (989) 386-2411 Calendar System: Semester

URL: www.midmich.edu

Established: 1965 Annual Undergrad Tuition & Fees (In-District): $7,364

Enrollment: 3,291 Coed

Affiliation or Control: State/Local IRS Status: 501(c)3

Highest Offering: Associate Degree

Accreditation: HLC, MAC, PTAA, RAD

01 President .... Mr. Tim HOOD
05 VP of Academic Affairs & Outreach .... Dr. Scott MERTES
10 VP of Finance & Administration .... Ms. Lillian FRICK
32 Vice President of Student Services .... Dr. Matt MILLER
102 Exec Director of the Mid Foundation .... Mr. Thomas OLVER
103 Assoc VP Economic & Workforce Dev .... Mr. Scott GOVITZ
15 Associate VP Human Resources .... Ms. Lori FASSETT
09 Asst VP Institutional Research .... Dr. Peter VELGUTH
04 Exec Asst to President & Trustees .... Ms. Amy LINCE

Monroe County Community College (C)

1555 S Raisinville Road, Monroe MI 48161-9746

County: Monroe FICE Identification: 002294

Unit ID: 171225

Telephone: (734) 242-7300 Carnegie Class: Assoc/MT-VT-Mix Trad/Non

FAX Number: (734) 242-9711 Calendar System: Semester

URL: www.monroeccc.edu

Established: 1964 Annual Undergrad Tuition & Fees (In-District): $5,600

Enrollment: 2,302 Coed

Affiliation or Control: Local IRS Status: 170(c)1

Highest Offering: Associate Degree

Accreditation: HLC, ADNUR, COARC, NAEYC

01 President .... Dr. Kojo QUARTEY
05 Vice President of Instruction .... Dr. Grace B. YACKEE
10 Vice Pres of Admin .... Ms. Suzanne M. WETZEL
32 Vice Pres Stdnt Success/Enroll Mgmt .... Mr. Scott BEHRENS
72 Dean of Applied Sci & Eng Tech .... Mr. Parmeshwar COOMAR
50 Dean of Business .... Mr. Leon LETTER
76 Dean of Health Sciences .... Ms. Kimberly LINDQUIST
79 Dean of Humanities/Social Science .... Vacant
81 Dean of Science/Mathematics .... Mr. Kevin COOPER
06 Registrar .... Ms. Tracy VOGT
07 Director of Admissions/Guidance .... Mr. Ryan RAFKO
88 Director of Upward Bound .... Mr. Anthony QUINN
88 Director of Respiratory Therapy .... Mr. Ijaz AHMED
21 Director of Financial Services .... Mr. Andrew FISCHER
18 Director Physical Plant .... Mr. Jack BURNS
109 Dir Auxiliary Services/Purchasing .... Ms. Kelly HEINZERLING
14 Director Data Processing Services .... Mr. James A. ROSS
37 Director of Financial Aid .... Ms. Valerie CULLER
36 Dir Business Devel/Employment Svcs .... Mr. Barry C. KINSEY
51 Director of Lifelong Learning .... Ms. Tina PILLARELLI
13 Manager Information Services .... Mr. Brian K. LAY
26 Director of Marketing/Communication .... Mr. Joseph VERKENNES
15 Director of Human Resources .... Ms. Linda TORBET
04 Executive Asst to President .... Ms. Penny R. DORCEY
09 Dir Inst Research/Eval/Accred .... Ms. Quri WYGONIK
102 Exec Director Foundation .... Mr. Joshua MYERS
19 Chief of Safety Services .... Mr. Charles ABEL

Montcalm Community College (D)

2800 College Drive, Sidney MI 48885-9723

County: Montcalm FICE Identification: 002295

Unit ID: 171234

Telephone: (989) 328-2111 Carnegie Class: Assoc/MT-VT-High Trad

FAX Number: (989) 328-2950 Calendar System: Semester

URL: www.montcalm.edu

Established: 1965 Annual Undergrad Tuition & Fees (In-District): $7,710

Enrollment: 1,414 Coed

Affiliation or Control: Local IRS Status: 501(c)3

Highest Offering: Associate Degree

Accreditation: HLC, MAC

01 President .... Dr. Stacy YOUNG
05 Vice Pres for Academic Affairs .... Mr. Robert SPOHR
10 VP Administrative Services .... Ms. Connie STEWART
102 Exec Dir Inst Advance/Foundation .... Ms. Lisa LUND
32 Dean Student & Enrollment Svcs .... Ms. Debra ALEXANDER
37 Director of Financial Aid .... Ms. Jessica HERRICK
13 Director Information Tech Svcs .... Mr. David KOHN
09 Research Analyst .... Mr. Vladimir EDELMAN
26 Communications Director .... Ms. Shelly SPRINGBORN
15 Director of Human Resources .... Ms. Riki JENSEN
21 Director of Accounting .... Ms. Kire WIERDA
18 Director of Facilities .... Mr. Taylor MALE
66 Dean of Nursing & Health Careers .... Ms. Danielle ANDERSON
07 Recruitment Director .... Ms. Emily DIMET
88 Dean Industrial Ed & Workforce Trng .... Ms. Susan HATTO
103 Director Workforce Development .... Ms. Susan HATTO
08 Librarian .... Ms. Katie ARWOOD

Moody Theological Seminary-Michigan (E)

41550 E Ann Arbor Trail, Plymouth MI 48170-4308

Telephone: (734) 207-9581 FICE Identification: 031353

Accreditation: &HLC, THEOL

† Regional accreditation is carried under the parent institution Moody Bible Institute, Chicago, IL.

Mott Community College (F)

1401 E Court Street, Flint MI 48503-2089

County: Genesee FICE Identification: 002261

Unit ID: 169275

Telephone: (810) 762-0200 Carnegie Class: Assoc/HT-High Trad

FAX Number: (810) 762-0257 Calendar System: Semester

URL: www.mcc.edu

Established: 1923 Annual Undergrad Tuition & Fees (In-District): $5,149

Enrollment: 5,920 Coed

Affiliation or Control: Local IRS Status: 501(c)3

Highest Offering: Associate Degree

Accreditation: HLC, ACBSP, ADNUR, COARC, DA, DH, NAEYC, OTA, PTAA

01 President .... Dr. Beverly WALKER-GRIFFEA
32 VP Stdnt Success/Int VP Acad Affs .... Mr. Jason WILSON
10 Chief Financial Officer .... Mr. Larry GAWTHROP
111 Assoc VP Institutional Advancement .... Mr. Dale WEIGHILL
15 Associate Vice President of HR .... Mr. Philip ESPINOSA
103 Assoc VP Workforce & Economic Dev ..... Mr. Robert MATTHEWS
37 Exec Dir Student Financial Svcs .... Mr. Richard BORUSZEWSKI
20 Exec Dir of Academic Operations .... Ms. Dolores SHARPE
84 Exec Dir of Enrollment Management .... Mr. Jon CALDERWOOD
124 Dean Enrollment Mgmt & Retention .... Mr. Chris ENGLE
81 Dean of Math & Science .... Dr. Charles WADE
76 Dean of Health Sciences .... Dr. Rebecca MYSZENSKI
83 Dean Social Sciences & Fine Arts .... Ms. Jennifer FILLION
50 Dean of Business .... Mr. Stephen SHUBERT
72 Dean of Technology .... Dr. Mark BANNATYNE
13 Chief Technology Officer .... Ms. Cheryl SHELTON
06 Registrar .... Ms. Michele TRAVER
36 Supervisor Student Employment Svcs .... Mr. Aron GERICS
62 Executive Director Library .... Mrs. Jill SODT
18 Int Exec Director Physical Plant .... Mr. Rodney WHITNEY
07 Director of Admissions .... Ms. Regina BROOMFIELD
41 Director Athletics/Campus Rec .... Mr. Al PERRY
09 Exec Dir Institutional Research .... Vacant
35 Student Life Coordinator .... Ms. Alexandria DOWDALL
96 Director of Purchasing .... Ms. Jody MICHAEL
04 Executive Asst to President .... Ms. Melody BARTHOLOMEW
101 Board Relations Coordinator .... Mr. Michael SIMON

Muskegon Community College (G)

221 S Quarterline Road, Muskegon MI 49442-1493

County: Muskegon FICE Identification: 002297

Unit ID: 171304

Telephone: (231) 773-9131 Carnegie Class: Assoc/MT-VT-Mix Trad/Non

FAX Number: (231) 777-0440 Calendar System: Semester

URL: www.muskegoncc.edu

Established: 1926 Annual Undergrad Tuition & Fees (In-District): $10,750

Enrollment: 3,456 Coed

Affiliation or Control: Local IRS Status: Exempt

Highest Offering: Associate Degree

Accreditation: HLC, ADNUR, COARC, MAC

01 President .... Dr. Dale K. NESBARY
03 Provost/Executive Vice President .... Dr. John SELMON
05 VP for Academic Affairs .... Ms. Kelley CONRAD
10 VP Finance/Chief Advancement Ofcr .... Mr. Kenneth LONG
32 Dean of Student Services .... Ms. Sally BIRKAM
20 Dean of Instruction & Assessment ...... Dr. Edward BREITENBACH
31 Dean of Community Outreach .... Ms. Trynette Lottie HARPS
06 Registrar .... Mr. Aaron RICHMAN
13 Chief Information Officer .... Dr. Steven WILSON
37 Director Financial Aid .... Mr. Bruce WIERDA
09 Dir Institutional Research & Grants .... Mr. Eduardo BEDOYA
45 Director of Strategic Initiatives .... Ms. Tina DEE
15 Executive Director of HR .... Ms. Kristine ANDERSON
41 Dean of College Svcs & AD .... Mr. Marty MCDERMOTT
18 Physical Plant Director .... Mr. David STURGEON
29 Alumni & Donor Relations Manager .... Ms. Rachel STEWART
04 Executive Assistant to President .... Ms. Cindy S. DEBOEF

North Central Michigan College (H)

1515 Howard Street, Petoskey MI 49770-8717

County: Emmet FICE Identification: 002299

Unit ID: 171395

Telephone: (231) 348-6600 Carnegie Class: Assoc/HT-Mix Trad/Non

FAX Number: (231) 348-6628 Calendar System: Semester

URL: www.ncmich.edu

Established: 1958 Annual Undergrad Tuition & Fees (In-District): $6,776

Enrollment: 1,748 Coed

Affiliation or Control: Local IRS Status: 501(c)3

Highest Offering: Associate Degree

Accreditation: HLC, EMT

01 President .... Dr. David R. FINLEY
05 VP Academic Affairs .... Dr. Stephen STROM
10 VP of Finance & Facilities .... Dr. Tom ZEIDEL
32 VP of Student Services .... Renee DEYOUNG
26 VP of Marketing .... Carol LAENEN
102 Executive Director Foundation .... Chelsea PLATTE
08 Librarian .... Kendra LAKE
37 Director of Financial Aid .... Katie MALONE
18 Director of Physical Plant .... Ernst RUSCHE
84 Dir Enrollment Services/Registrar .... Joseph BALINSKI
21 Director of Business Services .... Troy SLATER
39 Director of Campus Housing .... Leon NASH
15 Director of Human Resources .... Lynn ECKERLE
40 Bookstore Manager .... Debbie MORRISON
49 Dean Liberal Arts .... Dr. Sara GLASGOW
66 Dean Nurs/Allied Hlth/Sci .... Dr. Jamie PAGELS
50 Dean Business & Adjunct Faculty .... Michele ANDREWS
07 Director of Student Outreach .... Corey LANSING
13 Director of Information Services .... Vacant
88 Director of Resource Center .... Dallas CULVAHOUSE
04 Executive Asst to President .... Lea DIETZEL
06 Registrar .... Joseph BALINSKI
41 Athletic Director .... Ashley ANTONISHEN

Northern Michigan University (I)

1401 Presque Isle Avenue, Marquette MI 49855-5301

County: Marquette FICE Identification: 002301

Unit ID: 171456

Telephone: (906) 227-1000 Carnegie Class: Masters/M

FAX Number: (906) 227-2204 Calendar System: Semester

URL: www.nmu.edu

Established: 1899 Annual Undergrad Tuition & Fees (In-State): $12,402

Enrollment: 7,368 Coed

Affiliation or Control: State IRS Status: 501(c)3

Highest Offering: Doctorate

Accreditation: HLC, CAATE, CAEP, CGTECH, DMOLS, MLTAD, MT, MUS, NURSE, RAD, SURGT, SW

01 Interim President .... Dr. Kerri SCHUILING
05 Provost/VP Academic Affairs .... Vacant
10 VP for Finance & Administration .... Mr. R. Gavin LEACH
102 CEO NMU Foundation .... Mr. Brad CANALE
09 Asst Provost/Dir of Inst Research .... Mr. Jason NICHOLAS
106 VP Extended Lrng/Cmty Engagement .. Dr. Steve VANDENAVOND
20 Asc Provost Acad Affs/Undergrad Pgm .... Dr. Dale P. KAPLA
58 Dean Graduate Education .... Dr. Lisa ECKERT
08 Dean Library/Instructional Support .... Dr. Leslie A. WARREN
32 Assistant VP/Dean of Students .... Dr. Christine G. GREER
49 Dean of Arts & Sciences .... Dr. Rob WINN
50 Dean Walker L Cisler Col Bus .... Prof. Carol JOHNSON
72 Dean Col of Technology/Occ Science . Dr. Steve VANDENAVOND
06 Registrar .... Mr. Josh SANTIAGO

45 Asst to Pres Strategic Initiatives ... Ms. Cindy L. PAAVOLA
36 Dir of Acad & Career Advisement ... Mr. James G. GADZINSKI
37 Director of Financial Aid ... Mr. Michael R. ROTUNDO
38 Director Counseling Center ... Vacant
88 Director Glenn T Seaborg Center ... Mr. Chris STANDERFORD
41 Athletic Director ... Mr. Forrest KARR
19 Dir Public Safety/Police Services ... Mr. Michael J. BATH
39 Director Housing/Residence Life ... Ms. Catherine HARDENBERGH
07 Director of Admissions ... Ms. Gerri L. DANIELS
23 Chief of Staff/Physician ... Dr. Christopher KIRKPATRICK
15 Director of Human Resources ... Ms. Rhea DEVER
26 Asst VP Marketing & Communications ... Dr. Derek HALL
92 Director of Honors Program ... Dr. David H. WOOD
24 Director Broadcast & AV Services ... Mr. Eric L. SMITH
29 Exec Dir Alumni Ops/Annual Giving ... Ms. Robyn L. STILLE
40 Bookstore Manager ... Mr. Paul WRIGHT
18 Associate VP Eng & Plan/Facilities ... Ms. Kathy A. RICHARDS
13 Chief Technology Officer ... Mr. David W. MAKI
96 Manager of Purchasing ... Mr. Joseph OMBRELLO
86 Exec Dir of BOT & Govt Relations ... Ms. Deanna HEMMILA
04 Executive Assistant to President ... Ms. Laura GLOVER
101 Secretary Board of Trustees ... Ms. Cathy ANDREW
22 Dir Affirmative Action/EEO ... Ms. Janet KOSKI
53 Dean Teacher Educ/Dir of Educ ... Dr. Joe LUBIG
28 Chief Diversity Officer ... Vacant
103 Director Workforce Development ... Ms. Stephanie ZADROGA-LANGLOIS
105 Web Systems Director ... Mr. Eric JOHNSON
25 Director Grants & Contracts ... Vacant
104 Director International Programs ... Ms. Diana VREELAND
30 Director of Development ... Ms. Jane SURRELL
44 Assoc Director Annual Giving ... Mr. Andrew HILL

Northwestern Michigan College (A)

1701 E Front Street, Traverse City MI 49686-3061
County: Grand Traverse | FICE Identification: 002302
Unit ID: 171483
Telephone: (231) 995-1000 | Carnegie Class: Bac/Assoc-Assoc Dom
FAX Number: (231) 995-1339 | Calendar System: Semester
URL: www.nmc.edu
Established: 1951 | Annual Undergrad Tuition & Fees (In-District): $8,280
Enrollment: 3,278 | Coed
Affiliation or Control: Local | IRS Status: 501(c)3
Highest Offering: Baccalaureate
Accreditation: HLC, ACFEI, ADNUR, DA, PNUR, SURGT

01 President ... Dr. Nick NISSLEY
100 Exec Dir Pres Ofc & Board Ops ... Ms. Lynne M. MORITZ
05 VP for Educational Services ... Dr. Stephen N. SICILIANO
10 Special Assistant to the President ... Ms. Vicki COOK
15 Associate VP of Human Resources ... Mr. Mark LIEBLING
13 VP for Student Svcs & Technology ... Mr. Todd NEIBAUER
102 Assoc VP of Resource Dev & Found ... Ms. Rebecca M. TEAHEN
88 Exec Dir of Dennos Museum Center ... Mr. Craig A. HADLEY
107 VP Lifelong/Professional Learning ... Ms. Marguerite C. COTTO
75 Dir of Bus Dev/Marine Center ... Mr. Ed BAILEY
88 Director of Aviation ... Mr. Alex BLOYE
29 Director Alumni Relations ... Vacant
32 Dean of Students ... Ms. Lisa THOMAS
37 Director of Financial Aid ... Ms. Linda BERLIN
90 Director of Systems and LAN Mgmt ... Mr. Dan WASSON
50 Director of the Hagerty Center ... Mr. Chad SCHENKELBERGER
20 Dir Academic Business/Affairs Div ... Mr. Brian HEFFNER
08 Director of Library Services ... Ms. Kerrey WOUGHTER
92 Director of Learning Services ... Ms. Kari L. KAHLER
21 Controller ... Mr. Troy KIERCZYNSKI
24 Director Educational Media Tech ... Ms. Terri GUSTAFSON
26 Exec Dir of PR/Marketing/Comm ... Ms. Diana FAIRBANKS
56 Director Extended Educ Services ... Ms. Laura MATCHETT
18 Director of Campus Services ... Mr. Paul PERRY
12 Supt Great Lakes Maritime Academy ... RAdm. Gerard ACHENBACH, USMS
06 Registrar ... Ms. Cindy DEEMER
07 Director of Admissions ... Ms. Cathryn CLAERHOUT
09 Dir Research Planning Effectiveness ... Ms. Joy EVANS GOODCHILD
30 Director of Development ... Ms. Paris MORSE
88 Director of Water Studies Institute ... Mr. Hans VANSUMEREN
64 Director of Music Programs ... Mr. Jeffrey COBB
104 Director of International Services ... Mr. Jim BENSLEY
66 Director of Nursing Programs ... Ms. Amy JONES
23 Director of Health Services ... Ms. Renee R. JACOBSON
88 Director of Police Academy ... Mr. Gail KUROWSKI
39 Associate Dean of Campus & Res Life ... Dr. Marcus BENNETT
12 Director Great Lakes Culinary Inst ... Ms. Les ECKERT
36 Director of Advising ... Ms. Lindsey DICKINSON

Northwood University (B)

4000 Whiting Drive, Midland MI 48640-2398
County: Midland | FICE Identification: 004072
Unit ID: 171492
Telephone: (989) 837-4200 | Carnegie Class: Spec-4-yr-Bus
FAX Number: (989) 837-4111 | Calendar System: Semester
URL: www.northwood.edu
Established: 1959 | Annual Undergrad Tuition & Fees: $29,480
Enrollment: 2,541 | Coed
Affiliation or Control: Independent Non-Profit | IRS Status: 501(c)3
Highest Offering: Doctorate
Accreditation: HLC, ACBSP

01 President ... Dr. Kent MACDONALD
05 VP of Academics and Provost ... Dr. Kristin STEHOUWER
10 VP Finance & Administration ... Mr. Chip REEVES
88 Director of The McNair Center ... Dr. Timothy G. NASH
84 VP Enrollment & Marketing ... Mr. Chip REEVES
111 VP Advancement/Business Dev ... Mr. Justin W. MARSHALL
26 Senior Communications Officer ... Ms. Rachel VALDISERRI
51 Associate Dean Adult Degree Program ... Vacant
32 Dean of Student Affairs ... Mr. Andy CRIPE
96 Director of Asset Management ... Mr. David L. BENDER
06 Registrar ... Dr. Marisa HERNANDEZ
07 Director of Admissions ... Ms. Missy DEBOER
37 Financial Aid Director ... Mr. Mark A. MARTIN
15 Dir of Human Resources & Title IX ... Ms. Pamela L. CHRISTIE
21 Business Office Accountant ... Ms. Carrie A. PICKVET
29 Executive Director Alumni Relations ... Ms. Julie L. ADAMCZYK
19 Director Security and Safety ... Ms. April OWENS
39 Director Student & Residence Life ... Mr. Justin THOMASON

Oakland Community College (C)

2480 Opdyke Road, Bloomfield Hills MI 48304-2266
County: Oakland | FICE Identification: 002303
Unit ID: 171535
Telephone: (248) 341-2000 | Carnegie Class: Assoc/HT-High Non
FAX Number: (248) 341-2099 | Calendar System: Semester
URL: www.oaklandcc.edu
Established: 1964 | Annual Undergrad Tuition & Fees (In-District): $4,712
Enrollment: 14,511 | Coed
Affiliation or Control: State/Local | IRS Status: 501(c)3
Highest Offering: Associate Degree
Accreditation: HLC, ACFEI, ADNUR, COARC, DH, DMS, MAC, RAD, SURGT

01 Chancellor ... Mr. Peter PROVENZANO, JR.
05 Provost ... Dr. Jennifer I. BERNE
11 Vice Chanc Administrative Services ... Ms. Bobbie REMIAS
32 Vice Chanc for Student Services ... Ms. Lori PRZYMUSINSKI
15 Vice Chancellor for HR & DEI ... Mr. Andre' POPLAR
13 Vice Chanc Info Technologies/CIO ... Mr. Robert MONTGOMERY
26 Vice Chanc Marketing/ Communications ... Ms. Elizabeth R. SCHNELL
43 Vice Chanc for Legal Affairs ... Ms. Eileen K. HUSBAND
111 Vice Chancellor for Advancement ... Mr. Daniel J. JENUWINE
20 Associate Provost ... Mr. Joseph L. PETROSKY
04 Exec Administrator to Chancellor ... Ms. Cherie A. FOSTER
27 Dir of Marketing & Comm ... Ms. Shelia ACKER
35 Dean of Student Services ... Mr. Jahquan C. HAWKINS
35 Dean of Student Services ... Mr. Robert T. SPANN
35 Dean of Student Services ... Ms. Stacey N. JACKSON
66 Academic Dean Nursing/Health Prof ... Ms. Mary E. MILES
14 Exec Dir IT Infrastructure ... Mr. Chuck S. FLAGG
06 Registrar ... Mr. Stephen M. LINDEN
18 Director Physical Facilities ... Mr. Daniel P. CHEREWICK
19 Chief of Public Safety ... Mr. Paul J. MATYNKA
21 Controller ... Ms. Sharon K. CONVERSE
114 Director Budget & Financial Plng ... Mrs. Renee OSZUST
102 Exec Director OCC Foundation ... Mr. Daniel J. JENUWINE
36 Director of Career Svcs & Coop Ed ... Ms. Donna L. DUHAME-SCHMIDT
41 Athletic Director ... Ms. Jamie L. CORONA
96 Dir Purchasing/Auxiliary Svcs ... Ms. Sarah L. ROWLEY
37 Director Financial Res/Scholarships ... Ms. Wilma B. PORTER
81 Academic Dean Math & Sciences ... Mr. Ken M. WILLIAMS
80 Academic Dean Public Services/CREST ... Mr. David F. CECI
62 Academic Dean Learning Resources ... Ms. Mary Ann SHEBLE
83 Academic Dean Soc Sci & Human Svcs ... Mr. Kevin BRATTON
79 Academic Dean Comm/Art/Humanities ... Ms. Cindy L. CARBONE
89 Academic Dean College Readiness ... Ms. Beverly J. STANBROUGH
50 Acad Dean Bus & Info Technologies ... Mr. Tom M. HENDRICKS
88 Academic Dean EMIT ... Ms. Jolene J. CHAPMAN
106 Academic Dean of Distance Learning ... Ms. Kayla S. LEBLANC
88 Foundation Coordinator ... Ms. Candy GEETER
88 Director Law Enforcement Training ... Mr. David F. CECI
07 Director of Admissions ... Vacant
09 Chief Strategy Officer ... Dr. Steven M. SIMPSON
86 Director Government Relations ... Ms. Eunice M. JEFFRIES

Oakland Community College Auburn Hills (D)

2900 Featherstone Road, Auburn Hills MI 48326-2845
Telephone: (248) 232-4100 | Identification: 770281
Accreditation: &HLC, EMT

Oakland Community College Highland Lakes (E)

7350 Cooley Lake Road, Waterford MI 48327-4187
Telephone: (248) 942-3100 | Identification: 770285
Accreditation: &HLC

Oakland Community College Orchard Ridge (F)

27055 Orchard Lake Road, Farmington Hills MI 48334-4579
Telephone: (248) 522-3400 | Identification: 770282
Accreditation: &HLC

Oakland Community College Royal Oak (G)

739 South Washington Avenue, Royal Oak MI 48067-3898
Telephone: (248) 246-2400 | Identification: 770283
Accreditation: &HLC

Oakland Community College Southfield (H)

22322 Rutland Drive, Southfield MI 48075-4793
Telephone: (248) 341-2000 | Identification: 770284
Accreditation: &HLC

Oakland University (I)

371 Wilson Boulevard, Rochester MI 48309-4400
County: Oakland | FICE Identification: 002307
Unit ID: 171571
Telephone: (248) 370-2100 | Carnegie Class: DU-Higher
FAX Number: N/A | Calendar System: Semester
URL: www.oakland.edu
Established: 1957 | Annual Undergrad Tuition & Fees (In-State): $13,934
Enrollment: 18,552 | Coed
Affiliation or Control: State | IRS Status: 501(c)3
Highest Offering: Doctorate
Accreditation: HLC, ANEST, CACREP, CAEP, DANCE, MED, MUS, NURSE, PH, PTA, RAD, SPAA, SW, THEA

01 President ... Dr. Ora PESCOVITZ
05 Sr VP Academic Affairs/Provost ... Dr. Britt RIOS-ELLIS
32 VP Stdnt Affs/Chief Diversity Ofcr ... Mr. Glenn MCINTOSH
111 VP University Advancement ... Mr. Michael WESTFALL
10 VP Finance & Administration ... Mr. John W. BEAGHAN
86 VP Government & Comm Relations ... Ms. Rochelle A. BLACK
100 Chief of Staff ... Mr. Josh MERCHANT
12 Executive Director Outreach ... Ms. Julie DICHTEL
66 Dean School of Nursing ... Dr. Judy A. DIDION
54 Dean Engineering & Computer Science ... Dr. Louay M. CHAMRA
76 Dean School Health Sciences ... Dr. Kevin A. BALL
53 Dean Educ & Human Services ... Dr. Jon MARGERUM-LEYS
49 Dean College Arts & Sciences ... Dr. Kevin J. CORCORAN
50 Dean School of Business Admin ... Dr. Michael A. MAZZEO
63 Dean School of Medicine ... Dr. Duane MEZWA
08 Dean University Library ... Ms. Polly BORUFF-JONES
20 Associate Provost ... Dr. Anne HITT
46 VP for Research ... Dr. David A. STONE
24 Mgr Classroom Support/Tech Service ... Mr. John J. REESER
20 Asst VP Academic Affairs ... Ms. Peggy S. COOKE
88 Director Center for Excellence ... Dr. Judith ABLESER
88 Dir Eye Research Institute ... Dr. Frank GIBLIN
88 Director FAJRI ... Dr. Sayed NASSAR
21 Assoc VP Finance & Administration ... Mr. Thomas P. LEMARBE
18 Assoc VP Facilities Management ... Ms. Patricia A. ENGLE
15 VP Human Resources ... Vacant
102 AVP Princ Gifts/Campaign Strategy ... Ms. Alison K. GAUDREAU
35 Dean of Students ... Mr. Michael WADSWORTH
19 Chief of Police ... Mr. Mark B. GORDON
06 Registrar ... Ms. Tricia WESTERGAARD
44 Dir Annual Giving Program ... Ms. Kelly N. BRAULT
37 Director of Financial Aid ... Ms. Nancy FETZER
29 Sr Dir of Engagement ... Ms. Sue HELDEROP
26 VP Communications & Marketing ... Mr. John O. YOUNG
41 Athletics Director ... Mr. Steven WATERFIELD
16 AVP Academic Human Resources ... Ms. Joi M. CUNNINGHAM
39 Director of University Housing ... Mr. James R. ZENTMEYER
36 Senior Director Career Services ... Mr. Wayne J. THIBODEAU
38 Director Counseling Center ... Dr. David J. SCHWARTZ
85 Director International Students ... Mr. David J. ARCHBOLD
22 Director Disability Support Svcs ... Mr. Sarah GUADALUPE
96 Director of Purchasing ... Ms. Paula S. REYES
43 Interim VP General Counsel ... Mr. Boyd A. FARNAM
13 Interim Chief Information Officer ... Ms. Lori TIRPAK
84 VP Enrollment Management ... Ms. Dawn M. AUBRY
58 Dean Graduate Education ... Dr. Brandy RANDALL
09 Director of Institutional Research ... Ms. Song YAN
104 Exec Director Global Engagement ... Ms. Rosemary MAX
106 Director of e-learning ... Dr. Shaun A. MOORE
114 Director Internal Audit ... Mr. David P. VARTANIAN

Olivet College (J)

320 S Main Street, Olivet MI 49076-9406
County: Eaton | FICE Identification: 002308
Unit ID: 171599
Telephone: (269) 749-7000 | Carnegie Class: Bac-Diverse
FAX Number: (269) 749-7600 | Calendar System: Semester
URL: www.olivetcollege.edu
Established: 1844 | Annual Undergrad Tuition & Fees: $30,126
Enrollment: 1,023 | Coed
Affiliation or Control: Independent Non-Profit | IRS Status: 501(c)3
Highest Offering: Master's
Accreditation: HLC, NURSE

01 President ... Dr. Steven M. COREY
05 Provost and Dean of the College ... Dr. Maria DAVIS
10 Vice President and CFO ... Mr. Mark DERUITER
07 Vice Pres Admissions ... Mr. Doug KELLAR
32 Vice Pres/Dean Student Life ... Dr. Amy POPP-RADFORD
111 Vice Pres Advancement ... Ms. Vicki STOUFFER
13 Asst Vice President Technology ... Mr. Suresh ACHARYA
06 Registrar ... Ms. Leslie SULLIVAN
41 Athletic Director ... Ms. Haley HUNNEWELL
42 Director of Campus Ministries ... Mr. Michael F. FALES
36 Dir Career Services Network ... Vacant
37 Director of Student Financial Aid ... Ms. Libby JEAN
18 Director of Facilities ... Mr. Billy HASTINGS
94 Director of Women's Resource Center ... Ms. Cynthia NOYES
39 Student Housing ... Ms. Shawn HAGADON
15 Director of Human Resources ... Mrs. Terri GLASGOW

29 Director of Alumni Engagement ....Ms. Beth ROMEO
04 Executive Asst to President ....Ms. Barbara SPENCER
08 Head Librarian ....Ms. Julia FALES
19 Director Security/Safety ....Mr. Phil REED
100 Chief of Staff ....Mr. Ryan SHOCKEY
26 Chief Public Relations Officer ....Ms. Michele MCCAULEY
28 Director of Diversity ....Dr. Linda LOGAN

Puritan Reformed Theological Seminary (A)

2965 Leonard Street NE, Grand Rapids MI 49525
County: Kent Identification: 667099
Telephone: (616) 977-0599 Carnegie Class: Not Classified
FAX Number: (616) 285-3246 Calendar System: Semester
URL: www.prts.edu
Established: 1995 Annual Graduate Tuition & Fees: N/A
Enrollment: N/A Coed
Affiliation or Control: Independent Non-Profit IRS Status: 501(c)3
Highest Offering: Doctorate; No Undergraduates
Accreditation: THEOL

01 President ....Dr. Joel R. BEEKE
05 VP for Academics/Academic Dean ....Dr. Michael BARRETT
10 Vice President for Operations ....Mr. Henk KLEYN
32 Dean of Students/Spiritual Form ....Dr. Mark KELDERMAN
06 Registrar/Director of Admissions ....Dr. Jonathon BEEKE
04 Administrative Asst to President ....Ms. Ann C. DYKEMA
26 Chief Public Relations/Marketing ....Mr. Chris HANNA
08 Head Librarian ....Mrs. Laura LADWIG
106 Dir Online Education/E-learning ....Mr. Chris ENGELSMA
13 IT Director ....Mr. Seth HUCKSTEAD
24 Video Producer & Editor ....Mr. Darryl BRADFORD

Rochester University (B)

800 W Avon Road, Rochester Hills MI 48307-2764
County: Oakland FICE Identification: 002288
Unit ID: 170967
Telephone: (248) 218-2000 Carnegie Class: Bac-Diverse
FAX Number: (248) 487-9485 Calendar System: Semester
URL: https://rochesteru.edu/
Established: 1959 Annual Undergrad Tuition & Fees: $24,720
Enrollment: 1,231 Coed
Affiliation or Control: Independent Non-Profit IRS Status: 501(c)3
Highest Offering: Master's
Accreditation: HLC, NURSE

01 President ....Dr. Brian L. STOGNER
05 Provost ....Dr. Remylin BRUDER
101 Sr VP/Special Asst to President ....Mr. Klint A. PLEASANT
10 Exec VP/Chief Financial Officer ....Mr. Thomas D. RELLINGER
07 Vice President Admissions ....Mr. Scott SAMUELS
30 Vice Pres Development/Alumni Rels ....Mr. Steve MOORE
21 Controller ....Ms. Susan IDE
18 Director of Operations ....Mr. Jacob LAWLESS
50 Dir School of Business/Prof Studies ....Vacant
79 Dir School of Humanities ....Dr. Catherine PARKER
15 Director of Human Resources ....Mrs. Charity DAVIDSON
26 Dir of Communication Services ....Mr. Elliot JONES
32 Dean of Students ....Dr. Sharia HAYS
37 Director of Student Financial Svcs ....Mrs. Kara MILLER
08 Director of Library Services ....Mrs. Allison JIMENEZ
06 Registrar ....Ms. Rebekah PINCHBACK
108 Director of Assessment ....Dr. J. Mark MANRY
29 Director of Alumni ....Mr. Larry STEWART
121 Director of Advising ....Mrs. Debi RUTLEDGE
41 Director of Athletics ....Mr. Klint PLEASANT
42 Director of Spiritual Life ....Mr. Evan GREEN
19 Director of Safety & Security ....Mr. Jacob LAWLESS
13 Chief Information Technology Office ....Mr. Eric CAMPBELL
110 Director of Development ....Mrs. Jennifer PORTER
09 Director of Institutional Research ....Dr. Mark MANRY
104 GEO Coordinator ....Dr. Keith HUEY
53 Dir School of Education ....Dr. Melvin BLOHM
43 General Counsel ....Mr. Dennis VEARA
04 Admin Assistant to the President ....Mrs. Ginny A. MAY

Sacred Heart Major Seminary (C)

2701 Chicago Boulevard, Detroit MI 48206-1799
County: Wayne FICE Identification: 002313
Unit ID: 172033
Telephone: (313) 883-8501 Carnegie Class: Spec-4-yr-Faith
FAX Number: (313) 883-8685 Calendar System: Semester
URL: www.shms.edu
Established: 1919 Annual Undergrad Tuition & Fees: $21,107
Enrollment: 418 Coed
Affiliation or Control: Roman Catholic IRS Status: 501(c)3
Highest Offering: Master's
Accreditation: HLC, THEOL

01 Rector & President ....Rev. Stephen BURR
32 Vice Rector/Dean of Seminarians ....Rev. Charles FOX
05 Dean of Studies ....Rev. Timothy LABOE
73 Dean of the Inst for Lay Ministry ....Vacant
10 Director Finance/Treasurer ....Ms. Ann Marie CONNOLLY
06 Registrar ....Ms. Leslie JONES
35 Director Undergraduate Seminarians ....Rev. Clint MCDONELL
88 Graduate Spiritual Director ....Rev. Daniel TRAPP
08 Library Director ....Ms. Teresa LUBIENICKI
58 Dir Graduate Pastoral Formation ....Rev. Stephen PULLIS
111 Alumni Relations/Marketing ....Mrs. Emily BERSCHBACK
18 Facilities Director ....Mr. John DUNCAN
07 Director of Admissions ....Mr. Patrick CASSADY
106 Dir of Distance Ed/Online Learning ....Mr. Ryan CAHILL
58 Director of Graduate Seminarians ....Rev. Pieter VAN ROOYEN

Saginaw Chippewa Tribal College (D)

2274 Enterprise Drive, Mount Pleasant MI 48858-2335
County: Isabella FICE Identification: 037723
Unit ID: 441070
Telephone: (989) 317-4760 Carnegie Class: Tribal
FAX Number: (989) 317-4781 Calendar System: Semester
URL: www.sagchip.edu
Established: 1998 Annual Undergrad Tuition & Fees: $2,210
Enrollment: 96 Coed
Affiliation or Control: Tribal Control IRS Status: 501(c)3
Highest Offering: Associate Degree
Accreditation: HLC

01 President ....Ms. Carla SINEWAY
32 Dean of Student Services ....Ms. Amanda FLAUGHER
07 Admissions Officer/Registrar ....Ms. Jacqueline GRAVERATTE
09 Dean of Research ....Ms. Tracy REED
111 Dean of Institutional Advancement ....Ms. Gena QUALLS
05 Dean of Academics ....Ms. Mary PELCHER
04 Admin Assistant to the President ....Ms. Gladys GATES

Saginaw Valley State University (E)

7400 Bay Road, University Center MI 48710-0001
County: Saginaw FICE Identification: 002314
Unit ID: 172051
Telephone: (989) 964-4000 Carnegie Class: Masters/L
FAX Number: (989) 964-0180 Calendar System: Semester
URL: www.svsu.edu
Established: 1963 Annual Undergrad Tuition & Fees (In-State): $10,814
Enrollment: 8,028 Coed
Affiliation or Control: State IRS Status: 501(c)3
Highest Offering: Doctorate
Accreditation: HLC, CAEP, CEA, MT, MUS, NURSE, OT, SW

01 President ....Dr. Donald J. BACHAND
05 Provost/VP Academic Affairs ....Dr. Deborah R. HUNTLEY
10 Exec VP Admin & Business Affairs ....Mr. James G. MULADORE
29 Executive Director Alumni Relations ....Mr. James P. DWYER
32 Assoc Provost Student Affairs ....Vacant
28 Spec Asst to Pres Diversity Pgms ....Dr. Mamie T. THORNS
83 Assoc Dean Arts/Behavioral Sciences ....Dr. Carlos RAMET
49 Dean Arts/Behavioral Sciences ....Dr. Marc H. PERETZ
21 AVP Admin & Business Affairs/CBO ....Mr. Ronald E. PORTWINE
41 Athletic Director/AVP Legal Affairs ....Mr. John DECKER
114 AVP/Chief Budget Officer ....Ms. Susan L. CRANE
43 General Counsel ....Ms. Ellen E. CRANE
13 Exec Dir Information Tech Svcs ....Mr. Larry K. EMMONS
07 Director of Admissions ....Ms. Jennifer K. PAHL
06 Registrar ....Dr. Clifford DORNE
36 Director Career Services ....Mr. William R. STEC
21 Director Business Services ....Ms. Connie J. SCHWEITZER
08 Dir of Melvin J Zahnow Library ....Ms. Anita DEY
25 HHS Grant Project Manager ....Ms. Janet M. RENTSCH
15 Human Resources Manager ....Ms. Jennifer NEITZEL
37 Director Scholarships/Financial Aid ....Mr. Robert L. LEMUEL
15 Asst Director of Human Resources ....Mr. Eddie V. JONES
50 Dean Carmona College of Business ....Dr. Jayati GHOSH
88 Dir Environmental Health & Safety ....Mr. Robert J. TUTSOCK
88 Asst Dir Accessibility Resources ....Dr. Shawn WILSON
102 Executive Director SVSU Foundation ....Mr. Andrew J. BETHUNE
96 Purchasing Manager ....Mr. Joshua M. WEBB
76 Dean of Health & Human Services ....Dr. Judith P. RULAND
09 Dir of Institutional Effectiveness ....Dr. Nicholas J. WAGNER
101 Exec Asst to the Pres/Sec to Board ....Mrs. Mary A. KOWALESKI
20 Assoc Provost for Academic Affairs ....Dr. Joshua J. ODE
86 Director of Governmental Affairs ....Mr. John L. KACZYNSKI
39 Dir Resident Life/Student Housing ....Ms. Michele GUNKELMAN
54 Dean of Engineering ....Dr. Andrew M. CHUBB
19 Chief of University Police ....Mr. Clifford A. BLOCK

St. Clair County Community College (F)

323 Erie Street, PO Box 5015, Port Huron MI 48061-5015
County: St. Clair FICE Identification: 002310
Unit ID: 172291
Telephone: (810) 984-3881 Carnegie Class: Assoc/HT-Mix Trad/Non
FAX Number: (810) 984-4730 Calendar System: Semester
URL: www.sc4.edu
Established: 1923 Annual Undergrad Tuition & Fees (In-District): $8,845
Enrollment: 3,315 Coed
Affiliation or Control: Local IRS Status: 501(c)3
Highest Offering: Associate Degree
Accreditation: HLC, ADNUR, #COARC, RAD

01 President ....Dr. Deborah SNYDER
11 Exec VP/Chief Operating Officer ....Mr. Kirk KRAMER
05 Co-Chief Academic Officer ....Mr. Ethan FLICK
05 Co-Chief Academic Officer ....Ms. Tammy KENNY
32 VP of Student Services ....Mr. Pete LACEY
10 Chief Financial Officer ....Ms. Mary Kay BRUNNER
15 VP of Human Resources ....Ms. Bethany MAYEA
26 VP of Marketing & Communication ....Vacant
09 VP of Institutional Effectiveness ....Vacant
37 Dir of Financial Assistance/Svcs ....Ms. Josephine CASSAR
06 Registrar ....Ms. Carrie BEARSS
41 Director of Athletics ....Mr. Dale VOS
08 Assoc Dean Library Services ....Ms. Kendra LAKE

Schoolcraft College (G)

18600 Haggerty Road, Livonia MI 48152-2696
County: Wayne FICE Identification: 002315
Unit ID: 172200
Telephone: (734) 462-4400 Carnegie Class: Bac/Assoc-Assoc Dom
FAX Number: (734) 462-4340 Calendar System: Semester
URL: www.schoolcraft.edu
Established: 1961 Annual Undergrad Tuition & Fees (In-District): $5,364
Enrollment: 8,116 Coed
Affiliation or Control: Local IRS Status: Exempt
Highest Offering: Baccalaureate
Accreditation: HLC, ACFEI, ADNUR, CAHIIM, EMT, MAC, PNUR

01 President ....Dr. Glenn CERNY
10 Chief Financial Officer ....Mr. Jon LAMB
11 Chief Operations Officer ....Mr. Steven KAUFMAN
05 Chief Academic Officer ....Ms. Stacy WHIDDON
32 Chief Student Enrollment Officer ....Ms. Melissa SCHULTZ
13 Chief Technology Officer ....Mr. Jeff BORTON
32 Chief Student Services Officer ....Dr. Laurie KATTUAH-SNYDER
26 Chief Mktg & Communications Ofcr ....Ms. Van NGUYEN
19 Chief of Police ....Mr. Mark ENGSTROM
15 Chief HR & Risk Mgt Officer ....Ms. Brenda LEAVENS
30 Exec Director of Development ....Ms. Dawn MAGRETTA
35 Dean of Students ....Dr. Martin HEATOR
89 Dean New Student Experience ....Dr. Stacey STOVER
49 Dean Liberal Arts & Sciences ....Dr. Michele KELLY
75 Dean Occupational Pgm/Econ Dev ....Dr. Robert LEADLEY
108 Assoc Dn Opers/Curriculum/Assessmt ....Ms. Cindy CICCHELLI
66 Assoc Dean Nursing ....Dr. Deborah VENDITTELLI
88 Assoc Dean Public Safety Programs ....Dr. Gerald CHAMPAGNE
72 Assoc Dean Occupation Pgm/Engr Tech ....Ms. Amy JONES
76 Assoc Dean Health Professions ....Dr. David KESLER
53 Assoc Dean Occupational/Educ Pgms ....Dr. Dennis GENIG
36 Assoc Dean of Career Services ....Dr. Michael OLIVER
88 Assoc Dean of Student Relations ..Ms. Nicole WILSON-FENNELL
37 Director of Financial Aid ....Mr. Michael WILLIAMS
07 Director of Admissions ....Ms. Lisa BUSHAW
06 Registrar ....Ms. Tracy MILLER
51 Dir Personal & Prof Learning ....Ms. Jodie BECKLEY
85 Dir International Student Ctr ....Ms. Laura LESHOK
09 Dir Data Strategy & Effectiveness ....Ms. Michelle STANDO
112 Dir Major & Planned Gifts ....Mr. Christopher KELLY
44 Dir of Annual Gvg & Scholar Admin ....Ms. Carole BOOMS
121 Dir of Advising & Transfer ....Ms. Carol DWYER
41 Director of Athletics ....Ms. Cali CRAWFORD
117 Dir Risk Mgmt & HR Compliance ....Ms. Ann WHITE
18 Director Facilities ....Mr. Stephen GREEN
101 Dir Strat Opers & Board Liaison ....Ms. Beth LAFOREST
04 Ofc Mgr & SC Tech Coordinator ....Ms. Elizabeth NOVAK
40 Director of Bookstore ....Ms. Lyndsay TAGAREL
96 Chief Proc & Business Svcs Ofcr ....Mr. Matthew WILSON
90 Exec Dir Acad & Admin Info Sys ....Ms. Laura CULLEN
88 Director of Academic Innovation ....Mr. Adam AUTHIER

Siena Heights University (H)

1247 Siena Heights Drive, Adrian MI 49221-1796
County: Lenawee FICE Identification: 002316
Unit ID: 172264
Telephone: (517) 263-0731 Carnegie Class: Masters/S
FAX Number: (517) 264-7704 Calendar System: Semester
URL: www.sienaheights.edu
Established: 1919 Annual Undergrad Tuition & Fees: $27,642
Enrollment: 2,036 Coed
Affiliation or Control: Roman Catholic IRS Status: 501(c)3
Highest Offering: Beyond Master's But Less Than Doctorate
Accreditation: HLC, ART, CAEP, NURSE, SW

01 President ....Dr. Peg ALBERT, OP
10 Sr Vice Pres for Business/Finance ....Dr. Lee JOHNSON
111 Vice President for Advancement ....Mr. Daniel PENA
05 Vice President for Academic Affairs ....Dr. Sharon R. WEBER, OP
84 Vice Pres of Enrollment Mgmt Svcs ....Mr. George WOLF
107 Dean of Professional Studies/Grad ....Dr. Cheri BETZ
49 Dean College of Arts and Science ....Dr. Sharon WEBER, OP
32 Dean for Students ....Mr. Michael ORLANDO
06 Registrar ....Mr. Christopher COX
07 Director of Admissions ....Ms. Trudy MOHRE
08 Director of Library ....Mrs. Melissa SISSEN
13 Chief Information Officer ....Mr. Robert C. METZ
41 Director of Athletics ....Ms. Susan SYLJEBECK
15 Human Resource Director ....Mr. Michael L. KARABETSOS
42 Director of Campus Ministry ....Sr. Mary JONES, OP
38 Director of Counseling Services ....Mrs. Sandy MORLEY
121 Director of Academic Advising ....Vacant
18 Supt of Buildings & Grounds ....Mr. Brian BERTRAM
09 Director of Institutional Research ....Vacant
39 Director of Residence Life ....Ms. Samantha THACKER
19 Director of Campus Security ....Mrs. Cindy A. BIRDWELL
23 Director of Health Services ....Ms. Dawn E. MARSH
29 Director of Alumni Relations ....Mrs. Kate HAMILTON
36 Director of Career Services ....Ms. Sarah A. CHRENKO
28 Director of Immersion & Diversity ....Mrs. Sharese MATHIS
26 Dir of Integrated Univ Marketing ....Mr. Doug GOODNOUGH

37 Director Student Financial Aid Mrs. Lori KOSARUE
21 Controller Ms. Mary KRUSE
44 Coordinator of Annual Fund Mrs. Shawna WILSON
04 Executive Assistant to President Mrs. Krissie BARNES

Southwestern Michigan College (A)

58900 Cherry Grove Road, Dowagiac MI 49047-9793
County: Cass FICE Identification: 002317
Unit ID: 172307
Telephone: (269) 782-1000 Carnegie Class: Assoc/HT-High Trad
FAX Number: (269) 782-8414 Calendar System: Semester
URL: www.swmich.edu
Established: 1964 Annual Undergrad Tuition & Fees (In-District): $6,708
Enrollment: 1,759 Coed
Affiliation or Control: State/Local IRS Status: 501(c)3
Highest Offering: Associate Degree
Accreditation: HLC, ADNUR, CAHIIM

01 President Dr. Joseph ODENWALD
84 VP Enrollment Mgmt/Campus Life Mr. Brent BREWER
10 Senior VP Business Affairs & CFO Ms. Susan COULSTON
05 Provost Dr. David FLEMING
111 VP Institutional Advancement Mr. Michael O'BRIEN
12 Executive Director of Niles Campus Mr. Jason SMITH
13 Director of IT and CIO Mr. Mick VALERIS
66 Dean School Nursing/Health Services Dr. Melissa KENNEDY
49 Dean of Arts and Sciences Dr. Keith HOWELL
50 Dean of School of Business/Adv Tech Dr. Karen REILLY
32 Dean of Student Development Ms. Katie HANNAH
35 Executive Director of Student Life Mr. Jeffery HOOKS
18 Director of Buildings & Grounds Mr. John EBERHART
19 Director of Campus Security Mr. Lyndon PARRISH
07 Director Admission/Dir Career Partnership Ms. Heather ZILE
37 Director of Financial Aid Ms. Lauren MOW
88 Dir Educational Talent Search Pgm Ms. Maria KULKA
09 Director of Institutional Research Dr. Angela EVANS
15 Director of Human Resources Vacant
08 Director of Library Services Ms. Colleen WELSCH
06 Director of Records/Registrar Mr. Steven CARLSON
21 Controller Ms. Michelle KITE
103 Manager of Workforce Development Dr. Lucian LEONE
88 Manager of Accounting Ms. Christy MANGUS
121 Manager of Academic Advising Ms. Kathie GRIES
88 Manager of Dual Enrolled Students Mr. Brian DEVLESCHOWARD
26 Manager of Marketing Ms. Michelle ORLASKE
89 Manager First Year Exp/Testing Ctr Ms. Kristen LOWNDS
88 Manager of Theatre Operations Mr. Marcus ROLL
41 Asst Director Campus Life/Athletics Mr. Jordan PITRE
88 Asst Director Campus Life/Clubs Mr. Branden POMPEY

Southwestern Michigan College Niles Area Campus (B)

33890 U.S. Highway 12, Niles MI 49120
Telephone: (800) 456-8675 Identification: 770286
Accreditation: &HLC

Spring Arbor University (C)

106 E Main Street, Spring Arbor MI 49283-9799
County: Jackson FICE Identification: 002318
Unit ID: 172334
Telephone: (517) 750-1200 Carnegie Class: Masters/L
FAX Number: (517) 750-6620 Calendar System: Semester
URL: www.arbor.edu
Established: 1873 Annual Undergrad Tuition & Fees: $30,472
Enrollment: 3,118 Coed
Affiliation or Control: Free Methodist IRS Status: 501(c)3
Highest Offering: Doctorate
Accreditation: HLC, CACREP, CAEP, NURSE, SW

01 University President Dr. Brent D. ELLIS
03 Executive Vice President Dr. Douglas A. WILCOXSON
05 VP for Academic Affairs Dr. Carol C. GREEN
10 VP for Finance & Administration Ms. Dawn SCHNITKEY
32 VP Student Development/Success Mr. Corey ROSS
84 VP Enrollment & Marketing Mr. Jon BAHR
20 AVP Acad Affairs/Dean Engineering Dr. Ron A. DELAP
15 Assistant VP for Human Resources Mrs. Kerry J. KLEE-TIESMAN
88 Chief Strategy Officer Dr. Kimberly RUPERT
04 Exec Assistant to the President Ms. Julie MORSE
13 Chief Technology Officer Mr. Randy G. MELTON
66 Dean School of Nursing & Health Sci Dr. Alvin V. KAUFFMAN
79 Dean School of Humanities Mr. Kim T. BOWEN
83 Dean School of Social Sciences Dr. Terry DARLING
50 Dean School of Business Dr. Caleb K. CHAN
53 Interim Dean School of Education Mr. John M. WILLIAMS
60 Dean School of Communication Mrs. Dorie A. SHELBY
35 Asst VP Student Development Mr. Dan VANDERHILL
06 Registrar Mrs. Sherri HENDRIX
07 Director of Enrollment Operations Vacant
21 Assistant VP Financial Services Mrs. Dawn I. SCHNITKEY
30 Executive Director of Development Mrs. Linda SCHAUB
26 Exec Dir Mktg & Communication Ms. Bethany L. LANDIS
41 Athletic Director Mr. Ryan T. COTTINGHAM
42 Chaplain Dr. Brian S. KONO
37 Director of Financial Aid Mr. Herbert K. ROTICH
09 Director Institutional Research Mr. Thomas P. KORMAN
121 Dir of Student Success Initiative Mrs. Laura S. BRECKNER
108 Director of Assessment Vacant
08 Director Library Mr. Robert D. BOLTON
18 Director of Physical Plant Mr. Marty FORTRESS
124 Director Retention & Fresh Programs Mrs. Carrie L. WILLIAMS
104 Director Cross Cultural Studies Mrs. Diane L. KURTZ
23 Exec Dir Student Health/Wellness Mrs. Mary BRODA
39 Associate Dean of Students Mr. Robert C. PRATT
36 Career Development Advisor Mr. Chad W. MELTON
19 Director Campus Safety Mr. Scott L. KREBILL
106 Assoc Dean External/SAU Online Mr. Gary R. TUCKER
28 Chief Diversity Officer Mr. Kevin BROWN
29 Director Alumni Relations Mr. Brian R. KNAPP
105 Web Architect Mr. Ryan J. KELLY
44 Director Annual Giving Mrs. Tricia A. CRAMER

SS. Cyril and Methodius Seminary (D)

3535 Commerce Road, Orchard Lake MI 48324-1623
County: Oakland FICE Identification: 037384
Unit ID: 260211
Telephone: (248) 836-1271 Carnegie Class: Not Classified
FAX Number: (248) 738-6735 Calendar System: Semester
URL: www.sscms.edu
Established: 1885 Annual Graduate Tuition & Fees: N/A
Enrollment: N/A Coed
Affiliation or Control: Roman Catholic IRS Status: 501(c)3
Highest Offering: Master's; No Undergraduates
Accreditation: THEOL

01 Rector/President V.Rev. Miroslaw KROL
03 Vice Rector Rev. Przemyslaw NOWAK
32 Dean of Human Formation Rev. Damian CHRZANOWSKI
42 Dean of Spiritual Formation Rev. Lukasz IWANCZUK
05 Academic Dean Rev. Gregory A. BANAZAK

University of Detroit Mercy (E)

4001 W McNichols Road, Detroit MI 48221-3038
County: Wayne FICE Identification: 002323
Unit ID: 169716
Telephone: (313) 993-1000 Carnegie Class: DU-Mod
FAX Number: (313) 993-1229 Calendar System: Semester
URL: www.udmercy.edu
Established: 1877 Annual Undergrad Tuition & Fees: $29,562
Enrollment: 4,987 Coed
Affiliation or Control: Roman Catholic IRS Status: 501(c)3
Highest Offering: Doctorate
Accreditation: HLC, ANEST, ARCPA, CACREP, CAHIIM, CLPSY, DENT, DH, NURSE, SW

01 President Dr. Antoine M. GARIBALDI
05 Provost and VP for Academic Affairs Ms. Pamela ZARKOWSKI
10 VP for Business & Finance/CFO Mr. Thomas MANCEOR
111 VP for University Advancement Mr. Arnold D'AMBROSIO
84 VP Enrollment & Student Affairs Ms. Deborah STIEFFEL
101 University Secretary & Senior Atty Ms. Monica BARBOUR
18 Assoc Vice Pres Facil Management Ms. Tamara BATCHELLER
15 Associate Vice Pres Human Resources Ms. Netina ANDING-MOORE
26 Assoc VP Marketing & Communications Mr. Gary ERWIN
13 Associate Vice President ITS Mr. Edward TRACY, II
06 Associate VP/Registrar Ms. Diane M. PRAET
44 Exec Director of Annual Giving Ms. Judy WERNETTE
112 Exec Director of Major Gifts Mr. Dennis CARLESSO
32 Dean of Students Ms. Monica WILLIAMS
08 Dean of Libraries Dr. Jennifer DEAN
09 Director of Institutional Research Ms. Shelley WAGNON
37 Director Scholarships & Fin Aid Ms. Caren BENDES
35 Associate Director of Student Life Ms. Dorothy STEWART
41 Director of Athletics Mr. Robert VOWELS
49 Dean College of Liberal Arts/Ed Dr. Mark DENHAM
61 Dean School of Law Ms. Jelani JEFFERSON EXUM
54 Dean College Engr & Science Dr. Katherine SNYDER
48 Dean School of Architecture Mr. Daniel PITERA
50 Dean Col Business Admin Dr. Joseph EISENHAUER
52 Dean School of Dentistry Dr. Mert AKSU
76 Interim Dean CHP/Nursing Dr. Janet BAIARDI
36 Dir Center for Career & Prof Devel Vacant
39 Director Residence Life Ms. Lanae GILL
04 Exec Asst to the President Ms. Lisa MACDONNELL
85 Dir of International Services Ms. Lilymae SWAN
38 Director of Wellness Center Ms. Annamaria SILVERI
92 Co-Director of Honors Program Dr. Evan PETERSON
92 Co-Director of Honors Program Dr. Nicholas ROMBES
88 Coordinator of Advancement Systems Ms. Stephanie JONES
07 Executive Director of Admissions Ms. Tyra ROUNDS
108 Director of Assessment Vacant
19 Director Public Safety Mr. Joel GALLIHUGH
25 Dir of Sponsored Research Ms. Ann SERRA
53 Chair Education Department Dr. Alan GRIGG
106 Dir Online Education/E-learning Ms. Jennifer DEAN
102 Dir Foundation/Corporate Relations Ms. Yvonne LINDSTROM
22 Title IX & Equity/Compliance Coord Ms. Megan NOVELL
29 Director Alumni Relations Ms. Margaret PATTISON
96 Director of Purchasing Ms. Stacey KING

University of Detroit Mercy Corktown Campus (F)

2700 Martin Luther King Jr. Blvd, Detroit MI 48208-2576
Telephone: (313) 494-6700 Identification: 770291
Accreditation: &HLC

University of Detroit Mercy School of Law (G)

651 E Jefferson Avenue, Detroit MI 48226-4349
Telephone: (313) 596-0200 Identification: 770292
Accreditation: &HLC, LAW

University of Michigan-Ann Arbor (H)

500 S. State Street, Ann Arbor MI 48109
County: Washtenaw FICE Identification: 002325
Unit ID: 170976
Telephone: (734) 764-1817 Carnegie Class: DU-Highest
FAX Number: N/A Calendar System: Trimester
URL: umich.edu
Established: 1817 Annual Undergrad Tuition & Fees (In-State): $15,948
Enrollment: 47,907 Coed
Affiliation or Control: State IRS Status: 501(c)3
Highest Offering: Doctorate
Accreditation: HLC, ART, CAATE, CAEPT, CAMPEP, CLPSY, DANCE, DENT, DH, DIETD, DIETI, HSA, IPSY, LAW, LIB, LSAR, MED, MIDWF, MUS, NURSE, PCSAS, PDPSY, PH, PHAR, PLNG, SW

01 President Dr. Mark S. SCHLISSEL
05 Provost Dr. Susan M. COLLINS
10 Interim Exec Vice Pres/CFO Mr. Brian T. SMITH
17 Exec VP Medical Affairs/Dean Med Dr. Marschall S. RUNGE
30 Vice President Development Mr. Thomas A. BAIRD
32 VP Student Life Dr. Martino HARMON
46 Vice President for Research Dr. Rebecca M. CUNNINGHAM
86 Vice Pres Governmental Relations Mr. Chris KOLB
26 Vice Pres Communications Ms. Kallie B. MICHELS
43 Vice Pres/General Counsel Mr. Timothy G. LYNCH
101 Vice Pres/Sec of the University Ms. Sally J. CHURCHILL
04 Exec Asst to the President Ms. Erika J. HRABEC
100 Special Counsel to the President Ms. Liz M. BARRY
88 Special Counsel to the Provost Ms. Christine M. GERDES
114 Sr Vice Provost Acad/Budget Affairs Ms. Amy DITTMAR
20 Vice Provost Acad & Faculty Affairs Dr. Lori J. PIERCE
20 Vice Provost Acad & Faculty Affairs Dr. Sara B. BLAIR
58 V Prov Acad Affs/Dean Grad Studies Dr. Michael J. SOLOMON
88 Vice Provost Engaged Learning Dr. Valeria BERTACCO
85 Assoc VProv/Dir Global Engagement Dr. Amy CONGER
28 Vice Prov Diversity/Eqty/Inclusion Dr. Robert M. SELLERS
08 Vice Prov Acad Innov/Univ Librarian Dr. James L. HILTON
84 Int Vice Prov for Enrollment Mgmt Mr. Paul ROBINSON
09 Assoc Vice Provost & Exec Dir OBP Ms. Tammy C. BIMER
07 Director Undergrad Admissions Ms. Erica L. SANDERS
15 Int Assoc VProv/Sr Dir Acad HR/OIE Vacant
22 AVP for Institutional Equity Ms. Tamiko STRICKMAN
18 Assoc VP Facilities/Operations Mr. Henry D. BAIER
21 Assoc VP Finance Mr. Brian T. SMITH
115 Chief Investment Officer Mr. Erik LUNDBERG
88 AVP Research Nat Sciences/Engr Dr. Bradford ORR
88 Asst VP and Chief of Staff Research Dr. Nicholas WIGGINTON
88 Assoc VP for Research Dr. Michael J. IMPERIALE
88 Asst VP Reg and Comp Oversight Ms. Lois BRAKO
88 Assoc VP for Research Vacant
88 Asst VP Animal Resources Dr. William KING
88 Asst VP Animal Pgm Comp Oversight Mr. William GREER
88 Assoc VP for Research Vacant
88 Asst VP Fed Rel for Research Ms. Kristina KO
88 Assoc VP for Research Dr. Kelly B. SEXTON
35 Assoc VP Student Life/Dean Stdnts Ms. Laura B. JONES
35 Assoc VP Student Life Ms. Anjali N. ANTURKAR
35 Assoc VP Student Life Dr. Simone HIMBEAULT-TAYLOR
35 Assoc VP Student Life Mr. Kambiz KHALILI
16 Assoc VP for Human Resources Mr. Rich S. HOLCOMB
13 Chief Information Officer Dr. Ravi PENDSE
06 University Registrar Mr. Paul A. ROBINSON
96 Director Procurement Services Mr. Tony BURGER
38 Director Counseling & Psych Service Dr. Todd D. SEVIG
39 Director University Housing Mr. Rick GIBSON
23 Exec Dir University Health Service Dr. Robert D. ERNST
19 Exec Dir Pub Safety/Security Mr. Eddie L. WASHINGTON
37 Exec Director Financial Aid Ms. Tammie DURHAM
41 Director of Athletics Mr. Warde MANUEL
48 Dean Col Architecture/Urban Plng Dr. Jonathan MASSEY
49 Dean Col Literature/Science/Arts Dr. Anne L. CURZAN
54 Dean College of Engineering Dr. Alec D. GALLIMORE
61 Dean Law School Mr. Mark D. WEST
67 Dean College of Pharmacy Dr. Bruce MUELLER
65 Dean Sch Natural Resources/Environ Dr. Jonathan T. OVERPECK
64 Dean School Music/Theatre & Dance Dr. David GIER
57 Dean School of Art & Design Dr. Gunalan L. NADARAJAN
50 Dean School of Business Ms. Francine LAFONTAINE
52 Dean School of Dentistry Dr. Laurie K. MCCAULEY
53 Dean School of Education Dr. Elizabeth B. MOJE
62 Dean School of Information Dr. Thomas A. FINHOLT
68 Dean School of Kinesiology Dr. Lori PLOUTZ-SNYDER
66 Dean School of Nursing Dr. Patricia D. HURN
80 Dean School of Public Policy Mr. Michael S. BARR
70 Dean School of Social Work Dr. Lynn VIDEKA
69 Dean School of Public Health Dr. F. DuBois BOWMAN
29 President Alumni Association Mr. Steve C. GRAFTON
102 Director Foundation/Corporate Rels Ms. Maureen MARTIN
44 Director Annual Giving Ms. Megan F. DOUD

University of Michigan-Dearborn (I)

4901 Evergreen Road, Dearborn MI 48128-1491
County: Wayne FICE Identification: 002326
Unit ID: 171137
Telephone: (313) 593-5000 Carnegie Class: Masters/L
FAX Number: (313) 593-5452 Calendar System: Semester

URL: www.umdearborn.edu
Established: 1959 Annual Undergrad Tuition & Fees (In-State): $13,552
Enrollment: 8,783 Coed
Affiliation or Control: State IRS Status: 501(c)3
Highest Offering: Doctorate
Accreditation: HLC, CAEP, CEA

01 Chancellor .... Dr. Dominico GRASSO
05 Int Prov/Exec VC Academic Affairs .... Dr. Gabriella SCARLATTA
10 Vice Chancellor Business Affairs .... Mr. Bryan DADEY
84 Vice Prov Enrollment Management .... Ms. Melissa STONE
111 Vice Chanc Inst Advancement .... Dr. Casandra ULBRICH
26 Vice Chanc for External Relations .... Mr. Kenneth KETTENBEIL
21 Director of Financial Services .... Mr. Noel HORNBACHER
06 Registrar .... Mr. Timothy TAYLOR
27 Director Communications/Marketing .... Ms. Beth MARMARELLI
86 Government Relations Manager .... Vacant
15 Director of Human Resources .... Ms. Rima BERRY-HUNG
29 Alumni Engagement .... Ms. Cristina FRENDO
20 Associate Provost Undergraduate .... Dr. Mitchel SOLLENBERGER
58 Associate Provost Graduate .... Dr. Maureen LINKER
13 Dir IT Strategy/Operations .... Ms. Carrie SHUMAKER
08 Assoc Provost & Dir of Library .... Dr. Maureen LINKER
09 Exec Dir of Institutional Research .... Ms. Becky CHADWICK
07 Director of Admissions .... Ms. Deb PEFFER
32 Dean of Students .... Dr. Amy FINLAY
37 Director of Financial Aid .... Ms. Katherine ALLEN
38 Director of Counseling .... Dr. Sara BYCZEK
36 Director of Career Services .... Ms. Regina M. STORRS
85 Director of International Affairs .... Mr. Francisco LOPEZ
18 Exec Dir of Facilities Operations .... Ms. Carol GLICK
19 Chief of Police .... Mr. Gary GORSKI
22 Director Institutional Equity .... Ms. Pam HEATLIE
28 Sp Counsel to Chanc for Inclusion .... Dr. Ann LAMPKIN-WILLIAMS
49 Dean Col Arts/Science/Letters .... Dr. Martin HERSHOCK
54 Dean Col of Engr/Computer Science .... Dr. Ghassan KRIDLI
50 Dean College of Business .... Dr. Raju BALAKRISHNAN
53 Dean College of Educ/Health/HS .. Dr. Ann LAMPKIN-WILLIAMS
88 Director of Enrollment Research .... Mr. Dan MERIAN
41 Interim Athletic Director .... Mr. Bryan EARL
102 Dir Foundation/Corporate Relations .... Ms. Cheryl DONOHOE
44 Director Annual Giving .... Ms. Eva GOGOLA
90 Director Academic Computing .... Ms. Carrie SHUMAKER
04 Exec Assistant to the Chancellor .... Ms. Michelle BARNES
100 Chief of Staff .... Ms. Keisha BLEVINS

University of Michigan-Flint (A)

303 E Kearsley Street, Flint MI 48502-1950
County: Genesee FICE Identification: 002327
Unit ID: 171146
Telephone: (810) 762-3000 Carnegie Class: DU-Mod
FAX Number: (810) 762-5725 Calendar System: Semester
URL: www.umflint.edu
Established: 1956 Annual Undergrad Tuition & Fees (In-State): $12,744
Enrollment: 6,829 Coed
Affiliation or Control: State IRS Status: 501(c)3
Highest Offering: Doctorate
Accreditation: HLC, ANEST, ARCPA, CAEPN, #COARC, MUS, NURSE, PH, PTA, RTT, SW

01 Chancellor .... Dr. Debasish DUTTA
05 Provost/VC Academic Affairs .... Dr. Sonja FEIST-PRICE
32 VC Campus Inclusion & Student Life .... Dr. Christopher GIORDANO
111 VC University Advancement .... Ms. Shari SCHRADER
121 Asst VC for Student Success .... Vacant
35 Assoc VC & Dean of Students .... Dr. Julie SNYDER
20 Assoc Prov/Dean Undergrad Studies .... Ms. Shelby NEWPORT
26 Executive Dir External Relations .... Ms. Jennifer HOGAN
86 Director Government Relations .... Ms. Mia MCNEIL
28 Director of Educational Oppty .... Dr. Tiese ROXBURY
08 Interim Director of Library .... Mr. Mickey DOYLE
06 Registrar .... Ms. Karen A. ARNOULD
07 Admissions Director .... Mr. Joseph VAINNER
37 Director Financial Aid .... Ms. Lori VEDDER
15 Director Human Res/Affirm Action .... Ms. Beth MANNING
49 Dean College of Arts & Sciences ...... Dr. Susan GANO-PHILLIPS
50 Interim Dean School of Management .... Dr. Yener KANDOGAN
66 Dean School of Nursing .... Dr. Cynthia MCCURREN
76 Dean College of Health Studies .... Dr. Donna FRY
53 Interim Dean Educ & Human Services .... Dr. Sapna THWAITE
72 Dean College of Innovation & Tech .... Dr. Christopher A. PEARSON
106 Director of Online & Digital Educ .... Mr. Nicholas GASPAR
19 Director of Public Safety .... Mr. Raymond D. HALL
18 Dir Facilities Mgmt/Auxiliary Svcs .... Mr. George HAKIM
13 Director Info Technology Services .... Mr. Scott ARNST
121 Director Student Success Center .... Dr. Dawn MARKELL
46 Director of Research .... Dr. Kenneth SYLVESTER
21 Director of Financial Svcs & Budget .... Mr. Gerald GLASCO
88 Director Economic Development .... Ms. Paula NAS
96 Procurement Agent Senior .... Ms. Brenda ROTH
09 Director of Institutional Analysis .... Ms. Fawn SKARSTEN
04 Project Manager to the Chancellor .... Ms. Chelsea DUNCAN
29 Exec Director Alumni Relations .... Dr. Mary Jo SEKELSKY
92 Director Honors Program .... Dr. Maureen THUM
88 Asst Dir Stdnt Involvement/Ldrship .... Mr. Chris DEEULIS
88 Dir Center Gender & Sexuality .... Ms. Samara HOUGH
88 Dir Thompson Center for T&L .... Dr. Tracy WACKER

Van Andel Institute Graduate School (B)

333 Bostwick Avenue NE, Grand Rapids MI 49503
County: Kent Identification: 667085
Telephone: (616) 234-5708 Carnegie Class: Not Classified
FAX Number: (616) 234-5709 Calendar System: Semester
URL: vaigs.vai.org
Established: 2005 Annual Graduate Tuition & Fees: N/A
Enrollment: N/A Coed
Affiliation or Control: Independent Non-Profit IRS Status: 501(c)3
Highest Offering: Doctorate; No Undergraduates
Accreditation: HLC

01 President/Dean of VAIGS .... Dr. Steven J. TRIEZENBERG
05 Assistant Dean of Graduate School .... Dr. Brian HAAB
32 Director Student Support Services .... Ms. Allison ROMAN
07 Director of Enrollment and Records .... Ms. Christy MAYO
108 Director Assessment & Prof Devel .... Dr. John VASQUEZ
04 Executive Asst to President .... Mrs. Susanne MILLER-SCHACHINGER

Walsh College of Accountancy and Business Administration (C)

3838 Livernois Road, Troy MI 48083
County: Oakland FICE Identification: 004071
Unit ID: 172608
Telephone: (248) 689-8282 Carnegie Class: Spec-4-yr-Bus
FAX Number: (248) 689-9066 Calendar System: Semester
URL: www.walshcollege.edu
Established: 1922 Annual Undergrad Tuition & Fees: N/A
Enrollment: 1,744 Coed
Affiliation or Control: Independent Non-Profit IRS Status: 501(c)3
Highest Offering: Doctorate
Accreditation: HLC, ACBSP

01 President & CEO .... Dr. Michael P. LEVENS
05 Executive VP/Provost .... Dr. Suzanne SIEGLE
10 Vice President/CFO/Treasurer .... Ms. Teresa ESSHAKI
15 VP/Chief Human Resources/Admin Ofcr .... Ms. Elizabeth A. BARNES
26 VP/Chief Marketing Ofcr .... Ms. Patti SWANSON
84 VP/Chief Enrollment Mgmt Ofcr .... Mr. Jesus HERNANDEZ
100 Chief of Staff .... Mrs. Stephanie M. WHEELER
20 Asst VP Academic Admin .... Ms. Victoria R. SCAVONE
106 Director Office of Online Learning .... Mr. Drew SMITH
37 Director Financial Aid .... Ms. Heidi WISBY
18 Director Facilities/Auxiliary Svcs .... Ms. Christine STOUT
21 Controller .... Ms. Karen ST. ROMAIN
06 Director of Records/Registrar .... Ms. Stacy JOHNSON
13 Director of Info Technology .... Vacant
36 Director Career Services .... Ms. Brenda PAINE
20 Assoc Provost/Chair Doctoral Pgms .... Dr. Jenny TATSAK
29 Manager of Alumni Relations .... Ms. Melanie ESLAND
88 Chair Accounting .... Mr. John BLACK
88 Chair Finance & Economics .... Mr. John MOORE
88 Chair Decision Sciences .... Mr. Dave SCHIPPERS
88 Chair Taxation .... Mr. Richard DAVIDSON
08 Chief Library Officer .... Ms. Caryn NOEL
111 Interim Director of Advancement .... Mr. Scott TRUDELL

Washtenaw Community College (D)

4800 E Huron River Dr, Ann Arbor MI 48105-4800
County: Washtenaw FICE Identification: 002328
Unit ID: 172617
Telephone: (734) 973-3300 Carnegie Class: Assoc/HT-Mix Trad/Non
FAX Number: (734) 677-5413 Calendar System: Semester
URL: www.wccnet.edu
Established: 1965 Annual Undergrad Tuition & Fees (In-District): $4,176
Enrollment: 11,140 Coed
Affiliation or Control: Local IRS Status: 501(c)3
Highest Offering: Associate Degree
Accreditation: HLC, ACFEI, ADNUR, DA, NAEYC, PTAA, RAD, SURGT

01 President .... Dr. Rose B. BELLANCA
10 Exec VP & Chief Financial Officer .... Mr. William JOHNSON
05 VP for Instruction .... Dr. Kimberly HURNS
32 Exec VP Student & Academic Services .... Ms. Linda BLAKEY
111 AVP of College Advancement .... Mr. Phil SNYDER
51 VP Economic & College Dev .... Ms. Michelle MUELLER
84 VP of Strategic Enrollment Mgt .... Ms. Mika MCASKILL
45 Exec Dir Inst Effect Plng & Accred .... Dr. Julie MORRISON
121 Dean Supp Svcs & Student Advocacy .... Vacant
50 Dean Business & Computer Tech .... Ms. Eva SAMULSKI
81 Dean Math/Science/Engineering Tech .... Dr. Victor VEGA
76 Dean Health Science .... Dr. Valerie GREAVES
79 Dean Humanities/Social/Behavioral .... Dr. Scott BRITTEN
72 Dean ATP .... Dr. Jimmie BABER, III
36 Dean Career Svc/UA Programs .... Ms. Marilyn DONHAM
28 Dean Diversity & Inclusion .... Vacant
103 AVP Workforce & Community Dev .... Mr. Brandon TUCKER
10 Controller .... Mr. Ben HUNHOLZ
114 Dir Budget/Purchasing/Accts Payable .... Ms. Barbara FILLINGER
15 AVP Human Resource Svcs .... Ms. Christine MIHALY
37 Director Financial Aid .... Ms. Lori TRAPP
09 Director Institutional Research .... Dr. Roger MOURAD
19 Chief Public Safety .... Mr. Scott HILDEN
35 Dir Student Development/Activities .... Mr. Peter LESHKEVICH
86 Dir of Government Relations .... Vacant
43 General Counsel .... Mr. Larry BARKOFF
100 Chief of Staff .... Ms. Vanessa BROOKS
06 Study System Architect/Registrar .... Ms. Kathy CURRIE
106 Executive Director Online Education .... Mr. Peter BACCILE

Wayne County Community College District (E)

801 W Fort Street, Detroit MI 48226-3010
County: Wayne FICE Identification: 009230
Unit ID: 172635
Telephone: (313) 496-2600 Carnegie Class: Assoc/HT-Mix Trad/Non
FAX Number: (313) 961-9439 Calendar System: Semester
URL: www.wcccd.edu
Established: 1967 Annual Undergrad Tuition & Fees (In-District): $3,263
Enrollment: 10,748 Coed
Affiliation or Control: State/Local IRS Status: 501(c)3
Highest Offering: Associate Degree
Accreditation: HLC, ADNUR, AT, DA, DH, EMT, SURGT

01 Chancellor .... Dr. Curtis L. IVERY
05 Dist Lead Vice Chanc Educ Affairs .... Dr. David BEAUMONT
20 Dist VC Curriculum/Learning Pgm .... Dr. Patrick J. MCNALLY
88 Dist VC Acad Accountability/Policy .... Ms. CharMaine HINES
10 Deputy Chancellor/Chief Fiscal Ofcr .... Ms. Kim DICARO
15 Senior Vice Chancellor .... Mr. Furquan AHMED
09 Dist VC IE & Research .... Ms. Johnesa HODGE
32 Vice Chancellor for Student Svcs .... Mr. Brian SINGLETON
12 Campus President Downriver .... Mr. Anthony ARMINIAK
12 Campus President Downtown .... Ms. Denise SHANNON
12 Campus President Ted Scott Campus ...... Mr. Anthony ARMINIAK
12 Int Campus President Northwest .... Mr. Furquan AHMED
12 Campus President Eastern .... Mr. Mark SANFORD
17 District Provost Health Sciences .... Dr. Abby FREEMAN
26 Asst to Chanc for Communication .... Ms. Unbreen AMIR
28 Provost Diversity & Inclusion .... Dr. Fidelis D'CUNHA
13 Chief Technology Officer .... Mr. Yoseph DEMISSIE
19 Chief District Police Authority .... Mr. Darrick D. MUHAMMAD
104 Dist Dean International Programs .... Mr. David C. BUTTY

Wayne County Community College District Downriver Campus (F)

21000 Northline Road, Taylor MI 48180
Telephone: (734) 946-3500 Identification: 770297
Accreditation: &HLC

Wayne County Community College District Downtown Campus (G)

1001 West Fort Street, Detroit MI 48226
Telephone: (313) 496-2758 Identification: 770926
Accreditation: &HLC

Wayne County Community College District Eastern Campus (H)

5901 Conner, Detroit MI 48213
Telephone: (313) 922-3311 Identification: 770295
Accreditation: &HLC

Wayne County Community College District Northwest Campus (I)

8200 West Outer Drive, Detroit MI 48219
Telephone: (313) 943-4000 Identification: 770296
Accreditation: &HLC

Wayne County Community College District Ted Scott Campus (J)

9555 Haggerty Road, Belleville MI 48111
Telephone: (734) 699-7008 Identification: 770294
Accreditation: &HLC, SURGA

Wayne State University (K)

42 W. Warren Ave., Detroit MI 48202-4095
County: Wayne FICE Identification: 002329
Unit ID: 172644
Telephone: (313) 577-2424 Carnegie Class: DU-Highest
FAX Number: (313) 577-8154 Calendar System: Semester
URL: www.wayne.edu
Established: 1868 Annual Undergrad Tuition & Fees (In-State): $13,517
Enrollment: 26,241 Coed
Affiliation or Control: State IRS Status: 501(c)3
Highest Offering: Doctorate
Accreditation: HLC, ANEST, ARCPA, AUD, CAATE, CACREP, CAEP, CAMPEP, CEA, CLPSY, DANCE, DIETC, EXSC, FUSER, LAW, LIB, MED, MIDWF, MT, MUS, NURSE, OT, PA, PH, PHAR, PLNG, PTA, RAD, RTT, SP, SPAA, SW

01 President .... Dr. M. Roy WILSON
100 Chief of Staff/VP Marketing & Comm ..... Mr. Michael G. WRIGHT
05 Provost .... Dr. Mark KORNBLUH
10 VP Finance & Business/Treasurer/CFO .... Ms. Rebecca COOKE
43 Vice President and General Counsel .... Mr. Louis A. LESSEM
46 Vice President for Research .... Dr. Stephen M. LANIER
30 VP Development and Alumni Affairs .... Ms. Susan E. BURNS
86 VP Government and Community Affairs ... Mr. Patrick O. LINDSEY

20 Assoc Provost for Academic Affairs .... Dr. R. Darin ELLIS
88 VP for Economic Development .... Mr. Ned STAEBLER
84 Assoc VP for Enrollment Mgmt .... Ms. Dawn MEDLEY
101 VP & Secretary to the BOG .... Ms. Julie H. MILLER
04 Assistant to the President .... Ms. Allison GUILLIOM
29 Assoc VP Alumni Relations .... Mr. Peter CABORN
15 Asst VP of Human Resources .... Ms. Debra WILLIAMS
18 Assoc VP Facilities/Planning/Mgmt .... Mr. Robert DAVENPORT
114 Sr Director of University Budget .... Ms. Brelanda MANDIJA
44 Associate VP of Individual Gifts .... Dr. Stephen E. HENRIE
32 Dean of Students .... Dr. David J. STRAUSS
07 Director Undergraduate Admissions .... Ms. Ericka JACKSON
26 Director of Communications .... Mr. Matthew T. LOCKWOOD
25 Asst VP Sponsored Program Admin .... Ms. Gail L. RYAN
37 Director of Student Financial Aid .... Ms. Catherine KAY
62 Dean University Library System .... Dr. Jon G. CAWTHORNE
06 University Registrar .... Mr. Kurt KRUSCHINSKA
49 Dean College of Liberal Arts/Sci .... Dr. Stephanie HARTWELL
61 Dean Law School .... Mr. Richard BIERSCHBACH
63 Dean Sch of Medicine/VP Health Affs .... Dr. Mark SCHWEITZER
66 Interim Dean College of Nursing .... Dr. Ramona BENKERT
54 Dean College of Engineering .... Dr. Farshad FOTOUHI
50 Dean Ilitch School of Business .... Dr. Robert E. FORSYTHE
70 Dean School of Social Work .... Dr. Sheryl KUBIAK
67 Interim Dean College of Pharmacy .... Dr. Catherine LYSACK
53 Interim Dean College of Education .... Dr. Ingrid GUERRA-LOPEZ
57 Dean College Fine/Perf & Comm Arts .... Dr. Matthew SEEGER
92 Dean Honors College .... Dr. John CORVINO
58 Dean Graduate School .... Dr. Amanda BRYANT-FRIEDRICH
96 Assistant VP of Procurement .... Mr. Kenneth DOHERTY
104 Associate VP Outreach & Intl Pgms .... Dr. Ahmad EZZEDDINE
109 Assoc VP Business & Auxiliary Ops .... Mr. Timothy MICHAEL
88 Assoc VP Tech Commercialization .... Dr. Joan DUNBAR
41 Director of Athletics .... Mr. Robert FOURNIER
105 Director of Web Communications .... Mr. Nick DENARDIS
19 Chief of Police .... Mr. Anthony HOLT
22 Director Equal Opportunity .... Ms. Nikki WRIGHT
28 Assoc Provost Diversity & Inclusion .... Dr. Marquita CHAMBLEE
36 Director of Career Services .... Ms. Shawn PEWITT
39 Director Housing & Residential Life .... Ms. Nikki DUNHAM
108 Director Institutional Assessment .... Dr. Catherine BARRETTE
38 Director Student Counseling .... Dr. Jeffrey KUENTZEL
09 Assoc VP Institutional Research .... Dr. Meihua ZHAI
102 Assoc VP Principal Gifts .... Ms. Tracy UTECH
21 Controller .... Ms. Tamaka BUTLER
44 Director of Annual Giving .... Ms. Joye CLARK
106 Manager Online Education/E-Lrng .... Ms. Stacy N. JACKSON
90 Assoc VP Academic Computing .... Mr. Rob THOMPSON

West Shore Community College (A)

3000 N. Stiles Road, Scottville MI 49454-0277

County: Mason FICE Identification: 007950
Unit ID: 172671
Telephone: (231) 845-6211 Carnegie Class: Assoc/MT-VT-Mix Trad/Non
FAX Number: (231) 843-5803 Calendar System: Semester
URL: www.westshore.edu
Established: 1967 Annual Undergrad Tuition & Fees (In-District): $4,480
Enrollment: 1,058 Coed
Affiliation or Control: Local IRS Status: 501(c)3
Highest Offering: Associate Degree
Accreditation: HLC, MAC, NAEYC

01 President .... Mr. Scott WARD
05 VP of Academic & Student Services .... Dr. Mark KINNEY
04 Executive Assistant to President .... Ms. Lisa STANKOWSKI
26 Exec Director of College Relations .... Mr. Thomas A. HAWLEY
49 Dean of Arts and Sciences .... Vacant
13 Director of Information Technology .... Ms. Debra HINTZ
24 Media Svcs & Learning Tech Coord .... Mr. Craig PETERSON
119 Network Administrator .... Mr. Terrence JOHNSON
75 Dean of Occupational Programs .... Ms. Christy CHRISTMAS
32 Dean of Student Services .... Mr. Chad E. INABINET
06 Registrar .... Ms. Jill SWEET
09 Director of Institutional Research .... Mr. Steve SPARLING
40 Director of Bookstore & Food Svcs .... Ms. Cheryl HOGAN
37 Director Financial Aid .... Ms. Rebekah SCHAUB
91 Manager of Adm Computing Systems .... Mr. Ryan GREGORSKI
18 Director of Facilities & Recreation .... Mr. Michael A. MOORE
15 Director of Human Resources .... Ms. Debra CAMPBELL
16 Human Resources Specialist .... Ms. Jessica KEITH
08 Director of Library Services .... Ms. Renee SNODGRASS
23 Director of Wellness Center .... Ms. Julie PAGE-SMITH
10 Director of Accounting .... Ms. Conny BAX
84 Director of Enrollment Services .... Ms. Annie JACOBSON
04 Administrative Assistant .... Ms. Tasha DAULT
103 Dir of Business Opportunity Center .... Ms. Crystal YOUNG
120 Learning Management Systems Analyst .... Mr. Tom ALWAY
66 Director of Nursing .... Ms. Shelley BOES
105 Webmaster/Computer Technician .... Mr. Tim FINK

Western Michigan University (B)

1903 West Michigan Avenue, Kalamazoo MI 49008-5202

County: Kalamazoo FICE Identification: 002330
Unit ID: 172699
Telephone: (269) 387-1000 Carnegie Class: DU-Higher
FAX Number: (269) 387-0958 Calendar System: Semester
URL: wmich.edu
Established: 1903 Annual Undergrad Tuition & Fees (In-State): $13,017
Enrollment: 19,887 Coed
Affiliation or Control: State IRS Status: 501(c)3
Highest Offering: Doctorate
Accreditation: HLC, AAB, ABAI, #ARCPA, ART, AUD, #CAATE, CACREP, CAEP, CEA, CIDA, CLPSY, COPSY, DANCE, DIETD, DIETI, MUS, NURSE, OT, @PTA, SP, SPAA, SW, THEA

01 President .... Dr. Edward B. MONTGOMERY
05 Provost/Vice Pres Academic Affairs .... Dr. Jennifer P. BOTT
10 Vice Pres Business & Finance/CFO .... Ms. Jan VAN DER KLEY
32 VP Student Affairs .... Dr. Diane K. ANDERSON
46 Vice President for Research .... Dr. Terri G. KINZY
30 VP Development/Alumni Relations .... Ms. Kristen DEVRIES
43 General Counsel .... Dr. Carrick CRAIG
28 VP for Diversity and Inclusion .... Dr. Candy MCCORKLE
21 Assoc Vice Pres Business & Finance .... Ms. Colleen SCARFF
15 Assoc Vice Pres Human Resources .... Dr. Warren L. HILLS
18 Assoc Vice Pres Facilities Mgmt .... Mr. Peter J. STRAZDAS
35 Assoc VP of SA & Dean of Students .... Dr. Suzie NAGEL
35 Assoc VP for Student Affairs .... Mr. Vernon PAYNE
114 Exec Dir University Budgets .... Vacant
101 Chief of Staff/Sec Board Trustees .... Mr. Kahler B. SCHUEMANN
58 Dean Graduate College .... Dr. Christine BYRD-JACOBS
49 Dean of Arts & Sciences .... Dr. Carla M. KORETSKY
88 Dean of Aviation .... Capt. David M. POWELL
50 Dean of Business .... Dr. Satish DESHPANDE
53 Dean of Education & Human Dev .... Dr. Ming LI
54 Dean of Engineer & Applied Sciences .... Dr. Steven BUTT
57 Dean of Fine Arts .... Mr. Daniel GUYETTE
76 Dean Health & Human Services .... Dr. Ron CISLER
92 Dean of Lee Honors College .... Dr. Irma LOPEZ
08 Dean of Libraries .... Ms. Julie A. GARRISON
26 Vice Pres Marketing/Strategic Comm .... Mr. Tony PROUDFOOT
27 Director Strategic Communications .... Ms. Paula M. DAVIS
06 Registrar .... Ms. Carrie CUMMING
07 Director Admissions/Orientation .... Vacant
37 Dir Student Financial Aid .... Ms. Shashanta JAMES
38 Dir Counseling Services .... Dr. Brian J. FULLER
41 Dir Athletics .... Ms. Kathy B. BEAUREGARD
88 Assoc Prov for Global Education .... Dr. Paulo ZAGALO-MELO
85 Int Dir Intl Admissions & Services .... Ms. Soong Min CHOW
14 Chief Technology Officer .... Mr. Thomas WOLF, JR.
22 Exec Dir Institutional Equity .... Dr. Evelyn B. WINFIELD-THOMAS
104 Director Study Abroad .... Dr. Lee M. PENYAK
19 Dir Public Safety/Chief of Police .... Mr. Scott R. MERLO
25 Dir Grants/Contracts .... Ms. Betty J. MCKAIN
39 Director Residence Life .... Mr. Steven C. PALMER

Western Michigan University Cooley Law School (C)

300 S Capitol Avenue, Lansing MI 48933

County: Ingham FICE Identification: 012627
Unit ID: 172477
Telephone: (517) 371-5140 Carnegie Class: Spec-4-yr-Law
FAX Number: (517) 334-5718 Calendar System: Semester
URL: www.cooley.edu
Established: 1972 Annual Graduate Tuition & Fees: N/A
Enrollment: 972 Coed
Affiliation or Control: Independent Non-Profit IRS Status: 501(c)3
Highest Offering: First Professional Degree; No Undergraduates
Accreditation: HLC, LAW

01 President and Dean .... James MCGRATH
100 Chief of Staff .... Frank AIELLO
04 Executive Asst to the President .... Cherie BECK
10 Chief Financial Officer/COO .... Kathleen CONKLIN
08 Associate Dean Library/Info Svcs .... Duane STROJNY
108 Assoc Dean Planning/Accreditation .... Laura LEDUC
32 Assoc Dean Academics/Students .... Amy TIMMER
84 SVP/Assoc Dean for Enrol/Stdnt Svcs .... Paul ZELENSKI
12 Assoc Dean Experiential Education .... Tracey BRAME
88 Assistant Dean Lansing Campus .... Erika BRIETFELD
88 Assistant Dean Tampa Bay Campus .... Katherine GUSTAFSON
07 Asst Dean Admissions/Financial Aid .... Lena BAILEY
36 Asst Dean Career/Professional Devel .... Lisa FADLER
06 Registrar/Dir of Student Records .... Danielle HALL
40 Bookstore Manager .... Joelle TOPP
21 Controller .... Ronda BECK
29 Acting Dir Alumni Donor Relations .... Helen HAESSLY
26 Director Communications .... Terry CARELLA

Western Michigan University Homer Stryker MD School of Medicine (D)

1000 Oakland Dr, Kalamazoo MI 49008-8010

County: Kalamazoo Identification: 667287
Telephone: (269) 337-4400 Carnegie Class: Not Classified
FAX Number: N/A Calendar System: Semester
URL: med.wmich.edu
Established: 2012 Annual Graduate Tuition & Fees: N/A
Enrollment: N/A Coed
Affiliation or Control: Independent Non-Profit IRS Status: 501(c)3
Highest Offering: Doctorate; No Undergraduates
Accreditation: HLC, MED

01 Founding Dean .... Dr. Hal B. JENSON
05 Assoc Dean Educational Affairs .... Dr. Michael BUSHA
20 Assoc Dean for Faculty Affairs .... Dr. Lisa E. GRAVES
10 Assoc Dean Administration/Finance .... Ms. Lori STRAUBE
32 Assoc Dean Student Affairs .... Dr. Peter ZIEMKOWSKI
30 Assoc Dean Devel/Alumni Affairs .... Dr. Jack MOSSER
36 Asst Dean Career Development .... Dr. Kevin KAVANAUGH
28 Asst Dean Diversity/Inclusiveness .... Dr. Donovan ROY

Western Theological Seminary (E)

101 E 13th Street, Holland MI 49423-3622

County: Ottawa FICE Identification: 002331
Unit ID: 172705
Telephone: (616) 392-8555 Carnegie Class: Spec-4-yr-Faith
FAX Number: (616) 392-7717 Calendar System: Semester
URL: www.westernsem.edu
Established: 1866 Annual Graduate Tuition & Fees: N/A
Enrollment: 357 Coed
Affiliation or Control: Reformed Church In America IRS Status: 501(c)3
Highest Offering: Doctorate; No Undergraduates
Accreditation: THEOL

01 President .... Dr. Felix THEONUGRAHA
05 Academic Dean/VP Academic Affairs .... Dr. Kristen JOHNSON
10 Vice President of Finance .... Mr. Norman DONKERSLOOT
08 Director of the Library .... Vacant
06 Registrar .... Mr. Kyle WIGBOLDY
07 Director of Admissions .... Ms. Jill ENGLISH
15 Dir of Administration & Human Res .... Ms. Rayetta PEREZ
04 Executive Asst to the President .... Ms. Lannette ZYLMAN-TENHAVE
30 Director of Development .... Mr. Andy BAST

Yeshiva Beth Yehuda - Yeshiva Gedolah of Greater Detroit (F)

24600 Greenfield, Oak Park MI 48237-1544

County: Oakland FICE Identification: 023638
Unit ID: 247773
Telephone: (248) 968-3360 Carnegie Class: Spec-4-yr-Faith
FAX Number: (248) 968-8613 Calendar System: Semester
Established: 1985 Annual Undergrad Tuition & Fees: $7,800
Enrollment: 55 Male
Affiliation or Control: Independent Non-Profit IRS Status: 501(c)3
Highest Offering: Doctorate
Accreditation: RABN

01 Dean .... Rabbi Y. BAKST
05 Assistant Dean .... Rabbi M. S. BAKST
11 Executive Administrator .... Rabbi P. RUSHNAWITZ
37 Director of Financial Aid .... Rabbi Y. BLITZ

MINNESOTA

Academy College (G)

1600 W. 82nd Street, Suite 100, Bloomington MN 55431

County: Hennepin FICE Identification: 020503
Unit ID: 172866
Telephone: (952) 851-0066 Carnegie Class: Spec-4-yr-Other Tech
FAX Number: (952) 851-0094 Calendar System: Quarter
URL: www.academycollege.edu
Established: 1936 Annual Undergrad Tuition & Fees: $18,699
Enrollment: 95 Coed
Affiliation or Control: Proprietary IRS Status: Proprietary
Highest Offering: Baccalaureate
Accreditation: ACCSC

01 President .... Nancy GRAZZINI-OLSON
05 Director of Education .... Roger SAGE
37 Director of Financial Aid .... Kellye MACLEOD

Adler Graduate School (H)

10225 Yellow Circle Dr, Minnetonka MN 55343

County: Hennepin FICE Identification: 030519
Unit ID: 374024
Telephone: (612) 861-7554 Carnegie Class: Spec-4-yr-Other Health
FAX Number: (612) 861-7559 Calendar System: Semester
URL: www.alfredadler.edu
Established: 1969 Annual Graduate Tuition & Fees: N/A
Enrollment: 267 Coed
Affiliation or Control: Independent Non-Profit IRS Status: 501(c)3
Highest Offering: Master's; No Undergraduates
Accreditation: HLC

01 President .... Dr. Jeffrey ALLEN
05 Director of Academics .... Dr. Solange RIBEIRO
10 CFO .... Vacant
106 Director of Assessment .... Dr. Nicole RANDICK
07 Director of Admissions .... Ms. Christina HILPRE-FRISCHMAN
06 Registrar .... Ms. Debbie VELASCO
37 Director of Student Financial Aid .... Ms. Jeanette MAYNARD NELSON
08 Head Librarian .... Ms. Nicole MARCHAND
29 Director of Alumni Relations .... Ms. Evelyn HAAS
90 Director Academic Computing .... Mr. Laurencio LECHUGA

American Academy of Acupuncture and Oriental Medicine (I)

1925 W County Road B2, Roseville MN 55113-2703

County: Ramsey FICE Identification: 038333
Unit ID: 446002
Telephone: (651) 631-0204 Carnegie Class: Spec-4-yr-Other Health
FAX Number: (651) 631-0361 Calendar System: Trimester
URL: www.aaaom.edu
Established: 1997 Annual Graduate Tuition & Fees: N/A
Enrollment: 43 Coed

Affiliation or Control: Proprietary IRS Status: Proprietary
Highest Offering: Doctorate; No Undergraduates
Accreditation: #ACUP

01 President .... Dr. Changzhen GONG
11 Administrative Director .... Leila NIELSEN
37 Financial Aid Officer .... Cate LARSON

Augsburg University (A)

2211 Riverside Avenue, Minneapolis MN 55454-1398
County: Hennepin FICE Identification: 002334
Unit ID: 173045
Telephone: (612) 330-1000 Carnegie Class: Masters/L
FAX Number: (612) 330-1649 Calendar System: Semester
URL: www.augsburg.edu
Established: 1869 Annual Undergrad Tuition & Fees: $40,005
Enrollment: 3,346 Coed
Affiliation or Control: Evangelical Lutheran Church In America
IRS Status: 501(c)3
Highest Offering: Doctorate
Accreditation: HLC, #ACBSP, ARCPA, MUS, NURSE, SW

01 President .... Dr. Paul C. PRIBBENOW
05 Provost and Chief Academic Officer .... Dr. Karen KAIVOLA
10 CFO and Senior Director of Finances .... Mr. John COSKRAN
111 VP Institutional Advancement .... Ms. Heather RIDDLE
32 VP Student Affairs .... Vacant
11 VP and Chief Operating Officer .... Ms. Rebecca JOHN
84 VP Strategic Enrollment Management .... Mr. Robert GOULD
45 VP & Chief Strategy Officer .... Mr. Leif B. ANDERSON
110 AVP Institutional Advancement .... Ms. Amy ALKIRE
107 Dean of Professional Studies .... Dr. Monica C. DEVERS
49 Dean of Arts & Sciences .... Dr. Ryan HAALAND
88 Asst Provost of Global Education .... Mr. Patrick MULVIHILL
35 Dean of Students .... Dr. Sarah GRIESSE
121 Chief Student Success Officer .... Ms. Catherine BISHOP
12 Director Rochester Program .... Mr. Jeremy UPDIKE
41 Athletic Director .... Mr. Jeffrey F. SWENSON
42 Campus Pastor .... Rev. Justin LIND-AYRES
28 Chief Inclusion Officer .... Ms. Joanne REECK
37 Director of Financial Aid .... Ms. Amanda BURGESS
06 Asst Prov/Acad Admin & Registrar .... Ms. Marah JACOBSON-SCHULTE
07 Director Undergraduate Admissions .... Mr. Devon G. ROSS
18 Director of Facilities Mgmt .... Vacant
13 Chief Information Officer .... Mr. Scott KRAJEWSKI
26 Assoc Vice Pres & Chief Mktg Ofcr ... Mr. Stephen JENDRASZAK
38 Director Ctr Wellness & Counseling . Ms. Nancy G. GUILBEAULT
15 HR Director/CHRO .... Ms. Dawn MILLER
08 Director Library Services .... Ms. Mary HOLLERICH
19 Director Public Safety & Risk Mgmt .... Vacant
31 Director Community Relations .... Mr. Steve PEACOCK
88 Director StepUp Program .... Ms. Renee MOST
85 Director International Student Svc .... Vacant
114 Director of Budget .... Mr. Tom CARROLL
88 Director University Events .... Ms. Sarah CASH-DARVELL
27 Dir Public Rel & Internal Comm .... Ms. Gita SITARAMIAH
36 Exec Director Strommen Center .... Mr. Lee GEORGE
39 Director Residence Life .... Ms. Emily LONG
104 Director Global Initiatives .... Ms. Leah SPINOSA DE VEGA
25 Dir Research & Sponsored Programs .... Dr. Lauren CAUSEY
04 Executive Assistant to President .... Ms. Cyndi BERG
88 Dir Enrollment Systems & Analytics .... Ms. Stephanie RUCKEL
40 Bookstore Manager .... Ms. Chanti MILLER
09 Dir Inst Research & Effectiveness .... Ms. Kathryn HAHN
96 Manager of Purchasing/Central Svcs .... Vacant

Bethany Global University (B)

6820 Auto Club Road, Suite C, Bloomington MN 55438
County: Hennepin Identification: 667136
Unit ID: 486284
Telephone: (952) 222-0699 Carnegie Class: Spec-4-yr-Faith
FAX Number: (952) 829-2753 Calendar System: Semester
URL: https://bethanygu.edu/
Established: 1948 Annual Undergrad Tuition & Fees: $15,450
Enrollment: 359 Coed
Affiliation or Control: Interdenominational IRS Status: 501(c)3
Highest Offering: Master's
Accreditation: BI

01 President .... Dr. David HASZ
04 Executive Asst to President .... La'Tia COLEMAN
84 Director of Enrollment .... Kenneth FREIRE
05 Dean of Academic Operations .... Jason HACHÉ
103 Dean of Work Education .... Brian SCHWARZ
58 Dean of Graduate Studies .... Dr. Darin KINDLE
10 Chief Financial/Business Officer .... David ENTLER
101 Secretary of the Institution/Board .... Ron HAVE
30 Chief Development/Advancement .... Mike MINICH
26 Director of Marketing .... Kenneth FREIRE
18 Chief Facilities/Physical Plant .... Matthew ADAIR
88 Global Internship Director .... Doug GOODMUNDSON
106 Director Online Educ/Partnerships .... Kenneth ORTIZ
34 Dean of Women/Student Life .... Bethany FREIRE
33 Dean of Men/Student Life .... Derek BROKKE
13 Network/Computer Administrator .... Chris ERICKSON
15 Director Human Resources .... Noemi HEDRICK
19 Director Security/Safety .... Matthew ADAIR
44 Donor Communications Specialist .... Vacant
37 Director Financial Aid .... Anna BERGH
06 Registrar .... Hannah LEVIN

36 Director Career Development .... Dr. Elisabeth WILSON
08 Head Librarian .... Vacant

Bethany Lutheran College (C)

700 Luther Drive, Mankato MN 56001-6163
County: Blue Earth FICE Identification: 002337
Unit ID: 173142
Telephone: (507) 344-7000 Carnegie Class: Bac-A&S
FAX Number: (507) 344-7376 Calendar System: Semester
URL: www.blc.edu
Established: 1911 Annual Undergrad Tuition & Fees: $28,380
Enrollment: 769 Coed
Affiliation or Control: Evangelical Lutheran Synod IRS Status: 501(c)3
Highest Offering: Master's
Accreditation: HLC, NURSE

01 President .... Dr. Gene R. PFEIFER
42 Dir Campus Spiritual Life/Chaplain .... Rev. Donald L. MOLDSTAD
05 Vice President of Academic Affairs .... Dr. Jason H. LOWREY
32 Vice President of Student Affairs .... Dr. Theodore E. MANTHE
10 VP of Finance & Administration .... Mr. Daniel L. MUNDAHL
111 Vice President of Advancement .... Mr. Bruce A. GRATZ
37 Director of Financial Aid .... Mr. Jeffrey W. YOUNGE
06 Registrar .... Mr. Sergio SALGADO
07 VP of Admissions & Enrollment .... Dr. Jeffrey C. LEMKE
15 Manager of Human Resources .... Mr. Joshua PEDERSON
08 Director of Library Services .... Ms. Alyssa K. INNIGER
13 Director of Information Technology .... Mr. John M. SEHLOFF
26 Dir of Institutional Communication .... Mr. Lance W. SCHWARTZ
41 Director of Athletics .... Mr. Donald M. WESTPHAL
29 Manager of Alumni Relations .... Mr. Jacob C. KRIER
09 Mgr Acad & Institutional Research .... Ms. Lisa A. SHUBERT
40 Bookstore Manager .... Mr. Daniel GERDTS
21 Controller .... Mr. Gregory W. COSTELLO
28 Coord Ctr for Intercultural Develop .... Vacant
38 Coord of Student Counseling .... Vacant
18 Director of Facilities .... Mr. Patrick E. HULL
108 Director of Assessment .... Dr. Theodore E. MANTHE
04 Executive Asst to President .... Mrs. Barbara J. DRESSEN
106 Director Online Learning .... Mr. Kevin ZIMMERMAN

Bethel University (D)

3900 Bethel Drive, Saint Paul MN 55112-6999
County: Ramsey FICE Identification: 009058
Unit ID: 173160
Telephone: (651) 638-6400 Carnegie Class: DU-Mod
FAX Number: (651) 638-6001 Calendar System: Semester
URL: www.bethel.edu
Established: 1871 Annual Undergrad Tuition & Fees: $39,030
Enrollment: 3,814 Coed
Affiliation or Control: Baptist IRS Status: 501(c)3
Highest Offering: Doctorate
Accreditation: HLC, ACBSP, ARCPA, CAATE, MFCD, MIDWF, NURSE, SW, THEOL

01 President .... Mr. Ross ALLEN
100 Senior Assoc for the President .... Ms. Jeanne OSGOOD
05 University Provost .... Dr. Robin RYLAARSDAM
10 Vice Pres Finance .... Ms. Amy BLAZ
20 Assoc Provost/VP Academic Affairs .... Dr. Julie FINNERN
26 Chief Enrollment/Marketing Officer .... Mr. Michael VEDDERS
111 Vice Pres Univ Advancement .... Mr. Jim BENDER
46 Chief Inst Data/Research Officer .... Mr. Daniel NELSON
90 Chief Facilities/Technology Officer .... Mr. Mark POSNER
29 Exec Minister for Church Relations .... Dr. Dale DURIE
32 Vice Pres Student Experience .... Mr. John ADDLEMAN
20 Assoc Provost of CAS .... Dr. Deborah SULLIVAN-TRAINOR
73 Dean of Seminary .... Dr. Peter VOGT
49 Dean of Academic Programs .... Dr. Barrett FISHER
108 Assoc Dean Inst Assess/Accred .... Dr. Joel FREDERICKSON
66 Dean Nursing/CAPS-GS Health/Med .... Dr. Diane DAHL
107 Dean Faculty Dev/Professional Pgms .... Mr. Ray VAN ARRAGON
104 Assoc Dean Off-Campus Programs .... Mr. Vincent PETERS
35 Dean of Students .... Ms. Miranda POWERS
08 Director of Libraries .... Mr. David R. STEWART
15 Chief Human Resources/Strategy Ofcr .... Ms. Cara WALD
41 Athletic Director .... Mr. Robert B. BJORKLUND
37 Financial Aid Officer .... Mr. Jeffery D. OLSON
42 AVP Christian Formation/Church Rels .... Ms. Laurel BUNKER
07 Director of CAS Admissions .... Mr. Bret HYDER
07 Dir Seminary/CAPS/GS Admissions .... Ms. Kate GUNDERSON
06 University Registrar .... Ms. Diane KRUSEMARK
36 Dean Career Development .... Ms. Ann V. NGO
19 Director Risk Mgmt/Safety/Security .... Mr. Zach HILL
40 Director Campus Stores .... Ms. Jill SONSTEBY
23 Director of Health Services .... Mrs. Elizabeth K. MILLER
96 Director of Purchasing .... Vacant
38 Director Student Counseling .... Dr. Miriam HILL
109 Dir of Campus Svcs & Operations .... Mr. Barry HOLST
18 Director Facilities Tech Ops .... Mr. Glenn HOFER
28 VP Diversity/Equity/Inclusion .... Vacant
29 Director Alumni & Family Relations .... Ms. Jennifer SCOTT
110 Assoc Vice Pres of Development .... Vacant

† The marriage and family therapy master's program at Bethel Seminary San Diego is accredited by the Commission on Accreditation for Marriage and Family Therapy Education (COAMFTE) of the American Association for Marriage and Family Therapy (AAMFT)

Bethlehem College & Seminary (E)

720 13th Avenue South, Minneapolis MN 55415
County: Hennepin Identification: 667249
Unit ID: 486053
Telephone: (612) 455-3420 Carnegie Class: Spec-4-yr-Faith
FAX Number: N/A Calendar System: Semester
URL: bcsmn.edu
Established: 2009 Annual Undergrad Tuition & Fees: $6,560
Enrollment: 210 Coed
Affiliation or Control: Independent Non-Profit IRS Status: 501(c)3
Highest Offering: Master's
Accreditation: BI

01 President .... Dr. Joseph RIGNEY
05 Academic Dean .... Dr. Brian TABB
11 VP of Administration & CFO .... Jason ABELL
111 VP of Advancement .... Rick SEGAL
07 Dean of Admissions .... Jonathon WOODYARD
04 Assistant to President .... Lance M. KRAMER
06 Registrar/Bursar & Dir Inst Rsrch .... Connie KOPISCHKE

Capella University (F)

225 S 6th Street, 9th Floor, Minneapolis MN 55402-4319
County: Hennepin FICE Identification: 032673
Unit ID: 413413
Telephone: (888) 227-3552 Carnegie Class: DU-Mod
FAX Number: (612) 977-5066 Calendar System: Other
URL: www.capella.edu
Established: 1993 Annual Undergrad Tuition & Fees: $14,148
Enrollment: 38,930 Coed
Affiliation or Control: Proprietary IRS Status: Proprietary
Highest Offering: Doctorate
Accreditation: HLC, ACBSP, CACREP, CAEP, MFCD, NURSE, SW

01 President .... Dr. Richard SENESE
05 VP Academic Affairs/Provost .... Dr. Constance ST. GERMAIN
10 VP Finance .... Mike WICKARD

Carleton College (G)

1 N College Street, Northfield MN 55057-4001
County: Rice FICE Identification: 002340
Unit ID: 173258
Telephone: (507) 222-4000 Carnegie Class: Bac-A&S
FAX Number: N/A Calendar System: Trimester
URL: www.carleton.edu
Established: 1866 Annual Undergrad Tuition & Fees: $59,352
Enrollment: 1,940 Coed
Affiliation or Control: Independent Non-Profit IRS Status: 501(c)3
Highest Offering: Baccalaureate
Accreditation: HLC

01 President .... Ms. Alison R. BYERLY
05 Dean of the College .... Ms. Gretchen HOFMEISTER
10 VP Business & Finance/Treasurer .... Mr. Eric J. RUNESTAD
111 Vice President External Relations .... Mr. Tommy BONNER
32 VP for Student Dev/Dean of Students .. Ms. Carolyn LIVINGSTON
07 VP and Dean of Admissions/Fin Aid .... Mr. Art RODRIGUEZ
100 Vice President/Chief of Staff .... Ms. Elise ESLINGER
26 Assoc VP Ext Relations/Dir Col Comm .... Mr. Joe HARGIS
20 Associate Dean of the College .... Mr. Andrew FISHER
121 Assoc Dean Coll/Dir of Advising .... Mr. Alfred MONTERO
88 Director of Student Fellowships .... Ms. Marynel RYAN VAN ZEE
35 Associate Dean of Students .... Mr. Joseph BAGGOT
35 Associate Dean of Students .... Ms. Cathy CARLSON
37 Assoc Dean Admiss/Dir Stdnt Fin Svc .... Mr. Rod M. OTO
42 Chaplain .... Rev. Carolyn FURE-SLOCUM
06 Registrar .... Ms. Emy FARLEY
08 College Librarian .... Mr. Bradley SCHAFFNER
09 Asst VP Inst Research & Assessment .... Mr. Todd JAMISON
110 Asst VP for External Relations .... Ms. Becky ZRIMSEK
29 Director of Alumni Relations .... Mr. Michael THOMPSON
44 Director of Alumni Annual Fund .... Ms. Nicole SCHROEDER
30 Assoc VP for Development .... Mr. Dan RUSTAD
112 Director of Planned Giving .... Ms. Lynne WILMOT
13 Chief Technology Officer .... Ms. Janet SCANNELL
27 Dir Digital Strategy/Public Affairs .... Ms. Helen CLARKE EBERT
15 Director of Human Resources .... Ms. Kerstin CARDENAS
39 Director of Residential Life .... Ms. Andrea ROBINSON
85 Dir Intercult/International Life .... Ms. Brisa ZUBIA
104 Director of Off-Campus Studies .... Ms. Helena KAUFMAN
36 Director of the Career Center .... Mr. R.J HOLMES-LEOPOLD
23 Dir Student Health and Counseling .... Ms. Marit LYSNE
18 Dir of Facilities/Capital Planning .... Mr. Steven SPEHN
21 Comptroller .... Ms. Linda THORNTON
25 Director of the Grants Office .... Mr. Christopher TASSAVA
88 Dir of Educational Research .... Ms. Andrea NIXON
88 Dir Center for Learning/Teaching .... Ms. Melissa EBLEN-ZAYAS
109 Director of Auxiliary Services .... Mr. Jesse CASHMAN
41 Chair of Physical Educ/Athl/Rec .... Mr. Gerald YOUNG
19 Director of Security/Emergency Mgmt .... Mr. John BERMEL
105 Director of Web Services .... Ms. Julie ANDERSON
91 Dir of Enterprise Information Svcs .... Ms. Julie CREAMER
88 Director of Technology Support .... Mr. Austin ROBINSON-COOLIDGE

Central Baptist Theological Seminary of Minneapolis (A)

900 Forestview Lane N, Plymouth MN 55441-5934
County: Hennepin	Identification: 666050
Telephone: (763) 417-8250	Carnegie Class: Not Classified
FAX Number: (763) 417-8258	Calendar System: Semester
URL: www.centralseminary.edu
Established: 1956	Annual Undergrad Tuition & Fees: N/A
Enrollment: N/A	Coed
Affiliation or Control: Baptist	IRS Status: 501(c)3
Highest Offering: Doctorate
Accreditation: THEOL

01 President .... Dr. Matthew D. MORRELL
03 Provost/EVP .... Dr. Brett J. WILLIAMS
111 Vice Pres of Advancement .... Mr. Ron GOTZMAN
07 Director Recruitment/Retention .... Dr. Matt SHRADER
06 Registrar .... Dr. L. Mark BRUFFEY
08 Chief Library Officer .... Dr. L. Mark BRUFFEY

*College of Medicine, Mayo Clinic (B)

200 First Street, Rochester MN 55905-3712
County: Olmsted	Identification: 666719
Telephone: (507) 284-2511	Carnegie Class: N/A
FAX Number: (507) 284-0999
URL: www.mayo.edu

01 Chief Executive Officer .... Dr. John H. NOSEWORTHY
05 Exec Dean for Education Mayo Clinic .... Dr. Fredric B. MEYER
46 Exec Dean for Research Mayo Clinic .... Dr. Greg GORES
15 Chair of Human Resources .... Ms. Cathy FRASER
30 Exec Dean of Development .... Dr. Michael CAMILLERI

*Mayo Medical School (C)

200 1st Street, SW, Rochester MN 55905-0001
County: Olmsted	FICE Identification: 011732
Unit ID: 173957
Telephone: (507) 538-4897	Carnegie Class: Spec-4-yr-Med
FAX Number: (507) 284-2634	Calendar System: Other
URL: www.mayo.edu/mms
Established: 1971	Annual Undergrad Tuition & Fees: $7,290
Enrollment: 1,223	Coed
Affiliation or Control: Independent Non-Profit	IRS Status: 501(c)3
Highest Offering: First Professional Degree
Accreditation: HLC, MED

02 Dean .... Dr. Fredric B. MEYER
37 Director of Financial Aid .... Ms. Anne DAHLEN
06 Registrar .... Ms. Anne DAHLEN

*Mayo Clinic College of Medicine-Mayo Graduate School (D)

200 First Street, SW, Rochester MN 55905-0001
Telephone: (507) 538-1160	FICE Identification: 011516
Accreditation: &HLC, CAMPEP, DENT, PDPSY

† Regional accreditation is carried under College of Medicine, Mayo Clinic.

*Mayo Clinic School of Health Sciences (E)

200 First St. SW, Siebens Bldg 3,
Rochester MN 55905-0001
Telephone: (507) 284-3293	FICE Identification: 008182
Accreditation: &HLC, ACS, ANEST, #ARCPA, COARC, CVT, CYTO, DIETI, DMS, EMT, HT, MT, NDT, NMT, PAST, PTA, RAD, RTT, SURGA

† Regional accreditation is carried under College of Medicine, Mayo Clinic.

College of Saint Benedict (F)

37 S College Avenue, Saint Joseph MN 56374-2099
County: Stearns	FICE Identification: 002341
Unit ID: 174747
Telephone: (320) 363-5011	Carnegie Class: Bac-A&S
FAX Number: (320) 363-6099	Calendar System: Semester
URL: www.csbsju.edu
Established: 1913	Annual Undergrad Tuition & Fees: $48,444
Enrollment: 1,668	Coordinate
Affiliation or Control: Roman Catholic	IRS Status: 501(c)3
Highest Offering: Doctorate
Accreditation: HLC, DIETD, MUS, NURSE

01 Interim President .... Dr. Laurie HAMEN
05 Provost Academic Affairs .... Dr. Richard ICE
32 Vice President Student Development .... Ms. Mary A. GELLER
111 VP Institutional Advancement .... Ms. Kathy HANSEN
10 Vice Pres Finance/Administration .... Ms. Susan M. PALMER
84 VP Enrollment Management/Marketing .... Mr. Nate DEHNE
110 Assoc VP Institutional Advancement .... Ms. Heather PIEPER-OLSON
18 Exec Director Facilities .... Mr. Ryan GIDEON
26 Sr Director of Public Relations .... Mr. Michael HEMMESCH
20 Academic Dean .... Dr. Barbara MAY
34 Dean of Students .... Ms. Jody L. TERHAAR
06 Registrar .... Ms. Julie E. GRUSKA
08 Director Library .... Ms. Kathy PARKER
37 Exec Director Financial Aid .... Mr. Stuart PERRY
38 Director of Counseling .... Dr. Mike J. EWING
42 Interim Director of Campus Ministry .... Mr. Aaron VOTH
41 Athletic Director .... Ms. Kelly ANDERSON DIERCKS
13 Director of Info Technology Svc .... Ms. Casey GORDON
19 Director of Security .... Mr. Darren SWANSON
21 Controller .... Ms. Anne OBERMAN
36 Executive Director XPD .... Vacant
09 Assoc Dir of Institutional Research .... Ms. Karen KNUTSON
40 Director of Bookstores .... Ms. Tina STREIT
20 Dean of the Faculty .... Dr. Pamela BACON
07 Dean of Admission .... Ms. Karen BACKES

The College of Saint Scholastica (G)

1200 Kenwood Avenue, Duluth MN 55811-4199
County: Saint Louis	FICE Identification: 002343
Unit ID: 174899
Telephone: (218) 723-6000	Carnegie Class: DU-Mod
FAX Number: (218) 723-6290	Calendar System: Semester
URL: www.css.edu
Established: 1912	Annual Undergrad Tuition & Fees: $39,410
Enrollment: 3,712	Coed
Affiliation or Control: Roman Catholic	IRS Status: 501(c)3
Highest Offering: Doctorate
Accreditation: HLC, AAQEP, #ARCPA, CAATE, CAHIIM, NURSE, OT, PTA, SW

01 President .... Dr. Barbara MCDONALD
05 Vice President Academic Affairs .... Mr. Ryan SANDEFER
32 Vice President for Student Affairs .... Mr. Steve LYONS
10 Vice President of Finance & CFO .... Mr. Marty PARSONS
11 Chief Operating Officer .... Ms. Diane VERTIN
28 Chief Diversity Office .... Dr. Amy BERGSTROM
13 Chief Information Officer .... Vacant

Concordia College (H)

901 8th Street S, Moorhead MN 56562-0001
County: Clay	FICE Identification: 002346
Unit ID: 173300
Telephone: (218) 299-4000	Carnegie Class: Bac-A&S
FAX Number: (218) 299-3947	Calendar System: Semester
URL: www.cord.edu
Established: 1891	Annual Undergrad Tuition & Fees: $43,266
Enrollment: 1,973	Coed
Affiliation or Control: Evangelical Lutheran Church In America
IRS Status: 501(c)3
Highest Offering: Master's
Accreditation: HLC, CAEP, DIETD, DIETI, MUS, NURSE, SW

01 President .... Dr. William J. CRAFT
05 Provost and Dean of the College .... Dr. Susan J. LARSON
10 Vice Pres Finance/Treasurer .... Ms. Linda J. BROWN
84 Vice Pres Enrollment and Marketing .... Mr. Karl A. STUMO
111 Vice Pres Advancement .... Rev. Terry BRANDT
32 VP Student Dev and Campus Life .... Dr. Lisa SETHRE-HOFSTAD
28 Chief Diversity Officer .... Dr. Edward ANTONIO
20 Associate Provost .... Dr. Stephanie L. AHLFELDT
100 Deputy to the President .... Dr. Jill M. ABBOTT
13 Exec Dir of Information Technology .... Mr. Erik RAMSTAD
07 Dir of Admission Operations .... Ms. Samantha AXVIG
06 Registrar .... Ms. Lisa M. SJOBERG
37 Assoc VP Enrollment & Financial Aid .... Mr. Eric J. ADDINGTON
08 Library Director .... Mrs. Laura K. PROBST
15 Director Human Resources .... Ms. Peggy L. TORRANCE
29 Director Alumni Relations .... Mr. Eric P. JOHNSON
26 Assoc VP Comm/Chief Mktg Officer .... Mr. Josh D. LYSNE
18 Director of Facilities Management .... Mr. Dallas FOSSUM
41 Athletic Director .... Ms. Rachel D. BERGESON
42 Minister of Word and Sacrament .... Rev. Dave ADAMS
42 Minister Faith & Spirituality .... Mr. Jon LEISETH
19 Director of Security/Public Safety .... Mr. William MACDONALD
04 Exec Asst to the President .... Ms. Carrie ROGERS
104 Assoc Dean Global Learning .... Dr. Per M. ANDERSON
108 Dir Institutional Effectiveness .... Dr. Jasi O'CONNOR
25 Dir Found Rels/Research Grants .... Ms. Jillain VEIL-EHNERT
30 Director of Development .... Ms. Trina PISK HALL
39 Director Residence Life .... Ms. Mikal C. KENFIELD
117 Director Risk Management .... Mr. Roger T. OLSON
44 Director Annual Fund .... Ms. Rachel M. CLARKE
36 Director of Career Center .... Ms. Kris OLSON
38 Director of Counseling Center .... Mr. Matthew RUTTEN

Concordia University, St. Paul (I)

1282 Concordia Ave, Saint Paul MN 55104-5494
County: Ramsey	FICE Identification: 002347
Unit ID: 173328
Telephone: (651) 641-8278	Carnegie Class: Masters/L
FAX Number: (651) 659-0207	Calendar System: Semester
URL: www.csp.edu
Established: 1893	Annual Undergrad Tuition & Fees: $23,400
Enrollment: 5,585	Coed
Affiliation or Control: Lutheran Church - Missouri Synod
IRS Status: 501(c)3
Highest Offering: Doctorate
Accreditation: HLC, NURSE, OPE, PTA

01 President .... RevDr. Brian FRIEDRICH
11 Provost/SVP for Administration .... Dr. Eric E. LAMOTT
05 Vice President Academic Affairs .... Dr. Kevin HALL
10 Vice President for Finance .... RevDr. Michael H. DORNER
111 Vice President for Advancement .... Mr. Mark HILL
84 VP for Enrollment Management .... Dr. Kimberly CRAIG
07 Assoc Dir Undergraduate Admissions .... Vacant
32 Assoc VP Student Life .... Mr. Jason M. RAHN
108 Assoc VP for Assessment/Accred .... Dr. Miriam LUEBKE
28 Chief Diversity Officer .... Mr. Mychal THOM
53 Dean College of Education .... Mr. Lonn MALY
79 Dean Col of Humanities .... Dr. Paul HILLMER
83 Dean Col Human Svcs/Behavioral Sci .... Dr. Michael WALCHESKI
50 Dean College of Business .... Vacant
76 Dean College of Health & Science .... Dr. Katie J. FISCHER
28 Dean of Diversity .... Vacant
39 Asst Director of Residence Life .... Mr. Jake WAKEM
06 Registrar .... Ms. Lynn LUNDQUIST
08 Director of Library Services .... Mr. Jonathan B. NEILSON
26 Dir Univ Communications/Mrktng .... Mr. Brian EVANS
15 Director of Human Resources .... Ms. Milissa M. ORCHARD
37 Director of Financial Aid .... Ms. Jeanie PECK
42 University Pastor .... Rev. Thomas GUNDERMANN
88 Director of Traditional Advising .... Ms. Gretchen WALTHER
09 Director of Institutional Research .... Ms. Beth C. PETER
29 Director of Alumni Relations .... Mrs. Rhonda K. PALMERSHEIM
41 Director of Athletics .... Mrs. Regan M. MCATHIE
18 Director of Operations .... Mr. James P. ORCHARD
40 Bookstore Manager .... Mr. Chad L. MASTEL
90 Director of Computer Services .... Mr. Jonathan S. BREITBARTH
91 Director Administrative Computing .... Ms. Beth C. PETER
19 Risk Manager .... Mr. David GALLOWAY
24 Help Desk Coordinator .... Ms. Elizabeth GOODMAN
44 Director Annual Giving .... Ms. Staci POOLE
04 Admin Assistant to the President .... Mr. William SCHULTZ

Crown College (J)

8700 College View Drive, Saint Bonifacius MN 55375-9001
County: Carver	FICE Identification: 002383
Unit ID: 174862
Telephone: (952) 446-4100	Carnegie Class: Masters/S
FAX Number: (952) 446-4149	Calendar System: Semester
URL: www.crown.edu
Established: 1916	Annual Undergrad Tuition & Fees: $27,980
Enrollment: 1,485	Coed
Affiliation or Control: The Christian And Missionary Alliance
IRS Status: 501(c)3
Highest Offering: Master's
Accreditation: HLC, NURSE

01 President .... Dr. Andrew DENTON
04 Exec Assistant to the President .... Mrs. Emily HONEBRINK
10 VP Enrollment & Administration .... Mr. Michael PRICE
05 VP Academic Affairs .... Dr. Christopher MATHEWS
32 VP Student Development .... Dr. Bill KUHN
30 VP College Relations .... Mr. Travis WHIPPLE
58 AVP Sch Online Studies/Grad School .... Dr. Fawn MCCRACKEN
26 Chief Marketing & Comms Officer .... Mrs. Jen NISKA
15 Director of Human Resources .... Mrs. Amy LUESSE
21 Controller .... Mr. Ronald STRAKA
41 Athletic Director .... Vacant
66 Director of Nursing .... Mrs. Teresa NEWBY
06 Registrar .... Dr. Cheryl FISK
37 Director of Financial Aid .... Mrs. Allyson GILLETTE
124 Director Student Engagement .... Mrs. Martha SWIFT
123 Director of Graduate Admissions .... Ms. Maggie UNGER
18 Director of Facilities Services .... Mrs. Nancy DARBUT
40 Director of Campus Store .... Mrs. Sharie THOELKE
42 Chaplain .... Dr. Bill KUHN
36 Dir Counseling & Career Services .... Dr. Bill JOHNSON
13 Director of Technology Services .... Mr. Paul FLAGSTAD
121 Dir Inst Persistance/Completion .... Mrs. Patty PITTS
35 Dean of Students .... Mr. Ezra JOHNSON
93 Dir Intercultural Lrng/Experience .... Mr. Oliver FERGUSON
07 Director of Admission .... Mr. Mitch FISK

Dunwoody College of Technology (K)

818 Dunwoody Boulevard, Minneapolis MN 55403-1192
County: Hennepin	FICE Identification: 004641
Unit ID: 175227
Telephone: (612) 374-5800	Carnegie Class: Bac/Assoc-Mixed
FAX Number: (612) 381-9620	Calendar System: Semester
URL: www.dunwoody.edu
Established: 1914	Annual Undergrad Tuition & Fees: $23,122
Enrollment: 1,281	Coed
Affiliation or Control: Independent Non-Profit	IRS Status: 501(c)3
Highest Offering: Baccalaureate
Accreditation: HLC, CIDA, RAD

01 President .... Dr. Rich WAGNER
05 Provost .... Dr. Scott STALLMAN
84 Vice President Enrollment Mgmt .... Ms. Cynthia OLSON
111 VP of Institutional Advancement .... Mr. Brian NELSON
15 Vice President of Human Resources .... Ms. Patricia EDMAN
10 VP of Administrative Svcs & CFO .... Ms. Tammy MCGEE
100 Chief of Staff .... Ms. Katie MALONE

Free Lutheran Bible College and Seminary (L)

3134 East Medicine Lake Blvd, Plymouth MN 55441
County: Hennepin	Identification: 667235
Telephone: (763) 544-9501	Carnegie Class: Not Classified
FAX Number: (763) 412-2047	Calendar System: Semester
URL: www.flbc.edu

Established: 1964 Annual Graduate Tuition & Fees: N/A
Enrollment: N/A Coed
Affiliation or Control: Independent Non-Profit IRS Status: 501(c)3
Highest Offering: Master's; No Undergraduates
Accreditation: TRACS

01 President .... Dr. Wade MOBLEY
05 Chief Academic Officer/Dean .... Dr. James MOLSTRE
11 Vice President of Operations .... Larry MYHRER
03 Vice President/Dean .... Adam OSIER
06 Registrar .... Sarah BIERLE
07 Director of Admissions .... Josh JOHNSON
32 Director Student Life & Athletics .... Dr. Brad BIERLE

Gustavus Adolphus College (A)

800 W College Avenue, Saint Peter MN 56082-1498
County: Nicollet FICE Identification: 002353
Unit ID: 173647
Telephone: (507) 933-8000 Carnegie Class: Bac-A&S
FAX Number: (507) 933-7041 Calendar System: Semester
URL: www.gustavus.edu
Established: 1862 Annual Undergrad Tuition & Fees: $48,789
Enrollment: 2,230 Coed
Affiliation or Control: Evangelical Lutheran Church In America
IRS Status: 501(c)3
Highest Offering: Baccalaureate
Accreditation: HLC, CAATE, NURSE

01 President .... Ms. Rebecca M. BERGMAN
05 Provost and Dean of the College .... Dr. Brenda S. KELLY
10 VP for Finance/Treasurer/CFO .... Mr. Curtis J. KOWALESKI
07 AVP and Dean of Admission .... Mr. Richard S. AUNE
07 AVP for Enrollment .... Mr. Kirk CARLSON
111 VP for Institutional Advancement .... Mr. Thomas W. YOUNG
32 VP for Student Life .... Dr. JoNes R. VANHECKE
26 VP Marketing & Communication .... Mr. Timothy R. KENNEDY
88 VP Mission/Strategy/Innovation .... Dr. Kathi TUNHEIM
28 VP for Equity and Inclusion .... Mr. Doug THOMPSON
28 Director Diversity Center .... Mr. Thomas G. FLUNKER
09 Director Institutional Research .... Mr. David A. MENK
08 Head Librarian .... Ms. Michelle TWAIT
88 Director Church Relations .... Rev. Grady I. ST. DENNIS
29 Dir Alumni and Parent Engagement .... Ms. Angela ERICKSON
36 Exec Director Career Development .... Mr. Andrew COSTON
06 Registrar .... Ms. Deann SCHLOESSER
13 Dir Gustavus Technology Services .... Ms. Tami AUNE
18 AVP Facilities .... Mr. Travis JORDAN
37 Dean of Financial Aid .... Mr. Jesus O. HERNANDEZ MEJIA
39 Director Residential Life .... Mr. Anthony BETTENDORF
42 Chaplain .... Rev. Siri C. ERICKSON
35 Assistant VP for Student Life .... Ms. Megan RUBLE
35 Assistant VP for Student Life .... Mr. Charlie POTTS
41 Athletics Director .... Mr. Thomas W. BROWN
15 Director Human Resources .... Vacant
19 Director Campus Security .... Mr. Frederick SMITH
40 Manager Book Mark .... Ms. Molly L. YONKERS
27 Dir Media Relations/Internal Comm .... Mr. Jacob J. AKIN
04 Asst to the Pres & Sec of the Board .... Ms. Jolene D. CHRISTENSEN

Hamline University (B)

1536 Hewitt Avenue, Saint Paul MN 55104-1284
County: Ramsey FICE Identification: 002354
Unit ID: 173665
Telephone: (651) 523-2800 Carnegie Class: Masters/L
FAX Number: (651) 523-2899 Calendar System: 4/1/4
URL: www.hamline.edu
Established: 1854 Annual Undergrad Tuition & Fees: $45,145
Enrollment: 3,113 Coed
Affiliation or Control: United Methodist IRS Status: 501(c)3
Highest Offering: Doctorate
Accreditation: HLC, CAEP, CAEPN, MUS

01 President .... Dr. Fayneese S. MILLER
05 Interim Provost .... Dr. Andy RUNDQUIST
10 Sr VP Business/Finance/Technology .... Ms. Margaret TUNGSETH
111 VP Institutional Advancement .... Mr. Mike TOMPOS
32 VP/Dean of Students .... Ms. Patti KLEIN
43 VP/General Counsel .... Ms. Catherine WASSBERG
84 Vice Pres Enrollment Management .... Ms. Mai Nhia XIONG-CHAN
13 Assoc VP/Dir IT .... Vacant
26 Assoc VP Marketing/Communications .... Vacant
18 Assoc VP Facilities/Physical Plant .... Mr. Lowell BROMANDER
50 Dean School of Business .... Ms. Anne MCCARTHY
49 Dean College Liberal Arts .... Ms. Marcela KOSTIHOVA
85 Ast Dn/Dir Multicult/Intl Stdt Affs .... Mr. Carlos SNEED
06 University Registrar .... Ms. Gwen SHERBURNE
37 Sr Director Financial Aid .... Ms. Lynette WAHL
07 Director Undergraduate Admission .... Ms. Holly COLLINS
15 Director Human Resources .... Ms. Lisa TODD
36 Dir Career Dev Center .... Mr. Terry MIDDENDORF
41 Athletic Director .... Mr. Jason VERDUGO
19 Director of Safety & Security .... Ms. Melinda HEIKKINEN
23 Director Counseling & Health Center .... Ms. Hussein RAJPUT
35 Dir Student Leadership & Activities .... Mr. Patrick HAUGHT
42 Chaplain & Director .... Ms. Nancy M. VICTORIN-VANGERUD
96 Director of Purchasing .... Vacant
04 Exec Assistant to the President .... Ms. Elizabeth RADTKE
09 Director of Institutional Research .... Ms. Tracy WILLIAMS
08 Head Librarian .... Mr. Terry METZ
39 Director Student Housing .... Mr. Javier GUTIERREZ

Hazelden Betty Ford Graduate School of Addiction Studies (C)

PO Box 11 (CO9), Center City MN 55012-0011
County: Chisago FICE Identification: 040443
Unit ID: 173683
Telephone: (651) 213-4175 Carnegie Class: Spec-4-yr-Other Health
FAX Number: (651) 213-4710 Calendar System: Semester
URL: www.hazeldenbettyford.org
Established: 1999 Annual Graduate Tuition & Fees: N/A
Enrollment: 174 Coed
Affiliation or Control: Independent Non-Profit IRS Status: 501(c)3
Highest Offering: Master's; No Undergraduates
Accreditation: HLC

01 President and CEO .... Mr. Mark MISHEK
05 VP of Education & Research .... Dr. Valerie SLAYMAKER
88 Exec Asst to VP Education/Research .... Ms. Denell BELLE ISLE
20 Dean .... Dr. Roy KAMMER
07 Dir Enrollment & Student Services .... Ms. LeAnn BROWN
06 Registrar .... Ms. Debra MATTISON
88 Registrar of Administrative Service .... Ms. Twyla RAMSDELL

Herzing University (D)

435 Ford Rd, St. Louis Park MN 55426
Telephone: (763) 535-3000 FICE Identification: 011017
Accreditation: &HLC, DA, DH, NURSE, OTA, PTAA

† Regional accreditation is carried under the parent institution in Madison, WI.

Institute of Production and Recording (E)

300 N. 1st Avenue, Suite 500, Minneapolis MN 55401
County: Hennepin FICE Identification: 041302
Unit ID: 454616
Telephone: (612) 351-0631 Carnegie Class: Spec-4-yr-Arts
FAX Number: (612) 244-2801 Calendar System: Other
URL: www.ipr.edu
Established: 2002 Annual Undergrad Tuition & Fees: $22,635
Enrollment: 133 Coed
Affiliation or Control: Proprietary IRS Status: Proprietary
Highest Offering: Associate Degree
Accreditation: ACCSC

01 Executive Director .... Charlie BUEHLER
05 Associate Campus Director .... Trey WODELE
06 Associate Dean/Registrar .... Nathan O'BRIEN
07 Assoc Director of Admissions .... Lindsey MUNDY
36 Director of Career Services .... Kyle SHELSTAD
37 Financial Aid Manager .... Ben DOEHNE
08 Librarian .... Kalina KASTNER

Leech Lake Tribal College (F)

6945 Little Wolf Rd., NW, Cass Lake MN 56633
County: Cass FICE Identification: 030964
Unit ID: 413626
Telephone: (218) 335-4200 Carnegie Class: Tribal
FAX Number: (218) 335-4282 Calendar System: Semester
URL: www.lltc.edu
Established: 1990 Annual Undergrad Tuition & Fees: $4,850
Enrollment: 133 Coed
Affiliation or Control: Tribal Control IRS Status: 501(c)3
Highest Offering: Associate Degree
Accreditation: HLC

01 President .... Raymond L. BURNS
05 Dean of Academics .... Vikki HOWARD
10 Director of Finance .... Genny LOWRY
32 Dean of Student Services .... Jorge MENDOZA
09 Dir Institutional Rsrch/Assessment .... Helen ZAIKINA-MONTGOMERY
84 Dir Enrollment Services/Registrar .... Stacey LUNDBERG
37 Financial Aid Director .... Glen SAWA

Luther Seminary (G)

2481 Como Avenue, Saint Paul MN 55108-1496
County: Ramsey FICE Identification: 002357
Unit ID: 173896
Telephone: (651) 641-3456 Carnegie Class: Spec-4-yr-Faith
FAX Number: (651) 641-3425 Calendar System: Semester
URL: www.luthersem.edu
Established: 1869 Annual Graduate Tuition & Fees: N/A
Enrollment: 501 Coed
Affiliation or Control: Evangelical Lutheran Church In America
IRS Status: 501(c)3
Highest Offering: Doctorate; No Undergraduates
Accreditation: HLC, THEOL

01 President .... Rev.Dr. Robin STEINKE
05 VP of Academic Affairs .... Dr. Joy MOORE
10 VP Administration & Finance .... Mr. Michael MORROW
26 VP Seminary Relations .... Ms. Heidi DROEGEMUELLER
32 Dean of Students .... Dr. David FENRICK
28 Dir of Diversity/Equity/Inclusion .... Dr. Leon RODRIGUES
15 Director of Human Resources .... Vacant
07 Director of Admissions .... Vacant
06 Registrar .... Ms. Diane DONCITS
84 Director of Enrollment Services .... Ms. Jessi LECLEAR VACHTA
04 Admin Assistant to the President .... Ms. Gina LOTZER

Lutheran Brethren Seminary (H)

1036 Alcott Avenue W, Fergus Falls MN 56537
County: Otter Tail Identification: 666644
Telephone: (218) 739-3375 Carnegie Class: Not Classified
FAX Number: N/A Calendar System: Semester
URL: www.lbs.edu
Established: 1903 Annual Graduate Tuition & Fees: N/A
Enrollment: N/A Coed
Affiliation or Control: Other IRS Status: 501(c)3
Highest Offering: Master's; No Undergraduates
Accreditation: TRACS

01 President .... Dr. David VEUM
05 Dean of the Seminary/CAO .... Dr. Brad PRIBBENOW
06 Registrar/Director of Admissions .... Dr. Gaylan MATHIESEN

Macalester College (I)

1600 Grand Avenue, Saint Paul MN 55105-1801
County: Ramsey FICE Identification: 002358
Unit ID: 173902
Telephone: (651) 696-6000 Carnegie Class: Bac-A&S
FAX Number: (651) 696-6689 Calendar System: Semester
URL: www.macalester.edu
Established: 1874 Annual Undergrad Tuition & Fees: $58,478
Enrollment: 2,049 Coed
Affiliation or Control: Presbyterian Church (U.S.A.) IRS Status: 501(c)3
Highest Offering: Baccalaureate
Accreditation: HLC

01 President .... Dr. Suzanne M. RIVERA
05 Dean of the Faculty & Provost .... Dr. Karine F. MOE
115 Chief Investment Officer .... Mr. Gary D. MARTIN
111 VP Advancement .... Mr. Andrew BROWN
32 Int Student Affairs Leader .... Ms. Lisa A. TREVIRANUS
10 Int Vice President Admin/Finance .... Ms. Patricia LANGER
13 Associate VP ITS/CIO .... Ms. Jennifer HAAS
07 Vice Pres Admissions/Financial Aid .... Mr. Jeffrey S. ALLEN
85 Dean Annan Inst Global Citizenship .... Dr. Donna K. MAEDA
20 Director of Academic Programs .... Ms. Ann M. MINNICK
28 Dean of Multicultural Life .... Ms. Marjorie TRUEBLOOD
35 AVP Stdnt Affs/Dean of Students .. Dr. Kathryn KAY COQUEMONT
37 Director Student Financial Aid .... Ms. Jenae A. SCHMIDT
06 Registrar .... Mr. Timothy S. TRAFFIE
35 Assoc Dean of Students .... Mr. Andrew M. WELLS
15 Director Employment Services .... Mr. Bob GRAF
18 AVP of Facilities .... Mr. Nathan P. LIEF
41 Athletic Director .... Mr. Donnie A. BROOKS
04 Assist to President/Sec to Board .... Ms. Cynthia L. HENDRICKS
26 Associate VP Comm and Marketing .... Ms. Julie T. HURBANIS
29 Director Alumni Engagement .... Ms. Catie K. GARDNER SMITH
38 Director Health and Wellness Center .... Ms. Denise WARD
96 Dir Purchasing/Accounts Payable .... Mr. Matthew D. RUMPZA
105 Dir Digital Engagement & Ext Rel .... Ms. Sara C. SUELFLOW
84 Manager of Enrollment Systems .... Vacant
08 Head Librarian .... Ms. Angi FAIKS
102 Dir Foundation/Corporate Relations .... Ms. Michelle EPP
36 Dean of Career Exploration .... Ms. Mindy J. DEARDURFF
19 Director of Security .... Mr. James E. KURTZ
09 Director Institutional Research .... Dr. Bethany L. MILLER

Martin Luther College (J)

1995 Luther Court, New Ulm MN 56073-3300
County: Brown FICE Identification: 002361
Unit ID: 173452
Telephone: (507) 354-8221 Carnegie Class: Spec-4-yr-Other
FAX Number: (507) 354-8225 Calendar System: Semester
URL: www.mlc-wels.edu
Established: 1995 Annual Undergrad Tuition & Fees: $16,420
Enrollment: 968 Coed
Affiliation or Control: Wisconsin Evangelical Lutheran Synod
IRS Status: 501(c)3
Highest Offering: Master's
Accreditation: HLC

01 President .... Rev. Richard L. GURGEL
05 Vice President for Academics .... Dr. Jeffery P. WIECHMAN
11 Vice President for Administration .... Prof. Scott D. SCHMUDLACH
32 Vice President Student Life .... Prof. Jeffrey L. SCHONE
53 Academic Dean Educational Ministry .... Prof. Benjamin P. CLEMONS
73 Academic Dean Pastoral Ministry .... Prof. James N. DANELL
10 Director of Finance .... Mrs. Carla J. HULKE
08 Director of Library Services .... Mrs. Linda KRAMER
37 Director of Financial Aid .... Mr. Mark D. BAUER
07 Director of Admissions .... Prof. Theodore A. KLUG
58 Director Graduate Studies/Cont Educ .... Dr. John E. MEYER
88 Director of Clinical Experiences .... Vacant
41 Director of Athletics .... Prof. James M. UNKE
42 Campus Pastor .... Dr. John C. BOEDER
13 Director of Technology .... Mr. James A. RATHJE
26 Director of Public Relations .... Prof. William A. PEKRUL
40 Bookstore Manager .... Mrs. Linette M. SCHARLEMANN
90 Director of Academic Computing .... Prof. Rachel M. FELD
29 Director Alumni Relations .... Mr. Stephen J. BALZA

108 Director Student Assessment .... Prof. Rebecca L. COX
06 Registrar .... Mrs. Gwen L. KRAL
09 Director of Institutional Research .... Prof. Rachel R. FREDRICH
15 Chief Human Resources Officer .... Mrs. Andrea E. WENDLAND
104 Director Study Abroad .... Mrs. Megan R. KASSUELKE
30 Director of Development .... Vacant

Minneapolis College of Art and Design (A)

2501 Stevens Avenue, Minneapolis MN 55404-4343
County: Hennepin FICE Identification: 002365
Unit ID: 174127
Telephone: (612) 874-3700 Carnegie Class: Spec-4-yr-Arts
FAX Number: (612) 874-3704 Calendar System: Semester
URL: www.mcad.edu
Established: 1886 Annual Undergrad Tuition & Fees: $41,794
Enrollment: 760 Coed
Affiliation or Control: Independent Non-Profit IRS Status: 501(c)3
Highest Offering: Master's
Accreditation: HLC, ART

01 President .... Mr. Sanjit SETHI
04 Exec Asst to President/Sec Board .... Ms. Sarah HARDING
05 Vice President Academic Affairs .... Mr. Robert RANSICK
10 VP Finance/Chief Financial Officer .... Mr. Chuck SMITH
11 Vice President Administration .... Vacant
111 VP Institutional Advancement .... Ms. Cindy THEIS
84 Vice Pres Enrollment Management .... Ms. Melissa HUYBRECHT
32 Vice President of Student Affairs .... Ms. Jen ZUCCOLA
26 VP Communication/Marketing Strategy .... Ms. Annie G. CLEVELAND
18 Assoc VP Facilities/Public Safety .... Mr. Brock RASMUSSEN
06 Registrar .... Mr. River GORDON
51 Director of Continuing Education .... Ms. Lara ROY
08 Director of Library .... Ms. Amy BECKER
39 Director Student Housing .... Mr. Nate K. LUTZ
37 Director Student Financial Aid .... Ms. Laura LINK
108 Director Accreditation & Assessment .... Ms. Melissa RANDS
19 Director of Public Safety .... Mr. Steve MCLAUGHLIN

*Minnesota State Colleges and Universities System Office (B)

30 7th Street East, Suite 350, Saint Paul MN 55101-4901
County: Ramsey FICE Identification: 009346
Unit ID: 428453
Telephone: (651) 201-1800 Carnegie Class: N/A
FAX Number: (651) 297-5550
URL: https://www.minnstate.edu/

01 Chancellor .... Devinder MALHOTRA
15 Vice Chancellor Human Resources .... Eric DAVIS
05 Sr Vice Chanc Academic/Student Affs .... Ron ANDERSON
10 Vice Chanc Finance/Facilities & CFO .... William MAKI
13 Vice Chanc Information Tech/CIO .... Ramon PADILLA
26 Chief Marketing/Communications Ofcr .... Noelle HAWTON
18 Assoc Vice Chancellor Facilities .... Brian D. YOLITZ
46 Assoc Vice Chanc Research/Planning .... Vacant
32 Assoc Vice Chanc Student Affairs .... Brent GLASS
100 Chief of Staff .... Jaime SIMONSEN
16 Asst Dir Human Resources .... Jessica WHITE
28 Chief Diversity Officer .... Clyde WILSON PICKETT
102 Exec Dir System/Foundation Rels .... Vacant
43 General Counsel .... Gary CUNNINGHAM
45 System Dir Academic Pgms/Plng .... Jon DALAGER

*Alexandria Technical & Community College (C)

1601 Jefferson Street, Alexandria MN 56308-2796
County: Douglas FICE Identification: 005544
Unit ID: 172918
Telephone: (320) 762-4600 Carnegie Class: Assoc/HVT-High Non
FAX Number: (320) 762-4501 Calendar System: Semester
URL: www.alextech.edu
Established: 1961 Annual Undergrad Tuition & Fees (In-State): $5,649
Enrollment: 2,549 Coed
Affiliation or Control: State IRS Status: 501(c)3
Highest Offering: Associate Degree
Accreditation: HLC, MLTAD

02 President .... Mr. Michael SEYMOUR
10 Chief Financial Officer .... Mr. David BJELLAND
05 Sr Dean Academic Affairs & Students .... Mr. Gregg RAISANEN
32 Dean of Student Affairs .... Vacant
72 Dean of Technology .... Mr. Steve RICHARDS
66 Dean of Nursing and Health .... Ms. Merilee RETZLOFF
75 Dean of Law Enforcemnt/Transp/Manuf .... Mr. Scott BERGER
37 Financial Aid Director .... Mr. Jon ERICKSON
22 Human Rights Officer .... Ms. Tamzin BUKOWSKI
36 Director Student Placement .... Mr. Patrick RUNNING
102 Foundation Executive Director .... Mr. Jeffrey WILD
06 Registrar .... Mr. Patrick RUNNING
18 Director of Facilities .... Mr. Joel SEELA
15 Chief Human Resources Officer .... Ms. Shari MALONEY
09 Director of Institutional Research .... Ms. Heather RONDEAU
07 Director of Admissions .... Ms. Lynn ARNQUIST
35 Director of Student Activities .... Ms. Cynthia HAARSTAD
88 Director of K-12 Initiatives .... Ms. Mary LENZ
04 Asst to Pres/Dir of Office Services .... Ms. Annette PAVEK

21 Director of Financial Operations .... Ms. Julie FENLASON
40 Bookstore Manager .... Mr. David BJELLAND
30 Development Officer .... Ms. Christine HARRIS
121 Director of Support Services .... Ms. Kaye MADIGAN
28 Campus Diversity Officer .... Mr. Keith TURNER
26 Director Mktg & Communications .... Mr. Adam HAMMER
41 Athletic Director .... Mr. Tony VAN ACKER

*Anoka-Ramsey Community College (D)

11200 Mississippi Boulevard NW,
Coon Rapids MN 55433-3470
County: Anoka FICE Identification: 002332
Unit ID: 172963
Telephone: (763) 433-1100 Carnegie Class: Assoc/HT-High Non
FAX Number: (763) 433-1121 Calendar System: Semester
URL: www.anokaramsey.edu
Established: 1965 Annual Undergrad Tuition & Fees (In-State): $5,286
Enrollment: 8,482 Coed
Affiliation or Control: State IRS Status: 501(c)3
Highest Offering: Associate Degree
Accreditation: HLC, ACBSP, ADNUR, MUS, PTAA

02 President .... Dr. Kent HANSON
10 VP Finance & Administration .... Mr. Don LEWIS
05 Int VP Academic/Student Affairs .... Mr. Steve CRITTENDEN
32 Dean of Student Affairs .... Ms. Lisa HARRIS
50 Dean Business/World Lang/Soc Sci .... Mr. Scott STANKEY
09 Dean of Research & Assessment .... Ms. Nora MORRIS
66 Dean of Nursing and Allied Health .... Ms. Sandra KOHLER
81 Dean of STEM .... Ms. Becky KRYSTYNIAK
57 Dean of Arts & Letters .... Ms. Hannah OLIHA-DONALDSON
88 Dean of Academic/Community Outreach .... Ms. Shannon KIRKEIDE
20 Int Associate Dean .... Mr. Thom NORDIN
15 Chief HR Director .... Mr. Jay NELSON
26 Chief Marketing & Comm Officer .... Ms. Mary JACOBSON
13 Int Chief Information Officer .... Mr. Richard MALOTT
35 Dir Student Development/Engagement .... Mr. Michael OPOKU
114 Director of Budget Plng & Forecasts .... Mr. Dave AUNE
84 Director of Enrollment Management .... Mr. Ricky GONZALEZ
28 Director of Multicultural Affairs .... Ms. Venoreen BROWNE-BOATSWAIN
102 Director of Foundations .... Mr. Jamie BARTHEL
18 Director of Facilities .... Mr. Ken KARR
19 Director of Safety & Security .... Mr. Cliff ANDERSON
21 Director of Business Affairs .... Vacant
109 Director of Auxiliary Services .... Mr. Robert PEREZ
37 Director Financial Aid .... Ms. Brittany TWEED
04 Executive Asst to President .... Ms. Margie SCHLUETER
100 Special Assistant to the President .... Ms. Jessica MEDEARIS
06 Registrar .... Ms. Rhonda KERN
28 VP of Equity & Inclusion .... Mr. Brandyn WOODARD

*Anoka Technical College (E)

1355 W Highway 10, Anoka MN 55303-1590
County: Anoka FICE Identification: 007350
Unit ID: 172954
Telephone: (763) 576-4700 Carnegie Class: Assoc/HVT-High Trad
FAX Number: (763) 576-4715 Calendar System: Semester
URL: www.anokatech.edu
Established: 1967 Annual Undergrad Tuition & Fees (In-District): $5,812
Enrollment: 1,683 Coed
Affiliation or Control: State/Local IRS Status: 501(c)3
Highest Offering: Associate Degree
Accreditation: HLC, CAHIIM, MAC, OTA, PNUR, SURGT

02 President .... Dr. Kent HANSON
05 Vice Pres of Acad/Student Affs .... Dr. Elaina BLEIFIELD
10 Vice Pres Finance & Admin .... Donald LEWIS
28 Vice Pres Equity & Inclusion .... Brandyn WOODARD
20 Academic Dean .... Dawn EASLEY
04 Executive Asst to the President .... Margie SCHLUETER
15 Chief Human Resource Officer .... Jay NELSON
13 Chief Information Officer .... Richard MALOTT
26 Director of Marketing .... Mary JACOBSON
06 Director of Records .... Laura KITTELSON
32 Int Dean of Student Affairs .... Kevin LINDSTROM
37 Financial Aid Director .... Brittany TWEED
08 Head Librarian .... Susan BRETTSCHNEIDER
18 Chief Facilities/Physical Plant .... Kenneth KARR
19 Director Security/Safety .... Clifford ANDERSON
84 Director of Enrollment Services .... LeAnna WANGERIN
09 Director of Institutional Research .... Nora MORRIS
22 Director of Diversity .... Venoreen BROWNE-BOATSWAIN

*Bemidji State University (F)

1500 Birchmont Drive NE, Bemidji MN 56601-2699
County: Beltrami FICE Identification: 002336
Unit ID: 173124
Telephone: (218) 755-2001 Carnegie Class: Masters/S
FAX Number: N/A Calendar System: Semester
URL: www.bemidjistate.edu
Established: 1919 Annual Undergrad Tuition & Fees (In-State): $9,076
Enrollment: 4,577 Coed
Affiliation or Control: State IRS Status: 501(c)3
Highest Offering: Master's
Accreditation: HLC, AAQEP, IACBE, MUS, NAIT, NURSE, SW

02 President .... Dr. Faith C. HENSRUD
05 Provost/VP Academic Affairs .... Dr. Allen BEDFORD
10 VP Finance & Administration .... Ms. Karen SNOREK
84 Exec Dir of Enrollment Management .... Vacant
22 Affirmative Action & Accreditation .... Vacant
08 Library & Library Services .... Mr. Pete MCDONNELL
09 Director Inst Rsrch/Effectiveness .... Dr. Robert B. WILKINSON
103 Dir Center for Professional Devel .... Dr. Debbie GUELDA
92 Director Honors Program .... Dr. Season ELLISON
85 Director International Program Ctr .... Vacant
88 Co-Director Leadership Studies .... Dr. Anna CARLSON
88 Co-Director Leadership Studies .... Dr. Virgil BAKKEN
23 Int Dean Individual/Cmty Health .... Dr. Jim WHITE
50 Dean Business/Math & Sciences .... Dr. Marilyn YODER
88 Exec Dir MN Adv Manuf Ctr of Excell .... Mr. Jeremy LEFFELMAN
88 Director MARS Program .... Dr. Gabriel WARREN
79 Dean Arts/Education & Humanities .... Dr. Mary Theresa SEIG
32 VP for Student Life & Success .... Mr. Travis GREENE
20 Int Assoc VP for Academic Affairs .... Dr. Randy WESTHOFF
93 Director American Indian Center .... Ms. Chrissy DOWNWIND
93 Student Ctr/Diversity/Equity/Incl .... Dr. Ye (Solar) HONG
88 Director Campus Recreation .... Ms. Kierstin HOVEN
88 Director Hobson Memorial Union .... Ms. Nina JOHNSON
39 Director Housing & Res Life .... Dr. Randall LUDEMAN
38 Int Dir Center Health/Counseling .... Ms. Jennifer FRAIK
106 Director Distance Learning .... Ms. Lynn JOHNSON
21 Business Manager .... Mr. Ron BECKSTROM
18 Physical Plant Manager .... Mr. Travis BARNES
19 Director Public Safety .... Mr. Casey J. MCCARTHY
28 Campus Diversity Officer .... Mr. Steven PARKER
15 Chief Human Resources Officer .... Ms. Megan ZOTHMAN
13 Chief Information Officer .... Ms. Sherry LAWDERMILT
07 Director Admissions .... Mr. Andrew WRIGHT
37 Director Financial Aid .... Ms. Lesa LAWRENCE
06 Registrar .... Ms. Kim GOURNEAU
121 Director Advising Success Center .... Mr. Zak JOHNSON
36 Director Career Services .... Ms. Margie T. GIAUQUE
88 TRIO/SSS/UB/McNair .... Ms. Kelli STEGGALL
22 Accessibility Services .... Mr. Christian BRECZINSKI
26 Exec Dir Communications & Mktg .... Mr. Andy BARTLETT
41 Athletic Director .... Mr. Tracy DILL
111 Exec Dir for University Advancement .... Mr. Joshua CHRISTIANSON
29 Director Alumni Relations .... Mr. Brett BAHR
58 Director Graduate Studies .... Mr. George MCCONNELL

*Central Lakes College (G)

501 W College Drive, Brainerd MN 56401-3900
County: Crow Wing FICE Identification: 002339
Unit ID: 173203
Telephone: (218) 855-8000 Carnegie Class: Assoc/MT-VT-High Non
FAX Number: (218) 855-8057 Calendar System: Semester
URL: www.clcmn.edu
Established: 1938 Annual Undergrad Tuition & Fees (In-State): $5,759
Enrollment: 4,491 Coed
Affiliation or Control: State IRS Status: 501(c)3
Highest Offering: Associate Degree
Accreditation: HLC, DA, MAC

02 President .... Dr. Hara D. CHARLIER
05 VP Academic & Student Affairs .... Ms. Joy BODIN
11 VP Administrative Services .... Ms. Kari CHRISTIANSEN
12 Dean Staples Campus/CTE/Grants .... Mr. David ENDICOTT
12 Dean Brainerd CTE/Customized Trng .... Ms. Rebekah KENT
47 Dean of Agricultural Studies .... Mr. Keith OLANDER
84 Dean of Enrollment/Student Success .... Mr. Paul PREIMESBERGER
49 Dean of Liberal Arts .... Ms. Anne NELSON FISHER
30 Director of Res Develop/CLC Found .... Ms. Kate ADORNETTO
15 Director of Human Resources .... Ms. Kristi LANE
07 Director of Admissions/Recruitment .... Ms. Tambera GARZA
06 Registrar .... Ms. Susan RUMPCA
08 Librarian .... Mr. David BISSONETTE
37 Director Financial Aid .... Mr. Mike BARNABY
14 Director of Technology/Support .... Mr. Scott STREED
26 Director Marketing .... Mr. Kenn DOLS
109 Director of Business/Auxil Services .... Mr. Jonathan KNUTSON
88 Director of Trio Programs .... Mr. Charles BLACKLANCE
18 Director Physical Plant/Facilities .... Mr. James MCARDELL
28 Dean of Students/Equity/Inclusion .... Ms. Mary SAM
04 Executive Asst to President .... Ms. Jody LONGBELLA
09 Director of Institutional Research .... Ms. Wendy ADAMSON
88 Director Small Business Dev Center .... Ms. Rebecca ROWE
19 Director Security/Safety .... Mr. Matthew KRUEGER
32 Director of Student Life .... Mr. Erich HEPPNER

*Century College (H)

3300 Century Avenue North,
White Bear Lake MN 55110-1894
County: Ramsey FICE Identification: 010546
Unit ID: 175315
Telephone: (651) 779-3200 Carnegie Class: Assoc/MT-VT-High Trad
FAX Number: N/A Calendar System: Semester
URL: www.century.edu
Established: 1967 Annual Undergrad Tuition & Fees (In-State): $5,578
Enrollment: 8,203 Coed
Affiliation or Control: State IRS Status: 501(c)3
Highest Offering: Associate Degree
Accreditation: HLC, ADNUR, DA, DH, EMT, MAC, MUS, RAD

02 President .... Ms. Angelia MILLENDER

05 Provost/VP Academic & Student Affs .... Ms. Pakou YANG
10 VP Finance & Administration .... Mr. Patrick OPATZ
13 Assoc VP Information Tech/Admn Svcs .... Mr. John ROHLEDER
84 Assoc Dean Enrollment Management ... Ms. Ali PICKENS-OPOKU
96 Buyer Supervisor .... Vacant
21 Director of Finance .... Ms. Marilyn SMITH
102 Executive Director Foundation .... Ms. Nora SLAWIK
06 Registrar .... Ms. Kirsten FABOZZI
15 Director of Human Resources .... Ms. Jodean THRONSON
07 Associate Director of Admissions .... Mr. Robert BEAVER
37 Director of Financial Aid .... Ms. Pam ENGEBRETSON
18 Physical Building Supervisor .... Mr. Michael HOUFER
19 Director of Public Safety .... Mr. Jason PHILIPP
76 Dean of Human Svcs & Health Sci .... Ms. Beth HEIN
103 Dean Industry/English/Devel Ed//Lib .... Vacant
66 Dean Nursing/CETC/Online Lrng Excel .... Mr. Eric RIEDEL
81 Dean Science/Tech/Engr/Math .... Vacant
49 Dean of Liberal Arts .... Ms. Julie ZALOUDEK
35 Dean of Student Affairs .... Ms. Kristin HAGEMAN
09 Dean of Institutional Effectiveness .... Vacant
04 Executive Assistant to President .... Ms. Christine MCGING
26 Director of Marketing .... Mr. James STUMNE
28 Chief Diversity Officer .... Ms. Rosa RODRIGUEZ

*Dakota County Technical College (A)

1300 145th Street East, Rosemount MN 55068-2999
County: Dakota FICE Identification: 010402
Unit ID: 173416
Telephone: (651) 423-8000 Carnegie Class: Assoc/HVT-High Trad
FAX Number: (651) 423-8775 Calendar System: Semester
URL: www.dctc.edu
Established: 1970 Annual Undergrad Tuition & Fees (In-District): $5,941
Enrollment: 2,319 Coed
Affiliation or Control: State/Local IRS Status: 501(c)3
Highest Offering: Associate Degree
Accreditation: HLC, DA, MAC

02 President .... Mr. Michael D. BERNDT
05 Interim VP Academic Affairs .... Mr. Mike MENDEZ
10 VP/Chief Financial Officer .... Mr. David MILTON
09 Director Institutional Research .... Ms. Wendy MARSON
32 VP Student Affairs .... Ms. Anne JOHNSON
88 Dean Transportation/Construct/Manuf .... Mr. Jason WETZEL
49 Dean Arts & Sciences .... Mr. Nick WALLACE
50 Dean Business/Design/Hlth/Human Svc .... Mr. Ron ERICKSON
13 College Information Officer .... Mr. Todd JAGERSON
06 Registrar/Enrollment Director .... Ms. Jodie SWEARINGEN
18 Director of Operations .... Mr. Paul DEMUTH
35 Director Student Life/Activities .... Ms. Nicole MEULEMANS
07 Dir Recruitment & Admissions .... Mr. Heath BAUMGARD
37 Director Financial Aid .... Mr. Scott ROELKE
15 Director of Human Resources .... Ms. Laina CARLSON
26 Dir Strategic Mktg/Communication .... Ms. Lise FREKING
04 Executiv Assistant to the President .... Ms. Clarissa L. HERRERA
19 Director Security/Safety .... Mr. Anthony PANGAL

*Fond du Lac Tribal and Community College (B)

2101 14th Street, Cloquet MN 55720-2984
County: Carlton FICE Identification: 031291
Unit ID: 380368
Telephone: (218) 879-0800 Carnegie Class: Tribal
FAX Number: (218) 879-0814 Calendar System: Semester
URL: www.fdltcc.edu
Established: 1987 Annual Undergrad Tuition & Fees (In-State): $5,535
Enrollment: 1,639 Coed
Affiliation or Control: State IRS Status: 501(c)3
Highest Offering: Associate Degree
Accreditation: HLC, ADNUR

02 President .... Ms. Stephanie HAMMITT
05 Vice President of Academics .... Dr. Anna FELLEGY
10 Chief Financial Officer .... Mr. Bret BUSAKOWSKI
32 Dean of Student Affairs .... Ms. Anita HANSON
26 Dir Marketing/Communications .... Ms. Taylor WARNES
06 Registrar .... Ms. Erica GELO
88 Disability Services/Student Service .... Ms. Nancy OLSEN
13 Chief Information Officer .... Mr. Peter ANGELOS
37 Director of Financial Aid .... Mr. David SUTHERLAND
07 Director of Admissions .... Ms. Katie GUSTAFSON
09 Director of Institutional Research .... Mr. James EISENHAUER
124 Dir of Student Support Services .... Ms. Peggy POITRA
62 Library Services .... Mr. Keith CICH
30 Director of Development .... Ms. Stephanie HAMMITT
39 Director of Housing .... Mr. Jesse STIREWALT
15 Director of Human Resources .... Ms. Marisa HAGGY
18 Chief Facilities/Physical Plant .... Mr. Mark BERNHARDSON
40 Bookstore Coordinator .... Ms. Bonnie BERNHARDSON
04 Executive Assistant to President .... Ms. Mary SOYRING

*Hennepin Technical College (C)

9000 Brooklyn Boulevard, Brooklyn Park MN 55445-2399
County: Hennepin FICE Identification: 010491
Unit ID: 173708
Telephone: (952) 995-1300 Carnegie Class: Assoc/HVT-High Trad
FAX Number: (763) 488-2956 Calendar System: Semester
URL: www.hennepintech.edu
Established: 1972 Annual Undergrad Tuition & Fees (In-District): $5,494
Enrollment: 4,094 Coed
Affiliation or Control: State/Local IRS Status: 501(c)3
Highest Offering: Associate Degree
Accreditation: HLC, ACBSP, ACFEI, DA, MAC, PNUR

02 President .... Dr. Merrill IRVING, JR.
05 VP Academic Affairs .... Dr. Leanne ROGSTAD
10 Vice Pres Finance and Operations .... Joe WIGHTKIN
121 Vice President of Student Affairs .... Jess LAURITSEN
15 Vice Pres Human Resources .... Marybeth CHRISTENSON-JONES
84 Dean of Enrollment Services .... Debra NEWGARD
13 Dean of Tech & Inst Research .... Shannon THOMAS
28 Associate VP of Equity & Inclusion .... Jean MAIERHOFER
111 Assoc VP of Advancement .... Lisa YAEGER
09 Institutional Effectivenss Proj Mgr .... Elizabeth GIESEKE
37 Director of Financial Aid .... Tim JACOBSON
04 Executive Assistant to President .... Jessica SCHULTZ
22 Dir Affirmative Action/EEO .... Vacant
19 Director Security/Safety .... Randy ROEHRICK
32 Dir Student Life/Career Development .... Vacant
18 Director of Facilities .... Heidi RICCI

*Hibbing Community College, A Technical and Community College (D)

1515 E 25th Street, Hibbing MN 55746-3300
County: Saint Louis FICE Identification: 002355
Unit ID: 173735
Telephone: (218) 262-7200 Carnegie Class: Assoc/HVT-Mix Trad/Non
FAX Number: (218) 262-6717 Calendar System: Semester
URL: www.hibbing.edu
Established: 1916 Annual Undergrad Tuition & Fees (In-State): $5,525
Enrollment: 913 Coed
Affiliation or Control: State IRS Status: 501(c)3
Highest Offering: Associate Degree
Accreditation: HLC, ADNUR, DA, MLTAD

02 Interim President .... Dr. Michael RAICH
05 Interim Provost .... Mr. Aaron REINI
20 Interim Dean of Academics .... Ms. Jessalyn SABIN
10 VP Finance & Administration .... Ms. Karen KEDROWSKI
09 Institutional Research .... Ms. Tracey ROY
37 Director Student Financial Aid .... Ms. Jodi PONTINEN
18 Plant Maintenance Engineer .... Mr. David OLDS
26 Marketing Specialist/Public Info .... Ms. Jessica MATVEY
06 Registrar .... Ms. Kari DOUCETTE
13 Chief Info Technology Officer (CIO) .... Mr. Don BREARLEY
39 Director Student Housing .... Ms. Steffanie LYNN
41 Athletic Director .... Mr. Mike FLATEN
08 Head Librarian .... Ms. Rachel MILANI
28 Director of Diversity .... Ms. Miriam KERO
07 Director of Admissions .... Ms. Sarah MERHAR
121 Student Success Director .... Ms. Jen BOBEN
15 Chief Human Resource/Diversity Ofcr .... Ms. Carmen BRADACH
19 Safety & Emergency Management Coord .... Vacant

*Inver Hills Community College (E)

2500 80th Street E, Inver Grove Heights MN 55076-3224
County: Dakota FICE Identification: 009740
Unit ID: 173799
Telephone: (651) 450-3000 Carnegie Class: Assoc/HT-Mix Trad/Non
FAX Number: (651) 450-3679 Calendar System: Semester
URL: www.inverhills.edu
Established: 1970 Annual Undergrad Tuition & Fees (In-State): $5,558
Enrollment: 4,071 Coed
Affiliation or Control: State IRS Status: 501(c)3
Highest Offering: Associate Degree
Accreditation: HLC, ACBSP, ADNUR, EMT

02 President .... Mr. Michael BERNDT
05 VP Academic Affairs .... Dr. Derrick LINDSTROM
32 Interim Vice Pres Student Affairs .... Ms. Kari RUSCH-CURL
10 Vice Pres of Finance & Operations .... Mr. David MILTON
06 Registrar .... Mr. Scott KLAEHN
75 Dean of Career Programs .... Ms. Janica AUSTAD
76 Dean of Allied Health .... Mr. Christopher METSGAR
79 Dean of Liberal Arts .... Dr. Barb CURCHACK
81 Int Dean of STEM/Social Sciences .... Mr. Yohannes AGEGNEHU
102 Exec Dir Found & Advancement .... Ms. Kimberly SHAFF
15 Human Resources Director .... Ms. Laina CARLSON
08 Librarian .... Ms. Julie BENOLKEN
124 Interim Dean of Student Success .... Ms. Amanda BARKLIND
20 Director of Academic Affairs Opers .... Mr. JT BEALKA
18 Director Facilities Plng/Management .... Mr. Paul DEMUTH
88 Int Dir Emergency Health Svcs .... Mr. Kevin JOHNSON
37 Dir of Scholarship & Financial Aid .... Mr. Scott ROELKE
09 Director of Institutional Research .... Ms. Wendy MARSON
26 Dir of Strategic Marketing & Comm .... Ms. Lisa FREKING
13 College Information Officer .... Mr. Todd JAGERSON
106 Director of Teaching and Learning .... Mr. Martin SPRINGBORG
121 Assoc Dean/Dir of Acad Lrng Support .... Ms. Hilary DAHLMAN
103 Director of Workforce Training & CE ..... Mr. Robert TREWARTHA
84 Director of Outreach & Recruitment .... Mr. Aaron SALASEK
88 Dir of Student Support Services .... Mr. Matt KRUGER
36 Director of Career Development .... Ms. Emily JOHNSON
22 Dir of Accessibility Resources .... Ms. Randi GOETTL
88 Director of K12 Partnerships .... Ms. Mary Jo GARDNER
14 Director of Technology .... Mr. Abel ASFAW
19 Director of Safety & Security .... Mr. Anthony PANGAL
04 Admin Assistant to the President .... Ms. Clarissa L. HERRERA

*Itasca Community College (F)

1851 E Highway 169, Grand Rapids MN 55744-3397
County: Itasca FICE Identification: 002356
Unit ID: 173805
Telephone: (800) 996-6422 Carnegie Class: Assoc/HT-Mix Trad/Non
FAX Number: (218) 322-2332 Calendar System: Semester
URL: www.itascacc.edu
Established: 1922 Annual Undergrad Tuition & Fees (In-State): $5,540
Enrollment: 1,058 Coed
Affiliation or Control: State IRS Status: 501(c)3
Highest Offering: Associate Degree
Accreditation: HLC

02 President .... Dr. Michael RAICH
05 Provost/CAO .... Dr. Bart JOHNSON
32 Dean of Student & Admin Services .... Mr. Richard KANGAS
84 Dir of Enrollment Mgmt/Admissions .... Mr. William MARSHALL
06 Registrar .... Ms. Becky BOURQUIN
102 Director ICC Foundation/Alumni .... Mr. Charles BLACK
37 Director of Student Financial Aid .... Ms. Allison GEISLER
08 Head Librarian .... Mr. Steve BEAN
18 Director of Facilities & Info Tech .... Mr. Chad HAATVEDT
40 Bookstore Manager .... Ms. Faith MCBRIDE
28 Director of Diversity .... Mr. Harold ANNETTE
09 Director of Institutional Research .... Ms. Tracey ROY
39 Director Student Housing .... Mr. Richard KANGAS
04 Admin Assistant to the President .... Ms. Elise LIND
10 Chief Financial/Business Officer .... Ms. Stephanie POPE
15 Chief Human Resources Officer .... Ms. Carmen BRADACH

*Lake Superior College (G)

2101 Trinity Road, Duluth MN 55811-3399
County: Saint Louis FICE Identification: 005757
Unit ID: 173461
Telephone: (218) 733-7600 Carnegie Class: Assoc/MT-VT-High Non
FAX Number: (218) 733-5937 Calendar System: Semester
URL: www.lsc.edu
Established: 1995 Annual Undergrad Tuition & Fees (In-State): $5,334
Enrollment: 4,762 Coed
Affiliation or Control: State IRS Status: 501(c)3
Highest Offering: Associate Degree
Accreditation: HLC, ADNUR, COARC, DH, MAC, MLTAD, PNUR, PTAA, RAD, SURGT

02 President .... Dr. Patricia L. ROGERS
05 VP Academic/Student Affairs .... Dr. Linda KINGSTON
11 VP Administration .... Mr. Al FINLAYSON
111 VP Advancement & External Relations .... Mr. Daniel FANNING
20 Int Assoc VP of Acad/Student Affs .... Ms. LaNita ROBINSON
50 Dean of Business/Industry .... Mr. Brad VIETHS
49 Dean Liberal Arts/Sciences .... Ms. Hanna ERPESTAD
76 Dean Allied Health/Nursing .... Ms. Anna SACKETTE-URNESS
103 Dean of Workforce & Community Dev .... Mr. Erik SIMONSON
09 IR/Accred Assessment/Research .... Ms. Denise MILLS-LEMIRE
07 Director of Admissions .... Ms. Kayti STOLP
15 Director of Human Resources .... Ms. Jestina VICHOREK
06 Registrar .... Ms. Melissa LENO
18 Building Maintenance Foreman .... Mr. Mark CARDINAL
32 Dean of Students .... Mr. Wade GORDON
36 Director Career Services .... Ms. Kaitlyn STEFFEN
37 Director Student Financial Aid .... Vacant
21 Director Business Services .... Ms. Nickoel ANDERSON
13 Director Information Technology .... Mr. Steve FUDALLY
121 Director of Advising .... Mr. Keith TURNER
96 Purchasing Agent .... Mr. Michael FRANCISCO
04 Executive Asst to President .... Ms. Debbie JOHNSON
28 Director of Diversity .... Ms. Sarah LYONS

*Mesabi Range College (H)

1001 West Chestnut Street, Virginia MN 55792-3401
County: Saint Louis FICE Identification: 004009
Unit ID: 173993
Telephone: (218) 741-3095 Carnegie Class: Assoc/MT-VT-High Non
FAX Number: (218) 748-2419 Calendar System: Semester
URL: www.mesabirange.edu
Established: 1918 Annual Undergrad Tuition & Fees (In-State): $5,540
Enrollment: 926 Coed
Affiliation or Control: State IRS Status: Exempt
Highest Offering: Associate Degree
Accreditation: HLC, EMT

02 Interim President .... Mr. Michael RAICH
05 Provost/CAO .... Mrs. Shelly MCCAULEY JUGOVICH
10 Vice Pres Finance/Administration .... Mrs. Karen KEDROWSKI
32 Dir Student Support Services .... Ms. Jennifer WILLARD
15 Director Human Resources .... Mrs. Carmen BRADACH
37 Director Student Financial Aid .... Ms. Jodi PONTINEN
06 Registrar .... Mrs. Rebecca STEVINSON
07 Director of Admissions .... Ms. Brenda KOCHEVAR
09 Dir Tech/Inst Research & Effective .... Mr. Jim BOYD
38 Student Counseling .... Ms. Kelly BAKK
36 Student Placement .... Ms. Shari CHRISTENSON
13 Chief Info Technology Officer (CIO) .... Mrs. Shelly MCCAULEY-JUGOVICH
41 Athletic Director .... Mr. Brad SCOTT

*Metropolitan State University (I)

700 E 7th Street, Saint Paul MN 55106-5000
County: Ramsey FICE Identification: 010374
Unit ID: 174020

Telephone: (651) 793-1300 Carnegie Class: DU-Mod
FAX Number: (651) 793-1235 Calendar System: Semester
URL: www.metrostate.edu
Established: 1971 Annual Undergrad Tuition & Fees (In-State): $8,249
Enrollment: 7,552 Coed
Affiliation or Control: State IRS Status: 501(c)3
Highest Offering: Doctorate
Accreditation: HLC, ACBSP, ANEST, NURSE, SW

02 President .... Ms. Virginia ARTHUR
05 Prov/Exec VP Acad & Student Affs .... Dr. Amy GORT
10 VP for Finance and Operations/CFO .... Ms. Tracy HATCH
111 VP for University Advancement .... Ms. Rita DIBBLE
22 VP of Equity & Inclusion .... Dr. Josefina LANDRIEU
84 Exec Dir Strategic Enroll & Admiss .... Ms. Carrie CARROLL
32 Dean of Students .... Dr. Maya SULLIVAN
13 VP Info Tech & Inst Research .... Mr. Stephen REED
21 Business Manager .... Ms. Miliite GEBREMICHAEL
15 Int Chief Human Resources Officer .... Ms. Lori KINGSTON
06 Registrar .... Mr. Daryl JOHNSON
37 Director Financial Aid .... Ms. Lois LARSON
26 VP for Marketin/Comm & Recruitment .... Ms. Audrey BERGENGREN
29 Director Alumni Relations .... Ms. Kristine HANSEN
28 Chief Diversity Officer .... Vacant
81 Dean College of Sciences .... Dr. Kyle SWANSON
58 Dean College of Management .... Dr. Rassule HADIDI
88 Int Dean Col Individualized Stds .... Dr. Charles TEDDER
88 Int Dean School of Urban Education .... Dr. Jon DALAGER
49 Dean College of Liberal Arts .... Dr. Shirin EDWIN
66 Dean College of Nursing/Health Sci .... Dr. Doris HILL
08 Dean Library/Information Services .... Ms. Beth CLAUSEN
121 Assoc Provost for Student Success .... Ms. Roberta (Bobbie) ANDERSON

*Minneapolis Community and Technical College (A)

1501 Hennepin Avenue, Minneapolis MN 55403-9810
County: Hennepin FICE Identification: 002362
Unit ID: 174136
Telephone: (612) 659-6000 Carnegie Class: Assoc/MT-VT-High Trad
FAX Number: N/A Calendar System: Semester
URL: www.minneapolis.edu
Established: 1996 Annual Undergrad Tuition & Fees (In-State): $5,660
Enrollment: 6,429 Coed
Affiliation or Control: State IRS Status: 501(c)3
Highest Offering: Associate Degree
Accreditation: HLC, ADNUR, DA, POLYT

02 President .... Dr. Sharon PIERCE
05 Vice Pres Academic Affairs .... Dr. Gail O'KANE
10 Vice Pres Finance/Operations .... Mr. Christopher RAU
32 Vice President Student Affairs .... Mr. Patrick TROUP
28 VP Equity & Inclusion .... Dr. Trumanue LINDSEY, JR.
07 Director of Admissions .... Ms. Genna ANDERSON
49 Dean of Liberal Arts .... Vacant
81 Dean of Science & Mathematics .... Dr. Ben WENG
103 Director of Workforce Development .... Ms. Deanna KOENIG
66 Dean of Nursing & Allied Health .... Dr. Traci KRAUSE
35 Dean of Students .... Ms. Becky NORDIN
15 VP of Human Resources .... Ms. Dianna CUSICK
13 VP of Information Technology .... Ms. Tiffni DEEB
84 Dean of Enrollment Management .... Ms. Heidi ALDES
108 Assoc VP of Inst Effectiveness .... Mr. Thomas WILLIAMSON
06 Registrar .... Ms. Michele COPELAND
08 Librarian .... Mr. Tom ELAND
37 Financial Aid Director .... Ms. Angela CHRISTENSEN
09 Dir of Institutional Effectiveness .... Mr. Fernando FURQUIM
18 Director Facilities .... Mr. Roger BROZ
19 Director of Public Safety .... Mr. Curt SCHMIDT
26 VP Advancement/Marketing Comms .... Ms. Deanna SHEELY
35 Director Student Life .... Ms. Tara MARTINEZ
22 Dir of Diversity/Equity/Inclusion .... Ms. Nanette MISSAGHI

*Minnesota State College Southeast (B)

1250 Homer Road, Winona MN 55987-4897
County: Winona FICE Identification: 002393
Unit ID: 175263
Telephone: (507) 453-2700 Carnegie Class: Assoc/HVT-Mix Trad/Non
FAX Number: (507) 453-2715 Calendar System: Semester
URL: www.southeastmn.edu
Established: 1949 Annual Undergrad Tuition & Fees (In-District): $5,835
Enrollment: 1,912 Coed
Affiliation or Control: State/Local IRS Status: 501(c)3
Highest Offering: Associate Degree
Accreditation: HLC, PNUR, RAD

02 President .... Dr. Marsha DANIELSON
10 Vice Pres Finance/Administration .... Ms. Amy SCHMIDT
05 Vice President of Academic Affairs .... Mr. Chad DULL
32 VP of Student Affs/Dean of Students .... Mr. Josiah LITANT
13 Chief Information Officer .... Mr. Rick NAHRGANG
49 Int Dean of Liberal Arts & Sciences .... Ms. Jean EGBERT
72 Int Dean of Bus/Trade & Technology .... Ms. Dawn LUBHAN
15 Chief Human Resource Officer .... Ms. Megan ZECHES
84 Director of Secondary Relations .... Ms. Jeannie MEIDLINGER
07 Director of Admissions/Enrollment .... Dr. Tammy VONDRASEK
18 Plant Operations Supervisor .... Mr. Thomas HOFFMAN
29 Director of Alumni Relations .... Ms. Casie JOHNSON
26 Director of Marketing & Design .... Ms. Joanne THOMPSON
103 Director of Customized Training .... Vacant
27 Director of Communications .... Ms. Katryn CONLIN
21 Director of Business/Financial Svcs .... Ms. Lisa POZANC
16 HR Business Partner .... Ms. Alecia SPAGNOLETTI
19 Director of Security .... Mr. Chris CICHOSZ
04 Assistant to President .... Ms. Amy DRAZKOWSKI

*Minnesota State Community and Technical College (C)

1414 College Way, Fergus Falls MN 56537-1000
County: Otter Tail FICE Identification: 005541
Unit ID: 173559
Telephone: (218) 736-1500 Carnegie Class: Assoc/HVT-Mix Trad/Non
FAX Number: (218) 736-1510 Calendar System: Semester
URL: www.minnesota.edu
Established: 1960 Annual Undergrad Tuition & Fees (In-State): $5,560
Enrollment: 5,757 Coed
Affiliation or Control: State IRS Status: 501(c)3
Highest Offering: Associate Degree
Accreditation: HLC, CAHIIM, DA, MLTAD, RAD

02 President .... Dr. Carrie BRIMHALL
05 VP Academic & Student Affairs .... Dr. John MADUKO
15 Chief of Human Resources .... Mrs. Dacia JOHNSON
06 Registrar .... Ms. Sharlene ALLEN
13 Chief Information Officer .... Vacant
10 Chief Finance Officer .... Mr. Pat NORDICK
32 Dean of Student Affairs .... Mr. Shawn ANDERSON
81 Dean School Science & Mathematics .... Mr. Matthew BORCHERDING
76 Int Dean Health & Human Services .... Dr. John MADUKO
79 Dean of Liberal Arts & Humanities .... Ms. Anne THURMER
103 Exec Dir Workforce Dev Solutions .... Mr. G.L TUCKER
09 Dean of Inst Effect/Tech Solutions .... Mr. Steve ERICKSON
50 Dean School of Business/Info Tech .... Ms. Marsha WEBER
26 Assoc Dean of Marketing & Outreach .... Ms. Karen REILLY
72 Dean School of Applied Technology .... Mr. Matthew LOESLIE
30 Chief Development & Alum Officer .... Mr. Melvin WHITNEY
36 Career Services Director .... Ms. Sue ZURN
08 College Librarian .... Ms. Kari OANES
04 Exec Assistant to the President .... Ms. Alyssa CAMPION
19 Director Safety & ER Preparedness .... Ms. Paula PEDERSON
102 Exec Dir Fergus Area Col Foundation .... Ms. Lori LARSON
37 Director of Financial Aid .... Ms. Wendy OLDS
39 Dir Campus Life & Housing .... Ms. David ROBERTS
35 Dir of Student Engagement .... Ms. Teresa STOLFUS
28 Assoc Dir of Equity & Inclusion .... Ms. Madison JANSKY
88 Accessibility Resource Director .... Dr. Jon KRAGNESS
88 Accessibility Resource Director .... Ms. Jamie JENSEN
88 Compliance Officer .... Ms. Laura ZEIHER
88 Accessibility Res Dir/Acad Advisor .... Mr. Mark NELSON

*Minnesota State University, Mankato (D)

309 Wigley Administration Center,
Mankato MN 56001-6062
County: Blue Earth FICE Identification: 002360
Unit ID: 173920
Telephone: (507) 389-1111 Carnegie Class: Masters/L
FAX Number: (507) 389-6200 Calendar System: Semester
URL: www.mnsu.edu
Established: 1868 Annual Undergrad Tuition & Fees (In-State): $8,566
Enrollment: 14,761 Coed
Affiliation or Control: State IRS Status: Exempt
Highest Offering: Doctorate
Accreditation: HLC, AAB, ART, CAATE, CACREP, CAEP, CAPRT, CONST, DH, DIETD, MUS, NURSE, SP, SPAA, SW

02 President .... Dr. Edward INCH
05 Int Provost/SVP Academic Affairs .... Dr. Brian MARTENSEN
10 Vice Pres Finance & Administration .... Mr. Richard STRAKA
111 VP University Advancement .... Mr. Kent STANLEY
13 VP IT Solutions/CIO .... Mr. Mark JOHNSON
88 VP Strategic/Bus/Educ/Reg Prtnrshps .... Mr. Robert FLEISCHMAN
32 VP Student Affairs/Enrollment Mgmt .... Dr. David JONES
121 VP Stdnt Succ/Analytics/Integ Plng .... Ms. Lynn AKEY
100 Chief of Staff .... Ms. Sheri SARGENT
04 Exec Assistant to the President .... Ms. Juanita MILBRETT
20 Interim AVP for Undergrad Education .... Ms. Jennifer VELTSOS
28 Vice President Inst Diversity .... Mr. Henry MORRIS
18 Facilities Service Director .... Mr. David COWAN
06 University Registrar .... Mr. Marcius BROCK
07 Director of Admissions .... Mr. Brian JONES
08 Interim Dean Library Services .... Mr. Chris CORLEY
15 Director of Human Resources .... Mr. Steve BARRETT
36 Director Career Development .... Ms. Pamela WELLER-DENGEL
26 Director Media Relations .... Mr. Daniel BENSON
41 Dir of Intercollegiate Athletics .... Mr. Kevin BUISMAN
29 Director of Alumni Relations .... Mr. Ramon PINERO
22 Director Affirmative Action/Title I .... Ms. Linda ALVAREZ
37 Director Student Financial Services .... Ms. Jan MARBLE
58 AVP Graduate Studies/Research .... Dr. Stephen STOYNOFF
79 Interim Dean of Arts & Humanities .... Dr. Chris BROWN
53 Dean of Education .... Dr. Jean HAAR
50 Dean of Business .... Dr. Brenda FLANNERY
76 Dean Allied Health/Nursing .... Dr. Kristine RETHERFORD
81 Interim Dean CSET .... Dr. Aaron BUDGE
83 Dean Social/Behavioral Science .... Dr. Matt LAOYZA
104 Interim Dean Global Education .... Ms. Anne DAHLMAN
56 Dean University Extended Education .... Dr. Tom NORMAN
38 Director Student Counseling .... Ms. Kari MUCH
18 AVP Facilities Management .... Mr. Paul CORCORAN
114 AVP for Budget & Business Services .... Mr. Steve SMITH
19 Director Security/Safety .... Ms. Sandi SCHNORENBERG
39 Dean of Students/Res Life Director .... Ms. Cindy JANNEY

*Minnesota State University Moorhead (E)

1104 7th Avenue S, Moorhead MN 56563-2996
County: Clay FICE Identification: 002367
Unit ID: 174358
Telephone: (218) 477-4000 Carnegie Class: Masters/M
FAX Number: (218) 477-2168 Calendar System: Semester
URL: www.mnstate.edu
Established: 1887 Annual Undergrad Tuition & Fees (In-State): $8,980
Enrollment: 5,547 Coed
Affiliation or Control: State IRS Status: 501(c)3
Highest Offering: Doctorate
Accreditation: HLC, ART, CACREP, CAEPN, CONST, MUS, NAIT, NURSE, SP, SW

02 President .... Dr. Anne BLACKHURST
05 VP Academic Affairs .... Dr. Arrick L. JACKSON
10 VP Finance & Administration .... Ms. Jean HOLLAAR
84 VP Enrollment Mgmt/Student Affairs .... Dr. Brenda AMENSON-HILL
29 VP Alumni Foundation .... Mr. Gary HAUGO
04 Assistant to the President .... Ms. Kathleen J. MCNABB
20 AVP Academic Affairs .... Vacant
28 Campus Diversity Officer .... Mr. Jered PIGEON
09 Dir Institutional Effectiveness .... Vacant
13 Chief Information Officer .... Mr. Daniel A. HECKAMAN
21 Comptroller .... Ms. Karen K. LESTER
50 Int Dean Business & Innovation .... Mr. Josh J. BEHL
49 Dean Arts & Humanities .... Dr. Earnest LAMB
53 Dean Educ/Human Svcs/Grad Stds .... Dr. Ok-Hee LEE
83 Int Dean Science/Health/Environment .... Dr. Lisa NAWROT
106 Dean Graduate/Extended Learning .... Dr. Lisa KARCH
32 Dean of Students .... Ms. Kara GRAVLEY-STACK
15 VP Human Resources .... Ms. Ann HIEDEMAN
06 Registrar .... Ms. Heather M. SOLEIM
26 Chief Marketing Officer .... Mrs. Kirsten JENSEN
19 Director of Public Safety .... Mr. Ryan NELSON
37 Dir Financial Aid & Scholarships .... Ms. Melissa DINGMANN
23 Dir Hendrix Counseling Ctr .... Ms. Angela BELLANGER
22 Director of Accessibility Resources .... Mr. Chuck EADE
36 Director of Career Development .... Vacant
07 Director of Admissions .... Mr. Tom REBURN
35 Exec Dir Student Union .... Mr. Layne ANDERSON
39 Dir Housing & Residential Life .... Ms. Heather PHILLIPS
85 Global Engagement Director .... Ms. Kimberly GILLETTE
18 Interim Manager Physical Plant .... Ms. Jean HOLLAAR
40 Bookstore Supervisor .... Ms. Kim M. SAMSON

*Minnesota West Community and Technical College (F)

1593 11th Avenue, Granite Falls MN 56241
County: Yellow Medicine FICE Identification: 005263
Unit ID: 173638
Telephone: (800) 658-2330 Carnegie Class: Assoc/HVT-High Non
FAX Number: (507) 372-5803 Calendar System: Semester
URL: www.mnwest.edu
Established: 1985 Annual Undergrad Tuition & Fees (In-State): $5,936
Enrollment: 3,253 Coed
Affiliation or Control: State IRS Status: 501(c)3
Highest Offering: Associate Degree
Accreditation: HLC, ADNUR, DA, MAC, MLTAD, RAD, SURGT

02 President .... Dr. Terry GAALSWYK
05 College Provost .... Dr. Jeff WILLIAMSON
10 Vice Pres Finance/Facilities .... Ms. Jodi LANDGAARD
106 Dean Technology/Distance Learning .... Ms. Kayla WESTRA
66 Dean Science/Nursing .... Ms. Dawn GORDON
07 Director Admissions/Registration .... Ms. Katie HERONIMUS
18 Chief Facilities/Physical Plant .... Mr. Gordon HEITKAMP
37 Director Financial Aid .... Ms. Katie HERONIMUS
15 Director Human Resources .... Ms. Karen MILLER
102 Foundation Director .... Mr. Michael VAN KEULEN
08 Library Director .... Mr. Kip THORSON
10 Business Manager .... Ms. Kayla RICHTER
26 Dir Marketing/Enrollment/Comm .... Ms. Amber LUINENBURG

*Normandale Community College (G)

9700 France Avenue S, Bloomington MN 55431-4399
County: Hennepin FICE Identification: 007954
Unit ID: 174428
Telephone: (952) 358-8200 Carnegie Class: Assoc/HT-Mix Trad/Non
FAX Number: (952) 358-8101 Calendar System: Semester
URL: www.normandale.edu
Established: 1968 Annual Undergrad Tuition & Fees (In-State): $5,679
Enrollment: 9,420 Coed
Affiliation or Control: State IRS Status: 501(c)3
Highest Offering: Associate Degree
Accreditation: HLC, ACBSP, ADNUR, ART, DH, MUS, THEA

02 President .... Dr. Joyce C. ESTER

04 Executive Assistant to President Mrs. Kris CRAIG
11 Vice President Administration Mrs. Jill BOLDENOW
05 Provost/Vice Pres of Academic Affs Dr. Kristina KELLER
32 Vice President of Student Affairs Mrs. Dara HAGEN
15 Vice Pres Human Resources Mrs. Jodee MCCALLUM
111 Vice President Advancement Ms. Andrea SPECHT
09 Dir of Research & Planning Dr. Mark LEWIS
50 Dean of Business & Social Sci Mr. Michael KIRCH
79 Dean of Humanities Dr. Jeffrey JUDGE
81 Dean of STEM Dr. Cary KOMOTO
76 Dean of Health Sciences Dr. Colleen BRICKLE
08 Dean of Academic Svcs & Library Mrs. Erin DALY
10 Assoc VP Finance & Accounting Ms. Norma KONSCHAK
13 Chief Information Officer Mr. Stephen WINCKELMAN
18 Assoc Vice Pres of Operations Mr. Patrick BUHL
84 Dean of Recruitment and Outreach Mr. Charles FRAME
35 Dean of Students Mr. Jason CARDINAL
26 Chief Public Relations Officer Mr. Steve GELLER
06 Registrar Ms. Tonya HANSON
07 Director of Admissions Ms. Nancy PATES
37 Director of Financial Aid & Scholar Mrs. Susan ANT
38 Assoc Director of Advising & Couns Ms. Kari RUSCH-CURL
19 Director of Public Safety Mr. Erik BENTLEY
106 Director of Online Learning Vacant
27 Director of Marketing Communication Mrs. Jennifer LEFLER
88 Accounting Supervisor Mrs. Cindy LADD
40 Bookstore Manager Mr. Chris PETERSON
25 Grant Development Director Mrs. Angela ARNOLD
22 Equity & Inclusion Officer Mr. John PARKER-DER BOGHOSSIAN
109 Director of Auxiliary Services Mr. Chris MIKKELSEN

*North Hennepin Community College (A)

7411 85th Avenue N, Brooklyn Park MN 55445-2299
County: Hennepin FICE Identification: 002370
Unit ID: 174376
Telephone: (763) 424-0702 Carnegie Class: Assoc/HT-Mix Trad/Non
FAX Number: (763) 424-0929 Calendar System: Semester
URL: www.nhcc.edu
Established: 1966 Annual Undergrad Tuition & Fees (In-State): $4,596
Enrollment: 5,756 Coed
Affiliation or Control: State IRS Status: 501(c)3
Highest Offering: Associate Degree
Accreditation: HLC, ACBSP, ADNUR, MLTAD

02 President Dr. Rolando GARCIA
05 Provost Dr. Jesse MASON
10 Int VP Finance & Facilities Ms. Dawn BELKO
13 Chief Information Officer Mr. Joseph COLLINS
32 Dean Student Development Ms. Lindsay FORT
08 Librarian Mr. Craig LARSON
06 Director of Admissions & Records Ms. Melissa LEIMBEK
15 Chief Human Resources Officer Ms. Victoria DEFORD
18 Director of Facilities Mr. Joshua BLACKWELL
102 Foundation Executive Director Mr. Dale FAGRE
28 Assoc Vice Pres Equity/Inclusion Dr. Eda WATTS
26 Dir Marketing/Communications Ms. Liz HOGENSON
09 Director of Institutional Research Ms. Dena COLEMER
19 Director of Public Safety Mr. Ibuchwa KISONGO
21 Int Business Manager Ms. Kristen HARINEN
49 Dean of Liberal Arts Mr. Anthony MILLER
50 Dean Business & Career Programs Dr. Nerita HUGHES
81 Dean of Math/Science Mr. Jayant ANAND
76 Int Dean of Nursing & Allied Health Dr. Julia UGORJI
60 Dean of Comm/Language/Fine Arts Ms. Kathy HENDRICKSON
121 Director Student Advising Ms. Sarah DOMAN-FLYGARE
04 Executive Assistant to President Ms. Nicole CARLSON
36 Director Student Placement Ms. Deb ATKINS
37 Director Student Financial Aid Ms. Kristi L'ALLIER

*Northland Community and Technical College (B)

1101 Highway One East, Thief River Falls MN 56701
County: Pennington FICE Identification: 002385
Unit ID: 174473
Telephone: (218) 683-8800 Carnegie Class: Assoc/HVT-Mix Trad/Non
FAX Number: (218) 683-8980 Calendar System: Semester
URL: www.northlandcollege.edu
Established: 1965 Annual Undergrad Tuition & Fees (In-State): $5,793
Enrollment: 2,962 Coed
Affiliation or Control: State IRS Status: 501(c)3
Highest Offering: Associate Degree
Accreditation: HLC, ADNUR, COARC, EMT, OTA, PTAA, RAD, SURGT

02 President Dr. Dennis BONA
10 VP of Admin Services/CFO Ms. Shannon JESME
04 Asst to President Ms. Julie FENNING
05 Provost Dr. Brian HUSCHLE
15 Director of Human Resources Mr. Mike CURFMAN
103 Dean Workforce & Econ Development Mr. James RETKA
102 Executive Director NCTC Foundation Mr. Lars DYRUD
121 Academic Success Ctr Director Vacant
38 Counselor Ms. Kelsy BLOWERS
84 Dir of Enrollment Mgmt & Admission Ms. Nicki CARLSON
37 Director Student Financial Aid Ms. Lisa BOTTEM
32 Dean Student Affairs Dr. Mary FONTES
18 Chief Facilities/Physical Plant Mr. Clinton CASTLE
26 Director of Marketing/Communication Mr. Chad SPERLING
06 Registrar Mr. Ben HOFFMAN
13 Director of Technology Ms. Stacey HRON
41 Director of Athletics Mr. James RETKA
19 Director Security/Safety Mr. Cory FELLER

*Northwest Technical College (C)

905 Grant Avenue, SE, Bemidji MN 56601-4907
County: Beltrami FICE Identification: 005759
Unit ID: 173115
Telephone: (218) 333-6600 Carnegie Class: Assoc/HVT-High Non
FAX Number: (218) 333-6694 Calendar System: Semester
URL: www.ntcmn.edu
Established: 1966 Annual Undergrad Tuition & Fees (In-State): $5,731
Enrollment: 825 Coed
Affiliation or Control: State IRS Status: 501(c)3
Highest Offering: Associate Degree
Accreditation: HLC, ADNUR, DA, PNUR

02 President Dr. Faith HENSRUD
05 Chief Academic Officer Mr. Darrin STROSAHL

*Pine Technical and Community College (D)

900 Fourth Street, SE, Pine City MN 55063-2198
County: Pine FICE Identification: 005535
Unit ID: 174570
Telephone: (320) 629-5100 Carnegie Class: Assoc/HVT-High Non
FAX Number: (320) 629-5101 Calendar System: Semester
URL: www.pine.edu
Established: 1965 Annual Undergrad Tuition & Fees (In-State): $4,302
Enrollment: 1,724 Coed
Affiliation or Control: State IRS Status: 501(c)3
Highest Offering: Associate Degree
Accreditation: HLC

02 President Mr. Joe MULFORD
05 Vice Pres Academic/Student Affairs Ms. Denine ROOD
13 Chief Information Officer Ms. Janis WEGNER
10 Chief Financial Officer Ms. Janis WEGNER
51 Dean of Continuing Edu/Custom Trng Mr. Jason SPAETH
66 Dean Nursing/Health Science Vacant
06 Registrar Ms. Darla CALVERLEY
15 Chief Human Resources Officer Ms. Amy KRUSE
26 Director Marketing/Enrollment Ms. Katie KOPPY
32 Director Student Affairs Mr. Shawn REYNOLDS
18 Physical Plant Supervisor Mr. Steven LANGE
04 Executive Asst to President Ms. Sandi CARLISLE

*Rainy River Community College (E)

1501 Highway 71, International Falls MN 56649-2187
County: Koochiching FICE Identification: 006775
Unit ID: 174604
Telephone: (218) 285-7722 Carnegie Class: Assoc/HT-High Non
FAX Number: (218) 285-2239 Calendar System: Semester
URL: www.rainyriver.edu
Established: 1967 Annual Undergrad Tuition & Fees (In-State): $5,540
Enrollment: 173 Coed
Affiliation or Control: State IRS Status: 501(c)3
Highest Offering: Associate Degree
Accreditation: HLC

02 Interim President Dr. Michael RAICH
05 Provost Vacant
06 Registrar Ms. Stephanie TURBAN
37 Director of Financial Aid Ms. Jodi PONTINEN
13 Dir Information Technology Ms. Shelly JUGOVICH
10 Business Manager Mrs. Emily AHRENS

*Ridgewater College (F)

PO Box 1097, 2101 15th Ave NW, Willmar MN 56201-1097
County: Kandiyohi FICE Identification: 005252
Unit ID: 175236
Telephone: (320) 222-5200 Carnegie Class: Assoc/HVT-Mix Trad/Non
FAX Number: (320) 222-5212 Calendar System: Semester
URL: www.ridgewater.edu
Established: 1961 Annual Undergrad Tuition & Fees (In-State): $5,958
Enrollment: 3,176 Coed
Affiliation or Control: State IRS Status: 501(c)3
Highest Offering: Associate Degree
Accreditation: HLC, ADNUR, CAHIIM, EMT, MAC, PNUR

02 President Dr. Craig JOHNSON
05 Vice Pres Student Success Mr. Mike KUTZKE
10 Vice President Finance & Operations Mr. Daniel F. HOLTZ
51 Dean of Cust Trng & Cont Education Mr. Sam BOWEN
20 Dean of Instruction/Technical Pgms Mr. Matthew FEUERBORN
20 Dean Instruction/Liberal Arts/Sci Mr. Jeff MILLER
32 Dean of Student Services Ms. Heidi L. OLSON
21 Director of Business Services Ms. Cheryl A. NORLIEN
15 Chief Human Resource Officer Mr. Keith BALASKI
66 Director of Nursing Ms. Faith JOHNSON
37 Director of Financial Aid Mr. James W. RICE
22 Dir Equity/Inclusion/Stdnt Success Ms. Stacy GRIFFEY
07 Admissions/Academic Advisor Ms. Amy BIRKLAND
41 Athletic Coordinator Mr. Todd M. THORSTAD
06 Registrar Ms. Kelli S. KIENITZ
13 Chief Information Officer Vacant
26 Dir Communications/Mktg/Admissions Ms. Laura KUVAAS
102 VP Advancement/Foundation Exec Dir Ms. Kelly J. MAGNUSON
09 Director of Institutional Research Vacant
28 Multicultural Outreach/Academic Adv Ms. Jehana SCHWANDT
18 Physical Plant Director Mr. Kip R. OVESON

*Riverland Community College (G)

1900 8th Avenue, NW, Austin MN 55912-1473
County: Mower FICE Identification: 002335
Unit ID: 173063
Telephone: (507) 433-0600 Carnegie Class: Assoc/HT-High Non
FAX Number: (507) 433-0665 Calendar System: Semester
URL: www.riverland.edu
Established: 1940 Annual Undergrad Tuition & Fees (In-State): $5,826
Enrollment: 3,494 Coed
Affiliation or Control: State IRS Status: 501(c)3
Highest Offering: Associate Degree
Accreditation: HLC, ADNUR, MAC, PNUR, RAD

02 President Dr. Adenuga ATEWOLOGUN
05 VP of Academic & Student Affairs Ms. Barbara EMBACHER
10 VP of Finance & Operations Mr. Brad DOSS
15 VP of Employee Relations & HR Ms. Karen IRWIN
66 Dean of Nursing/Health & Wellness Ms. Laura BEASLEY
49 Dean Liberal Arts & Sciences Ms. Jen OUELLETTE-SCHRAMM
75 Dean Ag/Trans/Trade & Tech Mr. Ryan LANGEMEIER
32 Dean of Student Affairs Ms. Chelsea ANDERSON
111 Dean of Institutional Advancement Ms. Janelle KOEPKE
50 Dean of Business/SS/Safety & CT Vacant
06 Registrar Ms. Sue JECH
07 Dir of Admissions & New Student Rel Ms. Nel ZELLAR
26 Exec Dir Communications/Media/Mktg Mr. James DOUGLASS
37 Director of Financial Aid Ms. Patty HEMANN
36 Dir of College Partnerships & Trans Ms. Jean KYLE
13 VP Technology & Learning Resources Mr. Mark BAAS
18 Physical Plant Supervisor Mr. Shawn O'CONNOR
96 Purchasing Agent Ms. Page PETERSEN
28 Diversity Officer Ms. Dani HEINY
08 Librarian Ms. Jeannie (Carol) DIGGS
19 Safety Administrator Mr. Mike HOWE
29 Director Grants/Alumni Relations Ms. Kim NELSON
41 Athletic Director Mr. Derek HAHN
04 Exec Assistant to the President Ms. Holly SHERMAN
09 Director of Institutional Research Mr. Pawel BUDA
39 Director Residential Life & Housing Ms. Alexis PERSONS

*Rochester Community and Technical College (H)

851 30th Avenue, SE, Rochester MN 55904-4999
County: Olmsted FICE Identification: 002373
Unit ID: 174738
Telephone: (507) 285-7210 Carnegie Class: Assoc/MT-VT-High Trad
FAX Number: (507) 285-7496 Calendar System: Semester
URL: www.rctc.edu
Established: 1915 Annual Undergrad Tuition & Fees (In-State): $5,252
Enrollment: 5,115 Coed
Affiliation or Control: State IRS Status: 501(c)3
Highest Offering: Associate Degree
Accreditation: HLC, ACBSP, ADNUR, CAHIIM, DA, DH, PNUR, SURGT

02 President Dr. Jeffery BOYD
05 VP of Academic Affairs Ms. Michelle PYFFEROEN
10 Vice Pres Finance Mr. Steve SCHMALL
81 Dean Sciences & Health Professions Mr. Jason JADIN
49 Dean of Liberal Arts Dr. Brenda FRAME
75 Int Dean Career/Technical Education Dr. Matt BISSONETTE
18 Vice Pres Facilities Mr. Steve SCHMALL
15 Chief Human Resource Officer Vacant
13 Chief Information Officer Mr. Mir QADER
32 Chief Student Affairs Officer Dr. Teresa BROWN
103 Dir of Business/Workforce Dev Vacant
35 Student Life Coordinator Ms. Megan ROSS
06 Registrar Ms. Melanie CALLISTER
07 Director Admissions and Enrollment Ms. Alicia ZEONE
37 Director Financial Aid Ms. Beth DIEKMANN
09 Chief Inst Effectiveness Officer Mr. Peter WRUCK
04 Executive Assistant to President Mrs. Judy KINGSBURY
21 Business Office Supervisor Ms. Kelly PYFFEROEN
26 Chief Public Relations Officer Mr. Nate STOLTMAN
19 Director of Campus Safety/Security Mr. Scott MCCULLOUGH
40 Bookstore Coordinator Ms. Michelle DANIELSON
96 Purchasing Manager Ms. June MEITZNER
102 Foundation Executive Director Dr. Matt BISSONETTE
08 Head Librarian Ms. Mary DENNISON
22 Dir Affirmative Action/EEO Vacant
41 Athletic Director Mr. Mike LESTER
105 Director Web Services Mr. Darin HOFFMAN
30 Advancement Coordinator Ms. Kristin MANNIX

*St. Cloud State University (I)

720 4th Avenue S, Saint Cloud MN 56301-4498
County: Stearns FICE Identification: 002377
Unit ID: 174783
Telephone: (320) 308-0121 Carnegie Class: Masters/L
FAX Number: N/A Calendar System: Semester
URL: www.stcloudstate.edu
Established: 1869 Annual Undergrad Tuition & Fees (In-State): $8,779
Enrollment: 11,841 Coed
Affiliation or Control: State IRS Status: 501(c)3

Highest Offering: Doctorate
Accreditation: HLC, ABAI, ART, #CAATE, CACREP, HT, JOUR, MT, MUS, NAIT, NURSE, SP, SW

02 President — Dr. Robbyn R. WACKER
04 Executive Asst to President — Ms. Meredith L. ATHMAN
05 Provost/VP for Academic Affairs — Dr. Dan GREGORY
10 Vice Pres for Finance/Admin — Ms. Tressa C. RIES
84 VP Enrollment Management — Dr. Jason L. WOODS
45 VP for Planning & Engagement — Dr. Lisa H. FOSS
111 Vice Pres University Advancement — Mr. Matthew ANDREW
32 VP for Student Affairs — Dr. Katrina RODRIGUEZ
43 Special Advisor to the President — Dr. Judith P. SIMINOE
86 Director Univ/Legislative Relations — Mr. Bernie OMANN
22 Equity & Access Officer — Dr. Ellyn BARTGES
41 Director of Athletics — Ms. Heather WEEMS
15 Chief Human Resource Officer — Mr. Michael FREER
13 Deputy Chief Information Officer — Mr. Phil THORSON
21 Director of Business Services — Mr. Jeff WAGNER
26 Exec Dir Marketing & Communications — Dr. Kathryn KLOBY
50 Dean Herberger Business School — Dr. David HARRIS
53 Dean School of Education — Dr. Jennifer MUELLER
76 Dean School of Health/Human Service — Dr. Shonda M. CRAFT
49 Dean College of Liberal Arts — Dr. Mark SPRINGER
80 Dean School of Public Affairs — Dr. King BANAIAN
81 Dean Science & Engineering — Dr. Adel ALI
08 Dean University Library — Ms. Rhonda HUISMAN
46 AP for Research/Sponsored Pgms — Dr. Claudia TOMANY
97 Dean University College — Dr. Feng-Ling JOHNSON
20 Exec Dir of Academic Resources — Dr. Michele MUMM
35 Dean of Students — Ms. Jen SELL MATZKE
07 AVP Student Recruit & Enrollment — Vacant
06 Registrar and Student Records — Vacant
29 Dir Alumni/Constituent Engagement — Ms. Terri MISCHE
36 Executive Director Career Center — Ms. Michelle SCHMITZ
37 Director of Financial Aid — Mr. Mike T. URAN
38 Director of Counseling — Dr. Jennifer ROCHELEAU DORHOLT
117 AVP Safety/Risk Management — Vacant
09 Dir Analytics/Business Intelligence — Mr. Tony KUNKEL
18 AVP Facilities Management — Mr. Phil MOESSNER
88 Director American Indian Center — Ms. Barbara K. MILLER
88 Int Director LGBT Resource Center — Ms. Jane OLSEN
88 Director Lindgren Child Care Center — Vacant
22 Director Student Accessibility Svcs — Ms. Andria BELISLE
23 Director Student Health Services — Vacant
94 Director Womens Center — Ms. Jane OLSEN
19 Director Public Safety — Vacant
85 Int AVP Intl Studies/Dir MSS — Mr. Shahzad AHMAD

*Saint Cloud Technical and Community College (A)

1540 Northway Drive, Saint Cloud MN 56303-1240
County: Stearns — FICE Identification: 005534
Unit ID: 174756
Telephone: (320) 308-5000 — Carnegie Class: Assoc/MT-VT-High Trad
FAX Number: (320) 308-5981 — Calendar System: Semester
URL: www.sctcc.edu
Established: 1948 — Annual Undergrad Tuition & Fees (In-State): $5,631
Enrollment: 3,931 — Coed
Affiliation or Control: State — IRS Status: 501(c)3
Highest Offering: Associate Degree
Accreditation: HLC, CAHIIM, CVT, DA, DH, DMS, EMT, PNUR, SURGT

02 President — Dr. Annesa CHEEK
05 VP of Academic Affairs — Dr. Emmanuel AWUAH
32 Vice President Student Affairs — Mr. Andrew PFLIPSEN
04 Assistant to the President — Ms. Karen A. HIEMENZ
10 Vice Pres Admin/Chief Financial Ofc — Ms. Lori KLOOS
22 Vice Pres Equity & Inclusion — Ms. Debra LEIGH
75 Dean Trade/Industry — Vacant
81 Dean of Liberal Arts & Trans Stds — Ms. Melissa LINDSEY
50 Dean of Business/IT & Online Lrng — Ms. Shanda DAVIS
66 Dean of Nursing/Health — Mr. Robert MUSTER
06 Registrar — Ms. Bretta EDWARDS
15 Dir Personnel Svcs/Affirm Action — Ms. Deb A. HOLSTAD
84 Dir of Enroll Management/Admissions — Ms. Jodi M. ELNESS
08 Head Librarian — Ms. Mary JORDAN
19 Security/Safety Officer — Ms. Carol BREWER
37 Director Student Financial Aid — Ms. Anita G. BAUGH
36 Director Student Placement — Ms. Lisa MOHR
40 Director Bookstore — Mr. Aquirre REESE
41 Director of Athletics — Mr. Nathaniel HIESTAND
18 Chief Facilities/Physical Plant — Mr. Jason THEISEN
13 Chief Information Officer — Mr. Tim FURR
21 Business Officer — Ms. Diane ILLIES
96 Director of Purchasing — Ms. Susan MEYER
08 Director Library — Ms. Jennifer ERICKSON
22 Director Affirm Action/Equal Oppty — Ms. Deb HOLSTAD
30 Chief Devel/Dir Annual/Planned Giv — Vacant
09 Director of Institutional Research — Dr. Kenneth MATTHEWS

*Saint Paul College-A Community & Technical College (B)

235 Marshall Avenue, Saint Paul MN 55102-1800
County: Ramsey — FICE Identification: 005533
Unit ID: 175041
Telephone: (651) 846-1703 — Carnegie Class: Assoc/MT-VT-Mix Trad/Non
FAX Number: (651) 846-1451 — Calendar System: Semester
URL: www.saintpaul.edu
Established: 1910 — Annual Undergrad Tuition & Fees (In-State): $5,811
Enrollment: 5,823 — Coed
Affiliation or Control: State — IRS Status: 501(c)3
Highest Offering: Associate Degree
Accreditation: HLC, ACBSP, ACFEI, CAHIIM, COARC, MLTAD, PNUR, SURGT

02 President — Dr. Deidra PEASLEE
10 Vice President Finance & Operations — Mr. Scott WILSON
05 Vice President of Academic Affairs — Dr. Kristen RANEY
32 Vice President of Student Affairs — Dr. Laura KING
28 VP Diversity/Equity/Inclusion — Ms. Wendy ROBERSON
27 Director of TRIO — Ms. Mary VANG
103 Dean Workforce Trng/Continuing Educ — Ms. Jennifer HUSTON
07 Director of Admissions — Ms. Tarah BJORKLUND
15 Senior Human Resources Officer — Mr. Craig MORRIS
13 Chief Information Officer — Ms. Ellen ROSTER
06 Director Records/Registration — Ms. Tarah SACHDEV
09 Dean of Inst Research/Plng/Grants — Ms. Nichole SORENSON
29 Director of Alumni Relations — Mr. Logan SPINDLER
36 Director Student Placement — Ms. Sheryl SAUL
38 Director Student Counseling — Dr. Lisa HANES-GOODLANDER
96 Director of Purchasing — Ms. Teresa SORENSEN
18 Director Facilities/Physical Plant — Mr. Ben MARTINSON
21 Business Office Manager — Ms. Liz SCHMIDT
37 Director of Student Financial Aid — Mr. Adam JOHNSON
102 Exec Director of Foundation — Mr. David KLINE
26 Int Dir Marketing/Recruitment — Mr. Ryan MAYOR
76 Dean of Health Sciences/Services — Dr. Julia BARTLETT
81 Dean Science/Technology/Eng & Math — Dr. Enyinda ONUNWOR
50 Dean Business/Career Tech Educ — Dr. Rainer HAARBUSCH
57 Dean Liberal & Fine Arts — Dr. Andrew KUBAS
19 Director Pubic Safety — Mr. Thomas BERGS
108 Dean of Academic Effectiveness — Ms. Sarah CARRICO
88 Director OneStop Services — Mr. Daniel RIVERA

*South Central College (C)

1920 Lee Boulevard, PO Box 1920,
North Mankato MN 56003
County: Nicollet — FICE Identification: 005537
Unit ID: 173911
Telephone: (507) 389-7200 — Carnegie Class: Assoc/MT-VT-Mix Trad/Non
FAX Number: (507) 388-9951 — Calendar System: Semester
URL: www.southcentral.edu
Established: 1946 — Annual Undergrad Tuition & Fees (In-District): $5,491
Enrollment: 2,653 — Coed
Affiliation or Control: State/Local — IRS Status: 501(c)3
Highest Offering: Associate Degree
Accreditation: HLC, ADNUR, DA, EMT, MAC, MLTAD, PNUR

02 President — Dr. Annette PARKER
04 Exec Assistant to the President — Ms. Susan JAMESON
05 Vice Pres Academic/Student Affs — Dr. Jennifer FAGER
10 VP Finance/Operations — Ms. Roxy TRAXLER
15 Chief Human Resources Officer — Ms. Roxy TRAXLER
09 VP Research & Inst Effectiveness — Dr. Narren BROWN
32 Dean of Student Affairs — Ms. Judy ENDRES
49 Dean of Arts & Sciences — Dr. Rick KURTZ
103 Dean of Career & Technical Educ — Vacant
47 Dean of Agriculture — Mr. Brad SCHLOESSER
66 Dean of Allied Health & Nursing — Dr. Kim JOHNSON
26 Public Relations/Marketing Director — Ms. Shelly MEGAW
28 Dir of Diversity/Equity & Inclusion — Mr. John HARPER
37 Director of Financial Aid — Ms. Bonnie SCHEFFLER
08 Librarian — Ms. Heather BIEDERMANN
06 Registrar — Ms. Lisa MELCHIOR
102 Exec Director N Mankato Foundation — Ms. Erin AANENSON
19 Safety & Security Program Manager — Mr. Aronn OAKLAND
07 Director of Admissions — Mr. Edel FERNANDEZ

*Southwest Minnesota State University (D)

1501 State Street, Marshall MN 56258-1598
County: Lyon — FICE Identification: 002375
Unit ID: 175078
Telephone: (507) 537-7678 — Carnegie Class: Masters/M
FAX Number: (507) 537-7154 — Calendar System: Semester
URL: www.smsu.edu
Established: 1963 — Annual Undergrad Tuition & Fees (In-State): $9,058
Enrollment: 7,259 — Coed
Affiliation or Control: State — IRS Status: 501(c)3
Highest Offering: Master's
Accreditation: HLC, MUS, NURSE, SW

02 President — Dr. Kumara JAYASURIYA
05 Provost — Dr. Ross WASTVEDT
10 VP Finance and Admin — Ms. Debra KERKAERT
32 AVP Stdnt Affairs/Dean of Students — Mr. Scott CROWELL
111 Co-Exec Dir Advancement/Foundation — Mr. Nathan POLFLIET
111 Co-Exec Dir Advancement/Foundation — Ms. Stacy FROST
49 Interim Dean Arts/Letters/Sciences — Dr. Jeff BELL
50 Dean Bus/Ed/Grad/Prof Studies — Dr. Raphael ONYEAGHALA
41 Interim Athletic Director — Mr. Bruce SAUGSTAD
13 Chief Information Officer — Mr. Dan BAUN
07 Exec Dir of Admission — Mr. Rich SHEARER
14 Director of Computer Services — Mr. Shawn HEDMAN
06 Registrar — Ms. Patricia CARMODY
19 Director University Public Safety — Mr. Michael MUNFORD
28 Director Diversity & Inclusion — Vacant
15 Chief Human Resources/Affirm Action — Ms. Nancy OLSON
29 Director of Alumni — Mr. Michael VANDREHLE
18 Facilities & Physical Plant Manager — Mr. Tony NUBILE
36 Director of Career Services — Ms. Melissa SCHOLTEN
37 Director of Financial Aid — Ms. Connie SMISEK
38 University Counselor — Ms. Sara FIER
96 Buyer Supervisor — Ms. Barb BERKENPAS
21 Business Manager — Ms. Jackie TAUER
26 Dir Communications/Marketing — Mr. James TATE
04 Exec Admin Asst to President — Ms. Chris ANDERSON
09 Director of Institutional Research — Mr. Alan MATZNER
30 Director Development — Vacant
44 Director Annual Giving — Ms. Meredith HYATT

*Vermilion Community College (E)

1900 E Camp Street, Ely MN 55731-1998
County: Saint Louis — FICE Identification: 002350
Unit ID: 175157
Telephone: (218) 365-7200 — Carnegie Class: Assoc/HT-Mix Trad/Non
FAX Number: (218) 235-2173 — Calendar System: Semester
URL: www.vcc.edu
Established: 1922 — Annual Undergrad Tuition & Fees (In-State): $5,540
Enrollment: 554 — Coed
Affiliation or Control: State — IRS Status: 501(c)3
Highest Offering: Associate Degree
Accreditation: HLC

02 Interim President — Dr. Michael RAICH
05 Provost/Chief Academic Officer — Mr. Christopher KOIVISTO
07 Director of Admissions/Student Affs — Mr. Jeff NELSON
09 Director of Institutional Research — Ms. Heather HOHENSTEIN
32 Dir Student Life/Facil/Phy Plant — Mr. Dave MARSHALL
36 Director of Student Placement — Ms. Molly JOHNSTON
37 Director of Student Financial Aid — Mr. Ray PODOMINICK
38 Director of Student Counseling — Ms. Kate F. COWLEY
29 Director Alumni Relations — Ms. Sarah GUY-LEVAR
28 Director of Diversity — Mr. Timothy LONEY
26 Chief Pub Rel Officer/Enrollment — Mr. Jeff NELSON
06 Registrar/Instructional Services — Ms. Chris HEGENBARTH

*Winona State University (F)

PO Box 5838, Winona MN 55987-0838
County: Winona — FICE Identification: 002394
Unit ID: 175272
Telephone: (507) 457-5000 — Carnegie Class: Masters/S
FAX Number: (507) 457-5586 — Calendar System: Quarter
URL: www.winona.edu
Established: 1858 — Annual Undergrad Tuition & Fees (In-State): $9,780
Enrollment: 7,106 — Coed
Affiliation or Control: State — IRS Status: 501(c)3
Highest Offering: Doctorate
Accreditation: HLC, CAATE, CACREP, MUS, NURSE, SW, THEA

02 President — Dr. Scott R. OLSON
05 Provost/VP Academic Affairs/CAO — Dr. Darrell NEWTON
10 VP Finance & Administration — Mr. Scott ELLINGHUYSEN
111 VP University Advancement — Mr. Jon OLSON
32 VP Enrollment & Student Life & Dev — Ms. Denise MCDOWELL
13 AVP Academic Affairs/CIO — Mr. Kenneth JANZ
38 Director of Counseling Services — Dr. Benedict EZEOKE
54 Dean College of Science/Engineering — Dr. Charla MIERTSCHIN
49 Dean College of Liberal Arts — Dr. Peter MIENE
50 Interim Dean College of Business — Ms. Marianne COLLINS
53 Dean College of Education — Dr. Daniel KIRK
66 Dean Col of Nursing/Health Science — Dr. Julie ANDERSON
35 Dean of Students — Ms. Karen JOHNSON
06 Sr Associate Registrar — Ms. Tania SCHMIDT
84 Director Warrior Success Center — Mr. Ron STREGE
37 Assistant Director of Financial Aid — Ms. Charlene KREUZER
36 Associate Director Career Services — Ms. Deanna GODDARD
07 Interim Director of Admissions — Ms. Kendra WEBER
39 Residential College Program Coord — Ms. Sarah OLCOTT
51 Exec Dir Outreach/Continuing Educ — Vacant
29 Director of Alumni Engagement — Ms. Tracy HALE
40 Bookstore Manager — Ms. Karen KRAUSE
44 Director Development — Vacant
88 Director of International Svcs — Ms. Kemale PINAR
19 Director of Security — Mr. Christopher CICHOSZ
41 Athletic Director — Mr. Eric SCHOH
18 Asst VP for Facilities Management — Mr. James GOBLIRSCH
26 Director Marketing & Communications — Ms. Andrea NORTHAM
94 Director of Women's Studies — Dr. Tamara BERG
96 Director of Purchasing — Ms. Laura MANN
28 Director of Cultural Diversity — Mr. Jonathan LOCUST
15 Director of Human Resources — Ms. Lori REED
04 Exec Admin Assistant to President — Ms. Ingrid SPIES

*Anoka-Ramsey Community College Cambridge Campus (G)

300 Spirit River Drive South, Cambridge MN 55008-5704
Telephone: (763) 433-1100 — Identification: 770298
Accreditation: &HLC

*Hennepin Technical College (H)

131000 College View, Eden Prairie MN 55347
Telephone: (952) 995-1300 — Identification: 770299
Accreditation: &HLC

*Mesabi Range College Eveleth (I)

1100 Industrial Park Drive, Eveleth MN 55734
Telephone: (218) 741-3095 — Identification: 770300
Accreditation: &HLC

* Minnesota State Community and Technical College Detroit Lakes (A)
900 Highway 34 E, Detroit Lakes MN 56501
Telephone: (218) 846-3700 Identification: 770303
Accreditation: &HLC

* Minnesota State Community and Technical College Moorhead (B)
1900 28th Avenue S, Moorhead MN 56560
Telephone: (218) 299-6500 Identification: 770304
Accreditation: &HLC, CVT, DH, SURGT

* Minnesota State Community and Technical College Wadena (C)
405 Colfax Avenue SW, Wadena MN 56482
Telephone: (213) 631-7800 Identification: 770305
Accreditation: &HLC

* Minnesota West Community and Technical College Canby Campus (D)
1011 First Street West, Canby MN 56220
Telephone: (507) 223-7252 Identification: 770306
Accreditation: &HLC

* Minnesota West Community and Technical College Jackson Campus (E)
401 West Street, Jackson MN 56143
Telephone: (547) 847-7920 Identification: 770308
Accreditation: &HLC

* Minnesota West Community and Technical College Pipestone Campus (F)
1314 North Hiawatha Ave/PO Box 250, Pipestone MN 56164
Telephone: (507) 825-6800 Identification: 770309
Accreditation: &HLC, CAHIIM

* Minnesota West Community and Technical College Worthington Campus (G)
1450 Collegeway, Worthington MN 56187
Telephone: (507) 372-3464 Identification: 770310
Accreditation: &HLC, PNUR

* Northland Community and Technical College East Grand Forks Campus (H)
2022 Central Avenue NE, East Grand Forks MN 56721
Telephone: (218) 793-2800 Identification: 770311
Accreditation: &HLC, DIETT

* Riverland Community College Albert Lea Campus (I)
2200 Riverland Drive, Albert Lea MN 56007
Telephone: (507) 379-3300 Identification: 770313
Accreditation: &HLC

* South Central College Faribault Campus (J)
1225 Third Street SW, Faribault MN 55021
Telephone: (507) 332-5800 Identification: 770314
Accreditation: &HLC

* Winona State University-Rochester (K)
859 30th Avenue SE, Rochester MN 55904
Telephone: (800) 366-5418 Identification: 770317
Accreditation: &HLC

Mitchell Hamline School of Law (L)
875 Summit Avenue, Saint Paul MN 55105-3076
County: Ramsey FICE Identification: 002391
Unit ID: 175281
Telephone: (651) 227-9171 Carnegie Class: Spec-4-yr-Law
FAX Number: (651) 290-6414 Calendar System: Semester
URL: www.mitchellhamline.edu
Established: 1900 Annual Graduate Tuition & Fees: N/A
Enrollment: 1,242 Coed
Affiliation or Control: Independent Non-Profit IRS Status: 501(c)3
Highest Offering: First Professional Degree; No Undergraduates
Accreditation: LAW

01 President & Dean ....Mr. Anthony S. NIEDWIECKI
04 Exec Asst to President & Dean ....Ms. Lynette M. FRACTION
05 Vice Dean Academic & Faculty Affs ....Mr. Jim HILBERT
30 VP of Development & Alumni Affairs ....Ms. Leslie WRIGHT
15 Interim Director Human Resources ....Mr. Michael FREER
13 Director of Information Technology ....Mr. Andrew ALLEN
10 VP Finance & Administration ....Mr. Stephen KENT
11 VP Cmty Relations & Operations ....Ms. Christine SZAJ
84 Vice Pres of Enrollment ....Ms. Ann GEMMELL
08 Interim Director of Law Library ....Ms. Lisa HEIDENREICH
28 VP of DEI ....Mr. Michael BIRCHARD
36 Dean for Career Development ....Ms. Leanne FUITH
06 Registrar ....Ms. Colleen CLISH
37 Director of Financial Aid ....Mr. Nick ANDERSON
96 Purchasing Manager ....Ms. Paula B. MERTH
19 Director Facilities & Security ....Mr. John BENTFIELD
32 Dean of Student Affairs ....Ms. Lynn LEMOINE
121 Dean of Academic Excellence ....Ms. Dena SONBOL
26 Asst Director of Marketing ....Mr. Doug BELDEN

North Central University (M)
910 Elliot Avenue, Minneapolis MN 55404-1391
County: Hennepin FICE Identification: 002369
Unit ID: 174437
Telephone: (612) 343-4400 Carnegie Class: Bac-Diverse
FAX Number: (612) 343-4778 Calendar System: Semester
URL: www.northcentral.edu
Established: 1930 Annual Undergrad Tuition & Fees: $26,280
Enrollment: 1,062 Coed
Affiliation or Control: Assemblies Of God Church IRS Status: 501(c)3
Highest Offering: Master's
Accreditation: HLC, SW

01 President ....Rev. Scott A. HAGAN
03 Executive Vice President ....Dr. Andrew C. DENTON
04 Executive Assistant to President ....Mrs. Kristie KERR
05 Provost ....Dr. Don L. TUCKER
10 Vice Pres Business & Operations ....Dr. Tim HAGER
20 VP for Academic Affairs ....Dr. Jason WENSCHLAG
84 VP Enrollment/Student Development ..Mrs. Beth HARSHBARGER
42 Assoc Vice Pres of Spiritual Life ....Mr. Joshua EDMON
57 Dean of the College of Fine Arts ....Mr. Larry C. BACH
50 Dean of College of Business & Tech ....Mr. Bill TIBBETTS
49 Dean of College of Arts & Sciences ....Dr. Desiree LIBENGOOD
88 Dean of Col of Church Leadership ....Dr. Allen TENNISON
32 Dean of Students ....Mr. Jeremy WILLIAMSON
41 Interim Director of Athletics ....Mr. Mike KNIPE
37 Director of Financial Aid ....Mr. Alex HINTZ
08 Library Director ....Mrs. Judy PRUITT
13 Director of Information Technology ....Mr. Colin MILLER
06 Registrar ....Ms. Mary MURPHY
09 Dir Inst Research/Effectiveness ....Ms. Erin WHITE
121 Exec Dir of Student Development ....Mr. Todd MONGER
18 Executive Director of Operations ....Mr. Jordan ROBERTSON
58 Dean College of Grad & Prof Educ ... Dr. Renea C. BRATHWAITE
15 Director of Human Resources ....Ms. Kate KETTERLING
19 Director Security/Safety ....Mr. Brent PETERS
111 Executive Director of Advancement ....Vacant
108 Dean of Assessment & Accreditation ....Ms. LaToya BURRELL
26 Director of Communications ....Ms. Nancy ZUGSCHWERT
29 Director Alumni Affairs ....Ms. Tabby FINTON

Northwestern Health Sciences University (N)
2501 W 84th Street, Bloomington MN 55431-1599
County: Hennepin FICE Identification: 012328
Unit ID: 174507
Telephone: (952) 888-4777 Carnegie Class: Spec-4-yr-Other Health
FAX Number: (952) 888-6713 Calendar System: Trimester
URL: www.nwhealth.edu
Established: 1941 Annual Undergrad Tuition & Fees: $11,700
Enrollment: 1,132 Coed
Affiliation or Control: Independent Non-Profit IRS Status: 501(c)3
Highest Offering: First Professional Degree
Accreditation: HLC, ACUP, CHIRO, COMTA, MAC, MLTAD, MT, RTT

01 President and CEO ....Dr. Deborah BUSHWAY
05 VP of Academic Affairs ....Ms. Kim PEARCE
10 Chief Financial Officer ....Ms. Jakki EDWARDS
32 Dean of Students ....Mr. Anthony MOLINAR
15 VP of Human Resources ....Ms. Mary GALE
26 VP of Marketing & Events ....Ms. Kathy HAGENS
30 VP of Development ....Ms. Linda KEILLOR BERG
20 Int Sr Dean Academic/Student Affs ....Dr. Dale HEALEY
07 Director of Admissions ....Ms. Erin KAHN
08 Director of Library Services ....Ms. Anne MACKERETH
29 Manager Alumni Services ....Ms. Lilly MOKAMBA
51 Director of Continuing Education ....Vacant
13 Chief Information Officer ....Mr. Cory MILLER
38 University Counselor ....Ms. Becky LAWYER
18 Director Facilities Management ....Mr. Kevin WOLPERN
96 Director Bookstore & Purchasing ....Ms. Jan HALLEEN
04 Administrative Asst to President ....Ms. Nancy JOHNSON
37 Director of Student Financial Svcs ....Ms. Karen SAMSTAD
76 Dean College of Health & Wellness ....Dr. Dale HEALEY
88 Dean College of Chiropractic ....Dr. Katie BURNS-RYAN
88 Dean College Acup & Chinese Med ....Dr. Jessica FRIER
06 Registrar ....Ms. Susan NEPPL

Oak Hills Christian College (O)
1600 Oak Hills Road SW, Bemidji MN 56601-8826
County: Beltrami FICE Identification: 009992
Unit ID: 174525
Telephone: (218) 751-8670 Carnegie Class: Spec-4-yr-Faith
FAX Number: (218) 751-8825 Calendar System: Semester
URL: www.oakhills.edu
Established: 1946 Annual Undergrad Tuition & Fees: $17,334
Enrollment: 103 Coed
Affiliation or Control: Interdenominational IRS Status: 501(c)3
Highest Offering: Baccalaureate
Accreditation: BI

01 President ....Dr. Martin GIESE
05 Dean of the College ....Dr. Suellyn (Sue) GLIDDEN
11 Sr VP of Administration ....Dr. Rick WEINERT
111 VP of Inst Advancement & Marketing ....Ms. Leesa DRURY
32 Dean of Student Life ....Mr. Ron MAIXNER
07 Director of Admissions ....Mr. Brad SPAULDING
19 Campus Mgr Safety/Security ....Mr. Brad DEJAGER
06 Registrar ....Ms. Jenny HODGSON
08 Library Director/IT Director ....Mr. Keith BUSH
37 Director of Financial Aid ....Ms. Mishele MCKAIN
10 Chief Business Officer ....Mr. Bruce KAEHNE
41 Athletic Director ....Mr. Jeremy ANDERSON
31 Dir of Church/Community Relations ....Mr. Jim HODGSON

* Rasmussen University Corporate Office (P)
8300 Norman Center Drive, Suite 300, Bloomington MN 55437
County: Hennepin Identification: 667034
Unit ID: 17501405
Telephone: (952) 806-3910 Carnegie Class: N/A
FAX Number: (952) 831-0624
URL: www.rasmussen.edu

01 Interim President ....Dr. Ann LEJA
05 Vice President of Academic Affairs ....Carrie DANINHIRSCH
10 Chief Financial Officer ....Kevin DELANO
84 Chief Enrollment Management Officer ....Don DEVITO
13 Chief Information Officer ....Rich DEJONG
06 Registrar ....Ms. Juliana KLOCEK
07 VP Admissions/Student Experience ....Mr. Dwayne BERTOTTO
37 Director Student Financial Aid ....Ms. Catherine BREUER

* Rasmussen University - St. Cloud (Q)
226 Park Avenue South, Saint Cloud MN 56301-3713
County: Stearns FICE Identification: 008694
Unit ID: 175014
Telephone: (320) 251-5600 Carnegie Class: Bac/Assoc-Mixed
FAX Number: (320) 251-3702 Calendar System: Quarter
URL: www.Rasmussen.edu
Established: 1902 Annual Undergrad Tuition & Fees: $12,233
Enrollment: 3,927 Coed
Affiliation or Control: Proprietary IRS Status: Proprietary
Highest Offering: Doctorate
Accreditation: HLC, ADNUR, CAHIIM, MAAB, NURSE, PNUR, SURGT

02 Campus Director ....Ms. Naomi MOGARD

† Regional accreditation carried under the parent institution in Lake Elmo, MN.

* Rasmussen University - Bloomington (R)
4400 W 78th St, 6th Floor, Bloomington MN 55435
Telephone: (952) 545-2000 FICE Identification: 011686
Accreditation: &HLC, ADNUR, CAHIIM, MAAB

† Regional accreditation carried under the parent institution in Saint Cloud, MN. The tuition figure is an average, actual tuition may vary.

* Rasmussen University - Eagan (S)
3500 Federal Drive, Eagan MN 55122-1346
Telephone: (651) 687-9000 FICE Identification: 004648
Accreditation: &HLC, CAHIIM, MAAB, PNUR

† Regional accreditation carried under the parent institution in Saint Cloud, MN. The tuition figure is an average, actual tuition may vary.

* Rasmussen University - Mankato (T)
1400 Madison Ave, Suite 510, Mankato MN 56001
Telephone: (507) 625-6556 FICE Identification: 025033
Accreditation: &HLC, ADNUR, CAHIIM, MAAB, PNUR

† Regional accreditation carried under the parent institution in Saint Cloud, MN.

Red Lake Nation College (U)
15480 Migizi Dr PO Box 576, Red Lake MN 56671
County: Beltrami Identification: 667311
Telephone: (218) 679-2860 Carnegie Class: Not Classified
FAX Number: (218) 679-3870 Calendar System: Semester
URL: www.rlnc.edu
Established: 2014 Annual Undergrad Tuition & Fees: N/A
Enrollment: N/A Coed
Affiliation or Control: Tribal Control IRS Status: 501(c)3
Highest Offering: Associate Degree
Accreditation: HLC

01 President ....Dan KING
05 Vice Pres Ops & Academic Affairs ....Mandy SCHRAM
32 Vice Pres Student Success ....Shielen OMEN
10 CFO ....Tami NISWANDER
08 Director of Library Services ....Jacob STARKS

06 Registrar .... Brandon SPEARS
30 Director of Development .... Tammi JALOWIEC

St. Catherine University (A)

2004 Randolph Avenue, Saint Paul MN 55105-1789
County: Ramsey FICE Identification: 002342
Unit ID: 175005
Telephone: (651) 690-6000 Carnegie Class: DU-Mod
FAX Number: N/A Calendar System: 4/1/4
URL: www.stkate.edu
Established: 1905 Annual Undergrad Tuition & Fees: $42,594
Enrollment: 4,277 Female
Affiliation or Control: Roman Catholic IRS Status: 501(c)3
Highest Offering: Doctorate
Accreditation: HLC, ACBSP, ARCPA, COARC, DIETD, DMS, EXSC, LIB, NUR, OT, OTA, PH, PTA, PTAA RAD, RTT, SW

01 President .... Ms. ReBecca K. ROLOFF
05 EVP and Provost .... Dr. Anita THOMAS
10 SVP and Chief Financial Officer .... Ms. Tracey GRAN
111 EVP and Chief Advancement Officer .... Ms. Elizabeth HALLORAN
04 Exec Assistant to the President .... Ms. Cynthia CONLEY
49 Dean Sch Humanities/Arts/Sci .... Dr. Tarshia STANLEY
76 Dean Health Sciences .... Dr. Lisa DUTTON
66 Dean Nursing .... Dr. Laura FERO
50 Dean of Business .... Mr. Benson K. WHITNEY
08 Library Director .... Ms. Emily ASCH
84 SVP Enrollment Management/Athletics .... Mr. John PYLE
30 Director of Development .... Ms. Elizabeth RIEDEL CARNEY
13 SVP and Chief Information Ofcr .... Ms. Jean GUEZMIR
15 SVP for HR/Equity & Inclusion .... Ms. Patricia PRATT-COOK
06 Registrar .... Ms. Cynthia EGENESS
29 Director of Alumnae Relations .... Ms. Mandy IVERSON
26 VP Marketing & Communications .... Dr. Toccara STARK
20 Assistant Provost .... Dr. Denise BAIRD
07 Associate VP of Admissions .... Ms. Cory PIPER-HAUSWIRTH
35 Associate Provost of Student Affair .... Mr. Matthew GOODWIN
37 AVP Enrollment/Financial Aid .... Ms. Elizabeth STEVENS
27 AVP Admission/Market Development .... Mr. Greg STEENSON
36 VP of Career Development .... Ms. May THAO-SCHUCK
16 Director of Human Resources .... Ms. Sarah SCHNELL
38 Director of Student Counseling .... Ms. Heide MALAT
92 Director of Honors Program .... Dr. Rafael CERVANTES
94 Director of Women's Studies .... Dr. Sharon DOHERTY
96 Director of Purchasing .... Mr. Michael HARA
28 Dir Multicultural/Intl Pgms & Svcs .... Vacant
41 Athletic Director .... Mr. Eric STACEY
19 Director of Public Safety .... Mr. Victor JURAN
22 Director of Equity and Inclusion .... Ms. Sandra MITCHELL

Saint John's University (B)

2850 Abbey Plaza, Box 2000, Collegeville MN 56321-2000
County: Stearns FICE Identification: 002379
Unit ID: 174792
Telephone: (320) 363-2011 Carnegie Class: Bac-A&S
FAX Number: (320) 363-2504 Calendar System: Semester
URL: www.csbsju.edu
Established: 1857 Annual Undergrad Tuition & Fees: $48,166
Enrollment: 1,668 Male
Affiliation or Control: Roman Catholic IRS Status: 501(c)3
Highest Offering: Master's
Accreditation: HLC, DIETD, MUS, NURSE, THEOL

01 Interim President .... Dr. James MULLIN
05 Provost Academic Affairs .... Dr. Richard ICE
20 Academic Dean .... Dr. Barbara MAY
20 Dean of the Faculty .... Dr. Pamela BACON
111 Vice President for Inst Advancement .... Mr. Rob CULLIGAN
32 Vice Pres Student Development .... Mr. Michael CONNOLLY
84 Vice Pres Enrollment Mgmt/Marketing .... Mr. Nathan DEHNE
10 Vice Pres Finance/Admin Services .... Mr. Richard ADAMSON
73 Dean School Theology .... Fr. Dale LAUNDERVILLE, OSB
35 Dean of Students .... Mr. Michael CONNOLLY
08 Director of Library .... Ms. Kathleen PARKER
06 Registrar .... Ms. Julie GRUSKA
26 Exec Director of Public Relations .... Mr. Michael HEMMESCH
37 Exec Director of Financial Aid .... Mr. Stuart PERRY
29 Exec Dir of University Relations .... Mr. Adam HERBST
15 Director Human Resources .... Ms. Carol ABELL
13 Director of Info Technology Svcs .... Ms. Casey GORDON

Saint Mary's University of Minnesota (C)

700 Terrace Heights, Winona MN 55987-1399
County: Winona FICE Identification: 002380
Unit ID: 174817
Telephone: (507) 452-4430 Carnegie Class: Masters/L
FAX Number: (507) 457-1633 Calendar System: Semester
URL: www.smumn.edu
Established: 1912 Annual Undergrad Tuition & Fees: $38,280
Enrollment: 5,152 Coed
Affiliation or Control: Roman Catholic IRS Status: 501(c)3
Highest Offering: Doctorate
Accreditation: HLC, ANEST, COPSY, IACBE, MFCD, NMT, NURSE, @SW

01 President .... Rev. James P. BURNS, IVD
10 Executive Vice President & CFO .... Mr. Benjamin MURRAY
18 Vice President of Facilities .... Mr. James BEDTKE
111 VP for Advancement .... Mr. Gary KLEIN
32 VP for Student Affairs .... Dr. Timothy GOSSEN
43 Senior VP and General Counsel .... Ms. Ann E. MERCHLEWITZ
26 VP for Marketing and Communication .... Ms. Kelly SHANNON
22 VP for Inclusion & Human Dignity .... Mr. Leon DIXON
05 Provost and Dean of Faculties .... Dr. Brian SCHMISEK
20 Interim Vice Prov for Faculties .... Dr. Matt NOWAKOWSKI
84 Vice Provost for Enrollment Mgmt .... Mr. Timothy ALBERS
106 Vice Provost for Online Strategy . Ms. Andrea CARROLL-GLOVER
35 Assistant VP for Student Life .... Vacant
04 Exec Assistant to the President .... Ms. Peggy WALTERS
06 Registrar .... Mr. Christopher VERCH
37 Director of Financial Aid .... Mr. Paul TERRIO
88 Director of Conferencing & Camps .... Ms. Kathy PEDERSON
36 Dir Career Services & Internships .... Vacant
38 Director of Counseling Center .... Vacant
08 Director of Library Services .... Ms. Laura OANES
19 Director of Campus Safety .... Mr. Timothy KAUPHUSMAN
88 Facilities Manager .... Mr. Timothy STENSGARD
23 Director of Health Services .... Ms. Christina URIBE NITTI
29 Director Alumni Relations .... Mr. Robert FISHER
41 Director of Athletics .... Mr. Brian SISSON
15 Assistant VP for Human Resources .... Mr. David MILIOTIS
09 Director of Institutional Research .... Ms. Kara WENER
53 Dean School of Education .... Dr. Michael LOVORN
79 Dean of the College .... Dr. Susan COSBY RONNENBERG
108 Director Accreditation & Compliance .... Dr. Robin HEMENWAY
50 Dean School of Business .... Dr. Michelle WIESER
83 Dean Sciences & Health Professions .... Vacant
120 Director of Online Operations .... Vacant
13 Director Information Technology .... Ms. Tianna JOHNSON
112 Director of Major & Planned Giving .... Mr. Matt MUSEL
100 Chief of Staff .... Mr. Andrew DIRKSEN
07 Director of Admissions .... Ms. Kristina LEMMER
39 Dir Resident Life/Student Housing .... Ms. Nicole PETERSON

St. Olaf College (D)

1520 St. Olaf Avenue, Northfield MN 55057-1098
County: Rice FICE Identification: 002382
Unit ID: 174844
Telephone: (507) 786-2222 Carnegie Class: Bac-A&S
FAX Number: N/A Calendar System: 4/1/4
URL: wp.stolaf.edu
Established: 1874 Annual Undergrad Tuition & Fees: $51,450
Enrollment: 2,953 Coed
Affiliation or Control: Evangelical Lutheran Church In America
IRS Status: 501(c)3
Highest Offering: Baccalaureate
Accreditation: HLC, ART, DANCE, MUS, NURSE, SW, THEA

01 President .... Dr. David R. ANDERSON
05 Provost & Dean of the College .... Dr. Marci J. SORTOR
10 Vice Pres & Chief Financial Officer .... Ms. Janet K. HANSON
111 Vice Pres for Advancement .... Mr. Enoch BLAZIS
32 Vice Pres for Student Life .... Dr. Hassel Andre MORRISON
84 Vice Pres Enrollment/Col Relations .... Mr. Michael KYLE
88 Vice Pres for Mission .... Dr. Jo M. BELD
15 Vice Pres for Human Resources .... Ms. Leslie MOORE
43 General Counsel .... Mr. Carl CROSBY LEHMANN
28 Vice Pres for Equity & Inclusion . Ms. Maria C. PABON GAUTIER
20 Associate Provost .... Dr. Dan DRESSEN
06 Asst VP/Registrar .... Ms. Ericka K. PETERSON
89 Assoc Dean Interdisciplin/Gen Stds .... Dr. Karil KUCERA
81 Assoc Dean Natural Sciences & Math .... Dr. Jason ENGBRECHT
79 Assoc Dean Humanities .... Dr. Colin WELLS
57 Assoc Dean Fine Arts .... Dr. Irve DELL
83 Assoc Dean Social Sciences .... Dr. Susan SMALLING
115 Asst VP/Chief Investment Officer .... Mr. Mark GELLE
114 Asst VP/Budget & Auxiliary Ops .... Ms. Angela MATHEWS
07 Dean of Admissions & Financial Aid .... Mr. Chris GEORGE
35 Dean of Students .... Dr. Rosalyn EATON
35 Assoc Dean of Students .... Mr. Justin FLEMING
35 Assoc Dean of Students .... Mr. Timothy SCHROER
42 Campus Pastor .... Dr. Matthew MAROHL
13 Director of IT and Libraries .... Ms. Roberta LEMBKE
19 Director of Public Safety .... Mr. Fred C. BEHR
41 Director of Athletics .... Mr. Ryan A. BOWLES
29 Dir of Engage/Alum/Parent Relations .... Mr. Brad HOFF
44 Director of Annual Giving .... Ms. Sara ELDRIDGE
38 Director of Counseling .... Dr. Stephen O'NEILL
26 Chief Marketing Officer .... Ms. Katie WARREN
75 Dir Piper Ctr for Vocation & Career .... Ms. Leslie MOORE
36 Sr Assoc Dir Career Educ & Coaching .... Ms. Kirsten CAHOON
108 Assoc Dir of Eval & Assessment .... Ms. Kelsey THOMPSON
09 Director of Institutional Research .... Ms. Susan CANON
39 Director of Residence Life .... Ms. Pamela MCDOWELL
37 Director of Student Financial Aid .... Mr. Steve LINDLEY
102 Dir of Govt/Fndtn & Corp Relations .... Mr. Valeng CHA
104 Dir of Intl & Off-Campus Studies .... Dr. Jodi MALMGREN
04 Exec Assistant to the President .... Ms. Jennifer WHITSON

United Theological Seminary of the Twin Cities (E)

767 N. Eustis Street, Suite 140, St. Paul MN 55114
County: Ramsey FICE Identification: 002386
Unit ID: 175139
Telephone: (651) 633-4311 Carnegie Class: Spec-4-yr-Faith
FAX Number: (657) 309-8925 Calendar System: Trimester
URL: www.unitedseminary.edu
Established: 1962 Annual Graduate Tuition & Fees: N/A
Enrollment: 147 Coed
Affiliation or Control: United Church Of Christ IRS Status: 501(c)3
Highest Offering: Doctorate; No Undergraduates
Accreditation: HLC, THEOL

01 Interim President .... Dr. Molly T. MARSHALL
05 VP for Academic Affairs/Dean .... Dr. Kyle ROBERTS
10 VP for Finance/Admin & Strategy .... Mr. Jeff SWENSON
111 VP for Advancement .... Ms. Cindi Beth JOHNSON
26 Director of Marketing/Communication .... Ms. Laura LARSON
121 VP for Student Formation/Vocation .... Rev. Karen HUTT
84 Dir for Student Enrollment .... Ms. Ronny BRADTKE
08 Director of the Library .... Mr. Tim SENAPATIRATNE
88 Dir of Advanced Studies .... Mr. Demian WHEELER
73 Director of Theology and the Arts .... Ms. Jennifer AWES-FREEMAN
29 Dir of Alum Engagement/Giving .... Dr. Cindi Beth JOHNSON
88 Dir for Social Transformation .... Mr. Justin SABIA-TANIS
15 Dir Human Resources & Operations .... Ms. Vonda PEARSON
20 Dir Academic Ops & Distance Educ .... Mr. Matt STOLLENWERK
88 Dir of Formation .... Vacant
88 Dir Student Mentoring and Context .... Vacant
13 Director of Information Services .... Mr. Adam PFUHL
06 Registrar and Academic Advisor .... Ms. Hillary VAMSTAD
88 Operational Logistics/Special Event .... Vacant
04 Admin Assistant to the President .... Ms. Ashley HOVELL

University of Minnesota (F)

100 Church Street SE, 202 Morrill, Minneapolis MN 55455
County: Hennepin FICE Identification: 003969
Unit ID: 174066
Telephone: (612) 626-1616 Carnegie Class: DU-Highest
FAX Number: (612) 625-3875 Calendar System: Semester
URL: www.umn.edu
Established: 1851 Annual Undergrad Tuition & Fees (In-State): $15,027
Enrollment: 52,017 Coed
Affiliation or Control: State IRS Status: 501(c)3
Highest Offering: Doctorate
Accreditation: HLC, ANEST, AUD, CAMPEP, CEA, CIDA, CLPSY, DANCE, DENT, DH, DIETC, DIETD, DIETI, FUSER, HSA, IPSY, JOUR, LAW, LSAR, MED, MFCD, MIDWF, MT, MUS, NURSE, OT, PCSAS, PH, PHAR, PLNG, PTA, RTT, SCPSY, SP, SPAA, SW, VET

01 President .... Dr. Joan T. GABEL
100 Senior Assistant to President .... Dr. Bill HALDEMAN
05 EVP Academic Affairs/Provost .... Dr. Rachel CROSON
10 Sr VP Finance & Operations .... Mr. Myron FRANS
46 Int Vice President for Research .... Dr. Michael OAKES
58 Vice Prov/Dean Graduate Education .... Dr. Scott LANYON
20 Vice Prov/Dean Undergrad Education .... Dr. Robert MCMASTER
15 Int Vice President Human Resources .... Mr. Ken HORSTMAN
88 Vice Pres for University Services .... Mr. Michael BERTHELSEN
28 Vice Pres Equity and Diversity .... Dr. Michael GOH
13 VP/Chief Info Officer .... Mr. Jaime WASCALUS
43 General Counsel .... Mr. Doug PETERSON
102 President Univ Minnesota Foundation .... Vacant
25 Assoc VP Sponsored Projects Admin .... Ms. Pamela WEBB
26 Vice Pres for University Relations .... Mr. Matt KRAMER
18 Assoc VP/Chief of Facilities .... Mr. Bill PAULUS
32 VP Student Affairs/Dean of Students .... Mr. Calvin PHILLIPS
19 Chief of Police .... Vacant
08 University Librarian .... Dr. Wendy P. LOUGEE
06 Assoc Vice Provost/Registrar .... Ms. Sue N. VAN VOORHIS
07 Exec Director of Admissions .... Ms. Heidi MEYER
09 Director of Institutional Research .... Dr. John KELLOGG
22 Director Equal Oppty/Affirm Action .... Ms. Tina MARISAM
37 Director of Student Finance .... Ms. Tina FALKNER
40 Director of the U of M Bookstores .... Mr. Ross ROSATI
39 Dir of Housing & Residential Life .... Ms. Laurie L. MCLAUGHLIN
48 Dean College of Design .... Ms. Carol STROHECKER
86 Chief Government Relations Officer .... Mr. J.D BURTON
29 CEO Alumni Association .... Ms. Lisa LEWIS
38 Dir of Student Counseling Services .... Dr. Vesna HAMPEL-KOZAR
114 Associate VP for Budget/Finance .... Ms. Julie A. TONNESON
96 Director of Purchasing .... Ms. Beth TAPP
49 Dean of the College of Liberal Arts .... Mr. John COLEMAN
51 Dean Cont/Professional Studies .... Vacant
61 Dean of the Law School .... Mr. Garry JENKINS
74 Dean College of Veterinary Medicine .... Dr. Trevor R. AMES
63 Dean of the Medical School .... Dr. Jakub TOLAR
66 Dean of the School of Nursing .... Dr. Connie W. DELANEY
53 Dean College Education/Human Devel .... Dr. Jean K. QUAM
52 Dean of the School of Dentistry .... Dr. Gary C. ANDERSON
69 Dean of the School Public Health .... Dr. John FINNEGAN
54 Dean College of Science/Engineering .... Dr. Mostafa KAVEH
67 Dean of the College Pharmacy .... Dr. Lynda WELAGE
50 Dean Carlson School of Management .... Dr. Srilata A. ZAHEER
80 Dean Humphrey Sch of Pub Aff .... Dr. Laura BLOOMBERG
81 Dean College of Biological Science .... Dr. Valery E. FORBES
47 Dean Col Food/Agric/Natural Res Sci .... Mr. Brian BUHR
41 Director Intercollegiate Athletics .... Mr. Mark COYLE
27 Chief Public Relations Officer .... Mr. Chuck TOMBARGE
27 Chief Marketing Officer .... Ms. Ann ARONSON
21 Associate VP of Finance/Asst CFO .... Mr. Michael D. VOLNA
101 Secretary of the Institution/Board .... Mr. Brian STEEVES

University of Minnesota Duluth (G)

1049 University Drive, Duluth MN 55812-3011
County: Saint Louis FICE Identification: 002388
Unit ID: 174233
Telephone: (218) 726-8000 Carnegie Class: Masters/M
FAX Number: (218) 726-6254 Calendar System: Semester
URL: www.d.umn.edu
Established: 1947 Annual Undergrad Tuition & Fees (In-State): $13,576
Enrollment: 10,275 Coed

Affiliation or Control: State IRS Status: 501(c)3
Highest Offering: Doctorate
Accreditation: HLC, ART, MUS, SP, SW

01 Chancellor .... Dr. Lendley C. BLACK
05 Exec Vice Chanc Acad Affairs .... Dr. Fernando DELGADO
32 Vice Chanc Stdnt Life/Dean Stdnts .... Dr. Lisa ERWIN
10 Int Vice Chanc Finance/Operations .... Ms. Sue BOSELL
06 Registrar .... Ms. Carla L. BOYD
08 Director of Library .... Mr. Matt ROSENDAHL
37 Director Financial Aid .... Ms. Brenda H. HERZIG
36 Director Career Services .... Ms. Julie A. WESTLUND
13 Director Info Tech Sys/Services .... Dr. Jason DAVIS
09 Director Institutional Research .... Ms. Mary KEENAN
25 Senior Grant Administrator .... Ms. Elizabeth RUMSEY
41 Athletic Director .... Mr. Josh BERLO
15 Director Human Resources .... Mr. Mark YURAN
07 Director Admissions .... Mr. Scott SCHULZ
18 Dir Facilities/Physical Plant .... Mr. John RASHID
29 Director Alumni Relations .... Mr. Matthew DUFFY
30 Director Development .... Ms. Tricia BUNTEN
114 Director of Budget and Analysis .... Mr. Greg SATHER
86 Dir University Marketing Public Rel .... Ms. Lynne WILLIAMS
63 Dean School of Medicine .... Dr. Paula TERMUHLEN
81 Dean College Science/Engineering .... Dr. Wendy REED
49 Dean College Liberal Arts .... Dr. Jeremy YOUDE
53 Dean Col Education/Human Svc Prof .... Dr. Jill PINKNEY-PASTRANA
50 Dean School of Business & Economics .... Dr. Amy HIETAPELTO
67 Dean School of Pharmacy .... Dr. Mike SWANOSKI
58 Director of Grad Programs .... Dr. Erik BROWN
19 Chief of Police .... Mr. Sean HULS
04 Executive Asst to the Chancellor .... Ms. Jean CONNER
104 Director Study Abroad .... Mr. Karl MARKGRAF
39 Dir Resident Life/Student Housing .... Mr. Jeremy LEIFERMAN

University of Minnesota-Crookston (A)

2900 University Avenue, Crookston MN 56716-5001
County: Polk FICE Identification: 004069
Unit ID: 174075
Telephone: (218) 281-6510 Carnegie Class: Bac-Diverse
FAX Number: (218) 281-8040 Calendar System: Semester
URL: www.crk.umn.edu
Established: 1965 Annual Undergrad Tuition & Fees (In-State): $12,014
Enrollment: 2,530 Coed
Affiliation or Control: State IRS Status: 501(c)3
Highest Offering: Baccalaureate
Accreditation: HLC, ACBSP

01 Chancellor .... Dr. Mary HOLZ-CLAUSE
05 VC for Academic & Student Affairs .... Dr. John HOFFMAN
32 AVC Student Affairs/Enrollment .... Dr. Savala DEVOGE
18 Director Facilities/Operations .... Mr. Dave DANFORTH
10 Dir of Finance/University Services .... Ms. Tricia SANDERS
15 Director Human Resources .... Mr. Jonathon FULLER
37 Director Financial Aid .... Ms. Kayla PAHLEN
26 Director of Communications .... Vacant
30 Dir Development/Alumni Relations .... Ms. Brandy CHAFFEE
08 Director Library .... Ms. Keri YOUNGSTRAND
36 Director Career/Counseling .... Mr. Tim MENARD
49 Head of Arts/Humanities/Soc Sci .... Dr. Kevin THOMPSON
47 Head Agriculture & Nat Resources .... Dr. Tony KERN
81 Head Math/Science/Technology .... Dr. Tony KERN
50 Head Business .... Dr. Kevin THOMPSON
51 Director of Outreach .... Ms. Michelle CHRISTOPHERSON
06 Registrar .... Mr. Jason TANGQUIST
07 Director of Admissions .... Mr. Mike GRIFFIN
28 Director of Diversity .... Vacant
85 Dir of International Programs .... Ms. Sok Leng TAN

University of Minnesota-Morris (B)

600 E 4th Street, Morris MN 56267-2132
County: Stevens FICE Identification: 002389
Unit ID: 174251
Telephone: (320) 589-6035 Carnegie Class: Bac-A&S
FAX Number: (320) 589-6399 Calendar System: Semester
URL: www.morris.umn.edu
Established: 1959 Annual Undergrad Tuition & Fees (In-State): $13,578
Enrollment: 1,339 Coed
Affiliation or Control: State IRS Status: 501(c)3
Highest Offering: Baccalaureate
Accreditation: HLC

01 Acting Chancellor .... Dr. Janet S. ERICKSEN
05 Interim Vice Chanc Acad Affs/Dean .... Dr. Peh NG
32 Vice Chanc for Student Affairs .... Ms. Sandra OLSON-LOY
10 Vice Chanc for Finance & Facilities .... Mr. Bryan HERRMANN
21 Finance Manager .... Ms. Melissa WROBLESKI
08 Head Librarian .... Ms. LeAnn DEAN
06 Director of Registrar's Office .... Mr. Marcus MULLER
26 Director of Communications .... Vacant
29 Director of Alumni Relations .... Ms. Jennifer ZYCH HERRMANN
09 Director of Institutional Research .... Vacant
36 Assoc Director Career Services .... Ms. Cindy BOE
13 Information Technology Director .... Mr. Bill ZIMMERMAN
37 Director of Financial Aid .... Ms. Jill BEAUREGARD
93 Dir Multi Ethnic Student Program .... Ms. Tammy BERBERI
24 Director Educational Media .... Mr. Michael CIHAK
07 Director of Admissions .... Mr. Brian STUDEBAKER
108 Sr Dir Institutional Effectiveness .... Ms. Melissa BERT
53 Chair of Education Division .... Dr. Michelle PAGE
81 Chair of Science/Math Division .... Dr. Rachel JOHNSON
79 Chair of Humanities Division .... Dr. Stacey ARONSON
83 Chair of Social Science Division .... Dr. Jennifer DEANE

University of Minnesota Rochester (C)

111 South Broadway, Suite 300, Rochester MN 55904
Telephone: (800) 947-0117 Identification: 770316
Accreditation: &HLC, OT

University of Northwestern - St. Paul (D)

3003 Snelling Avenue N, Saint Paul MN 55113-1598
County: Ramsey FICE Identification: 002371
Unit ID: 174491
Telephone: (651) 631-5100 Carnegie Class: Masters/M
FAX Number: (651) 628-3339 Calendar System: Semester
URL: www.unwsp.edu
Established: 1902 Annual Undergrad Tuition & Fees: $33,200
Enrollment: 3,506 Coed
Affiliation or Control: Independent Non-Profit IRS Status: 501(c)3
Highest Offering: Master's
Accreditation: HLC, MUS, NURSE

01 President .... Dr. Alan S. CURETON
05 Senior Vice Pres Academic Affairs .... Dr. Janet B. SOMMERS
26 Senior Vice President Media .... Mr. Jason R. SHARP
32 Vice Pres Student Life & HR .... Ms. Nina M. BARNES
111 Vice President for Advancement .... Mrs. April L. MORETON
10 Vice President Finance/CFO .... Mr. Bryon D. KRUEGER
84 Vice President Enrollment Mgmt .... Vacant
18 Assoc VP Facility Ops & Planning .... Mr. Brian L. HUMPHRIES
79 Dean College of Arts & Humanities .... Vacant
83 Dean College Behavioral/Natural Sci .... Dr. Daniel R. CRANE
107 Dean College Professional Studies .... Dr. Susan E. JOHNSON
58 Dean Graduate/Online & Adult Lrng .... Mr. Todd R. HARMENING
13 CIO .... Mr. Chad N. MILLER
21 Controller .... Mr. Steven M. WHITEHOUSE
38 Director of Counseling Services .... Mr. Joseph M. BIANCARDI
28 Director of Disability Services .... Mrs. Ruth A. FRIES
37 Director of Financial Aid .... Ms. Hannah K. BLAHNIK
23 Director of Health Services .... Mrs. Alison L. PUTZ
08 Director of Library Services .... Mrs. Ruth A. MCGUIRE
19 Director of Public Safety .... Mr. Peter L. SOLA
96 Manager of Purchasing .... Ms. Cheryl A. GLASS
40 Manager Campus Store .... Mrs. Julienne N. ENTINGER
101 Exec Secy to Pres & Bd of Trustees .... Mrs. Kathy M. SPARKS
04 Executive Admin Asst to President .... Mrs. Rachel A. MORGAN
102 Asst VP Advance/VP of NW Foundation .... Vacant
103 Director of Career Development .... Mrs. April C. STENSGARD
88 Director of Enrollment Marketing .... Mrs. Sheri V. LUNN
06 Registrar .... Mr. Andy L. SIMPSON
110 Sr Director Advancement Relations .... Mr. Rich A. BRANHAM
29 Director Alumni & Public Relations .... Mr. Scott D. ANDERSON
07 Dir Trad Enrollment Management .... Mr. Andy B. GAMMONS
104 Director of Global Programs .... Ms. Kendra L. SUNDEEN
26 Associate VP of Marketing and Comm .... Mr. Greg L. JOHNSON
39 Dean of Students .... Mr. Jerod L. CORNELIUS
41 Athletic Director .... Mr. Mathew B. HILL
44 Director Annual Giving & Donor Svcs .... Ms. Teri L. NORBY
88 Assoc VP of Business Services .... Mrs. Marla K. DENNISON
90 Sr Director of Academic Technology .... Mr. Joel T. JOHNSON

† Formerly Northwestern College

University of Saint Thomas (E)

2115 Summit Avenue, Saint Paul MN 55105-1096
County: Ramsey FICE Identification: 002345
Unit ID: 174914
Telephone: (651) 962-5000 Carnegie Class: DU-Mod
FAX Number: (651) 962-6360 Calendar System: 4/1/4
URL: www.stthomas.edu
Established: 1885 Annual Undergrad Tuition & Fees: $47,383
Enrollment: 9,792 Coed
Affiliation or Control: Roman Catholic IRS Status: 501(c)3
Highest Offering: Doctorate
Accreditation: HLC, COPSY, HSA, IPSY, LAW, MUS, SW, THEOL

01 President .... Dr. Julie H. SULLIVAN
05 EVP & Provost .... Dr. Eddy M. ROJAS
20 Rector/VP School of Divinity .... Fr. Joseph C. TAPHORN
32 VP For Student Affairs .... Dr. Karen M. LANGE
10 VP For Business Affairs/CFO .... Mr. Mark D. VANGSGARD
100 Chief of Staff .... Ms. Amy G. MCDONOUGH
13 VP Innovation & Technology/CIO .... Dr. Edmund U. CLARK
20 Vice Provost for Academic Affairs .... Dr. Wendy N. WYATT
84 VP Enrollment Management .... Mr. Allan L. COTRONE
21 AVP & Controller .... Ms. Katelyn L. SHEHU
18 VP for Facilities .... Mr. James M. BRUMMER
88 Executive Director Dining Services .... Dr. Pamela L. PETERSON
49 Int Dean College Arts & Sciences .... Dr. Mark D. STANSBURY-O'DONNELL
50 Dean Opus College of Business .... Dr. Stefanie A. LENWAY
53 Dean School of Education .. Dr. Kathlene L. HOLMES CAMPBELL
76 VP/Dean Morrison Fam Col of Health .... Dr. MayKao Y. HANG
73 Academic Dean School of Divinity .... Dr. Christopher J. THOMPSON
61 Dean School of Law .... Mr. Robert K. VISCHER
35 Dean of Students .... Ms. Linda M. BAUGHMAN
54 Dean School of Engineering .... Dr. Donald H. WEINKAUF
111 VP University Advancement .... Mr. Erik J. THURMAN
06 AVP of Student Data & Registrar .... Ms. Karen M. JULIAN
37 Director of Financial Aid .... Ms. Kristin A. ROACH
35 Director Campus Life .... Ms. Margaret D. CAHILL
29 AVP Careers/Alumni/Corporate .... Ms. Karen A. MCCOY
26 VP of Marketing/Insight/Comm/CMCO .... Ms. Kymm MARTINEZ
41 VP/Director of Athletics .... Dr. Phil J. ESTEN
40 Director Bookstore .... Mr. Stephen L. GRIFFIN
42 Director Campus Ministry .... Fr. Lawrence BLAKE
19 Director Public Safety .... Mr. Daniel J. MEUWISSEN
38 Exec Dir Center For Well Being .... Ms. Madonna K. MCDERMOTT
96 AVP Procurement Services .... Ms. Karen M. HARTHORN
88 Int Dean Dougherty Family College .... Dr. Buffy SMITH
88 VP For Mission .... Fr. Christopher J. COLLINS
15 VP & Chief Human Resources Officer .... Ms. Kathy R. ARNOLD
43 General Counsel .... Ms. Sara E. GROSS METHNER
125 President Emeritus .... Fr. Dennis J. DEASE
39 Director Residence Life .... Dr. Aaron M. MACKE
28 AVP For Inclusive Excellence .... Ms. Kha A. YANG
109 AVP For Auxiliary Services .... Mr. Mitchell KARSTENS

Walden University (F)

100 Washington Ave S, Suite 900, Minneapolis MN 55401
County: Hennepin FICE Identification: 025042
Unit ID: 125231
Telephone: (866) 492-5336 Carnegie Class: DU-Mod
FAX Number: (612) 338-5092 Calendar System: Other
URL: www.waldenu.edu
Established: 1970 Annual Undergrad Tuition & Fees: $12,180
Enrollment: 49,695 Coed
Affiliation or Control: Proprietary IRS Status: Proprietary
Highest Offering: Doctorate
Accreditation: HLC, ACBSP, CACREP, CAEP, NURSE, SW

01 President .... Dr. Paula R. SINGER
11 Sr VP Commercial Operations .... Mr. Jeff TOGNOLA
88 Chief Transform Ofcr & Sr VP SE .... Mr. Steven TOM
05 Provost and Chief Academic Officer .... Dr. Sue SUBOCZ
13 CIO .... Mr. Karthik VENKATESH
10 CFO .... Mr. Roger MCKINNEY
20 Vice Provost .... Dr. Savitri DIXON-SAXON
20 Vice Provost .... Dr. Andrea LINDELL
20 Vice Provost .... Dr. Marilyn POWELL
28 VP of Diversity/Equity & Inclusion .... Dr. Denise BOSTON
43 VP Asst General Counsel .... Ms. Staci SHELLEY
86 VP Government Relations .... Vacant
06 Registrar & Vice Provost .... Ms. Devon EDMUND
88 Assoc Vice Provost & Director .... Dr. Maleka INGRAM
72 Dean College of Management and Tech ... Dr. Karlyn BARILOVITS
83 Dean Sch of Counseling/Human Svcs .... Dr. Bill BARKLEY
53 Dean Sch Higher Ed/Ldrshp & Policy .... Dr. Kelly COSTNER
121 Dean Ctr for Academic Excellence .... Ms. Susanna DAVIDSEN
82 Dean Sch Public Pol Admin/Psych/CJ .... Dr. Shana GARRETT
88 Dean of Research/Exec Dir .... Dr. Laura LYNN
32 Dean Student Affairs/Alumni Engage .... Dr. Walter MCCOLLUM
70 Dean School of Social Work .... Dr. Lisa MOON
88 Dean Prod Strategy/Innov & Design .... Ms. Kathy STRANG
51 Dean Learning Pathways & SLL .... Dr. Barry SUGARMAN
76 Dean School of Health Sciences .... Dr. Jorg WESTERMANN
66 Dean Sch of Nursing .... Dr. George ZANGARO
53 Assoc Dean Sch Educ/Prof License .... Dr. Steve CANIPE
97 Assoc Dean Ctr for Gen Ed .... Dr. Sara MAKRIS
88 Assoc Dean Ctr for Faculty Excel .... Dr. Annie MORGAN
50 Assoc Dean Educ/Mgmt & Tech .... Ms. Joanna PATTERSON
58 Assoc Dean Sch High Educ/Leadership .... Dr. Pat THURMOND
76 Assoc Dean Health/SBS/Nursing .... Ms. Kristi TRAPP
15 Exec Dir of Human Resources .... Ms. Ivanie BRONSON
106 Exec Dir Ctr Competency-Based Educ .... Dr. Steven DANVER
46 Exec Dir Inst Research/Assessment .... Dr. Jim LENIO
107 Exec Dir Student Experiential Learn .... Dr. Mary RAEKER-REBEK
07 Director of Admissions .... Vacant
113 Bursar .... Ms. Linda ANTHONY
121 Sr Director Academic Advising .... Ms. Mandy OLSEN
08 Director of Library Services .... Ms. Michelle HAJDER
37 Director of Financial Aid .... Ms. Melvina JOHNSON
108 Dir of University Assessment .... Dr. Shari JORISSEN
26 Director of External Relations .... Ms. Sabrina RAM
88 Director Ctr for Social Change .... Dr. William SCHULZ

White Earth Tribal and Community College (G)

PO Box 478, Mahnomen MN 56557-0478
County: Mahnomen FICE Identification: 039214
Unit ID: 434751
Telephone: (218) 935-0417 Carnegie Class: Tribal
FAX Number: (218) 936-5814 Calendar System: Semester
URL: www.wetcc.edu
Established: 1997 Annual Undergrad Tuition & Fees: $4,568
Enrollment: 141 Coed
Affiliation or Control: Tribal Control IRS Status: 501(c)3
Highest Offering: Associate Degree
Accreditation: HLC

01 President .... Lorna J. LAGUE
10 Finance Director .... Landa MOORE
05 Academic Dean .... Brian DINGMANN
32 Dean of Student Services .... Tracy DIEFENBACH
56 Director of Extension .... Lisa BRUNNER
07 Admissions Coordinator .... Amber FOX
06 Registrar .... Lorraine LUFKINS

37 Financial Aid Coordinator .... Michelle WARREN
15 Human Resources Technician .... Jessica ASHER-PHILLIPS
18 Facilities Manager .... Paul PEMBERTON
13 IT Director .... Jacob MCARTHUR
19 Security Coordinator .... Kurt HALVORSON
08 Head Librarian .... Jane BERG

MISSISSIPPI

Alcorn State University (A)

1000 ASU Drive, #359, Lorman MS 39096-7500
County: Claiborne FICE Identification: 002396
Unit ID: 175342
Telephone: (601) 877-6100 Carnegie Class: Masters/M
FAX Number: (601) 877-2975 Calendar System: Semester
URL: www.alcorn.edu
Established: 1871 Annual Undergrad Tuition & Fees (In-State): $7,290
Enrollment: 3,230 Coed
Affiliation or Control: State IRS Status: 501(c)3
Highest Offering: Doctorate
Accreditation: SC, ACBSP, ADNUR, CAEP, MUS, NAIT, NUR, SW

01 President .... Dr. Felecia M. NAVE
05 Provost/Sr VP for Academic Affairs .... Dr. Ontario S. WOODEN
11 Sr VP for Univ Operations/COO .... Vacant
04 Exec Asst to the President .... Ms. Karen R. SHEDRICK
116 Director of Internal Audit .... Ms. Tomeka L. MOORE
46 Chief Research Officer .... Dr. Keith MCGEE
10 SVP Finance/Admin Svcs/Opers/CFO .... Dr. Cornelius WOOTEN
32 VP for Student Affs & Enroll Mgmt .... Dr. Tracy M. COOK
111 VP Institutional Advancement .... Mr. Marcus D. WARD
26 VP Marketing/Communications .... Mr. Larry ORMAN
20 Assoc Prov Res/Innov & Grad Educ .... Dr. Keith MCGEE
18 Assoc VP for Facilities Management .... Mr. Robert WATTS
84 Asst VP for Enrollment Management .... Ms. Roslyn M. WHITE
39 Director of Residence Life .... Ms. Janelle WATTS
28 Dir of Educational Equity/Inclusion .... Mrs. Lljuna WEIR
21 Director of Accounting .... Vacant
96 Purchasing Agent .... Ms. Mertha V. GEORGE
07 Director of Admissions/Recruiting .... Ms. Katangela TENNER
37 Director of Financial Aid .... Mrs. Juanita RUSSELL-EDWARDS
06 Registrar .... Dr. Tracee SMITH
08 Dean University Libraries .... Dr. Blanche SANDERS
47 Dean School of Agriculture .... Dr. Edmund BUCKNER
49 Dean School of Arts & Science .... Dr. Babu P. PATLOLLA
50 Interim Dean School of Business .... Dr. Benedict UDEMGBA
53 Interim Dean School of Education .... Dr. Malinda BUTLER
66 Interim Dean School of Nursing .... Dr. Shirley EVERS-MANLY
89 Dean University College .... Dr. Valerie THOMPSON
13 Interim CIO Ctr for Info Tech Svcs .... Ms. Donna HAYDEN
15 AVP for Human Resources & Payroll .... Dr. Wanda FLEMING
36 Director Career Services .... Dr. Carolyn DAVIS
23 Director of Health & Disab Services .... Ms. Dorothy G. JACKSON-DAVIS
41 Director of Athletics .... Mr. Derek HORNE
40 Follett Book Store .... Ms. Roshae LACEY
38 Director of Counseling & Testing .... Dr. Barbara MARTIN
09 Dir Institutional Rsrch/Assessment .... Dr. LaDonna EANOCHS
108 Dir Institutional Effectiveness .... Vacant
19 Chief of Campus Police .... Mr. Douglas STEWART
88 General Manager Sodexo .... Mr. Brent DAVIDSON
102 Exec Dir ASU Foundation .... Mr. Marcus D. WARD
88 Exec Dir Ofc of Univ Compliance .... Mr. Alfred GALTNEY
92 Director of Honors Program .... Vacant
25 Grants/Contract Administrator .... Mrs. Sallie MCMILLIAN
104 Director of International Affairs .... Dr. Dovi ALIPOE
88 Sr Assoc AD/Asst VP Ath Cmpl & AS .... Mr. Cyrus K. RUSS
100 Chief of Staff .... Vacant

Belhaven University (B)

1500 Peachtree Street, Jackson MS 39202-1798
County: Hinds FICE Identification: 002397
Unit ID: 175421
Telephone: (601) 968-5940 Carnegie Class: Masters/L
FAX Number: (601) 968-9998 Calendar System: Semester
URL: www.belhaven.edu
Established: 1883 Annual Undergrad Tuition & Fees: $27,025
Enrollment: 4,999 Coed
Affiliation or Control: Presbyterian Church (U.S.A.) IRS Status: 501(c)3
Highest Offering: Doctorate
Accreditation: SC, ART, DANCE, IACBE, MUS, NURSE, SW, THEA

01 President .... Dr. Roger PARROTT
05 Provost/Vice Pres Academic Affairs .... Dr. Bradford SMITH
58 VP for Adult/Graduate & Online Educ .... Dr. Audrey KELLEHER
84 VP of Enrollment and Marketing .... Mr. Kevin RUSSELL
10 CFO & VP Business Affairs .... Vacant
111 VP for University Advancement .... Mr. Jeff RICKLES
41 VP of Athletics .... Mr. Scott LITTLE
32 VP of Student Development .... Dr. Shelley SMITH
11 Asst VP Campus Operations .... Mr. David POTVIN
84 Assoc VP for Enrollment .... Mrs. Suzanne SULLIVAN
51 AVP for Adult/Graduate/Online .... Dr. Rick UPCHURCH
13 AVP of IT and Systems Admin .... Mrs. Stephanie STEELMAN
106 Dean of Adult/Grad/Online Studies .... Dr. Kim PREISMEYER
50 Dean of the School of Business .... Dr. Chip MASON
53 Dean of the School of Education .... Dr. David HAND
66 Dean of the School of Nursing .... Dr. Amy REX SMITH
79 Dean of Worldview Studies .... Dr. Tracy FORD
20 Dean of Curriculum .... Dr. Ken ELLIOTT
07 Assoc Director of Admission .... Mr. Michael HAWKINS
06 Registrar .... Ms. Lea Ann BETHANY
26 Director of University Relations .... Mr. Bryant BUTLER
13 Director Information Technology .... Mr. Bo MILLER
19 Director of Security .... Mr. David POTVIN
41 Director of Athletics .... Mr. Scott LITTLE
09 Dir Institutional Research .... Mr. Aaron PRITCHETT
08 Director of Libraries .... Mr. Chris CULLNANE, II
15 Director of Human Resources .... Mrs. Virginia HENDERSON
37 Director of Financial Services .... Mrs. Debbi BRASWELL
121 Director of Student Care .... Ms. Rebecca ROMINE
110 Director of Advancement/Alumni .... Mr. Frank LAWS
04 Admin Assistant to the President .... Mrs. Lea PARTRIDGE
18 Chf Facilities/Physical Plant Ofcr .... Mr. Wayne GREEN
121 Assoc VP of Academic Support .... Dr. Vicki WOLFE

Blue Mountain College (C)

201 W Main Street, PO Box 160,
Blue Mountain MS 38610-0160
County: Tippah FICE Identification: 002398
Unit ID: 175430
Telephone: (662) 685-4771 Carnegie Class: Bac-Diverse
FAX Number: (662) 685-4776 Calendar System: Semester
URL: www.bmc.edu
Established: 1873 Annual Undergrad Tuition & Fees: $15,800
Enrollment: 952 Coed
Affiliation or Control: Southern Baptist IRS Status: 501(c)3
Highest Offering: Master's
Accreditation: SC

01 President .... Dr. Barbara C. MCMILLIN
04 Admin Assistant to the President .... Mrs. Pam BOWMAN
05 Provost and Vice President .... Dr. Sharon B. ENZOR
53 Dean of Education .... Dr. Jenetta WADDELL
50 Dean of Business .... Dr. Anthony BULLARD
09 Director of Institutional Research .... Mr. Robert E. RUCKER
08 Director of Library Services .... Ms. Hannah JOHNSON
06 Registrar .... Mrs. Sheila D. FREEMAN
121 Director Teaching & Learning Center .... Dr. Delise TEAGUE
32 Dean of Students .... Mr. Philip RITCHEY
07 Vice Pres for Enrollment Services .... Mr. Lynn GIBSON
30 VP Community Rels/Dir BMC Found .... Vacant
37 Director of Financial Aid .... Mrs. Beverly HICKEY
10 Chief Financial Officer .... Mr. Steve ROBBINS
11 Chief Operating Officer .... Mrs. Joyce PETERS
40 Campus Store Manager .... Mrs. Dot M. LOCKE
41 Athletic Director .... Mr. Will LOWREY
42 Director Baptist Student Union .... Mrs. Tracy S. MOSER
13 Director of Information Services .... Mr. Kevin BAREFIELD
26 Dir of PR/Publications .... Ms. Emma L. AINSWORTH
29 Director of Alumni Relations .... Mrs. Kayce BRAGG
88 Director of Church Relations .... Dr. Ronald MEEKS

Coahoma Community College (D)

3240 Friars Point Road, Clarksdale MS 38614-9700
County: Coahoma FICE Identification: 002401
Unit ID: 175519
Telephone: (662) 627-2571 Carnegie Class: Assoc/HVT-High Trad
FAX Number: (662) 627-9451 Calendar System: Semester
URL: www.coahomacc.edu
Established: 1949 Annual Undergrad Tuition & Fees (In-District): $3,003
Enrollment: 1,612 Coed
Affiliation or Control: State/Local IRS Status: 501(c)3
Highest Offering: Associate Degree
Accreditation: SC, ADNUR, COARC, EMT, POLYT

01 President .... Dr. Valmadge T. TOWNER
05 Dean of Academics .... Dr. Rolanda BROWN
10 Chief Financial Officer .... Ms. Deborah VALENTINE
32 Director of Student Services .... Mrs. Karen DONE
09 Dir Inst Effectiveness/SACS Liaison .... Mrs. Margaret DIXON
30 Coordinator for Federal Programs .... Mrs. Marilyn STARKS
75 Dean of Career/Technical Education .... Dr. Larry WEBSTER
06 Registrar .... Dr. Nakisha WATTS
08 Dir Library/Instructional Resources .... Mrs. Rose LOCKETT
13 Director Computer Services .... Mr. Rob STALDER
19 Director of Safety .... Mr. Charles JONES
26 Chief Communication Officer .... Mr. Marriel HARDY
37 Director of Financial Aid .... Mr. Joseph MCKEE
15 Director of Employee Services .... Mr. Michael HOUSTON
51 Director of Educational Outreach .... Mr. William WADE
29 Director Alumni Relations .... Vacant
36 Director Student Placement .... Mrs. Trina COX
38 Coordinator of Student Counseling .... Dr. Renee HALL
04 Administrative Asst to President .... Ms. Yolanda D. MILLER
100 Chief of Staff .... Mr. Jerone SHAW
103 Dir Workforce/Career Development .... Mr. Steven JOSSELL
105 Director Web Services .... Mr. Ezra HOWARD
106 Online Education/E-learning Coord .... Ms. Monica MOORE JOHNSON
41 Interim Athletic Director .... Mr. Reggie HANKERSON

Concorde Career College (E)

7900 Airways Boulevard, Suite 103, Southaven MS 38671
Telephone: (662) 429-9909 Identification: 770540
Accreditation: COE

† Branch campus of Concorde Career College, Memphis, TN

Copiah-Lincoln Community College (F)

PO Box 649, Wesson MS 39191-0649
County: Copiah FICE Identification: 002402
Unit ID: 175573
Telephone: (601) 643-5101 Carnegie Class: Assoc/HT-High Trad
FAX Number: (601) 643-8212 Calendar System: Semester
URL: www.colin.edu
Established: 1928 Annual Undergrad Tuition & Fees (In-State): $3,180
Enrollment: 2,907 Coed
Affiliation or Control: State IRS Status: 501(c)3
Highest Offering: Associate Degree
Accreditation: SC, ADNUR, COARC, MLTAD, RAD

01 President .... Dr. Jane HULON SIMS
04 Assistant to the President .... Mrs. Amber N. BRITT
10 Vice President Business Affairs .... Mr. Richard BAKER
03 Executive Vice President .... Dr. Dewayne MIDDLETON
12 Vice Pres of the Natchez Campus .... Dr. Sandra BARNES
12 Vice President of the Wesson Campus .... Mrs. Jackie MARTIN
05 Dean of Academic Instructions .... Dr. Stephanie DUGUID
32 Dean of Enroll/Student Services .... Vacant
75 Dean Career & Technical Educ .... Mr. Brent DUGUID
31 Dean of Community Programs .... Vacant
41 Athletic Dir/Asst Dean of Students .... Mr. Bryan NOBILE
37 Director Student Financial Aid .... Mrs. Leslie SMITH
40 Director Bookstore .... Mr. Charles HART
08 Director of Library Resources .... Mrs. Jacqueline QUINN
26 Director of Public Relations .... Mrs. Natalie DAVIS
13 Information Systems Specialist .... Ms. Deemie LETCHWORTH
19 Director of Security .... Mr. Thomas ROBERTS
09 Dir Inst Effectiv/Facilities Plng .... Mrs. Tiffany PERRYMAN
35 Dean of Students .... Vacant
102 Director of Foundation & Alumni Svc .... Mrs. Angela FURR
18 Director of Physical Plant .... Mr. Daniel CASE
66 Director of Assoc Degree Nursing .... Ms. Mary Ann FLINT
06 Student Records Manager .... Mrs. Gay LANGHAM
57 Chair Fine Arts Division .... Ms. Juanita PROFFITT
50 Chair Business Division .... Ms. Heather MARTIN
68 Chair Physical Education Division .... Ms. Dana HALE
77 Chair Math/Computer Science Div .... Mr. Eddie BRITT
79 Chair Humanities Division .... Mrs. Mary WARREN
82 Chair Social Science Division .... Mr. Keith STOVALL
81 Chair Science Division .... Dr. Kevin MCKONE
96 Director of Purchasing .... Mrs. Erin LIKENS
106 Director of E-learning .... Dr. Amanda HOOD
108 QEP Director .... Vacant
15 Human Resources Director .... Ms. Julia PARKER
39 Director Student Housing .... Mr. Allen KENT
91 Director of Technology/Info Systems .... Mr. James P. MCINNIS

Delta State University (G)

1003 W. Sunflower Rd., Cleveland MS 38733
County: Bolivar FICE Identification: 002403
Unit ID: 175616
Telephone: (662) 846-3000 Carnegie Class: Masters/L
FAX Number: (662) 846-4014 Calendar System: Semester
URL: www.deltastate.edu
Established: 1924 Annual Undergrad Tuition & Fees (In-State): $8,121
Enrollment: 2,999 Coed
Affiliation or Control: State IRS Status: 501(c)3
Highest Offering: Doctorate
Accreditation: SC, AAB, AAFCS, ACBSP, ART, CACREP, CAEPN, DIETC, MUS, NURSE, SW

01 President .... Mr. William (Bill) LAFORGE
05 Provost/VP Academic Affairs .... Dr. Andy NOVOBILSKI
10 Vice President for Finance .... Mr. James RUTLEDGE
32 Vice President for Student Affairs .... Dr. Eddie LOVIN
111 Vice Pres Univ Advance & Ext Rels .... Mr. Rick MUNROE
100 Chief of Staff/VP Univ Relations .... Dr. Michelle A. ROBERTS
15 Director of Human Resources .... Ms. Lisa GIGER
41 Director of Athletics .... Mr. Mike KINNISON
49 Interim Dean College of Arts & Sci .... Dr. Ellen GREEN
50 Dean College of Business .... Dr. Billy MOORE
53 Dean College of Education .... Dr. Leslie GRIFFIN
66 Dean School of Nursing .... Dr. Vicki L. BINGHAM
08 Dean Library Services .... Mr. Jeff SLAGELL
58 Dean Graduate/Continuing Studies .... Dr. Beverly MOON
06 Registrar .... Ms. Emily C. DABNEY
13 Chief Information Officer .... Mr. Edwin CRAFT
21 Director of Financial Reporting .... Mr. Kelvin DAVIS
116 Internal Auditor .... Mrs. Mary Helen VARNER
88 Executive Director BPAC .... Ms. Laura HOWELL
121 Executive Director Student Success .... Dr. Christy RIDDLE
37 Dir Student Financial Assistance .... Dr. Megan SMITH
38 Director Counsel/Stdnt Health Svcs .... Ms. Kashanta JACKSON
36 Director Career Services .... Ms. Nakikke JOHNSON
19 Director of Police Dept .... Mr. Jeffrey JOHNS
39 Director of Housing .... Ms. Julie JACKSON
26 Director of Media Relations .... Ms. Brittany DAVIS
25 Director Institutional Grants .... Ms. Heather MILLER
113 Director Student Business Svcs .... Mr. Mikhail COLLINS
106 Dir of Clinical Exp/Licensing/Acct .... Mrs. Anjanette POWERS
31 Director Delta Center Culture Learn .... Dr. Rolando HERTS
18 Director of Facilities Mgmt .... Mr. Gerald FINLEY
40 Manager of Bookstore .... Mr. James SOREY
109 Director of Food Services .... Mr. Gerald FRYE
07 Director of Admissions .... Mr. Merritt DAIN
09 Director of Institutional Research .... Ms. Chrisa MANSELL
30 Director of Development .... Dr. Lori SPENCER

East Central Community College (A)

PO Box 129, Decatur MS 39327-0129
County: Newton FICE Identification: 002404
Unit ID: 175643
Telephone: (601) 635-2111 Carnegie Class: Assoc/MT-VT-High Trad
FAX Number: (601) 635-4011 Calendar System: Semester
URL: www.eccc.edu
Established: 1928 Annual Undergrad Tuition & Fees (In-District): $3,150
Enrollment: 2,388 Coed
Affiliation or Control: Local IRS Status: 501(c)3
Highest Offering: Associate Degree
Accreditation: SC, ADNUR, SURGT

01 President ... Dr. Brent GREGORY
05 Vice President for Instruction ... Dr. Teresa L. MACKEY
10 Vice Pres for Business Operations ... Mr. Mickey VANCE
32 Vice President for Student Services ... Dr. Randall LEE
09 VP Institutional Research/Effective ... Mr. David CASE
26 VP for Public Information ... Mr. Bill WAGNON
106 Director of eLearning Education ... Ms. Alicia BEASLEY
08 Dean of Learning Resources ... Mr. Leslie HUGHES
51 Director of Adult Education/HSE ... Mrs. Alfreda THOMPSON
103 Director of Career & Tech Education ... Mr. Wayne EASON
07 Director Admissions and Records .. Dr. Stacey HOLLINGSWORTH
15 Director of Human Resources ... Mrs. Julie ROWZEE
18 Dir Facilities Planning & Project ... Mr. Artie FOREMAN
13 Dean of Information Technology ... Mr. Derek PACE
14 Assoc Dir Information Technology ... Mrs. Regena BOYKIN
37 Director of Financial Aid ... Mrs. Brenda B. CARSON
19 Chief of Police ... Mr. John HARRIS
39 Director of Hous/Student Activities ... Dr. Amanda WALTON
29 Dir of Alumni Relations/Foundation ... Vacant
57 Chairperson Fine Arts Division ... Mr. Chas EVANS
81 Chair Mathematics/Computer Science ... Ms. Cathryn MAY
83 Chairperson Social Sciences ... Mrs. Wanda HURLEY
76 Dean of Healthcare Education ... Dr. Sheryl ALLEN
81 Chairperson Science Division ... Mr. Curt SKIPPER
60 Chairperson Communications/ Language ... Mrs. Carol SHACKELFORD
04 Administrative Asst to President ... Mrs. Carole H. GERMANY
41 Director of Athletics ... Mr. Paul NIXON

East Mississippi Community College (B)

PO Box 158, Scooba MS 39358-0158
County: Kemper FICE Identification: 002405
Unit ID: 175652
Telephone: (662) 476-5000 Carnegie Class: Assoc/MT-VT-Mix Trad/Non
FAX Number: (662) 476-5058 Calendar System: Semester
URL: www.eastms.edu
Established: 1927 Annual Undergrad Tuition & Fees (In-District): $3,740
Enrollment: 3,392 Coed
Affiliation or Control: State/Local IRS Status: Exempt
Highest Offering: Associate Degree
Accreditation: SC, ADNUR, FUSER, SURGT

01 President ... Dr. Scott ALSOBROOKS
05 VP of Instruction ... Dr. James RUSH
11 VP of Operations ... Dr. Paul MILLER
10 Chief Financial Officer ... Ms. Tammie HOLMES
103 VP of Workforce/Economic Dev ... Dr. Courtney TAYLOR
84 VP for Enrollment Management ... Dr. Melanie SANDERS
04 Administrative Asst to President ... Ms. Nakisha WOODS
09 Director IR/E ... Mrs. Susan BAIRD
13 Director of Info Technology ... Mr. Michael TVARKUNAS
18 Director of Physical Plant ... Mr. Kyle YOUNGER
37 Director of Financial Aid ... Mr. Garry JONES
06 Registrar ... Mrs. Tammy PRATHER
88 Dir of Recruiting/GT Recruiter ... Mrs. Tawana BAUER
07 Director of Admissions ... Ms. Danielle HOPSON
40 Bookstore Manager ... Mrs. Ginnie CODY
26 Director of External Affairs ... Mrs. Julia MORRISON
76 Dean of Health Sciences ... Dr. Tonsha EMERSON
32 Dean of Students SC Campus ... Mr. Tony MONTGOMERY
32 Dean of Students GT Campus ... Dr. Melanie SANDERS
41 Athletic Director ... Ms. Sharon THOMPSON
19 Chief of Police ... Mr. Archer SALLIS
15 Director Human Resources ... Ms. Theresa HARPOLE
111 Exec Dir of CLG Advance/Athletics ... Mr. Marcus WOOD
20 Dean of Instruction GT ... Mr. Michael BUSBY
20 Dean of Instruction SC ... Dr. Jairus JOHNSON
106 Associate Dean of E-learning ... Mrs. Chris SQUARE
124 Dist Dir Advise/Retent/Stdnt Succ ... Dr. Nikita ASHFORTH-ASHWORTH
29 Director Alumni Affairs ... Mrs. Gina COTTON
91 Director Administrative Computing ... Mr. Elanthus WICKS

Hinds Community College (C)

PO Box 1100, Raymond MS 39154-1100
County: Hinds FICE Identification: 002407
Unit ID: 175786
Telephone: (601) 857-5261 Carnegie Class: Assoc/HVT-High Trad
FAX Number: (601) 857-3518 Calendar System: Semester
URL: www.hindscc.edu
Established: 1917 Annual Undergrad Tuition & Fees (In-District): $3,450
Enrollment: 11,181 Coed
Affiliation or Control: State/Local IRS Status: 501(c)3
Highest Offering: Associate Degree
Accreditation: SC, ADNUR, CAHIIM, COARC, DA, DMS, EMT, MLTAD, PTAA, RAD, SURGT

01 President ... Dr. Stephen VACIK
10 VP Finance & Administration ... Mr. Vic PARKER
05 VP Instruction/Academics ... Dr. Keri COLE
75 VP of Instruction & Career Tech Edu ... Ms. Sherry FRANKLIN
20 Academic Dean ... Ms. Shakira CAIN
20 Academic Dean ... Mr. Gary FOX
20 Academic Dean ... Ms. Melissa K. BUIE
32 VP Student Svcs/Chief Operations ... Mr. Randall HARRIS
103 VP Workforce/Community Development ... Dr. Chad STOCKS
18 VP for Auxiliary Services ... Mr. Marvin MOAK
15 VP for Human Resources ... Ms. Andrea JANOUSH
100 Chief of Staff ... Mrs. Renee COTTON
84 Director of Enrollment Services ... Ms. Kathryn B. COLE
08 Dean of Learning Resources ... Ms. Mary Beth APPLIN
66 Dean of Health Science ... Ms. Katharine ELLIOTT
37 Dir of Financial Aid & Veterans Svc ... Mrs. Deena MCINNIS
38 Director of Counseling Services ... Ms. Jennifer SCOTT-GILMORE
41 Athletic Director ... Mr. Nathan WERREMEYER
09 Dir of Institutional Effectiveness ... Dr. Christopher RUFFIN
26 Director of Publications ... Ms. Cathy C. HAYDEN
96 Director of Procurement ... Mr. Samuel LEMONIS
04 Executive Secretary to President ... Vacant
106 Dean of ELearning ... Mrs. Katherine PUCKETT
13 Exec Dir Information Technology ... Mr. Taylor ARMSTRONG
29 Alumni Coordinator ... Ms. Olivia POSEY
35 AVP Student Svcs/Dean of Students ... Mr. Deandre HOUSE
07 AVP Student Svcs/Admissions/Record ... Dr. Stephanie HUDSON
102 Executive Director Foundation ... Mrs. Jackie GRANBERRY
19 Director Campus Safety ... Mr. Britt THOMAS
86 Grants & Legislation Liaison ... Mrs. Colleen HARTFIELD

Holmes Community College (D)

Hill Street, PO Box 369, Goodman MS 39079-0369
County: Holmes FICE Identification: 002408
Unit ID: 175810
Telephone: (662) 472-2312 Carnegie Class: Assoc/HVT-Mix Trad/Non
FAX Number: (662) 472-9152 Calendar System: Semester
URL: www.holmescc.edu
Established: 1925 Annual Undergrad Tuition & Fees (In-District): $3,410
Enrollment: 5,409 Coed
Affiliation or Control: Local IRS Status: 501(c)3
Highest Offering: Associate Degree
Accreditation: SC, ADNUR, EMT, OTA, PTAA, SURGT

01 President ... Dr. Jim HAFFEY
03 Executive Vice President ... Mr. Sonny SPARKS
09 VP Inst Research & Student Affairs ... Dr. Lindy MCCAIN
05 Vice Pres for Academic Programs ... Dr. Jenny B. JONES
12 Vice President Ridgeland Campus ... Dr. Don BURNHAM
12 Vice President Grenada Center ... Dr. Michelle BURNEY
72 Vice President CareerTech Education ... Dr. Amy WHITTINGTON
10 Vice Pres of Financial Services ... Mr. Sonny SPARKS
08 Librarian ... Mr. James THOMPSON
26 Director of Communications & Assoc ... Mr. Steve DIFFEY
103 Vice President of Workforce Develop ... Dr. Mike BLANKENSHIP
37 Director Student Financial Aid ... Mr. Clate HOLLEMAN
15 Director Personnel Services ... Ms. Julia BROWN
09 Director of Institutional Research ... Dr. Stephanie DIFFEY
18 Chief Facilities/Physical Plant ... Vacant
96 Director of Purchasing ... Ms. Rosemary SELF
29 Director Alumni Relations ... Mrs. Katherine ELLARD
21 Business Manager ... Mr. Matt SURRELL
04 Exec Assistant to the President ... Mrs. Angie S. BURRELL
105 Director Marketing/Recruiting ... Mrs. Bronwyn MARTIN
106 Vice President Online Ed/E-learning ... Mrs. Tish STEWART
108 Director Institutional Research ... Dr. Stephanie DIFFEY
13 Director of Information Technology ... Mr. Kevin BAKER
19 Director of Public Safety ... Mr. Chris DILL
38 Student Academic Counselor ... Mrs. Simone MILLER
39 Dir Resident Life/Student Housing ... Mr. Terry FANCHER
41 Vice Pres/Director of Athletics ... Mr. Andy WOOD
50 VP/Academic Dean-Goodman ... Dr. Jenny BAILEY-JONES
53 Academic Dean-Ridgeland ... Dr. Tonya LAWRENCE

Itawamba Community College (E)

602 W Hill Street, Fulton MS 38843-1022
County: Itawamba FICE Identification: 002409
Unit ID: 175829
Telephone: (662) 862-8000 Carnegie Class: Assoc/HT-High Trad
FAX Number: (662) 862-8036 Calendar System: Semester
URL: www.iccms.edu
Established: 1948 Annual Undergrad Tuition & Fees (In-District): $3,160
Enrollment: 4,696 Coed
Affiliation or Control: Local IRS Status: 501(c)3
Highest Offering: Associate Degree
Accreditation: SC, ADNUR, CAHIIM, COARC, EMT, OTA, PTAA, RAD, SURGT

01 President ... Mr. Jay S. ALLEN
05 Vice President of Instruction ... Dr. Michelle SUMEREL
10 Exec Director of Finance ... Ms. Sandi SOUTH
07 Dean of Enrollment ... Dr. Melissa HAAB
32 Dean of Students ... Dr. Brad BOGGS
26 Director Community Relations ... Ms. Nina STROTHER
37 Director of Financial Aid ... Mr. Terry BLAND
24 Director of Library ... Ms. Holly GRAY
08 Librarian/Tupelo ... Ms. Megan PEARSON
51 Director of Adult & Continuing Educ ... Ms. Julia HOUSTON
41 Athletic Director ... Ms. Carrie BALL-WILLIAMSON
111 Director of Advancement ... Mr. Michael UPTON
18 Chief Facilities/Physical Plant ... Mr. Thomas BONDS
09 Director of Institutional Research ... Mrs. Elizabeth EDWARDS
15 Exec Director of Human Resources ... Mr. Timothy C. SENTER
106 Dean of eLearning ... Ms. Denise GILLESPIE
76 Dean of Health Sciences ... Ms. Rilla JONES
75 Dean of Career & Technical Educ ... Mr. Barry EMISON
108 Director Strategic Planning and IE ... Mrs. Amy CAPPLEMAN
39 Director Student Housing ... Mr. Chad CASE
06 Registrar ... Mr. Bobby SOLOMON

Jackson State University (F)

1400 J. R. Lynch Street, Jackson MS 39217
County: Hinds FICE Identification: 002410
Unit ID: 175856
Telephone: (601) 979-2121 Carnegie Class: DU-Higher
FAX Number: (601) 979-2358 Calendar System: Semester
URL: www.jsums.edu
Established: 1877 Annual Undergrad Tuition & Fees (In-State): $8,445
Enrollment: 6,921 Coed
Affiliation or Control: State IRS Status: 501(c)3
Highest Offering: Doctorate
Accreditation: SC, ART, CACREP, CAEPN, CLPSY, MUS, NAIT, PH, PLNG, SP, SPAA, SW

01 President ... Mr. Thomas HUDSON
05 Provost/Senior VP Academic Affairs ... Dr. Alisa MOSLEY
100 Vice President & Chief of Staff ... Dr. Debra MAYS-JACKSON
10 VP Business & Finance/CFO ... Mr. Howard BROWN
111 VP Institutional Advancement ... Ms. Veronica M. COHEN
41 VP & Director of Athletics ... Mr. Ashley ROBINSON
46 VP Research & Economic Dev ... Dr. Joseph A. WHITTAKER
84 Assoc VP Enrollment Management ... Vacant
32 Assoc VP for Student Life ... Dr. Susan E. POWELL
114 Exec Dir Budget & Fin Analysis ... Mrs. Tammiko HARRISON
21 Exec Dir Actg/Fin Rpts/Fiscal Comm ... Mrs. Tracy STAPLETON
13 Chief Information Officer ... Dr. Deborah DENT
15 Executive Director Human Resources ... Mrs. Robin SPANN-PACK
43 General Counsel ... Mr. Edward WATSON
50 Dean College of Business ... Dr. Fidelis M. IKEM
53 Int Dean College Educ/Human Devel ... Dr. Tracy HARRIS
49 Dean College of Liberal Arts ... Dr. K. B TURNER
72 Dean College of Sci/Engr/Tech ... Dr. Wilbur WALTERS
69 Dean College of Health Sciences ... Dr. Girmay BERHIE
58 Dean Division of Graduate Studies .. Dr. Preselfannie MCDANIELS
106 Executive Director JSU Online ... Ms. Andrea JONES
08 Int Dean Div of Library & Info Res ... Dr. Locord WILSON
88 Interim Dean University College ... Dr. Shirley BURNETT
92 Assoc Dean Div of Honors College ... Dr. Loria BROWN GORDAN
88 Assoc VP/Director of Title III ... Dr. Mitchell SHEARS
14 Assoc VP Information Tech ... Dr. Michael ROBINSON
35 Assoc VP Student Life/Dean Students ... Dr. Laquala DIXON
51 Director of Lifelong Learning ... Dr. Carlos WILSON
110 Asst VP Institutional Advancement ... Mrs. Gwen CAPLES
116 Internal Auditor ... Mr. Christopher THOMAS
85 Director JSU Global ... Dr. Huie J. CUNNINGHAM
29 Dir Alumni/Constituency Relations ... Mr. David HOWARD
18 Exec Dir for Business ... Mr. Michael BOLDEN
88 Associate University Physician ... Dr. Robert SMITH
37 Director of Financial Aid ... Mr. Ozie RATCLIFF
39 Exec Director Housing & Residence ... Vacant
06 Registrar ... Dr. Harrison P. JOHNSON
23 Director of Health Center Services ... Dr. Samuel JONES
88 Director MS Urban Research Ctr ... Dr. Sam MOZEE, JR.
19 Director Public Safety ... Mr. Thomas ALBRIGHT
26 Chief Communications Officer ... Ms. Alonda THOMAS
22 Assistant Dir of Disability Service ... Dr. Aaron RICHARDSON
40 Manager Bookstore ... Ms. Dyonne CONNER
09 AVP Inst Research/Planning/Effect ... Dr. La Toya HART
36 Executive Director Career Services ... Ms. Lashanda JORDAN
38 Director Student Counseling ... Ms. Shanice WHITE
21 Executive Director Business Office ... Ms. Jewell HARRIS
22 Dir of Legal Oper/EEO-AA Officer ... Ms. Tiffany DOCKINS
07 Dir Undergraduate Admissions ... Ms. Janieth ADAMS
90 Director Academic IT ... Mr. Gregory ANDERSON
109 Director Auxiliary Services ... Ms. Kameshia HILL
88 Ombudsman ... Dr. Floressa HANNAH-JEFFERSON
88 Director Veteran & Military Center ... Ms. Latoya REED
04 Admin Assistant to the President ... Ms. Joyce JORDAN-GOODEN

Jones County Junior College (G)

900 S Court Street, Ellisville MS 39437-3999
County: Jones FICE Identification: 002411
Unit ID: 175883
Telephone: (601) 477-4000 Carnegie Class: Assoc/MT-VT-High Trad
FAX Number: (601) 477-4875 Calendar System: Semester
URL: www.jcjc.edu
Established: 1927 Annual Undergrad Tuition & Fees (In-District): $3,870
Enrollment: 4,535 Coed
Affiliation or Control: State/Local IRS Status: Exempt
Highest Offering: Associate Degree
Accreditation: SC, ACBSP, ADNUR, EMT, RAD

01 President ... Dr. Jesse R. SMITH
05 Interim Chief Academic Officer ... Mr. Rick YOUNGBLOOD
10 EVP/Chief Financial Officer ... Mr. Rick YOUNGBLOOD
32 VP Student Affairs ... Dr. Tessa FLOWERS
111 VP of Institutional Advancement ... Mr. Joel CAIN
84 VP of Enrollment Management ... Mr. Paul SPELL
13 VP of Information Technology ... Mr. John Howard ROBERTSON

26 EVP/CMO/CIO/CEMO ... Dr. Finee RUFFIN
18 Asst to the Pres Facilities Mgmt ... Mr. Michael BRADSHAW
86 Asst to the Pres Govt Relations ... Mr. Jim WALLEY
88 Asst to the Pres Leadership Trng ... Dr. Sam JONES
04 Asst to the Pres Office Operations ... Ms. Teresa WELCH
35 VP of Advancement and Athletics and ... Mr. Joel CAIN
20 Dean of Academic Affairs ... Dr. Jason DEDWYLDER
103 Dir of the Advanced Tech Center ... Ms. Jennifer GRIFFITH
37 Director of Student Financial Aid ... Ms. Kari DEDWYLDER
39 Director of Housing ... Mr. Chuck ROBERTSON
40 Bookstore Manager ... Ms. Lisa SIMS
41 Director of Athletics ... Mr. Joel CAIN
15 Director of Human Resources ... Mr. Luke HAMMONDS
96 Director of Purchasing ... Ms. Daphne YEAGER
106 Dean of eLearning ... Ms. Kandi JOHNSON
08 Head Librarian ... Mr. Andrew SHARP
19 Chief Campus Police ... Mr. Stan LIVINGSTON

Meridian Community College (A)

910 Highway 19 North, Meridian MS 39307-5890
County: Lauderdale FICE Identification: 002413
Unit ID: 175935
Telephone: (601) 483-8241 Carnegie Class: Assoc/HVT-High Trad
FAX Number: (601) 481-1305 Calendar System: Semester
URL: www.meridiancc.edu
Established: 1937 Annual Undergrad Tuition & Fees (In-District): $3,478
Enrollment: 3,003 Coed
Affiliation or Control: Local IRS Status: 501(c)3
Highest Offering: Associate Degree
Accreditation: **SC**, ADNUR, CAHIIM, COARC, DA, DH, EMT, MAC, MLTAD, PNUR, PTAA, RAD, SURGT

01 President ... Dr. Thomas HUEBNER, JR.
04 Executive Assistant to President ... Mrs. Lauren CLAY
05 VP for Academic Affairs ... Mr. Michael THOMPSON
10 Chief Financial Officer ... Mrs. Pam HARRISON
21 Assistant Chief Financial Officer ... Mr. Drew EDWARDS
15 Director Human Resources ... Ms. Angie PICKARD
18 Director Physical Plant ... Mr. Adam FOREMAN
40 Bookstore Manager ... Mrs. Cher WARREN
32 Interim VP Student Success ... Mrs. Annette COOK
35 Dean of Student Services ... Mrs. Deanna SMITH
121 Director Advising & Retention ... Mrs. Kimberly RUSH
41 Athletic Director ... Mr. Sander ATKINSON
07 Director of Admissions ... Ms. Ashley TANKSLEY
124 Director Student Engagement ... Mr. Brandon DEWEASE
37 Director Financial Aid ... Ms. Nedra BRADLEY
06 Registrar ... Ms. Deborah OLDHAM
19 Chief of Police ... Mr. Nick KIRKLAND
39 Director Housing & Residence Life ... Mr. Reginald DAVIS
20 Associate Dean Academic Affairs ... Dr. Chad GRAHAM
13 Associate VP for Technology ... Dr. Kelley GONZALES
09 Dean Institutional Effectiveness ... Mrs. Valerie BISHOP
08 Director Library Services ... Mr. Doug JERNIGAN
103 VP for Workforce Solutions ... Mr. Joseph KNIGHT
103 Dean of Workforce Education ... Dr. Lori SMITH
66 Assoc VP Nursing/Health Education ... Dr. Lara COLLUM
25 Dir Workforce Grants & Development ... Mrs. Lucy LAMBERTH
36 Career Center Director ... Ms. Katrina GARRETT
111 VP Advancement/Exec Dir Foundation ... Mrs. Leia HILL
26 Director of Public Information ... Mrs. Kay THOMAS
105 Web Designer/Media Specialist ... Ms. Desi ROSS

Millsaps College (B)

1701 N State Street, Jackson MS 39210-0001
County: Hinds FICE Identification: 002414
Unit ID: 175980
Telephone: (601) 974-1000 Carnegie Class: Bac-A&S
FAX Number: (601) 974-1059 Calendar System: Semester
URL: www.millsaps.edu
Established: 1890 Annual Undergrad Tuition & Fees: $41,314
Enrollment: 712 Coed
Affiliation or Control: United Methodist IRS Status: 501(c)3
Highest Offering: Master's
Accreditation: **SC**, CAEP

01 President ... Dr. Rob PEARIGEN
05 Provost & Dean of the College ... Dr. Keith DUNN
10 Vice President of Finance ... Ms. Whitney EMRICH
111 VP for Institutional Advancement ... Ms. Hope CARTER
32 Dean of Students ... Ms. Megan JAMES
50 Dean of Else School of Management ... Mr. Harvey FISER
84 Vice Pres for Enrollment ... Ms. Beth CLARKE
79 Assoc Dean Arts & Humanities ... Dr. Holly SYPNIEWSKI
28 Assoc Dean Intercul Affs/Cmty Life ... Mr. Demetrius BROWN
81 Associate Dean Sciences Division ... Dr. Stan GALICKI
82 AVP for International Initiatives ... Ms. Molly WEST
37 Director of Financial Aid ... Mrs. Isabelle HIGBEE
20 Director Academic Support Services ... Dr. Jennifer LEWTON-YATES
51 Director of Continuing Education ... Dr. Nola R. GIBSON
08 College Librarian ... Ms. Jamie B. WILSON
36 Director of Career Center ... Mr. Ryan COLVIN
41 Director of Athletics ... Mr. Aaron PELCH
15 Dir of Human Resource Services ... Ms. Julie DANIELS
42 Chaplain/Director Church Relations ... Dr. Joey SHELTON
21 Controller ... Mrs. Whitney EMRICH
06 Registrar ... Dr. Ken THOMPSON
09 Director of Institutional Research ... Mr. Ken THOMPSON
18 Director of Physical Plant ... Mr. Michael SWITZER

29 Director Alumni Relations ... Ms. Maribeth KITCHINGS
19 Director Security/Safety ... Mr. John CONWAY
26 Director of Communications & Market ... Mr. John SEWELL
04 Executive Asst to President ... Mrs. Penta MOORE
100 Chief of Staff ... Mr. Kenneth TOWNSEND
102 Dir Foundation/Corporate Relations ... Mr. Lloyd GRAY
44 Director Annual Giving ... Mr. Jim BURKE

Mississippi College (C)

200 W College Street, Clinton MS 39058-0001
County: Hinds FICE Identification: 002415
Unit ID: 176053
Telephone: (601) 925-3000 Carnegie Class: DU-Mod
FAX Number: (601) 925-3276 Calendar System: Semester
URL: www.mc.edu
Established: 1826 Annual Undergrad Tuition & Fees: $19,308
Enrollment: 4,667 Coed
Affiliation or Control: Southern Baptist IRS Status: 501(c)3
Highest Offering: Doctorate
Accreditation: **SC**, ARCPA, CACREP, CAEP, CIDA, LAW, MUS, NAEYC, NURSE, SW

01 President ... Dr. Blake THOMPSON
04 Sr Exec Assistant to President ... Ms. Shelia CARPENTER
10 COO/Chief Financial Officer ... Ms. Laura JACKSON
05 Provost/Exec Vice President ... Dr. Keith ELDER
29 VP & Exec Dir Alumni Assn ... Dr. Jim TURCOTTE
58 Assoc Provost & Graduate Dean ... Dr. Debbie NORRIS
32 Assoc VP for the Student Experience ... Dr. Jonathan AMBROSE
06 Registrar ... Ms. Megan PRITCHETT
09 Director of Institutional Research ... Ms. Cassandra SESSOMS
08 Director of Library ... Ms. Claudia CONKLIN
21 Controller ... Ms. Ebby DEDEAUX
13 Chief Information Officer ... Mr. Bill CRANFORD
38 Exec Director of Student Counseling ... Dr. Morgan BRYANT
15 Director Human Resources ... Ms. Donna SMITH
26 Director Public Relations ... Ms. Tracey HARRISON
18 Director of Physical Plant ... Dr. Tom WILLIAMS
39 Coordinator of Residence Life ... Ms. Julie KERR
37 Director Student Financial Aid ... Ms. Karon MCMILLAN
07 Acting Dean of Enrollment ... Mr. Michael WRIGHT
88 Asst Dean Christian Leadership ... Ms. Becca BENSON
19 Director of Public Safety ... Mr. Mike WARREN
41 Director of Athletics ... Mr. Kenny BIZOT
96 Director of Purchasing ... Ms. Dana ELMORE
40 Manager Bookstore ... Mr. Daniel HOWARD
36 Director of Career Services ... Ms. Taylor ORMON
81 Dean School of Science/Mathematics ... Dr. Stan BALDWIN
50 Dean School of Business Admin ... Dr. Marcelo EDUARDO
79 Dean School of Humanities ... Dr. Jonathan RANDLE
53 Dean School of Education ... Dr. Cindy MELTON
73 Dean Sch Christian Studies/Fine Art ... Dr. Wayne VAN HORN
61 Dean School of Law ... Dr. Patricia BENNETT
58 Dean Grad School/Special Programs ... Dr. Debbie NORRIS
66 Dean School of Nursing ... Dr. Kimberly SHARP
30 Excecutive Director of Development ... Ms. Katrina PACE
43 VP Gen Counsel/Spec Asst to Pres ... Dr. Bill TOWNSEND

Mississippi Delta Community College (D)

PO Box 668, Moorhead MS 38761-0668
County: Sunflower FICE Identification: 002416
Unit ID: 176008
Telephone: (662) 246-6322 Carnegie Class: Assoc/MT-VT-High Trad
FAX Number: (662) 246-6321 Calendar System: Semester
URL: www.msdelta.edu
Established: 1926 Annual Undergrad Tuition & Fees (In-District): $3,140
Enrollment: 2,096 Coed
Affiliation or Control: Local IRS Status: 501(c)3
Highest Offering: Associate Degree
Accreditation: **SC**, ADNUR, DH, MLTAD, @PTAA, RAD

01 President ... Dr. Tyrone JACKSON
05 Vice President of Instruction ... Mrs. Teresa WEBSTER
10 Dean of Business Services ... Mrs. Staci MILLER
32 Dean of Student Services ... Mr. Derrick FIELDS
88 Dean of GHEC Operations ... Ms. Linda CLARK
103 VP of Workforce ... Mr. Todd DONALD
15 Director of Human Resources ... Ms. Carla JOHNSON
37 Director of Financial Aid ... Ms. Debra MARTIN
84 Dean of Enrollment Management ... Mr. Jay GARY
13 Director Computer & Info Tech Svcs ... Mr. Torrey MOORE
08 Director of Library Services ... Mrs. Kristi BARIOLA
124 Dean of Planning/Assessment ... Mrs. Kate FAILING
18 Director of Maintenance ... Vacant
108 VP of Enrollment & Effectiveness ... Dr. Benjamin CLOYD
11 VP of Administrative Services ... Dr. Steven JONES
04 Executive Asst to the President ... Mrs. Debra BAKER
41 Athletic Director ... Vacant
19 Director Security/Safety ... Mr. Clifton KING
76 Dean of Allied Health ... Mrs. Patricia KELLY
75 Dean of Career/Technical Education ... Mrs. Suzanne THOMPSON
106 Coordinator of E-learning ... Ms. Carmen BROWN
111 Exec Dir College Advancement/Alumni ... Mr. Jim AYCOCK

Mississippi Gulf Coast Community College (E)

PO Box 609, Perkinston MS 39573-0012
County: Stone FICE Identification: 002417
Unit ID: 176071
Telephone: (601) 928-5211 Carnegie Class: Assoc/MT-VT-High Trad
FAX Number: (601) 928-6386 Calendar System: Semester
URL: www.mgccc.edu
Established: 1911 Annual Undergrad Tuition & Fees (In-District): $3,750
Enrollment: 8,677 Coed
Affiliation or Control: Local IRS Status: Exempt
Highest Offering: Associate Degree
Accreditation: **SC**, ACFEI, ADNUR, #COARC, EMT, MAC, MLTAD, @OTA, PNUR, PTAA, RAD, SURGT

01 President ... Dr. Mary S. GRAHAM
05 Exec VP Teaching/Lrng/Cmty Campus ... Dr. Jonathan WOODWARD
10 Exec VP Administration/Finance ... Dr. Jason PUGH
12 VP Perkinston Campus (PC) ... Dr. Ladd TAYLOR
12 VP Harrison County Campus (JDC) ... Dr. Cedric BRADLEY
12 VP Jackson County Campus (JCC) ... Dr. Tammy FRANKS
32 Exec VP Student Svcs/Enroll Mgmt ... Dr. Phil BONFANTI
111 Exec VP Institutional Advancement ... Dr. Suzi BROWN
103 AVP Career & Tech Educ for CC ... Mr. Brock CLARK
15 Assoc VP Human Resources ... Mr. Jared BURNS
09 AVP Inst Research & Effectiveness ... Mr. Adam SWANSON
26 AVP Institutional Relations ... Ms. Christen DUHE
102 AVP Foundation & Alumni Relations ... Ms. Kady PIETZ
106 Director of eLearning ... Ms. Buffy MATTHEWS
96 Dir of Purchasing/Property Control ... Mr. Jay NEWTON
50 Dean of Business Services ... Mr. Wayne KUNTZ
50 Dean of Business Services PC ... Ms. Rebecca LAYTON
50 Dean of Business Services JC ... Mr. Jason FERGUSON
50 Dean of Business Services HCC ... Ms. Blythe KING
66 AVP School of Nursing & Health Prof ... Dr. Joan HENDRIX
75 Dean of Teaching & Learning PCC ... Mr. Bobby GHOSAL
75 Dean of Teaching & Learning HCC ... Dr. Emma MILLER
75 Dean of Teaching & Learning JCC ... Dr. Brad BAILEY
75 Dean of Career/Tech & Workforce JCC ... Mr. Brock CLARK
32 Dean Stdnt Svcs/Enroll Mgmt PC ... Dr. Jason BEVERLY
32 Dean Stdnt Svcs/Enroll Mgmt JCC ... Ms. Michelle SEKUL
20 AVP Teaching and Learning ... Dr. Erin RIGGINS
88 Dean George County Center ... Dr. Lisa RHODES
39 Director Residential/Student Life ... Mr. Trey ROBERTSON
07 Director of Admissions/Rec JCC ... Ms. Miranda HEDMAN
07 Director of Admissions/Rec HCC ... Mr. Christopher BAGWELL
07 Director of Admissions/Rec PCC ... Ms. Mollie BARGER
37 Financial Aid Director JCC ... Ms. Angela BRADLEY
37 Financial Aid Director PCC ... Ms. Heather DEARMAN
37 Financial Aid Director HCC ... Ms. LaShanda CHAMBERLAIN
84 Director of Enrollment Services JCC ... Ms. Beth LOVORN
84 Director of Enrollment Services HCC ... Ms. Dawn BUCKLEY
84 Director of Enrollment Services PCC ... Ms. Paula RAINEY
04 Sr Exec Assistant to the President ... Ms. Natasha BAUCUM
21 Assoc VP Finance/Comptroller ... Ms. Shelly BENTZ

Mississippi State University (F)

Lee Boulevard, Mississippi State MS 39762-5708
County: Oktibbeha FICE Identification: 002423
Unit ID: 176080
Telephone: (662) 325-2323 Carnegie Class: DU-Highest
FAX Number: (662) 325-7455 Calendar System: Semester
URL: www.msstate.edu
Established: 1878 Annual Undergrad Tuition & Fees (In-State): $8,910
Enrollment: 22,986 Coed
Affiliation or Control: State IRS Status: 501(c)3
Highest Offering: Doctorate
Accreditation: **SC**, AAFCS, #ARCPA, ART, CACREP, CAEPN, CIDA, CLPSY, CONST, DIETD, DIETI, IPSY, LSAR, MUS, SCPSY, SPAA, SW, VET

01 President ... Dr. Mark E. KEENUM
05 Provost/Executive VP ... Dr. David SHAW
46 VP Research & Econ Development ... Dr. Julie JORDAN
47 VP Agric/Forestry/Vet Med ... Dr. Keith COBLE
10 VP for Finance & Administration ... Mr. Don ZANT
32 VP for Student Affairs ... Dr. Regina HYATT
30 VP for Development and Alumni ... Mr. John P. RUSH
07 Assistant VP Enrollment ... Dr. John DICKERSON
41 Athletic Director ... Mr. John COHEN
43 General Counsel ... Ms. Joan LUCAS
28 VP for Access/Diversity & Inclusion ... Ms. Rasheda BODDIE-FORBES
15 Int Chief Human Resources Ofcr ... Ms. Leslie COREY
88 Special Assistant to the President ... Mr. Kyle STEWARD
26 Chief Communications Officer ... Mr. Sid SALTER
86 Special Assistant to the President ... Mr. Lee WEISKOPF
20 Executive Vice Provost ... Dr. Peter RYAN
13 Chief Information Officer ... Mr. Steve PARROTT
85 AVP International Institute ... Dr. Dan REYNOLDS
48 Dean Architecture/Art & Design ... Dr. Angi BOURGEOIS
49 Dean Arts & Sciences ... Dr. Rick TRAVIS
50 Dean Business ... Dr. Sharon OSWALD
53 Dean Education ... Dr. Teresa JAYROE
58 Dean Graduate School ... Dr. Peter RYAN
54 Dean Engineering ... Dr. Jason KEITH
65 Int Dean Forest Resources ... Dr. Wes BURGER
47 Int Dean Agric & Life Science ... Dr. Scott WILLARD
74 Dean Veterinary Medicine ... Dr. Kent H. HOBLET
12 Associate VP & Head of MSU-Meridian ... Dr. Terry CRUSE
08 Interim Dean Libraries ... Dr. Thomas ANDERSON
92 Dean Honors College ... Dr. Christopher SNYDER
56 Dir University Extension Service ... Dr. Gary JACKSON
88 Int Dir Ag Experiment Station ... Dr. Reuben MOORE
06 Registrar ... Dr. John R. DICKERSON
106 Exec Director Distance Education ... Dr. Susan SEAL
36 Interim Director Career Center ... Dr. Brent FOUNTAIN

35 Dean of Students ... Dr. Thomas BOURGEOIS
38 Director Counseling Services ... Ms. Luellyn SWITZER
37 Director Student Financial Aid ... Mr. Paul MCKINNEY
39 Exec Director Housing/Res Life ... Ms. Dei ALLARD
09 Director Institutional Research ... Dr. Tracey BAHAM
23 Interim Medical Director ... Dr. Katrina POE
29 Director of Alumni Association ... Mr. Jeffrey DAVIS
112 Director of Planned Giving ... Mr. Wes GORDON
25 Director Sponsored Projects ... Mr. Kevin ENROTH
116 Director Internal Audit ... Ms. Leisa ERVIN
96 Exec Director Procurement/Contracts ... Mr. Don BUFFUM
19 Police Chief ... Mr. Vance RICE

Mississippi University for Women (A)

1100 College Street, Columbus MS 39701-5800
County: Lowndes — FICE Identification: 002422
Unit ID: 176035
Telephone: (877) 462-8439 — Carnegie Class: Masters/M
FAX Number: (662) 329-7297 — Calendar System: Semester
URL: www.muw.edu
Established: 1884 — Annual Undergrad Tuition & Fees (In-State): $7,525
Enrollment: 2,704 — Coed
Affiliation or Control: State — IRS Status: 501(c)3
Highest Offering: Doctorate
Accreditation: SC, ACBSP, ADNUR, ART, CAEP, MUS, NURSE, SP

01 President ... Ms. Nora R. MILLER
05 Provost/VP Academic Affairs ... Dr. Scott TOLLISON
10 Sr Vice Pres Administration & CFO ... Mr. Mark D. ELLARD
26 Exec Dir of University Relations ... Ms. Anika M. PERKINS
32 VP Student Affs/Dean of Students ... Ms. Jessica HARPOLE
20 Assoc Vice Pres Academic Affairs ... Dr. Martin HATTON
43 University Counsel ... Ms. Karen CLAY
49 Dean College Arts/Sciences ... Dr. Brian ANDERSON
50 Dean Business/Professional Studies ... Dr. Marty A. BROCK
66 Dean College Nursing/SLP ... Dr. Tammie M. MCCOY
08 Dean of Library Services ... Ms. Amanda C. POWERS
35 Dean of Students ... Ms. Jessica HARPOLE
58 Director Graduate Studies ... Dr. Martin HATTON
88 Director Outreach & Innovation ... Ms. Melinda LOWE
27 Chief Information Officer ... Ms. Carla LOWERY
06 Acting Registrar ... Ms. Sherry DURKIN
09 Director Inst Research & Assessment ... Ms. Jennifer MOORE
92 Director Honors College ... Dr. Kim WHITEHEAD
29 Dir Alumni Rels/Donor Engagement . Ms. Lyndsay CUMBERLAND
30 Exec Dir Development & Alumni ... Ms. Andrea N. STEVENS
105 Dir Web Development/Univ Webmaster ... Mr. Rich SOBOLEWSKI
21 Director University Accounting ... Ms. Susan SOBLEY
116 Internal Auditor ... Mr. Kenneth WIDNER
13 Director of Information Systems ... Mr. Aaron BROOKS
07 Director of Admissions ... Ms. Ilka MCCARTER
37 Director Financial Aid ... Ms. Nicole PATRICK
15 Director Human Resources ... Ms. Laura QUINN
19 Chief of Police ... Mr. Randy G. VIBROCK
18 Director of Facilities Management ... Mr. Jody KENNEDY
96 Director Resources Management ... Ms. Angie S. ATKINS
35 Interim Director Student Life ... Ms. Mea ASHLEY
41 Dir Athletics & Recreation ... Ms. Jennifer CLAYBROOK
40 Director Bookstore ... Ms. Rita ROBINSON
121 Director Student Success Center ... Dr. David BROOKING
109 Int Gen Mgr MUW Dining Svcs ... Mr. Scott HAGER
84 Enrollment Certification Officer ... Ms. Jody PETERS
14 Director of Systems & Networks ... Mr. Rodney GODFREY
104 Coordinator Study Abroad ... Ms. Erinn HOLLOWAY
39 Director Housing & Residence Life ... Mr. Andrew MONEYMAKER

Mississippi Valley State University (B)

14000 Highway 82 W, Itta Bena MS 38941-1400
County: Leflore — FICE Identification: 002424
Unit ID: 176044
Telephone: (662) 254-9041 — Carnegie Class: Masters/S
FAX Number: (662) 254-6709 — Calendar System: Semester
URL: www.mvsu.edu
Established: 1950 — Annual Undergrad Tuition & Fees (In-State): $6,746
Enrollment: 2,032 — Coed
Affiliation or Control: State — IRS Status: 501(c)3
Highest Offering: Master's
Accreditation: SC, ACBSP, ART, CAEP, MUS, SW

01 President ... Dr. Jerryl BRIGGS, SR.
05 Provost/Sr VP Academic Affairs ... Dr. Kathie S. GOLDEN
32 VP Enrollment Mgmt/Student Affairs .. Dr. Thomas CALHOUN, JR.
20 Assoc VP Academic Affairs ... Dr. Abigail Sophia NEWSOME
09 Asst VP for IRE/Strat Planning ... Dr. Sharon FREEMAN
10 VP Business & Finance/CFO ... Ms. Joyce A. DIXON
100 Chief of Staff/Legislative Liaison ... Dr. LaShon F. BROOKS
111 Int Vice Pres for Univ Advancement ... Mr. Dameon SHAW
106 Asst VP for Distance & Online ... Dr. Kenneth DONE
39 Director Residence Life ... Mr. Raynaldo GILLUS
41 Director of Athletics ... Mrs. Dianthia FORD-KEE
06 Director of Student Records ... Mr. Jeffery LOGGINS
07 Director Admission/Recruitment ... Dr. Danisha WILLIAMS
08 Head Librarian ... Ms. Mantra HENDERSON
15 Director of Human Resources ... Mrs. Elizabeth HURSSEY
13 Director of Information Technology ... Vacant
37 Director of Financial Aid ... Mr. Letherio ZEIGLER
29 Manager of Alumni Relations ... Ms. Alyssa WEBB
26 Director of Comm/Mktg ... Mr. Donell MAXIE
19 Chief/Director University Police ... Mr. Xavier REDMOND
18 Director Facilities/Capital Project ... Mr. Terrence HURSSEY
36 Director Career Development ... Ms. Essie L. BRYANT
38 Dean of Student Development ... Dr. Yolanda JONES
50 Chair of Business Department ... Dr. Curressia BROWN
53 Acting Chair of Education Dept ... Dr. Theresa DUMAS
79 Chair English/Foreign Language ... Dr. John ZHENG
57 Acting Chair Fine Arts Department ... Dr. Kimberly BROADWATER
68 Chair Health/Phys Ed/Rec Dept ... Dr. Gloria ROSS
81 Chair of Math/Computer Science Dept ... Dr. Latonya GARNER
54 Acting Chair of Engineering Tech ... Mr. Antonio BROWNLOW
60 Chair Mass Communication Dept ... Vacant
88 Chair Criminal Justice ... Dr. Emmanual AMADI
70 Chair Social Work Department ... Dr. Catherine SINGLETON-WALKER
96 Director of Purchasing ... Ms. Carla M. WILLIAMS
04 Executive Asst to President ... Mrs. Auguster WALLACE
25 Director Sponsored Pgm/Title III ... Mr. Samuel MELTON, JR.
30 Director of Development ... Vacant

Northeast Mississippi Community College (C)

101 Cunningham Boulevard, Booneville MS 38829-1731
County: Prentiss — FICE Identification: 002426
Unit ID: 176169
Telephone: (662) 728-7751 — Carnegie Class: Assoc/MT-VT-High Trad
FAX Number: (662) 728-1165 — Calendar System: Semester
URL: www.nemcc.edu
Established: 1948 — Annual Undergrad Tuition & Fees (In-District): $4,036
Enrollment: 3,243 — Coed
Affiliation or Control: State/Local — IRS Status: 501(c)3
Highest Offering: Associate Degree
Accreditation: SC, ADNUR, COARC, DH, MAC, MLTAD, RAD

01 President ... Dr. Ricky G. FORD
03 Executive Vice President ... Dr. Craig-Ellis SASSER
103 VP Workforce Training/Economic Dev ... Nadara L. COLE
26 VP Marketing/Communications ... Will KOLLMEYER
10 Vice President of Finance ... Chris MURPHY
26 Vice Pres of Public Information ... Tony FINCH
05 Vice President of Instruction ... Dr. Michelle BARAGONA
32 Vice President of Student Services ... Ray SCOTT
12 Vice Pres Satellite Campuses ... Ben SHAPPLEY
35 Assoc Vice Pres of Student Service ... Rod COGGIN
08 Library Director ... Ellice YAGER
96 Director of Purchasing ... Amber GARNER
37 Director of Financial Aid ... Greg WINDHAM
13 Director Computer Center ... Gregory SMITH
18 Director Facilities/Maintenance ... Mark HATFIELD
84 Dir of Enrollment Svcs/Registrar ... Chassie KELLY
15 Human Resources Officer ... Wesley FLOYD
04 Administrative Asst to President ... Misty DEVAUGHN
102 Dir Foundation/Corporate Relations ... Patrick D. EATON
106 Dir Online Education/E-learning ... Kim HARRIS
19 Chief of Security/Safety ... Anthony ANDERSON
09 Director of Institutional Research ... Dr. Kelli HEFNER
121 Director of Student Success Center ... Britney WHITLEY
51 Director of Adult Education ... Laurie KESLER
108 Dir of Institutional Effectiveness ... Amber NELMS
41 Athletic Director ... Kent FARRIS
88 Director of Sports Information ... Blake LONG
88 New Albany Center Director/WIOA ... David GOODE

Northwest Mississippi Community College (D)

4975 Highway 51 N, Senatobia MS 38668-1703
County: Tate — FICE Identification: 002427
Unit ID: 176178
Telephone: (662) 562-3200 — Carnegie Class: Assoc/MT-VT-High Trad
FAX Number: (662) 562-3911 — Calendar System: Semester
URL: www.northwestms.edu
Established: 1927 — Annual Undergrad Tuition & Fees (In-State): $3,390
Enrollment: 7,092 — Coed
Affiliation or Control: State — IRS Status: 501(c)3
Highest Offering: Associate Degree
Accreditation: SC, ADNUR, COARC, EMT, FUSER

01 President ... Dr. Michael J. HEINDL
10 Vice President for Fiscal Affairs ... Mr. Jeff HORTON
31 VP for Community Relations ... Dr. Andrew DALE
05 Vice Pres for Educational Affairs ... Dr. Matthew DOMAS
103 AVP Wrkfce Sol/Career Tech Educ ... Mr. Dwayne CASEY
84 AVP Stdnt Svcs/Enrolllment Mgmt ... Dr. Tonyalle V. RUSH
22 Disability Student Svcs Coordinator ... Ms. Missy KELSAY
26 Director of Communications ... Ms. Kayleigh MCCOOL
37 Director of Financial Aid ... Ms. LeKeisha MURRY-HIBBLER
36 Dir Student Development Center ... Ms. Meg ROSS
08 Director of Learning Resources ... Dr. Melissa WRIGHT
13 Director of Information Tech ... Mrs. Amy LATHAM
07 Director of Recruiting ... Mrs. Jere HERRINGTON
09 AVP Inst Research/Effectiveness ... Dr. Carolyn WILEY
18 Director of Physical Plant Building ... Mrs. Mary AYERS
19 Chief of Campus Security ... Mr. Zabe DAVIS
30 Director of Development/Alumni Rels ... Ms. Patti GORDON
32 District Dean of Student Services ... Dr. Tommy (TJ) WALKER
40 Director Bookstore ... Mr. Joel BOYLES
41 Director of Athletics ... Mr. Brian OAKES
96 Director of Purchasing ... Mrs. Ruth DUNLAP
15 Director of Human Resources ... Mrs. Erica STANFORD
21 Director of Accounting ... Mr. Matt SELLERS
06 Registrar ... Mrs. Angela DORTCH
29 Director Alumni Affairs ... Ms. Patti GORDON

Pearl River Community College (E)

101 Highway 11 N, Poplarville MS 39470-2298
County: Pearl River — FICE Identification: 002430
Unit ID: 176239
Telephone: (601) 403-1000 — Carnegie Class: Assoc/MT-VT-Mix Trad/Non
FAX Number: (601) 403-1339 — Calendar System: Semester
URL: www.prcc.edu
Established: 1909 — Annual Undergrad Tuition & Fees (In-District): $3,500
Enrollment: 5,065 — Coed
Affiliation or Control: State/Local — IRS Status: 501(c)3
Highest Offering: Associate Degree
Accreditation: SC, ADNUR, COARC, DA, DH, MLTAD, OTA, PTAA, RAD, SURGT

01 President ... Dr. Adam J. BREERWOOD
04 Exec Assistant to the President ... Ms. Maghan SMITH
05 Sr VP Poplarville Campus/Provost ... Dr. Martha L. SMITH
07 Director of Admissions and Records ... Ms. Tonia SEAL
09 VP for Planning & Inst Research ... Dr. Jennifer SEAL
10 VP for College Operations ... Vacant
103 Dean of Workforce/Cmty Dev ... Ms. Rebecca BROWN
106 Director of eLearning ... Ms. Michele MITCHELL
105 Webmaster ... Mr. Eric REID
13 Chief Info Technology Officer (CIO) ... Mr. Matt LOGAN
15 Director of Human Resources ... Ms. Kelly REID
19 Director of Public Safety ... Mr. Don Butch RABY
26 Assoc VP Marketing/Comm ... Ms. Candace HARPER
29 Director Development/Alumni Rels ... Vacant
32 VP Poplarville Campus/Student Svcs ... Mr. Jeff LONG
121 Assoc VP Student Success ... Dr. Amy TOWNSEND
35 Dean of Student Services ... Vacant
86 Dir Government/Cmty Relations ... Ms. Angie KOTHMANN

Reformed Theological Seminary (F)

5422 Clinton Boulevard, Jackson MS 39209-3099
County: Hinds — FICE Identification: 009193
Unit ID: 176284
Telephone: (601) 923-1600 — Carnegie Class: Not Classified
FAX Number: (601) 923-1654 — Calendar System: 4/1/4
URL: www.rts.edu
Established: 1965 — Annual Graduate Tuition & Fees: N/A
Enrollment: N/A — Coed
Affiliation or Control: Independent Non-Profit — IRS Status: 501(c)3
Highest Offering: Doctorate; No Undergraduates
Accreditation: SC, THEOL

00 Chancellor Emeritus ... Dr. Robert C. CANNADA, JR.
01 Chancellor/CEO ... Dr. J. Ligon DUNCAN
10 Chief Operations Financial Officer ... Mr. Bradley TISDALE
05 Provost and Chief Academic Officer ... Dr. Robert CARA
30 Sr Vice President for Development ... Mr. Matthew S. BRYSON
12 President Charlotte Campus ... Dr. Michael J. KRUGER
12 President Orlando Campus ... Dr. Scott R. SWAIN
12 President Jackson Campus ... Dr. Guy L. RICHARDSON
12 Executive Director Atlanta Campus ... Dr. Guy RICHARD
106 Exec Dir RTS Global/Distance Educ ... Mr. David R. JOHN, III
12 President Washington DC ... Dr. Scott REDD
12 Executive Director Dallas Campus ... Dr. Mark MCDOWELL
12 Executive Director Houston Campus ... Dr. Mark MCDOWELL
12 Executive Director NYC Campus ... Dr. Jay HARVEY
26 VP for Institutional Communications ... Mr. Phillip HOLMES
84 VP for Enrollment Management ... Mr. David VELDKAMP
21 VP for Finance ... Vacant

Rust College (G)

150 Rust Avenue, Holly Springs MS 38635-2328
County: Marshall — FICE Identification: 002433
Unit ID: 176318
Telephone: (662) 252-8000 — Carnegie Class: Bac-A&S
FAX Number: (662) 252-7901 — Calendar System: Semester
URL: www.rustcollege.edu
Established: 1866 — Annual Undergrad Tuition & Fees: $9,900
Enrollment: 623 — Coed
Affiliation or Control: United Methodist — IRS Status: 501(c)3
Highest Offering: Baccalaureate
Accreditation: SC, SW

01 President ... Dr. Ivy R. TAYLOR
100 Chief of Staff ... Mrs. Tiffani PERRY
10 Vice President for Finance ... Dr. Daarel BURNETTE
05 Vice President for Academic Affairs ... Dr. Rolondus R. RICE
32 Vice Pres Student Engagement ... Dr. Dartell TREADWELL
84 Vice Pres Enrollment Management ... Dr. Jason K. JOHNSON
111 AVP Institutional Advancement ... Mrs. Tiffiney GRAY
06 Interim Dir of Registration Service ... Mrs. Marilyn CURRY
08 Interim Library Director ... Mrs. Wanda PEGUES
13 Director Computer Center ... Vacant
35 Director Student Activities ... Mr. Gino PIERRE
37 Director of Financial Aid ... Ms. Arlisha WALTON
25 Director Contracts & Grants ... Vacant
29 Director Alumni Development ... Ms. JoAnn SCOTT
89 Director FYE & Student Enrichment ... Ms. Talisa BOSWELL
21 Comptroller ... Mrs. Sandra C. DAWKINS
23 Director Student Health Services ... Ms. Jannie LUELLEN
39 Director Student Housing ... Vacant
36 Director of Career Pathways ... Ms. Sandra BURKE
18 Director Physical Plant ... Mr. Tracy HAMPTON
83 Division Chair Social Science ... Dr. Alfred J. STOVALL
15 Human Resources Manager ... Mrs. Angela WILLIAMS
19 Chief of Security ... Mr. Eric SCOTT

30	Director of Development	Ms. Jo Ann SCOTT
40	Bookstore Manager	Mrs. Patricia HARRIS
42	College Chaplain	Rev. Sapada THOMAS
96	Director of Purchasing	Vacant
50	Division Chair Business	Mr. Richard FREDERICK
53	Division Chair Education	Dr. Marrix SEYMORE
79	Division Chair Humanities	Dr. Margaret DELASHMIT
81	Chair Division Science & Math	Dr. Doris WARD
70	Chair Department of Social Work	Mrs. Debra BUTLER
105	Director Web Services	Mr. Gino PETERSON
41	Athletic Director	Mr. Jarvis STEPHEN
106	Dir Online Education/E-learning	Dr. Helen OLIVER
09	Director of Institutional Research	Vacant
91	Director Administrative Computing	Vacant
04	Admin Assistant to the President	Mrs. Willa J. TERRY
22	Dir Affirm Action/Equal Opportunity	Mrs. Angela WILLIAMS
26	Director of Public Relations	Ms. Mary LESUEUR
44	Director Annual Giving	Ms. Kimberly WOODS

Southeastern Baptist College (A)

4229 Highway 15 N, Laurel MS 39440-1096

County: Jones — FICE Identification: 002435 — Unit ID: 176336

Telephone: (601) 426-6346 — Carnegie Class: Spec-4-yr-Faith

FAX Number: (601) 426-6347 — Calendar System: Semester

URL: www.southeasternbaptist.edu

Established: 1948 — Annual Undergrad Tuition & Fees: $6,275

Enrollment: 62 — Coed

Affiliation or Control: Baptist — IRS Status: 501(c)3

Highest Offering: Baccalaureate

Accreditation: BI

01	President	Dr. Scott CARSON
05	Academic Dean	Mrs. Janice WALKER
06	Registrar	Mrs. Caroline ADAMS
07	Director of Admissions	Mrs. Anderle FOSTER
37	Director of Financial Aid	Mrs. Ginny SINGLETON
08	Director of Library	Mrs. Kathy ROBINSON
41	Director of Athletics	Mr. Richard LOPEZ
13	Director Information Technology	Mr. Hubert DYESS
09	Director of Institutional Research	Mrs. Christina LUCAS

Southwest Mississippi Community College (B)

1156 College Drive, Summit MS 39666-9029

County: Pike — FICE Identification: 002436 — Unit ID: 176354

Telephone: (601) 276-2000 — Carnegie Class: Assoc/MT-VT-High Trad

FAX Number: (601) 276-3888 — Calendar System: Semester

URL: www.smcc.edu

Established: 1918 — Annual Undergrad Tuition & Fees (In-District): $3,380

Enrollment: 1,888 — Coed

Affiliation or Control: Local — IRS Status: 501(c)3

Highest Offering: Associate Degree

Accreditation: SC, ADNUR, CAHIIM

01	President	Dr. Steve BISHOP
05	Vice President of Academic Affairs	Ms. Alicia SHOWS
10	Vice President of Financial Affairs	Mr. Andrew ALFORD
32	Vice President of Student Affairs	Mr. Blake BREWER
18	Vice Pres Physical Resources	Mr. Bill TUCKER
06	Vice President Admissions/Registrar	Mr. Matthew CALHOUN
75	Asst VP for CTE	Dr. Addie BOONE
37	Director Financial Aid	Ms. Amber KELLY
09	Director of Institutional Research	Mr. Matthew CALHOUN
08	Librarian	Ms. Natalie MCMAHON
39	Dir Student Activities/Housing	Mrs. Lauren WOODWORTH

Tougaloo College (C)

500 West County Line Road, Tougaloo MS 39174-9999

County: Madison — FICE Identification: 002439 — Unit ID: 176406

Telephone: (601) 977-7730 — Carnegie Class: Bac-A&S

FAX Number: (601) 977-7739 — Calendar System: Semester

URL: www.tougaloo.edu

Established: 1869 — Annual Undergrad Tuition & Fees: $10,861

Enrollment: 775 — Coed

Affiliation or Control: United Church Of Christ — IRS Status: 501(c)3

Highest Offering: Master's

Accreditation: SC

01	President	Dr. Carmen J. WALTERS
05	Provost/VP Academic Affairs	Dr. Leon C. WILSON
10	CFO/VP for Finance and Admin	Vacant
84	VP of Enroll Mgmt/Student Services	Dr. Whitney MCDOWELL-ROBINSON
111	VP Institutional Advancement	Mrs. Sandra HODGE
100	Chief of Staff	Dr. Linda DANIELS
18	Asst VP for Facilities/Real Prop	Mr. Claude E. BROWN
08	Int Director of Library Services	Ms. Stefanie TAYLOR
13	Chief Information Officer	Ms. LaMica JUSTICE
37	Director of Student Financial Aid	Vacant
06	Registrar	Vacant
15	Director Human Resources	Vacant
29	Director of Alumni Affairs	Mrs. Doris BRIDGEMAN
36	Int Director of Career Services	Dr. Melissa MCCOY
25	Int Dir of Sponsored Pgms/Research	Dr. Christina GLADNEY
88	Director of TRiO	Dr. Valvia WILSON
38	Director of Counseling Services	Vacant
96	Business Operations Manager	Ms. Tracey MINOR
19	Director Security/Safety	Ms. Edna DRAKE
39	Director Residential Life	Ms. Adrienne GREEN
104	Director Study Abroad Education	Vacant
105	Director Web Services	Mr. D'Cory OWENS
41	Athletic Director	Mr. Keith BARNES
04	Executive Asst to the President	Mrs. Latona BANKS
07	Director of Admissions	Mr. Paul SCOTT, SR.
09	Director of Institutional Research	Ms. Demetria WHITE HOWARD

University of Mississippi (D)

P.O. Box 1848, University MS 38677

County: Lafayette — FICE Identification: 002440 — Unit ID: 176017

Telephone: (662) 915-7211 — Carnegie Class: DU-Highest

FAX Number: (662) 915-7010 — Calendar System: Semester

URL: www.olemiss.edu

Established: 1844 — Annual Undergrad Tuition & Fees (In-State): $8,828

Enrollment: 21,014 — Coed

Affiliation or Control: State — IRS Status: 501(c)3

Highest Offering: Doctorate

Accreditation: SC, ART, CACREP, CAEPN, CAPRT, CEA, CLPSY, DIETC, DIETD, FEPAC, JOUR, LAW, MUS, PHAR, SP, SW, THEA

01	Chancellor	Dr. Glenn BOYCE
05	Provost/Exec Vice Chancellor	Dr. Noel E. WILKIN
10	Vice Chanc Administration & Finance	Mr. Steven HOLLEY
32	Vice Chancellor of Student Affairs	Dr. Charlotte FANT PEGUES
46	VC Research/Sponsored Programs	Dr. Josh GLADDEN
28	VC of Diversity/Cmty Engagement	Ms. Shawnboda MEAD
30	Vice Chanc Development	Mrs. Charlotte PARKS
26	Chief Marketing/Communications Ofcr	Mr. Jim ZOOK
35	Asst VC Student Affs/Dean Students	Dr. Brent MARSH
51	Assoc Prov/Dir Outreach/Cont Stds	Dr. Tony AMMETER
08	Dean of Libraries	Ms. Cecilia BOTERO
13	Chief Information Officer	Mr. Nishanth RODRIGUES
110	Exec Director Development	Mr. Denson HOLLIS
29	Exec Director of Alumni Affairs	Mr. Kirk PURDOM
37	Director of Financial Aid	Mrs. Laura DIVEN-BROWN
36	Director of Career Center	Ms. Toni D. AVANT
41	VC of Intercollegiate Athletics	Mr. Keith CARTER
15	AVC/Dir of Human Res & Contr Svcs	Vacant
18	Director of Facilities Management	Mr. Dean HANSEN
19	Dir/Chief Univ Police/Campus Safety	Mr. Ray HAWKINS
38	Dir of University Counseling Center	Dr. Quinton T. EDWARDS, JR.
23	Director University Health Services	Mr. Alex LANGHART
39	AVC Student Affairs/Housing	Mr. Lionel MATEN
09	Director Institutional Research	Dr. Katie BUSBY
22	Dir Equal Oppty/Reg Compliance	Ms. Rebecca B. BRESSLER
100	Special Assistant to the Chancellor	Mrs. Sue T. KEISER
43	General Counsel & Chief Legal Ofcr	Ms. Erica MCKINLEY
96	Director of Procurement Services	Ms. Rachel R. BOST
06	Interim Registrar	Mrs. Denise KNIGHTON
21	Controller	Mrs. Nina JONES
07	Interim Director of Admissions	Mrs. Jody LOWE
50	Dean School of Business Admin	Dr. Kendall B. CYREE
49	Dean College of Liberal Arts	Dr. Lee COHEN
81	Dean School of Applied Sciences	Dr. Peter W. GRANDJEAN
53	Dean School of Education	Dr. David ROCK
54	Dean School of Engineering	Dr. David PULEO
61	Dean School of Law	Dr. Susan DUNCAN
67	Dean of the School of Pharmacy	Dr. David D. ALLEN
88	Dean School of Accountancy	Dr. W. Mark WILDER
60	Int Dean Sch Journalism/New Media	Ms. Debora WENGER
58	Dean of the Graduate School	Dr. Annette KLUCK
92	Dean of SM Barksdale Honors College	Dr. Douglass SULLIVAN-GONZALEZ
86	Special Asst to Chanc for Govt Affs	Mr. Perry SANSING
88	University Ombudsman	Mr. Paul CAFFERA
116	Director of Audit	Ms. Tanya SATTERFIELD
104	Sr Intl Ofcr/Director Study Abroad	Ms. Blair MCELROY
44	Director Annual Giving	Mrs. Maura LANGHART
39	Director of Student Housing	Mr. John YAUN
84	Vice Chancellor Enrollment Mgmt	Mr. Eduardo PRIETO

University of Mississippi Medical Center (E)

2500 N State Street, Jackson MS 39216-4505

County: Hinds — FICE Identification: 004688 — Unit ID: 17601701

Telephone: (601) 984-1000 — Carnegie Class: Not Classified

FAX Number: (601) 984-1013 — Calendar System: Semester

URL: www.umc.edu

Established: 1955 — Annual Undergrad Tuition & Fees (In-State): N/A

Enrollment: N/A — Coed

Affiliation or Control: State — IRS Status: 501(c)3

Highest Offering: Doctorate

Accreditation: SC, CAHIIM, DENT, DH, HT, IPSY, MED, MT, NMT, NURSE, OT, PHAR, PTA, RAD, RADMAG

01	Vice Chancellor Health Affairs	Dr. LouAnn WOODWARD
05	Assoc VC for Academic Affairs	Dr. Ralph H. DIDLAKE
23	Assoc VC for Clinical Affairs	Dr. Alan E. JONES
46	Associate Vice Chanc Research	Dr. Richard SUMMERS
10	Chief Financial Officer	Mr. Nelson WEICHOLD
17	CEO Adult Hospitals	Mr. Britt H. CREWSE
17	CEO Children's of Mississippi	Dr. Guy B. GIESECKE
17	CEO Community Hospitals	Ms. Dodie T. MCELMURRAY
26	Exec Dir Communications & Mktg	Mr. Marc ROLPH
15	Chief Human Resources Officer	Ms. Molly A. BRASFIELD
63	Vice Dean for Medical Educ SOM	Dr. Loretta JACKSON-WILLIAMS
28	Chief Diversity & Inclusion Officer	Dr. Juanyce TAYLOR
100	Chief of Staff to Vice Chancellor	Dr. Brian RUTLEDGE
43	Chief Legal Officer	Mr. William C. SMITH, III
11	Chief Administrative Officer	Dr. Jonathan WILSON
76	Dean Sch Health Related Professions	Dr. Jessica H. BAILEY
69	Interim Dean School Pop Health	Dr. Natalie W. GAUGHF
58	Dean Sch Grad Stds Health Sciences	Dr. Joey GRANGER
66	Dean School of Nursing	Dr. Julie SANFORD
52	Dean of School of Dentistry	Dr. Sreenivas KOKA
67	Assoc Dean for Clinical Affs/SOPH	Dr. Leigh A. ROSS

University of Southern Mississippi (F)

118 College Drive, #5001, Hattiesburg MS 39406-0001

County: Forrest — FICE Identification: 002441 — Unit ID: 176372

Telephone: (601) 266-1000 — Carnegie Class: DU-Highest

FAX Number: (601) 266-5756 — Calendar System: Semester

URL: www.usm.edu

Established: 1910 — Annual Undergrad Tuition & Fees (In-State): $8,896

Enrollment: 14,606 — Coed

Affiliation or Control: State — IRS Status: 501(c)3

Highest Offering: Doctorate

Accreditation: SC, AAFCS, ANEST, ART, AUD, CAATE, CAEP, CIDA, CLPSY, CONST, COPSY, DANCE, DIETD, DIETI, JOUR, KIN, LIB, MFCD, MPCAC, MT, MUS, NURSE, PH, SCPSY, SP, SW, THEA

01	President	Dr. Rodney D. BENNETT
04	Executive Asst to the President	Dr. Steven MILLER
05	Provost & SVP for Academic Affairs	Dr. Steven MOSER
10	VP Finance & Administration	Ms. Allyson EASTERWOOD
32	VP Student Affairs	Dr. Deanna ANDERSON
12	Sr Assoc VP for Coastal Operations	Dr. Shannon CAMPBELL
20	Exec Vice Provost	Dr. Amy CHASTEEN
108	Sr Assoc Prov Inst Effectiveness	Dr. Doug MASTERSON
46	VP for Research	Dr. Gordon CANNON
50	Dean College Business	Dr. Bret BECTON
66	Dean College Nursing	Dr. Lachel STORY
49	Dean College Arts & Sciences	Dr. Chris WINSTEAD
92	Interim Dean of Honors College	Dr. Sabine HEINHORST
53	Dean College Educ & Human Sciences	Dr. Trent GOULD
58	Dean Graduate School	Dr. Karen COATS
08	Dean/University Librarian	Dr. John EYE
18	Assoc VP Planning & Facilities Mgmt	Dr. Chris CRENSHAW
13	Chief Information Officer	Mr. David SLIMAN
06	Registrar	Mr. Greg PIERCE
25	Asst VP for Research Administration	Ms. Marcia LANDEN
45	Dir of Institutional Effectiveness	Mrs. Kathryn LOWERY
29	Alumni Activities/Exec Director	Mr. Jerry DEFATTA
36	Director Career Services	Mr. Russell ANDERSON
22	Interim Title IX Coordinator	Ms. Cristin REYNOLDS
38	Interim Dir Counseling Center	Ms. April ESTILL
23	Director of Health Services	Dr. Melissa ROBERTS
35	Dean of Students	Ms. Sirena CANTRELL
15	Associate VP of Human Resources	Mrs. Krystyna VARNADO
96	Director Procurement & Contracts	Mr. Steve BALLEW
07	Asst Dir of Recruitment	Ms. Susan W. SCOTT
88	Dir of Vet & Military Student Svcs	Gen. Jeff HAMMOND
102	Exec Dir USM Foundation	Ms. Stace L. MERCIER
104	Assoc VP for Intl Programs	Dr. Daniel NORTON
106	Dir Office of Online Learning	Dr. Tom HUTCHINSON
43	Dir Legal Services/General Counsel	Mr. Robert D. GHOLSON
86	Vice President for External Affairs	Mr. Chad DRISKELL
37	Director Student Financial Aid	Mr. David WILLIAMSON
09	Director of Institutional Research	Dr. Megan MCCAY
19	Chief of Police	Chief Rusty KEYES
26	Chief Communications Officer	Mr. James P. COLL
41	Director of Athletics	Mr. Jeremy MCCLAIN
28	Chief Diversity Officer	Ms. Kimbaya BROWN

Wesley Biblical Seminary (G)

1880 E County Line Rd, Ridgeland MS 39157

County: Madison — FICE Identification: 025162 — Unit ID: 176451

Telephone: (601) 366-8880 — Carnegie Class: Spec-4-yr-Faith

FAX Number: (601) 510-9114 — Calendar System: Semester

URL: www.wbs.edu

Established: 1974 — Annual Graduate Tuition & Fees: N/A

Enrollment: 158 — Coed

Affiliation or Control: Interdenominational — IRS Status: 501(c)3

Highest Offering: Master's; No Undergraduates

Accreditation: THEOL

01	President	Dr. Matthew I. AYARS
05	VP Academic Affairs/Academic Dean	Dr. Andy MILLER, III
10	VP of Business Affairs	Mr. Ethan KELLY
84	VP of Enrollment	Mr. Elijah FRIEDEMAN
30	Director of Development	Mrs. Maribeth GIBSON
21	Director Business Affairs	Ms. Peggy PRICE
08	Director of Library Services	Ms. Grace ANDREWS
06	Registrar/Director Financial Aid	Mr. Karl LUMAN

William Carey University (H)

710 William Carey Parkway, Hattiesburg MS 39401

County: Forrest — FICE Identification: 002447 — Unit ID: 176479

Telephone: (601) 318-6051 — Carnegie Class: DU-Mod

FAX Number: N/A — Calendar System: Trimester

URL: www.wmcarey.edu
Established: 1892 Annual Undergrad Tuition & Fees: $13,650
Enrollment: 5,472 Coed
Affiliation or Control: Southern Baptist IRS Status: 501(c)3
Highest Offering: Doctorate
Accreditation: SC, CAEPN, CAHIIM, IACBE, MUS, NURSE, OSTEO, PHAR, PTA

01 President/Chief Executive Officer ....Dr. Tommy KING
03 Executive Vice President ....Dr. Benjamin BURNETT
05 Vice President of Academic Affairs ....Dr. Daniel CALDWELL
10 Vice Pres Business Affs/CFO ....Mr. Grant GUTHRIE
32 Vice Pres for Student Support ....Mrs. Valerie BRIDGEFORTH
46 Vice President Inst Effectiveness ....Dr. Bennie R. CROCKETT
88 VP for Spiritual Development ....Dr. Brett GOLSON
17 Associate VP for Health Programs ....Dr. Janet WILLIAMS
63 Dean College Osteopathic Medicine ....Dr. Italo SUBBARAO
12 Admin/Acad Dean Tradition Campus ....Dr. Cassandra CONNER
50 Dean School of Business ....Dr. Cheryl DALE
53 Dean School of Education ....Dr. Teresa POOLE
83 Dean Sch Natural/Behavioral Science ....Dr. Frank BAUGH
66 Dean School of Nursing ....Dr. Alicia LUNDSTROM
49 Dean School of Arts & Letters ....Dr. Myron NOONKESTER
64 Dean School of Music ....Dr. Wes DYKES
58 Dean of Graduate Studies ....Dr. Frank BAUGH
73 Dean School of Ministry Studies ....Dr. Brett GOLSON
06 Registrar ....Ms. Rachel SINGLETON
08 Dean Libraries & Learning Resource ....Mr. Reese POWELL
29 Alumni Director ....Mrs. Pam SHEARER
26 Coordinator of Media Relations ....Ms. Suzanne MONK
13 Chief Information Officer ....Mr. Jeff ANDREWS
92 Director of Honors Program ....Dr. David LOWERY
41 Athletic Director ....Mr. D. J PULLEY
18 Dir Facilities/Grounds/Maintenance ....Mr. Robert BLEVINS
15 Associate VP of Human Resources ....Dr. Deidre SHOWS
07 Director of Admissions ....Ms. Meagan E. SMITH
04 Administrative Asst to President ....Mrs. Charlotte GREEN
106 E-Learning Coordinator ....Ms. Shanna MURRAY-LUKE
102 Assoc VP for University Enhancement ....Dr. Angela HOUSTON
37 Director Student Financial Aid ....Mr. Bill CURRY
39 Director of Housing ....Mr. Jared ACKLEY
43 General Legal Counsel ....Mrs. Julie HAWKINS
44 Annual Fund Director ....Mrs. Karen GOLSON

MISSOURI

A. T. Still University of Health Sciences (A)

800 W Jefferson Street, Kirksville MO 63501-1497
County: Adair FICE Identification: 002477
Unit ID: 177834
Telephone: (660) 626-2391 Carnegie Class: Spec-4-yr-Med
FAX Number: (660) 626-2672 Calendar System: Semester
URL: www.atsu.edu
Established: 1892 Annual Graduate Tuition & Fees: N/A
Enrollment: 3,995 Coed
Affiliation or Control: Independent Non-Profit IRS Status: 501(c)3
Highest Offering: First Professional Degree; No Undergraduates
Accreditation: HLC, DENT, OSTEO, PH

01 President ....Dr. Craig PHELPS
05 Sr VP Academic Affairs ....Dr. Norman GEVITZ
63 Dean KCOM ....Dr. Margaret WILSON
32 VP Student Affairs ....Mrs. Lori HAXTON
111 VP University Advancement ....Dr. Shaun SOMMERER
43 VP & General Counsel ....Mr. Matthew HEEREN
10 VP Finance & Administration/CFO ....Ms. Dana FUNDERBURK
13 VP Info Technologies/Services ....Mr. Bryan KRUSNIAK
52 Dean MO Sch of Dentistry/Oral Hlth ....Dr. Dwight MCLEOD
58 Dean Col of Graduate Hlth Studies ....Dr. Don ALTMAN
52 Dean AZ Sch of Dentistry/Oral Hlth ....Dr. Robert TROMBLY
76 Dean AZ Sch of Health Sciences ....Dr. Ann Lee BURCH
63 Dean Sch of Osteo Med in AZ ....Dr. Jeffrey MORGAN
35 Assoc VP AZ Student Affairs ....Dr. Beth POPPRE
07 Asst VP Admissions ....Dr. David KOENECKE
88 VP Univ Strat Partnershps/Diversity ....Dr. Gary CLOUD
45 Sr VP Strat Planning & Univ Init ....Dr. O.T WENDEL
46 VP Research & Grants ....Mrs. Gaylah SUBLETTE
04 Asst to Pres & Secretary to BoT ....Mrs. Norine EITEL
06 Registrar ....Dr. Deanna HUNSAKER
08 University Librarian ....Mr. Harold BRIGHT
15 Asst VP Human Resources/AA Ofcr .Mrs. Donna BROWN WYATT
18 Director Facilities/Plant Operation ....Mr. Robert EHRLICH
96 Director Purchasing ....Mr. Corey LOUDER
19 Director Security ....Mr. Jim HUGHES
28 VP of Diversity/Inclusion ....Mr. Clinton NORMORE
20 SVP Academic Affairs ....Dr. Ann BOYLE
110 Associate VP University Advancement ....Mr. Bob BEHNEN
51 Assistant VP Continuing Education ....Dr. Lloyd CLEAVER
21 Assistant VP for Finance ....Mrs. Tonya GRIMM
09 Director AT Still Research Inst ....Dr. Brian DEGENHARDT
29 Assoc Director Alumni Relations ....Mrs. Melody CHAMBERS

† Arizona campus accreditation includes ARPCA, AUD, CAATE, DENT, OSTEO, OT, PTA.

American Business & Technology University (B)

1018 West Saint Maartens Drive, Saint Joseph MO 64506
County: Buchanan FICE Identification: 041187
Unit ID: 457688
Telephone: (816) 279-7000 Carnegie Class: Bac/Assoc-Mixed
FAX Number: (888) 890-8190 Calendar System: Other
URL: www.abtu.edu
Established: 2001 Annual Undergrad Tuition & Fees: N/A
Enrollment: 353 Coed
Affiliation or Control: Proprietary IRS Status: Proprietary
Highest Offering: Master's
Accreditation: DEAC

01 President ....Mr. Ramsey ATIEH
11 CEO ....Mr. Lute ATIEH
88 VP of Strategic Initiatives ....Mr. Eddie COLON
37 VP of Financial Aid/Compliance ....Dr. Michael CAMPBELL
05 Chief Academic Officer ....Dr. Luanne HAGGARD
13 Chief Information Officer ....Mr. Ramsey ATIEH
10 Chief Financial Officer ....Mr. Dan MARLOW
20 Program Development Officer ....Dr. Donald LADER
108 Accreditation/Compliance Officer ....Mr. Chad BREAZILE
06 Registrar ....Mrs. Kourtney DRAKE
07 Director of Admissions ....Mr. Richard LINGLE
29 Director Alumni/Career Services ....Ms. Debra HAYES

American Trade School (C)

3925 Industrial Drive, Saint Ann MO 63074
County: Saint Louis FICE Identification: 041748
Unit ID: 461573
Telephone: (314) 423-1900 Carnegie Class: Spec 2-yr-Tech
FAX Number: (314) 423-1911 Calendar System: Quarter
URL: www.americantradeschool.edu
Established: 2003 Annual Undergrad Tuition & Fees: N/A
Enrollment: 128 Coed
Affiliation or Control: Proprietary IRS Status: Proprietary
Highest Offering: Associate Degree
Accreditation: ACCSC

01 Ceo/President/Director ....Mr. John VATTEROTT, JR.

Aquinas Institute of Theology (D)

23 South Spring Avenue, Saint Louis MO 63108-3323
County: City of Saint Louis FICE Identification: 001632
Unit ID: 176600
Telephone: (314) 256-8800 Carnegie Class: Spec-4-yr-Faith
FAX Number: N/A Calendar System: Semester
URL: www.ai.edu
Established: 1951 Annual Graduate Tuition & Fees: N/A
Enrollment: 124 Coed
Affiliation or Control: Roman Catholic IRS Status: 501(c)3
Highest Offering: Doctorate; No Undergraduates
Accreditation: THEOL

01 President ....Rev. Mark WEDIG, OP
05 Academic Dean ....Rev. Michael MASCARI, OP
11 Exec Director of Operations ....Br. John STEILBERG, OP
20 Coordinator of Admin Affairs ....Ms. Mary URBANEK-MUELLER
84 Coordinator of Enrollment Mgmt ....Ms. Jessica ADAMS
06 Registrar ....Ms. Mary URBANEK-MUELLER
13 Coordinator of Inst Technology ....Mr. Tim ROESSLEIN
26 Coordinator of Marketing & Comm ....Mr. Michael WINTERS
10 Chief Financial/Business Officer ....Mrs. Donna THRO
30 Coordinator of Development ....Ms. Erin HAMMOND

Assemblies of God Theological Seminary (E)

1111 N Glenstone Avenue, Springfield MO 65802-2131
County: Greene FICE Identification: 012120
Unit ID: 176619
Telephone: (417) 268-1000 Carnegie Class: Spec-4-yr-Faith
FAX Number: (417) 268-1001 Calendar System: Semester
URL: www.agts.edu
Established: 1972 Annual Graduate Tuition & Fees: N/A
Enrollment: N/A Coed
Affiliation or Control: Assemblies Of God Church IRS Status: 501(c)3
Highest Offering: Doctorate; No Undergraduates
Accreditation: THEOL

05 Vice President/Dean of AGTS ....Dr. Timothy A. HAGER
84 Vice President of Enrollment ....Mr. Chris BELCHER
111 Vice President of Advancement ....Dr. Michael KOLSTAD
20 Associate Dean ....Dr. Paul W. LEWIS
58 Dir Intercultural Doctoral Studies ....Dr. Mike MCATEER
58 Dir PhD Biblical Interpr/Theology ....Dr. Paul W. LEWIS
58 Director DMin Program ....Dr. John A. BATTAGLIA
32 Student Life Coordinator ....Mr. Alex L. BRYANT
88 Veteran Center Coordinator ....Mr. Dane MOORE
08 Seminary & Instruction Librarian ....Mr. Matthew CLARK
06 Assistant Registrar Seminary ....Mrs. Kathy L. HARRISON
37 Financial Aid Counselor ....Mrs. Katie FINZO
29 Director Alumni Engagement ....Mr. Hector CRUZ
88 Executive Assistant to the Deans ....Mrs. Cara R. CROSS
26 Director of Public Relations & Adv ....Mrs. Erin HEDLUN
112 AGTS Major Gifts Officer ....Ms. Soncee PARTIDA

† The Seminary continues to offer its educational programs as a distinct unit within the consolidated Evangel University, Springfield, MO.

Avila University (F)

11901 Wornall Road, Kansas City MO 64145-9990
County: Jackson FICE Identification: 002449
Unit ID: 176628
Telephone: (816) 942-8400 Carnegie Class: Masters/M
FAX Number: (816) 942-3362 Calendar System: Semester
URL: www.avila.edu
Established: 1916 Annual Undergrad Tuition & Fees: $21,115
Enrollment: 1,414 Coed
Affiliation or Control: Roman Catholic IRS Status: 501(c)3
Highest Offering: Master's
Accreditation: HLC, CAEP, IACBE, MPCAC, NURSE, RAD, SW

01 President ....Dr. Ron SLEPITZA
05 Provost/VP of Academic Affairs ....Dr. Ted WHAPHAM
10 Vice Pres for Finance/Admin Svcs ....Mr. Tim KLOCKO
84 VP for Enrollment & Athletics ....Dr. Alexandra ADAMS
32 AVP Student Development/Success ....Ms. Darby GOUGH
13 VP for Information Services ....Mr. Jon GAMBILL
26 Sr Dir Marketing/Communications ....Mr. Darren ROUBINEK
111 Interim VP of Advancement ....Ms. Maggie MOHRFELD
06 Registrar/Director Student Records ....Ms. Michelle DRISCOLL
08 Director of Library ....Ms. Becky NICHOLS
37 Director of Financial Aid ....Mr. Michael PEPPLE
42 Dir Mission Effect/Campus Ministry ..Mr. David M. ARMSTRONG
21 Controller ....Mr. Joseph H. SJUTS
30 Sr Director of Development ....Ms. Bailey CARR
41 Director of Athletics ....Mr. Sean SUMME
15 Director of Human Resources ....Ms. Nancy BURFORD
18 Director Campus Services ....Vacant
40 Bookstore Manager ....Mr. John A. TARANTO
38 Coord Counseling & Career Services ....Ms. Taryn HODISON
04 University Executive Assistant ....Ms. Malissa TOLLIVER
07 Dir of Undergraduate Admissions ....Mr. Josh PARISSE
09 Director Institutional Research ....Mr. Rusty MCLOUTH

Baptist Bible College (G)

628 E Kearney St, Springfield MO 65803-3498
County: Greene FICE Identification: 013208
Unit ID: 176664
Telephone: (417) 268-6000 Carnegie Class: Spec-4-yr-Faith
FAX Number: (800) 819-8330 Calendar System: Semester
URL: www.gobbc.edu
Established: 1950 Annual Undergrad Tuition & Fees: $14,890
Enrollment: 222 Coed
Affiliation or Control: Baptist IRS Status: 501(c)3
Highest Offering: Master's
Accreditation: HLC, BI

01 President ....Mr. Mark L. MILIONI
05 Academic Dean ....Mr. Terry A. ALLCORN
10 Vice President of Financial Affairs ....Mr. Jason L. TODD
32 Vice President of Student Affairs ....Mr. Nathaniel S. HARMON
18 Chief Facilities/Physical Plant ....Mr. Chris C. WILLIAMS
06 Registrar ....Mr. Terry A. ALLCORN
84 Director of Enrollment Services ....Mr. Nathaniel S. HARMON
37 Director of Financial Aid ....Mr. Brian RAINS
33 Dean of Men ....Mr. Bill J. LEVERGOOD
34 Dean of Women ....Mrs. Tina L. EBERT
15 Director of Human Resources ....Miss Emily MILIONI
19 Director of Security/Safety ....Mr. Glenn COZZENS
08 Director of Library Services ....Mr. Jon JONES
04 Administrative Asst to President ....Mrs. Barbara MILIONI
09 Director of Institutional Research ....Mr. Shannon L. MULFORD
108 Dir of Institutional Effectiveness ....Mr. Roland Q. DUDLEY
41 Athletic Director ....Mr. Darin MEINDERS

Bolivar Technical College (H)

1135 North Oakland Avenue, Bolivar MO 65613
County: Polk FICE Identification: 042557
Unit ID: 490203
Telephone: (417) 777-5062 Carnegie Class: Spec 2-yr-Health
FAX Number: (417) 777-8908 Calendar System: Semester
URL: https://www.bolivarcollege.edu/
Established: 1996 Annual Undergrad Tuition & Fees: N/A
Enrollment: N/A Coed
Affiliation or Control: Independent Non-Profit IRS Status: 501(c)3
Highest Offering: Associate Degree
Accreditation: ABHES

02 President/Campus Director ....Ms. Charlotte GRAY
03 Vice President ....Dr. William GRAY
05 Academic Director/Admissions ....Mr. Nancy BRANNON
26 Marketing Director ....Ms. Rachael HENEISE

Brookes Bible College (I)

10257 St. Charles Rock Road, St Louis MO 63074
County: St. Louis Identification: 667137
Telephone: (314) 773-0083 Carnegie Class: Not Classified
FAX Number: (314) 736-6293 Calendar System: Semester
URL: www.brookes.edu
Established: 1909 Annual Undergrad Tuition & Fees: N/A
Enrollment: N/A Coed
Affiliation or Control: Independent Non-Profit IRS Status: 501(c)3
Highest Offering: Baccalaureate
Accreditation: BI

01 President ....Rev. Robert D. THURMAN, JR.
00 Chairman of the Board ....Dr. James CLARK
106 VP Online Learning and Cohorts ....Rev. Joshua CLUTTERHAM
05 Chief Academic Officer ....Vacant
10 Chief Financial Officer ....Mr. Brian TOENNIES
08 Librarian ....Mrs. Amy PEARCE
30 Chief Advancement Officer ....Dr. Robert B. RICKETT
32 Student Ministry Director ....Mr. Verle CLINES

Bryan University (A)

4255 Nature Center Way, Springfield MO 65804

County: Greene FICE Identification: 030663
Unit ID: 369516
Telephone: (417) 862-5700 Carnegie Class: Bac/Assoc-Mixed
FAX Number: (417) 865-7144 Calendar System: Other
URL: www.bryanu.edu
Established: 1982 Annual Undergrad Tuition & Fees: $15,782
Enrollment: 275 Coed
Affiliation or Control: Proprietary IRS Status: Proprietary
Highest Offering: Master's
Accreditation: ACICS

01 Executive Director ... Mr. Scott HAAR

Calvary University (B)

15800 Calvary Road, Kansas City MO 64147-1341

County: Cass FICE Identification: 002450
Unit ID: 176789
Telephone: (816) 322-0110 Carnegie Class: Spec-4-yr-Faith
FAX Number: (816) 331-4474 Calendar System: Semester
URL: www.calvary.edu
Established: 1932 Annual Undergrad Tuition & Fees: $11,164
Enrollment: 469 Coed
Affiliation or Control: Independent Non-Profit IRS Status: 501(c)3
Highest Offering: Doctorate
Accreditation: HLC, BI

01 President/CEO ... Dr. Alexander GRANADOS
11 Chief Operating Officer/VP ... Mr. Jeff CAMPA
10 Chief Financial Officer/VP ... Mr. Randy GRIMM
05 Chief Academic Officer/VP ... Dr. Teddy BITNER
111 Chief Development Officer/VP ... Mr. John MCGEE
41 Athletic Director ... Miss Jeanette REGIER
97 Dean of the College ... Dr. Luther SMITH
58 Dean of the Graduate School ... Dr. Germaine WASHINGTON
73 Dean of the Seminary ... Dr. Thomas BAURAIN
06 Registrar ... Mr. Gary ROGERS
13 Director Information Technology ... Mr. Aaron HEATH
19 Director of Security ... Mr. Allen PRODOEHL
37 Director of Financial Aid ... Mrs. Martha BYERS
08 Head Librarian ... Miss Tiffany SMITH
108 Director of Institutional Effective ... Dr. Allan HENDERSON
15 Human Resources Director ... Vacant
29 Alumni Relations Coordinator ... Mrs. Sara KLAASSEN
88 Director of Christian Ministries ... Mrs. Dawnita PHILLIPS
109 Director of Food Service ... Mr. Joe DAPRA
105 Director Web Services ... Vacant
32 Dean of Students ... Mr. Joshua JOHNSON
35 Associate Dean of Students ... Mrs. Jamie FRANZ
26 VP of Marketing & Communications ... Mr. Adam WEEKS
18 Director of Maintenance ... Mr. Anthony HARWELL
39 Residence Life Coordinator ... Mr. Samuel TSCHETTER

Carver Baptist Bible College, Institute & Theological Seminary (C)

8524 Blue Ridge Blvd, Kansas City MO 64138

County: Jackson Identification: 667418
Telephone: (816) 333-1577 Carnegie Class: Not Classified
FAX Number: N/A Calendar System: Semester
URL: carverbiblecollegekc.org
Established: 1942 Annual Undergrad Tuition & Fees: N/A
Enrollment: N/A Coed
Affiliation or Control: Independent Non-Profit IRS Status: 501(c)3
Highest Offering: Master's
Accreditation: @BI

01 President ... Dr. Antoine D. RICHARDSON

Central Christian College of the Bible (D)

911 E Urbandale Drive, Moberly MO 65270-1997

County: Randolph FICE Identification: 022664
Unit ID: 176910
Telephone: (660) 263-3900 Carnegie Class: Spec-4-yr-Faith
FAX Number: (660) 263-3936 Calendar System: Semester
URL: www.cccb.edu
Established: 1957 Annual Undergrad Tuition & Fees: $9,250
Enrollment: 186 Coed
Affiliation or Control: Christian Churches And Churches of Christ
IRS Status: 501(c)3
Highest Offering: Master's
Accreditation: BI

01 President ... Dr. David B. FINCHER
05 Vice President of Academics ... Dr. Jim ESTEP
10 Vice Pres of Business & Finance ... Mrs. Lara LAWRENCE
84 Vice Pres Enrollment Mgt/Marketing ... Mr. Brian TAYLOR
32 VP Student Development/Dean of Men ... Mr. Darryl C. AMMON
111 Vice Pres Advancement/Operations ... Mr. Janeil OWEN
07 Director of Admissions ... Mr. Jeremiah RATLIFF
04 Exec Assistant to the President ... Mrs. Sherry L. WALLIS
121 Dean of Student Success ... Dr. Eric A. STEVENS
06 Registrar/Assessment Coordinator ... Ms. Anne P. MENEAR
41 Athletic Director ... Mr. Jack DEFREITAS
08 Head Librarian ... Mrs. Patty A. AGEE
35 Dean of Students ... Mr. Joshua MILLER
37 Director of Financial Aid ... Ms. Veronica HAMBLIN
13 Director of Information Technology ... Mr. James WILLIAMSON
18 Physical Plant Manager ... Mr. Mark E. DUNHAM
40 Bookstore Manager ... Mrs. Tracey WILLIAMSON
39 Residence Director - Women ... Ms. Tina NIPPER
39 Residence Director - Men ... Mr. James WILLIAMSON
106 Director Online Education ... Mr. James FRANKE
30 Director of Development ... Mr. Kevin BROWN
107 Dean of Professional Studies ... Mr. Brandon BRADLEY

† Onsite students accepted into a degree or certificate program will receive Full-Tuition Scholarship which equals cost of tuition up to 18 hrs/semester. Scholarship may be reduced from deficiencies in grades, Christian service, or chapel attendance.

Central Methodist University (E)

411 Central Methodist Square, Fayette MO 65248-1198

County: Howard FICE Identification: 002453
Unit ID: 445267
Telephone: (660) 248-3391 Carnegie Class: Masters/S
FAX Number: (660) 248-2287 Calendar System: Semester
URL: www.centralmethodist.edu
Established: 1854 Annual Undergrad Tuition & Fees: $6,430
Enrollment: 3,429 Coed
Affiliation or Control: United Methodist IRS Status: 501(c)3
Highest Offering: Master's
Accreditation: HLC, CAATE, CACREP, MUS, NURSE, OTA, PTAA

01 President ... Dr. Roger D. DRAKE
05 Provost ... Dr. Rita GULSTAD
13 VP Technology & Planning ... Mr. Chad GAINES
111 VP Advancement/Alumni Rels ... Mr. William SHEEHAN
32 Dean of Students ... Mr. Brad DIXON
84 VP Enrollment Management ... Dr. Joseph PARISI
10 VP Finance & Administration ... Ms. Julee SHERMAN
08 Director of Information Resources ... Mr. Jordan RUSTEMEYER
37 Director of Financial Aid ... Ms. Brenda KREHBIEL
07 Director of Admissions ... Ms. Aimee SAGE
106 Asst Dean Online Programs ... Ms. Stephanie BRINK
09 Coordinator Institutional Research ... Ms. Amber MONNIG
26 Exec Dir Marketing Communications ... Mr. Scott QUEEN
04 Administrative Asst to President ... Ms. Whitney PARKS
15 Director of Human Resources ... Ms. Kimberly THOMSON
06 Registrar ... Ms. Brianne HILGEDICK
18 Chief Facilities/Physical Plant ... Mr. Derry WISWALL
19 Campus Safety Officer ... Mr. Don CLEAR
36 Dir Student Placement/Career Dev ... Ms. Nicolette YEVICH
40 Bookstore Manager ... Ms. Jill BARRINGHAUS
39 Coordinator of Residential Life ... Mr. Jordan SCHWELLENBACH
29 Director Alumni Affairs ... Ms. Stasia SHERMAN
41 Athletic Director ... Ms. Natasha WILSON

Chamberlain University-St. Louis (F)

11830 Westline Industrial, Ste 106, St. Louis MO 63146

Telephone: (314) 991-6200 Identification: 770494
Accreditation: &HLC, NURSE

† Branch campus of Chamberlain University-Addison, Addison, IL

City Vision University (G)

1100 E 11th Street, Kansas City MO 64106-3028

County: United States FICE Identification: 041191
Unit ID: 457697
Telephone: (816) 960-2008 Carnegie Class: Spec-4-yr-Other Health
FAX Number: (816) 256-8471 Calendar System: Other
URL: www.cityvision.edu
Established: 1998 Annual Undergrad Tuition & Fees: $6,000
Enrollment: 127 Coed
Affiliation or Control: Other IRS Status: 501(c)3
Highest Offering: Master's
Accreditation: DEAC

01 Executive Director/President ... Dr. Andrew SEARS
05 Chief Academic Officer ... Dr. Joshua REICHARD
83 Addiction Studies Department Chair ... Mrs. Lynda MITTON
10 Financial Aid/Accounting Manager ... Mrs. Traci HEDLUND
07 Director of Admissions ... Ms. Nancy YOUNG

† Mail address is 31 Torrey St, Dorchester, MA 02124-3543.

College of the Ozarks (H)

PO Box 17, Point Lookout MO 65726-0017

County: Taney FICE Identification: 002500
Unit ID: 178697
Telephone: (417) 334-6411 Carnegie Class: Bac-Diverse
FAX Number: N/A Calendar System: Semester
URL: www.cofo.edu
Established: 1906 Annual Undergrad Tuition & Fees: $19,960
Enrollment: 1,489 Coed
Affiliation or Control: Independent Non-Profit IRS Status: 501(c)3
Highest Offering: Baccalaureate
Accreditation: HLC, ACFEI, DIETD, NURSE, TRACS

01 President ... Dr. Jerry C. DAVIS
03 Vice President ... Dr. Howell W. KEETER
05 VP Academic Affairs/Dean of College ... Dr. Eric BOLGER
10 Chief Financial Officer ... Mr. Sam KETCHER
11 COO/VP Vocational Pgms ... Dr. Weston T. WIEBE
93 VP Cultural Affs/Dean Character Ed ... Dr. Sue HEAD
07 VP Patriotic Activities/Dean Admiss ... Dr. Marci LINSON
42 VP Christian Ministries/Dean Chapel ... Dr. Justin CARSWELL
30 Dean of Development ... Mrs. Natalie RASNICK
103 Dean of Work Education/Admin ... Mr. Bryan CIZEK
32 Dean of Students ... Dr. Nick SHARP
06 Registrar ... Mrs. Lacey MATTHEIS
29 Director of Alumni Affairs ... Mrs. Angela WILLIAMSON
36 Director of Career Center ... Mr. Jim FREEMAN
37 Director of Financial Aid ... Mr. Jeff FORD
26 Director of Public Relations ... Mrs. Valorie COLEMAN
96 Director of Purchasing ... Mr. Andy MCNEILL
38 Student Counseling ... Mrs. Pat MCLEAN
04 Assistant to the President ... Mrs. Tamara J. SCHNEIDER
04 Assistant to President Research ... Mrs. Elizabeth BLEVINS
13 Chief Info Technology Officer ... Mr. Jeffrey K. SCHNEIDER
18 Chief Facilities/Physical Plant ... Mr. Jody BRASWELL
41 Athletic Director ... Mr. Steve SHEPHERD
08 Librarian/Library Science ... Ms. Gwen SIMMONS
19 Director of Security ... Mr. Robert BRIDGES

Columbia College (I)

1001 Rogers Street, Columbia MO 65216-0001

County: Boone FICE Identification: 002456
Unit ID: 177065
Telephone: (573) 875-8700 Carnegie Class: Masters/L
FAX Number: (573) 875-7209 Calendar System: Semester
URL: www.ccis.edu
Established: 1851 Annual Undergrad Tuition & Fees: $24,320
Enrollment: 8,347 Coed
Affiliation or Control: Christian Church (Disciples Of Christ)
IRS Status: 501(c)3
Highest Offering: Master's
Accreditation: HLC, ADNUR, MAC, NURSE

01 Interim President ... Dr. David R. RUSSELL
05 Provost/Vice Pres Academic Affairs ... Dr. Piyusha SINGH
51 VP Adult Higher Education ... Dr. Jeff MUSGROVE
11 SVP/Chief Operations Officer ... Mr. Kevin PALMER
111 Vice President of Advancement ... Ms. Suzanne ROTHWELL
10 Chief Financial Officer ... Mr. Bruce E. BOYER
32 Dean of Student Affairs ... Mr. Dave ROBERTS
18 Exec Director of Plant/Facilities ... Mr. Cliff JARVIS
26 AVP of Marketing ... Mr. Brad WUCHER
07 AVP of Admissions ... Ms. Stephanie JOHNSON
06 Registrar ... Ms. Jennifer THORPE
29 Sr Director of Alumni Relations ... Ms. Ann MERRIFIELD
27 Sr Director of Public Relations ... Mr. Sam FLEURY
37 Int Director of Financial Aid ... Ms. Coleen BROWN
08 Director of Stafford Library ... Ms. Janet CARUTHERS
106 Dir Online Academic Programs ... Ms. Kate BOULERSOX
35 Director of Student Activities ... Ms. Kim COKE
36 Director Career Services Center ... Mr. Dan GOMEZ-PALACIO
15 Executive Director Human Resources ... Ms. Michelle MCCAULLEY
13 Chief Information Officer ... Mr. Gary STANOWSKI
55 Sr Dir Adult Higher Educ Acad Spprt ... Mr. Eric CUNNINGHAM
41 Director of Athletics ... Mr. Robert BURCHARD
09 Director Institutional Research ... Ms. Shonda IRELAND
19 Director of Campus Safety ... Mr. Robert KLAUSMEYER
113 Bursar ... Ms. Denise GELINA

Conception Seminary College (J)

37174 State Highway VV, PO Box 502, Conception MO 64433-0502

County: Nodaway FICE Identification: 002467
Unit ID: 177083
Telephone: (660) 944-3105 Carnegie Class: Spec-4-yr-Faith
FAX Number: (660) 944-2829 Calendar System: Semester
URL: www.conception.edu
Established: 1883 Annual Undergrad Tuition & Fees: $22,873
Enrollment: 42 Male
Affiliation or Control: Roman Catholic IRS Status: 501(c)3
Highest Offering: Baccalaureate
Accreditation: HLC

01 Rector & President ... VRev. Victor SCHINSTOCK, OSB
11 Director of Administration ... Mrs. Amy K. SCHIEBER
32 Vice Rector/Dean of Stdnts/ Chaplain ... Rev. Pachomius MEADE, OSB
05 Dean of Academic Affairs ... Dr. Elizabeth MCGRATH
10 Business Manager/Dir Auxiliary Svcs ... Bro. Jacob KUBAJAK
30 Development Director ... Mrs. Jenny HUARD
07 Director of Admissions/Registrar ... Mrs. Jeanette SCHIEBER
37 Director of Student Financial Aid ... Bro. Justin J. HERNANDEZ
29 Director of Alumni ... Bro. Thomas SULLIVAN, OSB
08 Librarian ... Mr. Chris BRITE
26 Director of Communications ... Mrs. Kaity HOLTMAN
13 Director of Information Technology ... Mr. Tony MEISTER
38 Director of Counseling Services ... Rev. Duane REINERT
41 Director of Wellness Program ... Mr. Skip SHEAR
18 Chief Facilities/Physical Plant ... Mr. Mark WIEDERHOLT

Concorde Career College (K)

3239 Broadway Street, Kansas City MO 64111-2407

County: Jackson FICE Identification: 023616
Unit ID: 155283
Telephone: (816) 531-5223 Carnegie Class: Spec-4-yr-Other Health
FAX Number: (816) 756-3231 Calendar System: Other
URL: https://www.concorde.edu/campus/kansas-city-missouri
Established: 1986 Annual Undergrad Tuition & Fees: N/A
Enrollment: 323 Coed

Affiliation or Control: Proprietary IRS Status: Proprietary
Highest Offering: Baccalaureate
Accreditation: ACCSC, COARC, DH, PTAA

01 Campus President ... Katherin PACKARD
05 Academic Dean ... Heather NICKEL
07 Director of Admissions ... Monte SCHAICH
32 Director of Student Affairs ... Dan GURULE
37 Asst Director of Financial Aid ... Samoa LE'AU

Concordia Seminary (A)

801 Seminary Place, Saint Louis MO 63105-3168
County: Saint Louis FICE Identification: 002457
Unit ID: 177092
Telephone: (314) 505-7000 Carnegie Class: Spec-4-yr-Faith
FAX Number: (314) 505-7001 Calendar System: Semester
URL: www.csl.edu
Established: 1839 Annual Graduate Tuition & Fees: N/A
Enrollment: 596 Coed
Affiliation or Control: Lutheran Church - Missouri Synod
IRS Status: 501(c)3
Highest Offering: Doctorate; No Undergraduates
Accreditation: HLC, THEOL

01 President ... Rev Dr. Thomas J. EGGER
03 Executive Vice President/COO ... Mr. Michael LOUIS
05 Provost ... Rev Dr. Douglas L. RUTT
10 Sr VP for Finance/Administration ... Mr. Chad A. CATTOOR
111 Senior VP for Advancement ... Mrs. Vicki BIGGS
58 Dean of Advanced Studies ... Rev Dr. Joel ELOWSKY
06 Registrar ... Mrs. Beth R. MENNEKE
110 Executive Director Seminary Support ... Mrs. Kathleen LUTHER
20 Associate Provost ... Rev Dr. Benjamin HAUPT
88 Director Center for Hispanic Study ... Rev Dr. Leopoldo A. SANCHEZ
15 Director of Human Resources ... Mr. Thomas MYERS
18 Director Campus Facilities ... Mr. Martin HAGUE
36 Director of Placement ... Rev Dr. Glenn NIELSEN
37 Director of Student Financial Aid ... Mrs. Laura HEMMER
13 Chief Information Officer ... Mr. John KLINGER
29 Sr Coord Alumni Relations ... Ms. Melodie BOSTIC
04 Executive Asst to President ... Ms. Pamela K. DAVITZ
09 Director of Institutional Research ... Rev Dr. Alan BORCHERDING
44 Director Gift Operations ... Ms. Megan DUNCAN
51 Director Continuing Education ... Ms. Erika BENNETT
88 Managing Editor Sem Publication ... Ms. Melanie APPLEBAUM
84 Director Recruitment ... Rev. Micah A. GLENN
08 Director Library Services ... Rev Dr. Paul ROBINSON

Cottey College (B)

1000 W Austin Boulevard, Nevada MO 64772-2763
County: Vernon FICE Identification: 002458
Unit ID: 177117
Telephone: (417) 667-8181 Carnegie Class: Bac/Assoc-Mixed
FAX Number: (417) 667-8103 Calendar System: Semester
URL: www.cottey.edu
Established: 1884 Annual Undergrad Tuition & Fees: $22,770
Enrollment: 283 Female
Affiliation or Control: Independent Non-Profit IRS Status: 501(c)3
Highest Offering: Baccalaureate
Accreditation: HLC, MUS

01 President ... Dr. Jann WEITZEL
05 VP Academic Affs/Dean of Faculty ... Dr. Joann BANGS
10 VP for Administration & Finance ... Mr. Terry (TJ) TUBBS
32 VP for Student Life ... Mr. Landon ADAMS
84 VP for Enrollment Mgmt & Marketing ... Mr. David HERINGER
42 Director Spiritual Life & Diversity ... Ms. Erica SIGAUKE
30 Director of Development ... Ms. Staci KEYS
88 Dir of Enrollment/Comm & Research ... Ms. Angela MOORE
06 Registrar ... Mr. William STANFILL
08 Director of the Library ... Ms. Courtney TRAUTWEILER
18 Director Physical Plant ... Mr. Todd HEFNER
19 Director Campus Security ... Mr. Mark BURGER
27 Director of Public Information ... Mr. Steve REED
15 Director of Human Resources ... Ms. McGee STOLLER
91 Director Administrative Computing ... Mr. Keith SPENCER
37 Director of Financial Aid ... Ms. Hannah MASTERS
90 Director Academic Computing ... Mr. Adam DEAN
39 Director of Housing ... Ms. Cindy SPENCER
41 Director of Athletics ... Ms. Maryann MITTS
40 Bookstore Manager ... Ms. Sherry PENNINGTON
09 Coordinator Institutional Research ... Ms. Nancy KERBS
111 Associate VP Inst Advancement ... Ms. Christi ELLIS
38 Director of Health & Counseling Svc ... Ms. Jeanna SIMPSON
88 Director of PEO Relations ... Ms. Margaret HAVERSTIC
121 Coordinator Academic Advising ... Ms. Stephanie MCGHEE
85 Coord International Student Svcs ... Mr. Bern MULVEY
04 Director of the President's Office ... Ms. Heather BROWNE
21 Controller ... Ms. Kimberly KROKROSKIA
108 Dir of Assessment & Inst Research ... Ms. Nancy KERBS
26 Director of Marketing ... Mr. Randon COFFEY
35 Director of Campus Activities & Cal ... Ms. Kristi KORB
36 Coord Career Svcs/Experiential Lrng ... Ms. Renee HAMPTON
109 Executive Chef & Director of Dining ... Ms. April MOSHER
88 Asst Dir Administrative Computing ... Mr. Justin MAYS

Covenant Theological Seminary (C)

12330 Conway Road, Saint Louis MO 63141-8697
County: Saint Louis FICE Identification: 004707
Unit ID: 177126
Telephone: (314) 434-4044 Carnegie Class: Spec-4-yr-Faith
FAX Number: (314) 434-4819 Calendar System: 4/1/4
URL: www.covenantseminary.edu
Established: 1956 Annual Graduate Tuition & Fees: N/A
Enrollment: 593 Coed
Affiliation or Control: Presbyterian Church In America IRS Status: 501(c)3
Highest Offering: Doctorate; No Undergraduates
Accreditation: HLC, THEOL

01 President ... RevDr. Thomas C. GIBBS
05 VP of Academics ... Dr. Jay SKLAR
10 VP of Business and Finance ... Ms. Alice EVANS
111 VP of Advancement ... Mr. John RANHEIM
03 VP at Large ... Dr. Daniel M. DORIANI
08 Library Director ... Mr. Steve JAMIESON
20 Dean of Academic Administration ... Ms. Jessica SWIGART
32 Dean of Students ... Mr. Mark MCELMURRY
07 Director of Admissions ... Mr. Stuart MCCLURE
30 Sr Director of Business Development ... Mr. Ken MCDONALD
37 Director of Financial Aid ... Ms. Lori BODE
13 Director of Information Technology ... Mr. Ryan JOHNS
06 Registrar ... Ms. Betsy GASOSKE
29 Alumni/Placement Services Director ... Dr. Joel HATHAWAY
21 Controller ... Mr. Jason ROBEY
88 Director of Field Education ... Mr. Jeremy MAIN
26 Sr Director of Communications ... Mr. Kent NEEDLER
38 Associate Dean of Counseling ... Mrs. Sabrina HICKEL
35 Associate Dean of Student Life ... Ms. Lindsey DEJONG
20 Associate Dean of Academic Services ... Ms. Diane PRESTON
15 Assoc Director of Human Resources ... Mrs. Meagan BUCHHOLZ
106 Assoc Director of Online Learning ... Mr. Aaron GOLDSTEIN

Cox College (D)

1423 N Jefferson Avenue, Springfield MO 65802-1917
County: Greene FICE Identification: 020682
Unit ID: 176770
Telephone: (417) 269-3401 Carnegie Class: Spec-4-yr-Other Health
FAX Number: (417) 269-3581 Calendar System: Semester
URL: www.coxcollege.edu
Established: 1907 Annual Undergrad Tuition & Fees: $12,600
Enrollment: 975 Coed
Affiliation or Control: Independent Non-Profit IRS Status: 501(c)3
Highest Offering: Master's
Accreditation: HLC, ADNUR, DIETI, DMS, NURSE, OT, RAD

01 President ... Dr. Amy DEMELO
05 Vice Pres Acad Affairs/Inst Effect ... Vacant
10 Vice Pres Business/Finance ... Jayne BULLARD
32 VP Student Affs/Marketing/Comm/Dev ... Dr. Sonya HAYTER
37 Director of Financial Aid ... Steve NICHOLS
06 Registrar ... Ms. Monica LEWIN
113 Bursar ... Lianna MARSHALL
106 Chair E-Learning/General Education ... Heather SADE

Crowder College (E)

601 Laclede Avenue, Neosho MO 64850-9165
County: Newton FICE Identification: 002459
Unit ID: 177135
Telephone: (417) 451-3223 Carnegie Class: Assoc/HT-Mix Trad/Non
FAX Number: (417) 455-5702 Calendar System: Semester
URL: www.crowder.edu
Established: 1963 Annual Undergrad Tuition & Fees (In-District): $5,328
Enrollment: 4,194 Coed
Affiliation or Control: Local IRS Status: 501(c)3
Highest Offering: Associate Degree
Accreditation: HLC, ADNUR, EMT, OTA

01 President ... Dr. Glenn COLTHARP
10 Vice President of Finance ... Mrs. Mickie MAHAN
05 Vice President of Academic Affairs ... Dr. Adam MORRIS
32 Vice President of Student Affairs ... Mrs. Tiffany SLINKARD
26 Assoc VP of Information Services ... Vacant
75 Assoc VP of Careers & Tech Educ ... Dr. Phillip WITT
20 Assoc VP of Academic Affairs ... Mr. Keith ZOROMSKI
07 Director of Admissions ... Mr. JP DICKEY
09 Director of Institutional Research ... Mr. Chett DANIEL
08 Director of Lee Library ... Mr. Eric DEATHERAGE
27 Director of Public Information ... Mrs. Cindy BROWN
41 Athletic Director ... Mr. John SISEMORE
37 Director of Financial Aid ... Mr. Jared BROWN
15 Director of Human Resources ... Mrs. Cassandra HALE
111 Dir of Institutional Advancement ... Mr. Jim CULLUMBER
40 Bookstore Manager ... Ms. Colleen HOLLAND
35 Assoc VP of Student Affairs ... Ms. Jamie WARD
13 Vice President of Info Services ... Mr. Al STADLER

Culver-Stockton College (F)

One College Hill, Canton MO 63435-1257
County: Lewis FICE Identification: 002460
Unit ID: 177144
Telephone: (573) 288-6000 Carnegie Class: Bac-Diverse
FAX Number: (573) 288-6611 Calendar System: Semester
URL: www.culver.edu
Established: 1853 Annual Undergrad Tuition & Fees: $27,740
Enrollment: 1,006 Coed
Affiliation or Control: Christian Church (Disciples Of Christ)
IRS Status: 501(c)3
Highest Offering: Master's
Accreditation: HLC, CAATE, IACBE, MUS

01 President ... Dr. Douglas PALMER
05 Provost/VPAA ... Dr. Lauren SCHELLENBERGER
32 Dean of Student Life ... Dr. Angela ROYAL
84 VP for Enrollment Management ... Dr. Kim GAITHER
111 VP for Advancement and Marketing ... Ms. Leslie PAYNE
06 Registrar/Director Inst Research ... Mrs. Chris HUEBOTTER
08 Librarian ... Dr. Katherine MARNEY
26 Dir of Communications & Marketing ... Ms. Alyssa HUMMEL
37 Director Financial Aid ... Mrs. Tina WISEMAN
29 Director of Alumni Programs ... Ms. Melissa DUBUQUE
91 Exec Dir Admin Systems/Services ... Dr. Joseph LIESEN
10 Chief Financial Officer ... Mrs. Diane BOZARTH
15 Exec Dir of Human Resources ... Mrs. Amy BAKER
35 Coordinator of Student Activities ... Mr. Bill BOXDORFER
42 Chaplain ... Rev. Wesley KNIGHT
41 Athletic Director ... Mr. Patrick ATWELL
40 Wildcat Warehouse Manager ... Mrs. Sharon FARR
04 Sr Assistant to the President ... Ms. Cindy FREELS
19 Director Campus Security & Facil ... Mr. Michael BRINGER
49 Chair Applied Liberal Arts/Sciences ... Dr. Scott GILTNER
50 Chair Business Education & Law ... Mrs. Julie STRAUS
57 Chair Fine Applied & Literary Arts ... Dr. Dylan MARNEY
58 Dean of Grad & Professional Studies ... Dr. Dell Ann JANNEY
92 Director of Honors Program ... Dr. Haidee HEATON
24 Circulation Coordinator ... Ms. Robyn LAMBERT
112 Dir Major Gifts & Estate Giving ... Ms. Courtney POURCIAUX
36 Dir of Career Services/Internship ... Ms. Robin JARVIS
124 Director of Retention ... Dr. Alissa BURGER
38 Dir Counseling/Student Wellness ... Ms. Susan MOON
09 Director of Institutional Research ... Mrs. Karla MCREYNOLDS
110 Director of Advancement Operations ... Mrs. Marjorie ELLISON
104 Director Study Abroad ... Dr. Melissa HOLT

Drury University (G)

900 N Benton Avenue, Springfield MO 65802-3791
County: Greene FICE Identification: 002461
Unit ID: 177214
Telephone: (417) 873-7879 Carnegie Class: Masters/M
FAX Number: (417) 873-7529 Calendar System: Semester
URL: www.drury.edu
Established: 1873 Annual Undergrad Tuition & Fees: $31,215
Enrollment: 1,691 Coed
Affiliation or Control: Independent Non-Profit IRS Status: 501(c)3
Highest Offering: Master's
Accreditation: HLC, CAEP, MUS

01 President ... Dr. Timothy CLOYD
05 Provost/EVP Academic Affairs ... Dr. Beth HARVILLE
10 EVP Administrative Services ... Vacant
32 EVP Student Affs/Dean of Students ... Dr. Tijuana S. JULIAN
43 Exec VP Univ Rels/General Counsel ... Mr. Aaron JONES
84 EVP Enrollment Management ... Mr. Kevin KROPF
111 EVP of University Advancement ... Mr. Wayne CHIPMAN
15 Dir Human Resources/D&I Officer ... Ms. Marilyn HARRIS
112 VP Stewardship/Principle Gifts ... Mrs. Judy THOMPSON
20 Assoc Provost Adult/Online/Grad ... Dr. Shannon CUFF
18 VP of Facilities Operations ... Mr. Brandon GAMMILL
41 VP & Director of Athletics ... Mr. Corey BRAY
06 University Registrar ... Ms. Salia MANIS
13 VP of Technology Services ... Mr. Val SERAFIMOV
26 Exec Dir Marketing/Communications ... Ms. Sarah NENNINGER
09 Dir Inst Research & Fin Analysis ... Mr. Rob FRIDGE
21 University Controller ... Ms. Stephanie MOSER
121 Assoc VP Ac Affrs/Dir Compass Cntr ... Dr. Jennifer JOSLIN
37 Director of Financial Aid ... Ms. Rebecca AHRENS
08 Director of FW Olin Library ... Mr. William GARVIN
36 Dir Career Planning & Development ... Mr. Brandon GASH
88 Dir Disability Support Services ... Ms. Lori SLATER
19 Director of Safety and Security ... Mr. Chris JOHNS
89 Dir Orientation/New Student Program ... Ms. Jennifer STEWART
39 Dir of Student Housing/Res Pgms ... Mr. Ethan SYKES
88 Director of Administrative Services ... Ms. Christie GARRISON
42 Chaplain ... Dr. Peter BROWNING
04 Executive Asst to President ... Ms. Bonnie WILCOX
104 Associate Dean Intl Programs ... Dr. Thomas RUSSO
106 Director of Online Education ... Ms. Alexis SLYTER
07 Director of Admission ... Ms. Lindsay TOBIN
110 Director of Advancement Services ... Ms. Teresa SKIDMORE
113 Director of Business Services ... Ms. Jill HOLMES
50 Dean School of Business ... Dr. Clifton PETTY
81 Dean Sch Natural & Math Sciences ... Mr. Albert KORIR
57 Dean School Comm/Fine & Perf Arts ... Dr. Allin SORENSON
83 Dean School of Hum & Soc Sciences ... Dr. Jennifer SILVA-BROWN
48 Dean Hammons School of Architecture ... Dr. Robert WEDDLE
53 Dean School Education & Child Dev ... Ms. Natalie PRECISE
35 Assoc Dean of Students ... Mr. Chip PARKER
28 Director of Diversity/Support Svcs ... Ms. Rosalyn THOMAS
29 Asst Director Alumni Relations ... Ms. Abbie BLISS
44 Dir Annual Giving & Donor Stwrdship ... Ms. Melanie EARL-REPLOGLE
40 Director Univ Bookstore ... Ms. Valerie RAINS
105 Director of Digital Communications ... Mrs. Chelsea BALTIMORE

Drury University Ft. Leonard Wood Campus (H)

4904 Constitution Drive, Ft. Leonard Wood MO 65473
Telephone: (573) 329-4400 Identification: 770319
Accreditation: &HLC

Drury University Rolla Campus (A)

1034 S. Bishop Avenue, Rolla MO 65401
Telephone: (573) 368-4959 Identification: 770321
Accreditation: &HLC

East Central College (B)

1964 Prairie Dell Road, Union MO 63084-0529
County: Franklin FICE Identification: 008862
Unit ID: 177250
Telephone: (636) 584-6500 Carnegie Class: Assoc/HT-Mix Trad/Non
FAX Number: (636) 583-1897 Calendar System: Semester
URL: www.eastcentral.edu
Established: 1968 Annual Undergrad Tuition & Fees (In-District): $4,272
Enrollment: 2,593 Coed
Affiliation or Control: Local IRS Status: 501(c)3
Highest Offering: Associate Degree
Accreditation: HLC, ACFEI, ART, CAHIIM, EMT, MAC, MLTAD, MUS, NAIT, OTA

01 President ... Dr. C. Jon BAUER
10 Vice Pres Finance/Administration ... Ms. DeAnna CASSAT
05 Vice President Academic Affairs ... Ms. Robyn WALTER
32 Vice President Student Development ... Ms. Sarah LEASSNER
26 VP External Relations ... Mr. Joel DOEPKER
12 Director ECC Rolla ... Ms. Christina M. AYRES
102 Exec Director Foundation ... Ms. Bridgette KELCH
18 Director Facilities & Grounds ... Mr. Tot PRATT
08 Director of Library Services ... Ms. Lisa M. FARRELL
96 Purchasing Manager ... Ms. Melissa D. POPP
79 Dean of Instruction ... Ms. Ann BOEHMER
75 Dean of Career & Technical Educ ... Mr. Richard HUDANICK
81 Department Chair Math & Education ... Dr. Reginald BRIGHAM
79 Dept Chair English & Humanities ... Mr. Joshua STROUP
54 Dept Chair Science & Engineering ... Dr. Parvadha GOVINDASWAMY
83 Department Chair Social Sciences ... Dr. William CUNNINGHAM
64 Dept Chair Fine & Performing Arts ... Vacant
15 Director Human Resources ... Ms. Wendy HARTMANN
76 Dean of Health Sciences ... Ms. Nancy MITCHELL
37 Director Financial Aid ... Mr. Jon GRUETT
06 Registrar ... Ms. Sarah SCROGGINS
21 Director Financial Svcs/Comptroller ... Ms. Annette MOORE
09 Director of Institutional Research ... Ms. Bethany L. LOHDEN
27 Director Communications/Marketing ... Mr. Gregg JONES
13 Director Information Technology ... Mr. Doug HOUSTON
40 Bookstore/Mail/Imaging Coordinator ... Mr. Doug A. AGEE
121 Director Advising & Counseling ... Mr. Paul LAMPE
103 Executive Director Workforce Devel ... Mr. Edward SHELTON
51 Coordinator Adult Educ & Literacy ... Ms. Alice WHALEN
24 Coordinator Instructional Design ... Mr. R. Chad BALDWIN
35 Coordinator Student Activities ... Ms. Carson MOWERY
04 Executive Asst to President ... Ms. Bonnie S. GARDNER
41 Athletic Director ... Mr. Jay MEHRHOFF
101 Secretary of the Institution/Board ... Ms. Bonnie GARDNER
07 Dir Early College & Admissions ... Ms. Megen STRUBBERG
30 Director of Development ... Ms. Bridgette KELCH
108 Director Institutional Assessment ... Dr. Michelle SMITH

Eden Theological Seminary (C)

475 E Lockwood Avenue,
Webster Groves MO 63119-3192
County: Saint Louis FICE Identification: 002462
Unit ID: 177278
Telephone: (314) 961-3627 Carnegie Class: Spec-4-yr-Faith
FAX Number: (314) 962-9918 Calendar System: 4/1/4
URL: www.eden.edu
Established: 1850 Annual Graduate Tuition & Fees: N/A
Enrollment: 117 Coed
Affiliation or Control: United Church Of Christ IRS Status: 501(c)3
Highest Offering: Doctorate; No Undergraduates
Accreditation: HLC, THEOL

01 President ... Ms. Deborah KRAUSE
05 Int Academic Dean ... Ms. Damayanthi NILES
06 Registrar ... Ms. Michelle WOBBE
04 Admin Asst to the President ... Ms. Danita CARTER
32 Dean of Students ... Dr. Sonja WILLIAMS
10 Director of Accounting ... Ms. Trina OWENS
30 Director of Development ... Ms. Sandi BOEHLEIN
26 Chief Public Rels/Mktg/Comm Ofcr ... Ms. Deanne SWARINGEN
101 Secretary of the Institution/Board ... Ms. Denise D. STAUFFER
18 Chief Facilities/Physical Plant ... Mr. John DONNELL

Evangel University (D)

1111 N Glenstone, Springfield MO 65802-2191
County: Greene FICE Identification: 002463
Unit ID: 177339
Telephone: (417) 865-2815 Carnegie Class: Masters/M
FAX Number: (417) 865-9599 Calendar System: Semester
URL: www.evangel.edu
Established: 1955 Annual Undergrad Tuition & Fees: $25,037
Enrollment: 1,999 Coed
Affiliation or Control: Assemblies Of God Church IRS Status: 501(c)3
Highest Offering: Doctorate
Accreditation: HLC, ACBSP, CACREP, MUS, SW

01 President ... Vacant
10 Vice Pres for Business/Finance ... Ms. Linda ALLEN
32 VP for Student Development ... Dr. Greg JOHNS
111 VP for University Advancement ... Dr. Michael KOLSTAD
05 VP for Academic Affairs/Provost ... Dr. Michael MCCORCLE
84 Vice Pres Enrollment Management ... Mr. Chris BELCHER
73 Vice President/Dean of AGTS ... Dr. Tim HAGER
26 Chief Marketing/Communication Ofcr ... Vacant
18 Director of Physical Plant ... Mr. Brian HAUFF
41 Director of Athletics ... Dr. Dennis MCDONALD
06 Registrar ... Mrs. Connie CROSS
08 Librarian ... Mr. Richard OLIVER
19 Director of Public Safety ... Mr. Brian KEYES
38 Director of Counseling Services ... Mr. Brian UPTON
29 Director Alumni Relations ... Mr. Hector CRUZ
37 Dir of Student Financial Services ... Mrs. Valerie SHARP
36 Career Development/Placement ... Mrs. Shannon MCCLURE
42 Campus Pastor ... Vacant
27 Director of Public Relations ... Mrs. Erin HEDLUN
23 Director of Health Services ... Ms. Susan BRYAN
21 Controller ... Mr. Dan EDWARDS
35 Director Student Life ... Miss Gina RENTSCHLER
15 Director of Human Resources ... Mrs. Samantha TYLER
39 Housing Coordinator ... Mrs. Danielle POULSON-JONES
09 Director of Institutional Research ... Dr. Linda WELLBORN
04 Executive Asst to President ... Mrs. Angela DENSE
101 Secretary of the Institution/Board ... Mrs. Angela DENSE

Fontbonne University (E)

6800 Wydown Boulevard, Saint Louis MO 63105-3098
County: Saint Louis FICE Identification: 002464
Unit ID: 177418
Telephone: (314) 862-3456 Carnegie Class: Masters/L
FAX Number: (314) 889-1451 Calendar System: Semester
URL: www.fontbonne.edu
Established: 1923 Annual Undergrad Tuition & Fees: $27,790
Enrollment: 1,112 Coed
Affiliation or Control: Roman Catholic IRS Status: 501(c)3
Highest Offering: Doctorate
Accreditation: HLC, ACBSP, DIETC, DIETD, SP, SW

01 President ... Dr. Nancy BLATTNER
05 Vice President Academic Affairs ... Dr. Adam WEYHAUPT
30 Vice President Advancement ... Ms. Kathleen BARNES
32 Vice President Student Affairs ... Ms. Heather FRENCH
10 Vice President Finance & Admin/CFO ... Mrs. Ann SPALL
84 Vice President Enrollment Mgmt ... Mr. Quinton CLAY
41 Vice President for Athletics ... Mrs. Maria BUCKEL
13 Director of Information Technology ... Ms. Julianne HAYES
35 Associate Vice Pres Student Affairs ... Dr. Janelle JULIAN
20 Associate VP Acad Affairs ... Vacant
35 Assistant VP for Student Affairs ... Vacant
49 Dean Arts & Sciences ... Dr. Gale RICE
50 Dean Global Business/Prof Studies ... Dr. Gale RICE
76 Dean Educ/Allied Health Prof ... Dr. Gale RICE
06 Registrar ... Ms. Katie PIACENTINI
15 Director Human Resources ... Mr. Steven LOHER
08 University Librarian ... Dr. Sharon MCCASLIN
22 Acad/Disabilities Resources Coord ... Mrs. Regina WADE JOHNSON
09 Director Institutional Research ... Mrs. Meaghan ONG
26 Director of Integrated Marketing ... Ms. Stephanie DANE
106 Director Online Programs ... Ms. Joanne MATTSON
121 Director Academic Advising ... Ms. Lee DELAET
85 Director International Affairs ... Ms. Caroline CLASBY
29 Director Alumni Relations ... Ms. Kate FLATLEY
28 Director Multicultural Affairs ... Ms. Deanna WILLIAMS
124 Dir Orientation & Stdnt Engagement ... Mr. Joel HERMANN
19 Director Public Safety ... Mr. Larry VERTREES
18 Director Physical Plant ... Vacant
04 Exec Asst Office of Pres/Board ... Mrs. Yvonne FARMER
121 Dir Student Success/Engagement ... Mr. Corey HAWKINS
36 Director Career Development ... Vacant
38 Director Counseling and Wellness ... Ms. Therese JACQUES
07 Associate VP Admission ... Ms. Jenny CHISM
37 Director Student Financial Aid ... Mr. Shawn MCCAW
39 Director Residential Life ... Mr. AJ FRIEDHOFF

Global University (F)

1211 South Glenstone Avenue,
Springfield MO 65804-1894
County: Greene Identification: 666687
Unit ID: 247296
Telephone: (800) 443-1083 Carnegie Class: Not Classified
FAX Number: (417) 865-7167 Calendar System: Other
URL: www.globaluniversity.edu
Established: 2000 Annual Undergrad Tuition & Fees: N/A
Enrollment: N/A Coed
Affiliation or Control: Assemblies Of God Church IRS Status: 501(c)3
Highest Offering: Doctorate
Accreditation: HLC

01 President ... Dr. Gary SEEVERS, JR.
03 Executive Vice President ... Rev. Keith HEERMANN
05 Provost ... Dr. David L. DEGARMO
20 Vice Provost Academic Effectiveness ... Dr. D. Bradley AUSBURY
58 Dean Graduate School/Theology ... Dr. Randy J. HEDLUN
73 Dean UG School Bible & Theology ... Dr. Kevin FOLK
13 VP Info Tech/Media Dept ... Mr. Wade W. PETTENGER
10 Vice President Finance ... Mr. Aram VAD
111 Vice President Advancement ... Vacant
07 Director of Enrollment Services ... Rev. Todd WAGGONER
06 Registrar ... Mrs. Lynne KROH
15 Director of Human Resources ... Ms. Jami NEMETI
04 Administrative Asst to President ... Mr. Gabriel RICHNER
08 Head Librarian ... Rev. Russ LANGFORD
09 Director of Institutional Research ... Dr. Brad AUSBURY
18 Chief Facilities/Physical Plant ... Mr. Bruce HAVENS

Goldfarb School of Nursing at Barnes-Jewish College (G)

4483 Duncan Avenue, Stop: 90-36-697,
Saint Louis MO 63110-1111
County: Saint Louis FICE Identification: 006389
Unit ID: 177719
Telephone: (314) 454-7055 Carnegie Class: Spec-4-yr-Other Health
FAX Number: (314) 362-9250 Calendar System: Trimester
URL: www.barnesjewishcollege.edu
Established: 1902 Annual Undergrad Tuition & Fees: N/A
Enrollment: 627 Coed
Affiliation or Control: Independent Non-Profit IRS Status: 501(c)3
Highest Offering: Doctorate
Accreditation: HLC, ANEST, NURSE

01 President ... Dr. Nancy RIDENOUR
10 Vice Dean for Finance/Admin ... Mr. Djuan COLEMAN
32 Vice Dean Student Affairs/Diversity ... Dr. Michael WARD
15 Vice Dean Human Res/Strat Effect ... Ms. Rosalynn BRYANT
05 Dean Academic Affairs ... Dr. Mayola ROWSER
46 Associate Dean for Research ... Vacant
08 Library & Info Services Director ... Ms. Renee GORRELL
21 Finance Director ... Ms. Linda STILLE
13 Director Information System ... Mr. Carlos PARDO
06 Registrar ... Dr. Samantha DEAN
84 Director Enrollment Management ... Ms. Stacy BOGIER
04 Administrative Asst to Dean ... Ms. Wanda CUMMINGS
29 Director Alumni Relations ... Dr. June COWELL-OATES
09 Dir Institutional Effectiveness ... Dr. George VINEYARD
26 Marketing Research Manager ... Ms. Angela WADE
100 Special Assistant to the President ... Deborah METTLACH

Graceland University (H)

1401 West Truman Road, Independence MO 64050-3434
Telephone: (816) 833-0524 Identification: 666262
Accreditation: &HLC, NURSE

† Regional accreditation is carried under the parent institution in Lamoni, IA.

Graduate School of the Stowers Institute for Medical Research (I)

1000 East 50th Street, Kansas City MO 64110
County: Jackson Identification: 667369
Telephone: (816) 926-4400 Carnegie Class: Not Classified
FAX Number: N/A Calendar System: Other
URL: www.stowers.org/gradschool
Established: 2012 Annual Graduate Tuition & Fees: N/A
Enrollment: N/A Coed
Affiliation or Control: Independent Non-Profit IRS Status: 501(c)3
Highest Offering: Doctorate; No Undergraduates
Accreditation: @HLC

01 President ... Dr. Betty M. DREES
05 Dean ... Dr. Matthew GIBSON
10 Chief Financial Officer ... Roderick STURGEON
11 Assoc Dean Administration/Registrar ... Susan WEIGEL
15 Human Resources Officer ... George SATTERLEE

Hannibal-LaGrange University (J)

2800 Palmyra Road, Hannibal MO 63401-1999
County: Marion FICE Identification: 009089
Unit ID: 177542
Telephone: (573) 221-3675 Carnegie Class: Bac-Diverse
FAX Number: (573) 221-6594 Calendar System: Semester
URL: www.hlg.edu
Established: 1858 Annual Undergrad Tuition & Fees: $24,000
Enrollment: 739 Coed
Affiliation or Control: Southern Baptist IRS Status: 501(c)3
Highest Offering: Master's
Accreditation: HLC, ADNUR, NURSE

01 President ... Dr. Anthony W. ALLEN
05 VP for Acad Admin/Dean of Faculty ... Dr. Robert MATZ
111 VP for Institutional Advancement ... Dr. Raymond W. CARTY
10 VP for Business & Finance ... Mrs. Betty L. ANDERSON
84 VP for Enrollment Management ... Mr. Tad WINGO
32 Dean of Students ... Mr. Josh PIERCE
06 Registrar/Director of Records ... Mr. Joseph GARNER, III
37 Director of Financial Aid ... Mr. Brice D. BAUMGARDNER
26 Director Public Relations ... Vacant
29 Dir Alumni Rels/Development ... Ms. Lauren YOUSE
36 Assoc Dean Academic/Career Services ... Dr. Karry D. RICHARDSON
08 Library Director ... Mrs. Julie A. ANDRESEN
19 Chief Public Safety/Compliance Ofcr ... Mr. Kyle BRENNEMANN
39 Director of Residential Life ... Mr. Joshua PIERCE
41 Athletic Director ... Mr. Jason D. NICHOLS
40 Campus Store Manager ... Mrs. Susan A. BOOTH
07 Director of Admissions ... Vacant

30 Director of Development ....Mr. David DEXHEIMER
58 Dir Adult/Graduate Division ....Dr. Jill ARNOLD

Harris-Stowe State University (A)

3026 Laclede Avenue, Saint Louis MO 63103-2199
County: Independent City FICE Identification: 002466
Unit ID: 177551
Telephone: (314) 340-3366 Carnegie Class: Bac-Diverse
FAX Number: (314) 340-3399 Calendar System: Semester
URL: www.hssu.edu
Established: 1857 Annual Undergrad Tuition & Fees (In-State): $5,484
Enrollment: 1,400 Coed
Affiliation or Control: State IRS Status: 501(c)3
Highest Offering: Baccalaureate
Accreditation: HLC, ACBSP, CAEP

01 Interim President ....Dr. LaTonia COLLINS SMITH
05 Interim Provost/VP Academic Affairs ....Dr. Edward HILL
10 Chief Financial Officer ....Dr. Terence FINLEY
13 Interim CIO ....Mr. Tahir YOUNAS
88 Spec Asst to Pres Spec Events/ Proj ....Mr. Bennie GILLIAM-WILLIAMS
111 VP of Institutional Advancement ....Mr. Jeffrey L. SHAW
06 Registrar ....Dr. Chauvette MCELMURRY-GREEN
07 Dir Admissions/Advise/Retention ....Ms. Iris TABB
08 Coordinator of Special Services ....Ms. Linda ORZEL
37 Director Financial Assistance ....Mr. James GREEN
15 Director of Human Resources ....Ms. Romney EDWARDS
38 Director Counseling Services ....Dr. Cammie CONNOR
25 Exec Dir Title III/Sponsored Pgms ....Vacant
20 Director of Academic Success ....Mr. Sean SPINKS
41 Director of Athletics ....Ms. Dorianne JOHNSON
21 Director of Business Services ....Ms. Barbara A. MORROW
36 Dir Career/Engage/Experiential Lrng ....Ms. Victoria HARRIS
53 Dean College of Education ....Dr. Edward HILL
50 Dean Anhauser Busch Sch of Business ....Dr. Stacy HOLLINS
49 Dean College of Arts & Sciences ....Dr. Terry Daily DAVIS
19 Director Security/Safety ....Chief Eric SULLIVAN
32 VP/Dean of Student Success ....Dr. Shawn BAKER
04 Executive Asst to the President ....Ms. Karen MAY
26 Int VP Marketing & Communications ....Dr. Alandrea STEWART
39 Dir Residential Life/Stdnt Conduct ....Mr. Virgil PEARSON
84 Dean of Enrollment Management ....Dr. Manicia FINCH

Heartland Christian College (B)

321 Mercy Street, Bethel MO 63434
County: Shelby Identification: 667091
Telephone: (660) 284-4800 Carnegie Class: Not Classified
FAX Number: (680) 284-4098 Calendar System: Semester
URL: www.heartlandcollege.edu
Established: 1992 Annual Undergrad Tuition & Fees: N/A
Enrollment: N/A Coed
Affiliation or Control: Non-denominational IRS Status: 501(c)3
Highest Offering: Associate Degree
Accreditation: BI

01 President ....Kris R. PALMER
05 Chief Academic Officer ....Martha PALMER
10 CFO ....Nathan MAYES
06 Registrar ....Christie RIHANEK
08 Head Librarian ....Molly NICKERSON

Jefferson College (C)

1000 Viking Drive, Hillsboro MO 63050-2441
County: Jefferson FICE Identification: 002468
Unit ID: 177676
Telephone: (636) 481-3000 Carnegie Class: Assoc/MT-VT-High Trad
FAX Number: (636) 789-4012 Calendar System: Semester
URL: www.jeffco.edu
Established: 1963 Annual Undergrad Tuition & Fees (In-District): $5,940
Enrollment: 3,740 Coed
Affiliation or Control: State/Local IRS Status: 501(c)3
Highest Offering: Associate Degree
Accreditation: HLC, CAHIIM, EMT, OTA, PTAA, RAD

01 President ....Dr. Dena MCCAFFREY
04 Exec Asst to the President & Board ....Ms. Lisa VINYARD
05 Acting VP/Dean of Instruction & CAO ....Dr. Chris DEGEARE
10 VP Finance & Administration ....Mr. Daryl GEHBAUER
32 VP Student Services ....Dr. Kimberly HARVEY-MANUS
20 Dean Integrated Plng/Academic Svcs ....Mr. Allan WAMSLEY
21 Controller ....Mr. Mark JANIESCH
15 Director of Human Resources ....Ms. Tasha WELSH
30 Exec Director of Development ....Mr. Blake TILLEY
26 Director of PR & Marketing ....Mr. Roger BARRENTINE
13 Director Information Technology ....Mr. Tracy JAMES
45 Dir Financial Reporting/Analysis ....Ms. Kathy KUHLMANN
06 Registrar ....Ms. Stacey WILSON
50 Assoc Dean Business/Social Science ....Dr. Terry KITE
79 Assoc Dean Humanities ....Dr. Michael BOOKER
76 Assoc Dean Science & Health ....Mr. Kenny WILSON
81 Assoc Dean Math/Physics/ Technology ....Ms. Maryanne ANGLIONGTO
37 Director Student Financial Services ....Ms. Sarah BRIGHT
84 Director Enrollment Services ....Ms. Holly LINCOLN
96 Director of Purchasing ....Ms. Sheree BELL
08 Director Library Services ....Ms. Lisa PRITCHARD
41 Director Athletics ....Mr. Robert DEUTSCHMAN
31 Director Business/Community Develop ....Vacant

18 Director Buildings & Grounds ....Mr. Dale RICHARDSON
19 Director Public Safety Programs ....Mr. Paul FERBER
66 Director of Nursing ....Ms. Amy MCDANIEL
121 Director Advising & Retention ....Ms. Kathy JOHNSTON
124 Director of Student Support Svcs ....Ms. Teresa SCHWARTZ
74 Director Veterinary Technology ....Ms. Dana NEVOIS
88 Director Child Care Center ....Ms. Stephanie CAGE
39 Director Residential & Student Life ....Vacant
55 Director Adult Educ/Literacy ....:. Ms. Julie JOHNS
07 Director of Admissions ....Ms. Carrie GREER
09 Director of Institutional Research ....Dr. Jude KYOORE

Kansas City Art Institute (D)

4415 Warwick Boulevard, Kansas City MO 64111-1874
County: Jackson FICE Identification: 002473
Unit ID: 177746
Telephone: (816) 472-4852 Carnegie Class: Spec-4-yr-Arts
FAX Number: (816) 472-3493 Calendar System: Semester
URL: www.kcai.edu
Established: 1885 Annual Undergrad Tuition & Fees: $40,100
Enrollment: 698 Coed
Affiliation or Control: Independent Non-Profit IRS Status: 501(c)3
Highest Offering: Baccalaureate
Accreditation: HLC, ART

01 The Nerman Family President ....Mr. Tony JONES
10 EVP for Administration/CFO ....Mr. Brian HENKE
05 EVP for Academic Affairs ....Dr. Bambi BURGARD
111 Exec VP for Advancement ....Ms. Nicolle RATLIFF
20 VP for Academic Affairs ....Dr. Milton KATZ
15 VP of Human Resources ....Vacant
13 Vice Pres/Chief Information Officer ....Vacant
32 VP/Dean of Student Affairs ....Ms. Gina GOLBA
110 VP for Advancement/General Counsel ....Ms. Emily HESS
20 Senior Academic Affairs Specialist ....Ms. Julia WELLES
26 Director of Communications and PR ....Mr. Whit BONES
06 Registrar .... Ms. Nancy EASTMAN
35 Assistant Dean of Student Affairs ....Mr. Joe TIMSON
38 Psychologist and Counseling Coord .... Ms. Elisabeth SUNDERMEIER
18 Facilities Director/Plant Services ....Ms. Roxie CURTIS
29 Manager of Alumni Relations ....Ms. Angelica DESIMIO
37 Director of Financial Aid ....Ms. Lori BAER
36 Dir of Acad Advising & Career Svcs ....Ms. Amanda HADJU
08 Director of Library ....Ms. M.J POEHLER
24 Director of Creative Media ....Mr. Aldo BACCHETTA
19 Director of Safety & Security ....Mr. Mike RAUNIG
109 Manager of Auxiliary Services ....Ms. Jennifer BOE
88 Director of H&R Block Artspace ....Ms. Raechell SMITH
21 Director of Finance & Accounting ....Ms. Breely BENNETT
04 Exec Admin Asst to President ....Ms. Sarah MCDONALD
39 Asst Dir of Housing & Student Activ ....Ms. Roxie KENNEDY
102 Dir Foundation/Corporate Relations ....Mr. Randy WILLIAMS
90 Director Academic Computing ....Ms. Evonne BRIONES
07 Director of Admissions ....Ms. Darcy DEAL
28 Director of Diversity ....Ms. Shawntae JONES

Kansas City University of Medicine & Biosciences (E)

1750 East Independence Avenue, Kansas City MO 64106
County: Jackson FICE Identification: 002474
Unit ID: 179812
Telephone: (816) 654-7000 Carnegie Class: Spec-4-yr-Med
FAX Number: (816) 654-7101 Calendar System: Semester
URL: www.kcumb.edu
Established: 1916 Annual Graduate Tuition & Fees: N/A
Enrollment: 1,275 Coed
Affiliation or Control: Independent Non-Profit IRS Status: 501(c)3
Highest Offering: First Professional Degree; No Undergraduates
Accreditation: HLC, CLPSY, OSTEO

01 President & CEO ....Dr. Marc B. HAHN
05 EVP Academic & Rsrch Affs/Provost .... Dr. Edward R. O'CONNOR
10 Exec VP Finance/Operations ....Mr. Joseph MASSMAN
31 Vice Pres Community Engagement ....Dr. Jane LAMPO
111 VP for Institutional Advancement ....Dr. Jane LAMPO
84 Vice Prov Student/Enrollment Svcs ....Dr. Kristine A. STEVENS
32 Assoc Provost Student Services ....Ms. Sara E. SELKIRK
17 Vice Pres Health Affairs ....Vacant
12 Dean Joplin Campus ....Dr. Laura ROSCH
76 Dean College of Biosciences ....Dr. Robert WHITE
20 Vice Dean/COM KCU ....Dr. G. Michael JOHNSON
35 Director Student Activities ....Dr. Catherine DOBSON
100 Chief of Staff/Dir Govt Relations ....Dr. Brooke YODER
26 Exec Dir University Relations ....Ms. Lisa CAMBRIDGE
08 University Library Director ....Ms. Lori FITTERLING
15 Director Human Resources ....Ms. Julie DEANE
13 Director of Information Technology ....Mr. Lance HUGGINS
37 Director of Financial Aid ....Ms. Kristi NICHOL
12 Campus Dean COM Kansas City ....Dr. Josh COX
19 Director Campus Operations ....Mr. James HERRINGTON
38 Director Counseling and Support Svc ....Dr. James DUGAN
29 Dir Alumni Dev/Annual Giving ....Mr. Alex HOPKINS
07 Assoc Director of Admissions ....Ms. Brooke SONGBIRD

Kenrick-Glennon Seminary, Kenrick School of Theology (F)

5200 Glennon Drive, Saint Louis MO 63119-4399
County: Saint Louis FICE Identification: 002476
Unit ID: 177816
Telephone: (314) 792-6100 Carnegie Class: Spec-4-yr-Faith
FAX Number: (314) 792-6500 Calendar System: Semester
URL: www.kenrick.edu
Established: 1893 Annual Undergrad Tuition & Fees: N/A
Enrollment: 68 Male
Affiliation or Control: Roman Catholic IRS Status: 501(c)3
Highest Offering: Master's
Accreditation: HLC, THEOL

01 President/Rector ....Rev. James MASON
03 Vice Rector for Formation ....Rev. Paul HOESING
73 Dir Pre-Theol & Asst Vice Rector ....Rev. Fadi AURO
05 Academic Dean ....Dr. Edward HOGAN
88 Director of Spiritual Formation ....Rev. Kristian TEATER
08 Director of Library ....Ms. Mary Ann AUBIN
42 Director of Worship ....Rev. Don ANSTOETTER
30 Director of Development ....Mrs. Kate SAUERBURGER
06 Registrar/Financial Aid ....Deacon Carl SOMMER
10 Director of Operations & Finance .... Mr. Greg NOVAK

Lincoln University (G)

820 Chestnut Street, Jefferson City MO 65101-3537
County: Cole FICE Identification: 002479
Unit ID: 177940
Telephone: (573) 681-5000 Carnegie Class: Bac-Diverse
FAX Number: (573) 681-5566 Calendar System: Semester
URL: www.lincolnu.edu
Established: 1866 Annual Undergrad Tuition & Fees (In-State): $8,370
Enrollment: 2,012 Coed
Affiliation or Control: State IRS Status: 501(c)3
Highest Offering: Beyond Master's But Less Than Doctorate
Accreditation: HLC, ACBSP, ADNUR, CAEPN, NUR, SW

01 Interim President ....Dr. John MOSELEY
100 Director Strategic Initiatives ....Mrs. Laura BENNETT-SMITH
05 Interim VP Academic Affairs/Provost ....Dr. Jennifer BENNE
10 Vice Pres Administration/Finance ....Mrs. Sandy KOETTING
111 VP Advancement/Athletics ....Mr. Kevin WILSON
19 VP Campus Culture & Chief of Police ....Mr. Gary HILL
21 Asst VP Admin/Finance & Controller ....Mrs. Stacey SCHULTE
32 Dean of Student Success ....Ms. Zakiya BROWN
84 Interim Dean Enrollment Management .... Mr. Darius WATSON
26 Director of University Relations .... Ms. Misty YOUNG
49 Interim Dean Arts/Sciences ...... Dr. Sunder BALASUBRAMANIAN
47 Dean of Ag/Natural Sciences .... Dr. Majed EL-DWEIK
107 Interim Dean Professional Studies ....Dr. Ann MCSWAIN
13 Chief Information Officer ....Mr. John BAX
08 University Librarian .... Ms. Waheedah BILAL
15 Director Human Resources ....Vacant
06 Registrar ....Mr. Blaine BREDEMAN
113 Bursar ....Vacant
114 Budget Officer .... Ms. Kathy MUENKS
96 Director of Purchasing ....Ms. Catherine FREDE
86 Governmental Liaison ....Mr. Carlos GRAHAM
36 Director of Career Services ....Mrs. Elizabeth JORDAN
25 Director of Grants/Sponsored Rsrch ....Ms. Tiffany NOLAN
09 Director of Institutional Research ....Mrs. Beth NOLTE
37 Director Financial Aid ....Ms. Kala SMITH
18 Director of Facilities and Planning .... Mr. Jeffrey TURNER
23 Director Student Health Services .... Mrs. Leasa WEGHORST
121 Director Student Success Center ......Ms. Lakeisha WASHINGTON
85 International Student Svcs Advisor .... Mr. Joshua WILLIAMS
22 Dir Affirmative Action/EEO ....Vacant
12 Director Fort Leonard Wood Site ....Dr. Rosalind PRIDE

Lindenwood University (H)

209 S Kingshighway, Saint Charles MO 63301-1695
County: Saint Charles FICE Identification: 002480
Unit ID: 177968
Telephone: (636) 949-2000 Carnegie Class: DU-Mod
FAX Number: (636) 949-4910 Calendar System: Semester
URL: www.lindenwood.edu
Established: 1827 Annual Undergrad Tuition & Fees: $18,100
Enrollment: 7,382 Coed
Affiliation or Control: Independent Non-Profit IRS Status: 501(c)3
Highest Offering: Doctorate
Accreditation: HLC, ACBSP, CAATE, CAEPT, SW

01 President ....Dr. John R. PORTER
05 Int Provost/SVP Academic Affairs ..... Dr. Bethany ALDEN-RIVERS
111 VP Advancement & Communications .... Mr. Orrie COVERT
15 Vice Pres Human Resources ....Dr. Deb AYRES
84 SVP Enroll Mgmt/Student Engagement .... Mr. Terry WHITTUM
10 Chief Financial Officer ....Mr. Rick BANIAK
11 VP Operations ....Dr. Diane MOORE
41 VP Athletics ....Mr. Brad WACHLER
13 VP Information Technology ....Mr. TJ RAINS
45 VP Strategy & Innovation ....Mr. Rob WESTERVELT
43 General Counsel ....Mr. Mark FALKOWSKI
32 Associate VP Student Affairs .... Ms. Kelly MOYICH
88 Assoc VP Operations .... Mr. Tim CRUTCHLEY
88 Assoc VP Enrollment Management ....Ms. Sara WIEDMAN
04 Executive Asst to the President .... Mrs. Nicole SULLIVAN
20 Assistant Provost ....Ms. Kate HERRELL
53 Dean School of Education .... Dr. Anthony SCHEFFLER
79 Dean School of Arts & Humanities ....Dr. Kathi VOSEVICH
50 Dean Business/Entrepreneurship ....Dr. Molly HUDGINS
81 Dean School of Sciences .... Dr. Cynthia SCHROEDER
08 Dean of Library Services .... Ms. Elizabeth MACDONALD
06 Registrar .... Ms. Christine HANNAR

108 Assoc VP/Chief Assessment Officer . Dr. Bethany ALDEN-RIVERS
07 Asst VP Enrollment Management .... Ms. Kara SCHILLI
110 Assistant VP Advancement .... Mr. Brian BRUNNER
16 Assistant VP HR .... Ms. Amanda PRICE
42 Chaplain .... Dr. Nichole TORBITZKY
21 Asst VP Fiscal Affairs .... Mr. John PLUNKETT
89 Director of First Year Programs .... Mrs. Sarah LEASSNER
106 Dir Online Education/E-learning .... Dr. Hannah KOHLER
19 Director Security/Safety .... Mr. Ryan ANDERSON
26 Director of Communications .... Ms. Julee MITSLER
38 Director Student Counseling .... Mr. Jonathan HUNN
09 Director of Institutional Research .... Dr. Peter WEITZEL
29 Director Alumni Relations .... Ms. Rachael HEUERMANN
104 Asst Director Study Abroad .... Ms. Elizabeth SNELL
105 Webmaster .... Mr. Jason WAACK
27 Director Marketing .... Ms. Jessica SCHROER
09 Director Research and Compliance .... Mr. Michael LEARY

Logan University (A)

1851 Schoettler Road, Chesterfield MO 63017

County: Saint Louis FICE Identification: 004703
Unit ID: 177986
Telephone: (636) 227-2100 Carnegie Class: Spec-4-yr-Other Health
FAX Number: N/A Calendar System: Trimester
URL: www.logan.edu
Established: 1935 Annual Undergrad Tuition & Fees: $6,700
Enrollment: 1,806 Coed
Affiliation or Control: Independent Non-Profit IRS Status: 501(c)3
Highest Offering: First Professional Degree
Accreditation: HLC, CHIRO, @DIETC

01 President .... Dr. Clay MCDONALD
05 Provost .... Dr. Kimberly PADDOCK-O'REILLY
29 VP Chiropractic/Alumni Relations .... Dr. Ralph BARRALE
07 VP Admissions/Financial Aid .... Dr. Natacha DOUGLAS
111 VP Institutional Advancement .... Ms. Theresa FLECK
13 VP Information Tech/CIO .... Dr. Brad HOUGH
10 VP Admin Services/CFO .... Mr. Adil KHAN
15 VP Human Resources .... Ms. Nichole NICHOLS
09 VP Strategic Perf/Cont Improv .... Dr. Lee VAN DUSEN

Maryville University of Saint Louis (B)

650 Maryville University Drive,
Saint Louis MO 63141-7299

County: Saint Louis FICE Identification: 002482
Unit ID: 178059
Telephone: (314) 529-9300 Carnegie Class: DU-Mod
FAX Number: (314) 529-9900 Calendar System: Semester
URL: www.maryville.edu
Established: 1872 Annual Undergrad Tuition & Fees: $27,166
Enrollment: 10,979 Coed
Affiliation or Control: Independent Non-Profit IRS Status: 501(c)3
Highest Offering: Doctorate
Accreditation: HLC, ACBSP, ART, CACREP, CAEPN, CIDA, MUS, NURSE, OT, PTA, SP, @SW

01 President .... Dr. Mark LOMBARDI
05 Vice Pres Academic Affairs .... Dr. Cherie FISTER
10 Vice Pres Finance & Facilities .... Dr. Steve MANDEVILLE
84 Vice President Enrollment .... Ms. Shani LENORE
86 VP Community/Gov Relations .... Ms. Laraine DAVIS
32 VP for Student Life .... Dr. Nina CALDWELL
121 VP for Student Success .... Dr. Jennifer MCCLUSKEY
26 VP Integrated Mktg & Communications ..... Ms. Marcia SULLIVAN
20 Associate VP Academic Affairs .... Ms. Laura ROSS
46 VP Strategic Trends .... Mr. Jeff MILLER
100 Chief of Staff .... Ms. Jessica NORRIS
50 Dean School of Business .... Dr. Tammy GOCIAL
53 Dean School of Education .... Dr. Mascheal SCHAPPE
76 Dean School Health Professions .... Dr. Michelle JENKINS
49 Int Dean College Arts & Sciences .... Ms. Jennifer YUKNA
106 Dean Adult & Online Education .... Ms. Katherine LOUTHAN
88 VP for Operational Excellence .... Dr. Stephanie ELFRINK
07 Asst Vice Pres Enrollment .... Ms. Melissa MACE
29 Director of Alumni Affairs .... Mr. Andrew FOX
42 Dir Campus Ministry & Comm Service .... Mr. Stephen DISALVO
35 Dean of Students .... Mr. Joseph FITZGERALD
36 Director Career & Prof Development .... Ms. Erin BOSWELL
21 Controller/Dir Finance .... Ms. Nikki PAYNE
37 Senior Director of Financial Aid .... Ms. Liesl FLANAGAN
23 Director of Health & Wellness .... Ms. Suzanne JAUDES
28 Sr Advisor to Pres for Access/Oppty .... Mr. Turan MULLINS
13 Chief Technology Officer .... Mr. Doug GLAZE
09 Dir Info Resources/Data Analytics .... Mr. Jonathan SCHLERETH
90 Dir Learning Design &
Technology .... Ms. Pamela BRYAN WILLIAMS
18 Senior Project Manager .... Ms. Angela WARNER
112 Director of Planned Gifts .... Mr. Michael SCHROEDER
102 Dir Foundation/Corp Relations .... Mr. Michael WHITLEY
19 Director of Public Safety .... Mr. Jair KOLLASCH
39 Director of Residential Life .... Mr. Ryan MCDONNELL
104 Assoc VP/Dir Ctr for Global Educ .... Dr. James HARF
88 Asst Athletic Dir Communications .... Mr. Charles YAHNG
88 AVP Ops Systems/Quality Assurance .... Ms. Elizabeth STACEY
88 Director Fresh Ideas Food Services .... Ms. Linda THACKER
38 Director Personal Counseling .... Ms. Jennifer HENRY
30 Exec Director Devel & Alumni Rels .... Ms. Fay FETICK
88 Assoc VP Ctr for Institution Values .... Dr. Alden CRADDOCK
04 Executive Asst to President .... Ms. Maria-Louisa KNIERIM
109 Director of Auxiliary Operations .... Mr. Damon MITCHELL

105 Assoc Director Web Strategy .... Ms. Kate BOELHAUF
41 Director of Athletics & Recreation .... Mr. Lonnie FOLKS
101 Secretary of the Board .... Ms. Jessica NORRIS
103 Chief of Corp Partnership Acquis .... Mr. Scott CHADWICK
15 Director of Human Resources .... Ms. April SANTOS

*Metropolitan Community College - Kansas City Administrative Center (C)

3200 Broadway, Kansas City MO 64111-2429

County: Jackson FICE Identification: 009137
Unit ID: 177995
Telephone: (816) 604-1000 Carnegie Class: N/A
FAX Number: (816) 759-1158
URL: www.mcckc.edu

01 Chancellor .... Dr. Kimberly BEATTY
101 Chancellor's Asst/Board Secretary .... Ms. Cindy K. JOHNSON
12 President Penn Valley .... Dr. Tyjaun LEE
12 President Blue River/Bus & Tech .... Dr. Thomas MEYER
12 President Longview .... Dr. Dan HOCOY
12 President MW .... Dr. Larry RIDEAUX
05 VC of Instruction & CAO .... Dr. Suzanne GOCHIS
32 VC Student Success/Engagement .... Dr. Kathrine SWANSON
10 Vice Chanc Admin Svcs/CFO .... Dr. Donald CHRUSCIEL
09 VC Inst Effectiveness/Research/Tech .... Dr. John CHAWANA
100 Chief Legal Officer .... Ms. Sandra GARCIA
20 AVC Academic Affairs .... Dr. Dreand JOHNSON
35 AVC Student Svcs/Enrollment .... Dr. Karen MOORE
18 Chief Facilities Officer .... Mr. Jeffrey ULLMANN
15 AVC/Chief Human Resources Officer .... Dr. Rosemary MARTIN
103 AVC Workforce & Economic Dev .... Dr. Alicia DICKENS
37 AVC Student Financial Services .... Ms. Dena NORRIS
21 AVC Financial Svcs & Admin Sys .... Ms. Patricia A. AMICK
111 AVC of Advancement .... Ms. Jessica RAMIREZ
13 AVC of Information Technology .... Dr. Barcus JACKSON
106 VP Online Instruction/Student Svcs .... Dr. Deanna SYNDER
108 Exec Dir Curriculum & Assessment .... Ms. Tammie MAY
19 Chief of Campus Police .... Mr. Londell JAMERSON, JR.
28 VP Diversity/Equity/Inclusion .... Mr. Warren HAYNES
09 Executive Director Inst Research .... Mrs. Melissa GIESE
114 Exec Director Budget and Planning .... Ms. Britney DOMANN
96 Executive Director of Procurement .... Mr. Mitch BORCHERS
26 Exec Dir Communications/Marketing .... Mr. Blake FRY
88 Dir of Support Services PS .... Mr. Domenick R. BROUILLETTE
22 Director Student Disability Svcs .... Ms. Kim FERNANDES
19 Director of Public Safety .... Mr. Rusty SULLIVAN
88 Dir of CTE Accountability & Comp .... Ms. Teresa A. LONEY
06 Registrar .... Mr. Ryan MEADOR
41 Athletic Director .... Mr. Brian BECHTEL
43 Associate General Counsel .... Ms. Andrea SCHATZ
88 Director of Enterprise/PM/P&IE .... Mr. Ed FOLEY

*Metropolitan Community College - Blue River (D)

20301 E 78 Highway, Independence MO 64057-2053

County: Jackson FICE Identification: 032613
Telephone: (816) 604-1000 Carnegie Class: Not Classified
FAX Number: N/A Calendar System: Semester
URL: www.mcckc.edu
Established: 1997 Annual Undergrad Tuition & Fees (In-District): N/A
Enrollment: N/A Coed
Affiliation or Control: State/Local IRS Status: 501(c)3
Highest Offering: Associate Degree
Accreditation: &HLC

02 President .... Dr. Thomas W. MEYER
03 Vice President .... Dr. Ryan CRIDER
04 Sr Exec Admin Asst to the President .... Mrs. Karla DEATHERAGE
05 Int Dean of Instruction .... Mrs. Cheryl WINTER
32 Dean of Student Development/Enroll .... Dr. Jonathan L. BURKE
11 Director of Campus Operations .... Mrs. Kimberly POINDEXTER
19 Campus Police Sergeant .... SGT. Larry MCCREA
18 Facilities Superintendent .... Mr. Clint JOHNSON

† Regional accreditation is carried under the parent institution Metropolitan Community College-Kansas City Administrative Center in Kansas City, MO.

*Metropolitan Community College - Business and Technology (E)

1775 Universal Avenue, Kansas City MO 64120-2429

County: Jackson Identification: 666295
Telephone: (816) 604-1000 Carnegie Class: Not Classified
FAX Number: (816) 482-5256 Calendar System: Semester
URL: www.mcckc.edu/btc
Established: 1995 Annual Undergrad Tuition & Fees (In-District): N/A
Enrollment: N/A Coed
Affiliation or Control: Local IRS Status: 501(c)3
Highest Offering: Associate Degree
Accreditation: &HLC

02 President .... Dr. Thomas MEYER
05 VP Instruction/Student Services .... Dr. Ryan CRIDER
20 Int Dean of Instruction .... Mrs. Cheryl WINTER
32 Dean Student Development/Enrollment .... Dr. Jon BURKE
10 Director of Campus Operations .... Mrs. Kim POINDEXTER
04 Sr Exec Admin Asst to the President .... Mrs. Karla DEATHERAGE

† Regional accreditation is carried under the parent institution Metropolitan Community College-Kansas City Administrative Center in Kansas City, MO.

*Metropolitan Community College - Longview (F)

500 SW Longview Road, Lee's Summit MO 64081-2105

County: Jackson FICE Identification: 009140
Telephone: (816) 604-2144 Carnegie Class: Not Classified
FAX Number: (816) 672-2025 Calendar System: Semester
URL: www.mcckc.edu
Established: 1969 Annual Undergrad Tuition & Fees (In-District): N/A
Enrollment: N/A Coed
Affiliation or Control: Local IRS Status: 501(c)3
Highest Offering: Associate Degree
Accreditation: &HLC

02 President .... Dr. Kathrine SWANSON
05 Vice Pres Instruction/Student Svcs .... Dr. David OEHLER
20 Interim Dean of Instruction .... Ms. Gretchen BLYTHE
32 Dean Student Devel/Enrollment
Mgmt .... Dr. Diana BOYD MCELROY
11 Interim Director Campus Operations ..... Ms. Tahmeka THOMPSON
37 Financial Aid Manager .... Ms. Lisa L. FANNAN
124 Student Retention Manager .... Dr. Joe BARNHILL

† Regional accreditation is carried under the parent institution Metropolitan Community College-Kansas City Administrative Center in Kansas City, MO.

*Metropolitan Community College - Maple Woods (G)

2601 NE Barry Road, Kansas City MO 64156-1299

County: Clay FICE Identification: 009139
Telephone: (816) 604-1000 Carnegie Class: Not Classified
FAX Number: (816) 437-3049 Calendar System: Semester
URL: www.mcckc.edu
Established: 1968 Annual Undergrad Tuition & Fees (In-District): N/A
Enrollment: N/A Coed
Affiliation or Control: Local IRS Status: 501(c)3
Highest Offering: Associate Degree
Accreditation: &HLC

02 President .... Dr. Laarry RIDEAUX, JR.
03 Executive Vice President .... Dr. Ellen CROWE
05 Dean Instruction .... Mr. James R. MOES
32 Dean Student Devel/Enrollment .... Mr. Terrell TIGNER
11 Director of Campus Operations .... Vacant
08 Librarian .... Mrs. Linda CARTER
41 Athletic Director .... Vacant
37 Financial Aid Manager .... Mrs. Robin STIMAC
18 Physical Facilities Superintendent .... Vacant

† Regional accreditation is carried under the parent institution Metropolitan Community College-Kansas City Administrative Center in Kansas City, MO.

*Metropolitan Community College - Penn Valley (H)

3201 Southwest Trafficway, Kansas City MO 64111-2764

County: Jackson FICE Identification: 002484
Telephone: (816) 604-1000 Carnegie Class: Not Classified
FAX Number: (816) 759-4161 Calendar System: Semester
URL: www.mcckc.edu
Established: 1915 Annual Undergrad Tuition & Fees (In-District): N/A
Enrollment: N/A Coed
Affiliation or Control: Local IRS Status: 501(c)3
Highest Offering: Associate Degree
Accreditation: &HLC, ADNUR, CAHIIM, DA, EMT, OTA, PTAA, RAD, SURGT

02 President .... Dr. Tyjaun LEE
05 VP of Instruction & Student Svcs .... Ms. Lesha GREGORY
20 Dean of Instruction .... Ms. Christine HOWELL
32 Dean of Student Development .... Ms. Chelsia B. POTTS
84 Dean of Enrollment Services .... Vacant
08 Librarian .... Mr. Michael KORKLAN
13 NUS Department Director .... Vacant
18 Facilities Services Superintendent .... Mr. Robert BURKEY
19 Campus Police Captain .... Cpt. Ronald REILLY
84 Enrollment Manager .... Mr. Carlton FOWLER
41 Athletic Programs Manager .... Mr. Marcus HARVEY
37 Student Financial Aid Manager .... Vacant
10 Business Office Supervisor .... Ms. Michele ALLEN
36 Career Coordinator .... Vacant
11 Director of Campus Operations .... Mr. Basil LISTER

† Regional accreditation is carried under the parent institution Metropolitan Community College-Kansas City Administrative Center in Kansas City, MO.

Midwest Institute (I)

2 Soccer Park Road, Fenton MO 63026

County: St. Louis FICE Identification: 021211
Unit ID: 178183
Telephone: (314) 965-8363 Carnegie Class: Spec 2-yr-Health
FAX Number: N/A Calendar System: Other
URL: www.midwestinstitute.com
Established: 1965 Annual Undergrad Tuition & Fees: N/A
Enrollment: 297 Coed
Affiliation or Control: Proprietary IRS Status: Proprietary
Highest Offering: Associate Degree
Accreditation: ABHES

05 Director of Education .... Vacant

Midwest Institute-Earth City (A)

4260 Shoreline Drive, Earth City MO 63045
County: Saint Louis Identification: 667074
Telephone: (314) 344-4440 Carnegie Class: Not Classified
FAX Number: (314) 344-0495 Calendar System: Other
URL: www.midwestinstitute.com
Established: 1970 Annual Undergrad Tuition & Fees: N/A
Enrollment: N/A Coed
Affiliation or Control: Proprietary IRS Status: Proprietary
Highest Offering: Associate Degree
Accreditation: ABHES, SURTEC

01 President .... Vacant

Midwest University (B)

851 Parr Road, Wentzville MO 63385-0365
County: Saint Charles FICE Identification: 035283
Telephone: (636) 327-4645 Carnegie Class: Not Classified
FAX Number: (636) 327-4715 Calendar System: Semester
URL: www.midwest.edu
Established: 1986 Annual Undergrad Tuition & Fees: N/A
Enrollment: N/A Coed
Affiliation or Control: Independent Non-Profit IRS Status: 501(c)3
Highest Offering: Doctorate
Accreditation: BI

01 President .... Dr. James SONG
04 Executive Assistant to President .... Ms. Taylor BUMILLER
05 Academic Dean .... Dr. Hee Cheol LEE
06 Registrar/Admission .... Mr. Jeoung H. HAM
08 Director of Library Services .... Mrs. Mi Kyoung HWANG
10 Director of Finance .... Mr. Kyong S. YEOM
21 Business Office Manager .... Mrs. Bokhee SONG
45 Director of Planning & Marketing .... Mr. Jae Pil SONG
12 Korea Office Regional Director .... Dr. Jae M. SONG
12 Washington DC Regional Director .... Dr. Yoo K. KO
07 Admission Counselor .... Mr. Sang Bae SEO
88 Dir Sch of Intl Aviation/Bus Ldrshp .... Dr. Soon C BYEON
73 Dir Col & Grad School of Theology .... Dr. Myeong Hwan OH
64 Director of School of Music .... Dr. Eunkyung SON
12 Dir of MIRI .... Dr. Joseph Y. PARK

Midwestern Baptist Theological Seminary (C)

5001 N Oak Trafficway, Kansas City MO 64118-4697
County: Clay FICE Identification: 002485
Unit ID: 178208
Telephone: (816) 414-3700 Carnegie Class: Spec-4-yr-Faith
FAX Number: (816) 414-3724 Calendar System: Semester
URL: www.mbts.edu
Established: 1957 Annual Undergrad Tuition & Fees: $8,410
Enrollment: 3,432 Coed
Affiliation or Control: Southern Baptist IRS Status: 501(c)3
Highest Offering: Doctorate
Accreditation: HLC, THEOL

01 President .... Dr. Jason K. ALLEN
05 Provost .... Dr. Jason DUESING
10 VP for Inst Administration/Fin Svcs ... Mr. James KRAGENBRING
30 VP of Institutional Relations .... Mr. Charles SMITH
20 Dean Spurgeon College .... Dr. Samuel BIERIG
58 Dean of Graduate Studies .... Dr. Thor MADSEN
09 Dean of Institutional Effectiveness .... Dr. Rodney A. HARRISON
73 Dean of Postgraduate Studies .... Dr. Rodney A. HARRISON
32 Dean of Students .... Dr. John Mark YEATS
20 Associate Dean .... Dr. Rustin UMSTATTD
13 Director of Info Technology .... Mr. David MEYER
06 Registrar .... Mr. Jared KATHCART
08 Librarian .... Ms. Kenette HARDER
84 Dir Student Recruitment & Admission .... Mr. Camden PULLIAM

Mineral Area College (D)

5270 Flat River Road, Park Hills MO 63601-2224
County: Saint Francois FICE Identification: 002486
Unit ID: 178217
Telephone: (573) 431-4593 Carnegie Class: Assoc/HT-High Trad
FAX Number: (573) 518-2164 Calendar System: Semester
URL: www.mineralarea.edu
Established: 1922 Annual Undergrad Tuition & Fees (In-District): $5,200
Enrollment: 2,410 Coed
Affiliation or Control: Local IRS Status: 501(c)3
Highest Offering: Associate Degree
Accreditation: HLC, EMT, MLTAD, PTAA, #RAD

01 President .... Dr. Joe GILGOUR
05 Provost .... Mr. Roger MCMILLIAN
32 Dean Student Services .... Ms. Julie SHEETS
10 Chief Financial Officer .... Ms. Lori CRUMP
06 Registrar .... Ms. Connie HOLDER
09 Director of Institutional Research .... Ms. Lisa EDBURG
26 Director of College Communications .... Ms. Danielle BASLER
30 Director of Development .... Mr. Kevin THURMAN
15 Director Human Resources .... Ms. Kathryn NEFF
37 Director Student Financial Aid .... Ms. Denise SEBASTIAN
38 Director Student Counseling .... Mr. Michael EASTER
18 General Services Director .... Mr. Rodney RESINGER
04 Administrative Asst to President .... Ms. Amy MCKENNA-JONES
08 Director of the Library .... Mr. Ryan HARRINGTON
19 Director Security/Safety .... Mr. Rich FLOTRON
39 Co-Director Student Housing .... Mr. Blake JONES
39 Co-Director Student Housing .... Ms. Julie CRABDREE
41 Athletic Director .... Mr. Jim GERWITZ

Missouri Baptist University (E)

One College Park Drive, Saint Louis MO 63141-8698
County: Saint Louis FICE Identification: 007540
Unit ID: 178244
Telephone: (314) 434-1115 Carnegie Class: Masters/L
FAX Number: (314) 434-7596 Calendar System: Semester
URL: www.mobap.edu
Established: 1964 Annual Undergrad Tuition & Fees: $29,360
Enrollment: 4,860 Coed
Affiliation or Control: Baptist IRS Status: 501(c)3
Highest Offering: Doctorate
Accreditation: HLC, CACREP, CAEP, EXSC, MUS, NURSE, @SW

01 President .... Dr. Keith L. ROSS
04 Assistant to the President .... Mrs. Janet MAYFIELD
05 Senior VP of Academic Affs/Provost .... Dr. Andy CHAMBERS
26 VP of Enroll/Mktg/Communications .... Mr. Bryce CHAPMAN
32 VP of Student Development .... Dr. Benjamin LION
10 VP for Business Affairs .... Mr. Oran WOODWORTH
20 Assoc VP for Academic Affs & Accred .... Dr. Lydia THEBEAU
58 Assoc VP for Grad Affairs .... Dr. Melanie BISHOP
29 Assoc Director for Alumni Relations .... Mrs. Abby KASSEBAUM
85 Director of International Services .... Ms. Marie TUDOR
09 Director Institutional Research .... Mr. Tim DELICATH
08 Director of Library Services .... Mrs. Zana SUEME
37 Director Financial Services .... Mr. Zach GREENLEE
111 Assoc VP for Univ Advancement .... Mrs. Ashlee JOHNSON
35 Assoc Dean Students .... Mrs. Amy GOODBERLET
41 Assoc VP & Director of Athletics .... Dr. Thomas SMITH
18 Director Campus Operations .... Mr. Andy HOUGH
06 Director of Records .... Mrs. Thea ABRAHAM
15 Director Personnel Services .... Mrs. Laurie WALLACE
13 Director of Information Systems .... Mr. Jerry MCKITTRICK
19 Director Public Safety .... Mr. Stephen HEIDKE
21 Controller .... Mrs. Pam SAVAGE
30 Development Officer .... Mrs. Ashlee JOHNSON
07 Exec Director of Admissions .... Mrs. Cynthia SUTTON
28 Diversity/Inclusion Initiative .... Vacant
66 Dean of School of Nursing .... Dr. Amber PYATT
106 Assoc VP for Extended Learning .... Dr. Amber HENRY
39 Dir of Student Life .... Mrs. Taira SCHERTZ
50 Dean of Business .... Dr. Karen KANNENBERG
53 Dean of Education .... Dr. Tammy COX

Missouri Southern State University (F)

3950 E Newman Road, Joplin MO 64801-1595
County: Jasper FICE Identification: 002488
Unit ID: 178341
Telephone: (417) 625-9300 Carnegie Class: Bac-Diverse
FAX Number: (417) 625-3121 Calendar System: Semester
URL: www.mssu.edu
Established: 1965 Annual Undergrad Tuition & Fees (In-State): $6,964
Enrollment: 5,045 Coed
Affiliation or Control: State IRS Status: 501(c)3
Highest Offering: Master's
Accreditation: HLC, ACBSP, CAEP, COARC, DH, EMT, MUS, NUR, RAD, SW

01 President .... Dr. Dean A. VAN GALEN
05 Int Provost/VP Academic Affairs .... Ms. Lorinda HACKETT
32 Int VP Student Affairs/Enrollment .... Dr. Julie WENGERT
10 Vice President Business Affairs .... Mr. Rob YUST
30 Exec Vice Pres for Development .... Dr. Brad HODSON
20 Prov/Vice Pres Academic Affairs .... Dr. Wendy MCGRANE
06 Registrar .... Ms. Faustina ABRAHAM
08 Library Director .... Mr. James CAPECI
37 Director Student Financial Aid .... Ms. Becca L. DISKIN
21 Treasurer .... Mrs. Linda EIS
15 Director Human Resources .... Mr. Evan JEWSBURY
18 Director Facilities/Physical Plant .... Mr. Bryan GOODWIN
76 Int Dean College of Health Sciences .... Ms. Erica WIGHT
49 Dean College of Arts & Sciences .... Dr. Marsi ARCHER
53 Interim Dean College of Education .... Dr. Holly HACKETT
50 Dean Plaster College of Business .... Dr. Jeff ZIMMERMAN
04 Administrative Asst to President .... Ms. Laura BOYD
07 Director of Admissions .... Dr. Shellie HEWITT
104 Director Study Abroad .... Dr. Chad STEBBINS
106 Director Distance Learning .... Mr. Scott SNELL
108 Dir Institutional Effectiveness .... Vacant
19 Chief of Campus Police .... Mr. Kenneth KENNEDY
41 Director of Athletics .... Mr. Robert MALLORY
44 Director of Annual Giving .... Ms. Elisa BRYANT
114 Dir Budget & Operations .... Mr. Jeff GIBSON
26 Dir University Relations/Marketing .... Ms. Heather LESMEISTER
29 Director Alumni Relations .... Ms. Lee ELLIFF POUND
28 Director of Diversity .... Ms. Stacey CLAY
13 Chief Info Technology Officer (CIO) .... Mr. Don MIHULKA
39 Director Student Housing .... Mr. Joshua M. DOAK

Missouri State University (G)

901 S National Avenue, Springfield MO 65897-0027
County: Greene FICE Identification: 002503
Unit ID: 179566
Telephone: (417) 836-8500 Carnegie Class: DU-Mod
FAX Number: (417) 836-7669 Calendar System: Semester
URL: www.missouristate.edu
Established: 1905 Annual Undergrad Tuition & Fees (In-State): $7,938
Enrollment: 23,505 Coed
Affiliation or Control: State IRS Status: 501(c)3
Highest Offering: Doctorate
Accreditation: HLC, ADNUR, ANEST, ARCPA, AUD, CAATE, CACREP, CAPRT, CEA, CONST, DIETD, DIETI, MUS, NURSE, OT, PH, PTA, SP, SW, THEA

01 President .... Mr. Clifton M. SMART, III
05 Provost .... Dr. Frank E. EINHELLIG
12 Chancellor West Plains Campus .... Dr. Dennis LANCASTER
46 VP for Research/Economic Devel .... Dr. James P. BAKER
11 Vice Pres Administrative Services .... Mr. Matthew MORRIS
111 Vice Pres University Advancement .... Mr. W. Brent DUNN
32 VP Student Affairs & Dean of Stdts .... Dr. Dee SISCOE
26 VP Marketing and Communications .... Ms. Suzanne SHAW
20 Deputy Provost .... Dr. Christopher J. CRAIG
20 Associate Provost .... Dr. Kelly WOOD
20 Associate Provost .... Dr. Joye NORRIS
58 Dean of Grad College .... Dr. Julie J. MASTERSON
10 Chief Financial Officer .... Mr. Steve FOUCART
84 Associate VP Enrollment Mgmt & Svcs .. Mr. Rob HORNBERGER
08 Dean Library Services .... Mr. Thomas A. PETERS
28 Chief Diversity Officer .... Mr. H. Wes PRATT
09 Director of Institutional Research .... Dr. Michelle D. OLSEN
29 Exec Dir of Alumni Relations .... Vacant
15 Director of Human Resources .... Mr. Scot SCOBEE
37 Director of Student Financial Aid .... Mr. Rob MOORE
19 Director of University Safety .... Mr. David A. HALL
36 Director of the Career Center .... Dr. Kelly E. RAPP
13 Chief Information Officer .... Mr. Jeff P. COINER
100 Chief of Staff .... Mr. Ryan DEBOEF
23 Director of Health & Wellness Svcs .... Dr. Dave MUEGGE
92 Director Honors College .... Dr. John F. CHUCHIAK
18 Director Facilities Management .... Mr. Brad B. KIELHOFNER
96 Director of Procurement .... Mr. Mike WILLS
07 Director of Admissions .... Ms. Teresa HANEY
06 Asst VP Enrollment Mgmt/Registrar .... Ms. Angela YOUNG
49 Dean College Arts & Letters .... Dr. Shawn T. WAHL
79 Dean Col Humanities/Public Affairs .... Dr. Victor MATTHEWS
76 Dean Col Health/Human Services .... Dr. Mark SMITH
81 Dean Col Natural/Applied Science .... Dr. Tamera S. JAHNKE
53 Dean College of Education .... Vacant
50 Dean College of Business .... Dr. David B. MEINERT
85 Director of International Services .... Mr. Patrick M. PARNELL
105 Dir of Web Strategy and Devel .... Ms. Jessica J. HEINZ
41 Athletic Director .... Mr. Kyle MOATS
43 General Counsel .... Ms. Rachael M. DOCKERY
04 Exec Assistant to the President .... Ms. Jessica L. SILVEY
101 Secretary of the Board .... Ms. Rowena STONE
102 Director Foundation/Corporate Rels .... Ms. Stephanie MATTHEWS
104 Director Study Abroad .... Ms. Elizabeth C. STRONG
108 Assoc Prov Public Affs & Assessment .... Ms. Keri FRANKLIN
39 Dir Resident Life/Student Housing .... Mr. Gary K. STEWART

Missouri State University - West Plains (H)

128 Garfield Avenue, West Plains MO 65775-2715
County: Howell FICE Identification: 031060
Unit ID: 179344
Telephone: (417) 255-7255 Carnegie Class: Assoc/HT-Mix Trad/Non
FAX Number: (417) 255-7962 Calendar System: Semester
URL: www.wp.missouristate.edu
Established: 1963 Annual Undergrad Tuition & Fees (In-State): $4,620
Enrollment: 1,920 Coed
Affiliation or Control: State IRS Status: 501(c)3
Highest Offering: Associate Degree
Accreditation: HLC

01 Chancellor .... Dr. Dennis LANCASTER
05 Interim Dean of Academics .... Dr. Michael ORF
32 Dean of Student Services .... Dr. Angela TOTTY
20 Assistant Dean of Academic Affairs .... Dr. Michael ORF
10 Director of Business/Support Svcs .... Mr. Crockett OAKS
30 Asst Director of Development/Alumni .... Ms. Amber CARR
26 Dir of Communications/Public Rels .... Mr. Ian CAMEJO
31 Director of Univ/Community Pgms .... Ms. Brenda POLYARD
06 Registrar .... Mrs. Laurie WALL
13 Dir Information Technology Services .... Mr. David YOUNG
18 Chief Facilities/Physical Plant .... Mr. Ron HENSLEY
04 Executive Asst to Chancellor .... Ms. Trish SMITH
08 Director Library Services .... Ms. Rebekah MCKINNEY
07 Coord of Admissions .... Mrs. Melissa JETT
09 Coord of Institutional Research .... Ms. Carrie STEEN
35 Coord Student Life and Development .... Mr. Jared CATES

Missouri Valley College (I)

500 E College, Marshall MO 65340-3197
County: Saline FICE Identification: 002489
Unit ID: 178369
Telephone: (660) 831-4000 Carnegie Class: Bac-Diverse
FAX Number: (660) 831-4039 Calendar System: Semester
URL: www.moval.edu
Established: 1889 Annual Undergrad Tuition & Fees: $21,500
Enrollment: 1,682 Coed
Affiliation or Control: Presbyterian Church (U.S.A.) IRS Status: 501(c)3
Highest Offering: Master's
Accreditation: HLC, NURSE

01 President .... Dr. Bonnie HUMPHREY
111 Vice Pres of External Relations .... Mr. Eric SAPPINGTON

32 Vice Pres Student Affairs .... Dr. Heath MORGAN
05 VP of Academic Affairs .... Dr. Diane BARTHOLOMEW
18 Vice Pres of Operations .... Mr. Tim SCHULTE
41 Exec Vice Pres/Athletic Director .... Mr. Tom FIFER
10 VP Business Svcs/Enrollment Mgmt .... Mr. Greg SILVEY
07 Director of Admissions .... Ms. Jessica GREEN
06 Registrar .... Ms. Marsha LASHLEY
21 Director Business Office .... Ms. Paula BURKE
08 Head Librarian .... Dr. Bryan CARSON
42 Director Campus Ministry .... Rev. Pam SEBASTIAN
09 Director of Institutional Research .... Dr. Tonia COMPTON
37 Director of Financial Aid .... Mr. Derek BOHNSACK
38 Director Counseling Center .... Ms. Teresa CESELSKI
13 Chief Information Officer .... Mr. Omar ALREFAE
26 Dir of Marketing & Public Relations .... Ms. Danielle DURHAM
19 Director of Public Safety .... Mr. Nick BOEHMER
29 Alumni Relations Director .... Ms. Jennifer SWIFT
04 Administrative Asst to President .... Ms. Brandy SCHULTE

Missouri Western State University (A)

4525 Downs Drive, Saint Joseph MO 64507-2294
County: Buchanan FICE Identification: 002490
Unit ID: 178387
Telephone: (816) 271-4200 Carnegie Class: Masters/M
FAX Number: N/A Calendar System: Semester
URL: www.missouriwestern.edu
Established: 1915 Annual Undergrad Tuition & Fees (In-State): $8,875
Enrollment: 4,911 Coed
Affiliation or Control: State IRS Status: 501(c)3
Highest Offering: Master's
Accreditation: HLC, CAEPN, CAHIIM, MUS, NURSE, PTAA, SW

01 President .... Dr. Elizabeth KENNEDY
100 Chief of Staff .... Ms. Chris DUNN
05 Int Provost .... Mr. Marc MANGANARO
111 Vice Pres Univ Advancement .... Vacant
10 VP Finance & Administration .... Mr. Darrell MORRISON
32 Vice Pres for Student Affairs .... Ms. Melissa MACE
20 Int Vice Provost Academic Affairs .... Ms. Elise HEPWORTH
21 Assoc VP Financial Plng/Admin .... Vacant
84 Vice Pres Enrollment Mgmt .... Ms. Melissa MACE
81 Interim Dean Science & Health .... Dr. Crystal HARRIS
57 Dean of Fine Arts .... Vacant
49 Dean Liberal Arts .... Dr. Joel HYER
51 Dean of Western Institute .... Vacant
50 Dean of Business & Prof Studies .... Dr. Logan JONES
35 AVP Student Affs & Dean of Students .... Mr. Brett BRUNER
06 Registrar .... Ms. Susan BRACCIANO
08 Director of Library .... Ms. Sally GIBSON
37 Director Student Financial Aid .... Ms. Cindy SPOTTS-CONRAD
13 Director of Information Technology .... Vacant
38 Director Student Counsel & Testing .... Mr. H. David BROWN
18 Director Physical Plant .... Mr. Bryan ADKINS
41 Vice President Intercol Athletics .... Vacant
15 Director of Human Resources .... Ms. Sara FREEMYER
86 Director of External Relations .... Vacant
26 Chief Communications Officer .... Ms. Becky DUNN
29 Exec Dir of Alumni Relations/Giving .... Ms. Kimberly WEDDLE
96 Director of Purchasing .... Mr. Tim KISSOCK
04 Executive Associate to President .... Ms. Betsy WRIGHT
36 Career Development Director .... Ms. Megan RANEY
39 Director Student Housing .... Mr. Nathan ROBERTS
19 Chief of University Police .... Ms. Jill VOLTMER

Moberly Area Community College (B)

101 College Avenue, Moberly MO 65270-1304
County: Randolph FICE Identification: 002491
Unit ID: 178448
Telephone: (660) 263-4100 Carnegie Class: Assoc/HT-Mix Trad/Non
FAX Number: (660) 263-6252 Calendar System: Semester
URL: www.macc.edu
Established: 1927 Annual Undergrad Tuition & Fees (In-District): $5,520
Enrollment: 4,878 Coed
Affiliation or Control: State/Local IRS Status: 501(c)3
Highest Offering: Associate Degree
Accreditation: HLC, MLTAD, OTA, SURGT

01 President .... Dr. Jeffery LASHLEY
10 Vice President for Finance .... Ms. Susan SPENCER
05 Vice President for Instruction .... Dr. Todd MARTIN
75 Dean Workforce Dev/Technical Educ .... Ms. Jo FEY
32 Dean Student Affairs & Enrollment .... Ms. Michele MCCALL
20 Dean of Academic Affairs .... Mr. Matthew CRIST
09 Dir Inst Reporting & Compliance .... Ms. Meghan HOLLERAN
21 Director Business Services .... Ms. Heather WITT
26 Dir Marketing and Public Relations .... Vacant
18 Director of Plant Operations .... Mr. Eric ROSS
13 Chief Information Officer .... Mr. Robert WIDEMAN
08 Dir Library & Academic Resources .... Ms. Donna MONNIG
15 Director of Human Resources .... Ms. Ann PARKS
14 Dir of Instructional Technology .... Ms. Susan BURDEN
37 Director of Financial Aid .... Ms. Amy HAGER
06 Registrar .... Ms. Julie PERKINS
29 Dir Inst Development & Alumni Svcs ...... Ms. Elizabeth GREGORY
36 Dir Career and Technical Programs .... Ms. Suzi MCGARVEY
88 Director of Academic Services .... Ms. Katelyn WILSON
04 Executive Asst to President .... Ms. Tammi RICHARDSON
103 Exec Dir of Workforce Development .... Ms. Brandi GLOVER
19 Director Security & Residence Life .... Ms. Lori PERRY
76 Dean of Health Sciences .... Ms. Michelle FREY

Nazarene Theological Seminary (C)

1700 E Meyer Boulevard, Kansas City MO 64131-1263
County: Jackson FICE Identification: 002494
Unit ID: 178518
Telephone: (816) 268-5400 Carnegie Class: Spec-4-yr-Faith
FAX Number: (816) 268-5500 Calendar System: Semester
URL: www.nts.edu
Established: 1945 Annual Graduate Tuition & Fees: N/A
Enrollment: 160 Coed
Affiliation or Control: Church Of The Nazarene IRS Status: 501(c)3
Highest Offering: Doctorate; No Undergraduates
Accreditation: THEOL

01 President .... Dr. Jeren ROWELL
05 Dean of the Faculty .... Dr. Josh SWEEDEN
11 Dean for Administration .... Dr. Glenn MILLER
08 Director Library Service .... Mrs. Debra BRADSHAW
37 Financial Aid Coordinator .... Mrs. Cindy HOWARD
26 Director of Communications .... Dr. Jason VEACH
111 Dean for Advancement .... Rev. Timothy MCPHERSON
04 Admin Assistant to the President .... Mrs. Nancy MCPHERSON
13 Chief Information Technology Ofcr .... Dr. Stephen PORTER
123 Director of Graduate Admissions .... Dr. Levi JONES
07 Director of Admissions .... Mr. Derek DAVIS
101 Secretary of the Institution/Board .... Mr. Allen BROWN
15 Dir HR/Controller .... Ms. Carol NOLTING
29 Director Alumni Affairs .... Rev. Dana PREUSCH
38 Director Student Counseling .... Dr. William KIRKEMO
18 Chief Facilities/Physical Plant Ofc .... Mr. Steve GARROW

North Central Missouri College (D)

1301 Main Street, Trenton MO 64683-1824
County: Grundy FICE Identification: 002514
Unit ID: 179715
Telephone: (660) 359-3948 Carnegie Class: Assoc/MT-VT-High Non
FAX Number: (660) 359-2211 Calendar System: Semester
URL: www.ncmissouri.edu
Established: 1925 Annual Undergrad Tuition & Fees (In-District): $5,670
Enrollment: 1,591 Coed
Affiliation or Control: Local IRS Status: 501(c)3
Highest Offering: Associate Degree
Accreditation: HLC, MLTAD, OTA

01 President .... Dr. Lenny KLAVER
05 Vice President of Academics .... Dr. Tristan LONDRE
10 Vice President of Finance .... Mr. Tyson OTTO
32 Vice President of Student Affairs .... Dr. Kristen ALLEY
20 Dean of Instruction .... Dr. Mitchell HOLDER
06 Registrar .... Ms. Joni OAKS
13 Chief Information Officer .... Ms. Jennifer TRIPLETT
08 Librarian .... Ms. Beth CALDARELLO
37 Director of Financial Aid .... Ms. Kimberly MEEKER
30 Director Development .... Ms. Alicia ENDICOTT
40 Director Bookstore .... Ms. Cecilia MARSH
39 Director Student Housing .... Mr. Donnie HILLERMAN
41 Athletic Director .... Mr. Nate GAMET
18 Director of Facilities .... Mr. Randy YOUNG
105 Director Web Services .... Ms. Tami CAMPBELL
09 Director of Institutional Research .... Ms. Tara NOAH
07 Director of Admissions .... Ms. Megan PESTER
26 Chief Public Relations Officer .... Ms. Kristi HARRIS

Northwest Missouri State University (E)

800 University Drive, Maryville MO 64468-6015
County: Nodaway FICE Identification: 002496
Unit ID: 178624
Telephone: (660) 562-1212 Carnegie Class: Masters/L
FAX Number: (660) 562-1900 Calendar System: Trimester
URL: www.nwmissouri.edu
Established: 1905 Annual Undergrad Tuition & Fees (In-State): $8,500
Enrollment: 7,267 Coed
Affiliation or Control: State IRS Status: 501(c)3
Highest Offering: Beyond Master's But Less Than Doctorate
Accreditation: HLC, AAQEP, ACBSP, CAPRT, DIETD, @DIETI, MUS

01 President .... Dr. John JASINSKI
05 Provost .... Dr. Jamie HOOYMAN
10 VP of Finance & Administration .... Ms. Stacy CARRICK
32 VP of Student Affairs .... Dr. Matt BAKER
111 VP Univ Advance/Dir NW Foundation ... Ms. Mitzi G. MARCHANT
19 Chief Univ Police/VP of Culture .... Dr. Clarence GREEN
58 Assoc Prov for Grad & Prof Studies .... Dr. Gregory HADDOCK
49 Assoc Prov Dean Col of Arts & Sci .... Dr. Michael STEINER
20 Assoc Prov Academic Ops & Dev .... Dr. Jay JOHNSON
53 Dean School of Education .... Dr. Timothy WALL
26 Exec Dir Marketing/Communications .... Mr. Brandon STANLEY
41 Director Athletics .... Mr. Andy PETERSON
15 AVP of Human Resources .... Ms. Krista BARCUS
13 AVP of IT .... Mr. Brennan LEHMAN
09 AVP of Institutional Research .... Mr. Egon HEIDENDAL
96 Director of Purchasing .... Ms. Alyssa PULLEY
21 AVP of Finance .... Ms. Mary COLLINS
18 AVP of Facility Services .... Mr. Dan HASLAG
84 AVP Admissions & Student Success .... Dr. Allison S. HOFFMANN
60 Director School of Comm/Mass Media .... Dr. Matt WALKER
47 Director School of Agriculture .... Mr. Rodney BARR
50 Director School of Business .... Dr. Ben BLACKFORD
77 Director School of Computer Science .... Ms. Joni ADKINS
76 Dir School of Health Sci & Wellness .... Dr. Terry LONG
04 Exec Asst to President/Sec BOR .... Ms. Melissa EVANS
06 Registrar .... Ms. Terri VOGEL
07 Director of Admissions-Operations .... Ms. Tamera J. GROW
22 AVP Student Affairs/Title IX/Equity .... Mr. William R. SABIO
28 AVP Diversity/Inclusion .... Dr. Justin MALLETT
29 Dir Alumni Relations/Annual Giving .... Vacant
102 Director Corp Relations/Major Gifts .... Ms. Jill BROWN
37 Director Financial Assistance .... Mr. Charles MAYFIELD
23 AVP Stdnt Affs/Hlth/Well-Being .... Mr. Chris DAWE
36 Director Career Services .... Ms. Hannah CHRISTIAN
104 Director Intl Involvement Center .... Dr. Philip R. HULL
105 Manager of Web Services .... Ms. Crystal D. WARD
106 Director NW Online & LTC .... Dr. Darla J. RUNYON
108 Assoc Dir Accreditation/Assessment .... Dr. Mike MCBRIDE
25 Grants Coordinator .... Mr. Ty T. PARSONS
38 Assistant Director Counseling .... Ms. Kristen S. PELTZ
39 Asst Director Residential Life .... Mr. Mike MILLER
14 Director Technology Services .... Mr. Merlin R. MILLER

Ozark Christian College (F)

1111 N Main Street, Joplin MO 64801-4804
County: Jasper FICE Identification: 022027
Unit ID: 178679
Telephone: (417) 626-1234 Carnegie Class: Spec-4-yr-Faith
FAX Number: (417) 624-0090 Calendar System: Semester
URL: occ.edu
Established: 1942 Annual Undergrad Tuition & Fees: $13,600
Enrollment: 629 Coed
Affiliation or Control: Independent Non-Profit IRS Status: 501(c)3
Highest Offering: Master's
Accreditation: HLC, BI

01 President .... Matt PROCTOR
03 Executive Vice President .... Damien SPIKEREIT
111 Exec VP of College Advancement .... Jim DALRYMPLE
05 Executive VP of Academics .... Chad RAGSDALE
20 Assoc Academic Dean .... Shane WOOD
106 Assc Dean Online Learning/Acad Tech .... Shawn LINDSAY
88 Director Academic Operations .... Lisa WITTE
09 VP Inst Research & Effectiveness .... Teresa ROBERTS
32 VP of Student Affairs .... Andy STORMS
11 VP of Campus Operations .... David MCMILLIN
84 VP of Enrollment Management .... Robert WITTE
26 Director Marketing & Communications .... Amy STORMS
43 General Counsel .... Doug MILLER

Ozarks Technical Community College (G)

1001 E Chestnut Expressway, Springfield MO 65802-3625
County: Greene FICE Identification: 030830
Unit ID: 177472
Telephone: (417) 447-7500 Carnegie Class: Assoc/MT-VT-High Trad
FAX Number: N/A Calendar System: Semester
URL: www.otc.edu
Established: 1990 Annual Undergrad Tuition & Fees (In-District): $4,924
Enrollment: 11,237 Coed
Affiliation or Control: State/Local IRS Status: 501(c)3
Highest Offering: Associate Degree
Accreditation: HLC, ACFEI, ADNUR, CAHIIM, COARC, DA, DH, EMT, IFSAC, MLTAD, NAEYC, NAIT, OTA, PTAA, SURGT

01 Chancellor .... Dr. Hal L. HIGDON
100 Chief of Staff .... Ms. Amy BACON
101 Secretary to the Chancellor .... Ms. Janel GRASSI
05 Vice Chancellor Academic Affairs .... Dr. Tracy MCGRADY
11 Vice Chancellor Admin Services .... Mr. Rob RECTOR
32 Vice Chancellor Student Affairs .... Ms. Joan BARRETT
10 Vice Chancellor Finance .... Ms. Sharon DAY
12 President Table Rock Campus .... Dr. Robert GRIFFITH
12 President Richwood Valley Campus .... Dr. Cliff DAVIS
13 Interim Chief Technology Officer .... Mr. Eric KYLE
15 Assoc VC Human Resources/Workforce .... Ms. Ocki HAAS
20 Dean of Academic Services .... Dr. Megan WEAVER
76 Dean of Allied Health Programs .... Dr. Aaron LIGHT
97 Dean of General Education .... Mr. Lance RENNER
72 Dean of Technical Education .... Dr. Matthew HUDSON
103 Exec Dir Workforce Development .... Ms. Sherry COKER
06 Asst Registrar Records/Registration .... Ms. Amy BERGANT
38 Director of Counseling Services .... Mr. James CARPENTER
26 Director Communications & Marketing .... Ms. Sarah BARGO
18 College Director Facilities/Grounds .... Mr. Raymond WADE
28 Title IX Coord/Col Dir Civil Rights .... Mr. Kevin LUEBBERING
37 College Director of Financial Aid .... Ms. Kim CARY
08 Director College Library .... Ms. Sarah FANCHER
88 Director College Library RVC/TRC .... Ms. Angela SWIFT
36 Director of Career Employment Svcs .... Vacant
102 Exec Director of OTC Foundation .... Ms. Amy BACON
30 Development Coordinator .... Ms. Kirsten BINDER
09 Chief Research/Govt Affairs Officer .... Mr. Matthew SIMPSON
19 College Director Safety & Security .... Mr. Scott LEVEN
35 Dean of Students .... Ms. Joyce BATEMAN
88 Director Dual Credit/HS Admissions .... Ms. Piper WILSON
105 Director Web Services .... Mr. George LAMELZA
106 Dean Online Education/Faculty Dev .... Dr. Julie COLTHARP
25 Chief Strategy Officer .... Dr. Abigail BENZ
96 Director of Procurement .... Ms. Katie HIGHFILL
07 Director of Admissions/Registrar .... Mr. Scott FIEDLER
88 Exec Dir Ctr for Advanced Mfg .... Mr. Robert RANDOLPH

121 College Dir of Student Success .... Mr. Steve FOUSE
88 Director Republic Education Center .... Mr. James ACKERMAN
28 Director Diversity/Equity/Inclusion .... Mr. Daniel OGUNYEMI

Ozarks Technical Community College Richwood Valley (A)

3369 W Jackson Street, Nixa MO 65714
Telephone: (417) 447-7700 Identification: 770324
Accreditation: &HLC

Ozarks Technical Community College Table Rock Campus (B)

10698 Historic Highway, MO 165, Hollister MO 65672
Telephone: (417) 336-6239 Identification: 770325
Accreditation: &HLC

Park University (C)

8700 River Park Drive, Parkville MO 64152-3795
County: Platte FICE Identification: 002498
Unit ID: 178721
Telephone: (816) 741-2000 Carnegie Class: Masters/L
FAX Number: (816) 746-6423 Calendar System: Semester
URL: www.park.edu
Established: 1875 Annual Undergrad Tuition & Fees: $11,929
Enrollment: 10,165 Coed
Affiliation or Control: Independent Non-Profit IRS Status: 501(c)3
Highest Offering: Master's
Accreditation: HLC, ACBSP, NURSE, SW

01 Interim President .... Mr. Shane SMEED
11 Interim VP/Chief Operating Officer .... Ms. Kena WOLF
05 Provost .... Dr. Michelle MYERS
10 Chief Financial Officer .... Mr. Gregg GIVENS
111 Chief Advancement Officer .... Mr. Nathan MARTICKE
20 Associate Provost .... Dr. Emily SALLEE
29 Assoc VP for External Relations .... Mr. Erik BERGRUD
32 Associate VP/Dean of Student Life .... Dr. Jayme UDEN
58 Director Graduate Student Success .... Ms. Joslyn CREIGHTON
06 Registrar .... Dr. Cynthia OTTS
37 Director Student Financial Service .... Ms. Brynn BOLOGNA
15 Chief Human Resources Officer .... Mr. Roger DUSING
41 Director of Athletics .... Mr. Claude ENGLISH
66 Director of Nursing Program .... Ms. Summer MASTERS
85 Sr Director International Students .... Mr. Kevin VICKER
13 Chief Information Officer .... Mr. David WHITTAKER
19 Director of Campus Safety .... Mr. William LONDON
04 Executive Asst to the President .... Ms. Bobbi SHAW
50 Dean College of Management .... Mr. Kirby BROWN
20 Associate VP Academic Operations .... Dr. Kathryn ERVIN
49 Dean Liberal Arts & Sciences .... Dr. James PASLEY
53 Dean School for Education .... Dr. Karen GARBER-MILLER
101 Asst Secretary to Board of Trustees .... Ms. Ami WISDOM
100 Chief of Staff .... Ms. Laure CHRISTENSEN
88 Assoc Dir International Recruitment ..... Ms. Lora ZAIDARHZAUVA
105 Director of Marketing/Digital .... Ms. Aimee PATTON
26 Dir Communications/Public Relations .... Mr. Brad BILES
36 Director of Career Development .... Ms. Leah FLETCHER
39 Director Student Housing .... Ms. Tonya WESSEL
21 Senior Director Financial Report .... Ms. Donna BAKER
09 Dir Institutional Effectiveness .... Ms. Jennifer HELLER
121 Sr Director Student Success .... Mr. Andrew DAVIS

Pinnacle Career Institute (D)

10301 Hickman Mills Drive, Kansas City MO 64137
County: Jackson FICE Identification: 010405
Unit ID: 177302
Telephone: (816) 331-5700 Carnegie Class: Assoc/HVT-High Trad
FAX Number: (816) 331-2026 Calendar System: Quarter
URL: www.pcitraining.edu
Established: 1953 Annual Undergrad Tuition & Fees: N/A
Enrollment: 508 Coed
Affiliation or Control: Proprietary IRS Status: Proprietary
Highest Offering: Associate Degree
Accreditation: ACCSC

01 Campus President .... Valerie BUJAK
05 Director of Education .... Kelly LAMB

Pinnacle Career Institute (E)

11500 Ambassador Dr Ste 221, Kansas City MO 64153
Telephone: (816) 331-5700 Identification: 770737
Accreditation: ACCSC

Ranken Technical College (F)

4431 Finney Avenue, Saint Louis MO 63113-2898
County: Saint Louis FICE Identification: 012500
Unit ID: 178891
Telephone: (314) 371-0236 Carnegie Class: Bac/Assoc-Assoc Dom
FAX Number: (314) 371-0241 Calendar System: Semester
URL: ranken.edu/
Established: 1907 Annual Undergrad Tuition & Fees: $15,947
Enrollment: 1,823 Coed
Affiliation or Control: Independent Non-Profit IRS Status: 501(c)3
Highest Offering: Baccalaureate
Accreditation: HLC, ACBSP

01 President .... Mr. Don J. POHL
10 Vice President for Finance & Admin ...... Mr. Peter T. MURTAUGH
00 Chief Executive Officer .... Mr. Stan SHOUN
22 VP Diversity/Student Success .... Ms. Crystal HERRON
51 Dean of Continuing Education .... Mr. Keyvan GERAMI
05 VP Educ/Dean Academic Affairs .... Mr. Dan KANIA
84 Dean of Enrollment Management/Mktg .... Ms. Frank MILLER

Research College of Nursing (G)

2525 E Meyer Boulevard, Kansas City MO 64132-1133
County: Jackson FICE Identification: 006392
Unit ID: 178989
Telephone: (816) 995-2800 Carnegie Class: Spec-4-yr-Other Health
FAX Number: (816) 995-2817 Calendar System: Semester
URL: www.researchcollege.edu
Established: 1980 Annual Undergrad Tuition & Fees: N/A
Enrollment: 420 Coed
Affiliation or Control: Proprietary IRS Status: Proprietary
Highest Offering: Master's
Accreditation: HLC, NURSE

01 President .... Dr. Thad R. WILSON
05 Dean .... Dr. Julie NAUSER
07 Director Admissions .... Ms. Leslie BURRY
32 Director Student Affairs .... Ms. Amanda GRAY
37 Director Financial Aid .... Ms. Stacie WITHERS
24 Director LRC .... Ms. Tobey STOSBERG
13 Senior Technology Analyst .... Mr. Bill HAMPSON
04 Administrative Asst to President .... Mrs. Sherry L. OWEN
06 Registrar .... Ms. Camelia WILLIAMS
08 Head Librarian .... Ms. Kitty SERLING
106 Dir Online Education/E-learning .... Ms. Sheryl MAX
111 Advancement & Development Officer .... Ms. Tiffany HAMLETT
39 Asst Director of Student Affairs .... Ms. Caelee LEHMAN
113 Coordinator of Student Accounts .... Ms. Marcy SACKMAN
88 Director of Resources .... Mr. Daniel ODER
09 Director of Institutional Research .... Ms. Christine HAMMOND
88 Director of Instructional Design .... Mr. Matthew LIVENGOOD

Rockbridge Seminary (H)

3111 East Battlefield Street, Springfield MO 65804
County: Greene Identification: 667151
Telephone: (866) 931-4300 Carnegie Class: Not Classified
FAX Number: (866) 931-4300 Calendar System: Semester
URL: www.rockbridge.edu
Established: 2002 Annual Graduate Tuition & Fees: N/A
Enrollment: N/A Coed
Affiliation or Control: Independent Non-Profit IRS Status: 501(c)3
Highest Offering: Doctorate; No Undergraduates
Accreditation: DEAC

01 President .... Tommy HILLIKER
05 Chief Academic Officer .... Dr. Mark SIMPSON
08 Head Librarian .... Seth ALLEN
04 Administrative Asst to President .... Brenda CIRTIN
121 Director of Academic Coaching .... Linda GRABER

Rockhurst University (I)

1100 Rockhurst Road, Kansas City MO 64110-2561
County: Jackson FICE Identification: 002499
Unit ID: 179043
Telephone: (816) 501-4000 Carnegie Class: Masters/L
FAX Number: (816) 501-4588 Calendar System: Semester
URL: www.rockhurst.edu
Established: 1910 Annual Undergrad Tuition & Fees: $39,780
Enrollment: 3,688 Coed
Affiliation or Control: Roman Catholic IRS Status: 501(c)3
Highest Offering: Doctorate
Accreditation: HLC, CAEP, NURSE, OT, PTA, SP

01 President .... Rev. Thomas B. CURRAN, SJ
28 Chief Inclusion Officer .... Dr. Leslie DOYLE
111 Vice President for Advancement .... Ms. Mary MOONEY BURNS
10 Chief Financial Officer .... Mr. Gerald MOENCH
05 Provost & Senior VP Acad Affairs .... Dr. Douglas N. DUNHAM
45 VP Strategy and Innovation .... Dr. Hubert BENITEZ
88 Vice Pres Mission & Ministry .... Ms. Cindy SCHMERSAL
32 VP Student Development/Athletics .... Dr. Matthew D. QUICK
13 Assoc VP Information Technology .... Mr. Bart KLEIN
18 Assoc VP Facilities Operations .... Mr. Jason RIORDAN
84 Assoc Provost Enrollment Services .... Dr. Paula SHORTER
108 Dir of Institutional Effectiveness .... Ms. Annalisa GRAMLICH
121 Assoc Provost of Student Success .... Ms. Melinda PETTEGREW
35 Director of Student Life .... Ms. Angie CARR ROBINETT
39 Assoc Dean of Students/Dir Res Life .... Mr. Mark HETZLER
04 Exec Assistant to the President .... Ms. Decla TYLER-SIMPSON
50 Interim Dean College of Business .... Dr. Myles GARTLAND
49 Dean Arts & Sciences .... Dr. Jennifer FRIEND
69 Dean College Health/Human Services .... Ms. Kris VACEK
66 Dean St Luke's School of Nursing .... Dr. Victoria GRANDO
76 Dean of Health Sciences .... Dr. Karla BRUNTZEL
08 Director Library .... Ms. Laurie E. HATHMAN
06 Registrar .... Ms. Brenda LANEY
37 Director Student Financial Aid .... Ms. Maureen MCKINNON
41 Director of Athletics .... Mr. Gary BURNS
15 Director of Human Resources .... Ms. Barbra UPTON-GARVIN
13 Director of Infrastructure Services .... Mr. Michael CRAIG
36 Director of Career Center .... Mr. Michael J. THEOBALD
30 Exec Director of Development .... Ms. Paula MOSS

26 Director of University Relations .... Ms. Katherine FROHOFF
110 Assistant Director Advancement .... Mr. Brent BLAZEK
42 Director of Campus Ministry .... Mr. Bill KRIEGE
19 Director Security/Safety .... Mr. Randy HOPKINS
38 Director of Student Counseling .... Dr. Elbert DARDEN
31 Dir Community Relations & Outreach ...... Ms. Alicia R. DOUGLAS
07 Director of Operations/Admission .... Ms. Annie LEHWALD
40 Director Bookstore .... Ms. Jami CADE
09 Project Manager Inst Data/Analytics .... Ms. Wendy PICKEL
14 Support Manager Computer Services .... Mr. Darnell JONES
21 Controller .... Ms. Kris PACE
104 Study Abroad Advisor .... Ms. Paivi BYBEE
106 Director Center for E-learning .... Ms. Laurena CALDERON
27 Director of Marketing .... Mr. Dave HUNT
88 Director of the Learning Center .... Mr. Kirk SKOGLUND
88 Director Center for Svc Learning .... Dr. Julia VARGAS

St. Charles Community College (J)

4601 Mid Rivers Mall Drive, Cottleville MO 63376-2865
County: Saint Charles FICE Identification: 025306
Unit ID: 262031
Telephone: (636) 922-8000 Carnegie Class: Assoc/HT-High Trad
FAX Number: (636) 922-8352 Calendar System: Semester
URL: www.stchas.edu
Established: 1986 Annual Undergrad Tuition & Fees (In-District): $4,152
Enrollment: 6,014 Coed
Affiliation or Control: State/Local IRS Status: 501(c)3
Highest Offering: Associate Degree
Accreditation: HLC, ADNUR, CAHIIM, CEA, CSHSE, EMT, OTA

01 President .... Dr. Barbara KAVALIER
05 VP Academic Affairs .... Dr. Holly MARTIN
11 VP Administrative Services/COO .... Mr. Todd GALBIERZ
32 VP Student Services .... Mr. Dave LEENHOUTS
15 VP Human Resources .... Ms. Terri EDRICH
26 VP Marketing/Student Life .... Ms. Heather MCDORMAN
20 AVP Academic Affairs .... Vacant
10 Asst VP Financial Services .... Ms. Susan RUBEMEYER
124 AVP Col Transitions/Support Svcs .. Ms. Kathy BROCKGREITENS
103 AVP Corporate & Community Dev .... Ms. Amanda SIZEMORE
35 Student Life Manager .... Mr. James BRATCHER
102 Exec Director of the Foundation .... Ms. Betsy SCHNEIDER
19 Exec Dir Public Safety/Facilities .... Mr. Bob RONKOSKI
37 Director Financial Aid .... Mr. David SEWARD
09 Director Institutional Research ..... Dr. Chris HUBBARD JACKSON
13 Exec Dir Information Technology .... Mr. Don POPHAM
21 Director Financial Services .... Ms. Barbara FUERST
121 Director Advising Svcs .... Ms. Diane AMZEN
41 Director Athletics .... Mr. Timothy BRIX
88 Director Technology Support .... Ms. Lisa MOUSER
50 Dean Bus/Sci/Ed/Math/CompSci .... Dr. Darren OSBURN
57 Dean Arts/Humanities/Soc Sci .... Dr. Mara VORACHEK-WARREN
103 Assoc Dean Workforce Pgm & Svcs .... Ms. Lauren DICKENS
36 Career Services Manager .... Ms. Jenny HAHN SCHNIPPER
96 Purchasing Manager .... Ms. Diana SCHOO
109 Asst Director Food Services .... Ms. Laura GRANT
40 Asst Director Bookstore .... Mr. Daniel GRANZOW
04 Sr Administrator Ofc of President .... Ms. Amy SNYDER

Saint Louis Christian College (K)

1360 Grandview Drive, Florissant MO 63033-6499
County: Saint Louis FICE Identification: 012580
Unit ID: 179256
Telephone: (314) 837-6777 Carnegie Class: Spec-4-yr-Faith
FAX Number: (314) 837-8291 Calendar System: Semester
URL: https://stlchristian.edu/
Established: 1956 Annual Undergrad Tuition & Fees: $13,280
Enrollment: 76 Coed
Affiliation or Control: Christian Churches And Churches of Christ
IRS Status: 501(c)3
Highest Offering: Baccalaureate
Accreditation: BI

01 President .... Mr. Terry STINE
10 VP of Finance/Administration .... Dr. Ron COOK
05 VP of Academics .... Dr. Scott WOMBLE
32 VP of Student Life .... Mr. Steve NAGLAK
111 VP of Advancement .... Mr. Dennis MCCONNAUGHHAY
04 Assistant to the President .... Ms. Deb PABARCUS
07 Director of Admissions .... Ms. Kelsey FORD
06 Registrar .... Ms. Cindy BINGAMON
37 Director of Financial Aid .... Ms. Cathi WILHOIT
08 Librarian .... Vacant
13 Dir IT/Tech Svcs Specialist .... Mr. Joshua BETTISON
40 Bookstore Manager .... Ms. Jeri Ann JERALDS

Saint Louis College of Health Careers-Fenton Campus (L)

1297 N Highway Drive, Fenton MO 63026-1909
Telephone: (636) 529-0000 Identification: 666274
Accreditation: ABHES, COARC, OTA, PTAA

† Branch campus of Saint Louis College of Health Careers-South Taylor, Saint Louis, MO.

Saint Louis College of Health Careers-South Taylor (M)

909 S Taylor Avenue, Saint Louis MO 63110-1511
County: Saint Louis FICE Identification: 023405
Unit ID: 179511

Telephone: (314) 652-0300 Carnegie Class: Spec 2-yr-Health
FAX Number: (314) 884-2838 Calendar System: Semester
URL: www.slchc.edu
Established: 1981 Annual Undergrad Tuition & Fees: N/A
Enrollment: 100 Coed
Affiliation or Control: Proprietary IRS Status: Proprietary
Highest Offering: Associate Degree
Accreditation: **ABHES**

11 Chief of Administration .... Dr. Rush ROBINSON
06 Registrar .... Ms. Teresa JACKSON
05 Director of Education .... Mr. Michael TRAAS

*Saint Louis Community College - Cosand Center (A)

3221 McKelvey Road, Bridgeton MO 63044
County: Saint Louis FICE Identification: 002471
Unit ID: 179308
Telephone: (314) 539-5000 Carnegie Class: N/A
FAX Number: (314) 539-5170
URL: www.stlcc.edu

01 Chancellor .... Dr. Jeff PITTMAN
05 Vice Chanc Academic Affairs .... Dr. Andrew LANGREHR
10 Vice Chanc Finance/Administration .... Mr. Paul ZINCK
32 Vice Chanc Student Affairs .... Dr. Christine DAVIS
103 Assoc VC Workforce Solutions .... Mr. Hart NELSON
13 Chief Information Officer .... Mr. Keith HACKE
15 Assoc Vice Chanc Human Resources .... Ms. Robin PHILLIPS
102 Executive Director STLCC Foundation .... Ms. Jo-Ann DIGMAN
26 Exec Dir Marketing/Communication .... Ms. Kedra TOLSON
09 Exec Dir of Inst Research/Planning .... Ms. Kelli BURNS
112 Director of Grants .... Vacant
06 Registrar .... Vacant
04 Administrative Assoc to Chancellor .... Ms. Yvonne BLOOM
101 Secretary of the Board .... Ms. Jessica GROVE
106 Mgr Online Student Services .... Ms. Stacey FOSTER
96 Assistant Controller .... Ms. Cindy GREEN
19 Dir Public Safety/Emergency Mgmt .... LtCol. Alfred ADKINS
43 Dir Legal Services/General Counsel .... Vacant

*Saint Louis Community College at Florissant Valley (B)

3400 Pershall Road, Saint Louis MO 63135-1499
Telephone: (314) 513-4200 FICE Identification: 002470
Accreditation: **&HLC**, ADNUR, ART

*Saint Louis Community College at Forest Park (C)

5600 Oakland Avenue, Saint Louis MO 63110-1393
Telephone: (314) 644-9100 Identification: 667353
Accreditation: **HLC**, ACFEI, ADNUR, CAHIIM, COARC, DA, DH, DMS, EMT, FUSER, MLTAD, RAD, SURGT

*Saint Louis Community College at Meramec (D)

11333 Big Bend Road, Kirkwood MO 63122-5720
Telephone: (314) 984-7500 FICE Identification: 002472
Accreditation: **&HLC**, ADNUR, ART, OTA, PTAA

*Saint Louis Community College at Wildwood (E)

2645 Generations Drive, Wildwood MO 63040-1168
Telephone: (636) 422-2000 Identification: 667084
Accreditation: **&HLC**

Saint Louis University (F)

One Grand Boulevard, Saint Louis MO 63103-2097
FICE Identification: 002506
Unit ID: 179159
Telephone: (314) 977-2500 Carnegie Class: DU-Higher
FAX Number: (314) 977-3874 Calendar System: Semester
URL: www.slu.edu
Established: 1818 Annual Undergrad Tuition & Fees: $47,124
Enrollment: 12,229 Coed
Affiliation or Control: Roman Catholic IRS Status: 501(c)3
Highest Offering: Doctorate
Accreditation: **HLC**, AAB, ARCPA, ART, CAATE, CAHIIM, CEA, CLPSY, DENT, DIETD, DIETI, HSA, LAW, MED, MFCD, MT, NMT, NURSE, OT, PH, PTA, RADMAG, RTT, SP, SW

01 President .... Dr. Fred P. PESTELLO
05 Provost .... Dr. Michael LEWIS
10 Vice Pres/Chief Financial Officer .... Mr. David F. HEIMBURGER
18 Assoc VP Facilities Management .... Mr. Michael LUCIDO
84 VP Enrollment/Retention Management .... Ms. Kathleen DAVIS
12 Director Madrid Campus .... Dr. Paul VITA
15 VP Human Resources .... Mr. Mickey LUNA
26 VP Marketing and Communications .... Mr. Jeffrey FOWLER
43 Vice President/General Counsel .... Mr. William R. KAUFFMAN
32 VP Student Development .... Dr. Sarah CUNNINGHAM
30 VP Development .... Ms. Sheila M. MANION
42 Vice President for Mission/Identity .... Fr. David SUWALSKY, SJ
13 VP Information Tech Svcs/CIO .... Mr. Kyle COLLINS
23 Vice President for Medical Affairs .... Dr. Robert WILMOTT
27 Asst VP Marketing & Communications .... Ms. Laura GEISER
29 Exec Development Director .... Ms. Mary CONNOLLY
21 Assistant Controller .... Mr. Fred R. WINKLER
35 Assistant Dean of Students .... Dr. Donna BESS MYERS
54 Int Dean Parks Col Engr/Aviation .... Dr. Scott DUELLMAN
49 Interim Dean Arts & Sciences .... Dr. Donna LAVOIE
50 Dean Cook School of Business .... Dr. Scott DUELLMAN
61 Dean of Law .... Mr. William P. JOHNSON
63 Acting Dean of Medical School .... Dr. Christine JACOBS
79 Dean Philosophy & Letters .... Dr. Randall ROSENBERG
53 Dean School of Education .... Dr. Gary RITTER
08 University Librarian .... Mr. David CASSENS
88 Director Ctr for Health Care Ethics .... Dr. Jason EBERL
52 Exec Dir Ctr Advanced Dental Educ .... Dr. John HATTON
46 Vice President for Research .... Dr. Kenneth OLLIFF
19 Asst Dir Pub Safety/Emergency Prep .... Mr. Darryl WALKER
06 University Registrar .... Mr. Jay HAUGEN
07 AVP and Dean of Admission .... Ms. Jean COX
37 AVP and Director Financial Aid .... Ms. Cari S. WICKLIFFE
41 Athletics Director .... Mr. Christopher V. MAY
85 Director International Services .... Ms. Rebecca BAHAN
92 Director Honors Program .... Mr. Robert PAMPEL
31 Director Community Svc & Engagement .... Dr. Bryan SOKOL
100 Chief of Staff .... Mr. Bob GAGNE
88 Director Univ Museums/Galleries .... Dr. Petruta LIPAN
110 Exec Development Director .... Mr. Kent G. LEVAN
20 Associate Provost Grad and UG Educ .... Dr. Robert WOOD
108 Associate Provost & Inst Assessment .... Dr. Steven SANCHEZ
09 Assoc Prov & Dir of Inst Research .... Ms. Stacey HARRINGTON
96 Director of Business Services .... Mr. Jeff HOVEY
22 Dir Ofc of Inst Equity & Diversity .... Ms. Michelle LEWIS
86 Director Government Relations .... Mr. Marc SCHEESSELE
28 Diversity/Community Engagement .... Dr. Amber JOHNSON
103 Executive Dir Workforce Development .... Ms. Katherine CAIN
105 Director Web Services .... Mr. Mark RIMAR
38 Director Student Counseling .... Dr. Steve BYRNES
101 Board & Council Administrator .... Ms. Amelia ARNOLD
39 Dir Resident Life/Student Housing .... Ms. Manisha FORD-THOMAS

Southeast Missouri Hospital College of Nursing and Health Sciences (G)

2001 William Street, Cape Girardeau MO 63703-5815
County: Cape Girardeau FICE Identification: 030709
Unit ID: 417734
Telephone: (573) 334-6825 Carnegie Class: Spec-4-yr-Other Health
FAX Number: (573) 339-7805 Calendar System: Semester
URL: www.sehcollege.edu
Established: 1990 Annual Undergrad Tuition & Fees: $13,301
Enrollment: 203 Coed
Affiliation or Control: Independent Non-Profit IRS Status: 501(c)3
Highest Offering: Baccalaureate
Accreditation: **HLC**, ADNUR, MT, NURSE, RAD, SURGT

01 President .... Dr. Steven D. LANGDON
05 Dean General Education/Student Svcs .... Dr. Dedria A. BLAKELY
66 Dean of Nursing .... Dr. Tonya BUTTRY
06 Registrar .... Ms. Erica URY
37 Financial Aid Director .... Ms. Cassandra HICKS
09 Inst Research Officer/Admissions .... Ms. Rhonda VANDERGRIFF
10 Business Officer .... Ms. Deanna SELLS

Southeast Missouri State University (H)

One University Plaza, Cape Girardeau MO 63701-4799
County: Cape Girardeau FICE Identification: 002501
Unit ID: 179557
Telephone: (573) 651-2000 Carnegie Class: Masters/L
FAX Number: (573) 651-2200 Calendar System: Semester
URL: www.semo.edu
Established: 1873 Annual Undergrad Tuition & Fees (In-State): $8,033
Enrollment: 10,001 Coed
Affiliation or Control: State IRS Status: 501(c)3
Highest Offering: Beyond Master's But Less Than Doctorate
Accreditation: **HLC**, ART, CAATE, CACREP, CAEP, CAEPN, CAPRT, CEA, CIDA, COSMA, DANCE, DIETC, DIETD, JOUR, MUS, NAIT, NURSE, SP, SW, THEA

01 President .... Dr. Carlos VARGAS
05 Provost .... Dr. Michael GODARD
10 VP Finance & Administration .... Mr. Brad SHERIFF
84 VP Enrollment Mgmt/Student Success .... Dr. Debbie BELOW
111 VP University Advancement .... Mrs. Trudy LEE
09 Director of Institutional Research .... Mr. Eric CHAMBERS
100 Chief of Staff & Asst to the Pres .... Mr. Chris MARTIN
22 VP Equity/Access & Behav Health .... Ms. Sonia RUCKER
58 Vice Provost & Dean Grad Studies .... Dr. Doug KOCH
13 Asst Vice Pres Information Tech .... Mr. Floyd DAVENPORT
32 AVP for Student Life .... Dr. Bruce SKINNER
50 Dean Harrison Col of Bus & Comp .... Dr. Alberto DAVILA
53 Dean Col of Educ/Hlth/Hum Stds .... Dr. Joe PUJOL
79 Int Dean Col of Humanities/Soc Sci .... Dr. Melissa ODEGARD-KOESTER
57 Dean Holland Col of Arts & Media .... Ms. Rhonda WELLER STILSON
81 Dean Col of Sci/Tech/Engr/Math .... Dr. Tamela RANDOLPH
35 Dean of Students .... Ms. Sonia RUCKER
08 Dean of Kent Library .... Ms. Barbara GLACKIN
07 Director of Admissions .... Ms. Lenell HAHN
35 Director of Campus Life & Event Svc .... Ms. Michele IRBY
26 Dir Univ Marketing .... Ms. Tonya WELLS
41 Director of Athletics .... Mr. Brady L. BARKE
29 Director Alumni Services .... Mr. George GASSER
85 Exec Dir Intl Education & Svcs .... Mr. Kevin TIMLIN
56 Dean of Extended Studies .... Mr. Nathan BULLOCK
18 Director of Facilities Management .... Ms. Angela MEYER
37 Director of Student Financial Svcs .... Mr. Matt KEARNEY
27 Director of Univ Communications .... Ms. Kathy HARPER
15 Director of Human Resources .... Ms. Alissa VANDEVEN
19 Dir of Public Safety/Trans .... Ms. Beth GLAUS
06 Registrar .... Ms. Sandy L. HINKLE
88 Director of Show Me Center .... Mr. Wil GORMAN
92 Int Dir Jane Stephens Honors Pgm .... Dr. Joe SNYDER
38 Dir Ctr Behav Health & Access .... Ms. Millicent ODHIAMBO
21 Asst VP Financial Svcs .... Ms. Sue WILDE
39 Director of Residence Life .... Dr. Kendra SKINNER

Southwest Baptist University (I)

1600 University Avenue, Bolivar MO 65613-2597
County: Polk FICE Identification: 002502
Unit ID: 179326
Telephone: (417) 328-5281 Carnegie Class: Masters/M
FAX Number: (417) 328-1514 Calendar System: Semester
URL: www.sbuniv.edu
Established: 1878 Annual Undergrad Tuition & Fees: $25,508
Enrollment: 3,039 Coed
Affiliation or Control: Southern Baptist IRS Status: 501(c)3
Highest Offering: Doctorate
Accreditation: **HLC**, ACBSP, ADNUR, MUS, NUR, PTA, RAD, SW

00 Chairman of the Board .... Dr. Eddie BUMPERS
01 Interim President .... Dr. Brad JOHNSON
05 Provost .... Dr. Lee SKINKLE
45 VP Strategic Initiative & Planning .... Dr. Allison LANGFORD
111 VP for Institutional Advancement .... Dr. Brad JOHNSON
11 Vice President Administration .... Mrs. Tara PARSON
84 Dean of Enrollment Management .... Mr. Darren CROWDER
41 Athletic Director .... Mr. Mike PITTS
32 Vice Pres for Student Development .... Dr. Rob HARRIS
20 Assistant Provost .... Dr. Dana STEWARD
73 Asst Provost of Spiritual Formation .... Dr. Matt KIMBROUGH
107 Dean College Professional Programs .... Dr. Troy BETHARDS
49 Dean College of Liberal Arts .... Dr. Holly HILL-STANFORD
76 Dean College of Health Professional .... Dr. Brittney HENDRICKSON
08 Dean of University Libraries .... Dr. Ed WALTON
13 Chief Technology Officer .... Mr. David BOLTON
37 Dir Student Financial Assistance .... Mrs. Karla GOUGHNOUR
91 Network Administrator .... Mr. Kevin KELLEY
19 Director Campus Security .... Mr. Mark GRABOWSKI
106 Sr Director of Teaching & Learning .... Ms. Angela CARR
42 Director University Ministries .... Mr. Kurt CADDY
18 Director Physical Plant .... Mr. Robbie BRYANT
06 Registrar .... Mrs. Roberta RASOR
39 Director Residence Life .... Ms. Michelle MARTIN
07 Director Undergraduate Admissions .... Mrs. Becky VAN STAVERN
36 Director of Career Services .... Mrs. Shonna FORE
29 Director of Alumni Engagement .... Mrs. Holly BRIDGE
35 Director Student Activities .... Dr. Nathan PENLAND
04 Executive Coordinator to President .... Mrs. Brittany EARL
108 Dir of Institutional Effectiveness .... Mr. Levi FOX
26 Chief Public Relations Officer .... Mrs. Charlotte MARSCH
123 Director of Graduate Admissions .... Dr. Todd EARL
38 Director Counseling Services .... Vacant
10 Controller .... Ms. Terri ROGERS
15 Director of Human Resources .... Mrs. Sunny FULLER
40 Book Store Manager .... Mrs. Debbie LEWIS
12 Director of Springfield Campus .... Mrs. Jeanie DAVIDSON
12 Director of Mtn View Campus .... Mrs. Shae MILLER
12 Director of Salem Campus .... Ms. Linda ARMER
105 Director Web Services .... Ms. Rebekah WRIGHT

Southwest Baptist University Mountain View Campus (J)

PO Box 489, Mountain View MO 65548
Telephone: (417) 934-2999 Identification: 770326
Accreditation: **&HLC**

Southwest Baptist University Salem (K)

501 S Grand, Salem MO 65560
Telephone: (573) 729-7071 Identification: 770327
Accreditation: **&HLC**

Southwest Baptist University Springfield (L)

4431 S Fremont, Springfield MO 65804
Telephone: (417) 820-2069 Identification: 770328
Accreditation: **&HLC**

State Fair Community College (M)

3201 W 16th Street, Sedalia MO 65301-2199
County: Pettis FICE Identification: 008080
Unit ID: 179539
Telephone: (660) 596-7222 Carnegie Class: Assoc/HT-High Trad
FAX Number: (660) 596-7335 Calendar System: Semester
URL: www.sfccmo.edu
Established: 1968 Annual Undergrad Tuition & Fees (In-District): $4,680
Enrollment: 3,928 Coed
Affiliation or Control: Local IRS Status: 501(c)3
Highest Offering: Associate Degree

Accreditation: **HLC**, CAHIIM, CONST, DH, DMS, MLTAD, OTA, RAD

01 President .... Dr. Joanna ANDERSON
05 VP for Educ/Student Support Svcs .... Dr. Brent BATES
10 VP for Finance/Administration & HR .... Mr. Keith ACUFF
20 Dean of Academic Affairs .... Mr. Jim CUNNINGHAM
75 Dean Vocational/Technical Studies .... Mr. Michael ROGG
121 Dean Student/Academic Support .... Mr. Daniel AVEGALIO
13 Chief Information Officer .... Mr. Mark HAVERLY
102 Exec Director SFCC Foundation .... Ms. Mary TREUNER
06 Registrar .... Mrs. Jennifer WILBANKS
37 Director of Financial Aid .... Mrs. Angel MEFFORD
18 Chief Facilities/Physical Plant .... Mr. Justin O'NEAL
21 Controller Business Officer .... Mrs. Diane BROCKMAN
26 Exec Dir Marketing/Communication .... Mr. Brad HENDERSON
04 Executive Asst to President .... Mrs. Jo Lynn TURLEY
41 Athletic Director .... Mr. Darren PANNIER
15 Exec Director Human Resources .... Ms. Rachel DAWSON
09 Exec Director Institutional Effect .... Mrs. Darci MCFAIL
19 Director Security/ Safety .... Mr. David HOCKADAY

State Technical College of Missouri (A)

One Technology Drive, Linn MO 65051-0479
County: Osage FICE Identification: 004711
Unit ID: 177977
Telephone: (573) 897-5000 Carnegie Class: Assoc/HVT-High Trad
FAX Number: N/A Calendar System: Semester
URL: www.statetechmo.edu
Established: 1961 Annual Undergrad Tuition & Fees (In-State): $6,510
Enrollment: 1,756 Coed
Affiliation or Control: State IRS Status: 501(c)3
Highest Offering: Associate Degree
Accreditation: **HLC**, DA, NAIT, PTAA, RAD

01 President .... Dr. Shawn STRONG
101 Board of Regents Secretary .... Ms. Nichole ENGELHARDT
05 Vice President of Academic Affairs .... Ms. Angie GAINES
32 Vice President of Student Affairs .... Dr. Chris BOWSER
10 Vice President of Finance .... Ms. Jenny JACOBS
111 Vice President of Advancement .... Ms. Shannon GRUS
100 Chief of Staff .... Ms. Amy AMES
04 Executive Asst to the President .... Ms. Nichole ENGELHARDT
18 Director of Facilities .... Mr. Brad CREDE
13 Director of IT .... Mr. Mike ELY
26 Director of Marketing .... Mr. Brandon MCELWAIN
09 Director of Institutional Research .... Mr. Aaron KLIETHERMES
20 Dean of Curriculum and Instruction .... Ms. Janet CLANTON
72 Dean of Technology .... Mr. Ben BERHORST
72 Dean of Technology .... Mr. Chris MEUNKS
97 Dean of Professional Studies .... Mr. Ken THOMPSON

Stephens College (B)

1200 E Broadway, Columbia MO 65215-0001
County: Boone FICE Identification: 002512
Unit ID: 179548
Telephone: (573) 442-2211 Carnegie Class: Masters/S
FAX Number: (573) 876-7248 Calendar System: Semester
URL: www.stephens.edu
Established: 1833 Annual Undergrad Tuition & Fees: $23,385
Enrollment: 622 Female
Affiliation or Control: Independent Non-Profit IRS Status: 501(c)3
Highest Offering: Master's
Accreditation: **HLC**, ARCPA, CAHIIM

01 President .... Dr. Dianne LYNCH
10 Vice Pres Finance/Business/CFO .... Mr. Dane FUHRMAN
05 Vice Pres Academic Affairs .... Dr. Leslie WILLEY
111 Vice Pres Institutional Advancement .... Ms. Gina SHOLTIS
32 Vice Pres Student Development .... Dr. Laura NUNNELLY
26 VP of Marketing/Public Relations .... Vacant
84 Vice President Enrollment Mgmt .... Vacant
06 Registrar .... Ms. Linda SHARP
13 IT Director .... Mr. Chris HERBOLD
41 Athletic Director .... Vacant
37 Sr Director of Financial Aid .... Vacant
04 Executive Asst to President .... Ms. Lita PISTONO
07 Director of Admissions .... Ms. Severin ROBERTS
08 Head Librarian .... Mr. Dan KAMMER
18 Director of Facilities Mgmt .... Vacant
19 Director Security/Safety .... Ms. Candy CORNMAN
39 Director of Residence Life .... Vacant
104 Study Abroad Coordinator .... Dr. James TERRY
108 Director Institutional Assessment .... Dr. Sharon SCHATTGEN
15 Director of Human Resources .. Ms. Kimberly SCHELLENBERGER

Stevens Institute of Business & Arts (C)

1521 Washington Avenue, Saint Louis MO 63103
County: Saint Louis FICE Identification: 008552
Unit ID: 178767
Telephone: (314) 421-0949 Carnegie Class: Spec-4-yr-Bus
FAX Number: (314) 421-0304 Calendar System: Quarter
URL: www.siba.edu
Established: 1947 Annual Undergrad Tuition & Fees: $12,285
Enrollment: 109 Coed
Affiliation or Control: Proprietary IRS Status: Proprietary
Highest Offering: Baccalaureate
Accreditation: **ACCSC**

01 President .... Ms. Cynthia A. MUSTERMAN
05 Academic Dean & Registrar .... Ms. Emilee SCHNEFKE
37 Financial Aid Director .... Ms. Christa SIAMPOS
07 Director of Admissions .... Ms. Sara DORN
36 Career Services Director .... Mr. Steve ASHER

Texas County Technical College (D)

6915 S Highway 63 PO Box 314, Houston MO 65483
County: Texas FICE Identification: 035793
Unit ID: 441487
Telephone: (417) 967-5466 Carnegie Class: Spec 2-yr-Health
FAX Number: (417) 967-4604 Calendar System: Semester
URL: www.texascountytech.edu
Established: 1986 Annual Undergrad Tuition & Fees: $18,240
Enrollment: 52 Coed
Affiliation or Control: Independent Non-Profit IRS Status: 501(c)3
Highest Offering: Associate Degree
Accreditation: **ABHES**

01 President .... Ms. Charlotte GRAY
06 Campus Director/Registrar .... Ms. Clarice CASEBEER
37 Admissions/Financial Aid .... Ms. Chelsye SCANTLIN

Three Rivers College (E)

2080 Three Rivers Boulevard,
Poplar Bluff MO 63901-2350
County: Butler FICE Identification: 004713
Unit ID: 179645
Telephone: (573) 840-9600 Carnegie Class: Assoc/HT-High Trad
FAX Number: (573) 840-9604 Calendar System: Semester
URL: www.trcc.edu
Established: 1966 Annual Undergrad Tuition & Fees (In-State): $5,490
Enrollment: 2,759 Coed
Affiliation or Control: State IRS Status: 501(c)3
Highest Offering: Associate Degree
Accreditation: **HLC**, ADNUR, EMT, MLTAD, OTA

01 President .... Dr. Wesley A. PAYNE
10 Chief Financial Officer .... Ms. Charlotte EUBANK
05 Chief Academic Officer .... Dr. Sherry A. PHELAN
08 Director Library Services .... Dr. John LADUE
37 Director Financial Aid .... Ms. Regina MORRIS
06 Registrar .... Ms. Melanie HAMANN
32 Dean of Student Services .... Ms. Ann MATTHEWS
09 Dean of Institutional Effectiveness .... Dr. Maribeth PAYNE
18 Chief Facilities/Physical Plant .... Mr. Rob TOMLINSON
15 Director Human Resources .... Ms. Kristina D. MCDANIEL
26 Chief Public Relations Officer .... Ms. Carrie FRANKLIN
30 Chief Development/Dir Alumni Rels .... Ms. Michelle REYNOLDS
84 Director Enrollment Management .... Mr. Chris ADAMS
96 Dir Procurement/Risk Management .... Ms. Cambrea HALCUMB
04 Executive Asst to President .... Ms. Janine HEATH
103 Dir Workforce/Career Development .... Mr. William COOPER
13 Chief Info Technology Officer .... Mr. Steve ATWOOD
22 Dir Affirmative Action/EEO .... Ms. Kristina D. MCDANIEL
39 Interim Director Student Housing .... Ms. Adrian CLYBURN
19 Director Security/Safety .... Mr. Chuck STRATTON

Truman State University (F)

100 E Normal, Kirksville MO 63501-4221
County: Adair FICE Identification: 002495
Unit ID: 178615
Telephone: (660) 785-4000 Carnegie Class: Masters/M
FAX Number: (660) 785-4030 Calendar System: Semester
URL: www.truman.edu
Established: 1867 Annual Undergrad Tuition & Fees (In-State): $8,299
Enrollment: 4,655 Coed
Affiliation or Control: State IRS Status: 501(c)3
Highest Offering: Master's
Accreditation: **HLC**, CAATE, CAEP, MUS, NURSE, SP

01 President .... Dr. Susan L. THOMAS
05 Exec VP Acad Affairs & Provost .... Dr. Janet L. GOOCH
111 Vice Pres for Univ Advancement .... Dr. Ernie T. HUGHES
10 VP for Admin Finance & Planning .... Mr. David RECTOR
84 VP for Enrollment Mgmt & Marketing .... Dr. Tyana LANGE
32 Dean of Student Life .... Ms. Janna STOSKOPF
43 General Counsel .... Ms. Amy CLENDENNEN
21 Comptroller .... Mr. Mike GARZANELLI
41 Director of Athletics .... Mr. Jerry WOLLMERING
15 Director of Human Resources .... Ms. Melissa GARZANELLI
37 Financial Aid Director .... Ms. Marla FERNANDEZ
06 Registrar .... Ms. Nancy ASHER
13 Chief Information Officer .... Ms. Donna LISS
26 Director of Public Relations .... Mr. Travis MILES
20 Associate Provost .... Dr. Kevin M. MINCH
83 Dean Sch Social & Cultural Studies .... Dr. Elizabeth M. CLARK
50 Dean School of Business .... Dr. Rashmi PRASAD
81 Dean Sch of Science & Math .... Dr. Tim WALSTON
53 Dean Sch of Health Sci & Educ .... Dr. Lance RATCLIFF
49 Dean School of Arts & Letters .... Dr. Steve PARSONS

University of Central Missouri (G)

Administration Building, Room 101,
Warrensburg MO 64093-5299
County: Johnson FICE Identification: 002454
Unit ID: 176965
Telephone: (660) 543-4255 Carnegie Class: Masters/L
FAX Number: (660) 543-4200 Calendar System: Semester
URL: www.ucmo.edu
Established: 1871 Annual Undergrad Tuition & Fees (In-State): $8,306
Enrollment: 9,959 Coed
Affiliation or Control: State IRS Status: 501(c)3
Highest Offering: Beyond Master's But Less Than Doctorate
Accreditation: **HLC**, AAB, AAFCS, ART, CACREP, CAEPN, CEA, CIDA, @DIETC, DIETD, MUS, NAIT, NURSE, SP, SW, THEA

01 President .... Dr. Roger BEST
101 Exec Asst to Pres/Asst Sec to Board .... Ms. Monica R. HUFFMAN
43 General Counsel .... Ms. Lindsay CHAPMAN
05 Provost & VP of Academic Affairs .... Dr. Phillip BRIDGMON
32 VP Student Experience/Engagement .... Dr. Sharlene GARBER BAX
10 Vice President Finance & Operations .... Mr. Bill HAWLEY
41 Vice Pres Intercollegiate Athletics .... Mr. Jerry M. HUGHES
20 Vice Prov Acad Pgms/Dean Grad Stds .... Dr. Lisa TOMS
26 Vice Pres Integrated Mktg & Comm .... Ms. Susan SMEDLEY
35 Assoc VP Student Services/Title IX .... Dr. Corey L. BOWMAN
84 Exec Vice Provost Enroll Mgmt .... Dr. Randall LANGSTON
111 VP Advancement/External Engagement .... Ms. Courtney GODDARD
08 University Librarian .... Dr. Janette KLEIN
49 Dean Arts/Humanities/Soc Sci .... Dr. Mike SAWYER
72 Interim Dean Health/Science/Tech .... Dr. Mark ARANT
50 Dean Business & Prof Studies .... Dr. Jose MERCADO
53 Dean of College of Education .... Dr. Ann MCCOY
13 Vice Provost for Technology & CIO .... Dr. James F. GRAHAM
06 Director of Registrar Office .... Dr. Lisa RUNYAN
121 Director Academic Success Advisor .... Mr. Kenneth SCHUELLER
37 Dir Student Financial Assistance .... Mr. Tony LUBBERS
19 Director of Public Safety .... Mr. Scott RHOAD
39 Sr Director of University Housing .... Dr. Brenda MOEDER
18 Assoc VP Capital Plng/Fac Mgmt .... Mr. Timothy CASTILAW
96 Director Purchasing .... Mr. Adam VIERBICKAS
15 Assoc VP Human Resources .... Ms. Ranea TAYLOR
40 Director of Univ Store & Textbooks .... Mr. Charles D. RUTT
106 Vice Prov Online & Learning Engage .... Dr. Laurel HOGUE
07 Associate Director Admissions .... Mr. Christopher LANG
38 Asst Director Counseling Center .... Dr. Jeanne WOON
36 Director Career Services .... Ms. Amber GOREHAM
09 Director of Institutional Research .... Dr. Meng CHEN
86 Director Governmental Relations .... Mr. David PEARCE

University of Health Sciences and Pharmacy in St. Louis (H)

4588 Parkview Place, Saint Louis MO 63110-1088
County: Independent City FICE Identification: 002504
Unit ID: 179265
Telephone: (314) 367-8700 Carnegie Class: Spec-4-yr-Other Health
FAX Number: (314) 446-8304 Calendar System: Semester
URL: www.uhsp.edu
Established: 1864 Annual Undergrad Tuition & Fees: $30,147
Enrollment: 998 Coed
Affiliation or Control: Independent Non-Profit IRS Status: 501(c)3
Highest Offering: First Professional Degree
Accreditation: **HLC**, PHAR

01 President .... Dr. John A. PIEPER
05 Exec Assoc Dean Academic Affairs .... Dr. Brenda GLEASON
67 Interim Dean of Pharmacy .... Dr. Brenda GLEASON
111 Vice Pres Devel/Alumni Relations .... Ms. Kathy GARDNER
10 VP Finance/Administration/CFO .... Ms. Lisa VANSICKLE
84 VP Enrollment Services/Marketing .... Ms. Beth KESERAUSKIS
28 Vice Pres Diversity & Inclusion .... Dr. Isaac BUTLER
32 Vice President of Student Affairs .... Dr. Heather FRENCH
46 Vice President of Research .... Dr. Thomas BURRIS
18 Vice President College Services .... Mr. Eric KNOLL
49 Dean Arts & Science/Student Affairs .... Dr. Kimberly J. KILGORE
15 Director of Human Resources .... Mr. Daniel C. BAUER
06 Registrar .... Ms. Laura KLOS
08 Library Director .... Ms. Jill NISSEN
37 Director of Financial Aid .... Mr. Daniel J. STIFFLER
41 Director of Athletics .... Ms. Jill HARTER
88 Special Assistant to the President .. Sr. Mary Louise DEGENHART
88 Special Assistant to the President .... Dr. Michael SASS
07 Director of Admissions .... Ms. Jill GEBKE
19 Director Security/Safety .... Mr. Scott PATTERSON
29 Director Alumni Relations .... Ms. Stephanie MAUZY
38 Director Counseling Center .... Ms. Michelle HASTINGS
43 General Counsel .... Mr. Kenneth FLEISCHMANN
44 Annual Giving Officer .... Mr. Vincent PIAZZA
04 Admin Assistant to the President .... Ms. Lynn FALLERT
13 Director Information Technology .... Mr. Zachary LEWIS

*University of Missouri System Administration (I)

105 Jesse Hall, Columbia MO 65211-3020
County: Boone FICE Identification: 002515
Unit ID: 178439
Telephone: (573) 882-2011 Carnegie Class: N/A
FAX Number: (573) 882-2721
URL: www.umsystem.edu

01 President .... Dr. Mun Y. CHOI
05 Provost/Exec VC Academic Affairs .... Dr. Latha RAMCHAND
10 Vice President Finance/CFO .... Mr. Ryan RAPP
28 Vice Chancellor of Incl/Div/Equity .... Dr. Maurice GIPSON
13 Vice President Info Technology .... Ms. Beth CHANCELLOR
15 Vice Pres Human Resource Svcs .... Ms. Marsha FISCHER
20 Sr Assoc Vice Pres Academic Affairs .... Vacant
88 Assistant Vice Chancellor .... Dr. John MIDDLETON

43 General Counsel .... Mr. Stephen J. OWENS
26 Chief Communications Officer .... Ms. Kamrhan FARWELL
17 CEO/COO UM Health Care .... Mr. Jonathan CARTRIGHT
21 Treasurer .... Mr. Tom F. RICHARDS
21 Controller .... Mr. Eric VOGELWEID
04 Executive Asst to President .... Ms. Janet WAIBEL
101 Secretary of the Board of Curators .... Ms. Cindy S. HARMON

*University of Missouri - Columbia (A)

Columbia MO 65211-0001
County: Boone FICE Identification: 002516
Unit ID: 178396
Telephone: (573) 882-2121 Carnegie Class: DU-Highest
FAX Number: (573) 882-9907 Calendar System: Semester
URL: www.missouri.edu
Established: 1839 Annual Undergrad Tuition & Fees (In-State): $10,723
Enrollment: 31,089 Coed
Affiliation or Control: State IRS Status: 501(c)3
Highest Offering: Doctorate
Accreditation: HLC, CAEP, CAPRT, CEA, CIDA, CLPSY, COARC, COPSY, DIETC, DMS, HSA, IPSY, JOUR, LAW, LIB, MED, MUS, NMT, NURSE, OT, PCSAS, PH, PHAR, PTA, RAD, SCPSY, SP, SPAA, SW, VET

02 President and Chancellor .... Dr. Mun Y. CHOI
100 Chief of Staff .... Dr. Christine J. HOLT
05 Prov/Exec Vice Chanc Acad Affs .... Dr. Latha RAMCHAND
111 Vice Chanc Advancement .... Ms. Jackie A. LEWIS
56 Vice Chanc Extension & Engagement .. Dr. Marshall M. STEWART
10 Vice Chanc Finance & CFO .... Dr. Rhonda K. GIBLER
15 Assoc Vice Chanc Human Resources .... Ms. Patty A. HABERBERGER
28 VC Inclusion/Diversty & Equity .... Dr. Maurice D. GIPSON
26 Vice Chanc/Chief Marketing & Comm .... Dr. Kamrhan M. FARWELL
11 Vice Chanc Operations .... Mr. Gary L. WARD
46 Int Vice Chanc Research/Econ Dev .... Dr. Thomas E. SPENCER
32 Vice Chanc Student Affairs .... Dr. William B. STACKMAN
110 Asst Vice Chanc Advancement .... Ms. Meichele A. FOSTER
22 Asst V Chanc Civil Rights/Title IX ..... Dr. Andrea (Andy) S. HAYES
29 Assoc Vice Chanc Alumni Relations .... Mr. Todd A. MCCUBBIN
17 Exec Vice Chanc Health Affairs .... Dr. Richard J. BAROHN
84 Vice Prov Enrollment Mgmt .... Ms. Kim A. HUMPHREY
09 Vice Prov Institutional Rsrch & QI .... Dr. Mardy T. EIMERS
85 Vice Prov International Programs .... Dr. Mary A. STEGMAIER
08 Interim Vice Prov Libraries .... Ms. Deb H. WARD
20 Vice Prov Undergraduate Studies .... Dr. James N. SPAIN
17 Chief Exec Officer MU Health Care . Dr. Jonathan W. CURTRIGHT
13 Chief Information Officer .... Ms. Beth C. CHANCELLOR
19 Police Chief University Police .... Mr. Brian WEIMER
35 Dean of Students .... Dr. Jeffrey R. ZEILENGA
23 Exec Dir Stdnt Health & Well-Being .... Dr. Jamie L. SHUTTER
06 University Registrar .... Ms. Brenda V. SELMAN
47 Dean Agri/Food & Natural Resources .... Dr. Christopher R. DAUBERT
49 Dean Arts & Science .... Dr. Cooper C. DRURY
50 Dean Business .... Dr. Ajay S. VINZE
53 Interim Dean Education .... Dr. Erica S. LEMBKE
54 Interim Dean Engineering .... Dr. Noah D. MANRING
58 Dean Graduate School .... Dr. Jeni L. HART
76 Dean Health Professions .... Dr. Kristofer HAGGLUND
59 Int Dean Human Environ Sciences .... Dr. Brenda J. LOHMAN
60 Dean Journalism .... Dr. David D. KURPIUS
61 Dean Law .... Dr. Lyrissa B. LIDSKY
63 Dean Medicine .... Dr. Steven C. ZWEIG
66 Dean Nursing .... Dr. Sarah A. THOMPSON
74 Dean Veterinary Medicine .... Dr. Carolyn J. HENRY
07 Director Admissions .... Mr. Charles A. MAY
41 Director Athletics .... Mr. Jim STERK
40 Director Campus Retail .... Mr. Dale B. SANDERS
36 Director Career Center .... Dr. Rob M. MCDANIELS
105 Director Digital Service .... Mr. Kevin S. BAILEY
88 Director Disability Center .... Ms. Ashley M. BRICKLEY
92 Director Honors College .... Dr. Jerome (J.D.) D. BOWERS
25 Director Sponsored Program Admin .... Mr. Craig A. DAVID
37 Exec Director Student Financial Aid .... Ms. Emily L. HAYNAM

*University of Missouri - Kansas City (B)

5100 Rockhill Road, Kansas City MO 64110-2499
County: Jackson FICE Identification: 002518
Unit ID: 178402
Telephone: (816) 235-1000 Carnegie Class: DU-Higher
FAX Number: (816) 235-1717 Calendar System: Semester
URL: www.umkc.edu
Established: 1929 Annual Undergrad Tuition & Fees (In-State): $10,145
Enrollment: 16,147 Coed
Affiliation or Control: State IRS Status: 501(c)3
Highest Offering: Doctorate
Accreditation: HLC, AA, ANEST, ARCPA, CAEP, CEA, CLPSY, COPSY, DANCE, DENT, DH, EMT, IPSY, LAW, MED, MPCAC, MUS, NURSE, OTA, PHAR, PLNG, SPAA, SW, THEA

02 Chancellor .... Dr. C. Mauli AGRAWAL
100 Chief of Staff .... Ms. Sheri GORMLEY
05 Provost .... Dr. Jennifer LUNDGREN
28 Int Vice Chanc Diversity/Inclusion .... Dr. Makini KING
10 Vice Chanc Finance/Administration .... Ms. Sharon LINDENBAUM
21 Director Budgeting and Planning .... Ms. Karen WILKERSON
113 Director Cashiering .... Mr. Paul SCHWARTZ
104 Director International Affairs .... Dr. Joy STEVENSON
102 Pres UMKC Foundation .... Ms. Lisa BARONIO
111 Vice Chanc External Relations .... Mr. Curt CRESPINO
41 Athletic Director .... Dr. Brandon MARTIN
13 Chief Information Officer .... Mr. Andrew GOODENOW
119 Information Security Officer .... Mr. Justin MALYN
15 Vice Chanc Human Resources .... Ms. Carol HINTZ
118 Employee Services .... Mr. Ted STAHL
20 Vice Provost Faculty Affairs .... Dr. Diane FILION
108 Vice Prov Curriculum & Assessment .... Dr. Kim MCNELEY
106 Asst Vice Provost Acad Innovation .... Dr. Molly MEAD
49 Int Dean College of Arts & Sciences .... Ms. Kati TOIVANEN
50 Dean Bloch School of Management .... Dr. Brian KLAAS
81 Dean Sch Bio and Chemical Sciences .... Dr. Theodore WHITE
92 Dean Honors College .... Dr. Jim MCKUSICK
64 Dean of UMKC Conservatory .... Vacant
52 Dean School of Dentistry .... Vacant
53 Interim Dean School of Education .... Dr. Carolyn BARBER
54 Dean Sch of Computing/Engineering .... Dr. Kevin Z. TRUMAN
61 Dean School of Law .... Ms. Barbara GLESNER FINES
63 Dean School of Medicine .... Dr. Mary Anne JACKSON
66 Int Dean Nursing & Health Studies .... Dr. Joy ROBERTS
67 Dean School of Pharmacy .... Dr. Russell B. MELCHERT
08 Interim Dean University Libraries .... Dr. Cindy THOMPSON
58 Dean of Graduate Studies .... Dr. Chris LIU
20 Vice Provost Inst Effectiveness .... Dr. Kelli COX
84 Asst Vice Prov Enroll Management .... Mr. Doug SWINK
124 Sr Vice Prov Student Success .... Dr. Kristi HOLSINGER
32 Vice Prov/Dean Student Affairs .... Vacant
88 Director Student Conduct .... Ms. Keishea BOYD
35 Director Student Involvement .... Mr. Todd WELLS
26 Vice Chanc Strategic Market & Comm .... Ms. Anne SPENNER
27 Director Media Relations .... Mr. John MARTELLARO
29 Director Alumni & Constituent Rels .... Ms. Kathryn HOUSTON
86 Asst Vice Chanc External Relations .... Mr. Troy LILLEBO
22 Title IX Coordinator .... Dr. KC ATCHINSON
121 Dir Academic Support & Mentoring .... Dr. Julie COLLINS
07 Director Admissions .... Ms. Elora THOMAS
37 Director Student Financial Aid .... Mr. Scott YOUNG
06 Registrar .... Ms. Amy COLE
19 Chief Campus Police .... Mr. Michael BONGARTZ
40 Director Bookstore .... Mr. Pete EISENTRAGER
38 Director Counseling Services .... Dr. Arnold ABELS
88 Director Women's Center .... Dr. Brenda BETHMAN
36 Int Director Career Services .... Ms. Tess SURPRENANT
39 Director Residential Life .... Ms. Kristen TEMPLE
93 Dir Multicultural Student Affairs . Ms. Keichanda DEES-BURNETT
109 Director Student Union .... Mr. Jody JEFFRIES
25 Business Manager for Admin Services .... Mr. Jeffery ROSS

*University of Missouri - Saint Louis (C)

1 University Boulevard, Saint Louis MO 63121-4400
County: Saint Louis FICE Identification: 002519
Unit ID: 178420
Telephone: (314) 516-5000 Carnegie Class: DU-Higher
FAX Number: (314) 516-5378 Calendar System: Semester
URL: www.umsl.edu
Established: 1963 Annual Undergrad Tuition & Fees (In-State): $10,573
Enrollment: 13,874 Coed
Affiliation or Control: State IRS Status: 501(c)3
Highest Offering: Doctorate
Accreditation: HLC, AAQEP, CACREP, CLPSY, IPSY, MUS, NURSE, OPT, OPTR, SPAA, SW

02 Chancellor .... Dr. Kristin SOBOLIK
05 Provost/Exec Vice Chanc Acad Affs .... Dr. Steven BERBERICH
10 Interim VC Finance/Admn & CFO .... Ms. Tanika BUSCH
111 VC Univ Advancement .... Ms. Rebecca COLE
26 Asst Vice Chanc Marketing/Comm .... Mr. Justin L. ROBERTS
28 VC Diversity/Equity/Inclusion .... Dr. Tanisha STEVENS
46 Vice Chancellor Research Admin .... Dr. Christopher SPILLING
32 Vice Provost .... Dr. Elizabeth ECKELKAMP
58 Sr Director Graduate School .... Dr. Teresa THIEL
13 Interim CIO .... Mr. Kenneth L. VOSS
88 AVP Center for Teaching & Learning .... Dr. Keeta HOLMES
85 Exec Dir International Studies .... Ms. Liane CONSTANTINE
49 Dean College Arts & Sciences .... Dr. Andrew KERSTEN
50 Dean College Business Admin .... Dr. Joan PHILLIPS
53 Dean College of Education .... Dr. Ann TAYLOR
66 Dean College of Nursing .... Dr. Roxanne K. VANDERMAUSE
92 Dean Honors College .... Dr. Edward MUNN SANCHEZ
88 Dean College of Optometry .... Dr. Larry J. DAVIS
08 Dean of Libraries .... Mr. Christopher DAMES
54 Dean Engineering Program .... Dr. Joseph O'SULLIVAN
04 Special Asst to the Chancellor .... Ms. Elizabeth VAN UUM
35 Dean of Students & AVP .... Dr. D'Andre BRADDIX
103 VP for Student Affs/Workforce Dev .... Dr. Natissia SMALL
41 Director of Athletics .... Ms. Lori FLANAGAN
84 AVC Strategic Enrollment .... Dr. Reggie HILL
40 Asst Director Bookstore .... Ms. Stephanie EATON
36 Director Career Services .... Ms. Teresa A. BALESTRERI
06 Registrar .... Ms. Theresa KEUSS
39 Director Residential Life .... Ms. Jacquelyn WARREN
37 Director Student Financial Aid .... Mr. Mitchell R. HESS
88 Dir MO Inst of Mental Health .... Dr. Robert H. PAUL
18 Exec Director Facilities Mgmt .... Mr. Daryl S. IVES
21 Director of Finance & Accounting .... Mr. Randall VOGAN
15 Executive Director Human Resources .... Ms. Jill H. WOOD
19 Director Institutional Safety .... Mr. Dan FREET
09 Manager Institutional Research .... Dr. Carol S. SHOLY
88 Interim GM St Louis Public Radio .... Mr. Tom LIVINGSTON
44 Assoc VC Engagement/Annual Giving .... Ms. Jennifer JEZEK-TAUSSIG
70 Dean Social Work .... Dr. Sharon JOHNSON
88 Dir of Ops-Touhill PAC .... Mr. Jason A. STAHR
88 Dir Comm Outreach/Leg Liason .... Ms. Patricia ZAHN
88 Dir Student Support/SUCCEED .... Mr. Jonathan LIDGUS
88 Dir Recreation/Wellness .... Ms. Yvette KELL
100 Chief of Staff .... Mr. Robert SAMPLES
102 Director Foundation/Corporate Rels . Ms. Elizabeth LANIER-SHIPP
29 Director Alumni Activities .... Mr. Phillip DONATO
30 AVC Univ Development .... Ms. Sharon FENOGLIO
86 AVC Comm/Econ Dev .... Mr. Karl GUENTHER

*Missouri University of Science & Technology (D)

300 W 13th Street, Rolla MO 65409-0001
County: Phelps FICE Identification: 002517
Unit ID: 178411
Telephone: (573) 341-4111 Carnegie Class: DU-Higher
FAX Number: (573) 341-4307 Calendar System: Semester
URL: www.mst.edu
Established: 1870 Annual Undergrad Tuition & Fees (In-State): $10,165
Enrollment: 7,642 Coed
Affiliation or Control: State IRS Status: 501(c)3
Highest Offering: Doctorate
Accreditation: HLC, CEA

02 Chancellor .... Dr. Mohammad DEHGHANI
05 Provost/Exec Vice Chanc Acad Affs .... Dr. Colin POTTS
10 Vice Chanc Finance/Operations .... Ms. Alysha M. O'NEIL
111 Vice Chanc University Advancement .... Ms. Joan M. NESBITT
32 Vice Chancellor Student Affairs .... Dr. Debra A G. ROBINSON
35 Assoc Vice Chanc Student Affairs .... Dr. James H. MURPHY
20 Int Deputy Provost Acad Excellence .... Dr. Richard K. BROW
121 Int Vice Provost Academic Support .... Dr. Kathryn NORTHCUT
84 Vice Provost Enrollment Mgmt .... Ms. Shobi SIVADASAN
54 VP/Dean Col Engr & Computing .... Dr. Richard WLEZIEN
49 Int VP/Dean Arts/Sciences/Business .... Dr. Kate DROWNE
08 Director of Library .... Dr. Oliver CHEN
13 Chief Information Officer .... Mr. Danny TANG
06 Registrar .... Ms. Deanne JACKSON
38 AVC Student Affairs/Support Svcs ...... Dr. Edna GROVER-BISKER
41 Director of Athletics .... Mr. Mark E. MULLIN
23 Senior Dir Student Health Services .... Dr. Dennis S. GOODMAN
36 Dir Career Opportunities Center .... Mr. William ZWIKELMAIER
85 AP International/Cultural Affairs .... Dr. Jeanie HOFER
35 Director Student Life .... Mr. John GALLAGHER
39 Director Residential Life .... Dr. Dorie PAINE
07 Interim Director of Admissions .... Ms. Cathy TIPTON
29 Asst Vice Chanc Advancement Svcs .... Ms. Darlene RAMSAY
37 Director Student Financial Aid .... Ms. Bridgette K. BETZ
26 Chief Marketing/Communications Ofcr ... Mr. Andrew P. CAREAGA
18 Asst Vice Chanc Facilities Svcs .... Mr. Ted RUTH
40 Manager of University Bookstore .... Mr. Mark GALLARDO
19 Director University Police .... Mr. Douglas P. ROBERTS
27 Assoc Dir Strategic Communications .... Ms. Cheryl A. MCKAY
112 Director Planned Giving .... Mr. John HELD, II
28 Acting Chief Diversity Officer .... Ms. Anitra RIVERA
15 Director Human Resources .... Ms. Rhonda BYERS
09 Director Inst Research Data Mgmt .... Dr. Wayne R. JONES

*Missouri University of Science & Technology Global-St. Louis (E)

12837 Flushing Meadows Dr., Ste 210,
St. Louis MO 63131
Telephone: (314) 835-9822 Identification: 770323
Accreditation: &HLC

Urshan College and Urshan Graduate School of Theology (F)

1151 Century Tel Dr., Wentzville MO 63385
County: St. Charles FICE Identification: 041461
Unit ID: 455099
Telephone: (314) 838-8858 Carnegie Class: Spec-4-yr-Faith
FAX Number: (636) 538-5317 Calendar System: Semester
URL: www.ugst.edu
Established: 2001 Annual Undergrad Tuition & Fees: N/A
Enrollment: 103 Coed
Affiliation or Control: Pentecostal/Charismatic Non-Denominational
IRS Status: 501(c)3
Highest Offering: Master's
Accreditation: HLC, THEOL

01 President .... Dr. Brent COLTHARP
03 Executive Vice President .... Rev. Jennie RUSSELL
05 Academic Dean .... Rev. David JOHNSON
32 Dean of Student Services .... Rev. Jonathan MCCLINTOCK
10 CFO .... Mrs. Ashley CHANCELLOR
06 Registrar .... Ms. Brook CROW
08 Head Librarian .... Dr. Gary ERICKSON
106 Director of Distance Learning .... Ms. Vinessa D'SA
26 Director of Marketing and Events .... Mr. David MOLINA
07 Director of Admissions .... Ms. Dinecia GATES
15 Chief Human Resources Officer .... Mrs. Marsha JOHNSTON
30 Development Ofcr/Dir Annual Giving .... Mrs. Phyllis JONES
36 Director Student Placement .... Ms. Amber WILLEFORD
37 Director Student Financial Aid .... Mr. Grant POLLARD
39 Director Student Housing .... Mrs. Alisha DUGAS

101 Secretary of the Institution/Board ....Rev. Terry BAUGHMAN
108 Dir Institutional Effectiveness ....Mrs. Wanda BAKER
09 Director of Institutional Research ....Dr. Cindy MILLER
18 Chief Facilities/Physical Plant ....Rev. Billy BABB
35 Assistant Dean of Student Services .....Mrs. Angela MCCLINTOCK
13 Chief Info Technology Officer ....Rev. Dewayne PRESSON

Washington University in St. Louis (A)

One Brookings Drive, Saint Louis MO 63130-4899
County: Saint Louis FICE Identification: 002520
Unit ID: 179867
Telephone: (314) 935-5100 Carnegie Class: DU-Highest
FAX Number: N/A Calendar System: Semester
URL: www.wustl.edu
Established: 1853 Annual Undergrad Tuition & Fees: $57,386
Enrollment: 15,449 Coed
Affiliation or Control: Independent Non-Profit IRS Status: 501(c)3
Highest Offering: Doctorate
Accreditation: HLC, ART, AUD, CLPSY, LAW, LSAR, OT, PCSAS, PH, PTA, SW

01 Chancellor ....Dr. Andrew D. MARTIN
05 Exec Vice Chancellor/Provost ....Dr. Beverly R. WENDLAND
45 EVC Civic Affairs/Strategic Plng ....Mr. Henry S. WEBBER
11 Exec VC Administration ....Dr. Shantay N. BOLTON
63 Exec Vice Chanc/Dean of Medicine ... Dr. David H. PERLMUTTER
43 Vice Chanc/General Counsel ....Ms. Monica J. ALLEN
111 Exec VC University Advancement ....Ms. Pamella A. HENSON
10 Vice Chancellor for Finance/CFO ....Ms. Amy B. KWESKIN
46 Vice Chancellor for Research ....Dr. Jennifer K. LODGE
15 Vice Chanc for Human Resources ....Ms. Legail P. CHANDLER
13 Interim VC & Chief Info Officer ....Ms. Stephanie L. REEL
32 VC for Student Affairs ....Dr. Anna K. GONZALEZ
26 VC for Marketing & Communications ....Ms. Julie FLORY
86 VC Government & Community Relations . Ms. Pamela S. LOKKEN
115 Chief Investment Officer ....Mr. Scott L. WILSON
21 Assoc VC for Finance and Treasurer ....Mr. Mark N. AMIRI
49 Dean Faculty of Arts & Sciences ....Dr. Feng Sheng HU
61 Dean School of Law ....Dr. Nancy STAUDT
54 Dean McKelvey School ....Dr. Aaron F. BOBICK
57 Dean Sam Fox Sch Design/Visual Arts ....Prof. Carmon COLANGELO
57 Dir College & Grad Sch of Art ....Prof. Amy G. HAUFT
50 Dean Olin School of Business ....Prof. Mark P. TAYLOR
58 Interim Dean The Graduate School ...... Prof. Laurie MAFFLY-KIPP
70 Dean Brown School of Social Work ....Prof. Mary M. MCKAY
97 Interim Dean University College .... Prof. Heather A. CORCORAN
48 Dir College of Architecture & Grad .... Prof. Heather WOOFTER
100 VC/Board Secretary/Chief of Staff ....Ms. Rebecca L. BROWN
07 Vice Prov Admissions/Financial Aid .... Ms. Ronne P. TURNER
110 Sr VC University Advancement .... Mr. William S. STOLL
27 Assoc VC Medical Public Affairs ......Ms. Joni L. WESTERHOUSE
28 Vice Prov & Dir Diversity/Inclusion ....Vacant
85 VC for International Affairs ....Prof. Kurt T. DIRKS
08 Int Vice Provost & Univ Librarian .... Mr. Leeland DEEDS
35 Assoc Vice Chanc for Students/Dean ....Dr. Robert M. WILD
92 Assoc VC & Dean Scholar Pgm ....Vacant
85 Asst VC/Dir International Students ...... Ms. Kathy STEINER-LANG
36 Assoc VC for Student Affairs ....Mr. Mark W. SMITH
18 Assoc VC Facilities Planning/Mgmt ....Mr. JD LONG, II
88 Asst VC Environ Health & Safety ....Mr. Bruce D. BACKUS
88 Assoc VC Real Estate .... Ms. Mary B. CAMPBELL
72 Director OTM ....Ms. Nichole R. MERCIER
23 Exec Dir Habif Health/Wellness Ctr .... Dr. Cheri LEBLANC
37 Director Student Financial Services ....Mr. Michael J. RUNIEWICZ
41 Director of Athletics ....Mr. Anthony J. AZAMA
19 Chief of Police ....Mr. Mark R. GLENN
06 University Registrar ....Ms. Keri A. DISCH
38 Director of Mental Health Services ....Dr. Thomas M. BROUNK

Washington University School of Medicine in St. Louis (B)

660 Euclid Avenue, Saint Louis MO 63110
Telephone: (314) 360-5000 Identification: 770329
Accreditation: &HLC, CAMPEP, MED

Webster University (C)

470 E Lockwood, Webster Groves MO 63119-3141
County: Saint Louis FICE Identification: 002521
Unit ID: 179894
Telephone: (800) 981-9801 Carnegie Class: Masters/L
FAX Number: N/A Calendar System: Semester
URL: www.webster.edu
Established: 1915 Annual Undergrad Tuition & Fees: $28,700
Enrollment: 8,197 Coed
Affiliation or Control: Independent Non-Profit IRS Status: 501(c)3
Highest Offering: Doctorate
Accreditation: HLC, ACBSP, ANEST, CACREP, CAEPN, MUS, NUR

00 Chancellor ....Dr. Elizabeth J. STROBLE
01 President ....Dr. Julian Z. SCHUSTER
10 Vice President & CFO ....Mr. Richard MEYER
13 Chief Information Officer ....Ms. Margie MUTHUKUMARU
101 Asst Chancellor/Univ Secretary ....Ms. Jeanelle WILEY
05 Vice President Academic Affairs ....Ms. Nancy HELLERUD
84 Interim VP of Enrollment Mgmt ....Dr. James LOFTUS
20 AVP for Academic Affairs .... Dr. Thao DANG-WILLIAMS
32 AVP Stdnt Affs/Dean of Students ....Dr. John BUCK
04 Executive Asst to the Chancellor .... Ms. Dana SPREHE
50 Dean School Business/Technology .... Dr. Simone CUMMINGS
53 Interim Dean School of Education ....Dr. Thomas CORNELL
57 Dean Leigh Gerdine Col of Fine Arts .... Mr. Paul STEGER
49 Interim Dean Col of Arts & Sciences .... Dr. Michael HULSIZER
60 Dean School of Communications ....Dr. Eric ROTHENBUHLER
08 Dean of University Libraries ....Ms. Eileen CONDON
15 Chief Human Resources Officer ....Ms. Cheryl FRITZ
27 AVP & Chief Comm Officer ....Dr. Rick ROCKWELL
12 AVP Extended US Campuses ....Dr. Donavan OUTTEN
37 AVP UG Admiss/Dir Financial Aid .... Mr. James MYERS
28 Chief Diversity Officer ....Mr. Vincent FLEWELLEN
06 Registrar ....Ms. Heidi AMORES MIRANDA
121 Senior Dir of Academic Advising .... Ms. Kyle MCCOOL
19 Director Public Safety ....Mr. Rick GERGER
26 Dir Public Relations .... Mr. Patrick GIBLIN
90 Dir of Media Center ....Mr. Marty (Dewey) MARTIN
36 Dir Career Planning & Dev Center ....Mr. John LINK
29 Dir of Alumni Rel & Annual Fund ....Ms. Kelly DOPMAN
41 Director Athletics ....Mr. Scott KILGALLON
23 Director Student Health Svcs ....Ms. Ann BROPHY
35 Director Student Engagement ....Ms. Jennifer STEWART
38 Director Counsel & Life Development ....Dr. Patrick STACK
96 AVP for Administrative Services .... Mr. Kenneth CREEHAN
09 Director of Inst Effectiveness ....Vacant
18 Manager of Facilities Operations ....Mr. Gilbert MORALES
104 Director of Study Abroad ....Ms. Kelly HEATH
111 Asst AVP Advancement ....Ms. Andrea SOTO
07 AVP of Undergraduate Admission ....Ms. Joanna FINCH
123 Director of Graduate Admission ....Ms. Sarah NANDOR
39 Dir Resident Life/Student Housing .... Ms. Anna DICKHERBER
44 AVP Advancement Services ....Mr. Ryan ELLIOT
86 AVP Govt Rels/Sponsored Research .... Ms. Carolyn CORLEY
106 AVP for Online Education ....Dr. Michelle LOYET
88 Sr Dir Military Campus Operations .... Mr. Ben BRINK

WellSpring School of Allied Health-Kansas City (D)

9140 Ward Pkwy Ste 100, Kansas City MO 64114
County: Jackson FICE Identification: 039704
Unit ID: 447999
Telephone: (816) 523-9140 Carnegie Class: Spec 2-yr-Health
FAX Number: (816) 523-0741 Calendar System: Other
URL: www.wellspring.edu
Established: 1988 Annual Undergrad Tuition & Fees: N/A
Enrollment: 173 Coed
Affiliation or Control: Proprietary IRS Status: Proprietary
Highest Offering: Associate Degree
Accreditation: ABHES

01 President ....Donald FARQUHARSON
11 VP of Campus Operations ....Robin O'CONNELL
05 Education Director .... Dan GERBER
10 Chief Financial/Business Officer ....Sandy DELAPP

Westminster College (E)

501 Westminster Avenue, Fulton MO 65251-1230
County: Callaway FICE Identification: 002523
Unit ID: 179946
Telephone: (573) 642-3361 Carnegie Class: Bac-A&S
FAX Number: (573) 592-5227 Calendar System: Semester
URL: www.wcmo.edu
Established: 1851 Annual Undergrad Tuition & Fees: $30,880
Enrollment: 609 Coed
Affiliation or Control: Independent Non-Profit IRS Status: 501(c)3
Highest Offering: Baccalaureate
Accreditation: HLC, ACBSP

01 President/Chief Transform Ofcr .... Mr. Donald P. LOFE, JR.
11 CFO/COO ....Dr. Steven TYRELL
05 VP of Academic Affairs ....Dr. David ROEBUCK
111 VP for Advancement ....Mr. JR ANDREWS
10 AVP Business/Controller ....Ms. Jennifer YELTON
26 Exec Dir Marketing/Communicationss .... Ms. Kristina BRIGHT
32 Dean of Student Life ....Dr. Kasi LACEY
84 VP of Enrollment Services ....Mr. Paul ORSCHELN
18 Exec Dir Plant Ops/Security ....Mr. Jack BENKE
20 Associate Dean of Faculty ....Dr. Cinnamon BROWN
121 Associate Dean of Student Success ....Dr. Ingrid ILINCA
06 Registrar ....Mrs. Phyllis MASEK
07 Director of Admissions ....Vacant
13 AVP of IT .... Mr. Nick WATSON
37 AVP Enroll Mgmt/Dir Financial Aid ....Ms. Aimee BRISTOW
30 Director of Advancement Services .... Ms. Jeni WHITTINGTON
15 Director of Human Resources ....Ms. Mandy MARCH
19 Director of Campus Safety/Security ....Mr. Jack BENKE
41 Athletic Director ....Mr. Matt MITCHELL
23 Exec Director Wellness Center ....Dr. Kasi LACEY
29 Dir Alumni Engagement ....Ms. Melanie BARGER
08 Director of Library Services ....Ms. Victoria KNIGHT
09 Dir of Inst Research/Assessment ....Mr. Matt KNUDTSON
42 Chaplain ....Rev. Kiva NICE-WEBB
04 Executive Asst to the President ....Mrs. Jessie JONES

William Jewell College (F)

500 College Hill, Liberty MO 64068-1896
County: Clay FICE Identification: 002524
Unit ID: 179955
Telephone: (816) 781-7700 Carnegie Class: Bac-Diverse
FAX Number: (816) 415-5027 Calendar System: Semester
URL: www.jewell.edu
Established: 1849 Annual Undergrad Tuition & Fees: $34,450
Enrollment: 751 Coed
Affiliation or Control: Independent Non-Profit IRS Status: 501(c)3
Highest Offering: Master's
Accreditation: HLC, MUS, NURSE

01 President ....Dr. Elizabeth MACLEOD WALLS
05 Provost ....Dr. Anne C. DEMA
10 Vice Pres for Finance & Operations .... Mr. Joseph GARCIA
111 Vice Pres Institutional Advancement .... Mr. Clark MORRIS
84 Vice Pres Enrollment & Marketing ....Mr. Eric BLAIR
28 Vice President Access & Engagement ....Dr. Rodney SMITH
45 Assoc VP Institutional Strategy ....Mr. Daniel HOLT
32 Dean of Student Life ....Ms. Shelly KING
07 Director of Student Recruitment .... Mr. William PALMER
06 Registrar ....Dr. Edwin H. LANE
08 Director of Library Services ....Ms. Rebecca HAMLETT
21 Director of Budget and Finance ....Ms. Deborah GREEN
13 Director of Information Technology ....Ms. Lan GUO
97 Assoc Dean Core Curriculum ....Dr. Gary ARMSTRONG
37 Asst VP & Director Financial Aid .... Mr. Thomas STUART
15 Director of Human Resources .... Ms. Julie DUBINSKY
18 Director of Facilities Management ....Ms. Stephany GUEST
57 Executive Director Harriman-Jewell ....Mr. Clark W. MORRIS
41 Director of Athletics .... Mr. Thomas EISENHAUER
36 Director of Career Development .... Ms. Marissa BLAND
38 Director of Counseling Services ....Ms. Tricia HAGER
29 Director of Alumni Relations .... Ms. Andrea MELOAN
104 Director of Global Studies ....Ms. Sara ROUND
04 Executive Asst to President ....Ms. Angela BASS
19 Director of Campus Safety .... Mr. Mike CRUTCHFIELD
26 Director of Marketing .... Ms. Cara DAHLOR
39 Director of Residence Life .... Mr. Ernie STUFFLEBEAN
90 Director of Teaching/Learning Tech ....Mr. Heath HASE
50 Chair Comm in Business & Leadership .... Dr. Kelli SCHUTTE
53 Chair Education ....Dr. Donna GARDNER
110 Assoc VP of Advancement .... Ms. Susan TIDEMAN
54 Chair of Engineering ....Dr. Will LINDQUIST

William Woods University (G)

One University Avenue, Fulton MO 65251-1098
County: Callaway FICE Identification: 002525
Unit ID: 179964
Telephone: (800) 995-3159 Carnegie Class: DU-Mod
FAX Number: (573) 592-1146 Calendar System: Semester
URL: www.williamwoods.edu
Established: 1870 Annual Undergrad Tuition & Fees: $25,930
Enrollment: 2,114 Coed
Affiliation or Control: Christian Church (Disciples Of Christ)
IRS Status: 501(c)3
Highest Offering: Doctorate
Accreditation: HLC, ACBSP, SW

01 President ....Dr. Jahnae H. BARNETT
03 University Vice President ....Scott GALLAGHER
84 Vice President of Enrollment ....Jennifer CRUMP
32 Vice President/Dean of Student Life ....Dr. Venita MITCHELL
26 Vice President of Strategic Comm ....John FOUGERE
05 Vice President/Dean for Acad Affs ....Dr. Aimee SAPP
111 Vice President of Advancement ....Kathy GROVES
10 Chief Financial Officer ....Julie HOUSEWORTH
13 Chief Information Officer ....Travis BOND

MONTANA

Aaniiih Nakoda College (H)

PO Box 159, Harlem MT 59526-0159
County: Blaine FICE Identification: 025175
Unit ID: 180203
Telephone: (406) 353-2607 Carnegie Class: Tribal
FAX Number: (406) 353-2898 Calendar System: Semester
URL: www.ancollege.edu
Established: 1984 Annual Undergrad Tuition & Fees: $2,410
Enrollment: 143 Coed
Affiliation or Control: Tribal Control IRS Status: 501(c)3
Highest Offering: Associate Degree
Accreditation: NW

01 President .... Dr. Sean CHANDLER
05 Co-Dean of Academic Affairs .... Mr. Daniel KINSEY
05 Co-Dean of Academic Affairs ....Ms. Krisi SYVERTSON
32 Dean of Student Affairs ....Ms. Clarena BROCKIE
10 Comptroller .... Ms. Debra EVE
06 Registrar/Admissions Officer .... Mr. Kimberly BARROWS
37 Financial Aid Director .... Ms. Toma CAMPBELL
08 Library Director ....Ms. Eva ENGLISH
25 Sponsored Programs Director ....Mr. Scott FRISKICS
13 Manager Information Systems ....Mr. Harold H. HEPPNER
40 Bookstore Manager ....Ms. Kim BROCKIE
04 Assistant to the President ....Ms. Michele BROCKIE
09 Institutional Research Assistant .... Ms. Danielle JACKSON

Apollos University (I)

600 Central Avenue, Ste 215, Great Falls MT 59401
County: Cascade Identification: 667096
Telephone: (406) 604-4300 Carnegie Class: Not Classified
FAX Number: (866) 287-1938 Calendar System: Quarter
URL: apollos.edu
Established: 2005 Annual Undergrad Tuition & Fees: N/A
Enrollment: N/A Coed
Affiliation or Control: Proprietary IRS Status: Proprietary

Highest Offering: Doctorate
Accreditation: DEAC

00 CEO .... Dr. Paul EIDSON
01 President .... Dr. Scott EIDSON
05 EVP/Provost and CAO .... Dr. Robin WESTERIK
32 Exec Vice Pres Student Services .... Dr. Michelle FOX
10 Sr Exec Vice President Admin/CFO .... Dr. Kelly LANCASTER
15 Vice President Human Resources .. Dr. Amanda CERAR-DERBISH
07 Dir Admissions/Student Engagement . Ms. Regina BURCKHALTER
06 Registrar/Dir of Office Admin .... Ms. Shirley CASTRO

Blackfeet Community College (A)

Box 819, Browning MT 59417-0819
County: Glacier FICE Identification: 025106
Unit ID: 180054
Telephone: (406) 338-5441 Carnegie Class: Tribal
FAX Number: (406) 338-3272 Calendar System: Semester
URL: www.bfcc.edu
Established: 1974 Annual Undergrad Tuition & Fees: $3,370
Enrollment: 417 Coed
Affiliation or Control: Independent Non-Profit IRS Status: 501(c)3
Highest Offering: Associate Degree
Accreditation: NW

01 President .... Dr. Karla BIRD
05 Dean Academic Affairs .... Mrs. Carol MURRAY
10 Vice Pres of Finance .... Ms. Lola WIPPERT
37 Director of Financial Aid .... Mrs. Gaylene DUCHARME
06 Registrar/Dir of Admissions .... Ms. Helen HORN
18 Chief Facilities/Physical Plant .... Mr. Smokey HENRIKSEN
15 Human Resources Director .... Ms. Shannon CONNELLY

Carroll College (B)

1601 N Benton Avenue, Helena MT 59625-0002
County: Lewis And Clark FICE Identification: 002526
Unit ID: 180106
Telephone: (406) 447-4300 Carnegie Class: Bac-Diverse
FAX Number: (406) 447-4533 Calendar System: Semester
URL: www.carroll.edu
Established: 1909 Annual Undergrad Tuition & Fees: $37,262
Enrollment: 1,108 Coed
Affiliation or Control: Roman Catholic IRS Status: 501(c)3
Highest Offering: Master's
Accreditation: NW, IACBE, NURSE

01 President .... Dr. John E. CECH
04 Sr Executive Asst to the President .... Ms. Kara PAUL
05 Senior VP for Academic Affairs .... Ms. Jennifer GLOWIENKA
10 VP for Finance & Administration .... Ms. Lori PETERSON
32 VP for Mission & Student Engagement ... Mr. Michael MCMAHON
111 Int VP for Inst Advancement .... Ms. Katherine RAMIREZ
42 Director Campus Ministry-Chaplain .... Rev. Marc LENNEMAN
41 Athletic Director .... Mr. Charles GROSS
121 Dean of Students & Retention .... Ms. Annette WALSTAD
09 Director of Institutional Research .... Mr. Erik ROSE
06 Registrar .... Ms. Cassie HALL
26 Director of Public Relations .... Ms. Sarah LAWLOR
37 Financial Aid Director .... Ms. Janet RIIS
36 Career Services & Internships .... Mr. Wes FEIST
15 Director Human Resources .... Ms. Karla SMITH
18 Director of Facilities .... Mr. Walter H. BISKUPIAK
35 Director Student Activities .... Mr. Patrick HARRIS
21 Controller .... Ms. Kari BRUSTKERN
13 Campus Computing/Info Tech Director ..... Ms. Loretta ANDREWS
29 Director Alumni Relations .... Ms. Renee WALL

Chief Dull Knife College (C)

One College Drive, PO Box 98, Lame Deer MT 59043
County: Rosebud FICE Identification: 025452
Unit ID: 180160
Telephone: (406) 477-6215 Carnegie Class: Tribal
FAX Number: (406) 477-6219 Calendar System: Semester
URL: www.cdkc.edu
Established: 1975 Annual Undergrad Tuition & Fees: $2,260
Enrollment: N/A Coed
Affiliation or Control: Independent Non-Profit IRS Status: 501(c)3
Highest Offering: Associate Degree
Accreditation: NW

01 President/Int Dean Cultural Affairs .... Dr. Richard LITTLEBEAR
05 Vice President Academic Affairs .... Mr. William BRIGGS
32 Vice President Student Affairs .... Mr. Zane SPANG
37 Director Financial Aid .... Ms. Sunshine WOODEN LEGS
08 Library Directory .... Ms. Adrienne VIOLETT
06 Registrar .... Mr. Joey DITONNO

Dawson Community College (D)

P.O. Box 421, Glendive MT 59330-0421
County: Dawson FICE Identification: 002529
Unit ID: 180151
Telephone: (406) 377-3396 Carnegie Class: Assoc/HT-High Non
FAX Number: (406) 377-8132 Calendar System: Semester
URL: www.dawson.edu
Established: 1940 Annual Undergrad Tuition & Fees (In-District): $5,580
Enrollment: 377 Coed
Affiliation or Control: State/Local IRS Status: 501(c)3
Highest Offering: Associate Degree
Accreditation: NW

01 President .... Dr. Scott R. MICKELSEN
05 VP Academic & Student Affairs .... Ms. Suela CELA
06 Registrar .... Ms. Virginia BOYSUN
08 Library Director .... Vacant
37 Director of Financial Aid .... Mr. Justin BEACH
13 Director of Information Technology .... Mr. Marc ROE
15 VP of Advancement & Human Resources ...... Ms. Leslie WELDON
103 Dir Workforce/Career Development .... Ms. Sara ENGLE
04 Assistant to the President .... Ms. Randi JOHNSON
10 Chief Financial/Business Officer .... Ms. Jennifer KING
41 Athletic Director .... Mr. Joe PETERSON
102 Exec Director of the Foundation .... Mr. Dennis HARP
18 Chief Facilities/Phys Plant Ofcr .... Mr. Todd THOMPSON
26 Dir Marketing & Public Relations .... Ms. Katy PETERSON
96 Director of Purchasing .... Ms. Tammy REED
32 Assoc Dean Student Success .... Mr. Jon LANGLOIS

Flathead Valley Community College (E)

777 Grandview Drive, Kalispell MT 59901
County: Flathead FICE Identification: 006777
Unit ID: 180197
Telephone: (406) 756-3822 Carnegie Class: Assoc/MT-VT-High Non
FAX Number: (406) 756-3815 Calendar System: Semester
URL: www.fvcc.edu
Established: 1967 Annual Undergrad Tuition & Fees (In-District): $6,377
Enrollment: 2,049 Coed
Affiliation or Control: Local IRS Status: 501(c)3
Highest Offering: Associate Degree
Accreditation: NW, EMT, MAC, MLTAD, PTAA, SURGT

01 President .... Dr. Jane A. KARAS
05 Vice President Academic Affairs .... Dr. Chris CLOUSE
10 VP Administration & Finance/CFO .... Ms. Beckie CHRISTIAENS
12 Prog Director Lincoln County Campus .... Ms. Megan RAYOME
32 Dean of Student Affairs .... Ms. Kelly MURPHY
51 Exec Dir Economic Dev/Cont Educ .... Mr. Luke LAVIN
111 Assoc Dir Institutional Advancement .... Ms. Susan EVANS
13 Exec Dir Mgmt Information Systems .... Mr. Duane ANDERSON
15 Exec Director of Human Resources .... Ms. Karen GLASSER
06 Registrar .... Ms. Sharon NAU
37 Dean Student Financial Svcs & Compl .... Ms. Brenda HANSON
55 Director of Adult Basic Education .... Ms. Jacqueline WROBLE
21 Controller/Business Services .... Ms. Dawn STEELE
26 Exec Dir Marketing & Communication .... Ms. Allison LINVILLE
96 Purchasing Coordinator .... Mr. Donald SKARE
18 Manager Maintenance Service .... Mr. David EVANS
24 Coord Instructional Media Services .... Ms. Malinda CRAWFORD
36 Career Advisor .... Ms. Cathy ALLARD
04 Administrative Asst to President .... Ms. Monica SETTLES

Fort Peck Community College (F)

PO Box 398, Poplar MT 59255-0398
County: Roosevelt FICE Identification: 023430
Unit ID: 180212
Telephone: (406) 768-6300 Carnegie Class: Tribal
FAX Number: (406) 768-6301 Calendar System: Semester
URL: www.fpcc.edu
Established: 1978 Annual Undergrad Tuition & Fees: $2,250
Enrollment: 328 Coed
Affiliation or Control: Tribal Control IRS Status: 501(c)3
Highest Offering: Associate Degree
Accreditation: NW

01 President .... Ms. Haven GOURNEAU
05 Int Vice Pres Academic Affairs .... Ms. Carrie SHUMACHER
32 Vice President Student Services .... Mr. Elijah HOPKINS
30 Vice Pres Institutional Development .... Mr. Craig SMITH
10 Business Manager .... Ms. Rose ATKINSON
06 Registrar .... Ms. Michelle DAY
37 Financial Aid Officer .... Ms. Lanette CLARK
08 Head Librarian .... Mrs. Anita A. SCHEETZ

Little Big Horn College (G)

PO Box 370, Crow Agency MT 59022-0370
County: Big Horn FICE Identification: 022866
Unit ID: 180328
Telephone: (406) 638-3104 Carnegie Class: Tribal
FAX Number: (406) 638-3169 Calendar System: Semester
URL: www.lbhc.edu
Established: 1980 Annual Undergrad Tuition & Fees: $3,200
Enrollment: 211 Coed
Affiliation or Control: Tribal Control IRS Status: 501(c)3
Highest Offering: Associate Degree
Accreditation: NW

01 President .... Dr. David YARLOTT, JR.
05 Dean of Academics .... Vacant
32 Dean of Student Affairs .... Miss Patricia WHITEMAN
11 Dean of Administration .... Ms. Shaleen OLD COYOTE
06 Registrar .... Mr. William OLD CROW
08 Director of Library .... Mr. Tim BERNARDIS
13 Chief Information Officer .... Mr. Franklin COOPER
10 Chief Finance Officer .... Ms. Aldean GOOD LUCK
15 Director Human Resources .... Vacant
97 Dept Head/General Stds/Crow Stds .... Dr. Tim MCCLEARY
81 Dept Head/Math/Science/Technology .... Vacant
25 Chief Contracts/Grants Admin .... Miss Eva FLYING
37 Financial Aid Director .... Ms. Beverly SNELL
41 Athletic Director .... Dr. Cheryl POLACEK

Miles Community College (H)

2715 Dickinson, Miles City MT 59301-4799
County: Custer FICE Identification: 002528
Unit ID: 180373
Telephone: (406) 874-6100 Carnegie Class: Assoc/MT-VT-Mix Trad/Non
FAX Number: (406) 874-6282 Calendar System: Semester
URL: www.milescc.edu
Established: 1939 Annual Undergrad Tuition & Fees (In-District): $5,910
Enrollment: 567 Coed
Affiliation or Control: State/Local IRS Status: 501(c)3
Highest Offering: Associate Degree
Accreditation: NW

01 President .... Mr. Ron SLINGER
05 Vice Pres of Academic Affairs .... Dr. Rita KRATKY
84 Dean of Enrollment Services .... Ms. Erin NIEDGE
32 Dean of Student Engagement .... Mr. Richard DESHIELDS
08 Director of Library .... Ms. Jerusha SHIPSTEAD
13 Director Information Technology .... Mr. Donald D. WARNER
37 Director Student Financial Aid .... Ms. Danielle DINGES
18 Chief Facilities/Physical Plant .... Mr. Ross LAWRENCE
21 Business Services Director .... Ms. Nancy AABERGE
06 Registrar .... Vacant
15 Dean of Admn Svcs & Human Resources .... Ms. Kylene PHIPPS
66 Nursing Program Director .... Ms. Diedre FITZGERALD
20 Associate Academic Officer .... Mr. Garth SLEIGHT
40 Manager Bookstore .... Ms. Michele TRIMBLE
04 Administrative Asst to President .... Ms. Candy LANEY
111 Dir of Institutional Advancement .... Ms. Elizabeth PATTEN
09 Dir of Institutional Research .... Mr. Loren LANCASTER

Montana Bible College (I)

20 Cornerstone Way, Bozeman MT 59718
County: Gallatin FICE Identification: 041403
Unit ID: 262165
Telephone: (406) 586-3585 Carnegie Class: Spec-4-yr-Faith
FAX Number: N/A Calendar System: Semester
URL: www.montanabiblecollege.edu
Established: 1987 Annual Undergrad Tuition & Fees: $9,040
Enrollment: N/A Coed
Affiliation or Control: Independent Non-Profit IRS Status: 501(c)3
Highest Offering: Baccalaureate
Accreditation: BI

01 President .... Mr. Ryan WARD
05 Vice President of Academic Affairs .... Dr. Andre GAZAL
06 Registrar .... Mrs. Louise TURNER
08 Librarian .... Mr. Cody GILLILAND
32 VP Col Relations/Dean of Students .. Mr. Glen SCHAUMLOEFFEL
10 Vice President of Finance .... Mrs. Leota FRED
84 Director of Enrollment Management .... Mr. Dan HOVESTOL
09 Dir Inst Effective/Dean of Women .... Ms. Jenni O'BRIAN
88 Discipleship Director .... Mr. Micah FORSYTHE

*Montana University System Office (J)

560 North Park Avenue, 4th Floor, Helena MT 59620
County: Lewis And Clark FICE Identification: 029072
Unit ID: 180470
Telephone: (406) 449-9124 Carnegie Class: N/A
FAX Number: (406) 449-9171
URL: www.mus.edu

01 Commissioner Higher Education .... Mr. Clayton T. CHRISTIAN
05 Deputy Cmsr Academic/Student Affs .... Dr. Brock TESSMAN
45 Deputy Cmsr Budget/Plng/Chief Staff .... Mr. Tyler TREVOR
15 Deputy Cmsr Human Resources .... Mr. Kevin MCRAE
43 MUS Chief Legal Counsel .... Ms. Ali BOVINGDON
100 Chief of Staff .... Mr. Tyler TREVOR
118 Director of Benefits .... Mrs. Mary LACHENBRUCH
117 Director of Work Comp Risk Mgmt .... Ms. Leah Jo TIETZ
93 Dir Minority/Amer Ind Achievement .... Ms. Angela MCLEAN
13 OCHE IT Manager .... Ms. Edwina MORRISON

*University of Montana - Missoula (K)

32 Campus Drive, Missoula MT 59812-0001
County: Missoula FICE Identification: 002536
Unit ID: 180489
Telephone: (406) 243-2311 Carnegie Class: DU-Higher
FAX Number: (406) 243-2797 Calendar System: Semester
URL: www.umt.edu
Established: 1893 Annual Undergrad Tuition & Fees (In-State): $7,430
Enrollment: 9,808 Coed
Affiliation or Control: State IRS Status: 501(c)3
Highest Offering: Doctorate
Accreditation: NW, ART, CAATE, CACREP, CAEPN, CLPSY, COARC, JOUR, LAW, MUS, PH, PHAR, PTA, SCPSY, SP, SPAA, SW, THEA

02 President .... Mr. Seth BODNAR
05 Interim Exec Vice President/Provost .... Dr. Reed HUMPHREY
100 Chief of Staff .... Ms. Kelly WEBSTER
10 Vice Pres for Admin & Finance .... Mr. Paul LASITER
84 VP Enroll/Strategic Communications .... Dr. Cathy COLE
26 VP Marketing & Communications .... Ms. Jenny PETTY

46 Vice Pres Research/Development Dr. Scott WHITTENBURG
45 AVP for Plng/Budget Analysis Ms. Dawn RESSEL
15 AVP Human Resource Services Ms. Terri PHILLIPS
20 Vice Provost for Academic Affairs Dr. Nathan LINDSAY
32 Vice Provost for Student Success Ms. Sarah SWAGER
121 Exec Dir Student Success Mr. Brian FRENCH
43 Legal Counsel Ms. Lucy FRANCE
12 Director Mansfield Center Ms. Deena MANSOUR
88 Dir Broadcast Media Center Mr. Ray EKNESS
22 Dir Equal Oppty & Title IX Coord Ms. Alicia ARANT
06 Registrar Ms. Maria MANGOLD
18 Director Facilities Svcs Mr. Kevin KREBSBACH
13 CIO Mr. Zach ROSSMILLER
38 Director Counseling Mr. Mike FROST
36 Int Dir Exper Lrng/Career Success Dr. Andrea VERNON
37 Director of Financial Aid Ms. Emily WILLIAMSON
29 Director of Alumni Office Mr. Jed LISTON
102 President & CEO/UM Foundation Ms. Cindy WILLIAMS
19 Director of Public Safety Vacant
23 Director Curry Health Center Dr. Rick CURTIS
39 Director Residence Life Ms. Sandra CURTIS
41 Athletic Director Mr. Kent HASLAM
85 Exec Director of Global Engagement Dr. Donna ANDERSON
08 Interim Dean Mansfield Library Dr. Barry BROWN
49 Dean Coll Humanities/Sciences Dr. Larry HUFFORD
61 Dean School of Law Mr. Paul KIRGIS
65 Int Dean Col Forestry/Conservation Dr. Chad BISHOP
50 Interim Dean College of Business Dr. Suzanne TILLEMAN
76 Dean Col Health Prof & Biomed Sci Dr. Marketa MARVANOVA
53 Dean College of Education Dr. Adrea LAWERANCE
57 Int Dean Col of Arts/Media Dr. John DEBOER
67 Dean School of Pharmacy Dr. Marketa MARVANOVA
75 Dean Missoula College Dr. Thomas GALLAGHER
92 Dean Honors College Dr. Timothy NICHOLS
04 Admin Assistant to the President Ms. Jessica SHONTZ
07 Director of Admissions Ms. Emily FERGUSON STEGER
106 Director Online Education Ms. Maricel LAWRENCE

*The University of Montana Western (A)

710 S Atlantic St, Dillon MT 59725-3598
County: Beaverhead FICE Identification: 002537
Unit ID: 180692
Telephone: (406) 683-7011 Carnegie Class: Bac-Diverse
FAX Number: (406) 683-7493 Calendar System: Other
URL: www.umwestern.edu
Established: 1893 Annual Undergrad Tuition & Fees (In-State): $5,747
Enrollment: 1,334 Coed
Affiliation or Control: State IRS Status: 501(c)3
Highest Offering: Baccalaureate
Accreditation: NW, CAEP, IACBE

02 Chancellor Mr. Michael L. REID
05 Interim Provost Dr. Ashley CARLSON
10 Int Vice Chancellor Admin/Finance Mrs. Susan BRIGGS
26 Director of Communications Mr. Matt RAFFETY
25 Dean of Outreach/Grants Ms. Anneliese RIPLEY
06 Registrar Ms. Charity WALTERS
07 Director of Admissions Mr. Matt ALLEN
08 Librarian Ms. Anne KISH
36 Director of Field Learning Vacant
41 Director of Athletics Mr. Bill WILSON
13 Director of Information Technology Mr. Mel EWING
32 Dean of Students Ms. Nicole HAZELBAKER
102 Director of Foundation/Alumni Ms. Roxanne ENGELLANT
37 Director of Student Financial Aid Ms. Louise DRIVER
38 Dir of Student Counseling/Wellness Mrs. Heidi PETERSON
15 Human Resources Ms. Patti LAKE
04 Administrative Asst to Chancellor Mrs. Hillary LOWELL
21 Dir Business Services/Controller Ms. Debra RICHARDSON
18 Director of Facilities Services Mr. Michael (Embee) BROWN
109 Senior Director Auxiliary Services Mr. Mike PIAZZOLA
39 Assistant Director Residence Life Ms. Bonita BONTRAGER
88 Dir Conference & Event Services Ms. Kathy SIMKINS
106 Director E-learning/Moodle Mr. Justin MASON

*Helena College University of Montana (B)

1115 N Roberts, Helena MT 59601-3098
County: Lewis and Clark FICE Identification: 007570
Unit ID: 180276
Telephone: (406) 447-6900 Carnegie Class: Assoc/HVT-Mix Trad/Non
FAX Number: (406) 447-6395 Calendar System: Semester
URL: www.HelenaCollege.edu
Established: 1939 Annual Undergrad Tuition & Fees (In-State): $3,507
Enrollment: 1,324 Coed
Affiliation or Control: State IRS Status: 501(c)3
Highest Offering: Associate Degree
Accreditation: NW, ADNUR

02 Acting Dean/CEO Dr. Sandra BAUMAN
04 Exec Assistant to Dean/CEO Ms. Paige PAYNE
97 Exec Dir of Gen Educ/Transfer Ms. Robyn KIESLING
75 Exec Dir of Career Tech Educ Ms. Tammy BURKE
84 Exec Dir of Enrollment Ms. Sarah DELLWO
11 Asst Dean of Admin Affairs Vacant
26 Director of Marketing/Communication Ms. Donna BREITBART
37 Exec Dir of Compliance/Fin Aid Ms. Valerie CURTIN
108 Dir of IR/Effectiveness Ms. Jessie PATE
18 Dir of Maintenance & Facilities Mr. John RUTHERFORD

13 Director of IT Services Mr. Mike HAUSLER
08 Director of Library Learning Hub Ms. Della DUBBE
106 Dir eLearning & Faculty Development Ms. Amy KONG
66 Director of Nursing Ms. Sandra SACRY
88 Director of K12 Partnerships Ms. Stephanie HUNTHAUSEN
124 Director of Retention Initiatives Ms. Ann WILLCOCKSON
16 Human Resources Specialist Ms. Mary TWARDOS
21 Director of Business Services Ms. Cari SCHWEN
40 Bookstore Director Vacant
51 Director of CEWD/SBDC Mr. Ryan LOOMIS

*Montana State University (C)

PO Box 172190, Bozeman MT 59717-2190
County: Gallatin FICE Identification: 002532
Unit ID: 180461
Telephone: (406) 994-2452 Carnegie Class: DU-Highest
FAX Number: (406) 994-1923 Calendar System: Semester
URL: www.montana.edu
Established: 1893 Annual Undergrad Tuition & Fees (In-State): $7,371
Enrollment: 16,218 Coed
Affiliation or Control: State IRS Status: 501(c)3
Highest Offering: Doctorate
Accreditation: NW, ART, CACREP, CAEP, DIETD, DIETI, IPSY, MT, MUS, NURSE

02 President Dr. Waded CRUZADO
05 Exec VP Academic Affairs/Provost Dr. Robert MOKWA
20 Senior Vice Provost Dr. Durwood SOBEK
88 Vice Provost Dr. Steven SWINFORD
10 Vice Pres Admin/Finance Mr. Terry LEIST
32 Vice Pres Student Success Dr. Chris KEARNS
56 Executive Director Extension Dr. Cody STONE
46 VP Research & Econ Development Dr. Jason CARTER
13 Vice Pres for Information Tech/CIO Mr. Ryan KNUTSON
18 Assoc Vice Pres University Services Mr. John HOW
15 Assoc VP HR/Chief HR Officer Ms. Jeannette GREY GILBERT
102 President/CEO MSU Foundation Mr. Christopher D. MURRAY
104 Actg Vice Prov/Dean Internat'l Pgm Dr. Deborah C. HAYNES
26 Vice Pres Univ Communications Mr. Tracy ELLIG
88 Exec Dir Museum of the Rockies Mr. Chris DOBBS
50 Interim Dean and Professor JJCB Dr. Daniel MILLER
53 Dean Education/Health/Human Dev Dr. Alison HARMON
54 Dean Engineering Dr. Brett GUNNINK
49 Dean Letters & Science Dr. Yves IDZERDA
66 Dean Nursing Dr. Sarah SHANNON
08 Dean Libraries Mr. Kenning ARLITSCH
35 Dean Students Dr. Matthew CAIRES
58 Dean Graduate School Dr. Craig OGILVIE
92 Dean Honors College Dr. Ilses-Mari LEE
47 VP and Dean Agriculture Dr. Sreekala BAJWA
48 Dean Arts/Architecture Dr. Royce SMITH
63 Dir WWAMI Medical Educ Program Dr. Martin TEINTZE
07 Director Admissions Mr. Mike OUERT
22 Director Institutional Equity Vacant
41 Director Athletics Mr. Leon COSTELLO
109 Assoc VP Auxiliary Services Mr. Tom STUMP
36 Dir Allen Yarnell Center Dr. Carina BECK
38 Dir Counseling/Psych Services Dr. Elizabeth ASSERSON
56 Exec Director Extended University Dr. Kim OBBINK
37 Director Financial Aid Mr. James BROSCHEIT
43 Legal Counsel Ms. Kellie PETERSON
45 Director Planning & Analysis Dr. Chris FASTNOW
96 Director Procurement Mr. Brian O'CONNOR
06 Registrar Mr. Tony CAMPEAU
27 Director Marketing/Creative Service Ms. Julie KIPFER
19 Chief of University Police Mr. Kevin GILLILAN
100 Exec Assistant to the President Ms. Amber VESTAL
105 Director Web Communications Mr. Justin ARNDT
25 Asst Vice Pres for Research Ms. Leslie SCHMIDT
39 Director Housing/Residence Life Mr. Jeff BONDY
14 Assoc Chief IT/CSO Mr. Adam EDELMAN
16 Dir Employee & Labor Relations Ms. Susan ALT
114 Dir University Budget Office Ms. Megan LASSO
88 Director Women's Center Ms. Elizabeth DANFORTH

*Montana State University Billings (D)

1500 University Drive, Billings MT 59101-0245
County: Yellowstone FICE Identification: 002530
Unit ID: 180179
Telephone: (406) 657-2011 Carnegie Class: Masters/M
FAX Number: (406) 657-2302 Calendar System: Semester
URL: www.msubillings.edu
Established: 1927 Annual Undergrad Tuition & Fees (In-State): $5,980
Enrollment: 4,000 Coed
Affiliation or Control: State IRS Status: 501(c)3
Highest Offering: Master's
Accreditation: NW, ABAI, ART, CAATE, CACREP, CAEP, EMT, IFSAC, MUS, NURSE, RAD

02 Chancellor Dr. Stefani HICSWA
10 Vice Chanc Administration/Finance Ms. Susan SIMMERS
05 Provost/Vice Chanc Academic Affairs Dr. Sepehr ESKANDARI
32 Vice Chanc Student Access & Success Dr. Kimberly HAYWORTH
102 President/CEO Foundation Mr. Bill KENNEDY
29 Director Alumni Relations Vacant
08 Director Library Services Ms. Darlene HERT
06 Registrar Dr. Cheri JOHANNES
07 Director Admissions Mr. Ed BROWN
15 Director Human Resources Ms. Jody STAHL
36 Director Career Services Dr. Becky LYONS

121 Dir Advising & Stdnt Support Svcs Ms. Laura GITTINGS-CARLSON
13 Chief Information Officer Mr. Brett WEISZ
25 Dir Grants & Sponsored Pgms Ms. Cindy BELL
26 Dir University Comm & Marketing Ms. Maureen BRAKKE
09 Director Institutional Research Ms. Joann STRYKER
18 Int Director Facility Services Mr. Brian MACKEY
58 Director Graduate Studies Dr. Jana MARCETTE
41 Athletic Director Vacant
19 Interim Chief of Campus Police Mr. Brandon GATLIN
37 Director Financial Aid Mr. Thomas VALLES
40 Interim Director Campus Store Ms. Lorie HAACKE
35 Dean of Student Engagement Ms. Kathy KOTECKI
114 Assistant Vice Chancellor Finance Ms. Heather HANNA
96 Director of Business Services Ms. Barb SHAFER
121 Director Academic Support Center Dr. Stephen FOGGATT
28 Dir Montana Ctr for Inclusive Educ Dr. Tom MANTHEY
89 Director New Student Services Ms. Kristin PETERMAN
88 Dir Native American Achievement Ctr Ms. Sunny Day REAL BIRD
85 Exec Dir Intl Studies/Outreach Dr. Paul FOSTER
106 Director e-Learning Vacant
92 Dir of University Honors Program Dr. Jana MARCETTE
104 Specialist Intl Marketing/Outreach Vacant
49 Int Dean Liberal Arts & Social Sci Ms. Tami HAALAND
53 Dean of Education Vacant
50 Interim Dean of Business Mr. Ed GARDING
12 Dean City College Dr. Vicki TRIER
97 Associate Dean City College Vacant
76 Dean Health Professions & Science Dr. Kurt TOENJES
04 Exec Assistant to the Chancellor Vacant
39 Director Center for Engagement Ms. Brandee SOENS
108 Director Assessment & Accreditation Ms. Kathleen THATCHER

*Montana State University - Northern (E)

PO Box 7751, Havre MT 59501-7751
County: Hill FICE Identification: 002533
Unit ID: 180522
Telephone: (406) 265-3700 Carnegie Class: Bac-Diverse
FAX Number: N/A Calendar System: Semester
URL: www.msun.edu
Established: 1929 Annual Undergrad Tuition & Fees (In-State): $5,955
Enrollment: 1,024 Coed
Affiliation or Control: State IRS Status: 501(c)3
Highest Offering: Master's
Accreditation: NW, ADNUR, NUR

02 Chancellor Mr. Gregory D. KEGEL
05 Provost/VC Academic Affairs Dr. Neil MOISEY
10 VC Finance & Administration Vacant
102 Executive Director of Foundation Ms. Shantel CRONK
72 Dean College Technical Sciences Dr. Dave KRUEGER
32 Dean of Students Mr. Corey KOPP
53 Int Dean Col Educ/Arts & Sciences Dr. Darlene SELLERS
06 Director Admissions/Student Records Ms. Alisha SCHROEDER
66 Int Dean of Col of Health Sciences Ms. Jaime DUKE
21 Controller Mr. Chris WENDLAND
41 Athletic Director Mr. Christian OBERQUELL
36 Director Career Center Vacant
13 Interim Chief Info Tech Officer Ms. Marianne HOPPE
37 Director of Financial Aid Ms. Cindy SMALL
26 Director of University Relations Mr. James POTTER
08 Director of Library Ms. Vicki GIST
121 Director Student Support Services Vacant
84 Exec Director Enrollment Mgmt Ms. Maura GATCH
15 Director of Human Resources Ms. Suzanne HUNGER
18 Facilities Manager Mr. Dan ULMEN
29 Outreach Specialist Ms. Lee LOUNDER
100 Chief of Staff Ms. Rachel DEAN

*Great Falls College Montana State University (F)

2100 16th Avenue South, Great Falls MT 59405-4909
County: Cascade FICE Identification: 009314
Unit ID: 180249
Telephone: (406) 771-4300 Carnegie Class: Assoc/MT-VT-Mix Trad/Non
FAX Number: (406) 771-4317 Calendar System: Semester
URL: gfcmsu.edu
Established: 1969 Annual Undergrad Tuition & Fees (In-State): $3,450
Enrollment: 1,071 Coed
Affiliation or Control: State IRS Status: 501(c)3
Highest Offering: Associate Degree
Accreditation: NW, CAHIIM, COARC, DA, DH, EMT, PTAA, SURGT

02 CEO/Dean Dr. Stephanie ERDMANN
05 Exec Director of Instruction Dr. Leanne FROST
32 Chief Student Affairs & HR Officer Ms. Mary Kay BONILLA
26 Dir Communications & Marketing Mr. Scott THOMPSON
13 Chief Technology Officer Mr. David BONILLA
18 Director of Facilities Services Mr. Gary SMART
36 Director Advising & Career Center Mr. Troy STODDARD
37 Director Student Financial Aid Ms. Leah HABEL
40 Bookstore Manager Mr. Steve HALSTED
11 Exec Director of Operations Ms. Carmen ROBERTS
09 Research Analyst Ms. Eleazar ORTEGA
88 Trades Division Director Mr. Joel SIMS
97 Director of General Studies Dr. Leanne FROST
76 Director of Health Sciences Mr. Russell MOTSCHENBACHER
06 Registrar Ms. Dena WAGNER-FOSSEN
84 Director Recruitment & Enrollment Ms. Shannon MARR
108 Dir Teaching & Learning Innovation Ms. Mandy WRIGHT

* Montana Technological University (A)

1300 W Park Street, Butte MT 59701-8997
County: Silver Bow FICE Identification: 002531
Unit ID: 180416
Telephone: (800) 445-8324 Carnegie Class: Masters/S
FAX Number: (406) 496-4710 Calendar System: Semester
URL: www.mtech.edu
Established: 1900 Annual Undergrad Tuition & Fees (In-State): $7,390
Enrollment: 1,650 Coed
Affiliation or Control: State IRS Status: 501(c)3
Highest Offering: Doctorate
Accreditation: NW, IACBE, NURSE

02 Chancellor ... Dr. Les COOK
05 Provost/Vice Chanc Academic Affairs ... Dr. Steve GAMMON
10 Business Officer/Controller ... Ms. Carleen CASSIDY
11 VC for Administration & Finance ... Mr. Michael VAN ALSTYNE
30 VC for Development & Univ Relations ... Mr. Joseph MCCLAFFERTY
84 Exec Dir Admissions/Enrollment ... Ms. Leslie DICKERSON
46 VC Research & Dean Grad Sch ... Vacant
65 Director Bureau of Mines & Geology ... Dr. John J. METESH
88 Dir Inst of Educational Opportunity ... Ms. Amy VERLANIC
36 Director Career Services ... Ms. Sarah RAYMOND
08 Director Library ... Mr. Scott JUSKIEWICZ
37 Director of Financial Aid ... Ms. Shauna SAVAGE
18 Director of Physical Facilities ... Mr. Layne SESSIONS
29 Director Alumni Affairs ... Vacant
41 Athletic Director ... Mr. Matt STEPAN
72 Int Dean College of Technology ... Ms. Karen VAN DAVEER
49 Dean Col Letters/Sci/Prof Studies ... Dr. Michele HARDY
54 Dean School of Mines & Engineering ... Dr. Dan TRUDNOWSKI
110 Director of Development ... Mr. Michael BARTH
39 Director Residence Life ... Mr. Scott FORTHOFER
26 Director Public Relations ... Ms. Amanda BADOVINAC
40 Bookstore Director ... Ms. Laurie VANDEL
09 Director Institutional Research ... Ms. Melissa KUMP
06 Registrar ... Ms. Janet FRIESZ
105 Webmaster ... Ms. Diane WARTHEN
106 Director of Distance Learning ... Vacant
13 Director of Information Technology ... Ms. Jennifer SIMON
96 Dir Purchasing & Budgets ... Ms. Marissa BENTLEY
15 Dir Human Resources ... Ms. Vanessa VAN DYK
25 Dir of Sponsored Programs ... Ms. Joanne LEE
38 Director Student Counseling ... Ms. Amy LORANG
100 Chief of Staff ... Ms. Jodie DELAY

* *City College at Montana State University Billings* (B)

3803 Central Avenue, Billings MT 59102-4398
Telephone: (406) 247-3000 FICE Identification: 010166
Accreditation: &NW

† Regional accreditation is carried under the parent institution Montana State University-Billings, Billings, MT.

* *Highlands College of Montana Tech* (C)

25 Basin Creek Road, Butte MT 59701-9704
Telephone: (406) 496-3701 FICE Identification: 009282
Accreditation: &NW

† Regional accreditation is carried under the parent institution Montana Tech of The University of Montanna, Butte, MT.

* *Missoula College-University of Montana* (D)

1205 East Broadway Street, Missoula MT 59802
Telephone: (406) 243-7811 FICE Identification: 007561
Accreditation: &NW, ACFEI, ADNUR, SURGT

† Regional accreditation is carried under the parent institution The University of Montana-Missoula, Missoula, MT.

Rocky Mountain College (E)

1511 Poly Drive, Billings MT 59102-1796
County: Yellowstone FICE Identification: 002534
Unit ID: 180595
Telephone: (406) 657-1000 Carnegie Class: Masters/S
FAX Number: (406) 259-9751 Calendar System: Semester
URL: www.rocky.edu
Established: 1878 Annual Undergrad Tuition & Fees: $30,586
Enrollment: 1,014 Coed
Affiliation or Control: Interdenominational IRS Status: 501(c)3
Highest Offering: Doctorate
Accreditation: NW, AAB, ARCPA, OT

01 President ... Dr. Robert WILMOUTH
05 Provost ... Mr. Anthony PILTZ
32 Vice President for Student Life ... Mr. Bradley A. NASON
111 Vice President of Advancement ... Vacant
84 Vice President of Enrollment ... Mr. Austin MAPSTON
20 Academic Vice President ... Dr. Erin RESER
10 Chief Financial Officer ... Ms. Melodie MILROY
88 Director of Educational Leadership ... Dr. Stevie SCHMITZ
08 Director of the Library ... Ms. Bobbi OTTE
112 Director of Major Gifts ... Ms. Heather OHS
13 Director of Information Technology ... Mr. Daniel WOLTERS
18 Director of Campus Facilities ... Mr. Keith NORTH
41 Director of Athletics ... Mr. Jeff MALBY
44 Director of Annual Fund ... Ms. Jill HIRSCHI
09 Director of Student Records ... Ms. Erica JOHNSON
37 Director of Financial Assistance ... Ms. Jessica FRANCISCHETTI
39 Director of Residence Life ... Ms. Shaydean SAYE
04 Executive Assistant to the Pres ... Ms. Tracy DAVIDSON
29 Director of Alumni Relations ... Ms. Sarah CLARK
19 Director Security/Safety ... Mr. Donald LAUX
91 Director Administrative Computing ... Ms. Kellee PIERCE
15 Chief Human Resources Officer ... Ms. Marcella BUSTER
07 Director of Admissions ... Mr. Sean COLEMAN

Salish Kootenai College (F)

PO Box 70, Pablo MT 59855-0070
County: Lake FICE Identification: 021434
Unit ID: 180647
Telephone: (406) 275-4800 Carnegie Class: Tribal
FAX Number: (406) 275-4801 Calendar System: Quarter
URL: www.skc.edu
Established: 1977 Annual Undergrad Tuition & Fees: $6,399
Enrollment: 716 Coed
Affiliation or Control: Independent Non-Profit IRS Status: 501(c)3
Highest Offering: Baccalaureate
Accreditation: NW, ADNUR, DA, NUR, SW

01 President ... Dr. Sandra BOHAM
05 Vice President of Academic Affairs ... Mr. Dan DURGLO
10 Vice Pres Business Affairs ... Ms. Audrey PLOUFFE
32 Vice President of Student Affairs ... Mr. Antony BERTHELOTE
06 Registrar ... Ms. Cleo KENMILLE
07 Director of Admissions ... Mr. Juan PEREZ
08 Library Director ... Mr. Fred NOEL
37 Financial Aid Director ... Ms. Jackie SWAIN
09 Dir Institutional Effectiveness ... Vacant
15 HR Generalist/Title IX Coord ... Ms. Tommie LINSEBIGLER
102 College Foundation Director ... Mr. William N. ROBERTS
13 Chief Information Officer ... Mr. Al ANDERSON
18 Physical Plant Operations Manager ... Vacant
04 Admin Assistant to President ... Ms. Anita BIG SPRING
100 Chief of Staff ... Ms. Brandy COUTURE
25 Chief Contract/Grants Administrator ... Mr. Greg GOULD
38 Director Student Counseling ... Ms. Kellie CALDBECK
39 Dir Resident Life/Student Housing ... Ms. Nihtawneemiw BOHAM
41 Athletic Director ... Ms. Melissa TIENSVOLD
50 Dean of Business ... Ms. Rachel ANDREWS-GOULD
53 Dean of Education ... Mr. Douglas RUHMAN

Stone Child College (G)

8294 Upper Box Elder Road, Box Elder MT 59521-9796
County: Hill FICE Identification: 026109
Unit ID: 366340
Telephone: (406) 395-4875 Carnegie Class: Tribal
FAX Number: (406) 395-4836 Calendar System: Semester
URL: www.stonechild.edu/
Established: 1984 Annual Undergrad Tuition & Fees: $2,645
Enrollment: 311 Coed
Affiliation or Control: Tribal Control IRS Status: 501(c)3
Highest Offering: Associate Degree
Accreditation: NW

01 President ... Ms. Cory SANGREY-BILLY
05 Dean of Academics ... Ms. Wilma TYNER
32 Dean of Student Services ... Ms. Helen WINDY BOY
10 Chief Financial Officer ... Ms. Tiffany GALBARY
15 Personnel Officer ... Ms. Wanda ST. MARKS
06 Registrar ... Ms. Gaile TORRES
13 Network Systems Administrator ... Mr. Paul GARCIA
40 Bookstore Manager ... Mr. Colton GALBAVY
37 Financial Aid Officer ... Ms. Jolin SUN CHILD
18 Facilities/Maintenance Supervisor ... Mr. Gus BACON
08 Head Librarian ... Ms. Joy BRIDWELL
41 Athletic Director ... Mr. Cameron BILLY

University of Providence (H)

1301 20th Street S, Great Falls MT 59405-4996
County: Cascade FICE Identification: 002527
Unit ID: 180258
Telephone: (800) 856-9544 Carnegie Class: Bac-Diverse
FAX Number: (406) 791-5209 Calendar System: Semester
URL: www.uprovidence.edu
Established: 1932 Annual Undergrad Tuition & Fees: $26,662
Enrollment: 1,005 Coed
Affiliation or Control: Roman Catholic IRS Status: 501(c)3
Highest Offering: Master's
Accreditation: NW, CACREP, NURSE

01 President ... Rev. Oliver J. DOYLE
05 Provost ... Dr. Matthew REDINGER
10 CFO ... Vacant
100 Chief of Staff to the President ... Ms. Kylie CARRANZA
84 VP for Enrollment Management ... Ms. Mackenzie STICK
88 VP for Athletics ... Mr. Dave GANTT
76 Executive Dean SHP ... Dr. Jonas NGUH
03 Interim Mission Officer ... Mr. Nicolas ESTRADA
111 VP for Advancement ... Vacant
41 Athletics Director ... Mr. Douglas HASHLEY
121 Dir of Academic Success Center ... Mr. Greg STIVERS
21 Financial Controller ... Ms. Jillian EHNOT
15 Director of Human Resources ... Mrs. Melanie HOUGE
06 Registrar ... Ms. Brittany BUDESKI
09 Director of Institutional Research ... Dr. Gregory MADSON
106 Director of Distance Learning ... Mr. Jim GRETCH
108 Director of Inst Effectiveness ... Mr. Greg MADSON
88 Director of Campus Ministry ... Mr. Nicolas ESTRADA
18 Director Physical Plant ... Mr. Chet PIETRYKOWSKI
08 Senior Librarian ... Ms. Susan LEE
04 Executive Asst to the President ... Ms. Trudi COLE
88 Executive Assistant to the Provost ... Ms. Lindsay BERG
26 Dir of Marketing & COmmunications ... Mr. Colton SCHANG

Yellowstone Christian College (I)

1605 Danielson Rd, Kalispell MT 59901
County: Flathead Identification: 667254
Telephone: (406) 656-9950 Carnegie Class: Not Classified
FAX Number: N/A Calendar System: Semester
URL: www.yellowstonechristian.edu
Established: 1974 Annual Undergrad Tuition & Fees: N/A
Enrollment: N/A Coed
Affiliation or Control: Independent Non-Profit IRS Status: 501(c)3
Highest Offering: Baccalaureate
Accreditation: BI

01 President ... Vacant
05 Provost & Dean of Academics ... Mr. John RAMOS
84 Dean of Enrollment ... Mr. Max SOFT
10 Chief Financial/Operations Officer ... Dr. Robert ESHLEMAN
32 Associate Dean of Students ... Miss Miranda CARTER
06 Registrar ... Mrs. Cheryl ANDERSON
41 Athletic Director ... Mr. Kyle SPENCER

NEBRASKA

Bellevue University (J)

1000 Galvin Road S, Bellevue NE 68005-3098
County: Sarpy FICE Identification: 009743
Unit ID: 180814
Telephone: (402) 293-2000 Carnegie Class: Masters/L
FAX Number: (402) 293-2020 Calendar System: Other
URL: www.bellevue.edu
Established: 1966 Annual Undergrad Tuition & Fees: $7,851
Enrollment: 13,059 Coed
Affiliation or Control: Independent Non-Profit IRS Status: 501(c)3
Highest Offering: Doctorate
Accreditation: HLC, CACREP, IACBE, NURSE

01 President ... Dr. Mary B. HAWKINS
03 Executive Vice President ... Ms. Sherrye HUTCHERSON
11 Exec VP Administrative Services ... Mr. Matthew DAVIS
18 Vice President Facilities ... Mr. Jerry A. BLASIG
72 Dean of College of Science & Tech ... Dr. Mary DOBRANSKY
50 Dean College of Business ... Dr. Rebecca MURDOCK
49 Dean College of Arts & Sciences ... Dr. Clif MASON
51 Dean Continuing/Professional Educ ... Dr. Michelle EPPLER
04 Exec Assistant to the President ... Ms. Christine HOW
32 AVP Community & Student Affairs ... Mr. Scott BIERMAN
37 Director Student Financial Aid ... Ms. Janet SOLBERG
08 Sr Dir Library Services ... Ms. Robin BERNSTEIN
102 Foundation CEO ... Mr. Russ RUPIPER
41 Director of Athletics ... Mr. Ed LEHOTAK
40 Director Bookstore ... Mr. Mark RIGGERT
88 Director of Buildings & Grounds ... Mr. Ralph (Sam) J. BORER
30 VP Development Programs ... Ms. Dorothy MORROW
10 Controller ... Ms. Brooke LAMBERT
19 Director of Security/Safety ... Mr. Greg ALLEN
108 Quality Assurance Programs Director ... Mr. Pete HEINEMAN
26 Sr Dir Marketing Operations ... Ms. Geri MASON
06 Registrar ... Ms. Colette LEWIS

Bryan College of Health Sciences (K)

1535 S 52nd St., Lincoln NE 68506
County: Lancaster FICE Identification: 006399
Unit ID: 180878
Telephone: (402) 481-3801 Carnegie Class: Spec-4-yr-Other Health
FAX Number: (402) 481-8421 Calendar System: Semester
URL: www.bryanhealthcollege.edu
Established: 2001 Annual Undergrad Tuition & Fees: $18,216
Enrollment: 778 Coed
Affiliation or Control: Independent Non-Profit IRS Status: 501(c)3
Highest Offering: Doctorate
Accreditation: HLC, ANEST, CVT, DMS, NUR

01 President ... Dr. Richard LLOYD
05 Provost ... Dr. Kelsi ANDERSON
97 Dean of Educational Development ... Dr. Kristy PLANDER
11 Dean of Operations ... Dr. Bill EVANS
66 Dean of Undergraduate Nursing ... Dr. Theresa DELAHOYDE
58 Dean of Graduate Studies ... Dr. Marcia KUBE
76 Dean of Healthcare Studies ... Dr. Amy KNOBBE
88 Dean of Nurse Anesthesia ... Dr. Sharon HADENFELDT
32 Dean of Students ... Dr. Alethea STOVALL
08 Director of Library Services ... Ms. Heather ST. CLAIR
06 Registrar ... Ms. Deann BAYNE
29 Student/Alumni Services Director ... Ms. Brenda NEEMANN
37 Financial Aid Director ... Ms. Maggie HACKWITH
113 Student Accounts Coordinator ... Ms. Alicia ARNOLD
106 Director of Digital Education ... Ms. Deb MAEDER
84 Dean of Enrollment Management ... Ms. Stacy DAM

Central Community College (A)

PO Box 4903, Grand Island NE 68802-4903
County: Hall FICE Identification: 020995
Unit ID: 180902
Telephone: (308) 398-4222 Carnegie Class: Assoc/HVT-High Non
FAX Number: (308) 398-7398 Calendar System: Semester
URL: www.cccneb.edu
Established: 1966 Annual Undergrad Tuition & Fees (In-District): $3,210
Enrollment: 5,974 Coed
Affiliation or Control: Local IRS Status: 501(c)3
Highest Offering: Associate Degree
Accreditation: HLC, ADNUR, CAHIIM, DA, DH, EMT, MAC, MLTAD, OTA

01 College President .... Dr. Matthew GOTSCHALL
05 VP of Innovation & Instruction .... Dr. Candace WALTON
10 Vice President of Admin Services .... Mr. Joel KING
15 Vice President of Human Resources .... Dr. Chris WADDLE
12 Grand Island Campus President .... Dr. Marcie KEMNITZ
12 Columbus Campus President .... Dr. Kathy FUCHSER
12 Hastings Campus President .... Dr. Jerry WALLACE
102 Foundation Executive Director .... Mr. Dean MOORS
20 Assoc Dean of Instruction .... Dr. Kyle STERNER
50 Dean of Business & Entrepreneurship .... Ms. Roxann HOLLIDAY
76 Dean of Health Sciences .... Ms. Paulette WOODS-RAMSEY
88 Dean of Skilled & Technical Science .... Dr. Nate ALLEN
84 Dean of Enrollment Management .... Ms. Janel WALTON
32 Dean of Student Success .... Dr. Beth PRZYMUS
56 Dean of Ext Learning Services .... Mr. Ron KLUCK
75 Dean of Training .... Dr. Kelly CHRISTENSEN
13 IT Services Manager .... Mr. Tom PETERS
06 Registrar .... Ms. Barb LARSON
29 Alumni Director .... Ms. Cheri BEDA
37 Area Director Student Financial Aid .... Ms. Victoria KUCERA
41 Athletic Director .... Ms. Mary YOUNG
09 Director Institutional Research .... Mr. Brian MCDERMOTT
28 Equity and Compliance Manager .... Ms. Lauren SLAUGHTER
26 Sr Dir College Communications .... Mr. Scott MILLER
07 Admissions Director Columbus .... Ms. Kristin HOESING
07 Admissions Director Grand Island .... Ms. Erin LESIAK
07 Admissions Director Hastings .... Ms. Regina SOMER
96 Purchasing Manager .... Ms. Carmen TAYLOR
04 Communications Asst to President .... Ms. Joni RANSOM

Central Community College Columbus Campus (B)

PO Box 1027, 4500 63rd Street,
Columbus NE 68602-1027
Telephone: (402) 564-7132 Identification: 770331
Accreditation: &HLC

Central Community College Hastings Campus (C)

550 S Technical Blvd, PO Box 1024,
Hastings NE 68902-1024
Telephone: (402) 463-9811 Identification: 770332
Accreditation: &HLC

CHI Health School of Radiologic Technology (D)

6901 North 72nd Street, Omaha NE 68122
County: Douglas FICE Identification: 008492
Unit ID: 181145
Telephone: (402) 572-3650 Carnegie Class: Spec 2-yr-Health
FAX Number: (402) 398-6650 Calendar System: Semester
URL: www.chihealth.com/school-of-radiologic-technology
Established: 1953 Annual Undergrad Tuition & Fees: N/A
Enrollment: 15 Coed
Affiliation or Control: Independent Non-Profit IRS Status: 501(c)3
Highest Offering: Associate Degree
Accreditation: RAD

01 Int CEO CHI Health .... Jeanett WOJTALEWICZ
10 Int Chief Financial Officer .... Nick O'TOOL
05 Chief Medical Officer .... Dr. Cary WARD

Clarkson College (E)

101 S 42nd Street, Omaha NE 68131-2739
County: Douglas FICE Identification: 009862
Unit ID: 180832
Telephone: (402) 552-3100 Carnegie Class: Spec-4-yr-Other Health
FAX Number: (402) 552-3369 Calendar System: Semester
URL: www.clarksoncollege.edu
Established: 1888 Annual Undergrad Tuition & Fees: $14,496
Enrollment: 1,169 Coed
Affiliation or Control: Independent Non-Profit IRS Status: 501(c)3
Highest Offering: Doctorate
Accreditation: HLC, ANEST, CAHIIM, NUR, PTAA, RAD

01 President .... Dr. Gary PACK
05 VP of Academic Affairs .... Dr. Andriea NEBEL
11 Vice Pres Operations .... Jina PAUL
10 Controller .... Megan WICKLESS-MULDER
06 Registrar .... Natalie VRBKA
15 Director Human Resources .... Daniel WOJTALEWICZ
13 Director Technology Services .... Ryan SCHURMAN
37 Director Student Financial Services .... Laura THAYER-MENCKE
08 Director Library Services .... Anne HEIMANN
38 Manager Success Center .... Kitty CAPPELLANO
97 Director General Education .... Lori BACHLE
50 Dir Health Care Business .... Carla DIRKSCHNEIDER
76 Dir Medical Imaging/Radiologic Tech .... Shelli WEDDUM
76 Dir Physical Therapist Asst Pgm .... Jessica NIEMANN
84 Director Enrollment/Advising .... Ken ZEIGER
51 Director of Professional Dev .... Judi B. DUNN
111 Director College Advancement .... Chris SHIVES
106 Coordinator Online Education .... Vacant
09 Coord Inst Effect/Quality Assurance .... Chris SWANSON

College of Saint Mary (F)

7000 Mercy Road, Omaha NE 68106-2606
County: Douglas FICE Identification: 002540
Unit ID: 181604
Telephone: (402) 399-2400 Carnegie Class: Masters/M
FAX Number: (402) 399-2647 Calendar System: Semester
URL: www.csm.edu
Established: 1923 Annual Undergrad Tuition & Fees: $21,370
Enrollment: 1,024 Female
Affiliation or Control: Roman Catholic IRS Status: 501(c)3
Highest Offering: Doctorate
Accreditation: HLC, #ARCPA, NUR, OT, @PTA

01 President .... Dr. Maryanne STEVENS, RSM
05 Provost .... Dr. Sarah KOTTICH
10 Vice Pres Finance/Administration .... Ms. Bridgette RENBARGER
05 Vice Pres Academic Affairs .... Dr. Kimbery ALLEN
84 Vice President Enrollment .... Mr. John FROST
26 Vice Pres Marketing/Athletics/IT .... Mr. Nate NEUFIND
111 Vice Pres Alumnae/Donor Relations .... Ms. Terri CAMPBELL
124 Assistant Dean of Student Success .... Ms. Daniela ROJAS
38 Asst Dean Student Support Services .... Ms. Barbara TREADWAY
32 Assistant Dean of Student LIfe .... Mr. Kristofer CZERWIEC
08 Director of Library .... Vacant
88 Vice President Mission Integration .... Dr. Andrea STAPLETON
19 Director Security/Safety .... Mr. David FERBER
06 Registrar .... Vacant
37 Chief Student Financial Aid Officer .... Ms. Beth SISK
28 Director of Multicultural Affairs .... Ms. Alexis SHERMAN
27 AVP for Marketing/Public Relations .... Ms. Brittney LONG
21 Controller .... Vacant
11 Chief of Administration .... Ms. Kim SAVICKY
15 Chief HR Officer .... Ms. Jessica HOCHSTEIN
40 Director Bookstore .... Mr. Steve WESTENBROEK
29 Senior Director Alumnae Relations .... Ms. Katty PETAK
39 Director Residence Life .... Ms. Larissa BUSTER
112 Director of Major Gifts .... Ms. Susan MEDINA
44 Director of Annual Giving & Alumna .... Ms. Megan COLE
41 Athletic Director .... Mr. Peter HARING
18 Director Physical Plant .... Mr. Dan SPARGEN
42 Director Campus Ministry .... Vacant
13 Chief IT Officer .... Mr. Kevin SHOLL
04 Executive Asst to the President .... Ms. Robyn KNIFFEN

Concordia University (G)

800 N Columbia Avenue, Seward NE 68434-1599
County: Seward FICE Identification: 002541
Unit ID: 180984
Telephone: (402) 643-3651 Carnegie Class: Masters/L
FAX Number: (402) 643-4073 Calendar System: Other
URL: www.cune.edu
Established: 1894 Annual Undergrad Tuition & Fees: $34,900
Enrollment: 3,224 Coed
Affiliation or Control: Lutheran Church - Missouri Synod
IRS Status: 501(c)3
Highest Offering: Master's
Accreditation: HLC, CAEP, CAEPN, IACBE, MUS

01 President .... Dr. Bernard BULL
05 Provost .... Dr. Timothy PREUSS
111 Vice President Inst Advancement .... Mr. Kurth BRASHEAR
84 VP Enrollment & Marketing .... Mr. Gary MCDANIEL
32 VP for Student Affairs & Athletics .... Mr. Gene BROOKS
10 Chief Financial Officer .... Mr. David KUMM
13 Chief Information Officer .... Mr. Curt SHERMAN
53 Dean of Educ/Health & Human Science .... Dr. Lorinda SANKEY
49 Dean of Arts & Sciences .... Dr. Brent ROYUK
50 Dean College of Business .... Mr. Jonathon MOBERLY
14 Dir Special IT Projects .... Dr. Kent EINSPAHR
08 Director of Library Services .... Mr. Philip HENDRICKSON
88 Dir of Education/Synodical Careers .... Mr. William SCHRANZ
29 Director Alumni/University Rels .... Mrs. Jennifer FURR
36 Dir Career Development & Retention .... Mr. Corey GRAY
41 Athletic Director .... Mr. Devin SMITH
06 University Registrar .... Mr. Ed SIFFRING
42 Campus Pastor .... Rev. Ryan MATTHIAS
37 Director of Financial Aid .... Mr. Scott JENKINS
18 Facilities Director/Maintenance .... Mr. Dale NOVAK
15 Director of Human Resources .... Mrs. Connie BUTLER
07 Director Admission Operations .... Mr. Aaron ROBERTS
27 Director of Marketing/Communication .... Mr. Seth MERANDA
115 Sr Dir Strategic Initiatives/Invest .... Mr. Curt SHERMAN
110 Sr Dir of Advancement Operations .... Mrs. Leigh LEWIS
106 Dir Classroom Innov & Online Educ .... Ms. Angie WASSENMILLER
121 Sr Director of Student Success Ctr .... Mrs. Lori READ
19 Director Security/Safety .... Mr. Ron DOWN
35 Director Student Development .... Ms. Rebekah FREED
43 Assoc VP Legal Affairs/Gen Counsel .... Mr. Kirby KLAPPENBACK
28 Multicult Spec/Asst Dir Stdnt Life .... Mr. Von THOMAS
30 Sr Dir Development & Engagement .... Mr. Scott SEEVERS

Creighton University (H)

2500 California Plaza, Omaha NE 68178-0001
County: Douglas FICE Identification: 002542
Unit ID: 181002
Telephone: (402) 280-2700 Carnegie Class: DU-Mod
FAX Number: N/A Calendar System: Semester
URL: www.creighton.edu
Established: 1878 Annual Undergrad Tuition & Fees: $43,018
Enrollment: 8,770 Coed
Affiliation or Control: Roman Catholic IRS Status: 501(c)3
Highest Offering: Doctorate
Accreditation: HLC, #ARCPA, CAEP, CAMPEP, DENT, EMT, LAW, MED, NURSE, OT, PHAR, PTA, SW

01 President .... Rev. Daniel S. HENDRICKSON, SJ
00 Chairman Creighton University Board .... Mr. Nizar GHOUSSAINI
05 Provost .... Dr. Mardell A. WILSON
100 Spec Asst to Pres & Board Liaison .... Vacant
04 Sr Exec Assistant President Office .... Ms. Lori L. VANDER MOLEN
04 Exec Assistant President Office .... Mr. David L. BARNUM
101 Corporate Secretary .... Mr. James S. JANSEN
03 Executive Vice President .... Ms. Jan E. MADSEN
88 Vice President Mission & Ministry .... Dr. Eileen C. BURKE-SULLIVAN
88 Sr Dir Ignation Formation/Ministry .... Ms. Susan NAATZ
42 Interim Director Campus Ministry .... Ms. Kelly TADEO ORBIK
88 Director Ctr for Service & Justice .... Mr. Kenneth REED-BOULEY
88 Director Retreat Center .... Ms. Amy K. HOOVER
111 Vice President University Relations .... Mr. Matthew C. GERARD
112 Assistant VP Principal Gifts .... Mr. Mike T. FINDLEY
110 Asst VP University Relations .... Fr. Tom MERKEL, SJ
30 AVP Development AZ HSC Campus .... Ms. Meghan S. FROST
30 Assistant VP of Development .... Ms. Cortney A. BAUER
88 AVP Athletic Development .... Mr. Adrian E. DOWELL
30 AVP Advancement Svcs & Dev Prog .... Ms. Amy M. MCELHANEY
29 Assistant VP Alumni Relations .... Ms. Diane M. GLOW
88 Sr Philanthropic Advisor .... Mr. Steven A. SCHOLER
08 Asst Vice Provost Library Services .... Ms. Elizabeth J. KISCADEN
106 Assoc VP Teaching & Learning Center .... Dr. Debra FORD
09 Director Institutional Research .... Dr. Kristin BUSCHER
06 Registrar .... Ms. Melinda J. STONER
22 Director Disability Accommodations .... Ms. Jacque KNEDLER
36 Director Career Center .... Mr. Jeremy M. FISHER
43 General Counsel .... Mr. James S. JANSEN
32 Vice Provost Student Life .... Dr. Tanya C. WINEGARD
35 AVP Student Retention/Development .... Dr. Wayne YOUNG
35 Assoc VP Student Engagement .... Dr. Michele K. BOGARD
41 Athletic Director .... Mr. Bruce D. RASMUSSEN
39 Sr Dir Housing & Auxiliary Service .... Mr. Lucas NOVOTNY
39 Director of Residential Life .... Ms. Michael LORENZ
88 Sr Dir Community Stdrds & Wellbeing .... Ms. Desiree NOWNES
93 Dir Creighton Intercultural Center .... Ms. Becky NICKERSON
88 Director of Recreation and Wellness .... Mr. Greg DURHAM
89 Dir Student Ldrshp/Involvement Ctr .... Ms. Katie M. KELSEY
84 VP Enrollment Mgmt & Univ Planning .... Dr. Mary E. CHASE
07 Director Admissions/Scholarships .... Ms. Sarah D. RICHARDSON
123 Dir Graduate and Adult Recruitment .... Ms. Elizabeth CHURCHICH
37 Director Student Financial Aid .... Ms. Janet SOLBERG
121 Sr Dir Acad Success & Educ Oppty .... Dr. Joe ECKLUND
49 Dean College of Arts & Sciences .... Dr. Bridget M. KEEGAN
50 Dean Heider College of Business .... Dr. Anthony R. HENDRICKSON
58 Interim Dean Graduate School .... Fr. Kevin FITZGERALD, SJ
52 Dean School of Dentistry .... Dr. Jillian WALLEN
61 Dean School of Law .... Mr. Joshua P. FERSHEE
63 Dean School of Medicine .... Dr. Robert W. DUNLAY
66 Dean College of Nursing .... Dr. Catherine M. TODERO
67 Dean Sch of Pharmacy & Health Prof .... Dr. Evan T. ROBINSON
26 Vice Pres Univ Comm & Marketing .... Ms. Heidi GRUNKEMEYER
27 Director Communication .... Mr. Rick C. DAVIS
105 Interim Director Web Strategy .... Ms. Beth CAVANAUGH
18 Assoc VP Facility Mgmt & Planning .... Mr. Derek SCOTT
19 Director Public Safety .... Mr. Michael D. REINER
21 Assoc VP Finance .... Mr. John J. JESSE, III
113 Assoc Director Business Office .... Ms. Ann M. O'DOWD
21 Assoc VP Finance .... Ms. Tara S. MCGUIRE
116 Director Internal Audit .... Mr. T. Paul TOMOSER
117 Risk Manager .... Ms. Katie BOOTON
88 Manager of Tax and GAAP .... Mr. Jason T. MCGILL
96 Sr Director Procurement .... Mr. Eric J. GILMORE
15 Assoc VP Human Resources .... Ms. Judi SZATKO
118 Sr Director Benefits & Compensation .... Ms. Molly BILLINGS
13 Vice Pres Information Technology .... Mr. Russ B. PEARLMAN
14 AVP Solution Delivery .... Dr. David RAMCHARAN
90 AVP Planning .... Mr. Scott TAYLOR
91 Senior Director IT Operations .... Mr. Mark MONGAR
119 Information Security Officer .... Mr. Bryan S. MCLAUGHLIN
24 IT Solutions Architect Learning Env .... Vacant
22 Exec Director Equity & Inclusion .... Ms. Allison S. TAYLOR
23 Medical Dir Student Health Services .... Vacant
25 Director Sponsored Programs Admin .... Ms. Beth J. HERR
28 Interim VP Inst Diversity/Inclusion .... Dr. Sarah WALKER
38 Director Counseling Services .... Dr. Jennifer PETER
40 Bookstore Manager .... Mr. Cory DAVIS
85 Vice Provost Global Engagement .... Dr. Rene L. PADILLA
86 Director Comm & Govt Relationships .... Mr. Chris T. RODGERS
92 Director Honors Program .... Dr. Jeffrey P. HAUSE

104 Global Programs Coordinator .... Ms. Lizzy E. CURRAN
104 Global Programs Coordinator .... Ms. Krista CUPICH
20 Vice President Compliance .... Ms. Tricia SHARRAR
20 VP Learning & Assessment .... Dr. Gail M. JENSEN

Doane University (A)

1014 Boswell Avenue, Crete NE 68333
County: Saline FICE Identification: 002544
Unit ID: 181020
Telephone: (800) 333-6263 Carnegie Class: Bac-A&S
FAX Number: (402) 826-8600 Calendar System: 4/1/4
URL: www.doane.edu
Established: 1872 Annual Undergrad Tuition & Fees: $36,800
Enrollment: 2,281 Coed
Affiliation or Control: United Church Of Christ IRS Status: 501(c)3
Highest Offering: Doctorate
Accreditation: HLC, CAEP, CAEPN, MUS, NURSE

01 President .... Dr. Roger HUGHES
05 Interim Chief Academic Officer .... Dr. Lorie COOK-BENJAMIN
10 Interim Chief Financial Officer .... Mr. Ned TUCKER
111 Vice President for Advancement .... Mr. Marty FYE
84 Vice Pres Enroll/Student Experience .... Mr. Jake HOY-ELSWICK
13 Chief Information Officer .... Mr. Derek BIERMAN
53 Dean College of Education .... Dr. Tim FREY
50 Dean of the College of Business .... Ms. Jennifer BOSSARD
20 Assoc Dean of Academic Affairs .... Mr. Kristopher WILLIAMS
49 Dean College of Arts/Sciences .... Dr. Pedro MALIGO
06 Registrar .... Ms. Denise ELLIS
37 Director of Financial Aid .... Mr. Federico PENA, JR.
07 Director of Admissions .... Mr. Kyle MCMURRAY
08 Interim Director of the Library .... Ms. Cali BIAGGI
88 Director of Enrollment .... Ms. Lauren ERICKSON
21 Controller .... Mr. Bryce ENGELBERT
26 Chief Marketing Officer .... Mr. Dan KOHLER
29 Director of Alumni Relation .... Mr. Michael STEHLIK
15 Director of Human Resources .... Ms. Anne ZIOLA
18 Dir of Facilities & Constr Proj .... Mr. Brian FLESNER
12 Director of Lincoln Campus .... Ms. Angie KLASEK
32 Dean of Students .... Ms. Megan FAILOR
12 Director of Omaha Campus .... Mr. Chris BRADY
41 Athletic Director .... Mr. Mark WATESKA
42 Dir of Religious & Spiritual Life .... Dr. Leah REDIGER
28 VP for Diversity/Equity & Inclusion .... Mr. Luis SOTELO
23 Director of Student Health .... Ms. Kelly JIROVEC
38 Director of Campus Wellness .... Vacant
121 Director of Student Support Service .... Ms. Anita HARKINS
09 Director of Institutional Research .... Dr. Raja TAYEH
19 Dir of Campus Safety/Assoc Dean .... Mr. Russ HEWITT
04 Executive Assistant to President .... Ms. Jenei SKILLETT
30 Senior Director of Development .... Ms. Jacqueline HINRICHSEN
44 Executive Director Annual Giving .... Ms. Julie RASGORSHEK

Doane University (B)

303 North 52nd Street, Lincoln NE 68504
Telephone: (402) 466-4774 Identification: 770334
Accreditation: &HLC

Hastings College (C)

710 N Turner Avenue, Box 269, Hastings NE 68902-0269
County: Adams FICE Identification: 002548
Unit ID: 181127
Telephone: (402) 463-2402 Carnegie Class: Bac-Diverse
FAX Number: (402) 461-7490 Calendar System: 4/1/4
URL: www.hastings.edu
Established: 1882 Annual Undergrad Tuition & Fees: $32,770
Enrollment: 982 Coed
Affiliation or Control: Presbyterian Church (U.S.A.) IRS Status: 501(c)3
Highest Offering: Master's
Accreditation: HLC, CAEP, MUS

01 Executive President .... Dr. Rich LLOYD
00 Chairman of the Board .... Mr. Roger DOERR
102 Executive Director of Foundation .... Mr. Gary FREEMAN
10 VP for Finance/CFO .... Ms. Stephanie OURADA
84 EVP Enrollment/Student Experience .... Vacant
05 VP of Academic Affairs .... Vacant
41 Athletic Director .... Mr. B.J PUMROY
32 Assoc VP for Student Affairs .... Vacant
112 Assoc VP for Planned & Major Gifts .... Mr. Michael KARLOFF
110 Assoc VP for Development .... Ms. Judee L. KONEN
06 Registrar .... Mr. Jim BOEVE
37 Director of Financial Aid .... Ms. Traci BOEVE
18 Director of Facilities .... Vacant
15 Director of Human Resources .... Ms. Ana LUZ
26 Director of Marketing .... Mr. Michael HOWIE
29 AVP of External Relations .... Mr. Matt FONG
13 Director of IT .... Ms. Patty KINGSLEY
14 Network Administrator .... Mr. Josh KELLEY
18 Director Physical Plant Services .... Mr. Ron GRIGGS
93 Minority Students .... Dr. Moses DOGBEVIA
28 Pushkin Institute Director .... Dr. Rob BABCOCK
36 Director of Career Services .... Ms. Kimberly K. GRAVIETTE
23 Director Campus Health Services .... Vacant
42 Chaplain .... Vacant
35 Dean of Student Engagement .... Dr. Lisa SMITH
19 Director of Security/Safety .... Mr. Brian HESSLER
38 Director of Counseling Services .... Mr. Jon LOETTERLE
40 Bookstore Manager .... Ms. Brianna WEICHEL

88 Graphic Designer/Publisher .... Mrs. Camille KASTL
85 International Program Director .... Mr. Grant HUNTER
04 Executive Asst to President & VPAA .... Ms. Marin SUHR
07 Director of Admissions .... Ms. Chris SCHUKEI
09 Director of Institutional Research .... Dr. Kristin CHARLES
44 Director Annual Giving .... Ms. Alicia O'DONNELL

Little Priest Tribal College (D)

601 East College Drive, PO Box 270,
Winnebago NE 68071-0270
County: Thurston FICE Identification: 033233
Unit ID: 434016
Telephone: (402) 878-2380 Carnegie Class: Tribal
FAX Number: (402) 878-2380 Calendar System: Semester
URL: www.littlepriest.edu
Established: 1996 Annual Undergrad Tuition & Fees: $5,140
Enrollment: 113 Coed
Affiliation or Control: Independent Non-Profit IRS Status: 501(c)3
Highest Offering: Associate Degree
Accreditation: HLC

01 President .... Mr. Manoj PATIL
05 VP of Teaching and Learning .... Ms. Loretta BROBERG
10 VP of Finance and Operations .... Mr. Mark VASINA
07 Director of Admissions .... Ms. Alyssa TURNQUIST
37 Director of Financial Aid .... Ms. Yatty MOHAMMAD
15 Human Resource Coordinator .... Mrs. Angela KENT
32 Director of Student Support Service .... Ms. Trisha WEGNER
13 IT Director .... Mr. Morri CONWAY
25 Director of Grants .... Ms. Kathleen DOY
09 Institutional Research/Data Analyst .... Ms. Kavya MARIBOYINA
04 Exec Assistant to the President .... Ms. Carla KAI
19 Director Security/Safety .... Mr. Justin MCCAULEY

Mary Lanning Healthcare School of Radiology (E)

715 North St. Joseph Avenue, Hastings NE 68901
County: Adams FICE Identification: 004431
Unit ID: 181251
Telephone: (402) 461-5177 Carnegie Class: Not Classified
FAX Number: (402) 460-5059 Calendar System: Other
URL: www.marylanning.org
Established: 1952 Annual Undergrad Tuition & Fees: N/A
Enrollment: N/A Coed
Affiliation or Control: Independent Non-Profit IRS Status: 501(c)3
Highest Offering: Associate Degree
Accreditation: RAD

01 President and CEO .... Eric BARBER
05 Chief Medical Officer .... Dr. Abel LUKSAN
10 Chief Financial Officer .... Shawn NORDBY
11 Chief Operating Officer .... Mark CALLAHAN
15 Vice Pres Human Resources .... Bruce CUTRIGHT

McCook Community College (F)

1205 East Third Street, McCook NE 69001
Telephone: (308) 345-8100 Identification: 770337
Accreditation: &HLC, EMT

Metropolitan Community College (G)

PO Box 3777, Omaha NE 68103-0777
County: Douglas FICE Identification: 012586
Unit ID: 181303
Telephone: (531) 622-2400 Carnegie Class: Assoc/HT-High Non
FAX Number: (402) 457-2395 Calendar System: Quarter
URL: www.mccneb.edu
Established: 1974 Annual Undergrad Tuition & Fees (In-District): $3,195
Enrollment: 13,244 Coed
Affiliation or Control: State/Local IRS Status: Exempt
Highest Offering: Associate Degree
Accreditation: HLC, ACBSP, ACFEI, ADNUR, CAHIIM, COARC, CSHSE, DA, EMT, MAC

01 President .... Mr. Randy SCHMAILZL
05 Vice President Academic Affairs .... Dr. Tom MCDONNELL
28 Assoc Vice Pres Equity/Diversity . Dr. Cynthia GOOCH-GRAYSON
15 Assoc Vice Pres of Human Resources .... Ms. Melissa BEBER
45 VP for Strategic Initiatives .... Mr. William OWEN
32 Vice Pres for Student Affairs .... Dr. Marie VAZQUEZ
10 College Business Officer .... Ms. Brenda SCHUMACHER
26 Assoc VP Marketing Brand & Commun .... Ms. Nannette RODRIGUEZ
18 Director Facilities Management .... Mr. Bernard SEDLACEK
37 Director of Financial Aid .... Ms. Wilma HJELLUM
96 Director Administrative Management .... Ms. KT NELSON
19 Chief of Police/Dir Emergency Mgmt .... Mr. Dave FRIEND
84 Dean of Enrollment Management .... Dr. Charles CHEVALIER
27 Chief Information Officer .... Mr. Chad LYNCH
06 Registrar .... Ms. Albertha SCHMID
43 Dir Legal Services/General Counsel .... Mr. Jim THIBODEAU
30 Director of Development .... Ms. Amy RECKER
91 Director Administrative Computing .... Ms. Jodie SNIDER
04 Executive Assistant to President .... Ms. Rita EYERLY
100 Senior Aide to the President .... Ms. Patricia CRISLER

Metropolitan Community College Elkhorn Valley Campus (H)

829 North 204th Street, Elkhorn NE 68022
Telephone: (531) 622-5231 Identification: 770335
Accreditation: &HLC

Metropolitan Community College South Omaha Campus (I)

2909 Edward Babe Gomez Avenue, Omaha NE 68107
Telephone: (531) 622-5231 Identification: 770336
Accreditation: &HLC

Mid-Plains Community College (J)

601 W State Farm Road, North Platte NE 69101-9491
County: Lincoln FICE Identification: 002557
Unit ID: 181312
Telephone: (800) 658-4308 Carnegie Class: Assoc/MT-VT-High Non
FAX Number: (308) 535-3794 Calendar System: Semester
URL: www.mpcc.edu
Established: 1926 Annual Undergrad Tuition & Fees (In-District): $3,360
Enrollment: 2,075 Coed
Affiliation or Control: State/Local IRS Status: 501(c)3
Highest Offering: Associate Degree
Accreditation: HLC, ADNUR, DA, MLTAD

01 President .... Mr. Ryan PURDY
12 VP North Platte Community College .... Dr. Jody TOMANEK
12 Vice Pres McCook Community College .... Ms. Kelly RIPPEN
11 VP for Administrative Services .... Mr. Michael STEELE
05 VP for Academic Affairs .... Dr. Jody TOMANEK
09 Dir Institutional Effectiveness .... Mr. Tad PFEIFER
32 Dean of Student Life .... Dr. Brian OBERT
56 Associate Dean of Outreach .... Ms. Gail KNOTT
36 Director of Career Services .... Ms. Becky BARNER
84 Dir of Recruiting & Admissions .... Ms. Mindy HOPE
06 Registrar .... Ms. Lana STEWART
26 Dir Public Info/Marketing .... Mr. Daniel STINMAN
15 Director of Human Resources .... Ms. Rebecca WRAGE
13 Dir Information Tech Svcs .... Mr. Trent WIESE
37 Dir of Student Financial Aid .... Ms. Erinn BROWN
04 Exec Assistant to the President .... Ms. Karen HALLER
106 Ctr for Teaching Excellence Coord .... Mrs. Cathy NUTT
108 Director Institutional Assessment .... Ms. Holly ANDREWS
18 Chief Fac/Physical Plant Ofcr .... Mr. Shawn ATEN
19 Director Security/Safety .... Mrs. Rebecca SINSEL
111 Director Institutional Advancement .... Mr. Jacob RISSLER
39 Dir Resident Life/Student Housing .... Mr. Jason OSMOTHERLY
41 Athletic Director .... Mr. Kevin O'CONNOR
07 Director of Admissions .... Ms. Donna MENKE

Mid-Plains Community College North Platte - North Campus (K)

1101 Halligan Drive, North Platte NE 69101
Telephone: (308) 535-3600 Identification: 770338
Accreditation: &HLC

Midland University (L)

900 N Clarkson, Fremont NE 68025-4395
County: Dodge FICE Identification: 002553
Unit ID: 181330
Telephone: (402) 721-5480 Carnegie Class: Masters/S
FAX Number: (402) 721-0250 Calendar System: 4/1/4
URL: www.midlandu.edu
Established: 1883 Annual Undergrad Tuition & Fees: $35,528
Enrollment: 1,765 Coed
Affiliation or Control: Evangelical Lutheran Church In America
IRS Status: 501(c)3
Highest Offering: Master's
Accreditation: HLC, CAATE, NUR

01 President .... Ms. Jody HORNER
05 Vice Pres Academic Affairs .... Ms. Susan KRUML
32 VP Stdnt Affs/Chief Diversity Ofcr .... Mr. Lawrence CHATTERS
10 Vice Pres Finance & Administration .... Ms. Jodi BENJAMIN
111 Vice Pres for Inst Advancement .... Ms. Jessica JANSSEN WOLFORD
84 VP Enrollment Management/Marketing .... Mr. Merritt NELSON
15 Director Human Resources .... Ms. Caryl JOHANNSEN
06 Director Academic Services .... Mr. Eric MACZKA
07 Assoc VP Undergraduate Admissions .... Ms. Lori ETHIER
37 Director of Financial Aid .... Mr. Douglas WATSON
21 Controller & AVP Finance/Fac Plng .... Mr. Joe HARNISCH
41 Athletic Director .... Mr. Dave GILLESPIE
66 Director of Nursing .... Dr. Linda QUINN
13 Chief Information Officer .... Mr. Shane PERRIEN
18 Director Facilities Management .... Vacant
44 Annual Giving Officer .... Ms. Katie CHATTERS

Myotherapy Institute (M)

245 S. 84th Street #100, Lincoln NE 68510
County: Lancaster FICE Identification: 032793
Unit ID: 434432
Telephone: (402) 421-7410 Carnegie Class: Spec 2-yr-Health
FAX Number: (402) 421-6736 Calendar System: Other
URL: www.myotherapy.edu
Established: 1992 Annual Undergrad Tuition & Fees: $16,750

Enrollment: 13 Coed
Affiliation or Control: Proprietary IRS Status: Proprietary
Highest Offering: Associate Degree
Accreditation: ACCSC

01 Director .... Ms. Sue KOZISEK

Nebraska Indian Community College (A)

1111 Hwy 75 - PO Box 428, Macy NE 68039-0428
County: Thurston FICE Identification: 025508
Unit ID: 181419
Telephone: (402) 494-2311 Carnegie Class: Tribal
FAX Number: (402) 837-4183 Calendar System: Semester
URL: www.thenicc.edu
Established: 1973 Annual Undergrad Tuition & Fees: $4,080
Enrollment: 210 Coed
Affiliation or Control: Tribal Control IRS Status: Exempt
Highest Offering: Associate Degree
Accreditation: HLC

01 President .... Dr. Michael OLTROGGE
05 Academic Dean .... Dr. Kristine SUDBECK
32 Dean Student Services .... Dawne PRICE
13 Chief Information Officer .... Justin KOCIAN
06 Registrar .... Troy MUNHOFEN
15 Human Resources Director .... Marcia ROBERTSON
08 Library Director .... Susan TYNDALL

Nebraska Methodist College (B)

720 N 87th Street, Omaha NE 68114-2852
County: Douglas FICE Identification: 006404
Unit ID: 181297
Telephone: (402) 354-7000 Carnegie Class: Spec-4-yr-Other Health
FAX Number: (402) 354-7090 Calendar System: Semester
URL: www.methodistcollege.edu
Established: 1891 Annual Undergrad Tuition & Fees: $16,708
Enrollment: 1,212 Coed
Affiliation or Control: Independent Non-Profit IRS Status: 501(c)3
Highest Offering: Doctorate
Accreditation: HLC, COARC, DMS, NURSE, OT, PTAA, RAD, SURGT

01 President .... Dr. Deb CARLSON
05 Vice President Academic Affairs .... Dr. Amy CLARK
108 VP Institutional Effectiveness .... Ms. Lindsay SNIPES
84 Chief Enrollment/Bus Mgmt Officer .... Mrs. Jillian KRUMBACH
32 Chief Student Officer .... Ms. Sarah MURPHY
66 Dean of Nursing .... Dr. Susie WARD
66 Pgm Director Undergrad Nursing .... Ms. Colleen WOODWARD
76 Dean Health Professions .... Ms. Kendra CRAVEN
58 Program Director Master's Nursing .... Dr. Marla KNIEWEL
49 Dean of Arts & Sciences .... Dr. Dean MANTERNACH
76 Director Physical Therapist Asst .... Ms. Shannon STRUBY
76 Director Respiratory Care .... Ms. Lisa FUCHS
88 Director Radiologic Technology .... Ms. Kate ROLLINS
88 Program Director Sonography .... Ms. Jody BERG
88 Director Surgical Technology .... Ms. Janet MCADAMS
08 Director John Moritz Library .... Ms. Emily MCILLECE
42 Coordinator Spiritual Development .... Ms. Kim HAIZLIP
29 Alumni Engagement Director .... Ms. Julie RAETHER
07 Director Enrollment Services .... Ms. Megan KOKENGE
06 Dir Student Records/Registration .... Mr. Shawn BAKER
37 Director Financial Aid .... Ms. Penny JAMES
09 Director of Institutional Research .... Ms. Megan DREESZEN
121 Chief Student/Inst Success Ofcr .... Ms. Lindsay SNIPES
04 Administrative Coordinator .... Ms. Lily KEOGH
26 Dir Marketing/Communications .... Ms. Emily PEKLO

*Nebraska State College System (C)

1327 H Street, Suite 200, Lincoln NE 68508
County: Lancaster FICE Identification: 033441
Telephone: (402) 471-2505 Carnegie Class: N/A
FAX Number: (402) 471-2669
URL: www.nscs.edu

01 Chancellor .... Dr. Paul D. TURMAN
43 General Counsel/VC for Empl Rels .... Ms. Kristin DIVEL
10 Vice Chancellor Finance/Admin .... Dr. Monte KRAMER
32 VC Student Affairs & Risk Mgmt .... Ms. Angela MELTON
18 Vice Chanc Facilities & Info Tech .... Mr. Steve HOTOVY
05 VC Acad Planning/Partnerships .... Dr. Jodi KUPPER
21 Director of Financial Operations .... Mr. Robert HALADA
21 Director of Systemwide Accounting . Ms. Christina WUNDERLICH
13 System Data Analyst/Reports Devel .... Mr. Mike DUNKLE
26 Sys Dir Ext Rels/Communications .... Ms. Judi YORGES
22 System Director for Title IX .... Ms. Taylor SINCLAIR
15 Human Resource Specialist .... Ms. Kara VOGT

*Chadron State College (D)

1000 Main Street, Chadron NE 69337-2690
County: Dawes FICE Identification: 002539
Unit ID: 180948
Telephone: (308) 432-6000 Carnegie Class: Masters/M
FAX Number: (308) 432-6464 Calendar System: Semester
URL: www.csc.edu
Established: 1911 Annual Undergrad Tuition & Fees (In-State): $7,634
Enrollment: 2,330 Coed
Affiliation or Control: State IRS Status: 501(c)3
Highest Offering: Master's
Accreditation: HLC, ACBSP, CAEP, MUS, SW

02 President .... Dr. Randy RHINE
05 Vice President Academic Affairs .... Dr. James POWELL
10 Vice Pres Administration & Finance .... Ms. Kari GASWICK
32 VP Student Svcs/Enroll Mgmt .... Mr. Jon HANSEN
13 Chief Information Officer .... Ms. Ann M. BURK
58 Dean Graduate Studies/BEAMS .... Dr. Wendy WAUGH
49 Dean Essential Studies/Liberal Art .... Dr. James MARGETTS
107 Dean Prof Studies/Applied Sciences .... Vacant
21 Comptroller .... Ms. Melany HUGHES
09 Director Institutional Research .... Ms. Malinda LINEGAR
102 Chief Exec Officer CS Foundation .... Mr. Ben WATSON
06 Registrar .... Ms. Melissa MITCHELL
35 Assoc VP Student Services .... Vacant
07 Director of Admissions .... Ms. Lisa STEIN
15 Assoc VP Human Resources .... Ms. Anne DEMERSSEMAN
39 Director of Housing .... Mr. Austen STEPHENS
41 Athletics Director .... Mr. Joel SMITH
36 Director of Internships/Career Svcs .... Ms. Deena KENNELL
114 Budget Director .... Ms. Jordan HEITING
26 Director College Relations .... Mr. Alex HELMBRECHT
18 Director Facilities .... Mr. Harold MOWRY

*Peru State College (E)

PO Box 10, Peru NE 68421-0010
County: Nemaha FICE Identification: 002559
Unit ID: 181534
Telephone: (402) 872-3815 Carnegie Class: Masters/M
FAX Number: (402) 872-2407 Calendar System: Semester
URL: www.peru.edu
Established: 1867 Annual Undergrad Tuition & Fees (In-State): $7,920
Enrollment: 1,902 Coed
Affiliation or Control: State IRS Status: 501(c)3
Highest Offering: Master's
Accreditation: HLC, CAEPN

02 President .... Dr. Michael EVANS
05 Vice Pres Academic Affairs .... Dr. Tim BORCHERS
10 Vice Pres Administration & Finance .... Ms. Debbie WHITE
84 Vice Pres Enroll Mgmt & Stdnt Affs .... Dr. Jesse DORMAN
102 Exec Director PSC Foundations .... Vacant
41 Director of Athletics .... Mr. Wayne ALBURY
26 Dir of Marketing & Communications .... Mr. Jason HOGUE
06 Dir Student Records/Col Registrar .... Ms. Heather RINNE
37 Director of Financial Aid .... Ms. Sarah ROGERS
08 Director of Library .... Ms. Veronica MEIER
15 Director of Human Resources .... Ms. Eulanda CADE
18 Director Campus Services .... Mr. Darrin REEVES
21 Director of Business Services .... Mr. Keith ELLIS
07 Director of Admissions .... Ms. Cindy CAMMACK
38 Licensed Student Counselor .... Ms. Jamie EBERLY
108 Director Institutional Assessment .... Mr. Paul TRANA
13 Chief Info Technology Officer (CIO) .... Mr. Gene BEARDSLEE
19 Director Security/Safety .... Mr. Tim ROBERTSON
04 Admin Assistant to the President .... Ms. Amy MINCER

*Wayne State College (F)

1111 Main Street, Wayne NE 68787-1172
County: Wayne FICE Identification: 002566
Unit ID: 181783
Telephone: (402) 375-7000 Carnegie Class: Masters/M
FAX Number: (402) 375-7204 Calendar System: Semester
URL: www.wsc.edu
Established: 1909 Annual Undergrad Tuition & Fees (In-State): $7,428
Enrollment: 4,202 Coed
Affiliation or Control: State IRS Status: 501(c)3
Highest Offering: Beyond Master's But Less Than Doctorate
Accreditation: HLC, ART, CACREP, CAEP, CSHSE, IACBE, MUS

02 President .... Dr. Marysz RAMES
05 Vice President Academic Affairs .... Mr. Steven ELLIOTT
10 Vice Pres Admin/Finance .... Ms. Angela FREDRICKSON
102 CEO Foundation Office .... Mr. Kevin ARMSTRONG
32 Vice President of Student Affairs .... Mr. C.D DOUGLAS
13 VP for Information Technology .... Mr. John DUNNING
20 Assoc VP for Academic Affairs .... Dr. Anne MCCARTHY
37 Director Financial Aid .... Ms. Tiffany REED
07 Director of Admissions .... Mr. Kevin HALLE
38 Director of Counseling .... Ms. Alicia DORCEY MCINTOSH
39 Director of Residence Life .... Mr. Pete RIZZO
36 Director of Career Services .... Ms. Jason BARELMAN
26 Director College Relations .... Mr. Jay COLLIER
41 Director of Athletics .... Mr. Mike POWICKI
18 Director of Facility Services .... Mr. Kyle NELSEN
08 Director of Library Services .... Mr. David GRABER
06 Registrar .... Ms. Rebeka WILSON
112 Director of Major Gifts .... Ms. Laura ROBINETT
29 Director of Alumni Relations .... Ms. Amber SPERRY
15 Director of Human Resources .... Ms. Candace TIMMERMAN
79 Dean School of Arts & Humanities .... Dr. Yasuko TAOKA
50 Dean Sch of Business & Technology .... Dr. Anne POWER
53 Dean Sch of Educ/Behavioral Science .... Dr. Nicholas SHUDAK
83 Dean Sch of Sci/Health/Crim Justice .... Dr. Ron LOGGINS
93 International/Multicultural Coord .... Mr. Edi HERNANDEZ
09 Director Institutional Research .... Ms. Jeannette BARRY
04 Admin Assistant to the President .... Ms. Joni BACKER
19 Campus Security Manager .... Mr. Jason MRSNY
51 Dir of Continuing Educ & Outreach .... Ms. Judith SCHERER CONNEALY
78 Exec Dir Coop Educ & Indust Liaison .... Mr. Michael KEIBLER

Nebraska Wesleyan University (G)

5000 St. Paul Avenue, Lincoln NE 68504-2794
County: Lancaster FICE Identification: 002555
Unit ID: 181446
Telephone: (402) 466-2371 Carnegie Class: Masters/M
FAX Number: (402) 465-2179 Calendar System: Semester
URL: www.nebrwesleyan.edu
Established: 1887 Annual Undergrad Tuition & Fees: $36,854
Enrollment: 1,924 Coed
Affiliation or Control: United Methodist IRS Status: 501(c)3
Highest Offering: Master's
Accreditation: HLC, CAATE, CAEPN, MUS, NURSE, SW

01 President .... Dr. Darrin S. GOOD
00 Chair of the Board .... Ms. Cori VOKOUN
100 Chief of Staff .... Ms. Sara OLSON
05 Provost .... Dr. Graciela CANEIRO-LIVINGSTON
10 Vice Pres Finance/Administration .... Ms. Tish GADE-JONES
84 Vice President Enrollment Mgmt .... Mr. Bill MOTZER
111 Vice President Advancement .... Mr. John GREVING
32 Vice President Student Life .... Dr. Sarah KELEN
42 Univ Minister/Church Relations .... Rev. Eduardo BOUSSON
58 Dean of Graduate Programs .... Dr. Jennifer ZIEGLER
20 Dean of Undergraduate Programs .... Dr. Jodi RYTER
88 Assoc Prov Integral/Exper Learning .... Dr. Patrick HAYDEN-ROY
06 Asst Provost & Univ Registrar .... Ms. Brooke GLENN
21 Asst VP & Controller .... Mr. Greg D. MASCHMAN
121 Asst Dean Stdnt Success/Engagement .... Ms. Karri SANDERSON
124 Asst Dean Stdnt Success/Persistence .... Ms. Candice HOWELL
39 Asst Dean Stdnt Success/Res Educ .... Ms. Brandi SESTAK
88 Asst Dean Stdnt Success/Campus Comm .. Ms. Janelle ANDREINI
41 Athletic Director .... Dr. Ira A. ZEFF
08 University Librarian .... Ms. Julie PINNELL
09 Data Analyst/IR Specialist .... Mr. Ricky HULL
38 Director Counseling Services .... Dr. Kimberly CORNER
07 Director of Admissions .... Mr. Gordie COFFIN
104 Director of Global Engagement .... Ms. Sarah BARR
102 Director of Foundation Relations .... Ms. Tara GREGG
23 Director Student Health Services .... Ms. Karri AHLSCHWEDE
13 Director of Computer Services .... Mr. Steven R. DOW
24 Director Instructional Technology .... Mr. Jay L. KAHLER
91 Director Administrative Systems .... Mr. Mark MURPHY
92 Director Wesleyan Honors Academy .... Dr. Marian BORGMANN-INGWERSEN
30 Director of Development .... Ms. Mary HAWK
36 Director Career Development .... Ms. Kim AFRANK
37 Director of Financial Aid .... Mr. Tom J. OCHSNER
15 Director of Human Resources .... Ms. Maria HARDER
18 Director of Physical Plant .... Mr. Jim RUZICKA
26 Director of Marketing .... Ms. Peggy S. HAIN
27 Director of Public Relations .... Vacant
105 Director Web Services .... Mr. Eric ASPEGREN
29 Director of Alumni Relations .... Ms. Shelley MCHUGH
04 Exec Asst to President .... Mr. Matt TEWES
28 Asst Director Diversity & Inclusion .... Ms. Wendy HUNT
44 Manager Annual Giving .... Ms. Ashley MURRAY-HANSEN
112 Planned Giving Officer .... Vacant

Northeast Community College (H)

801 E Benjamin, PO Box 469, Norfolk NE 68702-0469
County: Madison FICE Identification: 011667
Unit ID: 181491
Telephone: (402) 371-2020 Carnegie Class: Assoc/MT-VT-High Non
FAX Number: (402) 844-7400 Calendar System: Semester
URL: www.northeast.edu
Established: 1973 Annual Undergrad Tuition & Fees (In-District): $3,750
Enrollment: 5,105 Coed
Affiliation or Control: Local IRS Status: 501(c)3
Highest Offering: Associate Degree
Accreditation: HLC, ADNUR, CAHIIM, EMT, PTAA

01 President .... Dr. Leah BARRETT
10 VP Administrative Services .... Mr. Scott GRAY
13 VP Technology Services .... Mr. Paul FEILMEIER
32 Vice President of Student Services .... Mrs. Amanda NIPP
30 VP of Development/External Affairs .... Dr. Tracy L. KRUSE
05 VP Educational Services .... Dr. Michele GILL
15 Asst VP of Human Resources .... Vacant
75 Dean of Applied Technology .... Ms. Shanelle GRUDZINSKI
50 Dean of Business .... Dr. Wade HERLEY
76 Dean of Health/Public Services .... Dr. Jeff HOFFMAN
81 Dean Science/Tech/Agric/Math .... Mrs. Tara SMYDRA
45 Dean of Institutional Effectiveness .... Mrs. Michela KEELER-STROM
18 Exec Director of Physical Plant .... Mr. Brandon MCLEAN
121 Dean of Student Success .... Ms. Shelley LAMMERS
61 Dean of Workforce Development .... Dr. Cyndi HANSON
06 Registrar .... Mrs. Makala MAPLE
37 Financial Aid Director .... Ms. Stacy DIECKMAN
96 Director of Purchasing .... Mr. Chris RUTTEN
66 Director of Nursing Programs .... Mrs. Karen K. WEIDNER
26 Director of Public Relations .... Mr. James CURRY
40 Retail Services Manager .... Mrs. Julie CARLSON
07 Director of Recruitment .... Mr. Anthony FAUST
35 Director of Student Activities .... Ms. Carissa KOLLATH
39 Director of Residence Life .... Ms. Emily NORMAN
114 Director of Budgeting .... Mrs. Chris MCKIBBON
09 Dir of Inst Research & Analytics .... Mrs. Jody GIBSON
16 Dir of HR/Talent and HR Compliance .... Mrs. Jessica DVORAK
104 Dir of Ctr for Global Engagement .... Ms. Pam SAALFELD
19 Dir of Safety/Emer Preparedness .... Mr. Brian PAULSEN

25 Chief Contract/Grants Administrator .... Mr. Kent WARNEKE
11 Exec Director Administrative Svcs .... Mrs. Coleen BRESSLER
08 Director of Library Services .... Vacant
38 Counselor .... Ms. Stephanie BRUNDIECK
27 Exec Dir of Marketing/Recruitment .... Mrs. Jennifer GREVE
36 Director of Career Services .... Mrs. Terri HEGGEMEYER
04 Executive Assistant to President .... Mrs. Diane REIKOFSKI

Saint Gregory the Great Seminary (A)

800 Fletcher Road, Seward NE 68434-8145
County: Seward Identification: 667027
Unit ID: 486114
Telephone: (402) 643-4052 Carnegie Class: Not Classified
FAX Number: (402) 643-6964 Calendar System: Semester
URL: www.sggs.edu
Established: 1998 Annual Undergrad Tuition & Fees: N/A
Enrollment: N/A Male
Affiliation or Control: Roman Catholic IRS Status: 501(c)3
Highest Offering: Baccalaureate
Accreditation: HLC

01 Rector/President .... VRev. Jeffrey EICKHOFF
05 Academic Dean .... Rev. Matthew ROLLING
13 Vice Rector/Director of Technology .... Rev. John ROONEY

Southeast Community College (B)

4771 West Scott Road, Beatrice NE 68310-7042
Telephone: (402) 228-3468 Identification: 770341
Accreditation: &HLC

Southeast Community College (C)

301 S 68 Street Place, Lincoln NE 68510-2449
County: Lancaster FICE Identification: 025083
Unit ID: 181640
Telephone: (402) 323-3400 Carnegie Class: Assoc/MT-VT-High Non
FAX Number: (402) 323-3420 Calendar System: Semester
URL: www.southeast.edu
Established: 1973 Annual Undergrad Tuition & Fees (In-District): $2,664
Enrollment: 9,328 Coed
Affiliation or Control: State/Local IRS Status: 501(c)3
Highest Offering: Associate Degree
Accreditation: HLC, ACBSP, ACFEI, ADNUR, COARC, CSHSE, DA, EMT, MAC, MLTAD, NAEYC, PNUR, POLYT, PTAA, RAD, SURGA, SURGT

01 President .... Dr. Paul ILLICH
05 VP for Instruction .... Dr. Joel MICHAELIS
22 VP Access/Equity/Diversity .... Mr. Jose SOTO
11 VP Admin Svcs/Resource Devel .... Ms. Amy G. JORGENS
32 Vice Pres Student Services .... Ms. Bev CUMMINS
46 VP Research/Planning/Technology .... Mr. Ed KOSTER
15 Vice Pres Human Resources/Safety .... Mr. Bruce TANGEMAN
88 VP for Program Development .... Dr. Brett BRIGHT
106 Dean of Virtual Learning .... Mr. Bruce EXSTROM
35 Dean of Students .... Ms. Stacy RILEY
35 Dean of Students .... Ms. Toni LANDENBERGER
35 Dean of Students .... Ms. Theresa WEBSTER
84 Dean Student Enrollment .... Mr. Mike PEGRAM
37 Director of Financial Aid .... Ms. Melissa TROYER
06 Admin Director Registration .... Ms. Nancy MCCONKEY
07 Admin Director Admissions .... Ms. Kat KREIKEMEIER
26 Dir of Public Information/Marketing .... Mr. Stu OSTERTHUN
09 Admin Dir Institutional Research .... Ms. Robin MOORE
102 Foundation Director .... Ms. Michelle BIRKEL
90 Information Services Manager .... Mr. Alan BRUNKOW
04 Assistant to the President .... Ms. Katy NOVAK
88 Operations Assistant .... Ms. Amy BASSEN
51 Dean Continuing Education .... Ms. Amy CHESLEY
18 Director of Facilities .... Mr. Aaron EPPS
45 Admin Director Planning & Accred .... Ms. Shawna HERWICK

Southeast Community College (D)

600 State Street, Milford NE 68405-8498
Telephone: (402) 761-2131 Identification: 770342
Accreditation: &HLC

Summit Christian College (E)

2025 21st Street, Gering NE 69341
County: Scotts Bluff Identification: 667209
Unit ID: 181543
Telephone: (308) 632-6933 Carnegie Class: Spec-4-yr-Faith
FAX Number: N/A Calendar System: Semester
URL: www.summitcc.edu
Established: 1951 Annual Undergrad Tuition & Fees: $7,570
Enrollment: 34 Coed
Affiliation or Control: Independent Non-Profit IRS Status: 501(c)3
Highest Offering: Baccalaureate
Accreditation: BI

01 President .... David K. PARRISH
05 Academic Dean .... Scott GRIBBLE
06 Registrar .... Kayleen COLLOPY
07 Director of Admissions .... Emilie YATES

Union College (F)

3800 S 48th Street, Lincoln NE 68506-4300
County: Lancaster FICE Identification: 002563
Unit ID: 181738
Telephone: (402) 486-2600 Carnegie Class: Bac-Diverse
FAX Number: (402) 486-2895 Calendar System: Semester
URL: www.ucollege.edu
Established: 1891 Annual Undergrad Tuition & Fees: $25,340
Enrollment: 757 Coed
Affiliation or Control: Seventh-day Adventist IRS Status: 501(c)3
Highest Offering: Master's
Accreditation: HLC, ARCPA, CAEP, NURSE, OTA, SW

01 President .... Dr. Vinita SAUDER
05 Vice President for Academic Admin .... Vacant
10 Vice President for Financial Admin .... Mr. Steve TRANA
32 Vice President Student Life .... Ms. Kim CANINE
111 Vice President for Advancement .... Ms. LuAnn DAVIS
42 Vice President for Spiritual Life .... Mr. David KABANJE
08 Library Director .... Ms. Bliss KUNTZ
13 Director of Information Systems .... Mr. Richard HENRIQUES
33 Dean of Men .... Mr. Daniel FORCE
06 Director Records/Registrar .... Ms. Rachael BOYD
07 Director Enrollment & Admissions .... Mr. Kevin ERICKSON
26 Director of Public Relations .... Mr. Ryan TELLER
29 Director Alumni Relations .... Ms. Peggy CARLSON
37 Director Student Financial Aid .... Ms. Laurie WHEELER
15 Human Resources Director .... Ms. Lisa R. FORBES
36 Career Center Coordinator .... Ms. Trina CRESS
09 Director of Institutional Research .... Mr. Tim SIMON
19 Director Security/Safety .... Mr. Dustin SAUDER
39 Dir Resident Life/Student Housing .... Mr. Chris CANINE

Universal College of Healing Arts (G)

8702 N 30th Street, Omaha NE 68112-1810
County: Douglas FICE Identification: 038214
Unit ID: 446598
Telephone: (402) 556-4456 Carnegie Class: Spec 2-yr-Health
FAX Number: N/A Calendar System: Semester
URL: www.ucha.edu
Established: 1995 Annual Undergrad Tuition & Fees: $11,327
Enrollment: 29 Coed
Affiliation or Control: Proprietary IRS Status: Proprietary
Highest Offering: Associate Degree
Accreditation: ABHES

01 President .... Ms. Paulette GENTHON

*University of Nebraska Central Administration (H)

3835 Holdrege, Lincoln NE 68583-0745
County: Lancaster FICE Identification: 008025
Unit ID: 181747
Telephone: (402) 472-8636 Carnegie Class: N/A
FAX Number: (402) 472-1237
URL: www.nebraska.edu

01 President .... Mr. Ted E. CARTER
05 Exec Vice President & Provost .... Dr. Jeffrey GOLD
10 Sr Vice Pres Business & Finance .... Mr. Chris KABOUREK
43 VP/General Counsel .... Mr. James POTTORFF
47 VP Agriculture/Natural Res .... Dr. Michael J. BOEHM
100 Chief of Staff .... Mr. Phillip BAKKEN
13 Assoc VP/CIO .... Mr. Bret R. BLACKMAN
86 Interim VP University Affairs .... Mr. Heath M. MELLO
18 Asst VP/Dir Facility Plng/Mgmt .... Mr. Ryan SWANSON
09 Asst VP/Dir Inst Research/Planning .... Dr. Kristin YATES
88 Asst VP P-16 Initiatives .... Dr. Steven T. DUKE
85 Asst VP Global Strategy/Intl .... Vacant
26 Asst VP Univ Affs/Dir Comm & Mktg .... Ms. Jacqueline M. OSTROWICKI
28 Assistant VP Diversity/Inclusion .... Ms. Stancia J. JENKINS
04 Exec Assistant to the President .... Ms. Jayne SUTTON

*University of Nebraska at Kearney (I)

2504 9th Avenue, Kearney NE 68849
County: Buffalo FICE Identification: 002551
Unit ID: 181215
Telephone: (308) 865-8208 Carnegie Class: Masters/L
FAX Number: (308) 865-8665 Calendar System: Semester
URL: www.unk.edu
Established: 1903 Annual Undergrad Tuition & Fees (In-State): $7,962
Enrollment: 6,225 Coed
Affiliation or Control: State IRS Status: 501(c)3
Highest Offering: Beyond Master's But Less Than Doctorate
Accreditation: HLC, CAATE, CACREP, CAEP, CIDA, MACTE, MUS, NAIT, SP, SW

02 Chancellor .... Mr. Douglas A. KRISTENSEN
05 Sr VC Academic & Student Affairs .... Dr. Charles J. BICAK
10 Vice Chanc Business & Finance .... Mr. Jon C. WATTS
84 VC for Enrollment Mgmt & Marketing ..... Ms. Kelly H. BARTLING
30 Vice President Development .... Mr. Lucas DART
13 Asst Vice Chanc Info Technology .... Ms. Andrea CHILDRESS
21 Assoc Vice Chanc Business & Finance .... Ms. Jane SHELDON
49 Dean Arts & Sciences .... Dr. Ryan L. TETEN
50 Dean Business/Technology .... Dr. Tim E. JARES
53 Dean of Education .... Dr. Mark REID
58 Dean Graduate Studies .... Dr. Mark ELLIS
32 Dean of Student Affairs .... Dr. Gilbert HINGA
04 Exec Assistant to the Chancellor .... Dr. John FALCONER
06 Dir Student Records/Registration .... Ms. Lisa NEAL
08 Dean of the Library .... Ms. Janet S. WILKE
36 Director Academic & Career Services .. Ms. Amy L. RUNDSTROM
07 Dir UG Recruitment/Admissions .... Ms. Jody HOLT
18 Int Dir Facilities Mgmt & Planning .... Mr. Michael CREMERS
19 Director Police .... Mr. James F. DAVIS
22 Dir Affirm Action/Equal Opportunity .... Ms. Mary J. CHINNOCK PETROSKI
09 Director Academic Resources .... Ms. Megan M. FRYDA
26 Sr Dir Communications & Marketing .... Mr. Todd GOTTULA
29 Director Alumni Services .... Mr. Lucas DART
35 Director Student Life .... Ms. Sharon PELC
23 Director Counseling & Health Care .... Ms. Wendy L. SCHARDT
39 Director Residence Life .... Mr. George HOLMAN
40 Director Bookstore .... Mr. Len J. FANGMEYER
41 Director Intercollegiate Athletics .... Dr. Marc BAUER
88 Director Finance .... Ms. Jill PURDY
108 Director Assessment .... Dr. Beth D. HINGA
25 Asst Vice Chanc Sponsored Programs .... Mr. Richard A. MOCARSKI
85 Asst Vice Chanc for Intl Affairs .... Dr. Tim J. BURKINK
114 Budget Officer .... Ms. Chris MORAN
37 Director Financial Aid .... Ms. Mary SOMMERS
93 Director Multicultural Affairs .... Mr. Juan GUZMAN
92 Director Honors Program .... Ms. Angela HOLLMAN
15 Director Human Resources .... Mr. Scott A. BENSON
109 Director Business Services .... Mr. Michael T. CHRISTEN

*University of Nebraska - Lincoln (J)

14th and R Streets, Lincoln NE 68588-0002
County: Lancaster FICE Identification: 002565
Unit ID: 181464
Telephone: (402) 472-7211 Carnegie Class: DU-Highest
FAX Number: (402) 472-2410 Calendar System: Semester
URL: www.unl.edu
Established: 1869 Annual Undergrad Tuition & Fees (In-State): $9,690
Enrollment: 25,108 Coed
Affiliation or Control: State IRS Status: 501(c)3
Highest Offering: Doctorate
Accreditation: HLC, ART, AUD, CAATE, CAEP, CIDA, CLPSY, COPSY, DANCE, DIETC, DIETD, JOUR, LAW, LSAR, MFCD, MUS, PLNG, SCPSY, SP, THEA

02 Chancellor .... Dr. Ronnie D. GREEN
05 EVC for Academic Affairs .... Dr. Elizabeth SPILLER
10 VC Business & Finance .... Dr. William NUNEZ
32 VC Student Affairs .... Dr. Laurie BELLOWS
65 Vice Chanc Agric/Nat Resources .... Dr. Michael BOEHM
46 VC Rsrch/Economic Development .... Mr. Robert WILHELM
13 AVP Information Technology & CIO .... Mr. Heath TUTTLE
28 Vice Chanc Diversity/Inclusion .... Dr. Marco BARKER
124 Asst VC Academic Services .... Mr. James VOLKMER
86 Asst to Chanc Govt & Mil Relations .... Ms. Michelle WAITE
15 Asst Vice Chanc for Human Resources .... Mr. Bruce A. CURRIN
20 Sr Assoc Vice Chanc & Dean .... Dr. Amy GOODBURN
84 Int Asst VC for Enrollment Mgmt .... Mr. James S. VOLKMER
08 Dean University Libraries .... Ms. Claire STEWART
58 Assoc VC & Dean Grad Studies .... Dr. Timothy CARR
49 Dean Arts & Sciences .... Dr. Mark BUTTON
54 Dean Engineering .... Dr. Lance PEREZ
61 Dean of Law .... Dr. Richard MOBERLY
47 Dean Agric Science/Nat Resources .... Dr. Tiffany HENG-MOSS
50 Dean Business .... Dr. Kathy FARRELL
60 Dean Journalism/Mass Communications .... Dr. Shari VEIL
53 Dean Education & Human Sciences .... Dr. Sherri JONES
48 Dean College Architecture .... Dr. Katherine ANKERSON
47 Dean Agricultural Research Division .... Dr. Archie CLUTTER
56 Int Dean/Dir Cooperative Extension .... Dr. David VARNER
93 Director Educ Access & TRIO Pgms .. Ms. Catherine YAMAMOTO
57 Dean Fine & Performing Arts .... Dr. Charles D. O'CONNOR
37 Dir Scholarships/Financial Aid .... Mr. Justin C. BROWN
09 Dir Research/Analytics .... Mr. Jason CASEY
92 Director Honors Program .... Dr. Patrice MCMAHON
94 Director Women's Studies .... Dr. Marie-Chantal KALISA
06 University Registrar .... Mr. Steven BOOTON
36 Director Career Services Center .... Mr. Bill WATTS
19 Chief University Police Services .... Mr. Hassan RAMZAH
22 Equity/Compliance Investigator .... Ms. Meagan COUNLEY
23 Director University Health Center .... Ms. Jill LYNCH-SOSA
39 Director Housing & Dining .... Mr. Charlie FRANCIS
41 Director of Athletics .... Mr. William MOOS
106 Dir Distance Education Services .... Dr. Nancy ADEN-FOX
29 Exec Director Alumni Association .... Ms. Shelley ZABOROWSKI
26 Chief Communication/Mktg Ofcr .... Ms. Deb FIDDELKE
30 Chief Development .... Mr. Brian HASTINGS
38 Director Student Counseling .... Dr. Robert N. PORTNOY
96 Director of Procurement Services .... Ms. Maggie L. WITT
07 Director of Admissions .... Ms. Abby FREEMAN
100 Chief of Staff .... Dr. Michael ZELENY
104 Director Education Abroad .... Ms. Rebecca BASKERVILLE

*University of Nebraska Medical Center (K)

987020 Nebraska Medical Center, Omaha NE 68198-7020
County: Douglas FICE Identification: 006895
Unit ID: 181428
Telephone: (402) 559-4000 Carnegie Class: Spec-4-yr-Med
FAX Number: (402) 559-4396 Calendar System: Semester
URL: www.unmc.edu
Established: 1869 Annual Undergrad Tuition & Fees (In-State): N/A
Enrollment: 3,699 Coed
Affiliation or Control: State IRS Status: 501(c)3
Highest Offering: Doctorate

Accreditation: HLC, ABAI, ARCPA, CAMPEP, CYTO, DENT, DH, DIETC, DMS, MED, MT, NURSE, PERF, PH, PHAR, PTA, RAD, RADMAG, RTT

02 Chancellor ... Dr. Jeffery P. GOLD
05 Sr Vice Chancellor Acad Affairs ... Dr. H. Dele O. DAVIES
10 Vice Chanc Business/Fin & Bus Dev ... Mr. Douglas EWALD
46 Vice Chancellor Research ... Dr. Jennifer LARSEN
86 Vice Chancellor External Affairs ... Mr. Robert BARTEE
32 Vice Chanc Student Success/Acad Aff ... Dr. Daniel SHIPP
20 Assoc Vice Chanc Academic Affairs ... Dr. Gary YEE
20 Assoc Vice Chancellor iEXCEL ... Dr. Pamela BOYERS
20 Assoc Vice Chanc Global/Stdnt Supp ... Dr. Jane MEZA
88 Assoc Vice Chanc Basic Sci Rsch ... Dr. Kenneth BAYLES
88 Assoc Vice Chancellor Research ... Dr. Christopher KRATOCHVIL
88 Assoc Vice Chanc Bus Development ... Dr. Rodney MARKIN
18 Assoc Vice Chanc Facilities ... Mr. Kenneth HANSEN
13 Assoc Vice Chancellor ITS ... Dr. Michael ASH
20 Asst Vice Chanc Acad Affs/Reg Comp ... Dr. Bruce GORDON
88 Asst VC Health Security Train/Educ ... Dr. John-Martin LOWE
23 Asst Vice Chanc Campus Wellness ... Dr. Steven WENGEL
20 Asst Vice Chanc Acad Affs ... Dr. Philip COVINGTON
21 Asst Vice Chanc Business & Finance ... Mr. William LAWLOR
15 Asst Vice Chanc for Human Resources ... Ms. Aileen WARREN
08 Asst Vice Chanc & Director Library ... Ms. Emily J. MCELROY
58 Dean Graduate Studies ... Dr. H. Dele O. DAVIES
52 Dean College of Dentistry ... Dr. Janet GUTHMILLER
63 Dean College of Medicine ... Dr. Bradley E. BRITIGAN
66 Dean College of Nursing ... Dr. Juliann SEBASTIAN
67 Dean College of Pharmacy ... Dr. Keith OLSEN
69 Dean College of Public Health ... Dr. Ali KHAN
76 Dean College of Allied Health Prof ... Dr. Kyle P. MEYER
88 Dir Eppley Cancer Research Inst ... Dr. Kenneth H. COWAN
88 Director Munroe-Meyer Institute ... Dr. Karoly MIRNICS
43 Assoc Gen Counsel Hlth Sci ... Ms. Tara SCROGIN
37 Director Financial Aid Office ... Ms. Paula KOHLES
26 Director of Public Relations ... Mr. William O'NEILL
29 Director Alumni Relations ... Ms. Catherine MELLO
38 Exec Dir Counseling & Student Dev ... Dr. David S. CARVER
28 Director of Diversity ... Ms. Linda CUNNINGHAM
96 Director Procurement & Mtrls Mgt ... Mr. Robert JENNINGS
09 Director Institutional Research ... Ms. Jeanne FERBRACHE
19 Asst Vice Chanc/Chief of Police ... Ms. Charlotte EVANS

*University of Nebraska at Omaha (A)

6001 Dodge Street, Omaha NE 68182-0001
County: Douglas FICE Identification: 002554
Unit ID: 181394
Telephone: (402) 554-2262 Carnegie Class: DU-Higher
FAX Number: (402) 554-3555 Calendar System: Semester
URL: www.unomaha.edu
Established: 1908 Annual Undergrad Tuition & Fees (In-State): $8,136
Enrollment: 15,892 Coed
Affiliation or Control: State IRS Status: 501(c)3
Highest Offering: Doctorate
Accreditation: HLC, AAB, ART, CAATE, CACREP, CAEPN, MUS, SP, SPAA, SW

02 Chancellor ... Dr. Joanne LI
05 Sr Vice Chanc Acad/Student Affs ... Dr. Sacha E. KOPP
10 Vice Chanc Business & Finance ... Mr. Doug A. EWALD
13 Chief Information Officer ... Mr. Bret BLACKMAN
32 Vice Chanc Student Affairs ... Dr. Daniel SHIPP
84 Assoc Vice Chanc Enroll Mgmt Svcs ... Mr. Omar CORREA
58 Dean Graduate Studies ... Dr. Deb SMITH-HOWELL
57 Dean Fine Arts/Communication/Media ... Dr. Michael HILT
53 Dean of Education ... Dr. Nancy EDICK
50 Dean of Business Administration ... Dr. Michelle TRAWICK
49 Dean of Arts & Sciences ... Dr. David J. BOOCKER
104 Associate Vice Chancellor Global ... Dr. Jane L. MEZA
72 Dean Info Science/Technology ... Dr. Martha GARCIA-MURILLO
80 Dean Public Affairs/Community ... Dr. John R. BARTLE
62 Dean of Library Services ... Mr. David E. RICHARDS
09 Dir Institutional Effectiveness ... Dr. T. Hank ROBINSON
35 Chief Student Life Officer ... Vacant
15 Assoc VC Human Resources ... Ms. Aileen WARREN
18 Director Facilities Mgmt/Planning ... Mr. Larry MORGAN
06 Registrar ... Mr. Matt SCHILL
07 Director of Admissions ... Dr. Lina STOVER
37 Director Financial Aid ... Mr. Marty HABROCK
88 Director Student Testing Center ... Mr. John GOLKA
41 Vice Chanc Athletic Leadership/Mgmt ... Mr. Trev ALBERTS
29 President/CEO Alumni Association ... Vacant
26 Exec Dir University Communications ... Ms. Makayla MCMORRIS
96 Procurement Systems Coordinator ... Ms. Lynn MCALPINE
40 Manager Book Store ... Ms. Chelsie HANSEN
19 Director of Public Safety ... Ms. Charlotte EVANS
106 Director Online Educ/E-learning ... Dr. Jaci LINDBURG
28 Assoc Vice Chanc of Diversity ... Mr. Cecil HICKS, JR.

*University of Nebraska - Nebraska College of Technical Agriculture (B)

404 E 7th Street, Curtis NE 69025-9502
County: Frontier FICE Identification: 007358
Unit ID: 181765
Telephone: (308) 367-4124 Carnegie Class: Spec 2-yr-Other
FAX Number: (308) 367-5203 Calendar System: Semester
URL: www.ncta.unl.edu
Established: 1913 Annual Undergrad Tuition & Fees (In-State): $5,483
Enrollment: 282 Coed
Affiliation or Control: State IRS Status: 501(c)3
Highest Offering: Associate Degree
Accreditation: HLC

02 Dean ... Dr. Larry GOSSEN
10 Assoc Dean Finance/Ops/Student Svcs ... Mrs. Jennifer A. MCCONVILLE
21 Business Manager ... Ms. Jan GILBERT
04 Administrative Associate to Dean ... Ms. Josi ARNOLD
06 Registrar ... Mrs. Victoria LUKE
08 Head Librarian ... Mr. Mo KHAMOUNA
09 Director of Institutional Research ... Ms. Mary RITTENHOUSE
39 Residence Life Manager ... Ms. Erika ARAMBULA

Western Nebraska Community College (C)

1601 E 27th Street, Scottsbluff NE 69361-1815
County: Scotts Bluff FICE Identification: 002560
Unit ID: 181817
Telephone: (308) 635-3606 Carnegie Class: Assoc/MT-VT-High Non
FAX Number: (308) 635-6100 Calendar System: Semester
URL: www.wncc.edu
Established: 1926 Annual Undergrad Tuition & Fees (In-District): $2,976
Enrollment: 1,625 Coed
Affiliation or Control: State/Local IRS Status: 501(c)3
Highest Offering: Associate Degree
Accreditation: HLC, CAHIIM, MLTAD, PNUR, SURGT

01 Interim President ... Mr. John MARRIN
05 Vice President of Educational Svcs ... Dr. Grant WILSON
10 Vice Pres Administrative Services ... Ms. Lynne KOSKI
84 Vice President of Enrollment ... Mr. William KNAPPER
15 Executive Director of HR ... Ms. Kathy AULT
88 Executive Director of Partnerships ... Ms. Paula ABBOTT
102 Foundation Executive Director ... Ms. Jennifer REISIG
108 Executive Director Assessment & IR ... Dr. Patrick FORTNEY
103 Dean of Instruction & Workforce Dev ... Dr. Charlie GREGORY
32 Executive Dean of Students ... Dr. Norman COLEY, JR.
121 Assoc Dean Instruct Support Svcs ... Ms. Ellen DILLON
35 Assistant Dean of Students ... Ms. Brynn ELLIOTT
06 Registrar ... Mr. Brian ELKINS
37 Financial Aid Director ... Ms. Sheila JOHNS
26 Public Relations & Marketing Dir ... Ms. Allison JUDY
38 Counseling Director ... Mr. Norman STEPHENSON
21 Accounting Services Director ... Mr. David KOEHLER
41 Athletic Director ... Mr. Ryan BURGNER
51 Lifelong Learning Director ... Ms. Lori STROMBERG
07 Admissions Director ... Ms. Gretchen FOSTER
29 Director Alumni Relations/Steward ... Ms. Mary SHEFFIELD
124 Student Engagement Director ... Ms. Megan WESCOAT
39 Residence Life Director ... Ms. Molly BONUCHI
13 Information Technology Director ... Mr. Loren MOENCH
40 Bookstore Operations Director ... Mr. Rich RIDDICK
19 Safety/Environmental Mgmt Director ... Mr. Josh VESPER
09 Institutional Research Officer ... Mr. Dustin EICKE
106 Instructional Tech Coordinator ... Ms. Heidi JACKSON
88 Academic Testing & Tutoring Coord ... Ms. Tammie KLEICH
08 Chief Library Officer ... Ms. Allison REISIG
28 Inclusion Coordinator ... Ms. Maricia GUZMAN
83 Div Chair Soc Sciences & Human Perf ... Ms. Jacklyn CAWIEZEL
76 Division Chair Health Sciences ... Vacant
81 Division Chair Math & Science ... Ms. Amy WINTERS
72 Division Chair Applied Tech ... Mr. Daniel JOPPA
79 Div Chair Acad Enrich/Lang/Fine Art ... Vacant
66 Nursing Program Director ... Ms. Rebecca KAUTZ
88 Surg Tech Program Director ... Ms. Marcene ELWELL
88 Health Info Technology Program Dir ... Ms. Nicole DANIELZUK
66 BNA Program Director ... Ms. Sherri YORGES
88 Med Lab Tech Program Director ... Vacant
88 EMS Program Director ... Mr. Ken BOSTON
04 Admin Assistant to the President ... Ms. Susan VERBECK

York College (D)

1125 E 8th Street, York NE 68467-2699
County: York FICE Identification: 002567
Unit ID: 181853
Telephone: (402) 363-5600 Carnegie Class: Bac-Diverse
FAX Number: (402) 363-5623 Calendar System: Semester
URL: www.york.edu
Established: 1890 Annual Undergrad Tuition & Fees: $19,810
Enrollment: 652 Coed
Affiliation or Control: Churches Of Christ IRS Status: 501(c)3
Highest Offering: Master's
Accreditation: HLC, CAEP

01 President ... Dr. Sam SMITH
05 Provost ... Dr. Shane MOUNTJOY
10 Vice President Finance & Operations ... Mr. Todd SHELDON
111 Vice Pres Advancement ... Mr. Jared STARK
42 VP for Spiritual Development ... Dr. Sam GARNER
32 VP for Student Development ... Mrs. Catherine SEUFFERLEIN
21 Business Manager ... Mr. Dan COLE
06 Registrar ... Mr. Jared LEINEN
35 Dean of Students ... Ms. Meghan SHRUCK
08 Director of Information Commons ... Vacant
26 Director of Publications ... Mr. Steddon L. SIKES
37 Financial Aid Director ... Mr. Brien ALLEY
40 Campus Store Manager ... Mrs. Janet RUSH
18 Supervisor Buildings & Grounds ... Mr. Bob GAVER
73 Chair Bible ... Dr. Frank E. WHEELER
88 Chair History ... Mr. Tim D. MCNEESE
50 Chair English ... Dr. Aleshia O'NEAL
81 Chair Math/Sciences ... Dr. Bryan KRETZ
57 Chair Performing Arts/Communication ... Dr. Clark A. ROUSH
29 Alumni Relations Officer ... Mr. Brent MAGNER
04 Executive Asst to President ... Mrs. Gayle A. GOOD
13 Chief Info Technology Officer (CIO) ... Mr. Joel COEHOORN
39 Director Student Housing ... Ms. Jennifer OTTE
106 Dir Online Education/E-learning ... Dr. Cheryl COUCH
07 Director of Admissions ... Mr. David ODOM

NEVADA

Career College of Northern Nevada (E)

1421 Pullman Drive, Sparks NV 89434
County: Washoe FICE Identification: 026215
Unit ID: 181941
Telephone: (775) 241-4445 Carnegie Class: Assoc/HVT-High Trad
FAX Number: (775) 856-0935 Calendar System: Quarter
URL: www.ccnn.edu
Established: 1984 Annual Undergrad Tuition & Fees: N/A
Enrollment: 385 Coed
Affiliation or Control: Proprietary IRS Status: Proprietary
Highest Offering: Associate Degree
Accreditation: ACCSC

01 President ... Mr. L. Nathan N. CLARK
05 Academic Dean ... Mr. Robert MCLAUGHLIN

Carrington College - Las Vegas (F)

5740 S Eastern Avenue, Suite 140, Las Vegas NV 89119
Telephone: (702) 688-4300 Identification: 770742
Accreditation: &WJ, COARC, PTAA

† Regional accreditation is carried under the parent institution in Sacramento, CA.

Carrington College - Reno (G)

5580 Kietzke Lane, Reno NV 89511
Telephone: (775) 335-2900 Identification: 770743
Accreditation: &WJ, ADNUR

† Regional accreditation is carried under the parent institution in Sacramento, CA.

Chamberlain University-Las Vegas (H)

9901 Covington Cross Drive, Las Vegas NV 89144
Telephone: (702) 786-1660 Identification: 770852
Accreditation: &HLC, NURSE

† Branch campus of Chamberlain University-Addison, Addison, IL

Las Vegas College (I)

170 North Stephanie Street, Henderson NV 89074
County: Clark FICE Identification: 022375
Unit ID: 182148
Telephone: (702) 567-1920 Carnegie Class: Assoc/HVT-High Trad
FAX Number: (702) 566-9725 Calendar System: Semester
URL: https://www.lvcollege.edu/
Established: 2004 Annual Undergrad Tuition & Fees: $14,903
Enrollment: 399 Coed
Affiliation or Control: Independent Non-Profit IRS Status: 501(c)3
Highest Offering: Associate Degree
Accreditation: ACCSC, ADNUR

01 CEO/CFO ... Peter MIKHAIL
03 Executive Vice President ... Bob ALLEN
05 Campus Director/Academic Dean ... David DOLBOW
06 Registrar ... Marjorie ZELAYA
07 Director of Admissions ... George VEGERANO

*Nevada System of Higher Education (J)

2601 Enterprise Road, Reno NV 89512-1666
County: Washoe FICE Identification: 008026
Unit ID: 182519
Telephone: (775) 784-4901 Carnegie Class: N/A
FAX Number: (775) 784-1127
URL: www.nevada.edu

01 Chancellor ... Dr. Melody ROSE
05 VC Academic & Student Affairs ... Ms. Crystal ABBA
10 Chief Financial Officer ... Mr. Andrew CLINGER
101 Chief of Staff of Board of Regents ... Mr. Michael FLORES
43 Chief General Counsel ... Mr. Joseph REYNOLDS
86 VC Govt and Community Affairs ... Vacant
12 VC Community Colleges ... Mr. Nate MACKINNON

*College of Southern Nevada (K)

6375 W Charleston Boulevard, Las Vegas NV 89146-1139
County: Clark FICE Identification: 010362
Unit ID: 182005
Telephone: (702) 651-5000 Carnegie Class: Bac/Assoc-Assoc Dom
FAX Number: N/A Calendar System: Semester
URL: www.csn.edu
Established: 1971 Annual Undergrad Tuition & Fees (In-State): $3,878
Enrollment: 29,965 Coed
Affiliation or Control: State IRS Status: 501(c)3
Highest Offering: Baccalaureate

Accreditation: NW, ACBSP, ACFEI, ADNUR, CAHIIM, CEA, COARC, DA, DH, DMS, EMT, MAC, MLTAD, MT, OPD, PNUR, PTAA, SURGT

Code	Title	Name
02	President	Dr. Federico ZARAGOZA
04	Executive Assistant	Ms. Annette LORD
100	Chief of Staff	Mr. Lawrence WEEKLY
10	VP for Finance & Administration	Ms. Mary Kaye BAILEY
32	VP for Student Affairs	Ms. Juanita CHRYSANTHOU
05	VP Academic Affairs	Mr. James MCCOY
12	VP/Provost Henderson Campus	Ms. Patricia A. CHARLTON
12	VP/Provost Charleston Campus	Dr. Sonya PEARSON
12	VP/Provost North Las Vegas Campus	Dr. Clarissa COTA
102	Exec Director CSN Foundation	Vacant
18	AVP Facilities/Opers/Maint	Ms. Sylvia KIM
43	Legal Counsel	Mr. James MARTINES
06	Dir Student Affairs/Registrar	Ms. Bernadette LOPEZ-GARRETT
103	Exec Dir Workforce Education	Vacant
72	Dean Adv & Applied Technologies	Dr. Michael SPANGLER
81	Dean Science & Math	Dr. Douglas SIMS
83	Dean Social Sciences & Education	Dr. Charles OKEKE
79	Interim Dean Arts & Letters	Dr. Vartouhi ASHERIAN
76	Dean Health Sciences	Ms. Janice GLASPER
50	Dean of Business	Dr. Marcus JOHNSON
96	Associate VP of Purchasing	Mr. Rolando MOSQUEDA
41	Director of Athletics	Mr. L. Dexter IRVIN
114	Assoc Vice Pres Budget Services	Ms. Lisa BAKKE
09	Exec Dir of Institutional Research	Mr. John BEARCE
08	Interim Dir Library Services	Ms. Emily KING
37	Associate VP for Financial Aid	Mr. Tyler HEU
19	Chief of Police	Mr. Adam GARCIA
13	Technology CIO	Mr. Mugunth VAITHYLINGAM
15	Chief HR Officer	Dr. Bill DIAL
28	Executive Director of Diversity	Mr. Lawrence WEEKLY
106	Dir Online Education/E-learning	Mr. Terry NORRIS
22	Director of Institutional Equity	Dr. Armen ASHERIAN
86	Director Government Relations	Ms. Mariana KIHUEN

*Great Basin College (A)

1500 College Parkway, Elko NV 89801-5032

County: Elko — FICE Identification: 006977 — Unit ID: 182306

Telephone: (775) 327-5002 — Carnegie Class: Bac/Assoc-Mixed

FAX Number: (775) 327-5131 — Calendar System: Semester

URL: www.gbcnv.edu

Established: 1967 — Annual Undergrad Tuition & Fees (In-State): $3,248

Enrollment: 3,772 — Coed

Affiliation or Control: State — IRS Status: 501(c)3

Highest Offering: Baccalaureate

Accreditation: NW, ADNUR, CSHSE, EMT, NUR, RAD

Code	Title	Name
02	President	Ms. Joyce HELENS
05	VP for Student & Academic Affairs	Dr. Jake HINTON-RIVERA
10	Vice President for Business Affairs	Ms. Sonja SIBERT
111	Exec Dir Advancement/Communications	Ms. Jennifer SPROUT
04	Assistant to the President	Ms. Mardell DORSA
66	Dean of Health Sciences/Human Svcs	Dr. Amber DONNELLI
49	Dean of Arts and Sciences	Ms. Mary DOUCETTE
75	Dean of Applied Science	Mr. Bret MURPHY
106	Dean of Distance Education	Mr. Karl STEVENS
09	Dir Institutional Rsrch/Effective	Dr. William BROWN
37	Dir Student Financial Svcs & VA	Mr. Scott NIELSEN
07	Director Enrollment Services	Ms. Jennifer BROWN
12	Director Ely Center	Ms. Veronica NELSON
12	Director Winnemucca Center	Ms. Becky COLEMAN
12	Director Pahrump Valley Center	Ms. Diane WRIGHTMAN
51	Director Continuing Education	Mrs. Angie DEBRAGA
19	Director Safety and Security	Ms. Patricia ANDERSON
25	Director Grants	Vacant
43	General Counsel	Mr. John ALBRECHT

*Nevada State College (B)

1300 Nevada State Drive, Henderson NV 89002-9455

County: Clark — FICE Identification: 041143 — Unit ID: 441900

Telephone: (702) 992-2000 — Carnegie Class: Bac-Diverse

FAX Number: (702) 992-2226 — Calendar System: Semester

URL: www.nsc.edu

Established: 2002 — Annual Undergrad Tuition & Fees (In-District): $6,075

Enrollment: 7,289 — Coed

Affiliation or Control: State/Local — IRS Status: 501(c)3

Highest Offering: Master's

Accreditation: NW, NURSE, SP

Code	Title	Name
02	President	Bart PATTERSON
05	Provost/Exec Vice President	Dr. Vickie SHIELDS
28	VP of College/Cmty Engagement	Dr. Edith FERNANDEZ
10	SVP Finance & Business Operations	Kevin BUTLER
53	Dean of Education	Dr. Dennis POTTHOFF
49	Dean of Liberal Arts & Sciences	Vacant
66	Dean of Nursing	Dr. June EASTRIDGE
20	Executive Vice Provost	Dr. Tony SCINTA
121	Vice Provost Student Success	Dr. Gregory ROBINSON
06	Registrar	Adelfa SULLIVAN
08	Director of Library Services	Nathaniel KING
09	Director of Institutional Research	Dr. Sandip THANKI
37	Director Student Financial Aid	Anthony MORRONE

*Truckee Meadows Community College (C)

7000 Dandini Boulevard, Reno NV 89512-3999

County: Washoe — FICE Identification: 021077 — Unit ID: 182500

Telephone: (775) 673-7000 — Carnegie Class: Assoc/MT-VT-Mix Trad/Non

FAX Number: (775) 673-7108 — Calendar System: Semester

URL: www.tmcc.edu

Established: 1971 — Annual Undergrad Tuition & Fees (In-State): $2,862

Enrollment: 10,249 — Coed

Affiliation or Control: State — IRS Status: 501(c)3

Highest Offering: Associate Degree

Accreditation: NW, ACFEI, ADNUR, DA, DH, DIETT, EMT, NAEYC, RAD

Code	Title	Name
02	President	Dr. Karin HILGERSOM
04	Executive Assistant to President	Ms. Lisa FARMER
05	VP Academic Affairs	Dr. Jeffrey ALEXANDER
26	Assoc VP Research/Mktg & Web Svcs	Ms. Elena BUBNOVA
09	Director Institutional Research	Ms. Cheryl SCOTT
32	VP Student Services & Diversity	Ms. Estela LEVARIO GUTIERREZ
102	Exec Dir Foundation/Development	Mrs. Gretchen SAWYER
07	Director Admissions & Records	Mr. Andrew HUGHES
21	Controller Accounting Services	Mr. Rich WILLIAMS
37	Director Financial Aid	Ms. Leslie JIA
124	Exec Dir Retention and Support Svcs	Ms. Joan STEINMAN
114	Exec Director Budget & Planning	Ms. Elise BUNKOWSKI
15	Interim Director Human Resources	Ms. Kim STUDEBAKER
103	Dir Workforce Devel/Cmty Education	Ms. Bruncha MILASZEWSKI
08	Learning Commons Director	Ms. Brandy SCARNATI
13	Chief Information Technology Office	Mr. Thomas DOBBERT
19	Asst Vice Pres/Chief of Police	Mr. Todd RENWICK
28	Director of Diversity	Ms. YeVonne ALLEN
41	Athletic Director	Ms. Tina RUFF
18	Executive Director Facilities	Dr. Ayodele AKINOLA

† Granted candidacy at the Baccalaureate level.

*University of Nevada, Las Vegas (D)

4505 S Maryland Parkway, Las Vegas NV 89154-1001

County: Clark — FICE Identification: 002569 — Unit ID: 182281

Telephone: (702) 895-3201 — Carnegie Class: DU-Highest

FAX Number: (702) 895-1088 — Calendar System: Semester

URL: www.unlv.edu

Established: 1957 — Annual Undergrad Tuition & Fees (In-State): $8,685

Enrollment: 31,142 — Coed

Affiliation or Control: State — IRS Status: 501(c)3

Highest Offering: Doctorate

Accreditation: NW, ART, CAATE, CAMPEP, CIDA, CLPSY, CONST, DENT, DIETD, DIETI, HSA, IPSY, LAW, LSAR, MED, MFCD, MUS, NURSE, PH, PTA, RAD, SPAA, SW

Code	Title	Name
02	President	Dr. Keith E. WHITFIELD
100	Chief of Staff	Dr. Fred TREDUP
05	Executive Vice President & Provost	Dr. Chris HEAVEY
10	Vice Pres Finance & Business & CFO	Mrs. Jean VOCK
41	Director of Athletics	Mrs. Desiree REED-FRANCOIS
32	Vice President for Student Affairs	Dr. Juanita FAIN
19	Vice Pres Public Safety	Mr. Adam GARCIA
46	VP Research & Economic Development	Dr. Lori OLAFSON
88	VP University Compliance	Mr. Robert CORREALES
30	VP Philanthropy & Alumni	Mr. Rickey MCCURRY
86	VP Govt & Community Affairs	Mrs. Sabra NEWBY
26	VP Brand & Chief Marketing Officer	Mr. Vince ALBERTA
28	Chief Diversity Officer	Dr. Barbee OAKES
43	General Counsel	Mrs. Elda SIDHU
45	Exec Dir Strategic Initiatives	Dr. Kyle KAALBERG
88	Senior Advisor to the President	Dr. Tod FITZPATRICK
07	AVP Enrollment & Student Services	Dr. Steve MCKELLIPS
88	Asst VP Student Affairs/Finance	Ms. Summer MUDD
35	Assoc VP for Student Affairs	Dr. Renee WATSON
29	Sr Dir for Alumni Programs & Events	Mr. Blake DOUGLAS
31	Int Exec Dir of Community Relations	Mrs. Sue DIBELLA
15	VP Human Resources Officer	Dr. Ericka SMITH
87	Vice Provost Educational Outreach	Mr. Joseph MIERA
20	Vice Provost Academic Programs	Dr. Javier RODRIGUEZ
20	Vice Provost for Undergraduate Educ	Dr. Laurel PRITCHARD
09	Vice Provost Decision Support	Dr. Brent DRAKE
13	Vice Provost Information Technology	Dr. Lori TEMPLE
58	Dean of Graduate College	Dr. Kate H. KORGAN
50	Interim Dean Business	Dr. Paulette TANDY
49	Dean Liberal Arts	Dr. Jennifer KEENE
53	Interim Dean of Education	Dr. Danica HAYS
54	Dean of Engineering	Dr. Rama VENKAT
66	Dean of Nursing	Dr. Angela AMAR
63	Dean School of Medicine	Dr. Marc J. KAHN
52	Dean School of Dental Medicine	Dr. Lily T. GARCIA
61	Dean School of Law	Mr. Daniel W. HAMILTON
81	Dean of Sciences	Dr. Eric CHRONISTER
88	Dean College of Hotel Admin	Dr. Stowe SHOEMAKER
57	Dean Fine Arts	Dr. Nancy USCHER
08	Dean of Libraries	Ms. Maggie FARRELL
88	Dean Urban Affairs	Dr. Robert R. ULMER
92	Dean Honors College	Dr. Andrew HANSON
121	Dean Academic Success Center	Dr. Ann MCDONOUGH
88	Dean Community Health Sciences	Dr. Shawn GERSTENBERGER
76	Dean Sch Allied Health Sciences	Dr. Ronald T. BROWN
06	Registrar	Dr. Sam FUGAZZOTTO
37	Dir Financial Aid & Scholarships	Mr. Norm BEDFORD
39	Executive Director Residential Life	Mr. Richard CLARK
38	AVP Student Wellness	Dr. Jamie DAVIDSON
23	Director Student Health	Ms. Kathy A. UNDERWOOD
96	Director Purchasing	Ms. Sharrie MAYDEN
85	Dir International Students/Scholars	Ms. Marianna PANOSSI
25	Director Sponsored Programs	Ms. Lori CICCONE

*University of Nevada, Reno (E)

1664 N. Virginia Street, Reno NV 89557

County: Washoe — FICE Identification: 002568 — Unit ID: 182290

Telephone: (775) 784-1110 — Carnegie Class: DU-Highest

FAX Number: (775) 784-1300 — Calendar System: Semester

URL: www.unr.edu

Established: 1874 — Annual Undergrad Tuition & Fees (In-State): $8,366

Enrollment: 20,722 — Coed

Affiliation or Control: State — IRS Status: 501(c)3

Highest Offering: Doctorate

Accreditation: NW, ABAI, #ARCPA, CACREP, CAEPN, CLPSY, DIETD, DIETI, IPSY, JOUR, MED, MUS, NURSE, PH, SP, SW

Code	Title	Name
02	President	Mr. Brian SANDOVAL
05	Interim Exec Vice Pres & Provost	Dr. Jeff THOMPSON
11	Vice Pres Administration & Finance	Mr. Victor REDDING
63	VP Health Sci/Dean Sch of Medicine	Dr. Thomas L. SCHWENK
30	Int VP Devel/Alumni Relations	Ms. Lynda BUHLIG
32	Vice President for Student Services	Dr. Shannon ELLIS
46	Vice President for Research	Dr. Mridul GAUTAM
08	Dean of Libraries	Dr. Kathlin D. RAY
20	Vice Prov Instr/Undergrad Programs	Dr. David SHINTANI
20	Vice Provost Faculty Affairs	Dr. Jill HEATON
58	Vice Provost/Dean Grad School	Dr. David ZEH
10	Assoc VP Business & Finance	Ms. Sheri MENDEZ
84	Assoc VP Enrollment Services	Dr. Melisa N. CHOROSZY
32	Dean of Students	Dr. Leilani KUPO
45	Assoc VP Plng/Budget/Analysis	Mr. Rashawn NORMAN
18	Asst Vice Pres Facilities Svcs	Mr. Sean MCGOLDRICK
21	Controller	Ms. Kara GRIFFIN
41	Director Athletics	Mr. Doug KNUTH
96	Director Purchasing	Mr. Raymond MORAN
19	Director University Police Svcs	Mr. Eric JAMES
22	Dir Equal Opportunity & Title IX	Ms. Maria DOUCETTPERRY
37	Director Student Financial Svcs	Mr. Timothy WOLFE
39	Director Resident Life & Housing	Mr. Rodney L. AESCHLIMANN
23	Director Student Health Svcs	Dr. Cheryl HUG-ENGLISH
09	Manager of Decision Support	Mr. Cody CRIGG
86	Dir Govt Affairs & Ext Relations	Mr. Michael FLORES
65	Dir Mackay Sch Mines/Earth Science	Dr. Anna HUHTA
66	Dean of Nursing	Dr. Debera THOMAS
57	Director School of the Arts	Dr. Larry ENGSTROM
25	Director Sponsored Projects	Ms. Charlene HART
40	Director Wolf Shop	Ms. Amy LEWIS
49	Dean Liberal Arts	Dr. Debra MODDELMOG
47	Dean Agriculture/Biotech/Nat Res	Dr. William PAYNE
50	Dean Business Administration	Dr. Gregory MOSIER
53	Dean of Education & Human Dev	Dr. Donald EASTON-BROOKS
54	Dean Engineering	Dr. Emmanuel MARAGAKIS
60	Dean School of Journalism	Mr. Alan STAVITSKY
81	Int Dean College of Science	Dr. Katherine MCCALL
70	Dean School of Social Work	Dr. Shadi MARTIN
07	Director of Admissions	Dr. Stephen MAPLES
29	Director Alumni Relations	Ms. Amy CAROTHERS
06	Associate Registrar	Ms. Heather TURK FIECOAT
26	Exec Dir Marketing & Comm	Ms. Kerri GARCIA
04	Executive Asst to President	Ms. Aubrey FLORES
100	Chief of Staff	Ms. Patricia RICHARD
104	Dir/CEO Univ Study Abroad Consort	Dr. Alyssa NOTA
13	Chief Info Technology Officer (CIO)	Mr. Steven SMITH
28	Dir Ctr for Student Cultural Dev	Mr. Jose M. PULIDO LEON
43	General Counsel	Ms. Mary DUGAN
112	Director of Planned Giving	Ms. Lisa RILEY
69	Dean School of Public Health	Dr. Trudy LARSON

*Western Nevada College (F)

2201 W College Parkway, Carson City NV 89703-7316

County: Carson — FICE Identification: 010363 — Unit ID: 182564

Telephone: (775) 445-3000 — Carnegie Class: Bac/Assoc-Assoc Dom

FAX Number: (775) 445-3051 — Calendar System: Semester

URL: www.wnc.edu

Established: 1971 — Annual Undergrad Tuition & Fees (In-State): $3,548

Enrollment: 3,495 — Coed

Affiliation or Control: State — IRS Status: 501(c)3

Highest Offering: Baccalaureate

Accreditation: NW, ADNUR

Code	Title	Name
02	President	Dr. Vincent R. SOLIS
04	Assistant to the President	Ms. Deb CONRAD
05	Provost/VP of Finance	Dr. Kyle DALPE
43	VP Special Projects/Legal Counsel	Mr. Mark GHAN
32	VP of Student Success & Support	Mr. Jeffrey DOWNS
10	Chief Financial Officer	Ms. Coral LOPEZ
88	Director Child Development Center	Ms. Linda JACOBSEN
38	Director of Counseling/Advising	Ms. Piper MCCARTHY
18	Director Facilities Mgmt/Planning	Mr. Kevin GAFFNEY
37	Director Financial Aid	Mr. John (JW) LAZZARI
08	Director of Learning & Innovation	Ms. Denise FROHLICH
07	Director of Admissions	Ms. Dianne HILLIARD
102	Exec Director of WNC Foundation	Ms. Niki GLADYS

09 Director of Institutional Research .... Ms. Cathy FULKERSON
13 Director of Computing Services .... Mr. Ryan SWAIN
15 Director Human Resources .... Ms. Melody DULEY
35 Student Life Coord/Asst to Pres .... Ms. Heather RIKALO
49 Academic Director Liberal Arts .... Mr. Scott MORRISON
72 Academic Director Career & Tech Div .... Dr. Georgia WHITE
66 Int Director Nursing/Allied Health .... Ms. Deborah INGRAFFIA STRONG
114 Budget Officer .... Ms. Darla DODGE
19 Police Services Commander .... Mr. Tod MILLER

Northwest Career College (A)

7398 Smoke Ranch Road, Las Vegas NV 89128
County: Clark — FICE Identification: 038385
Unit ID: 445948
Telephone: (702) 254-7577 — Carnegie Class: Spec 2-yr-Other
FAX Number: (702) 256-9181 — Calendar System: Other
URL: www.northwestcareercollege.edu
Established: 1997 — Annual Undergrad Tuition & Fees: N/A
Enrollment: 1,723 — Coed
Affiliation or Control: Proprietary — IRS Status: Proprietary
Highest Offering: Associate Degree
Accreditation: ABHES

01 President/Founder .... Dr. John KENNY
05 Director of Education .... Dr. Thomas KENNY
13 Chief Operating Officer .... Patrick KENNY
10 Chief Financial Officer .... Stephanie KENNY
37 Senior Financial Aid Officer .... Guillermo BALDERAS
36 Director of Career Services .... Tina SPENCER
09 Director of Compliance .... Thomas KENNY
07 Director of Admissions .... Grace PEREA
13 Director of Technology .... Pablo CHACON
06 Registrar .... Century LEIGH

Pima Medical Institute-Las Vegas (B)

3333 E Flamingo Road, Las Vegas NV 89121-4329
Telephone: (702) 458-9650 — Identification: 666273
Accreditation: ABHES, COARC, OTA, #PTAA

† Branch campus of Pima Medical Institute, Tucson, AZ.

Roseman University of Health Sciences (C)

11 Sunset Way, Henderson NV 89014-2333
County: Clark — FICE Identification: 040653
Unit ID: 445735
Telephone: (702) 990-4433 — Carnegie Class: Spec-4-yr-Other Health
FAX Number: (702) 990-4435 — Calendar System: Other
URL: www.roseman.edu
Established: 1999 — Annual Undergrad Tuition & Fees: N/A
Enrollment: 1,554 — Coed
Affiliation or Control: Independent Non-Profit — IRS Status: 501(c)3
Highest Offering: Doctorate
Accreditation: NW, DENT, IACBE, NURSE, PHAR

01 President .... Dr. Renee COFFMAN
12 Chancellor Henderson Campus .... Dr. Eucharia E. NNADI
10 VP Business & Finance .... Vacant
11 VP of Operations .... Mr. Terrell SPARKS
03 Vice President Executive Affairs .... Dr. Charles F. LACY
26 VP Communications & Partnerships .... Mr. Jason ROTH
09 VP Qual Assurance/Intercampus Cons .... Dr. Thomas METZGER
32 VP for Student Services .... Dr. Michael DEYOUNG
45 VP Strategic Implementation/Engage .... Ms. Vanessa MANIAGO
67 Dean College of Pharmacy .... Dr. Larry FANNIN
66 Dean College of Nursing .... Dr. Brian OXHORN
52 Dean College of Dental Medicine .... Dr. Frank LICARI
50 Director MBA Program .... Dr. Okeleke NZEOGWU
37 Director of Financial Aid .... Ms. Sally MICKELSON
15 Director of Human Resources .... Ms. Saralyn BARNES
08 Director of Library Services .... Ms. Karen CANEPI

Sierra Nevada University (D)

999 Tahoe Boulevard, Incline Village NV 89451-9500
County: Washoe — FICE Identification: 009192
Unit ID: 182458
Telephone: (775) 831-1314 — Carnegie Class: Masters/M
FAX Number: (775) 832-1696 — Calendar System: Semester
URL: www.sierranevada.edu
Established: 1969 — Annual Undergrad Tuition & Fees: $35,508
Enrollment: 617 — Coed
Affiliation or Control: Independent Non-Profit — IRS Status: 501(c)3
Highest Offering: Master's
Accreditation: NW

00 Chairman Board of Trustees .... Dr. Atam LALCHANDANI
05 Executive Vice President/Provost .... Dr. Jill HEATON
111 Interim VP for Advancement .... Ms. Dianne SEVERANCE
10 Exec VP for Finance/Administration .... Ms. Susan JOHNSON
07 Interim Director of Admissions .... Mr. Kyle KELLY
37 Director of Financial Aid .... Ms. Maia ROWLAND
26 Director of Marketing .... Mr. Daniel KELLY
15 Director of Human Resources .... Vacant
18 Chief Facilities/Physical Plant .... Mr. Thayne CHRISTENSEN
06 Registrar .... Ms. Rose WEHBY
53 Statewide Dir Teacher Education .... Dr. Winship VARNER

13 Director Information Technology .... Mr. Franklin ARMSTRONG
16 Human Resources Coordinator .... Ms. Christin WILCOX
04 Exec Asst & Secretary to the Board .... Ms. Kristine YOUNG
41 Athletic Director .... Mr. Christian DELEON
08 Chief Library Officer .... Ms. Lara SCHOTT

Touro University Nevada (E)

874 American Pacific Drive, Henderson NV 89014
Telephone: (702) 777-8687 — Identification: 770966
Accreditation: &WC, ARCPA, NURSE, &OSTEO, OT, PTA

† Branch campus of Touro University California, Vallejo, CA

University of Phoenix Las Vegas Campus (F)

3755 Breakthrough Way, Ste. 100,
Las Vegas NV 89135-3047
Telephone: (702) 352-2944 — Identification: 770220
Accreditation: &HLC, ACBSP

† Branch campus of University of Phoenix, Tempe, AZ

Wongu University of Oriental Medicine (G)

8620 S Eastern Avenue, Las Vegas NV 89123
County: Clark — Identification: 667262
Unit ID: 488907
Telephone: (702) 463-2122 — Carnegie Class: Spec-4-yr-Other Health
FAX Number: (702) 946-5050 — Calendar System: Quarter
URL: www.wongu.edu
Established: 2012 — Annual Graduate Tuition & Fees: N/A
Enrollment: 45 — Coed
Affiliation or Control: Independent Non-Profit — IRS Status: 501(c)3
Highest Offering: Master's; No Undergraduates
Accreditation: ACUP

01 President .... Dr. Daniel DAVIES
05 Academic Dean .... Dr. Vim OSATHANUGRAH
10 Chief Financial Officer/HR .... Carolyn YANAI
06 Registrar .... Chau NGUYEN
07 Director Admissions/Marketing .... Michael GIAMPAOLI

NEW HAMPSHIRE

Colby-Sawyer College (H)

541 Main Street, New London NH 03257-7835
County: Merrimack — FICE Identification: 002572
Unit ID: 182634
Telephone: (603) 526-3000 — Carnegie Class: Bac-Diverse
FAX Number: (603) 526-3500 — Calendar System: Semester
URL: www.colby-sawyer.edu
Established: 1837 — Annual Undergrad Tuition & Fees: $44,930
Enrollment: 910 — Coed
Affiliation or Control: Independent Non-Profit — IRS Status: 501(c)3
Highest Offering: Master's
Accreditation: EH, ACBSP, CAATE, NURSE

01 President .... Dr. Susan D. STUEBNER
05 Academic Vice Pres/Dean of Faculty .... Dr. Laura A. SYKES
10 Vice Pres for Finance and Admin .... Ms. Karen I. BONEWALD
32 Vice Pres Stdnt Dev/Dean of Stdnts .... Ms. Robin BURROUGHS DAVIS
111 Vice President Advancement .... Mr. Daniel B. PARISH
07 Vice Pres Admissions/Financial Aid .... Ms. Anna D. MINER
26 Vice Pres Marketing/Communications .... Mr. Gregg MAZZOLA
101 Secretary of the College .... Ms. Rachel A. PARSONS
21 Controller/Assistant Treasurer .... Ms. Megan M. MILLER
09 Director Institutional Research .... Vacant
39 Director Residential Education .... Mr. Dave ZAMANSKY
37 Director of Financial Aid .... Ms. Beth W. RENZULLI
08 Director Library .... Ms. Malia M. EBEL
06 Registrar .... Ms. Siobhan SWANSON
13 Director Information Technology .... Mr. William ST. CYR
41 Director of Athletics .... Mr. Mitchell CAPELLE
88 Dir Student Lrng Collaborative .... Ms. Caren L. BALDWIN-DIMEO
44 Dir Annual Giving/Operations .... Mr. Luke GORMAN
29 Dir Alumni/Community Relations .... Ms. Tracey M. AUSTIN
19 Director of Campus Safety .... Mr. Peter L. BERTHIAUME
18 Director of Facilities .... Mr. Domenic GIOIOSO, JR.
40 Bookstore Manager .... Ms. Alison SEWARD
23 Dir of Baird Health & Counsel Ctr .... Ms. Pamela A. SPEAR
92 Director Wesson Honors Program .... Mr. Russell MEDBERY
04 Admin Assistant to the President .... Ms. Rachel A. PARSONS

*Community College System of New Hampshire (I)

26 College Drive, Concord NH 03301-7407
County: Merrimack — Identification: 666462
Telephone: (603) 230-3500 — Carnegie Class: N/A
FAX Number: (603) 271-2725
URL: www.ccsnh.edu

01 Interim Chancellor .... Dr. Susan HUARD
11 Chief Operating Officer .... Scott FIELDS
15 Interim Chief HR Officer .... Monica BRADLEY
26 Director of Communications .... Shannon REID
111 Chief Advancement Officer .... Tim ALLISON

*Great Bay Community College (J)

320 Corporate Drive, Portsmouth NH 03801-2879
County: Rockingham — FICE Identification: 002583
Unit ID: 183150
Telephone: (603) 427-7600 — Carnegie Class: Assoc/MT-VT-Mix Trad/Non
FAX Number: (603) 334-6308 — Calendar System: Semester
URL: www.greatbay.edu
Established: 1945 — Annual Undergrad Tuition & Fees (In-State): $7,200
Enrollment: 1,565 — Coed
Affiliation or Control: State — IRS Status: 501(c)3
Highest Offering: Associate Degree
Accreditation: EH, ACBSP, ADNUR, SURGT

02 President .... Dr. Cathryn ADDY
05 Vice President Academic Affairs .... Ms. Lisa MCCURLEY
32 VP Student Success/Enroll Mgmt .... Ms. Tina FAVARA
37 Director Financial Aid .... Ms. Susan PROULX
06 Registrar .... Ms. Sandra HO
07 Director Admissions .... Mr. Steven GORMAN
08 Library Director .... Ms. Rebecca CLERKIN

*Lakes Region Community College (K)

379 Belmont Road, Laconia NH 03246-1364
County: Belknap — FICE Identification: 007555
Unit ID: 183123
Telephone: (603) 524-3207 — Carnegie Class: Assoc/HVT-Mix Trad/Non
FAX Number: (603) 527-2042 — Calendar System: Semester
URL: www.lrcc.edu
Established: 1967 — Annual Undergrad Tuition & Fees (In-District): $6,738
Enrollment: 697 — Coed
Affiliation or Control: State/Local — IRS Status: 501(c)3
Highest Offering: Associate Degree
Accreditation: EH, ADNUR

02 President .... Dr. Larissa BAIA
05 VP of Academic & Student Affairs .... Mr. Patrick CATE
10 Chief Financial Officer .... Ms. Marsha BOURDON
04 Executive Asst to President .... Ms. Elizabeth LAWTON
06 Registrar .... Vacant
102 Exec Director Foundation .... Mr. Tim ALLISON
07 Director of Admissions .... Mrs. Shawna YOUNG
37 Director Student Financial Aid .... Ms. Kristen PURRINGTON
26 Public Information Officer .... Ms. Carlene ROSE
103 Director Workforce Development .... Mr. Andrew DUNCAN
18 Chief Facilities/Physical Plnt Ofcr .... Mr. Roger LAJOIE
19 Director Security/Safety .... Mr. David STEVENS
21 Associate Business Officer .... Ms. Linda JENNINGS
35 Associate Student Affairs Officer .... Ms. Laura LEMIEN
39 Residence Director .... Mr. Eric WALSH

*Manchester Community College (L)

1066 Front Street, Manchester NH 03102-8518
County: Hillsborough — FICE Identification: 002582
Unit ID: 183132
Telephone: (603) 206-8000 — Carnegie Class: Assoc/MT-VT-Mix Trad/Non
FAX Number: (603) 668-5354 — Calendar System: Semester
URL: www.mccnh.edu
Established: 1945 — Annual Undergrad Tuition & Fees (In-State): $7,090
Enrollment: 2,263 — Coed
Affiliation or Control: State — IRS Status: 501(c)3
Highest Offering: Associate Degree
Accreditation: EH, ACBSP, ADNUR, CAHIIM, MAC, NAEYC

02 President .... Dr. Brian BICKNELL
05 Vice President Academic Affairs .... Dr. Adriane LECHE
32 VP Students/Community Development .... Megan CONN
07 Director of Admissions .... Miho BEAN
26 Director of Marketing .... Victoria JAFFE
37 Financial Aid Officer .... Stephanie J. WELDON
06 Registrar .... Evelyn R. PERRON
08 Library Director .... Deb BAKER
09 Director Institutional Research .... Dr. Jere TURNER
10 Business Affairs Officer .... Kelly MARR
15 Human Resources Officer .... Vacant
40 Bookstore Manager .... Cindy CORLISS
66 Nursing Director .... Charlene WOLFE-STEPRO
21 Accountant I .... Carol DESPATHY
13 Director Information Technology .... Jean POTILLO
35 Director Student Life .... Aileen CLAY
113 Bursar .... Nathalie FERNS
04 Administrative Asst to President .... Karen KEELER
103 Dir Workforce/Career Development .... Kristine DUDLEY
106 Dir Online Education/E-learning .... Brian CHICK
18 Chief Facilities/Physical Plant .... Joshua MURPHY
29 Director Alumni Relations .... Vacant
19 Director of Campus Safety .... Ronald PEDDLE

*Nashua Community College (M)

505 Amherst Street, Nashua NH 03063-1092
County: Hillsborough — FICE Identification: 009236
Unit ID: 183141
Telephone: (603) 578-8900 — Carnegie Class: Assoc/MT-VT-Mix Trad/Non
FAX Number: (603) 882-8690 — Calendar System: Semester
URL: www.nashuacc.edu
Established: 1967 — Annual Undergrad Tuition & Fees (In-State): $7,140
Enrollment: 1,352 — Coed
Affiliation or Control: State — IRS Status: 501(c)3
Highest Offering: Associate Degree

Accreditation: EH, ACBSF, ADNUR

02 President ....Ms. Lucille A. JORDAN
05 Vice Pres Academic Affairs ....Ms. Robyn GRISWOLD
32 Vice Pres Student & Community Affs ....Ms. Lizbeth GONZALEZ
09 Assoc VP Inst Research/Acad Affs ....Mr. Phil FRANKLAND
10 Business Office Manager/Bursar ....Ms. Laurie BERNA
06 Registrar-Nashua ....Ms. Jennifer OLISZCZAK
37 Financial Aid Officer ....Ms. Anne EULE
08 Director Library Services ....Ms. Fran KEENAN
15 Human Resources Director ....Ms. Catherine BARRY
18 Plant Maintenance Engineer ....Mr. Scott BIENVENUE
19 Director of Security ....Mr. Kyle METCALF
26 Director Marketing/Public Relations ....Mr. Barry MEEHAN
04 Administrative Asst to President ....Ms. Lucy JENKINS

*NHTI-Concord's Community College (A)

31 College Drive, Concord NH 03301-7412
County: Merrimack FICE Identification: 002581
Unit ID: 183099
Telephone: (603) 271-6484 Carnegie Class: Assoc/MT-VT-High Trad
FAX Number: (603) 230-9311 Calendar System: Semester
URL: www.nhti.edu
Established: 1965 Annual Undergrad Tuition & Fees (In-State): $7,200
Enrollment: 2,945 Coed
Affiliation or Control: State IRS Status: 501(c)3
Highest Offering: Associate Degree
Accreditation: EH, ADNUR, DA, DH, DMS, EMT, NAEYC, RAD, RTT

02 President ....Dr. Gretchen MULLIN-SAWICKI
32 VP Student Affairs ....Dr. Laura PANTANO
05 Vice President Academic Affairs ....Dr. Andrew FISHER
10 Business Operations Officer ....Vacant
08 Coordinator of Library ....Ms. Christine CHO
84 AVP Student Success/Enrollment Mgmt ....Ms. Rebecca DEAN
06 Registrar ....Ms. Michele KARWOCKI
13 Enterprise Technology Manager ....Mr. Todd BEDELL
26 Director of Communications ....Dr. Anni JONES
36 Dir Residence Life/Career Counsel ....Ms. Trish LORING
38 Counseling ....Ms. Samantha ROBERTSON
37 Financial Aid Director ....Ms. Sheri GONTHIER
19 Interim Director of Campus Safety ....Mr. Jason WOVKANECH
41 Athletic Director ....Mr. Paul HOGAN
15 Director Human Resources ....Ms. Susan MAKEE
28 Dir Cross-Cultural Education/ESOL ....Ms. Dawn HIGGINS
96 Director of Purchasing ....Mr. Robert BOWEN
106 Dir Online Learning ....Ms. Trisha DIONNE
09 Director of Institutional Research ....Mr. Gary GONTHIER
29 Director Alumni & Development ....Ms. Laura A. SCOTT
39 Director Residence Life/Aux Srvs ....Ms. Trish LORING

*River Valley Community College (B)

1 College Place, Claremont NH 03743-9707
County: Sullivan FICE Identification: 007560
Unit ID: 183114
Telephone: (603) 542-7744 Carnegie Class: Assoc/HVT-Mix Trad/Non
FAX Number: (603) 543-1844 Calendar System: Semester
URL: www.rivervalley.edu
Established: 1968 Annual Undergrad Tuition & Fees (In-State): $7,160
Enrollment: 694 Coed
Affiliation or Control: State IRS Status: 501(c)3
Highest Offering: Associate Degree
Accreditation: EH, ACBSP, ADNUR, COARC, MAC, MLTAD, OTA, PTAA, RAD

02 President ....Alfred WILLIAMS
05 VP of Academic & Student Affairs ....Jennifer COURNOYER
20 AVP of Academic & Student Affairs ....Morgan SAILER
04 Exec Assistant to the President ....Kate CROCKER
10 Chief Accounting Officer ....Michelle LOCKWOOD
06 Registrar ....Jillian DAVIS
84 Director of Enrollment ....Suzanne GROENEWOLD
37 Director of Financial Aid ....Julia DOWER
08 Director of Library Services ....Sarah HEBERT
13 IT Manager ....Shubhashish MATHEMA
15 Human Resource Coordinator ....Connie SAMPSON

*White Mountains Community College (C)

2020 Riverside Drive, Berlin NH 03570-3799
County: Coos FICE Identification: 005291
Unit ID: 183105
Telephone: (603) 752-1113 Carnegie Class: Assoc/HVT-High Non
FAX Number: (603) 752-6335 Calendar System: Semester
URL: www.wmcc.edu
Established: 1966 Annual Undergrad Tuition & Fees (In-State): $7,050
Enrollment: 649 Coed
Affiliation or Control: State IRS Status: 501(c)3
Highest Offering: Associate Degree
Accreditation: EH, ADNUR, MAC

02 President ....Dr. Charles LLOYD
05 Vice President Academic Affairs ....Dr. Kristen MILLER
32 Vice President Student Affairs ....Dr. Mark DESMARAIS
10 Chief Financial Officer ....Vacant
15 Human Resources Officer ....Gretchen TAILLON
88 Director of Academic Centers ....Melanie ROBBINS
08 Director of Library Services ....Melissa LAPLANTE
13 Director Computer Center ....Vacant
06 Registrar ....Laura PROVOST
18 Chief Facilities/Physical Plant ....Scott LOCKE
40 Director Bookstore ....Melissa COTE
22 Dir Affirmative Action/Equal Oppty ....Vacant
91 Director Administrative Computing ....Tammy VASHAW
07 Director of Admissions ....Amanda GAEB
105 Director Web Services ....Matthew MALKIN
37 Asst Director Student Financial Aid ....Angela LABONTE
09 Director of Institutional Research ....Dr. Suzanne WASILESKI
38 Director Student Counseling ....Jeff SWAYZE
04 Admin Assistant to the President ....Gretchen TAILLON
19 Director Security/Safety ....James ASTUTO
103 Coordinator Workforce Development ....Tamara ROBERGE
50 Chair of Business Dept ....Nikolaus NUTTING
53 Chair of Education Dept ....Robin SCOTT
96 Coordinator of Purchasing ....Cynthia MACKAY
26 Chief Public Relations Officer ....Matthew MALKIN

Dartmouth College (D)

Hanover NH 03755-4030
County: Grafton FICE Identification: 002573
Unit ID: 182670
Telephone: (603) 646-1110 Carnegie Class: DU-Highest
FAX Number: N/A Calendar System: Quarter
URL: www.dartmouth.edu
Established: 1769 Annual Undergrad Tuition & Fees: $60,117
Enrollment: 6,292 Coed
Affiliation or Control: Independent Non-Profit IRS Status: 501(c)3
Highest Offering: Doctorate
Accreditation: EH, CAMPEP, IPSY, MED, PAST, PH

01 President ....Dr. Philip J. HANLON
03 Executive Vice President ....Mr. Richard G. MILLS
101 Secretary to Board of Trustees ....Ms. Laura H. HERCOD
05 Interim Provost ....Dr. David F. KOTZ
111 Sr Vice President for Advancement ....Mr. Robert W. LASHER
46 Vice Provost for Research ....Dr. Dean R. MADDEN
10 CFO and Vice Pres Finance ....Mr. Michael F. WAGNER
26 VP Communications ....Mr. Justin ANDERSON
28 SVP/Senior Diversity Officer ....Dr. Shontay DELALUE
15 Chief Human Resources Officer ....Mr. Scot R. BEMIS
29 Vice President Alumni Relations ....Ms. Cheryl A. BASCOMB
63 Dean Geisel Sch of Medicine ....Dr. Duane A. COMPTON
18 VP of Campus Services ....Mr. Josh KENISTON
43 General Counsel ....Ms. Sandhya L. IYER
20 Dean of the College ....Dr. Kathryn J. LIVELY
06 Registrar ....Mr. Eric PARSONS
07 VProv Enroll/Dean Admiss & Fin Aid ....Mr. Lee A. COFFIN
37 Director of Financial Aid ....Mr. Gordon D. KOFF
13 VP and Chief Information Officer ....Mr. Mitchel W. DAVIS
08 Dean of Libraries ....Ms. Susanne MEHRER
49 Dean of Faculty of Arts & Sciences ....Dr. Elizabeth F. SMITH
50 Dean of Amos Tuck School ....Dr. Matthew J. SLAUGHTER
54 Dean of the Thayer School ....Dr. Alexis R. ABRAMSON
58 Dean of Graduate Studies ....Dr. F. Jon KULL
42 Dean of Tucker Ctr/Col Chaplain ....Rabbi Daveen H. LITWIN
41 Interim Director of Athletics ....Mr. Peter ROBY
117 Int Dir Risk/Internal Control Svcs ....Mr. David F. FOSTER
23 Director of the Health Services ....Dr. Mark H. REED
36 Dir Center for Prof Development ....Ms. Monica WILSON
25 Dir Office of Sponsored Projects ....Ms. Jill M. MORTALI
32 Vice Provost for Student Affairs ....Vacant
19 Director Safety & Security ....Mr. Keiselim A. MONTAS
09 Assoc Prov Institutional Research ....Dr. Elizabeth A. BARLOW
38 Dir Counseling/Human Development ....Dr. Heather A. EARLE
22 Dir Equal Opportunity/Affirm Action ....Vacant
96 Director of Procurement ....Ms. Tammy L. MOFFATT
115 Chief Investment Officer ....Ms. Alice A. RUTH
35 Sr Assoc Dean for Student Affairs ....Vacant
21 Controller ....Ms. Dianne J. INGALLS
04 Senior Executive Asst to President .....Ms. Jennifer A. SHEPHERD
100 Chief of Staff ....Ms. Laura H. HERCOD
103 Dir Workforce/Career Development ....Mr. Roger W. WOOLSEY
104 Director Study Abroad ....Ms. John G. TANSEY
105 Director Web Services ....Mr. Jonathan CHIAPPA
106 Dir Digital Learning Initiatives ....Mr. Joshua M. KIM
39 Director Residential Life ....Mr. Michael W. WOOTEN

Franklin Pierce University (E)

40 University Drive, Rindge NH 03461-5046
County: Cheshire FICE Identification: 002575
Unit ID: 182795
Telephone: (603) 899-4000 Carnegie Class: Masters/M
FAX Number: (603) 899-6448 Calendar System: Semester
URL: www.franklinpierce.edu
Established: 1962 Annual Undergrad Tuition & Fees: $40,680
Enrollment: 1,928 Coed
Affiliation or Control: Independent Non-Profit IRS Status: 501(c)3
Highest Offering: Doctorate
Accreditation: EH, ARCPA, IACBE, NUR, PTA

01 President ....Dr. Kim MOONEY
05 Interim VP Academic Affairs/Provost ....Dr. David STARRETT
10 Vice President Finance & CFO ....Ms. Sandra QUAYE
111 VP for University Advancement ....Ms. Julie ZAHN
84 VP Enrollment & Univ Communications ....Ms. Linda QUIMBY
32 Dean of Student Affairs ....Dr. Andrew POLLOM
37 Assoc VP for Student Financial Svcs ....Mr. Kenneth FERREIRA
41 Athletic Director ....Ms. Rachel BURLESON
15 Interim Director of Human Resources ......Ms. Dawn BROUSSARD
06 University Registrar ....Ms. Charlee EATON
08 University Librarian ....Dr. Paul JENKINS
20 Exec Dean Assessment and Acad Aff ....Dr. Sarah DANGELANTONIO
09 Executive Director of IR ....Dr. Karen J. BROWN
79 Dean Coll Liberal Arts & Social Sci ....Dr. Matthew KONIECZKA
76 Dean Coll of Health & Natural Sci ....Dr. Maria R. ALTOBELLO
50 Dean College of Business ....Dr. Norman FAIOLA
36 Exec Director of Career Services ....Mr. Pierre MORTON
110 Assc VP for University Advancement .....Ms. Crystal NEUHAUSER
26 Director University Communication ....Mr. Kenneth PHILLIPS
88 Asst Dean of Student Involvement ......Mr. Scott ANSEVIN-ALLEN
39 Asst Dean Res Life & Comm Standard ....Ms. Kathleen DOUGHERTY
21 Director of Finance & Accounting ....Ms. Suzanne CARPENTER
18 Director of Plant Operations ....Mr. Doug LEAR
124 Dir of Diversity & Retention ....Mr. Derek SCALIA
96 Director of Purchasing ....Ms. Chere HALLETT-ADAMS
104 Director Study Abroad ....Ms. Patti VORFELD
13 Director of IT ....Mr. Thomas TOLBERT
04 Executive Asst to the President ....Ms. Heather RINGWALD

MCPHS-Manchester Campus (F)

1260 Elm Street, Manchester NH 03101
Telephone: (603) 314-0210 Identification: 770113
Accreditation: &EH, ARCPA, OT, PHAR

† Branch campus of MCPHS University, Boston, MA

New England College (G)

98 Bridge Street, Henniker NH 03242-3244
County: Merrimack FICE Identification: 002579
Unit ID: 182980
Telephone: (603) 428-2000 Carnegie Class: Masters/L
FAX Number: (603) 428-7230 Calendar System: Semester
URL: www.nec.edu
Established: 1946 Annual Undergrad Tuition & Fees: $39,648
Enrollment: 4,483 Coed
Affiliation or Control: Independent Non-Profit IRS Status: 501(c)3
Highest Offering: Doctorate
Accreditation: EH

01 President ....Dr. Michele D. PERKINS
05 Provost ....Dr. Wayne LESPERANCE
88 Sr VP Academic Alliances ....Dr. James MURTHA
10 Sr Vice President/CFO ....Dr. Paula A. AMATO
08 Library Director ....Ms. Chelsea HANRAHAN
108 Assoc Dean for Inst Effectiveness ....Ms. Cynthia MARTIN
04 Assistant to President ....Ms. Betsy MEDVETZ
13 VP Technology ....Mr. David RUBIN
06 Registrar ....Ms. Beth DOWLING
32 Dean of Students ....Mr. Jason BUCK
37 Director Student Financial Svcs ....Ms. Kristen BLASE
21 Controller ....Mr. Brian BOYER
36 Sr Assoc Dir Career/Life Planning ....Ms. Lindsay COATS
111 VP for Advancement ....Mr. Bill DEPTULA
15 Director of Human Resources ....Mr. David HARRINGTON
102 Director Legacy/Campaign Giving ....Mr. Gregory PALMER
18 AVP of Capital and Facilities Mgmt ....Mr. Dan GEARAN
19 Director Campus Safety ....Mr. Kevin COVEY
35 Assoc Dean of Students ....Ms. Doreen LONG
41 Athletic Director ....Mr. Dave DECEW
09 Institutional Researcher ....Mr. Frank HALL
26 Director Marketing/Communications ....Ms. Jen ROBERTSON
38 Director Mentoring ....Ms. Erin BROOKS
97 Dean of Undergraduate Programs ....Ms. Patricia CORBETT
14 Director Technology Services ....Mr. Eric SAWYER
28 Director of Diversity ....Ms. India BARROWS
29 Director Alumni Relations ....Ms. Lorella VOLPE
50 Assoc Dean of Management ......Dr. Erin WILKINSON HARTUNG

Magdalen College of the Liberal Arts (H)

511 Kearsarge Mountain Road, Warner NH 03278-4012
County: Merrimack FICE Identification: 022233
Unit ID: 182917
Telephone: (603) 456-2656 Carnegie Class: Bac-A&S
FAX Number: (603) 456-2660 Calendar System: Semester
URL: https://magdalen.edu/
Established: 1973 Annual Undergrad Tuition & Fees: $24,000
Enrollment: 71 Coed
Affiliation or Control: Roman Catholic IRS Status: 501(c)3
Highest Offering: Baccalaureate
Accreditation: EH

01 President ....Dr. Ryan MESSMORE
05 Academic Dean ....Dr. Brian FITZGERALD
32 Dean of Students ....Ms. Mazel BELT
07 Director of Admissions ....Mrs. Michele MCKENNA
37 Director of Financial Aid ....Mrs. Marie LASHER
08 Librarian ....Mrs. Marie LASHER

Rivier University (I)

420 S Main Street, Nashua NH 03060-5086
County: Hillsborough FICE Identification: 002586
Unit ID: 183211
Telephone: (603) 888-1311 Carnegie Class: Masters/L
FAX Number: (603) 897-8811 Calendar System: Semester
URL: www.rivier.edu
Established: 1933 Annual Undergrad Tuition & Fees: $34,510

Enrollment: 2,178 Coed
Affiliation or Control: Roman Catholic IRS Status: 501(c)3
Highest Offering: Doctorate
Accreditation: EH, ACBSP, ADNUR, NUR, PSPSY

01 President ... Sr. Paula Marie BULEY
05 Vice President for Academic Affairs ... Dr. Brian ERNSTING
10 Vice Pres Finance & Administration ... Mr. Steven PERROTTA
32 Vice President Student Affairs ... Mr. Kurt STIMELING
84 Vice Pres Enrollment Management ... Mr. Paul BROWER
111 Vice Pres University Advancement ... Ms. Karen COOPER
35 Asst Vice Pres Student Affairs ... Ms. Paula RANDAZZA
13 Chief Information Officer ... Ms. Heidi CROWELL
21 Controller ... Mr. Norman SMITH
06 Registrar ... Ms. Dina BROWN
08 Library Director ... Mr. Daniel SPEIDEL
36 Exec Dir Career Development Center ... Vacant
37 Director Student Financial Aid ... Vacant
15 Human Resources Manager ... Vacant
18 Director Facilities Management ... Mr. Richard PERRINE
14 Director Instructional Computing ... Sr. Martha VILLENEUVE
41 Athletic Director ... Ms. Joanne MERRILL
42 Chaplain Campus Ministry ... Vacant
28 Director Multicultural Affairs ... Vacant
29 Dir Alumni Relations/Special Events ... Ms. Joanne YOUNG
26 Director Marketing/Communication ... Ms. Sky CROSWELL

Saint Anselm College (A)

100 Saint Anselm Drive, Manchester NH 03102-1310
County: Hillsborough FICE Identification: 002587
Unit ID: 183239
Telephone: (603) 641-7000 Carnegie Class: Bac-A&S
FAX Number: (603) 641-7116 Calendar System: Semester
URL: www.anselm.edu
Established: 1889 Annual Undergrad Tuition & Fees: $42,840
Enrollment: 2,019 Coed
Affiliation or Control: Roman Catholic IRS Status: 501(c)3
Highest Offering: Master's
Accreditation: EH, NURSE

01 President ... Dr. Joseph A. FAVAZZA
03 Executive Vice President ... Bro. Isaac MURPHY, OSB
05 Interim Vice Pres Academic Affairs ... Dr. Mark W. CRONIN
111 Sr VP College Advancement ... Mr. James P. FLANAGAN
125 President Emeritus ... Fr. Jonathan P. DEFELICE
20 Dean of the College ... Dr. Mark W. CRONIN
26 Exec Dir Col Comm & Mktg ... Mr. Paul PRONOVOST
10 Chief Financial Ofcr/Sr VP Finance ... Mr. William FURLONG
28 Chief Diversity Officer ... Dr. Ande DIAZ
29 Assistant VP Alumni & Programs ... Ms. Patrice RUSSELL
06 Registrar ... Ms. Tracy MORGAN
07 Dean of Admissions/VP Enrollment ... Mr. Steven GOETSCH
08 Interim Librarian ... Mr. John DILLON
37 Director of Financial Aid ... Ms. Elizabeth KEUFFEL
35 Dean of Students ... Dr. Alicia A. FINN
89 Dean of Freshmen ... Dr. Benjamin HORTON
121 Dean of Academic Excellence ... Dr. Christine A. GUSTAFSON
66 Exec Director of Nursing ... Dr. Maureen A. O'REILLY
04 Assistant to the President ... Ms. Valerie S. DIAZ
18 Director of Physical Plant ... Mr. Jonathan WOODCOCK
23 Director of Health Services ... Ms. Maura MARSHALL
41 Director of Athletics ... Mr. Daron MONTGOMERY
42 Director of Campus Ministry ... Dr. Susan S. GABERT
09 Director of Institutional Research ... Vacant
13 Chief Information Officer ... Mr. Steven MCDEVITT
15 Director Human Resources ... Ms. Molly MCKEAN
19 Director Security/Safety ... Mr. Robert BROWNE
53 Director Education Planning ... Dr. Laura WASIELEWSKI
28 Director Multicultural Center ... Dr. Wayne CURRIE
39 Director Student Housing ... Ms. Susan WEINTRAUB
104 Assoc Dir Study Abroad ... Ms. Jane BJERKLIE-BARRY
25 Dir Sponsored Programs & Research ... Ms. Mary MADER
44 Asst VP Individual Giving ... Mr. John DAVIS
86 Director Government Relations ... Mr. Neil LEVESQUE
102 Dir Foundation/Corporate Rels ... Ms. Sharon SWEET

St. Joseph School of Nursing (B)

5 Woodward Avenue, Nashua NH 03060
County: Hillsborough FICE Identification: 021404
Unit ID: 183248
Telephone: (603) 594-2567 Carnegie Class: Spec 2-yr-Health
FAX Number: (603) 578-5028 Calendar System: Semester
URL: www.sjson.edu
Established: 1908 Annual Undergrad Tuition & Fees: $22,764
Enrollment: 92 Coed
Affiliation or Control: Roman Catholic IRS Status: 501(c)3
Highest Offering: Associate Degree
Accreditation: ACCSC, ADNUR

01 Dean ... Vickie K. FIELER

Southern New Hampshire University (C)

2500 North River Road, Manchester NH 03106-1045
County: Hillsborough FICE Identification: 002580
Unit ID: 183026
Telephone: (603) 626-9100 Carnegie Class: Masters/L
FAX Number: (603) 645-9665 Calendar System: Semester
URL: www.snhu.edu
Established: 1932 Annual Undergrad Tuition & Fees: $9,650
Enrollment: 134,345 Coed
Affiliation or Control: Independent Non-Profit IRS Status: 501(c)3
Highest Offering: Doctorate
Accreditation: EH, ACBSP, CACREP, CAEPT, CAHIIM, NURSE

01 President ... Dr. Paul LEBLANC
04 Executive Assistant to President ... Ms. Alycia AVERY
03 Executive Vice President ... Dr. Adrian HAUGABROOK
05 Sr VP/Chief Academic Officer ... Dr. Kimberly BOGLE JUBINVILLE
11 Chief Operating Officer ... Ms. Amelia MANNING
15 Exec VP Human Resources ... Ms. Danielle STANTON
13 Exec VP Technology & Transformation ... Mr. Thomas DIONISIO
14 Exec VP Digital Transformation ... Mr. John JIBILIAN
54 EVP Col Engr/Tech/Aeronautics ... Dr. Kirk KOLENBRANDER
10 EVP F&A/Chief Financial Ofcr ... Mr. Kenneth LEE
100 Sr VP of IA/Chief of Staff ... Mr. Donald BREZINSKI
26 SVP External Affairs/Communications ... Ms. Libby MAY
88 Sr VP Campus Transformation ... Dr. Steven JOHNSON
27 Chief Marketing Officer ... Ms. Alana BURNS
88 Chief Product Officer ... Mr. Travis WILLARD
43 Sr VP/General Counsel ... Ms. Yvette CLARK
28 SVP/Chief Diversity/Inclusion Ofcr ... Ms. Jada HEBRA
103 Sr VP Workforce Partnerships ... Ms. Sarah NORMAND
85 Sr VP Global Education Movement ... Dr. Chrystina RUSSELL
20 VPAA University College ... Dr. Michael EVANS
20 Interim Sr VP Global Campus ... Dr. Jennifer BATCHELOR
06 VP University Registrar ... Ms. Deanna BECHARD
32 VP Student Affairs Univ College ... Dr. Heather LORENZ
35 Chief Experience Officer ... Ms. Susan NATHAN
84 VP Enroll Mgmt/Stdnt Success ... Ms. Carey GLINES
88 Executive Director LRNG ... Ms. Megan STILES

The Thomas More College of Liberal Arts (D)

6 Manchester Street, Merrimack NH 03054-4805
County: Hillsborough FICE Identification: 030431
Unit ID: 183275
Telephone: (603) 880-8308 Carnegie Class: Bac-A&S
FAX Number: (603) 880-9280 Calendar System: Semester
URL: www.thomasmorecollege.edu
Established: 1978 Annual Undergrad Tuition & Fees: $24,600
Enrollment: 80 Coed
Affiliation or Control: Independent Non-Profit IRS Status: 501(c)3
Highest Offering: Baccalaureate
Accreditation: EH

01 President ... Dr. William E. FAHEY
30 Exec VP/Director Inst Advancement ... Mr. Paul JACKSON
05 Academic Dean ... Dr. Walter THOMPSON
32 Dean of Students ... Mr. Denis KITZINGER
10 Director of Business ... Ms. Pamela BERNSTEIN
35 Director of Collegiate Life ... Dr. Sara KITZINGER
04 Executive Asst President's Office ... Ms. Valerie BURGESS
06 Registrar ... Ms. Pamela BERNSTEIN
07 Director of Admissions ... Mr. Zachary NACCASH
08 Librarian ... Ms. Alexis ROHLFING
18 Director of Buildings & Grounds ... Mr. Clark INGRAM

*University System of New Hampshire (E)

5 Chenell Drive, Suite 301, Concord NH 03301
County: Merrimack FICE Identification: 008027
Unit ID: 183327
Telephone: (603) 862-0700 Carnegie Class: N/A
FAX Number: (603) 862-0908
URL: usnh.edu

01 Chief Administrative Officer ... Ms. Catherine A. PROVENCHER
43 General Counsel ... Mr. Ronald F. RODGERS
09 Dir of Institutional Research ... Ms. Heidi HEDEGARD
15 Chief Human Resource Officer ... Mr. James MCGRAIL
04 Admin Assistant to the President ... Ms. Tia MILLER
13 Chief Info Technology Officer (CIO) ... Mr. Bill POIRIER
26 Chief Public Relations Officer ... Ms. Lisa THORNE

*University of New Hampshire (F)

105 Main Street, Durham NH 03824
County: Strafford FICE Identification: 002589
Unit ID: 183044
Telephone: (603) 862-1234 Carnegie Class: DU-Highest
FAX Number: N/A Calendar System: Semester
URL: www.unh.edu
Established: 1866 Annual Undergrad Tuition & Fees (In-State): $18,938
Enrollment: 14,348 Coed
Affiliation or Control: State IRS Status: 501(c)3
Highest Offering: Doctorate
Accreditation: EH, #CAATE, CAEP, CAEPT, CAPRT, CARTE, DIETD, DIETI, IPSY, LAW, MFCD, MT, MUS, NURSE, OT, PH, SP, SW

02 President ... Dr. James W. DEAN, JR.
05 Provost & VP for Academic Affairs ... Dr. Wayne E. JONES, JR.
10 Interim Chief Financial Officer ... Mr. Jay CALHOUN
13 Chief Information Officer ... Mr. Bill POIRIER
11 VP Administration/COO ... Mr. Christopher D. CLEMENT
111 VP Advancement ... Ms. Deborah DUTTON COX
41 Dir Intercollegiate Athletics ... Mr. Martin SCARANO
28 Assoc VP Cmty/Equity/Diversity ... Ms. Nadine PETTY
100 Chief of Staff ... Ms. Megan W. DAVIS
20 Sr Vice Prov Academic Affairs ... Dr. Katherine ZIEMER
46 Sr Vice Provost for Research ... Dr. Marian MCCORD
32 Sr Vice Provost/Dean Students ... Mr. Kenneth HOLMES
25 Asst Prov Contract Administration ... Mr. John WALLIN
47 Dean Life Sciences/Agriculture ... Dr. Jon M. WRAITH
49 Dean Liberal Arts ... Dr. Michele M. DILLON
54 Dean Engineering/Physical Sci ... Dr. Charles K. ZERCHER
50 Dean Paul College of Business ... Dr. Deborah M. MERRILL-SANDS
76 Dean Health & Human Services ... Dr. Michael FERRARA
61 Dean UNH School of Law ... Ms. Megan M. CARPENTER
12 Dean UNH at Manchester ... Dr. Michael P. DECELLE
88 Director Institute for EOS ... Dr. Harlan SPENCE
58 Dean Graduate School ... Dr. Cari A. MOORHEAD
08 Dean University Library ... Dr. Tara Lynn FULTON
56 Vice Provost University Outreach ... Dr. Kenneth J. LAVALLEY
84 Vice Provost Enrollment Management ... Dr. Pelema ELLIS
21 Assoc VP Business Affairs ... Mr. David J. MAY
18 Assoc VP Facilities ... Mr. William P. JANELLE
15 Assoc VP/Chief HR Officer ... Ms. Kathleen A. NEILS
21 Assoc VP for Finance ... Ms. Kerry L. SCALA
19 Assoc VP Public Safety & Risk Mgt ... Chief Paul M. DEAN
26 Assoc VP Univ Communications ... Mr. Mica B. STARK
91 Sr Director for Center of Data ... Ms. Jackie SNOW
30 Assoc VP for Development ... Mr. Troy FINN
29 Assoc VP Alumni Affairs ... Ms. Susan ENTZ
88 Exec Dir Media Relations ... Ms. Erika MANTZ
39 Director Residential Life ... Ms. Ruth E. ABELMANN
23 Exec Director Health & Wellness ... Dr. Kevin E. CHARLES
25 Dir Sponsored Programs ... Ms. Louise GRIFFIN
22 Dir Affirmative Action & Equity ... Ms. Donna Marie SORRENTINO
06 Registrar ... Mr. Andrew G. COLBY
37 Dir Financial Aid ... Mr. Joel B. CARSTENS
38 Dir Psychological Services ... Dr. Shari A. ROBINSON
102 Sr Exec Dir Advance Fin/Foundation ... Mr. Erik E. GROSS
88 Dir Housing/Conf Services ... Ms. Katherine M. IRLA-CHESNEY
85 Dir Intl Students & Scholars ... Ms. Leila L. PAJE-MANALO
92 Dir Honors Program ... Dr. Lisa MACFARLANE
09 Dir Inst Research & Assessment ... Dr. Anne SHATTUCK
88 Dir Writing Program ... Dr. Edward A. MUELLER
07 Director of Admissions ... Vacant
16 Asst VP Human Resources ... Ms. Sari M. BENNETT
88 Asst VP Enterprise Comp ... Mr. William J. HALL
88 Sr VProv Engagement & Faculty Dev ... Dr. Leslie COUSE
90 Asst Vice Prov Digital Lrng & Comm ... Ms. Terri S. WINTERS

*Granite State College (G)

25 Hall Street, Concord NH 03301-7317
County: Merrimack FICE Identification: 031013
Unit ID: 183257
Telephone: (603) 228-3000 Carnegie Class: Masters/S
FAX Number: (603) 513-1389 Calendar System: Quarter
URL: www.granite.edu
Established: 1972 Annual Undergrad Tuition & Fees (In-State): $7,791
Enrollment: 1,879 Coed
Affiliation or Control: State IRS Status: 501(c)3
Highest Offering: Master's
Accreditation: EH, CAEPT, NURSE

02 President ... Dr. Mark RUBINSTEIN
05 Provost/VP Academic Affairs ... Dr. Scott A. STANLEY
10 VP Finance & Administration ... Ms. Lisa L. SHAWNEY
84 VP Enrollment Management ... Ms. Tara PAYNE
53 Dean of School of Education ... Mr. Nick MARKS
24 Director of Educational Technology ... Ms. Reta CHAFFEE
08 Librarian ... Ms. Lia HORTON
04 Administrative Asst to Provost ... Ms. Susan L. ORR
15 Asst VP of Human Resources ... Ms. Maggie HYNDMAN
21 Asst VP of Finance ... Mr. Steve PERROTTA
18 Dir of Facilities/Safety/Sustain ... Mr. Peter CONKLIN
07 Asst VP of Enrollment Operations ... Ms. Christine WILLIAMS
121 Sr Dir of Advising/Stdnt Engagement ... Ms. Nicole HORNE
37 Director Student Financial Aid ... Mr. Mac BRODERICK
36 Director of Career Services ... Ms. Jan COVILLE
06 Registrar ... Ms. Cortney FRENCH
108 Dir Inst Effectiveness/Compliance ... Mr. Todd SLOVER
124 Director of Student Affairs ... Ms. Tiffany DOHERTY

*Keene State College (H)

229 Main Street, Keene NH 03435-0001
County: Cheshire FICE Identification: 002590
Unit ID: 183062
Telephone: (603) 352-1909 Carnegie Class: Bac-Diverse
FAX Number: (603) 358-2257 Calendar System: Semester
URL: www.keene.edu
Established: 1909 Annual Undergrad Tuition & Fees (In-State): $14,638
Enrollment: 3,210 Coed
Affiliation or Control: State IRS Status: 501(c)3
Highest Offering: Master's
Accreditation: EH, CAEPN, DIETD, DIETI, MUS, NURSE

02 President ... Dr. Melinda TREADWELL
05 Provost/VP Academic Affairs ... Dr. James BEEBY
84 VP Enrollment/Student Engagement ... Dr. MB LUFKIN
10 VP Finance & Administration ... Ms. Nathalie HOUDER
28 AVP Diversity & Inclusion ... Dr. Dottie MORRIS
111 VP Advancement/Constituent Rels ... Ms. Veronica ROSA
15 Director Human Resources ... Ms. Karen CRAWFORD
81 Dean of Sciences/Sustain & Health ... Dr. Karrie KALICH
57 Dean Arts/Education & Humanities ... Dr. Kirsti SANDY
08 Dean of Library ... Dr. Celia E. RABINOWITZ

13 Chief Information Officer .... Vacant
26 Director Strategic Communications .... Ms. Kelly RICAURTE
20 Associate Provost .... Dr. Sue CASTRIOTTA
39 Assoc Dean Students/Dir Res Life .... Vacant
07 Director of Admissions .... Ms. Peggy RICHMOND
06 Registrar .... Vacant
37 Dir of Financial Aid/Scholarships .... Ms. Cathy MULLINS
38 Exec Dir Wellness Center .... Dr. Brian QUIGLEY
41 Athletic Director .... Mr. Philip RACICOT
09 Dir Inst Effectiveness & IR .... Vacant
18 Director Physical Plant .... Vacant
96 Campus Purchasing Director .... Ms. Renee HARLOW

*Plymouth State University (A)

17 High Street, Plymouth NH 03264-1595
County: Grafton FICE Identification: 002591
Unit ID: 183080
Telephone: (603) 535-5000 Carnegie Class: Masters/L
FAX Number: (603) 535-2654 Calendar System: Semester
URL: www.plymouth.edu
Established: 1871 Annual Undergrad Tuition & Fees (In-State): $14,492
Enrollment: 4,491 Coed
Affiliation or Control: State IRS Status: 501(c)3
Highest Offering: Doctorate
Accreditation: EH, AAQEP ACBSP, CAATE, CACREP, CAEP, CAEPN, NURSE, PTA, SW

02 President .... Dr. Donald L. BIRX
05 Int Provost/VP for Academic Affairs .... Dr. Ann K. MCCLELLAN
10 VP for Finance & Administration .... Ms. Tracy L. CLAYBAUGH
111 Director of Development .... Mr. John E. SCHEINMAN
26 Int VP of Comm/Enroll/Student Life .. Mr. Marlin COLLINGWOOD
13 USNH/UNH Chief Information Officer .... Mr. Bill POIRIER
21 Assoc VP Finance & Administration .... Ms. Laurie WILCOX
07 Interim Director of Admissions .... Mr. Matthew L. WALLACE
39 Dir Residence Life/Dining Svcs .... Ms. Amanda GRAZIOSO
32 Dean of Students .... Mr. Jeffrey C. FURLONE
108 Dir Institutional Effectiveness .... Ms. Melissa K. CHRISTENSEN
06 Registrar .... Ms. Tonya B. LABROSSE
30 Director of Development/Major Gifts ..... Mr. John E. SCHEINMAN
29 Director of Alumni Relations .... Mr. Rodney EKSTROM
113 Director Student Financial Services ..... Mr. Matthew N. DALLAIRE
15 Director of Human Resources .... Ms. Caryn L. INES
19 Dir Public Safety and Emer Planning . Mr. Steven H. TEMPERINO
41 Director of Athletics .... Ms. Kim M. BOWNES
18 Director of Physical Plant .... Mr. Stephen P. FOSTER
38 Dir of Counseling/Human Rel Center .... Dr. Robert W. ORF
88 Coordinator Title IX/504 .... Ms. Janette T. WIGGETT
08 Outreach Librarian .... Ms. Anne M. JUNG-MATHEWS
40 Bookstore Manager .... Mr. Steve RHEAUME
09 Director Inst Research/Innovation .... Vacant

Upper Valley Educators Institute (B)

194 Dartmouth College Hwy, Lebanon NH 03766
County: Grafton FICE Identification: 034373
Unit ID: 440004
Telephone: (603) 678-4888 Carnegie Class: Not Classified
FAX Number: (603) 678-4899 Calendar System: Other
URL: www.uvei.edu
Established: 1969 Annual Graduate Tuition & Fees: N/A
Enrollment: N/A Coed
Affiliation or Control: Independent Non-Profit IRS Status: 501(c)3
Highest Offering: Master's; No Undergraduates
Accreditation: @EH

01 Executive Director .... Dr. Page TOMPKINS

NEW JERSEY

Assumption College for Sisters (C)

200A Morris Avenue, Denville NJ 07834
County: Morris FICE Identification: 002595
Unit ID: 183600
Telephone: (973) 957-0188 Carnegie Class: Assoc/HT-High Trad
FAX Number: (973) 957-0190 Calendar System: Semester
URL: www.acs350.org
Established: 1953 Annual Undergrad Tuition & Fees: $5,773
Enrollment: 45 Female
Affiliation or Control: Roman Catholic IRS Status: 501(c)3
Highest Offering: Associate Degree
Accreditation: M

01 President/Chief of Development .... Sr. Joseph SPRING, SCC
05 Academic Dean .... Sr. Teresa BRUNO, SC
10 Treasurer/Institutional Advancement .... Mrs. Patricia MCGRADY
32 Chief Student Life Officer .... Sr. Monique ELOIZARD, SCC
06 Registrar .... Mrs. Barbara KELLY-VERGONA
13 Chf Information Technology Officer .... Mrs. Jean WEDEMEIER

Atlantic Cape Community College (D)

5100 Black Horse Pike, Mays Landing NJ 08330-2699
County: Atlantic FICE Identification: 002596
Unit ID: 183655
Telephone: (609) 343-4900 Carnegie Class: Assoc/HT-High Trad
FAX Number: (609) 343-4917 Calendar System: Semester
URL: www.atlantic.edu
Established: 1964 Annual Undergrad Tuition & Fees (In-District): $6,840
Enrollment: 4,464 Coed
Affiliation or Control: State/Local IRS Status: 501(c)3
Highest Offering: Associate Degree
Accreditation: M, ACFEI, ADNUR

01 President .... Dr. Barbara GABA
05 Vice President Academic Affairs .... Dr. Josette KATZ
11 Chief Business Officer .... Mr. George BOOSKOS
100 Chief of Staff/Chief Advance Ofcr .... Ms. Jean MCALISTER
10 Chief Financial Officer .... Ms. Leslie JAMISON
46 Dean Institutional Research ..Dr. Vanessa O'BRIEN-MCMASTERS
26 Executive Director Marketing .... Ms. Laura BATCHELOR
12 Dean Worthington Atlantic City .... Dr. Natalie DEVONISH
12 Dean Cape May County Campus .... Ms. Maria KELLETT
88 Dean Academy of Culinary Arts .... Ms. Kelly MCCLAY
49 Dean Liberal Studies .... Dr. Denise COULTER
06 Registrar .... Ms. Heather PETERSON
07 Director Admissions & Recruitment .... Vacant
37 Director Financial Aid .... Ms. Victoria DELAURENTIS
35 Dir Student Dev & Judicial Officer .... Ms. Nancy PORFIDO
09 Director Institutional Research .... Mr. Luis MONTEFUSCO
96 Director Business Services .... Ms. Carol MELKONIAN
13 Chief Information Officer .... Mr. John PIAZZA
15 Director Human Resources .... Ms. Cindy DEFALCO
19 Director Security/Safety .... Mr. Clifton SUDLER

Bais Medrash Mayan Hatorah (E)

101 Milton Avenue, Lakewood NJ 08701
County: Ocean Identification: 667280
Unit ID: 490513
Telephone: (732) 367-9900 Carnegie Class: Spec-4-yr-Faith
FAX Number: N/A Calendar System: Other
Established: Annual Undergrad Tuition & Fees: $10,650
Enrollment: 41 Male
Affiliation or Control: Independent Non-Profit IRS Status: 501(c)3
Highest Offering: Baccalaureate
Accreditation: AIJS

05 Dean .... Rabbi Abraham NEWMAN

Bais Medrash Toras Chesed (F)

910 Monmouth Avenue, Lakewood NJ 08701-1921
County: Ocean FICE Identification: 040813
Unit ID: 449658
Telephone: (732) 364-1220 Carnegie Class: Spec-4-yr-Faith
FAX Number: (732) 886-2323 Calendar System: Semester
Established: 1999 Annual Undergrad Tuition & Fees: $7,200
Enrollment: 150 Male
Affiliation or Control: Independent Non-Profit IRS Status: 501(c)3
Highest Offering: Baccalaureate
Accreditation: RABN

01 Dean .... Rabbi N. STEIN
37 Director of Financial Aid .... Mrs. H. WEISS

Bais Medrash Zichron Meir (G)

1500 Vermont Ave, Lakewood NJ 08701
County: Ocean Identification: 667259
Telephone: (732) 370-1560 Carnegie Class: Not Classified
FAX Number: (732) 363-7864 Calendar System: Semester
Established: 2013 Annual Undergrad Tuition & Fees: N/A
Enrollment: N/A Male
Affiliation or Control: Independent Non-Profit IRS Status: 501(c)3
Highest Offering: First Talmudic Degree
Accreditation: @RABN

01 CEO .... Zev MINTZ
10 CFO .... Nissim BASALA
37 Dir Student Financial Aid/Registrar .... Lipa EIDELMAN

Bergen Community College (H)

400 Paramus Road, Paramus NJ 07652-1595
County: Bergen FICE Identification: 004736
Unit ID: 183743
Telephone: (201) 447-7100 Carnegie Class: Assoc/HT-High Trad
FAX Number: (201) 447-9042 Calendar System: Semester
URL: www.bergen.edu
Established: 1965 Annual Undergrad Tuition & Fees (In-District): $8,281
Enrollment: 11,409 Coed
Affiliation or Control: State/Local IRS Status: 501(c)3
Highest Offering: Associate Degree
Accreditation: M, ADNUR, COARC, DH, DMS, EMT, MAC, RAD, RTT, SURGT

01 President .... Dr. Eric M. FRIEDMAN
05 Vice President of Academic Affairs .... Dr. Brock FISHER
32 Int Vice Pres Student Affairs .... Dr. Ralph CHOONOO
50 Int Dean Business/Arts/Social Sci .... Mr. Adam GOODELL
79 Dean of Humanities .... Mr. Adam GOODELL
76 Dean Health Professions .... Dr. Susan BARNARD
81 Dean Science/Math & Technology .... Ms. Emily VANDALOVSKY
51 Exec Dir of Cont Educ/Workforce Dev .... Ms. Christine GILLESPIE
08 Dean Library Services .... Mr. David MARKS
12 Dean of Off-Campus Sites .... Ms. Linda EMR
121 Dean of Student Support Services .... Ms. Jennifer REYES
15 Director of Human Resources .... Vacant
18 Managing Director Physical Plant .... Mr. Michael HYJECK
19 VP Fac Ops/Plng & Public Safety .... Vacant
13 Exec Dir of Info Technology/CIO .... Mr. Ronald SPAIDE
06 Managing Dir Registration/Records .... Ms. Jacqueline OTTEY
31 Director of Community/Cultural Affs .... Mr. Peter LEDONNE
101 Exec Asst Board of Trustees/Pres .... Ms. Maria FERRARA
29 Managing Director of Alumni Affairs .... Vacant
37 Managing Dir Stdnt Financial Ops .... Ms. Caroline OFODILE
102 Exec Dir Foundation/Development .... Mr. Ronald MILLER
25 Dir Grants Admin/Inst Effectiveness .... Dr. William YAKOWICZ
96 Director of Purchasing & Services .... Ms. Barbara HAMILTON-GOLDEN
26 Exec Dir Pub Rels & Community Cult ... Dr. Lawrence HLAVENKA
07 Managing Dir of Admissions .... Ms. Kathryn BRUNETTO

Berkeley College (I)

44 Rifle Camp Road, Woodland Park NJ 07424-3367
County: Passaic FICE Identification: 007502
Unit ID: 183789
Telephone: (973) 278-5400 Carnegie Class: Bac-Diverse
FAX Number: N/A Calendar System: Semester
URL: www.berkeleycollege.edu
Established: 1931 Annual Undergrad Tuition & Fees: $27,000
Enrollment: 2,625 Coed
Affiliation or Control: Proprietary IRS Status: Proprietary
Highest Offering: Master's
Accreditation: M, CIDA, IACBE, MAC, SURGT

00 Chairman of the Board .... Mr. Kevin L. LUING
01 President .... Mr. Michael J. SMITH
05 Provost .... Dr. Marsha POLLARD
84 Executive VP .... Mr. Tim LUING
32 Senior VP Student Success .... Dr. Diane RECINOS
10 VP Finance .... Mr. Dino KASAMIS
88 Vice President .... Mr. Brian MAHER
35 VP Student Development/Campus Life .... Dr. Dallas F. REED
36 VP Career Services .... Ms. Amy SORICELLI
37 VP Financial Aid &alE .... Mr. Will MOYA
114 VP Budget & Student Accounts .... Ms. Eileen LOFTUS-BERLIN
13 Senior VP/Chief Information Officer .... Mr. Leonard DE BOTTON
88 VP Financial Aid Compliance .... Mr. Howard LESLIE
20 Asst Prov Curriculum/Instruct/Tech .... Ms. Dana HEIMLICH
50 Dean School of Business .... Dr. Joseph SCURALLI
76 Dean School Health Studies .... Dr. Eva SKUKA
107 Dean School of Professional Studies .... Dr. Marianne VAKALIS
106 Dean Online .... Dr. Joseph SCURALLI
58 Director MBA Program .... Dr. David GLAZER
49 Director General Education .... Dr. Gregory HOTCHKISS
25 Executive Dir Academic Partnerships .... Ms. Michelle R. WHITE
11 Campus Operating Officer .... Ms. LaTysha GAINES
37 Assoc VP Financial Aid .... Mr. Alejandro GUIRAL
15 VP Human Resources .... Ms. Karen J. CARPENTIERI
26 VP Communications & Ext Relations .. Ms. Angela HARRINGTON
86 Senior VP Government Relations NJ .... Ms. Teri DUDA
06 Registrar .... Ms. Deborah PALICIA
29 AVP Alumni Relations & Career Svcs .... Mr. Michael IRIS
26 Director Marketing .... Mr. Michael ROMAN
22 Director Disability Services .... Ms. Gail KRIEGER
88 Asst VP Military & Veterans Affairs .... Mr. Edward J. DENNIS
38 Sr Director Personal Counseling .... Dr. Sandra COPPOLA
41 Director Athletics .... Mr. Andrew DESTEPHANO
84 VP Undergraduate Enrollment .... Mr. David J. BERTONE
85 VP International Operations .... Dr. Nori JAFFER
45 Dir Institutional Analysis & Plng .... Ms. Janan JOHNSTON
123 Director Graduate Admissions .... Mr. Michael LINCOLN
18 Sr Vice President Operations .... Mr. Thomas ALESSANDRELLO
19 Asst VP Pub Safety/Emergency Mgmt .... Mr. Robert MAGUIRE
109 Senior Director Auxiliary Services .... Mr. Luis COLLAZO
119 Info Systems Security Manager .... Mr. Dana KILCREASE
09 Director of Institutional Research .... Ms. Rebecca J. DRENNEN

Best Care College (J)

68 South Harrison St, East Orange NJ 07018
County: Essex FICE Identification: 041814
Unit ID: 461865
Telephone: (973) 673-3900 Carnegie Class: Not Classified
FAX Number: (973) 673-0597 Calendar System: Trimester
URL: bestcarecollege.edu
Established: 1997 Annual Undergrad Tuition & Fees: N/A
Enrollment: 31 Coed
Affiliation or Control: Proprietary IRS Status: Proprietary
Highest Offering: Associate Degree
Accreditation: ACICS

01 President .... Theodore FAYETTE

Beth Medrash Govoha (K)

617 Sixth Street, Lakewood NJ 08701-2797
County: Ocean FICE Identification: 007947
Unit ID: 183804
Telephone: (732) 367-1060 Carnegie Class: Spec-4-yr-Faith
FAX Number: (732) 367-7487 Calendar System: Semester
URL: www.yeshivanotices.org
Established: 1943 Annual Undergrad Tuition & Fees: N/A
Enrollment: 7,159 Male
Affiliation or Control: Independent Non-Profit IRS Status: 501(c)3
Highest Offering: Master's
Accreditation: RABN

01 President/Chief Executive Officer .... Rabbi Aaron KOTLER
05 Chairman Academic Council .... Rabbi A. Malkiel KOTLER
10 Chief Financial Officer .... Mr. Isaac LEVINE
43 VP Finance/Corporate/Legal Affairs .... Rabbi Eli KUPERMAN

11 Vice President Admin/Campus Life ......Rabbi Yitzchok S. KOTLER
33 Dean of Students ....Rabbi Mattisyahu SALOMON
58 Dean of Graduate Studies ....Rabbi Yisroel NEUMAN
30 Vice President of Fundraising ......Rabbi Mordechai HERSKOWITZ
86 Director Government Affairs ....Mrs. Chanie JACOBOWITZ
06 Registrar ....Rabbi Moshe ROCKOVE
84 Director Enrollment Management ....Rabbi Gedalya A. GREEN
07 Director of Admissions ....Rabbi Avraham FEUER
08 Director Library/Research Programs ....Rabbi Benjamin SPIEGEL
36 Director of Placement ....Rabbi Yaakov SHULMAN
39 Director of Residence Halls ....Rabbi Yosef HOUSMAN
15 Director of Human Resources ....Mrs. Dina YELLIN
18 Director of Facilities ....Mr. Mottie MOSESON

Bloomfield College (A)

467 Franklin Street, Bloomfield NJ 07003-3425
County: Essex — FICE Identification: 002597
Unit ID: 183822
Telephone: (973) 748-9000 — Carnegie Class: Bac-A&S
FAX Number: (973) 743-3998 — Calendar System: Semester
URL: www.bloomfield.edu
Established: 1868 — Annual Undergrad Tuition & Fees: $30,680
Enrollment: 1,533 — Coed
Affiliation or Control: Presbyterian Church (U.S.A.) — IRS Status: 501(c)3
Highest Offering: Master's
Accreditation: M, CAEPT, NURSE

01 President ....Dr. Marcheta P. EVANS
10 Vice President Finance/Admin ....Ms. Cynthia MCDANIEL
04 Administrative Asst to President ....Vacant
05 Vice President Academic Affairs ....Dr. Michael PALLADINO
84 VP Enrollment Mgmt ....Mr. Kevin CAVANAGH
32 VP Student Affairs ....Vacant
111 VP for Advancement ....Ms. Sarah LACZ
107 VP Global Affairs/Prof Studies ....Vacant
06 Registrar and Director of Advising .... Ms. Annette RAYMOND
09 Director Inst Research/Assessment .... Mr. Craigon CAMPBELL
79 Chair Div of Humanities ....Dr. Brandon FRALIX
83 Chair Div Social/Behavioral Science ....Dr. Daniel SKINNER
66 Chair Div of Nursing ....Dr. Frances MAL
81 Chair Div of Natural Science/Math ....Dr. Jim MURPHY
57 Chair Div Creative Arts Technology ..... Prof. Yuichiro NISHIZAWA
50 Chair Div of Business ....Dr. Steven KREUTZER
53 Chair Div of Education ....Dr. Karen FASANELLA
08 Library Director ....Mr. Gregory REID
13 Director Enterprise Tech Services .... Mr. Andrew GERSTMAYR
36 Director of Ctr for Career Develop ....Vacant
37 Interim Director of Financial Aid ....Ms. Quincina LITTLEJOHN
35 Asst VP for Student Affairs ....Vacant
15 Assoc Director Human Resources ....Ms. Susan DACEY
07 Assoc Director Of Admissions .... Ms. Julia DELBAGNO
18 Supervisor of Buildings & Grounds ....Mr. Peter DOYLE
85 Coord Intl Admissions/Student Svcs .... Mr. Jorge FERNANDEZ
38 Director Personal Counseling .... Ms. Nicole PALAGANO
42 Dir Spiritual Life/College Chaplain ....Vacant
41 Director of Athletics ....Ms. Sheila WOOTEN
121 Dir Center Academic Development .Ms. Leah BROWN-JOHNSON
19 Director of Security ....Mr. David REILLY
39 Director Res Educ & Housing ....Mr. Derrick HICKS
105 Webmaster ....Mr. Matt SHILLITANI
14 Director Institutional Technology ....Mr. Yifeng BAI

Brookdale Community College (B)

Newman Springs Road, Lincroft NJ 07738-1597
County: Monmouth — FICE Identification: 008404
Unit ID: 183859
Telephone: (732) 842-1900 — Carnegie Class: Assoc/MT-VT-High Trad
FAX Number: (732) 224-2242 — Calendar System: Other
URL: www.brookdalecc.edu
Established: 1967 — Annual Undergrad Tuition & Fees (In-District): $8,804
Enrollment: 10,438 — Coed
Affiliation or Control: State/Local — IRS Status: 501(c)3
Highest Offering: Associate Degree
Accreditation: M, ACFEI, ADNUR, COARC, CSHSE, RAD

01 President ....Dr. David M. STOUT
05 Vice President for Academic Affairs ....Dr. Matthew REED
10 VP of Finance & Operations .... Ms. Teresa MANFREDA
86 Exec Dir Govt & Comm Rels .... Mr. Edward JOHNSON
32 Assoc VP of Student Affairs ....Dr. Yesenia MADAS
15 Assoc VP HR & Organizational Safety .... Ms. Patricia SENSI
08 Director of Library ....Mr. Steven CHUDNICK
45 Assoc VP Plng & Inst Effectiveness .... Dr. Nancy KEGELMAN
26 Int Exec Director College Relations .... Ms. Kathy KAMATANI
111 VP of Advancement ....Ms. Nancy KAARI
88 Dir of Student Life & Activities .... Ms. Lauren BRUTSMAN
37 Director of Financial Aid .... Ms. Stephanie FITZSIMMONS
25 Director Grants & Institutional Dev ..... Ms. Laura V. QAISSAUNEE
35 Exec Dir Student Services ....Mr. Christopher JEUNE
06 Registrar ....Ms. Eleanor GLAZEWSKI
09 Dir of Inst Research/Evaluation ....Dr. Laura LONGO
104 Director of International Center .... Ms. Janice THOMAS
13 Chief Information Officer (CIO) .... Mr. George SOTIRION
19 Police Chief ....Mr. Robert KIMLER
41 Dir Athletics & Recreation ....Ms. Katelyn AMUNDSON
76 Dean of Health Sciences ....Dr. Jayne EDMAN
50 Dean Business/Social Science ....Dr. Norah KERR-MCCURRY
81 Int Dean of STEM ....Dr. Jim CROWDER
106 Assoc VP Educ Access/Innovation .... Dr. William BURNS
79 Dean Humanities Inst ....Dr. Christine WEBSTER-HANSEN
04 Senior Asst to President & BOT ....Ms. Cynthia GRUSKOS
18 Mgr Facilities/Construction .... Mr. Michael NAPARLO
84 Exec Dir Enrollment Services ....Ms. Mary Beth REILLY
51 Dean of Cont & Prof Studies ....Dr. Joan SCOCCO
43 Exec Assoc of Legal Services ....Ms. Bonnie PASSARELLA
36 Exec Dir Career & Transfer Pathways .... Dr. Sarah MCELROY
28 Dir Diversity/Inclusion & CCOG ....Ms. Angela KARIOTIS
07 Director of Admissions ....Ms. Kristin WORTHLEY

Brookdale Community College Freehold Campus (C)

3680 US Highway 9 South, Freehold NJ 07728
Telephone: (732) 780-0020 — Identification: 770125
Accreditation: &M

Caldwell University (D)

120 Bloomfield Avenue, Caldwell NJ 07006-5310
County: Essex — FICE Identification: 002598
Unit ID: 183910
Telephone: (973) 618-3000 — Carnegie Class: Masters/M
FAX Number: (973) 618-3300 — Calendar System: Semester
URL: www.caldwell.edu
Established: 1939 — Annual Undergrad Tuition & Fees: $36,700
Enrollment: 2,274 — Coed
Affiliation or Control: Roman Catholic — IRS Status: 501(c)3
Highest Offering: Doctorate
Accreditation: M, ABAI, ACBSP, CACREP, CAEP, NURSE

01 President ....Dr. Matt WHELAN
05 Vice President for Academic Affairs ....Dr. Peter UBERTACCIO
15 Vice President Operations ....Mrs. Sheila N. O'ROURKE
32 Vice President for Student Affairs ....Sr. Kathleen TUITE
84 VP for Enrollment Management ....Mr. Stephen QUINN
30 Vice Pres Development/Alumni Affs ....Mr. Kevin BOYLE
10 Vice President Finance ....Mr. Shin MOON
50 Associate Dean School of Business ....Ms. Virginia RICH
53 Associate Dean School of Education ....Dr. Kevin BARNES
85 Director International Student Svcs ....Mr. Maulin JOSHI
112 Philanthropy Officer ....Ms. Christina HALL
06 University Registrar ....Mr. Ian K. WHITE
08 Director of Library ....Ms. Victoria SWANSON
58 Associate VP for Academic Affairs ....Dr. Ellina CHERNOBILSKY
38 Executive Director of Counseling .... Ms. Robin DAVENPORT
39 Assistant Dean Residence Life .... Ms. Crystal LOPEZ
13 Assistant Vice President and CIO ....Mr. Anthony YANG
36 Dir Career Plng & Development ....Ms. Geraldine PERRET
37 Director Financial Aid ....Ms. Eileen FELSKE
41 Asst Vice Pres & Dir of Athletics ....Mr. Mark A. CORINO
26 Director News and Media Relations ....Ms. Colette LIDDY
19 Executive Director Campus Safety ....Mr. Glenn GATES
91 Exec Director Application Support ....Mr. David BOHNY
16 Asst VP of Human Resources ....Mrs. Michelle STAUSS
35 Asst Dean Student Engagement .. Mr. Timothy KESSLER-CLEARY
106 Dir Online Education ....Ms. Soheila KOBLER
04 Administrative Asst to President .... Ms. Sharon KIEVIT
09 Exec Dir of Inst Research/Planning ....Dr. Susan HAYES
124 Asst Dean Advisement and Retention ....Ms. Henrieta GENFI
102 Dir Foundation/Corporate Relations ....Ms. Pat LEVINS
105 Director Web Services ....Mr. Matt NETTER
42 Director of Campus Ministry ....Ms. Colleen O'BRIEN
29 Director Alumni Affairs ....Ms. Meghan MORAN
07 Director of Admissions ....Mr. Jan Marco JIRAS
18 Chief Facilities/Physical Plnt Ofcr ....Mr. Raymond WILLIAMS

Camden County College (E)

PO Box 200, Blackwood NJ 08012-0200
County: Camden — FICE Identification: 006865
Unit ID: 183938
Telephone: (856) 227-7200 — Carnegie Class: Assoc/MT-VT-Mix Trad/Non
FAX Number: (856) 374-4894 — Calendar System: Semester
URL: www.camdencc.edu
Established: 1967 — Annual Undergrad Tuition & Fees (In-District): $4,680
Enrollment: 8,122 — Coed
Affiliation or Control: State/Local — IRS Status: 501(c)3
Highest Offering: Associate Degree
Accreditation: M, CAHIIM, DA, DH, DIETT, DNUR, OPD

01 President ....Mr. Donald BORDEN
45 VP Institutional Effectiveness .... Dr. Lovell PUGH-BASSETT
05 Vice Pres Academic Affairs .... Dr. David EDWARDS
32 Exec Dean Student Affairs ....Ms. Anne DALY-EIMER
10 Exec Dir Finance & Planning ....Ms. Helen ANTONAKAKIS
11 Exec Dir Financial Admin Svcs ....Mr. Maris KUKAINIS
15 Executive Director Human Resources ....Ms. Kathleen KANE
61 Exec Dean School/Cmty Academic Pgm ...... Ms. Margo VENABLE
13 Chief Info Technology Officer (CIO) ....Mr. Jack POST
43 Dir Legal Services/General Counsel .... Mr. Karl MCCONNELL
108 Dean Academic Affairs ....Dr. Teresa A. SMITH
09 Dean Inst Research/Plng/ Grants .... Dr. Rebecca FIDLER-SHEPPARD
81 Dean Math/Science/Health Careers ....Mr. John STEINER
79 Dean Liberal Arts/Profess Studies .... Dr. Michael NESTER
12 Exec Dean Camden City Campus ....Vacant
07 Dir Admissions/Registration Svcs .... Mr. Steve D'AMBROSIO
37 Executive Director of Financial Aid ....Ms. Felicia BRYANT
19 Director Public Safety ....Mr. John SCHUCK
29 External Resources Devel Associate ....Ms. Melissa DALY
88 Director of Testing ....Mr. Daniel MCMASTERS
26 Director of Communications ....Mr. Ronald TOMASELLO
08 Director Library Services ....Ms. Isabel GRAY
41 Athletic Director ....Mr. William BANKS

Camden County College Camden City Campus (F)

200 N Broadway, Camden NJ 08102-1185
Telephone: (856) 338-1817 — Identification: 770126
Accreditation: &M

Centenary University (G)

400 Jefferson Street, Hackettstown NJ 07840-2100
County: Warren — FICE Identification: 002599
Unit ID: 183974
Telephone: (908) 852-1400 — Carnegie Class: Masters/M
FAX Number: (908) 850-9508 — Calendar System: Semester
URL: www.centenaryuniversity.edu
Established: 1867 — Annual Undergrad Tuition & Fees: $34,498
Enrollment: 1,629 — Coed
Affiliation or Control: Independent Non-Profit — IRS Status: 501(c)3
Highest Offering: Doctorate
Accreditation: M, CAEPT, IACBE, SW

01 President ....Dr. Bruce MURPHY
05 VP for Academic Affairs ....Dr. Amy D'OLIVO
10 VP for Business & Finance ....Mr. Denton STARGEL
84 VP for Enrollment Mgmt & Marketing . Dr. Robert L. MILLER, JR.
32 VP for Student Life/Dean of Stdnts ....Ms. Kerry MULLINS
15 Director for Human Resources ....Ms. Christine ROSADO
18 Director of Facilities ....Mr. Jonathan MIRABAL
09 Coordinator Institutional Research ....Ms. Ying WANG
35 Sr Director Student Engagement ....Ms. Tiffany KUSHNER
06 Registrar .... Ms. Christine VANDENBERG
08 Int Dir Taylor Memorial Library ....Ms. Maryanne FEGAN
36 Asst Director Career Development ....Mr. Aaron RATZAN
41 Director of Athletics ....Mr. Travis SPENCER
19 Chief of Campus Safety ....Mr. Leonard KUNZ
38 Director of Counseling Center ....Vacant
13 Chief Information Officer ....Ms. Sharon AINSLEY
04 Exec Assistant to the President ....Ms. Diane LYNCH

Chamberlain University-North Brunswick (H)

630 US Highway One, North Brunswick NJ 08902
Telephone: (732) 875-1300 — Identification: 770850
Accreditation: &HLC, NURSE

† Branch campus of Chamberlain University-Addison, Addison, IL

The College of New Jersey (I)

2000 Pennington Road, Ewing NJ 08628-1104
County: Mercer — FICE Identification: 002642
Unit ID: 187134
Telephone: (609) 771-1855 — Carnegie Class: Masters/L
FAX Number: (609) 637-5191 — Calendar System: Semester
URL: www.tcnj.edu
Established: 1855 — Annual Undergrad Tuition & Fees (In-State): $16,029
Enrollment: 7,783 — Coed
Affiliation or Control: State — IRS Status: 501(c)3
Highest Offering: Master's
Accreditation: M, ART, CACREP, CAEPN, MUS, NURSE

01 President ....Dr. Kathryn A. FOSTER
05 Provost/VP Academic Affairs ....Mr. Jeffrey OSBORN
10 Vice President & Treasurer ....Mr. Lloyd RICKETTS
43 Vice President & General Counsel .... Mr. Thomas MAHONEY
111 Vice Pres for College Advancement ....Mr. John DONOHUE
32 Vice President Student Affairs ....Mr. Sean STALLINGS
28 Vice Pres Inclusive Excellence .... Mr. James FELTON, III
84 Vice Pres Enrollment Management ....Ms. Lisa ANGELONI
11 VP for Operations ....Dr. Sharon BLANTON
100 Chief of Staff/Secy to Board ....Ms. Heather FEHN
30 Assoc Vice President of Development .... Mr. Charles WRIGHT
35 Asst Vice Pres Student Services ....Dr. Kelly HENNESSY
20 Vice Provost .... Dr. Timothy CLYDESDALE
57 Dean School of The Arts & Comm .... Dr. Maurice HALL
50 Dean School of Business .... Dr. Kathryn JERVIS
79 Dean Sch Humanities/Soc Sci ....Dr. Jane WONG
53 Dean School of Education ....Dr. Suzanne MCCOTTER
54 Interim Dean School of Engineering ....Dr. Steve O'BRIEN
66 Dean Nursing/Health/Exercise Sci .... Dr. Carole KENNER
81 Interim Dean School of Science .... Dr. Amanda NORVELL
58 Director for Grad Studies ....Mr. Michael ELLARD
37 Exec Dir of Student Fin Assistance .... Mr. Wil CASAINE
09 Assoc Provost Ctr Inst Effective ....Vacant
41 Exec Director of Athletics ....Ms. Amanda DEMARTINO
29 Director of Alumni Engagement .... Ms. Amy WALTON
26 Assoc VP Comm/Mktg/Brand Mgmt ....Mr. David MUHA
18 Director of Campus Construction .... Mr. William RUDEAU
23 Director for Health Services .... Ms. Janice VERMEYCHUK
06 Exec Director Records/Registration ....Mr. Frank COOPER
19 Director of Campus Police ....Chief Timothy GRANT
96 Exec Dir Procurement Services ....Mr. Anup KAPUR
07 Exec Dir Admissions/Enrollment Mgmt ...... Ms. Grecia MONTERO
36 Director Career Center ....Ms. Shannon CONKLIN
38 AVP/Director Counseling/Psych Svcs .... Dr. Mark FOREST

County College of Morris (J)

214 Center Grove Road, Randolph NJ 07869-2086
County: Morris — FICE Identification: 007729
Unit ID: 184180
Telephone: (973) 328-5000 — Carnegie Class: Assoc/HT-High Trad
FAX Number: (973) 328-1282 — Calendar System: Semester
URL: www.ccm.edu

Established: 1965 Annual Undergrad Tuition & Fees (In-District): $9,720
Enrollment: 6,697 Coed
Affiliation or Control: State/Local IRS Status: 501(c)3
Highest Offering: Associate Degree
Accreditation: M, ACBSP, ADNUR, COARC, RAD

01 President .... Dr. Anthony J. IACONO
05 Vice President of Academic Affairs .... Dr. John MARLIN
10 Vice President of Business/Finance .... Ms. Karen VANDERHOOF
32 VP of Student Development .... Dr. Bette M. SIMMONS
102 Exec Dir Foundation .... Ms. Katie OLSEN
15 VP Human Resources & Labor Rels .... Ms. Vivyen RAY
09 Dean Inst Research .... Ms. Phebe SOLIMAN
114 Director Budget & Business Services .... Vacant
25 Director Resource Development .... Dr. Katrina BELL
07 Admissions Officer .... Ms. Donna TATARKA
37 Director Financial Aid .... Mr. Harvey WILLIS
06 Registrar .... Ms. Laura Lee BOWENS
26 Chief Public Relations Officer .... Ms. Kathleen BRUNET
29 Director Alumni Office .... Ms. Barbara CAPSOURAS
13 VP Institutional Effectiveness/CIO .... Mr. Robert STIRTON
08 Dean Learning Resource Ctr .... Ms. Heather CRAVEN
36 Director Career Svcs/Coop Education .... Ms. Denise SCHMIDT
38 Counseling Services Coordinator .... Ms. Janique CAFFIE
49 Interim Dean Liberal Arts .... Ms. Nieves GRUNEIRO
50 Dean Business/Math/Eng/Tech .... Dr. Kathleen NAASZ
76 Dean Health Prof/Natural Sciences .... Dr. Maria ISAZA
103 VP Workforce Dev/Prof Studies .... Mr. Patrick ENRIGHT
19 Director Security & Safety .... Mr. Steven ACKERMAN
41 Director Athletics .... Mr. Jack SULLIVAN
23 Health Services Coordinator .... Ms. Elizabeth HOBAN
18 Director of Plant & Maintenance .... Vacant
96 Manager of Purchasing .... Ms. Joanne KEARNS
40 Bookstore Manager .... Mr. Jeff LUBNOW

Drew University (A)

36 Madison Avenue, Madison NJ 07940-1493
County: Morris FICE Identification: 002603
Unit ID: 184348
Telephone: (973) 408-3000 Carnegie Class: Bac-A&S
FAX Number: N/A Calendar System: 4/1/4
URL: www.drew.edu
Established: 1866 Annual Undergrad Tuition & Fees: $40,960
Enrollment: 2,229 Coed
Affiliation or Control: Independent Non-Profit IRS Status: 501(c)3
Highest Offering: Doctorate
Accreditation: M, CAEP, THEOL

01 President .... Mr. Thomas SCHWARZ
05 Chief Academic Officer .... Dr. Jessica LAKIN
111 Vice Pres Advancement .... Mr. Bret SILVER
10 Interim Vice Pres Finance .... Mr. Michael WARD
73 Interim Dean Theological School .... Dr. Melanie JOHNSON-DEBAUFRE
08 University Librarian .... Mr. Andrew BONAMICI
32 Vice President Student Life .... Dr. Frank MERCKX
26 Director Communications & Marketing .... Ms. Kristen WILLIAMS
15 Director of Human Resources .... Ms. Maria FORCE
22 Title IX Coordinator .... Dr. Frank MERCKX
18 Director Facilities Operations .... Mr. Greg SMITH
07 Dean of Admissions .... Ms. Colby MCCARTHY
19 Director Public Safety .... Vacant
23 Director Health Services .... Ms. Joan GALBRAITH
35 Dean of Student Activities .... Ms. Michelle BRISSON
88 Director Theological Admissions .... Mr. Kevin D. MILLER
123 Director Graduate Admissions .... Mr. Kevin D. MILLER
09 Director Institutional Research .... Ms. Nadine HYLTON
41 Director Athletics .... Ms. Christa RACINE
06 Registrar .... Ms. Stephanie CALDWELL
40 Manager Bookstore .... Ms. Marie JOYNER
04 Administrative Asst to President .... Ms. Kathleen SUTHERLAND
100 Chief of Staff .... Ms. Barb BRESNAHAN
104 Director Study Abroad .... Ms. Stacy FISCHER
105 Webmaster .... Mr. Justin JACKSON
13 Interim Chief Technology Officer .... Mr. Christopher DARRELL
29 Director Alumni Relations .... Ms. Carol BASSIE
43 Director Legal Services .... Ms. Meredith PALMER
39 Dir Resident Life/Student Housing .... Ms. Stephanie PELHAM
20 Assoc Prov Exp Educ & Career .... Dr. Daniel PASCOE AGUILAR

Eastern International College (B)

684 Newark Avenue, Jersey City NJ 07306
County: Hudson FICE Identification: 031226
Unit ID: 421878
Telephone: (201) 216-9901 Carnegie Class: Spec-4-yr-Other Health
FAX Number: (201) 533-1027 Calendar System: Semester
URL: www.eicollege.edu
Established: 1990 Annual Undergrad Tuition & Fees: $16,442
Enrollment: 292 Coed
Affiliation or Control: Proprietary IRS Status: Proprietary
Highest Offering: Baccalaureate
Accreditation: M, ADNUR, CVT, DH

01 CEO/President .... Dr. Bashir MOHSEN
05 VP of Academic Affairs .... Vacant
06 Registrar/Bursar .... Mrs. Tina HAMILTON
11 Campus Director .... Ms. Agnieszka DRUPKA
36 Corporate Director of Career Svcs .... Ms. Jennifer GONZALEZ
37 Director Student Financial Aid .... Ms. Ashley KENDE
20 Dean of Academic Affairs .... Dr. Kristine SOUTHARD
13 Chief Info Technology Officer (CIO) .... Ms. Brynn DEPREY
32 Student Student Services .... Ms. Jennifer GONZALEZ
38 Student Counseling Officer .... Ms. Maria BILLINGS
08 Head Librarian .... Ms. Kelsey GALLAGHER
22 Chief EEO Officer & Legal Liaison .... Mr. George CACERES

Eastern International College-Belleville Campus (C)

251 Washington Avenue, Belleville NJ 07109
Telephone: (973) 751-9051 Identification: 770580
Accreditation: &M

Eastwick College (D)

250 Moore Street, Hackensack NJ 07601
County: Bergen Identification: 667131
Unit ID: 183488
Telephone: (201) 488-9400 Carnegie Class: Assoc/HVT-High Non
FAX Number: (201) 488-1007 Calendar System: Quarter
URL: www.eastwick.edu
Established: 1985 Annual Undergrad Tuition & Fees: $16,797
Enrollment: 533 Coed
Affiliation or Control: Proprietary IRS Status: Proprietary
Highest Offering: Baccalaureate
Accreditation: ACCSC, FUSER

01 President .... Thomas M. EASTWICK
11 Director Hackensack Campus .... Joyce MARCHIONE-TRAINA
05 Dean of Academics .... Dawood GUIRGUIS

Eastwick College (E)

103 Park Avenue, Nutley NJ 07110
County: Essex FICE Identification: 020923
Unit ID: 185721
Telephone: (973) 661-0600 Carnegie Class: Assoc/HVT-Mix Trad/Non
FAX Number: (973) 661-2954 Calendar System: Quarter
URL: www.eastwick.edu
Established: 2014 Annual Undergrad Tuition & Fees: $15,806
Enrollment: 455 Coed
Affiliation or Control: Proprietary IRS Status: Proprietary
Highest Offering: Associate Degree
Accreditation: ACCSC

01 President .... Thomas EASTWICK
11 Vice Pres of Operations .... Bhavna TAILOR
05 Dean of Academics .... Sameh FARAGALLA
06 Registrar .... Rocio SANCHEZ
13 Chief Information Technology Office .... Joseph NEYMAN
37 Director Student Financial Aid .... Marlyn RABELO

Eastwick College (F)

10 South Franklin Turnpike, Ramsey NJ 07446
County: Bergen FICE Identification: 020537
Unit ID: 184959
Telephone: (201) 327-8877 Carnegie Class: Spec-4-yr-Other Health
FAX Number: (201) 327-9054 Calendar System: Other
URL: www.eastwick.edu
Established: 1968 Annual Undergrad Tuition & Fees: $16,882
Enrollment: 781 Coed
Affiliation or Control: Proprietary IRS Status: Proprietary
Highest Offering: Baccalaureate
Accreditation: ACCSC, CVT, OTA, SURGT

01 President .... Thomas EASTWICK
03 Executive Vice President .... Rafael CASTILLA
05 Vice President Academic Affairs .... Joyce TRAINA
11 Vice Pres Operations .... Bhavna TAILOR
07 Director of Admissions .... Letitia BURKE
36 Director Career Development .... Jennifer BATE
37 Corp Director of Financial Aid .... Christy DELAGUERRA

Essex County College (G)

303 University Avenue, Newark NJ 07102-1798
County: Essex FICE Identification: 007107
Unit ID: 184481
Telephone: (973) 877-3000 Carnegie Class: Assoc/MT-VT-High Trad
FAX Number: (973) 877-3044 Calendar System: Other
URL: www.essex.edu
Established: 1966 Annual Undergrad Tuition & Fees (In-District): $8,790
Enrollment: 6,360 Coed
Affiliation or Control: State/Local IRS Status: 501(c)3
Highest Offering: Associate Degree
Accreditation: M, ACBSP, ADNUR, OPD, PTAA, RAD

01 Interim President .... Dr. Augustine A. BOAKYE
04 Liaison to the President/BOT .... Ms. Jonell CONGLETON
10 Chief Financial Officer .... Mr. George PETERSON
21 Deputy Chief Financial Officer .... Mr. Evens WAGNAC
05 Exec Dean of Faculty & Academics .... Dr. Alvin WILLIAMS
108 Exec Dir Inst Planning/Assessment .... Mr. John RUNFELDT
111 Exec Dir Inst Advancement .... Mr. Alfred BUNDY
15 Exec Director Human Resources .... Ms. Yvette HENRY
13 Exec Dean/CIO Admin & Learning Tech .... Mr. Mohamed SEDDIKI
32 Dean Student Affairs .... Dr. Keith KIRKLAND
106 Assoc Dean Online Learning Resource .... Dr. Leigh BELLO-DECASTRO
09 Director Institutional Research .... Dr. Jinsoo PARK
51 Dean Cmty/Continuing Educ/Wkfce Dev .... Dr. Elvira VIEIRA
08 Director MLK Library .... Vacant
35 Assoc Dean Student Life/Development .... Ms. Patricia SLADE
18 Director Facilities Mgmt .... Mr. Jeff SHAPIRO
19 Director Public Safety .... Mr. Anthony CROMARTIE
96 Director Purchasing .... Vacant
37 Director Financial Aid .... Mr. David SMEDLEY
113 Director Bursar's Office .... Ms. Darlene MILLER
36 Director Student Devel & Counsel .... Dr. S. Aisha STEPLIGHT JOHNSON
88 Director Child Development Center .... Ms. Virginia FLANIGAN
41 Director Athletics .... Mr. Michael DOUGHTIE
24 Chief of Operations Media Prod Tech .... Mr. Eugene JACKSON
00 President Emeritus .... Dr. A. Zachary YAMBA
06 Registrar .... Mrs. Zewdnesh KASSA
43 General Counsel .... Ms. Joy TOLLIVER
84 Director Enrollment Management .... Vacant
88 Director Men & Women of Excellence .... Mr. Ledawn HALL
88 Deputy General Counsel & CCO .... Mr. Syrion JACK
102 Director Foundation/Corporate Rels .... Ms. Yvette JEFFERIES
103 Director Workforce Development .... Mrs. Sanghamitra CHOUDHURY
104 Director Study Abroad .... Dr. Akil KHALFANI

Essex County College-West Essex Branch Campus (H)

730 West Bloomfield Avenue, West Caldwell NJ 07006
Telephone: (973) 877-6590 Identification: 770127
Accreditation: &M

Fairleigh Dickinson University (I)

1000 River Road, Teaneck NJ 07666-1996
County: Bergen FICE Identification: 002607
Unit ID: 184603
Telephone: (201) 692-2000 Carnegie Class: Masters/L
FAX Number: N/A Calendar System: Semester
URL: www.fdu.edu
Established: 1942 Annual Undergrad Tuition & Fees: $42,240
Enrollment: 7,479 Coed
Affiliation or Control: Independent Non-Profit IRS Status: 501(c)3
Highest Offering: Doctorate
Accreditation: M, CACREP, CAEP, CLPSY, NURSE, PHAR, @SW

01 President .... Dr. Christopher CAPUANO
43 General Counsel & CCO .... Mr. Edward SILVER
05 University Provost/Sr VP Acad Affs .... Dr. Gillian SMALL
03 Sr VP for University Operations .... Dr. Robert PIGNATELLO
111 Sr Vice Pres University Advancement .... Mr. Jason AMORE
10 Senior VP for Finance & COO .... Ms. Hania FERRARA
18 VP for Facilities & Auxiliary Svcs .... Mr. Richard A. FRICK
84 VP Enrollment/Planning & Effect .... Dr. Luke D. SCHULTHEIS
13 VP/Chief Information Officer .... Mr. Neal M. STURM
32 VP for Student Affairs/DOS .... Dr. Uchenna BAKER
07 AVP Admissions/Fin Aid/Enrollment .... Ms. Traci BANKS
26 Associate VP Communications .... Mr. Angelo CARFAGNA
15 Associate VP Human Resources .... Ms. Rose D'AMBROSIO
06 AVP Enrollment Services/Registrar .... Ms. Carol CREEKMORE
21 Assoc VP for Finance .... Mr. Frank BARRA
104 Vice Provost for International Affs .... Dr. Jason SCORZA
44 Manager of Donor Relations .... Mr. Richard DATZKO-BANTA
49 Interim Dean Becton Col Arts & Sci .... Dr. David ROSEN
50 Dean College Business Admin .... Dr. Pierre BALTHAZARD
08 Assoc University Librarian-Florham .... Ms. Brigid BURKE
08 University Librarian .... Ms. Ana M. FONTOURA
88 Dir Public Administration Institute .... Dr. William ROBERTS
116 Director Internal Audit .... Ms. Agnes SCAGLIONE
53 Dir School of Education .... Dr. Vicki COHEN
66 Director Sch of Nurs/Allied Health .... Dr. Minerva GUTTMAN
41 Director of Athletics-Metro .... Mr. Bradford D. HURLBUT
41 Director of Athletics-Florham .... Ms. Jennifer NOON
07 Univ Dir of Undergrad Admissions .... Mr. Andrew IPPOLITO
09 Director of Institutional Research .... Dr. Sam MICHALOWSKI
37 University Director Financial Aid .... Ms. Renee VOLAK
19 Dir Public Safety-Florham Campus .... Mr. Joseph VITIELLO
19 Director Public Safety-Metro Campus .... Mr. David A. MILES
12 Assoc VP Univ Operations Metro .... Dr. Steven NELSON
12 Exec Dir Florham Campus Operations .... Dr. Brian MAURO
96 Director of Purchasing .... Ms. Juliette BROOKS
04 Assistant to the President .... Ms. Jeanne MAZZOLLA
25 Univ Dir Grants/Sponsored Projects .... Ms. Jane TSAMBIS
36 University Dir Career Development .... Ms. Donna ROBERTSON
117 Risk Manager .... Ms. Gail LEMAIRE
88 Florham Assoc Dean of Students .... Ms. Pamela MESSINA
88 Metro Assoc Dean of Students .... Mr. Vidal LOPEZ-MARRERO

Felician University (J)

262 S Main Street, Lodi NJ 07644-2198
County: Bergen FICE Identification: 002610
Unit ID: 184612
Telephone: (201) 559-6000 Carnegie Class: Masters/M
FAX Number: (201) 559-6188 Calendar System: Semester
URL: www.felician.edu
Established: 1942 Annual Undergrad Tuition & Fees: $35,000
Enrollment: 2,556 Coed
Affiliation or Control: Roman Catholic IRS Status: 501(c)3
Highest Offering: Doctorate
Accreditation: M, CAEPT, COPSY, IACBE, MPCAC, NURSE

01 President .... Mr. James W. CRAWFORD, III

05 Acting Vice Pres Academic Affairs .... Dr. Christine CLOUTIER MIHAL
20 Asst VP Academic Support Services .... Dr. Ann V. GUILLORY
10 VP for Business/Finance/CFO .... Mr. Thomas TRUCHAN
111 Vice Pres University Advancement .... Ms. Maura DENICOLA
84 VP Enroll Mgmt/Mktg & Registrar .... Ms. Priscilla KLYMENKO
11 Vice Pres Administration .... Vacant
32 VP Student Affairs/Dean of Students .... Dr. Ronald A. GRAY
123 Assoc Vice Pres Grad & Intl Enroll .... Mr. Michael SZAREK
13 Asst VP of Information Technology .... Mr. Christopher FINCH
07 AVP of Admissions .... Ms. Camile BRAKER-BALKUM
04 Exec Asst to Pres/Sec to Board .... Ms. Stephanie CACHEZ
15 Director of Human Resources .... Ms. Virginia TOPOLSKI
37 Exec Director Student Financial Aid .... Ms. Cynthia MONTALVO
39 Director of Residence Life .... Ms. Laura PIEROTTI
36 Director of Career Development Ctr .... Ms. Tiffany AUSTIN
24 Director Audio Visual Services .... Mr. Anthony KLYMENKO
88 Assoc Director Center for Learning .... Mr. Hamdi SHAHIN
53 Dean School of Education .... Dr. Stephanie MCGOWAN
49 Dean School of Arts/Science .... Dr. Mildred MIHLON
66 Dean School of Nursing .... Dr. Christine CLOUTIER MIHAL
50 Dean School of Business .... Dr. Heather PFLEGER
121 Dean Academic Success Programs .... Dr. Dolores HENCHY
23 Director Health Services .... Ms. Carolyn LEWIS
41 Director of Athletics .... Mr. Benjamin DINALLO, JR.
92 Director Honors Program .... Dr. Jeffrey BLANCHARD

Georgian Court University (A)

900 Lakewood Avenue, Lakewood NJ 08701-2697
County: Ocean FICE Identification: 002608
Unit ID: 184773
Telephone: (732) 987-2200 Carnegie Class: Masters/M
FAX Number: N/A Calendar System: Semester
URL: www.georgian.edu
Established: 1908 Annual Undergrad Tuition & Fees: $33,640
Enrollment: 2,231 Coed
Affiliation or Control: Roman Catholic IRS Status: 501(c)3
Highest Offering: Master's
Accreditation: M, ACBSP, CACREP, CAEPT, NURSE, SW

01 President .... Dr. Joseph R. MARBACH
05 Provost .... Dr. Janice WARNER
10 VP Finance/Chief Financial Officer .... Ms. Amy BOSIO
111 Vice Pres Institutional Advancement .... Mr. Matthew MANFRA
84 VP of Enrollment & Retention .... Mr. Chris KRZAK
20 Assoc Provost Academic Pgm Devel .... Dr. Michael GROSS
124 Associate VP for Student Retention .... Ms. Kathleen BOODY
32 Dean of Students .... Dr. Amani JENNINGS
42 Director of Campus Ministry .... Mr. Jeff SCHAFFER
41 Director Athletics/Recreation .... Ms. Laura LIESMAN
50 Dean School of Business .... Dr. Jennifer EDMONDS
53 Dean of School of Education .... Dr. Amuhelang MAGAYA
49 Dean School of Arts & Sciences .... Dr. Mary CHINERY
09 Director of Institutional Research .... Mr. Wayne ARNDT
08 Director of Library Services .... Mr. Jeffrey DONNELLY
06 Registrar .... Ms. Kathleen BOODY
21 Controller .... Ms. Kristen NAGLE
15 Director of Human Resources .... Ms. Dianna SOFO
13 Chief Information Officer .... Mr. AJ LACOMBA
37 Director of Financial Aid .... Ms. Cynthia MCCARTHY
26 Exec Dir of Marketing & Comm .... Ms. Gail TOWNS
88 Dir Conferences & Special Events .... Ms. Mary CRANWELL
29 Director of Alumni/Donor Relations .... Ms. Alicia SMITH
36 Director Career Services .... Ms. Ceceilia O'CALLAGHAN
38 Director of Counseling .... Dr. Robin SOLBACH
23 Director of Health Services .... Ms. Robin SOLBACH
18 Director of Facilities .... Mr. Michael PUTNAM
19 Director of Security .... Mr. Charles TIGHE
123 Director Graduate Admissions .... Mr. Jerred THOMPSON
39 Director of Residence Life .... Mr. Seth RICHARDS
04 Executive Asst to President .... Ms. Stephanie TEDESCO
105 Web Administrator .... Mr. Richard BERARDI
108 Asst VP for University Assessment .... Sr. Janet THIEL
96 Purchasing Coordinator .... Ms. Julie PARLACOSKI
30 Asst Vice Pres for Development .... Mr. Frank MASCIA
102 Dir Foundation/Corporate Relations .... Ms. Lori THOMAS

Hackensack Meridian School of Medicine (B)

123 Metro Blvd, Nutley NJ 07110
County: Essex FICE Identification: 042933
Unit ID: 495314
Telephone: (973) 542-6500 Carnegie Class: Not Classified
FAX Number: N/A Calendar System: Other
URL: www.hmsom.org
Established: 2020 Annual Undergrad Tuition & Fees: N/A
Enrollment: N/A Coed
Affiliation or Control: Independent Non-Profit IRS Status: 501(c)3
Highest Offering: First Professional Degree
Accreditation: @M, #MED

01 Founding Dean .... Dr. Bonita STANTON

Hudson County Community College (C)

70 Sip Avenue, Jersey City NJ 07306
County: Hudson FICE Identification: 012954
Unit ID: 184995
Telephone: (201) 714-7100 Carnegie Class: Assoc/HT-High Trad
FAX Number: (201) 656-1799 Calendar System: Semester
URL: www.hccc.edu
Established: 1974 Annual Undergrad Tuition & Fees (In-District): $8,390
Enrollment: 7,039 Coed
Affiliation or Control: State/Local IRS Status: 501(c)3
Highest Offering: Associate Degree
Accreditation: M, ACFEI, ADNUR, EMT, RAD

01 President .... Dr. Christopher M. REBER
05 Vice President Academic Affairs .... Dr. Darryl JONES
10 Vice Pres Business/Finance & CFO .... Ms. Veronica ZEICHNER
111 Vice Pres Planning/Development .... Dr. Nicholas CHIARAVALLOTI
15 Vice President Human Resources .... Ms. Anna KRUPITSKIY
32 VP for Student Affairs/Enrollment .... Mrs. Lisa DOUGHERTY
50 Assoc Dean Business and Science .... Ms. Catherine SIRANGELO-ELBADAWY
37 Executive Director Financial Aid .... Ms. Sylvia F. MENDOZA
88 Assoc Dean English and ESL .... Ms. Jenny BOBEA
06 Registrar .... Ms. Victoria ORELLANA
13 Chief Information Officer .... Ms. Patricia CLAY
07 Director of Admissions .... Mr. Matthew FESSLER
81 Dean of Instruction/Sciences .... Mr. Burl YEARWOOD
88 Director Testing & Assessment .... Ms. Darlery FRANCO
88 Interim Assoc Dean Culinary Arts .... Mr. Ara KARAKASHIAN
51 Assoc VP Cont Educ & Workforce Dev .... Ms. Lori MARGOLIN
21 Controller .... Mr. Geoffrey SIMS
25 Director of Grants .... Mr. Sean KERWICK
08 Librarian .... Vacant
35 Asst Dean Student Life & Leadership .... Ms. Veronica GEROSIMO
26 Director of Communications .... Ms. Jennifer CHRISTOPHER
121 Associate Dean Student Success .... Dr. Sheila DYNAN
40 Manager HCCC Bookstore .... Mr. Jose ORTIZ
96 Dir of Contracts and Procurement .... Mr. Jeff ROBERSON
19 Director Security/Safety .... Mr. John QUIGLEY
04 Executive Admin Asst to President .... Ms. Alexa RIANO
18 Exec Dir Engineering Operations .... Mr. Ilya ASHMYAN
08 Interim Dean of College Libraries .... Mr. James COX
106 Exec Dir Center for Online Learning .... Mr. Matthew LABRAKE
45 Exec Dir Institutional Research .... Mr. John SCANLON
28 VP Diversity/Equity and Inclusion .... Mr. Yeurys PUJOLS
29 Alumni Manager .... Ms. Maria LITA SARMIENTO

Jersey College (D)

546 US Highway 46, Teterboro NJ 07608
County: Bergen FICE Identification: 041341
Unit ID: 455196
Telephone: (201) 489-5836 Carnegie Class: Spec 2-yr-Health
FAX Number: (201) 525-0986 Calendar System: Quarter
URL: jerseycollege.edu
Established: 2003 Annual Undergrad Tuition & Fees: N/A
Enrollment: 3,514 Coed
Affiliation or Control: Proprietary IRS Status: Proprietary
Highest Offering: Associate Degree
Accreditation: COE, ADNUR

00 Chancellor .... Greg KARZHEVSKY
01 President .... Steven B. LITVACK
05 Provost .... Colette GARGIULO

Kean University (E)

1000 Morris Avenue, Union NJ 07083-0411
County: Union FICE Identification: 002622
Unit ID: 185262
Telephone: (908) 737-5326 Carnegie Class: Masters/L
FAX Number: (908) 737-4636 Calendar System: Semester
URL: www.kean.edu
Established: 1855 Annual Undergrad Tuition & Fees (In-State): $12,445
Enrollment: 14,064 Coed
Affiliation or Control: State IRS Status: 501(c)3
Highest Offering: Doctorate
Accreditation: M, #ARCPA, ART, #CAATE, CACREP, CAEP, CAEPN, CIDA, MUS, NUR, OT, PSPSY, PTA, SP, SW, THEA

01 President .... Dr. Lamont REPOLLET
10 SVP for Finance .... Mr. Andrew BRANNEN
11 SVP of Administration .... Dr. Michael SALVATORE
111 SVP of External Affairs .... Dr. Joseph YOUNGBLOOD
46 SVP for Research .... Dr. Jeffrey TONEY
05 Provost/VP Academic Affairs .... Vacant
32 Acting VP for Student Affairs .... Mr. Matthew CARUSO
26 VP University Relations .... Ms. Karen SMITH
100 Chief of Staff .... Ms. Audrey KELLY
45 SVP of Planning/Special Counsel .... Ms. Felice VAZQUEZ
12 Exec Vice Chancellor WKU .... Vacant
43 Assoc VP/Chief University Counsel .... Ms. Kristin GANLEY
84 VP Enrollment Services .... Ms. Marsha MCCARTHY
12 Assoc VP/Dean Kean Ocean .... Vacant
12 Acting Assoc VPAA Kean Wenzhou .... Mr. Yixin YANG
13 AVP Information Technology .... Mr. Joseph MARINELLO
20 Asst VP Academic Affairs .... Ms. Joy MOSKOVITZ
39 Asst VP Residential Stdnt Services .... Ms. Maximina RIVERA
18 Assoc VP Planning/Facilities .... Mr. Steve REMOTTI
08 Assoc VP University Library .... Mr. Paul CROFT
37 Asst VP Student Financial Services .... Mr. Faruque CHOWDHURY
58 Dean Nathan Weiss Grad Col .... Dr. Christine THORPE
53 Dean Col Education .... Dr. Barbara RIDENER
79 Acting Dean Col Liberal Arts .... Dr. Jonathan MERCANTINI
50 Dean Col Business & Public Mgt .... Dr. Jin WANG
81 Dean Col Nat & Applied Hlth Sci .... Dr. George CHANG
48 Dean Michael Graves Col .... Dr. David MOHNEY
106 Dean Online Learning .... Mr. Corey VIGDOR
15 Exec Dir Human Services .... Ms. Jennifer PETERS
108 Assoc Dir Accredit & Assessment .... Mr. Mukul ACHARYA
09 Dir Institutional Research .... Vacant
07 Dir of Admissions .... Mr. Carlos NAZARIO
114 Director Budget .... Ms. Jennifer STRAHAN
21 Dir General Accounting .... Mr. Joseph ANTONOWICZ
37 Dir Financial Aid .... Ms. Cheryl ZHANG
06 Registrar .... Ms. Aylin BRANDON
25 Dir Research & Sponsored Pgms .... Vacant
27 Assoc Dir University Relations .... Ms. Margaret MCCORRY
96 Dir for Procurement/Business Svcs .... Mr. Faruque CHOWDHURY
38 Dir Counseling & Disability Svcs .... Mr. Vidal ANNAN
65 Director for Sustainability .... Ms. Suzanne KUPIEC
104 Dir Center International Studies .... Ms. Katsumi KISHIDA
35 Asst VP for Student Affairs .... Mr. Scott SNOWDEN
19 Dir of Campus Police .... Mr. Anthony MONTICELLO
23 Dir for Health Services .... Ms. Robin MANSFIELD
88 Dir Veterans Student Services .... Mr. Vito ZAJDA
22 Dir Affirmative Action .... Vacant
04 Admin Assistant to the President .... Ms. Maris HENSON
28 Director of Diversity .... Dr. Alberta T. QUICK
41 Athletic Director .... Mr. David K. WILLIAMS
86 Director Government Relations .... Ms. Kelley LEDET

Mercer County Community College (F)

1200 Old Trenton Road, PO Box 17202, West Windsor NJ 08550
County: Mercer FICE Identification: 004740
Unit ID: 185509
Telephone: (609) 586-4800 Carnegie Class: Assoc/MT-VT-High Trad
FAX Number: (609) 570-3870 Calendar System: Semester
URL: www.mccc.edu
Established: 1966 Annual Undergrad Tuition & Fees (In-District): $5,814
Enrollment: 6,342 Coed
Affiliation or Control: State/Local IRS Status: 501(c)3
Highest Offering: Associate Degree
Accreditation: M, AAB, ADNUR, FUSER, MACTE, MLTAD, PTAA, RAD

01 President .... Dr. Jianping WANG
111 Vice President College Advancement .... Mr. Joseph CLAFFEY
05 Vice President for Academic Affairs .... Dr. Robert SCHREYER
10 Vice President for Admin & Finance .... Ms. Laura SCHEPPS
32 Interim Dean Student Support Svcs .... Dr. Tonia PERRY-CONLEY
15 Vice President for Human Resources .... Ms. Barbara BASEL
76 Dean Health Professions .... Mr. Kevin DUFFY
49 Interim Dean of Liberal Arts .... Dr. Dylan WOLFE
50 Interim Dean Business/Technology .... Ms. Laura SOSA
12 Dean of James Kerney Campus .... Dr. Tonia PERRY-CONLEY
13 Chief Information Officer .... Mr. Inder SINGH
21 Exec Dir of Finance .... Vacant
26 Director Marketing .... Mr. Francis PAIXAO
06 Registrar .... Vacant
37 Director of Financial Aid .... Mr. Thomas FOGA
09 Senior Dir Institutional Research .... Ms. Nina MAY
18 Chief Facilities/Physical Plant .... Mr. Bryon MARSHALL
96 Director of Purchasing .... Mr. Steven QUATTRO
84 Dean Student Enrollment Management .... Ms. Savita BAMBHROLIA
08 Director of Library Services .... Ms. Pam PRICE
101 Exec Asst to the President/Board .... Ms. Beth BROWER
104 Coord of Global Education .... Dr. Andrea LYNCH
106 Dean Innov/Online Educ/Stdnt Suc .... Dr. Gonzalo PEREZ
25 Chief Contracts/Grants Admin .... Ms. Eileen SWIATKOWSKI
36 Director Transfer & Career Services .... Vacant
41 Athletic Director .... Mr. John SIMONE
108 Dean Inst Effectiveness .... Dr. Elizabeth ANDERSON
19 Director Security/Safety .... Mr. Bryon MARSHALL
29 Director Alumni Affairs .... Vacant

Middlesex College (G)

2600 Woodbridge Avenue, Edison NJ 08818-3050
County: Middlesex FICE Identification: 002615
Unit ID: 185536
Telephone: (732) 548-6000 Carnegie Class: Assoc/MT-VT-High Trad
FAX Number: (732) 494-8244 Calendar System: Semester
URL: www.middlesexcc.edu
Established: 1964 Annual Undergrad Tuition & Fees (In-District): $7,416
Enrollment: 10,084 Coed
Affiliation or Control: State/Local IRS Status: 501(c)3
Highest Offering: Associate Degree
Accreditation: M, ADNUR, DH, DIETT, RAD

01 President .... Dr. Mark MCCORMICK
05 VP Academic Affairs .... Dr. Linda SCHERR
10 Chief Financial Officer .... Mr. Frank MALTINO
111 VP for Institutional Advancement .... Ms. Michelle CAMPBELL
108 VP Institutional Effectiveness .... Dr. Jeffrey HERRON
103 Exec Dir Workforce Dev/Lifelong Lrn .... Ms. Joanie COFFARO
18 Exec Director Facilities Management .... Mr. Donald DROST
84 Exec Dean Student & Enrollment Svcs .... Mr. José LAUREANO
13 Exec Director Information Tech .... Mr. John MATTALIANO
21 Controller .... Ms. Caryl CERQUA
07 Director Admissions & Recruitment .... Ms. Lisa RODRIGUEZ-GREGORY
06 Registrar .... Mr. Richard COLE
37 Financial Aid Director .... Ms. Taina MORALES
26 Chief Public Relations Officer .... Mr. Thomas PETERSON
96 Director of Purchasing .... Ms. Madeline CATERINICCHIO
09 Dean Inst Research/Assessment .... Ms. Meghan ALAI
25 Director Grants Development .... Ms. Yamillet FEBO-GOMEZ
29 Dir Development & Alumni Relations .... Ms. Lisa KELLY

04 Interim Admin Asst to President .... Ms. Bernadette ROA
15 Exec Director of Human Resources .... Mr. Joseph MORGAN
08 Director Library .... Ms. Marilyn OCHOA
49 Assistant Dean Liberal Arts .... Dr. Theresa OROSZ

Monmouth University (A)

400 Cedar Avenue, West Long Branch NJ 07764-1898
County: Monmouth　FICE Identification: 002616
Unit ID: 185572
Telephone: (732) 571-3400　Carnegie Class: Masters/L
FAX Number: (732) 571-3629　Calendar System: Semester
URL: www.monmouth.edu
Established: 1933　Annual Undergrad Tuition & Fees: $40,680
Enrollment: 5,674　Coed
Affiliation or Control: Independent Non-Profit　IRS Status: 501(c)3
Highest Offering: Doctorate
Accreditation: M, ARCPA, CACREP, CAEP, NURSE, SP, SW

01 President .... Dr. Patrick F. LEAHY
04 Exec Asst to President & BOT .... Ms. Annette GOUGH
05 Provost/SVP Academic Affairs .... Dr. Pamela SCOTT-JOHNSON
104 Director of Global Education .... Ms. MyKellann MALONEY
45 AVP Inst Research & Effectiveness ....Ms. Christine BENOL
06 Registrar .... Ms. Gloria SCHOPF
79 Int Dean Sch Humanities/Soc Sci ....Dr. Richard VEIT
50 Dean Leon Hess Business Sch .... Dr. Raj DEVASAGAYAM
53 Dean School of Education ....Dr. John HENNING
81 Dean Sch of Science .... Dr. Steven BACHRACH
66 Dean School of Nursing/Health Stds ....Dr. Ann Marie MAURO
70 Dean School of Social Work ....Dr. Robin MAMA
92 Dean Honors School .... Dr. Nancy MEZEY
08 University Librarian ....Mr. Kurt WAGNER
10 Vice President Finance .... Mr. William G. CRAIG
21 Assoc VP for Finance/Budgets ....Mr. Joseph A. PINGITORE
96 Director of Purchasing .... Mr. Mark MIRANDA
43 Vice President & General Counsel .... Mr. John J. CHRISTOPHER
117 Dir of Compliance/Risk Mgr .... Mr. Michael WUNSCH
22 Director Equity and Diversity .... Ms. Nina ANDERSON
18 Exec Dir Campus Plng & Facilities .... Mr. William SIEMER
19 Director/Chief of Police ....Capt. Dean VOLPE
15 Director of Human Resources ....Ms. Robyn SALVO
32 VP Student Life & Ldrshp Engagement ...... Mrs. Mary Anne NAGY
35 Assoc VP for Student Life .... Mr. James PILLAR
35 Dir Student Activities/Student Ctr ....Ms. Amy BELLINA
111 VP University Advancement .... Ms. Amanda KLAUS
26 Assoc VP Univ Mktg/Communications .... Ms. Tara PETERS
110 Assoc VP for Univ Advancement ....Mrs. Lucille FLYNN
84 Vice Pres Enrollment Management ....Dr. Robert MC CAIG
37 Assoc VP Enr Mgmt/Dir Fin Aid .... Ms. Claire ALASIO
07 Assoc VP for UG & GR Admission ... Ms. Lauren VENTO-CIFELLI
41 Director of Athletics .... Mr. Jeff STAPLETON
13 Vice Pres Information Management .....Dr. Edward CHRISTENSEN
36 Exec Director Career Development .... Ms. Beth M. RICCA
86 Dir of Government & Community Rels .... Mr. Paul DEMENT
27 Exec Director of Univ Communication .... Mr. Michael MAIDEN
39 Assoc Dir Res Life/Housing Ops ....Ms. Megan JONES
29 Sr Dir Alum Engage/Annual Giving ....Ms. Lindsay S. WOOD
38 Director Counseling & Psych Svcs .... Mr. Andrew LEE
100 Chief of Staff .... Ms. Emily B. MILLER-GONZALEZ
28 Director of Diversity ....Ms. Zaneta RAGO-CRAFT
44 Dir Alumni Engage/Annual Giving .... Ms. Laura MACDONALD

Montclair State University (B)

1 Normal Avenue, Montclair NJ 07043-9987
County: Essex and Passaic　FICE Identification: 002617
Unit ID: 185590
Telephone: (973) 655-4000　Carnegie Class: DU-Higher
FAX Number: N/A　Calendar System: Semester
URL: www.montclair.edu
Established: 1908　Annual Undergrad Tuition & Fees (In-State): $13,073
Enrollment: 21,005　Coed
Affiliation or Control: State　IRS Status: 501(c)3
Highest Offering: Doctorate
Accreditation: M, ART, AUD, #CAATE, CACREP, CAEPN, CLPSY, DANCE, DIETD, DIETI, MUS, NURSE, PH, SP, SW, THEA

01 President .... Dr. Jonathan KOPPELL
05 Acting Provost/VP Academic Affairs ....Dr. Kimberly HOLLISTER
10 Vice Pres Finance & Treasurer .... Ms. Donna MCMONAGLE
32 Vice Pres Student Devel/Campus Life ... Dr. Dawn M. SOUFLERIS
84 Vice Pres Enrollment Management ....Dr. Wendy LIN-COOK
18 Vice Pres Univ Facilities .... Mr. Shawn M. CONNOLLY
13 Vice Pres Info Technology .... Ms. Candace C. FLEMING
30 Vice Pres Development .... Ms. Colleen COPPLA
26 Vice Pres Communications/Marketing .....Dr. Joseph A. BRENNAN
15 Vice Pres Human Resources .... Mr. David VERNON
114 Exec Director Budget and Planning .... Mr. David JOSEPHSON
43 University Counsel .... Mr. Mark FLEMING
46 Vice Prov Research/Dean Grad School ....Dr. Scott HERNESS
89 Assoc Prov UG Ed/Dean Univ College ....Dr. David HOOD
79 Dean Col Humanities & Soc Sciences ....Dr. Peter KINGSTONE
81 Dean Col Science & Mathematics ....Dr. Lora BILLINGS
53 Acting Dean Col Educ & Human Svcs ....Dr. Katrina BULKLEY
57 Dean College of the Arts .... Mr. Daniel A. GURSKIS
50 Dean School of Business ....Dr. Kimberly HOLLISTER
66 Dean School of Nursing .... Dr. Janice SMOLOWITZ
60 Dir School of Communication & Media .... Dr. Keith STRUDLER
64 Director School of Music ....Mr. Anthony MAZZOCCHI
08 Dean Library Services .... Ms. Danianne MIZZY
35 Dean of Students ....Ms. Margaree COLEMAN-CARTER

20 Assoc Provost Academic Affairs .... Dr. Kenneth SUMNER
20 Assoc Provost Academic Affairs .. Dr. Joanne F. COTE-BONANNO
21 Associate VP Finance .... Mr. Michael GALVIN
121 Assoc VP Student Acad Services ....Vacant
88 Assoc VP Campus Planning/Proj Mgmt ....Mr. Michael ZANKO
14 Assoc VP Enterprise Tech Services .... Mr. Jeff GIACOBBE
14 Assoc VP Enterprise Application Svc ....Ms. Donna SADLON
88 Assoc VP Program Management Office ....Mr. Samir BAKANE
110 Assoc VP Development ....Ms. Lisa HOYT
109 Assoc VP Campus Business Services ....Mr. Ed MIDGLEY
102 Assoc VP Foundation Adm & Finance ....Mr. Jeffrey CAMPO
88 Assoc University Counsel .... Ms. Maria ANDERSON
07 Director Undergraduate Admissions ....Ms. Jordanna MAZIARZ
37 Director Financial Aid ....Mr. James T. ANDERSON
09 Asst VP Institutional Research ....Ms. Klavdiya HAMMOND
06 University Registrar .... Ms. Leslie SUTTON-SMITH
19 Chief of Police .... Mr. Paul M. CELL
41 Athletic Director .... Mr. Robert CHESNEY
100 Chief of Staff .... Mr. Keith D. BARRACK
86 Director Government Relations ....Vacant
04 Exec Asst to President ....Ms. Karen M. AIELLO

New Brunswick Theological Seminary (C)

35 Seminary Place, New Brunswick NJ 08901
County: Middlesex　FICE Identification: 002619
Unit ID: 185758
Telephone: (732) 247-5241　Carnegie Class: Spec-4-yr-Faith
FAX Number: (732) 249-5412　Calendar System: Semester
URL: www.nbts.edu
Established: 1784　Annual Graduate Tuition & Fees: N/A
Enrollment: 121　Coed
Affiliation or Control: Reformed Church In America　IRS Status: 501(c)3
Highest Offering: Doctorate; No Undergraduates
Accreditation: @M, THEOL

01 President .... Dr. Micah L. MCCREARY
100 Chief of Staff/Exec Asst to Pres .... Ms. Amanda BRUEHL
10 Exec VP Operations/CFO .... Mr. Kenneth TERMOTT
13 VP Communications/Technology .... Mr. Steve MANN
111 VP Seminary Advancement/Relations .... Ms. Cathy PROCTOR
05 Dean of Academic Affairs ....Dr. Beth LANEEL TANNER
21 Manager/Bursar .... Ms. Tara HAMILL
08 Director of the Library ....Mr. T. Patrick MILAS
06 Registrar ....Ms. Jeanette CARRILLO
32 Dean of Students/Title IX Coord .... Ms. Joan MARSHALL
108 Assoc Dean of Assessment .... Dr. Terry SMITH
07 Director of Admissions .... Dr. JerQuentin SUTTON
18 Facilities Manager .... Mr. Paul KUHN
36 Director of Field Education .... Dr. Faye TAYLOR
37 Financial Aid Coordinator .... Ms. Rachel SEFCIK

New Jersey City University (D)

2039 Kennedy Boulevard, Jersey City NJ 07305-1597
County: Hudson　FICE Identification: 002613
Unit ID: 185129
Telephone: (201) 200-2000　Carnegie Class: Masters/L
FAX Number: (201) 200-2352　Calendar System: Semester
URL: www.njcu.edu
Established: 1927　Annual Undergrad Tuition & Fees (In-State): $14,738
Enrollment: 7,550　Coed
Affiliation or Control: State　IRS Status: 501(c)3
Highest Offering: Doctorate
Accreditation: M, ACBSP, ART, CACREP, CAEP, MUS, NURSE

01 President .... Dr. Sue HENDERSON
05 Provost/Sr VP Academic Affairs .... Dr. Tamara JHASHI
11 Vice Pres & Chief Operating Officer .... Dr. Aaron ASKA
111 Vice Pres & Chief Strategy Officer .... Mr. Jason KROLL
100 Chief of Staff to the President .... Dr. Andres ACEBO
10 Vice Pres/Chief Financial Officer .... Mr. James WHITE
32 Int Assoc VP Student Affairs ....Ms. Jodi BAILEY
84 Assoc VP Enrollment/Student Success .... Mr. Benjamin ROHDIN
26 Assoc VP Marketing/Communications .... Ms. Faith JACKSON
15 Assoc VP Human Resources ....Ms. Julia BASILE
88 Assoc VP Real Estate/Capital Proj .... Mr. Jeff LIVINGSTON
20 Assoc Provost for Academic Affairs .... Dr. Nurdan S. DUZGOREN-AYDIN
13 Assoc VP Information Technology ....Ms. Phyllis SZANI
102 Chief Devel Officer/Exec Dir Found .... Mr. Kwi BRENNAN
85 Assoc VP Global Initiatives ....Ms. Tamara CUNNINGHAM
21 Controller ....Ms. Rosemary TAVARES
49 Dean College of Arts & Sciences .... Dr. Joao SEDYCIAS
53 Dean College of Education .... Dr. Donna BREAVLT
50 Dean School of Business ....Dr. Bernard MCSHERRY
107 Dean Prof Educ & Lifelong Learning ... Dr. Michael EDMONDSON
108 Assoc VP Inst Effectiveness ....Dr. Sue GERBER
08 Director Library Services .... Mr. Frederick SMITH
07 Director Admissions .... Mr. Jose BALDA
06 Registrar ....Mr. Navin SAIBOO
36 Director Career Planning/Placement ....Vacant
19 Associate VP Public Safety ....Dr. Ronald HURLEY
41 Assoc VP & Director Athletics .... Mr. Shawn TUCKER
18 Assoc VP Building Services ....Mr. Andre PEARSON
29 Director Donor/Alumni Engagement .... Ms. Jane MCCLELLAN
38 Director Counseling & Wellness Svcs ....Vacant
96 Associate VP Business Services .... Ms. Edie DELVECCHIO
43 University Counsel .... Mr. Alfred E. RAMEY, JR.
37 Director Financial Aid .... Mr. Robert MACAULEY
117 Budget Officer & Risk Manager ....Mr. David R. RIDER

39 Assistant Dean for Residence Life ....Ms. Jennifer K. LUCIANO
106 Director Online Learning ....Vacant
25 Executive Director Grants Office ....Mr. Todd REGN
04 Admin Assistant to the President ....Mr. Michael SIMS
104 Dir Intl Programs & Study Abroad .... Mr. Craig KATZ
28 Director EEO/AA/Diversity .... Ms. Lisa NORCIA MARSHALL
116 Internal Auditor .... Ms. Alice BLOUNT-FENNEY

New Jersey Institute of Technology (E)

University Heights, Newark NJ 07102-1982
County: Essex　FICE Identification: 002621
Unit ID: 185828
Telephone: (973) 596-3000　Carnegie Class: DU-Highest
FAX Number: (973) 642-4380　Calendar System: Semester
URL: www.njit.edu
Established: 1881　Annual Undergrad Tuition & Fees (In-State): $17,674
Enrollment: 11,652　Coed
Affiliation or Control: State　IRS Status: 501(c)3
Highest Offering: Doctorate
Accreditation: M, ART, CIDA

01 President ....Dr. Joel S. BLOOM
05 Provost and Senior Executive VP ....Dr. Fadi P. DEEK
10 Sr VP Finance/CFO .... Ms. Catherine BRENNAN
88 Sr VP for Real Estate & Capital Dev ....Mr. Andrew P. CHRIST
30 VP Development & Alumni Relations ...... Dr. Kenneth ALEXO, JR.
15 VP for Human Resources .... Mr. Dale A. MCLEOD
26 Chief Strategy Officer ....Dr. Matthew GOLDEN
10 VP/Chief Commercial Officer ....Dr. Simon NYNENS
43 General Counsel/VP Legal Affairs ....Ms. Holly C. STERN
20 Sr Vice Prov Acad Affs & Stdnt Svcs .... Dr. Basil BALTZIS
54 Dean Newark College of Engineering ....Dr. Moshe KAM
48 Dean Col Architecture & Design ....Dr. Branko R. KOLAREVIC
49 Dean Col Science/Liberal Arts ....Dr. Kevin D. BELFIELD
50 Dean School of Management .... Dr. Oya I. TUKEL
22 Dean A Dorman Honors College ....Dr. Louis I. HAMILTON
77 Dean Ying Wu College of Computing .... Dr. Craig GOTSMAN
46 Sr Vice Provost for Research ....Dr. Atam P. DHAWAN
21 AVP Accounting & Treasury Mgmt ..... Mr. Brian J. KIRKPATRICK
58 Vice Provost Graduate Studies .... Dr. Sotirios G. ZIAVRAS
13 Vice Provost & CIO .... Ms. Kamalika SANDELL
84 AVP Enrollment Mgmt/Academic Svcs ....Vacant
41 Assoc VP/Director of Athletics ....Mr. Leonard I. KAPLAN
32 VP/Dean of Students & Campus Life ....Dr. Marybeth BOGER
29 Assoc VP for Constituent Relations .... Mr. Michael A. WALL
04 Sr Assistant to President .... Ms. Renee WATKINS
88 Exec Dir Ctr for Pre-College Pgms ...... Dr. Jacqueline L. CUSACK
36 Exec Director Career Devel Svcs .... Mr. Gregory MASS
09 Exec Director Inst Effectiveness .... Dr. Eugene P. DEESS
08 University Librarian ....Ms. Ann D. HOANG
06 Registrar ....Dr. Jerry TROMBELLA
37 Exec Dir Student Financial Aid Svcs ....Ms. Ivon NUNEZ
22 Exec Director EOP .... Dr. Crystal SMITH
38 Dir Counseling & Psych Services .... Dr. Phyllis BOLLING
19 Chief of Police ....Mr. Joseph S. MARSWILLO
24 Dir Media & Technology Support Svcs .... Mr. Joseph BONCHI
85 Exec Director Global Initiatives .... Dr. Marieta CHEMISHANOVA
88 Sr Dir Events & Conference Svcs ....Ms. Lorie BROWN
96 Executive Director Purchasing ....Ms. Eugenia REGENCIO
86 Chief External Affairs Officer ....Ms. Angela R. GARRETSON
105 Director Web Services ....Mr. Ersal ASLAM
07 Exec Dir of University Admissions .... Mr. Stephen M. ECK
106 Assoc CIO Digital Lrng/Campus Supp ....Mr. Blake HAGGERTY
25 Exec Director Sponsored Research ... Dr. Eric D. HETHERINGTON
35 Assoc Dean of Students ....Mr. Sean R. DOWD

Ocean County College (F)

PO Box 2001, Toms River NJ 08754-2001
County: Ocean　FICE Identification: 002624
Unit ID: 185873
Telephone: (732) 255-0400　Carnegie Class: Assoc/HT-Mix Trad/Non
FAX Number: (732) 255-0444　Calendar System: Semester
URL: www.ocean.edu
Established: 1964　Annual Undergrad Tuition & Fees (In-District): $5,790
Enrollment: 7,480　Coed
Affiliation or Control: State/Local　IRS Status: 501(c)3
Highest Offering: Associate Degree
Accreditation: M, ADNUR, EMT

01 President ....Dr. Jon H. LARSON
10 Exec VP of Finance & Administration ..... Ms. Sara WINCHESTER
32 VP Student Affairs .... Dr. Gerald RACIOPPI
05 VP of Academic Affairs .... Dr. Joseph KONOPKA
88 VP e-Learning & Lrng Enterprises .... Dr. Eileen GARCIA
15 Asst VP Human Resources .... Ms. Tracey DONALDSON
20 Asst VP for Academic Affairs ....Dr. Antoinette M. CLAY
18 Asst VP Facilities ....Mr. Matthew KENNEDY
57 Dean Language and the Arts ....Ms. Heidi SHERIDAN
81 Dean Math/Science & Tech .... Dr. Sylvia RIVIELLO
66 Dean of Nursing .... Ms. Teresa WALSH
83 Dean of Social Science .... Ms. Rosann BAR
104 Assoc VP of Intl Programs Academic ....Dr. Maysa HAYWARD
102 Exec Dir OCC Foundation .... Mr. Kenneth MALAGIERE
103 Dir Cont Educ/Workforce Devel ....Ms. Kaitlin EVERETT
08 Director of Library Services .... Ms. Donna ROSINSKI-KAUS
13 Chief Information Officer .... Mr. James ROSS
37 Director of Financial Aid .... Ms. Yessica GARCIA-GUZMAN
06 Registrar ....Ms. Janine EMMA
121 Dir of Academic Advising Services ....Ms. Anna REGAN

19 Director of College Security .... Mr. John LOPEZ
26 Exec Director of College Relations .... Ms. Jan KIRSTEN
07 Director of Admissions .... Mr. A.J TRUMP
93 Director of EOF & OMS .... Ms. Laura RICKARDS
18 Director of Facilities .... Mr. James CALAMIA
41 Exec Dir of Athletics .... Ms. Ilene COHEN
45 Exec Dir of Institutional Planning .... Ms. Alexa BESHARA
35 Director of Student Life .... Ms. Jennifer FAZIO
29 Alumni & Advancement Director .... Ms. Kimberly MALONEY
38 Dir Counseling/Student Development .... Dr. Kathryn PANDOLPHO
84 Director Enrollment Services .... Ms. Sheenah HARTIGAN
105 Assoc Director Web Services .... Ms. Maureen CONLON
25 Manager of Grants .... Ms. Kayci CLAYTON
96 Director Purchasing & Payables .... Ms. Christine HEALEY
106 Dean of e-Learning .... Ms. Vivian LYNN

Passaic County Community College (A)

1 College Boulevard, Paterson NJ 07509-1179
County: Passaic FICE Identification: 009994
Unit ID: 186034
Telephone: (973) 684-6868 Carnegie Class: Assoc/MT-VT-High Trad
FAX Number: (973) 684-5843 Calendar System: Semester
URL: www.pccc.edu
Established: 1968 Annual Undergrad Tuition & Fees (In-District): $7,350
Enrollment: 5,549 Coed
Affiliation or Control: State/Local IRS Status: 501(c)3
Highest Offering: Associate Degree
Accreditation: M, ADNUR, CAHIIM, RAD

01 President .... Dr. Steven ROSE
05 Vice Pres Academic/Student Affairs .... Dr. Jacqueline KINEAVY
10 Vice Pres Finance/Adm Services .... Mr. Steven HARDY
13 Vice Pres Information Technology .... Mr. Bradley MORTON
15 Associate Vice Pres Human Resources ...... Mr. Jose FERNANDEZ
20 Dean Academic Affairs .... Dr. Bassel STASSIS
08 Associate Dean Learning Resources .... Mr. Greg FALLON
66 Assoc Dean Nurse Educ/Health Scis ..... Dr. Donna STANKIEWICZ
121 Assoc Dean Academic Support Svc .... Mr. Peter HYNES
09 Dir Institutional Research .... Dr. Justin HULL
88 Ex Dir Cultural Affs/The Poetry Ctr .... Ms. Maria GILLAN
111 Vice President Inst Advancement .... Mr. Todd SORBER
84 Dean Enrollment Management .... Ms. Tonya ANDERSON
88 Dn Academic Initiative Policy Mgmt .... Ms. Betsy MARINACE
18 Assoc VP Facilities/Planning .... Mr. Brian EGAN
37 Director Financial Aid .... Ms. Linda GAYTON
06 Registrar .... Ms. Lorriane SMITH
19 Director Security .... Mr. Glenn BROWN
35 Director Student Activities .... Ms. Maria MARTE
41 Athletic Director .... Mr. Wayne MARTIN
07 Director of Admissions .... Ms. Stephanie DECKER
29 Director Alumni Relations .... Vacant
32 Chief Student Life Officer .... Dr. Sharon GOLDSTEIN
26 Chief Public Relations Officer .... Mr. Todd SORBER
96 Director of Purchasing .... Mr. Michael D'AGATI
101 Dir Board Affairs/Asst to President .... Ms. Evelyn DEFEIS
103 Exec Dir Workforce/Career Dev .... Ms. Janet ALBRECHT

Pillar College (B)

60 Park Place, Suite 701, Newark NJ 07102
County: Essex FICE Identification: 036663
Unit ID: 440794
Telephone: (973) 803-5000 Carnegie Class: Spec-4-yr-Faith
FAX Number: (973) 242-3282 Calendar System: Semester
URL: www.pillar.edu
Established: 1908 Annual Undergrad Tuition & Fees: $22,756
Enrollment: 534 Coed
Affiliation or Control: Other IRS Status: 501(c)3
Highest Offering: Master's
Accreditation: M, BI

01 President .... Dr. David E. SCHROEDER
30 VP Business Development/Operations .... Mr. Kelvin THOMAS
05 VP Academic Affairs/Dean of College .... Ms. Amy HUBER
11 Chf Operating Ofcr/Exec Vice Pres ..... Mr. Rupert A. HAYLES, JR.
88 VP Strategic Alliances .... Dr. Wayne R. DYER
58 VP Academic Development .... Dr. Ralph GRANT
06 Registrar .... Mr. Brian SCHROEDER
37 Director of Financial Aid .... Ms. Betzi SCHROEDER
07 Assoc VP of Admissions .... Mr. Dominic DIGIOACCHINO
08 Assoc Dean Information Resources .... Ms. Vinell SPIED
26 VP Institutional Outreach & Mktg .... Ms. Erica OLIVER
32 Assoc Dean Student Development .... Mr. Nishanth THOMAS
04 Admin Assistant to the President .... Ms. Alexandra MADRIGAL
09 Director Institutional Research .... Mr. Brian SCHROEDER
13 Chief Information Technology Office .... Vacant
15 Director of Human Resources .... Ms. Samantha ARES

Princeton Theological Seminary (C)

PO Box 821, 64 Mercer Street, Princeton NJ 08542-0803
County: Mercer FICE Identification: 002626
Unit ID: 186122
Telephone: (609) 497-7990 Carnegie Class: Spec-4-yr-Faith
FAX Number: (609) 924-2973 Calendar System: Semester
URL: www.ptsem.edu
Established: 1812 Annual Graduate Tuition & Fees: N/A
Enrollment: 350 Coed
Affiliation or Control: Presbyterian Church (U.S.A.) IRS Status: 501(c)3
Highest Offering: Doctorate; No Undergraduates
Accreditation: M, THEOL

01 President .... Dr. M. Craig BARNES
111 EVP for External Relations .... Mr. Shane A. BERG
10 VP Finance/CFO/Treasurer .... Mr. Kurt A. GABBARD
26 VP for External Relations .... Ms. Anne WHITAKER STEWART
05 Dean and VP of Academic Affairs .... Dr. Jacqueline E. LAPSLEY
32 Dean Student Life & VP Stdnt Rels .... Rev. John E. WHITE
20 Senior Assoc Academic Dean .... Dr. Shawn OLIVER
78 Int Dir Vocational/Field Education .... RevDr. Catherine C. DAVIS
51 Assoc Dean of Continuing Educ .... Rev. Dayle G. ROUNDS
06 Registrar .... Ms. Brenda D. WILLIAMS
07 Dir Admissions/Enrollment Mgmt .... Mr. Joel David ESTES
08 Managing Dir of the Library .... Ms. Evelyn FRANGAKIS
110 Assoc VP for Advancement .... Vacant
15 Int Director of Human Resources .... Ms. Pamela WHITT
13 Director of Information Tech/CIO .... Mr. Jeffrey SIEBEN
18 Director of Facilities/Construction .... Mr. German MARTINEZ
09 Dir of Institutional Research .... Mr. Matthew WITKOWSKI
88 Business Office Consultant .... Mr. John W. GILMORE
96 Director Contracts/Procurement .... Mr. Stephen CARDONE
20 Assoc Dean for Academic Admin .... Dr. Rose Ellen DUNN
38 Director of Student Counseling .... Ms. Wanda Marie SEVEY
42 Minister of the Chapel .... Rev. Janice S. AMMON
28 Assoc Dean of Inst Diversity .... Rev. Victor ALOYO, JR.
04 Deputy to the President .... Ms. Catherine AHMAD
37 Assoc Director Financial Aid .... Mr. Michael D. LIVIO
44 Director of Annual Giving .... Ms. Cheryl ALI
112 Director of Planned Giving .... Vacant
29 Director of Alumni Relations .... Rev. Ann-Henley NICHOLSON

Princeton University (D)

Princeton NJ 08544-1098
County: Mercer FICE Identification: 002627
Unit ID: 186131
Telephone: (609) 258-3000 Carnegie Class: DU-Highest
FAX Number: N/A Calendar System: Semester
URL: www.princeton.edu
Established: 1746 Annual Undergrad Tuition & Fees: $48,502
Enrollment: 7,853 Coed
Affiliation or Control: Independent Non-Profit IRS Status: 501(c)3
Highest Offering: Doctorate
Accreditation: M, CAEP

01 President .... Cristopher L. EISGRUBER
03 Executive Vice President .... Treby WILLIAMS
05 Provost .... Deborah PRENTICE
04 Vice President & Secretary .... Hilary PARKER
10 Vice Pres for Finance & Treasurer .... Jim MATTEO
111 Vice President for Advancement .... Kevin B. HEANEY
26 Vice Pres Comm/Public Affairs .... Brent COLBURN
32 Vice President of Campus Life .... Rochelle CALHOUN
18 Vice President for Facilities .... KyuJung E. WHANG
13 Vice President Info Technology/CIO .... Jay DOMINICK
15 Vice President for Human Resources .... Lianne C. SULLIVAN-CROWLEY
109 Vice Pres for University Services .... Chad L. KLAUS
116 VP/Chief Audit & Compliance Officer .... Nilufer K. SHROFF
43 VP & General Counsel .... Ramona E. ROMERO
20 Vice Provost Academic/Budget Plng .... Richard MYERS
22 Vice Provost Inst Equity/Diversity .... Michelle MINTER
09 Vice Provost Institutional Research .... Jed MARSH
88 Vice Prov Space Programming/Plng .... Paul LAMARCHE
114 Budget Dir/Vice Provost Finance .... Steven GILL
85 Actg Vice Provost Intl Initiatives .... Aly KASSAM-REMTULLA
29 Deputy VP Alumni Engagement .... Alexandra H. DAY
44 AVP Annual Giving/Advancement .... Susan E. WALSH
88 AVP Capital Projects/Construction .... Jim KAZDA
88 Assoc Vice Pres University Services .... Andrew KANE
30 AVP for Development .... Kerstin LARSEN
39 AVP Univ Svcs/Housing .... Andrew KANE
46 Chair Univ Rsrch Bd/Dean Research .... Pablo DEBENEDETTI
88 President PRINCO .... Andrew K. GOLDEN
58 Dean of the Graduate School .... Sarah-Jane LESLIE
20 Dean of the Faculty .... Sanjeev KULKARNI
49 Dean of the College .... Jill S. DOLAN
54 Dean School of Engineering .... Andrea J. GOLDSMITH
82 Int Dean Sch of Public/Intl Affairs .... Nolan MCCARTY
48 Dean of School of Architecture .... Monica PONCE DE LEON
42 Dean of Religious Life .... Alison BODEN
35 Dean of Undergraduate Students .... Kathleen DEIGNAN
07 Dean of Admission .... Karen RICHARDSON
17 Exec Director Health Services .... John KOLLIGIAN
08 University Librarian .... Anne JARVIS
06 Registrar .... Polly WINFREY GRIFFIN
37 Dir Undergraduate Financial Aid .... Robin A. MOSCATO
86 Director Government Affairs .... Joyce A. RECHTSCHAFFEN
31 Dir Community & Regional Affairs .... Kristin APPELGET
41 Director of Athletics .... Mollie D. MARCOUX
96 Director of Procurement Svcs .... Mohamed ELA
38 Dir of Counseling & Psych Services .... Calvin R. CHIN
16 Director Human Resources .... John J. MARTIN
85 Director Davis International Center .... Albert RIVERA
90 Assoc CIO/Dir Academic Services OIT .... Serge J. GOLDSTEIN
14 Assoc CIO/Dir Support Services OIT .... David MORREALE
91 Dir Enterprise Infrastructure OIT .... Donna E. TATRO
104 Sr Assoc Dean for Intl Pgms .... Rebecca GRAVES-BAYAZITOGLU
19 Executive Director Public Safety .... Paul OMINSKY
36 Exec Dir Center for Career Dev .... Kimberly BETZ

Rabbi Jacob Joseph School (E)

1 Plainfield Avenue, Edison NJ 08817-4494
County: Middlesex FICE Identification: 030775
Unit ID: 384421
Telephone: (732) 985-6533 Carnegie Class: Spec-4-yr-Faith
FAX Number: (732) 985-6553 Calendar System: Semester
Established: 1982 Annual Undergrad Tuition & Fees: $11,950
Enrollment: 73 Male
Affiliation or Control: Independent Non-Profit IRS Status: 501(c)3
Highest Offering: Baccalaureate
Accreditation: RABN

01 President .... Mr. Avi SCHICK
03 Rosh Yeshiva .... Rabbi Yaakov BUSEL
05 Rosh Yeshiva .... Rabbi Joseph EICHENSTEIN
37 Financial Aid Director .... Rabbi Yitzchok WEINTRAUB

Rabbinical College of America (F)

226 Sussex Avenue, Morristown NJ 07960-3600
County: Morris FICE Identification: 008609
Unit ID: 186186
Telephone: (973) 267-9404 Carnegie Class: Spec-4-yr-Faith
FAX Number: (973) 553-6957 Calendar System: Trimester
URL: www.rca.edu
Established: 1956 Annual Undergrad Tuition & Fees: $12,000
Enrollment: 258 Male
Affiliation or Control: Independent Non-Profit IRS Status: 501(c)3
Highest Offering: Baccalaureate
Accreditation: RABN

01 Dean .... Rabbi Moshe HERSON
04 Admin Assistant to the Dean .... Rabbi Mendy HERSON
26 Public Relations Officer .... Mrs. Chana TUNK
06 Registrar .... Mrs. Shoshana SOLOMON
88 Director New Direction Program .... Rabbi Zalman DUBINSKY
10 Chief Business Officer .... Vacant
37 Director Student Financial Aid .... Rabbi Yisroel GOLDBERG
08 Chief Librarian .... Rabbi Sholom SPALTER
51 Dir Continuing Educ/Alumni Rels .... Rabbi Boruch HECHT
88 Director Semicha Program .... Rabbi Chaim SCHAPIRO
18 Director Building and Grounds .... Rabbi Hershel LIPSKIER

Rabbinical Seminary M'kor Chaim (G)

160 Locust Street, Lakewood NJ 08701
County: Ocean FICE Identification: 008617
Unit ID: 194718
Telephone: (718) 851-0183 Carnegie Class: Spec-4-yr-Faith
FAX Number: (718) 853-2967 Calendar System: Semester
Established: 1965 Annual Undergrad Tuition & Fees: $8,300
Enrollment: 34 Male
Affiliation or Control: Independent Non-Profit IRS Status: 501(c)3
Highest Offering: Second Talmudic Degree
Accreditation: AIJS

Ramapo College of New Jersey (H)

505 Ramapo Valley Road, Mahwah NJ 07430-1680
County: Bergen FICE Identification: 009344
Unit ID: 186201
Telephone: (201) 684-7500 Carnegie Class: Masters/M
FAX Number: (201) 684-7508 Calendar System: Semester
URL: www.ramapo.edu
Established: 1969 Annual Undergrad Tuition & Fees (In-State): $14,952
Enrollment: 6,042 Coed
Affiliation or Control: State IRS Status: 501(c)3
Highest Offering: Doctorate
Accreditation: M, CAEP, NUR, SW

01 President .... Dr. Cindy R. JEBB
05 Interim Provost/VP Academic Affairs .... Dr. Susan GAULDEN
10 VP Admin & Fin/Chief of Operations . Ms. Kirsten LOEWRIGKEIT
43 VP and General Counsel .... Mr. Michael A. TRIPODI
111 Int VP Inst Advance/Dir Foundation .... Dr. Angela CRISTINI
84 VP Enrollment Mgmt/Student Affairs .... Mr. Christopher ROMANO
45 Chief Planning Officer .... Vacant
100 Chief of Staff/Board Liaison .... Dr. Brittany A. WILLIAMS-GOLDSTEIN
116 Director of Internal Audit .... Ms. Patricia CHAVEZ
20 Vice Prov Curriculum & Assessment .... Dr. Susan GAULDEN
88 Director of Capital Planning .... Mr. Daniel ROCHE
13 AVP/Chief Information Officer .... Mr. Robert DOSTER
86 Government Relations Officer .... Mr. Patrick W. O'CONNOR
105 Asst VP Mktg/Comm & Web Admin .... Ms. Melissa HORVATH-PLYMAN
08 Interim College Librarian/Dean .... Ms. Leigh-Cregan KELLER
06 Registrar .... Ms. Fernanda PAPALIA
07 Interim Director of Admissions .... Mr. Anthony DOVI
37 Director of Financial Aid .... Mr. F. Shawn O'NEILL
21 Controller .... Ms. Colleen O'KEEFE
15 Asst VP of HR & Benefits .... Ms. Viriginia GALDIERI
78 Dir Exper Learning/Career Svcs .... Ms. Beth RICCA
32 Dean of Students .... Ms. Melissa VAN DER WALL
41 Director of Athletics .... Mr. Harold CROCKER
18 Director of Facilities .... Mr. Michael CUNNINGHAM
19 Director Public Safety .... Vacant
88 Director Educ Opportunity Program .... Ms. Barbara HARMON-FRANCIS
50 Dean Anisfield School of Business .... Dr. Edward PETKUS

79 Int Dean Sch Humanities/Global Stds .... Dr. Susan HANGEN
57 Interim Dean Sch of Contemp Arts .... Mr. Peter CAMPBELL
83 Dean Sch Soc Science & Human Svc .... Dr. Aaron S. LORENZ
81 Int Dn Sch Theoretical/Applied Sci .... Dr. Edward SAIFF
53 Asst Dean for Teacher Education .... Dr. Brian CHINNI
38 Director Ctr for Health/Counseling .... Dr. Judith GREEN
29 Dir Alumni Relations .... Vacant
04 Executive Assistant to President .... Ms. Sara GAZZILLO
23 Coordinator Health Services .... Ms. Debbie LUKACSKO
09 Director of Institutional Research .... Dr. Gurvinder KHANEJA
22 Dir Affirmative Action/EEO .... Vacant
40 Bookstore Manager .... Ms. Theresa KING
85 Dir Intl Education/Study Abroad .... Mr. Ben LEVY
36 Asst Dir Career Dev & Placement .... Ms. Debra STARK
96 Director of Procurement .... Mr. Shawn LAIDLAW
103 Manager of Learning/Devel & Perf .... Mr. Roger JANS
25 Asst VP of Grants/Sponsor Programs .... Ms. Angela CRISTINI
28 Chief Diversity & Equity Officer ...... Ms. Nicole MORGAN AGARD
35 Director of Student Conduct .... Ms. Kathleen HALLISSEY
121 Asst VP of Student Success .... Mr. Joseph CONNELL
114 Chief Budget Officer .... Ms. Beth WALKLEY
113 Director of Student Accounts .... Ms. Debra SCHULTES
118 Benefits Manager .... Vacant
119 Network Administrator .... Vacant
39 Dir Resident Life/Student Housing .... Ms. Lisa GONSISKO
110 Asst Dir of Institutional Advance .... Mr. David TERDIMAN
102 Sr Director Constituent Relations .... Mr. Peter RICE
112 Director Major Gifts .... Vacant

Raritan Valley Community College (A)

118 Lamington Road, Branchburg NJ 08876
County: Somerset FICE Identification: 007731
Unit ID: 186645
Telephone: (908) 526-1200 Carnegie Class: Assoc/MT-VT-High Trad
FAX Number: (908) 526-0253 Calendar System: Semester
URL: www.raritanval.edu
Established: 1966 Annual Undergrad Tuition & Fees (In-District): $6,672
Enrollment: 7,080 Coed
Affiliation or Control: State/Local IRS Status: 501(c)3
Highest Offering: Associate Degree
Accreditation: M, ADNUR, CAHIIM, MAC, OPD, OTA

01 President .... Dr. Michael MCDONOUGH
05 Provost & VP Academic Affairs .... Dr. Deborah PRESTON
10 Vice President Finance/Facilities .... Mr. John TROJAN
15 Exec Dir HR & Labor Relations .... Ms. Cheryl WALLACE
32 VP for Student Affairs & Outreach .... Ms. Jacki BELIN
49 Dean Liberal/Fine Arts/Bus/Pub Svc .... Dr. Patrice MARKS
81 Dean STEM & Health Science .... Dr. Sarah IMBRIGLIO
121 Dean Academic Support & Ed Partners .... Dr. Audrey LOERA
18 Exec Director Facilities/Grounds .... Mr. Brian O'ROURKE
92 Dir Honors Pgm & Alumni Outreach .... Mr. Greg DESANCTIS
24 Director Media Relations .... Ms. Donna STOLZER
102 Executive Director Foundation .... Mr. Michael MARION
14 Exec Dir Technology Services .... Mr. Robert PESCINSKI
21 Controller/Exec Dir of Finance .... Ms. Violet J. WILLENSKY
57 Director of Theatre .... Vacant
09 Dir of Inst Research/Assessment .... Ms. Sarah DONNELLY
88 Director of Planetarium .... Ms. Amie GALLAGHER
88 Director of Child Care Center .... Ms. Cathy GRIFFIN
37 Director of Financial Aid .... Mr. Lenny MESONAS
06 Registrar .... Mr. John WHEELER
96 Director of Purchasing .... Mr. Michael DEPINTO
35 Director of Student Life .... Mr. Russell BAREFOOT
36 Director Transfer/Career Services .... Mr. Paul MICHAUD
84 Exec Dir Enrollment Management .... Ms. Carolyn WHITE
35 Dean of Student Affairs .... Mr. Jason FREDERICKS
19 Director Security/Safety .... Mr. Robert SZKODNEY
106 Dir Online Educ/Distance Learning .... Mr. Brett COUP

Rider University (B)

2083 Lawrenceville Road, Lawrenceville NJ 08648-3099
County: Mercer FICE Identification: 002628
Unit ID: 186283
Telephone: (609) 896-5000 Carnegie Class: Masters/L
FAX Number: (609) 895-5681 Calendar System: Semester
URL: www.rider.edu
Established: 1865 Annual Undergrad Tuition & Fees: $45,860
Enrollment: 4,636 Coed
Affiliation or Control: Independent Non-Profit IRS Status: 501(c)3
Highest Offering: Doctorate
Accreditation: M, CACREP, CAEP, CAEPN, NURSE

01 President .... Dr. Gregory DELL'OMO
05 Provost/Vice Pres Academic Affairs .... Dr. DonnaJean A. FREDEEN
10 Vice President Finance/Treasurer .... Mr. James HARTMAN
111 Vice Pres University Advancement .... Ms. Karin KLIM
32 Vice President Student Affairs .... Dr. Leanna FENNEBERG
84 Vice Pres Enrollment Management .... Mr. Drew C. AROMANDO
43 VP Legal Affs/General Counsel .... Mr. Mark SOLOMON
18 VP Facilities/Auxiliary Services .... Mr. Michael F. RECA
15 VP HR/Affirmative Action .... Mr. Robert STOTO
45 VP Strategic Initiatives & Planning .... Ms. Debbie STASOLLA
13 CIO & Assoc VP Info Tech .... Mr. Douglas MCCREA
26 Assoc VP for Univ Mktg/Comm .... Ms. Kristine A. BROWN
21 Associate Vice President/Controller .... Vacant
20 Associate Provost/Legal Counsel .... Dr. Matt STIEGLITZ
57 Dean Westminster Col of the Arts .... Dr. Marshall ONOFRIO
49 Dean Col Liberal Arts & Sciences .... Dr. Kelly BIDLE
53 Dean Col of Educ & Human Svcs .... Dr. Jason BARR
50 Dean Norm Brodsky Col of Business .... Dr. Gene KUTCHER

35 AVP Student Affairs/Dean of Stdnts .... Ms. Cindy THREATT
09 Director Institutional Research .... Dr. Brad LITCHFIELD
37 Exec Director One Stop .... Mr. Jim CONLON
06 Registrar .... Ms. Susan A. STEFANICK
19 Director of Public Safety .... Mr. James WALDON
29 Director of Alumni Relations .... Ms. Natalie M. POLLARD
41 Director of Athletics .... Mr. Donald P. HARNUM
36 Exec Director Career Dev & Success .... Ms. Kim BARBERICH
28 Exec Director Diversity & Inclusion .... Dr. Pamela PRUITT
38 Director of Counseling .... Vacant
96 Director of Procurement .... Ms. Ann Marie MEAD
07 Director for UG & Transfer Adm .... Ms. Susan MAKOWSKI
40 Manager College Store .... Ms. Catherine RUSSOMANNO

Rowan College at Burlington County (C)

900 College Circle, Mt. Laurel NJ 08054
County: Burlington FICE Identification: 007730
Unit ID: 183877
Telephone: (856) 222-9311 Carnegie Class: Assoc/HT-Mix Trad/Non
FAX Number: (609) 894-0183 Calendar System: Semester
URL: www.rcbc.edu
Established: 1966 Annual Undergrad Tuition & Fees (In-District): $5,159
Enrollment: 7,316 Coed
Affiliation or Control: State/Local IRS Status: 501(c)3
Highest Offering: Associate Degree
Accreditation: M, ADNUR, CAHIIM, DH, DMS, NAIT, RAD

01 President .... Dr. Michael A. CIOCE
04 Exec Asst to the President .... Ms. Lynne Marie DEVERICKS
05 Sr Vice President/Provost .... Dr. David SPANG
03 Sr VP Admin and Operations .... Mr. Thomas J. CZERNIECKI
103 VP WDI and Lifelong Learning ...... Ms. Anna PAYANZO COTTON
84 VP Enroll Mgmt and Student
Success .... Dr. Karen ARCHAMBAULT
13 Chief Information Officer .... Mr. Mark MEARA
15 Exec Dir Budget/Purchasing/HR .... Mr. Harry METZINGER
11 Chief Operations Officer .... Mr. Matthew FARR
102 Director of RCBC Foundation .... Ms. Lindsey DANIELLO
26 Exec Dir Marketing/Communications .... Mr. Greg VOLPE
15 Asst Director of HR .... Ms. Michelle RUSSELL
49 Dean of Liberal Arts .... Dr. Donna VANDERGRIFT
81 Dean of STEM .... Dr. Edem TETTEH
76 Dean of Health Sciences .... Dr. Karen MONTALTO
106 Dean of Learning Resources .... Dr. Martin A. HOFFMAN, SR.
07 Interim Dean of Enrollment Mgmt .... Mr. Jarrett KEALEY
32 Dean of Student Success .... Dr. Catherine R. BRIGGS
06 Registrar .... Ms. LacyJane RYMAN-MESCAL
41 Director of Athletics .... Ms. Heather CONGER
88 Director of Culinary Arts .... Mr. James BRUDNICKI
88 Director of EOF Program .... Ms. Edith CORBIN
19 Director of Public Safety .... Mr. Andrew EATON

Rowan College of South Jersey (D)

1400 Tanyard Road, Sewell NJ 08080-9518
County: Gloucester FICE Identification: 006901
Unit ID: 184791
Telephone: (856) 468-5000 Carnegie Class: Assoc/HT-High Trad
FAX Number: N/A Calendar System: 4/1/4
URL: www.rcsj
Established: 1966 Annual Undergrad Tuition & Fees (In-District): $5,400
Enrollment: 6,369 Coed
Affiliation or Control: State/Local IRS Status: 501(c)3
Highest Offering: Associate Degree
Accreditation: M, ACBSP, ADNUR, DMS, NMT, PTAA

01 President .... Dr. Frederick KEATING
05 VP Academic Services/Provost .... Dr. Brenden RICKARDS
11 Vice President & COO .... Mr. Dominick BURZICHELLI
32 Vice President Student Svcs .... Ms. Judith ATKINSON
13 Vice President/CIO .... Mr. Josh R. PIDDINGTON
10 Exec Director Financial Services .... Ms. Cheryl LEWIS
15 Exec Director Human Resource .... Vacant
04 Sr Exec Assistant to the President .... Ms. Meg RESUE
28 Exec Dir Diversity and Equity .... Mrs. Almarie JONES
09 Dean Inst Research & Assessment .... Ms. Karen DURKIN
66 Dean Nursing & Allied Health .... Dr. Susan HALL
49 Dean Liberal Arts .... Dr. Paul RUFINO
81 Dean STEM .... Dr. Christina NASE
20 Dean Academic Compliance ..Dr. Danielle ZIMECKI-FENNIMORE
61 Dean Law and Justice .... Mr. Fred H. MADDEN
50 Dean Business Studies .... Ms. Patricia CLAGHORN
07 Exec Director Admissions/Registrar .... Ms. Sandra HOFFMAN
36 Director Career & Academic Planning .... Ms. Megan RUTTLER
35 Exec Director Student Engagement .... Ms. Samantha VAN KOOY
08 Director Library Services .... Mrs. Jane S. CROCKER
19 Director Security/Safety .... Mr. Joseph GETSINGER
37 Exec Dir Financial Aid & Admission .... Mr. Michael CHANDO
96 Controller/Purchasing .... Mr. Mark ZORZI

Rowan College of South Jersey Cumberland Campus (E)

3322 College Drive, PO Box 1500,
Vineland NJ 08362-1500
Telephone: (856) 691-8600 FICE Identification: 002601
Accreditation: &M, RAD

Rowan University (F)

201 Mullica Hill Road, Glassboro NJ 08028-1700
County: Gloucester FICE Identification: 002609
Unit ID: 184782
Telephone: (856) 256-4000 Carnegie Class: DU-Higher
FAX Number: (856) 256-4929 Calendar System: Semester
URL: www.rowan.edu
Established: 1923 Annual Undergrad Tuition & Fees (In-State): $12,939
Enrollment: 19,678 Coed
Affiliation or Control: State IRS Status: 501(c)3
Highest Offering: Doctorate
Accreditation: M, ART, CAATE, CACREP, CAEPN, CLPSY, DIETC, MED, MUS, NURSE, OSTEO, THEA

01 President .... Dr. Ali HOUSHMAND
05 Provost/Sr VP for Academic Affairs .... Dr. Anthony LOWMAN
10 Senior Vice Pres of Finance/CFO .... Mr. Joseph F. SCULLY
32 SVP for Student Affairs .... Dr. Jeffrey HAND
111 Int VP Univ Advance/Exec Dir Fndn .... Mr. Jesse R. SHAFER
11 SVP Administration/Operations .... Vacant
35 VP Student Life/Dean Students .... Dr. Kevin S. KOETT
86 VP Govt Rels/External Relationships .... Mr. Sean KENNEDY
18 VP for Facilities & Operations .... Dr. Joseph CAMPBELL
15 VP Human Resources/CHRO .... Ms. Theresa DRYE
44 VP & Chief Growth Officer .... Mr. Ronald J. TALLARIDA
20 VP Academic Affairs .... Dr. Roberta HARVEY
13 VP Information Resources/CIO .... Dr. Mira LALOVIC-HAND
26 VP for University Relations .... Dr. Joe CARDONA
46 Vice President for Research .... Dr. Tabbetha DOBBINS
43 General Counsel .... Ms. Melissa WHEATCROFT
88 Chief Audit/Compliance/Privacy Ofcr .... Mr. Ray BRAEUNIG
88 Asst VP Facilities/Planning/Opers ....Mr. Arijit DE
84 VP for Strategic Enrollment Mgmt .... Mr. Jimmy JUNG
88 VP for Student Affairs .... Ms. Rory MCELWEE
28 VP Diversity/Equity/Inclusion .. Ms. Penny MCPHERSON-MYERS
14 Assoc VP Info Resources/Technology .... Ms. Jackie RING
20 Vice Provost for Faculty Affairs .... Mr. Mariano SAVELSKI
19 Asst VP Public Safety/Emerg Mgmt .... Mr. Michael KANTNER
63 Dean of Cooper Medical School of RU .... Dr. Annette REBOLI
50 Dean Rohrer College of Business .... Dr. Susan LEHRMAN
81 Dean College of Science/Mathematics . Dr. Vojislava POPHRISTIC
53 Dean of Education .... Dr. Gaetane JEAN-MARIE
57 Dean of Performing Arts .... Dr. Rick DAMMERS
88 VP Strategic Ventures/Initiatives .... Dr. Horacio SOSA
54 Interim Dean of Engineering .... Dr. Stephanie FARRELL
60 Dean Communication & Creative Arts .... Dr. Sanford M. TWEEDIE
83 Dean Humanities & Social Sciences .... Dr. Nawal H. AMMAR
63 Dean School of Osteopathic Medicine ...... Dr. Thomas CAVALIERI
20 AVP Academic Affairs .... Dr. Lorraine RICCHEZZA
16 Asst VP Employee Equity/Labor Rels .... Mr. Henry OH
22 SVP Diversity/Equity/Inclusion .... Dr. Monika SHEALEY
41 Director of Athletics .... Dr. John GIANNINI
88 Dir University Events .... Ms. Linda DIGENNARO
07 Director of Admissions .... Mr. Dan P. REIGEL
36 Asst Dir Ofc Career Advancement .... Dr. Alicia MONROE
96 Sr Dir Contracting & Procurement ...... Ms. Christina BRASTETER
27 Asst VP University Relations .... Ms. Lori MARSHALL
105 Dir Strategic Planning/Management .... Dr. Rihab SAADEDDINE
85 Assoc Director International Center .... Ms. Ghina MAHMOUD
100 Chief of Staff/BOT Liaison .... Dr. Joanne M. CONNOR

Rutgers University - Camden (G)

303 Cooper Street, Camden NJ 08102
County: Camden FICE Identification: 004741
Unit ID: 186371
Telephone: (856) 225-6095 Carnegie Class: DU-Higher
FAX Number: (856) 225-6495 Calendar System: Semester
URL: www.camden.rutgers.edu
Established: 1926 Annual Undergrad Tuition & Fees (In-State): $14,877
Enrollment: 7,076 Coed
Affiliation or Control: State IRS Status: 501(c)3
Highest Offering: Doctorate
Accreditation: &M, CAEPT, LAW, NURSE, PTA, SPAA

00 President Rutgers University .... Dr. Jonathan HOLLOWAY
88 Chief of Staff to Pres/SVP
Admin .... Dr. Andrea CONKLIN BUESCHEL
02 Chancellor Rutgers Camden .... Dr. Antonio TILLIS
100 Chief of Staff Rutgers Camden .... Mr. Michael J. SEPANIC
05 Provost .... Dr. Michael PALIS
11 Sr Vice Chancellor Admin & Finance .... Mr. Larry GAINES
03 Sr Vice Chancellor .... Dr. Daniel HART
20 Int Vice Chancellor Student Success .... Dr. Marsha BESONG
32 Vice Chancellor Student Affairs .... Ms. Mary Beth DAISEY
46 Vice Chancellor Research .... Dr. Benedetto PICCOLI
84 Vice Chancellor Enrollment Mgmt .... Dr. Craig WESTMAN
111 Acting Vice Chancellor Advancement .... Mr. Scott D. OWENS
28 Assoc Chancellor Diversity .... Dr. Nyemma WATSON
06 Assoc Registrar .... Ms. Diana KEOUGH
50 Dean School of Business .... Dr. Monica ADYA
61 Int Co-Dean Rutgers Law School .. Ms. Rose CUISON-VILLAZOR
61 Co-Dean Rutgers Law School .... Ms. Kimberly MUTCHERSON
35 Dean of Students .... Mr. Thomas J. DIVALERIO
49 Dean Fac Arts & Sciences .... Dr. Howard MARCHITELLO
66 Dean School of Nursing .... Dr. Donna NICKITAS
58 Assoc Dean Grad School .... Dr. Michelle MELOY
39 Assoc Dean Students .... Ms. Allison WISNIEWSKI
85 Asst Dean International Students .... Ms. Elizabeth A. ATKINS
36 Asst Dean Career Center .... Ms. Cheryl A. HALLMAN
37 Exec Director Financial Aid .... Ms. Danielle BARBEE
18 Exec Director Space Management .... Mr. Christopher PYE

30 Sr Director Development .... Ms. Kate BRENNAN
105 Sr Director Office of Creative Svcs ... Ms. Joanne DUS-ZASTROW
110 Director of Development .... Ms. Akua ASIAMAH-ANDRADE
53 Director MA Teaching Program .... Dr. Sara M. BECKER
41 Director Athletics & Recreation ....Mr. Jeffrey L. DEAN
103 Director Economic Development ....Mr. Gregory GAMBLE
08 Director Paul Robeson Library ....Ms. Regina KOURY
25 Director Sponsored Research .... Ms. Cammie MORRISON
106 Director Instructional Design ....Mr. William PAGAN
10 Director Finance and Administration ....Ms. Rosa M. RIVERA
07 Director Enrollment Communications ....Dr. Yosmeriz ROMAN
13 Director Information Technology ....Mr. Thomas J. RYAN
23 Director Student Wellness Center .... Dr. Neuza SERRA
94 Director Gender Studies ....Dr. Shauna SHAMES
92 Director Honors College ....Dr. Lee Ann WESTMAN
104 Assoc Director International Stdnts ....Ms. Elizabeth ATKINS
90 Assoc Director IT ....Mr. Timothy DIVITO
22 Asst Director EOF ....Ms. Randi FERGUSON
51 Asst Director Continuing Studies .... Ms. Dalynn KNIGGE
29 Asst Director Alumni Engagement ....Ms. Mary Clare VENUTO
88 Chair Economic Department ....Dr. I-Ming CHIU
82 Chair Political Science Department .... Dr. Maureen DONAGHY
57 Chair Fine Arts Department ....Dr. Kenneth ELLIOTT
88 Chair English Department ....Dr. Richard EPSTEIN
81 Chair Mathematics Department ....Dr. Siqi FU
81 Chair Chemistry Department ....Dr. Catherine GRGICAK
79 Chair World Languages & Cultures ....Dr. Tyler HOFFMAN
73 Chair Philosophy and Religion Dept .... Dr. Nicole KARAPANAGIOTIS
80 Chair Public Policy Department ....Dr. Lorraine MINNITE
81 Chair Physics ....Dr. Sean M. O'MALLEY
77 Chair Computer Science Department ... Dr. Suneeta RAMASWAMI
81 Chair Biology Department ....Dr. Daniel SHAIN
88 Chair Childhood Studies Department ....Dr. Lynne VALLONE
83 Chair Psychology Department ....Dr. Bill WHITLOW
83 Chair Sociology/Anthro Department ....Dr. Wojtek WOLFE
88 Chair History Department .... Dr. Wendy WOLOSON
19 Chief Campus Police ....Mr. Richard DINAN
39 Manager Housing & Residence Life .... Mr. Brandon CHANDLER
15 Manager Human Resources .... Ms. Roxanne HUERTAS
96 Sr Analyst University Procurement ....Mr. Christian AHA
09 Research Analyst ....Ms. Emily WOOD
38 Staff Psychologist ....Dr. Rachel THUER
101 Secretary of the University ....Ms. Kimberlee PASTVA

† Regional accreditation is carried under Rutgers the State University of New Jersey New Brunswick.

Rutgers University - New Brunswick (A)

57 US Highway 1, New Brunswick NJ 08901-8554
County: Middlesex FICE Identification: 002629
Unit ID: 186380
Telephone: (848) 932-7821 Carnegie Class: DU-Highest
FAX Number: (732) 932-5532 Calendar System: Semester
URL: https://newbrunswick.rutgers.edu/
Established: 1766 Annual Undergrad Tuition & Fees (In-State): $15,003
Enrollment: 50,411 Coed
Affiliation or Control: State IRS Status: 501(c)3
Highest Offering: Doctorate
Accreditation: M, ART, CACREP, CAEPT, CEA, CLPSY, DANCE, DIETD, HSA, IPSY, LIB, LSAR, MUS, PCSAS, PH, PHAR, PLNG, SCPSY, SPAA, SW

00 President Rutgers University ....Dr. Jonathan HOLLOWAY
88 Chief of Staff Pres & SVP Admin ....Dr. Andrea CONKLIN BUESCHEL
02 Chancellor/Provost New Brunswick .... Dr. Francine CONWAY
17 Chancellor Rutgers RBHS ....Dr. Brian J. STROM
100 Chief of Staff Rutgers RBHS ....Mr. Steven ANDREASSEN
76 Provost Rutgers RBHS ....Dr. Jeffrey CARSON
76 Provost Rutgers RBHS ...... Dr. Patricia FITZGERALD-BOCARSLY
88 CEO Univ Behavioral Health Care ....Dr. Frank GHINASSI
28 Senior VP Equity ....Dr. Enobong (Anna) BRANCH
30 Sr Assoc VP Development .... Ms. Andrianni VOLLAS VISCARIELLO
111 Vice Provost Faculty Advancement ....Dr. Ingrid FULMER
46 Vice Provost Research ....Dr. Denise HIEN
20 Vice Provost UG Education .... Dr. Carolyn MOEHLING
20 Vice Provost Academic Affairs ....Dr. Saundra TOMLINSON-CLARKE
10 Sr Vice Chancellor Fin & Admin RBHS .... Ms. Kathleen BRAMWELL
23 Sr Vice Chanc Clinical Affs RBHS .... Dr. Vicente H. GRACIAS
20 Sr Vice Chancellor Acad Affs RBHS ....Dr. M. Bishr OMARY
21 Vice Chancellor Finance ....Ms. Romayne BOTTI
26 Vice Chancellor Comm & Marketing .... Ms. Jennifer HOLLINGSHEAD
88 Vice Chancellor Grad Medical Educ ....Dr. Sherry HUANG
88 Vice Chanc Diversity & Inclusion ....Dr. Sangeeta LAMBA
88 Vice Chancellor Cancer Pgms RBHS ....Dr. Steven K. LIBUTTI
84 Vice Chancellor Enroll Management ....Mr. Courtney MCANUFF
32 Vice Chancellor Student Affairs ....Dr. Salvador MENA
88 Vice Chancellor Faculty Development .... Dr. Maral MOURADIAN
88 Vice Chanc Translational Med RBHS ..... Dr. Reynold PANETTIERI
88 Vice Chanc Interprofessional Pgm .... Dr. Denise V. RODGERS
88 Assoc Vice Chanc Technology & Instr .... Dr. Paul HAMMOND
27 Assoc Vice Chanc Comm & Marketing .... Mr. Zach HOSSEINI
88 Assoc Vice Chanc Admin & Engagement ....Ms. Keisha DABROWSKI
35 Assoc Vice Chanc Student Affairs .... Dr. Anne NEWMAN
06 University Registrar ....Ms. Kelley BRENNAN-SOKOLOWSKI
47 Int Exec Dean Agri & Nat Resources .... Dr. Laura LAWSON
49 Exec Dean School Arts & Sciences ....Dr. Peter MARCH
67 Dean Ernest Mario Sch Pharm .... Dr. Joseph BARONE
53 Dean Graduate School of Educ ....Dr. Wanda BLANCHETT
88 Dean Life Sciences SAS ....Dr. Lori COVEY
88 Dean Sch Mgmt Labor Relations .... Dr. Adrienne EATON
54 Dean School of Engineering ....Dr. Thomas N. FARRIS
52 Dean Rutgers School of Dental Med ....Dr. Cecile FELDMAN
66 Dean Division of Nursing Science ....Dr. Linda FLYNN
57 Dean Mason Gross School of Art ....Dr. Jason GEARY
92 Admn Dean New Brunswick Honors Col .... Dr. Paul GILMORE
69 Dean School of Public Health .... Dr. Perry N. HALKITIS
63 Dean New Jersey Medical School .... Dr. Robert JOHNSON
88 Int Dean Grad Sch App & Prof Psych .... Dr. Ryan J. KETTLER
50 Dean Sch of Business Newark/NB .... Dr. Lei LEI
97 Dean Douglass Residential College .... Dr. Jacquelyn S. LITT
76 Dean School of Health Professions ..... Dr. Gwendolyn M. MAHON
92 Academic Dean Honors College .... Dr. Matt MATSUDA
58 Int Dean School of Grad Studies .... Dr. Henrik PEDERSEN
70 Dean School of Social Work ....Dr. Cathryn C. POTTER
62 Dean Sch Communication & Info .... Dr. Jonathan POTTER
80 Dean EJB Sch Plng/Public Policy .... Dr. Piyushimita THAKURIAH
12 Asst Dean College Avenue Campus ....Ms. Cynthia SANCHEZ GÓMEZ
12 Asst Dean Livingston Campus ....Dr. Mahasti HASHEMI
12 Asst Dean Busch Campus ....Dr. Jennifer KIM-LEE
88 Vice Dean School of Graduate Stds .... Dr. Kathleen SCOTTO
19 Exec Director Police Services/Chief ....Mr. Kenneth B. COP
39 Exec Director of Residence Life ....Mr. Dan MORRISON
109 Exec Director Student Centers ....Mr. William O'BRIEN
18 Exec Director Space Management .... Mr. Christopher PYE
88 Exec Director Center for Org Leader ....Dr. Brent D. RUBEN
105 Sr Director Office of Creative Svcs ... Ms. Joanne DUS-ZASTROW
31 Sr Director Community Affairs .... Ms. Melissa SELESKY
122 Dir Fraternity & Sorority Affairs ....Ms. JoAnn ARNHOLT
88 Dir Advanced Biotech/Medicine ....Dr. Martin J. BLASER
07 Director Undergrad Admissions .... Ms. Kate BRITTAIN
123 Director Graduate Admissions ....Ms. Linda J. COSTA
88 Director Inst Health/Health Policy .... Dr. XinQi DONG
88 Dir Center Org Dev & Leadership ....Dr. Ralph GIGLIOTTI
09 Director Data Analytics & Mgmt .... Ms. Tina GRYCENKOV
41 Director Intercollegiate Athletics ....Mr. Patrick E. HOBBS
13 Director IT ....Mr. Brian LUPER
08 Director New Brunswick Libraries .... Ms. Dee MAGNONI
60 Director UG Studies Journalism .... Mr. Steven MILLER
85 Dir International Student Services .... Ms. Mohini MUKHERJEE
25 Director Research Financial Service ....Mr. Lamar OGLESBY
96 Director Strategic Sourcing .... Ms. Susan PANACEK
106 Director Instructional Design .... Mr. William PAGAN
22 Director SAS Equal Opp Fund Program .. Dr. Michelle SHOSTACK
38 Director of CAPS Counseling .... Dr. Steven SOHNLE
104 Director Study Abroad ....Dr. Dan WAITE
37 Director Financial Aid .... Ms. Sherrell WATSON-HALL
75 Dir Occupational Hlth Sciences Inst .... Dr. Helmut ZARBL
74 Program Director UG Animal Sciences .... Dr. Aparna M. ZAMA
36 Int Director Career Exploration ....Mr. William JONES
64 Int Director Music Education .... Dr. Steven KEMPER
103 Asst Director Continuing Studies .... Ms. Dalynn KNIGGE
87 Asst Director NB Summer Session .... Ms. Barbara RUSEN
94 Chair Dept Women's/Gender Studies .... Dr. Ethel BROOKS
65 Chair Dept of Ecol/Evol/Natural Res .... Dr. Julie LOCKWOOD
73 Chair Dept of Religion ....Dr. Tao JIANG
82 Chair Political Sciences Dept .... Dr. Daniel KELEMAN
81 Chair Math Department .... Dr. Michael SAKS
29 Sr Alumni Engagement Associate .... Mr. Elijah ROSENTHAL
101 Secretary of the University ....Ms. Kimberlee PASTVA

Rutgers University - Newark (B)

123 Washington St., Newark NJ 07102
County: Essex FICE Identification: 002631
Unit ID: 186399
Telephone: (973) 353-5541 Carnegie Class: DU-Higher
FAX Number: (973) 353-1048 Calendar System: Semester
URL: https://www.newark.rutgers.edu/
Established: 1908 Annual Undergrad Tuition & Fees (In-State): $14,502
Enrollment: 13,231 Coed
Affiliation or Control: State IRS Status: 501(c)3
Highest Offering: Doctorate
Accreditation: &M, ANEST, CAEPT, IPSY, LAW, NURSE, @SP, SPAA, SW

00 President Rutgers University .... Dr. Jonathan HOLLOWAY
88 Chief of Staff Pres & SVP Admin ....Dr. Andrea CONKLIN BUESCHEL
02 Chancellor Rutgers Newark .... Dr. Nancy E. CANTOR
05 Exec Vice Chancellor & Provost .... Dr. Ashwani MONGA
03 Exec Vice Chancellor .... Dr. Sherri-Ann P. BUTTERFIELD
26 Sr Vice Chancellor Public Affairs ....Mr. Peter ENGLOT
46 Sr Vice Chancellor Research ....Dr. Piotr PIOTROWIAK
10 Sr Vice Chancellor Admin & CFO .... Ms. Amber RANDOLPH
32 Sr Vice Chancellor Student Affairs .... Dr. Corlisse THOMAS
86 Vice Chanc External & Govt Rels ....Dr. Marcia W. BROWN
20 Vice Chancellor Acad Pgms/Strategy ....Dr. John GUNKEL
30 Vice Chancellor for Development ....Dr. Irene O'BRIEN
84 Assoc VC Enroll Svcs & Experience ....Dr. Bil LEIPOLD
31 Asst Chancellor Cmty Partnerships .... Dr. Diane HILL
84 Asst Chancellor Enroll Management .... Ms. LaToya BATTLE-BROWN
114 Asst Provost Budget Admin .... Dr. Mary TAMASCO
06 Registrar ....Ms. Marie DIAZ-TORRES
61 Int Co-Dean Rutgers Law School .. Ms. Rose CUISON-VILLAZOR
61 Co-Dean Rutgers Law School ....Ms. Kimberly MUTCHERSON
66 Dean Division of Nursing Science ....Dr. Linda FLYNN
58 Dean Graduate School Newark ....Dr. Taja-Nia HENDERSON
50 Dean Business Newark/New Bruns .... Dr. Lei LEI
49 Dean Arts & Science ....Dr. Jacqueline MATTIS
80 Dean Sch Public Affairs & Admin .... Dr. Charles MENIFIELD
88 Dean School Criminal Justice .... Dr. William MCCARTHY
39 Assoc Dean Housing & Residence Life ....Dr. Angelita BONILLA
88 Exec Director Newark Learn Collabor ..... Ms. Robyn BRADY INCE
18 Exec Director Space Management .... Mr. Christopher PYE
36 Exec Director Career Services ....Ms. Bernadette SO
38 Exec Dir Student Health & Wellness ....Dr. Anice THOMAS
85 Exec Dir Global Engage/Exp Lrng .... Dr. Clayton WALTON
45 Director Admin & Strategic Dev ....Dr. Margaret BRENNAN-TONETTA
13 Director IT ....Ms. Shelley COUSINS
88 Director Express Newark .... Dr. Frances BARTKOWSKI
94 Director Women's & Gender Studies ..Dr. Catherine FITZPATRICK
60 Director Journalism Program ....Ms. Robin GABY FISHER
41 Director of Athletics & Recreation .... Mr. Mark GRIFFIN
29 Director Alumni Relations ....Mr. Terranze GRIFFIN
64 Director RU Chorus ....Mr. Brian HARLOW
19 Director Public Safety Newark .... Mr. Carmelo V. HUERTAS
15 Director Human Resources .... Ms. Candace JOSEPH
90 Director Acad Technology Services .... Ms. Joy MCDONALD
37 Director Financial Aid ....Ms. Natalia MORISSEAU
25 Director Research Financial Svcs ....Mr. Lamar OGLESBY
106 Director Instructional Design ....Mr. William PAGAN
87 Director Summer Session .... Ms. Carmen PARDO
88 Director Center for Metro Research ....Dr. Charles M. PAYNE
81 Director UG Mathematics .... Dr. Robert PUHAK
23 Director Health Services .... Dr. Sandra SAMUELS
92 Director Honors College ....Dr. Laura TROIANO
104 Director Study Abroad ....Mr. Dan WAITE
27 Dir Communications/Marketing ....Ms. Kimberlee S. WILLIAMS
09 Director Inst Effectiveness .... Mr. Chengbo YIN
96 Assoc Director Univ Procurement ....Mr. Wes COLEMAN
103 Asst Director Continuing Studies .... Ms. Dalynn KNIGGE
08 Int Assoc Univ Librarian Newark ....Ms. Rhonda MARKER
21 Manager Business Office ....Ms. Rosann RICHARDS
57 Chair Arts/Culture/Media .... Mr. Ned DREW
83 Chair Sociology Department ....Dr. Christopher DUNCAN
82 Chair Political Science Department ....Dr. Elizabeth HULL
88 Chair African American Studies .... Mr. John KEENE
53 Chair Urban Education Program ....Dr. Arthur B. POWELL
22 Program Coordinator EOF .... Mr. Amir MALCOLM
04 Sr Exec Associate to Chancellor ....Ms. Carla HAILEY PENN
101 Secretary of the University ....Ms. Kimberlee PASTVA

† Regional accreditation is carried under Rutgers the State University of New Jersey New Brunswick.

Rutgers New Jersey Medical School (C)

185 South Orange Avenue, Newark NJ 07103
Telephone: (973) 972-4538 FICE Identification: 002620
Accreditation: &M, MED

Rutgers - Robert Wood Johnson Medical School (D)

675 Hoes Lane West, Piscataway NJ 08854
Telephone: (732) 235-6300 FICE Identification: 024549
Accreditation: &M, CAMPEP, IPSY, MED, PAST

Rutgers School of Dental Medicine (E)

110 Bergen Street, Suite B812, Newark NJ 07103
Telephone: (973) 972-4440 FICE Identification: 024635
Accreditation: &M, DENT

Rutgers School of Health Professions (F)

65 Bergen Street, Room 149, Newark NJ 07107
Telephone: (973) 972-4276 FICE Identification: 020668
Accreditation: &M, ARCPA, CACREP, CAHIIM, CYTO, DIETC, DIETI, DMS, MT, OTA, PTA

Rutgers School of Nursing (G)

180 University Avenue, Newark NJ 07102
Telephone: (973) 353-5293 Identification: 666970
Accreditation: &M, MIDWF, NURSE

Rutgers School of Public Health (H)

683 Hoes Lane West, Piscataway NJ 08854
Telephone: (732) 235-9700 Identification: 666991
Accreditation: &M, PH

Saint Elizabeth University (I)

2 Convent Road, Morristown NJ 07960-6989
County: Morris FICE Identification: 002600
Unit ID: 186618
Telephone: (973) 290-4000 Carnegie Class: Masters/M
FAX Number: N/A Calendar System: Semester
URL: www.steu.edu
Established: 1899 Annual Undergrad Tuition & Fees: $34,876
Enrollment: 1,272 Coed
Affiliation or Control: Roman Catholic IRS Status: 501(c)3
Highest Offering: Doctorate
Accreditation: M, #ARCPA, CAEPT, COPSY, DIETD, DIETI, NUR, SW

01 President ....Dr. Gary B. CROSBY

Code	Title	Name
05	VP for Academic Affairs	Dr. Anne BARTLETT
32	VP Student Life	Ms. Katherine BUCK
10	VP Finance Admin/Treasurer	Mr. Michael FESCOE
111	VP Institutional Advancement	Mr. Joseph ERCKERT
84	VP Enrollment Management	Ms. Joanne LANDERS
21	Controller	Ms. Julia PEREZ
06	Registrar	Ms. Marybeth OBRYCKI
09	Dir Inst Research & Acad Assessment	Dr. Michele YURECKO
08	Director Mahoney Library	Mr. Mark FERGUSON
42	Campus Minister	Ms. Clare ETTENSOHN
18	Director of Facilities & Security	Mr. James GERRISH
37	Director of Financial Aid	Ms. Rebecca E. REES
26	Director Marketing/ Communications	Ms. Denise G. PANYIK-DALE
22	Director EOF Program	Mr. David HILL
78	Coord Experiential Lrng & Mentoring	Ms. Mayelin TORRES
38	Director of Counseling	Ms. Zsuzsanna NAGY
88	Dir Volunteerism & Svc Learning	Ms. Jayne I. MURPHY-MORRIS
35	Director of Student Engagement	Ms. Naima K. RICKS
41	Director of Athletics	Mr. Thomas WAGENBLAST
29	Dir Alumni Engagement/Alumni Assoc	Ms. Jennifer SANCHEZ
15	Director Human Resources	Vacant
109	C-Store/Dining Services	Mr. Dean PIACENTINI
110	Asst VP Institutional Advancement	Vacant
105	Director IT-Web	Mr. David B. RABINOWITZ
13	Chief Info Technology Officer	Ms. Margie ROHR
107	Dean of Professional Studies	Dr. Patricia HEINDEL
49	Dean of Arts and Sciences	Dr. Anthony SANTAMARIA
19	Director Bi-Campus Security	Mr. Richard WALL
39	Director Residence Life	Ms. Deborah J. PAWLIKOWSKI
04	Exec Asst to President	Mrs. Meghan AITKEN
07	Director of Admissions	Ms. Nadine HAWKINS
108	Director Institutional Assessment	Ms. Michele YURECKO
86	Director Government Relations	Vacant
90	Director Academic Computing	Dr. Jeffrey GUTKIN
91	Director Administrative Computing	Ms. Angela IANNELLI

Saint Peter's University (A)

2641 Kennedy Boulevard, Jersey City NJ 07306-5997

County: Hudson | FICE Identification: 002638 | Unit ID: 186432

Telephone: (201) 761-6000 | Carnegie Class: Masters/L

FAX Number: (201) 761-7801 | Calendar System: Semester

URL: www.saintpeters.edu

Established: 1872 | Annual Undergrad Tuition & Fees: $38,760

Enrollment: 3,197 | Coed

Affiliation or Control: Roman Catholic | IRS Status: 501(c)3

Highest Offering: Doctorate

Accreditation: M, CAEPT, IACBE, NURSE

Code	Title	Name
01	President	Dr. Eugene J. CORNACCHIA
45	Spec Asst to Pres for Inst Plng	Dr. Virginia BENDER
100	Special Assistant to the President	Dr. Eileen POIANI
04	Exec Admin Asst to President	Ms. Jane HALMA
05	Provost/VP Academic Affairs	Dr. Frederick BONATO
10	VP of Finance & Business	Mr. Paul CIRAULO
32	VP Stdnt Life & Development	Ms. Erin MCCANN
42	Vice Pres for Mission & Ministry	Fr. Andrew DOWNING, SJ
84	VP Enrollment Mgmt & Marketing	Ms. Elizabeth SULLIVAN
13	CIO of Information Technology/Ops	Mr. Michael DE VARTI
111	Vice President Advancement	Ms. Leah LETO
20	Asst VP Academic Affairs	Dr. Nicole DECAPUA-RINCK
66	Dean of Nursing	Dr. Lauren O'HARE
50	KPMG Dean School of Business	Dr. Mary Kate NAATUS
53	Dean Caufield School of Education	Dr. Joseph DORIA
49	Dean College of Arts & Sciences	Dr. WeiDong ZHU
78	Exec Dir Career Engagement/Exp Lrng	Mr. Crescenzo FONZO
123	Exec Dir Admission Graduate	Vacant
26	Exec Dir University Communications	Ms. Sarah MALINOWSKI-FERRARY
37	Director of Student Fin Aid	Ms. Jennifer RAGSDALE
08	Director of the Library	Ms. Daisy DECOSTER
09	Executive Director of IR	Mr. Ben SCHOLZ
19	Director of Campus Safety	Mr. Scott TORRE
15	Director of Human Resources	Ms. Elena SERRA
29	Director Alumni Engagement	Ms. Claudia POPE-BAYNE
44	Director of Annual Giving	Mr. Scott DONOVAN
38	Dir of Counseling & Psyc Service	Ms. Colleen SZEFINSKI
39	Director of Residence Life	Mr. Willie LEE
41	Director of Athletics	Ms. Rachelle PAUL
42	Director of Campus Ministry	Rev. Andrew DOWNING
14	Director of Network Services	Mr. Bert VABRE
51	Director of Center Global Learning	Mr. Scott KELLER
18	Dir of Facility & Univ Services	Ms. Anna DE PAULA
102	Dir Foundation/Corp & Govt Rels	Mr. Emory EDWARDS
105	Dir of Web Strategies & Comm	Vacant
36	Director of Student Placement	Ms. Laura PAKHMANOV
06	Registrar	Ms. Kamla SINGH
43	General Counsel	Mr. Eugene T. PAOLINO

Salem Community College (B)

460 Hollywood Avenue, Carneys Point NJ 08069-2799

County: Salem | FICE Identification: 005461 | Unit ID: 186469

Telephone: (856) 299-2100 | Carnegie Class: Assoc/MT-VT-High Trad

FAX Number: (856) 351-2634 | Calendar System: Semester

URL: www.salemcc.edu

Established: 1972 | Annual Undergrad Tuition & Fees (In-District): $6,360

Enrollment: 865 | Coed

Affiliation or Control: State/Local | IRS Status: 501(c)3

Highest Offering: Associate Degree

Accreditation: M, ADNUR

Code	Title	Name
01	President	Dr. Michael GORMAN
05	Dean of Academic Affairs	Mr. Kenneth ROBEL
10	Chief Financial/Business Ofcr	Mr. Kevin KUTCHER
04	Exec Asst to the President	Ms. Maria FANTINI
20	Assoc Dean of Academic Affairs	Mrs. Maura CAVANAGH-DICK
84	Dean of Enrollment/Admissions	Mr. Kevin CATALFAMO
06	Registrar	Ms. Jill JAMES
108	Dir of Institutional Effectiveness	Mr. Marc ROY
19	Director of Security/Safety	Mr. John MORRISON
09	Asst Dean Inst Research & Planning	Mr. Ronald BURKHARDT
30	Dir of Inst Advancement/Alumni	Mr. William CLARK
37	Director of Financial Aid	Mrs. Heather STITH
66	Dir of Nursing/Allied Health	Mrs. Terri COVELLO
88	Director of Academic & Info Svcs	Ms. Jennifer PIERCE
13	Director of Information Technology	Mr. Larry MCKEE
102	Executive Director SCC Foundation	Ms. Ceil SMITH
21	Manager of Finance	Ms. Lynn MCCOSKER
121	Manager of Advising	Mrs. Laura GREEN
88	Accounts Manager	Ms. Adrienne MUSUMECI
07	Director of Admissions	Mrs. Kelly SCHIMPF
15	Manager Human Resources	Ms. Barbara QUAILE
41	Athletic Director	Mr. Bob BUNNELL

Seton Hall University (C)

400 S Orange Avenue, South Orange NJ 07079-2697

County: Essex | FICE Identification: 002632 | Unit ID: 186584

Telephone: (973) 761-9000 | Carnegie Class: DU-Higher

FAX Number: N/A | Calendar System: Semester

URL: www.shu.edu

Established: 1856 | Annual Undergrad Tuition & Fees: $45,290

Enrollment: 9,814 | Coed

Affiliation or Control: Roman Catholic | IRS Status: 501(c)3

Highest Offering: Doctorate

Accreditation: M, ARCPA, CAATE, CAEP, CAEPN, COPSY, HSA, LAW, MFCD, NURSE, OT, PTA, SP, SPAA, SW, THEOL

Code	Title	Name
01	President	Dr. Joseph E. NYRE
05	Provost & Executive Vice President	Dr. Katia PASSERINI
20	Senior Associate Provost	Ms. Amy NEWCOMBE
20	Assoc Prov Undergrad Ed/Assessment	Dr. Peter SHOEMAKER
10	Interim Vice Pres for Finance/CFO	Mr. Robert MCLAUGHLIN
11	EVP Operations & Chief of Staff	Mr. Patrick G. LYONS
101	VP for Board Affairs/Univ Strategy	Dr. Michelle NELSON
43	General Counsel	Ms. Kimberly A. CAPADONA
110	Vice Pres for Advancement	Mr. Jon PAPARSENOS
111	Vice Pres for University Relations	Mr. Matthew BOROWICK
32	Interim VP for Student Services	Dr. Monica BURNETTE
84	Sr Vice Pres for Enrollment Mgmt	Dr. Alyssa MCCLOUD
42	Vice Pres for Mission & Ministry	Rev. Colin KAY
15	Assoc Vice Pres Human Resources	Mr. Michael SILVESTRO
29	Assoc VP Alumni/Engage/ Philanthropy	Mr. Anthony D. BELLUCCI
112	Sr Dir Principal Gifts/Gift Plng	Mr. Joseph GUASCONI
18	Assoc VP for Facilities & Operation	Mr. John SIGNORELLO
35	Assoc VP/Dean of Students	Ms. Karen VAN NORMAN
45	Dir Advising Tech Integration	Dr. Anna CALKA
88	Assoc Provost for Strategy/Finance	Mr. Erik LILLQUIST
20	Assoc Provost for Academic Affairs	Dr. Christopher CUCCIA
88	Special Advisor to Provost	Rev. Forrest PRITCHETT
88	Special Advisor to Provost	Dr. Jonathan FARINA
88	Special Advisor to Provost	Dr. Kurt ROTTHOFF
19	Asst VP Security	Mr. Patrick LINFANTE
49	Dean of Arts & Sciences	Dr. Georita FRIERSON
50	Dean School of Business	Dr. Joyce A. STRAWSER
60	Dean Communication & the Arts	Ms. Deirdre YATES
66	Dean of Nursing	Dr. Marie FOLEY
53	Interim Dean Education Svcs	Dr. Joseph MARTINELLI
73	Rector/Dean School of Theology	Msgr. Joseph R. REILLY
63	Dean School of Health & Med Science	Dr. Brian SHULMAN
82	Interim Dean Diplomacy/Intl Rels	Dr. Courtney SMITH
61	Dean of Law School	Ms. Kathleen BOOZANG
08	Dean of University Libraries	Dr. John E. BUSCHMAN
51	Dean Cont Educ/Professional Studies	Ms. Karen PASSARO
22	Assoc Dean/Director of EOP	Dr. Majid WHITNEY
88	Director Upward Bound	Ms. Shanetta S. LILLARD
21	Director of Business Affairs	Mr. Peter TRUNK
13	Chief Information Officer	Dr. Stephen LANDRY
28	Director Compliance & Risk Mgmt	Ms. Lori A. BROWN
37	Director for Financial Aid	Ms. Javonda ASANTE
39	Interim Dir of Housing/Res Life	Ms. Jessica PROANO
06	University Registrar	Ms. Autumn BUCIOR
36	Director of the Career Center	Ms. Reesa GREENWALD
41	Dir Athletics/Recreational Services	Mr. Bryan FELT
18	Director of Facilities Engineering	Mr. Leon VANDEMEULEBROEKE
38	Director of Counseling	Dr. Dianne AGUERO-TROTTER
42	Director of Campus Ministry	Rev. Colin KAY
88	Minister to Priest Community	Fr. Gerard BUONOPANE
09	Dir Plng Inst Research & Assessment	Ms. Connie L. BEALE
07	Dir of Undergraduate Admissions	Ms. Mary Clare CULLUM
96	Director of Procurement	Mr. Martin E. KOELLER
23	Director Health Services	Ms. Diane LYNCH
88	Director Core Curriculum	Dr. Nancy ENRIGHT
102	Dir Foundation/Corporate Relations	Mr. Steven SMITH
104	Director International Programs	Ms. Maria BOUZAS
58	Director Graduate Affairs/Info Svcs	Mr. Israel CHIA
86	Director Government Relations	Mr. Matthew BOROWICK

Stevens Institute of Technology (D)

1 Castle Point Terrace, Hoboken NJ 07030

County: Hudson | FICE Identification: 002639 | Unit ID: 186867

Telephone: (201) 216-5000 | Carnegie Class: DU-Higher

FAX Number: (201) 216-8341 | Calendar System: Semester

URL: www.stevens.edu

Established: 1870 | Annual Undergrad Tuition & Fees: $55,952

Enrollment: 7,257 | Coed

Affiliation or Control: Independent Non-Profit | IRS Status: 501(c)3

Highest Offering: Doctorate

Accreditation: M

Code	Title	Name
01	President	Dr. Nariman FARVARDIN
04	Exec Assistant to the President	Ms. Phyllis RUIZ
05	Provost/VP Academics	Dr. Christophe PIERRE
30	VP Development/Alumni Engagement	Ms. Laura ROSE
10	CFO/VP for Finance/Treasurer	Dr. Louis MAYER
84	VP Enrollment Mgt/Student Affairs	Ms. Marybeth MURPHY
15	Vice President Human Resources	Mr. Warren PETTY
43	Vice President General Counsel	Ms. Kathy L. SCHULZ
13	VP for Information Technology & CIO	Mr. Tej PATEL
26	VP Univ Relations/Chief of Staff	Ms. Beth MCGRATH
18	VP for Facilities/Campus Operations	Mr. Robert MAFFIA
32	Assistant VP Student Affairs	Ms. Sara KLEIN
21	AVP for Financial Planning/Budgets	Ms. Theresa PASCOE
35	Dean of Students	Mr. Kenneth NILSEN
39	Dean for Residential & Dining Svcs	Ms. Trina BALLANTYNE
20	Assoc Dean Undergraduate Academics	Dr. Erol CESMEBASI
29	AVP Alumni Engagement & ED/SAA	Mr. Matthew GWIN
36	Exec Director of Stevens Career Ctr	Ms. Cherena WALKER
19	Chief & Director of Campus Police	Mr. Timothy GRIFFIN
41	Athletic Director	Mr. Russell ROGERS
85	Director of Intl Student & Scholars	Ms. Jean LEE
38	Director of Student Counseling	Dr. Eric D. ROSE
25	Exec Director Sponsored Research	Ms. Barbara DEHAVEN
54	Dean School of Engr & Science	Dr. Jean ZU
50	Dean School of Business	Dr. Gregory PRASTACOS
49	Dean College of Arts & Letters	Dr. Kelland THOMAS
77	Dean School Systems & Enterprise	Dr. Yehia MASSOUD
07	Dean of UG Admissions	Ms. Jacqueline WILLIAMS
09	Director of Institutional Research	Ms. Minghui WANG
28	Exec Director Diversity & Inclusion	Ms. Susan METZ
58	Vice Provost for Graduate Education	Dr. Constantin CHASSAPIS
20	Vice Prov Acad Innov & Faculty Affs	Dr. Xiangwu ZENG
46	Vice Provost for Research	Dr. Dilhan KALYON
06	Registrar	Ms. Anna-Lize HARRIS
08	Director of Library & Info Svcs	Ms. Linda BENINGHOVE
104	Director International Programs	Ms. Susan RACHOUH
106	Assistant Dean WebCampus	Mr. Robert ZOTTI
37	AVP for Financial Aid/UG Admissions	Ms. Susan GROSS
96	Director of Procurement	Mr. Brian SEABOLD
108	Asst Director for Assessment	Dr. Jie ZHANG

Stockton University (E)

101 Vera King Farris Drive, Galloway NJ 08205-9441

County: Atlantic | FICE Identification: 009345 | Unit ID: 186876

Telephone: (609) 652-1776 | Carnegie Class: Masters/L

FAX Number: N/A | Calendar System: Semester

URL: www.stockton.edu

Established: 1969 | Annual Undergrad Tuition & Fees (In-State): $14,329

Enrollment: 9,893 | Coed

Affiliation or Control: State | IRS Status: 501(c)3

Highest Offering: Doctorate

Accreditation: M, CAEP, NURSE, OT, PTA, SP, SW

Code	Title	Name
01	President	Dr. Harvey KESSELMAN
05	Provost & VP for Academic Affairs	Dr. Leamor KAHANOV
03	Exec VP and Chief of Staff	Dr. Susan C. DAVENPORT
10	Vice Pres Admin/Finance & CFO	Ms. Jennifer POTTER
32	Vice President Student Affairs	Dr. Christopher C. CATCHING
20	Assoc VP Academic Affairs, CAO/AC	Dr. Michelle MCDONALD
20	Assistant VP for Academic Affairs	Ms. AmyBeth GLASS
96	Dir Procurement/Contract & Risk Mgt	Mr. Christopher HOWARD
13	Chief Information Officer	Mr. Scott HUSTON
18	VP Facilities & Operations	Mr. Donald M. HUDSON
28	Chief Ofcr Inst Diversity/Inclusion	Dr. Valerie HAYES
88	Exec Dir WJ Hughes Ctr Pub Policy	Mr. John FROONJIAN
30	Chief Dev Ofcr/Exec Dir Found	Mr. Daniel P. NUGENT
26	Exec Dir Univ Relations/Marketing	Mr. Geoffrey PETTIFER
84	Chief Enrollment Management Officer	Mr. Robert HEINRICH
07	Director of Admissions	Ms. Heather MEDINA
06	Registrar	Mr. Joseph LOSASSO
53	Dean School of Education	Dr. Claudine KEENAN
97	Dean School of General Studies	Dr. Robert S. GREGG
79	Dean School Arts & Humanities	Dr. Lisa HONAKER
50	Dean School of Business	Dr. Alphonso OGBUEHI
81	Dean School of Natural Sci/Math	Dr. Peter STRAUB
83	Dean Sch Social/Behav Sciences	Dr. Marissa LEVY
76	Dean School of Health Sciences	Dr. Margaret SLUSSER
09	Director Institutional Research	Ms. Jessica KAY
08	Director of Library Services	Mr. Joseph TOTH
88	Director SRI & ETTC	Ms. Patricia WEEKS
37	Director of Financial Aid	Mr. Christopher CONNORS
19	Director of Campus Public Safety	Mr. Adrian WIGGINS
88	Manager Performing Arts Center	Vacant
41	Exec Dir Athletics & Recreation	Mr. Kevin MCHUGH
39	Executive Director Residential Life	Mr. Steven E. RADWANSKI
124	Asst VP Transitions & Retention	Mr. Walter L. TARVER, III
43	General Counsel	Mr. Brian KOWALSKI

121 Interim Director Academic Advising ....Dr. Kate SPALDING
114 Director of Budget/Fiscal Planning .... Ms. Diane GARRISON
29 Director Alumni Relations ....Ms. Sara FAUROT
110 Assoc Chf Devel Ofcr/Campaign Mgr ....Ms. Cindy CRAGER
12 COO Atlantic City Campus ....Mr. Brian K. JACKSON
04 Admin Assistant to the President .... Ms. Kathryn MASON
25 Exec Dir Research & Spons Programs ....Vacant
45 Chief Institutional Planning Office ....Mr. Peter BARATTA
38 Asst VP Student Health & Wellness ....Mr. Stephen DAVIS
86 VP Personnel/Labor/Govt Relations ....Mr. Michael ANGULO
104 Director Global Engagement .... Dr. Jiangyuan ZHOU
22 Director Title IX/EEO ....Ms. Brittany MEDIO

Sussex County Community College (A)

One College Hill Road, Newton NJ 07860-1146
County: Sussex FICE Identification: 025688
Unit ID: 247603
Telephone: (973) 300-2100 Carnegie Class: Assoc/HT-High Trad
FAX Number: (973) 579-9351 Calendar System: Semester
URL: www.sussex.edu
Established: 1982 Annual Undergrad Tuition & Fees (In-District): $7,080
Enrollment: 2,190 Coed
Affiliation or Control: State/Local IRS Status: 501(c)3
Highest Offering: Associate Degree
Accreditation: M, MAC

01 President ....Dr. Jon H. CONNOLLY
10 CFO/Vice Pres Administrative Svcs .... Ketan GANDHI
05 SVP of Academic & Student Affairs ....Dr. Kathleen OKAY
15 Dir of Human Resources ....Beth MULLER
26 Dir of Marketing/Public Info .... Kathleen PETERSON
88 Assistant Director of Testing Svcs ....Kathleen CARR
09 AVP Student Success/Inst Effective .... Cory HOMER
41 Dir of Athletics/Dean Student Affs ....John KUNTZ
21 Director of Accounting .... Manal MESEHA
19 Director Campus Safety & Security .... Fred MAMAY
113 Dir of Bursar/Financial Services .... Kimberly RYAN
08 Director of College Library ....Stephanie COOPER
07 Director of Admissions .... Todd POLTERSDORF
37 Director of Financial Aid .... Diane PIENTA-LETTA
06 Registrar ....Solweig DIMINO
101 Exec Asst to Pres/Board of Trustees .... Wendy FULLEM
04 President's Office Assistant ....Melissa DEJOSEPH
102 Exec Director of Foundation ....Stan KULA
13 Director Information Technology ....Judy LOVAS
38 Director Student Counseling ....Kathy GALLICHIO
18 Chf Facilities/Physical Plant Ofcr ....Charlene PETERSON
107 Dean of Prof Studies/SS & STEM ....Nancy GALLO
49 Assoc VPAA/Dean Liberal Arts ....Sherry FITZGERALD
88 Dean of Technical Occupations ....Jason FRUGE
96 Director of Purchasing .... Heather GALLAGHER

Talmudical Academy of New Jersey (B)

Route 524, Adelphia NJ 07710-9999
County: Monmouth FICE Identification: 011989
Unit ID: 186900
Telephone: (732) 431-1600 Carnegie Class: Spec-4-yr-Faith
FAX Number: (732) 431-3951 Calendar System: Semester
URL: https://talmudicalacademynj.com/
Established: 1971 Annual Undergrad Tuition & Fees: $13,900
Enrollment: 63 Male
Affiliation or Control: Independent Non-Profit IRS Status: 501(c)3
Highest Offering: Baccalaureate
Accreditation: RABN

01 President .... Mr. Charles SEMAH
05 Dean/Registrar ....Rabbi Yeruchim SHAIN
10 Chief Financial/Business Officer ....Mr. Neal GOTTLIEB

Thomas Edison State University (C)

111 W State Street, Trenton NJ 08608-1176
County: Mercer FICE Identification: 021922
Unit ID: 187046
Telephone: (609) 984-1100 Carnegie Class: Masters/M
FAX Number: (609) 292-9000 Calendar System: Other
URL: www.tesu.edu
Established: 1972 Annual Undergrad Tuition & Fees (In-State): $7,182
Enrollment: 10,495 Coed
Affiliation or Control: State IRS Status: 501(c)3
Highest Offering: Doctorate
Accreditation: M, ACBSP, CAEPT, NURSE, POLYT

01 President ....Dr. Merodie A. HANCOCK
05 Provost/SVP Academic Affairs .... Dr. Cynthia BAUM
10 Senior Vice President & CFO .... Mr. Christopher STRINGER
26 Vice President Public Affairs ....Mr. John P. THURBER
31 Vice Pres Cmty & Govt Affairs .... Ms. Robin WALTON
84 VP Enrollment Management ....Dr. Dennis DEVERY
51 Vice Prov/Dean Watson Sch Cont Stds ....Dr. Joseph YOUNGBLOOD, II
88 Assoc VP Military/Veteran Education ....Mr. Louis MARTINI
09 Assoc VP for Planning & Research ....Dr. Ann Marie SENIOR
27 Senior Director of Communications ...Ms. Victoria A. MONAGHAN
88 Assoc Provost Learning Technology .... Mr. Matthew COOPER
21 Treasurer .... Mr. Steve D. ALBANO
100 Chief of Staff .... Mr. Michael MANCINI
88 Director Market Research/ Assessment ....Ms. Marie R. POWER-BARNES
43 General Counsel ....Ms. Jennifer HOFF
66 Dean School of Nursing .... Dr. Filomela MARSHALL
49 Dean Heavin Sch of Arts & Sciences ....Dr. John WOZNICKI
50 Dean School of Business & Mgmt ....Dr. Michael WILLIAMS
06 Assoc Vice Pres/Univ Registrar ....Ms. Catharine PUNCHELLO-COBOS
72 Dean School of Applied Sci/Tech .... Dr. John AJE
21 Controller ....Mr. John SCHAIBLE
13 Chief Information Officer ....Mr. Drew W. HOPKINS
88 Senior Dir Office of Testing ....Mr. Maureen WOODRUFF
29 Director of Alumni Affairs ....Ms. Meg FRANTZ
37 Director of Financial Aid ....Mr. James OWENS
18 Director Facilities & Operations .... Ms. Mary C. HACK
30 Associate VP for Development ....Ms. Misty ISAK
102 Director Corporate Relations ....Mr. Frederick BRAND
08 State Librarian ....Ms. Mary CHUTE
105 Dir Website/Multimedia Productivity ...... Mr. Jeffery LUSHBAUGH
111 Chief Advanc Ofcr/VP TESU Fndn .... Ms. Deb D'ARCANGELO
44 Dir Annual Fund/Donor Relations ....Ms. Jennifer GUERRERO
88 Executive Director Watson Institute .... Ms. Barbara JOHNSON
22 ADA Coordinator ....Ms. Laura BRENNER-SCOTTI
88 Sr Fellow/Dir Ctr Leadership/Govt ...... Ms. Melissa A. MASZCZAK
03 Chief of Staff/Chief Operating Ofcr ....Michael MANCINI
04 Executiv Assistant to the President ....Jamie ADAMS
101 Secretary of the Institution/Board ....Michael MANCINI

† The Thomas Edison State University 12-month enrollment is 17,511.

Union County College (D)

1033 Springfield Avenue, Cranford NJ 07016-1598
County: Union FICE Identification: 002643
Unit ID: 187198
Telephone: (908) 709-7000 Carnegie Class: Assoc/HT-High Trad
FAX Number: (908) 709-0527 Calendar System: Semester
URL: www.ucc.edu
Established: 1933 Annual Undergrad Tuition & Fees (In-District): $10,562
Enrollment: 8,298 Coed
Affiliation or Control: State/Local IRS Status: 501(c)3
Highest Offering: Associate Degree
Accreditation: M, PTAA

01 President .... Dr. Margaret M. MCMENAMIN
05 Vice President Academic Affairs .... Dr. Maris LOWN
10 Vice Pres Financial Affs/Treasurer ....Ms. Lynne A. WELCH
32 Vice President Student Development ..Dr. Demond T. HARGROVE
11 Vice President Admin Services ....Vacant
88 Associate VP Administration .... Mr. Vincent LOTANO
21 Associate VP Finance ....Ms. Lori WILKIN
20 Assoc VPAA & Dean Scotch Plains ....Dr. Bernard POLNARIEV
121 Asst VP SD & Dean Student Success ....Ms. Rebecca ROYAL
09 Exec Dir of Institutional Research ....Dr. Elizabeth COONER
102 Exec Director Foundation ....Mr. Douglas ROUSE
51 Exec Dir Cont Educ & Workforce Dev .... Dr. Lisa HISCANO
26 Exec Dir Col Relations & Board Sec ....Dr. Jaime M. SEGAL
43 Assc Gen Couns/Exec Dir Procurement ....Dr. Marlene WHITE
12 Dean Plainfield Campus ....Dr. Victoria UKACHUKWU
12 Interim Dean Elizabeth Campus ....Dr. Melinda NORELLI
79 Dean of Humanities ....Dr. Melissa SANDE
81 Interim Dean of STEM ....Mr. William DUNSCOMBE
83 Dean Social Sciences & Business ....Vacant
116 Dir Financial Operations & Grants .... Ms. Jane KANE
96 Director of Purchasing ....Mr. Mark ANDERSON
13 Chief Information Officer .... Mr. Eric WINCH
18 Director Facilities .... Mr. Robert HOGAN
19 Director Public Safety .... Mr. Joseph HINES
25 Director of Grants .... Ms. Cheryl SHIBER
15 Director of Human Resources ....Vacant
41 Dean of College Life .... Ms. Tamalea SMITH
35 Dean of Students ....Vacant
88 Asst Dean of Students ....Ms. Beatriz RODRIGUEZ
06 Registrar .... Ms. Nina HERNANDEZ
36 Asst Dean & Director Advising .... Ms. Heather KEITH
37 Director of Financial Aid ....Mr. Dayne CHANCE
113 Director of Student Accounts ....Ms. Kathryn VELLIOS
07 Director of Admissions ....Mr. Gregory BENEDICT, JR.
28 Director EOF ....Mr. Samuel CASIMIR
41 Director of Athletics ....Vacant
24 Director Media Services .... Mr. Patrick GALLAGHER
106 Director of Instructional Design ....Ms. Gaby ANGULO
08 Director of Libraries ....Ms. Jane JIANG
88 Dir Acad Learning Center ....Mr. Jose PAEZ-FIGUEROA
14 Technical Director .... Mr. Kevin TSAKONAS
14 Enterprise Applications Director ....Mr. Wisam SHAHIN
04 Executive Assistant to President .... Ms. Susan MATIKA
40 Manager Bookstore ....Ms. Christine SALZMAN
21 Assistant VP of Finance ....Ms. Marlene SOUSA

Union County College Elizabeth Campus (E)

40 W Jersey Street, Elizabeth NJ 07202-2314
Telephone: (908) 965-6000 Identification: 770134
Accreditation: &M, DNUR, EMT

Union County College Plainfield Campus (F)

232 E 2nd Street, Plainfield NJ 07060
Telephone: (908) 412-3599 Identification: 770135
Accreditation: &M, #COARC

University of Phoenix Jersey City Campus (G)

88 Town Square Place, Jersey City NJ 07310-1756
Telephone: (201) 610-1408 Identification: 770218
Accreditation: &HLC, ACBSP

† No longer accepting campus-based students.

Warren County Community College (H)

475 Route 57 W, Washington NJ 07882-4343
County: Warren FICE Identification: 025039
Unit ID: 245625
Telephone: (908) 835-9222 Carnegie Class: Assoc/HT-High Non
FAX Number: (908) 689-9262 Calendar System: Semester
URL: www.warren.edu
Established: 1981 Annual Undergrad Tuition & Fees (In-District): $5,490
Enrollment: 3,251 Coed
Affiliation or Control: State/Local IRS Status: 501(c)3
Highest Offering: Associate Degree
Accreditation: M, ADNUR, MAC

01 President ....Dr. William AUSTIN
10 Vice Pres Finance & Operations .... Ms. Barbara PRATT
51 Vice Pres Corporate/Continuing Educ ....Ms. Eve AZAR
11 Dean of Administration ....Mr. Dennis FLORENTINE
07 VP of Student Services .... Mr. Jeremy BEELER
05 VP of Academics ....Dr. Marianne VANDEURSEN
37 Director of Financial Aid ....Ms. Jacqueline DALY
15 Director Human Resources ....Ms. Sharon HINTZ
04 Administrative Asst to President ....Ms. Genevieve VASKO
08 Head Librarian ....Ms. Lisa STOLL
09 Director of Institutional Research ....Ms. Nikki DADARRIA
102 Dir Foundation/Corporate Relations ......Ms. Samir ELBASSIOUNY

Westminster Choir College (I)

2083 Lawrenceville Road, Lawrenceville NJ 08648
Telephone: (609) 896-5000 Identification: 770128
Accreditation: &M, MUS

William Paterson University of New Jersey (J)

300 Pompton Road, Wayne NJ 07470-2152
County: Passaic FICE Identification: 002625
Unit ID: 187444
Telephone: (973) 720-2000 Carnegie Class: Masters/L
FAX Number: N/A Calendar System: Semester
URL: www.wpunj.edu
Established: 1855 Annual Undergrad Tuition & Fees (In-State): $13,770
Enrollment: 9,635 Coed
Affiliation or Control: State IRS Status: 501(c)3
Highest Offering: Doctorate
Accreditation: M, ART, CAATE, CACREP, CAEP, CLPSY, MPCAC, MUS, NURSE, PH, SP

01 President ....Dr. Richard HELLDOBLER
05 Senior Vice President/Provost ....Dr. Joshua POWERS
100 Chief of Staff to President/ BOT ....Ms. Loretta MCLAUGHLIN VIGNIER
10 Sr VP Administration/Finance ....Vacant
111 Vice Pres Institutional Advancement .... Ms. Pamela FERGUSON
32 Vice President Student Development .... Dr. Miki CAMMARATA
84 VP of Enrollment Management ....Dr. Reginald ROSS
20 Assoc Provost Academic Development .....Ms. Danielle LIAUTAUD
114 Director of University Budgets .... Mr. Timothy LEVER
11 Assoc VP for Administration ....Mr. Kevin GARVEY
26 VP Marketing & Public Relations .... Mr. Stuart GOLDSTEIN
15 Vice Pres Human Resources .... Ms. Allison BOUCHER-JARVIS
19 Dir Public Safety & Univ Police ....Mr. Charles LOWE
35 Assoc VP for Student Development ....Mr. Francisco DIAZ
35 Assoc VP/Dean Student Development .... Dr. Glen SHERMAN
60 Interim Dean Col Arts/ Comm ....Dr. Loretta C. MCLAUGHLIN VIGNIER
53 Dean College of Education .... Dr. Amy GINSBERG
66 Dean College of Science & Health ....Dr. Venkatanarayanan SHARMA
79 Dean Col of Arts/Humanities/Soc Sci .... Dr. Wartyna DAVIS
50 Dean College of Business ....Dr. Anthony BOWRIN
08 Dean D & L Cheng Library .... Dr. Edward OWUSU-ANSAH
21 Assoc VP Finance & Controller .... Ms. Samantha GREEN
28 Dir Empl Rels/Ethics/Title IX Coord ....Ms. Regina A. TINDALL
51 Exec Dir Cont Educ/Distance Lrng ....Dr. Bernadette TIERNAN
20 Associate Provost ....Ms. Kara M. RABBITT
20 Associate Provost Academic Affairs ....Dr. Sandra B. HILL
20 Assoc Prov for Curriculum & Intl Ed ....Dr. Jonathan LINCOLN
86 Assoc VP Govt & External Relations ....Mr. Guillermo DE VEYGA
27 Sr Director Public Relations ....Ms. Mary Beth ZEMAN
29 Executive Director Alumni .... Ms. Jenna VILLANI
108 Exec Dir Inst Research & ASMT ....Dr. Sesime ADANU
13 Chief Information Officer ....Mr. Eric ROSENBERG
43 General Counsel ....Ms. Melissa REARDON HENRY
16 Director of Human Resources ...... Ms. Denise ROBINSON-LEWIS
07 Assoc Vice President Admissions .... Mr. Ken SCHNEIDER
37 Director Financial Aid .... Mr. Michael CORSO
06 Registrar .... Ms. Susan ASTARITA
88 Director Athletic Communications ....Ms. Heather BROCIOUS
36 Director of Career Dev & Advisement ...Ms. Sharon ROSENGART
39 Director of Residence Life ....Ms. Rebecca BAIRD

23 Dir Counseling/Health & Wellness .... Dr. Jill GUZMAN
40 Director Bookstore .... Mr. Scott DUNLAP
85 Director International Student Svcs .... Ms. Cinzia RICHARDSON
94 Director of Women's Center .... Dr. Librada SANCHEZ
96 Director of Purchasing .... Mr. Stephen SONDEY
89 Director of New Student Programs .... Ms. Amanda VASQUEZ
92 Dean of Honors College .... Dr. Barbara ANDREW
35 Dir Campus Activ/Svc & Leadership .... Ms. Donna MINNICH SPUHLER
88 Assoc Dir Instruction/Research Tech .... Mr. Patrick RYAN
04 Exec Assistant to President .... Ms. Sherry WASHINGTON
88 Director of Communications .... Mr. Gregory CANNON

Yeshiva Bais Aharon (A)

905 Park Avenue, Lakewood NJ 08701

County: Ocean — Identification: 667291
Unit ID: 490319
Telephone: (732) 367-7604 — Carnegie Class: Spec-4-yr-Faith
FAX Number: (732) 367-1777 — Calendar System: Semester
Established: 2012 — Annual Undergrad Tuition & Fees: $9,250
Enrollment: 24 — Male
Affiliation or Control: Independent Non-Profit — IRS Status: 501(c)3
Highest Offering: Baccalaureate
Accreditation: AIJS

Yeshiva Chemdas Hatorah (B)

950 Massachusetts Avenue, Lakewood NJ 08701

County: Ocean — Identification: 667281
Telephone: (732) 363-7110 — Carnegie Class: Not Classified
FAX Number: (732) 961-5220 — Calendar System: Other
URL: https://yeshivachemdashatorah.com/
Established: — Annual Undergrad Tuition & Fees: N/A
Enrollment: N/A — Male
Affiliation or Control: Independent Non-Profit — IRS Status: 501(c)3
Highest Offering: Baccalaureate
Accreditation: AIJS

01 Dean .... Rabbi Aron PRUZANSKY

Yeshiva Gedolah of Cliffwood (C)

200 Center Street, Keyport NJ 07735

County: Monmouth — Identification: 667322
Telephone: (732) 765-9126 — Carnegie Class: Not Classified
FAX Number: (732) 865-7247 — Calendar System: Semester
Established: 2004 — Annual Undergrad Tuition & Fees: N/A
Enrollment: N/A — Male
Affiliation or Control: Independent Non-Profit — IRS Status: 501(c)3
Highest Offering: First Talmudic Degree
Accreditation: RABN

01 CEO .... Samuel ALSTER
06 Registrar .... Baruch SEGEL
10 CFO .... Shimon ALSTER
37 Financial Aid Administrator .... Aryeh BRODSKY

Yeshiva Gedolah Keren Hatorah (D)

1083 Brook Road, Lakewood NJ 08701

County: Ocean — Identification: 667282
Telephone: (732) 942-1811 — Carnegie Class: Not Classified
FAX Number: (732) 994-4222 — Calendar System: Other
URL: yeshivagedolahkerenhatorah.com
Established: 2009 — Annual Undergrad Tuition & Fees: N/A
Enrollment: N/A — Male
Affiliation or Control: Independent Non-Profit — IRS Status: 501(c)3
Highest Offering: Baccalaureate
Accreditation: AIJS

Yeshiva Gedolah Shaarei Shmuel (E)

511 Ocean Ave, Lakewood NJ 08701

County: Ocean — Identification: 667260
Unit ID: 488350
Telephone: (732) 363-2164 — Carnegie Class: Spec-4-yr-Faith
FAX Number: (732) 364-3331 — Calendar System: Other
URL: https://yeshivagedolahshaareishmuel.com/
Established: 2008 — Annual Undergrad Tuition & Fees: $8,800
Enrollment: 77 — Male
Affiliation or Control: Independent Non-Profit — IRS Status: 501(c)3
Highest Offering: First Talmudic Degree
Accreditation: @RABN

Yeshiva Gedolah Tiferes Boruch (F)

21 Rockview Avenue, North Plainfield NJ 07060

County: Union — Identification: 667283
Telephone: (908) 753-2600 — Carnegie Class: Not Classified
FAX Number: (908) 753-4243 — Calendar System: Semester
URL: yeshivagedolahtiferesboruch.com
Established: 1989 — Annual Undergrad Tuition & Fees: N/A
Enrollment: N/A — Male
Affiliation or Control: Independent Non-Profit — IRS Status: 501(c)3
Highest Offering: Baccalaureate
Accreditation: AIJS

05 Rosh Yeshiva .... Rabbi Elya Meir SOROTZKIN

Yeshiva Gedolah Zichron Leyma (G)

2035 Vauxhall Road, Union NJ 07083

County: Union — FICE Identification: 041924
Unit ID: 476692
Telephone: (908) 587-0502 — Carnegie Class: Spec-4-yr-Faith
FAX Number: (908) 349-3111 — Calendar System: Semester
URL: www.yzl.edu
Established: 1999 — Annual Undergrad Tuition & Fees: $10,750
Enrollment: 34 — Male
Affiliation or Control: Independent Non-Profit — IRS Status: 501(c)3
Highest Offering: First Talmudic Degree
Accreditation: RABN

Yeshiva Toras Chaim (H)

999 Ridge Avenue, Lakewood NJ 08701-2120

County: Ocean — FICE Identification: 041311
Unit ID: 451398
Telephone: (732) 414-2834 — Carnegie Class: Spec-4-yr-Faith
FAX Number: (732) 414-2838 — Calendar System: Semester
Established: 2000 — Annual Undergrad Tuition & Fees: $12,250
Enrollment: 218 — Male
Affiliation or Control: Independent Non-Profit — IRS Status: 501(c)3
Highest Offering: Baccalaureate
Accreditation: RABN

05 Chief Academic Officer .... Rabbi Mendel SLOMOVITS
06 Registrar .... Mrs. Devoiry DURST
10 Bookkeeper .... Mrs. Michal GROSSMAN

Yeshiva Yesodei Hatorah (I)

2 Yesodei Court, Lakewood NJ 08701

County: Ocean — Identification: 667109
Unit ID: 481438
Telephone: (732) 370-3360 — Carnegie Class: Spec-4-yr-Faith
FAX Number: (732) 886-2659 — Calendar System: Semester
Established: 1995 — Annual Undergrad Tuition & Fees: $12,500
Enrollment: 52 — Male
Affiliation or Control: Independent Non-Profit — IRS Status: 501(c)3
Highest Offering: First Talmudic Degree
Accreditation: RABN

05 Dean .... Rabbi Shaya TREFF
10 Chief Financial/Business Officer .... Rabbi Shaya UNGAR
20 Associate Academic Officer .... Rabbi Yisroel Meir TREFF

Yeshivas Be'er Yitzchok (J)

1391 North Avenue, Elizabeth NJ 07208

County: Union — FICE Identification: 041234
Unit ID: 451370
Telephone: (908) 354-6057 — Carnegie Class: Spec-4-yr-Faith
FAX Number: (908) 820-0431 — Calendar System: Semester
URL: https://yeshivasbeeryitzchok.org/
Established: 1999 — Annual Undergrad Tuition & Fees: $10,900
Enrollment: 57 — Male
Affiliation or Control: Independent Non-Profit — IRS Status: 501(c)3
Highest Offering: Baccalaureate
Accreditation: AIJS

01 Chief Executive Officer .... Rabbi Avrohom SCHULMAN
37 Director of Student Financial Aid .... Mrs. Chana MILLER

NEW MEXICO

Brookline College (K)

4201 Central Avenue NW Ste J, Albuquerque NM 87015

Telephone: (505) 880-2877 — Identification: 666724
Accreditation: ABHES

† Branch campus of Brookline College, Phoenix, AZ

Burrell College of Osteopathic Medicine (L)

3501 Arrowhead Drive, Las Cruces NM 88001

County: Dona Ana — Identification: 667248
Unit ID: 488554
Telephone: (575) 674-2266 — Carnegie Class: Not Classified
FAX Number: (575) 674-2267 — Calendar System: Semester
URL: www.bcomnm.org
Established: 2013 — Annual Graduate Tuition & Fees: N/A
Enrollment: 645 — Coed
Affiliation or Control: Other — IRS Status: Proprietary
Highest Offering: Doctorate; No Undergraduates
Accreditation: OSTEO

01 President .... Mr. John L. HUMMER
05 Dean & Chief Academic Officer .... Dr. William PIERATT
10 CFO/VP Admin & Finance .... Ms. Jennifer TAYLOR
13 Chief Information Officer/AVP Admin .... Mr. Jeff HARRIS
84 AVP Enroll Svcs/Inst Effectiveness .... Ms. Nina NUNEZ
06 Interim Registrar .... Ms. Keziah GARCIA
07 Director of Admissions .... Ms. Courtney LEWIS
37 Director of Financial Aid .... Dr. Marlene MELENDEZ
32 Exec Dir of Student Affairs .... Ms. Vanessa RICHARDSON
15 Director of Human Resources .... Ms. Dawn M. LEAKE
111 VP of Institutional Advancement .... Ms. Victoria PINEDA
26 Dir Communications & Marketing .... Ms. Summer MASOUD
28 AVP of Diversity & Inclusion .... Mr. Justin MCHORSE
09 Asst Dean for Research .... Dr. Joseph BENOIT
08 Library Director .... Ms. Erin PALAZZOLO
04 Admin Assistant to the President .... Ms. Linda KUTINAC

Carrington College - Albuquerque (M)

1001 Menaul Boulevard NE, Albuquerque NM 87107

Telephone: (505) 254-7777 — Identification: 666014
Accreditation: &WJ, ADNUR

† Regional accreditation is carried under the parent institution in Sacramento, CA.

Central New Mexico Community College (N)

900 University Boulevard SE, Albuquerque NM 87106

County: Bernalillo — FICE Identification: 004742
Unit ID: 187532
Telephone: (505) 224-3000 — Carnegie Class: Assoc/HT-Mix Trad/Non
FAX Number: N/A — Calendar System: Semester
URL: www.cnm.edu
Established: 1965 — Annual Undergrad Tuition & Fees (In-District): $1,650
Enrollment: 21,398 — Coed
Affiliation or Control: State/Local — IRS Status: 501(c)3
Highest Offering: Associate Degree
Accreditation: HLC, ACBSP, ACFEI, ADNUR, CAHIIM, COARC, CONST, DA, DMS, EMT, MLTAD, NDT, PTAA, RAD, SURGT

01 President .... Ms. Tracy HARTZLER
05 Vice President for Academic Affairs ... Dr. Sydney D. GUNTHORPE
32 Vice President for Student Services .... Ms. Nireata SEALS
10 Vice Pres for Finance & Operations .... Mrs. Olivia PADILLA JACKSON
84 Assoc Vice Pres Enrollment Mgmt .... Vacant
35 Dean of Students .... Mr. Christopher CAVAZOS
08 Director Learning Resources ...... Ms. Poppy JOHNSON RENVALL
13 Chief Information Officer .... Mr. Victor LEON
103 Sr Director of Programs .... Ms. Mary GALLIVAN
36 Job Connection Services .... Ms. Stacey COOLEY
30 Exec Director of Development .... Mr. Clinton WELLS
21 Exec Dir Fiscal Ops/Comptroller .... Ms. Christine DUNCAN
07 Director of Admissions .... Ms. Andrea GURROLA
26 Exec Dir Mktg & Public Relations .... Mrs. Angela SIMS
27 Dir Communications/Media Relations .... Mr. Brad MOORE
37 Sr Director Student Financial Aid .... Mr. Joseph RYAN
15 Executive Director Human Resources .... Ms. Juliane ZITER
81 Dean Sch of Math/Sci/Engr .... Mr. Philip LISTER
50 Dean School of Bus/Info Technology .... Ms. Kalynn PIRKL
72 Dean Sch of Applied Technology .... Ms. Amy BALLARD
97 Dean Sch of Adult & Gen Educ .... Ms. LouAnne LUNDGREN
83 Dean Comm/Humanities/Soc Sciences .... Ms. Melanie VIRAMONTES
76 Dean Health/Wellness/Public/Safety .... Ms. Carol ASH
06 Registrar .... Ms. Rosenda MINELLA
18 Exec Dir Physical Plant .... Mr. Marvin MARTINEZ
35 Director of Student Life .... Mr. Kristofer GAUSSOIN
96 Director of Purchasing .... Ms. Gerrie BECKER
19 Chief of Safety & Security .... Mr. John CORVINO
04 Exec Asst to President .... Ms. Erin BRADSHAW
09 Dir Assess/Institutional Research .... Ms. Linda MARTIN
29 Director Alumni Relations .... Vacant
43 Dir Legal Svcs/General Counsel .... Mr. Michael ANAYA

Clovis Community College (O)

417 Schepps Boulevard, Clovis NM 88101-8381

County: Curry — FICE Identification: 004743
Unit ID: 187639
Telephone: (575) 769-2811 — Carnegie Class: Assoc/MT-VT-High Non
FAX Number: (575) 769-4190 — Calendar System: Semester
URL: www.clovis.edu
Established: 1971 — Annual Undergrad Tuition & Fees (In-State): $1,616
Enrollment: 2,321 — Coed
Affiliation or Control: State — IRS Status: 501(c)3
Highest Offering: Associate Degree
Accreditation: HLC, ADNUR, PTAA, RAD

01 President .... Dr. Charles NWANKWO
05 EVP Academic Affairs/Student Svcs .... Dr. Robin JONES
10 Chief Financial Officer .... Ms. Heather LOVATO
13 VP of IT and Operations .... Mr. Norman KIA
21 Comptroller .... Ms. Katrina WALLEY
07 Dir Admissions/Records/Registrar .... Ms. Kari SMITH
37 Director of Financial Aid .... Ms. April CHAVEZ
08 Director Library/Learning Resources .... Mr. Paul MOORE
121 Dir Center for Student Success .... Ms. Emily GLIKAS
86 Dir of Advising & Govt Relations .... Mr. Marcus SMITH
15 Director of Human Resource Services .... Ms. Regina DART
88 Director Small Business Development .... Ms. Sandra TAYLOR-SAWYER
91 Administrative Info Systems Manager .... Mr. Ronald WILDER
84 AVP Enrollment Mgmt/Student Affs .... Dr. Robin KUYKENDALL
36 Director Student Placement .... Vacant
111 Dir of Institutional Advancement .... Ms. Kolby RAINS
18 Director of Physical Plant .... Mr. Paul ARAGON
76 Div Chair Allied Health Programs .... Ms. Shawna MCGILL
79 Div Chair Languages/History/Theater .... Mr. Gregory RAPP

50 Div Chair Business Admin/Accounting .... Ms. Monica TURNER
81 Div Chair Math/Science/Hum/HPE .... Mr. Don SCROGGINS
77 Div Chair CIS/Art/Comm .... Mr. Ray WALKER
04 Executive Asst to President .... Ms. Beverly ARAGON
09 Director of Institutional Research .... Ms. Courtney TEMPEL
19 Director of Campus Security .... Mr. Freddie SALAZAR
105 Marketing & Website Manager .... Vacant
25 Exec Dir Plng/Sponsored Projects .... Dr. Mindy WATSON
36 Career & Development Coordinator .... Ms. Sarah FULMER
90 Director of User Services .... Mr. Ricky FUENTES
96 Director of Purchasing .... Mr. Steve BROOKS

Dine College Shiprock Branch (A)

1228 Yucca St., PO Box 580, Shiprock NM 87420
Telephone: (505) 368-3500 Identification: 770007
Accreditation: &HLC

† Branch campus of Dine College, Tsaile, AZ

Eastern New Mexico University Main Campus (B)

1500 S Avenue K, Portales NM 88130-7400
County: Roosevelt FICE Identification: 002651
Unit ID: 187648
Telephone: (575) 562-1011 Carnegie Class: Masters/L
FAX Number: (575) 562-2980 Calendar System: Semester
URL: www.enmu.edu
Established: 1927 Annual Undergrad Tuition & Fees (In-State): $6,648
Enrollment: 5,266 Coed
Affiliation or Control: State IRS Status: 501(c)3
Highest Offering: Master's
Accreditation: HLC, ACBSP, MUS, NUR, SP, SW

01 President/System Chancellor .... Dr. Patrice CALDWELL
05 Vice President Academic Affairs .... Dr. Jamie LAURENZ
10 Vice Prest Business Affairs/CFO .... Mr. Scott SMART
32 Vice President for Student Affairs .... Dr. Jeff LONG
13 Vice President of Technology .... Mr. Clark ELSWICK
45 VP Planning/Analysis/Inst Research .... Vacant
20 Asst Vice Pres for Academic Affairs .... Dr. Suzanne BALCH-LINDSAY
58 Asst VP Research/Graduate Dean .... Dr. John MONTGOMERY
111 AVP Advancement/Exec Dir Foundation .... Ms. Noelle BARTL
26 Asst Vice Pres of Communications .... Mr. John HOUSER
21 Comptroller .... Mrs. Carol FLETCHER
53 Dean Education/Technology .... Dr. Lee HURREN
50 Dean Business .... Dr. Herbert SNYDER
57 Dean Fine Arts .... Dr. Jeff GENTRY
49 Dean Liberal Arts & Science .... Dr. Mary AYALA
22 Affirmative Action Officer .... Ms. Jessica SMALL
08 Director of Library .... Vacant
06 Registrar .... Ms. DeLynn BARGAS
37 Director Student Financial Aid .... Mr. Brent SMALL
84 Director Enrollment Services .... Mr. Cody SPITZ
15 Exec Director of Human Resources .... Mr. Benito GONZALES
88 Director of Broadcasting .... Mr. Duane RYAN
18 Director Physical Plant .... Mr. John KANMORE
41 Athletic Director .... Mr. Paul WEIR
19 Chief of University Police .... Mr. Brad MAULDIN
36 Dir Counseling Center/Career Svcs .... Ms. Susan LARSEN
39 Director Student Housing .... Mr. Steven ESTOCK
09 Director Institutional Research .... Mr. Brendan HENNESSEY
96 Director of Purchasing .... Mr. Scott DAVIS
29 Coordinator of Alumni .... Ms. Annamaria SHORT
106 Dir of Distance Learning/Outreach .... Mr. Ryan ROARK
35 Director Campus Life .... Mr. Reydecel COSS

Eastern New Mexico University-Roswell (C)

52 University Blvd., Roswell NM 88203
County: Chaves FICE Identification: 002661
Unit ID: 187666
Telephone: (575) 624-7000 Carnegie Class: Assoc/HVT-High Non
FAX Number: (575) 624-7342 Calendar System: Semester
URL: www.roswell.enmu.edu
Established: 1958 Annual Undergrad Tuition & Fees (In-State): $2,424
Enrollment: 1,698 Coed
Affiliation or Control: State IRS Status: 501(c)3
Highest Offering: Associate Degree
Accreditation: HLC, ADNUR, COARC, EMT, MAC, OTA

01 President .... Dr. Shawn POWELL
05 VP of Academic & Student Affairs .... Ms. Annemarie OLDFIELD
10 SVP/Chief Operations Officer .... Mr. Robert ROESCHNTHALER
08 Director Learning Resource Center .... Dr. Jennifer HUGHES
06 Registrar .... Mr. Chris MEEKS
30 Director College Development .... Vacant
07 Director Admissions and Records .... Vacant
13 Director of Computer Services .... Vacant
15 Human Resources Supervisor .... Ms. Stephanie VENEGAS
18 Director of Physical Plant .... Vacant
19 Director of Security .... Mr. Brad MCFADIN
96 Director of Purchasing .... Mr. Nate HOPKINS
09 Exec Dir Inst Effectiveness .... Mr. Todd DEKAY
04 Administrative Asst to President .... Mrs. Linde NEWMAN
49 AVP of Arts & Science Education .... Mr. Robert MOORE
76 AVP of Health Education .... Dr. Laurie JENSEN
72 Interim AVP of Technical Education .... Mr. Ron FLURY
22 Dir Affirmative Action/Equal Opp .... Ms. Jessica SMALL
28 Director of Diversity .... Vacant

EC-Council University (D)

101C Sun Avenue NE, Albuquerque NM 87109
County: Bernalillo Identification: 667232
Telephone: (505) 922-2889 Carnegie Class: Not Classified
FAX Number: (505) 856-8267 Calendar System: Other
URL: www.eccu.edu
Established: 2003 Annual Undergrad Tuition & Fees: N/A
Enrollment: N/A Coed
Affiliation or Control: Proprietary IRS Status: Proprietary
Highest Offering: Master's
Accreditation: DEAC

00 CEO .... Sanjay BAVISI
01 President .... Lata BAVISI
03 Vice President .... David OXENHANDLER
05 Dean .... Charline NIXON
06 Registrar .... Greg CIMINO
32 Student Support Executive .... David VALDEZ

Institute of American Indian Arts (E)

83 Avan Nu Po Road, Santa Fe NM 87508-1300
County: Santa Fe FICE Identification: 021464
Unit ID: 187745
Telephone: (505) 424-2300 Carnegie Class: Tribal
FAX Number: (505) 424-4500 Calendar System: Semester
URL: www.iaia.edu
Established: 1962 Annual Undergrad Tuition & Fees: $4,726
Enrollment: 693 Coed
Affiliation or Control: Federal IRS Status: Exempt
Highest Offering: Master's
Accreditation: HLC

01 President .... Dr. Robert MARTIN

Luna Community College (F)

366 Luna Drive, Las Vegas NM 87701-1510
County: San Miguel FICE Identification: 009962
Unit ID: 363633
Telephone: (505) 454-2500 Carnegie Class: Assoc/MT-VT-High Non
FAX Number: (505) 454-2519 Calendar System: Semester
URL: www.luna.edu
Established: 1970 Annual Undergrad Tuition & Fees (In-District): $1,370
Enrollment: 720 Coed
Affiliation or Control: State/Local IRS Status: 501(c)3
Highest Offering: Associate Degree
Accreditation: HLC, ACBSP, ADNUR, DA

01 President .... Dr. Rolando RAEL
05 VP of Instruction/Student Services .... Dr. Kenneth PATTERSON
10 Vice Pres of Finance/Administration .... Ms. Donna FLORES-MEDINA
09 Institutional Research Admin .... Ms. Denise GIBSON
07 Director of Admissions .... Mr. Moses MARQUEZ
06 Registrar .... Ms. Geraldine SAAVEDRA
18 Manager Physical Plant .... Mr. Matthew CORDOVA
37 Director Student Financial Aid .... Mr. Michael MONTOYA
15 Director Human Resources .... Ms. Carolyn CHAVEZ
08 Learning Resource Center Manager .... Ms. Linda SALAZAR
13 Director of Computer Services .... Mr. Matthew BOWIE

Mesalands Community College (G)

911 S 10th Street, Tucumcari NM 88401-3352
County: Quay FICE Identification: 032063
Unit ID: 188261
Telephone: (575) 461-4413 Carnegie Class: Assoc/MT-VT-High Non
FAX Number: (575) 461-1901 Calendar System: Semester
URL: www.mesalands.edu
Established: 1980 Annual Undergrad Tuition & Fees (In-District): $2,136
Enrollment: 709 Coed
Affiliation or Control: State/Local IRS Status: 501(c)3
Highest Offering: Associate Degree
Accreditation: HLC

01 President .... Dr. Gregory T. BUSCH
04 Executive Asst to President .... Ms. Margaret RAGLAND
32 Vice President Student Affairs .... Dr. Aaron KENNEDY
05 Vice President of Academic Affairs .... Ms. Natalie GILLARD
26 Vice President Public Relations .... Mr. Josh MCVEY
11 Vice President of Campus Affairs .... Mr. Jim MORGAN
121 Vice President of Student Success .... Ms. Hazel ROUNTREE
06 Registrar .... Dr. Forrest KAATZ

National College of Midwifery (H)

1041 Reed Street, Suite C, Taos NM 87571
County: Taos Identification: 666251
Telephone: (575) 758-8914 Carnegie Class: Not Classified
FAX Number: N/A Calendar System: Trimester
URL: www.midwiferycollege.edu
Established: 1989 Annual Undergrad Tuition & Fees: N/A
Enrollment: N/A Coed
Affiliation or Control: Independent Non-Profit IRS Status: 501(c)3
Highest Offering: Doctorate
Accreditation: MEAC

01 CEO/President .... Marcy ANDREW
11 Chief Operations Officer .... Clorinda ROMERO
30 Chief Development Officer .... Cassaundra JAH
06 Registrar .... Jennifer HELSEL

Navajo Technical University (I)

PO Box 849, Crownpoint NM 87313-0849
County: McKinley FICE Identification: 023576
Unit ID: 187596
Telephone: (505) 387-7401 Carnegie Class: Tribal
FAX Number: (505) 786-5644 Calendar System: Semester
URL: www.navajotech.edu
Established: 1979 Annual Undergrad Tuition & Fees: $4,070
Enrollment: 1,350 Coed
Affiliation or Control: Tribal Control IRS Status: 501(c)3
Highest Offering: Master's
Accreditation: HLC, ACFEI

01 President .... Dr. Elmer GUY
32 Dean of Student Services .... Ms. Jerlynn HENRY
10 Finance Director .... Ms. Cheryl THOMPSON
05 Dean of Undergraduate Studies .... Dr. Casmir AGBARAJI
06 Registrar/Director of Admissions .... Mr. Kelly CHIQUITO
37 Student Financial Aid Officer .... Mr. Gary SEGAY
04 Executive Assistant .... Ms. Tonilee BECENTI
13 IT Director .... Mr. Jared RIBBLE
41 Athletic Director .... Mr. George LAFRANCE
15 Human Resource Director .... Ms. Wanda COOKE

† Tuition figure is for a student enrolled in a federally recognized Indian tribe.

New Mexico Highlands University (J)

Box 9000, Las Vegas NM 87701-9000
County: San Miguel FICE Identification: 002653
Unit ID: 187897
Telephone: (877) 850-9064 Carnegie Class: Masters/L
FAX Number: N/A Calendar System: Semester
URL: www.nmhu.edu
Established: 1893 Annual Undergrad Tuition & Fees (In-State): $6,558
Enrollment: 2,777 Coed
Affiliation or Control: State IRS Status: 501(c)3
Highest Offering: Master's
Accreditation: HLC, ACBSP, CACREP, CAEP, MPCAC, NURSE, SW

01 President .... Dr. Sam MINNER
05 Provost/VP for Academic Affairs .... Dr. Roxanne GONZALES
10 VP Finance & Admin .... Mr. Max BACA
32 Dean of Students .... Dr. Kimberly BLEA
36 Director Center Prof Development .... Mr. Reynaldo MAESTAS
06 Registrar .... Ms. Henrietta ROMERO
09 Dir Inst Effectiveness & Research .... Dr. Heather TILSON
13 Director of Information Technology .... Mr. Joe GIERI
15 Director Human Resources .... Mr. Faron VALENCIA
18 Director of Facilities Mgmt .... Ms. Sylvia BACA
19 Chief Police/Security .... Mr. Clarence ROMERO
26 Director of University Relations .... Mr. Sean WEAVER
29 Alumni Director .... Ms. Juli SALMAN
111 Vice President for Advancement .... Dr. Theresa LAW
70 Dean School of Social Work .... Dr. Cristina DURAN
49 Dean College of Arts & Science .... Dr. Brandon KEMPNER
37 Director of Financial Aid .... Ms. Susan CHAVEZ
40 Bookstore Manager .... Ms. Naomi VILLANUEVA
50 Dean School of Business .... Dr. Veena PARBOTEEAH
53 Dean School of Education .... Dr. Mary EARICK
39 Director Student Housing .... Ms. Yvette WILKES
04 Sr Exec Admin to President .... Ms. Maria SENA
08 Chief Library Officer .... Mr. Ruben ARAGON
106 Director Online/Extended Learning .... Dr. Patrick WILSON
41 Athletic Director .... Mr. Andrew EHLING
96 Director of Purchasing .... Mr. Adam BUSTOS
84 Dir of Strategic Enrollment Mgmt .... Mr. Benito PACHECO
25 Chief Contract/Grants Administrator .... Dr. Ian WILLIAMSON
100 Special Assistant to the President .... Mr. Leon BUSTOS
86 Assoc VP for Govt Relations .... Dr. Denise MONTOYA

New Mexico Institute of Mining and Technology (K)

801 Leroy Place, Socorro NM 87801-4796
County: Socorro FICE Identification: 002654
Unit ID: 187967
Telephone: (575) 835-5434 Carnegie Class: Masters/S
FAX Number: (575) 835-6329 Calendar System: Semester
URL: www.nmt.edu
Established: 1889 Annual Undergrad Tuition & Fees (In-State): $8,361
Enrollment: 1,686 Coed
Affiliation or Control: State IRS Status: 501(c)3
Highest Offering: Doctorate
Accreditation: HLC

01 President .... Dr. Stephen G. WELLS
04 Executive Asst to the President .... Ms. Vanessa M. GRAIN
10 Vice Pres Administration & Finance .... Mr. Cleve MCDANIEL
05 Vice President Academic Affairs .... Dr. Doug WELLS
46 Vice Pres Research .... Dr. Van D. ROMERO
32 Acting Vice Pres of Student Life .... Dr. Peter PHAIAH
20 Assoc Vice Pres Academic Affairs .... Dr. Peter MOZLEY
88 Assoc VP Research .... Mr. Carlos REY ROMERO
86 Director of Government Affairs .... Mr. David MANZANO
15 Director of Human Resources .... Ms. JoAnn SALOME

22 Director Affirm Action & Compliance ....Mr. Randy SAAVEDRA
111 Director Office for Advancement ....Ms. Colleen FOSTER
26 Communications/Marketing Director ....Mr. Dave LEPRE
30 Director of OIC ....Dr. Peter ANSELMO
65 Director Bur Geology & Mineral Res ....Dr. Nelia DUNBAR
12 Director Petro Recovery Res Ctr ....Dr. Robert BALCH
13 Director of Information Services ....Mr. Joseph FRANKLIN
58 Dean of Graduate Studies ....Dr. Aly EL-OSERY
35 Dir Student Affairs/Coord Intl Pgms ....Mr. Michael VOEGERL
06 Registrar ....Mr. James SCOTT
07 Director of Admission ....Mr. Gregory STRINGER
37 Director of Financial Aid ....Mr. Kenneth AERTS
109 Asst Director Auxiliary Services ....Mr. Mitch TAPPEN
38 Dir Counseling/Disabilities Svcs ....Ms. Angela GAUTIER
23 Director of Health Center ....Ms. Hannah QUIGG
08 Director Library ....Mr. David COX
19 Director of Campus Police ....Mr. Scott SCARBOROUGH
68 Director of Physical Education ....Mr. Melissa BEGAY
18 Co-Director Facilities Management ..... Mr. Robby MONTGOMERY
18 Co-Director Facilities Management ....Mr. Jason HEBERT
96 Chief Procurement Officer ....Ms. Kimela MILLER

New Mexico Junior College (A)

1 Thunderbird Circle, Hobbs NM 88240-9123

County: Lea FICE Identification: 002655
Unit ID: 187903

Telephone: (575) 392-4510 Carnegie Class: Assoc/HT-Mix Trad/Non
FAX Number: (575) 492-2732 Calendar System: Semester
URL: www.nmjc.edu
Established: 1965 Annual Undergrad Tuition & Fees (In-District): $2,072
Enrollment: 1,406 Coed
Affiliation or Control: Local IRS Status: 501(c)3
Highest Offering: Associate Degree
Accreditation: HLC, ADNUR

01 President ....Dr. Kelvin SHARP
05 Vice President Instruction ....Dr. Larry SANDERSON
10 Vice President Finance ....Joshua MORGAN
32 Vice President Student Services ....Cathy MITCHELL
103 Vice President Training & Outreach ....Jeff MCCOOL
43 General Counsel/Admin Services ....Scotty HOLLOMAN
13 Dir Computer Information System ....Bill KUNKO
26 Director of Communications ....Genevieve CAVANAUGH
04 Executive Asst to the President ....Norma FAUGHT
37 Director Financial Aid ....Kerrie MITCHELL
66 Director of Allied Health/Nursing ....Cammie ARMSTRONG
18 Chief Facilities/Physical Plant ....Dr. Charley CARROLL
81 Dean Applied Sciences ....Dr. Stephanie FERGUSON
08 Dean Academic Studies/Library ....Dianne MARQUEZ
84 Dean of Students ....Sarah PATTERSON
40 Director of Bookstore Services ....Julie BUCHANAN
19 Director of Public Safety ....Walter COBURN
08 Director of Library Services ....Vacant
96 Coordinator of Purchasing ....JoeMike GOMEZ
41 Director of Athletics ....Deron CLARK
102 Acct/Controller-NMJC Foundation ....Tina KUNKO
21 Controller ....Stacey WYNN
39 Director of Resident Life ....Eric GARCIA
88 Dir Western Heritage Museum/LCCHF ....Erin ANDERSON
88 Dir NMJC Research Foundation ....Dennis HOLMBERG
06 Registrar ....Rebecca WHITLEY
19 Director of Campus Security/Safety ....Dennis KELLEY
30 Director of Development ....Vacant

New Mexico Military Institute (B)

101 W College, Roswell NM 88201-5173

County: Chaves FICE Identification: 002656
Unit ID: 187912

Telephone: (575) 622-6250 Carnegie Class: Assoc/HT-High Trad
FAX Number: (575) 624-8058 Calendar System: Semester
URL: www.nmmi.edu
Established: 1891 Annual Undergrad Tuition & Fees (In-State): $6,616
Enrollment: 493 Coed
Affiliation or Control: State IRS Status: 501(c)3
Highest Offering: Associate Degree
Accreditation: HLC

01 Superintendent/President ....MGen. Jerry W. GRIZZLE
32 Commandant ....Col. Thomas TATE
100 Chief of Staff ....Col. David WEST
10 Chief Financial Officer ....Col. Deana CURNUTT
05 Dean ....Dr. Orlando GRIEGO
41 Athletic Director/Dir Physical Educ ....Col. Jose BARRON
116 Internal Auditor ....Vacant
88 Professor of Military Science ....LtCol. Ryan L. EISENHAUER
20 Vice Dean & High School Princ ....Col. Jose PORRAS
15 Assistant Human Resources Director ....Ms. Dori CAMERON
50 Assoc Dean Social Science/Business ..... LtCol. Cody NORTHRUP
81 Assoc Dean Science/Mathematics ....Col. John R. MCVAY
79 Assoc Dean Humanities ....LtCol. Patricia MATCHIN
64 Director of Music ....Mr. Matthew BRADY
08 Director of the Library ....LtCol. Kalith SMITH
18 Chief Facilities/Physical Plant ....Mr. Kent TAYLOR
06 Registrar ....Maj. Chris WRIGHT
37 Director of Financial Aid ....Maj. Monica L. GARCIA
88 Mil Services Academies Prep Dir ....SCPO. Charles SCOTT
19 Chief of Campus Police ....Mr. Jerrold LONOWSKI
38 Director of Cadet Counseling Center ....Vacant
29 Director Alumni Relations ....LtCol. Danny ARMIJO
04 Executive Secretary to President ....Ms. Bernadette BEATTY
09 Director of Institutional Research ....Ms. Michele BATES

102 Dir Foundation/Corporate Relations ....Mr. Jimmy BARNES
13 Chief Info Technology Officer ....Mr. Todd LUPIEN
07 Director of Admissions ....LtCol. Kris WARD

New Mexico State University Main Campus (C)

Box 30001, 3Z, Las Cruces NM 88003-8001

County: Dona Ana FICE Identification: 002657
Unit ID: 188030

Telephone: (575) 646-2035 Carnegie Class: DU-Higher
FAX Number: (575) 646-6334 Calendar System: Semester
URL: www.nmsu.edu
Established: 1888 Annual Undergrad Tuition & Fees (In-State): $7,301
Enrollment: 14,227 Coed
Affiliation or Control: State IRS Status: 501(c)3
Highest Offering: Doctorate
Accreditation: HLC, #CAATE, CACREP, CAEP, CAEPN, COPSY, DIETD, DIETI, IPSY, MUS, NURSE, PH, SP, SPAA, SW

01 President ....Dr. John FLOROS
00 Chancellor ....Dr. Dan ARVIZU
11 Vice Chancellor ....Dr. Ruth JOHNSTON
05 Provost & Exec VP ....Ms. Carol PARKER
10 Sr VP Administration/Finance ....Dr. Andrew BURKE
111 VP Univ Advance/Pres NMSU Found ....Mr. Derek DICTSON
32 VP Student Success/Enroll Mgmt ....Dr. Renay SCOTT
26 Assoc VP Marketing/Communications ....Mr. Justin BANNISTER
21 Assoc VP Admin & Finance ....Ms. D'Anne STUART
15 Asst VP Human Resources Svcs ....Ms. Gena W. JONES
20 Assoc VP/Deputy Provost ....Ms. Rebecca CAMPBELL
09 Int Asst VP Institutional Analysis ....Mr. Calixto MELERO
86 Asst VP Government Relations ....Mr. Ricardo REL
49 Dean College of Arts & Sciences ....Dr. Enrico PONTELLI
50 Dean Business College ....Dr. James HOFFMAN
53 Dean College of Education ....Dr. Henrietta PICHON
54 Dean College of Engineering ....Dr. Lakshmi REDDI
58 Dean Graduate School ....Dr. Luis CIFUENTES
76 Int Dean Col Health & Social Svcs ....Vacant
35 Dean of Students ....Dr. Ann GOODMAN
13 Interim Chief Information Officer ....Mr. Chris KIELT
06 University Registrar ....Ms. Dacia SEDILLO
43 General Counsel ....Mr. Roy COLLINS
08 Dean University Library ....Ms. Katherine TERPIS
29 AVP Marketing & Strat Initiatives ....Mrs. Lynn SCHLEMEYER
21 University Controller ....Ms. Norma NOEL
39 Acting Director Student Housing ....Ms. Ophelia WATKINS
23 Exec Director Health & Wellness ....Ms. Lori MCKEE
41 Director Athletics ....Mr. Mario MOCCIA
35 Asst VP Student Affairs ....Dr. Anthony S. MARIN
96 Dir Procurement Services ....Ms. Javier CORDERO
22 Dir Institutional Equity/EEO ....Ms. Laura CASTILLE
07 Director Admissions ....Ms. Seth MINER
18 Assoc VP Facilities Services ....Mr. Luis CAMPOS
27 Dir of Marketing/Creative Svcs ....Dr. Melissa CHAVIRA
47 Dean College of Agric ....Dr. Rolando FLORES
92 Dean Honors College ....Dr. Phame CAMARENA
12 President NMSU-DACC ....Dr. Monica TORRES
12 Branch Executive Director ....Dr. Ken VAN WINKLE
100 Chief of Staff ....Mrs. Leslie CERVANTES
37 Director Student Financial Aid ....Dr. Vandeen MCKENZIE
102 Dir Foundation/Corporate Relations ....Vacant
28 Director of Diversity ....Dr. Teresa Maria Linda SCHOLZ

New Mexico State University at Alamogordo (D)

2400 N Scenic Drive, Alamogordo NM 88310-4239

County: Otero FICE Identification: 002658
Unit ID: 187994

Telephone: (575) 439-3600 Carnegie Class: Assoc/HT-High Non
FAX Number: (575) 439-3643 Calendar System: Semester
URL: www.nmsua.edu
Established: 1958 Annual Undergrad Tuition & Fees (In-State): $2,424
Enrollment: 941 Coed
Affiliation or Control: State IRS Status: 501(c)3
Highest Offering: Associate Degree
Accreditation: HLC

12 Branch Exec Director ....Dr. Ken VAN WINKLE
05 Vice President for Academic Affairs ....Dr. Mark CAL
32 Vice President for Student Services ...... Mrs. Anne RICKSECKEER
10 Vice President for Business/Finance .... Mr. Antonio SALINAS
08 Librarian ....Ms. Emily ANDERSON
37 Financial Aid Representative ....Vacant
09 Director of Institutional Research ....Mr. Greg HILLIS
15 Director Human Resources ....Vacant
96 Senior Buyer ....Mr. Lee M. KINNEY
106 Dir Online Education/E-learning ....Mrs. Sherrell WHEELER
108 Director Institutional Assessment ....Dr. Joyce HILL

New Mexico State University at Carlsbad (E)

1500 University Drive, Carlsbad NM 88220-3598

County: Eddy FICE Identification: 002659
Unit ID: 188003

Telephone: (575) 234-9200 Carnegie Class: Assoc/MT-VT-High Non
FAX Number: (575) 885-4951 Calendar System: Semester
URL: https://carlsbad.nmsu.edu/
Established: 1950 Annual Undergrad Tuition & Fees (In-State): $2,068
Enrollment: 1,203 Coed

Affiliation or Control: State IRS Status: 501(c)3
Highest Offering: Associate Degree
Accreditation: HLC, ADNUR

01 Campus Exec Director ....Dr. Ken VAN WINKLE
05 VP Acad Affs/Assoc Campus Director ....Dr. Andrew I. NWANNE
20 Int AVP Academic Affairs ....Dr. Monty HARRIS
32 Vice Pres Student Services ....Ms. Juanita GARCIA
10 VP Business & Finance ....Dr. Karla VOLPI
37 Director Financial Aid ....Ms. Diana CAMPOS
15 Human Resources Specialist ....Ms. Amihan TY
26 Director Marketing & Publications ....Ms. Sky KLAUS
04 Administrative Asst to President ....Ms. Merdia THERAGOOD
18 Chief Facilities/Physical Plant ....Mr. Kelly JOHNSON
09 Director of Institutional Research ....Ms. Bright BORKORM

New Mexico State University Dona Ana Community College (F)

2800 Sonoma Ranch Boulevard, Las Cruces NM 88011

County: Dona Ana Identification: 666649
Unit ID: 187620

Telephone: (575) 527-7500 Carnegie Class: Assoc/MT-VT-Mix Trad/Non
FAX Number: (575) 528-7300 Calendar System: Semester
URL: dacc.nmsu.edu
Established: 1973 Annual Undergrad Tuition & Fees (In-State): $2,160
Enrollment: 7,028 Coed
Affiliation or Control: State IRS Status: 501(c)3
Highest Offering: Associate Degree
Accreditation: HLC, ACBSP, ADNUR, COARC, DA, DH, DMS, EMT, IFSAC, RAD

01 President ....Dr. Monica TORRES
05 VP Academic Affairs ....Vacant
10 VP Business & Finance ....Ms. Kelly BROOKS
32 VP Student Services ....Mr. Amadeo LEDESMA
26 VP External Relations ....Vacant
20 AVP Acad Affairs/Assessment & Accr ....Vacant
84 Assoc VP Acad Affairs/Enroll Mgt ....Dr. Rusty FOX
49 Division Dean Arts/Hum/Social Sci ....Ms. Shannon BRADLEY
50 Division Dean Business/Public Svcs ....Vacant
76 Division Dean Health Sciences ....Ms. Josefina CARMONA
72 Division Dean Advanced Technologies ....Mr. Chipper MOORE
103 Exec Director Workforce Dev/Trng ....Dr. Fred OWENSBY
08 Director Library Services ....Vacant
121 Director Academic Advising ....Mr. Brad MAZDRA
09 Director Institutional Analysis ....Ms. Mary Beth WORLEY
55 Director Adult Education ....Ms. Maria ETHIER
31 Director Community Education ....Ms. Mary ULRICH
21 Manager Business Office ....Ms. Diane PIERCE
15 Manager Human Resources Operation .... Ms. Yvette BENITIZ
90 Director Computer Support ....Ms. Lori ALLEN
18 Manager Facilities Services ....Mr. Michael LUCHAU
07 Director Admissions ....Ms. Geraldine MARTINEZ
37 Director Financial Aid ....Ms. Michelle LOPEZ
22 Director Student Accessibility Svcs ....Mr. Jesse HAAS

New Mexico State University Grants (G)

1500 Third Street, Grants NM 87020-2025

Telephone: (505) 287-6678 FICE Identification: 008854
Accreditation: &HLC

† Regional accreditation is carried under the parent institution in Las Cruces, NM.

Northern New Mexico College (H)

921 N Paseo de Onate, Espa´ola NM 87532-2649

County: Rio Arriba FICE Identification: 020839
Unit ID: 188058

Telephone: (505) 747-2100 Carnegie Class: Bac/Assoc-Mixed
FAX Number: (505) 747-2170 Calendar System: Semester
URL: www.nnmc.edu
Established: 1909 Annual Undergrad Tuition & Fees (In-State): $4,952
Enrollment: 1,234 Coed
Affiliation or Control: State IRS Status: 501(c)3
Highest Offering: Baccalaureate
Accreditation: HLC, ACBSP, ADNUR, CAEPN, NURSE

01 President ....Dr. Richard J. BAILEY, JR.
10 Vice President Finance & Admin ....Mr. Ricky A. BEJARANO
05 Provost/VP Academic Affairs .... Dr. Ivan LOPEZ-HURTADO
32 Interim Dean of Students ....Mr. Frank ORONA
06 Registrar ....Mr. Gerald WHEELER
08 Head Librarian ....Ms. Courtney BRUCH
07 Acting Director Admissions ....Ms. Sara MCCORMICK
37 Director of Financial Aid ....Ms. Kathy LEVINE
13 Director Information Technologies ....Mr. Jimi MONTOYA
15 Director of Human Resources ....Mr. Kenneth LUCERO
102 Dir Foundation/Corporate Relations .....Dr. Richard J. BAILEY, JR.
28 Director of Equity & Diversity ....Vacant
18 Director of Facilities/Security ....Mr. Andy ROMERO
09 Director of Institutional Research ....Ms. Carmella SANCHEZ
21 Dir Small Business Development ....Ms. Julianna BARBEE
121 Dir Inst Advise/Student Success ....Vacant
41 Athletic Director/Coach ....Mr. Ryan CORDOVA
101 Executive Office Director ....Ms. Amy F. PEÑA
51 Coordinator Continuing Education ....Ms. Cecilia ROMERO
53 Chair Dept of Education ....Dr. Sandra RODRIGUEZ
76 Chair Dept of Nursing/Health Sci ....Ms. Ellen TRABKA
50 Chair Dept Business Administration ....Dr. Lori BACA
54 Chair Dept Engineering/Technology ....Dr. Sadia AHMED

26	Creative Dir Communications/Mktg	Ms. Sandy KROLICK
96	Chief Procurement Officer	Ms. Cheryl JAMES

Pima Medical Institute-Albuquerque (A)

4400 Cutler Avenue NE, Albuquerque NM 87110-3935
Telephone: (505) 881-1234 FICE Identification: 036783
Accreditation: **ABHES**, COARC, DH, PTAA

† Branch campus of Pima Medical Institute-Tucson, Tucson, AZ

Ruidoso Branch Community College (B)

709 Mechem Drive, Ruidoso NM 88345
Telephone: (575) 257-7222 Identification: 770345
Accreditation: **&HLC**

St. John's College (C)

1160 Camino de la Cruz Blanca,
Santa Fe NM 87505-4599
County: Santa Fe FICE Identification: 002093
Unit ID: 245652
Telephone: (505) 984-6000 Carnegie Class: Bac-A&S
FAX Number: (505) 984-6003 Calendar System: Semester
URL: www.sjc.edu
Established: 1964 Annual Undergrad Tuition & Fees: $35,760
Enrollment: 355 Coed
Affiliation or Control: Independent Non-Profit IRS Status: 501(c)3
Highest Offering: Master's
Accreditation: **HLC**

01	President	Mr. Mark ROOSEVELT
05	Dean of the College	Mr. J. Walter STERLING
30	Vice Pres for Dev/Alumni Affairs	Ms. Phelosha COLLAROS
10	Treasurer/Finance Officer	Mr. Michael S. DURAN
58	Assoc Dean Graduate Programs	Mr. Edward WALPIN
06	Registrar	Ms. Julie ROMERO
08	Library Director	Ms. Jennifer SPRAGUE
07	Director of Admissions	Ms. Caroline RANDALL
09	Director of Institutional Research	Ms. Alethea SCALLY
15	Director of Human Resources	Mr. Aaron YOUNG
18	Chief Facilities/Physical Plant	Mr. Phillip KANIATOBE
29	VP of Development/Alumni Relations	Ms. Phelosha COLLAROS
36	Director Career Services	Mr. Charles BERGMAN
37	Director Student Financial Aid	Ms. Darlene SANDOVAL
13	Chief Information Technology Office	Mr. Mehmet GORGULU

† Affiliated with St. John's College, Maryland.

San Juan College (D)

4601 College Boulevard, Farmington NM 87402-4699
County: San Juan FICE Identification: 002660
Unit ID: 188100
Telephone: (505) 326-3311 Carnegie Class: Assoc/HVT-Mix Trad/Non
FAX Number: (505) 566-3385 Calendar System: Semester
URL: www.sanjuancollege.edu
Established: 1956 Annual Undergrad Tuition & Fees (In-District): $1,618
Enrollment: 5,240 Coed
Affiliation or Control: Local IRS Status: 501(c)3
Highest Offering: Associate Degree
Accreditation: **HLC**, ADNUR, CAHIIM, COARC, DH, EMT, OTA, PTAA, SURGA, SURGT

01	President	Dr. Toni PENDERGRASS
03	Executive Vice President	Mr. Edward DESPLAS
05	Vice Pres for Learning	Dr. Adrienne FORGETTE
32	Vice Pres for Student Services	Dr. Boomer APPLEMAN
04	Executive Asst to President	Ms. Donna ELLIS
20	Associate VP for Learning	Mr. Sandy GILPIN
15	VP of Human Resources/Legal Action	Ms. Kerri LANGONI
102	Executive Director Foundation	Ms. Gayle DEAN
21	Controller	Mr. Kristie ELLIS
26	Director Marketing/Public Relations	Ms. Rhonda SCHAEFER
124	Director of Retention	Dr. Jenniffer VALORA
84	Sr Dir Enrollment Management	Vacant
50	Dean School of Business & IT	Mr. Eddy RAWLINSON
79	Dean School of Humanities	Ms. Lisa SNYDER
76	Dean School of Health Sciences	Ms. Sherrie PAXSON
65	Dean School of Energy	Ms. Alicia CORBELL
72	Dean School Trades & Technology	Mr. Ruben JOHNSON
81	Dean Math/Science & Engineering	Dr. Michael OTTINGER
16	Asst Dir HR Equity/Diversity	Ms. Stacey ALLEN
28	Director Native American Programs	Mr. Byron TSABETSAYE
08	Director Library Services	Ms. Samanthi HEWAKAPUGE
37	Sr Director of Financial Aid	Ms. Mindi-Kim SCHRUM
18	Director Physical Plant	Mr. Chris HARRELSON
19	Director Security/Safety	Mr. Kenneth HIBNER
35	Director Student Activities	Ms. Amanda ROBLES
96	Director Purchasing	Mr. Frank COLE
38	Director Student Advising Center	Ms. Christy FERRATO
74	Director Vet-Tech Program	Ms. Laura BLACK
06	Registrar	Ms. Sherri SCHAAF
09	Sr Dir of Institutional Research	Mr. Ron JERNIGAN
13	Chief Info Technology Officer (CIO)	Mr. Roy LYTLE
103	AVP of Workforce & Economic Devel	Dr. Lorenzo REYES

Santa Fe Community College (E)

6401 Richards Avenue, Santa Fe NM 87508-4887
County: Santa Fe FICE Identification: 022781
Unit ID: 188137
Telephone: (505) 428-1000 Carnegie Class: Assoc/MT-VT-High Non
FAX Number: (505) 428-1296 Calendar System: Semester
URL: www.sfcc.edu
Established: 1983 Annual Undergrad Tuition & Fees (In-State): $2,505
Enrollment: 3,459 Coed
Affiliation or Control: State IRS Status: 501(c)3
Highest Offering: Associate Degree
Accreditation: **HLC**, ADNUR, COARC, DA, EMT, MAC

01	President	Dr. Becky ROWLEY
05	Vice Pres Academic Affairs	Ms. Margaret PETERS
10	Vice Pres Finance/CFO	Mr. Nick TELLES
32	Vice President for Student Affairs	Ms. Margaret PETERS
09	Asc VP Planning/Inst Effectiveness	Mr. Yash MORIMOTO
121	Assoc VP for Student Success	Ms. Thomasinia ORTIZ-GALLEGOS
51	Dir Cont Educ/Contract Training	Ms. Kris SWEDIN
26	Exec Dir Marketing/Public Rels	Mr. Todd LOVATO
102	Exec Dir SFCC Foundation	Ms. Deborah BOLDT
06	Registrar	Ms. Diana BACA
13	Chief Information Officer	Ms. Cori BERGEN
37	Financial Aid Director	Ms. Kelly DURBIN
66	Director of Nursing Education	Ms. Terri TEWART
08	Library Director	Ms. Valerie NYE
15	Human Resources Manager	Ms. Michelle HARDING
88	Director Small Business Development	Mr. Brian DUBOFF
18	Director of Facilities	Mr. Dobby SCHMIDT
12	Executive Director HEC	Ms. Rebecca ESTRADA
101	Executive Asst to the President	Ms. Patricia NEWMAN
96	Director of Purchasing	Mr. John APODACA
25	Director of Grants	Ms. Ann BLACK
49	Dean School of Liberal Arts	Dr. James WYSONG
54	Dean Sch Health/Engineering & Math	Dr. Terri TEWART
76	Dean School of Fitness Education	Dr. Jenny LANDEN
57	Dean Sch Arts/Design & Media Arts	Dr. James WYSONG
75	Int Dean Trades/Tech/Sustainability	Ms. Julia DEISLER
50	Dean School of Business & Educ	Dr. Joseph COOKE

Southwest Acupuncture College (F)

2100 Calle de la Vuelta, Santa Fe NM 87505-6351
County: Santa Fe FICE Identification: 026220
Unit ID: 366605
Telephone: (505) 438-8884 Carnegie Class: Spec-4-yr-Other Health
FAX Number: (505) 438-8883 Calendar System: Semester
URL: www.acupuncturecollege.edu
Established: 1980 Annual Undergrad Tuition & Fees: N/A
Enrollment: 33 Coed
Affiliation or Control: Proprietary IRS Status: Proprietary
Highest Offering: Master's; No Lower Division
Accreditation: **ACUP**

01	CEO	Dr. Anthony ABBATE
03	Executive Director	Dr. Skya ABBATE
10	Chief Fiscal Officer	Ms. Piper KING
12	Campus Director Santa Fe	Dr. Paul ROSSIGNOL
17	Clinical Director Santa Fe	Dr. Pamela BARRETT
05	Academic Dean Santa Fe	Ms. Susan CHANEY
37	Financial Aid Director	Ms. Angela ANAYA
07	Director of Admissions & Alumni	Ms. Sophia BUNGAY
08	Chief Library Officer	Ms. Elizabeth MARTINEZ
04	Administrative Assistant	Ms. Sandy SZABAT

Southwest University of Naprapathic Medicine (G)

2006 Botulph Road, Ste A, Sante Fe NM 87505
County: Santa Fe Identification: 667420
Telephone: (505) 467-8777 Carnegie Class: Not Classified
FAX Number: N/A Calendar System: Quarter
URL: sunm.edu
Established: 2006 Annual Graduate Tuition & Fees: N/A
Enrollment: N/A Coed
Affiliation or Control: Proprietary IRS Status: Proprietary
Highest Offering: Doctorate; No Undergraduates
Accreditation: **DEAC**

01	President	Dr. Patrick NUZZO

Southwestern College (H)

3960 San Felipe Road, Santa Fe NM 87507
County: Santa Fe FICE Identification: 030761
Unit ID: 188207
Telephone: (505) 471-5756 Carnegie Class: Spec-4-yr-Other Health
FAX Number: (505) 471-4071 Calendar System: Quarter
URL: www.swc.edu
Established: 1979 Annual Graduate Tuition & Fees: N/A
Enrollment: 164 Coed
Affiliation or Control: Independent Non-Profit IRS Status: 501(c)3
Highest Offering: Master's; No Undergraduates
Accreditation: **HLC**

01	President	Dr. Ann FILEMYR
03	Exec VP/Dir New Earth Institute SWC	Ms. Katherine NINOS
05	Dean of the College	Dr. Virginia P. VIGIL
84	Director of Enrollment Services	Ms. Dru PHOENIX
06	Registrar	Ms. Andrea PACHECO
10	Chief Finance Officer	Ms. Allison FRANK
13	Chief Technology Officer	Ms. Donna HARRINGTON
32	Director of Student & Career Svcs	Ms. Lily GUTIERREZ
08	Chief Library Officer	Mr. Larry HARKCOM
11	Chief of Operations/ Administration	Ms. Dianne DELOREN
15	Chief Human Resources Officer	Ms. Esperanza GRIEGO
37	Director Student Financial Aid	Ms. Christy MARTINEZ

Southwestern Indian Polytechnic Institute (I)

9169 Coors Boulevard, NW, Albuquerque NM 87120
County: Bernalillo FICE Identification: 025110
Unit ID: 188216
Telephone: (505) 346-2348 Carnegie Class: Tribal
FAX Number: (505) 346-2343 Calendar System: Trimester
URL: www.sipi.edu
Established: 1971 Annual Undergrad Tuition & Fees: $1,095
Enrollment: 450 Coed
Affiliation or Control: Federal IRS Status: 501(c)3
Highest Offering: Associate Degree
Accreditation: **HLC**, OPD

01	President	Dr. Sherry ALLISON
10	Vice Pres College Operations	Mr. Eric CHRISTENSEN
05	Vice President Academic Programs	Ms. Valerie MONTOYA
09	Dir Institutional Rsch/Effect/Plng	Mr. Edward HUMMINGBIRD
32	Supervisory Student Services Spec	Dr. Cecelia COMETSEVAH
07	Director Admissions/Registrar	Vacant
15	Human Resources Specialist	Ms. Dawn AMI
18	Facilities Director	Ms. Renee ALLEN
37	Director Student Financial Aid	Vacant

University of New Mexico Main Campus (J)

1 University of New Mexico, Albuquerque NM 87131-0001
County: Bernalillo FICE Identification: 002663
Unit ID: 187985
Telephone: (505) 277-0111 Carnegie Class: DU-Highest
FAX Number: (505) 277-6019 Calendar System: Semester
URL: www.unm.edu
Established: 1889 Annual Undergrad Tuition & Fees (In-State): $8,161
Enrollment: 22,311 Coed
Affiliation or Control: State IRS Status: 501(c)3
Highest Offering: Doctorate
Accreditation: **HLC**, ARCPA, CAATE, CACREP, CAEPN, CAMPEP, CLPSY, DANCE, DENT, DH, DIETD, DIETI, EMT, IPSY, LAW, LSAR, MED, MIDWF, MT, MUS, NMT, NURSE, OT, PCSAS, PH, PHAR, PLNG, PTA, SP, SPAA, THEA

01	President	Garnett S. STOKES
05	Provost	Dr. James HOLLOWAY
17	Vice Chancellor of Clinical Affairs	Dr. Michael RICHARDS
10	SVP Finance & Administration	Dr. Teresa COSTANTINIDIS
100	Chief of Staff	Dr. Terry BABBITT
20	Sr Vice Prov for Academic Affairs	Dr. Barbara L. RODRIGUEZ
46	Vice President Research	Dr. Ellen FISHER
25	AVP Research Administration	Patricia HENNING
32	Vice President Student Affairs	Dr. Eliseo S. TORRES
28	Vice Chancellor HSC Diversity	Dr. John Paul SANCHEZ
84	Vice Prov Enrollment & Analytics	Dan GARCIA
15	Vice President Human Resources	Dorothy ANDERSON
21	University Controller	Elizabeth METZGER
13	Chief Information Officer	Duane ARRUTI
14	Int Deputy Chief Information Ofcr	Brian PIETREWICZ
43	Chief Legal Counsel	Loretta MARTINEZ
29	Int AVP Alumni Relations	Connie BEIMER
20	Dir Financial Ops Academic Affairs	Nicole DOPSON
35	AVP Student Life	Vacant
35	AVP Student Services	Dr. Tim GUTIERREZ
50	Dean Anderson School of Mgmt	Dr. Mitzi MONTOYA
48	Dean Sch of Architecture & Planning	Robert A. GONZALEZ
49	Dean College of Arts & Sciences	Dr. Mark PECENY
53	Dean College of Education	Hansel E. BURLEY
54	Dean School of Engineering	Dr. Christos CHRISTODOULOU
57	Dean College of Fine Arts	Dr. Harris SMITH
61	Dean School of Law	Sergio PAREJA
63	Exec Vice Dean School of Medicine	Dr. Martha MCGREW
66	Dean College of Nursing	Dr. Christine KASPER
67	Dean College of Pharmacy	Dr. Donald A. GODWIN
80	Dir School of Public Admin	Dr. Bruce J. PERLMAN
97	Dean University College	Dr. Eric LAU
58	Dean Office of Graduate Studies	Dr. Julie COONROD
51	Exec Director Continuing Education	Audrey ARNOLD
08	Dean University Libraries	Dr. Richard CLEMENT
26	Chief Univ Marketing & Comm Officer	Cinnamon BLAIR
27	HSC Comm/Marketing/Public Info Ofcr	Alex SANCHEZ
27	University Media Relations Officer	Daniel JIRON
105	Mgr University Web Communications	Matt CARTER
86	Director Government Affairs	Dr. Barbara DAMRON
09	Director Institutional Analytics	Dr. Heather S. MECHLER
88	University Architect	Amy COBURN
18	Director Facilities Management	Al SENA
19	Interim Chief of Police	Joseph SILVA
96	Chief Procurement Officer	Bruce E. CHERRIN
23	Exec Dir Student Health/Counseling	Dr. James WILTERDING
22	Chief Compliance Officer	Francie CORDOVA
56	Director Extended Learning	Debby KNOTTS
35	Dean of Students	Nasha TORREZ
07	Director Admissions and Recruitment	Matt HULETT
06	Registrar	Sheila JURNAK
37	Director Student Financial Aid	Brian MALONE
36	Director Career Services	Dr. Jenna S. CRABB
39	Int Dir Res Life & Student Housing	Megan CHIBANGA
40	Interim Director Bookstore	Lisa WALDEN

108 Director of Assessment .... Julie SANCHEZ
102 UNM Foundation President and CEO .... Jeff TODD
30 VP for Development .... Larry RYAN
30 VP Development Health Sciences Ctr .... Bill UHER
88 CEO UNM Hospital .... Kate BECKER
04 Administrative Asst to President .... Mitch GARRITY
101 Special Asst to Board of Regents .... Mallory REVIERE

University of New Mexico-Gallup (A)

705 Gurley Avenue, Gallup NM 87301

Telephone: (505) 863-7500 FICE Identification: 006881

Accreditation: &HLC, ADNUR, CAHIIM, DA, MLTAD

† Regional accreditation is carried under the parent institution in Albuquerque, NM.

University of New Mexico-Los Alamos (B)

4000 University Drive, Los Alamos NM 87544-2233

Telephone: (505) 662-5919 Identification: 666742

Accreditation: &HLC

† Regional accreditation is carried under the parent institution in Albuquerque, NM.

University of New Mexico-Taos (C)

1157 Country Road 110, Ranchos de Taos NM 87557

Telephone: (575) 737-6215 Identification: 666743

Accreditation: &HLC, ADNUR

† Regional accreditation is carried under the parent institution in Albuquerque, NM.

University of New Mexico-Valencia (D)

280 La Entrada Road, Los Lunas NM 87031-7633

Telephone: (505) 925-8500 Identification: 666741

Accreditation: &HLC, ADNUR

† Regional accreditation is carried under the parent institution in Albuquerque, NM.

University of St. Francis (E)

1500 N. Renaissance Blvd, NE, Ste C,
Albuquerque NM 87107

Telephone: (505) 266-5565 Identification: 770099

Accreditation: &HLC, ARCPA

† Branch campus of University of St. Francis, Joliet, IL

University of the Southwest (F)

6610 Lovington Highway, Hobbs NM 88240-9129

County: Lea FICE Identification: 002650
Unit ID: 188182

Telephone: (575) 392-6561 Carnegie Class: Masters/M
FAX Number: N/A Calendar System: Semester
URL: www.usw.edu
Established: 1962 Annual Undergrad Tuition & Fees: $16,200
Enrollment: 904 Coed
Affiliation or Control: Independent Non-Profit IRS Status: 501(c)3
Highest Offering: Doctorate
Accreditation: HLC, CACREP

01 President .... Dr. Quint THURMAN
05 Provost .... Dr. Ryan TIPTON
10 VP for Financial Services/CFO .... Mr. Steven RACHEL
37 Executive Director of Financial Aid .... Mrs. Dawny KRINGEL
18 Campus Steward .... Dr. David ARNOLD
41 Athletic Director .... Mr. Steve APPEL
32 Director of Student Affairs .... Ms. Amanda GUZMAN
15 Asst VP HR & Regulatory Compliance .... Mrs. Veronica TORREZ
49 Dean College of Arts & Sciences .... Dr. Daniel KIRKPATRICK
50 Dean College of Business .... Dr. Ryan TIPTON
53 Dean College of Education .... Dr. Laura HUNT
07 Director Admissions .... Dr. Ryan TIPTON
06 University Registrar .... Ms. Lissete TERRAZAS
58 Director Graduate Programs .... Mrs. Sandy WILKINSON
13 Director Resource Systems .... Mr. Josh FORD
39 Director Student Housing .... Ms. Catarina GARCIA
38 University Counselor .... Mr. Brian ARNOLD
42 Campus Pastor/Christian Ministry .... Mr. David BLACKWOOD
105 Instructional Design Technician .... Mr. David WILLIS
26 Dir of Mktg/Stakeholder Rels Coord .... Ms. Maria DUARTE
29 Director of Alumni Affairs .... Ms. Maria DUARTE
04 Administrative Asst to President .... Mrs. Linda WOODFIN
08 Student Learning Resource Director .... Ms. Corina MADRID
88 Maintenance Supervisor .... Mr. Lonnie HARRISON

Western New Mexico University (G)

PO Box 680, Silver City NM 88062-0680

County: Grant FICE Identification: 002664
Unit ID: 188304

Telephone: (575) 538-6238 Carnegie Class: Masters/L
FAX Number: (575) 538-6364 Calendar System: Semester
URL: wnmu.edu
Established: 1893 Annual Undergrad Tuition & Fees (In-State): $6,574
Enrollment: 2,896 Coed
Affiliation or Control: State IRS Status: 501(c)3
Highest Offering: Beyond Master's But Less Than Doctorate
Accreditation: HLC, ACBSP, CAEP, NAEYC, NURSE, SW

01 President .... Dr. Joseph SHEPARD
05 Provost/Vice Pres Academic Affairs .... Dr. Jack CROCKER
32 VP Student Affairs/Enrollment Mgmt .... Dr. Isaac BRUNDAGE
10 VP Business Affairs .... Ms. Kelley RIDDLE
30 VP External Affairs .... Dr. Magdaleno MANZANAREZ
20 Assoc Vice Pres Academic Affairs .... Dr. Steven CHAVEZ
06 Registrar .... Ms. Betsy MILLER
08 University Librarian .... Dr. Gilda BAEZA-ORTEGO
37 Director Student Financial Aid .... Ms. Debra REYES
07 Director Admissions & Recruitment .... Mr. Andrew LUNT
09 Director of Institutional Research .... Vacant
15 Director of Human Resources .... Ms. Michelle HALT
18 Asst VP of Facilities .... Mr. Kevin MATTHES
26 Director of Marketing .... Mr. Mario SANCHEZ
29 Director of Alumni Affairs .... Ms. Amanda MOFFETT LANE
36 Coord of Career/Student Svcs .... Ms. Janine SOHLER
35 Asst Dean of Student Life & Develop .... Ms. Jessica MORALES
96 Director Materials/Resources .... Ms. Amy BACA
100 Chief of Staff .... Ms. Julie MORALES
19 Director Campus Police .... Mr. Eddie FLORES
41 Athletic Director .... Mr. Scott NOBLE
53 Interim Dean of Education .... Dr. Debra DIRKSEN
04 Admin Assistant to the President .... Ms. Mary Rae MCDONALD
22 Affirmative Action/Equal Oppty .... Ms. Debra NOBLE

NEW YORK

Academy for Jewish Religion (H)

28 Wells Avenue, Yonkers NY 10701

County: Westchester Identification: 667403
Telephone: (914) 709-0900 Carnegie Class: Not Classified
FAX Number: (914) 709-0901 Calendar System: Trimester
Established: 1956 Annual Graduate Tuition & Fees: N/A
Enrollment: N/A Coed
Affiliation or Control: Jewish IRS Status: 501(c)3
Highest Offering: Master's; No Undergraduates
Accreditation: THEOL

01 CEO & Academic Dean .... Dr. Ora HORN PROUSER

Adelphi University (I)

One South Avenue, PO Box 701,
Garden City NY 11530-0701

County: Nassau FICE Identification: 002666
Unit ID: 188429

Telephone: (516) 877-3000 Carnegie Class: DU-Mod
FAX Number: (516) 877-3545 Calendar System: Semester
URL: www.adelphi.edu
Established: 1896 Annual Undergrad Tuition & Fees: $41,435
Enrollment: 7,584 Coed
Affiliation or Control: Independent Non-Profit IRS Status: 501(c)3
Highest Offering: Doctorate
Accreditation: M, AUD, CAEP, CLPSY, IPSY, NURSE, SP, SW

01 President .... Dr. Christine M. RIORDAN
05 Provost/Executive VP .... Dr. Chris K. STORM, JR.
10 EVP of Finance & Operations .... Mr. James J. PERRINO
28 VP of Diversity/Equity/Inclusion ... Ms. Jacqueline JONES LAMON
111 AVP Advancement/External Relations .... Ms. Maggie YOON GRAFER
84 VP Enrollment Mgmt/Communications .... Ms. Kristen CAPEZZA
26 AVP Branding Strategy & Univ Comm .. Ms. Joanna TEMPLETON
100 Chief of Staff .... Ms. Maggie YOON GRAFER
20 Deputy Provost .... Vacant
32 Assoc Provost for Student Success .... Dr. R. Sentwali BAKARI
20 Assoc Provost Fac Adv & Research .... Vacant
21 CFO & Assoc VP .... Mr. Robert L. DECARLO
13 Chief Information Officer .... Ms. Carol Ann BOYLE
15 Chief Human Resource Officer .... Ms. Lucinda J. DONNELLY
11 VP Wellness/Safety/Administration .... Mr. Eugene PALMA
09 Assistant Provost for IR .... Dr. Nava LERER
18 Asst VP for Facilities Management .... Mr. Robert J. SHIPLEY
37 Asst VP Student Financial Services .... Ms. Sheryl L. MIHOPULOS
49 Dean College of Arts & Sciences .... Dr. Vincent WANG
53 Dean Col of Educ & Health Sciences .... Dr. Xiao-lei WANG
66 Dean Col of Nursing & Public Health .... Dr. Elaine L. SMITH
70 Dean School of Social Work .... Mr. Manoj PARDASONI
83 Dean GF Derner Sch of Psychology .... Dr. Jacques BARBER
50 Dean RB Willumstad Sch of Business .... Dr. Rajib N. SANYAL
92 Dean Honors College .... Dr. Susan DINAN
107 Dean Col of Prof & Cont Studies .... Mr. Andy ATZERT
08 Interim Dean University Libraries .... Ms. Debbi SMITH
35 Dean of Student Affairs/Asst VP .... Vacant
22 Exec Dir Diversity/Equity/Inclusion .... Ms. Chotsani WEST
16 Dir Talent Mgmt & Labor Relations .... Ms. Jane FISHER
41 Director of Athletics .... Mr. Daniel MCCABE
36 Exec Dir Center Career & Prof Dev .... Mr. Thomas J. WARD, JR.
06 University Registrar .... Mr. Steven E. SMITH
104 Director International Education .... Ms. Shannon HARRISON
23 Director Health Services .... Ms. Jacqueline JOHNSTON
38 Director Counseling & Support Svcs .... Dr. Carol A. LUCAS
39 Director Residential Life/Housing .... Mr. Guy SENEQUE
29 Exec Director Alumni Relations .... Ms. Jodie SPERICO
114 Dir of Financial Ops & Assoc VP .... Mr. Michael J. MCLEOD
96 Director of Procurement .... Ms. Elizabeth F. KASH
108 Director Institutional Assessment .... Vacant
105 Director of Web Development .... Ms. Tara A. COYLE
101 Director of Board Relations .... Ms. Mary ALDRIDGE
91 Director of Postmodern ERP .... Mr. Michael DICRESCIO
44 Director of Participation .... Ms. Jennifer WALSH
88 Spec Asst to Provost for Strat Init .... Dr. Sam GROGG
46 Director Research & Sponsored Pgms .... Ms. Mary CORTINA
88 Dir Faculty Ctr for Prof Excellence .... Ms. Nathalie ZARISFI

Albany College of Pharmacy and Health Sciences (J)

106 New Scotland Avenue, Albany NY 12208-3492

County: Albany FICE Identification: 002885
Unit ID: 188526

Telephone: (518) 694-7200 Carnegie Class: Spec-4-yr-Other Health
FAX Number: (518) 694-7202 Calendar System: Semester
URL: www.acphs.edu
Established: 1881 Annual Undergrad Tuition & Fees: $36,745
Enrollment: 1,118 Coed
Affiliation or Control: Independent Non-Profit IRS Status: 501(c)3
Highest Offering: Doctorate
Accreditation: M, CYTO, MT, PH, PHAR

01 President .... Greg DEWEY
05 Dean/VP of Academic Affairs .... Anuja GHORPADE
46 Director of Research .... Martha HASS
12 Interim Regional Dean for VT Campus .... Abby BOIRE
32 VP of Student Affairs .... John FELIO
10 VP of Finance .... Michele VIEN
111 VP of Institutional Advancement .... Vicki DILORENZO
84 VP of Enrollment Management .... Tiffany GUTIERREZ
13 Chief Information Officer .... Joshua SINGLETARY
11 VP of Administrative Operations .... Packy MCGRAW
07 Director of Admissions .... Kevin RIVENBURG
06 Registrar .... Jeff DUFOUR
26 Director of Public Relations .... Shannon HUTTON
41 Director of Athletics & Rec .... Robert COLEMAN
15 VP of Human Resources .... Susan KARAVOLAS
110 AVP of Development .... Deanna ENNELLO-BUTLER
37 Director of Financial Aid .... Kathleen MONTAGUE

Albany Law School (K)

80 New Scotland Avenue, Albany NY 12208-3494

County: Albany FICE Identification: 002886
Unit ID: 188535

Telephone: (518) 445-2311 Carnegie Class: Spec-4-yr-Law
FAX Number: (518) 445-2315 Calendar System: Semester
URL: www.albanylaw.edu
Established: 1851 Annual Undergrad Tuition & Fees: N/A
Enrollment: 566 Coed
Affiliation or Control: Independent Non-Profit IRS Status: 501(c)3
Highest Offering: First Professional Degree
Accreditation: @M, LAW

01 President & Dean .... Dean Alicia OUELLETTE
05 Assoc Dean Academic Affairs .... Dean Connie MAYER
10 Vice President Finance & Business .... Mr. Victor E. RAUSCHER
08 Director of Library .... Mr. David WALKER
111 Vice President Inst Advancement .... Dr. Jeffrey SCHANZ
32 Associate Dean for Student Affairs .... Prof. Rosemary QUEENAN
06 Assistant Dean and Registrar .... Ms. Joanne FITZSIMMONS
36 Asst Dean Career Center .... Ms. Mary WALSH FITZPATRICK
26 Director Communications .... Mr. Tom TORELLO
04 Executive Assistant to the Dean .... Ms. Barbara JORDAN-SMITH
07 Assistant Dean of Admissions .... Ms. Amy MANGIONE
88 Director Clinical Program .... Prof. Connie MAYER
29 Director Alumni Engage/Inst Events .... Mr. Geoffrey SEBER
15 Director Human Resources .... Ms. Sherri DONNELLY
37 Director Student Financial Aid .... Ms. Andrea WEDLER
18 Director of Facilities & Admin Svcs .... Mr. Brian LAPLANTE
36 Director of Career Services .... Ms. Joanne CASEY
108 Director Institutional Assessment .... Mr. Will TREVOR

Albany Medical College (L)

47 New Scotland Avenue, Mail #34,
Albany NY 12208-3479

County: Albany FICE Identification: 002887
Unit ID: 188580

Telephone: (518) 262-6008 Carnegie Class: Spec-4-yr-Med
FAX Number: (518) 262-6515 Calendar System: Semester
URL: www.amc.edu
Established: 1839 Annual Graduate Tuition & Fees: N/A
Enrollment: 835 Coed
Affiliation or Control: Independent Non-Profit IRS Status: 501(c)3
Highest Offering: Doctorate; No Undergraduates
Accreditation: M, ANEST, ARCPA, IPSY, MED, PAST

01 Dean/Exec VP Health Affairs .... Dr. Vincent P. VERDILE
10 EVP/COO/Chief Financial Officer .. Ms. Frances SPREER-ALBERT
05 Vice Dean for Academic Admin .... Dr. Ellen COSGROVE
17 Vice Dean Clinical Affairs .... Dr. Ferdinand VENDITTI
32 Assoc Dean for Acad & Student Affs .... Vacant
63 Assoc Dean Graduate Medical Educ .... Dr. Joel BARTFIELD
22 Assoc Dean Cmty Outreach/Medical Ed .... Dr. Ingrid M. ALLARD
08 Asc Dn Info Resrcs/Tech/Dir Library .... Ms. Enid GEYER
88 Asst Dean Medical Education .... Dr. Rebecca KELLER
58 Assoc Dean for Graduate Studies .... Dr. Peter VINCENT
06 Registrar .... Ms. Krista REYNOLDS-STUMP
58 Director Graduate Medical Education .... Ms. Catherine RIDDLE
76 Director Physician Asst Program .... Mr. Nathan GARDNER
29 Executive Director Alumni Relations .... Ms. Sandra DINOTO

26 Director Communications .... Ms. Sue FORD
30 Chief Development .... Vacant
51 Director Cont Medical Education .... Ms. Jennifer PRICE
15 Director Human Resources .... Ms. Sandra CASTILLA
37 Director Student Financial Aid .... Ms. Ann LOUGHMAN
28 Chief Diversity Officer .... Dr. Angela ANTONIKOWSKI
96 Director of Purchasing .... Ms. Ann CRISLIP
27 Marketing Manager .... Mr. Eli FANNING
03 Executive Assoc Dean .... Mr. John DEPAOLA
09 Director of Institutional Research .... Dr. Paul FEUSTEL
85 Director Foreign Students .... Ms. Marianne R. WILLIAMS
13 Chief Info Technology Officer (CIO) .... Mr. George HICKMAN
18 Chief Facilities Physical Plant .... Mr. Donald STICHTER
19 Director Security/Safety .... Mr. Charles DAY
38 Director Student Counseling .... Dr. Jeffrey WINSEMAN
43 Dir Legal Services/General Counsel .... Mr. Lee HESSBERG
45 Chief Institutional Planning .... Ms. Courtney BURKE
76 Director Nurse Anesthesia Pgm .... Dr. Jodi DELLA ROCCA
07 Director of Admissions .... Ms. Julia SALTANOVICH

Albert Einstein College of Medicine (A)

1300 Morris Park Avenue, Bronx NY 10461
FICE Identification: 042797
Telephone: (718) 430-2000 Carnegie Class: Not Classified
FAX Number: N/A Calendar System: Semester
URL: www.einsteinmed.org
Established: 1953 Annual Undergrad Tuition & Fees: N/A
Enrollment: N/A Coed
Affiliation or Control: Independent Non-Profit IRS Status: 501(c)3
Highest Offering: First Professional Degree
Accreditation: M, MED

01 Dean/EVP/CAO .... Dr. Gordon F. TOMASELLI
63 Executive Dean .... Dr. Edward R. BURNS
10 CFO & Assoc Vice President .... Mr. James GERAGHTY
32 Assoc Dean for Student Affairs .... Dr. Allison LUDWIG
07 Associate Dean of Admissions .... Ms. Noreen KERRIGAN

Alfred University (B)

One Saxon Drive, Alfred NY 14802-1205
County: Allegany FICE Identification: 002668
Unit ID: 188641
Telephone: (607) 871-2111 Carnegie Class: Masters/L
FAX Number: (607) 871-2339 Calendar System: Semester
URL: www.alfred.edu
Established: 1836 Annual Undergrad Tuition & Fees: $34,960
Enrollment: 2,187 Coed
Affiliation or Control: Independent Non-Profit IRS Status: 501(c)3
Highest Offering: Doctorate
Accreditation: M, AAQEP, ART, CAATE, CACREP, SCPSY

01 President .... Dr. Mark A. ZUPAN
05 Int Provost/VP for Academic Affairs .... Dr. Elizabeth A. DOBIE
10 VP for Business & Finance/Treasurer .... Ms. Giovina LLOYD
30 Interim VP for University Relations .... Mr. Mark H. RIORDAN
84 VP for Enrollment Management .... Mr. Jonathan KENT
32 VP for Student Affairs .... Vacant
57 Dean School of Art & Design .... Ms. Lauren LAKE
49 Dean Col of Lib Arts & Sciences .... Dr. Robert STEIN
107 Dean College of Business .... Mr. Mark LEWIS
54 Dean School of Engineering .... Dr. Gabrielle G. GAUSTAD
35 Dean Student Wellbeing .... Dr. Tamara KENNEY
29 Alumni Engagement Officer .... Ms. Janet MARBLE
37 Exec Dir Student Financial Aid Svcs .... Ms. Jane A. GILLILAND
07 Director of Admissions .... Ms. Kristen VARGASON
06 Interim Registrar .... Ms. Tammy JURSZA-WILLIAMS
19 Chief of Public Safety .... Ms. Jessica M. MIDDAUGH
26 Exec Dir of Mktg & Communication .... Mr. Michael KOZLOWSKI
39 Dir Residence Communities .... Mr. Max KOSKOFF
13 Director Information Tech Svcs .... Mr. Gary O. ROBERTS
36 Int Director Career Development Ctr .... Ms. Jill CRANDALL
41 Athletic Director .... Mr. Paul VECCHIO
23 Dir Counseling & Wellness Center .... Vacant
08 Dean of Libraries .... Mr. Brian T. SULLIVAN
15 Director of Human Resources .... Mr. Mark A. GUINAN
21 Controller .... Ms. Amanda R. AZZI
92 Director of the Honors Program .... Dr. Julianna R. GRAY
94 Dir of Women's Leadership Center .... Vacant
18 Dir Facilities/Capital Projects .... Mr. Jamie T. BABCOCK
101 Secretary to the Corporation .... Ms. Mary C. MCALLISTER
104 Dir Study Abroad Programs .... Vacant
40 Bookstore Manager .... Mrs. Marcy K. BRADLEY
87 Dir of Summer/Parent Programs .... Vacant
09 Director of Institutional Research .... Mr. Frederick B. RODGERS
28 Chief Diversity Officer .... Dr. Brian SALTSMAN
102 Dir Foundation/Corporate Relations .... Mr. Brian SHANAHAN
96 Director of Procurement .... Mrs. Melissa BADEAU

American Academy of Dramatic Arts (C)

120 Madison Avenue, New York NY 10016-7089
County: New York FICE Identification: 007465
Unit ID: 188678
Telephone: (212) 686-9244 Carnegie Class: Spec 2-yr-A&S
FAX Number: (212) 545-7934 Calendar System: Other
URL: www.aada.edu
Established: 1884 Annual Undergrad Tuition & Fees: $37,230
Enrollment: 159 Coed
Affiliation or Control: Independent Non-Profit IRS Status: 501(c)3
Highest Offering: Associate Degree
Accreditation: M, THEA

01 President .... Ms. Susan ZECH
111 Sr VP Institutional Advancement .... Vacant
10 Chief Financial Officer .... Mr. Joel BLOCK
05 Director of Instruction .... Mr. Constantine SCOPAS
07 Director of Admissions .... Ms. Kerin REILLY
27 Sr Director of Marketing .... Mr. James LUBIN
08 Librarian .... Ms. Deborah PICONE
21 Controller .... Ms. Linda VIALA
11 Senior Director of Operations .... Mr. Peter TUFEL
26 Director External Affairs .... Vacant
37 Director of Financial Aid .... Ms. Lisa SHAHEEN
04 Exec Assistant to the President .... Mr. Jimmy WILSON

American Academy McAllister Institute of Funeral Service (D)

619 W 54th Street, 2nd Floor, New York NY 10019
County: New York FICE Identification: 010813
Unit ID: 188687
Telephone: (212) 757-1190 Carnegie Class: Spec 2-yr-A&S
FAX Number: (212) 765-5923 Calendar System: Semester
URL: www.funeraleducation.org
Established: 1926 Annual Undergrad Tuition & Fees: $18,292
Enrollment: 463 Coed
Affiliation or Control: Independent Non-Profit IRS Status: 501(c)3
Highest Offering: Associate Degree
Accreditation: #FUSER

01 President .... Dr. George CONNICK
05 Program Director/Academic Affairs .... Ms. Tracy LENTZ
10 Bursar .... Mr. Jay TSO
37 Financial Aid Officer .... Ms. Natalie GIVAN
06 Registrar .... Mr. Andre RAMPAUL
07 Dir of Admissions/Enrollment Mgmt .... Ms. Tracy LENTZ
20 Academic Advisor .... Ms. Charlotte RERRICK
20 Academic Advisor .... Ms. Karen CARR
43 Legal Counsel .... Mr. Charles MAURER

ASA College (E)

151 Lawrence Street, Brooklyn NY 11201
County: Kings FICE Identification: 030955
Unit ID: 404994
Telephone: (718) 522-9073 Carnegie Class: Assoc/MT-VT-High Trad
FAX Number: (718) 532-1433 Calendar System: Semester
URL: www.asa.edu
Established: 1985 Annual Undergrad Tuition & Fees: $12,528
Enrollment: 2,965 Coed
Affiliation or Control: Proprietary IRS Status: Proprietary
Highest Offering: Baccalaureate
Accreditation: M, MAC

01 Interim President .... Mr. Alex SHCHEGOL
05 Provost .... Dr. Shanthi KONKOTH
26 Vice President Marketing/Admissions .. Ms. Victoria KOSTYUKOV
29 VP Placement/Alumni Services .... Ms. Lesia WILLIS
37 VP Financial Aid Services .... Ms. Victoriya SHTAMLER
11 VP Planning & Operations .... Ms. Maritza MERCADO
86 VP Govt & Community Relations .... Mr. Roberto DUMAUAL
10 Controller .... Mr. Mark MIRENBERG
20 Academic Dean .... Dr. Edward KUFUOR
106 Director of Distance Learning .... Mr. Joel ALMORADIE
08 Head Librarian .... Mr. Brook STOWE
06 Registrar .... Ms. Mariana ZINDER
13 IT Director .... Mr. David ESTRIN
108 Director Institutional Assessment .... Ms. Ksenia KASIMOVA
09 Director Institutional Research .... Ms. Anna BOUKHMAN
15 Director of Human Resources .... Vacant
18 Chief Facilities/Physical Plant .... Mr. Walter KRUMER
50 Dean of Business .... Ms. Bridget UDEH
61 Dean of Legal Studies .... Vacant
49 Dean of Arts and Sciences .... Mr. Lizhi (Frank) ZHU
79 Director for Language Studies .... Ms. Ludmilla DRAGUSHANSKAYA
36 Director College/Career Prep .... Ms. Denise DUBRON
76 Dean of Health Disciplines .... Dr. Nasser SEDHOM
66 Dean of Nursing .... Ms. Donna M. REID
54 Dean Div Engineering & Technology .... Vacant
20 Dean Academic & Program Development ... Ms. Deborah HUGHES
88 Ombudsperson .... Dr. Jennifer ROSS
32 Asst Dean for Student Success .... Ms. Lillian GRANILLO
16 Title IX Coordinator .... Dr. Jayne WEINBERGER
38 Director Student Counseling .... Ms. Tatyana KRYZHANOVSKAYA
41 Athletic Director .... Dr. Jody KING
39 Director Student Housing .... Vacant

Bais Binyomin Academy, Inc (F)

51 Carlton Road, Monsey NY 10952
County: Rockland FICE Identification: 029120
Unit ID: 128586
Telephone: (845) 207-0330 Carnegie Class: Spec-4-yr-Faith
FAX Number: N/A Calendar System: Semester
Established: 1976 Annual Undergrad Tuition & Fees: $9,650
Enrollment: 35 Male
Affiliation or Control: Independent Non-Profit IRS Status: 501(c)3
Highest Offering: First Talmudic Degree
Accreditation: RABN

01 Rosh Hayeshiva .... Rabbi Meyer HERSHKOWITZ
04 Associate Rosh Hayeshiva .... Rabbi Yeruchom ZEILBERGER
05 Dean .... Rabbi Michael BENDER

Bais Medrash Ateres Shlomo (G)

220 Bennett Avenue, New York NY 10040
County: New York Identification: 667321
Telephone: (212) 419-5758 Carnegie Class: Not Classified
FAX Number: (914) 736-1055 Calendar System: Semester
URL: baismedrashateresshlomo.com
Established: 2016 Annual Undergrad Tuition & Fees: N/A
Enrollment: N/A Male
Affiliation or Control: Jewish IRS Status: 501(c)3
Highest Offering: First Talmudic Degree
Accreditation: AIJS

Bank Street College of Education (H)

610 W 112 Street, New York NY 10025-1898
County: New York FICE Identification: 002669
Unit ID: 189015
Telephone: (212) 875-4400 Carnegie Class: Spec-4-yr-Other
FAX Number: (212) 875-4759 Calendar System: Semester
URL: www.bankstreet.edu
Established: 1916 Annual Graduate Tuition & Fees: N/A
Enrollment: 599 Coed
Affiliation or Control: Independent Non-Profit IRS Status: 501(c)3
Highest Offering: Master's; No Undergraduates
Accreditation: M, AAQEP

01 President .... Shael POLAKOW-SURANSKY
100 Chief of Staff .... Katherine CONNELLY
11 Chief Operating Officer .... Justin TYACK
10 Chief Financial Officer .... Aparna MURALIDHARAN
30 VP Development .... Marcela HAHN
05 VP Bank Street Education Center .... Tracy FRAY-OLIVER
28 VP Governance/Social Justice/Equity .... Akilah ROSADO
58 Dean of the Graduate School .... Cecelia TRAUGH
88 Dean of Children's Programs .... Doug KNECHT
123 Director of Graduate Admissions .... Stephen OSTENDORFF
06 Registrar .... Meghan CHVIRKO
37 Director of Student Financial Aid .... Emmett COOPER
29 Director of Alumni Relations .... Eric GUTIERREZ
15 Chief Human Resources Officer .... Elyse MATTHEWS
13 Chief Information Officer .... Judith JOHNSON
18 Dir of Facilities/Security/Safety .... Carlos ESQUIVEL
08 Director of Library Services .... Kristin FREDA
36 Director of Student Placement .... Susan LEVINE
04 Executive Assistant to President .... Regina WRIGHT

Bard College (I)

PO Box 5000, Annandale-On-Hudson NY 12504-5000
County: Dutchess FICE Identification: 002671
Unit ID: 189088
Telephone: (845) 758-6822 Carnegie Class: Bac-A&S
FAX Number: (845) 758-4294 Calendar System: Semester
URL: www.bard.edu
Established: 1860 Annual Undergrad Tuition & Fees: $56,036
Enrollment: 2,465 Coed
Affiliation or Control: Independent Non-Profit IRS Status: 501(c)3
Highest Offering: Doctorate
Accreditation: M, CAEP

01 President .... Dr. Leon BOTSTEIN
03 Executive Vice President of College .... Vacant
05 EVP/VP Acad Affs/Dir Civic Engage .... Dr. Jonathan BECKER
10 SVP/Chief Financial Officer .... Mr. Taun TOAY
30 VP Alumni/ae Affairs/Development .... Ms. Debra R. PEMSTEIN
11 Vice President for Administration .... Ms. Coleen MURPHY ALEXANDER
20 Associate VP for Academic Affairs .... Dr. David SHEIN
100 Chief of Staff .... Ms. Malia DU MONT
32 VP for Student Affairs .... Ms. Erin CANNAN
09 VP for Institutional Research .... Dr. Mark D. HALSEY
35 Dean of Student Affairs .... Ms. Bethany NOHLGREN
20 Associate Dean of the College .... Ms. Deirdre D'ALBERTIS
57 Dir Milton Avery Grad Sch of Arts .... Mr. Arthur GIBBONS
88 Dir Bard Grad Ctr Decorative Arts .... Dr. Susan WEBER
88 Exec Dir Ctr Curatorial Studies .... Mr. Tom ECCLES
110 Asst VP Dir of Inst Support .... Ms. Karen UNGER
88 Director Ctr Environmental Policy .... Dr. Eban GOODSTEIN
37 Director Financial Aid .... Ms. Denise ACKERMAN
06 Registrar .... Mr. Peter GADSBY
26 Associate VP of Communications .... Mr. Mark PRIMOFF
15 Director of Human Resources .... Ms. Kimberly ALEXANDER
21 Associate VP for Finance .... Vacant
88 Director Inst Writing/Thinking .... Ms. Erica KAUFMAN
18 Director of Buildings & Grounds .... Mr. Randy CLUM
13 Director Mgmt Info Systems .... Mr. Michael TOMPKINS
29 Director Alumni/ae Affairs .... Ms. Jane BRIEN
36 Assoc Director Career Development ... Ms. Maureen AURIGEMMA
19 Director Safety & Security .... Mr. John GOMEZ
09 Director of Institutional Research .... Mr. Joseph F. AHERN
24 Director of Audio/Video Services .... Mr. Paul LABARBERA
28 Director of Multicultural Affairs .... Dr. Ann SEATON
41 Director of Athletics .... Ms. Kristin E. HALL
40 Bookstore Manager .... Ms. Merry MEYER
23 Director Student Health Services .... Ms. Barbara BRISKEY
38 Director Student Counseling .... Ms. Tamara TELBERG
07 Director of Admission .... Ms. Mackie SIEBENS

39 Director of Housing .... Ms. Nancy W. SMITH
90 Chief Information Officer .... Mr. David BRANGAITIS

Barnard College (A)

3009 Broadway, New York NY 10027-6598
County: New York FICE Identification: 002708
Unit ID: 189097
Telephone: (212) 854-5262 Carnegie Class: Bac-A&S
FAX Number: (212) 854-6220 Calendar System: Semester
URL: www.barnard.edu
Established: 1889 Annual Undergrad Tuition & Fees: $57,479
Enrollment: 2,744 Female
Affiliation or Control: Independent Non-Profit IRS Status: 501(c)3
Highest Offering: Baccalaureate
Accreditation: M

01 President .... Sian L. BEILOCK
43 VP Legal Affairs/Chief of Staff .... Jomysha STEPHEN
05 Provost & Dean of Faculty .... Linda BELL
11 VP Campus Svcs/Int VP Operations .... Roger MOSIER
30 Vice President for Development .... Lisa YEH
10 CFO & Vice Pres for Finance .... Eileen M. DI BENEDETTO
13 Int Exec Dir Info Technology .... Victoria SWANN
15 Exec Director Human Resources .... Kathleen VETERI
84 VP for Enrollment & Communications .... Jennifer FONDILLER
28 VP Diversity/Equity & Inclusion .... Ariana GONZÁLEZ STOKAS
32 Dean of the College .... Leslie GRINAGE
20 Interim Dean of Studies .... Christina KUAN TSU
06 Registrar .... Vacant
37 Director of Financial Aid .... Nanette DILAURO
35 Associate Dean for Student Life .... Emy CARDOZA
39 Interim Exec Dir Res Life & Housing .... Lizeth JARAMILLO
23 Exec Director of Student Health Svc .... Mary Joan MURPHY
36 Dean Beyond Barnard .... A-J ARONSTEIN
36 Dean Beyond Barnard .... Nikki YOUNGBLOOD GILES
29 Exec Director of Alumnae Relations .... Karen SENDLER
08 Interim Co-Dean Library .... Melanie HIBBERT
08 Interim Co-Dean Library .... Kristen HOGAN
08 Interim Co-Dean Library .... Miriam NEPTUNE
101 Secretary to the Board of Trustees .... Virginia RYAN
19 Interim Exec Director Public Safety .... Amy ZAVADIL
109 Director of Business Operations .... Douglas MAGET
18 Director Facilities Services .... Daniel DAVIS
09 Exec Dir Institutional Assessment .... Nikisha WILLIAMS
88 Spec Asst to Pres/Dir Family Engage .... Katelyn DUTTON
102 Asst VP for Development .... Kate MARTINEZ
104 Assoc Provost Inst Initiatives .... Giorgio DIMAURO
38 Director Student Counseling .... Mary COMMERFORD
44 Director Annual Giving .... Sally VALLIMARESCU
96 Director of Purchasing .... Douglas MAGET
100 Chief of Staff .... Jomysha STEPHEN
07 Dean of Admissions .... Christina LOPEZ
22 Dir Ctr Access Res/Disability Svcs .... Holly TEDDER

† Affiliated with Columbia University in the City of New York.

Be'er Yaakov Talmudic Seminary (B)

12 Truman Avenue, Spring Valley NY 10977
County: Rockland FICE Identification: 041928
Unit ID: 476717
Telephone: (845) 362-3053 Carnegie Class: Spec-4-yr-Faith
FAX Number: (845) 406-3699 Calendar System: Semester
URL: www.byts.edu
Established: 1995 Annual Undergrad Tuition & Fees: $10,460
Enrollment: 565 Male
Affiliation or Control: Independent Non-Profit IRS Status: 501(c)3
Highest Offering: Special 5-year Faith
Accreditation: RABN

01 CEO .... Mr. Jacob UNGER
05 Dean .... Rabbi Israel EISENBERGER
06 Registrar/Administrator .... Rabbi Yitzchok SOIFER
37 Financial Aid Administrator .... Mrs. Chana NOTIS

Beis Medrash Heichal Dovid (C)

211 Beach 17th Street, Far Rockaway NY 11691-4433
County: Queens FICE Identification: 037133
Unit ID: 444413
Telephone: (718) 868-2300 Carnegie Class: Spec-4-yr-Faith
FAX Number: (718) 868-0517 Calendar System: Semester
URL: heichaldovid.org
Established: 1999 Annual Undergrad Tuition & Fees: $10,000
Enrollment: 183 Male
Affiliation or Control: Independent Non-Profit IRS Status: 501(c)3
Highest Offering: Second Talmudic Degree
Accreditation: RABN

01 Dean .... Rabbi Yaakov BENDER
05 Rosh Yeshiva .... Rabbi Shlomo Avidgor ALTUSKY
37 Financial Aid Officer .... Rabbi Aaron STEINBERG

The Belanger School of Nursing (D)

650 McClellan Street, Schenectady NY 12304
County: Schenectady FICE Identification: 006448
Unit ID: 190956
Telephone: (518) 243-4471 Carnegie Class: Spec 2-yr-Health
FAX Number: (518) 243-4470 Calendar System: Semester
URL: www.ellisbelangerschoolofnursing.org
Established: 1903 Annual Undergrad Tuition & Fees: $10,664
Enrollment: 143 Coed
Affiliation or Control: Independent Non-Profit IRS Status: 501(c)3
Highest Offering: Associate Degree
Accreditation: ADNUR

01 Director .... Ms. Michele HEWITT
37 Financial Aid Coordinator/Registrar .... Ms. Patricia BRUNDIGE
22 ADA Coordinator .... Ms. Ellen GRAY
08 Head Librarian .... Ms. Emily SPINNER
07 Director of Admissions .... Ms. Cathy BIESTY
19 Director Security/Safety .... Mr. Keith EDWARDS
26 Sr Dir Marketing/Communications .... Mr. Philip SCHWARTZ

Berkeley College (E)

3 East 43rd Street, New York NY 10017-4604
County: New York FICE Identification: 007394
Unit ID: 189228
Telephone: (212) 986-4343 Carnegie Class: Spec-4-yr-Bus
FAX Number: (212) 818-1169 Calendar System: Semester
URL: www.berkeleycollege.edu
Established: 1931 Annual Undergrad Tuition & Fees: $27,000
Enrollment: 2,376 Coed
Affiliation or Control: Proprietary IRS Status: Proprietary
Highest Offering: Baccalaureate
Accreditation: M, IACBE

00 Chairman of the Board .... Mr. Kevin L. LUING
01 President .... Mr. Michael J. SMITH
05 Provost .... Dr. Marsha POLLARD
84 Executive VP .... Mr. Tim LUING
32 Senior VP Student Success .... Dr. Diane RECINOS
10 VP Finance .... Mr. Dino KASAMIS
03 Vice President .... Mr. Brian MAHER
35 VP Student Development/Campus Life .... Dr. Dallas REED
36 VP Career Services .... Ms. Amy SORICELLI
37 VP Financial Aid &AIE .... Mr. Will MOYA
114 VP Budget & Student Accounts .... Ms. Eileen LOFTUS-BERLIN
13 Senior VP/Chief Information Officer .... Mr. Leonard DE BOTTON
88 VP Financial Aid Compliance .... Mr. Howard LESLIE
20 Asst Prov Curriculum/Instruction .... Ms. Dana HEIMLICH
50 Dean School of Business .... Dr. Joseph SCURALLI
76 Dean School Health Studies .... Dr. Eva SKUKA
107 Dean School of Professional Studies .... Dr. Marianne VAKALIS
106 Dean Online .... Dr. Joseph SCURALLI
97 Director General Education .... Dr. Gregory HOTCHKISS
11 Campus Operating Officer .... Ms. Linda MAURO
25 Exec Dir of Academic Partnerships .... Ms. Michelle R. WHITE
15 VP Human Resources .... Ms. Karen J. CARPENTIERI
31 VP Communications & Ext Relations .... Ms. Angela HARRINGTON
86 VP Government Relations NY .... Mr. Gbubemi OKOTIEURO
06 Registrar .... Ms. Deborah PALICIA
29 AVP Alumni Relation & Career Svcs .... Mr. Michael IRIS
26 Director Marketing .... Mr. Michael ROMAN
22 Director Disability Services .... Dr. Sharon M. MCLENNON-WIER
88 Asst VP Military & Veterans Affairs .... Mr. Edward J. DENNIS
38 Sr Director Personal Counseling .... Dr. Sandra E. COPPOLA
41 Director Athletics .... Mr. Andrew DESTEPHANO
07 VP Undergraduate Enrollment .... Mr. David J. BERTONE
85 VP International Operations .... Dr. Nori JAFFER
45 Dir Institutional Analysis & Plng .... Ms. Janan JOHNSTON
18 Sr Vice Pres Operations .... Mr. Thomas ALESSANDRELLO
19 Assistant VP Public Safety .... Mr. Robert MAGUIRE
109 Senior Director Auxiliary Services .... Mr. Luis COLLAZO
119 Director of Information Security .... Mr. Dana KILCREASE
09 Director Institutional Research .... Ms. Rebecca J. DRENNEN

Bet Medrash Gadol Ateret Torah (F)

901 Quentin Road, Brooklyn NY 11223
County: Kings Identification: 667146
Unit ID: 485999
Telephone: (347) 394-1036 Carnegie Class: Spec-4-yr-Faith
FAX Number: (347) 394-1096 Calendar System: Semester
Established: 1992 Annual Undergrad Tuition & Fees: $10,050
Enrollment: 142 Male
Affiliation or Control: Independent Non-Profit IRS Status: 501(c)3
Highest Offering: Second Talmudic Degree
Accreditation: @RABN

01 President/CEO .... Rabbi Joseph HARARI-RAFUL
05 Executive Director .... Irwin SHAMAH
06 Registrar .... Mrs. Ruchana MANSOUR
11 Chief of Operations/Administration .... Zev KLEINER

Beth Hamedrash Shaarei Yosher Institute (G)

4102-10 16th Avenue, Brooklyn NY 11204-1099
County: Kings FICE Identification: 011192
Unit ID: 189273
Telephone: (718) 854-2290 Carnegie Class: Spec-4-yr-Faith
FAX Number: (718) 854-2292 Calendar System: Semester
Established: 1962 Annual Undergrad Tuition & Fees: $10,350
Enrollment: 97 Male
Affiliation or Control: Independent Non-Profit IRS Status: 501(c)3
Highest Offering: Second Talmudic Degree
Accreditation: RABN

01 Chief Executive Officer .... Rabbi Pinches KAFF
05 Chief Academic Officer .... Rabbi Chaim ROSENBERG
29 Director Alumni Association .... Rabbi Eliyohu ROSENBLUM
15 Director Personnel Services .... Rabbi Mordechai MARGULIES
37 Director Student Financial Aid .... Rabbi Aaron ROTTENBERG
06 Registrar .... Rabbi Sol ROSENBERG

Beth Medrash Meor Yitzchok (H)

65 Dykstra's Way East, Monsey NY 10952
County: Rockland Identification: 667111
Unit ID: 486196
Telephone: (845) 426-3488 Carnegie Class: Spec-4-yr-Faith
FAX Number: (845) 425-5415 Calendar System: Semester
Established: 2007 Annual Undergrad Tuition & Fees: $10,400
Enrollment: 187 Male
Affiliation or Control: Independent Non-Profit IRS Status: 501(c)3
Highest Offering: First Talmudic Degree
Accreditation: RABN

37 Financial Aid Administrator .... Isreal WEINGARTEN

Bill and Sandra Pomeroy College of Nursing at Crouse Hospital (I)

736 Irving Avenue, Syracuse NY 13210
County: Onondaga FICE Identification: 006445
Unit ID: 190451
Telephone: (315) 470-7481 Carnegie Class: Spec 2-yr-Health
FAX Number: (315) 470-5774 Calendar System: Semester
URL: www.crouse.org/nursing
Established: 1913 Annual Undergrad Tuition & Fees: $17,148
Enrollment: 245 Coed
Affiliation or Control: Independent Non-Profit IRS Status: 501(c)3
Highest Offering: Associate Degree
Accreditation: ADNUR

05 Dean .... Patricia MORGAN
20 Assistant Dean for Faculty .... David FALCI
07 Assistant Dean for Enrollment .... Amy GRAHAM
32 Assistant Dean for Students .... Ryan BARKER
06 Registrar/Bursar .... Jeanne CELSO
37 Financial Affairs Officer .... Kenny KENDALL
88 Instruction/Technology Coordinator .... Kelly DUFFY
08 Head Librarian .... Ellen OWENS

Boricua College (J)

3755 Broadway, New York NY 10032-1599
County: New York FICE Identification: 013029
Unit ID: 189413
Telephone: (212) 694-1000 Carnegie Class: Bac-Diverse
FAX Number: (212) 694-1015 Calendar System: Semester
URL: www.boricuacollege.edu
Established: 1974 Annual Undergrad Tuition & Fees: $11,025
Enrollment: 588 Coed
Affiliation or Control: Independent Non-Profit IRS Status: 501(c)3
Highest Offering: Master's
Accreditation: M

01 President .... Dr. Victor G. ALICEA
04 Exec Assistant to the President .... Ms. Sandra BELLAMY
05 VP Academic Affairs .... Dr. Shivaji SENGUPTA
13 VP Information & Tech/Facil Mgmt .... Mr. Irving RAMIREZ
20 VP Academic Planning & Programming .... Dr. John GUZMAN
15 VP Personnel/Human Resources .... Ms. Francia L. CASTRO
43 Legal Counsel .... Mr. Jorge BATISTA
10 Director Finance .... Mr. Elias OYOLA
113 Director Bursar Office .... Mr. Jose R. MANSO
07 Dir Admissions Bronx Campus Ctr .... Mr. Teofilo SANTIAGO
07 Dir Admissions Manhattan Campus .... Mr. Ismael SANCHEZ
07 Dir Admissions Brooklyn Cam Ctr .... Ms. Aurea MORALES
06 Director Registration & Assessments .... Ms. Beatriz AHORRIO
37 Director Financial Aid .... Ms. Rosalia CRUZ
08 Director Library/Learning Resources .... Ms. Liza RIVERA
18 Dir Environment Svcs Manhattan Camp .... Mr. Carlos ANDUJAR
18 Dir Environment Svcs Brooklyn .... Mr. Juan RIVERA PAGAN
18 Dir Environment Svcs Bronx Camp .... Mr. Jose VAZQUEZ
30 Director of Development .... Vacant
20 Dean Acad Affairs Manhattan Campus .... Mr. Moises PEREYRA
20 Dean Academic Affairs Bronx Campus .... Vacant

Brooklyn Law School (K)

250 Joralemon Street, Brooklyn NY 11201-3798
County: Kings FICE Identification: 002677
Unit ID: 189501
Telephone: (718) 625-2200 Carnegie Class: Spec-4-yr-Law
FAX Number: (718) 780-0393 Calendar System: Semester
URL: www.brooklaw.edu
Established: 1901 Annual Graduate Tuition & Fees: N/A
Enrollment: 1,162 Coed
Affiliation or Control: Independent Non-Profit IRS Status: 501(c)3
Highest Offering: First Professional Degree; No Undergraduates
Accreditation: LAW

01 President/Dean .... Dean Michael T. CAHILL
00 Dean and President Emerita .... Dean Joan G. WEXLER
05 Vice Dean of Academic Affairs .... Dean Christina MULLIGAN
20 Assoc Dean for Experiential Educ .... Dean Stacy CAPLOW
20 Assoc Dn Faculty/Rsrch/Scholarship .... Dean Edward JANGER
32 Dean of Students .... Dean Jennifer R. LANG
10 EVP Admin/Finance & Chief Bus Ofcr .... Mr. Marc C. HAMPTON
21 Treasurer .... Ms. Shoshanna M. CAMPBELL

07 Dean of Admissions .... Dean Eulas BOYD, JR.
36 Dean of Career Development .... Dean Karen EISEN
08 Director of Library .... Prof. Janet SINDER
111 Chief Advancement Officer .... Ms. Annie NIENABER
29 Director of Alumni Relations .... Ms. Caitlin MONCK
06 Registrar .... Ms. Julie BROWN
37 Director of Financial Aid .... Ms. Nancy L. ZAHZAM
11 Chief Operating Officer .... Ms. Linda HARVEY
18 Director of Facilities .... Mr. Steven OLEKSIW
15 Director of Human Resources .... Mr. Matthew BURNS
13 Chief Info Technology Officer (CIO) .... Vacant
19 Director of Public Safety .... Ms. Mercedes RAVELO
43 Gen Counsel/Chf Compliance Officer .... Ms. Stephanie VULLO

*Bryant & Stratton College System Office (A)

200 Redtail Rd., Orchard Park NY 14127
County: Erie Identification: 666828
Telephone: (716) 250-7500 Carnegie Class: N/A
FAX Number: (716) 250-7510
URL: www.bryantstratton.edu

01 President & CEO .... Dr. Francis J. FELSER
11 VP/Chief Operating Officer .... Mr. David VADEN
10 VP/Chief Financial Officer .... Mr. Christopher GERACE
13 VP/Online Division and CIO .... Ms. Doreen JUSTINGER
84 VP/Chief Enrollment Officer .... Ms. Tracy NANNERY
108 VP Research/Planning & Assessment .... Ms. Anne LORIA

*Bryant & Stratton College (B)

110 Broadway, 2nd Floor, Buffalo NY 14203
County: Erie FICE Identification: 002678
Unit ID: 189583
Telephone: (716) 884-9120 Carnegie Class: Bac/Assoc-Mixed
FAX Number: (716) 884-0091 Calendar System: Semester
URL: www.bryantstratton.edu
Established: 1854 Annual Undergrad Tuition & Fees: $17,833
Enrollment: 855 Coed
Affiliation or Control: Proprietary IRS Status: Proprietary
Highest Offering: Baccalaureate
Accreditation: M, MAC, NURSE

02 Campus Director .... Dr. Marvel E. ROSS-JONES
05 Dean of Instruction .... Mr. Brantley TAYLOR
07 Director of Admissions .... Mr. Kevin MUSE
36 Director of Career Services .... Mrs. Angelette BODDIE
10 WNY Business Office Director .... Ms. Kathleen OWCZARCZAK

*Bryant & Stratton College (C)

1259 Central Avenue, Albany NY 12205-5230
Telephone: (518) 437-1802 FICE Identification: 004749
Accreditation: &M, MAC

*Bryant & Stratton College (D)

854 Long Pond Road, Rochester NY 14612-3049
Telephone: (585) 720-0660 FICE Identification: 012470
Accreditation: &M, MAC, OTA

*Bryant & Stratton College (E)

953 James Street, Syracuse NY 13203-2502
Telephone: (315) 472-6603 FICE Identification: 008276
Accreditation: &M, MAC, OTA, PTAA

Canisius College (F)

2001 Main Street, Buffalo NY 14208-1098
County: Erie FICE Identification: 002681
Unit ID: 189705
Telephone: (716) 883-7000 Carnegie Class: Masters/L
FAX Number: (716) 888-2525 Calendar System: Semester
URL: www.canisius.edu
Established: 1870 Annual Undergrad Tuition & Fees: $30,230
Enrollment: 2,820 Coed
Affiliation or Control: Roman Catholic IRS Status: 501(c)3
Highest Offering: Master's
Accreditation: M, #ARCPA, CACREP

01 President .... Mr. John J. HURLEY
05 VP Academic Affairs .... Dr. Sara R. MORRIS
10 Vice Pres Business/Finance .... Mr. Timothy P. BALKIN
32 Int VP for Student Affairs .... Dr. Sandra M. ESTANEK
111 VP Institutional Advancement .... Ms. Kimberly A. VENTI
84 VP for Enrollment Management .... Dr. Danielle D. IANNI
04 AVP/Assistant to the President .... Ms. Erica C. SAMMARCO
20 Assoc VP for Academic Affairs .... Vacant
113 Asst VP/Dir Stdnt Rec & Fin Svcs .... Mr. Kevin M. SMITH
26 Asst VP Mktg & Communications .... Mr. Matther Z. WOJICK
88 Assoc Dean/Director Griff Center .... Dr. Mark R. HARRINGTON
08 Director of Library .... Ms. Kristine E. KASBOHM
07 Director Undergrad Admissions .... Vacant
112 Director of Principal Gifts .... Mr. J. Patrick GREENWALD
21 Controller .... Mr. Ronald J. HABERER
50 Dean School of Business .... Dr. Denise M. ROTONDO
37 Assoc Dir of Stdnt Records/Fin Svcs .... Ms. Mary A. KOEHNEKE
06 Registrar/Asst Dir Stdnt Rec & FA .... Ms. Deborah W. PROHN
26 Chief Communications Officer .... Ms. Eileen C. HERBERT
15 Assoc VP for HR and Compliance .... Ms. Linda M. WALLESHAUSER
53 Interim Dean School Educ/Human Svcs .... Dr. Nancy WALLACE
25 Director of Sponsored Programs .... Ms. Mary Ann LANGLOIS
18 Director Facilities Management .... Mr. Thomas E. CIMINELLI
23 Director Student Health Center .... Ms. Patricia H. CREAHAN
38 Director Counseling Center .... Ms. Eileen A. NILAND
39 Assoc Dean of Stdnts/Dir Resid Life .... Mr. Matthew H. MULVILLE
104 Director Study Abroad .... Mr. Brian SMITH
40 Course Materials Manager/Bookstore .... Mr. Andrew J. THOMAS
41 Director Athletics .... Mr. William J. MAHER
42 Director Campus Ministry .... Vacant
90 Director of User Services .... Mr. Scott D. CLARK
94 Dir of Women's Business Center .... Ms. Sara L. VESCIO
92 Director of All College Honors Pgm .... Dr. Janet M. MCNALLY
24 Director Media Center .... Mr. Daniel J. DREW
91 Director Administrative Computing .... Ms. Michele FOLSOM
108 Dir Inst & Research Effectiveness .... Ms. Lauren YOUNG
102 Dir Foundation/Corporate Relations .... Mrs. Sandy A. MILLER
19 Director Public Safety .... Mrs. Kimberly L. BEATY
29 Director Alumni Engagement .... Ms. Erin M. ZACK
44 Director Canisius Fund .... Ms. Summer L. HANDZLIK
28 Assoc Dean for Diversity/ Inclusion .... Ms. Fatima L. RODRIGUEZ JOHNSON

Cayuga Community College (G)

197 Franklin Street, Auburn NY 13021-3099
County: Cayuga FICE Identification: 002861
Unit ID: 189839
Telephone: (315) 255-1743 Carnegie Class: Assoc/HT-High Non
FAX Number: (315) 255-2117 Calendar System: Semester
URL: www.cayuga-cc.edu
Established: 1953 Annual Undergrad Tuition & Fees (In-District): $5,884
Enrollment: 2,906 Coed
Affiliation or Control: State/Local IRS Status: 501(c)3
Highest Offering: Associate Degree
Accreditation: M, ADNUR, OTA

01 President .... Mr. Brian M. DURANT
04 Assistant to President/Board .... Ms. Pamela A. HELEEN
05 Provost/Vice Pres Academic Affairs .... Dr. Ronald G. CANTOR
32 Vice President Student Affairs .... Mr. Jeffrey E. ROSENTHAL
10 Vice Pres Administration/Treasurer .... Vacant
102 Executive Director Foundation .... Vacant
07 Director of Admissions .... Mr. Bruce M. BLODGETT
09 Director Institutional Research .... Ms. Virginia RUDNICK
08 Library Director .... Ms. Sara DAVENPORT
41 Director Athletics .... Mr. Peter E. LIDDELL
15 Director Human Resources .... Mr. Thomas CORCORAN
35 Director Student Activities .... Mr. Norman LEE
19 Director Public Safety .... Mr. Doug KINNEY

Cazenovia College (H)

22 Sullivan Street, Cazenovia NY 13035
County: Madison FICE Identification: 002685
Unit ID: 189848
Telephone: (800) 654-3210 Carnegie Class: Bac-Diverse
FAX Number: (315) 655-4143 Calendar System: Semester
URL: www.cazenovia.edu
Established: 1824 Annual Undergrad Tuition & Fees: $36,668
Enrollment: 800 Coed
Affiliation or Control: Independent Non-Profit IRS Status: 501(c)3
Highest Offering: Baccalaureate
Accreditation: M, ART, IACBE

01 President .... Dr. Ronald D. CHESBROUGH
03 Executive Vice President .... Dr. David BERGH
05 VP Academic Affs/Dean of Faculty .... Dr. Sharon A. DETTMER
32 Vice Pres for Student Affairs .... Dr. Karey PINE
10 VP Financial Affs/Chief Fin Officer .... Mr. Mark H. EDWARDS
26 Director Marketing/Communications .... Mr. Timothy D. GREENE
07 Sr Assoc Director of Admissions .... Ms. Kristen BOWERS
15 Director Human Resources .... Ms. Janice ROMAGNOLI
111 Int Dir Institutional Advancement .... Ms. Samantha HARMON
89 Dean First Year Program .... Mr. Jesse LOTT
08 Director of Library Services .... Ms. Heather C. WHALEN-SMITH
37 Financial Aid Coordinator .... Mr. Nicholas M. KORDEK
06 Registrar .... Ms. Sherri J. BENEDICT
23 Director Health Services .... Ms. Deborah FRANK
36 Dir Career/Extended Learning Svcs .... Ms. Katherine GEORGE
41 Director Intercollegiate Athletics .... Mr. Pete WAY
13 Director of Technology Development .... Mr. David PALMER
09 Dir Institutional Rsrch/Assessment .... Dr. Jon C. DALY
18 Dir of Physical Plant Operations .... Mr. Jeff SLOCUM
29 Director Alumni Relations .... Ms. Shari WHITAKER
04 Exec Assistant to the President .... Ms. Judy L. PAPAYANAKOS
51 Dir for Adult/Continuing Educ .... Ms. Carla M. DESHAW
58 Assoc Dir for Graduate & Intl Pgms .... Mr. Charles F. HARCOURT
19 Director of Campus Safety .... Ms. Roberta COMERFORD
28 Director for Multicultural Affairs .... Ms. Katiuzca LOAIZA-ESPINOZA
96 Payroll & Purchasing Coordinator .... Ms. Kelli GRAHAM
44 Director Annual Giving .... Ms. Cary RUEPPEL
113 Bursar .... Ms. Abby BERRY

Central Yeshiva Beth Joseph (I)

1502 Avenue N, Brooklyn NY 11230
County: Kings Identification: 667157
Unit ID: 488004
Telephone: (718) 269-4080 Carnegie Class: Spec-4-yr-Faith
FAX Number: (718) 269-4080 Calendar System: Semester
Established: 1942 Annual Undergrad Tuition & Fees: $11,000
Enrollment: 23 Male
Affiliation or Control: Independent Non-Profit IRS Status: 501(c)3
Highest Offering: First Talmudic Degree
Accreditation: RABN

01 Chief Executive Officer .... Rabbi Moshe JOFEN
05 Dean .... Rabbi Mordechai JOFEN
37 Director Student Financial Aid .... Rabbi Yechezkel MOSCOVITZ
06 Registrar .... Rabbi Baruch MILLER

Central Yeshiva Tomchei Tmimim Lubavitch America (J)

841-853 Ocean Parkway, Brooklyn NY 11230-2798
County: Kings FICE Identification: 004776
Unit ID: 189857
Telephone: (718) 774-3430 Carnegie Class: Spec-4-yr-Faith
FAX Number: N/A Calendar System: Semester
URL: centralyeshiva.com/registration/choose-yeshiva
Established: 1941 Annual Undergrad Tuition & Fees: $7,700
Enrollment: 594 Male
Affiliation or Control: Independent Non-Profit IRS Status: 501(c)3
Highest Offering: Second Talmudic Degree
Accreditation: AIJS

01 Principal and Director .... Rabbi Mendel BLAU
05 Dean .... Rabbi Zalman LABKOWSKI

*City University of New York (K)

205 E. 42nd Street, New York NY 10017
County: New York FICE Identification: 025061
Unit ID: 190035
Telephone: (646) 664-9100 Carnegie Class: N/A
FAX Number: (646) 664-3868
URL: www2.cuny.edu

01 Chancellor .... Dr. Felix V. MATOS RODRIGUEZ
05 Int Exec VC/University Provost .... Dr. Daniel E. LEMONS
10 Sr Vice Chancellor/CFO .... Mr. Matthew SAPIENZA
101 Secretary of the Board of Trustees .... Ms. Gayle HORWITZ
43 General Counsel/SVC Legal Affs .... Mr. Derek DAVIS
11 Exec VC/Chief Operating Officer .... Mr. Hector BATISTA
18 VC Facility Plng/Construction Mgmt .... Mr. Mohamed ATTALLA
13 VC/Chief Information Officer .... Mr. Brian COHEN
32 Int VC Student Affairs/Enrollment .... Dr. Denise B. MAYBANK
88 Sr Vice Chanc for Labor Relations . Ms. Pamela S. SILVERBLATT
09 Vice Provost for Research .... Mr. Dan E. MCCLOSKEY
15 Vice Chanc for Human Resources Mgmt .... Ms. Dorianne K. GLORIA
111 Int VC for Univ Advancement .... Ms. Andrea SHAPIRO DAVIS
20 Sr Dean for Academic Affairs .... Mr. John MOGULESCU
09 Dean Institutional Research .... Mr. David CROOK
28 Dean Diversity/Recruitment .... Ms. Arlene TORRES
26 Vice Chanc Communications/Marketing .... Ms. Maite JUNCO

*Baruch College/City University of New York (L)

One Bernard Baruch Way, New York NY 10010-5526
County: New York FICE Identification: 007273
Unit ID: 190512
Telephone: (646) 312-1000 Carnegie Class: Masters/L
FAX Number: N/A Calendar System: Semester
URL: www.baruch.cuny.edu
Established: 1968 Annual Undergrad Tuition & Fees (In-District): $7,462
Enrollment: 19,740 Coed
Affiliation or Control: State/Local IRS Status: 501(c)3
Highest Offering: Doctorate
Accreditation: M, IPSY, SPAA

02 President .... Dr. S. David WU
05 Provost/SVP Academic Affairs .... Dr. Linda ESSIG
10 Vice Pres Administration/Finance .... Ms. Katharine COBB
84 VP Enroll Mgmt/Strategic Init .... Ms. Mary GORMAN
111 VP for College Advancement .... Mr. David SHANTON
13 VP for Information Services .... Mr. Arthur DOWNING
26 VP for Comm/Ext Rels & Econ Dev .... Ms. Christina LATOUF
32 VP Student Affairs/Dean of Students .... Dr. Art KING
21 Asst Vice President Finance .... Ms. Mary FINNEN
43 Asst VP Legal Counsel .... Ms. Olga DAIS
20 Assoc Provost .... Dr. Dennis SLAVIN
102 President Baruch College Fund .... Vacant
50 Dean Zicklin School of Business .... Dr. Fenwick HUSS
49 Int Dean Weissman School .... Dr. Jessica LANG
80 Int Dean School Public/Intl Affairs .... Dr. Nancy ARIES
08 Dean of Library .... Mr. Arthur DOWNING
100 Chief of Staff .... Ms. Kenya N. LEE
25 Director of Sponsored Programs .... Ms. Zolicia ABOTSI
15 Exec Dir of Human Resources .... Ms. Andrea CAVINESS
36 Director Career Development Center .... Ms. Ellen STEIN
90 Asst Dir Client Svcs/Fac Liaison .... Vacant
85 Director Intl Student Office .... Ms. Rosa KELLEY
19 Director Public Safety .... Mr. Robert CURRY
09 Dir Institutional Rsrch/Pgm Assess .... Mr. John CHOONOO
29 Director Alumni Relations .... Ms. Janet ROSSBACH
96 Director of Purchasing .... Dr. Diane OQUENDO
28 Exec Chief Diversity Officer .... Mr. Elliott DAWES
41 Athletic Director .... Ms. Heather MACCULLOCH
86 Dir of Govt and Community Relations .... Mr. Eric LUGO

06 Senior Registrar ... Mr. Edward ADAMS
104 Director Study Abroad ... Dr. Richard MITTEN
37 Director of Financial Aid Services ... Ms. Elizabeth RIQUEZ
07 Dir of Undergraduate Admissions ... Ms. Marisa DELACRUZ
108 Asst Provost for Assessment/Accred ... Dr. Rachel FESTER

*City University of New York Borough of Manhattan Community College (A)

199 Chambers Street, New York NY 10007-1047
County: New York FICE Identification: 002691
Unit ID: 190521
Telephone: (212) 220-1230 Carnegie Class: Assoc/HT-High Trad
FAX Number: (212) 220-1244 Calendar System: Semester
URL: www.bmcc.cuny.edu
Established: 1963 Annual Undergrad Tuition & Fees (In-District): $5,170
Enrollment: 22,496 Coed
Affiliation or Control: State/Local IRS Status: 501(c)3
Highest Offering: Associate Degree
Accreditation: M, ADNUR, CAHIIM, COARC, EMT

02 President ... Dr. Anthony MUNROE
05 Acting Provost/SVP Academic Affairs ... Dr. Erwin WONG
11 Vice President Administration/Plng ... Vacant
43 Spec Legal Counsel/Labor Designee ... Ms. Meryl R. KAYNARD
32 Vice President of Student Affairs ... Dr. Marva CRAIG
111 Vice Pres of Inst Advancement ... Ms. Lorna A. MALCOLM
84 Vice Pres Enrollment Management ... Dr. Sanjay RAMDATH
10 Asst Vice Pres of Finance ... Ms. Elena SAMUELS
51 Dean Ctr for Cont Ed/Workforce Dev ... Mr. Anthony WATSON
25 Dean Office of Sponsored Programs ... Ms. Aleksandra CATARUZOLO
20 Dean for Instruction/Curriculum ... Vacant
20 Assoc Dean of Faculty ... Dr. David BARNET
121 Asst Dean Academic Support ... Ms. Janice ZUMMO
37 Director Financial Aid ... Ms. Albina KHASIDOVA
15 Director Human Resources ... Ms. Gloria CHAO
07 Director of Admissions ... Ms. Lisa KASPER
06 Senior Registrar ... Mr. Mohammad ALAM
08 Dir Learning Resource Center ... Mr. Gregory FARRELL
09 Dean Inst Effective/Strategic Plng ... Dr. Christopher SHULTS
28 Chief Diversity Officer ... Ms. Odelia LEVY
18 Asst VP Planning/Facilities ... Mr. Jorge YAFAR
26 Exec Director Public Affairs ... Mr. Manuel ROMERO
41 Director of Athletics ... Vacant
102 Dir Foundation/Corporate Relations ... Mr. Brian HALLER
36 Dir Academic Advise/Transfer Center ... Ms. Carei THOMAS
38 Director Counseling Center ... Vacant
96 Director of Procurement ... Ms. Leonore GONZALEZ
86 Director Government Relations ... Mr. Douglas ISRAEL

*City University of New York Bronx Community College (B)

2155 University Avenue, Bronx NY 10453-2895
County: Bronx FICE Identification: 002692
Unit ID: 190530
Telephone: (718) 289-5100 Carnegie Class: Assoc/HT-High Trad
FAX Number: (718) 289-6011 Calendar System: Semester
URL: www.bcc.cuny.edu
Established: 1957 Annual Undergrad Tuition & Fees (In-District): $5,206
Enrollment: 8,370 Coed
Affiliation or Control: State/Local IRS Status: 501(c)3
Highest Offering: Associate Degree
Accreditation: M, ACBSP, ADNUR, MLTAD, NMT, RAD

02 President ... Dr. Thomas A. ISEKENEGBE
05 Provost/VP Academic Affairs ... Dr. Lester RAPALO
86 Government Rels and Ext Affairs Dir ... Mr. David W. LEVERS
32 VP for Student Affairs ... Ms. Irene R. DELGADO
111 VP for Advance/Comm & Ext Rels ... Dr. Eddy BAYARDELLE
26 Asst VP Comm & Marketing ... Mr. Richard GINSBERG
35 Dean of Student Services ... Mr. Bernard GANTT
11 AVP for Campus Operations ... Mr. David A. TAYLOR
30 Asst VP for Development ... Ms. Angela WAMBUGU COBB
103 Int Dean for Workforce & Econ Dev ... Ms. Karla R. WILLIAMS
45 Dean for Research/Plng & Assessment ... Dr. Nancy RITZE
20 Assoc Dean AA for Curr & Fac Dev ... Dr. Alexander OTT
10 Dir for Financial & Business Svcs ... Ms. Gina UGARTE
06 Registrar/Dir Enrollment ... Ms. Karen THOMAS
13 Interim Chief Information Officer ... Ms. Luisa MARTICH
37 Financial Aid Director ... Ms. Margaret NELSON
07 Director for Admission/Recruitment ... Ms. Patricia A. RAMOS
15 Human Resources Director ... Ms. Marta CLARK
08 Chief Librarian ... Prof. Michael J. MILLER
19 Public Safety Director ... Mr. James VERDICCHIO
41 Student Athletics Director ... Mr. Ryan MCCARTHY
18 Chief Super Physical Plant Svcs ... Vacant
29 Alum Rel/Plan Giv/Indiv Donors Mgr ... Mr. Robert WHELAN
88 Mgr of College Discovery ... Ms. Cynthia SUAREZ-ESPINAL
43 Int Exec Counsel & Deputy to Pres ... Ms. Susan FIORE
96 Director of Purchasing ... Ms. Kelema K. BRADFORD
28 Chief Diversity/Affirm Act Ofcr ... Ms. Jessenia PAOLI
14 Deputy Chief Technology Officer ... Ms. Luisa MARTICH
108 Academic Assessment Manager ... Dr. Richard LAMANNA
20 Dean for Academic Affairs ... Dr. Luis MONTENEGRO
90 Dir for Academic Comp Svcs Desk ... Ms. Wanda SANTIAGO
91 Manager of Admin Systems & Svcs ... Mr. Rolly WILTSHIRE
51 Manager Continuing/Prof Education ... Vacant
25 Dir of Grants Development ... Ms. Judith EISENBERG
22 Affirmative Action Specialist ... Mr. Oluwafemi AKINSANYA
102 Dev Corp and Foundation Rel Mgmt ... Ms. Julia OLIVA
104 Dir Intl Educ and Study Abroad Pgm ... Vacant
09 OIR Inst Research Specialist ... Mrs. Chelsea RAMOS
46 Director of Research & Testing ... Mr. Chris EFTHIMIOU
106 Dir IT Academic App/CTLT ... Mr. Mark LENNERTON
36 Dir Transfer and Job Placement ... Mr. Alan FUENTES
04 Administrative Asst to President ... Ms. Amirah COUSINS
100 Chief of Staff ... Ms. Susan FIORE
38 Director Student Counseling ... Vacant

*City University of New York Brooklyn College (C)

2900 Bedford Avenue, Brooklyn NY 11210-2889
County: Kings FICE Identification: 002687
Unit ID: 190549
Telephone: (718) 951-5000 Carnegie Class: Masters/L
FAX Number: N/A Calendar System: Semester
URL: www.brooklyn.cuny.edu
Established: 1930 Annual Undergrad Tuition & Fees (In-District): $7,440
Enrollment: 17,735 Coed
Affiliation or Control: State/Local IRS Status: 170(c)1
Highest Offering: Master's
Accreditation: M, AUD, CACREP, DIETD, DIETI, SP

02 President ... Ms. Michelle J. ANDERSON
05 Provost/Sr Vice Pres Acad Affairs ... Dr. Anne LOPES
10 Sr VP for Finance & Administration ... Mr. Alan GILBERT
111 Vice Pres Institutional Advancement ... Mr. Todd GALITZ
32 Vice President for Student Affairs ... Dr. Ronald JACKSON
84 VP Enroll Management and Retention ... Ms. Lillian O'REILLY
100 Chief of Staff to Pres & Exec Dir ... Vacant
43 Chief Legal/Labor Relations Officer ... Mr. Tony THOMAS
108 Assoc Prov & AVP Inst Effectiveness ... Dr. Tammie CUMMING
20 Assoc Provost for Faculty & Admin ... Dr. Tammy LEWIS
53 Dean School of Education ... Dr. April BEDFORD
57 Dean Schl Visual Media & Perf Arts ... Dr. Maria A. CONELLI
83 Int Dean Sch Humanities & Soc Sci ... Dr. Kenneth GOULD
81 Dean Schl Natural & Behav Sciences ... Dr. Kleanthis PSARRIS
50 Dean Koppelman Sch Business ... Dr. Susanne SCOTT
13 Asst VP Info Technology Services ... Vacant
08 Assoc Dn Lib/Ex Dir Acad Info Tech ... Dr. Mary MALLERY
88 Assoc Dean Sch of Business ... Dr. Herve QUENEAU
88 Asst Dean Academic Programs ... Dr. Lucas RUBIN
35 Assistant Dean for Student Services ... Mr. Dave BRYAN
35 Assistant Dean for Student Life ... Ms. Moraima SMITH
28 Chief Diversity Officer ... Mr. Anthony BROWN
113 Exec Dir Student Fin Svcs & Bursar ... Ms. Yasmin ALI
07 Exec Director Enrollment Services ... Ms. Natalie COOMBS
45 Exec Director Budget & Planning ... Mr. Emir GANIC
121 Exec Dir Student Success Center ... Ms. Tracy NEWTON
18 Executive Director of Operations ... Vacant
21 Comptroller ... Ms. Beatrice GILLING RAYNOR
15 Exec Dir Human Resource Services ... Ms. Renita W. SIMMONS
26 Assoc Dir Communications/Marketing ... Ms. Anita BULAN
112 Managing Dir Campaign & Leader Gift ... Ms. Emily MOQTADERI
09 Sr Dir Inst Rsrch & Data Analysis ... Dr. Michael AYERS
25 Dir Research & Sponsored Programs ... Ms. Robin NESBY
96 Dir Procurement & Support Services ... Ms. Madonna CHARLES
29 Director of Alumni Affairs ... Ms. Lisa DICCE
06 Interim Registrar ... Ms. Natalie COOMBS
41 Dir Rec Intramurals/Intercol Athl ... Mr. Bruce FILOSA
36 Dir Magner Ctr/Career Dev & Interns ... Ms. Natalia GUARIN-KLEIN
38 Director Personal Counseling ... Dr. Gregory KUHLMAN
114 Director of Budget ... Mr. Michael LANZA
37 Director Financial Aid ... Mr. Antonio MARRERO
88 Testing & Transfer Evaluation Ofcr ... Ms. Monica RIVERA
92 Dir Scholars Pgm & Honors Academy ... Dr. Lisa SCHWEBEL
90 Dir Acad Information Technologies ... Mr. Howard SPIVAK
19 Director Safety & Security ... Mr. Donald A. WENZ

*City University of New York The City College (D)

160 Convent Avenue, New York NY 10031-9198
County: New York FICE Identification: 002688
Unit ID: 190567
Telephone: (212) 650-7000 Carnegie Class: DU-Higher
FAX Number: (212) 650-7680 Calendar System: Semester
URL: www.ccny.cuny.edu
Established: 1847 Annual Undergrad Tuition & Fees (In-District): $7,340
Enrollment: 15,227 Coed
Affiliation or Control: State/Local IRS Status: 501(c)3
Highest Offering: Doctorate
Accreditation: M, ARCPA, CLPSY, LSAR, #MED

02 President ... Dr. Vincent G. BOUDREAU
05 Provost/Sr VP Academic Affairs ... Mr. Tony LISS
102 VP & Exec Dir Fndn/Comms/Sr Advisor ... Ms. Dee Dee MOZELESKI
10 Vice Pres Finance & CFO ... Mr. Felix LAM
84 VP Student Affairs/Enrollment Mgmt ... Ms. Celia P. LLOYD
18 AVP Facilities Mgmt ... Mr. David ROBINSON
86 VP Governmental/Community Affairs ... Ms. Karen WITHERSPOON
11 VP Campus Administration ... Mr. Kenneth IHRER
63 Interim Dean CUNY Sch of Medicine ... Ms. Erica FRIEDMAN
54 Int Dean of Engineering ... Dr. Alex COUZIS
53 Int Dean School of Education ... Mr. Edwin LAMBOY
47 Dean School of Architecture ... Ms. Lesley LOKKO
88 Dean of CWE-Div of Interdiscip Stds ... Dr. Juan Carlos MERCADO
81 Dean of Science ... Dr. Susan L. PERKINS
82 Dean School of Civic/Global Ldrshp ... Dr. Andrew RICH
79 Dean of Humanities & The Arts ... Mr. Erec KOCH
43 Executive Counsel to the President ... Mr. Paul F. OCCHIOGROSSO
15 Asst Vice Pres of Human Resources ... Vacant
23 Exec Director Health and Wellness ... Vacant
06 Senior Registrar ... Mr. Thomas CASTIGLIONE
35 Exec Dir of Student Affairs at CWE ... Ms. Sophia DEMETRIOU
102 Exec Director of Foundation ... Ms. Dee Dee MOZELESKI
08 Assoc Dean & Chief Librarian ... Dr. Charles STEWART
25 Dir for Grants & Sponsored Pgms ... Dr. Alan SHIH
09 Director of Institutional Research ... Vacant
37 Director of Financial Aid ... Ms. Arshaw RAMKARAN
27 Public Relations Coordinator ... Ms. Ashley AROCHO
28 Chief Diversity Officer ... Ms. Diana COUZZO
36 Director of Career Services ... Ms. Katie NAILLER
19 Exec Dir Public Safety/Security ... Mr. Pat MORENA
24 Director of Instructional Media ... Mr. Nana ABEYIE
07 Exec Director of Admissions ... Mr. Joseph FANTOZZI
96 Director of Business Services ... Vacant

*College of Staten Island CUNY (E)

2800 Victory Boulevard, Staten Island NY 10314-6600
County: Richmond FICE Identification: 002698
Unit ID: 190558
Telephone: (718) 982-2000 Carnegie Class: Masters/L
FAX Number: N/A Calendar System: Semester
URL: www.csi.cuny.edu
Established: 1976 Annual Undergrad Tuition & Fees (In-District): $7,490
Enrollment: 12,797 Coed
Affiliation or Control: State/Local IRS Status: 501(c)3
Highest Offering: Doctorate
Accreditation: M, ADNUR, CAEP, MPCAC, MT, NUR, PTA, SW

02 President ... Dr. William J. FRITZ
05 Sr VP Acad Affairs/Provost ... Dr. J. Michael PARRISH
32 VP Student Affairs ... Ms. Jennifer S. BORRERO
111 Executive Dir Inst Advancement ... Ms. Cheryl ADOLPH
10 AVP for Finance & Budget/CFO ... Mr. Carlos A. SERRANO
18 Int VP Campus Planning/Facilities ... Ms. Hope BERTE
84 AVP for Enrollment Services ... Mr. Alexander SCOTT
20 Assoc Provost for Undergrad Studies ... Dr. Ralf PEETZ
13 AVP & CIO Info Technology Services ... Dr. Patricia KAHN
81 Dean of Science & Technology ... Dr. Michael J. CAVAGNERO
79 Dean Humanities & Social Sci ... Dr. Sarolta A. TAKACS
08 Associate Dean & Chief Librarian ... Ms. Amy STEMPLER
114 Interim VP for Budget Strategy ... Mr. Robert WALLACE
35 Executive Dir Student Svcs ... Ms. Danielle E. DIMITROV
50 Dean School of Business ... Dr. Susan L. HOLAK
76 Dean School of Health Sciences ... Dr. Marcus C. TYE
53 Dean School of Education ... Dr. Marcus C. TYE
58 Assoc Provost Grad Studies/Research ... Vacant
28 Int Chief Diversity Office/Title IX ... Ms. Catherine FERRARA
100 Int Chief of Staff/Dir Employee Res ... Ms. Jessica COLLURA

*City University of New York Graduate Center (F)

365 Fifth Avenue, New York NY 10016-4309
County: New York FICE Identification: 004765
Unit ID: 190576
Telephone: (212) 817-7000 Carnegie Class: DU-Highest
FAX Number: N/A Calendar System: Semester
URL: www.gc.cuny.edu
Established: 1961 Annual Undergrad Tuition & Fees (In-District): N/A
Enrollment: 9,300 Coed
Affiliation or Control: State/Local IRS Status: 501(c)3
Highest Offering: Doctorate
Accreditation: M, AUD, CAHIIM, CLPSY, DIETI, JOUR, NURSE, PH

02 President ... Dr. Robin L. GARRELL
05 Provost & SVP Graduate Center ... Mr. Steve EVERETT
10 Int SVP Finance & Administration ... Mr. Brian A. PETERSON
13 AVP Information Technology/CIO ... Ms. Elaine MONTILLA
111 Int VP Institutional Advancement ... Ms. Wendy DEMARCO FUENTES
26 VP Communications ... Ms. Wendy DEMARCO FUENTES
32 VP Student Affairs ... Mr. Matthew G. SCHOENGOOD
22 Int VP Inst Equity/Human Resources ... Ms. Pinar OZGU
21 Asst Vice President Finance ... Vacant
81 Dean for Science ... Dr. Joshua BRUMBERG
20 Assoc Provost & Dean Academic Affs ... Dr. David OLAN
08 Chief Librarian ... Ms. Polly THISTLETHWAITE
100 Chief of Staff ... Vacant
19 Exec Dir Security & Public Safety ... Mr. John FLAHERTY
15 Exec Dir of Human Resources ... Mr. David BOXILL
46 Exec Dir Research & Sponsored Pgm ... Dr. Edith GONZALEZ
37 Exec Dir Fellowships/Financial Aid ... Ms. Phyllis SCHULZ
20 Exec Director of Academic Affairs ... Ms. Patti MYATT
06 Dir Stdnt Services/Senior Registrar ... Mr. Vincent J. DELUCA
85 Director International Students ... Ms. Linda ASARO
43 Legal Counsel & Labor Designee ... Ms. Lynette M. PHILLIPS
18 Director Facilities ... Mr. Charles SCOTT
07 Director Admissions ... Mr. Les GRIBBEN
25 Director Sponsored Research ... Vacant
38 Dir Well Ctr/Psy Coun Svc/Adult Dev ... Dr. Robert HATCHER
04 Administrative Asst to President ... Ms. Alexandra ROBINSON

*City University of New York Herbert H. Lehman College (A)

250 Bedford Park Boulevard W, Bronx NY 10468-1589

County: Bronx | FICE Identification: 007022
Unit ID: 190637
Telephone: (718) 960-8000 | Carnegie Class: Masters/L
FAX Number: N/A | Calendar System: Semester
URL: www.lehman.edu
Established: 1968 | Annual Undergrad Tuition & Fees (In-District): $7,410
Enrollment: 15,091 | Coed
Affiliation or Control: State/Local | IRS Status: 501(c)3
Highest Offering: Doctorate
Accreditation: M, CACREP, CAEPN, DIETD, DIETI, NURSE, SP, SW

02 President ... Dr. Fernando DELGADO
100 COS/Deputy to Pres Strategic Init ... Ms. Gladys MALDOON
05 Provost/SVP Academic Affairs ... Dr. Peter O. NWOSU
84 VP Enrollment Mgmt/Assoc Provost ... Dr. Reine SARMIENTO
10 VP Administration/Finance ... Ms. Rene M. ROTOLO
111 Vice Pres Institutional Advancement ... Ms. Susan EBERSOLE
32 Vice President Student Affairs ... Dr. Germaine A. WRIGHT
13 Vice Pres/Chief Info Officer ... Mr. Ronald BERGMANN
28 VP Diversity/Human Resources ... Ms. Dawn EWING-MORGAN
79 Dean School of Arts/Humanities ... Dr. James MAHON
83 Int Dean School of Nat & Soc Sci ... Dr. Pamela MILLS
20 Dean of Academic Affairs ... Dr. Daniel LEMONS
76 Dean Sch Hlth Sci/Hum Svc/Nurs ... Dr. Elgloria HARRISON
51 Dean School Cont Educ/Prof Studies ... Dr. Jane MACKILLOP
53 Int Assoc Dean School of Education ... Ms. Serigne GNINGUE
08 Chief Librarian ... Dr. Kenneth SCHLESINGER
43 Exec Counsel to Pres/Labor Designee ... Ms. Bridget BARBERA
18 Dir Campus Planning/Facilities ... Ms. Robin AUCHINCLOSS
45 AVP Strategy/Policy & Analytics ... Dr. Jonathan GAGLIARDI
26 AVP for Marketing & Communications ... Vacant
35 Dean of Student Affairs ... Dr. Stanley BAZILE
21 Asst VP for Financial Operations ... Ms. Gina HARWOOD
14 Asst VP Information Technology ... Ms. Ediltrudys RUIZ
06 Senior Registrar ... Ms. Yvette ROSARIO
07 Director of Admissions/Recruitment ... Ms. Laurie AUSTIN
29 Assoc Director of Alumni Relations ... Mr. Robert PAGAN
88 Director of the Art Gallery ... Mr. Bartholomew F. BLAND
36 Director of Career Services ... Ms. Bascilla TOUSSAINT
38 Director Counseling Center ... Ms. Karen SMITH MOORE
37 Dir Financial Aid/Enroll Mgmt ... Ms. Vera SENESE
89 Director Freshman Year Initiative ... Dr. Steven WYCKOFF
46 Dir Research & Sponsored Programs ... Mr. Brandon J. BEGARLY
92 Director of Honors College Program ... Dr. Gary SCHWARTZ
15 Director of Human Resources ... Mr. Eric WASHINGTON
09 Director of Institutional Research ... Vacant
121 Sr Dir Acad Pgms/SEEK Pgm ... Ms. Althea FORDE
27 Int Asst VP Media Rels/Publications ... Ms. Colleen LUTOLF
88 Exec Dir Performing Arts Center ... Ms. Eva BORNSTEIN
19 Director of Public Safety ... Mr. Fausto RAMIREZ
109 Director of Auxiliary Services ... Ms. Andrea PINNOCK
41 Athletic Director ... Dr. Martin ZWIREN
40 Bookstore Manager ... Mr. Dominique WEST
120 Dir Online Education/E-learning ... Dr. Olena ZHADKO
114 Director of Budget ... Ms. Bethania ORTEGA
44 Director Advancement Initiatives ... Ms. Tara REGIST TOMLINSON

*Hostos Community College-City University of New York (B)

500 Grand Concourse, Bronx NY 10451-5323

County: Bronx | FICE Identification: 008611
Unit ID: 190585
Telephone: (718) 518-4300 | Carnegie Class: Assoc/HT-High Trad
FAX Number: (718) 518-4294 | Calendar System: Semester
URL: www.hostos.cuny.edu
Established: 1970 | Annual Undergrad Tuition & Fees (In-District): $5,208
Enrollment: 6,136 | Coed
Affiliation or Control: State/Local | IRS Status: 501(c)3
Highest Offering: Associate Degree
Accreditation: M, DH, RAD

02 Interim President ... Dr. Daisy COCCO DE FILIPPIS
05 Acting Provost/VP Academic Affairs ... Dr. Charles I. DRAGO
10 Senior Vice Pres for Admin/Finance ... Ms. Esther RODRIGUEZ-CHARDAVOYNE
32 VP Student Development/Enroll Mgmt ... Mr. Nathaniel CRUZ
100 Assist to President/Dir Pres Ofc ... Ms. Diana KREYMER
111 Vice Pres Institutional Advancement ... Ms. Ana MARTINEZ
103 Dean Cont Educ & Workforce Dev ... Mr. Peter MERTENS
13 Asst Vice Pres Info Technology ... Mr. Varun SEHGAL
114 Finance/Budget Director ... Ms. Fanny DUMANCELA
18 Exec Dir Facil Plng Des Mgmt ... Ms. Elizabeth FRIEDMAN
31 Associate Dean for Community Rels ... Ms. Ana I. GARCIA-REYES
20 Asst Dean of Academic Affairs ... Mr. Felix CARDONA
84 Asst Dean of Enrollment Management ... Vacant
35 Assistant Dean of Student Life ... Ms. Johanna GOMEZ
43 Exec Counsel & Labor Designee ... Mr. Eugene SOHN
26 Director of Communication ... Ms. Soldanela RIVERA LOPEZ
38 Director of Counseling ... Ms. Linda ALEXANDER-WALLACE
15 Exec Director Human Resources ... Ms. Christina DIAS-SINGH
86 Dir Government/External Affairs ... Vacant
06 Registrar ... Mr. David PRIMAK
07 Dir of Admissions & Recruitment ... Mr. Carlos RIVERA
37 Director of Financial Aid ... Ms. Leslie KING
19 Director of Campus Security ... Mr. Arnaldo BERNABE
25 Director Grants & Contracts ... Ms. Kelba SOSA
09 Director Institutional Research ... Mr. Piotr KOCIK
08 Head Librarian ... Ms. Madeline FORD
28 Chief Diversity Officer ... Ms. Lauren GRETINA
29 Development/Alumni Relations Mgr ... Mr. Felix SANCHEZ
36 Director Student Career Programs ... Ms. Lisanette ROSARIO
35 Director Student Activities ... Mr. Jerry ROSA
96 Director of Procurement ... Mr. Kevin CARMINE
108 Asst Dn Inst Eff/Strat Plng/Assess ... Ms. Babette AUDANT
21 Exec Director Business & Finance ... Mr. Ken ACQUAH

*City University of New York Hunter College (C)

695 Park Avenue, New York NY 10065

County: New York | FICE Identification: 002689
Unit ID: 190594
Telephone: (212) 772-4000 | Carnegie Class: Masters/L
FAX Number: N/A | Calendar System: Semester
URL: www.hunter.cuny.edu
Established: 1870 | Annual Undergrad Tuition & Fees (In-District): $7,382
Enrollment: 24,052 | Coed
Affiliation or Control: State/Local | IRS Status: 501(c)3
Highest Offering: Doctorate
Accreditation: M, AUD, CACREP, CAEPN, CYTO, DIETC, DIETD, DIETI, NURSE, PLNG, PTA, #SP, SPAA, SW

02 President ... Ms. Jennifer J. RAAB
100 Chief of Staff ... Ms. Anne LYTLE
10 Acting Vice Pres Finance/Budget ... Ms. Livia CANGEMI
05 Provost/Vice Pres Academic Affairs ... Mr. Lon KAUFMAN
32 VP Student Affs/Dean of Stdnts ... Ms. Eija AYRAVAINEN
43 General Counsel/Dean of Faculty ... Ms. Carol ROBLES-ROMAN
26 Asst VP & Dir Communication ... Vacant
13 Asst Vice Pres Information Tech ... Vacant
21 Executive Director Business Svcs ... Ms. Livia CANGEMI
28 Dean Diversity and Compliance ... Mr. John ROSE
49 Dean School of Arts & Sciences ... Dr. Andrew POLSKY
70 Acting Dean School of Social Work ... Ms. Mary CAVANAUGH
53 Dean School of Education ... Mr. Michael MIDDLETON
66 Dean School of Nursing ... Dr. Gail C. MCCAIN
08 Dean of Libraries/Chief Librarian ... Mr. Brian LYM
06 Registrar ... Vacant
09 Director of Institutional Research ... Ms. Joan LAMBE
15 Director of Human Resources ... Ms. Galia GALANSKY
110 Vice President Student Affairs ... Mr. Brian MAASJO
36 Director Student Placement ... Ms. Susan MCCARTY
29 Director Alumni Relations ... Vacant
19 College Security Director ... Mr. Joseph FOELSCH
07 Director of Admissions ... Ms. Lori JANOWSKI
41 Athletic Director ... Ms. Terry WANSART
84 Dir Enrollment Mgmt/Recruit ... Ms. Sarah FARSAD

*City University of New York John Jay College of Criminal Justice (D)

524 West 59th Street, New York NY 10019-1093

County: New York | FICE Identification: 002693
Unit ID: 190600
Telephone: (212) 237-8000 | Carnegie Class: Masters/L
FAX Number: (212) 237-8607 | Calendar System: Semester
URL: www.jjay.cuny.edu
Established: 1964 | Annual Undergrad Tuition & Fees (In-District): $7,470
Enrollment: 15,766 | Coed
Affiliation or Control: State/Local | IRS Status: 501(c)3
Highest Offering: Master's
Accreditation: M, CLPSY, FEPAC, SPAA

02 President ... Ms. Karol V. MASON
05 Provost ... Dr. Yi LI
32 Vice Pres Student Affairs ... Vacant
111 Vice Pres Institutional Advancement ... Ms. Robin MERLE
84 VP Enrollment Management ... Vacant
04 Executive Assoc to President ... Ms. Raeanne DAVIS
121 Academic Advising Director ... Ms. Rulisa GALLOWAY-PERRY
46 Associate Provost/Dean of Research ... Dr. Anthony CARPI
10 Int Vice Pres & COO ... Mr. Mark FLOWER
20 Assoc Prov & Dean of Undergrad Stds ... Dr. Dara BYRNE
08 Chief Librarian ... Dr. Lawrence SULLIVAN
37 Director of Financial Aid ... Ms. Sylvia CRESPO-LOPEZ
35 Director Student Activities ... Ms. Danielle OFFICER
25 Director of Funded Research ... Ms. Susy MENDES
09 Director of Institutional Research ... Mr. Ricardo ANZALDUA
89 Director of First Year Experience ... Ms. Katalin SZUR
06 Registrar ... Mr. Daniel MATOS
88 Director of CRJ Research & Eval ... Dr. Jeffrey BUTTS
07 Director of Admissions ... Mr. Vincent PAPANDREA
13 Chief Information Officer ... Mr. Joe LAUB
19 Director of Public Safety ... Mr. Diego REDONDO
26 Director of Media Relations ... Mr. Richard RELKIN
27 Chief Communications Officer ... Ms. Rama SUDHAKAR
36 Dir of Career Development Svcs ... Ms. Chantelle WRIGHT
38 Director of Counseling ... Dr. Gerard BRYANT
41 Athletic Director ... Ms. Carol KASHOW
21 Associate Business Officer ... Ms. Emily KARP
29 Dir Alumni Relations/Annual Giving ... Mr. Steve DERCOLE
96 Director of Purchasing ... Mr. Daniel DOLAN
88 Senior International Officer ... Ms. Mayra NIEVES
18 Director Facilities/Physical Plant ... Mr. Anthony BRACCO
43 Vice President & Exec Counsel ... Mr. Tony BALKISSOON
86 Exec Dir of External Relations ... Ms. Mindy BOCKSTEIN
121 Dir of Academic Advisement ... Ms. Katherine MUNET-PABON
22 Int Dir of Accessibility Services ... Ms. Malaine CLARKE
104 Director Study Abroad ... Mr. Kenneth YANES
28 Int Director Diversity/Compliance ... Ms. Gabriela LEAL
39 Director Student Housing ... Ms. Jessica CARSON
102 Dir Foundation/Corporate Relations ... Ms. Rona LANE
106 Dir Online Education/E-learning ... Ms. Judith CAHN
15 Exec Director of Human Resources ... Vacant

† The Clinical Psychology PhD is awarded through the CUNY Graduate Center.

*City University of New York Kingsborough Community College (E)

2001 Oriental Boulevard, Brooklyn NY 11235-2333

County: Kings | FICE Identification: 002694
Unit ID: 190619
Telephone: (718) 368-5109 | Carnegie Class: Assoc/HT-Mix Trad/Non
FAX Number: (718) 368-5003 | Calendar System: Other
URL: www.kbcc.cuny.edu
Established: 1963 | Annual Undergrad Tuition & Fees (In-District): $5,252
Enrollment: 15,116 | Coed
Affiliation or Control: State/Local | IRS Status: 501(c)3
Highest Offering: Associate Degree
Accreditation: M, ADNUR, EMT, POLYT, PTAA, SURGT

02 President ... Dr. Claudia V. SCHRADER
05 Vice Pres Academic Affs/Provost ... Dr. Joanne RUSSELL
10 Vice Pres Finance/Administration ... Mr. Eduardo RIOS
100 Executive Chief of Staff ... Dr. Tasheka SUTTON-YOUNG
32 Vice Pres of Student Affairs ... Mr. Peter COHEN
51 Dean Continuing Education ... Ms. Christine BECKNER
35 Director of Student Life ... Ms. Maria PATESTAS
84 Vice Pres Enrollment Management ... Dr. Johana RIVERA
09 Vice Pres Inst Effectiveness ... Dr. Richard FOX
111 Vice Pres Institutional Advancement ... Dr. Tasheka SUTTON-YOUNG
15 Director of Human Resources ... Ms. Micheline DRISCOLL
22 Dir Affirmative Action/EO Officer ... Mr. Michael VALENTE
19 Director of Security & Safety ... Mr. Kenneth GREENE
08 Chief Librarian ... Ms. Tina KOPEL
06 Registrar ... Ms. Colleen RUSSO
18 Campus Facilities Officer ... Mr. Albert TROCHE
37 Financial Aid Officer ... Mr. Sinu JACOB
13 Chief Information Officer ... Mr. Asif HUSSAIN
36 Director Career Services ... Ms. Melissa MERCED
24 Director of Educational Media ... Mr. Michael ROSSON
41 Director of Athletics ... Mr. Damani THOMAS
96 Director of Purchasing ... Ms. Kiesha STEWART
29 Director Alumni Relations ... Ms. Laura GLAZIER-SMITH
38 Director Student Counseling ... Ms. Ilona FRIDSON

*LaGuardia Community College/ City University of New York (F)

31-10 Thomson Avenue, Long Island City NY 11101-3083

County: Queens | FICE Identification: 010051
Unit ID: 190628
Telephone: (718) 482-7200 | Carnegie Class: Assoc/HT-High Trad
FAX Number: (718) 609-2000 | Calendar System: Semester
URL: www.lagcc.cuny.edu
Established: 1971 | Annual Undergrad Tuition & Fees (In-District): $5,218
Enrollment: 16,971 | Coed
Affiliation or Control: State/Local | IRS Status: 501(c)3
Highest Offering: Associate Degree
Accreditation: M, ADNUR, EMT, OTA, PTAA

02 President ... Mr. Kenneth ADAMS
05 Provost/Senior Vice President ... Dr. Paul ARCARIO
04 Senior Advisor to President ... Mr. Robert JAFFE
11 Vice President of Administration ... Mr. Shahir ERFAN
111 VP of Institutional Advancement ... Vacant
13 Vice Pres Information Technology ... Mr. Henry SALTIEL
32 Vice President Student Affairs ... Vacant
51 Vice Pres Continuing Education ... Mr. Sunil B. GUPTA
20 Assoc Dean for Academic Affairs ... Ms. Dion MILLER
121 Int Assoc Dean for Student Success ... Dr. Fay BUTLER
84 Int Assoc Dean Enrollment Mgmt ... Dr. Gail BAKSH-JARRETT
103 Int Asst Dean of Workforce Dev ... Dr. Assuanta HOWARD
18 Exec Dir Facilities Mgmt/Planning ... Mr. Kenneth CAMPANELLI
15 Exec Director of Human Resources ... Mr. Ronald EDWARDS
10 Exec Director Finance & Business ... Vacant
08 Acting Chief Librarian ... Mr. Steve OVADIA
37 Director Student Financial Services ... Vacant
07 Director of Admissions ... Ms. LaVora DESVIGNE
26 Dir Marketing/Communications ... Ms. Georgina TARASKEWICH
21 Associate Business Manager ... Ms. Carmen LUONG
36 Director Employment/Career Svc Ctr ... Ms. Claudia BALDONEDO
96 Director Procurement/Contracts ... Ms. Tawanikka SMITH
86 Government Relations Manager ... Ms. Claudia CHAN
30 Int Exec Director of Development ... Ms. Laura BARTOVICS

*City University of New York Medgar Evers College (G)

1650 Bedford Avenue, Brooklyn NY 11225-2010

County: Kings | FICE Identification: 010097
Unit ID: 190646
Telephone: (718) 270-4900 | Carnegie Class: Bac/Assoc-Mixed
FAX Number: (718) 270-5126 | Calendar System: Semester
URL: www.mec.cuny.edu
Established: 1970 | Annual Undergrad Tuition & Fees (In-District): $7,352
Enrollment: 5,237 | Coed
Affiliation or Control: State/Local | IRS Status: 501(c)3
Highest Offering: Baccalaureate

Accreditation: M, ACBSP, ADNUR, CAEP, NUR, SW

02 President .... Dr. Patricia RAMSEY
11 Chief Operating Officer .... Ms. Jacqueline CLARK
05 Interim Provost/Senior VP .... Dr. Ronald SHEEHY
10 VP Finance & Administration .... Ms. Jacqueline CLARK
20 Asst VP & Assoc Provost .... Dr. Heyward M. DREHER
18 Asst Vice President of Facilities .... Mr. Thomas CHING
32 SVP for Student Success .... Mr. Jesse KANE
20 Dean of Academic Affairs .... Dr. Hollie JONES
51 Dean Sch Professional & Comm Dev .... Dr. Evelyn CASTRO
50 Dean of the School of Business .... Dr. Jo-Ann ROLLE
49 Dean of the School of Liberal Arts .... Dr. Ethan GOLOGAR
72 Dean School of Science/Health/Tech .... Dr. Mohsin PATWARY
100 SVP for Strategy/Chief of Staff .... Dr. Kimberly WHITEHEAD
43 Chief Legal Officer .... Vacant
04 Exec Assistant to the President .... Mrs. Lisa ANDERSON
22 Director of Affirmative Action .... Vacant
06 Registrar .... Vacant
86 Exec Dir Govt Affs/Comm & Mktg .... Ms. Jennifer N. JAMES
13 Asst VP/CIO .... Mr. Xavier BARRETO
37 Director of Financial Aid .... Vacant
38 Director of Counseling .... Dr. JoAnn JOYNER-GRAHAM
19 Director of Security .... Mr. Jerry HOFFMAN
41 Director of Athletics .... Ms. Chetara MURPHY
25 Grants Officer .... Mr. Chi KOON
89 Dir Freshman Year Program .... Ms. Deborah CHARLES
55 Director Evening/Weekend Programs .... Ms. Yvette WALL
36 Sr Director of Career Development .... Ms. Antoinette ROBERSON
111 Vice Pres Inst Advancement .... Vacant
84 Exec Dir Enrollment Management .... Mrs. Shannon CLARKE-ANDERSON
29 Director of Alumni Relations .... Ms. Marsha ESCAGY
07 Director Admissions .... Ms. Jo-Ann JACOBS
09 Director of Institutional Research .... Dr. Eva CHAN
08 Interim Chief Librarian .... Dr. Judith SCHWARTZ
66 Chair Dept of Nursing .... Dr. Jean GUMBS
50 Chair Dept of Business Admin .... Ms. Sambhavi LAKSHMINARAYANAN
53 Chair Multi-Early Child & Elem Educ .... Dr. Rupam SARAN
60 Chair Dept of Mass Comm .... Dr. Clinton CRAWFORD
88 Chair Department Accounting .... Dr. Rosemary WILLIAMS
81 Chair Department of Mathematics .... Dr. Joshua SUSSAN
77 Chair Dept Physics/Computer Sci .... Dr. Armando HOWARD
81 Chair Department of Biology .... Vacant
83 Chair Dept of Social/Behavioral Sci .... Dr. Maria DELONGORIA
83 Chair Department of Psychology .... Dr. Maudry LASHLEY
80 Chair Dept of Public Administration .... Dr. Zulema BLAIR
77 Chair Computer Info Systems .... Dr. David AHN
88 Chair Department Economics/Finance .... Dr. Emmanuel EGBE
79 Chair Department of English .... Dr. Keming LIU
73 Chair Dept of Philosophy & Religion .... Dr. Vivaldi JEAN MARIE
88 Chair Dept of World Lang & Culture .... Dr. Maria-Luisa RUIZ
88 Chair Chemistry/Environmental Sci .... Dr. Alicia REID
88 Chair Dev & Special Education .... Dr. Donna WRIGHT
35 Director of Student Life .... Ms. Amani REECE
15 Human Resources Manager .... Ms. Kareema MONROE
113 Director Office of the Bursar .... Ms. Thais PILIERI
104 Director Study Abroad .... Ms. Rachelle TAYLOR

*New York City College of Technology/City University of New York (A)

300 Jay Street, Brooklyn NY 11201-1909
County: Kings | FICE Identification: 002696
Unit ID: 190655
Telephone: (718) 260-5000 | Carnegie Class: Bac/Assoc-Mixed
FAX Number: (718) 260-5198 | Calendar System: Semester
URL: www.citytech.cuny.edu
Established: 1946 | Annual Undergrad Tuition & Fees (In-District): $7,320
Enrollment: 15,513 | Coed
Affiliation or Control: State/Local | IRS Status: 501(c)3
Highest Offering: Baccalaureate
Accreditation: M, ADNUR, ART, CSHSE, DH, DT, NUR, OPD, RAD

02 President .... Dr. Russell K. HOTZLER
05 Int Provost/VP Academic Affairs .... Dr. Pamela BROWN
10 Vice Pres Finance/Administration .... Dr. Miguel CAIROL
84 VP Enrollment/Student Affairs .... Mr. Michel HODGE
20 Associate Provost Academic Affairs .... Dr. Pamela BROWN
22 Counsel/Affirmative Action Officer .... Ms. Gilen CHAN
07 Director of Admissions .... Ms. Alexis CHACONIS
06 Registrar .... Ms. Tasha RHODES
37 Director of Financial Aid .... Ms. Sandra HIGGINS
08 Librarian .... Ms. Maura SMALE
13 AVP/Chief Information Officer .... Ms. Rita UDDIN
107 Dean of Professional Studies .... Mr. David SMITH
72 Int Dean of Technology/Design .... Ms. Gerarda M. SHIELDS
49 Dean of Arts & Science .... Mr. Justin VASQUEZ-PORITZ
51 Dean Continuing Education .... Dr. Carol SONNENBLICK
55 Director Evening Session .... Mr. James LAP
15 OFSR Exec Dir/Labor Designee/HR .... Ms. Sandra GORDON
25 Grants Officer .... Ms. Barbara BURKE
24 Director of Inst Tech/Media Svcs .... Ms. Karen LUNDSTREM
09 Director of Assessment .... Vacant
26 AVP Public Relations .... Ms. Faith CORBETT
29 Director Alumni Relations .... Vacant
38 Director Student Counseling .... Ms. Cynthia BINK
96 Director of Purchasing .... Mr. Wayne ROBINSON
18 Chief Facilities/Physical Plant .... Mr. James VASQUEZ
30 Chief Development/Spec Asst to Pres .... Dr. Stephen SOIFFER
21 Executive Dir of Business Mgmt .... Mr. Wayne ROBINSON

*City University of New York Queens College (B)

65-30 Kissena Boulevard, Flushing NY 11367-1597
County: Queens | FICE Identification: 002690
Unit ID: 190664
Telephone: (718) 997-5000 | Carnegie Class: Masters/L
FAX Number: (718) 997-5598 | Calendar System: Semester
URL: www.qc.cuny.edu
Established: 1937 | Annual Undergrad Tuition & Fees (In-District): $7,538
Enrollment: 19,700 | Coed
Affiliation or Control: State/Local | IRS Status: 501(c)3
Highest Offering: Master's
Accreditation: M, CAEP, CLPSY, DIETD, DIETI, LAW, LIB, MUS, SP

02 President .... Mr. Frank H. WU
05 Provost & VP Academic Affairs .... Dr. Elizabeth HENDREY
10 VP Finance/Administration .... Vacant
32 Vice President for Student Affairs .... Vacant
26 VP Comm/Mktg/Sr Advisor to Pres .... Mr. Jay HERSHENSON
84 VP Enrollment & Student Retention .... Mr. Richard ALVAREZ
111 VP Inst Advancement/Alumni Rels .... Ms. Laurie DORF
43 AVP/General Counsel .... Ms. Sandy A. CURKO
100 Chief of Staff .... Ms. Meghan MOORE-WILK
27 Director of Communications .... Ms. Leslie JAY
13 AVP/CIO Information Tech .... Mr. Troy HAHN
20 Assoc Provost Res/Faculty Programs .... Dr. Alicia ALVERO
20 Assoc Provost Res and Intl Programs .... Vacant
21 AVP Budget and Finance .... Mr. Joseph LOUGHREN
88 Assistant Provost .... Dr. Eva FERNANDEZ
57 Dean of Arts & Humanities .... Dr. William MCCLURE
81 Dean of Math & Natural Sciences .... Dr. Daniel WEINSTEIN
53 Interim Dean of Education .... Dr. Dana FUSCO
58 Dean of Graduate Studies .... Vacant
83 Interim Dean of Social Sciences .... Dr. Ekaterina PECHENKINA
15 AVP Human Resources .... Ms. Lee KELLY
41 Director of Athletics .... Mr. Robert TWIBLE
88 Director of Events .... Ms. Sylvia HERNANDEZ
18 AVP Facilities .... Mr. Zeco KRCIC
07 Executive Director for the QC Hub .... Vacant
38 Director of Counseling & Advisement .... Vacant
06 Int Director QC Hub/Registrar .... Mr. James CURRY
09 Dean of Inst Effectiveness .... Ms. Rachel FESTER
08 Chief Librarian .... Ms. Kristin HART
37 Co-Director QC Hub/Financial Aid .... Mr. Clifford COULOUTE
29 Manager Alumni Affairs .... Ms. Laura ABRAMS
19 Director of Security/Safety .... Dr. Anastasia KOUTSIDIS
28 Int Chief Diversity Officer .... Vacant
96 Director of Purchasing .... Mr. Surinder VIRK
86 AVP Ext Affairs & Govt Relations .... Mr. Jeffrey ROSENSTOCK
26 Director of Marketing .... Ms. Lillian ZEPEDA
88 Deputy Chief of Staff .... Vacant
104 Director of Study Abroad .... Vacant
25 Chief Contract/Grants Administrator .... Ms. Poline PAPOULIS
39 Director of Student Housing .... Mr. Sean PIERCE

† The Clinical Psychology PhD is awarded through the CUNY Graduate Center.

*City University of New York Queensborough Community College (C)

222-05 56th Avenue, Bayside NY 11364-1497
County: Queens | FICE Identification: 002697
Unit ID: 190673
Telephone: (718) 631-6262 | Carnegie Class: Assoc/HT-High Trad
FAX Number: N/A | Calendar System: Semester
URL: www.qcc.cuny.edu
Established: 1958 | Annual Undergrad Tuition & Fees (In-District): $5,210
Enrollment: 12,405 | Coed
Affiliation or Control: State/Local | IRS Status: 501(c)3
Highest Offering: Associate Degree
Accreditation: M, ACBSP, ADNUR, ART, DANCE, THEA

02 President .... Dr. Christine MANGINO
05 Sr Vice Pres Academic Affs/Provost .... Dr. Timothy LYNCH
10 Vice Pres Finance & Admin .... Mr. William FAULKNER
111 Vice Pres Institutional Advancement .... Vacant
32 Vice President Student Affairs .... Dr. Brian KERR
20 Dean of Faculty .... Dr. Sandra PALMER
15 Dean Human Resource/Labor Rels .... Ms. Liza LARIOS
108 VP Strategic Plng/Assessment .... Vacant
51 VP Continuing Ed/Workforce Dev .... Vacant
88 Dean Accred Assessment .... Dr. Arthur CORRADETTI
26 VP/Chief Communications/Mktg Ofcr .... Mr. Stephen DI DIO
13 Chief Information Technology Ofcr .... Mr. Ralph ROMANELLI
06 Registrar .... Ms. Emiko SANCHEZ
08 Chief Librarian .... Ms. Jeanne GALVIN
07 Asst Dean of New Student Enrollment .... Ms. Patricia RAMOS
09 Director of Institutional Research .... Ms. Elisabeth LACKNER
16 Director of Human Resources .... Ms. Sangeeta NOEL
19 Director of Safety & Security .... Mr. John TRIOLO
22 Chief Diversity Officer .... Ms. Josephine PANTALEO
04 Executive Asst to President .... Ms. Elaine IOANNOU
104 Dir Ctr for Intl Stds/Study Abroad .... Ms. Lampeto (Betty) EFTHYMIOU
84 Dean of Enrollment Management .... Ms. Veronica LUKAS
36 Director of Career Services .... Ms. Constance PELUSO
18 Chief Admin Superintendent .... Mr. Joseph CARTOLANO
30 Development Officer .... Ms. Saji SHEERAZI
21 Exec Dir Finance/Admin Operations .... Mr. David WASSERMAN
114 Exec Dir Budget/Resource Planning .... Mr. Mark CARPENTIER
35 Asst Dean of Student Dev/Conduct .... Ms. Tikola RUSSELL
103 Dean Continuing Educ/Workforce Dev .... Ms. Hui-Yin HSU

*City University of New York Stella and Charles Guttman Community College (D)

50 West 40th Street, New York NY 10018
County: New York | Identification: 667126
Unit ID: 475565
Telephone: (646) 313-8000 | Carnegie Class: Assoc/HT-High Trad
FAX Number: N/A | Calendar System: Semester
URL: www.guttman.cuny.edu
Established: 2011 | Annual Undergrad Tuition & Fees (In-District): $5,194
Enrollment: 1,021 | Coed
Affiliation or Control: State/Local | IRS Status: 501(c)3
Highest Offering: Associate Degree
Accreditation: M

02 President .... Larry JOHNSON
05 Provost and Vice President .... Vacant
10 Vice Pres Admin & Finance .... Mary COLEMAN
32 VP Student Engagement .... Charles PRYOR
09 Director of Institutional Research .... Elisa HERTZ
100 Chief of Staff .... Linda MERIANS
13 Chief Info Technology Officer (CIO) .... John STROUD
15 Director Human Resources .... Nila BHAUMIK
18 Director Facilities Planning .... Shirley LAW
19 Director Public Safety .... Vacant
37 Director Student Financial Aid .... Cristina ORTIZ-HARVEY
06 Registrar .... Cortes MARISOL
07 Director of Admissions .... So SOPHEA
86 Director Government Relations .... Vacant
04 Administrative Asst to President .... Brady GALAN
29 Director Alumni Relations .... LaToya JACKSON
08 Chief Library Officer .... Vacant
28 Chief Diversity Officer .... Jaclyn HELMS
38 Director Student Counseling .... Courtney STEVENSON
43 Director Legal Services .... Lori FOX

*City University of New York York College (E)

94-20 Guy Brewer Boulevard, Jamaica NY 11451-0001
County: Queens | FICE Identification: 004759
Unit ID: 190691
Telephone: (718) 262-2000 | Carnegie Class: Bac-Diverse
FAX Number: (718) 262-2352 | Calendar System: Semester
URL: www.york.cuny.edu
Established: 1966 | Annual Undergrad Tuition & Fees (In-District): $7,358
Enrollment: 7,784 | Coed
Affiliation or Control: State/Local | IRS Status: 501(c)3
Highest Offering: Master's
Accreditation: M, ARCPA, CAEP, EXSC, MT, NUR, OT, SW

02 President .... Dr. Berenecea J. EANES
05 Interim Sr VP & Provost .... Dr. Derrick BRAZILL
10 VP of Administration & Finance/COO .... Mr. Charles BOZIAN
32 Int VP Enroll Mgmt & Student Aff .... Dr. Karen WILLIAMS
111 Int VP Institutional Advancement .... Ms. Dana TRIMBOLI
49 Interim Dean Sch of Arts & Sciences .... Dr. George WHITE
50 Int Dean Sch of Bus & Info Systems .... Dr. Maureen BECKER
83 Dean Sch of Health Sci & Prof Pgms .... Dr. Maureen BECKER
43 Labor & Legal Affairs .... Mr. Russell PLATZEK
15 Exec Director HR .... Ms. Sabrina JOHNSON-CHANDLER
19 Exec Dir Facilities & Planning .... Mr. Kachi AKOMA
21 Exec Dir Bus Oper & Compliance .... Ms. Vivian FEBUS
13 Interim Chief Information Officer .... Mr. Claudio LINDOW
09 AVP Inst Effective/Strategic Plng .... Dr. Lori HOEFFNER
100 Chief of Staff .... Ms. Dana TRIMBOLI
06 Registrar .... Ms. Sharon DAVIDSON
08 Chief Librarian .... Ms. Njoki KINYATTI
90 Director of Academic Computing .... Dr. Che-Tsao HUANG
86 Exec Dir Govt/Strategic Initiative .... Dr. Earl G. SIMONS
19 Director of Security .... Vacant
37 Director of Financial Aid .... Ms. Beverly BROWN
18 Director Campus Planning .... Mr. Noel GAMBOA
35 Director Student Activities .... Dr. Jean PHELPS
36 Director Career Services .... Ms. Linda H. CHESNEY
25 Dir Research/Sponsored Programs .... Ms. Dawn HEWITT
38 Director of Counseling Cntr .... Dr. Jayoung CHOI
41 Director of Athletics .... Mr. Carl CHRISTIAN
04 Executive Assoc to the President .... Ms. Sandra BELL ADAMS
28 Director of Diversity .... Vacant
96 Director of Purchasing .... Ms. Christine WEITHERS
07 Director of Admissions .... Mr. Anthony DAVIS
103 Director Workforce Development .... Vacant

Clarkson University (F)

8 Clarkson Ave, Potsdam NY 13699
County: St. Lawrence | FICE Identification: 002699
Unit ID: 190044
Telephone: (315) 268-6400 | Carnegie Class: DU-Higher
FAX Number: (315) 268-7647 | Calendar System: Semester
URL: www.clarkson.edu
Established: 1896 | Annual Undergrad Tuition & Fees: $52,724
Enrollment: 4,025 | Coed
Affiliation or Control: Independent Non-Profit | IRS Status: 501(c)3
Highest Offering: Doctorate

Accreditation: M, AAQEP, ARCPA, HSA, OT, PTA

01 President ... Dr. Anthony G. COLLINS
05 Provost ... Dr. Robyn HANNIGAN
111 VP External Relations ... Dr. Kelly O. CHEZUM
10 Interim Chief Financial Officer ... Mr. William MCGARRY
84 VP Enrollment & Student Advancement ... Mr. Brian T. GRANT
30 VP Development & Alumni Relations ... Mr. Matthew DRAPER
15 Chief Human Resources Officer ... Ms. Amy MCGAHERAN
28 Chief Inclusion Officer ... Dr. Jennifer BALL
41 Athletics Director ... Mr. Scott J. SMALLING
13 Chief Information Officer ... Mr. Joshua A. FISKE
04 Assistant to the President ... Ms. Carrie CAPELLA
16 Asst Dir Human Resources ... Ms. Diana LETOURNEAU
45 Assoc Vice Provost Research & Tech ... Ms. Shannon ROBINSON
88 Assoc Provost Faculty Achievement ... Dr. Christopher ROBINSON
20 Exec Dir Academic Affairs ... Ms. Amanda PICKERING
49 Dean of Arts & Sciences ... Dr. Darryl SCRIVEN
50 Interim Dean of Business ... Dr. Diego NOCETTI
54 Dean of Engineering ... Dr. William JEMISON
76 Founding Dean of Health Sciences ... Dr. Lennart JOHNS
08 Dean of Libraries ... Ms. Michelle L. YOUNG
65 Dir Inst for a Sustainable Environ ... Dr. Susan POWERS
58 Dean of Graduate School ... Dr. Michelle CRIMI
12 Pres & CEO Beacon Institute ... Mr. Michael WALSH
88 Head of The Clarkson School ... Dr. Benjamin GALLUZZO
88 Dir of Inst for STEM Education ... Dr. Kathleen KAVANAGH
92 Director Honors Program ... Dr. Kate KRUEGER
88 Managing Director Clarkson Ignite ... Ms. Erin DRAPER
09 Assoc Dir Institutional Research ... Ms. Jenna STONE
25 Contract & Grant Administrator ... Ms. Anna Marie DAWLEY
21 Controller ... Mr. Keith ROSSER
88 Director of Project Management ... Ms. Anastasia THOMAS
18 Director Facilities & Services ... Mr. Michael TREMPER
114 Director Budget & Planning ... Ms. Paula STURGE
117 Dir Legal Affairs/Compliance/Risk ... Ms. Debra DRESCHER
88 Dir Student Administrative Services ... Ms. Suzanne E. DAVIS
06 Registrar ... Ms. Jen J. STOKES
07 Director of Admissions ... Ms. Trish DOBBS
37 Director Financial Aid ... Ms. Kara PITTS
88 Dir of Clarkson School Admission ... Mr. Matthew RUTHERFORD
121 AVP Stdnt Success Ctr & Int Rel ... Ms. Cathy MCNAMARA
32 Dean of Students ... Mr. James PITTMAN
35 AVP Student Affairs & Global Init ... Mr. Jeffrey D. TAYLOR
19 Director Campus Safety & Security ... Mr. David W. DELISLE
23 Director Student Health Center ... Ms. Amanda ROSS
36 Director Career Center ... Ms. Heather DIFINO
104 Study Abroad Advisor ... Ms. Christine BAILEY
38 Director of Counseling ... Ms. Coreen BOHL
85 Director Intl Students & Scholars ... Ms. Tess C. CASLER
29 AVP Engagement & Operations ... Ms. Teresa PLANTY
110 AVP Development ... Mr. Steven SMALLING
102 Dir Donor Engmnt/Stwrdshp/Found Rel ... Ms. Erin LONDRAVILLE
44 Director Annual Giving Programs ... Ms. Nichole THOMAS
91 Director Administrative Computing ... Mr. Chris CUTLER
119 Dir Net Services & Info Security ... Mr. Brian HUNTLEY
90 Dir Academic Technology & Support ... Ms. Laura PERRY
105 Director Web Development ... Ms. Julie DAVIS
26 Director of Media Relations ... Ms. Melissa M. LINDELL
27 Director of Interactive Marketing ... Ms. Jessica CARISTA
88 Dir of Creative Services & Proj Mgt ... Mr. David HOMSEY
40 Bookstore Manager ... Mr. Evan HITCHMAN

Clinton Community College (A)

136 Clinton Point Drive, Plattsburgh NY 12901-9573
County: Clinton FICE Identification: 006787
Unit ID: 190053
Telephone: (518) 562-4200 Carnegie Class: Assoc/HT-Mix Trad/Non
FAX Number: (518) 561-4890 Calendar System: Semester
URL: www.clinton.edu
Established: 1966 Annual Undergrad Tuition & Fees (In-District): $6,831
Enrollment: 1,060 Coed
Affiliation or Control: State/Local IRS Status: 501(c)3
Highest Offering: Associate Degree
Accreditation: M, ADNUR

01 President ... Mr. Ray DI PASQUALE
05 Vice President for Academic Affairs ... Dr. John KOWAL
10 Vice Pres for Admin/Business Affs ... Vacant
32 Dean of Student Affairs ... Mr. John BORNER
111 Vice Pres Institutional Advancement ... Dr. Wendy BAKER
20 Assoc Vice Pres Academic Affairs ... Vacant
37 Director of Financial Aid ... Ms. Mary LA PIERRE
84 Dean of Enrollment Management ... Mrs. Anna MIARKA-GRZELAK
06 Registrar ... Mr. Jonathan REID
13 Director Information Technology ... Vacant
15 Human Resource/Affirm Act Officer ... Vacant
18 Director of Buildings/Grounds ... Mr. Robert TROMBLEY
04 Administrative Asst to President ... Mrs. Tammy M. VILLANUEVA
21 Controller ... Mr. Antonio MAGLIONE

Cochran School of Nursing (B)

967 North Broadway, Yonkers NY 10701-1399
County: Westchester FICE Identification: 006443
Unit ID: 190071
Telephone: (914) 964-4282 Carnegie Class: Spec 2-yr-Health
FAX Number: (914) 964-4266 Calendar System: Semester
URL: www.cochranschoolofnursing.us
Established: 1894 Annual Undergrad Tuition & Fees: N/A
Enrollment: 94 Coed
Affiliation or Control: Independent Non-Profit IRS Status: 501(c)3
Highest Offering: Associate Degree
Accreditation: ADNUR

01 Dean ... Dr. Patrick REINHARD
08 Director of CSN Learning Resource ... Ms. Andria CLEGHORN
32 Director Student Services/Finances ... Ms. Alphonsa ITTOOP
06 Registrar ... Ms. Lisa PEGUES
07 Admissions Counselor ... Ms. Haaneen EL JAMAL
88 Information Literacy Officer ... Ms. Diana KRPIC
37 Financial Aid Officer ... Ms. Maria GONCALVES

Cold Spring Harbor Laboratory, School of Biological Sciences (C)

PO Box 100, One Bungtown Road,
Cold Spring Harbor NY 11724-0100
County: Suffolk FICE Identification: 034563
Unit ID: 436377
Telephone: (516) 367-6890 Carnegie Class: Not Classified
FAX Number: (516) 367-6919 Calendar System: Other
URL: www.cshl.edu
Established: 1890 Annual Graduate Tuition & Fees: N/A
Enrollment: N/A Coed
Affiliation or Control: Independent Non-Profit IRS Status: 501(c)3
Highest Offering: Doctorate; No Undergraduates
Accreditation: NY

01 President ... Dr. Bruce STILLMAN
05 Dean of Academic Affairs ... Dr. Terri I. GRODZICKER
10 Chief Financial Officer ... Ms. Lari C. RUSSO
30 VP Development/Cmty Relations ... Mr. Charles V. PRIZZI
13 VP Information Technology/CIO ... Mr. Hans-Erik ARONSON
15 Vice Pres Human Resources ... Ms. Katherine G. RAFTERY
26 Vice Pres Communications ... Ms. Dagnia ZEIDLICKIS
43 Vice Pres General Counsel ... Ms. Debra ARENARE
81 Dean ... Dr. Alexander GANN
06 Registrar ... Dr. Alyson KASS-EISLER
25 Chief Contract/Grants Administrator ... Mr. Walter GOLDSCHMIDTS
28 Director of Diversity ... Ms. Charla LAMBERT

Colgate Rochester Crozer Divinity School (D)

320 North Goodman Street, Ste 207, Rochester NY 14607
County: Monroe FICE Identification: 002700
Unit ID: 190080
Telephone: (585) 271-1320 Carnegie Class: Spec-4-yr-Faith
FAX Number: (585) 271-8013 Calendar System: Semester
URL: www.crcds.edu
Established: 1817 Annual Graduate Tuition & Fees: N/A
Enrollment: 46 Coed
Affiliation or Control: Independent Non-Profit IRS Status: 501(c)3
Highest Offering: Doctorate; No Undergraduates
Accreditation: THEOL

01 President ... Dr. Angela D. SIMS
11 VP Institutional Effectivenss/COO ... Rev. Paula B. BLUE
10 VP Finance/Administration ... Ms. Patty KEENAHAN
05 VP Academic Affairs ... Dr. Deborah ROGERS
111 VP Institutional Advancement ... Dr. Courtney WILEY-HARRIS
94 Dean of Women & Gender Studies ... Dr. Hilary J. SCARSELLA
07 Director of Admissions ... Ms. Polly BUSH
30 Director of Development ... Ms. Lisa BORS
06 Registrar/Coord Financial Aid ... Ms. Qhamora KIMBROUGH
04 Executive Administrator ... Ms. Lydia CRIM

Colgate University (E)

13 Oak Drive, Hamilton NY 13346-1386
County: Madison FICE Identification: 002701
Unit ID: 190099
Telephone: (315) 228-1000 Carnegie Class: Bac-A&S
FAX Number: (315) 228-7798 Calendar System: Semester
URL: www.colgate.edu
Established: 1819 Annual Undergrad Tuition & Fees: $60,015
Enrollment: 3,054 Coed
Affiliation or Control: Independent Non-Profit IRS Status: 501(c)3
Highest Offering: Master's
Accreditation: M

01 President ... Brian W. CASEY
05 Interim Dean of Faculty & Provost ... Ellen KRALY
10 Sr VP for Finance & Admin ... Joseph S. HOPE
100 Chief of Staff/Sec to the BOT ... Hanna RODRIGUEZ-FARRAR
88 Sr Advisor to the President ... Christopher WELLS
32 VP & Dean of the College ... Paul J. MCLOUGHLIN, II
41 VP & Director of Athletics ... Nicki MOORE
101 VP/Sr Philanthropic Advisor ... Robert L. TYBURSKI
07 VP of Admission & Fin Aid ... Gary L. ROSS
26 Acting CDO/VP for Communications ... Laura JACK
111 VP for Advancement ... Karl W. CLAUSS
04 Assistant to the President ... Debbie PILS
21 Associate Vice Pres/Controller ... Thomas O'NEILL
114 Assoc VP Budget & Financial Plg ... John COLLINS
21 AVP for Finance & Administration ... Dan PARTIGIANONI
18 Assoc VP for Facilities ... Stephen HUGHES
20 Associate Dean of the Faculty ... Doug JOHNSON
20 Associate Dean of the Faculty ... Krista INGRAM
20 Associate Dean of the Faculty ... Martin WONG
45 Vice Provost Admin & Planning ... Trish ST. LEGER
28 Assoc Provost Equity & Diversity ... Marilyn RUGG
06 Registrar ... Neil ALBERT
35 Dean of Students ... Dorsey SPENCER
07 Dean of Admission ... Tara BUBBLE
08 University Librarian ... Courtney YOUNG
13 Chief Information Officer ... Niranjan DAVRAY
112 AVP Advancement/Planned Giving ... Andrew CODDINGTON
110 AVP Advancement Admin & Planning ... Thirza MORREALE
88 Asst VP Advancement/Dir Prof Net ... Jennifer STONE
29 Director of Alumni Relations ... Vacant
37 Director of Financial Aid ... Gina M. SOLIZ
109 AVP Cmty Affairs/Auxiliary Services ... Joanne BORFITZ
19 Assoc VP for Campus Safety ... Vacant
40 Sr General Merchandise Manager ... Craig WILSON
42 University Chaplain ... Barry BARON
38 Director Counseling/Psych Services ... Dawn LAFRANCE
96 Director of Purchasing ... Simon FRITZ
23 Director Student Health Services ... Merrill MILLER
94 Director Women's Studies ... Susan THOMSON
88 Director Relationship Development ... Sara GROH
88 Director Advancement Operations ... Lindsey HOHAM
44 Director Annual Giving ... Catherine MARHENKE
39 Director of Residential Housing ... Danielle NIED
09 Dir Institutional Planning/Research ... Neil ALBERT
22 Dir EEO & Affirmative Action ... Tamala FLACK
102 Dir of Corp Foundation & Govt Rels ... Bruce MOSELEY
104 Director of Off-Campus Study ... Joanna HOLVEY BOWLES

College of Mount Saint Vincent (F)

6301 Riverdale Avenue, Riverdale NY 10471-1093
County: Bronx FICE Identification: 002703
Unit ID: 193399
Telephone: (718) 405-3200 Carnegie Class: Masters/S
FAX Number: (718) 601-6392 Calendar System: Semester
URL: www.mountsaintvincent.edu
Established: 1847 Annual Undergrad Tuition & Fees: $40,980
Enrollment: 2,663 Coed
Affiliation or Control: Independent Non-Profit IRS Status: 501(c)3
Highest Offering: Master's
Accreditation: M, ACBSP, NURSE

01 President ... Dr. Susan R. BURNS
05 Provost/Dean of Faculty ... Vacant
20 Vice Provost & Dean of the College ... Dr. Lynne BONGIOVANNI
07 Sr VP for Admission/External Rels ... Ms. Madeleine MELKONIAN
10 Executive VP/Treasurer/CFO ... Mr. Abed ELKESHK
11 VP for Operations ... Mr. Kevin DEGROAT
13 VP Information Technology/CIO ... Mr. W. Adam WICHERN, III
32 Vice President for Student Affairs ... Ms. Kelli SMITH
88 Director Mission Integration ... Mr. Matthew SHIELDS
06 Registrar ... Mrs. Jeannette PICHARDO
08 Director of Library ... Mr. Joseph LEVIS
09 Director of Institutional Research ... Sr. Carol M. FINEGAN, SC
36 Director Career Education ... Mr. Robson CHERETTA
37 Director of Financial Aid ... Vacant
42 Dir Campus Ministry/Act Dir Mission ... Mr. Mathew SHIELDS
35 Dir of Student Affairs/Assoc Dean ... Dr. Gabrielle OCCHIOGROSSO
41 Dir Athletics & Recreation ... Mr. Phil STERN
38 Director Counseling Services ... Ms. Rebecca HALPERIN
23 Director of Health Services ... Mrs. Eileen MCCABE
26 Director for Public Relations/Mktg ... Ms. Leah MUNCH
19 Dir Campus Safety/Security ... Mr. Thomas VASSALLO
66 Dean College of Nursing ... Ms. Annemarie MCALLISTER
44 Assoc Dir Alumnae Rels/Annual Giv ... Ms. Kristin YANNIELLO
15 Director of Human Resources ... Vacant
21 Controller ... Mr. James WONG
04 Assistant to the President ... Ms. Mary BAUER
18 Director of Facilities ... Mr. Ryan ANDERSON
07 Director of Admissions ... Vacant
92 Director of Honors Program ... Dr. Rosita VILLAGOMEZ
97 Director of Core Curriculum ... Dr. Robert JACKLOSKY

The College of Saint Rose (G)

432 Western Avenue, Albany NY 12203-1490
County: Albany FICE Identification: 002705
Unit ID: 195234
Telephone: (518) 454-5111 Carnegie Class: Masters/L
FAX Number: (518) 438-3293 Calendar System: Semester
URL: www.strose.edu
Established: 1920 Annual Undergrad Tuition & Fees: $34,354
Enrollment: 3,863 Coed
Affiliation or Control: Independent Non-Profit IRS Status: 501(c)3
Highest Offering: Master's
Accreditation: M, ACBSP, ART, MUS, SP, SW

01 Interim President ... Ms. Marcia WHITE
100 Chief of Staff ... Ms. Lisa HALEY-THOMSON
05 Interim Provost/VP Academic Affairs ... Dr. Margaret MCLANE
58 Assoc Provost for Grad & Prof Study ... Vacant
32 VP for Student Development ... Vacant
10 VP for Finance & Administration ... Ms. Debra L. POLLEY
111 Interim VP Inst Advancement ... Mr. Robert DIVITO
15 Assoc Vice Pres Human Res/Risk Mgt ... Mr. Jeffrey KNAPP
21 AVP Financial Reporting/Comptroller ... Ms. Valerie MYERS
114 Assistant VP for Financial Planning ... Ms. Christina BARBER
07 Interim Assoc VP for Admissions ... Mr. Daniel GALLAGHER
37 Asst VP of Financial Aid ... Mr. Steven W. DWIRE
42 Dir Spiritual Life/Interfaith Init ... Ms. Joan HORGAN
13 Associate Vice President for IT ... Mr. John ELLIS
35 AVP Stdnt Devel/Compliance/ Wellness ... Ms. Jennifer RICHARDSON

18 Assoc VP for Facilities Operations .... Mr. Gary GOSS
06 Registrar .... Mr. Craig TYNAN
08 Director of Library Services .... Vacant
39 Director Residence Life .... Ms. Phylicia COLEY
36 Assistant Director Career Center .... Ms. Emily NICHOLSON
41 Assoc VP & Director of Athletics .... Ms. Lori ANCTIL
19 Director of Safety/Security .... Mr. Steven STELLA
121 Director of Academic Advisement .... Ms. Jennifer HANKIN
109 Director Purchasing/Auxiliary Svcs .... Ms. Patricia BUCKLEY
09 Assoc VP of Institutional Effective .... Mrs. Lisa KEATING
40 Manager of Campus Store .... Mr. Austin ANTLE
24 Technology Support Services Manager .... Ms. Rachel RAMSEY
04 Exec Admin Asst to the President .... Ms. Maria RUSSO
50 Dean School of Business .... Dr. Rajarshi AROSKAR
79 Dean Arts & Humanities .... Dr. Gerald LORENTZ
81 Dean Math & Sciences .... Dr. Ian MACDONALD
53 Interim Dean School of Education .... Dr. Theresa WARD
112 Director of Major Gifts .... Ms. Therese STILLMAN
29 Director of Alumni Engagement .... Ms. Frances VORSKY
26 AVP of Marketing & Communications .... Ms. Jennifer GISH
28 Chief Diversity Ofcr/Dir Leadership .... Ms. Yolanda CALDWELL
23 Dir of Counseling/Health Services .... Mr. Mark PARISI
113 Bursar .... Ms. Deana BIZZARRO
27 Dir of Marketing & Communications .... Mr. Michael HICKLING
44 Director Annual Giving .... Ms. Colleen KEATING

The College of Westchester (A)

325 Central Avenue, White Plains NY 10606

County: Westchester   FICE Identification: 005208
Unit ID: 197285
Telephone: (914) 948-4442   Carnegie Class: Bac/Assoc-Mixed
FAX Number: (914) 948-5441   Calendar System: Semester
URL: www.cw.edu
Established: 1915   Annual Undergrad Tuition & Fees: $22,410
Enrollment: 934   Coed
Affiliation or Control: Proprietary   IRS Status: Proprietary
Highest Offering: Baccalaureate
Accreditation: M

01 President & CEO .... Mrs. Mary Beth DEL BALZO
05 Provost/VP Academic Affairs .... Dr. Warren ROSENBERG
88 Vice President Special Projects .... Mr. Dale T. SMITH
84 VP of Enrollment Management .... Mr. Matt CURTIS
36 Director of Career Services .... Ms. Joann SONDEY
32 VP of Student Services & Retention .... Mrs. Maria GANGI
37 Dir of Student Financial Services .... Mrs. Dianne PEPITONE

Columbia-Greene Community College (B)

4400 Route 23, Hudson NY 12534-9543

County: Columbia   FICE Identification: 006789
Unit ID: 190169
Telephone: (518) 828-4181   Carnegie Class: Assoc/HT-Mix Trad/Non
FAX Number: (518) 822-2015   Calendar System: Semester
URL: www.sunycgcc.edu
Established: 1966   Annual Undergrad Tuition & Fees (In-District): $5,616
Enrollment: 1,445   Coed
Affiliation or Control: State/Local   IRS Status: 501(c)3
Highest Offering: Associate Degree
Accreditation: M, ADNUR

00 Chairman of the Board .... Dr. Edward SCHNEIER, JR.
01 President .... Dr. Carlee DRUMMER
05 Provost/VP Acad & Student Affairs .... Dr. George TIMMONS
10 VP Administration/Chief Fin Ofcr .... Ms. Dianne TOPPLE
20 Dean of Academic Affairs .... Dr. Casey O'BRIEN
18 Director Building & Grounds .... Ms. Alison MURPHY
26 Director Marketing & Communications ... Ms. Jaclyn STEVENSON
37 Director of Financial Aid .... Ms. Joel PHELPS
06 Registrar .... Ms. Ann BRUNO
13 Director Information Systems .... Mr. Gino RIZZI
15 Director of Human Resources .... Ms. Melissa FANDOZZI
22 Affirmative Action Officer .... Ms. Melissa FANDOZZI
31 Director of Community Services .... Ms. Amanda KARCH
41 Athletic Director .... Mr. Nicolas DYER
121 Director Academic Support Center .... Vacant
103 Director of Workforce Development .... Ms. Christopher NARDONE
07 Asst Director of Admissions .... Mr. Kevin KROPP
102 Exec Dir of CG Community Foundation .... Ms. Joan KOWEEK
113 Bursar .... Ms. Christy WARD
19 Director of Security .... Mr. John LEONE
96 Purchasing Officer .... Ms. Patricia DAY
04 Assistant to the President .... Ms. Mary GARAFALO
29 Director Alumni Relations .... Ms. Christine PERRY
84 Assistant Dean of Enrollment Mgmt .... Mr. Matthew GREEN

Columbia University in the City of New York (C)

615 West 131st Street, New York NY 10027-6902

County: New York   FICE Identification: 002707
Unit ID: 190150
Telephone: (212) 854-1754   Carnegie Class: DU-Highest
FAX Number: (212) 851-7022   Calendar System: Semester
URL: www.columbia.edu
Established: 1754   Annual Undergrad Tuition & Fees: $61,671
Enrollment: 30,135   Coed
Affiliation or Control: Independent Non-Profit   IRS Status: 501(c)3
Highest Offering: Doctorate
Accreditation: M, ANEST, CAMPEP, CEA, DENT, HSA, IPSY, JOUR, LAW, MED, MIDWF, NURSE, OT, PH, PLNG, PTA, SPAA, SW

01 President .... Mr. Lee C. BOLLINGER
05 Provost .... Dr. Mary C. BOYCE
03 Senior Exec Vice President .... Mr. Gerald M. ROSBERG
49 EVP/Dean Arts & Sciences .... Dr. Amy HUNGERFORD
76 Exec VP Health/Biomed Sciences .... Dr. Lee GOLDMAN
09 Exec Vice President Research .... Dr. Jeanette M. WING
43 General Counsel .... Ms. Jane E. BOOTH
26 Exec Vice President Public Affairs .... Ms. Shailagh J. MURRAY
101 Secretary of the University .... Mr. Jerome DAVIS
10 Exec Vice President for Finance .... Ms. Anne R. SULLIVAN
18 Exec Vice President Facilities .... Mr. David GREENBERG
85 Exec Vice President Global Dev .... Mr. Safwan M. MASRI
30 Exec Vice Pres Development & Alumni .... Ms. Amelia J. ALVERSON
32 Exec Vice President University Life .... Mr. Dennis A. MITCHELL
41 Athletic Director .... Mr. Peter E. PILLING
88 Ombuds Officer .... Ms. Joan WATERS
100 Chief of Staff to President .... Ms. Susan K. GLANCY
20 Vice Provost Academic Programs .... Dr. Julie KORNFELD
20 Vice Provost Faculty Affairs .... Ms. Latha VENKATARAMAN
11 Vice Provost Administration .... Mr. Troy EGGERS
88 Vice Provost Teaching & Learning .... Mr. Soulaymane KACHANI
28 Vice Provost Diversity & Inclusion .... Dr. Dennis MITCHELL
08 Vice Provost & Univ Librarian .... Ms. Ann D. THORNTON
48 Dean Grad School Arch/Plng/Preserv .... Ms. Amale ANDRAOS
57 Dean School of the Arts .... Dr. Carol BECKER
58 Dean Grad School of Arts & Science .... Dr. Carlos J. ALONSO
50 Dean Graduate School of Business . Dr. Constantinos MAGLARAS
49 Dean Columbia College .... Dr. James J. VALENTINI
107 Dean School of Professional Studies .... Mr. Jason M. WINGARD
54 Dean Sch Engr/Applied Science .... Dr. Mary C. BOYCE
82 Dean School Intl/Public Affairs .... Ms. Merit E. JANOW
97 Dean School General Studies .... Dr. Lisa ROSEN-METSCH
60 Dean Graduate School Journalism .... Mr. Stephen W. COLL
61 Dean School of Law .... Ms. Gillian LESTER
70 Dean School of Social Work .... Dr. Melissa BEGG
63 Int EVP/Dean Faculty of Medicine .... Dr. Anil RUSTGI
52 Dean Sch Dental & Oral Surgery .... Dr. Christian S. STOHLER
66 Dean School of Nursing .... Dr. Bobbie BERKOWITZ
69 Dean School of Public Health .... Dr. Linda P. FRIED
38 Exec Director Student Counseling .... Dr. Richard EICHLER
37 Assoc VP Student Financial Svcs .... Dr. Jane HOJAN-CLARK
06 Assoc Vice Pres & Registrar .... Mr. Barry S. KANE
07 Dean of Undergraduate Admissions .... Ms. Jessica MARINACCIO

† Parent institution of Barnard College and Teachers College, Columbia University.

Congregation Talmidei Mesivta Tiferes Schmiel Aleksander (D)

1535 63rd Street, Brooklyn NY 11219

County: Kings   FICE Identification: 042769
Unit ID: 493600
Telephone: (718) 435-2105   Carnegie Class: Not Classified
FAX Number: (917) 410-7477   Calendar System: Semester
Established: Annual Undergrad Tuition & Fees: $19,000
Enrollment: 173   Male
Affiliation or Control: Independent Non-Profit   IRS Status: 501(c)3
Highest Offering: First Talmudic Degree
Accreditation: @RABN

01 CEO .... Rabbi Abraham SINGER

Cooper Union (E)

30 Cooper Square, New York NY 10003-7120

County: New York   FICE Identification: 002710
Unit ID: 190372
Telephone: (212) 353-4100   Carnegie Class: Bac-Diverse
FAX Number: (212) 353-4244   Calendar System: Semester
URL: www.cooper.edu
Established: 1859   Annual Undergrad Tuition & Fees: $46,820
Enrollment: 887   Coed
Affiliation or Control: Independent Non-Profit   IRS Status: 501(c)3
Highest Offering: Master's
Accreditation: M, ART

01 President .... Laura SPARKS
05 Assoc Dean Academic Affairs .... Ruben SAVIZKY
10 Vice President Finance and Admin .... John RUTH
84 Vice President for Enrollment .... Mark CAMPBELL
111 VP for Development/Alumni Affairs .... Terri COPPERSMITH
07 Assoc Dir of Admissions .... Hilary FERNANDEZ
57 Dean School of Art .... Michael (Mike) ESSL
88 Associate Dean School of Art .... Adriana FARMIGA
48 Dean School of Architecture .... Nader TEHRANI
54 Dean School of Engineering .... Barry SHOOP
32 Dean of Students .... Christopher CHAMBERLIN
88 Asst Dean School of Architecture .... Hayley EBER
79 Assoc Dean Humanities/Social Sci .... Nada AYAD
15 Chief Talent Officer .... Natalie BROOKS
88 Creative Director .... Mindy LANG
45 VP Strategic Initiatives/Effective .... Antoinette (Toni) TORRES
27 Media Relations Manager .... Kim NEWMAN
88 Assoc Dean Educational Innovation .... Lisa SHAY
101 Secretary of the Institution/Board .... Charlotte WESSELL
06 Assoc Registrar .... David CHENKIN
19 Dir Campus Safety/Security .... Thomas TRESSELT
29 Deputy Dir of Alumni Affairs .... Jennifer DURST
30 Development Associate .... Adam D'ALEXANDER
37 Sr Dir Student Financial Svcs .... Charlie XU
15 Dir of Human Resources .... Mary Ann NISSEN

† Every student receives a full-tuition scholarship.

Cornell University (F)

Day Hall, Ithaca NY 14850

County: Tompkins   FICE Identification: 002711
Unit ID: 190415
Telephone: (607) 255-2000   Carnegie Class: DU-Highest
FAX Number: (607) 255-5396   Calendar System: Semester
URL: www.cornell.edu
Established: 1865   Annual Undergrad Tuition & Fees: $59,282
Enrollment: 23,620   Coed
Affiliation or Control: Independent Non-Profit   IRS Status: 501(c)3
Highest Offering: Doctorate
Accreditation: M, CIDA, DIETD, DIETI, HSA, LAW, LSAR, PH, PLNG, VET

01 President .... Martha E. POLLACK
05 Provost .... Michael I. KOTLIKOFF
63 Prov Medical Affairs/Dean Med Col .... Augustine M.K CHOI
20 Deputy Provost .... John A. SILICIANO
10 Executive VP Financial Affairs/CFO .... Joanne M. DESTEFANO
46 VP for Research and Innovation .... Emmanuel P. GIANNELLIS
58 Vice Prov & Dean Grad School .... Kathryn J. BOOR
85 Vice Prov for International Affairs .... Wendy WOLFORD
20 Vice Provost .... Katherine MCCOMAS
114 Vice Pres Budget & Planning .... Laura E. SYER
29 VP Alumni Affairs/Development .... Fred VAN SICKLE
15 VP and Chief Human Resources .... Mary George OPPERMAN
32 VP Student & Campus Life .... Ryan T. LOMBARDI
26 Vice Pres for University Relations .... Joel M. MALINA
86 Associate VP for Govt Relations .... Charles KRUZANSKY
72 Dean/Vice Prov Cornell NYC Tech .... J. Gregory MORRISETT
43 VP and General Counsel .... Donica T. VARNER
13 VP & CIO for Info Technology .... David LIFKA
115 Chief Investment Officer .... Kenneth M. MIRANDA
18 VP for Facilities and Campus Svcs .... Frederick BURGESS
97 Vice Provost Undergrad Educ .... Lisa NISHI
84 Vice Provost Enrollment .... Jonathan BURDICK
21 Assoc VP and University Controller .... William SIBERT
21 Assoc Vice President/Treasurer .... Michelle BENEDICT-JONES
116 Interim University Auditor .... Steven CHADWICK
20 Dean of Faculty .... Eve DE ROSA
47 Dean Col Agriculture/Life Sciences .... Benjamin Z. HOULTON
48 Dean College Arch/Art/Planning .... J. Meejin YOON
49 Dean College Arts & Science .... Ray JAYAWARDHANA
54 Dean College of Engineering .... Lynden A. ARCHER
88 Dean School Hotel Admin .... Kate D. WALSH
59 Dean College Human Ecology .... Rachel DUNIFUN
50 Dean SC Johnson College of Business .... Mark NELSON
88 Dean Dyson School Applied Economics .... Jinhua ZHAO
50 Dean Industrial/Labor Rel .... Alexander J. COLVIN
61 Dean Law School .... Jens D. OHLIN
74 Dean College Veterinary Medicine .... Lorin D. WARNICK
77 Dean of Computing and Info Science .... Kavita BALA
51 Dean Cont Education/Summer Session .... Charles W. JERMY
50 Dean of the Weill Graduate School .... Barbara L. HEMPSTEAD
08 University Librarian .... Gerald R. BEASLEY
07 Dir Undergraduate Admissions .... Shawn FELTON
37 Director Financial Aid .... Kevin JENSEN
35 Interim Dean of Students .... Marla LOVE
06 University Registrar .... Rhonda K. KITCH
41 Director Athletics/Physical Educ .... J. Andrew NOEL, JR.
36 Interim Director of Career Svcs .... Greg FOSTER
28 Assoc Vice Prov Faculty Diversity .... Yael LEVITTE
42 Dir Cornell United Religious Works .... Oliver GOODRICH
25 Sr Director Sponsored Fin Svcs .... Jeffrey A. SILBER
19 Chief Cornell Police .... David HONAN
29 Vice Pres Alumni Affairs .... Fred VAN SICKLE
09 AVP Inst Research/Planning .... Marin E. CLARKBERG
80 Dean Johnson Grad School of Mgmt .... Andrew KAROLYI
104 Dir Office of Global Learning .... Brandon LANNERS

† Parent institution of Weill Medical College of Cornell University.

The Culinary Institute of America (G)

1946 Campus Drive, Hyde Park NY 12538-1499

County: Dutchess   FICE Identification: 007304
Unit ID: 190503
Telephone: (845) 905-4288   Carnegie Class: Spec-4-yr-Other
FAX Number: (845) 452-0165   Calendar System: Semester
URL: www.ciachef.edu
Established: 1946   Annual Undergrad Tuition & Fees: $34,650
Enrollment: 3,231   Coed
Affiliation or Control: Independent Non-Profit   IRS Status: 501(c)3
Highest Offering: Master's
Accreditation: M

01 President .... Dr. Tim RYAN
10 VP Finance and Administration .... Ms. Maria KRUPIN
111 VP Advancement .... Mr. Kevin ALLAN
05 Provost .... Mr. Mark ERICKSON
20 VP Academic Affairs .... Dr. Michael SPERLING
26 VP Mktg & Communications .... Mr. Dan VINH
45 VP Strategic Init & Industry Ldrsp .... Mr. Greg DRESCHER
32 AVP & Dean of Student Affairs .... Dr. Kathleen MERGET
12 AVP Branch Campuses .... Ms. Susan CUSSEN
84 Assoc VP Enrollment Management .... Ms. Rachel BIRCHWOOD
100 Associate VP/Chief of Staff .... Mr. Rick TIETJEN

84 Assoc VP Enrollment Mgmt ... Ms. Rachel BIRCHWOOD
35 Assistant Director Student Life ... Mr. Nathan FLINTJER
38 Director Counseling & Psych Svcs ... Ms. Mueller CHRISTIANE
09 Dir Inst Research & Effectiveness ... Ms. Betsy CARROLL
23 Director Health Services ... Ms. Margot SCHINELLA
21 Director Finance ... Mr. Steven STROM
96 Director Purchasing & Storeroom ... Mr. Gower LANE
19 Director Campus Safety ... Mr. William CAREY
37 Director Student Financial Planning ... Ms. Kathleen GAILOR
88 Dean Academic Engagement & Admin ... Ms. Carolyn TRAGNI
88 Dean School of Culinary Arts ... Mr. Brendan WALSH
49 Dean School of Lib Arts & Food Std ... Ms. Denise BAUER
108 Dir Accreditation and Assessment ... Ms. Maureen ERICKSON
06 Registrar ... Mr. Chet KOULIK
36 Director Career & Academic Advising ... Ms. Crystal DECAROLIS
08 Director Library & Information Sys ... Mr. Jon GRENNAN
15 Senior Director Human Resources ... Ms. Shay GARRIOCH
04 Executive Asst to President ... Ms. Shannon CAMPER
110 Senior Advancement Officer ... Ms. Elly ERICKSON
50 Dean School of Business & Mgmt Stds ... Ms. Annette GRAHAM
88 Acting Dean School of Cul Science ... Mr. Ted RUSSIN
88 Sr Director Faculty Relations ... Mr. Joe MORANO
88 Director Creative Services ... Ms. Terri TOTTEN
39 Assoc Dean Campus Life/Stdnt Dev ... Mr. James MANLEY
41 Asst Dir Recreation & Wellness ... Mr. Serge NALYWAYKO

Daemen College (A)

4380 Main Street, Amherst NY 14226-3592

County: Erie FICE Identification: 002808
Unit ID: 190725
Telephone: (716) 839-3600 Carnegie Class: DU-Mod
FAX Number: (716) 839-8516 Calendar System: Semester
URL: www.daemen.edu
Established: 1947 Annual Undergrad Tuition & Fees: $30,360
Enrollment: 2,536 Coed
Affiliation or Control: Independent Non-Profit IRS Status: 501(c)3
Highest Offering: Doctorate
Accreditation: M, ARCPA, CAATE, CYTO, IACBE, NUR, PTA, SW

01 President ... Dr. Gary A. OLSON
05 SVP Academic Affs/Dean of College ... Dr. Michael S. BROGAN
10 VP for Business Affairs & Treasurer ... Dr. Robert ROOD
111 VP Institutional Advancement ... Ms. Emily BURNS PERRYMAN
32 VP Student Affairs ... Dr. Greg J. NAYOR
20 Assoc VP Academic Affairs ... Ms. Doris MURPHY
21 VP for Business Affairs/Comptroller ... Ms. Lisa A. ARIDA
13 VP & Chief Information Officer ... Ms. Melaine KENYON
09 Director of Institutional Research ... Mr. Lee ALLARD
35 Dean of Students ... Ms. Kerry SPICER
108 Assoc VP of Inst Effectiveness ... Ms. Irene HOLOHAN-MOYER
08 Director of RIC & Library Service ... Ms. Melissa PETERSON
06 Registrar ... Ms. Tiffany SHADDEN
100 Chief of Staff ... Ms. Amanda R. GROSS
121 Asst Dean for Academic Advisement ... Ms. Sabrina FENNELL
37 Director of Financial Aid ... Mr. Jeffrey M. PAGANO
15 Director of Human Resources ... Ms. Tracy MASSE
26 Dir of Institutional Communications ... Mr. Daniel ROBISON
39 Dir of Housing & Residence Life ... Ms. Emilee YORMICK
35 Director of Student Activities ... Mr. Michael PAGLICCI
18 Director of Facilities ... Mr. Don PHILLIPS
19 Director of Campus Safety ... Mr. Douglas SMITH
41 Director of Athletics ... Ms. Traci MURPHY
96 Dir of Purchasing/Central Services ... Ms. Mary HARTNETT
92 Director of Honors Program ... Mr. Jay WENDLAND
29 Director Alumni Relations ... Ms. Kathryn HAMMER
40 Bookstore Manager ... Ms. Jaclyn HERNE
88 Dir of New Program Development ... Ms. Susan M. MARCHIONE
04 Admin Assoc Office of the President ... Ms. Sarah PORZUCEK
104 Director Study Abroad ... Ms. Ann ROBINSON
106 Exec Dir of Web Communications ... Mr. Thomas WOJCIECHOWSKI
38 Clinical Director of Counseling ... Ms. Danielle EADIE
84 Dean of Enrollment ... Ms. Julie ZULEWSKI

Davis College (B)

400 Riverside Drive, Johnson City NY 13790-2714

County: Broome FICE Identification: 021691
Unit ID: 194569
Telephone: (607) 729-1581 Carnegie Class: Spec-4-yr-Faith
FAX Number: (607) 729-2962 Calendar System: Semester
URL: www.davisny.edu
Established: 1900 Annual Undergrad Tuition & Fees: $17,150
Enrollment: 79 Coed
Affiliation or Control: Independent Non-Profit IRS Status: 501(c)3
Highest Offering: Baccalaureate
Accreditation: #M, BI

01 Interim President ... Dr. Doug BLANC
05 Vice Pres Academic Affairs ... Dr. George SNYDER, JR.
32 Vice Pres of Student Affairs ... Vacant
10 Financial Officer ... Mr. Larry ELLIS
04 Assistant to the President ... Ms. Naomi SARAVANAPAVAN
06 Registrar ... Ms. Naomi SARAVANAPAVAN
08 Librarian ... Mrs. Shelley BYRON
37 Director Financial Aid ... Ms. Naomi SARAVANAPAVAN
108 Dir Institutional Effectiveness ... Ms. Shelley BYRON
18 Chief Facilities/Physical Plant ... Vacant
41 Athletic Director ... Vacant
106 Dir Online Education/E-learning ... Dr. JoAnna OSTER

Dominican College of Blauvelt (C)

470 Western Highway, Orangeburg NY 10962-1210

County: Rockland FICE Identification: 002713
Unit ID: 190761
Telephone: (845) 848-7800 Carnegie Class: Masters/S
FAX Number: (845) 359-2313 Calendar System: Semester
URL: www.dc.edu
Established: 1952 Annual Undergrad Tuition & Fees: $30,720
Enrollment: 1,724 Coed
Affiliation or Control: Independent Non-Profit IRS Status: 501(c)3
Highest Offering: Doctorate
Accreditation: M, IACBE, NURSE, OT, PTA, SW

01 President ... Sr Dr. Mary Eileen O'BRIEN
00 Chancellor ... Sr. Kathleen SULLIVAN
05 Vice Pres/Dean Academic Affairs ... Dr. Thomas S. NOWAK
84 Vice Pres of Enrollment Management ... Mr. Brian FERNANDES
32 Dean of Students ... Mr. John BURKE
10 Director of Fiscal Affairs ... Mr. Anthony CIPOLLA
06 Registrar ... Ms. Mary MCFADDEN
07 Director of Admissions ... Mr. Douglas MCNABB
08 Head Librarian ... Ms. Mary-Elizabeth SCHAUB
111 Director of Inst Advancement ... Mr. Joseph VALENTI
15 Director Human Resources ... Ms. Marybeth BRODERICK
26 Chief Public Relations Officer ... Ms. Susan CERRA
29 Director Alumni Relations ... Ms. Mary MCHUGH
35 Director Student Activities ... Ms. Rachel MCGINTY
09 Inst Research/Plng/Assessment Ofcr ... Mr. Fredric COHEN
37 Director Student Financial Aid ... Ms. Stacy SALINAS
36 Director Student Placement ... Ms. Evelyn FISKAA
38 Director Student Counseling ... Ms. Alise COHEN
21 Controller ... Mr. Kenneth FLUG
13 Director Information Technology ... Mr. Russell DIAZ
18 Chief Facilities/Physical Plant ... Mr. Agron GASHI
20 Associate Academic Officer ... Vacant
39 Director Student Housing ... Mr. Joseph DRATCH
41 Athletic Director ... Mr. Joseph CLINTON
42 Director Campus Ministry ... Sr. Barbara MCENEANY
96 Director of Purchasing ... Mr. Peter PABON
28 Director of Diversity ... Vacant
19 Director of Security/Safety ... Mr. John LENNON
42 Chaplain ... Vacant
31 Dir Cmty Engagemt/Ldrship Devel ... Ms. Kathryn STROBEL

Dutchess Community College (D)

53 Pendell Road, Poughkeepsie NY 12601-1595

County: Dutchess FICE Identification: 002864
Unit ID: 190840
Telephone: (845) 431-8000 Carnegie Class: Assoc/HT-Mix Trad/Non
FAX Number: (845) 431-8984 Calendar System: Semester
URL: www.sunydutchess.edu
Established: 1957 Annual Undergrad Tuition & Fees (In-District): $4,896
Enrollment: 8,034 Coed
Affiliation or Control: State/Local IRS Status: 501(c)3
Highest Offering: Associate Degree
Accreditation: M, ADNUR, EMT, MLTAD

01 President ... Dr. Peter G. JORDAN
32 Dean of Student Services ... Dr. Colleen M. TROGISCH
10 VP & Dean of Administration ... Dr. Ellen M. GAMBINO
05 Dean of Academic Affairs ... Ms. Maria F. BOADA
20 Associate Dean of Academic Affairs ... Dr. Susan ROGERS
20 Acting Assoc Dean of Academic Affs ... Dr. Angela L. RIOS
31 Assoc VP & Dean Comm Svcs Spec Pgms ... Vacant
21 Associate VP Administration ... Ms. Donna ROCAP
06 Registrar ... Ms. Angela ROMANO
84 Assoc Dean Stdnt Svcs/Enrollment ... Mr. Michael ROE
08 Director of the Library ... Ms. Bonnie GALLAGHER
111 Exec Dir Institutional Advancement ... Ms. Diana POLLARD
09 Director Planning/Inst Research ... Mr. Scott SCHNACKENBERG
37 Director Financial Aid ... Mr. Robert ZASSO
38 Director Counseling ... Dr. Mark BALABAN
15 Interim Director of Human Resources ... Ms. Ruth SPENCER
18 Assoc VP of Admin Facilities Mgmt ... Ms. Bridgette ANDERSON
19 Chief of Campus Safety & Security ... Ms. Nilda HOFFMAN
13 Acting Assoc Dean Admin Info Tech ... Mr. Michael SOLTISH
35 Director of Student Life ... Vacant
26 Director of Marketing/Social Media ... Ms. Gail GLOVER
106 Dir of Instrctional Tech/e-Learning ... Ms. Chrisie MITCHELL
88 Director of Scheduling ... Ms. Danielle WILLIAMS
12 Director DCC Fishkill Branch ... Mr. Timothy DECKER
04 Exec Assistant to the President ... Ms. AnneMarie ANDREWS
101 Exec Asst to the Board of Trustees ... Ms. Linda M. BEASIMER
39 Director Residence Life ... Ms. Kaitlin YOUNG
25 Chief Contract/Grants Administrator ... Mr. Martin SCHNEIDER
28 Chief Diversity Officer ... Ms. Jackie GOFFE-MCNISH
96 Director of Purchasing ... Mr. Thomas DUFFY

D'Youville College (E)

320 Porter Avenue, Buffalo NY 14201-1084

County: Erie FICE Identification: 002712
Unit ID: 190716
Telephone: (716) 829-8000 Carnegie Class: DU-Mod
FAX Number: (716) 829-7820 Calendar System: Semester
URL: www.dyc.edu
Established: 1908 Annual Undergrad Tuition & Fees: $28,886
Enrollment: 2,785 Coed
Affiliation or Control: Independent Non-Profit IRS Status: 501(c)3
Highest Offering: Doctorate
Accreditation: M, ARCPA, CHIRO, DIETC, IACBE, NURSE, OT, PHAR, PTA

01 President ... Dr. Lorrie CLEMO
05 VP for Academic Affairs ... Dr. Natalia BLANK
10 Chief Financial Officer ... Ms. Karen COSTA
45 VP for Inst Effectiv & Planning ... Mr. Joggeshwar DAS
84 VP Enrollment Mgmt/Student Life ... Ms. Ona HALLADAY
18 VP of Operations ... Mr. Nathan MARTON
111 VP of Institutional Advancement ... Ms. Kimberly PIETRO
88 VP for Mission Integration ... Mr. Nathan MARTON
66 Dean School of Nursing ... Dr. Deborah GARRISON
32 Chief Student Affairs Officer ... Mr. Benjamin GRANT
67 Dean School of Pharmacy ... Dr. Canio MARASCO
76 Dean School of Health Professions ... Dr. Lisa RAFALSON
106 Dean of Online Learning ... Dr. Jeremiah GRABOWSKI
35 Assistant VP for Student Life ... Mr. Anthony SPINA
114 Dir of Budgets/Planning and Assess ... Mr. John CIPOLLITTI
88 Executive Director Kavinoky Theatre ... Ms. Loraine O'DONNELL
13 Director Information Technology ... Mr. Joseph GUNNELLS
06 Registrar ... Mr. Daryl SMITH
113 Bursar ... Ms. Andrea ADDISON
09 Director Inst Rsrch/Assess Support ... Dr. Henry BOATENG
108 Assistant Dean of Assessment ... Mr. Salvatore D'AMATO
91 Director Administrative Computing ... Mr. Robert HALL
44 Director Annual Giving ... Ms. LeeAnn PETRONSKY
41 Director Athletics ... Ms. Ona HALLADAY
36 Director Career Services Center ... Ms. Christine DEMCIE
15 Director of Human Resources ... Ms. Tammy MASTON
88 Dir of HEOP & Transfer Services ... Ms. Christina SPINK-FORMANSKI
08 Director of the Library ... Mr. Rand BELLAVIA
28 Chief Diversity Officer ... Dr. Rachel ERSING
38 Interim Dir Mental Hlth Counselor ... Ms. Juanita GREEN-JOHNSON
26 Dir of Marketing and Brand Mgmt ... Ms. Sarah SIGNORELLI
19 Director Security ... Mr. Keith BOVA
37 Director Student Financial Aid ... Ms. Nitasha SETH
88 Director of Veteran Affairs ... Mr. Mark MARTINEZ
88 Director CRPASH ... Dr. Renee CADZOW
88 Director Ctr Health Behav Rsrch ... Dr. Brian WROTNIAK
88 Dir of Int Affs VA & Mil Rsrch Ctr ... Dr. Bonnie FOX-GARRITY
88 Dir of Ext Aff VA & Mil Rsrch Ctr ... Dr. Dion DALY
96 Director of Purchasing ... Ms. Tammy DISTEFANO

Elim Bible Institute and College (F)

7245 College Street, Lima NY 14485

County: Livingston Identification: 667245
Unit ID: 488305
Telephone: (585) 582-1230 Carnegie Class: Spec 2-yr-Other
FAX Number: (585) 582-8130 Calendar System: Semester
URL: www.elim.edu
Established: 1924 Annual Undergrad Tuition & Fees: $9,980
Enrollment: 103 Coed
Affiliation or Control: Independent Non-Profit IRS Status: 501(c)3
Highest Offering: Baccalaureate
Accreditation: TRACS

01 President ... Dr. Fred ANTONELLI
03 Executive Vice President & Provost ... Danuta CASE
32 Dean of Students ... Stacy CLINE
10 Chief Financial Officer ... Mary Lynne KNILEY
07 Associate Admissions Director ... Krista VANN
73 Program Chair ... John MILLER
35 Campus Life Director ... Emily SANDERS
06 Registrar ... Cana FUEST
26 Marketing Director ... Leah WILSON

The Elmezzi Graduate School of Molecular Medicine (G)

350 Community Drive, Manhasset NY 11030-3828

County: Nassau Identification: 666671
Unit ID: 486080
Telephone: (516) 562-3405 Carnegie Class: Spec-4-yr-Other Health
FAX Number: (516) 562-1022 Calendar System: Other
URL: https://www.northwell.edu/
Established: 1999 Annual Graduate Tuition & Fees: N/A
Enrollment: 9 Coed
Affiliation or Control: Independent Non-Profit IRS Status: 501(c)3
Highest Offering: Doctorate; No Undergraduates
Accreditation: NY

01 President ... Dr. Kevin J. TRACEY
03 Provost ... Dr. Bettie M. STEINBERG
05 Dean ... Dr. Annette LEE
20 Associate Dean ... Dr. Christine METZ
10 Chief Financial Officer ... Ms. Michele FRANKEL
11 Chief of Administration ... Ms. Emilia HRISTIS
19 Director Security/Safety ... Mr. Robert KIKEL
25 Director Contracts/Grants Admin ... Ms. Diane MARBURY

Elmira College (H)

One Park Place, Elmira NY 14901-2099

County: Chemung FICE Identification: 002718
Unit ID: 190983
Telephone: (607) 735-1800 Carnegie Class: Bac-Diverse
FAX Number: (607) 735-1758 Calendar System: Other
URL: www.elmira.edu
Established: 1855 Annual Undergrad Tuition & Fees: $36,228
Enrollment: 768 Coed
Affiliation or Control: Independent Non-Profit IRS Status: 501(c)3
Highest Offering: Master's

Accreditation: M, NUR

01 President .... Dr. Charles W. LINDSAY
10 VP of Finance and Administration .... Mr. C. Edward ASHLEY
05 Provost .... Dr. Patricia IRELAND
30 Vice Pres of External Relations .... Mr. Michael B. ROGERS
32 VP Campus Life/Chief Retention Ofcr .... Dr. Elizabeth LAMBERT
09 VP of IR/Planning & Assessment .... Vacant
26 VP of Communications & Marketing .... Ms. Jennifer L. SWAIN
20 Dean of Academic Affairs .... Dr. Lynn L. GILLIE
37 Director of Financial Aid .... Mrs. Lorraine MOTHERSHED
06 Registrar .... Mr. Michael HALPERIN
51 Director of Prof & Continuing Educ .... Mr. Alan YECK
08 Dir of the Gannett-Tripp Library .... Ms. Margaret KAPPANADZE
41 AVP of Athletics .... Ms. Renee CARLINEO
36 Director of Career Services .... Ms. Brenna WESTON
50 Chair of Business/Economics .... Dr. Mariam KHAWAR
79 Chair of Creative Arts/Humanities .... Dr. Mitchell R. LEWIS
81 Chair of Math/Natural Sciences .... Dr. Daniel KJAR
83 Chair of Soc/Behavioral Science .... Dr. Christopher TERRY
53 Chair of Teacher Ed/Dir of Grad Ed .... Dr. Deborah D. OWENS
88 Dir of Comm Sciences/Disorders .... Prof. Cathy M. THORNTON
66 Director of Nurse Education .... Dr. Milissa VOLINO
29 Director of Alumni Relations .... Ms. Ellen HIMMELREICH
39 Director of Residence Life .... Mr. Nathan FRIESEMA
40 Dir of Bookstore & Special Projects .... Ms. Shannon MOYLAN
15 Director of Human Resources .... Ms. Jessica CARPENTER
13 Chief Information Officer .... Vacant
19 Director of Campus Safety .... Mr. Steve VANN
112 Director of Major and Planned Gifts .... Ms. Adriana GIANCOLI
44 Director of Annual Giving .... Vacant
102 Director of Grants .... Mrs. Valerie R. ROSPLOCK
23 Director of Health Services .... Mrs. Wendy FISCUS
04 Exec Assistant to the President .... Mrs. Mary C. BARRETT
38 Assoc Dean of Students .... Dr. Kevin MURPHY
90 Director of User Services .... Ms. Kim WIEHE
96 Purchasing Coordinator .... Ms. Kathy KNAPP

Elyon College (A)

1400 West 6th Street, Brooklyn NY 11204
County: Kings — Identification: 667290
Unit ID: 490346
Telephone: (718) 259-5600 — Carnegie Class: Spec 2-yr-Other
FAX Number: (218) 259-8024 — Calendar System: Trimester
URL: elyoncollege.org
Established: — Annual Undergrad Tuition & Fees: $14,020
Enrollment: 47 — Coed
Affiliation or Control: Independent Non-Profit — IRS Status: 501(c)3
Highest Offering: Associate Degree
Accreditation: CNCE

01 President .... Rabbi Chaim A. WALDMAN
05 Dean Academic &Student Affairs .... Rabbi Samuel KOHN

Erie Community College (B)

121 Ellicott Street, Buffalo NY 14203-2698
County: Erie — FICE Identification: 010684
Unit ID: 191083
Telephone: (716) 842-2770 — Carnegie Class: Assoc/MT-VT-High Non
FAX Number: (716) 851-1129 — Calendar System: Semester
URL: www.ecc.edu
Established: 1971 — Annual Undergrad Tuition & Fees (In-District): $5,722
Enrollment: 8,364 — Coed
Affiliation or Control: State/Local — IRS Status: 501(c)3
Highest Offering: Associate Degree
Accreditation: M, ACFEI, ADNUR, CAHIIM, COARC, DH, DIETT, DT, EMT, MAC, MLTAD, OPD, OTA, RTT

01 Interim President .... Mr. William REUTER
111 EVP Inst Advancement & Efficiency .... Vacant
11 EVP Administration & Finance .... Vacant
05 Int Provost/EVP Academic Affs .... Dr. Adiam TSEGAI
84 Vice President Enrollment Mgmt .... Vacant
32 VP Student Affairs .... Vacant
35 Dean of Students City .... Ms. Petrina HILL-CHEATOM
35 Dean of Students North .... Mr. Jason PERRI
35 Dean of Students South .... Ms. Amy YODER
13 Interim Chief Information Officer .... Mr. Scott ERMER
76 Vice Provost Health Sciences .... Vacant
14 Director of ERP Sys & Info Svcs .... Mr. David L. ARLINGTON
18 Vice President Facilities/Security .... Mr. Mark PACHOLEC
109 Coordinator Institutional Services .... Mr. Joel J. DAMIANI
15 Associate Vice Pres Human Resources .... Ms. Tracey CLEVELAND
16 Employee Relations Manager .... Vacant
49 Dean Liberal Arts & Science North .... Vacant
49 Dean Liberal Arts & Science South .... Ms. Joanne COLMERAUER
50 Dean Business/Public Service .... Mr. Juan MARTINEZ
56 Dir Dist Learning/Alternative Pgms .... Mr. Patrick RYAN
72 Dean Engineering/Technology .... Ms. Adiam TSEGAI
28 Chief Diversity Officer .... Ms. Tracey ARCHIE
06 Director of Registration .... Vacant
07 Director of Admissions .... Mr. Philip STRUEBEL
08 Librarian City .... Ms. Kathleen POWERS
08 Librarian North .... Mr. Matthew BEST
08 Librarian South .... Ms. Taheera SHAHEED-SONUBI
40 Bookstore Manager City .... Ms. Susan SCHMITTENDORF
40 Bookstore Manager North .... Ms. Teresa KALINOWSKI
40 Bookstore Manager South .... Mr. Michael FOX
23 Health Services Nurse South .... Ms. Frances WILLIAMS
23 Health Services Nurse North .... Ms. Lisa GRAZIANO
23 Health Services Nurse City .... Ms. Kelly ROCKWELL
36 Career Resource Center Director .... Ms. Katherine MARSHALL
09 Director Institutional Research .... Ms. Marlene ARNO
45 Vice Provost .... Dr. Fabio ESCOBAR
27 Exec Dir of Marketing/Communication .... Ms. Paula SANDY
41 Director of Athletics .... Mr. Steven MULLEN
37 Director of Financial Aid .... Mr. Scott WELTJEN
21 Business Manager .... Mr. Paul F. DANIEU
24 Audio Visual Coordinator City .... Mr. Mark DZIELSKI
24 Audio Visual Coordinator North .... Mr. Ryan NOGLE
24 Audio Visual Coordinator North .... Mr. Nicholas SONRICKER
24 Audio Visual Coordinator South .... Mr. David SEIFERT
103 Coordinator of Corporate Training .... Vacant
25 Grants Coordinator .... Mr. Michael J. BIGGANE
29 Coordinator of Alumni Affairs .... Ms. Sarah LASKY
22 Dir of Student Access/Veteran Affs .... Mr. Daniel FRONTERA
88 Advanced Studies Coordinator .... Ms. Deborah F. SCHMITT

Excelsior College (C)

7 Columbia Circle, Albany NY 12203-5159
County: Albany — FICE Identification: 002834
Unit ID: 196680
Telephone: (518) 464-8500 — Carnegie Class: Masters/L
FAX Number: (518) 464-8777 — Calendar System: Other
URL: www.excelsior.edu
Established: 1971 — Annual Undergrad Tuition & Fees: N/A
Enrollment: 21,974 — Coed
Affiliation or Control: Independent Non-Profit — IRS Status: 501(c)3
Highest Offering: Master's
Accreditation: M, ADNUR, IACBE, NUR

01 President .... Dr. David SCHEJBAL
43 Deputy Counsel .... Mr. Michael DISIENA
05 Provost/VP Academic Affairs .... Dr. John CARON
10 VP Finance/CFO .... Mr. Richard HANNMANN
11 Chief Operating Officer .... Mr. James LETTKO
117 Exec Dir of Risk Management .... Ms. Holly ROGERS
13 Chief Technology Officer .... Mr. Saul MORSE
15 VP Human Resources .... Mr. Mark HOWE
46 AVP Analytics/Decision Support .... Dr. Lisa DANIELS
108 Exec Dir Outcomes Assessment .... Mr. Andre FOISY
21 Controller .... Ms. Hillary KOLDIN
97 Dean of Undergraduate Studies .... Dr. Catherine SEAVER
66 Dean of Nursing .... Dr. Mary Lee POLLARD
58 Dean of Graduate Studies .... Dr. Scott DOLAN
88 Ombudsperson .... Ms. Kathy MORAN
88 Exec Dir of Test Development .... Ms. Mika HOFFMAN
26 Chief Marketing/Bus Dev Officer .... Ms. Dawn GERRAIN
91 Deputy CIO of Enterprise Systems .... Mr. Donn AIKEN
88 Exec Dir Enterprise Ops .... Mr. Dan MERKT
88 Director of Creative Services .... Ms. Maria SPARKS
28 Diversity Coordinator .... Ms. Toby HAMLIN
37 Exec Dir Financial Aid .... Ms. Susan MERCHANT
14 Chief Operations Officer for IT .... Ms. Andrea LALA
88 Exec Dir of Enterprise Apps Support .... Mr. Jim WALL
88 Exec Director Transcript Analysis .... Ms. Kat MCGRATH
07 Exec Director of Admissions .... Ms. Patti HOEG
101 Asst to Pres for Trustee .... Ms. Laurie KEENAN

Fashion Institute of Technology (D)

Seventh Avenue at 27 Street, New York NY 10001-5992
County: New York — FICE Identification: 002866
Unit ID: 191126
Telephone: (212) 217-7999 — Carnegie Class: Masters/S
FAX Number: N/A — Calendar System: Semester
URL: www.fitnyc.edu
Established: 1944 — Annual Undergrad Tuition & Fees (In-District): $5,913
Enrollment: 8,191 — Coed
Affiliation or Control: State/Local — IRS Status: 501(c)3
Highest Offering: Master's
Accreditation: M, ACBSP, ART, CIDA

01 President .... Dr. Joyce F. BROWN
10 Treasurer/VP Finance/Administration .... Ms. Sherry F. BRABHAM
101 Secy of College/General Counsel .... Mr. Stephen P. TUTTLE
05 Interim Vice Pres, Academic Affairs .... Dr. Yasemin JONES
26 Vice Pres Comm/External Rels .... Ms. Loretta LAWRENCE KEANE
84 VP Enrollment/Student Success .... Ms. Catherine O'ROURKE
15 VP Human Res Mgmt/Labor Rels .... Dr. Cynthia M. GLASS
30 VP Advancement/Exec Dir FIT Fdn .... Mr. Philips R. MCCARTY
13 Acting VP of Information Technology .... Mr. Laurence A. BAACH
88 Deputy to Pres Industry/Partnership .... Ms. Joanne ARBUCKLE
100 Deputy to the President .... Ms. Jennifer LOTURCO
28 Chief Diversity Officer .... Dr. Ronald A. MILON
45 Acting Exec Dir Strategic Planning .... Ms. Jacqueline JENKINS
88 Associate General Counsel .... Mr. Eric ODIN
20 Assoc VP, Acad Affairs Operations .... Mr. Sidney A. GRIMES
20 Interim Assoc VP Academic Affairs .... Dr. Deborah KLESENSKI-RISPOLI
21 Assoc Vice Pres, Finance & Admin .... Mr. Bayard KING
27 Assistant VP Comm/External Rels .... Ms. Carol LEVEN
14 AVP Business Intelligence .... Doris BERGER
88 Asst VP Enrollment Management .... Mr. Terence PEAVY
32 Asst VP Student Success/Dean Stdnts .... Dr. Shadia A. SACHEDINA
119 AVP & Chief Info Security Officer .... Mr. Walter KERNER
58 Interim Dean, Graduate Studies .... Dr. Brooke CARLSON
50 Dean School Business & Technology .... Ms. Shannon MAHER
49 Dean School of Liberal Arts .... Dr. Patrick KNISLEY
104 Dean for International Education .... Dr. Deirdre C. SATO
51 Exec Dir Continuing & Prof Studies .... Mr. Daniel GERGER
57 Dean School of Art & Design .... Mr. Troy RICHARDS
121 Assoc Dean Student Acad Support .... Dr. Tardis JOHNSON
88 Acting Associate Dean Art & Design .... Ms. Melanie REIM
09 Asst Dean Inst Research & Effect .... Dr. Darrell GLENN
20 Asst Dean Curriculum & Instruction .... Ms. Deborah KLESENSKI-RISPOLI
35 Assistant Dean of Students .... Ms. Suzanne MCGILLICUDDY
88 Assistant Dean for International Ed .... Dr. Helen GAUDETTE
08 Acting Director G Marcus Library .... Ms. Greta EARNEST
88 Director of The Museum at FIT .... Dr. Valerie STEELE
88 Exec Dir FIT/Infor DTech Lab .... Mr. Michael FERRARO
18 Executive Director of Facilities .... Mr. George JEFREMOW
108 Exec Dir Management Analysis .... Mr. Joseph IANNINI
07 Director of Admissions .... Mr. Richard S. SUNDAY
22 Affirmative Action Officer .... Ms. Deliwe KEKANE
38 Director Counseling Center .... Dr. Susan BRETON
39 Director of Residential Life .... Ms. Christina DIGGS
37 Acting Director of Financial Aid .... Mr. Barry FISCHER
06 Director of Registration & Records .... Ms. Rita CAMMARATA
36 Director Career & Internship Svcs .... Mr. Frantz L. ALCINDOR
35 Director of Student Life .... Ms. Michelle VAN-ESS
19 Director of Public Safety .... Mr. Mario CABRERA
86 Director Govt & Community Relations .... Ms. Lisa WAGER
41 Director Athletics & Recreation .... Mr. Keith HERON
96 Director of Budget .... Ms. Nancy SU
88 Dir of Educational Opportunity Pgms .... Ms. Taur D. ORANGE
21 Controller .... Ms. Shelci GRAHAM
88 Dir Envir Health/Safety Compliance .... Mr. Paul DEBIASE
29 Dir Alumni Engagement/Giving/Fndn .... Ms. Amy GARAWITZ
105 Manager Digital Strategy .... Ms. Taryn REJHOLEC
55 Dir Evening/Weekend/Pre-College Pgm .... Ms. Michele NAGEL
96 Director of Procurement Services .... Mr. Walter WINTER
85 Acting Director, Intl Student Svcs .... Ms. Marie MEKARI
90 Director Educ Tech/Desktop Svcs .... Ms. Meredith PERKINS
106 Director Online Learning .... Ms. Tamara CUPPLES
16 Director, Employee & Labor Relns .... Ms. Esther OLIVERAS
92 Exec Dir President'l Scholars Pgm .... Ms. Yasemin C. LEVINE
88 Director of Policy and Compliance .... Ms. Griselda GONZALEZ
116 Internal Auditor .... Mr. Harold LEDERMAN
04 Assistant to the President .... Ms. Beverly SOLOCHEK
04 Special Assistant to the President .... Ms. Alin BABASOLOUKIAN

Fei Tian College (E)

140 Galley Hill Road, Cuddebackville NY 12729
County: Orange — Identification: 667205
Telephone: (845) 672-0550 — Carnegie Class: Not Classified
FAX Number: (845) 977-0481 — Calendar System: Semester
URL: www.feitian.edu
Established: — Annual Undergrad Tuition & Fees: N/A
Enrollment: N/A — Coed
Affiliation or Control: Independent Non-Profit — IRS Status: 501(c)3
Highest Offering: Baccalaureate
Accreditation: NY

01 President .... Ms. Vina LEE

Finger Lakes Community College (F)

3325 Marvin Sands Drive, Canandaigua NY 14424-8405
County: Ontario — FICE Identification: 007532
Unit ID: 191199
Telephone: (585) 394-3522 — Carnegie Class: Assoc/HT-High Non
FAX Number: (585) 394-5005 — Calendar System: Semester
URL: www.flcc.edu
Established: 1965 — Annual Undergrad Tuition & Fees (In-District): $5,534
Enrollment: 5,640 — Coed
Affiliation or Control: State/Local — IRS Status: 501(c)3
Highest Offering: Associate Degree
Accreditation: M, ADNUR

01 President .... Dr. Robert NYE
05 Provost/VP Academic & Student Affs .... Mr. Jonathan M. KEISER
10 Vice President of Admin/Finance .... Mr. Adam RATHBUN
84 Vice Pres Enrollment Management .... Ms. Carol S. URBAITIS
32 Assoc Vice Pres of Student Affairs .... Ms. Sarah WHIFFEN
108 VP Strategic Init/Assessment .... Ms. Debora ORTLOFF
20 Assoc VP Instruction & Assessment .... Dr. Cassy KENT
15 Chief Human Resources Officer .... Ms. Michelle POLOWCHAK
111 Chief Advancement Officer .... Mr. Louis NOCE
19 Dir Campus Security Ops/Act Chf Pol .... Mr. Derrick SMITH
21 Controller .... Ms. Christine PALACE-NEININGER
18 Director of Facilities & Grounds .... Ms. Catherine AHERN
07 Director of Admissions .... Mr. Matthew STEVER
06 Registrar/AVP Enrollment Mgmt .... Mr. Michael FISHER
37 Director of Financial Aid .... Ms. Megan KENNERKNECHT
35 Director of Student Life .... Ms. Jennie ERDLE
13 Chief Information Officer .... Mr. John TAYLOR
38 Dir Educ Planning/Career Services .... Ms. Tomas GONZALEZ
36 Career Services Coordinator .... Ms. Tammie WOODY
08 Director Library Learning Resources .... Ms. Sarah MOON
26 Director of Marketing .... Ms. Christen ACCARDI
23 Director of Student Health Services .... Ms. Janette ARUCK
24 Dir Instructional Technology .... Vacant
29 Director of Alumni Relations .... Ms. Lisa L. SCOTT
72 Chair Science & Technology .... Ms. Jennifer CARNEY
50 Interim Chair Business .... Mr. Gary SLOAN
65 Chair Environment Conservation Hort .... Mr. John FOUST
57 Chair Visual/Performing Arts .... Ms. Catherine JOHNSON
66 Chair Nursing .... Ms. Mary CORIALE
68 Chair Physical Education .... Mr. Eric MARSH
81 Chair Computer Science .... Mr. William MCLAUGHLIN
79 Chair Humanities .... Ms. Maureen MASS-FEARY
83 Chair Social Science .... Mr. Joshua W. HELLER

81 Chair Mathematics ..... Ms. Theresa GAUTHIER
09 Director of Institutional Research ..... Ms. Debora ORTLOFF
103 Director Workforce Development ..... Mr. Todd SLOANE
106 Director of Online Learning ..... Mr. Ryan MCCABE
28 Chief Diversity Officer ..... Mr. Sim COVINGTON
04 Admin Assistant to the President ..... Ms. Penny HAMILTON
30 Director of Development ..... Ms. Brie CHUPALIO
41 Athletic Director ..... Ms. Samantha BOCCACINO

Finger Lakes Health College of Nursing and Health Sciences (A)

196 North Street, Geneva NY 14456
County: Ontario — Identification: 667154
Unit ID: 475422
Telephone: (315) 787-4005 — Carnegie Class: Spec 2-yr-Health
FAX Number: (313) 787-4275 — Calendar System: Semester
URL: www.flhcon.edu
Established: 2008 — Annual Undergrad Tuition & Fees: $12,690
Enrollment: 115 — Coed
Affiliation or Control: Independent Non-Profit — IRS Status: 501(c)3
Highest Offering: Associate Degree
Accreditation: ABHES, ADNUR, PNUR

01 Interim Dean ..... Kathy MILLS
32 Student Services Coordinator ..... Ann SPAYD

Five Towns College (B)

305 North Service Road, Dix Hills NY 11746-6055
County: Suffolk — FICE Identification: 012561
Unit ID: 191205
Telephone: (631) 656-2157 — Carnegie Class: Bac-Diverse
FAX Number: (631) 656-2172 — Calendar System: Semester
URL: www.ftc.edu
Established: 1972 — Annual Undergrad Tuition & Fees: $25,595
Enrollment: 632 — Coed
Affiliation or Control: Proprietary — IRS Status: Proprietary
Highest Offering: Doctorate
Accreditation: M, CAEPN, MUS, THEA

01 President ..... Dr. David COHEN
05 Provost ..... Ms. Carolann MILLER
10 Vice Pres Finance/Administration ..... Mr. Hubert STACHURA
32 Dean of Students ..... Ms. Angela JASUR
06 Registrar ..... Mr. Eric FARAHANI
37 Director of Financial Aid ..... Mr. Jason LABONTE
08 Library Director ..... Mr. John VANSTEEN
38 College Counselor ..... Mr. Randy GEIBEL
64 Chair of Music Division ..... Dr. Jill MILLER-THORN
50 Chair of Business Division ..... Ms. Kate KIMMEL
49 Chair of Liberal Arts Division ..... Dr. Jennifer DARDZINSKI
53 Chair of Music Education Department ..... Dr. Margaret THIELE
57 Chair of Theatre Arts ..... Dr. David KRASNER
36 Director Student Placement ..... Ms. Krysti O'ROURKE
18 Interim Director of Facilities ..... Mr. Russell ROXBURGH
19 Interim Director of Public Safety ..... Mr. Brandon MORAN
39 Director of Residential Life ..... Mr. Thomas O'BOYLE
07 Interim Director of Admissions ..... Ms. Maureen WALTON
09 Director of Institutional Research ..... Dr. Joshua DINSMAN
13 Chief Information Technology Office ..... Mr. Craig HEALY
41 Athletic Director ..... Mr. Matthew GUERCIO

Fordham University (C)

441 East Fordham Road, Bronx NY 10458-9993
County: Bronx — FICE Identification: 002722
Unit ID: 191241
Telephone: (718) 817-1000 — Carnegie Class: DU-Higher
FAX Number: (718) 817-4925 — Calendar System: Semester
URL: www.fordham.edu
Established: 1841 — Annual Undergrad Tuition & Fees: $56,161
Enrollment: 16,364 — Coed
Affiliation or Control: Independent Non-Profit — IRS Status: 501(c)3
Highest Offering: Doctorate
Accreditation: M, CAEPN, CLPSY, COPSY, LAW, MPCAC, SCPSY, SW

01 President ..... Rev. Joseph M. MCSHANE, S.J.
100 Assoc VP Pres Operations ..... Mrs. Dorothy MARINUCCI
04 Asst Univ Sec/Spec Asst to Pres ..... Mr. Michael R. TREROTOLA
05 Provost/SVP ..... Dr. Dennis C. JACOBS
10 SVP/CFO and Treasurer ..... Ms. Martha K. HIRST
32 Sr Vice President Student Affairs ..... Mr. Jeffrey L. GRAY
84 Sr Vice President for Enrollment ..... Dr. Peter A. STACE
21 Vice President for Finance ..... Mr. Nicholas B. MILOWSKI
13 Vice President and CIO ..... Mr. Anand PADMANABHAN
12 Vice President for Lincoln Center ..... Mr. Frank SIMIO
30 Vice President for Development ..... Mr. Roger A. MILICI, JR.
88 Vice President for Mission ..... Rev. John CECERO, S.J.
11 Vice President for Administration ..... Mr. Marco VALERA
15 Vice President for HR ..... Ms. Kay TURNER
43 General Counsel/Sec of University ..... Ms. Margaret T. BALL
20 Vice Provost ..... Dr. Jonathan CRYSTAL
20 Assoc Vice Pres Academic Affairs ..... Dr. Benjamin CROOKER
20 Assoc Vice Pres Academic Affairs ..... Dr. Ellen FAHEY-SMITH
28 CDO/AVP Academic Affairs ..... Mr. Rafael ZAPATA
20 Assoc Vice Pres Academic Affairs ..... Dr. Ron JACOBSON
29 AVP/Director of Alumni Relations ..... Mr. Michael GRIFFIN
37 Vice Pres Financial Aid/Admission ..... Mr. John W. BUCKLEY
06 Asst Vice Pres Enrollment/Registrar ..... Dr. Gene FEIN
86 Assoc Vice Pres for Government Rels ..... Ms. Lesley A. MASSIAH-ARTHUR
35 Assoc VP Student Affairs ..... Ms. Michele BURRIS
35 Asst VP and Dean of Students ..... Mr. Christopher RODGERS
35 Asst VP/Dean of Student Services ..... Mr. Keith ELDREDGE
35 Dean of Students LC ..... Dr. Jenifer CAMPBELL
12 Dean Fordham College at Rose Hill ..... Dr. Maura B. MAST
49 AVP Arts & Sci Educ/Dean A&S Fac ..... Dr. Eva BADOWSKA
58 Dean Grad Arts and Sciences ..... Dr. Tyler STOVALL
73 Dean Graduate Religious Education ..... Rev. Faustino M. CRUZ
50 Dean Gabelli School of Business ..... Dr. Donna RAPACCIOLI
107 Dean Sch of Prof and Cont Studies ..... Dr. Anthony R. DAVIDSON
12 Dean Fordham College LC ..... Dr. Laura AURICCHIO
53 Dean Graduate Education LC ..... Dr. Jose Luis ALVARADO
61 Dean School of Law LC ..... Mr. Matthew DILLER
70 Dean Graduate Social Service LC ..... Dr. Debra MCPHEE
09 Director Institutional Research ..... Dr. Peter FEIGENBAUM
42 Executive Director Campus Ministry ..... Rev. Jose-Luis SALAZAR, S.J.
21 Assoc Vice Pres/Controller ..... Mr. Anthony GRONO
19 AVP Public Safety ..... Mr. John CARROLL
22 Title IX Coordinator ..... Mr. Kareem PEAT
46 Chief Research Officer/AVP ..... Dr. Z. George HONG
08 Director of University Libraries ..... Ms. Linda LOSCHIAVO
23 Director of Health Center ..... Ms. Maureen KEOWN
88 Asst Dean Student Involvement ..... Mr. Cody ARCURI
88 AVP of Athletic Alumni Relations ..... Mr. Francis X. MCLAUGHLIN
96 Director of Strategic Sourcing ..... Ms. Diana LULGJURAJ
38 Director of Psychological Svcs ..... Dr. Jeffrey NG
28 Asst Dean/Dir Multicultural Affairs ..... Mr. Juan Carlos MATOS
36 Director Career Services ..... Ms. Annette MCLAUGHLIN
39 Asst Dean/Dir Residential Life ..... Vacant
07 Dean of Admission ..... Dr. Patricia PEEK
41 Interim Athletic Director ..... Mr. Edward KULL
26 Asst VP Communications ..... Mr. Bob HOWE

Fulton-Montgomery Community College (D)

2805 State Highway 67, Johnstown NY 12095-3790
County: Montgomery — FICE Identification: 002867
Unit ID: 191302
Telephone: (518) 736-3622 — Carnegie Class: Assoc/HT-High Trad
FAX Number: (518) 762-5693 — Calendar System: Semester
URL: www.fmcc.edu
Established: 1963 — Annual Undergrad Tuition & Fees (In-District): $5,718
Enrollment: 1,946 — Coed
Affiliation or Control: State/Local — IRS Status: 501(c)3
Highest Offering: Associate Degree
Accreditation: M, ADNUR, RAD

01 President ..... Dr. Greg TRUCKENMILLER
05 Provost/Vice Pres Academic Affairs ..... Ms. Diana PUTNAM
10 Vice Pres Finance & Administration ..... Mr. Gregg WILBUR
32 Vice President of Student Affairs ..... Ms. Jane KELLEY
101 Administrative Assistant ..... Ms. Diane BOSLET
20 Associate VP of Academic Affairs ..... Ms. Jacqueline SNYDER
35 Associate Dean ..... Ms. Arlene SPENCER
18 Director of Facilities ..... Mr. Paul MARSHALL
21 Accounting Supervisor ..... Ms. Chasity HULSAVER
07 Associate Dean for Admissions ..... Ms. Laura LAPORTE
113 Bursar ..... Mr. Jared DEMAGISTRIS
15 Human Resources Manager ..... Ms. Connie GRANT
06 Registrar ..... Mr. Scott COLLINS
08 Librarian ..... Mr. Daniel TOWNE
36 Director of Career Planning ..... Ms. Andrea SCRIBNER
121 Director of Advisement ..... Ms. Mary-Jo FERRAUILO-DAVIS
30 Chief Development ..... Ms. Lesley LANZI
37 Coordinator Financial Aid ..... Ms. Rebecca COZZOCREA
04 Administrative Asst to President ..... Ms. Diane BOSLET
19 Director of Public Safety ..... Mr. Mark PIERCE
25 Director of Opportunity Grants ..... Ms. Jean KARUTIS
41 Athletic Director ..... Mr. Kevin JONES
13 Chief Information Officer ..... Mr. Romeyn PRESCOTT

General Theological Seminary (E)

440 West 21st Street, New York NY 10011-2981
County: New York — FICE Identification: 002726
Unit ID: 191320
Telephone: (212) 243-5150 — Carnegie Class: Spec-4-yr-Faith
FAX Number: (212) 727-3907 — Calendar System: Semester
URL: www.gts.edu
Established: 1817 — Annual Graduate Tuition & Fees: N/A
Enrollment: 56 — Coed
Affiliation or Control: Protestant Episcopal — IRS Status: 501(c)3
Highest Offering: Master's; No Undergraduates
Accreditation: THEOL

01 Acting Dean and President ..... Rev Dr. Michael DELASHMUTT
05 VP & Dean of Academic Affairs ..... Vacant
10 VP & Controller ..... Mr. Robert ELLIOT
11 Vice President of Operations ..... Mr. Anthony KHANI
111 VP for Institutional Advancement ..... Ms. Donna ASHLEY
07 Director of Admissions ..... Vacant
06 Director of Acad Mgmt & Registrar ..... Ms. Stacie WARING
15 Director of HR & Financial Aid ..... Ms. Trecia O'SULLIVAN
26 Director of Communications ..... Mr. Joshua BRUNER
30 Director of Development ..... Mr. Jonathan SILVER

Genesee Community College (F)

One College Road, Batavia NY 14020-9704
County: Genesee — FICE Identification: 006782
Unit ID: 191339
Telephone: (585) 343-0055 — Carnegie Class: Assoc/MT-VT-High Non
FAX Number: (585) 343-4541 — Calendar System: Semester
URL: www.genesee.edu
Established: 1966 — Annual Undergrad Tuition & Fees (In-District): $5,040
Enrollment: 4,735 — Coed
Affiliation or Control: State/Local — IRS Status: 501(c)3
Highest Offering: Associate Degree
Accreditation: M, ADNUR, COARC, PTAA

01 President ..... Dr. James SUNSER
05 Provost/Exec VP Academic Affairs ..... Dr. Kathleen SCHIEFEN
81 Dean Math/Science/Career Education ..... Dr. Rafael ALICEA-MALDONADO
83 Dean Human Communication/Behavior ..... Mr. Timothy TOMCZAK
56 Dean of Distributed Learning ..... Dr. Craig LAMB
20 Asc Dean Accelerated Col Enrol Pgms ..... Mr. Edward LEVINSTEIN
06 Registrar ..... Ms. Karlyn BACKUS
57 Director Fine & Performing Arts ..... Ms. Maryanne ARENA
68 Director of Health & Physical Educ ..... Ms. Rebecca DZIEKAN
10 Acting VP for Finance & Operations ..... Ms. Gina WEAVER
09 Assoc VP Inst Rsrch & Assessment ..... Ms. Carol MARRIOTT
15 Executive Director Human Resources ..... Mr. Lawrence MANCUSO
88 Director Business Skills Training ..... Mr. John MCGOWAN
21 Controller ..... Ms. Kristin L. YUNKER
13 Director of Computer Services ..... Ms. Cindy DELMAR
18 Director of Buildings & Grounds ..... Mr. Levi OLSEN
32 VP for Student & Enrollment Svcs ..... Dr. Shelitha WILLIAMS
35 Dean of Students ..... Ms. Patricia CHAYA
07 Assistant Dean of Admissions ..... Ms. Lyndsay GERHARDT
37 Director of Financial Aid ..... Mr. Joseph A. BAILEY
88 Dir of Student Engagement & Inclus ..... Vacant
41 Director of Athletics ..... Ms. Kristen SCHUTH
30 VP Devel & External Affairs ..... Mr. Justin JOHNSTON
04 Administrative Asst to President ..... Ms. Bethany ARADINE
19 Director Security/Safety ..... Mr. Stephen WISE
08 Chief Library Officer ..... Ms. Jessica HIBBARD

Glasgow Caledonian New York College (G)

64 Wooster Street, New York NY 10012
County: New York — Identification: 667340
Telephone: (646) 768-5300 — Carnegie Class: Not Classified
FAX Number: N/A — Calendar System: Semester
URL: www.gcnyc.com
Established: 2017 — Annual Graduate Tuition & Fees: N/A
Enrollment: N/A — Coed
Affiliation or Control: Independent Non-Profit — IRS Status: 501(c)3
Highest Offering: Master's; No Undergraduates
Accreditation: @M

01 President/Vice Chancellor ..... Dr. Pamela GILLIES
05 Vice President/Provost ..... Dr. Jacqueline LEBLANC
06 Registrar ..... Mr. Stephen LOPEZ
11 Dir of Operations/Title IX Coord ..... Ms. Jessica CHANG-RUSSELL
07 Dir Admissions/Recruitment ..... Ms. Dominique STUDER

Hamilton College (H)

198 College Hill Road, Clinton NY 13323-1218
County: Oneida — FICE Identification: 002728
Unit ID: 191515
Telephone: (315) 859-4011 — Carnegie Class: Bac-A&S
FAX Number: (315) 859-4991 — Calendar System: Semester
URL: www.hamilton.edu
Established: 1812 — Annual Undergrad Tuition & Fees: $58,510
Enrollment: 1,902 — Coed
Affiliation or Control: Independent Non-Profit — IRS Status: 501(c)3
Highest Offering: Baccalaureate
Accreditation: M

01 President ..... David WIPPMAN
05 VPAA/Dean of Faculty ..... Suzanne KEEN
11 Vice Pres Administration/Finance ..... Karen L. LEACH
111 Vice Pres Advancement ..... Lori R. DENNISON
13 Vice Pres Information Technology ..... Joseph SHELLEY
07 VP/Dean Admission & Financial Aid ..... Monica C. INZER
32 Vice Pres/Dean of Students ..... Terry MARTINEZ
26 VP Communications/Marketing ..... Melissa RICHARDS
20 Associate Dean of Faculty ..... Nathan GOODALE
20 Associate Dean of Faculty ..... Penny YEE
41 Athletic Director ..... Jonathan T. HIND
39 Director Residential Life ..... Travis R. HILL
10 AVP of Finance and Controller ..... Carol GABLE
08 Dir of Library/Info Technology ..... Joe SHELLLEY
27 Sr Director Content Communications ..... Stacey J. HIMMELBERGER
37 Director of Financial Aid ..... K. Cameron FEIST
36 Exec Director of the Career Center ..... Sam WELCH
06 Registrar ..... Kristin M. FRIEDEL
15 Director of Human Resources ..... Stephen STEMKOSKI
18 Associate VP for Facilities ..... Roger F. WAKEMAN
19 Director of Campus Safety ..... Frank COOTS
38 Director Counseling/Psych Services ..... David WALDEN
42 Catholic Chaplain ..... Peter EL HACHEM
24 Director Audiovisual Services ..... Timothy J. HICKS
09 Director of Institutional Research ..... Jasmine X. YANG

26 Associate VP of Communications … Michael J. DEBRAGGIO
28 Chief Diversity Officer … Terry M. MARTINEZ
29 Director Alumni Relations … Sharon T. RIPPEY
96 Director of Procurement/Admin … Lucy BURKE
40 Manager College Store … Jennifer PHILLIPS
100 Chief of Staff … Gillian M. KING

Hartwick College (A)

One Hartwick Drive, Oneonta NY 13820-1790
County: Otsego FICE Identification: 002729
Unit ID: 191533
Telephone: (607) 431-4000 Carnegie Class: Bac-A&S
FAX Number: (607) 431-4206 Calendar System: 4/1/4
URL: www.hartwick.edu
Established: 1797 Annual Undergrad Tuition & Fees: $48,364
Enrollment: 1,209 Coed
Affiliation or Control: Independent Non-Profit IRS Status: 501(c)3
Highest Offering: Master's
Accreditation: M, ART, MUS, NURSE

01 President … Dr. Margaret L. DRUGOVICH
05 Executive Vice President & Provost … Dr. Barbara FELDMAN
10 Vice President Finance/CFO … Ms. karen ZUILL
111 VP for College Advancement … Ms. Paula Lee HOBSON
84 VP Enrollment Mgmt & Student Exper … Ms. Karen MCGRATH
04 Senior Assistant to the President … Ms. Lisa CORBETT
15 Chief Human Resource Officer … Ms. Suzanne JANITZ
39 Director Residence Life & Housing … Dr. Colleen BUNN
06 Registrar … Mr. Matthew SANFORD
20 Asst Provost Academic Affairs … Dr. Kellie BEAN
37 Director of Financial Aid … Ms. Melissa ALLEN
08 Interim Director of Libraries … Mr. David HEYDUK
28 Chief Diversity Officer … Mr. Rory SMITH
13 Director Inst Info Systems Services … Ms. Deb B. HILTS
91 Director Technologies Services … Mr. Bryan DEL BENE
18 Director of Facilities Services … Mr. Joseph MACK
41 Director of Athletics … Mr. John CZARNECKI
38 Director of Counseling Services … Mr. Gary ROBINSON
23 Director of Student Health Center … Ms. Amy GARDNER
26 Marketing Communications Manager … Mr. David LUBELL
07 Director Admissions … Ms. Lisa STARKEY-WOODS
12 Director Pine Lake Campus … Ms. Erin TOAL
21 Director Financial Svcs/Controller … Mr. James CHATTERTON
09 Director of Institutional Research … Mr. J. R BJERKLIE
19 Director of Campus Safety … Mr. Donald DEPASS
40 Manager of B&N Bookstore … Mr. Frank WERDANN
102 Dir Foundation/Corporate Relations … Ms. Lisa IANNELLO
105 Assoc Dir Comm for Web Services … Ms. Stephanie BRUNETTA
108 Director Institutional Assessment … Mr. Joseph BJERKLIE
29 Director Alumni Relations … Ms. Jennifer JANES

Hebrew Union College-Jewish Institute of Religion (B)

1 West 4th Street, New York NY 10012-1186
County: New York FICE Identification: 004054
Unit ID: 203067
Telephone: (212) 674-5300 Carnegie Class: Spec-4-yr-Faith
FAX Number: (212) 388-1720 Calendar System: Semester
URL: www.huc.edu
Established: 1875 Annual Graduate Tuition & Fees: N/A
Enrollment: 335 Coed
Affiliation or Control: Jewish IRS Status: 501(c)3
Highest Offering: Doctorate; No Undergraduates
Accreditation: M, PAST

01 President … Dr. Andrew REHFELD
05 Provost/Dean … Rabbi Andrea WEISS
10 Chief Financial Officer … Ms. Amy GOLDBERG
101 Exec Sec to Board of Governors … Ms. Andrea KANN
26 AVP National Dir Public Affs/Comm … Ms. Jean B. ROSENSAFT
44 Director of Institutional Giving … Ms. Cheryl SLAVIN
08 Librarian … Mr. Yoram BITTON
07 Director Recruitment/Admission … Mr. Adam ALLENBERG
13 Director of Information Systems … Mr. John H. BRUGGEMAN
37 National Director of Financial Aid … Ms. Roseanne ACKERLEY

Helene Fuld College of Nursing (C)

24 East 120th Street, New York NY 10035
County: New York FICE Identification: 010153
Unit ID: 191597
Telephone: (212) 616-7200 Carnegie Class: Spec-4-yr-Other Health
FAX Number: (212) 616-7299 Calendar System: Quarter
URL: www.helenefuld.edu
Established: 1945 Annual Undergrad Tuition & Fees: N/A
Enrollment: 525 Coed
Affiliation or Control: Independent Non-Profit IRS Status: 501(c)3
Highest Offering: Baccalaureate
Accreditation: M, ADNUR, NURSE

01 President … Dr. Joyce P. GRIFFIN-SOBEL
05 Exec Vice President/Provost … Dr. Sandy CAROLLO
10 Head of Finance … Mrs. Galina VILKINA
100 Chief of Staff … Ms. Leslie FOUNTAIN WILLIAMS
32 Director of Student Services … Vacant
08 Director of Library … Mr. Indrajeet SINGH CHAUHAN
35 Assoc Director of Student Services … Ms. Gladys PINEDA
26 Assistant Dean of External Affairs … Ms. Cathy DOLAN
15 Director Human Resources … Jamar WILSON
38 College Counselor … Ms. Dana GOLIN
04 Executive Assistant … Ms. Kadia DARBY
13 Director Information Technology … Mr. Eickel ORTIZ
07 Interim Director of Admissions … Ms. Gladys PINEDA
29 Director Alumni Relations … Vacant

Herkimer County Community College (D)

100 Reservoir Road, Herkimer NY 13350-1598
County: Herkimer FICE Identification: 004788
Unit ID: 191612
Telephone: (315) 866-0300 Carnegie Class: Assoc/HT-Mix Trad/Non
FAX Number: (315) 866-5539 Calendar System: Semester
URL: www.herkimer.edu
Established: 1966 Annual Undergrad Tuition & Fees (In-District): $5,706
Enrollment: 2,224 Coed
Affiliation or Control: State/Local IRS Status: 501(c)3
Highest Offering: Associate Degree
Accreditation: M, PTAA

01 President … Dr. Cathleen C. MCCOLGIN
10 Sr VP for Admin & Finance … Mr. Nicholas LAINO
05 Provost … Mr. Michael ORIOLO
32 Dean of Students … Mr. Donald DUTCHER
20 Associate Dean Academic Affairs BH … Mr. William MCDONALD
83 Assoc Dean Academic Affs Social Sci … Dr. Robin RIECKER
20 Assoc Dean of Academic Affairs … Mrs. Linda LAMB
15 Director of Human Resources … Mr. James SALAMY
41 Director of Athletics … Mr. Donald DUTCHER
08 Director of Library Services … Mr. Alfred BEROWSKI
09 Director Institutional Research … Ms. Karen AYOUCH
100 Assistant to the President … Mr. Daniel SARGENT
18 Director Facilities Operations … Mr. Robert WOUDENBERG
37 Director Student Financial Aid … Ms. Maureen BOUFAS
26 Director of Public Relations … Ms. Rebecca RUFFING
36 Career Services Counselor … Mrs. Suzanne PADDOCK
96 Purchasing Agent … Mr. Nicholas LAINO
102 Dir Foundation/Corporate Relations … Mr. Robert FOWLER
19 Director of Campus Safety … Mr. Timothy ROGERS
39 Director Residence Life … Mr. Jason RATHBUN
04 Admin Assistant to the President … Ms. Shari HUNT
07 Director of Admissions … Dr. Denver STICKROD
38 Director Student Counseling … Ms. Wendy MARCHESE
06 Registrar … Ms. Jaclyn HARRINGTON
13 Chief Information Technology Ofcr … Mr. Edris NOORI
104 Director Study Abroad … Vacant
108 Assoc Dean Institution Assessment … Ms. Mary Ann CARROLL

Hilbert College (E)

5200 South Park Avenue, Hamburg NY 14075-1597
County: Erie FICE Identification: 002735
Unit ID: 191621
Telephone: (716) 649-7900 Carnegie Class: Bac-Diverse
FAX Number: (716) 649-0702 Calendar System: Semester
URL: www.hilbert.edu
Established: 1957 Annual Undergrad Tuition & Fees: $24,530
Enrollment: 801 Coed
Affiliation or Control: Independent Non-Profit IRS Status: 501(c)3
Highest Offering: Master's
Accreditation: M

01 President … Dr. Michael S. BROPHY
05 Provost/Vice Pres Academic Affs … Dr. Maureen FINNEY
111 Vice Pres Inst Advancement … Ms. Kathleen CHRISTY
10 Vice Pres for Finance and Admin … Ms. Jean BOLAND
84 VP Enrollment Management … Mr. Randyll BOWEN
32 Vice President & Dean of Stdnts … Mr. Gregory ROBERTS
42 VP Mission Intgrtn/Campus Ministry … Mr. Jeff PAPIA
26 Dir Marketing & Communications … Mr. Matthew HEIDT
92 Director Honors Program … Dr. Amy E. SMITH
39 Dir Residence Life/Judicial Affairs … Ms. Jill COLE
41 Athletic Director … Ms. Megan VALENTINE
19 Director Security/Safety … Mr. Vito CZYZ
29 Asst Dir Annual Giving/Alum Engage … Ms. Carol BERNAT
08 Director of McGrath Library … Ms. Colleen DIPPOLD
07 Director of Admissions … Ms. Meghan HARMON
36 Director Placement/Career Services … Mr. Chris SIUTA
37 Director Financial Aid … Ms. Nicole GRIFFO
06 Director of Student Records … Ms. Katelyn LETIZIA
38 Director Student Counseling … Mr. Chris SIUTA
09 Director of Institutional Research … Dr. John WISE
15 Director of Human Resources … Ms. Maura FLYNN
28 Director of Multicultural Affairs … Vacant
35 Director of Student Activities … Ms. Jill COLE
96 Director of Purchasing … Mr. Gary DILLSWORTH
21 Asst Vice Pres Business/Finance … Mr. Anthony WIERTEL
18 Chief Facilities/Physical Plant … Mr. Gary DILLSWORTH
04 Administrative Asst to President … Ms. Eileen STACK

Hobart and William Smith Colleges (F)

300 Pulteney Street, Geneva NY 14456-3397
County: Ontario FICE Identification: 002731
Unit ID: 191630
Telephone: (315) 781-3000 Carnegie Class: Bac-A&S
FAX Number: (315) 781-3654 Calendar System: Semester
URL: www.hws.edu
Established: 1822 Annual Undergrad Tuition & Fees: $58,650
Enrollment: 1,833 Coordinate
Affiliation or Control: Independent Non-Profit IRS Status: 501(c)3
Highest Offering: Master's
Accreditation: M

01 President … Dr. Joyce P. JACOBSEN
04 Assistant to the President … Ms. Amanda BLOWERS
05 Provost & Dean of Faculty … Dr. Sarah KIRK
10 VP for Finance & Administration/CFO … Ms. Carolee WHITE
32 Vice President for Campus Life … Mr. Robert FLOWERS
100 Chief of Staff President's Office … Ms. Kathleen REGAN
111 Vice President for Advancement … Mr. Robert O'CONNOR
15 Director of Human Resources … Ms. Deborah DRAIN
07 VP of Admissions … Mr. John YOUNG
26 VP for Marketing & Communications … Ms. Cathy WILLIAMS
13 VP for Strategic Initiatives/CIO … Mr. Fred DAMIANO
43 Vice President and General Counsel … Mr. Louis GUARD
28 VP Diversity/Equity/Inclusion … Dr. Khuram HUSSAIN
19 Associate VP of Campus Safety … Mr. Martin CORBETT
20 Assoc Dean Faculty & Development … Dr. Joseph RUSINKO
35 Asst VP/Dean Student Engagement … Mr. Brandon BARILE
42 Chaplain … Rev. Nita BYRD
14 Deputy CIO/Dir Enterprise Solutions … Mr. Jeremy TRUMBLE
08 Director of the Library … Mr. Vincent BOISSELLE
06 Registrar … Mr. Peter SARRATORI
104 Dean of Global Education … Dr. Thomas D'AGOSTINO
108 Dean Teach/Learn & Assessment … Dr. Susan PLINER
41 Director of Athletics … Ms. Deborah STEWARD
33 Dean of Hobart College … Dr. Scott BROPHY
34 Dean of William Smith College … Ms. Lisa KAENZIG
110 Associate VP for Advancement … Mr. Jared WEEDEN
29 Dir of Alumni & Alumnae Relations … Ms. Chevy DEVANEY
21 Controller … Ms. Carol GROVER
88 Associate Dean for Curriculum … Dr. Jamie MAKINSTER
36 Director Center for Career Services … Ms. Brandi FERRARA
88 Director of Admissions … Mr. Alan PAYNTER
37 Director of Financial Aid … Ms. Beth NEPA
39 Assistant Dean Student Engagement … Ms. Shelle BASILIO
35 Director of Student Activities … Ms. Kristen TOBEY
88 Director of Intercultural Affairs … Dr. Alejandra MOLINA
88 Director Conferences/Events … Mr. Chad DUPUIS
38 Director Counseling Center … Ms. Jennifer HOGAN
85 Director of International Students … Ms. Marilyn O'HORA UHNAK
102 Dir Corp/Foundation Rels/Legal Affs … Mr. Gerard BUCKLEY
113 Assoc Controller/Student Accounts … Ms. Rebecca BARNES
91 Dir Network/Systems Infrastructure … Mr. Derek LUSTIG
106 Director of Digital Learning … Ms. Juliet BOISSELLE
27 Associate VP of Communications … Ms. Mary LECLAIR
105 Director Web Development … Mr. Michael DIMAURO
88 Director Athletic Communications … Mr. Ken DEBOLT
12 Director Finger Lakes Institute … Dr. Lisa CLECKNER
31 Dir Community Engagement … Ms. Kathleen FLOWERS
88 Director Academic Opportunity Pgm … Ms. Renee GRANT
88 Director of Parent Program … Ms. Jennifer MURRAY
88 Director Stewardship Programs … Ms. Kelly YOUNG
44 Director Annual & Athletic Giving … Ms. Dulcie MEYER
96 Director Procurement/Auxiliary Svcs … Ms. Claudette KILLIAN
88 Sr Dir Development for Athletics … Mr. Michael CRAGG
27 Director of Marketing … Ms. Gina KANE
25 Director of Sponsored Programs … Ms. Roberta TRUSCELLO
30 Director Advancement Services … Ms. Karen REUSCHER
09 Director of Institutional Research … Mr. Chris CALIENES

Hofstra University (G)

100 Hofstra University, Hempstead NY 11549-1000
County: Nassau FICE Identification: 002732
Unit ID: 191649
Telephone: (516) 463-6600 Carnegie Class: DU-Mod
FAX Number: (516) 463-4848 Calendar System: Semester
URL: www.hofstra.edu
Established: 1935 Annual Undergrad Tuition & Fees: $49,410
Enrollment: 10,444 Coed
Affiliation or Control: Independent Non-Profit IRS Status: 501(c)3
Highest Offering: Doctorate
Accreditation: M, ACATE, ANEST, ARCPA, AUD, #CAATE, CACREP, CAMPEP, CLPSY, HSA, IPSY, JOUR, LAW, MED, NURSE, OT, PERF, PH, SCPSY, SP

01 President … Dr. Susan POSER
05 Interim Provost … Dr. Janet A. LENAGHAN
20 Special Advisor to the Provost … Dr. Margaret ABRAHAM
43 SVP Legal Affairs/General Counsel … Ms. Dolores FREDRICH
10 Sr VP Financial Affairs/Treasurer … Ms. Catherine HENNESSY
18 VP for Facilities and Operations … Mr. Joseph BARKWILL
41 VP & Director of Athletics … Mr. Rick COLE, JR.
26 Vice President University Relations … Ms. Melissa A. CONNOLLY
32 Vice President for Student Affairs … Mr. W. Houston DOUGHARTY
84 Vice Pres Enrollment Management … Ms. Jessica L. EADS
13 VP Digital Innovation & Technology … Mr. Steve FABIANI
30 Vice President for Development … Mr. Alan J. KELLY
28 Chief Diversity & Inclusion Officer … Mr. Cornell CRAIG
92 Dean Honors College … Dr. Warren FRISINA
66 Dean Sch Nursing & Health Prof … Dr. Kathleen GALLO
60 Dean School of Communication … Mr. Mark LUKASIEWICZ
61 Dean Law School … Hon. A. Gail PRUDENTI
54 Dean School of Engineering … Dr. Sina Y. RABBANY
49 Int Dean Col Liberal Arts/Science … Dr. Daniel E. SEABOLD
63 Dean Health Prof & Human Services … Dr. Holly J. SEIRUP
63 Dean Medical School … Dr. Lawrence SMITH
50 Int Dean Zarb Sch of Business … Dr. K.G VISWANATHAN
09 Exec Dir Inst Rsrch/Admin Assessmnt … Ms. Chavon STUPARICH
114 Vice Provost Budget & Planning … Mr. Richard M. APOLLO
25 Vice Provost Rsrch/Sponsored Pgms … Ms. Sofia KAKOULIDIS
08 Director Library & Info Services … Mr. Howard E. GRAVES
35 Dean of Students … Dr. Gabrielle ST. LEGER
36 Exec Dir Career Center … Ms. Michelle KYRIAKIDES
38 Dir Student Counseling Services … Dr. John C. GUTHMAN

39 Assoc Dir Residential Programs ... Ms. Novia P. WHYTE
23 Dir Health & Wellness Center ... Dr. Robert STAHL
29 Exec Director Alumni Affairs ... Ms. Amy R. REICH
40 Manager Bookstore ... Mr. Will GILER
06 Registrar/Dir of Academic Records ... Mr. Evan S. KOEGL
121 Dean for University Advisement ... Ms. Anne M. MONGILLO
15 Director of Human Resources ... Ms. Denise S. CUNNINGHAM
22 Equal Rights/Opportunity Ofcr ... Ms. Jennifer MONE
19 Director Public Safety ... Ms. Geraldine HART
96 Director of Purchasing Contracts ... Mr. David DALE
37 Director Student Financial Aid ... Ms. Sandra MERVIUS
04 Admin Assistant to the President ... Ms. Isabel D. FREY

Holy Trinity Orthodox Seminary (A)

PO Box 36, Jordanville NY 13361-0036
County: Herkimer — FICE Identification: 002733
Telephone: (315) 858-0945 — Carnegie Class: Not Classified
FAX Number: (315) 858-0945 — Calendar System: Semester
URL: www.hts.edu
Established: 1948 — Annual Undergrad Tuition & Fees: N/A
Enrollment: N/A — Male
Affiliation or Control: Russian Orthodox — IRS Status: 501(c)3
Highest Offering: Baccalaureate
Accreditation: NY

01 Rector/CEO ... M.Rev. Luke MURIANKA
05 Dean ... Dr. Nicholas SCHIDLOVSKY
32 Dean of Students ... V.Rev. Archimandrite HARDING
30 Director of Development ... V.Deac. Michael PAVUK
07 Director of Admissions/Registrar ... Rev. Ephraim WILLMARTH
08 Librarian ... Mr. Michael PEREKRESTOV
13 Information Technology Manager ... Mr. Benjamin MARQUARDT

Houghton College (B)

One Willard Avenue, Houghton NY 14744-0128
County: Allegany — FICE Identification: 002734
Unit ID: 191676
Telephone: (585) 567-9200 — Carnegie Class: Bac-A&S
FAX Number: (585) 567-9572 — Calendar System: Semester
URL: www.houghton.edu
Established: 1883 — Annual Undergrad Tuition & Fees: $34,466
Enrollment: 902 — Coed
Affiliation or Control: Wesleyan Church — IRS Status: 501(c)3
Highest Offering: Master's
Accreditation: M, AAQEP, MUS

01 President ... Dr. Wayne D. LEWIS, JR.
05 Chief Academic Ofcr/Dean of Faculty ... Dr. Cathy FREYTAG
32 Dean of Student Life ... Mr. Marc SMITHERS
10 Vice President for Finance ... Mr. Dale WRIGHT
111 Vice President for Advancement ... Mr. Karl SISSON
84 Vice President for Enrollment ... Mr. Jason TOWERS
06 Registrar ... Mr. Kevin KETTINGER
37 Director of Financial Aid ... Ms. Marianne LOPER
08 Director of the Library ... Mr. David STEVICK
29 Dir Alumni & Community Relations ... Ms. Phyllis GAERTE
42 Dean of the Chapel ... Dr. Michael JORDAN
09 Director of Data Management ... Mr. Kurt HABECKER
36 Director of VOCA ... Ms. Rachel WRIGHT
15 Director of Human Resources ... Ms. Nancy STANLEY
26 Dir Marketing & Communications ... Mr. Michael BLANKENSHIP
13 Director of Technology ... Mr. Donald HAINGRAY
18 Director of Facilities ... Mr. Chad PLYMALE
19 Chief Security Officer ... Mr. Ray M. PARLETT
23 Director of Health Services ... Dr. David BRUBAKER
41 Executive Director of Athletics ... Mr. Matthew WEBB
21 Controller ... Ms. Danae FORREST
39 Director Residence Life ... Ms. Katie BREITIGAN
38 Director Counseling Services ... Dr. William BURRICHTER
92 Director of Honors Program ... Dr. Benjamin LIPSCOMB
07 Director of Admissions ... Vacant
28 Director of Mosaic Center ... Ms. P. Nuk KONGKAW ODEN
30 Director of Advancement Services ... Mr. John ODEN
100 Chief of Staff ... Dr. Gregory BISH

Hudson Valley Community College (C)

80 Vandenburgh Avenue, Troy NY 12180-6096
County: Rensselaer — FICE Identification: 002868
Unit ID: 191719
Telephone: (518) 629-4822 — Carnegie Class: Assoc/MT-VT-Mix Trad/Non
FAX Number: (518) 629-4576 — Calendar System: Semester
URL: www.hvcc.edu
Established: 1953 — Annual Undergrad Tuition & Fees (In-District): $5,964
Enrollment: 8,933 — Coed
Affiliation or Control: State/Local — IRS Status: 501(c)3
Highest Offering: Associate Degree
Accreditation: M, ADNUR, COARC, DH, DMS, EMT, FUSER, NAEYC, POLYT, SURGT

01 President ... Dr. Roger A. RAMSAMMY
04 Executive Asst to the President ... Ms. Suzanne K. KALKBRENNER
10 VP for Administration & CFO ... Mr. Donal CHRISTIAN
05 Vice President for Academic Affairs ... Ms. Judith DILORENZO
32 Vice President for Student Affairs ... Mr. Louis COPLIN
50 Acting Dean Business/Liberal Arts ... Ms. Ronalyn WILSON
81 Dean of STEM ... Dr. Jonathan ASHDOWN
103 Dean Econ/Workforce Development ... Ms. Penny HILL
76 Dean School of Health Sciences ... Dr. Patricia KLIMKEWICZ
08 Dir of College Learning Centers ... Ms. Marcy PENDERGAST
07 Director of Admissions ... Ms. Julie PANZANARO
06 Registrar ... Mr. Ian LACHANCE
13 Chief Information Officer ... Mr. Jonathan BRENNAN
18 Director Physical Plant ... Vacant
45 Exec Dir Institutional Effective ... Ms. Kathleen PETLEY
37 Interim Director of Financial Aid ... Ms. Heather HENRY
36 Dir Center For Careers & Transfer ... Dr. Gayle HEALY
15 Exec Director of Human Resources ... Ms. Karen PAQUETTE
19 Director of Public Safety ... Mr. Fred ALIBERTI
23 Coordinator Health Services ... Ms. Claudine POTVIN-GIORDANO
22 Director of Disability Resources ... Ms. DeAnne MARTOCCI
09 Director Planning & Research ... Ms. Vaidehi AGASHE
35 Director of Student Life ... Mr. Alfredo BALARIN
85 International Student Advisor ... Dr. Jay DEITCHMAN
40 Bookstore Manager ... Ms. Stephanie DANZ
41 Director of Athletics ... Mr. Justin HOYT
20 Asst VP of Academics ... Ms. Ronalyn WILSON
96 Dir Business Services/Purchasing ... Ms. Patricia GASTON
21 Comptroller ... Mr. John BRAUNGARD
26 Exec Dir Communications/Marketing ... Mr. Dennis KENNEDY
86 Exec Dir External & Govt Affairs ... Ms. Regina LAGATTA
25 Director of Grants ... Ms. Cheryl L. BEAUCHAMP
29 Alumni Relations/Annual Giving ... Ms. Jana PUTZIG
106 Interim Dir of Distance Learning ... Ms. Elissa BAKER
108 Dean Institutional Assessment ... Dr. Margaret GEEHAN
105 Web Coordinator ... Ms. Sandra EYERMAN
28 Chief Diversity Officer ... Mr. Ainsley THOMAS
30 Dir of Development/Donor Relations ... Ms. Angela D. O'NEAL
16 Director of Human Resources ... Ms. Deborah RICHEY

Icahn School of Medicine at Mount Sinai (D)

One Gustave L. Levy Place, New York NY 10029-6500
County: New York — FICE Identification: 007026
Unit ID: 193405
Telephone: (212) 241-6500 — Carnegie Class: Spec-4-yr-Med
FAX Number: (212) 241-7146 — Calendar System: Other
URL: www.icahn.mssm.edu
Established: 1963 — Annual Graduate Tuition & Fees: N/A
Enrollment: 1,298 — Coed
Affiliation or Control: Independent Non-Profit — IRS Status: 501(c)3
Highest Offering: Doctorate; No Undergraduates
Accreditation: M, CAMPEP, DENT, IPSY, MED, PH

01 President & CEO ... Dr. Kenneth L. DAVIS
05 Exec Vice Pres/Dean Sch of Medicine ... Dr. Dennis S. CHARNEY
10 Sr Vice Pres for Finance ... Mr. Stephen HARVEY
63 Dean for Medical Education ... Dr. David MULLER
11 Dean for Operations ... Mr. Jeffrey SILBERSTEIN
13 Dean for Information Technology ... Ms. Kristin MYERS
28 Director of Diversity ... Dr. Gary BUTTS

Iona College (E)

715 North Avenue, New Rochelle NY 10801-1890
County: Westchester — FICE Identification: 002737
Unit ID: 191931
Telephone: (914) 633-2000 — Carnegie Class: Masters/L
FAX Number: (914) 633-2642 — Calendar System: Semester
URL: www.iona.edu
Established: 1940 — Annual Undergrad Tuition & Fees: $41,580
Enrollment: 3,590 — Coed
Affiliation or Control: Independent Non-Profit — IRS Status: 501(c)3
Highest Offering: Master's
Accreditation: M, MFCD, OT, SP, SW

01 President ... Dr. Seamus CAREY
05 Provost/Sr VP Academic Affairs ... Dr. Darrell WHEELER
10 Sr Vice President Finance & Admin ... Ms. Anne Marie SCHETTINI-LYNCH
111 Sr VP Advancement/External Affairs ... Mr. Paul J. SUTERA
100 VP Strat Initiatives & Board Secy ... Ms. MaryEllen CALLAGHAN
84 VP Enrollment Mgmt/Stdnt Affairs ... Mr. Kevin O'SULLIVAN
13 Vice Provost Info Technology/CIO ... Ms. Joanne STEELE
37 Assoc VP Student Financial Services ... Ms. Eileen DOYLE
14 Asst Vice Provost for Info Tech ... Mr. Dimitris HALARIS
20 Assoc Vice Provost Academic Affairs ... Vacant
88 Assc Prov Strategic Acad Initiative ... Dr. Tricia MULLIGAN
32 Asst Vice Prov Student Life ... Ms. Elizabeth OLIVIERI-LENAHAN
49 Dean School Arts & Sciences ... Dr. Joseph STABILE
50 Dean School of Business ... Dr. Lynne RICHARDSON
43 General Counsel ... Ms. Kathleen MCELROY
18 Director of Facilities Management ... Mr. Richard MURRAY
39 Director Residential Life ... Mr. Aaron HARMAN
15 Director of HR & Title IX Coord ... Ms. Denise SMITH
38 Director of Counseling Center ... Dr. Brielle STARK-ADLER
36 Assoc Vice Prov Career Development ... Mr. Matthew CARDIN
08 Director of Libraries ... Mr. Richard PALLADINO
42 Director of Campus Ministries ... Mr. Carl PROCARIO-FOLEY
06 Registrar ... Ms. Beverly AZURE
41 Director of Athletics ... Mr. Matthew T. GLOVASKI
86 Director of Govt Relations/Grants ... Vacant
09 Dir of Inst Effectiveness/Planning ... Mr. Jason DIFFENDERFER
21 Director of Business Services ... Ms. Nancy MORANO
26 VP for Marketing & Communications ... Ms. Mary Clare REILLEY
19 Dir of Campus Safety & Security ... Mr. Adrian NAVARRETE
23 Director of Health Services ... Ms. Patty FURLONG
96 Asst Director of Business Services ... Ms. Carol Ann KENNY
92 Director of Honors Program ... Dr. Kim PAFFENROTH
123 Director of Graduate Admissions ... Vacant
04 Executive Asst to President ... Ms. Laura PROSTANO
105 Webpage Designer/Developer ... Mr. Peter MACELI
29 Director Alumni Relations ... Vacant
11 Chief Operating Officer ... Mr. Kevin CURNIN
28 Chief Diversity Officer ... Dr. Sumita FURLONG

Island Drafting and Technical Institute (F)

128 Broadway, Amityville NY 11701-2704
County: Suffolk — FICE Identification: 007375
Unit ID: 191959
Telephone: (631) 691-8733 — Carnegie Class: Spec 2-yr-Tech
FAX Number: (631) 691-8738 — Calendar System: Semester
URL: www.idti.edu
Established: 1957 — Annual Undergrad Tuition & Fees: $16,950
Enrollment: 68 — Coed
Affiliation or Control: Proprietary — IRS Status: Proprietary
Highest Offering: Associate Degree
Accreditation: ACCSC

01 President ... Mr. James G. DI LIBERTO
03 Vice President ... Mr. John G. DI LIBERTO
05 Dean ... Ms. Patricia HAUSFELD
37 Director Student Financial Aid ... Mr. Daniel GREENER

Ithaca College (G)

953 Danby Road, Ithaca NY 14850-7001
County: Tompkins — FICE Identification: 002739
Unit ID: 191968
Telephone: (607) 274-3011 — Carnegie Class: Masters/L
FAX Number: N/A — Calendar System: Semester
URL: www.ithaca.edu
Established: 1892 — Annual Undergrad Tuition & Fees: $46,610
Enrollment: 5,354 — Coed
Affiliation or Control: Independent Non-Profit — IRS Status: 501(c)3
Highest Offering: Doctorate
Accreditation: M, #ARCPA, CAATE, CAPRT, MUS, OT, PTA, SP, THEA

01 Interim President ... Dr. La Jerne T. CORNISH
100 Chief of Staff ... Ms. Odalys DIAZ PINEIRO
05 Interim Provost/VP Academic Affairs ... Ms. Melanie STEIN
10 VP of Finance & Admin ... Mr. Timothy DOWNS
43 General Counsel ... Ms. Emily ROCKETT
84 VP Marketing & Enrollment Strategy ... Ms. Laurie KOEHLER
111 VP Institutional Advancement ... Ms. Wendy KOBLER
15 VP Human & Org Development/Plng ... Ms. Hayley HARRIS
32 VP Student Affairs/Campus Life ... Dr. Rosanna FERRO
26 Exec Director of Strategic Comm ... Mr. Robert WAGNER
13 Assoc VP Information Technology ... Mr. David WEIL
18 Assoc VP for Facilities Management ... Mr. Tim CAREY
21 Assoc VP Business & Finance ... Mr. Marc ISRAEL
20 Associate Provost Academic Program ... Dr. Jeane COPENHAVER-JOHNSON
58 Assoc Provost Grad & Prof Studies ... Ms. Christina MOYLAN
79 Interim Dean Sch Humanities/Science ... Dr. Claire GLEITMAN
64 Interim Dean of School of Music ... Ms. Ivy WALZ
76 Dean Sch Health Sciences/Human Perf ... Ms. Linda PETROSINO
50 Interim Dean School of Business ... Dr. Alka BRAMHANDKAR
60 Int Dean School of Communication ... Dr. Jack POWERS
06 Registrar ... Ms. Vikki LEVINE
09 Director Analytics & Inst Research ... Ms. Claire BORCH
07 Director of Admission ... Ms. Nicole EVERSLEY BRADWELL
12 Director London Center ... Ms. Catherine WEIDNER
38 Director Counseling/Health/Wellness ... Dr. Ellyn SELLERS-SELIN
37 Exec Dir Student Financial Services ... Ms. Shana GORE
35 Dean of Students ... Ms. Bonnie S. PRUNTY
08 Interim College Librarian ... Ms. Karin WIKOFF
41 Dir Intercol Athletics/Rec Sports ... Ms. Susan BASSETT
114 Director of Budget ... Ms. Beth REYNOLDS
27 Director of Public Relations ... Mr. David C. MALEY
40 Manager of College Stores ... Mr. Rick WATSON
28 Exec Dir Student Equity & Belonging ... Mr. Hierald OSORTO
85 Dir International Student Services ... Ms. Diana DIMITROVA
88 Dir Center for Faculty Excellence ... Mr. Gordon ROWLAND
04 Exec Assistant to the President ... Ms. Jaimie M. VOORHEES
96 Director Procurement ... Mr. Douglas FREEMAN
101 Secretary & Legal Counsel to Board ... Ms. Nancy PRINGLE
104 Director Study Abroad ... Ms. Rachel GOULD
19 Exec Dir Public Safety & Emer Mgmt ... Mr. Bill KERRY
39 Dir Resident Life/Judicial Affairs ... Ms. Marsha DAWSON

Jamestown Business College (H)

7 Fairmount Avenue, Box 429, Jamestown NY 14702-0429
County: Chautauqua — FICE Identification: 008495
Unit ID: 192004
Telephone: (716) 664-5100 — Carnegie Class: Spec-4-yr-Bus
FAX Number: (716) 664-3144 — Calendar System: Quarter
URL: www.jbc.edu
Established: 1886 — Annual Undergrad Tuition & Fees: $12,645
Enrollment: 284 — Coed
Affiliation or Control: Proprietary — IRS Status: Proprietary
Highest Offering: Baccalaureate
Accreditation: M

01 President ... Mr. David CONKLIN
05 Dean ... Ms. Pamela REESE
07 Director Admissions ... Ms. Christina CONKLIN
06 Registrar ... Ms. Erica SHEESLEY
37 Director of Financial Aid ... Ms. Victoria BARAN

Jamestown Community College (A)

525 Falconer Street, Jamestown NY 14701
County: Chautauqua FICE Identification: 002869
Unit ID: 191986
Telephone: (716) 338-1000 Carnegie Class: Assoc/HT-High Non
FAX Number: (716) 338-1466 Calendar System: Semester
URL: www.sunyjcc.edu
Established: 1950 Annual Undergrad Tuition & Fees (In-District): $6,336
Enrollment: 3,430 Coed
Affiliation or Control: State/Local IRS Status: 501(c)3
Highest Offering: Associate Degree
Accreditation: M, ADNUR, OTA

01 President .... Dr. Daniel T. DEMARTE
05 Vice Pres of Academic Affairs .... Dr. Marilyn A. ZAGORA
11 Vice Pres of Administration .... Mr. Michael MARTELLO
32 Vice Pres of Student Affairs .... Dr. Kirk YOUNG
103 Vice Pres of Workforce Readiness .... Mr. Holger EKANGER
12 Exec Dir of Catt County Campus .... Ms. Paula SNYDER
09 Chief Inst Research/Planning Ofcr .... Ms. Katie CARPEN
06 Registrar .... Ms. Tracy KELLY
07 Director Admission .... Ms. Corrine CASE
08 Library Director .... Mr. Timothy ARNOLD
37 Exec Dir Student Finance/Records .... Ms. Michelle SCHRAM
15 Exec Director Human Resources .... Ms. Nicolette RICZKER
41 Athletic Director .... Mr. George SISSON
43 Legal Counsel .... Vacant
18 Director Facilities/Physical Plant .... Mr. David JOHNSON
04 Administrative Asst to President .... Ms. Marsha L. HERN
19 Director Security/Safety .... Mr. Barry SWANSON
30 Chief Development/Advancement .... Vacant
39 Director Student Housing .... Mr. Tyler SILAGYI
105 Director Web Services .... Ms. Karli CHAMP
13 Int Exec Dir of Technology .... Mr. Kyle BROWN
29 Director Alumni Relations .... Ms. Heather MORRIS
21 Exec Director Administrative Svcs .... Ms. Karen FULLER
96 Financial Analyst/Business Office .... Ms. Jennifer BEEBE
36 Director Student Placement .... Vacant
38 Director Student Counseling .... Ms. Tammy SMITH
102 Exec Dir Foundation/Corporate Rels .... Ms. Maria KINDBERG
22 Dir Affirmative Action/Equal Opp .... Ms. Nickey RICZKER
25 Chief Contract & Grants Admin .... Ms. Katrina JONES
44 Director Annual Giving .... Ms. Maria KINDBERG

Jamestown Community College Cattaraugus County Campus (B)

260 North Union Street, PO Box 5901,
Olean NY 14760-5901
Telephone: (716) 376-7504 Identification: 770138
Accreditation: &M

Jefferson Community College (C)

1220 Coffeen Street, Watertown NY 13601-1897
County: Jefferson FICE Identification: 002870
Unit ID: 192022
Telephone: (315) 786-2200 Carnegie Class: Assoc/HT-Mix Trad/Non
FAX Number: (315) 786-0158 Calendar System: Semester
URL: www.sunyjefferson.edu
Established: 1961 Annual Undergrad Tuition & Fees (In-District): $5,688
Enrollment: 2,658 Coed
Affiliation or Control: State/Local IRS Status: 501(c)3
Highest Offering: Associate Degree
Accreditation: M, ADNUR

01 President .... Dr. Ty A. STONE
05 Interim Vice Pres Academic Affairs .... Dr. Maryrose EANNACE
10 Executive VP Admin/Finance/Enroll .... Dr. Daniel J. DUPEE
32 VP for Student Engagement/Retention .... Dr. Corey A. CAMPBELL
49 Associate VP for Liberal Arts .... Ms. Jerilyn FAIRMAN
81 Associate VP for STEM .... Vacant
04 Assistant to the President .... Vacant
08 Library Director .... Vacant
84 Dean of Enrollment Services .... Mr. James AMBROSE
86 Spec Asst to President/Govt Affairs .... Ms. Karen FREEMAN
37 Director Financial Aid .... Ms. Robyn RHYNER
06 Registrar .... Ms. Deborah M. ELLIOTT
88 Director Small Business Center .... Ms. Elizabeth LONERGAN
09 Associate VP Strategic Initiatives .... Dr. Megan STADLER
18 Chief Facilities/Physical Plant .... Mr. Bruce ALEXANDER
29 Alumni Development Officer .... Ms. Edie ROGGIE
35 Dir of Student Activities/Inclusion .... Ms. Margaret TAYLOR
36 Coord Career Planning/Placement .... Ms. Michele D. GEFELL
88 Dir of Educ Planning/Veteran Svcs .... Ms. Rebecca SMALL KELLOGG
26 Dir of Marketing/Communications .... Ms. Gillian MAITLAND
15 Associate VP for Human Resources .... Ms. Kerry A. YOUNG
30 College Development Officer .... Mr. Ben FOSTER
119 Chief Security Information Officer .... Mr. Donald HORTON
19 Director Security/Safety .... Mr. Wesley HISSONG
41 Athletic Director .... Mr. Jeffrey WILEY
88 Director Opportunity Programs .... Ms. Gabrielle THOMPSON
07 Director of Admissions .... Ms. Chelsea MARRA

Jewish Theological Seminary of America (D)

3080 Broadway, New York NY 10027-4649
County: New York FICE Identification: 002740
Unit ID: 192040
Telephone: (212) 678-8000 Carnegie Class: Spec-4-yr-Faith
FAX Number: (212) 678-8947 Calendar System: Semester
URL: www.jtsa.edu
Established: 1886 Annual Undergrad Tuition & Fees: $58,703
Enrollment: 360 Coed
Affiliation or Control: Independent Non-Profit IRS Status: 501(c)3
Highest Offering: Doctorate
Accreditation: M, PAST

01 Chancellor .... Dr. Shuly SCHWARTZ
10 Vice Chanc Finance/Administration .... Ms. Clare PEETERS
30 Vice Chanc/Chief Development Ofcr .... Ms. Bonnie EPSTEIN
05 Provost .... Dr. Jeffrey KRESS
10 Chief Financial Officer .... Mr. Jeffrey S. JACOB
43 General Counsel .... Mr. Keath BLATT
49 Dean List College Jewish Studies .... Dr. Amy KALMANOFSKY
53 Dean Davidson School of Education .... Dr. Shira EPSTEIN
58 Dean of The Graduate School .... Dr. Amy KALMANOFSKY
64 Director Miller Cantorial School .... Cantor Nancy ABRAMSON
73 Dean of Religious Leadership .... Rabbi Jan UHRBACH
32 Dean of Student Life .... Ms. Sara HOROWITZ
08 Librarian .... Dr. David KRAEMER
15 Director of Human Resources .... Ms. Diana TORRES-PETRILLI
18 Director of Operations .... Mr. James ESPOSITO
13 Director Information Technology .... Mr. Ray MORALES
26 Vice Chancellor for Communications .... Ms. Elise DOWELL
06 Registrar/Director Financial Aid .... Ms. Amy S. FEINFELD
39 Director of Residence Life .... Mr. Bradley MOOT
84 Director of Enrollment Management .... Ms. Melissa PRESENT
35 Director of Student Life .... Ms. Sara HOROWITZ
38 Director Student Counseling .... Dr. David DAVAR
29 Director of Alumni Affairs .... Mrs. Melissa FRIEDMAN
31 Director of Community Engagement .... Rabbi Julia ANDELMAN
04 Executive Asst to Chancellor .... Ms. Chava BLUMENTHAL
19 Director Security/Safety .... Chief Anthony VAUGHAN

The Juilliard School (E)

60 Lincoln Center Plaza, New York NY 10023-6588
County: New York FICE Identification: 002742
Unit ID: 192110
Telephone: (212) 799-5000 Carnegie Class: Spec-4-yr-Arts
FAX Number: (212) 724-0263 Calendar System: Semester
URL: www.juilliard.edu
Established: 1905 Annual Undergrad Tuition & Fees: $49,260
Enrollment: 961 Coed
Affiliation or Control: Independent Non-Profit IRS Status: 501(c)3
Highest Offering: Doctorate
Accreditation: M

01 President .... Mr. Damian WOETZEL
05 Provost & Dean .... Mr. Adam MEYER
10 Vice Pres/Chief Financial Officer .... Ms. Christine TODD
08 VP for Library/Info Resources .... Ms. Jane GOTTLIEB
111 VP & Chief Advancement Officer .... Ms. Alexandra WHEELER
18 AVP for Facilities Management .... Mr. Cameron CHRISTENSEN
84 VP Enrollment Mgmt/Student Dev .... Ms. Joan D. WARREN
43 Vice Pres Admin/General Counsel .... Mr. Maurice F. EDELSON
100 Vice President & Chief of Staff .... Ms. Ciaran ESCOFFERY
26 Vice Pres for Public Affairs .... Ms. Rosalie CONTRERAS
32 Dean for Student Development .... Mr. Barrett HIPES
20 Dean of Academic Affairs .... Mr. Jose GARCIA-LEON
64 Deputy Dean/Director Music Division .... Vacant
64 Asst Dean/Dir of Chamber Music .... Ms. Barli NUGENT
35 Asst Dean of Student Affairs .... Ms. Sabrina TANBARA
57 Dir Richard Rodgers Drama Div .... Mr. Evan YIONOULIS
57 Artistic Director of Dance Division .... Ms. Alicia Graf MACK
57 Artistic Director of Vocal Arts .... Mr. Brian ZEGER
88 Director of Performance Activities .... Ms. Anna ROYZMAN
88 Artistic Dir Pre-College Division .... Ms. Yoheved KAPLINSKY
06 Registrar .... Ms. Katherine GERTSON
07 Assoc Dean Enrollment Management .... Dr. Kathleen TESAR
112 Director of Major Gifts .... Ms. Katie MURTHA
15 Director of Human Resources .... Ms. Katie GERMANA
38 Director of Counseling Services .... Mr. William BUSE
37 Director Student Financial Aid .... Ms. Tina GONZALEZ
88 Director of Juilliard Jazz .... Mr. Wynton MARSALIS
36 Director Career Services .... Ms. Rachel CHRISTENSEN
13 Chief Information Officer .... Mr. Carl YOUNG
14 Chief Technology Officer .... Mr. Steve DOTY
19 Director Security/Safety .... Mr. Adam GAGAN
29 Director Alumni Relations .... Ms. Rebecca VACCARELLI
39 Director of Residence Life .... Mr. Todd PORTER

Kehilath Yakov Rabbinical Seminary (F)

638 Bedford Avenue, Brooklyn NY 11211-8007
County: Kings FICE Identification: 010549
Unit ID: 192165
Telephone: (718) 963-1212 Carnegie Class: Spec-4-yr-Faith
FAX Number: (718) 387-8586 Calendar System: Semester
Established: 1948 Annual Undergrad Tuition & Fees: $10,300
Enrollment: 158 Male
Affiliation or Control: Independent Non-Profit IRS Status: 501(c)3
Highest Offering: First Talmudic Degree
Accreditation: RABN

01 President .... Mr. Sandor SCHWARTZ

Keuka College (G)

141 Central Avenue, Keuka Park NY 14478
County: Yates FICE Identification: 002744
Unit ID: 192192
Telephone: (315) 279-5000 Carnegie Class: Masters/M
FAX Number: (315) 279-5216 Calendar System: Semester
URL: www.keuka.edu
Established: 1890 Annual Undergrad Tuition & Fees: $34,032
Enrollment: 1,535 Coed
Affiliation or Control: Independent Non-Profit IRS Status: 501(c)3
Highest Offering: Master's
Accreditation: M, IACBE, NURSE, OT, SW

01 President .... Mrs. Amy STOREY
05 Provost/VP for Academic Affairs .... Dr. Bradley FUSTER
10 VP for Finance/Administration .... Mr. Robert BAUMET
84 VP for Enroll Mgmt/Student Devel .... Mr. Mark PETRIE
111 AVP for Advancement/External Affs .... Mr. Peter BEKISZ
32 VP for Student Development .... Dr. Heather MALDONADO
20 Assoc Provost for Acad Innovation .... Dr. Timothy SELLERS
20 Assistant Provost .... Dr. Laurel HESTER
08 Director of Library .... Ms. Linda PARK
29 Sr Dir Alumni Relations/Advancement .... Mrs. Billy Jo JAYNE
15 Interim AVP of Human Resources .... Ms. Colleen BERTRAND
37 Director Financial Aid .... Ms. Catherine BUZANSKI
21 Controller .... Mr. Philip CATALANO
13 Asst VP/Chief Information Officer .... Ms. Andrea CAMPBELL
19 Director of Campus Safety .... Mr. James CUNNINGHAM
23 Coordinator of Health Services .... Ms. Cindy CHRISTIE
38 Director of Counseling Services .. Ms. Mary MARTINI-HAUSNER
07 Director of Admissions on Campus .... Ms. Megan PERKINS
41 AVP/Director of Athletics .... Mr. Jon ACCARDI
42 College Chaplain .... Mr. Eric DETAR
06 Registrar .... Ms. Jill BIRD
26 Sr Director of Marketing .... Ms. Tammy SWALES
96 Purchasing Liaison .... Ms. Brenda DEUCK
76 Div Chair Occupational Therapy .... Dr. Christopher ALTERIO
83 Div Chair Basic Soc & Applied Sci .... Dr. Rich MARTIN
50 Div Chair Business & Management .... Dr. Ed SILVERMAN
53 Div Chair of Education .... Dr. Klaudia LORINCZOVA
79 Div Chair Humanities/Fine Arts .... Dr. Jennie JOINER
81 Div Chair Natural Sciences/Math .... Dr. Mark SUGALSKI
66 Div Chair Nursing .... Dr. Elizabeth RUSSO
70 Div Chair Social Work .... Dr. Jason MCKINNEY
44 Director of Annual Giving .... Ms. Kaitlyn CARHART
88 Senior Dir of Conference Services .... Ms. Karen MANN
104 Assoc Director Intercultural Affs .... Ms. Jamyra YOUNG
85 Dean of International Program/Asia .... Mr. Gary GISS
119 Director of Info Systems & Security .... Mr. Thomas FLICKER
27 Director of Comm & Media Relations .... Mr. Kevin FRISCH
31 Dir of Community Relations/Events .... Ms. Katharine WAYE
88 Dir of Field Period Pgm/Internships .... Ms. Tara BLOOM
88 Senior Accountant .... Ms. Kayla ROBINSON
08 Director of HEOP .... Ms. Lisa THOMPSON
113 Director of Student Accounts .... Ms. Mary Ellen GRIFFITHS
35 Dir Student Activities/New Students .... Ms. Eva ROBBINS
88 Program & Org Management .... Dr. Deborah GREGORY
09 Director of Institutional Research .... Vacant

The King's College (H)

56 Broadway, New York NY 10004-1613
County: New York FICE Identification: 040953
Unit ID: 454184
Telephone: (212) 659-7200 Carnegie Class: Bac-A&S
FAX Number: (212) 659-7210 Calendar System: Semester
URL: www.tkc.edu
Established: 1938 Annual Undergrad Tuition & Fees: $37,690
Enrollment: 442 Coed
Affiliation or Control: Independent Non-Profit IRS Status: 501(c)3
Highest Offering: Baccalaureate
Accreditation: M

00 Chairman of the Board of Trustees .... Mr. Timothy DUNN
01 President .... Dr. Tim GIBSON
03 Executive Vice President .... Mr. Brian BRENBERG
05 Interim Provost .... Dr. Matthew PARKS
10 Chief Financial Officer .... Mr. Frank TORINO
32 Vice President Student Development .... Mr. David LEEDY
07 Vice Pres Admissions .... Mr. Mat MARQUEZ
35 Dean of Students .... Mr. David LEEDY
21 Asst VP & Controller .... Ms. Judy BARRINGER
84 Assoc VP Enrollment Management .... Ms. Whitney CLARK
06 Registrar .... Mr. Paul MIDDLEKAUFF
37 Director of Financial Aid .... Ms. Anna PETERS
100 Chief of Staff .... Ms. Megan DISHMAN
09 Director of Institutional Research .... Dr. Kimberly THORNBURY
26 Dir Strategic Communication .... Ms. Rebecca AU-MULLANEY
29 Exec Director of Alumni Affairs .... Ms. Sophia COSTON
18 Director Facilities .... Mr. Rich SWITZER
30 Chief Development Officer .... Ms. Bridget ROGERS
36 Director Career Development .... Mr. Matthew PERMAN
38 Director Student Counseling .... Ms. Esther JHUN
08 Director Library Services .... Ms. Christina ROGERS
39 Director Resident Life .... Ms. Leticia MOSQUEDA
41 Athletic Director .... Mr. Bryan FINLEY
15 Director Human Resources .... Ms. Grace GLEASON
102 Director Grants and Foundation .... Mr. Michael TOSCANO
13 Director of Information Technology .... Mr. Bracey FUENZALIDA

Le Moyne College (I)

1419 Salt Springs Road, Syracuse NY 13214-1301
County: Onondaga FICE Identification: 002748
Unit ID: 192323
Telephone: (315) 445-4100 Carnegie Class: Masters/L
FAX Number: (315) 445-4540 Calendar System: Semester
URL: www.lemoyne.edu

Established: 1946 Annual Undergrad Tuition & Fees: $35,910
Enrollment: 3,409 Coed
Affiliation or Control: Independent Non-Profit IRS Status: 501(c)3
Highest Offering: Doctorate
Accreditation: M, ARCPA, NURSE, OT

01 President ... Dr. Linda M. LEMURA
05 Int Prov/VP Acad Affs & Stdnt Dev ... Dr. James HANNAN
10 Senior VP Fin & Admin & Treasurer ... Mr. Roger W. STACKPOOLE
111 Vice Pres Comm & Advancement ... Mr. Bill BROWER
84 Vice Pres of Enrollment ... Dr. Timothy LEE
88 Vice Pres Mission Integration & DEI ... Rev. Charles ODUKE, SJ
88 Rector of the Jesuit Community ... Rev. Donald KIRBY, SJ
49 Interim Dean of Arts & Sciences ... Dr. Beth MITCHELL
50 Dean School of Business ... Mr. James E. JOSEPH
58 Dean of Graduate & Prof Studies ... Dr. Meega WELLS
20 Assoc Provost ... Dr. Mary K. COLLINS
21 Controller ... Ms. Nicole BROWN
15 Asst VP for HR and Org Dev ... Ms. Karin BOTTO
41 Director of Athletics ... Mr. Bob BERETTA
18 Asst VP Facilities Mgmt & Planning ... Mr. Jed S. SCHNEIDER
32 Int Assoc Provost for Student Devel ... Ms. Barb KARPER
35 Asst Dean for Student Development ... Mr. Mark G. GODLESKI
121 Asst Dean for Academic Advising ... Ms. Allison FARRELL
88 Asst Dean/Dir CSTEP & STEP ... Ms. Darshini ROOPNARINE
07 Senior Director of Admission ... Ms. Mary CHANDLER
51 Director of Continuing Education ... Vacant
88 Dir of Transfer Admission ... Ms. Cathy ANDERSON
13 Director of Info Technology ... Mr. Shaun C. BLACK
09 Director of Institutional Research ... Dr. Daniel L. SKIDMORE
22 EEO/Affirmative Action Officer ... Ms. Karin BOTTO
06 Registrar ... Ms. Natasha FARRELL
08 Director of the Library ... Ms. Inga BARNELLO
42 Director of Campus Ministry ... Mr. Thomas ANDINO
27 Director of Communications ... Mr. Joseph B. DELLA POSTA
88 Director Campus Life & Leadership ... Mr. John R. HALEY
19 Director of Security ... Mr. Mark J. PETTERELLI
110 AVP Advancement ... Mr. Samuel MCCRIMMON
39 Dir of Campus Life & Leadership ... Mr. John HALEY
36 Dir Career Advising/Development ... Ms. Meredith TORNABENE
04 Assistant to the President ... Ms. Carly J. COLBERT
28 Asst to the Provost for Diversity ... Dr. Tabor FISHER
86 Director Govt/Foundation Relations ... Mr. Steven W. KULICK
88 Director of Advancement Services ... Mr. Paul F. LYNCH
29 Director of Alumni Engagement ... Ms. Kasha GODLESKI
23 Dir Wellness Ctr for Health & Couns ... Ms. Maria RANDAZZO
88 Director of HEOP and AHANA ... Ms. Kelsi-Leandra LANE
40 Bookstore Manager ... Vacant

LIM College (A)

12 E 53rd Street, New York NY 10022-5268
County: New York FICE Identification: 007466
Unit ID: 192271
Telephone: (212) 752-1530 Carnegie Class: Spec-4-yr-Bus
FAX Number: (212) 832-6109 Calendar System: Semester
URL: www.limcollege.edu
Established: 1939 Annual Undergrad Tuition & Fees: $28,756
Enrollment: 1,681 Coed
Affiliation or Control: Proprietary IRS Status: Proprietary
Highest Offering: Master's
Accreditation: M, ACBSP

01 President ... Elizabeth S. MARCUSE
05 Provost ... Lisa SPRINGER
10 Exec VP Finance & Operations/Treas ... Michael T. DONOHUE
26 VP of Marketing and Communications ... Jacquelyn NEALON
84 VP of Enrollment Services ... Kristina ORTIZ
86 VP of Govt Relations/Cmty Affairs ... Christopher E. BARTO
21 VP of Finance and Controller ... Erik PAULSON
32 Vice President of Student Affairs ... Curtis HOOVER
58 Chair of Graduate Studies ... John KEANE
20 Assoc Dean of Academic Affairs ... Patricia FITZMAURICE
35 Assistant Dean of Student Affairs ... Erica MONNIN
08 Director of Library Services ... Lou ACIERNO
06 College Registrar ... Carolyn DISNEW
36 AVP of Career and Internship Svcs ... Nina FIDDIAN-GREEN
38 Sr Dir Counseling & Accessibility ... Jodi N. LICHT
07 Director of Admissions ... Laura HEALY
09 Director of Institutional Research ... Eugene MULLER
21 Accounting Manager ... Svetlana KANEVSKAYA
96 Purchasing Director ... Eric MARTIN
30 Sr VP for External Relations ... Gail NARDIN
27 Director of Communications ... Meredith FINNIN
27 Director of Marketing ... Laura CIOFFI
13 Chief Technology Officer ... Maurice MORENCY
14 Director of Information Technology ... Nelson LEON
18 Manager of Facilities ... Kwamina AFFUL
88 Dean of Academic Administration ... Gilbert STACK
40 Director of the Bookstore ... Kerri ZIEMBA
121 Director of Academic Advising ... Jackie CORAGGIO
16 Asst Dir of Human Resources ... Carolyn HIGGINS
104 Study Abroad Coordinator ... Tiffany GOLDING
88 Director of Learning Innovation ... Deepa RAO-SISARIO
123 Assoc Director of Grad Admissions ... George TOLEDO
35 Director of Student Life ... M.T TELOKI

Long Island Business Institute (B)

6500 Jericho Turnpike, Commack NY 11725
Telephone: (631) 499-7100 Identification: 770746
Accreditation: NY

Long Island Business Institute (C)

136-18 39th Avenue 5th Floor, Flushing NY 11354
County: Queens FICE Identification: 020937
Unit ID: 192509
Telephone: (718) 939-5100 Carnegie Class: Spec 2-yr-Other
FAX Number: (718) 939-9235 Calendar System: Semester
URL: www.libi.edu
Established: 1968 Annual Undergrad Tuition & Fees: $10,416
Enrollment: 1,186 Coed
Affiliation or Control: Proprietary IRS Status: Proprietary
Highest Offering: Associate Degree
Accreditation: NY

01 President ... Ms. Monica W. FOOTE
05 Provost ... Ms. Stacey JOHNSON
11 Asst Campus Program Director ... Ms. Michelle HOUSTON
10 Assoc Dir Administration/Finance ... Mr. Li ZHU
37 Financial Aid Director ... Ms. Yun Lin (Cynthia) LIU
08 Sr Librarian Flushing Campus ... Ms. Adrianna ARGUELLES
07 Director of Admissions ... Mr. Keith BROTHERSON

*Long Island University (D)

700 Northern Boulevard, Brookville NY 11548-1327
County: Nassau FICE Identification: 002751
Unit ID: 192457
Telephone: (516) 299-2501 Carnegie Class: N/A
FAX Number: N/A
URL: www.liu.edu

01 President ... Dr. Kimberly R. CLINE
13 VP for Information Technology & CIO ... Mr. George BAROUDI
10 Vice President Finance & Treasurer ... Mr. Christopher N. FEVOLA
07 VP of Admissions ... Ms. Deirdre WHITMAN
43 Chief University Counsel ... Mr. Michael BEST
45 Chief of Strategic Planning ... Mr. Andy PERSON
16 Exec Dir Human Resources ... Ms. Shannon SHAKESPEARE
96 Dir Sourcing/Procurement Svcs ... Ms. Joan MICELI
05 Senior VP for Academic Affairs ... Dr. Randy BURD
21 Assoc Vice Pres/Controller ... Mr. Keith VOSS
111 Vice President of Univ Advancement ... Mr. Charles RASBERRY
11 Chief Administrative Officer ... Mr. Joseph SCHAEFER

*Long Island University - LIU Post (E)

720 Northern Boulevard, Brookville NY 11548
County: Nassau FICE Identification: 002754
Unit ID: 192448
Telephone: (516) 299-2900 Carnegie Class: DU-Mod
FAX Number: (516) 299-2137 Calendar System: Semester
URL: www.liu.edu/post
Established: 1954 Annual Undergrad Tuition & Fees: $39,136
Enrollment: 15,066 Coed
Affiliation or Control: Independent Non-Profit IRS Status: 501(c)3
Highest Offering: Doctorate
Accreditation: M, ACATE, CACREP, CLPSY, DIETC, DIETD, DIETI, LIB, MT, NURSE, RAD, SP, SPAA, SW, #VET

02 President ... Dr. Kimberly R. CLINE
05 Vice President for Academic Affairs ... Dr. Ed WEIS
07 VP of Admissions ... Ms. Deirdre WHITMAN
49 Dean College Lib Arts/Science ... Vacant
66 Dean Sch Health Prof/Nursing ... Dr. Denise WALSH
50 Dean College of Management ... Vacant
53 Dean College of Educ/Info & Tech ... Dr. Laura SEINFELD
88 Dean of School of Comm & Design ... Dr. Jennifer HOLMES
32 Dean of Students/LIU Promise ... Mr. Michael BERTHEL
41 Director of Athletics ... Dr. Willam MARTINOV
18 University Facilities Officer ... Mr. Roy FERGUS
19 University Dir of Public Safety ... Mr. Michael FEVOLA

Long Island University - LIU Brentwood (F)

1001 Crooked Hill Rd, Brentwood NY 11717
Telephone: (631) 287-8500 Identification: 666076
Accreditation: &M

Long Island University - LIU Brooklyn (G)

1 University Plaza, Brooklyn NY 11201
Telephone: (718) 488-1011 FICE Identification: 004779
Accreditation: &M, ARCPA, CLPSY, COARC, DMS, NURSE, OT, PH, PHAR, PTA, SP, SPAA, SW

Long Island University - LIU Hudson (H)

735 Anderson Hill Road, Purchase NY 10577
Telephone: (914) 831-2700 Identification: 666078
Accreditation: &M

Long Island University - LIU Riverhead (I)

121 Speonk Riverhead Road, Riverhead NY 11901-3499
Telephone: (631) 287-8010 Identification: 666174
Accreditation: &M

Louis V. Gerstner Jr. Graduate School of Biomedical Sciences, Memorial Sloan Kettering Cancer Center (J)

1275 York Avenue, P.O. Box 441, New York NY 10065
County: New York Identification: 666643
Telephone: (646) 888-6639 Carnegie Class: Not Classified
FAX Number: (646) 422-2351 Calendar System: Semester
URL: www.sloankettering.edu
Established: 2004 Annual Graduate Tuition & Fees: N/A
Enrollment: N/A Coed
Affiliation or Control: Independent Non-Profit IRS Status: 501(c)3
Highest Offering: Doctorate; No Undergraduates
Accreditation: NY

01 President ... Dr. Craig B. THOMPSON
05 Provost ... Dr. Joan MASSAGUE
20 Dean ... Dr. Michael H. OVERHOLTZER
88 Associate Dean ... Ms. Linda BURNLEY
81 VP Scientific Education & Training ... Dr. Ushma S. NEILL
06 Registrar ... Mr. David L. MCDONAGH
08 Director of Library Services ... Ms. Donna S. GIBSON
88 Assistant Dean ... Dr. Thomas G. MAGALDI
28 Assoc Dir Trainee Diversity Init ... Dr. Yaihara M. FORTIS SANTIAGO
22 Title IX Coordinator ... Ms. Lindsay CORNACCHIA
22 Title IX Coordinator ... Ms. Leslie M. BALLANTYNE

Machzikei Hadath Rabbinical College (K)

5407 16th Avenue, Brooklyn NY 11204-1805
County: Kings FICE Identification: 013026
Unit ID: 192624
Telephone: (718) 854-8777 Carnegie Class: Spec-4-yr-Faith
FAX Number: (718) 851-1265 Calendar System: Semester
URL: mhrc.edu
Established: 1956 Annual Undergrad Tuition & Fees: $11,650
Enrollment: 158 Male
Affiliation or Control: Independent Non-Profit IRS Status: 501(c)3
Highest Offering: Special 5-year Faith
Accreditation: RABN

01 President ... Mr. Alexander SCHAECHTER

Mandl School - The College of Allied Health (L)

254 W 54th Street, 9th Floor, New York NY 10019
County: New York FICE Identification: 007401
Unit ID: 192688
Telephone: (212) 247-3434 Carnegie Class: Spec 2-yr-Health
FAX Number: (212) 247-3617 Calendar System: Semester
URL: www.mandl.edu
Established: 1924 Annual Undergrad Tuition & Fees: $14,600
Enrollment: 493 Coed
Affiliation or Control: Proprietary IRS Status: Proprietary
Highest Offering: Associate Degree
Accreditation: ABHES, COARC, SURTEC

01 President ... Mr. Melvyn P. WEINER
05 Vice President of Academic Affairs ... Dr. Orsete DIAS
11 VP Operations/Dir Financial Aid ... Mr. Stuart WEINER
36 Vice President of Career Services ... Mr. James FLANAGAN
06 Vice Pres Records & Registration ... Mr. Marc WEINER
84 Vice Pres Enrollment Management ... Ms. Randie SENSER
10 Chief Financial Officer ... Mrs. Nettie WEINER
07 Director of Recruitment ... Ms. Racquel GARCIA

Manhattan College (M)

Manhattan College Parkway, Bronx NY 10471-4099
County: Bronx FICE Identification: 002758
Unit ID: 192703
Telephone: (718) 862-8000 Carnegie Class: Masters/L
FAX Number: (718) 862-8014 Calendar System: Semester
URL: www.manhattan.edu
Established: 1853 Annual Undergrad Tuition & Fees: $45,880
Enrollment: 3,965 Coed
Affiliation or Control: Independent Non-Profit IRS Status: 501(c)3
Highest Offering: Master's
Accreditation: M, #NMT

01 President ... Dr. Brennan O'DONNELL
05 Provost & VP Academic Affairs ... Dr. Steven SCHREINER
10 VP for Finance & CFO ... Mr. Matthew S. MCMANNESS
32 Interim Vice President Student Life ... Dr. Esmilda ABREU-HORBOSTEL
111 Vice President College Advancement ... Mr. Thomas MAURIELLO
15 Vice President for Human Resources ... Ms. Barbara A. FABE
18 Vice President for Facilities ... Vacant
84 Vice President Enrollment Mgmt ... Dr. Colette GEARY
88 Vice President for Mission ... Br. Jack CURRAN
20 Associate Provost ... Dr. Rani ROY
35 Assistant VP of Student Life ... Dr. Emmanuel AGO
35 Dean of Students ... Dr. Esmilda ABREU-HORNBOSTEL
06 Registrar ... Mr. Carlos TONCHE
07 Dir of Undergraduate Admissions ... Ms. Tara FAY-REILLY

08 Director of Libraries Dr. William WALTERS
13 Director of Information Tech Svcs Mr. Jake HOLMQUIST
19 Director of Public Safety Mr. Peter DECARO
29 Director of Alumni Relations Mr. Louis CALVELLI
26 Assistant VP Marketing & Comm Mrs. Lydia E. GRAY
36 Director Ctr Career Development Ms. Rachel CIRELLI
38 Dir of Counseling & Health Services Ms. Jennifer MCARDLE
39 Director of Residence Life Mr. Charles CLENCY
41 Director of Athletics Ms. Marianne REILLY
42 Director of Campus Ministry Vacant
30 Director of Development/Advancement Mr. Stephen WHITE
78 Director Opportunity Pgms Mr. Andrew BURNS
40 Director of Campus Bookstore Mr. Henry CASTILLO
22 Dir of Personnel/Affirm Action Ofcr Ms. Vickie M. COWAN
09 Dir Institutional Research Dr. Soohong KIM
21 Controller Mr. Dennis LONERGAN
21 Business Manager Mr. Kenneth WALDHOF
85 International Student Advisor Ms. Debra L. DAMICO
37 Director of Financial Aid Admin Ms. Denise SCALZO
49 Interim Dean of Liberal Arts Dr. Cory BLAD
50 Dean of O'Malley School of Business Dr. Donald GIBSON
53 Dean of Education & Health Dr. Karen NICHOLSON
54 Dean of Engineering Dr. Tim WARD
51 Dean of Sch Cont & Prof Studies Dr. Steven GOSS
121 Director Ctr for Academic Success Ms. Marisa PASSAFIUME
81 Interim Dean of Science Dr. Janet MCSHANE
88 Dir of Specialized Resource Center Ms. Anne VACCARO
88 Asst Dir Grad/Fellowship Advisement Br. Daniel GARDNER
123 Director of Graduate Admissions Mr. Kevin TAYLOR
88 Director of Transfer Admissions Vacant
88 Dir Acad Support Svcs/HE Opp Pgm Ms. Marilyn CARTER-STEVENS
104 Director Study Abroad Dr. Ricardo DELLO BUONO
43 VP External/Legal Affs/Chf of Staff Ms. Tamara BRITT
28 Director Equity/Diversity/Title IX Ms. Sheetal KALE
88 Sr Advisor Strategic Partnerships Mr. Robert WALSH
108 Director of Assessment Dr. Edward DEE

Manhattan School of Music (A)

130 Claremont Avenue, New York NY 10027-4631
County: New York FICE Identification: 002759
Unit ID: 192712
Telephone: (212) 749-2802 Carnegie Class: Spec-4-yr-Arts
FAX Number: (212) 749-5471 Calendar System: Semester
URL: www.msmnyc.edu
Established: 1918 Annual Undergrad Tuition & Fees: $49,270
Enrollment: 939 Coed
Affiliation or Control: Independent Non-Profit IRS Status: 501(c)3
Highest Offering: Doctorate
Accreditation: M

01 President Dr. James GANDRE
05 Executive VP and Provost Dr. Joyce GRIGGS
10 Sr VP and CFO Ms. Tangella MADDOX
111 VP for Advancement Ms. Susan MADDEN
84 VP/Dean of Enrollment Management Ms. Melissa COCCO
26 VP for Media and Communications Mr. Jeff BREITHAUPT
15 VP for Human Relations & Admin Ms. Carol MATOS
20 Dean of Academic Affairs Ms. Kelly SAWATSKY
32 Dean of Students Dr. Monica CHRISTENSEN
88 Dean of Performance/Production Ops Mr. Henry VALORIS
100 Chief of Staff Ms. Alexa SMITH
18 Dir of Facilities & Campus Safety Mr. Bryan GREANEY
13 Chief Information Officer Mr. Ray MORALES
06 Registrar Mr. Thomas ZARKOS
106 Dir of Distance Learning & Rec Arts Mr. Chris SHADE
37 Director of Financial Aid Ms. Anna CHRISSOTIMOS
07 Director of Admissions Ms. Christina QUENTAL
35 Director of Student Engagement Ms. Melanie DORSEY
39 Director of Residence Life Ms. Samantha TYMCHYN
31 Director of Community Partnerships Ms. Rebecca CHARNOW
29 Assoc Dir for Alumni Engagement Vacant
08 Director of Library Services Mr. Peter CALEB
44 Assoc Dir of Annual Giving Ms. Julie WALLIN
40 Campus Store Manager Ms. Katherine COPLAND
85 Director of Intl Student Services Mr. Michael LOCKHART
88 Ctr for Music Entrepreneurship Mr. Chris VAUGHN
21 Assoc VP of Finance and Controller Mr. Hector PAREDES
04 Admin Asst Office of the President Ms. Nicole WEIGELT

Manhattanville College (B)

2900 Purchase Street, Purchase NY 10577-2132
County: Westchester FICE Identification: 002760
Unit ID: 192749
Telephone: (914) 694-2200 Carnegie Class: Masters/L
FAX Number: (914) 694-2386 Calendar System: Semester
URL: www.mville.edu
Established: 1841 Annual Undergrad Tuition & Fees: $40,330
Enrollment: 2,408 Coed
Affiliation or Control: Independent Non-Profit IRS Status: 501(c)3
Highest Offering: Doctorate
Accreditation: M, CAEP, CAEPN, RAD

01 President Dr. Michael E. GEISLER
04 Exec Admin Asst to the President Ms. Deborah A. FALLONE
05 Int Provost/VP of Academic Affairs Ms. Christine DEHNE
10 VP Finance/Operations Ms. Jean HALL
84 Vice Pres Admissions/Enrollment Vacant
111 Vice Pres Inst Advancement Ms. Sarah E. KELLY
18 Director of Physical Plant Mr. Daniel HANNON
32 Vice Pres of Student Affairs Dr. Cindy L. PORTER
49 Dean School of Arts & Sciences Dr. Rebecca LAFLEUR
13 CIO/VP Digital Strategy & Planning Mr. Jim RUSSELL
107 Assoc Dean School of Prof Studies Ms. Laura PERSKY
53 Dean School of Education Dr. Shelley WEPNER
26 AVP for Communications & Marketing Ms. Cara CEA
06 Registrar Ms. Jeneen KELLY
08 Director of the Library Mr. Jeff ROSEDALE
37 Director of Financial Aid Mr. Robert GILMORE
38 Assoc Dean Stdnt Health/Counseling Ms. Melissa BOSTON
35 Dean of Students Ms. Sharlise SMITH-RODRIGUEZ
41 Director of Athletics Ms. Julene CAULFIELD
36 Director Center for Career Devel Ms. Meghan MAKARCZUK
19 Director of Security Mr. Anthony HERRMANN
07 Director of Admissions Vacant
15 Director of Human Resources Vacant
35 Asst Dir Student Involvement/Ldrshp Mr. Alexander BARKLEY
96 Director of Purchasing Mr. Matthew HYLAND
104 Dir Intl Student Svcs/Study Abroad Ms. L.A ADAMS
23 Assoc Dn Student Health/Counseling Ms. Melissa BOSTON
100 Special Assistant to the President Ms. Loren MCDERMOTT
30 Dir of Advance Svcs & Prospect Mgmt Ms. Elizabeth FIORE
39 Dir Resident Life/Conf Svcs Ms. Juls WHITE
44 Director Annual Giving Ms. Meghan CASEY

Maria College of Albany (C)

700 New Scotland Avenue, Albany NY 12208-1798
County: Albany FICE Identification: 002763
Unit ID: 192785
Telephone: (518) 438-3111 Carnegie Class: Spec-4-yr-Other Health
FAX Number: (518) 438-7170 Calendar System: 4/1/4
URL: www.mariacollege.edu
Established: 1958 Annual Undergrad Tuition & Fees: $15,610
Enrollment: 864 Coed
Affiliation or Control: Independent Non-Profit IRS Status: 501(c)3
Highest Offering: Baccalaureate
Accreditation: M, ADNUR, NUR, OTA

01 President Dr. Thomas J. GAMBLE
05 VP for Academic Affairs Dr. Anne S. JUNG
10 Vice Pres Finance/Enrollment Mgmt Dr. Joseph M. MCDONALD
11 VP for Administration Mr. Joel D. NUDI
111 Sr VP Inst Advance/Marketing/Comm Ms. Victoria L. BATTELL
110 Assoc VP Advancement Mr. Drew D. LEDOUX
37 Director Financial Aid Mr. Richard F. SABBIA
06 Registrar Ms. Karen CONRAD
07 AVP Enroll Mgmt/Dir of Admissions Ms. Katie COONEY-LESKO
08 Librarian Ms. Krista ROBBIN
13 Director of Information Technology Ms. Robin DELORENZO
18 Superintendent Physical Plant Mr. Andrew PEREZ
36 Director Career Services Dr. Jason COLEY
15 Manager of Human Resources Ms. Rosalyn VAZQUEZ
20 Dean of College Dr. Anne S. JUNG
09 Director or Institutional Research Dr. Kim SPEERSCHNEIDER
04 Admin Assistant to the President Mrs. Sandra K. GRADY
30 Director of Development Ms. Katelyn PAULY
32 AVP Student Affairs/Dean of Stdnts Ms. Barbara RUSLANDER

Marist College (D)

3399 North Road, Poughkeepsie NY 12601-1387
County: Dutchess FICE Identification: 002765
Unit ID: 192819
Telephone: (845) 575-3000 Carnegie Class: Masters/L
FAX Number: (845) 471-6213 Calendar System: Semester
URL: www.marist.edu
Established: 1929 Annual Undergrad Tuition & Fees: $42,290
Enrollment: 6,600 Coed
Affiliation or Control: Independent Non-Profit IRS Status: 501(c)3
Highest Offering: Doctorate
Accreditation: M, ARCPA, CAATE, MT, PTA, SPAA, SW

01 President Dr. Dennis J. MURRAY
03 EVP/Chief Strategy/Innovation Ofcr Dr. Geoffrey L. BRACKETT
05 Vice President for Academic Affairs Dr. Thomas S. WERMUTH
84 VP Enrollment/Mktg & Communications Mr. Sean P. KAYLOR
111 Vice President College Advancement Mr. Christopher M. DELGIORNO
13 VP Information Technology/CIO Mr. Michael CAPUTO
32 VP/Dean for Student Affairs Mrs. Deborah A. DICAPRIO
10 Vice President Business Affairs/CFO Mr. John P. PECCHIA
15 VP for Human Resources Mrs. Christina DANIELE
20 Assoc VP/Dean Academic Affairs Dr. John RITSCHDORFF
07 Asst VP Enroll Mgmt/Dean UG Admiss Mr. Kent W. RINEHART
123 Dean Graduate Admission Mrs. Kelly HOLMES
35 Assoc Dean of Student Affairs Mr. Steve SANSOLA
43 College Counsel Ms. Sima Saran AHUJA
29 Executive Director Alumni Relations Ms. Amy K. WOODS
09 Director Inst Research & Planning Vacant
06 Assoc Dean Stdnt Acad Aff/Registrar Mrs. Judith IVANKOVIC
37 Exec Dir Student Financial Services Mr. Joseph R. WEGLARZ
08 Director of Library Ms. Becky ALBITZ
18 Director of Physical Plant Mr. Justin BUTWELL
26 Asst VP Marketing & Communications Mrs. Elisabeth W. TAVAREZ
96 Director of Purchasing Mr. Stephen J. KOCHIS
36 Director Career Services Dr. Mary O. JONES
19 Director of Safety & Security Mr. John BLAISDELL
39 Director of Housing & Resident Life Mrs. Sarah H. ENGLISH
41 Director of Athletics Mr. Timothy S. MURRAY
24 Director of Media & Instruct Tech Ms. Joey WALL
23 Director of Health Services Dr. Claudia ZEGANS
38 Director of Counseling Dr. Naomi A. FERLEGER
42 Director Campus Ministry Bro. Francis E. KELLY
44 Director of Annual Giving Ms. Hannah ALLEY-KELLER
105 Director Web Services Vacant
50 Dean School of Management Vacant
60 Dean School of Communication/Arts Dr. Jacqueline REICH
77 Dean School of Comp Sci/Mathematics Dr. Roger L. NORTON
49 Dean School of Liberal Arts Dr. Martin B. SHAFFER
81 Dean School of Science Dr. Alicia SLATER
107 Dean School of Professional Pgms Vacant
83 Dean Sch of Social/Behavioral Sci Dr. Deborah GATINS
104 Dean International Programs Mr. John PETERS
101 Chief of Staff & Secy to Board Mrs. Emily V. SALAND
25 Director of Academic Grants Mrs. Donna S. BERGER
28 Diversity/Inclusion/Engagement Ofcr Vacant

Marymount Manhattan College (E)

221 E 71st Street, New York NY 10021-4597
County: New York FICE Identification: 002769
Unit ID: 192864
Telephone: (212) 517-0400 Carnegie Class: Bac-A&S
FAX Number: (212) 517-0541 Calendar System: Semester
URL: www.mmm.edu
Established: 1936 Annual Undergrad Tuition & Fees: $37,410
Enrollment: 1,722 Coed
Affiliation or Control: Independent Non-Profit IRS Status: 501(c)3
Highest Offering: Master's
Accreditation: M

01 President Dr. Kerry WALK
05 Int VP Acad Aff/Dean of Faculty Dr. Peter NACCARATO
10 Vice Pres Finance & Admin/CFO Ms. Maisha WILLIAMS
111 VP Institutional Advancement Mr. Graham CIRAULO
84 VP for Student Success/Engagement Mr. Todd HEILMAN
32 AVP Student Success/Engagement Ms. Eammalyn YAMRICK
15 Associate VP for Human Resources Ms. Bree BULLINGHAM
45 Associate VP Strategic Initiatives Dr. Kathleen LEBESCO
21 Associate Controller & Dir Finance Ms. Sun A. YOON
20 AVP for Academic Administration Mr. Richard SHELDON
13 Chief Information Officer Ms. Dale HOCHSTEIN
28 Chief Diversity Off/Title IX Coord Ms. Rebecca MATTIS-PINARD
36 Exec Dir of Career Svcs Ms. Robin E. NACKMAN
88 Int Controller for Financial Oper Ms. Felisa COLEMAN
07 Dean of Admissions Mr. Christian ANDRADE
121 Asst VP and Dean of CAE Mr. Michael G. SALMON
88 Associate VP Enrollment Management Ms. Maria DEINNOCENTIIS
06 Registrar Ms. Regina CHAN
09 Dir Institutional Research Vacant
35 Dir of Student Dev and Activities Dr. Dayne HUTCHINSON
89 Asst Dean of Student Success Ms. Melissa WEEKES-STOUTE
08 Director of the Library Mr. Brian ROCCO
22 Dir of Acad Access/Disability Srvs Ms. Diana NASH
38 Dir Counseling & Wellness Center Ms. Deborah GUORDANO
12 Dir of Bedford Hills College Prog Ms. Aileen BAUMGARTNER
96 Director of Administrative Services Ms. Maria MARZANO
114 Asst Controller for Recon/Reporting Vacant
19 Assoc Director of Campus Safety Mr. Charles HENDERSON
26 Sr Director of Strategic Comm Mr. Stephen EICHINGER
35 Dean of Students Ms. Emmalyn YAMRICK
109 Exec Dir of Business Operations Ms. Diana ZAMBROTTA-SHEETZ
102 Sr Dir Inst Giving/Advance Svcs Vacant
44 Sr Dir Indiv Giving/Donor Rel Ms. Lisha BODDEN
112 Director of Major Gifts/Parent Prog Ms. Rita MURRAY
04 Special Assistant to the President Ms. Tunisia WRAGG

Mechon L'Hoyroa (F)

168 Maple Avenue, Monsey NY 10952
County: Rockland FICE Identification: 042615
Unit ID: 490328
Telephone: (845) 425-9565 Carnegie Class: Spec-4-yr-Faith
FAX Number: (845) 425-2094 Calendar System: Other
Established: 1990 Annual Undergrad Tuition & Fees: N/A
Enrollment: 57 Male
Affiliation or Control: Jewish IRS Status: 501(c)3
Highest Offering: First Talmudic Degree
Accreditation: AIJS

01 Rosh Kollel Reb. Yitzchok M. TAUBER

Medaille College (G)

18 Agassiz Circle, Buffalo NY 14214-2695
County: Erie FICE Identification: 002777
Unit ID: 192925
Telephone: (716) 880-2000 Carnegie Class: Masters/L
FAX Number: (716) 884-0291 Calendar System: Semester
URL: www.medaille.edu
Established: 1875 Annual Undergrad Tuition & Fees: $31,500
Enrollment: 2,076 Coed
Affiliation or Control: Independent Non-Profit IRS Status: 501(c)3
Highest Offering: Doctorate
Accreditation: M, CACREP, CAHIIM, IACBE

01 President Dr. Kenneth M. MACUR
05 Vice President Academic Affairs Dr. Janel M. CURRY
10 Vice President Business/Finance Ms. Lori A. MITERKO
30 Vice Pres for College Relations Mr. John P. CRAWFORD
07 VP Enroll Mgmt/Marketing/Admiss Mr. Christopher P. LARUSSO
09 Director of Institutional Research Dr. Mary M. TODD

32 VP for Student Development ... Ms. Amy M. DEKAY
41 Athletic Director ... Ms. Susan M. ROARKE
36 Director Career Planning/Placement ... Ms. Carol CULLINAN
13 Chief Information Officer ... Mr. Robert D. CHYKA
06 Registrar ... Ms. Tracey KONGATS
08 Library Director ... Mr. Andrew YEAGER
37 Director Financial Aid ... Mr. James P. AYERS
15 Director of Human Resources ... Ms. Barbara J. BILOTTA
35 Director of Student Involvement ... Mr. Daniel P. PUCCIO
38 Director Counseling Services ... Ms. Rosalina B. RIZZO
19 Director of Campus Public Safety ... Ms. Debra D. KELLY
29 Coordinator of Alumni Relations ... Mr. John P. CRAWFORD

Medaille College Rochester Campus (A)

1880 S Winton Road, Suite 1, Rochester NY 14618
Telephone: (585) 272-0030 Identification: 770140
Accreditation: &M

Memorial College of Nursing (B)

714 New Scotland, 111 Marian Hall, Albany NY 12208
County: Albany FICE Identification: 012203
Unit ID: 192961
Telephone: (518) 525-6850 Carnegie Class: Spec 2-yr-Health
FAX Number: (518) 525-6852 Calendar System: Semester
URL: www.sphp.com/memorial-college-of-nursing
Established: 1901 Annual Undergrad Tuition & Fees: $13,911
Enrollment: 135 Coed
Affiliation or Control: Independent Non-Profit IRS Status: 501(c)3
Highest Offering: Associate Degree
Accreditation: ADNUR

01 Dean ... Ms. Mary Ellen GIAMBONA
32 Dean of Student Services ... Ms. Angela COX

† Relocated to Maria College of Albany Campus

Mercy College (C)

555 Broadway, Dobbs Ferry NY 10522-1189
County: Westchester FICE Identification: 002772
Unit ID: 193016
Telephone: (800) 637-2969 Carnegie Class: Masters/L
FAX Number: (914) 674-5978 Calendar System: Semester
URL: www.mercy.edu
Established: 1950 Annual Undergrad Tuition & Fees: $20,558
Enrollment: 9,547 Coed
Affiliation or Control: Independent Non-Profit IRS Status: 501(c)3
Highest Offering: Doctorate
Accreditation: M, ARCPA, CAEP, EXSC, MT, NURSE, OT, OTA, PTA, SP, SW

01 President ... Mr. Timothy HALL
05 Interim Provost ... Dr. Peter WEST
20 Associate Provost ... Dr. Saul FISHER
32 Vice President of Student Affairs ... Mr. Kevin JOYCE
50 Dean School of Business ... Dr. Lloyd GIBSON
53 Interim Dean School of Education ... Dr. Eric MARTONE
83 Dean School Soc/Behav Sci ... Dr. Stuart SIDLE
76 Dean School Health/Natural Sci ... Dr. Joan TOGLIA
66 Associate Dean of Nursing ... Dr. Deborah HUNT
66 Associate Dean of Nursing ... Dr. Miriam FORD
49 Interim Dean School of Liberal Arts ... Dr. Andres MATIAS-ORTIZ
15 Director of Human Resources ... Ms. Annette PIECORA
11 VP Operations & Facilities ... Mr. Thomas SIMMONDS
10 VP Finance & Chief Financial Ofcr ... Mr. Brett CARROLL
84 VP for Enrollment Management ... Mr. Adam CASTRO
111 Chief Advancement Officer ... Ms. Bernadette WADE
100 Chief of Staff ... Ms. Jessica HABER
04 Exec Assistant Office of President ... Ms. Grace CREIGHTON
108 Director of Learning Assessment ... Ms. Victoria FERRARA
43 General Counsel ... Ms. Kristen BOWES
37 Director of Financial Aid ... Mr. Paul LORENZONI
07 Executive Director of Admissions ... Mrs. Allison GURDINEER
09 Interim Dir Institutional Research ... Ms. Joanne DEMARCO
121 Exec Dir Student Success ... Mr. Rajesh KUMAR
39 Interim Dir Residence Life ... Mr. Alexander COLON
13 Chief Information Officer ... Ms. Camille SHELLEY
14 Director of Information Technology ... Mr. Todd PRATTELLA
06 Registrar ... Mrs. Danielle QUILLIGAN
45 Exec Dir Inst Planning & Assessment ... Mr. Matthew PRESSER
113 Exec Director of Student Accounts ... Ms. Felicia BRANDON
21 Controller ... Ms. Narda ROMERO
19 Exec Dir Safety & Emergency Mgmt ... Mr. Konrad MOTYKA
114 Director Budget & Planning ... Ms. Claire HOWARD-COSTER
18 Director of Operations ... Ms. Orla FITZSIMONS
96 Director of Purchasing ... Ms. Patricia SABATINO
08 Interim Director of Libraries ... Dr. Moddie BRELAND
41 Director of Athletics ... Mr. Matt KILCULLEN
26 AVP Marketing & Analytics ... Mr. Christian CONNELLY
27 Director of Communications ... Ms. Jessica BAILY
30 Exec Director of Development ... Ms. Katherine COPPINGER
29 Director of Alumni Relations ... Ms. Alexis MCGRATH-ROTHENBERG
25 Dir Sponsored Programs ... Ms. Janet PARTENZA
85 Sr Dir International Student Svcs ... Ms. Bogdana VLADESCU
104 Sr Dir International Student Svcs ... Ms. Bogdana VLADESCU
106 Director Online Learning ... Dr. Mary LOZINA
103 Exec Director of Career & Prof Dev ... Ms. Jill HART
101 Secretary of the Institution/Board ... Ms. Jessica HABER
112 Assoc Dir Donor Rels/Annual Giving ... Ms. Heather APOLLONIO
23 Director Health & Wellness ... Ms. Colleen POWERS
38 Director Student Counseling Center ... Dr. Ori SHINAR

Mesivta of Eastern Parkway Rabbinical Seminary (D)

510 Dahill Road, Brooklyn NY 11218-5559
County: Kings FICE Identification: 009335
Unit ID: 193061
Telephone: (718) 438-1002 Carnegie Class: Spec-4-yr-Faith
FAX Number: (718) 438-2591 Calendar System: Semester
Established: 1947 Annual Undergrad Tuition & Fees: $9,450
Enrollment: 45 Male
Affiliation or Control: Independent Non-Profit IRS Status: 501(c)3
Highest Offering: Second Talmudic Degree
Accreditation: RABN

01 President ... Rabbi Issac HEIMOVITZ
32 Dean of Students ... Rabbi Shlomo Z. EPSTEIN
37 Director of Student Financial Aid ... Rabbi Ira LIBERMAN
46 Director of Research ... Rabbi Hersch BASCH
10 Chief Fiscal Officer ... Rabbi Joseph HALBERSTADT

Mesivta Torah Vodaath Seminary (E)

425 E Ninth Street, Brooklyn NY 11218-5299
County: Kings FICE Identification: 007264
Unit ID: 193052
Telephone: (718) 941-8000 Carnegie Class: Spec-4-yr-Faith
FAX Number: (718) 941-8032 Calendar System: Semester
Established: 1918 Annual Undergrad Tuition & Fees: $12,360
Enrollment: 525 Male
Affiliation or Control: Independent Non-Profit IRS Status: 501(c)3
Highest Offering: First Talmudic Degree
Accreditation: AIJS

01 Dean ... Rabbi Yisroel REISMAN
03 Executive Director ... Rabbi Yitzchok GOTTDIENER
33 Dean of Men ... Rabbi Elya KATZ

Mesivtha Tifereth Jerusalem of America (F)

145 E Broadway, New York NY 10002-6301
County: New York FICE Identification: 003974
Unit ID: 193070
Telephone: (212) 964-2830 Carnegie Class: Spec-4-yr-Faith
FAX Number: (212) 349-5213 Calendar System: Semester
Established: 1907 Annual Undergrad Tuition & Fees: $12,000
Enrollment: 62 Male
Affiliation or Control: Independent Non-Profit IRS Status: 501(c)3
Highest Offering: Second Talmudic Degree
Accreditation: RABN

01 President & Dean Faculties ... Rabbi David FEINSTEIN
06 Registrar ... Chana YAMPOLSKY
37 Director Student Financial Aid ... E. GOLD

Metropolitan College of New York (G)

60 West Street, New York NY 10006
County: New York FICE Identification: 009769
Unit ID: 190114
Telephone: (212) 343-1234 Carnegie Class: Masters/L
FAX Number: (212) 343-7399 Calendar System: Semester
URL: www.metropolitan.edu
Established: 1964 Annual Undergrad Tuition & Fees: $20,188
Enrollment: 856 Coed
Affiliation or Control: Independent Non-Profit IRS Status: 501(c)3
Highest Offering: Master's
Accreditation: M, ACBSP

01 President ... Dr. Joanne PASSARO
10 VP Finance & Admin/CFO ... Ms. Michelle BLANKENSHIP
05 VP for Academic Affairs ... Mr. Humphrey CROOKENDALE
84 VP Enrollment Mgmt/Student Svcs ... Ms. Amy GREENSTEIN
13 Chief Information Officer ... Mr. Adrian SMITH
15 Director Human Resources ... Ms. Judith SANTIAGO
30 Interim Chief Development Officer ... Mr. David F A. WALKER
80 Dean Human Svcs & Public Admin ... Dr. Joanne ARDOVINI
07 Director of Admissions/Recruitment ... Ms. Shawana SINGLETARY
32 Dean of Students ... Ms. Clotilde IBARRA
12 Exec Director of MCNY Bronx Campus ... Mr. John EDWARDS
37 Dir of Financial Aid/Scholarships ... Mr. Lakhbir SINGH
06 Assc Dir Stdnt Records/Registration ... Ms. Joanna BOSTON
08 Director of Library Services ... Ms. Kate ADLER
09 Dir Institutional Rsrch/Assessment ... Mr. Anthony WILLIAMS
26 Director Public/Alumni Relations ... Ms. Tina GEORGIOU
113 Bursar ... Mr. Taurean KENNEDY
04 Exec Assistant to the President ... Ms. Isabel CABRERA

Mildred Elley (H)

855 Central Avenue, Albany NY 12206
County: Albany FICE Identification: 022195
Unit ID: 193201
Telephone: (518) 786-0855 Carnegie Class: Assoc/HVT-High Trad
FAX Number: (518) 786-0898 Calendar System: Other
URL: www.mildred-elley.edu
Established: 1917 Annual Undergrad Tuition & Fees: $13,509
Enrollment: 466 Coed
Affiliation or Control: Proprietary IRS Status: Proprietary
Highest Offering: Associate Degree
Accreditation: ABHES

01 Chairwoman of the Board ... Ms. Faith A. TAKES

Mildred Elley-New York City (I)

25 Broadway, 16th Floor, New York NY 10004
Telephone: (212) 380-9004 Identification: 770747
Accreditation: ABHES

Mirrer Yeshiva Central Institute (J)

1795 Ocean Parkway, Brooklyn NY 11223-2010
County: Kings FICE Identification: 004798
Unit ID: 193247
Telephone: (718) 645-0536 Carnegie Class: Spec-4-yr-Faith
FAX Number: (718) 645-9251 Calendar System: Semester
Established: 1947 Annual Undergrad Tuition & Fees: $10,170
Enrollment: 156 Male
Affiliation or Control: Independent Non-Profit IRS Status: 501(c)3
Highest Offering: Second Talmudic Degree
Accreditation: RABN

00 Chancellor ... Rabbi Avrohom Yaakov NELKENBAUM
01 President and Dean ... Rabbi Osher KALMANOWITZ
05 Vice President & Dean ... Rabbi Asher BERENBAUM
33 Dean of Men ... Rabbi Esrael ERLANGER
03 Executive Director ... Rabbi Pinchas HECHT
06 Registrar-Administrator ... Rabbi Eli ADLIN
08 Director of the Library ... Rabbi Aaron SAPOZNICK
38 Director of Guidance ... Rabbi Yisroel FISHMAN
37 Financial Aid Director ... Mrs. Devorah BERENBAUM

Mohawk Valley Community College (K)

1101 Sherman Drive, Utica NY 13501-5394
County: Oneida FICE Identification: 002871
Unit ID: 193283
Telephone: (315) 792-5400 Carnegie Class: Assoc/HT-Mix Trad/Non
FAX Number: (315) 792-5666 Calendar System: Semester
URL: www.mvcc.edu
Established: 1946 Annual Undergrad Tuition & Fees (In-District): $5,500
Enrollment: 5,704 Coed
Affiliation or Control: State/Local IRS Status: 501(c)3
Highest Offering: Associate Degree
Accreditation: M, ADNUR, CAHIIM, COARC, RAD, SURTEC

01 President ... Dr. Randall J. VAN WAGONER
04 Assistant to the President ... Ms. Gloria KAROL
88 Exec Dir Org Culture & Wellness ... Ms. Jill HEINTZ
09 Dir Institutional Research/Analysis ... Ms. Marie MIKNAVICH
05 Vice Pres Learning/Academic Affairs ... Dr. Lewis J. KAHLER
32 Vice Pres Student Affairs ... Ms. Stephanie C. REYNOLDS
10 Vice Pres Administrative Services ... Mr. Thomas SQUIRES
111 VP Cmty Devel/Exec Dir MVCC Found ... Mr. Frank DUROSS
20 Asst VP Learning/Academic Affairs ... Mr. James LYNCH
108 Dean Curriculum/Assessment ... Ms. Julie DEWAN
20 Asst VP Learning/Academic Affairs ... Mr. Timothy THOMAS
81 Dean School of STEM Transfer ... Mr. Jake MIHEVC
57 Dean School of Art ... Mr. Todd BEHRENDT
50 Dean School of Business/Hospitality ... Ms. Christine VANNAMEE
54 Dean School of STEM Career ... Dr. Robert WOODROW
79 Dean School of Humanities ... Mr. Jim ROBERTS
76 Dean School of Health Sciences ... Ms. Melissa COPPERWHEAT
83 Dean School of Public/Human Service ... Vacant
08 Director College Libraries ... Mr. Stephen FRISBEE
84 Dean Enrollment ... Mrs. Jennifer DEWEERTH
121 Dean Student Support ... Mr. James MAIO
39 Dean Student & Residence Life ... Mr. Dennis GIBBONS
103 Assoc VP of Workforce Development ... Ms. Franca ARMSTRONG
30 Dir of Development ... Ms. Deanna FERRO-AURIENCE
96 Coord Expend/Fixed Asset Procure ... Ms. Joyce PALMER
13 Exec Dir of Information Technology ... Ms. Mary Jane PARRY
88 Dir Ctr Community/Economic Dev ... Ms. Sarah LAM
15 Exec Director of Human Resources ... Mrs. Crystal MARCEAU
26 Director Marketing/Communications ... Mr. Alen SMAJIC
07 Director of Admissions ... Mr. Daniel IANNO
37 Director of Financial Aid ... Mr. Michael PEDE
06 Dir of Student Records/Registrar ... Mrs. Rosemary V. SPETKA
18 Dir of Facilities and Operations ... Mr. Michael MCHARRIS
19 Exec Dir Pub Safety/Emergency Mgmt ... Mr. David AMICO
21 Business Office Controller ... Mr. Brian MOLINARO
41 Dean of Athletics ... Mr. Gary BROADHURST
28 Director of Diversity ... Dr. Todd MARSHALL

Mohawk Valley Community College Rome Campus (L)

1101 Floyd Avenue, Rome NY 13440
Telephone: (315) 339-3470 Identification: 770141
Accreditation: &M

Molloy College (M)

1000 Hempstead Avenue, PO Box 5002,
Rockville Centre NY 11571-5002
County: Nassau FICE Identification: 002775
Unit ID: 193292
Telephone: (516) 323-3000 Carnegie Class: Masters/L
FAX Number: N/A Calendar System: 4/1/4
URL: www.molloy.edu
Established: 1955 Annual Undergrad Tuition & Fees: $32,550

Enrollment: 5,115 Coed
Affiliation or Control: Independent Non-Profit IRS Status: 501(c)3
Highest Offering: Doctorate
Accreditation: M, CACREP, CAEP, CAEPN, COARC, CVT, IACBE, MUS, NMT, NURSE, SP, SW

01 President ... Dr. James P. LENTINI
05 VP Academic Affairs/Dean of Faculty ... Dr. Ann Z. BRANCHINI
10 Vice Pres for Finance & Treasurer ... Ms. Susan WILLIAMS
84 Vice Pres Enrollment Management ... Ms. Linda ALBANESE
111 VP for Advancement ... Mr. Edward J. THOMPSON
32 VP for Student Affairs ... Dr. Janine BRANCINI
45 VP Tech & Inst Effectiveness ... Mr. Michael TORRES
42 VP for Mission & Ministry ... Ms. Catherine MUSCENTE
30 Dir Development & Special Projects ... Ms. Angela ZIMMERMAN
37 Director Student Financial Services ... Ms. Debra OCONNOR
36 Asst Director of Career Services ... Ms. Cristen D'ACCORDO
41 Director of Athletics ... Ms. Susan CASSIDY
07 Asst VP for Enrollment Management ... Ms. Marguerite LANE
37 Director of Financial Aid ... Mrs. Ana C. LOCKWARD
21 Asst VP for Finance ... Ms. Barbara CALISSI
06 Registrar ... Ms. Susan FORTMAN
09 Sr Dir Institutional Effectiveness ... Ms. Christina CAPPELLANO
15 Asst VP for HR & Title IX Coord ... Ms. Lisa MILLER
18 Asst VP for Facilities ... Mr. James MULTARI
26 Asst VP of Marketing & PR ... Mr. Ken YOUNG
29 Director of Alumni Relations ... Ms. Mary Jane REILLY
19 Director of Public Safety ... Mr. Brian CONNORS
85 Director of International Education ... Ms. Kimberly LANGENMAYR
105 Director of Web Technologies ... Vacant
20 Asst VP for Academic Affairs ... Dr. Barbara T. SCHMIDT
13 Sr Director of IT ... Mr. Michael OLIVO
91 Dir Networking/Infrastructure ... Mr. Sean LAURIE
08 Head Librarian ... Ms. Judith BRINK-DRESCHER
100 Chief of Staff ... Ms. Diane K. FORNIERI
106 Dean Innovative Delivery Methods ... Ms. Amy GAIMARO
04 Executive Asst to the President ... Ms. Ann Marie LUONGO

Monroe College (A)

2501 Jerome Avenue, Bronx NY 10468-5407
County: Bronx FICE Identification: 004799
Unit ID: 193308
Telephone: (718) 933-6700 Carnegie Class: Masters/L
FAX Number: (718) 295-5861 Calendar System: Semester
URL: www.monroecollege.edu
Established: 1933 Annual Undergrad Tuition & Fees: $16,536
Enrollment: 6,541 Coed
Affiliation or Control: Proprietary IRS Status: Proprietary
Highest Offering: Master's
Accreditation: M, ACBSP, ACFEI, ADNUR, CAEP, NUR, PNUR

01 President ... Marc M. JEROME
05 SVP of Academic/Student Affairs ... Dr. Karenann CARTY
21 Controller ... Olesia TIAGI
12 SVP/Bronx Campus Dean ... Anthony ALLEN
12 SVP/New Rochelle Campus Dean ... David DIMOND
26 Executive Director Public Affairs ... Jacqueline RUEGGER
58 SVP King Graduate School ... Alex EPHREM
32 VP Academic/Student Affairs ... Carol GENESE
86 Asst Vice Pres Governmental Affairs ... Dr. Donald E. SIMON
108 Asst VP Inst Research & Effective ... Dr. Edward S. SCHNEIDERMAN
27 Executive Director of Marketing ... Lauren ROSENTHAL
06 Registrar ... Abigail THORPE
09 Dir Institutional Research ... Peter NWAKEZE
07 Dean Admissions NR Campus ... Michael NIEDZWIECKI
21 AVP Student Financial Services ... Daniel SHARON
113 Bursar ... Scott STERN
35 Dean of Intl Student Services ... Mark SONNENSTEIN
07 Dean of International Admissions ... Gersom LOPEZ
07 Vice President Online Admissions ... Craig PATRICK
37 Director Student Financial Aid ... Calette FAGAN-MURDOCK
36 VP Corporate & Community Outreach ... Pamela DELLAPORTA
08 Director of Library Services BX ... Christine ARTIS
08 Director of Library Services NR ... Tom GORDON
39 Director of Residential Life ... Romario DACOSTA
29 Director of Alumni Relations ... Leslie JEROME
13 Chief Info Technology Officer (CIO) ... Michael MCGOVERN
04 Executive Assistant to President ... Jennifer NACCARI
15 Director of Human Resources ... Kerry MCLAUGHLIN
19 Director of Public Safety ... Clifford HOLLINGSWORTH
41 Athletic Director ... Luis MELENDEZ

Monroe Community College (B)

1000 E Henrietta Road, Rochester NY 14623-5780
County: Monroe FICE Identification: 002872
Unit ID: 193326
Telephone: (585) 292-2000 Carnegie Class: Assoc/HT-Mix Trad/Non
FAX Number: (585) 427-2749 Calendar System: Semester
URL: www.monroecc.edu
Established: 1961 Annual Undergrad Tuition & Fees (In-District): $5,662
Enrollment: 10,161 Coed
Affiliation or Control: State/Local IRS Status: 501(c)3
Highest Offering: Associate Degree
Accreditation: M, ADNUR, CAHIIM, DH, EMT, MLTAD, RAD, SURGT

01 President ... Dr. DeAnna R. BURT-NANNA
05 Provost & VP Academic Svcs ... Dr. Andrea C. WADE
84 Assoc VP Enrollment Mgmt ... Ms. Christine CASALINUOVO-ADAMS
32 Acting VP Student Services ... Dr. Kimberly MCKINSEY-MABRY
10 Int CFO & VP Admin Svcs ... Mr. Darrell JACHIM-MOORE
103 Acting VP Econ Dev/Workforce Svc ... Ms. Kristin M. SINE-KINZ
102 VP Advancement/Dir MCC Foundation ... Ms. Gretchen D. WOOD
12 Exec Dean Downtown Campus ... Dr. Joel L. FRATER
35 Assoc Vice Pres Student Services ... Mr. John J. DELATE
13 AVP Technology Svcs/CIO ... Ms. Eileen M. WIRLEY
18 Assoc Vice Pres Facilities ... Mr. Blaine D. GRINDLE
88 Assoc Vice Pres Instructional Svc ... Mr. Terrance KEYS
20 Assoc Vice Pres Academic Services ... Ms. Kimberley COLLINS
88 Director Financial Aid Compliance ... Mr. Jerome S. ST. CROIX
09 Director Institutional Research ... Mr. William DIXON
08 Director ETS Libraries ... Ms. Katherine E. GHIDIU
36 Director Career & Veteran Services ... Ms. Michelle P. MAYO
21 Assoc Vice President Admin Svcs ... Mr. Darrell K. JACHIM-MOORE
28 Chief Diversity Officer ... Dr. Calvin J. GANTT
06 Director Registrar & Records ... Ms. Sarah HAGREEN
30 Director of Development ... Mr. Mark J. PASTORELLA
38 Dir Counseling & Disability Svcs ... Ms. Aubrey ZAMIARA
19 Director Public Safety ... Mr. Melvin (Tony) A. PEREZ
41 Director Athletics ... Mr. Aaron M. BOUYEA
25 Director Grants ... Vacant
23 Director of Health Services ... Ms. Jacqueline M. CARSON
21 Controller ... Mr. Michael G. QUINN
79 Dean Humanities & Social Services ... Mr. Michael JACOBS
81 Dean STEM and Health ... Ms. Margaret I. KAMINSKY
88 Dean Academic Foundations ... Ms. Medea RAMBISH
19 Dean Public Safety Training Ctr ... Mr. Michael S. KARNES
35 Director Student Svcs DC ... Ms. Kimberly F. DELARGE
20 Dean Acad Svcs DC ... Dr. Kimberly MCKINSEY-MABRY
15 Director Human Resources ... Ms. Kristen M. LOWE
40 Manager Bookstore ... Ms. Charlene SUTER
22 Director Educ Opportunity Program ... Ms. Brenda A. SMITH
121 Director Advise/Transfer Services ... Vacant
43 Legal Counsel ... Vacant
37 Dir Financial Aid Opers ... Ms. Melissa M. JARKOWSKI
96 Director of Purchasing ... Mr. Patrick M. BATES
39 Director Housing/Residence Life ... Ms. Jamia DANZY
04 Executive Asst to President ... Ms. Sheila M. STRONG
07 Director of Admissions ... Vacant
101 Secy to the Board of Trustees/Pres ... Ms. Linda M. HALL
108 Asst Director Assessment/Curriculum ... Dr. Susan L. HALL
29 Coord Alumni & Annual Giving ... Ms. Karen A. SHAW
45 Director Institutional Planning ... Ms. Valarie L. AVALONE
90 Assoc Dir Comm and Network Services ... Mr. James F. CLEMENT
86 Asst to the Pres Govt/Cmty Rels ... Mr. Clayton W. JONES

Montefiore School of Nursing (C)

53 Valentine Street, Mount Vernon NY 10550
County: Westchester FICE Identification: 022178
Unit ID: 193380
Telephone: (914) 361-6221 Carnegie Class: Not Classified
FAX Number: (914) 665-7047 Calendar System: Semester
URL: www.montefioreschoolofnursing.org
Established: 2014 Annual Undergrad Tuition & Fees: $12,067
Enrollment: 88 Coed
Affiliation or Control: Independent Non-Profit IRS Status: 501(c)3
Highest Offering: Associate Degree
Accreditation: ADNUR

05 Dean ... Dr. Rebecca GREER
20 Assistant Dean ... Susan JOSEPH
32 Coordinator of Student Services ... Chanelle HYDE

Mount Saint Mary College (D)

330 Powell Avenue, Newburgh NY 12550-3412
County: Orange FICE Identification: 002778
Unit ID: 193353
Telephone: (845) 561-0800 Carnegie Class: Masters/M
FAX Number: (845) 562-6762 Calendar System: Semester
URL: www.msmc.edu
Established: 1959 Annual Undergrad Tuition & Fees: $34,412
Enrollment: 2,125 Coed
Affiliation or Control: Independent Non-Profit IRS Status: 501(c)3
Highest Offering: Master's
Accreditation: M, CAEP, IACBE, NURSE

01 President ... Dr. Jason N. ADSIT
05 Vice President for Academic Affairs ... Dr. George ABAUNZA
10 Vice Pres Finance & Admin/Treasurer ... Mr. Art GLASS
111 Vice Pres for College Advancement ... Mrs. Nikki KHURANA-BAUGH
32 Vice President for Students ... Mrs. Elaine O'GRADY
20 Assistant VP for Academic Affairs ... Mrs. Barbara W. PETRUZZELLI
84 Dean of Admissions ... Mrs. Susana BRISCOE-ALBA
38 Asst Dean of Support Services ... Vacant
06 Registrar ... Ms. Jannelle HAUG
07 Director of Admissions ... Ms. Eileen BARDNEY
08 Director of the Library ... Ms. Vivian MILCZARSKI
37 Director of Financial Aid ... Ms. Thalia MCFARLANE
09 Asst VP of Inst Research/CDO ... Mr. Ryan WILLIAMS
15 Director of Human Resources ... Mrs. Sharnie CANARY
42 Chaplain ... Fr. Gregoire J. FLUET
35 Director of Student Activities ... Ms. Barbara MULLIGAN
29 Director of Alumni Affairs ... Ms. Michelle A. IACUESSA
41 Director of Athletics & Recreation ... Ms. Jessica MUSHEL
36 Director of the Career Center ... Ms. Ellen BOURHIS NOLAN
13 Chief Information Officer ... Mr. Dennis RUSH
96 Purchasing Manager ... Mr. Brian MOORE
106 Director of Online Learning ... Ms. Kristen DELLASALA
39 Director of Residence Life ... Ms. Amy R. WEIT
18 Exec Director of Facilities & Space ... Ms. Maryann PILON
26 Exec Dir of Marketing/Communication ... Mr. Dean DIMARZO
04 Executive Asst to the President ... Ms. Barbara CONNOLLY
19 Director Security/Safety ... Mr. Richard J. ALGARIN
44 Director Annual Giving ... Ms. Margaret TREACY
50 Dean School of Business ... Ms. Tiffany N. GAGLIANO
66 Dean School of Nursing ... Vacant
88 Asst to Pres Mission Integration ... Dr. Charles ZOLA

Nassau Community College (E)

1 Education Drive, Garden City NY 11530-6793
County: Nassau FICE Identification: 002873
Unit ID: 193478
Telephone: (516) 572-7501 Carnegie Class: Assoc/HT-High Trad
FAX Number: (516) 572-7750 Calendar System: Semester
URL: www.ncc.edu
Established: 1959 Annual Undergrad Tuition & Fees (In-District): $6,330
Enrollment: 13,864 Coed
Affiliation or Control: State/Local IRS Status: 501(c)3
Highest Offering: Associate Degree
Accreditation: M, ADNUR, CAHIIM, COARC, FUSER, MLTAD, PTAA, RTT, SURGT

01 President ... Dr. Jermaine F. WILLIAMS
05 VP Academic Affairs ... Dr. Mark C. LAUSCH
18 VP Facilities Management ... Dr. Joseph V. MUSCARELLA
10 VP Finance/CFO ... Mr. Julio IZQUIERDO
21 Asst VP Office of Comptroller ... Vacant
32 VP Academic Student Services ... Ms. Maria P. CONZATTI
20 AVP Academic/Student Services ... Mr. David FOLLICK
111 VP Institutional Advancement ... Mr. Adrian KERRIGAN
22 Assoc VP Equity/Inclusion & AA/CDO ... Dr. Craig J. WRIGHT
28 Dir Affirm Action & Compliance ... Ms. Nardos HAMILTON
51 Assoc Vice Pres Lifelong Learning ... Dr. Janet CARUSO
43 General Counsel ... Ms. Donna M. HAUGEN
103 Asst Dir Workforce Development ... Ms. Katherine WAGNER
88 Asst VP Labor Relations ... Ms. Laurie PEZZULLO
103 Director of Workforce Development ... Ms. Dawn NOLAN
88 Asst Dir Community Pgms/Testing ... Ms. Maureen RAMERT
113 Dir Student Financial Affairs ... Ms. Annmarie WELCH
21 AVP Finance ... Ms. Lisa HAHN
15 Associate VP Human Resources ... Ms. Dorlena DUNBAR
93 Director EOP ... Mr. William CLYDE, JR.
113 Assoc VP Student Financial Affairs ... Ms. Sandra V. FRIEDMAN
45 AVP Inst Effectiveness & Strat Plng ... Dr. John D. OSAE-KWAPONG
96 Director Procurement ... Mr. Phillip CAPPELLO
35 Dean of Students ... Dr. Charmian SMITH
18 Acting Asst VP Design & Construct ... Mr. Robert JAROCKI
88 Asst Dean Judicial Affairs ... Dr. Adeoba (David) OYERO
88 Asst Dean Judicial Affairs ... Ms. Jacqueline CUFFEY
79 Dean Arts & Humanities ... Vacant
83 Dean Soc & Behavioral Sciences ... Ms. Genette ALVAREZ-ORTIZ
81 Dean Math & Science ... Vacant
66 Dean Nursing & Health Sciences ... Vacant
107 Dean Professional Studies ... Dr. Jerry KORNBLUTH
108 Asst VP Acad Assess Program Review ... Vacant
37 Director Financial Aid ... Ms. Patricia NOREN
25 Asst VP Sponsored Programs ... Mr. Edmund KOEPPEL
16 Asst VP HR Operations ... Ms. Deborah REED-SEGRETI
106 Asst VP Distance Education ... Dr. Deborah SPIRO
88 Dir Environmental Health & Safety ... Mr. Robert RAMIREZ
26 Dir Marketing/Communications ... Ms. Lindsey ANGIOLETTI
08 Chairperson Library ... Ms. Christine FARADAY
41 Director Athletics/PED ... Ms. Kerri-Ann MCTIERNAN
06 Registrar ... Mr. Chester BARKAN
19 Director Public Safety ... Mr. Martin RODDINI
23 Director Student Health Services ... Dr. Neil SINGHANI
121 Director Academic Advisement ... Ms. Amanda FOX
13 Asst VP/CIO ... Vacant
91 IT Manager Network Services ... Ms. Maryam MIRZA
102 Executive Dir NCC Foundation ... Ms. Joy DEDONATO
04 Exec Asst to Pres/Board of Trustees ... Ms. Anne E. BRANDI
36 Dir Placement Testing ... Ms. Noreen WADE
09 Asst Dir Institutional Effectivenes ... Ms. Tina S. WYNDER
85 Dean International Education ... Vacant

Nazareth College of Rochester (F)

4245 East Avenue, Rochester NY 14618-3790
County: Monroe FICE Identification: 002779
Unit ID: 193584
Telephone: (585) 389-2525 Carnegie Class: Masters/L
FAX Number: (585) 586-2452 Calendar System: Semester
URL: www.naz.edu
Established: 1924 Annual Undergrad Tuition & Fees: $36,735
Enrollment: 2,791 Coed
Affiliation or Control: Independent Non-Profit IRS Status: 501(c)3
Highest Offering: Doctorate
Accreditation: M, AAQEP, ACATE, ART, MT, MUS, NURSE, OT, PTA, SP, SW

01 President ... Dr. Elizabeth L. PAUL
04 Executive Assistant to President ... Ms. Cathleen M. STEVENS
05 Vice President Academic Affairs ... Dr. Andrea TALENTINO
111 Vice Pres Institutional Advancement ... Mr. Darrell BELL
10 Vice President Finance & Admin ... Mr. Patrick RICHEY
84 Vice Pres Enrollment & Student Exp ... Mr. Frank WILLIAMS
28 Vice President Diversity/Inclusion ... Dr. Lisa DURANT-JONES
26 VP Marketing & Communications ... Ms. Elizabeth CRONIN

15 Assoc VP Human Resources ....Ms. Deborah J. WINSLOW-SCHABER
32 Assoc VP Student Engagement ....Ms. Kim HARVEY
20 Asst VP Academic Affairs ....Dr. Mary Ellen VORE
06 Registrar ....Vacant
37 Director Student Financial Aid ....Ms. Janice SCHEUTZOW
13 Director Information Tech Svcs ....Ms. Karen KUPPINGER
08 Director of Library ....Ms. Catherine DOYLE
19 Director of Security ....Ms. Terri STEWART
29 Director of Alumni Relations ....Vacant
41 Director of Athletics ....Mr. Peter G. BOTHNER
42 Director Center for Spirituality ....Mr. Jamie FAZIO
36 Director of Career Services ....Vacant
18 Director Buildings/Grounds ....Mr. Peter LANA
09 Director of Institutional Research ....Vacant
23 Director of Health Services ....Ms. Susan QUINN
121 Director of Academic Advisement ....Ms. Linda SEARING
113 Bursar ....Mr. John GARBE
49 Dean of Col of Arts and Sciences ....Dr. Dianne OLIVER
76 Dean School of Health & Human Svcs ....Dr. Catherine RASMUSSIN
53 Dean School of Education ....Dr. Kathleen DABOLL-LAVOIE
50 Dean Sch of Business & Leadership ....Dr. Kenneth RHEA
88 Exec Dir of Ctr International Educ ....Dr. Nevan FISHER
88 Dir of Center for Service Learning ....Ms. Shirley SOMMERS
89 Dir Stdnt Transition/First Year Ctr ....Mr. Andrew MORRIS
96 Director of Purchasing ....Ms. Joanne FITZGERALD
88 Dir Center for Civic Engagement ....Ms. Nuala BOYLE
123 Dir Graduate Admissions/Transfer ....Ms. Judith G. BAKER
86 Director Government Relations ....Ms. Mary Kay BISHOP

The New School (A)

66 W 12th Street, New York NY 10011-8603

County: New York — FICE Identification: 020662
Unit ID: 193654
Telephone: (212) 229-5600 — Carnegie Class: DU-Higher
FAX Number: N/A — Calendar System: Semester
URL: www.newschool.edu
Established: 1919 — Annual Undergrad Tuition & Fees: $51,022
Enrollment: 9,047 — Coed
Affiliation or Control: Independent Non-Profit — IRS Status: 501(c)3
Highest Offering: Doctorate
Accreditation: M, CLPSY, SPAA

01 President ....Dr. Dwight A. MCBRIDE
101 Sr VP Admin/Univ Sec/Chief of Staff ....Dr. Jennifer HOBBS
04 Executive Assistant to President ....Ms. Mary KARMELEK
05 Exec VP Academic Affairs/Provost ....Dr. Renée T. WHITE
88 Sr Director/Chief of Strategy ....Ms. Jane MCNAMARA
10 Exec VP Business & Operations ....Mr. Tokumbo SHOBOWALE
11 Asst VP Business & Operations/COS ....Ms. Lisa BONNER
48 Exec Dean Parsons School for Design ....Dr. Rachel SCHREIBER
82 Exec Dean Pub Engage & Dean Milano ....Dr. Mary WATSON
64 Exec Dean Perf Arts and Dean Mannes ....Mr. Richard KESSLER
83 Dean New School for Social Research ....Dr. William MILBERG
49 Dean Eugene Lang College ....Dr. Jennifer WILSON
12 Dean Parsons Paris ....Ms. Florence LECLERC-DICKLER
30 Sr VP Development/Alumni Engagement ....Mr. Jonah NIGH
26 Sr VP Marketing and Business Dev ....Ms. Anne ADRIANCE
43 Sr VP and General Counsel ....Mr. Jerry CUTLER
28 Sr VP EISJ/Chief Diversity Officer ....Ms. Melanie HART
20 Sr Vice Prov for Faculty Affairs ....Dr. Michael SCHOBER
20 Dep Prov Academic Planning & Admin ....Ms. Jin KIM
84 Sr Vice Prov Enrollment Management ....Ms. Carol KIM
20 Vice Provost Curriculum & Learning ....Ms. Maggie KOOZER
46 Vice Provost Research ....Dr. Adam BROWN
09 Vice Prov Inst Rsrch Decison Sup ....Dr. Paula MAAS
32 Interim Vice Prov Student Success ....Ms. Xenia MARKOWITT
88 Assoc Dean/Dean Fashion ....Dr. Ben BARRY
88 Assc Dn/Dean Art/Design Hist/Theory ....Dr. Rhonda GARELICK
88 Assoc Dean/Dean Art/Media & Tech ....Dr. Shana AGID
88 Assoc Dean/Dean Constructed Envir ....Mr. David LEWIS
88 Assoc Dean/Dean Media Studies ....Mr. Vladan NIKOLIC
48 Assoc Dean/Dean Design Strategies ....Ms. Cynthia LAWSON
88 Assoc Dean/Dean Undergrad Stds ....Ms. Erin CHO
88 Assoc Dean/Dean School of Drama ....Mr. Pippin PARKER
64 Assoc Dean/Dean School of Jazz ....Mr. Keller COKER
88 Director Creative Writing ....Mr. Luis JARAMILLO
06 VP & University Registrar ....Ms. Rebecca HUNTER
20 Assoc Provost Faculty Affairs ....Dr. Eleni LITT
08 Assoc Prov Libraries/Archives & Ac ....Mr. Ed SCARCELLE
35 Assoc Prov for Student Life ....Ms. Susan AUSTIN
121 Assoc Prov Acad Advising/Career Dev ....Ms. Lorenley BAEZ
88 Assoc VP Community Engagement ....Ms. Deborah BOGOSIAN
88 Sr VP Corporate Partnerships ....Ms. Deborah GIBB
15 VP Human Resources ....Ms. Sonya WILLIAMS
27 VP University Marketing ....Ms. Lisa PRESTON
31 Asst VP Cmty and Public Affairs ....Ms. Amy MALSIN
86 Sr Dir Government and Ext Affairs ....Vacant
43 Deputy General Counsel ....Ms. Junea WILLIAMS-EDMUND
13 Sr VP & Chief Information Officer ....Mr. Lin ZHOU
14 Assoc VP Foundation Technology ....Mr. Chris BREZIL
91 Asst VP Enterprise Applications/BI ....Mr. Shawn OGIBA
90 Sr Director Academic Technology ....Mr. Marcus LONGMUIR
14 Sr Director Operations (IT) ....Ms. Jennifer SMITH
119 Director Info Security and Privacy ....Vacant
21 Asst VP Finance & Controller ....Ms. Natalie PRESSEY
114 Asst VP Budget & Planning ....Ms. Loretta FERRARI
96 Director of Business Operations ....Mr. Gregory HERRERA
22 VP EEO/Affirmative Action ....Ms. Rhonnie JAUS
16 Asst VP Human Resources ....Mr. Irwin KROOT
118 Asst VP Benefits ....Ms. Andrea YENCO
18 Asst VP Facilities Management ....Mr. Thomas WHALEN
88 Asst VP Design & Construction ....Ms. Jo GOLDBERGER
19 Director Security ....Mr. Thomas ILICETO
102 Asst VP Inst Giving/Acad Initiative ....Ms. Laura CRONIN
112 Asst VP of Development Parsons ....Mr. André ALLAIRE
112 Asst VP of Development NSSR ....Ms. Meg KAUFMAN
23 Assoc Provost Student Health Svcs ....Ms. Tracy ROBIN
38 Sr Director Counseling Services ....Dr. Jerry FINKELSTEIN
124 Asst Prov for Student Engagement ....Mr. Zach HARRELL
93 Asst Prov for Student Advocacy ....Ms. Shondrika MERRITT
25 Asst Provost Research Support ....Dr. Cheryl GREEN
37 Sr Director Financial Aid ....Ms. Deirdre BAIRSTOW-ALLEN
22 Director Student Disability Svcs ....Mr. Nicholas FARANDA

New York Academy of Art (B)

111 Franklin Street, New York NY 10013

County: New York — FICE Identification: 026001
Unit ID: 366368
Telephone: (212) 966-0300 — Carnegie Class: Spec-4-yr-Arts
FAX Number: N/A — Calendar System: Semester
URL: www.nyaa.edu
Established: 1982 — Annual Graduate Tuition & Fees: N/A
Enrollment: 97 — Coed
Affiliation or Control: Independent Non-Profit — IRS Status: 501(c)3
Highest Offering: Master's; No Undergraduates
Accreditation: M, ART

01 President ....Mr. David KRATZ
05 Provost ....Mr. Peter DRAKE
30 Vice Pres of Development ....Mr. Gregory THORNBURY
32 Director of Student Services ....Ms. Noelle TIMMONS
11 Director of Operations ....Mr. Michael SMITH
06 Registrar/Director of Admissions ....Ms. Katie HEMMER

New York Automotive and Diesel Institute (C)

178-18 Liberty Avenue, Jamaica NY 11433

County: Queens — FICE Identification: 035373
Telephone: (718) 658-0006 — Carnegie Class: Not Classified
FAX Number: (718) 658-4044 — Calendar System: Semester
URL: nyadi.edu
Established: — Annual Undergrad Tuition & Fees: N/A
Enrollment: N/A — Coed
Affiliation or Control: Proprietary — IRS Status: Proprietary
Highest Offering: Associate Degree
Accreditation: ACCSC

01 College President ....Patrick HART
05 Dean of Academic Affairs ....Joseph SANTORA

New York College of Health Professions (D)

6801 Jericho Turnpike, Syosset NY 11791-4413

County: Nassau — FICE Identification: 025994
Unit ID: 418126
Telephone: (516) 364-0808 — Carnegie Class: Spec-4-yr-Other Health
FAX Number: (516) 364-6645 — Calendar System: Trimester
URL: www.nycollege.edu
Established: 1981 — Annual Undergrad Tuition & Fees: $14,226
Enrollment: 367 — Coed
Affiliation or Control: Independent Non-Profit — IRS Status: 501(c)3
Highest Offering: Master's
Accreditation: NY, #ACUP

01 President ....Dr. A Li SONG
10 Chief Financial Officer ....Mr. Errol VIRASAWMI
63 Dean Grad Sch Oriental Medicine ....Dr. Lizel STOVER
05 Dean of Academic Affairs ....Vacant
06 Registrar ....Ms. Amy KOTOWSKI
08 Dir Library/Information Services ....Ms. Cynthia CAYEA
09 Director of Institutional Research ....Mr. Timothy BOUDREAU
113 Bursar ....Ms. Jacqueline MCINTYRE
13 Manager Information Technology ....Mr. Peter WANG
32 Student Services Administrator ....Mr. Brian ALVAREZ
88 Dean Sch of Massage Therapy ....Dr. Steven HAFFNER

New York College of Podiatric Medicine (E)

53 E 124th Street, New York NY 10035-1815

County: New York — FICE Identification: 002749
Unit ID: 194073
Telephone: (212) 410-8000 — Carnegie Class: Spec-4-yr-Med
FAX Number: (212) 876-7670 — Calendar System: Semester
URL: www.nycpm.edu
Established: 1911 — Annual Undergrad Tuition & Fees: N/A
Enrollment: 337 — Coed
Affiliation or Control: Independent Non-Profit — IRS Status: 501(c)3
Highest Offering: First Professional Degree
Accreditation: POD

01 President ....Mr. Louis L. LEVINE
05 Vice Pres Academic Affairs/Dean ....Dr. Michael J. TREPAL
11 Chief Operating Ofcr/VP Admin ....Mr. Joel STURM
10 Sr Director of Finance ....Mr. Avi COHEN
13 Vice Pres Info Systems & Technology ....Mr. Aman SAFAEI
63 VP Medical Education/Medical Dir ....Dr. Mark SWARTZ
20 Dean Clinical Educ/Dir Res Pgms ....Dr. Ronald SOAVE
09 Dean Institutional Research ....Dr. Eileen CHUSID
32 Dean Student Affairs ....Ms. Lisa LEE
07 Asst Dean Academic Administration ....Mr. Alain SILVERIO
88 Asst Clinical Clerkships/Affairs ....Ms. Maxiel MEDINA
26 Director Public Affairs/Development ....Ms. Ellen LUBELL
08 Director of Library ....Mr. Paul TREMBLAY
06 Registrar ....Ms. Doreen D'AMICO
19 Director Security/Safety ....Mr. James WARREN
39 Housing Manager ....Ms. Natasha PEELE
15 Chief Human Resources Officer ....Ms. Sandra DANIELS

New York College of Traditional Chinese Medicine (F)

200 Old Country Road, Suite 500, Mineola NY 11501-4204

County: Nassau — FICE Identification: 034433
Unit ID: 439783
Telephone: (516) 739-1545 — Carnegie Class: Spec-4-yr-Other Health
FAX Number: (516) 873-9622 — Calendar System: Trimester
URL: www.nyctcm.edu
Established: 1996 — Annual Undergrad Tuition & Fees: N/A
Enrollment: 213 — Coed
Affiliation or Control: Independent Non-Profit — IRS Status: 501(c)3
Highest Offering: Master's
Accreditation: ACUP

01 President ....Dr. Yemeng CHEN
10 Administrative Dean ....Ms. Megan HAUNGS
05 Academic Dean ....Dr. Sunny SHEN
07 Admissions Manager ....Ms. Lynn BAI
23 Clinic Director ....Ms. Mona LEE-YUAN
88 Clinic Manager ....Ms. Yiping ZHAO
06 Records Manager ....Ms. Susan SU
37 Financial Aid/Admin Coordinator ....Ms. Elise MA
21 Financial Manager ....Ms. Lily ZOU
08 Operations Manager ....Ms. Ling Ling CHANG
32 Student Services Coordinator ....Ms. Lois GROSS

The New York Conservatory for Dramatic Arts (G)

39 West 19th Street, New York NY 10011

County: New York — FICE Identification: 031207
Unit ID: 421841
Telephone: (212) 645-0030 — Carnegie Class: Spec 2-yr-A&S
FAX Number: (212) 645-0039 — Calendar System: Semester
URL: www.nycda.edu
Established: 1980 — Annual Undergrad Tuition & Fees: $34,400
Enrollment: 257 — Coed
Affiliation or Control: Proprietary — IRS Status: Proprietary
Highest Offering: Associate Degree
Accreditation: THEA

00 CEO ....Mike Vishol DABIDAT
01 President/Artistic Director ....Richard OMAR
05 Director of Education ....Jay GOLDENBERG
06 Registrar ....Nazig TCHAKARIAN
08 Head Librarian ....Martha REPPETTO
07 Director of Admissions ....Bryce RUSSELL
10 Chief Business Officer ....Emily CHOU
37 Director Student Financial Aid ....Alexander VO

New York Graduate School of Psychoanalysis (H)

16 West Tenth Street, New York NY 10011

Telephone: (212) 260-7050 — Identification: 770116
Accreditation: &EH

† Branch campus of Boston Graduate School of Psychoanalysis, Brookline, MA

New York Institute of Technology (I)

Northern Boulevard, Old Westbury NY 11568-8000

County: Nassau — FICE Identification: 004804
Unit ID: 194091
Telephone: (516) 686-7516 — Carnegie Class: Masters/L
FAX Number: (516) 686-7613 — Calendar System: Semester
URL: www.nyit.edu
Established: 1955 — Annual Undergrad Tuition & Fees: $39,760
Enrollment: 6,851 — Coed
Affiliation or Control: Independent Non-Profit — IRS Status: 501(c)3
Highest Offering: Doctorate
Accreditation: M, ARCPA, CACREP, CAEP, CIDA, NURSE, OSTEO, OT, PTA

01 President ....Dr. Henry FOLEY
05 Provost/Vice Pres Academic Affairs ....Dr. Junius GONZALEZ
11 EVP & COO ....Dr. Jerry BALENTINE
20 Associate Provost ....Dr. Michaela ROME
111 Vice Pres Advancement/Alumni Rels ....Mr. Patrick MINSON
26 Vice Pres Strategic Communications ....Dr. Nada ANID
10 VP Financial Affs/CFO & Treasurer ....Ms. Barbara HOLAHAN
21 Controller ....Ms. Eileen VALERIO
43 General Counsel ....Ms. Catherine FLICKINGER
13 CIO & VP Information Tech ....Ms. Pennie TURGEON
84 VP Enrollment Management ....Mr. Joseph POSILLICO
18 Chief Arch/VP RE & Sus Cap Plng ....Ms. Suzanne MUSHO
06 Registrar ....Ms. Kristen SMITH
76 Dean School of Health Professions ....Dr. Gordon SCHMIDT

48 Dean Sch Architecture & Design ... Ms. Maria PERBELLINI
54 Dean School of Engr/Computer Sci ... Dr. Babak DASTGHEIB-BEHESHTI
49 Dean School Arts & Sciences ... Dr. Daniel QUIGLEY
50 Dean School of Management ... Dr. Jess BORONICO
32 Dean of Students/Student Life ... Mr. Felipe HENAO
36 Director Career Services ... Ms. Laurie HOLLISTER
09 Sr Director Rsrch/Assess/Dec Supp ... Mr. Michael LANE
22 Director Compliance/Title IX Coord ... Ms. Cheryl MONTICCIOLO
07 Dean Admissions & Financial Aid ... Ms. Karen VAHEY
27 Exec Dir of Strategic Comm ... Ms. Bobbie DELL'AQUILO
29 Asst Director of Alumni Relations ... Ms. Sabrina POLIDORO
88 Assoc Dir Operations RE & Sus Cap ... Mr. Spiros DANDOURAS
19 Director Security ... Mr. John ESPINA
25 Sr Dir Sponsored Pgm & Research ... Ms. Dawn GRZAN
121 Asst Dean Advising & Enrichment ... Ms. Monika ROHDE
15 Executive Director Human Resources ... Ms. Carol JABLONSKY
14 Director Academic Tech Svcs ... Ms. Laurie HARVEY
91 Director Systems & Network ... Mr. Brian MAROLDO
04 Special Assistant to President ... Mr. Michael SCHIAVETTA
105 Director Web Services ... Mr. Bobby SAHA
96 Assistant Director of Purchasing ... Ms. Kelly CASTILLO

New York Law School (A)

185 West Broadway, New York NY 10013-2959
County: New York FICE Identification: 002783
Unit ID: 193821
Telephone: (212) 431-2100 Carnegie Class: Spec-4-yr-Law
FAX Number: (212) 965-8833 Calendar System: Semester
URL: www.nyls.edu
Established: 1891 Annual Graduate Tuition & Fees: N/A
Enrollment: 1,076 Coed
Affiliation or Control: Independent Non-Profit IRS Status: 501(c)3
Highest Offering: Doctorate; No Undergraduates
Accreditation: LAW

01 Dean and President ... Dean Anthony CROWELL
05 Assoc Dean Academic/Student Engage . Dean William P. LAPIANA
10 Sr Vice President & CFO ... Mr. Plachikkat (PV) ANANTHARAM
26 Asst VP of Marketing/Communications ... Ms. Regina CHUNG
08 Director of Law Library/Assoc Dean ... Prof. Camille BROUSSARD
111 Assoc Dean Institutional Advancemnt ... Mr. Jeffery BECHERER
07 Asst Dean of Admissions & Finan Aid ... Ms. Ella Mae ESTRADA
36 Assoc Dean Acad Plng and Career Dev ... Ms. Erin BOND
21 Vice Pres Financial Plng & Mgmt ... Ms. Susan REDLER
18 Chief Maintenance/Operations/Secur ... Mr. Paul REPETTO
15 Vice President Human Resources ... Ms. Jody PARIANTE
09 Sr Dir Institutional Research ... Ms. Jill BEZEL
32 Assistant Dean for Student Life ... Ms. Sally HARDING
88 Senor Asst VP Project Management ... Mr. George HAYES
30 Director of Development ... Vacant
06 Assistant Dean and Registrar ... Mr. Oral HOPE
13 Chief Information Officer ... Mr. Thomas SOCASH
35 Sr Director of Student Life ... Ms. Shani DARBY
96 Purchasing Coordinator ... Mr. Norman DAWKINS
104 Director Study Abroad ... Mr. Michael RHEE
86 Director Government Relations ... Mr. Ariel DVORKIN
37 Director Student Financial Aid ... Mr. David WOODS
04 Exec Assistant to the President ... Mr. Frank CHIAPPETTA
43 Asst Dean & General Counsel ... Mr. Matthew GEWOLB

New York Medical College (B)

40 Sunshine Cottage Road, Valhalla NY 10595-1690
County: Westchester FICE Identification: 002784
Unit ID: 193830
Telephone: (914) 594-4900 Carnegie Class: Spec-4-yr-Med
FAX Number: (914) 594-4145 Calendar System: Other
URL: www.nymc.edu
Established: 1860 Annual Graduate Tuition & Fees: N/A
Enrollment: 1,604 Coed
Affiliation or Control: Jewish IRS Status: 501(c)3
Highest Offering: Doctorate; No Undergraduates
Accreditation: M, DENT, MED, PAST, PH, PTA, SP

00 President ... Dr. Alan H. KADISH
01 Chancellor and CEO ... Dr. Edward C. HALPERIN
100 Chief of Staff ... Ms. Vilma BORDONARO
63 Dean School of Medicine ... Dr. Jerry NADLER
10 Vice Pres Financial Operations ... Mr. Adam D. HAMMERMAN
26 Vice Pres Communications ... Ms. Jennifer RIEKERT
46 Vice President for Research ... Dr. Salomon AMAR
43 Vice Pres/Chief Counsel ... Mr. Nicholas JANIGA
58 Dean Grad Sch Basic Medical Science ... Dr. Marina HOLZ
76 Dean Sch Health Sciences & Practice ... Dr. Robert W. AMLER
30 Chief Development Officer ... Ms. Bess CHAZHUR
86 Vice President Government Affairs ... Dr. Robert W. AMLER
21 Controller ... Ms. Irene CRASTRO-BOLIN
13 Dir Information Tech Services ... Mr. James CURRAN
32 VC Stdnt Svcs/Vice Dean Grad Med Ed ... Dr. Richard G. MCCARRICK
35 Sr Assoc Dean Student Affairs ... Dr. Jane PONTERIO
37 Asc Dn Stdnt Affs/Dir Finan Plng ... Mr. Anthony M. SOZZO
08 Assoc Dean/Dir Health Sci Library ... Ms. Marie ASCHER
07 Director of Admissions ... Ms. Karen MURRAY
06 College Registrar ... Ms. Eileen ROMERO
39 Director Student Housing ... Ms. Katherine E. DILLON
18 Dir Capital Planning/Facilities ... Ms. Sarah COTTET
19 Director of Security ... Mr. William ALLISON
85 Intl Student/Scholar Advisor ... Ms. Elizabeth WARD
23 Director Health Services ... Ms. Marisa MONTECALVO
38 Director Student Counseling ... Dr. Mark SINGER

105 Director Web Communications ... Mr. Kevin R. CUMMINGS
24 Head Educational Media ... Mr. Michael COTTER
14 Coord of Instruct Computing Tech ... Mr. Jason DI NARDI
04 Admin Assistant to the President ... Ms. Ashley MCCARRICK
22 Dir Affirm Action/Equal Opportunity ... Ms. Lisa TRONAZANO
29 Director Alumni Affairs ... Ms. Tara ALFANO
96 Director of Purchasing ... Ms. Maribel GIRALDO

The New York School for Medical and Dental Assistants (C)

33-10 Queens Blvd, Long Island City NY 11101-2327
County: Queens FICE Identification: 010551
Unit ID: 193858
Telephone: (718) 793-2330 Carnegie Class: Not Classified
FAX Number: (718) 793-0619 Calendar System: Semester
URL: nysmda.com
Established: 1967 Annual Undergrad Tuition & Fees: N/A
Enrollment: 381 Coed
Affiliation or Control: Proprietary IRS Status: Proprietary
Highest Offering: Associate Degree
Accreditation: ACCSC

05 Vice President of Academic Affairs ... Ms. Marina KLEBANOV
06 Director of Registrar ... Ms. Shannon NELSON

New York School of Interior Design (D)

170 East 70th Street, New York NY 10021-5110
County: New York FICE Identification: 020690
Unit ID: 194116
Telephone: (212) 472-1500 Carnegie Class: Spec-4-yr-Arts
FAX Number: (212) 472-3800 Calendar System: 4/1/4
URL: www.nysid.edu
Established: 1916 Annual Undergrad Tuition & Fees: $26,322
Enrollment: 621 Coed
Affiliation or Control: Independent Non-Profit IRS Status: 501(c)3
Highest Offering: Master's
Accreditation: M, ART, CIDA

01 President ... Mr. David SPROULS
05 VP Academic Affairs/Dean ... Dr. Ellen FISHER
10 VP for Finance & Administration ... Ms. Jane CHEN
100 Chief of Staff ... Mr. David OWENS-HILL
15 Assistant VP of Administration ... Ms. Yvonne MORAY
20 Associate Dean ... Ms. Barbara LOWENTHAL
32 Dean of Students ... Ms. Karen HIGGINBOTHAM
07 Director of Admissions ... Mr. Brett CIONE
18 Director of Facilities ... Mr. Zeke KOLENOVIC
30 Director of Development ... Ms. Joy COOPER
08 Director of the Library ... Mr. Billy KWAN
06 Registrar ... Ms. Jennifer MELENDEZ
37 Financial Aid Manager ... Mr. Russie ALLEN
113 Bursar ... Mr. Joseph FANTOZZI
13 Dir of Network & Tech Support Svcs ... Mr. Dan TRUONG
38 Director of Counseling Services ... Dr. Penny MORGANSTEIN
09 Director of Institutional Research ... Mr. Christopher VINGER
04 Admin Assistant to the President ... Ms. Jeanne KO

New York Theological Seminary (E)

475 Riverside Drive, Suite 500, New York NY 10115-0083
County: New York FICE Identification: 002674
Unit ID: 193894
Telephone: (212) 870-1211 Carnegie Class: Spec-4-yr-Faith
FAX Number: (212) 870-1236 Calendar System: Semester
URL: www.nyts.edu
Established: 1900 Annual Graduate Tuition & Fees: N/A
Enrollment: 272 Coed
Affiliation or Control: Independent Non-Profit IRS Status: 501(c)3
Highest Offering: Doctorate; No Undergraduates
Accreditation: #THEOL

01 President ... Dr. LaKeesha WALROND
30 VP Inst Advancement & Research ... Vacant
05 VP Academic Affairs/Dean ... Dr. Tamara HENRY
10 Chief Financial Officer/Controller ... Mr. Craig KING
08 Librarian ... Dr. Rafael REYES
06 Registrar ... Ms. Gina L. GREEN
37 Director Financial Aid ... Ms. Tamisia WHITE
105 Director Web Services ... Mr. Ahsan RAZA
108 Director Institutional Assessment ... Vacant
29 Director Alumni Relations ... Mr. Cassius RUDOLPH
38 Director of Student Counseling ... Vacant
07 Director Admissions/Student Svcs ... Dr. Adriane HILL
11 Chief Operations Officer ... Ms. Lenier THOMAS
106 Dean of Online Education/E-learning ... Dr. Jin HAN

New York University (F)

70 Washington Square South, New York NY 10012-1092
County: New York FICE Identification: 002785
Unit ID: 193900
Telephone: (212) 998-1212 Carnegie Class: DU-Highest
FAX Number: N/A Calendar System: Semester
URL: www.nyu.edu
Established: 1831 Annual Undergrad Tuition & Fees: $54,880
Enrollment: 52,775 Coed
Affiliation or Control: Independent Non-Profit IRS Status: 501(c)3
Highest Offering: Doctorate
Accreditation: M, AAQEP, ACATE, ART, CAMPEP, COPSY, DENT, DH, DIETD, DIETI, HSA, IPSY, JOUR, LAW, MED, MIDWF, MPCAC, NURSE, OT, PAST, PH, PLNG, PTA, SP, SPAA, SURGT, SW

01 President ... Dr. Andrew HAMILTON
100 Chief of Staff to President ... Mr. Richard BAUM
05 Provost ... Dr. Katherine FLEMING
03 Executive Vice President ... Dr. Martin DORPH
26 SVP Univ Relations/Public Affairs ... Dr. Lynne BROWN
30 Sr VP Development/Alumni Relations ... Mr. Robert CASHION
32 Sr Vice Pres for Student Affairs ... Dr. Marc L. WAIS
28 SVP Global Inclusion/Diversity Ofcr ... Dr. Lisa COLEMAN
10 SVP Finance and Budget/CFO ... Ms. Stephanie PIANKA
43 SVP/General Counsel & Secretary .. Ms. Aisha OLIVER-STANLEY
46 Vice Provost for Research ... Dr. Stacie GROSSMAN BLOOM
35 VC Global Pgms/Univ Life at NYU ... Dr. Linda G. MILLS
18 VP Capital Projects/Facilities ... Ms. Linda CHIARELLI
27 SVP Public Affairs/Strategic Comm ... Mr. John H. BECKMAN
84 Sr Vice Pres Enrollment ... Ms. MJ KNOLL-FINN
15 Vice Pres Human Resources ... Ms. Sabrina ELLIS
13 VP and Chief Information Officer ... Mr. Len PETERS
45 Vice Provost for Resource Planning ... Mr. Anthony JIGA
19 VP Global Campus Safety ... Mr. Fountain WALKER
06 University Registrar ... Ms. Elizabeth A. KIENLE-GRANZO
20 Deputy Provost ... Dr. C. Cybele RAVER
104 VP for Global Programs ... Dr. Nancy J. MORRISON
07 AVP for Undergrad Admissions ... Mr. Jonathan WILLIAMS
20 Asst Provost Academic Pgm Review ... Dr. Diana L. KARAFIN
41 Asst VP Stdnt Affairs/Dir Athletics ... Mr. Christopher BLEDSOE
23 Assoc VP Stdnt Hlth/Exec Dir SHC ... Dr. Carlo CIOTOLI
37 Asst VP Financial Aid ... Ms. Lynn E. HIGINBOTHAM
22 AVP Ofc of Equal Opportunity ... Ms. Mary SIGNOR
08 Dean of Libraries ... Mr. H. Austin BOOTH
39 Sr Director Housing Services ... Mr. Neil S. HANRAHAN
09 Exec Dir of Institutional Research ... Mr. David P. VINTINNER

Niagara County Community College (G)

3111 Saunders Settlement Road, Sanborn NY 14132-9460
County: Niagara FICE Identification: 002874
Unit ID: 193946
Telephone: (716) 614-6200 Carnegie Class: Assoc/MT-VT-High Trad
FAX Number: (716) 614-6700 Calendar System: Semester
URL: www.niagaracc.suny.edu
Established: 1962 Annual Undergrad Tuition & Fees (In-District): $5,501
Enrollment: 4,389 Coed
Affiliation or Control: State/Local IRS Status: 501(c)3
Highest Offering: Associate Degree
Accreditation: M, ACFEI, ADNUR, MAC, PTAA, RAD, SURGT

01 President ... Dr. William MURABITO
05 Int Vice President Academic Affairs ... Ms. Lydia ULATOWSKI
103 VP Workforce Development ... Ms. Karen KWANDRANS
10 Int Vice Pres of Finance/Info Tech ... Ms. Patrice ELNICKI
32 Vice President of Student Services ... Ms. Julia PITMAN
11 Vice President Operations ... Mr. Wayne LYNCH
09 Coordinator of Inst Research Data ... Ms. Emily RADER
15 Asst VP of Human Resources ... Ms. Catherine BROWN
84 Asst VP of Enrollment Management ... Mr. Robert MCKEOWN
21 Director of Business Services ... Mr. John EICHNER
04 Assistant to President ... Ms. Barbara WALCK
06 Registrar ... Ms. Julie SCHUCKER
35 Director of Student Development ... Vacant
37 Director of Financial Aid ... Mr. James TRIMBOLI
26 Director Public Relations ... Ms. Barbara DESIMONE
18 Assistant Director of Facilities ... Mr. Donald SAPH
08 Head Librarian ... Ms. Nancy KENNEDY
105 Director Web Services ... Mr. Cory WRIGHT
106 Dir Online Education/E-learning ... Ms. Lisa DUBUC
13 Asst VP of Information Technology ... Mr. Dennis MICHAELS
19 Director Security/Safety ... Mr. Ross ANNABLE
102 Foundation Director ... Ms. Deborah BREWER
39 Assistant Director Student Housing ... Ms. Jill FADDOUL
41 Athletic Director ... Ms. Amanda HASELEY
91 Dir User & Administrative Tech ... Mr. Brian ZELLI
29 Alumni Development Specialist ... Ms. Allison KORTA
07 Director of Admissions ... Mr. Douglas MCNABB
108 Director Institutional Assessment ... Vacant
25 Director of Grants ... Mr. Brian MICHEL
104 Director Study Abroad ... Ms. Alissa SHUGATS-CUMMINGS
36 Dir Career and Transitional Svcs ... Ms. Alissa SHUGATS-CUMMINGS
38 Director Student Counseling ... Vacant

Niagara University (H)

5795 Lewiston Road, Niagara University NY 14109
County: Niagara FICE Identification: 002788
Unit ID: 193973
Telephone: (716) 285-1212 Carnegie Class: Masters/L
FAX Number: (716) 286-8710 Calendar System: Semester
URL: www.niagara.edu
Established: 1856 Annual Undergrad Tuition & Fees: $35,240
Enrollment: 3,544 Coed
Affiliation or Control: Roman Catholic IRS Status: 501(c)3
Highest Offering: Doctorate
Accreditation: M, CACREP, CAEP, NURSE, SW

01 President ... Rev. James MAHER, CM
03 Executive Vice President ... Dr. Debra COLLEY
05 Provost/VP for Academic Affairs ... Dr. Timothy IRELAND

11 Senior VP Operations & Facilities ..... Ms. Mary E. BORGOGNONI
32 VP Student Affairs ....Mr. Christopher R. SHEFFIELD
85 VP for International Relations .... Dr. Deborah CURTIS
111 Int VP Institutional Advancement ....Ms. Jaclyn ROSSI
42 VP Mission Integration ....Rev. Aidan R. ROONEY, CM
84 VP Undergrad Enrollment & Mktg ....Mr. Michael J. FREEDMAN
20 Associate Provost ....Dr. Henrik C. BORGSTROM
26 AVP of Public/External/Govt Rels .... Mr. Thomas BURNS
110 Assoc VP for Inst Advancement .... Mr. David GREENMAN
43 General Counsel ....Mr. Jeremy COLBY
10 Chief Financial/Innovation Ofcr ....Mr. Robert MORREALE
35 Dean of Student Affairs ....Mrs. Averl HARBIN
49 Dean Col of Arts & Science ....Dr. Peter BUTERA
66 Dean Col of Nursing ....Dr. Christine VERNI
50 Dean Col of Business Admin ....Dr. Mark FRASCATORE
53 Dean Col of Education ....Dr. Chandra FOOTE
88 Dean Col Hospitality/Tourism Mgt ....Ms. Bridget NILAND
09 Exec Dir Inst Effect & Assessment .... Dr. Vennessa L. WALKER
88 Asst Dir of Facility Oper & Plng .... Mr. Daniel MCMANN
07 Director of Transfer Enrollment ....Mr. Mark E. WOJNOWSKI
07 Director of First Year Enrollment .... Mr. Benjamin ASCHER
07 Director of First Year Enrollment .....Ms. Stephanie BUCZKOWSKI
08 Director of Libraries .... Mr. David SCHOEN
19 Director of Campus Safety ....Mr. John F. BARKER
37 Director of Financial Aid .... Ms. Katie L. KOCSIS
39 Director of Residence Life ....Ms. Kimberly FENTON
35 Director of Campus Activities ....Mrs. Mati ORTIZ
13 Director Information Technology .... Mr. Richard P. KERNIN
15 Director of Human Resources ....Vacant
23 Dir of Student Health & Wellness ....Ms. Adrienne KASBAUM
41 Director of Athletics .... Mr. Simon GRAY
18 Interim Dir of Facility Services ....Mrs. Lori CACCAMISE
20 Dean of Academic Services .... Ms. Antonia KNIGHT
121 Director Academic Success Center .... Mrs. Diane STOELTING
86 Exec Dir Inst for Civic Engagement .... Mrs. Patricia WROBEL
88 Dir Rec & Intramurals/Kiernan Ctr ....Mr. Derek PUFF
29 Director Alumni Relations ....Ms. Jaclyn ROSSI
21 Controller ....Ms. Christina HOVEN
123 Dir of Strategic Enrollment Oper ....Mr. Evan F. PIERCE
92 Honors Program Coordinator .... Dr. Michael BARNWELL
93 Assoc Dir Multicultural
Affairs .... Ms. Simone MCKINSON-BECKFORD
28 Title IX Coordinator .... Mrs. Megan ALTMAN-COSGROVE
06 University Registrar ....Mr. Harry GONG
113 Director of Student Accounts .... Mr. Jacob KOPERA
25 Dir Sponsored Pgms & Fndn Rels ....Ms. Jill SHUEY
102 Asst VP Spons Pgms & Found Rels ....Ms. Adrienne STANFILL
36 Director of Career Services .... Ms. Stephanie MORRIS
45 Dir of Strategic Initiatives ....Vacant
88 Veterans Services Program Director ..... Mr. Karl HINTERBERGER
04 Executive Asst to President ....Ms. Maritza MULREADY

North Country Community College (A)

23 Santanoni Avenue, PO Box 89,
Saranac Lake NY 12983-0089
County: Essex FICE Identification: 007111
Unit ID: 194028
Telephone: (518) 891-2915 Carnegie Class: Assoc/HVT-High Non
FAX Number: (518) 891-2915 Calendar System: Semester
URL: www.nccc.edu
Established: 1967 Annual Undergrad Tuition & Fees (In-District): $6,562
Enrollment: 1,602 Coed
Affiliation or Control: State/Local IRS Status: 501(c)3
Highest Offering: Associate Degree
Accreditation: M

01 President ....Mr. Joe KEEGAN
05 Vice Pres of Academic Affairs .... Mrs. Sarah MAROUN
10 Chief Financial Officer ....Mr. Erik HARVEY
21 Director of Financial Operations .... Mrs. Lisa SYMONDS
84 VP of Marketing & Enrollment ....Mr. Kyle JOHNSTON
06 Registrar/Records Officer ....Mrs. Shelly ST. LOUIS
09 Asst Dean Inst Research/Support .... Mr. Scott HARWOOD
32 Dean of Campus & Student Life .... Ms. Kim IRLAND
29 Director Alumni Relations ....Mrs. Diana FORTUNE
04 Executive Asst to the President ....Mrs. Stacie HURWITCH
37 Director of Financial Aid ....Mrs. MaryEllen CHAMBERLAIN
41 Athletic Director .... Mr. Chad LADUE

Northeast College of Health Sciences (B)

2360 State Route 89, Seneca Falls NY 13148-0800
County: Seneca FICE Identification: 012277
Unit ID: 193751
Telephone: (315) 568-3000 Carnegie Class: Spec-4-yr-Other Health
FAX Number: (315) 568-3012 Calendar System: Trimester
URL: www.nycc.edu
Established: 1919 Annual Undergrad Tuition & Fees: N/A
Enrollment: 676 Coed
Affiliation or Control: Independent Non-Profit IRS Status: 501(c)3
Highest Offering: First Professional Degree
Accreditation: M, CHIRO

01 President ....Dr. Michael A. MESTAN
05 Exec Vice Pres of Academic Affairs ....Dr. Anne KILLEN
10 Vice Pres of Finance/Admin Svcs .... Mr. Sean ANGLIM
111 VP Stakeholder Engagement .... Dr. J. Todd KNUDSEN
84 Vice Pres Enrollment & Planning ....Dr. Jen SESSLER
96 VP of Admin Services .... Mr. Chris B. MCQUEENEY
20 Asst VP of Academic Affairs .... Dr. J. Nicolas POIRIER

17 Asst VP of Clinical Education .... Mr. Scott BOOTH
06 Registrar .... Mr. Kevin MCCARTHY
37 Director Financial Aid .... Mr. Darrin ROOKER
107 Director of Bachelor Prof Studies ....Vacant
46 Dean of Faculty & Research .... Dr. Jeanmarie R. BURKE
12 Depew Health Center Administrator .... Dr. Ana STEARNS
12 Levittown Health Ctr Chief of Staff ....Vacant
88 Director of Clinical Education ....Dr. Wendy L. MANERI
51 Director Post Grad & Cont Educ ....Dr. Owen PAPUGUA
08 Director of the Library ....Ms. Bethyn BONI
29 Alumni & Stakeholder Svcs Coord ....Ms. Tracy JONES
108 Dir of Ed Effectiveness/
Compliance .... Dr. Suellen CHRISTOPOULUS-NUTTING
09 Quality Engineer .... Ms. Patricia MERKLE
15 Human Resources Manager ....Ms. Christine MCDERMOTT
14 Information Tech Administrator .... Mr. Shane SHOWERS
19 Director Facilities/Security .... Mr. William WAYNE
106 Dean of Online Education .... Dr. Peter NICKLESS
88 Dir MS Diagnostic Imaging Program ....Dr. Chad WARSHEL
90 Sr Systems Administrator .... Mr. Miles SINICROPI
24 Educational Tech Administrator .... Mr. Bernard CECCHINI
23 Director Health Center Operations .... Mrs. Melissa BAXTER
21 Controller .... Ms. Karen QUEST
88 Dir MS Hum Anat Phys Instructn Pgm ..... Dr. William GERMANO
04 Admin Assistant to the President ....Mrs. Laurie REYNOLDS

Northeastern Seminary (C)

2265 Westside Drive, Rochester NY 14624-1932
County: Monroe FICE Identification: 034194
Unit ID: 439817
Telephone: (585) 594-6800 Carnegie Class: Spec-4-yr-Faith
FAX Number: (585) 594-6801 Calendar System: Semester
URL: www.nes.edu
Established: 1998 Annual Graduate Tuition & Fees: N/A
Enrollment: 206 Coed
Affiliation or Control: Independent Non-Profit IRS Status: 501(c)3
Highest Offering: Doctorate; No Undergraduates
Accreditation: M, THEOL

01 President ....Dr. Deana L. PORTERFIELD
05 Academic Vice President and Dean ....Dr. Douglas CULLUM
32 VP Student/Organizational Dev .... Ms. Kristen BROWN
07 AVP for Seminary Enrollment .... Mr. JP ANDERSON
04 Administrative Asst to President ....Mrs. Mimi WHEELER
06 Registrar ....Ms. Lesa KOHR
10 VP Finance/Chief Financial Officer ....Ms. Laurie LEO
111 VP for Institutional Advancement .... Mr. Alexander JONES
13 AVP Information Technology .... Mr. Peter SAXENA
102 Dir Foundation/Corporate Relations ....Vacant
11 Associate Dean ....Vacant
30 Director of Inst Advancement ....Mrs. Carrie STARR

† The Seminary is affiliated with Roberts Wesleyan College.

Nyack College (D)

2 Washington Street, New York NY 10004
County: Manhattan FICE Identification: 002790
Unit ID: 194161
Telephone: (646) 378-6100 Carnegie Class: Masters/L
FAX Number: N/A Calendar System: Semester
URL: www.nyack.edu
Established: 1882 Annual Undergrad Tuition & Fees: $25,500
Enrollment: 2,063 Coed
Affiliation or Control: The Christian And Missionary Alliance
IRS Status: 501(c)3
Highest Offering: Doctorate
Accreditation: M, CAEP, MFCD, MUS, NURSE, SW, THEOL

01 President .... Mr. Rajan G. MATHEWS
04 Assistant to the President ....Mrs. Bonita D'AMIL
10 Exec Vice President & Treasurer .... Mr. David C. JENNINGS
05 Provost/VP for Academic Affairs .... Dr. David F. TURK
73 VP/Dean Alliance Seminary .... Dr. Ronald WALBORN
50 Dean School of Business & Ldrshp .... Dr. Anita UNDERWOOD
64 Dean School of Music ....Dr. Sue Lane TALLEY
53 Dean School of Education ....Dr. JoAnn LOONEY
66 Dean School of Nursing ....Dr. Inseon HWANG
121 Dean Student Success ....Dr. Gwen PARKER AMES
32 Vice Pres of Student Development ....Mrs. Wanda VELEZ
42 Vice President of Church Relations .... Dr. Charles HAMMOND
06 Institutional Registrar .... Ms. Evangeline COUCHEY
37 Dir of Fin Svcs Undergrad ....Mr. Isaac FOSTER
41 Director of Athletics .... Mr. Keith A. DAVIE
15 Director of Human Resources .... Mrs. Karen DAVIE
13 Director of Information Technology ....Mr. Kevin A. BUEL
09 Director of Institutional Research .... Mr. Greg BEEMAN
18 Director of Operations/Aramark .... Mr. Doug WALKER
26 Dir of Public & Media Relations .... Mrs. Deborah WALKER
105 Webmaster .... Mr. Joshua WAY
108 Director Institutional Assessment ....Ms. Kristen LUBA
07 Director of Admissions .... Mr. Kevin WHITE

Ohr Hameir Theological Seminary (E)

141 Furnace Woods Road,
Cortlandt Manor NY 10567-6112
County: Westchester FICE Identification: 011984
Unit ID: 194189
Telephone: (914) 736-1500 Carnegie Class: Spec-4-yr-Faith
FAX Number: (914) 736-1055 Calendar System: Semester
Established: 1962 Annual Undergrad Tuition & Fees: $12,250
Enrollment: 92 Male
Affiliation or Control: Independent Non-Profit IRS Status: 501(c)3
Highest Offering: Second Talmudic Degree
Accreditation: RABN

01 President ....Rabbi E. KANAREK
30 Chief Devel Ofcr/Dir Financial Aid .... Rabbi Jacob ROTHBERG
06 Registrar ....Rabbi Berel KANAREK

Onondaga Community College (F)

4585 West Seneca Turnpike, Syracuse NY 13215-4585
County: Onondaga FICE Identification: 002875
Unit ID: 194222
Telephone: (315) 498-2622 Carnegie Class: Assoc/HT-Mix Trad/Non
FAX Number: (315) 492-9208 Calendar System: Semester
URL: www.sunyocc.edu
Established: 1962 Annual Undergrad Tuition & Fees (In-District): $5,754
Enrollment: 8,545 Coed
Affiliation or Control: State/Local IRS Status: 501(c)3
Highest Offering: Associate Degree
Accreditation: M, ADNUR, CAHIIM, NAEYC, PTAA, SURGT

01 President .... Dr. Casey CRABILL
05 Interim Provost ....Dr. Anastasia URTZ
10 Sr Vice Pres & CFO ....Mr. Mark MANNING
03 VP Governance and Compliance ....Ms. Anastasia URTZ
30 Vice President Development .... Ms. Kathleen STRESS
84 VP Enrollment Development & Comm ....Ms. Amy KREMENEK
09 VP Inst Planning/Assess/Research ....Dr. Agatha AWUAH
13 Chief Information Officer ....Mr. Dwight FISCHER
20 Asst VP Academic & Support Svcs ....Ms. Kathleen D'APRIX
28 VP/Chief Diversity Officer ....Ms. Eunice WILLIAMS
37 Director Financial Aid .... Mr. Kevin SAPIO
41 Athletic Director ....Mr. Michael BORSZ
08 Chair Library .... Dr. Fantasia THORNE-ORTIZ
19 Director Campus Safety & Security .... Dr. Andrea MOUREY
22 Director Disability Services .... Ms. Nancy CARR
06 Interim Registrar .... Ms. Wendy TARBY
113 Assistant Director Student Accounts .... Ms. Sally LUTON
96 Assistant VP Management Services ....Mr. Michael MCMULLEN
88 Director of Sustainability .... Dr. Sean VORMWALD
04 Assistant to the President .... Ms. Julie HART
25 AVP Research & Grants .... Ms. Nicole SCHLATER
29 Assistant Director Alumni Comm .... Mr. Russ CORBIN
45 AVP Inst Effectiveness & Planning .... Ms. Wendy TARBY
26 AVP Advancement Communications ....Ms. Susan TORMEY
15 Chief Human Resources Officer .... Ms. Bridget SCHOLL
44 Director Annual Giving .... Ms. Steffani WILLIAMS
39 Director Resident Life/Student Hous .... Mr. Shawn EDIE

Orange County Community College (G)

115 South Street, Middletown NY 10940-6437
County: Orange FICE Identification: 002876
Unit ID: 194240
Telephone: (845) 344-6222 Carnegie Class: Assoc/HT-High Trad
FAX Number: (845) 343-1228 Calendar System: Semester
URL: www.sunyorange.edu
Established: 1950 Annual Undergrad Tuition & Fees (In-District): $6,094
Enrollment: 5,862 Coed
Affiliation or Control: State/Local IRS Status: 501(c)3
Highest Offering: Associate Degree
Accreditation: M, ACBSP, ADNUR, DH, MLTAD, OTA, PTAA, RAD

01 President ....Dr. Kristine M. YOUNG
05 Vice Pres Academic Affairs ....Ms. Erika HACKMAN
32 Vice Pres Student Services ....Ms. Gerianne BRUSATI
10 VP Administration/Finance ....Mr. Paul MARTLAND
111 Vice Pres Institutional Advancement ....Vacant
13 Chief Information Officer ....Mr. Michael THARP
84 Assoc VP for Enrollment Management ....Vacant
76 Assoc VP Health Professions .... Dr. Michael GAWRONSKI, JR.
102 Int Executive Director Foundation .... Ms. Dawn ANSBRO
50 Assoc VP Business/Math/Sci/Tech .... Ms. Anne PRIAL
35 Assoc Vice Pres Stdnt Engagemt/
Comp .... Ms. Madeline TORRES-DIAZ
15 Assoc Vice Pres Human Resources .... Ms. Iris MARTINEZ-DAVIS
08 Library Director ....Mr. Andrew HEIZ
51 Dir Continuing/Professional Educ .... Mr. David KOHN
19 Int Director Campus Security/Safety ..... Mr. Anthony JACKLITSCH
09 Inst Plng/Assessment/Research Ofcr ....Ms. Christine WORK
18 Director Administrative Services ....Mr. Michael WORDEN
37 Director of Financial Aid ....Vacant
06 Registrar .... Ms. Darlene BENZENBERG
26 Communications Officer .... Mr. Mike ALBRIGHT
121 Director Academic Advising ....Ms. Talia LLOSA
07 Director of Admissions ....Mr. Maynard SCHMIDT
35 Director Student Activities .... Mr. Steve HARPST
04 Exec Asst to President .... Ms. Carol MURRAY
41 Athletic Director .... Mr. Wayne SMITH
28 Chief Diversity Officer .... Ms. Lorraine LOPEZ-JANOVE
29 Dir Alumni Engagement/Cmty Rels ....Ms. Jennifer D'ANDREA

Orange County Community College Newburgh Branch Campus (H)

1 Washington Center, Newburgh NY 12550
Telephone: (845) 562-2454 Identification: 770144
Accreditation: &M

Pace University (A)

1 Pace Plaza, New York NY 10038-1598

County: New York FICE Identification: 002791
Unit ID: 194310
Telephone: (212) 346-1200 Carnegie Class: DU-Mod
FAX Number: (212) 346-1933 Calendar System: Semester
URL: www.pace.edu
Established: 1906 Annual Undergrad Tuition & Fees: $47,684
Enrollment: 12,835 Coed
Affiliation or Control: Independent Non-Profit IRS Status: 501(c)3
Highest Offering: Doctorate
Accreditation: M, ARCPA, CACREP, @DIETC, IPSY, LAW, NURSE, OT, PSPSY, @SP

01 President ..... Mr. Marvin KRISLOV
10 Exec Vice President/CFO ..... Mr. Robert C. ALMON
05 Provost ..... Dr. Vanya QUINONES
84 Vice Pres Enrollment/Placement ..... Ms. Robina C. SCHEPP
111 VP Development/Alumni Relations ..... Mr. Gary LAERMER
13 VP Information Tech/CIO ..... Mr. Paul DAMPIER
26 VP/Chief Marketing Ofcr Univ Rels ..... Ms. Mary BAGLIVO
15 Assoc Vice Pres Human Resources ..... Vacant
09 Asst Vice Pres Plng/Assess/Inst Res ..... Ms. Nancy DERIGGI
19 Associate VP General Services ..... Mr. Frank MCDONALD
50 Dean Lubin School of Business ..... Mr. Lawrence SINGLETON
49 Dean Dyson College Arts/Sci ..... Vacant
53 Dean School of Education ..... Vacant
76 Dean College Health Professions ..... Dr. Marcus TYE
77 Dean School of CSIS ..... Dr. Jonathan H. HILL
32 Dean of Students New York ..... Ms. Rachel CARPENTER
32 Dean of Students Westchester ..... Vacant
61 Dean School of Law ..... Mr. Horace E. ANDERSON, JR.
107 Asst VP Continuing/Professional Ed ..... Dr. Christine SHAKESPEARE
06 Graduate Registrar ..... Ms. Margaret JONES
06 Law School Registrar ..... Ms. Nilda RODRIGUEZ
06 Associate University Registrar ..... Ms. Barbara MCCARTHY
88 Asst Director Adult Education NY ..... Ms. Nicola FOSTER
21 Interim Comptroller ..... Mr. William VOLL
43 University Counsel ..... Mr. Stephen BRODSKY
113 University Bursar ..... Ms. Susan WEYGANT
07 Dir of Admissions NY/Westchester ..... Ms. Joanna BRODA
22 Affirmative Action Officer ..... Ms. Arletha MILES
14 Asst VP Information Technology Svcs ..... Mr. Chris ELARDE
84 Director Adult Enroll Svcs/New York ..... Ms. Janet KIRTMAN
38 Director Counseling Services ..... Dr. Richard SHADICK
39 Director of Residential Life ..... Mr. A. Patrick ROGER-GORDON
40 Executive Director Bookstore ..... Ms. Mary LIETO
85 Assoc Dir Intl Pgms & Services ..... Mr. Kraig WALKUP
96 Director of Purchasing - Contracts ..... Ms. Alice SEIFERT
18 Director Facilities/Physical Plant ..... Mr. Abdul JABAR
28 Director of Diversity ..... Ms. Shanelle HENRY ROBINSON

Pacific College of Health and Science (B)

110 William Street, 19th Floor, New York NY 10038

Telephone: (212) 982-3456 Identification: 666139
Accreditation: &WC, ACUP, NUR

† Branch campus of Pacific College of Health and Science, San Diego CA.

Paul Smith's College (C)

PO Box 265, Paul Smiths NY 12970-0265

County: Franklin FICE Identification: 002795
Unit ID: 194392
Telephone: (518) 327-6000 Carnegie Class: Bac-Diverse
FAX Number: N/A Calendar System: Semester
URL: www.paulsmiths.edu
Established: 1937 Annual Undergrad Tuition & Fees: $30,194
Enrollment: 681 Coed
Affiliation or Control: Independent Non-Profit IRS Status: 501(c)3
Highest Offering: Master's
Accreditation: M

01 President ..... Dr. Scott DALRYMPLE
05 Provost ..... Dr. Nicholas HUNT-BULL
111 Vice President Inst Advancement ..... Mr. Steven FREDERICK
84 VP Enrollment Management ..... Mr. Robert HERR
32 Dean of Students ..... Ms. Courtney BRINGLEY
29 Director of Alumni Relations ..... Ms. Heather TUTTLE
13 Director Information Technology ..... Mr. Michael MAGURK
06 Registrar ..... Dr. Jeffrey WALTON
19 Lead Campus Safety Officer ..... Ms. Holly PARKER
09 Director Institutional Research ..... Dr. Jeffrey WALTON
22 Director HEOP ..... Ms. Kate MULLEN
41 Director of Athletics ..... Mr. James TUCKER
10 Comptroller ..... Ms. Lauren POEHLMAN
40 Manager of College Store ..... Ms. Diana L. LYNG-GLIDDI
96 Purchasing Coordinator ..... Ms. Cynthia LEMERY
36 Career Services Coordinator ..... Ms. Lydia WRIGHT
20 Assoc Academic Officer/Provost ..... Dr. Catherine LALONDE
04 Admin Assistant to the President ..... Ms. Kathleen KECK
15 Director of Human Resources ..... Ms. Gwen GOODMAN
26 Chief Marketing Officer ..... Ms. Sarah WHEELER
37 Director Student Financial Aid ..... Ms. Sonya STEIN
38 Director Student Counseling ..... Ms. Najla HRUSTANOVIC
39 Director Residence Life ..... Mr. Lou KAMINSKI
18 Chief Facilities/Physical Plant ..... Mr. Jeremy ASMUS
08 Director of Library Services ..... Mr. Andrew KELLY

Phillips School of Nursing at Mount Sinai Beth Israel (D)

148 East 126th Street, New York NY 10035

County: New York FICE Identification: 006438
Unit ID: 189282
Telephone: (212) 614-6110 Carnegie Class: Spec-4-yr-Other Health
FAX Number: (212) 614-6109 Calendar System: Semester
URL: https://www.mountsinai.org/locations/beth-israel/pson
Established: 1904 Annual Undergrad Tuition & Fees: N/A
Enrollment: 254 Coed
Affiliation or Control: Independent Non-Profit IRS Status: 501(c)3
Highest Offering: Baccalaureate
Accreditation: NY, ADNUR, NURSE

01 Dean ..... Dr. Todd AMBROSIA
05 Sr Associate Dean ..... Dr. Laly JOSEPH
09 Asst Dean Inst Effectiveness ..... Mrs. Bernice PASS-STERN
32 Director Student Services ..... Mr. Ashni PATEL
30 Dir Development/Communications ..... Ms. Linda FABRIZIO

Plaza College (E)

118-33 Queens Boulevard, Forest Hills NY 11375

County: Queens FICE Identification: 012358
Unit ID: 194499
Telephone: (718) 779-1430 Carnegie Class: Bac/Assoc-Mixed
FAX Number: (718) 779-7423 Calendar System: Semester
URL: www.plazacollege.edu
Established: 1916 Annual Undergrad Tuition & Fees: $13,450
Enrollment: 914 Coed
Affiliation or Control: Proprietary IRS Status: Proprietary
Highest Offering: Baccalaureate
Accreditation: M, CAHIIM, DH, MAC

01 President ..... Charles E. CALLAHAN, III
10 Vice Pres of Financial Services ..... Vacant
11 Chief Operating Officer ..... Charles E. CALLAHAN, IV
05 Dean of Academic Affairs ..... Marie DOLLA
06 Registrar ..... Carol GARCIA
21 Comptroller ..... Linda ROCKHILL
07 Director of Admissions ..... Vanessa LOPEZ
20 Dean Curriculum Development ..... Marianne C. ZIPF
08 College Librarian ..... Eva BABALIS
23 Director Health Services ..... Candice CALLAHAN
37 Director Financial Aid ..... Peggy CHUNG
32 Dean of Students ..... Dawn VETRANO
35 Dean of Student Activities ..... Jonathan HOWLE
15 Director of HR/HR Officer ..... Correne CAVALIERI
09 Assoc Dean Institutional Research ..... Edward DEE
13 Chief Technology Officer ..... David COLUCCI
88 Director of ARC/Library ..... Allison KRAMPF
14 Manager Information Technology ..... Norman ALVARADO
76 Program Director Medical Assisting ..... Daryl ANDERSON
26 Director of Communications ..... Brittany TRAVIS
38 Freshman Counseling ..... Caroline CALLAHAN
36 Director of Career Services ..... Regina POKIDAYLO

Pratt Institute (F)

200 Willoughby Avenue, Brooklyn NY 11205-3899

County: Kings FICE Identification: 002798
Unit ID: 194578
Telephone: (718) 636-3600 Carnegie Class: Spec-4-yr-Arts
FAX Number: (718) 636-3670 Calendar System: Semester
URL: www.pratt.edu
Established: 1887 Annual Undergrad Tuition & Fees: $53,814
Enrollment: 4,353 Coed
Affiliation or Control: Independent Non-Profit IRS Status: 501(c)3
Highest Offering: Master's
Accreditation: M, CIDA, LIB, PLNG

01 President ..... Ms. Frances BRONET
100 Chief of Staff ..... Ms. Nicole HAAS
05 Provost ..... Vacant
32 Vice President for Student Life ..... Ms. Delmy LENDOF
10 Vice Pres Finance/Administration ..... Ms. Cathleen KENNY
111 Vice Pres for Inst Advancement ..... Ms. Daphne HALPERN
84 Vice President for Enrollment ..... Mr. Rick LONGO
28 VP for Diversity/Equity/Inclusion ..... Ms. Nsombi B. RICKETTS
26 Vice Pres Communications/Marketing ..... Mr. James KEMPSTER
20 Interim Provost ..... Dr. Donna HEILAND
88 Assoc Provost Strat Partnerships ..... Dr. Allison DRUIN
11 Assistant to Pres Administration ..... Ms. Josie CAPORUSCIO
06 Registrar ..... Mr. Luke PHILLIPS
08 Director of the Library ..... Mr. Russ ABELL
15 Assistant VP of Human Resources ..... Mr. Steve RICCOBONO
51 Dean Continuing Education ..... Ms. Maira SEARA
35 Asst VP for Student Affairs ..... Ms. Rhonda SCHALLER
37 Exec Director Student Financial Svc ..... Mr. Nedzad GOGA
09 Exec Dir Strat Planning & Inst Eff ..... Vacant
43 Director of Legal Affairs ..... Mr. Thomas GREENE
57 Dean of Art ..... Mr. Jorge OLIVER
49 Interim Dean Liberal Arts/Science ..... Dr. Helio TAKAI
48 Dean School of Architecture ..... Dr. Harriet HARRISS
62 Dean Information/Library Sci ..... Dr. Anthony COCCIOLO
88 Dean of Design ..... Ms. Anita COONEY
13 Chief Info Technology Officer (CIO) ..... Mr. Joseph HEMWAY
18 Chief Facilities Officer ..... Mr. Christopher GAVLICK
19 Asst VP for Campus Safety ..... Mr. Dennis MAZONE
39 Director Student Housing ..... Mr. Christopher KASIK
41 Athletic Director ..... Mr. Walter RICKARD
90 Director Academic Computing ..... Mr. Ellery MATTHEWS

Rabbinical Academy Mesivta Rabbi Chaim Berlin (G)

1605 Coney Island Avenue, Brooklyn NY 11230-4715

County: Kings FICE Identification: 003976
Unit ID: 194657
Telephone: (718) 377-0777 Carnegie Class: Spec-4-yr-Faith
FAX Number: (718) 338-5578 Calendar System: Semester
Established: 1939 Annual Undergrad Tuition & Fees: $12,450
Enrollment: 336 Male
Affiliation or Control: Independent Non-Profit IRS Status: 501(c)3
Highest Offering: Second Talmudic Degree
Accreditation: RABN

01 Provost ..... Rabbi Abraham H. FRUCHTHANDLER
05 President of the Faculty ..... Rabbi Aaron M. SCHECHTER
03 Executive Director ..... Rabbi Y. Mayer LASKER
29 Director of Alumni Association ..... Mendel SCHECHTER
45 Chief Planning Officer ..... Rabbi Tuvia M. OBERMEISTER
20 Associate Director ..... Eli RABINOWITZ
37 Financial Aid Administrator ..... Michael A. REISS

Rabbinical College Beth Shraga (H)

28 Saddle River Road, Monsey NY 10952-3035

County: Rockland FICE Identification: 010943
Unit ID: 194693
Telephone: (845) 356-1980 Carnegie Class: Spec-4-yr-Faith
FAX Number: (845) 425-2604 Calendar System: Semester
Established: 1965 Annual Undergrad Tuition & Fees: $14,250
Enrollment: 40 Male
Affiliation or Control: Independent Non-Profit IRS Status: 501(c)3
Highest Offering: Second Talmudic Degree
Accreditation: RABN

01 President ..... Rabbi Emanuel SCHIFF

Rabbinical College Bobover Yeshiva B'nei Zion (I)

1577 48th Street, Brooklyn NY 11219-3293

County: Kings FICE Identification: 008614
Unit ID: 194666
Telephone: (718) 438-2018 Carnegie Class: Spec-4-yr-Faith
FAX Number: (718) 871-9031 Calendar System: Semester
Established: 1947 Annual Undergrad Tuition & Fees: $8,500
Enrollment: 418 Male
Affiliation or Control: Independent Non-Profit IRS Status: 501(c)3
Highest Offering: First Talmudic Degree
Accreditation: RABN

01 President ..... Rabbi Boruch Avrohom HOROWITZ

Rabbinical College of Long Island (J)

205 W Beech Street, Long Beach NY 11561-0630

County: Nassau FICE Identification: 010378
Unit ID: 194736
Telephone: (516) 255-4700 Carnegie Class: Spec-4-yr-Faith
FAX Number: (516) 255-4701 Calendar System: Semester
Established: 1965 Annual Undergrad Tuition & Fees: $9,100
Enrollment: 160 Male
Affiliation or Control: Independent Non-Profit IRS Status: 501(c)3
Highest Offering: First Talmudic Degree
Accreditation: RABN

01 President ..... Rabbi Yitzchok FEIGELSTOCK
06 Registrar ..... Rabbi Dovid N. ROTHSCHILD
32 Dean of Students ..... Rabbi Yeruchem PITTER
07 CEO and Director of Admissions ..... Rabbi Chaim HOBERMAN
37 Financial Aid Administrator ..... Rabbi Shlomo TEICHMAN
06 Assistant Registrar ..... Mrs. Toni TURNER

Rabbinical College Ohr Shimon Yisroel (K)

215-217 Hewes Street, Brooklyn NY 11211-8102

County: Kings FICE Identification: 031292
Unit ID: 405854
Telephone: (718) 855-4092 Carnegie Class: Spec-4-yr-Faith
FAX Number: (646) 448-2272 Calendar System: Semester
Established: Annual Undergrad Tuition & Fees: $14,600
Enrollment: 211 Male
Affiliation or Control: Independent Non-Profit IRS Status: 501(c)3
Highest Offering: First Talmudic Degree
Accreditation: RABN

01 President ..... Rabbi Shulem WALTER

Rabbinical College Ohr Yisroel (L)

8800 Seaview Avenue, Brooklyn NY 11236

County: Kings Identification: 667145
Unit ID: 484871
Telephone: (718) 633-4715 Carnegie Class: Spec-4-yr-Faith
FAX Number: (347) 702-5436 Calendar System: Semester
Established: 2009 Annual Undergrad Tuition & Fees: $9,000
Enrollment: 115 Male

Affiliation or Control: Independent Non-Profit IRS Status: 501(c)3
Highest Offering: First Talmudic Degree
Accreditation: @RABN

01 President ... Rabbi Daniel GELDZAHLER

Rabbinical Seminary of America (A)

76-01 147th Street, Flushing NY 11367-3148
County: Queens FICE Identification: 003978
Unit ID: 194763
Telephone: (718) 268-4700 Carnegie Class: Spec-4-yr-Faith
FAX Number: (718) 268-4684 Calendar System: Semester
Established: 1933 Annual Undergrad Tuition & Fees: $9,900
Enrollment: 502 Male
Affiliation or Control: Independent Non-Profit IRS Status: 501(c)3
Highest Offering: Second Talmudic Degree
Accreditation: RABN

01 President ... Rabbi David HARRIS
01 President ... Rabbi Akiva GRUNBLATT
03 Executive Vice President ... Rabbi Hayim SCHWARTZ
11 Director of Operation ... Rabbi Meir GLAZER
06 Registrar ... Rabbi Abraham SEMMEL
05 Executive Director ... Rabbi Yehuda JEGER
30 Director Development ... Rabbi Yossi SINGER
37 Director of Financial Aid ... Mrs. Laya EISENSTEIN
18 Chief Physical Plant ... Mr. Ariel WOLFARTH
88 Director of Special Projects ... Vacant
91 Director of Admin Computing ... Mr. Jonathan PLATOVSKY
39 Director Student Housing ... Rabbi Elisha FEINBERG
46 Director Research & Development ... Vacant

Relay Graduate School of Education (B)

25 Broadway, 3rd Floor, New York NY 10004
County: New York Identification: 667117
Unit ID: 475033
Telephone: (212) 228-1888 Carnegie Class: Spec-4-yr-Other
FAX Number: (212) 228-1855 Calendar System: Other
URL: www.relay.edu
Established: 2011 Annual Graduate Tuition & Fees: N/A
Enrollment: 3,790 Coed
Affiliation or Control: Independent Non-Profit IRS Status: 501(c)3
Highest Offering: Master's; No Undergraduates
Accreditation: M, CAEP

01 President ... Dr. Mayme HOSTETTER
05 Vice Provost ... Dr. Jonathan PAUL
11 Executive Vice President ... Ms. Pamela INBASEKARAN
10 Chief Financial Officer ... Ms. Piper EVANS
32 Chief Student Services Officer ... Ms. Kelly BOUCHER MORRIS
20 Senior Dean ... Ms. Jennifer RAMOS

Rensselaer Polytechnic Institute (C)

110 8th Street, Troy NY 12180-3590
County: Rensselaer FICE Identification: 002803
Unit ID: 194824
Telephone: (518) 276-6000 Carnegie Class: DU-Highest
FAX Number: N/A Calendar System: Semester
URL: www.rpi.edu
Established: 1824 Annual Undergrad Tuition & Fees: $57,012
Enrollment: 7,501 Coed
Affiliation or Control: Independent Non-Profit IRS Status: 501(c)3
Highest Offering: Doctorate
Accreditation: M

01 President ... Dr. Shirley Ann JACKSON
05 Provost ... Dr. Prabhat HAJELA
11 Vice President for Administration ... Mr. Claude ROUNDS
26 VP Strategic Comm/External Rels ... Ms. Richie C. HUNTER
10 Vice President for Finance/CFO ... Ms. Barbara J. HOUGH
45 Acting Vice Pres for Research ... Dr. Robert HULL
111 Vice Pres Institutional Advancement ... Mr. Graig R. EASTIN
32 Vice President Student Life ... Dr. Peter KONWERSKI
15 Vice Pres Human Resources ... Mr. Curtis N. POWELL
13 Vice Pres for Info Services & CIO ... Mr. John E. KOLB
84 Vice Pres Enrollment Management ... Dr. Jonathan D. WEXLER
43 Secretary of Inst/General Counsel ... Mr. Craig A. COOK
27 Assoc VP Marketing/Communications ... Ms. Pamela S. SMITH
41 Assoc Vice Pres/Director Athletics ... Dr. Lee MCELROY
19 AVP Public Safety/Emergency Mgmt ... Mr. Vadim THOMAS
21 Asst Vice Pres for Administration ... Mr. Paul W. MARTIN
29 Asst Vice Pres Alumni Relations ... Vacant
35 Asst Vice Pres & Dean of Students ... Mr. Travis APGAR
121 Asst Vice Pres of Student Success ... Ms. Lisa TRAHAN
54 Dean School of Engineering ... Dr. Shekhar GARDE
81 Dean School of Science ... Dr. Curt BRENEMAN
79 Dean Sch of Humanities/Arts/Soc Sci ... Dr. Mary SIMONI
50 Acting Dean Lally School Management ... Dr. Chanaka EDIRISINGHE
48 Dean School of Architecture ... Mr. Evan DOUGLIS
107 Dean Acad & Admin Affs Hartford ... Dr. Aric KRAUSE
58 Vice Provost/Dean Graduate Educ ... Dr. Stanley DUNN
20 Vice Provost/Dean Undergrad Educ ... Dr. Keith MOO-YOUNG
06 Registrar ... Ms. Rajni Etka SOHARU
37 Director Financial Aid ... Mr. Martin C. DANIELS
09 Director of Institutional Research ... Dr. Judith STODDARD
08 Director of Libraries ... Mr. Andrew C. WHITE
25 Director of Research Finance ... Mr. Niels HANSEN
36 Director Career Development Center ... Mr. Philip BRUCE
07 Director Undergrad Admissions ... Ms. Karen S. LONG
123 Director Graduate Admissions ... Mr. Jarron P. DECKER
18 Director Physical Plant ... Mr. Ernest J. KATZWINKEL
23 Exec Director Student Health Center ... Dr. Leslie LAWRENCE
38 Director Counseling Center ... Ms. Anita CHU
96 Director Procurement Services ... Vacant
105 Director Web Services ... Mr. Andrew C. WHITE
44 Director Annual Giving ... Vacant
90 Director Client Info Services ... Ms. Jacqueline B. STAMPALIA
91 Director Enterprise Info Services ... Ms. Mary Alice O'BRIEN
39 Dean Student Living & Learning ... Mr. John LAWLER
30 Assoc VP Development & Fundraising ... Mr. Joel B. KINCART

Richard Gilder Graduate School at the American Museum of Natural History (D)

200 Central Park West, New York NY 10024
County: New York Identification: 667003
Unit ID: 458548
Telephone: (212) 769-5055 Carnegie Class: Not Classified
FAX Number: (212) 769-5257 Calendar System: Other
URL: www.amnh.org/our-research/richard-gilder-graduate-school
Established: 2006 Annual Graduate Tuition & Fees: N/A
Enrollment: N/A Coed
Affiliation or Control: Independent Non-Profit IRS Status: 501(c)3
Highest Offering: Doctorate; No Undergraduates
Accreditation: NY, CAEP

01 Dean ... Dr. John J. FLYNN

Roberts Wesleyan College (E)

2301 Westside Drive, Rochester NY 14624-1997
County: Monroe FICE Identification: 002805
Unit ID: 194958
Telephone: (585) 594-6000 Carnegie Class: Masters/L
FAX Number: (585) 594-6371 Calendar System: Semester
URL: www.roberts.edu
Established: 1866 Annual Undergrad Tuition & Fees: $33,500
Enrollment: 1,706 Coed
Affiliation or Control: Independent Non-Profit IRS Status: 501(c)3
Highest Offering: Doctorate
Accreditation: M, IACBE, MUS, NURSE, PSPSY, SW

01 President ... Dr. Deana L. PORTERFIELD
05 Sr VP & Chief Academic Officer ... Dr. David BASINGER
10 Sr Vice President & Treasurer ... Ms. Laurie LEO
32 VP for Student & Org Development ... Ms. Kristen BROWN
111 VP Institutional Advancement ... Mr. Alexander JONES
84 VP for Enrollment Management ... Mrs. Kimberley WIEDEFELD
07 Exec Director of UG Admissions ... Ms. Mary SASSO
112 Assoc VP for Major Gifts ... Mr. Maurice (Max) MCGINNIS
26 AVP for Brand/Marketing Comm ... Ms. Donna MCLAREN
13 Assoc VP for Information Technology ... Mr. Pradeep SAXENA
40 Director of Bookstore Services ... Mr. Neal FAHEY
41 Director of Athletics ... Mr. Robert SEGAVE
37 Director of Student Financial Svcs ... Ms. Tayler KREUTTER
09 Dir Institutional Research/Assess ... Dr. Paul W. KENNEDY
42 Chaplain ... Rev. Gerald COLEMAN
06 Registrar ... Mrs. Lesa J. KOHR
04 Administrative Asst to President ... Mrs. Mimi WHEELER
15 Director Personnel Services ... Mrs. Diane WILEY
18 Chief Facilities/Physical Plant ... Mr. T. Richard GREER
19 Director Security/Safety ... Mr. Rick BILLITIER
25 Chief Contracts/Grants Admin ... Vacant
29 Director Alumni Relations ... Mr. Kirk KETTINGER
103 Dir Workforce/Career Development ... Ms. Mary FLAHERTY
104 Director International Engagement ... Ms. Julie RUSHIK
50 Dean School of Business ... Vacant
28 Director of Diversity & Equity ... Mr. Herbert ALEXANDER

† Parent institution of Northeastern Seminary.

Rochester Institute of Technology (F)

1 Lomb Memorial Drive, Rochester NY 14623-5604
County: Monroe FICE Identification: 002806
Unit ID: 195003
Telephone: (585) 475-2411 Carnegie Class: DU-Higher
FAX Number: (585) 475-7049 Calendar System: Quarter
URL: www.rit.edu
Established: 1829 Annual Undergrad Tuition & Fees: $51,240
Enrollment: 16,158 Coed
Affiliation or Control: Independent Non-Profit IRS Status: 501(c)3
Highest Offering: Doctorate
Accreditation: M, ARCPA, ART, CAEP, CEA, CIDA, DIETD, DMS, IPSY

01 President ... Dr. David C. MUNSON, JR.
05 Provost/SVP Academic Affairs ... Dr. Ellen GRANBERG
100 Chief of Staff ... Mrs. Karen A. BARROWS
10 Sr Vice Pres Finance/Administration ... Dr. James H. WATTERS
84 VP Enrollment Management ... Mr. Ian MORTIMER
32 Sr Vice President Student Affairs ... Dr. Sandra S. JOHNSON
12 President NTID/RIT Vice Pres & Dean ... Dr. Gerard J. BUCKLEY
12 President RIT Kosovo ... Dr. Kamal SHAHRABI
12 President RIT Croatia ... Mr. Donald HUDSPETH
12 President RIT Dubai ... Dr. Yousef AL-ASSAF
111 VP for University Advancement ... Mr. Phillip CASTLEBERRY
26 VP/Chief Marketing Officer ... Mr. John K. TRIERWEILER
86 Vice President Govt/Cmty Relations ... Ms. Vanessa HERMAN
46 Vice President Research ... Dr. Ryne RAFFAELLE
28 VP/Provost Diversity/Inclusion ... Dr. Keith JENKINS
76 Dean Col Health Sciences/Tech ... Dr. Yong Tai WANG
20 Vice Provost Academic Affairs ... Dr. Christine M. LICATA
36 Director Coop Educ/Career Svcs ... Ms. Maria RICHART
27 AVP University Communications ... Mr. Bob FINNERTY
110 Assoc VP Univ Advancement ... Ms. Cathy HAIN
20 Assoc Provost AA & Director CIMS ... Dr. Nabil NASR
08 Director of RIT Libraries ... Ms. Marcia TRAVERNICHT
29 Exec Director Alumni/Const Engage ... Mr. Jon RODIBAUGH
21 Assoc VP/Controller/Asst Treasurer ... Ms. Milagros CONCEPCION
18 Assoc VP Facilities Management Svcs ... Mr. John MOORE
06 Assoc VP/Registrar ... Mr. Joe LOFFREDO
07 Asst VP/Dean of Admissions ... Ms. Marian NICOLETTI
37 Exec Dir Fin Aid & Scholarship ... Ms. Meaghan M. DRUMM
88 Exec Director Corp Relations ... Ms. Natalie ANDERSON
88 Sr AVP/Dir Grad/PT Enroll Svcs ... Ms. Diane ELLISON
112 Dir Planned Giving/Major Gifts ... Mr. Hallett BURRALL
09 Asst VP Inst Research ... Dr. Joan E. GRAHAM
15 Assoc VP/Chief Human Resources Ofcr ... Ms. Jo Ellen PINKHAM
44 Executive Director Annual Giving ... Ms. Marisa PSAILA
35 Assoc VP Student Development ... Dr. Heath BOICE-PARDEE
85 Director International Student Svcs ... Mr. Jeffrey W. COX
96 Exec Director Procurement Services ... Ms. Debra KUSSE
102 Exec Director Foundation Relations ... Ms. Barbara HOERNER
107 Dean/Director Univ Studies ... Dr. James HALL
50 Dean Saunders Col of Business ... Dr. Jacqueline MOZRALL
54 Dean Gleason Col of Engineering ... Dr. Doreen EDWARDS
72 Dean of Engineering Technology ... Dr. S. Manian RAMKUMAR
49 Dean College of Liberal Arts ... Dr. Anna WESTERSTANL STENPORT
81 Dean College of Science ... Dr. Sophia MAGGELAKIS
57 Dean College of Art & Design ... Dr. Todd JOKL
77 Dean Col Computer/Info Science ... Dr. Anne HAAKE
58 Dean/Assoc Provost Graduate Educ ... Dr. Twyla CUMMINGS
04 Exec Admin Asst to President ... Ms. Sonia RODRIGUEZ
11 Chief of Administration ... Mrs. Karen A. BARROWS
13 Assoc VP/Chief Info Tech Officer ... Ms. Jeanne CASARES
41 Exec Dir Intercollegiate Athletics ... Ms. Jacqueline NICHOLSON
103 Direcctor of Talent Management ... Ms. Natosha MCDONALD
104 Assoc Provost Intl Educ/Global Pgms ... Dr. James A. MYERS
105 AVP Univeristy Web Services ... Mr. Raman S. BHALLA
106 Exec Dir Innovative Learning Inst ... Dr. Neil F. HAIR
108 Asst Prov Assessment/Accreditation ... Dr. Anne G. WAHL
19 Director Public Safety ... Mr. Gary D. MOXLEY
38 Director Counseling & Psych Svcs ... Dr. David R. REETZ
39 AVP Student Auxiliary Svcs ... Mr. Kory SAMUELS

Rockefeller University (G)

1230 York Avenue, New York NY 10065-6399
County: New York FICE Identification: 002807
Unit ID: 195049
Telephone: (212) 327-8000 Carnegie Class: DU-Higher
FAX Number: (212) 327-8699 Calendar System: Trimester
URL: www.rockefeller.edu
Established: 1901 Annual Graduate Tuition & Fees: N/A
Enrollment: 255 Coed
Affiliation or Control: Independent Non-Profit IRS Status: 501(c)3
Highest Offering: Doctorate; No Undergraduates
Accreditation: NY

01 President ... Dr. Richard P. LIFTON
03 Executive Vice President ... Dr. Timothy O'CONNOR
43 Vice President & General Counsel ... Ms. Deborah YEOH
05 Vice President Academic Affairs ... Mr. Michael W. YOUNG
10 Vice President Finance ... Mr. James H. LAPPLE
30 Sr Vice President Development ... Ms. Maren E. IMHOFF
17 Vice President for Medical Affairs ... Dr. Barry S. COLLER
20 Dean & Vice Pres of Educ Affairs ... Dr. Sidney STRICKLAND
18 Assoc Vice Pres Plant Operations ... Mr. Alexander KOGAN
45 Assoc Vice Pres Plng & Constr ... Mr. George B. CANDLER
13 Chief Information Officer ... Mr. Anthony CARVALLOZA
25 Dir Pgm Dev & Sponsored Research ... Ms. Collette L. RYDER
08 University Librarian ... Dr. Matthew V. COVEY
19 Director Security ... Mr. James ROGERS
26 Assoc VP Communications/Public Affs ... Mr. Franklin HOKE

Rockland Community College (H)

145 College Road, Suffern NY 10901-3699
County: Rockland FICE Identification: 002877
Unit ID: 195058
Telephone: (845) 574-4000 Carnegie Class: Assoc/HT-High Trad
FAX Number: (845) 574-4463 Calendar System: Semester
URL: www.sunyrockland.edu
Established: 1959 Annual Undergrad Tuition & Fees (In-District): $5,618
Enrollment: 5,735 Coed
Affiliation or Control: State/Local IRS Status: 501(c)3
Highest Offering: Associate Degree
Accreditation: M, ADNUR, OTA

01 President ... Dr. Michael A. BASTON
10 Int Chief Financial Officer ... Dr. Daniel DOBELL
05 Provost/Exec Vice President ... Dr. Susan DEER
84 VP Enrollment & Student Affairs ... Dr. Helen BREWER
13 Chief Information Officer ... Mr. Michael SALEM
32 Dean Student Development ... Vacant
37 Director Financial Aid ... Ms. Madelene APONTE
06 Registrar ... Ms. Robin CONKLIN
28 Dir Equity/Compliance/Affirm Act ... Ms. Melissa ROY
09 Director of Institutional Research ... Dr. Jim ROBERTSON

20 Asst to Vice Pres Academic Affairs .... Ms. Patricia KOBES
04 Administrative Asst to President ....Mr. Ben NAYLOR
101 Secretary of the Board ....Mr. Ben NAYLOR
106 Dir Online Education/E-learning .... Ms. Lilia JUELE
11 Dir Administrative Services .... Mr. Dennis CALLINAN
19 Director Public Safety .... Mr. William MURPHY

Russell Sage College (A)

65 First Street, Troy NY 12180-4199

County: Rensselaer FICE Identification: 002810
Unit ID: 195128

Telephone: (518) 244-2000 Carnegie Class: DU-Mod
FAX Number: (518) 244-2460 Calendar System: Semester
URL: www.sage.edu
Established: 1916 Annual Undergrad Tuition & Fees: $32,950
Enrollment: 2,389 Coed
Affiliation or Control: Independent Non-Profit IRS Status: 501(c)3
Highest Offering: Doctorate
Accreditation: M, AAQEP, ART, CAEPN, DIETD, DIETI, IACBE, MPCAC, NURSE, OT, PTA

01 President .... Dr. Christopher AMES
05 Provost ....Dr. Theresa HAND
111 VP for Institutional Advancement ....Ms. Kate ADAMS
84 VP Marketing/Enrol Mgmt ....Mr. Thomas NESBITT
20 Dean Russell Sage College .... Dr. Deborah LAWRENCE
10 VP for Finance & Treasurer .... Mr. Rick BARTHELMAS
32 Vice Pres for Campus Life ....Ms. Patricia CELLEMME
35 Dean of Students-RSC .... Ms. Stacy GONZALEZ
35 Dean of Students-SCA .... Ms. Sharon MURRAY
76 Dean of Health Sciences .... Dr. Kathleen KELLY
06 Registrar .... Ms. Kathy SCOVILLE
94 Exec Dir of Women's Institute-RSC ....Ms. Shelly CALABRESE
26 Sr Dir of Marketing/Communications .... Mr. Douglas GRUSE
07 Director of UG Admission .... Ms. Sarah BARRETT
50 Dean School of Management ....Dr. John PELIZZA
53 Dean School of Education ....Dr. John PELIZZA
29 Dir of Alumni Relations SCA/SGS .... Ms. Katie FALSO
29 Director Alumnae Relations RSC ....Ms. Joan CLIFFORD
123 Dir of Graduate & Adult Admissions .... Mr. Michael JONES
37 Director of Financial Aid .... Ms. Kelley ROBINSON
15 Director of Human Resources .... Ms. Laura D'AGOSTINO
09 Director of Institutional Research .... Ms. Lori PIZER
18 Director Facilities Management .... Mr. John ZAJACESKOWSKI
121 Dir of Academic Advisement-SCA .... Ms. Karen SCHELL
121 Dir of Academic Advisement-RSC .... Ms. Beth MANEY
92 Director of Honors Programs .... Dr. Tonya MOUTRAY
04 Exec Admin Asst to President .... Ms. Janet RONDEAU
08 Head Librarian .... Ms. Lisa C. BRAINARD
105 Webmaster ....Mr. Kurt EYE
108 Dir Institutional Effectiveness ....Mr. Kirk ROBINSON
19 Associate Director Public Safety .... Mr. Charles MCDONALD
39 Director of Residence Life .... Ms. Shylah ADDANTE
41 Athletic Director ....Ms. Sandy AUGESTINE-COLLINS
44 Sr Director of Annual Giving ....Ms. Kathleen DANICA
91 Director of IT/Network Services ....Mr. John HARRIS
106 Director of Online Education .... Ms. Kimberly TAYLOR
28 Director of Diversity & Inclusion ....Ms. Barbara COCKFIELD
25 Asst Provost for Grants & Community .... Dr. Kimberly FREDERICKS

Saint Bernard's School of Theology & Ministry (B)

120 French Road, Rochester NY 14618-3822

County: Monroe FICE Identification: 002815
Unit ID: 195155

Telephone: (585) 271-3657 Carnegie Class: Spec-4-yr-Faith
FAX Number: (585) 271-2045 Calendar System: Semester
URL: www.stbernards.edu
Established: 1893 Annual Graduate Tuition & Fees: N/A
Enrollment: 91 Coed
Affiliation or Control: Roman Catholic IRS Status: 501(c)3
Highest Offering: Master's; No Undergraduates
Accreditation: THEOL

01 President .... Dr. Stephen J. LOUGHLIN
05 Academic Dean ....Dr. Matthew KUHNER
04 Exec Asst to the President .... Mrs. Kelly BRUNACINI
10 Finance Manager ....Mr. Tom KUBUS
07 Director of Admissions/Fin Aid .... Mr. Matthew BROWN
18 Chief Facilities/Physical Plant Ofc .... Mr. Patrick SWEENEY
30 Development Coordinator & Registrar .. Mrs. Sophia ZDANOWSKI

St. Bonaventure University (C)

P.O. Box A, St. Bonaventure NY 14778

County: Cattaraugus FICE Identification: 002817
Unit ID: 195164

Telephone: (716) 375-2000 Carnegie Class: Masters/M
FAX Number: N/A Calendar System: Semester
URL: www.sbu.edu
Established: 1858 Annual Undergrad Tuition & Fees: $36,515
Enrollment: 2,540 Coed
Affiliation or Control: Roman Catholic IRS Status: 501(c)3
Highest Offering: Master's
Accreditation: M, #ARCPA, CACREP, CAEPN, JOUR, NURSE

01 Acting President ....Dr. Joseph E. ZIMMER
05 Provost and VP for Academic Affairs .... Dr. David HILMEY
32 Vice Pres for Student Affairs .... Ms. Kathryn O'BRIEN
10 VP Finance & Administration/CFO ..Mr. H. Daniel HUNGERFORD
26 Chief Communications Officer .... Mr. Thomas MISSEL
111 Vice Pres for Advancement .... Mr. Robert VAN WICKLIN
84 Vice President for Enrollment .... Mr. Bernard VALENTO
57 Exec Dir of Q Arts Center .... Mr. Ludwig BRUNNER
100 Assoc VP & Chief of Staff .... Ms. Ann LEHMAN
15 Director of Human Resources .... Ms. Leslie CARLSON
07 Director of Recruitment .... Mr. Douglas BRADY
37 Director of Financial Aid .... Mr. Christopher CARTMILL
06 Registrar ....Mr. George B. SWINDOLL
13 Assoc Provost/Chief Info Officer ....Dr. Michael HOFFMAN
08 Director Friedsam Memorial Library ....Ms. Ann TENGLUND
101 Director of Board/Govt/Cmty Rels .... Mr. Thomas BUTTAFARRO, JR.
29 Director of Alumni Services ....Mr. Joseph FLANAGAN
36 Director of Career Services .... Ms. Pamela FERMAN
43 University Counsel ....Mr. Jeff REISNER
23 Assoc Dean Stdnt & Cmty Wellbeing ... Ms. Del Rey HONEYCUTT
18 Director of Facilities Operations .... Mr. Jared SMITH
21 Controller .... Ms. Nancy K. TAYLOR
19 Director of Safety and Security .... Mr. Gary SEGRUE
40 Manager Bookstore .... Ms. Annette DONAVON
44 Director Annual Giving Program .... Mr. Alan RIDDLE
92 Director of Honors Program .... Dr. Megan WALSH
49 Dean School of Arts & Sci .... Dr. David HILMEY
50 Dean School of Business .... Dr. Matricia JAMES
58 Dean School of Graduate Studies ....Dr. Michael HOFFMAN
53 Interim Dean School of Education .... Dr. Latoya PIERCE
60 Dean Jandoli Sch of Communication ....Mr. Aaron CHIMBLE
76 Dean School of Health Professions .... Dr. Douglas PISANO
26 Director Marketing and Promotions ....Mr. Seth JOHNSON
41 Acting Director of Athletics .... Ms. Barb QUESTA

St. Elizabeth College of Nursing (D)

2215 Genesee Street, Utica NY 13501-5998

County: Oneida FICE Identification: 006461
Unit ID: 195702

Telephone: (315) 801-8253 Carnegie Class: Spec 2-yr-Health
FAX Number: (315) 801-8271 Calendar System: Semester
URL: www.secon.edu
Established: 1904 Annual Undergrad Tuition & Fees: $18,570
Enrollment: 155 Coed
Affiliation or Control: Independent Non-Profit IRS Status: 501(c)3
Highest Offering: Associate Degree
Accreditation: M, ADNUR

01 President .... Dr. Varinya SHEPPARD
32 Dean of Student/Faculty Devel .... Mrs. Kimberly PANKO
06 Registrar & Bursar .... Mr. Joseph CASCELLA
10 Director of Finance & Enrollment .... Ms. Sherry WOJNAS

St. Francis College (E)

180 Remsen Street, Brooklyn NY 11201-4398

County: Kings FICE Identification: 002820
Unit ID: 195173

Telephone: (718) 522-2300 Carnegie Class: Bac-Diverse
FAX Number: (718) 522-1274 Calendar System: Semester
URL: www.sfc.edu
Established: 1859 Annual Undergrad Tuition & Fees: $26,798
Enrollment: 2,735 Coed
Affiliation or Control: Independent Non-Profit IRS Status: 501(c)3
Highest Offering: Master's
Accreditation: M, NURSE

01 President .... Dr. Miguel MARTINEZ-SAENZ
10 Chief Financial Officer ....Ms. Maureen LAWRENCE
86 Vice Pres Govt/Community Relations .... Ms. Linda WERBEL DASHEFSKY
30 Vice President of Development .... Mr. Thomas FLOOD
84 Asst VP Enrollment Mgmt/Dir Admiss ....Mr. Robert OLIVA
18 VP Facilities Mgmt/Capital Projects ....Mr. Kevin O'ROURKE
104 VP Internationalization Initiative .... Mr. Reza FAKHARI
05 VP Academic Affairs/Academic Dean ...... Dr. Jennifer LANCASTER
20 AVP Academic Affs/Dean Curriculum ....Dr. Kathleen GRAY
58 Assoc Dean Grad Pgms/Adult Educ ....Vacant
121 Assoc Dean for Student Success ....Ms. Monica MICHALSKI
15 Exec Director of Human Resources .... Mr. Richard GRASSO
13 Exec Dir Information Technology .... Mr. Matthew HOGAN
06 Registrar ....Ms. Susan E. WEISMAN
32 Dean of Students .... Dr. Jose RODRIGUEZ
08 Director Library Services .... Ms. Mona WASSERMAN
36 Director of Career Development ....Ms. Naomi KINLEY
29 Director of Alumni Relations ....Vacant
41 Director of Athletics .... Ms. Irma GARCIA
42 Director Campus Ministry ....Dr. Joel WARDEN
09 Director of Institutional Research .... Mr. Steven CATALANO
100 Chief of Staff .... Ms. Monique PRYOR
26 Exec Dir Marketing/Communications .... Ms. Tearanny STREET
106 AVP of Online Learning & Program .... Dr. Gale GIBSON-GAYLE
19 Asst Director of Campus Security .... Mr. Edward EVANS
25 Chief Contract/Grants Administrator .... Ms. Emily WARD
23 Director of Student Health Services ....Ms. Natasha EDWARDS
39 Dir Student Engagement/Resid Life .... Ms. Anilsa NUNEZ

St. John Fisher College (F)

3690 East Avenue, Rochester NY 14618-3597

County: Monroe FICE Identification: 002821
Unit ID: 195720

Telephone: (585) 385-8000 Carnegie Class: DU-Mod
FAX Number: (585) 899-3870 Calendar System: Semester
URL: www.sjfc.edu
Established: 1948 Annual Undergrad Tuition & Fees: $35,150
Enrollment: 3,610 Coed
Affiliation or Control: Independent Non-Profit IRS Status: 501(c)3
Highest Offering: Doctorate
Accreditation: M, CACREP, CAEP, COSMA, NURSE, PHAR

01 President .... Dr. Gerard J. ROONEY
04 Senior Executive Assistant .... Ms. Mary M. MCGOWAN
05 Provost/VP for Academic Affairs .... Dr. Kevin RAILEY
84 VP Enrollment Management ....Mr. Jose J. PERALES
10 VP Finance/CFO .... Ms. Linda M. STEINKIRCHNER
32 VP Student Affairs/Dean of Students .... Dr. Matha THORNTON
111 VP Institutional Advancement .... Mr. Christopher M. BIEHN
49 Dean School of Arts/Sciences .... Dr. Ann Marie FALLON
50 Interim Dean School of Business .... Dr. Carol WITTMEYER
53 Dean School of Education ....Dr. Joellen MAPLES
66 Dean School of Nursing ....Dr. Patricia GATLIN
67 Dean School of Pharmacy ....Dr. Christine R. BIRNIE
28 Director Multicultural Affairs .... Mr. Yantee SLOBERT
06 Registrar ....Mr. Jason WELCH
15 Asst Vice Pres Human Resources .... Ms. Valerie C. BENJAMIN
28 Senior Diversity Officer .... Dr. Marlowe WASHINGTON
26 Director Marketing & Communications .... Ms. Kate M. TOROK
08 Director of the Library .... Ms. Melissa JADLOS
13 Chief Information/Computing Officer ....Mr. Stacy S. SLOCUM
16 Director of Payroll & Accts Payable ....Ms. Mary R. POWLEY
37 Director Student Financial Aid .... Ms. Marie FICO
42 Director Campus Ministry .... Fr. Kevin MANNARA
19 Interim Director Safety & Security ....Mr. Russell REYNOLDS
41 Athletic Director .... Mr. Robert A. WARD
18 Director of Facilities Services .... Mr. Kenneth WIDANKA
21 Controller ....Ms. Diane MARTZ
23 Dir of Health & Wellness Center .... Ms. Rebecca KIEFFER
104 Director of Global Education .... Ms. Maria S. PLUTINO
07 Director of Freshman Admissions ....Ms. Stacy A. LEDERMANN
123 Dir of Transfer/Grad Admissions ....Ms. Michelle GOSIER
09 Director Institutional Research ....Ms. Elizabeth A. LACHANCE
35 Director Student Affairs .... Ms. Amanda METZGER
36 Director Career Services .... Dr. Julia OVERTON-HEALY
105 Webmaster ....Ms. Jocy C. BENEDICT
96 Director of Purchasing .... Ms. Susan WISNIEWSKI
101 Secretary to the Board ....Ms. Stephanie WILLIAMS
29 Director Alumni Affairs .... Ms. Teah TERRANCE
30 Asst VP for Development ....Mr. Adam PARE
39 Director Residential Life ....Mr. Derick WIGLE

St. John's University (G)

8000 Utopia Parkway, Queens NY 11439-0001

County: Queens FICE Identification: 002823
Unit ID: 195809

Telephone: (718) 990-6161 Carnegie Class: DU-Mod
FAX Number: (718) 990-2314 Calendar System: Semester
URL: www.stjohns.edu
Established: 1870 Annual Undergrad Tuition & Fees: $44,760
Enrollment: 20,143 Coed
Affiliation or Control: Roman Catholic IRS Status: 501(c)3
Highest Offering: Doctorate
Accreditation: M, ARCPA, ART, AUD, CACREP, CLPSY, EMT, LAW, LIB, MT, PHAR, RAD, SCPSY, SP

01 President ....Rev. Brian J. SHANLEY, OP
04 Presidential Asst Administration .... Ms. Carolyn MADAIO
03 Executive VP Mission .... Rev. Bernard M. TRACEY, CM
05 Provost/VP Academic Affairs ....Dr. Simon MOLLER
10 VP Business Affairs/CFO/ Treasurer ....Ms. Sharon HEWITT WATKINS
11 VP Admin/Secretary & Gen Counsel ....Mr. Joseph E. OLIVA
32 VP Student Affairs .... Dr. Kathryn T. HUTCHINSON
111 VP University Advancement/Relations .....Dr. Christian P. VAUPEL
13 Chief Information Officer .... Ms. Anne R. PACIONE
41 Director of Athletics .... Mr. Michael CRAGG
49 Interim Dean St John's College ....Dr. Gina FLORIO
53 Int Dean The School of Education ....Dr. Aliya E. HOLMES
61 Dean School of Law ....Mr. Michael A. SIMONS
50 Dean The Tobin College of Business ....Dr. Norean R. SHARPE
67 Dean Pharmacy/Health Sciences .... Dr. Russell J. DIGATE
107 Dean Collins Col Prof Studies .... Dr. Glenn GERSTNER
08 University Librarian ....Ms. Caroline FUCHS
12 Vice Provost - SI ....Dr. James O'KEEFE
31 VP Community Relations ....Mr. Joseph A. SCIAME
18 Assoc VP Campus Facilities/Services .... Mr. Brian BAUMER
91 Assoc VP Bus Process & Applications ...... Ms. Maura A. WOODS
27 Assoc VP Marketing & Communications ....Ms. Caren BATZER
42 Assoc VP University Ministry .... Ms. Victoria R. SANTANGELO
15 Int Assoc VP fot Human Resources ....Ms. Keaton WONG
21 Asst VP Business Affairs .... Dr. Judy CHEN
88 Asst VP University Events .... Ms. Nunziatina A. MANULI
20 Vice Prov Acad Sup/Int Chief Div Of ....Dr. Andre A. MCKENZIE
100 Vice Provost & Chief of Staff .... Ms. Linda A. SHANNON
104 Assoc Provost Global Studies ....Dr. Matthew PUCCIARELLI
121 Assoc Provost Student Success ....Dr. Jacqueline H. GROGAN
20 Asst Provost Acad Res & Mgmt Plng ....Ms. Geraldine AMERA
07 Executive Director Admissions ....Mrs. Samantha R. WRIGHT
106 Exec Dir CTL/Online Learning ....Dr. Cynthia R. PHILLIPS
19 Exec Dir Public Safety ....Ms. Denise VENCAK
36 Exec Dir University Career Services ....Ms. Paulette B. GONZALEZ
86 Exec Dir Univ Rel/Asst VP Gov Rels .... Mr. Brian BROWNE
90 Exec Dir Operations/ Infrastructure .... Mr. Kenneth J. MAHLMEISTER
88 Exec Director Vincentian Center .... Rev. Patrick J. GRIFFIN, CM
06 University Registrar ....Ms. Joanne A. LLERANDI

39 Sr Director Residence Life .... Mr. Eric M. FINKELSTEIN
29 Director Alumni Relations .... Mr. Mark A. ANDREWS
38 Director Counseling Center .... Vacant
105 Director Digital Communications .... Ms. Linda ROMANO
37 Director Financial Aid/Research .... Ms. Maryanne H. TWOMEY
25 Dir Grants & Sponsored Research .... Mr. Jared E. LITTMAN
92 Director Honors Program .... Dr. Robert J. FORMAN
16 Director Human Resources Services ...... Ms. Cynthia F. SIMPSON
09 Director Institutional Research .... Dr. Christine M. GOODWIN
116 Director Internal Audit .... Mr. Jorge J. OSORIO
85 Dir Int Students/Scholar Svcs .... Ms. Amy R. SCHOENFELD
112 Director of Gift Planning .... Ms. Susan M. DAMIANI
88 Dir Pre-Admin/Asst to VP S&O P .... Mrs. Cecelia M. RUSSO
23 Director Student Health Services .... Ms. Sharon MACARTHUR
20 Assoc Provost Academic - SI .... Dr. Robert FANUZZI
35 Assoc Dean Student Affairs - SI .... Mr. David GACHIGO
07 Sr Assoc Director Admissions - SI .... Mr. David A. PIERRE
37 Asst Director Financial Aid - SI .... Mr. Thomas J. MARLOW
40 Manager of Bookstore .... Mrs. Denise SERVIDIO

Saint Joseph's College, New York (A)

245 Clinton Avenue, Brooklyn NY 11205-3688
County: Kings FICE Identification: 002825
Unit ID: 195544
Telephone: (718) 940-5300 Carnegie Class: Masters/M
FAX Number: (718) 636-7245 Calendar System: Semester
URL: www.sjcny.edu
Established: 1916 Annual Undergrad Tuition & Fees: $29,200
Enrollment: 5,012 Coed
Affiliation or Control: Independent Non-Profit IRS Status: 501(c)3
Highest Offering: Master's
Accreditation: M, ADNUR, CAPRT, NUR

01 President .... Dr. Donald R. BOOMGAARDEN
05 Provost/VP Academic Affairs .... Dr. Robert RILEY
26 VP of Marketing &d Communications .... Ms. Jessica MCALEER
10 Chief Financial Officer .... Mr. John C. ROTH
20 Executive Dean - BK .... Dr. Phillip DEHNE
13 VP IT and Chief Information Officer .... Ms. Michelle PAPAJOHN
32 VP for Student Life - BK .... Ms. Shantey HILL-HANNA
111 VP for Institutional Advancement ...... Ms. Rory SHAFFER-WALSH
84 VP for Enrollment Management - BK .... Ms. Christine MURPHY
41 VP for Athletics & Campus Services .... Ms. Shantey HILL-HANNA
19 Director Security/Safety .... Mr. Michael MCGRANN
88 Director of Child Study Center ...... Dr. Susan STRAUT COLLARD
90 Exec Director Client Services .... Ms. Lichele ABEAR
37 Director of Financial Aid .... Ms. Amy THOMPSON
36 Exec Director Career Development .... Ms. Ellen BURTI
15 Exec Director of Human Resources .... Ms. D'adra CRUMP
18 Director Physical Plant .... Ms. Linda VIGNATO
21 Controller .... Ms. Marion KOWALSKI
14 Exec Director Network Operations .... Mr. Ted DEC
06 College Registrar .... Mr. Robert PERGOLIS
08 Director of Library .... Dr. Elizabeth POLLICINO MURPHY
27 Director of Public Affairs .... Mr. Michael BANACH
28 Coordinator of Diversity .... Vacant
112 Planned Giving Officer .... Ms. Susan LOUCKS
38 Director of Counseling .... Dr. Cynthia CABRAL
29 Director of Alumni Engagement .... Ms. Paulina MELIN
09 Director of Institutional Research .... Ms. Allison LIST
102 Director Foundation Relations .... Vacant
86 Director Government Relations .... Mr. Michael BANACH
04 Executive Admin Asst to President .... Ms. Kimberly MAILLEY
84 VP for Enrollment Management - LI .... Ms. Gigi LAMENS
108 Director Institutional Assessment .... Ms. Heather BARRY

St. Joseph's College of Nursing (B)

206 Prospect Avenue, Syracuse NY 13203-1806
County: Onondaga FICE Identification: 006467
Unit ID: 195191
Telephone: (315) 448-5040 Carnegie Class: Spec 2-yr-Health
FAX Number: (315) 448-5745 Calendar System: Semester
URL: www.sjhcon.org
Established: 1898 Annual Undergrad Tuition & Fees: $22,156
Enrollment: 383 Coed
Affiliation or Control: Independent Non-Profit IRS Status: 501(c)3
Highest Offering: Associate Degree
Accreditation: M

01 VP/Dean .... Dr. Marianne MARKOWITZ
05 Dean of Academic Affairs .... Dr. Sarah J. LORMAND

Saint Joseph's Seminary (C)

201 Seminary Avenue, Yonkers NY 10704-1852
County: Westchester FICE Identification: 002826
Telephone: (914) 968-6200 Carnegie Class: Not Classified
FAX Number: (914) 376-2019 Calendar System: Semester
URL: www.dunwoodie.edu
Established: 1896 Annual Graduate Tuition & Fees: N/A
Enrollment: N/A Coed
Affiliation or Control: Roman Catholic IRS Status: 501(c)3
Highest Offering: Master's; No Undergraduates
Accreditation: M, THEOL

01 Rector .... Bishop James MASSA
03 Vice Rector .... Rev. William CLEARY
05 Academic Dean .... Rev. Matthew S. ERNEST
32 Dean of Students .... Rev. Michael BRUNO
08 Director Library Services .... Mr. Connor FLATZ

06 Registrar .... Ms. Roenice GONZALEZ
18 Director of Buildings & Grounds .... Mr. Joseph DI LELLO
26 Dir of Communications/Technology ..... Ms. Cynthia F. HARRISON
108 Director Institutional Assessment .... Rev. Michael BRUNO
70 Director of Admissions .... Rev. Thomas BERG

St. Lawrence University (D)

23 Romoda Drive, Canton NY 13617-1423
County: St. Lawrence FICE Identification: 002829
Unit ID: 195216
Telephone: (315) 229-5011 Carnegie Class: Bac-A&S
FAX Number: (315) 229-5502 Calendar System: Other
URL: www.stlawu.edu
Established: 1856 Annual Undergrad Tuition & Fees: $58,750
Enrollment: 2,319 Coed
Affiliation or Control: Independent Non-Profit IRS Status: 501(c)3
Highest Offering: Master's
Accreditation: M, CAEPT

01 President .... Dr. Kathryn A. MORRIS
05 Vice Pres/Dean Academic Affairs .... Dr. Karl K. SCHONBERG
111 Vice Pres University Advancement .... Mr. Thomas PYNCHON
10 VP Finance/Administration & Treas .... Mr. Stephen HIETSCH
32 Vice Pres/Dean Student Life .... Mr. Earlhagi BRADLEY
07 VP & Dean for Admissions/Fin Aid .... Ms. Florence HINES
26 VP University Communications .... Mr. Paul REDFERN
89 Associate Dean of the First-Year .... Dr. Sarah BARBER
35 Associate Dean of Student Life .... Mr. Rance DAVIS
06 Registrar .... Ms. Lorie MACKENZIE
37 Director of Financial Aid .... Mrs. Patricia J B. FARMER
36 Director of Career Services ...... Ms. Jillian MCKERNAN-WALLEY
09 Director of Institutional Research .... Ms. Christine ZIMMERMAN
18 Chief Facilities/Physical Plant .... Mr. Daniel B. SEAMAN
20 Assoc Dean of Academic Admin .... Ms. Lorie R. MACKENZIE
29 Director Alumni Relations .... Mr. Joseph C. KENISTON
39 Director Residence Life .... Mr. Christopher MARQUARDT
23 Director of Health & Counseling .... Mr. Timothy CORBITT
84 Exec Director Enrollment Management .... Mr. Jeremy FREEMAN
96 Director of Purchasing .... Mr. Nickolas ORMASEN
15 Director Personnel Services .... Mrs. Colleen MANLEY
38 Director Student Counseling .... Mr. Timothy CORBITT
04 Exec Assistant to the President .... Ms. Cheryl CASEY-ROSE
19 Director Security/Safety .... Mr. Patrick GAGNON
28 Director of Diversity .... Dr. Kimberly FLINT-HAMILTON
41 Athletic Director .... Mr. Robert DUROCHER
13 Exec Dir Enterprise/Infrastructure .... Mr. Darrin GOODROW
14 Exec Dir Campus Svcs & Outreach IT .... Ms. Rene THATCHER

Saint Paul's School of Nursing-Queens (E)

97-77 Queens Boulevard, Queens NY 11374
County: Queens FICE Identification: 012364
Unit ID: 189811
Telephone: (718) 357-0500 Carnegie Class: Spec 2-yr-Health
FAX Number: (718) 357-4683 Calendar System: Semester
URL: www.stpaulsschoolofnursing.edu
Established: 1969 Annual Undergrad Tuition & Fees: $20,871
Enrollment: 747 Coed
Affiliation or Control: Proprietary IRS Status: Proprietary
Highest Offering: Associate Degree
Accreditation: ABHES

01 Campus President .... Paul FERRISE

Saint Paul's School of Nursing-Staten Island (F)

2 Teleport Dr Ste 203, Corp Comm 2,
Staten Island NY 10311
County: Richmond FICE Identification: 009479
Unit ID: 195784
Telephone: (718) 818-6470 Carnegie Class: Spec 2-yr-Health
FAX Number: (718) 818-6020 Calendar System: Semester
URL: www.stpaulsschoolofnursing.edu
Established: 1904 Annual Undergrad Tuition & Fees: $17,731
Enrollment: 746 Coed
Affiliation or Control: Proprietary IRS Status: Proprietary
Highest Offering: Associate Degree
Accreditation: ABHES

01 President .... Mr. David SMITH
05 Director of Education .... Dr. Christine RAGHEB
66 Dean of Nursing .... Dr. Keven O'NEILL
06 Registrar .... Ms. Sat KAUR
10 Business Office Manager .... Ms. Olga FORINA
07 Director of Admissions .... Mr. Deshun TAYLOR
36 Director of Career Services .... Ms. Lynn SALVAGE
37 Director of Financial Aid .... Ms. Nayamka WARD
08 LRC Manager .... Ms. Judy LEE

St. Thomas Aquinas College (G)

125 Route 340, Sparkill NY 10976-1050
County: Rockland FICE Identification: 002832
Unit ID: 195243
Telephone: (845) 398-4000 Carnegie Class: Masters/S
FAX Number: (845) 359-8136 Calendar System: 4/1/4
URL: www.stac.edu
Established: 1952 Annual Undergrad Tuition & Fees: $34,200
Enrollment: 1,779 Coed
Affiliation or Control: Independent Non-Profit IRS Status: 501(c)3
Highest Offering: Master's
Accreditation: M, IACBE

01 President .... Dr. Kenneth D. DALY
10 SVP/VP Administration & Finance .... Mr. Joseph DONINI
05 Provost/Vice Pres Academic Affairs .... Dr. Robert MURRAY
32 Vice Pres/Dean Student Development .... Dr. Kirk MANNING
15 Director Human Resources .... Mrs. Maria COUPE
07 Director Admissions .... Ms. Samantha BAZILE
09 Dir Inst Research/Program Develop .... Dr. Renee QUINTYNE
21 Controller .... Ms. Jennifer MAZZA
44 Dir Annual Giving & Alumni Affairs .... Mr. James ERRICO
35 Director Student Activities .... Mr. Nicholas MIGLIORINO
38 Director Student Counseling .... Dr. Louis MUGGEO
06 Registrar .... Ms. Eileen MURPHY
36 Director Career Development .... Mrs. Maureen MULHERN
37 Director Financial Aid .... Mrs. Joanne SULLIVAN
13 Director of Computing Services .... Mr. Sunny ANTHWAL
18 Dir Facilities & Construction .... Mr. Patrick LAMBERT
26 Dir Campus Communications/Enr Mktg ..... Ms. Annie LOMBARDI
50 Dean School of Business .... Mr. Michael MURPHY
53 Dean School of Education .... Dr. Meenakshi GAJRIA
49 Dean School of Arts & Sciences .... Dr. Heath BOWEN
04 Executive Asst to President .... Ms. Lee TAUSSI

Saint Vladimir's Orthodox Theological Seminary (H)

575 Scarsdale Road, Yonkers NY 10707
County: Westchester FICE Identification: 002833
Unit ID: 195580
Telephone: (914) 961-8313 Carnegie Class: Spec-4-yr-Faith
FAX Number: (914) 961-4507 Calendar System: Semester
URL: www.svots.edu
Established: 1938 Annual Graduate Tuition & Fees: N/A
Enrollment: 79 Coed
Affiliation or Control: Independent Non-Profit IRS Status: 501(c)3
Highest Offering: Doctorate; No Undergraduates
Accreditation: THEOL

01 President .... V.Rev. Chad HATFIELD
05 Academic Dean .... Dr. Ionut Alexandru TUDORIE
10 Chief Financial Officer .... Mrs. Melanie RINGA
13 Chief Technology Officer .... Mr. Georgios KOKONAS
42 Director of Spiritual Formation .... Rev. Nicholas ROTH
06 Registrar .... Mrs. Gabrielle RUSSIN
08 Librarian .... Mrs. Danielle EARL
32 Student Affairs Administrator .... Mrs. Gabrielle RUSSIN
108 Dir Institutional Assessment .... Dr. Ionut Alexandru TUDORIE
111 Sr Advisor Advancement .... Mr. Ted BAZIL
26 Director of Marketing .... Ms. Sarah WERNER
30 Director of Development .... Ms. Sharon ROSS
04 Admin Assistant to President .... Ms. Ann SANCHEZ
07 Director of Admissions .... Mr. Alexandru POPOVICI
18 Chf Facilities/Physical Plant Ofcr .... Mr. Rafael RIVERA

Salvation Army College for Officer Training (I)

201 Lafayette Avenue, Suffern NY 10901-4707
County: Rockland Identification: 666020
Telephone: (845) 368-7200 Carnegie Class: Not Classified
FAX Number: (845) 357-6644 Calendar System: Other
URL: www.use.salvationarmy.org
Established: 1905 Annual Undergrad Tuition & Fees: N/A
Enrollment: N/A Coed
Affiliation or Control: Independent Non-Profit IRS Status: 501(c)3
Highest Offering: Associate Degree
Accreditation: NY

01 Principal .... LtCol. David E. KELLY
11 Asst Principal for Administration .... Major Ron STARNES
05 Director of Curriculum .... Major Sun-Kyung SIMPSON
09 Coord Inst Research/Accred
Liaison .... Dr. Dennis A. VANDER WEELE
10 Chief Business Officer .... Major Paul CORNELL
15 Director Personnel Services .... Major Alberto SUAREZ
20 Associate Academic Officer .... Capt. Sheila WILLIAMS-GAGE
72 Education Tech Coordinator .... Mr. Marcos A. LOPEZ
13 Director of IT & Communications .... Mr. Daniel MACHADO

Samaritan Hospital School of Nursing (J)

1300 Massachusetts Avenue, Troy NY 12180
County: Rensselaer FICE Identification: 009248
Unit ID: 195289
Telephone: (518) 268-5010 Carnegie Class: Spec 2-yr-Health
FAX Number: (518) 268-5040 Calendar System: Semester
URL: www.nehealth.com
Established: 1903 Annual Undergrad Tuition & Fees: $14,292
Enrollment: 152 Coed
Affiliation or Control: Independent Non-Profit IRS Status: 501(c)3
Highest Offering: Associate Degree
Accreditation: ADNUR, PNUR

01 Dean/Director .... Ms. Patti CANNISTRACI

Sarah Lawrence College (A)

1 Meadway, Bronxville NY 10708-5999

County: Westchester FICE Identification: 002813
Unit ID: 195304
Telephone: (914) 337-0700 Carnegie Class: Bac-A&S
FAX Number: N/A Calendar System: Semester
URL: www.slc.edu
Established: 1926 Annual Undergrad Tuition & Fees: $57,520
Enrollment: 1,506 Coed
Affiliation or Control: Independent Non-Profit IRS Status: 501(c)3
Highest Offering: Master's
Accreditation: M

01 President .... Dr. Cristle COLLINS JUDD
05 Provost and Dean of Faculty .... Dr. Kanwal SINGH
10 Vice Pres Finance/Operations .... Vacant
111 VP for Advancement/External Rels .... Patricia GOLDMAN
09 AVP Inst Research & Govt Relations .... Thomas L. BLUM
84 VP Enrollment & Dean of Admission .... Kevin MCKENNA
20 Associate Dean of the College .... Melissa FRAZIER
32 Dean of Studies & Student Life .... Daniel TRUJILLO
35 Dean of Student Affairs .... Vacant
58 Dean Graduate Studies .... Kim FERGUSON
06 Registrar .... Daniel LICHT
08 Director of Libraries .... Bobbie SMOLOW
13 Chief Technology Officer .... Sean JAMESON
29 Director of Alumni .... Christina CAMARDELLA
36 Director Career Counseling .... Angela CHERUBINI
44 Individual Giving Officer .... Elisa BALESTRA
28 Assoc Dean Engage/Div/EquityInclus .... Amada SANDOVAL
18 Asst Vice President of Facilities .... Maureen GALLAGHER
19 Director of Campus Safety .... James VERDICCHIO
04 Executive Asst to President .... Donna WATSON
104 Asst Dean Study Abroad .... Prema SAMUEL
37 Director Student Financial Aid .... Nick SALINAS
102 Director Foundation/Corporate Rels .... Vacant
15 VP for Human Resources .... Danielle COSCIA
41 Athletic Director .... Kristin MAILE
96 Director of Purchasing .... Jennifer MELENDEZ
101 Secretary of the Institution/Board .... Thomas BLUM

Schenectady County Community College (B)

78 Washington Avenue, Schenectady NY 12305

County: Schenectady FICE Identification: 006785
Unit ID: 195322
Telephone: (518) 381-1200 Carnegie Class: Assoc/MT-VT-High Non
FAX Number: (518) 346-0379 Calendar System: Semester
URL: www.sunysccc.edu
Established: 1967 Annual Undergrad Tuition & Fees (In-District): $5,524
Enrollment: 4,015 Coed
Affiliation or Control: State/Local IRS Status: 501(c)3
Highest Offering: Associate Degree
Accreditation: M, ACFEI, MUS

01 President .... Dr. Steady MOONO
05 Vice Pres for Academic Affairs .... Dr. Cheryl GOOCH
10 Vice President of Administration .... Mr. Patrick RYAN
30 Vice Pres Development/External Affs .... Ms. Stacy MCILDUFF
45 Vice Pres for Strategic Initiatives .... Dr. David CLICKNER
103 Exec Dir Workforce Dev/Cmty Educ .... Ms. Sarah WILSON-SPARROW
13 Chief Information Officer .... Vacant
20 Dean of Academic Affairs .... Ms. Jessica GILBERT
32 Interim Dean of Student Affairs .... Mr. Stephen FRAGALE
37 Asst Dean of Financial Aid .... Mr. Mark BESSETTE
06 Registrar .... Ms. Cynthia ZIELASKOWSKI
07 Director of Admissions .... Ms. Laura SPRAGUE
08 Director Library Services .... Ms. Jacqueline KELEHER-HUGHES
18 Director of Facilities .... Mr. Anthony SCHWARTZ
36 Exec Dir Sche Col/Career Outreach .... Dr. DeShawn MCGARRITY
15 Human Resources Specialist .... Ms. Carianne TROTTA
09 Director Institutional Research .... Mr. Dale MILLER
22 Dir Educ Opp Pgms/Access .... Mr. Jeff ARANDA
10 Controller .... Ms. Aimee S. WARFIELD
100 Chief of Staff .... Ms. Paula OHLHOUS
26 Director Marketing/Public Relations .... Vacant
27 Public Rels/Publications Specialist .... Ms. Heather L. MEANEY
19 Director Security/Safety .... Mr. Michael MUNGER

School of Visual Arts (C)

209 E 23rd Street, New York NY 10010-3994

County: New York FICE Identification: 007468
Unit ID: 197151
Telephone: (212) 592-2000 Carnegie Class: Spec-4-yr-Arts
FAX Number: (212) 725-3587 Calendar System: Semester
URL: www.sva.edu
Established: 1947 Annual Undergrad Tuition & Fees: $43,400
Enrollment: 3,692 Coed
Affiliation or Control: Proprietary IRS Status: Proprietary
Highest Offering: Master's
Accreditation: M, CIDA

01 President .... David J. RHODES
03 Executive Vice President .... Anthony P. RHODES
05 Provost .... Christopher J. CYPHERS
10 Chief Financial Officer .... Gary SHILLET
32 Exec Dir of Student Affairs/Admiss .... Javier VEGA
26 Exec Director of External Relations .... Susan MODENSTEIN
13 Chief Information Officer .... Cosmin TOMESCU
06 Registrar .... Jason KOTH
07 Director Admission .... Matthew R. FARINA
35 Director of Student Affairs .... Bill MARTINO
08 Director Visual Arts Library .... Caitlin KILGALLEN
37 Director Financial Aid .... William BERRIOS
36 Director Career Development .... Angie WOJAK
30 Director Development/Alumni Affairs .... Jane NUZZO
19 Director Security .... Nick AGJMURATI
15 Exec Director of Human Resources .... Frank AGOSTA
09 Director of Institutional Research .... Jerold DAVIS
26 Director of Communication .... Joyce KAYE

Sh'or Yoshuv Rabbinical College (D)

1 Cedarlawn Avenue, Lawrence NY 11559-1714

County: Nassau FICE Identification: 025059
Unit ID: 195438
Telephone: (516) 239-9002 Carnegie Class: Spec-4-yr-Faith
FAX Number: (516) 239-9003 Calendar System: Semester
URL: www.shoryoshuv.org
Established: 1963 Annual Undergrad Tuition & Fees: $10,560
Enrollment: 183 Male
Affiliation or Control: Independent Non-Profit IRS Status: 501(c)3
Highest Offering: Second Talmudic Degree
Accreditation: RABN

01 Dean .... Rabbi Naftali JAEGER
05 Executive Director .... Mr. Moshe RUBIN
32 Director of Student Affairs .... Rabbi Elysha SANDLER
06 Registrar .... Mrs. Hindie FRIED
37 Director SFA .... Rabbi Chaim MAJEROVIC
11 Administrator .... Mr. Mendel M. JAROSLAWICZ

Siena College (E)

515 Loudon Road, Loudonville NY 12211-1462

County: Albany FICE Identification: 002816
Unit ID: 195474
Telephone: (518) 783-2300 Carnegie Class: Masters/S
FAX Number: (518) 783-4280 Calendar System: Semester
URL: www.siena.edu
Established: 1937 Annual Undergrad Tuition & Fees: $40,175
Enrollment: 3,425 Coed
Affiliation or Control: Independent Non-Profit IRS Status: 501(c)3
Highest Offering: Master's
Accreditation: M, NURSE, SW

01 President .... Dr. Christopher P. GIBSON
05 Provost & Senior Vice President .... Dr. Margaret MADDEN
32 Vice President for Student Life .... Dr. Maryellen GILROY
10 Vice President for Finance & Admin .... Mr. Paul T. STEC
84 VP for Enrollment Management .... Mr. Ned J. JONES
30 VP for Development & Ext Affairs .... Mr. David B. SMITH
100 Special Assistant to the President .... Mr. Jason RICH
88 VP for Mission .... Fr. Mark REAMER, OFM
41 VP & Director of Athletics .... Mr. John D'ARGENIO
13 Chief Information Officer .... Mr. Mark A. BERMAN
49 Dean of Liberal Arts .... Dr. Christiane FARNAN
50 Dean of Business .... Dr. Charles SEIFERT
81 Dean of Science .... Dr. John CUMMINGS
124 Assoc VP Stdnt Retention & Success .... Dr. Glenn BRADDOCK
37 Assoc Vice Pres Financial Aid .... Ms. Mary K. LAWYER
35 Assoc VP Student Life .... Mr. Michael PAPADOPOULOS
15 Asst VP for Human Resources .... Ms. Cynthia B. KING-LEROY
21 Asst VP for Finance & Admin .... Ms. Mary C. STRUNK
18 Asst VP for Facilities Management .... Mr. Mark FROST
19 Asst VP Stdnt Life/Dir Public Safe .... Mr. Ron MATOS
20 Asst VP Academic Affairs .... Ms. Laurie FAY
06 Registrar .... Ms. Kari A. BENNETT
07 Director of Admissions .... Ms. Katie SZALDA
08 Dir of Library/Audio Visual Svcs .... Ms. Loretta EBERT
92 Director of Honors Program .... Dr. Lois K. DALY
39 Director of Community Living .... Mr. Adam CASLER
36 Dir Ofc of Career Dev & Prof Educ .... Ms. Debra DELBELSO
26 Deputy Chief Information Officer .... Ms. Mary W. PARLETT-SWEENEY
42 Chaplain of the College .... Fr. Lawrence ANDERSON, OFM
38 Director of Counseling Center .... Dr. Nathan PRUITT
29 Director of Alumni Relations .... Ms. Mary Beth FINNERTY
09 Dir of Institutional Research .... Ms. Tara COPE
94 Dir Sr Thea Bowman Ctr for Women .... Ms. Beth DEANGELIS
23 Director of Health Services .... Ms. Carrie HOGAN
110 Director of Development .... Mr. Brad R. BODMER
28 Dir of Damietta Cross-Cultural Ctr .... Br. George CAMACHO
104 Director of Study Abroad/Intl Pgms .... Br. Brian C. BELANGER, OFM
109 Dir of Auxiliary Svcs & Procurement .... Ms. Laura S. ZOCCO
43 Legal Services/General Counsel .... Ms. Rose SEGGOS
20 Director of Academic Programs .... Ms. Lynn ROGERS
121 Dir of Siena Enhanced Edu Dev/SEED .... Ms. Holly CHEVERTON
88 Director HEOP .... Ms. Yasmin FISHER
25 Dir Grants & Sponsored Pgms .... Ms. Sally SOUTHWICK
22 Title IX Coord/EEO Specialist .... Ms. Lois GOLAND
88 Dir Office of Accessibility .... Ms. Julie GOLD
04 Admin Assistant to the President .... Mr. Zachary BRIMMER
101 Secretary of the Institution/Board .... Mrs. Kathleen KIERNAN
108 Dir Institutional Effectiveness .... Dr. Mohua BOSE

Skidmore College (F)

815 N Broadway, Saratoga Springs NY 12866-1632

County: Saratoga FICE Identification: 002814
Unit ID: 195526
Telephone: (518) 580-5000 Carnegie Class: Bac-A&S
FAX Number: (518) 580-5936 Calendar System: Semester
URL: www.skidmore.edu
Established: 1911 Annual Undergrad Tuition & Fees: $58,278
Enrollment: 2,582 Coed
Affiliation or Control: Independent Non-Profit IRS Status: 501(c)3
Highest Offering: Baccalaureate
Accreditation: M, ART, SW

01 President .... Dr. Marc C. CONNER
05 VP Academic Affairs/Dean of Faculty .... Dr. Michael T. ORR
10 Vice Pres Finance/Admin/Treasurer .... Ms. Donna NG
111 Vice President for Advancement .... Ms. Carey Anne ZUCCA
15 Interim Director for HR .... Ms. Sarah DELANEY VERO
32 Vice President/Dean of Students .... Dr. Adrian BAUTISTA
35 Assistant VP for Student Affairs .... Ms. Gail L. CUMMINGS-DANSON
07 VP & Dean of Admiss & Fin Aid .... Ms. Mary Lou W. BATES
88 Managing Dir of Special Programs .... Dr. Auden THOMAS
06 Registrar .... Mr. David DECONNO
20 Assoc Dean for Stdnt Acad Affairs .... Dr. Michael F. ARNUSH
28 Assoc Dn for Diversity/Faculty Affs .... Dr. Janet G. CASEY
88 Assoc Dean Infrastructure/Fac Affs .... Dr. Patricia FEHLING
89 Dir of First Year Experience .... Dr. Amon EMEKA
35 Assoc Dean Student Affs/Campus Life .... Ms. Mariel MARTIN
39 Assoc Dean Res Life/Student Conduct .... Ms. Ann Marie PRZYWARA
88 Dir Student Academic Services .... Mr. Jamin TOTINO
45 VP Strategic Plng & Inst Diversity .... Dr. Joshua C. WOODFORK
26 VP Communications & Mktg .... Vacant
09 Director of Institutional Research .... Mr. Joseph STANKOVICH
102 Dir Foundation & Corporate Rels .... Mr. Barry PRITZKER
46 Director of Sponsored Research .... Ms. Mary HOEHN
13 Chief Technology Officer .... Mr. Dwane M. STERLING
27 Director of Marketing & Engagement .... Mr. Luke MEYERS
88 Dir Acad Pgm/Resid/Inst & Cmty Pgms .... Dr. Auden THOMAS
88 Dir Ctr for Leadership/Teach/Lrng .... Dr. Kristie A. FORD
22 Asst Dir EEO & Workforce Diversity .... Vacant
91 Director IT-Enterprise Systems .... Mr. Kevin L. CRIDER
104 Dir of Off-Campus Study & Exchanges .... Ms. Cori FILSON
44 Sr Assoc Dir Donor Engagement .... Ms. Barb CASEY
30 Assoc VP Advancement & Campaign Dir .... Ms. Lori EASTMAN
29 Exec Dir Alumni Rels/Col Events .... Mr. Michael SPOSILI
36 Assoc Dean Stdnt Affs/Career Dev .... Ms. Kim CRABBE
37 Director of Financial Aid .... Ms. Beth POST
38 Assoc Dn Stdnt Affs/Health/Wellness .... Dr. Julia C. ROUTBORT
21 Asst VP for Finance & Controller .... Mr. Kyle BERNARD
109 Asst VP for Fin Planning & Aux Svcs .... Ms. Kelley A. PATTON-OSTRANDER
23 Director of Health Services .... Ms. Patricia BOSEN
18 Director of Facilities Services .... Mr. Daniel RODECKER
19 Director of Campus Safety .... Mr. Timothy J. MUNRO
08 College Librarian .... Ms. Marta BRUNNER
96 Director of Purchasing .... Mrs. Carol N. SCHNITZER
42 Dir Religious & Spiritual Life .... Ms. Parker DIGGORY
24 Asst Director Media Services .... Mr. DJ WALKER
40 Skidmore Shop Sales Manager .... Ms. Dawn J. ARIA
88 Special Assistant to the President .... Ms. Jeanne M. SISSON
101 Board Coordinator .... Ms. Kathleen A. GRIMES
41 Assoc Dean Stdnt Affs/Athletics Dir .... Ms. Gail L. CUMMINGS-DANSON
108 Inst Effectiveness Specialist .... Dr. Amy J. TWEEDY

Sotheby's Institute of Art (G)

570 Lexington Ave, 6th Floor, New York NY 10022

County: New York Identification: 667007
Unit ID: 481094
Telephone: (212) 517-3929 Carnegie Class: Spec-4-yr-Arts
FAX Number: (212) 517-6568 Calendar System: Semester
URL: www.sothebysinstitute.com
Established: 2006 Annual Graduate Tuition & Fees: N/A
Enrollment: 135 Coed
Affiliation or Control: Proprietary IRS Status: Proprietary
Highest Offering: First Professional Degree; No Undergraduates
Accreditation: ART

01 Interim Director/CEO .... Ms. Ann-Marie RICHARD
10 Jr Accountant .... Mr. Philip LAM
08 Head Librarian .... Mr. Eric WOLF
32 Chief Student Affairs/Student Life .... Ms. Sara MOORE
06 Registrar .... Mr. Giovanni PALOMO
56 Director Non-Degree Programs .... Ms. Kay CHUBBUCK

*State University of New York System Office (H)

State University Plaza, Albany NY 12246-0001

County: Albany FICE Identification: 008788
Unit ID: 195827
Telephone: (518) 320-1100 Carnegie Class: N/A
FAX Number: (518) 320-1561
URL: www.suny.edu

01 Chancellor .... Dr. Jim MALATRAS
11 Sr Vice Chancellor & COO .... Mr. Robert L. MEGNA
15 SVP/Chief Human Resources Officer .... Mr. Paul N. PATTON

28 SVC Strat Init/Chief Diversity Ofcr ... Ms. Teresa MILLER
05 Provost & SVC for Academic Affairs ... Dr. Tod LAURSEN
10 Vice Chancellor for Finance & CFO ... Ms. Eileen MCLOUGHLIN
46 Vice Chanc Research & Econ Devel ... Dr. Grace WANG
43 General Counsel in Charge ... Ms. Sandra CASEY
22 System Affirmative Action Officer ... Ms. Jennie Marie DURAN
18 SVC for Cap Facil/GM Constr Fund ... Mr. Robert HAELEN
17 AVC Acad Health & Univ Hospital ... Dr. Stephanie FARGNOLI
88 Sr VC for Cmty Col & Educ Pipeline ... Ms. Johanna DUNCAN-POITIER
88 University Faculty Senate President ... Ms. Gwen KAY
20 Sr Assoc VC and Vice Prov Acad Affs ... Vacant
84 Assoc VC for Enrollment Management ... Vacant

*University at Albany, SUNY (A)

1400 Washington Avenue, Albany NY 12222-1000
County: Albany FICE Identification: 002835
Unit ID: 196060
Telephone: (518) 442-3300 Carnegie Class: DU-Highest
FAX Number: N/A Calendar System: Semester
URL: www.albany.edu
Established: 1844 Annual Undergrad Tuition & Fees (In-State): $10,160
Enrollment: 17,688 Coed
Affiliation or Control: State IRS Status: 501(c)3
Highest Offering: Doctorate
Accreditation: M, AAQEP, CAEPT, CLPSY, COPSY, IPSY, LIB, MPCAC, PH, PLNG, SCPSY, SPAA, SW

02 President ... Havidán RODRÍGUEZ
05 Provost/Sr VP Academic Affairs ... Carol KIM
46 Vice President for Research ... James DIAS
10 Vice Pres Finance & Administration ... Todd FOREMAN
30 VP Univ Dev & Exec Dir UA Found ... Fardin SANAI
32 Vice President Student Affairs ... Michael N. CHRISTAKIS
41 Director of Athletics ... Mark BENSON
43 Senior Counsel ... Janet THAYER
86 VP Govt & Community Relations ... Sheila SEERY
28 Int Chief Diversity Officer ... Samuel CALDWELL
21 Assoc VP Office of Risk Mgmt ... Kevin WILCOX
35 Assoc VP Enrollment Mgmt ... Ed ENGELBRIDE
100 Chief of Staff ... Bruce SZELEST
49 Dean College of Arts & Sciences ... Jeanette ALTARRIBA
53 Interim Dean School of Education ... Virginia GOATELY
50 Dean School of Business ... Sen NILANJAN
69 Dean School of Public Health ... David HOLTGRAVE
77 Dean Col Emer Prep/Homeland/Cyber ... Robert GRIFFIN
80 Interim Dean Rockefeller College ... Julie NOVKOV
70 Dean School of Social Welfare ... Lynn WARNER
54 Dean Engineering & Applied Sci ... Kim L. BOYER
58 Vice Provost & Dean Grad Educ ... Kevin WILLIAMS
08 Dean of Libraries ... Rebecca MUGRIDGE
06 College Registrar ... Karen CHICO HURST
29 Exec Director Alumni Association ... Lee SERRAVILLO, JR.
38 Dir Counsel/Psych Svcs/Asst VP SA ... Estela RIVERO
20 Sr Vice Prov/AVP Academic Affairs ... William B. HEDBERG
104 Int VP Ctr for Intl Ed/Global Strat ... Gilbert VALVERDE
20 Asst Vice Prov Faculty/Acad Affairs ... Benjamin WEAVER
106 Assoc Provost for Online Learning ... Peter J. SHEA
100 Vice Provost & Chief of Staff ... Steve GALIME
07 Director of Admissions ... Michael MCKEON
09 Int Dir of Institutional Research ... Jeffrey GERKEN

*State University of New York at Binghamton (B)

4400 Vestal Parkway E, Binghamton NY 13902
County: Broome FICE Identification: 002836
Unit ID: 196079
Telephone: (607) 777-2000 Carnegie Class: DU-Highest
FAX Number: (607) 777-4000 Calendar System: Semester
URL: www.binghamton.edu
Established: 1946 Annual Undergrad Tuition & Fees (In-State): $10,014
Enrollment: 18,148 Coed
Affiliation or Control: State IRS Status: 501(c)3
Highest Offering: Doctorate
Accreditation: M, AAQEP, CLPSY, MUS, NURSE, PHAR, SPAA, SW

02 President ... Dr. Harvey G. STENGER, JR.
100 Chief of Staff ... Ms. Darcy FAUCI
05 Exec VP for Academic Affs/Provost ... Dr. Donald NIEMAN
10 Vice President Operations ... Ms. JoAnn NAVARRO
26 Vice Pres Univ Comm/Mktg ... Mr. Gregory DELVISCIO
32 Vice President Student Affairs ... Mr. Brian T. ROSE
46 Vice President for Research ... Dr. Bahgat SAMMAKIA
22 VP Diversity/Equity/Inclusive ... Dr. Karen JONES
111 Vice President Advancement ... Mr. John KOCH
104 Exec Vice Prov Intl Initiatives ... Dr. Hari SRIHARI
20 Senior Vice Provost ... Dr. Michael F. MCGOFF
58 Interim Dean of Graduate School ... Dr. Donald NIEMAN
35 Assistant VP for Students ... Dr. Randall EDOUARD
102 Exec Dir of Bing Foundation ... Ms. Sheila DOYLE
13 Chief Information Officer ... Dr. Niyazi BODUR
04 Exec Assistant to the President ... Ms. Laura L. O'NEIL
15 Asst Vice Pres for Human Resources ... Mr. Joseph P. SCHULTZ
07 Int Asst Vice Prov & Dir of Admiss ... Ms. Krista MEDIONTE-PHILIPS
08 Dean of Libraries ... Dr. Curtis KENDRICK
85 Director Intl Students/Scholar Svcs ... Ms. Patricia MARRAPESE
37 Dir Financial Aid/Stdnt Records ... Ms. Amber STALLMAN
38 Director Health & Counseling ... Ms. Johann FIORE CONTE
36 Director Career Development Center ... Ms. Kelli SMITH
19 Director Public Safety ... Mr. Timothy FAUGHANAN
41 Director Athletics ... Mr. Patrick ELLIOTT
88 Director Educ Opportunities Pgm ... Mr. Calvin GANTT
28 Director Multi-Cultural Res Ctr ... Ms. Nicole SIRJU-JOHNSON
92 Director Binghamton Univ Scholars ... Dr. William ZIEGLER
94 Exec Director of Women's Studies ... Ms. Dara J. SILBERSTEIN
96 Director of Procurement ... Mr. Matthew SCHOFIELD
09 Asst Provost Institutional Research ... Ms. Nasrin FATIMA
49 Int Dean Arts & Science Harpur Col ... Dr. Celia KLIN
50 Dean School of Management ... Dr. Upinder S. DHILLON
54 Dn Watson Sch Engr/Applied Science ... Dr. Hari SRIHARI
66 Dean Decker School of Nursing ... Dr. Mario ORTIZ
31 Dean Community & Public Affairs ... Dr. Laura BRONSTEIN
43 Campus Atty/General Counsel ... Ms. Barbara SCARLETT

*University at Buffalo-SUNY (C)

3435 Main Street, Buffalo NY 14214
County: Erie FICE Identification: 002837
Unit ID: 196088
Telephone: (716) 645-2000 Carnegie Class: DU-Highest
FAX Number: N/A Calendar System: Semester
URL: www.buffalo.edu
Established: 1846 Annual Undergrad Tuition & Fees (In-State): $10,526
Enrollment: 32,347 Coed
Affiliation or Control: State IRS Status: 501(c)3
Highest Offering: Doctorate
Accreditation: M, ANEST, AUD, CAATE, CACREP, CAMPEP, CLPSY, DA, DENT, DIETC, DIETI, IPSY, LAW, LIB, MED, MPCAC, MT, NMT, NURSE, OT, PCSAS, PH, PHAR, PLNG, PSPSY, PTA, SP, SW

02 President ... Dr. Satish K. TRIPATHI
05 Provost/Exec VP Academic Affs ... Dr. A. Scott WEBER
10 Vice Pres Finance & Administration ... Ms. Laura E. HUBBARD
32 Vice President Student Life ... Mr. Brian F. HAMLUK
17 Vice President Health Sciences ... Dr. Michael E. CAIN
111 Vice Pres Univ Advancement ... Mr. Rodney M. GRABOWSKI
46 Vice Pres for Research/Econ Develop ... Dr. Venugopal GOVINDARAJU
84 Vice Provost of Enrollment ... Mr. Lee H. MELVIN
15 Assoc VP Human Resources ... Mr. Mark COLDREN
58 Vice Provost Educational Affairs ... Dr. Graham L. HAMMILL
20 Vice Provost for Faculty Affairs ... Dr. Robert GRANFIELD
104 Vice Provost for International Educ ... Dr. Nojin KWAK
08 Vice Provost for Univ Libraries ... Ms. Evviva LAJOIE
13 VP & Chief Information Officer ... Mr. Brice J. BIBLE
37 Director Financial Aid ... Mr. John GOTTARDY
09 Vice Provost Inst Analysis & Plng ... Mr. Craig W. ABBEY
88 Assoc VP Academic Planning ... Mr. William J. MCDONNELL
96 Asst Vice Pres Procurement Services ... Mr. Daniel T. VIVIAN
26 VP Univ Communications ... Mr. John DELLACONTRADA
22 Vice Provost Inclusive Excellence ... Dr. Despina M. STRATIGAKOS
28 Dir Equity/Diversity/Inclusion ... Ms. Sharon E. NOLAN-WEISS
41 Vice President & Dir of Athletics ... Mr. Mark M. ALNUTT
91 Director Enterprise Application Svc ... Ms. Susan A. HUSTON
07 Director of UG Admissions ... Mr. Troy A. MILLER
19 Chief of Police ... Mr. Chris J. BARTOLOMEI
39 Director of Campus Living ... Mr. Tom R. TIBERI
38 Director of Counseling Services ... Dr. Sharon L. MITCHELL
23 Director Health Services ... Ms. Susan M. SNYDER
36 Director Career Design Center ... Ms. Arlene F. KAUKUS
85 Director Intl Students/Scholar Svc ... Ms. Kathryn E. TUDINI
40 Manager University Bookstores ... Mr. Gregory NEUMANN
92 Director Univ Honors College ... Dr. Dalia A. MULLER
29 Assoc VP Alumni Eng & Annual Giving ... Ms. Cynthia KHOO-ROBINSON
27 Assoc VP Marketing & Digital Comm ... Mr. Jeffrey N. SMITH
18 Assoc Vice Pres Univ Facilities ... Ms. Tonga PHAM
48 Dean School Arch & Planning ... Dr. Robert G. SHIBLEY
49 Dean College of Arts/Sciences ... Dr. Robin G. SCHULZE
52 Dean School Dental Medicine ... Dr. Joseph J. ZAMBON
53 Dean Graduate Sch of Education ... Dr. Suzane N. ROSENBLITH
54 Dean School Engr/Applied Science ... Dr. Kemper E. LEWIS
61 Dean School of Law ... Ms. Aviva ABRAMOVSKY
50 Dean School of Management ... Dr. Paul E. TESLUK
63 Dean School Medicine/Biomed Sci ... Dr. Michael E. CAIN
66 Dean School of Nursing ... Dr. Marsha L. LEWIS
67 Dean School Pharmacy/Pharm Sciences ... Dr. Gary M. POLLACK
76 Dean Sch Public Hlth/Hlth Prof ... Dr. Jean WACTAWSKI-WENDE
70 Dean School of Social Work ... Dr. Keith A. ALFORD
97 Dean Undergraduate Education ... Dr. Ann M. BISANTZ
06 Registrar ... Dr. Kara C. SAUNDERS
88 Exec Dir Educ Opportunity Ctr ... Dr. Julius G. ADAMS
100 Chief of Staff ... Dr. Beth DEL GENIO

*State University of New York at Fredonia (D)

280 Central Avenue, Fredonia NY 14063-1136
County: Chautauqua FICE Identification: 002844
Unit ID: 196158
Telephone: (716) 673-3111 Carnegie Class: Masters/M
FAX Number: N/A Calendar System: Semester
URL: www.fredonia.edu
Established: 1826 Annual Undergrad Tuition & Fees (In-State): $8,492
Enrollment: 4,055 Coed
Affiliation or Control: State IRS Status: 501(c)3
Highest Offering: Master's
Accreditation: M, ART, CAEP, MUS, SP, SW, THEA

02 President ... Dr. Stephen KOLISON
05 Provost/VP for Academic Affairs ... Dr. David STARRETT
10 VP for Finance & Admin ... Mr. Michael D. METZGER
84 VP for Enrollment & Student Svcs ... Dr. Cedric B. HOWARD
102 Exec Dir for the College Foundation ... Ms. Betty GOSSETT
20 Assoc VP Curriculum/Assessment/Ac ... Vacant
49 Dean College of Liberal Arts & Sci ... Dr. Andy KARAFA
88 VP Engagement & Economic Dev ... Dr. Kevin KEARNS
57 Dean College of Visual & Perf Arts ... Vacant
58 Assoc Provost for Graduate Studies ... Dr. Judy HOROWITZ
50 Interim Dean School of Business ... Dr. Mojtaba SEYEDIAN
53 Dean College of Education ... Vacant
18 Director Facilities Services ... Mr. Kevin P. CLOOS
07 Executive Dir of Admissions ... Mr. Cory M. BEZEK
06 Registrar ... Mr. Scott D. SAUNDERS
88 Director of Admissions ... Ms. Dana M. BEARER
08 Director Library Services ... Mr. Randolph Lee GADIKIAN
09 Dir Institutional Research/Planning ... Dr. Xiao Y. ZHANG
36 Director of Career Development ... Ms. Tracy COLLINGWOOD
19 Chief University Police ... Mr. Brett ISAACSON
39 Director Residence Life ... Mrs. Kathy FORSTER
41 Athletic Director ... Mr. Gerald FISK
23 Director of Health Services ... Ms. Deborah A. DIBBLE
38 Director Counseling Center ... Dr. Tracy L. STENGER
13 CIO/Associate VP ... Mr. Benjamin HARTUNG
15 Director of Human Resources ... Ms. Maria CARROLL
26 Director of Public Relations ... Mr. Jeffrey WOODARD
85 Director of Intercultural Center ... Dr. Khristian J. KING
92 Director of Honors Program ... Dr. Natalie GERBER
94 Coordinator of Women's Studies ... Mr. Jeffry J. IOVANNONE
96 Director of Purchasing ... Mrs. Shari K. MILLER
28 Chief Diversity Officer ... Dr. Vicki T. SAPP
29 Director Alumni Affairs ... Ms. Patricia A. FERALDI
04 Administrative Asst to President ... Mrs. Denise M. SZALKOWSKI
104 Director Office International Educ ... Dr. Naomi BALDWIN
105 Web Content Manager ... Mr. Jonathan WOOLSON
106 Online Learning Coordinator ... Ms. Lisa MELOHUSKY
22 Dir Affirm Action/Equal Opportunity ... Vacant
37 Director of Financial Aid ... Mr. Brandon M. GILLILAND

*State University of New York at New Paltz (E)

1 Hawk Drive, New Paltz NY 12561-2443
County: Ulster FICE Identification: 002846
Unit ID: 196176
Telephone: (845) 257-7869 Carnegie Class: Masters/L
FAX Number: (845) 257-3009 Calendar System: Semester
URL: www.newpaltz.edu
Established: 1823 Annual Undergrad Tuition & Fees (In-State): $8,416
Enrollment: 7,489 Coed
Affiliation or Control: State IRS Status: 501(c)3
Highest Offering: Beyond Master's But Less Than Doctorate
Accreditation: M, ART, CACREP, MUS, SP, THEA

02 President ... Dr. Donald P. CHRISTIAN
100 Chief of Staff/VP Communication ... Ms. Shelly A. WRIGHT
05 Interim Provost ... Dr. Barbara G. LYMAN
10 Vice Pres Administration & Finance ... Ms. Michele HALSTEAD
30 VP Development/Alumni Relations ... Ms. Erica MARKS
32 Student Affairs Vice President ... Dr. Stephanie BLAISDELL
84 Vice Pres Enrollment Management ... Mr. Jeffrey D. GANT
20 Assoc Provost ... Dr. Laurel GARRICK DUHANEY
13 Asst Vice Pres Tech/Info Systems ... Mr. John REINA
21 Asst Vice President Administration ... Ms. Julieta MAJAK
114 Asst VP Budget ... Ms. Julie WALSH
09 Asst VP Inst Research/Planning ... Ms. Lucy WALKER
18 Asst VP Facilities Management ... Mr. John SHUPE
58 Assistant VP Grad & Ext Learning ... Ms. Shala MILLS
53 Dean of Education ... Dr. René ANTROP-GONZÁLEZ
57 Dean Fine & Performing Arts ... Dr. Jennifer MOKREN
49 Dean Liberal Arts & Sciences ... Dr. Laura BARRETT
50 Dean School of Business ... Dr. Kristin BACKHAUS
54 Dean Science & Engineering ... Dr. Daniel FREEDMAN
07 Dean of Admissions ... Ms. Lisa JONES
08 Dean Sojourner Truth Library ... Mr. W. Mark COLVSON
86 Ex Dir Compliance/Camp Clm/Title IX ... Ms. Tanhena PACHECO DUNN
07 Assoc Dean/Dir Freshmen Admissions ... Ms. Kimberly STRANO
15 Director Human Resources ... Ms. Tanhena PACHECO DUNN
37 Director of Financial Aid ... Ms. Maureen LOHAN-BREMER
06 Registrar ... Ms. Stella TURK
29 Director Alumni Relations ... Mr. Chris BROWN
38 Director Student Counseling ... Dr. Gweneth LLOYD
26 Media Relations Manager ... Ms. Melissa KACZMAREK
96 Director of Purchasing/Procurement ... Mr. David FARBANIEC
19 Chief of Police ... Ms. Mary RITAYIK
41 Interim Athletic Director ... Mr. Matt GIUFRE
39 Dir Resident Life/Student Housing ... Ms. Corinna CARACCI

*State University of New York at Oneonta (F)

108 Ravine Parkway, Oneonta NY 13820-4015
County: Otsego FICE Identification: 002847
Unit ID: 196185
Telephone: (607) 436-3500 Carnegie Class: Masters/M
FAX Number: N/A Calendar System: Semester
URL: www.oneonta.edu
Established: 1889 Annual Undergrad Tuition & Fees (In-State): $8,740
Enrollment: 6,718 Coed
Affiliation or Control: State IRS Status: 501(c)3
Highest Offering: Master's
Accreditation: M, AAFCS, DIETC, DIETD, IPSY, MUS, THEA

02 Acting President .... Mr. Dennis CRAIG
100 Chief of Staff .... Ms. Danielle MCMULLEN
05 Interim Provost/VP Academic Affairs .... Dr. Richard LEE
10 VP Finance/Administration .... Ms. Julie PISCITELLO
32 Interim VP Student Development .... Dr. Bernadette TIAPO
111 Vice President College Advancement .... Mr. Paul J. ADAMO
26 VP External Affairs .... Dr. Franklin D. CHAMBERS
20 Assoc Provost Academic Programs .... Dr. Eileen MORGAN-ZAYACHEK
83 Dean School of Liberal Arts .... Dr. Elizabeth DUNN
50 Int Dean Sch of Economics/Business .... Dr. Elizabeth DUNN
53 Dean School of Educ & Human Ecology .... Dr. Mark DAVIES
81 Dean School of Sciences .... Dr. Tracy ALLEN
58 Director of Graduate Studies .... Vacant
35 Assoc Vice Pres Student Development .... Ms. Amanda FINCH
18 Chief Facilities/Safety Officer .... Mr. Lachlan SQUAIR
19 Chief of Police .... Ms. Jennifer FILA
15 Chief Human Resources Officer .... Ms. Dia M. CARLETON
26 Chief Communication/Mktg Officer .... Mr. Hal S. LEGG
28 AVP/Chief Diversity Officer .... Ms. Bernadette TIAPO
07 Exec Director of Admissions .... Ms. Karen A. BROWN
29 Director of Alumni Engagement .... Ms. Laura MADELONE LINCOLN
110 Director Advancement Services .... Mr. Benjamin WENDROW
44 Director Fund for Oneonta .... Ms. Kim NOSTROM
41 Associate Athletic Director .... Mr. Ryan HOOPER
114 Budget Control Officer/Director .... Ms. Kimberly DEVLIN
25 Director Business Services .... Ms. Betty M. TIRADO
36 Director Career Development .... Vacant
13 Chief Information Officer .... Mr. Steven MANISCALCO
23 Dir Health & Counseling Services . Dr. Melissa A. FALLON-KORB
24 Director Creative Media Services .... Mr. David W. GEASEY
37 Associate Director Financial Aid .... Ms. Barbara PLEDGER
09 Dir Institutional Research .... Ms. Caitlin ALLEN
85 Director International Education .... Ms. Katherine STANLEY
89 Director Orientation/First Year Exp .... Ms. Monica C. GRAU
96 Procurement/Travel Office Manager .... Ms. Terri THOMAS
06 College Registrar .... Ms. Maureen P. ARTALE
93 Director Access/Opportunity Pgms .... Ms. Pathy LEIVA
22 Affirmative Action Officer .... Mr. Andrew STAMMEL
04 Assistant to the President .... Ms. Kathleen WEBSTER
08 Chief Library Officer .... Mr. Darren CHASE

*Stony Brook University (A)

310 Administration Building, Stony Brook NY 11794-0701
County: Suffolk FICE Identification: 002838
Unit ID: 196097
Telephone: (631) 632-6265 Carnegie Class: DU-Highest
FAX Number: (631) 632-6621 Calendar System: Semester
URL: www.stonybrook.edu
Established: 1957 Annual Undergrad Tuition & Fees (In-State): $10,091
Enrollment: 26,782 Coed
Affiliation or Control: State IRS Status: 501(c)3
Highest Offering: Doctorate
Accreditation: M, ARCPA, CAATE, CAMPEP, CLPSY, COARC, COARCP, DENT, DIETI, EMT, HSA, IPSY, JOUR, MED, MIDWF, MT, NURSE, OT, PCSAS, PH, PTA, RADDOS, @SP, SW

02 President/CEO .... Dr. Maurie MCINNIS
05 EVP/Provost .... Dr. Paul M. GOLDBART
63 Sr VP HSC .... Vacant
11 Sr VP for Administration .... Ms. Kathleen BYINGTON
46 Vice President Research .... Dr. Richard REEDER
32 VP Student Affairs .... Dr. Richard GATTEAU
10 VP Finance .... Mr. Lyle GOMES
111 Sr VP University Advancement .... Vacant
86 SVP Government & Community Rels .... Ms. Judith GREIMAN
100 Chief Deputy .... Ms. Judith GREIMAN
114 Sr VP for Budget & Finance .... Vacant
26 Int VP Communications & Marketing .... Ms. Teresa FLANNERY
28 VP for Equity and Inclusion .... Dr. Judith B. CLARKE
17 CEO University Hospital .... Ms. Carol GOMES
13 Int SVP of Info Techonolgy & CIO .... Mr. Charlie MCMAHON
43 Senior Counsel in Charge .... Ms. Susan BLUM
49 Dean College of Arts & Sciences .... Dr. Nicole SAMPSON
81 Dean Sch of Marine/Atmospheric Sci .... Dr. Paul SHEPSON
52 Int Dean School of Dental Medicine .... Dr. Allan R. KUCINE
41 Athletic Director .... Mr. Shawn R. HEILBRON
58 Dean Grad Sch/VProv Grad Stds .... Dr. Eric WERTHEIMER
76 Dean School Health Tech & Mgmt .... Dr. Stacy JAFFE GROPACK
66 Dean School of Nursing .... Dr. Annette WYSOCKI
70 Dean School of Social Welfare .... Dr. Jacqueline MONDROS
50 Dean College of Business .... Dr. Manuel LONDON
60 Dean School of Journalism .... Ms. Laura LINDENFELD
08 Int Dean of Libraries .... Mr. Shafeek FAZAL
88 Exec Dir LI State Vets Home .... Mr. Fred SGANGA
19 Int Chief of Police .... Mr. Neil FARRELL
15 VP Human Resource Svcs .... Ms. Lynn JOHNSON
28 Dir Diversity/AA/Equal Employ Oppty .... Ms. Marjolie LEONARD
09 AVP Inst Rsrch/Plng/Effectiveness .... Dr. Braden J. HOSCH
85 Int Dean International Programs .... Ms. Lindsi WALKER
23 Director University Health Services .... Dr. Rachel BERGESON
38 Dir Counseling/Psych Services .... Dr. Julian PESSIER
36 Director Career Placement Center .... Ms. Marianna SAVOCA
06 Registrar .... Ms. Diane BELLO
27 University Media Relations Officer .... Ms. Lauren SHEPROW
96 Director of Purchasing/Procurement .... Vacant
04 Executive Asst to President .... Ms. Lorraine RUBINO

*SUNY Downstate Health Sciences University (B)

450 Clarkson Avenue, Brooklyn NY 11203-2098
County: Kings FICE Identification: 002839
Unit ID: 196255
Telephone: (718) 270-1000 Carnegie Class: Spec-4-yr-Med
FAX Number: (718) 270-4092 Calendar System: Semester
URL: www.downstate.edu
Established: 1860 Annual Undergrad Tuition & Fees (In-State): N/A
Enrollment: 2,118 Coed
Affiliation or Control: State IRS Status: 501(c)3
Highest Offering: Doctorate
Accreditation: M, #ARCPA, DMS, MED, MIDWF, NURSE, OT, PH, PTA

02 President .... Dr. Wayne J. RILEY
10 VP/Chief Financial Officer .... Dr. Richard MILLER
11 COO/Exec VP Administration .... Ms. Heidi J. ARONIN
05 Sr Vice Pres for Academic Affairs .... Dr. Pascal IMPERATO
63 SVP/Dean College of Medicine .... Dr. F. Charles BRUNICARDI
32 VP Academic & Student Affairs .... Dr. Jeffrey S. PUTMAN
26 AVP Communications & Marketing . Ms. Dawn SKEETE-WALKER
13 VP/Chief Information Officer .... Ms. Michele SCAGGIANTE
121 AVP Academic Support Services .... Dr. Seth LANGLEY
07 Director of Admissions .... Dr. Shushawna DEOLIVEIRA
06 Registrar .... Ms. Anne SHONBRUN
37 Director Student Financial Aid .... Ms. Farah BURNETT
27 Dir Media & Public Relations .... Mr. John GILLESPIE
04 Executive Asst to President .... Ms. Reina ALFRED
08 Interim Librarian .... Dr. Mohamed HUSSAIN
09 Director of Institutional Research .... Ms. Charis NG
15 VP Human Resources .... Ms. Judith DORSEY
18 VP Facilities Mgmt/Development .... Mr. James MINTO
19 Interim Chief University Police .... Mr. Israel MALDONADO
28 AVP Diversity & Inclusion .... Ms. Victoria AJIBADE
25 Chief Contracts/Grants Admin .... Ms. Maureen CRYSTAL
39 Director Student Housing .... Ms. Margaret O'SULLIVAN
43 Dir Legal Services/General Counsel .... Mr. Kevin O'MARA
45 Chief Institutional Planning .... Vacant
53 Dean College of Nursing .... Dr. Lori A. ESCALLIER
76 Dean School of Health Professions .... Dr. Allen LEWIS
69 Dean School of Public Health .... Dr. Kitaw DEMISSIE
58 Dean School of Graduate Studies .... Dr. Mark STEWART
86 Director Government Relations .... Mr. Jelanie DESHONG
90 Asst Director Academic Computing .... Dr. Jim NEILL
96 Exec Dir of Contracts & Purchasing .... Mr. Raul TOSADO
113 Bursar .... Mr. Peter LJUTIC
100 Chief of Staff .... Dr. Keydron GUINN
108 Director Institutional Assessment .... Dr. Bonnie GRANAT
36 Director Student Placement .... Vacant

*State University of New York Upstate Medical University (C)

750 E Adams Street, Syracuse NY 13210-2375
County: Onondaga FICE Identification: 002840
Unit ID: 196307
Telephone: (315) 464-5540 Carnegie Class: Spec-4-yr-Med
FAX Number: (315) 464-8823 Calendar System: Semester
URL: https://www.upstate.edu
Established: 1834 Annual Undergrad Tuition & Fees (In-State): N/A
Enrollment: 1,528 Coed
Affiliation or Control: State IRS Status: 501(c)3
Highest Offering: Doctorate
Accreditation: M, ARCPA, COARC, DENT, DMOLS, EMT, IPSY, MED, MT, NURSE, PAST, PERF, PH, PTA, RAD, RTT

02 President .... Dr. Mantosh DEWAN
63 Dean College of Medicine .... Dr. Lawrence CHIN
17 CEO University Hospital .... Dr. Robert CORONA
10 Vice President Finance & Management .... Mr. Eric SMITH
05 Vice President Academic Affairs .... Dr. Lynn CLEARY
46 Vice President for Research .... Dr. David AMBERG
58 Dean College Graduate Studies .... Dr. Mark SCHMITT
66 Dean College of Nursing .... Dr. Tammy AUSTIN-KETCH
76 Dean College of Health Professions .... Dr. Katherine BEISSNER
102 Exec Director HSC Foundation .... Ms. Eileen PEZZI
100 Interim Chief of Staff .... Ms. Linda VEIT
32 Dean Student Affairs .... Dr. Julie R. WHITE
43 Senior Managing Counsel .... Ms. Lisa ALEXANDER
29 Director of Medical Alumni Affairs .... Mr. Paul W. NORCROSS
15 Assoc VP Human Resources .... Mr. Eric FROST
13 Chief Information Officer .... Mr. Mark ZEMAN
28 Chief Diversity Officer .... Dr. Daryll DYKES
108 Director Evaluation/Assessment .... Dr. Lauren GERMAIN
06 Registrar/Dir Inst Research .... Ms. Jennifer MARTIN TSE
08 Director of Libraries .... Ms. Christina POPE
07 Assoc Dean Admissions/Financial Aid .... Ms. Jennifer C. WELCH
106 Director E-Learning .... Dr. Pamela YOUNGS-MAHER
18 Chief Facilities/Physical Plant .... Mr. Bob LOTKOWICTZ
21 Assistant Vice President Finance .... Mr. David ANTHONY
37 Director Student Financial Aid .... Ms. Nicole MORGANTE

*SUNY Broome Community College (D)

PO Box 1017, Binghamton NY 13902-1017
County: Broome FICE Identification: 002862
Unit ID: 189547
Telephone: (607) 778-5000 Carnegie Class: Assoc/HT-Mix Trad/Non
FAX Number: (607) 778-5310 Calendar System: Semester
URL: www.sunybroome.edu
Established: 1946 Annual Undergrad Tuition & Fees (In-District): $6,136
Enrollment: 5,386 Coed
Affiliation or Control: State/Local IRS Status: 501(c)3
Highest Offering: Associate Degree
Accreditation: M, ADNUR, CAHIIM, DH, MAC, MLTAD, PTAA, RAD

02 President .... Dr. Kevin DRUMM
05 VP/Chief Academic Officer .... Dr. Penny HAYNES
11 Vice Pres Admin/Financial Affairs .... Mr. Michael SULLIVAN
32 VP Student Development & CDO .... Dr. Carol ROSS-SCOTT
10 Associate Vice Pres & Controller .... Ms. Jeanette TILLOTSON
49 Assoc VP & Dean of LA & Bus .... Dr. Michael KINNEY
51 Dir Continuing Education .... Ms. Danielle BRITTON
81 Assoc Vice Pres & Dean STEM/HS .... Dr. Michele SNYDER
35 Interim Dean of Students .... Ms. Shelli CORDISCO
102 Executive Director BCC Foundation .. Ms. Catherine R. WILLIAMS
08 Director Learning Resource Center .... Ms. Robin PETRUS
07 Director of Admissions .... Ms. Maja SZOSTAK
15 Human Resources Officer .... Ms. Lynn FEDORCHAK
06 Registrar .... Mr. Martin GUZZI
36 Director of Placement Services .... Vacant
108 Dean Inst Effectiveness .... Dr. Kimberly MCLAIN
18 Interim Campus Operations Director .... Mr. David LIGEIKIS
37 Director of Financial Aid .... Ms. Laura HODEL
13 Interim Dir IT Services .... Mr. Fermin ROMERO, III
19 Director of Public Safety .... Mr. Nick BREY
25 Director of Sponsored Programs .... Ms. Shelli CORDISCO
41 Director of Athletics .... Mr. Brett CARTER
40 Bookstore Manager .... Ms. Kristin DEMPSEY
88 Dir Educational Opportunity Pgm .... Ms. Venessa RODRIGUEZ
96 Director of Purchasing .... Mr. Randy CAMPBELL
26 Dir of Marketing/Communications .... Mr. Jesse WELLS
85 Ast Dir Intl Admiss/Intl Stdnt Stds .... Ms. Susan WELLINGTON
104 Coordinator Study Abroad Program .... Ms. Maria BASUALDO
38 Student Counseling .... Mr. Joseph SPENCE
22 Dir Affirmative Action/EEO .... Ms. Paige SEDLACEK
39 Director Student Housing .... Ms. Amy ZIEZIULA
04 Assistant to the President .... Ms. Diana D. LENZO
84 Exec Enrollment Management Officer .... Mr. Jesse WELLS
103 Director Workforce Development .... Ms. Danielle BRITTON
30 Director of Development .... Ms. Lisa SCHAPPERT
106 Asst Dean of Distance Learning .... Dr. Stephanie MALMBERG

*State University of New York, The College at Brockport (E)

350 New Campus Drive, Brockport NY 14420-2914
County: Monroe FICE Identification: 002841
Unit ID: 196121
Telephone: (585) 395-2211 Carnegie Class: Masters/L
FAX Number: (585) 395-2401 Calendar System: Semester
URL: www.brockport.edu
Established: 1835 Annual Undergrad Tuition & Fees (In-State): $8,624
Enrollment: 7,592 Coed
Affiliation or Control: State IRS Status: 501(c)3
Highest Offering: Doctorate
Accreditation: M, CAATE, CACREP, CAEP, CAPRT, DANCE, EXSC, NURSE, SPAA, SW, THEA

02 President .... Dr. Heidi R. MACPHERSON
05 Provost & VP Academic Affairs .... Dr. Katy HEYNING
10 VP Administration & Finance .... Mr. James WALL
84 VP Enrollment Mgmt/Student Affairs .... Dr. Kathryn WILSON
111 VP Advancement .... Mr. Michael ANDRIATCH
26 VP for University Relations .... Mr. David MIHALYOV
20 Vice Provost .... Dr. Eileen DANIEL
28 Interim Chief Diversity Officer .... Dr. Lorraine ACKER
18 Director of Physical Plant .... Mr. Kevin RICE
32 AVP EMSA - Student Affairs .... Dr. Lorraine ACKER
21 Asst VP Finance & Management .... Ms. Karen M. RIOTTO
13 CIO .... Mr. Robert CUSHMAN
49 Dean Arts and Sciences .... Dr. Jose MALIEKAL
50 Dean Business and Management .... Dr. Dan GOEBEL
53 Dean Educ/Health & Hum Svcs .... Dr. Thomas J. HERNANDEZ
14 Director of Info Tech System .... Mr. Stephen COOK
07 Dir of Undergrad Admissions .... Mr. Robert WYANT
58 Dir Center for Grad Studies .... Mr. Michael HARRISON
104 Dir Global Educ and Engagement .... Ms. Lindsay CRANE
37 Dir Financial Aid Daily Ops .... Dr. Kimberley WILLIS
36 Int Director of Career Services .... Ms. Stephanie LEARN
19 Chief of University Police .... Mr. Daniel VASILE
06 College Registrar .... Mr. Peter DOWE
15 Director of Human Resources .... Ms. Tammy GOUGER
22 Int Affirmative Action Officer .... Ms. Denine CARR
124 AVP EMSA - Plng/Assess/Retention .... Dr. Sara KELLY
23 Director Student Health/Counseling .... Ms. Cheryl VAN LARE
39 Dir Residential Life .... Ms. Monique REW-BIGELOW
41 Director of Athletics .... Mr. Erick HART
25 Director of Grants Development .... Ms. Justine BRIGGS
92 Director of Honors Program .... Dr. Austin BUSCH
09 Dir Inst Research & Analysis .... Mr. Richard DIRMYER
96 Director of Procurement & Payment .... Mr. Mark W. STACY
94 Chair Women and Gender Studies .... Dr. Milo OBOURN
29 Director Alumni Relations .... Mr. Kerry GOTHAM
04 Assistant to the President .... Ms. Julie A. PRUSS
08 Director of Library Services .... Ms. Diane FULKERSON
88 Title IX & College Compliance Ofcr .... Ms. Denine CARR

*State University of New York College at Buffalo (F)

1300 Elmwood Avenue, Buffalo NY 14222-1091
County: Erie FICE Identification: 002842
Unit ID: 196130
Telephone: (716) 878-4000 Carnegie Class: Masters/L
FAX Number: (716) 878-3039 Calendar System: Semester

URL: www.buffalostate.edu
Established: 1871 Annual Undergrad Tuition & Fees (In-State): $8,428
Enrollment: 8,339 Coed
Affiliation or Control: State IRS Status: 501(c)3
Highest Offering: Master's
Accreditation: M, ART, CAEPN, CIDA, DIETC, DIETD, FEPAC, JOUR, MUS, NAIT, SP, SW, THEA

02 President .... Dr. Katherine S. CONWAY-TURNER
100 Chief of Staff/Chief Diversity Ofcr .... Ms. Crystal J. RODRIGUEZ-DABNEY
05 Provost/VP Academic Affairs .... Dr. James MAYROSE
10 Vice President Finance & Management .... Ms. Laura J. BARNUM
32 Vice President Student Affairs .... Dr. Timothy W. GORDON
111 VP Inst Advance & FNDN Exec Dir .... Dr. James M. FINNERTY
84 Interim VP Enrollment Management .... Dr. David P. LORETO
19 Interim Chief University Police .... Ms. Amy M. PEDLOW
21 Assoc Vice President & Comptroller .... Mr. James A. THOR
15 Officer in Charge HR Management .... Mrs. Jamie E. WARNES
88 Int AVP Inst Effectiveness .... Dr. Eric J. KRIEG
14 Deputy CIO .... Mr. Khaleel M. GATHERS
108 Associate Provost .... Dr. Amitra A. WALL
30 Assoc VP Development .... Mr. R. Scott BURNS
86 AVP Govt Rels/Alumni Engagement .... Mr. William J. BENFANTI
51 Int Dir Continuing Prof Studies .... Ms. Kristin E. FIELDS
53 Dean School of Education .... Dr. Wendy A. PATERSON
49 Dean School of Arts and Sciences .... Dr. Brian C. CRONK
107 Int Dean School of the Professions .... Dr. Rita M. ZIENTEK
58 Dean Graduate School .... Dr. Kevin J. MILLER
88 Resident Manager Chartwells .... Mr. Glenn R. BUCELLO
88 Director Liberty Partnership .... Ms. Patrice A. CATHEY
88 Director STEP .... Mr. Darryl CARTER
88 Director Upward Bound .... Mr. Donald A. PATTERSON
36 Director of Career Development .... Ms. Denise M. HARRIS
26 Interim Exec Dir Marketing/Comm .... Mr. Jerod T. DAHLGREN
07 Director Undergraduate Admissions .... Vacant
06 Registrar .... Dr. Nigel R. MARRINER
37 Director of Financial Aid .... Ms. Connie F. COOKE
39 Asst Dean Residence Life .... Dr. Philip BADASZEWSKI
113 Dir Student Accounts/Parking Svcs .... Mrs. Jayme S. RITER
41 Director Intercollegiate Athletics .... Ms. Renee M. CARLINEO
23 AVP Weigel Wellness Center .... Dr. Rock D. DOYLE
35 Dean of Students .... Ms. Sarah M. YOUNG
85 Int Dir Student Global Engagement .... Ms. Joy A. GUARINO
25 AVP for Sponsored Program Operation .... Mrs. Donna L. SCUTO
124 Asst Dean Student Ldrshp/Engagement .... Mr. David W. COX
09 Director Institutional Research .... Mr. Yves M. GACHETTE
29 Director of Alumni Engagement .... Ms. Mary-Jo JAGORD
96 Director of Contract Management .... Mr. Steven M. OLSEN
40 Manager College Bookstore .... Ms. Lynn M. PUMA
88 Operations Manager .... Mr. Dominic HANNON
22 Director Accessibility Service .... Ms. Lisa T. MORRISON-FRONCKOWIAK
88 Asst Dean Stdnt Conduct/Cmty Stand .... Ms. Janelle BROOKS
18 Dir Facilities/Constr/Maintenance .... Mr. Steven E. SHAFFER
38 Clinical Manager Student Counseling .... Dr. Charlene J. VETTER

*State University of New York College at Cortland (A)

PO Box 2000, Cortland NY 13045-0900
County: Cortland FICE Identification: 002843
Unit ID: 196149
Telephone: (607) 753-2011 Carnegie Class: Masters/L
FAX Number: (607) 753-5999 Calendar System: Semester
URL: www.cortland.edu
Established: 1868 Annual Undergrad Tuition & Fees (In-State): $8,677
Enrollment: 6,832 Coed
Affiliation or Control: State IRS Status: 501(c)3
Highest Offering: Master's
Accreditation: M, CAATE, CAEP, CAPRT, PH, SP

02 President .... Dr. Erik J. BITTERBAUM
05 Provost .... Dr. Mark PRUS
32 Vice Pres Student Affairs .... Mr. C. Gregory SHARER
111 Vice Pres Inst Advancement .... Mr. Peter PERKINS
10 Vice Pres for Finance & Admin .... Vacant
18 Assoc VP Facilities Management .... Mr. Zach NEWSWANGER
20 Assoc Prov for Academic Affairs .... Dr. Carol VAN DER KARR
84 Asst Vice Pres Enrollment Mgmt .... Mr. Mark YACAVONE
09 Director Inst Rsrch/Assessment .... Mr. Stephen CUNNINGHAM
08 Director of Libraries .... Ms. Jennifer KRONENBITTER
06 Registrar .... Mr. Thomas HANFORD
36 Director of Career Services .... Ms. Nanette PASQUARELLO
15 Assoc VP Human Resources .... Mr. Gary EVANS
29 Exec Director Alumni Engagement .... Ms. Erin BOYLAN
38 Dir Counseling/Student Devel .... Dr. Carolyn BERSHAD
37 Dir of Student Financial Aid .... Ms. Karen GALLAGHER
19 Chief of University Police .... Mr. Mark DEPAULL
28 Chief Diversity/Equity/Incl Ofcr .... Ms. Lorraine LOPEZ-JANOVE
91 Director Admin Computing Svcs .... Vacant
13 Assoc VP and Chief Info Officer .... Ms. Lisa KAHLE
107 Dean Professional Studies .... Dr. John COTTONE
49 Dean Arts & Sciences .... Dr. Bruce MATTINGLY
26 Director of Communications .... Mr. Frederic PIERCE
53 Dean of Education .... Dr. Andrea LACHANCE
93 Dir Educational Opportunity Program .... Dr. Lewis ROSENGARTEN
92 Director of Honors Program .... Dr. Sebastian PURCELL
94 Coord Women/Gender/Sexual Studies .... Dr. Jena CURTIS
96 Director of Purchasing .... Ms. Melissa FOX
22 Affirmative Action Officer .... Ms. Melanie WOODWARD
88 Director Multicult Life/Diversity .... Ms. AnnaMaria CIRRINCIONE
41 Athletic Director .... Mr. Mike URTZ

104 Director International Programs .... Dr. Mary SCHLARB
25 Assoc Dir Research & Sponsored Pgms .... Mr. Thomas FRANK
39 Director Student Housing .... Vacant
07 Director of Admissions .... Mr. Mark YACAVONE
04 Admin Assistant to the President .... Ms. Lori PORTER
100 Chief of Staff .... Dr. Laura J. DAVIES

*State University of New York College at Geneseo (B)

1 College Circle, Geneseo NY 14454-1401
County: Livingston FICE Identification: 002845
Unit ID: 196167
Telephone: (585) 245-5000 Carnegie Class: Masters/S
FAX Number: (585) 245-5005 Calendar System: Semester
URL: www.geneseo.edu
Established: 1871 Annual Undergrad Tuition & Fees (In-State): $8,856
Enrollment: 4,911 Coed
Affiliation or Control: State IRS Status: 501(c)3
Highest Offering: Master's
Accreditation: M, CAEP

02 President .... Dr. Denise A. BATTLES
05 Provost .... Dr. Stacey ROBERTSON
20 Vice Provost for Academic Affairs .... Dr. Glenn GEISER-GETZ
11 Vice President for Finance & Admin .... Ms. Julie BUEHLER
32 Vice Pres for Student & Campus Life .... Mr. Michael TABERSKI
111 VP College Advancement/Geneseo Fndn .... Ms. Ellen LEVERICH
84 Vice Pres Enrollment Mgmt .... Dr. Costas SOLOMOU
10 Assoc VP Administration/Controller .... Vacant
26 Chief Comm & Marketing Officer .... Ms. Kerri HOWELL
100 Chief of Staff .... Ms. Wendi KINNEY
15 Asst Vice Pres Human Resources .... Ms. Julie A. BRIGGS
29 Interim Director Alumni Relations .... Ms. Michelle WORDEN
20 Int Asst Prov Curriculum/Assessment .... Dr. Melanie BLOOD
35 Dean of Students .... Dr. Leonard SANCILIO
07 Director of Admissions .... Ms. Christie SMITH
08 Library Director .... Mr. Corey HA
13 Director Computing/Info Technology .... Ms. Susan E. CHICHESTER
37 Director of Financial Aid .... Ms. Susan ROMANO
25 Director of Sponsored Research .... Dr. Anne E. BALDWIN
09 Director of Institutional Research .... Dr. Julie M. RAO
06 Registrar .... Ms. Keely BIELAT SOLTOW
36 Director of Career Development .... Ms. Jessie STACK LOMBARDO
28 Chief Diversity Officer .... robbie ROUTENBERG
88 Dir Multicultural Pgms & Services .... Dr. Sasha ELOI-EVANS
19 Chief of University Police .... Mr. Christopher PRUSAK
18 Asst VP Facilities & Planning .... Mr. Robert M. AMES
114 Dir of Acct & Budgeting Services .... Mr. Jeffrey NORDLAND
38 Director of Counseling Services .... Dr. Emma WOLFORD
38 Asst Director of Counseling Svcs .... Dr. Beth K. CHOLETTE
96 Director of Purchasing .... Ms. Rebecca E. ANCHOR
04 Asst to President .... Ms. Susan MOORE
121 Dean of Acad Planning & Advising .... Dr. Celia A. EASTON
41 Dir of Intercollegiate Athletics .... Mr. Michael C. MOONEY
50 Dean of School of Business .... Dr. Mary Ellen ZUCKERMAN
53 Interim Dir School of Education .... Dr. Dennis SHOWERS
90 Director Educational Technology .... Ms. Laurie FOX
14 Assoc Director & Manager Info Sys .... Mr. Paul JACKSON
104 Director Study Abroad .... Mr. Samuel CARDAMONE
39 Director of Residence Life .... Ms. Sarah FRANK

*State University of New York College at Old Westbury (C)

P.O. Box 210, 223 Store Hill Road, Old Westbury NY 11568-0210
County: Nassau FICE Identification: 007109
Unit ID: 196237
Telephone: (516) 876-3000 Carnegie Class: Masters/S
FAX Number: (516) 876-3209 Calendar System: Semester
URL: www.oldwestbury.edu
Established: 1965 Annual Undergrad Tuition & Fees (In-State): $8,122
Enrollment: 5,007 Coed
Affiliation or Control: State IRS Status: 501(c)3
Highest Offering: Master's
Accreditation: M, PH

02 President .... Dr. Timothy SAMS
100 Chief of Staff .... Dr. Jo-Ann ROBINSON
05 Provost/Sr VP Acad Affairs .... Dr. Duncan QUARLESS
84 Acting VP for Enrollment Services .... Mr. Frank PIZZARDI
32 VP Stdnt Affs/Chief Diversity Ofcr .... Mr. Usama SHAIKH
10 Sr VP Div Business & Finance/CFO .... Mr. Len L. DAVIS
15 Asst to Pres for Admin/Dir HR .... Mr. William P. KIMMINS
111 VP Inst Advance/Exec Dir Foundation .... Dr. Wayne EDWARDS
26 Vice Pres Communications .... Mr. Michael G. KINANE
21 Assoc VP Business Affs/Controller .... Mr. Pat LETTINI
20 Acting Associate Provost .... Dr. Barbara HILLERY
21 Assoc VP of Business Compliance .... Mr. Arthur H. ANGST, JR.
20 Asst Vice Pres Academic Affairs .... Mr. Anthony BARBERA
09 Asst VP Inst Effectiveness & Admin .... Dr. Jacob HELLER
49 Acting Dean Sch of Arts & Sciences .... Dr. Amanda FRISKEN
50 Dean School of Business .... Dr. Raj DEVASAGAYAM
35 Dean of Students .... Ms. Claudia L. MARIN ANDRADE
53 Acting Dean School of Education .... Dr. Diana P. SUKHRAM
107 Director School of Prof Studies .... Dr. Edward BEVER
19 Chief of Police .... Mr. Steven SIENA
13 Chief Information Officer .... Mr. Evan KOBOLAKIS
06 Acting Registrar .... Ms. Regina SCARBROUGH
89 Director First-Year Experience .... Dr. Laura M. ANKER

31 Director of Community Relations .... Ms. Carolyn BENNETT
29 Director of Alumni Affairs .... Ms. Penny J. CHIN
22 Dir Ofc Svcs for Stdnts/Disability .... Ms. Stacey DEFELICE
92 Director Honors College .... Dr. Anthony L. DELUCA
08 Library Director .... Ms. Antonia DIGREGORIO
88 Coordinator of Scholarships .... Ms. Pritpal KAINTH
108 Dir Inst Research & Assessment .... Ms. Sandra KAUFMANN
109 Exec Dir Auxiliary Svc Corp .... Ms. Carol KAUNITZ
88 Dir Ofc of Student Conduct .... Ms. Kathleen LIEBLICH
88 Director of Capital Planning .... Mr. Ray MAGGIORE
88 Dir Spec Programs Acad Affairs .... Mr. Yves M. MAGLOIRE
36 Dir Career Plng & Development .... Ms. Jerilyn MARINAN
18 Director of Facilities .... Mr. Timothy MCGARRY
35 Director of Student Activities .... Ms. Suzanne MCLOUGHLIN
25 Director of Sponsored Programs .... Mr. Thomas MURPHY
96 Director of Purchasing .... Mr. James MWAURA
37 Director Financial Aid .... Ms. Mildred O'KEEFE
88 Dir Educational Opportunity Program .... Dr. Jerrell W. ROBINSON
38 Dir Counseling/Psych Wellness Svcs .... Dr. Oren SHEFET
39 Director Residential Life .... Mr. Gareth SHUMACK
23 Dir Student Health Services .... Ms. Cristine TESORIERO
89 Dir Orientation & Special Events .... Ms. Jaclyn VENTO
41 Director of Athletics .... Ms. Lenore J. WALSH
07 Director of Admissions .... Mr. Frank PIZZARDI

*State University of New York College at Oswego (D)

7060 State Route 104, Oswego NY 13126-3501
County: Oswego FICE Identification: 002848
Unit ID: 196194
Telephone: (315) 312-2500 Carnegie Class: Masters/L
FAX Number: (315) 312-5799 Calendar System: Semester
URL: www.oswego.edu
Established: 1861 Annual Undergrad Tuition & Fees (In-State): $8,651
Enrollment: 7,636 Coed
Affiliation or Control: State IRS Status: 501(c)3
Highest Offering: Master's
Accreditation: M, ART, CACREP, CAEPN, MUS, THEA

02 President .... Dr. Deborah F. STANLEY
05 VP Academic Affairs/Provost .... Dr. Scott R. FURLONG
10 Interim VP Admin/Finance .... Ms. Victoria L. FURLONG
32 VP Student Affairs .... Dr. Kathleen KERR
30 VP Devel/Alumni Engagement .... Ms. Mary CANALE
100 Chief of Staff .... Ms. Kristi ECK
88 Dpty to Pres Ext Prtnr/Econ Dev .... Ms. Pamela CARACCIOLI
28 Chief Diversity & Inclusion Officer .... Dr. Rodmon KING
04 EA to Pres/Affirm Action Ofcr .... Dr. Mary TOALE
26 Chief Communication Officer .... Mr. Wayne WESTERVELT
84 Exec Dir of Enrollment Mgmt .... Ms. Ebony DIXON
18 Asst VP for Facilities Services .... Mr. Mitch FIELDS
20 Associate Provost .... Dr. Rameen MOHAMMADI
25 Assoc Provost Research Dev & Admin .... Mr. William BOWERS
35 Interim Dean of Students .... Ms. Christy HUYNH
94 Director Gender & Women's Studies .... Dr. Joanna GOPLEN
06 Registrar .... Mr. Jerret LEMAY
08 Director of Libraries .... Ms. Sarah CONRAD WEISMAN
91 Assoc Dir Campus Tech Services .... Mr. Michael C. PISA
37 Director of Financial Aid .... Mr. Rodrick ANDREWS
09 Director Inst Research & Assessment .... Dr. Deborah FURLONG
36 Director Career Services .... Mr. Gary MORRIS
38 Director Counseling Services Center .... Ms. Katherine WOLFE-LYGA
15 Director Human Resources .... Ms. Amy PLOTNER
19 University Police Chief .... Mr. Kevin VELZY
23 Director of Health Services .... Ms. Angela BROWN
39 Asst VP Residence Life & Housing .... Mr. Shaun N. CRISLER
41 Interim Director of Athletics .... Mr. Daniel KANE
96 Purchasing Associate .... Ms. Karen HURD
13 Chief Technology Officer .... Mr. Sean MORIARTY
29 Exec Dir Alum Rels/Dir Alum Engage .... Ms. Laura KELLY
40 College Store Manager .... Ms. Susan RABY
49 Dean Col Lib Arts & Science .... Dr. Kristin CROYLE
53 Dean School of Education .... Dr. Pamela MICHEL
58 Dean Grad Studies .... Dr. Kristen C. EICHHORN
50 Dean School of Business .... Dr. Prabakar KOTHANDARAMAN
51 Dean of Extended Learning .... Ms. Jill PIPPIN
60 Dean of Comm/Media & the Arts .... Dr. Julie PRETZAT
121 VP Academic Support .... Dr. Kathleen EVANS
109 Interim General Mgr Auxiliary Svcs .... Mr. Stephen MCAFEE
104 Assoc Provost Intl Educ & Programs .... Dr. Joshua S. MCKEOWN

*State University of New York College at Plattsburgh (E)

101 Broad Street, Plattsburgh NY 12901-2637
County: Clinton FICE Identification: 002849
Unit ID: 196246
Telephone: (518) 564-2000 Carnegie Class: Masters/M
FAX Number: (518) 564-3932 Calendar System: Semester
URL: www.plattsburgh.edu
Established: 1889 Annual Undergrad Tuition & Fees (In-State): $8,574
Enrollment: 5,109 Coed
Affiliation or Control: State IRS Status: 501(c)3
Highest Offering: Master's
Accreditation: M, AAQEP, CACREP, DIETD, NURSE, SP, SW

02 President .... Dr. Alexander ENYEDI
05 Provost/VP Academic Affairs .... Dr. Anne HERZOG
10 Vice Pres Administration/Finance .... Ms. Josee LAROCHELLE
111 Vice Pres Institutional Advancement .... Ms. Anne W. HANSEN

32 VP Student Success/Enrollment ... Ms. R. Lizzie WAHAB
49 Interim Dean of Arts & Sciences ... Dr. Genie BABB
53 Dean Educ/Health/Human Svcs ... Dr. Denise SIMARD
50 Int Dean of Business/Economics ... Dr. Brian NEUREUTHER
12 Dean Branch Campus at Queensbury ... Mr. Stephen DANNA
08 Dean Library/Info Services ... Ms. Holly B. HELLER-ROSS
28 VP Inst Diversity/Equity/Inclusion ... Dr. Michelle CROMWELL
88 Title IX Coordinator ... Ms. Butterfly L. BLAISE
20 AVP Academic Affairs ... Dr. JoAnn GLEESON KREIG
11 Asst VP Administration/Finance ... Mr. Sean B. DERMODY
15 Director of Human Resources ... Ms. Sarah REYELL
110 Asst VP for Institutional Advanc ... Mr. David P. GREGOIRE
06 Registrar ... Ms. Pamela MUNSON
114 Dir Budget/Financial Reporting ... Ms. Magen M. RENADETTE
19 Chief University Police ... Mr. Patrick RASCOE
07 Executive Director or Admissions ... Ms. Carrie WOODWARD
109 Exec Dir College Auxiliary Services ... Ms. Dana KELLERMAN
100 Chief of Staff ... Mr. Kennith KNELLY
121 Director of Academic Advising ... Ms. Suzanne L. DALEY
29 Director of Alumni Relations ... Ms. Kerry CHAPIN-LAVIGNE
41 Director of Athletics ... Mr. Michael P. HOWARD
36 Director of Career Development Ctr ... Ms. Tobi HAY
40 Director of College Store ... Ms. Michelle MARCIL
30 Director of Development ... Ms. Faith M. LEACH
18 Director of Facilities ... Mr. William A. CIRCELLI
37 Director of Financial Aid ... Mr. Todd A. MORAVEC
39 Director of Housing ... Mr. Stephen P. MATTHEWS
09 Dir of Institutional Effectiveness ... Ms. Sara PHILLIPS
96 Director of Purchasing ... Ms. Jenna BEAUREGARD
46 Dir Sponsored Research/Programs ... Mr. Michael E. SIMPSON
88 Director of Student Conduct ... Mr. Larry K. ALLEN
23 Dir Ctr for Stdnt Hlth & Psych Svcs ... Dr. Kathleen M. CAMELO
91 Programming Manager ... Mr. Thomas J. HIGGINS
04 Executive Asst to the President ... Ms. Cherice GRANGER
13 Dean Info Technology Services ... Ms. Holly B. HELLER-ROSS

*State University of New York College at Potsdam (A)

44 Pierrepont Avenue, Potsdam NY 13676-2294
County: Saint Lawrence FICE Identification: 002850
Unit ID: 196200
Telephone: (315) 267-2000 Carnegie Class: Masters/M
FAX Number: (315) 267-2496 Calendar System: Semester
URL: www.potsdam.edu
Established: 1816 Annual Undergrad Tuition & Fees (In-State): $8,554
Enrollment: 3,084 Coed
Affiliation or Control: State IRS Status: 501(c)3
Highest Offering: Master's
Accreditation: M, CAEPN, MUS, THEA

02 President ... Dr. Kristin G. ESTERBERG
05 Provost ... Dr. Bette S. BERGERON
10 Interim VP for Business Affairs ... Mr. Keith B. KAPLAN
111 VP College Advancement ... Mr. Sal CANIA
84 Vice President for Enrollment ... Mr. Patrick A. QUINN
100 Chief of Staff ... Ms. Nicole A. FEML
11 Asst VP for Administration & HR ... Mrs. Melissa E. PROULX
18 Asst Vice Pres for Facilities ... Vacant
13 Chief Information Officer ... Vacant
53 Dean Educ & Prof Studies ... Dr. Allen C. GRANT
49 Dean of Arts and Sciences ... Dr. Gretchen GALBRAITH
64 Interim Dean of Music ... Dr. David D. HEUSER
08 Director of Libraries ... Ms. Lauren A. JACKSON-BECK
06 Registrar ... Ms. Stephanie L. CLAXTON
37 Director of Financial Aid ... Ms. Tommiann R. RUSSELL
36 Director of Career Planning ... Vacant
38 Director of Counseling Center ... Mrs. Gena C. NELSON
15 Director of Human Resources Opers ... Ms. Jennifer MURRAY
19 Chief of University Police ... Mr. Tim M. ASHLEY
29 Director of Alumni Relations ... Ms. Mona O. VROMAN
109 Executive Dir of Auxiliary Corp ... Mr. Daniel J. HAYES
23 Director of Health Services ... Ms. Tracy J. HARCOURT
32 Interim Dean of Students ... Mr. Eric D. DUCHSCHERER
40 Director of College Bookstore ... Mr. Lyndon J. LAKE
41 Interim Athletic Director ... Mr. Mark J. MISIAK
25 Director Research & Sponsored Pgms ... Mr. Jack MCGUIRE
92 Director of Honors Program ... Dr. Thomas N. BAKER
94 Director of Women's Studies ... Dr. Christine M. DORAN
27 Asst VP Marketing/Communications ... Mrs. Mindy E. THOMPSON
58 Director of Graduate and Cont Educ ... Dr. Alan L. HERSKER
28 Interim Chief Diversity Officer ... Dr. Claudia J. FORD
09 Director of Institutional Research ... Mrs. Judith R. SINGH
104 Director Study Abroad ... Vacant
96 Director of Purchasing ... Vacant
39 Director of Residence Life ... Ms. Julie DOLD
44 Director Annual Giving ... Ms. Rebecca WEISSMAN
26 Director of Public Relations ... Ms. Alexandra JACOBS WILKE

*Purchase College, State University of New York (B)

735 Anderson Hill Road, Purchase NY 10577-1402
County: Westchester FICE Identification: 006791
Unit ID: 196219
Telephone: (914) 251-6000 Carnegie Class: Bac-A&S
FAX Number: (914) 251-6014 Calendar System: Semester
URL: www.purchase.edu
Established: 1967 Annual Undergrad Tuition & Fees (In-State): $8,953
Enrollment: 3,685 Coed
Affiliation or Control: State IRS Status: 501(c)3
Highest Offering: Master's
Accreditation: M, ART

02 President ... Dr. Milly PENA
10 CFO/VP Operations ... Ms. Judy NOLAN
05 Provost/VP Academic Affairs ... Mr. Barry PEARSON
32 Int VP Student Affs & Enroll Mgmt ... Ms. Patricia BICE
111 VP of Institutional Advancement ... Vacant
19 Chief of University Police ... Mr. Dayton TUCKER
57 Director Conservatory Theatre Arts ... Vacant
81 Dean Sch Natural/Social Sciences ... Dr. Linda BASTONE
79 Chair School of Humanities ... Dr. Aviva TAUBENFELD
20 Assoc Provost Academic Affairs ... Dr. Gregory TAYLOR
88 Dir Performing Arts Center ... Mr. Seth SOLOWAY
88 Director Neuberger Museum of Art ... Dr. Tracy FITZPATRICK
08 Interim Director of the Library ... Mr. Keith LANDA
64 Dir Conservatory of Music ... Dr. Jennifer UNDERCOFLER
13 Director Campus Technology Services ... Mr. Bill JUNOR
37 Director Student Financial Services ... Corey YORK
38 Director of Counseling Center ... Dr. Cathie CHESTER
36 Director Career Development ... Ms. Wendy MOROSOFF
15 Director of Human Resources ... Ms. Kathleen FARRELL
41 Athletic Director ... Mr. Chris BISIGNANO
35 Dean of Student Affairs ... Ms. Patricia BICE
09 Director of Institutional Research ... Ms. Barbara MOORE
18 Sr Dir Capital Facilities Planning ... Mr. Michael KOPAS
22 Title IX Officer/Affirm Action Ofcr ... Ms. Jerima DEWESE
88 Environmental Health/Safety Officer ... Mr. Edward MUSAL
44 Director Annual Giving ... Ms. Carla WEILAND-ZALEZNAK

*State University of New York College of Agriculture and Technology at Cobleskill (C)

106 Suffolk Circle, Cobleskill NY 12043
County: Schoharie FICE Identification: 002856
Unit ID: 196033
Telephone: (518) 255-5011 Carnegie Class: Bac-Diverse
FAX Number: (518) 255-5333 Calendar System: Semester
URL: www.cobleskill.edu
Established: 1911 Annual Undergrad Tuition & Fees (In-State): $8,591
Enrollment: 2,079 Coed
Affiliation or Control: State IRS Status: 501(c)3
Highest Offering: Baccalaureate
Accreditation: M, ACFEI, EMT, HT

02 President ... Dr. Marion TERENZIO
05 Provost & Vice Pres Academic Affs ... Dr. Susan ZIMMERMANN
100 Chief of Staff ... Ms. Amy HEALY
32 VP for Student Development ... Dr. Anne HOPKINS-GROSS
10 Vice Pres Business & Finance ... Ms. Wendy GILMAN
11 Vice Pres Operations ... Ms. Bonnie MARTIN
30 Vice Pres for Development ... Mr. John J. ZACHAREK
47 Dean Agriculture/Natural Res ... Dr. Timothy MOORE
49 Dean Liberal Arts & Sciences ... Dr. Gail WENTWORTH
08 Dean Library/Information Svcs ... Vacant
26 Assoc Dir Strategic Communications ... Mr. Jason POLITI
06 Registrar ... Ms. Christine JOHANNESEN
21 Interim Chief Business Officer ... Ms. Laura GROSS
29 Finance & Alumni Engagement Coord ... Ms. Shannon M. MANCHESTER
07 AVP Enroll/Marketing/Communications ... Mr. Caleb GRANT
39 Asst Vice Pres for Student Dev ... Dr. Matthew LALONDE
36 Director of Student Success Ctr ... Ms. Donna PESTA
23 Interim Co-Director Wellness Center ... Ms. Cheryl PEROG
23 Co-Director Wellness Center ... Ms. Lynn ONTL
37 Director of Financial Aid ... Ms. Louise BIRON
41 Director of Athletics ... Ms. Marie CURRAN-HEADLEY
13 Director Information Tech Services ... Vacant
19 Chief University Police Dept ... Mr. Richard BIALKOWSKI
09 Chief Strat Plng/Inst Effectiveness ... Dr. Tara WINTER
15 Human Resource Manager ... Ms. Nicole FIELD
18 Director Facilities/Physical Plant ... Mr. Joseph BATCHELDER
40 Manager Bookstore ... Ms. Jeri USATCH
85 Director of International Programs ... Dr. Susan JAGENDORF
25 Dir of Grants and Sponsored Program ... Mr. Barry GELL
22 Asc Dir Campus Outreach/Programming ... Mr. Jeffrey C. FOOTE
113 Dir of Student Accounts ... Ms. Sarah LEDERMANN
105 Web/Social/New Media Coordinator ... Mr. Mohamed BALIGH

*State University of New York College of Environmental Science and Forestry (D)

1 Forestry Drive, Syracuse NY 13210-2778
County: Onondaga FICE Identification: 002851
Unit ID: 196103
Telephone: (315) 470-6500 Carnegie Class: DU-Higher
FAX Number: (315) 470-6779 Calendar System: Semester
URL: www.esf.edu
Established: 1911 Annual Undergrad Tuition & Fees (In-State): $9,130
Enrollment: 2,127 Coed
Affiliation or Control: State IRS Status: 501(c)3
Highest Offering: Doctorate
Accreditation: M, LSAR

02 President ... Ms. Joanie MAHONEY
05 Int Provost/VP for Academic Affairs ... Dr. David NEWMAN
10 CFO/Vice Pres for Administration ... Mr. Joseph RUFO
11 Executive Operating Officer ... Mr. Mark LICHTENSTEIN
100 Chief of Staff/Chief Sust Officer ... Mr. Mark LICHTENSTEIN
04 Asst to the President ... Ms. Ragan A. SQUIER
86 VP for Govt & External Relations ... Vacant
45 Exec Dir for Strategic Initiatives ... Mr. Matthew J. MILLEA
30 Asst VP for Development ... Ms. Brenda T. GREENFIELD
46 Vice President for Research ... Dr. John STELLA
58 Assoc Prov & Dean Grad School ... Mr. S. Scott SHANNON
32 Vice Provost/Dean Student Affairs ... Dr. Anne E. LOMBARD
21 Director Business Affairs ... Mr. David R. DZWONKOWSKI
13 Chief Information Officer ... Vacant
15 Director Human Resources ... Mr. Timothy BLEHAR
26 AVP Communications/Marketing ... Vacant
19 Acting Chief of University Police ... Mr. Robert DUGAN
28 Chief Diversity Officer ... Dr. Malika CARTER
08 Director of College Libraries ... Mr. Matthew R. SMITH
07 Director of Admissions ... Mrs. Susan H. SANFORD
37 Director of Financial Aid ... Mr. Mark J. HILL
29 Director of Alumni Affairs ... Ms. Debbie J. CAVINESS
18 Dir Facil Planning/Design & Constr ... Mr. Gary S. PEDEN
36 Dir of Career Services ... Mr. John TURBEVILLE
38 Dir of Counseling Services ... Ms. Ruth LARSON
35 Dir Stdnt Involvement & Leadership ... Mrs. Laura CRANDALL
41 Dir of Intercollegiate Athletics ... Mr. Daniel RAMIN
43 Associate Counsel ... Ms. Kelly BERGER
104 Dir of International Education ... Mr. Thomas E. CARTER
44 Development Officer - Annual Giving ... Ms. Tammy SCHLAFER
91 Manager of Information Systems ... Mr. Kenneth J. STVAN
06 Registrar ... Ms. Leslie A. RUTKOWSKI
09 Asst Dir Assessment & Inst Research ... Dr. Sophie A. GUBLO-JANTZEN
22 Title IX Coord & Affirm Action Ofcr ... Ms. Rebecca A. HODA-KEARSE
84 Asst Provost for Enrollment Mgmt ... Ms. Katherine M. MCCARTHY
106 Director ESF Open Academy ... Dr. Tondelaya K. GEORGE

*State University of New York College of Optometry (E)

33 W 42nd Street, New York NY 10036-8003
County: New York FICE Identification: 009929
Unit ID: 196228
Telephone: (212) 938-4000 Carnegie Class: Spec-4-yr-Other Health
FAX Number: (212) 938-5696 Calendar System: Semester
URL: www.sunyopt.edu
Established: 1971 Annual Graduate Tuition & Fees: N/A
Enrollment: 402 Coed
Affiliation or Control: State IRS Status: 501(c)3
Highest Offering: Doctorate; No Undergraduates
Accreditation: M, OPT, OPTR

02 President ... Dr. David A. HEATH
05 Dean/VP Academic Affairs ... Dr. David TROILO
10 VP For Administration and Finance ... Mr. David A. BOWERS
32 Vice Pres Student Affairs ... Dr. Guilherme ALBIERI
17 Vice Pres for Clinical Admin ... Ms. Liduvina MARTINEZ-GONZALEZ
111 Vice Pres Institutional Advancement ... Ms. Dawn RIGNEY
04 Assistant to the President ... Ms. Ayana WINT
09 Dir Institutional Research/Planning ... Dr. Suresh VISWANATHAN
08 Director Library Services ... Ms. Elaine WELLS
15 Asst Vice Pres of Human Resources ... Ms. Guerda FILS
37 Financial Aid Officer ... Mr. Vito CAVALLARO
06 Registrar ... Ms. Jacqueline MARTINEZ
58 Assoc Dean Rsrch/Graduate Studies ... Dr. Stewart BLOOMFIELD
26 Director of Communications ... Ms. Adrienne STOLLER
13 Chief Info Technology Officer ... Mr. Robert PELLOT
84 Director Enrollment Management ... Dr. Guilherme ALBIERI
96 Director of Purchasing ... Ms. Maureen MORLEY
07 Director of Admissions ... Mr. Christian ALBERTO
29 Assoc Vice Pres of Alumni Affairs ... Ms. Jennifer Kelly CAMPBELL

*Alfred State College (F)

10 Upper College Drive, Alfred NY 14802-1196
County: Allegany FICE Identification: 002854
Unit ID: 196006
Telephone: (607) 587-4215 Carnegie Class: Bac/Assoc-Mixed
FAX Number: N/A Calendar System: Semester
URL: www.alfredstate.edu
Established: 1908 Annual Undergrad Tuition & Fees (In-State): $8,726
Enrollment: 3,667 Coed
Affiliation or Control: State IRS Status: 501(c)3
Highest Offering: Baccalaureate
Accreditation: M, ADNUR, CAHIIM, CONST, FEPAC, IACBE, NURSE, RAD

02 President ... Vacant
05 Provost ... Dr. Kristin POPPO
32 Vice President Student Affairs ... Dr. Gregory S. SAMMONS
111 Exec Dir Institutional Advancement ... Ms. Danielle M. WHITE
09 Dir Inst Research/Planning/Effect ... Mr. Daniel D. JARDINE
84 VP for Enrollment Mgmt ... Ms. Betsy PENROSE
13 Director Computer Services ... Mr. Michael A. CASE
100 Chief of Staff ... Ms. Wendy DRESSER-RECKTENWALD
37 Sr Dir Student Financial Services ... Mrs. Julie ROSE
29 Int Director Alumni Relations ... Ms. Roxana SAMMONS
18 Director of Facilities ... Mr. Jon NICKERSON
14 Asst Director of Computing Services ... Mr. Carl H. RAHR, JR.
23 Sr Director Health Svcs/Wellness ... Ms. Hollie M. HALL
121 Assoc VP of Academic Services ... Ms. Kathleen CASEY
19 Chief of University Police ... Mr. Scott RICHARDSON
96 Director of Purchasing ... Mrs. Michelle MCCARTHY
10 Chief Financial Officer ... Mr. Joseph T. GREENTHAL
36 Director of Career Planning ... Ms. Elaine MORSMAN
49 Dean School of Arts & Sciences ... Mr. Dan KATZ

54 Dean School of Mgmt & Engr Tech ... Dr. John WILLIAMS
75 Int Dean Sch Applied Technology ... Mr. Jeff STEVENS
41 Athletic Director ... Mr. Jason DOVIAK
04 Executive Assistant to President ... Ms. Trish HAGGERTY

*SUNY Adirondack (A)

640 Bay Road, Queensbury NY 12804-1498
County: Warren FICE Identification: 002860
Unit ID: 188438
Telephone: (518) 743-2200 Carnegie Class: Assoc/HT-High Trad
FAX Number: (518) 745-1433 Calendar System: Semester
URL: www.sunyacc.edu
Established: 1960 Annual Undergrad Tuition & Fees (In-District): $5,832
Enrollment: 2,994 Coed
Affiliation or Control: State/Local IRS Status: 501(c)3
Highest Offering: Associate Degree
Accreditation: M, ADNUR

02 President ... Dr. Kristine DUFFY
05 Vice Pres Academic Affairs ... Mr. John JABLONSKI
10 Vice Pres Admin Services ... Ms. Ann Marie SCHEIDEGGER
84 VP for Enrollment & Student Affairs ... Mr. Rob PALMIERI
20 AVP Academic Affairs ... Ms. Diane WILDEY
32 Dean for Student Affairs ... Vacant
09 Director of Inst Research/Planning ... Ms. Carol RUNGE
13 Chief Information Officer ... Ms. Mary HAND
15 AVP of Human Resources ... Ms. Mindy WILSON
51 Asst Dean Cont Educ & Workforce ... Mrs. Caelynn PRYLO
40 Director Bookstore ... Mr. Tom KENT
21 Dir of Business/Financial Affairs ... Ms. Lisa DESTER
18 AVP of Facilities ... Mr. Anthony PALANGI
37 Director Financial Aid/Marketing ... Ms. Colleen WISE
06 Registrar ... Ms. Mary ALDOUS
07 Asst Director of Admissions ... Mr. Shaughn G. CLANCY
08 Director of Library Services ... Ms. Teresa RONNING
35 Dir of Student Engagement/Diversity ... Ms. Barbara COCKFIELD
04 Exec Assist to President ... Ms. Brooke TOMA
19 Asst Director of Public Safety ... Mr. Richard CONINE

*SUNY Canton-College of Technology (B)

34 Cornell Drive, Canton NY 13617-1098
County: Saint Lawrence FICE Identification: 002855
Unit ID: 196015
Telephone: (315) 386-7011 Carnegie Class: Bac-Diverse
FAX Number: (315) 386-7930 Calendar System: Semester
URL: www.canton.edu
Established: 1906 Annual Undergrad Tuition & Fees (In-State): $8,689
Enrollment: 3,135 Coed
Affiliation or Control: State IRS Status: 501(c)3
Highest Offering: Baccalaureate
Accreditation: M, ADNUR, COSMA, FUSER, IACBE, NUR, PNUR, PTAA

02 President ... Dr. Zvi SZAFRAN
05 Provost ... Dr. Peggy A. DE COOKE
11 Vice Pres for Administration ... Ms. Shawn MILLER
10 Chief Financial Officer ... Ms. Shawn MILLER
111 Vice Pres for Advancement ... Ms. Tracey THOMPSON
32 Vice President for Student Affairs ... Ms. Courtney D. BISH
35 Dean of Students ... Ms. Courtney D. BISH
72 Dean Canino Sch Eng Tech ... Mr. Michael J. NEWTOWN
76 Dean Sch Sci/Health/Crim Justice ... Dr. Michelle CURRIER
50 Dean Sch Business/Liberal Arts ... Dr. Phil NEISSER
20 Associate Provost ... Dr. Molly MOTT
41 Director of Athletics ... Mr. Randy B. SIEMINSKI
100 Exec Dir for University Relations ... Dr. Lenore VANDERZEE
101 College Council Secretary ... Ms. Michaela J. YOUNG
04 Exec Assistant to the President ... Ms. Michaela J. YOUNG
35 Director Student Activities ... Ms. Priscilla LEGGETTE COLLINS
28 Co-Chief Diversity Officer/AAO ... Ms. Lashawanda T. INGRAM
28 Co-Chief Diversity Officer/AAO ... Ms. Emily HAMILTON-HONEY
96 Director of Purchasing ... Ms. Bethany A. MARTIN
37 Director of Financial Aid ... Ms. Heather M. ADNER
21 College Accountant ... Ms. Amanda CRUMP
15 Director of Human Resources ... Ms. Suzan MCDERMOTT
36 Director of Career Services ... Ms. Julie PARKMAN
06 Registrar ... Ms. Aimee WALKER
08 Director of Library Services ... Ms. Cori WILHELM
18 Director of Physical Plant ... Mr. Patrick G. HANSS
18 Plant Superintendent ... Mr. Martin D. AVERY
19 Chief of University Police ... Mr. Alan MULKIN
23 Director of Health Services ... Ms. Shanna WHITE
26 Dir Public Rels/Web Coord ... Mr. Travis SMITH
40 Manager Campus Store ... Mr. Corey JORDAN
39 Director of Residence Life ... Mr. John M. KENNEDY
09 Dir of Inst Research/Assessment ... Ms. Sarah E. TODD
13 Assistant VP IT/CIO ... Mr. Kyle BROWN
29 Director of Alumni Affairs ... Ms. Peggy S. LEVATO
38 Director of Counseling ... Ms. Melinda A. MILLER
07 Director of Admissions ... Ms. Melissa EVANS
88 Director of Facilities ... Mr. Michael R. MCCORMICK
30 Director of Development ... Ms. Peggy S. LEVATO
90 Help Desk Manager ... Mr. Benjamin MATOTT
104 Coord Intl Student Initiatives ... Ms. Erin LASSIAL
88 Dir CREST Center/Veterans Coord ... Mr. Patrick MASSARO
25 Dir of Research & Sponsored Pgms ... Ms. Betsy ROHR ADAMS

*SUNY Corning Community College (C)

One Academic Drive, Corning NY 14830-3297
County: Steuben FICE Identification: 002863
Unit ID: 190442
Telephone: (607) 962-9000 Carnegie Class: Assoc/HT-Mix Trad/Non
FAX Number: (607) 962-9456 Calendar System: Semester
URL: www.corning-cc.edu
Established: 1956 Annual Undergrad Tuition & Fees (In-District): $5,824
Enrollment: 4,063 Coed
Affiliation or Control: State/Local IRS Status: 501(c)3
Highest Offering: Associate Degree
Accreditation: M, ADNUR

01 President ... Dr. William P. MULLANEY
10 Executive Director of Finance/CFO ... Ms. Susan CHANDLER
05 Provost ... Dr. Barbara CANFIELD
30 Exec Dir CCC Development Foundation ... Ms. Angela FLEMING
06 Registrar ... Ms. Loretta HENDRICKSON
84 Director of Enrollment Operations ... Mr. Christian KULL
15 Exec Dir of HR and Ch Div Officer ... Ms. Connie PARK
18 Chief Facilities/Physical Plant ... Mr. Calvin WILLIAMS
37 Director Student Financial Aid ... Ms. Shalena CLARY
09 Director of Institutional Research ... Mr. Paul ANDREWS
04 Exec Office Mgr/Asst to Pres ... Ms. Nogaye KA-TANDIA
103 Exec Dir Workforce Development ... Ms. Jeanne ESCHBACH
19 Director Public Safety ... Mr. Michael FRIEBIS
13 Chief Information Officer ... Mr. John PETKASH
09 Director of Library ... Ms. Rejoice SCHERRY

*State University of New York College of Technology at Delhi (D)

454 Delhi Drive, Delhi NY 13753-4454
County: Delaware FICE Identification: 002857
Unit ID: 196024
Telephone: (607) 746-4000 Carnegie Class: Bac/Assoc-Mixed
FAX Number: (607) 746-4208 Calendar System: Semester
URL: www.delhi.edu
Established: 1913 Annual Undergrad Tuition & Fees (In-State): $8,640
Enrollment: 3,077 Coed
Affiliation or Control: State IRS Status: 501(c)3
Highest Offering: Master's
Accreditation: M, ACFEI, ADNUR, CONST, NUR, NURSE

02 President ... Dr. Michael R. LALIBERTE
05 Provost ... Dr. Thomas T. JORDAN
32 VP for Student Life ... Mr. Tomas A. AGUIRRE
10 VP for Finance & Administration ... Ms. Carol M. BISHOP
111 Vice Pres for College Advancement ... Mr. Michael A. SULLIVAN
36 Career Planning & Devel Associate ... Ms. Kristin A. DEFOREST
07 Director of Admissions ... Mr. Robert C. PIUROWSKI
13 Chief Information Officer ... Mr. Shawn P. BRISLIN
19 Chief of University Police ... Mr. Martin A. PETTIT
39 Asst Vice Pres Housing/Aux Svcs ... Mr. John J. PADOVANI
08 Director of the Resnick Library ... Ms. Carrie J. FISHNER
36 Dir Career & Business Development ... Vacant
31 Sr Staff Assoc Ctr for Cmty Engage ... Ms. Michele T. DEFREECE
18 Director of Physical Plant ... Mr. David A. LOVELAND
41 Director of Athletics ... Mr. Robert H. BACKUS
06 Registrar ... Ms. Nancy L. SMITH
37 Director of Financial Aid ... Ms. Elizabeth D. BERRY
23 Director of Health Services ... Ms. Karen GABRIEL
29 Director of Alumni/Annual Giving ... Ms. Lucinda C. BRYDON
21 Controller ... Ms. Amy L. BROWN
26 Vice Pres Communications/Marketing ... Ms. Dawn R. SOHNS
09 Asst for Institutional Research ... Ms. JoAnna M. BROSNAN
04 Administrative Asst to President ... Mr. George L. SPIELMAN
102 Exec Dir College Foundation ... Vacant
22 Dir Human Resources/Affirm Action ... Ms. Mary B. MORTON
25 Grants Specialist ... Ms. Ellen A. LIBERATORI

*State University of New York Empire State College (E)

2 Union Avenue, Saratoga Springs NY 12866-4390
County: Saratoga FICE Identification: 010286
Unit ID: 196264
Telephone: (518) 587-2100 Carnegie Class: Masters/L
FAX Number: (518) 587-2886 Calendar System: Other
URL: www.esc.edu
Established: 1971 Annual Undergrad Tuition & Fees (In-State): $7,630
Enrollment: 10,724 Coed
Affiliation or Control: State IRS Status: 501(c)3
Highest Offering: Doctorate
Accreditation: M, AAQEP, IACBE, NURSE

02 Officer in Charge ... Dr. Nathan GONYEA
100 Int Chief of Staff ... Ms. Leigh YANNUZZI
11 EVP Administration & COO ... Vacant
05 Acting Provost ... Dr. Tai ARNOLD
111 Int AVP of Advancement ... Ms. Sue EPSTEIN
84 VP for Enrollment Management ... Dr. Clayton STEEN
10 Chief Financial Officer/Int COO ... Ms. Alexandra BONITATIBUS
26 AVP for Communications/Marketing ... Mr. Solomon SYED
15 Asst VP for Human Resources ... Ms. Tracey MEEK
20 Dean Academic/Instructional Svcs ... Dr. Lisa D'ADAMO-WEINSTEIN
20 Int VP Academic Stdnt Succes ... Dr. Tai ARNOLD
20 Int Vice Provost Academic Affairs ... Dr. Nikki SHRIMPTON
70 Associate Dean Social Science ... Dr. Frank VANDER VALK
50 Associate Dean Business ... Dr. Julie GEDRO
79 Associate Dean Humanities ... Dr. Megan MULLEN
58 Assoc Dean School for Grad Studies ... Dr. Nathan GONYEA
66 Dean School of Nursing ... Dr. Kim STOTE
28 Int Chief Diversity Officer ... Dr. Audeliz MATIAS
12 Co-Int Exec Director Metro Center ... Dr. Christopher WHANN
91 Director Admin Applications ... Mr. Mark CLAVERIE
110 Director Advancement Services ... Ms. Vicki SCHAAKE
29 Dir Alumni and Student Relations ... Ms. Maureen WINNEY
44 Director of the Fund ... Ms. Stephanie CORP
21 Director Business Office ... Ms. Becky PALMIERI
108 Dir Collegewide Academic Review ... Dr. Nan TRAVERS
27 Director of Communications ... Mr. David HENAHAN
88 Director of Academic Development ... Mr. Brian GOODALE
88 Dir Compliance/Environment Sustain ... Ms. Sadie ROSS
18 Senior Director of Facilities ... Mr. Rick REIMANN
30 Director of Development ... Mr. Toby TOBROCKE
88 Director College Project Management ... Mr. Walter LEWIS
96 Director Procurement ... Mr. Charley SUMMERSELL
24 Director Publications ... Mr. Kirk STARCZEWSKI
19 Director of Safety & Security ... Mr. Mark JANKOWSKI
113 Director Student Accounts ... Ms. Pamela MALONE
88 Int Dir Veteran & Military Educ ... Ms. Desiree DRINDAK
06 Registrar ... Ms. Pamela ENSER
07 Sr Director Admissions ... Ms. Jennifer D'AGOSTINO

*Farmingdale State College (F)

2350 Broadhollow Road, Farmingdale NY 11735-1021
County: Suffolk FICE Identification: 002858
Unit ID: 196042
Telephone: (934) 420-2000 Carnegie Class: Bac-Diverse
FAX Number: N/A Calendar System: Semester
URL: www.farmingdale.edu
Established: 1912 Annual Undergrad Tuition & Fees (In-State): $8,395
Enrollment: 10,018 Coed
Affiliation or Control: State IRS Status: 501(c)3
Highest Offering: Master's
Accreditation: M, AAB, ART, DH, MT, NURSE

02 President ... Dr. John S. NADER
05 Provost/SVP for Academic Affairs ... Dr. Laura JOSEPH
10 Executive VP & CFO ... Mr. Gregory O'CONNOR
32 VP Student Affairs & CDO ... Dr. Kevin JORDAN
111 VP Inst Advancement/Enrollment Mgmt ... Vacant
30 VP Development & Alumni Engagement ... Mr. Matthew COLSON
20 Associate Provost ... Dr. Michael GOODSTONE
11 Asst VP Administration & Finance ... Ms. Dorothy HUGHES
35 Dean of Students ... Vacant
84 Dir Enrollment Svc/Partnership Pgm ... Mr. Jim HALL
19 Chief University Police ... Mr. Daniel DAUGHERTY
18 Director of Physical Plant ... Mr. John S. DZINANKA
26 Sr Director of Communications ... Vacant
06 Registrar ... Ms. Cindy MCCUE
07 Director of Admissions ... Mr. Jeffrey LEVINE
08 Head Librarian ... Ms. Karen GELLES
15 Director Human Resources ... Ms. Marybeth INCANDELA
13 Director of Information Technology ... Mr. Jeffrey BORAH
36 Director Career Development ... Ms. Dolores CIACCIO
37 Director Student Financial Services ... Ms. Diane KAZANECKI-KEMPTER
09 Chief Inst Research Officer ... Ms. Patricia LIND-GONZALEZ
23 Director of Campus Heath & Wellness ... Mr. Kevin MURPHY
41 Dir Athletics Admin & Ext Affairs ... Mr. Michael HARRINGTON
41 Dir of Athletics Comp & Operations ... Mr. Thomas AZZARA
39 Dir Student Activities/Campus Ctr ... Ms. Eunice RO
102 President Farmingdale Foundation ... Mr. Robert VAN NOSTRAND
24 Director Media Resources ... Mr. Martin BRANDT
29 Director Alumni Relations ... Ms. Michelle JOHNSON
40 Manager Bookstore ... Mr. Matthew DAVID
21 Controller ... Vacant
96 Purchasing Manager ... Ms. Lisa BRUNS
75 Interim Exec Director LIEOC ... Mr. Charles MIRANDA
50 Dean School of Business ... Dr. Richard VOGEL
76 Dean School Health Sciences ... Dr. Denny RYMAN
49 Dean School of Arts & Sciences ... Dr. Charles ADAIR
54 Dean School of Engineering Tech ... Dr. Barbara CHRISTIE
104 Study Abroad Specialist ... Ms. Elizabeth HAMBERGER
105 Director Web Program & Developement ... Ms. Sylvia NAVARRO-NICOSIA
85 Acting Dir International Education ... Mr. James HALL
04 Executive Assistant to President ... Ms. Carolyn FEDDER

*State University of New York Maritime College (G)

6 Pennyfield Avenue, Throggs Neck NY 10465-4198
County: Bronx FICE Identification: 002853
Unit ID: 196291
Telephone: (718) 409-7200 Carnegie Class: Masters/S
FAX Number: (718) 409-7392 Calendar System: Semester
URL: www.sunymaritime.edu
Established: 1874 Annual Undergrad Tuition & Fees (In-State): $8,522
Enrollment: 1,671 Coed
Affiliation or Control: State IRS Status: 501(c)3
Highest Offering: Master's
Accreditation: M, IACBE

02 President ... Dr. Michael A. ALFULTIS
05 Provost/Vice Pres Academic Affairs ... Dr. Jennifer K. WATERS
10 Vice Pres Finance/Admin ... Mr. Scott DIETERICH
111 Vice President Advancement ... Mr. Douglas HASBROUCK
20 Academic Dean ... Vacant
100 Chief of Staff ... CAPT. Mark WOOLLEY
07 Dean of Admissions ... Mr. Rohan HOWELL
32 Assoc Provost/Dean of Students ... Mr. William IMBRIALE
27 Director of External Affairs ... CAPT. Mark WOOLLEY

15 AVP Human Resources/Chief Div Ofcr ... Ms. Lu-Ann AUGUSTINE-PLAISANCE
19 University Police Chief ... Mr. Myron PRYJMAK
37 Director Financial Aid ... Ms. Andrea DAMAR
41 Interim Director of Athletics ... Mr. Mike BERKUN
06 Registrar ... Ms. Sarah GRADY
09 Dir Inst Research/Assessment ... CAPT. Mark WOOLLEY
08 Library Director ... Ms. Jillian KEHOE
88 Dean Maritime Educ/Training ... CAPT. Ernest FINK
54 Dean School of Engineering ... Dr. Carl DELO
50 Dean Sch of Business/Sci/Humanities ... Dr. Joseph HOFFMAN

*SUNY Morrisville (A)

PO Box 901, Morrisville NY 13408-0901

County: Madison FICE Identification: 002859
Unit ID: 196051
Telephone: (315) 684-6000 Carnegie Class: Bac/Assoc-Mixed
FAX Number: (315) 684-6116 Calendar System: Semester
URL: www.morrisville.edu
Established: 1908 Annual Undergrad Tuition & Fees (In-State): $8,740
Enrollment: 2,486 Coed
Affiliation or Control: State IRS Status: 501(c)3
Highest Offering: Baccalaureate
Accreditation: M, ACBSP, ADNUR, DIETT, NUR

02 President ... Dr. David E. ROGERS
05 Provost ... Dr. Barry A. SPRIGGS
10 Chief Financial Officer ... Mr. Jamie CYR
84 Chief Enrollment Officer ... Dr. Robert C. BLANCHET
32 Int VP Student Affairs ... Dr. Mary BONDEROFF
47 Dean School Agric/Business/Tech ... Vacant
49 Dean Liberal Arts/Sciences/Society ... Dr. Dean P. O'GRADY
111 VP for Inst Advancement ... Ms. Theresa R. KEVORKIAN
07 Director of Admission ... Ms. Kaylynn C. INGLESIAS
37 Director of Financial Aid ... Ms. Dacia L. BANKS
09 Director of Institutional Research ... Ms. Marian D. WHITNEY
08 Director of Library ... Ms. Christine A. RUDECOFF
23 Director Student Health Center ... Ms. Debra P. BABOWICZ
15 Director Human Resources ... Ms. Dawn NORCROSS
29 Alumni Engagement Coordinator ... Ms. Rhiannon L. DACUNHA
26 Exec Director Communication Mktg ... Vacant
06 Registrar ... Ms. Marian D. WHITNEY
13 Director of Technology Svcs ... Mr. Kyle A. CAMPANARO
18 Exec Director of Facilities ... Mr. Christopher S. MARONEY
19 Chief of Police ... Mr. Paul G. FIELD
36 Career Planning/Development Ofcr ... Ms. Barbara A. ROBACK
39 Director Student Housing ... Ms. Elizabeth R. ACKMAN
41 Athletic Director ... Vacant
108 Associate Provost of Assessment ... Dr. Jason P. ZBOCK
28 Director of Diversity ... Dr. Mary BONDEROFF

*SUNY Polytechnic Institute (B)

100 Seymour Road, Utica NY 13502

County: Oneida FICE Identification: 011678
Unit ID: 196112
Telephone: (315) 792-7100 Carnegie Class: Masters/M
FAX Number: (315) 792-7222 Calendar System: Semester
URL: www.sunypoly.edu
Established: 1966 Annual Undergrad Tuition & Fees (In-State): $8,427
Enrollment: 3,044 Coed
Affiliation or Control: State IRS Status: 501(c)3
Highest Offering: Doctorate
Accreditation: M, CAHIIM, NURSE

02 Acting President ... Dr. Tod LAURSEN
11 Chief Operating Officer ... Mr. Michael FRAME
04 Assistant to the President ... Ms. Laurie HARTMAN
46 Int VP for Research Advancement ... Dr. Shadi SHAHEDIPOUR-SANDVIK
15 VP for Human Resources ... Ms. Rhonda HAINES
32 VP for Student Affairs ... Ms. Marybeth LYONS
30 AVP for Development ... Mrs. Andrea LAGATTA
05 Provost ... Dr. Steven SCHNEIDER
84 AVP for Enrollment Mgmt ... Ms. Maryrose RAAB
49 Dean Arts & Sciences ... Dr. Andrew RUSSELL
50 Dean Business ... Dr. Arthur LU
54 Dean Engineering ... Dr. Michael CARPENTER
81 Dean Nanoscale Science & Engr ... Dr. Andre MELENDEZ
76 Dean Health Professions ... Dr. Joanne JOSEPH
19 Chief of Police ... Mr. Gary BEAN
18 Director of Facilities ... Mr. Matt PUTNAM
41 Director Athletics ... Mr. Kevin M. GRIMMER
21 Associate VP of Business Affairs ... Ms. Susan HEAD
88 Director of Student Conduct ... Ms. Megan WYETT
36 Director Career Services ... Mr. Jose Miguel LONGO
23 Director Health & Wellness Center ... Ms. Jo RUFFRAGE
09 Assistant VP Institutional Research ... Ms. Valerie FUSCO
35 AVP Student Affairs ... Mrs. Jennifer ADAMS
37 Director Student Financial Aid ... Mr. Michael ALSHEIMER
06 Registrar ... Mrs. Meghan GETMAN
123 Coordinator Graduate Center ... Ms. Alicia FOSTER
43 Associate Counsel ... Mr. Mark LEMIRE
13 Chief Information Officer ... Mr. Andrew BELLINGER
28 Chief Diversity Officer ... Dr. Mark MONTGOMERY
07 Director of Admissions ... Ms. Gina LISCIO
08 Director of Library Services ... Ms. Rebecca HEWITT
120 Dir Online Education/E-learning ... Mr. Rick SHELTON
29 Director Alumni Relations ... Vacant
96 Director of Purchasing ... Mr. David MANORE

*Suffolk County Community College Central Administration (C)

533 College Road, Selden NY 11784-2899

County: Suffolk Identification: 666658
Unit ID: 366395
Telephone: (631) 451-4000 Carnegie Class: N/A
FAX Number: (631) 451-4715
URL: www.sunysuffolk.edu

01 President ... Mr. Edward BONAHUE
27 College Communications Director ... Mr. Drew BIONDO
43 College General Counsel ... Mr. Louis J. PETRIZZO
05 VP Academic Affairs ... Dr. Paul M. BEAUDIN
10 VP Business/Financial Affairs ... Mr. Mark HARRIS
30 Vice Pres Institutional Advancement ... Ms. Mary Lou ARANEO
45 VP Planning/Inst Effectiveness ... Ms. Kaliah GREENE
32 Int Asst VP of Student Affairs ... Dr. Patty MUNSCH
13 VP Computer Information Systems ... Mr. Shady AZZAM-GOMEZ
103 Assoc VP Workforce/Econ Development ... Mr. John LOMBARDO
84 College Dean Enrollment Management ... Ms. Joanne E. BRAXTON
06 Assoc Dean Master Sched/Registrar ... Ms. Anna FLACK
35 Assistant Dean Student Services ... Ms. Katherine AGUIRRE
37 College Director of Financial Aid ... Ms. Nancy A. BREWER
28 Col Coord Multicultural Affairs ... Mr. James W. BANKS
102 Executive Director Foundation ... Dr. Sylvia DIAZ
30 Col Assoc Dean Inst Advancement ... Mr. Andrew FAWCETT
104 Col Assoc Dean Spec Prog & Ext Part ... Dr. Iaroslava BABENCHUK
106 Asst Dean Instructional Technology ... Mr. Douglas KAHN
14 Assoc Dean Computer Info Systems ... Vacant
19 Director Fire/Public Safety ... Mr. Baycan FIDELI
22 Chief Diversity Officer/Title IX ... Ms. Christina VARGAS
25 Assoc Dean Grants Development ... Dr. William T. TUCKER
26 Dir College Relations/Publications ... Ms. Mary M. FEDER
29 Director Alumni Relations ... Mr. Russell MALBROUGH
41 College Assoc Director of Athletics ... Mr. Joseph KOSINA
86 Col Director Legislative Affairs ... Mr. Benjamin ZWIRN
96 Admin Director Business Operations ... Ms. Beatriz CASTANO
36 Director Career Services ... Ms. Tania VELAZQUEZ
18 Executive Director Facilities ... Mr. Paul COOPER

*Suffolk County Community College (D)

533 College Road, Selden NY 11784-2899

County: Suffolk FICE Identification: 002878
Telephone: (631) 451-4000 Carnegie Class: Not Classified
FAX Number: (631) 451-4015 Calendar System: Semester
URL: www.sunysuffolk.edu
Established: 1959 Annual Undergrad Tuition & Fees (In-District): N/A
Enrollment: N/A Coed
Affiliation or Control: State/Local IRS Status: 501(c)3
Highest Offering: Associate Degree
Accreditation: M, ADNUR, CAHIIM, DIETT, EMT, OTA, PNUR, PTAA

02 Interim Campus CEO/Executive Dean ... Dr. Irene RIOS
05 Assoc Dean of Academic Affairs ... Dr. Sandra SPROWS
05 Assoc Dean of Academic Affairs ... Dr. Fara AFSHAR
32 Assoc Dean of Student Affairs ... Dr. Edward MARTINEZ
37 Director of Financial Aid ... Ms. Renee NUNZIATO
35 Assistant Dean of Student Affairs ... Dr. Katherine AGUIRRE
08 Interim Head Librarian ... Ms. Dana ANTONUCCI-DURGAN
13 Director of Enterprise Applications ... Mr. Christopher T. BLAKE
18 Director Facilities/Physical Plant ... Mr. Steve HARTMANN
36 Asst Dean Stdnt Affs/Dir Career Svc ... Ms. Tania VELAZQUEZ
92 Coordinator Honors Program ... Mr. Albin COFONE
10 Admin Director of Business Affairs ... Mr. John CIENSKI
90 Coord of Instructional Technology ... Vacant
91 Assoc Director Data Center ... Mr. John GANNON

Sullivan County Community College (E)

112 College Road, Loch Sheldrake NY 12759-5721

County: Sullivan FICE Identification: 002879
Unit ID: 195988
Telephone: (845) 434-5750 Carnegie Class: Assoc/MT-VT-Mix Trad/Non
FAX Number: (845) 434-4806 Calendar System: Semester
URL: www.sunysullivan.edu
Established: 1962 Annual Undergrad Tuition & Fees (In-District): $6,310
Enrollment: 1,701 Coed
Affiliation or Control: State/Local IRS Status: 501(c)3
Highest Offering: Associate Degree
Accreditation: M, ACBSP, COARC

01 President ... Mr. John (Jay) QUAINTANCE
05 Int VP Academic & Student Affs ... Mr. Lawrence WEILL
10 Chief Financial Officer/Controller ... Ms. Faith DEMING
32 Dean Student Development Services ... Mr. Chris DEPEW
49 Dean of Liberal Arts & Sciences ... Ms. Rosemarie HANOFEE
31 Dean of Community Outreach ... Vacant
07 Director Admissions & Recruiting ... Ms. Christina BUCKLER
84 Student Enrollment Specialist ... Mr. Frank SINIGAGLIA
41 Director of Athletics ... Mr. Chris DEPEW
15 Director of Human Resources ... Ms. Stephanie GREENO
09 Director Institutional Research ... Dr. Jeffrey KEEFER
38 Director Student Counseling ... Vacant
13 Director Institutional Technology ... Mr. Quazi RAHMAN
19 Director Public Safety ... Mr. Matt LASPISA
06 Dir Registration Services/Registrar ... Ms. Anne MARCHAL
26 Dean of Communications ... Ms. Eleanor DAVIS
04 Dir Executive Operations/AA to BOT ... Ms. Maura CAYCHO
37 Director Student Financial Aid ... Ms. Keri WHITEHEAD

Swedish Institute-College of Health Sciences (F)

226 W 26th Street, New York NY 10001-6700

County: New York FICE Identification: 021700
Unit ID: 196389
Telephone: (212) 924-5900 Carnegie Class: Spec 2-yr-Health
FAX Number: (212) 924-7600 Calendar System: Semester
URL: www.swedishinstitute.edu
Established: 1916 Annual Undergrad Tuition & Fees: $24,040
Enrollment: 765 Coed
Affiliation or Control: Proprietary IRS Status: Proprietary
Highest Offering: Associate Degree
Accreditation: ACCSC, ADNUR, SURGT

01 President ... Ms. Erin SHEA
10 Director of Finance ... Mr. Nathan FIELDS
05 Chief Academic Officer ... Dr. Joseph BALATBAT
07 Director of Admissions ... Mr. Derrick RUFFIN
88 VP for Program Development ... Mr. John KATOMSKI
88 Dean of Advanced Personal Training ... Mr. Vincent METZO
88 Dean for Massage Therapy ... Ms. Ericka CLINTON
66 Dean of Nursing ... Ms. Hillory THORPE
13 Director of Information Technology ... Mr. Rob SIEFKEN
32 Director of Student Services ... Ms. Theresa ROBBINSON
26 Director of Public Relations ... Vacant
37 Financial Aid Director ... Ms. Anuvita PARBHU
08 Director of Library Services ... Mr. Matthew FORTINO
06 Registrar ... Ms. Qiana HORTON
113 Bursar ... Ms. Beatriz ACEVEDO
51 Director of Continuing Education ... Ms. Tania OGULLUKIAN
40 Bookstore Manager ... Mr. Dan YUEN
36 Director of Career Services ... Mr. Richard GARDNER

Syracuse University (G)

900 South Crouse Avenue, Syracuse NY 13244

County: Onondaga FICE Identification: 002882
Unit ID: 196413
Telephone: (315) 443-1870 Carnegie Class: DU-Highest
FAX Number: (315) 443-3503 Calendar System: Semester
URL: www.syr.edu
Established: 1870 Annual Undergrad Tuition & Fees: $55,926
Enrollment: 21,322 Coed
Affiliation or Control: Independent Non-Profit IRS Status: 501(c)3
Highest Offering: Doctorate
Accreditation: M, AAQEP, ART, AUD, CACREP, CIDA, CLPSY, DIETD, DIETI, FEPAC, JOUR, LAW, LIB, MFCD, MUS, PH, SCPSY, SP, SPAA, SW

01 Chancellor & President ... Mr. Kent SYVERUD
05 Vice Chancellor/Provost/CAO ... Dr. Gretchen RITTER
10 Int Sr Vice President & CFO ... Ms. Gwenn JUDGE
43 Sr VP and General Counsel ... Mr. Daniel J. FRENCH
100 Sr VP and Chief of Staff ... Ms. Candace CAMPBELL JACKSON
111 Chief Advancement Officer/SVP ... Mr. Matthew TER MOLEN
32 Sr VP Student Experience ... Mr. Allen GROVES
101 SVP/Secretary Board of Trustees ... Ms. Lisa A. DOLAK
88 SVP for Academic Operations ... Mr. Steve BENNETT
41 Athletic Director ... Mr. John WILDHACK
26 SVP & Chief Marketing Officer ... Ms. Dara J. ROYER
21 Comptroller ... Ms. Jean B. GALLIPEAU
15 Sr VP/Chief Human Resources Officer ... Mr. Andrew GORDON
20 Assoc Provost Faculty Affairs ... Ms. LaVonda REED
20 Assoc Prov for Academic Affairs ... Dr. Chris JOHNSON
13 VP Information Technology/CIO ... Mr. Samuel SCOZZAFAVA
46 Vice Pres for Research ... Dr. Ramesh RAINA
48 Dean School of Architecture ... Dr. Michael A. SPEAKS
49 Dean College of Arts & Sciences ... Dr. Karin RUHLANDT
58 Assoc Prov Grad Stds/Dean Grad Sch ... Dr. Peter VANABLE
08 Dean of University Libraries ... Mr. David SEAMAN
53 Dean School of Education ... Dr. Joanna O. MASINGILA
76 Dean Col of Sport & Human Dynamics ... Dr. Diane LYDEN MURPHY
54 Dean Col Engineering/Computer Sci ... Dr. J. Cole SMITH
62 Dean iSchool ... Mr. Rajiv DEWAN
61 Dean College of Law ... Dr. Craig M. BOISE
50 Dean Whitman School of Management ... Dr. Eugene ANDERSON
60 Dean Newhouse Sch Public Comm ... Mr. Mark LODATO
57 Dean Col Visual & Performing Arts ... Dr. Michael TICK
51 Dean University College ... Dr. Michael FRASCIELLO
07 Dean of Admissions ... Dr. Maurice A. HARRIS
42 Dean Hendricks Chapel ... Rev. Brian KONKOL
88 Vice Chancellor Strat Init & Innov ... Dr. Michael HAYNIE
18 VP and Chief Facilities Officer ... Mr. Pete SALA
19 SVP Safety/Chief Law Enforce Ofcr ... Mr. Anthony CALLISTO
28 Chief Diversity Officer ... Dr. Keith ALFORD

Talmudical Institute of Upstate New York (H)

769 Park Avenue, Rochester NY 14607-3046

County: Monroe FICE Identification: 025506
Unit ID: 196440
Telephone: (585) 473-2810 Carnegie Class: Spec-4-yr-Faith
FAX Number: (585) 442-0417 Calendar System: Semester
URL: tiuny.org
Established: 1974 Annual Undergrad Tuition & Fees: $6,150
Enrollment: 8 Male
Affiliation or Control: Independent Non-Profit IRS Status: 501(c)3

Highest Offering: Second Talmudic Degree
Accreditation: RABN

01 Dean ... Rabbi Menachem DAVIDOWITZ
03 Executive Vice President ... Rabbi Shlomo NOBLE

Talmudical Seminary of Bobov (A)

5120 New Utrecht Avenue, Brooklyn NY 11204-1108
County: Kings FICE Identification: 041155
Unit ID: 451404
Telephone: (718) 854-8700 Carnegie Class: Spec-4-yr-Faith
FAX Number: (718) 854-8707 Calendar System: Semester
Established: 2005 Annual Undergrad Tuition & Fees: $10,200
Enrollment: 423 Male
Affiliation or Control: Independent Non-Profit IRS Status: 501(c)3
Highest Offering: First Talmudic Degree
Accreditation: RABN

01 Dean ... Rabbi Joshua RUBIN
37 Director Student Financial Aid ... Josef DEUTSCH
06 Registrar ... Solomon GORDON

Talmudical Seminary Oholei Torah (B)

667 Eastern Parkway, Brooklyn NY 11213-3397
County: Kings FICE Identification: 012011
Unit ID: 196431
Telephone: (718) 774-5050 Carnegie Class: Spec-4-yr-Faith
FAX Number: (718) 778-0784 Calendar System: Semester
URL: tsot.edu/
Established: 1956 Annual Undergrad Tuition & Fees: $10,300
Enrollment: 331 Male
Affiliation or Control: Independent Non-Profit IRS Status: 501(c)3
Highest Offering: First Talmudic Degree
Accreditation: RABN

01 Chief Executive Officer ... Mr. Zalman CHEIN
05 Dean ... Elchonon LESCHES
10 Business Officer ... Dov KLYNE
37 Financial Aid Officer ... Sholom ROSENFELD

Teachers College, Columbia University (C)

525 West 120th Street, New York NY 10027
County: New York FICE Identification: 003979
Unit ID: 196468
Telephone: (212) 678-3000 Carnegie Class: DU-Higher
FAX Number: (212) 678-4048 Calendar System: Semester
URL: www.tc.columbia.edu
Established: 1887 Annual Graduate Tuition & Fees: N/A
Enrollment: 4,547 Coed
Affiliation or Control: Independent Non-Profit IRS Status: 501(c)3
Highest Offering: Doctorate; No Undergraduates
Accreditation: M, AAQEP, ABAI, CLPSY, COPSY, DIETC, DIETI, MPCAC, PH, SCPSY, SP

01 President ... Dr. Thomas R. BAILEY
05 Provost & VP for Academic Affairs ... Dr. Stephanie ROWLEY
30 Vice Pres for Development ... Ms. Kelly MOODY
10 Vice Pres Finance & Operations ... Mr. Henry PERKOWSKI
22 Vice Pres for Diversity/Cmty Affs ... Ms. Janice S. ROBINSON
88 VP Sch/Cmty Prtnrshp/Spec Adviser ... Dr. Nancy STREIM
21 Assoc Vice Pres/Controller ... Ms. Elisha RODRIGUEZ
18 Asst VP Facilities ... Mr. Brian ALFORD
13 Chief Information Officer ... Mr. Dan ARACENA
08 Library Director ... Ms. Jennifer GOVAN
19 Director Public Safety ... Mr. John DEANGELIS
43 General Counsel ... Mr. Michael FEIERMAN
29 Director Alumni Relations ... Ms. Rosella GARCIA
11 Vice Pres for Administration ... Ms. Lisa SEALES

† Affiliated with Columbia University in the City of New York.

Tompkins Cortland Community College (D)

170 North Street, PO Box 139, Dryden NY 13053-8504
County: Tompkins FICE Identification: 006788
Unit ID: 196565
Telephone: (607) 844-8211 Carnegie Class: Assoc/HT-High Non
FAX Number: (607) 844-9665 Calendar System: Semester
URL: www.TompkinsCortland.edu
Established: 1968 Annual Undergrad Tuition & Fees (In-District): $6,547
Enrollment: 4,764 Coed
Affiliation or Control: State/Local IRS Status: 501(c)3
Highest Offering: Associate Degree
Accreditation: M, ADNUR

01 President ... Dr. Orinthia T. MONTAGUE
05 Provost and VP of Academic Affairs ... Dr. Paul REIFENHEISER
10 VP for Finance and Administration ... Mr. Bill TALBOT
32 Vice President for Student Services ... Mr. Greg MCCALLEY
15 VP for Human Resources ... Ms. Sharon CLARK
31 Asst VP for College Relations ... Ms. Deb MOHLENHOFF
20 Associate Provost ... Dr. Malvika TALWAR
21 Comptroller ... Ms. Kathleen MCCONNELL
08 Library Director ... Mr. Gregg KIEHL
84 Associate Dean for Enrollment Mgmt ... Ms. LaSonya GRIGGS
121 Director of Student Success Service . Ms. Michelle NIGHTINGALE
37 Director of Financial Aid ... Ms. Tamara OLIVER
26 Director of Communications ... Mr. Bryan CHAMBALA
07 Assoc Director of Admissions ... Mr. Kar-Leam TOXEY
13 Chief Information Officer ... Mr. Timothy DENSMORE
19 Director of Safety & Security ... Mr. John GEBO
41 Athletic Director ... Mr. Mick R. MCDANIEL
39 Director of Residence Life ... Vacant
18 Director of Facilities ... Vacant
28 Chief Diversity Officer/Dir ODESS ... Mr. Seth THOMPSON
04 Exec Assistant to the President ... Ms. Jan BRHEL
102 Exec Director Foundation ... Ms. Julie GERG

Torah Temimah Talmudical Seminary (E)

3323 Richmond Avenue, Staten Island NY 10312
County: Kings FICE Identification: 021916
Unit ID: 196583
Telephone: (718) 853-8500 Carnegie Class: Spec-4-yr-Faith
FAX Number: (718) 854-0872 Calendar System: Semester
Established: 1978 Annual Undergrad Tuition & Fees: $11,050
Enrollment: 45 Male
Affiliation or Control: Independent Non-Profit IRS Status: 501(c)3
Highest Offering: Second Talmudic Degree
Accreditation: RABN

01 President & Dean ... Rabbi L. MARGULIES
06 Registrar ... Rabbi Moshe SCHACHAR
37 Financial Aid Administrator ... Mr. Martin WALDMAN
10 Chief Financial Officer ... Rabbi Tzvi MARGULIES
11 Administrator ... Rabbi Betzalel BUSEL

*Touro College Executive Offices (F)

500 7th Avenue, New York NY 10018
County: New York Identification: 667405
Unit ID: 196592
Telephone: (646) 565-6000 Carnegie Class: N/A
FAX Number: N/A
URL: www.touro.edu

01 President/Chief Executive Officer ... Dr. Alan KADISH
03 Executive Vice President ... Rabbi Moshe D. KRUPKA
10 Senior Vice President & CFO ... Mr. Melvin M. NESS
05 Senior Vice President and Provost ... Ms. Patricia SALKIN
43 Senior VP of Legal Affairs ... Mr. Michael NEWMAN
11 Sr Vice Pres/Chief Admin Officer ... Mr. Jeffrey ROSENGARTEN
13 VP of Operations & Info Systems ... Dr. Franklin STEEN
86 Assoc VP of Govt Affairs ... Mr. Clifford METH
116 Institutional Auditor ... Ms. Sabine CHARLES
05 Provost for Biomedical Research ... Dr. Salomon AMAR
84 VP Student Administrative Services ... Mr. Matthew BONILLA
20 VP Undergrad Acad Affs/Dean of Fac ... Dr. Stanley L. BOYLAN
32 VP Plng & Assessment/Dean of Stdnts ... Mr. Robert GOLDSCHMIDT
53 Dean Grad School Education ... Dr. Jacob EASLEY, II
58 Vice Pres of Grad Studies ... Dr. Nadja GRAFF
05 Touro Provost for Biomedical Affair ... Dr. Edward HALPERIN
88 Vice Pres of Community Engagement ... Rabbi Alan CINER
88 Liaison European Branch Campuses ... Dr. Simcha FISHBANE
31 VP of Community Affairs ... Dr. Martin KATZENSTEIN
56 Vice President IPE/Dean NYSCAS ... Dr. Judah WEINBERGER
111 Vice Pres Institutional Advancement ... Mr. Paul GLASSER
106 VP Online Educ/Dn Women's Division ... Dr. Marian STOLTZ-LOIKE
85 VP for International Affairs ... Dr. Israel SINGER
09 Director Institutional Research ... Mr. Evan HOBERMAN
52 Dean College of Dental Medicine ... Dr. Ronnie MYERS
63 Dean Col of Osteopathic Med ... Dr. Kenneth STEIER
61 Dean Touro Law Center ... Ms. Elena LANGAN
67 Dean College of Pharmacy ... Dr. Henry COHEN
76 Dean of School of Health Sciences ... Dr. Louis H. PRIMAVERA
58 Dean Grad School Jewish Studies ... Dr. Michael A. SHMIDMAN
72 Dean Grad School of Technology ... Dr. Issac HERSKOWITZ
70 Dean Graduate School of Social Work ... Dr. Steven HUBERMAN
70 Acting Dean School of Social Work ... Dr. Nancy GALLINA
12 Dean Lander College for Men ... Dr. Moshe Z. SOKOL
49 Dean-Lander Coll of Arts & Sciences ... Dr. Henry ABRAMSON
50 Dean Grad School of Business ... Dr. Mary LO RE
38 Dean of Advising & Counseling ... Dr. Avery HOROWITZ
51 Asst Dean School Lifelong Education ... Dr. Briendy STERN
06 University Registrar ... Ms. Lidia MEINDL
37 Dir Reg Compliance/Financial Aid ... Mr. Matthew LIEBERMAN
08 Director of Libraries ... Ms. Bashe SIMON
07 Director of Admissions ... Dr. Benjamin ENOMA
76 Director Physician Asst Program ... Dr. Joseph TOMMASINO
75 Director of Occupational Therapy ... Dr. Stephanie DAPICE-WONG
76 Director of Physical Therapy ... Ms. Jill HORBACEWICZ
88 Pgm Dir Speech/Lang Path Grad Pgm ... Ms. Hindy LUBINSKY
110 AVP Institutional Advancement ... Ms. Beth GORIN
110 AVP Institutional Advancement ... Ms. Linda HOWARD-WEISSMAN
91 Chief Info Security Officer ... Ms. Patricia CIUFFO
19 Director of Security ... Ms. Lydia PEREZ
19 Dir of Emergency Preparedness ... Ms. Shoshana YEHUDAH
15 Director of Human Resources ... Mr. Thomas MODERO
96 Director of Purchasing ... Ms. Wanda HERNANDEZ
18 Dir of Facilities/Real Estate ... Mr. Mark GOODMAN
21 Controller ... Mr. Stuart LIPPMAN
26 Dir of Communication/External Rels ... Ms. Elisheva SCHLAM
36 Director Student Placement ... Mrs. Jodi SMOLEN
25 Director Office Sponsored Pgm ... Mr. Glenn DAVIS
04 Administrative Asst to President ... Ms. Elaine GOLDBERG
88 Asst to Exec Vice President ... Ms. Amy JACOBS
104 Director Study Abroad ... Dr. Chana SOSEVSKY
105 Director Web Services ... Ms. Lisa HALBERSTAM
41 Athletic Director ... Mr. Irv BADER
114 Director of Budget & Planning ... Mr. David BELL

*Touro College Main Campus (G)

320 West 31st St, New York NY 10001
County: New York FICE Identification: 010142
Telephone: (212) 463-0400 Carnegie Class: DU-Mod
FAX Number: N/A Calendar System: Semester
URL: www.touro.edu
Established: 1971 Annual Undergrad Tuition & Fees: N/A
Enrollment: N/A Coed
Affiliation or Control: Independent Non-Profit IRS Status: 501(c)3
Highest Offering: Doctorate
Accreditation: M, ARCPA, CAEP, NURSE, OT, PTA, RAD, SP, SW

58 Vice President Graduate Division ... Dr. Nadja GRAFF
35 VP Student Admin Services ... Mr. Matthew F. BONILLA
85 Vice Pres International Affairs ... Dr. Israel SINGER
56 VP IPE/Dean NYSCAS ... Dr. Judah WEINBERGER
53 Dean Graduate Sch of Education ... Dr. Jacob EASLEY, II
58 Dean Graduate Sch of Jewish Studies ... Dr. Michael A. SHMIDMAN
72 Dean Grad Sch of Tech ... Dr. Issac HERSKOWITZ
06 University Registrar ... Ms. Lidia MEINDL
08 Director of Libraries ... Ms. Bashe SIMON
88 Assoc Dean Grad Sch Jewish Studies ... Dr. Moshe SHERMAN
88 Assoc Dean Grad Sch of Education ... Dr. Marcella BULLMASTER-DAY
88 Assoc Dean Sch of Health Sciences ... Dr. Rivka MOLINSKY
88 Assoc Dean Grad Sch of Education ... Dr. Yuriy KARPOV
88 Associate Dean NYSCAS ... Mr. Lenin ORTEGA
88 Associate Dean NYSCAS ... Ms. Elvira TSIRULNIK
07 Director Undergraduate Admissions ... Mr. Arthur WIGFALL
123 Director Graduate Admissions ... Dr. Benjamin ENOMA
88 Asst Dean Grad Sch Ed/Chair/Lead ... Dr. Nilda SOTO-RUIZ
88 Chair Grad Sch Ed Disabilities ... Dr. Laurie BOBLEY
88 Chair Grad Sch Ed Sch Counseling ... Dr. Yair MAMAN
88 Dir Grad Sch Ed Lander Center ... Dr. Velma L. COBB
88 Ch Grad Sch Ed Early Child/Sp Ed ... Dr. Susan COUREY
88 Chair Grad Sch Ed Child Ed/Sp Ed . Dr. Elina LAMPERT-SHEPEL
88 Chair Grad Sch Ed Jewish Chld/Sp Ed ... Dr. Jeffrey LICHTMAN
88 Chair Grad Sch Ed Literacy ... Dr. Elaine NIKOLAKAKOS
76 Chair Sch Hlth Sci Physical Therapy ... Dr. Jill HORBACEWICZ
88 Chair Grad Sch Ed TESOL ... Dr. Olga DEJESUS
88 Chair Grad Sch Ed Math Ed ... Dr. Brenda STRASSFELD
75 Chair Sch Hlth Sci OccupTherapy .. Dr. Stephanie DAPICE-WONG
88 Dir Grad Sch Ed Clinical Practice ... Dr. Ruth BEST
88 Director Physician Assistant ... Ms. Paula PASHKOFF
01 President/Chief Executive Officer ... Dr. Alan KADISH
03 Executive Vice President ... Rabbi Moshe D. KRUPKA
10 Senior Vice President & CFO ... Mr. Mevin M. NESS
05 Senior Vice President and Provost ... Ms. Patricia SALKIN
43 Senior Vice President Legal Affairs ... Mr. Michael NEWMAN
11 Senior Vice Pres/Chief Admin Office . Mr. Jeffrey ROSENGARTEN
13 VP Operations & Info Systems ... Dr. Franklin STEEN
86 Assoc Vice Pres Government Affairs ... Mr. Clifford METH
116 Institutional Auditor ... Ms. Sabine CHARLES
05 Provost for Biomedical Research ... Dr. Salomon AMAR
20 VP Undergrad Ed/Dean Facilities ... Dr. Stanley BOYLAN
32 VP Plng Assessment/Dean Students ... Dr. Robert GOLDSCHMIDT
05 Touro Provost Biomedical Affairs ... Dr. Edward HALPERIN
31 VP Community Engagement ... Rabbi Alan CINER
88 Liaison European Branch Campuses ... Dr. Simcha FISHBANE
31 VP Community Affairs ... Mr. Martin KATZENSTEIN
111 VP Institutional Advancement ... Mr. Paul GLASSER
106 VP Online Educ/Dean Womens Division ... Dr. Marian STOLTZ-LOIKE
09 Director Institutional Research ... Mr. Evan HOBERMAN
52 Dean College of Dental Medicine ... Dr. Ronnie MYERS
63 Dean College Osteopathic Medicine ... Dr. Kenneth STEIER
61 Dean Touro Law Center ... Ms. Elena LANGAN
67 Dean College of Pharmacy ... Dr. Henry COHEN
76 Dean School of Health Sciences ... Dr. Louis H. PRIMAVERA
70 Acting Dean Grad Sch of Social Work ... Dr. Nancy GALLINA
12 Dean Lander College for Men ... Dr. Moshe SOKOL
49 Dean Lander College Arts & Sciences ... Dr. Henry ABRAMSON
38 Dean Advising & Counseling ... Dr. Avery HOROWITZ
50 Dean Grad School Business ... Dr. Mary LO RE
51 Asst Dean School Lifelong Education ... Dr. Briendy STERN
37 Dir Reg Compliance/Financial Aid ... Mr. Matthew LIEBERMAN
76 AVP Physician Assistant Program ... Dr. Joseph TOMMASINO
88 Chair SHS Speech Language Pathology ... Ms. Hindy LUBINSKY
83 Chr Sch Hlth Sci Behavioral Science ... Dr. Faye FRIED-WALKENFELD
110 AVP Institutional Advancement ... Ms. Beth GORIN
110 AVP Institutional Advancement ... Ms. Linda HOWARD-WEISSMAN
91 Chief Info Security Officer ... Ms. Patricia CIUFFO
19 Director of Security ... Ms. Lydia PEREZ
117 Director Emergency Preparedness ... Ms. Shoshana YEHUDAH
15 Director of Human Resources ... Mr. Thomas MODERO
96 Director of Purchasing ... Ms. Wanda HERNANDEZ
18 Director Facilities/Real Estate ... Mr. Mark GOODMAN
21 Controller ... Mr. Stuart LIPPMAN
26 Dir Communications/External Rels ... Ms. Elisheva SCHLAM
36 Director of Student Placement ... Ms. Jodi SMOLEN
25 Director Office Sponsored Programs ... Mr. Glenn DAVIS
04 Admin Asst to President ... Ms. Elaine GOLDBERG
88 Asst to Exec VP ... Ms. Amy JACOBS

104 Director Study Abroad .... Ms. Chana SOSEVSKY
105 Director Web Services .... Ms. Lisa HALBERSTAM
41 Athletic Director .... Mr. Irv BADER
114 Director Budget & Planning .... Mr. David BELL

* Touro College Flatbush (A)
1602 Avenue J, Brooklyn NY 11230
Telephone: (718) 252-7800 Identification: 770146
Accreditation: &M, SP

* Touro College Harlem (B)
230 West 125th Street, New York NY 10027
Telephone: (646) 981-4500 Identification: 770989
Accreditation: &M, OSTEO, PHAR

* Touro College Jacob D. Fuchsberg Law Center (C)
225 Eastview Drive, Central Islip NY 11722
Telephone: (631) 761-7000 Identification: 770148
Accreditation: &M, LAW

* Touro College Kew Gardens Hills (D)
75-31 150th Street, Kew Gardens Hills NY 11367
Telephone: (718) 820-4800 Identification: 770992
Accreditation: &M

* Touro College of Dental Medicine (E)
19 Skyline Dr, Hawthorne NY 10532
Telephone: (914) 594-3865 Identification: 770991
Accreditation: &M, DENT

* Touro College of Osteopathic Medicine - Middletown Campus (F)
60 Prospect Avenue, Middletown NY 10940
Telephone: (845) 648-1100 Identification: 770990
Accreditation: &M, #ARCPA, &OSTEO

Trocaire College (G)
360 Choate Avenue, Buffalo NY 14220-2094
County: Erie FICE Identification: 002812
Unit ID: 196653
Telephone: (716) 826-1200 Carnegie Class: Spec-4-yr-Other Health
FAX Number: (716) 828-6109 Calendar System: Semester
URL: www.trocaire.edu
Established: 1958 Annual Undergrad Tuition & Fees: $18,340
Enrollment: 1,376 Coed
Affiliation or Control: Independent Non-Profit IRS Status: 501(c)3
Highest Offering: Baccalaureate
Accreditation: M, ADNUR, CAHIIM, NUR, RAD, SURGT

01 President .... Dr. Bassam M. DEEB
03 Senior Vice President .... Dr. Richard T. LINN
10 VP for Finance .... Mr. Michael CUCINOTTA
05 Vice President for Academic Affairs .... Dr. Allyson M. LOWE
32 Chief Student Affairs Officer .... Ms. Kathleen SAUNDERS
111 Exec Director of Advancement .... Ms. Dianna CIVELLO
13 AVP Technology/Information Svcs .... Vacant
88 Special Asst to Pres External Affs .... Ms. Jacqueline MATHENY
66 Dean McAuley School Nursing .... Dr. Ann-Marie JOHN
15 Chief Human Resources Officer .... Ms. Janet PETERS
07 Interim Director of Admissions .... Ms. Danielle SCHMIDT
37 Director of Financial Aid .... Mr. Sean HUDSON
25 Grant Coordinator .... Vacant
06 Registrar .... Ms. Dorothy WORRALL
121 Dir Advisement & Student Support .... Dr. Christine RYAN
88 Director Learning Center .... Dr. Verjaun GORDON
124 Director of Student Engagement .... Ms. Lauren RECZEK
18 Facilities Director .... Mr. Richard MCGILVRAY
30 Director of Development .... Ms. Monica STAGE
84 Interim Chief Enrollment Officer .... Mrs. Mollie A. BALLARO
40 Manager Bookstore .... Mr. Connor CLARKE
76 Dean of Allied Health & Professions .... Dr. Linda KERWIN
108 Coordinator of Assessment/Research .... Ms. Kate LEVY
103 VP for Innovation/Workforce Devel .... Dr. Gary SMITH
36 Coord of Career Services .... Mr. David FERRIS, JR.

Ulster County Community College (H)
491 Cottekill Road, PO Box 557, Stone Ridge NY 12484
County: Ulster FICE Identification: 002880
Unit ID: 196699
Telephone: (845) 687-5000 Carnegie Class: Assoc/HT-High Non
FAX Number: (845) 687-5083 Calendar System: Semester
URL: www.sunyulster.edu
Established: 1961 Annual Undergrad Tuition & Fees (In-District): $5,740
Enrollment: 3,089 Coed
Affiliation or Control: State/Local IRS Status: 501(c)3
Highest Offering: Associate Degree
Accreditation: M, ADNUR

01 President .... Dr. Alan P. ROBERTS
84 Acting Dean of Enrollment Mgmt .... Ms. Megan SHEELEY
05 VP for Academic Affairs .... Mr. Kevin STONER
51 AVP of Continuing & Prof Educ .... Mr. Christopher MARX
10 VP for Administrative Services .... Ms. Jamie CAPUANO
13 Chief Info Technology Officer .... Mr. Dennis MICHAELS
111 Exec Dir of Inst Advance & Ext Rels .... Ms. Lorraine SALMON
100 Acting Chief of Staff .... Ms. Jennifer ZELL
08 Director of Library Services .... Ms. Kari MACK
37 Director of Financial Aid .... Mr. Christopher CHANG
06 Registrar .... Ms. Sarah FAJARDO
41 Asst Dean Students/Athletic Dir .... Mr. Matthew BRENNIE
19 Director of Safety & Security .... Mr. Wayne FREER
26 Director of Marketing & Media .... Ms. Deborah KAUFMAN
36 Dir Student Place/Acad Support Svcs .... Ms. Jane KITHCART
32 Coordinator of Campus Life .... Ms. Megan SHEELEY
18 Director of Plant Operations .... Mr. Donald STEWARD, III
09 Director of Institutional Research .... Ms. Laura FOSS
103 AVP Workforce Development .... Mr. Christopher MARX
15 Director of Personnel Services .... Mrs. Debra DELANOY
11 Dean of Admin Services - Finance .... Ms. Amy WINTERS
28 Dean for Admin Op & Title IX Coord .... Mr. Kenneth JURAS
96 Coord Procurement/General Services .... Vacant
101 Secretary of the Institution/Board .... Ms. Jennifer ZELL
121 Assistant Dean of Student Success .... Ms. Wendy BEESLEY
78 Asst Dean Workforce/Career/Apprent .... Mrs. Barbara REER
22 Dir Affirmative Action/Equal Opty .... Ms. Jamie CAPUANO

Unification Theological Seminary (I)
4 West 43rd Street 2nd Floor, New York NY 10036
County: Manhattan FICE Identification: 032163
Unit ID: 246789
Telephone: (212) 563-6647 Carnegie Class: Spec-4-yr-Faith
FAX Number: (212) 563-6431 Calendar System: Semester
URL: www.uts.edu
Established: 1975 Annual Undergrad Tuition & Fees: N/A
Enrollment: 130 Coed
Affiliation or Control: Unification Church IRS Status: 501(c)3
Highest Offering: Doctorate
Accreditation: M

01 President .... Dr. Thomas WARD
05 Academic Dean .... Dr. Keisuke NODA
11 Vice President .... Dr. Michael MICKLER
88 Director of Field Education .... Dr. Thomas WARD
10 Director of Finances .... Mr. Frank ZOCHOL
06 Registrar .... Mrs. Ute DELANEY
08 Librarian .... Mr. Robert WAGNER
37 Student Financial Aid Director .... Mr. Henry CHRISTOPHER
18 Plant Director .... Mr. Carl VERDERBER
84 Dean of Enrollment Management .... Mr. Steven BOYD
32 Chief Student Affairs/Student Life .... Mr. Steven BOYD
13 Chief Info Technology Officer .... Mr. Robert PUMPHREY
04 Admin Assistant to the President .... Ms. Christina MIYAKE

Union College (J)
807 Union Street, Schenectady NY 12308-3181
County: Schenectady FICE Identification: 002889
Unit ID: 196866
Telephone: (518) 388-6000 Carnegie Class: Bac-A&S
FAX Number: (518) 388-6800 Calendar System: Trimester
URL: www.union.edu
Established: 1795 Annual Undergrad Tuition & Fees: $59,502
Enrollment: 2,047 Coed
Affiliation or Control: Independent Non-Profit IRS Status: 501(c)3
Highest Offering: Baccalaureate
Accreditation: M

01 President .... Dr. David R. HARRIS
05 Int Vice Pres Academic Affairs .... Dr. Michele P. ANGRIST
111 Vice President College Relations .... Dr. Robert J. PARKER, JR.
10 AVP for Finance & Administration .... Ms. Marsha R. ANDERSON-BEWERSDORF
07 VP Admissions/Fin Aid/Enrollment ... Mr. Matthew J. MALATESTA
100 Chief of Staff .... Ms. Darcy CZAJKA
22 Chief Diversity Officer .... Vacant
32 VP Student Affairs/Dean of Students .... Dr. Fran 'Cee BROWN-MCCLURE
20 Dean of Studies .... Vacant
13 Chief Information Officer .... Ms. Ellen YU
06 Senior Registrar .... Ms. Katherine A. YAUNEY
08 College Librarian .... Ms. Frances J. MALOY
26 Director of Media and Public Rels .... Mr. Phillip J. WAJDA
37 Director of Financial Aid .... Ms. Linda M. PARKER
38 Director of Student Counseling .... Mr. Marcus S. HOTALING
36 Assoc Director of Career Center .... Mr. Peter A. FOWLER
15 Chief Human Resources Officer .... Mr. Tye A. DIENES
41 Assoc Director of Athletics .... Ms. Beth TIFFANY
19 Director Campus Safety .... Mr. Christopher M. HAYEN
39 Director Residence Life .... Ms. Amanda J. IVERSON
09 Director of Institutional Research .... Mr. Len SCHLEGEL
108 Director Institutional Assessment .... Mr. Ashok RAMASUBRAMANIAN

† Tuition figure is a comprehensive fees figure.

Union Theological Seminary (K)
3041 Broadway, New York NY 10027-5792
County: New York FICE Identification: 002890
Unit ID: 196884
Telephone: (212) 662-7100 Carnegie Class: Spec-4-yr-Faith
FAX Number: (212) 280-1416 Calendar System: Semester
URL: www.utsnyc.edu
Established: 1836 Annual Graduate Tuition & Fees: N/A
Enrollment: 226 Coed
Affiliation or Control: Independent Non-Profit IRS Status: 501(c)3
Highest Offering: Doctorate; No Undergraduates
Accreditation: M, THEOL

01 President .... Dr. Serene JONES
03 Executive Vice President .... Mr. Fred DAVIE
10 VP Finance & Operations .... Mr. Brent DICKMAN
30 VP for Development .... Ms. Rita WALTERS
05 VP of Academic Affairs and Dean ..... Dr. Pamela COOPER-WHITE
32 Dean of Students .... Ms. Charlene VISCONTI
78 Senior Director of Integrative Educ .... Dr. Su Y. PAK
07 VP for Admissions and Financial Aid .... Ms. Vanessa HUTCHINSON
06 Registrar .... Ms. Nicole MIRANDO
18 Deputy Vice Pres Building/Grounds .... Mr. Michael MALONEY
39 Director Housing/Campus Services . Mr. Michael ORZECHOWSKI
15 Director Personnel Services .... Ms. Diana TORRES-PETRILLI
100 Chief of Staff .... Mr. Jody WEST
13 Chief Info Technology Officer (CIO) .... Mr. Donald JOSHUA
29 Manager Alumni Relations/Ind Giving .... Mr. Kevin BENTLEY
37 Director Student Financial Aid .... Ms. Melissa DESRAVINES

United Talmudical Seminary (L)
191 Rodney Street, Brooklyn NY 11211-7900
County: Kings FICE Identification: 011189
Unit ID: 197018
Telephone: (718) 963-9770 Carnegie Class: Spec-4-yr-Faith
FAX Number: (718) 963-9775 Calendar System: Semester
Established: 1949 Annual Undergrad Tuition & Fees: $15,300
Enrollment: 3,118 Male
Affiliation or Control: Independent Non-Profit IRS Status: 501(c)3
Highest Offering: Second Talmudic Degree
Accreditation: RABN

01 Dean .... Rabbi Zalman TEITLBAUM
05 Assoc Dean Scholastic Services .... Rabbi Yeruchem DEUTSCH
37 Financial Aid Administrator .... Mr. Bernard KATZ
10 Business Officer .... Mr. Solomon GREENFELD

University of Rochester (M)
500 Joseph C. Wilson Boulevard, Rochester NY 14627
County: Monroe FICE Identification: 002894
Unit ID: 195030
Telephone: (585) 275-2121 Carnegie Class: DU-Highest
FAX Number: (585) 275-0359 Calendar System: Semester
URL: www.rochester.edu
Established: 1850 Annual Undergrad Tuition & Fees: $58,241
Enrollment: 11,741 Coed
Affiliation or Control: Independent Non-Profit IRS Status: 501(c)3
Highest Offering: Doctorate
Accreditation: M, CACREP, CLPSY, DENT, IPSY, MED, MFCD, MT, MUS, NURSE, PAST, PDPSY, PH

01 President .... Mrs. Sarah C. MANGELSDORF
05 Interim Provost .... Ms. Sarah PEYRE
10 Sr Vice Pres Admin & Fin/CFO .... Ms. Holly G. CRAWFORD
17 Sr Vice Pres Health Sci/Med Ctr CEO ...... Dr. Mark B. TAUBMAN
115 Sr Vice Pres/Chief Investment Ofcr .... Mr. Douglas PHILLIPS
111 SVP & Chief Advancement Officer .... Mr. Thomas FARRELL
43 Vice Pres & General Counsel .... Ms. Donna G. PAYNE
28 Vice Pres Equity & Inclusion/CDO .... Mrs. Mercedes RAMÍREZ FERNÁNDEZ
26 Vice Pres Communications .... Ms. Elizabeth STAUDERMAN
13 Vice Pres/CIO for the University .... Mr. David E. LEWIS
58 Vice Provost/Univ Dean of Grad Ed .... Ms. Melissa STURGE-APPLE
100 Pres Chief of Staff/Board Secretary .... Mr. Tony GREEN
32 Dean of Students Arts/Sci & Engr .... Mr. Matthew BURNS
08 Dean River Campus Libraries .... Ms. Mary Ann MAVRINAC
49 Dean of School of Arts & Sciences .... Ms. Gloria CULVER
88 Dean of Arts/Sci & Engr Faculty .... Mr. Donald HALL
54 Dean of Hajim Engineering School .... Ms. Wendi HEINZELMAN
07 Dir of AS&E Undergrad Admissions .... Mr. Jason NEVINGER
37 Director of Financial Aid .... Ms. Samantha VEEDER
108 Assoc Provost Academic Admin .... Ms. Jane Marie SOUZA
114 Sr Assoc VP Budgets & Planning .... Mr. Michael W. ANDREWS
63 Dean School of Medicine & Dentistry .... Dr. Mark B. TAUBMAN
64 Dean of Eastman School of Music .... Mr. Jamal ROSSI
66 Dean of School of Nursing .... Ms. Kathy RIDEOUT
50 Dean of Simon Business School .... Mr. Andrew AINSLIE
53 Dean Warner Grad Sch Educ & Hum Dev .... Vacant
35 Assoc Dean Students Arts/Sci & Engr .... Ms. Anne-Marie ALGIER
23 Chief Medical Officer .... Dr. Michael J. APOSTOLAKOS
52 Dir Eastman Institute Oral Health .... Dr. Eli ELIAV
25 Assoc VP Research & Project Admin .... Ms. Gunta LIDERS
18 Sr AVP Facilities & Services .... Mr. Michael CHIHOSKI
29 AVP Alumni & Constituent Relations .... Dr. Karen CHANCE MERCURIUS
86 Vice Pres Govt/Community Relations .... Mr. Peter J. ROBINSON
96 Assoc Vice Pres Purchasing & Supply .... Mr. Carl TIETJEN
04 Executive Asst to the President .... Ms. Deb DALE
06 University Registrar .... Ms. Tina STURGIS
19 Director of Public Safety .... Mr. Mark T. FISCHER
15 VP/Chief Human Resources Officer .... Ms. Kathleen GALLUCCI
88 Dir of the Memorial Art Gallery .... Mr. Jonathan BINSTOCK
41 Director of Athletics & Recreation .... Mr. George VANDERZWAAG
39 Exec Dir Res Life & Housing Svcs .. Ms. Laurel CONTOMANOLIS
36 Assoc Vice Provost Career Education .... Mr. Joe TESTANI
101 Administrator to Board of Trustees .... Ms. Jackie E. KING
42 Director Religious & Spiritual Life .... Rev. Denise YARBROUGH

104 Director Study Abroad ....Ms. Tynelle STEWART
22 AVP Equity & Inclusion ....Ms. Adrienne MORGAN
09 Sr Univ Dir Institutional Research ....Mr. John PODVIN

U.T.A. Mesivta of Kiryas Joel (A)

PO Box 2009, Monroe NY 10949-8509
County: Orange FICE Identification: 038023
Unit ID: 446604
Telephone: (845) 783-9901 Carnegie Class: Spec-4-yr-Faith
FAX Number: (845) 782-3620 Calendar System: Semester
Established: 1999 Annual Undergrad Tuition & Fees: $13,500
Enrollment: 2,268 Male
Affiliation or Control: Independent Non-Profit IRS Status: 501(c)3
Highest Offering: First Talmudic Degree
Accreditation: RABN

00 Chief Executive Officer ....David GOLDBERGER
01 President ....Elias HOROWITZ
05 Rosh Yeshiva .... Rabbi Aharon TEITELBAUM
37 Financial Aid Director ....David SCHWARTZ

Utica College (B)

1600 Burrstone Road, Utica NY 13502-4892
County: Oneida FICE Identification: 002883
Unit ID: 197045
Telephone: (315) 792-3111 Carnegie Class: Masters/L
FAX Number: (315) 792-3292 Calendar System: Semester
URL: www.utica.edu
Established: 1946 Annual Undergrad Tuition & Fees: $22,110
Enrollment: 4,613 Coed
Affiliation or Control: Independent Non-Profit IRS Status: 501(c)3
Highest Offering: Doctorate
Accreditation: M, ACBSP, CONST, @DIETC, NURSE, OT, PTA

01 President .... Dr. Laura CASAMENTO
05 Provost & Vice Pres Academic Aff .... Dr. Todd PFANNESTIEL
10 Vice Pres Financial Affs/Treasurer ....Ms. Pamela SALMON
32 SVP Student Life & Enrollment ....Dr. Jeffrey GATES
04 Executive Assistant to President ....Ms. Elizabeth CRANE
111 VP of Advancement ....Mr. George NEHME
13 VP for Infrastructure and CIO ....Mr. Matthew S. CARR
28 VP DEI Chief Diversity Officer .... Dr. Anthony M. BAIRD
20 Associate Provost ....Dr. Robert M. HALLIDAY
26 Asst VP Marketing/Communication ....Mr. Kelly L. ADAMS
76 Dean for Health Professions/Educ ....Dr. Ahmed Y. RADWAN
49 Dean for Arts & Sciences ....Dr. Sharon H. WISE
50 Dean for Business & Justice Studies ....Dr. Stephanie R. NESBITT
35 Dean of Students ....Mr. Scott NONEMAKER
113 Dir of Student Accounting .... Ms. Susan BOUCHER
36 Director Career Services ....Vacant
37 Director of Financial Aid ....Ms. Karolina HOLL
06 Registrar ....Mr. Craig DEWAN
30 Director of Development ....Ms. Ashlea SCHAD
41 Director of Physical Educ/Athletics .... Mr. David FONTAINE
39 Director of Student Living ....Ms. Marissa FINCH
13 Dir College Info & Application Svcs .... Mr. Scott HUMPHREY
15 Director of Human Resources ....Ms. Lisa GREEN
107 Exec Dir Corp/Professional Pgms .... Ms. Joni L. PULLIAM
85 Dean of International Education .... Ms. Deborah WILSON-ALLAM
18 Director Facilities Management ....Mr. Daniel C. BOLLANA
19 Director of Campus Safety .... Mr. Musco MILLNER
92 Director Honors Program .... Dr. Lawrence DAY
28 Dir Office of Opportunity Programs ....Mr. John OSSOWSKI
96 Manager of Purchasing ....Ms. Bobbi H. SMOROL
101 Secretary to the Board ....Ms. Elizabeth CRANE
108 Dean of Academic Assessment .... Dr. Ann DAMIANO
08 Head Librarian ....Mr. James K. TELIHA
106 Assoc Prov/VP E-learning ....Dr. Polly SMITH
43 Dir Legal Services/General Counsel ..... Mr. Andrew W. BEAKMAN
09 Assoc Director of Inst Research ....Ms. Brandy GRAY
117 VP for Emergency Management .... Mr. Shad M. CROWE

Vassar College (C)

124 Raymond Avenue, Poughkeepsie NY 12604-0001
County: Dutchess FICE Identification: 002895
Unit ID: 197133
Telephone: (845) 437-7000 Carnegie Class: Bac-A&S
FAX Number: (845) 437-7187 Calendar System: Semester
URL: www.vassar.edu
Established: 1861 Annual Undergrad Tuition & Fees: $60,930
Enrollment: 2,435 Coed
Affiliation or Control: Independent Non-Profit IRS Status: 501(c)3
Highest Offering: Master's
Accreditation: M

01 President .... Dr. Elizabeth BRADLEY
05 Dean of the Faculty .... Mr. William HOYNES
20 Dean of the College .... Mr. Carlos ALAMO
10 Vice Pres Finance & Administration ....Mr. Bryan SWARTHOUT
13 VP CIS/Chief Information Officer .... Mr. Carlos GARCIA
07 Dean Admission/Financial Aid ....Ms. Sonya SMITH
49 Dean of Studies ....Dr. Benjamin LOTTO
20 Sr Assoc Dean College Prof Dev ....Mr. Edward L. PITTMAN
35 Assoc Dean Col/Dir Campus Activit .... Ms. Teresa QUINN
06 Registrar .... Ms. Colleen MALLET
08 Director of the Libraries ....Mr. Andrew ASHTON
36 Director Career Development
Center ....Ms. Stacy Lee SCHNEIDER BINGHAM
15 AVP Human Resources .... Ms. Sarah BAKKE

18 Exec Dir of Facilities Operations .... Mr. William PEABODY
38 Director of Psychological Services ....Dr. Wendy A. FREEDMAN
96 Director of Purchasing .... Ms. Rosaleen CARDILLO
04 Exec Asst to President .... Ms. Veronica PECCIA
104 Director Study Abroad .... Dr. Tracey HOLLAND
19 Director Security/Safety .... Ms. Arlene SABO
29 VP Alumni Relations/Exe Dir AAVC .... Ms. Lisa TESSLER
41 Athletic Director .... Ms. Michelle WALSH

Vaughn College of Aeronautics and Technology (D)

86-01 23rd Avenue, Flushing NY 11369
County: Queens FICE Identification: 002665
Unit ID: 188340
Telephone: (718) 429-6600 Carnegie Class: Bac/Assoc-Mixed
FAX Number: (718) 429-0671 Calendar System: Semester
URL: www.vaughn.edu
Established: 1932 Annual Undergrad Tuition & Fees: $26,150
Enrollment: 1,442 Coed
Affiliation or Control: Independent Non-Profit IRS Status: 501(c)3
Highest Offering: Master's
Accreditation: M, AAB, IACBE

01 President ....Dr. Sharon B. DEVIVO
10 Vice Pres for Business & Finance ......Mr. Robert G. WALDMANN
84 Vice President Enrollment Services ....Vacant
15 Assoc VP College Services/Human Res ....Ms. Mary DURKIN
05 Vice Pres of Academic Affairs ....Dr. Paul LAVERGNE
32 VP Student Affairs .... Ms. Kelli SMITH
35 Assoc VP/Dean Student Affairs .... Ms. Elaine T. WHITE
30 Asst VP Development/Alumni Affair ....Mr. Stephen DESALVO
37 Director of Financial Aid .... Ms. Tameika BENNETT
06 Registrar/Assoc VP Enrollment ....Mrs. Beatriz CRUZ
08 Librarian ....Vacant
26 Assoc VP of Public Affairs ....Ms. Maureen KIGGINS
96 Coordinator of Purchasing .... Mr. Manuel ADRIANZEN
09 Manager of Inst Effectiveness ....Vacant
07 Assoc VP Enrollment ....Mr. Celso ALVAREZ
18 Director of Facilities ....Mr. Justin BURMEISTER
38 Dir Student Counseling/Wellness .... Ms. Stacey DUTIL
13 Asst Director Computer Operations ..... Mr. Hamwant (Neil) SINGH
88 Vice Pres Training .... Mr. Domenic PROSCIA
04 Administrative Asst to President .... Ms. Barbara LOCKE
103 Dir Workforce/Career Development ....Mr. Phil MEADE
106 Dir Online Education/E-learning ....Vacant
41 Athletic Director .... Mr. Ricky MCCOLLUM
29 Director Alumni Relations ....Vacant
19 Director Security/Safety ....Mr. Martin CAPUNAY
101 Secretary of the Institution/Board ....Vacant
39 Director Resident Life/Student Hous ....Ms. Becky FALTO

Villa Maria College of Buffalo (E)

240 Pine Ridge Road, Buffalo NY 14225-3999
County: Erie FICE Identification: 002896
Unit ID: 197142
Telephone: (716) 896-0700 Carnegie Class: Bac/Assoc-Mixed
FAX Number: (716) 896-0705 Calendar System: Semester
URL: www.villa.edu
Established: 1960 Annual Undergrad Tuition & Fees: $25,400
Enrollment: 508 Coed
Affiliation or Control: Independent Non-Profit IRS Status: 501(c)3
Highest Offering: Baccalaureate
Accreditation: M, CIDA, MUS, OTA, PTAA

01 President .... Dr. Matthew GIORDANO
05 Vice President for Academic Affairs .... Dr. Ryan HARTNETT
10 Vice President for Finance .... Mr. Richard PINKOWSKI
30 Vice President for Development .... Mrs. Mary ROBINSON
84 VP for Enrollment Mgmt & Operations .... Mr. Brian EMERSON
88 Vice President for Mission ....Dr. Donald MONNIN
20 Dean of Faculty ....Dr. Ann RIVERA
06 Registrar ....Mrs. Erin PAWLAK
07 Director of Admissions ....Ms. Becky STRATHEARN
08 Director of Library Services .... Ms. Lucy WAITE
37 Director of Financial Aid .... Ms. Aimee MURCH
09 Director of Institutional
Research ....Sr. Mary Albertine STACHOWSKI
38 Director of the Care Center ....Ms. Karen ZGODA
13 Director of Computer Services ....Vacant
18 Plant & Grounds Manager ....Mr. David WISNER
25 Director of Grants .... Mrs. Mary ROBINSON
88 Instructional Design & Program Dev .... Dr. Ryan HARTNETT
36 Dir Career Svcs & Internships .... Mrs. Judith PISKUN
42 Campus Minister ....Vacant
85 Director of Foreign Students ....Vacant
26 Communications Specialist .... Ms. Kristen SCHOBER
32 Director of Student Affairs ....Mr. DJ (Donald) SCHIER
22 Affirmative Action Officer ....Ms. Diane M. HANDZLIK
29 Director of Alumni Relations ....Ms. Rachel TABAK
121 Director Student Success Center ....Mrs. Elizabeth KERR
57 Art Department Chair ....Mr. Robert GRIZANTI
76 Health Sciences Chair ....Dr. Kim KOTZ
79 Humanities & Social Sci Chair ....Dr. Will MEYERS
64 Music Department Chair ....Mr. Anthony CASUCCIO
81 Natural Sciences/Prof Studies Chair ....Vacant
108 Director Institutional Assessment .... Dr. Matthew GIORDANO
04 Administrative Asst to President ....Ms. Michaelene KARPINSKI
103 Dir Workforce/Career Development .... Dr. Ryan HARTNETT
41 Director of Athletics .... Ms. Amanda JANOSKY
15 Director of Human Resources .... Dr. Carleen FLOREA

88 Director of Achieve ....Mrs. Jennifer CORNACCHIO
21 Accounting Manager ....Ms. Mary DETTELIS
88 Special Events Coordinator ....Mrs. Tracy ROZLER

Wagner College (F)

1 Campus Road, Staten Island NY 10301-4479
County: Richmond FICE Identification: 002899
Unit ID: 197197
Telephone: (718) 390-3100 Carnegie Class: Masters/M
FAX Number: (718) 390-3467 Calendar System: Semester
URL: www.wagner.edu
Established: 1883 Annual Undergrad Tuition & Fees: $50,010
Enrollment: 2,070 Coed
Affiliation or Control: Independent Non-Profit IRS Status: 501(c)3
Highest Offering: Doctorate
Accreditation: M, AAQEP, ACBSP, ARCPA, NUR

01 President ....Dr. Joel W. MARTIN
05 Provost/VP Academic Affairs .... Dr. Jeffrey KRAUS
84 Sr VP for Planning & Enrollment ....Mr. Angelo G. ARAIMO
11 VP Administration ....Vacant
04 Assistant to the President ....Ms. Ria CARNAVAS
32 VP Internationalization/Campus Life .....Ms. Ruta SHAH-GORDON
10 CFO/VP for Finance & Administration ....Mr. John CARRESCIA
108 Assoc Provost for Assessment ....Vacant
20 Assoc Provost for Academic Affairs ....Dr. Nicholas RICHARDSON
06 Registrar ....Ms. Athena TURNER-FREDERICK
13 Chief Information Officer ....Mr. Frank CAFASSO
42 Chaplain ....Ms. Elaine SCHENK
29 Director Alumni Relations .... Ms. Nicolina ASTORINA
39 Director Residential Educ ....Mr. Thomas TRESSLER-GELOK
30 Exec Director Development ....Ms. Kaitlin GIRTON
18 Director of Campus Operations ....Mr. Daniel SWITZER
41 Director of Athletics ....Mr. Walter HAMELINE
23 Dean of Health & Wellness ....Ms. Kathleen OBERFELDT
19 Security Supervisor .... Mr. Robert LARSON
15 Chief HR Officer & Title IX
Coord ....Ms. Jazzmine CLARKE-GLOVER
37 Director of Financial Aid .... Ms. Theresa WEIMER
58 Director of Graduate Studies ....Ms. Kathleen AHERN
07 Dean of Enrollment ....Vacant
09 IR Director/Asst Dir of Enrollment ....Ms. Patricia CLANCY
35 Assistant Dean Campus Life ....Ms. Ange CONCEPCION
36 Dean & Director CACE ....Dr. Matthew KUBACKI
08 Director of the Horrman Library .... Mr. Dennis SCHAUB
101 Secretary to BOT/Dir Planned Giving ....Mr. David MARTIN

Webb Institute (G)

298 Crescent Beach Road, Glen Cove NY 11542-1398
County: Nassau FICE Identification: 002900
Unit ID: 197221
Telephone: (516) 671-2213 Carnegie Class: Spec-4-yr-Eng
FAX Number: (516) 674-9838 Calendar System: Semester
URL: www.webb.edu
Established: 1889 Annual Undergrad Tuition & Fees: $52,880
Enrollment: 101 Coed
Affiliation or Control: Independent Non-Profit IRS Status: 501(c)3
Highest Offering: Baccalaureate
Accreditation: M

01 President ....Mr. R. Keith MICHEL
05 Director Academic Services .... Ms. Jocelyn WILSON
20 Assistant Dean ....Prof. Richard C. HARRIS
08 Librarian ....Ms. Patricia M. PRESCOTT
30 Director of Development ....Mr. Anthony ZIC
10 Director of Financial Affairs ....Ms. Rhonda LIGHTCAP
09 Director of Institutional Research ....Prof. Richard A. ROYCE
32 Director of Student Affairs ....Ms. Lauren CARBALLO
18 Director of Facilities ....Mr. John FERRANTE
84 Director of Admissions ....Ms. Lauren CARBALLO
29 Director of Alumni Relations ....Ms. Gailmarie SUJECKI
26 Chief Public Relations Officer ....Ms. Kerri ALLEGRETTA
13 Director of Information Tech ....Mr. Peter MILLER
06 Registrar ....Ms. Jocelyn M. WILSON
04 Administrative Asst to President ....Ms. Gailmarie SUJECKI
15 Director Personnel Services ....Ms. Svetlana MILLER
37 Director of Financial Aid ....Ms. Jocelyn M. WILSON

Weill Cornell Medicine (H)

1300 York Avenue, New York NY 10065-4805
Telephone: (212) 746-5454 FICE Identification: 004762
Accreditation: &M, ARCPA, DENT, IPSY, MED

† Regional accreditation is carried under the parent institution Cornell University, Ithaca, NY.

Wells College (I)

170 Main Street, Aurora NY 13026-0500
County: Cayuga FICE Identification: 002901
Unit ID: 197230
Telephone: (315) 364-3266 Carnegie Class: Bac-A&S
FAX Number: (315) 364-3227 Calendar System: Semester
URL: www.wells.edu
Established: 1868 Annual Undergrad Tuition & Fees: $31,800
Enrollment: 357 Coed
Affiliation or Control: Independent Non-Profit IRS Status: 501(c)3
Highest Offering: Baccalaureate
Accreditation: M, AAQEP

01 President .... Dr. Jonathan GIBRALTER
05 Provost and Dean of the College .... Dr. Cindy SPEAKER
10 Vice President and CFO .... Mr. Robert A. CREE
21 Controller .... Ms. Susan WEATHERBY
111 Vice President for Advancement .... Mr. Larry JEROME
32 Dean of Students .... Dr. Charles B. KENYON
84 Vice President for Enrollment Svcs .... Mr. Gerard TURBIDE
06 Assistant Registrar .... Ms. Melanie CULLEN
08 Assistant Library Director .... Ms. Tiffany RAYMOND
37 Director Financial Aid .... Ms. Laura BURNS
44 Director of Annual Giving .... Ms. Jessica CORTER
26 Dir of Communications/Marketing .... Mr. Christopher POLLOCK
112 Dir Planned/Leadership Giving .... Ms. Pamela SHERADIN
19 Interim Dir of Campus Safety .... Mr. John SAUL
18 Dir of Facilities/Physical Plant .... Mr. Brian BROWN
15 Manager of Human Resources .... Ms. Kit VAN ORMAN

Westchester Community College (A)

75 Grasslands Road, Valhalla NY 10595-1636
County: Westchester FICE Identification: 002881
Unit ID: 197294
Telephone: (914) 606-6600 Carnegie Class: Assoc/HT-Mix Trad/Non
FAX Number: (914) 606-6780 Calendar System: Semester
URL: www.sunywcc.edu
Established: 1946 Annual Undergrad Tuition & Fees (In-District): $5,036
Enrollment: 10,072 Coed
Affiliation or Control: State/Local IRS Status: 501(c)3
Highest Offering: Associate Degree
Accreditation: M, ADNUR, COARC, EMT, RAD

01 President .... Dr. Belinda S. MILES
05 Provost & VP Academic Affairs .... Dr. Vanessa MOREST
32 VP Stdnt Access/Involve/Success .... Vacant
10 VP/Dean Administrative Svcs/CFO .... Mr. Brian MURPHY
102 VP Ext Affairs/Exec Dir Foundation .... Vacant
103 VP Workforce Dev & Comm Education .... Ms. Teresita WISELL
100 VP Strategic Opers/Chief of Staff .... Dr. Shawn BROWN
81 Dean School of Math/Science/Engr .... Dr. Raymond HOUSTON
76 Dean School of Health Careers/Tech .... Dr. Ronald BLOOM
50 Dean School of Bus & Prof Careers .... Dr. Carmen Leonor MARTINEZ-LOPEZ
79 Dean School Arts/Hum/Soc Science .... Dr. Karen TAYLOR
22 Associate Dean & Director of EOC .... Dr. Gina GAINES
35 Assoc Dean Student Personnel Svcs .... Ms. Ellen ZENDMAN
08 Asc Dn Lrng Res/Dist Lrng/Inst Tech .... Ms. Pamela POLLARD
26 Director of College/Cmty Relations .... Mr. Mark STOLLAR
06 Registrar .... Mr. Christopher WESTBY
37 Dir of Student Financial Assistance .... Mr. Jason FRANKY
13 Vice President of IT .... Mr. Anthony SCORDINO
07 Director of Admissions .... Ms. Gloria DE LA PAZ
84 Assoc Dean Enrollment Management .... Dr. Ruben BARATO
15 Director Human Resources .... Ms. Aurora WORKMAN
88 Dir Faculty Student Assoc .... Mr. Joseph POPPA
45 Asst Dean Planning and Inst Effect .... Ms. Yelizaveta ADAMS
19 Director of Security .... Mr. Scott SULLIVAN
24 Director Media Services .... Mr. Gennaro MASELLI
41 Athletic Director .... Mr. Michael BELFIORE
21 Assoc Business Officer/Controller .... Ms. Dawn GILLINS
18 Director Physical Plant .... Mr. Robert CIRILLO
96 Deputy Purchasing Agent .... Mr. Stewart GLASS
27 Publications Manager .... Mr. Edward TATTON
23 Coordinator Student Health Services .... Ms. Janice GILROY
88 Coord of Transfer Services .... Ms. Robin GRAFF
101 Secretary of the Institution/Board .... Ms. Yolanda HOWELL
105 Director Web Services .... Mr. Patrick DANNENHOFFER
25 Chief Contract/Grants Administrator .... Dr. Laurie MILLER-MCNEILL
28 Director of Diversity .... Dr. Rinardo REDDICK
29 Director Alumni Affairs .... Ms. Michelle SCHLEIBAUM
44 Director Annual Giving .... Ms. Jessica DENARO

Yeshiva Derech Chaim (B)

1573 39th Street, Brooklyn NY 11218-4413
County: Kings FICE Identification: 022651
Unit ID: 197647
Telephone: (718) 438-5476 Carnegie Class: Spec-4-yr-Faith
FAX Number: (718) 435-9285 Calendar System: Semester
URL: https://ydc.edu/
Established: 1975 Annual Undergrad Tuition & Fees: $12,100
Enrollment: 127 Male
Affiliation or Control: Independent Non-Profit IRS Status: 501(c)3
Highest Offering: Second Talmudic Degree
Accreditation: RABN

01 President .... Rabbi Chaim RENNERT
01 President .... Rabbi Moshe PLUTCHOK

Yeshiva D'Monsey Rabbinical College (C)

2 Roman Boulevard, Monsey NY 10952-3106
County: Rockland FICE Identification: 031473
Unit ID: 420325
Telephone: (845) 426-3276 Carnegie Class: Spec-4-yr-Faith
FAX Number: (845) 352-1119 Calendar System: Semester
Established: 1984 Annual Undergrad Tuition & Fees: $7,500
Enrollment: 71 Male
Affiliation or Control: Independent Non-Profit IRS Status: 501(c)3
Highest Offering: Second Talmudic Degree
Accreditation: RABN

01 Rosh Yeshiva .... Rabbi Sholom GREEN
05 Rosh Yeshiva .... Rabbi Ruvain GREEN
37 Financial Aid Director .... Rabbi Aron BERGER

Yeshiva of Far Rockaway (D)

802 Hicksville Road, Far Rockaway NY 11691-5219
County: Queens FICE Identification: 041196
Unit ID: 190752
Telephone: (718) 327-7600 Carnegie Class: Spec-4-yr-Faith
FAX Number: (718) 327-1430 Calendar System: Semester
URL: https://www.yofr.org/
Established: 1969 Annual Undergrad Tuition & Fees: $13,750
Enrollment: 43 Male
Affiliation or Control: Independent Non-Profit IRS Status: 501(c)3
Highest Offering: First Talmudic Degree
Accreditation: RABN

01 President .... Rabbi Yechiel I. PERR
03 Executive Director .... Rabbi Shayeh KOHN
32 Dean of Students .... Rabbi Dovid KLEINKAUFMAN
06 Registrar .... Mrs. Tamara MASLOW

Yeshiva Gedolah Imrei Yosef D'Spinka (E)

1466 56th Street, Brooklyn NY 11219-4696
County: Kings FICE Identification: 030001
Unit ID: 375230
Telephone: (718) 851-8721 Carnegie Class: Spec-4-yr-Faith
FAX Number: (718) 686-8849 Calendar System: Semester
Established: 1987 Annual Undergrad Tuition & Fees: $9,500
Enrollment: 187 Male
Affiliation or Control: Independent Non-Profit IRS Status: 501(c)3
Highest Offering: First Talmudic Degree
Accreditation: RABN

01 President .... Joseph SOLOMON

Yeshiva Gedolah Kesser Torah (F)

50 Cedar Lane, Monsey NY 10952
County: Rockland Identification: 667112
Unit ID: 481410
Telephone: (845) 406-4308 Carnegie Class: Spec-4-yr-Faith
FAX Number: (845) 406-4199 Calendar System: Semester
Established: 2004 Annual Undergrad Tuition & Fees: $11,300
Enrollment: 85 Male
Affiliation or Control: Independent Non-Profit IRS Status: 501(c)3
Highest Offering: First Talmudic Degree
Accreditation: RABN

00 CEO .... Rabbi David FISHMAN
01 President .... David BERNSTEIN
06 Registrar .... Rabbi Ephraim SALB
37 Director Student Financial Aid .... Yaakov BERGER

Yeshiva Gedolah Ohr Yisrael (G)

2899 Nostrand Avenue, Brooklyn NY 11229
County: Kings Identification: 667077
Unit ID: 486017
Telephone: (718) 382-8702 Carnegie Class: Spec-4-yr-Faith
FAX Number: (718) 382-8703 Calendar System: Semester
URL: www.ohryisroel.org
Established: 1999 Annual Undergrad Tuition & Fees: $8,250
Enrollment: 36 Male
Affiliation or Control: Independent Non-Profit IRS Status: 501(c)3
Highest Offering: First Talmudic Degree
Accreditation: RABN

01 Rosh Yeshiva .... Avraham ZUCKER
10 Treasurer .... Avi KAHN

Yeshiva Karlin Stolin Beth Aaron V'Israel Rabbinical Institute (H)

1818 54th Street, Brooklyn NY 11204-1545
County: Kings FICE Identification: 025058
Unit ID: 197601
Telephone: (718) 232-7800 Carnegie Class: Spec-4-yr-Faith
FAX Number: (718) 331-4833 Calendar System: Semester
Established: 1948 Annual Undergrad Tuition & Fees: $11,800
Enrollment: 132 Male
Affiliation or Control: Independent Non-Profit IRS Status: 501(c)3
Highest Offering: First Talmudic Degree
Accreditation: RABN

01 Chief Executive Officer .... Rabbi Yochanan PILCHICK
05 Dean Theology/Chief Acad Officer .... Rabbi Chaim WOLPIN, OBM
06 Registrar .... Rabbi Aryeh WOLPIN
08 Librarian .... Rabbi Yochanan GOLDHABER
10 Fiscal Officer .... Rabbi Irving PERRES
37 Financial Aid Director .... Rabbi David STEIN
33 Dean of Men .... Rabbi Gedelyah MACHLIS

Yeshiva of Kasho (I)

590 Smith Street, Brooklyn NY 11231
County: Kings FICE Identification: 043017
Telephone: (718) 522-6646 Carnegie Class: Not Classified
FAX Number: (718) 310-3333 Calendar System: Semester
Established: 1995 Annual Undergrad Tuition & Fees: N/A
Enrollment: N/A Male
Affiliation or Control: Independent Non-Profit IRS Status: 501(c)3
Highest Offering: First Talmudic Degree
Accreditation: RABN

01 Director .... Aron BLUM
32 Financial Aid Administrator .... Juda NEWUMAN

Yeshiva Kollel Tifereth Elizer (J)

1227 47th Street, Brooklyn NY 11219
County: Kings Identification: 667367
Telephone: (718) 600-8897 Carnegie Class: Not Classified
FAX Number: (718) 889-7033 Calendar System: Semester
URL: https://yeshivakolleltiferethelizer.com/
Established: 1987 Annual Undergrad Tuition & Fees: N/A
Enrollment: N/A Male
Affiliation or Control: Independent Non-Profit IRS Status: 501(c)3
Highest Offering: First Talmudic Degree
Accreditation: RABN

01 Chief Executive Officer .... Rabbi Avrum Yehuda LOW
10 Chief Financial Officer .... Rabbi Hershel LOW
37 Financial Aid Administrator .... Rabbi Yesoscher MEISELS
06 Registrar .... Mrs. Rochel LOW

Yeshiva of Machzikai Hadas (K)

1301 47th Street, Brooklyn NY 11219
County: Kings FICE Identification: 041381
Unit ID: 455257
Telephone: (718) 853-2442 Carnegie Class: Spec-4-yr-Faith
FAX Number: (718) 853-2504 Calendar System: Semester
Established: 2001 Annual Undergrad Tuition & Fees: $10,100
Enrollment: 457 Male
Affiliation or Control: Independent Non-Profit IRS Status: 501(c)3
Highest Offering: First Talmudic Degree
Accreditation: RABN

01 Rosh Yeshiva .... Rabbi Yidel MONHEIT

Yeshiva of Nitra Rabbinical College (L)

194 Division Avenue, Brooklyn NY 11211-7199
County: Kings FICE Identification: 011670
Unit ID: 197674
Telephone: (718) 387-0422 Carnegie Class: Spec-4-yr-Faith
FAX Number: (718) 387-9400 Calendar System: Semester
URL: yeshivaofnitra.org/
Established: 1946 Annual Undergrad Tuition & Fees: $12,750
Enrollment: 197 Male
Affiliation or Control: Independent Non-Profit IRS Status: 501(c)3
Highest Offering: Second Talmudic Degree
Accreditation: RABN

01 President .... Mr. Alfred SCHOENBERGER
03 Vice President .... Mr. Mendel KLEIN
05 Dean .... Rabbi Samuel D. UNGAR
11 Administrative Officer .... Mr. Ernest SCHWARTZ

Yeshiva Ohr Naftoli (M)

701 Blooming Grove Turnpike, New Windsor NY 12553
County: Orange Identification: 667284
Unit ID: 490504
Telephone: (845) 784-4020 Carnegie Class: Spec-4-yr-Faith
FAX Number: (845) 784-2028 Calendar System: Other
URL: www.ohrnaftoli.org
Established: Annual Undergrad Tuition & Fees: $9,926
Enrollment: 37 Male
Affiliation or Control: Independent Non-Profit IRS Status: 501(c)3
Highest Offering: First Talmudic Degree
Accreditation: AIJS

01 Executive Director .... Rabbi Yitzchok KRAUSZ

Yeshiva Shaar Ephraim (N)

178 Maple Avenue, Monsey NY 10952
County: Rockland FICE Identification: 042590
Unit ID: 490276
Telephone: (845) 426-3110 Carnegie Class: Spec-4-yr-Faith
FAX Number: (845) 425-4721 Calendar System: Semester
URL: shaarephraim.org
Established: 2012 Annual Undergrad Tuition & Fees: $14,175
Enrollment: 83 Male
Affiliation or Control: Independent Non-Profit IRS Status: 501(c)3
Highest Offering: First Talmudic Degree
Accreditation: RABN

01 President .... Rabbi Yehuda OSHRY
33 Dean of Men .... Rabbi Moshe GREENBURG
37 Director of Financial Aid .... Mr. Dov KRESCH

Yeshiva Shaar HaTorah-Grodno (O)

83-96 117th Street, Kew Gardens NY 11415
County: Queens FICE Identification: 021520
Unit ID: 197692

Telephone: (718) 846-1940 Carnegie Class: Spec-4-yr-Faith
FAX Number: (718) 850-7916 Calendar System: Semester
URL: shaarhatorah.edu/
Established: 1976 Annual Undergrad Tuition & Fees: $17,160
Enrollment: 106 Male
Affiliation or Control: Independent Non-Profit IRS Status: 501(c)3
Highest Offering: Second Talmudic Degree
Accreditation: RABN

01 Administrator .... Rabbi Yoel YANKELEWITZ

Yeshiva Shaarei Torah of Rockland (A)

91 W Carlton Road, Suffern NY 10901-4013
County: Rockland FICE Identification: 034963
Unit ID: 441609
Telephone: (845) 352-3431 Carnegie Class: Spec-4-yr-Faith
FAX Number: (845) 352-3433 Calendar System: Semester
URL: https://www.yst.edu/
Established: 1977 Annual Undergrad Tuition & Fees: $13,750
Enrollment: 90 Male
Affiliation or Control: Independent Non-Profit IRS Status: 501(c)3
Highest Offering: First Talmudic Degree
Accreditation: AIJS

01 President .... Dr. Don ZWICKLER
05 Rosh Hayeshiva .... Rabbi Mordechai WOLMARK
37 Financial Aid Administrator .... Mr. Elimelech SCHWARTZ
06 Registrar .... Mrs. Rachel CELNIK

Yeshiva Sholom Shachna (B)

401 Elmwood Avenue, Brooklyn NY 11230
County: Kings Identification: 667147
Unit ID: 486026
Telephone: (718) 252-6333 Carnegie Class: Spec-4-yr-Faith
FAX Number: (718) 338-2536 Calendar System: Semester
URL: yeshivasholomshachna.com
Established: 2005 Annual Undergrad Tuition & Fees: $10,750
Enrollment: 106 Male
Affiliation or Control: Independent Non-Profit IRS Status: 501(c)3
Highest Offering: First Talmudic Degree
Accreditation: @RABN

01 Chief Executive Officer .... Rabbi Meir Chaim GUTFREUND
10 Chief Financial/Business Officer .... Mrs. Dina GUTFREUND
05 Chief Academic Officer/Registrar .... Rabbi Simcha OLEN
37 Director for Financial Aid .... Mrs. Esther FARKAS

Yeshiva of the Telshe Alumni (C)

4904 Independence Avenue, Riverdale NY 10471
County: Bronx FICE Identification: 025463
Unit ID: 431983
Telephone: (718) 601-3523 Carnegie Class: Spec-4-yr-Faith
FAX Number: (718) 601-2141 Calendar System: Semester
URL: https://yeshivatelshealumni.com/
Established: 1981 Annual Undergrad Tuition & Fees: $10,700
Enrollment: 75 Male
Affiliation or Control: Independent Non-Profit IRS Status: 501(c)3
Highest Offering: First Talmudic Degree
Accreditation: RABN

01 President .... Rabbi Avrohom AUSBAND
03 Executive Director .... Rabbi Noson JOSEPH
29 Director Alumni Relations .... Rabbi Moshe FERBER

Yeshiva University (D)

500 W 185th Street, New York NY 10033-3201
County: New York FICE Identification: 002903
Unit ID: 197708
Telephone: (212) 960-5400 Carnegie Class: DU-Higher
FAX Number: (212) 960-0055 Calendar System: Semester
URL: www.yu.edu
Established: 1886 Annual Undergrad Tuition & Fees: $46,475
Enrollment: 5,524 Coordinate
Affiliation or Control: Independent Non-Profit IRS Status: 501(c)3
Highest Offering: Doctorate
Accreditation: M, #ARCPA, CLPSY, IPSY, LAW, PSPSY, SP, SW

01 President .... Dr. Ari BERMAN
05 Provost/Sr VP Academic Affairs .... Dr. Selma BOTMAN
88 Chief of Staff to the Provost .... Dr. Timothy STEVENS
100 Chief of Staff to the President .... Ms. Julie SCHREIER
10 Vice Pres/Chief Financial Officer .... Mr. Jacob HARMAN
111 Vice Pres Institutional Advancement .... Mr. Adam GERDTS
11 Vice President University Affairs .... Dr. Herbert C. DOBRINSKY
13 Chief Information Officer .... Mr. Jim VASQUEZ
43 VP Legal Affs/Secretary/Gen Counsel .... Mr. Andrew J. LAUER
32 Vice Pres Univ & Cmty Life .... Vacant
26 Exec Dir Communications/Public Affs .... Mr. Doron STERN
04 Exec Assistant to President .... Vacant
08 Director of University Libraries .... Mr. Paul GLASSMAN
35 Vice Provost & Dean of Students .... Dr. Chaim NISSEL
73 Dn Undergrad Torah Stds/REITS .... Rabbi Yosef KALINSKY
49 Dean YU Undergrad Fac Arts Sci .... Dr. Karen BACON
50 Dean Sy Syms School of Business .... Dr. Noam WASSERMAN
58 Dean Ferkauf Graduate School Psych .... Dr. Leslie F. HALPERN
58 Dean Bernard Revel Graduate School .... Dr. Daniel RHYNHOLD
58 Dean Azrieli Grad Sch Jewish Educ .... Dr. Rona NOVICK
70 Dean Wurzweiler School Social Work .... Dr. Danielle WOZNIAK
81 Dean Katz School of Sci & Health .... Dr. Paul RUSSO
37 Director of Student Finances .... Mr. Robert FRIEDMAN
07 Acting Dir Undergraduate Admissions .... Mr. Marc ZHARNEST
29 Director of Alumni Engagement .... Ms. Aliza ABRAMS KONIG
06 University Registrar .... Ms. Jennifer SPIEGEL
09 Director of Institutional Research .... Mr. Yuxiang LIU
96 Director of Procurement .... Mr. Thomas CANNON
15 Chief Human Resources Officer .... Ms. Julie AUSTER
38 Director Student Counseling .... Dr. Yael MUSKAT
22 Dir Affirmative Action/EEO .... Ms. Renee COKER
41 Athletic Director .... Mr. Joe BENDARSH
19 Director Security/Safety .... Mr. Donald SOMMERS
36 Executive Director Career Center .... Ms. Susan BAUER
18 Chief Facilities & Admin Officer .... Mr. Randy APFELBAUM
84 Chief Enrollment Management Officer .... Mr. Chad K. AUSTEIN
86 Director Government Relations .... Mr. Jon GREENFIELD

Yeshiva Yesoda Hatorah Vetz Chaim (E)

505 Bedford Avenue, Brooklyn NY 11211
County: Kings Identification: 667368
Telephone: (718) 302-7500 Carnegie Class: Not Classified
FAX Number: N/A Calendar System: Semester
Established: 2013 Annual Undergrad Tuition & Fees: N/A
Enrollment: N/A Male
Affiliation or Control: Independent Non-Profit IRS Status: 501(c)3
Highest Offering: First Talmudic Degree
Accreditation: RABN

01 President .... Mr. Samuel FISCHER
37 Director of Financial Aid .... Mr. Getzel FALKOWITZ

Yeshiva Zichron Aryeh (F)

1213 Bay 25th Street, Far Rockaway NY 11691
County: Queens Identification: 667110
Unit ID: 487746
Telephone: (347) 619-9074 Carnegie Class: Spec-4-yr-Faith
FAX Number: (516) 295-5737 Calendar System: Semester
Established: 1992 Annual Undergrad Tuition & Fees: $8,750
Enrollment: 28 Male
Affiliation or Control: Independent Non-Profit IRS Status: 501(c)3
Highest Offering: First Talmudic Degree
Accreditation: RABN

03 Executive Vice President .... Rabbi Shaya COHEN
10 Controller .... Rabbi Ari DERDIK
06 Registrar/Dir of Admissions .... Rabbi Yehuda COHEN
37 Financial Aid Admin .... Mr. Yaakov JAFFE
18 Chief Facilities .... Mr. Danny SCHUSTER
08 Head Librarian .... Mr. Yechezkel MOSKOWITZ

Yeshivas Maharit Dsatmar (G)

475 County Rt. 105, Monroe NY 10950
County: Orange Identification: 667204
Unit ID: 488101
Telephone: (845) 782-1380 Carnegie Class: Spec-4-yr-Faith
FAX Number: (845) 302-1093 Calendar System: Semester
URL: yeshivasmaharit.org/
Established: 2011 Annual Undergrad Tuition & Fees: $11,500
Enrollment: 143 Male
Affiliation or Control: Independent Non-Profit IRS Status: 501(c)3
Highest Offering: First Talmudic Degree
Accreditation: @RABN

01 CEO .... Yitzchok TYRNAUER
06 Registrar .... Joel BRAVER
10 Associate Business Officer .... Libi WITRIOL
37 Director of Financial Aid .... Yoel KESTENBAUM

Yeshivas Novominsk (H)

1690 60th Street, Brooklyn NY 11204-2138
County: Kings FICE Identification: 031271
Unit ID: 405058
Telephone: (718) 438-2727 Carnegie Class: Spec-4-yr-Faith
FAX Number: (718) 438-2472 Calendar System: Semester
URL: https://yeshivasnovominsk.com/
Established: 1988 Annual Undergrad Tuition & Fees: $10,300
Enrollment: 165 Male
Affiliation or Control: Independent Non-Profit IRS Status: 501(c)3
Highest Offering: First Talmudic Degree
Accreditation: RABN

01 Executive Director .... Rabbi Lipa BRENNAN
32 Dean of Students .... Rabbi Yehoshua PERLOW
32 Dean of Students .... Rabbi Yisroel PERLOW
11 Administrator .... Rabbi Boruch TWERSKI

Yeshivath Viznitz (I)

PO Box 446, Monsey NY 10952-0446
County: Rockland FICE Identification: 013027
Unit ID: 197735
Telephone: (845) 731-3700 Carnegie Class: Spec-4-yr-Faith
FAX Number: (845) 356-7359 Calendar System: Semester
Established: 1946 Annual Undergrad Tuition & Fees: $8,640
Enrollment: 842 Male
Affiliation or Control: Independent Non-Profit IRS Status: 501(c)3
Highest Offering: Second Talmudic Degree
Accreditation: RABN

01 President .... Gershon NEIMAN
10 Chief Fiscal Officer .... Rabbi David ROSENBERG

Yeshivath Zichron Moshe (J)

PO Box 580, South Fallsburg NY 12779-0580
County: Sullivan FICE Identification: 011821
Unit ID: 197744
Telephone: (845) 434-5240 Carnegie Class: Spec-4-yr-Faith
FAX Number: (845) 434-1009 Calendar System: Semester
URL: https://yeshivathzichronmoshe.com/
Established: 1969 Annual Undergrad Tuition & Fees: $13,450
Enrollment: 240 Male
Affiliation or Control: Independent Non-Profit IRS Status: 501(c)3
Highest Offering: First Talmudic Degree
Accreditation: AIJS

01 President .... Rabbi Ephraim Y. SHER
37 Director Student Financial Aid .... Rabbi Dov PERECMAN
06 Registrar .... Mrs. Miryom R. MILLER

NORTH CAROLINA

Barton College (K)

400 Atlantic Christian College Dr, Wilson NC 27893
County: Wilson FICE Identification: 002908
Unit ID: 197911
Telephone: (252) 399-6300 Carnegie Class: Bac-Diverse
FAX Number: (252) 399-6374 Calendar System: Semester
URL: www.barton.edu
Established: 1902 Annual Undergrad Tuition & Fees: $32,590
Enrollment: 1,177 Coed
Affiliation or Control: Christian Church (Disciples Of Christ)
IRS Status: 501(c)3
Highest Offering: Master's
Accreditation: SC, NURSE, SW

01 President .... Dr. Douglas N. SEARCY
05 Provost/VP Acad Affs/Stdnt Engage .... Dr. Gary DAYNES
10 Vice Pres Finance & Administration .... Mr. David A. BROWNING
111 Vice President Inst Advancement .... Vacant
84 Vice President for Enrollment Mgmt .... Mr. Dennis T. MATTHEWS
07 Asst VP for Enrollment Mgmt .... Ms. Amanda METTS
30 Asst VP for Leadership Giving .... Mr. Tom MAZE
20 Assistant Provost Integrative Lrng .... Ms. Blythe TAYLOR
50 Dean School of Business .... Mr. Ron EGGERS
66 Dean School of Nursing .... Dr. Sharon SARVEY
53 Dean School of Education .... Dr. Jackie ENNIS
79 Dean School of Humanities .... Dr. Liz KISER
32 Dean of Student Life .... Mr. Joseph DLUGOS
81 Assoc Provost/Dean School Sciences .... Dr. Kevin PENNINGTON
76 Dean Allied Health & Sport Studies .... Dr. Steve FULKS
70 Director of Social Work Program .... Ms. Trinette B. LANGLEY
57 Dean Visual/Performing & Comm Arts .... Ms. Susan FECHO
58 Dean Graduate/Professional Studies .... Vacant
21 Controller .... Mr. Chris D. MCKENZIE
41 Athletic Director .... Mr. Todd WILKINSON
106 Dir Online Education/E-learning .... Ms. Lorraine RAPER
36 Asst Provost Academic/Career Plng .... Ms. Angie WALSTON
06 Registrar .... Ms. Sheila MILNE
37 Director Student Financial Aid .... Mr. Thomas WELCH
26 Director of Public Relations .... Mrs. Kathy DAUGHETY
08 Director of the Library .... Mr. Robert CAGNA
15 Asst VP of Human Resources .... Mrs. Vicky MORRIS
23 Director of Health Services .... Mrs. Jennifer HIGH
110 Exec Director of Inst Advancement .... Mr. Archer BANE
13 Sr Director Technology Services .... Mr. David GRAYBEAL
18 Director of Facilities Services .... Mr. Mark A. TERRELL
42 Chaplain .... Vacant
40 Bookstore Manager .... Vacant
04 Executive Asst to President .... Mrs. Sheila WILSON
88 Director of Publications .... Mr. Keith TEW
105 Director Web Services .... Mr. Ken DOZIER
09 Director of Institutional Research .... Ms. Lorie A. DALOLA
39 Asst Dean Campus Life/Residential .... Vacant
28 Director of Diversity .... Ms. Vicky A. MORRIS

Belmont Abbey College (L)

100 Belmont Mount Holly Road, Belmont NC 28012-1802
County: Gaston FICE Identification: 002910
Unit ID: 197984
Telephone: (704) 461-6701 Carnegie Class: Bac-Diverse
FAX Number: (704) 461-6670 Calendar System: Semester
URL: belmontabbeycollege.edu/
Established: 1876 Annual Undergrad Tuition & Fees: $18,500
Enrollment: 1,467 Coed
Affiliation or Control: Roman Catholic IRS Status: 501(c)3
Highest Offering: Master's
Accreditation: SC

01 President .... Dr. William K. THIERFELDER
10 SVP Finance/Admin/Operations .... Mr. Allan MARK
05 Provost .... Dr. Travis FEEZELL
20 Vice Provost for Academic Affairs .... Dr. David WILLIAMS

26 VP College Relations ... Mr. Philip BRACH
92 Dean of the Honors College ... Dr. Joseph WYSOCKI
30 Development Officer ... Ms. Chris PEELER
29 Director of Alumni Relations ... Ms. Bridget CONBOY
08 Director of the Library ... Mr. Donald BEAGLE
06 Registrar ... Ms. Margot RHOADES
09 Vice Prov Assessment/Rsrch/Accred ... Ms. Karen PRICE
36 Director Career Counseling/Placemnt ... Vacant
27 Exec Dir Marketing/Communications ... Mr. Rolando RIVAS
37 Dir Student Financial Services ... Mrs. Julie HODGE
38 Director of Wellness Center ... Mrs. Melanie ECKSTEIN
41 Athletic Director ... Mr. Stephen MISS
21 Controller ... Ms. Beth RUNSER
19 Chief of Campus Police ... Mr. Andy LEONARD
42 Director of Campus Ministry ... Mr. Wesley NELSON
15 Exec Director of Human Resources ... Ms. Cheryl TROTTER
07 Vice Provost and Dean of Admissions ... Mr. Martin C. AUCOIN
13 Chief Info Technology Officer (CIO) ... Mr. Nash HASAN
32 Vice President and Dean of Students ... Mr. Tom MACALESTER
04 Sr Executive Assistant to the Pres ... Ms. Maria DIMURA

Bennett College (A)

900 E Washington Street, Greensboro NC 27401-3239
County: Guilford FICE Identification: 002911
Unit ID: 197993
Telephone: (336) 273-4431 Carnegie Class: Bac-A&S
FAX Number: (336) 370-8688 Calendar System: Semester
URL: www.bennett.edu
Established: 1873 Annual Undergrad Tuition & Fees: $18,513
Enrollment: 232 Female
Affiliation or Control: United Methodist IRS Status: 501(c)3
Highest Offering: Baccalaureate
Accreditation: @TRACS, SW

01 President ... Ms. Suzanne E. WALSH
05 Vice Pres Academic Affairs ... Dr. Laura COLSON
10 VP Business & Finance ... Vacant
111 Vice Pres Inst Advancement ... Mr. LaDaniel GATLING, II
11 Sr Advisor/Assoc VP Admin Services ... Dr. Anne C. HAYES
21 Interim CFO ... Mr. George LATTER
84 VP Enrollment Mgmt/Stdnt Svcs ... Ms. Catherine HURD
32 Exec Dir Student Affairs ... Dr. Kimberly DRYE-DANCY
26 Dir Public Relations & Publication ... Vacant
09 Dir Inst Plng/Assess/Effect/Rsrch ... Mr. Brian AURITI
08 Director of Holgate Library ... Ms. Joan WILLIAMS
07 Director of Admissions ... Mr. James CRAWFORD
37 Director of Financial Aid ... Ms. Pam DOUGLAS
29 Int Exec Director Alumnae Relations ... Ms. Deborah LOVE
36 Director Career Services ... Mr. Darryl JOHNSON
38 Dir Coun Svcs/Supervisor Health Svc ... Ms. Robin CAMPBELL
15 Director of Human Resources ... Ms. Ebony KENDRICK
42 Chaplain/Director Campus Ministry ... Rev Dr. Natalie MCLEAN
88 Chair Curriculum & Instruction ... Dr. Annette WILSON
79 Interim Chair Humanities ... Ms. Penny SPEAS
81 Int Chair Biological & Chemical Sci ... Dr. Michael COTTON
19 Director Campus Safety ... Mr. Keifer BRADSHAW
13 Assoc Dir Information Tech Svcs ... Mr. William MORRIS
04 Executive Asst to the President ... Vacant
104 Director Center for Global Studies ... Ms. Kelly MALLARI
106 Dean or Director Online Education ... Mr. Tom LIPSCOMB
108 Director Institutional Assessment ... Dr. Sonya RICKS
25 Dir Title III & Sponsored Programs ... Ms. Sylvia NICHOLSON
39 Dir Campus Life/Student Activities ... Ms. Rachel PRIDGEN
50 Dept Chair Bus/Econ & Entre Studies ... Dr. Christopher WALSON
20 Dean of Faculty ... Dr. Willietta GIBSON

Brevard College (B)

One Brevard College Drive, Brevard NC 28712-3306
County: Transylvania FICE Identification: 002912
Unit ID: 198066
Telephone: (828) 641-0641 Carnegie Class: Bac-Diverse
FAX Number: N/A Calendar System: Semester
URL: www.brevard.edu
Established: 1853 Annual Undergrad Tuition & Fees: $30,250
Enrollment: 828 Coed
Affiliation or Control: United Methodist IRS Status: 501(c)3
Highest Offering: Master's
Accreditation: SC, MUS

01 President ... Dr. David C. JOYCE
05 VP Academic Affairs/Dean of Faculty ... Dr. Scott SHEFFIELD
10 VP for Finance & Operations ... Mr. Juan C. MASCARO
30 VP for Alumni Affairs & Development ... Ms. Kathryn HOLTEN
07 Vice Pres Admissions/Financial Aid ... Dr. Ryan C. HOLT
32 VP Student Life/Dean of Students ... Dr. Debora D'ANNA
04 Executive Asst to the President ... Ms. Katherine T. PARNELL
13 Dir of Information Technology ... Mr. William DEWITT
06 Registrar ... Mr. Quintin OVEROCKER
21 Associate VP Finance/Controller ... Mr. Mitchell RADFORD
08 Director of Library ... Dr. Marie JONES
30 Director of Development ... Mr. Jeff JOYCE
19 Dir of Safety/Security/Risk Mgmt ... Mr. Stan JACOBSEN
41 Director of Athletics ... Ms. Myranda NASH
18 Director of Facilities/Grounds ... Mr. Burke ULREY
121 Assoc Dean Student Support/Advising ... Ms. Shirley E. ARNOLD
36 Assoc Dir of Career Exploration/Dev ... Ms. Nacole POTTS
92 Director of Honors Program ... Dr. Robert J. CABIN
38 Assoc Dean/Dir of Counseling ... Ms. Deanne DASBURG
57 Chair Division of Fine Arts ... Dr. Kathryn GRESHAM
79 Chair Division of Humanities ... Dr. Tom J. BELL
83 Chair Div of Social Sciences ... Dr. Laura VANCE
81 Chair Div Env Stds/Math/Nat Science ... Dr. Jennifer E. FRICK-RUPPERT
88 Chair Division of WLEE ... Dr. Jennifer L. KAFSKY
26 Director of Public Information ... Ms. Christie CAUBLE
108 Dir of Institutional Effectiveness ... Mr. Michael COHEN
37 Dir of Admissions & Financial Aid ... Mr. David VOLRATH
15 Director of Human Resources ... Mrs. Myra COOPER
09 Director of Institutional Research ... Vacant
29 Director Alumni Affairs ... Ms. Megan SHINA
39 Dir of Housing & Student Conduct ... Mr. Christopher CENTER

Cabarrus College of Health Sciences (C)

401 Medical Park Drive, Concord NC 28025-3959
County: Cabarrus FICE Identification: 006477
Unit ID: 198109
Telephone: (704) 403-1555 Carnegie Class: Spec-4-yr-Other Health
FAX Number: (704) 403-1764 Calendar System: Semester
URL: www.cabarruscollege.edu
Established: 1942 Annual Undergrad Tuition & Fees: $13,966
Enrollment: 526 Coed
Affiliation or Control: Independent Non-Profit IRS Status: 501(c)3
Highest Offering: Master's
Accreditation: SC, ADNUR, MAC, NURSE, OT, OTA, SURGT

01 President ... Dr. Cam CRUICKSHANK
05 Provost ... Dr. Meg PATCHETT
32 Dean Student Affs/Enrollment Mgmt ... Ms. Christine L. CORSELLO
10 Chief Financial Officer ... Mrs. Sandra HARVEY
66 ADN Program Chair ... Dr. Kim PLEMMONS
88 OT Assistant Program Chair ... Ms. Nancy GREEN
88 Master OT Program Chair ... Dr. Jacqueline MAYO
88 Medical Assisting Program Chair ... Ms. Rachel HOUSTON
88 Surgical Technology Program Chair ... Ms. Michelle GAY
88 Medical Imagining Program Chair ... Mrs. Rhonda WEAVER
97 General Education Program Chair ... Mrs. Zinat HASSANPOUR
66 Dean of Nursing ... Dr. Delores BENN
26 Manager Marketing & Events ... Vacant
37 Director of Financial Aid ... Mrs. Valerie RICHARD
06 Dir Student Records & Info Mgmt ... Mrs. Mary ELMORE
07 Dir of Admissions & Recruitment ... Mrs. Lorri B. CONNOR
04 Administrative Asst to President ... Mrs. Heather PENINGER
08 Head Librarian ... Mrs. Cassie DIXON
09 Dir Inst Research & Effectiveness ... Mrs. Tripti DEVKOTA

Campbell University (D)

PO Box 127, Buies Creek NC 27506-0097
County: Harnett FICE Identification: 002913
Unit ID: 198136
Telephone: (910) 893-1200 Carnegie Class: DU-Mod
FAX Number: (910) 893-1424 Calendar System: Semester
URL: www.campbell.edu
Established: 1887 Annual Undergrad Tuition & Fees: $36,740
Enrollment: 5,964 Coed
Affiliation or Control: Baptist IRS Status: 501(c)3
Highest Offering: Doctorate
Accreditation: SC, ACBSP, ARCPA, CACREP, CAEP, LAW, NURSE, OSTEO, PH, PHAR, PTA, SW, THEOL

00 Chancellor ... Dr. Jerry WALLACE
01 President ... Dr. J. Bradley CREED
03 Executive Vice President ... Dr. John ROBERSON
05 Vice Pres Academic Affs & Provost ... Dr. Mark HAMMOND
111 Vice President for Advancement ... Dr. Britt DAVIS
32 Vice President for Student Life ... Dr. Dennis BAZEMORE
84 Vice Pres Enrollment Management ... Dr. David MEE
10 VP for Business/CFO ... Ms. Sandra CONNOLLY
49 Dean of College of Arts & Science ... Dr. Michael WELLS
61 Dean of the Law School ... Mr. J. Rich LEONARD
50 Dean Lundy-Fetterman Sch Business ... Dr. Kevin O'MARA
53 Dean School of Education ... Dr. Alfred BRYANT
67 Dean College of Pharmacy/Health Sci ... Dr. Michael ADAMS
63 Dean of Osteopathic Medical School ... Dr. Brian KESSLER
54 Dean School of Engineering ... Dr. Jenna CARPENTER
35 Dean of Campus Life ... Ms. Kellie NOTHSTINE
06 Registrar ... Ms. Karen PORE
29 AVP of Alumni Engagement ... Ms. Sarah SWAIN
08 Dean of Library ... Ms. Sarah STEELE
37 Director of Financial Aid ... Mr. Preston DODSON
13 CIO/Assoc VP for IT ... Ms. Sherri YERK-ZWICKL
26 AVP Communications/Marketing ... Ms. Haven HOTTEL
15 Director Human Resources ... Mr. Trent ELMORE
18 Asst Director Facilities Management ... Mr. Jason WANGELIN
38 Director Student Counseling ... Ms. Laura RICH
96 Director of Procurement ... Mr. Thomas PHAM
92 Director of Honors Program ... Dr. Sherry TRUFFIN
09 Asst Provost for Inst Effectiveness ... Mrs. Maren HESS
106 Dean of Adult & Online Education ... Dr. Beth RUBIN
41 Athletic Director ... Dr. Omar BANKS
43 Dir Legal Services/General Counsel ... Ms. Gina CALABRO
04 Exec Assistant to the President ... Ms. Suzanne CREWS
07 Director of Admissions ... Vacant
104 Dean of Global Engagement ... Dr. Donna WALDRON
19 Director Security/Safety ... Mr. Chase BANKER
44 Director Annual Giving ... Ms. Tammi FRIES

Carolina Christian College (E)

PO Box 777, Winston-Salem NC 27102
County: Forsyth FICE Identification: 035703
Unit ID: 199971
Telephone: (336) 744-0900 Carnegie Class: Spec-4-yr-Faith
FAX Number: (336) 744-0901 Calendar System: Semester
URL: www.carolina.edu
Established: 1945 Annual Undergrad Tuition & Fees: $8,930
Enrollment: 74 Coed
Affiliation or Control: Independent Non-Profit IRS Status: 501(c)3
Highest Offering: Doctorate
Accreditation: BI

01 President ... Dr. LaTanya V. TYSON
05 VP of Academics/Graduate Studies ... Dr. Derrick THORPE
32 Dean of Students ... Mr. Tyrone TYSON
10 Chief Business Officer ... Ms. Jennifer CLAVER
08 Library Director ... Ms. Sarah TAYLOR
37 Financial Aid Director ... Ms. Garriell LUCAS
06 Registrar ... Ms. Daneisha DESMOND
26 Chief Public Relations Officer ... Vacant
09 Director of Institutional Research ... Ms. Nneka FORSMAN
07 Director of Admissions ... Ms. Qiana Anngel BAZEMORE

Carolina College of Biblical Studies (F)

817 S. McPherson Church Road, Fayetteville NC 28303
County: Cumberland FICE Identification: 041542
Unit ID: 461032
Telephone: (910) 323-5614 Carnegie Class: Spec-4-yr-Faith
FAX Number: (910) 323-0425 Calendar System: Semester
URL: www.ccbs.edu
Established: 1973 Annual Undergrad Tuition & Fees: $5,964
Enrollment: 167 Coed
Affiliation or Control: Non-denominational IRS Status: 501(c)3
Highest Offering: Master's
Accreditation: BI

01 President ... Dr. Bill KORVER
05 Provost ... Dr. Chris DICKERSON
30 Vice Pres Strategic Development ... Mr. Gary BARRETT
10 Vice Pres of Finance ... Mr. Richard HOVATER
84 VP Enrollment/Student Services ... Dr. Rodney PHILLIPS

Carolinas College of Health Sciences (G)

2110 Water Ridge Parkway, Charlotte NC 28217
County: Mecklenburg FICE Identification: 031042
Unit ID: 433174
Telephone: (704) 355-5043 Carnegie Class: Spec 2-yr-Health
FAX Number: (704) 355-9336 Calendar System: Semester
URL: www.CarolinasCollege.edu
Established: 1990 Annual Undergrad Tuition & Fees (In-District): $15,424
Enrollment: 514 Coed
Affiliation or Control: State/Local IRS Status: 501(c)3
Highest Offering: Baccalaureate
Accreditation: SC, ADNUR, HT, MT, NURSE, RAD, RTT

01 President ... Dr. T. Hampton HOPKINS
05 Provost ... Dr. Lori BEQUETTE
10 Dean Administrative/Financial Svcs ... Ms. Sandra HARVEY
32 Dean Student Affs/Enrollment Mgmt ... Vacant
06 Registrar ... Ms. Paige LEVESQUE
30 Dir Development/Alumni Relations ... Ms. Ruthie MIHAL
07 Director Admissions & Recruitment ... Mr. Jameson DONNELL
37 Interim Director Financial Aid ... Mr. Gary BYERS
90 Director Teaching/Learning & Tech ... Dr. Jared SMITH
09 Institutional Research Coordinator ... Ms. Cheryl PULLIAM
04 Admin Assistant to President ... Ms. Pat LEWIS

Carolina University (H)

420 S Broad Street, Winston-Salem NC 27101-5197
County: Forsyth FICE Identification: 002956
Unit ID: 489937
Telephone: (336) 725-8344 Carnegie Class: Spec-4-yr-Faith
FAX Number: (336) 725-5522 Calendar System: Semester
URL: www.carolinau.edu
Established: 1945 Annual Undergrad Tuition & Fees: $14,580
Enrollment: 951 Coed
Affiliation or Control: Independent Non-Profit IRS Status: 501(c)3
Highest Offering: Doctorate
Accreditation: TRACS

01 President ... Dr. Charles W. PETITT
32 Chancellor/Dean of Students ... Dr. Steve CONDON
05 Exec Vice President Academic Affs ... Dr. Sandeep GOPALAN
73 VP/Dir of Ministry Program ... Dr. Byron EDENS
10 Chief Financial Officer ... Dr. Chris RONK
13 Chief Info Technology Officer ... Vacant
37 Financial Aid Director ... Mrs. Mandy MCLAIN
41 Athletic Director ... Dr. Steve CONDON
108 Dir Inst Effectiveness/Registrar ... Vacant
30 Asst to Chanc Univ Advancement ... Ms. Shealynn MILLER
18 Chf Facilities/Physical Plant Ofcr ... Vacant

Catawba College (I)

2300 W Innes Street, Salisbury NC 28144-2488
County: Rowan FICE Identification: 002914
Unit ID: 198215
Telephone: (704) 637-4111 Carnegie Class: Bac-Diverse
FAX Number: (704) 637-4444 Calendar System: Semester
URL: www.catawba.edu
Established: 1851 Annual Undergrad Tuition & Fees: $31,436

Enrollment: 1,371 Coed
Affiliation or Control: United Church Of Christ IRS Status: 501(c)3
Highest Offering: Master's
Accreditation: SC, ACBSP, NURSE

01 President Dr. David NELSON
42 Senior Vice President/Chaplain Dr. Kenneth W. CLAPP
05 Provost Dr. Constance ROGERS-LOWERY
30 VP of Development Ms. Meg K. DEES
07 Vice Pres for Admissions Vacant
04 Assistant to President Mrs. Amy H. WILLIAMS
09 Dir Institutional Research Dr. Sharon SULLIVAN
10 Chief Financial Officer Ms. Lauren COX
15 Chief Human Resources Officer Mr. Drew DAVIS
13 Chief Information Tech Officer Vacant
32 Senior VP/Dean of Students Dr. Jared TICE
88 Director of Student Conduct Ms. Laura GILLAND
08 Library Director Mr. Earl GIVENS
06 Registrar Ms. Chrisanne RANCATI
37 Director of Financial Assistance Ms. Kelli HAND
36 Director of Placement Vacant
88 Director Sports Info & Promotion Mr. Jim D. LEWIS
40 Director Bookstore Mrs. Stephanie TAYLOR
41 Athletic Director Vacant
18 Chief Facilities/Physical Plant Mr. Billy WHITE
29 Director Alumni Relations Ms. Savannah SHAVER
19 Director Security/Safety Mr. David NAJARIAN
44 Director Annual Giving Ms. Mindy MILLER
101 Secretary of the Institution/Board Mrs. Amy H. WILLIAMS
106 Dean of Distance & Online Education Vacant
39 Director Housing & Residence Life Mr. Marcus WASHINGTON
50 Dean of Business Dr. Eric HAKE
26 Chief Public Relations Officer Ms. Jodi BAILEY

Chamberlain University-Charlotte (A)

2015 Ayrsley Town Blvd, Ste 204, Charlotte NC 28273
Telephone: (980) 939-6241 Identification: 770979
Accreditation: &HLC, NURSE

† Branch campus of Chamberlain University-Addison, Addison, IL

Charlotte Christian College and Theological Seminary (B)

PO Box 790106, Charlotte NC 28227-9446
County: Mecklenburg FICE Identification: 038273
Unit ID: 444778
Telephone: (704) 334-6882 Carnegie Class: Spec-4-yr-Faith
FAX Number: (704) 334-6885 Calendar System: Semester
URL: www.charlottechristian.edu
Established: 1996 Annual Undergrad Tuition & Fees: N/A
Enrollment: 182 Coed
Affiliation or Control: Independent Non-Profit IRS Status: 501(c)3
Highest Offering: Doctorate
Accreditation: TRACS

01 President Dr. Eddie G. GRIGG
05 VP of Academic/Student Affairs Dr. Adiaha STRANGE
10 Business Office Manager/CFO Mr. Al WITT
111 Director of Advancement Vacant
06 Registrar/Dir International Student Ms. Nancy RAY
08 Head Librarian Dr. Gwendolyn PEART
07 Director of Admissions Mr. George SHEARS, III
37 Financial Aid Officer Mr. Kenneth ROACH
04 Admin Assistant to the President Mr. Matt RUSSELL

Chowan University (C)

One University Place, Murfreesboro NC 27855-1844
County: Hertford FICE Identification: 002916
Unit ID: 198303
Telephone: (252) 398-6500 Carnegie Class: Bac-A&S
FAX Number: (252) 398-1190 Calendar System: Semester
URL: www.chowan.edu
Established: 1848 Annual Undergrad Tuition & Fees: $25,880
Enrollment: 1,100 Coed
Affiliation or Control: Baptist IRS Status: 501(c)3
Highest Offering: Master's
Accreditation: SC, MUS

01 President Dr. Kirk E. PETERSON
05 Vice President Academic Affairs Dr. Danny B. MOORE
20 Associate Provost Academic Affairs Dr. John DILUSTRO
20 Assoc Provost External Relations Dr. Brenda S. TINKHAM
10 Vice President Business Affairs Mr. Danny R. DAVIS
32 Vice President Student Affairs Dr. Montrose STREETER
111 Vice President for Advancement Mr. Andy WILSON
07 Vice President Admissions Dr. Daniel WILSON
41 Vice Pres/Director for Athletics Mr. Patrick M. MASHUDA
13 Assistant VP Information Technology Mr. James R. HOWELL
112 Executive Director of Major Gifts Mr. John TAYLOE
15 Director of Human Resources Mrs. Emily TERRY
06 Registrar Mr. Richard TODD
26 Dir of Univ Rels/Communications Mrs. Kimberly BAILEY
08 Head Librarian Mrs. Georgia E. WILLIAMS
37 Director of Financial Aid Ms. Ruth CASPER
42 Campus Minister Ms. Mari E. WILES
18 Director Physical Plant Mr. Alex CHAPPELL
19 Chief of Security Mr. Derek A. BURKE
35 Director Student Life Mr. Bradley CASH
36 Director Counseling/Career Services Ms. Yolanda MAJETTE
39 Director Housing and Residence Life Ms. Sher-Ron LAUD
09 Director Institutional Research Vacant
88 Director Upward Bound Mr. E. Frank STEPHENSON
21 Director Business Services Mrs. Julie W. EMORY
29 Director Alumni Services Mrs. Kay M. THOMAS
49 Dean School of Arts/Sciences Dr. Jennifer PLACE
50 Dean School of Business and Design Dr. Hunter TAYLOR
53 Dean School of Educ & Profess Stds Dr. Ella E. BENSON
88 Dean School Accessibility Services Vacant
58 Dean School of Graduate Studies Dr. John DILUSTRO
40 Bookstore Manager Vacant

Daoist Traditions College of Chinese Medical Arts (D)

382 Montford Avenue, Asheville NC 28801
County: Buncombe FICE Identification: 041464
Unit ID: 455178
Telephone: (828) 225-3993 Carnegie Class: Spec-4-yr-Other Health
FAX Number: (828) 255-3306 Calendar System: Semester
URL: www.daoisttraditions.edu
Established: 2003 Annual Graduate Tuition & Fees: N/A
Enrollment: 110 Coed
Affiliation or Control: Proprietary IRS Status: Proprietary
Highest Offering: Doctorate; No Undergraduates
Accreditation: ACUP

01 President/Financial Director Dr. Mary Cissy MAJEBE
04 Administrative Asst to President Jennifer MOORE
05 Academic Dean Megan BURNS
07 Director of Admissions/Financial Ai Juliet DANIEL
08 Librarian Emily FADER

Davidson College (E)

PO Box 5000, Davidson NC 28035-5000
County: Mecklenburg FICE Identification: 002918
Unit ID: 198385
Telephone: (704) 894-2000 Carnegie Class: Bac-A&S
FAX Number: (704) 894-2005 Calendar System: Semester
URL: www.davidson.edu
Established: 1837 Annual Undergrad Tuition & Fees: $55,175
Enrollment: 1,983 Coed
Affiliation or Control: Independent Non-Profit IRS Status: 501(c)3
Highest Offering: Baccalaureate
Accreditation: SC

01 President Dr. Carol E. QUILLEN
05 Vice Pres Acad Affs/Dean of Faculty Dr. Philip N. JEFFERSON
26 Vice President College Relations Ms. Eileen M. KEELEY
10 Vice Pres Finance & Administration Ms. Ann MCCORVEY
32 VP Student Life/Dean of Students Dr. Byron P. MCCRAE
07 VP & Dean Admissions/Financial Aid Mr. Christopher J. GRUBER
09 VP Planning/Institutional Research Ms. Linda M. LEFAUVE
43 VP and General Counsel Ms. Sarah L. PHILLIPS
111 Exec Dir of Advancement Opers Vacant
20 Assoc Dean Academic Administration Vacant
45 VP for Strategic Initiatives Vacant
20 Assoc Dean of Faculty Dr. Fuji P. LOZADA
30 Assoc VP of Development Mr. Brad MARTIN
31 Assoc VP Campus/Community Relations Ms. Stephanie GLASER
06 Registrar Ms. Angela B. DEWBERRY
13 Chief Information Officer Mr. Kevin DAVIS
37 Director Financial Aid Mr. Chad A. SPENCER
15 Director of Human Resources Dr. Kim BALL
41 Director of Athletics Mr. Chris CLUNIE
08 Director of the Library Ms. Lisa FORREST
29 Director Alumni Relations Ms. Marya L. HOWELL
21 Controller/Director Business Svcs Ms. Lori GASTON
18 Director Facilities & Engineering Mr. David M. HOLTHOUSER
19 Chief of Campus Police Mr. Julian COAXUM
36 Exec Dir Career Development Mr. Jamie STAMEY
35 Director of College Union Mr. Mike GOODE
39 Dir Resid Life/Assoc Dean Students Mr. Jason S. SHAFFER
42 College Chaplain Dr. Robert C. SPACH
88 Dir Ctr for Interdisciplinary Stds Dr. Jane MANGAN
82 Assoc Dean Intl Programs/Studies Dr. Jonathan BERKEY
25 Director of Grants & Contracts Dr. Mary W. MUCHANE
24 Director of Digital Innovation Ms. Kristen ESHLEMAN
38 Director Student Counseling Mr. David GRAHAM
44 Exec Dir of Engagement Ms. Lisa H. COMBS
96 Director of Purchasing Vacant
40 College Store General Manager Mr. William T. REILLY
04 Executive Asst to President Mrs. Traci L. RUSS-WILSON
27 Chief Comm & Marketing Officer Mr. Mark JOHNSON

Duke University (F)

Durham NC 27706-8001
County: Durham FICE Identification: 002920
Unit ID: 198419
Telephone: (919) 684-8111 Carnegie Class: DU-Highest
FAX Number: (919) 684-3200 Calendar System: Semester
URL: www.duke.edu
Established: 1838 Annual Undergrad Tuition & Fees: $57,633
Enrollment: 16,172 Coed
Affiliation or Control: Independent Non-Profit IRS Status: 501(c)3
Highest Offering: Doctorate
Accreditation: SC, ANEST, ARCPA, CAEP, CAMPEP, CLPSY, CYTO, DIETC, DIETI, IPSY, LAW, MED, NURSE, PA, PAST, PCSAS, PTA, THEOL

01 President Vincent PRICE
03 Executive Vice President Daniel ENNIS
05 Provost Sally KORNBLUTH
17 Chancellor for Health Affairs A. Eugene WASHINGTON
10 Interim Vice Pres Financial Svcs Rachel SATTERFIELD
15 Vice President for Administration Kyle CAVANAUGH
07 Dean Undergraduate Admissions Christoph O. GUTTENTAG
21 Exec Vice Provost Finance & Admin Jennifer FRANCIS
13 Vice Prov Information Technology Tracy FUTHEY
88 Vice Prov Interdisciplinary Studies Edward BALLEISEN
88 Vice Provost Faculty Advancement Abbas BENMAMOUN
46 Int Vice Pres Research/Innovation R. Sanders WILLIAMS
08 Librarian/Vice Prov Library Affairs Deborah JAKUBS
37 Asst Vice Provost/Dir Financial Aid Miranda MCCALL
65 Dean Sch of the Environment Toddi R. STEELMAN
61 Dean of Law School Kerry ABRAMS
63 Dn Sch Med/Sr Vice Chanc Acad Affs Mary E. KLOTMAN
50 Dean Fuqua School of Business William BOULDING
73 Dean of the Divinity School Edgardo COLON-EMERIC
58 Dean Grad Sch/Vice Prov Grad Educ Paula D. MCCLAIN
49 Dean Faculty Arts/Science Valerie ASHBY
66 Dean School of Nursing Vincent GUILAMO-RAMOS
54 Interim Dean of Engineering Jeff GLASS
80 Dean Sanford Sch of Public Policy Judith KELLEY
88 Director Duke University Press Dean SMITH
18 Vice President for Facilities John NOONAN
06 Registrar Frank BLALARK
09 Director of Institutional Research David JAMIESON-DRAKE
04 Executive Asst to the President Sarah BRAMAN
101 VP & University Secretary Margaret W. EPPS
102 Asst VP Foundation Relations Beth EASTLICK
105 Senior Manager Web Services Ryn NASSER
22 Vice President Institutional Equity Kimberly HEWITT
26 Chief Public Relations/Marketing Michael SCHOENFELD
29 Director Alumni Relations Sterly WILDER
32 Vice President Student Affairs Mary Pat MCMAHON
36 Executive Director Career Center Gregory J. VICTORY
41 VP and Director Athletics Nina E. KING
43 Vice President and General Counsel Pamela BERNARD
44 Asst VP Annual Giving Jennifer SPISAK-CAMERON
20 Vice Provost Undergrad Education Gary BENNETT
57 Vice Provost for the Arts John V. BROWN
86 Assoc VP Federal Relations Christopher SIMMONS
96 VP Supply Chain Jim CHURCHMAN
104 Executive Director Global Education Amanda KELSO
30 VP Alumni Affairs/Development David KENNEDY
88 Vice President Durham Affairs Stelfanie WILLIAMS
19 Chief of Police John DAILEY
39 Interim Dir Residential Life Deb LOBIONDO

ECPI University-Charlotte (G)

4800 Airport Center Pkwy #100, Charlotte NC 28208
Telephone: (704) 399-1010 Identification: 770951
Accreditation: &SC, MAAB

† Branch campus of ECPI University, Virginia Beach, VA

ECPI University-Greensboro (H)

7802 Airport Center Drive, Greensboro NC 27409
Telephone: (336) 792-7594 Identification: 770952
Accreditation: &SC, MAAB

† Branch campus of ECPI University, Virginia Beach, VA

ECPI University-Raleigh (I)

4101 Doie Cope Road, Raleigh NC 27613
Telephone: (919) 283-5748 Identification: 770953
Accreditation: &SC, MAAB

† Branch campus of ECPI University, Virginia Beach, VA

Elon University (J)

2700 Campus Box, Elon NC 27244-2010
County: Alamance FICE Identification: 002927
Unit ID: 198516
Telephone: (336) 278-2000 Carnegie Class: DU-Mod
FAX Number: N/A Calendar System: 4/1/4
URL: www.elon.edu
Established: 1889 Annual Undergrad Tuition & Fees: $37,921
Enrollment: 7,117 Coed
Affiliation or Control: Independent Non-Profit IRS Status: 501(c)3
Highest Offering: Doctorate
Accreditation: SC, ARCPA, CAEPN, JOUR, LAW, PTA

01 President Dr. Connie LEDOUX BOOK
05 Provost/Exec VP Academic Affairs Dr. Aswani VOLETY
45 VP for Strategic Iniatives Mr. Jeff STEIN
100 Chief of Staff/Sec to Bd Trustees Mr. Patrick NOLTEMEYER
03 Executive Vice President Dr. Steven HOUSE
88 SVP & Special Asst to President Mr. Gerald O. WHITTINGTON
88 Asst to Pres/VP Emeritus Stdnt Life Dr. Smith JACKSON
84 VP for Enrollment Mr. Greg ZAISER
32 Vice Pres for Student Life Dr. Jon DOOLEY
26 Vice Pres University Communications Mr. Daniel J. ANDERSON
22 VP/Assoc Prov Inclusive Excellence Dr. Randy WILLIAMS
111 Vice Pres University Advancement Mr. James B. PIATT
41 Director of Athletics Mr. Dave L. BLANK
88 VP for Access & Success Dr. Jean RATTIGAN-ROHR
20 Sr Assoc Provost for Faculty Affs Dr. Tim PEEPLES
20 Assoc Prov Acad Excellence/Opers Dr. Paul MILLER

20 Assoc Provost for Academic Affairs ... Dr. Jennifer PLATANIA
10 VP for Finance & Administration ... Mrs. Janet WILLIAMS
21 AVP Finance & Administration ... Ms. Susan M. KIRKLAND
49 Dean College of Arts & Sciences ... Dr. Gabie SMITH
50 Dean Love School of Business ... Dr. Raghu TADEPALLI
60 Dean of School of Communications ... Dr. Rochelle FORD
53 Dean of School of Education ... Dr. Ann BULLOCK
61 Dean of School of Law ... Mr. Luke BIERMAN
76 Dean of School of Health Sciences ... Dr. Becky NEIDUSKI
85 Dean of Global Studies ... Dr. Nick GOZIK
35 Associate VP of Student Life ... Mrs. Jana Lynn F. PATTERSON
08 Dean and University Librarian ... Ms. Joan RUELLE
06 Registrar ... Dr. Rodney PARKS
42 University Chaplain ... Vacant
37 Asst VP for Financial Aid ... Dr. M. Patrick MURPHY
110 Assoc VP University Advancement ... Mr. John BARNHILL
30 Assoc VP/Dir Principal Gifts ... Mr. Brian BAKER
29 Asst VP Annual Giv/Alum Engagement ... Mr. Brian FEELEY
110 Asst VP Univ Advancemt Parent Engmt . Ms. Jozi SNOWBERGER
121 Assoc Dean of Academic Support ... Dr. Anne BRYAN
36 Exec Director of Std Prof Dev Ctr ... Mr. Tom BRINKLEY
88 Dir of Planning/Design/Construction ... Mr. Brad D. MOORE
18 Asst VP of Physical Plant ... Mr. Tom FLOOD
15 Assoc VP Human Resources ... Ms. Kelli SHUMAN
109 Asst VP for Auxiliary Services ... Ms. Carrie RYAN
19 Chief of Campus Safety/Police ... Mr. Joe LEMIRE
23 Dir Student Health/Univ Physician ... Dr. Ginette ARCHINAL
38 Director Counseling Services ... Ms. Anita HODNETT
11 Asst VP for Admin Services ... Mr. Christopher D. FULKERSON
108 Dir Accreditation and Assessment ... Dr. Maurice LEVESQUE
09 Exec Director Institutional Rsrch ... Dr. Robert I. SPRINGER
13 Assoc VP for InfoTechnology and CIO ... Mr. Christopher C. WATERS
25 Director of Sponsored Programs ... Ms. Bonnie BRUNO
92 Director of Honors Program ... Dr. Lynn HUBER
94 Director Women's/Gender Studies ... Ms. Shayna MEHAS
96 Director of Purchasing ... Mr. Jeff HENDRICKS
88 Director of Sustainability ... Ms. Elaine DURR
104 Exec Dir of Global Engagement ... Ms. Rhonda WALLER
28 Dir Inclusive Excellence/Educ/Dev ... Ms. Carla FULLWOOD
39 Asst Dean Campus Life/Dir Res Life ... Mrs. MarQuita BARKER
102 Director Foundation/Corporate Rels ... Ms. Chris ESTERS
44 Director Annual Giving ... Ms. Chandler THOMPSON

Gardner-Webb University (A)

PO Box 897 (110 South Main Street),
Boiling Springs NC 28017-0897

County: Cleveland
FICE Identification: 002929
Unit ID: 198561
Telephone: (704) 406-2361
Carnegie Class: DU-Mod
FAX Number: (704) 406-4329
Calendar System: Semester
URL: www.gardner-webb.edu
Established: 1905
Annual Undergrad Tuition & Fees: $32,180
Enrollment: 3,536
Coed
Affiliation or Control: Baptist
IRS Status: 501(c)3
Highest Offering: Doctorate
Accreditation: SC, ACBSP, ADNUR, ARCPA, CACREP, CAEP, EXSC, MUS, NUR, THEOL

01 President ... Dr. William M. DOWNS
05 Provost & Executive Vice President ... Dr. Benjamin C. LESLIE
04 Sr Assistant to the President ... Mrs. Stephanie L. STEARNS
11 Vice President for Administration ... Mr. Timothy SHUEY
26 VP of Marketing ... Mr. Richard K. MCDEVITT
111 VP for External Affairs/Advancement ... Mr. Nate EVANS
32 Vice Pres Student Development ... Mrs. Lesley VILLAROSE
84 Vice Pres Enrollment Management ... Ms. Kristen SETZER
41 Vice President for Athletics ... Mr. Chuck S. BURCH
45 VP Planning & Inst Effectiveness ... Dr. Jeffrey L. TUBBS
18 Director of Operations ... Mr. David WACASTER
13 Asst VP for Technology Services ... Ms. Didi LEDBETTER
20 Assoc Provost Prof/Graduate Studies ... Dr. Bruce BOYLES
49 Assoc Provost for Arts & Sciences ... Dr. David YELTON
21 Assoc VP for Business & Finance ... Ms. Robin G. HAMRICK
07 Assoc VP for Undergrad Admissions ... Ms. Julie FLEMING
37 Asst VP for Financial Planning ... Ms. Anita ELLIOTT
06 Registrar ... Mrs. LouAnn P. SCATES
20 Assoc Provost Academic Development ... Ms. Carmen BUTLER
19 Chief of University Police ... Mr. Barry JOHNSON
27 Assoc VP for Marketing/Comm ... Mr. Noel T. MANNING
08 Director of the Library ... Ms. Pam DENNIS
38 Director of Counseling Services ... Ms. Stephanie ALLEN
89 Director of First-Year Programs ... Ms. Tammy BASS
58 Dean of Graduate School ... Dr. Elizabeth PACK
73 Dean of Divinity School ... Dr. Robert W. CANOY
66 Dean of Nursing School ... Dr. Tracy ARNOLD
92 Director of Honors Program ... Dr. Thomas H. JONES
88 Director Program for Blind/Deaf ... Mrs. Cheryl J. POTTER
21 Comptroller ... Ms. Haley KENDRICK
35 Director Student Activities ... Mr. Brian ARNOLD
42 Minister to the University ... Dr. Tracy C. JESSUP
39 Director of Residence Life ... Mr. John R. JOHNSON, JR.
50 Dean of Business School ... Ms. Mischia TAYLOR
15 Director Human Resources ... Mr. Eric PLEMMONS
09 Director of Institutional Research ... Ms. Lisa KINDLER
29 Director Alumni Relations ... Mrs. Leah CLEVENGER
44 Director of Annual Campaign ... Ms. Sara MCCALL
40 Bookstore Manager ... Ms. Jane POWELL
109 Director of Operations Support ... Mr. Brian SPEER
102 Dir Foundation/Corporate Relations ... Mr. Aaron HINTON
103 Director Workforce Development ... Mr. Micah MARTIN
106 Director of Digital Learning ... Dr. Emily ROBERTSON

108 Director Institutional Assessment ... Dr. Lucas STERN
28 Director of Diversity ... Vacant
53 Dean School of Education ... Dr. Prince BULL
105 AVP Web & Digital Communications .. Ms. Theandra THOMPSON
43 University Counsel ... Mr. Steve SERCK

Grace Communion Seminary (B)

3120 Whitehall Park Drive, Charlotte NC 28273-3335

County: Mecklenburg
Identification: 667115
Telephone: (980) 495-3978
Carnegie Class: Not Classified
FAX Number: (844) 350-3419
Calendar System: Semester
URL: www.gcs.edu
Established: 2008
Annual Graduate Tuition & Fees: N/A
Enrollment: N/A
Coed
Affiliation or Control: Independent Non-Profit
IRS Status: 501(c)3
Highest Offering: Master's; No Undergraduates
Accreditation: DEAC

01 President/CEO ... Dr. Gary DEDDO
05 Dean of Faculty ... Dr. Michael MORRISON
06 Registrar ... Ms. Georgia MCKINNON
10 CFO/Liaison Officer ... Dr. Russell DUKE

Greensboro College (C)

815 W Market Street, Greensboro NC 27401-1875

County: Guilford
FICE Identification: 002930
Unit ID: 198598
Telephone: (336) 272-7102
Carnegie Class: Bac-Diverse
FAX Number: (336) 217-6634
Calendar System: Semester
URL: www.greensboro.edu
Established: 1838
Annual Undergrad Tuition & Fees: $18,960
Enrollment: 944
Coed
Affiliation or Control: United Methodist
IRS Status: 501(c)3
Highest Offering: Master's
Accreditation: SC, ACBSP, MUS

00 Chairman of the Board ... Mr. Kevin GREEN
01 President ... Dr. Lawrence D. CZARDA
04 Exec Asst to President/Clerk to BoT ... Ms. Susan J. BARRINGER
100 Chief of Staff ... Ms. Emily M. SCOTT
05 VP Academic Affairs ... Dr. Daniel MALOTKY
10 VP Business & Finance ... Mr. Chris ELMORE
111 VP Advancement & Admissions ... Ms. Anne J. HURD
20 Assoc VP Academic Admin ... Ms. Martha M. BUNCH
20 Dean of the Faculty ... Dr. Jessica SHARPE
57 Dean School of Arts ... Prof. Jo HALL
50 Dean School of Business ... Dr. William K. MACREYNOLDS
53 Dean School of Soc Sci & Education ... Dr. Natasha VEALE
79 Dean School of Humanities ... Dr. Michelle PLAISANCE
81 Dean School of Science & Mathematic ... Dr. Stuart DAVIDSON
07 Dean of Admissions ... Ms. Julianne SCHATZ
13 Information Technology Director ... Vacant
14 Network Support Supervisor ... Ms. Stephanie FULLER
37 Financial Aid Director ... Ms. Lindsay S. LATHAM
113 Student Accounts Director ... Ms. Marilyn WOODS
26 Sr Dir Marketing & Communications ... Mr. Tom SAITTA
06 Registrar ... Mr. Travis MICKEY
32 Dean of Students ... Ms. Shana PLASTERS
39 Residence Life Coordinator ... Ms. Megan WHITCOMB
89 First Year Experience Director ... Ms. Jenna AVENT
36 Career Services Director ... Ms. Caryn ATWATER
104 Study Abroad Director ... Ms. Georgiann BOGDAN
09 Institutional Research Director ... Mr. Travis MICKEY
108 Director Institutional Assessment ... Dr. Dana L. DALTON
121 Academic Success Director ... Ms. Tica D. GREEN
124 Student Retention Director ... Ms. D'andre HARDY
28 Diversity Equity Inclusion Director ... Ms. Tasha M. MYERS
15 Human Resources Director ... Ms. Sonia HOFFMAN
18 Facilities Director ... Mr. Justin LISZKA
19 Security Director ... Mr. Calvin L. GILMORE
23 Student Health Director ... Ms. Lauren T. CHILDREY
38 Counseling Services Director ... Ms. Bernette JONES
92 George Ctr/Honors Studies Director ... Prof. Brittany SONDBERG
30 Asst VP Development ... Ms. Ellie P. YEARNS
29 Alumni Giving & Programs Director ... Ms. Destiney S. ALLEN
08 Library Director ... Mr. Will RITTER
41 Athletic Director ... Mr. Kim STRABLE
42 Campus Chaplain ... Rev. Robert W. BREWER
40 Bookstore Manager ... Mr. Cliff BRALY, JR.
21 Controller ... Ms. Michelle STILES
88 Title IX Coordinator ... Ms. Emily SCOTT

Guilford College (D)

5800 W Friendly Avenue, Greensboro NC 27410-4173

County: Guilford
FICE Identification: 002931
Unit ID: 198613
Telephone: (336) 316-2000
Carnegie Class: Bac-A&S
FAX Number: (336) 316-2950
Calendar System: Other
URL: www.guilford.edu
Established: 1837
Annual Undergrad Tuition & Fees: $40,120
Enrollment: 1,429
Coed
Affiliation or Control: Friends
IRS Status: 501(c)3
Highest Offering: Master's
Accreditation: SC, ACBSP

01 President ... Dr. Jim W. HOOD
05 Interim Provost ... Dr. Rob WHITNELL
04 Exec Administrator to Pres & CFO ... Dr. Meredeth D. SUMMERS
10 CFO/VP Administration & Finance ... Mr. John WILKINSON

26 Vice Pres Marketing/Enrollment ... Mr. Roger DEGERMAN
111 Vice Pres Advancement ... Dr. Ara SERJOIE
22 VP Diversity/Equity/Inclusion ... Dr. Barbara LAWRENCE
29 Assoc VP Alumni/Constituent Rels ... Mr. R. Ty BUCKNER
28 Assoc VP Diversity/Equity/Inclusion ... Dr. Krishauna HINES-GAITHER
32 Dean of Students ... Dr. Steven MENCARINI
20 Associate Academic Dean ... Dr. Kathryn SHIELDS
20 Interim Academic Dean ... Dr. Kyle DELL
37 Director of Financial Aid ... Ms. Char BEDILLION
06 Registrar ... Dr. Alfred MOORE
08 Director of the Library ... Ms. Suzanne M. BARTELS
41 Director of Athletics ... Dr. Bill FOTI
19 Director of Public Safety ... Mr. Jermaine THOMAS
15 Director Human Resources ... Ms. Janet GOULD
09 Dir Inst Research/Assessment ... Dr. Stephanie HARGRAVE
13 Director Info Technology & Services ... Ms. Gloria THORNTON
42 WR Rogers Dir of Friends Center ... Dr. C. Wess DANIELS
38 Director Student Counseling ... Ms. Taleisha BOWEN
92 Director Honors Program ... Dr. Heather HAYTON
96 Director of Purchasing ... Ms. Tracy A. HALL
104 Director Study Abroad ... Mr. Daniel DIAZ
88 Exec Coordinator to the Provost ... Ms. Lisa DEMERS
44 Director Annual Giving ... Vacant
07 Director of Admissions ... Mr. Kyle WOODEN

Heritage Bible College (E)

PO Box 1628, Dunn NC 28335-1628

County: Harnett
FICE Identification: 030893
Unit ID: 198677
Telephone: (910) 892-3178
Carnegie Class: Spec-4-yr-Faith
FAX Number: (910) 491-9790
Calendar System: Semester
URL: www.heritagebiblecollege.edu
Established: 1971
Annual Undergrad Tuition & Fees: $8,328
Enrollment: 43
Coed
Affiliation or Control: Other
IRS Status: 501(c)3
Highest Offering: Baccalaureate
Accreditation: TRACS

01 President ... Mr. Stephen RZONCA
05 Academic Dean ... Mrs. Dana SCHAEFER
10 Business Administrator ... Mrs. LeAnne PAGE
09 Dir Inst Effectiveness/Dir Library ... Ms. Janet PARKER
13 Chief Info Technology Officer (CIO) ... Mr. Wesley JOHNSON
07 Director Admissions/Financial Aid ... Mr. Sterling THARRINGTON
06 Registrar ... Mr. Matt CLARK

High Point University (F)

One University Parkway, High Point NC 27268-0001

County: Guilford
FICE Identification: 002933
Unit ID: 198695
Telephone: (336) 841-9000
Carnegie Class: Bac-Diverse
FAX Number: (336) 841-4599
Calendar System: Semester
URL: www.highpoint.edu
Established: 1924
Annual Undergrad Tuition & Fees: $38,080
Enrollment: 5,617
Coed
Affiliation or Control: United Methodist
IRS Status: 501(c)3
Highest Offering: Doctorate
Accreditation: SC, ARCPA, ART, CAATE, CAEP, CIDA, PHAR, PTA

01 President ... Dr. Nido R. QUBEIN
05 SVP for Academic Affairs/Provost ... Dr. Daniel E. ERB
10 Sr VP for Business Affairs ... Mr. Brad CALLOWAY
84 Sr VP for Graduate Enrollment ... Mr. Andy BILLS
26 Sr VP for Communications ... Mr. Roger D. CLODFELTER, JR.
32 SVP Student Life/Health/Wellness ... Mrs. Gail C. TUTTLE
30 Sr VP for Development ... Mr. Christopher H. DUDLEY
07 SVP for Undergrad Admissions ... Mr. Kerr C. RAMSAY
46 VP for Research and Planning ... Dr. Jeffrey M. ADAMS
18 VP for Facilities & Auxiliary Svcs ... Mr. Barry S. KITLEY
21 VP for Financial Affairs ... Ms. Debi S. BUTT
88 VP for Exp Learning & Career Dev ... Dr. Stephanie O. CROFTON
13 VP for Enterprise IT ... Mr. Curtis BARKER
41 VP for Athletics and AD ... Mr. Dan HAUSER
123 Assoc VP of Graduate Admissions ... Mr. Andrew S. MODLIN
35 Asst VP for Student Life ... Dr. Tara K. SHOLLENBERGER
35 Asst VP for Student Life ... Mr. Scott WOJCIECHOWSKI
35 Asst VP for Student Life ... Ms. Erica D. LEWIS
88 Asst VP for Graduate Admissions ... Mr. Lars C. FARABEE
27 Asst VP for Communication Mgt ... Ms. Hillary C. KOKAJKO
27 Asst VP for Communications ... Ms. Pamela J. HAYNES
110 Asst VP for Development ... Mr. McKennon SHEA
88 Asst VP for Facility Operations ... Mr. Troy J. THOMPSON
49 Dean of College of Arts & Science ... Mr. Ken D. ELSTON
57 Dean of School of Art and Design ... Dr. John C. TURPIN
50 Dean of School of Business ... Dr. James B. WEHRLEY
60 Dean of School of Communication . Dr. Virginia M. MCDERMOTT
53 Dean of School of Education ... Dr. Kristy P. DAVIS
54 Dean of the School of Engineering ... Dr. Michael OUDSHOORN
76 Dean of School of Health Sciences ... Dr. Daniel E. ERB
81 Dean of School of Natural Sciences ... Dr. Angela C. BAUER
67 Dean of School of Pharmacy ... Dr. Earl W. LINGLE
20 Assistant Dean Academic Services ... Ms. Karen C. NAYLON
08 Director of Library Services ... Mr. David L. BRYDEN
23 Medical Director ... Dr. Marnie S. MARLETTE
19 Chief of Security ... Mr. Derek S. STAFFORD
06 Registrar ... Mr. Danny K. BROOKS
15 AVP of Human Resources ... Mr. Marc SEARS
88 Sr Director of University Events ... Ms. Melissa L. ANDERSON
29 Director of Alumni Engagement ... Mr. Bradley G. TAYLOR
37 Sr Dir Student Financial Services ... Mr. Jonathan M. MADOR

25 Director of Sponsored Programs .... Ms. Leanna NICKS
38 Director of Counseling Services .... Dr. M.J RALEIGH
09 Dir of Inst Research & Assessment .... Mr. James S. LOWREY
113 Assoc Director of Student Accounts .... Ms. Megan INCH
96 Mgr Contracts & Procurement .... Mr. Gene BUNTING
40 Manager Bookstore .... Mr. William HOLSTON
85 Director of International Students .... Ms. Marjorie R. CHURCH
36 Director of Career Development .... Dr. William A. GENTRY
104 Director of Global Education .... Dr. Jeffrey M. PALIS
88 Director of Service Learning .... Dr. Joseph D. BLOSSER
88 Director of Undergraduate Research .... Dr. Joanne D. ALTMAN
04 Admin Assistant to President .... Ms. Judy K. RAY
88 Manager of University Mail Center .... Mr. Michael R. HALL
20 VP for Academic Affairs .... Dr. Angela C. BAUER

Hood Theological Seminary (A)

1810 Lutheran Synod Drive, Salisbury NC 28144-5768
County: Rowan FICE Identification: 036633
Unit ID: 443076
Telephone: (704) 636-7611 Carnegie Class: Spec-4-yr-Faith
FAX Number: (704) 636-7685 Calendar System: Semester
URL: www.hoodseminary.edu
Established: 1904 Annual Undergrad Tuition & Fees: N/A
Enrollment: 142 Coed
Affiliation or Control: African Methodist Episcopal Zion Church
IRS Status: 501(c)3
Highest Offering: Doctorate
Accreditation: THEOL

01 President .... Dr. Vergel L. LATTIMORE
05 Academic Dean .... Dr. Trevor EPPEHIMER
32 Dean of Students .... Dr. Dora R. MBUWAYESANGO
10 Chief Financial Officer .... RevDr. Regina M. DANCY
26 Dir Communication/Info/Pub .... Ms. Kelly BRYANT
111 Dir Institutional Advancement .... Mr. John C. EVERETT
06 Registrar .... Ms. Nancy BAKER
19 Chief of Security .... Mr. James MILTON
07 Director of Admissions .... RevDr. Reginald BOYD, JR.
08 Director of the Library .... Ms. Patricia COMMANDER
37 Director Student Financial Aid .... Ms. Angela DAVIS-BAXTER

Hosanna Bible College (B)

3519 Fayetteville St, Durham NC 27707
County: Durham Identification: 667373
Telephone: (919) 267-1640 Carnegie Class: Not Classified
FAX Number: (888) 392-4968 Calendar System: Semester
URL: www.hosannabc.org
Established: 1992 Annual Undergrad Tuition & Fees: N/A
Enrollment: N/A Coed
Affiliation or Control: Independent Non-Profit IRS Status: 501(c)3
Highest Offering: Doctorate
Accreditation: @TRACS

01 President .... Dr. Sherman R. TRIBBLE
03 Executive Vice President .... Keith ANDRESON
05 Provost/VP Academic Affairs .... Dr. LaTonya AGARD
10 Chief Financial Officer .... Darrin ALBRITTON
11 Vice President of Operation .... Angel HARVEY
13 Chief Technology Officer .... Debra HAMILTON
06 Registrar .... Mary FARRINGTON
18 Director of Physical Plant .... Clayton JOHNSON

Johnson & Wales University-Charlotte (C)

801 W Trade Street, Charlotte NC 28202-1122
Telephone: (980) 598-1000 Identification: 666375
Accreditation: &EH

† Regional accreditation is carried under the parent institution in Providence, RI.

Johnson C. Smith University (D)

100 Beatties Ford Road, Charlotte NC 28216-5398
County: Mecklenburg FICE Identification: 002936
Unit ID: 198756
Telephone: (704) 378-1000 Carnegie Class: Bac-A&S
FAX Number: (704) 372-1242 Calendar System: Semester
URL: www.jcsu.edu
Established: 1867 Annual Undergrad Tuition & Fees: $18,784
Enrollment: 1,306 Coed
Affiliation or Control: Independent Non-Profit IRS Status: 501(c)3
Highest Offering: Master's
Accreditation: SC, LC, SW

01 President .... Mr. Clarence (Clay) D. ARMBRISTER
05 Sr VP for Academic Affairs .... Dr. Karen MORGAN
10 Sr Vice Pres for Finance/Admin .... Mr. Greg PETZKE
111 Vice President for Inst Advancement .... Ms. Tami SIMMONS
86 VP Government Sponsored Pgms .... Dr. Diane BOWLES
15 VP Admin Svcs/Chief HR Officer ..... Ms. Latrelle P. MCALLISTER
32 Vice Pres Student Affairs .... Dr. Davida HAYWOOD
84 AVP Enrollment Management .... Dr. Rhonda MOSES
81 Dean College of STEM .... Dr. Vijaya L. GOMPA
49 Interim Dean of Arts and Letters .... Dr. Matthew DEFORREST
70 Dean of School of Social Work .... Dr. Helen CALDWELL
35 Dean of Students .... Mr. Takeem DEAN
89 Assoc Dean of First-Year Experience .... Dr. Cathy JONES
97 Dean of the University College .... Dr. Antonio HENLEY
107 Int Dean Metro College Prof Studies .Dr. Melita POPE MITCHELL
121 Dean of Academic Support Services .... Mr. John NORRIS
08 Director of the Library .... Ms. Monika RHUE
13 Chief Information Officer .... Mr. John NORRIS
09 Dir Assessment/Effect/Inst Rsrch .... Mrs. Sharell CANNADY
26 Director of Comm and Marketing .... Ms. Sherri BELFIELD
29 Director Alumni Affairs .... Mrs. Wanda FOY-BURROUGHS
37 Director Financial Aid .... Ms. Rochelle D. KING
41 Athletic Director .... Mr. Stephen JOYNER, SR.
06 Registrar .... Mrs. Keisha WILSON
40 Manager of Bookstore .... Ms. Kathy DEVLIN
117 Manager Risk Management .... Mrs. Debra HOLLIS
39 Coordinator of Housing Services .... Ms. Ashley SMITH
23 Health Center Coordinator .... Ms. Marian JONES
19 Dir Security/Safety/Chief Police .... Mr. Jermaine CHERRY
18 Director Facilities .... Ms. Erna JONES

Lees-McRae College (E)

191 Main Street, Banner Elk NC 28604-0128
County: Avery FICE Identification: 002939
Unit ID: 198808
Telephone: (828) 898-5241 Carnegie Class: Bac-Diverse
FAX Number: (828) 898-8814 Calendar System: Semester
URL: www.lmc.edu
Established: 1900 Annual Undergrad Tuition & Fees: $27,390
Enrollment: 838 Coed
Affiliation or Control: Presbyterian Church (U.S.A.) IRS Status: 501(c)3
Highest Offering: Master's
Accreditation: SC, NURSE

01 President .... Dr. Herbert L. KING
04 Exec Assistant to the President .... Ms. Michelle TAIT
05 Provost & Dean of Faculty .... Dr. Alyson GILL
45 VP Planning & External Relations .... Mr. Blaine J. HANSEN
10 VP Finance/Business Affairs .... Mr. Jon KOKOS
84 VP Enrollment Management .... Mr. Kevin PHILLIPS
111 VP for Institutional Advancement .... Mr. Edward ROBERTS
41 VP Athletics/Club Sports .... Mr. Craig MCPHAIL
32 VP for Student Affairs .... Dr. Melanie HULBERT
66 Dean Nursing/Health Sciences .... Dr. Kimberly S. PRIODE
79 Dean Arts/Humanities/Education .... Dr. Pamela VESELY
81 Dean Natural & Behavioral Sciences .... Vacant
50 Dean Business & Management .... Ms. Amy ANDERSON
111 Director of Advancement Services .... Ms. Mary TAYLOR
121 Dir Burton Ctr for Student Success .... Ms. Beth BEGGS
08 Director Libraries .... Ms. Jess BELLEMER
06 Registrar .... Ms. Lynn HINSHAW
19 Director Security/Safety .... Mr. H.D STEWART
13 Director Technology Services .... Vacant
15 Director Human Resources .... Ms. Mary FURST
21 Controller .... Ms. Susan STEPHENSON
35 Associate Dean of Students .... Vacant
26 Director Marketing & Design .... Ms. Lauren FOSTER
07 Director Admissions .... Ms. Amanda MERRITT
37 Director Financial Aid .... Ms. Karen KING
36 Director Career Services .... Ms. Grace CHAMPION
38 Director Counseling Services .... Ms. Marla GENTILE
113 Bursar .... Ms. Denise DYER
23 Director of Health Services .... Mr. Carl GRIEWISCH
121 Director of Tutoring Services .... Ms. Sue MCGUIRE
112 Major Gifts Officer .... Mr. Samuel STEPHENSON
09 Director of Institutional Research .... Ms. Taylor BARRY
18 Chief Facilities/Physical Plnt Ofcr .... Mr. James LEENHOUTS
29 Director Alumni Affairs .... Dr. Katie TALBERT
106 Dean of Online Education/E-learning .... Dr. Jennifer LOPES
28 Director of Diversity .... Vacant
39 Dir Resident Life/Student Housing .... Ms. Erin SMITH

Lenoir-Rhyne University (F)

625 7th Avenue NE, Hickory NC 28601-3984
County: Catawba FICE Identification: 002941
Unit ID: 198835
Telephone: (828) 328-1741 Carnegie Class: Masters/L
FAX Number: (828) 328-7368 Calendar System: Semester
URL: www.lr.edu
Established: 1891 Annual Undergrad Tuition & Fees: $39,900
Enrollment: 2,686 Coed
Affiliation or Control: Evangelical Lutheran Church In America
IRS Status: 501(c)3
Highest Offering: Doctorate
Accreditation: SC, ACBSP, CAATE, CACREP, DIETI, NURSE, OT, PH, THEOL

01 President .... Dr. Fred WHITT
05 Provost .... Dr. Gary JOHNSON
10 Sr Vice President Finance/Admin .... Mr. Jeremy SHREVE
111 Vice Pres Institutional Advancement .... Mrs. Catherine NIEKRO
84 Vice President for Enrollment Mgmt .... Ms. Rachel NICHOLS
32 Asst Provost/Dean of Students .... Dr. Katie FISHER
28 Vice President for DEI .... Mr. Avery STALEY
58 Dean Grad Studies/Lifelong Learning .... Dr. Amy WOOD
06 Registrar .... Mr. Stacey BRACKETT
08 Librarian .... Mr. Frank QUINN
15 Director of Human Resources .... Ms. Angelene FORTUNE
40 Director of Bookstore .... Vacant
18 Director of Facilities/Plant .... Mr. Jesse CHILDERS
41 Athletic Director .... Ms. Kim PATE
42 Campus Pastor .... Rev. Todd CUTTER
19 Director of Security .... Mr. Norris YODER
92 Director of Honors Program .... Dr. Joshua RING
13 Chief Information Officer .... Ms. Cherie WHIPPLE
26 Dir of Marketing/Athletics .... Ms. Leah CLAYTON
88 Director of Conferences & Events .... Ms. Jessica STEWART
07 Director of Enrollment Services .... Mr. Eric BRANDON
09 Dir of Inst Research/Assess .... Vacant
37 Director Student Financial Aid .... Ms. Courtney THOMPSON-BALLARD
38 Dir Student Counseling/Placement .... Ms. Jenny SMITH
88 Dir Liberal Arts/Visiting Writers .... Dr. Rand BRANDES
28 Director Multicultural Affairs .... Vacant
88 Director Solmaz Institute .... Ms. Kimberly PENNINGTON
65 Co-Director Reese Institute .... Dr. John BRZORAD
85 Dir of International Programs .... Dr. Laura DOBSON
53 Dean Col of Education/Human Svcs .... Dr. Hank WEDDINGTON
76 Dean College of Health Sciences .... Dr. Michael MCGEE
49 Dean College of Arts & Sciences .... Dr. Dan KISER
81 Dean Col of Profess/Math Studies .... Dr. Mary LESSER
36 Director Student Placement .... Ms. Katie WOHLMAN
39 Director Student Housing .... Mr. Jonathan RINK
43 Dir of Compliance/Title IX .... Ms. Dawn FLOYD
04 Admin Assistant to the President .... Ms. Cameron WOMACK
29 Director Alumni Affairs .... Ms. Mary Ellen SHERRILL
44 Director Annual Giving .... Ms. Tatum POTTENGER

Living Arts College @ School of Communication Arts (G)

3000 Wakefield Crossing Drive, Raleigh NC 27614-7076
County: Wake FICE Identification: 031090
Unit ID: 421832
Telephone: (919) 488-8500 Carnegie Class: Bac-Diverse
FAX Number: (919) 488-8490 Calendar System: Quarter
URL: www.living-arts-college.edu
Established: 1992 Annual Undergrad Tuition & Fees: $16,600
Enrollment: 171 Coed
Affiliation or Control: Proprietary IRS Status: Proprietary
Highest Offering: Baccalaureate
Accreditation: ACICS

01 Campus President .... James RAMSEY, III

Livingstone College (H)

701 W Monroe Street, Salisbury NC 28144-5298
County: Rowan FICE Identification: 002942
Unit ID: 198862
Telephone: (704) 216-6000 Carnegie Class: Bac-Diverse
FAX Number: (704) 216-6217 Calendar System: Semester
URL: www.livingstone.edu
Established: 1879 Annual Undergrad Tuition & Fees: $18,296
Enrollment: 845 Coed
Affiliation or Control: African Methodist Episcopal Zion Church
IRS Status: 501(c)3
Highest Offering: Baccalaureate
Accreditation: SC, IACBE, SW

01 President .... Dr. Jimmy R. JENKINS, SR.
04 Exec Asst to the President .... Dr. State W. ALEXANDER
05 Vice Pres Academic Affairs .... Dr. Kelli V. RANDALL
10 Vice Pres Business & Finance/Ops .... Mr. Reginald DICKENS
32 Vice President Student Affairs .... Dr. Orlando LEWIS
111 VP Inst Advance/College Rels/COO .... Dr. Anthony J. DAVIS
35 Assoc Vice Pres of Student Affairs .... Dr. Tony BALDWIN
20 Asst Vice Pres Academic Affairs .... Vacant
38 Dean of Counseling Services .Mrs. Elizabeth ALSTON-PINCKNEY
06 Registrar .... Mrs. Wendy JACKSON
08 Director Library Services .... Ms. Laura JOHNSON
26 Vice Pres Communications & PR .... Dr. State W. ALEXANDER
37 Director of Financial Aid .... Ms. Stephanie MCNEIL
36 Director of Career Services .... Ms. Brenda MITCHELL
13 Director of Computer Info Systems .... Mr. Chong DAN
15 Director of Human Resources .... Mr. Avery STALEY
29 Director Alumni Affairs .... Ms. Vincia MILLER
09 Director of Institutional Research .... Mr. Robert L. MCINNIS
84 Assoc VP of Enrollment Management .... Dr. Tony BALDWIN
07 Director of Admissions .... Vacant
40 Bookstore & Retail Coordinator .... Mr. Timothy GRAY
41 Athletic Director .... Mr. Lamonte J. MASSEY-SAMPSON
27 Director Public Relations .... Ms. Kimberly HARRINGTON

Louisburg College (I)

501 N. Main Street, Louisburg NC 27549-7705
County: Franklin FICE Identification: 002943
Unit ID: 198871
Telephone: (919) 496-2521 Carnegie Class: Assoc/HT-High Trad
FAX Number: (919) 496-7141 Calendar System: Semester
URL: www.louisburg.edu
Established: 1787 Annual Undergrad Tuition & Fees: $19,795
Enrollment: 490 Coed
Affiliation or Control: United Methodist IRS Status: 501(c)3
Highest Offering: Associate Degree
Accreditation: SC

01 President .... Dr. Gary M. BROWN
05 VP of Academic Life .... Dr. Calandra LOCKHART
10 Chief Financial Officer .... Ms. Anna FAATILIGA
84 Senior VP of Enrollment Management .... Ms. Stephanie B. TOLBERT
44 Director of Annual Giving .... Ms. Jamie PATRICK
06 Registrar .... Ms. Carla A. WASHINGTON
08 Librarian .... Ms. Kristine JONES
38 Director of Counseling Services .... Ms. Fonda PORTER

37 Director of Financial Aid ..... Ms. Ashley SCHREINER
18 Associate VP of Facilities ..... Mr. Nathan BIEGENZAHN
04 Administrative Asst to President ..... Vacant
07 Director of Admissions ..... Ms. Timyra STANTON
09 Director of Institutional Research ..... Vacant
19 Director of Campus Safety ..... Mr. Chris ADKINS
41 Athletic Director ..... Mr. Mike HOLLOMAN
13 Chief Technology Officer ..... Mr. Adam SNELL
15 Director of Human Resources ..... Ms. Terry WRIGHT

Lumbee River Christian College (A)

PO Box 248, Shannon NC 28386
County: Hoke Identification: 667092
Telephone: (910) 843-5304 Carnegie Class: Not Classified
FAX Number: N/A Calendar System: Semester
URL: lumbeeriver.edu
Established: 1968 Annual Undergrad Tuition & Fees: N/A
Enrollment: N/A Coed
Affiliation or Control: Assemblies Of God Church IRS Status: 501(c)3
Highest Offering: Baccalaureate
Accreditation: BI

01 President ..... James A. KEYS
05 Acting Academic Dean ..... Tony BUCHANAN
11 Vice Pres Administration ..... Justin NICHOLS
32 Vice Pres Student Life ..... John DAVIS
08 Chief Librarian ..... Liisa KELLY
06 Registrar/Dir Financial Aid ..... Carolee NICHOLS
108 Director Institutional Assessment ..... Gay DAVIS
10 Chief Financial Officer ..... Tracy KEYS
07 Director of Admissions ..... Justin NICHOLS
21 Associate Financial Officer ..... Candace BUCHANAN

Manna University (B)

5117 Cliffdale Road, Fayetteville NC 28314
County: Cumberland FICE Identification: 041737
Unit ID: 461528
Telephone: (910) 221-2224 Carnegie Class: Spec-4-yr-Faith
FAX Number: N/A Calendar System: Semester
URL: https://manna.edu/
Established: 2000 Annual Undergrad Tuition & Fees: $6,200
Enrollment: 247 Coed
Affiliation or Control: Other Protestant IRS Status: 501(c)3
Highest Offering: Doctorate
Accreditation: BI

01 President ..... Dr. Steven CROWTHER
11 Vice President of Administration ..... Ms. Cathy LUCAS
05 Academic Dean ..... Mr. Ron MCBRIDE
84 Dean of Enrollment Management ..... Mr. Frank BRAZELL
32 Dean of Students ..... Mr. John MCINTYRE
106 Dean of Online Education/E-Learning ..... Ms. Stefanie ERTEL
10 Chief Financial Officer ..... Ms. Omayra COON
30 Director of Development ..... Dr. Diane AXON
08 Librarian ..... Ms. Elsa MCBRIDE
108 Director of Assessment & Planning ..... Ms. Sharyn J. TEAGUE
06 Registrar ..... Ms. Dahly ALLUP

Mars Hill University (C)

PO Box 370, Mars Hill NC 28754-0370
County: Madison FICE Identification: 002944
Unit ID: 198899
Telephone: (828) 689-1307 Carnegie Class: Bac-Diverse
FAX Number: (828) 689-1478 Calendar System: Semester
URL: www.mhu.edu
Established: 1856 Annual Undergrad Tuition & Fees: $35,052
Enrollment: 1,049 Coed
Affiliation or Control: Independent Non-Profit IRS Status: 501(c)3
Highest Offering: Master's
Accreditation: SC, AAQEP, MUS, NURSE, SW

01 President ..... Dr. Tony FLOYD
111 Vice President for Inst Advancement ..... Mr. Harold (Bud) G. CHRISTMAN
05 Provost & VP of Enrollment Mgmt ..... Dr. Tracy PARKINSON
10 Vice President for Finance ..... Mr. Roger SLAGLE
32 VP for Student Life ..... Dr. David ROZEBOOM
07 Director of Admissions ..... Ms. Kristie VANCE
06 University Registrar ..... Ms. Marie NICHOLSON
08 Director of Library Services ..... Vacant
26 Sr Dir of Marketing/Communications ..... Ms. Samantha FENDER
11 Sr Director of Planning & Strategy ..... Dr. Grainger CAUDLE
42 University Chaplain ..... Rev. Stephanie MCLESKEY
41 Athletic Director ..... Mr. Rick BAKER
37 Director of Financial Aid ..... Ms. Nichole BUCKNER
85 Director International Education ..... Dr. Greg CLEMMONS
09 Director Institutional Research ..... Dr. Kim REIGLE
38 Director of Counseling ..... Vacant
13 Chief Information Officer ..... Mr. Ted BRUNER
18 Director of Facilities ..... Vacant
109 Director of Auxiliary Services ..... Vacant
19 Director of Security/Safety ..... Mr. Kevin WEST
28 Dir of Diversity/Equity/Inclusion ..... Mr. Jonathan MCCOY
29 Ex Dir of Alumni & Board Relations ..... Dr. Joy KISH
112 Director of Donor Relations ..... Mr. John CHASTAIN
44 Director of the Mars Hill Fund ..... Ms. Erin MAENNLE
102 Foundations Engagement ..... Ms. Stacey SPARKS
04 Admin Assistant to the President ..... Ms. Danielle HAGERMAN
108 Dir Inst Effectiveness/Assessment ..... Vacant
36 Director of Career Services ..... Mr. James KNIGHT

Meredith College (D)

3800 Hillsborough Street, Raleigh NC 27607-5298
County: Wake FICE Identification: 002945
Unit ID: 198950
Telephone: (919) 760-8600 Carnegie Class: Bac-A&S
FAX Number: (919) 760-2828 Calendar System: Semester
URL: www.meredith.edu
Established: 1891 Annual Undergrad Tuition & Fees: $39,952
Enrollment: 1,802 Female
Affiliation or Control: Independent Non-Profit IRS Status: 501(c)3
Highest Offering: Master's
Accreditation: SC, CAEPN, CIDA, DIETD, DIETI, MUS, SW

01 President ..... Dr. Jo ALLEN
05 Sr Vice Pres and Provost ..... Dr. Matthew POSLUSNY
111 Vice Pres Institutional Advancement ..... Dr. Charles (Lennie) BARTON
10 Vice Pres for Business & Finance ..... Dr. Tammi JACKSON
32 Vice President for College Programs ..... Dr. Jean JACKSON
26 Vice President of Marketing ..... Ms. Kristi EAVES-MCLENNAN
35 Dean of Students ..... Ms. Ann C. GLEASON
58 Director of Graduate Programs ..... Dr. Monica MCKINNEY
06 Registrar ..... Ms. Shelly MCMAHON
09 Dir Research/Planning & Assessment ..... Dr. C. Dianne RAUBENHEIMER
08 Director Library Info Services ..... Ms. Laura DAVIDSON
07 Director of Admissions ..... Ms. Shery BOYLES
37 Director of Financial Assistance ..... Mr. Kevin MICHAELSEN
35 Dir Student Activ/Leadership Devel ..... Ms. Cheryl S. JENKINS
28 Assistant Dean of Students ..... Ms. Tomecca SLOANE
36 Director Office of Career Planning ..... Ms. Dana SUMNER
29 Dir of Alumnae & Parent Relations ..... Ms. Hilary ALLEN
38 Director of Counseling Center ..... Ms. Beth A. MEIER
121 Director of Academic Advising ..... Dr. Alex DAVIS
31 Director Campus Events ..... Mr. Bill BROWN
23 Director Health Services ..... Dr. Mary JOHNSON
42 Campus Minister ..... Rev. Stacy PARDUE
13 Chief Information Officer ..... Mr. Jeffrey HOWLETT
19 Chief Campus Police ..... Mr. Al WHITE
15 Director of Human Resources ..... Ms. Pamela GALLOWAY
18 Chief Facilities/Physical Plant ..... Ms. Sharon CAMPBELL
21 Director of Accounting ..... Ms. Susan WILLIAMS
88 Director of Learning Center ..... Ms. Tina ROMANELLI
104 Director of International Programs ..... Dr. Brooke SHURER
124 Dir Retention & Student Success ..... Mr. Brandon STOKES
88 Director of Strong Points ..... Ms. Candice WEBB

Methodist University (E)

5400 Ramsey Street, Fayetteville NC 28311-1498
County: Cumberland FICE Identification: 002946
Unit ID: 198969
Telephone: (910) 630-7005 Carnegie Class: Masters/S
FAX Number: (910) 630-7317 Calendar System: Semester
URL: www.methodist.edu
Established: 1956 Annual Undergrad Tuition & Fees: $36,076
Enrollment: 1,773 Coed
Affiliation or Control: United Methodist IRS Status: 501(c)3
Highest Offering: Doctorate
Accreditation: SC, ACBSP, ARCPA, #CAATE, NURSE, OT, PTA, SW

01 President ..... Dr. Stanley T. WEARDEN
05 Provost ..... Dr. Suzanne BLUM MALLEY
11 VP Planning and Administration ..... Ms. Sheila C. KINSEY
10 VP Business Affairs/Controller ..... Ms. Dawn AUSBORN
32 VP for Student Affairs ..... Mr. William WALKER
84 VP Enrollment Management ..... Mr. Rick D. LOWE
111 VP Institutional Advancement ..... Mr. Greg SWANSON
42 VP Campus Ministry/Cmty Engagement ..... Rev. Kelli W. TAYLOR
41 VP/Director of Athletics ..... Mr. Dave EAVENSON
106 Vice Prov Online/Extended Learning ..... Dr. Beth CARTER
13 Chief Information Officer ..... Dr. Mary LEARY MCCANTS
28 Chief Diversity Officer ..... Dr. Quincy MALLOY, SR.
07 Dean of Admissions ..... Mr. Jamie W. LEGG
35 Assoc Dean Student Services ..... Mr. Todd D. HARRIS
36 Assoc Dean Student/Career Services . Ms. Antoinette P. BELLAMY
29 Director Alumni Affairs ..... Ms. Taylor MURPHY
26 Director Marketing/Communication ..... Mr. Brad JOHNSON
88 Director of Accreditation ..... Dr. Donald L. LASSITER
37 Director of Financial Aid ..... Ms. Bonnie J. ADAMSON
06 Registrar ..... Ms. Jasmin K. BROWN
08 Head Librarian ..... Ms. Tracey PEARSON
104 Dir Intl Programs/Study Abroad ..... Ms. Minnu PAUL
19 Director Police/Public Safety ..... Mr. Mark BREWINGTON
15 Director Human Resources ..... Mrs. Debra YEATTS
18 Director of Facilities ..... Mr. Bill YOUNG
38 Director Student Counseling ..... Dr. Deirdre JACKSON
96 Director of Purchasing ..... Ms. Mckenzie JACKSON
04 Exec Assistant to the President ..... Ms. Jessica W. HOBBS
105 Director Web Services ..... Mr. Michael MOLTER
25 Chief Contract/Grants Administrator ..... Ms. Wendy HUSTWIT
39 Director Housing & Residence Life ..... Ms. Barb MORGAN
90 Director Academic Computing ..... Mr. Bruce MORGAN

Mid-Atlantic Christian University (F)

715 N Poindexter, Elizabeth City NC 27909-4054
County: Pasquotank FICE Identification: 022809
Unit ID: 199458
Telephone: (252) 334-2000 Carnegie Class: Spec-4-yr-Faith
FAX Number: (252) 334-2071 Calendar System: Semester
URL: www.macuniversity.edu
Established: 1948 Annual Undergrad Tuition & Fees: $16,490
Enrollment: 165 Coed
Affiliation or Control: Churches Of Christ IRS Status: 501(c)3
Highest Offering: Baccalaureate
Accreditation: SC

01 President ..... Mr. John W. MAURICE, JR.
05 Vice President Academic Affairs ..... Dr. Kevin W. LARSEN
32 Vice President Student Life ..... Dr. E. Jay BANKS
84 Vice President Enrollment Services ..... Mr. Marty RILEY
111 Director Inst Advancement ..... Mrs. Elizabeth H. CROSS
10 Vice President Finance ..... Mrs. Sara SHEPHERD
09 Director of Institutional Research ..... Dr. Kevin W. LARSEN
06 Registrar ..... Miss Yolanda K. TESKE
08 Director of Library ..... Vacant
38 Counselor ..... Dr. David S. KING
37 Financial Aid Administrator ..... Mrs. Emily MENEELY
35 Student Life Administrator ..... Mr. Charles MABE
49 Chair of Arts and Sciences ..... Dr. Robert W. SMITH
42 Chair of Bible & Christian Ministry ..... Dr. Claudio F. DIVINO
88 Chair of Marketplace Ministry ..... Dr. David S. KING
41 Athletic Director ..... Mr. J. Andy MENEELY

Miller-Motte College (G)

3725 Ramsey Street, Fayetteville NC 28311
Telephone: (910) 354-1900 Identification: 770728
Accreditation: ACCSC

† Branch campus of Platt College, Tulsa, OK.

Miller-Motte College (H)

105 New Frontier Way, Jacksonville NC 28546
Telephone: (910) 478-4300 Identification: 770729
Accreditation: ACCSC

† Branch campus of Platt College, Tulsa, OK.

Miller-Motte College (I)

3901 Capital Boulevard, Suite 151, Raleigh NC 27604
Telephone: (919) 230-6471 Identification: 770727
Accreditation: ACCSC, DA, MAC

† Branch campus of Platt College, Tulsa, OK.

Miller-Motte Technical College (J)

5000 Market Street, Wilmington NC 28405-3430
Telephone: (910) 442-3525 FICE Identification: 030632
Accreditation: ACCSC, DA, MAC

† Branch campus of Platt College, Tulsa, OK.

Montreat College (K)

PO Box 1267, 310 Gaither Circle,
Montreat NC 28757-1267
County: Buncombe FICE Identification: 002948
Unit ID: 199032
Telephone: (828) 669-8012 Carnegie Class: Masters/S
FAX Number: (828) 669-9554 Calendar System: Semester
URL: www.montreat.edu
Established: 1916 Annual Undergrad Tuition & Fees: $28,750
Enrollment: 950 Coed
Affiliation or Control: Non-denominational IRS Status: 501(c)3
Highest Offering: Master's
Accreditation: SC, CACREP

01 President ..... Dr. Paul J. MAURER
10 VP for Finance and Administration ..... Mr. Josh TRUSCHEL
58 VP and Dean for Adult/Grad Studies ..... Dr. Dave POOLE
05 VP and Dean for Academic Affairs ..... Ms. Ashley RHYMER
84 VP for Enrollment Mgmt & Athletics ..... Mr. Jose LARIOS
32 VP & Dean for Student Services ..... Dr. Daniel BENNETT
111 Chief Advancement Officer ..... Mr. Joe KIRKLAND
26 VP Marketing/Communications ..... Ms. Sara BAUGHMAN
108 Director of Assessment ..... Mr. Brad FAIRCLOTH
41 Athletic Director ..... Mr. Jose LARIOS
29 Director Alumni Relations ..... Ms. Samantha NORTHEY
37 Director of Student Financial Svcs ..... Mr. Jeremy HURSE
38 Director of Counseling ..... Mr. Wesley DAVIS
110 Director for Advancement Services ..... Ms. Kristine BUCKWALTER
08 Library Director ..... Mr. Nathan KING
21 Controller ..... Mrs. Patti GUFFEY
04 Executive Assistant to President ..... Ms. Catherine RYBIOKI
42 Dean of Spiritual Formation ..... Rev. Rachel TOONE
06 Registrar ..... Mr. Fred MILLER
40 Bookstore Manager ..... Mrs. Carly LEE
19 Director of Campus Security ..... Mr. Bill HENSLEY
18 Chief Facilities/Physical Plant ..... Mr. Alan EDWARDS
13 Chief Information Technology Office ..... Mr. Paul HAWKINSON
07 Director of Admissions ..... Mrs. Erin CHAPMAN
15 Human Resources Officer ..... Ms. Mickie KELLY

*North Carolina Community College System (L)

200 W Jones Street, 5001 MSC, Raleigh NC 27699-5001
County: Wake FICE Identification: 033445
Telephone: (919) 807-7100 Carnegie Class: N/A
FAX Number: (919) 807-7166
URL: www.nccommunitycolleges.edu

01 President ....Mr. Thomas STITH, III
05 Sr Vice Pres/Chief Academic Officer ....Dr. Kimberly GOLD
100 Chief of Staff/EVP ....Ms. Jennifer HAYGOOD
10 Vice Pres/Chief Financial Officer ....Ms. Elizabeth GROVENSTEIN
13 SVP/CIO Technology Solutions ....Mr. Jim PARKER
46 Assoc VP for STEM Innovation ....Dr. Matthew MEYER
101 Exec Director State Board Affairs ....Mr. Bryan JENKINS
04 Exec Assistant to the President ....Ms. Kelly BARRETTO

*Alamance Community College (A)

1247 Jimmie Kerr Road/PO Box 8000,
Graham NC 27253-8000

County: Alamance FICE Identification: 005463
Unit ID: 199786
Telephone: (336) 578-2002 Carnegie Class: Assoc/MT-VT-Mix Trad/Non
FAX Number: (336) 578-1987 Calendar System: Semester
URL: www.alamancecc.edu
Established: 1958 Annual Undergrad Tuition & Fees (In-District): $2,492
Enrollment: 4,037 Coed
Affiliation or Control: State/Local IRS Status: 501(c)3
Highest Offering: Associate Degree
Accreditation: SC, ACFEI, DA, EMT, HT, MAC, MLTAD

02 President ....Dr. Algie C. GATEWOOD
03 Executive Vice President ....Dr. Constance WOLFE
10 VP Admin & Fiscal Svcs ....Mr. Christopher D. CREPPS
111 VP Institutional Advancement ....Ms. Carolyn RHODE
05 VP of Instruction ....Dr. Lisa JOHNSON
103 VP Workforce Development ....Mr. Gary SAUNDERS
32 VP Student Success ....Dr. Carol DISQUE
50 Dean Business/Arts & Sciences ....Ms. Sonya MCCOOK
72 Dean Industrial Technologies ....Mr. Justin SNYDER
69 Dean Health & Public Svcs ....Mr. David FRAZEE
21 Controller ....Ms. Steffanie VAUGHAN
06 Registrar ....Mr. Kenneth DOBBINS
11 AVP Administrative Services ....Mr. Thomas HARTMAN
15 Interim Director Human Resources ....Ms. Valerie FEARRINGTON
13 Director Information Services ....Mr. Shawn O'HARA
08 Director Learning Resources Center ....Ms. Sara THYNNE
26 Director Public Information/Mktg ....Ms. Sarah HARDIN
56 Director Occupational Ext Program ....Vacant
84 Director Enrollment Management ....Ms. Elizabeth BREHLER
37 Director Financial Aid ....Ms. Sabrina DEGAIN
36 Director Counseling & Career Svcs ....Ms. Ilona OWENS
38 Special Needs/Counseling Svcs Coord ....Ms. Monica ISBELL
121 Academic Support Specialist ....Ms. Jennifer BROWNELL
09 Institutional Researcher ....Dr. Jessica HARRELL
19 Director Security/Safety ....Vacant
04 Admin Assistant to the President ....Ms. Darian RADER
28 Director of Diversity & Inclusion ....Mr. Josefvon JONES

*Asheville - Buncombe Technical Community College (B)

340 Victoria Road, Asheville NC 28801-4897

County: Buncombe FICE Identification: 004033
Unit ID: 197887
Telephone: (828) 398-7900 Carnegie Class: Assoc/MT-VT-High Non
FAX Number: (828) 281-9696 Calendar System: Semester
URL: www.abtech.edu
Established: 1959 Annual Undergrad Tuition & Fees (In-District): $2,632
Enrollment: 6,601 Coed
Affiliation or Control: State/Local IRS Status: 501(c)3
Highest Offering: Associate Degree
Accreditation: SC, ACFEI, DA, DH, DMS, EMT, MAC, MLTAD, OTA, RAD, SURGT

02 President ....Dr. John GOSSETT
10 VP Business & Finance/CFO ....Dr. Dirk WILMOTH
13 Vice Pres Information Technology ....Mr. Brian WILLIS
05 VP Instructional Services ....Dr. Beth STEWART
20 Associate VP Instructional Services ....Dr. Gene LOFLIN
32 VP Student Services ....Dr. Terry BRASIER
15 Exec Dir Human Resources & OD ....Ms. Shanna CHAMBERS
103 VP Econ/Workforce Dev/Cont Educ ....Ms. Deborah WRIGHT
04 Executive Administrative Assistant ....Ms. Carolyn RICE
111 Exec Director College Advancement ....Ms. Amanda EDWARDS
49 Dean Arts & Sciences ....Mr. Kenet ADAMSON
50 Dean Business & Hospitality Educ ....Ms. Brenda MCFARLAND
54 Dean Engineering & Applied Tech ....Mr. Vernon D. DAUGHERTY
35 Director Student Life/Development ....Ms. Michele HATHCOCK
21 Exec Director Business Services ....Ms. Melissa VALKO
37 Director of Financial Aid ....Ms. Cynthia ANDERSON
06 Associate Registrar ....Mr. Jason HECHT
84 Director Enrollment Services ....Ms. Lisa F. BUSH
24 Director Library Services ....Mr. Russell TAYLOR
12 Director Madison County Campus ....Ms. Sherri DAVIS
18 Director Plant Operations ....Mr. Lee PACK
19 Chief of Police/Security ....Ms. Kara WALKER
31 Director Community Services Program ....Ms. Brinda W. CALDWELL
08 Librarian ....Mr. Russell TAYLOR
09 Exec Director Research & Planning ....Ms. Anne OXENREIDER
26 Exec Dir Community Rels/Marketing ....Ms. Kerri GLOVER
28 Director of Diversity ....Vacant
40 Bookstore Manager ....Mr. Taylor NORRIS
96 Purchasing Agent ....Ms. Rebecca R. WATKINS
72 Dir Cust Rels/Technology Services ....Mr. Cris HARSHMAN

*Beaufort County Community College (C)

5337 US Hwy 264 East, Washington NC 27889-7889

County: Beaufort FICE Identification: 008558
Unit ID: 197966
Telephone: (252) 946-6194 Carnegie Class: Assoc/HT-High Trad
FAX Number: (252) 940-6234 Calendar System: Semester
URL: www.beaufortccc.edu
Established: 1967 Annual Undergrad Tuition & Fees (In-District): $2,518
Enrollment: 1,382 Coed
Affiliation or Control: State/Local IRS Status: 501(c)3
Highest Offering: Associate Degree
Accreditation: SC, MLTAD

02 President ....Dr. David LOOPE
05 VP of Academic Affairs ....Dr. Jay SULLIVAN
10 VP of Administrative Services ....Mr. Mark NELSON
32 VP of Student Services ....Dr. LaTonya NIXON
51 VP of Continuing Education ....Mrs. Stacey GERARD
111 VP of Institutional Advancement ....Ms. Serena SULLIVAN
09 Dean Inst Effectiveness ....Ms. Erica S. CARACOGLIA
26 Mktg & PR Coordinator ....Mr. Attila NEMECZ
31 Dir of Community Partnerships ....Mr. Clay CARTER
66 Dean of Nursing & Allied Health ....Mr. Kent DICKERSON
49 Dean Arts & Sciences ....Dr. Lisa HILL
50 Dean of Business & Industrial Tech ....Mr. Ben MORRIS
08 Director of Library ....Mrs. Paula HOPPER
14 Network Administrator ....Mr. Whiting TOLER
91 System Administrator ....Mr. Brandon BUNCH
15 Director of Human Resources ....Ms. Nicole HAM
19 Chief of Campus Police ....Mr. Todd ALLIGOOD
37 Director of Financial Aid ....Ms. Crystal TAYLOR
06 Registrar ....Ms. Melissa A. FRANCIS
07 Director of Admissions ....Mrs. Michele MAYO
103 Dir of Business & Industry Svcs ....Mr. Lentz STOWE
04 Executive Asst to President & Board ....Mrs. Jennie SINGLETON
96 Purchasing Coordinator ....Ms. Rebecca ADAMS
38 Director of Counseling ....Mrs. Kimberly JACKSON
105 Webmaster ....Mr. Patrick ROHRMAN
18 Dir Campus Operations ....Mr. Jason SQUIRES
13 Chief Technology Officer/Info Tech ....Mr. Arthur RICHARD
21 Controller ....Ms. Gay EDWARDS

*Bladen Community College (D)

PO Box 266, Dublin NC 28332-0266

County: Bladen FICE Identification: 007987
Unit ID: 198011
Telephone: (910) 879-5500 Carnegie Class: Assoc/MT-VT-Mix Trad/Non
FAX Number: (910) 879-5564 Calendar System: Semester
URL: www.bladencc.edu
Established: 1967 Annual Undergrad Tuition & Fees (In-State): $2,558
Enrollment: 1,057 Coed
Affiliation or Control: State IRS Status: 501(c)3
Highest Offering: Associate Degree
Accreditation: SC

02 President ....Dr. Amanda LEE
04 Exec Admin Asst to the President ....Ms. Melissa HESTER
05 VP and Chief Academic Officer ....Ms. Cynthia MCKOY
111 VP for Institutional Advancement ....Ms. Sondra GUYTON
32 Vice President for Student Services ....Mr. Barry PRIEST
10 Vice President for Finance ....Mr. Jay STANLEY
21 Controller ....Mr. Roy THOMPSON
08 Director Student Resource Center ....Ms. Sherwin RICE
09 Dir Institutional Effect & Planning ....Ms. Lisa DEVANE
37 Director of Financial Aid ....Ms. Samantha BENSON
106 Director of Distance Learning ....Mr. Ray SHEPPARD
15 Director of Human Resources ....Ms. Tiina MUNDY
18 Director of Facilities ....Mr. Junior RIDEOUT
26 POI/Marketing Coordinator ....Vacant
102 Foundation Director ....Ms. Linda BURNEY
06 Registrar ....Ms. Andrea CARTER-FISHER

*Blue Ridge Community College (E)

180 W Campus Drive, Flat Rock NC 28731-4728

County: Henderson FICE Identification: 009684
Unit ID: 198039
Telephone: (828) 694-1700 Carnegie Class: Assoc/MT-VT-Mix Trad/Non
FAX Number: (828) 694-1690 Calendar System: Semester
URL: www.blueridge.edu
Established: 1969 Annual Undergrad Tuition & Fees (In-District): $2,651
Enrollment: 2,399 Coed
Affiliation or Control: State/Local IRS Status: 501(c)3
Highest Offering: Associate Degree
Accreditation: SC, EMT, NAEYC, SURGT

02 President ....Dr. Laura B. LEATHERWOOD
05 VP for Instruction ....Ms. Katherine ALLEN
32 VP for Student Services ....Ms. Kirsten BUNCH
103 VP Economic/Workforce Development ....Dr. Scott QUEEN
10 AVP for Finance/CFO ....Ms. Carolyn W. ALLEY
11 Vice Pres General Administration ....Dr. Chad MERRILL
111 VP Institutional Advancement ....Ms. Lisa ADKINS
49 Dean for Arts and Sciences ....Mr. Aaron COOK
72 Dean for Advanced Technology ....Mr. Joe SHOOK
76 Dean for Health Sciences ....Ms. Leigh ANGEL
97 Dean for Basic Skills ....Ms. Robin NORRIS-PAULISON
50 Dean for Business/Service Careers ....Ms. Brenda BLACKBURN

44 Institutional Advance/Rsrch Coord ....Ms. Carol Ann LYDON
06 Registrar ....Ms. Sara SCHUMACHER
08 Director for Library Services ....Ms. Ali NORVELL
37 Director Financial Aid ....Ms. Lisanne MASTERSON
13 Assoc Vice Pres Technology/CIO ....Mr. Steven YOUNG
18 Director of Facilities ....Mr. Peter HEMANS
26 Dir of Marketing & Communications ....Ms. Lee Anna HANEY
84 Director of Enrollment Management ....Ms. Laura SIMMONS
15 Director of Human Resources ....Ms. Lorri ALLISON
19 Chief of Police/Dir Public Safety ....Mr. Daran DODD
04 Admin Assistant to the President ....Ms. Tammy L. PRYOR

*Brunswick Community College (F)

50 College Road, Bolivia NC 28422

County: Brunswick FICE Identification: 021707
Unit ID: 198084
Telephone: (910) 755-7300 Carnegie Class: Assoc/HT-High Non
FAX Number: (910) 754-9609 Calendar System: Semester
URL: www.brunswickcc.edu
Established: 1979 Annual Undergrad Tuition & Fees (In-State): $2,532
Enrollment: 1,553 Coed
Affiliation or Control: State IRS Status: 501(c)3
Highest Offering: Associate Degree
Accreditation: SC, CAHIIM, MAC

02 President ....Dr. Gene SMITH
05 Exec Vice Pres/Chief Academic Ofcr ....Dr. Lois SMITH
10 Vice President Budget and Finance ....Ms. Sheila GALLOWAY
32 Vice Pres of Student Affairs .. Dr. Denise A. HOUCHEN-CLAGETT
09 Director of Institutional Planning ....Dr. Michael COBB
08 Dir Learning Resources/Acad Support ....Mrs. Carmen ELLIS
06 Registrar/Dir Enrollment ....Ms. Christine DYE
15 Director Human Resources ....Ms. Nancy DISBROW
18 AVP/Physical Plant Director ....Mr. Jack LUCIANO
102 Director Resource Development ....Ms. Elizabeth WASSUM
26 Director of Marketing & Public Info ....Ms. London SCHMIDT
37 Financial Aid/Veterans Affs Coord ....Ms. Tracy SOMERLAD
72 Dean Professional Technical Service ....Mr. Eric HOLLOMAN
49 Dean Arts & Sciences ....Dr. John GRAY
04 Executive Asst to President ....Ms. Cynthia STERLING
13 Chief Info Officer ....Mr. Dave SORENSON
41 Athletic Director ....Mr. Robert ALLEN
36 Career Counselor ....Ms. Leslie WILDER

*Caldwell Community College and Technical Institute (G)

2855 Hickory Boulevard, Hudson NC 28638-1399

County: Caldwell FICE Identification: 004835
Unit ID: 198118
Telephone: (828) 726-2200 Carnegie Class: Assoc/HT-High Non
FAX Number: (828) 726-2216 Calendar System: Semester
URL: www.cccti.edu
Established: 1964 Annual Undergrad Tuition & Fees (In-District): $2,528
Enrollment: 3,845 Coed
Affiliation or Control: State/Local IRS Status: 501(c)3
Highest Offering: Associate Degree
Accreditation: SC, ADNUR, DMS, EMT, MAC, NMT, PTAA, RAD

02 President ....Dr. Mark POARCH
32 Vice President Student Services ....Mrs. Dena HOLMAN
103 Dean Cont Ed/Workforce Development ....Mrs. Brandy DUNLAP
11 Vice President of Operations ....Mr. Donnie BASSINGER
12 Executive Director Watauga Campus ....Mr. Steve MELTON
05 Vice President of Instruction ....Mr. Randy LEDFORD, JR.
84 Dir Enrollment Mgmt Services ....Mr. Dennis SEAGLE
08 Director Learning Resources Center ....Ms. Alison BEARD
37 Director Financial Aid ....Vacant
36 Dir Custom Training/Work Based Lrng ....Mr. Rick SHEW
15 Director Human Resources ....Mrs. Rose MOON
10 Controller ....Mrs. Rashelle PENLEY
09 Dir Inst Effectiveness/Research ....Mrs. Liz SILVERS
26 Public Relations Officer ....Mr. Edward TERRY
102 Director Foundation Office ....Ms. Marla CHRISTIE
38 Director Student Counseling ....Mr. Shannon BROWN
96 Purchasing Agent ....Mrs. Barbara DAY
40 Director of College Stores ....Mrs. Trina CURTIS
04 Exec Assistant to the President ....Mrs. Donna CHURCH
18 Director Facility Services ....Mr. Jeff HERMAN
06 Registrar ....Ms. Beth HOLLAND
13 Chief Info Technology Officer (CIO) ....Ms. Susan WOOTEN
105 Director Web Services ....Mr. Gary WILSON
28 Director of Diversity ....Mr. Jimmy GRIFFITH

*Cape Fear Community College (H)

411 N Front Street, Wilmington NC 28401-3993

County: New Hanover FICE Identification: 005320
Unit ID: 198154
Telephone: (910) 362-7000 Carnegie Class: Assoc/HT-High Trad
FAX Number: (910) 763-2279 Calendar System: Semester
URL: www.cfcc.edu
Established: 1958 Annual Undergrad Tuition & Fees (In-District): $2,748
Enrollment: 8,680 Coed
Affiliation or Control: State/Local IRS Status: 501(c)3
Highest Offering: Associate Degree
Accreditation: SC, ADNUR, DA, DH, DMS, NAEYC, OTA, RAD, SURGT

02 President ....Mr. James P. MORTON
32 VP Student Svcs & Enrollment Mgmt ....Ms. Joanne CERES

05 Vice Pres Academic Affairs ... Dr. Jason CHAFFIN
10 Vice President Business Services ... Ms. Christina GREENE
111 VP Advancement & Arts ... Mr. Lionel FERNANDO
103 VP Economic & Workforce Development ... Mr. John DOWNING
06 Registrar ... Ms. Angela MURPHY
102 Director Philanthropy & Foundation ... Mr. Logan THOMPSON
31 Exec Dir Community Relations ... Ms. Sonja JOHNSON
84 Dean of Enrollment Management ... Ms. Jackie FOSTER
08 Dean Learning Resources Center ... Ms. Catherine LEE
37 Director of Financial Aid ... Ms. Rachel CAVANAUGH
13 Director Information Technology Svc ... Mr. Jakim FRIANT
15 Director Human Resources ... Ms. Anne SMITH
35 Dean of Student Affairs ... Mr. Robby MCGEE
75 Dean Career/Technical Education ... Mr. Mark COUNCIL
49 Dean Arts & Sciences ... Ms. Lynn CRISWELL
96 Director of Purchasing/Inventory ... Ms. Liz MANTOOTH
76 Dean Health Sciences ... Dr. Mary NAYLOR
105 Web Services Analyst ... Ms. Christina HEIKKILA
100 Exec Dir Pres Office/Board Liaison ... Ms. Michelle LEE
19 Director Campus Safety/Training ... Ms. Lynn SYLVIA
25 Director of Grant Development ... Ms. Val CLEMMONS
22 Dir of Disability Support Services ... Ms. Aimee HELMUS
41 Dir Student Activities/Athletics ... Mr. Ryan MANTLO
18 Exec Dir Capital Projects & Maint ... Mr. David KANOY
88 Director Customized Training ... Ms. Jan YOKELEY
07 Sr Director of Admissions ... Mr. Jeremy GIBBONS
09 VP of Institutional Effectiveness ... Mr. Michael COBB

*Carteret Community College (A)

3505 Arendell Street, Morehead City NC 28557-2989
County: Carteret FICE Identification: 008081
Unit ID: 198206
Telephone: (252) 222-6000 Carnegie Class: Assoc/MT-VT-High Trad
FAX Number: (252) 222-2514 Calendar System: Semester
URL: www.carteret.edu
Established: 1963 Annual Undergrad Tuition & Fees (In-District): $2,640
Enrollment: 1,347 Coed
Affiliation or Control: State/Local IRS Status: 501(c)3
Highest Offering: Associate Degree
Accreditation: SC, ADNUR, COARC, MAC, RAD

02 President ... Dr. Tracy MANCINI
05 VP for Instruction/Student Support ... Dr. Maggie BROWN
10 VP Finance/Administrative Services ... Vacant
31 VP Corp/Community Education ... Mr. Perry L. HARKER
04 Exec Dir Office of the President ... Ms. Jo Ann CANNON
08 Director of the Library ... Ms. Elizabeth BAKER
32 Dean of Student Services ... Mr. Dana MERCK
84 Director Admissions & Enrollment ... Ms. Elizabeth NEW
13 Dir Network/Info Systems/Security ... Mr. John GREEN
15 Director of Human Resources ... Ms. Amanda BRYANT
102 Exec Director of the Foundation ... Ms. Brenda REASH
49 Dean Arts & Sciences ... Ms. Doree HILL
76 Dean of Health Sciences ... Ms. Laurie A. FRESHWATER
88 Dean of Applied Science ... Ms. Nicole THOMPSON
37 Director/Financial Aid Officer ... Ms. Brenda J. LONG
06 Director Enrollment Svcs/Registrar ... Ms. Jennifer FOX
09 Exec Dir Inst Rsrch/Effectiveness ... Ms. Kristy CRAIG
18 VP of Plant Operations/Facilities ... Mr. Steve SPARKS
26 Director Marketing/Public Affairs ... Ms. Logan OKUN
96 Director of Business Operations ... Ms. Donna L. CUMBIE
106 Dir of Instruct Support/Dist Lrng ... Mr. Ed LADENBURGER

*Catawba Valley Community College (B)

2550 Highway 70, SE, Hickory NC 28602-9699
County: Catawba FICE Identification: 005318
Unit ID: 198233
Telephone: (828) 327-7000 Carnegie Class: Assoc/HT-Mix Trad/Non
FAX Number: (828) 327-7276 Calendar System: Semester
URL: www.cvcc.edu
Established: 1960 Annual Undergrad Tuition & Fees (In-District): $2,367
Enrollment: 4,328 Coed
Affiliation or Control: State/Local IRS Status: 501(c)3
Highest Offering: Associate Degree
Accreditation: SC, ADNUR, CAHIIM, COARC, DH, EMT, NDT, POLYT, RAD, SURGT

02 President ... Dr. Garrett D. HINSHAW
03 Executive Vice President ... Dr. Larry PUTNAM
05 Chief Academic Officer ... Ms. Brice MELTON
10 Sr VP Business Affairs/Operations ... Mr. Wes BUNCH
32 Dean of Student Access/Development ... Mrs. Cindy COULTER
15 Chief Human Resources Officer ... Mr. Roger IRVIN
07 Director of Admissions ... Ms. Laurie WEGNER
21 Chief Business Administrator ... Ms. Jennifer HAMM
37 Director Scholarships/Financial Aid ... Ms. Carolyn BRANDON
09 Chief Ofcr Accountability/Research ... Mr. Kevin ROUSE
88 Associate Dean ... Ms. Crystal GLENN
88 Sr Director Small Business Center ... Mr. Jeff NEUVILLE
50 Director Business/Technology Ext ... Ms. Susan BLAKE
88 Director Manufacturing Sol Center ... Ms. Jodi GEIS
13 Chief Technology Officer ... Mr. Daniel CLANTON
19 Chief of Staff/Safety/Security ... Mr. Steve HUNT
51 Associate Dean ... Dr. Chanell MORELLO
103 Exec Dir Strat Business Partnership ... Ms. Tammy MULLER
76 Dean Sch of Health & Public Service ... Ms. Robin ROSS
04 Special Asst to Pres/Board Liaison ... Mr. John WATTS
29 Director Events/Tours/Alumni ... Ms. Melanie ZIMMERMAN
41 Director of Athletics ... Mr. Nick SCHROEDER

26 Public Information Officer ... Mr. Cody DALTON
30 Exec Director of Development ... Ms. Jennifer JONES

*Central Carolina Community College (C)

1105 Kelly Drive, Sanford NC 27330-9000
County: Lee FICE Identification: 005449
Unit ID: 198251
Telephone: (919) 775-5401 Carnegie Class: Assoc/MT-VT-Mix Trad/Non
FAX Number: (919) 718-7380 Calendar System: Semester
URL: www.cccc.edu
Established: 1958 Annual Undergrad Tuition & Fees (In-District): $2,554
Enrollment: 5,154 Coed
Affiliation or Control: State/Local IRS Status: 501(c)3
Highest Offering: Associate Degree
Accreditation: SC, CAHIIM, DA, DH, DMS, EMT, MAC

02 President ... Dr. Lisa M. CHAPMAN
05 Interim Chief Academic Officer ... Dr. Delanie DAUGHTRY
10 Exec Vice Pres/Chief Financial Ofcr ... Dr. Philip PRICE
32 Vice President Student Services ... Mr. Ken R. HOYLE
09 VP Assessment/Planning/Research ... Dr. Linda SCUILETTI
26 Assoc VP Marketing/External Rels ... Dr. Marcie DISHMAN
12 Provost Chatham Campus ... Dr. Mark HALL
35 Dean of Student Support Svcs ... Ms. Heather WILLETT
04 Exec Asst to Pres/Secretary to BOT ... Ms. Lorraine WHITAKER
12 Principal Harnett Early College ... Dr. Walter MCPHERSON
08 Director of Library Services ... Ms. Samantha O'CONNOR
102 Exec Director of CCCC Foundation ... Dr. Emily HARE
06 Dean of Enrollment/Registrar ... Ms. Jamie TYSON-CHILDRESS
15 Director Human Resources ... Ms. Trinity FAUCETT
07 Director of Admissions ... Mr. Adam WADE
37 Director Financial Aid ... Ms. Amber WERKHEISER
18 Physical Plant Manager ... Mr. Ronnie MEASAMER
75 Dean Career/Technical Programs ... Mr. Drew GOODSON
76 Dean Health Sciences/Human Services ... Ms. Denise MARTIN
49 Dean Arts & Sciences/Advising ... Mr. Scott BYINGTON

*Central Piedmont Community College (D)

PO Box 35009, Charlotte NC 28235-5009
County: Mecklenburg FICE Identification: 002915
Unit ID: 198260
Telephone: (704) 330-2722 Carnegie Class: Assoc/HT-High Trad
FAX Number: N/A Calendar System: Semester
URL: www.cpcc.edu
Established: 1963 Annual Undergrad Tuition & Fees (In-District): $2,792
Enrollment: 16,668 Coed
Affiliation or Control: State/Local IRS Status: 501(c)3
Highest Offering: Associate Degree
Accreditation: SC, ACFEI, ADNUR, CAHIIM, COARC, CSHSE, CVT, CYTO, DA, DH, EMT, MAC, MLTAD, NAEYC, OTA, POLYT, PTAA, SURGT

02 President ... Dr. Kandi W. DEITEMEYER
111 EVP Institutional Advancement ... Dr. Kevin MCCARTHY
05 VP Academic Affairs ... Dr. Heather HILL
32 VP Student Affairs ... Dr. Chris CATHCART
45 VP Strategy/Org Excellence ... Dr. Tracie CLARK
10 VP Finance & Admin Services ... Mr. Mike WHITEMAN
15 VP Talent & Org Engagement ... Mr. Mark SHORT
26 VP Comm/Marketing/Public Relations ... Mr. Jeff LOWRANCE
13 VP for Technology & CIO ... Mr. David KIM
21 AVP Finance/Admin Services ... Ms. Jessica BOYCE
20 AVP Academic Affairs ... Dr. Edith MCELROY
102 AVP Foundation/Inst Advancement ... Ms. Katie JONES
20 AVP Academic Affairs ... Mr. George HENDERSON
25 Assoc VP Government Rels & Grants ... Mr. Michael HORN
18 Assoc VP Facilities & Construction ... Ms. Vicki SAVILLE
04 Admin Assistant to the President ... Vacant
116 Exec Director Compliance/Audit ... Ms. Kelley HORTON
19 Exec Dir College Security ... Mr. Charles WRIGHT
22 Executive Director Institution/EEO ... Mr. Leon MATTHEWS
88 Dean Educational Partnership ... Mr. Chris PAYNTER
124 Dean Retention Services ... Dr. Clint MCELROY
35 Dean Student Life/Service Learning ... Mr. Mark HELMS
84 Dean Enrollment Management ... Dr. Daniel (JJ) MCEACHERN
08 Dean Libraries ... Ms. Gloria KELLEY
121 Dean College & Career Readiness ... Ms. Karen PAULY
06 Dean Admissions & Registration ... Mr. Greg STANLEY
76 Dean Health Professions/Human Svcs ... Ms. Karen SUMMERS

*Cleveland Community College (E)

137 S Post Road, Shelby NC 28152-6296
County: Cleveland FICE Identification: 008082
Unit ID: 198321
Telephone: (704) 669-6000 Carnegie Class: Assoc/MT-VT-Mix Trad/Non
FAX Number: (704) 669-4202 Calendar System: Semester
URL: www.clevelandcc.edu
Established: 1965 Annual Undergrad Tuition & Fees (In-District): $2,602
Enrollment: 2,269 Coed
Affiliation or Control: State/Local IRS Status: 501(c)3
Highest Offering: Associate Degree
Accreditation: SC, EMT, IFSAC, MAC, NAEYC, RAD, SURGT

02 President ... Dr. Jason HURST
05 Vice President of Academic Affairs ... Dr. Becky SAIN
32 Vice President of Student Affairs ... Dr. Andy GARDNER
10 Vice Pres Business Operations/CFO ... Mr. Bruce COLE

102 Executive Director CCC Foundation ... Dr. Mary CARLSON
09 Dean of Plng & Institutional Effect ... Dr. Laura BOWEN
121 Dean of Equity & Student Support ... Ms. Nedra MADDOX
84 Dean of Enrollment ... Dr. Emily HURDT
08 Director of Library Services ... Ms. Leslie QUEEN
96 Purchasing Officer ... Mr. Lance ASHLEY
18 Director of Physical Plant ... Mr. Mark FOX
19 Campus Security Supervisor ... Mr. Michael HAWKINS
15 Director Human Resources/Safety ... Mr. Allen KNICELEY
13 Chief Information Officer ... Mr. Jonathan DAVIS
14 Network Administrator ... Mr. Robin DYER
24 Audiovisual Coordinator ... Mr. Rodger PERRY
26 Public Relations & Comm Coordinator ... Mrs. Paula VESS
88 Dean of College Transfer ... Dr. Starr CAMPER
103 VP Econ/Workforce Development ... Mr. Tony FOGLEMAN
41 Athletic Director/Dean of CCR ... Dr. Chris NANNEY
100 Chief of Staff ... Mrs. Kristin BLANTON
106 Director of E-learning ... Dr. Chance WITHERSPOON
76 Dean Health Sciences & Public Svcs ... Mrs. Christina HILL
103 Dean of Workforce Development ... Ms. Amy DULIN
27 Marketing Coordinator ... Mrs. Kendra HANELINE

*Coastal Carolina Community College (F)

444 Western Boulevard, Jacksonville NC 28546-6816
County: Onslow FICE Identification: 005316
Unit ID: 198330
Telephone: (910) 455-1221 Carnegie Class: Assoc/HT-Mix Trad/Non
FAX Number: (910) 455-7027 Calendar System: Semester
URL: www.coastalcarolina.edu
Established: 1963 Annual Undergrad Tuition & Fees (In-District): $2,462
Enrollment: 3,571 Coed
Affiliation or Control: State/Local IRS Status: 501(c)3
Highest Offering: Associate Degree
Accreditation: SC, DA, DH, EMT, MLTAD, NAEYC, SURGT

02 President ... Mr. David L. HEATHERLY
05 VP for Instruction ... Ms. Ginger TUTON
09 VP Inst Effective & Student Success ... Ms. Sharon R. MCGINNIS
11 VP Administrative Support Svcs ... Dr. Annette HARPINE
32 Division Chair for Student Services ... Mr. Matthew HERRMANN
15 Personnel Officer ... Ms. Cindy BURKHART
26 Pub Info Ofcr/Ex Dir Col Foundation ... Ms. Emily ELLIS
07 Director for Admissions ... Ms. Heather CALIHAN
18 Dir Physical Plant/Auxiliary Svcs ... Ms. Carol LURZ
37 Director for Financial Aid Services ... Ms. Tammy LYON
88 Director for Veterans Services ... Mr. Devere P. MICHEAU
103 Director Economic Development ... Ms. Anne C. SHAW
04 Assistant to the President and BOT ... Ms. Lora TAYLOR
06 Registrar ... Ms. Mishelle DUPUIS

*College of the Albemarle (G)

1208 North Road Street, Elizabeth City NC 27906-2327
County: Pasquotank FICE Identification: 002917
Unit ID: 197814
Telephone: (252) 335-0821 Carnegie Class: Assoc/HT-High Non
FAX Number: (252) 335-2011 Calendar System: Semester
URL: www.albemarle.edu
Established: 1960 Annual Undergrad Tuition & Fees (In-District): $2,270
Enrollment: 2,508 Coed
Affiliation or Control: State/Local IRS Status: 501(c)3
Highest Offering: Associate Degree
Accreditation: SC, ADNUR, MAC, MLTAD, SURGT

02 President ... Dr. Jack BAGWELL
10 Chief Financial Officer ... Mrs. Susan GENTRY
05 Vice President for Learning ... Dr. Evonne CARTER
11 VP Business & Admin Services ... Vacant
32 VP Student Success & Enroll Mgmt ... Vacant
12 Dean Dare County Campus ... Mr. Timothy SWEENEY
30 Executive Director Foundation & Dev ... Mrs. Amy ALCOCER
37 Director Admissions & Financial Aid ... Ms. Angela R. GODFREY-DAWSON
35 Coord Student Life & Leadership ... Ms. Dawn ALLEN
06 Registrar ... Ms. Andrea DANCE
88 Director Small Business Center ... Ms. Ginger H. O'NEAL
78 Work-Based Learning Liaison ... Mrs. Lynn JENNINGS
04 Exec Assistant to the President ... Mrs. Valerie MUELLER
08 Director Library ... Mr. Rodney WOOTEN
12 Campus Admin Edenton-Chowan Campus ... Mrs. Robin ZINSMEISTER
13 Director Mgmt Information Services ... Mr. Wayman WHITE
15 Director Human Resources ... Ms. Ella BUNCH
18 Director Physical Facilities ... Mr. James DAVISON
23 Dean Health & Wellness ... Ms. Robin HARRIS
40 Administrative Services Manager ... Mr. William DEFEO
09 Director of Inst Effectiveness ... Vacant
88 Coord Prison Education Programs ... Mr. Andre WILLIAMS
88 Coordinator Secondary Education ... Mr. Derek MEREDITH
49 Dean Arts and Sciences ... Mr. Dean ROUGHTON
50 Dean Business & Applied Tech ... Mrs. Michelle WATERS
81 Dept Chair Sciences ... Mr. Todd KRUEGER
83 Department Chair Social Sciences ... Mr. Brian EDWARDS
60 Dept Chair English & Comm ... Mrs. Laura MORRISON
54 Dept Chair Math and Engineering ... Mrs. Lisa MEADS
76 Dept Chair Allied Health ... Mr. Jeffrey CARTER
77 Dept Chair Bus & Computer Sys Tech ... Ms. Sharon BROWN
57 Department Chair Human & Fine Arts ... Ms. Christina WEISNER
66 Dept Chair ADN ... Mrs. Katie MILLER
19 Dir Public Safety & Preparedness ... Mr. Dennis SMITH

36 Dir College and Career Readiness ... Mrs. Kimberly GREGORY
121 Director Advising & Student Success ... Mrs. Eushekia HEWITT
103 Dean Workforce Dev/Pub Svc/Career .. Mrs. Robin ZINSMEISTER
106 Coordinator Distance Education ... Dr. Susan PECK

*Craven Community College (A)

800 College Court, New Bern NC 28562-4984
County: Craven FICE Identification: 006799
Unit ID: 198367
Telephone: (252) 638-7200 Carnegie Class: Assoc/MT-VT-Mix Trad/Non
FAX Number: (252) 638-4232 Calendar System: Semester
URL: www.cravencc.edu
Established: 1965 Annual Undergrad Tuition & Fees (In-District): $2,114
Enrollment: 2,629 Coed
Affiliation or Control: State/Local IRS Status: 501(c)3
Highest Offering: Associate Degree
Accreditation: SC, ACBSP, CAHIIM, MAC, NAEYC, PTAA

02 President ... Dr. Raymond STAATS
05 VP for Instruction ... Dr. Kathleen GALLMAN
11 VP for Administration ... Mr. Jim MILLARD
32 VP for Students ... Mr. Gery BOUCHER
49 Dean Liberal Arts & Univ Transfer ... Dr. Betty K. HATCHER
36 Dean Career Programs ... Mr. Ricky MEADOWS
09 Exec Director Inst Effectiveness ... Dr. David L. TOWNSEND
06 Registrar ... Ms. Yuko BOYD
111 Executive Director Inst Advancement .. Mr. Charles WETHINGTON
12 Dean Havelock-Cherry Point Campus ... Ms. Tanya MCGHEE
37 Executive Director Financial Aid ... Ms. Susie GAMES
31 Dir Community Workforce Relations ... Mr. Greg SINGLETON
88 Director Basic Skills Programs ... Ms. Sandy BAYLISS-CARR
08 Director Library Services ... Mrs. Wendy WHITE
10 Exec Dir Financial Services ... Mrs. Cynthia A. PATTERSON
88 Director TRIO Student Support Svcs ... Ms. Sandra HUNTER
15 Exec Director Human Resources ... Ms. Denise HORNE
103 Dean Workforce Development ... Mr. Robin MATTHEWS
18 Executive Director Facilities ... Mr. John MELVILLE
13 Dean Technology Services ... Dr. Julia HAMILTON
96 Procurement & Fixed Assets Officer ... Mr. Hiram Todd MURPHREY
84 Dean Enrollment Management ... Ms. Zomar PETER
25 Director Grants/Strategic Partners ... Ms. Monica MINUS
04 Exec Asst to Pres/Board of Trustees ... Ms. Cynthia ENSLEY
19 Director Security & Emergency Mgmt ... Mr. Timothy HALL
121 Exec Director Academic Support ... Ms. Jennifer BUMGARNER
76 Dean Health Programs ... Dr. J. Alec NEWTON
07 Director Admissions & Records ... Mrs. Tina PROCTOR
26 Director Communications ... Mr. Craig RAMEY

*Davidson-Davie Community College (B)

PO Box 1287, Lexington NC 27293-1287
County: Davidson FICE Identification: 002919
Unit ID: 198376
Telephone: (336) 249-8186 Carnegie Class: Assoc/MT-VT-Mix Trad/Non
FAX Number: (336) 249-0379 Calendar System: Semester
URL: www.davidsondavie.edu
Established: 1958 Annual Undergrad Tuition & Fees (In-District): $2,588
Enrollment: 3,765 Coed
Affiliation or Control: State/Local IRS Status: 501(c)3
Highest Offering: Associate Degree
Accreditation: SC, ADNUR, CAHIIM, DA, EMT, MAC, MLTAD, NAEYC, SURGT

02 President ... Dr. Darrin L. HARTNESS
05 EVP Academic & Student Affairs ... Dr. Susan D. BURLESON
10 VP Financial/Administrative Svcs ... Ms. Laura L. YARBROUGH
102 VP Ext Affairs/Exec Dir Foundation ... Ms. Jenny M. VARNER
76 Dean Health Sciences ... Ms. Holly MYERS
20 AVP Academic Programs/Studies ... Dr. Christy FORREST
103 AVP Workforce Dev & Cmty Engagement ... Dr. Jonathan BROWN
35 Director Student Support Services ... Ms. Shareka BROWN
84 Dean Enrollment Services ... Mr. Bryan MCCULLOUGH
108 Dean IE & Innovations ... Vacant
07 Director Recruitment & Admissions ... Ms. Cailin ASIP
36 Director Career Development ... Mr. Charles MAYER
18 Director Physical Plant Services ... Mr. Keith RAKER
15 Director Human Resources ... Ms. Adrienne FRIDDLE
04 Executive Asst to President ... Ms. Elle KING
08 Head Librarian ... Mr. Jason SETZER
37 Director Student Financial Aid ... Mr. Brian DE YOUNG
41 Athletic Director ... Mr. Matthew RIDGE
09 Director of Institutional Research ... Mr. Mark PUTERBAUGH
111 Dir Development/Advancement ... Ms. Kristin BRIGGS
124 Dean Student Engagement/Completion ... Ms. Keisha JONES
13 Director Information Technology ... Mr. Donald BECK

*Durham Technical Community College (C)

1637 East Lawson Street, Durham NC 27703-5023
County: Durham FICE Identification: 005448
Unit ID: 198455
Telephone: (919) 536-7200 Carnegie Class: Assoc/MT-VT-Mix Trad/Non
FAX Number: (919) 686-3601 Calendar System: Semester
URL: www.durhamtech.edu
Established: 1961 Annual Undergrad Tuition & Fees (In-District): $1,958
Enrollment: 4,672 Coed
Affiliation or Control: State/Local IRS Status: 501(c)3
Highest Offering: Associate Degree
Accreditation: SC, ADNUR, CAHIIM, CEA, COARC, CR, DT, EMT, MAC, NAEYC, OPD, OTA, PNUR, SURGT

02 President ... Mr. John B. BUXTON
05 Exec VP Academics/Stdnt Engagement ... Mr. Tom JAYNES
20 VP/Chief Academic Officer ... Ms. Susan PARIS
10 VP Finance/Administration ... Mr. Andrew KLEITSCH, II
32 VP Student Engage/Dev/Support ... Dr. Christine KELLY KLEESE
100 Chief of Staff ... Ms. Tina B. RUFF
04 Executive Asst to the President ... Ms. Toni BROWN
35 Dean Student Development/Support ... Ms. Lisa D. INMAN
06 Asst Dean Admissions/Registrar ... Mr. Abraham DONES
13 Exec Dir Information Tech Svcs ... Mr. Patrick HINES
09 Dir Institutional Research/Eval ... Dr. Melanie RIESTER
15 Exec Director Human Resources ... Ms. Kathy MCKINLEY
08 Director Library ... Ms. Julie HUMPHREY
37 Dir Financial Aid/Veteran Svcs ... Ms. Nadine FORD
109 Director Auxiliary Services ... Ms. Yolanda V. MOORE-JONES
18 Director Facility Services ... Mr. Marshall R. FULLER
26 Dir Marketing/Comm/Public Info Ofcr ... Mr. Nathan HARDIN

*Edgecombe Community College (D)

2009 W Wilson Street, Tarboro NC 27886-9399
County: Edgecombe FICE Identification: 008855
Unit ID: 198491
Telephone: (252) 823-5166 Carnegie Class: Assoc/MT-VT-High Trad
FAX Number: N/A Calendar System: Semester
URL: www.edgecombe.edu
Established: 1967 Annual Undergrad Tuition & Fees (In-District): $2,640
Enrollment: 1,459 Coed
Affiliation or Control: State/Local IRS Status: 501(c)3
Highest Offering: Associate Degree
Accreditation: SC, ADNUR, CAHIIM, COARC, MAC, PNUR, RAD, SURGT

02 President ... Dr. Gregory MCLEOD
05 Vice President of Instruction ... Mr. Bruce PANNETON
11 Vice Pres Administrative Services ... Ms. Debbie BATTEN
32 Vice President Student Services ... Mr. Michael J. JORDAN
84 Dean Enrollment Management ... Mr. Tony ROOK
35 Dean of Students ... Ms. Samanthia PHILLIPS
108 Director of Inst Effectiveness ... Ms. Sheila HOSKINS
26 Director of Public Information ... Ms. Mary T. BASS
08 Director of Library Services ... Ms. Deborah PARISHER
06 Registrar ... Ms. Kienesha EBRON
15 Director Personnel Services ... Ms. Susan BARKALOW
18 Chief Facilities/Physical Plant ... Mr. John BUTTS
37 Director Student Financial Aid ... Mr. Sherlock MCDOUGALD
04 Executive Asst to President ... Mrs. Adrian C. RAMSEY-FRANCO
13 Director Computer Services ... Mr. Brad HILL
30 Director of Development ... Mr. Lynwood ROBERSON

*Fayetteville Technical Community College (E)

PO Box 35236, 2201 Hull Road,
Fayetteville NC 28303-0236
County: Cumberland FICE Identification: 007640
Unit ID: 198534
Telephone: (910) 678-8400 Carnegie Class: Assoc/MT-VT-Mix Trad/Non
FAX Number: (910) 678-8269 Calendar System: Semester
URL: www.faytechcc.edu
Established: 1961 Annual Undergrad Tuition & Fees (In-State): $2,544
Enrollment: 10,932 Coed
Affiliation or Control: State IRS Status: 501(c)3
Highest Offering: Associate Degree
Accreditation: SC, ADNUR, COARC, DA, DH, EMT, FUSER, PTAA, RAD, SURGA, SURGT

02 President ... Dr. Larry KEEN
05 Sr VP Academic/Student Svcs ... Dr. Mark SORRELLS
10 Sr VP Business and Finance ... Mrs. Robin DEAVER
15 VP Human Res/Inst Effect/Assessment ... Mr. Carl MITCHELL
11 VP for Administrative Services ... Mr. Joseph W. LEVISTER, JR.
13 VP Learning Technologies ... Vacant
43 VP for Legal Services ... Mr. David SULLIVAN
26 Exec Dir Marketing/Public Relations ... Ms. Catherine PRITCHARD
102 Executive Director of Foundation ... Ms. Sandy AMMONS
84 Dean Enrollment Mgmt/Financial Aid ... Ms. Misty LYON
51 Assoc Vice Pres for Cont Educ ... Dr. Jolee MARSH
32 Assoc Vice Pres Student Services ... Dr. Rosemary KELLY
06 Registrar ... Ms. Melissa A. JONES
21 Assoc Vice Pres Business & Finance ... Mr. Charles SMITH
07 Director of Admissions ... Dr. Louanna CASTLEMAN
20 Assoc Vice Pres of Academic Support ... Ms. DeSandra WASHINGTON
14 Director Management Information Svc ... Mrs. Pamela SCULLY
18 Director of Facility Services ... Mr. Richard LEE
96 Procurement Manager Business/Financ ... Ms. Amy SAMPERTON
50 Dean of Business Programs ... Mrs. Cindy BURNS
66 Dean of Nursing ... Dr. Murtis WORTH
49 Dean of Arts/Humanities ... Mr. Antonio JACKSON
76 Dean of Health Programs ... Ms. Michelle WALDEN
54 Dean Engr/Applied Tech Pgms ... Mrs. Pamela GIBSON
81 Dean of Sciences & Mathematics ... Dr. Melissa HARMON
80 Dean of Public Service ... Mrs. Linda NOVAK
77 Dean of Computer Technologies ... Mrs. Tenette PREVATTE
08 Chief Library Officer ... Mr. Laurence GAVIN
09 Dean of Institutional Effectiveness ... Dr. Vincent CASTANO
19 Director Security/Safety ... Mr. Joseph BAILER
37 Director Student Financial Aid ... Mrs. Regina ANGLIN
41 Athletic Director ... Dr. Shannon YATES

*Forsyth Technical Community College (F)

2100 Silas Creek Parkway,
Winston-Salem NC 27103-5197
County: Forsyth FICE Identification: 005317
Unit ID: 198552
Telephone: (336) 723-0371 Carnegie Class: Assoc/MT-VT-High Trad
FAX Number: (336) 761-2399 Calendar System: Semester
URL: www.forsythtech.edu
Established: 1960 Annual Undergrad Tuition & Fees (In-State): $2,152
Enrollment: 7,587 Coed
Affiliation or Control: State IRS Status: 501(c)3
Highest Offering: Associate Degree
Accreditation: SC, CAHIIM, COARC, CVT, DA, DH, DMS, MAC, NMT, RAD, RTT

02 President ... Dr. Janet N. SPRIGGS
05 VP Student Academic Success/CAO ... Dr. Jacob SURRATT
103 VP Economic & Workforce Development .. Mr. Alan K. MURDOCK
10 VP Business Services & CFO ... Ms. Kizzy LEA
22 VP Incl Excellence & Employee Supp ... Vacant
13 VP Information Technology & CIO ... Mr. Chris PEARCE
45 VP for Strategic Innovation ... Mr. Kevin OSBORNE
32 VP Student Success Services ... Ms. Masonne SAWYER
84 VP for Strategy & Outreach ... Ms. Paula DIBLEY
15 Assoc VP Human Resources ... Ms. Rachel SCHROEDER
102 Exec Director Foundation ... Mr. William GREEN
50 Dean Business & Info Tech ... Ms. Pamela SHORTT
49 Dean Arts & Sciences ... Dr. Torry REYNOLDS
53 Dean Education & Human Services ... Ms. Anu WILLIAMS
54 Dean of Engineering Tech Div ... Mr. John CARSTENS
76 Dean of Health Technologies ... Ms. Linda LATHAM
88 Dean Cmty & Workforce Development ... Mr. Joshua BURCHAM
08 Dean of Learning Resources ... Mr. J. Randel CANDELARIA
88 Dean College and Career Readiness ... Dr. Sydney RICHARDSON
66 Dept Chair Practical Nursing ... Ms. Angie LUNDGREN
66 Dept Chair Assoc Degree Nursing ... Ms. Renee HARRISON
07 Director of Admissions & Records ... Ms. Heather AZZU
21 Exec Director Financial Services ... Ms. Demetria BURTON
37 Director Student Financial Services ... Ms. Adina LONG
06 Registrar ... Ms. Gwen D. WHITAKER
18 Executive Director Facilities ... Mr. Scott BOOTH
19 Chief of Police ... Ms. Carolyn MCMACKIN
88 Director Small Business Center ... Mr. Allan YOUNGER
35 Director Student Life & Engagement ... Ms. Beverly N. LEWIS
96 Exec Director Purchasing/Aux Svcs ... Mr. Keith BLYTHE
109 Director Auxiliary Services ... Mr. Brian A. HICKS
88 Exec Director National Ctr Biotech ... Mr. Russel READ
88 Exec Dir Div Operations/Support ... Ms. Michelle DANCHO
12 Director Stokes County Center ... Ms. Sally ELLIOTT
88 AVP Business Partnerships ... Ms. Jennifer B. COULOMBE
88 Dean of Public Safety ... Mr. Konrad WALSH
88 Dir Transportation Technology Ctr ... Ms. Kirsten SEAMSTER
88 AVP Transformative Learning Center ... Dr. James COOK
29 Director Donor Relations ... Ms. Angela COOK
25 Director Grant Writing & Dev ... Mr. Mike MASSOGLIA
44 Director Development & Annual Fund ... Ms. Patricia VAUGHN
34 Director Shugarts Women's Center ... Ms. Kenyetta RICHMOND
36 Director Career Services ... Ms. Jessica LONG
26 Director College Relations ... Mr. Devin PURGASON
121 Exec Director Student Support Svcs .. Dr. Stacy WATERS-BAILEY

*Gaston College (G)

201 Highway 321 South, Dallas NC 28034-1499
County: Gaston FICE Identification: 002973
Unit ID: 198570
Telephone: (704) 922-6200 Carnegie Class: Assoc/MT-VT-High Trad
FAX Number: (704) 922-2323 Calendar System: Semester
URL: www.gaston.edu
Established: 1964 Annual Undergrad Tuition & Fees (In-District): $2,704
Enrollment: 5,345 Coed
Affiliation or Control: State/Local IRS Status: 501(c)3
Highest Offering: Associate Degree
Accreditation: SC, ACBSP, ADNUR, DIETT, EMT, IFSAC, MAC, NAEYC, PNUR

02 President ... Dr. John HAUSER
03 EVP Academic/Student Affairs ... Dr. Dewey DELLINGER
103 Int VP Econ & Workforce Development ... Mr. Greg SMITH
10 VP Finance/Operations & Facilities ... Ms. Shelly ALMAN
102 Chief Dev Ofcr/Dir Foundation ... Mr. Luke UPCHURCH
04 Exec Admin Assistant to Pres ... Ms. Mary Ellen DILLON
11 VP Admin Services/CHRO ... Mr. Todd BANEY
88 VP/GM Man & Textiles Innov Network ... Mr. Sam BUFF
05 VP Academic Affairs ... Dr. Heather WOODSON
32 VP Student Affairs/Enrollment Mgmt ... Dr. Audrey SHERRILL
88 VP Educational Partnerships ... Dr. Jennifer NICHOLS
21 Controller ... Ms. Tracy BARRETT
26 Exec Dir Marketing/Communication ... Ms. Julie OSTROWSKI
103 Dean Career & Tech Education ... Dr. Lisa ALBRIGHT-JURS
49 Dean Arts & Sciences ... Ms. Tonia BROOME
76 Dean Health & Human Services ... Dr. Allison ABERNATHY
12 Dean Lincoln/Kimbrell Campus ... Dr. John MCHUGH
35 Dean Student Development ... Ms. Renita JOHNSON
88 Dean Learning Resources ... Mr. Calvin CRAIG
06 Dir Registration & Records ... Ms. Alisa ROY
18 Dir Facilities Management ... Mr. Russell SMYRE
37 Dir Financial Aid/Veterans Affairs ... Ms. Ungina PERKINS
25 Dir Grants/Special Projects ... Mr. Luke UPCHURCH
09 Dir Institutional Effectiveness ... Vacant
124 Dir Student Success & Retention ... Mr. Damon MURRAY
08 Dir Libraries ... Dr. Harry COOKE

121 Dir Advising/Testing .... Mr. Zach KENDRA-DILL
07 Dir Admissions .... Ms. Tanisha WILLIAMS
40 Dir Bookstore/Vending Services .... Mr. Charles WILSON
75 Dir Textile Technology Ctr .... Mr. Dan RUSCH
19 Chief Campus Police & Security .... Mr. Talmadge MCINNIS
13 Chief Technology Services Officer .... Ms. Savonne MCNEILL
15 Dir Human Resources .... Ms. Carol DENTON
88 Dir Customized Training .... Ms. Emily HANSLEY
51 Dir Cont Educ & Bus/Industry Trng .... Ms. Jodi HUFFMAN
88 Dir Life Skills .... Ms. Rebecca MCLAIN
78 Dir Apprentice/Work-Based Learning .... Ms. Jill HENDRIX
66 Dir of Nursing .... Ms. Leslie PRESSLEY
88 Dir Fire Rescue .... Mr. Josh CRISP

*Guilford Technical Community College (A)

PO Box 309, Jamestown NC 27282-0309
County: Guilford FICE Identification: 004838
Unit ID: 198622
Telephone: (336) 334-4822 Carnegie Class: Assoc/MT-VT-High Trad
FAX Number: (336) 454-2745 Calendar System: Semester
URL: www.gtcc.edu
Established: 1958 Annual Undergrad Tuition & Fees (In-State): $2,319
Enrollment: 10,821 Coed
Affiliation or Control: State IRS Status: 501(c)3
Highest Offering: Associate Degree
Accreditation: SC, ACFEI, CAHIIM, DA, DH, EMT, IFSAC, MAC, NAEYC, PTAA, RAD, SURGT

02 President .... Dr. Anthony CLARKE
05 Sr Vice Pres Instruction .... Dr. Beth PITONZO
32 VP Student Services .... Dr. James EDWARDS
11 VP Operations & Facilities .... Mr. Mitchell JOHNSON
10 VP of Business & Finance/CFO .... Ms. Nancy B. SOLLOSI
121 AVP Student Services .... Mr. Kirby MOORE
103 VP Workforce & Continuing Educ .... Dr. Manuel DUDLEY
50 Dir Business & Industry Training .... Mr. Stephen CASTELLOE
15 AVP Human Resources/CHRO .... Ms. Cheryl BRYANT-SHANKS
13 Chief Information Officer .... Mr. Ron HORN
18 Director of Construction .... Mr. Charles YOUNG
09 Director of Institutional Research .... Dr. Kristen CORBELL
07 Director of Admissions .... Mr. Jesse CROSS
35 Director of Student Life .... Ms. Berri V. CROSS
37 Director Financial Aid .... Ms. Lisa A. KORETOFF
19 Interim Chief of Campus Police .... Mr. Raymond REESE
06 Registrar .... Mr. Keith KARRIKER
21 AVP Business & Finance/Controller .... Ms. Angela M. CARTER
40 Bookstore Manager .... Mr. Shawn G. DEE
36 Coordinator Career Services .... Vacant
38 Director Counseling & Assessment .... Dr. Ernest LAWSON
30 AVP Mktg Comm & Foundatioin .... Ms. Jan KNOX
08 Dir of Library Services .... Ms. Monica YOUNG
41 Athletic Director .... Mr. Kirk CHANDLER
96 Director of Purchasing .... Mr. Michael STOUT
88 Dir of Organizational Development .... Dr. Jackie GREENLEE

*Halifax Community College (B)

PO Drawer 809, Weldon NC 27890-0809
County: Halifax FICE Identification: 007986
Unit ID: 198640
Telephone: (252) 536-2551 Carnegie Class: Assoc/MT-VT-High Non
FAX Number: (252) 536-4144 Calendar System: Semester
URL: www.halifaxcc.edu
Established: 1967 Annual Undergrad Tuition & Fees (In-District): $2,608
Enrollment: 988 Coed
Affiliation or Control: State/Local IRS Status: 501(c)3
Highest Offering: Associate Degree
Accreditation: SC, DH, MLTAD, NAEYC

02 President .... Dr. Michael A. ELAM
04 Exec Assistant to the President .... Ms. Lisa C. BARKLEY
05 Vice Pres Academic Affairs .... Dr. Jeffery B. FIELDS
10 Vice President Admin Services .... Mr. David FORESTER
111 VP Inst Effectiveness/Advancement .... Dr. Edwin IMASUEN
32 VP Student Svcs & Enrollment Mgmt .... Dr. Barbara BRADLEY-HASTY
20 Dean of Curriculum Programs .... Ms. Allisha HICKS
06 Registrar .... Ms. Dawn VELIKY
07 Director of Admissions/Enrol Mgmt .... Vacant
08 Director Learning Resources .... Mr. Derrick FLOOD
09 Dir of Institutional Research .... Mr. Marcus LEWIS
26 Dir Public Relations & Marketing .... Vacant
38 Director Counseling Services .... Ms. Charice ROSSER
18 Director Facilities/Physical Plant .... Mr. Jeremy WEBB
36 Director Career/College Promise .... Ms. Jennifer JONES
37 Director of Financial Aid .... Mrs. Tara KEETER
96 Purchasing Agent .... Ms. Nicole BOONE
15 Director Human Resources .... Mrs. Margaret MURGA
13 Information Systems Manager .... Ms. Caroline HARRIS
49 Div Chair Arts & Sciences/Business .... Mr. Eugene TINKLEPAUGH
76 Div Chr Health Sciences/Humanities .... Ms. Allisha HICKS
75 Div Chair Vocation/Industrial Tech .... Vacant
106 Director of Distance Learning .... Ms. Ellen GRANT
19 Chief Campus Security .... Lt. Emmett SMITH
25 Chief Contracts/Grants Admin .... Mr. Victor MARROW
30 Director of Development .... Mr. Allen PURSER
103 Director Workforce Development .... Mr. Jerry EDMONDS, III
86 Director Government Relations .... Ms. Kimberly J. MACK

*Haywood Community College (C)

185 Freedlander Drive, Clyde NC 28721-9453
County: Haywood FICE Identification: 008083
Unit ID: 198668
Telephone: (828) 627-2821 Carnegie Class: Assoc/MT-VT-High Trad
FAX Number: (828) 627-3606 Calendar System: Semester
URL: www.haywood.edu
Established: 1965 Annual Undergrad Tuition & Fees (In-State): $2,580
Enrollment: 1,440 Coed
Affiliation or Control: State IRS Status: 501(c)3
Highest Offering: Associate Degree
Accreditation: SC, MAC, NAEYC

02 President .... Dr. Shelley Y. WHITE
05 Vice President of Instruction .... Mrs. Wendy HINES
32 Vice President Student Services .... Dr. Michael COLEMAN
10 Vice President Business Operations .... Mrs. Karen DENNEY
18 Director of Campus Development .... Mr. Brek LANNING
111 Exec Dir College Advancement .... Ms. Hylah BIRENBAUM
26 Director Marketing & Communications .... Mrs. Michelle HARRIS
15 Director of Human Resources .... Mrs. Sara J. PHILLIPS
84 Dir of Enrollment Mgmt/Registrar .... Mrs. Danielle HARRIS
37 Sr Dir Student Enrollment/Fin Aid .... Mrs. Tracy RAPP
09 Dir Inst Excellence/Research/Grants .... Mr. David ONDER
103 Dean of Workforce Dev/Cont Educ .... Mr. Doug BURCHFIELD

*Isothermal Community College (D)

PO Box 804, Spindale NC 28160-0804
County: Rutherford FICE Identification: 002934
Unit ID: 198710
Telephone: (828) 395-1292 Carnegie Class: Assoc/MT-VT-High Non
FAX Number: (828) 286-1120 Calendar System: Semester
URL: www.isothermal.edu
Established: 1964 Annual Undergrad Tuition & Fees (In-District): $1,994
Enrollment: 2,042 Coed
Affiliation or Control: State/Local IRS Status: 501(c)3
Highest Offering: Associate Degree
Accreditation: SC

02 President .... Dr. Margaret H. ANNUNZIATA
11 COO & Vice Pres .... Mr. Stephen MATHENY
05 Vice Pres Academic & Student Affs .... Dr. Greg THOMAS
103 Vice Pres Cmty/Workforce Educ .... Dr. Thad HARRILL
32 Dean of Student Affairs .... Ms. Sandra LACKNER
49 Dean of Arts & Sciences .... Dr. Kathy ACKERMAN
51 Dean of Continuing Education .... Ms. Donna HOOD
12 Director of Polk Campus & HRD .... Ms. Karen MARSHALL
08 Director Library Services .... Mr. Charles WIGGINS
10 Controller .... Ms. Amy M. PENSON
37 Financial Aid Officer .... Ms. Pamela ELLIS
26 Dir Marketing/Community Relations .... Mr. Mike GAVIN
18 Dir Plant Operations/Maintenance .... Mr. Bill DOLL
84 Director of Enrollment Management .... Ms. Diane DICKERSON
06 Registrar .... Ms. Rachel MERCANTINI
96 Director of Purchasing .... Ms. Trish HUNTSINGER
13 Director of Information Technology .... Mr. Robby WALTERS
40 Bookstore Manager .... Ms. Danielle ALEY
04 Executive Asst to President .... Ms. DeeDee BARNARD
09 Director of Institutional Research .... Mr. Adam PETIT

*James Sprunt Community College (E)

PO Box 398, Kenansville NC 28349-0398
County: Duplin FICE Identification: 007687
Unit ID: 198729
Telephone: (910) 296-2400 Carnegie Class: Assoc/MT-VT-High Trad
FAX Number: (910) 296-1636 Calendar System: Semester
URL: www.jamessprunt.edu
Established: 1964 Annual Undergrad Tuition & Fees (In-State): $2,570
Enrollment: 1,202 Coed
Affiliation or Control: State IRS Status: 501(c)3
Highest Offering: Associate Degree
Accreditation: SC

02 President .... Dr. Jay CARRAWAY
05 VP of Curriculum Services .... Dr. Dustin WALSTON
103 AVP Workforce Development/Cont Ed .... Ms. Gloria WIGGINS
10 VP of Admin & Fiscal Services .... Ms. Jessica MCMAHON
32 Associate VP of Student Services .... Dr. Shakeena WHITE
13 Assoc VP of Information Technology .... Mr. Jeff TAYLOR
100 Chief of Staff .... Mrs. Renee SUTTON
06 Registrar .... Ms. Kelly ENGLISH
07 Admissions Specialist .... Ms. Wanda EDWARDS
37 Director Financial Aid/Vet Affairs .... Ms. Tracy WARD
38 Director of Student Counseling .... Ms. Amber FERRELL
08 Director Library Services .... Mrs. Colleen R. KEHOE-ROBINSON
15 Dir Human Resources/Title IX Coord .... Ms. Tonya KENAN
97 Director of General Education .... Mr. Andy CAVENAUGH
09 Dir Research/Plng/Inst Effective .... Mrs. Norma Jean HATCHER
26 Director of Public Info/Print Media .... Vacant
18 Chief Facilities/Physical Plant .... Mr. Dennis SUTTON
96 Director of Purchasing .... Mrs. Amanda FARINA
55 Instr/Coord Evening/Weekend Svcs .... Vacant
19 Director Security/Safety .... Mr. Richard WHITMAN
04 Admin Assistant to the President .... Ms. Jeanette RACKLEY

*Johnston Community College (F)

PO Box 2350, 245 College Road,
Smithfield NC 27577-2350
County: Johnston FICE Identification: 009336
Unit ID: 198774
Telephone: (919) 934-3051 Carnegie Class: Assoc/MT-VT-High Non
FAX Number: (919) 209-2142 Calendar System: Semester
URL: www.johnstoncc.edu
Established: 1969 Annual Undergrad Tuition & Fees (In-District): $2,657
Enrollment: 4,182 Coed
Affiliation or Control: State/Local IRS Status: 501(c)3
Highest Offering: Associate Degree
Accreditation: SC, ADNUR, DMS, EMT, MAC, NAEYC, RAD

02 President .... Dr. David N. JOHNSON
10 VP Facilities & Finance .... Mr. Michael BARALDI
05 Vice Pres of Instruction .... Dr. Linda SMITH
32 Vice Pres of Student Services .... Dr. Pamela J. HARRELL
09 VP of IE & Strategic Initiatives .... Dr. Terri S. LEE
111 VP Advancement/Community Rels .... Dr. Twyla C. WELLS
13 Assoc VP/Chief Information Officer .... Mr. Jeff PICKERING
08 Library Administrator .... Mrs. Jennifer SEAGRAVES
105 Dir of Digital Comm & Webmaster .... Mr. Dustin H. GURLEY
06 Registrar .... Ms. Deena H. HENRY
37 Director Financial Aid .... Mrs. Betty C. WOODALL
109 Assoc VP of Auxiliary Services .... Mr. Ken H. MITCHELL
15 Assoc VP of Human Resources .... Mr. Harlan FRYE
07 Dir of Enrollment & Student Success .... Mrs. Megan L. SHANER
103 Exec Dir Econ Dev & Corp Partners .... Mrs. Danielle T. KROEGER
76 AVP Health/Wellness & Human Svcs .... Mrs. Angela P. SWANK
49 AVP of University Studies/Educ Tech .... Mrs. Dawn S. DIXON
50 AVP Business/Applied Tech .... Dr. Jennifer SERVI-ROBERTS
26 Sr Dir Commnications & Marketing .... Vacant
18 Director of Facility Services .... Mr. Michael MASSEY
96 Director of Purchasing .... Mrs. Brandi MITCHELL
88 Director Campus Police & Security .... Ms. Sarah GIBBS
04 Exec Asst to the President .... Mrs. Sandy MILLARD

*Lenoir Community College (G)

231 Highway 58 South, Kinston NC 28502-0188
County: Lenoir FICE Identification: 002940
Unit ID: 198817
Telephone: (252) 527-6223 Carnegie Class: Assoc/MT-VT-High Non
FAX Number: (252) 233-6879 Calendar System: Semester
URL: www.lenoircc.edu
Established: 1958 Annual Undergrad Tuition & Fees (In-District): $2,568
Enrollment: 2,361 Coed
Affiliation or Control: State/Local IRS Status: 501(c)3
Highest Offering: Associate Degree
Accreditation: SC, EMT, MAC, POLYT, RAD, SURGT

02 President .... Dr. Rusty HUNT
11 Senior VP Administrative Services .... Ms. Deborah SUTTON
05 SVP Instruction/Student Services .... Dr. Deborah GRIMES
20 VP of Instruction .... Dr. John Paul BLACK
32 VP of Student Services & IE .... Dr. Stanley ELLIOTT
37 Director of Financial Aid .... Ms. Shelia WIGGINS
84 Director Enrollment Mgmt/Admissions .... Mr. Dusk STROUD
35 Dean of Student Services .... Mrs. Kimberly HILL
10 Controller .... Mr. J. D GIBBS
13 Chief Info Ofcr/Dean Admin Svcs .... Mr. Lee WETHERINGTON
09 Director Innovation & Effectiveness .... Mr. Jonathan TYNDALL
15 Director Human Resources .... Mrs. Tasha JOHNSON
18 Director of Maintenance .... Vacant
41 Athletic Director .... Mrs. Shelly BARNES
06 Registrar .... Ms. Kamesha WILSON
96 Purchasing Agent .... Ms. Cindy JONES
26 Director of Mktg/Recruiting/Comm .... Ms. Richy HUNEYCUTT
111 Director Institutional Advancement .... Mrs. Jeanne KENNEDY
103 Work-Based Lrng Coord .... Mrs. Sherry IRSIK
08 Director of Learning Resources .... Mr. Rich GARAFOLO
50 Dean of Business & Industry .... Mr. Warren MOORE
20 Associate VP of Instruction .... Dr. Timothy MADDOX
76 Dean of Health Sciences & Nursing .... Dr. Alexis WELCH
103 Dean of Workforce Dev & Pub Safety .... Dr. Justin TILGHMAN
35 Director Student Activities .... Mrs. Shelly BARNES

*Martin Community College (H)

1161 Kehukee Park Road, Williamston NC 27892-9988
County: Martin FICE Identification: 007988
Unit ID: 198905
Telephone: (252) 792-1521 Carnegie Class: Assoc/MT-VT-High Non
FAX Number: (252) 792-0826 Calendar System: Semester
URL: www.martincc.edu
Established: 1967 Annual Undergrad Tuition & Fees (In-State): $1,915
Enrollment: 944 Coed
Affiliation or Control: State IRS Status: 501(c)3
Highest Offering: Associate Degree
Accreditation: SC, MAC, PTAA

02 President .... Mr. Wesley BEDDARD
03 Executive Vice President .... Dr. Brian BUSCH
05 AVP of Academic Affairs .... Dr. Tabitha MILLER
10 Chief Financial Officer .... Ms. Tammy BAILEY
11 AVP of Operations .... Mr. Billy BARBER
37 Financial Aid Director .... Ms. Terri LEGGETT
07 Counselor and Admissions .... Ms. Vanessa TRIPP
06 Registrar .... Ms. Eileen JARMUL
51 AVP Continuing Education .... Mr. Nathan MIZELL

18 Director of Facilities ....Mr. Walter WHEELER
15 Human Resource Director ....Ms. Morgan ROBERSON
13 Director of IT ....Mr. Jason FREEMAN
09 Director of Institutional Research ....Ms. Maureen GREEN
96 Director of Purchasing ....Ms. Jennifer CHERRY
12 Director of Bertie Campus ....Ms. Deborah THOMPSON
08 Library Director ....Ms. Mary Anne CAUDLE
04 Assistant to President ....Ms. Blair MAJOR
26 Dir Communications/PIO ....Ms. Judy JENNETTE
106 Director Online Education ....Ms. Kim BARBER
102 Director Foundation/Corporate Rels ....Ms. Kismet MATTHEWS

*Mayland Community College (A)

PO Box 547, Spruce Pine NC 28777-0547
County: Mitchell FICE Identification: 011197
Unit ID: 198914
Telephone: (828) 765-7351 Carnegie Class: Assoc/MT-VT-Mix Trad/Non
FAX Number: (828) 765-0728 Calendar System: Semester
URL: www.mayland.edu
Established: 1971 Annual Undergrad Tuition & Fees (In-District): $2,558
Enrollment: 441 Coed
Affiliation or Control: State/Local IRS Status: 501(c)3
Highest Offering: Associate Degree
Accreditation: SC, MAC

02 President ....Dr. John C. BOYD
04 Assistant to the President ....Ms. Brooke BURLESON
10 Vice President Administrative Svcs ....Mrs. Amanda BUCHANAN
05 Vice Pres Academics & Workforce Dev ....Mrs. Rita EARLEY
32 Dean of Students ....Ms. Michelle MUSICH
76 Dean of Health Sciences Programs ....Mrs. Kim BURR
49 Dean of Arts & Sciences ....Ms. Sherry SHERMAN
72 Dean of Career Technologies ....Ms. Brenda MCFEE
08 Director Learning Resources Center ....Mr. Jon WILMESHERR
09 Dir Institutional Effectiveness ....Mr. Ryan RAY
06 Registrar ....Vacant
88 Dean of Basic Skills Programs ....Mr. Steve GUNTER
12 Dean Avery County EWD ....Mrs. Melissa C. PHILLIPS
12 Dean Mitchell County EWD ....Mr. Chris HELMS
103 Associate VP Workforce Dev & CE ....Dr. Monica S. CARPENTER
37 Director Student Financial Aid ....Ms. Sonja PETERSON
18 Director Facilities/Physical Plant ....Mr. Lee WHITTINGTON
13 Dir Management Information Systems ....Mr. Tommy R. LEDFORD
15 Director Personnel Services ....Mr. Judy MCCLURE
96 Coordinator of Purchasing/Equipment ....Mr. William ELLIS

*McDowell Technical Community College (B)

54 College Drive, Marion NC 28752-8728
County: McDowell FICE Identification: 008085
Unit ID: 198923
Telephone: (828) 652-6021 Carnegie Class: Assoc/MT-VT-High Non
FAX Number: (828) 652-1014 Calendar System: Semester
URL: www.mcdowelltech.edu
Established: 1964 Annual Undergrad Tuition & Fees (In-District): $1,926
Enrollment: 1,048 Coed
Affiliation or Control: State/Local IRS Status: 501(c)3
Highest Offering: Associate Degree
Accreditation: SC, CAHIIM

02 President ....Dr. Brian S. MERRITT
05 Vice Pres for Learning/Student Svcs ....Dr. Penny CROSS
10 Vice Pres Finance/Administration ....Mr. Ryan GARRISON
20 Dean Curriculum Programs ....Dr. James BENTON
09 Director of Inst Effectiveness ....Mr. Ladelle HARMON
26 Director of External Relations ....Mr. Michael K. LAVENDER
13 Director of Technology/Info Systems ....Mr. Elmer R. MACOPSON
08 Director of Library Services ....Ms. Ramona DEANGELUS
88 Director of Industrial Training ....Mr. Eddie SHUFORD
49 Dean Arts & Sciences ....Mrs. Judy MELTON
06 Registrar ....Ms. Aprille BAILEY
37 Director Student Financial Aid ....Vacant
36 Director of Student Enrichment Ctr ....Mr. Wingate CAIN
97 Director College/Career Readiness ....Mrs. Teresa VALENTINO
22 Director VA & Disability Services ....Vacant
51 Director of Continuing Education ....Vacant
88 Director Law Enforcement Trng ....Mr. Alan MOORE
15 Human Resources Manager ....Ms. Breanna WILSON
102 Foundation Director ....Mr. Chip CROSS
88 Director MTCC Small Business Center ....Mr. Frank SILVER
04 Exec Assistant to the President ....Ms. Madalyn GAITO

*Mitchell Community College (C)

500 W Broad Street, Statesville NC 28677-5293
County: Iredell FICE Identification: 002947
Unit ID: 198987
Telephone: (704) 878-3200 Carnegie Class: Assoc/HT-High Non
FAX Number: (704) 878-0872 Calendar System: Semester
URL: www.mitchellcc.edu
Established: 1852 Annual Undergrad Tuition & Fees (In-State): $2,651
Enrollment: 3,373 Coed
Affiliation or Control: State IRS Status: 501(c)3
Highest Offering: Associate Degree
Accreditation: SC, ADNUR, MAC, MUS, NAEYC

02 President ....Dr. Tim BREWER
05 Vice President for Instruction ....Dr. Camille REESE
10 Vice Pres of Finance/Administration ....Mr. Gerald HYDE
103 Vice Pres Workforce Development/CEC ....Ms. Carol JOHNSON
111 Vice President for Advancement ....Mr. James HOGAN
32 Vice President for Student Services ....Vacant
12 Exec Director of Mooresville Campus ....Mr. Robert LESLIE
09 Exec Director Research & Planning ....Ms. Eva GIFFORD
121 Director Student Academic Success ....Vacant
37 Director of Financial Aid ....Ms. Candace COOPER
18 Director of Facilities ....Mr. Chad LACKEY
88 Director of Educational Partnership ....Ms. Amanda RHEA
06 Registrar ....Ms. Betsy PATTERSON
19 Director of Public Safety ....Mr. David BULLINS
121 Director of Academic Advising ....Ms. Myra LEWIS
15 Director of Human Resources ....Mr. Paul SANTOS
97 Dean of College Transfer ....Ms. Tia COLEMAN
50 Dean of Bus/Agriculture/Public Svc ....Vacant
66 Dean of Nursing and Sciences ....Ms. Linda WIERSCH

*Montgomery Community College (D)

1011 Page Street, Troy NC 27371-0787
County: Montgomery FICE Identification: 008087
Unit ID: 199023
Telephone: (910) 898-9600 Carnegie Class: Assoc/HVT-High Non
FAX Number: (910) 576-2176 Calendar System: Semester
URL: www.montgomery.edu
Established: 1967 Annual Undergrad Tuition & Fees (In-District): $2,537
Enrollment: 679 Coed
Affiliation or Control: State/Local IRS Status: 501(c)3
Highest Offering: Associate Degree
Accreditation: SC, CSHSE, DA, MAC

02 President ....Dr. Chad A. BLEDSOE
05 VP of Instruction/Student Services ....Lee PROCTOR
11 VP of Administrative Services ....Jeanette MCBRIDE
32 Dean of Student Services ....Dr. Michelle AHERON
51 Dean of Continuing Education ....Andrew GARDNER
102 Executive Director Foundation/Grant ....Korrie ERVIN
26 Dir of Communications/Marketing ....Kelly MORGAN
09 Dir Institutional Effectiveness ....Greg TAYLOR
13 Dir of Information Technology ....Stephanie WEISHNER
04 Assistant to the President ....Courtney B. ATKINS
06 Director of Records ....Karen FRYE
37 Director of Financial Aid ....Doni S. HATCHEL
15 Director Of Human Resources ....Melinda HILL
10 Accountant ....Tonya LUCK
18 Director of Facilities ....Wanda FRICK
07 Admissions Counselor/Recruiter ....Jessica LATHAM
08 Head Librarian ....Touger VANG

*Nash Community College (E)

522 N Old Carriage Road, Rocky Mount NC 27804-0488
County: Nash FICE Identification: 008557
Unit ID: 199087
Telephone: (252) 443-4011 Carnegie Class: Assoc/MT-VT-Mix Trad/Non
FAX Number: (252) 451-8201 Calendar System: Semester
URL: www.nashcc.edu
Established: 1967 Annual Undergrad Tuition & Fees (In-District): $2,666
Enrollment: 2,623 Coed
Affiliation or Control: State/Local IRS Status: 501(c)3
Highest Offering: Associate Degree
Accreditation: SC, MAC, NAEYC, PTAA

02 President ....Dr. Lew K. HUNNICUTT
04 Executive Assistant to President ....Mrs. Odell P. HOLLIDAY
103 VP Corporate/Economic Dev ....Mrs. Wendy C. MARLOWE
111 VP Institutional Advancement ....Ms. Pamela H. BALLEW
05 Vice President for Instruction ....Dr. Tammie L. CLARK
10 Vice President of Finance ....Mrs. Adrienne S. COVINGTON
13 Vice President Technology & CIO ....Dr. Jonathan S. VESTER
32 Vice President Student Services ....Mr. Mike LATHAM
26 Dean of Marketing/Strategic Engage ....Mrs. Kelley P. DEAL
09 Assoc Dean Institutional Effective ....Ms. Farley A. PHILLIPS
88 Director Small Business Center ....Ms. Tierra NORWOOD
07 Director of Admissions/Recruitment ....Mrs. Tammie WEBB
37 Director of Financial Aid ....Ms. Tammy LESTER
15 Director Human Resources ....Ms. Morgan H. ROBERSON
18 Director of Facilities ....Mr. Greg DEANS
06 Registrar/Director of Records ....Mrs. Kathy S. ADCOX
08 Chief Library Officer ....Mr. Robert JAMES
19 Director Security/Safety ....Ms. Sara WIGGINS
25 Chief Contract/Grants Administrator ....Ms. Lucrecia A. HIGH
29 Director Alumni Affairs ....Mrs. Denise BEAMER
38 Director Student Counseling ....Ms. Sonya SMALL

*Pamlico Community College (F)

PO Box 185, Grantsboro NC 28529-0185
County: Pamlico FICE Identification: 007031
Unit ID: 199263
Telephone: (252) 249-1851 Carnegie Class: Assoc/MT-VT-Mix Trad/Non
FAX Number: (252) 249-2377 Calendar System: Semester
URL: www.pamlicocc.edu
Established: 1962 Annual Undergrad Tuition & Fees (In-District): $1,867
Enrollment: 362 Coed
Affiliation or Control: State/Local IRS Status: 501(c)3
Highest Offering: Associate Degree
Accreditation: SC, #MAC, NDT

02 President ....Dr. Jim ROSS
10 CFO ....Ms. Sherry RABY
05 Vice Pres Instructional Svcs ....Ms. Michelle WILLIS KRAUSS
32 Vice Pres of Student Services ....Mr. Jamie GIBBS
13 CIO ....Mr. Scott FRAZER
09 Dir of Institutional Effectiveness ....Dr. Rebecca PESKO
06 Registrar ....Ms. Gretchen STEIGER
37 Director of Financial Aid ....Ms. Meredith BEEMAN
21 Controller ....Ms. Karan SMITH
26 Director of Public Affairs ....Mr. Sandy WALL
04 Executive Asst to President ....Ms. Michelle NOEVERE
106 Coordinator of Distance Learning ....Ms. Kathy MAYO
08 Chief Library Officer ....Mr. Paul GOODSON
18 Chf Facilities/Physical Plant Ofcr ....Mr. George WILLEY
96 Director of Purchasing ....Ms. Sue FORE

*Piedmont Community College (G)

1715 College Dr, Roxboro NC 27573-1197
County: Person FICE Identification: 009646
Unit ID: 199324
Telephone: (336) 599-1181 Carnegie Class: Assoc/MT-VT-Mix Trad/Non
FAX Number: (336) 597-3817 Calendar System: Semester
URL: www.piedmontcc.edu
Established: 1970 Annual Undergrad Tuition & Fees (In-District): $2,546
Enrollment: 1,329 Coed
Affiliation or Control: State/Local IRS Status: 501(c)3
Highest Offering: Associate Degree
Accreditation: SC, EMT, MAC

02 President ....Dr. Pamela G. SENEGAL
05 Vice Pres Instruction/CAO ....Dr. Barbara BUCHANAN
11 Vice Pres Administrative Services ....Ms. Beverly J. MURPHY
32 Vice President Student Development ....Ms. Shelly T. STONE-MOYE
111 Vice Pres Advancement & Comm ....Ms. Elizabeth R. TOWNSEND
76 Dean Health & Wellness ....Ms. Alisa L. MONTGOMERY
106 Dean Distance Lrng/Learning Commons ....Dr. Don M. MILLER
50 Dean Business Studies/Emerging Tech ....Mr. Walter C. MONTGOMERY
72 Dean Technical & Manufacturing ....Mr. Jody B. BLACKWELL
84 Dean Enrollment Services ....Ms. Paulita N. WILLIAMS
97 Dean Univ Transfer & Gen Educ ....Vacant
13 Chief Information Officer ....Vacant
06 Registrar ....Ms. Swanita FULLER
18 Director Facility Services ....Mr. Ed MORRAH
15 Director Human Resources & Org Dev ....Dr. Julie GILLIAM
09 Dir Research/Inst Effectiveness ....Ms. Michele W. MATHIS
19 Dir College Safety/Title IX Coord ....Mr. Adam W. IRBY
04 Executive Asst to President ....Ms. Felicia P. HOLT
10 Controller ....Vacant
12 Dir Caswell Co Campus Operations ....Ms. Emily B. BUCHANAN
07 Director Admissions & Recruitment ....Ms. Patricia A. HATCHETT

*Pitt Community College (H)

PO Drawer 7007, Greenville NC 27835-7007
County: Pitt FICE Identification: 004062
Unit ID: 199333
Telephone: (252) 493-7200 Carnegie Class: Assoc/MT-VT-Mix Trad/Non
FAX Number: (252) 321-4458 Calendar System: Semester
URL: www.pittcc.edu
Established: 1961 Annual Undergrad Tuition & Fees (In-State): $1,940
Enrollment: 7,688 Coed
Affiliation or Control: State IRS Status: 501(c)3
Highest Offering: Associate Degree
Accreditation: SC, CAHIIM, COARC, CSHSE, DA, DMS, EMT, MAC, OTA, POLYT, RAD, RADDOS, RTT

02 President ....Dr. Lawrence L. ROUSE
05 VP Academic Affairs & Student Svcs ....Dr. Thomas GOULD
11 Vice Pres Administrative Services ....Mr. Rick OWENS
26 Vice Pres Strategic Initiatives ....Dr. Johnny SMITH
111 Vice Pres Institutional Advancement ....Mrs. Marianne COX
20 Asst Vice Pres Academic Affairs ....Ms. Lori PREAST
13 AVP Information Technology/Services ....Mr. Ernest SIMONS
10 Vice President of Finance ....Mr. Ricky BROWN
04 Executive Admin Asst to President ....Mrs. Kathy M. CARNES
08 Director Library ....Ms. Leigh RUSSELL
09 Exec Dir of Planning & Research ....Dr. Brian MILLER
15 Vice President of Human Resources ....Dr. Ina RAWLINSON
91 Director of Admin Computing ....Mr. Wes WOOTEN
06 Registrar ....Ms. Angela CLINE
38 Director of Counseling ....Dr. Kimberly WILLIAMSON
88 Director Basic Skills Program ....Ms. Laurie WESTON
18 Director of Facilities ....Mr. Timothy STRICKLAND
41 Athletic Director ....Ms. Dawn MANNING
29 Director of Alumni Relations ....Mr. John BACON
96 Director of Purchasing ....Ms. Jane ALLIGOOD
19 Chief Public Safety/Campus Police ....Mr. Tyrone TURNAGE
88 Director Small Business Svcs ....Mr. Jerry ENSOR
104 Director Study Abroad ....Vacant
37 Director Financial Aid ....Ms. Lee BRAY
40 Manager of College Store ....Ms. Holly BARBEE
106 Coord Instructional Tech/Dist Educ ....Mr. Mike CLENDENEN
55 Coord/Counselor Evening Programs ....Mr. Alton WADFORD
50 Division Dean of Business ....Ms. Katherine CLYDE
76 Division Dean Health Sciences ....Ms. Donna V. NEAL
49 Division Dean of Art & Sciences ....Dr. Stephanie MANLEY-ROOK
75 Div Dean Construct/Indus Tech ....Mr. Steven MATHEWS
61 Div Dean Legal Sci/Public Svc ....Dr. Dan MAYO
07 Director of Admissions ....Vacant
102 Dir Foundation/Corporate Relations ....Ms. Georgia SIGMON
105 Director Web Services ....Vacant
25 Director Grants Management ....Ms. Julia CRIPPEN

27 Marketing Director Ms. Jane POWER
84 Asst VP Enrollment Management Mr. Brian JONES

*Randolph Community College (A)

629 Industrial Park Avenue, Asheboro NC 27205
County: Randolph FICE Identification: 005447
Unit ID: 199421
Telephone: (336) 633-0200 Carnegie Class: Assoc/HT-Mix Trad/Non
FAX Number: (336) 629-4695 Calendar System: Semester
URL: www.randolph.edu
Established: 1962 Annual Undergrad Tuition & Fees (In-District): $2,386
Enrollment: 2,548 Coed
Affiliation or Control: State/Local IRS Status: 501(c)3
Highest Offering: Associate Degree
Accreditation: SC, EMT, MAC, RAD

02 President Dr. Robert S. SHACKLEFORD, JR.
10 Vice Pres Administrative Services Ms. Daffie H. GARRIS
05 Vice Pres Instructional Services Ms. Suzanne Y. ROHRBAUGH
32 Vice President Student Services Mr. Chad WILLIAMS
103 VP Workforce Development/Cont Educ Mr. Elbert J. LASSITER
111 VP Institutional Advancement Ms. Shelley W. GREENE
08 Dean Library Services Ms. Deborah S. LUCK
12 Director Archdale Center Ms. Tonya C. MONROE
26 Director Marketing Ms. Felicia R. BARLOW
18 Director Facilities Operations Ms. Cindi J. GOODWIN
13 Director Information Tech Svcs Ms. Tara A. WILLIAMS
09 Planning & Assessment Specialist Ms. Stacy C. SCHMITT
15 Director of Human Resources Ms. Melanie AVELINO
37 Director Financial Aid & Veteran Af Mr. Joel TROGDON
07 Dir Admissions/Records & Registrar Ms. Hillary D. PRITCHARD
88 Director of ABE and AHS Ms. Jordan H. WILLIAMSON
88 Director Public Safety Programs Ms. Regina L. BREWER
96 Purchasing Agent Mr. Christopher G. HUSSEY
04 Exec Asst to Pres/Board of Trustees Ms. Heather O. CLOUSTON
19 Dir Safety/Emergency Preparedness Mr. Matthew R. NEEDHAM
30 Director of Development Ms. Lorie L. MCCROSKEY

*Richmond Community College (B)

Box 1189, Hamlet NC 28345-1189
County: Richmond FICE Identification: 005464
Unit ID: 199449
Telephone: (910) 410-1700 Carnegie Class: Assoc/MT-VT-Mix Trad/Non
FAX Number: (910) 582-7028 Calendar System: Semester
URL: www.richmondcc.edu
Established: 1964 Annual Undergrad Tuition & Fees (In-District): $2,536
Enrollment: 2,226 Coed
Affiliation or Control: State/Local IRS Status: 501(c)3
Highest Offering: Associate Degree
Accreditation: SC, MAC

02 President Dr. W. Dale MCINNIS
32 Vice President for Student Services Ms. Sharon GOODMAN
05 Vice President for Instruction/CAO Mr. Kevin PARSONS
10 Executive VP and CFO Mr. Brent BARBEE
26 Assoc VP of Mktg & Strategic Plng Ms. Sheri DUNN-RAMSAY
30 Assoc VP of Development Dr. Hal SHULER
09 Director of Institutional Research Ms. Chihoko TERRY
15 Director of Human Resources Ms. Gaye CLARK
27 Dir of Marketing & Communications Ms. Wylie BELL
21 Controller Ms. Debbie CASHWELL
36 Director of Career and Transfer Svc Ms. Patsy STANLEY
37 Director of Student Financial Aid Ms. Jenelle HANDCOX
96 Purchasing Officer Mr. Martin BRIDGES
18 Director of Facility Services Mr. Scotty MABE
38 Director Student Counseling Mr. Chris GARDNER
04 Executive Asst to President Ms. Teena PARSONS
06 Registrar Ms. Cayce HOLMES
106 Director of Distance Learning Ms. Katelynn ARNER
13 Chief Information Officer Mr. Lee MONTROSE
54 Dean of Applied Sciences & Engr Dr. Devon HALL
49 Dean of Arts & Sciences Mr. Lee BALLENGER
88 Dean Adult Education & Immured Pgm Mr. John KESTER
76 Dean Allied Health & Human Services Ms. Janet SIMS

*Roanoke-Chowan Community College (C)

109 Community College Road, Ahoskie NC 27910
County: Hertford FICE Identification: 008613
Unit ID: 199467
Telephone: (252) 862-1200 Carnegie Class: Assoc/HT-High Non
FAX Number: (252) 862-1358 Calendar System: Semester
URL: www.roanokechowan.edu
Established: 1967 Annual Undergrad Tuition & Fees (In-District): $2,642
Enrollment: 525 Coed
Affiliation or Control: State/Local IRS Status: 501(c)3
Highest Offering: Associate Degree
Accreditation: SC

02 President Dr. Murray J. WILLIAMS
05 VP of Instruction Ms. Jami WOODS
10 VP of Administration/Fiscal Svcs Mr. Daniel J. FIGLER
20 Assoc VP of Instruction Ms. Kim HARRELL
51 Assoc Dean Continuing Education Ms. Wendy VANN
76 Director Allied Health Programs Ms. Jamie BURNS
32 AVP of Student Services Dr. Tanya W. OLIVER
21 Controller Ms. Angela BAGLEY
18 Director of Facilities Mr. Timothy LASSITER
106 Director Distance Learning Ms. Melanie TEMPLE
37 Director Financial Aid Mrs. Ruchelle RICKS
13 Director of Information Systems Vacant
08 Director of Library Services Ms. Carol A. HANKINSON
84 Director Enrollment Svcs/Curric Reg Mrs. Amy F. WIGGINS
121 Director Student Support Services Vacant
15 Director Human Resources Ms. Andrea A. WRIGHT
06 Registrar/Continuing Educ/Workforce Ms. Sharda D. BRITT
102 Director R-CCC Foundation Vacant
09 Director of Institutional Research Mrs. Jaime P. HECKSTALL
88 Director of Small Business Center Mr. Derrick ARMSTEAD
30 Vice President External Affairs Mrs. Wendy P. VANN
96 Purchasing Agent/Equipment Coord Ms. Susan B. MELTON
04 Exec Assistant to the President Ms. Renicka VAUGHAN
19 Director Security/Safety Mr. Timothy LASSITER
07 Director Admission/Student Life Ms. Rushelle D. SAXBY

*Robeson Community College (D)

5160 Fayetteville Road, Lumberton NC 28360
County: Robeson FICE Identification: 008612
Unit ID: 199476
Telephone: (910) 272-3700 Carnegie Class: Assoc/MT-VT-Mix Trad/Non
FAX Number: (910) 272-3546 Calendar System: Semester
URL: www.robeson.edu
Established: 1965 Annual Undergrad Tuition & Fees (In-District): $2,563
Enrollment: 1,828 Coed
Affiliation or Control: State/Local IRS Status: 501(c)3
Highest Offering: Associate Degree
Accreditation: SC, COARC, NAEYC, RAD, SURGT

02 President Ms. Melissa SINGLER
05 VP Instruction/Sppt Svcs/CAO Ms. Patrena ELLIOTT
103 VP Workforce Devel/Continuing Educ Mr. Steven HUNT
10 VP Business/Institutional Services Ms. Tami GEORGE
13 VP Information Sys/Chief Info Ofcr Mr. Dustin LONG
76 Asst VP Univ Transfer/Hlth Sci Pgms Ms. LaRonda LOWERY
32 Asst VP Student Services Mr. Ronnie LOCKLEAR
07 Director of Admissions/Enroll Svcs Ms. Patricia LOCKLEAR
08 Director of Learning Resource Svcs Ms. Maryellen O'BRIEN
06 Dir Records/Registration/Registrar Ms. Sherry MARTIN
37 Director of Financial Aid Ms. Zilma LOPES
18 Director of Facilities Vacant
102 Director Foundation & Development Ms. Jessica BULLARD
36 Counseling & Career Services Ms. Susan MOORE
15 Director of Human Resources Ms. Sally CARR
96 Purchasing Specialist Ms. Christy MUSSELWHITE
04 Executive Assistant to President Ms. Courtney JACOBS
09 Dir of Institutional Effectiveness Ms. Jamee FREEMAN
19 Director of Security Ms. Patricia CLARK
26 Chief Public Relations Officer Ms. Cheryl HEMRIC

*Rockingham Community College (E)

PO Box 38, Wentworth NC 27375-0038
County: Rockingham FICE Identification: 002958
Unit ID: 199485
Telephone: (336) 342-4261 Carnegie Class: Assoc/HT-High Trad
FAX Number: (336) 349-9986 Calendar System: Semester
URL: www.rockinghamcc.edu
Established: 1963 Annual Undergrad Tuition & Fees (In-District): $1,966
Enrollment: 1,922 Coed
Affiliation or Control: State/Local IRS Status: 501(c)3
Highest Offering: Associate Degree
Accreditation: SC, COARC, SURGT

02 President Dr. Mark O. KINLAW
05 Vice President for Academic Affairs Ms. Sheila REGAN
11 VP of Administrative Services Mr. Steven W. WOODRUFF
32 Vice Pres for Student Development Dr. Robert S. LOWDERMILK
18 AVP Facilities/External Affairs Dr. E. Anthony GUNN
103 Dean Workforce Development Mr. Christopher BROOKS
49 Dean of Arts & Sciences Ms. Celeste H. ALLIS
76 Dean of Health & Public Services Ms. Vickie CHITWOOD
88 Director Testing Services Ms. Kimberly SHIREMAN
13 AVP Technology/Inst Effectiveness Ms. Gretchen PARRISH
06 Registrar Ms. Carla MOORE
08 Director Library Services/Archivist Ms. Mary GOMEZ
30 Dir Development/Exec Dir Foundation Ms. Kim PRYOR
37 Director of Financial Aid Ms. Carol PERRY
84 Director of Enrollment Services Mr. Derick SATTERFIELD
35 Director Student Life Ms. Maggie MURRAY
40 Bookstore Manager Ms. Angie PURGASON
15 Director Human Resources Ms. Joy G. CHAPPELL
26 Director Public Information Ms. Gerri HUNT
96 Purchasing Ofcr/Capital Projects Mr. Caleb RORRER

*Rowan-Cabarrus Community College (F)

1333 Jake Alexander Blvd., South, Salisbury NC 28145
County: Rowan FICE Identification: 005754
Unit ID: 199494
Telephone: (704) 216-7222 Carnegie Class: Assoc/HT-Mix Trad/Non
FAX Number: N/A Calendar System: Semester
URL: www.rccc.edu
Established: 1963 Annual Undergrad Tuition & Fees (In-State): $2,632
Enrollment: 7,109 Coed
Affiliation or Control: State IRS Status: 501(c)3
Highest Offering: Associate Degree
Accreditation: SC, ADNUR, DA, EMT, OTA, PNUR, PTAA, RAD

02 President Dr. Carol SPALDING
05 Vice President Academic Programs Dr. Michael QUILLEN
51 VP Corporate & Continuing Education Mr. Craig LAMB
32 Vice President Student Success Ms. Natasha LIPSCOMB
13 Chief Officer Information Svcs Mr. Kenneth INGLE, III
18 Chief Officer Civility/Environment Mr. Jonathan CHAMBERLAIN
20 Assoc Academic Vice President Ms. Debra NEESMITH
20 Assoc Academic Vice President Mr. Angelo MARKANTONAKIS
76 Dean Health & Education Dr. Wendy BARNHARDT
49 Dean Arts and Sciences Ms. Carol SCHERCZINGER
72 Dean Technical Programs Mr. Zackary HUBBARD
120 Director Distance Education Mrs. Faith JELLEY
36 Exec Dir College & Career Readiness Mr. Jay TAYLOR
08 Director Library Services Mr. Timothy HUNTER
25 Director Grants Ms. Rebecca HOOKS
121 Exec Dir Students Success Svc Ms. Crytsal RYERSON
96 Purchasing Manager Ms. Kathy PIPER
37 Director of Student Financial Aid Ms. Allison SCOTT
06 Registrar/Dir Admission & Records Mr. Phillip LOPP
35 Director Student Life Mrs. Barb MEIDL
15 Chief Officer Human Resources Mrs. Nekita EUBANKS
09 Exec Dir Inst Effectiveness & Rsch Ms. Xiana SANTOS-SMITHHART
19 Director Campus Safety & Security Mr. Paul DUPREE
69 Dean Public Services Mr. Chris NESBITT
124 Director Recruitment & Retention Dr. A'Lelianne WARREN
102 Foundation Director Ms. Connie RHEINECKER
119 Dir Info Security/IT Const & Comp Mr. Steven SAINE
38 Director TRIO/Wellness & Access Svc Mrs. Misty MOLER

*Sampson Community College (G)

PO Box 318, Clinton NC 28329-0318
County: Sampson FICE Identification: 007892
Unit ID: 199625
Telephone: (910) 592-8081 Carnegie Class: Assoc/MT-VT-High Trad
FAX Number: (910) 592-8048 Calendar System: Semester
URL: www.sampsoncc.edu
Established: 1967 Annual Undergrad Tuition & Fees (In-District): $2,830
Enrollment: 1,492 Coed
Affiliation or Control: State/Local IRS Status: 501(c)3
Highest Offering: Associate Degree
Accreditation: SC, ADNUR, MAC, PNUR

02 President Dr. Bill STARLING
05 Vice Pres Academic & Student Affs Mrs. Blair HAIRR
10 Vice Pres Finance/Auxiliary Svcs Mrs. Kelly JACKSON
32 Acting Dean of Student Services Dr. Marvin RONDON
111 Dean Advance/Exec Dir Foundation Mrs. Lisa TURLINGTON
103 Dean of Wkfc Dev/Continuing Educ Mrs. Amanda BRADSHAW
07 Dir Enrollment & Student Success Ms. Amelia ELMORE
09 Director of Academic Svcs/IE Dr. Marvin RONDON
13 Int Dir of Information Technology Mr. Paul RUGGLES
06 Registrar Ms. Billie Jo PITTMAN
19 Director of Security Mr. Darryl GRADY
37 Dir Financial Aid/Veteran Services Ms. Marleen POWELL
08 Director Library Services Ms. Michelle MILLIKEN
106 Director of Distance Learning Ms. Marion POPE
15 Director of Personnel Mrs. Frankie SUTTER

*Sandhills Community College (H)

3395 Airport Road, Pinehurst NC 28374-8283
County: Moore FICE Identification: 002961
Unit ID: 199634
Telephone: (910) 692-6185 Carnegie Class: Assoc/MT-VT-Mix Trad/Non
FAX Number: (910) 695-1823 Calendar System: Semester
URL: www.sandhills.edu
Established: 1963 Annual Undergrad Tuition & Fees (In-State): $2,764
Enrollment: 3,990 Coed
Affiliation or Control: State IRS Status: 501(c)3
Highest Offering: Associate Degree
Accreditation: SC, COARC, EMT, MLTAD, RAD, SURGT

02 President Dr. John R. DEMPSEY
11 Chief Operating Officer Ms. Brenda JACKSON
05 SVP of Academic Affairs Dr. Rebecca ROUSH
32 VP of Student Services Mrs. Kellie SHOEMAKE
35 AVP for Student Services Dr. David FARMER
51 VP of Continuing Education Ms. Andrea KORTE
88 VP College Initiatives Mr. Ron LAYNE
15 Assoc VP Human Resources Ms. Wendy B. DODSON
04 Exec Assistant to the President Ms. Heather LYONS
20 Dean of Instruction Dr. Julie VOIGT
09 Dean of Planning & Research Ms. Lindsey FARMER
102 VP of Institutional Advancement Ms. Germaine ELKINS
08 Dean of Learning Resources Vacant
06 Director of Records & Registration Ms. Jean BLUE
37 Director of Financial Aid Ms. Shenika WARD
106 Dean of Academic Support Ms. Wendy KAUFFMAN
13 Chief Information Officer Mr. Roderick BROWER
19 Director of Security/Safety Mr. Dwight THREET
18 Director of Facilities Mr. Doug SMITH
57 Exec Dir Bradshaw Perform Arts Ctr Mr. Joseph BROWN
26 Director of Marketing and PR Ms. Karen MANNING
40 Bookstore Manager Ms. Sandra DALES
07 Director of Admissions Ms. Cary GREENE

*South Piedmont Community College (I)

PO Box 126, Polkton NC 28135-0126
County: Anson/Union FICE Identification: 007985
Unit ID: 197850

Telephone: (704) 272-5300 Carnegie Class: Assoc/MT-VT-High Non
FAX Number: (704) 272-5350 Calendar System: Semester
URL: www.spcc.edu
Established: 1999 Annual Undergrad Tuition & Fees (In-District): $2,015
Enrollment: 3,019 Coed
Affiliation or Control: State/Local IRS Status: 501(c)3
Highest Offering: Associate Degree
Accreditation: SC, DMS, EMT, MAC, NAEYC

02 President .... Dr. Maria PHARR
05 Vice Pres Acad & Stdnt Affs/CAO .... Mr. Carl BISHOP
10 VP Finance/Administrative Svcs/CFO .... Ms. Michelle BROCK
111 VP Inst Advancement/SPCC Foundation .... Ms. Bonnie COTTER
04 Exec Assistant to President .... Mrs. Elizabeth HAMRICK
15 Assoc VP Human Res/Payroll/Org Dev .... Ms. Lauren SELLERS
21 Assoc Vice Pres Finance/Admin Svcs .... Mr. Richard ASHLEY
13 Assoc VP Info Tech Svcs/CIO .... Ms. Natisha GIVENS
20 Assoc VP of Academic Affairs .... Dr. Makena STEWART
35 Assoc VP of Student Affairs .... Mr. Brandon DYER
18 Executive Director of Facilities .... Mr. Thomas SUGGS
108 Assoc VP Planning/IE .... Ms. Jill MILLARD
49 Dean School of Arts & Science .... Dr. Diane PAIGE
76 Dean Health & Public Safety .... Mr. Ryan ANTHONY
72 Dean Applied Science & Technology .... Dr. Maria LANDER
88 Dean College & Career Readiness .... Ms. Kelly STEGALL
06 Registrar .... Ms. Cathy HORNE
121 Director Academic Advising .... Ms. Laura GREGO
07 Director of Admissions .... Ms. Amanda SECREST
37 Director Student Financial Aid .... Ms. Emily JARRELL
102 Director Foundation .... Ms. Shelley JARMAN
96 Director of Purchasing .... Mr. Anthony BARBOUR
88 Director Learning Commons .... Ms. Kamisha KIRBY
19 Director Safety & Security .... Mr. William KILGO

*Southeastern Community College (A)

4564 Chadbourn Highway, PO Box 151,
Whiteville NC 28472-0151
County: Columbus FICE Identification: 002964
Unit ID: 199722
Telephone: (910) 642-7141 Carnegie Class: Assoc/MT-VT-Mix Trad/Non
FAX Number: (910) 642-5658 Calendar System: Semester
URL: www.sccnc.edu
Established: 1964 Annual Undergrad Tuition & Fees (In-State): $2,600
Enrollment: 1,271 Coed
Affiliation or Control: State IRS Status: 501(c)3
Highest Offering: Associate Degree
Accreditation: SC, MLTAD

02 President .... Dr. Chris ENGLISH
05 Exec VP & Chief Academic Officer .... Dr. Sylvia COX
11 VP Administrative Services/COO .... Ms. Lacie JACOBS
32 Dean of Student Services .... Vacant
66 Dean Nursing & Healthcare Training .... Ms. Kimberly FINE
19 Dean of Public Safety .... Ms. Stephanie KRINER
20 Dean of Student Lrng & Innovation .... Ms. Elizabeth HIGH
103 Dean Careers & Technical Training .... Ms. Angela RANSOM
09 Dean of Inst Effectiveness .... Dr. Natalie HINSON
08 Librarian .... Ms. Kay HOUSER
102 SCC Foundation Director .... Vacant
15 Director Human Resources .... Mr. Bill MAULTSBY
21 Controller .... Ms. Donna TURBEVILLE
26 Dir Marketing & Outreach .... Ms. Haylee DAMATO
13 Director of Information Technology .... Mr. Jason STRICKLAND
37 Director of Financial Aid .... Ms. Sheila DOCKERY
06 Dir of Student Records/Registrar .... Vacant
36 Director of Counseling .... Ms. Julia ROBERTS
04 Admin Assistant to the President .... Ms. Terrie H. PRIEST

*Southwestern Community College (B)

447 College Drive, Sylva NC 28779-8581
County: Jackson FICE Identification: 008466
Unit ID: 199731
Telephone: (828) 339-4000 Carnegie Class: Assoc/MT-VT-Mix Trad/Non
FAX Number: (828) 586-3129 Calendar System: Semester
URL: www.southwesterncc.edu
Established: 1964 Annual Undergrad Tuition & Fees (In-District): $2,337
Enrollment: 2,259 Coed
Affiliation or Control: State/Local IRS Status: 501(c)3
Highest Offering: Associate Degree
Accreditation: SC, CAHIIM, COARC, DMS, EMT, MAC, MLTAD, OTA, PTAA, RAD

02 President .... Dr. Don L. TOMAS
05 Exec VP Instructional/Student Svcs .... Dr. Thom R. BROOKS
10 VP for Financial & Admin Services .... Mr. William BROTHERS
13 VP Information Technology .... Mr. Scott BAKER
103 Dean of Workforce/Cont Education .... Mr. Scott SUTTON
12 Dean Macon Campus .... Dr. Cheryl DAVIDS
06 Dir Student Records/Registrar .... Ms. Clyanne HYDE
08 Library Director .... Ms. Tina ADAMS
09 Director Inst Research & Planning .... Mr. Jonathan E. DEAN
26 Director of Public Relations .... Mr. Tyler GOODE
102 Director of SCC Foundation .... Mr. Brett L. WOODS
84 Director of Enrollment Management .... Dr. Mark ELLISON
18 Director of Human Resources .... Ms. Lisa SIZEMORE

*Stanly Community College (C)

141 College Drive, Albemarle NC 28001-7458
County: Stanly FICE Identification: 011194
Unit ID: 199740
Telephone: (704) 982-0121 Carnegie Class: Assoc/MT-VT-Mix Trad/Non
FAX Number: (704) 982-0819 Calendar System: Semester
URL: www.stanly.edu
Established: 1971 Annual Undergrad Tuition & Fees (In-District): $2,674
Enrollment: 2,432 Coed
Affiliation or Control: State/Local IRS Status: 501(c)3
Highest Offering: Associate Degree
Accreditation: SC, COARC, EMT, MAC, MLTAD, NAEYC, RAD

02 President .... Dr. John ENAMAIT
45 VP of Strategic Planning/Compliance .... Mrs. Carmen NUNALEE
05 VP of Academic Affairs/CAO .... Mr. Jeff PARSONS
32 VP Student Success .... Dr. Myra FURR
10 VP Administrative Services/CFO .... Mrs. Kimberly BRADSHAW
76 Assoc VP Health & Public Svcs .... Dr. Tammy CRUMP
50 Assoc VP Transfer & Business .... Mrs. Tammi MCILWAINE
75 Assoc VP AMIT .... Mr. Devin BAUCOM
13 Chief Technical Officer .... Mr. Jeff DRAKE
14 Director of Enterprise Applications .... Mr. Joel ALLEN
119 Director of Network Services .... Mr. Heath LUQUIRE
90 Senior Network Administrator .... Mr. Terry MCMANUS
120 Dean of Center for Teaching & Lrng .... Mr. Joe POLLARD
04 Exec Aide to President .... Mrs. Abby ELKINS
103 Director of Econ/Workforce Dev .... Mrs. Krista BOWERS
37 Dean Financial Aid Management .... Ms. Petra FIELDS
84 Dean of Enrollment Management .... Mr. Patrick HOLYFIELD
35 Dean of Students .... Mr. Marcus PRYOR
121 Dean of Advising .... Mrs. Jennifer HATLEY
06 Curriculum Associate Registrar .... Ms. Michelle POPLIN
38 Director Counseling/Special Svcs .... Ms. Megan BREHUN
26 Director Marketing & Communications .... Mrs. Michelle PEIFER
07 Director of Admissions .... Ms. April HARPER
21 Dean of Business Services .... Mr. Michael SPERLING
18 Director Admin/Facilities Services .... Mr. Blake BOSTIC
102 Exec Director of SCC Foundation .... Ms. Jeania MARTIN
15 Director of Human Resources .... Mrs. Lori POPLIN
08 LRC Director .... Mr. Joel FERDON
24 Director of Media Services .... Mr. Mark SAMPLE
96 Purchasing Agent .... Mrs. Shelley OSBORNE
19 Director of Security .... Mr. Michael HINSON
09 Director Inst Research/Planning .... Dr. Cindy DEAN

*Surry Community College (D)

630 S Main Street, Dobson NC 27017-0304
County: Surry FICE Identification: 002970
Unit ID: 199768
Telephone: (336) 386-8121 Carnegie Class: Assoc/MT-VT-Mix Trad/Non
FAX Number: (336) 386-8951 Calendar System: Semester
URL: www.surry.edu
Established: 1964 Annual Undergrad Tuition & Fees (In-State): $2,663
Enrollment: 3,103 Coed
Affiliation or Control: State IRS Status: 501(c)3
Highest Offering: Associate Degree
Accreditation: SC, EMT, MAC, PTAA

02 President .... Dr. David R. SHOCKLEY
10 Chief of Finance .... Mr. Tony L. MARTIN
05 Chief Academic/Tech Officer .... Dr. Candace HOLDER
09 Exec Dir of Analytics & Research .... Mr. Michael FAULKNER
15 Director of Human Resources .... Ms. Melonie WEATHERS
18 Chief Facilities/Physical Plant .... Mr. Randy ROGERS
19 Chief of Police/Safety Director .... Mr. Marty SHROPSHIRE
26 Director of Mktg/PIO .... Ms. Julie PHARR
41 Athletic Director .... Mr. Mark TUCKER

*Tri-County Community College (E)

21 Campus Circle, Murphy NC 28906-7919
County: Cherokee FICE Identification: 009430
Unit ID: 199795
Telephone: (828) 837-6810 Carnegie Class: Assoc/HT-High Non
FAX Number: (828) 837-0028 Calendar System: Semester
URL: www.tricountycc.edu
Established: 1964 Annual Undergrad Tuition & Fees (In-State): $2,363
Enrollment: 991 Coed
Affiliation or Control: State IRS Status: 501(c)3
Highest Offering: Associate Degree
Accreditation: SC, EMT

02 President .... Dr. Donna TIPTON-ROGERS
05 VP for Teaching & Learning .... Dr. Steve WOOD
10 VP for Business & Finance .... Mr. Bill VESPASIAN
13 Dir of Computing & Information Mgt .... Mr. Jason OUTEN
124 Coordinator Advising/Career Center .... Ms. Samantha Major JONES
103 Exec Dir Workforce/Govt Relations .... Mr. Paul WORLEY
09 Dean Planning & Research/EC Liaison .... Dr. Jason CHAMBERS
15 Director of Human Resources .... Ms. Connie IVEY
91 Systems Administrator/Data Base Mgr .... Mr. Randy GUYETTE
106 Learning Mgt Systems Administrator .... Mr. Donnie MORROW
108 Dean Institutional Effectiveness .... Mr. Roarke ARROWOOD
06 Registrar Curriculum .... Ms. Holly HYDE
37 Director of Financial Aid .... Ms. Diane OWL
96 Director of Purchasing .... Ms. Joy KEPHART
32 Director of Student Services .... Ms. Kelly HEMBREE
18 Director of Facilities .... Mr. Tim NICHOLSON
04 Senior Assistant to the President .... Ms. Helen KILPATRICK
26 Director of Communications .... Ms. Grace CHESHIRE
08 Director of Learning Resources .... Ms. Rachel WHITENER

*Vance-Granville Community College (F)

PO Box 917, Henderson NC 27536-0917
County: Vance FICE Identification: 009903
Unit ID: 199838
Telephone: (252) 492-2061 Carnegie Class: Assoc/MT-VT-Mix Trad/Non
FAX Number: (252) 430-0460 Calendar System: Semester
URL: www.vgcc.edu
Established: 1969 Annual Undergrad Tuition & Fees (In-State): $1,948
Enrollment: 2,963 Coed
Affiliation or Control: State Related IRS Status: 501(c)3
Highest Offering: Associate Degree
Accreditation: SC, CSHSE, HT, MAC, RAD

02 President .... Dr. Rachel M. DESMARAIS
05 VP Learning/Engagement/Success .... Dr. Levy BROWN
10 VP for Finance & Operations .... Mr. Steve GRAHAM
103 VP Workforce & Cmty Engagement .... Dr. Jerry EDMONDS, II
09 VP of Institutional Research & Tech .... Dr. Kenneth A. LEWIS, JR.
88 Dean of Corp Learning & Prof Dev .... Ms. Cherrelle LAWRENCE
50 Dean of Bus & Industry Solutions .... Ms. Tanya WEARY
88 Dean K12 Partnerships/Warren Campus .... Mr. Lyndon HALL
26 Director of Marketing .... Mr. Chris LA ROCCA
37 Director of Financial Aid .... Mr. Robert LEONARD
15 Director of Human Resources .... Mr. Kevin TOMPKINS
08 Director Learning Resources Center .... Ms. Elaine STEM
09 Director of Planning & Research .... Ms. Julie HICKS
18 Director of Plant Operations .... Mr. Ashley ROBERSON
121 Dir of Advising & College Success .... Ms. Amy O'GEARY
36 Director of Career Services .... Ms. Linda FLETCHER
06 Registrar .... Ms. Kathy KTUL
84 Dean Student Access/Support .... Ms. Kali BROWN

*Wake Technical Community College (G)

9101 Fayetteville Road, Raleigh NC 27603-5696
County: Wake FICE Identification: 004844
Unit ID: 199856
Telephone: (919) 866-5000 Carnegie Class: Assoc/HT-High Trad
FAX Number: (919) 779-3360 Calendar System: Semester
URL: www.waketech.edu
Established: 1958 Annual Undergrad Tuition & Fees (In-District): $2,432
Enrollment: 21,760 Coed
Affiliation or Control: State/Local IRS Status: 501(c)3
Highest Offering: Associate Degree
Accreditation: SC, ACFEI, ADNUR, DA, DH, EMT, MAC, MLTAD, RAD

02 President .... Dr. Scott RALLS
03 Executive Vice President .... Dr. Gayle GREENE
03 Executive Vice President .... Dr. Nicole REAVES
30 VP of Devel & Strategic Partnership .... Mr. Matthew B. SMITH
05 VP Curriculum Education Svcs .... Mrs. Sandra L. DIETRICH
103 VP Workforce Continuing Education .... Mr. Anthony CAISON
10 VP of Financial & Business Svcs .... Ms. Marla L. TART
26 VP Communications/Public Relations .... Mrs. Laurie C. CLOWERS
15 VP Human Resources/College Safety .... Ms. Benita I. CLARK
84 VP Enrollment and Student Services .... Dr. Brian GANN
18 Vice Pres Facilities .... Mr. Jeffrey J. CARTER
13 VP Information Technology Svcs .... Dr. Ryan SCHWIEBERT
88 AVP Enrollment Services .... Mr. John W. SAPARILAS
35 AVP Student Services .... Mr. Kevin A. BROWN
88 AVP Military Veteran Spec Program .... Mrs. Scarlet EDWARDS
88 AVP CE Operations/CCO Assessment .... Mrs. Monica P. GEMPERLEIN
04 Strategic Projects Coord/Exec Asst .... Mrs. Savannah VINCE
19 Chief of Police .... Mr. Michael A. PENRY
88 Dean of Curriculum Support .... Mr. John BAKKEN
108 Dean IE/Accreditation & Research .... Dr. John B. BOONE
14 Dean Information Technology .... Ms. Cindy LUTTRELL
76 Dean Health Sciences .... Ms. Angela WASHINGTON
88 Dean Student Life/Student Conduct .... Dr. Jonathan WIRT
88 Dean of Enrollment/Student Services .... Ms. Wendy COOK
75 Dean Occupational Services .... Ms. Lonette MIMS
88 Dean of Professional Services .... Ms. Pamela LITTLE
124 Dean of Student Engagement & Impact .... Mr. Michael COLEMAN
08 Dean of Library Services .... Dr. Carenado DAVIS
07 Dean Admissions and Outreach .... Ms. Santrell CAISON
30 COO/Sr Dir Foundation Rels/Admin .... Mrs. Stephanie S. LAKE
25 Dean Sponsored Programs .... Mrs. Amy MACDONALD
06 Sr Dean Curriculum/Registrar .... Ms. Holly Elaine SWART
72 Dean Tech Training & Career Dev .... Mr. Jeffrey MERRITT
37 Dean Financial Aid/Veterans Affairs .... Mrs. Regina M. HUGGINS
88 Sr Dean Strat Innovations/Spec Proj .... Mrs. Karen B. PHINAZEE
88 Associate Dean Admissions .... Ms. Tina P. CARTER
88 Associate Dean Health Sciences .... Dr. Barbara COLES
27 Dir Communications Ops/Brand Mgmt .... Mrs. Francie W. SANDERSON
36 Dean Career & Employment Resources .... Mrs. Lynn E. KAVCSAK
121 Associate Dean of Academic Advising .... Davis SMITH
12 Dean Public Safety Education Campus .... Mr. Jeffrey B. ROBINSON
88 Provost Health Sci Campus .... Dr. Angela BALLENTINE
81 Dean Mathematics/Sciences Div .... Ms. Sharon L. WELKER
49 Sr Dean Liberal Arts .... Dr. Micheal BECK
50 Dean Business & Public Svcs Tech .... Ms. Catherine LASSITER
75 Dean Applied Engr & Technologies .... Ms. Lora EDDINGTON
88 Dean Transportation .... Mr. David FAVRE
77 Dean/Provost Computer Technologies .... Mr. Keith BABUSZCZAK
88 Sr Dean Strategic Innovations .... Dr. Kai WANG

*Wayne Community College (H)

3000 Wayne Memorial Drive Box 8002,
Goldsboro NC 27533-8002
County: Wayne FICE Identification: 002980
Unit ID: 199892
Telephone: (919) 735-5151 Carnegie Class: Assoc/MT-VT-High Trad
FAX Number: (919) 739-7137 Calendar System: Semester
URL: www.waynecc.edu

Established: 1957 Annual Undergrad Tuition & Fees (In-District): $2,524
Enrollment: 2,701 Coed
Affiliation or Control: State/Local IRS Status: 501(c)3
Highest Offering: Associate Degree
Accreditation: SC, ADNUR, DA, DH, MAC, MLTAD, NAEYC, PNUR

02 President ... Dr. Thomas A. WALKER, JR.
05 VP Academic/Student Services ... Dr. Patty PFEIFFER
10 VP Finance/Chief Financial Officer ... Mrs. Joy KORNEGAY
11 VP of Operations ... Mr. Derek HUNTER
45 AVP Inst Effectiveness/COS ... Mrs. Dorothy MOORE
32 AVP Academic and Student Services ... Ms. Joanna MORRISETTE
51 VP of Workforce/Continuing Educ ... Ms. Renita DAWSON
15 AVP Human Res/Safety/Compliance ... Mr. Charles GAYLOR, IV
72 Division Dean Applied Technologies ... Dr. Ernie WHITE
49 Division Dean Arts & Sciences ... Dr. Brandon JENKINS
101 Asst Sec to the Board of Trustees ... Mrs. Amber TYLER
50 Div Dean Business & Computer Tech ... Dr. Tracy SCHMELTZER
76 Div Dean Allied Health/Public Svc ... Mrs. Janeil MARAK
88 Division Dean Public Safety ... Ms. Beverly DEANS
08 Director Library Services ... Dr. Ruth Aletha ANDREW
12 Coordinator Seymour Johnson AFB ... Mrs. Dori FRASER
92 Honors Program Coordinator ... Mrs. Deniz TUCK
106 Distance Education Specialist ... Mr. Randall SHEARON
26 Director Office of Communications ... Mr. Ken JONES
13 Director Information Technology ... Mr. Matt BAUER
18 Facility Operations Superintendent ... Mr. Chris SCHOTT
19 Chief Campus Police & Security ... Chief Willie L. BRINSON
40 Manager Bookstore ... Ms. DiAnna BARBER
103 Ex Dir Wayne Bus/Indus Ctr & WORKS ... Mr. Craig FOUCHT
07 Director Admissions & Records ... Ms. Jennifer MAYO
37 Director Student Financial Aid ... Ms. Katrina LEE
36 Director College & Career Promise ... Mrs. Lorie WALLER
78 Director Cooperative Programs ... Ms. Lorie WALLER
35 Student Activities Coordinator ... Ms. Paige HAM
96 Director of Purchasing ... Mr. Wade QUINN
102 Executive Director of Foundation .. Mrs. Adrienne NORTHINGTON
27 Public Information Officer ... Ms. Tara HUMPHRIES
16 Director Human Resources ... Ms. Melanie BELL
04 Senior Executive Asst to President ... Mrs. Amber TYLER
38 Director of Counseling ... Mrs. Melanie JENKINS
04 Executive Administrative Assistant ... Mrs. Shelbra JACKSON
88 Director of Inventory Management ... Mr. Wade QUINN
124 Director College Transfer Advising ... Ms. Peyton OVERBEE

*Western Piedmont Community College (A)

1001 Burkemont Avenue, Morganton NC 28655-4504
County: Burke FICE Identification: 002982
Unit ID: 199908
Telephone: (828) 448-3500 Carnegie Class: Assoc/HT-Mix Trad/Non
FAX Number: (828) 438-6015 Calendar System: Semester
URL: www.wpcc.edu
Established: 1964 Annual Undergrad Tuition & Fees (In-State): $2,577
Enrollment: 1,792 Coed
Affiliation or Control: State IRS Status: 501(c)3
Highest Offering: Associate Degree
Accreditation: SC, ADNUR, DA, MAC, MLTAD

02 President ... Dr. Joel D. WELCH
05 VP Academic Affairs ... Vacant
10 VP Admin Svcs/Chief Financial Ofcr ... Ms. Sandra K. HOILMAN
121 VP Stdnt Success/Support Svcs ... Ms. Susan A. BERLEY
32 Dean of Student Services ... Ms. Susan WILLIAMS
08 Library Director ... Ms. Nancy DANIEL
54 Dean Applied Technologies ... Mr. Michael DANIELS
49 Dean Arts & Sciences ... Ms. Ann Marie MCNEELY
06 Director Records & Registration ... Mr. Tou VANG
15 Director Human Resources ... Ms. Lisa H. SESSIONS
84 Director Enrollment Management ... Mrs. Jennifer PROPST
37 Director Student Financial Aid ... Ms. Dori BARRON
13 Director Management Info Systems ... Ms. Nancy E. NORRIS
96 Director of Purchasing ... Ms. Robin HALL
18 Director Facility Services ... Mr. Ronald GRAY
04 Exec Asst to President ... Ms. Stacey SHOLAR
19 Director Security/Safety ... Mr. Zebedee GRAHAM

*Wilkes Community College (B)

1328 S Collegiate Drive, Wilkesboro NC 28697-0120
County: Wilkes FICE Identification: 002983
Unit ID: 199926
Telephone: (336) 838-6100 Carnegie Class: Assoc/MT-VT-Mix Trad/Non
FAX Number: (336) 903-3219 Calendar System: Semester
URL: www.wilkescc.edu
Established: 1965 Annual Undergrad Tuition & Fees (In-State): $2,572
Enrollment: 2,435 Coed
Affiliation or Control: State IRS Status: 501(c)3
Highest Offering: Associate Degree
Accreditation: SC, COARC, DA, MAC, RAD

02 President ... Dr. Jeff A. COX
05 VP of Instruction ... Dr. Yolanda WILSON
10 Senior VP of Administration ... Mr. D. Morgan FRANCIS, JR.
32 VP of Instr Support/Student Svcs ... Ms. Kim E. FAW
13 Assoc VP Information Technology ... Mr. Mike WINGLER
103 VP WDCE/Ashe Campus ... Mr. Christopher D. ROBINSON
12 Director Alleghany Center ... Ms. Susan NILO
09 Inst Effectiveness Exec Director ... Ms. Nicole FOGLE
72 Dean Applied Career Technologies ... Mr. Ronald DOLLYHITE
50 Dean Business/Public Svc Tech Div ... Mrs. Kristen MACEMORE
76 Dean Health Sciences Division ... Mr. Billy WOODS
18 Exec Director/Facilities Services ... Mr. Morgan FRANCIS
30 Exec Director Development ... Ms. Allison PHILLIPS
15 Director of Human Resources ... Ms. Sherry P. COX
06 Registrar ... Mr. Michael WARD
35 Dean of Student Services ... Mr. Scott JOHNSON
37 Director of Financial Aid ... Ms. Roberta HARLESS
38 Director Counseling & Career Svcs ... Dr. Lynda K. BLACK
36 Coord Occup/Business/Spec Careers ... Ms. Marina BRANNOCK
08 Director Learning Resources ... Ms. Christy EARP
38 Director SAGE ... Mr. Jon HUTCHINS
40 Bookstore Manager ... Ms. Kelly CHURCH
26 Public Info & Relations Officer ... Ms. Patty PARSONS
19 Chief of Police/Campus Police Dept ... Mr. Jamie MCGUIRE
04 Executive Asst to President ... Ms. Cynthia ALFORD
96 Purchasing Agent ... Ms. Amber BLACKBURN
07 Director of Admissions ... Ms. Elisabeth BLEVINS

*Wilson Community College (C)

PO Box 4305, Wilson NC 27893-0305
County: Wilson FICE Identification: 004845
Unit ID: 199953
Telephone: (252) 291-1195 Carnegie Class: Assoc/MT-VT-High Non
FAX Number: (252) 243-7148 Calendar System: Semester
URL: www.wilsoncc.edu
Established: 1958 Annual Undergrad Tuition & Fees (In-State): $2,642
Enrollment: 1,862 Coed
Affiliation or Control: State IRS Status: 501(c)3
Highest Offering: Associate Degree
Accreditation: SC, SURGT

02 President ... Dr. Tim WRIGHT
05 Vice Pres for Academic Affairs ... Mr. Robert HOLSTEN
10 Vice Pres for Finance & Admin Svcs ... Ms. Jessica JONES
09 Director of Institutional Effective ... Mr. Andrew WALKER
32 Exec Dean of Student Development ... Ms. Amy NOEL
76 Dean of Allied Health & Sciences ... Ms. Becky STRICKLAND
50 Dean of Business & Applied Tech ... Mr. Wes HILL
72 Dean of Industrial Technologies ... Mr. Travis FLEWELLING
15 Director of Human Resources ... Ms. Cindy ALLEN
08 Head Librarian ... Ms. Lola BRADLEY
21 Controller ... Ms. Deborah WHITE
06 Dir of Enrollment Svcs/Registrar ... Ms. Jennifer GONYEA
07 Dir of Admissions/Student Success ... Ms. Leigh GOROSKI
18 Director of Facilities ... Mr. Ray OWENS
37 Dir of Financial Aid/Vet Affairs ... Ms. Lisa BAKER
111 Director Institutional Advancement ... Ms. Jessica GRIFFIN
13 Director of IT ... Ms. Susan WEEKLEY
96 Purchasing & Capital Projects Mgr ... Ms. Donna A. TURNER
40 Bookstore Manager ... Ms. Kaschia SPELLS
04 Exec Asst to the President ... Ms. Tracy LANE
106 Director of Inst Support Svcs ... Ms. Angela HERRING

North Carolina Wesleyan College (D)

3400 N Wesleyan Boulevard,
Rocky Mount NC 27804-8630
County: Nash FICE Identification: 002951
Unit ID: 199209
Telephone: (252) 985-5100 Carnegie Class: Bac-Diverse
FAX Number: (252) 985-5231 Calendar System: 4/1/4
URL: www.ncwc.edu
Established: 1956 Annual Undergrad Tuition & Fees: $32,750
Enrollment: 1,720 Coed
Affiliation or Control: United Methodist IRS Status: 501(c)3
Highest Offering: Master's
Accreditation: SC, CAEPN, EXSC

01 President ... Dr. Evan DUFF
05 Interim Provost ... Dr. Molly WYATT
11 Vice President of Administration ... Ms. Suzanne BRACKETT
111 Vice President of Advancement ... Mr. Eddie COATS
07 Interim Dean of Admissions ... Mr. Michael DREW
32 Dean of Stdnts/Stdnt Affairs Admin ... Mr. Jason MODLIN
88 Dean of Accreditation ... Mr. Jarrod KELLY
06 Registrar ... Mrs. Candace CASHWELL
08 Interim Director of Library ... Ms. Rachel MCWILLIAMS
26 Director Marketing Communications ... Ms. Crystal HILL
23 Director Health Services ... Ms. Jessica BRYS-WILSON
36 Dean of Career Services ... Ms. Gena MESSER-KNODE
19 Director of Campus Security ... Mr. J. W. SEARS
41 Director of Athletics ... Mr. Aaron DENTON
10 Controller ... Mr. Andrew VOTIPKA
37 Director of Financial Aid ... Ms. Leah HILL
15 Director of Human Resources ... Mr. Darrell S. WHITLEY
18 Director of Facilities ... Mr. David FRYAR
88 Assistant Director of Admissions ... Ms. Megan BRABBLE
38 Director of Counseling Services ... Ms. Quenetta JOHNSON
40 Manager College Store ... Mr. Marcus RICH
20 Associate Academic Officer ... Dr. Molly WYATT
85 Director International Services ... Ms. Dawn TURNER
13 Chief Info Technology Officer (CIO) ... Mr. Gregory BOYKIN
39 Director of Residence Life ... Mr. Steve BURRELL
50 Chair Business ... Dr. Jackie LEWIS

Pfeiffer University (E)

48380 US Highway 52 N / PO Box 960,
Misenheimer NC 28109-0960
County: Stanly FICE Identification: 002955
Unit ID: 199306
Telephone: (704) 463-1360 Carnegie Class: Masters/L
FAX Number: (704) 463-1363 Calendar System: Semester
URL: www.pfeiffer.edu
Established: 1885 Annual Undergrad Tuition & Fees: $31,840
Enrollment: 1,185 Coed
Affiliation or Control: United Methodist IRS Status: 501(c)3
Highest Offering: Master's
Accreditation: #SC, #ACBSP, #ARCPA, CAEPN, MFCD, MUS, NURSE

01 President ... Dr. Scott W. BULLARD
04 Executive Assistant to President ... Ms. Teena P. MAULDIN
13 CIO ... Vacant
10 Vice President for Finance/CFO ... Mrs. Robin LESLIE
05 Provost/VP Academic Affairs ... Dr. Daniel MYNATT
32 VP Student Affairs/Dean of Students ... Mr. Ron LAFFITTE
84 VP for Enrollment ... Ms. Emily CARELLA
15 Director of Human Resources ... Ms. Ramanda MEDLIN
41 Director of Athletics ... Ms. Danielle LAFFERTY
06 Registrar ... Ms. Robin LISTERMAN
09 Exec Director IR/Plng & Research ... Ms. Julia KENNEDY
26 Director of Inst Communications ... Mr. Casey HABICH
38 Director of Counseling ... Vacant
08 Director of the Library ... Ms. Lara LITTLE
37 Director of Financial Aid ... Ms. Amy BROWN
121 Dir of Academic Support Services ... Dr. Jim E. GULLEDGE
19 Dir of Campus Safety & Security ... Mr. Erik MCGINNIS
18 Director of Facilities ... Ms. Sharon K. BARD
42 University Chaplain ... Rev. Maegan HABICH
36 Director of Career Development ... Ms. Caroline SAWYER
39 Director of Residence Life ... Ms. Regina SIMMONS
58 Director of MCE Program ... Vacant
111 Exec Dir of Inst Advancement ... Ms. JoEllen NEWSOME
29 Director of Alumni Affairs ... Vacant
40 Bookstore Manager ... Ms. Dechelle ELLIS
104 Coord of Intl Studies/Study Abroad ... Ms. Rebecca HRACZO
50 Dean of the Undergraduate College ... Dr. Michael THOMPSON
53 Dean of the Graduate College ... Dr. Chris BOE

Queens University of Charlotte (F)

1900 Selwyn Avenue, Charlotte NC 28274-0001
County: Mecklenburg FICE Identification: 002957
Unit ID: 199412
Telephone: (704) 337-2200 Carnegie Class: Masters/L
FAX Number: (704) 337-2517 Calendar System: Semester
URL: www.queens.edu
Established: 1857 Annual Undergrad Tuition & Fees: $37,332
Enrollment: 2,338 Coed
Affiliation or Control: Presbyterian Church (U.S.A.) IRS Status: 501(c)3
Highest Offering: Master's
Accreditation: SC, CAEPN, MUS, NURSE

01 President ... Dr. Daniel G. LUGO
05 VP Academic Affairs & Provost ... Dr. Sarah FATHERLY
30 VP Univ Advancement & Athletics ... Ms. Jennifer ERIKSEN
26 VP Stdnt Engagement/Dean of Stdnts . Ms. Maria FLORES-MILLS
10 CFO & VP for Administration ... Ms. Mary Alice BOYD
13 AVP/Chief Information Officer ... Mr. Brian BAUTE
49 Int Dean Col A & S/Cato School Educ ... Dr. Jeremiah WILLS
50 Dean of McColl School of Business ... Dr. Rick MATHIEU
60 Dean Knight School of Communication ... Vacant
76 Dean Blair College of Health ... Dr. Tama MORRIS
06 Registrar ... Ms. Linda FLEISCHMAN
15 Director of Human Resources ... Ms. Teri ORSINI, SPHR

Reformed Theological Seminary (G)

2101 Carmel Road, Charlotte NC 28226-6399
Telephone: (704) 366-5066 Identification: 666785
Accreditation: &SC, THEOL

† Regional accreditation is carried under the parent institution in Jackson, MS.

St. Andrews University (H)

1700 Dogwood Mile, Laurinburg NC 28352-5598
Telephone: (910) 277-5555 FICE Identification: 002967
Accreditation: &SC

† Regional accreditation is carried under the parent institution, Webber International University, Babson Park, FL.

Saint Augustine's University (I)

1315 Oakwood Avenue, Raleigh NC 27610-2298
County: Wake FICE Identification: 002968
Unit ID: 199582
Telephone: (919) 516-4000 Carnegie Class: Bac-Diverse
FAX Number: (919) 828-0817 Calendar System: Semester
URL: www.st-aug.edu
Established: 1867 Annual Undergrad Tuition & Fees: $16,884
Enrollment: 1,110 Coed
Affiliation or Control: Protestant Episcopal IRS Status: 501(c)3
Highest Offering: Baccalaureate
Accreditation: SC

01 President ... Dr. Christine MCPHAIL
111 VP Inst Advancement & External Affs ... Ms. Caroline CARTER
100 VP & Chief of Staff ... Mr. Bernardo I. DARGAN
05 Provost/VP Academic Affairs ... Dr. Josiah SAMPSON, III
10 SVP for Business & Administration ... Mr. Edward PATRICK
20 Vice Provost for Academic Services ... Dr. Orlando E. HANKINS
88 VP for Special Projects ... Mr. Eugene NICHOLSON
30 VP of Development ... Ms. Veronica CREECH

32	AVP Student Affairs	Dr. Cindy LOVE
22	ADA Coordinator	Ms. Tiffany TUMA
15	Director Human Resources	Ms. Norma P. SMITH
35	Dean of Students	Ms. Ann BROWN
42	Chaplain	Rev. Hershey M. STEPHENS
13	Chief Information Officer	Mr. Farooq AGHA
41	Interim Director Athletics	Mr. David BOWSER
06	Registrar	Ms. Martarash TORAIN
50	Dean Business/Mgmt & Technology	Mr. Van SAPP
83	Dean Social and Behavioral Sciences	Vacant
81	Dean Sciences/Math/Public Health	Dr. Mark A. MELTON
79	Dean Humanities/Educ/Soc Sci	Dr. Wanda B. CONEAL
97	Dean General College	Dr. Kengie R. BASS
37	Director Financial Aid	Ms. Sharon R. GRIFFIN
08	Director of Library Service	Ms. Tiawanna S. NEVELS
19	Director of Public Safety	Mr. Charles L. SIMPSON, JR.
18	Director Physical Plant	Vacant
29	Director Alumni Affairs	Ms. Sheryl H. XIMINES
39	Dir Student Life/Housing	Mr. Jarron MORTIMER
90	Director Academic Computing	Ms. Carlene J. MORGAN
07	Dean of Enroll Mgmt/Admissions	Mr. Paul VANDERGRIFT
106	Director Online Education	Vacant
25	Chief Contract/Grants Administrator	Ms. Linda GUNN-JONES
26	Int Chief Marketing Officer	Mr. Demarcus WILLIAMS

Salem College (A)

601 South Church Street, Winston-Salem NC 27101

County: Forsyth | FICE Identification: 002960 | Unit ID: 199607
Telephone: (336) 721-2600 | Carnegie Class: Bac-A&S
FAX Number: (336) 917-5339 | Calendar System: 4/1/4
URL: www.salem.edu
Established: 1772 | Annual Undergrad Tuition & Fees: $31,016
Enrollment: 636 | Female
Affiliation or Control: Moravian Church | IRS Status: 501(c)3
Highest Offering: Master's
Accreditation: SC, MUS

01	President	Dr. Summer MCGEE
100	Chief of Staff	Ms. Renee GARCIA-PRAJER
84	Vice President for Enrollment Mgmt	Mr. James MCCOY
05	VP Acad/Stdnt Affs/Dean of Col	Dr. Daniel PROSTERMAN
111	VP for Inst Advancement	Ms. Kathryn M. BARNES
45	VP for Strategic Planning	Ms. Katherine K. WATTS
10	Interim VP Finance & Admin/CFO	Mr. David BROWNING
32	Dean of Students	Ms. Laurie NEFF
58	Dean of Graduate Studies	Dr. Sheryl LONG
20	Dean Undergraduate Studies	Dr. Richard VINSON
08	Director of Libraries	Ms. Elizabeth NOVICKI
44	Dir Annual Fund/Alum Engagement	Ms. Felicia CAREY
13	Director Information Technology	Mr. Kris KELLEY
15	Director of Payroll & Benefits	Ms. Debbie SULLIVAN
38	Director Counseling Services	Ms. Robin CAMPBELL
37	Asst VP Student Financial Aid	Mr. Paul COSCIA
36	Exec Dir Career Innovation	Ms. Collier LUMPKIN
41	Athletic Director	Ms. Patricia HUGHES
19	Director Security/Safety	Mr. Jerry BOLES

Shaw University (B)

118 East South Street, Raleigh NC 27601

County: Wake | FICE Identification: 002962 | Unit ID: 199643
Telephone: (919) 546-8300 | Carnegie Class: Bac-Diverse
FAX Number: (919) 546-8301 | Calendar System: Semester
URL: www.shawu.edu
Established: 1865 | Annual Undergrad Tuition & Fees: $16,480
Enrollment: 1,283 | Coed
Affiliation or Control: Baptist | IRS Status: 501(c)3
Highest Offering: Master's
Accreditation: SC, CAEP, SW, THEOL

01	President	Dr. Paulette DILLARD
05	VP for Academic Affairs	Dr. Renata DUSENBURY
10	VP for Finance & Administration	Mr. David BYRD
111	VP Institutional Advancement	Ms. Marilyn RICHARDS
32	VP for Student Affairs	Dr. Keith POWELL
84	VP Enrollment Mgmt/Student Success	Mr. Terrance DIXON
88	VP Real Estate/Strat Development	Mr. Kevin SULLIVAN
13	Chief Information Officer	Mr. David ALEXANDER
73	Dean Divinity School	Dr. Johnny HILL
101	Exec Asst to Pres/Board Liaison	Ms. Cynthia TRAYNHAM
15	Director Human Resources/Title IX	Mr. Richard BARNES
07	Director Admissions/Recruitment	Dr. Oscar RODRIQUEZ
06	Registrar	Ms. Jody HAMILTON
51	Assoc Director Adult Degree Pgms	Dr. Oscar A. RODRIQUEZ
08	Director of Library Services	Vacant
41	Director of Athletics	Mr. George KNOX
38	Director Counseling Center	Ms. Jerelene CARVER
88	Director Judicial Services	Ms. Agnes BAXTER
121	Director Academic Success	Ms. Rishard WEDDERBURN
36	Dir Exper Learning/Career Devel	Mrs. Amy HEDGEPETH
50	Dean Business & Prof Studies	Dr. Lynette WOOD
49	Dean Arts/Sciences & Humanities	Dr. Valerie JOHNSON
121	Dean Academic Support	Dr. Vanessa RAYNOR
53	Dept Head Education & Child Develop	Dr. Lucy WILSON
81	Dept Head General/Interdisciplinary	Mr. Jason MORGAN
76	Dept Head Health/Human/Life Science	Dr. Kimberly RAIFORD
60	Dept Head Mass Comm & Digital Tech	Dr. Cassandra MITCHELL
83	Dept Head Social & Justice Studies	Ms. MaNina MCNEILL
19	Chief Campus Police & Security	Mr. Steven LESANE

09	Director of Institutional Research	Mr. Brian CUMBERBATCH
26	Director Public Relations	Mr. Jeff TIPPETT
105	Digital Media Manager	Vacant
25	Dir Sponsored Programs/Title III	Ms. Tori WILLIS
124	Director Student Retention	Vacant
29	Director Alumni Relations	Ms. Kristen BROWN
37	Director Student Financial Aid	Mr. Ibrahim BAH
106	Dir Digital Teaching & Learning	Dr. Alesheia BACCOUS
96	Director Procurement	Ms. Dana MONROE
102	Dev Officer Corp/Found Relations	Mr. Brian ALLEN
108	Senior Assessment Coordinator	Ms. Elysia LASH
30	Senior Director Development	Vacant
44	Director of Donor Relations	Ms. Melodie CARTER

Shepherds Theological Seminary (C)

6051 Tryon Road, Cary NC 27518-9316

County: Wake | FICE Identification: 041730 | Unit ID: 461485
Telephone: (919) 573-5350 | Carnegie Class: Spec-4-yr-Faith
FAX Number: (919) 573-1438 | Calendar System: Semester
URL: www.shepherds.edu
Established: 2003 | Annual Graduate Tuition & Fees: N/A
Enrollment: 136 | Coed
Affiliation or Control: Non-denominational | IRS Status: 501(c)3
Highest Offering: Doctorate; No Undergraduates
Accreditation: THEOL

01	President	Dr. Stephen DAVEY
05	Provost/Dean	Dr. Tim M. SIGLER
20	Vice Pres Academic Affairs/CAO	Mr. Thomas PITTMAN
10	Chief Financial Officer	Mr. Ewart HODGINS
32	Dean of Students	Dr. Peter GOEMAN
06	Registrar/Financial Aid Officer	Mrs. Lucy BURGGRAFF
26	Director of Church Relations	Dr. Les LOFQUIST
56	Director of the West Institute	Dr. Clayton SCHULTZ
56	Director of Texas Teaching Site	Dr. Thomas BABER
27	Director of Communications	Mrs. Marilyn FITCH
108	Director of Assessment	Mr. Edward GELB
111	Director of Advancement	Mr. Brett INGALLS
56	Director of Shepherds Institute	Mr. Jimmy CARTER

Southeastern Baptist Theological Seminary (D)

Box 1889, Wake Forest NC 27588-1889

County: Wake | FICE Identification: 002963 | Unit ID: 199759
Telephone: (919) 761-2100 | Carnegie Class: Masters/L
FAX Number: N/A | Calendar System: Semester
URL: www.sebts.edu
Established: 1950 | Annual Undergrad Tuition & Fees: $9,562
Enrollment: 3,343 | Coed
Affiliation or Control: Southern Baptist | IRS Status: 501(c)3
Highest Offering: Doctorate
Accreditation: SC, THEOL

01	President	Dr. Daniel L. AKIN
05	Provost/Dean of Faculty/CAO	Dr. Keith WHITFIELD
03	Executive Vice President (COO)	Mr. Ryan HUTCHINSON
20	VP Academic Administration	Mr. Chris THOMPSON
111	Vice Pres Institutional Advancement	Mr. Art RAINER
32	VP Student Services/Dean Students	Dr. Mark LIEDERBACH
10	Chief Financial/Business Officer	Mr. Chris HLAVACEK
18	Chief Facilities/Physical Plnt Ofcr	Mr. Travis WILLIAMS
04	Administrative Asst to President	Mrs. Kim HUMPHREY
06	Registrar	Mr. Trevor KING
07	Director of Admissions	Dr. Sam MORRIS
29	Dir Financial/Alumni Development	Mr. Jonathan SIX
37	Director of Financial Aid	Mr. Jesse PARKER
08	Director Library Services	Mr. Jason FOWLER
106	Dir Online Education	Mr. Jerry LASSETTER
09	Institutional Researcher	Mr. Will JOHNSTON
13	Director Information Technologies	Mr. Wayne JENKS
15	Director Human Resources	Mrs. Dawn SATTERWHITE
39	Director Student Housing	Mr. Doug NALLEY
43	General Counsel	Mr. George HARVEY
19	Director Security/Safety	Dr. Michael S. LAWSON
30	Director of Development	Dr. Jonathan SIX

Southeastern Free Will Baptist College (E)

532 Eagle Rock Rd, Box 1960, Wendell NC 27591

County: Wake | Identification: 667309
Telephone: (919) 365-7711 | Carnegie Class: Not Classified
FAX Number: (919) 365-4940 | Calendar System: Semester
URL: sfwbc.edu
Established: 1983 | Annual Undergrad Tuition & Fees: N/A
Enrollment: N/A | Coed
Affiliation or Control: Free Will Baptist | IRS Status: 501(c)3
Highest Offering: Baccalaureate
Accreditation: TRACS

01	President	Rev. Nate ANGE
05	College Dean	Dr. Russ MOOTS
30	Director of Development	Rev. Steve BERRY
32	Dean of Students	Mr. Timothy GAYNOR
06	Academic Dean	Mr. Marc HOLLOMAN
10	Business Manager	Mr. Daniel OSBORNE
04	Admin Assistant to the President	Mrs. Lynnette GAYNOR
08	Chief Library Officer	Mrs. Catherine PENDLEY

Southern Evangelical Seminary (F)

15009 Lancaster Hwy, Charlotte NC 28277

County: Mecklenburg | FICE Identification: 036115
Telephone: (704) 847-5600 | Carnegie Class: Not Classified
FAX Number: (704) 845-1747 | Calendar System: Semester
URL: www.ses.edu
Established: 1992 | Annual Undergrad Tuition & Fees: N/A
Enrollment: N/A | Coed
Affiliation or Control: Independent Non-Profit | IRS Status: 501(c)3
Highest Offering: Doctorate
Accreditation: TRACS

01	President of the Seminary	Dr. Richard D. LAND
05	Academic Dean	Dr. J. Thomas BRIDGES
07	Dir Recruiting and Admissions	Mr. Adam TUCKER
10	Chief Operating Officer/CFO	Mr. Steven V. HASE
32	Dean of Students	Dr. Mel WINSTEAD
08	Acting Dir Library Services	Mr. Matt WASIELEWSKI
06	Registrar	Dr. Douglas E. POTTER
04	Executive Asst to President	Mrs. Christina S. WOODSIDE
106	Dir Online Education/E-learning	Mr. Alex JOSEPH
30	Dir of Institutional Advancement	Mr. Eric GUSTAFSON
12	Director of Bible College	Dr. Timothy BROWN

University of Mount Olive (G)

634 Henderson Street, Mount Olive NC 28365-1263

County: Wayne | FICE Identification: 002949 | Unit ID: 199069
Telephone: (919) 658-2502 | Carnegie Class: Masters/S
FAX Number: (919) 658-7180 | Calendar System: Semester
URL: www.umo.edu
Established: 1951 | Annual Undergrad Tuition & Fees: $22,194
Enrollment: 2,536 | Coed
Affiliation or Control: Original Free Will Baptist Church | IRS Status: 501(c)3
Highest Offering: Master's
Accreditation: SC, ACBSP, NURSE

01	President	Dr. H. Edward CROOM
03	Executive Vice President	Dr. Carol G. CARRERE
05	Interim VP for Academic Affairs	Dr. Kenneth D. HINES
10	Senior VP for Business & Finance	Mr. Jeremy SHREVE
84	VP for Enrollment	Mr. Tim WOODARD
32	Senior VP for Student Affairs	Dr. Dan SULLIVAN
111	VP for Institutional Advancement	Mr. Jason GIPE
20	Associate VP for Academic Admin	Dr. David DOMMER
49	Dean School of Arts and Sciences	Dr. Gerald SEATON
50	Dean Tillman School of Business	Dr. Kathy BEST
88	Dean of Learning Commons	Dr. Delight YOKLEY
123	AVP for Adult & Graduate Enrollment	Dr. Lisa M. NUESELL
08	Director of Library Services	Ms. Pamela R. WOOD
09	Director Inst Research & Planning	Dr. Juliane SANTIAGO
06	Registrar	Ms. Vicky WARRICK
35	Director of Campus Life	Ms. Nicole L. GARRETT
36	Director of Career Center	Ms. Laurica YANCEY
26	Director of Public Relations	Ms. Rhonda E. JESSUP
102	Dir Foundation & Sponsored Programs	Mr. Dustin BANNISTER
37	Director of Financial Aid	Mr. Brian BLACKBURN
15	Director of Human Resources	Ms. Cordelia A. WILCOX
18	Director Building & Grounds	Mr. Jeff D. BROGDEN
13	Director Technology Services	Mr. Kenneth M. DAVIS, JR.
14	Director Technology Support	Mr. Robert R. PRUETT
41	VP for Athletics	Mr. Jeffrey M. EISEN

*University of North Carolina General Administration (H)

Box 2688, 910 Raleigh Road, Chapel Hill NC 27515-2688

County: Orange | FICE Identification: 002971 | Unit ID: 199175
Telephone: (919) 962-1000 | Carnegie Class: N/A
FAX Number: (919) 962-2751
URL: www.northcarolina.edu

01	President	Mr. Peter HANS
05	Sr Vice Pres Academic Affairs/CAA	Dr. Kimberly VAN NOORT
10	SVP Finance/Administration & CFO	Mr. Clinton P. CARTER
100	Chief of Staff/Sr Vice President	Ms. Chris MCCLURE
11	Int Chief Operating Officer	Mr. Peter BRUNSTETTER
20	VP Academic Affairs	Vacant
13	VP for Information Tech & CIO	Mr. Keith E. WERNER
32	VP Student Affairs	Ms. Bethany MEIGHEN
111	Vice Pres for Advancement	Mr. Timothy A. MINOR
14	Assoc Vice Pres Data & Analytics	Ms. Diane E. MARIAN
43	SVP & General Counsel	Mr. Thomas SHANAHAN
46	VP Academic Pgms/Faculty/Research	Mr. David J. ENGLISH
101	Asst VP/Sec of the University	Ms. Meredith STEADMAN
86	Vice Pres State Govt Relations	Mr. Drew MORETZ
86	Vice Pres Federal Relations	Ms. Elizabeth MORRA
26	Vice President for Communications	Mr. Earl D. WHIPPLE
15	Vice Pres for Human Resources	Mr. Matthew BRODY
31	Sr VP for External Affairs	Vacant

*Appalachian State University (I)

287 Rivers Street, Boone NC 28608-0001

County: Watauga | FICE Identification: 002906 | Unit ID: 197869
Telephone: (828) 262-2000 | Carnegie Class: Masters/L
FAX Number: (828) 262-2347 | Calendar System: Semester
URL: www.appstate.edu
Established: 1899 | Annual Undergrad Tuition & Fees (In-State): $7,410

Enrollment: 20,023 Coed
Affiliation or Control: State IRS Status: 501(c)3
Highest Offering: Doctorate
Accreditation: SC, ART, CAATE, CACREP, CAEPN, CAPRT, CIDA, DANCE, DIETD, DIETI, IPSY, MFCD, MUS, NURSE, PH, SP, SPAA, SW, THEA

02 Chancellor ... Dr. Sheri EVERTS
100 Chief of Staff/Vice Chancellor ... Mr. Hank T. FOREMAN
05 Provost/Exec Vice Chancellor ... Dr. Heather NORRIS
10 Vice Chanc Business Affairs ... Mr. Paul D. FORTE
32 Vice Chanc Student Development ... Mr. J.J BROWN
111 Vice Chanc Univ Advancement ... Ms. Jane BARGHOTHI
20 Vice Provost for Undergrad Educ ... Dr. Mark GINN
46 Interim Vice Provost for Research ... Dr. Ece KARATAN
26 Assc VC Advance/Chief Comm Ofcr ... Mrs. Megan HAYES
84 Assoc VC for Enrollment Management ... Ms. Cindy BARR
29 Exec Director of Alumni Affairs ... Mrs. Stephanie L. BILLINGS
43 General Counsel ... Mr. Paul MEGGETT
13 Interim Chief Information Officer ... Mr. Tom VAN GILDER
06 University Registrar ... Ms. Debbie RACE
38 Dir Counseling/Psychological Svcs ... Dr. Christopher J. HOGAN
37 Director of Financial Aid ... Mr. Wesley ARMSTRONG
15 Director of Human Resources ... Mr. Mark BACHMEIER
09 Exec Dir Inst Research/Planning ... Mrs. Heather H. LANGDON
51 Exec Director of Distance Education ... Dr. Terry RAWLS
41 Director of Athletics ... Mr. Douglas P. GILLIN
49 Dean for College of Arts & Sciences ... Dr. Neva J. SPECHT
50 Acting Dean for College of Business ... Dr. Sandra VANNOY
53 Dean for College of Education ... Dr. Melba C. SPOONER
57 Dean for College Fine/Applied Arts ... Dr. Janice POPE
64 Dean for the School of Music ... Dr. James DOUTHIT
58 Dean of Graduate School ... Dr. Michael MCKENZIE
08 Interim Dean of Libraries ... Mr. Paul ORKISZEWSKI
18 Dir of the Physical Plant ... Mr. Jeff PIERCE
114 Budget Director ... Mr. John E. ADAMS
96 Director of Materials Management ... Mr. John WALL
28 Dir Multicultural Student Devel ... Vacant

*East Carolina University (A)

1000 East Fifth Street, Greenville NC 27858-4353
County: Pitt FICE Identification: 002923
Unit ID: 198464
Telephone: (252) 328-6212 Carnegie Class: DU-Higher
FAX Number: (252) 328-4155 Calendar System: Semester
URL: www.ecu.edu
Established: 1907 Annual Undergrad Tuition & Fees (In-State): $7,239
Enrollment: 28,798 Coed
Affiliation or Control: State IRS Status: 501(c)3
Highest Offering: Doctorate
Accreditation: SC, AAFCS, ANEST, ARCPA, ART, AUD, CAATE, CACREP, CAEPN, CAHIIM, CAMPEP, CAPRT, CARTE, CEA, CIDA, CLPSY, CONST, DENT, DIETD, DIETI, LIB, MED, MFCD, MIDWF, MT, MUS, NAIT, NURSE, OT, PH, PLNG, PTA, SCPSY, SP, SPAA, SW, THEA

02 Chancellor ... Dr. Philip ROGERS
100 Chief of Staff ... Dr. Chris LOCKLEAR
05 Interim Provost & Sr VC AA ... Dr. Grant HAYES
32 Vice Chancellor for Student Affairs ... Dr. Virginia HARDY
17 Interim VC Health Sciences ... Dr. Ron MITCHELSON
10 Interim VC Administration & Finance ... Ms. Stephanie COLEMAN
111 Vice Chanc Univ Advancement ... Mr. Christopher DYBA
46 Int VC Research/Econ Dev/Engagement ... Dr. Mike VAN SCOTT
39 Assoc VC Camp Liv/Dining ... Mr. William L. MCCARTNEY, JR.
35 Assoc Vice Chanc & Dean of Stdnts ... Dr. Lynn M. ROEDER
22 Assoc Provost Equity/Diversity ... Dr. Lakesha ALSTON FORBES
43 Vice Chancellor for Legal Affairs ... Mr. Paul ZIGAS
09 Associate Provost IPAR ... Dr. Ying ZHOU
41 Athletic Director ... Mr. Jon GILBERT
13 CIO & Assoc Vice Chanc ITCS ... Mr. Zach LOCH
15 Assoc VC Human Resources ... Ms. Kitty WETHERINGTON
18 Assoc VC for Campus Opers ... Mr. William BAGNELL
88 Assoc VC Environ Health & Safety ... Mr. Bill KOCH
88 Assistant VC of Global Affairs ... Dr. Jon REZEK
45 Dir of Institutional Plng & Accred ... Dr. Cynthia BELLACERO
88 Dir of Campus Rec & Wellness ... Mr. William EHLING
26 Exec Dir Comm/Public Affs/Mktg ... Ms. Jeannine HUTSON
07 Assistant VC/Director of Admissions ... Ms. Stephanie WHALEY
06 Registrar ... Ms. Angela R. ANDERSON
08 Director JY Joyner Library ... Ms. Jan LEWIS
88 Dir Health Sciences Library ... Ms. Beth KETTERMAN
101 Asst Secretary to Board of Trustees ... Ms. Megan AYERS
37 Director of Financial Aid ... Ms. Julie POORMAN
19 Chief of Police ... Mr. Jon R. BARNWELL
51 Exec Dir Acad Out/Cont & Dist Educ ... Dr. Regis M. GILMAN
27 Director of Marketing Strategy ... Mr. Clint BAILEY
27 Project Manager Vendor Relations ... Mr. Jimmy ROSTAR
96 Director of Purchasing/Real Estate ... Mr. Kevin CARRAWAY
36 Director Career Services ... Mr. Tom HALASZ
116 Chief Audit Officer ... Mr. Wayne B. POOLE
21 AVC for Financial Services ... Ms. Dee BOWLING
49 Dean College of Arts & Sciences ... Dr. Allison DANELL
76 Dean College of Allied Health ... Dr. Robert ORLIKOFF
68 Dean Col Health/Human Performance ... Dr. Anisa ZVONKOVIC
66 Dean College of Nursing ... Dr. Sylvia BROWN
50 Dean College of Business ... Dr. Paul SCHWAGER
57 Int Dean Col Fine Arts/Comm ... Dr. Linda KEAN
53 Int Dean College of Education ... Dr. Art ROUSE
72 Dean Col of Engineering and Tech ... Dr. Harry PLOEHN
58 Dean Graduate School ... Dr. Paul GEMPERLINE
92 Dean Honors College ... Dr. David WHITE
63 Int Dean Brody School of Medicine ... Dr. Jason HIGGINSON
52 Dean School of Dental Medicine ... Dr. Gregory CHADWICK
04 Assistant to Chancellor ... Ms. Christy DANIELS
25 Dir of Grants and Contracts ... Ms. Julie COLE
86 Director of Strategic Initiatives ... Vacant
102 President/CEO ECU Foundation ... Mr. Chris DYBA
54 Chairperson Engineering ... Dr. Barbara MULLER-BORER
108 Director Institutional Assessment ... Dr. Kristen DREYFUS

*Elizabeth City State University (B)

1704 Weeksville Road, Elizabeth City NC 27909-7806
County: Pasquotank FICE Identification: 002926
Unit ID: 198507
Telephone: (252) 335-3400 Carnegie Class: Bac-Diverse
FAX Number: (252) 335-3731 Calendar System: Semester
URL: www.ecsu.edu
Established: 1891 Annual Undergrad Tuition & Fees (In-State): $3,260
Enrollment: 2,002 Coed
Affiliation or Control: State IRS Status: 501(c)3
Highest Offering: Master's
Accreditation: SC, CAEP, CAEPN, MUS, SW

02 Chancellor ... Dr. Karrie G. DIXON
05 Provost/VC Acad Affairs ... Dr. Farrah J. WARD
03 Vice Chanc/Chief of Staff ... Dr. Derrick L. WILKINS
11 VC for Operations/General Counsel ... Mr. Alyn GOODSON
10 VC for Business & Finance/CFO ... Ms. Lisa R. MCCLINTON
32 Vice Chancellor for Student Affairs ... Mr. Gary L. BROWN
111 VC for University Advancement ... Ms. Anita B. WALTON
116 Director of Internal Audit ... Ms. Sharnita I. WILSON-PARKER
86 Special Asst Government Relations ... Mr. Carson D. RICH
100 Deputy Chief of Staff ... Ms. Gwendolyn SANDERS
04 Executive Asst to Chancellor ... Ms. Sandra F. POWERS
13 Chief Information Officer ... Vacant
41 Athletic Director ... Mr. George L. BRIGHT
15 Chief Human Resources Officer ... Ms. Shamica LANE
26 Exec Dir Strategic Communications ... Vacant
20 Interim Assoc VC Academic Affairs ... Dr. Gloria E. PAYNE
20 Interim Assoc VC Academic Affairs ... Dr. Melinda R. ANDERSON
06 Assoc VC Academic Affairs/Registrar ... Dr. Althea A. RIDDICK
21 Controller ... Ms. Gina R. KNIGHT
96 Director of Business Services ... Vacant
114 Director of Budget ... Mr. Robert J. THIBEAULT
109 Director of Auxiliary Services ... Ms. Sherron D. WHITE
113 Accountant/Bursar ... Ms. Thelma R. WILLIAMS
14 Deputy Chief Information Officer ... Mr. Eric V. ZARGHAMI
90 IT Client Services Manager ... Vacant
91 IT Systems Administrator ... Ms. Angela W. BAILEY
09 Dir Institutional Effectiveness ... Dr. Fred M. OKANDA
35 Assoc Vice Chanc Student Affairs ... Mr. Kevin J. WADE
08 Director of Library Services ... Dr. Juanita M. SPENCE
121 Exec Dir Student Success/Retention ... Vacant
07 Interim Director of Admissions ... Mr. Darius D. EURE
38 Director Counseling Center ... Ms. Jody GRANDY
36 Interim Director of Career Services ... Ms. Yolanda S. CARCANA
37 Director Student Financial Aid ... Mr. Jeremi WATKINS
102 Dir Foundation and Corp Relations ... Vacant
29 Dir Alumni Relations and Engagement ... Mr. Enoch D. BOND
112 Major and Planned Gifts Officer ... Ms. Teresa C. LASSITER
18 Interim Dir of Facilities/Planning ... Mr. Harley G. GRIMES
26 Director of Marketing ... Ms. Rhonda HAYES
87 Director of Summer School ... Dr. Chyna N. CRAWFORD
104 Director of International Programs ... Dr. Andre P. STEVENSON
58 Director of Graduate Education ... Dr. Timothy A. GOODALE
106 Dir Distance/Continuing Educ ... Dr. Kimberley N. STEVENSON
19 Director of Public Safety ... Mr. John MANLEY
39 Director Housing/Resident Life ... Ms. Sabrina R. WILLIAMS
121 Chair of University Studies ... Dr. Tarsha M. ROGERS
23 Director of Student Health Services ... Ms. Gloria M. BROWN
25 Director of Sponsored Programs ... Ms. AnneMarie DELGADO

*Fayetteville State University (C)

1200 Murchison Road, Fayetteville NC 28301-4298
County: Cumberland FICE Identification: 002928
Unit ID: 198543
Telephone: (910) 672-1111 Carnegie Class: Masters/M
FAX Number: (910) 672-1769 Calendar System: Semester
URL: https://www.uncfsu.edu/
Established: 1867 Annual Undergrad Tuition & Fees (In-State): $5,309
Enrollment: 6,726 Coed
Affiliation or Control: State IRS Status: 501(c)3
Highest Offering: Doctorate
Accreditation: SC, ART, CAEPN, FEPAC, MUS, NAEYC, NURSE, SW

02 Chancellor ... Mr. Darrell T. ALLISON
100 Chief of Staff ... Ms. Samantha HARGROVE
05 Provost/Vice Chanc Academic Affs ... Dr. Monica TERRELL LEACH
10 Vice Chancellor Business/Finance ... Mr. Carlton SPELLMAN
32 Vice Chancellor Student Affairs ... Dr. Juanette COUNCIL
111 Vice Chancellor of Advancement ... Mr. Bruce ROSENGRANT
13 Vice Chanc Info Technology/CIO ... Vacant
35 Assoc Vice Chanc Student Affairs ... Vacant
18 Assoc Vice Chanc Facilities Mgmt ... Mr. Jon PARSONS
15 Assoc Vice Chanc Human Resources ... Ms. Terri TIBBS
20 Sr Assoc Vice Chanc Academic Affair ... Dr. Perry A. MASSEY
45 Assoc VC Pgms/Plng/Assessment ... Vacant
92 Acting Program Director Honors ... Dr. Erin WHITE
06 Registrar ... Ms. Sarah BAKER
26 AVC Communications/Public Relations ... Mr. Jeff WOMBLE
08 Director of Library Services ... Vacant
07 Exec Director of Admissions ... Ms. Ulisa BOWLES
39 Director of Residence Life ... Ms. Adrina RUSSELL
37 Exec Director Student Financial Aid ... Mrs. Kamesia HOUSE
43 General Counsel ... Mrs. Wanda LESSANE JENKINS
41 Athletic Director ... Mr. Anthony T. BENNETT
96 Director of Purchasing ... Ms. Willie MCINTYRE
28 Director of Diversity ... Vacant
89 Dean University College ... Dr. John I. BROOKS
66 Department Chair Nursing ... Dr. Afua ARHIN
50 Int Dean Sch Business/Economics ... Dr. J. Lee BROWN
53 Dean School of Education ... Dr. Marion GILLIS-OLION
49 Dean College Arts and Sciences ... Dr. Samuel ADU-MIREKU
101 Secretary of Univ/Board Liaison ... Ms. Suzetta M. PERKINS
04 Executive Asst to President ... Ms. Treva BENTLEY
86 Director Government Relations ... Mr. Wesley FOUNTAIN
25 Chief Contracts/Grants Admin ... Ms. Chrystal COOPER-JOHNSON
84 AVC Director Enrollment Management ... Dr. Thalia WILSON
29 Interim Director of Alumni Affairs ... Ms. Jasmin B. SESSOMS

*North Carolina Agricultural and Technical State University (D)

1601 East Market Street, Greensboro NC 27411-0001
County: Guilford FICE Identification: 002905
Unit ID: 199102
Telephone: (336) 334-7500 Carnegie Class: DU-Higher
FAX Number: (336) 334-7136 Calendar System: Semester
URL: www.ncat.edu
Established: 1891 Annual Undergrad Tuition & Fees (In-State): $6,657
Enrollment: 12,753 Coed
Affiliation or Control: State IRS Status: 501(c)3
Highest Offering: Doctorate
Accreditation: SC, AAFCS, CACREP, CAEPN, CONST, JOUR, LC, LSAR, MUS, NAIT, NUR, SW, THEA

02 Chancellor ... Dr. Harold L. MARTIN, SR.
05 Provost/Exec VC Academic Affairs ... Dr. Beryl MCEWEN
10 VC Business & Finance ... Mr. Robert POMPEY, JR.
100 Chief of Staff ... Ms. Erin HART
46 VC Research & Economic Dev ... Vacant
32 VC Student Affairs ... Dr. Melody C. PIERCE
15 Interim VC Human Resources ... Ms. Erickia ELBERT
13 VC ITS & CIO ... Mr. Tom JACKSON
43 General Counsel ... Ms. Melissa HOLLOWAY
111 VC University Advancement ... Mr. Kenneth E. SIGMON, JR.
20 AVP Academic Budget/Operations ... Dr. Sharon G. NEAL
26 AVC University Relations ... Mr. Todd H. SIMMONS
114 AVC for Budget & Planning ... Mrs. Chartarra JOYNER
58 VP Grad Research/Dean Grad College ... Dr. Clay GLOSTER
45 VP Strategic Planning & Inst Effect ... Vacant
18 AVC for Bus/Finance/Facilities ... Mr. Andrew M. PERKINS, JR.
19 Int AVC Police/Public Safety ... Mr. Jack MOORMAN
08 Dean Library Services ... Ms. Vicki COLEMAN
47 Dean Agriculture/Environmental Sci ... Dr. Mohamed AHMEDNA
49 Dean Arts/Human/Soc Sciences ... Dr. Frances WARD-JOHNSON
53 Dean College of Education ... Dr. Paula PRICE
54 Dean College of Engineering ... Dr. Robin N. COGER
66 Dean College Health & Hum Sci ... Dr. Lenora CAMPBELL
50 Dean College of Business/Economics ... Dr. Kevin L. JAMES
72 Dean College Science and Technology ... Dr. Abdellah AHMIDOUCH
54 Dean Joint Sch Nanosci/Nanoeng ... Dr. Sherine O. OBARE
06 University Registrar ... Mrs. Kelly A. ROWETT JAMES
84 AVP for Enrollment Management ... Ms. Jacque POWERS
37 Director Financial Aid ... Mrs. Sherri M. AVENT
36 Exec Director Career Services ... Ms. Cynthia DOWNING
29 AVC for Alumni Relations ... Ms. Teresa DAVIS
85 Dir International Student Affairs ... Ms. Loreatha D. GRAVES
88 Dir Multicultural Student Center ... Mr. Gerald SPATES
41 Director of Athletics ... Mr. Earl M. HILTON, III
39 Interim Exec Dir Housing ... Ms. Elfrida MENSAH
23 Dir Student Health Services ... Dr. David H. WAGNER
38 Director of Counseling Service ... Dr. Vivian D. BARNETTE
25 Director of Contracts/Grants ... Ms. Natalie TEAGLE
92 Director of Honors Program ... Dr. Margaret KANIPES
96 Director of Procurement Services ... Ms. Martinique WILLIAMS
27 Director of Media Relations ... Vacant
40 Bookstore Manager ... Ms. Michaele WIGGINS
106 Dir of ITS/Distance Education ... Dr. Tracie O. LEWIS
108 Int Dir Inst Research/Assessment ... Ms. Thelma WOODARD
22 Director Affirmative Action/EEO ... Ms. Linda MANGUM
112 AVC for Major Gifts/Annual Giving ... Mr. P. Kevin WILLIAMSON
86 Director External Affairs ... Mr. Ray TRAPP
07 Director of Admissions ... Ms. Jameia TENNIE
101 Secretary to the Board ... Ms. Shannon BENNETT

*North Carolina Central University (E)

1801 Fayetteville Street, Durham NC 27707-3129
County: Durham FICE Identification: 002950
Unit ID: 199157
Telephone: (919) 530-6100 Carnegie Class: Masters/L
FAX Number: (919) 530-5014 Calendar System: Semester
URL: www.nccu.edu
Established: 1910 Annual Undergrad Tuition & Fees (In-State): $6,629
Enrollment: 8,078 Coed
Affiliation or Control: State IRS Status: 501(c)3
Highest Offering: Doctorate
Accreditation: SC, CACREP, CAEPN, CAPRT, DIETC, DIETD, DIETI, LAW, LIB, NUR, SP, SPAA, SW, THEA

02 Chancellor ... Dr. Johnson O. AKINLEYE
05 Provost & VCAA ... Dr. David H. JACKSON, JR.
100 Chief of Staff ... Dr. Al ZOW
43 General Counsel ... Mrs. Fenita T. MORRIS-SHEPARD

10 VC Admin & Finance ....Ms. Akua J. JOHNSON MATHERSON
32 VC for Student Affairs ....Dr. Angela COLEMAN
111 Vice Chanc Inst Advancement ....Dr. Gia SOUBLET
20 Assoc Provost for Academic Programs ....Dr. Michelle L. MAYO
11 Assoc VC Administration/Finance ....Vacant
15 Chief Human Resources Officer ....Mr. Michael E. HILL
85 AVC Innovative/Engaged/Global Educ ....Vacant
45 Assoc VC Strategic Planning ....Mr. Johnnie SOUTHERLAND
35 Assistant VC of Student Affairs ....Mr. William CLEMM, II
13 Chief Information Officer ....Mrs. Leah KRAUS
07 Director Undergraduate Admissions ....Vacant
30 Director of External Affairs ....Dr. Michael PAGE
06 Registrar ....Dr. Jerome GOODWIN
91 Interim Student Systems Manager ....Mr. Damond L. NOLLAN
29 Director of Alumni Relations ....Mrs. LaMisa M. FOXX
26 Assoc VC for Public Relations ....Mrs. Ayana D. HERNANDEZ
37 Director of Financial Aid ....Ms. Sharon J. OLIVER
08 Director Library Services ....Dr. Theodosia T. SHIELDS
19 Chief of University Police ....Mr. Damon WILLIAMS
121 Exec Dir Student Academic Success ....Dr. Kesha T. REED
88 Director Art Museum ....Ms. Brenda FAISON
39 Director Residential Life ....Vacant
41 Director Athletics ....Dr. Ingrid L. WICKER-MCCREE
111 Assoc VC Inst Advancement ....Ms. Susan HESTER
96 Director of Purchasing ....Mr. James TANZOSCH
92 Director of Honors Program ....Dr. Ansel E. BROWN
38 Exec Director of Counseling Center ....Vacant
22 Director of EEO & Employee Relation ....Ms. Delores R. HARRIS
84 Assoc VC Enrollment Management ....Vacant
109 Dir Auxiliaries/Business Services ....Vacant
40 Manager Bookstore ....Ms. Jacqueline MCDOWELL
58 Dean Sch Grad Stds/Asc VC Grad Rsch ....Dr. Jaleh REZAIE
61 Dean of the Law School ....Ms. Browne C. LEWIS
62 Dean School of Library/Info Science ....Dr. Jon P. GANT
50 Dean School of Business ....Mr. Anthony C. NELSON
97 Dean of University College ....Dr. Joseph GREEN
49 Dean College of Arts and Sciences ....Dr. Carlton E. WILSON
83 Dean College Behavioral/Social Sci ....Dr. La Verne M. REID
53 Dean School of Education ....Dr. Audrey W. BEARD
04 Executive Asst to Chancellor ....Ms. Zelda STANFIELD
102 Executive Director NCCU Foundation ....Mr. Ernest JENKINS
104 Asst Director International Affairs ....Dr. Olivia JONES
105 Director Web Services ....Mr. Damond NOLLAN
106 Director Division Extended Studies ....Mrs. Kimberly C. PHIFER-MCGHEE
108 Director of Surveys & Evaluations ....Ms. Tia M. DOXEY
25 Director Contracts/Grants Admin ....Vacant
36 Director Career Services ....Mrs. Catrina S. DOSREIS
44 Director Annual Giving ....Ms. Kara ENDSLEY

*North Carolina State University (A)

20 Watauga Club Drive, Raleigh NC 27695

County: Wake | FICE Identification: 002972 | Unit ID: 199193

Telephone: (919) 515-2011 | Carnegie Class: DU-Highest

FAX Number: (919) 515-7740 | Calendar System: Semester

URL: www.ncsu.edu

Established: 1887 | Annual Undergrad Tuition & Fees (In-State): $9,101

Enrollment: 36,042 | Coed

Affiliation or Control: State | IRS Status: 501(c)3

Highest Offering: Doctorate

Accreditation: SC, ART, CACREP, CAEP, CAPRT, IPSY, LSAR, SCPSY, SPAA, SW, VET

02 Chancellor ....Dr. William Randy WOODSON
05 Provost/Exec Vice Chancellor ....Dr. Warwick A. ARDEN
43 Vice Chanc & General Counsel ....Ms. Allison NEWHART
10 Vice Chanc Finance & Admin ....Mr. Charles MAIMONE
46 Vice Chanc Research & Innovation ....Dr. Mladen VOUK
32 Vice Chan/Dean Div Acad & Stdnt Aff ....Dr. Lisa ZAPATA
111 Vice Chanc Univ Advancement ....Mr. Brian C. SISCHO
13 Vice Chanc Information Technology ....Dr. Marc I. HOIT
86 VC Ext Affs/Partnerships/Econ Dev ....Mr. Kevin D. HOWELL
100 Chief of Staff/Sec of University ....Ms. Paula GENTIUS
88 Sr Vice Provost for Acad Strategy ....Dr. Duane K. LARICK
106 Sr Vice Prov Acad Outreach/Entrepre ....Dr. Thomas K. MILLER
08 Vice Provost/Director of Libraries ....Mr. Greg RASCHKE
22 VP Inst Equity & Diversity ....Ms. Sheri SCHWAB
18 Assoc Vice Chanc Facilities ....Mr. Doug MORTON
39 Assoc Vice Chanc Housing and Living ....Dr. Barry OLSON
26 Assoc Vice Chanc Univ Communication ....Mr. Brad BOHLANDER
29 Assoc Vice Chanc Alumni Relations ....Mr. Benny SUGGS
15 Assoc Vice Chanc Human Resources ....Vacant
19 Chief of Public Safety ....Mr. Dan HOUSE
09 Sr Vice Prov Inst Rsrch & Planning ....Ms. Mary K. LELIK
07 AVP & Director of UG Admissions ....Mr. Jon WESTOVER
06 Sr Vice Provost & Univ Registrar ....Dr. Louis D. HUNT
25 Director Contracts & Grants ....Mr. Justo TORRES
37 Director of Financial Aid ....Ms. Krista RINGLER
38 Director of Counseling Center ....Dr. Monica OSBURN
41 Director Athletics ....Mr. Boo CORRIGAN
21 Assoc Vice Chancellor & Treasurer ....Ms. Mary T. PELOQUIN-DODD
88 Director of Materials Management ....Mrs. Sharon LOOSMAN
79 Dean Humanities/Social Sciences ....Dr. Jeffery P. BRADEN
48 Dean of Design ....Dr. Mark HOVERSTEN
54 Dean of Engineering ....Dr. Louis A. MARTIN-VEGA
47 Dean Agriculture/Life Sciences ....Dr. Richard H. LINTON
65 Dean of Natural Resources ....Dr. Myron FLOYD
53 Int Dean College of Education ....Dr. Paola SZTAJN
50 Dean of Poole College of Management ....Dr. Frank BUCKLESS
81 Dean College of Sciences ....Dr. Chris MCGAHAN
88 Dean of Textiles ....Dr. David HINKS
74 Dean of Veterinary Medicine ....Dr. D. Paul LUNN
58 Dean of Graduate School ....Dr. Peter J. HARRIES

*University of North Carolina at Asheville (B)

1 University Heights, Asheville NC 28804-8503

County: Buncombe | FICE Identification: 002907 | Unit ID: 199111

Telephone: (828) 251-6600 | Carnegie Class: Bac-A&S

FAX Number: (828) 251-6495 | Calendar System: Semester

URL: www.unca.edu

Established: 1927 | Annual Undergrad Tuition & Fees (In-State): $7,244

Enrollment: 3,363 | Coed

Affiliation or Control: State | IRS Status: 501(c)3

Highest Offering: Master's

Accreditation: SC, CAEP

02 Chancellor ....Dr. Nancy J. CABLE
100 Chief of Staff ....Ms. Shannon C. EARLE
05 Provost/VC Academic Affairs ....Dr. Kai CAMPBELL
10 Vice Chancellor Admin & Finance ....Mr. John PIERCE
111 Vice Chancellor Advancement ....Mr. Kirk I. SWENSON
32 Vice Chanc for Student Affairs ....Dr. Bill HAGGARD
15 Vice Chanc HR/Inst Equity/Gen Couns ....Ms. Heather PARLIER
41 Director of Athletics ....Ms. Janet R. CONE
09 Dir IR/Effectiveness/Planning ....Mr. Deaver TRAYWICK
81 Dean Natural Science ....Dr. Herman HOLT
79 Dean Humanities ....Dr. Tracey RIZZO
83 Dean Social Science ....Dr. Melissa HIMELEIN
08 University Librarian ....Ms. Brandy BOURNE
13 Chief Information Officer ....Mr. Scott COWDREY
07 Sr Dir Admissions/Financial Aid ....Ms. Sarah HUMPHRIES
06 Registrar ....Ms. Lynne HORGAN
21 Assoc VC of Finance/Controller ....Ms. Mary HALL
19 Asst VC for Public Safety ....Mr. Eric BOYCE
96 Purchasing Officer ....Mr. Joel KNISLEY
26 Chief Communication/Mktg Ofcr ....Ms. Sarah BROBERG
27 Public Communication Spec ....Mr. Steve PLEVER
23 Dir Student Health/Counseling ....Mr. John CUTSPEC
88 Assoc Dean of Students ....Dr. Melanie FOX
39 Dir of Housing/Student Life Opers ....Mr. Vollie BARNWELL
36 Dir Ctr for Career Development ....Ms. Lisa TANDAN
35 Dean of Students ....Ms. Jackie MCHARGUE
04 Exec Asst to Chancellor ....Ms. Jennifer MENNELL

*University of North Carolina at Chapel Hill (C)

Chapel Hill NC 27599-0001

County: Orange | FICE Identification: 002974 | Unit ID: 199120

Telephone: (919) 962-2211 | Carnegie Class: DU-Highest

FAX Number: (919) 962-5604 | Calendar System: Semester

URL: www.unc.edu

Established: 1789 | Annual Undergrad Tuition & Fees (In-State): $8,980

Enrollment: 30,092 | Coed

Affiliation or Control: State | IRS Status: 501(c)3

Highest Offering: Doctorate

Accreditation: SC, ACAE, #ARCPA, AUD, CAATE, CACREP, CAEP, CAEPN, CAMPEP, CLPSY, DENT, DH, DIETC, DMOLS, HSA, IPSY, JOUR, LAW, LC, LIB, MED, MT, NMT, NURSE, OT, PAST, PCSAS, PH, PHAR, PTA, RAD, RADDOS, RTT, SCPSY, SP, SPAA, SW

02 Chancellor/CEO ....Dr. Kevin M. GUSKIEWICZ
05 Provost & Exec Vice Chancellor ....Dr. Bob A. BLOUIN
20 Exec Vice Provost ....Dr. Ronald STRAUSS
10 Vice Chancellor Finance/Operations ....Mr. Nathan K. PRUITT
32 Vice Chancellor Student Affairs ....Dr. Amy JOHNSON
13 VC Info Technology/Chief Info Ofcr ....Dr. Michael BARKER
46 Vice Chancellor for Research ....Dr. Terry MAGNUSON
17 CEO UNC Health Care/VC Medical Affs ....Dr. A. Wesley BURKS
26 Vice Chancellor Univ Communications ....Mr. Joel CURRAN
106 Vice Prov Digital/Lifelong Learning ....Mr. Todd NICOLET
08 Vice Provost/University Librarian ....Ms. Elaine WESTBROOKS
114 Assoc Vice Chanc Finance/Budget ....Mr. Stephen AGOSTINI
21 Asst Provost Finance ....Mr. Barron MATHERLY
20 Int Vice Prov Acad/Cmty Engagement ....Mr. Joseph JORDAN
88 Assoc Prov Strategy/Spec Projects ....Ms. Debbi CLARKE
88 Senior Advisor & Chief Strategist ....Vacant
18 Assoc Vice Chanc Facilities Svcs ....Ms. Anna WU
88 Asst Prov/Dir Acad Support Athletes ....Ms. Michelle BROWN
22 Vice Provost Equity & Inclusion ....Vacant
28 Int Chief Diversity Officer ....Dr. Sibby ANDERSON-THOMPKINS
09 Asst Prov/Dir Inst Rsch/Assessment ....Dr. Lynn E. WILLIFORD
39 Exec Dir Carolina Housing ....Mr. Allan BLATTNER
41 Director of Athletics ....Mr. Lawrence (Bubba) R. CUNNINGHAM
06 Asst Prov/Univ Registrar ....Ms. Lauren DIGRAZIA
07 Int Vice Prov Enroll/Ugrad Admiss ....Ms. Rachelle FELDMAN
29 President General Alumni Assoc ....Mr. Douglas S. DIBBERT
37 Int Assoc Provost Student Aid ....Ms. Jackie COPELAND
88 Assoc Provost Rural Innovation ....Ms. Giselle CORBIE-SMITH
27 Assoc Vice Chanc Communications ....Ms. Beth KEITH
27 Assoc Vice Chanc Communications ....Ms. Tanya MOORE
16 Int Asst Provost Academic Personnel ....Mr. Linc BUTLER
88 Asst Prov Interprofessional Educ ....Ms. Meg ZOMORODI
36 Int Exec Dir University Career Svcs ....Dr. Tierney BATES
38 Dir Counseling & Psychological Svcs ....Dr. Allen H. O'BARR
44 Exec Director of Annual Giving ....Ms. Darlene GOOCH
19 Asst Vice Chanc/Chief of Police ....Chief David L. PERRY
51 Int Dir Center Continuing Education ....Ms. Jessica BRINKER
27 Director University Relations ....Mr. Mike MCFARLAND
88 Chief Sustainability Officer ....Dr. Michael PIEHLER
96 Chief Ofcr/Exec Dir Procurement ....Mr. Beau JIMMERSON
100 Chief of Staff ....Ms. Amy LOCKLEAR HERTEL
35 Assoc Vice Chanc Student Affairs ....Dr. Bettina SHUFORD
11 Sr Vice Prov Business Operations ....Mr. Rick WERNOSKI
87 Dean of the Summer School ....Ms. Sherry SALYER
21 Business Ofcr ....Ms. Emma DEHNE
49 Dean College Arts & Sciences ....Dr. Terry RHODES
85 Vice Prov Global Affairs ....Ms. Barbara STEPHENSON
61 Dean School of Law ....Mr. Martin BRINKLEY
63 Dean School of Medicine ....Dr. A. Wesley BURKS
52 Interim Dean School of Dentistry ....Dr. Julie S. BYERLEY
66 Dean School of Nursing ....Ms. Nilda PERAGALLO MONTANO
58 Dean of Graduate School ....Dr. Suzanne W. BARBOUR
50 Dean Kenan-Flagler Business School ....Dr. Douglas SHACKLEFORD
70 Dean School of Social Work ....Dr. Gary L. BOWEN
67 Dean School of Pharmacy ....Dr. Angela KASHUBA
60 Dean School of Journalism/Media ....Ms. Susan R. KING
62 Dean School of Info/Library Science ....Dr. Gary MARCHIONINI
69 Dean School of Public Health ....Dr. Barbara K. RIMER
53 Dean School of Education ....Dr. Fouad ABD-EL-KHALICK
80 Dean School of Government ....Dr. Michael R. SMITH
23 Exec Dir Campus Health Services ....Mr. Keith PITTMAN
92 Associate Dean for Honors ....Dr. James L. LELOUDIS
104 Assoc Provost Global Affairs ....Ms. Heather WARD
116 Chief Audit Officer ....Mr. Dean WEBER
57 Int Dir Carolina Performing Arts ....Mr. James MOESER
15 Vice Chancellor Human Resources/EEO ....Ms. Becci MENGHINI
88 Assoc Vice Provost Innovation ....Ms. Michelle BOLAS
00 Chair Board of Trustees ....Mr. Richard Y. STEVENS
86 Vice Chancellor Public Affairs ....Mr. Clayton SOMERS
30 Vice Chancellor Univ Development ....Mr. David ROUTH
117 Vice Chancellor Risk Management ....Mr. George BATTLE, III
43 Vice Chancellor & General Counsel ....Mr. Charles MARSHALL

*University of North Carolina at Charlotte (D)

9201 University City Boulevard, Charlotte NC 28223-0001

County: Mecklenburg | FICE Identification: 002975 | Unit ID: 199139

Telephone: (704) 687-8622 | Carnegie Class: DU-Higher

FAX Number: N/A | Calendar System: Semester

URL: https://www.uncc.edu/

Established: 1946 | Annual Undergrad Tuition & Fees (In-State): $7,096

Enrollment: 30,146 | Coed

Affiliation or Control: State | IRS Status: 501(c)3

Highest Offering: Doctorate

Accreditation: SC, ANEST, ART, CAATE, CACREP, CAEP, CEA, CLPSY, #COARC, DANCE, EXSC, HSA, IPSY, MUS, NURSE, PH, POLYT, SPAA, SW, THEA

02 Chancellor ....Dr. Sharon L. GABER
100 Chief of Staff ....Ms. Kim S. BRADLEY
05 Provost/Vice Chanc Academic Affairs ....Dr. Joan F. LORDEN
20 Senior Associate Provost ....Dr. Jay RAJA
88 Assoc Prov Urban Rsrch/Cmty Engage ....Mr. Byron WHITE
10 Int VC Business Affairs ....Mr. Lawrence KELLEY
111 Vice Chancellor Univ Advancement ....Mr. Niles F. SORENSEN
86 Spec Asst for Constituent Relations ....Ms. Betty DOSTER
32 Vice Chancellor Student Affairs ....Dr. Kevin BAILEY
46 Vice Chanc Research/Econ Dev ....Dr. Richard A. TANKERSLEY
13 Vice Chanc Info Tech Svcs/CIO ....Dr. Michael CARLIN
18 Assoc Vice Chanc Facilities Mgmt ....Mr. Jon VARNELL
08 Dean Atkins Library ....Dr. Anne C. MOORE
114 Assoc Prov Budget & Personnel ....Ms. Lori MCMAHON
82 Asst Provost for Intl Programs ....Mr. Joel A. GALLEGOS
88 Assistant Provost ....Dr. Leslie ZENK
26 Assoc VC for Univ Communications ....Ms. Colleen PENHALL
117 Chief Risk Officer ....Mr. Steven DUNHAM
106 Dir Distance Educ/Summer School ....Mr. Jody CEBINA
51 Dir Continuing Education ....Mr. Asher HAINES
31 Sr Dir Community Relations ....Ms. Joy P. SPRINGS
39 Assoc VC/Dir Residence Life ....Dr. Casey TULLOS
21 Assoc Vice Chancellor for Finance ....Ms. Anne BROWN
21 Assoc Vice Chanc Business Svcs ....Mr. Richard STEELE
58 Assoc Provost/Dean Graduate School ....Dr. Thomas L. REYNOLDS
84 Assoc Provost Enrollment Mgmt ....Ms. Claire KIRBY
43 VC for Inst Integrity/Gen Counsel ....Mr. James E. HUMPHREY, IV
07 Director Undergraduate Admissions ....Ms. Claire J. KIRBY
35 Dean of Students/Assoc VC Stdnt Aff ....Ms. Christine REED DAVIS
37 Director of Financial Aid ....Mr. Bruce BLACKMON
38 Int Assoc VC Health & Wellbeing ....Dr. Dennis WIESE
36 Director University Career Center ....Dr. Patrick MADSEN
40 Bookstore Manager ....Ms. Cheri GRIFFITH-KLINE
29 Exec Director Alumni Affairs ....Ms. Sallie HUTTON SISTARE
88 Assoc VC Safety and Security ....Mr. John BOGDAN
19 Chief/Dir Police & Public Safety ....Mr. Jeffrey A. BAKER
09 Asst Provost Institutional Research ....Mr. Stephen A. COPPOLA
41 Director of Athletics ....Mr. Mike HILL
96 Director of Purchasing ....Mr. Randy DUNCAN
93 Dir Acad Diversity/Inclusion ....Mrs. Regena BROWN
23 Int Director Student Health Svcs ....Ms. Emily STEWART
15 Assoc Vice Chanc Human Res/Aff Act ....Mr. Gary W. STINNETT
85 Dir Intl Student/Scholar Svcs ....Mr. Tarek A. ELSHAYEB
104 Director Study Abroad ....Mr. Brad SEKULICH
48 Dean College of Arts/Architecture ....Mr. Brook MULLER
50 Dean College of Business ....Dr. Jennifer TROYER
54 Dean College of Engineering ....Dr. Robert S. KEYNTON

53 Dean College of Education ....Dr. Teresa PETTY
49 Dean Col of Liberal Arts & Sciences ....Dr. Nancy A. GUTIERREZ
76 Dean Col of Health & Human Svcs ....Dr. Catrine TUDOR-LOCKE
72 Dean College Computing/Informatics ....Dr. Fatma MILI
97 Dean University College ....Dr. John SMAIL
121 Asst Dean for UG Educ/Advising ....Dr. David DEARDEN
92 Exec Director of Honors College ....Dr. Malin PEREIRA
06 University Registrar ....Mr. Jonathan REECE
44 Director of Planning Giving ....Ms. Amy SHEHEE
44 Director of Annual Giving ....Ms. Stacie G. YOUNG
04 Executive Asst to President ....Ms. Shari DUNN
108 Exec Dir Assessment & Accreditation ....Dr. Christine ROBINSON
25 Exec Dir Contracts/Grants Admin ....Ms. Valerie CRICKARD
28 Director Faculty Affairs/Diversity ....Dr. Yvette HUET
119 Chief Info Security Officer ....Mr. Mac MCGAUGHY

*University of North Carolina at Greensboro (A)

PO Box 26170, Greensboro NC 27402-6170

County: Guilford FICE Identification: 002976
Unit ID: 199148
Telephone: (336) 334-5000 Carnegie Class: DU-Higher
FAX Number: (336) 256-0408 Calendar System: Semester
URL: www.uncg.edu
Established: 1891 Annual Undergrad Tuition & Fees (In-State): $7,403
Enrollment: 19,764 Coed
Affiliation or Control: State IRS Status: 501(c)3
Highest Offering: Doctorate
Accreditation: SC, ANEST, ART, CAATE, CACREP, CAEPN, CAPRT, CIDA, CLPSY, DANCE, DIETD, DIETI, LIB, MUS, NURSE, PH, SP, SPAA, SW, THEA

02 Chancellor ....Dr. Franklin D. GILLIAM
100 Chief of Staff ....Ms. Waiyi TSE
05 Provost/Exec VC Academic Affairs ....Dr. Terri SHELTON
10 VC Business Affairs ....Mr. Bob SHEA
13 Vice Chanc Info Tech Services ....Ms. Donna R. HEATH
32 Vice Chanc for Student Affairs ....Dr. Cathy AKENS
84 Vice Chancellor Enrollment Mgmt ....Ms. Tina MCENTIRE
111 VC University Advancement ....Dr. Beth FISCHER
26 Int VC Strategic Communications ....Ms. Kimberly OSBORNE
43 University General Counsel ....Mr. Jerry D. BLAKEMORE
20 Senior Vice Provost ....Dr. Alan J. BOYETTE
88 AVP Academic Resources ....Ms. Mitzi W. BURCHINAL
88 Associate Vice Provost ....Ms. Andrea WHITLEY
97 AVP Univ Teaching/Learning Commons ....Dr. David J. TEACHOUT
121 AVP Stdnt Success Strategy & Innov ....Dr. Samantha RAYNOR
46 Vice Chanc Research & Engagement ....Dr. Terri L. SHELTON
104 Assoc Provost Intl Programs ....Dr. Maria ANASTASIOU
15 Assoc VC Human Resources ....Ms. Jeanne MADORIN
35 Assoc VC/Dean Students ....Dr. Brett CARTER
21 Int Assoc VC Financial Services ....Mr. Steven HONEYCUTT
88 Assoc VC Learning Tech Client Svcs ....Mr. Todd SUTTON
18 Associate Vice Chanc for Facilities ..Mr. Sameer KAPILESHWARI
09 AVP/Dir Inst Research Analytics ....Dr. Larry D. MAYES
88 Assoc Dir Opers & Ext Reporting ....Dr. William B. ZHANG
35 Associate VC for Student Affairs ....Ms. Adrienne M. CRAIG
91 Assoc VC for Administrative Systems ....Mr. Lee NORRIS
45 Assoc VC Strategy & Policy ....Dr. Julia JACKSON-NEWSOM
20 Assoc VP Dean Undergrad Studies ....Dr. Andrew HAMILTON
58 Vice Prov/Dean Graduate Education ....Dr. Kelly J. BURKE
49 Dean of Arts & Sciences ....Dr. John Z. KISS
50 Dean of Business & Economics ....Dr. McRae BANKS
53 Dean of Education ....Dr. Randall D. PENFIELD
68 Dean of Health & Human Sciences ....Dr. Carl G. MATTACOLA
64 Dean of Visual & Performing Arts ....Dr. bruce d. MCCLUNG
66 Int Dean of Nursing ....Dr. Heidi KROWCHUK
54 Dean Joint Sch NanoScience/Engineer ....Dr. Sherine O. OBARE
106 Dean UNCG Online ....Dr. Karen BULL
08 Int Dean of University Libraries ....Mr. Michael A. CRUMPTON
06 Director Registration & Records ....Mr. Chris PARTRIDGE
108 AVP/Dir Assessment/Accreditation ....Dr. Jodi E. PETTAZZONI
07 Director of Admissions ....Mr. Christopher J. KELLER
29 Dir Alumni Assn & Annual Giving ....Ms. Mary G. LANDERS
88 Director of Recreation and Wellness ....Dr. Jill BEVILLE
23 Director Student Health Services ....Ms. Kathleen BABER
36 Director Career & Prof Development ....Ms. Nicole HALL
106 Dean Division of Online Learning ....Ms. Karen Z. BULL
92 Dean Lloyd International Honors Col ....Mr. Omar ALI
25 Dir Contracts and Grants ....Mr. William D. WALTERS
37 Director of Financial Aid ....Ms. Deborah TOLLEFSON
39 Director Housing & Residence Life ....Mr. Timothy JOHNSON
41 Director Intercollegiate Athletics ....Ms. Kim RECORD
89 Dir New Stdnt Transitions/First Yr ....Dr. Kim SOUSA-PEOPLES
19 Director Safety/Emergency Mgmt ....Mr. Zachary SMITH
28 Director Intercultural Engagement ....Mr. Agusto E. PENA
96 Director Purchasing ....Mr. Michael F. LOGAN
40 University Bookstore Manager ....Mr. Brad LIGHT
04 Exec Assistant to the Chancellor ....Ms. Kristi CROWTHER
105 University Webmaster ....Mr. Chris WATERS
38 Director Counseling Center ....Dr. Jennifer M. WHITNEY
44 Director Annual Giving ....Mr. Randy HOLDEN
86 Dir Federal & External Affairs ....Ms. Nikki M. BAKER
90 Director Tech Support & Svcs ....Ms. Sherry L. WOODY
86 Dir State & External Affairs ....Mr. Andrew R. CAGLE
22 Dir Affirm Action/Equal Opportunity ....Ms. Patricia LYNCH

*University of North Carolina at Pembroke (B)

One University Drive, PO Box 1510,
Pembroke NC 28372-1510

County: Robeson FICE Identification: 002954
Unit ID: 199281
Telephone: (910) 521-6000 Carnegie Class: Masters/L
FAX Number: (910) 521-6176 Calendar System: Semester
URL: www.uncp.edu
Established: 1887 Annual Undergrad Tuition & Fees (In-State): $3,456
Enrollment: 8,262 Coed
Affiliation or Control: State IRS Status: 501(c)3
Highest Offering: Master's
Accreditation: SC, ART, CAATE, CACREP, CAEPN, MUS, NURSE, SW

02 Chancellor ....Dr. Robin G. CUMMINGS
43 General Counsel ....Mr. Kelvin JACOBS
05 Int Provost/VC Academic Affairs ....Dr. Zoe LOCKLEAR
100 Chief of Staff ....Mr. Mark GOGAL
10 Vice Chanc Finance & Admin ....Mrs. Virginia TEACHEY
116 Chief Audit Officer ....Ms. Megan FEES
32 Vice Chanc Student Affairs ....Dr. Lisa L. SCHAEFFER
41 Director of Athletics ....Mr. Dick CHRISTY
111 Vice Chanc for Advancement ....Mr. Steve VARLEY
26 Chief Univ Communications/Mktg Ofcr ....Ms. Jodi PHELPS
22 Director Title IX and Clery Act Co ....Ms. Ronette SUTTON GERBER
88 Asst to Chancellor Rsrch/Comm ....Ms. Tabi CAIN
04 Executive Asst to the Chancellor ....Ms. Jocelyn GRAHAM
20 Assoc Vice Provost ....Dr. Scott BILLINGSLEY
85 Assoc VC Global Engagement ....Ms. Cathy Lee ARCUINO
84 Assoc Vice Chanc for Enrollment Mgt ....Ms. Lois H. WILLIAMS
45 Assoc VC for Planning/Accreditation ....Dr. Elizabeth NORMANDY
25 Assoc VC Research and Sponsored ....Vacant
53 Interim Dean of School of Education ....Dr. Zoe LOCKLEAR
50 Dean of School of Business ....Dr. Barry O'BRIEN
49 Dean of Arts & Sciences ....Dr. Jeff FREDERICK
08 Dean of Library Services ....Dr. Dennis SWANSON
58 Dean of The Graduate School ....Dr. Irene AIKEN
89 Dean of University College ....Ms. Beth HOLDER
92 Dean of Honors College ....Dr. Mark MILEWICZ
76 Dean College of Health Sciences ....Vacant
88 Director for Academic Resources ....Ms. Leslie T. BELL
09 Director Institutional Research ....Dr. Chunmei YAO
06 Registrar ....Ms. Christina REEVES
07 Director of Admissions ....Ms. Engle REVELS
37 Director Financial Aid ....Ms. Jenelle HANDCOX
121 Dir Center for Student Success ....Dr. Derek OXENDINE
88 Director Accessibility Resource ....Dr. Nicolette CAMPOS
106 Int Dir Online/Distance Education ....Dr. Ki Byung CHAE
25 Dir Sponsored Research/Grant ....Ms. Lisa HUNT
21 Assoc Vice Chancellor for Finance ....Vacant
13 Int Assoc VC Info Resources/CIO ....Mr. Kevin PAIT
15 Asst Vice Chanc for Human Resources ....Ms. Angela REVELS
18 Asst VC for Facilities ....Vacant
16 Assoc Dir Human Resources ....Ms. Donna STRICKLAND
16 Dir Employee Relations and Dev ....Mr. Benjamin SIMMONS
88 Facilities Superintendent ....Mr. Mark VESELY
119 Chief Information Security Officer ....Mr. Don BRYANT
14 Deputy CIO Infrastructure and Opers ....Mr. Kevin PAIT
14 Dir IT Support Services ....Ms. Liz CUMMINGS
96 Director of Business Services ....Ms. Karen SWINEY
21 Controller ....Ms. Jennifer ADDISON
113 Bursar ....Ms. Cynthia REVELS
114 Director Budget & Planning ....Ms. Kristy NANCE
35 Asst Vice Chanc Student Affairs ....Ms. Cynthia OXENDINE
38 Director Counseling/Testing Center ....Ms. LynnDee HORNE
32 Dir of Campus Engagement/Leadership ....Mr. Abdul GHAFFAR
39 Director Housing and Resident Life ....Mr. Paul POSENER
28 Dir Office of Diversity/Inclusion ....Dr. Lawrence LOCKLEAR
36 Director Career Services Center ....Mr. Bradley MERRITT
88 Sports Information Director ....Mr. Todd ANDERSON
80 Director Public Administration Pgm ....Dr. Emily NEFF-SHARUM
23 Director of Student Health Services ....Ms. Cora BULLARD
44 Assistant Director of Annual Fund ....Mr. Paris ROEBUCK
110 Dir Advancement Services ....Vacant
27 Director of Creative Services ....Mr. David YBARRA
31 Director of Community Relations ....Mr. Paul JOLICOEUR
19 Director Security/Safety ....Mr. McDuffie CUMMINGS, JR.
88 Faculty Senate Chair ....Dr. Mitu ASHRAF
104 Director Study Abroad ....Mr. Alexander BRANDT

*University of North Carolina Wilmington (C)

601 S College Road, Wilmington NC 28403-5931

County: New Hanover FICE Identification: 002984
Unit ID: 199218
Telephone: (910) 962-3030 Carnegie Class: DU-Higher
FAX Number: (910) 962-4050 Calendar System: Semester
URL: www.uncw.edu
Established: 1947 Annual Undergrad Tuition & Fees (In-State): $7,181
Enrollment: 17,915 Coed
Affiliation or Control: State IRS Status: 501(c)3
Highest Offering: Doctorate
Accreditation: SC, CAATE, CAEPN, CARTE, CEA, CLPSY, #COARC, MUS, NURSE, PH, SPAA, SW

02 Chancellor ....Dr. Jose V. SARTARELLI
05 Provost/Vice Chanc Academic Affairs ....Dr. James WINEBRAKE
10 Vice Chancellor Business Affairs ....Mr. Miles LACKEY
32 Vice Chanc for Student Affairs ....Dr. Lowell DAVIS
111 Vice Chanc University Advancement ....Mr. Eddie STUART
110 Assoc Vice Chanc Univ Advancement ....Ms. Missy KENNEDY
21 Assoc Vice Chanc Business Services ....Ms. Sharon H. BOYD
21 Assoc VC Business Affs/Facilities ....Mr. Mark D. MORGAN
31 Assoc Vice Chanc Cmty Engagement ....Ms. Jeanine MINGE
106 Assoc VC for Distance Education ....Dr. Jeremy DICKERSON
46 Assoc Provost for Research ....Dr. Stuart BORRETT
28 Interim Chief Diversity Officer ....Dr. Donyell ROSEBORO
26 Int Chief Communications Officer ....Ms. Andrea WEAVER
09 Assoc Provost Inst Research/Plng ....Dr. Andy MAUK
35 Assoc VC/Dean of Students ....Dr. Michael A. WALKER
85 Assoc VC International Programs ....Dr. Michael WILHELM
15 Interim Assoc VC Human Resources ....Ms. Elaine DOELL
100 Chief of Staff ....Mr. Bradley BALLOU
06 University Registrar ....Ms. Amanda FLEMING
08 University Librarian ....Ms. Lucy HOLMAN
37 Director Financial Aid/Scholarships ....Mr. Frederick HOLDING
18 Director of Physical Plant ....Mr. David OLSON
19 Assoc Dir Envir Health & Safety ....Mr. Jeffrey CAMPBELL
23 Dir Student Health/Wellness Center ....Ms. Katrin WESNER
109 Director of Auxiliary Services ....Mr. Brian DAILEY
41 Director of Athletics ....Mr. Jimmy BASS
36 Director of the Career Center ....Ms. Nadirah PIPPEN
29 Director of Alumni Relations ....Mrs. Lindsay LEROY
96 Director of Purchasing ....Mr. John ROBINSON
38 Dir Counseling Center/Univ Testing ....Dr. Mark PEREZ-LOPEZ
40 Manager Bookstore ....Ms. Mee So YIM
49 Interim Dean Col Arts & Sciences ....Dr. Michelle SCATTON-TESSIER
50 Dean Cameron School of Business ....Dr. Robert BURRUS
53 Dean Watson School of Education ....Dr. Van O. DEMPSEY
66 Director School of Nursing ....Dr. Linda HADDAD
58 Dean of Graduate School ....Dr. Chris FINELLI
76 Dean Col Health & Human Svcs ....Dr. Charles HARDY
04 Executive Assistant to the Chanc ....Ms. Carolyn S. HARTMAN
07 Director Admissions ....Dr. Lauren FRANKLIN
13 Chief Info Technology Officer (CIO) ....Ms. Sharyne MILLER
25 Dir Sponsored Pgms/Rsrch/Compliance ....Ms. Leanne PRETE
43 General Counsel ....Mr. John SCHERER
54 Director Engineering ....Dr. Amy REAMER
90 Consulting Services Support Dir ....Ms. Beverly VAGNERINI
101 Asst to the Chancellor/Trustees ....Mr. Mark LANIER
39 Interim Director Housing ....Mr. Larry WRAY
108 Dir Office of Inst Effectiveness ....Dr. Andy MAUK
30 Director of Development ....Ms. Dawn CARTER
102 Dir Foundation/Corporate Relations ....Ms. Megan GORHAM

*University of North Carolina School of the Arts (D)

1533 S Main Street, Winston-Salem NC 27127-2738

County: Forsyth FICE Identification: 003981
Unit ID: 199184
Telephone: (336) 770-3399 Carnegie Class: Spec-4-yr-Arts
FAX Number: (336) 770-3375 Calendar System: Semester
URL: www.uncsa.edu
Established: 1963 Annual Undergrad Tuition & Fees (In-State): $9,358
Enrollment: 1,070 Coed
Affiliation or Control: State IRS Status: 501(c)3
Highest Offering: Master's
Accreditation: SC

02 Chancellor ....Mr. Brian COLE
05 Provost & Exec Vice Chancellor ....Mr. Patrick SIMS
10 Vice Chanc for Finance & Admin ....Mr. Michael SMITH
111 Int Vice Chanc for Advancement ....Mr. Rich WHITTINGTON
26 Vice Chanc Strategic Communication ....Ms. Claire MACHAMER
43 Vice Chanc/General Counsel ....Mr. David HARRISON
32 Vice Provost & Dean Student Affairs ....Dr. Tracey FORD
88 Vice Chanc Economic Development ....Mr. Jim DECRISTO
18 Assoc Vice Chancellor Facilities ....Mr. Steve MARTIN
09 Director of Institutional Research ....Mr. Jeff PATON
07 Director of Admissions ....Mr. Paul RAZZA
08 University Librarian ....Ms. Sarah FALLS
27 Director of Communications ....Ms. Marla CARPENTER
06 Registrar ....Vacant
15 AVC/Chief Human Resources ....Ms. Angela MAHONEY
37 Director of Financial Aid ....Mrs. Jane KAMIAB
49 Interim Dean of Liberal Arts ..Ms. Martine Kei GRREEN-ROGERS
64 Dean School of Music ....Mr. Saxton ROSE
57 Dean School of Dance ....Ms. Endalyn TAYLOR
48 Dean Sch of Design/Production ....Mr. Michael KELLEY
88 Dean School of Drama ....Mr. Scott ZIGLER
13 Chief Technology Officer ....Mr. Terrence HARMON
19 Chief of Police ....Mr. Frank BRINKLEY
38 Dir of Counseling & Testing Svcs ....Vacant
96 Director of Purchasing ....Ms. Jeanette VALENTINE
57 Exec Dir Kenan Inst for the Arts ....Mr. Kevin BITTERMAN
88 Dean School of Filmmaking ....Ms. Deborah LAVINE
88 Headmaster/Dean HS Academic Program ....Mr. Martin FERRELL
35 Director of Student Engagement ....Mr. Steve GALLAGHER
87 Dir Educ Outreach & Summer Programs ..Ms. Suzanna WATKINS
23 Director of Health Services ....Ms. Sharon SUMMER
100 Chief of Staff ....Mr. James DECRISTO
102 Foundation Director ....Ms. Cynthia LIBERTY
108 Director of Inst Effectiveness ....Mr. Jeff PATON

*Western Carolina University (E)

One University Drive, HFR 501,
Cullowhee NC 28723-9646

County: Jackson FICE Identification: 002981
Unit ID: 200004
Telephone: (828) 227-7100 Carnegie Class: Masters/L
FAX Number: (828) 227-7176 Calendar System: Semester
URL: www.wcu.edu
Established: 1889 Annual Undergrad Tuition & Fees (In-State): $4,285
Enrollment: 12,243 Coed
Affiliation or Control: State IRS Status: 501(c)3
Highest Offering: Doctorate

Accreditation: SC, ANEST, ART, CAATE, CACREP, CAEPN, CARTE, CIDA, DIETD, DIETI, EMT, IPSY, MUS, NURSE, PTA, SP, SPAA, SW, THEA

02 Chancellor .... Dr. Kelli R. BROWN
05 Provost/Vice Chanc Academic Affs .... Dr. Richard STARNES
20 Vice Provost for Academic Affairs .... Dr. Carol BURTON
10 Vice Chanc Admin & Finance .... Mr. Mike BYERS
32 Vice Chancellor/Student Affairs .... Dr. H. Samuel MILLER, JR.
121 Int Asst Vice Chanc Student Success .... Dr. Jeffrey LAWSON
35 Asst Vice Chanc/Student Affairs .... Ms. Kellie MONTEITH
111 Interim Vice Chancellor Advancement .... Mrs. Jamie RAYNOR
18 Assoc VC for Facilities Management .... Mr. Joe WALKER
100 Chief of Staff .... Dr. Melissa WARGO
04 Assistant to the Chancellor .... Ms. Jessica WOODS
43 General Counsel .... Mr. Shea BROWNING
38 Director of Counseling Services .... Dr. Kimberly GORMAN
06 Registrar .... Mr. Larry HAMMER
84 Asst Vice Chanc/Undergrad Enrollmnt .... Mr. Phil CAULEY
09 Asst Vice Chancellor of OIPE .... Mr. Tim METZ
37 Director of Financial Aid .... Ms. Trina ORR
15 Assoc VC of Human Resources .... Dr. Cory CAUSBY
13 Chief Information Officer .... Mr. Craig FOWLER
29 Director of Alumni Affairs .... Mr. Marty RAMSEY
08 Dean of Library Services .... Dr. Farzaneh RAZZAGHI
88 Exec Director Education Outreach .... Dr. Carolyn CALLAGHAN
109 Director Campus Services .... Mr. Bryant BARNETT
41 Athletic Director .... Mr. Alex GARY
23 Director University Health Services .... Ms. Pamela BUCHANAN
96 Director of Business Operations .... Mr. Bruce BARKER
40 Int Director Book & Supply Store .... Ms. Jennifer THOMAS
38 Director of Advising Center .... Mr. Travis BULLUCK
36 Director of Career Services .... Ms. Theresa C. PAUL
26 Exec Director of Communications .... Mr. Benny SMITH
50 Dean College of Business .... Dr. AJ GRUBE
57 Dean of Fine & Performing Arts .... Dr. George H. BROWN
58 Dean Grad School & Research .... Dr. Brian KLOEPPEL
49 Dean Arts & Sciences .... Dr. David KINNER
72 Dean Kimmel School Constr Mgmt/Tech .... Dr. Jeffrey RAY
53 Dean Educ & Allied Professions .... Dr. Kim WINTER
76 Dean Health & Human Sciences .... Dr. Lori ANDERSON
92 Dean of Honors College .... Dr. Jill GRANGER
88 Executive Creative Director .... Ms. Tiffany WYSOCKI
86 Deputy COS/Dir of External Rels .... Ms. Meredith WHITFIELD
27 Executive Director of Marketing .... Vacant
88 Chief Marketing & Comm Officer .... Mr. Brian MULLEN
28 Director of Diversity .... Dr. Ricardo NIZARIO-COLON

*Winston-Salem State University (A)

601 MLK Jr. Drive, 200 Blair Hall,
Winston-Salem NC 27110-0001
County: Forsyth FICE Identification: 002986
Unit ID: 199999
Telephone: (336) 750-2000 Carnegie Class: Masters/M
FAX Number: (336) 750-2049 Calendar System: Semester
URL: www.wssu.edu
Established: 1892 Annual Undergrad Tuition & Fees (In-State): $5,941
Enrollment: 5,169 Coed
Affiliation or Control: State IRS Status: 501(c)3
Highest Offering: Doctorate
Accreditation: SC, CACREP, CAEPN, CAPRT, MT, MUS, NURSE, OT, PTA, SW

02 Chancellor .... Dr. Elwood L. ROBINSON
05 Provost/VC Academic Affairs .... Dr. Anthony GRAHAM
32 Assoc Prov/VC Student Development .... Dr. Melvin NORWOOD
20 Associate Provost .... Dr. Carolynn BERRY
45 Assoc Prov Administration/Plng .... Mrs. Letitia C. WALL
10 Vice Chanc Finance & Admin .... Mrs. Constance MALLETTE
111 Vice Chanc Univ Advancement .... Mrs. LaTanya D. AFOLAYAN
100 Int Vice Chancellor/Chief of Staff .... Ms. Letitia WALL
18 Assoc Vice Chanc Facilities Mgmt .... Mr. Timothy MCMULLEN
13 Assoc Prov/Chief Information Ofcr .... Mrs. Raisha COBB
116 Int Dir Internal Audit/Compliance .... Mr. Santonius R. ISOM
19 Dir of Police/Campus Safety .... Chief Amir HENRY
08 Director of Library Services .... Ms. Wanda BROWN
39 Director Hous/Residence Life .... Ms. Chantal BOUCHEREAU
37 Int Director of Financial Aid .... Ms. Jill POWELL
15 Assoc Vice Chanc Human Resources .... Dr. August MEBANE
26 Dir of Public Relations .... Ms. Haley N. GINGLES
84 Dir Enrollment Communications .... Ms. Cathy HOOTS
102 Exec Director Univ Donor Events .... Mrs. Kimberly REESE
35 Asst Dean of Students .... Mr. Mitch MITCHELL
23 Dir of Student Health Center .... Dr. Leticia E. HELLEBY
41 Athletic Director .... Ms. Etienne M. THOMAS
07 Director of Admissions .... Dr. Kerwin GRAHAM
43 Chief Legal Counsel .... Dr. Ivey BROWN
96 Director Purchasing .... Mr. Alan IRELAND
90 Director Academic Computer Center .... Mr. Cuthrell JOHNSON
79 Dean University College LLL .... Dr. Darryl SCRIVEN
76 Int Dean School of Health Science .... Dr. Leslee S. BATTLE
88 Director of Title III .... Dr. Everette L. WITHERSPOON
06 Registrar .... Ms. Marquita J. GRAVES
108 Director Institutional Assessment . Dr. Becky MUSSAT-WHITLOW

University of Phoenix Charlotte Campus (B)

3800 Arco Corporate Drive, Charlotte NC 28273-3409
Telephone: (704) 504-5409 Identification: 770216
Accreditation: &HLC

† No longer accepting campus-based students.

Wake Forest University (C)

1834 Wake Forest Road, Winston-Salem NC 27109-8758
County: Forsyth FICE Identification: 002978
Unit ID: 199847
Telephone: (336) 758-5000 Carnegie Class: DU-Higher
FAX Number: (336) 758-6074 Calendar System: Semester
URL: www.wfu.edu
Established: 1834 Annual Undergrad Tuition & Fees: $57,760
Enrollment: 8,789 Coed
Affiliation or Control: Independent Non-Profit IRS Status: 501(c)3
Highest Offering: Doctorate
Accreditation: SC, ANEST, ARCPA, CACREP, CAEP, DENT, IPSY, LAW, MED, THEOL

01 President .... Dr. Susan R. WENTE
43 SVP/General Counsel/Sec BOT .... Mr. J. Reid MORGAN
10 Exec Vice Pres/Chief Financial Ofcr .... Mr. B. Hofler MILAM
05 Provost .... Mr. Rogan KERSH
11 Vice President for Administration .... Mr. John SHENETTE
111 Vice Pres University Advancement .... Mr. Mark A. PETERSEN
32 Vice Pres Campus Life .... Dr. Penny RUE
115 Vice Pres/Chief Investment Officer .... Mr. James J. DUNN
100 Chief of Staff .... Ms. Mary E. PUGEL
35 Assoc Vice Pres/Dean of Students .... Mr. Adam GOLDSTEIN
44 Asst VP/Dir Parent & Donor Rels .... Ms. Minta A. MCNALLY
30 Sr AVP of Development .... Mr. Robert T. BAKER
13 Vice Pres Info Tech/CIO .... Mr. Mur MUCHANE
46 Assoc Provost for Research .... Dr. Keith BONIN
49 Dean of the College .... Dr. Michele K. GILLESPIE
61 Dean School of Law .... Ms. Jane AIKEN
50 Int Dean of Business .... Ms. Michelle ROEHM
73 Dean of Divinity .... Dr. Jonathan L. WALTON
107 Dean School of Professional Studies .... Dr. Charles L. IACOVOU
09 Assist Provost Inst Research .... Mr. Phil HANDWERK
08 Dir of the Z Smith Reynolds Library .... Mr. Tim PYATT
07 Dean of Admissions .... Ms. Karen VARGAS
37 Director of Financial Aid .... Mr. William T. WELLS
36 VP Innovation & Career Dev .... Mr. Andy CHAN
06 Registrar .... Mr. Harold PACE
41 Director of Athletics .... Mr. John D. CURRIE
15 VP Human Resources .... Ms. Dedee I. DELONGPRE JOHNSTON
18 Director Facilities Management .... Mr. John SHENETTE
38 Dir University Counseling Center .... Dr. Marianne A. SCHUBERT
23 Director Student Health Service .... Dr. Cecil D. PRICE
42 Chaplain .... Rev. Timothy L. AUMAN
19 Chief University Police .... Ms. Regina G. LAWSON
22 EEO Mgr/Diversity & Compliance Dir .... Ms. Angela CULLER
94 Director Women's & Gender Studies .... Dr. Wanda BALZANO
26 Sr AVP Comm/External Relations .... Mr. Brett EATON
104 Director Study Abroad .... Mr. David F. TAYLOR
29 Director Alumni Engagement .... Mrs. Kelly MCCONNICO

Warren Wilson College (D)

PO Box 9000, Asheville NC 28815-9000
County: Buncombe FICE Identification: 002979
Unit ID: 199865
Telephone: (828) 771-2000 Carnegie Class: Bac-A&S
FAX Number: (828) 771-7097 Calendar System: Semester
URL: www.warren-wilson.edu
Established: 1894 Annual Undergrad Tuition & Fees: $38,350
Enrollment: 703 Coed
Affiliation or Control: Presbyterian Church (U.S.A.) IRS Status: 501(c)3
Highest Offering: Master's
Accreditation: SC, SW

01 President .... Dr. Lynn M. MORTON
05 Provost/Dean of Faculty .... Dr. Jay ROBERTS
10 VP Administration & Finance/CFO .... Ms. Belinda BURKE
111 Vice Pres for Advancement .... Ms. Zanne GARLAND
32 Vice Pres Student Life .... Mr. Paul C. PERRINE
84 Vice Pres Enrollment/Marketing .... Mr. Brian LIECHTI
103 Vice Pres Applied Learning .... Ms. Cathy KRAMER
37 Director Financial Aid .... Ms. Lori LEWIS
44 Director WWC Fund .... Ms. Mary HAY
26 Director of Marketing/Operations .... Ms. Morgan DAVIS
38 Director of Counseling .... Mr. Arthur SHUSTER
36 Director Career Services .... Ms. Wendy SELIGMANN
42 Dir of Spiritual Life & Chaplain .... Rev. Brian AMMONS
07 Director of Admission .... Mr. Nathan WYRICK
19 Director Public Safety .... Mr. Justin GILDNER
28 VP Inclusion/Diversity/Equity .... Ms. Kartet MENSAH
121 Assoc Dean Integrated Advising .... Ms. Brooke MILLSAPS

William Peace University (E)

15 E Peace Street, Raleigh NC 27604-1194
County: Wake FICE Identification: 002953
Unit ID: 199272
Telephone: (919) 508-2000 Carnegie Class: Bac-Diverse
FAX Number: (919) 508-2326 Calendar System: Semester
URL: www.peace.edu
Established: 1857 Annual Undergrad Tuition & Fees: $32,450
Enrollment: 830 Coed
Affiliation or Control: Presbyterian Church (U.S.A.) IRS Status: 501(c)3
Highest Offering: Baccalaureate
Accreditation: SC, NURSE

01 President .... Dr. Brian C. RALPH
100 Dir of Presidential Operations .... Ms. Kelley DIETZ
05 Vice President for Academic Affairs .... Dr. Charles DUNCAN
111 Vice Pres University Advancement .... Ms. Jodi STAMEY
32 Vice President for Student Life .... Mr. Frank RIZZO
10 Vice Pres Administration/ CFO .... Mr. George (Rocky) A. YEARWOOD
84 VP Enrollment Mgmt/Marketing .... Ms. Colleen MURPHY
20 Assoc VP Academic Affairs .... Ms. Carolyn BLATTNER
15 Assoc Vice Pres for Human Resources .... Ms. Kathy LAMBERT
18 Assoc VP for Buildings and Grounds .... Mr. John B. CRANHAM
13 Chief Information Officer .... Mr. Darryl MCGRAW
06 Registrar .... Ms. Melanie FULLER
37 Director of Financial Aid .... Ms. Valerie CLEM-BROWN
41 Director of Athletics .... Mr. Thomas CURLE
29 Director Alumni Relations .... Ms. Ellie BARKER
07 Interim Director of Admissions .... Ms. Ashley MURRAY
19 Director of Public Safety .... Mr. Michael Andrew JOHN
26 Dir Communications/Donor Relations .... Ms. Elizabeth EDWARDS
28 Director of Diversity/Equity .... Ms. Leah YOUNG

Wingate University (F)

220 N. Camden Road, Wingate NC 28174-0159
County: Union FICE Identification: 002985
Unit ID: 199962
Telephone: (704) 233-8000 Carnegie Class: DU-Mod
FAX Number: (704) 233-8014 Calendar System: Semester
URL: www.wingate.edu
Established: 1896 Annual Undergrad Tuition & Fees: $38,896
Enrollment: 3,653 Coed
Affiliation or Control: Southern Baptist IRS Status: 501(c)3
Highest Offering: Doctorate
Accreditation: SC, ACBSP, ARCPA, #CAATE, MUS, NUR, PHAR, PTA

01 President .... Dr. T. Rhett BROWN
05 Provost .... Dr. Jeff FREDERICK
41 VP & Director of Athletics .... Mr. R. Stephen POSTON
10 SVP Business and Finance .... Vacant
26 SVP/Chief of Staff .... Dr. Heather C. MILLER
11 Vice President .... Mr. Scott E. HUNSUCKER
111 SVP for University Advancement .... Mr. James R. BULLOCK
15 VP for Human Resources .... Ms. Sherri SATTERFIELD
88 VP Strategic Partnerships .... Mr. Vincent TILSON
115 VP Business .... Mr. William H. DURHAM
109 AVP for Auxiliary Services .... Mr. Cameron JACKSON
88 Associate Vice Pres of Campus Opers .... Ms. Glenda H. BEBBER
67 Dean School of Pharmacy .... Dr. Susan BRUCE
49 Dean School Arts & Sciences .... Dr. Carrie HOEFFERLE
50 Dean School of Business .... Dr. Sergio CASTELLO
53 Dean School of Education .... Vacant
08 Interim Director of Library .... Mr. Keith LASSITER
39 Assoc Dean Res Life & Involvement .... Ms. Jessica HEAD
37 Director Student Financial Planning .... Ms. Teresa G. WILLIAMS
91 Director Administrative Computing .... Mr. Timothy D. HERRIN
29 Asst Director of Alumni Relations .... Ms. Brittany BUMGARNER
42 Minister to Stdnts/Sr Dir CVICS .... Rev. A. Dane JORDAN
40 Director of Campus Store .... Ms. Sherri SHANK
19 Campus Safety Chief .... Mr. Mike EASLEY
38 Director of Counseling Services .... Ms. Corrine HARRIS
13 Director of Information Technology .... Ms. Jeanette K. BUJAK
36 Dir of Internships and Career Svcs .... Ms. Sharon ROBINSON
32 Dean of Campus Life/Student Life .... Mr. Michael REYNOLDS
06 Registrar .... Ms. Maria TAYLOR
07 Director of Admissions .... Ms. Elizabeth BIGGERSTAFF
123 Director of Graduate Admissions .... Dr. Eva BAUCOM
04 Executive Assistant to President .... Ms. Tammy T. BRITT
13 CIO .... Mr. Steve SHANK
20 Vice Provost Student Engagement .... Dr. Nancy RANDALL
84 VP Enrollment Management .... Dr. Eva BAUCOM
43 SVP General Counsel .... Mr. Ben SIDBURY

NORTH DAKOTA

Cankdeska Cikana Community College (G)

PO Box 269, 214 First Avenue,
Fort Totten ND 58335-0269
County: Benson FICE Identification: 022365
Unit ID: 200208
Telephone: (701) 766-4415 Carnegie Class: Tribal
FAX Number: (701) 766-4077 Calendar System: Semester
URL: www.littlehoop.edu
Established: 1974 Annual Undergrad Tuition & Fees: $3,300
Enrollment: 182 Coed
Affiliation or Control: Independent Non-Profit IRS Status: 501(c)3
Highest Offering: Associate Degree
Accreditation: HLC

01 President .... Dr. Cynthia A. LINDQUIST
05 CO-Academic Dean .... Ms. Jackie LAMPERT
05 Co-Academic Dean .... Ms. Kim KREBSBACH
10 CFO .... Mrs. Chelly VEER
11 Dean of Administration .... Mr. Stuart YOUNG
06 Registrar .... Mr. Chris DAHLEN
15 Human Resources Director .... Ms. Vanessa THOMAS
37 Director Financial Aid .... Ms. Tina PLOIUM

*North Dakota University System Office (A)

600 E Boulevard Avenue, Dept. 215,
Bismarck ND 58505-0230

County: Burleigh　FICE Identification: 033434
Telephone: (701) 328-2960　Carnegie Class: N/A
FAX Number: (701) 328-2961
URL: www.ndus.edu

01	Chancellor	Mark HAGEROTT
100	Chief of Staff	Terry MEYER
05	VC Acad/Student Affairs	Lisa JOHNSON
10	VC Administrative Affairs/CFO	Tammy DOLAN
13	VC IT/Chief Information Officer	Darin KING
45	VC Strategy/Strategic Engagement	Jerry ROSTAD
37	Director of Financial Aid	Brenda ZASTOUPIL
21	Director of Finance	David KREBSBACH
09	Dir of Institutional Research	Jennifer WEBER
26	Dir of Communications & Media Rels	Billie Jo LORIUS
88	Director of Financial Reporting	Robin PUTNAM
20	Dir of Acad Aff & Workforce Innovat	Claire GUNWALL
32	Director of Student Affairs	Katie FITZSIMMONS
18	Director Facilities Planning	Rick TONDER
15	Director of Human Resources	Jane GRINDE

*University of North Dakota (B)

264 Centennial Drive, Grand Forks ND 58202

County: Grand Forks　FICE Identification: 003005
Unit ID: 200280
Telephone: (701) 777-3000　Carnegie Class: DU-Higher
FAX Number: (701) 777-2696　Calendar System: Semester
URL: www.und.edu
Established: 1883　Annual Undergrad Tuition & Fees (In-State): $10,276
Enrollment: 13,615　Coed
Affiliation or Control: State　IRS Status: 501(c)3
Highest Offering: Doctorate
Accreditation: HLC, AAB, ANEST, ARCPA, ART, CAATE, CAEPN, CLPSY, COPSY, DIETC, HT, LAW, MED, MT, MUS, NURSE, OT, PH, PTA, SP, SPAA, SW, THEA

02	President	Dr. Andrew ARMACOST
100	Chief of Staff	Mr. Robert CAROLIN
05	VP Academic Affairs/Provost	Dr. Eric LINK
10	Vice Pres Finance/Operations & CFO	Mr. Jed SHIVERS
32	Int Vice Pres Stdnt Affs/Diversity	Dr. Cara HALGREN
17	Vice President Health Affairs	Dr. Joshua WYNNE
46	Int VP Research/Economic Devel	Dr. John MIHELICH
26	VP Marketing/Communications	Ms. Meloney LINDER
27	Director of Communications	Mr. David L. DODDS
27	Dir of Marketing & Creative Svcs	Ms. Jennifer SWANGLER
21	Assoc VP Finance	Ms. Karla MONGEON-STEWART
18	Assoc VP Facilities	Mr. Michael PIEPER
45	AVP Research & Economic Dev/RDC	Dr. Barry MILAVETZ
88	AVP Rsrch & Econ Dev/Capacity Bldg	Dr. Mark HOFFMANN
84	Vice Provost/Enrollment Management	Ms. Janelle KILGORE
13	Chief Information Officer	Dr. Madhavi MARASINGHE
20	Senior Vice Provost	Vacant
28	Assoc VP Diversity & Inclusion	Vacant
08	Dean of Libraries & Info Res	Ms. Stephanie WALKER
06	Registrar	Mr. Scott CORRELL
15	AVP Human Resources/Payroll Svcs	Ms. Peggy VARBERG
19	AVP Public Safety/Police Chief	Vacant
38	Director Univ Counseling Center	Mr. Thomas SOLEM
20	Director Instructional Development	Dr. Anne KELSCH
22	Director EEO/Affirmative Action	Ms. Donna SMITH
37	Int Director Student Financial Aid	Ms. Chelsea LARSON
39	Director Housing	Mr. Troy NOELDNER
23	Director of Student Health	Ms. Jessica DOTY
43	General Counsel	Mr. Jason JENKINS
41	Director Athletics	Mr. William CHAVES
21	Controller	Ms. Sharon LOILAND
88	Dir Student Rights/Responsibilities	Mr. Alex POKORNOWSKI
96	Director Financial Operations	Ms. Jana THOMPSON
92	Int Director Honors Program	Dr. A. Rebecca ROZELLE-STONE
114	Assoc Dir Resource Plng/Alloc	Ms. Cindy FETSCH
49	Dean of Arts & Sciences	Dr. Brad RUNDQUIST
58	Int Dean School of Graduate Studies	Dr. John MIHELICH
61	Dean School of Law	Mr. Michael MCGINNISS
66	Int Dn Col Nursing/Prof Discipline	Dr. Diana KOSTRZEWSKI
50	Dean Business/Public Admin	Dr. Amy HENLEY
54	Dean College of Engr/Mines	Dr. Brian TANDE
53	Dean Col Education/Human Devel	Dr. Cindy JUNTUNEN
88	Dean of Aerospace Sciences	Dr. Robert KRAUS
63	Dean Sch Medicine/Health Science	Dr. Joshua WYNNE
35	Assoc Dean of Students	Dr. Cassie GERHARDT
88	Executive Director Memorial Union	Ms. Cheryl GREW-GILLEN
109	Director Dining Services	Mr. Orlynn ROSAASEN
88	Director TRIO Programs	Mr. Derek SPORBERT
88	Student Account Relations Mgr	Mr. Matt LUKACH
07	Director Admissions	Ms. Jennifer AAMODT
09	Dir University Analytics/Planning	Ms. Amanda MOSKE
105	Director Web Services	Ms. Tera BUCKLEY
106	Vice Prov Online Educ/Strat Plng	Dr. Jeffrey HOLM
25	Export Control/Contract Officer	Mr. Michael SADLER

*Dickinson State University (C)

291 Campus Drive, Dickinson ND 58601-4896

County: Stark　FICE Identification: 002989
Unit ID: 200059
Telephone: (701) 483-2507　Carnegie Class: Bac-Diverse
FAX Number: (701) 483-2006　Calendar System: Semester
URL: www.dickinsonstate.edu
Established: 1918　Annual Undergrad Tuition & Fees (In-State): $8,122
Enrollment: 1,441　Coed
Affiliation or Control: State　IRS Status: 501(c)3
Highest Offering: Master's
Accreditation: HLC, CAEP, IACBE, MUS, NUR, PNUR

02	President	Dr. Stephen D. EASTON
05	Provost/VP Academic Affairs	Dr. Debora DRAGSETH
10	Chief Financial Officer	Mr. Kent ANDERSON
32	Int VP Student Affairs/Univ Rels	Mr. Mark JASTORFF
29	Exec Dir Alumni Assoc/Foundation	Mr. Ty ORTON
41	Director of Intercollege Athletics	Mr. Pete STANTON
12	Programming Specialist DSU Bismarck	Ms. Nicky KADRMAS
06	Director of Academic Records	Ms. Kathy MEYER
08	Head of Library Services	Ms. Staci GREEN
13	Director of Information Technology	Mr. Todd HAUF
37	Director of Financial Aid	Mr. Christopher MEEK
121	Tutoring Center Specialist/Advisor	Ms. Monica WATSON
109	Director of Food Service	Mr. Aaron ZUMMER
85	Intl/Multicultural Affairs Coord	Ms. Wynter MILLER
39	Housing/Director of Student Life	Mr. Keith JAMES
15	Director of Human Resources	Ms. Krissy KILWEIN
18	Director of Facility Operations	Mr. Trent MYRAN
19	Director of Public Safety	Mr. Ed STRIEFEL
04	Executive Asst to President	Ms. Kari HANSTAD
22	Title IX Coordinator	Mr. Keith JAMES

*Mayville State University (D)

330 3rd Street, NE, Mayville ND 58257-1299

County: Traill　FICE Identification: 002993
Unit ID: 200226
Telephone: (701) 788-2301　Carnegie Class: Bac-Diverse
FAX Number: (701) 788-4748　Calendar System: Semester
URL: www.mayvillestate.edu
Established: 1889　Annual Undergrad Tuition & Fees (In-State): $7,381
Enrollment: 1,168　Coed
Affiliation or Control: State　IRS Status: 501(c)3
Highest Offering: Master's
Accreditation: HLC, CAEP, NURSE

02	President	Dr. Brian VAN HORN
05	Interim VPAA/Dean of Nursing	Ms. Tami SUCH
10	Interim VP for Business Affairs	Mr. Steven BENSEN
32	VP Student Affairs & Inst Research	Dr. Andrew J. PFLIPSEN
102	Executive Foundation Director	Mr. Lon JORGENSEN
41	Athletic Director	Vacant
04	Exec Assistant to the President	Ms. Mary L. TRUDEAU
26	Dir Public Relations & Marketing	Ms. Beth I. SWENSON
07	Director Recruitment/Outreach	Mr. James R. MOROWSKI
06	Dir Academic Records/Registrar	Ms. Heather HOYT
106	Director of Extended Learning	Ms. Misti L. WUORI
37	Director of Financial Aid	Ms. Susan CORDAHL
08	Director of Library Services	Ms. Kelly J. KORNKVEN
35	Director of Student Life	Dr. Jeffrey A. POWELL
40	Director of Bookstore	Ms. Pam B. SOHOLT
18	Director of Physical Plant	Mr. Dan P. LORENZ
18	Director of Facilities Services	Mr. Bob J. KOZOJED
15	Director of Human Resources	Ms. Sarah GASEVIC
13	Chief Information Officer	Mr. Robert R. FREDERICK
21	Controller	Ms. Courtney PETERSON
38	Director of Counseling Services	Ms. Hanna KASTER
121	Dir Student Success/Disability Svc	Ms. Katie J. RICHARDS
28	Dir Diversity/Inclusion	Ms. Bella HETTICH
36	Director of Career Services	Ms. Megan VIG
25	Director Grants & Research	Dr. Robert D. MIESS
108	Int Dir Inst Accred/Assessment	Dr. Erin KUNZ
50	Division Chair Business	Ms. Rhonda L. NELSON
53	Dean/Div Chair Education	Dr. Pamela L. JOHNSON
68	Division Chair Physical Education	Mr. Scott B. PARKER
81	Division Chair Science/Math	Dr. Joseph MEHUS
66	Interim Div Chair Nursing	Dr. Collette CHRISTOFFERS
49	Division Chair Liberal Arts	Dr. Erin KUNZ

*Minot State University (E)

500 University Avenue W, Minot ND 58707-0001

County: Ward　FICE Identification: 002994
Unit ID: 200253
Telephone: (701) 858-3000　Carnegie Class: Masters/M
FAX Number: (701) 839-6933　Calendar System: Semester
URL: www.minotstateu.edu
Established: 1913　Annual Undergrad Tuition & Fees (In-State): $7,896
Enrollment: 2,920　Coed
Affiliation or Control: State　IRS Status: 501(c)3
Highest Offering: Beyond Master's But Less Than Doctorate
Accreditation: HLC, CAEP, CAEPN, IACBE, MUS, NURSE, SP, SW

02	President	Dr. Steven SHIRLEY
05	VP for Academic Affairs	Dr. Laurie GELLER
10	Vice President for Finance/Admin	Mr. Brent WINIGER
111	Vice President for Advancement	Mr. Rick HEDBERG
32	Vice President for Student Affairs	Mr. Kevin HARMON
21	AVP Business Services/Controller	Ms. Jonelle WATSON
84	Assoc VP Enrollment/Grad/Marketing	Dr. Jacek MROZIK
07	Director Enrollment Services	Ms. Katie TYLER
18	Facilities Management	Mr. Brian SMITH
06	Registrar	Ms. Rebecca RINGHAM
08	Chair of Library Services	Ms. Jane LAPLANTE
23	Director of Student Wellness	Mr. Paul BREKKE
37	Director of Financial Aid	Ms. Laurie WEBER
29	Director Alumni Relations	Ms. Janna MCKECHNIE
13	Director Computer Services	Mr. George WITHUS
40	Director Bookstore	Ms. Tiffany HETH
41	Athletic Director	Mr. Andy CARTER
26	Director University Communications	Mr. Michael LINNELL
15	Director of Human Resources	Ms. Laurie DAVIS
12	Dean of Dakota College at Bottineau	Dr. Jerry MIGLER
36	Director of Campus Career Services	Ms. Lynda BERTSCH
25	Grants & Contracts Accountant	Ms. Sheila LATHAM
09	Director of Institutional Research	Ms. Cari OLSON
04	Executive Asst to President	Ms. Deb WENTZ
39	Director Student Housing	Ms. Karina STANDER
27	Director of Marketing	Vacant
104	Director International Programs	Ms. Libby CLAERBOUT
19	Director Security/Safety	Mr. Gary ORLUCK
88	Director of Veterans Services	Mr. Andrew HEITKAMP
22	Title IX Coordinator	Ms. Lisa DOOLEY
56	Director of CEL	Dr. Robert NORMAN

*North Dakota State University Main Campus (F)

P.O. Box 6050, Fargo ND 58108-6050

County: Cass　FICE Identification: 002997
Unit ID: 200332
Telephone: (701) 231-8011　Carnegie Class: DU-Higher
FAX Number: (701) 231-8722　Calendar System: Semester
URL: www.ndsu.edu
Established: 1890　Annual Undergrad Tuition & Fees (In-State): $10,168
Enrollment: 12,846　Coed
Affiliation or Control: State　IRS Status: 501(c)3
Highest Offering: Doctorate
Accreditation: HLC, ART, CAATE, CACREP, CAEP, CAEPN, CIDA, COARC, CONST, DIETC, DIETD, EXSC, LSAR, MUS, NURSE, PH, PHAR, THEA

02	President	Dr. Dean BRESCIANI
05	Provost	Dr. Margaret FITZGERALD
10	Vice President Business & Finance	Mr. Bruce BOLLINGER
46	Vice Pres Research & Creative Act	Dr. Jane SCHUH
56	Vice President Ag/Univ Extension	Mr. Greg LARDY
102	Pres/CEO Fdn/Alumni Assn	Mr. John GLOVER
13	VP IT/Chief Information Officer	Mr. Marc WALLMAN
84	Vice Prov Student Affs/Enroll Mgmt	Ms. Laura OSTER-AALAND
20	Vice Provost Faculty/Title IX	Ms. Canan BILEN-GREEN
25	Assoc VP Sponsored Programs Admin	Ms. Valrey V. KETTNER
26	Assoc VP University Relations	Ms. Laura MCDANIEL
06	University Registrar	Mr. Philip HUNT
91	Director Administrative Systems	Mr. Joel BESELER THOMPSON
08	Dean of Libraries	Vacant
51	Int Dir Distance/Continuing Educ	Dr. Stacy DUFFIELD
37	Director Financial Aid/Scholarships	Dr. Matt SANCHEZ
36	Director Career Center	Vacant
50	Dean Business	Dr. Scott BEAULIER
54	Dean Engineering/Architecture	Dr. Michael KESSLER
59	Int Dean Human Dev/Family Science	Ms. Jill NELSON
49	Dean Arts/Humanities/Social Science	Dr. David BERTOLINI
81	Dean of Science & Mathematics	Dr. Kimberly WALLIN
67	Dean of Pharmacy/Nursing/Allied Sci	Dr. Charles D. PETERSON
47	Dean of Agric/Food Sys & Nat Res	Dr. Greg LARDY
58	Interim Dean Graduate School	Dr. Benton DUNCAN
114	Director of Budget	Ms. Cynthia ROTT
18	Director Facilities Management	Mr. Mike ELLINGSON
19	Dir of Univ Police/Safety Officer	Mr. Mike BORR
38	Director Counseling Center	Dr. William BURNS
23	Director Wellness Center	Mr. Jobey LICHTBLAU
39	Director of Residence Life	Mr. Rian NOSTRUM
40	Director Bookstore	Ms. Kimberly ANVINSON
41	Director of Athletics	Mr. Matt LARSEN
57	Director Fine Arts	Dr. E. John MILLER
09	Dir Institutional Research/Analysis	Ms. Emily BERG
96	Director of Purchasing	Ms. Stacey O. WINTER
07	Interim Director of Admissions	Ms. Seinquis LEINEN
04	Executive Asst to President	Ms. Stephanie WAWERS
15	Director HR/Payroll	Mr. John WOOLSEY
88	Dir Grant & Contract Accounting	Ms. Ann YOUNG
100	Chief of Staff	Mr. Christopher WILSON
104	Director Study Abroad	Ms. Alicia KAUFFMAN
04	Assoc Executive Asst to President	Ms. La Donna K. DE GELDERE

*Valley City State University (G)

101 College Street, SW, Valley City ND 58072-4098

County: Barnes　FICE Identification: 003008
Unit ID: 200572
Telephone: (701) 845-7122　Carnegie Class: Bac-Diverse
FAX Number: (701) 845-7104　Calendar System: Semester
URL: www.vcsu.edu
Established: 1889　Annual Undergrad Tuition & Fees (In-State): $7,942
Enrollment: 1,676　Coed
Affiliation or Control: State　IRS Status: 501(c)3
Highest Offering: Master's
Accreditation: HLC, #CAATE, CAEPN, MUS

02	President	Dr. Alan LAFAVE
05	Vice Pres Academic Affairs	Dr. Margaret DAHLBERG
10	Vice President Business Affairs	Mr. Wesley WINTCH
32	Interim Dean Student Affairs	Dr. Erin KLINGENBERG
53	Dean Sch of Education/Graduate Stds	Vacant
08	Library Director	Ms. Jennier JENNESS
20	Director Student Academic Services	Ms. Kaleen PETERSON
37	Director Student Financial Aid	Ms. Marcia PRITCHERT

13 Chief Information Officer .... Mr. Joseph TYKWINSKI
41 Athletic Director .... Ms. Jill DEVRIES
84 Director of Enrollment Services .... Ms. Charlene STENSON
111 Exec Dir of University Advancement .... Mr. Corey ANDERSON
18 Asst Director Facilities Services .... Mr. Pat HORNER
15 Human Resources Director .... Ms. Jennifer LARSON
29 Asst Dir Univ Advance/Alumni Rels .... Ms. Kim HESCH
38 Director of Student Counseling .... Ms. Erin KLINGENBERG
26 Director Marketing/Communications .... Ms. Tamara Jo TAFT
40 Director Bookstore .... Mr. Todd ROGELSTAD
06 Registrar .... Vacant
09 Director Inst Research/Assessment .... Ms. Kerry GREGORYK
36 Career Services Coordinator .... Ms. Kari KLETTKE
19 Director Security/Safety .... Ms. Jessica GORTMAKER

*Bismarck State College (A)

PO Box 5587, Bismarck ND 58506-5587
County: Burleigh FICE Identification: 002988
Unit ID: 200022
Telephone: (701) 224-5400 Carnegie Class: Bac/Assoc-Assoc Dom
FAX Number: (701) 224-5550 Calendar System: Semester
URL: bismarckstate.edu
Established: 1939 Annual Undergrad Tuition & Fees (In-State): $4,731
Enrollment: 3,716 Coed
Affiliation or Control: State IRS Status: 501(c)3
Highest Offering: Baccalaureate
Accreditation: HLC, ADNUR, EMT, MLTAD, SURGT

02 President .... Dr. Douglas J. JENSEN
10 VP Operations/CFO .... Ms. Rebecca COLLINS
05 VP Academic Affairs .... Mr. Dan LEINGANG
111 VP College Advance/Exec Dir Found .... Ms. Kari KNUDSON
32 VP Student Affairs .... Ms. Kaylyn BONDY
88 Dean Nat Energy Ctr of Excell .... Mr. Bruce EMMIL
84 Dean of Enrollment Management .... Ms. Karen ERICKSON
72 Dean Current & Emerging Technology .... Ms. Mari VOLK
13 Chief Information Officer .... Ms. Carol FLAA
15 Chief Human Resources Officer .... Vacant
21 Chief Accounting Officer .... Ms. Sonya KOBLE
106 Chief Dist Learning/Military Affs .... Vacant
26 Chief College Relations Officer .... Vacant
51 Dean Continuing Education .... Ms. Sara VOLLMER
08 Director of Library Services .... Ms. Marlene ANDERSON
18 Chief Buildings/Grounds Officer .... Mr. Don ROETHLER
41 Director of Athletics .... Mr. Buster GILLISS
37 Director of Financial Aid .... Mr. Scott LINGEN
39 Director Student & Residence Life .... Ms. Heather SHEEHAN
06 Director Academic Records/Registrar .... Ms. Sandy FRIED
121 Director of Student Success .... Ms. Kate MILLNER
108 Director IE & Strategic Planning .... Dr. John CARROLL
88 Program Manager NECE .... Mr. Dan SCHMIDT
88 Program Manager NECE .... Mr. Kyren MILLER
88 Polytechnic Program Outreach Dir .... Ms. Alicia UHDE
30 Resource Development Manager .... Vacant
40 Bookstore Manager/Purchasing Coord .... Ms. Debra SANDNESS
04 Executive Assistant to President .... Ms. Janell CAMPBELL
19 Campus Safety & Security Manager .... Mr. Matthew GIDDINGS
07 Director of Admissions .... Ms. Retha MATTERN

*Dakota College at Bottineau (B)

105 Simrall Boulevard, Bottineau ND 58318-1198
County: Bottineau FICE Identification: 002995
Unit ID: 200314
Telephone: (701) 228-2277 Carnegie Class: Assoc/HT-High Non
FAX Number: (701) 228-5468 Calendar System: Semester
URL: www.dakotacollege.edu
Established: 1906 Annual Undergrad Tuition & Fees (In-State): $5,106
Enrollment: 1,060 Coed
Affiliation or Control: State IRS Status: 501(c)3
Highest Offering: Associate Degree
Accreditation: HLC, EMT

02 Campus Dean .... Dr. Jerry MIGLER
10 Director of Business Affairs .... Ms. Lisa MOCK
05 Assoc Dean Academic/Student Affairs .... Mr. Larry BROOKS
08 Librarian .... Ms. Hattie ALBERTSON
06 Registrar .... Ms. Heidi KIPPENHAN
37 Director Financial Aid .... Ms. April ABRAHAMSON
41 Athletic Director .... Mr. Corey GORDER
30 Director of Development .... Ms. Leslie STEVENS
39 Housing Director .... Ms. Bridget GUSTAFSON
28 Director of Diversity .... Vacant
40 Bookstore Manager .... Ms. Christina ENNA
18 Chief Facilities/Physical Plant .... Mr. Christopher NERO
38 Director Student Counseling .... Ms. Corey GORDER
04 Administrative Asst to President .... Ms. Sandy HAGENESS
106 Dir Online Education/E-learning .... Ms. Kayla O'TOOLE
25 Chief Contracts/Grants Admin .... Dr. Indrani SASMAL
07 Director of Admissions .... Ms. Beth MACDONALD
13 Chief Information Technology Ofcr .... Mr. Brad GANGL

*Lake Region State College (C)

1801 College Drive N, Devils Lake ND 58301-1598
County: Ramsey FICE Identification: 002991
Unit ID: 200192
Telephone: (701) 662-1600 Carnegie Class: Assoc/MT-VT-High Non
FAX Number: (701) 662-1570 Calendar System: Semester
URL: www.lrsc.edu
Established: 1941 Annual Undergrad Tuition & Fees (In-State): $4,843
Enrollment: 1,771 Coed
Affiliation or Control: State IRS Status: 501(c)3
Highest Offering: Associate Degree
Accreditation: HLC, ADNUR

02 President .... Dr. Douglas D. DARLING
05 VP Academic/Student Affairs .... Mr. Lloyd HALVORSON
10 VP Administrative Affairs .... Mr. Corry G. KENNER
12 Director of GFAFB Branch Campus .... Mr. John COWGER
102 Executive Director Foundation .... Ms. Elonda NORD
32 Director of Student Services .... Mr. Steven SHARK
37 Dir Financial Aid/Placemnt Svcs .... Ms. Kelsey WALTERS
109 Director Food Service .... Ms. Rosalie SEIBEL
18 Director Physical Plant .... Mr. Chad ESTENSON
08 Librarian .... Vacant
41 Director Athletics .... Mr. Daniel MERTENS
13 Director of Information Technology .... Mr. Gary HAUGLAND
15 HR Risk Mgmt/Placement Svcs .... Mrs. Sandi LILLEHAUGEN
40 Director of Bookstore .... Ms. Melissa STOTTS
06 Registrar .... Mr. Daniel JOHNSON
26 Director of Public Relations/Mktg .... Ms. Erin WOOD
31 Dir Distance Educ/Outreach Svcs .... Mr. Daniel DRIESSEN
09 Director of Institutional Research .... Ms. Brandi NELSON
28 Director of Diversity .... Vacant
38 Counseling Services .... Ms. Jessica DIMITCH
21 Controller .... Ms. Joann KITCHENS
04 Administrative Asst to President .... Ms. Bobbi J. LUNDAY
29 Director Alumni Relations .... Ms. Elonda NORD
39 Director Student Housing .... Mr. Scott DUNBAR

*North Dakota State College of Science (D)

800 N Sixth Street, Wahpeton ND 58076-0002
County: Richland FICE Identification: 002996
Unit ID: 200305
Telephone: (800) 342-4325 Carnegie Class: Assoc/HVT-Mix Trad/Non
FAX Number: (701) 671-2145 Calendar System: Semester
URL: www.ndscs.edu
Established: 1903 Annual Undergrad Tuition & Fees (In-State): $5,450
Enrollment: 2,829 Coed
Affiliation or Control: State IRS Status: 501(c)3
Highest Offering: Associate Degree
Accreditation: HLC, ADNUR, CAHIIM, DA, DH, EMT, OTA, PNUR

02 President .... Dr. John RICHMAN
05 Vice Pres Academic Affairs .... Vacant
11 Vice Pres Administrative Affairs .... Vacant
32 Vice Pres Student Affairs .... Dr. Jane VANGSNESS FRISCH
103 Vice Pres Workforce Development .... Vacant
10 Chief Financial Officer .... Mr. Keith JOHNSON
13 Chief Information Officer .... Mr. Cloy TOBOLA
37 Director Financial Aid .... Mrs. Shelley BLOME
29 Exec Dir of Alumni Foundation .... Mrs. Kim NELSON
41 Athletic Director .... Mr. Stuart ENGEN
15 Exec Dir Human Resources .... Mrs. Sandi GILBERTSON
18 Director Facilities/Physical Plant .... Mr. Andrew PEDERSEN
39 Exec Director of Residence Life .... Mrs. Melissa JOHNSON
49 Dean Arts Sciences/Business .... Mr. Ken KOMPELIEN
64 Director of Music .... Mr. Bryan POYZER
04 Exec Assistant to the President .... Mrs. Vivian BERNOTAS
08 Chief Library Officer .... Ms. Patricia DUBOSKY
19 Director Security/Safety .... Mrs. Whitney LINK
26 Communications Manager .... Dr. Jane VANGNESS FRISCH

*Williston State College (E)

1410 University Avenue, Williston ND 58801-1326
County: Williams FICE Identification: 003007
Unit ID: 200341
Telephone: (701) 774-4200 Carnegie Class: Assoc/HT-Mix Trad/Non
FAX Number: (701) 774-4211 Calendar System: Semester
URL: www.willistonstate.edu
Established: 1961 Annual Undergrad Tuition & Fees (In-State): $5,528
Enrollment: 959 Coed
Affiliation or Control: State IRS Status: 501(c)3
Highest Offering: Associate Degree
Accreditation: HLC

02 President .... Dr. Bernell HIRNING
05 Vice President Academic Affairs .... Kimberli WRAY
10 Chief Financial Officer .... Riley YADON
32 Dean of Students .... Megan KASNER
102 Exec Director WSC Foundation .... Hunter BERG
103 Regional Director for Technical Pgm .... Kenley NEBEKER
37 Coord for Student Financial Aid .... Andrea CARVER
06 Registrar .... Jennifer NEBEKER
41 Athletic Director .... Jayden OLSON

Nueta Hidatsa Sahnish College (F)

PO Box 490, New Town ND 58763-0490
County: Mountrail FICE Identification: 025537
Unit ID: 200086
Telephone: (701) 627-4738 Carnegie Class: Tribal
FAX Number: (701) 627-3609 Calendar System: Semester
URL: www.nhsc.edu
Established: 1973 Annual Undergrad Tuition & Fees: $3,870
Enrollment: 179 Coed
Affiliation or Control: Independent Non-Profit IRS Status: 501(c)3
Highest Offering: Baccalaureate
Accreditation: HLC

01 President .... Dr. Twyla BAKER-DEMARAY
05 Vice Pres Academic Affairs .... Mr. Robert RAINBOW
32 Vice Pres Student Services .... Dr. Constance FRANKBERRY
10 Comptroller .... Mr. Jeremy LEWIS
20 Academic Dean .... Dr. Kerry HARTMAN
25 Director Grants/Accreditation .... Dr. Stacey MORTENSEN
06 Registrar .... Ms. Joetta MCLEOD
37 Director Financial Aid .... Ms. Jacquelyn ZELTINGER
08 Director Library Services .... Ms. Amy SOLIS
124 Student Devel Retention Counselor .... Ms. Deanna RAINBOW
40 Bookstore Manager .... Ms. Iona LITTLE WHITEMAN

Rasmussen University - Fargo/Moorhead (G)

4012 19th Avenue South, Fargo ND 58103-7196
Telephone: (701) 277-3889 FICE Identification: 004846
Accreditation: &HLC

† Regional accreditation is carried under parent institution in Saint Cloud, MN. The tuition figure is an average, actual tuition may vary.

Sitting Bull College (H)

9299 Highway 24, Fort Yates ND 58538-9706
County: Sioux FICE Identification: 021882
Unit ID: 200466
Telephone: (701) 854-8000 Carnegie Class: Tribal
FAX Number: (701) 854-8197 Calendar System: Semester
URL: www.sittingbull.edu
Established: 1973 Annual Undergrad Tuition & Fees: $4,010
Enrollment: 229 Coed
Affiliation or Control: Tribal Control IRS Status: 501(c)3
Highest Offering: Master's
Accreditation: HLC, @SW

01 President .... Dr. Laurel VERMILLION
05 Vice President .... Dr. Koreen RESSLER
37 Director Financial Student Aid .... Ms. Donna SEABOY
06 Registrar .... Ms. Lisa MCLAUGHLIN
08 Head Librarian .... Mr. Mark HOLMAN
40 Director of Bookstore .... Mrs. Tracy MAHER

Trinity Bible College & Graduate School (I)

50 S 6th Avenue, Ellendale ND 58436-7150
County: Dickey FICE Identification: 012059
Unit ID: 200484
Telephone: (701) 349-3621 Carnegie Class: Spec-4-yr-Faith
FAX Number: (701) 349-5786 Calendar System: Semester
URL: www.trinitybiblecollege.edu
Established: 1948 Annual Undergrad Tuition & Fees: $17,340
Enrollment: 231 Coed
Affiliation or Control: Assemblies Of God Church IRS Status: 501(c)3
Highest Offering: Doctorate
Accreditation: BI

01 President .... Dr. Paul ALEXANDER
03 Executive Vice President .... Rev. Ian O'BRIEN
05 Vice President of Academic Affairs .... Dr. Bill HENNESSY
32 Vice President of Student Affairs .... Ms. Twyla KUNTZ
84 Director of Enrollment .... Rev. Matthew PAYNE
58 Dean of Graduate School .... Dr. Carol ALEXANDER
06 Academic Registrar .... Ms. Sara BEST
08 Librarian .... Mrs. Phyllis KUNO
18 Director of Facility Services .... Mr. Mike FERGEL
41 Athletic Director .... Mr. Jordan NOWELL
04 Admin Assistant to the President .... Mrs. Jessica M. SAYLOR
26 Director of Marketing .... Mrs. Maggie PAYNE
38 Director Student Counseling .... Ms. Amanda BELMONT
29 Director Alumni Affairs .... Mr. Bryan JACOBSON

Turtle Mountain Community College (J)

Box 340, Belcourt ND 58316-0340
County: Rolette FICE Identification: 023011
Unit ID: 200527
Telephone: (701) 477-7862 Carnegie Class: Tribal
FAX Number: (701) 477-7870 Calendar System: Semester
URL: www.tm.edu
Established: 1972 Annual Undergrad Tuition & Fees: $2,250
Enrollment: 586 Coed
Affiliation or Control: Independent Non-Profit IRS Status: 501(c)3
Highest Offering: Baccalaureate
Accreditation: HLC, MLTAD

01 Interim President .... Dr. Donna BROWN
03 Vice President .... Dr. Kellie M. HALL
05 Academic Dean .... Dr. Terri MARTIN PARISIEN
32 Dean of Student Affairs .... Wanda LADUCER
10 Comptroller .... Tracy AZURE
75 Director Vocational/Education .... Sheila TROTTIER
06 Registrar .... Angel GLADUE
51 Dir of Community/Adult Education .... Sandra LAROCQUE
07 Admissions Records Officer .... Joni LAFONTAINE
37 Financial Aid Director .... Sheila MORIN
40 Director of Bookstore .... Shirley MORIN
22 Title III Director .... Dave RIPLEY
04 Executive Assistant to President .... Vacant
101 Secretary of the Institution/Board .... Candace LONGIE
38 Director Student Counseling .... Dr. Andrea LAVERDURE

41 Athletic Director Pete DAVIS
09 Director of Institutional Research Ace CHARETTE
19 Safety/Compliance Officer Chris PARISIEN
08 Library Director Laisee ALLERY
13 IT Director Chad DAVIS
36 Placement Center Coordinator Mike VANDAL
53 Director of Teacher Education Dr. Teresa DELORME
15 Human Resources Manager Holly CAHILL
18 Facilities/Physical Plant Manager Wesley DAVIS

United Tribes Technical College (A)

3315 University Drive, Bismarck ND 58504-7596
County: Burleigh FICE Identification: 022429
Unit ID: 200554
Telephone: (701) 255-3285 Carnegie Class: Tribal
FAX Number: (701) 530-0605 Calendar System: Semester
URL: www.uttc.edu
Established: 1969 Annual Undergrad Tuition & Fees: $4,252
Enrollment: 326 Coed
Affiliation or Control: Independent Non-Profit IRS Status: 501(c)3
Highest Offering: Baccalaureate
Accreditation: **HLC**

01 President Dr. Leander MCDONALD
05 Vice Pres Academic Affairs Dr. Lisa AZURE
11 Vice Pres Campus Services Ms. Jolene DECOTEAU
10 Chief Financial Officer Mrs. Katina DECOTEAU
84 Dean of Enrollment Management Mr. Darko DRAGANIC
06 Registrar Ms. Aja BAKER
15 Human Resources Director Mrs. Rae GUNN
41 Athletic Director Mr. Pete CONWAY
19 Safety and Security Director Mr. Joely HEAVY RUNNER
04 Exec Assistant to the President Ms. Courtney LAWRENCE
08 Librarian Mrs. Charlene WEIS
20 Dean of Instruction Ms. Leah HAMANN
37 Financial Aid Director Mr. Scott SKARRO
106 Director Distance Education Vacant
09 Director Institutional Research Ms. Leah WOODKE
39 Director Student Housing Ms. Melissa PLENTY CHIEF
18 Facilities Director Mr. Melvin MINER
26 College Relations Director Mr. Brent KLEINJAN
13 Information Technology Supervisor Mr. Brian DECOTEAU

University of Jamestown (B)

6000 College Lane, Jamestown ND 58405-0001
County: Stutsman FICE Identification: 002990
Unit ID: 200156
Telephone: (701) 252-3467 Carnegie Class: Bac-Diverse
FAX Number: (701) 253-4318 Calendar System: Semester
URL: www.uj.edu
Established: 1883 Annual Undergrad Tuition & Fees: $23,498
Enrollment: 1,147 Coed
Affiliation or Control: Presbyterian Church (U.S.A.) IRS Status: 501(c)3
Highest Offering: Doctorate
Accreditation: **HLC**, NURSE, PTA

01 President Dr. Polly PETERSON
05 Provost Dr. Paul OLSON
32 VP Student Affairs Mr. Dustin JENSEN
20 Assoc Prov/Dean Undergraduate Col Dr. Christopher REDFEARN
84 Vice President of Enrollment Mgmt Mr. Greg ULLAND
30 VP Development and Alumni Relations Mr. Brett MOSER
26 Executive VP Ms. Tena LAWRENCE
101 Asst to Pres/Secy to Bd of Trustees Ms. Erin KLEIN
06 Registrar Mr. Michael P. WOODLEY
37 Director of Financial Aid Ms. Judy HAGER
08 Librarian Mrs. Tuya DUTTON
78 Director Experiential Education Dr. Heidi LARSON
27 Director of Design & Publications Ms. Donna SCHMITZ
41 Athletic Director Mr. Sean JOHNSON
13 Chief Information Officer Mr. Chris HOKE
18 Chief Facilities/Physical Plant Mr. Ramone GUNKE
105 Director Web Services Vacant
19 Director Security/Safety Ms. Nicole HEINLE
22 Dir Affirmative Action/EEO Ms. Becky KNODEL
39 Director Student Housing Vacant
108 Director of Assessment Ms. Anna ENGDAHL
29 Director of Alumni Relations Ms. Setareh CAMPION
44 Director Annual Giving Mr. Jim KLEMANN
88 Executive VP UJAccelerated Mr. Scott MEYER
10 Chief Financial/Business Officer Ms. Kresha WIEST

University of Mary (C)

7500 University Drive, Bismarck ND 58504-9652
County: Burleigh FICE Identification: 002992
Unit ID: 200217
Telephone: (701) 255-7500 Carnegie Class: DU-Mod
FAX Number: (701) 255-7687 Calendar System: Semester
URL: www.umary.edu
Established: 1959 Annual Undergrad Tuition & Fees: $19,830
Enrollment: 3,799 Coed
Affiliation or Control: Roman Catholic IRS Status: 501(c)3
Highest Offering: Doctorate
Accreditation: **HLC**, CAATE, COARC, EXSC, IACBE, MUS, NURSE, OT, PTA, @SP, SW

01 President Msgr. James P. SHEA
03 Executive Vice President Mr. Jerome J. RICHTER
05 Vice President for Academic Affairs Dr. Diane FLADELAND
10 Vice President Financial Affairs Mrs. Christi SCHAEFBAUER
32 Vice President Student Development Dr. Timothy SEAWORTH
26 Vice President for Public Affairs Mrs. Brenda K. NAGEL
30 Director of Mission Advancement Vacant
06 Registrar Ms. Melissa MCDOWALL
08 Librarian Ms. Nicole ECKROTH
37 Director of Financial Aid Mrs. Karrie K. HUBER
07 Director of Admissions Mr. Joseph KITTELL
09 Director of Institutional Research Mr. James SORENSON
15 Director Human Resources Mrs. Tonya LINK
18 Chief Facilities/Physical Plant Mr. Luke SEIDLING
20 Associate Academic Officer Dr. Alyssa MARTIN
35 Associate Student Affairs Officer Mrs. Sarah D. EBERLE
04 Assistant to the President Mr. Austin J. HOLGARD

OHIO

Allegheny Wesleyan College (D)

2161 Woodsdale Road, Salem OH 44460-8920
County: Columbiana FICE Identification: 034573
Unit ID: 200873
Telephone: (330) 337-6403 Carnegie Class: Spec-4-yr-Faith
FAX Number: (424) 228-3006 Calendar System: Semester
URL: www.awc.edu
Established: 1956 Annual Undergrad Tuition & Fees: $6,800
Enrollment: 67 Coed
Affiliation or Control: Wesleyan Church IRS Status: 501(c)3
Highest Offering: Baccalaureate
Accreditation: **BI**

01 President Rev. Daniel R. HARDY, SR.
05 Academic Dean Mrs. Jeanne W. ZVARITCH
10 Business Manager Miss Katrina KAUFMAN
32 Dean of Students Rev. Timothy FORRIDER
30 Director of Development Mr. Tom SANDERS
06 Registrar & Director Admissions Mr. James DENTLER
08 Head Librarian Mrs. Crystal WHITHAM
37 Financial Aid Administrator Mrs. Esther PHELPS
09 Dir of Institutional Effectiveness Mrs. Jeanne ZVARITCH
40 Bookstore Manager Rev. Daniel GILES
33 Dean of Men Mr. Timothy HARTLEY
34 Dean of Women Mrs. Beth MILLER
07 Director of Admissions Mr. James DENTLER
18 Chief Facilities/Physical Plant Mr. Darrin PATTERSON
29 Director Alumni Relations Rev. Douglas STRAWN
38 Director Student Counseling Mrs. Kimberly FORD
04 Admin Assistant to the President Mr. Paul DUNCAN
13 Chief Information Tech Officer Mr. Matt DAVIS
84 Director Enrollment Management Mr. Tom SANDERS
105 Director Web Services Mr. Matt DAVIS
15 Chief Human Resources Officer Miss Katrina KAUFMAN
19 Director Security/Safety Mr. Darrin PATTERSON

American Institute of Alternative Medicine (E)

6685 Doubletree Avenue, Columbus OH 43229-1113
County: Franklin FICE Identification: 035344
Unit ID: 441636
Telephone: (614) 825-6255 Carnegie Class: Spec-4-yr-Other Health
FAX Number: (614) 825-6279 Calendar System: Quarter
URL: www.aiam.edu
Established: 1994 Annual Undergrad Tuition & Fees: $14,338
Enrollment: 341 Coed
Affiliation or Control: Proprietary IRS Status: Proprietary
Highest Offering: Master's
Accreditation: **ACCSC**, ACUP

00 Chief Executive Officer Diane SATER-WEE
01 Campus President Dr. Ralynn ERNEST
10 Chief Financial Officer Helen YEE
05 Academic Dean Dr. Elaine HIATT
36 Director Student Success Melissa FISCHER
21 Controller Barry COOK
37 Financial Aid Officer Debbie BREWER
06 Registrar James BROOKS
66 Director of Nursing Pamela FROST
08 Chief Library Officer Melissa FISCHER

American Winds College of Aeronaautics (F)

1461 Exeter Rd., Ste A, Akron OH 44306
County: Summit Identification: 667401
Telephone: (320) 733-2500 Carnegie Class: Not Classified
FAX Number: (320) 733-2501 Calendar System: Quarter
URL: www.americanwinds.edu
Established: Annual Undergrad Tuition & Fees: N/A
Enrollment: N/A Coed
Affiliation or Control: Proprietary IRS Status: Proprietary
Highest Offering: Associate Degree
Accreditation: **CNCE**

01 President Denise HOBART

Antioch College (G)

One Morgan Place, Yellow Springs OH 45387
County: Greene Identification: 667214
Unit ID: 483018
Telephone: (937) 767-1286 Carnegie Class: Bac-A&S
FAX Number: N/A Calendar System: Quarter
URL: www.antiochcollege.edu
Established: 1853 Annual Undergrad Tuition & Fees: $37,143
Enrollment: 116 Coed
Affiliation or Control: Independent Non-Profit IRS Status: 501(c)3
Highest Offering: Baccalaureate
Accreditation: **HLC**

01 President Dr. Jane FERNANDES
05 Vice Pres Academic Affairs Dr. David KAMMLER
111 Acting VP Advancement/Dir Alum Rels Ms. April WOLFORD
32 Vice Pres Student Affairs/Diversity Ms. Mila COOPER
84 Vice Pres Enrollment/Stdnt Success Dr. Gariot LOUIMA
06 Registrar Ms. Donna EVANS
10 Vice Pres Operations & Business Ms. Hannah SPIRRISON MONTGOMERY
13 Dir Information Technology Mr. Kevin STOKES
37 Director of Financial Aid Mr. Matthew DEC
04 Exec Asst to President/BOT Ms. Anita BROWN

Antioch University (H)

900 Dayton Street, Yellow Springs OH 45387-1635
County: Greene FICE Identification: 003010
Unit ID: 442392
Telephone: (937) 769-1800 Carnegie Class: Spec-4-yr-Bus
FAX Number: (937) 769-1806 Calendar System: Semester
URL: www.antioch.edu
Established: Annual Undergrad Tuition & Fees: N/A
Enrollment: 157 Coed
Affiliation or Control: Independent Non-Profit IRS Status: 501(c)3
Highest Offering: Doctorate
Accreditation: **HLC**, CACREP, CLPSY, MFCD

01 Chancellor Mr. William GROVES
05 Vice Chancellor Academic Affairs Dr. Chet HASKELL
10 Vice Chancellor/CFO Dr. Allan GOZUM
15 Vice Chancellor Human Resources Ms. Maria-Judith RODRIGUEZ
13 Director IT/Chief Information Ofcr Mr. Rodney FOWLKES
04 Exec Asst to the Executive Team Ms. Judy OWENS
06 Registrar Ms. Maureen HEACOCK
08 Head Librarian Ms. Dana KNOTT
101 Exec Asst to Chancellor & Board Ms. Leslie BATES
111 Director Institutional Advancement Ms. Laura ANDREWS
37 Director Student Financial Aid Mr. Donald RONAN
26 Dir Mktg Content/Communications Ms. Karen HAMILTON

† Parent institution of Antioch University Midwest in OH; Antioch University Seattle in WA; Antioch University New England in NH; and Antioch University Los Angeles and Antioch University Santa Barbara in CA.

Art Academy of Cincinnati (I)

1212 Jackson Street, Cincinnati OH 45202-7106
County: Hamilton FICE Identification: 003011
Unit ID: 201061
Telephone: (513) 562-6262 Carnegie Class: Spec-4-yr-Arts
FAX Number: (513) 562-8778 Calendar System: Semester
URL: www.artacademy.edu
Established: 1869 Annual Undergrad Tuition & Fees: $34,854
Enrollment: 235 Coed
Affiliation or Control: Independent Non-Profit IRS Status: 501(c)3
Highest Offering: Master's
Accreditation: **HLC**, ART

01 President Mr. Joe GIRANDOLA
05 VP for Academic Affairs/CAO Ms. Paige WILLIAMS
84 VP Marketing/Enrollment Ms. Amanda PARKER-WOLERY
37 Director of Financial Aid Ms. Rebecca CARR
06 Director of Registrar Services Mr. Alex SIEBERT
21 Accounting Specialist Mrs. Rose EMORY
15 Human Resources Generalist Ms. Linda KOLLMANN
32 Director of Student Services Ms. Kelsey NIHISER
113 Student Accounts Specialist Mrs. Cheryl SCHNEBELT
04 Executive Assistant to President Ms. Lacey HASLAM
105 Website Manager Mr. Jimmy BAKER
13 Lead Systems Engineer Mr. Kyle GRIZZELL
10 Business Office Manager Mrs. Katie HYKLE
07 Director of Admissions Mr. Jack WIRTH
28 Associate Director of Diversity Ms. Anissa LEWIS
29 Alumni Coordinator Mrs. Caroline BELL
36 Assoc Director of Professional Dev Ms. Audrey BERTAUX
38 Mental Health Counselor Ms. Casey RIORDAN

Ashland University (J)

401 College Avenue, Ashland OH 44805
County: Ashland FICE Identification: 003012
Unit ID: 201104
Telephone: (419) 289-4142 Carnegie Class: Masters/L
FAX Number: (419) 289-5099 Calendar System: Semester
URL: www.ashland.edu
Established: 1878 Annual Undergrad Tuition & Fees: $23,060
Enrollment: 4,447 Coed
Affiliation or Control: Brethren Church IRS Status: 501(c)3
Highest Offering: Doctorate
Accreditation: **HLC**, ACBSP, #ARCPA, CAATE, CACREP, CAEP, DIETD, MUS, NURSE, SW, THEOL

01 President Dr. Carlos CAMPO
73 Dean of the Seminary Dr. John BYRON

05 Provost .... Dr. Amiel JARSTFER
32 Vice President Student Affairs .... Dr. Robert POOL
111 Vice President Inst Advancement .... Mrs. Margaret POMFRET
84 Vice President Enrollment Mgmt/Mktg .... Mr. Keith RAMSDELL
18 Vice Pres Facilities/Mgmt & Plng .... Mr. Rick M. EWING, II
88 Vice President of Correctional Educ .... Dr. Todd MARSHALL
10 CFO .... Mr. Marc PASTERIS
13 Chief Tech & Info Officer .... Vacant
42 Director Religious Life .... Dr. Charles NEFF
37 Director Student Financial Aid .... Mr. Stephen C. HOWELL
29 Director Alumni Engagement .... Mr. Jeff ALIX
26 Director Marketing/Communications .... Ms. Karen MARTIN
15 Director of Human Resources/Legal .... Mr. Joshua A. HUGHES
36 Director Career Services .... Vacant
26 Director Public Relations .... Vacant
41 Director Athletics .... Mr. Albert KING
88 Exec Director Ashbrook Center .... Dr. Jeff SIKKENGA
09 Director Inst Research & Assessment .... Dr. Larry BUNCE
07 Director Admissions .... Mr. Wray BLAIR
123 Director Graduate Admissions .... Mr. Bernard BANNIN
49 Dean College Arts & Sciences .... Dr. Dawn WEBER
106 Interim Dean Online & Adult Studies .... Ms. Shawn ORR
50 Dean College Business/Econ .... Dr. Elad GRANOT
53 Dean College Education .... Dr. Donna BREAULT
66 Dean Col Nursing & Health Sci .... Dr. Carrie KEIB
51 Exec Director Prof Development .... Dr. James POWELL
19 Director Security/Safety .... Mr. David B. MCLAUGHLIN
38 Director Counseling .... Dr. Oscar MCKNIGHT
112 Associate Director Planned Giving .... Mrs. Amy CLARK
39 Director Residence Life .... Mrs. Christy GRUNDY
102 Chief Corporate Relations Officer .... Dr. Dan LAWSON
104 Director Study Abroad .... Ms. Rebecca PARILLO
122 Assistant Director Greek Life .... Mr. Dustin HARGIS
25 Dir Univ Grants & Foundation Rels .... Mrs. Sharon LOWE
06 Registrar .... Mr. Mark BRITTON
08 Director Library .... Mr. Scott SAVAGE
109 Director Auxiliary Services .... Mr. Matthew PORTNER
40 Bookstore Manager .... Ms. Amanda BROWN
85 Director Foreign Students .... Mr. Scott PARILLO
121 Director Academic Support .... Ms. Megan SHERAR
04 Director Office of the President .... Mr. Aaron ROSS
28 Director Diversity .... Vacant
30 Associate VP Development .... Mr. Jason MILLER
44 Interim Director Annual Giving .... Ms. Allison GOURNIAK

ATA College (A)

225 Pictoria Drive Suite 200, Cincinnati OH 45246
Telephone: (513) 671-1920 Identification: 666673
Accreditation: ABHES

† Branch campus of ATA College, Florence, KY.

Athenaeum of Ohio (B)

6616 Beechmont Avenue, Cincinnati OH 45230-5900
County: Hamilton FICE Identification: 003013
Unit ID: 201140
Telephone: (513) 231-2223 Carnegie Class: Spec-4-yr-Faith
FAX Number: (513) 231-3254 Calendar System: Semester
URL: www.athenaeum.edu
Established: 1829 Annual Graduate Tuition & Fees: N/A
Enrollment: 160 Coed
Affiliation or Control: Roman Catholic IRS Status: 501(c)3
Highest Offering: Master's; No Undergraduates
Accreditation: HLC, THEOL

01 President & Rector .... V.Rev. Anthony R. BRAUSCH
05 Academic Dean .... Rev. David ENDRES
111 VP Development/Advancement .... Dr. Lori RASSATI
08 Head Librarian .... Mrs. Connie SONG
06 Registrar .... Mr. Nicholas JOBE
42 Director of Lay Ecclesial Formation .... Dr. Susan MCGURGAN
108 Director of Assessment .... Mr. Nicholas JOBE
13 Chief Information Technology Office .... Mr. Ken BIRCK

Aultman College of Nursing and Health Sciences (C)

2600 Sixth Street SW, Canton OH 44710-1799
County: Stark FICE Identification: 006487
Unit ID: 201177
Telephone: (330) 363-6347 Carnegie Class: Spec-4-yr-Other Health
FAX Number: (330) 580-6654 Calendar System: Semester
URL: www.aultmancollege.edu
Established: 2004 Annual Undergrad Tuition & Fees: $18,950
Enrollment: 355 Coed
Affiliation or Control: Independent Non-Profit IRS Status: 501(c)3
Highest Offering: Baccalaureate
Accreditation: HLC, ADNUR, NURSE, RAD, @SW

01 President .... Dr. Jean PADDOCK
10 VP Business & Student Affairs .... Jeannine SHAMBAUGH
05 VP Academic Affairs .... Dr. Brock REIMAN
30 VP Community Engagement .... Vi LEGGETT
09 Director IE and Compliance .... Lyn SABINO
06 Registrar .... Christine COURT
13 Chief Info Technology Officer/CIO .... Jacqui KRUMPELMAN
84 Director Enrollment Management .... Sue SHEPHERD
37 Director Student Financial Aid .... Wendy DAVIS
49 Dean of Arts & Sciences .... Dr. Theresa BENZEL
66 Dean of Nursing .... Dr. Joann DONNENWIRTH

Baldwin Wallace University (D)

275 Eastland Road, Berea OH 44017-2088
County: Cuyahoga FICE Identification: 003014
Unit ID: 201195
Telephone: (440) 826-2900 Carnegie Class: Masters/L
FAX Number: (440) 826-3777 Calendar System: Semester
URL: www.bw.edu/
Established: 1845 Annual Undergrad Tuition & Fees: $34,504
Enrollment: 3,399 Coed
Affiliation or Control: Independent Non-Profit IRS Status: 501(c)3
Highest Offering: Master's
Accreditation: HLC, ARCPA, #CAATE, CAEP, CAEPN, EXSC, MUS, NURSE, SP

01 President .... Dr. Robert C. HELMER
05 Provost .... Dr. Stephen D. STAHL
10 Vice President for Finance & Admin .... Mr. William M. RENIFF
32 Vice Pres of Student Affairs .... Dr. Timeka RASHID
84 Vice Pres of Enrollment Management .... Dr. Scott SCHULZ
111 Vice Pres for Advancement .... Mr. Patrick DUNLAVY
26 Asst VP/Director College Relations .... Mr. Dan KARP
20 Associate Provost .... Dr. Lisa HENDERSON
89 Dean of First Year Students .... Mr. Marc WEST
51 Director of Adult Learning .... Ms. Nancy JIROUSEK
08 Director of Ritter Library .... Mr. Charles VESEI
13 Chief Information Officer .... Mr. Greg G. FLANIK
44 Director Annual Giving .... Ms. Ann MILLER
29 Assoc Director Alumni Relations .... Ms. Lisa JUDGE
30 Senior Advancement Officer .... Mrs. Ellen ZEGARRA
37 Director of Financial Aid .... Mr. William MCGINLEY
15 Chief Talent Officer .... Mr. Jeremy SHORT
38 Director of Counseling Services .... Ms. Sophia D. KALLERGIS
121 Coordinator of Academic Advising .... Ms. Dianna SPYCHER
06 Registrar .... Mr. Tim SEITZ
07 Director UG Enrollment .... Ms. Joyce CENDROSKI
123 Assoc Dir Tr/Adult & Grad Admission .... Ms. Katelyn GLASER
18 Director of Buildings & Grounds .... Mr. Randy HUDAK
88 Director of Intercultural Education .... Dr. Javier MORALES-ORTIZ
96 Director of Purchasing .... Ms. Karen STENGER
28 Director Campus Diversity Affairs .... Mr. CJ HARKNESS
04 Administrative Asst to President .... Ms. Kimberlee A. KUHAJDA
09 Director of Institutional Research .... Ms. Susan T. WARNER
104 Director Study Abroad .... Ms. Christy L. SHREFLER
39 Director Student Housing .... Mr. Robin W. GAGNOW
102 Dir Foundation/Corporate Relations .... Ms. Ellen ZEGARRA
19 Director Security/Safety .... Mr. Gary BLACK
41 Athletic Director .... Mr. Steve THOMPSON
50 Dean of School of Business .... Dr. Frank BRAUN
53 Dean of School of Education .... Dr. Michael SMITH
36 Director Career Services .... Mr. Patrick KEEBLER

Belmont College (E)

68094 Hammond Road, Saint Clairsville OH 43950-9766
County: Belmont FICE Identification: 009941
Unit ID: 201283
Telephone: (740) 695-9500 Carnegie Class: Assoc/HVT-Mix Trad/Non
FAX Number: (740) 695-2247 Calendar System: Semester
URL: www.belmontcollege.edu
Established: 1969 Annual Undergrad Tuition & Fees (In-State): $4,218
Enrollment: 802 Coed
Affiliation or Control: State IRS Status: 501(c)3
Highest Offering: Associate Degree
Accreditation: HLC, EMT, MAC, RAD

01 President & CEO .... Dr. Paul F. GASPARRO
05 VP of Academic & Student Affairs .... Dr. Jeremy VITTEK
11 Vice Pres of Administrative Affairs .... Vacant
15 Interim VP Human Resources .... Mrs. Judi MCMULLEN
26 Mgr of Marketing & Strategic Comm .... Mrs. Julie L. KECK
32 Dean of Student Affairs .... Mrs. Bridgette DAWSON
20 Dean of Academic Affairs .... Dr. Jesse GIPKO
09 Dir of Institutional Research/Plng .... Vacant
06 Registrar .... Ms. Jennifer NIPPERT
37 Assoc Dean of Financial Aid .... Ms. Susan NELSON-HENSLEY
121 Transfer/Articulat/Academic Advisor .... Vacant
13 Exec Dir of Info Svcs & Security .... Mr. Troy CALDWELL
04 Exec Asst to President .... Ms. Kristy KOSKY
11 Director of Operations .... Vacant

Bluffton University (F)

1 University Drive, Bluffton OH 45817-2104
County: Allen FICE Identification: 003016
Unit ID: 201371
Telephone: (419) 358-3000 Carnegie Class: Bac-Diverse
FAX Number: (419) 358-3323 Calendar System: Semester
URL: www.bluffton.edu
Established: 1899 Annual Undergrad Tuition & Fees: $34,502
Enrollment: 750 Coed
Affiliation or Control: Mennonite Church IRS Status: 501(c)3
Highest Offering: Master's
Accreditation: HLC, CAEP, DIETD, MUS, SW

01 President .... Dr. Jane WOOD
10 Vice President for Fiscal Affairs .... Mr. Art WOODRUFF
111 Vice Pres Advancement & Enroll Mgmt .... Ms. Robin BOWLUS
05 Vice Pres & Dean Academic Affairs .... Dr. Lamar NISLY
32 VP Student Life & Athletics .... Mr. Phillip TALAVINIA
08 Director of Libraries .... Ms. Carrie PHILLIPS
06 Registrar .... Ms. Iris NEUFELD
29 Alumni Relations Mgr & Mktg Coord .... Ms. Claire CLAY
18 Director Building/Grounds .... Mr. Steven HEINZE
15 Director Human Resources .... Ms. Tracey JORDAN
04 Director of President's Office .... Ms. Karen BONTRAGER
13 Chief Info Technology Officer (CIO) .... Vacant
36 Director Student Placement .... Vacant
39 Director of Residence Life .... Mr. Tyson GOINGS
44 Annual Fund Coordinator .... Ms. Jessi SAMUEL
105 Director Web Services .... Ms. Sara KISSEBERTH
37 Director of Financial Aid .... Mr. Lawrence MATTHEWS

Bowling Green State University (G)

220 McFall Center, Bowling Green OH 43403-0001
County: Wood FICE Identification: 003018
Unit ID: 201441
Telephone: (419) 372-2211 Carnegie Class: DU-Higher
FAX Number: (419) 372-6050 Calendar System: Semester
URL: www.bgsu.edu
Established: 1910 Annual Undergrad Tuition & Fees (In-State): $11,573
Enrollment: 18,142 Coed
Affiliation or Control: State IRS Status: 501(c)3
Highest Offering: Doctorate
Accreditation: HLC, AAB, ART, CACREP, CAEPN, CLPSY, CONST, COSMA, DIETD, DIETI, EXSC, IPSY, JOUR, MT, MUS, NAIT, NURSE, SP, SPAA, SW, THEA

01 President .... Dr. Rodney K. ROGERS
05 Sr VP Academic Affairs/Provost .... Dr. Joe B. WHITEHEAD, JR.
10 CFO/VP Finance & Admin .... Ms. Sherideen S. STOLL
100 VP Partnerships/Chief of Staff .... Dr. Sue HOUSTON
32 Vice President Student Affairs .... Vacant
04 Executive Asst to President .... Ms. Laurel E. ZAWODNY
111 VP Univ Advancement .... Ms. Pam CONLIN
84 VP Enrollment Management .... Ms. Cecilia CASTELLANO
20 Vice Provost Academic Affairs .... Dr. Glenn DAVIS
35 Dean of Students .... Mr. Chris BULLINS
11 Asst VP for Campus Operations .... Dr. Andrea DEPINET
26 Asst VP for Mktg & Brand Stratgy .... Ms. Amy WEST
30 Exec Dir Donor Rels & Stewardship .... Ms. Laura J. MOORE
46 VP Research & Econ Engagement .... Dr. Michael Y. OGAWA
88 Dir Recreation and Wellness .... Mr. David HOLLINGER
41 Director of Athletics .... Mr. Bob MOOSBRUGGER
15 Chief Human Resources Officer .... Ms. Viva MCCARVER
39 Director of Residence Life .... Mr. Joshua LAWRIE
45 VP Capital Planning/Campus Ops .... Ms. April SMUCKER
13 Chief Information Officer .... Mr. John M. ELLINGER
43 General Counsel .... Ms. Natalie JACKSON
58 Interim Dean Graduate College .... Dr. Alex GOBERMAN
49 Int Dean College Arts/Sciences .... Dr. Dale KLOPFER
50 Dean College Business Admin .... Mr. Raymond BRAUN
88 Director Service Learning .... Dr. Virginia J. ROSSER
53 Dean Col of Educ & Human Dev .... Dr. Dawn SHINEW
12 Dean Firelands College .... Dr. Andrew KURTZ
69 Dean College Hlth/Human Svcs .... Dr. James CIESLA
08 Dean University Libraries .... Ms. Sara BUSHONG
64 Dean College of Musical Arts .... Dr. William MATHIS
72 Dean College of TAAE .... Dr. Jennie GALLIMORE
57 Director of School of Art .... Mr. Charlie KANWISCHER
60 Dir Sch of Media & Communication .... Dr. Laura STAFFORD
88 Dir Sch Human Move/Sport/Leisure .... Dr. Ray SCHNEIDER
88 Dir Sch Family & Consumer Sciences .... Dr. Deborah G. WOOLDRIDGE
88 Dir Sch Educ Fnds/Leadership/Policy .... Dr. Patrick PAUKEN
53 Dir Sch of Teaching & Learning .... Dr. Mark SEALS
92 Dean Honors College .... Dr. Simon MORGAN-RUSSELL
106 Assoc Director eCampus .... Dr. Sheri ORWICK OGDEN
85 Exec Dir International Student Svcs .... Dr. Marcia SALAZAR-VALENTINE
21 Exec Dir of Business Operations .... Mr. Bradley K. LEIGH
07 Director Admissions .... Ms. Adrea SPOON
114 Dir Budgeting & Resource Planning .... Ms. Sharon SWARTZ
06 University Registrar .... Ms. Michelle RABLE
40 Retail Sales/Cust Svc Mgr Bookstore .... Ms. Lori NAUGLE
19 Director Public Safety .... Mr. Michael A. CAMPBELL
36 Director Career Center .... Ms. Danielle DIMOFF
38 Int Director/Training Director .... Dr. Denise LITTERER
37 Dir Student Financial Aid .... Dr. Betsy JOHNSON
23 Asst Director Center for Health .... Ms. Marlene REYNOLDS
44 Director of Annual Giving .... Vacant
101 Secretary to the Board .... Dr. Patrick PAUKEN
88 Co-Gen Manager WBGU Public Media .... Vacant
88 Co-Gen Manager WBGU Public Media .... Ms. Tina L. SIMON
88 Director Trio Programs .... Ms. Victoria AMPIAW
116 Internal Auditing & Adv Svcs .... Mr. James LAMBERT
88 Director Women's Center .... Vacant
22 Director Accessibility Svcs .... Ms. Peggy DENNIS
88 Director Marvin Center/Leadership .... Dr. Jacob E. CLEMENS
109 Director Dining Services .... Mr. Michael L. PAULUS
96 Director of Business Operations .... Mr. Phillip WORLEY
88 Director Student Employment .... Ms. Dawn FRIESON
88 Director Learning Commons .... Mr. Travis BROWN
121 Director Advising Services .... Mr. Dermot M. FORDE
88 Asst VP Non-Trad & Transfer Svcs .... Dr. Barbara L. HENRY
09 Director Institutional Research .... Dr. Oyebanjo A. LAJUBUTU
65 Dir Sch Earth/Environ & Society .... Dr. Jeffrey SNYDER
112 AVP for Development .... Ms. Robin STOCK
28 AVP Equity/Div/Incl/Title IX Coord .... Ms. Jennifer Q. MCCARY
35 Assoc VP Student Affairs .... Ms. Jodi WEBB

Bowling Green State University Firelands College (H)

One University Drive, Huron OH 44839-9719
Telephone: (419) 433-5560 FICE Identification: 007856
Accreditation: &HLC, COARC, DMS

† Regional accreditation is carried under the parent institution in Bowling Green, OH.

Bryant & Stratton College (A)

12955 Snow Road, Parma OH 44130-1013
Telephone: (216) 265-3151 FICE Identification: 022744
Accreditation: &M, ADNUR, MAC, NURSE, PNUR, PTAA

† Regional accreditation is carried under the parent institution (corporate office) in Buffalo, NY.

Capital University (B)

1 College and Main Street, Columbus OH 43209-2394
County: Franklin FICE Identification: 003023
Unit ID: 201548
Telephone: (614) 236-6011 Carnegie Class: Masters/M
FAX Number: N/A Calendar System: Semester
URL: www.capital.edu
Established: 1850 Annual Undergrad Tuition & Fees: $38,298
Enrollment: 3,020 Coed
Affiliation or Control: Evangelical Lutheran Church In America
IRS Status: 501(c)3
Highest Offering: First Professional Degree
Accreditation: HLC, ACBSP, CAATE, CAEP, LAW, MUS, NURSE, SW, THEOL

01 President ... Mr. David L. KAUFMAN
05 Provost & VP for Learning ... Dr. Jody FOURNIER
10 Vice President Business & Finance ... Mr. William MEA
43 University Counsel & Vice President ... Dr. Tanya J. POTEET
84 VP Strategic Enrollment Mgmt & Mktg ... Mr. Jean-Paul SPAGNOLO
111 Vice Pres Inst Advancement ... Ms. Jennifer PATTERSON
04 Exec Assistant to President ... Ms. Melissa LUNG
20 Sr Assoc Provost ... Dr. Terry D. LAHM
21 Asst VP Business & Finance ... Mr. Erin DELFFS
30 Assoc Vice President Development ... Ms. April NOVOTNY
26 Director of Communications ... Ms. Denise RUSSELL
09 Director of Institutional Research ... Dr. Larry T. HUNTER
06 Associate Registrar ... Ms. Cindy LAH
07 Assoc Director of Admissions ... Ms. Deanna BOND
29 Assoc Director of Alumni Engagement ... Ms. Kyrsten ROBINETTE
36 Director of Career Services ... Mr. Eric R. ANDERSON
08 Head of Library ... Mr. Matt COOK
121 Director Academic Success ... Mr. Bruce EPPS
41 Assoc Athletic Director ... Ms. Dixie JEFFERS
13 Assoc Director Client Services ... Mr. Rob AHERN
85 Director Intl Education & ESL ... Ms. Jennifer ADAMS
32 Dean Engagement & Success ... Ms. Deanna WAGNER
18 Director Facilities Management ... Mr. Paul MATTHEWS
15 Director Human Resources ... Mr. Mark PRINGLE
38 Dir Univ Counseling/Health Svcs ... Dr. Cathy MCDANIELS WILSON
28 Director Diversity and Inclusion ... Mr. Ralph COCHRAN
40 Manager Bookstore ... Ms. Cassandra STRALEY
42 University Pastor ... Mr. Andrew TUCKER
61 Dean of Law School ... Mr. Reynaldo VALENCIA
64 Interim Dean of the Conservatory ... Dr. Tom ZUGGER
53 Chair Department of Education ... Dr. James WIGHTMAN
66 Dean School of Nursing ... Dr. Renee DUNNINGTON
102 Dir Foundation/Corporate Relations ... Mr. Gregory WINSLOW
108 Assoc Provost Accred & Analytics ... Dr. Jens HEMMINGSEN
22 Asst Provost/Title IX Coordinator ... Ms. Jennifer SPEAKMAN
19 Director Security/Safety ... Mr. Frank FERNANDEZ
105 Assoc Director Web & Digital Svcs ... Mr. Russel PEPPER
39 Director Residential & Comm Life ... Mr. Jon GEYER
50 Dean School of Management & Ldrshp ... Dr. Sherry PECK
37 Director Financial Aid ... Mr. John BROWN

Capital University Law School (C)

303 East Broad Street, Columbus OH 43215
Telephone: (614) 236-6500 Identification: 770347
Accreditation: &HLC

Case Western Reserve University (D)

10900 Euclid Avenue, Cleveland OH 44106-7001
County: Cuyahoga FICE Identification: 003024
Unit ID: 201645
Telephone: (216) 368-2000 Carnegie Class: DU-Highest
FAX Number: N/A Calendar System: Semester
URL: www.case.edu
Established: 1826 Annual Undergrad Tuition & Fees: $52,948
Enrollment: 11,465 Coed
Affiliation or Control: Independent Non-Profit IRS Status: 501(c)3
Highest Offering: Doctorate
Accreditation: HLC, AA, ANEST, ARCPA, CAEPT, CAMPEP, CLPSY, DENT, DIETD, DIETI, IPSY, LAW, MED, MIDWF, MUS, NURSE, PH, SP, SW

01 President ... Dr. Eric W. KALER
100 Chief of Staff ... Ms. Katie M. BRANCATO
05 Provost/Executive Vice President ... Dr. Ben VINSON, III
10 Senior Vice Pres for Finance & CFO ... Mr. John F. SIDERAS
11 Senior Vice Pres for Administration ... Ms. Elizabeth J. KEEFER
30 Sr VP Univ Relations & Development ... Ms. Carol L. MOSS
17 Sr VP Medical Affairs/Dean Medicine ... Dr. Stanton L. GERSON
46 Int Vice President for Research ... Dr. Mitch DRUMM
13 VP for Information Services/CIO ... Ms. Sue B. WORKMAN
84 Vice Pres for Enrollment ... Mr. Richard W. BISCHOFF
32 Vice President for Student Affairs ... Mr. Louis W. STARK
18 Sr VP Campus Planning/Facil Mgmt ... Mr. Stephen M. CAMPBELL
15 Vice President for Human Resources ... Ms. Carolyn GREGORY
43 General Counsel/Secretary ... Mr. Peter G. POULOS
19 Vice President for Campus Services ... Mr. Richard J. JAMIESON
26 VP Univ Marketing & Communications ... Ms. Chris SHERIDAN
86 Exec Director Government Relations ... Ms. Jennifer RUGGLES
31 Exec Dir Local Govt & Community Rel ... Mr. Julian ROGERS
29 Sr Exec Director Alumni Relations ... Mr. Bradford CREWS
45 Assoc VP Univ Plng & Administration ... Ms. Victoria WRIGHT
28 VP Inclusion/Diversity/Equal Oppty ... Mr. Robert L. SOLOMON
22 Asst Vice Pres & Director of Equity ... Vacant
27 Dir Media Relations/Communications ... Mr. Bill LUBINGER
21 Treasurer ... Mr. Michael J. LEE
115 Deputy Chief Investment Officer ... Mr. Timothy R. MILANICH
20 Vice Provost Undergrad Education ... Dr. Donald L. FEKE
82 Vice Prov International Affairs ... Mr. David FLESHLER
97 Dean of Undergraduate Studies ... Dr. Jeffrey WOLCOWITZ
21 Controller ... Ms. Patricia L. KOST
06 Registrar ... Ms. Amy S. HAMMETT
37 Director of Financial Aid ... Ms. Venus PULIAFICO
07 Director Undergraduate Admissions ... Mr. Robert R. MCCULLOUGH
08 University Librarian & Assoc Prov ... Mr. Arnold HIRSHON
121 Vice Provost of Student Success ... Dr. Thomas MATTHEWS
85 Dir International Student Svcs ... Ms. Marielena MAGGIO
38 Exec Dir Univ Health & Counsel Svcs ... Dr. Sara LEE
09 Int Dir of Institutional Research ... Dr. Edward BOLDEN
96 Dir Procurement/Distribution Svcs ... Ms. Mandy CARTE
41 Athletic Director ... Ms. Amy BACKUS
61 Co-Dean of Law ... Mr. Michael P. SCHARF
61 Co-Dean of Law ... Ms. Jessica W. BERG
49 Dean of Arts & Sciences ... Ms. Joy K. WARD
66 Dean of Nursing ... Dr. Carol M. MUSIL
52 Dean of Dental Medicine ... Dr. Kenneth B. CHANCE
50 Dean of Management ... Dr. Manoj MALHOTRA
70 Dean Applied Social Science ... Dr. Grover C. GILMORE
54 Dean of Engineering ... Dr. Venkataramanan BALAKRISHNAN
58 Dean of Graduate Studies ... Dr. Charles E. ROZEK
04 Executive Asst to President ... Ms. Jane M. VONDRAK
102 Asst VP Corporate Rels ... Ms. Anne M. BORCHERT
25 Associate VP for Research ... Ms. Stephanie ENDY

Cedarville University (E)

251 N Main Street, Cedarville OH 45314-0601
County: Greene FICE Identification: 003025
Unit ID: 201654
Telephone: (937) 766-2211 Carnegie Class: Masters/S
FAX Number: (937) 766-2760 Calendar System: Semester
URL: www.cedarville.edu
Established: 1887 Annual Undergrad Tuition & Fees: $32,564
Enrollment: 4,461 Coed
Affiliation or Control: Baptist IRS Status: 501(c)3
Highest Offering: Doctorate
Accreditation: HLC, ACBSP, CAATE, CAEPN, MUS, NURSE, PHAR, SW

01 President ... Dr. Thomas WHITE
05 Vice President for Academics ... Dr. Thomas MACH
10 Vice President for Business/CFO ... Mr. Christopher SOHN
111 Vice President for Advancement ... Dr. Rick MELSON
32 VP Stdnt Life/Christian Ministries ... Dr. Jon WOOD
26 VP for Marketing and Communications ... Dr. Janice SUPPLEE
84 Vice President for Enrollment Mgmt ... Dr. Scott VAN LOO
41 Athletic Director ... Dr. Alan GEIST
43 General Counsel ... Mr. John HART
20 Assistant VP for Academics ... Dr. Randall MCKINION
15 VP for Human Resources ... Mr. John DAVIS
21 Associate VP for Finance/Controller ... Mr. Phillip GRAFTON
18 Associate VP for Operations ... Mr. Rodney JOHNSON
13 Associate VP for Technology/CIO ... Mr. Micah COOPER
42 Associate VP Christian Ministries ... Mr. Jim CATO
06 University Registrar ... Mrs. Fran CAMPBELL
97 Dean Undergraduate Programs ... Dr. Pamela D. JOHNSON
08 Dean Library Services ... Mr. Josh MICHAEL
73 Dean School of Biblical/Theological ... Dr. Jason LEE
53 Dean School of Education ... Vacant
50 Dean School of Business ... Dr. Jeffrey HAYMOND
67 Dean School of Pharmacy ... Dr. Marc SWEENEY
66 Dean School of Nursing ... Mrs. Angelia MICKLE
54 Dean School Engineering/Comp Sci ... Dr. Robert CHASNOV
34 Dir Stdt Development/Dean of Women ... Miss Mindy MAY
33 Assc Dean Stdnt Devel/Dean of Men ... Mr. Brad D. SMITH
26 Exec Director of Public Relations ... Mr. Mark WEINSTEIN
37 Exec Director of Financial Aid ... Mr. Kim JENERETTE
29 Exec Director Alumni ... Mr. Jeff BESTE
19 Director of Campus Safety ... Mr. Douglas W. CHISHOLM
105 Director Web Services ... Mr. Mark MAZELIN
108 Director Assessment & Accreditation ... Mr. Tom BETCHER
36 Director Career Services ... Mr. Jeff REEP
40 Manager of Retail Services ... Mrs. Tammy L. SLONE
04 Executive Asst to the President ... Dr. Zach BOWDEN
101 Admin Assoc to Pres/Asst Secy BOT ... Mrs. Angela MCINTOSH

Central Ohio Technical College (F)

1179 University Drive, Newark OH 43055-1767
County: Licking FICE Identification: 011046
Unit ID: 201672
Telephone: (740) 366-1351 Carnegie Class: Assoc/HVT-High Non
FAX Number: (740) 366-5047 Calendar System: Semester
URL: www.cotc.edu
Established: 1971 Annual Undergrad Tuition & Fees (In-State): $4,776
Enrollment: 3,029 Coed
Affiliation or Control: State IRS Status: 501(c)3
Highest Offering: Associate Degree
Accreditation: HLC, ACBSP, ACFEI, ADNUR, CSHSE, DMS, IFSAC, NAEYC, RAD, SURGT

01 President ... Dr. John BERRY
10 Vice President Business & Finance ... Mr. David BRILLHART
05 Provost ... Dr. Eric HEISER
97 Dean for General Educ/Transfer Pgms ... Dr. Chad WEIRICK
32 Dean of Students ... Ms. Holly MASON
100 Vice President & Chief of Staff ... Dr. Jacqueline PARRILL
08 Director of Library ... Ms. Katie BLOCKSIDGE
06 Records Manager/Registrar ... Ms. Veronica RINE
26 Director Marketing/Public Relations ... Ms. Suzanne BRESSOUD
37 Director Student Financial Services ... Ms. Faith PHILLIPS
19 Director Public Safety ... Mr. Adam FEATHERLING
111 Director of Advancement ... Ms. Kim MANNO
35 Asst Dean of Students ... Ms. Hannah BARNEY
13 Chief Information Officer ... Vacant
22 Program Mgr Learn Asst Ctr Disabled ... Ms. Connie ZANG
96 Manager of Purchasing ... Ms. Kimberley SIBERT
18 Facilities Superintendent ... Mr. Brian BOEHMER
51 Coord of Community Svc/Learning ... Ms. Vorley TAYLOR
36 Dir Career Dev & Experiential Lrng ... Mr. Derek THATCHER
04 Assistant to the President ... Ms. Jan TOMLINSON
09 Director of Institutional Research ... Mr. Christopher DOLL
50 Dean for Business/Engineering/IT ... Vacant
84 Dean of Enrollment Management ... Ms. Sarah MORRISON
101 Secretary of the Institution/Board ... Ms. Jan TOMLINSON
103 VP Econ Dev/Workforce Solutions ... Vacant

Central Ohio Technical College Coshocton Campus (G)

200 North Whitewoman Street, Coshocton OH 43812
Telephone: (740) 622-1408 Identification: 770348
Accreditation: &HLC

Central Ohio Technical College Knox Campus (H)

236 South Main Street, Mount Vernon OH 43050
Telephone: (740) 392-2526 Identification: 770350
Accreditation: &HLC

Central Ohio Technical College Pataskala Campus (I)

8660 East Broad Street, Reynoldsburg OH 43068
Telephone: (740) 755-7090 Identification: 770351
Accreditation: &HLC

Central State University (J)

PO Box 1004, 1400 Brush Row Road, Wilberforce OH 45384-1004
County: Greene FICE Identification: 003026
Unit ID: 201690
Telephone: (937) 376-6332 Carnegie Class: Bac-Diverse
FAX Number: (937) 376-6138 Calendar System: Semester
URL: www.centralstate.edu
Established: 1887 Annual Undergrad Tuition & Fees (In-State): $6,726
Enrollment: 4,021 Coed
Affiliation or Control: State IRS Status: 501(c)3
Highest Offering: Master's
Accreditation: HLC, ACBSP, ART, CAEP, MUS, SW

01 President ... Dr. Jack THOMAS
100 Chief of Staff ... Mr. Charles SHAHID
05 Provost/VP Academic Affairs ... Dr. F. Eric BROOKS
10 Vice President Admin & Finance ... Mr. Curtis PETTIS
111 Vice Pres Institutional Advancement ... Mr. Jahan CULBREATH
32 Vice President Student Affairs ... Mrs. Wendy HAYES
13 Director/Chief Information Officer ... Vacant
20 Assoc Vice Pres Academic Affairs ... Vacant
06 Interim University Registrar ... Ms. Amanda PAYTON
08 Director of Hallie Q Brown Library ... Ms. Carolin STERLING
89 Exec Director of University College ... Dr. Gene MOORE
12 Director of CSU Dayton ... Mrs. Lesa DEVOND
09 Director Assessment/Inst Research ... Mr. Mohammad ALI
19 Chief of Police ... Chief Stephanie HILL
26 Director Public Relations ... Vacant
23 Medical Director ... Dr. Karen MATHEWS
29 Director Alumni Relations ... Mr. Keith PERKINS
36 Director Career Services ... Ms. Karla HARPER
37 Director Student Financial Aid ... Mrs. Demarus CRAWFORD-WHITE
39 Director of Residence Life ... Mr. Justyn FRY
41 Athletic Director ... Ms. Tara OWENS
42 Director Campus Ministry ... Rev. Kima CUNNINGHAM
46 Director Sponsored Pgms/Research ... Mr. Morakinyo KUTI
49 Dean Coll Humanities/Arts & Sci ... Dr. George ARASIMOWICZ
50 Dean College of Business ... Dr. Gurupdesh PANDHER
53 Dean College of Education ... Dr. Zaki SHARIF
54 Dean Col of Science and Engineering ... Dr. Michelle CORLEY
15 Director of Human Resources ... Ms. Tonya TURNER
21 Director Business Svcs/Capital Dev ... Ms. Cynthia MICHAEL
25 Director Grants Accounting ... Vacant
92 Exec Director Honors College ... Dr. Paul A. SCHLAG
21 Controller ... Ms. Candy CARR
114 Budget Director ... Ms. Sheila BROWN
38 Director of Counseling Services ... Ms. Sonia HUNT
104 Director of Global Education ... Dr. Fahmi ABBOUSHI
106 Dir Online Learning ... Dr. Jean-Jacques MEDASTIN

18 Director Facilities Management .... Mr. Milton THOMPSON
43 General Counsel .... Ms. Laura WILSON
86 Chief Ofcr of Government Relations .... Mr. Charles SHAHID
07 Director of Admissions .... Mrs. Isabelle CAYO-SANDERS
108 Director Institutional Assessment .... Dr. Rebecca ERTEL

Chamberlain University-Cleveland (A)

6700 Euclid Avenue, Suite 201, Cleveland OH 44103
Telephone: (216) 361-6005 Identification: 770505
Accreditation: &HLC, NURSE

† Branch campus of Chamberlain University-Addison, Addison, IL

Chamberlain University-Columbus (B)

4111 Worth Avenue, Columbus OH 43219
Telephone: (614) 252-8890 Identification: 770499
Accreditation: &HLC, NURSE

† Branch campus of Chamberlain University-Addison, Addison, IL

Chatfield College (C)

20918 State Route 251, Saint Martin OH 45118-9059
County: Brown FICE Identification: 010880
Unit ID: 201751
Telephone: (513) 875-3344 Carnegie Class: Assoc/HT-High Non
FAX Number: (513) 875-3912 Calendar System: Semester
URL: www.chatfield.edu
Established: 1971 Annual Undergrad Tuition & Fees: $14,957
Enrollment: 170 Coed
Affiliation or Control: Independent Non-Profit IRS Status: 501(c)3
Highest Offering: Associate Degree
Accreditation: HLC

01 President .... Mr. Robert ELMORE
11 Vice President/COO .... Ms. Kelly GRAMLING
05 Chief Academic Officer/Dean .... Dr. Peter HANSON
10 Director of Finance .... Ms. Mary R. JACOBS
111 Director of Advancement .... Mrs. Kelly WATSON
07 Director of Admissions & Marketing .... Ms. Christina MULLIS
20 Assoc Dean/Cinci Site Director .... Ms. Tausha ROSS
04 Executive Asst to President .... Ms. Kimberly A. MONACO
06 Registrar .... Ms. Shelia YATES-MATTINGLY
08 Head Librarian .... Ms. Emilia KNISLEY
37 Financial Aid Manager .... Ms. Amy ROTH

The Christ College of Nursing and Health Sciences (D)

2139 Auburn Avenue, Cincinnati OH 45219
County: Hamilton FICE Identification: 006489
Unit ID: 201821
Telephone: (513) 585-2401 Carnegie Class: Spec-4-yr-Other Health
FAX Number: (513) 585-3540 Calendar System: Semester
URL: www.thechristcollege.edu
Established: 2006 Annual Undergrad Tuition & Fees: $15,381
Enrollment: 1,015 Coed
Affiliation or Control: Independent Non-Profit IRS Status: 501(c)3
Highest Offering: Baccalaureate
Accreditation: HLC, NURSE

01 President .... Dr. Gail E. KIST-KLINE
05 Chief Academic Officer/Dean of HS .... Mr. Rob KALLMEYER
66 Dean of Nursing .... Dr. Connie MCFADDEN CHASE
121 Dean Student Success/Col Spprt Svcs .... Dr. Meghan E. HOLLOWELL
84 Dean of Enrollment Management .... Mr. Bradley A. JACKSON
04 Executive Assistant to President .... Ms. Jessica L. DUNKLEY
10 Senior Financial Analyst .... Ms. Laura WEHBY
37 Director of Financial Aid .... Mr. Tim RING
06 Registrar .... Ms. Susan MACK
07 Director Admissions & Recruitment .... Ms. Kendal SCHWAB
28 Director of Diversity .... Ms. Anita FRAZIER
111 Ofcr of Advance/Strategic Ptnership .... Ms. Tiffany PORTER SHABAZZ

Cincinnati College of Mortuary Science (E)

645 W North Bend Road, Cincinnati OH 45224-1462
County: Hamilton FICE Identification: 010906
Unit ID: 201867
Telephone: (513) 761-2020 Carnegie Class: Spec-4-yr-Other
FAX Number: (513) 761-3333 Calendar System: Semester
URL: www.ccms.edu
Established: 1882 Annual Undergrad Tuition & Fees: N/A
Enrollment: 84 Coed
Affiliation or Control: Independent Non-Profit IRS Status: 501(c)3
Highest Offering: Baccalaureate
Accreditation: HLC, FUSER

01 President & CEO .... Mr. Jack E. LECHNER, JR.
11 Vice President & COO .... Mr. Mark D. IVEY
84 Dean of Enrollment Management .... Mr. Kevin BRINKMAN
37 Financial Aid Director .... Mr. Russ ROMANDINI
108 Dir Institutional Effectiveness .... Mrs. Beth WILLIAMS
05 Academic Chair .... Ms. Teresa DUTKO
08 Director Library/IT .... Ms. Molly JONES
88 Office Manager .... Mr. Randy ANDERSON
06 Registrar .... Ms. Brooke BOLTON
30 Director of Development .... Mr. Ken COGGESHALL

Cincinnati State Technical and Community College (F)

3520 Central Parkway, Cincinnati OH 45223-2690
County: Hamilton FICE Identification: 010345
Unit ID: 201928
Telephone: (513) 569-1500 Carnegie Class: Assoc/HVT-Mix Trad/Non
FAX Number: (513) 569-1495 Calendar System: Other
URL: www.cincinnatistate.edu
Established: 1966 Annual Undergrad Tuition & Fees (In-State): $5,040
Enrollment: 6,873 Coed
Affiliation or Control: State IRS Status: 501(c)3
Highest Offering: Baccalaureate
Accreditation: HLC, ACFEI, ADNUR, CAHIIM, COARC, CONST, DIETT, DMS, EMT, MAC, MLTAD, NAEYC, OTA, SURGT

01 President .... Dr. Monica POSEY
05 Provost .... Mr. Robbin HOOPES
13 Vice Pres for Technology/CIO .... Mr. Frankie BAKER
103 Vice Pres Workforce Development .... Ms. Amy WALDBILLIG
84 VP Enrollment/Student Development .... Dr. Soni HILL
72 Dean of Innovative Technology .... Mr. Doug BOWLING
50 Dean of Business Technologies .... Ms. Yvonne BAKER
76 Dean Health/Public Safety .... Ms. Janelle MCCORD
81 Dean Humanities/Sciences .... Ms. Angela HAENSEL
06 Registrar .... Mr. Jason A. MOORE
08 Library Director .... Mrs. Cindy SEFTON
35 Director Student Activities .... Ms. Andrea MILANI
15 Director of Human Resources .... Ms. Lawra BAUMANN
102 Executive Director CS Foundation .... Mr. Elliot RUTHER
04 Executive Administrative Associate .... Mrs. Lachanna JACKSON
19 Dean Health & Public Safety .... Ms. A. Janelle MCCORD
101 Secretary to the Board of Trustees .... Mrs. Nancy STUBBEMAN
88 Director Pathways to Employment .... Ms. Regina LIVERS
07 Director of Admissions .... Ms. Deborah POWELEIT
111 Chief Institutional Advancement .... Mr. Elliott V. RUTHER
10 Chief Financial/Business Officer .... Mr. Christopher CALVERT
37 Director Student Financial Aid .... Ms. Penny PARSONS

Clark State College (G)

570 E Leffel Lane, PO Box 570,
Springfield OH 45501-0570
County: Clark FICE Identification: 004852
Unit ID: 201973
Telephone: (937) 325-0691 Carnegie Class: Assoc/MT-VT-Mix Trad/Non
FAX Number: (937) 328-6142 Calendar System: Semester
URL: www.clarkstate.edu
Established: 1966 Annual Undergrad Tuition & Fees (In-State): $4,032
Enrollment: 5,396 Coed
Affiliation or Control: State IRS Status: 501(c)3
Highest Offering: Baccalaureate
Accreditation: HLC, ADNUR, EMT, MAC, MLTAD, PTAA

01 President .... Dr. Jo A. BLONDIN
05 Provost/Vice Pres Academic Affairs .... Dr. Tiffany HUNTER
10 VP for Business Affairs .... Doug SCHANTZ
32 VP of Student Affairs .... Dr. Dawayne KIRKMAN
102 Foundation Director .... Toni OVERHOLSER
21 Controller .... Kathy NELSON
07 Dean Enrollment Services .... Dr. Ronald GORDON
124 Dean Student Engagemt/Support Svcs .... Nina WILEY
49 Dean Arts & Sciences .... Naomi LOUIS
50 Dean Business/Applied Technologies .... Dr. Sharon BOMMER
76 Dean Health/Human/Public Services .... Dr. Rhoda SOMMERS
37 Financial Aid Director .... Victoria OWENS
06 Registrar .... Diane SEAMAN
13 Senior VP IT/Safety/Strategic Init .... Dr. Matt FRANZ
15 Director of Human Resources .... Laura WHETSTONE
57 Exec Dir Performing Arts Center .... Adele ADKINS
08 Director Library Services .... Dr. Sterling J. COLEMAN, JR.
18 Dir Facilities/Oper/Maint .... Daniel AYARS
41 Dir Athletics and Student Life .... Justin MCCULLA
103 Dir Workforce & Business Solutions .... Gerritt SMITH
88 Dir Commercial Trans Training Ctr .... Duane HODGE
106 Interim Dir Ctr Teaching/Learning .... Brittany BRIGGS
26 VP Marketing/Diversity/Community .... Crystal JONES
04 Executive Asst to the President .... Mellanie TOLES
09 Institutional Research Technician .... Kelly NERIANI

Cleveland Institute of Art (H)

11610 Euclid Avenue, Cleveland OH 44106-1710
County: Cuyahoga FICE Identification: 003982
Unit ID: 202046
Telephone: (216) 421-7000 Carnegie Class: Spec-4-yr-Arts
FAX Number: (216) 421-7438 Calendar System: Semester
URL: www.cia.edu
Established: 1882 Annual Undergrad Tuition & Fees: $44,385
Enrollment: 599 Coed
Affiliation or Control: Independent Non-Profit IRS Status: 501(c)3
Highest Offering: Baccalaureate
Accreditation: HLC, ART

01 President & CEO .... Mr. Grafton J. NUNES
04 Exec Assistant to CEO & VP IA .... Ms. Colleen SWEENEY
05 VP Academic/Dean Fac Affairs/CAO .... Ms. Kathryn HIEDEMANN
84 VP Enrollment & Marketing .... Mr. David SIGMAN
111 VP Institutional Advancement .... Ms. Malou MONAGO
10 VP Business Affairs & CFO .... Ms. Julie MELVIN
15 VP Human Resources & Inclusion .... Ms. Charise REID
13 Dir of Information Technology .... Mr. Matthew MCKENNA
32 Dean of Student Affairs .... Mr. Jesse GRANT
06 Registrar .... Ms. Marty MONDELLO-HENDREN
121 Director of Academic Services .... Ms. Elisaida MENDEZ
39 Director of Student Life & Housing .... Mr. Matthew SMITH
36 Director of Career Center .... Vacant
08 Director of Library .... Ms. Laura PONIKVAR
51 Dir Continuing Ed & Community .... Ms. Gabrielle BURRAGE
07 Assoc Director of Admissions .... Mr. Tom GREEN
37 Director of Financial Aid .... Mr. Marlon JONES
44 Dir of Annual Giving & Stewardship .... Ms. Anna GALIPO
102 Director of Foundation Relations .... Ms. Kate MACEK
29 Director Alumni & Scholarships .... Ms. Alexandra BURRAGE
26 Director of Communications .... Mr. Michael BUTZ
27 Director of Enrollment Marketing .... Mr. Richard SARIAN
21 Controller .... Ms. Sally PALMER
19 Chief of Public Safety .... Mr. Steve HAMMETT
18 Director Facilities Mgmt & Safety .... Mr. Joe FERRITTO
119 Assoc Dir of Network Administration .... Mr. Greg SLABY
120 Assoc Dir of Online Services .... Mr. Matthew MINNICH
16 Assoc Director of HR .... Ms. Lisa SCHUMANN
88 Dir of Admissions Systems .... Mr. Eric REITZ

Cleveland Institute of Music (I)

11021 East Boulevard, Cleveland OH 44106-1776
County: Cuyahoga FICE Identification: 003031
Unit ID: 202073
Telephone: (216) 791-5000 Carnegie Class: Spec-4-yr-Arts
FAX Number: (216) 791-3063 Calendar System: Semester
URL: www.cim.edu
Established: 1920 Annual Undergrad Tuition & Fees: $42,040
Enrollment: 381 Coed
Affiliation or Control: Independent Non-Profit IRS Status: 501(c)3
Highest Offering: Doctorate
Accreditation: HLC, MUS

01 President/CEO .... Mr. Paul HOGLE
11 Senior Vice President .... Mr. Eric BOWER
05 Interim Dean of Academic Affairs .... Dr. Dean SOUTHERN
10 Controller .... Mr. Daniel HOUT-REILLY
13 Chief Technology Officer .... Mr. John MALCOLM
84 Interim Dean Enrollment/Pathways .... Mr. Jerrod PRICE
32 Int Assoc Dean of Student Affairs .... Ms. Cicely SCHONBERG
37 Director Financial Aid .... Ms. Kristine GRIPP
06 Assoc Dean Acad Affs/Registrar .... Mrs. Hallie MOORE
15 Sr Director Human Resources .... Mrs. Tammie BELTON
08 Director of the Library .... Dr. Kevin MCLAUGHLIN
04 Executive Admin Asst to President .... Ms. Nancy SNELL
09 Institutional Research Analyst .... Vacant

Cleveland State University (J)

2121 Euclid Avenue, Cleveland OH 44115-2214
County: Cuyahoga FICE Identification: 003032
Unit ID: 202134
Telephone: (216) 687-2000 Carnegie Class: DU-Higher
FAX Number: (216) 687-9366 Calendar System: Semester
URL: www.csuohio.edu
Established: 1964 Annual Undergrad Tuition & Fees (In-State): $11,185
Enrollment: 15,247 Coed
Affiliation or Control: State IRS Status: 501(c)3
Highest Offering: Doctorate
Accreditation: HLC, CACREP, CAEP, CAMPEP, CEA, COPSY, IPSY, LAW, MUS, NURSE, OT, PH, PLNG, PTA, SP, SPAA, SW

01 President .... Mr. Harlan M. SANDS
05 Provost/Sr VP Academic Affairs .... Dr. Laura J. BLOOMBERG
10 SVP Business Affairs/CFO .... Mr. David N. JEWELL
84 VP Enrollment & Student Svcs .... Mr. Jonathan D. WEHNER
100 Chief of Staff/VP Administration .... Ms. Jeanell N. HUGHES
46 SVP Research Innovation/Chief Hlth .... Vacant
111 VP Univ Advanc/Exec Dir Foundation .... Dr. Julie REHM
32 Int Dean of Students .... Ms. Ali MARTIN SCOUFIELD
28 VP Campus Engagement/DEI .... Dr. Phillip A. COCKRELL
20 Vice Provost for Academic Planning .... Dr. Marius BOBOC
20 Int Vice Provost Academic Programs .... Dr. John HOLCOMB
26 Assoc VP University Mktg .... Vacant
15 Chief Human Resources Ofcr .... Vacant
35 Assoc VP Student Affairs .... Vacant
21 Controller/Asst VP Finance .... Ms. Nicole ADDINGTON
49 Dean Col Liberal Arts/Soc Sci .... Dr. Allyson ROBICHAUD
81 Dean College of Science .... Dr. Meredith R. BOND
50 Dean College of Business .... Dr. Kenneth B. KAHN
53 Dean College Education & Human Svcs .... Dr. Sajit ZACHARIAH
54 Dean Washkewicz Col Engineering .... Dr. Joanne BELOVICH
58 Dean College Graduate Studies .... Dr. John P. HOLCOMB
61 Dean of College of Law .... Mr. Lee FISHER
80 Dean College Urban Affairs .... Dr. Roland ANGLIN
92 Dean Honors College .... Dr. Elizabeth LEHFELDT
43 General Counsel .... Ms. Sonali B. WILSON
08 Director of Libraries .... Mr. David LODWICK
22 Dir Office of Institutional Equity .... Ms. Rachel LUTNER
07 Director Undergraduate Admissions .... Ms. Cristina WAYTON
09 Director Institutional Research .... Mr. Tom GEAGHAN
85 Director International Programs .... Dr. Joshladd KWAI
38 Director Counseling Center .... Dr. Brittany SOMMERS
37 Director Student Financial Aid .... Ms. Rachel SCHMIDT
06 Asst Vice President/Registrar .... Ms. Janet STIMPLE

41 Director of Athletics Mr. Scott GARRETT
29 Asst VP Alumni Relations Ms. Anne-Marie E. CONNORS
18 Exec Dir Facilities Services Vacant
96 Assoc Director Purchasing Ms. Laurie WOLOHAN
04 Director Office of the President Vacant
114 Exec Dir Budget & Operations Ms. Bonnie KALNASY
106 Director Center for E-learning Ms. Caryn LANZO
13 Chief Info Technology Ofcr (CIO) Vacant
39 Dir Resident Life/Student Housing Ms. Allison HEURING
86 Pres Advisor Government Relations Vacant
19 Director Security/Safety Mr. Anthony TRASKA

The College of Wooster (A)

1189 Beall Avenue, Wooster OH 44691-2363
County: Wayne FICE Identification: 003037
Unit ID: 206589
Telephone: (330) 263-2000 Carnegie Class: Bac-A&S
FAX Number: (330) 263-2427 Calendar System: Semester
URL: www.wooster.edu
Established: 1866 Annual Undergrad Tuition & Fees: $54,000
Enrollment: 1,924 Coed
Affiliation or Control: Independent Non-Profit IRS Status: 501(c)3
Highest Offering: Baccalaureate
Accreditation: HLC, CAEP, MUS

01 President Dr. Sarah BOLTON
05 Provost Dr. Lisa PERFETTI
10 Vice Pres Finance/Bus/Treasurer Mr. James PRINCE
111 Vice President for Advancement Mr. Wayne WEBSTER
84 Vice Pres Enrollment/College Rels Ms. Jennifer WINGE
32 VP Student Affairs/Dean of Students Ms. Myrna HERNANDEZ
04 Executive Asst to President Ms. Sally WHITMAN
18 Assoc VP Facilities Mgmt & Planning Mr. Mike TAYLOR
109 Assoc VP Auxiliaries Ms. Sheila WILSON
20 Dean Curriculum/Academic Engagement Dr. Jennifer BOWEN
20 Dean for Faculty Development Dr. Christa CRAVEN
28 Chief Div/Equity/Inclusion Ofcr Vacant
13 Chief Information Planning Officer Dr. Ellen FALDUTO
06 Registrar Mr. Nicholas SZYMANSKI
08 Librarian of the College Vacant
37 Director of Financial Aid Ms. Dana KENNEDY
27 Chief Comm/Marketing Officer Ms. Melissa ANDERSON
29 Dir of Alumni Rels & Wooster Fund Mr. Thomas MCARTHUR
36 Director Career Services Ms. Lisa KASTOR
19 Director Security/Protective Svcs Mr. Joe KIRK
101 Secretary of College/Chief Staff Ms. Angela JOHNSTON

Columbus College of Art & Design (B)

60 Cleveland Avenue, Columbus OH 43215-1758
County: Franklin FICE Identification: 003039
Unit ID: 202170
Telephone: (614) 224-9101 Carnegie Class: Spec-4-yr-Arts
FAX Number: N/A Calendar System: Semester
URL: www.ccad.edu
Established: 1879 Annual Undergrad Tuition & Fees: $37,370
Enrollment: 1,009 Coed
Affiliation or Control: Independent Non-Profit IRS Status: 501(c)3
Highest Offering: Master's
Accreditation: HLC, ART

01 President Dr. Melanie CORN
04 Exec Assistant to the President Ms. Sheri LUCAS
05 Provost Ms. Julie TAGGART
10 Chief Fiscal Officer Mr. Tom DOTSON
11 VP Planning & Administration Vacant
30 VP for Institutional Engagement Mr. Chris MUNDELL
84 VP for Enrollment Management Ms. D. Jean HESTER
32 AVP for Student Affairs Ms. Athena SANDERS
20 Dean of Undergraduate Studies Mr. Tom GATTIS
26 VP Marketing & Communications Ms. Jill MOORHEAD
58 Dean of Graduate Studies Ms. Jennifer SCHLUETER
06 Registrar Ms. Michele KIBLER
13 Chief Information Officer Mr. Matt GARDZINA
15 Director of Human Resources Ms. Beverly THOMAS
08 Director of Library Services Ms. Leslie JANKOWSKI NIEMCZURA
19 Director of Safety & Security Mr. Wallace TANKSLEY
18 Director of Facilities Mr. Dan PARRA
38 Director of Counseling & Wellness Ms. Erin VLACH
37 AVP of Financial Aid & Registration Ms. Susan KANNENWISCHER
36 Director Career Resources Ms. Tiffany SPERRING
21 Controller Mr. Roger ESCOLAS
51 Director of Career Education Ms. Jessi WALKER
39 Director of Residence Life Ms. Liz GORDON-CANLAS
109 AVP for Operations Ms. Richelle SIMONSON

Columbus State Community College (C)

Box 1609, Columbus OH 43216-1609
County: Franklin FICE Identification: 006867
Unit ID: 202222
Telephone: (614) 287-5353 Carnegie Class: Assoc/MT-VT-High Non
FAX Number: (614) 287-5113 Calendar System: Semester
URL: www.cscc.edu
Established: 1963 Annual Undergrad Tuition & Fees (In-State): $4,888
Enrollment: 27,621 Coed
Affiliation or Control: State IRS Status: 501(c)3
Highest Offering: Associate Degree
Accreditation: HLC, ACBSP, ACFEI, ADNUR, CAHIIM, COARC, CONST, CSHSE, DH, DIETT, EMT, MAC, MLTAD, RAD, SURGT

01 President Dr. David T. HARRISON
05 Interim VP Academic Affairs Dr. Martin MALIWESKY
10 VP Business Svcs/CFO/Treasurer Ms. Aletha SHIPLEY
26 VP Enrollment Svcs & Marketing Mr. Allen KRAUS
13 VP Information Technology Dr. Michael BABB
11 VP Administration Mr. Richard HATCHER
32 VP Student Affairs Dr. Desiree POLK-BLAND
111 VP Office of Advancement Ms. Kathryn TROMBITAS
20 Associate VP Academic Affairs Dr. Curt LAIRD
03 Executive Vice President Dr. Rebecca BUTLER
12 Dean of Delaware Campus Dr. Tina DIGGS
49 Dean of Arts & Sciences Dr. Allysen TODD
76 Dean Health and Human Services Mr. Kirk DICKERSON
50 Dean Business & Engineering Tech Ms. Carmen DANIELS
32 Administrator II EMSS/Student Life Vacant
91 Director IT Budget/Planning Mr. Etienne MARTIN
21 Director II Controller Ms. Jan ELLIS
06 Director Office of the Registrar Dr. Regina RANDALL
37 Director Financial Aid Ms. Deneene MERCHANT
19 Chief of Police Chief Sean ASBURY
18 Senior Director Facilities Mgmt Mr. Mark DUDGEON
28 VP DEI/Chief Diversity Officer Mr. Almar WALTER
09 Associate VP Inst Effectiveness Dr. Jennifer ANDERSON
08 Director Library Ms. Tracy KEMP
07 Director of Admissions Mr. Justin GROTE
40 Director Operations/Bookstore Ms. Stacey MULINEX
96 Director Procurement/College Svcs Mr. Bradley FARMER
100 Chief of Staff Mr. Charles NOBLE, III

Columbus State Community College-Delaware (D)

5100 Cornerstone Drive, Delaware OH 43015
Telephone: (740) 203-8345 Identification: 770353
Accreditation: &HLC

Cuyahoga Community College (E)

700 Carnegie Avenue, Cleveland OH 44115-2878
County: Cuyahoga FICE Identification: 003040
Unit ID: 202356
Telephone: (216) 987-4000 Carnegie Class: Assoc/MT-VT-Mix Trad/Non
FAX Number: (216) 566-5977 Calendar System: Semester
URL: www.tri-c.edu
Established: 1963 Annual Undergrad Tuition & Fees (In-District): $4,322
Enrollment: 18,754 Coed
Affiliation or Control: State/Local IRS Status: 501(c)3
Highest Offering: Associate Degree
Accreditation: HLC, ACFEI, ADNUR, CAHIIM, COARC, DH, DIETT, DMS, EMT, MAC, MLTAD, NAEYC, NDT, NMT, OTA, PTAA, RAD, SURGT

01 President Dr. Alex JOHNSON
05 Exec VP & Provost Dr. Karen MILLER
10 Exec VP Administration & Finance Mr. David KUNTZ
103 Exec VP Workforce/Comm & Econ Dev Mr. William GARY
12 Campus President East Campus Dr. Lisa WILLIAMS
12 President/CEO Corporate College Vacant
12 Int Campus President Metro Campus Dr. Denise MCCORY
12 Campus President Westshore Campus Dr. Terri POPE
12 Campus President West Campus Dr. Donna IMHOFF
21 Vice Pres Finance & Business Svcs Ms. Jennifer DEMMERLE
15 Vice Pres/Chief Human Res Officer Ms. Lillian WELCH
30 Vice Pres Development/Foundation Ms. Megan O'BRYAN
27 Chief Innovation/Strategy Ofcr Mr. Standish STEWART
86 Vice Pres Govt Affs/Comm Outreach Ms. Claire ROSACCO
84 VP Inst Research/Enrollment Mgmt Ms. Angela JOHNSON
26 Vice Pres Integrated Communications Ms. Jenny FEBBO
43 Vice Pres Legal Services Ms. Renee RICHARD
20 VP/Asst Provost Learning Engagement Ms. Lindsay ENGLISH
108 AVP Program Accreditation Ms. Chandra ARTHUR
88 VP/Dean Pub Safety/Criminal Justice Chief Clayton HARRIS
88 Vice Pres Manufacturing Ms. Alicia BOOKER
22 Assoc VP Access & Cmty Engagement Dr. JaNice MARSHALL
88 Exec Dir Access Learning & Success Dr. Sandra MCKNIGHT
88 Deputy Gen Counsel & Exec Dir Mr. Jason CARTER
88 Exec Director Media Engineering Mr. Robert (Bob) BRYAN
13 Exec Director EIS Mr. Jon DOLINAR
18 Exec Director Plant Operations Mr. Shehadeh ABDELKARIM
88 Exec Dir Veteran Services/Programs Ms. Marjorie MORRISON
88 Exec Dir College Services & Retail Mr. Chris MOIR
88 Exec Dir Supplier Managed Services Mr. Stephen HILBERT
96 VP Capital Const & Supply Mgmt Ms. Cynthia LEITSON
88 Dean GM Hospitality Management Mr. Michael HUFF
88 Exec Director Talent Management Mr. Barry ROYKO
20 Dean Learning & Engagement East Ms. Holly CRAIDER
20 Dean Learning & Engagement West Dr. Janice TAYLOR HEARD
20 Dean Learning & Engagement Metro Ms. Amy PARKS
20 Dean Lrng & Engagement Westshore Vacant
32 Dean of Student Affairs Ms. Ralonda ELLIS-HILL
35 Dean Access & Completion West Dr. Tim DORSEY
35 Dean Access & Completion East Mr. Andrew CRAWFORD
35 Dean Access & Completion Westshore Dr. Kristine WALZ
66 Dean Nursing Dr. Vivian YATES
88 Program Director Dietary Technology Ms. Judith KAPLAN
76 Assoc Dean Health Careers & Science Mr. Gregory MALONE
81 Assoc Dean STEM West Mr. Ormond BRATHWAITE
83 Assoc Dean Social Sciences West Ms. Courtney CLARKE
49 Assoc Dean Liberal Arts East Dr. William CUNION
49 Assoc Dean Creative Arts Ms. Amy PARKS
49 Assoc Dean Liberal Arts West Dr. Felisa EAFFORD
50 Assoc Dean Bus/Math & Tech East Dr. Ann CONRAD
72 Assoc Dean Bus IT Applied Tech West Ms. Pamela GRANT
54 Dean Manufacturing Engineer Mr. Lam WONG
88 Assoc Dean Hospitality Management Ms. Karen MONATH
88 Assoc Dean Nursing Ms. Ebony DRUMMER
100 Chief of Staff/Exec Asst to Pres Ms. Ronna MCNAIR
23 Assoc Dean Public Safety & EMT Dr. James PLOSKONKA
28 Exec Dir of Diversity & Inclusion Ms. Magda GOMEZ
110 Exec Director Development Ms. Sharon COON
09 Exec Director Evidence Inquiry Mr. G. Rob STUART
38 Dean Access Completion Mrs. Ralonda ELLIS-HILL
38 Assistant Dean Counseling-East Ms. Kate VODICKA
38 Assistant Dean Counseling-West Mr. Christopher JOHNSTON
04 Executive Admin Associate Ms. Barbara BELL
102 Exec Director Development Office Ms. Kate MCDADE
41 Athletic Director West Mr. Mark RODRIGUEZ
88 Mgr Transfer Res Ctr Metro Campus Ms. Melissa SWAFFORD
41 Dir Student Life/Athletics/Rec Ms. Jennifer DAVIS
88 Dean Creative Arts Dr. G. Paul COX
14 Int VP Workforce Innov/Dean IT Ms. Standish STEWART
91 Director Network Services Mr. Peter ANDERSON

Cuyahoga Community College Eastern Campus (F)

4250 Richmond Road, Highland Hills OH 44122
Telephone: (216) 987-6000 Identification: 770355
Accreditation: &HLC

Cuyahoga Community College Metropolitan Campus (G)

2900 Community College Avenue, Cleveland OH 44115
Telephone: (800) 954-8742 Identification: 770354
Accreditation: &HLC

Cuyahoga Community College Western Campus (H)

11000 Pleasant Valley Road, Parma OH 44130
Telephone: (800) 954-8742 Identification: 770356
Accreditation: &HLC

Cuyahoga Community College Westshore (I)

31001 Clemens Road, Westlake OH 44145
Telephone: (800) 954-8742 Identification: 770357
Accreditation: &HLC

Davis College (J)

433 North Summit Street, Suite 202,
Toledo OH 43623-4389
County: Lucas FICE Identification: 004855
Unit ID: 202435
Telephone: (419) 473-2700 Carnegie Class: Assoc/HVT-High Trad
FAX Number: (419) 473-2472 Calendar System: Quarter
URL: www.daviscollege.edu
Established: 1858 Annual Undergrad Tuition & Fees: $14,130
Enrollment: 109 Coed
Affiliation or Control: Proprietary IRS Status: Proprietary
Highest Offering: Associate Degree
Accreditation: HLC

01 President Diane BRUNNER
05 VP Academic & Student Services Mary RYAN BULONE
26 VP of Marketing Tim BRUNNER
37 Director Student Financial Aid Nancy POWERS
07 Director of Admissions Amy BERG
113 Bursar Barb HELMLINGER
36 Career Services Coordinator Brittany GUNNETT

The Defiance College (K)

701 N Clinton Street, Defiance OH 43512-1695
County: Defiance FICE Identification: 003041
Unit ID: 202514
Telephone: (419) 784-4010 Carnegie Class: Bac-Diverse
FAX Number: (419) 784-4101 Calendar System: Semester
URL: www.defiance.edu
Established: 1850 Annual Undergrad Tuition & Fees: $33,910
Enrollment: 607 Coed
Affiliation or Control: United Church Of Christ IRS Status: 501(c)3
Highest Offering: Master's
Accreditation: HLC, CAEP, IACBE, NURSE, SW

01 President Dr. Richanne C. MANKEY
05 VP for Academic Affairs Dr. Agnes CALDWELL
10 Vice Pres for Finance & Management Mr. Timothy PRUETT
32 VP Student Affs/Dean of Students Mrs. Lisa MARSALEK
84 Vice President for Enrollment Mgmt Mrs. Tracey D. FORD
88 Dean McMaster Sch Adv Hum Mrs. Mary Ann STUDER
15 Director of Human Resources Mrs. Mary E. BURKHOLDER
08 Dir of Library and Instr Resource Mrs. Lisa CRUMIT-HANCOCK
26 Director Public Relations/Marketing Mr. Ryan IMBROCK
13 Director of Computer Services Mr. Ryan NUNN
06 Registrar Dr. Robert DETWILER
37 Director of Financial Aid Mr. Ron HERRELL
41 Athletic Director Mr. Derek WOODLEY
28 Director Intercultural Relations Ms. Mercedes CLAY
39 Director of Residence Life Ms. Jennifer WALTON

18 Director of Physical Plant ... Mr. Ted CZARTOSKI
21 Director of Accounting ... Mrs. Kristine BOLAND
04 Administrative Asst to President ... Mrs. Judy LYMANSTALL
103 Dir Workforce/Career Development ... Ms. Sally BISSELL
50 Dean of Business ... Mr. William SHOLL
53 Dean of Education ... Dr. Carla HIGGINS
38 Director Student Counseling ... Ms. Lynn BRAUN
44 Director of Annual Giving ... Vacant
30 Director of Development ... Mrs. Brittanie KUHR

Denison University (A)

100 W College Street, Granville OH 43023-1359
County: Licking FICE Identification: 003042
Unit ID: 202523
Telephone: (740) 587-0810 Carnegie Class: Bac-A&S
FAX Number: (740) 587-6417 Calendar System: Semester
URL: www.denison.edu
Established: 1831 Annual Undergrad Tuition & Fees: $56,680
Enrollment: 2,258 Coed
Affiliation or Control: Independent Non-Profit IRS Status: 501(c)3
Highest Offering: Baccalaureate
Accreditation: HLC

01 President ... Dr. Adam S. WEINBERG
05 Provost ... Dr. Kimberly A. COPLIN
100 VP/Chief of Staff ... Dr. Rajesh BELLANI
10 VP Finance & Management/CFO ... Mr. David A. ENGLISH
111 VP Institutional Advancement ... Mr. Greg BADER
32 VP of Student Life ... Mr. Alexander MILLER
84 VP Enrollment Management ... Mr. Gregory W. SNEED
89 Dean of First-Year Students ... Dr. Mark MOLLER
88 Special Asst to Pres & Provost ... Dr. Joyce MEREDITH
41 Assoc VP of Athletics ... Ms. Nan CARNEY-DEBORD
115 Chief Investment Officer ... Ms. Kathleen BROWNE
04 Executive Asst to President ... Ms. Nancy BERG

Eastern Gateway Community College - Jefferson County Campus (B)

110 John Scott Hwy, Steubenville OH 43952
County: Jefferson FICE Identification: 007275
Unit ID: 203331
Telephone: (740) 264-5591 Carnegie Class: Assoc/MT-VT-High Non
FAX Number: N/A Calendar System: Semester
URL: www.egcc.edu
Established: 1966 Annual Undergrad Tuition & Fees (In-District): $4,026
Enrollment: 40,036 Coed
Affiliation or Control: State/Local IRS Status: 501(c)3
Highest Offering: Associate Degree
Accreditation: HLC, CAHIIM, COARC, DA, EMT, RAD

01 President ... Mr. Michael GEOGHEGAN
05 Sr VP of Academic Affairs ... Dr. John CROOKS
11 SVP & Chief Operations Officer .. Mr. Robert ROESCHENTHALER
32 SVP/Chief Student Affairs Ofcr ... Ms. Christina WANAT
12 Sr VP of Youngstown Campus ... Mr. Arthur DALY
09 VP Institutional Effectiveness/Rsch ... Mr. Christopher BIRD
28 Sr VP of Inst Diversity & Aspire ... Ms. Karla MARTIN
20 Dean of Academics ... Dr. Thomas GRAHAM
37 Director of Financial Aid ... Mr. Kurt PAWLAK
15 Exec Director of Human Resources ... Mr. Joshua MARTIN
88 Compliance Officer ... Ms. Stephanie SEVERIN
10 Controller ... Mr. Robert SEMICH
76 Dean Health Science/Public Service ... Ms. Gina AUGUSTINE
18 Director Building & Grounds ... Mr. Julius J. DZIEWATKOSKI
06 Registrar ... Ms. Marlise SIPES
21 Deputy CFO ... Ms. Jennifer REED
20 Assoc VP Curriculum/Academic Effect ... Ms. Vanessa BIRNEY

Eastern Gateway Community College - Youngstown Campus (C)

101 East Federal Street, Youngstown OH 44503
Telephone: (800) 682-6553 Identification: 770987
Accreditation: &HLC

† Branch campus of Eastern Gateway Community College in Steubenville, OH.

Edison State Community College (D)

1973 Edison Drive, Piqua OH 45356-9239
County: Miami FICE Identification: 012750
Unit ID: 202648
Telephone: (937) 778-8600 Carnegie Class: Assoc/MT-VT-High Non
FAX Number: (937) 778-1920 Calendar System: Semester
URL: www.edisonohio.edu
Established: 1973 Annual Undergrad Tuition & Fees (In-State): $5,050
Enrollment: 4,202 Coed
Affiliation or Control: State IRS Status: 501(c)3
Highest Offering: Associate Degree
Accreditation: HLC, ADNUR, MAC, MLTAD, PTAA

01 President ... Dr. Doreen LARSON
04 Executive Asst to the President ... Ms. Heather LANHAM
05 Provost ... Mr. Chris SPRADLIN
10 VP of Administration & Finance ... Mr. James LEHMKUHL
32 Dean of Student Affairs ... Ms. Jessica CHAMBERS
31 VP Business/Cmty Partnerships ... Mr. Rick HANES
13 Chief Information Officer ... Ms. Amy CROW
15 Exec Director Human Resources ... Ms. Kara MYERS
35 Director of Student Services ... Ms. Loleta COLLINS
49 Dean of Arts & Sciences ... Dr. Paul HEINTZ
09 Assoc Prov Planning/Effectiveness ... Ms. Mona WALTERS
21 Controller ... Mr. James LEHMKUHL
41 Director Athletics ... Mr. Nathan COLE
37 Director of Financial Aid ... Ms. Chris CUMMINGS
26 Dir of Marketing & Communications ... Mr. Bruce MCKENZIE
84 Enrollment Manager ... Ms. Stacey BEAN
06 Registrar ... Ms. Mary BORNHORST
08 Director of Library/Learning Center ... Ms. Lisa HOOPS
18 Dir of Physical Plant/Facilities ... Mr. Harold HITCHCOCK

ETI Technical College of Niles (E)

2076-86 Youngstown-Warren Road, Niles OH 44446-4398
County: Trumbull FICE Identification: 030790
Unit ID: 200590
Telephone: (330) 652-9919 Carnegie Class: Assoc/HVT-Mix Trad/Non
FAX Number: (330) 652-4399 Calendar System: Semester
URL: www.eticollege.edu
Established: 1989 Annual Undergrad Tuition & Fees: $10,460
Enrollment: 121 Coed
Affiliation or Control: Proprietary IRS Status: Proprietary
Highest Offering: Associate Degree
Accreditation: ACCSC

01 Director ... Mrs. Renee ZUZOLO
07 Director of Admissions ... Mrs. Diane MARSTELLER
37 Director Financial Aid ... Ms. Kay MADIGAN

Felbry College School of Nursing (F)

6055 Cleveland Avenue, Columbus OH 43231
County: Franklin FICE Identification: 042350
Unit ID: 487861
Telephone: (614) 781-1085 Carnegie Class: Not Classified
FAX Number: (614) 929-3816 Calendar System: Semester
URL: felbrycollege.edu
Established: 2007 Annual Undergrad Tuition & Fees: $30,315
Enrollment: 288 Coed
Affiliation or Control: Proprietary IRS Status: Proprietary
Highest Offering: Baccalaureate
Accreditation: ABHES

01 CEO/On Site Administrator ... Feyi TOLANI
05 Dean/Dir of Nursing ... Dr. Cathryn BAACK
88 Compliance ... Vanessa STAFFORD
06 Registrar ... Vacant
18 Chf Facilities/Physical Plant Ofcr ... Brains BANDA

Fortis College (G)

555 E Alex-Bell Road, Centerville OH 45459-6120
County: Montgomery FICE Identification: 021907
Unit ID: 205179
Telephone: (937) 433-3410 Carnegie Class: Assoc/HVT-High Trad
FAX Number: (937) 435-6516 Calendar System: Semester
URL: https://www.fortis.edu/campuses/ohio/centerville.html
Established: 1970 Annual Undergrad Tuition & Fees: $14,543
Enrollment: 559 Coed
Affiliation or Control: Proprietary IRS Status: Proprietary
Highest Offering: Associate Degree
Accreditation: ACCSC, ADNUR

01 College President ... Gregory SHIELDS
05 Dean of Education ... Lisa MAYS
09 Registrar ... Andrea BEHR
07 Director Admissions ... Chris BROWN
37 Director Financial Aid ... Rachel KARMON

Fortis College (H)

2545 Bailey Road, Cuyahoga Falls OH 44221-2949
County: Summit FICE Identification: 009412
Unit ID: 204307
Telephone: (330) 923-9959 Carnegie Class: Spec 2-yr-Health
FAX Number: (330) 923-0886 Calendar System: Other
URL: www.fortis.edu
Established: 1922 Annual Undergrad Tuition & Fees: N/A
Enrollment: N/A Coed
Affiliation or Control: Proprietary IRS Status: Proprietary
Highest Offering: Associate Degree
Accreditation: ACCSC

01 Campus President ... Mr. Brian PARKER
05 Academic Dean ... Ms. Shannon MCMANAMON

Franciscan University of Steubenville (I)

1235 University Boulevard, Steubenville OH 43952-1763
County: Jefferson FICE Identification: 003036
Unit ID: 205957
Telephone: (740) 283-3771 Carnegie Class: Masters/M
FAX Number: (740) 283-6472 Calendar System: Semester
URL: www.franciscan.edu
Established: 1946 Annual Undergrad Tuition & Fees: $30,180
Enrollment: 3,304 Coed
Affiliation or Control: Roman Catholic IRS Status: 501(c)3
Highest Offering: Master's
Accreditation: HLC, CACREP, CAEP, IACBE, NURSE, SW

01 President ... Rev. Dave PIVONKA, TOR
88 VP of Franciscan Life ... Rev. Jonathan ST. ANDRE, TOR
10 VP of Finance ... Mr. Richard ROLLINO
05 VP for Academic Affairs ... Dr. Daniel KEMPTON
31 Exec Dir of Community Relations ... Mr. Mike FLORAK
45 Exec Dir of Institutional Effect ... Dr. James MELLO
11 Vice Pres of Operations ... Mr. Brenan PERGI
15 VP of Human Resources ... Ms. Sara DRODDY
32 Vice President of Student Life ... Dr. Daniel DENTINO
84 Vice Pres of Enrollment Management ... Mr. Joel S. RECZNIK
111 VP for Advancement ... Mr. Thomas PAPPALARDO
88 Local Minister ... Rev. Luke ROBERTSON, TOR
42 University Chaplain ... Rev. Shawn ROBERSON, TOR
79 Dean of Humanities & Soc Sciences ... Dr. Regina BOERIO
107 Dean of Professional Programs ... Dr. Christin JUNGERS
81 Dean of Natural & Applied Science ... Dr. Daniel KUEBLER
73 Dean of Philosophy and Theology ... Dr. Paul SYMINGTON
121 Dean of Advising & Acad Operations ... Ms. Ann DULANY
105 Director Infrastructure Services ... Mr. Dennis BREEN
08 Director of Library ... Ms. Amy LEONI
88 VP of Center for Evangelization ... Mr. Mark JOSEPH
29 Dir of Alumni & Constituent Rels ... Mr. Timothy J. DELANEY
26 Dir Marketing & Communications ... Ms. Lisa M. FERGUSON
07 Director of Admissions ... Mr. Christopher KRIVONIAK
06 Registrar ... Vacant
84 Exec Dir of Enrollment Services ... Mr. John L. HERRMANN
09 Director of Institutional Research ... Dcn. Mark A. ERSTE, SR.
21 Controller ... Mr. Timothy HEFFRON
40 Director of Bookstore ... Ms. Dreama THOMPSON
91 Dir Enterprise Application Services ... Mrs. Pam SHANE
18 Director Physical Plant Services ... Mr. Joseph P. MCGURN
88 Director of Missionary Outreach ... Mr. Rhett YOUNG
88 Director of Chapel Ministries ... Mr. Robert PALLADINO
35 Dir Student Activities/Programming ... Mrs. Kathy L. MATTIOLI
38 Director of Wellness Center ... Mr. Matthew BURRISS
19 Director Campus Security ... Vacant
106 Dean of Online Programs ... Dr. Cory MALONEY
108 Director Institutional Assessment ... Vacant
04 Project Manager to President ... Mr. Daniel MILES
37 Director of Financial Aid ... Mr. Jody PEELER
26 Exec Dir Marketing & Communications ... Ms. Kimberly SPONSELLER
101 Corporate Secretary of University ... Ms. Janine MURDOCK
117 Dir of Risk Mgmt & Compliance ... Mr. John PIZZUTI
41 Director of Athletics ... Mr. Scott GREVE
35 Dean of Students ... Mr. Matthew SCHAEFER
88 Director of Academic Effectiveness ... Dr. David BURTON
44 Director Annual Giving ... Mr. Benjamin GESSLER
23 Assoc Dir of Wellness Ctr ... Ms. Charlotte JONES
30 Exec Dir Philanthropic Giving ... Mr. Michael ANDREOLA
106 Director of Franciscan Life Online ... Ms. Lindsey SCHROCK
88 Dean of Personal Vocation ... Mr. David SCHMIEISING
20 Director of Teaching Excellence ... Dr. Matthew BREUNINGER

Franklin University (J)

201 S Grant Avenue, Columbus OH 43215-5399
County: Franklin FICE Identification: 003046
Unit ID: 202806
Telephone: (614) 797-4700 Carnegie Class: Spec-4-yr-Bus
FAX Number: N/A Calendar System: Trimester
URL: www.franklin.edu
Established: 1902 Annual Undergrad Tuition & Fees: $9,577
Enrollment: 5,926 Coed
Affiliation or Control: Independent Non-Profit IRS Status: 501(c)3
Highest Offering: Doctorate
Accreditation: HLC, #CAEP, CAHIIM, IACBE, NURSE

01 President ... Dr. David R. DECKER
11 Sr VP Administration/Chief of Staff ... Ms. Christi L. CABUNGCAL
05 SVP/Provost Academic Affairs ... Dr. Christopher WASHINGTON
26 VP Marketing ... Ms. Linda M. STEELE
111 VP University Advancement ... Vacant
32 SVP Student Affs & Enrollment Mgmt ... Dr. Lynne HULL
108 Exec Director Accreditation & Auth ... Ms. Kelly EVANS WILSON
10 SVP/Chief Financial Officer ... Dr. Marvin BRISKEY
45 VP Planning & University Services ... Vacant
04 Executive Assistant to President ... Ms. Bonnie MCCANN
35 Dean of Students ... Dr. Blake RENNER
13 SVP/Chief Information Officer ... Mr. Rick SUNDERMAN
88 Dir of Accreditation & Inst Effect ... Ms. Susanne SMITH
09 Director Inst Effectiveness ... Mr. Kristopher COBLE
06 Registrar ... Mr. Frank YANCHAK
08 Director of Library Services ... Ms. Alyssa DARDEN
37 Director of Financial Aid ... Vacant
121 Exec Dir Student Affairs Operations ... Ms. Wendi ROBINSON
88 Dean/VP Acad Quality & Planning ... Dr. Patrick BENNETT
88 SVP/Exec Dir Domestic Partnership ... Mr. Bill CHAN
18 Director of Facilities ... Mr. Carl BROWN
26 Director of Public Relations ... Ms. Sherry MERCURIO
29 Director of Alumni Engagement & Dev ... Ms. Sherry MERCUIRIO
96 Director of Purchasing ... Mr. Bob DONAHUE
118 Director of Benefits ... Ms. Brenda LISTON
88 Director Teaching Excellence ... Dr. Meghan RAEHLL
49 Dean Arts/Science & Technology ... Dr. Kody KUEHNL
50 Dean College of Business ... Dr. Alyncia BOWEN
69 Dean College of Health & Public Adm ... Dr. Jonathan MCCOMBS
53 Dean School of Education ... Dr. Patrick BENNETT
85 SVP Global Programs ... Dr. Godfrey MENDES
15 Director of Human Resources ... Ms. Molly MILLER
88 Director of Accounting ... Mr. Sean HUNTER
21 Exec Dir of Financial Services ... Mr. Randolph SNYDER
19 Director Security/Safety ... Mr. Clifton SPINNER

Galen College of Nursing **(A)**
100 E Business Way, Suite 200, Cincinnati OH 45241
Telephone: (513) 475-3600 Identification: 770537
Accreditation: &SC, ADNUR, NURSE

† Branch campus of Galen College of Nursing, Louisville, KY

Global Tech College (B)
4346 Secor Rd, Toledo OH 43623
County: Lucas Identification: 667346
Telephone: (567) 200-6829 Carnegie Class: Not Classified
FAX Number: (567) 200-6841 Calendar System: Quarter
URL: www.globaltech.edu
Established: 2012 Annual Undergrad Tuition & Fees: N/A
Enrollment: N/A Coed
Affiliation or Control: Proprietary IRS Status: Proprietary
Highest Offering: Associate Degree
Accreditation: CNCE

01 President .... Dr. Joseph G. HOSNY
11 Dir Admin & Financial Affs .... Dr. Ramsey ATIEH
05 Dir Academic Affs & Student Svcs .... Dr. Michelle CHEASTY
07 Dir of Admissions & Marketing .... John REESE

God's Bible School and College (C)
1810 Young Street, Cincinnati OH 45202-6838
County: Hamilton FICE Identification: 022205
Unit ID: 202903
Telephone: (513) 721-7944 Carnegie Class: Spec-4-yr-Faith
FAX Number: (513) 763-6649 Calendar System: Semester
URL: www.gbs.edu
Established: 1900 Annual Undergrad Tuition & Fees: $7,150
Enrollment: 335 Coed
Affiliation or Control: Interdenominational IRS Status: 501(c)3
Highest Offering: Master's
Accreditation: HLC, BI

01 President .... Rodney S. LOPER
05 Vice President for Academic Affairs .... Aaron PROFITT
32 Vice President for Student Affairs .... Sonja VERNON
30 Vice President for Donor Relations .... Vacant
06 Registrar .... Kent STETLER
08 Head Librarian .... Stephanie OWENS
10 Vice President for Finance .... David FREDERICK
13 Dir of UX and Digital Strategies .... Jason WEED
84 Vice Pres for Enrollment Services .... Matt HALLAM
37 Financial Aid Coordinator .... Valorie QUESENBERRY

Good Samaritan College of Nursing and Health Science (D)
375 Dixmyth Avenue, Cincinnati OH 45220-2489
County: Hamilton FICE Identification: 006494
Unit ID: 202912
Telephone: (513) 862-2743 Carnegie Class: Spec-4-yr-Other Health
FAX Number: (513) 862-3572 Calendar System: Semester
URL: www.gscollege.edu
Established: 2001 Annual Undergrad Tuition & Fees: $15,470
Enrollment: 372 Coed
Affiliation or Control: Independent Non-Profit IRS Status: 501(c)3
Highest Offering: Baccalaureate
Accreditation: HLC, ADNUR, NUR

01 President .... Dr. Judy KRONENBERGER
05 Dean Academic Affairs/Allied Health .... Dr. Pryze SMITH
66 Academic Dean of Nursing .... Dr. Michelle ROA
10 College Business Administator .... Vacant
11 Associate Dean of Campus Operations .... Dr. Beth MOORE
09 Dir of Inst Assessment/Educ Tech .... Dr. Terri PULLEN
84 Dean of Enrollment .... Dr. Trent HAYES
06 Registrar .... Ms. Isabelle CAYO SANDERS

Heidelberg University (E)
310 E Market Street, Tiffin OH 44883-2462
County: Seneca FICE Identification: 003048
Unit ID: 203085
Telephone: (419) 448-2000 Carnegie Class: Bac-Diverse
FAX Number: (419) 448-2124 Calendar System: Semester
URL: www.heidelberg.edu
Established: 1850 Annual Undergrad Tuition & Fees: $32,300
Enrollment: 1,230 Coed
Affiliation or Control: United Church Of Christ IRS Status: 501(c)3
Highest Offering: Master's
Accreditation: HLC, ACBSP, CAATE, CACREP, CAEP, MUS

01 President .... Dr. Robert HUNTINGTON
05 Int VP for Academic Affairs/Provost .... Dr. Bryan SMITH
10 VP for Admin & Business Affairs .... Mr. Hoa NGUYEN
84 VP for Enrollment Mgmt & Marketing .... Dr. Anthony BOURNE
111 VP Univ Advancement & Alumni Affs .... Mr. Phil NESS
29 Exec Dir Alumni Engage/Major Gifts .. Ms. Ashley HELMSTETTER
13 Assoc VP for Information Resources .... Mr. Kurt HUENEMANN
18 Assoc VP for Facilities & Engr .... Mr. Rod MORRISON
06 Registrar .... Mr. Leroy MORGAN
50 Dean of Business & Technology .... Dr. Scott JOHNSON
108 Dir of Acad Assessment & Effect .... Ms. Jordan KAUFMAN
104 Director Intl Affairs & Studies .... Ms. Julie ARNOLD
26 Dir of Marketing & Communications .... Mr. Rick SHERLOCK
36 Exec Dir of HYPE & Placement .... Mr. Mark MCKEE
121 Exec Dir of Owen Center .... Dr. Courtney DEMAYO PUGNO
08 Director of Library .... Ms. Laurie REPP
41 Athletic Director .... Mr. Matt PALM
21 Business Officer .... Ms. Barb GABEL
30 Exec Dir for Development .... Mr. James MINEHART
32 Dean of Student Affairs .... Dr. Chris ABRAMS
39 Asst Dn Stdnt Affs for Campus Life .... Mr. Mark ZENO
124 Dir Student Engagement .... Ms. Jacqueline SIRONEN
15 Chief Human Resources Officer .... Vacant
22 Title IX Coord & HR Generalist .... Ms. Monica VERHOFF
21 Controller .... Mr. Joel WILKINS
04 Exec Asst to President & Provost .... Ms. April RUSSELL
42 Director of Campus Ministry .... Rev. Paul STARK
19 Director Security/Safety .... Mr. Jeff RHOADES
28 Coord of Multicultural Student Affs .... Mr. Shaun GUNNELL
105 Director Web Services .... Mr. Neil CARRIER
37 Director of Financial Aid .... Ms. Cathy BELFIORE

Herzing University-Akron **(F)**
1600 S Arlington Street, 100, Akron OH 44306-3958
Telephone: (330) 724-1600 FICE Identification: 020695
Accreditation: &HLC, ADNUR, NURSE

† Regional accreditation is carried under the parent institution in Madison, WI.

Hiram College (G)
Box 67, Hiram OH 44234-0067
County: Portage FICE Identification: 003049
Unit ID: 203128
Telephone: (330) 569-3211 Carnegie Class: Bac-Diverse
FAX Number: (330) 569-5494 Calendar System: Other
URL: www.hiram.edu
Established: 1850 Annual Undergrad Tuition & Fees: $24,500
Enrollment: 1,110 Coed
Affiliation or Control: Independent Non-Profit IRS Status: 501(c)3
Highest Offering: Master's
Accreditation: HLC, CAEP, NURSE

01 President .... Dr. David P. HANEY
05 VP Academic Affairs/Dean of College .... Dr. Judy A. MUYSKENS
10 CFO/VP Business and Finance .... Ms. Nancy G. RUBIN
30 VP Development & Alumni Relations . Ms. Jennifer N. SCHULLER
32 Senior VP & Dean of Students .... Dr. Elizabeth M. OKUMA
84 VP of Enrollment Management .... Vacant
20 Associate Dean of the College .... Dr. Ella W. KIRK
20 Associate Dean Academic Affairs .... Dr. Jeffrey C. SWENSON
106 Exec Dir Adult & Online Programs .... Dr. LaShon N. SAWYER
06 Registrar .... Vacant
08 Director Library .... Ms. Janet VOGEL
111 Assoc VP Development & Alumni Rels .... Ms. Aimee B. BELL
102 Dir Foundation/Corp/Govt Relations .... Ms. Mary K. LANG
29 Exec Dir Development/Alumni Rels .... Ms. Jackie K. CRANDALL
07 Director of Admission .... Mr. Sherman C. DEAN
112 Director of Planned Giving .... Ms. Peggy A. PAINLEY
37 Director Financial Services .... Ms. Andrea L. CAPUTO
36 Director of Career Services .... Ms. Bethani M. BURKHART
121 Coordinator of Academic Development .... Mr. Adam D. SANTAVY
13 Executive Director IT .... Mr. Peter E. MAHONEY
108 Director of Institutional Research .... Dr. Laura A. VAN WORMER
23 Director of Health Services .... Ms. Asha L. GOODNER
41 Director of Athletics .... Mr. Todd W. HIBBS
15 Director Human Resources .... Ms. Karen HOLLAND
18 Director of the Physical Plant .... Mr. Ryan OLSZEWSKI
21 Controller .... Mr. Brett RIEBAU
35 Director of Campus Involvement .... Mr. D. Ellis RATES
38 Director Student Counseling .... Dr. Kevin P. FEISTHAMEL
28 Assoc Dean/Dir Diversity & Inclus .... Ms. Detra E. WEST
96 Director of Purchasing .... Ms. Martha A. SCHETTLER
26 Dir Strategic Marketing/Media Rels .... Ms. Jenelle BAYUS
27 Director of Communications .... Mr. Philip J. EAVES
105 Website Administrator .... Mr. Adam M. KALCIC
04 Executive Asst to President .... Ms. Candice K. PAINLEY
104 Study Away Coordinator .... Dr. Matthew F. NOTARIAN
19 Director Security/Safety .... Mr. Daniel FYNES
39 Dir Residential and Citizenship Edu .... Mr. Ed FRATO-SWEENEY
42 Chaplain .... Rev. Christopher J. MCCREIGHT

Hocking College (H)
3301 Hocking Parkway, Nelsonville OH 45764-9704
County: Athens FICE Identification: 007598
Unit ID: 203155
Telephone: (740) 753-3591 Carnegie Class: Assoc/MT-VT-Mix Trad/Non
FAX Number: (740) 753-7005 Calendar System: Semester
URL: www.hocking.edu
Established: 1968 Annual Undergrad Tuition & Fees (In-State): $5,180
Enrollment: 2,431 Coed
Affiliation or Control: State IRS Status: 501(c)3
Highest Offering: Associate Degree
Accreditation: HLC, ACBSP, ACFEI, ADNUR, DH, EMT, MAC, MLTAD, PTAA

01 President .... Dr. Betty YOUNG
10 Exec Director Finance/Treasurer .... Mr. Mark FULLER
32 VP Student Affairs/Campus Relations . Ms. Jacqueline HAGEROTT
15 Director Human Resources .... Ms. Elizabeth DENNIS
04 Executive Assistant to President .... Mr. Kyle FULLER
37 Interim Exec Director Financial Aid .... Ms. Mary RUSSELL
26 Exec Dir Mktg/Public Rels/Enrol Mgt .... Mr. Joshua MOORE
19 Chief Hocking College Police .... Ms. Tiffany TIMS
06 Registrar .... Ms. Kensey LOVE
18 Exec Dir Facilities/Skill Trades .... Mr. Bryan LUTZ
102 Director Foundation .... Mr. Douglas WELLS
100 Exec VP & Chief of Staff .... Mr. Jeff DAUBENMIRE

Hocking College Perry Campus **(I)**
5454 State Route 37, New Lexington OH 43764
Telephone: (740) 342-3337 Identification: 770359
Accreditation: &HLC

Hondros College of Nursing **(J)**
1810 Successful Drive, Fairborn OH 45324
Telephone: (937) 879-1940 Identification: 770751
Accreditation: ABHES

Hondros College of Nursing **(K)**
5005 Rockside Road, Suite 130, Independence OH 44131
Telephone: (216) 524-1143 Identification: 770750
Accreditation: ABHES

Hondros College of Nursing **(L)**
7600 Tyler's Place Boulevard, West Chester OH 45069
Telephone: (513) 508-3005 Identification: 770749
Accreditation: ABHES

Hondros College of Nursing (M)
4140 Executive Parkway, Westerville OH 43081-3855
County: Franklin FICE Identification: 040743
Unit ID: 203386
Telephone: (614) 508-7277 Carnegie Class: Spec-4-yr-Other Health
FAX Number: (614) 508-7280 Calendar System: Quarter
URL: www.hondros.edu
Established: 1981 Annual Undergrad Tuition & Fees: $18,847
Enrollment: 2,159 Coed
Affiliation or Control: Proprietary IRS Status: Proprietary
Highest Offering: Baccalaureate
Accreditation: ABHES

00 CEO .... Harry WILKINS
01 Campus Executive Director .... Kelly CAVANAGH
66 Dean/Director of Nursing .... Dr. Carol SULLIVAN
07 Director of Admission .... Robert MINTO
37 Financial Aid Manger .... Bakary SIDIBETH

International College of Broadcasting (N)
6 S Smithville Road, Dayton OH 45431-1898
County: Montgomery FICE Identification: 013132
Unit ID: 203289
Telephone: (937) 258-8251 Carnegie Class: Spec 2-yr-A&S
FAX Number: (937) 258-8714 Calendar System: Semester
URL: www.icb.edu
Established: 1968 Annual Undergrad Tuition & Fees: $15,520
Enrollment: 60 Coed
Affiliation or Control: Proprietary IRS Status: Proprietary
Highest Offering: Associate Degree
Accreditation: ACCSC

01 President/School Director .... J. Michael LEMASTER
05 Director of Education .... Ronda DOSTER
36 Dir Career Student Services .... Kenny PYLES
07 Director of Admissions .... Ben NEWLAND

John Carroll University (O)
1 John Carroll Boulevard, University Heights OH 44118
County: Cuyahoga FICE Identification: 003050
Unit ID: 203368
Telephone: (216) 397-1886 Carnegie Class: Masters/M
FAX Number: (216) 397-4256 Calendar System: Semester
URL: www.jcu.edu
Established: 1886 Annual Undergrad Tuition & Fees: $44,406
Enrollment: 3,278 Coed
Affiliation or Control: Roman Catholic IRS Status: 501(c)3
Highest Offering: Beyond Master's But Less Than Doctorate
Accreditation: HLC, CACREP, CAEP, CAEPN

01 President .... Dr. Alan MICIAK
88 Title IX Coordinator .... Dan FOTOPLES
04 Exec Assistant to the President .... Maura JOCHUM
88 VP for Univ Mission & Identity .... Dr. Edward PECK
43 General Counsel .... Colleen TREML
05 Provost & Academic Vice President .... Dr. Steven HERBERT
10 VP Finance & Administration .... Lauri STRIMKOVSKY
32 Vice President for Student Affairs .... Dr. Sherri CRAHEN
111 VP for University Advancement .... Doreen RILEY
84 VP for Enrollment Management .... Stephanie LEVENSON
26 AVP for Integrated Marketing & Comm .... Michael SCANLAN
18 Associate VP for Facilities .... Vacant
20 Vice Provost Academic Affairs .... Dr. James KRUKONES
108 Asst Provost Assessment & IE .... Dr. R. Todd BRUCE
121 Asst Provost Academic Advising .... Patrick MULLANE
37 Asst VP Enrollment/Financial Svcs .... Claudia WENZEL

30 AVP for Development ... Richard DAY
15 AVP Human Resources ... Jennifer RICK
84 AVP Enrollment Operations ... Steve VITATOE
08 Director of the Library ... Michelle MILLET
13 Chief Information Officer ... James BURKE
50 Acting Dean Boler College ... Dr. Scott MOORE
49 Dean College of Arts & Sciences ... Dr. Bonnie GUNZENHAUSER
58 Dean of Graduate Studies ... Dr. Rebecca DRENOVSKY
83 Assoc Dean Humanities & Soc Sci ... Dr. Rodney HESSINGER
81 Assoc Dean Sciences & Mathematics ... Dr. Michael MARTIN
109 Director of Auxiliary Services ... Rory HILL
21 Controller ... John CLIFFORD
25 Director of Sponsored Research ... Erica KENNEDY
114 Dir of Budget & Financial Analysis ... Jennifer DILLON
112 Senior Director of Major Gifts ... Mary RYCYNA
29 Exec Dir of Alumni Rel & Annual Giv ... David VITATOE
31 Dir Ctr for Service & Social Action ... Katherine FEELY, SND
102 Dir Foundation Rels & Grant Writing ... Pamela GEORGE-MERRILL
86 Manager of Govt & Comm Relations ... Kate MALONE
19 Director & Chief of JCUPD ... Brian HURD
09 Director of Institutional Research ... Maria O'CONNOR
117 Dir Regulatory Affairs & Risk Mgmt ... Garry HOMANY
22 Affirm Action Officer for Faculty ... Dr. James KRUKONES
91 Director Enterprise Applications ... John SULLY
24 Center Digital Media Fac Liaison ... Dr. Jay TARBY
119 Data Security Engineer ... James SPITZNAGEL
93 Dir Ctr for Student Div & Inclusion ... Vacant
23 Dir of Student Health & Wellness ... Janet KREVH
92 Director Honors Program ... Dr. Angela CANDA
06 Registrar ... Michelle REYNARD
38 Director Univ Counseling Services ... Dr. Mark ONUSKO
39 Director of Residence Life ... Lisa BROWN CORNELIUS
41 Sr Director Athletics & Recreation ... Michelle MORGAN
42 Director of Campus Ministry ... John SCARANO

Kent State University Kent Campus (A)

PO Box 5190, Kent OH 44242-0001
County: Portage FICE Identification: 003051
Unit ID: 203517
Telephone: (330) 672-3000 Carnegie Class: DU-Higher
FAX Number: (330) 672-2190 Calendar System: Semester
URL: www.kent.edu
Established: 1910 Annual Undergrad Tuition & Fees (In-State): $11,009
Enrollment: 26,822 Coed
Affiliation or Control: State IRS Status: 501(c)3
Highest Offering: Doctorate
Accreditation: HLC, AAB, ART, AUD, CAATE, CACREP, CAEPN, CAPRT, CIDA, CLPSY, CONST, DANCE, DIETD, DIETI, EXSC, JOUR, LIB, LSAR, MUS, NAIT, NURSE, PH, POD, SCPSY, SP, SPAA, THEA

01 President ... Dr. Todd DIACON
05 Senior Vice President/Provost ... Dr. Melody TANKERSLEY
10 Senior Vice Pres Finance & Admin ... Dr. Mark M. POLATAJKO
15 Vice Pres Human Resources ... Mr. Jack WITT
111 Interim VP Inst Advancement ... Ms. Valoree VARGO
32 Vice Pres Student Affairs ... Dr. Lamar R. HYLTON
84 Interim VP Enrollment Management ... Dr. Sean BROGHAMMER
26 Interim VP University Relations ... Ms. Rebecca MURPHY
46 Interim VP Research ... Dr. Doug DELAHANTY
13 Vice Pres Information Services/CIO ... Mr. John M. RATHJE
28 VP Diversity/Equity/Inclusion ... Dr. Amoaba GOODEN
20 Dean Undergraduate Studies ... Dr. Eboni PRINGLE
35 Student Ombuds ... Ms. Amy QUILLIN
124 Assoc VP Univ Outreach & Engagement ... Dr. Dana LAWLESS-ANDRIC
20 Assoc Provost Faculty Affairs ... Mr. Kevin WEST
29 Asst Vice Pres Alumni Affairs ... Mrs. Lori RANDORF
16 Human Resources Director-CPM ... Mr. David DIXON
06 Registrar ... Mr. Chris DORSTEN
43 Vice Pres General Counsel ... Mr. Willis WALKER
100 VP and University Secretary ... Ms. Charlene K. REED
41 Director Intercollegiate Athletics ... Mr. Randale RICHMOND
118 Director of Compliance & Benefits ... Vacant
37 AVP Enroll Mgmt/Student Fin Aid ... Ms. Brenda BURKE
07 Assoc VP Enroll Mgmt/Admissions ... Mr. Sean BROGHAMMER
19 Director of Public Safety ... Mr. Dean TONDIGLIA
12 Interim Dean Trumbull Campus ... Dr. Daniel PALMER
96 Director of Procurement ... Mr. Timothy J. KONCZAL
49 Interim Dean Arts & Sciences ... Dr. Mandy MUNRO-STASIUK
50 Dean of Business Administration ... Dr. Deborah F. SPAKE
53 Dean EHHS ... Dr. James HANNON
57 Dean of the Arts ... Dr. John R. CRAWFORD-SPINELLI
66 Interim Dean College of Nursing ... Dr. Denice SHEEHAN
51 Asst VP Continuing & Distance Educ ... Ms. Valerie I. KELLY
92 Dean Honors College ... Dr. Alison SMITH
08 Dean of University Libraries ... Mr. Kenneth BURHANNA
48 Dean Architecture/Environ Design ... Mr. Mark MISTUR
60 Dean Col of Comm & Information ... Dr. Amy REYNOLDS
54 Dean Aeronautics & Engineering ... Dr. Christina BLOEBAUM
88 Dean College of Podiatric Medicine ... Dr. Allan BOIKE
21 Director Business Admin Svcs ... Mr. Mark M. MATEJCIK
08 Library Director-CPM ... Mrs. Donna M. PERZESKI
18 Dir Opers Satellite Facilities CPM ... Mr. Dan RIDGWAY
04 Assistant to the President ... Ms. Diana BOLDON
101 Board Ops Mgr/Asst to EO ... Ms. Charlene NICHOL
86 Director Government Relations ... Mr. Nicholas GATTOZZI

Kent State University at Ashtabula (B)

3300 Lake Road W, Ashtabula OH 44004-2299
Telephone: (440) 964-3322 FICE Identification: 003052
Accreditation: &HLC, ADNUR, COARC, OTA, PTAA, RAD

† Regional accreditation is carried under the parent institution in Kent, OH.

Kent State University East Liverpool Campus (C)

400 E Fourth Street, East Liverpool OH 43920-3497
Telephone: (330) 385-3805 FICE Identification: 003056
Accreditation: &HLC, ADNUR, OTA, PTAA

† Regional accreditation is carried under the parent institution in Kent, OH.

Kent State University Geauga Campus (D)

14111 Claridon-Troy Road,
Burton Township OH 44021-9500
Telephone: (440) 834-4187 FICE Identification: 003059
Accreditation: &HLC, ADNUR

† Regional accreditation is carried under the parent institution in Kent, OH.

Kent State University Salem Campus (E)

2491 State Route 45 South, Salem OH 44460-9412
Telephone: (330) 332-0361 FICE Identification: 003061
Accreditation: &HLC, RAD, RTT

† Regional accreditation is carried under the parent institution in Kent, OH.

Kent State University Stark Campus (F)

6000 Frank Avenue NW, North Canton OH 44720-9988
Telephone: (330) 499-9600 FICE Identification: 003054
Accreditation: &HLC

† Regional accreditation is carried under the parent institution in Kent, OH.

Kent State University Trumbull Campus (G)

4314 Mahoning Avenue, NW, Warren OH 44483-1998
Telephone: (330) 847-0571 FICE Identification: 003064
Accreditation: &HLC

† Regional accreditation is carried under the parent institution in Kent, OH.

Kent State University Tuscarawas Campus (H)

330 University Drive, NE,
New Philadelphia OH 44663-9403
Telephone: (330) 339-3391 FICE Identification: 003062
Accreditation: &HLC, ADNUR

† Regional accreditation is carried under the parent institution in Kent, OH.

Kenyon College (I)

106 College-Park Street, Gambier OH 43022-9623
County: Knox FICE Identification: 003065
Unit ID: 203535
Telephone: (740) 427-5000 Carnegie Class: Bac-A&S
FAX Number: (740) 427-3077 Calendar System: Semester
URL: www.kenyon.edu
Established: 1824 Annual Undergrad Tuition & Fees: $55,020
Enrollment: 1,615 Coed
Affiliation or Control: Independent Non-Profit IRS Status: 501(c)3
Highest Offering: Baccalaureate
Accreditation: HLC

01 President ... Dr. Sean DECATUR
05 Provost ... Dr. Jeff BOWMAN
111 Vice President Advancement ... Ms. Colleen GARLAND
10 Vice President for Finance ... Mr. Todd E. BURSON
08 Vice Pres Library & Info Svcs ... Mr. Ronald K. GRIGGS
100 Chief of Staff ... Ms. Susan MORSE
112 Assoc VP for Planned Giving ... Mr. Kyle W. HENDERSON
32 Dean of Students ... Ms. Robin HART RUTHENBECK
07 Dean of Admissions/Fin Aid ... Ms. Diane ANCI
20 Associate Provost ... Dr. Sheryl HEMKIN
06 Registrar/Dean Academic Support ... Ms. Ellen K. HARBOURT
26 Vice President for Communications ... Ms. Janet MARSDEN
29 Assoc VP Alumni & Parent Engagement ... Mr. Shawn DAILEY
37 Director of Financial Aid ... Mr. Craig SLAUGHTER
38 Dir Cox Health & Counseling Center ... Mr. Christopher SMITH
15 Director of Human Resources ... Ms. Jennifer G. CABRAL
42 Director of Religious/Spiritual ... Rabbi Marc BRAGIN
18 VP Facility/Planning/Sustainability ... Mr. Ian SMITH
22 Civil Rights/Title IX Coordinator ... Ms. Samantha HUGHES
19 Director of Campus Safety ... Mr. Michael SWEAZEY
09 Director of Institutional Research ... Ms. Erika M. FARFAN
21 Manager of Business Services ... Mr. Frederick S. LINGER
28 Director Diversity/Equity/Inclusion ... Mr. A. Chris KENNERLY
101 Director of Board Relations ... Ms. Kathryn LAKE
04 Executive Asst to President ... Ms. Mary Ellen O'MEARA
41 Athletic Director ... Ms. Jill MCCARTNEY

Kettering College (J)

3737 Southern Boulevard, Kettering OH 45429-1299
County: Montgomery FICE Identification: 007035
Unit ID: 203544
Telephone: (937) 395-8601 Carnegie Class: Spec-4-yr-Other Health
FAX Number: (937) 395-8106 Calendar System: Semester
URL: www.kc.edu
Established: 1967 Annual Undergrad Tuition & Fees: $13,824
Enrollment: 763 Coed
Affiliation or Control: Seventh-day Adventist IRS Status: 501(c)3
Highest Offering: Doctorate
Accreditation: HLC, ARCPA, COARC, DMS, NUR, OT, PAST, RAD

00 Chairman of the Board ... Mr. Walter SACKETT
01 President ... Dr. Nate BRANDSTATER
15 Vice President Human Resources ... Mr. Timothy DUTTON
05 Dean for Academic Affairs ... Dr. Rafael CANIZALES
32 Dean of Student Success ... Mr. Adam BROWN
102 President of Foundation ... Mr. Rick THIE, II
84 Assoc Dean Enrollment Mgmt ... Mrs. Jessica BEANS
121 Assoc Dean Student Success ... Mr. Ben HOTELLING
10 Chief Business Officer ... Mrs. Wendi BARBER
21 Director of Finance/Administration ... Mr. Nicholas HENSON
06 Registrar ... Mrs. Robin VANDERBILT
37 Director Student Financial Aid ... Mrs. Kim RAWLINS
40 Manager Bookstore ... Mrs. Jessica OLDFIELD
42 Campus Chaplain ... Mr. Steve CARLSON
32 Director Student Life ... Mr. Kris HARTER
26 Public Relations Officer ... Ms. Lauren BROOKS
08 Director of Library ... Ms. Pamela STEVENS
07 Director of Admissions ... Mrs. Katrina HILL
36 Director Career Services ... Mr. Benjamin HOTELLING
13 Senior Information Officer ... Mr. Jim NESBIT

Lake Erie College (K)

391 W Washington Street, Painesville OH 44077-3389
County: Lake FICE Identification: 003066
Unit ID: 203580
Telephone: (440) 375-7000 Carnegie Class: Masters/M
FAX Number: (440) 375-7005 Calendar System: Semester
URL: www.lec.edu
Established: 1856 Annual Undergrad Tuition & Fees: $33,172
Enrollment: 949 Coed
Affiliation or Control: Independent Non-Profit IRS Status: 501(c)3
Highest Offering: Master's
Accreditation: HLC, ARCPA, CAEPT, IACBE

01 President ... Dr. Brian POSLER
05 Vice Pres for Academic Affairs/CAO ... Bryan DEPOY
10 Vice Pres Administration & Finance ... Brian DIRK
111 VP for Institutional Advancement ... Jennifer SCHULLER
07 VP Admission ... Mike BROWN
53 Dean School of Educ & Prof Studies ... Dr. Katharine DELAVAN
50 Dean School of Business ... Dr. Jennifer KINNAIRD
88 Dean School of Equine Studies ... Dr. Pam HESS
79 Dean School of Arts/Human & SS ... Dr. Jennifer SWARTZ-LEVINE
81 Dean School of Nat Sci & Math ... Dr. Jonathan TEDESCO
06 Registrar ... Amanda FORDYCE
107 Director Prof Development ... Lisa STRAUSBAUGH
88 Director Physician Assistant Pgm ... Sean KRAMER
36 Dir Career Dev/Experiential Lrng ... Eric EVANS
13 Director of Information Technology ... Brad LUHTA
38 Director Student Success Center ... Dr. John SPIESMAN
18 Director Physical Plant ... Herb DILL
29 Director Alumni Relations ... Debra REMINGTON
41 Director of Athletics ... Molly HOFFMAN
08 Director Lincoln Library ... Jeanna PURSES
19 Director Security ... Richard KLINE
40 Bookstore Manager ... Natalie SCALA
04 President's Office Manager ... Leah JACKSON
31 Director College Events ... Catherine BEISEL
30 Director of Development ... John MCCREERY
37 Director Student Financial Aid ... Tricia PANGONIS
26 Exec Dir Public Relations/Marketing ... Angela DELPRETE
39 Dir Resident Life/Student Housing ... Kimberly ROBARE

Lakeland Community College (L)

7700 Clocktower Drive, Kirtland OH 44094-5198
County: Lake FICE Identification: 006804
Unit ID: 203599
Telephone: (440) 525-7000 Carnegie Class: Assoc/HT-High Non
FAX Number: (440) 525-7651 Calendar System: Semester
URL: www.lakelandcc.edu
Established: 1967 Annual Undergrad Tuition & Fees (In-District): $4,347
Enrollment: 5,331 Coed
Affiliation or Control: State/Local IRS Status: 501(c)3
Highest Offering: Associate Degree
Accreditation: HLC, ADNUR, CAHIIM, COARC, DH, EMT, HT, MAC, MLTAD, NAEYC, OTA, POLYT, RAD, SURGT

01 President ... Dr. Morris W. BEVERAGE, JR.
05 Exec VP & Provost ... Dr. Laura BARNARD
10 Exec Vice Pres/Treasurer ... Mr. Michael E. MAYHER
100 Chief of Staff/Sr VP Inst Effectiv ... Ms. Catherine BUSH
26 Chief Commun Ofcr/VP College Rels ... Ms. Dawn M. PLANTE
20 Assoc Provost Teach & Learn ... Dr. Deborah L. HARDY
32 Assoc VP Student Dev/Dean of Stdnts ... Mr. Richard J. NOVOTNY
81 Dean of Arts and Sciences ... Mr. Adam CLOUTIER
76 Dean of Health Technologies ... Dr. Deborah L. HARDY
88 Int Dir for Articulation & Transfer ... Ms. Barbara FRIEDT
21 Deputy Treasurer & Dir for Budget ... Mr. Thomas REYNOLDS
13 CIO Administrative Technologies ... Mr. Rick PENNY
21 Controller ... Mr. Michael GRAFF

18 Director for Facilities Management Mr. Bert DIEHL
19 Chief of Police Mr. Stephen GAGLIARDI
124 Asst Provost Strategic Retention Ms. Stephanie BROWN
84 Senior Dir Enrollment Operations Ms. Melissa A. AMSPAUGH
35 Director of Student Activities Mr. Mario PETITTI
30 Dir Development/Alumni Relations Mr. Gregory SANDERS
96 Director of Purchasing Mr. Tom A. KIRCHNER
43 General Legal Counsel Mr. Michael FISHER
86 Director Government Relations Ms. Amy SABATH
37 Dir for Financial Aid & Enrollment Ms. Ann Marie GRUBER

Lakewood University (A)

2231 North Taylor Road, Cleveland Heights OH 44112
County: Cuyahoga Identification: 666715
Telephone: (800) 517-0857 Carnegie Class: Not Classified
FAX Number: (216) 803-9899 Calendar System: Other
URL: www.lakewood.edu
Established: 1998 Annual Undergrad Tuition & Fees: N/A
Enrollment: N/A Coed
Affiliation or Control: Independent Non-Profit IRS Status: 501(c)3
Highest Offering: Associate Degree
Accreditation: DEAC

00 President and Founder Ms. Tanya HAGGINS
05 Academic Dean Mr. James GEPPERTH
30 Vice President of Business Develop Mr. Isaac HAGGINS
11 Vice President of Operations Mr. Tommy SUTTON-LOVETT

Lorain County Community College (B)

1005 N Abbe Road, Elyria OH 44035-1691
County: Lorain FICE Identification: 003068
Unit ID: 203748
Telephone: (440) 365-5222 Carnegie Class: Assoc/HT-Mix Trad/Non
FAX Number: (440) 365-6519 Calendar System: Semester
URL: www.lorainccc.edu
Established: 1963 Annual Undergrad Tuition & Fees (In-District): $4,400
Enrollment: 10,138 Coed
Affiliation or Control: State/Local IRS Status: 501(c)3
Highest Offering: Baccalaureate
Accreditation: HLC, ADNUR, ART, DH, DMS, EMT, MAC, MLTAD, OTA, PNUR, PTAA, RAD, SURGT

01 President Dr. Marcia J. BALLINGER
46 VP Strategic & Institutional Devel Ms. Tracy A. GREEN
05 Provost/VP Acad & Learner Svcs Dr. Jonathan N. DRYDEN
10 Vice President Admin Svcs/Treasurer Mr. Jonathan VOLPE
88 Assoc Prov University Partnership Vacant
08 Dean Library/Instruction Media Vacant
84 Assoc Prov Enroll/Fin Career Svcs Ms. Marisa VERNON WHITE
13 Chief Information Tech Officer Mr. Donald HUFFMAN
15 Director Human Resources Mr. Keith BROWN
88 Dir Talent and Business Innovation Ms. Terri B. SANDU
18 Director of Physical Plant Mr. Leo MAHONEY
57 Dir Stocker Humanit/Fine Arts Ctr Ms. Janet HERMAN-BARLOW
54 Dean Engr/Business & Info Tech Ms. Kelly ZELESNIK
76 Int Dean Allied Health & Wellness Dr. Hope MOON
79 Int Dean Arts/Humanities Dr. Karin HOOKS
81 Dean Science/Mathematics Mr. Aaron WEISS
83 Dean Social Science/Human Svc Dr. Denise DOUGLAS
06 Registrar Ms. Sun Kyong JAMERSON
101 Executive Assoc Board Liaison Ms. Jocelyn WIESER
19 Director of Campus Security Mr. Ken COLLINS
26 Dir School & Community Partnership Ms. Cynthia KUSHNER
102 LCC Foundation Exec Director Ms. Lisa BROWN
31 Director Strategic Cmty Engagement Ms. Alison MUSSER

Lourdes University (C)

6832 Convent Boulevard, Sylvania OH 43560-2898
County: Lucas FICE Identification: 003069
Unit ID: 203757
Telephone: (419) 885-3211 Carnegie Class: Masters/S
FAX Number: (419) 882-3987 Calendar System: Semester
URL: www.lourdes.edu
Established: 1958 Annual Undergrad Tuition & Fees: $25,644
Enrollment: 1,253 Coed
Affiliation or Control: Roman Catholic IRS Status: 501(c)3
Highest Offering: Doctorate
Accreditation: HLC, ANEST, CAEPT, IACBE, NURSE, SW

01 President Dr. Mary Ann GAWELEK
00 President Emerita Sr. Ann Francis KLIMKOWSKI
04 Exec Admin Asst to the President Ms. Theresa HOLUP
05 Provost Dr. Terry KELLER
10 Vice President of Finance Mr. Randy ROTHENBUHLER
42 VP for Mission & Ministry Sr. Barbara VANO, OSF
111 Vice President for Inst Advancement Ms. Mary SABIN
84 VP of Enrollment Management Mr. Jeffrey LILES
49 Dean College of Arts & Sciences Dr. Kate BEUTEL
53 Dean College of Social Services Dr. Jami CURLEY
66 Dean College of Nursing Vacant
50 Dean Col Business & Leadership Dr. David BURKITT
32 VP Student Affairs/Dean of Students Mr. Greg KNESER
39 Asst Dean of Residence Life Mr. T. Todd MASMAN
37 Director of Financial Aid Ms. Callie ZAKE
26 Director of University Relations Ms. Helene SHEETS
08 Director of Library Services Sr. Sandra RUTKOWSKI
06 Registrar Vacant
13 Chief Information Officer Mr. David MASSEY
15 Director of Human Resources Ms. Chantell CARGILE

36 Director of Career Services Ms. Andrea BROWN
21 Director of Finance Mr. Michael DETER
30 Director of Donor Relations Ms. Brittany TELANDER
18 Director of Facilities & Grounds Mr. Michael CRAVENS
22 Title IX Coordinator Mr. Terry STRODE
19 Director of Campus Security Mr. Benjamin TUCKER
07 Director of Undergrad Admissions Ms. Callie ZAKE
41 VP of Athletics Ms. Janet EATON
121 Dean of Student Success Ms. Alisa SMITH
102 Grants and Strategic Initiatives Ms. Cindy JEWELL

Malone University (D)

2600 Cleveland Avenue NW, Canton OH 44709-3308
County: Stark FICE Identification: 003072
Unit ID: 203775
Telephone: (330) 471-8100 Carnegie Class: Masters/M
FAX Number: (330) 471-8478 Calendar System: Semester
URL: www.malone.edu
Established: 1892 Annual Undergrad Tuition & Fees: $32,416
Enrollment: 1,463 Coed
Affiliation or Control: Friends IRS Status: 501(c)3
Highest Offering: Master's
Accreditation: HLC, ACBSP, CACREP, CAEP, MUS, NURSE, SW

01 President Dr. David A. KING
10 Vice Pres for Finance/CFO Mrs. Katie A. ROBBINS
05 Provost Dr. Gregory J. MILLER
32 Chief Student Development Officer Ms. Melody K. SCOTT
111 Vice Pres for Advancement Dr. Patrick S. ROBERTS
26 Vice Pres for Marketing & Comm Mr. Timothy A. BRYAN
84 Vice Pres for Enrollment Management Dr. Jason R. MOYER
66 Chair of Nursing/Chief Nurse Admin Dr. Debra A. LEE
21 Controller Ms. Shari A. APPEL
06 Registrar Mr. Gary L. PHELPS
07 Director of Admissions Mrs. Linda A. KURTZ HOFFMAN
29 Dir Alumni/Constituent Engagement Ms. Megan J. MAUCK
110 Dir of Adv Rsrch/Foundation Grants Mrs. Paula M. CALHOUN
09 Director of Institutional Research Dr. Matthew P. PHELPS
37 Director of Financial Aid Mrs. Pamela S. PUSTAY
41 Athletic Director Ms. Tanya C. HOCKMAN
08 Director of Library Ms. Rebecca L. FORT
106 Exec Director of Distance Learning Mr. John W. KOSHMIDER, III
93 Director of Multicultural Services Vacant
104 Dir Ctr for Intercultural Studies Dr. Elizabeth P. ROE
19 Director Security/Safety Mr. David W. BURNIP
13 Chief Information Officer Mr. M. Adam KLEMANN
90 Senior Network Engineer Mr. James M. SHAFFER
42 Director of Spiritual Formation Rev Dr. Linda J. LEON
105 Webmaster/Photo/Videographer Mr. Joshua C. MCMANAWAY
40 Bookstore Manager Mrs. Kathy L. SECREST
04 Exec Asst to Pres/Asst to Board Mrs. Teresa L. PITTINGER
88 Dir of Inst Reporting & Data Mgmt Mrs. Sara K. BURKE
92 Director of Honors Program Dr. Steven M. JENSEN
89 Dir of the College Experience Pgm Dr. Marcia K. EVERETT
38 Director of Counseling Center Mr. Timothy T. MORBER
23 Health Center Director Ms. Rebecca K. RODAK
15 Director of Human Resources Ms. Patrice D. YACKO

Marietta College (E)

215 Fifth Street, Marietta OH 45750-4033
County: Washington FICE Identification: 003073
Unit ID: 203845
Telephone: (740) 376-4000 Carnegie Class: Bac-Diverse
FAX Number: (800) 331-7896 Calendar System: Semester
URL: www.marietta.edu
Established: 1835 Annual Undergrad Tuition & Fees: $36,764
Enrollment: 1,254 Coed
Affiliation or Control: Independent Non-Profit IRS Status: 501(c)3
Highest Offering: Master's
Accreditation: HLC, ARCPA, CAATE, CAEP, MUS

01 President Dr. William N. RUUD
05 Provost/Dean of Faculty Dr. Janet L. BLAND
10 VP for Administration & Finance Ms. Michele L. MARRA
111 VP for Advancement Dr. Joshua JACOBS
32 VP Student Life/Chf Diversity Ofcr Dr. Richard K. DANFORD
84 VP for Enrollment Mgmt Mr. Scot SCHAEFER
88 Dean McDonough Ctr for Leadership Dr. Robert MCMANUS
101 Secretary to the Board of Trustees Dr. Mark MILLER
08 Director of Library Dr. N. Douglas ANDERSON
07 Director of Admissions Ms. Katie FENNELL
18 Director of Physical Plant Mr. Rodney WOOD
06 Registrar Ms. Tina K. PERDUE
15 Director of Human Resources Vacant
19 Chief of Campus Police Mr. James S. WEAVER
26 Exec Dir of Strategic Comm & Mktg Mr. Thomas D. PERRY
09 Institutional Researcher Mr. William (Bill) CLARK
36 Director of the Career Center Ms. Betsy KNOTT
41 Director of Athletics Mr. Larry R. HISER
13 Director of Information Technology Mr. Aaron COWDERY
63 PA Program Director Mr. David SAMS
104 Director of Education Abroad Ms. Christy BURKE
25 Grants Officer Ms. Chantal CENTOFANTI-FIELDS
51 Continuing Education Ms. Tina K. HICKMAN
35 Associate Dean of Students Ms. KJ MCCONNELL
04 Executive Coordinator to President Ms. Paula LEWIS
29 Alumni Relations Dr. Joshua JACOBS
28 Assoc Dean of Stdnts/Chief Div Ofcr Mr. Tony MAYLE
30 Director of Development Mr. Josh JACOBS
37 Assistant VP for Student Enrollment Ms. Emily SCHUCK

44 Senior Director Annual Giving Ms. Kathryn GLOOR
38 Director Student Counseling Ms. Andrea EUSER
39 Dir Resident Life/Student Housing Ms. KJ MCCONNELL
86 Director Government Relations Mr. Tom PERRY

Marion Technical College (F)

1467 Mount Vernon Avenue, Marion OH 43302-5694
County: Marion FICE Identification: 010736
Unit ID: 203881
Telephone: (740) 389-4636 Carnegie Class: Assoc/HVT-High Non
FAX Number: (740) 389-6136 Calendar System: Semester
URL: www.mtc.edu
Established: 1971 Annual Undergrad Tuition & Fees (In-State): $5,565
Enrollment: 2,147 Coed
Affiliation or Control: State IRS Status: 501(c)3
Highest Offering: Associate Degree
Accreditation: HLC, ADNUR, CAHIIM, DMS, MAC, MLTAD, OTA, PTAA, RAD, SURGT

01 President Dr. Ryan MCCALL
05 VP Academic Affairs & Student Svcs Vacant
111 Vice Pres Planning & Advancement Dr. Amy ADAMS
10 VP Business Affairs & CFO Ms. Rhonda WARD
45 Chief Strategy Officer Dr. Bob HAAS
100 Chief of Staff & Govt Relations Ms. Laura WOUGHTER
13 Executive Director IT Operations Mr. Steve DUVALL
26 Director of Marketing Mr. Justin DEAN
06 Registrar Ms. Kristy TAYLOR
37 Director Student Financial Aid Ms. Deb LANGDON
07 Director of Admissions Mr. Tony BOX
102 Director of Foundation Mr. Mike STUCKEY
121 Director of Student Advising Ms. Laura EMERICK
15 Director of Human Resources Ms. Cretia JOHNSON
103 Director of Workforce Solutions Mr. Mike AUGENSTEIN
88 Director Student Support Programs Ms. Kathy RICE
54 Director of Engineering Technology Dr. Elizabeth AZHIKANNICKAL
72 Dean Tech & Professional Programs Ms. Debbie STARK
49 Dean of Arts & Sciences Vacant
66 Director of Nursing Technology Ms. Cynthia HARTMAN
76 Dir Physical Therapist Asst Pgm Mr. Chad HENSEL
76 Dir Occupational Therapy Mr. Josh LINE
88 Director of College Credit Plus Ms. Callum MORRIS
18 Coord Facil Improvements/Operations Ms. Leeann GRAU

Mercy College of Ohio (G)

2221 Madison Avenue, Toledo OH 43604
County: Lucas FICE Identification: 030970
Unit ID: 203960
Telephone: (419) 251-1313 Carnegie Class: Spec-4-yr-Other Health
FAX Number: N/A Calendar System: Semester
URL: www.mercycollege.edu
Established: 1992 Annual Undergrad Tuition & Fees: $18,950
Enrollment: 1,561 Coed
Affiliation or Control: Roman Catholic IRS Status: 501(c)3
Highest Offering: Master's
Accreditation: HLC, ADNUR, ARCPA, CAHIIM, EMT, NURSE, POLYT, RAD

01 President Dr. Susan WAJERT
05 VP Acad Affs/Dean of Faculty Dr. Kenneth RYALLS
32 VP Student Affs/Dean of Student Mr. Marc ADKINS
66 Dean Nursing and Allied Hlth Dr. Elizabeth SPRUNK
76 Dean of Arts and Sciences Dr. Barbara STOOS
58 Dean of Graduate Studies Dr. Kim WATSON
117 Dir of Compliance/Risk Mgmt Ms. Leslie ERWIN
13 Dir of College Info Tech Services Mr. Jeff METZGER
10 Chief Financial Officer Ms. Andrea FLEMING
111 Int Director College Advancement Ms. Sandy SNYDER
84 VP Strategic Plng/Enroll Mgmt & IE Ms. Lori EDGEWORTH
08 Director Library/Resource Services Ms. Rebecca DANIELS
09 Dir Inst Research/Registrar Mr. Mark MCKELLIP
37 Financial Aid Director Ms. Julie LESLIE
26 Director of Communication Ms. Denise HUDGIN
42 Dir Campus Ministry & Svcs Learning Ms. Annie DEVINE
21 Business Manager Ms. Diane RAHN
18 Manager of Operations Ms. Sherri BOGGS
29 Coordinator Alumni Relations Ms. Hannah BOHN
121 Assistant Dean of Student Success Ms. Lisa SANCRANT
36 Dir of Career/Prof Dev & Retention Ms. Kristen PORTER
106 Dir of Distance Education Dr. Dan FRENCH
28 Dir of Diversity & Inclusion Vacant
04 Administrative Asst to President Ms. Andrea RAFTERY
07 Director of Admissions Ms. Amy MERGEN

Methodist Theological School in Ohio (H)

3081 Columbus Pike, Delaware OH 43015-3211
County: Delaware FICE Identification: 003075
Unit ID: 203997
Telephone: (740) 363-1146 Carnegie Class: Spec-4-yr-Faith
FAX Number: (740) 362-3135 Calendar System: 4/1/4
URL: www.mtso.edu
Established: 1958 Annual Graduate Tuition & Fees: N/A
Enrollment: 139 Coed
Affiliation or Control: United Methodist IRS Status: 501(c)3
Highest Offering: Doctorate; No Undergraduates
Accreditation: HLC, THEOL

01 President ... Rev. Jay A. RUNDELL
05 Dean and VP for Academic Affairs ... Dr. Valerie BRIDGEMAN
20 Associate Dean ... Dr. Yvonne ZIMMERMAN
11 Dir Strategic Init & Operations ... Ms. Leigh PRECISE
10 Controller ... Ms. Sarah MOUCH
26 Director of Communications ... Mr. Danny RUSSELL
84 Director of Enrollment Management ... Rev. Benjamin HALL
30 Director of Development ... Rev. Claudine LEARY
08 Director of the Library ... Ms. Elonda CLAY
06 Registrar ... Mr. Lee RICHARDS
37 Director of Financial Aid ... Ms. Molly HOFFMAN
32 Director of Student Services ... Ms. Kristin LOFRUMENTO
13 Director Information Technology ... Mr. Matthew REHM
18 Facilities Manager ... Mr. Keith HUFFMAN
15 Coordinator of Human Resources ... Ms. Erin WIGGINS

Miami University (A)

501 E High Street, Oxford OH 45056-1846
County: Butler FICE Identification: 003077
Unit ID: 204024
Telephone: (513) 529-1809 Carnegie Class: DU-Higher
FAX Number: (513) 529-3841 Calendar System: Semester
URL: www.miamioh.edu
Established: 1809 Annual Undergrad Tuition & Fees (In-State): $16,223
Enrollment: 18,880 Coed
Affiliation or Control: State IRS Status: 501(c)3
Highest Offering: Doctorate
Accreditation: HLC, ART, CAATE, CAEP, CIDA, CLPSY, DIETD, DIETI, IPSY, MUS, NURSE, SP, SW, THEA

01 President ... Dr. Gregory CRAWFORD
05 Provost/VP Academic Affairs ... Dr. Jason OSBORNE
10 Sr VP Finance & Bus Svcs/Treasurer ... Dr. David CREAMER
32 Vice President Student Affairs ... Dr. Jayne E. BROWNELL
111 VP University Advancement ... Mr. Tom HERBERT
13 VP Information Technology/CIO ... Mr. David SEIDL
15 Assoc VP Academic Personnel ... Ms. Ruth GROOM
20 Assoc Provost for Undergrad Studies ... Dr. Carolyn A. HAYNES
35 Dean of Students ... Dr. Kimberly MOORE
26 VP/Chief Mktg/Communications Ofcr ... Ms. Michele G. SPARKS
18 Assoc VP Facilities Planning & Op ... Mr. Cody J. POWELL
84 VP Enroll Mgmt/Student Success ... Mr. Brent SHOCK
28 VP Inst Diversity ... Vacant
09 Asst VP Institutional Research ... Dr. William E. KNIGHT
29 Assoc Vice Pres Alumni Relations ... Mrs. Kim TAVARES
88 Director Institutional Relations ... Mr. Randi Malcolm THOMAS
27 Dir Univ Communications ... Ms. Claire M. WAGNER
100 Secy Board/Exec Asst to President ... Mr. Ted O. PICKERILL
49 Dean College Arts & Science ... Dr. Christopher A. MAKAROFF, JR.
53 Dean Education/Health & Society ... Dr. Michael DANTLEY
50 Dean Farmer Sch of Business ... Dr. Marc A. RUBIN
57 Dean College of Creative Arts ... Dr. Elizabeth R. MULLENIX
54 Dean College of Engr & Computing ... Dr. Beena SUKUMARAN
08 Dean University Libraries ... Mr. Jerome CONLEY
58 Dean Graduate School/VP Research ... Dr. James T. ORIS
49 Dean Col of Lib Arts & Applied Sci ... Dr. Catherine U. BISHOP-CLARK
07 Assoc VP Strat Enroll Mgt/Mrkting ... Vacant
51 Asst Provost Global Init & Cont Ed ... Ms. Cheryl D. YOUNG
108 Dir Center for Teaching Excellence ... Dr. Ellen J. YEZIERSKI
88 Univ Dir Liberal Educ/ Assessment ... Dr. Shelly JARRETT BROMBERG
92 Univ Dir Honors & Scholars Program ... Dr. Zeb BAKER
16 Assoc VP Human Resources ... Ms. Dawn FAHNER
23 Medical Director Student Health Svc ... Vacant
104 Dir Intl Student & Scholar ... Ms. Molly HEIDEMANN
06 University Registrar ... Ms. Mandy L. EUEN
36 Asst VP Career Exploration/Success ... Ms. Jen FRANCHAK
38 Director Student Counseling Service ... Dr. John A. WARD
19 Chief of Police/Dir Public Safety ... Mr. John MCCANDLESS
96 Chief Procurement Officer ... Mr. Mark TAYLOR
43 University General Counsel ... Ms. Robin L. PARKER
22 Director Equity & Equal Opportunity ... Ms. Kenya D. ASH
41 Director Intercollegiate Athletics ... Mr. David A. SAYLER
17 Director Student Wellness ... Ms. Rebecca BAUDRY YOUNG
04 Assistant to the President ... Ms. Dawn TSIRELIS
37 Student Financial Aid Director ... Vacant
102 Asst Dir Corporate/Foundation Rels ... Mr. Ryan GILLEY
109 Assoc VP Auxiliaries ... Vacant
44 Asst VP Dev Ind/Annual Giving ... Ms. Emily BERRY
114 Assoc VP Budgeting & Analysis ... Dr. David A. ELLIS
105 Univ Web Content Manager ... Ms. Jeri MOORE
25 Dir Research & Sponsored Pgms ... Ms. Anne P. SCHAUER
39 Director of Residence Life ... Dr. Vicka BELL-ROBINSON

Miami University Middletown (B)

4200 N University Boulevard, Middletown OH 45042-3497
Telephone: (513) 727-3200 FICE Identification: 003080
Accreditation: &HLC

† Regional accreditation is carried under the parent institution in Oxford, OH.

Miami University Regionals (C)

1601 University Boulevard, Hamilton OH 45011-3399
Telephone: (513) 785-3000 FICE Identification: 003079
Accreditation: &HLC

† Regional accreditation is carried under the parent institution in Oxford, OH.

The Modern College of Design (D)

1725 E David Road, Dayton OH 45440-1612
County: Montgomery FICE Identification: 025530
Unit ID: 205391
Telephone: (877) 300-9866 Carnegie Class: Spec 2-yr-A&S
FAX Number: (937) 294-5869 Calendar System: Semester
URL: https://themodern.edu
Established: 1983 Annual Undergrad Tuition & Fees: $33,164
Enrollment: 190 Coed
Affiliation or Control: Proprietary IRS Status: Proprietary
Highest Offering: Baccalaureate
Accreditation: ACCSC

01 Owner/President/Creative Director ... Ms. Jessica BARRY
26 Vice Pres of Industry Relations ... Mr. Matt FLICK
32 Vice President of Student Affairs ... Ms. Melissa FERGUSON
05 Chief Academic Officer ... Ms. Korrine TOADVINE
36 Director of Career Services ... Mr. Rick WILLITS
37 Director of Financial Aid ... Ms. Veronica DAVIDSON
07 Director of Admissions ... Ms. Samira ZACHARIAS

Mount Carmel College of Nursing (E)

127 S Davis Avenue, Columbus OH 43222-1504
County: Franklin FICE Identification: 030719
Unit ID: 204176
Telephone: (614) 234-5800 Carnegie Class: Spec-4-yr-Other Health
FAX Number: (614) 234-2875 Calendar System: Semester
URL: www.mccn.edu
Established: 1990 Annual Undergrad Tuition & Fees: $14,675
Enrollment: 903 Coed
Affiliation or Control: Roman Catholic IRS Status: 501(c)3
Highest Offering: Doctorate
Accreditation: HLC, NURSE

01 President ... Dr. Kathleen WILLIAMSON
05 Assoc Dean Academic Affairs ... Dr. Jami NININGER
88 Assoc Dean Innovation/Partnerships ... Dr. Scott DOLAN
103 Assoc Dean Ldrshp-Clinical Practice ... Dr. Jerry MANSFIELD
32 Assoc Dean Student Svcs ... Dr. Todd EVERETT
12 Asst Dean Regional Campus ... Ms. Cora ARLEDGE
04 Senior Executive Assistant ... Ms. Colleen MURPHY
107 Dir Doctor-Nurse Practice Pgm ... Dr. Thelma PATRICK
58 Director Graduate Programs ... Dr. Roxanne OLIVER
66 Director Accelerated Programs ... Dr. Folorunso LADIPO
88 Director Compliance & Safety ... Mr. Mitch JOSEPH-KEMPLIN
10 Deputy Chief Financial Officer ... Ms. Libby MELZER
21 Director Business Affairs ... Ms. Kathy SMITH
06 Director Records & Registration ... Ms. Michelle LIVINGSTON
07 Director Admissions & Recruitment ... Dr. Kim CAMPBELL
108 Dir Institutional Effectiveness ... Ms. Susannah TOWNSEND
30 Director of Development ... Ms. Alyssa FRY
37 Senior Financial Aid Advisor ... Mr. Steve WETZ
08 Regional Director Library Services ... Mr. Stevo ROKSANDIC
26 Marketing/Communication Strategist ... Ms. Alexandra REESE
121 Student Success Coordinator ... Ms. Nancy HANN

Mount St. Joseph University (F)

5701 Delhi Road, Cincinnati OH 45233-1670
County: Hamilton FICE Identification: 003033
Unit ID: 204200
Telephone: (513) 244-4200 Carnegie Class: Masters/L
FAX Number: (513) 244-4654 Calendar System: Semester
URL: www.msj.edu
Established: 1920 Annual Undergrad Tuition & Fees: $32,200
Enrollment: 2,031 Coed
Affiliation or Control: Roman Catholic IRS Status: 501(c)3
Highest Offering: Doctorate
Accreditation: HLC, #ACBSP, #ARCPA, CAEP, NURSE, PTA, SW

01 President ... Dr. H. James WILLIAMS
111 VP of Institutional Advancement ... Mr. Joseph CORNELY
26 VP of Marketing & Communications ... Mr. Jeff WAMPLER
05 Provost ... Dr. Diana DAVIS
10 Chief Financial Officer ... Mr. Jeffrey C. BRIGGS
43 VP Compliance Risk/General Counsel ... Ms. Paige L. ELLERMAN
20 Assoc Provost for Academic Support ... Ms. Heather CRABBE
20 Associate Provost Academic Affairs ... Dr. Christa CURRY
13 AVP Campus Technology ... Mr. Alex NAKONECHNYI
15 Director of Human Resources ... Ms. Lisa KOBMAN
32 Dean of Students ... Ms. Janet COX
06 Registrar ... Ms. Ginny TAYLOR
37 Director Student Admin Services ... Ms. Kathy KELLY
36 Director Career/Exper Educ ... Ms. Linda POHLGEERS
102 Dir of Corp & Foundation Relations ... Ms. Michael HECKMAN
110 Director of Advancement ... Mr. Joe CORNELY
30 Dir of Development/Campaign Mgmt ... Ms. Michelle OLMSTED
44 Senior Philanthropy Officer ... Ms. Nancy HERZOG
29 Director of Alumni Engagement ... Mr. Matt TASKE
110 Director of Advancement Services ... Ms. Colleen PFEIFFENBERGER
18 Director Buildings & Grounds ... Mr. Michael DITTMER
09 Director Institutional Research ... Ms. Whitney KESSINGER
07 VP for Recruitment & Admissions ... Dr. Christopher POWERS
21 Controller ... Ms. Kristi BENGEL
38 Director Wellness Center ... Ms. Patsy SCHWAIGER
08 Director Library ... Mr. Scott LLOYD
13 Director Instructional Technology ... Ms. Kim HUNTER
19 Director of Campus Police ... Mr. Kevin KOO
41 Director of Athletics ... Ms. Melanee WAGENER
88 Dir Learning Center/Disability Svcs ... Ms. Stacy MUELLER
42 Director of Mission Integration ... Sr. Karen ELLIOTT, CPPS
109 Director of Auxiliary Services ... Ms. Katrina KENTON
76 Dean of Health Sciences ... Dr. Darla VALE
79 Dean of Arts & Humanities ... Dr. Michael SONTAG
50 Dean of Business ... Dr. Sharon WAGNER
53 Dean of Education ... Dr. Laura SAYLOR
83 Dean Behavioral & Natural Sciences ... Dr. Gene KRITSKY
91 Director Administrative Computing ... Mr. Dan LUKAC
105 Webmaster ... Ms. Carolyn BOLAND
23 Coordinator Health Services ... Ms. Amy DEMKO
39 Coordinator of Residence Life ... Mr. Jeff HURLEY
04 Exec Asst to the President ... Ms. Jacque MEYER
28 Chief Diversity & Inclusion Officer ... Mr. Rayshawn EASTMAN
121 Director Academic Advising ... Ms. Mary E. MAZUK

Mount Vernon Nazarene University (G)

800 Martinsburg Road, Mount Vernon OH 43050-9500
County: Knox FICE Identification: 007085
Unit ID: 204194
Telephone: (740) 392-6868 Carnegie Class: Masters/M
FAX Number: (740) 397-2769 Calendar System: Semester
URL: www.mvnu.edu
Established: 1968 Annual Undergrad Tuition & Fees: $31,610
Enrollment: 2,140 Coed
Affiliation or Control: Church Of The Nazarene IRS Status: 501(c)3
Highest Offering: Master's
Accreditation: HLC, ACBSP, CAEPN, MUS, NURSE, SW

01 President/CEO ... Dr. Henry W. SPAULDING, II
10 Vice Pres for Finance/CFO ... Mr. Scott L. CAMPBELL
05 Vice Pres for Academic Affairs/CAO ... Dr. B. Barnett COCHRAN
26 VP for University Relations ... Rev. James SMITH
32 Vice President Student Life ... Rev. Tracy WAAL
58 VP for Graduate and Prof Studies ... Rev. Eric STETLER
42 Campus Pastor ... Rev. Stephanie LOBDELL
21 Director of Business Services ... Mr. Steven JENKINS
84 Assoc VP Enroll Mgmt/Marketing ... Ms. Beth DALONZO
88 Director of Faculty Services GPS ... Mr. Kevin CHANEY
06 University Registrar ... Mr. Mel SEVERNS
15 Director of Human Resources ... Mr. Alan SHAFFER
38 Director Counseling and Wellness ... Dr. Eric BROWNING
13 Director of Information Tech ... Mr. John WALCHLE
29 Director of Alumni Relations ... Rev. Brad A. KOCHIS
40 Director of the Bookstore ... Mrs. Gina A. BLANCHARD
27 Coord Communications & Pub Rels ... Ms. Samantha SCOLES
53 Dir Teacher Education/Certification ... Dr. Sharon METCALFE
37 Dir of Student Fin Services ... Mr. Jared SPONSELLER
18 Director of Facilities Operations ... Mr. Tony EDWARDS
21 Controller ... Ms. Debra DEVORE
35 Director of Campus Life ... Ms. Rochel FURNISS
28 Director Intercultural Affairs ... Mr. Tavaris TAYLOR
04 Assistant to President ... Mrs. Lisa L. VAN NEST
08 Director of the Library ... Mr. Timothy RADCLIFFE
105 Director Web Services ... Mr. Carlos SERRAO
106 Dir Online Education/E-learning ... Vacant
50 Dean of the School of Business ... Dr. Melanie TIMMERMAN
81 Dean School of Natural & Social Sci ... Dr. LeeAnn COUTS
09 Director of Institutional Research ... Mrs. Krissta HADSELL
07 Director of Admissions ... Mr. Robert STANLEY
104 Director Study Abroad ... Ms. Krissta HADSELL
41 Athletic Director ... Mr. Chip WILSON
54 Dept Chair Engineering ... Dr. Jose OOMMEN
30 Assistant VP for Development ... Mr. Justin NOWICKI
39 Dir Resident Life/Student Housing ... Mr. Joshua KUSCH
108 AVP of Institutional Effectiveness ... Dr. Brenita NICHOLAS-EDWARDS
124 AVP for Student Success & Retention ... Mrs. Joy STRICKLAND
121 Director of Student Success ... Mrs. Lee BJORNSEN
79 Dean of School of Arts & Humanities ... Dr. Yvonne SCHULTZ
66 Dean of School of Nursing ... Dr. Carol DOROUGH
73 Dean School of Christian Ministry ... Dr. Douglas VAN NEST

Muskingum University (H)

163 Stormont Street, New Concord OH 43762-1199
County: Muskingum FICE Identification: 003084
Unit ID: 204264
Telephone: (740) 826-8211 Carnegie Class: Masters/S
FAX Number: (740) 826-8404 Calendar System: Semester
URL: www.muskingum.edu
Established: 1837 Annual Undergrad Tuition & Fees: $29,490
Enrollment: 2,231 Coed
Affiliation or Control: Presbyterian Church (U.S.A.) IRS Status: 501(c)3
Highest Offering: Beyond Master's But Less Than Doctorate
Accreditation: HLC, #CAATE, CAEP, CAEPN, MUS, NURSE, OT

01 President ... Dr. Susan SCHNEIDER HASSELER
05 Provost ... Dr. Nancy J. EVANGELISTA
10 VP Business/Finance & Treasurer ... Mr. Philip LAUBE
30 Vice Pres of Inst Advancement ... Mr. Paul MCCLELLAND
84 Vice Pres of Enrollment/Mktg ... Vacant
32 Assoc VP for Student Affairs ... Mr. Michael MALONE
08 Director of Library ... Dr. Nainsi HOUSTON
06 Registrar ... Mr. Daniel B. WILSON
36 Assistant Director Career Services ... Mrs. Jacquelyn L. VASCURA
13 Director of Computer Services ... Mr. Ryan D. HARVEY
26 Exec Dir Strategic Comm/Marketing ... Ms. Michelle BALL
29 Director Alumni Relations ... Ms. Jennifer L. BRONNER
07 Director of Admissions ... Mrs. Marcy RITZERT

19 Director of Public Safety ... Mr. Danny E. VINCENT
42 College Minister ... Rev. Julia WRIGHT
18 Supt of Building & Grounds ... Mr. Kevin J. WAGNER
41 Director of Athletics ... Mr. Steve BROCKELBANK
21 Associate Business Officer ... Vacant
37 Director of Student Financial Aid ... Mrs. Amber GUMP
38 Director of Student Counseling ... Mrs. Tracy F. BUGGLIN
40 Manager of Bookstore ... Mrs. Amber RODLAND
15 Human Resources Manager ... Vacant
28 Director of Diversity ... Ms. Danyelle GREGORY

MyComputerCareer (A)

380 Polaris Pkwy Suite 110, Westerville OH 43082

County: Delaware — FICE Identification: 041245
Telephone: (866) 606-6922 — Carnegie Class: Not Classified
FAX Number: N/A — Calendar System: Quarter
URL: mycomputercareer.edu
Established: 2007 — Annual Undergrad Tuition & Fees: N/A
Enrollment: N/A — Coed
Affiliation or Control: Proprietary — IRS Status: Proprietary
Highest Offering: Associate Degree
Accreditation: CNCE

01 Campus Director ... Teresa GARY
07 Admissions Director ... Michael BROWN
37 Financial Aid Director ... Susan BORGESI
36 Sr Career Services Director ... Tricia MOSHER

North Central State College (B)

2441 Kenwood Circle, Mansfield OH 44906

County: Richland — FICE Identification: 005313
Unit ID: 204422
Telephone: (419) 755-4800 — Carnegie Class: Assoc/HVT-High Non
FAX Number: (419) 755-4750 — Calendar System: Semester
URL: www.ncstatecollege.edu
Established: 1961 — Annual Undergrad Tuition & Fees (In-State): $4,468
Enrollment: 2,729 — Coed
Affiliation or Control: State — IRS Status: 501(c)3
Highest Offering: Associate Degree
Accreditation: HLC, ACBSP, ADNUR, COARC, EMT, PTAA, RAD

01 President ... Dr. Dorey DIAB
04 Exec Assistant to the President ... Mr. Stephen R. WILLIAMS
05 Vice President Academic Services ... Dr. Kelly A. GRAY
32 Vice President Student Svcs & IE ... Mr. Thomas PRENDERGAST
10 VP/CFO of Business Services ... Ms. Lori L. MCKEE
26 Exec Dir Marketing & Public Rels ... Mr. Keith STONER
07 Director of Admissions ... Ms. Amanda SHEETS
15 Director of Human Resources ... Mr. R. Douglas HANUSCIN
37 Director of Financial Aid ... Ms. Amanda KALTENBAUGH
08 Head Librarian ... Ms. Andrea WITTMER
22 Coord Disability Services ... Mr. Doug HESTAND
20 Dean Academic Services ... Dr. Toni JOHNSON
49 Dean of Liberal Arts ... Dr. Howard WALTERS
88 Asst Dean Liberal Arts ... Dr. Steven HAYNES
50 Dean of Business Ind & Technology ... Mr. Daniel WAGNER
51 Asst Dean of Business Ind & Tech ... Dr. Vincent PALOMBO
54 Dir/Chair Engineering BSMET ... Mr. Daniel O. WAGNER
76 Dean Health Sciences/Dir Nursing ... Ms. Melinda ROEPKE
66 Asst Dean Health Sciences ... Ms. Leesa COX
13 Director of IT ... Mr. Major PRICE, JR.
06 Registrar ... Mr. Mark J. MONNES
18 Manager of Facilities ... Mr. Kevin KLINE
88 Director Accounting Services ... Ms. Michele SCHAAD
102 Vice President College Foundation ... Ms. Christine COPPER
121 Dir of Student Success & Transition ... Ms. Monica DURHAM
88 Phi Theta Kappa Advisor ... Ms. Barb KEENER
40 Campus Bookstore Manager ... Ms. Carla BUTDORFF
21 Controller ... Ms. Lori L. MCKEE
105 Web Master ... Vacant
41 Athletics & Student Engagement ... Ms. Jennifer RACER
29 Coord of Alumni/Employer Relations ... Mr. Randy BLANKENSHIP
36 Career Development Counselor ... Ms. Paula WALDRUFF
108 Director Institutional Assessment ... Dr. Gina KAMWITHI
19 Director Security/Safety ... Sgt. Jeffrey HOFFER
28 Director of Diversity ... Dr. Toni JOHNSON

The North Coast College (C)

11724 Detroit Avenue, Lakewood OH 44107-3002

County: Cuyahoga — FICE Identification: 012896
Unit ID: 206394
Telephone: (216) 221-8584 — Carnegie Class: Bac/Assoc-Assoc Dom
FAX Number: (216) 221-2311 — Calendar System: Semester
URL: www.thencc.edu
Established: 1966 — Annual Undergrad Tuition & Fees: $22,800
Enrollment: 48 — Coed
Affiliation or Control: Proprietary — IRS Status: Proprietary
Highest Offering: Baccalaureate
Accreditation: ACCSC

01 President ... Dr. Milan MILASINOVIC
05 Dean of Academic Affairs ... Mr. Patrick MELNICK
37 Financial Aid Administrator ... Ms. Donna TURNBULL

Northeast Ohio Medical University (D)

4209 State Route 44, PO Box 95,
Rootstown OH 44272-0095

County: Portage — FICE Identification: 024544
Unit ID: 204477
Telephone: (330) 325-2511 — Carnegie Class: Spec-4-yr-Med
FAX Number: (330) 325-7943 — Calendar System: Other
URL: www.neomed.edu
Established: 1973 — Annual Graduate Tuition & Fees: N/A
Enrollment: 985 — Coed
Affiliation or Control: State — IRS Status: 501(c)3
Highest Offering: First Professional Degree; No Undergraduates
Accreditation: HLC, MED, PH, PHAR

01 President ... Dr. John LANGELL
100 Chief of Staff ... Ms. Michelle M. MULHERN
26 VP Govt & External Affairs ... Mr. John J. STILLIANA
46 VP Research/Sponsored Programs ... Dr. Steven P. SCHMIDT
05 VP Academic Affairs ... Dr. Richard J. KASMER
17 VP Health Affairs ... Dr. Elisabeth H. YOUNG
10 VP Operations & Finance ... Ms. Mary TAYLOR
111 VP Advancement ... Vacant
28 VP HR & Diversity ... Mr. Andre L. BURTON
26 VP Comm/Chief Marketing Officer . Mr. Roderick L. INGRAM, SR.
63 Dean College of Medicine ... Dr. Elisabeth H. YOUNG
58 Dean College of Graduate Studies ... Dr. Steven P. SCHMIDT
67 Dean College of Pharmacy ... Dr. Richard J. KASMER
43 General Counsel ... Ms. Maria R. SCHIMER
32 Sr Exec Dir Acad Affs & Stdnt Svcs ... Dr. Sandra M. EMERICK
88 Sr Ex Dir Wasson Ctr & Interprof Ed ... Dr. Holly A. GERZINA
25 Exec Dir Research & Sponsored Pgms ... Ms. Rebecca L. HAYES
09 Exec Dir Institutional Research ... Dr. Deborah LOYET
84 Sr Exec Dir Strategic Enroll Init ... Mr. James F. BARRETT
88 Dir Comparative Medicine Unit ... Dr. Stanley D. DANNEMILLER
29 Dir Alumni Rels & Annual Giving ... Mr. Craig S. EYNON
38 Dir Counseling Services ... Dr. Jennifer L. DOUGALL
13 Sr Ex Dir Information Technology ... Mr. Ronald L. MCGRADY
15 Dir Human Resources ... Ms. Charity DAVIS
18 Dir Campus Operations ... Mr. Dale A. HLUCH
24 Dir Academic Technology Services ... Mr. Michael G. WRIGHT
08 Dir Learning Center ... Mr. Craig R. THEISSEN
19 Dir Public Safety/Police Chief ... Ms. Kali A. MEONSKE
124 Exec Dir Academic Services ... Dr. Terri E. ROBINSON
114 Dir of Budget & Accounting ... Ms. Jacalyn E. KOVACH
40 Supervisor Bookstore ... Ms. Christine L. KOVACICH
06 Registrar ... Ms. Katherine M. MIRANDA
37 Dir Financial Aid ... Mr. Michael A. KEMPE

Northwest State Community College (E)

22-600 State Route 34, Archbold OH 43502-9542

County: Henry — FICE Identification: 008677
Unit ID: 204440
Telephone: (419) 267-5511 — Carnegie Class: Assoc/HVT-High Non
FAX Number: (419) 267-3688 — Calendar System: Semester
URL: www.northweststate.edu
Established: 1968 — Annual Undergrad Tuition & Fees (In-State): $4,338
Enrollment: 3,736 — Coed
Affiliation or Control: State — IRS Status: 501(c)3
Highest Offering: Associate Degree
Accreditation: HLC, ACBSP, ADNUR, MAC

01 President ... Dr. Todd HERNANDEZ
03 Executive Vice President ... Mr. Albert LEWIS, JR.
05 VP for Academics ... Dr. Daniel BURKLO
84 VP Enrollment Mgmt/Student Affairs ... Ms. Lana SNIDER
49 Dean of Arts & Sciences ... Ms. Jamilah TUCKER
66 Dean of Nursing & Allied Health ... Dr. Kathy KEISTER
50 Dean Business & Public Services ... Mr. Jason RICKENBERG
54 Dean STEM & IND Technologies ... Dr. Ryan HAMILTON
06 Registrar ... Ms. Connie KLINGSHIRN
18 Director of Plant Operations ... Mr. Kevin GERKEN
15 VP Human Resources ... Ms. Kathryn MCKELVEY
10 Chief Fiscal & Admin Officer ... Ms. Jennifer THOME
21 Director of Accounting & Finance ... Ms. Lynn SPEISER
07 Director of Admissions ... Mr. Austin FLORES
102 Executive Director Foundation ... Ms. Robbin WILCOX
37 Director Student Financial Aid ... Ms. Amber YOCOM
26 Marketing & Communications ... Mr. James BELLAMY
40 Bookstore Manager ... Mr. Kemp STAPLETON
08 Director Library ... Ms. Kristi ROTROFF
121 Dean of Learner Services ... Ms. Cassie RICKENBERG
103 VP Workforce Development ... Mr. James DREWES
13 Dir Network Systems/Tech Support ... Mr. Robert DUNCAN
14 Director Data Systems ... Mr. Terry KING
88 Director CTS/AMTC ... Mr. David CONOVER
04 Executive Assistant ... Ms. Megan BATT

Notre Dame College (F)

4545 College Road, South Euclid OH 44121-4293

County: Cuyahoga — FICE Identification: 003085
Unit ID: 204468
Telephone: (216) 381-1680 — Carnegie Class: Masters/S
FAX Number: (216) 381-3802 — Calendar System: Semester
URL: www.notredamecollege.edu
Established: 1922 — Annual Undergrad Tuition & Fees: $30,750
Enrollment: 1,585 — Coed
Affiliation or Control: Roman Catholic — IRS Status: 501(c)3
Highest Offering: Master's
Accreditation: HLC, CAEP, CAEPN, NURSE

01 President ... Dr. J. Michael PRESSIMONE
10 Vice Pres Finance and CFO ... Vacant
111 Vice Pres for Advancement ... Ms. Culeen CAREY
05 Interim Provost and Dean of Faculty ... Dr. David OROSZ
124 Dean of Retention & Acad Support ... Ms. Sandy GRASSMAN
88 Chief Mission Officer ... Mr. Ted STEINER
66 Nursing Division Chair ... Dr. Colleen SWEENEY
53 Education Division Chair ... Dr. Sue CORBIN
81 Math & Science Division Chair ... Dr. Sharon BALCHAK
50 Business Division Chair ... Ms. Natalie STROUSE
79 Arts and Humanities Division Chair ... Mr. Kenneth PALKO
84 Vice Pres for Enrollment ... Ms. Beth FORD
07 Asst Dean for Enrollment ... Ms. Amanda MEANS
06 Registrar ... Ms. Tracy SABRANSKY
37 Director of Financial Aid ... Ms. Allison MCBRADY
113 Director of Student Accounts ... Vacant
19 Director of Security/Safety ... Mr. Joseph GRECOL
18 Director of Physical Plant ... Mr. Tom MEEKS
13 Director of Information Technology ... Mr. Michael KIEC
15 Director of Human Resources ... Ms. Judy WEST
08 Director of Library ... Ms. Karen ZOLLER
42 Director of Campus Ministry ... Mr. Ted STEINER
38 Director of Counseling Center ... Mr. Jerry HAYES
32 Dean of Students ... Dr. D. Chris GILL
39 Director of Residence Life ... Mr. Shane YOUNG
29 Director Alumni Relations ... Ms. Nakeysha HAMILTON
04 Assistant to the President ... Sr. Carol ZIEGLER, SND
106 Dean Adult/Online/Graduate Educ ... Dr. Florentine HOELKER
41 Athletic Director ... Mr. Scott SWAIN

Oberlin College (G)

173 West Lorain Street, Oberlin OH 44074-1057

County: Lorain — FICE Identification: 003086
Unit ID: 204501
Telephone: (440) 775-8121 — Carnegie Class: Bac-A&S
FAX Number: (440) 775-8886 — Calendar System: 4/1/4
URL: www.oberlin.edu
Established: 1833 — Annual Undergrad Tuition & Fees: $58,554
Enrollment: 2,658 — Coed
Affiliation or Control: Independent Non-Profit — IRS Status: 501(c)3
Highest Offering: Master's
Accreditation: HLC

01 President ... Ms. Carmen T. AMBAR
10 VP for Finance & Admin ... Ms. Rebecca VASQUEZ-SKILLINGS
111 VP for Advancement ... Mr. Michael GRZESIAK
26 Vice President College Relations ... Mr. Ben JONES
49 Dean of Arts & Sciences ... Dr. David KAMITSUKA
64 Dean Conservatory Music ... Dr. William QUILLEN
32 VP & Dean of Students ... Ms. Karen GOFF
35 Spec Asst for Student Affairs ... Ms. Clare RAHM
07 Dean Admissions/Financial Aid ... Dr. Manuel CARBALLO
43 Interim VP/GC and Secretary ... Mr. Josh NOLAN
21 Asst Vice President Finance ... Ms. Nicole ADDINGTON
29 Exec Director Alumni Assoc ... Mr. Terry KURTZ
88 Assoc Dean of College of Arts & Sci ... Dr. Michael PARKIN
13 Chief Information Tech Officer ... Mr. Ben HOCKENHULL
08 Azariah Smith Root Dir of Libraries ... Vacant
07 Int Dir Admissions Conservatory ... Ms. Beth WEISS
38 Director of Counseling Center ... Dr. John HARSHBARGER
57 Director of Allen Art Museums ... Dr. Andria DERSTINE
06 Registrar ... Dr. Trecia POTTINGER
37 Director of Financial Aid ... Ms. Michele KOSBOTH
09 Director of Institutional Research ... Mr. Ross PEACOCK
18 Assistant VP of Facility Operations ... Mr. James S. KLAIBER
36 Exec Dir Career Dev Center ... Vacant
42 Director Religious and Spiritual Li ... Rev. David F. DORSEY
39 Asst VP/Strategic Initiatives ... Mr. Adrian BATISTA
41 Director of Physical Educ/Athletics ... Ms. Natalie WINKELFOOS
19 Director of Safety & Security ... Mr. Michael MARTINSEN
28 Director Multicultural Affairs ... Ms. Zahida SHERMAN
96 Institutional Buyer ... Mr. Rick SNODGRASS
15 Chief Human Resources Officer ... Mr. Joseph VITALE, JR.
04 Assistant to President ... Mrs. Jennifer S. BRADFIELD
100 Interim Chief of Staff ... Mr. David HERTZ
102 Exec Dir Office of Foundations ... Ms. Pamela SNYDER
44 Sr Philanthropic Advisor ... Ms. Catherine GLETHEROW

Ohio Business College (H)

5202 Timber Commons Drive, Sandusky OH 44870-5894

Telephone: (419) 627-8345 — Identification: 666467
Accreditation: COE

† Branch campus of Ohio Business College, Sheffield Village, OH.

Ohio Business College (I)

5095 Waterford Drive, Sheffield Village OH 44035

County: Lorain — FICE Identification: 021585
Unit ID: 203720
Telephone: (440) 934-3101 — Carnegie Class: Assoc/HVT-High Trad
FAX Number: (440) 934-3105 — Calendar System: Quarter
URL: www.ohiobusinesscollege.edu
Established: 1903 — Annual Undergrad Tuition & Fees: $9,385
Enrollment: 184 — Coed
Affiliation or Control: Proprietary — IRS Status: Proprietary
Highest Offering: Associate Degree
Accreditation: COE, MAC

01 Campus Director ... Mr. Jim ZINSMEISTER
05 Director of Education ... Mr. Greg SCHULTZ
07 Master Admissions Rep ... Ms. Nicole SMITH
37 Lead Financial Aid Administrator ... Ms. Christine TODD
36 Career Services Director ... Ms. Tanya FOOSE
06 Registrar ... Ms. Rhonda HIGGINS

Ohio Christian University (A)

1476 Lancaster Pike, Circleville OH 43113-0458
County: Pickaway FICE Identification: 003030
Unit ID: 201964
Telephone: (740) 474-8896 Carnegie Class: Masters/M
FAX Number: (740) 477-7755 Calendar System: Semester
URL: www.ohiochristian.edu
Established: 1948 Annual Undergrad Tuition & Fees: $21,990
Enrollment: 2,186 Coed
Affiliation or Control: Other Protestant IRS Status: 501(c)3
Highest Offering: Master's
Accreditation: HLC, CAEPT

01 President ....Dr. Jon KULAGA
05 Provost ....Dr. Bradford SAMPLE
10 Vice President of Finance ....Mr. Ted PERRY
111 Vice President for Advancement ....Mr. Matt HUNNELL
84 Vice President for Enrollment ....Mr. Kevin JONES
13 Executive Director of IT ....Mr. Jerad BADER
09 AVP for Institutional Effectiveness ....Dr. Cynthia TWEEDELL
50 Dean of Business ....Dr. Jon TOMLINSON
53 Dean of Education ....Dr. Valerie JONES
49 Dean of School of Arts and Sciences ....Dr. Krista STONEROCK
83 Dean of Social and Behavioral Scien ....Dr. Larry OLSON
06 Registrar ....Mr. Dustin EPPERLY
35 Director of Student Engagement ....Mr. Eric FEHR
42 Director of Spiritual Formation ....Mr. Kevin BENNIE
121 Director of Advising ....Ms. Michelle SAMPLE
08 Director of Library Services ....Vacant
37 Director Student Financial Services ....Mr. Brandon RITCHEY
41 Athletic Director ....Mr. David BIRELINE
15 Director for Human Resources ....Ms. Allison BROWNING
26 Chief Marketing Officer ....Mr. Dave HIRSCHLER
106 PSEO Director ....Mrs. Beth ASH
18 Director of Physical Plant ....Mr. Jerry SPARKS
19 Director of Security ....Mr. Anthony DILLARD
04 Executive Asst to President ....Ms. Lois J. TAYLOR
29 Director Alumni Affairs ....Ms. Michelle BLANTON

Ohio Dominican University (B)

1216 Sunbury Road, Columbus OH 43219-2099
County: Franklin FICE Identification: 003035
Unit ID: 204617
Telephone: (614) 251-4500 Carnegie Class: Masters/L
FAX Number: (614) 251-4634 Calendar System: Semester
URL: www.ohiodominican.edu
Established: 1911 Annual Undergrad Tuition & Fees: $32,880
Enrollment: 1,415 Coed
Affiliation or Control: Roman Catholic IRS Status: 501(c)3
Highest Offering: Doctorate
Accreditation: HLC, ACBSP, ARCPA, CAEPN, SW

01 President ....Ms. Connie GALLAHER
05 Vice President Academic Affairs ....Dr. Manuel MARTINEZ
10 Vice Pres Finance & Admin/CFO ....Mr. Alvin RODACK
84 Vice Pres Enrollment Management ....Mr. John NAUGHTON
111 VP for Advancement & External Rels ....Mr. Mark COOPER
04 Exec Asst to President/Vice Pres ....Ms. Heather MORRIS
32 Assoc Vice Pres Student Success ....Ms. Sharon REED
26 AVP Marketing/Public Relations ....Mr. Tom BROCKMAN
123 Assoc VP of Grad & Adult Admissions ....Mr. John NAUGHTON
110 Assoc VP for Advancement ....Ms. Christie FLOOD-WEINER
121 Dir of Advising & Student Success ....Mr. Adam HIRSCHFELD
07 Director Undergraduate Admissions ....Ms. Alecia DENNIS
114 Controller ....Ms. Vicki STEELE
13 Chief Information Officer ....Mr. Chris THEVE
37 Director of Financial Aid ....Ms. Tara SCHNEIDER
08 Director of the Library ....Ms. Michelle SARFF
36 Director Career Services ....Ms. Jessica HALL
15 Director of Human Resources ....Ms. Amy THOMAS
42 Director of Campus Ministry ....Fr. Paul COLLOTON
39 Director of Resident Life ....Ms. Lara CONRAD
41 Athletic Director ....Mr. Jeff BLAIR
19 Director of Safety ....Mr. Robin OLSON
06 Registrar ....Ms. Happiness MAPIRA
29 Director Alumni Relations ....Ms. Christie FLOOD-WEINER

Ohio Northern University (C)

525 S Main Street, Ada OH 45810-1599
County: Hardin FICE Identification: 003089
Unit ID: 204635
Telephone: (419) 772-2000 Carnegie Class: Bac-Diverse
FAX Number: (419) 772-1932 Calendar System: Semester
URL: www.onu.edu
Established: 1871 Annual Undergrad Tuition & Fees: $34,440
Enrollment: 2,817 Coed
Affiliation or Control: United Methodist IRS Status: 501(c)3
Highest Offering: First Professional Degree
Accreditation: HLC, CAEP, EXSC, LAW, MT, MUS, NAIT, NURSE, PHAR

01 President ....Dr. Daniel A. DIBIASIO
05 Interim Provost &d Vice President ....Dr. Juliet K. HURTIG
10 Vice President Financial Affairs ....Mr. Jason M. BROGE
111 Vice Pres of University Advancement .Ms. Shannon M. SPENCER
84 Vice Pres Enrollment Management ....Dr. William T. EILOLA
32 VP Student Affairs/Dean of Students ....Dr. Adriane L. THOMPSON-BRADSHAW
43 Vice President & General Counsel ....Mr. Andrew C. HUGHEY
49 Dean of Arts & Sciences ....Dr. Holly L. BAUMGARTNER
54 Dean of Engineering ....Dr. John-David S. YODER
67 Dean of Pharmacy ....Dr. Steven J. MARTIN
50 Dean Business Administration ....Dr. John C. NAVIN
61 Dean of the College of Law ....Dr. Charles H. ROSE, III
110 Assistant VP for Advancement ....Mr. Scott D. WILLS
08 Director of Heterick Library ....Ms. Kathleen T. BARIL
39 Dir of Res Life/Int Dir Career Svcs ....Mr. Justin F. COURTNEY
38 Director of Counseling ....Mr. Anthony C. RIVERA
29 Director of Alumni Relations ....Mrs. Kirsten E. OSBUN-MANLEY
08 Director of the Law Library ....Vacant
42 University Chaplain ....Rev Dr. David E. MACDONALD
18 Director of Facilities ....Mr. Marc E. STALEY
13 Director of Technology ....Mr. Jeff A. RIEMAN
09 Director of Institutional Research ....Mr. Joshua W. DEANS
15 Director of Human Resources ....Ms. Tonya D. PAUL
20 Interim Assoc VP Academic Affairs ....Dr. Lynda NYCE
37 Asst VP for Enroll Mgt/Dir Fin Aid ....Mrs. Melanie K. WEAVER
21 University Controller ....Mr. Mark A. RUSSELL
26 Exec Dir Communications & Marketing ....Mrs. Amy M. PRIGGE
07 Director of Admissions ....Ms. Deborah L. MILLER
06 University Registrar ....Ms. Melanie J. HOUGH
28 Int Dir Multicultural Development ....Dr. Albertina L. WALKER
41 Director of Athletics ....Mr. Thomas E. SIMMONS
44 Dir Annual Pgm & Donor Relations ....Ms. Ellie F. MCMANUS
96 Director of Business Services ....Ms. Vicki J. NIESE
101 Secretary to the Board ....Ms. Jennifer L. ROBY
19 Director of Public Safety ....Mr. Greg R. HORNE

The Ohio State University Main Campus (D)

281 W. Lane Ave., Columbus OH 43210-1358
County: Franklin FICE Identification: 003090
Unit ID: 204796
Telephone: (614) 292-6446 Carnegie Class: DU-Highest
FAX Number: (614) 292-9180 Calendar System: Semester
URL: www.osu.edu
Established: 1870 Annual Undergrad Tuition & Fees (In-State): $11,518
Enrollment: 61,369 Coed
Affiliation or Control: State IRS Status: 501(c)3
Highest Offering: Doctorate
Accreditation: HLC, AAB, ABAI, ACAE, ART, AUD, CAATE, CACREP, CAEP, CAEPN, CAHIIM, CAMPEP, CIDA, CLPSY, COARC, CONST, DANCE, DENT, DH, DIETC, DIETD, DIETI, DMS, HSA, IPSY, LAW, LSAR, MED, MFCD, MIDWF, MT, MUS, NURSE, OPT, OPTR, OT, PCSAS, PH, PHAR, PLNG, PTA, RAD, RTT, SCPSY, SP, SPAA, SW, THEA, VET

01 President ....Dr. Kristina M. JOHNSON
05 Executive Vice Pres/Provost ....Dr. Bruce MCPHERON
10 Sr VP Business & Finance/CFO ....Mr. Michael PAPADAKIS
43 Sr VP & General Counsel ....Ms. Anne GARCIA
32 Vice President for Student Life ....Dr. Melissa SHIVERS
20 Vice Provost for Academic Programs ....Mr. W. Randy SMITH
26 Sr VP Marketing & Communications ..Ms. Elizabeth PARKINSON
46 EVP Research Innovation & Knowledge ....Dr. Grace WANG
86 Vice Pres of Govt Affairs ....Ms. Stacy RASTAUKAS
23 Exec VP/Chancellor Health Affairs ....Dr. Harold L. PAZ
47 Vice Pres Ag Admin & Dean FAES ....Dr. Cathann KRESS
111 Sr VP for Advance/Pres OSU Found ....Mr. Michael EICHER
28 Vice Prov Diversity & Inclusion ....Dr. James L. MOORE
58 Vice Provost/Dean Grad School ....Dr. Alicia L. BERTONE
41 Sr VP/Athletics Director ....Mr. Gene D. SMITH
18 Assoc VP Facilities Op/Dev ....Mr. Mark E. CONSELYEA
84 Assoc VP Strategic Enroll Planning ....Vacant
13 Int Vice President & CIO ....Ms. Diane DAGEFOERDE
08 Vice Provost/Director of Libraries ....Mr. Damon E. JAGGARS
100 Chief of Staff ....Mr. JR BLACKBURN
101 Secretary Board of Trustees ....Ms. Jessica A. EVELAND
17 COO Medical Center ....Mr. David P. MCQUAID
85 Vice Prov Glob Strat/Intl Affs ....Dr. Gil I. LATZ, II
90 Exec Dir Ohio Supercomp Ctr ....Mr. David HUDAK
29 President/CEO Alumni Assoc ....Ms. Molly RANZ CALHOUN
12 Exec Dean of Reg Campuses ....Dr. Gregory S. ROSE
49 Vice Prov/Exec Dean Arts & Sci ....Dr. Gretchen RITTER
50 Dean Fisher Col of Business ....Dr. Anil K. MAKHIJA
52 Dean College of Dentistry ....Dr. Patrick M. LLOYD
53 Dean College of Educ & Hum Ecology ....Dr. Donald L. POPE-DAVIS
54 Dean College of Engineering ....Dr. Ayanna HOWARD
61 Dean College of Law ....Dr. Lincoln L. DAVIES
63 Dean College of Medicine ....Dr. Carol R. BRADFORD
88 Dean College of Optometry ....Dr. Karla S. ZADNIK
67 Dean College of Pharmacy ....Dr. Henry J. MANN
69 Dean College of Public Health ....Dr. Amy L. FAIRCHILD
70 Dean College of Social Work ....Dr. Tom GREGOIRE
74 Dean Col Veterinary Medicine ....Dr. Rustin MOORE
66 Dean College of Nursing ....Dr. Bernadette MELNYK
09 Asst VP Inst Research/Planning ....Vacant
37 Exec Dir Student Financial Aid ....Ms. Amy J. WHEELER
06 University Registrar ....Ms. Adrienne BRICKER
88 Exec Dir OSAS Analysis & Reporting ....Ms. Linda S. KATUNICH
96 Sr Director of Purchasing ....Mr. Nathan ANDRIDGE
11 Sr Vice Pres Admin & Planning ....Mr. Jay D. KASEY
19 Director of Public Safety ....Ms. Monica MOLL
39 Dir STEP Ops Housing Administration ....Ms. Toni GREENSLADE-SMITH
80 Dean JG College of Public Affairs ....Dr. Trevor L. BROWN
15 Sr VP Talent/Culture/HR ....Vacant

The Ohio State University Agricultural Technical Institute (E)

1328 Dover Road, Wooster OH 44691-4000
Telephone: (330) 264-3911 FICE Identification: 010687
Accreditation: &HLC

† Regional accreditation is carried under the parent institution in Columbus, OH.

The Ohio State University at Lima Campus (F)

4240 Campus Drive, Lima OH 45804-3597
Telephone: (419) 995-8600 FICE Identification: 003092
Accreditation: &HLC

† Regional accreditation is carried under the parent institution in Columbus, OH.

The Ohio State University Mansfield Campus (G)

1760 University Drive, Mansfield OH 44906-1599
Telephone: (419) 755-4011 FICE Identification: 003093
Accreditation: &HLC

† Regional accreditation is carried under the parent institution in Columbus, OH.

The Ohio State University at Marion (H)

1465 Mount Vernon Avenue, Marion OH 43302-5628
Telephone: (740) 389-6786 FICE Identification: 003094
Accreditation: &HLC

† Regional accreditation is carried under the parent institution in Columbus, OH.

The Ohio State University Newark Campus (I)

1179 University Drive, Newark OH 43055-9990
Telephone: (740) 366-3321 FICE Identification: 003095
Accreditation: &HLC

† Regional accreditation is carried under the parent institution in Columbus, OH.

Ohio Technical College (J)

1374 E 51st Street, Cleveland OH 44103-1269
County: Cuyahoga FICE Identification: 011745
Unit ID: 204608
Telephone: (216) 881-1700 Carnegie Class: Spec 2-yr-Tech
FAX Number: (216) 881-9145 Calendar System: Quarter
URL: www.ohiotech.edu
Established: 1969 Annual Undergrad Tuition & Fees: N/A
Enrollment: 426 Coed
Affiliation or Control: Proprietary IRS Status: Proprietary
Highest Offering: Associate Degree
Accreditation: ACCSC

01 President ....Mr. Bill HANTL
32 VP of Student Engagement ....Ms. Bonnie LACORTE
19 Director Security/Safety ....Mr. Glenn BODIFORD
37 Director Student Financial Aid ....Mr. Michael CAMPBELL
06 Registrar ....Ms. Sarah MANCINI
07 Director of Admissions ....Mr. Jordan BRENNER

Ohio University Main Campus (K)

1 Ohio University, Athens OH 45701-2979
County: Athens FICE Identification: 003100
Unit ID: 204857
Telephone: (740) 593-1000 Carnegie Class: DU-Higher
FAX Number: N/A Calendar System: Semester
URL: www.ohio.edu
Established: 1804 Annual Undergrad Tuition & Fees (In-State): $12,612
Enrollment: 25,714 Coed
Affiliation or Control: State IRS Status: 501(c)3
Highest Offering: Doctorate
Accreditation: HLC, AAFCS, ADNUR, ARCPA, AUD, CAATE, CACREP, CAEPN, CAPRT, CEA, CIDA, CLPSY, COSMA, DANCE, DIETD, DIETI, FEPAC, IPSY, JOUR, MUS, NAIT, NURSE, OSTEO, PH, PTA, SP, SW, THEA

01 President ....Dr. Hugh SHERMAN
100 Chief of Staff ....Ms. Jennifer KIRKSEY
05 Executive VP & Provost ....Dr. Elizabeth SAYRS
10 SVP for Finance & Administration ....Vacant
32 Interim VP for Student Affairs ....Dr. Jenny HALL-JONES
111 VP for University Advancement ....Mr. Nico KARAGOSIAN
13 Chief Information Officer ....Mr. Christopher AMENT
46 VP Research & Dean Grad College ....Dr. Joseph SHIELDS
84 Vice Pres Enrollment Management ....Ms. Candace BOENINGER
102 CEO University Foundation ....Mr. Nico KARAGOSIAN
43 General Counsel ....Ms. Stacey BENNETT
26 VP Univ Communications/Marketing ....Ms. Robin OLIVER
89 Interim Dean University College ....Dr. Carey BUSCH
49 Dean College of Arts & Sciences ....Dr. Florenz PLASSMANN
50 Dean College of Business ....Dr. Jackie REESE-ULMER
60 Dean Scripps Col Communication ....Dr. Scott TITSWORTH
53 Int Dn Patton College of Education ....Dr. Sarah HELFRICH
54 Dean Russ Col Engineering/Tech ....Dr. Mei WEI

57 Dean College of Fine Arts .... Dr. Matthew SHAFTEL
69 Int Dean Col Health/Human Services .... Dr. John MCCARTHY
92 Dean Honors Tutorial College .... Dr. Donal SKINNER
63 Dean Heritage Col Osteopathic Med .... Dr. Kenneth JOHNSON
62 Dean University Libraries .... Dr. Neil ROMANOSKY
35 Interim AVP/Dean of Students .... Dr. Patti MCSTEEN
12 Exec Dean Regional Higher Educ .... Dr. Nicole PENNINGTON
12 Dean Campus/Cmty Relations Eastern .... Dr. David ROHALL
12 Dean Southern Campus .... Dr. Nicole PENNINGTON
12 Dean Campus/Cmty Rels Chillicothe .... Dr. Roberta MILLIKEN
12 Dean Campus/Cmty Rels Lancaster .... Dr. Jarrod TUDOR
12 Dean Campus/Cmty Rels Zanesville .... Dr. Hannah NISSEN
20 Associate Provost Academic Affairs .... Dr. Katie HARTMAN
58 Asst Dean Graduate College .... Dr. Katherine TADLOCK
09 Assoc Prov Institutional Research .... Dr. Loralyn TAYLOR
41 Director of Athletics .... Ms. Julie CROMER
06 University Registrar .... Mrs. Debra M. BENTON
15 Chief Human Resources Officer .... Ms. Colleen BENDL
29 Asst Vice Pres Alumni Relations .... Ms. Erin ESSAK KOPP
36 Exec Dir Career/Leadership Dev Ctr .... Mr. Imants JAUNARAJS
07 Asst VProv/Dir Undergrad Admission .... Mr. Mateo REMSBURG
38 Dir Counseling/Psychological Svcs .... Dr. Paul CASTELINO
112 Exec Director of Gift Planning .... Ms. Kelli KOTOWSKI
37 Dir Student Fin Aid/Scholarships .... Ms. Valerie MILLER
106 Chief Strategy/Innovation Officer .... Dr. Brad COHEN
19 Chief of Police .... Chief Andrew POWERS
85 Dir International Svcs/Operations .... Dr. Diane CAHILL
39 Int Exec Dir Residential Housing .... Ms. Jneanne HACKER
28 VP for Diversity & Inclusion .... Dr. Gigi SECUBAN
24 Media Library Manager .... Ms. Robin WOOTEN
113 Bursar .... Ms. Sherry ROSSITER
101 Secretary to Board of Trustees .... Dr. David MOORE
86 Director of Government Relations .... Mr. Eric BURCHARD
88 Ombudsman .... Mr. Mac STRICKLEN
04 Presidential Assistant .... Ms. Joanna STOLTZFUS

Ohio University Chillicothe Campus (A)

101 University Drive, Chillicothe OH 45601-0629

Telephone: (740) 774-7200 FICE Identification: 003102

Accreditation: &HLC

† Regional accreditation is carried under the parent institution in Athens, OH.

Ohio University Eastern Campus (B)

45425 National Road, Saint Clairsville OH 43950-9724

Telephone: (740) 695-1720 FICE Identification: 003101

Accreditation: &HLC

† Regional accreditation is carried under the parent institution in Athens, OH.

Ohio University Lancaster Campus (C)

1570 Granville Pike, Lancaster OH 43130-1097

Telephone: (740) 654-6711 FICE Identification: 003104

Accreditation: &HLC, MAC

† Regional accreditation is carried under the parent institution in Athens, OH.

Ohio University Southern Campus (D)

1804 Liberty Avenue, Ironton OH 45638-2279

Telephone: (740) 533-4600 Identification: 666000

Accreditation: &HLC

† Regional accreditation is carried under the parent institution in Athens, OH.

Ohio University Zanesville (E)

1425 Newark Road, Zanesville OH 43701-2695

Telephone: (740) 453-0762 FICE Identification: 003108

Accreditation: &HLC

† Regional accreditation is carried under the parent institution in Athens, OH.

Ohio Valley College of Technology (F)

15258 State Route 170, East Liverpool OH 43920

County: Columbiana FICE Identification: 023014

Unit ID: 204884

Telephone: (330) 385-1070 Carnegie Class: Spec 2-yr-Health

FAX Number: (330) 385-4606 Calendar System: Semester

URL: www.ovct.edu

Established: 1886 Annual Undergrad Tuition & Fees: $14,497

Enrollment: 170 Coed

Affiliation or Control: Proprietary IRS Status: Proprietary

Highest Offering: Associate Degree

Accreditation: ABHES

01 President .... Mrs. Courtney E. MARTIN
37 Director of Financial Aid .... Ms. Sarah FERGUSON
36 Director Career Management .... Ms. Megan TINKLEPAUGH

Ohio Wesleyan University (G)

61 S Sandusky Street, Delaware OH 43015-2398

County: Delaware FICE Identification: 003109

Unit ID: 204909

Telephone: (740) 368-2000 Carnegie Class: Bac-A&S

FAX Number: (740) 368-3299 Calendar System: Semester

URL: www.owu.edu

Established: 1842 Annual Undergrad Tuition & Fees: $47,130

Enrollment: 1,426 Coed

Affiliation or Control: United Methodist IRS Status: 501(c)3

Highest Offering: Baccalaureate

Accreditation: HLC, CAEP, MUS

01 President .... Dr. Rockwell F. JONES
05 Provost .... Dr. Karlyn A. CROWLEY
10 VP for Finance/Admin/Treasurer .... Ms. Maura S. DONAHUE
111 VP for University Advancement .... Ms. Natalie MILBURN DOAN
84 Vice President for Enrollment .... Dr. Stefanie D. NILES
32 VP for Student Engagement/Success .... Dr. Dwayne K. TODD
26 Chief Communications Officer .... Mr. Will E. KOPP
09 Assoc Provost for Inst Research .... Dr. Dale E. SWARTZENTRUBER
108 Asst Prov Assessment/Accreditation .... Dr. Barbara S. ANDERECK
28 Interim Chief Diversity Officer .... Dr. Dawn M. CHISEBE
37 Director Student Financial Aid .... Mr. Kevin F. PASKVAN
36 Director of Career Services .... Ms. Leslie J. MELTON
06 Int Registrar .... Ms. Jaime E. MILBURN
13 Assoc Provost Academic Support .... Dr. Brian A. RELLINGER
19 Director of Public Safety .... Mr. Sean R. BOLENDER
29 Director Alumni Relations .... Ms. Katie P. WEBSTER
124 Admin Director OWU Connections .... Mr. Darrell J. ALBON
18 Director Physical Plant .... Mr. Jay E. SCHEFFEL
15 Director of Human Resources .... Ms. Imogene G. JOHNSON
31 Director Community Svc Learning .... Ms. Sally S. LEBER
04 Exec Asst to President/Board Secy .... Ms. Tammy A. LOWKS
23 Director Wellness Center .... Ms. Marsha A. TILDEN
39 Director Residential Life .... Mr. Brian J. EMERICK
41 Director of Athletics .... Mr. Doug W. ZIPP
42 Int Chaplain .... Rev. Chad E. JOHNS
35 Dean of Student Services .... Mr. Brad T. PULCINI
92 Honors Program Director .... Dr. Mark A. ALLISON
102 Foundation Relations Manager .... Ms. Sue E. HAIDLE
07 Director of Admission .... Ms. Laurie S. PATTON
96 Director of Purchasing .... Ms. Melanie T. KALB

Otterbein University (H)

1 South Grove Street, Westerville OH 43081-2006

County: Franklin FICE Identification: 003110

Unit ID: 204936

Telephone: (614) 890-3000 Carnegie Class: Masters/M

FAX Number: (614) 823-3114 Calendar System: Semester

URL: www.otterbein.edu

Established: 1847 Annual Undergrad Tuition & Fees: $33,074

Enrollment: 2,652 Coed

Affiliation or Control: United Methodist IRS Status: 501(c)3

Highest Offering: Doctorate

Accreditation: HLC, ANEST, CAATE, CAEPN, MUS, NURSE, THEA

01 President .... Dr. John L. COMERFORD
100 Vice President/Chief of Staff .... Ms. Kristine ROBBINS
05 Provost/VPAA .... Dr. Wendy R. SHERMAN HECKLER
32 Vice President Student Affairs .... Ms. Dawn STEWART
10 VP for Business Affairs/CFO .... Ms. Susan BOLT
111 VP Institutional Advancement .... Mr. Michael MCGREEVEY
84 Vice President for Enrollment .... Mr. Jefferson BLACKBURN-SMITH
13 Exec Director of Information Tech .... Mr. Willie NEUMANN
08 Director of the Library .... Ms. Tiffany LIPSTREU
06 Registrar .... Mr. David SCHNEIDER
36 Director Career Planning/Placement .... Mr. Ryan BRECHBILL
37 Director of Financial Aid .... Mrs. Kirsten CROTTE
41 Athletic Director .... Ms. Dawn STEWART
42 Chaplain .... Dr. Judy GUION-UTSLER
107 Dean School of Prof Studies .... Dr. Barbara H. SCHAFFNER
49 Dean School of Arts/Sciences .... Dr. Paul EISENSTEIN
07 Executive Director of Admissions .... Mr. Mark MOFFITT
15 Director Human Resources .... Mr. Scott FITZGERALD
18 Director/Physical Plant .... Mr. Troy A. BONTE
29 Director Alumni Relations .... Mr. Steve CRAWFORD
28 Director of Diversity .... Mr. James PRYSOCK
21 Assistant Controller .... Mr. Christopher A. HAYTER
09 Director of Institutional Research .... Dr. Sean M. MCLAUGHLIN
19 Director of Security .... Mr. Larry BANASZAK
04 Executive Assistant to President .... Ms. Becky SMITH
39 Director Student Housing .... Ms. Tracy BENNER
38 Director Student Counseling .... Dr. Kathleen RYAN
44 Director Annual Giving .... Vacant

Owens Community College (I)

30335 Oregon, PO Box 10000, Toledo OH 43699-1947

County: Wood FICE Identification: 005753

Unit ID: 204945

Telephone: (567) 661-7000 Carnegie Class: Assoc/HVT-High Non

FAX Number: N/A Calendar System: Semester

URL: www.owens.edu

Established: 1965 Annual Undergrad Tuition & Fees (In-State): $5,702

Enrollment: 7,536 Coed

Affiliation or Control: State IRS Status: 501(c)3

Highest Offering: Associate Degree

Accreditation: HLC, ACBSP, ACFEI, ADNUR, CAHIIM, DH, DIETT, DMS, EMT, MAC, NAEYC, NAIT, OTA, PTAA, RAD, RADMAG, SURGT

01 President .... Dr. Dione SOMERVILLE
101 Secretary to the Board of Trustees .... Ms. Patricia JEZAK
04 Executive Assistant to President .... Vacant
05 VP Academic Affairs/Provost .... Dr. Denise SMITH
10 Treasurer .... Mr. Jeff GANUES
11 VP Administration .... Ms. Lisa NAGEL
84 VP Enrollment Mgmt/Student Svcs .... Ms. Amy GIORDANO
103 Dean Workforce/Comm Service .... Mr. Quinton ROBERTS
12 Dean Findlay Campus .... Ms. Julie BAKER
21 Controller .... Ms. Katie FEHER
13 Chief Information Officer .... Mr. Jared BABER
19 Chief of Police .... Chief Steven HARRISON
37 Director Financial Aid .... Ms. Andrea MORROW
26 Director Mktg & Communications .... Mr. Jason GRIFFIN
18 Executive Director Operations .... Ms. Danielle TRACY
09 Director Inst Research .... Ms. Anne FULKERSON
81 Dean School of STEM .... Vacant
66 Dean School of Nursing/Health Prof .... Ms. Cathy FORD
50 Dean Sch Business/Info/Public Svc .... Dr. Michael PFAHL
57 Dean School of Liberal Arts .... Mr. Michael SANDER
08 Director Library Services .... Ms. Jane BERGER
106 Director eLearning .... Mr. Mark KARAMOL
32 Exec Dir Student Services .... Mr. David SHAFFER
102 Exec Dir Found/Govt & Cmty Rels .... Ms. Jennifer FEHNRICH
35 Director Student Life/Stdnt Conduct .... Ms. Danielle FILIPCHUK
109 Director Business Operations .... Mr. David WAHR
85 Manager Intl Stdnt Services .... Ms. Annette SWANSON
43 Legal Services Coordinator .... Ms. Jammie CASSONI
41 Director Athletics .... Vacant

Owens Community College Findlay Campus (J)

3200 Bright Road, Findlay OH 45840

Telephone: (567) 429-3500 Identification: 770360

Accreditation: &HLC

Payne Theological Seminary (K)

PO Box 474, Wilberforce OH 45384-0474

County: Greene FICE Identification: 010017

Unit ID: 204990

Telephone: (937) 376-2946 Carnegie Class: Spec-4-yr-Faith

FAX Number: (937) 250-7956 Calendar System: 4/1/4

URL: www.payneseminary.edu

Established: 1844 Annual Graduate Tuition & Fees: N/A

Enrollment: 177 Coed

Affiliation or Control: African Methodist Episcopal IRS Status: 501(c)3

Highest Offering: Doctorate; No Undergraduates

Accreditation: THEOL

01 President .... Dr. Michael BROWN
05 Academic Dean .... Dr. Betty HOLLEY
04 Executive Assistant to President .... Mr. Kim KING
111 Director of Inst Advancement .... Mr. Kim KING
10 Director of Finance .... Mr. Raymond INGRAM
06 Registrar .... Ms. Maryjo LEWIS
07 Admissions Officer .... Ms. Althea SMOOT

Pontifical College Josephinum (L)

7625 N High Street, Columbus OH 43235-1498

County: Franklin FICE Identification: 003113

Unit ID: 205027

Telephone: (614) 885-5585 Carnegie Class: Spec-4-yr-Faith

FAX Number: (614) 885-2307 Calendar System: Semester

URL: www.pcj.edu

Established: 1888 Annual Undergrad Tuition & Fees: $25,262

Enrollment: 86 Male

Affiliation or Control: Roman Catholic IRS Status: 501(c)3

Highest Offering: Beyond Master's But Less Than Doctorate

Accreditation: HLC, THEOL

01 Rector/President .... V.Rev. Steven P. BESEAU
10 VP for Administration/Treasurer .... Mr. John O. ERWIN
111 Vice President for Advancement .... Mr. Douglas H. STEIN
73 Vice Rec Sch Theology/Dn of Men .... Rev. Ervens MENGELLE
49 Vice Rector College Liberal Arts .... Rev. Mike LUMPE
88 Academic Dean School of Theology .... Dr. Perry J. CAHALL
88 Academic Dean College Liberal Arts .... Dr. Eric GRAFF
06 Registrar .... Mr. Samuel J. DEAN
08 Director Library Services .... Mrs. Beverly LANE
37 Director Financial Aid .... Mr. Samuel DEAN
108 Dir of Inst Plng/Assessment/Accred .... Mr. Eric S. GRAFF
26 Director of Communications .... Ms. Carolyn DINOVO
07 Admissions Coordinator .... Ms. Arminda CRAWFORD
105 Web Developer .... Ms. Tracy BROCKMAN

Professional Skills Institute (M)

1505 Holland Road, Maumee OH 43537

County: Lucas FICE Identification: 023377

Unit ID: 205054

Telephone: (419) 720-6670 Carnegie Class: Spec 2-yr-Health

FAX Number: (419) 720-6674 Calendar System: Quarter

URL: www.proskills.edu

Established: 1984 Annual Undergrad Tuition & Fees: $12,767

Enrollment: 350 Coed

Affiliation or Control: Proprietary IRS Status: Proprietary

Highest Offering: Associate Degree

Accreditation: ABHES, PTAA

00 CEO .... Michael MARINO
01 Campus President .... Elizabeth FOGLE
05 Dean of Education .... Susan LIPPENS
07 Director of Admissions .... Vacant

Rabbinical College of Telshe (A)

28400 Euclid Avenue, Wickliffe OH 44092-2584
County: Lake FICE Identification: 003115
Unit ID: 205124
Telephone: (440) 943-5300 Carnegie Class: Spec-4-yr-Faith
FAX Number: (440) 943-5303 Calendar System: Quarter
Established: 1941 Annual Undergrad Tuition & Fees: $13,400
Enrollment: 59 Male
Affiliation or Control: Independent Non-Profit IRS Status: 501(c)3
Highest Offering: Doctorate
Accreditation: RABN

01 President .... Rabbi Dovid GOLDBERG
06 Registrar .... Rabbi Abraham MATITIA

Remington College Cleveland Campus (B)

14801 Broadway Avenue, Maple Heights OH 44137
County: Cuyahoga FICE Identification: 007777
Unit ID: 375416
Telephone: (216) 475-7520 Carnegie Class: Assoc/HVT-Mix Trad/Non
FAX Number: (866) 630-4091 Calendar System: Other
URL: www.remingtoncollege.edu
Established: 1990 Annual Undergrad Tuition & Fees: $15,561
Enrollment: 401 Coed
Affiliation or Control: Independent Non-Profit IRS Status: 501(c)3
Highest Offering: Associate Degree
Accreditation: ACCSC

01 Dir of Campus Administration/Dean .... Mr. Terhan FREEMAN
06 Registrar/Retention .... Ms. Lisa ALESSANDRO
07 Director of Admissions .... Ms. Alicia CHET

Rhodes State College (C)

4240 Campus Drive, Lima OH 45804-3597
County: Allen FICE Identification: 010027
Unit ID: 203678
Telephone: (419) 995-8200 Carnegie Class: Assoc/HVT-High Non
FAX Number: (419) 221-0450 Calendar System: Semester
URL: www.rhodesstate.edu
Established: 1971 Annual Undergrad Tuition & Fees (In-State): $4,325
Enrollment: 3,324 Coed
Affiliation or Control: State IRS Status: 501(c)3
Highest Offering: Associate Degree
Accreditation: HLC, ACBSP, ADNUR, COARC, COARCP, CSHSE, DH, EMT, MAC, MAC, OTA, PTAA, RAD

01 President .... Dr. Cynthia E. SPIERS
10 Vice President Business & Finance .... Mr. Russ LITKE
05 SVP for Academic/Student Affairs .... Dr. Antoinette BALDIN
111 VP for Institutional Advancement .... Mr. Kevin L. REEKS
103 SVP Workforce Development .... Dr. Antoinette BALDIN
84 Int VP Enrollment Management .... Dr. Brendan GREANEY
45 Exec Dir Inst Effectiveness/Plng .... Dr. Nanette SMITH
20 Dean of Academic Affairs .... Dr. Eric MASON
32 Dean of Student Affairs .... Dr. Jeannette PASSMORE
21 Controller/Asst Treasurer .... Mr. David BRUNS
37 Director Financial Aid .... Ms. Pamela HUGHES
09 Director Institutional Research .... Mr. Eric SPONSELLER
36 Director of Career Development .... Ms. Krista RICHARDSON
08 Head Librarian .... Ms. Tina SCHNEIDER
15 Exec Director Human Resources .... Ms. Andrea GOINGS
49 Dean Technology & Liberal Studies .... Dr. Andrea FABER
76 Dean Health Sciences & Public Svc .... Ms. Angela HEATON
18 Chief Facilities/Physical Plant .... Vacant
26 Dir Mktg & Public Relations .... Ms. Paula SIEBENECK
04 Exec Admin Asst to the President .... Ms. Sandy KORTOKRAX

Rosedale Bible College (D)

2270 Rosedale Road, Irwin OH 43029-9517
County: Madison FICE Identification: 034253
Unit ID: 439899
Telephone: (740) 857-1311 Carnegie Class: Spec 2-yr-Other
FAX Number: (877) 857-1312 Calendar System: Semester
URL: www.rosedale.edu
Established: 1952 Annual Undergrad Tuition & Fees: $8,756
Enrollment: 71 Coed
Affiliation or Control: Mennonite Church IRS Status: 501(c)3
Highest Offering: Associate Degree
Accreditation: BI

01 President .... Mr. Jeremy MILLER
05 Academic Dean .... Mr. Phil WEBER
32 Dean of Students .... Mr. Matthew SHOWALTER
84 Director of Enrollment Services .... Mr. Hans SHENK
08 Director of Library Services .... Mr. Reuben SAIRS
06 Registrar .... Ms. Heather MAUST
10 Chief Financial Officer .... Mr. Lynford SCHROCK
26 Chief Public Relations Officer .... Mr. Kenneth MILLER
04 Administrative Asst to President .... Vacant
18 Chief Facilities/Physical Plant .... Mr. Darnell BRENNEMAN
37 Financial Aid Coordinator .... Mrs. Twila WEBER
30 Director of Development .... Ms. Jewel SHOWALTER

Saint Mary Seminary and Graduate School of Theology (E)

28700 Euclid Avenue, Wickliffe OH 44092-2585
County: Lake FICE Identification: 004061
Telephone: (440) 943-7600 Carnegie Class: Not Classified
FAX Number: (440) 943-7577 Calendar System: Semester
URL: www.stmarysem.edu
Established: 1848 Annual Graduate Tuition & Fees: N/A
Enrollment: N/A Coed
Affiliation or Control: Roman Catholic IRS Status: 501(c)3
Highest Offering: Doctorate; No Undergraduates
Accreditation: HLC, THEOL

01 President/Rector .... Rev. Mark A. LATCOVICH
03 Vice President/Vice Rector .... Rev. Joseph KOOPMAN
05 Academic Dean .... Sr. Mary MCCORMICK, OSU
32 Student Dean .... Rev. Michael G. WOOST
42 Spiritual Director .... Rev. David BLINE
06 Registrar/Assistant Dean .... Sr. Brendon ZAJAC, SND
08 Librarian .... Mr. Alan K. ROME
10 CFO/Treasurer .... Mr. Philip GUBAN
04 Administrative Asst to President .... Mrs. Angie PAVLIK
90 Director Academic Computing .... Sr. Brendon ZAJAC
18 Chief Facilities/Physical Plant .... Mr. Philip GUBAN
108 Director Institutional Assessment .... Dr. Edward KACZUK
13 Chief Info Technology Officer (CIO) .... Mr. Alan K. ROME
19 Director Security/Safety .... Mr. Philip GUBAN
105 Director Web Services .... Vacant

Shawnee State University (F)

940 Second Street, Portsmouth OH 45662-4344
County: Scioto FICE Identification: 009942
Unit ID: 205443
Telephone: (740) 351-3205 Carnegie Class: Masters/S
FAX Number: (740) 351-3470 Calendar System: Semester
URL: www.shawnee.edu
Established: 1975 Annual Undergrad Tuition & Fees (In-State): $8,604
Enrollment: 3,485 Coed
Affiliation or Control: State IRS Status: 501(c)3
Highest Offering: Doctorate
Accreditation: HLC, ADNUR, CAEPN, COARC, DH, EMT, MLTAD, NUR, OT, OTA, PTAA, RAD

01 President .... Dr. Jeffrey BAUER
05 Provost/VP Academic & Student Affs .... Dr. Sunil AHUJA
20 Associate Provost .... Vacant
10 Vice President for Finance & Admin .... Dr. Elinda BOYLES
111 VP for Advancement & Enrollment Mgt .... Mr. Eric BRAUN
43 General Counsel .... Mr. Michael MCPHILLIPS
26 Director Communications .... Ms. Elizabeth BLEVINS
107 Dean College Professional Studies .... Dr. Paul MADDEN
49 Int Dean College Arts & Sciences .... Dr. Jennifer PAULEY
08 Director of Library Services .... Ms. Suzanne JOHNSON-VARNEY
13 Director Univ Information Systems .... Mr. Charles WARNER
30 Executive Director of Development .... Mr. Chris MOORE
07 Director of Admission .... Ms. Amanda MEANS
06 Registrar .... Ms. Tamara SHEETS
32 Dean of Students .... Ms. Marcie SIMMS
15 Director of Human Resources .... Ms. Malonda JOHNSON
41 Athletic Director .... Mr. Jeff HAMILTON
37 Director of Financial Aid .... Ms. Nicole NEAL
36 Director Career Svcs & Workforce .... Ms. Angie DUDUIT
38 Director of Counseling & Psych Svcs .... Dr. Linda KOENIG
85 Director for International Pgms .... Mr. Ryan WARNER
18 Director of Facilities .... Mr. Butch KOTCAMP
97 Director General Education Program .... Dr. Michael BARNHART
09 Dir Inst Research/Spec Proj .... Mr. Christopher SHAFFER
21 Controller .... Mr. Greg BALLENGEE
19 Chief of Police .... Mr. Jon PETERS
04 Executive Asst to President .... Ms. Pamela OTWORTH
109 Exec Dir Auxiliary & Business Svcs .... Mr. Bill ROCKWELL
25 Chief Grants Administrator .... Ms. Susie RATCLIFF
108 Director Institutional Assessment .... Dr. Marc SCOTT
103 Director Workforce Development .... Ms. Angie DUDUIT
28 Dir of Diversity/Equity/Inclusion .... Ms. Malonda JOHNSON

Sinclair Community College (G)

444 W Third Street, Dayton OH 45402-1460
County: Montgomery FICE Identification: 003119
Unit ID: 205470
Telephone: (937) 512-3000 Carnegie Class: Assoc/MT-VT-Mix Trad/Non
FAX Number: (937) 512-4596 Calendar System: Semester
URL: www.sinclair.edu
Established: 1887 Annual Undergrad Tuition & Fees (In-District): $4,329
Enrollment: 18,687 Coed
Affiliation or Control: State/Local IRS Status: 501(c)3
Highest Offering: Baccalaureate
Accreditation: HLC, ACBSP, ACFEI, ADNUR, ART, CAHIIM, COARC, DH, DIETT, EMT, MAC, MLTAD, MUS, NDT, OTA, PTAA, RAD, SURGT, THEA

01 President .... Dr. Steven L. JOHNSON
22 VP Equity/Anti-Racism/Title IX .... Ms. Janet JONES
05 Interim Provost & Sr VP .... Dr. Kathleen CLEARY
10 Sr VP & CFO .... Mr. Jeff BOUDOURIS
103 SVP for Workforce Development .... Dr. Dave COLLINS
15 Director of HR/EEO Officer .... Mr. Nathaniel NEWMAN
84 VP Enroll Mgmt & Student Affairs .... Dr. Scott MARKLAND
111 VP for Advancement .... Ms. Madeline ISELI
100 VP External Affairs/Chief of Staff .... Mr. Adam MURKA
13 Chief Information Officer .... Mr. Scott MCCOLLUM
88 Chief School Partnership Officer .... Ms. Melissa TOLLE
106 Dean of eLearning .... Ms. Christina AMATO
20 Interim Director Student Completion .... Ms. Carol BONNER
20 Associate Provost .... Ms. Jennifer KOSTIC
81 Dean of Science/Math/Engineering .... Dr. Anthony PONDER
76 Dean Health Sciences .... Dr. Rena SEBOR
50 Interim Dean Business/Public Svc .... Ms. Angela FERNANDEZ
83 Dean Arts/Commun & Social Science .... Dr. Lisa MAHLE-GRISEZ
43 General Counsel .... Ms. Lauren ROSS
06 Registrar .... Dr. Tina HUMMONS
07 AVP for Enrollment Operations .... Mr. Matthew MOORE
104 Director International Education .... Ms. Deborah GAVLIK
121 Director Academic Advising .... Ms. Karla KNEPPER
04 Admin Assistant to the President .... Ms. Angela MILLER
08 Chief Library Officer .... Ms. Debra OSWALD
18 Chf Facilities/Physical Plant Ofcr .... Mr. Robert WOODRUFF
19 Director Security/Safety .... Mr. John HUBER
25 Chief Contract/Grants Administrator .... Ms. Karla HIBBERT-JONES
26 Marketing Director .... Dr. Deann HURTADO
28 Director of Diversity .... Mr. Michael CARTER
30 Director of Development .... Mr. Zach BECK
32 Director of Student Affairs .... Ms. Alicia SCHROEDER
41 Athletic Director .... Mr. Jeff PRICE
96 Director of Purchasing .... Mr. Paul MURPHY

Southern State Community College (H)

100 Hobart Drive, Hillsboro OH 45133-9488
County: Highland FICE Identification: 012870
Unit ID: 205966
Telephone: (937) 393-3431 Carnegie Class: Assoc/MT-VT-High Non
FAX Number: (937) 393-9370 Calendar System: Semester
URL: www.sscc.edu
Established: 1975 Annual Undergrad Tuition & Fees (In-State): $5,312
Enrollment: 2,018 Coed
Affiliation or Control: State IRS Status: 501(c)3
Highest Offering: Associate Degree
Accreditation: HLC, ADNUR, MAC

01 President .... Dr. Kevin S. BOYS
05 Vice President Academic Affairs .... Dr. Nicole ROADES
10 Chief Financial Officer .... Mr. Daniel SCHALL
32 Vice Pres Student Svcs/Enroll Mgmt .... Mr. James BLAND
12 Director of Fayette Campus .... Dr. Jessica WISE
12 Director of Central Campus .... Mr. Jeff MONTGOMERY
12 Director of Brown County Campus .... Ms. Amy MCCLELLAN
103 Dean Workforce Dev/Community Svcs .... Ms. Amy MCCLELLAN
15 Director of Human Resources .... Ms. Mindy MARKEY-GRABILL
55 Director Adult Opportunity Center .... Ms. Susan ARMSTRONG
91 Information Systems Coordinator .... Ms. Katy MARKEY
06 Registrar .... Ms. Amanda THOMPSON
66 Director of Nursing .... Dr. Julianne KREBS
08 Librarian .... Ms. Angel MOOTISPAW
37 Director of Financial Aid .... Ms. Suzanne HARMON
07 Director Recruitment & Admissions .... Mr. Jim BARNETT, III
13 Executive Director of IT Services .... Mr. Brian RICE
04 Executive Asst to President .... Ms. Robin THOLEN

† Enrollment figure encompasses all 4 campuses.

Southern State Community College Brown County Campus (I)

351 Brooks-Malott Rd, Mt Orab OH 45154
Telephone: (937) 444-7722 Identification: 770361
Accreditation: &HLC

Southern State Community College Fayette Campus (J)

1270 US Route 62 SW,
Washington Court House OH 43160
Telephone: (740) 333-5115 Identification: 770362
Accreditation: &HLC

Stark State College (K)

6200 Frank Avenue, NW, North Canton OH 44720-7299
County: Stark FICE Identification: 010881
Unit ID: 205841
Telephone: (330) 494-6170 Carnegie Class: Assoc/HVT-Mix Trad/Non
FAX Number: (330) 497-6313 Calendar System: Semester
URL: www.starkstate.edu
Established: 1960 Annual Undergrad Tuition & Fees (In-District): $4,310
Enrollment: 10,772 Coed
Affiliation or Control: State/Local IRS Status: 501(c)3
Highest Offering: Associate Degree
Accreditation: HLC, ACBSP, ACFEI, ADNUR, CAHIIM, COARC, DH, DIETT, EMT, MAC, MLTAD, OTA, PTAA, SURGA, SURGT

01 President .... Dr. Para M. JONES
05 Provost and Chief Academic Officer .... Dr. Lada GIBSON-SHREVE
10 VP for Business and Finance .... Mr. Thomas A. CHIAPPINI
84 VP for Enrollment Management .... Dr. Stephanie SUTTON
15 Director of Human Resources .... Ms. Melissa A. GLANZ
53 Dean Ed/Liberal Arts/Math/Science .... Mr. Andrew STEPHAN
76 Dean Health/Human Services .... Ms. Kelly REINSEL
50 Dean Business/Engr & IT .... Dr. Donald BALL

21 Controller .... Mr. Scott ANDREANI
37 Dir Financial Aid & Scholarships .... Mr. Lucas BREWER
18 Dir Physical Plant/Construction .... Mr. Steve SPRADLING
40 Bookstore Manager .... Ms. Kathryn FEICHTER
06 Registrar .... Ms. Pam ARRINGTON
111 Exec Dir Advance & SSC Foundation .... Ms. Marisa ROHN
114 Director of Budget .... Mr. Bruce WYDER
09 Director of Institutional Research .... Mr. Peter TRUMPOWER
54 Dean Engineering Technologies .... Dr. Don BALL
106 Director eStarkState .... Ms. Linda MOROSKO
08 Head Librarian .... Ms. Marcia ADDISON
04 Exec Admin Asst to President .... Ms. Teri ROSS
07 Exec Director of Admissions .... Mr. J.P COONEY
26 Director of Marketing .... Ms. Robyn STEINMETZ
19 Director Security/Safety .... Mr. Gregory BOUDREAUX

Stautzenberger College (A)

8001 Katherine Boulevard, Brecksville OH 44141
Telephone: (440) 838-1999　Identification: 770760
Accreditation: **ACCSC**, DMS, SURTEC

Stautzenberger College (B)

1796 Indian Wood Circle, Maumee OH 43537-4007
County: Lucas　FICE Identification: 004866
Unit ID: 205887
Telephone: (419) 866-0261　Carnegie Class: Assoc/HVT-Mix Trad/Non
FAX Number: (419) 867-9821　Calendar System: Other
URL: https://www.sctoday.edu
Established: 1926　Annual Undergrad Tuition & Fees: $16,699
Enrollment: 551　Coed
Affiliation or Control: Proprietary　IRS Status: Proprietary
Highest Offering: Associate Degree
Accreditation: **ACCSC**, MLTAB, SURTEC

01 Campus President .... Ms. Amy BEAUREGARD
05 Academic Dean .... Mr. Carlton ELLIS, III
37 Financial Aid Director .... Mrs. Mari L. HUFFMAN
36 Career Services Director .... Mr. Robert A. GARVER
06 Registrar .... Ms. Terri KINDER
08 Head Librarian .... Ms. Lori VAN LIERE
32 Director of Sstudent Services .... Mr. Cameron MILLER

Terra State Community College (C)

2830 Napoleon Road, Fremont OH 43420-9670
County: Sandusky　FICE Identification: 008278
Unit ID: 206011
Telephone: (419) 334-8400　Carnegie Class: Assoc/HVT-High Non
FAX Number: (419) 355-1247　Calendar System: Semester
URL: www.terra.edu
Established: 1968　Annual Undergrad Tuition & Fees (In-State): $5,338
Enrollment: 2,057　Coed
Affiliation or Control: State　IRS Status: 501(c)3
Highest Offering: Associate Degree
Accreditation: **HLC**, ADNUR, CAHIIM, MAC, PTAA

01 President .... Dr. Ron SCHUMACHER
111 VP Inst Advancement/Exec Dir Fdn .... Dr. Cory STINE
10 VP Financial Affairs .... Ms. Jacque FOOS
05 VP Academic Affairs .... Mr. William TAYLOR
32 VP Student Affairs/Enrollment Svcs .... Dr. Garien HUDSON
49 Dean Lib Arts/Bus/Hlthcare/Nursing .... Ms. Ann SERGENT
72 Dean Technology/Skilled Trades .... Mr. Andrew SHELLA
41 Athletic Director .... Mr. Gregory HEDDEN
09 Dir Planning/Inst Effectiveness .... Ms. Ellen WARDZALA
06 Registrar .... Mr. Eric STEINBERGER
13 Manager Information Technology .... Mr. Wayne YERDON
08 Librarian .... Ms. Amy KREILICK
04 Executive Assistant to President .... Ms. Lisa SHUEY
106 Instructional Technologist .... Ms. Melinda YERDON
35 Associate Dean of Students .... Mr. Todd LONG
19 Director Security/Safety .... Ms. Jen KIN

Tiffin University (D)

155 Miami Street, Tiffin OH 44883-2161
County: Seneca　FICE Identification: 003121
Unit ID: 206048
Telephone: (419) 447-6442　Carnegie Class: Masters/L
FAX Number: N/A　Calendar System: Semester
URL: www.tiffin.edu
Established: 1888　Annual Undergrad Tuition & Fees: $27,610
Enrollment: 2,933　Coed
Affiliation or Control: Independent Non-Profit　IRS Status: 501(c)3
Highest Offering: Doctorate
Accreditation: **HLC**, ACBSP

01 President .... Dr. Lillian SCHUMACHER
05 Provost & Chief Academic Ofcr .... Dr. Peter HOLBROOK
84 VP Enrollment Management .... Dr. Amy WOOD
111 VP University Advancement .... Mr. Mitchell BLONDE
10 VP Finance/Administration .... Ms. Donna FRANK
15 AVP Human Resources .... Ms. Nadia LEWIS
108 VP Inst Planning & Effectiveness .... Dr. Teresa SHAFER
26 Exec Dir Marketing/Communications .... Ms. Deborah ROSZMAN
04 Exec Assistant to the President .... Ms. Ellen LUCIUS
32 Dean of Students .... Mr. Mike HERDLICK
13 Chief Information Officer .... Mr. Jason MARSON
07 Director Undergrad Admissions .... Ms. Sarah JOHNSON
27 Exec Dir Media Rels/Publications .... Ms. Lisa WILLIAMS
06 Registrar & Assoc Provost .... Ms. Melissa WEININGER
41 Director Athletics .... Mr. Lonny ALLEN
21 Controller .... Ms. Julie ALFORD
08 Head Librarian .... Ms. Luanne EDWARDS
29 Director Alumni Relations .... Ms. Vickie WILKINS
36 Exec Director of Career Services .... Ms. Amanda HUMMEL
18 Director of Physical Plant .... Mr. Mike HERDLICK
39 Assoc Dean of Stdnts/Resident Life .... Mr. Jacob SIMON
44 Director of Annual Fund .... Ms. Mikki KING
28 AVP Equity/Access/Opp/Title IX .... Dr. Sharon PERRY-FANTINI
37 Exec Director Student Financial Aid .... Ms. Andrea FABER
49 Dean of Arts & Sciences .... Dr. Joyce HALL-YATES
50 Dean of Business .... Dr. Terry SULLIVAN
83 Dean Criminal Justice/Social Sci .... Mr. David SELNICK
09 Director of Institutional Research .... Ms. Holly ALLGOOD
121 Dir Undergrad Advising/Retention .... Mr. Jonathan BEARD
19 Director Security/Safety .... Mr. Sean DUROCHER
106 Vice Provost/Online & Extended Lrng .... Dr. Daniel CLARK

Tri-State Bible College (E)

506 Margaret Street, PO Box 445,
South Point OH 45680-8402
County: Lawrence　FICE Identification: 034754
Unit ID: 206154
Telephone: (740) 377-2520　Carnegie Class: Spec-4-yr-Faith
FAX Number: (740) 377-0001　Calendar System: Semester
URL: www.tsbc.edu
Established: 1970　Annual Undergrad Tuition & Fees: $9,100
Enrollment: 20　Coed
Affiliation or Control: Independent Non-Profit　IRS Status: 501(c)3
Highest Offering: Master's
Accreditation: **BI**

01 President .... Mr. Rex HOWE
05 VP Academic Affairs .... Vacant
10 Director of Finance .... Ms. Jeana GRAVES
11 VP Admin/Fin Aid Dir/Reg/Chief HR .... Ms. Roberta MERCER
32 Vice Pres Student Affairs .... Mr. Leroy FULFORD
18 Vice President Operations .... Mr. Manfred LANGER
20 Academic Dean Online Programs .... Mr. David LAMBERT

Union Institute & University (F)

2090 Florence Avenue, Cincinnati OH 45206-1947
County: Hamilton　FICE Identification: 010923
Unit ID: 206279
Telephone: (513) 861-6400　Carnegie Class: DU-Mod
FAX Number: (513) 861-0779　Calendar System: Semester
URL: www.myunion.edu
Established: 1964　Annual Undergrad Tuition & Fees: $15,686
Enrollment: 809　Coed
Affiliation or Control: Independent Non-Profit　IRS Status: 501(c)3
Highest Offering: Doctorate
Accreditation: **HLC**, CACREP, @DIETC, LC, SW

01 President .... Dr. Karen SCHUSTER-WEBB
05 Vice President Academic Affairs .... Dr. Nelson SOTO
04 Executive Assistant to President .... Ms. Susan GRACE
10 Chief Financial Officer .... Ms. Sandra MILLS
15 Vice President Human Resources .... Ms. Patty BURKE
111 VP Inst Innovation/Economic Dev .... Dr. Shanda GORE
20 Associate VP of Academic Affairs .... Dr. Arlene SACKS
06 Registrar .... Ms. Lew Rita MOORE
13 Director Information Technology .... Mr. Anthony KENDALL
18 Director Facilities Management .... Mr. Ray BOLIN
88 Special Assistant to the President .... Dr. Rhonda BRINKLEY-KENNEDY
108 AVP for Institutional Effectiveness .... Dr. Peter CACCAVERI
08 Director Library Services .... Mr. Matthew PAPPATHAN
37 Director Financial Aid .... Ms. Jean POHLMAN
29 Director Alumni Relations .... Ms. Carolyn KRAUSE
32 Director Student Success .... Dr. Jay KEEHN
106 Dir Center for Teaching & Learning .... Dr. Bob COTTER
30 Director of Development .... Vacant

United Theological Seminary (G)

4501 Denlinger Road, Dayton OH 45426-2308
County: Montgomery　FICE Identification: 003122
Unit ID: 206288
Telephone: (937) 529-2201　Carnegie Class: Spec-4-yr-Faith
FAX Number: (866) 359-9350　Calendar System: Semester
URL: www.united.edu
Established: 1871　Annual Graduate Tuition & Fees: N/A
Enrollment: 412　Coed
Affiliation or Control: United Methodist　IRS Status: 501(c)3
Highest Offering: Doctorate; No Undergraduates
Accreditation: **HLC**, THEOL

01 President .... Dr. Kent MILLARD
05 Vice Pres Academic Affairs & Dean .... Dr. David WATSON
10 Vice Pres Finance/Treasurer .... Mr. Steven SWALLOW
84 Vice Pres for Enrollment .... Dr. Bridget WEATHERSPOON
30 Vice Pres Development .... Ms. Callie PICARDO
101 Exec Asst to President/Corp Secy .... Ms. Laura WEBER
20 Assoc Dean Academic Affairs .... Dr. Vivian JOHNSON
06 Registrar .... Ms. Karen CLARK
13 Director of Information Technology .... Vacant
08 Librarian .... Mr. Ken S. COCHRANE
42 Dean of the Chapel .... Dr. Tesia MALLORY
26 Director of Communications .... Ms. Rachel HURLEY
37 Director Financial Aid .... Ms. Marcia BYRD
29 Coordinator of Alumni/ae Relations .... Ms. Dawn GREENWALT
18 Facility Manager .... Mr. Steve SWALLOW
108 Chf Strategy/Admin/Assessment Ofcr .... Ms. Karen E. PAYNE
07 Senior Dir Admissions .... Dr. Bridget WEATHERSPOON
32 Director of Student Services .... Rev. Chad CLARK
106 Director of Distance Learning .... Ms. Heather SHELLABARGER

The University of Akron, Main Campus (H)

302 Buchtel Common, Akron OH 44325
County: Summit　FICE Identification: 003123
Unit ID: 200800
Telephone: (330) 972-7111　Carnegie Class: DU-Higher
FAX Number: (330) 972-6990　Calendar System: Semester
URL: www.uakron.edu
Established: 1870　Annual Undergrad Tuition & Fees (In-State): $11,881
Enrollment: 16,094　Coed
Affiliation or Control: State　IRS Status: 501(c)3
Highest Offering: Doctorate
Accreditation: **HLC**, ANEST, ART, AUD, CACREP, CAEP, CAEPN, CIDA, COARC, COPSY, DANCE, DIETC, IFSAC, IPSY, LAW, MFCD, MUS, NURSE, PH, SP, SW

01 President .... Dr. Gary L. MILLER
05 Exec Vice President & Provost .... Dr. John WIENCEK
100 VP/Chief of Staff .... Mr. Wayne R. HILL
20 Sr Vice Provost .... Dr. Cher HENDRICKS
10 Sr VP Finance & Administration/CFO .... Mr. Dallas A. GRUNDY
43 Vice President & General Counsel .... Ms. M. Celeste COOK
32 VP for Student Affairs .... Dr. John A. MESSINA
13 Chief Information Officer .... Mr. John T. CORBY
32 Dean of Students .... Mr. Michael A. STRONG
30 Vice President of Development .... Mrs. Kimberly M. COLE
18 Chief Planning & Facilities .... Mr. Stephen L. MYERS
88 Communications & Content Mgr .... Mr. Nicholas B. NUSSEN
21 Controller .... Mr. Sameer ALRAMAHI
46 Actg VP Research & Business Engmt .... Dr. Philip A. ALLEN
22 VP Inclusion/Equity & CDO .... Dr. Sheldon B. WRICE
15 Assoc VP Talent Dev/Human Resources .... Mrs. Sarah J. KELLY
26 VP/Chief Comm and Marketing Officer .... Mrs. Tammy EWIN
19 Chief of Police & Campus Safety .... Chief Dale E. GOODING, JR.
43 Assoc VP & Deputy General Counsel .... Mr. John J. REILLY
06 Registrar .... Mr. Ronald L. BOWMAN, JR.
07 Director of Admissions .... Ms. Kim GENTILE
09 Lead Inst Research Info Officer .... Vacant
14 Acting Director Technology Transfer .... Ms. Kelly A. BIALEK
08 Dean University Libraries .... Dr. Aimee L. DECHAMBEAU
49 Dean Buchtel College Arts & Sci .... Dr. Mitchell S. MCKINNEY
54 Int Dean College of Engineering .... Dr. Craig C. MENZEMER
12 Director of Regional Campuses .... Vacant
50 Dean College of Business .... Dr. Susan C. HANLON
76 Acting Dean Health Professions .... Dr. Timothy M. MCCARRAGHER
61 Dean School of Law .... Mr. Christopher J. PETERS
58 Interim Director of Graduate School .... Dr. Marnie M. SAUNDERS
54 Int Dir of Polymer Sci/Engineer .... Dr. Ali DHINOJWALA
37 Director Student Financial Aid .... Mrs. Jennifer E. HARPHAM
29 Asst VP Alumni Relations .... Mr. Willy KOLLMAN
96 Director of Purchasing .... Ms. Luba CRAMER
88 Senior Director Integrated Comm .... Mr. Robert C. KROPFF
105 Director of Web Services .... Mr. Anthony W. SERPETTE
92 Interim Dean Honors College .... Dr. Joseph R. URGO
88 Director UA Adult Focus .... Mrs. Laura H. CONLEY
41 Director Athletics .... Mr. Charles D. GUTHRIE, JR.
36 Ex Dir Counseling/Test/Career Ctr .... Dr. Juanita K. MARTIN
39 Dir of Residence Life and Housing .... Dr. Melinda F. GROVE
25 Assoc Dir IRB Administration .... Ms. Kathryn A. WATKINS
85 Exec Dir Center for Intl Stds & Sch .... Ms. Nicola KILLE
23 Director Health Services .... Ms. Lisa L. RITENOUR
86 Spec Asst Gov Rels/Assoc Dir RCBIAP .... Dr. Matthew P. AKERS
91 Director IT Support Services .... Mr. Neal L'AMOREAUX
27 Director of Media Relations .... Ms. Cristine BOYD
104 Exec Dir Global Engagement .... Ms. Robyn K. BROWN

The University of Akron-Wayne College (I)

1901 Smucker Road, Orrville OH 44667-9758
Telephone: (330) 683-2010　FICE Identification: 010818
Accreditation: **&HLC**

† Regional accreditation is carried under the parent institution in Akron, OH.

University of Cincinnati Main Campus (J)

2624 Clifton Avenue, Cincinnati OH 45221-0001
County: Hamilton　FICE Identification: 003125
Unit ID: 201885
Telephone: (513) 556-6000　Carnegie Class: DU-Highest
FAX Number: (513) 556-3237　Calendar System: Semester
URL: www.uc.edu
Established: 1819　Annual Undergrad Tuition & Fees (In-State): $12,138
Enrollment: 40,826　Coed
Affiliation or Control: State　IRS Status: 501(c)3
Highest Offering: Doctorate
Accreditation: **HLC**, ANEST, ART, AUD, CACREP, CAEP, CAHIIM, CAMPEP, CIDA, CLPSY, COARC, CONST, DANCE, DENT, DIETC, DIETD, LAW, MED, MIDWF, MT, MUS, NMT, NURSE, OT, PH, PHAR, PLNG, PTA, RADMAG, SCPSY, SP, SW, THEA

01 President ....Dr. Neville G. PINTO
05 Exec VP/Provost Academic Affairs ....Dr. Valerio FERME
11 Sr VP for Administration & Finance ....Mr. Robert AMBACH
03 Executive VP ....Dr. Ryan HAYS
46 Vice President for Research ....Dr. Patrick A. LIMBACH
63 Dean Med/Sr VP Health Affairs ....Dr. Andrew FILAK
111 VP Univ Advancement/Alumni Rels ....Mr. Peter LANDGREN
86 Chief Marketing Officer ....Ms. Nicola ZIADY
32 Vice Pres Student Affairs & Svcs ....Ms. Debra S. MERCHANT
10 Vice President for Finance ....Mr. Patrick A. KOWALSKI
13 Chief Information Officer ....Vacant
43 General Counsel ....Ms. Lori A. ROSS
15 Sr Assoc VP/Chief HR Officer ....Ms. Tamie L. GRUNOW
84 Vice Provost Enrollment ....Mr. Jack D. MINER
31 Director Community Development ....Ms. Megan SMITH
26 Exec Dir/Spokesperson Public Rels ....Ms. M. B REILLY
07 Asst Vice Prov Admissions ....Ms. Yosmeriz ROMAN
110 Vice Pres for Development ....Mr. Stephen ROSFELD
76 Dean Allied Health Sciences ....Dr. Tina WHALEN
49 Int Dean Arts & Sciences ....Dr. Margaret HANSON
50 Dean Business ....Dr. Marianne W. LEWIS
64 Dean Col Conservatory of Music ....Dr. Stanley E. ROMANSTEIN
48 Dean Design/Architecture/Art & Plng ....Dr. Timothy J. JACHNA
53 Dean Education/Crim Justice & HS ....Dr. Lawrence J. JOHNSON
54 Dean Engineering & Applied Sci ....Dr. John W. WEIDNER
61 Dean Law ....Ms. Verna L. WILLIAMS
66 Interim Dean Nursing ....Dr. Denice GORMLEY
67 Interim Dean Pharmacy ....Dr. Pamela C. HEATON
58 Int Dean Graduate School ....Dr. Raj MEHTA
70 Director School Social Work ....Dr. Ruth Anne VAN LOON
08 Dean Library ....Mr. Xuemao WANG
29 VP Alumni Affairs ....Ms. Jennifer HEISEY
28 VP Equity/Inclusion/Cmty Impact ....Dr. Bleuzette MARSHALL
41 Director Athletics ....Mr. John A. CUNNINGHAM
40 Regional Manager of the Bookstore ....Mr. Shane ZALESKI
20 Vice Provost Undergrad Studies ....Dr. Gisela ESCOE
38 Director Counseling Center ....Dr. Tara H. SCARBOROUGH
39 Sr Assoc VP Campus Services ....Mr. Todd DUNCAN
37 Director Student Financial Aid ....Mr. Randy ULSES
09 Director Institutional Research ....Mrs. Suzana H. LUZURIAGA VOIGHT
19 Director Public Safety/Police Chief ....Mr. James L. WHALEN
06 Registrar ....Dr. Douglas BURGESS
96 Assoc VP Purchasing ....Mr. Thomas B. GUERIN
45 Co-Dir Institute for Policy Rsrch ....Dr. Eric RADEMACHER
45 Co-Dir Institute for Policy Rsrch ....Dr. Kimberly DOWNING
104 Vice Provost International Affs ....Dr. Raj MEHTA
18 Chief Facilities/Physical Plant ....Mr. Joseph H. HARRELL
101 Exec Director Board of Trustees ....Ms. Nicole BLOUNT
88 Chief Innovation Officer ....Mr. David J. ADAMS
25 Assoc VP Sponsored Research ....Mr. Patrick E. CLARK
88 Asst VP eLearning ....Mr. Paul C. FOSTER
04 Administrative Asst to President ....Mr. Lawrence P. LAMPE
100 Chief of Staff ....Dr. Ryan HAYS
106 Vice Prov/Dean Cincinnati Online ....Dr. Jason E. LEMON
108 Vice Prov Institutional Assessment ....Dr. Gigi ESCOE
102 Dir Foundation/Corporate Relations ....Ms. Carol G. RUSSELL
105 Director Web Services ....Mr. Jeremy A. MARTIN

University of Cincinnati Blue Ash College (A)

9555 Plainfield Road, Blue Ash OH 45236-1096

County: Hamilton | FICE Identification: 004868 | Unit ID: 201955

Telephone: (513) 745-5600 | Carnegie Class: Bac/Assoc-Assoc Dom
FAX Number: (513) 745-5780 | Calendar System: Semester
URL: www.ucblueash.edu
Established: 1967 | Annual Undergrad Tuition & Fees (In-State): $6,256
Enrollment: 7,239 | Coed
Affiliation or Control: State | IRS Status: 501(c)3
Highest Offering: Baccalaureate
Accreditation: HLC, ADNUR, ART, DH, MAC, RAD

01 Dean ....Dr. Robin LIGHTNER
05 Assoc Dean Academic Affairs ....Dr. Tracy HERRMANN
10 Director Business Affairs ....Ms. Diane WHITE
20 Asst Dean Academic Affairs ....Dr. Gregory METZ
18 Director Facilities & Campus Plan ....Mr. Rob KNARR
13 Director Information Technology ....Mr. Dale HOFSTETTER
07 Director Admissions ....Mr. Brad TATE
09 Director Institutional Research ....Mr. Steve MILLER
30 Director Development ....Ms. Jennifer BERIGAN
08 Library Director ....Ms. Heather MALONEY
26 Director Mktg/Communication ....Mr. Pete GEMMER
32 Director Student Engagement ....Ms. Sarah WOLFE
121 Associate Dir of Academic Advising ....Ms. Laurie MALONE
35 Director One Stop Student Services ....Ms. Martha GEIGER
15 HR Manager ....Ms. Amy SMITH
22 Director Accessibility Resources ....Ms. Pamela GOINES

University of Cincinnati-Clermont College (B)

4200 Clermont College Drive, Batavia OH 45103-1785

County: Clermont | FICE Identification: 010805 | Unit ID: 201946

Telephone: (513) 732-5200 | Carnegie Class: Bac/Assoc-Mixed
FAX Number: (513) 732-5275 | Calendar System: Semester
URL: www.ucclermont.edu
Established: 1972 | Annual Undergrad Tuition & Fees (In-State): $5,864
Enrollment: 7,504 | Coed
Affiliation or Control: State | IRS Status: 501(c)3
Highest Offering: Baccalaureate
Accreditation: HLC, CAHIIM, PTAA, SURGA, SURGT

01 Dean ....Dr. Jeffrey C. BAUER
05 Assoc Dean Academic Affairs ....Vacant
20 Sr Assistant Dean Academic Affairs ....Mr. Richard STACKPOLE
32 Sr Asst Dean Student Services ....Ms. Mae HANNA
08 Director Library ....Ms. Catherine CARLSON
09 Asst Dean Acad Init & Inst Effect ....Ms. Susan RILEY
10 Business Officer ....Mr. Daniel SOLAZZO
35 Assistant Dean of Student Affairs ....Ms. Jennifer RADT
07 Assoc Director Recruitment ....Mr. Blaine KELLY
22 Director Accessibility & Testing ....Ms. Meghann LITTRELL
41 Athletic Director ....Mr. Brian SULLIVAN
30 Director of Development ....Ms. Dana PARKER
84 Assoc Director of Enrollmnt Svcs ....Vacant
106 Dir Online Education/E-learning ....Ms. Karen LANKISCH
28 Chief Diversity Officer ....Ms. Jennifer RADT

University of Dayton (C)

300 College Park, Dayton OH 45469-0001

County: Montgomery | FICE Identification: 003127 | Unit ID: 202480

Telephone: (937) 229-1000 | Carnegie Class: DU-Higher
FAX Number: (937) 229-4000 | Calendar System: Semester
URL: www.udayton.edu
Established: 1850 | Annual Undergrad Tuition & Fees: $44,890
Enrollment: 11,650 | Coed
Affiliation or Control: Roman Catholic | IRS Status: 501(c)3
Highest Offering: Doctorate
Accreditation: HLC, ARCPA, ART, CACREP, CAEP, CEA, DIETD, LAW, MUS, PTA, SPAA

01 President ....Dr. Eric F. SPINA
05 Provost ....Dr. Paul H. BENSON
32 VP Student Development ....Mr. William M. FISCHER
10 EVP Finance & Admin Services ....Mr. Andrew E. HORNER
111 VP Univ Advancement ....Ms. Jennifer L. HOWE
26 VP Marketing & Communications ....Ms. Molly WILSON
41 VP/Director of Athletics ....Mr. Neil G. SULLIVAN
15 VP Human Resources ....Mr. Troy W. WASHINGTON
28 VP Diversity & Inclusion ....Dr. Lawrence A. BURNLEY
84 VP for Strategic Enrollment Mgmt ....Dr. Jason K. REINOEHL
42 VP for Mission and Rector ....Rev. James F. FITZ, SM
46 VP for Research ....Dr. John E. LELAND
30 Sr Dir Development/Principal Gifts ....Mr. James F. BROTHERS
42 Exec Director Campus Ministry ....Ms. Crystal C. SULLIVAN
31 Dir Ctr for Ldrshp in Cmty ....Ms. Hunter P. GOODMAN
20 Assoc Provost Faculty & Admin Affs ....Dr. Carolyn ROECKER-PHELPS
88 Asc Prov Lrng Spprt/Dir Rch Tch Ctr ....Dr. Deborah J. BICKFORD
06 Registrar ....Ms. Jennifer M. CREECH
07 Asst VP/Dean of Admission & Fin Aid ....Vacant
19 Exec Director/Chief of Police ....Mr. Savalas KIDD
09 Director Institutional Studies ....Ms. Susan K. SEXTON
21 Comptroller ....Ms. Angela K. BUECHELE
35 Assoc VP/Dean of Students ....Ms. Christine M. SCHRAMM
36 Director Career Services ....Mr. Jason C. ECKERT
38 Asst VP Student Dev/Dir Counseling ....Vacant
18 VP for Facilities/Management/Plng ....Mr. Richard KRYSIAK, JR.
23 Medical Director Univ Health Ctr ....Dr. Mary P. BUCHWALDER
08 Dean University Libraries ....Ms. Kathleen M. WEBB
49 Dean College A&S ....Dr. Jason L. PIERCE
61 Dean School of Law ....Mr. Andrew L. STRAUSS
50 Dean Sch of Business Admin ....Dr. John MITTELSTAEDT
58 Assoc Prov Graduate Acad Affairs ....Dr. Paul M. VANDERBURGH
13 Assoc Provost & Chief Info Officer ....Dr. Thomas D. SKILL
53 Interim Dean SOE & Health Sci ....Dr. Corinne DAPRANO
54 Dean School of Engineering ....Dr. Eddy M. ROJAS
29 Alumni Engagement Officer ....Ms. Catherine GRADY
35 Dir Student Life & Kennedy Union ....Ms. Amy L. LOPEZ-MATTHEWS
37 Exec Dir Flyers First/Dir Fin Aid ....Ms. Catherine MIX
39 Asst Dean Students & Dir Res Life ....Mr. Steven T. HERNDON
40 Manager UD Bookstore ....Ms. Julie M. BANKS
43 Univ Counsel/Dir Legal Affairs ....Ms. Mary A. RECKER
96 Dir Univ Purchases/Business Service ....Vacant
92 Dir University Honors/Scholars Pgm ....Dr. John P. MCCOMBE
94 Chair Women's/Gender Studies ....Vacant
22 Dir Affirmative Action & Compliance ....Ms. Patricia BERNAL-OLSON
86 Exec Dir Govt/Regional Relations ....Mr. S. Ted BUCARO
27 Dir Marketing & Creative Services ....Ms. Kim B. LALLY
04 Asst to President ....Ms. Annette MITCHELL
100 Executive Director ....Mr. Thomas U. WECKESSER
101 Secretary of the Board of Trustees ....Ms. Lisa S. RISMILLER

The University of Findlay (D)

1000 North Main Street, Findlay OH 45840-3653

County: Hancock | FICE Identification: 003045 | Unit ID: 202763

Telephone: (419) 422-8313 | Carnegie Class: DU-Mod
FAX Number: (419) 434-4822 | Calendar System: Semester
URL: www.findlay.edu
Established: 1882 | Annual Undergrad Tuition & Fees: $36,484
Enrollment: 4,829 | Coed
Affiliation or Control: Church Of God | IRS Status: 501(c)3
Highest Offering: Doctorate
Accreditation: HLC, ACBSP, ARCPA, CAEP, CEA, NMT, NURSE, OT, PHAR, PTA, SW

01 President ....Dr. Katherine R. FELL
05 Vice President for Academic Affairs ....Dr. Darin FIELDS
10 VP Business Affairs/CFO/Treasurer ....Mr. Thomas LAUSE
84 VP Enrollment Management ....Mr. Dave EMSWELLER
111 Vice Pres University Advancement ....Dr. Marcia SLOAN LATTA
32 Vice President for Student Affairs ....Mr. David W. EMSWELLER
20 Assoc VP Academic Affairs ....Dr. C. Damon OSBORNE
04 Assistant to the President ....Ms. Liz DITTO
81 Dean College of Sciences ....Dr. Jeffrey FRYE
50 Interim Dean College of Business ....Dr. Kirby OVERTON
49 Dean Col of Arts/Hum & Social Sci ....Dr. Ronald TULLEY
76 Dean College Health Professions ....Dr. Richard STATES
67 Dean College of Pharmacy ....Dr. Debra PARKER
53 Dean College of Education ....Dr. Julie MCINTOSH
18 Director of Physical Plant ....Mr. Orion JONES
06 Registrar/Dir of Inst Research ....Mr. Anthony SILECCHIA
41 Athletic Director ....Ms. Brandi LAURITA
08 Director of Shafer Library ....Mr. Andrew WHITIS
37 Director of Financial Aid ....Mr. Joseph F. SPENCER
13 VP of Information Tech Services ....Dr. Raymond MCCANDLESS
29 Director of Alumni/Parents/Friends ....Ms. Julie KLINGER
26 Asst VP of Enrollment Mgt/Marketing ....Ms. Rebecca JENKINS
36 Dir Career/Professional Development ....Mr. Bradley C. HAMMER
15 Director of Human Resources ....Mr. Robert LINK
23 Director of Health Services ....Ms. Tara SMITH
38 Director Counseling Services ....Ms. Jodi FIRSDON
40 Manager of Bookstore ....Mr. Jay CANTERBURY
42 Director Christian Ministries ....Mr. Matthew GINTER
19 Chief of Police/Dir of Security ....Mr. William SPRAW
104 Asst VP Intl/Intercult/Svc Engage ....Mr. Christopher SIPPEL
101 Secretary to the Board of Trustees ....Ms. Liz DITTO
25 Grants Manager ....Ms. Juliann REINEKE
88 Asst Dir International Admissions ....Vacant
21 Controller ....Ms. Megan SCHULTE
39 Asst Director of Housing ....Ms. Shari HELLMAN
35 Assistant Dean of Students ....Mr. Johnathan FERRARO
44 Director Annual Giving ....Ms. Kelly M. WARNER
30 Asst VP for Development ....Mr. Tyson PINION
07 Director of Admissions/Operations ....Ms. Kelli E. WAGES
07 Director of Admissions/Events ....Ms. DeeDee SPRAW

University of Mount Union (E)

1972 Clark Avenue, Alliance OH 44601-3993

County: Stark | FICE Identification: 003083 | Unit ID: 204185

Telephone: (330) 821-5320 | Carnegie Class: Bac-Diverse
FAX Number: (330) 829-2811 | Calendar System: Semester
URL: www.mountunion.edu
Established: 1846 | Annual Undergrad Tuition & Fees: $32,600
Enrollment: 2,178 | Coed
Affiliation or Control: Independent Non-Profit | IRS Status: 501(c)3
Highest Offering: Doctorate
Accreditation: HLC, ACBSP, ARCPA, CAEP, COSMA, MUS, NURSE, PTA

01 President ....Dr. Thomas J. BOTZMAN
05 Vice Pres Acad Affs/Provost ....Dr. Jeffrey R. BREESE
10 Vice Pres Business Affs/Treasurer ....Mr. Patrick D. HEDDLESTON
111 Vice President Univ Advancement ....Mr. Gregory KING
32 Vice Pres Student Affs/Dean Stdnts ....Mr. John FRAZIER
84 Vice President for Enrollment Mgmt ....Ms. Lindajean WESTERN
26 Vice President for Marketing ....Ms. Melissa GARDNER
08 Librarian ....Ms. Carla SARRAT
06 University Registrar ....Dr. Bryan BOATRIGHT
07 Director of Admission ....Dr. Eric YOUNG
112 Director of Planned Giving ....Ms. Bethany LESLIE
13 Director of Information Technology ....Ms. Tina STUCHELL
110 Director of Advancement ....Mr. Joseph D. MONTGOMERY
29 Director Alumni/College Activities ....Ms. Audra YOUNGEN
85 Director Center for Global Educ ....Dr. Jennifer HALL
18 Director of Physical Plant ....Mr. Lee SMITH
15 Director of Human Resources ....Ms. Marci CRAIG
39 Director of Residence Life ....Ms. Sara SHERER
42 Interim University Chaplain ....Mr. Stephen DAGES
36 Assistant Dean for Student Success ....Ms. Jessica CUNION
40 Manager of University Store ....Ms. Aimee SCHULLER
41 Interim Athletic Director ....Mr. Michael PARNELL
04 Exec Assistant to the President ....Ms. Heather HICKMAN
45 Assoc VP Planning Implementation ....Mr. Ronald CROWL
35 Associate Dean of Students ....Ms. Michelle GAFFNEY
96 Purchasing and Risk Manager ....Mr. Shawn BAGLEY
19 Director Security/Safety ....Mr. William KETJEN
28 Director of Diversity & Inclusion ....Mr. Ronald HOLDEN
38 Director of Counseling Services ....Ms. Francine PACKARD
44 Director of the Mount Union Fund ....Ms. Bethany LESLIE
37 Director Student Financial Aid ....Ms. Kathleen THOMAS
79 Dean of Arts & Humanities ....Dr. Heather DUDA
76 Dean of Natural & Health Sciences ....Dr. Sandra MADAR
83 Dean of Applied & Social Sciences ....Dr. Kristine STILL
09 Director of Institutional Research ....Ms. Suzette BURLINGAME

University of Northwestern Ohio (F)

1441 N Cable Road, Lima OH 45805-1498

County: Allen | FICE Identification: 004861 | Unit ID: 204486

Telephone: (419) 227-3141 | Carnegie Class: Bac/Assoc-Mixed
FAX Number: (419) 229-6926 | Calendar System: Quarter
URL: www.unoh.edu
Established: 1920 | Annual Undergrad Tuition & Fees: $11,550
Enrollment: 3,009 | Coed
Affiliation or Control: Independent Non-Profit | IRS Status: 501(c)3
Highest Offering: Master's

Accreditation: HLC, ACBSP, CAHIIM, MAC

01 President ... Dr. Jeffrey A. JARVIS
05 Vice Pres Academic Affairs/Provost ... Dr. Dean HOBLER
10 Vice President Finance ... Mrs. Marcia EICKHOLT
07 Dir of Admissions-Coll of Business ... Mr. Tony AZZARELLO
18 Vice Pres of Property Management ... Vacant
26 VP Public Relations/Marketing ... Mrs. Stephanie MALLOY
15 Exec Director of Human Resources ... Ms. Geri MORRIS
21 Controller ... Mr. James S. BRONDER
37 Director of Financial Aid ... Mr. Wendell SCHICK
04 Executive Assistant to President ... Mrs. Jennifer BENDELE
72 Dean College of Technologies ... Mr. Kevin MEAGER
06 Director of Registration ... Ms. Traci WELLS

University of Rio Grande (A)

218 N College Avenue, PO BOX 500,
Rio Grande OH 45674-3100
County: Gallia FICE Identification: 003116
Unit ID: 205203
Telephone: (740) 245-5353 Carnegie Class: Bac/Assoc-Mixed
FAX Number: (740) 245-5266 Calendar System: Semester
URL: www.rio.edu
Established: 1876 Annual Undergrad Tuition & Fees: $27,481
Enrollment: 1,551 Coed
Affiliation or Control: Independent Non-Profit IRS Status: 501(c)3
Highest Offering: Master's
Accreditation: HLC, ADNUR, CAEP, CAEPN, COARC, DMS, IACBE, NUR, RAD, SW

01 President ... Mr. Ryan SMITH
05 Provost/VP of Academic Affairs ... Dr. Richard SAX
10 CFO/VP of Finance ... Vacant
32 COO/VP Student & Admin Affairs ... Mrs. Rebecca LONG
45 Associate Provost Inst Effective ... Dr. David A. LAWRENCE
15 Director of Human Resources ... Mr. Chris NOURSE
26 Director of Marketing ... Ms. Renee DELAWDER
49 Interim Dean Col of Arts & Science ... Ms. Lynley CAREY
107 Dean College Prof/Tech Studies ... Dr. Donna MITCHELL
06 Registrar ... Ms. Olivia BEVAN
07 Director of Recruitment ... Ms. Kristie RUSSELL
88 Dir Cmty Ptnrshp/Admission Process ... Mrs. Amanda EHMAN
111 Exec Dir Institutional Advancement ... Vacant
41 Athletic Director ... Mr. Jeff LANHAM
08 Director of Davis Library ... Ms. Amy R. WILSON
13 Chief Information Officer ... Mr. Scott HUGHES
14 Management Information Systems Adm ... Mr. Eric LOLLATHIN
29 Director of Alumni Relations ... Vacant
04 Acting Board of Trustees Prof ... Ms. Susan HAFT
19 Campus Police Chief ... Mr. Scott BORDEN
37 Director Financial Aid ... Mrs. Meghann FRALEY
89 Dir New Student Adv/Testing/Career ... Mrs. Susan HAFT
121 Director of Student Success ... Dr. Stephanie ALEXANDER

University of Toledo (B)

2801 W Bancroft, Toledo OH 43606-3390
County: Lucas FICE Identification: 003131
Unit ID: 206084
Telephone: (419) 530-4636 Carnegie Class: DU-Higher
FAX Number: (419) 530-4984 Calendar System: Semester
URL: www.utoledo.edu
Established: 1872 Annual Undergrad Tuition & Fees (In-State): $11,082
Enrollment: 18,319 Coed
Affiliation or Control: State IRS Status: 501(c)3
Highest Offering: Doctorate
Accreditation: HLC, ARCPA, ART, CAATE, CACREP, CAEP, CAHIIM, CAMPEP, CAPRT, CEA, CLPSY, COARC, DENT, EMT, LAW, MED, MT, MUS, NURSE, OT, PA, PH, PHAR, PTA, SP, SW, THEA

01 President ... Dr. Gregory C. POSTEL
100 Chief of Staff ... Ms. Diane MILLER
05 EVP Academic Affairs/Provost ... Dr. Karen BJORKMAN
63 EVP for Clin Affs/Dean COMLS ... Dr. Christopher COOPER
10 EVP Finance & Admin/CFO ... Mr. Matt SCHROEDER
43 Vice President/General Counsel ... Mr. Charles JAKE
32 VP for Student Affairs ... Dr. Phillip COCKRELL
111 AVP for Advancement ... Ms. Cheryl ZWYER
84 Int VP Enrollment Management ... Mr. David MEREDITH
46 Vice President Research ... Dr. Frank J. CALZONETTI
13 Vice President CIO/CTO ... Mr. William MCCREARY
41 Vice Pres and Director of Athletics ... Mr. Michael E. O'BRIEN
28 VP for Diversity and Inclusion ... Dr. Willie MCKETHER
17 CEO Univ Toledo Med Ctr ... Mr. Richard SWAINE
86 VP Government Relations ... Ms. Diane MILLER
26 VP Marketing/Communications ... Dr. Adrienne KING
06 University Registrar ... Ms. Julie R. QUINONEZ
58 Int Dean Graduate Studies ... Dr. Barry SCHEUERMANN
50 Dean Business & Innovation ... Dr. Anne BALASZ
53 Dean J Herb College of Educ ... Dr. Raymond WITTE
54 Dean Engineering ... Dr. Michael TOOLE
76 Dean Health & Human Services ... Dr. Mark MERRICK
79 Dean Arts & Letters ... Dr. Charlene GILBERT
61 Dean Law ... Mr. Ben BARROS
81 Dean NSM ... Dr. Marcus SEIGAR
66 Dean Nursing ... Dr. Linda LEWANDOWSKI
67 Int Dean Pharmacy & Pharm Sciences ... Dr. Monica HOLIDAY-GOODMAN
92 Dean Jesup Scott Honors College ... Dr. Heidi APPEL
89 Dean University College ... Dr. Barbara KOPP-MILLER
35 AVP & Dean of Students ... Dr. Sammy SPANN
39 AVP Residence Life ... Ms. Valerie WALSTON
37 AVP Financial Aid/Enrollment Svcs ... Mr. Gina ROBERTS
15 Sr Director Faculty Labor Relations ... Vacant
102 President Foundation ... Ms. Brenda LEE
29 Assoc Vice Pres Alumni Relations ... Mr. William PIERCE
36 Dir Exp Lrng and Career Svcs ... Ms. Shelly DROUILLARD
85 Director Ctr for Intl Studies ... Ms. Sara CLARK
116 Director Internal Audit ... Mr. David CUTRI
19 Chief of Police ... Mr. Jeff NEWTON
40 General Manager Bookstore SU ... Ms. Colleen STRAYER
18 AVP Facilities/Physical Plant ... Mr. Jason TOTH
08 Director University Libraries ... Dr. Beau CASE
04 Sr Dir of Admin Operations ... Ms. Katie DEBENEDICTIS
07 Director of Admissions ... Mr. Collin PALMER
101 Secretary of the Institution/Board ... Ms. Katie DEBENEDICTIS
96 Director of Supply Chain Management ... Ms. Jennifer PASTOREK

Ursuline College (C)

2550 Lander Road, Cleveland OH 44124-4398
County: Cuyahoga FICE Identification: 003134
Unit ID: 206349
Telephone: (440) 449-4200 Carnegie Class: Masters/M
FAX Number: (440) 646-8318 Calendar System: Semester
URL: www.ursuline.edu
Established: 1871 Annual Undergrad Tuition & Fees: $34,630
Enrollment: 1,100 Female
Affiliation or Control: Roman Catholic IRS Status: 501(c)3
Highest Offering: Doctorate
Accreditation: HLC, ACATE, CACREP, CAEP, IACBE, NURSE, SW

01 President ... Sr. Christine DEVINNE
05 Vice President Academic Affairs ... Dr. Kathryn LAFONTANA
10 Vice Pres & Chief Financial Officer ... Mr. Robert HAMILL
111 Vice Pres Institutional Advancement ... Mr. Richard KONISIEWICZ
32 Vice President of Student Affairs ... Ms. Deanne HURLEY
84 Vice Pres of Enrollment Management ... Ms. Susan DILENO
49 Dean Arts/Sciences & Prof Studies ... Dr. Elizabeth KAVRAN
66 Dean College of Nursing ... Dr. Patricia SHARPNACK
88 Exec Dir Prof Dev/Degree Completion ... Ms. Brooke SCHARLOTT
08 Director of Library & Acad Support ... Ms. Suzanna SCHROEDER-GREEN
06 Registrar & Dir Academic Ops ... Ms. Barbara HELMS
21 Controller ... Ms. Kimberly LAKOTA
30 Director of Development ... Ms. Erin GAY MIYOSHI
37 Director of Financial Aid ... Ms. Mary Lynn PERRI
29 Dir Alumnae Relations/Annual Fund ... Ms. Lynne DEWYRE
26 Dir of Marketing/Communications ... Ms. Ann MCGUIRE
15 Director of Human Resources ... Ms. Kelli KNAUS
13 Dir of Information Technology ... Mr. Matt BOOS
39 Director of Residence Life ... Ms. Gina DEMART-KRAUS
42 Director Campus Ministry ... Ms. Paula FITZGERALD
28 Asst Dean of Diversity ... Ms. Yolanda KING
106 Dir Online Education/E-learning ... Vacant
41 Athletic Director ... Ms. Cynthia MCKNIGHT
04 Sr Executive Asst to President ... Ms. Julie HERBERT
19 Director Security/Safety ... Mr. James KRZYWICKI
22 Dir Compliance/Title IX/Disability ... Ms. Deborah KAMAT
07 Director of Admissions ... Ms. Emily HAGGERTY

Valor Christian College (D)

PO Box 800, Columbus OH 43216
County: Franklin Identification: 667093
Unit ID: 486257
Telephone: (614) 837-4088 Carnegie Class: Spec 2-yr-Other
FAX Number: (614) 837-6904 Calendar System: Semester
URL: www.valorcollege.edu
Established: 1990 Annual Undergrad Tuition & Fees: $8,410
Enrollment: 289 Coed
Affiliation or Control: Independent Non-Profit IRS Status: 501(c)3
Highest Offering: Baccalaureate
Accreditation: BI

01 President ... Ken GRUNDEN
05 Vice Pres Academic Affairs ... Laquetta CORTNER
32 Dean of Students ... Horace SIMONS
42 Campus Pastor ... Ashton PARSLEY
04 Exec Asst to VP Academic Affairs ... Vonnetta KING
37 Director of Financial Aid ... Norm STOPPENBRINK

Walsh University (E)

2020 East Maple Street, North Canton OH 44720
County: Stark FICE Identification: 003135
Unit ID: 206437
Telephone: (330) 490-7090 Carnegie Class: Masters/M
FAX Number: (330) 499-7165 Calendar System: Other
URL: www.walsh.edu
Established: 1958 Annual Undergrad Tuition & Fees: $31,725
Enrollment: 2,651 Coed
Affiliation or Control: Roman Catholic IRS Status: 501(c)3
Highest Offering: Doctorate
Accreditation: HLC, CACREP, CAEP, CAEPN, NURSE, OT, PTA

01 President ... Dr. Tim COLLINS
10 Vice Pres Finance/Business Affairs ... Ms. Laurel LUSK
05 Vice Pres Academic Affairs ... Dr. Michael DUNPHY
111 Vice Pres of Advancement ... Mr. Eric BELDEN
41 Vice Pres for Athletics ... Mr. Dale S. HOWARD
26 VP for Marketing/Communications ... Ms. Teresa FOX
13 VP of Administration/CIO ... Dr. Brian GREENWELL
07 Vice Pres for Enrollment ... Ms. Rebecca CONEGLIO
20 Assoc VP & Dean of Academic Admin ... Ms. Edna MCCULLOH
09 Dean Inst Effectiveness ... Dr. Ute LAHAIE
32 VP Student Affairs/Dean of Students ... Mr. Bryan BADAR
18 Director of Facilities & Grounds ... Mr. John SCHISSLER
91 Database Administrator ... Ms. Hope STANCIU
22 Director of Compliance ... Mr. Jason FAUTAS
78 Assoc Dean of Experiential Learning ... Dr. Rachel HOSLER
42 Senior Chaplain ... Fr. Thomas CEBULA
38 Director Counseling Services ... Ms. Frances MORROW
42 Director of Campus Ministry ... Mr. Ben WALTHER
31 Dir Campus & Community Programs ... Ms. Jacqueline M. MANSER
37 Director Financial Aid ... Mrs. Holly VAN GILDER
15 Director of Human Resources ... Ms. Kristin HANNON
29 Director of Alumni Relations ... Ms. Stephanie KOONTZ
25 Director of Grants ... Dr. Rachel HAMMEL
19 Chief of Campus Police ... Mr. Ron PERDUE
08 Director of Library Services ... Ms. LuAnn BORIS
83 Dean School of Behav/Health Science ... Dr. Pamela RITZLINE
49 Int Dean School of Arts & Science ... Dr. Katherine BROWN
66 Dean Byers School of Nursing ... Ms. Judy KREYE
92 Director Honors Program ... Ms. Katherine BROWN
04 Administrative Asst to President ... Ms. Christine SCHEETZ
06 Registrar ... Ms. Stacie HERMAN
50 Dean DeVille School of Business ... Dr. Rajshekhar JAVALGI
53 Chair Div of Education ... Dr. Jeannie DEFAZIO
104 Director of Global Learning ... Mr. Michael CINSON
39 Assoc Dean of Students ... Ms. Tiffany KINNARD-PAYTON
96 Director of Purchasing ... Ms. Rebecca MIMA
106 Director Digital Campus ... Ms. Christine LYNN
27 Director of University Relations ... Ms. Andrea MCCAFFREY

Washington State Community College (F)

710 Colegate Drive, Marietta OH 45750-9225
County: Washington FICE Identification: 010453
Unit ID: 206446
Telephone: (740) 374-8716 Carnegie Class: Assoc/HVT-High Non
FAX Number: (740) 374-9562 Calendar System: Semester
URL: www.wscc.edu
Established: 1971 Annual Undergrad Tuition & Fees (In-State): $3,960
Enrollment: 1,809 Coed
Affiliation or Control: State IRS Status: 501(c)3
Highest Offering: Associate Degree
Accreditation: HLC, COARC, MLTAD

01 President ... Dr. Vicky WOOD
10 Chief Financial Officer ... Ms. Angela LANG
111 VP of Institutional Advancement ... Ms. Amanda K. HERB
05 VP for Academic Affairs ... Ms. Sarah PARKER
03 VP of Organizational Effectiveness ... Mr. Gary BARBER
102 Exec Dir Foundation & Grants Dev ... Vacant
76 Dean of Health Sciences/Sciences ... Dr. Heather KINCAID
49 Dean of Public Services & Transfer ... Dr. Jona HALL
54 Dean of Engineering ... Mr. George BILOKONSKY
06 Registrar ... Ms. Dustin TAYLOR
07 Director of Admissions ... Ms. Carrie THRASH
26 Dir of Marketing & Communications ... Vacant
37 Director of Financial Aid ... Ms. Reba BARTRUG
08 Director Library Services ... Mr. Jeffrey GRAFFIUS
22 Director of College Access and ETS ... Ms. Donna MUNTZ
04 Admin Assistant to the President ... Ms. Cecily B. FYFFE
103 Director Workforce Development ... Vacant
18 Chief Facilities/Physical Plant Ofc ... Mr. Brandon HERB

Wilberforce University (G)

PO Box 1001, Wilberforce OH 45384-1001
County: Greene FICE Identification: 003141
Unit ID: 206491
Telephone: (937) 376-2911 Carnegie Class: Bac-Diverse
FAX Number: (937) 376-2627 Calendar System: Semester
URL: www.wilberforce.edu
Established: 1856 Annual Undergrad Tuition & Fees: $13,250
Enrollment: 453 Coed
Affiliation or Control: African Methodist Episcopal IRS Status: 501(c)3
Highest Offering: Master's
Accreditation: #HLC

01 President ... Dr. Elfred A. PINKARD
84 SVP of Enrollment/Student Affairs ... Dr. Tashia BRADLEY
10 Sr VP of Administration & Finance ... Mr. William WOODSON
15 VP of Administration and HR . Mrs. Anita R. JEFFERSON-GOMEZ
05 Int Provost/VP Academic Affairs ... Dr. Johnny JONES
111 VP of Institutional Advancement ... Mrs. Natalie COLES
32 VP Student Engagement & Success ... Mr. Parris CARTER
49 Dean of Arts & Sciences ... Dr. Sharon TIPPINS
107 Int Dean of Professional Studies ... Dr. Anuradha VENKATESWARAN
07 Director of Admissions ... Ms. Jocelyn NEELY
06 Registrar ... Mrs. Rudell MOORE
113 Bursar ... Ms. Debra OLIVER
41 Athletic Director ... Mr. Dereck WILLIAMS
51 Director of CLIMB Program ... Ms. Kimberly HARDY-PORTER
25 Director Title III/Sponsored Pgms ... Mrs. Mary MORALE
19 Chief of Campus Police & Safety ... Mr. Jon CROSS
04 Executive Asst to the President ... Mrs. Danita PEARL
18 Director of Plant Logistics ... Mr. Kevin FRYE
37 Director Student Financial Aid ... Mrs. Andrea SANDERS
08 Director of Library Services ... Ms. Stephanie ROSTRON

13 Director of IT Mr. Andrew MONCE
29 Director Alumni Affairs Mr. Albert BAILEY
21 Controller Mr. Jason COOK
09 Director of Institutional Research Dr. Michael ROBINSON

Wilmington College (A)

1870 Quaker Way, Wilmington OH 45177-2499
County: Clinton FICE Identification: 003142
Unit ID: 206507
Telephone: (937) 382-6661 Carnegie Class: Bac-Diverse
FAX Number: (937) 383-8574 Calendar System: Semester
URL: www.wilmington.edu
Established: 1870 Annual Undergrad Tuition & Fees: $27,400
Enrollment: 1,165 Coed
Affiliation or Control: Friends IRS Status: 501(c)3
Highest Offering: Master's
Accreditation: HLC, CAATE, CAEP, COSMA

01 President Dr. Trevor M. BATES
04 Assistant to the President Mrs. Leslie A. NICHOLS
05 Provost Dr. Erika GOODWIN
20 Academic Dean/Dean Faculty Dr. Kenneth PATTERSON
10 Vice President Business/Finance Ms. Beatriz IBANEZ
111 Interim VP for College Advancement Mr. Joe BULL
88 Vice President External Programs Ms. Sylvia STEVENS
32 Vice Pres Student Affs/Stdnt Life Ms. Sigrid B. SOLOMON
41 Vice President Athletic Admin Dr. Terry A. RUPERT
84 Chief Enrollment Officer/Admissions Mr. Dennis KELLY
124 AVP of Student Retention/Success Ms. Deanna VATAN
09 Dir Institutional Effectiveness Mr. Daniel MCCAMISH
26 Sr Dir of Pub Relations/Admissions Mr. Randall F. SARVIS
06 Registrar/Academic Records Ms. Sue HUTCHENS
08 Director of Watson Library Ms. Lucinda CHANDLER
15 Director of Human Resources Ms. Libby HAYES
36 Director of Career Services Dr. Nina TALLEY
18 Director of Physical Plant Mr. Randy GERBER
29 Director of Alumni Engagement Mr. John SCHRANTZ
37 Dir Financial Aid/One Stop Center Ms. Cheryl LOUALLEN
07 Director of Admission Mr. Adam LOHREY
21 Controller Ms. Kelly DUFFY
102 Director Leadership Giving Ms. Amie DENKENBERGER
105 Assoc Director Digital Marketing Ms. Ashleigh WELLMAN
13 Director of Information Technology Mr. George DIMIDIK
28 Director of Multicultural Affairs Mr. Chip MURDOCK
38 Director of Counseling Ms. Kazi MCDOWELL
39 Dir Resident Life/Student Housing Mr. Nick HOOVER
44 Annual Fund Coordinator Ms. Sarah HOLTSCLAW
114 Budget Director Ms. Sara SCOTT

Wilmington College Cincinnati (B)

3520 Central Pkwy, 181 Main Bldg, Cincinnati OH 45223
Telephone: (513) 569-4580 Identification: 770364
Accreditation: &HLC

Winebrenner Theological Seminary (C)

950 N. Main Street, Second Floor, Findlay OH 45840
County: Hancock FICE Identification: 004060
Unit ID: 206516
Telephone: (419) 434-4200 Carnegie Class: Spec-4-yr-Faith
FAX Number: N/A Calendar System: Trimester
URL: www.winebrenner.edu
Established: 1942 Annual Graduate Tuition & Fees: N/A
Enrollment: 67 Coed
Affiliation or Control: Independent Non-Profit IRS Status: 501(c)3
Highest Offering: Doctorate; No Undergraduates
Accreditation: HLC, CACREP, THEOL

01 President/CEO Dr. Brent C. SLEASMAN
05 VP of Academic Advancement Dr. Bruce COATS
10 Director of Finance Mr. Tom WEAVER
08 College Librarian Mrs. Margaret HIRSCHY
06 Registrar Vacant
04 Assistant to the President Vacant
108 Director Institutional Assessment Dr. Kathryn HELLEMAN
84 Director Enrollment Management Mrs. Amy J. KINNEY
30 Director of Development Ms. Katerina HINKLE

Wittenberg University (D)

PO Box 720, Springfield OH 45501-0720
County: Clark FICE Identification: 003143
Unit ID: 206525
Telephone: (937) 327-6231 Carnegie Class: Bac-A&S
FAX Number: (937) 327-6340 Calendar System: Semester
URL: www.wittenberg.edu
Established: 1845 Annual Undergrad Tuition & Fees: $41,476
Enrollment: 1,488 Coed
Affiliation or Control: Evangelical Lutheran Church In America
IRS Status: 501(c)3
Highest Offering: Master's
Accreditation: HLC, CAEPN, MUS, NURSE

01 President Dr. Michael FRANDSEN
05 Provost Dr. Michelle MATTSON
10 Vice Pres Finance/Administration Mr. Rob YOUNG
84 Vice Pres Enrollment Management Ms. Carola THORSON
111 VP University Advancement Ms. Rebecca KOCHER
26 Vice Pres Marketing/Communications Ms. Karen GERBOTH
41 VP/Director Athletics/Recreation Mr. Brian AGLER
35 Vice Pres/Dean of Students Ms. Casey GILL
09 Assoc Prov Acad Affs/Inst Research Dr. Darby L. HILLER-FREUND
124 Sr Assoc Dean Stdnt Success/Retent Mr. Jonathan DURAJ
85 Director International Education Ms. JoAnn BENNETT
20 Director of Academic Services Ms. Grace WHITELEY SEVER
42 Pastor to the University Rev. Rachel SANDUM TUNE
08 Interim Library Director Ms. Kristin PETERS
13 Chief Information Officer Mr. Richard MICKOOL
31 Director Community Service Ms. Kristen L. COLLIER
06 Registrar Ms. Debra LOVELESS
07 Sr Assoc Dir of Admissions Ms. Linda BEALS
58 Director Graduate Studies in Educ Dr. Amy MCGUFFEY
94 Director of Women's Studies Dr. Heather H. WRIGHT
29 Dir of Alumni/Lifelong Engagement Ms. Holly GERSBACHER
27 Sports Information Director Mr. AJ MEYER
105 Sr Writer/Web Communications Spec Mr. Ryan MAURER
39 Associate Dean for Residence Life Ms. Sherri SADOWSKI
38 Director Student Counseling Mr. Matthew WEST
88 Director Student Involvement Ms. Liz ARTZ
28 Assoc Dean Students/Dir Diversity Ms. Corrine WITHERSPOON
37 Exec Director of Financial Aid Ms. Amy BARNHART
15 Director Human Resources Ms. Mary Beth WALTER
19 Chief of Police Mr. Jim HUTCHINS
40 Manager of Bookstore Ms. Amy GARNER

Wright State University Main Campus (E)

3640 Colonel Glenn Highway, Dayton OH 45435-0001
County: Greene FICE Identification: 003078
Unit ID: 206604
Telephone: (937) 775-3333 Carnegie Class: DU-Higher
FAX Number: (937) 775-3301 Calendar System: Semester
URL: www.wright.edu
Established: 1964 Annual Undergrad Tuition & Fees (In-State): $10,012
Enrollment: 10,936 Coed
Affiliation or Control: State IRS Status: 501(c)3
Highest Offering: Doctorate
Accreditation: HLC, #CAATE, CACREP, CAEPN, CLPSY, EXSC, IPSY, MED, MT, MUS, NURSE, PH, SPAA, SW

01 President Dr. Susan L. EDWARDS
05 Interim Provost Dr. Oliver H. EVANS
11 Chief Operation Officer/EVP Mr. Gregory P. SAMPLE
32 Dean of Students Dr. Chris TAYLOR
46 Interim Vice Pres Research Dr. Madhavi KADAKIA
111 Int Vice Pres Univ Advancement Mr. Bill BIGHAM
84 Chief Recruitment and Admissions Ms. Jennifer MCCAMIS
20 Vice Prov Acad Aff/Dean Grad School Dr. Barry MILLIGAN
08 University Librarian Ms. Karen WILHOIT
15 Assoc Vice Pres for Human Resources Ms. Shari MICKEY-BOGGS
50 Dean Raj Soin Col of Business Dr. Thomas L. TRAYNOR
53 Dean Health/Education/Human Svcs Vacant
54 Dean Engr/Computer Science Dr. Brian RIGLING
12 Interim Dean WSU Lake Campus Dr. Dan KRANE
49 Dean Liberal Arts Dr. Linda CARON
66 Interim Chair Sch Nursing & Health Dr. Ann M. STALTER
63 Dean Boonshoft School of Medicine Dr. Valerie WEBER
83 Int Chair Sch of Prof Psychology Dr. LaTrelle JACKSON
81 Int Dean Science/Mathematics Dr. Kathy ENGISCH
06 Registrar Dr. Mary HOLLAND
13 Int Chief Information Officer Mr. Michael STANKAS
36 Director Career Services Ms. Cheryl STUART
37 Director of Financial Aid Ms. Kim EVERHART
38 Director Counsel/Wellness Svcs Dr. Robert A. RANDO
29 Exec Director Alumni Relations Mr. Gregory SCHARER
28 Vice Pres Inclusive Excellence Dr. Matthew C. CHANEY
22 Director Disability Services Mr. Tom WEBB
41 Director of Athletics Mr. Bob GRANT
85 Director Univ Center for Intl Educ Ms. Michelle STREETER-FERRARI
39 Director Residence Services Mr. Daniel BERTSOS
19 Director of Public Safety Mr. Kurt A. HOLDEN
92 Director Honors Program Dr. Susan CARRAFIELLO
94 Director Womens Studies Program Dr. Julianne WEINZIMMER
09 Director Institutional Research Dr. Aaron SKIRA
04 Executive Asst to President Ms. Rebecca TRAXLER
102 CFO WSU Foundation Mr. Robert BATSON
44 Director Annual Giving Ms. Amy N. SHOPE JONES
101 Secretary of the Board Ms. Shari MICKEY-BOGGS
26 Director Communications Mr. Seth BAUGUESS
27 Director Marketing Mr. Mark D. ANDERSON

Wright State University Lake Campus (F)

7600 Lake Campus Drive, Celina OH 45822-2952
Telephone: (419) 586-0300 FICE Identification: 009169
Accreditation: &HLC

† Regional accreditation is carried under the parent institution in Dayton, OH.

Xavier University (G)

3800 Victory Parkway, Cincinnati OH 45207-1096
County: Hamilton FICE Identification: 003144
Unit ID: 206622
Telephone: (513) 745-3000 Carnegie Class: Masters/L
FAX Number: (513) 745-4223 Calendar System: Semester
URL: www.xavier.edu
Established: 1831 Annual Undergrad Tuition & Fees: $42,460
Enrollment: 7,061 Coed
Affiliation or Control: Roman Catholic IRS Status: 501(c)3
Highest Offering: Doctorate
Accreditation: HLC, CAATE, CACREP, CAEPT, CLPSY, HSA, MACTE, MUS, NURSE, OT, RAD, SW

01 President Dr. Colleen M. HANYCZ
05 Provost/Chief Academic Officer Dr. Melissa J. BAUMANN
10 VP Financial Admin/CBO Mr. Phil CHICK
26 Vice Pres for University Relations Mr. Gary R. MASSA
88 Vice Pres Mission & Identity/CMO Dr. Debra MOONEY
13 Exec Dir Information Technologies Mr. Mark BROCKMAN
28 VP Inst Diversity/Inclusion & CDIO Dr. Janice B. WALKER
27 Director Strategic Communications Vacant
30 Assoc VP for University Relations Ms. Susan ABEL
32 Assoc Prov/Chief Student Affs Ofcr Dr. David J. JOHNSON
20 Associate Provost & CIO Mr. Jeff EDWARDS
18 Vice President for Facilities Mr. Robert M. SHEERAN
11 VP for Admin/Director Athletics Mr. Greg CHRISTOPHER
15 Assoc Vice Pres for Human Resources Ms. Jenni DRAMIS
84 Vice Pres Enrollment Management Mr. Aaron MEIS
44 Exec Dir Gifts & Estate Planning Mr. Mark MCLAUGHLIN
42 Dir Center for Mission/Identity Mr. Joseph P. SHADLE
06 Registrar Dr. Andrea WAWRZUSIN
121 Exec Dir of Student Support Svcs Ms. Lea MINNITI
27 Assoc VP Marketing & Communications Mr. Doug RUSCHMAN
39 Sr Dir Student Affairs/Ofc Res Life Ms. Lori A. LAMBERT
40 Director of Bookstore Mr. Steve EAGLE
86 Director of Government Relations Mr. Sean COMER
83 Dean College Prof Sciences Dr. Cynthia GEER
07 Dir Enr Prospect Mgmt/Parent Rels Ms. Mary KNIFFIN
35 Sr Dir Student Affairs/Involvement Ms. Leah BUSAM KLENOWSKI
49 Dean College Arts & Sciences Dr. David MENGEL
66 Interim Dean College of Nursing Dr. Judith LEWIS
19 Dir Public Safety/Chief of Police Chief Robert WARFEL
37 Director of Financial Aid Vacant
43 General Counsel/Sec of the Board Ms. Becky CULL
29 Dir Alumni Rels/Ex Dir Athletic Dev Mr. Brian MALEY
09 Dir Office Institutional Research Mrs. Emily SHIPLEY
50 Dean Williams College of Business Dr. Thomas HAYES
51 Dir Adult & Prof Educ at Xavier Ms. Patricia MEYER
96 Dir Purchasing & Supply Management Mr. John MERCER
88 Dir TRIO Student Support Services Dr. Daniel L. MCSPADDEN
36 Director Career Development Office Ms. Valarie JACOBSEN
04 Admin Assistant to the President Ms. Nancy DOWNING
38 Director Counseling Services Ms. Jamie BAXTER

Youngstown State University (H)

One University Plaza, Youngstown OH 44555-0001
County: Mahoning FICE Identification: 003145
Unit ID: 206695
Telephone: (330) 941-3001 Carnegie Class: Masters/L
FAX Number: (330) 941-7169 Calendar System: Semester
URL: www.ysu.edu
Established: 1908 Annual Undergrad Tuition & Fees (In-State): $9,656
Enrollment: 11,835 Coed
Affiliation or Control: State IRS Status: 501(c)3
Highest Offering: Doctorate
Accreditation: HLC, ANEST, ART, CAATE, CACREP, CAEP, COARC, DH, DIETC, DIETD, EMT, EXSC, MLTAD, MT, MUS, NUR, NURSE, PH, PTA, SW

01 President Mr. James P. TRESSEL
05 Provost/VP Academic Affairs Dr. Brien N. SMITH
10 Vice Pres Finance & Business Op Mr. Neal P. MCNALLY
09 Vice Pres for Institutional Effect Dr. Mike SHERMAN
32 Assoc VP for Student Experience Mrs. Joy POLKABLA BYERS
43 Vice President and General Counsel Ms. Holly A. JACOBS
26 Assoc VP for University Relations Ms. Shannon TIRONE
13 AVP/Chief Information Officer Mr. James YUKECH
50 Dean of Business Administration Dr. Betty Jo LICATA
53 Dean of Education Dr. Charles HOWELL
81 Dean of Science/Tech/Eng/Math Dr. Wim F. STEELANT
57 Dean Creative Arts & Communication Dr. Phyllis M. PAUL
76 Dean Health & Human Services Dr. Jeffery ALLEN
58 Dean College of Graduate Studies Dr. Salvatore A. SANDERS
20 Assoc Provost Acad Pgms/Planning Dr. Kevin BALL
41 Exec Director of Athletics Mr. Ronald A. STROLLO
08 Manager Library Operations Ms. Anna TORRES
29 Dir University Events & Protocol Ms. Jacquelyn LEVISEUR
07 Director Admissions Ms. Christine HUBERT
06 Registrar Ms. Jeanne HERMAN
19 Chief of University Police Mr. Shawn V. VARSO
18 Associate Vice President Facilities Mr. John P. HYDEN
23 Dir Environ/Occup Health & Safety Ms. Julie GENTILE
84 AVP Enrollment & Business Services Ms. Elaine RUSE
21 AVP Finance and Controller Ms. Katrena J. DAVIDSON
88 Cash Management Officer Mr. David EDWARDS
88 Director Support Services Mr. Danny J. O'CONNELL
90 Director Media/Acad Computing Mr. Michael S. HRISHENKO
88 Director WYSU-FM Mr. Gary SEXTON
04 Exec Assistant to President Ms. Cynthia M. BELL
106 Dir Online Education/E-learning Ms. Jessica CHILL
104 Assoc Provost Intl Programs Dr. Nathan MYERS
108 Director Institutional Assessment Ms. Hillary FUHRMAN
22 Director EEO and Policy Ms. Dana LANTZ
38 Director Student Counseling Dr. Ann JARONSKI
15 Chief Human Resources Officer Ms. Cynthia KRAVITZ
103 Exec Director Workforce Development Mrs. Jennifer ODDO
28 Assoc Provost Diversity & Inclusion Ms. Carol BENNETT

Zane State College (A)
9900 Brick Church Road, Cambridge OH 43725
Telephone: (740) 432-6568 Identification: 770365
Accreditation: &HLC

Zane State College (B)
1555 Newark Road, Zanesville OH 43701-2626
County: Muskingum FICE Identification: 008133
Unit ID: 204255
Telephone: (740) 454-2501 Carnegie Class: Assoc/MT-VT-High Non
FAX Number: (740) 454-0035 Calendar System: Semester
URL: www.zanestate.edu
Established: 1969 Annual Undergrad Tuition & Fees (In-State): $5,456
Enrollment: 2,223 Coed
Affiliation or Control: State IRS Status: 501(c)3
Highest Offering: Associate Degree
Accreditation: HLC, ACBSP, ACFEI, CAHIIM, MAC, MLTAD, OTA, PTAA, RAD

01 President .... Dr. Chad M. BROWN
30 Director of Development .... Mrs. Katlyn PORTER
05 Provost/Chief Academic Officer .... Vacant
10 Chief Financial Officer .... Ms. Terri M. BALDWIN
84 Sr Dir Enrollment/Outreach/Recruit .... Mrs. Molly DUNN
50 Dean of Business & Engineering .... Mrs. Marcie MOORE
103 Assoc Dean Workforce Development .... Ms. Tracey HOOPER-PORTER
15 Chief Human Resources Officer .... Dr. James KEMPER
13 Dir of ITS Operations .... Mr. Bryan BAKER
09 Dir of Institutional Research .... Mr. Andrew MORRISON
25 Director of Grants & Contracts .... Vacant
26 Director of Marketing .... Mrs. Jenn FOLDEN
32 Chief Student Affairs Officer .... Dr. Elizabeth KLINE
21 Comptroller .... Ms. Tammy S. HUFFMAN
40 Director of Bookstore Operations .... Ms. Vicki MITCHELL
76 Dean Health/Public Svc .... Mrs. Shelley ZIMMERMAN
06 Asst Dean Curriculum/Registrar .... Ms. Theresa KOLK-CONNER
18 Director of Facilities .... Mr. Joseph KEATING
04 Exec Asst to Pres/Coord Annual Giv .... Mrs. Julie A. MACLAINE
49 Dean of Arts and Sciences .... Dr. Elizabeth KLINE

OKLAHOMA

Bacone College (C)
2299 Old Bacone Road, Muskogee OK 74403-1568
County: Muskogee FICE Identification: 003147
Unit ID: 206817
Telephone: (918) 683-4581 Carnegie Class: Bac-Diverse
FAX Number: (918) 781-7422 Calendar System: Semester
URL: www.bacone.edu
Established: 1880 Annual Undergrad Tuition & Fees: $14,700
Enrollment: 321 Coed
Affiliation or Control: American Baptist IRS Status: 501(c)3
Highest Offering: Baccalaureate
Accreditation: #HLC, IACBE, #RAD

01 President .... Dr. Ferlin CLARK
05 VP of Academic Affairs .... Ms. Wambli SINA WIN
32 VP of Student Affairs .... Dr. Kelly LACHANCE
10 VP of Finance/CFO .... Ms. Mary Jo PRATT
45 VP Strategic Initiatives & Projects .... Dr. Nicole BEEN
30 VP of Development .... Vacant
15 Director Human Resources .... Mr. William LOWE
57 Director School of Indian Art .... Mr. Gerald COURNOYER
88 Director Ctr for American Indians .... Mr. Aaron ADSON
41 Athletic Director .... Mr. Mike GONZALES
26 Director of College Relations/Tech .... Ms. Wendy BURTON
04 Assistant to President .... Ms. Marcia TAYLOR
06 Registrar .... Mrs. Linda MILAM
07 Director of Admissions .... Vacant
08 Director/Head Librarian .... Mr. David MCMILLIAN
13 Director of Network Systems .... Mr. Chris EHLERS
37 Director of Financial Aid .... Mr. Josh CHAPMAN
19 Chief of Campus Police .... Mr. John LINDSEY
40 Bookstore Manager .... Ms. Elizabeth KALER
88 Executive Director Indigenous Study .... Dr. Nicky MICHAEL
76 Director Radiography Program .... Ms. Shawn DIXON
68 Interim Chair Exercise Sciences .... Dr. Jyoti ABRAHAM
61 Dean Tribal Law & Criminal Justice .... Ms. Wambli WIN
50 Chair School of Business & Finance .... Dr. John WINTERS
121 Director Student Support Services .... Ms. Patricia FARRELL
107 Chair of Professional Studies .... Dr. Rebecca TRUELOVE
49 Chair of Liberal Arts .... Ms. Linda JORDAN
88 Director Ctr for Christian Ministry .... Dr. Stephen WILEY
59 Chair of Family Studies .... Dr. Donna SHARP
88 Assistant to VP Student Affairs .... Ms. Jana TAYLOR
39 Director of Campus Housing .... Mr. Kendall SCOTT

Cameron University (D)
2800 W Gore Boulevard, Lawton OK 73505-6377
County: Comanche FICE Identification: 003150
Unit ID: 206914
Telephone: (580) 581-2200 Carnegie Class: Masters/M
FAX Number: (580) 581-2867 Calendar System: Semester
URL: www.cameron.edu
Established: 1908 Annual Undergrad Tuition & Fees (In-State): $6,450
Enrollment: 3,771 Coed
Affiliation or Control: State IRS Status: 501(c)3
Highest Offering: Master's
Accreditation: HLC, ACBSP, CAEPN, COARC, MUS, RAD

01 President .... Dr. John M. MCARTHUR
05 Vice President for Academic Affairs .... Dr. Ronna J. VANDERSLICE
10 Vice Pres for Business & Finance .... Dr. Scott SCHNEIDER
111 Vice Pres University Advancement .... Mr. Albert D. JOHNSON, JR.
84 VP for Enroll Mgmt & Stdnt Success .... Dr. Jerrett PHILLIPS
20 Assoc Vice Pres Academic Affairs .... Dr. Margery KINGSLEY
20 Asst Vice Pres Academic Affairs .... Ms. Susan CAMP
49 Dean School of Arts and Sciences .... Dr. Von E. UNDERWOOD
58 Dean School of Grad & Prof Studies .... Dr. Jennifer DENNIS
21 Controller .... Ms. Amanda KOLL
26 Senior Director of Public Affairs .... Mr. Keith MITCHELL
30 Director of Development .... Ms. Julie CUNNINGHAM
29 Director of Alumni Relations .... Ms. Jonna TURNER
41 Director Athletic Administration .... Mr. Jim C. JACKSON
07 Director of Admissions .... Ms. Brenda DALLY
06 Registrar .... Mrs. Linda PHILLIPS
09 Dir Inst Rsrch/Assess/Accountability .... Dr. Karla OTY
37 Director of Financial Assistance .... Mr. Justin STREATER
13 Director Information Tech Services .... Mr. Kelly MCCLURE
15 Director of Human Resources .... Ms. Jamie SMITH
36 Director of Student Development .... Dr. Jennifer PRUCHNICKI
32 Dean of Students .... Dr. Zeak NAIFEH
19 Director Public Safety .... Mr. John DEBOARD
18 Director Physical Facilities .... Mr. Robert HANEFIELD
96 Purchasing Agent .... Ms. Laura KANE
22 EEO Officer/Title IX Coordinator .... Ms. Christi WILLIAMS

Carl Albert State College (E)
1507 S McKenna, Poteau OK 74953-5208
County: Le Flore FICE Identification: 003176
Unit ID: 206923
Telephone: (918) 647-1200 Carnegie Class: Assoc/HT-High Trad
FAX Number: (918) 647-1201 Calendar System: Semester
URL: www.carlalbert.edu
Established: 1933 Annual Undergrad Tuition & Fees (In-State): N/A
Enrollment: N/A Coed
Affiliation or Control: State IRS Status: 501(c)3
Highest Offering: Associate Degree
Accreditation: HLC, ADNUR, PTAA

01 President .... Mr. Jay FALKNER
32 VP for Student Affairs/Athletic Dir .... Mr. Randy GRAVES
05 Vice President of Academic Affairs .... Mr. Marc WILLIS
10 Chief Financial Officer .... Mr. Brian ROBERTS
84 VP of Enrollment Management .... Mr. Bill NOWLIN
13 Director Information Technology .... Mr. Jerry ELLIS
101 Admin Assistant to Pres Office .... Ms. Cortney SMITH
26 Dir Marketing/Community Relations .... Ms. Holly BORMANN
06 Registrar/VA Coordinator .... Ms. Dee Ann DICKERSON
37 Director of Financial Aid .... Mr. Jeremy MINOR
88 TRIO Director .... Ms. Michelle WHITE
18 Director of Physical Plant .... Mr. Chuck LEWIS
15 Human Resources Dir/Title IX Coord .... Ms. Vicki SULLIVAN
21 Business Office Manager .... Ms. Amanda WILSON
108 Inst Effect/Assessment Officer .... Ms. Kelly KELLOGG
102 Exec Dir of CASC Dev Foundation .... Ms. Mandy ROBERTS
106 Coord for Virtual Campus/English .... Ms. Sarah BROWN
19 Instructor/Campus Police Coord .... Mr. Chad BROWN

Carl Albert State College Sequoyah County Campus (F)
1601 S. Opdyke St, Sallisaw OK 74955
Telephone: (918) 775-6977 Identification: 770366
Accreditation: &HLC

Central Oklahoma College (G)
14820 Serenita Ave, Oklahoma City OK 73134
County: Oklahoma FICE Identification: 022385
Unit ID: 206941
Telephone: (405) 609-6622 Carnegie Class: Masters/L
FAX Number: N/A Calendar System: Quarter
URL: www.centraloc.edu
Established: 1975 Annual Undergrad Tuition & Fees: $7,817
Enrollment: 14,132 Coed
Affiliation or Control: Proprietary IRS Status: Proprietary
Highest Offering: Associate Degree
Accreditation: ACCSC, SURGT

00 President .... Michael PUGLIESE
01 Chief Executive Officer .... Carol FISHER

College of the Muscogee Nation (H)
PO Box 917, 2170 Raven Circle, Okmulgee OK 74447
County: Okmulgee Identification: 667122
Unit ID: 480967
Telephone: (918) 549-2800 Carnegie Class: Tribal
FAX Number: (918) 759-6930 Calendar System: Trimester
URL: www.CMN.edu
Established: 1994 Annual Undergrad Tuition & Fees: $6,600
Enrollment: 252 Coed
Affiliation or Control: Tribal Control IRS Status: 501(c)3
Highest Offering: Associate Degree
Accreditation: HLC

01 President .... Mr. Robert BIBLE
05 Dean of Academic Affairs .... Dr. Monte RANDALL

Community Care College (I)
4242 S Sheridan Road, Tulsa OK 74145-1119
County: Tulsa FICE Identification: 033674
Unit ID: 439570
Telephone: (918) 610-0027 Carnegie Class: Spec 2-yr-Health
FAX Number: (918) 610-0029 Calendar System: Other
URL: www.communitycarecollege.edu
Established: 1995 Annual Undergrad Tuition & Fees: N/A
Enrollment: 658 Coed
Affiliation or Control: Independent Non-Profit IRS Status: 501(c)3
Highest Offering: Associate Degree
Accreditation: ACCSC, MAAB, SURGT

01 President .... Dr. Raye MAHLBERG
04 Exec Assistant to the President .... Brandi PACKARD
06 Registrar .... Brigitte KURR
07 Director of Admissions .... Vacant
10 Chief Financial/Business Officer .... Pallavi AGARWAL
15 Chief Human Resources Officer .... Brenda KNOX
36 Director Career Services .... Linda DEWITT
37 Director Student Financial Aid .... Karissa MANCARGELI

Connors State College (J)
700 College Road, Warner OK 74469-9700
County: Muskogee FICE Identification: 003153
Unit ID: 206996
Telephone: (918) 463-2931 Carnegie Class: Assoc/HT-High Trad
FAX Number: (918) 463-2233 Calendar System: Semester
URL: www.connorsstate.edu
Established: 1908 Annual Undergrad Tuition & Fees (In-State): $3,672
Enrollment: 2,069 Coed
Affiliation or Control: State IRS Status: 501(c)3
Highest Offering: Associate Degree
Accreditation: HLC, ADNUR, OTA, PTAA

01 President .... Dr. Ronald S. RAMMING
05 VP for Academic Affairs .... Dr. Makenna GARRISON
10 VP for Fiscal Services .... Mr. Mike LEWIS
26 Assoc VP for External Affairs .... Vacant
37 Director of Financial Aid .... Ms. Mattie KEYS
08 Director of Learning Center .... Ms. Ona BRITTON-SPEARS
13 Director of Information Technology .... Mr. Heath HODGES
06 Registrar .... Mr. John NORWOOD
07 Director of Recruitment .... Ms. Jessica LANGSTON
15 Director of Human Resources .... Ms. Nicole MOTE
09 Director of Institutional Research .... Vacant
41 Athletic Director .... Mr. Bill MUSE
32 Dean of Students .... Mr. Mike JACKSON
35 Asst Dean of Students .... Mr. Jacob LAWSON
19 Chief of Police .... Mr. James MENDENHALL
04 Executive Asst to the President .... Ms. Derotha RIVENBARK
20 Asst VP Acad/Stdt Affs/Acad Support .... Ms. Robin O'QUINN
102 Director of Development Foundation .... Dr. Krystle LANE

East Central University (K)
1100 E 14th Street, Ada OK 74820-6899
County: Pontotoc FICE Identification: 003154
Unit ID: 207041
Telephone: (580) 332-8000 Carnegie Class: Masters/L
FAX Number: (580) 332-1623 Calendar System: Semester
URL: www.ecok.edu
Established: 1909 Annual Undergrad Tuition & Fees (In-State): $7,052
Enrollment: 3,608 Coed
Affiliation or Control: State IRS Status: 501(c)3
Highest Offering: Master's
Accreditation: HLC, ACBSP, CACREP, CAEP, CAEPN, MUS, NUR, SW

01 President .... Dr. Katricia PIERSON
05 Provost/VP Academic Affairs .... Dr. Jeffrey GIBSON
20 Interim Associate Provost .... Dr. Sarah PETERS
32 VP Student Development .... Dr. Brandon HILL
10 Exec VP Administration/Finance .... Ms. Jessica KILBY
111 VP Institutional Advancement .... Ms. Amy FORD
21 Asst VP Administration/Finance .... Mr. Ty ANDERSON
53 Dean College of Educ & Psych .... Dr. Phyllis ISAACS
50 Dean School of Business .... Mr. Wendell GODWIN
81 Dean College of Health & Sciences .... Dr. Kenneth ANDREWS
49 Dean College of Lib Arts & Soc Sci .... Dr. Katherine LANG
58 Int Dean of College Graduate Stds .... Dr. Sarah PETERS
06 Registrar .... Ms. ADeidra SIMMONS
13 Director Information Technology .... Mr. Jeremy BENNETT
09 Director Inst Effectiveness .... Ms. Meredith JONES
26 Director Mktg & Communication .... Ms. Amy FORD
41 Interim Director Athletics .... Mr. Al JOHNSON
18 Director Facilities Mgmt .... Mr. Darryl OVERSTREET
15 Director Employment Services .... Mr. Ty ANDERSON
29 Director Alumni Relations .... Ms. Ashia TODD
07 Director Admissions .... Ms. ADeidra SIMMONS
96 Director Purchasing .... Ms. Chandra MILLER
37 Director Financial Aid .... Ms. Becky ISAACS
08 Director Library .... Ms. Dana BELCHER
23 Director Stdnt Health Services .... Ms. Lisa LETELLIER
35 Dean of Students .... Mr. Nicholas BUCKLEY
121 Dir Academic Success Center .... Dr. Haley MATLOCK
20 Coordinator Academic Services .... Ms. Haley VICKERS
38 Director Stdnt Counseling Ctr .... Ms. Jennifer COX
85 Director Intl Student Pgms & Svcs .... Ms. Jessika BAILEY
108 Director Assessment .... Dr. Robin ROBERSON
25 Director Grants & Research .... Ms. Leah LYON

22 Dir Testing/Accessibility Services .... Ms. Kim ROGERS
21 Controller .... Ms. Kelly DICKEY
113 Bursar .... Ms. Amy SCHLUP
19 Chief of University Police .... Mr. Bert MILLER
04 Admin Assistant to the President .... Ms. Brandi SCHUR
39 Director Residence Life .... Ms. Leena RUDOLPH

Eastern Oklahoma State College (A)

1301 W Main Street, Wilburton OK 74578-4999
County: Latimer FICE Identification: 003155
Unit ID: 207050
Telephone: (918) 465-2361 Carnegie Class: Assoc/HT-High Trad
FAX Number: (918) 465-2431 Calendar System: Semester
URL: www.eosc.edu
Established: 1909 Annual Undergrad Tuition & Fees (In-State): $4,767
Enrollment: 1,342 Coed
Affiliation or Control: State IRS Status: 501(c)3
Highest Offering: Associate Degree
Accreditation: HLC, ADNUR, #COARC

01 President .... Dr. Janet WANSICK
05 VP of Academic Affairs .... Dr. Patricia RATLIFF
32 VP for Student/External Affairs .... Dr. Trish MCBEATH
12 Dean of McAlester Campus .... Ms. Anne BROOKS
35 Director of Student Life .... Ms. London WHITE
41 Athletic Director .... Mr. Matt PARKER
26 Dir Marketing/Communications .... Mrs. Trish MCBEATH
13 Chief Technical Officer .... Mr. George LARSON
08 Director Library & Media Services .... Ms. Maria MARTINEZ
15 VP for Administrative Services/HR .... Mrs. Amy ARMSTRONG
06 Registrar/Admissions .... Mrs. Jennifer LABOR
18 Director Physical Plant Operations .... Mr. Alan MOSS
37 Financial Aid Director .... Ms. Mimi KELLEY
19 Campus Police Chief .... Mr. Alton JONES
04 Exec Assistant to the President .... Ms. Candace RANEY
10 Director of Finance .... Ms. Trisha WHITE
102 Exec Dir EOSC Found & Alumni Rels .... Ms. Teresa BRADY

Family of Faith Christian University (B)

PO Box 1805, Shawnee OK 74802-1805
County: Pottawatomie FICE Identification: 036763
Unit ID: 443058
Telephone: (405) 695-5533 Carnegie Class: Spec-4-yr-Faith
FAX Number: (405) 273-8535 Calendar System: Semester
URL: https://familyoffaith.edu/
Established: 1992 Annual Undergrad Tuition & Fees: $7,920
Enrollment: 148 Coed
Affiliation or Control: Independent Non-Profit IRS Status: 501(c)3
Highest Offering: Doctorate
Accreditation: BI

01 President .... Dr. Samuel W. MATTHEWS
05 Provost .... Mrs. Elaine W. PHILLIPS
10 Vice Pres Operations/Finance .... Mr. Daniel MATTHEWS
32 Vice Pres Student Affairs .... Mrs. Dara GILLIAM
42 Director of Spiritual Life .... Mr. Daniel J. MATTHEWS
108 Dir of Accreditation/Assessment .... Mrs. Elaine W. PHILLIPS
104 Director of International Studies .... Mrs. Dara GILLIAM

Langston University (C)

PO Box 1500, Langston OK 73050
County: Logan FICE Identification: 003157
Unit ID: 207209
Telephone: (405) 466-2231 Carnegie Class: Masters/S
FAX Number: N/A Calendar System: Semester
URL: www.langston.edu
Established: 1897 Annual Undergrad Tuition & Fees (In-State): $6,509
Enrollment: 2,038 Coed
Affiliation or Control: State IRS Status: 501(c)3
Highest Offering: Doctorate
Accreditation: HLC, ACBSP, CACREP, CAEPN, NAEYC, NUR, PTA

01 President .... Dr. Kent J. SMITH, JR.
11 VP for Operations .... Mrs. Theresa D. POWELL
10 VP Fiscal/Admin Affairs .... Vacant
111 VP Inst Development/External Affs .... Mrs. Mautra JONES
05 Vice President Academic Affairs .... Dr. Ruth JACKSON
13 Chief Information Officer .... Mr. Pritchard MONCRIFFE
20 Executive Director of LU-Tulsa .... Dr. Dytisha DAVIS
21 Comptroller .... Mrs. Karlon JAMES
32 Dean of Students .... Mr. Joshua BUSBY
29 Director Alumni Affairs .... Mrs. Vonnie WARE-ROBERTS
26 Director Public Relations .... Vacant
07 Director of Admissions .... Mr. Carlos ROBINSON
37 Director Financial Aid .... Ms. Shelia R. MCGILL
15 Director of Human Resources .... Mrs. Cynthia S. BUCKLEY
09 Director Inst Research & Planning .... Dr. Sheilynda STEWART
06 Registrar .... Vacant
41 Athletic Director .... Mrs. Donnita ROGERS
19 Chief of Police .... Mr. Mario HOLLAND
96 Purchasing Manager .... Ms. Chaste COPPAGE
49 Dean School of Arts & Sciences .... Dr. Alonzo F. PETERSON
50 Dean School of Business .... Dr. Joshua M. SNAVELY
47 Dean School Agric/Applied Science .... Dr. Wesley L. WHITTAKER
66 Dean School of Nursing/Hlth Profess .... Dr. Teressa HUNTER
53 Dean School of Education/Behav Sci .... Dr. Emily PATTERSON HARRIS
88 Dean School of Physical Therapy .... Dr. Elicia L. POLLARD
84 Exec Director Enrollment Mgmt .... Mrs. Sheila MCGILL
04 Executive Asst to President .... Ms. Elaine C. PRESTON
39 Director Student Housing .... Mr. Kavaris SIMS
44 Annual Giving Officer .... Ms. Jillian B. WHITAKER
38 Director Student Counseling .... Dr. Eartha W. COLLIER
08 Chief Library Officer .... Dr. Lynne SIMPSON

Mid-America Christian University (D)

3500 SW 119th Street, Oklahoma City OK 73170-4500
County: Cleveland FICE Identification: 006942
Unit ID: 245953
Telephone: (405) 691-3800 Carnegie Class: Masters/M
FAX Number: (405) 692-3165 Calendar System: Semester
URL: www.macu.edu
Established: 1953 Annual Undergrad Tuition & Fees: $18,838
Enrollment: 2,083 Coed
Affiliation or Control: Church Of God IRS Status: 501(c)3
Highest Offering: Master's
Accreditation: HLC

01 President .... Dr. John D. FOZARD
03 Executive VP .... Dr. Bobbie SPURGEON-HARRIS
05 Vice Pres for Academic Affairs .... Dr. Sharon LEASE
32 VP Student Engagement/Success .... Vacant
45 VP for University Advancement .... Mr. Steve SEATON
13 Chief Information Officer .... Mr. Jody ALLEN
15 Director of Human Resources .... Mrs. Darwina MARSHALL
108 Dir Institutional Effectiveness .... Mr. Ray DILLMAN
42 Exec Director of Church Relations .... Rev. Morgan ALSIP
06 Registrar .... Ms. Stephanie DAVIDSON
37 Director Office of Financial Aid .... Ms. Deaun MAAS-STEED
07 Asst VP of Enrollment Services .... Vacant
18 Director of Facilities .... Ms. Connie GALL
29 Director Alumni Relations .... Vacant
04 Executive Asst to President .... Ms. Ladonna TYNER
08 Director of Library Services .... Ms. Marsha KENDRICK
10 Chief Financial Officer .... Ms. Kristin JASPER
19 Director of Public Safety .... Mr. Tim GIBSON
41 Athletic Director .... Mr. Marcus MOELLER

Murray State College (E)

One Murray Campus, Tishomingo OK 73460-3130
County: Johnston FICE Identification: 003158
Unit ID: 207236
Telephone: (580) 387-7000 Carnegie Class: Assoc/HT-High Trad
FAX Number: (580) 371-9844 Calendar System: Semester
URL: www.mscok.edu
Established: 1908 Annual Undergrad Tuition & Fees (In-State): $6,231
Enrollment: 2,172 Coed
Affiliation or Control: State IRS Status: 501(c)3
Highest Offering: Associate Degree
Accreditation: HLC, ADNUR, OTA, PTAA

01 President .... Ms. Joy MCDANIEL
05 VP Acad Affs/Institutional Effect .... Ms. Becky HENTHORN
04 Exec Assistant to President/Board .... Mrs. Amy CASKEY
10 VP Finance/Administration/CFO .... Mr. Justin CELLUM
32 Vice Pres for Student Affairs .... Ms. Michaelle GRAY
20 Dean of Instruction .... Ms. Ginger COTHRAN
18 AVP Facilities/Safety .... Mr. Sam HOLT
102 Exec Director MSC Foundation .... Vacant
37 Dir Financial Aid .... Ms. Traci FRANKS
08 Director of Library .... Mr. Stephen FINLAY
74 Veterinary Tech Program Director .... Ms. Laura SANDMANN
66 Director of Nursing .... Ms. Robin COPPEDGE
07 Registrar .... Mr. Aaron BESHEARS
15 Director of Human Resources .... Ms. Michaelle GRAY
35 Director Student Support Services .... Ms. Ronda PICKENS
21 Comptroller .... Ms. Sherry GRAY-DEVINE

Northeastern Oklahoma Agricultural and Mechanical College (F)

200 I Street, NE, Miami OK 74354-6434
County: Ottawa FICE Identification: 003160
Unit ID: 207290
Telephone: (918) 542-8441 Carnegie Class: Assoc/MT-VT-High Trad
FAX Number: (918) 542-9759 Calendar System: Semester
URL: www.neo.edu
Established: 1919 Annual Undergrad Tuition & Fees (In-State): $4,913
Enrollment: 1,769 Coed
Affiliation or Control: State IRS Status: 501(c)3
Highest Offering: Associate Degree
Accreditation: HLC, ADNUR, MLTAD, PTAA

01 President .... Dr. Kyle STAFFORD
05 Vice President Academic Affairs .... Mr. Dustin GROVER
10 Vice President for Fiscal Affairs .... Mrs. Terry DECOSTER
32 VP Student Affairs/Enrollment Svcs .... Mrs. Amy ISHMAEL
20 Asst VP for Academic Affairs .... Vacant
37 Director of Financial Aid .... Mr. David FISHER
26 Chief Public Relations Officer .... Mr. Jordan ADAMS
15 Human Resources Generalist .... Ms. Hollie SNYDER
18 Director Facilities/Physical Plant .... Mr. Jeff BOMAN
13 Coord Instructional Technology .... Mr. Matt WESTPHAL
30 Exec Dir Development Foundation .... Ms. Jennifer WALKER
121 Director Academic Advising Center .... Mrs. Rachel LLOYD
41 Athletic Director .... Mr. Joe RENFRO
105 Webmaster .... Mr. David FRAZIER
06 Registrar .... Mrs. Shay CLAPP
21 AVP for Fiscal Affairs/Controller .... Mrs. Cheryl MOUDY
40 Bookstore Manager .... Mrs. Kathryn VANOVER
08 Director Library Services .... Ms. Leslie HAYES
47 Department Chair Agriculture .... Dr. Mary BOOTH
83 Department Chair Social Science .... Dr. Jeff BIRDSONG
81 Dept Chair Mathematics/Science .... Mr. Steve DIXON
66 Dept Chr Nurs/Allied Hlth/Phys Educ .... Mrs. Deborah MORGAN
50 Dept Chair Business and Technology .... Mrs. Joy BAUER
04 Executive Asst to President .... Mrs. Kendra CUMMINS
19 Director Security/Safety .... Mr. Buddy LAMBERT
39 Director Student Housing .... Mr. Jim ROWLAND
96 Coordinator of Purchasing .... Mr. Charlie WILMONTH

Northeastern State University (G)

600 N Grand Avenue, Tahlequah OK 74464-2399
County: Cherokee FICE Identification: 003161
Unit ID: 207263
Telephone: (918) 456-5511 Carnegie Class: Masters/L
FAX Number: (918) 458-2015 Calendar System: Semester
URL: www.nsuok.edu
Established: 1909 Annual Undergrad Tuition & Fees (In-State): $6,915
Enrollment: 7,349 Coed
Affiliation or Control: State IRS Status: 501(c)3
Highest Offering: First Professional Degree
Accreditation: HLC, ACBSP, #ARCPA, CACREP, CAEP, CAEPN, DIETD, MT, MUS, NUR, OPT, OPTR, SP, SW

01 President .... Dr. Steve TURNER
10 Chief Financial/Business Officer .... Mrs. Christy LANDSAW
05 Provost & VP Academic Affairs .... Dr. Debborah LANDRY
11 VP for Administration/Finance .... Ms. Christy LANDSAW
86 Dir Community/Government Relations .... Vacant
26 VP University Relations .... Mr. Dan MABERY
32 Vice President Student Affairs .... Dr. Jerrid FREEMAN
21 Director Business Affairs .... Mr. Austin ROSENTHAL
20 Asst VP Academic Affairs .... Dr. Carla SWEARINGEN
20 Asst VP Academic Affairs Admin .... Dr. Pam FLY
12 Dean Broken Arrow Campus .... Dr. Roy WOOD
12 Dean Muskogee Campus .... Dr. Kimberly WILLIAMS
49 Dean College of Liberal Arts .... Dr. Mike CHANSLOR
50 Dean College of Business/Technology .... Dr. Janet BUZZARD
53 Dean College of Education .... Dr. Vanessa ANTON
81 Dean Science & Health Professions .... Dr. Pamela HATHORN
88 Dean Optometry .... Dr. Douglas PENISTEN
08 Exec Director of NSU Libraries .... Dr. Michael JONES
108 Exec Director Inst Effectiveness .... Dr. Julia SAWYER
30 Director of Development .... Ms. Peggy GLENN
15 Director of Human Resources .... Mrs. Jean LOGUE
37 Director Student Financial Services .... Dr. Teri COCHRAN
06 Registrar .... Ms. Janet KELLEY
07 Director Admissions/Recruitment .... Mr. Brandon MILLER
84 Asst VP Enrollment Management .... Dr. Kelly Jo LARSEN
18 Assistant VP Facilities .... Mr. Jonathan ASBILL
41 Director of Athletics .... Mr. Matt COCHRAN
19 Director of Public Safety .... Mr. James BELL
22 Sr Coord Stdnt Disability Svcs .... Mrs. Donna AGEE
29 Director Alumni Services .... Mr. Daniel JOHNSON
109 Director of Auxiliary Services .... Mr. Chris ADNEY
39 Director of Housing .... Mr. Craig REINEHR
35 Asst VP Student Affairs Admin .... Ms. Sheila SELF
96 Director Purchasing Contr Payments .... Mr. Austin ROSENTHAL
44 Stewards/Annual Giving Coordinator .... Ms. Cami HIGHERS
04 Administrative Asst to President .... Ms. Robin HUTCHINS
13 Chief Info Tech Officer/Director IT .... Dr. Richard REIF
28 Diversity and Inclusion Coord .... Mrs. Kasey RHONE

Northeastern State University (H)

3100 East New Orleans St, Broken Arrow OK 74014
Telephone: (918) 449-6000 Identification: 770372
Accreditation: &HLC

Northeastern State University at Muskogee (I)

2400 W Shawnee, Muskogee OK 74401
Telephone: (918) 683-0040 Identification: 770373
Accreditation: &HLC, OT

Northern Oklahoma College (J)

1220 E Grand Avenue, PO Box 310,
Tonkawa OK 74653-0310
County: Kay FICE Identification: 003162
Unit ID: 207281
Telephone: (580) 628-6200 Carnegie Class: Assoc/MT-VT-High Non
FAX Number: (580) 628-6209 Calendar System: Semester
URL: www.noc.edu
Established: 1901 Annual Undergrad Tuition & Fees (In-State): $3,648
Enrollment: 3,374 Coed
Affiliation or Control: State IRS Status: 501(c)3
Highest Offering: Associate Degree
Accreditation: HLC, ACBSP, ADNUR, COARC

01 President .... Dr. Clark HARRIS
05 Vice President for Academic Affairs .... Dr. Pam STINSON
10 Vice President Financial Affairs .... Mrs. Anita SIMPSON
12 Vice President for NOC Enid .... Mr. Jeremy HISE
12 Vice President for NOC Stillwater .... Ms. Diana WATKINS

32 Vice President for Student Affairs .... Mr. Jason JOHNSON
30 Vice President for Devel/Cmty Rels .... Mrs. Sheri SNYDER
13 Director Information Technology .... Mr. Michael MACHIA
15 Director Human Resources .... Ms. Shannon CRANFORD
84 Vice Pres Enroll Mgmt/Registrar .... Dr. Rick EDGINGTON
08 Director of Library Services .... Mr. Benjamin HAINLINE
18 Assoc Vice Pres of Physical Plant .... Mr. Larry DYE
41 Athletic Director .... Mr. Alan FOSTER
37 Director Student Financial Aid .... Ms. Holly LEE
40 Manager Student Bookstore .... Mrs. Jimilea JANSSON

Northwestern Oklahoma State University (A)

709 Oklahoma Boulevard, Alva OK 73717-2799
County: Woods FICE Identification: 003163
Unit ID: 207306
Telephone: (580) 327-1700 Carnegie Class: Masters/S
FAX Number: (580) 327-1881 Calendar System: Semester
URL: www.nwosu.edu
Established: 1897 Annual Undergrad Tuition & Fees (In-State): $8,173
Enrollment: 1,833 Coed
Affiliation or Control: State IRS Status: 501(c)3
Highest Offering: Doctorate
Accreditation: HLC, ACBSP, CAEP, NUR, NURSE, SW

01 President .... Dr. Janet L. CUNNINGHAM
03 EVP for Academic Affairs .... Dr. Bo S. HANNAFORD
11 Vice President for Administration .... Dr. David M. PECHA
20 Assoc VP for Academics .... Dr. James L. BELL
26 Director Marketing/Univ Relations .... Ms. Kelsey A. MARTIN
32 Dean of Student Affairs .... Mr. Calleb N. MOSBURG
41 Athletic Director .... Mr. Brad FRANZ
06 Registrar .... Ms. Sheri K. LAHR
37 Director Financial Aid .... Ms. Tara HANNAFORD
113 Bursar .... Ms. Paige FISCHER
07 Asst Dean of Students & Recruitment .... Mr. Matt ADAIR
18 Chief Facilities/Physical Plant .... Mr. Doug CHAFFIN
15 Human Resource Director .... Ms. Cheryl ELLIS
29 Director Alumni Relations .... Mr. John W. ALLEN
58 Assoc Dean of Graduate Studies .... Dr. Shawn P. HOLLIDAY
08 Director of Libraries .... Mrs. Shannon LEAPER
09 Institutional Research Specialist .... Ms. Ashley FISCHER

Oklahoma Baptist University (B)

500 W University, Shawnee OK 74804-2590
County: Pottawatomie FICE Identification: 003164
Unit ID: 207403
Telephone: (405) 585-4000 Carnegie Class: Bac-Diverse
FAX Number: N/A Calendar System: Semester
URL: www.okbu.edu
Established: 1910 Annual Undergrad Tuition & Fees: $31,352
Enrollment: 1,763 Coed
Affiliation or Control: Southern Baptist IRS Status: 501(c)3
Highest Offering: Master's
Accreditation: HLC, ACBSP, CAEP, MUS, NURSE

01 President .... Dr. Heath THOMAS
05 Provost .... Dr. Susan DEWOODY
10 Exec VP Business Affs/Admin Svcs .... Mr. Randy SMITH
111 VP for Advancement .... Mr. Tim RASNIC
32 VP of Campus Life/Dean of Students .... Mr. Brandon PETERSEN
28 Interim VP for University Culture .... Ms. B.J GLOVER
84 VP for Enrollment Management .... Mr. Will BRANTLEY
41 Athletic Director .... Mr. Robert DAVENPORT
13 VP of Tech/Digital Innovation/CTO .... Mr. Britton BUSS
26 Assoc VP Marketing & Communication .... Ms. Paula GOWER
21 Asst VP Finance/Admin Svcs .... Vacant
37 Director Student Financial Services .... Ms. Danielle WELLMAN
06 Dir Academic Records/Registrar .... Ms. Marcia MCQUERRY
21 Controller .... Ms. Shannon HESTER
15 Director of Human Resources .... Mr. Steven JONES
19 Chief of University Police .... Mr. David SHANNON
18 Mgr of Facility Services .... Mr. Robert MARQUARDT
36 Dir of Career Services & Alumni Eng .... Ms. Lori HAGANS
73 Dean of Theology/Arts/Humanities .... Dr. Matthew EMERSON
50 Dean Business/Health Sci/Educ .... Dr. Larinee DENNIS
88 Chair School of Business .... Dr. David HOUGHTON
66 Chair School of Nursing .... Dr. Robbie HENSON
73 Chair School of Theology/Ministry .... Dr. Bobby KELLY
53 Chair School of Education .... Dr. Elizabeth JUSTICE
09 Dir of Institutional Research .... Mr. Marcus BREWER
07 Director of Admissions .... Ms. Kalyn FULLBRIGHT
04 Exec Secretary to the President .... Vacant
39 Director Student Housing .... Ms. Erin GULESERIAN
88 Dir of Conf/Camps & Events .... Ms. Tracy MALLORY
08 Chief Library Officer .... Ms. Julie RANKIN
29 Director Alumni Affairs .... Vacant

Oklahoma Christian University (C)

PO Box 11000, Oklahoma City OK 73136-1100
County: Oklahoma FICE Identification: 003165
Unit ID: 207324
Telephone: (405) 425-5000 Carnegie Class: Masters/L
FAX Number: (405) 425-5090 Calendar System: Semester
URL: www.oc.edu
Established: 1950 Annual Undergrad Tuition & Fees: $25,090
Enrollment: 2,055 Coed
Affiliation or Control: Independent Non-Profit IRS Status: 501(c)3
Highest Offering: Master's
Accreditation: HLC, ACBSP, CAEP, CIDA, MT, MUS, NURSE

01 President .... Mr. John DESTEIGUER
11 Chief Operating Officer .... Mr. John HERMES
05 Chief Academic Officer .... Dr. Jeff MCCORMACK
26 Chief Communications Officer .... Mrs. Risa FORRESTER
111 Chief Advancement Officer .... Mr. Kent ALLEN
43 Chief Legal Officer .... Mr. Stephen ECK
32 Chief Student Life Officer & Dean .... Mr. Neil ARTER
09 Chief Data & Analytics .... Mr. Jeff DIMICK
100 Chief of Staff .... Mr. Kent ALLEN
50 Dean The Professional College .... Dr. Jennifer GRAY
73 Dean College of Humanities & Bible .... Dr. Charles RIX
49 Dean The New College .... Dr. Sada KNOWLES
06 Registrar .... Dr. Stephanie BAIRD
08 Dean of Library/Instructional Supp .... Dr. LeeAnne PARIS
19 Chief of Police Dept .... Mr. Greg GILTNER
41 Athletic Director .... Mr. David LYNN
18 Director of Physical Plant Services .... Mr. Cary FALLING
37 Exec Dir Financial Svcs & Budgets .... Mr. Clint LARUE
104 Director of International Programs .... Mr. John OSBORNE
15 Chief Human Resources Officer .... Mr. Terry WINN
42 Dean for Spiritual Life .... Mr. Jeff MCMILLON
89 Dir of Freshman Experience .... Mr. Trent DOBBS
88 Director of Creative Services .... Mrs. Tessa WRIGHT
36 Dir of Calling and Career Services .... Mrs. Susan HOOVER
85 International Student Advisor .... Mrs. Joslyn HILL
38 Director of Counseling Services .... Mr. Sheldon ADKINS
121 Director of Student Success .... Mrs. Amy JANZEN
35 Assistant Dean of Students .... Mr. Gary JONES
04 Executive Assistant to President .... Mrs. Teri MUELLER
39 Director Student Housing .... Mrs. Candace BASS
10 Chief Financial Officer .... Mrs. Jennifer RAY
30 Sr Gifts Ofcr/Dir Advancement Ops .... Mrs. Christine MERIDETH

Oklahoma City Community College (D)

7777 S May Avenue, Oklahoma City OK 73159-4444
County: Oklahoma FICE Identification: 010391
Unit ID: 207449
Telephone: (405) 682-1611 Carnegie Class: Assoc/HT-High Trad
FAX Number: (405) 682-7585 Calendar System: Semester
URL: www.occc.edu
Established: 1972 Annual Undergrad Tuition & Fees (In-District): $4,059
Enrollment: 12,227 Coed
Affiliation or Control: State/Local IRS Status: 501(c)3
Highest Offering: Associate Degree
Accreditation: HLC, ACBSP, ADNUR, EMT, NAEYC, OTA, PTAA

01 Interim President .... Dr. Jeremy THOMAS
03 Executive Vice President .... Ms. Danita ROSE
04 Exec Assistant to the President .... Ms. Kim VELLECA
101 Exec Asst to the Board of Regents .... Ms. Roshell ROBERTS
11 Vice Pres Operations .... Mr. Greg GARDNER
05 Vice President Academic Affairs .... Dr. Vincent BRIDGES
32 Interim VP Student Affairs .... Dr. Liz LARGENT
10 Chief Financial Officer .... Ms. Cynthia GARY
88 Director of Cultural Programs .... Mr. Lemuel BARDEGUEZ
15 Vice Pres/Dir Human Resources .... Dr. Regina SWITZER
13 VP of IT Infrastructure .... Mr. Tim WHISENHUNT
20 Associate VP Academic Affairs .... Dr. Glenne WHISENHUNT
35 Associate VP Student Affairs .... Mr. Chris SNODDY
18 Exec Dir of Facilities Management .... Mr. Chris SNOW
79 Dean of Arts English/Humanities .... Dr. Joe MOFFETT
76 Dean of Health Professions .... Dr. Kathy WHEAT
81 Dean Math/Engineering/Phys Science .... Dr. Max SIMMONS
83 Interim Dean of Social Sciences .... Mr. John CASTREE
50 Dean of Bus & Information Tech .... Mr. John CLAYBON
30 Chief Development Officer .... Mr. Von ALLEN
26 Exec Director of Marketing & PR .... Mr. Erick WORRELL
25 Director of Grants & Contracts .... Mr. Von ALLEN
09 Dir Institutional Effectiveness .... Dr. Adam MOLNAR
37 Director of Student Financial Aid .... Ms. Sonya GORE
21 Director of Financial Accounting .... Ms. Billie Jo BERGERON
114 Dir of Budgeting/Fiscal Planning .... Mr. David CHURCHILL
19 Chief of Police .... Mr. Daniel PIAZZA
113 Bursar .... Ms. Samantha OLAH
40 Director of Bookstore .... Mr. Woodie COLEMAN
117 Emergency Manager .... Mr. Patrick SOLINSKI
96 Director of Purchasing .... Mr. Craig SISCO
88 Dir Recreation and Fitness .... Mr. Michael SHUGART
36 Director Career Transitions Program .... Ms. Lisa BROWN
22 Director of Equity and Compliance .... Mr. Jade CARTER
91 Dir Enterprise Resource Planning .... Ms. Connie DRUMMOND
08 Director of Library Services .... Ms. Ann RAIA
88 Dir of Ctr for Learning/Teaching .... Vacant
07 Dir of Recruitment & Admiss .... Mr. Michael HOGGATT
121 Director of Academic Advising .... Ms. Stephanie MILLER
06 Registrar .... Ms. Amanda WILLIAMS-MIZE

Oklahoma City University (E)

2501 N Blackwelder, Oklahoma City OK 73106-1493
County: Oklahoma FICE Identification: 003166
Unit ID: 207458
Telephone: (405) 208-5000 Carnegie Class: DU-Mod
FAX Number: (405) 208-5916 Calendar System: Semester
URL: www.okcu.edu
Established: 1904 Annual Undergrad Tuition & Fees: $32,744
Enrollment: 2,617 Coed
Affiliation or Control: United Methodist IRS Status: 501(c)3
Highest Offering: Doctorate
Accreditation: HLC, ARCPA, CAEP, LAW, MUS, NUR, @PTA

01 President .... Mr. Kenneth R. EVANS
05 Interim Provost/VPAA .... Dr. George SIMS
111 VP University Advancement .... Ms. Lynnann STERK-BROOKS
10 Chief Financial Officer .... Mr. Kevan BUCK
32 VP Student Affairs/Dean of Students .... Dr. Amy AYRES
15 VP for Human Resources .... Ms. Joey CROSLIN
84 Asst VP/Dean Enrollment Services .... Mr. Kevin WINDHOLZ
41 Asst Vice Pres of Athletics .... Mr. Jim ABBOTT
19 Chief of Police .... Mr. Dexter NELSON
13 Chief Info Officer (CIO) .... Mr. Gerry HUNT
06 Registrar .... Mr. Charles MONNOT
09 Director of Institutional Research .... Vacant
08 Director Dulaney-Browne Library .... Dr. Victoria SWINNEY
37 Director of Student Financial Svcs .... Mr. Kurt GRAU
27 Director of Communications .... Ms. Leslie BERGER
92 Director of Honors Program .... Dr. Karen YOUMANS
07 Director of Undergrad Admissions .... Ms. Tasha CASEY-LOVELESS
18 Chief Facilities/Physical Plant .... Mr. Mark CLOUSE
29 Director Alumni Engagement .... Ms. Megan HORNBEEK ALLEN
36 Director of Career Services .... Ms. Kanika BROWN
49 Dean of Arts & Sciences .... Dr. Amy E. CATALDI
50 Interim Dean School of Business .... Dr. Russell EVANS
61 Dean School of Law .... Mr. James ROTH
64 Dean School of Music .... Mr. Mark PARKER
66 Interim Dean of School of Nursing .... Dr. Gina CRAWFORD
73 Director School of Religion .... Dr. Sharon BETSWORTH
88 Dean Sch of American Dance/Arts Mgt .... Mr. John BEDFORD
104 Director Study Abroad .... Ms. Rachel BROWN
108 Director Institutional Assessment .... Vacant
38 Director of Counseling Services .... Ms. Mindy WINDHOLZ
39 Director University Housing .... Mr. Casey KREGER
43 University General Counsel .... Ms. Casey ROSS
44 Director Annual Giving .... Ms. Carrie SAUER
04 Administrative Asst to President .... Ms. Sarah POWERS
28 Dir Stdnt Engage/Incl/Multicult Pgm .... Mr. Russ TALLCHIEF
105 Web Services Manager .... Mr. Brian BYRNE

Oklahoma Panhandle State University (F)

Box 430, Goodwell OK 73939-0430
County: Texas FICE Identification: 003174
Unit ID: 207351
Telephone: (580) 349-2611 Carnegie Class: Bac-Diverse
FAX Number: (580) 349-2302 Calendar System: Semester
URL: www.opsu.edu
Established: 1909 Annual Undergrad Tuition & Fees (In-State): $7,384
Enrollment: 1,337 Coed
Affiliation or Control: State IRS Status: 501(c)3
Highest Offering: Baccalaureate
Accreditation: HLC, CAEP, NUR

01 President .... Dr. Tim FALTYN
05 Provost .... Dr. Julie DINGER
10 AVP of Fiscal Affairs .... Ms. Elizabeth MCMURPHY
111 Vice President of Operations .... Dr. Ryan BLANTON
20 AVP of Academic Affairs .... Dr. Brad DUREN
47 Dean Agriculture/Science/Nursing .... Ms. Shawna TUCKER
50 Dean Business & Technology .... Mr. Davin WINGER
32 Dean of Student Services .... Ms. Amber GLASS
06 Int Registrar/Dir of Admissions .... Ms. Olivia ROBINSON
37 Director Student Financial Aid .... Ms. Erin MOORE
09 Director Institutional Research .... Mr. Dillon SCHOENHALS
13 Director of Technology .... Mr. Howard HENDERSON
15 Director Human Resources .... Ms. Dana COLLINS
08 Director of Library .... Mr. Alton (Tony) HARDMAN
21 Comptroller .... Ms. Tiffany MURLEY
38 Director Counseling/Career Services .... Ms. Deanna Rene RAMON
26 Director Campus Communications .... Ms. Natasha EIDSON
41 Athletic Officer .... Mr. Victor ESPARZA
40 Bookstore Manager .... Ms. Heather UTT
18 Director Physical Plant .... Mr. Robby JOHNSON
29 Director Alumni Relations/Webmaster .... Mr. Nick TUTTLE
96 Director of Purchasing .... Ms. Carol HILL
04 Administrative Asst to President .... Ms. Calandra ROSE

Oklahoma State University (G)

Stillwater OK 74078
County: Payne FICE Identification: 003170
Unit ID: 207388
Telephone: (405) 744-5000 Carnegie Class: DU-Highest
FAX Number: N/A Calendar System: Semester
URL: osu.okstate.edu/
Established: 1890 Annual Undergrad Tuition & Fees (In-State): $9,019
Enrollment: 24,535 Coed
Affiliation or Control: State IRS Status: 501(c)3
Highest Offering: Doctorate
Accreditation: HLC, CAATE, CACREP, CAEPN, CARTE, CIDA, CLPSY, COPSY, DIETD, DIETI, JOUR, LSAR, MFCD, MUS, NURSE, PCSAS, SCPSY, SP, THEA, VET

01 President .... Dr. Burns HARGIS
04 Exec Assistant to the President .... Ms. Deborah LANE
102 President & CEO OSU Foundation .... Mr. Kirk JEWELL
43 Sr Vice President & General Counsel .... Mr. Gary C. CLARK
05 Provost & Sr Vice President .... Dr. Gary SANDEFUR
10 Sr Vice Pres Admin & Finance .... Mr. Joseph B. WEAVER, JR.
47 VP/Dean/Director Ag Sci & Nat Res .... Dr. Thomas COON
41 Vice President Athletic Programs .... Mr. Mike HOLDER

26 Vice Pres Enroll Mgmt/Univ Mktg .... Mr. Kyle WRAY
46 Vice President for Research .... Dr. Kenneth SEWELL
32 Vice President Student Affairs .... Dr. Lee E. BIRD
09 Assoc VP/Dir Inst Res/Info Mgmt .... Dr. Christie HAWKINS
20 Prov/Sr VP Academic Affairs .... Dr. Pamela FRY
58 Assoc Provost/Dean Graduate College .... Dr. Sheryl TUCKER
21 Assoc Vice President & Controller .... Ms. Tammy ECK
28 Assoc VP Institutional Diversity .... Dr. Jason KIRKSEY
24 Asst Prov/Dir Inst Tch/Lrng Excel .... Dr. Christine ORMSBEE
13 Chief Information Officer .... Ms. Darlene HIGHTOWER
18 Chief Facilities Officer .... Mr. Ron TARBUTTON
96 Chief Procurement Officer .... Mr. Scott SCHLOTTHAUER
19 Chief Public Safety Officer .... Mr. Michael ROBINSON
36 Director Career Services .... Dr. Pam EHLERS
27 Director Communication Services .... Vacant
25 Dir Grants/Contracts/Financial Admn .... Dr. Robert DIXON
37 Director Scholarships/Financial Aid .... Mr. Chad BLEW
39 Director of University Housing .... Dr. Leon MCCLINTON
108 Director Univ Assessment & Testing .... Mr. James KNECHT
38 Director University Counseling Svcs ..... Dr. Trevor RICHARDSON
23 Director University Health Services .... Mr. Christopher BARLOW
88 Assoc Dir Institutional Research .... Mr. Doug REED
40 Dir Student Union Bookstore .... Mr. Lance HINKLE
39 Asst Director Resident Life .... Ms. Tanya MASSEY
85 Asst Dir Intl Students & Scholars .... Mr. Tim T. HUFF
53 Dean College of Education .... Dr. John ROMANS
54 Dean Engineering .... Dr. Paul J. TIKALSKY
92 Dean Honors College .... Dr. Keith GARBUTT
59 Dean Human Sciences .... Dr. Stephan M. WILSON
08 Dean Library .... Dr. Sheila G. JOHNSON
50 Dean Spears School of Business .... Dr. Ken EASTMAN
74 Dean Veterinary Medicine .... Dr. Christopher R. ROSS
06 Registrar .... Ms. Rita PEASTER

Oklahoma State University Center for Health Sciences (A)

1111 W 17th Street, Tulsa OK 74107-1898
Telephone: (918) 582-1972 FICE Identification: 011282
Accreditation: &HLC, #ARCPA, FEPAC, OSTEO

† Regional accreditation is carried under the parent institution in Stillwater, OK.

Oklahoma State University Institute of Technology-Okmulgee (B)

1801 E Fourth Street, Okmulgee OK 74447-3901
County: Okmulgee FICE Identification: 003172
Unit ID: 207564
Telephone: (918) 293-4678 Carnegie Class: Bac/Assoc-Mixed
FAX Number: (918) 293-4644 Calendar System: Trimester
URL: www.osuit.edu
Established: 1946 Annual Undergrad Tuition & Fees (In-State): $5,774
Enrollment: 2,349 Coed
Affiliation or Control: State IRS Status: 501(c)3
Highest Offering: Baccalaureate
Accreditation: HLC, ADNUR

01 President .... Dr. Bill PATH
10 VP Fiscal Services .... Mr. Jim SMITH
05 Provost/VP Academic Affairs .... Dr. Scott NEWMAN
32 VP Student Services .... Dr. Ina AGNEW
20 Associate VP Academic Affairs .... Ms. Jody GRAMMER
103 Assoc VP Workforce & Econ Dev .... Mr. Charles HARRISON
49 Dean Arts/Sciences & Health Science .... Dr. Lisa WEIS
54 Dean Engineering/Construction Tech .... Mr. Steve OLMSTEAD
88 Dean Transportation & Heavy Equip .... Mr. Terryl LINDSEY
57 Dean Creative & Information Tech .... Mr. Christian BRADLEY
37 Dir Student Financial Services .... Mr. Matt SHORT
13 Associate VP Technology Services .... Mr. Kevin HULETT
07 Director of Admissions/ Registrar .... Ms. Crystal BOWLES PALACIOZ
106 Dir Acad Excellence & Distance Lrng .. Mr. Dominic CHRISTISON
15 Director of Human Resources .... Ms. Paula NORTH
09 Director of Institutional Research .... Ms. Michelle CANAN
18 Dir Physical Plant Services .... Mr. Mark PITCHER
35 Dean of Students .... Mr. Devin DEBOCK
109 Dir Student Union & Auxiliary Svcs .... Mr. James BYRD
35 Director of Student Life .... Ms. Kamie RASH
39 Director of Residential Life .... Mr. Bo HUDSON
08 Director of Library .... Ms. Jenny DUNCAN
96 Director of Purchasing .... Ms. Jalynda BAILEY
38 Counselor .... Ms. Kathy AVERY
40 Manager Bookstore .... Ms. Shayla KING
26 Director of Marketing .... Ms. Shari ERWIN
19 Campus Police Chief .... Mr. Matt WOOLIVER
04 Admin Asst to President .... Ms. Claudette BUTCHER
88 Dir Tutoring Ctr/Acad Accommodation .... Mr. Chad SPURLOCK
29 Director Alumni Relations .... Vacant
30 Director Development .... Ms. Mae BARTEL

Oklahoma State University - Oklahoma City (C)

900 N Portland Ave, Oklahoma City OK 73107-6195
County: Oklahoma FICE Identification: 009647
Unit ID: 207397
Telephone: (405) 947-4421 Carnegie Class: Bac/Assoc-Assoc Dom
FAX Number: (405) 945-3289 Calendar System: Semester
URL: www.osuokc.edu
Established: 1961 Annual Undergrad Tuition & Fees (In-State): $5,070
Enrollment: 4,949 Coed
Affiliation or Control: State IRS Status: 501(c)3
Highest Offering: Baccalaureate
Accreditation: HLC, ADNUR, DMS, EMT

01 President .... Dr. Brad WILLIAMS
04 Exec Assistant to the President .... Ms. Paige LANDRETH
05 Vice President Academic Affairs .... Dr. Joey FRONHEISER
10 Vice President Budget & Finance .... Ms. Ronda REECE
20 Associate VP Academic Affairs .... Mr. Tracy EDWARDS
32 Vice Pres of Student Experience .... Mr. Darioush YASSERI
30 Associate Dir Development .... Mr. Donovan WOODS
11 Vice Pres of Operations .... Mr. Mike WIDELL
08 Director Library Services .... Ms. Elaine REGIER
37 Director Financial Aid .... Ms. Bessie CARTER
15 Director Human Resources .... Ms. Melissa HERREN
18 Dir of Building Maint/Energy Mgr .... Mr. Mickey FULLER
26 Sr Dir Marketing/Communications .... Vacant
121 Director Academic Advisement .... Ms. Krystle DICK
07 Dir Recruitment & Admissions .... Ms. Brandee MORGAN
96 Director of Purchasing .... Ms. Sharon FITZPATRICK
113 Director Business Services .... Ms. Kim BEAUCOURT
06 Registrar .... Mr. Kyle BROWN
25 Sr Director Institutional Grants .... Ms. Jackie WESTON
19 Sr Director Safety & Security .... Mr. Darvin GORE
108 Sr Dir Institutional Effectiveness .... Ms. Virginia SMITH
88 Sr Dir Community Engagement .... Dr. Lisa FISHER
13 Chief Information Officer .... Mr. Richard BARR
28 Director Disability/Inclusion .... Ms. Emily CHENG
93 Director Upward Bound .... Mr. Donovan KELSO

Oklahoma State University - Tulsa (D)

700 N Greenwood Avenue, Tulsa OK 74106-0702
Telephone: (918) 594-8000 Identification: 666053
Accreditation: &HLC

† Regional accreditation is carried under the parent institution in Stillwater, OK.

Oklahoma Wesleyan University (E)

2201 Silver Lake Road, Bartlesville OK 74006-6299
County: Washington FICE Identification: 003151
Unit ID: 206835
Telephone: (800) 468-6219 Carnegie Class: Masters/M
FAX Number: N/A Calendar System: Semester
URL: www.okwu.edu
Established: 1905 Annual Undergrad Tuition & Fees: $28,924
Enrollment: 934 Coed
Affiliation or Control: Wesleyan Church IRS Status: 501(c)3
Highest Offering: Doctorate
Accreditation: HLC, CAEPN, IACBE, NURSE

01 President .... Dr. Jim DUNN
05 Provost/VP for Academic Affairs .... Dr. Mark WEETER
10 Vice President for Business Affairs .... Dr. Kirk JACKSON
32 Vice Pres for Student Development .... Mr. Kyle WHITE
84 Vice President for Enrollment Svcs .... Dr. Kevin OSBORN
35 Assoc VP for Student Dev .... Rev. Ben ROTZ
53 Dean School of Educ & Exercise Sci .... Dr. Keri BOSTWICK
73 Dean Sch of Ministry/Christ Theol .... Dr. Jerome VAN KUIKEN
49 Dean of School of Arts & Sciences .... Dr. Dalene FISHER
50 Dean of School of Business .... Dr. Wendel WEAVER
66 Dean of School of Nursing .... Dr. Jessica JOHNSON
58 Dir of Grad & Professional Studies .... Dr. Brett ANDREWS
21 Director of Accounting .... Mrs. Tabitha BENBROOK
06 Exec Dir of Student Services .... Mrs. Kandi MOLDER
13 Director of Information Technology .... Mr. Alex JOHNSON
08 Head Librarian .... Mrs. Cheryl SALERNO
37 Director of Financial Aid .... Mrs. Tirzah KNIGHT
15 Director of Human Resources ...... Mrs. Rachel GLASS-SHOWLER
41 Athletic Director .... Mr. Kirk KELLEY
04 Executive Assistant to President .... Ms. Leeann LITTLE
39 Director of Residential Life .... Mrs. Megan YOUNG
124 Dir of Student Engagement .... Mr. Aaron BUNKER
18 Director of Buildings and Grounds .... Mr. Dalton HIGGINS
19 Director of Campus Safety .... Mr. Stevan DJUKIC
101 Secretary of the Institution/Board .... Mr. Trevor SHAKIBA
26 VP of Creative Impact .... Mr. Kory PENCE
29 Dir of Alumni Rel & Grant Writing .... Ms. Charissa DUNN
43 General Counsel .... Dr. David PRESTON

Oral Roberts University (F)

7777 S Lewis Avenue, Tulsa OK 74171-0003
County: Tulsa FICE Identification: 003985
Unit ID: 207582
Telephone: (918) 495-6161 Carnegie Class: Bac-Diverse
FAX Number: (918) 495-6033 Calendar System: Semester
URL: https://oru.edu/
Established: 1965 Annual Undergrad Tuition & Fees: $30,930
Enrollment: 4,317 Coed
Affiliation or Control: Independent Non-Profit IRS Status: 501(c)3
Highest Offering: Doctorate
Accreditation: HLC, ACBSP, CAEPN, MUS, NURSE, SW, THEOL

01 President .... Dr. William M. WILSON
05 Provost .... Dr. Kathaleen REID-MARTINEZ
10 Chief Financial Officer .... Mr. Neal STENZEL
11 Chief Operations Officer .... Mr. Tim PHILLEY
111 VP of External Affairs .... Dr. Charles SCOTT
88 VP for Enrollment Management .... Vacant
43 University Counsel .... Mr. Terry KOLLMORGEN
32 Vice President Student Life .... Dr. Clarence BOYD
13 VP of Technology & Innovation .... Mr. Michael MATHEWS
84 AVP Of Enrollment Management - Res ..... Mrs. Alison VUJNOVIC
84 AVP of Enrollment Management-Online .... Mr. Nathan CARSON
14 AVP of Technology & Innovation .... Mr. Vinay MANDA
21 Controller .... Ms. Michelle MCMILLAN
08 Dean of the University Library .... Dr. Mark ROBERTS
104 Director Study Abroad .... Mrs. Jessica TENORIO
106 AD of Online & Lifelong Learning .... Dr. Jay GARY
54 Dean Col of Science & Engineering .... Dr. Kenneth WEED
49 Dean Col of Arts & Cultural Studies .... Dr. William C. ELLIS
73 Dean College Theology/Ministry .... Dr. Wonsuk MA
50 Dean College of Business .... Dr. Julie HUNTLEY
76 Dean College of Health Sciences .... Dr. Dean PRENTICE
53 Dean College of Education .... Dr. Kim BOYD
35 Dean of Student Development .... Mrs. Lori COOK
35 Director of Student Services .... Mrs. Juli ATKINSON
41 Director for Athletics .... Mr. Tim JOHNSON
25 Grants Facilitator .... Ms. Andrea STOGUE
38 Director of Student Counseling .... Ms. Haley FRENCH
92 Director of Honors Program .... Dr. John KORSTAD
113 Director Student Accounts .... Ms. Karen BAUER
96 Director of Purchasing .... Mr. Mark PEPIN
06 University Registrar .... Dr. Connie SJOBERG
89 Director of New Student Relations .... Ms. Stephanie OTTMAN
07 Exec Director Intl Admissions .... Mrs. Jenny FANG
37 Director of Financial Aid .... Ms. Emily ATKERSON
19 Director of Security/Safety .... Mr. Bill (William) HUNT
15 Human Resources Director .... Dr. Kathryn LENTZ
04 Executive Asst to President .... Mrs. Lisa BOWMAN
101 Secretary of the Institution/BOT .... Ms. Alyssa SANDERS
30 VP Development & Alumni Relations .... Mrs. Natalie ADAMS

Phillips Theological Seminary (G)

901 N Mingo Road, Tulsa OK 74116-5612
County: Tulsa FICE Identification: 025602
Unit ID: 414966
Telephone: (918) 610-8303 Carnegie Class: Spec-4-yr-Faith
FAX Number: (918) 610-8404 Calendar System: Semester
URL: www.ptstulsa.edu
Established: 1906 Annual Graduate Tuition & Fees: N/A
Enrollment: 170 Coed
Affiliation or Control: Christian Church (Disciples Of Christ)
IRS Status: 501(c)3
Highest Offering: Doctorate; No Undergraduates
Accreditation: THEOL

01 President .... Nancy C. PITTMAN
125 President Emeritus .... Gary PELUSO-VERDEND
05 VP Academic Affairs & Dean .... Lee H. BUTLER, JR.
10 Vice Pres Finance & Admin .... Karen MCMILLAN
111 Vice Pres Advancement .... Terry EWING
108 Assoc Dean Assessment & Faculty Dev .... Joseph A. BESSLER
20 Assoc Dn Contextual Ed/Church Rels .... Vacant
73 Director Doctor of Ministry Program .... Kathleen D. MCCALLIE
37 Financial Aid Officer .... Todd MANTOCK
08 Dean of Library .... Sandy SHAPOVAL
29 Sr Dir Stewardship & Alumni Rels .... Malisa PIERCE
26 Sr Director Seminary Relations .... Kurt GWARTNEY
06 Registrar .... Virginia THOMPSON
04 Executive Assistant to President .... Ashley M. GIBSON

Platt College (H)

201 N Eastern Avenue, Moore OK 73160
Telephone: (405) 445-6329 Identification: 770585
Accreditation: ACCSC

Platt College (I)

3801 S Sheridan, Tulsa OK 74145-1132
County: Tulsa FICE Identification: 023068
Unit ID: 245962
Telephone: (918) 663-9000 Carnegie Class: Spec 2-yr-Health
FAX Number: (918) 622-1240 Calendar System: Other
URL: www.plattcolleges.edu
Established: 1979 Annual Undergrad Tuition & Fees: N/A
Enrollment: 167 Coed
Affiliation or Control: Proprietary IRS Status: Proprietary
Highest Offering: Associate Degree
Accreditation: ACCSC

01 Executive Director of Campus .... Cheryl BEESE
07 Director of Admissions .... Kristen O'BRIEN
05 Director of Education .... Amy MOORE

Randall University (J)

3701 S. I-35 Service Road, Moore OK 73160
County: Cleveland FICE Identification: 010266
Unit ID: 207157
Telephone: (405) 912-9000 Carnegie Class: Bac-A&S
FAX Number: (405) 912-9050 Calendar System: Semester
URL: www.ru.edu
Established: 1959 Annual Undergrad Tuition & Fees: $16,547
Enrollment: 311 Coed
Affiliation or Control: Free Will Baptist IRS Status: 501(c)3
Highest Offering: Master's
Accreditation: TRACS

00 Chancellor ... Dr. Timothy W. EATON
01 President ... Rev. Robert G. THOMPSON
10 Chief Financial Officer ... Mr. Todd JENSON
05 Chief Academic Officer ... Dr. Brent SYKES
21 Chief Business Officer ... Ms. Pat MILLER
32 Dean of Students ... Ms. Jody BLACKWELL
42 Director of Church Engagement ... Rev. Mason POLK
07 Admissions Coordinator ... Mr. Evan ALDRIDGE
37 Financial Aid Coordinator ... Mr. Cliff BRISTOW
08 LRC Director ... Ms. Nancy J. DRAPER
13 Director of MIS ... Mr. Quentin C. LOOP
06 Registrar ... Ms. Patti ASHBY
41 Athletic Director ... Mr. Todd JENSON
106 Director of Online Learning ... Mrs. Michelle COFFMAN

Redlands Community College (A)

1300 S Country Club Road, El Reno OK 73036-5304
County: Canadian FICE Identification: 003156
Unit ID: 207069
Telephone: (405) 262-2552 Carnegie Class: Assoc/HT-High Non
FAX Number: (405) 422-1200 Calendar System: Semester
URL: www.redlandscc.edu
Established: 1938 Annual Undergrad Tuition & Fees (In-District): $5,360
Enrollment: 1,917 Coed
Affiliation or Control: State/Local IRS Status: 501(c)3
Highest Offering: Associate Degree
Accreditation: HLC, ADNUR

01 President ... Mr. Jack BRYANT
05 Chief Academic & Compliance Officer ... Ms. Rose Marie MOORE
10 Exec Vice Pres of Admin & Finance ... Ms. Jena MARR
47 Dept Head of Agriculture ... Ms. Annie PEARSON
18 Director Physical Plant ... Mr. Richard BUCHHOLZ
08 Director Learning Resource Center ... Mrs. Sharon RILEY
06 Registrar/Director Student Records ... Ms. Holly AVILA
37 Director Financial Aid ... Ms. Paris PRZEKURAT
41 Athletic Director ... Mr. Eli ZUCKSWORTH
13 Director of Information Technology ... Mr. Jon FIELDS
22 Director of Upward Bound ... Mrs. Kacey DANIELS
09 Coord of Institutional Research ... Mr. Troy MILLIGAN
32 Exec Director of Student Services ... Mrs. Tricia HOBSON
21 Business Office Supervisor ... Mrs. Brenda HARKINS
15 Coordinator Personnel/Payroll ... Mrs. Kim ANDRADE
26 Exec Director of External Affairs ... Mrs. Dayna ROWE
39 Coordinator of Resident Life ... Ms. Tina JACOBS

Rogers State University (B)

1701 W Will Rogers Boulevard,
Claremore OK 74017-3252
County: Rogers FICE Identification: 003168
Unit ID: 207661
Telephone: (918) 343-7777 Carnegie Class: Bac-Diverse
FAX Number: (918) 343-7898 Calendar System: Semester
URL: www.rsu.edu
Established: 1909 Annual Undergrad Tuition & Fees (In-State): $7,470
Enrollment: 3,400 Coed
Affiliation or Control: State IRS Status: 501(c)3
Highest Offering: Master's
Accreditation: HLC, NUR

01 President ... Dr. Larry RICE
05 Vice President for Academic Affairs ... Dr. Richard BECK
10 VP for Administration & Finance ... Dr. Mark RASOR
30 Vice President for Development ... Mr. Steve VALENCIA
32 Vice Pres for Student Affairs ... Dr. Robert GOLTRA
84 Int Vice President Enrollment Mgmt ... Dr. Robert GOLTRA
12 Director Bartlesville Campus ... Ms. Ronda RIDEN
20 Assoc VP for Academic Affairs ... Dr. Mary MILLIKIN
21 Comptroller/Asst Vice Pres Bus Affs ... Mr. Michael ALLGOOD
12 Director Pryor Campus ... Mr. Brett ROWH
107 Dean School of Professional Studies ... Dr. Susan WILLIS
49 Dean School of Arts and Sciences ... Dr. Keith MARTIN
35 Director of Student Development ... Ms. Jeana Rae CONN
08 Interim Director of the Library ... Ms. Kaitlyn CROTTY
07 Director of Admissions ... Mr. Lee JOHNSON
29 Director of Alumni Engagement ... Mr. Travis PECK
04 Exec Assistant to the President ... Ms. Alyssa CRAVENS
18 Director Physical Plant ... Mr. Karl REYNOLDS
19 Director Campus Police ... Mr. Louis ROSS
26 Director of Marketing ... Mr. Brandon IRBY
37 Director of Financial Aid ... Ms. LaKeitta MATOS
91 Director Administrative Computing ... Ms. Cathy BURNS
13 Director Information Technology ... Mr. Brian REEVES
15 Director of Human Resources ... Ms. Jamil HAYNES
41 Director of Athletics ... Mr. Chris RATCLIFF
39 Director Residential Life ... Ms. Kyla SHORT
23 Director Student Health Clinic ... Vacant
09 Director of Institutional Research ... Ms. Shelly BORGSTROM

Rogers State University-Bartlesville (C)

401 South Dewey Avenue, Bartlesville OK 74003
Telephone: (918) 338-8000 Identification: 770379
Accreditation: &HLC

Rogers State University-Pryor (D)

2155 Highway 69A, Pryor Creek OK 74361
Telephone: (918) 825-6117 Identification: 770380
Accreditation: &HLC

Rose State College (E)

6420 SE 15th, Midwest City OK 73110-2799
County: Oklahoma FICE Identification: 009185
Unit ID: 207670
Telephone: (405) 733-7673 Carnegie Class: Assoc/HT-Mix Trad/Non
FAX Number: (405) 733-7399 Calendar System: Semester
URL: www.rose.edu
Established: 1970 Annual Undergrad Tuition & Fees (In-District): $4,754
Enrollment: 6,722 Coed
Affiliation or Control: State/Local IRS Status: 501(c)3
Highest Offering: Associate Degree
Accreditation: HLC, ADNUR, CAHIIM, COARC, DA, DH, MLTAD, NAEYC, RAD

01 President ... Dr. Jeanie WEBB
10 Exec Vice President and CFO ... Dr. Kent LASHLEY
05 Vice President for Academic Affairs ... Ms. Isabelle BILLEN
32 Vice President for Student Affairs ... Mr. Lance NEWBOLD
26 Exec Dir PR & Comm/Govt Liaison ... Dr. Bradley BARRICK
13 Vice President for Info Technology ... Mr. John PRIMO
41 Exec Dir Athletic Programs ... Mr. Coty COOPER
102 Vice Pres Foundation & Resource Dev ... Ms. Cindy MIKEMAN
20 AVP Acad Affs & Inst Effectiveness ... Mr. Travis HURST
35 Assoc Vice Pres for Student Life ... Ms. Kirby HARZMAN
21 Sr Dir Fiscal Operations ... Mr. Raymond BLANKE
15 AVP Human Res/Affirm Action Ofcr ... Ms. Alberta NUTTER
109 Assoc VP for Campus Operations ... Mr. Richard ANDREWS
84 Assoc VP Enrollment Mgmt/ Registrar ... Ms. Mechelle AITSON-ROESSLER
37 Director Financial Aid ... Mr. Steve DAFFER
18 Director Operations ... Mr. Ardie RODGERS
41 Dir Health & Wellness Activities ... Mr. Chris LELAND
88 Director Special Services ... Dr. Joanne STAFFORD
08 Dean Learning Resources Center ... Mr. Chris MEYER
50 Dean Business & Info Tech Division ... Dr. Mark TIPPIN
54 Dean Engineering & Science Division ... Dr. Ryan STODDARD
79 Dean Liberal Arts Division ... Ms. Toni CASTILLO
76 Dean Health Sciences Division ... Ms. Barbara BAUMEISTER
88 Exec Dir Faculty Staff Advancement ... Dr. Juanita ORTIZ
101 Exec Asst to the President & Board ... Ms. Michelle NUTTER
19 Coord of Safety/Security/Risk Mgmt ... Mr. Joedon HUGHES
39 Director of Residence Life ... Ms. Kim QUERI
28 Exec Dir Diversity & Cultural Affs ... Dr. Monique BRUNER
118 Director Payroll & Employee Benefit ... Ms. Krista NORTON
04 Sr Exec Admin Asst to the President ... Ms. Emily FISHER
88 Dir Student Union & Event Services ... Dr. Anita POOLE-ENDSLEY
103 Director Workforce Development ... Mr. Joe PEARSON
106 Dean of E-learning & Acad Outreach ... Ms. Dana LINDON-BURGETT
108 Director Data Research ... Mr. John CAIN

Seminole State College (F)

PO Box 351, Seminole OK 74818-0351
County: Seminole FICE Identification: 003178
Unit ID: 207740
Telephone: (405) 382-9950 Carnegie Class: Assoc/HT-High Trad
FAX Number: (405) 382-3122 Calendar System: Semester
URL: www.sscok.edu
Established: 1931 Annual Undergrad Tuition & Fees (In-District): $5,190
Enrollment: 1,476 Coed
Affiliation or Control: State/Local IRS Status: 501(c)3
Highest Offering: Associate Degree
Accreditation: HLC, ADNUR, MLTAD, PTAA

01 President ... Ms. Lana REYNOLDS
05 Vice President Academic Affairs ... Dr. Linda GOELLER
10 Vice President Fiscal Affairs ... Vacant
32 Vice President of Student Affairs ... Dr. Bill KNOWLES
13 Director Mgmt Information Systems ... Mr. Marc HUNTER
66 Director of Nursing ... Ms. Crystal BRAY
06 Registrar ... Mrs. Sheila MORRIS
15 Director Human Resources ... Mrs. Holly WILSON-BYRD
26 Director of Public Relations ... Ms. Kristin DUNN
04 Administrative Asst to President ... Ms. Mechell DOWNEY
37 Director Student Financial Aid ... Ms. Edie CATHEY
39 Director Student Housing ... Ms. Melinda SIMS
41 Athletic Director ... Mr. Mike ST. JOHN

Southeastern Oklahoma State University (G)

425 W University Blvd, Durant OK 74701-3330
County: Bryan FICE Identification: 003179
Unit ID: 207847
Telephone: (580) 745-2000 Carnegie Class: Masters/L
FAX Number: N/A Calendar System: Semester
URL: www.se.edu
Established: 1909 Annual Undergrad Tuition & Fees (In-State): $6,750
Enrollment: 5,607 Coed
Affiliation or Control: State IRS Status: 501(c)3
Highest Offering: Master's
Accreditation: HLC, AAB, CAEP, MUS

01 President ... Dr. Thomas NEWSOM
05 Vice Pres Academic Affairs ... Dr. Teresa GOLDEN
10 Vice Pres Business Affairs/CFO ... Mr. Dennis WESTMAN
32 Vice President of Student Affairs ... Ms. Liz MCCRAW
07 Assoc Dean Admissions/Registrar ... Ms. Kristie LUKE
58 Dean Graduate School ... Vacant
37 Director Student Financial Aid ... Mr. Tony LEHRLING
08 Library Director ... Ms. Sandra THOMAS
41 Director of Athletics ... Mr. Keith BAXTER
26 Dir Univ Comm/Spec Asst Pres ... Mr. Alan BURTON
21 Director Finance/Controller ... Ms. Crystal CHEEK
18 Director Facilities/Physical Plant ... Mr. Dan SIMMONS
28 Director of Compliance and Safety ... Mr. Mike DAVIS
96 Purchasing Agent ... Ms. Dana BELL
40 Book Store Manager ... Ms. Jackie CODNER
29 Director Alumni Rels & Univ Develop ... Mr. Mark WEBB
106 Dir Online Education/E-learning ... Ms. Christala SMITH
19 Chief of Police ... Mr. Durwood COOK
39 Director Student Housing ... Dr. Kelly D'ARCY
04 Exec Asst to President ... Ms. Terri ROGERS
06 Registrar ... Ms. Rachel TOEWS

Southern Nazarene University (H)

6729 NW 39 Expressway, Bethany OK 73008-2694
County: Oklahoma FICE Identification: 003149
Unit ID: 206862
Telephone: (405) 789-6400 Carnegie Class: Masters/L
FAX Number: (405) 491-6381 Calendar System: Semester
URL: www.snu.edu
Established: 1899 Annual Undergrad Tuition & Fees: $26,000
Enrollment: 2,208 Coed
Affiliation or Control: Church Of The Nazarene IRS Status: 501(c)3
Highest Offering: Doctorate
Accreditation: HLC, ACBSP, CAEP, CAEPN, MUS, NURSE

01 President ... Dr. J. Keith NEWMAN
05 Provost & VP Academic Affairs ... Dr. Timothy EADES
03 Executive Vice President ... Dr. Mike REDWINE
10 Vice President Financial Affairs ... Dr. Scott STRAWN
88 VP Intercultural Lrng/Engagement ... Dr. Lena CROUSO
26 VP External Relations ... Mr. Larry MORRIS
84 VP for Trad Enrollment & Marketing ... Dr. Marian REDWINE
42 Univ Pastor/Dean of the Chapel ... Dr. Blair SPINDLE
21 Assoc VP for Financial Services ... Mr. Chris PETERSON
79 VP Acad Affairs Traditional ... Dr. Steve BETTS
81 VP Academic Affairs PGS ... Dr. Mark WINSLOW
06 Registrar ... Mr. Charles CHITWOOD
37 Director Student Financial Aid ... Mr. Perry DIEHM
37 Dir of Financial Aid/Traditional ... Mrs. Jamie SALAZAR
32 Dean of Students ... Mrs. Katy BRADLEY
38 Director Student Counseling ... Dr. Scott SECOR
36 Director Career Planning/Placement ... Mrs. Michelle MULLENS
08 Director Learning Resources Center ... Mr. Joshua ACHIPA
29 Exec Dir Alumni Relations ... Mr. Todd BRANT
13 Director Information Technology ... Mr. Keith CUMMINGS
121 Assoc VP for Student Success ... Mrs. Twyler EARL
09 Director Institutional Research ... Dr. Kirstin KRUG
58 VP Enrollment/Marketing PGS ... Mrs. Johnna VANOVER
66 Director of Nursing ... Dr. Brittany CUMMINGS
15 Director Human Resources ... Mrs. Gail COLLIER
18 Director of Physical Plant ... Mr. Ron LESTER
24 Director Network ... Mrs. Chichi FREELANDER
88 Social Media Coordinator ... Mrs. Hailee THOMPSON
40 Bookstore Manager ... Vacant
41 Athletic Director ... Mr. Daniel THOMASON
53 VP Strategy & Innovation ... Dr. Dennis WILLIAMS
04 Executive Asst to President ... Mrs. Tollya SPINDLE
19 Director Security/Safety ... Mr. Dan HANSEN
25 Chief Contracts/Grants Admin ... Dr. Gwen HACKLER
39 Director Student Housing ... Mrs. Katy BRADLEY
28 Director of Diversity ... Dr. Lena CROUSO

Southwestern Christian University (I)

PO Box 340, 7210 NW 39th Expressway,
Bethany OK 73008-0340
County: Oklahoma FICE Identification: 003180
Unit ID: 207856
Telephone: (405) 789-7661 Carnegie Class: Bac-Diverse
FAX Number: (405) 495-0078 Calendar System: Semester
URL: www.swcu.edu
Established: 1946 Annual Undergrad Tuition & Fees: $19,114
Enrollment: 486 Coed
Affiliation or Control: Pentecostal Holiness Church IRS Status: 501(c)3
Highest Offering: Master's
Accreditation: HLC

01 President ... Dr. Tom L. MURRAY
05 VP Academic Affairs ... Dr. Adrian HINKLE
10 VP for Business and Finance ... Mr. Kyle TAYLOR
32 Vice President for Student Services ... Mr. Brad DAVIS
41 Vice President of Athletics ... Mr. Mark ARTHUR
84 Director of Enrollment Management ... Mr. Joe BLACKWELL
37 Director of Financial Aid ... Mrs. Rita PALMER
07 Director of Admissions ... Mr. Kris JACKSON
08 Director of Library Services ... Mr. Michael LOWDER
06 Registrar ... Ms. Emily GROVES
58 Director of Graduate Studies ... Mrs. Shelley GROVES
35 Dean of Students ... Mr. Zach SHERRILL
20 Dean of Academics ... Vacant
30 Chief Development Officer ... Ms. April BLACK
18 Director of Plant/Property Mgmt ... Mr. Robert PALMER
26 Director of Sports Information/PR ... Mr. Philip YOUNTS
13 Director of Information Technology ... Mr. Scott KLEPPER
106 Director of Online Education ... Ms. Misty FOSTER
15 Director of Human Resources ... Vacant
04 Executive Asst to President ... Ms. Erin BROWN
19 Director Security/Safety ... Mr. Darin DAVIS

39 Director Student Life/Resident Dir ... Ms. Kaylee BISHOP
09 Director of Institutional Research ... Mr. Jesse HEATH
108 Director of Assessment ... Ms. Patty CLOUSE

Southwestern Oklahoma State University (A)

100 Campus Drive, Weatherford OK 73096-3098

County: Custer FICE Identification: 003181
Unit ID: 207865
Telephone: (580) 772-6611 Carnegie Class: Masters/L
FAX Number: (580) 774-3795 Calendar System: Semester
URL: www.swosu.edu
Established: 1901 Annual Undergrad Tuition & Fees (In-State): $7,913
Enrollment: 4,898 Coed
Affiliation or Control: State IRS Status: 501(c)3
Highest Offering: First Professional Degree
Accreditation: **HLC**, ACBSP, CAEP, CAHIIM, IACBE, MLTAD, MUS, NAIT, NUR, OTA, PHAR, PTAA, RAD

01 President ... Dr. Diana LOVELL
10 VP Business and Finance ... Ms. Brenda K. BURGESS
05 VP for Academic Affairs/Provost ... Dr. Joel KENDALL
32 VP Student Affairs ... Dr. Ruth BOYD
20 Assoc Provost Acad Affairs ... Vacant
26 VP for Marketing/Public Relations ... Mr. Brian D. ADLER
111 Asst Vice Pres Inst Advancement ... Mr. Garrett KING
35 Dean of Students ... Mr. Joshua ENGLE
21 Business Affairs Dir/Comptroller ... Mr. Steve JOHNSON
13 Information Technology Services Dir ... Ms. Dian RAY
06 Registrar ... Mr. Shamus MOORE
08 Library Dir ... Mr. Jason M. DUPREE
37 Student Financial Services Dir ... Mr. Jerome L. WICHERT
15 VP Human Resources/Affirm Action ... Mr. David MISAK
84 Enrollment Mgmt/Career Services Dir ... Mr. Todd BOYD
41 Athletics Director ... Mr. Todd HELTON
06 Registrar Sayre Campus ... Ms. Terry BILLEY
38 Counseling Services Dir ... Ms. Susan ELLIS
18 Physical Plant Dir ... Mr. James SKINNER
57 Facilities Dir FAC & PCEC ... Mr. Nate DOWNS
36 Career Exploration Coordinator ... Ms. Heather HUMMEL
58 Dean College of Prof/Grad Studies ... Dr. Chad L. KINDER
49 Dean College of Arts/Sciences ... Dr. Jason JOHNSON
67 Dean College of Pharmacy ... Dr. David RALPH
12 Dean College of Assoc/Applied Prog ... Mr. Bill SWARTWOOD
53 Assoc Dean Sch of Behavioral Sci ... Dr. Randy BARNETT
50 Assoc Dean Sch of Business/Tech ... Dr. Patsy PARKER
66 Assoc Dean Sch of Nursing ... Dr. Darryl BARNETT
04 Exec Assistant to the President ... Ms. Misty ZINK
105 Web Services Dir ... Ms. Susan MCELHANEY
106 CETL Dir ... Ms. Lisa FRIESSEN
108 Assessment & Testing Dir ... Ms. Jan KLIEWER
19 Public Safety Dir ... Ms. Kendra BROWN
25 Office of Sponsored Programs Dir ... Dr. Lori GWYN
39 Residence Life & Housing Dir ... Mr. Chad MARTIN
88 Univ Press Mgr ... Ms. Kandy HOUSE
88 Business Enterprise Center Dir ... Mr. Doug MISAK
40 Univ Bookstore Dir ... Ms. Ashley HANCOCK
88 Upward Bound Dir ... Ms. Jamie NOVEY
23 Wellness Center Dir ... Mr. Scott MILLER
88 Student Union Dir ... Ms. Jackie REAGAN
88 Food Services Dir ... Ms. Radonna SAWATZKY
104 International Student Affairs Dir ... Vacant
124 Retention Management Coordinator ... Dr. Wendy YODER
07 Director of Admissions ... Mr. Todd BOYD

† Campus at Sayre offers a two-year degree and is regionally accredited (NH) under parent institution.

Spartan College of Aeronautics and Technology (B)

8820 E Pine Street, Tulsa OK 74115

County: Tulsa FICE Identification: 007678
Unit ID: 207254
Telephone: (918) 836-6886 Carnegie Class: Spec-4-yr-Other Tech
FAX Number: (918) 831-5287 Calendar System: Other
URL: www.spartan.edu
Established: 1928 Annual Undergrad Tuition & Fees: $21,915
Enrollment: 708 Coed
Affiliation or Control: Proprietary IRS Status: Proprietary
Highest Offering: Baccalaureate
Accreditation: **ACCSC**

00 CEO ... Mr. Rob POLSTON
01 President ... Ms. Kari PAHNO
05 Chief Academic & Operations Ofcr ... Dr. Todd CELLINI
10 CFO ... Vacant
11 Campus Director ... Mr. Marc SHERROD
32 Dean of Student Affairs ... Ms. Alessia CUMMINGS
18 Dean of Operations ... Mr. Damon BOWLING
04 Executive Asst to President ... Ms. Catherine LOEPER
07 Director of Admissions ... Mr. Jeff STOLTENBERG
37 Director Student Financial Aid ... Ms. Megan COKER
06 Registrar ... Ms. Kari CAGLE

Tulsa Community College (C)

909 S. Boston Avenue, Tulsa OK 74119

County: Tulsa FICE Identification: 009763
Unit ID: 207935
Telephone: (918) 595-7000 Carnegie Class: Assoc/MT-VT-High Trad
FAX Number: (918) 595-7092 Calendar System: Semester
URL: www.tulsacc.edu
Established: 1968 Annual Undergrad Tuition & Fees (In-State): $3,445
Enrollment: 15,568 Coed
Affiliation or Control: State IRS Status: 501(c)3
Highest Offering: Associate Degree
Accreditation: **HLC**, ADNUR, CAHIIM, COARC, CVT, DH, MLTAD, OTA, PTAA, RAD

01 President/CEO ... Dr. Leigh GOODSON
05 Sr VP and Chief Academic Officer ... Dr. Angela SIVADON
111 VP Advancement & Found Pres ... Ms. Kari SHULTS
11 VP Administration and COO ... Mr. Sean A. WEINS
103 VP Workforce Development ... Mr. Pete SELDEN
43 General Counsel ... Ms. MacKenzie WILFONG
45 Chief Strategy Officer ... Dr. Lindsay WHITE
32 VP Student Success & Equity ... Ms. Eunice TARVER
20 AVP Academic Affairs ... Dr. Greg STONE
20 AVP Academic Affairs ... Dr. Kristopher COPELAND
10 Chief Financial Officer ... Mr. Mark MCMULLEN
13 AVP Admin Operations & CTO ... Mr. Michael SIFTAR
15 Actg Chief Human Resources Officer ... Ms. Mary SIRKEL
84 Assoc VP Enrollment & Retention ... Ms. Eileen KENNEY
26 Dir Marketing/Communications ... Ms. Laurie TILLEY
60 Dean Comm/English/World Lang ... Dr. Paula WILLYARD
08 Dean Libraries ... Ms. Paula SETTOON
49 Dean Liberal Arts & Public Service ... Vacant
81 Dean Science & Aeronautics ... Ms. Julie PORTERFIELD
57 Dean Visual & Performing Arts ... Ms. Kelly CLARK
76 Dean Health Sciences ... Ms. Jenny FIELDS
54 Dean Mathematics & Engineering ... Ms. Lyn KENT
88 Dean Center for Creativity ... Ms. Annina COLLIER
89 Dean Engaged Learning ... Ms. Cindy SHANKS
50 Dean Business & IT ... Mr. Travis WHITE
28 Dean Student Success & Equity ... Mr. Nate TODD
18 Dir Physical Facilities Operations ... Mr. Steven COX
18 Dir Facilities Plng/Constr Mgmt ... Mr. Jim CLENNAN
22 Dir Civil Rights Compl/Title IX ... Ms. Heather HANCOCK
37 Director Financial Aid ... Vacant
96 Dir Purch & Inventory Control ... Mr. Bill CREECH
09 Director Institutional Research ... Vacant
19 Chief Campus Police ... Mr. Melvin MURDOCK
25 Dir Sponsored Programs ... Dr. Barbara WAXMAN
104 Dir Fac Dev & Global Learning ... Dr. Douglas PRICE
106 Faculty Coord Online Learning ... Ms. Jennifer CAMPBELL
51 Dir Continuing Education ... Ms. Beth WILD
06 College Registrar ... Ms. Lindsay FIELDS
07 Dir Admissions/Prosp Stdnt Svcs ... Ms. Rachael ACHIVARE-HILL
36 Dir Career & Retention Programs ... Ms. Laura MCNEESE
30 Dir of Development ... Vacant
112 Chief Development Officer ... Ms. Megan KORN
105 Web Manager ... Ms. Melissa CLOUD
92 Honors Program Coord ... Mr. Allen CULPEPPER
04 Exec Asst to President ... Ms. Carrie BATESON
108 Assessment Manager ... Dr. Allison TIFFT
38 Director Wellness Services ... Ms. Jessica HEAVIN

Tulsa Community College Metro Campus (D)

909 South Boston Avenue, Tulsa OK 74119
Telephone: (918) 595-7224 Identification: 770383
Accreditation: **&HLC**, DMS

Tulsa Community College Northeast Campus (E)

3727 East Apache Street, Tulsa OK 74115
Telephone: (918) 595-7524 Identification: 770384
Accreditation: **&HLC**, EMT

Tulsa Community College Southeast Campus (F)

10300 East 81st Street, Tulsa OK 74133
Telephone: (918) 595-7724 Identification: 770385
Accreditation: **&HLC**

Tulsa Community College West Campus (G)

7505 W 41st Street, Tulsa OK 74107-8633
Telephone: (918) 595-8060 Identification: 770386
Accreditation: **&HLC**

Tulsa Welding School (H)

2545 E 11th Street, Tulsa OK 74104-3909

County: Tulsa FICE Identification: 009618
Unit ID: 207962
Telephone: (918) 587-6789 Carnegie Class: Spec 2-yr-Tech
FAX Number: (918) 587-8170 Calendar System: Other
URL: www.tws.edu
Established: 1949 Annual Undergrad Tuition & Fees: N/A
Enrollment: 785 Coed
Affiliation or Control: Proprietary IRS Status: Proprietary
Highest Offering: Associate Degree
Accreditation: **ACCSC**

01 Campus President ... Mr. Carlton SMITH
05 Director of Student Outcomes ... Ms. Frances HEASTON
07 Director of Adult Admissions ... Mr. Otis HALL
37 Director of Financial Aid ... Ms. Tiffany TYRRELL

University of Central Oklahoma (I)

100 N University Drive, Edmond OK 73034-5209

County: Oklahoma FICE Identification: 003152
Unit ID: 206941
Telephone: (405) 974-2000 Carnegie Class: Masters/L
FAX Number: (405) 359-5841 Calendar System: Semester
URL: www.uco.edu
Established: 1890 Annual Undergrad Tuition & Fees (In-State): N/A
Enrollment: N/A Coed
Affiliation or Control: State IRS Status: 501(c)3
Highest Offering: Master's
Accreditation: **HLC**, ART, CAATE, CAEPN, CIDA, DIETD, DIETI, EXSC, FEPAC, FUSER, #MPCAC, MUS, NURSE, SP, SPAA

01 President ... Ms. Patti NEUHOLD-RAVIKUMAR
05 Provost ... Dr. Charlotte SIMMONS
11 Vice Pres for Operations ... Mr. Kevin FREEMAN
32 Vice President ESS ... Mr. Christopher LYNCH
13 Chief Information Officer ... Ms. Sonya WATKINS
26 Vice Pres University Relations ... Ms. Adrienne NOBLES
30 Vice Pres Development ... Mrs. Anne HOLZBERLEIN
06 Associate Vice President/Registrar ... Dr. Adam JOHNSON
20 Assoc VP Academic Affairs ... Vacant
108 Assoc VP Inst Effectiveness ... Dr. Gary STEWARD
21 Asst VP Financial Operations ... Ms. Lisa HARPER
18 Asst Vice Pres Facilities Mgt ... Mr. Mark RODOLF
35 Asst Vice Pres Student Affairs ... Mr. Cole STANLEY
88 Asst Vice Pres Operations ... Mr. Benjamin HASTINGS
41 Athletic Director ... Mr. Stan WAGNON
09 Exec Dir Institutional Research ... Ms. Cindy BOLING
08 Exec Director University Libraries ... Dr. Habib TABATABAI
37 Director Student Financial Services ... Mr. Jason PRIDEAUX
29 Director Alumni Relations ... Ms. Lauri MONETTI
85 Exec Dir Global Affairs ... Dr. Dennis DUNHAM
19 Exec Dir Public Safety/Trans ... Mr. Jeff HARP
15 VP People & Culture ... Ms. Diane FEINBERG
88 Exec Director Leadership Central ... Dr. Jarrett JOBE
07 Dir of Undergraduate Admissions ... Mr. Dallas CALDWELL
28 Director of Diversity & Inclusion ... Ms. MeShawn GREEN
96 Director of Purchasing ... Mr. David YOUNG
50 Dean of Business Administration ... Dr. Jeremy OLLER
53 Dean College Education ... Dr. Donna COBB
49 Dean College of Liberal Arts ... Dr. Catherine WEBSTER
81 Dean College Math/Science ... Dr. Gloria CADDELL
58 Dean Graduate Studies ... Dr. Jeanetta SIMS
57 Dean of College Fine Arts & Design ... Ms. Charleen WEIDELL

University of Oklahoma Health Sciences Center (J)

1100 N. Lindsay, Oklahoma City OK 73104
Telephone: (405) 271-4000 FICE Identification: 005889
Accreditation: **&HLC**, ARCPA, AUD, CAMPEP, DENT, DH, DIETC, DIETI, DMS, HSA, IPSY, MED, NMT, NURSE, OT, PDPSY, PH, PHAR, PTA, RAD, RTT, SP

† Regional accreditation is carried under the parent institution in Norman, OK.

University of Oklahoma Norman Campus (K)

660 Parrington Oval, Norman OK 73019-3070

County: Cleveland FICE Identification: 003184
Unit ID: 207500
Telephone: (405) 325-0311 Carnegie Class: DU-Highest
FAX Number: (405) 325-7605 Calendar System: Semester
URL: www.ou.edu
Established: 1890 Annual Undergrad Tuition & Fees (In-State): $11,688
Enrollment: 27,772 Coed
Affiliation or Control: State IRS Status: 501(c)3
Highest Offering: Doctorate
Accreditation: **HLC**, AAB, CAEP, CIDA, CONST, COPSY, JOUR, LAW, LIB, LSAR, MUS, PLNG, SPAA, SW

01 President ... Mr. Joseph HARROZ, JR.
10 SVP & Chief Financial Officer ... Mr. Kenneth D. ROWE
11 VP/COO ... Mr. Eric W. CONRAD
05 Int Sr Vice President/Provost ... Dr. Jill IRVINE
43 VP of Univ/General Counsel ... Mr. Anil V. GOLLAHALLI
32 VP Student Affairs/Dean of Students ... Dr. David SURRATT
101 VP Univ Governance/Exec Sec ... Dr. Chris A. PURCELL
30 Interim VP University Development ... Ms. Jill HUGHES
88 Interim Sr Assoc VP Univ Outreach ... Dr. Belinda P. BISCOE
58 Dean Graduate College ... Dr. Randy S. HEWES
46 Vice Pres for Research ... Vacant
26 VP for Marketing/Communications ... Ms. Mackenzie DILBECK
13 Associate VP and CIO ... Mr. David HORTON
86 Exec Dir of Governmental Affairs ... Mr. John P. WOODS
20 Assoc Provost/Dir of Acad Integrity ... Dr. Gregory M. HEISER
121 Assoc Prov for Acad Advising ... Dr. Kathleen S. SMITH
09 Assoc Provost/Dir Inst Research ... Ms. Susannah B. LIVINGOOD
18 Director Facilities Management ... Mr. Brian F. ELLIS
109 Director of Food Services ... Mr. Frank M. HENRY
41 VP for Intercollegiate Athletics ... Mr. Joseph R. CASTIGLIONE
21 Assistant VP & Controller ... Ms. Karen SMITH
23 AVP for Student Affs/Health Svcs ... Dr. William R. WAYNE
36 Director Career Services ... Ms. Robin E. HUSTON
19 Chief of Police ... Ms. Elizabeth G. WOOLLEN
15 Sr VP & Chief Human Resources Ofcr ... Vacant
22 Equal Opportunity Officer ... Mr. Bobby J. MASON
84 Sr Assoc VP for Enrollment ... Mr. Jeffrey J. BLAHNIK

25 Assoc VP for Research Services .... Ms. Andrea D. DEATON
85 Dir International Student Services .... Ms. Robyn D. ROJAS
104 Director Education Abroad .... Ms. Whitney R. FRANCA
37 Dir of Financial Aid & Scholarships .... Mr. Bradley T. BURNETT
51 Dean College of PACS .... Dr. Martha L. BANZ
48 Dean Col of Architecture .... Mr. Hans W. BUTZER
49 Dean Col of Arts & Sciences .... Dr. David R. WROBEL
53 Dean Jeannine Rainbolt Col of Educ .... Dr. Gregg A. GARN
54 Dean Gallogly Col of Engineering .... Vacant
57 Dean Weitzenhoffer Col Fine Arts .... Ms. Mary Margaret HOLT
61 Interim Dean College of Law .... Ms. Katheleen GUZMAN
08 Interim Dean Univ Libraries .... Mr. Carl GRANT
65 Dean Col Atmospheric/Geographic Sc .... Dr. Berrien MOORE, III
50 Dean Price Col of Business .... Dr. Corey PHELPS
92 Interim Dean Honors College .... Dr. Douglas D. GAFFIN
60 Dean Gaylord Col Journal/Mass Comm .... Mr. Ed KELLEY
89 Dean University College .... Dr. Nicole J. CAMPBELL
65 Dean Mewborne Col of Earth & Energy .... Dr. J. Michael STICE
82 VP/Interim Dean Col Intl Studies .... Dr. Jill IRVINE
28 VP of Diversity & Inclusion .... Dr. Belinda HIGGS HYPPOLITE
04 Administrative Asst to President .... Ms. Sherry L. EVANS
102 Dir Foundation/Corporate Relations .... Mr. Guy L. PATTON
105 Assoc VP/Director Web Services .... Ms. Erin A. YARBROUGH
96 Director of Purchasing .... Vacant
112 Exec Dir Planned Giving/Development .... Mr. Eric E. MELTON
116 Chief Audit Executive .... Mr. Charles D. WRIGHT
35 Assoc Provost Fac & Student Affairs .... Mr. Christopher O. WALKER
14 Exec Dir of Technology Advancement .... Mr. Aaron A. BIGGS
88 Assoc Provost Academic Engagement ...... Ms. Michelle A. EODICE
88 Assoc Prov/Dir Acad Financial Plng .... Mr. Stewart M. BERKINSHAW

† Tuition is based on 30 credit hour per year.

University of Oklahoma Schusterman Center (A)

4502 E 41st Street, Tulsa OK 74135-2512
Telephone: (918) 660-3000 Identification: 770387
Accreditation: &HLC, ARCPA, OT

University of Science and Arts of Oklahoma (B)

1727 W Alabama, Chickasha OK 73018-5322
County: Grady FICE Identification: 003167
Unit ID: 207722
Telephone: (405) 224-3140 Carnegie Class: Bac-A&S
FAX Number: (405) 574-1220 Calendar System: Trimester
URL: www.usao.edu
Established: 1908 Annual Undergrad Tuition & Fees (In-State): $8,040
Enrollment: 733 Coed
Affiliation or Control: State IRS Status: 501(c)3
Highest Offering: Baccalaureate
Accreditation: HLC, CAEP, MUS

01 President .... Dr. John H. FEAVER
05 Vice President for Academic Affairs .... Dr. Donna MILES
10 Vice Pres for Business & Finance .... Mr. Mick D. COPONITI
32 VP Student Success/Human Resources .... Ms. Monica TREVINO
13 VP Univ Advancement/Info Technology .... Mr. Sid HUDSON
30 Vice President for Development .... Mr. JP AUDAS
08 Director of Library .... Ms. Nicole MCMONAGLE
06 Registrar/Dir of Enrollment/Records .... Ms. Chelsea PHILLIPS
26 Dir of Communications/Marketing .... Ms. Amy GODDARD
37 Director of Financial Aid .... Ms. Laura I. COPONITI
32 Dean of Students/Dir Student Svcs .... Ms. Nancy HUGHES
29 Director of Alumni Development .... Vacant
18 Director of Physical Plant .... Mr. Mike COPONITI
09 Institutional Research Analyst .... Ms. Kristi JOHN
15 Director Personnel Services .... Ms. Monica TREVINO
07 Dean of Admissions & Recruitment ... Mr. Sheppard MCCONNELL
38 Director Student Counseling .... Dr. Misty STEELE
49 Chair Div of Arts & Humanities .... Dr. Stephen WEBER
50 Chair Div of Social Sci & Business .... Dr. James VAUGHN
53 Chair Division of Education .... Dr. Sarah LAYMAN
81 Chair Div of Science/Physical Educ .... Dr. J.C SANDERS
88 Chair Interdisciplinary Studies .... Dr. Shelley REES
41 Athletic Director .... Mr. Brisco MCPHERSON
19 Emergency Preparedness/Security .... Mr. Russell POOL

University of Tulsa (C)

800 S Tucker, Tulsa OK 74104
County: Tulsa FICE Identification: 003185
Unit ID: 207971
Telephone: (918) 631-2000 Carnegie Class: DU-Higher
FAX Number: (918) 631-2033 Calendar System: Semester
URL: www.utulsa.edu
Established: 1894 Annual Undergrad Tuition & Fees: $43,985
Enrollment: 3,960 Coed
Affiliation or Control: Independent Non-Profit IRS Status: 501(c)3
Highest Offering: Doctorate
Accreditation: HLC, ANEST, CAATE, CLPSY, LAW, MUS, NUR, SP

01 President .... Mr. Brad CARSON
04 Exec Assistant to the President .... Ms. Doreen GRIFFITHS
41 Director of Athletics .... Mr. Rick DICKSON
05 Interim Provost .... Mr. Dean SMITH
20 Vice Provost .... Ms. Elizabeth SMITH
08 RM & Ida McFarlin Dean of Library ... Mr. Adrian W. ALEXANDER
49 Dean Arts & Sciences .... Dr. Karen PETERSEN
50 Dean of the Collins College of Bus .... Ms. Kathy TAYLOR
54 Dean Engineering/Natural Sciences ...... Dr. James R. SOREM, JR.
61 Dean Law .... Ms. Elizabeth MCCORMICK
111 Vice Pres Institutional Advancement .... Dr. Kayla HALE
29 Exec Director Alumni Relations .... Ms. Amy M. FREIBERGER
26 Sr Exec Dir Marketing/Communication .. Ms. Mona CHAMBERLIN
31 Dir True Blue Neighbors/Public Aff .... Ms. Danielle HOVENGA
10 Interim Chief Financial Officer .... Mr. Michael THESENVITZ
21 Assoc VP & Controller .... Mr. Michael D. THESENVITZ
114 Dir of Univ Budgets for Exec VP .... Ms. Mindi FUSER
113 Bursar .... Mr. Susan EVERETT
96 Director Purchasing .... Ms. Stephanie EYLER
15 VP & Chief Human Resources Officer .... Ms. Barbara ABERCROMBIE
118 Employee Benefits Coordinator .... Ms. Stacy KIZLINZKI
09 VP of Institutional Research .... Mr. Victor SOE
46 Vice Prov Research/Dean Grad School .... Dr. Brenton MCLAURY
108 Director Institutional Assessment .... Ms. Monica VARNER
22 Dir Acad Support/504 Coordinator .... Dr. Tawny RIGSBY
28 VP Diversity/Equity & Inclusion ... Ms. Kelli MCLOUD-SCHINGEN
43 General Counsel .... Ms. Elizabeth BULLOCK
19 Interim Director Campus Security .... Ms. Julie FRIEDEL
18 Assoc VP Operations & Facilities .... Mr. John HOLDERMAN
86 VP Public Affairs .... Ms. Susan NEAL
13 VP Info Services & CIO .... Mr. Paige FRANCIS
90 Dir of Academic & Learning Tech .... Ms. Janet CAIRNS
91 Dir ERP Operations .... Mr. Martin PAGE
105 Director of Web Systems .... Mr. Matthew CASTEEL
35 Interim Dean of Students .... Mr. Michael MCCLENDON
84 Sr Vice Provost for Enroll Mgmt .... Ms. Casey REED
07 Dean of Admission .... Ms. Patricia DEBOLT
06 Registrar .... Ms. Hope GEIGER
37 Director Student Financial Svcs .... Ms. Vicki A. HENDRICKSON
39 Assoc VP for Campus Student Housing ... Ms. Melissa H. FRANCE
36 Exec Director Career Services .... Ms. Christy CAVES
38 Director Counseling & Psych Svcs ...... Dr. Michael MCCLENDON
121 Director Student Success Coach .... Ms. Joey ONEAL
42 University Chaplain .... Dr. Jeffrey FRANCIS
104 Vice Provost Global Education .... Dr. Jane KUCKO
122 Director of Greek Life .... Mr. Will DEVINEY
44 Dir of Annual & Affinity Giving .... Ms. Mary HASTINGS
88 Assistant Director of Purchasing .... Ms. Natalie GILBERT
119 Chief Information Security Officer .... Mr. Jonathan KIMMITT
117 Vice Pres for Risk Mgmt .... Mr. Matt WARREN
76 Dean of Oxley College of Health Sci .... Dr. Robin PLOEGER
100 Interim Chief of Staff .... Ms. Jen BENNETT

Western Oklahoma State College (D)

2801 N Main Street, Altus OK 73521-1397
County: Jackson FICE Identification: 003146
Unit ID: 208035
Telephone: (580) 477-2000 Carnegie Class: Assoc/MT-VT-High Trad
FAX Number: (580) 477-7777 Calendar System: Semester
URL: www.wosc.edu
Established: 1926 Annual Undergrad Tuition & Fees (In-State): $4,978
Enrollment: 1,353 Coed
Affiliation or Control: State IRS Status: 501(c)3
Highest Offering: Associate Degree
Accreditation: HLC, NAEYC

01 President .... Dr. Chad WIGINTON
05 VP for Academic Affairs .... Ms. Chrystal OVERTON
10 Vice President for Business Affairs .... Ms. Melissa MCMAHON
32 Vice Pres Student Support Services .... Ms. Terri PEARSON
09 Assist Dir of Inst Effectiveness .... Ms. Anita MILLER
26 Director of Public Relations .... Ms. Maegan MARTIN
07 Director of Admissions & Registrar .... Ms. Lana SCOTT
37 Director of Financial Aid .... Ms. SaVana DENTON
30 Dir Development/Alumni Relations .... Ms. Debbie VALERIO
41 Director Athletics .... Vacant
08 Director of Learning Resources .... Ms. Suzanne ROOKER
15 Director Personnel Services .... Ms. April NELSON
18 Director Physical Plant .... Mr. Doyle JENCKS
38 Counselor .... Ms. Cheryl ORR

OREGON

American College of Healthcare Sciences (E)

5005 S Macadam, Portland OR 97239
County: Multnomah FICE Identification: 041944
Unit ID: 443599
Telephone: (503) 244-0726 Carnegie Class: Spec-4-yr-Other Health
FAX Number: (503) 244-0727 Calendar System: Semester
URL: www.achs.edu
Established: 1978 Annual Undergrad Tuition & Fees: $11,640
Enrollment: 856 Coed
Affiliation or Control: Proprietary IRS Status: Proprietary
Highest Offering: Master's
Accreditation: DEAC

01 President/CEO .... Tracey ABELL
05 Chief Academic Officer .... Dr. Tiffany RODRIGUEZ
11 Chief Operating Officer .... Brooke PILLSBURY
07 Interim Dean of Admissions .... Amanda HELLER
29 Director of Alumni & Career Svcs .... Amy SWINEHART
06 Registrar .... Jennifer MORRISON
26 Chief Marketing Officer .... Kate HARMON
37 Director of Financial Aid .... Stephanie NORTH
08 Director of Library Services .... Ashley EHMIG
22 Title IX Coordinator .... Brooke PILLSBURY

American Denturist College (F)

145 E. 12th Alley, Eugene OR 97401
County: Lane Identification: 667421
Telephone: (541) 654-5885 Carnegie Class: Not Classified
FAX Number: N/A Calendar System: Other
URL: adc.edu
Established: 2011 Annual Undergrad Tuition & Fees: N/A
Enrollment: N/A Coed
Affiliation or Control: Proprietary IRS Status: Proprietary
Highest Offering: Baccalaureate
Accreditation: DEAC

05 Director of Education .... Todd YOUNG

Birthingway College of Midwifery (G)

4550 SW Betts Avenue #142, Beaverton OR 97075
County: Washington FICE Identification: 036683
Unit ID: 442949
Telephone: (503) 760-3131 Carnegie Class: Spec-4-yr-Other Health
FAX Number: N/A Calendar System: Quarter
URL: www.birthingway.edu
Established: 1993 Annual Undergrad Tuition & Fees: N/A
Enrollment: 2 Coed
Affiliation or Control: Independent Non-Profit IRS Status: 501(c)3
Highest Offering: Baccalaureate
Accreditation: MEAC

01 President .... Ms. Holly SCHOLLES
10 Finance Coordinator .... Ms. Elizabeth BRAGG
37 Financial Aid Officer .... Ms. Stace MAURER
06 Registrar .... Ms. Claire HOFFMAN
05 Midwifery Program Coordinator ..... Ms. Heather HACK-SULLIVAN
21 Business Coordinator .... Ms. Nina THOMPSON
04 Admin Assistant to the President .... Ms. Claire E. HOFFMAN

Blue Mountain Community College (H)

PO Box 100, Pendleton OR 97801-0100
County: Umatilla/Morrow/Baker FICE Identification: 003186
Unit ID: 208275
Telephone: (541) 276-1260 Carnegie Class: Assoc/HT-High Non
FAX Number: (541) 278-5886 Calendar System: Quarter
URL: www.bluecc.edu
Established: 1962 Annual Undergrad Tuition & Fees (In-District): $6,300
Enrollment: 1,292 Coed
Affiliation or Control: State/Local IRS Status: 501(c)3
Highest Offering: Associate Degree
Accreditation: NW

01 President .... Mr. Mark BROWNING
05 Vice President of Instruction .... Mr. John FIELDS
32 Vice Pres Student Affairs .... Vacant
11 Chief Operating Officer .... Mr. David SHELLBERG
08 Director of Library & Media Svcs .... Ms. Brittany YOUNG
102 Executive Director Foundation .... Mr. Ken DANIEL
37 Director of Student Financial Aid .... Ms. Danielle HODGEN
04 Administrative Asst to President .... Ms. Shannon FRANKLIN
10 Chief Financial Officer .... Ms. Celeste TATE
106 Dir Online Education/E-learning .... Vacant
13 Chief Info Technology Officer (CIO) .... Mr. Brad HOLDEN
38 Director Student Counseling .... Vacant
15 Chief Human Resources Officer ...... Ms. Norma JAIME-SANCHEZ
41 Athletic Director .... Ms. Dawn MCCLENDON
103 Dean Workforce Development .... Ms. Tammy KRAWCZYK
124 Dean Student Retention .... Mr. Wade MULLER
84 Director Enrollment Svcs/Registrar .... Ms. Theresa BOSWORTH
18 Chief Facilities/Physical Plant .... Mr. Dwayne WILLIAMS
20 Dean Student Learning & Success .... Mr. Daniel G. ANDERSON
44 Director Annual Giving .... Mr. Ken DANIEL

Bushnell University (I)

828 E. 11th Ave., Eugene OR 97401-3745
County: Lane FICE Identification: 003208
Unit ID: 209409
Telephone: (541) 343-1641 Carnegie Class: Masters/M
FAX Number: (541) 343-9159 Calendar System: Semester
URL: www.bushnell.edu
Established: 1895 Annual Undergrad Tuition & Fees: $32,320
Enrollment: 717 Coed
Affiliation or Control: Christian Church (Disciples Of Christ)
IRS Status: 501(c)3
Highest Offering: Master's
Accreditation: NW, CACREP, IACBE, NURSE

01 President .... Dr. Joseph WOMACK
04 Exec Admin Asst to President .... Ms. Jennifer BOX
05 VP Academic Affairs/Dean of Faculty .... Dr. Dennis LINDSAY
10 VP Finance & Administration .... Mr. Gene DE YOUNG
32 VP Student Development/Enrollment .... Mr. Michael FULLER
111 VP Advancement .... Dr. Keith POTTER
26 Senior Director of Public Affairs .... Mr. Patrick WALSH
07 Dean of Admission .... Ms. Kacie GERDRUM
21 Asst VP for Financial Services .... Ms. Jocelyn HUBBS
41 Athletic Director .... Mr. Corey ANDERSON
42 Campus Pastor .... Mr. Troy DEAN

39 Director of Residence Life ....Ms. Jennifer LITTLE
35 Director Student Programs ....Mr. Paul WRIGHT
121 Dean of Career & Academic Resources ....Ms. Angela DOTY
06 Registrar ....Dr. John D'AGUANNO
108 Director of Assessment ....Mr. Brian MILLS
44 Director of Annual Giving ....Ms. Bethany DILLA
30 Director of Development ....Ms. Corynn GILBERT
107 Assoc Dean of Professional Studies ....Vacant
50 Dean Business/Leadership/Tech ....Vacant
73 Assoc Dean Bible/World Christianity ....Mr. Agametochukwu IHEANYI-IGWE
49 Assoc Dean of Arts & Sciences ....Ms. Constance WILMARTH
64 Assoc Dean Music & Performing Arts ....Mr. Kelly BALLARD
83 Dean of Psychology and Counseling ....Dr. Ryan MELTON
53 Associate Dean of Education ....Ms. Suzanne PRICE
66 Associate Dean of Nursing ....Dr. Linda VELTRI
13 Director Tech & Physical Operations ....Mr. Stead HALSTEAD
37 Director of Financial Aid ....Mr. Nathan ICENHOWER

Central Oregon Community College (A)

2600 NW College Way, Bend OR 97703
County: Deschutes FICE Identification: 003188
Unit ID: 208318
Telephone: (541) 383-7700 Carnegie Class: Assoc/HT-High Trad
FAX Number: N/A Calendar System: Quarter
URL: www.cocc.edu
Established: 1949 Annual Undergrad Tuition & Fees (In-District): $6,111
Enrollment: 4,304 Coed
Affiliation or Control: Local IRS Status: 501(c)3
Highest Offering: Associate Degree
Accreditation: NW, ACFEI, ADNUR, CAHIIM, COMTA, DA, EMT, IFSAC, MAC

01 President ....Dr. Laurie CHESLEY
05 Vice President for Instruction ....Dr. Betsy JULIAN
10 Chief Financial Officer ....Mr. David DONA
20 Instructional Dean ....Dr. Julie DOWNING
20 Instructional Dean ....Dr. Annemarie HAMLIN
20 Instructional Dean ....Dr. Michael FISHER
32 VP Student Affairs ....Dr. Alicia MOORE
07 Director of Admissions/Registrar ....Mr. Tyler HAYES
08 Director of Library Services ....Dr. Tina HOVEKAMP
26 Director College Relations/Comm ....Ms. Jenn KOVITZ
18 Director Campus Services ....Mr. Joe VIOLA
15 Director Human Resources ....Ms. Naomi ROUNDTREE
35 Director of Student and Campus Life ....Mr. Andrew DAVIS
09 Dir Institutional Effectiveness ....Ms. Brynn PIERCE
38 Director Student Counseling ....Ms. Diane PRITCHARD
40 Director Bookstore/Auxiliary Svcs ....Ms. Lori BENEFIEL
108 Director Curriculum & Assessment ....Mr. Franklin CLARK
19 Director Security/Safety ....Vacant
25 Director Contracts/Risk Management ....Ms. Sharla ANDRESEN
102 CAO/Executive Director Foundation ....Mr. Zak BOONE
51 Director of Continuing Education ....Ms. Glenda LANTIS
04 Admin Assistant to the President ....Ms. Deena COOK
13 Chief Information Officer ....Dr. Laura BOEHME
106 Director of E-learning ....Ms. Kristine ROSHAU
28 Director of Diversity ....Ms. Christy WALKER
37 Director Student Financial Aid ....Ms. Breana SYLWESTER

Chemeketa Community College (B)

PO Box 14007, Salem OR 97309-7070
County: Marion FICE Identification: 003218
Unit ID: 208390
Telephone: (503) 399-5000 Carnegie Class: Assoc/HT-Mix Trad/Non
FAX Number: (503) 399-5214 Calendar System: Quarter
URL: www.chemeketa.edu
Established: 1962 Annual Undergrad Tuition & Fees (In-District): $5,670
Enrollment: 8,328 Coed
Affiliation or Control: Local IRS Status: 501(c)3
Highest Offering: Associate Degree
Accreditation: NW, ADNUR, CAHIIM, DA, EMT, IFSAC

01 President/Chief Executive Officer ....Dr. Jessica HOWARD
05 VP Academic Officer ....Dr. Michael VARGO
11 VP Governance & Administration ....Mr. David HALLETT
32 VP Student Affairs ....Dr. Bruce CLEMETSEN
13 Interim VP/CIO ....Mr. Michael KINKADE
107 Exec Dean Gen Educ/Transfer Studies ....Mr. Don BRASE
75 Interim Exec Dean CTE ....Mr. Marshall ROACH
121 Exec Dean Student Dev/Learning Res ....Mr. Manuel GUERRA
88 Exec Dean Regional Ed & Acad Dev ....Ms. Holly NELSON
88 Interim Executive Assistant ....Ms. Amy EARLY
83 Dean Liberal Arts & Social Sciences ....Dr. Keith RUSSELL
76 Dean Health Services ....Ms. Sandra KELLOGG
37 Director Financial Aid ....Mr. Ryan WEST
38 Dean Counseling/Career Services ....Mr. Christopher POTTS
72 Interim Dean Applied Technologies ....Mr. Nol COBB
81 Dean Science/Eng/Math/Comp Science ....Mr. Timor SAFFARY
50 Dn Bus/Tech/Early Chld Ed/Vis Comm ....Dr. R. TAYLOR
27 Dir Marketing/Public Relations ....Dr. Marie HULETT
88 Interim Dean Curric Instr/Accred ....Ms. Julie PETERS
47 Dir Agric Innov/Prod Tech ....Mr. Larry CHEYNE
08 Director Library/Learning Resources ....Ms. Natalie BEACH
88 Director Northwest Innovations ....Mr. Brian RADER
10 Interim Chief Financial Officer ....Mr. Rich MCDONALD
18 Dir Capital Projects/Facilities ....Mr. Rory ALVAREZ
15 Associate VP Human Resources ....Ms. Alice SPRAGUE
19 Director Public Safety ....Mr. Tony MOORE
109 Director Auxiliary/Contracted Svcs ....Ms. Meredith SCHREIBER
41 Dean Health/Human Perf/Athletics ....Ms. Cassie BELMODIS
50 Exec Dir Chemeketa Ctr Bus/Industry ....Vacant
88 Coordinator Prof Tech Educ ....Mr. Ed WOODS
28 Chief Diversity & Equity Officer ....Ms. Vivi CALEFFI-PRICHARD
124 Dean Student Retention/College Life ....Mr. Mike EVANS
06 Registrar/Dir Enrollment Services ....Ms. Melissa FREY
102 Executive Director Foundation ....Dr. Marie HULETT
25 Grants Coordinator ....Vacant
09 Director of Institutional Research ....Ms. Heidi GILLIARD
43 General Counsel/Legal Resources ....Ms. Rebecca HILLYER
12 Dean Woodburn Center ....Mr. Elias VILLEGAS
12 Director Polk Center ....Mr. Glen MILLER
12 Director Yamhill Valley Campus ....Ms. Danielle HOFFMAN
04 Exec Coordinator to the President ....Ms. Julie DEUCHARS

Clackamas Community College (C)

19600 Molalla Avenue, Oregon City OR 97045-7998
County: Clackamas FICE Identification: 004878
Unit ID: 208406
Telephone: (503) 594-6000 Carnegie Class: Assoc/HT-High Non
FAX Number: N/A Calendar System: Quarter
URL: www.clackamas.edu
Established: 1966 Annual Undergrad Tuition & Fees (In-District): $5,334
Enrollment: 5,555 Coed
Affiliation or Control: Local IRS Status: 501(c)3
Highest Offering: Associate Degree
Accreditation: NW, MAC, NAEYC

01 President ....Dr. Tim COOK
05 VP Instruct & Stdnt Svcs/Provost ....Dr. David PLOTKIN
11 Vice Pres College Services ....Ms. Alissa MAHAR
04 Executive Asst to the President ....Ms. Denice BAILEY
102 Executive Director Foundation ....Mr. John CHANG
26 Public Information Officer ....Ms. Lori HALL
06 Registrar/Enrol Svcs/Operations Mgr ....Mr. Chris SWEET
32 Assoc Dean Acad Found/Connect Div ....Ms. Jennifer ANDERSON
13 Dean/CIO Information Technology ....Mr. Saby WARAICH
49 Dean Arts & Sciences ....Ms. Sue GOFF
46 Dean Inst Effectiveness & Planning ....Mr. Jason KOVAC
72 Assoc Dn Tech/Hlth Occup/Wrkfc Div ....Ms. Shalee HODGSON
15 Dean Human Resources ....Ms. Melissa RICHARDSON
88 Dir Office Education Partnerships ....Ms. Jaime CLARKE
10 Dean Business Services ....Mr. Jeff SHAFFER
11 Dean Campus Services ....Mr. Bob COCHRAN
18 Director Campus Services ....Vacant
41 Director Health/PE/Athletics ....Mr. Jim MARTINEAU
13 Director IT Operations ....Vacant
09 Director of Institutional Research ....Ms. Ashley SEARS
37 Director Student Financial Aid ....Vacant
19 Director Security/Safety ....Mr. Thomas SONOFF

Clatsop Community College (D)

1651 Lexington Avenue, Astoria OR 97103
County: Clatsop FICE Identification: 003189
Unit ID: 208415
Telephone: (503) 325-0910 Carnegie Class: Assoc/HVT-High Non
FAX Number: (503) 325-5738 Calendar System: Quarter
URL: www.clatsopcc.edu
Established: 1958 Annual Undergrad Tuition & Fees (In-District): $4,230
Enrollment: 754 Coed
Affiliation or Control: State/Local IRS Status: 501(c)3
Highest Offering: Associate Degree
Accreditation: NW

01 President ....Mr. Chris BREITMEYER
05 Vice President Academic Affairs ....Dr. Peter WILLIAMS
10 Vice President Finance & Operations ....Ms. JoAnn ZAHN
32 Vice President of Student Success ....Mr. Jerad SORBER
06 Registrar ....Ms. Jiang Fei KOCH
26 Director Communication & Marketing ....Ms. Julie KOVATCH
13 Director Computer Services ....Mr. Greg RIEHL
15 Director Human Resources ....Ms. Desiree NOAH
37 Director Student Financial Aid ....Mr. Lloyd MUELLER
09 Director of Institutional Research ....Vacant
18 Dir Physical Plant/Sr Project Mgr ....Mr. Shaun MARTIN
21 Interim Director Accounting Svcs ....Ms. Stephanie HOMER
102 Director College Foundation ....Ms. Angela HUNT
08 Director of Library ....Mr. Dan MCCLURE
04 Executive Coordinator to President ....Ms. Patricia SCHULTE
106 Distance Education Coordinator ....Mrs. Kirsten HORNING
103 Dean Workforce Educ & Training ....Ms. Kristen WILKIN
88 Dean Transfer Education ....Ms. Teena TOYAS

College of Emergency Services (E)

12438 SE Capps Road, Clackamas OR 97015
County: Clackamas Identification: 667128
Telephone: (971) 236-9231 Carnegie Class: Not Classified
FAX Number: (971) 653-9239 Calendar System: Semester
URL: www.collegeofems.com
Established: 1995 Annual Undergrad Tuition & Fees: N/A
Enrollment: N/A Coed
Affiliation or Control: Proprietary IRS Status: Proprietary
Highest Offering: Associate Degree
Accreditation: ABHES, EMT

01 Program Medical Director ....Dr. David LEHRFELD
05 Lead Instructor ....Lauren ENRIGHT

Columbia Gorge Community College (F)

400 East Scenic Drive, The Dalles OR 97058
County: Wasco FICE Identification: 041519
Unit ID: 420556
Telephone: (541) 506-6000 Carnegie Class: Assoc/HT-High Non
FAX Number: N/A Calendar System: Quarter
URL: www.cgcc.edu
Established: 1977 Annual Undergrad Tuition & Fees (In-District): $4,752
Enrollment: 825 Coed
Affiliation or Control: State/Local IRS Status: 501(c)3
Highest Offering: Associate Degree
Accreditation: NW, MAC

01 President ....Dr. Marta CRONIN
05 VP of Instructional Services ....Jarett GILBERT
10 VP of Financial Services ....Michael MALLERY
32 Chief Student Services Officer ....Gerardo CIFUENTES
26 Manager Marketing & Cmty Outreach ....Dan SPATZ
13 Exec Director of Infrastructure ....Danny DEHAZE
06 Registrar/Veteran Svcs ....Mary MARTIN
07 Director of Admissions ....Vacant
08 Dean of Library & Learning Commons ....Dylan MCMANUS
108 Dir Curriculum & Assessment ....Susan LEWIS
15 Director Human Resources ....Courtney JUDAH
18 Director of Facilities Services ....Vacant
37 Director Financial Aid ....Mike JOHNSON
102 Foundation Director ....Vacant
39 Dir of Housing/Student Life ....Tiffany PRINCE

Concorde Career College (G)

1425 NE Irving Street, Portland OR 97232
County: Multnomah FICE Identification: 008887
Unit ID: 208479
Telephone: (503) 281-4181 Carnegie Class: Spec 2-yr-Health
FAX Number: (503) 281-6739 Calendar System: Other
URL: www.concorde.edu/campus/portland
Established: 1996 Annual Undergrad Tuition & Fees: N/A
Enrollment: 466 Coed
Affiliation or Control: Proprietary IRS Status: Proprietary
Highest Offering: Associate Degree
Accreditation: ACCSC, COARC, MAC, POLYT, SURGT

07 Director of Admissions ....Vacant
01 Campus President ....Kim IERIEN

Corban University (H)

5000 Deer Park Drive SE, Salem OR 97317
County: Marion FICE Identification: 001339
Unit ID: 210331
Telephone: (503) 581-8600 Carnegie Class: Bac-Diverse
FAX Number: (503) 585-4316 Calendar System: Semester
URL: www.corban.edu
Established: 1935 Annual Undergrad Tuition & Fees: $34,188
Enrollment: 1,160 Coed
Affiliation or Control: Independent Non-Profit IRS Status: 501(c)3
Highest Offering: Master's
Accreditation: NW, CACREP

01 President ....Dr. Sheldon C. NORD
05 Provost/Executive Vice President ....Dr. Thomas CORNMAN
10 Vice President for Business ....Ms. Dee WENDLER
32 Vice President For Student Life ....Dr. Brenda ROTH
26 Vice Pres for Strategic Initiatives ....Mr. Steve SAMMONS
84 Vice Provost for Enrollment ....Dr. Chris VETTER
111 Chief Advancement Officer ....Mr. Ken DRIVER
35 Dean of Students ....Mr. Nathan GEER
85 Associate Provost Global Engagement ....Dr. Janine ALLEN
49 Dean of Arts and Sciences ....Dr. Felicia SQUIRES
50 Dean Hoff School of Business ....Mr. Shawn HUSSEY
53 Dean of Education and Counseling ....Dr. Kristin DIXON
73 Dean School of Ministry ....Dr. Gregory TRULL
42 Assoc Dean of Service/Operations ....Mr. Eugene EDWARDS
13 Director Information Services ....Ms. Brenda GIBSON
88 Director of DMin Program ....Dr. Leroy GOERTZEN
18 Campus Care Project Manager ....Mr. Troy CROFF
08 Librarian ....Mr. Garrett TROTT
06 University Registrar ....Ms. Karen GOERTZEN
41 Athletic Director ....Ms. Sue ROTH
27 Director of Communication ....Ms. Rebekah BENHAM
121 Director of Student Support ....Mr. Daren MILIONIS
21 Sr Director of Accounting ....Mrs. Ellen ZARFAS
37 Director of Financial Aid ....Ms. Mary MCGLOTHLAN
40 Bookstore Manager ....Mr. Larry HULTBERG
123 Asst Dir Grad/Online Admissions ....Ms. Allison SMALL
04 Executive Asst to President ....Ms. Susan COLEMAN
104 Director Study Abroad ....Mr. Sam PEARSON
106 Director of Academic Services ....Mr. Dan CHRISTENSEN
15 Interim Director of Human Resources ....Ms. Lisa HINMAN
29 Director Alumni/Parent Relations ....Ms. Shirley TURNER
118 Payroll & Benefits Manager ....Ms. Kathy GALLAGHER
19 Chief of Campus Safety/Security ....Mr. Mike ROTH
38 Clinical Director ....Dr. Mary AGUILERA
07 Director of Admissions ....Mr. Jordan LINDSEY

Eastern Oregon University (I)

One University Boulevard, La Grande OR 97850-2807
County: Union FICE Identification: 003193
Unit ID: 208646

Telephone: (541) 962-3672 Carnegie Class: Masters/M
FAX Number: (541) 962-3493 Calendar System: Quarter
URL: www.eou.edu
Established: 1929 Annual Undergrad Tuition & Fees (In-State): $9,405
Enrollment: 2,853 Coed
Affiliation or Control: State IRS Status: 501(c)3
Highest Offering: Master's
Accreditation: **NW**, AAQEP, IACBE

01 President Mr. Thomas INSKO
05 Provost/Sr VP Academic Affairs Dr. Sarah WITTE
32 Vice President for Student Affairs Dr. Lacy KARPILO
10 Vice President Finance & Admin Ms. Lara MOORE
30 Vice Pres UA Mr. Tim SEYDEL
49 Dean Col Arts/Humanities/Social Sci Mr. Nathan LOWE
50 Dean Colleges of Business Dr. Ed HENNINGER
53 Dean Colleges of Education Dr. Matt SEIMEARS
37 Director of Financial Aid Ms. Sandy HENRY
08 Director of Pierce Library Ms. Karen CLAY
07 Director of Admissions Ms. Genesis MEADERDS
06 Registrar Ms. Emily SHARRATT
15 Director of Human Resources Mr. Chris MCLAUGHLIN
29 Dir of Alumni Relations Ms. Jessie BOWMAN
41 Director of Athletics Ms. Anji WEISSENFLUH
39 Director of Residence Life Mr. Jeremy JONES
18 Director of Facilities & Planning Mr. John GARLITZ
38 Director Counseling Center Dr. Marianne WEAVER
04 Exec Assistant to the President Ms. Katelyn WINKLER
21 Director of Business Affairs Vacant
88 Learning Center Operations Manager Ms. Kathryn SHORTS
35 Dir of Student Relations/Title IX Ms. Colleen DUNNE-CASCIO
19 Campus Security/Public Safety Ofcr Mr. Jim HOFFMAN

George Fox University (A)

414 N Meridian, Newberg OR 97132-2697
County: Yamhill FICE Identification: 003194
Unit ID: 208822
Telephone: (503) 538-8383 Carnegie Class: DU-Mod
FAX Number: (503) 554-3880 Calendar System: Semester
URL: www.georgefox.edu
Established: 1891 Annual Undergrad Tuition & Fees: $38,370
Enrollment: 4,106 Coed
Affiliation or Control: Friends IRS Status: 501(c)3
Highest Offering: Doctorate
Accreditation: **NW**, AAQEP, ACBSP, #ARCPA, CAATE, CACREP, CLPSY, IPSY, MUS, NURSE, PTA, SW, THEOL

01 President Dr. Robin E. BAKER
05 Provost Dr. Andrea SCOTT
10 Exec VP Finance/CFO Ms. Vicki PIERSALL
111 Int Vice President for Advancement Mr. Kyle DICKINSON
32 Vice President Student Life Dr. Bradley A. LAU
84 VP Enrollment & Marketing Ms. Lindsay KNOX
28 AVP Intercultural Engagement Dr. Rebecca HERNANDEZ
21 Asst VP of Finance/Controller Ms. Cris BANTON
100 Chief of Staff Ms. Melissa D. TERRY
08 Dean of Libraries Mr. Alexander ROLFE
07 Director of Undergrad Admissions Ms. Lindsay KNOX
06 Registrar Ms. Melissa THOMAS
36 Dir of Career Services/IDEA Center Ms. Wendy FLINT
18 Director of Plant Services Mr. Jeremiah HORTON
37 Director of Financial Aid Ms. Johanna KAYE
96 Director Purchasing/Admin Services Mr. Matt HAMMAR
41 Director of Athletics Mr. Adam PUCKETT
105 Director of Web Development Mr. Peter CRACKENBERG
15 Exec Dir Human Res/Title IX Coord Ms. Nichole DREW
42 Univ Pastor/Dean of Spiritual Life Ms. Jamie NOLING-AUTH
26 Director of Executive Communication Mr. Rob FELTON
13 Chief Information Officer Mr. Tim GOODFELLOW
19 Director Security Services Mr. Ed GIEROK
35 Dean Stdnt Svcs/Dir Hlth/Counseling Dr. William C. BUHROW
73 Dean of Portland Seminary Dr. MaryKate MORSE
83 Dean Sch Behavioral/Health Sci Dr. David CIMBORA
53 Dean School of Education Mr. Marc SHELTON
54 Dean of Engineering Dr. Robert HARDER
09 Chief Data Officer Mr. Tyler SUSMILCH
04 Executive Asst to the President Ms. Jennifer MCCOLLUM
100 Chief of Staff Ms. Melissa TERRY
103 Recruiting and Training Manager Ms. Kara HOLCOMBE
104 Director Study Abroad Dr. David J. MARTINEZ
108 Director Institutional Assessment Mr. Rob BOHALL
29 Director Alumni Affairs Ms. Sara REAMY
30 Executive Director of Development Mr. Kyle DICKINSON
39 Director University Housing Ms. Kayin GRIFFITH
44 Director Annual Giving Mr. Gene CHRISTIAN
90 Director Academic Computing Mr. Josh NAUMAN

Gutenberg College (B)

1883 University Street, Eugene OR 97403-1368
County: Lane FICE Identification: 039324
Telephone: (541) 683-5141 Carnegie Class: Not Classified
FAX Number: (541) 683-6997 Calendar System: Quarter
URL: www.gutenberg.edu
Established: 1994 Annual Undergrad Tuition & Fees: N/A
Enrollment: N/A Coed
Affiliation or Control: Independent Non-Profit IRS Status: 501(c)3
Highest Offering: Baccalaureate
Accreditation: **TRACS**

01 President Chris SWANSON
10 Vice President Finance Mark BRAISHER
05 Dean Thomas DEWBERRY
07 Vice President Eliot GRASSO
06 Registrar Chris SWANSON
39 Dir Resident Life/Student Housing Gil GRECO

Klamath Community College (C)

7390 S 6th Street, Klamath Falls OR 97603-7121
County: Klamath FICE Identification: 034283
Unit ID: 428392
Telephone: (541) 882-3521 Carnegie Class: Assoc/MT-VT-High Non
FAX Number: (541) 885-7758 Calendar System: Quarter
URL: www.klamathcc.edu
Established: 1996 Annual Undergrad Tuition & Fees (In-District): $4,497
Enrollment: 1,492 Coed
Affiliation or Control: State/Local IRS Status: 501(c)3
Highest Offering: Associate Degree
Accreditation: **NW**

01 President Dr. Roberto GUTIERREZ
11 Vice Pres Administrative Svcs Ms. Tricia FISCUS
05 Vice Pres Academic Affairs Ms. Jamie JENNINGS
32 Interim Vice Pres Student Affairs Mr. Bill JENNINGS
103 Exec Director External Programs Mr. Charles MASSIE
15 Exec Dir HR & General Counsel Mr. Michael SWANZY
20 Dean of Instruction Dr. Jeanne LAHAIE
20 Dean of Instruction Mr. Christopher STICKLES
103 Director of Workforce Mr. Michael CARGILL
13 Director Information Services Mr. Paul BREEDLOVE
06 Registrar Mr. M. SHABBIR
26 Director of Communications Ms. Lacey JARRELL
18 Facilities Director Mr. Mike HOMFELDT
10 Director Business Services Mr. Goeffrey LAHAIE
37 Financial Aid Director Mr. Nathan HENDRICKSON
04 Executive Admin Asst to President Ms. Shannon CHILDS
09 Institutional Researcher Mr. Bill JENNINGS
25 Grants Program Manager Mr. Peter LAWSON

Lane Community College (D)

4000 E 30th Avenue, Eugene OR 97405-0640
County: Lane FICE Identification: 003196
Unit ID: 209038
Telephone: (541) 463-3000 Carnegie Class: Assoc/HT-High Trad
FAX Number: (541) 463-5201 Calendar System: Quarter
URL: www.lanecc.edu
Established: 1964 Annual Undergrad Tuition & Fees (In-District): $5,153
Enrollment: 7,702 Coed
Affiliation or Control: Local IRS Status: 501(c)3
Highest Offering: Associate Degree
Accreditation: **NW**, ACFEI, CAHIIM, DA, DH, EMT, MAC, PTAA

01 President Dr. Margaret HAMILTON
05 Provost & Executive VP Dr. Paul JARRELL
10 VP Finance & College Operations Vacant
49 AVP Academic & Student Affairs Dr. Jennifer FREI
103 AVP CTE/Workforce Development Mr. Grant MATTHEWS
28 AVP Diversity/Equity/Inclusion Mr. Greg EVANS
32 Associate VP of Student Affairs Dr. Mindie DIEU
15 Chief Human Resources Officer Mr. Shane TURNER
18 Director Facilities Mgmt & Planning Ms. Jennifer HAYWARD
19 Director Public Safety Ms. Lisa RUPP
08 Library Dean Mr. Ian CORONADO
26 Public Information Officer Vacant
102 Foundation Director Ms. Wendy JETT
04 Executive Asst to President/Board Ms. Donna ZMOLEK
104 Director International Programs Ms. Jennifer FALZERANO
06 Registrar Ms. Dawn WHITING
45 Chief Strategy & Planning Officer Dr. Richard PLOTT
113 Director Student Financial Services Mr. Matt FADICH
100 Chief of Staff Ms. Deborah BUTLER
43 Director Legal Services Mr. Michael BLADE

Lewis and Clark College (E)

0615 SW Palatine Hill, Portland OR 97219-7899
County: Multnomah FICE Identification: 003197
Unit ID: 209056
Telephone: (503) 768-7000 Carnegie Class: Bac-A&S
FAX Number: (503) 768-7055 Calendar System: Semester
URL: www.lclark.edu
Established: 1867 Annual Undergrad Tuition & Fees: $55,266
Enrollment: 3,157 Coed
Affiliation or Control: Independent Non-Profit IRS Status: 501(c)3
Highest Offering: Doctorate
Accreditation: **NW**, ACATE, CACREP, CAEP, LAW, MFCD

01 President Dr. Wim WIEWEL
03 VP/Secretary and General Counsel Mr. David REESE
07 Vice Pres Admiss & Financial Aid Mr. Eric STAAB
05 Chief Academic Officer/Dean Dr. Bruce SUTTMEIER
58 Dean Grad Sch Education/Counseling Dr. Scott FLETCHER
61 Dean of the Law School Ms. Jennifer JOHNSON
28 Dean of Diversity and Inclusion Mr. Mark FIGUEROA
10 Vice Pres Opers/Chief Finance Ofcr Ms. Andrea DOOLEY
111 Vice Pres Institutional Advancement Mr. Josh WALTER
32 Vice President of Student Life Dr. Robin HOLMES-SULLIVAN
09 Assoc VP Research & Planning Dr. Mark FIGUEROA
26 Exec Dir of Public Affairs & Comm Mr. Joe BECKER
13 Assoc VP & Chief Information Ofcr Mr. Adam BUCHWALD
15 Assoc VP/Director Human Resources Mrs. Heyke KIRKENDALL-BAKER
18 Assoc Vice Pres Facilities Mr. Michel GEORGE
06 Registrar College of Arts/Sciences Ms. Judy FINCH
06 Registrar Law School Mr. Seneca GRAY
06 Registrar Graduate School Ms. Courtney WHETSTINE
37 Director of Financial Aid Ms. Anastacia DILLON
08 Director of Watzek Library Mr. Mark DAHL
85 Assoc Dean Intl Stdnts & Scholars Mr. Brian WHITE
30 Assoc VP & Director of Development Mr. Aaron WHITEFORD
29 Senior Director Alumni/Parent Pgms Mr. Andrew MCPHEETERS
19 Interim Director of Campus Safety Mr. John HARVEY
42 Dean of Religious & Spiritual Life Dr. Mark DUNTLEY
41 Director of PE & Athletics Mr. Mark PIETROK
39 Interim Director of Campus Living Mr. Joe Barry GARDNER
14 Director of IT Operations Mr. Patrick RYALL
23 Assoc Dean Stdnt Health & Wellness Dr. John HANCOCK
101 Executive Asst Board Relations Ms. Moira DOMANN
04 Executive Asst to the President Ms. Rachel MARTINEZ
102 Director Corp/Foundation Relations Vacant
104 Director Overseas & Off Campus Pgms Ms. Blythe KNOTT

Linfield University (F)

900 SE Baker Street, McMinnville OR 97128-6894
County: Yamhill FICE Identification: 003198
Unit ID: 209065
Telephone: (503) 883-2200 Carnegie Class: Bac-A&S
FAX Number: (503) 883-2472 Calendar System: 4/1/4
URL: www.linfield.edu
Established: 1858 Annual Undergrad Tuition & Fees: $45,132
Enrollment: 1,392 Coed
Affiliation or Control: American Baptist IRS Status: 501(c)3
Highest Offering: Master's
Accreditation: **NW**, CAEP, MUS, NURSE

01 President Dr. Miles DAVIS
05 Vice Pres Academic Affairs/Provost Ms. Susan AGRE-KIPPENHAN
10 Vice Pres Finance/Admin/CFO Ms. Mary Ann RODRIGUEZ
111 Vice Pres University Advancement Mr. Joseph HUNTER
32 VP Student Affairs Ms. Susan HOPP
66 Dean of Nursing Dr. Kim DUPREE JONES
35 Dean of Students Mr. Jeff MACKAY
15 Director of Human Resources Ms. Lynn JOHNSON
18 Director Facilities & Auxiliary Svc Ms. Allison HORN
85 Director International Programs Mr. Shaik ISMAIL
06 Registrar Ms. Diane CRABTREE
07 Director of Admission Ms. Lisa KNODLE-BRAGIEL
08 Library Director Ms. Ginny BLACKSON
09 Director of Institutional Research Ms. Jennifer BALLARD
37 Director of Financial Aid Ms. Keri BURKE
13 Chief Information Officer Mr. Sam WILLIAMS
105 Webmaster Mr. Jonathan PIERCE
51 Director of Continuing Education Vacant
19 Director of Public Safety Mr. Dennis MARKS
38 Director of Student Health Ms. Patricia HADDELAND
26 AVP Strat Comm/Chief Mktg Officer Mr. Scott Bernard NELSON
44 Director of Annual Giving Ms. Lisa GOODWIN
30 Director of Development Mr. Craig HAISCH
29 Director of Constituent Engagement Ms. Joni CLAYPOOL
36 Director of Career Development Mr. Michael HAMPTON
42 Chaplain Vacant
41 Athletic Director Mr. Garry KILLGORE
40 Bookstore Manager Ms. Amber SIMMONS
04 Exec Assistant to the President Ms. Allison XAVIER
39 Asst Director of Student Housing Ms. Keri DIXON
50 Dean of Business Ms. Jennifer MADDEN
49 Dean College of Arts & Sciences Mr. Joe WILFERTH

Linn-Benton Community College (G)

6500 Pacific Boulevard, SW, Albany OR 97321-3774
County: Linn FICE Identification: 006938
Unit ID: 209074
Telephone: (541) 917-4999 Carnegie Class: Assoc/MT-VT-Mix Trad/Non
FAX Number: (541) 917-4445 Calendar System: Quarter
URL: www.linnbenton.edu
Established: 1966 Annual Undergrad Tuition & Fees (In-District): $5,487
Enrollment: 4,956 Coed
Affiliation or Control: State/Local IRS Status: 501(c)3
Highest Offering: Associate Degree
Accreditation: **NW**, DA, MAC, OTA, POLYT, SURGT

01 President Dr. Lisa AVERY
05 Vice Pres Academic Affs/Wrkfce Dev Dr. Ann BUCHELE
10 Vice Pres Finance & Operations Mr. Sheldon FLOM
12 Regional Director Benton County Mr. Jeff DAVIS
15 Dir Human Resources/Affirm Act Ofcr Mr. Scott ROLEN
41 Director of Athletics Mr. Mark MAJESKI
81 Dean Science/Engr & Math Ms. Kristina HOLTON
49 Dean Arts/Soc Sci/Humanities Div Ms. Meg ROLAND
20 Dean of Instruction Ms. Katie WINDER
111 Exec Dir Institutional Advancement Ms. Jennifer BOEHMER
04 Executive Asst to President Ms. Amanda KLIEVER
06 Dir Registrar/Admissions Mr. Danny AYNES
13 Chief Info Technology Officer (CIO) Mr. Michael QUINER
18 Chief Facilities/Physical Plant Mr. Terrell LANGLEY
28 Dir Equity/Diversity/Inclusion Mr. Javier CERVANTES
09 Director of Institutional Research Mr. Justin SMITH
37 Dir Financial Aid/Veterans Affairs Ms. Elaine ROBINSON

Mount Angel Abbey & Seminary (A)

1 Abbey Drive, Saint Benedict OR 97373-0505
County: Marion FICE Identification: 003203
Unit ID: 209241
Telephone: (503) 845-3951 Carnegie Class: Spec-4-yr-Faith
FAX Number: (503) 845-3128 Calendar System: Semester
URL: www.mountangelabbey.org
Established: 1889 Annual Undergrad Tuition & Fees: $24,770
Enrollment: 127 Coed
Affiliation or Control: Roman Catholic IRS Status: 501(c)3
Highest Offering: Doctorate
Accreditation: NW, THEOL

01 President-Rector .... Msgr. Joseph V. BETSCHART
05 Academic Dean .... Dr. Shawn KEOUGH
11 VP of Admin/Dir Human Formation .... Rev. Stephen CLOVIS
20 Associate Dean .... Dr. Andrew CUMMINGS
06 Registrar/Director of Financial Aid .... Mr. Terence MERRITT
07 Director of Admissions .... Fr. Teresio CALDWELL, OSB
04 Exec Asst to the President-Rector .... Mrs. Nancy BROSTROM
10 Procurator .... Fr. Martin GRASSEL, OSB
30 Director of Development .... Ms. Jodi KILCUP
26 Communications Manager .... Ms. Theresa MYERS
08 Librarian .... Dr. Brian MORIN
29 Alumni Relations .... Ms. Maurissa FISHER
112 Director of Planned Giving .... Ms. Susan GALLAGHER
44 Director of Annual Giving .... Ms. Melissa EDDINGS
15 Chief Human Resources Officer .... Ms. Colette BLAKELY

Mt. Hood Community College (B)

26000 SE Stark, Gresham OR 97030-3300
County: Multnomah FICE Identification: 003204
Unit ID: 209250
Telephone: (503) 491-6422 Carnegie Class: Assoc/HT-Mix Trad/Non
FAX Number: (503) 491-7389 Calendar System: Quarter
URL: www.mhcc.edu
Established: 1965 Annual Undergrad Tuition & Fees (In-District): $5,286
Enrollment: 6,812 Coed
Affiliation or Control: Local IRS Status: 501(c)3
Highest Offering: Associate Degree
Accreditation: NW, COARC, DH, FUSER, PTAA, SURGT

01 President .... Dr. Lisa SKARI
05 Vice President of Instruction .... Mr. Alfred MCQUARTERS
15 Associate VP of Human Resources .... Mr. Travis BROWN
88 Dir Child Dev/Family Support Pgms .... Dr. Josi KISA
10 VP of Finance and Administration .... Ms. Jennifer DEMENT
09 Associate VP Institutional Research .... Mr. Sergey SHEPELOV
35 Dir Student Development/Tech .... Ms. Christi HART
32 Vice President of Student Services .... Mr. John HAMBLIN
13 Associate VP Information Technology .... Ms. Linda VIGESAA
111 Vice Pres of College Advancement .... Mr. Al SIGALA
76 Dean Allied Health & Nursing .... Dr. Carri CLAYCOMB
81 Dean of Mathematics/Science .... Mr. Peter SZUCS
79 Dean Humanities/Math/Social Science .... Ms. Sara RIVARA
50 Dean Business/Engr/Applied Tech .... Ms. Kay LOPEZ
103 Exec Dean Workforce/CTE/Partner .... Ms. Joy JEROME TURTOLA
04 Executive Asst to the President .... Ms. Felisha BREWER
101 Executive Asst to the Board .... Ms. Laurie POPP
106 Director Online Learning .... Ms. Cat SCHLEICHERT
41 Athletic Director .... Dr. Kim HYATT
84 Director of Enrollment Services .... Ms. Dawn SALLEE-JUSTESEN
18 Associate Vice Pres Facilities .... Mr. Charles GEORGE
19 Manager of Public Safety .... Mr. Wayne FEAGLE
28 Associate VP of DEI .... Ms. Traci SIMMONS
37 Director of Financial Aid .... Mr. Christopher NATELBORG

Multnomah University (C)

8435 NE Glisan Street, Portland OR 97220-5898
County: Multnomah FICE Identification: 003206
Unit ID: 209287
Telephone: (503) 255-0332 Carnegie Class: Spec-4-yr-Faith
FAX Number: (503) 254-1268 Calendar System: Semester
URL: www.multnomah.edu
Established: 1936 Annual Undergrad Tuition & Fees: $28,000
Enrollment: 623 Coed
Affiliation or Control: Independent Non-Profit IRS Status: 501(c)3
Highest Offering: Doctorate
Accreditation: NW, THEOL

01 President .... Dr. G. Craig WILLIFORD
84 VP Enrollment Management/IT .... Ms. Gina BERQUIST
11 Executive Vice President/COO .... Mr. Ted ALLEN
111 Vice President of Advancement .... Dr. Robert LARSON
28 VP Diversity/Inclusive Development .... Dr. Jessica L. TAYLOR
05 Chief Academic Officer .... Mr. Alin VRANCILA
49 Dean School of Arts and Sciences .... Dr. Daniel SCALBERG
73 Dean School of Bible & Theology .... Dr. Derek CHINN
107 Dean School of Prof Studies .... Dr. Steven HOLLER
32 Dean of Students & Athletics .... Dr. Joseph SLAVENS
42 Assoc Dean Spiritual Life .... Mr. Renjy ABRAHAM
35 Associate Dean of Student Success .... Mrs. Christy MARTIN
108 Dir of Institutional Effectiveness .... Mrs. Lydia GILLESPIE
06 Registrar .... Ms. Amy M. STEPHENS
21 Controller .... Mrs. Debbie WHITEHEAD
08 Librarian .... Mrs. Pamela MIDDLETON
37 Director Student Financial Aid .... Mr. Stephen BUCKLAND
13 Director Information Technology .... Mr. Sudha PEETHALA
15 Director of Human Resources .... Ms. Tracy L. MORESCHI

41 Athletic Director .... Mr. Mike ANDERSON
26 Dir of Marketing/Communications .... Vacant
18 Executive Director of Operations .... Mr. Eric LINMAN
04 Assistant to the President .... Mrs. Denise STONE
19 Director of Campus Safety .... Mr. Josh HARPER
38 Director Student Counseling .... Mrs. Rebecca JONES
121 Associate Dean of Student Success .... Mrs. Christy MARTIN
106 Learning Mgmt Systems Specialist .... Ms. Alyssa CHARLES

National University of Natural Medicine (D)

49 South Porter Street, Portland OR 97201-4878
County: Multnomah FICE Identification: 025340
Unit ID: 209296
Telephone: (503) 552-1555 Carnegie Class: Spec-4-yr-Other Health
FAX Number: (503) 499-0022 Calendar System: Quarter
URL: nunm.edu
Established: 1956 Annual Undergrad Tuition & Fees: N/A
Enrollment: 485 Coed
Affiliation or Control: Independent Non-Profit IRS Status: 501(c)3
Highest Offering: Doctorate
Accreditation: NW, ACUP, NATUR

01 President .... Dr. Melanie HENRIKSEN
10 EVP/Chief Finance Officer .... Mr. Gerald BORES
05 Chief Academics/VP Inst Effective .... Ms. Cheryl MILLER
32 VP Student Engagement & Innovation .... Dr. Glenn C. SMITH
15 VP of Human Resources .... Ms. Kathy STANFORD
84 VP of Enrollment Management .... Ms. Beth WOODWARD
88 VP Health Centers & Aux Ops .... Ms. Nora SANDE
88 Director Helfgott Research Inst .... Dr. Ryan BRADLEY
11 Administrative Dean .... Dr. Charles KUNERT
63 Int Dir Naturopathic Medicine .... Dr. Kelly BALTAZAR
88 Director of Curriculum Innovation .... Dr. Shehab EL-HASHEMY
58 Director Graduate Medical Education .... Dr. Dee SAUNDERS
88 Interim Director CCM .... Mr. Andrew MCINTYRE
20 Director Undergrad & Grad Studies .... Dr. Tim IRVING
88 Department Chair Nutrition .... Dr. Erlandsen ANDREW
76 Department Chair Health Sciences .... Dr. Heather ZWICKEY
35 Dean of Students .... Ms. Rachael ALLEN
08 University Librarian .... Ms. Noelle STELLO
23 Director of Health Centers .... Dr. Brooke LINN
28 Director of Equity & Inclusion .... Ms. Ayasha SHAMSUD-DIN
06 Registrar .... Ms. Kelly GAREY
07 Director of Admissions .... Vacant
26 Director Marketing & Communication .... Ms. Sherrie MARTEL
37 Director of Financial Aid .... Ms. Sally KALSTROM
121 Director of Student Success .... Ms. Morgan CHICARELLI
120 Director Instructional Design/Tech .... Mr. Justin FOWLER
13 IT Manager .... Mr. Steve FONG
19 Chief of Campus Security .... Mr. Mike HALE
100 Chief of Staff & Strategic Engage .... Mr. Jeremy ANDERSON-SLOAN
88 Associate Dean Administration .... Ms. Heather SCHIFFKE
38 Interim Director Counseling Service .... Dr. Jason RIBNER
88 Laboratory Director .... Dr. Sonia KAPUR
18 Manager of Facilities .... Mr. Dave MCALLISTER
17 Chief Medical Officer/Dean Clinics .... Dr. Jessica NAGELKIRK

New Hope Christian College (E)

2155 Bailey Hill Road, Eugene OR 97405-1194
County: Lane FICE Identification: 021597
Unit ID: 208725
Telephone: (541) 485-1780 Carnegie Class: Spec-4-yr-Faith
FAX Number: (541) 343-5801 Calendar System: Semester
URL: www.newhope.edu
Established: 1925 Annual Undergrad Tuition & Fees: $15,700
Enrollment: 52 Coed
Affiliation or Control: Other IRS Status: 501(c)3
Highest Offering: Baccalaureate
Accreditation: BI

01 President .... Dr. Wayne CORDEIRO
05 Academic Dean .... Mr. Donald GRAFTON
11 Vice President of Operations .... Mr. Thomas KIRST
04 Executive Assistant to President .... Mrs. Lori HIGASHI
13 Chief Technology Officer .... Mr. Peter THOURSON
32 Dean of Student Services .... Mr. Aaron CORDEIRO
35 Director of Student Life .... Mr. Paul WRIGHT
29 Director of Alumni Relations .... Vacant
84 Enrollment Management .... Mr. Christopher KIRIAKOS
37 Director of Financial Aid .... Ms. Sayaka MEARIG
06 Registrar .... Mrs. Floria GRAFTON
10 Director Financial Services .... Ms. Elaine NAULU
08 Librarian .... Mrs. Uilani CORDEIRO
07 Admissions Assistant .... Ms. Leslie KIRIAKOS

Oregon Coast Community College (F)

400 SE College Way, Newport OR 97366
County: Lincoln FICE Identification: 032132
Unit ID: 423652
Telephone: (541) 867-8501 Carnegie Class: Assoc/MT-VT-High Trad
FAX Number: (541) 265-3820 Calendar System: Quarter
URL: www.oregoncoast.edu
Established: 1987 Annual Undergrad Tuition & Fees (In-District): $5,148
Enrollment: 417 Coed
Affiliation or Control: State/Local IRS Status: 501(c)3
Highest Offering: Associate Degree
Accreditation: NW

01 President .... Dr. Birgitte RYSLINGE
05 VP of Academic Affairs .... Dan LARA
32 VP Student Affairs .... Dr. Andres OROZ
11 VP Administrative Services .... Robin GINTNER
26 VP Engagement & Entrepreneurship .... Dave PRICE
04 Exec Assistant to the President .... Kathleen ANDREWS
06 Registrar .... Ann HOVEY
08 Director of Library and Media Svcs .... Darci ADOLF
15 Director of Human Resources .... Joy GUTKNECHT
18 Director of Facilities .... Chris ROGERS

Oregon College of Oriental Medicine (G)

75 NW Couch Street, Portland OR 97209-4018
County: Multnomah FICE Identification: 026037
Unit ID: 369659
Telephone: (503) 253-3443 Carnegie Class: Spec-4-yr-Other Health
FAX Number: (503) 253-2701 Calendar System: Quarter
URL: www.ocom.edu
Established: 1983 Annual Graduate Tuition & Fees: N/A
Enrollment: 236 Coed
Affiliation or Control: Independent Non-Profit IRS Status: 501(c)3
Highest Offering: Doctorate; No Undergraduates
Accreditation: ACUP

01 President/CEO .... Dr. Sherri GREEN
10 CFO/VP of Finance .... Neville WELLMAN
05 Vice President of Academic Affairs .... Dr. Valerie HOBBS
11 Vice Pres Planning & Operations .... Dr. Phil LUNDBERG
58 Dean of Postgraduate Studies .... Dr. Beth BURCH
88 Associate Dean of Doctoral Studies .... Dr. Zhaoxue LU
46 Interim Director of Research .... Vacant
15 Director of Human Resources .... Amber APPLETON
06 Registrar .... Carol ACHESON
07 Director of Admissions .... Anna GRACE
37 Director Student Financial Aid .... Katrina HITZEMAN
44 Director of Annual Giving .... Vacant
08 Director of Library Services .... Candise BRANUM
13 Director of Facilities and IT .... Chris LANGFORD
38 Director Student Counseling .... Elizabeth MILES
32 Dir of Student and Alumni Affairs .... Mike LAW

Oregon Health & Science University (H)

3181 SW Sam Jackson Park Road, Portland OR 97239-3098
County: Multnomah FICE Identification: 004882
Unit ID: 209490
Telephone: (503) 494-8311 Carnegie Class: Spec-4-yr-Med
FAX Number: (503) 494-5738 Calendar System: Quarter
URL: www.ohsu.edu
Established: 1887 Annual Undergrad Tuition & Fees (In-State): N/A
Enrollment: 3,035 Coed
Affiliation or Control: State IRS Status: 501(c)3
Highest Offering: Doctorate
Accreditation: NW, ANEST, ARCPA, CAHIIM, CAMPEP, DENT, DIETI, EMT, IPSY, MED, MIDWF, MT, NURSE, PH, RTT

01 President .... Dr. Danny O. JACOBS
03 Executive Vice Provost .... Dr. David W. ROBINSON
05 Provost Education & Research .... Dr. Elena ANDRESEN
18 Assoc VP Facilities/Physical Plant .... Mr. Scott PAGE
84 Vice Prov Enroll & Academic Program .... Ms. Cherie HONNELL
46 Chief Research Officer .... Dr. Peter BARR-GILLESPIE
63 Dean School of Medicine .... Dr. Sharon ANDERSON
52 Dean School of Dentistry .... Dr. Phillip T. MARUCHA
69 Dean Joint School of Public Health .... Dr. David BANGSBERG
66 Dean School of Nursing .... Dr. Susan BAKEWELL-SACHS
06 Registrar .... Ms. Gwen HYATT
17 Director University Hospital .... Mr. Peter RAPP
88 Director Vollum Inst Adv Biomed Res .. Dr. Richard H. GOODMAN
15 Vice Provost of Human Resources .... Mr. Greg MOAWAD
08 University Librarian .... Ms. Kristine ALPI
26 VP and Chief Marketing Officer .... Ms. Kimberly OVITT
88 Director Child Devel/Rehab Center .... Dr. Brian ROGERS
37 Director Student Financial Aid .... Ms. Rachel DURBIN
28 Vice Pres for Equity & Inclusion .... Dr. Derick DU VIVIER
108 Vice Prov Educ Improve/Innovation .... Dr. Constance TUCKER

Oregon Institute of Technology (I)

3201 Campus Drive, Klamath Falls OR 97601-8801
County: Klamath FICE Identification: 003211
Unit ID: 209506
Telephone: (541) 885-1000 Carnegie Class: Bac-Diverse
FAX Number: (541) 885-1101 Calendar System: Quarter
URL: www.oit.edu
Established: 1947 Annual Undergrad Tuition & Fees (In-State): $11,269
Enrollment: 5,323 Coed
Affiliation or Control: State IRS Status: 501(c)3
Highest Offering: Master's
Accreditation: NW, COARC, DH, DMS, EMT, IACBE, MT, POLYT

01 President .... Dr. Nagi G. NAGANATHAN
05 Provost/Vice Pres Academic Affairs .... Ms. Joanna MOTT
10 VP Finance/Administration .... Mr. John HARMON
32 VP Student Affairs/Dean of Students .... Dr. Erin FOLEY
37 Director of Financial Aid .... Ms. Tracey A. LEHMAN
15 Associate VP Human Resources .... Vacant

07 Director of Admissions .... Mr. Erik JOHNSON
06 Registrar .... Ms. Wendy IVIE
21 Assistant VP Financial Operations .... Vacant
13 Assoc VP/Chief Information Officer .... Ms. Connie ATCHLEY
26 Executive Director of Marketing .... Mr. Marcus POPIOLEK
23 Director Student Health Services .... Mrs. Gaylyn MAURER
18 Director Facilities Svcs .... Mr. Thom DARRAH
41 Athletic Director .... Mr. John VANDYKE
35 Director Campus Life .... Ms. Holly ANDERSON
88 Assoc Director Campus Life .... Ms. Josie HUDSPETH
36 Assoc Director of Career Services .... Ms. Sarah MOORE
09 Institutional Research Analyst .... Mr. Farooq SULTAN
30 VP Institutional Advanc/Development .... Mr. Ken FINCHER
04 Sr Exec Assistant to the President .... Mrs. Adria D. PASCHAL
19 Director Security/Safety .... Mr. Edward DANIELS
39 Dir Resident Life/Student Housing .... Ms. Mandi CLARK
43 Director of Legal Services .... Mr. David GROFF
84 Assoc VP Strategic Enrollment .... Vacant
96 Director of Procurement Contracts .... Ms. Vivian CHEN
100 Senior Advisor to the President .... Ms. Sandra FOX
49 Dean of Health/Arts & Sciences .... Mr. Dan PETERSON
54 Dean of Engineering .... Dr. Tom KEYSER

Oregon State University (A)

1500 SW Jefferson Avenue, Corvallis OR 97331-8507
County: Benton FICE Identification: 003210
Unit ID: 209542
Telephone: (541) 737-0123 Carnegie Class: DU-Highest
FAX Number: N/A Calendar System: Quarter
URL: www.oregonstate.edu
Established: 1868 Annual Undergrad Tuition & Fees (In-State): $11,858
Enrollment: 32,312 Coed
Affiliation or Control: State IRS Status: 501(c)3
Highest Offering: Doctorate
Accreditation: NW, CAATE, CACREP, CAEPN, CEA, CONST, DIETD, DIETI, IPSY, PH, PHAR, SPAA, VET

01 Interim President .... Dr. Rebecca JOHNSON
05 Provost/Exec Vice President .... Dr. Ed FESER
10 Vice Pres Finance/Admin .... Mr. Mike GREEN
111 Vice Pres University Advancement .... Mr. Steve CLARK
46 Vice President for Research .... Dr. Irem TUMER
20 Vice Provost for Faculty Affairs .... Dr. Richard SETTERSTEN
32 Assoc Vice Provost Student Affairs .... Mr. Dan LARSON
12 V Prov/Campus Ex Ofcr OSU-Cascades .. Dr. Andrew KETSDEVER
102 President & CEO OSU Foundation .... Mr. Shawn SCOVILLE
11 Sr Assoc VP for Administration .... Mr. Paul ODENTHAL
106 Assoc Provost for Ecampus .... Ms. Lisa TEMPLETON
47 Dean of Agricultural Sciences .... Dr. Alan SAMS
50 Dean of Business .... Dr. James COAKLEY
54 Dean of Engineering .... Dr. Scott ASHFORD
65 Dean of Forestry .... Dr. Thomas DELUCA
68 Dean of Health & Human Sciences .... Dr. Javier NIETO
65 Dean of Earth/Ocean/Atmospheric Sci ...... Dr. Roberta MARINELLI
67 Dean of Pharmacy .... Dr. Mark ZABRISKIE
81 Dean of Science .... Dr. Roy HAGGERTY
74 Dean of Veterinary Medicine .... Dr. Susan TORNQUIST
51 Assoc Provost Extended Campus .... Ms. Lisa TEMPLETON
35 Dean of Student Life .... Dr. Kevin DOUGHERTY
92 Dean University Honors College .... Dr. Toni DOOLEN
53 Dean of Education .... Dr. Susan GARDNER
08 University Librarian .... Ms. Faye CHADWELL
22 Director Equity & Inclusion .... Dr. Charlene ALEXANDER
43 General Counsel .... Ms. Becca GOSE
41 Director Intercollegiate Athletics .... Mr. Scott BARNES
37 Dir of Financial Aid/Scholarship .... Mr. Keith RAAB
23 Dir Student Health Services .... Ms. Jenny HAUBENREISER
38 Dir Univ Counseling/Psych Svcs .... Dr. Ian KELLEMS
39 Director Univ Housing/Dining Svcs .... Mr. Stephen JENKINS
06 Registrar .... Ms. Rebecca MATHERN
07 Director of Admissions .... Mr. Noah BUCKLEY
24 Director Media & Outreach Services .... Mr. John GREYDANUS
14 Dir of Enterprise Computing Service .... Mr. Kent KUO
15 Director of Human Resources .... Ms. Kathy HASENPFLUG
19 Chief of Police .... Ms. Shanon ANDERSON
29 Exec Dir of Alumni Association .... Mr. John VALVA
86 Director Government Relations .... Ms. Katie FAST
27 Dir News/Comm Svcs/Asst Vice Pres .... Ms. Annie HECK
26 Director of University Marketing .... Ms. Melody K. OLDFIELD
105 Asst Director Web Communications .... Mr. David A. BAKER
28 Chief Diversity Officer .... Ms. Charlene ALEXANDER
09 Director of Institutional Research .... Mr. Salvador CASTILLO
84 Director Enrollment Management .... Mr. Jon BOECKENSTEDT
40 General Mgr & CEO OSU Bookstores .... Mr. Steve E. ECKRICH
96 Manager Procurement/Contract Svcs .... Ms. Kelly L. KOZISEK
101 Secretary of the Institution/Board .... Ms. Debbie COLBERT
45 Chief Institutional Planning Office .... Dr. Sherm BLOOMER

Pacific Bible College (B)

28 S. Fir St., Suite 212, Medford OR 97501
County: Jackson Identification: 667252
Unit ID: 407610
Telephone: (541) 776-9942 Carnegie Class: Spec 2-yr-Other
FAX Number: (541) 770-9065 Calendar System: Semester
URL: https://pacificbible.edu/
Established: 1991 Annual Undergrad Tuition & Fees: $4,370
Enrollment: 47 Coed
Affiliation or Control: Non-denominational IRS Status: 501(c)3
Highest Offering: Baccalaureate
Accreditation: BI

01 President .... Mr. Mike ROBINSON
05 Chief Academic Officer .... Mr. Matthew MCAULIFFE
08 Chief Library Officer .... Mr. Terry PRUETT
37 Student Financial Aid Coordinator .... Ms. Amy STONEHILL
04 Administrative Assistant .... Ms. Kathy CURRAN

Pacific University (C)

2043 College Way, Forest Grove OR 97116-1797
County: Washington FICE Identification: 003212
Unit ID: 209612
Telephone: (503) 357-6151 Carnegie Class: DU-Mod
FAX Number: (503) 352-2242 Calendar System: Semester
URL: www.pacificu.edu
Established: 1849 Annual Undergrad Tuition & Fees: $48,095
Enrollment: 3,808 Coed
Affiliation or Control: Independent Non-Profit IRS Status: 501(c)3
Highest Offering: Doctorate
Accreditation: NW, #ACBSP, ARCPA, AUD, CAATE, CLPSY, DH, IPSY, MPCAC, MUS, OPT, OPTR, OT, PHAR, PTA, SP, SW

01 President .... Dr. Lesley M. HALLICK
05 Vice Pres Academic Affairs/Provost ..... Dr. Ann BARR-GILLESPIE
10 Vice Pres Finance & Administration .... Mr. Jim LANGSTRAAT
111 Vice Pres University Advancement .... Ms. Cassie WARMAN
84 Vice Pres Enrollment Management .... Ms. Sarah PHILLIPS
15 VP Human Resources/Legal Affairs .... Ms. Jennifer YRUEGAS
32 Vice Pres Student Affairs .... Mr. Narce RODRIGUEZ
26 Assoc VP of Marketing/Comm .... Ms. Jenni LUCKETT
110 Sr AVP for University Advancement .... Ms. Jan STRICKLIN
21 Int Assoc VP for Finance/Admin .... Ms. Alecia NEUMAN
07 Assoc Vice Pres of Admissions .... Ms. Karen DUNSTON
123 AVP Grad & Prof Admiss/Enroll .... Mr. Jon-Erik LARSEN
29 AVP Engagement Ops/Advancement .Ms. Martha CALUS-MCLAIN
20 Vice Provost Academic Affairs .... Dr. Lisa CARSTENS
20 Int Vice Provost/Exec Dean .... Dr. Mary VON
06 Registrar .... Ms. Anne KENNEDY
18 Director of Facilities .... Ms. Cindy SCHUPPERT
37 Director Financial Aid .... Ms. Leslie LIMPER
13 Interim Chief Information Officer .... Mr. Ted KRUPICKA
76 Exec Dean Col of Health Professions .. Dr. Ann BARR-GILLESPIE
49 Dean of Arts & Sciences .... Dr. Sarah PHILLIPS
63 Dean College of Optometry .... Dr. Fraser C. HORN
67 Dean School of Pharmacy .... Dr. Reza KARIMIGEVARI
53 Dean College of Education .... Dr. Leif GUSTAVSON
83 Dean School of Grad Psych .... Dr. Joaquin BORREGO
08 Dean of University Libraries .... Mr. Isaac GILMAN
50 Dean of College of Business .... Dr. Jennifer YRUEGAS
41 Dir of Intercollegiate Athletics .... Mr. Keith BUCKLEY
75 Dir Sch Physical/Occup Therapy .... Dr. Kevin CHUI
23 Director of Health Services .... Vacant
35 Dir Univ Center/Student Activities .... Mr. Steve KLEIN
52 Director Dental Hygiene Studies .... Ms. Amy COPLEN
40 Manager Bookstore .... Vacant
38 Director of the Counseling Center .... Vacant
09 Director of Institutional Research .... Mr. William O'SHEA
04 Executive Asst to President .... Ms. Sue WEINBENDER
100 Chief of Staff .... Ms. Karla STAIHAR
112 Major Gift Ofcr Found/Corp Rels .... Mr. Orhan K. BELDING
104 Director International Programs .... Dr. Stephen PRAG
28 Director Equity/Diversity/Inclusion ..... Ms. Narcedalia RODRIGUEZ

Portland Community College (D)

PO Box 19000, Portland OR 97280-0990
County: Multnomah FICE Identification: 003213
Unit ID: 209746
Telephone: (971) 722-6111 Carnegie Class: Assoc/HT-Mix Trad/Non
FAX Number: (971) 722-4960 Calendar System: Quarter
URL: www.pcc.edu/
Established: 1961 Annual Undergrad Tuition & Fees (In-District): $4,810
Enrollment: 22,904 Coed
Affiliation or Control: Local IRS Status: 501(c)3
Highest Offering: Associate Degree
Accreditation: NW, ADNUR, CAHIIM, DA, DH, EMT, IFSAC, MAC, MLTAD, NAEYC, RAD

01 President .... Mr. Mark MITSUI
03 Executive Vice President .... Ms. Sylvia KELLEY
100 Program Administrator .... Dr. Traci FORDHAM
05 Vice President of Academic Affairs .... Ms. Katy W. HO
32 Interim Vice Pres Student Affairs .... Dr. Heather LANG
10 Vice Pres Finance/Administration .... Mr. Eric BLUMENTHAL
21 Assoc VP Financial Services .... Ms. Dina FARRELL
15 Associate VP Human Resources .... Ms. Lisa BLEDSOE
13 Chief Information Officer .... Mr. Michael NORTHOVER
20 Dean of instruction .... Ms. Jennifer PIPER
20 Dean Instruction Sylvania .... Dr. Karen PAEZ
20 Dean Instruction Cascade Campus .... Mr. Kurt SIMONDS
20 Dean Instruction Rock Creek Campus .... Dr. Cheryl SCOTT
20 Dean Instruct Southeast Campus .... Ms. Sarah TILLERY
32 Dean Student Dev Sylvania
Campus .... Ms. Vicky LOPEZ-SANCHEZ
32 Dean Stdnt Dev Rock Creek Campus .... Mr. Ryan A. AIELLO
121 Dean of Student Success .... Ms. Sonya BEDIENT
32 Dean Student Dev Cascade
Campus .... Ms. Vivian MIRANDA-WENDELKEN
84 Dean of Enrollment Management .... Mr. Ryan CLARK
18 Director Facilities Management .... Mr. Brad ORTMAN
08 Dean Library Services .... Ms. Michelle M. BAGLEY
09 Dir Institutional Effectiveness .... Ms. Laura MASSEY
19 Director Public Safety .... Mr. Derrick FOXWORTH

37 Director Financial Aid .... Mr. Peter GOSS
28 Chief Diversity Officer .... Ms. Tricia BRAND
30 Director of Development .... Vacant
06 Manager of Registration Services .... Ms. Darilis GARCIA
31 Director of Community Engagement .... Ms. Kate CHESTER
96 Manager Purchasing .... Mr. Mike MATHEWS

Portland State University (E)

PO Box 751, Portland OR 97207-0751
County: Multnomah FICE Identification: 003216
Unit ID: 209807
Telephone: (503) 725-3000 Carnegie Class: DU-Higher
FAX Number: (503) 725-4882 Calendar System: Quarter
URL: www.pdx.edu
Established: 1946 Annual Undergrad Tuition & Fees (In-State): $10,112
Enrollment: 23,640 Coed
Affiliation or Control: State IRS Status: 501(c)3
Highest Offering: Doctorate
Accreditation: NW, CACREP, CAEP, CEA, HSA, LC, MUS, PH, PLNG, SP, SPAA, SW, THEA

01 President .... Dr. Stephen PERCY
43 General Counsel & Board Secretary .... Ms. Cindy STARKE
05 Provost & VP Academic Affairs .... Dr. Susan JEFFORDS
10 Vice President Finance/Admin .... Dr. Kevin REYNOLDS
102 CEO PSU Foundation .... Ms. Sarah SCHWARZ
100 Chief of Staff .... Ms. Clair C. PINKERTON
84 Vice Pres Enrollment Mgmt .... Dr. Chuck KNEPFLE
46 Interim VP Research & Grad Studies .... Dr. Jason PODRABSKY
28 VP Global Diversity & Inclusion .... Dr. Ame LAMBERT
32 Vice Provost for Student Affairs .... Dr. Michele TOPPE
20 Vice Provost Acad Pers Ldrshp & Dev .... Dr. Shelly CHABON
26 Interim Assoc VP Communications .... Ms. Julie SMITH
09 Director Inst Research/Planning .... Dr. Kathi A. KETCHESON
19 Director Campus Public Safety .... Mr. Willie HALIBURTON
13 VP & Chief Information Officer .... Mr. Kirk KELLY
86 VP for Public Affairs .... Mr. Kevin NEELY
08 Interim Dean University Librarian .... Dr. Michael BOWMAN
41 Athletics Director .... Ms. Valerie CLEARY
49 Dean of CLAS .... Dr. Todd ROSENSTIEL
50 Dean School of Business .... Mr. Clifford ALLEN
53 Dean Graduate Sch of Education .... Dr. Marvin LYNN
54 Dean Col Engr/Computer Science .... Dr. Richard CORSI
57 Dean College of the Arts .... Dr. Leroy BYNUM
70 Dean School of Social Work .... Dr. Jose COLL
80 Int Dean Col Urban/Public Affairs .... Dr. Sy ADLER
06 AVP & University Registrar .... Ms. Cindy BACCAR
23 Exec Dir Stdnt Health & Counseling .... Dr. Dana TASSON
58 Dean Graduate Studies .... Ms. Rossitza WOOSTER

Process Work Institute (F)

2049 NW Hoyt Street, Portland OR 97209
County: Multnomah Identification: 667297
Telephone: (503) 223-8188 Carnegie Class: Not Classified
FAX Number: (503) 227-7003 Calendar System: Quarter
URL: www.processwork.edu
Established: 1989 Annual Graduate Tuition & Fees: N/A
Enrollment: N/A Coed
Affiliation or Control: Independent Non-Profit IRS Status: 501(c)3
Highest Offering: Master's; No Undergraduates
Accreditation: ACICS

01 Executive Director/Dean .... Dr. Hellene GRONDA

Reed College (G)

3203 SE Woodstock Boulevard, Portland OR 97202-8199
County: Multnomah FICE Identification: 003217
Unit ID: 209922
Telephone: (503) 771-1112 Carnegie Class: Bac-A&S
FAX Number: (503) 777-7769 Calendar System: Semester
URL: www.reed.edu
Established: 1908 Annual Undergrad Tuition & Fees: $60,620
Enrollment: 1,385 Coed
Affiliation or Control: Independent Non-Profit IRS Status: 501(c)3
Highest Offering: Master's
Accreditation: NW

01 President .... Dr. Audrey BILGER
111 Vice President College Relations .... Mr. Hugh E. PORTER
05 Dean of the Faculty .... Dr. Kathryn C. OLESON
10 Vice President & Treasurer .... Dr. Lorraine ARVIN
32 Vice Pres for Student Life . Dr. Karnell MCCONNELL-BLACK
04 Exec Asst to the President .... Ms. Dawn G. THOMPSON
28 Dean for Institutional Diversity .... Dr. Mary B. JAMES
35 Dean of Students .... Vacant
23 Director Health & Counseling .... Ms. Carrie BALDWIN-SAYRE
07 Vice Pres/Dean Admission & Fin Aid .... Mr. Milyon TRULOVE
06 Registrar .... Ms. Nora MCLAUGHLIN
08 College Librarian .... Ms. Dena HUTTO
30 Executive Director of Development .... Ms. Sarah PANETTA
37 Director of Financial Aid .... Ms. Sandy SUNDSTROM
09 Director of Institutional Research .... Mr. Mike TAMADA
26 Exec Dir Comm & Public Affairs .... Ms. Mandy HEATON
13 Chief Information Officer .... Dr. Martin D. RINGLE
105 Director of Web Support Services ...Ms. Marianne M. COLGROVE
91 Director Administrative Computing .... Ms. Kerri A. CREAGER
21 Associate Treasurer & Controller .... Mr. Rob TUST
15 Director of Human Resources .... Ms. Michelle VALINTIS
29 Sr Dir Alumni Pgms & Annual Fund ..... Ms. Mary M. ASKELSON

102 Dir Corporate/Foundation Support .... Mr. Jeremy NICULESCU
104 Director International Programs .... Dr. Paul D. DEYOUNG
36 Dean of Stdnts/Dir Life Beyond Reed ....Ms. Alice HARRA
58 Assoc Dean Graduate & Special Pgms ....Ms. Ashley HUDSON
18 Director Facilities Operations .... Mr. Steven W. YEADON
19 Director Community Safety .... Mr. Gary GRANGER
41 Director of Athletics/Fitness ....Mr. Michael LOMBARDO
40 Director Bookstore & Auxiliary Svcs .... Ms. Jessica VALESKE
39 Asst Dean of Students for Res Life .... Ms. Amy SCHUCKMAN

Rogue Community College (A)

3345 Redwood Highway, Grants Pass OR 97527-9298
County: Josephine FICE Identification: 010182
Unit ID: 209940
Telephone: (541) 956-7500 Carnegie Class: Assoc/HT-Mix Trad/Non
FAX Number: (541) 471-3591 Calendar System: Quarter
URL: www.roguecc.edu
Established: 1970 Annual Undergrad Tuition & Fees (In-District): $5,040
Enrollment: 3,765 Coed
Affiliation or Control: Local IRS Status: 501(c)3
Highest Offering: Associate Degree
Accreditation: NW, EMT

01 College President ....Dr. Cathy KEMPER-PELLE
05 VP Academic Affairs ....Ms. Juliet LONG
32 VP Student Affairs/CSSO/ADA ....Ms. Kori EBENHACK
10 VP Operations & Finance/CFO .... Ms. Lisa STANTON
76 Director SOHOPE .... Ms. Lisa PARKS
88 Director Small Bus Dev Center ....Ms. Ruth SWAIN
81 Dean of Instuction Art/Science/Tech ....Ms. Kimberly FREEZE
08 Head Librarian .... Mr. Robert FELTHOUSEN
102 Executive Director Foundation ....Ms. Judy BASKER
15 Dir People/Culture & Safety .... Ms. Jamee HARRINGTON
117 Director Risk Mgmt/Title IX .... Mr. Sean TAGGART
24 Director Instructional Media ....Mr. Josh OGLE
109 Director Auxiliary Svcs/Ship/Rec ....Ms. Laura HAGA-DUFFY
26 Dir Marketing/Call Center ....Ms. Carmen SUMNER
37 Dir Student Financial Aid ....Ms. Frankie EVERETT
13 Director IT Network Services ....Mr. Mike MCCLURE
88 Director TRiO-EOC/ETS .... Ms. Janet BASNEY
88 Director TRiO-SSS Programs ....Ms. Colletta YOUNG
09 Director of Institutional Research .... Ms. Laurie ROE
88 Director Apprenticeship .... Ms. Andrea ANDERSON
96 Dir Contract and Procurement .... Ms. Jodie FULTON
91 Director of IT Programming & QA ....Mr. Al SHELDON
18 Director of Facilities/Operations .... Mr. Grant LAGORIO
20 Data Mgmt Specialist Curriculum/Sch ....Ms. Marita WILDER
124 Director of Student Engagement .... Ms. Rene MCKENZIE
06 Director Enrollment Svcs/Registrar .... Ms. Dani CROUCH
07 Director Admissions & Recruitment .... Ms. Nicole SAKRAIDA
04 Assistant to the Pres Operationss ....Ms. Vicki MCCRARY
35 Dean of Student Success ....Ms. August FARNSWORTH
22 Dir of Advising & Comp/Title IX ....Ms. April HAMLIN
108 Outcomes & Assessment Coordinator ....Ms. Terrie SANDLIN
28 Diversity Programming Coordinator .... Ms. Sally SNYDER
38 Faculty/Chair Student Counseling ....Ms. Michelle GRAY
50 Faculty/Dept Chair Bus Tech ....Ms. Melissa POLEN
06 Registrar .... Ms. Dani CROUCH
51 Director of Continuing Educ ....Ms. Diane HOOVER
76 Director Allied Health Occupations .... Ms. Lisa PARKS
41 Athletic Director ....Mr. Darren VAN LEHN
101 Secretary of the Institution/Board ....Ms. Rachelle BROWN
20 Dean of Academic Affairs .... Mr. Navarro CHANDLER

Southern Oregon University (B)

1250 Siskiyou Boulevard, Ashland OR 97520-5001
County: Jackson FICE Identification: 003219
Unit ID: 210146
Telephone: (541) 552-7672 Carnegie Class: Masters/L
FAX Number: (541) 552-6329 Calendar System: Quarter
URL: www.sou.edu
Established: 1872 Annual Undergrad Tuition & Fees (In-State): $10,710
Enrollment: 5,140 Coed
Affiliation or Control: State IRS Status: 501(c)3
Highest Offering: Master's
Accreditation: NW, ACBSP, CACREP, MUS

01 President ....Dr. Linda SCHOTT
05 Provost .... Dr. Susan WALSH
10 VP for Finance & Administration .... Mr. Greg PERKINSON
111 Vice President Advancement .... Ms. Janet FRATELLA
86 Vice Pres Government Relations ....Ms. Jeanne STALLMAN
32 VP Student/Academic Affs/Enrollment .... Mr. Neil WOOLF
15 Director for Human Resource Svcs .... Ms. Kelly SZOTT
26 Ex Dir Interactive Mktg/Media Rels ....Ms. Nicolle ALEMAN
18 Dir of Facilities Mgmt & Planning .... Mr. Leon CROUCH
21 Director of Business Services .... Mr. Jeremy CARLTON
08 University Librarian ....Vacant
19 Director of Campus Public Safety .... Mr. Robert GIBSON
29 Director of Alumni Affairs .... Mr. Mike BEAGLE
88 Director of Schneider Museum of Art .... Mr. Scott MALBAURN
28 Director of Diversity & Inclusion ....Ms. Sabrina PRUD'HOMME
57 Director Center for the Arts .... Dr. David HUMPHREY
83 Director Social Sciences ....Dr. Dan DENEUI
97 Director Undergraduate Studies ....Dr. Lee AYERS
81 Director STEM ....Dr. Sherry ETTLICH
50 Dir Business Comm & Environment .... Mr. Vincent SMITH
79 Director Humanities & Culture .... Dr. Scott REX
88 Director Educ Health & Leadership ....Dr. John KING
06 Registrar .... Dr. Matt STILLMAN
07 Director of Admissions ....Mr. Zac OLSON

09 Director of Institutional Research ....Mr. Chris STANEK
41 Athletic Director ....Mr. Matt SAYRE
101 University Board Secretary .... Ms. Sabrina PRUD'HOMME
39 Director Student Housing ....Ms. Staci BUCHWALD
35 Director of Student Life .... Ms. Carrie VATH

Southwestern Oregon Community College (C)

1988 Newmark Avenue, Coos Bay OR 97420-2911
County: Coos FICE Identification: 003220
Unit ID: 210155
Telephone: (541) 888-2525 Carnegie Class: Assoc/MT-VT-High Trad
FAX Number: (541) 888-7285 Calendar System: Quarter
URL: www.socc.edu
Established: 1961 Annual Undergrad Tuition & Fees (In-District): $6,260
Enrollment: 1,537 Coed
Affiliation or Control: Local IRS Status: 501(c)3
Highest Offering: Associate Degree
Accreditation: NW, ACFEI, EMT, NAEYC

01 President ....Dr. Patty SCOTT
11 VP Administrative Services ....Mr. Jeff WHITEY
05 VP Instructional Services .... Dr. Ali MAGEEHON
84 VP Enrollment & Student Services ....Ms. Meredith STONE
12 Executive Dean Curry Campus .... Mr. Doug BUNN
72 Dean of Career and Technical Educ ....Mr. Daniel KOOPMAN
20 Dean of LDC .... Mr. Mike WINSTON
84 Dean of Enrollment Services ....Vacant
111 Dean of Advancement/Alumni Rels ....Ms. Elise HAMNER
37 Dean Financial Aid/Registration .... Ms. Avena SINGH
121 Dean Student Success/Transfer .... Mr. Jared GARDNER
13 Exec Director Integrated Technology ....Mr. Carl GERISCH
88 Exec Director OCCI (Culinary) ....Mr. Randy TORRES
41 Athletic Director .... Dr. Mike HERBERT
19 Director Campus Safety .... Mr. Joe THOMAS
18 Director Facilities Services .... Ms. Emerald BRUNETT
06 Registrar .... Ms. Avena SINGH
15 Chief Human Resources Officer ....Ms. Rachele LYON
10 Executive Director Business Office ....Ms. Kathy DIXON
66 Director Nursing ....Ms. Joannie MILLER
39 Director Residence Life .... Mr. Joe BELTER
88 Director SOCC Business Dev Center .... Mr. John BACON
38 Director Student Support Services .... Ms. Michele BENOIT
40 Manager Bookstore ....Ms. Clarissa RICKELS
09 Dir Institutional Effectiveness ....Ms. Ciera MILKEWICZ
04 Exec Asst to the Pres/Board of Educ ....Ms. Dina LASKEY
26 Chief Public Relations/Marketing ....Ms. Anne MATTHEWS

Sumner College (D)

8338 NE Alderwood Road, Ste 100, Portland OR 97220
County: Multnomah FICE Identification: 021049
Unit ID: 208512
Telephone: (503) 972-6230 Carnegie Class: Spec 2-yr-Health
FAX Number: (503) 952-0010 Calendar System: Other
URL: www.sumnercollege.edu
Established: 1974 Annual Undergrad Tuition & Fees: N/A
Enrollment: 464 Coed
Affiliation or Control: Proprietary IRS Status: Proprietary
Highest Offering: Baccalaureate
Accreditation: ABHES

01 President ....Joanna S. RUSSELL

Tillamook Bay Community College (E)

4301 3rd Street, Tillamook OR 97141
County: Tillamook Identification: 666647
Unit ID: 420723
Telephone: (503) 842-8222 Carnegie Class: Assoc/HT-High Non
FAX Number: (503) 842-8336 Calendar System: Quarter
URL: www.tillamookbaycc.edu
Established: 1981 Annual Undergrad Tuition & Fees (In-District): $4,176
Enrollment: 497 Coed
Affiliation or Control: State/Local IRS Status: 501(c)3
Highest Offering: Associate Degree
Accreditation: NW

01 President ....Dr. Ross L. TOMLIN
05 VP of Instruction .... Dr. Teresa RIVENES
10 VP of Finance ....Ms. Kyra WILLIAMS
30 Exec Dir Development/Col Advance .... Mrs. Heidi LUQUETTE
32 VP of Student Services .... Mrs. Rhoda HANSON
15 Dir Hum Resources/Facilities/Safety ....Mr. Pat RYAN
09 Dir of Institutional Effectiveness .... Ms. Erin MCCARLEY

Treasure Valley Community College (F)

650 College Boulevard, Ontario OR 97914-3423
County: Malheur FICE Identification: 003221
Unit ID: 210234
Telephone: (541) 881-8822 Carnegie Class: Assoc/HT-Mix Trad/Non
FAX Number: (541) 881-5510 Calendar System: Quarter
URL: www.tvcc.cc
Established: 1961 Annual Undergrad Tuition & Fees (In-District): $5,760
Enrollment: 1,470 Coed
Affiliation or Control: Local IRS Status: 501(c)3
Highest Offering: Associate Degree
Accreditation: NW, ADNUR

01 President .... Dr. Dana YOUNG
05 Vice President of Academic Affairs .... Mr. Eddie ALVES
11 Vice Pres Admin Services ....Ms. Shirley HAIDLE
32 Vice President of Student Services .... Mr. Travis MCFETRIDGE
08 Librarian .... Ms. Tara DOMINICK
26 Assoc VP College/Public Relations ....Ms. Abby LEE
37 Financial Aid Director ....Ms. Diahann DERRICK
13 Director Information Technology .... Mr. Scott CARPENTER
07 Director of Admissions .... Ms. Stephanie OESTER
15 Director of Human Resources ....Ms. Anne-Marie KELSO
51 Director of Continuing Education .... Ms. Andrea TESTI
41 Athletic Director .... Mr. Andy WARD
09 Dir of Institutional Effectiveness ....Ms. Nino KALATOZI
102 TVCC Foundation Exec Dir ....Ms. Cathy YASUDA
40 Bookstore Manager ....Mr. Kjetil ROM
04 Executive Asst to President .... Ms. Gina ROPER
39 Director Student Housing ....Ms. Kristine NEEDS
07 Director Admissions/Student Success .... Mr. Travis MCFETRIDGE

Umpqua Community College (G)

1140 Umpqua College Road, Roseburg OR 97470
County: Douglas FICE Identification: 003222
Unit ID: 210270
Telephone: (541) 440-4600 Carnegie Class: Assoc/MT-VT-High Non
FAX Number: (541) 440-4637 Calendar System: Quarter
URL: www.umpqua.edu
Established: 1964 Annual Undergrad Tuition & Fees (In-District): $5,297
Enrollment: 2,140 Coed
Affiliation or Control: Local IRS Status: 501(c)3
Highest Offering: Associate Degree
Accreditation: NW, DA, EMT

01 President .... Dr. Rachel POKRANDT
05 Provost .... Dr. Kacy CRABTREE
10 CFO .... Ms. Natalya BROWN
20 Asst Vice President of Academics ....Ms. Danielle HASKETT
84 Asst VP Enrollment/Student Services .... Ms. Missy OLSON
37 Director of Financial Aid .... Ms. Michelle BERGMANN
13 Director Informational Technology ....Mr. Tim HILL
08 Director of Library Services ....Ms. Mireille KOTOKLO
103 Dean Community Educ & Partnership .... Ms. Robin VAN WINKLE
09 Director Institutional Research ....Mr. Steve ROGERS
15 Director of Human Resources ....Ms. Kelley PLUEARD
04 Executive Asst to President & Board ....Ms. Robynne WILGUS
06 Director of Registration & Records .... Ms. Brenna HOBBS
18 Director of Facilities & Security ....Mr. Jess MILLER
111 Chief Advancement Officer .... Ms. Tiffany COLEMAN
41 Athletic Director ....Mr. Craig JACKSON
96 Purchasing Manager ....Mr. Jules DEGIULIO

University of Oregon (H)

1585 E. 13th Avenue, Eugene OR 97403
County: Lane FICE Identification: 003223
Unit ID: 209551
Telephone: (541) 346-1000 Carnegie Class: DU-Highest
FAX Number: N/A Calendar System: Quarter
URL: www.uoregon.edu
Established: 1876 Annual Undergrad Tuition & Fees (In-State): $13,857
Enrollment: 21,752 Coed
Affiliation or Control: State IRS Status: 501(c)3
Highest Offering: Doctorate
Accreditation: NW, AAQEP, ART, CEA, CIDA, CLPSY, COPSY, IPSY, JOUR, LAW, LSAR, MFCD, MUS, PCSAS, PLNG, SCPSY, SP, SPAA

01 President .... Mr. Michael H. SCHILL
100 Sr Advisor/Chief of Staff to Pres ....Mr. Greg J. STRIPP
05 Provost & Senior Vice President ....Dr. Patrick PHILLIPS
10 VP Finance & Admin & CFO .... Ms. Jamie H. MOFFITT
32 VP Student Life ....Dr. Kevin MARBURY
111 VP University Advancement .... Mr. Michael C. ANDREASEN
46 Interim VP Research & Innovation .... Dr. Cassandra MOSELEY
26 VP University Communications .... Ms. Richie HUNTER
43 Vice President and General Counsel .... Mr. Kevin REED
20 VProv Undergrad Educ/Stdnt Success ...... Dr. Kimberly JOHNSON
28 VP Equity & Inclusion ....Dr. Yvette M. ALEX-ASSENSOH
84 VP Student Svcs & Enrollment Mgmt ....Dr. Roger J. THOMPSON
13 Vice Prov Information Services/CIO .... Ms. Jessie MINTON
85 Dean/Vice Provost Global Engagement ....Dr. Dennis C. GALVAN
86 Assoc Vice Pres Federal Affairs ....Ms. Betsy A. BOYD
86 Assoc VP State & Cmty Affairs ....Mr. Hans BERNARD
29 AVP Alumni Affairs/Exec Dir UOAA ....Mr. Raphe BECK
06 University Registrar ....Ms. Julia POMERENK
07 Director of Admissions ....Mr. Jim H. RAWLINS
08 Vice Provost & University Librarian ....Ms. Alicia SALAZ
21 Dir Business Affairs and Controller ....Mr. Kelly B. WOLF
37 Director Student Financial Aid .... Mr. Jim J. BROOKS
36 Director of Career Center .... Mr. Paul TIMMINS
15 Chief Human Resources Officer .... Mr. Mark SCHMELZ
18 Assoc VP Planning & Facilities Mgmt .... Mr. Mike HARWOOD
22 AVP/Chief Civil Rights & Title IX ...... Ms. Nicole COMMISSIONG
41 Director Intercollegiate Athletics ....Mr. Rob A. MULLENS
56 Executive Dir UO Academic Extension .... Ms. Sandra K. GLADNEY
49 Dean College Arts & Science .... Dr. Bruce BLONIGEN
48 Dean College of Design ....Dr. Adrian PARR
50 Dean College of Business ....Dr. Sarah NUTTER
53 Dean College of Education ....Dr. Randy W. KAMPHAUS
60 Dean School of Journalism/Comm ...... Dr. Juan-Carlos MOLLEDA
58 Vice Provost for Graduate Studies .... Ms. Krista CHRONISTER
61 Dean School of Law .... Ms. Marcilynn BURKE

64 Dean School of Music & Dance ...... Dr. Sabrina MADISON-CANNON
92 Interim Dean Clark Honors College ...... Ms. Carol STABILE
09 Director of Institutional Research ...... Dr. JP MONROE
38 Dir Counseling & Testing Center ...... Dr. Shelly K. KERR
96 Chief Procurement Officer ...... Mr. Greg SHABRAM
101 Secretary of the University/Board ...... Mr. Tim INMAN
19 Chief of Police ...... Mr. Matthew CARMICHAEL
39 Director Student Housing ...... Mr. Michael M. GRIFFEL
114 Vice Provost Budget & Planning ...... Dr. Brad SHELTON
90 Director Academic Technology ...... Vacant
106 Assoc VP Online & Distance Educ ...... Ms. Carol GERING
30 Senior Assoc VP for Development ...... Mr. Paul ELSTONE
86 Senior Director State Affairs ...... Ms. Jenna ADAMS-KALLOCH

University of Portland (A)

5000 N Willamette Boulevard, Portland OR 97203-5798
County: Multnomah FICE Identification: 003224
Unit ID: 209825
Telephone: (503) 943-8000 Carnegie Class: Masters/M
FAX Number: (503) 943-7491 Calendar System: Semester
URL: www.up.edu
Established: 1901 Annual Undergrad Tuition & Fees: $49,644
Enrollment: 3,999 Coed
Affiliation or Control: Independent Non-Profit IRS Status: 501(c)3
Highest Offering: Doctorate
Accreditation: NW, CAEP, MUS, NURSE, SW, THEA

01 President ...... Rev. Mark L. POORMAN, CSC
05 Provost ...... Dr. Herbert A. MEDINA
41 Vice President for Athletics ...... Mr. Scott R. LEYKAM
10 Int Vice Pres for Financial Affairs ...... Mr. Eric C. BARGER
43 Vice Pres & General Counsel ...... Ms. Andrea M. BARTON
15 Vice President for Human Resources ...... Vacant
26 Vice Pres for Mktg & Communications ...... Mr. Michael E. LEWELLEN
32 Vice President for Student Affairs ...... Rev. John J. DONATO, CSC
11 Vice Pres for University Operations ...... Mr. James B. RAVELLI
111 Vice Pres for Univ Relations ...... Mr. Bryce STRANG
20 Associate Provost ...... Ms. Elise M. MOENTMANN
85 Asst Provost Intl Educ/Diver/Inclus ...... Dr. Eduardo R. CONTRERAS
35 Assoc VP for Student Development ...... Dr. Matthew J. RYGG
88 Special Asst to President ...... Mr. Evan LEADEM
07 Dean of Admissions ...... Mr. Jason S. MCDONALD
49 Interim Dean of Arts & Sciences ...... Dr. Laura A. MCLARY
50 Interim Dean of Business ...... Dr. Gary L. MALECHA
53 Dean of Education ...... Dr. John L. WATZKE
54 Dean of Engineering ...... Dr. Brian FABIEN
08 Dean of Library ...... Ms. Xan ARCH
66 Dean of Nursing ...... Dr. Casey R. SHILLAM
18 Assoc VP Const & Facilities ...... Mr. David HOBBS
30 Assoc VP for Development ...... Ms. Amy EATON
88 Assoc VP for Land Use & Planning ...... Ms. Trang LAM
29 Director Alumni Relations ...... Ms. Gina AMATO YAZZOLINO
40 Director Bookstore ...... Ms. Erin L. CAVE
42 Director Campus Ministry ...... Rev. James T. GALLAGHER, CSC
36 Director Career Services ...... Ms. Amy E. CAVANAUGH
112 Dir Gift Planning & Major Gifts ...... Ms. Sharon K. HOGAN
09 Director Institutional Research ...... Ms. Elizabeth LEE
18 Director Facilities Planning Constr ...... Mr. Paul J. LUTY
27 Director Marketing and Comm ...... Vacant
19 Director Public Safety ...... Ms. Sara WESTBROOK
39 Director Residence Life ...... Mr. Andrew WEINGARTEN
37 Director Student Financial Aid ...... Ms. Janet K. TURNER
104 Director of Studies Abroad ...... Ms. Kallan PICHA
35 Director Student Activities ...... Mr. Jeromy A. KOFFLER
88 Director University Events ...... Mr. Joe D. KALEEL
23 Director University Health Center ...... Ms. Carol A. DELL'OLIVER
25 Associate Director of Grants ...... Ms. Annie M. KAFFEN
21 Interim Controller ...... Ms. Lori WATSON
06 Registrar ...... Ms. Roberta D. LINDAHL
13 Chief Info Technology Officer ...... Mr. Curtis R. PEDERSON
04 Administrative Asst to President ...... Ms. Kathy M. SIMEK
04 Admin Asst to Office of President ...... Ms. Kristin S. NIELSEN

University of Western States (B)

8000 NE Tillamook Street, Portland OR 97213
County: Multnomah FICE Identification: 012309
Unit ID: 210438
Telephone: (503) 256-3180 Carnegie Class: Spec-4-yr-Other Health
FAX Number: (503) 251-5723 Calendar System: Quarter
URL: www.uws.edu
Established: 1904 Annual Undergrad Tuition & Fees: N/A
Enrollment: 1,195 Coed
Affiliation or Control: Independent Non-Profit IRS Status: 501(c)3
Highest Offering: Doctorate
Accreditation: NW, CHIRO

01 President ...... Dr. Joseph BRIMHALL
03 Executive Vice President ...... Dr. Rosalia MESSINA
11 Sr VP of Finance and Administration ...... Mr. Glenn FORD
10 Chief Business Officer ...... Ms. Lisa LOPEZ
05 Provost/VP Academic Affairs ...... Dr. Dana SIMS
88 Special Assistant to the President ...... Dr. Patrick BROWNE
23 Chief Medical Officer ...... Dr. Bill MOREAU
45 VP Innovation/Strategic Initiative ...... Dr. Sara MATHOV
88 Associate Dean Clinical Internship ...... Dr. Stanley EWALD
13 Interim Chief Technology Officer ...... Mr. Mark STALEY
20 Dean of Teaching and Learning ...... Dr. Denise DALLMANN
32 Assoc Vice Pres of Student Affairs ...... Ms. Elena HOWELLS
26 AVP University Comm & Marketing ...... Ms. Megan NUGENT
15 Director Human Resources ...... Ms. Kathleen CANNON
06 Registrar ...... Ms. Michelle DODGE
08 University Librarian ...... Ms. Stephanie DEBNER
63 Dean College of Chiropractic ...... Dr. Kathleen GALLIGAN
58 Dean College of Graduate Studies ...... Dr. Alisa BATES
108 Director Academic Assessment ...... Dr. Cecelia MARTIN
10 Exec Dir Clinic Business Operation ...... Ms. Monika MAJCHRZAK
07 Executive Director of Admissions ...... Mr. Joshua CIVIELLO
117 Executive Director of Emergency Mgt ...... Mr. Sean SPELLECY
114 Exec Dir of Budget & Resource Plng ...... Ms. Tonja HODGKINSON
88 Director of Capital Planning/Devel ...... Mr. Chris ADAMS
37 Director Financial Aid ...... Ms. Kim LAMBORN
31 Director Community Engagement ...... Ms. Alisa FAIRWEATHER
26 Director of Marketing ...... Ms. Jennifer ROSENBERGER
30 Development Officer ...... Ms. Amy LODHOLZ
29 Alumni Relations Manager ...... Ms. Chelsea NORDBY
09 AVP Institutional Effectiveness ...... Dr. Rachael PANDZIK
108 Dir Inst Appraisal and Accred ...... Dr. Susan DONOFF
38 Dir Clinical Mental Hlth Counseling ...... Dr. Michelle COX
28 Dir of Diversity/Equity & Inclusion ...... Ms. Abolade MAJEKOBAJE
35 Director of Student Svcs Online ...... Ms. Rachel HASSE
117 Director of Risk Management ...... Mr. David MUSIAL
35 Director of Student Svcs On-Campus ...... Ms. Jenna GERACITANO
109 Director of Auxiliary Services ...... Ms. Amber LYSIAK
04 Exec Assistant Office of the Pres ...... Ms. Miranda HOLTMANN
25 Research/Inst Review Board Admin ...... Ms. Leslie TAKAKI

Warner Pacific University (C)

2219 SE 68th Avenue, Portland OR 97215
County: Multnomah FICE Identification: 003225
Unit ID: 210304
Telephone: (503) 517-1020 Carnegie Class: Bac-Diverse
FAX Number: (503) 517-1350 Calendar System: Semester
URL: www.warnerpacific.edu
Established: 1937 Annual Undergrad Tuition & Fees: $19,860
Enrollment: 466 Coed
Affiliation or Control: Church Of God IRS Status: 501(c)3
Highest Offering: Master's
Accreditation: NW, SW

01 President ...... Dr. Brian L. JOHNSON
05 Vice Pres Acad Affs/Dean of Faculty ...... Dr. Luke GOBLE
10 VP Finance/Chief Financial Officer ...... Mr. Doug WADE
111 VP Inst Advancement/External Rels ...... Ms. Wendy MARSH
32 VP Student Life/Dean of Students ...... Dr. Ashlee SPEARMAN
84 VP for Enrollment and Marketing ...... Dr. Molly S. SMITH
20 Assoc VP for Academic Affairs ...... Dr. Lori K. JASS
37 Ex Dir Stdnt Financial Svcs/Fin Aid ...... Ms. Nancy DRUMMOND
07 Director of Admissions ...... Mr. Andrew R. WRIGHT
41 Athletics Director ...... Mr. Michael WILSON
08 Director of Library Services ...... Dr. Lishi KWASITSU
06 Registrar ...... Dr. Marlo WATERS
13 Director Information Technology ...... Dr. Max SIGANDER
29 Dir Alumni Relations/Annual Giving ...... Ms. Stephanie HARVEY
42 Campus Pastor ...... Ms. Michelle LANG-RAYMOND
35 Associate Dean of Students ...... Ms. Felita SINGLETON
18 Director of Facilities ...... Mr. Dean JENKS
15 Director of Human Resources ...... Mrs. Rachel LEA
09 Dir of Assessment/Inst Research ...... Mr. Ben MOLL
26 Dir Marketing/Communications ...... Dr. Molly S. SMITH
38 Director Student Counseling ...... Mr. Gene HALL
21 Controller ...... Mrs. Cheryl ANDERSON
121 Director of Academic Success ...... Dr. Jonathan MANZ
04 Admin Assistant to the President ...... Ms. Joy HOWARD
19 Director of Campus Safety ...... Mr. Daniel ROBLES

Western Oregon University (D)

345 N Monmouth Avenue, Monmouth OR 97361-1394
County: Polk FICE Identification: 003209
Unit ID: 210429
Telephone: (503) 838-8000 Carnegie Class: Masters/L
FAX Number: (503) 838-8474 Calendar System: Quarter
URL: www.wou.edu
Established: 1856 Annual Undergrad Tuition & Fees (In-State): $10,194
Enrollment: 4,554 Coed
Affiliation or Control: State IRS Status: 501(c)3
Highest Offering: Beyond Master's But Less Than Doctorate
Accreditation: NW, CACREP, CAEPN

01 President ...... Dr. Jay KENTON
03 Vice President & General Counsel ...... Mr. Ryan HAGEMANN
05 Provost ...... Dr. Rob WINNINGHAM
32 Vice President Student Affairs ...... Dr. Gary DUKES
10 VP Finance & Administration ...... Dr. Ana KARAMAN
20 Interim Assoc VP Academic Programs ...... Dr. Erin BAUMGARTNER
15 VP Human Resources/Dir AAEO ...... Vacant
32 Asst VP Student Engagement ...... Mr. Patrick MOSER
86 Associate VP for Public Affairs ...... Mr. Dave MCDONALD
108 Assoc Provost Program Development ...... Ms. Sue MONAHAN
35 Dean of Students ...... Ms. Tina M. FUCHS
49 Dean Col Liberal Arts & Sciences ...... Dr. Kathy CASSITY
53 Dean College of Education ...... Dr. Mark GIROD
43 Deputy General Counsel ...... Mr. Carson CAMPBELL
06 Registrar ...... Ms. Amy CLARK
111 Executive Director of Advancement ...... Ms. Erin MCDONOUGH
08 Dean Hamersly Library/Acad Innov ...... Chelle BATCHELOR
13 Dir University Computing Solutions ...... Mr. William KERNAN
18 Director Facilities Services ...... Mr. Michael SMITH
19 Director University Public Safety ...... Ms. Rebecca CHILES
23 Dir Student Health/Counseling Ctr ...... Ms. Beth SCROGGINS
26 Dir Public Relations/Communications ...... Ms. Denise VISUANO
37 Director Financial Aid ...... Ms. Kella HELYER
41 Athletic Director ...... Ms. Randi LYDUM
46 Dir of Teaching Research Institute ...... Vacant
28 Asst Dir Multicultural Student Svcs ...... Ms. Luanne CARRILLO
04 Executive Asst to President ...... Mrs. LouAnn VICKERS
21 Controller/Business Services ...... Mr. Gabe DOUGHERTY
07 Director of Admissions ...... Mr. Rob FINDTNER
09 Director of Institutional Research ...... Dr. Abdus SHAHID

Western Seminary (E)

5511 SE Hawthorne Boulevard, Portland OR 97215-3399
County: Multnomah FICE Identification: 007178
Unit ID: 210368
Telephone: (503) 517-1800 Carnegie Class: Spec-4-yr-Faith
FAX Number: (503) 517-1801 Calendar System: Semester
URL: https://www.westernseminary.edu/
Established: 1927 Annual Graduate Tuition & Fees: N/A
Enrollment: 826 Coed
Affiliation or Control: Independent Non-Profit IRS Status: 501(c)3
Highest Offering: Doctorate; No Undergraduates
Accreditation: NW, CACREP, THEOL

01 President ...... Dr. Charles CONNIRY
10 Interim COO ...... Ms. Carolyn RAYBACK
05 VP Academic Affairs/Dean of Faculty ...... Dr. Josh MATHEWS
111 VP of Advancement ...... Mr. Robert JONES
32 Chief Student Affairs/Life Officer ...... Ms. Rebekah BUCHTERKIRCHEN
20 Associate Academic Dean ...... Ms. Julia MAYO
06 Registrar ...... Cynthia MATHAI
21 Controller ...... Mr. Jonathan GIBSON
35 Director of Student Services ...... Mr. Andy PELOQUIN
13 Director of Information Services ...... Mr. Sean GORDON
37 Financial Aid Director ...... Mr. Luke TODD
106 Asst Director of Distance Education ...... Mr. Jon RAIBLEY
15 Human Resources Director ...... Ms. Ashley MITCHELL
08 Library Director ...... Mr. Matthew THIESEN
26 Director of Marketing ...... Mr. Ben HOFFMAN
18 Chief Facilities/Physical Plant ...... Mr. Cliff STEIN
106 Director of Distance Education ...... Mr. Andrew PACK
07 Director of Admissions ...... Ms. Allison MURPHY
04 Admin Assistant to the President ...... Ms. Kelly BORROR

Willamette University (F)

900 State Street, Salem OR 97301-3930
County: Marion FICE Identification: 003227
Unit ID: 210401
Telephone: (503) 370-6300 Carnegie Class: Bac-A&S
FAX Number: (503) 370-6148 Calendar System: Semester
URL: www.willamette.edu
Established: 1842 Annual Undergrad Tuition & Fees: $53,834
Enrollment: 1,866 Coed
Affiliation or Control: Independent Non-Profit IRS Status: 501(c)3
Highest Offering: Doctorate
Accreditation: NW, CEA, LAW, MUS, SPAA

01 President ...... Dr. Stephen THORSETT
05 Sr VP for Academic/Student Affairs ...... Dr. Carol LONG
10 VP for Finance and Treasurer ...... Mr. Dan VALLES
111 Vice President for Advancement ...... Ms. Shelby RADCLIFFE
07 VP & Dean of Admission ...... Ms. Mary RANDERS
13 Vice President and CIO ...... Ms. Jacqueline BARRETTA
32 VP Student Affairs/Dean of Students ...... Ms. Lisa LANDREMAN
49 Dean of the College Liberal Arts ...... Dr. Ruth P. FEINGOLD
61 Dean of the College of Law ...... Mr. Brian GALLINI
50 Dean Graduate School Management ...... Dr. Orn BODVARSSON
42 Chaplain ...... Rev. Ineda ADENSANYA
23 Director of Bishop Wellness Center ...... Mr. Donald A. THOMSON
88 Director Center Dispute Resolution ...... Dr. Aaron SIMOWITZ
91 Director Administrative Computing ...... Mr. Harvey J. PRUDHOMME
37 Director Student Financial Aid ...... Ms. Patricia K. HOBAN
09 Director of Institutional Research ...... Dr. Kelley STRAWN
06 University Registrar ...... Ms. Laura JACOBS ANDERSON
08 University Librarian ...... Mr. Craig MILBERG
21 Controller ...... Mr. Kenneth PIFER
40 Bookstore Manager ...... Mr. Dan C. VALLES
104 Director of International Education ...... Mr. Kris LOU
41 Athletic Director ...... Mr. Rob PASSAGE
29 Assoc VP Alumni & Parent Relations ...... Mr. Tyler REICH
112 Assoc Dir of Dev for Gift Planning ...... Ms. Cathy M. GASKIN
15 VP Human Resources/Risk Management ...... Ms. Shana SECHRIST
35 Assoc Dean Stdnts/Stdnt Activities ...... Ms. Lisa C. HOLLIDAY
36 Director Career Development ...... Ms. Mandy DEVEREUX
28 Director of Multicultural Affairs ...... Mr. Gordon K. TOYAMA
18 Director Facilities Management ...... Mr. Gary GRIMM
26 Chief Communications Officer ...... Mr. Tim COBB
19 Director Security/Safety ...... Mr. Ross STOUT
04 Executive Assistant to President ...... Ms. Elizabeth GARLAND
100 Chief of Staff ...... Ms. Colleen KAWAHARA
22 Title IX Coordinator ...... Ms. Darci HEROY
39 Director of Housing & Conferences ...... Mr. Scott ETHERTON
43 General Counsel ...... Ms. Yvonne TAMAYO

PENNSYLVANIA

Albright College (G)

N 13th & Bern Streets, PO Box 15234,
Reading PA 19612-5234
County: Berks FICE Identification: 003229
Unit ID: 210571

Telephone: (610) 921-2381 Carnegie Class: Bac-A&S
FAX Number: (610) 921-7530 Calendar System: 4/1/4
URL: www.albright.edu
Established: 1856 Annual Undergrad Tuition & Fees: $26,688
Enrollment: 1,584 Coed
Affiliation or Control: United Methodist IRS Status: 501(c)3
Highest Offering: Master's
Accreditation: M

01 President Dr. Jacquelyn S. FETROW
05 Provost/SVP Academic Affairs Dr. Karen CAMPBELL
10 Vice Pres Administration/Finance Mr. Gregory L. FULMER
111 Vice President Advancement Ms. Wendy PARSONS
32 SVP Student & Campus Life/CHO Ms. Samantha WESNER
26 Vice President for Communications Ms. Jennifer STOUDT
13 VP DSI & Chief Information Officer Mr. Jason HOERR
89 Assoc Dean First Yr Exp/Acad Affs Dr. Robert SEESENGOOD
08 Interim Director Library Services Ms. Sandy STUMP
102 Dir of The Fund for Albright/ADV Ms. Caitlin KAMERER
21 AVP & Controller/F&SP Mr. Rick W. MELCHER
37 Director of Financial Aid Ms. Chris HANLON
35 Actg Dean of Stdnts/Title IX Coord Ms. Becky ACHEY
06 Associate Registrar Ms. Debra BAVER
36 Director Career Development/AA Ms. Laura KLINE
39 Director of Residential Life/SCL Ms. Amanda HIGGINBOTHAM
38 Director of Counseling/SCL Dr. Brenda J. INGRAM-WALLACE
18 Director Facilities/Svcs/Opers Mr. Chuck MURPHY
41 Co-Athletic Director Mr. Richard E. FERRY
41 Co-Athletic Director Ms. Janice J. LUCK
19 Director of Public Safety Mr. Michael L. GROSS
40 Book Store Manager Ms. Heather SHERMAN
42 Chaplain/SCL RevDr. Sudha ALLITT
42 Chaplin/SCL Rev. Melvin SENSENIG
42 Chaplain/SCL Rev. Ibrahim BANGURA
15 Director of Human Resources Ms. Kim HUBRIC
85 Dir of OSIL/Coord Multicultural Mr. Keith WALLS
09 Director of Institutional Research Vacant
25 Dir of Grants & Sponsored Programs Ms. Julie SWEITZER
92 Director Honors Program Dr. Julia F. HEBERLE
92 Director Honors Program Mr. Christopher J. CATONE
07 Director of Admission/EM Ms. Jennifer WILLIAMSON
88 Dir of Conferences/Pres Office Ms. Lois A. KUBINAK
100 Chief of Staff/President's Office Ms. Kathy L. CAFONCELLI
88 Director of Schumo Center/SCL Ms. Alison BURKE
22 Dir of Stdnt Accessibility/Advocacy Ms. Sherry YOUNG
109 General Manager Dining Services/SCL Mr. Heath MCCORMICK
106 Dir Digital Learning & Innovation Vacant
112 Sr Dir Prospect Rsrch/Stewardship Ms. Jessica MORRIS
108 Dir Assessment/Inst Effectiveness Ms. Maria QUEERY

Allegheny College (A)

520 N Main Street, Meadville PA 16335-3902
County: Crawford FICE Identification: 003230
Unit ID: 210669
Telephone: (814) 332-3100 Carnegie Class: Bac-A&S
FAX Number: (814) 332-2796 Calendar System: Semester
URL: www.allegheny.edu
Established: 1815 Annual Undergrad Tuition & Fees: $50,980
Enrollment: 1,667 Coed
Affiliation or Control: United Methodist IRS Status: 501(c)3
Highest Offering: Baccalaureate
Accreditation: M

01 President Dr. Hilary L. LINK
03 Exec Vice President and COO Vacant
05 Provost & Dean of the College Dr. Ronald B. COLE
111 Vice Pres Institutional Advancement Mr. Matthew P. STINSON
84 Vice Pres for Enrollment Mgmt Ms. Ellen V. JOHNSON
32 VP Student Life/Dean of Students Ms. April THOMPSON
10 VP Finance & Administration/CFO Ms. Linda S. WETSELL
04 Assistant to the President Ms. Pamela S. HIGHAM
110 AVP Development & Alumni Affairs Mr. Philip R. FOXMAN
26 Vice President College Relations Ms. Susan SALTON
28 Dean for Institutional Diversity Ms. Kristin Nicole DUKES
20 Associate Provost Dr. Terry BENSEL
37 Senior Assoc Dir Financial Aid Ms. Natasha ECKART
108 VP for Info Svcs & Assessment Dr. Richard A. HOLMGREN
06 Assoc Provost/Int Registrar Ms. Jennifer DEARDEN
08 Director of the Library Dr. Richard A. HOLMGREN
15 Director of Human Resources Ms. Jennifer PADLAN
19 Director of Public Safety Mr. Jim BASINGER
44 Director of Annual Giving Ms. Sara PINEO
18 Director Physical Plant Vacant
13 Director of Enterprise Services Mr. Jason M. RAMSEY
41 Director of Athletics Mr. William ROSS
31 Director of Civic Engagement Dr. David RONCOLATO
38 Director of Counseling Center Dr. Trae YECKLEY
09 Director of Institutional Research Vacant
36 Director Career Education Mr. James FITCH
88 Associate Dean for Wellness Educ Ms. Gretchen BECK
42 Chaplain Dr. Jane Ellen NICKELL
88 Dir Center Political Participation Dr. Brian HARWARD
22 Director of Disability Services Mr. John J. MANGINE
57 Director of Art & Publications Ms. Penny M. DREXEL
27 Assoc Dir Marketing & Communication Mr. Jason ANDRACKI
40 Manager of Bookstore Vacant
96 Purchasing & Student Services Coord Ms. Kathleen M. CONAWAY

Allegany College of Maryland Bedford County Campus (B)

18 North River Lane, Everett PA 15537-1410
Telephone: (814) 652-9528 Identification: 770124
Accreditation: &M

† Branch campus of Allegany College of Maryland, Cumberland, MD

Alvernia University (C)

400 Saint Bernardine Street, Reading PA 19607-1799
County: Berks FICE Identification: 003233
Unit ID: 210775
Telephone: (610) 796-8200 Carnegie Class: Masters/M
FAX Number: (610) 777-6632 Calendar System: Semester
URL: www.alvernia.edu
Established: 1958 Annual Undergrad Tuition & Fees: $38,030
Enrollment: 2,560 Coed
Affiliation or Control: Roman Catholic IRS Status: 501(c)3
Highest Offering: Doctorate
Accreditation: M, ACBSP, CAATE, CACREP, NURSE, OT, PTA, SW

01 President Dr. John R. LOYACK
05 SVP & Provost Dr. Glynis FITZGERALD
10 VP/Chief Financial Officer Mr. Joshua HOFFMAN
111 VP for Institutional Advancement Mr. Thomas MINICK
84 SVP Enrollmt Managemt/Student Affs Ms. Mary-Alice OZECHOSKI
100 SVP & Chief of Staff Dr. John R. MCCLOSKEY, JR.
42 Asst to Pres/VP Mission & Ministry Vacant
26 VP Mktg & Comms/Chief PR Ofcr Vacant
31 Vice Pres for Cmty Engagement Dr. Rudy RUTH
13 Vice Pres & CIO Vacant
32 Dean of Students Ms. Karolina DREHER
35 Associate Dean of Students Ms. Abby SWATCHICK
06 Registrar Ms. Beki STEIN
21 Controller Vacant
92 Director Honors Program Dr. Victoria WILLIAMS
41 Director Athletics & Recreation Mr. Bill STILES
07 Dean of UG Admissions Vacant
09 Dean of Institutional Research Dr. Evelina PANAYOTOVA
15 Executive Director Human Resources Mrs. Allyson MULLIN
18 Dir of Facilities Planning Vacant
11 Director of Campus Operations Mr. Matthew BOARDER
36 Career Development Director Mrs. Megan ADUKAITIS
37 Sr Dir of Student Financial Svcs Ms. Christine SAADI
96 Procurement Manager Ms. Ann NAWROCKI
28 Dir of Multicultural Initiatives Vacant
113 Director of Student Billing Vacant
58 Dean of Graduate & Cont Studies Vacant
49 Dean College of HSS Dr. Elizabeth MATTEO
107 Dean of Professional Programs Ms. Karen S. THACKER
04 Executive Admin Assistant Ms. Sherry SHADE-REENOCK
19 Director of Public Safety Mr. Edward HEIM
08 Director of Library Ms. Christina STEFFY
25 Director of Grants Mr. Andrew REID
101 Secretary of the Institution/Board Dr. John R. MCCLOSKEY
104 Director Intl Student Recruitment Dr. Sibel AHI
108 Director Institutional Assessment Dr. Evelina PANAYOTOVA

The American College of Financial Services (D)

630 Allendale Rd, King of Prussia PA 19406
County: Montgomery FICE Identification: 033173
Unit ID: 210809
Telephone: (610) 526-1000 Carnegie Class: Spec-4-yr-Bus
FAX Number: (610) 526-1310 Calendar System: Other
URL: www.theamericancollege.edu
Established: 1927 Annual Undergrad Tuition & Fees: N/A
Enrollment: 5,723 Coed
Affiliation or Control: Independent Non-Profit IRS Status: 501(c)3
Highest Offering: Doctorate
Accreditation: M

01 President & CEO Mr. George NICHOLS, III
05 Executive Vice President & Provost Dr. Gwen HALL
20 Assoc Provost Faculty & Curriculum Dr. Kathleen IRWIN
111 VP Advancement/Alumni Rel Mr. Stephen J. GROURKE
15 VP Admin & Chief HR Officer Ms. Deborah GLENN
45 VP Organizational Effectiveness Mr. Bryan JOHNSON
32 Assoc VP Student Experience Mr. Rob HUGHES
04 Assistant to the President Ms. Jean C. MEYER
117 Chief Financial and Risk Officer Mr. Mark MONTGOMERY
26 Chief Marketing Officer Vacant
13 Chief Technology Officer Mr. Ed M. MCEVOY
88 AVP Accreditation Dr. Lynn WALLACE
06 Registrar Mr. Will JACOBS
08 Library Services Ms. Shiloa THOMAS
88 AVP/Director Assessments & Exams Ms. Diane M. HAMMONDS

Arcadia University (E)

450 S Easton Road, Glenside PA 19038-3295
County: Montgomery FICE Identification: 003235
Unit ID: 211088
Telephone: (215) 572-2900 Carnegie Class: Masters/L
FAX Number: (215) 572-0240 Calendar System: Semester
URL: www.arcadia.edu
Established: 1853 Annual Undergrad Tuition & Fees: $45,340
Enrollment: 3,300 Coed
Affiliation or Control: Independent Non-Profit IRS Status: 501(c)3
Highest Offering: Doctorate
Accreditation: M, ACBSP, ARCPA, ART, FEPAC, MPCAC, PH, PTA

01 President Dr. Ajay NAIR
05 Provost & VP Academic Affairs Dr. Jeff RUTENBECK
84 VP Enrollment Management Mr. Rakin HALL
10 VP of Finance and CFO Ms. Joan SINGLETON
43 General Counsel Ms. Margaret CALLAHAN
13 VP and Chief Information Officer Ms. Rashmi RADHAKRISHNAN
30 VP Development/Alumni Engagement Ms. Brigette BRYANT
26 VP for Marketing and Communications Ms. Laura BALDWIN
32 Dean of Students Mr. Andrew GORETSKY
18 Assoc VP Facilities/Capital Plng Mr. Thomas J. MACCHI
88 VP/Exec Dir Col of Global Studies Ms. Lorna STERN
21 Assoc VP Finance & COO TCGS Ms. Colleen BURKE
15 Assoc VP Human Resources Ms. Mary SWEENEY
20 Deputy Provost Dr. Thomas EGAN
06 Registrar Mr. William ELNICK
88 Sr Associate Registrar Mrs. Nicole M. ZUCKER
49 Dean College Arts & Sciences Dr. Rebecca KOHN
76 Dean College of Health Sciences Dr. Rebecca L. CRAIK
51 Coord Office of Continuing Studies Ms. Kathryn PHILLIPS
50 Dean School of Global Business Mr. Thomas M. BRINKER, JR.
58 Dean Graduate & Undergrad Studies Dr. Nancy ROSOFF
82 Dean International Affairs Dr. Warren HAFFAR
28 Assoc Dean Institutional Diversity Ms. Judith DALTON
35 Dean of Students Dr. Andrew GORETZKY
20 Assoc Dean Undergraduate Studies Mr. Bruce KELLER
88 Asst Dean Graduate Studies Ms. Mary Kate MCNULTY
109 Director Auxiliary Services Ms. Mimi BASSETTI
29 Director Alumni Relations Vacant
88 Director University Art Gallery Mr. Richard TORCHIA
41 Director Athletics & Recreation Mr. Brian GRANATA
88 Director Campus Visits and EM Ms. Kathleen BEARDSLEY
36 Director Career Education Ms. Marissa DEITCH
38 Director Counseling Services Ms. Amy HENNING
37 Exec Dir Financial Aid & Enroll Mgt Ms. Holly R. KIRKPATRICK
25 Director Sponsored Research Ms. Nataliia SHABLIA
88 Director of Academic Administration Ms. Kristin O. JUDGE
96 Purchasing Coordinator Ms. Jennifer SUDLOW
88 Payroll Manager Ms. Heather MAJOR
19 Director of Public Safety Ms. Ruth EVANS
88 Title IX Coordinator Ms. Nora NELLE
101 Executive Dir Board of Trustees Mr. Kevin MULDOON
88 Assoc Dean International Affairs Ms. Janice FINN
45 Director of Strategic Initiatives Mr. Joseph S. SUN
07 Asst Vice Pres of Admissions Ms. Collene PERNICELLO
04 Exec Assistant to the President Ms. April WANSER
09 Director of Institutional Research Ms. Bridget MILLER

Aspira City College (F)

4322 North 5th Street, Philadelphia PA 19140
County: Philadelphia FICE Identification: 031091
Unit ID: 214023
Telephone: (215) 455-2300 Carnegie Class: Spec 2-yr-Tech
FAX Number: N/A Calendar System: Semester
URL: www.aspiracitycollege.edu
Established: 1974 Annual Undergrad Tuition & Fees: $12,097
Enrollment: 5 Coed
Affiliation or Control: Independent Non-Profit IRS Status: 501(c)3
Highest Offering: Associate Degree
Accreditation: ACCSC

01 President Mr. Alfredo B. CALDERON
11 Int Campus Director Ms. Nerissa CONN
10 Chief Operating Officer Mr. Thomas DARDEN
90 Director of Education - IT Vacant
21 Controller Mr. Xinyan YI
37 Financial Aid Director Ms. Madeline SARGENT
07 Admissions Representative Mr. Karl ARNEY
36 Career Manager Vacant

Berks Technical Institute (G)

2205 Ridgewood Road, Wyomissing PA 19610-1168
County: Berks FICE Identification: 022539
Unit ID: 213534
Telephone: (610) 372-1722 Carnegie Class: Assoc/HVT-Mix Trad/Non
FAX Number: (610) 376-4863 Calendar System: Other
URL: www.berks.edu
Established: 1974 Annual Undergrad Tuition & Fees: N/A
Enrollment: 429 Coed
Affiliation or Control: Proprietary IRS Status: Proprietary
Highest Offering: Associate Degree
Accreditation: ACCSC

01 Executive Director Ms. Elizabeth VLASTOS
05 Dean Academic Affairs Mr. James REECE
07 Director of Admissions Mr. Eric SNYDER
37 Director Financial Aid Ms. Val WESSNER

Bidwell Training Center (H)

1815 Metropolitan Street, Pittsburgh PA 15233-2200
County: Allegheny FICE Identification: 031015
Unit ID: 211149
Telephone: (412) 323-4000 Carnegie Class: Spec 2-yr-Tech
FAX Number: (412) 325-7378 Calendar System: Quarter
URL: bidwelltraining.edu
Established: 1968 Annual Undergrad Tuition & Fees: N/A
Enrollment: N/A Coed
Affiliation or Control: Independent Non-Profit IRS Status: 501(c)3
Highest Offering: Associate Degree

Accreditation: ACCSC, MAC

01 Executive Director ... Dr. Kimberly RASSAU
11 Sr Dir Operations/Financial Aid ... Mr. Ken HUSELTON
06 Registrar ... Ms. Patricia THOMAS

Bryn Athyn College of the New Church (A)

PO Box 717, Bryn Athyn PA 19009-0717
County: Montgomery
FICE Identification: 003228
Unit ID: 210492
Telephone: (267) 502-2400
Carnegie Class: Bac-A&S
FAX Number: (215) 938-2658
Calendar System: Trimester
URL: www.brynathyn.edu
Established: 1876
Annual Undergrad Tuition & Fees: $25,449
Enrollment: 287
Coed
Affiliation or Control: Church of New Jerusalem
IRS Status: 501(c)3
Highest Offering: Master's
Accreditation: M

01 President ... Mr. Brian BLAIR
10 Chief Financial Officer ... Mr. Daniel T. ALLEN
05 Dean of Academics/Faculty ... Dr. Wendy CLOSTERMAN
73 Dean of Theological School ... Rev. Andrew M T. DIBB
32 Dean of Student Affairs ... Dr. Suzanne NELSON
84 VP Enrollment Management/ Admissions ... Mr. William LARROUSSE
08 Director of Swedenborg Library ... Mrs. Carol TRAVENY
41 Director of Athletics ... Dr. Suzanne NELSON
13 Chief Information Officer ... Ms. Lelia HOWARD
15 Director of Human Resources ... Ms. Melissa GAMBA
19 Director of Public Safety ... Mr. James KALAVIK
42 Chaplain ... Rev. Grant SCHNARR
04 Executive Asst to President ... Ms. Melodie GREER
14 Director Information Technology ... Mr. Richard DAUM
06 Registrar ... Ms. Casey SCHAUDER
37 Asst Director of Financial Aid ... Ms. Ashley MCCARRIE

Bryn Mawr College (B)

101 N Merion Avenue, Bryn Mawr PA 19010-2899
County: Montgomery
FICE Identification: 003237
Unit ID: 211273
Telephone: (610) 526-5000
Carnegie Class: Bac-A&S
FAX Number: (610) 526-7450
Calendar System: Semester
URL: www.brynmawr.edu
Established: 1885
Annual Undergrad Tuition & Fees: $54,440
Enrollment: 1,634
Female
Affiliation or Control: Independent Non-Profit
IRS Status: 501(c)3
Highest Offering: Doctorate
Accreditation: M, SW

01 President ... Kimberly CASSIDY
05 Provost ... Tim HARTE
49 Dean Undergraduate College ... Jennifer WALTERS
10 Chief Financial/Admin Officer ... Kari FAZIO
30 Chief Development Officer ... Bob MILLER
84 Chief Enrollment Officer ... Cheryl Lynn HORSEY
26 Chief Communications Officer ... Jesse GALE
08 Director Libraries/Chief Info Ofcr ... Gina SIESING
58 Dean of Graduate Studies ... Sharon BURGMAYER
28 Asst Dean Col of Access/Cmty Devel ... Vanessa CHRISTMAN
06 Registrar ... Kirsten O'BEIRNE
37 Director of Financial Aid ... Susan CHADWICK
19 Director of Public Safety ... Tom KING
41 Dir Athletics & Physical Education ... Kathleen TIERNEY
21 Controller ... Tijana STEFANOVIC
09 Director of Institutional Research ... Richard BARRY
18 Director of Facilities ... Nina BISBEE
07 Director of Admissions ... Marissa TURCHI
15 Director of Human Resources ... Martin MASTASCUSA
29 Director of Alumnae Relations ... Millie BOND
101 Secretary of the Institution/Board ... Ruth LINDEBORG

Bucknell University (C)

1 Dent Drive, Lewisburg PA 17837
County: Union
FICE Identification: 003238
Unit ID: 211291
Telephone: (570) 577-2000
Carnegie Class: Bac-A&S
FAX Number: (570) 577-3760
Calendar System: Semester
URL: www.bucknell.edu
Established: 1846
Annual Undergrad Tuition & Fees: $58,202
Enrollment: 3,726
Coed
Affiliation or Control: Independent Non-Profit
IRS Status: 501(c)3
Highest Offering: Master's
Accreditation: M, MUS

01 President ... Dr. John C. BRAVMAN
100 Chief of Staff ... Vacant
04 Exec Director President Office ... Ms. Carol M. KENNEDY
41 Director Athletics & Recreation ... Mr. Jermaine M. TRUAX
05 Provost ... Dr. Elisabeth MERMANN-JOZWIAK
20 Vice Provost ... Dr. Robert MIDKIFF
20 Assoc Provost ... Dr. Karen M. MORIN
49 Dean of Arts & Sciences ... Dr. Karl VOSS
50 Dean Freemen College of Management ... Dr. Raquel M. ALEXANDER
54 Dean of Engineering ... Dr. Erin JABLONSKI
92 Honors Council Chair ... Dr. Robert W. JACOB
88 Dir/Provost Business Operations ... Ms. Pamela A. BENFER
88 Dir Small Business Development Ctr ... Mr. Steven V. STUMBRIS
57 Exec Dir Weis Ctr Performing Arts ... Ms. Kathryn L. MAGUET
111 VP University Advancement ... Dr. Scott G. ROSEVEAR
30 Assoc VP University Advancement ... Mr. Joshua L. GRILL
30 Assoc VP University Advancement ... Ms. Kathleen GRAHAM
88 Executive Dir Leadership Gifts ... Mr. Mark SHARER
88 Senior Development Adviser ... Mr. Mark ELLIOTT
88 Exec Dir Adv Strategy Integration ... Ms. Lucille TARIN
88 Dir Parents Fund & Family Programs ... Vacant
88 Sr Adviser University Advancement ... Vacant
88 Dir Prospect Research & Mgmt ... Ms. Cynthia D. JANESCH
88 Dir Adv Marketing/Research/Strategy ... Ms. Tasha WILLIAMS
110 Dir Stewardship & Donor Relations ... Vacant
29 Executive Director Alumni Relations ... Ms. Kristin STETLER
44 Dir Annual Fund Individual Giving ... Ms. Abbey SCHECKTER
112 Director of Gift Planning ... Ms. Melissa M. DIEHL
102 Dir Corporate & Foundation Rels ... Mr. Edmond CLARKE
26 VP for Communications ... Ms. Heather JOHNS
27 Director of Media Relations ... Mr. Mike FERLAZZO
88 Senior Director Creative Services ... Vacant
10 VP Finance & Administration ... Ms. Eileen E. PETULA
21 Assoc VP/Treasurer and Controller ... Ms. Elizabeth D. STEWART
45 Director Business Planning ... Vacant
115 Dir of Investments ... Ms. Angela MOTTO
25 Executive Dir Sponsored Projects ... Mr. Robert GUTIERREZ
88 Assoc Controller Financial Services . Mr. Ronald E. STAUFFER, II
109 Director of Business Services ... Ms. Lori J. WILSON
114 Dir of Budget & Financial Modeling ... Vacant
88 Asst Controller ... Ms. Michelle M. HENDRICKS
88 Assoc Controller Accounting Svcs ... Mr. William D. GEORGE
88 Dir Financial Information Systems ... Ms. Pamela K. NOONE
113 Director of Disbursement Services ... Mr. Jody D. GRAYBILL
113 Bursar Services Manager ... Ms. Carol YOST
96 Director of Procurement Services ... Vacant
88 Exec Dir Events Management Office ... Ms. Dana M. MIMS
116 Director of Internal Audit ... Mr. Robert L. HOSTER
117 Dir Risk Management & Insurance ... Vacant
15 VP Human Resources ... Mr. Pierre D. JOANIS
16 Dir of Recruitment & Compensation ... Ms. Marcia J. COONEY
118 Director of HRIS & Benefits ... Ms. Cindy L. BILGER
09 Asst Prov Inst Research/Assessment ... Mr. Kevork T. HORISSIAN
28 Interim Assoc Provost Diversity ... Dr. Thelathia N. YOUNG
43 General Counsel ... Ms. Karin RILLEY
19 Chief of Public Safety ... Mr. Stephen J. BARILAR
18 AVP Facilities & Sustainability ... Mr. Jeffrey LOSS
88 Dir of Construction & Design ... Mr. Dominic SILVERS
13 VP Library & Information Technology ... Mr. Param S. BEDI
14 Exec Dir Enterprise Technologies ... Mr. Kevin WILLEY
105 Director of Web Services ... Vacant
119 Info Security Program Manager ... Mr. Brandon SEYMORE
32 Dean of Students ... Ms. Amy A. BADAL
35 Associate Dean of Students ... Ms. Lena CRAIN
35 Associate Dean of Students ... Ms. Denelle BROWN
35 Associate Dean of Students ... Ms. Kari M. CONRAD
35 Associate Dean of Students ... Ms. Jane GRASSADONIA
84 VP Enrollment Management ... Ms. Lisa KEEGAN
07 Dean of Admissions ... Mr. Kevin MATHES
37 Director Financial Aid ... Ms. Andrea C. LEITHNER STAUFFER
39 Dir of Housing Services ... Mr. Stephen J. APANEL
88 Dir Card Svcs & Student Transit ... Vacant
36 Exec Director Career Services ... Ms. Pamela G. KEISER
38 Dir Counseling & Stdnt Dev Ctr ... Dr. Kelly KETTLEWELL
22 Dir of Disability Services ... Ms. Heather L. FOWLER
42 University Chaplain ... Rev. Kurt D. NELSON
85 Dir International Student Services ... Ms. Jennifer E. FIGUEROA
104 Dir Global & Off-Campus Education ... Mr. Stephen K. APPIAH-PADI
88 Title IX Coord Clery Act Comp ... Ms. Samatha HART
88 Dir of Civic Engagement ... Ms. Theresa CUSIMANO
88 Director Women's Resource Center ... Vacant
88 Director Office of LGBTQ Resources ... Mr. William K. MCCOY
88 Director of Writing Center ... Ms. Deirdre M. O'CONNOR

Bucks County Community College (D)

275 Swamp Road, Newtown PA 18940-4106
County: Bucks
FICE Identification: 003239
Unit ID: 211307
Telephone: (215) 968-8000
Carnegie Class: Assoc/HT-Mix Trad/Non
FAX Number: (215) 968-8129
Calendar System: Semester
URL: www.bucks.edu
Established: 1964
Annual Undergrad Tuition & Fees (In-District): $9,098
Enrollment: 6,988
Coed
Affiliation or Control: Local
IRS Status: 501(c)3
Highest Offering: Associate Degree
Accreditation: M, ACBSP, ADNUR, ART, IFSAC, MLTAD, MUS, RAD

01 President ... Dr. Felicia L. GANTHER
05 Provost ... Ms. Lisa ANGELO
10 VP for Administrative Affairs & CFO ... Mr. Dennis W. MATTHEWS
121 VP Student Success ... Dr. Kelly KELLEWAY
13 VP Tech & Innovation/CIO ... Mr. Brant STEEN
21 Assoc VP Finance ... Mr. David JERDAN
88 Int Assoc VP Strategic Partnership ... Ms. Tracy TIMBY
28 Assoc VP Govt Rels & CDO ... Mr. Kevin ANTOINE
114 Exec Dir Budget & Internal Audit ... Ms. Loren HERBERT
09 Exec Dir Research/Assess/Analytics ... Dr. Maureen MCCARTHY
103 Exec Dir Workforce Development ... Ms. Susan HERRING
18 Exec Director Physical Plant ... Mr. Martin SNYDER
26 Exec Dir Marketing/Public Relations ... Ms. Megan SMITH
100 Chief of Staff & Board Liaison ... Ms. Kathleen C. FEDORKO
15 Exec Director Human Resources ... Dr. Patricia BRINING
96 Director of Purchasing ... Mr. Eric GULI
106 Associate Dean Bucks Online ... Ms. Susan DARLINGTON
37 Director Financial Aid ... Ms. Donna M. WILKOSKI
36 Director Career Services ... Ms. Sharon STEPHENS
32 Director Student Life & Athletics ... Mr. Matt J. CIPRIANO
19 Exec Dir Security & Safety ... Mr. Dennis MCCAULEY
08 Director Library Services ... Ms. Monica KUNA
07 Director of Admissions ... Ms. Joyce WHEATLEY
06 Registrar ... Ms. Rebecca BREUNINGER
102 Executive Director Foundation ... Ms. Christina MCGINLEY
68 Dean Kinesiology & Sport Studies ... Dr. Priscilla RICE
81 Dean STEM ... Dr. Shawn WILD
50 Interim Dean Business & Innovation ... Mr. Greg LUCE
57 Dean Arts ... Mr. John MATHEWS
83 Dean Social & Behavioral Sci ... Dr. Lynn DELLAPIETRA
76 Dean Health Sciences ... Dr. Constance CORRIGAN
79 Dean Language & Literature ... Ms. Nicole TRACEY
88 Dean Learning Resources ... Mr. Bill HEMMIG

Butler County Community College (E)

107 College Drive, Butler PA 16002
County: Butler
FICE Identification: 003240
Unit ID: 211343
Telephone: (724) 287-8711
Carnegie Class: Assoc/MT-VT-High Trad
FAX Number: (724) 285-6047
Calendar System: Semester
URL: www.bc3.edu
Established: 1965
Annual Undergrad Tuition & Fees (In-District): $8,250
Enrollment: 2,984
Coed
Affiliation or Control: Local
IRS Status: 501(c)3
Highest Offering: Associate Degree
Accreditation: M, ACBSP, ADNUR, MAC, PTAA

01 President ... Dr. Nicholas C. NEUPAUER
05 VP for Academic Affairs ... Dr. Belinda M. RICHARDSON
11 VP for Administration & Finance ... Mr. James A. HRABOSKY
32 VP Student Affairs/Enrollment Mgt ... Dr. G. Case WILLOUGHBY
10 Chief Business Officer ... Mr. Wm. Jake FRIEL
50 Interim Dean of Business ... Ms. Sherri MACK
83 Dean Social Science/Humanities ... Mr. Stephen M. JOSEPH
66 Dean of Nursing/Allied Health ... Dr. Patricia T. ANNEAR
72 Dean of Nat Science/Tech ... Mr. Matt KOVAC
106 Dean of Education Technology ... Ms. Ann MCCANDLESS
08 Dean of Library Services ... Mr. Martin J. MILLER
35 Dean of Students ... Dr. Joshua NOVAK
103 Dean of Workforce Development ... Ms. Lisa M. CAMPBELL
15 Exec Director Human Resources ... Ms. Christina M. FLEEGER
26 Exec Director of Comm & Marketing .. Ms. Jessica M. MATONAK
51 Director of Lifelong Learning ... Mr. Paul M. LUCAS
07 Dean of Admissions ... Ms. Amy PIGNATORE
13 Director of Information Technology ... Mr. Matt MILLER
32 Director of Student Life ... Mr. Rob A. SNYDER
09 Asst Dean of Institutional Research ... Ms. Sharla M. ANKE
18 Exec Director of Operations ... Mr. Brian R. OPITZ
12 Director of BC3 at Armstrong ... Ms. Karen ZAPP
12 Dir of BC3 at Lawrence Crossing ... Mr. Sean M. CARROLL
12 Director of BC3 at Cranberry ... Mr. Ryan KOCIELA
12 Director of BC3 at LindenPointe ... Ms. Lauren A. BUCHANAN
12 Director of BC3 at Brockway ... Dr. Jill MARTIN-REND
37 Director of Financial Aid ... Ms. Julianne E. LOUTTIT
41 Athletic Director ... Mr. Rob A. SNYDER
75 Coord of Business/Industry Trng ... Ms. Kathy STROBEL
102 Exec Director of the Foundation ... Vacant
19 Director of Campus Police/Security ... Mr. K. Scott RICHARDSON
88 Director of Children's Center ... Ms. Judith A. ZUZACK
88 Associate Director Admissions ... Ms. Morgan M. RIZZARDI
40 Bookstore Manager ... Mr. Richard A. BENKO
96 College Services/Purchasing Agent ... Ms. Nicole BARNES
105 Web Manager ... Mr. R. Dennis BIRKES
30 Int Assoc Dir of the Foundation ... Ms. Lynn ISMAIL
04 Administrative Asst to President ... Ms. Juliann SHEPTAK
22 Dir Affirmative Action/EEO ... Ms. Christina M. FLEEGER
06 Registrar ... Ms. Amy PIGNATORE
29 Director Alumni Affairs ... Ms. Bobbi Jo CORNETTI

Byzantine Catholic Seminary of Ss. Cyril and Methodius (F)

3605 Perrysville Avenue, Pittsburgh PA 15214-2229
County: Allegheny
FICE Identification: 041180
Unit ID: 444103
Telephone: (412) 321-8383
Carnegie Class: Spec-4-yr-Faith
FAX Number: (412) 321-9936
Calendar System: Semester
URL: www.bcs.edu
Established: 1950
Annual Graduate Tuition & Fees: N/A
Enrollment: 47
Coed
Affiliation or Control: Other
IRS Status: 501(c)3
Highest Offering: Master's; No Undergraduates
Accreditation: THEOL

01 Rector ... V.Rev. Robert M. PIPTA
32 Director of Human Formation ... Rev. Joel I. BARSTAD
05 Academic Dean ... Rev. Christiaan KAPPES
08 Director of Information Services ... Dr. Sandra COLLINS
11 Registrar/Dir of Seminary Opers ... Ms. Carol PRZYBORSKI
108 Director of Assessment ... Dr. Matthew K. MINERD
10 Chief Financial Officer ... Dcn. Robert SHALHOUB
15 Human Resources Administrator ... Ms. Helen KENNEDY

Cabrini University (G)

610 King of Prussia Road, Radnor PA 19087-3698
County: Delaware
FICE Identification: 003241
Unit ID: 211352
Telephone: (610) 902-8200
Carnegie Class: Masters/L

FAX Number: (610) 902-8204 Calendar System: Semester
URL: www.cabrini.edu
Established: 1957 Annual Undergrad Tuition & Fees: $33,845
Enrollment: 2,009 Coed
Affiliation or Control: Roman Catholic IRS Status: 501(c)3
Highest Offering: Doctorate
Accreditation: M, #ACBSP, SW

01 President Dr. Donald TAYLOR
05 Provost/VP Academic Affairs Dr. Chioma UGOCHUKWU
10 VP Finance & Treasurer Mr. Eric OLSON
111 VP Advancement & External Rels Mr. Stephen HIGHSMITH
32 VP Mission/DEI/Student Engagement Dr. Angela CAMPBELL
84 VP of Enrollment Management Mr. George WALTER
100 Chief of Staff/Sr VP Strat Init Mr. Brian EURY
26 Exec Dir Marketing & Communication Ms. Linda BOYK
35 Dean of Students Dr. Stephen RUPPRECHT
50 Dean School Business & Prof Studies Dr. Tim MANTZ
53 Dean School of Education Dr. Beverly BRYDE
49 Dean School of Arts & Sciences Dr. Richard THOMPSON
04 Exec Asst to the President & VPIA Ms. Claire CLUTE
06 Registrar Mr. Gerard DONAHUE
08 Library Director Ms. Anne SCHWELM
91 Director Administrative Computing Mr. Rob GETZ
19 Director Public Safety Mr. Joseph FUSCO
18 Director of Facilities Ms. Patty SMITH
29 Dir Alumni Engagement/Annual Giving Ms. Jackie MARCIANO
37 Director of Financial Aid Ms. Susan WENDLING
36 Dir of Career & Professional Dev Ms. Erin GABRIELE
41 Director of Athletics & Recreation Mr. Bradley KOCH
15 Director Human Resources Ms. Gina CAMPBELL
21 Controller Ms. Diane SCUTTI
24 Coord of Education Resources Center Ms. Mary BUDZILOWICZ
40 Bookstore Manager Mr. Bill BRIDDES
105 Director of Content Marketing Ms. Molly HARTY
20 Associate Provost Dr. Michelle FILLING-BROWN
35 Dean Student Engage/Leadership Ms. Anne FILIPPONE
92 Director of the Honors Program Dr. Jennifer BULCOCK
28 Dir Student Diversity Initiatives Mr. Jose RODRIGUEZ
38 Director Counseling/Psych Service Dr. Sara MAGGITTI
39 Director of Residence Life Mr. Brett BUCKRIDGE
07 Dean Univ Admissions & Fin Aid Ms. Kimberley LEWIS
101 Dir Trustee Admin & Pres Initiative Mrs. Nancy OLLINGER
102 Dir Grants & Foundation Relations Ms. Laura CHISHOLM
88 Creative Director Mr. Kevin HAUGH
96 Procurement Manager Ms. Elizabeth KANARAS

Cairn University (A)

200 Manor Avenue, Langhorne Manor PA 19047-2990
County: Bucks FICE Identification: 003351
Unit ID: 215114
Telephone: (215) 752-5800 Carnegie Class: Masters/S
FAX Number: (215) 702-4341 Calendar System: Semester
URL: www.cairn.edu
Established: 1913 Annual Undergrad Tuition & Fees: $29,853
Enrollment: 1,229 Coed
Affiliation or Control: Independent Non-Profit IRS Status: 501(c)3
Highest Offering: Master's
Accreditation: M, BI, IACBE, MUS, SW

01 President & Provost Dr. Todd J. WILLIAMS
32 Sr VP Student Affairs & Admin Mr. J. Scott CAWOOD
111 Sr VP Advancement & Communications Mr. Paul NEAL
10 Sr VP Finance Mr. Yunn KANG
15 Sr VP Human Resources Ms. Mary BOYER
88 Special Assistant to President Dr. Timothy HUI
06 Registrar Dr. Steven SCHLENKER
35 Dean Student Life Mr. Adam PORCELLA
73 Dean School of Divinity Dr. Keith PLUMMER
49 Dean School of Liberal Arts & Sci Dr. Aneesh KHUSHMAN
50 Dean School of Business Mr. Yunn KANG
53 Dean School of Education Dr. Stacey BOSE
64 Dean School of Music Dr. Benjamin HARDING
08 Director Library Ms. Stephanie KACELI
106 Dir Educ Tech & Distance Learning Mr. Sali KACELI
29 Vice President Alumni/Cmty Affairs Mr. Nathan WAMBOLD
84 Assistant VP Enrollment Mr. Thomas SHERF
41 Director Athletics Mr. Jay BUTLER
18 Director Campus Services Mr. Andrew NORTON
39 Director Community Life Mr. Andrew GORDON
38 Director Counseling Services Dr. Jeffrey S. BLACK
37 Director Financial Aid Mr. Stephen CASSEL
23 Director Health Services Ms. Alison KIKENDALL
09 Director Research & Analytics Ms. Cheryl STUM
19 Director Safety & Security Mr. Chris LLOYD
13 Director Tech Svcs/Data Governance Mr. David HUI
108 Asst Prov Assessment/Accreditation Dr. Timothy HUI
14 Director Information Systems Mr. Vimul ROS
21 Director Business Services Mr. Andrew HUI
26 Director Marketing Mr. John MULVANEY
04 Administrative Asst to President Ms. Lori MILLER

Carlow University (B)

3333 Fifth Avenue, Pittsburgh PA 15213-3165
County: Allegheny FICE Identification: 003303
Unit ID: 211431
Telephone: (800) 333-2275 Carnegie Class: Masters/L
FAX Number: (412) 578-6668 Calendar System: Semester
URL: www.carlow.edu
Established: 1929 Annual Undergrad Tuition & Fees: $31,446
Enrollment: 1,976 Coed
Affiliation or Control: Roman Catholic IRS Status: 501(c)3
Highest Offering: Doctorate
Accreditation: M, CACREP, #COARC, COPSY, IACBE, NURSE, @SP, SW

01 President Dr. Kathy W. HUMPHREY
05 Provost/VP Academic Affairs Dr. Sibdas GHOSH
10 CFO/SVP Finance & Admin Services Mr. David J. MEADOWS
84 VP Enrollment Mgmt & Mktg Ms. Mollie E. CECERE
111 VP Advancement Ms. Caralynn KASSABOV
32 VP Student Affairs/Dean of Students Dr. Timothy P. PHILLIPS
101 Chief of Staff/Secretary of Board Ms. Lisa FISCHETTI
88 Special Asst to Pres/Mercy Heritage Sr. Sheila A. CARNEY, RSM
106 Asst Prov Online & Acad Operations Mr. Jason KRALL
15 VP Human Res/Diversity/Inclusion Ms. Bridgette N. COFIELD
66 Dean Health and Wellness Dr. Lynn E. GEORGE
49 Dean Arts & Science Dr. Matthew E. GORDLEY
13 Chief Information Officer Ms. Laurie CAPOZZA
26 Exec Dir Marketing/Comm & Brand Ms. Beth M. FAZZINI
21 Controller Ms. Nancy DEGENHARDT
09 Sr Dir Inst Research/Effect/Plng Dr. Edith L. COOK
103 Prog Dir Innovation & Workforce Dev Dr. Rae A. HIRSH
06 Registrar Ms. Elizabeth A. MCCLINTOCK
88 Head of Campus Laboratory School Ms. Jessica WEBSTER
84 Director Enrollment Management Mr. Joel W. MULLNER
123 Dir Adult/Grad/Regional Admissions Ms. Wendy S. PHILLIPS
36 Director Career Development Ms. Jennifer A. O'TOOLE
113 Dir Student Accounts Mr. James V. SHANKEL
08 Exec Dir Library & Lrng Commons Ms. Alexius SMITH-MACKLIN
35 Asst Dean of Students Ms. Erin I. BOYLES
39 Director Residence Life Mr. Keith CERRONI
23 Director Health Services Ms. Carla R. BERGAMASCO
41 Director Athletics Mr. Lou ZADECKY
88 Director Wellness & Fitness Svcs Ms. Julie M. GAUL
18 Manager of Facility Services Mr. Eric SWAGGER
19 Chief of Police Ms. Corrin M. CULHANE
37 Director Financial Aid Ms. Natalie L. WILSON
112 Director of Major Gifts Mr. Mitchel COATES
102 Dir Corp/Found Rels/Advancement Ms. Jennifer FICARRI
27 Director Media & Public Rels Mr. Sean MCFARLAND
42 Campus Ministry Ms. Siobhan K. DEWITT
04 Exec Asst to the President Ms. Juliet A. CREEHAN
28 Director of Equity and Inclusion Dr. Maleea D. JOHNSON
43 Director of Annual Giving Ms. Regan GIBNEY

Carnegie Mellon University (C)

5000 Forbes Avenue, Pittsburgh PA 15213-3890
County: Allegheny FICE Identification: 003242
Unit ID: 211440
Telephone: (412) 268-2000 Carnegie Class: DU-Highest
FAX Number: (412) 268-2330 Calendar System: Semester
URL: www.cmu.edu
Established: 1900 Annual Undergrad Tuition & Fees: $58,810
Enrollment: 13,519 Coed
Affiliation or Control: Independent Non-Profit IRS Status: 501(c)3
Highest Offering: Doctorate
Accreditation: M, MUS

01 President Dr. Farnam JAHANIAN
05 Provost/Chief Academic Officer Dr. James H. GARRETT, JR.
10 Vice President and CFO Ms. Angela BLANTON
111 VP for University Advancement Mr. Scott MORY
46 Int VP for Research Mr. Daryl WEINERT
43 Vice President/General Counsel Ms. Mary Jo DIVELY
26 VP Marketing & Communications Mr. Nicholas SCIBETTA
101 Secretary of the Corporation Ms. Cathy A. LIGHT
04 Exec Asst to President/Office Mgr Ms. Kelly ELDER
20 Vice Provost for Education Dr. Amy L. BURKERT
11 Vice President for Operations Mr. Daryl WEINERT
100 Chief of Staff/VP Strategic Init Mr. Daryl WEINERT
32 VP Student Affairs/Dean of Students Ms. Gina CASALEGNO
13 VP Info Tech/Chief Information Ofcr Mr. Stan M. WADDELL
15 AVP & Chief Human Resources Officer Mrs. Michelle PIEKUTOWSKI
29 Asst VP Alumni Relations Ms. Theresa TROMBETTA
18 Asc VP Campus Design/Facility Devel Mr. Ralph R. HORGAN
27 Sr Dir For News & Media Relations Mr. Jason MADERER
28 Asst Vice Pres for Diversity & EOS Mr. Everett L. TADAMY
41 Dir Athletics & Physical Education Mr. Josh CENTOR
19 Director Security/Chief Univ Police Mr. Thomas A. OGDEN
84 AVP & Dir of Enrollment Services Ms. Lisa M. KRIEG
14 Director Software Engr Inst Dr. Paul D. NIELSEN
07 Dean of Admissions Mr. Michael STEIDEL
08 Dean of University Libraries Mr. Keith WEBSTER
06 Registrar Mr. John R. PAPINCHAK
09 Director of Institutional Research Vacant
36 Assoc Dean for Career/Prof Dev Mr. Kevin MONAHAN
38 Dir Counseling & Psychological Svcs Dr. Kurt KUMLER
54 Dean Carnegie Inst of Technology Vacant
57 Dean College Fine Arts Dr. Dan J. MARTIN
49 Dean Dietrich College Dr. Richard SCHEINES
50 Dean Tepper School of Business Dr. Robert DAMMON
81 Dean Mellon College of Science Dr. Rebecca W. DOERGE
80 Dean Heinz Sch Publ Policy/Mgmt Dr. Ramayya KRISHNAN
77 Dean School of Computer Sciences Vacant
35 Asst Dean of Student Affairs Ms. Renee CAMERLENGO
102 Dir Foundation Relations Ms. Jennifer SOBOL
104 Director of International Education Ms. Linda GENTILE
25 Chief Contracts/Grants Admin Mr. Matthew D'EMILIO
37 Director Student Financial Aid Mr. Brian HILL
39 Director Housing Services Mr. Thomas COOLEY
30 Sr Assoc Vice Pres for Development Ms. Pamela EAGER
86 Assoc VP Government Relations Mr. Timothy MCNULTY
96 Director University Procurement Vacant

Cedar Crest College (D)

100 College Drive, Allentown PA 18104-6196
County: Lehigh FICE Identification: 003243
Unit ID: 211468
Telephone: (610) 437-4471 Carnegie Class: Masters/S
FAX Number: (610) 437-5955 Calendar System: Semester
URL: www.cedarcrest.edu
Established: 1867 Annual Undergrad Tuition & Fees: $41,567
Enrollment: 1,433 Female
Affiliation or Control: Non-denominational IRS Status: 501(c)3
Highest Offering: Doctorate
Accreditation: M, ACBSP, ANEST, DIETD, DIETI, FEPAC, NUR, NURSE, SW

01 President Dr. Elizabeth MEADE
05 Provost Dr. Robert A. WILSON
10 Chief Financial Officer/Treasurer Ms. Audra J. KAHR
111 VP Institutional Advancement Ms. Valerie DOWNING
84 VP Enrollment Mgmt/Student Affairs Dr. Erika DAVIS
06 Registrar Vacant
29 Exec Director for Alumnae Affairs Ms. Lori GALLAGHER
19 Chief of Campus Safety and Security Mr. Mark VITALOS
18 Director of Facilities Mr. Michael STANTON
08 Library Director Dr. Stephani GOMEZ
13 Director Information Technology Mr. Bruce SARTE
09 Dir of Institutional Research Ms. Lyn WILLIAMS
04 Assistant to the President Ms. Erin FENSTERMACHER
37 Dir Student Financial Services Ms. Valerie KREISER
22 Director Health/Counseling Services Ms. Nancy ROBERTS
26 Dir Marketing/Communication Dr. Erika DAVIS
40 Manager Bookstore Ms. Breanna GANTHER
28 Director of Diversity Dr. Leon JOHN
41 Athletic Director Mr. Allen SNOOK
101 Secretary of the Institution/Board Ms. Meghan GRADY
104 Director Study Abroad Dr. Kelly HALL
15 Chief Human Resources Officer Ms. Lisa GARBACIK
32 Chief Student Affairs/Life Officer Dr. Kyle DAILEY

Central Penn College (E)

600 Valley Road, Summerdale PA 17093-0309
County: Cumberland FICE Identification: 004890
Unit ID: 211477
Telephone: (800) 759-2727 Carnegie Class: Bac-Diverse
FAX Number: (717) 732-5254 Calendar System: Quarter
URL: www.centralpenn.edu
Established: 1881 Annual Undergrad Tuition & Fees: $18,714
Enrollment: 963 Coed
Affiliation or Control: Proprietary IRS Status: Proprietary
Highest Offering: Master's
Accreditation: M, MAC, OTA, PTAA

01 President Dr. Linda FEDRIZZI-WILLIAMS
05 VPAA/Provost Dr. Krista WOLFE
10 VP of Admin & Finance Mr. Shawn FARR
111 VP of Advncmnt & Strat Initiatives Mr. Michael FEDOR
15 VP of People & Culture Ms. Maggie LEBO
26 AVP Advncmnt & Strategic Initiative Mrs. Mary E. WETZEL
06 Registrar Mrs. Jen CORRELL
18 Facilities Director Mr. Robert WHITCOMB, III
37 Financial Aid Director Ms. Kathy J. SHEPARD
41 Athletic Director Ms. Kasey HICKS
36 Dean of Career Services & Devel Mr. Steven HASSINGER
39 Dir of Student Housing & Res Life Ms. Lindsay GARBER
108 Dir of Institutional Effectiveness Vacant

Central Pennsylvania Institute of Science and Technology (F)

540 North Harrison Rd, Pleasant Gap PA 16823
County: Centre FICE Identification: 005335
Unit ID: 369668
Telephone: (814) 359-2793 Carnegie Class: Not Classified
FAX Number: (814) 359-3489 Calendar System: Quarter
URL: www.cpi.edu
Established: 1969 Annual Undergrad Tuition & Fees (In-District): N/A
Enrollment: 113 Coed
Affiliation or Control: State/Local IRS Status: 501(c)3
Highest Offering: Associate Degree
Accreditation: ACCSC

01 President Dr. Richard C. MAKIN

Chatham University (G)

Woodland Road, Pittsburgh PA 15232-2826
County: Allegheny FICE Identification: 003244
Unit ID: 211556
Telephone: (412) 365-1100 Carnegie Class: DU-Mod
FAX Number: (412) 365-1505 Calendar System: Other
URL: www.chatham.edu
Established: 1869 Annual Undergrad Tuition & Fees: $39,902
Enrollment: 2,353 Coed
Affiliation or Control: Independent Non-Profit IRS Status: 501(c)3
Highest Offering: Doctorate
Accreditation: M, ARCPA, CAATE, CIDA, COPSY, IACBE, MPCAC, NURSE, OT, PTA, SW

01 President Dr. David FINEGOLD
10 Vice Pres Finance/Administration Mr. Walter B. FOWLER

05 Vice President Academic Affairs ....Dr. Jenna TEMPLETON
84 Vice Pres Enrollment Management .... Ms. Amy BECHER
26 Vice Pres for Mktg & Communications .... Mr. Bill CAMPBELL
111 Vice Pres University Advancement .... Ms. Carey MILLER
106 Director Chatham Online .... Mr. Mark KASSEL
88 Dn Falk Sch Sustainability/Environ .... Mr. Lou LEONARD
21 Assoc VP Finance/Admin ....Ms. Jennifer HOERSTER
45 Vice Pres of Planning ....Mr. Sean COLEMAN
09 Director of IR & Effectiveness ....Mr. Giovanni GAROFALO
06 Registrar ....Ms. Maria KRONISER
37 Asst Vice Pres Financial Aid .... Ms. Jennifer A. BURNS
08 Director of Library ....Ms. Jill AUSEL
29 Director of Alumni Engagement ....Ms. Lauren TUDOR
44 Director of Annual Giving .... Ms. Brianna BROWN
30 Asst VP of Development ....Ms. Amanda KILE
15 Asst VP of Human Resources ....Mr. Frank M. GRECO
18 Asst VP of Facilities Management .... Mr. Robert R. DUBRAY
19 Chief of Police .... Ms. Valerie TOWNSEND
41 Director of Athletics ....Mr. Leonard TREVINO
36 Asst Dean of Students .... Mr. Chris PURCELL
38 Director of Student Counseling ....Dr. Elsa M. ARCE
32 Dean of Students .... Ms. Heather BLACK
49 Dean School Arts/Science/Business .... Dr. Darlene MOTLEY
76 Dean School of Health Sciences .... Dr. Patricia DOWNEY
04 Exec Assistant to the President ....Ms. Brittany TYLER
13 CIO/Director of Info Technology .... Mr. Paul STEINHAUS
39 Director Residence Life .... Mr. Shawn A. MCQUILLAN
88 Dir University Sustainability .... Ms. Mary WHITNEY
102 Grants Manager .... Mr. Thomas MCGEE
104 Study Abroad Coordinator .... Ms. Karin CHIPMAN
28 Asst VP Diversity/Inclusion ....Dr. Randi CONGLETON
50 Chair/Director Business .... Mr. James PIERSON
53 Director of Education ....Dr. Kristin HARTY
105 Web Content Manager .... Ms. Sara POLETTI

Chestnut Hill College (A)

9601 Germantown Avenue, Philadelphia PA 19118-2693
County: Philadelphia FICE Identification: 003245
Unit ID: 211583
Telephone: (215) 248-7000 Carnegie Class: Masters/M
FAX Number: (215) 248-7155 Calendar System: Semester
URL: www.chc.edu
Established: 1924 Annual Undergrad Tuition & Fees: $38,200
Enrollment: 1,528 Coed
Affiliation or Control: Roman Catholic IRS Status: 501(c)3
Highest Offering: Doctorate
Accreditation: M, CLPSY, IPSY, MACTE, MPCAC

01 President ....Sr. Carol Jean VALE, SSJ
05 VP Academic Affairs/Dean of Faculty ....Dr. Christopher DOUGHERTY
10 Int Vice Pres for Financial Affairs .... Mr. Robert WALLETT
30 Vice President for Inst Advancement .... Ms. Erin WOOLEY
32 Vice President for Student Life .... Dr. Lynn ORTALE
84 Vice Pres Enrollment Management ....Mr. Troy MILLER
11 Asst to Pres for Administration .... Sr. Kathryn MILLER, SSJ
58 Dean School of Graduate Studies .... Dr. William CUNNINGHAM
97 Int Dean School Undergrad Studies .... Dr. Jacqueline REICH
51 Dean Continuing/Professional Stds ....Dr. Elaine GREEN
08 Dean Library/Information Resources ....Sr. Mary Josephine LARKIN, SSJ
28 Chief Officer for Diversity/Equity .... Dr. LaKeisha THORPE
26 Chief Communications Officer .... Mr. Chris SPANGLER
42 Director of Campus Ministry .... Ms. Anna RYAN-BENDER
35 Dean of Student Life .... Dr. Krista BAILEY MURPHY
20 Director Campus Life Operations .... Ms. Chelsea FARREN
06 Registrar ....Mr. Michael REIG
38 Director Counseling Center ....Sr. Sheila KENNEDY, SSJ
85 Int Coord of Global Education .... Dr. Walter PERRY
13 Director of IT Services ....Mr. Rich MACINTYRE
23 Director Health Services ....Ms. Deirdre HORAN
36 Director of Career Development .... Ms. Nancy DACHILLE
07 Dir Admission/Sch Graduate Studies .... Ms. Ariel EDWARDS
07 Director Accelerated Admissions .... Ms. April FOWLKES
21 Controller ....Mr. Mitch BILKER
37 Director Financial Aid ....Ms. Yolanda COLE
09 Director of Institutional Research .... Sr. Patricia O'DONNELL, SSJ
102 Dir Corporate/Found/Govt Relations .... Ms. Rebecca POWERS
29 Director of Alumnae/i Affairs .... Ms. Maureen MCLAUGHLIN
41 Director of Athletics .... Mr. Jesse BALCER
15 Director Human Resources ....Ms. Sharon DOUGHERTY
19 Dir Security/Safety/Bldgs/Grounds ....Ms. Polly TETI
18 Director of Facilities .... Mr. Mark MCGRATH
88 Financial Systems Analyst .... Ms. Meg O'BRIEN
39 Director Residence Life ....Mr. William WHITE
04 Administrative Asst to President ....Ms. Bianca HART
40 Manager of Campus Store .... Ms. Jennifer WARING

Clarks Summit University (B)

538 Venard Road, S. Abington Twp. PA 18411-1297
County: Lackawanna FICE Identification: 002670
Unit ID: 211024
Telephone: (570) 586-2400 Carnegie Class: Spec-4-yr-Faith
FAX Number: (570) 585-9226 Calendar System: Semester
URL: www.clarkssummitu.edu
Established: 1932 Annual Undergrad Tuition & Fees: $26,082
Enrollment: 768 Coed
Affiliation or Control: Baptist IRS Status: 501(c)3
Highest Offering: Doctorate
Accreditation: M, BI

01 President ....Dr. James R. LYTLE
04 Executive Assistant to President .... Ms. Darlene CATLETT
05 VP of Academics ....Dr. William J. HIGLEY
32 VP of Student Development ....Mr. Ted BOYKIN
34 Associate Dean of Women ....Mrs. Faye MOORE
11 Exec Dir of Administrative Svcs .... Mr. Allen R. DREYER
37 Director of Financial Aid ....Mr. Larry ELLIS
84 Exec Dir On-Campus Enrollment Mgmt ....Mr. Frank JUDSON
13 Director of Information Technology .... Mr. David BOSKET
06 Registrar .... Mr. Chris WELMAN
09 Director of Institutional Research .... Mr. Robert PLANTZ
29 Exec Dir Alumni & Development ....Mr. Paul GOLDEN
73 Assoc Dean of School of Theology .... Mr. James BUCHANAN
53 Dean of School of Education ....Dr. Ritch KELLEY
49 Dean of School of Arts & Sciences .... Dr. Janet K. HICKS
106 Exec Dir Online Learning .... Ms. Erica YOUNG
10 Controller ....Mr. Daniel KING
26 Exec Dir Marketing/Communications .... Ms. Dena CAMBRA

Commonwealth Technical Institute at the Hiram G. Andrews Center (C)

727 Goucher Street, Johnstown PA 15905-3092
County: Cambria FICE Identification: 025366
Unit ID: 212975
Telephone: (814) 255-8200 Carnegie Class: Assoc/HVT-High Non
FAX Number: (814) 255-5709 Calendar System: Semester
URL: www.dli.pa.gov/Individuals/Disability-Services/hgac/
Established: 1959 Annual Undergrad Tuition & Fees: $7,664
Enrollment: 133 Coed
Affiliation or Control: Proprietary IRS Status: Proprietary
Highest Offering: Associate Degree
Accreditation: ACCSC

01 Center Director ....Jill MORICONI
11 Center Deputy Director ....James MARKER
05 Director of Education ....James THOMAS
07 Director of Admissions .... Martin TRAN
32 Chief Student Life Officer .... Stacie ANDREWS
37 Director Student Financial Aid .... Chris ZAKRAYSEK

Community College of Allegheny County (D)

800 Allegheny Avenue, Pittsburgh PA 15233-1895
County: Allegheny FICE Identification: 003231
Unit ID: 210605
Telephone: (412) 237-4413 Carnegie Class: Assoc/MT-VT-Mix Trad/Non
FAX Number: (412) 237-4420 Calendar System: Semester
URL: www.ccac.edu
Established: 1966 Annual Undergrad Tuition & Fees (In-District): $8,323
Enrollment: 13,217 Coed
Affiliation or Control: State/Local IRS Status: 501(c)3
Highest Offering: Associate Degree
Accreditation: M, ADNUR, CAHIIM, COARC, DIETT, DMS, EMT, MAC, MLTAD, NAEYC, NMT, OTA, PTAA, RTT, SURGT

01 President ....Dr. Quintin B. BULLOCK
05 Provost/Exec Vice Pres Acad Affairs ....Dr. Stuart BLACKLAW
10 Vice President Finance .... Dr. Brian MCKLOSKEY
43 Vice President and General Counsel ......Mr. Anthony DITOMMSO
84 VP Enrollment Management .... Dr. Brian SAJKO
12 Northwest Regional President ....Dr. Evon WALTERS
12 Southeast Regional President .... Ms. Charlene NEWKIRK
103 Interim VP Workforce Development .... Ms. Deborah KILLMYER
15 VP Human Resources .... Ms. Kimberly MANIGAULT
102 CEO Educational Foundation ....Mr. James MCMAHON
13 VP & Chief Information Officer .... Mr. Chuck GRAHAM
06 Registrar .... Dr. Diane JACOBS
18 VP & Chief Facilities Management .... Mr. Carlo VAZQUEZ
21 Controller ....Mr. James FLYNN
25 Executive Director Grants ....Ms. Natasha WALTON
96 Director Purchasing/Contracts Admin .... Mr. Mike CVETIC
28 Chief Diversity/Equity/Inclusion . Dr. Angelica PEREZ-JOHNSTON
26 Executive Director Public Relations .... Ms. Elizabeth JOHNSTON
04 Exec Asst to the President & BoT ..... Ms. Bonita L RICHARDSON
100 Chief of Staff .... Dr. Frank SARGENT
19 Exec Director Security/Safety .... Mr. Andre HENDERSON

Community College of Allegheny County Boyce Campus (E)

595 Beatty Road, Monroeville PA 15146-1396
Telephone: (724) 327-1327 Identification: 770150
Accreditation: &M

Community College of Allegheny County North Campus (F)

8701 Perry Highway, Pittsburgh PA 15237-5353
Telephone: (412) 366-7000 Identification: 770151
Accreditation: &M

Community College of Allegheny County, South Campus (G)

1750 Clairton Road, West Mifflin PA 15122-3029
Telephone: (412) 237-2222 Identification: 770152
Accreditation: &M

Community College of Beaver County (H)

1 Campus Drive, Monaca PA 15061-2588
County: Beaver FICE Identification: 006807
Unit ID: 211079
Telephone: (724) 480-2222 Carnegie Class: Assoc/HVT-Mix Trad/Non
FAX Number: (724) 480-3573 Calendar System: Semester
URL: www.ccbc.edu
Established: 1966 Annual Undergrad Tuition & Fees (In-District): $12,630
Enrollment: 1,713 Coed
Affiliation or Control: State/Local IRS Status: 501(c)3
Highest Offering: Associate Degree
Accreditation: M, ADNUR

01 President .... Dr. Roger W. DAVIS
05 Executive Vice President & Provost ....Dr. Shelly MOORE
10 VP Finance/Operations and IT .... Mr. Glenn NATALI
15 VP Human Resources ....Ms. Sally MERCER
32 VP Student Affairs & Enrollment .... Dr. Sutonia BOYKIN
13 AVP of IT ....Mr. Brandon BERG
26 Assoc VP Communications .... Ms. Leslie A. TENNANT
35 Assoc VP of Student Affairs .... Ms. Angela M. HAMILTON
103 Dean Workforce & Continuing Educ .... Mr. John S. GOBERISH
37 Director Student Financial Services ....Mr. Steve PLANEY
04 Assistant to the President & Board .... Ms. Roni GILES
76 Dean Nursing & Allied Health .... Ms. Elaine STROUSS
49 Senior Dean .... Dr. John HIGGS
88 Dean Aviation Sciences .... Dr. John HIGGS
88 Dean HS Academies & Dual Enroll .... Ms. Joyce CIRELLI
111 Exec Dir Advance & Sponsored Pgms .... Mr. Kolton CODNER
35 Director of Student Life ....Mr. Colin SISK
88 Associate Dean ....Dr. Katie THOMAS
88 Associate Dean ....Dr. Chet THOMPSON
06 Registrar .... Ms. Rose WHELPLEY
08 Chief Library Officer .... Ms. Terri GALLAGHER
09 Exec Dir of Plng/Assessment/Imp .... Ms. Sara LEIGH
21 Director of Financial Operations .... Mr. Matthew ZELEZNIK

Community College of Philadelphia (I)

1700 Spring Garden Street, Philadelphia PA 19130-3991
County: Philadelphia FICE Identification: 003249
Unit ID: 215239
Telephone: (215) 751-8000 Carnegie Class: Assoc/HT-High Trad
FAX Number: (215) 751-8762 Calendar System: Semester
URL: www.ccp.edu
Established: 1965 Annual Undergrad Tuition & Fees (In-District): $8,592
Enrollment: 13,672 Coed
Affiliation or Control: State/Local IRS Status: 501(c)3
Highest Offering: Associate Degree
Accreditation: M, ADNUR, COARC, DH, MLTAD, NAEYC, RAD

01 President .... Dr. Donald GENERALS
10 Vice President Business & Finance ....Mr. Jacob EAPEN
45 VP Strategic Initiatives and COS ....Vacant
111 Vice Pres Institutional Advancement .... Ms. Mellissia ZANJANI
05 VP Academic and Student Success .... Dr. Samuel HIRSCH
103 VP Workforce Dev & Economic Innova ....Ms. Carol DE FRIES
43 General Counsel ....Ms. Victoria ZELLERS
13 Interim Chief Information Officer .... Mr. William BROMLEY
32 Dean of Students .... Dr. David ASENCIO
84 Dean of Enrollment Services .... Dr. Donna RICHEMOND
49 Dean Liberal Studies ....Dr. Chae SWEET
51 Dean Div Adult/Community Education .... Dr. David E. THOMAS
72 Div Dean of Business/Technology ....Dr. Pam CARTER
09 Director Institutional Research ....Dr. Dawn SINNOT
06 Director Stdnt Records/Registration ..... Ms. Bonnie HARRINGTON
18 Int AVP Facilities/Construction Mgt .... Mr. John WIGGINS
28 Affirmative Action Director .... Mr. Simon BROWN
07 Director of Recruitment/Admissions .... Mr. Jason HAND
37 Director Financial Aid ....Vacant
96 Director of Purchasing .... Ms. Marsia HENLEY
38 Dept Head Student Counseling .... Ms. Carmen COLON
36 Coord Career Info/Placement Svcs .... Ms. Tracy HANTON
29 Coord Alumni Rels/Annual Giving ....Ms. Lyvette BROOKS
25 Coord Grants/Prospect Research .... Ms. Anne GRECO
86 Government Relations Officer .... Ms. Jasmine SESSOMS

Curtis Institute of Music (J)

1726 Locust Street, Philadelphia PA 19103-6187
County: Philadelphia FICE Identification: 003251
Unit ID: 211893
Telephone: (215) 893-5252 Carnegie Class: Spec-4-yr-Arts
FAX Number: (215) 893-9065 Calendar System: Semester
URL: www.curtis.edu
Established: 1924 Annual Undergrad Tuition & Fees: $3,015
Enrollment: 145 Coed
Affiliation or Control: Independent Non-Profit IRS Status: 501(c)3
Highest Offering: Master's
Accreditation: M, MUS

01 President & Chief Executive Officer .... Mr. Roberto DIAZ
11 Sr Vice Pres Administration .... Mr. Larry BOMBACK
111 Vice President Inst Advancement .... Mr. Christopher MOSSEY
05 Dean of Academics/Students .... Mr. Paul BRYAN
13 Chief Technology Officer .... Mr. Matt MORGAN
06 Registrar ....Mr. Darin KELLY
07 Admissions Officer ....Mr. Christopher HODGES
08 Library Director .... Ms. Michelle OSWELL

Delaware County Community College (A)

901 S Media Line Road, Media PA 19063-1094
County: Delaware FICE Identification: 007110
Unit ID: 211927
Telephone: (610) 359-5000 Carnegie Class: Assoc/MT-VT-High Trad
FAX Number: (610) 359-5343 Calendar System: Semester
URL: www.dccc.edu
Established: 1967 Annual Undergrad Tuition & Fees (In-District): $9,710
Enrollment: 9,989 Coed
Affiliation or Control: State/Local IRS Status: 501(c)3
Highest Offering: Associate Degree
Accreditation: M, ADNUR, ART, COARC, EMT, MAC, NAEYC, SURGT

01 President Dr. L. Joy GATES BLACK
10 VP Finance/Admin & Treasurer Dr. Patricia BENSON
05 Vice Pres Academic Affairs Dr. Marian MCGORRY
111 Vice President for Advancement Ms. Rachael HUNSINGER PATTEN
12 Vice Provost & Vice Pres Chester Co Dr. Mary Jo BOYER
84 Vice President of Enrollment Mgmt Dr. Mitch MURTHA
15 VP Human Resources Ms. Sara EVANS
103 VP Workforce Dev & Cmty Educ Ms. Karen KOZACHYN
13 CIO Information Technology Ms. Bianca VALENTE
32 Vice Provost Student/Instr Support Dr. Grant S. SNYDER
88 Director Municipal Police Academy Mr. William DAVIS
106 Dean Distance Learning Services Dr. Alexandra SALAS
37 Director of Financial Aid Mr. Raymond L. TOOLE
07 Asst VP Enrollment Svcs & Registrar Ms. Hope L. DIEHL
108 Assoc Vice Prov Inst Effectiveness Dr. Christopher TOKPAH
91 Director Admin Computing Mr. Bob HARDCASTLE
29 Director Alumni Programs Mr. Douglas J. FERGUSON
89 Director of First Year Experience Dr. Kendrick MICKENS
25 Director Grants Management Vacant
31 Director Community Education Ms. Patricia S. SCEPANSKY
35 Director Campus Life Ms. Allyson GLEASON
19 Director Safety & Security Mr. Matthew BRENNER
88 Dir Dual Enrollment HS Initiatives Ms. Patricia SHANNON
12 Director Southeast Center Ms. Jane SCHURMAN
88 Director Assessment Center Mr. Christos THEODOROPULOS
18 Director Facilities Mr. Nate SIMCOX
81 Interim Dean STEM Dr. Terri AMLONG
50 Dean Business & Social Science Dr. Richard MCFADDEN
79 Dean Comm/Arts & Humanities Dr. Terri AMLONG
76 Interim Dean Health/Nursing/EMS Dr. Genny CAVANAUGH
40 Manager Bookstore Mr. Jamar ABDULLAH
04 Executive Assistant to President Ms. Diane FOSTER
26 Executive Dir of Marketing & Comm Mr. Daniel KANAK
100 Chief of Staff Mr. Harry COSTIGAN
86 Director Govt Relations/Comm Mr. Anthony TWYMAN
06 Registrar Ms. Hope DIEHL
28 Chief Diversity & Inclusion Officer Ms. Simmuelle MEYERS
41 Athletic Director Vacant

Delaware Valley University (B)

700 E Butler Avenue, Doylestown PA 18901-2697
County: Bucks FICE Identification: 003252
Unit ID: 211981
Telephone: (215) 345-1500 Carnegie Class: Masters/S
FAX Number: (215) 345-5277 Calendar System: Semester
URL: www.delval.edu
Established: 1896 Annual Undergrad Tuition & Fees: $40,620
Enrollment: 2,303 Coed
Affiliation or Control: Independent Non-Profit IRS Status: 501(c)3
Highest Offering: Doctorate
Accreditation: M, ACBSP, LSAR, MPCAC

01 Interim President Dr. Benjamin RUSILOSKI
04 Executive Asst to the President Ms. Kristen OLSZEWSKI
100 Chief of Staff Vacant
05 VP Academic Affairs/Dean of Faculty Dr. Benjamin RUSILOSKI
32 VP Campus Life & Inclusive Excel Dr. April VARI
10 VP for Finance & Admin/CFO Mr. Randy BARFIELD
30 VP for Development & Alumni Affairs Mr. Keith RICHARDSON
09 Exec Dir of Institutional Research Ms. Regina BENASUTTI
84 VP for Enrollment Management Ms. Kathy PAYNE
81 Dean of Life & Physical Sciences Dr. Jean SMOLEN
47 Dean Agriculture & Environ Science Dr. Broc SANDELIN
50 Dean Business & Humanities Dr. Tanya CASAS
58 Dean of Graduate & Prof Studies Dr. John WOZNICKI
06 Registrar Mr. James SLIZEWSKI
41 Athletic Director Mr. David DUDA
26 Assoc VP Marketing & Communications Ms. Kathy HOWELL
21 Asst VP Finance & Administration Vacant
07 Executive Director of Admission Dr. Thomas SPEAKMAN
13 Exec Director Technology Services Mr. Mike DAVIS
36 Exec Dir Ctr for Student Prof Dev Dr. Benjamin RUSILOSKI
08 Librarian Mr. Peter A. KUPERSMITH
37 Director Student Financial Aid Mrs. Joan HOCK
107 Dir Graduate & Professional Studies Ms. Yolonda UDVARDY
38 Director Counseling/Learn Support Ms. Sharon DONNELLY
23 Director Health Services Ms. Meredyth VANVREEDE
14 Assoc Dir of Help Desk Operations Vacant
35 Asst Dean of Stdnts/Dir Stdnt Inv Mr. Andrew MOYER
19 Director Security/Public Safety Mr. Michael LYNSKY
15 Director of Human Resources Ms. Jennifer BRENNAN
18 Director of Facilities & Grounds Mr. Pat CALLAHAN
44 Director Annual Giving & Adv Svcs Mr. Kevin LADDEN
96 Director of Purchasing Mr. William LYLE
102 Dir Foundation/Corporate Relations Ms. Wendy CONNUCK
88 Experiential Learning Advisor Ms. Darrah MUGRAUER
104 Director Study Abroad Vacant
106 Dir Online Education/E-learning Ms. Cynthia RENNER
29 Director Alumni Engagement Ms. Rachel MAUER
28 Asst Dean Stdnt Dev/Div & Incl Ms. Evie HUNTER
39 Dir Resident Life/Student Housing Ms. Carey HADDOCK

DeSales University (C)

2755 Station Avenue, Center Valley PA 18034-9568
County: Lehigh FICE Identification: 003986
Unit ID: 210739
Telephone: (610) 282-1100 Carnegie Class: Masters/L
FAX Number: (610) 282-2254 Calendar System: Semester
URL: www.desales.edu
Established: 1965 Annual Undergrad Tuition & Fees: $39,500
Enrollment: 3,302 Coed
Affiliation or Control: Roman Catholic IRS Status: 501(c)3
Highest Offering: Doctorate
Accreditation: M, ACBSP, ARCPA, NURSE, PTA

01 President V.Rev. James J. GREENFIELD, OSFS
04 Executive Asst President's Office Ms. Nancy SEIER
03 Executive Vice President Dr. Gerard JOYCE
88 Vice President for Mission Rev. Kevin NADOLSKI, OSFS
10 VP for Admin & Finance Mr. Robert SNYDER
45 VP for Strategic Planning Vacant
111 Vice Pres Institutional Advancement Ms. Cheryl MURPHY
05 Provost Bro. Daniel WISNIEWSKI, OSFS
06 Registrar Mr. Thomas MANTONI
84 Assoc VP for Enrollment Management Mr. Derrick WETZEL
28 AVP Diversity/Equity/ Inclusion Mr. Scott BLAIR
08 Librarian Ms. Deborah MALONE
51 Asst Dean Adult & Continuing Educ Mr. Michael YERGEY
20 Assoc Provost of Academic Pgm Dr. Robert BLUMENSTEIN
36 Exec Dir of Career Development Ms. Kristin EICHOLTZ
86 Director of Government Relations Vacant
102 Director Corp/Foundation Relations Mrs. Kathy DIAMANDOPOULOS
26 Executive Director of Communication Mr. Thomas MCNAMARA
44 Assoc VP for Annual Giving Ms. Lina BARBIERI
29 Director of Alumni Relations Mr. Michael RITCHIE
11 Assoc VP for Admin & Planning Mr. Peter RAUTZHAN
21 Director of Finance/Treasurer Mr. Michael SWEETANA
19 Chief of Police Chief Steven MARSHALL
09 Dir of Institutional Rsrch/Analysis Ms. Lisa PLUMMER
88 VP of Campus Environment Mr. Marc ALBANESE
18 Director of Facilities Mr. Jim MOLCHANY
40 Campus Store Manager Mr. Joseph JUDGE
15 Exec Dir of Human Resources Ms. Margie GRANDINETTI
16 HR Generalist Ms. Lisa LIGHTCAP
13 Director of Information Technology Mr. James MAZUROWSKI
32 Vice President for Student Life Mrs. Linda ZERBE
35 Dean of Students Vacant
39 Director of Residence Life Vacant
07 Director of Admissions Ms. Kate MCNALLY
37 Director of Student Financial Aid Mrs. Joyce FARMER
42 Chaplain Rev. Dan LANNEN
38 Asst Dean of Students for Wellness Ms. Wendy KRISAK
41 Athletic Director Mr. Scott COVAL
58 Dean of Graduate Education Mr. Ron NORDONE
96 Director of Campus Environment Mr. Jeffrey RICHTER
104 Exec Dir of International Learning Mr. Brian MACDONALD
50 Division Head of Business Dr. Christopher COCOZZA
53 Chair of Education Dr. Katrin BLAMEY
105 Director Web Communications Ms. Kristin LAUDENSLAGER
106 Dean of Online Education Dr. Eric HAGAN

Dickinson College (D)

Box 1773, College & Louther Street,
Carlisle PA 17013-2896
County: Cumberland FICE Identification: 003253
Unit ID: 212009
Telephone: (800) 644-1773 Carnegie Class: Bac-A&S
FAX Number: N/A Calendar System: Semester
URL: www.dickinson.edu
Established: 1783 Annual Undergrad Tuition & Fees: $56,523
Enrollment: 1,932 Coed
Affiliation or Control: Independent Non-Profit IRS Status: 501(c)3
Highest Offering: Master's
Accreditation: M

01 Interim President Mr. John E. JONES, III
05 Provost/Dean of the College Dr. Neil B. WEISSMAN
84 VP Enrollment Mgmt/Dean Admissions Ms. Catherine M. DAVENPORT
10 VP Finance & Administration Dr. Bronté BURLEIGH-JONES
111 VP College Advancement Mr. Carlo ROBUSTELLI
32 VP Student Life Dr. George H. STROUD
13 VP & Chief Information Officer Vacant
09 VP Inst Effectiveness Dr. Brenda K. BRETZ
15 Assoc VP Human Resource Services Ms. Debra HARGROVE
43 General Counsel/Chief Legal Officer Mr. Kendall ISAAC
100 Chief of Staff/Secretary of College Ms. Karen N. FARYNIAK
18 Assoc VP Sustain & Facilities Plng Mr. Kenneth E. SHULTES
20 Sr Assoc Provost Academic Affairs Dr. Catrina HAMILTON-DRAGER
20 Asst Provost for Curriculum Ms. Deb L. BOLEN
110 Assoc VP College Advancement Ms. Jessica J. WILSON
109 Assoc VP Auxil Svcs & Budget Mgmt Vacant
26 VP Marketing & Communications Ms. Connie MCNAMARA
06 Registrar Vacant
41 Athletic Director Mr. Joel M. QUATTRONE
09 Dir Institutional Effectiveness Mr. Lester D. KO
37 Director of Financial Aid Ms. Leah YOUNG
104 Assoc Provost/Exec Dir Global Stdy Ms. Samantha C. BRANDAUER
31 Assoc Provost/Exec Dir CCLA Dr. Gary R. KIRK
88 Asc Prov/Dir Ctr Sustainability Ed Dr. Neil A. LEARY
36 Asst Provost/Dir Career Development Ms. Annie KONDAS
23 Exec Dir Wellness Center Ms. Lauren STRUNK
21 Assoc VP Fin Ops & Controller Mr. Sean WITTE
90 Director Academic Computing Ms. Patricia A. PEHLMAN
27 Director of Media Relations Ms. Christine BAKSI
29 Director of Alumni Relations Ms. Liz TOTH
114 Director Planning & Budget Vacant
08 Director Library Services Ms. Eleanor MITCHELL
40 Dir Col Bookstore/Central Svcs Ms. Lori COLEMAN
19 Asst VP Compliance/Campus Safety Ms. Dolores A. DANSER
91 Assoc VP Enterprise Systems Ms. Jill M. FORRESTER
102 Dir Academic & Foundation Relations Ms. Cheryl E. KREMER
39 Assoc Dean/Dir Res Life & Housing Ms. Amanda GEORGE
35 Assoc VP Student Life Ms. Angie HARRIS
112 Executive Director Donor Relations Ms. Tara C. RENAULT
113 Bursar Financial Operations Ms. Sally HECKENDORN
105 Director Online Marketing Ms. Sarah M. SHERIFF
42 Director Cmty Svcs/Religious Life Dr. Cody NIELSEN
28 Title IX Coordinator Ms. Katharina MATIC

Douglas Education Center (E)

130 Seventh Street, Monessen PA 15062-1097
County: Westmoreland FICE Identification: 020683
Unit ID: 212045
Telephone: (724) 684-3684 Carnegie Class: Spec 2-yr-A&S
FAX Number: (724) 684-7463 Calendar System: Semester
URL: www.dec.edu
Established: 1904 Annual Undergrad Tuition & Fees: $17,750
Enrollment: 207 Coed
Affiliation or Control: Proprietary IRS Status: Proprietary
Highest Offering: Associate Degree
Accreditation: ACCSC

01 President Mr. Jeffrey D. IMBRESCIA
05 Vice President of Academic Affairs Mr. Julian IMBRESCIA
10 Director of Financial Services Mr. Jeffrey FEDOREK
20 Senior Academic Affairs Coordinator Ms. N. Renee MCDOWELL
07 Executive Director of Admissions Mr. Tony BAEZ MILAN
11 Executive Director of Operations Ms. Amanda PHILLIPS
26 Chief Marketing Officer Mr. Kevin G. FEAR
88 Supervisor of Cosmetology Ms. Karen NELSON
36 Director of Career Services Ms. Dana MELVIN
32 Student Life/Social Media Ms. Janelle IMBRESCIA
13 Exec Dir of Information Technology Mr. John SECHRIST

Drexel University (F)

3141 Chestnut Street, Philadelphia PA 19104-2875
County: Philadelphia FICE Identification: 003256
Unit ID: 212054
Telephone: (215) 895-2000 Carnegie Class: DU-Highest
FAX Number: (215) 895-1414 Calendar System: Quarter
URL: www.drexel.edu
Established: 1891 Annual Undergrad Tuition & Fees: $56,238
Enrollment: 23,589 Coed
Affiliation or Control: Independent Non-Profit IRS Status: 501(c)3
Highest Offering: Doctorate
Accreditation: M, ANEST, ARCPA, ART, CAHIIM, CEA, CIDA, CLPSY, CONST, DIETC, DIETD, HT, IPSY, LAW, LC, LIB, MED, MFCD, NURSE, PA, PH, PTA

01 President Mr. John A. FRY
05 Provost/Executive Vice President Dr. Paul E. JENSEN
111 SVP Inst Advancement Mr. David L. UNRUH
10 Exec Vice Pres/Treasurer/COO Mrs. Helen Y. BOWMAN
84 SVP Enrollment Mgmt/Student Success Ms. Evelyn THIMBA
26 AVP Communications/Marketing Mr. Craig KAMPES
43 Sr VP & General Counsel Mr. Michael J. EXLER
86 Sr VP Govt & Community Relations Mr. Brian T. KEECH
20 Vice Prov Undergraduate Education Dr. Shivanthi ANANDAN
13 Vice Pres IT & CIO Mr. Thomas DECHIARO
88 Exec Dir/VProv Cultural Partnership Dr. Rosalind REMER
88 VP & Exec Dir Applied Innovation Mr. Shintaro KAIDO
46 Sr Vice Provost for Research Dr. Aleister SAUNDERS
32 SVP Stdnt Success/Dean Student Life Dr. Subir SAHU
09 Vice Provost Institutional Research Dr. Sujoy DAS
108 VP Compliance/Privacy & IA Ms. Kim UPSHAW
115 Vice President Investments Ms. Catherine B. ULOZAS
88 Sr Vice Provost Partnerships Dr. Lucy E. KERMAN
15 Vice Pres Human Resources & PMOE Ms. Megan E. WEYLER
49 Int Dean College Arts & Sciences Dr. Kelly JOYCE
50 Dean LeBow College of Business Dr. Vibhas MADAN
54 Dean College of Engineering Dr. Sharon WALKER
77 Dean Col of Computing & Informatics Dr. Yi DENG
92 Dean of Pennoni Honors College Dr. Paula COHEN
81 SVP/CSO/Dean Grad Sch of Biomed Sci Dr. Elisabeth VANBOCKSTAELE
62 Dean of Libraries Dr. Danuta A. NITECKI
88 Dean Close Sch of Entrepreneurship Dr. Donna M. DECAROLIS
61 Dean Kline School of Law Mr. Daniel M. FILLER
60 Dean Col of Media Arts & Design Mr. Jason SCHUPBACH
53 Dean School of Education Dr. Penny HAMMRICH
63 Sr VP & Dean College of Medicine Dr. Charles B. CAIRNS
66 Dean Col Nursing/Health Prof Dr. Laura N. GITLIN

69 Dean Dornsife Sch of Public Health ... Dr. Ana V. DIEZ ROUX
81 Dean School Biomed Engineering ... Dr. Paul BRANDT-RAUF
19 Vice President Public Safety ... Ms. Eileen W. BEHR
41 Athletic Director ... Ms. Maisha KELLY
36 Vice Prov Career Development Ctr ... Mr. Ian SLADEN
22 Title IX Coordinator ... Mr. Paul APICELLA
85 Vice Provost Global Engagement ... Dr. Rogelio MIÑANA
88 Chair Faculty Senate ... Dr. Kevin G. OWENS
83 Director AJ Drexel Autism Institute ... Dr. Diana ROBINS
06 Registrar ... Dr. Giuseppe SALOMONE
104 Senior Director Education Abroad ... Ms. Ahaji SCHREFFLER
18 VP Real Estate & Facilities ... Mr. Alan GREENBERGER
28 AVP HR/Chief Diversity Officer ... Ms. Kim GHOLSTON
39 Senior Exec Director Resident Life ... Dr. Melissa DEPRETTO-BEHAN
96 VP/Chief Procurement Officer ... Ms. Julie JONES

Duquesne University (A)

600 Forbes Avenue, Pittsburgh PA 15282-0001
County: Allegheny FICE Identification: 003258
Unit ID: 212106
Telephone: (412) 396-6000 Carnegie Class: DU-Higher
FAX Number: (412) 396-4186 Calendar System: Semester
URL: www.duq.edu
Established: 1878 Annual Undergrad Tuition & Fees: $41,892
Enrollment: 8,830 Coed
Affiliation or Control: Roman Catholic IRS Status: 501(c)3
Highest Offering: Doctorate
Accreditation: M, ARCPA, CAATE, CACREP, CAEP, CEA, CLPSY, FEPAC, LAW, MUS, NURSE, OT, PHAR, PTA, SCPSY, SP

01 President ... Mr. Kenneth G. GORMLEY
04 Assistant to the President ... Ms. Margaret EISEMAN
05 Provost/Exec Vice Pres ... Dr. David J. DAUSEY
10 Sr Vice Pres for Finance & Business ... Dr. Matthew J. FRIST
32 Sr Vice Pres for Student Life ... Dr. Douglas FRIZZELL
111 Sr VP for University Advancement ... Mr. Jim MILLER
88 Sr Vice Pres Mission/Identity ... Rev. Raymond FRENCH, CSSP
43 VP Legal Affairs & General Counsel ... Ms. Madelyn REILLY
26 VP Marketing and Communications ... Mr. Gabriel WELSCH
41 Vice Pres of Athletics ... Mr. David HARPER
20 Assoc Academic Vice President ... Dr. Darlene WEAVER
20 Assoc Academic Vice President ... Dr. Jeffrey A. MILLER
13 Vice Pres Information Tech/CIO ... Dr. Charles R. BARTEL
84 Vice Pres Enrollment Management ... Mr. Joel BAUMAN
109 Director Auxiliary Services ... Mr. Scott RICHARDS
85 Exec Dir International Programs ... Dr. Joseph DECROSTRA
06 Registrar ... Dr. Kimberly HOERITZ
08 Librarian ... Dr. Sara BARON
29 Asst Vice Pres Alumni Relations ... Ms. Sarah SPERRY
09 Director of Institutional Research ... Mr. Matthew NORTH
37 AVP for Financial Aid ... Mr. Richard C. ESPOSITO
15 Asst Vice Pres/CHRO ... Mr. John G. GREENO
19 Director of Security ... Mr. Thomas HART
88 Dir Environmental Health/Safety ... Ms. Paula D. SWEITZER
18 Asst VP/Chief Facilities Officer ... Mr. Rodney W. DOBISH
36 Director of Career Services ... Ms. Nicole FELDHUES
22 Dir Anti-discrimination/Risk Mgmt ... Mr. Sean F. WEAVER
23 Director Health Service ... Ms. Dessa MRVOS
38 Dir University Counseling Center ... Dr. Ian C. EDWARDS
39 Director Residence Life ... Mrs. Sharon G. OELSCHLAGER
42 Director Campus Ministry ... Rev. William CHRISTY
28 AVP Diversity/Inclus/Stdnt Advance ... Mr. Jeff MALLORY
50 Dean Business & Administration ... Dr. Dean B. MCFARLIN
63 Dean Col of Osteopathic Medicine ... Dr. John M. KAUFFMAN
66 Dean of Nursing ... Dr. Mary Ellen S. GLASGOW
67 Interim Dean of Pharmacy ... Dr. James K. DRENNEN III
64 Interim Dean of Music ... Dr. David Allen WEHR
53 Dean of Education ... Dr. Cindy M. WALKER
76 Dean of Health Sciences ... Dr. Fevzi AKINCI
61 Dean of Law ... Ms. April BARTON
49 Dean of Liberal Arts/Graduate ... Dr. Kristine BLAIR
65 Dean of Natural/Environment Sci ... Dr. Philip P. REEDER
40 Bookstore Manager ... Mr. John KACHUR
07 AVP Undergraduate Admissions ... Ms. Debra A. ZUGATES
100 Chief of Staff/AVP Ofc of President ... Ms. Mary Ellen SOLOMON
30 Asst VP for External Relations ... Ms. Mary Beth FORD
106 Dir Online Education/E-learning ... Dr. Michael W. BRIDGES

Eastern University (B)

1300 Eagle Road, Saint Davids PA 19087-3696
County: Delaware FICE Identification: 003259
Unit ID: 212133
Telephone: (610) 341-5800 Carnegie Class: Masters/L
FAX Number: N/A Calendar System: Semester
URL: www.eastern.edu
Established: 1925 Annual Undergrad Tuition & Fees: $34,706
Enrollment: 3,504 Coed
Affiliation or Control: American Baptist IRS Status: 501(c)3
Highest Offering: Doctorate
Accreditation: M, #ACBSP, EXSC, MPCAC, NURSE, SW, THEOL

01 President ... Dr. Ronald A. MATTHEWS
10 Vice Pres for Finance/Operations ... Mr. J. Pernell JONES
05 Provost/VP Academic Affairs ... Dr. Kenton SPARKS
06 Registrar ... Ms. Sarah ROCHE
32 Vice Prov for Student Development ... Dr. Jacqueline IRVING
45 VP for Inst Planning/Effectiveness ... Dr. Christine P. MAHAN
111 Interim Vice President Advancement ... Mr. Tom RIDINGTON
110 Associate VP Advancement ... Ms. Natissa KULTAN-PFAUTZ
15 Chief Human Resources Officer ... Ms. Kacey BERNARD
118 Sr Dir of Benefits Admin & Trng ... Ms. Patti MCHUGH
04 Exec Asst to the President ... Ms. Heather NORCINI
12 Executive Dean Esperanza College ... Ms. Marilyn MARSH
76 Dean College of Health and Sciences ... Dr. Patricia REGER
73 Dean Palmer Theological Seminary ... Dr. F. David BRONKEMA
50 Dean Col of Business Leadership ... Dr. Al SOCCI
92 Dean College Arts/Humanities/Honors ... Dr. Brian WILLIAMS
53 Dean College of Education ... Dr. Susan EDGAR-SMITH
18 Exec Dir Facilities Services ... Mr. Jeffrey GROMIS
105 Senior Web Manager ... Ms. Allison MARSHALECK
09 Asst VP/Dir Institutional Research ... Mr. Thomas A. DAHLSTROM
26 Assoc VP Marketing/Enroll & Comm ... Dr. Michael THOMAS
113 Senior Director Student Accounts ... Ms. Lisa WELLER
08 Director of University Library ... Ms. Joy DLUGOSZ
42 University Chaplain ... Rev Dr. Joseph B. MODICA
37 Director of Financial Aid ... Ms. Andrea RUTH
13 Chief Information Officer ... Mr. Eric MCCLOY
24 Media Services Supervisor ... Mr. Paul THORPE
36 Director of Talent & Career Dev ... Ms. Sarah TODD
41 Director of Athletics ... Mr. Eric MCNELLEY
19 Director of Public Safety ... Mr. Michael BICKING
88 Exec Dir Conferences/Spec Events ... Ms. Meggin CAPERS
38 Dir Counseling/Academic Support ... Dr. Lisa M. HEMLICK
85 Dir Intl Student & Scholar Services ... Ms. Augusta ALLEN
39 Dir of Student Conduct & Comm Stand ... Ms. Ashlee WILLIAMS
40 Follett Bookstore Manager ... Mr. Christopher HOAGLAND
93 Int Dir Multicultural Student Init ... Ms. Theresa NOYE
109 Director Auxiliary Services ... Mr. Byron MCMILLAN
120 Mgr Instruct Design & Lrng Tech ... Ms. Susan YAVOR
44 Exec Dir Adv Mktg & Ext Const Eng ... Ms. Elizabeth LOCHNER
104 Sr Assc Reg/Coord Off-Campus Pgm ... Ms. Lori BRISTOL
106 Dir Center Teach/Learn/Tech ... Dr. Rebecca GIDJUNIS
96 Financial Asst/Purchasing Mgr ... Ms. Heather SYKES
07 Director of Admissions ... Vacant
101 Asst to the Office of the BOT ... Ms. Amanda KELLY
28 Spec Asst to the Pres for Diversity ... Mr. Randolph WALTERS
29 Assoc VP for Alumni & Family Engage ... Mr. Timothy WORTHAM

† Parent institution of Palmer Theological Seminary.

Elizabethtown College (C)

1 Alpha Drive, Elizabethtown PA 17022-2298
County: Lancaster FICE Identification: 003262
Unit ID: 212197
Telephone: (717) 361-1000 Carnegie Class: Bac-A&S
FAX Number: (717) 361-1207 Calendar System: Semester
URL: www.etown.edu
Established: 1899 Annual Undergrad Tuition & Fees: $32,960
Enrollment: 1,881 Coed
Affiliation or Control: Other IRS Status: 501(c)3
Highest Offering: Doctorate
Accreditation: M, ACBSP, MUS, OT, SW

01 President ... Ms. Cecilia M. MCCORMICK
05 Sr Vice Pres Acad Affs/Dn Faculty ... Dr. Elizabeth (Betty) RIDER
10 Vice Pres Finance/Strategy ... Mr. Gerald SILBERMAN
111 VP Advancement/Cmty Relations ... Mr. David C. BEIDLEMAN
84 Vice Pres Enrollment Management ... Mr. John F. CHAMPOLI
32 Vice Pres Student Life ... Vacant
51 Dean of SGPS/Prof of Educ ... Mr. Jack RICE
07 Sr Director Admissions ... Mr. Adam D. SMITH
35 Asst Dean of Students & Dir of CSS ... Ms. Stephanie A. RANKIN
26 Exec Dir Marketing/Communications ... Ms. Keri B. STRAUB
102 Exec Dir Foundation/Govt Relations ... Ms. Lesley M. FINNEY
09 Director Institutional Research ... Ms. Debra K. SHEESLEY
37 Director of Financial Aid ... Ms. Melodie R. JACKSON
08 Director The High Library ... Ms. Sarah PENNIMAN
29 Exec Director Alumni Devel/Programs ... Mr. Mark A. CLAPPER
19 Director of Campus Security ... Mr. Andrew L. POWELL
41 Director of Athletics ... Mr. Chris MORGAN
42 Chaplain/Director Religious Life ... Ms. Amy SHORNER-JOHNSON

Erie Institute of Technology (D)

940 Millcreek Mall, Erie PA 16565-1002
County: Erie FICE Identification: 022039
Unit ID: 212434
Telephone: (814) 868-9900 Carnegie Class: Spec 2-yr-Tech
FAX Number: (814) 868-9977 Calendar System: Semester
URL: www.erieit.edu
Established: 1958 Annual Undergrad Tuition & Fees: $14,839
Enrollment: 282 Coed
Affiliation or Control: Proprietary IRS Status: Proprietary
Highest Offering: Associate Degree
Accreditation: ACCSC

01 Director ... Mr. Paul FITZGERALD
05 Director of Education ... Ms. Kate HUSHON
07 Admissions Director ... Ms. Barb BOLT

Esperanza College (E)

4261 North 5th Street, Philadelphia PA 19140
Telephone: (215) 324-0746 Identification: 770153
Accreditation: &M

† Branch campus of Eastern University, Saint Davids, PA

Evangelical Theological Seminary (F)

121 S College Street, Myerstown PA 17067-1299
County: Lebanon FICE Identification: 003263
Unit ID: 212443
Telephone: (717) 866-5775 Carnegie Class: Spec-4-yr-Faith
FAX Number: (717) 866-4667 Calendar System: 4/1/4
URL: www.evangelical.edu
Established: 1953 Annual Graduate Tuition & Fees: N/A
Enrollment: 179 Coed
Affiliation or Control: Evangelical Congregational Church
IRS Status: 501(c)3
Highest Offering: Doctorate; No Undergraduates
Accreditation: M, MFCD, THEOL

01 President ... Dr. Anthony L. BLAIR
111 Exec Dir Institutional Advancement ... Rev. Ann E. STEEL
10 Vice President Finance & Operations ... Mr. Kevin C. HENRY
26 Director of Marketing ... Mr. Mike DONGHIA
05 EVP/Dean of Academic Services ... Mr. James E. EHRMAN
08 Director Library Services ... Mr. James SAURER
18 Director of Buildings & Grounds ... Mr. William J. ROBERTSON
91 Database Manager ... Mrs. Marsha A. CONLEY
04 Executive Asst to President ... Mrs. Jayne SENSENIG

Fortis Institute (G)

166 Slocum Street, Forty Fort PA 18704-2347
County: Luzerne FICE Identification: 030115
Unit ID: 249609
Telephone: (570) 288-8400 Carnegie Class: Spec 2-yr-Health
FAX Number: (570) 287-7936 Calendar System: Other
URL: www.fortis.edu
Established: 1984 Annual Undergrad Tuition & Fees: $13,921
Enrollment: 182 Coed
Affiliation or Control: Proprietary IRS Status: Proprietary
Highest Offering: Associate Degree
Accreditation: ACCSC

01 Campus President ... Madeline LEVY CRUZ
05 Director of Education ... Christopher JONES
07 Director of Admissions ... Jane AUSTIN
37 Director Financial Aid ... Ruth BRUMAGIN

Fortis Institute (H)

517 Ash Street, Scranton PA 18509
County: Lackawanna FICE Identification: 030116
Unit ID: 385503
Telephone: (570) 558-1818 Carnegie Class: Spec 2-yr-Health
FAX Number: (570) 342-4537 Calendar System: Other
URL: www.fortis.edu/scranton-pennsylvania.php
Established: 1986 Annual Undergrad Tuition & Fees: $28,087
Enrollment: 279 Coed
Affiliation or Control: Proprietary IRS Status: Proprietary
Highest Offering: Associate Degree
Accreditation: ACCSC, DH

01 Campus President ... Ms. Madeline LEVY CRUZ
06 Registrar ... Mr. Art BOBBOUINE
07 Director of Admissions ... Ms. Rachel SCOTCH
36 Director Career/Student Services ... Ms. Heather CONTARDI
37 Director Student Financial Aid ... Ms. Stacie TAROLI

† Tuition varies by degree program.

Franklin & Marshall College (I)

PO Box 3003, Lancaster PA 17604-3003
County: Lancaster FICE Identification: 003265
Unit ID: 212577
Telephone: (717) 358-3971 Carnegie Class: Bac-A&S
FAX Number: (717) 358-4183 Calendar System: Semester
URL: www.fandm.edu
Established: 1787 Annual Undergrad Tuition & Fees: $61,062
Enrollment: 2,254 Coed
Affiliation or Control: Independent Non-Profit IRS Status: 501(c)3
Highest Offering: Baccalaureate
Accreditation: M

01 President ... Dr. Barbara K. ALTMANN
10 VP for Finance/Admin & Treasurer ... Mr. Michael TODD
111 Vice Pres for College Advancement ... Mr. Matthew EYNON
84 VP for Enrollment Management ... Mr. Jimmie FOSTER
26 Vice Pres for College Communication ... Ms. Barbara STAMBAUGH
05 Provost/Dean of Faculty ... Dr. Cameron WESSON
32 VP and Dean of Student Affairs ... Ms. Margaret HAZLETT
88 Acting Director of the Klehr Center ... Ms. Amy ZYLBERMAN
11 Associate VP for Administration ... Mr. Barry BOSLEY
45 VP for Strategic Initiatives ... Dr. Alan S. CANIGLIA
100 Interim Dir Ofc of the President ... Dr. Deb MORIARTY
08 College Librarian ... Mr. Scott VINE
85 Assoc Dean International Programs ... Ms. Sue MENNICKE
20 Associate Dean of Faculty ... Dr. Annalisa CRANNELL
20 Associate Dean of Faculty ... Dr. Amelia RAUSER
28 Assoc Dir of Multicultural Affairs ... Ms. Xay CHONGTUA
88 Assistant Dean/College House Dean ... Ms. Melissa GIESS
88 Assistant Dean/College House Dean ... Ms. Courtnee N. JORDAN-COX
88 Assistant Dean/College House Dean ... Dr. Beth PROFFITT
88 Assistant Dean/College House Dean ... Mr. Todd DEKAY
88 Assistant Dean/College House Dean ... Mr. Jedrek DINEROS
21 Asst VP for Treasury & Controller ... Mr. Sean GALLOWAY
15 Assistant VP Human Resources ... Vacant
18 Associate VP/Facilities Management ... Mr. Mike WETZEL
19 Assoc VP Public Safety ... Mr. William MCHALE, JR.
23 Managing Physician Student Wellness ... Dr. Amy A. MYERS

13 VP and Chief Information Officer ..... Ms. Carrie RAMPP
37 Director Financial Aid ..... Mr. Clarke C. PAINE
38 Head of Counseling Services ..... Dr. Lauren A. FIRESTONE
90 Dir Instruct/Emerging Technology ..... Mr. Teb LOCKE
06 College Registrar ..... Ms. Laura A. MEDVIC
29 Asst VP/Alumni Engagement ..... Ms. Amy T. LAYMAN
07 Dean of Admission ..... Vacant
41 Athletic Director ..... Ms. Lauren PACKER
43 VP and General Counsel ..... Vacant
101 Secretary of the Board ..... Dr. Deb MORIARTY
102 Dir Corp/Found/Cmty Partners ..... Vacant
44 Director Annual Giving ..... Mr. Ramy RAHAL
39 Dir Resident Life/Student Housing ..... Ms. Lori N. FOUST
09 Director of Institutional Research ..... Ms. Chris D. ALEXANDER

Gannon University (A)

University Square, Erie PA 16541-0001
County: Erie FICE Identification: 003266
Unit ID: 212601
Telephone: (814) 871-7000 Carnegie Class: DU-Mod
FAX Number: (814) 871-7338 Calendar System: Other
URL: www.gannon.edu
Established: 1925 Annual Undergrad Tuition & Fees: $34,526
Enrollment: 4,251 Coed
Affiliation or Control: Roman Catholic IRS Status: 501(c)3
Highest Offering: Doctorate
Accreditation: M, ACBSP, ANEST, ARCPA, CAATE, CACREP, CEA, COARC, COARCP, EXSC, NURSE, OT, PTA, RAD, @SP, SW

01 President ..... Dr. Keith TAYLOR
05 Provost & VP Student Experience ..... Dr. Walter IWANENKO, JR.
10 Vice Pres Planning and Finance ..... Ms. Valerie BACIK
111 Vice Pres University Advancement ..... Ms. Barbara BEUSCHER
88 Assoc Vice President for Mission ..... Rev. Michael KESICKI
84 Vice President for Enrollment ..... Mr. William EDMONDSON
32 VP Student Development & Engagement ..... Vacant
11 VP Strategy & Campus Operations ..... Dr. Steven A. MAURO
04 Assistant to the President ..... Ms. Darlene A. MCMICHAEL
79 Dean Col Humanities/Educ/Soc Sci ..... Dr. Lori LINDLEY
54 Dean Col Engineering/Business ..... Dr. Karinna VERNAZA
76 Dean Morosky Col Health Prof/Sci ..... Dr. Sarah EWING
49 Director of Liberal Studies ..... Dr. Megan WOLLER
08 Director Nash Library ..... Mr. Ken BRUNDAGE
37 Director of Financial Aid ..... Mr. Andrew TEETS
06 Registrar ..... Mr. Zachary HOPKINS
36 Assoc Dir Career Dev/Employment Svc ..... Ms. Erin HART
39 Director of Residence Life ..... Ms. Denise GOLDEN
88 Dir Stdnt Org/Leadership Dev ..... Ms. Jaime MCCASLIN
30 Associate VP for Development ..... Ms. Almi CLERKIN
100 Chief of Staff/Dir Marketing/Comm ..... Mr. Douglas OATHOUT
102 Dir of Research/Foundation Rels ..... Vacant
21 Controller ..... Mr. Jeffrey TAYLOR
114 Assoc Vice President Budget ..... Ms. Mary Kathleen LEONARD
15 Exec Director of Human Resources ..... Mr. Robin WILLIAMS
41 Director of Athletics ..... Ms. Lisa GODDARD MCGUIRK
19 Director Campus Police & Safety ..... Mr. Les FETTERMAN
13 Director of Computing/Telecomm ..... Mr. Mark JORDANO
42 University Chaplain ..... Rev. Michael KESICKI
07 Director of Admissions ..... Mr. Thomas P. CAMILLO
09 Director of Institutional Research ..... Mr. Dana BAGWELL
18 Director Physical Plant/Maintenance ..... Ms. Ashley SPEARS
27 Chief Media Relations Officer ..... Vacant
38 Director Student Counseling ..... Dr. Jodi GIACOMELLI
86 Dir Community/Government Relations ..... Ms. Erika A. RAMALHO
96 Director of Purchasing ..... Ms. Bridget SETH
40 Bookstore Manager ..... Ms. Amber COOK
29 Director Alumni Affairs ..... Ms. Allison MOSIER

Geisinger Commonwealth School of Medicine (B)

525 Pine Street, Scranton PA 18509
County: Lackawanna FICE Identification: 041672
Unit ID: 456542
Telephone: (570) 504-7000 Carnegie Class: Spec-4-yr-Med
FAX Number: (570) 504-9660 Calendar System: Semester
URL: https://www.geisinger.edu/education
Established: 2009 Annual Graduate Tuition & Fees: N/A
Enrollment: 607 Coed
Affiliation or Control: Independent Non-Profit IRS Status: 501(c)3
Highest Offering: Doctorate; No Undergraduates
Accreditation: M, MED

01 President and Dean ..... Dr. Steven J. SCHEINMAN
10 VP for Finance & Admin/CFO ..... Ms. Anna ARVAY
28 VP Cmty Engage/Chf Diversity Ofcr ..... Dr. Ida L. CASTRO
05 VP Acad Affairs/Vice Dean Med Ed ..... Dr. William JEFFRIES
45 VP Strat Plng Com/Vice Dean Grad Ed .. Dr. Venard S. KOERWER
32 Dean Student Affairs ..... Dr. Tanja ADONIZIO
20 Assoc Dean Educ Admin ..... Dr. Andrea DIMATTIA
07 Assoc Dean Admission/Enrol/Fin Aid ..... Dr. Michelle SCHMUDE
21 Senior Dir Opers/Acad Affairs ..... Mr. Sam DIAZ
35 Asst Dean of Students ..... Ms. Jacquelyn GHORMOZ
06 Registrar ..... Mr. Edward LAHART
37 Director of Financial Aid ..... Ms. Sue MCNAMARA
29 Director Alumni Relations ..... Vacant

Geneva College (C)

3200 College Avenue, Beaver Falls PA 15010-3557
County: Beaver FICE Identification: 003267
Unit ID: 212656
Telephone: (724) 846-5100 Carnegie Class: Masters/M
FAX Number: (724) 847-6687 Calendar System: Semester
URL: www.geneva.edu
Established: 1848 Annual Undergrad Tuition & Fees: $29,040
Enrollment: 1,349 Coed
Affiliation or Control: Reformed Presbyterian Church IRS Status: 501(c)3
Highest Offering: Master's
Accreditation: M, ACBSP, CACREP

01 President ..... Dr. Calvin L. TROUP
05 Provost ..... Dr. Melinda R. STEPHENS
111 Vice Pres of Advancement ..... Dr. Marvin L. DEWEY
10 VP Business/Finance ..... Mr. Timothy R. BAIRD
84 VP Enrollment & Marketing ..... Vacant
13 CIO & VP Information Technology ..... Vacant
21 Controller ..... Mrs. Kami S. GREENE
07 Assoc VP for Enrollment ..... Mr. Dave B. LAYTON
32 VP of Student Dev/Title IX Coord ..... Ms. Jamie R. SWANK
124 Director of Student Engagement ..... Mr. Randon T. WILLARD
58 Dean Grad/Adult & Online Programs ..... Mr. John D. GALLO
06 Registrar ..... Mr. William M. STARKE
37 Director of Student Financial Svcs ..... Vacant
08 Librarian ..... Mr. Steve P. KENNEALLY
26 Director Public Relations ..... Mrs. Cheryl L. JOHNSTON
29 Alumni Relations Coordinator ..... Ms. Kelly J. SANZARI
41 Chief Athletic Officer ..... Mr. Van G. ZANIC
18 Director of Physical Plant ..... Vacant
36 Director of Career Development ..... Ms. Krista M. AUTREY
85 International Admissions Counselor ..... Ms. Sarah A. MURISON
40 Campus Store Manager ..... Ms. Rachael E. VAN DERVEER
19 Director of Security ..... Mr. Dennis E. DAMAZO
28 Interim Coordinator of Diversity ..... Mrs. Kristie A. MARTEL
92 Director of Honors Program ..... Dr. Eric MILLER
39 Director of Residence Life ..... Mrs. Kelsey L. MURPHY
23 Health Services Director ..... Mrs. Beth L. CARLSON
96 Purchasing Coordinator ..... Ms. Heid J. SRAY
88 Accounting and Payroll Manager ..... Mr. William NICHOLS
121 Director of Student Success ..... Mr. Thomas C. PYLE
04 Executive Asst to President ..... Mrs. Andrea KAMICKER
09 Director of Institutional Research ..... Mr. Jordan BOUSCHER
50 Business Dept Chair ..... Ms. Christen S. ADELS
53 Education Dept Chair ..... Mrs. Adel G. AIKEN
54 Engineering Dept Chair ..... Dr. Anthony C. COMER
90 Director of Technology Services ..... Mr. Jeremy T. YERSE
104 Dir Crossroads/Ctr Special Programs ..... Dr. Jeffrey S. COLE
105 Online Marketing/Webmaster ..... Mr. Michael W. DUNCAN
106 Dean Grad/Adult/Online Programs ..... Mr. John D. GALLO
15 Chief Human Resources Officer ..... Mrs. Sue THOMPSON
30 Director of Development ..... Ms. Kelli J. MCKEE
38 Director Student Counseling ..... Ms. Amy L. SOLMAN

Gettysburg College (D)

300 N Washington Street, Gettysburg PA 17325-1486
County: Adams FICE Identification: 003268
Unit ID: 212674
Telephone: (717) 337-6000 Carnegie Class: Bac-A&S
FAX Number: (717) 337-6008 Calendar System: Semester
URL: www.gettysburg.edu
Established: 1832 Annual Undergrad Tuition & Fees: $58,500
Enrollment: 2,507 Coed
Affiliation or Control: Evangelical Lutheran Church In America
IRS Status: 501(c)3
Highest Offering: Baccalaureate
Accreditation: M, MUS

01 President ..... Mr. Robert IULIANO
05 Provost ..... Dr. Christopher ZAPPE
30 Vice Pres Dev/Alumni/Parent Rels ..... Mr. Clarence (Tres) MULLIS
10 Vice President Finance/Treasurer ..... Mr. Daniel T. KONSTALID
32 Vice President for College Life ..... Ms. Anne EHRLICH
84 Vice Pres Enrollment/Education Svcs ..... Mr. Carey THOMPSON
13 Vice President Information Tech ..... Dr. Rod TOSTEN
45 Assoc Provost for Plng/Fac & Tech ..... Mrs. Rhonda GOOD
28 Interim Chief Diversity Officer ..... Mr. Darrien DAVENPORT
100 Chief of Staff/Strat Adv to Pres ..... Ms. Kristin J. STUEMPFLE
21 Associate Vice President/Treasurer ..... Mr. Christopher DELANEY
26 Exec Dir Communications/Marketing ..... Ms. Jamie YATES
35 Associate Dean of College Life ..... Mr. James P. DUFFY
85 Dir International Student Services ..... Mr. Brad LANCASTER
06 Registrar ..... Mr. Brian REESE
37 Director of Financial Aid ..... Ms. Kathryn F. ADAMS
07 Dean of Admissions ..... Ms. Gail M. SWEEZEY
42 Chaplain ..... Vacant
09 Director for Institutional Analysis ..... Ms. Suhua DONG
38 Exec Dir of Health & Counseling ..... Ms. Kathy BRADLEY
08 Dean of the Library ..... Ms. Robin WAGNER
29 Exec Director of Alumni Relations ..... Mr. Joe LYNCH
41 Exec Director for Athletics ..... Mr. Mike M. MATIIA
19 Asst VP Col Life/Exec Dir Safety ..... Mr. William J. LAFFERTY
18 Exec Dir Facilities Plng & Mgmt ..... Mr. James BIESECKER
21 Sr Dir of Financial Svcs/Controller ..... Ms. Sharon S. DAYHOFF
80 Director Center for Public Service ..... Ms. Gretchen NATTER
39 Dir Res Life & First Yr Programs ..... Ms. Danielle PHILLIPS
121 Dean of Academic Advising ..... Ms. Charmaine T. CRUISE
122 Dir Student Activities & Greek Life ..... Mr. Jonathan ALLEN
40 Director of College Bookstore ..... Mr. Michael J. KOTLINSKI
94 Dir Women's Center ..... Ms. Valentina CUCUZZA
96 Asst Director of Procurement ..... Ms. Patricia K. VERDEROSA
15 Exec Director Human Resources ..... Ms. Jennifer R. LUCAS
16 Asst Director Human Resources ..... Ms. Cassandra FOCKLER
102 Dir Foundation/Govt & FAC Grants ..... Vacant
104 Dir Global Init/Ctr Global Educ ..... Ms. Rebecca A. BERGREN
04 Administrative Asst to President ..... Ms. Pamela EISENHART
109 Exec Dir Aux Svcs/Life Safety Mgr ..... Vacant
36 Exec Dir Ctr for Career Engagement ..... Mr. Marc GOLDMAN
101 Asst Secy to Board of Trustees ..... Mr. Darrien DAVENPORT

Gratz College (E)

7605 Old York Road, Melrose Park PA 19027-3010
County: Montgomery FICE Identification: 004058
Unit ID: 212771
Telephone: (215) 635-7300 Carnegie Class: Spec-4-yr-Faith
FAX Number: (215) 635-1046 Calendar System: Trimester
URL: www.gratz.edu
Established: 1895 Annual Undergrad Tuition & Fees: N/A
Enrollment: 454 Coed
Affiliation or Control: Independent Non-Profit IRS Status: 501(c)3
Highest Offering: Doctorate
Accreditation: M

01 President ..... Dr. Zev ELEFF
05 Dean of Gratz College ..... Dr. Honour MOORE
26 Chief Public Relations Officer ..... Ms. Dodi KLIMOFF
84 Director of Enrollment Management ..... Mr. Dave MALTER
06 Registrar ..... Mr. Scott MINKOFF
13 Manager Information Technoloy ..... Ms. Suzette QUILES
15 Personnel Services ..... Ms. Yaffa HOWARD
111 Dir Institutional Advancement ..... Ms. Naomi HOUSMAN
07 Assoc Director of Enroll Mgmt ..... Ms. Mindy BLECHMAN
88 Director of Gratz Advance ..... Ms. Deborah LEON
37 Student Financial Services Advisor ..... Vacant
106 Online Education/E-learning ..... Dr. Philip MOORE
08 Dir of Library/Info Tech Svcs ..... Ms. Donna GUERIN
18 Chief Facilities/Physical Plant ..... Mr. Ernest COLLINS
04 Administrative Asst to President ..... Ms. Dodi KLIMOFF
10 Mgr Business Operations/Facilities ... Mr. Thomas CIPRIANO, JR.
101 Secretary of the Institution/Board ..... Ms. Sharon LIEBHABER
19 Director Security/Safety ..... Ms. Suzette QUILES

Great Lakes Institute of Technology (F)

5100 Peach Street, Erie PA 16509
County: Erie FICE Identification: 021122
Unit ID: 213181
Telephone: (814) 864-6666 Carnegie Class: Spec 2-yr-Health
FAX Number: (814) 868-1717 Calendar System: Other
URL: www.glit.edu
Established: 1965 Annual Undergrad Tuition & Fees: N/A
Enrollment: 429 Coed
Affiliation or Control: Proprietary IRS Status: Proprietary
Highest Offering: Associate Degree
Accreditation: ACCSC, DMS, SURGT

01 Director/CEO ..... Eric BERRIOS
07 Director of Admissions ..... Mark STOTTS
37 Director Student Financial Aid ..... Andrew DICK
05 Director of Education ..... Vickie CLEMENTS
10 Director of Finance ..... Andrea CAMPBELL
36 Director Career Services ..... Carl ROZENEK

Grove City College (G)

100 Campus Drive, Grove City PA 16127-2104
County: Mercer FICE Identification: 003269
Unit ID: 212805
Telephone: (724) 458-2000 Carnegie Class: Bac-A&S
FAX Number: (724) 458-2190 Calendar System: Semester
URL: www.gcc.edu
Established: 1876 Annual Undergrad Tuition & Fees: $18,930
Enrollment: 2,277 Coed
Affiliation or Control: Non-denominational IRS Status: 501(c)3
Highest Offering: Master's
Accreditation: M, ACBSP, EXSC, SW

01 President ..... Hon. Paul J. MCNULTY
05 Provost and VP Academic Affairs ..... Dr. Peter M. FRANK
10 Vice Pres for Business & Finance ..... Mr. Michael R. BUCKMAN
32 Vice Pres For Student Life/Learning ..... Mr. Larry E. HARDESTY
111 Vice President for Inst Advancement .. Mr. Jeffrey D. PROKOVICH
11 Vice President for Operations ..... Mr. James M. LOPRESTI
13 Vice Pres/Chief Information Officer ..... Dr. Vincent F. DISTASI
84 VP of Enrollment Svcs & Registrar ..... Dr. John G. INMAN
88 Vice Pres for Student Recruitment ..... Mr. Lee S. WISHING, III
100 Assistant to the President ..... Ms. Betty L. TALLERICO
49 Dean Sch of Arts/Letters ..... Dr. Paul C. KEMENY
81 Dean Sch of Sci/Engr/Math ..... Dr. Richard N. SAVAGE
66 Director of Nursing ..... Dr. Janey A. ROACH
21 Director of Financial Services ..... Mrs. Michelle M. WILLIAMS
15 Director of Human Resources ..... Mrs. Marci K. WAGNER
35 Assistant Dean of Students ..... Dr. John M. COYNE
07 Director of Admissions ..... Vacant
36 Director of Career Services ..... Ms. Amanda L. SPOSATO
08 Librarian ..... Mrs. Barbra M. MUNNELL
37 Director of Financial Aid ..... Vacant
88 Dir Stdnt Rec/Club Sports/Frat Life ... Mr. Andrew A. TONCIC, JR.
35 Director Stdnt Activities/Programs ..... Mr. T. Scott GORDON
19 Director of Campus Safety ..... Mr. Seth J. VAN TIL
23 Director of Health & Wellness Ctr ..... Mrs. Amy E. PAGANO
40 Bookstore Manager ..... Mrs. Carrie J. ROSE
41 Athletic Director ..... Mr. Todd D. GIBSON
42 Chaplain ..... Rev Dr. Donald D. OPITZ
29 Sr Dir Alumni & College Relations ..... Ms. Melissa A. MACLEOD

30 Sr Director of Development .... Mr. Brian M. POWELL
26 Sr Director of Communications ....Mrs. Jacquelyn P. MULLER
38 Director of College Counseling ....Dr. Suzanne N. HOUK
39 Director of Residence Life ....Mr. Jonathan J. DIBENEDETTO

Gwynedd Mercy University (A)

1325 Sumneytown Pike, PO Box 901,
Gwynedd Valley PA 19437-0901
County: Montgomery FICE Identification: 003270
Unit ID: 212832
Telephone: (215) 646-7300 Carnegie Class: Masters/M
FAX Number: (215) 641-5596 Calendar System: Semester
URL: www.gmercyu.edu
Established: 1948 Annual Undergrad Tuition & Fees: $35,430
Enrollment: 2,737 Coed
Affiliation or Control: Roman Catholic IRS Status: 501(c)3
Highest Offering: Doctorate
Accreditation: M, COARC, IACBE, NURSE, OT, RTT, SW

01 President ....Ms. Deanne H. D'EMILIO
05 Provost & VP Academic Affairs ....Dr. Mary H. VAN BRUNT
10 Vice Pres Finance/Administration ....Mr. James E. TRUSDELL
111 Int VP University Advancement ....Mr. Keith RICHARDSON
32 VP Stdnt Svcs/Dean of Students ....Mr. Joshua STERN
42 VP Mission Integration ....Dr. James GALLO
84 VP for Mktg & Enroll Mgmt ....Ms. Kelly STATMORE
108 AVP for Assessment & Compliance .... Dr. Dawn HAYWARD
06 Registrar ....Ms. Joanna RAUDENBUSH
08 Director of Library ....Ms. Jing Feng XIA
37 Director of Student Financial Aid ....Mr. Joseph ALAIMO
13 Chief Information Officer ....Mr. Joseph PUPO
29 Director Alumni Relations ....Ms. Gianna QUINN
09 Director of Institutional Research ....Dr. Jing GAO
15 AVP Human Resources ....Mr. Matthew LASECKI
21 Controller ....Ms. Jennifer GINNETTI
38 Director Counseling ....Ms. Pamela MOORE
07 Director of Undergrad Admissions ...... Mr. Alexander SPERRAZZA
96 Director of Procurement ....Mr. Frank PETKA
102 Dir Foundation/Corporate Relations ....Ms. Josephina BANNER
19 Director Campus Safety/Security .... Ms. Joanna GALLAGHER
41 Athletic Dir/Head Women's Bsktbl ....Mr. Keith MONDILLO
39 Director Student Housing .... Mr. Bryan DUNPHY-CULP

HACC, Central Pennsylvania's Community College (B)

1 HACC Drive, Harrisburg PA 17110-2999
County: Dauphin FICE Identification: 003273
Unit ID: 212878
Telephone: (800) 222-4222 Carnegie Class: Assoc/MT-VT-High Trad
FAX Number: (717) 909-1491 Calendar System: Semester
URL: www.hacc.edu
Established: 1964 Annual Undergrad Tuition & Fees (In-District): $8,160
Enrollment: 15,376 Coed
Affiliation or Control: State/Local IRS Status: 501(c)3
Highest Offering: Associate Degree
Accreditation: M, ACBSP, ACFEI, ADNUR, ART, COARC, CSHSE, CVT, DA, DH, DMS, EMT, MLTAD, NAEYC, PNUR, RAD, SURGT

01 President/CEO ....Dr. John J. SYGIELSKI
05 VP Academic Affairs ....Dr. Al GRISWOLD
32 VP Student Affairs/Enroll Mgmt ....Dr. Chrissy DAVIS JONES
10 Vice Pres Finance/CFO ....Mr. Timothy SANDOE
111 VP College Advancement ....Dr. Linnie S. CARTER
20 Assoc Provost Academic Affairs ....Dr. Kathleen T. DOHERTY
103 Assoc Provost Workforce Development .... Mr. Victor RODGERS
15 Int VP Human Resources ....Ms. Ellen HORSCH
28 Chief Inclusion/Diversity Officer ....Dr. Armenta HINTON
106 Associate Provost Virtual Learning .... Ms. Doreen FISHER-BAMMER
06 Registrar ....Dr. Genita D. MANGUM
13 VP Information Technology/CIO ....Mr. Robert H. MESSNER
96 Director Procurement and Contracts .... Mr. Lee W. HAYES
19 Director Safety and Security ....Vacant
40 Director College Bookstores ....Mr. Kyle J. DIBRITO
21 Controller ....Mr. Rich CARDAMONE
09 Exec Dir Inst Effectiveness .... Mr. Bob MESSNER
37 Director Financial Aid ....Vacant
102 Executive Director HACC Foundation .... Dr. Linnie S. CARTER
04 Executive Asst to the President .... Mrs. Kristin GRAESER

HACC Gettysburg Campus (C)

731 Old Harrisburg Road, Gettysburg PA 17325
Telephone: (717) 337-3855 Identification: 770156
Accreditation: &M

Harcum College (D)

750 Montgomery Avenue, Bryn Mawr PA 19010-3476
County: Montgomery FICE Identification: 003272
Unit ID: 212869
Telephone: (610) 525-4100 Carnegie Class: Assoc/HVT-High Trad
FAX Number: (610) 526-6009 Calendar System: Semester
URL: www.harcum.edu
Established: 1915 Annual Undergrad Tuition & Fees: $26,000
Enrollment: 1,150 Coed
Affiliation or Control: Independent Non-Profit IRS Status: 501(c)3
Highest Offering: Associate Degree
Accreditation: M, ADNUR, DA, DH, HT, MLTAD, NAEYC, OTA, PTAA, RAD

01 President ....Dr. Jon Jay DETEMPLE
05 EVP/VP of Academic & Legal Affairs ....Dr. Julia INGERSOLL
10 SVP/Chief Financial Officer ....Mr. Dario BELLOT
32 Dean of Student Life ....Mr. Edward KOVACS
84 VP of Enrollment Management ....Ms. Rachel BOWEN
111 VP of Institutional Advancement ....Ms. Brooke WALKER
15 Assoc VP HR/CHRO ....Mr. Hunt BARTINE
20 Asst VP Academic Support Services ....Vacant
37 Asst VP Financial Aid ....Ms. Melissa WALSH
51 Exec Dir of Partnership Sites ....Ms. Evelyn SANTANA
18 Facilities Manager ....Mr. Nikolay KARPALO
06 Registrar ....Ms. Beth MCMICHAEL
08 Director of Library Services ....Ms. Katie MCGOWAN
85 Director of International Programs .... Ms. Michelle STANZIANO
26 Exec Dir of Communications & Mktg .... Ms. Gale MARTIN
29 Director of Alumni Relations ....Ms. Melissa SAMANGO
38 Director of Counseling Services ....Ms. Kathy ANTHONY
36 Interim Dir Career & Transfer Svcs ....Mr. Trevor GULLEDGE
39 Assistant Dean of Student Life ....Mr. Jameel TUCKER
35 Director of Campus Activities ....Ms. Brittany SHAW
21 Director of Business Services ....Mr. Stephen KLEPONIS
19 Director of Campus Safety ....Mr. Rick SANFILIPPO
41 Associate VP for Athletics ....Mr. Drew KELLY
04 Dir President's Office Operations ....Ms. Tricia FLEMING
13 Chief Information Officer ....Mr. John SUPPLEE
09 Exec Dir of Inst Rsrch/Strat Plng ....Mr. Tim ELY
106 Dir Online Education/E-learning ....Mr. Stephen PIPITONE
108 Director Institutional Assessment ....Mr. Tim ELY
50 Director of Business Mgmt Program ....Mr. Mike PRUSHAN
86 External Affairs ....Dr. Jon Jay DETEMPLE

Harrisburg Area Community College Lancaster Campus (E)

1641 Old Philadelphia Pike, Lancaster PA 17602
Telephone: (717) 293-5000 Identification: 770157
Accreditation: &M

Harrisburg Area Community College Lebanon Campus (F)

735 Cumberland Street, Lebanon PA 17042
Telephone: (717) 270-4222 Identification: 770158
Accreditation: &M

Harrisburg Area Community College York Campus (G)

2010 Pennsylvania Avenue, York PA 17404
Telephone: (717) 718-0328 Identification: 770159
Accreditation: &M

Harrisburg University of Science and Technology (H)

326 Market Street, Harrisburg PA 17101-2116
County: Dauphin FICE Identification: 039483
Unit ID: 446640
Telephone: (717) 901-5100 Carnegie Class: Masters/L
FAX Number: (717) 901-3152 Calendar System: Trimester
URL: www.harrisburgu.edu
Established: 2001 Annual Undergrad Tuition & Fees: $23,900
Enrollment: 3,997 Coed
Affiliation or Control: Independent Non-Profit IRS Status: 501(c)3
Highest Offering: Doctorate
Accreditation: M, NURSE

01 President/CEO ....Dr. Eric D. DARR
05 Provost/Chief Academic Officer ....Dr. Bilita S. MATTES
10 COO/Chief Financial Officer ....Mr. Duane F. MAUN
103 VP Strategic Workforce Dev/Univ Ctr .Ms. Kelly POWELL LOGAN
26 Assoc VP Comm/Marketing/Alum Rels .....Mr. Steven M. INFANTI
13 Assoc VP/Chief Technology Officer ....Mr. Alex C. PITZNER
108 Director of Assessment ....Ms. Penny L. WEIDNER
37 Director Financial Aid ....Mr. Vincent P. FRANK
06 Registrar ....Ms. Sandra NELSON
07 Director of Admissions ....Ms. Laurie BARROW
08 University Librarian ....Mr. David RUNYON
32 Director of Student Services ....Ms. Melissa MORGAN

Haverford College (I)

370 Lancaster Avenue, Haverford PA 19041-1392
County: Delaware & Montgomery FICE Identification: 003274
Unit ID: 212911
Telephone: (610) 896-1000 Carnegie Class: Bac-A&S
FAX Number: (610) 896-4202 Calendar System: Semester
URL: www.haverford.edu
Established: 1833 Annual Undergrad Tuition & Fees: $59,162
Enrollment: 1,307 Coed
Affiliation or Control: Independent Non-Profit IRS Status: 501(c)3
Highest Offering: Master's
Accreditation: M

01 President ....Dr. Wendy E. RAYMOND
05 Provost ....Dr. Linda STRONG-LEEK
10 SVP Finance/Chief Admin Officer ....Mitchell L. WEIN
111 Acting VP for Inst Advancement ....Deborah STRECKER
32 Dean of the College ....Dr. John MCKNIGHT
07 VP & Dean of Admission ....Jess LORD
104 Director of Intl Academic Programs ....Rebecca AVERY
115 Chief Investment Officer ....Michael CASEL
110 Asst VP Institutional Advancement ....Diane WILDER
100 VP & Chief of Staff ....Dr. Jesse LYTLE
41 Director of Athletics ....Wendall SMITH
26 Asst VP College Communications ....Chris MILLS
09 Director of Institutional Research ....Catherine FENNELL
08 Librarian ....Dr. Terry SNYDER
15 Director of Human Resources ....T. Muriel BRISBON
21 Asst VP & Controller ....Terri ALBERTSON
96 Director of Purchasing ....Nikoletta MILLAS
18 Director of Physical Plant ....Donald CAMPBELL
19 Director of Safety & Security ....Thomas KING
88 Director Conferences/Dir Campus Ctr ....Geoffey LABE
109 Assoc Director of Dining Services ....Vacant
40 Bookstore Manager ....Lydia WHITELAW
39 Director of Student Housing ....Nathan DIEHL
23 Director of Health Services ....Kathy MCGOVERN
38 Director Counseling/Disability Svcs ....Dr. Philip ROSENBAUM
36 Dean of Career/Prof Advising ....Amy FEIFER
06 Registrar ....James KEANE
37 Director of Financial Aid ....Michael COLAHAN
29 Director of Alumni & Parent Rels ....Lauren PORTNOY
44 Director of Gift Planning ....Olga BRIKER
20 Director for Academic Resources ....Brian CUZZOLINA
35 Asst Dean of Student Activities ....Michael ELIAS
13 Chief Information Officer ....Megan FITCH
04 Administrative Asst to President ....Joan WANKMILLER

Holy Family University (J)

9801 Frankford Avenue, Philadelphia PA 19114-2009
County: Philadelphia FICE Identification: 003275
Unit ID: 212984
Telephone: (215) 637-7700 Carnegie Class: Masters/L
FAX Number: (215) 637-3787 Calendar System: Semester
URL: www.holyfamily.edu
Established: 1954 Annual Undergrad Tuition & Fees: $31,640
Enrollment: 3,087 Coed
Affiliation or Control: Roman Catholic IRS Status: 501(c)3
Highest Offering: Doctorate
Accreditation: M, ACBSP, IFSAC, NURSE, RAD

01 President ....Dr. Anne PRISCO
10 VP for Finance & Administration ....Mr. Eric NELSON
05 Provost/VP for Academic Affairs ....Dr. Michael MARKOWITZ
42 VP for Mission ....Sr. Rita FANNING
13 VP for Information Technology .... Mr. Eugene KOVALCHICK
32 VP for Student Affairs/Enroll Mgmt ....Dr. Abigail WERNICKI
111 VP for University Advancement ....Dr. James GARVEY
26 VP Marketing/Communications ....Ms. Sherrie MADIA
06 Assoc VP Academic Svcs/Registrar ....Dr. Ann Marie VICKERY
35 Dean of Students/Title IX Coord ....Ms. Marianne PRICE
35 Assoc VP of Student Life ....Mr. Michael MCNULTY
37 Director Student Financial Aid ....Ms. Janice HETRICK
21 Assoc VP/Controller ....Ms. Anne MCMAHON
15 Assoc VP for Human Resources ....Ms. Jennifer LULING
30 Asst VP for Development ....Mr. Joshua LISS
102 Asst VP Corp Foundation & Govt Rels ....Ms. Kim CAULFIELD
08 Exec Director Library Services ....Ms. Shannon BROWN
38 Director Counseling Services ....Ms. Lisa SPATAFORE
42 Director of Campus Ministry ....Rev. James MACNEW
07 Director Undergraduate Admissions .... Ms. Lauren CAMPBELL
41 Director of Athletics ....Mr. Timothy HAMILL
107 Dean of Professional Studies ....Dr. Kristi RINGEN
66 Dean of Nursing/Allied Health Prof ....Vacant
49 Dean of School of Arts & Sciences ....Dr. Rochelle ROBBINS
58 Assoc Dean Graduate/Prof Studies ....Dr. Karen GALARDI
29 Asst Dir Alumni & Parent Relations ....Ms. Julie REMPFER
09 Director of Institutional Research ....Mr. Mark GREEN
18 Director Campus Operations ....Mr. Edward MCLAUGHLIN
39 Director Residence Life ....Mr. Troy YOUNG
101 Board Liaison & Special Asst ....Ms. Kate BRESLIN
19 Director Security/Safety-Allied ....Mr. Dave NEUMAN
85 Dir International Student Affairs ....Vacant
108 Dir Inst Assessment/Accreditation ....Vacant
44 Director of Development ....Ms. Christina BENDER
23 Director of Health Services ....Dr. Tracy BOYLE
105 Website Manager ....Mr. Christopher LAMBERT
04 Admin Assistant to the President ....Ms. Patricia TOWNSEND

Hussian College (K)

1500 Spring Garden Street, Philadelphia PA 19130
County: Philadelphia FICE Identification: 007469
Unit ID: 212993
Telephone: (215) 574-9600 Carnegie Class: Spec-4-yr-Arts
FAX Number: (267) 831-6054 Calendar System: Semester
URL: www.hussiancollege.edu
Established: 1946 Annual Undergrad Tuition & Fees: $21,428
Enrollment: 101 Coed
Affiliation or Control: Proprietary IRS Status: Proprietary
Highest Offering: Baccalaureate
Accreditation: ACCSC

01 President ....Dr. Jeremiah STAROPOLI
05 Chief Academic Officer (Provost) ....Sylvia MCCRAY
07 Director of Admissions ....Quincy GILES
37 Director of Financial Aid ....Susan COHEN

Immaculata University (L)

1145 King Road, Immaculata PA 19345-0654
County: Chester FICE Identification: 003276
Unit ID: 213011

Telephone: (610) 647-4400 Carnegie Class: DU-Mod
FAX Number: (610) 251-1668 Calendar System: Semester
URL: www.immaculata.edu
Established: 1920 Annual Undergrad Tuition & Fees: $27,750
Enrollment: 2,563 Coed
Affiliation or Control: Roman Catholic IRS Status: 501(c)3
Highest Offering: Doctorate
Accreditation: M, ACBSP, CACREP, CLPSY, DIETD, DIETI, IPSY, MUS, NURSE

01 President ... Ms. Barbara LETTIERE
05 VP Academic Affairs & Provost ... Dr. Angela TEKELY
10 VP Finance/Administration ... Mr. Bruce FRIEDMAN
111 VP Institutional Advancement ... Ms. Susan ARNOLD
32 VP Student Development & UG Admiss . Ms. Patricia CANTERINO
26 VP Marketing & Communications ... Sr. Monica SICILIA, IHM
42 VP Mission and Ministry ... Sr. Mary HENRICH, IHM
06 Registrar ... Ms. Collette DELANEY
26 Exec Director of Communications ... Ms. Melissa KUSHNER
15 Exec Director of Human Resources ... Ms. Claudine VITA
08 Executive Director of Library ... Dr. Jeffrey ROLLISON
13 Exec Director of Info Tech Services ... Mr. Bryan STEINBERG
07 Director of Admissions ... Ms. Christine RHINE
91 Director Network Operations ... Mr. Robert MARSDEN
14 Director of Technology Services ... Mr. Robert POTTER
37 Director Student Financial Aid ... Ms. Dina STERN
88 Director Curriculum & Instruction ... Ms. Dorothy (Darcy) DOYLE
29 Director Alumni Relations ... Ms. Karen MATWEYCHUK
36 Director Career & Prof Development ... Ms. Heidi HARRISON
104 Director Study Abroad ... Vacant
85 International Student Services ... Sr. Janet WALTERS, IHM
20 Dean of Academic Affairs ... Ms. Mary Kate BOLAND
58 Dean College of Graduate Studies ... Dr. Marcia PARRIS
88 Dean College of Undergrad Studies ... Dr. Jean SHINGLE
107 Dean College of Adult Prof Studies ... Dr. Jean SHINGLE
21 Director of Finance/Controller ... Ms. Joanne CRISTINZIO
19 Director Campus Safety & Protection ... Mr. Dennis DOUGHERTY
22 Title IX Coordinator ... Ms. Janelle CRONMILLER
38 Director Counseling Services ... Ms. Jessica GILPERT
18 Director of Facilities ... Mr. Kevin CONVERY
25 Director of Sponsored Research ... Vacant
45 Director of Strategic Initiatives .. Sr. M. Carroll ISSELMANN, IHM
110 Director of Advancement Services ... Ms. Martha BORRACCINI
39 Director Res Life & Student Housing ... Ms. Jenny LINDSAY
09 Office Inst Research/Effectiveness ... Ms. Cecelia OSWALD
04 Administrative Asst to President ... Ms. Leslie BOKOSKI
106 Online Education/E-learning ... Dr. Angela TEKELY
121 Exec Dir of Learning Support ... Ms. Jennifer PERUSO
28 Director of Diversity & Inclusion ... Vacant

Institute of Medical and Business Careers (A)

133 Jefferson Rd, Ste 101, Pittsburgh PA 15235
County: Allegheny FICE Identification: 041551
Telephone: (412) 244-3240 Carnegie Class: Not Classified
FAX Number: (412) 244-3241 Calendar System: Other
URL: www.imbc.edu
Established: Annual Undergrad Tuition & Fees: N/A
Enrollment: N/A Coed
Affiliation or Control: Proprietary IRS Status: Proprietary
Highest Offering: Associate Degree
Accreditation: ABHES

01 Director ... Mr. Zack LESAK

International Institute for Restorative Practices (B)

531 Main Street, Bethlehem PA 18018
County: Northampton FICE Identification: 042061
Unit ID: 448691
Telephone: (610) 807-9221 Carnegie Class: Spec-4-yr-Other
FAX Number: (610) 807-0423 Calendar System: Trimester
URL: www.iirp.edu
Established: 2005 Annual Graduate Tuition & Fees: N/A
Enrollment: 185 Coed
Affiliation or Control: Independent Non-Profit IRS Status: 501(c)3
Highest Offering: Master's; No Undergraduates
Accreditation: M

01 President ... Dr. John W. BAILIE
05 Provost ... Dr. Craig ADAMSON
11 Vice President for Administration ... Ms. Linda B. KLIGMAN
10 Chief Financial Officer ... Ms. Robin TURNER-TOLLEY
32 Director of Student Services ... Ms. Jamie KAINTZ

JNA Institute of Culinary Arts (C)

1212 S Broad Street, Philadelphia PA 19146-3119
County: Philadelphia FICE Identification: 031033
Unit ID: 419341
Telephone: (215) 468-8800 Carnegie Class: Spec 2-yr-A&S
FAX Number: (215) 468-8838 Calendar System: Quarter
URL: www.culinaryarts.edu
Established: 1988 Annual Undergrad Tuition & Fees: $14,575
Enrollment: 14 Coed
Affiliation or Control: Proprietary IRS Status: Proprietary
Highest Offering: Associate Degree
Accreditation: ACCSC

01 Director ... Mr. Joseph DIGIRONIMO

Johnson College (D)

3427 North Main Avenue, Scranton PA 18508-1495
County: Lackawanna FICE Identification: 021142
Unit ID: 213233
Telephone: (570) 702-8856 Carnegie Class: Assoc/HVT-High Trad
FAX Number: (570) 348-2181 Calendar System: Semester
URL: www.johnson.edu
Established: 1912 Annual Undergrad Tuition & Fees: $20,025
Enrollment: 497 Coed
Affiliation or Control: Independent Non-Profit IRS Status: 501(c)3
Highest Offering: Associate Degree
Accreditation: M, PTAA, RAD

01 President & CEO ... Dr. Katie LEONARD
10 Chief Financial Officer ... Ms. Liz RENDA
15 VP of Human Resources & Sr Advisor ... Ms. Stephenie VERGNETTI
32 VP of Student & Academic Affairs ... Mr. William BURKE
11 Chief Administrative Officer ... Mr. Mike NOVAK
88 Associate VP of Faculty ... Ms. Barb BYRNE
05 Chief Academic Officer ... Dr. Kellyn WILLIAMS
09 Director of Inst Effectiveness ... Dr. Laura LITTLE
04 Exec Assistant to President ... Ms. Ann SPARACINO
21 Associate Director of Finance ... Ms. Kristin MASCI
16 Asst Director of Human Resources ... Ms. Heather BUCK
08 Resource Officer ... Ms. Ashley HASSENBEIN
32 Director of Student Engagement ... Mr. Nolan RENZ
38 Counselor/Manager Disability Svcs ... Ms. Melissa SAXON-PRICE
13 Director of Information Technology ... Mr. Jerry MARSH
18 Director of Facilities ... Mr. Joseph MUSHENO
26 Sr Dir of Marketing/Communications ... Mr. Doug COOK
111 Sr Director of Advancement ... Ms. Karen BAKER
36 Career Services Manager ... Ms. Dana HEALEY
37 Director of Financial Aid ... Vacant
124 Associate Dir of Student Success ... Mr. Mike MCGURL
06 Registrar ... Vacant
103 Manager of Continuing Education ... Ms. Felicia ENNES
84 Director Enrollment Management ... Vacant

Juniata College (E)

1700 Moore Street, Huntingdon PA 16652-2119
County: Huntingdon FICE Identification: 003279
Unit ID: 213251
Telephone: (814) 641-3000 Carnegie Class: Bac-A&S
FAX Number: (814) 641-3199 Calendar System: Semester
URL: www.juniata.edu
Established: 1876 Annual Undergrad Tuition & Fees: $49,175
Enrollment: 1,356 Coed
Affiliation or Control: Independent Non-Profit IRS Status: 501(c)3
Highest Offering: Master's
Accreditation: M, IACBE, SW

01 President ... Dr. James A. TROHA
05 Provost ... Dr. Lauren BOWEN
84 VP Enrollment ... Mr. Jason E. MORAN
32 VP Student Life & Dean of Students ... Dr. Matthew DAMSCHRODER
111 VP for Advancement ... Mr. James R. WATT
13 Asst VP/Chief Information Officer ... Ms. Anne WOOD
10 Controller/Chief Financial Officer ... Ms. Karla D. WISER
28 Dean Equity/Diversity & Inclusion . Dr. Crystal SELLERS BATTLE
85 Acting Dean International Programs ... Ms. Caitlin MURPHY
06 Registrar ... Ms. Dawn SCIALABBA
37 Dir Student Financial Plng ... Ms. Tracie M. PATRICK
15 Director of Human Resources ... Ms. Tracy L. GRAJEWSKI
18 Director of Facilities Services ... Mr. Tristan S. DEL GIUDICE
35 Assistant Dean of Students ... Mr. Jesse W. LEONARD
41 Athletic Director ... Mr. Greg M. CURLEY
90 Dir Technology Solutions Center ... Mr. Joel C. PHEASANT
113 Bursar ... Ms. Lauren A. PEROW
114 Assistant Controller ... Mr. Jeremy M. KOLLER
124 Asst Dean of Students Campus Life ... Ms. Erin PASCHAL
88 Director of Conferences & Events ... Ms. Lorri P. SHIDELER
07 Senior Associate Dean of Admission ... Ms. Terri L. BOLLMAN-DALANSKY
36 Executive Director of Career Devel ... Mr. David D. MEADOWS
04 Executive Asst to President ... Mrs. Bethany D. SHEFFIELD
43 College Counsel ... Mr. David P. ANDREWS
19 Director of Public Safety ... Mr. Timothy LAUNTZ

Keystone College (F)

One College Green, P.O. Box 50, La Plume PA 18440-0200
County: Lackawanna FICE Identification: 003280
Unit ID: 213303
Telephone: (570) 945-8000 Carnegie Class: Bac-Diverse
FAX Number: (570) 945-8962 Calendar System: Semester
URL: www.keystone.edu
Established: 1868 Annual Undergrad Tuition & Fees: $17,000
Enrollment: 1,386 Coed
Affiliation or Control: Independent Non-Profit IRS Status: 501(c)3
Highest Offering: Master's
Accreditation: M, IACBE

01 President ... Dr. Tracy BRUNDAGE
05 Interim Provost/VP Academic Affairs ... Dr. David ARNOLD
10 Vice Pres Finance & Administration ... Mr. Stuart RENDA
111 Vice President for Advancement ... Ms. Frances LANGAN
84 Interim Vice Pres Enrollment ... Dr. Nicole LANGAN
32 Associate VP Student Life ... Dr. Nicole LANGAN
08 Associate Dean of Miller Library ... Ms. Mari FLYNN
07 Director of Admissions ... Ms. Jennifer SEKOL
06 Associate Dean/Registrar ... Ms. Kate OWENS
37 Director Financial Aid ... Vacant
13 Chief Information Officer ... Mr. Charles L. PROTHERO
15 Director of Human Resources ... Ms. Melanie SMITH
26 Senior Director College Relations ... Mr. Fran CALPIN
29 Director of Alumni Engagement ... Vacant
09 Director Institutional Research ... Ms. Robyn DICKINSON
41 Director of Athletics ... Mr. Ryan NOVITSKY

King's College (G)

133 N River Street, Wilkes-Barre PA 18711-0801
County: Luzerne FICE Identification: 003282
Unit ID: 213321
Telephone: (570) 208-5900 Carnegie Class: Masters/M
FAX Number: (570) 825-9049 Calendar System: Semester
URL: www.kings.edu
Established: 1946 Annual Undergrad Tuition & Fees: $40,080
Enrollment: 2,320 Coed
Affiliation or Control: Roman Catholic IRS Status: 501(c)3
Highest Offering: Master's
Accreditation: M, ARCPA, CAATE, NURSE

01 President ... Rev. Thomas P. LOONEY, CSC
05 Provost & VP for Academic Affairs ... Dr. Joseph EVAN
10 Exec VP for Business Affairs ... Ms. Janet KOBYLSKI
111 Vice President for Inst Advancement ... Mr. Frederick PETTIT
32 Vice President for Student Affairs ... Vacant
84 Interim VP for Enrollment Mgmt ... Dr. Barry WILLIAMS
04 Exec Assistant to the President ... Ms. Anne NOONE
13 Associate VP/Chief Info Officer ... Mr. Paul MORAN
26 Exec Dir College Marketing/Comm ... Ms. Wendy HINTON
08 Director of Library ... Mr. David SCHAPPERT
35 Assoc Vice Pres Student Affairs ... Mr. Robert MCGONIGLE
50 Dean Wm G McGowan Sch Business ... Dr. Barry WILLIAMS
06 Registrar ... Mr. Daniel CEBRICK
37 Director of Financial Aid ... Mr. Jared MENGHINI
42 Chaplain/Director Campus Ministry ... Rev. Brogan RYAN, CSC
36 Director Career Planning & Placemnt ... Mr. Christopher SUTZKO
15 Associate VP Human Resources ... Ms. Regina CORCHADO
29 Senior Director of Engagement ... Ms. Patrice PERSICO
18 Executive Director of Facilities ... Mr. Thomas BUTCHKO
19 Director of Security/Safety ... Mr. James GILGALLON
41 Dir of Intercollegiate Athletics ... Ms. Cheryl ISH
21 Associate VP Finance ... Ms. Holly KULP
39 Assoc Dean of Students Res Life ... Ms. Megan CASEY
09 Director of Institutional Research ... Ms. Marian PALMERI
28 Director of College Diversity ... Ms. Jasmine TABRON-GIDDINGS
90 Managing Dir of User Services ... Mr. Raymond PRYOR
91 Managing Director for MIS ... Mr. William CORCORAN
112 Major Gifts Officer ... Mr. Richard LANAHAN
104 Director Study Abroad ... Ms. Margaret KOWALSKY
25 Dir of Inst and Academic Grants ... Ms. Michelle GIOVAGNOLI
44 Director Annual Giving ... Ms. Desiree VOITEK

La Roche University (H)

9000 Babcock Boulevard, Pittsburgh PA 15237-5898
County: Allegheny FICE Identification: 003987
Unit ID: 213358
Telephone: (412) 367-9300 Carnegie Class: Masters/S
FAX Number: (412) 536-1062 Calendar System: Semester
URL: www.laroche.edu
Established: 1963 Annual Undergrad Tuition & Fees: $30,320
Enrollment: 1,292 Coed
Affiliation or Control: Roman Catholic IRS Status: 501(c)3
Highest Offering: Doctorate
Accreditation: M, ACBSP, ADNUR, ANEST, ART, CIDA, NUR

01 President ... Sr. Candace INTROCASO, CDP
04 Exec Asst to the President ... Ms. Karen P. WILLOUGHBY
05 Provost & SVP for Academic Affairs ... Dr. Howard J. ISHIYAMA
84 VP for Enrollment Mgmt ... Dr. James (Chip) E. WEISGERBER
10 VP for Finance & Administration ... Mr. Stephen LIPPIELLO
32 VP for Student Life/Dean Stdnts ... Ms. Colleen RUEFLE
111 VP for University Advancement ... Ms. Michele A. HUFNAGEL
20 Assoc VP Academic Affairs ... Dr. Rosemary MCCARTHY
121 Assoc Dean Academic/Student Support ... Ms. Marie DEEM
35 Director of Student Development ... Mr. David DAY
83 Div Chair Natural & Behavioral Sci ... Dr. Rebecca BOZYM
79 Div Chair Humanities ... Dr. Edward BOBINCHOCK
50 Div Co-Chair Management ... Dr. Lynn ARCHER
50 Div Co-Chair Management ... Ms. Shelia MUELLER
57 Div Chair Design ... Ms. Lisa KAMPHAUS
53 Div Co-Chair Education & Nursing ... Dr. Kathryn SILVIS
66 Div Co-Chair Education & Nursing ... Dr. Terri LIBERTO
06 Registrar ... Ms. Katie ELVERSON
08 Director Library/Learning Center ... Ms. Alecia KERR
07 Executive Director for Enrollment ... Ms. Hope SCHIFFGENS
26 Assoc VP Mktg & Media Relations ... Mr. Brady BUTLER
37 Director of Financial Aid ... Ms. Sharon PLATT
41 Director of Athletics ... Mr. Jim TINKEY
42 Director of Mission & Ministry ... Sr. Elena ALMENDAREZ
39 Director Residence Life ... Ms. Ashley TESTA
13 Director Information Technology ... Ms. Terri BALLARD
85 Director International Student Svcs ... Dr. Natasha GARRETT
29 Executive Director Alumni Relations ... Vacant
21 Director of Finance ... Ms. Cathleen JACOBS
09 Director of Institutional Research ... Mr. John INGRAM
18 Assoc VP of Facilities Management ... Mr. J.R YOUNG

38 Director Counseling Services ... Vacant
19 Director Public Safety ... Mr. Mark WILCOX
15 Assoc VP of Human Resources ... Ms. Eileen PETRONE
40 Bookstore Manager ... Ms. Michelle JAMES
113 Director of Student Accounts ... Ms. Danya TINKEY
101 Secretary of the Institution/Board ... Ms. Karen WILLOUGHBY
104 Coordinator Study Abroad ... Ms. Nicole GABLE
44 Dir Annual Giving/Advancement Srvs ... Vacant
105 Director Web Services ... Mr. David SIROKI
28 Director of Diversity ... Ms. Sarah WHITE

La Salle University (A)

1900 W Olney Avenue, Philadelphia PA 19141-1199
County: Philadelphia | FICE Identification: 003287
Unit ID: 213367
Telephone: (215) 951-1000 | Carnegie Class: Masters/L
FAX Number: N/A | Calendar System: Semester
URL: www.lasalle.edu
Established: 1863 | Annual Undergrad Tuition & Fees: $32,425
Enrollment: 4,624 | Coed
Affiliation or Control: Roman Catholic | IRS Status: 501(c)3
Highest Offering: Doctorate
Accreditation: M, ANEST, CACREP, CLPSY, DIETC, DIETD, MFCD, NURSE, PH, SP, SW

01 President ... Dr. Colleen M. HANYCZ
05 Int Provost/VP Academic Affairs ... Dr. Steven SICONOLFI
10 VP Finance and Administration ... Mrs. Stephanie PRICKEN
32 VP Student Affairs & Enrollment Mgt ... Dr. Dawn M. SOUFLERIS
43 Vice President and General Counsel ... Mr. Kevin DOLAN
20 Assistant Provost ... Bro. John MCGOLDRICK
30 Asst VP Development ... Mr. Daniel JOYCE
49 Dean School of Arts & Sciences ... Dr. Lynne A. TEXTER
50 Dean School of Business Admin . Ms. MarySheila A. MCDONALD
66 Dean School of Nursing/Health Sci ... Dr. Kathleen CZEKANSKI
22 Affirmative Action Officer/Title IX ... Ms. Rose Lee PAULINE
26 AVP Marketing and Communication ... Dr. Angela M. POLEC
29 AVP Alumni Relations ... Mr. Trey P. ULRICH
58 Dir Grad Ctr/East European Studies ... Vacant
77 Director MS/CIS ... Ms. Margaret MCCOEY
53 Director Grad Education Program ... Dr. Greer RICHARDSON
60 Dir Grad Communication ... Dr. Michael SMITH
66 Director Undergraduate Nursing ... Vacant
66 Dir Grad Nursing RN-MSN Pgm ... Dr. Patricia DILLON
69 Dir Master Public Health Program ... Dr. Candace ROBERTSON-JAMES
88 Dir Grad Econ Crime Forensics ... Ms. Margaret MCCOEY
58 Dir Grad Pgm Nonprofit Leadership ... Dr. Laura OTTEN
39 Asst VP Res Life Community Dev ... Mr. Alan B. WENDELL
35 Asst VP for Campus Life ... Ms. Anna M. ALLEN
42 Director Univ Ministry & Service ... Bro. Robert J. KINZLER
92 Dir University Honors Program ... Bro. Michael MCGINNISS
13 Chief Information Officer ... Mr. Karl HORVATH
08 Director of the Library ... Ms. Sarah CLARK
18 Asst VP Facilities Mgmt ... Mr. Dennis SHORES, JR.
19 Asst VP Public Safety ... Ms. Amanda GUTHORN
15 Asst VP Human Resources ... Ms. Kristin HEASLEY
41 Dir Intercollegiate Athletics ... Mr. Brian BAPTISTE
112 Director of Major Gifts ... Ms. Theresa MALANDRA
07 Executive Director of Admission ... Mr. James C. PLUNKETT
37 Director Financial Aid ... Ms. Jennifer HOUSEMAN
06 Registrar ... Ms. Jean W. LANDIS
83 Dir Doctorate in Psych Program ... Dr. Megan SPOKAS
88 Dir Academic Partnerships ... Dr. Elizabeth LANGEMAK
72 Graduate Director Instruct Tech Mgt ... Ms. Margaret MCCOEY
88 Director Full-time MBA Program ... Ms. Elizabeth SCOFIELD
28 Multicultural Education Coordinator ... Ms. Cherylyn L. RUSH
105 Director of Web Communication ... Mr. Gregory FALA
66 Dir Doctor of Nursing Practice Pgm ... Dr. Patricia BICKNELL
88 Director Graduate History ... Dr. George B. STOW
88 Director of Athletic Development ... Mr. Brian QUINN
100 Chief of Staff/Dir of Gov Affairs ... Mr. Joseph MEADE
101 Secretary of the Institution/Board ... Ms. Lisa WILLIE
106 Director Online/Hybrid Learning ... Mr. David LEES
25 Chief Contract/Grants Administrator ... Ms. Wendy ARDAGNA
38 Director Student Counseling ... Ms. Jessica BRANNAN

Lackawanna College (B)

501 Vine Street, Scranton PA 18509-3206
County: Lackawanna | FICE Identification: 003283
Unit ID: 213376
Telephone: (570) 961-7810 | Carnegie Class: Bac/Assoc-Assoc Dom
FAX Number: (570) 961-7858 | Calendar System: 4/1/4
URL: www.lackawanna.edu
Established: 1894 | Annual Undergrad Tuition & Fees: $16,130
Enrollment: 2,043 | Coed
Affiliation or Control: Independent Non-Profit | IRS Status: 501(c)3
Highest Offering: Baccalaureate
Accreditation: M, DMS, OTA, PTAA, SURGT

01 President ... Dr. Jill A. MURRAY
11 Chief Operating Officer ... Mr. TJ ELTRINGHAM
10 Vice President of Finance/Admin ... Mr. John RISBOSKIN
05 Provost/Chief Academic Officer ... Dr. Erica PRICCI
32 Associate VP for Student Engagement ... Mr. Dan LAMAGNA
07 Regional Director of Admissions ... Mr. Tom BOGUSH
111 Vice Pres for College Advancement ... Mr. Brian COSTANZO
15 VP for Human Resources ... Ms. Renee MUNDY
35 Dean of Students ... Mr. Kris LIEBEGOTT
20 Associate Dean of Faculty Affairs ... Mrs. Adrienne ASBURY

29 Mgr of Special Events/Alumni Rels ... Ms. Megan MOULD
113 Director of Student Financial Svcs ... Ms. Joya WHITTINGTON
26 Director of External Relations ... Vacant
41 Director of Athletics ... Mr. Erik LARSON
121 Director of Advising & Transfer Svc . Mrs. Barbara NOWOGORSKI
06 Registrar ... Mrs. Theresa SCOPELLITI
19 Director of Public Safety ... Mr. Carl GRAZIANO
116 Audit Officer ... Vacant
25 Grant Administrator ... Ms. Laurel RADZIESKI
39 Director Housing & Residence Life ... Mr. Jeff KRISIAK
18 Director of Facilities ... Mr. Derek GREGORY
37 Director of Financial Aid ... Mr. Matthew PETERS
13 Director of MIS ... Mrs. Melanie KOWALSKI
124 Director of Student Retention ... Mrs. Denise LARSON
04 Executive Asst to President ... Ms. Mary A. OLIVERI
106 Dir Online Education/E-learning ... Mr. Gopu KIRON
101 Assistant Secretary for the Board ... Ms. Mary A. OLIVERI
86 Director Government Relations ... Mrs. Cathy WECHSLER

Lafayette College (C)

730 High Street, Markle Hall Suite, Easton PA 18042-1798
County: Northampton | FICE Identification: 003284
Unit ID: 213385
Telephone: (610) 330-5000 | Carnegie Class: Bac-A&S
FAX Number: (610) 330-5127 | Calendar System: Semester
URL: www.lafayette.edu
Established: 1826 | Annual Undergrad Tuition & Fees: $55,742
Enrollment: 2,514 | Coed
Affiliation or Control: Independent Non-Profit | IRS Status: 501(c)3
Highest Offering: Baccalaureate
Accreditation: M

01 President ... Dr. Alison R. BYERLY
05 Provost ... Dr. John MEIER
30 Vice Pres Dev/College Relations ... Ms. Kimberly SPANG
32 VP Campus Life ... Dr. Annette DIORIO
15 Vice President Human Resources ... Ms. Leslie F. MUHLFELDER
26 VP Marketing/Communications ... Mr. Mark EYERLY
13 VP and Chief Information Officer ... Mr. John L. O'KEEFE
10 VP Finance & Administration ... Mr. Roger DEMARESKI
54 Director of Engineering ... Dr. Scott R. HUMMEL
100 VP & Liaison to Board of Trustees ... Dr. Melissa STARACE
84 Vice Pres for Enrollment Management ... Mr. Gregory MACDONALD
121 Dean Advising & Co-Curricular Pgms ... Dr. Mike OLIN
08 Dean of Libraries ... Ms. Anne HOUSTON
35 Dean of Students ... Dr. Annette DIORIO
07 Dean of Admissions ... Mr. Matthew HYDE
37 Assoc VP of Financial Aid ... Dr. Forrest STUART
09 Director of Institutional Research ... Dr. Simon T. TONEV
06 Registrar ... Ms. Kara HOWE
41 Director of Athletics ... Ms. Sherryta FREEMAN
36 Asst VP of Career Services ... Mr. Mike SUMMERS
23 Director Health Services ... Dr. Jeffrey E. GOLDSTEIN
38 Director Counseling Center ... Dr. Melissa GARRISON
19 Director of Public Safety ... Mr. Jeffrey E. TROXELL
18 Dir Physical Planning & Plant Oper ... Mr. Bruce S. FERRETTI
29 Executive Director Alumni Relations ... Ms. Rachel NELSON MOELLER
16 Director of HR/Employment ... Ms. Lisa Youngkin REX
96 Manager of Procurement ... Ms. Patricia REICH
88 Title IX Coordinator ... Ms. Amanda HANINCIK
20 Dean of Faculty ... Dr. Jamila BOOKWALA
115 Interim Chief Investment Officer ... Mr. Merv BURTON
04 Executive Assistant to President ... Ms. Katherine D. KANEPS

Lake Erie College of Osteopathic Medicine (D)

1858 W Grandview Boulevard, Erie PA 16509-1025
County: Erie | FICE Identification: 030908
Unit ID: 407629
Telephone: (814) 866-6641 | Carnegie Class: Spec-4-yr-Med
FAX Number: (814) 866-8123 | Calendar System: Semester
URL: www.lecom.edu
Established: 1992 | Annual Graduate Tuition & Fees: N/A
Enrollment: 4,336 | Coed
Affiliation or Control: Independent Non-Profit | IRS Status: 501(c)3
Highest Offering: First Professional Degree; No Undergraduates
Accreditation: M, OSTEO, PHAR

01 President/CEO ... Dr. John M. FERRETTI
05 Provost/Sr Vice Pres/Dean Acad Affs ... Dr. Silvia M. FERRETTI
10 Vice Pres of Fiscal Affairs/CFO ... Mr. Steve G. INMAN
12 Vice Pres for LECOM at Seton Hill ... Dr. Irving FREEMAN
52 Dean School of Dental Medicine ... Dr. Mathew BATEMAN
20 Assoc Dean Acad Affairs Bradenton ... Dr. Mark KAUFFMAN
63 Asst Dean Clinical Educ Bradenton ... Dr. Steven MA
63 Assoc Dean of Clinical Education ... Dr. Michael ROWANE
63 Asst Dean of Clinical Education ... Dr. Regan SHABLOSKI
63 Asst Dean Preclinical Ed Bradenton ... Dr. James GNARRA
63 Assoc Dean Preclinical Educ Erie ... Dr. Jon KALMEY
81 Assoc Dean Biomedical Sciences ... Dr. Randy KULESZA
58 Dean Graduate Studies ... Dr. Timothy NOVAK
67 Dean School of Pharmacy ... Dr. Rachel OGDEN
88 Asst Dean of Florida Pathway ... Dr. Tatiana YERO
88 Asst Dean of Clin Education Dental ... Dr. Thomas YOON
88 Asst Dean Cir and Assessment ... Dr. Katie DINH
88 Asst Dean of Pre-Clinical Educ ... Dr. Todd NOLAN
26 VP of External Affairs ... Msgr. David RUBINO
32 Director of Student Affairs ... Mr. Jamie MURPHY

09 Inst Dir Plng/Assess/Accred/Rsrch ... Dr. Mathew BATEMAN
43 Dir Legal Services/General Counsel ... Mr. Richard E. FERRETTI
27 Acting Inst Dir Comm/Marketing ... Mr. Eric NICASTRO
08 Inst Dir of Learning Resources ... Mr. Dan WELCH
38 Director of Behavioral Health ... Dr. Melanie DUNBAR
13 Director of Information Technology ... Mr. Randy HARRIS
46 Asst Dean of Research ... Dr. Bertalan DUDAS
88 Director of Research Medical Col ... Dr. Diana SPEELMAN
15 Inst Dir of HR/EEO and Title IX ... Mr. Aaron E. SUSMARSKI
19 Inst Dir of Police & Security ... Mr. Kevin GOODE
88 Asst Dean Med Educ/Fac Dev ... Dr. Mark TERRELL
18 Facilities Director ... Mr. Brian KING
37 Director of Financial Aid ... Ms. Shari GOULD
06 Institutional Registrar ... Mr. Jeremy SIVILLO
96 Inst Director of Purchasing ... Ms. Naz KROL
04 Exec Assistant to the President ... Ms. Helen R. MCKENZIE

Lancaster Bible CollegelCapital Seminary & Graduate School (E)

901 Eden Road, Lancaster PA 17601-5036
County: Lancaster | FICE Identification: 003285
Unit ID: 213400
Telephone: (717) 569-7071 | Carnegie Class: Masters/S
FAX Number: (717) 560-8260 | Calendar System: Semester
URL: www.lbc.edu
Established: 1933 | Annual Undergrad Tuition & Fees: $27,370
Enrollment: 2,038 | Coed
Affiliation or Control: Independent Non-Profit | IRS Status: 501(c)3
Highest Offering: Doctorate
Accreditation: M, BI, COSMA, MUS, SW

01 President ... Dr. Thomas L. KIEDIS
04 Assistant to the President ... Mrs. Judith M. HECKAMAN
03 Executive Vice President ... Dr. Lee DEREMER
05 Provost ... Mrs. Tricia WILSON
111 VP of Advancement ... Mr. Scott KEATING
10 VP of Finance ... Mr. Matthew MASON
88 VP of Institutional Alignment ... Rev. Zachary RITVALSKY
88 VP of Global Education ... Dr. Beau WALKER
58 VP of Seminary & Graduate Education ... Dr. Brian PINZER

Lancaster County Career and Technology Center (F)

1730 Hans Herr Drive, Willow Street PA 17584
County: Lancaster | FICE Identification: 023108
Unit ID: 418533
Telephone: (717) 464-7050 | Carnegie Class: Spec 2-yr-Health
FAX Number: (717) 464-9518 | Calendar System: Semester
URL: www.lancasterctc.edu
Established: 1970 | Annual Undergrad Tuition & Fees (In-District): N/A
Enrollment: 348 | Coed
Affiliation or Control: State/Local | IRS Status: 501(c)3
Highest Offering: Associate Degree
Accreditation: COE, DH

01 Superintendent of Record ... Dr. April HERSHEY
11 Administrative Director ... Dr. Stuart SAVIN
05 Supervisor of Curriculum ... Mike MOELLER
32 Supervisor of Student Services ... Darla GETTLE
15 Human Resources Director ... Kristin SMITH
10 Business Manager ... Dr. Michael DELPRIORE

Lancaster Theological Seminary (G)

555 W James Street, Lancaster PA 17603-2812
County: Lancaster | FICE Identification: 003286
Unit ID: 213446
Telephone: (717) 393-0654 | Carnegie Class: Spec-4-yr-Faith
FAX Number: (717) 393-4254 | Calendar System: Trimester
URL: www.lancasterseminary.edu
Established: 1825 | Annual Graduate Tuition & Fees: N/A
Enrollment: 99 | Coed
Affiliation or Control: United Church Of Christ | IRS Status: 501(c)3
Highest Offering: Doctorate; No Undergraduates
Accreditation: M, THEOL

01 President ... Dr. Bryon GRIGSBY
10 Vice President Business & Finance ... Ms. Elizabeth P. BENNETT
05 Vice Pres Academic Affairs & Dean ... Dr. Vanessa LOVELACE
111 Vice Pres of Development/Alumni ... Ms. Jill ANDERSON
07 Dir of Admissions & Financial Aid ... Rev. Diane BOGUES
08 Seminary Librarian ... Mrs. Myka K. STEPHENS
06 Registrar ... Mrs. Teresa BENNEIAN
13 Director Computing/Information Mgmt ... Mr. Augustine APPREY
04 Exec Assistant to the President ... Ms. Rachel GOODRICH

Lansdale School of Business (H)

290 Wissahickon Ave, North Wales PA 19454-4114
County: Montgomery | FICE Identification: 007779
Unit ID: 213473
Telephone: (215) 699-5700 | Carnegie Class: Assoc/HVT-High Trad
FAX Number: (215) 699-8770 | Calendar System: Semester
URL: www.LSB.edu
Established: 1918 | Annual Undergrad Tuition & Fees: $11,850
Enrollment: 119 | Coed
Affiliation or Control: Proprietary | IRS Status: Proprietary
Highest Offering: Associate Degree
Accreditation: ACCSC

01 President .... Mr. Marlon D. KELLER
03 Executive Director .... Mrs. Marianne H. JOHNSON
32 Student Services Coordinator .... Ms. Jacklyn G. WHEELER
08 Librarian .... Mrs. Marie B. WALCROFT
37 Financial Aid Coordinator .... Mr. David E. SOUZA
36 Career Services Coord/Dean Students .... Ms. Kellyann R. GERIA

Laurel Business Institute (A)

11 East Penn Street, Uniontown PA 15401-3453
County: Fayette FICE Identification: 025462
Unit ID: 250027
Telephone: (724) 439-4900 Carnegie Class: Assoc/HVT-Mix Trad/Non
FAX Number: (724) 439-3607 Calendar System: Semester
URL: www.laurel.edu
Established: 1985 Annual Undergrad Tuition & Fees: $10,912
Enrollment: 238 Coed
Affiliation or Control: Proprietary IRS Status: Proprietary
Highest Offering: Associate Degree
Accreditation: ACCSC, COARC

01 President .... Mrs. Nancy M. DECKER
11 Executive Director .... Mrs. Bonnie MARSH
10 Vice President of Finance .... Ms. Vicki M. JOLLIFFE
15 Vice President of Human Resources .... Mr. Chuck SANTORE, JR.
13 Director of IT .... Mr. Ken LAPIKAS
37 Vice President of Financial Aid .... Ms. Stephanie M. MIGYANKO
07 Director of Admission .... Mr. Douglas S. DECKER
20 Academic Coordinator .... Ms. Sandi FIELD

Laurel Technical Institute (B)

2370 Broadway Avenue, Hermitage PA 16148
County: Mercer FICE Identification: 020925
Unit ID: 215992
Telephone: (724) 983-0700 Carnegie Class: Assoc/HVT-Mix Trad/Non
FAX Number: (724) 983-8355 Calendar System: Semester
URL: www.laurel.edu
Established: 1925 Annual Undergrad Tuition & Fees: $10,912
Enrollment: 122 Coed
Affiliation or Control: Proprietary IRS Status: Proprietary
Highest Offering: Associate Degree
Accreditation: ACCSC, COARC

01 President .... Ms. Nancy DECKER
11 Director/Exec VP of Operations .... Mr. Douglas DECKER
07 Director of Admission .... Ms. Kelly RUSSO
05 Director of Education .... Ms. Michele TOTA

Lebanon Valley College (C)

101 N College Avenue, Annville PA 17003-1400
County: Lebanon FICE Identification: 003288
Unit ID: 213507
Telephone: (717) 867-6161 Carnegie Class: Masters/S
FAX Number: (717) 867-6124 Calendar System: Semester
URL: www.lvc.edu
Established: 1866 Annual Undergrad Tuition & Fees: $46,030
Enrollment: 1,959 Coed
Affiliation or Control: United Methodist IRS Status: 501(c)3
Highest Offering: Doctorate
Accreditation: M, ACBSP, CAATE, MUS, PTA, @SP

01 President .... Dr. James M. MACLAREN
05 Provost/Vice Pres Academic Affairs .... Dr. Monica R. COWART
111 Vice President of Advancement .... Mr. Matthew WEAVER
10 Vice Pres Finance/Administration .... Mr. Shawn P. CURTIN
84 Vice President of Enrollment .... Mr. Edwin R. WRIGHT
32 VP Stdnt Affs/Dean of Students .... Dr. Robert L. MIKUS
26 VP of Marketing/ Communications .... Mrs. Molly O'BRIEN-FOELSCH
13 Senior Director of Information Tech .... Mr. David W. SHAPIRO
15 Sr Dir of Human Res/TitleIX Coord .... Mrs. Ann C. HAYES
20 Dean of Faculty .... Dr. Marc HARRIS
09 Assoc Prov Institutional Research .... Ms. Susan TAMMARO
58 Assoc Prov Grad & Prof Studies .... Dr. Renee NORRIS
06 Assistant Dean and Registrar .... Mr. Jeremy A. MAISTO
41 Director of Athletics .... Mr. Richard L. BEARD
114 Dir of Finance/Chief Budget Officer .... Ms. Wendy ALBERT
21 Controller .... Mr. Gabriel PAZ
37 Director of Financial Aid .... Mrs. Kendra M. FEIGERT
36 Associate Dean of the Breen Center .... Dr. Kimberlee JOSEPHSON
28 Director of Intercultural Affairs .... Vacant
19 Director of Public Safety .... Mr. Brent OBERHOLTZER
104 Director of Global Education .... Mrs. Jill T. RUSSELL
39 Director of Residential Life .... Ms. Caitlin LENKER
22 Director of Accessibility Resources .... Mrs. Erin E. HANNAFORD
50 Director of the MBA Program .... Dr. Treva CLARK
08 Director of the Bishop Library .... Mrs. Maureen A. BENTZ
30 Director of Individual Giving .... Ms. Jordan EVANGELISTA
18 Director of Facilities Management .... Mr. Michael MUMPER
35 Assoc Dean Student Affairs .... Vacant
42 Chaplain .... Vacant
27 Director Campus Communications .... Dr. Thomas M. HANRAHAN
91 Dir Enterprise Information Systems .... Mr. Robert J. DILLANE
90 Director of Client Services .... Mr. Michael C. ZEIGLER
24 Director of Audiovisual Technology .... Mr. Andrew S. GREENE
38 Director of Counseling Services .... Mr. James FELTY
88 Director of Student Activities .... Mrs. Jennifer M. EVANS
88 Assistant Controller .... Mr. Todd M. LATSHAW
29 Director Alumni & Parent Engagement .... Mrs. Susan SARISKY JONES
04 Admin Assistant to the President .... Mrs. Wendy CARFAGNO

Lehigh Carbon Community College (D)

4525 Education Park Drive, Schnecksville PA 18078-2598
County: Lehigh FICE Identification: 006810
Unit ID: 213525
Telephone: (610) 799-2121 Carnegie Class: Assoc/MT-VT-Mix Trad/Non
FAX Number: (610) 799-1527 Calendar System: Semester
URL: www.lccc.edu
Established: 1966 Annual Undergrad Tuition & Fees (In-District): $8,070
Enrollment: 6,205 Coed
Affiliation or Control: Local IRS Status: 501(c)3
Highest Offering: Associate Degree
Accreditation: M, ACBSP, ADNUR, CAHIIM, CSHSE, NAEYC, OTA, PNUR, PTAA

01 President .... Dr. Ann D. BIEBER
05 VP Academic/Student Dev .... Ms. Larissa M. VERTA
10 VP Finance & Admin Svcs .... Ms. Stefanie E. NESTER
84 VP Enrollment Management .... Ms. Cindy M. HANEY
04 Exec Asst to President and Board .... Ms. Tracy BEAN
32 Dean of Student Development .... Ms. Peggy M. HEIM
106 Dean Online Lrng/Org Devel/CS/Tech .... Ms. Kelly TRAHAN
13 Chief Information Security Officer .... Mr. Joshua MITCHELL
79 Int Dean Humanities/Arts/Social Sci .... Mr. Eike REICHARDT
76 Dean Healthcare Sciences .... Mr. Craig A. KOLLER
103 Int Dean Workfrc/Cmty Educ/Tech Ed .... Dr. Andrea K. GRANNUM-MOSLEY
26 Exec Dir College Relations .... Ms. Linda BAKER
09 Exec Dir Inst Research & Effectiv .... Dr. Fawad RAFI
50 Dean Business/Educ/Legal/Social Svc .... Dr. Cecelia A. CONNELLY-WEIDA
114 Dir Budgets & Purchasing .... Ms. Shannon HELMER
102 Executive Director Foundation .... Ms. Silvia VARGAS
07 Exec Dir Recruitment & Enroll .... Ms. Ellia SABLAN-ZEBEDY
36 Dir Career Development .... Ms. Christina L. MOYER
108 Dn Accred/Compliance/Curric/Assess .... Mr. Scott W. AQUILA
88 Exec Dir of High School Connections .... Ms. Jennifer K. AQUILA
15 Dir HR/Title IX/Equity Coord .... Ms. Donna M. WILLIAMS
88 Dir Org & Faculty Development .... Vacant
66 Director Nursing Programs .... Dr. Tina VANBUREN
35 Director Student Life .... Ms. Gene F. EDEN
14 Asst Dir Technical Architect .... Mr. Ervin J. MEASE
18 Dir Facilities Mgmt & Public Safety .... Mr. George CALABA
37 Exec Dir Fin Aid & Scholarship .... Ms. Tracey RICHARDS
88 Dir Academic Grants .... Ms. Linda L. MESICS
41 Director Athletics .... Mr. Andrew JOHNSON
88 Dir Early Learning Center .... Ms. Elizabeth D. LIPMAN
88 Grant Writer .... Ms. Mary KOVALCHICK
74 Dir Veterinary Tech Program .... Ms. Lisa A. MARTINI-JOHNSON
27 Dir Marketing & Publications .... Mr. Shane BAGLINI
06 Dir Registration/Student Records .... Mr. Gregory J. GOLETZ, JR.
40 Bookstore Manager .... Mr. Zachary POTTER
38 Dir Counseling & Cmty Standards .... Mr. Brian C. DELONG
19 Public Safety Supervisor .... Mr. Gary D. OLEWINE
113 Dir Student Accounts .... Ms. Ann L. BOYLE
121 Dean of Academic Support & Success .... Dr. Dorothy COLLINS
21 Controller .... Ms. Stacey BETZ

Lehigh University (E)

27 Memorial Drive W, Bethlehem PA 18015-3094
County: Northampton FICE Identification: 003289
Unit ID: 213543
Telephone: (610) 758-3000 Carnegie Class: DU-Higher
FAX Number: (610) 691-5420 Calendar System: Semester
URL: www.lehigh.edu
Established: 1865 Annual Undergrad Tuition & Fees: $55,260
Enrollment: 7,067 Coed
Affiliation or Control: Independent Non-Profit IRS Status: 501(c)3
Highest Offering: Doctorate
Accreditation: M, COPSY, IPSY, MPCAC, SCPSY, THEA

01 President .... Dr. John D. SIMON
05 Provost & VP for Academic Affairs .... Dr. Nathan N. URBAN
10 Vice Pres Finance & Administration .... Ms. Patricia A. JOHNSON
88 VP for International Affairs .... Dr. Cheryl A. MATHERLY
30 VP Development and Alumni Relations .... Mr. Joseph E. BUCK
46 VP/Assoc Prov Research/Grad Studies .... Dr. Alan J. SNYDER
26 VP Communications & Public Affairs .... Mr. Frederick J. MCGRAIL
28 VP Diversity/Inclusion & Equity .... Dr. Donald A. OUTING
115 Chief Investment Officer .... Ms. Kristin AGATONE
09 Vice Provost Institutional Research .... Dr. Yenny ANDERSON
32 Vice Provost Student Affairs .... Dr. Ricardo HALL
13 Vice Provost Library & Tech Svcs .... Dr. Greg REIHMAN
88 Vice Provost for Academic Diversity .... Mr. Henry U. ODI
86 Assoc VP for Govt Relations .... Mr. Christopher C. CARTER
21 Assoc VP Finance/Asst Secy Board .... Vacant
15 Assoc VP for Human Resource .... Mr. Chris HALLADAY
18 Assoc VP Facilities Svcs/Architect .... Mr. Brent STRINGFELLOW
20 Deputy Provost Academic Affairs .... Ms. Jennifer M. JENSEN
35 Dean of Students .... Ms. Katherine W. LAVINDER
29 Asst VP of Alumni Engagement .... Ms. Jennifer L. CUNNINGHAM
31 Asst VP Community & Regional Affs .... Ms. Adrienne J. WASHINGTON
54 Dean Engr & Applied Science .... Dr. Stephen P. DEWEERTH
49 Dean of Arts & Sciences .... Dr. Robert FLOWERS
50 Dean of Business/Economics .... Dr. Georgette C. PHILLIPS
53 Dean of Education .... Dr. William GAUDELLI
69 Interim Dean College of Health .... Dr. Elizabeth DOLAN
07 Vice Provost Admiss/Financial Aid .... Mr. Dan WARNER
41 Murray H Goodman Dean of Athletics .... Mr. Joseph D. STERRETT
06 Registrar .... Mr. Steven H. WILSON
37 Director Financial Aid .... Ms. Jennifer L. MERTZ
106 Director Distance Education .... Ms. Margaret A. PORTZ
36 Director Career Services .... Ms. Lori B. KENNEDY
23 Inaugural Exec Dir Health Center .... Mr. David RUBENSTEIN
39 Director Residential Services .... Mr. Ozzie BREINER
40 Director Bookstore .... Mr. Brian ADLER
19 Chief University Police .... Mr. Jason D. SCHIFFER
38 Interim Dir of Counseling Svcs .... Dr. Aaron STERBA
42 Chaplain .... Rev. Lloyd H. STEFFEN
43 General Counsel .... Mr. Frank A. ROTH
114 Director of Budget .... Mr. Stephen J. GUTTMAN
96 Manager Strategic Sourcing .... Ms. Jane ALTEMOSE
84 Director Enrollment Management .... Ms. Jennifer E. O'BRIEN-KNOTTS
100 Chief of Staff .... Mr. Erik J. WALKER
04 Executive Asst to the President .... Ms. Donna L. FEIST
104 Director Study Abroad .... Ms. Katie W. RADANDE

Lincoln Technical Institute (F)

5151 Tilghman Street, Allentown PA 18104-3298
County: Lehigh FICE Identification: 007759
Unit ID: 213570
Telephone: (610) 398-5300 Carnegie Class: Assoc/HVT-High Trad
FAX Number: (610) 395-2706 Calendar System: Semester
URL: www.lincolntech.edu
Established: 1946 Annual Undergrad Tuition & Fees: N/A
Enrollment: 599 Coed
Affiliation or Control: Proprietary IRS Status: Proprietary
Highest Offering: Associate Degree
Accreditation: ACCSC

01 Campus President .... Mrs. Angela REPPERT
05 Director of Education .... Ms. Hollie ESTES
66 Director of Nursing .... Mrs. Michelle DAVIS
11 Director of Administrative Services .... Mrs. Rebecca DRAYTON
07 Director of Admissions .... Mr. Vincent SALVATORIELLO
36 Director of Career Services .... Mrs. Charmain BRODY
37 Financial Aid Manager .... Ms. Erica BRANDI

Lincoln Technical Institute (G)

9191 Torresdale Avenue, Philadelphia PA 19136-1595
County: Philadelphia FICE Identification: 007832
Unit ID: 213589
Telephone: (215) 335-0800 Carnegie Class: Spec 2-yr-Tech
FAX Number: (215) 335-1443 Calendar System: Other
URL: www.lincolntech.com
Established: 1946 Annual Undergrad Tuition & Fees: N/A
Enrollment: 389 Coed
Affiliation or Control: Proprietary IRS Status: Proprietary
Highest Offering: Associate Degree
Accreditation: ACCSC

01 Campus President .... Mr. Jim KUNTZ
32 Director of Admissions .... Ms. Michele GRANT
05 Director of Education .... Mrs. Jennifer MCLAUGHLIN
11 Director Administration .... Ms. Gina ALTSHULER
36 Director of Career Services .... Ms. Emily MATTHEWS

Lincoln University (H)

1570 Baltimore Pike, Lincoln University PA 19352-0999
County: Chester FICE Identification: 003290
Unit ID: 213598
Telephone: (484) 365-8000 Carnegie Class: Masters/M
FAX Number: (484) 365-7316 Calendar System: Semester
URL: www.lincoln.edu
Established: 1854 Annual Undergrad Tuition & Fees (In-State): $11,266
Enrollment: 2,077 Coed
Affiliation or Control: State Related IRS Status: 501(c)3
Highest Offering: Master's
Accreditation: M, NURSE

01 President .... Dr. Brenda A. ALLEN
111 AVP for Institutional Advancement .... Ms. Samira MALIK
100 Chief of Staff/Mgr Board Trustees .... Ms. Diane M. BROWN
05 Provost and VP for Academic Affairs .... Vacant
10 Vice Pres Fiscal Affairs/Treasurer .... Mr. Charles GRADOWSKI
32 VP Student Success/Dean of College .... Dr. Lenetta LEE
15 Vice President Human Resources .... Mr. Jake TANKSLEY
13 Chief Information Officer .... Mr. Justin MCKENZIE
42 Chaplain .... Rev Dr. Frederick FAISON
09 Asst Prov Inst Effect/Research/Plng .... Ms. Tiffany LEE
08 Int Director of Library .... Ms. Sophia SOTILLEO
35 Assoc Dean of College/Students .... Rev Dr. Frederick FAISON
84 Assoc Provost Enrollment Management .... Dr. Kimberly TAYLOR-BENNS
26 Manager of Comm & Public Relations .... Mr. Terrance J. YOUNG
29 Assoc VP of Alumni Relations .... Ms. Deborah JOHNSON
35 AVP Stdnt Success/Dean of Students .... Mr. Brian DUBENION
06 Registrar .... Ms. Catherine RUTLEDGE
36 Director Career Development .... Vacant
41 Director of Athletics .... Mr. Harry STINSON
21 Controller .... Mr. Jay SIMMONS
85 Director of International Services .... Ms. Dafina BLACKSHER DIABATE
23 Director Health Services .... Ms. Velva GREENE-RAINEY
123 Dir Graduate Student Svcs/Admission .... Ms. Jernice LEA
37 Director Financial Aid .... Ms. Kim ANDERSON
96 Director of Purchasing .... Ms. Lynn POWELL
20 Dean of the Faculty .... Dr. Patricia JOSEPH

121 Assoc VP Academic Support ....Ms. Evelyn POE
07 Director of Admissions ....Mrs. Nokoia FORDE
19 Director Security/Safety ....Mr. Marc PARTEE
22 Director Title III ....Ms. Marion BERNARD-AMOS
38 Director Student Counseling ....Ms. Rachel MANSON
44 Director Annual Giving ....Mr. Rich LANCASTER
90 Proj Manager Academic Computing ....Ms. Nancy EVANS

Luzerne County Community College (A)

1333 S Prospect Street, Nanticoke PA 18634-3899
County: Luzerne FICE Identification: 006811
Unit ID: 213659
Telephone: (570) 740-0200 Carnegie Class: Assoc/HVT-High Trad
FAX Number: (570) 740-0750 Calendar System: Semester
URL: www.luzerne.edu
Established: 1966 Annual Undergrad Tuition & Fees (In-District): $10,020
Enrollment: 4,454 Coed
Affiliation or Control: Local IRS Status: 501(c)3
Highest Offering: Associate Degree
Accreditation: M, ACBSP, ADNUR, COARC, DH, EMT, NAEYC, SURGT

01 President ....Mr. Thomas P. LEARY
101 Executive Asst to President/BOT ....Ms. Paula LABENSKI
05 Vice Pres Academic Affairs ....Dr. Cheryl LESSER
32 VP of Enrollment Mgmt/Student Dev ....Ms. Rosana REYES
103 VP of Applied Tech/Workforce Devel ....Ms. Susan SPRY
15 Dean Human Resources ....Mr. John SEDLAK
66 Dean of Nursing/Health Sciences ....Ms. Deborah VILEGI PAYNE
13 Chief Information Officer ....Ms. Patricia YENCHA
10 VP of Finance ....Ms. Cheryl BAUR
07 Assistant Director Admissions ....Mr. Ed HENNIGAN
37 Director of Student Financial Aid ....Mr. Mark CARPENTIER
08 Director of Library ....Ms. Katherine CUMMINGS
38 Dir Counseling/Stdnt Support Svcs ....Mrs. Janine KELLEY
35 Dir Student Life/Athletics ....Ms. Kristen CORCORAN
09 Director Inst Research/Planning ....Ms. Graceann PLATUKUS
18 Director of Physical Plant ....Mr. Keith GRAHAM
30 Exec Dir of Institutional Advance ....Ms. Rebecca BROMINSKI
84 Director Enrollment Management ....Mr. Jim DOMZALSKI
26 Director of College Relations ....Ms. Lisa NELSON
29 Director Alumni Relations ....Ms. Bonnie LAUER
28 Diversity Coordinator ....Ms. Judi MYERS
19 Director of Public Safety/Security ....Mr. Douglas FAWBUSH

Lycoming College (B)

700 College Place, Williamsport PA 17701-5192
County: Lycoming FICE Identification: 003293
Unit ID: 213668
Telephone: (570) 321-4000 Carnegie Class: Bac-A&S
FAX Number: (570) 321-4337 Calendar System: Semester
URL: www.lycoming.edu
Established: 1812 Annual Undergrad Tuition & Fees: $42,939
Enrollment: 1,065 Coed
Affiliation or Control: United Methodist IRS Status: 501(c)3
Highest Offering: Baccalaureate
Accreditation: M

01 President ....Dr. Kent C. TRACHTE
05 Provost and Dean of the College ....Dr. Philip W. SPRUNGER
10 VP for Finance and Admin/Treasurer ....Mr. Jeffrey L. BENNETT
111 Executive Vice President ....Dr. Charles W. EDMONDS
84 VP for Enrollment Management ....Mr. Michael J. KONOPSKI
21 Controller ....Ms. Dawn HENDRICKS
32 Vice President for Student Life ....Dr. Daniel P. MILLER
20 Vice Provost ....Dr. Susan ROSS
89 Assistant Dean First Year Students ....Ms. Mallory L. WEYMER
08 Director of Snowden Library ....Vacant
06 Registrar ....Ms. Jilliane BOLT-MICHEWICZ
37 Director of Financial Aid ....Mr. James LAKIS
13 Chief Information Officer ....Mr. Robert L. DUNKLEBERGER
29 Director Alumni Relations ....Ms. Amy S. REYES
112 Sr Dir for Major Planned Gifts ....Mr. Robb DIETRICH
39 Assoc Dean of Students ....Ms. Kate HUMMEL
41 Director of Athletics ....Mr. Michael CLARK
110 Assoc Dir of Major Gifts ....Mr. Gregory J. BELL
44 Director of Annual Giving ....Ms. Lesley LARSON
15 Director of Human Resources ....Ms. Kacy HAGAN
18 Chief Facilities/Physical Plant ....Mr. F. Douglas KUNTZ
23 Director of Health Services ....Vacant
38 Director Student Counseling ....Mr. Townsend VELKOFF
40 Campus Store Manager ....Ms. Patricia E. BAUSINGER
92 Lycoming Scholars ....Dr. Cullen CHANDLER
94 Women's Studies ....Dr. Kerry RICHMOND
118 Human Resources Benefits Coord ....Ms. Cathleen A. LUTZ
04 Assistant to the President ....Ms. Diane CARL
09 Director of Institutional Research ....Dr. Chiaki KOTORI
108 Associate Provost ....Dr. Amy ROGERS
90 Dir of IT Core Services ....Ms. Nicole KUNTZ
91 Director Administrative Computing ....Ms. Janet PAYNE
07 Director of Admissions ....Ms. Jessica A. QUINTANA HESS
102 Foundations Relations Officer ....Mrs. Melanie TAORMINA
104 Coordinator of Study Abroad ....Ms. Allison HOLLADAY
105 Director Web Services ....Mr. Robert BROWN
19 Director Security/Safety ....Ms. Holly BLEAM
26 Sr Dir of Marketing & Comm ....Ms. Marla KRAMER

Manor College (C)

700 Fox Chase Road, Jenkintown PA 19046-3399
County: Montgomery FICE Identification: 003294
Unit ID: 213774
Telephone: (215) 885-2360 Carnegie Class: Assoc/MT-VT-High Trad
FAX Number: (215) 576-6564 Calendar System: Semester
URL: www.manor.edu
Established: 1947 Annual Undergrad Tuition & Fees: $18,530
Enrollment: 834 Coed
Affiliation or Control: Independent Non-Profit IRS Status: 501(c)3
Highest Offering: Baccalaureate
Accreditation: M, ACBSP, DA, DH

01 President ....Dr. Jonathan PERI
05 Provost and VPAA ....Dr. Marc MINNICK
06 Registrar ....Ms. Dianne I. SARIDAKIS
13 Information Technology Manager ....Mr. Brian WHELAN
15 Director of Human Resources ....Ms. Christine COLELLA
111 VP of Institutional Advancement ....Ms. Kelly PEIFFER
10 VP of Finance & Facilities ....Ms. Janice SALERNO
19 Chief of Public Safety ....Mr. David CARISTO
26 VP of Marketing/Communications ....Ms. Kelly PEIFFER
32 VP and Dean of Student Affairs ....Ms. Allison C. MOOTZ
84 VP of Enrollment Management ....Dr. Joseph GILLESPIE
37 Director Financial Aid ....Mr. Chris T. HARTMAN
38 Director Counseling ....Ms. Christine B. PRINCE
39 Assistant Director Residence Life ....Ms. Shamika FORD
41 Director Athletics ....Mr. John DEMPSTER
79 Humanities and Social Science Chair ....Dr. Matthew SMALARZ
08 Head Librarian ....Mr. Richard JUTKIEWICZ
09 Director of Institutional Research ....Mr. John T. KREBS
04 Exec Assistant to the President ....Mrs. Katharina M. KILMER
49 Sr Dean Arts & Sciences ....Dr. Julie SENECOFF
53 Dean/Dir Instruct Learning Init ....Dr. Cherie CROSBY
103 Dean Academic Services ....Mr. Nick RUDNYTZKY
105 Web Services ....Ms. Emily CARROLL
108 Director Institutional Assessment ....Mr. John KREBS
96 Director of Purchasing ....Mrs. Janice SALERNO
29 Institutional Advancement Officer ....Mr. Tom SIMS

Marywood University (D)

2300 Adams Avenue, Scranton PA 18509-1598
County: Lackawanna FICE Identification: 003296
Unit ID: 213826
Telephone: (570) 348-6211 Carnegie Class: Masters/L
FAX Number: (570) 961-4769 Calendar System: Semester
URL: www.marywood.edu
Established: 1915 Annual Undergrad Tuition & Fees: $36,928
Enrollment: 2,613 Coed
Affiliation or Control: Roman Catholic IRS Status: 501(c)3
Highest Offering: Doctorate
Accreditation: M, ACATE, ACBSP, ARCPA, ART, CAATE, CACREP, CLPSY, COARC, DIETD, DIETI, MUS, NURSE, SP, SW

01 President ....Sr. Mary PERSICO, IHM
05 Provost ....Dr. Christina A. CLARK
10 VP for Finance and Administration ....Mr. William MCDONALD
111 Vice Pres University Advancement ....Dr. Renee G. ZEHEL
84 VP Enrollment Svcs/Student Success ....Ms. Ann BOLAND-CHASE
15 Exec Director of Human Resources ....Ms. Molly BARON
26 Exec Dir Marketing/Communication ....Mr. James M. BROWN
18 VP of Operations ....Ms. Wendy YANKELITIS
49 Dean College of Arts/Science ....Dr. Jeffrey JOHNSON
76 Dean Col Health/Human Svcs ....Dr. Lori E. SWANCHAK
107 Dean Col of Prof Studies ....Mr. James J. SULLIVAN
70 Director School of Social Work ....Sr. Angela KIM
08 University Librarian ....Dr. Susan M. FREY
06 Registrar ....Ms. Rosemary BURGER
07 Dir of UG Admissions ....Ms. Rachel HARTZ
21 Interim Controller/Asst Treasurer ....Ms. Melissa SADDLEMIRE
37 Director of Financial Aid ....Ms. Barbara L. SCHMITT
113 Manager of Cashier's Office ....Ms. Darlene J. SEDLAK
44 Leadership Annual Giving Officer ....Ms. Patricia H. ROSETTI
20 Associate Provost ....Ms. Leslie W. CHRISTIANSON
30 Sr Dir Development & Annual Giving ....Ms. Christina M. MACE
121 Asst Provost for Student Success ....Dr. Paul J. BALLARD
27 Public Relations Director ....Ms. Juneann GRECO
32 Interim Exec Dir Student Services ....Sr. Elizabeth A. MCGILL
41 Exec Director Athletics/Recreation ....Mr. Patrick MURPHY
36 Career Engagement Specialist ....Dr. Christina BRUNDAGE
42 VP for Mission Services ....Sr. Catherine LUXNER
88 Dir of Dining Services ....Mr. Louis MAZZA
13 Chief Information Officer ....Dr. David HUNTER
19 Chief Campus Safety ....Mr. Michael C. PASQUALICCHIO
23 Director of Student Health Services ....Ms. Maura K. SMITH
38 Director Counseling & Student Devel ....Dr. Robert S. SHAW
110 Dir Advancement Services ....Ms. Elizabeth M. STIRES
29 Director of Alumni Engagement ....Mr. Kevin FARRELL
35 Dean of Students ....Mr. Ross NOVAK
22 Dir of Student Equity/Inclusion ....Dr. Lia Richards PALMITER
09 Asst Dir for Research & Spons Pgms ....Dr. Diane KELLER
109 Exec Dir Confer/Events/Auxil Svcs ....Mr. John J. COVAL
04 Exec Secretary to the President ....Ms. Robyn M. KRUKOVITZ
43 Secretary Univ & General Counsel ....Ms. Mary T. GARDIER PATERSON
28 Exec Dir Equity & Inclus/Title IX ....Dr. Yerodin LUCAS

McCann School of Business & Technology (E)

2200 North Irving Street, Allentown PA 18109
Telephone: (484) 223-4600 Identification: 770768
Accreditation: ACCSC, MLTAD

† Branch campus of Platt College, Tulsa, OK.

McCann School of Business & Technology (F)

7495 Westbranch Highway, Lewisburg PA 17837
Telephone: (570) 497-8014 Identification: 666485
Accreditation: ACCSC, SURGT

† Branch campus of Platt College, Tulsa, OK.

Mercyhurst University (G)

501 E 38th Street, Erie PA 16546-0001
County: Erie FICE Identification: 003297
Unit ID: 213987
Telephone: (814) 824-2000 Carnegie Class: Masters/M
FAX Number: (814) 824-2438 Calendar System: Semester
URL: www.mercyhurst.edu
Established: 1926 Annual Undergrad Tuition & Fees: $41,350
Enrollment: 2,790 Coed
Affiliation or Control: Roman Catholic IRS Status: 501(c)3
Highest Offering: Doctorate
Accreditation: M, ADNUR, ARCPA, CAATE, COARC, DANCE, IACBE, MLTAD, MUS, OTA, PTAA, SW

01 Acting President ....Mr. Joseph NECASTRO
05 Interim Provost ....Dr. Joanne M. HOSEY-MCGURK
10 Vice Pres Finance & Administration ....Mr. David P. MYRON
30 Vice Pres University Development ....Vacant
32 Vice Pres of Student Life ....Dr. Laura ZIRKEL
84 Interim VP for Enrollment ....Ms. Dionne VEITCH
13 Chief Information Officer ....Ms. Jeanette BRITT
18 Director Facilities/Physical Plant ....Mr. David MYRON
38 Director Student Counseling Service ....Ms. Judy SMITH
07 Director Undergraduate Admissions ....Mr. Christian BEYER
06 Registrar ....Ms. Michele WHEATON
08 Dir Univ Libraries/Online Learning ....Ms. Darci JONES
39 Dir Residential Life/Stdnt Conduct ....Vacant
19 Director of Public Safety Programs ....Mr. Donald J. FUHRMANN
29 Dir Alumni Engagement ....Ms. Lindsay FRANK
42 Director of Campus Ministry ....Fr. James PISZKER
37 Director of Student Financial Svcs ....Ms. Carrie NEWMAN
41 Director of Athletics ....Mr. Bradley DAVIS
09 Director of Institutional Research ....Mrs. Sheila W. RICHTER
15 Director Human Resources ....Vacant
93 Coordinator Multicultural Affairs ....Vacant
04 Administrative Asst to President ....Ms. Stacey WILEY
104 Director Study Abroad ....Dr. Heidi HOSEY
26 Chief Public Relations/Marketing ....Mr. Sean P. CUNEO
43 Dir Legal Services/General Counsel ....Mrs. Meredith BOLLHEIMER

Messiah University (H)

One University Avenue, Mechanicsburg PA 17055
County: Cumberland FICE Identification: 003298
Unit ID: 213996
Telephone: (717) 766-2511 Carnegie Class: Masters/M
FAX Number: (717) 691-6025 Calendar System: Semester
URL: www.messiah.edu
Established: 1909 Annual Undergrad Tuition & Fees: $37,180
Enrollment: 3,370 Coed
Affiliation or Control: Interdenominational IRS Status: 501(c)3
Highest Offering: Doctorate
Accreditation: M, ACBSP, ART, CAATE, CACREP, DIETD, DIETI, MUS, NURSE, OT, @PTA, SW, THEA

01 President ....Dr. Kim S. PHIPPS
05 Provost ....Dr. Randall G. BASINGER
10 Vice Pres for Finance & Planning ....Mr. David S. WALKER
11 Vice President for Operations ....Mrs. Kathrynne G. SHAFER
111 Vice President for Advancement ....Mr. Barry G. GOODLING
84 Vice Pres for Enrollment Management ....Mr. John A. CHOPKA
15 VP for Human Res & Compliance ....Ms. Amanda A. COFFEY
28 VP for Diversity Affairs ....Dr. Todd ALLEN
121 Vice Provost for Student Success ....Dr. Kristin M. HANSEN-KIEFFER
58 Asst Provost/Dean of Grad Studies ....Dr. Robert PEPPER
79 Dean School of Humanities ....Dr. Peter K. POWERS
81 Dean School of Science/Engr/Health ....Dr. Angela HARE
32 Dean of Students ....Mr. Kevin VILLEGAS
35 Associate Dean of Students ....Mr. Douglas M. WOOD
30 Exec Director of Development ....Dr. Jon C. STUCKEY
93 Dir of Intercultural Office ....Vacant
07 Director of Admissions ....Mrs. Dana J. BRITTON
37 Director of Financial Aid ....Mr. Gregory L. GEARHART
39 Asst Dir of Residence Life/Housing ....Mr. Bryce WATKINS
21 Dir Financial Operations/Controller ....Mrs. Christine HARTMAN
06 Registrar ....Ms. Carrie WIDDOWSON
08 Director of the Murray Library ....Ms. Linda POSTON
91 Director Information Services ....Mr. John P. LUFT
90 Dir Learning Technology Services ....Mrs. Susan K. SHANNON
09 Director of Institutional Research ....Ms. Laura M. MILLER
42 Campus Pastor ....Vacant
26 Exec Director Communications ....Mrs. Carla E. GROSS
29 Director Alumni & Parent Relations ....Mr. Jay W. MCCLYMONT
38 Director of the Engle Center ....Ms. Eleanor MUIR
41 Athletics Director ....Ms. Sarah GUSTIN HAMROCK
92 Dir of the College Honors Program ....Dr. James LAGRAND
18 Director of Facility Services ....Mr. Bradley A. MARKLEY
36 Dir Career/Profess Development ....Mrs. Christina R. HANSON
40 Campus Store Manager ....Vacant
19 Director Safety/Dispatch Services ....Ms. Cindy L. BURGER
04 Executive Coordinator for President ....Mrs. Karin BISBEE
96 Purchasing Manager ....Mrs. Daisy ANDERSON

23 Coordinator of Health Services .... Mrs. Michelle LUCAS
105 Web Services Manager .... Ms. Ramona FRITSCHI
108 Director of Assessment .... Ms. Kate WILKINS
20 Associate Provost .... Dr. Alison NOBLE

Missio Seminary (A)

421 N. 7th St., Philadelphia PA 19123
County: Philadelphia FICE Identification: 023230
Unit ID: 211130
Telephone: (215) 368-5000 Carnegie Class: Spec-4-yr-Faith
FAX Number: (215) 368-2301 Calendar System: Semester
URL: www.missio.edu
Established: 1971 Annual Graduate Tuition & Fees: N/A
Enrollment: 223 Coed
Affiliation or Control: Independent Non-Profit IRS Status: 501(c)3
Highest Offering: Doctorate; No Undergraduates
Accreditation: M, THEOL

01 President .... Dr. Frank JAMES, III
03 Executive Vice President .... Mr. Charles BLACHFORD
05 Dean of the Faculty .... Dr. David LAMB
04 Executive Assistant to the Pres .... Mrs. Beatrice L. BARKLEY
88 Director of DMin Program .... Dr. Kyuboem LEE
37 Director Student Financial Aid .... Mr. Jermaine HARRINGTON
08 Director of Library Services .... Ms. Rachel MCCONNELL
06 Registrar/Dir of Academic Services .... Ms. Julie COWEN
07 Director of Admissions .... Dr. Michael HEATH
13 Chief Info Technology Officer .... Mr. Gregg ALDERFER
29 Director Alumni Affairs .... Ms. Wendy WALTERS

Misericordia University (B)

301 Lake Street, Dallas PA 18612-1098
County: Luzerne FICE Identification: 003247
Unit ID: 214069
Telephone: (570) 674-6400 Carnegie Class: DU-Mod
FAX Number: (570) 675-2441 Calendar System: Semester
URL: www.misericordia.edu
Established: 1924 Annual Undergrad Tuition & Fees: $35,940
Enrollment: 2,374 Coed
Affiliation or Control: Roman Catholic IRS Status: 501(c)3
Highest Offering: Doctorate
Accreditation: M, #ARCPA, DMS, IACBE, NURSE, OT, PTA, RAD, SP, SW

01 President .... Dr. Daniel J. MYERS
10 Vice Pres Finance & Administration .... Mr. Mark VAN ETTEN, JR.
05 Vice President Academic Affairs .... Dr. David REHM
111 VP of Institutional Advancement .... Ms. Susan M. HELWIG
88 Vice Pres of Mission Integration .... Ms. Amy LAHART
45 Sec to BOT/VP Plng/External Rels .... Dr. Barbara SAMUEL
32 Vice President of Student Life .... Ms. Kathleen FOLEY
84 Vice President of Enrollment Mgmt .... Mr. Glenn BOZINSKI
21 Assoc Vice Pres of Finance .... Mr. Ronald S. HROMISIN
102 AVP of Advancement .... Mr. Larry PELLEGRINI
100 Chief of Staff .... Mr. James ROBERTS
06 Registrar .... Mr. Joseph REDINGTON
35 Dean of Students .... Ms. Callie RIMPFEL
29 Director Alumni Relations .... Ms. Lailani AUGUSTINE
08 Librarian .... Ms. Jennifer LUKSA
04 Exec Assistant to the President .... Ms. Lisa BORCHERT
96 Director of Purchasing .... Mr. Thomas F. KANE
121 Director of Student Success Center .... Ms. Jessica NELSON
42 Director Campus Ministry .... Ms. Christine SOMERS
41 Director of Athletics .... Mr. Charles EDKINS
39 Director of Residence Life .... Mr. Angelo NUDO
14 Manager Applications Development .... Mr. Matt MIHAL
13 Director of Information Technology .... Mr. Val APANOVICH
88 Director of Student Engagement .... Ms. Darcy BRODMERKEL
36 Dir Insalaco Ctr Career Development .... Ms. Bernadette RUSHMER
51 Director of Adult Education/CACE .... Mr. Paul NARDONE
15 Director of Human Resources .... Ms. Pamela PARSNIK
04 Special Assistant to President .... Ms. Barbara SAMUEL
37 Assoc Director of Financial Aid .... Ms. Karen COLE
19 Director Security/Safety .... Ms. Ruth ANDERIKA
18 Director of Facilities .... Mr. Taras MIHALKO
09 Director of Institutional Research .... Ms. Sharon HUDAK
90 Manager of User Services .... Mr. David A. JOHNDROW
07 Director of Admissions .... Mr. Stephen SECORA
104 Director Study Abroad .... Vacant

Montgomery County Community College (C)

340 Dekalb Pike, Blue Bell PA 19422-1400
County: Montgomery FICE Identification: 004452
Unit ID: 214111
Telephone: (215) 641-6300 Carnegie Class: Assoc/MT-VT-Mix Trad/Non
FAX Number: (215) 461-1460 Calendar System: Semester
URL: www.mc3.edu
Established: 1964 Annual Undergrad Tuition & Fees (In-District): $10,350
Enrollment: 9,827 Coed
Affiliation or Control: State/Local IRS Status: 501(c)3
Highest Offering: Associate Degree
Accreditation: M, ADNUR, CSHSE, DH, MLTAD, NAEYC, PTAA, RAD, SURGT

01 President .... Dr. Victoria BASTECKI-PEREZ
04 Exec Asst to the Office of the Pres .... Ms. Deborah A. ROGERS
05 VP for Academic Affairs .... Dr. Gloria OIKELOME
103 VP of Workforce Development .... Vacant
13 VP for Information Technology .... Dr. Celeste M. SCHWARTZ
10 VP for Finance & Administration .... Mr. Charles SOMERS
111 Vice Pres for Advancement .... Mr. Jay BROWNING
32 VP of Student Services .... Mr. Philip NEEDLES
06 Registrar .... Ms. Sherry PHILLIPS
15 Executive Director Human Resources .... Ms. Diane O'CONNOR
21 Controller .... Ms. Heather MEIER
30 Director of Development .... Ms. Traci CONNELLY GOIDAS
19 Director of Campus Safety .... Mr. David CARISTO
37 Director of Financial Aid .... Ms. Christal CHATMAN
09 Exec Dir of Inst Research .... Mr. David KOWALSKI
28 Dir Equity & Diversity Initiatives .... Ms. Rose MAKOFSKE
29 Dir of Alumni Rel & Major Gifts .... Vacant
26 Director of Strategic Communication .... Ms. Diane VANDYKE
07 Dir of Enrollment Services .... Ms. Maureen CARVER
08 Director of Libraries .... Ms. Robin BOWLES
18 Director of Facilities Mgmt .... Mr. Michael BILLETTA
102 Dir of Corp & Found Rels & Grants .... Mr. Donald SMITH
35 Dean of Student Affairs .... Vacant
96 Director of Procurement .... Ms. Jenny RARIG
50 Dean of Business/Entrepreneurship .... Vacant
86 Director Government Relations .... Mr. Michael BETTINGER
41 Dir Athletics & Campus Recreation .... Ms. Kelly DUNBAR
84 Exec Director Enrollment Management .... Ms. Michelle BROWN
100 Special Assistant to the President .... Dr. Jenna MEEHAN

Montgomery County Community College Pottstown Campus (D)

101 College Drive, Pottstown PA 19464
Telephone: (610) 718-1800 Identification: 770162
Accreditation: &M

Moore College of Art and Design (E)

1916 Race Street, Philadelphia PA 19103-1179
County: Philadelphia FICE Identification: 003300
Unit ID: 214148
Telephone: (215) 965-4000 Carnegie Class: Spec-4-yr-Arts
FAX Number: (215) 568-8017 Calendar System: Semester
URL: www.moore.edu
Established: 1848 Annual Undergrad Tuition & Fees: $44,806
Enrollment: 389 Female
Affiliation or Control: Independent Non-Profit IRS Status: 501(c)3
Highest Offering: Master's
Accreditation: M, CIDA

01 President .... Ms. Cecelia FITZGIBBON
10 SVP Finance & Administration .... Mr. William L. HILL, II
111 VP Institutional Advancement .... Ms. Elizabeth CAHILL
05 Academic Dean/CAO .... Ms. Lynn TOMASZEWSKI
32 Dean of Students .... Mr. Joshua WILKIN
09 Assoc Dean/Director Inst Research .... Ms. Claudine THOMAS
39 Director Residence Life/Housing .... Ms. Kimberley FOX
88 Director of Galleries .... Ms. Gabrielle LAVIN
51 Assoc Dean Cont Educ/Grad Studies .... Dr. Joanna JENKINS
26 Chief Mktg & Communications Ofcr .... Ms. Nicole STEINBERG
110 Assoc Director of Advancement .... Ms. Patricia MA
29 Assoc Dir Alumnae Affs/Annual Fund .... Ms. Laura KOCHMAN
08 Library Director .... Ms. Kimberly LESLEY
07 Dean of Admissions .... Mr. Jonathan SQUIRE
37 Director of Financial Aid .... Ms. Ashley SLOWE
06 Registrar .... Mr. Michael MCHUGH
15 Director Human Resources .... Ms. Rachel PHILLIPS
36 Director Career Center .... Ms. Belena CHAPP
90 Academic Computing Manager .... Mr. Dennis DAWTON
100 Chief of Staff .... Ms. Alysson CWYK

Moravian College (F)

1200 Main St., Bethlehem PA 18018-6650
County: Northampton FICE Identification: 003301
Unit ID: 214157
Telephone: (610) 861-1300 Carnegie Class: Bac-A&S
FAX Number: (610) 625-7918 Calendar System: Semester
URL: www.moravian.edu
Established: 1742 Annual Undergrad Tuition & Fees: $47,367
Enrollment: 2,605 Coed
Affiliation or Control: Moravian Church IRS Status: 501(c)3
Highest Offering: Doctorate
Accreditation: M, ACBSP, CAATE, MUS, NURSE, OT, @PTA, @SP, THEOL

01 President .... Dr. Bryon L. GRIGSBY
05 Provost .... Dr. Cynthia KOSSO
10 VP Finance & Administration .... Mr. Mark F. REED
15 VP Human Resources .... Mr. Jon B. CONRAD
30 VP Development and Alumni .... Ms. Jill C. ANDERSON
32 VP Student Affairs Dean of Students .... Dr. Nicole L. LOYD
84 VP for Enrollment and Marketing .... Mr. Scott DAMS
13 Chief Information Officer .... Mr. David BRANDES
100 Chief of Staff .... Mrs. Elaine C. DEITCH
106 Dean Online Education/E-learning .... Dr. Bernardo CANTENS
121 Dean of Student Success .... Dr. Kevin HARTSHORN
76 Dean of Natural & Health Sci .... Dr. Diane HUSIC
79 Dean of Arts/Humanities/SS .... Dr. Daniel JASPER
73 Dean of the Seminary .... Dr. Heather VACEK
35 Asst VP Student Affairs .... Ms. Amy SAUL
20 Assoc Provost .... Dr. Carol TRAUPMAN-CARR
21 Director of Finance .... Mr. Wilson GONZALEZ
39 Assoc Dean of Students .... Ms. Liz YATES SEAMAN
113 Director of Student Accounts .... Ms. Dawn SNOOK
06 Institutional Registrar .... Ms. Monique DAVIS
88 Dir Business/Financial Operations .... Ms. Rachel LYALL
18 Dir Facilities Mgt Plng/Construct .... Ms. Yasmin BUGAIGHIS
19 Chief of Police .... Mr. Richard BLAKE
26 Dir of Marketing & Communications .... Mr. Michael CORR
08 Library Director .... Ms. Janet OHLES
37 Interim Exec Dir of Financial Aid .... Ms. Evelynne BLATT
41 Director of Athletics .... Ms. Mary Beth SPIRK
42 Chaplain .... Rev. Jennika BORGER
88 Director of the Payne Gallery .... Dr. David LEIDICH
23 Nurse Coordinator .... Mrs. Stephanie C. DILLMAN
105 Webmaster .... Ms. Christie JACOBSEN
09 Director of Institutional Research .... Ms. Sharon MAUS
28 Director of Diversity .... Vacant

Mount Aloysius College (G)

7373 Admiral Peary Highway, Cresson PA 16630-1999
County: Cambria FICE Identification: 003302
Unit ID: 214166
Telephone: (814) 886-6383 Carnegie Class: Bac-Diverse
FAX Number: (814) 886-2978 Calendar System: Semester
URL: www.mtaloy.edu
Established: 1853 Annual Undergrad Tuition & Fees: $24,370
Enrollment: 2,806 Coed
Affiliation or Control: Independent Non-Profit IRS Status: 501(c)3
Highest Offering: Master's
Accreditation: M, ACBSP, ADNUR, DMS, MLTAD, NUR, PTAA, SURGT

01 President .... Mr. John N. MCKEEGAN
05 VP Academic Affairs .... Dr. David HASCHAK
32 VP Student Affairs .... Dr. Tracy B. MCFARLAND
84 VP for Enrollment Management .... Mr. Jacob YALE
07 Dean of Admissions .... Mr. Andrew D. CLOUSE
111 VP Institutional Advancement .... Dr. John FARKAS
10 SVP Administration & Strategy/CFO .... Mr. Michael BAKER
06 Registrar .... Ms. Janna KOHLER
08 Director of Library .... Vacant
37 Director of Financial Aid .... Ms. Stacy L. SCHENK
15 VP People & Mission/CHRO .... Ms. Tonia J. GORDON
26 Assoc VP Marketing & Comm .... Mr. Sam WAGNER
13 Director of Information Technology .... Mr. Rich J. SHEA
23 Director of Health Services .... Ms. Shannon D. GROVE
40 Director of Bookstore .... Ms. Christine M. CLINTON
41 Director of Athletics .... Mr. Kevin KIME
19 Chief of Police .... Mr. Troy WRIGHT
18 Director of Physical Plant .... Mr. Gerald RUBRITZ
09 Institutional Researcher .... Mr. Bryan J. PEARSON
121 Dir Student Success & Persistence . Ms. Kimberly WASHINGTON
38 Dir Student Counseling/Disabilities .... Ms. Marisa L. EVANS
39 Director of Residence Life .... Ms. Andrea MANTILLA
42 Director Campus Ministry .... Ms. Amy KANICH
44 Manager of Annual Giving .... Ms. Sally GORDON
04 Administrative Asst to President .... Ms. Carla NELEN

Muhlenberg College (H)

2400 West Chew Street, Allentown PA 18104-5586
County: Lehigh FICE Identification: 003304
Unit ID: 214175
Telephone: (484) 664-3100 Carnegie Class: Bac-A&S
FAX Number: (484) 664-3234 Calendar System: Semester
URL: www.muhlenberg.edu
Established: 1848 Annual Undergrad Tuition & Fees: $54,600
Enrollment: 2,067 Coed
Affiliation or Control: Evangelical Lutheran Church In America
IRS Status: 501(c)3
Highest Offering: Master's
Accreditation: M

01 President .... Dr. Kathleen HARRING
05 Provost .... Dr. Laura FURGE
10 Treasurer & Chief Finance Officer .... Mr. Kent DYER
26 Vice President Communications .... Mr. Brian SPEER
111 Vice President of Advancement .... Ms. Rebekkah L. BROWN
15 Vice President for Human Resources .... Dr. Jill WALSH
32 Vice President of Student Affairs .... Ms. Allison GULATI
58 VP/Exec Dir Grad Continuing Educ .... Dr. A.J LEMHENEY
04 Exec Asst to the President & BoT .... Ms. Sonya CONRAD
30 Senior Assoc VP for Development .... Mr. Mike GARDNER
35 Dean of Students .... Ms. Allison GULATI
20 Dean of Academic Life .... Dr. Michele DEEGAN
104 Dean of Global Education .... Dr. Donna M. KISH-GOODLING
37 Assoc Dean Admission/Dir Finan Aid ...... Mr. Gregory S. MITTON
22 Asst Dean Acad Res/Disability Svcs .... Mr. David HALLOWELL
29 Asst VP Alumni Affairs/Career Svc .... Ms. Natalie HAND
51 Dean Continuing Studies/CGE .... Ms. Jane E. HUDAK
84 VP of Enrollment Management .... Ms. Megan RYAN
08 Director of Trexler Library .... Ms. Tina L. HERTEL
06 Registrar .... Ms. Ginger YAVORSKI
13 Chief Information Officer .... Mr. Jose DIEUDONNE
19 Dir/Chief of Campus Safety/Security .... Mr. Brian FIDATI
124 Assoc Dean Stdnts/Dir Stdnt Engage .... Ms. Ellen LENTINE
36 Executive Director Career Svcs .... Mr. Sean SCHOFIELD
114 Chief Budget/Accting Ofcr .... Mr. Jason FEIERTAG
23 Exec Dir Health/Counseling Svcs .... Ms. Brynnmarie DORSEY
38 Director Counseling Services .... Dr. Timothy SILVESTRI
42 Chaplain .... Rev. Janelle NEUBAUER
09 Dir Institutional Research/Records .... Ms. Cheryl ARNDT
18 Director Plant Operations .... Mr. James BOLTON
96 Director of Business Svcs .... Mr. Brian BLENIS
40 Bookstore Manager .... Ms. Karen R. NORMANN

Neumann University (A)

One Neumann Drive, Aston PA 19014-1298

County: Delaware FICE Identification: 003988
Unit ID: 214272
Telephone: (610) 459-0905 Carnegie Class: Masters/L
FAX Number: (610) 459-1370 Calendar System: Semester
URL: www.neumann.edu
Established: 1965 Annual Undergrad Tuition & Fees: $32,960
Enrollment: 2,506 Coed
Affiliation or Control: Roman Catholic IRS Status: 501(c)3
Highest Offering: Doctorate
Accreditation: M, ACBSP, CAATE, CACREP, MT, NUR, PTA, SW

01 President .... Dr. Chris E. DOMES
05 Vice President Academic Affairs .... Dr. Lawrence DIPAOLO
100 Chief of Staff .... Mr. Brad BAKER
32 Vice Pres Student Affairs .... Dr. Christopher HAUG
10 Vice Pres Finance/Administration .... Mr. Gene MCWILLIAMS
42 Vice President Mission/Ministry .... Sr. Linda DECERO, OSF
111 Vice Pres University Advancement .... Ms. Carrie SNYDER
84 VP of Enrollment Mgmt & Marketing .... Ms. Francesca REED
15 Vice President HR & Risk Management .... Mr. David W. BROWNLEE
13 CIO & Assoc VP of IR and Planning .. Dr. Richard H. HARTWELL
49 Dean School of Arts & Science .... Dr. Alfred G. MUELLER, II
50 Dean School of Business .... Dr. Eric R. WELLINGTON
53 Dean School of Educ/Human Svcs .... Dr. Amy HOYLE
66 Dean School Nursing/Health Sciences .... Dr. Kathleen HOOVER
35 Dean of Students .... Ms. Stephanie JONES
04 Assistant to President .... Ms. Connie GALLAGHER
06 Registrar .... Mr. Joel A. NATALE
18 Facilities Director .... Mr. William J. LEONARD
19 Director Safety & Security .... Mr. Leon J. FRANCIS
08 Director Library .... Ms. Tiffany MCGREGOR
26 Director Media Relations .... Mr. Stephen T. BELL
42 Chaplain .... Fr. Suresh RAJ, OFM CAP
51 Exec Dir of Adult Continuing Educ .... Dr. Jilian DONNELLY
29 Dir Alumni Rels/Special Programs .... Ms. Judi STANAITIS
38 Director Counseling .... Ms. Georgette HALL-PETERSON
39 Director Housing & Residence Life .... Ms. Alexandria L. THOMAS
112 Dir Major Gifts & Planned Giving .... Mr. Fran WALMSLEY
44 Director Annual Giving .... Vacant
41 Director Athletics .... Mr. Chuck SACK
36 Dir Career & Personal Development .... Ms. Preeti SINGH
121 Dean Academic Support Services .... Mr. Michael MULLEN
88 Director Child Development Center .... Mr. John SPERDUTO
21 Controller .... Mr. John YOUHOUSE
37 Director Financial Assistance .... Ms. Eileen TUCKER
23 Director Health Services .... Ms. Faith CELLA
07 Dir of Undergraduate Admissions .... Mr. Edward WRIGHT
31 Coordinator of Cultural Programming ..... Mr. Nicholas DIMARINO
88 Director Conference/Scheduling Svcs .... Ms. Jess WEBSTER
40 Director University Bookstore .... Ms. Natalie VAN WYK
88 Director Developmental Education .... Ms. Lori BLOUNT
124 Dir Student Engagement & Ldrshp .... Mr. Matt FULLMER
105 Director Web Services .... Ms. Rachel SPINA

New Castle School of Trades (B)

4117 Pulaski Road, New Castle PA 16101

County: Lawrence FICE Identification: 007780
Unit ID: 214290
Telephone: (724) 964-8811 Carnegie Class: Assoc/HVT-High Trad
FAX Number: (724) 202-6147 Calendar System: Other
URL: www.ncstrades.edu
Established: 1945 Annual Undergrad Tuition & Fees: N/A
Enrollment: 606 Coed
Affiliation or Control: Proprietary IRS Status: Proprietary
Highest Offering: Associate Degree
Accreditation: ACCSC

01 President .... Mr. Rex SPALDING
05 Director of Education .... Mr. Tony GIOVANNELLI
07 Director of Admissions .... Mr. John MEISSNER
88 Veteran Affairs Director .... Mr. Jim CATHELINE
10 Fiscal Director .... Mrs. Donna DAVIS
36 Director Student Placement .... Mrs. Carrie KRAYNAK
37 Director Student Financial Aid .... Mrs. Trudy SOTTER

Northampton Community College (C)

3835 Green Pond Road, Bethlehem PA 18020-7599

County: Northampton FICE Identification: 007191
Unit ID: 214379
Telephone: (610) 861-5300 Carnegie Class: Assoc/MT-VT-High Trad
FAX Number: (610) 861-5070 Calendar System: Semester
URL: www.northampton.edu
Established: 1967 Annual Undergrad Tuition & Fees (In-District): $10,080
Enrollment: 8,951 Coed
Affiliation or Control: State/Local IRS Status: 170(c)1
Highest Offering: Associate Degree
Accreditation: M, ACBSP, ADNUR, DH, DMS, FUSER, NAEYC, PNUR, RAD

01 President .... Dr. Mark H. ERICKSON
05 Vice President Academic Affairs .... Dr. Carolyn BORTZ
100 Chief of Staff .... Dr. David RUTH
10 Vice President Finance & Operations .... Mr. James F. DUNLEAVY
30 Vice Pres Institutional Advancement .... Ms. Sharon BEALES
32 Vice Pres Enroll/Student Affairs .... Mr. Sedwick HARRIS
31 Vice President Community Education .... Ms. Lauren LOEFFLER
12 Dean Monroe Campus .... Dr. Allison FITZPATRICK
79 Dean Humanities & Social Sciences .... Dr. Christine PENSE
53 Dean Education/Academic Success .... Dr. Elizabeth BUGAIGHIS
50 Dean Business & Technology .... Dr. Denise FRANCOIS-SEENY
76 Dean Allied Health & Sciences .... Dr. Judith REX
13 Assoc VP/Chief Information Officer .... Dr. Deborah BURAK
26 Exec Dir Marketing & Communications .... Mr. Brad DREXLER
06 Registrar .... Vacant
84 Asst VP Enrollment Mgmt/Retention .... Mr. Robert MCGANN
37 Director Financial Aid .... Ms. Sarah FEVIG
108 Dir of Institutional Effectiveness .... Ms. Dorothy SCHRAMM
15 Exec Dir Human Resources/Title IX .... Ms. Karen ANGENY
09 Director of Institutional Research .... Mr. Marco ANGLESIO
18 Director Buildings & Grounds .... Mr. Mark K. CULP
29 Dir Alumni Engagement/Annual Fund .... Ms. Karen GLOSE
36 Director Career Services .... Ms. Karen VERES
35 Dean of Students .... Mr. Eric ROSENTHAL
07 Senior Assoc Dir of Enrollment Svcs .... Ms. Mary S. MANCINO
28 VP Diversity/Equity/Inclusion .... Dr. Robert ROBINSON

Northampton Community College Monroe Campus (D)

2411 Route 715, Tannersville PA 18372
Telephone: (570) 369-1800 Identification: 770164
Accreditation: &M

Peirce College (E)

1420 Pine Street, Philadelphia PA 19102-4699

County: Philadelphia FICE Identification: 003309
Unit ID: 214883
Telephone: (215) 545-6400 Carnegie Class: Bac-Diverse
FAX Number: (215) 670-9366 Calendar System: Semester
URL: www.peirce.edu
Established: 1865 Annual Undergrad Tuition & Fees: $15,060
Enrollment: 1,046 Coed
Affiliation or Control: Independent Non-Profit IRS Status: 501(c)3
Highest Offering: Master's
Accreditation: M, ACBSP, CAHIIM

01 President & CEO .... Ms. Mary Ellen CARO
10 VP Finance/Administration .... Ms. Elizabeth M. KRAPP
05 VP Academic Advancement .... Dr. Rita J. TOLIVER-ROBERTS
103 VP Workforce Dev & Career Partnrshp .... Mr. Hassan CHARLES
26 Vice President Integrated Marketing .... Mr. Joseph GUZZARDO
84 VP Enrollment Mgmt/Student Services .... Mr. Brad K. HODGE
15 AVP Human Res/Chief Diversity Ofcr .... Ms. Carrie ROBINSON
108 Asst VP Institutional Assessment .... Ms. Debra S. SCHRAMMEL
13 Chief Information Officer .... Mr. James T. BURNS
08 Chief Library Officer .... Ms. Kristin INCIARDI
109 Chief Auxiliary Services Officer .... Mr. Vito R. CHIMENTI
04 Administrative Asst to President .... Ms. Tara E. MCBRIDE
06 Registrar .... Dr. Shannon BEGLEY
07 Director of Admissions .... Dr. Stephanie GIBBS-EMENAKA
37 Director Student Financial Aid .... Ms. Ruthann WYATT
86 Director Government Relations .... Ms. Amanda HILL

Penn Commercial Business/ Technical School (F)

242 Oak Spring Road, Washington PA 15301-6822

County: Washington FICE Identification: 004902
Unit ID: 214892
Telephone: (724) 222-5330 Carnegie Class: Assoc/HVT-High Trad
FAX Number: (724) 222-4722 Calendar System: Quarter
URL: www.penncommercial.edu
Established: 1929 Annual Undergrad Tuition & Fees: $17,313
Enrollment: 238 Coed
Affiliation or Control: Proprietary IRS Status: Proprietary
Highest Offering: Associate Degree
Accreditation: ACCSC

01 President/Owner .... Mr. Robert S. BAZANT
11 Vice President of Operations .... Ms. Marianne ALBERT
04 Assistant to the President .... Vacant
07 Asst Director of Admissions .... Mr. Michael BERRY
32 Director of Student Services .... Ms. Kristine GORBY
37 Director of Financial Aid .... Ms. Jayme TUITE
05 Director of Education .... Ms. Anita ROSSELL
09 Director of Reports & Statistics .... Mrs. Melissa PAPSON
36 Director of Career Services .... Mr. Jeff MANUKIN

Penn State University Park (G)

201 Old Main, University Park PA 16802-1503

County: Centre FICE Identification: 003329
Unit ID: 214777
Telephone: (814) 865-4700 Carnegie Class: DU-Highest
FAX Number: (814) 863-7590 Calendar System: Semester
URL: www.psu.edu
Established: 1855 Annual Undergrad Tuition & Fees (In-State): N/A
Enrollment: N/A Coed
Affiliation or Control: State Related IRS Status: 501(c)3
Highest Offering: Doctorate
Accreditation: M, ART, CAATE, CACREP, #CAEP, CAEPN, CEA, CLPSY, DIETC, DIETD, FEPAC, HSA, IPSY, JOUR, LAW, LSAR, MUS, NURSE, PCSAS, SCPSY, SP, THEA

01 President .... Dr. Eric J. BARRON
05 Executive Vice President & Provost .... Dr. Nicholas P. JONES
46 Vice President for Research .... Dr. Lora G. WEISS
32 Vice President for Student Affairs .... Dr. Damon R. SIMS
26 Vice Pres Strategic Communications .... Mr. Lawrence H. LOKMAN
30 Vice Pres Devel/Alumni Relations .... Mr. O. Richard BUNDY, III
10 Sr Vice Pres Finance & Bus/Treas .... Dr. Sara F. THORNDIKE
106 Vice President for Outreach .... Ms. Tracey D. HUSTON
11 Vice President for Administration .... Mr. Frank GUADAGNINO
104 Vice Provost for Global Programs .... Dr. Roger N. BRINDLEY
43 Vice President & General Counsel .... Dr. Stephen S. DUNHAM
49 Vice Pres & Dean Undergrad Educ .... Dr. Yvonne GAUDELIUS
20 Vice Provost Faculty Affairs .... Dr. Kathleen BIESCHKE
28 Vice Provost Educational Equity ...... Dr. Marcus A. WHITEHURST
12 Vice Pres Commonwealth Campuses .... Dr. Madlyn L. HANES
13 Vice Pres Info Tech/CIO .... Mr. Donald J. WELCH
45 Vice Provost Plng/Assessment/ IR .... Dr. Lance C. KENNEDY-PHILLIPS
09 Asst VP Institutional Research .... Dr. Karen VANCE
108 Director of Assessment .... Dr. Geoff MAMEROW
45 Asst VP for Strategic Planning .... Dr. Daniel NEWHART
22 Assoc Vice Pres Affirmative Action .... Dr. Suzanne C. ADAIR
114 University Budget Officer .... Ms. Mary Lou D. ORTIZ
21 Assoc Vice Pres Finance/Corp Cont ..... Mr. Joseph J. DONCSECZ
21 Assoc Vice Pres Finance & Business .... Vacant
15 Vice Pres Human Resources .... Ms. Lorraine GOFFE
18 Assoc Vice President Physical Plant .... Mr. William E. SITZABEE, JR.
109 Assoc VP Auxiliary & Business Svcs ...... Mr. John PAPAZOGLOU
106 Vice Prov Online Education .... Dr. Renata S. ENGEL
27 Director News/Media Relations .... Ms. Lisa M. POWERS
39 Asst VP for Housing & Food Svcs .... Ms. Cheryl FABRIZI
37 Asst VP UG Ed/Exec Dir Stdnt Aid .... Ms. Melissa J. KUNES
29 AVP Alumni Rels/CEO PS Alum Assoc .... Mr. Paul J. CLIFFORD
115 Exec Director Office of Investment .... Mr. Joseph M. CULLEN
07 Asst VP UG Admissions .... Mr. Rob SPRINGALL
38 Director Counseling/Psych Services .... Dr. Benjamin D. LOCKE
41 Athletic Director .... Ms. A. Sandy BARBOUR
86 Vice Pres for Govt & Cmty Rels .... Mr. Zachery MOORE
06 University Registrar .... Mr. Robert A. KUBAT
36 Senior Director Career Services .... Dr. Robert M. ORNDORFF
17 CEO Penn State Health .... Mr. Stephen M. MASSINI
08 Dean Univ Libraries/Scholar Comm .... Ms. Faye A. CHADWELL
47 Dean Agricultural Sciences .... Dr. Richard T. ROUSH
48 Dean Arts & Architecture .... Dr. B. Stephen CARPENTER
50 Dean Business .... Dr. Charles H. WHITEMAN
60 Dean Communications .... Dr. Marie HARDIN
65 Dean Earth & Mineral Sciences .... Dr. Lee KUMP
53 Dean Education .... Dr. Kimberly LAWLESS
54 Dean Engineering .... Dr. Justin SCHWARTZ
58 V Prov Grad Educ/Dean Grad School .... Dr. Regina VASILATOS-YOUNKEN
76 Dean Health & Human Dev .... Dr. Craig J. NEWSCHAFFER
66 Dean School of Nursing .... Ms. Laurie A. BADZEK
56 Assoc Dean/Dir Coop Extension .... Dr. Brent HALES
81 Dean Science .... Dr. Tracy LANGKILDE
72 Dean Info Sciences and Technology .... Dr. Andrew L. SEARS
92 Dean Honors College .... Dr. Peggy A. JOHNSON
61 Dean Penn State Law .... Dr. Hari M. OSOFSKY
63 Dean College of Medicine .... Dr. Kevin BLACK
75 Chief Penn College of Technology .... Dr. Davie J. GILMOUR
88 Assoc Vice President for Research .... Dr. John W. HANOLD
19 Chief Op Univ Police/Public Safety .... Mr. Joseph MILEK
23 Director University Health Services .... Dr. Robin E. OLIVER-VERONESI
96 Director Procurement Services .... Mr. R. Duane ELMORE
04 Exec Admin Assistant to President .... Ms. Carmella MULROY-DEGENHART
116 Director of Internal Audit .... Mr. Daniel P. HEIST
119 Chief Information Security Officer .... Mr. Donald J. WELCH, JR.
101 Secretary of the Institution/Board .... Ms. Shannon S. HARVEY

† The legal name of Penn State and all its campuses is The Pennsylvania State University. For communication purposes, the name is shortened to Penn State followed by the name of the campus.

Penn State Abington (H)

1600 Woodland Road, Abington PA 19001-3918
Telephone: (215) 881-7300 FICE Identification: 003342
Accreditation: &M, ART

† Regional accreditation is carried under the parent institution in University Park, PA.

Penn State Altoona (I)

3000 Ivyside Park, Altoona PA 16601-3777
Telephone: (814) 949-5000 FICE Identification: 003331
Accreditation: &M

† Regional accreditation is carried under the parent institution in University Park, PA.

Penn State Beaver (J)

100 University Drive, Monaca PA 15061-2764
Telephone: (724) 773-3800 FICE Identification: 003332
Accreditation: &M

† Regional accreditation is carried under the parent institution in University Park, PA.

Penn State Berks (K)

Tulpehocken Road, PO Box 7009, Reading PA 19610-1016
Telephone: (610) 396-6000 FICE Identification: 003334

Accreditation: &M, OTA

† Regional accreditation is carried under the parent institution in University Park, PA.

Penn State Brandywine (A)

25 Yearsley Mill Road, Media PA 19063-5522
Telephone: (610) 892-1200 FICE Identification: 006922
Accreditation: &M

† Regional accreditation is carried under the parent institution in University Park, PA.

Penn State Dickinson Law (B)

150 South College Street, Carlisle PA 17013-2861
Telephone: (717) 240-5000 FICE Identification: 003254
Accreditation: &M, LAW

† Part of Penn State University. Regional accreditation is carried under the parent institution in University Park, PA.

Penn State DuBois (C)

One College Place, DuBois PA 15801-2549
Telephone: (814) 375-4700 FICE Identification: 003335
Accreditation: &M, OTA, #PTAA

† Regional accreditation is carried under the parent institution in University Park, PA.

Penn State Erie, The Behrend College (D)

4701 College Drive, Erie PA 16563-0001
Telephone: (814) 898-6000 FICE Identification: 003333
Accreditation: &M

† Regional accreditation is carried under the parent institution in University Park, PA.

Penn State Fayette, The Eberly Campus (E)

2201 University Drive, Lemont Furnace PA 15456-1025
Telephone: (724) 430-4100 FICE Identification: 003336
Accreditation: &M, EMT, PTAA

† Regional accreditation is carried under the parent institution in University Park, PA.

Penn State Great Valley School of Graduate Professional Studies (F)

30 E Swedesford Road, Malvern PA 19355-1488
Telephone: (610) 648-3200 FICE Identification: 003348
Accreditation: &M

† Regional accreditation is carried under the parent institution in University Park, PA.

Penn State Greater Allegheny (G)

4000 University Drive, McKeesport PA 15132-7644
Telephone: (412) 675-9000 FICE Identification: 003339
Accreditation: &M

† Regional accreditation is carried under the parent institution in University Park, PA.

Penn State Harrisburg (H)

777 West Harrisburg Pike, Middletown PA 17057-4846
Telephone: (717) 948-6250 FICE Identification: 006814
Accreditation: &M, SPAA

† Regional accreditation is carried under the parent institution in University Park, PA.

Penn State Hazleton (I)

76 University Drive, Hazleton PA 18202-8025
Telephone: (570) 450-3000 FICE Identification: 003338
Accreditation: &M, MLTAD, PTAA

† Regional accreditation is carried under the parent institution in University Park, PA.

Penn State Lehigh Valley (J)

2809 Saucon Valley Road, Center Valley PA 18034-8447
Telephone: (610) 285-5000 FICE Identification: 003330
Accreditation: &M

† Regional accreditation is carried under the parent institution in University Park, PA.

Penn State Milton S. Hershey Medical Center College of Medicine (K)

500 University Drive, Hershey PA 17033-2360
Telephone: (717) 531-8563 FICE Identification: 006813
Accreditation: &M, #ARCPA, IPSY, MED, MT, PAST, PH

† Regional accreditation is carried under the parent institution in University Park, PA.

Penn State Mont Alto (L)

One Campus Drive, Mont Alto PA 17237-9700
Telephone: (717) 749-6000 FICE Identification: 003340
Accreditation: &M, OTA, PTAA

† Regional accreditation is carried under the parent institution in University Park, PA.

Penn State New Kensington (M)

3550 Seventh Street Road, Route 780,
New Kensington PA 15068-1765
Telephone: (724) 334-5466 FICE Identification: 003341
Accreditation: &M, RAD

† Regional accreditation is carried under the parent institution in University Park, PA.

Penn State Schuylkill (N)

200 University Drive, Schuylkill Haven PA 17972-2202
Telephone: (570) 385-6000 FICE Identification: 003343
Accreditation: &M, RAD

† Regional accreditation is carried under the parent institution in University Park, PA.

Penn State Scranton (O)

120 Ridge View Drive, Dunmore PA 18512-1602
Telephone: (570) 963-2500 FICE Identification: 003344
Accreditation: &M

† Regional accreditation is carried under the parent institution in University Park, PA.

Penn State Shenango (P)

147 Shenango Avenue, Sharon PA 16146-1537
Telephone: (724) 983-2803 FICE Identification: 003345
Accreditation: &M, OTA, PTAA

† Regional accreditation is carried under the parent institution in University Park, PA.

Penn State Wilkes-Barre (Q)

44 University Drive, Dallas PA 18612
Telephone: (570) 675-2171 FICE Identification: 003346
Accreditation: &M

† Regional accreditation is carried under the parent institution in University Park, PA.

Penn State York (R)

1031 Edgecomb Avenue, York PA 17403-3326
Telephone: (717) 771-4000 FICE Identification: 003347
Accreditation: &M

† Regional accreditation is carried under the parent institution in University Park, PA.

Pennco Tech (S)

3815 Otter Street, Bristol PA 19007-3696
County: Bucks FICE Identification: 009449
Unit ID: 214944
Telephone: (215) 785-0111 Carnegie Class: Spec 2-yr-Tech
FAX Number: (215) 785-1945 Calendar System: Other
URL: www.penncotech.edu
Established: 1973 Annual Undergrad Tuition & Fees: N/A
Enrollment: 511 Coed
Affiliation or Control: Proprietary IRS Status: Proprietary
Highest Offering: Associate Degree
Accreditation: ACCSC

01 CEO .... Michael S. HOBYAK
05 Director of Education/School Dir .... Fred PARCELLS
07 Director of Admissions .... Karl MANCUSO
06 Registrar .... Sondra KOOB
32 Director Student Services .... Hakien COLES
37 Director Student Financial Aid .... Debbie KEILFRIDER
36 Director Career Services .... Teresa SCHEERER

Pennsylvania Academy of the Fine Arts (T)

128 N Broad Street, Philadelphia PA 19102-1424
County: Philadelphia FICE Identification: 021073
Unit ID: 214971
Telephone: (215) 972-7600 Carnegie Class: Spec-4-yr-Arts
FAX Number: (215) 569-0153 Calendar System: Semester
URL: www.pafa.edu
Established: 1805 Annual Undergrad Tuition & Fees: $40,376
Enrollment: 188 Coed
Affiliation or Control: Independent Non-Profit IRS Status: 501(c)3
Highest Offering: Master's
Accreditation: M, ART

01 Interim President & CEO .... Ms. Elizabeth B. WARSHAWER
10 Chief Financial Officer .... Ms. Maryanne MURPHY
84 SVP Enrollment Mgmt .... Mr. Ryan BURTON-ROMERO
15 SVP Human Res/Int Chief of Staff .... Ms. Lisa BIAGAS
05 Exec Dean School of Fine Arts .... Mr. Clint A. JUKKALA
32 Dean of Students .... Mr. Ryan BURTON-ROMERO
35 Director of Student Services .... Ms. Morgan HOBBS
37 Director of Financial Aid .... Ms. Celeste FRANKLIN
36 Director of Career Services .... Mr. Gregory MARTINO
08 Director of Library Services .... Mr. Brian DUFFY
06 Registrar .... Mr. Peter MEDWICK
18 Director of Facilities Management .... Mr. Ed POLETTI
19 Director of Security and Safety .... Mr. Jimmie GREENO
13 Director of Information Technology .... Mr. Kevin MARTIN
04 Exec Assistant to President and CEO .... Ms. Sheryl KESSLER
58 Director of Grad Program Services .... Mr. Steven CONNELL
20 Academic Services Coordinator .... Mr. C.J STAHL
38 Student Care Coordinator .... Ms. Juliana FOMENKO
88 Executive Assistant to the Dean .... Ms. Katharine S. PEPPLE

Pennsylvania College of Art & Design (U)

204 N Prince Street, Box 59, Lancaster PA 17608-0059
County: Lancaster FICE Identification: 022699
Unit ID: 215053
Telephone: (717) 396-7833 Carnegie Class: Spec-4-yr-Arts
FAX Number: (717) 396-1339 Calendar System: Semester
URL: www.pcad.edu
Established: 1982 Annual Undergrad Tuition & Fees: $27,650
Enrollment: 242 Coed
Affiliation or Control: Independent Non-Profit IRS Status: 501(c)3
Highest Offering: Master's
Accreditation: M, ART

01 President .... Mr. Michael MOLLA
05 Provost .... Ms. Carissa MASSEY
10 VP of Finance and Administration .... Ms. Elizabeth P. BENNETT
32 Dean of Students .... Ms. Jessica EDONICK
28 Dean Diversity/Equity & Inclusion .... Ms. Debbie BAZARSKY
30 Dir Development/Strat Initiatives .... Mr. Todd SNOVEL
26 Director Strategic Communications .... Ms. Daina SAVAGE
07 Director of Enrollment/Admissions .... Ms. Jenn RENKO
35 Director Student Life .... Mr. Jeff BINGEMAN
18 Director of Facilities .... Mr. Dan FREILER
113 Bursar .... Ms. Lisa GOOD
04 Exec Asst to the President .... Ms. Amy GASTON
37 Director of Financial Aid .... Mr. J. David HERSHEY
51 Director of Continuing Education .... Ms. Natalie LASCEK
13 Director of IT .... Mr. Alex LEONHART
88 Dir Institute Entrepreneurship .... Vacant
06 Registrar .... Mr. Christopher WAGENHEIM
08 Dir Ctr for Teaching/Learning .... Ms. Mariah POSTLEWAIT
90 Director Academic Computing .... Mr. Hylon PLUMB
15 Human Resources Manager .... Ms. Michele WHERLEY

Pennsylvania College of Health Sciences (V)

850 Greenfield Road, Lancaster PA 17601
County: Lancaster FICE Identification: 009863
Unit ID: 442356
Telephone: (800) 622-5443 Carnegie Class: Spec-4-yr-Other Health
FAX Number: (717) 947-6250 Calendar System: Semester
URL: www.pacollege.edu
Established: 1903 Annual Undergrad Tuition & Fees: $29,922
Enrollment: 2,011 Coed
Affiliation or Control: Independent Non-Profit IRS Status: 501(c)3
Highest Offering: Doctorate
Accreditation: M, ADNUR, COARC, CVT, DMS, MT, NMT, NURSE, RAD, SURGT

01 President .... Dr. Mary Grace SIMCOX
05 AVP Academic Affairs .... Dr. Jean HERSHEY
108 VP Institutional Effectiveness .... Dr. Penni LONGENECKER
10 VP Finance & Administration .... Mr. Thomas HULSTINE
111 VP Advancement .... Ms. Ellen WILEY
15 VP Human Resources .... Ms. Nancy FLOREY
13 Chief Information Officer .... Mr. Kevin BALSBAUGH
84 AVP Enrollment Management .... Dr. Erika WILKINSON
04 Administrative Asst to President .... Ms. Susan GARDINA
06 Registrar .... Mr. Edwin ADDIS
109 Director of Campus & Auxiliary Svcs .... Mr. Kyle MOORE
07 Director of Admissions .... Mr. William RHINIER

Pennsylvania College of Technology (W)

One College Avenue, Williamsport PA 17701-5799
County: Lycoming FICE Identification: 003395
Unit ID: 366252
Telephone: (570) 326-3761 Carnegie Class: Bac/Assoc-Mixed
FAX Number: (570) 327-4503 Calendar System: Semester
URL: www.pct.edu
Established: 1989 Annual Undergrad Tuition & Fees (In-State): $17,610
Enrollment: 4,565 Coed
Affiliation or Control: State IRS Status: 501(c)3
Highest Offering: Master's
Accreditation: M, ACBSP, ACFEI, ADNUR, ARCPA, CAHIIM, CONST, DH, EMT, NAIT, NUR, OTA, PNUR, PTAA, RAD, SURGT

01 President .... Dr. Davie Jane GILMOUR

05 VP for Academic Affairs/Provost .... Dr. Michael J. REED
10 Senior VP for Finance/CFO .... Ms. Suzanne T. STOPPER
111 Vice Pres Institutional Advancement ....Ms. Loni N. KLINE
84 VP Enrollment Mgmt & Assoc Provost ....Dr. Carolyn R. STRICKLAND
32 VP for Student Affairs ....Mr. Elliott STRICKLAND, JR.
103 VP for Workforce Development .... Ms. Shannon M. MUNRO
15 VP for Human Resources ....Ms. Hillary E. HOFSTROM
20 Dean of Curriculum & Instruction .... Ms. Joanna K. FLYNN
88 Dean of Academic Operations ....Mr. Anthony J. PACE
04 Administrative Asst to President ....Mrs. Valerie A. BAIER
66 Dean of Nursing & Health Sciences ..... Dr. Sandra L. RICHMOND
54 Dean of Engineering Technologies .... Dr. Bradley M. WEBB
50 Dean of Business/Arts & Sciences .... Dr. Sue A. KELLEY
102 Exec Dir of Penn College Foundation .... Mr. Kyle A. SMITH
109 Exec Dir General Services ....Mr. Timothy O. RISSEL
88 Director of Construction & Planning ....Mr. Jason K. BOGLE
18 Director of Facilities Operations ....Mr. Don J. LUKE
08 Director of the Madigan Library .... Ms. Tracey AMEY
14 Dir of Educational Technologies ....Mr. Walter J. SHULTZ, JR.
09 Exec Dir Assessment/Research/Plng .... Dr. Brian L. CYGAN
06 Registrar .... Ms. Maria N. PISELLI
35 Associate Dean of Student Affairs .... Dr. Jennifer MCLEAN
39 Dir Residence Life/Student Conduct .... Mr. Jon D. WESCOTT
19 Chief of Police ....Mr. Chris E. MILLER
26 Assoc VP Public Rels & Marketing .... Mr. Joseph S. YODER
29 Director Alumni Relations .... Ms. Kimberly R. CASSEL
102 Director of Corporate Relations .... Ms. Elizabeth A. BIDDLE
88 Director Children Learning Center .... Ms. Linda A. REICHERT
41 Director of Athletics ....Mr. John D. VANDEVERE
124 Director of Student Engagement ....Ms. Allison A. GROVE
22 Director of Disability Services .... Ms. Dawn M. DICKEY
96 Director/Procurement Services .... Ms. Karen P. FESSLER
07 Director of Admissions .... Ms. Audriana L. EMPET
89 Director of College Transitions .... Ms. Tanya BERFIELD
38 Director of Counseling .... Dr. Kathy W. ZAKARIAN
100 Chief of Staff ....Mr. Patrick MARTY
30 Director of Development ....Ms. Heather M. SHUEY
24 Director of Academic Success Center .... Ms. Kathleen V. MCNAUL
37 Director Student Financial Aid ....Ms. Jessica S. HUNTER
90 Director Academic Computing ....Mr. Jim R. DOUGHERTY, III

† Affiliate of Pennsylvania State University.

Pennsylvania Highlands Community College (A)

101 Community College Way, Johnstown PA 15904-2949
County: Cambria FICE Identification: 031804
Unit ID: 414911
Telephone: (814) 262-6400 Carnegie Class: Assoc/MT-VT-High Non
FAX Number: (814) 269-9700 Calendar System: Semester
URL: www.pennhighlands.edu
Established: 1994 Annual Undergrad Tuition & Fees (In-District): $8,640
Enrollment: 2,456 Coed
Affiliation or Control: State/Local IRS Status: 501(c)3
Highest Offering: Associate Degree
Accreditation: M, MAC

01 President ....Dr. Steve NUNEZ
32 VP of Student Services .... Trish CORLE
10 VP of Finance/Administration .... Lorraine DONAHUE
05 VP of Academic Affairs .... Robert FARINELLI
15 Assistant VP of Human Resources ....Susan FISHER
09 Asst VP of Inst Effectiveness ....Gary BOAST
13 Chief Information Officer .... Matthew HOFFMAN
12 Regional Center Director .... Robert SEKERAK
12 Director Blair Center ....Chris FARRELL
12 Director Huntingdon Center ....Marissa DAVIS
12 Director Somerset Center .... Landon LOYA
08 Dean Library Svcs/Special Projects ..... Dr. Barbara ZABOROWSKI
06 Dean Enrollment Services/Registrar ....Michelle STUMPF
20 Dean of Faculty .... Erica REIGHARD
111 Exec Dir of Inst Advancement ....Kathleen MORRELL
18 Director of Facilities Operation ....Reb BROWNLEE
07 Director Admissions and Recruiting ....Matthew BODENSCHATZ
21 Director of Finance/Administration ....Christopher PRIBULSKY
37 Director of Student Financial Svcs ....Ashley KRINJECK
26 Director of Marketing/Communication ....Raymond WEIBLE, JR.
19 Director of Security and Safety ....Cregg DIBERT
35 Dir of Student Activities/Athletics .... Suzanne BRUGH
121 Director of Student Success Center .... Mindy NITCH
04 Assistant to the President ....Nicole ROBSON

Pennsylvania Institute of Technology (B)

800 Manchester Avenue, Media PA 19063-4098
County: Delaware FICE Identification: 010998
Unit ID: 214582
Telephone: (610) 892-1500 Carnegie Class: Spec 2-yr-Health
FAX Number: (610) 892-1510 Calendar System: Quarter
URL: www.pit.edu
Established: 1953 Annual Undergrad Tuition & Fees: $13,905
Enrollment: 454 Coed
Affiliation or Control: Independent Non-Profit IRS Status: 501(c)3
Highest Offering: Baccalaureate
Accreditation: M, PTAA

01 Executive Vice President/CEO ....Mr. Harry (Matt) M. MEYERS
05 Dean of Academic Affairs ....Ms. Kimberly MARUCCI
10 Chief Financial Officer ....Ms. Annamarie CASSIDY
32 Director of Student Services ....Ms. Kamira EVANS
06 Dir of Inst Research/Registrar ....Mr. Craig M. JACOBS
07 Director of Admissions ....Ms. Laura BLOMGREN
37 Financial Aid Director ....Ms. Laura BLOMGREN
18 Director of Facilities .... Mr. Frederick FIVECOAT
13 Dir of Information Technology ....Mr. Michael TESTA
08 Director of the Library ....Ms. Kristin BERNET
20 Assoc Dean of Academic Affairs .... Ms. Rachelle CHAYKIN

*Pennsylvania's State System of Higher Education, Office of the Chancellor (C)

Dixon University Ctr, 2986 N 2nd St, Harrisburg PA 17110-1201
County: Dauphin FICE Identification: 029371
Unit ID: 214661
Telephone: (717) 720-4000 Carnegie Class: N/A
FAX Number: (717) 720-4011
URL: www.passhe.edu

01 Chancellor ....Dr. Daniel GREENSTEIN
03 Deputy Chancellor ....Mr. Randy GOIN, JR.
10 Vice Chancellor Admin/Finance .... Ms. Sharon MINNICH
05 Vice Chancellor/CAO ....Dr. Donna WILSON
26 Chief Strategic Relations Officer ....Mr. Cody JONES
43 Chief Legal Counsel ....Mr. Andrew LEHMAN
88 System Redesign Project Manager ....Ms. Rosa LARA

*Bloomsburg University of Pennsylvania (D)

400 E Second Street, Bloomsburg PA 17815-1399
County: Columbia FICE Identification: 003315
Unit ID: 211158
Telephone: (570) 389-4000 Carnegie Class: Masters/L
FAX Number: (570) 389-3700 Calendar System: Semester
URL: www.bloomu.edu
Established: 1839 Annual Undergrad Tuition & Fees (In-State): $10,958
Enrollment: 8,427 Coed
Affiliation or Control: State IRS Status: 501(c)3
Highest Offering: Doctorate
Accreditation: M, ANEST, ART, AUD, CAEP, EXSC, MUS, NURSE, #SP, SW, THEA

02 President ....Dr. Bashar W. HANNA
05 Sr VP & Provost Acad Affairs ......Dr. Diana ROGERS-ADKINSON
10 Vice Pres Finance/Administration ....Ms. Claudia THRUSH
32 Acting Vice Pres Student Affairs .... Mr. Jim MCCORMACK
111 Vice Pres University Advancement ....Mr. Erik EVANS
84 Vice Pres Stdnt Success/Enroll Mgmt ...... Mr. Thomas FLETCHER
86 Director External & Govt Relations .... Mr. Dan KNORR
100 Chief of Staff ....Dr. Peter T. KELLY
20 Interim Vice Provost/Dean UG Educ .... Dr. Kara SHULTZ
58 Int Assoc Vice Prov/Dean Grad Stds .... Dr. Heather FELDHAUS
13 Chief Technology Officer ....Mr. Samuel JOSUWEIT
108 Asst VP Planning & Assessment ....Vacant
18 Asst VP for Facilities Management .... Mr. Eric NESS
21 Asst VP Finance/Budget & Bus Svcs ....Ms. Claudia THRUSH
35 Dean of Students ....Mr. Scott KANE
26 AVP Marketing/Communications .... Ms. Jennifer UMBERGER
29 AVP Alumni/Professional Engagement .... Ms. Lynda MICHAELS
07 AVP for Undergraduate Admissions .... Mr. Christopher LAPOS
09 AVP of Institutional Research ....Dr. Mary Lou D'ALLEGRO
121 AVP Student Success .... Ms. Marty WYGMANS
49 Dean College of Liberal Arts .... Dr. James BROWN
50 Dean Zeigler College of Business ....Dr. Todd SHAWVER
81 Dean College of Science/Tech .... Dr. Latha RAMAKRISHNAN
53 Dean College of Education .... Dr. Daryl E. FRIDLEY
15 Assoc VP Human Resources ....Ms. Tena MAURER
46 Director Research Programs ....Ms. Sadie HAUCK
06 Registrar/Dir Enrollment Services ....Ms. Linda L. SWISHER
104 Director Global & Multicultural Ed ....Vacant
37 Director Financial Aid .... Ms. Amanda KISHBAUGH
36 Dir Career/Professional Development ....Dr. Wren FRITSKY
41 Director of Athletics .... Mr. Michael S. MCFARLAND
42 Director Protestant Campus Ministry ....Rev. Jill YOUNG
42 Director Catholic Campus Ministry ....Fr. Richard MOWERY
19 Dir Bloomsburg University Police .... Mr. Leo SOKOLOSKI
92 Director University Honors Program ....Dr. Julie VANDIVERE
96 Director Procurement & Operations ....Mr. Jeffrey MANDEL
08 Director Library Services ....Ms. Charlotte DROLL
91 Dir Applications Development ....Ms. Frances DONAHOE
102 Executive Director BU Foundation ....Mr. Jerome DVORAK
90 Manager Technology Support Services ....Mr. David S. CELLI
40 Manager University Store ....Ms. Laura HEGER

*California University of Pennsylvania (E)

250 University Avenue, California PA 15419-1394
County: Washington FICE Identification: 003316
Unit ID: 211361
Telephone: (724) 938-4000 Carnegie Class: Masters/L
FAX Number: (724) 938-4138 Calendar System: Semester
URL: www.calu.edu
Established: 1852 Annual Undergrad Tuition & Fees (In-State): $11,108
Enrollment: 6,885 Coed
Affiliation or Control: State IRS Status: 501(c)3
Highest Offering: Doctorate
Accreditation: M, ACBSP, ART, #CAATE, CACREP, CAEPN, CAPRT, NURSE, PTAA, RAD, SP, SW, THEA

02 Interim President ....Mr. Robert THORN
100 Chief of Staff to the President ....Vacant
04 Interim Exec Asst to the President ....Mrs. Anna STEWART
05 Int Provost/Sr VP for Acad Affairs .... Dr. Dan M. ENGSTROM
10 Interim VP Administration & Finance .... Ms. Fawn PETROSKY
84 VP for Enrollment Management .... Mr. T. David GARCIA
09 Director of Institutional Research ....Mr. Steve ZIDEK
58 Dean of Graduate Studies .... Dr. Yugo IKACH
121 Int Director of Academic Success ....Ms. Jill LOOP
30 VP for Development & Alumni Rels ....Mr. Anthony MAURO
32 Interim VP for Student Affairs .... Mr. Lawrence SEBEK
13 Assoc VP and Chief Info Officer ....Mr. Paul ALLISON
72 Dean Eberly College of Sci & Tech ....Dr. Brenda FREDETTE
49 Dean College of Educ & Liberal Arts .... Dr. Kristen MAJOCHA
08 Dean Library Svcs & UG Researc .... Mr. Douglas HOOVER
07 Dean of Admissions ....Ms. Tracey SHEETZ
123 Director Graduate Admissions ....Mr. Ben BRUDNOCK
37 Director of Financial Aid .... Mr. Jeff DERUBBO
06 Registrar ....Mr. Shayne GERVAIS
36 Dir Career & Prof Dev Center .... Ms. Rhonda GIFFORD
92 Director Honors Program ....Mr. Mark AUNE
29 Director of Alumni Relations ....Dr. Ryan BARNHART
39 Facilities & Occupancy Manager .... Mrs. Jackie THORN
94 Director Women's Studies ....Dr. Marta MCCLINTOCK-COMEAUX
104 Study Abroad/Asst Dir Admissions ....Ms. Kristen LOUTTIT
41 Athletic Director ....Dr. Karen HJERPE
15 Director Human Resources ....Mr. Eric GUISER
22 Dir Equity/Compliance & Title IX ....Dr. John BURNETT
19 Chief of Police ....Mr. Ed MCSHEFFERY
18 Director of Facilities Mgmt ....Mr. Mike KANALIS
26 VP for Communications & Marketing .... Mrs. Christine KINDL
27 Director of Marketing ....Mrs. Keli HENDERSON
88 Director of Creative Services ....Mr. Greg SOFRANKO
40 Bookstore Manager ....Ms. Amy NASH
96 Purchasing Agent Supervisor .... Ms. Melissa WALKER
108 Assoc Prov for Assessment & Accred .... Dr. Leonard COLELLI
28 Int Chief Diversity/Equity/Incl .... Ms. Sheleta CAMARDA-WEBB
113 Acting Director of Student Accounts .... Mr. Jack ROGERS
85 Intl Stdnt Advis/Asst Dir Welc Ctr ....Mr. Kevin EGGLESTON

*Cheyney University of Pennsylvania (F)

1837 University Circle PO Box 200, Cheyney PA 19319-0200
County: Delaware FICE Identification: 003317
Unit ID: 211608
Telephone: (610) 399-2000 Carnegie Class: Bac-A&S
FAX Number: (610) 399-2415 Calendar System: Semester
URL: www.cheyney.edu
Established: 1837 Annual Undergrad Tuition & Fees (In-State): $10,904
Enrollment: 623 Coed
Affiliation or Control: State IRS Status: 501(c)3
Highest Offering: Master's
Accreditation: M

02 President ....Mr. Aaron A. WALTON
05 Provost ....Ms. Kizzy MORRIS
10 Exec Dir Finance & Admin ....Ms. Cynthia MOULTRIE
21 Controller ....Ms. Victoria ATKINS
38 Chairperson Guidance & Counseling ....Ms. Jolly MALICKEL
06 Interim Registrar ....Ms. Stephanie STEVENS
37 Director Student Financial Services ....Ms. Tonya WILLIAMS
09 Exec Dir Institutional Research .... Dr. Erika SHEHATA
18 Exec Director of Operations ....Mr. James LEWIS
19 Dir of Campus & Public Safety .... Mr. Mark CORBIN
41 Athletic Director ....Ms. Tammy A. BAGBY
17 College Physician ....Dr. Manijeh BAHREMAND
43 University Legal Counsel ....Ms. Cathleen MCCORMICK
32 Interim Exec Dir Student Affairs .... Mr. Gregory SMITH
39 Director of Housing ....Ms. Ramona DIXON
103 Dir Title III/Grants Administration ....Ms. Mamie STEPHENS
113 Bursar ....Ms. Lauronda FLETCHER
92 Director of Keystone Honors Academy ..... Dr. Eric SCHUMACHER
84 Exec Dir Enrollment Management ....Mr. Jeffrey JONES
25 Grant and Contract Accountant ....Mr. George JONES
04 Executive Associate to President ....Vacant
15 Exec Director of Human Resources ....Mr. John GRUENWALD
07 Interim Director of Admissions ....Ms. Jacqueline GOODE

*Clarion University of Pennsylvania (G)

840 Wood Street, Clarion PA 16214-1232
County: Clarion FICE Identification: 003318
Unit ID: 211644
Telephone: (814) 393-2000 Carnegie Class: Masters/L
FAX Number: (814) 393-1826 Calendar System: Semester
URL: www.clarion.edu
Established: 1867 Annual Undergrad Tuition & Fees (In-State): $11,199
Enrollment: 4,465 Coed
Affiliation or Control: State IRS Status: 501(c)3
Highest Offering: Doctorate
Accreditation: M, ART, CAEP, CSHSE, LIB, NAEYC, NURSE, SP

02 President .... Dr. Dale-Elizabeth PEHRSSON
05 Provost/AVP .... Dr. Pamela GENT
32 Vice Pres Student & University Affs ....Dr. Susanne FENSKE
10 Vice Pres Finance/Administration ....Mr. Leonard CULLO
111 Vice President Univ Advancement ....Mr. James GEIGER

100 Chief of Staff ... Ms. Kelly C. MORAN
11 Assoc VP for Administration ... Mr. Timothy P. FOGARTY
84 AVP of Enrollment Management ... Mr. David DOLLINS
21 Assoc VP for Finance ... Ms. Tamara B. VARSEK
13 Assoc VP for Information Technology ... Mr. Samuel T. PULEIO
36 Dean Career/Workforce Development ... Ms. Hope E. LINEMAN
08 Dean of Libraries ... Dr. Terry S. LATOUR
49 Dean of Arts & Sciences ... Dr. Laura DELBRUGGE
50 Dean of Business Administration ... Dr. Philip FRESE
06 University Registrar ... Ms. Lisa L. HEPLER
22 Director of Social Equity ... Ms. Amy SALSGIVER
46 Director Faculty Research ... Dr. Amy ESTERHUIZEN
26 Dir of Marketing & Communications ... Ms. Tina HORNER
37 Director of Student Financial Svcs ... Ms. Sue BLOOM
18 Director of Facilities Management ... Mr. Chad THOMAS
29 Director of Alumni Engagement ... Ms. Ann THOMPSON
39 Director of Residence Life Services ... Ms. Jennifer GRAHAM
19 Director of Public Safety ... Mr. Jason HENDERSHOT
41 Athletic Director ... Dr. Wendy SNODGRASS
96 Director of Purchasing ... Vacant
09 Institutional Research Director ... Mr. Robert GATESMAN
112 Director of Planned Giving ... Mr. Larry W. JAMISON

*East Stroudsburg University of Pennsylvania (A)

200 Prospect Street, East Stroudsburg PA 18301-2999
County: Monroe — FICE Identification: 003320
Unit ID: 212115
Telephone: (570) 422-3211 — Carnegie Class: Masters/L
FAX Number: (570) 422-3777 — Calendar System: Semester
URL: www.esu.edu
Established: 1893 — Annual Undergrad Tuition & Fees (In-State): $11,559
Enrollment: 5,835 — Coed
Affiliation or Control: State — IRS Status: 501(c)3
Highest Offering: Doctorate
Accreditation: M, CAATE, CAEPN, COSMA, EXSC, NUR, PH, SP, SW

02 Interim President ... Mr. Kenneth A. LONG
05 Provost/Vice Pres Academic Affairs ... Ms. Joanne Z. BRUNO
32 VP Camp Life/Inclulsive Excellence ... Dr. Santiago SOLIS
10 Vice Pres Administration & Finance ... Vacant
46 VP Economic Devel/ Entrepreneurship ... Ms. Mary Frances POSTUPACK
84 Vice Pres Enrollment Management ... Ms. Karen E. LUCAS
58 Director Graduate/Extended Studies ... Dr. William BAJOR
49 Dean of Arts & Sciences ... Dr. Andra BASU
76 Dean of Health Sciences ... Dr. Denise SEIGART
53 Acting Dean of Education ... Dr. Brooke LANGAN
50 Dean of Business & Management ... Dr. Sylvester WILLIAMS
20 Assoc Provost ... Dr. Margaret BALL
35 Dean of Student Life ... Vacant
100 Chief of Staff & Governmental Rels ... Mr. Miguel BARBOSA
07 Director of Admissions ... Mr. Alexander SPERRAZZA
06 Registrar/Dir Enrollment Services ... Ms. Karen JOHNSON
37 Director Financial Aid ... Ms. Kary TEJEDA
36 Dir Career/WF & Econ Dev/ Entrepren ... Mr. Christopher S. LANDINO
38 Director Counseling Center ... Dr. Linda L. VAN METER
41 Director of Athletics ... Dr. Gary GRAY
39 Dir Residential/Dining Services ... Mr. Curtis DUGAR
88 Dir of Student Activity Association ... Mr. Joe AKOB
21 Controller ... Ms. Donna R. BULZONI
13 Chief Information Officer ... Mr. James M. DUTCHER
15 Director of Human Resources ... Vacant
18 Director of Facilities Management ... Mr. John BLOSHINSKI
96 Asst Dir of Procurement/Contracting ... Ms. Denise AYLWARD
29 Director of Alumni Engagement ... Vacant
26 Director University Relations ... Dr. Brenda FRIDAY
09 Dir Inst Effect/Planning/Assessment ... Vacant
28 Ctr for Multicul Affs/Inclusive Ed ... Ms. Lyesha J. FLEMING

*Edinboro University (B)

219 Meadville Street, Edinboro PA 16444-0001
County: Erie — FICE Identification: 003321
Unit ID: 212160
Telephone: (814) 732-2000 — Carnegie Class: Masters/L
FAX Number: (814) 732-2880 — Calendar System: Semester
URL: www.edinboro.edu
Established: 1857 — Annual Undergrad Tuition & Fees (In-State): $10,544
Enrollment: 4,319 — Coed
Affiliation or Control: State — IRS Status: 501(c)3
Highest Offering: Doctorate
Accreditation: M, ACATE, ACBSP, ART, CACREP, CAEP, NUR, NURSE, SP, SW

02 Interim President ... Dr. Dale-Elizabeth PEHRSSON
05 Provost/VP Acad/Student Affairs ... Dr. Michael HANNAN
10 VP Finance/Administration ... Mr. John HYNES
26 VP for Marketing & Communications ... Ms. Angela BURROWS
111 VP University Advancement ... Ms. Marilyn GOELLNER
15 AVP Human Resources/Faculty Rels ... Mr. Wayne PATTERSON
84 VP for Enrollment Management ... Dr. William EDMONDS
09 Dir Inst Research & Assessment ... Mr. Matthew CETTIN
18 Dir Facilities Management/Planning ... Ms. Ashley SPEARS
27 Director of Marketing ... Mr. William BERGER
37 Director of Student Financial Aid ... Ms. Kelly VITELLI
92 Director Honors College ... Dr. Roger SOLBERG
22 Title IX Coordinator ... Mr. Andrew MATT
79 Dean Col Arts/Humanities/Soc Sci ... Dr. Scott MILLER
81 Dean College of Science & Health ... Dr. Denise OHLER
58 Exec Director of Graduate Studies ... Dr. Erinn LAKE
53 Dean School of Education ... Dr. Erinn LAKE
50 Dean School of Business ... Dr. Scott MILLER
06 Registrar ... Mr. Tim W. PILEWSKI
36 Dir Office of Career Development ... Ms. Monica CLEM
29 Dir Alumni Engagement/Fund Devel ... Ms. Amanda SISSEM
41 Athletic Director ... Vacant
19 Chief of Police ... Ms. Angela VINCENT
23 Medical Dir Student Health Services ... Dr. Thomas MITCHELL
109 Director Auxiliary Operations ... Vacant
85 Dir Global Education Office ... Ms. Linda KIGHTLINGER
25 Dir Grant & Sponsored Programs ... Ms. Rosmari GRAHAM
14 Dir Networks & Telecommunications ... Ms. Karen MURDZAK
90 Director Client Support Services ... Mr. Dennis J. BRADLEY
13 Director of Information Services ... Ms. Sallie A. TERPACK
96 Director Purchasing & Contracts ... Ms. Darla SPAID
30 Director of Development ... Mr. Jon PULICE
114 Director of Budget and Payroll ... Ms. Theresa VILLELLA
07 Director of Admissions ... Ms. Diane RAYBUCK
113 Bursar ... Ms. Shari GOULD
17 Director of Health & Wellness Ctr ... Ms. Darla ELDER
106 Manager of Online Programs ... Dr. James BOULDER
24 Learning Technology Specialist ... Ms. Jill LINTON
56 Coordinator Non-Credit Programs ... Ms. Beth ZEWE
32 Associate Student Affairs Officer ... Vacant

*Indiana University of Pennsylvania (C)

1011 South Drive, Indiana PA 15705-0001
County: Indiana — FICE Identification: 003277
Unit ID: 213020
Telephone: (724) 357-2100 — Carnegie Class: DU-Mod
FAX Number: (724) 357-6213 — Calendar System: Semester
URL: www.iup.edu
Established: 1875 — Annual Undergrad Tuition & Fees (In-State): $13,144
Enrollment: 10,037 — Coed
Affiliation or Control: State — IRS Status: 501(c)3
Highest Offering: Doctorate
Accreditation: M, ACFEI, ART, CACREP, CAEP, CAEPN, CLPSY, COARC, DIETC, DIETD, EMT, EXSC, MUS, NURSE, PLNG, SP, THEA

02 President ... Dr. Michael A. DRISCOLL
05 Interim Provost & VP Acad Affairs ... Dr. Lara LUETKEHANS
11 Vice Pres Administration/Finance ... Dr. Debra L. FITZSIMMONS
32 Vice President Student Affairs ... Dr. Thomas SEGAR
84 VP Enrollment Management ... Ms. Patricia MCCARTHY
111 Vice Pres University Advancement ... Dr. Khatmeh OSSEIRAN-HANNA
10 Assoc Vice President for Finance ... Mr. William BUTTZ
20 Assoc VP Academic Administration ... Dr. John N. KILMARX
58 Int Dean Grad Studies & Research ... Dr. Hilliary CREELY
15 Assoc Vice Pres Human Resources ... Mr. Craig BICKLEY
50 Int Dean Eberly Col of Business ... Dr. Geofrey MILLS
53 Int Dean Col Educ & Communication ... Dr. Sue RIEG
81 Dean Col Natural Science & Math ... Dr. Steve HOVAN
57 Dean College of Arts & Humanities ... Dr. Curt SCHEIB
66 Dean College Health & Human Svcs ... Dr. Sylvia GAIKO
08 Dean of Libraries & University Col ... Dr. Yaw ASAMOAH
06 Registrar ... Dr. Michael POWELL
13 Chief Information Officer ... Mr. William S. BALINT
45 Exec Dir of Planning & Assessment ... Mr. Chris KITAS
14 Exec Dir of Technology Services Ctr ... Mr. Todd D. CUNNINGHAM
26 Exec Dir of Marketing/Communication ... Dr. Michael POWERS
19 Director of Public Safety & Police ... Mr. Anthony CLEMENT
36 Director Career Development Ctr ... Dr. Tammy P. MANKO
29 Director Alumni Relations ... Vacant
44 Director Annual Giving ... Vacant
85 Asst VP Intl Education & Global ... Dr. Michele L. PETRUCCI
46 Assistant Dean for Research ... Vacant
39 Director Housing/Residential Living ... Ms. Valerie BARONI
40 Co-op Store Director ... Mr. Tim L. SHARBAUGH
41 Athletic Director ... Mr. Todd GARZARELLI
23 Nurse Director ... Ms. Melissa L. DICK
12 Director of Regional Campuses ... Mr. Richard J. MUTH
43 Staff Attorney ... Ms. Cathleen MCCORMACK
27 Exec Director of Media Relations ... Ms. Michelle S. FRYLING
96 Procurement Svcs PASSHE -Western ... Ms. Jennifer LEWIS
37 Director of Financial Aid ... Ms. Ragan K. GRIFFIN
07 Executive Director of UG Admissions ... Ms. Stacy HOPKINS
26 Chief Marketing Officer ... Mr. Chris NOAH
18 Director of Facilities Operations ... Mr. Laurence MILLER
28 Diversity/Inclusion/Title IX Coord ... Ms. Elise GLENN
38 Director Student Counseling ... Dr. Jessica MILLER

*Kutztown University of Pennsylvania (D)

15200 Kutztown Road, Kutztown PA 19530-0730
County: Berks — FICE Identification: 003322
Unit ID: 213349
Telephone: (610) 683-4000 — Carnegie Class: Masters/L
FAX Number: (610) 683-4693 — Calendar System: Semester
URL: www.kutztown.edu
Established: 1866 — Annual Undergrad Tuition & Fees (In-State): $11,156
Enrollment: 7,890 — Coed
Affiliation or Control: State — IRS Status: 501(c)3
Highest Offering: Doctorate
Accreditation: M, ART, CACREP, CAEPN, COSMA, MUS, SW

02 President ... Dr. Kenneth S. HAWKINSON
05 Provost/VP Academic Affairs ... Dr. Anne ZAYAITZ
10 Interim VP Administration & Finance ... Ms. Sharon M. PICUS
84 VP Enrollment Management ... Dr. Warren HILTON
22 VP Compliance/Equity ... Mr. Jesus PENA
102 Executive Director KU Foundation ... Mr. Alex OGEKA
26 VP University Relations & Athletics ... Mr. Matt SANTOS
20 Vice Prov Acad Affs/Dean Grad Stds ... Dr. Carole WELLS
21 Asst VP Finance & Business Services ... Mr. Matthew DELANEY
32 Asst VP/Dean of Students ... Dr. Donavan MCCARGO
13 Asst Vice Pres/Info Technology ... Mr. Troy VINGOM
15 Asst VP for Human Resources ... Ms. Sharon M. PICUS
57 Dean College Visual/Perf Arts ... Dr. Michele KIEC
49 Dean College Liberal Arts/Sci ... Dr. David BEOUGHER
50 Dean College of Business ... Dr. Anne CARROLL
53 Dean College Education ... Dr. John WARD
62 Director of Library Services ... Ms. Martha STEVENSON
09 Director Institutional Research ... Ms. Natalie CARTWRIGHT
06 Registrar ... Mr. Ted WITRYK
37 Director of Financial Aid ... Mr. Bernard L. MCCREE
38 Director Counseling & Psych Svcs ... Dr. Lisa COULTER
96 Purchasing Manager ... Vacant
07 Spec Asst Enrl Mgmt/Div Recr Admis ... Vacant
19 Chief of Police ... Mr. John DILLON
36 Director Career/Community Services ... Ms. Kerri GARDI
04 Sr Executive Assoc to President ... Ms. Toyia HEYWARD
108 Assoc Prov Accreditation/Acad Affs ... Dr. Karen RAUCH
106 Dir Online Education/E-learning ... Mr. Douglas SCOTT

*Lock Haven University (E)

401 N Fairview Street, Lock Haven PA 17745-2390
County: Clinton — FICE Identification: 003323
Unit ID: 213613
Telephone: (570) 484-2011 — Carnegie Class: Masters/M
FAX Number: (570) 484-2432 — Calendar System: Semester
URL: www.lockhaven.edu
Established: 1870 — Annual Undergrad Tuition & Fees (In-State): $10,878
Enrollment: 3,163 — Coed
Affiliation or Control: State — IRS Status: 170(c)1
Highest Offering: Master's
Accreditation: M, ACBSP, ADNUR, ARCPA, CAATE, CACREP, CAEPN, CAPRT, NUR, SW

02 Interim President ... Dr. Bashar W. HANNA
05 Provost & Executive Vice President ... Dr. Ron DARBEAU
11 Chief Administration/Finance Ofcr ... Ms. Deana HILL
32 Dean of Student Affairs ... Dr. Dwayne ALLISON
84 VP for Enrollment Management ... Dr. Stephen LEE
111 VP for University Advancement ... Mr. Joseph FIOCHETTA
49 Dean of Liberal Arts & Education ... Vacant
83 Dean Natural/Behavioral/Health Sci ... Dr. Jonathan LINDZEY
50 Dean Business/Info Sys/Human Svcs ... Vacant
12 Director Clearfield Branch Campus ... Ms. Valerie DIXON
85 Director of International Studies ... Ms. Rosana CAMPBELL
09 Director Institutional Research ... Mr. John (Mike) ABPLANALP
15 Associate VP of Human Resources ... Vacant
07 Interim Director of Admissions ... Ms. Jaimee KESTER
06 Interim Registrar ... Ms. Meisha MCDERMIT
22 Dir Affirm Action/Equal Opportunity ... Ms. Sherry MOORE
37 Interim Director of Financial Aid ... Mr. Michael HALL
36 Director of Career Services ... Ms. Maryjo CAMPANA
26 Exec Director of Communications ... Ms. Elizabeth ARNOLD
19 Director of Public Safety ... Mr. Timothy STRINGER
18 Director of Facilities ... Mr. Scott MCCALL
41 Director of Athletics ... Dr. Tom GIOGLIO
66 Director of Nursing Program ... Dr. Darlene ARDARY
38 Director of Counseling ... Dr. Lynn BRUNER
90 Dir Computing/Instructional Tech ... Mr. Boise MILLER
88 Director of Physician Asst Program ... Ms. Anna Mae SMITH
92 Director Honors Program ... Dr. Elizabeth GRUBER
94 Director Women's Studies ... Dr. Holle CANATELLA
28 Director of DEI ... Mr. Kenneth HALL
40 Manager University Bookstore ... Ms. Tanya HARPSTER
29 Director Alumni Relations ... Ms. Ashley KOSER
103 Interim Director of Workforce Dev ... Ms. Angelic HARDY
04 Admin Assistant to the President ... Ms. Bianca HOFFMAN
13 Chief Info Technology Officer ... Mr. Boise MILLER

*Mansfield University of Pennsylvania (F)

Academy Street, Mansfield PA 16933-1697
County: Tioga — FICE Identification: 003324
Unit ID: 213783
Telephone: (570) 662-4000 — Carnegie Class: Bac-A&S
FAX Number: (570) 662-4995 — Calendar System: Semester
URL: www.mansfield.edu
Established: 1857 — Annual Undergrad Tuition & Fees (In-State): $10,660
Enrollment: 1,784 — Coed
Affiliation or Control: State — IRS Status: 501(c)3
Highest Offering: Master's
Accreditation: M, ACBSP, COARC, DIETD, MUS, NUR, RAD, SW

02 Acting President ... Dr. John ULRICH
10 Interim VP Finance/Administration ... Ms. Amy DICELLOW
05 Provost/VP Academic Affairs ... Mr. John ULRICH
08 Director Library/Info Resource Svcs ... Mr. Scott R. DIMARCO
18 Director of Facilities Management ... Mr. Kenneth B. LAWTON
26 Dir of Marketing and Communications ... Mr. Ryan MCNAMARA
32 Interim Dean of Students ... Mr. Scott KANE
37 Director of Student Financial Aid ... Ms. Pamela KATHCART
19 Dir University Police & Safety ... Mr. Scott HENRY
41 Director of Athletics ... Ms. Peggy CARL
09 Dir Institutional Rsrch/Assess Data ... Dr. John COSGROVE
29 Dir of Alumni Affairs & Advancement ... Ms. Casey WOOD

06 Registrar .... Ms. Lori CASS
38 Director Counseling Services .... Ms. Jolene MEISNER
07 Director of Admissions .... Ms. Rachel GREEN
13 Director of Campus Technologies .... Mr. Nicholas ANDRE

*Millersville University of Pennsylvania (A)

PO Box 1002, Millersville PA 17551-0302
County: Lancaster FICE Identification: 003325
Unit ID: 214041
Telephone: (717) 871-4636 Carnegie Class: Masters/L
FAX Number: (717) 871-7930 Calendar System: 4/1/4
URL: www.millersville.edu
Established: 1855 Annual Undergrad Tuition & Fees (In-State): $11,665
Enrollment: 7,456 Coed
Affiliation or Control: State IRS Status: 501(c)3
Highest Offering: Doctorate
Accreditation: M, ACBSP, ART, CAEP, CAEPN, COARC, MUS, NAIT, NURSE, SW

02 President .... Dr. Daniel A. WUBAH
05 Vice Pres Academic Affs/Provost .... Dr. Gail GASPARICH
10 VP Finance & Administration .... Mr. Guilbert BROWN
111 Vice Pres for Advancement .... Mr. Victor RAMOS
32 VP Student Affs & Enrollment Mgmt .... Mr. Brian HAZLETT
28 Chief Diversity Officer .... Dr. Felicia BROWN-HAYWOOD
100 Chief of Staff .... Mr. Christopher J. STEUER
20 Associate Provost Academic Admin .... Dr. James A. DELLE
108 Acting Asst VP Inst Assess/Plng .... Dr. Kyle VERBOSH
13 Chief Technology Officer .... Mr. Stephen J. DIFILIPO, JR.
15 Exec Director of Human Resources .. Ms. Diane L. COPENHAVER
37 Assoc VP Student Financial Services .... Mr. Dwight G. HORSEY
35 AVP Student Affs/Enrollment Mgmt .... Mr. Renardo A. HALL
84 Assoc VP SA & Enrollment Mgmt .. Mr. Thomas J. RICHARDSON
26 Asst VP Communications/Marketing . Mr. Gregory E. FREEDLAND
18 Assistant VP Facilities .... Mr. Thomas A. WALTZ, JR.
53 Dean Education & Human Services ...... Dr. George P. DRAKE, JR.
79 Dean Arts/Human & Social Sci .... Dr. Ieva ZAKE
81 Dean Science & Technology .... Dr. Mike JACKSON
58 Dean Col of Grad Stds & Adult Lrng .... Dr. James DELLE
86 VP External Rels/Chief of Staff .... Dr. Victor S. DESANTIS
06 Registrar .... Ms. Alison M. HUTCHINSON
07 Director of Admissions .... Ms. Katy A. CHARLES
121 Dir Student Access/Support Services .... Ms. Darlene R. NEWMAN
36 Director Exp Learn & Career Mgmt ...... Ms. Melissa WARDWELL
38 Director Counseling/Human Devel .... Dr. Kelsey K. BACKELS
19 Chief of University Police .... Mr. Peter J. ANDERS
41 Director of Intercollegiate Ath .... Mr. Miles P. GALLAGHER
40 University Store Manager .... Ms. Audrey HERR
42 Campus Minister .... Rev. Trip BEANS
110 Assoc VP for Advancement .... Ms. Alice R. MCMURRY
09 Int AVP Inst Assessment/Planning .... Dr. Kyle W. VERBOSH
112 Major Gift Officer .... Mr. Robert L. BENTLEY
102 Dir Sponsored Pgms & Research Admin .... Dr. Rene MUNOZ
96 Procurement Manager .... Ms. Ruth SHEETZ
57 Director Visual & Performing Arts .... Ms. Robin D. ZAREMSKI
27 Director of Communications .... Ms. Janet E. KACSKOS
106 Director of Online Programs .... Ms. Janice R. MOORE
29 Int Director Alumni Engagement .... Ms. Gabrielle BUZGO
43 Dir Legal Services/General Counsel .... Mr. Jeffrey HAWKINS
04 Admin Assistant to the President .... Ms. Madelyn MATIAS
08 Chief Library Officer .... Mr. Andrew WELAISH
101 Secretary of the Institution/Board .... Mrs. Jennifer HART
104 Director Study Abroad .... Dr. Patriece CAMPBELL
50 Dean Lombardo College of Business .... Dr. Marc I. TOMLJANOVICH

*Shippensburg University of Pennsylvania (B)

1871 Old Main Drive, Shippensburg PA 17257-2200
County: Cumberland FICE Identification: 003326
Unit ID: 216010
Telephone: (717) 477-7447 Carnegie Class: Masters/L
FAX Number: (717) 477-1273 Calendar System: Semester
URL: www.ship.edu
Established: 1871 Annual Undergrad Tuition & Fees (In-State): $13,544
Enrollment: 6,130 Coed
Affiliation or Control: State IRS Status: 501(c)3
Highest Offering: Doctorate
Accreditation: M, CACREP, CAEPN, JOUR, SW

02 President .... Dr. Charles E. PATTERSON
05 Sr Exec VP Acad Affairs & Provost .... Dr. Tom ORMOND
45 Sr VP Strategy & Student Success .... Dr. Sue MUKHERJEE
84 Sr VP Enr Mgmt/Stdnt Affs/Stdnt Svc .... Vacant
10 Sr VP Administration & Finance .... Mr. Scott BARTON
26 VP External Rels/Communications .... Dr. Kim GARRIS
15 Director Human Resources .... Ms. Laurie PORTER
102 Pres Shippensburg Univ Foundation .... Dr. Leslie CLINTON
21 Assoc VP for A&F/CFO .... Dr. Melinda D. FAWKS
11 AVP Operations .... Mr. Christopher CLARKE
13 Deputy CITO/Exec Dir Ac Tech & User .... Dr. Justin SENTZ
20 Assoc Provost & Interim Dean .... Dr. Tracy SCHOOLCRAFT
51 Exec Dir CMDPC .... Ms. Lorelee ISBELL
35 Dean of Students .... Ms. Lorie DAVIS
06 Registrar .... Ms. Cathy J. SPRENGER
36 Dir Career & Community Engagement . Ms. Victoria BUCHBAUER
37 Director Financial Aid .... Ms. Trina SNYDER
29 Dir Alumni Outreach & Data Mgmt .... Ms. Lori SMITH
39 AVP for Student Affairs .... Mr. Barry MCCLANAHAN
08 Dean of Libraries .... Ms. Michelle FOREMAN
28 Chief Diversity Officer .... Ms. Stephanie JIRARD
88 Director Womens Center .... Ms. Arielle CATRON
09 Exec Dir Research/Assessment/Plng .... Mr. Eric ZEGLEN
25 Dir Institute for Public Service .... Mr. Christopher WONDERS
38 Director of Counseling Services .... Dr. Christopher CARLTON
88 Director of Conference Services .... Ms. Melinda BENDER
53 Dean College Education & Human Svcs .... Dr. Nicole R. HILL
49 Dean College Arts & Science .... Dr. Leslie BROWN
50 Dean College of Business .... Dr. John KOOTI
121 AVP & Dean for Student Success .... Vacant
18 Chief Facilities/Physical Plant .... Mr. Jeffrey KUGLER
96 Director of Purchasing/Contracting .... Mr. Wesley LIGHT
07 AVP for Enrollment Management .... Dr. Jennifer A. HAUGHIE
19 Director Public Safety .... Mr. Michael LEE
41 Athletic Director .... Mr. Jeff A. MICHAELS
04 Exec Associate to the President .... Mr. Scott BROWN
104 Assoc Dean Stdnts/Dir Intl Programs .... Ms. Mary BURNETT
100 Chief of Staff .... Vacant

*Slippery Rock University of Pennsylvania (C)

1 Morrow Way, Slippery Rock PA 16057-1326
County: Butler FICE Identification: 003327
Unit ID: 216038
Telephone: (724) 738-9000 Carnegie Class: Masters/L
FAX Number: (724) 738-2169 Calendar System: Semester
URL: www.sru.edu
Established: 1889 Annual Undergrad Tuition & Fees (In-State): $9,984
Enrollment: 8,860 Coed
Affiliation or Control: State IRS Status: 501(c)3
Highest Offering: Doctorate
Accreditation: M, ART, #ARCPA, CAATE, CAEPN, CAHIIM, CARTE, COSMA, DANCE, EXSC, MUS, NURSE, OT, PTA, SW, THEA

02 President .... Dr. William BEHRE
05 Provost/VP Acad & Student Affs .... Dr. Abbey ZINK
11 Sr VP for Admin & Economic Devel .... Dr. Amir MOHAMMADI
111 Vice Pres for Univ Advancement .... Dr. Dennis WASHINGTON
18 Asst Vice Pres for Facilities/Plng .... Mr. Scott ALBERT
15 Chief Human Resources Officer .... Ms. Lynne M. MOTYL
28 Asst VP Div & Compliance/Title IX .... Ms. Holly M. MCCOY
100 Chief of Staff .... Ms. Tina L. MOSER
10 Chief Financial & Data Officer .... Ms. Carrie J. BIRCKBICHLER
84 Chief Enrollment Mgmt Officer .... Dr. Amanda A. YALE
32 Chief Student Affairs Officer .... Mr. David WILMES
13 Assoc Provost Info Technology .... Dr. John ZIEGLER
102 Exec Director SRU Foundation Inc .... Dr. Edward BUCHA
26 Chief Comm/Public Affairs Officer .... Mr. Robert KING
37 Director Student Financial Aid .... Ms. Alyssa DOBSON
19 Director Public Safety .... Mr. Paul NOVAK
19 Director University Police .... Mr. Kevin SHARKEY
08 Manager of Library Operations .... Ms. Jennifer J. BARTEK
14 Director of Info & Admin Tech Svcs .... Mr. Henry MAGUSIAK
06 Director Acad Records & Registrar .... Ms. Connie EDWARDS
07 Director Undergraduate Admissions .... Mr. Michael MAY
23 Director Health Services .... Ms. Kristina BENKESER
36 Assistant Director Career Services .... Ms. Renee COYNE
29 Director Alumni Affairs .... Ms. Kelly BAILEY
81 Interim Dean Col Health/Engr/Sci .... Dr. Michael ZIEG
123 Director Graduate Admissions ... Ms. Brandi WEBER-MORTIMER
41 Athletic Director .... Ms. Roberta PAGE
39 Director of Residence Life .... Mr. Patrick T. BESWICK
25 Director Grants & Sponsored Rsrch .... Ms. Casey HYATT
38 Director of Student Counseling .... Dr. Chris CUBERO
93 Director of Inclusive Excellence .... Vacant
96 Int Dir of Contracts & Purchasing .... Ms. Terri LEASE
88 Assoc Provost Trans Exper .... Dr. Bradley WILSON
49 Dean College Liberal Arts .... Dr. Dan BAUER
50 Dean College of Business .... Dr. Lawrence SHAO
53 Dean College of Education .... Dr. Keith DILS
04 Admin Assistant to the President .... Ms. Kelli RENSEL

*West Chester University of Pennsylvania (D)

University & High Street, West Chester PA 19383-0001
County: Chester FICE Identification: 003328
Unit ID: 216764
Telephone: (610) 436-1000 Carnegie Class: Masters/L
FAX Number: (610) 436-3115 Calendar System: Semester
URL: www.wcupa.edu
Established: 1871 Annual Undergrad Tuition & Fees (In-State): $10,471
Enrollment: 17,719 Coed
Affiliation or Control: State IRS Status: 501(c)3
Highest Offering: Doctorate
Accreditation: M, #ARCPA, ART, CAATE, CACREP, CAEPN, CLPSY, COARC, DIETD, @DIETI, EXSC, FEPAC, MUS, NURSE, PH, SP, SPAA, SW, THEA

02 President .... Dr. Chris FIORENTINO
100 Vice President University Affairs .... Dr. John VILLELLA
04 Sr Assoc to the President .... Ms. Megan FAHEY
28 Chief Diversity & Inclusion Officer .... Dr. Tracey RAY
05 Executive VP & Provost .... Dr. R. Lorraine BERNOTSKY
10 Vice President Admin/Finance .... Mr. Todd MURPHY
13 Chief Information Officer .... Mr. Jatinder SINGH
119 Information Security Officer .... Mr. Frank PISCITELLO
32 Vice President Student Affairs .... Dr. Zebulun DAVENPORT
35 Asst VP for Student Development .... Ms. Judy KAWAMOTO
88 AVP for Identity/Health/Wellness .... Mr. Antonio DELGADO
49 Dean College Arts & Humanities .... Dr. Jen BACON
20 Vice Provost .... Vacant
58 Senior Vice Provost .... Dr. Jeffery OSGOOD
07 Asst VP Admissions .... Ms. Sarah FREED
53 Dean College of Education .... Dr. Desha WILLIAMS
50 Dean College Business/Public Mgmt .... Dr. Evan LEACH
81 Dean College Science & Math .... Dr. Radha PYATI
76 Dean College Health Science .... Dr. Scott HEINERICHS
64 Dean School of Music .... Dr. Chris HANNING
25 Assoc VP Sponsored Research .... Dr. Nicole BENNETT
23 Director Student Health Center .... Vacant
15 AVP Human Resources .... Mr. William HELZLSOUER
11 AVP for Admin Svcs/Spec Projects .... Ms. Sara HINKLE
35 AVP Student Life/Dean of Students .... Mr. Gerald MARTIN
21 AVP Finance/Business Svcs .... Vacant
84 Asst Prov/VP Enrollment Mgmt .... Vacant
85 Interim Dir International Programs .... Dr. Vishal SHAH
102 Chief Exec Officer WCU Foundation .... Mr. Christopher MOMINEY
18 Assoc Vice President for Facilities .... Mr. Gary BIXBY
88 Dir Facilities Finance/Support Svcs .... Ms. Susan MILLER
21 Controller .... Ms. Jennifer COFFEY
09 AVP Institutional Research .... Ms. Lisa YANNICK
113 Bursar/Director Student Finan Svcs .... Ms. Colleen CORRADO
114 Director Budget .... Ms. Ilene MATES
26 Asst VP Communications & Marketing .... Ms. Nancy GAINER
24 Director Publications/Printing Svcs .... Mr. Matthew BORN
31 Director Cultural/Community Affairs .... Mr. John RHEIN
88 Director Conference Services .... Ms. Mary Beth KURIMAY
08 University Librarian .... Ms. Mary PAGE
88 Director Teacher Education Center .... Dr. James B. PRICE
36 Director Career Devel Center .... Ms. Jennifer ROSSI-LONG
88 Dir Acad Development Pgm .... Dr. John CRAIG
88 Dir Learning Asst/Resource .... Dr. Jocelyn MANIGO
37 Director Financial Aid .... Mr. Daniel MCILHENNEY
38 Director Counseling Center .... Dr. Rachel DALTRY
29 Director Alumni Relations .... Ms. Jenna BIRCH
41 Director Athletics .... Dr. Terry BEATTIE
88 Director Sports Information .... Mr. James ZUHLKE
93 Dir Multicultural Affairs .... Dr. Dametraus JAGGERS
88 Sr Director Women & Gender Equity .... Ms. Sendy ALCIDONIS
19 Dir Public Safety .... Mr. Raymond STEVENSON
96 Director Business Services .... Mr. Jeff BAUN
91 AVP & Deputy CIO .... Mr. Kevin PARTRIDGE
88 Asst Dir Sourcing/Planning/Project .... Ms. Chaw-ye CHANG
105 Exec Dir Application Development .... Vacant
89 Director New Student Programs .... Dr. Kristin AUSTIN
88 Asst Dean of Students .... Mr. Peter GALLOWAY
39 Senior Director Residence Life .... Ms. Marion MCKINNEY
88 Asst Dean of Student Conduct .... Ms. Christina BRENNER
88 Dir Student Leadership/Involve .... Mr. Charles WARNER
109 Senior Director Sykes Student Union .... Dr. Clayton KOLB
122 Senior Dir Fraternity & Sorority .... Ms. Cara JENKINS
121 Sr Vice Provost Student Success .... Ms. Kathleen HOWLEY
88 Dir Pre-major Academic Advising .... Dr. Ann COLGAN
92 Director Honors College .... Dr. Kevin DEAN
104 Asst VP for International Programs .... Vacant
106 Exec Director Distance Educ Svcs .... Dr. Rui LI
88 Exec Dir Student Service Inc .... Ms. Donna SNYDER
40 Student Svcs Inc Bookstore Manager ..... Mr. Stephen MANNELLA
06 Registrar .... Ms. Megan JERABEK

*Clarion University - Venango (E)

1801 W First Street, Oil City PA 16301-3297
Telephone: (814) 676-6591 FICE Identification: 003319
Accreditation: &M, ADNUR, COARC, NAIT, NUR

*Lock Haven University Clearfield Branch Campus (F)

201 University Drive, Clearfield PA 16830
Telephone: (814) 768-3405 Identification: 770186
Accreditation: &M

Philadelphia College of Osteopathic Medicine (G)

4170 City Avenue, Philadelphia PA 19131-1694
County: Philadelphia FICE Identification: 003352
Unit ID: 215123
Telephone: (215) 871-6100 Carnegie Class: Spec-4-yr-Med
FAX Number: (215) 871-6719 Calendar System: Trimester
URL: www.pcom.edu
Established: 1899 Annual Graduate Tuition & Fees: N/A
Enrollment: 3,133 Coed
Affiliation or Control: Independent Non-Profit IRS Status: 501(c)3
Highest Offering: Doctorate; No Undergraduates
Accreditation: M, ARCPA, CLPSY, IPSY, OSTEO, SCPSY

01 President & CEO .... Dr. Jay S. FELDSTEIN
05 Provost/Sr VP Academic Affairs/Dean .... Dr. Kenneth J. VEIT
10 Vice Pres Finance/Treasurer/CFO .... Mr. Peter DOULIS
17 Chief Acad Ofcr-PCOM Mednet-Opti .... Dr. David KUO
43 Chief Legal Affairs Officer .... Mr. David F. SIMON
63 Dean Osteopathic Med Pgm-GA Campus .... Dr. William CRAVER, III
67 Dean School of Pharmacy .... Dr. Shawn SPENCER
20 Assoc Dean Graduate Medical Educ .... Dr. David KUO
20 Dean/Chief Academic Officer .... Dr. Andrea MANN
20 Assoc Dean Curriculum .... Dr. Kerin FRESA
20 Assoc Dean Curriculum .... Dr. Bonnie BUXTON
12 Chief Campus Officer-Georgia Campus .... Mr. Bryan GINN

46 Chief Science Officer .... Dr. Mindy GEORGE-WEINSTEIN
32 Chief Student Affairs Officer .... Ms. Patience MASON
26 Chief Marketing/Communications Ofcr ... Ms. Wendy W. ROMANO
37 Chief Student Financial Aid Officer ....Mr. Samuel MATHENY
15 Chief Human Resources Officer .... Ms. Christina MAZZELLA
07 Chief Admissions Officer .... Ms. Adrianne JONES
28 Chief Diversity/Cmty Relations Ofcr .... Dr. Marcine PICKRON-DAVIS
13 Chief Technology Officer .... Mr. Richard SMITH
88 Chief Compliance Officer .... Ms. Margaret MCKEON
18 Chief Facilities/Plant Operations .... Mr. Frank H. WINDLE
111 Chief Advancement Officer .... Ms. Carrie COLLINS
08 Chair of Library/Exec Director .... Ms. Stephanie FERRETTI
06 Registrar .... Ms. Maureen O'MARA CARVER
19 Director Security/Safety .... Mr. Richard KRALLE
117 Risk Manager .... Mr. Isaiah LOPEZ
96 Purchasing Manager .... Ms. LaVerne MAYES
04 Executive Asst to the President .... Ms. Lynn A. KUSH

PITC Institute (A)

827 Glenside Ave, Wyncote PA 19095
County: Montgomery FICE Identification: 037813
Unit ID: 444811
Telephone: (215) 392-2938 Carnegie Class: Not Classified
FAX Number: (215) 576-5652 Calendar System: Other
URL: www.pitc.edu
Established: 1998 Annual Undergrad Tuition & Fees: N/A
Enrollment: 347 Coed
Affiliation or Control: Proprietary IRS Status: Proprietary
Highest Offering: Associate Degree
Accreditation: ABHES

01 President .... Dr. Shahid AHMED

Pittsburgh Career Institute (B)

421 Seventh Avenue, Pittsburgh PA 15219-1907
County: Allegheny FICE Identification: 022023
Unit ID: 216782
Telephone: (412) 281-2600 Carnegie Class: Spec 2-yr-Health
FAX Number: (412) 209-0419 Calendar System: Other
URL: www.pci.edu
Established: 2014 Annual Undergrad Tuition & Fees: $15,064
Enrollment: 217 Coed
Affiliation or Control: Proprietary IRS Status: Proprietary
Highest Offering: Associate Degree
Accreditation: ACICS, COARC, DMS

01 Campus President .... Patti L. YAKSHE
05 Chief Academic Officer .... Peggy BRINTON
09 Director of Institutional Research .... Cindy SMITH
36 Director Student Placement .... Patty O'ROURKE

Pittsburgh Institute of Aeronautics (C)

PO Box 10897, Pittsburgh PA 15236-0897
County: Allegheny FICE Identification: 005310
Unit ID: 215381
Telephone: (412) 346-2100 Carnegie Class: Spec 2-yr-Tech
FAX Number: (412) 466-0513 Calendar System: Quarter
URL: www.pia.edu
Established: 1929 Annual Undergrad Tuition & Fees: $16,650
Enrollment: 567 Coed
Affiliation or Control: Independent Non-Profit IRS Status: 501(c)3
Highest Offering: Associate Degree
Accreditation: ACCSC

01 President/CEO .... Ms. Suzanne L. MARKLE
05 Director of Student Affairs .... Mr. Jason S. MONGAN
37 Director of Financial Aid .... Ms. Donata CLARK
26 Director of Marketing/IT .... Mr. Steven D. SABOLD
07 Director of Admissions .... Ms. Roxanne OBER
18 Director of Campus Operations .... Mr. Gary E. HOYLE

Pittsburgh Institute of Mortuary Science (D)

5808 Baum Boulevard, Pittsburgh PA 15206-3706
County: Allegheny FICE Identification: 010814
Unit ID: 215390
Telephone: (412) 362-8500 Carnegie Class: Spec 2-yr-A&S
FAX Number: (412) 362-1684 Calendar System: Trimester
URL: www.pims.edu
Established: 1939 Annual Undergrad Tuition & Fees: N/A
Enrollment: 191 Coed
Affiliation or Control: Independent Non-Profit IRS Status: 501(c)3
Highest Offering: Associate Degree
Accreditation: FUSER

01 President/CEO/Dean of Admin .... Mr. Eugene C. OGRODNIK
05 Program Director .... Dr. Barry T. LEASE
32 Dean of Faculty/Students .... Mr. Michael BURNS
06 Registrar/Dir Admin Services .... Ms. Nicole ELACHKO
07 Admissions Advisor .... Ms. Maria SPROULL
113 Bursar/Financial Aid .... Ms. Karen S. ROCCO

Pittsburgh Technical College (E)

1111 McKee Road, Oakdale PA 15071-3205
County: Allegheny FICE Identification: 007437
Unit ID: 215415
Telephone: (412) 809-5100 Carnegie Class: Bac/Assoc-Assoc Dom
FAX Number: (412) 809-5320 Calendar System: Quarter
URL: www.ptcollege.edu
Established: 1946 Annual Undergrad Tuition & Fees: $16,460
Enrollment: 1,559 Coed
Affiliation or Control: Independent Non-Profit IRS Status: 501(c)3
Highest Offering: Baccalaureate
Accreditation: M, ACFEI, MAC, PNUR, SURGT

01 President .... Dr. Alicia B. HARVEY-SMITH
04 Executive Assistant to President .... Christine RAIZIN
111 Chief of Staff/Exec Dir Advancement .... Brenda PSOTKA
28 Chief DEI Officer .... Marsha N. LINDSAY
43 General Counsel .... Gretchen GARDNER
14 Supervisor of Network Operations .... Jon BUHAGIAR
102 Exec Director Corporate College .... Sunjay BALI
13 Chief Information Officer .... William SHOWERS
21 Vice President Financial Services .... Connie VANCAMP
10 VP of Administration/CFO .... Jay CLAYTON
50 Dean of Business/Online .... Dr. Melissa WERTZ
06 Registrar .... Samantha BYCURA
66 Dean of Nursing/Health Professions .... Teresa DUCSAY
53 Dean of Education Services .... Dr. Bonnie ORDONEZ
09 Exec. Director Inst. Research .... Nancy FEATHER
25 Grants Mgr/Foundation Relations .... Julie THROCKMORTON
26 VP of Marketing/Communication .... Barry SHEPARD
84 Director of Enrollment Marketing .... Jennifer DONOVAN
101 Executive Assistant/Sec to Board .... Jayme HOLLOWAY
05 Vice President of Academic Affairs .... Dr. Eileen STEFFAN
36 Director of Career Services .... Kristy SWEGMAN
32 Vice President of Student Affairs .... Rodney CLARK
29 Alumni Coordinator .... Christine IOLI
15 Director of HR/Title IX Coordinator .... Nancy STARR
19 Director of Public Safety .... Gregory BOLYARD
39 Director of Resident Life .... Gloria RITCHIE
18 Director of Facilities Services .... Tom VUCELICH
37 Assoc VP Student Financial Aid .... Jill BITTEL
86 Manager of Compliance .... Melissa BROWN
40 Campus Store Manager .... Cynthia KLEIN
07 AVP Admissions and Advising .. Dr. Rebecca DUNCAN-RAMIREZ

Pittsburgh Theological Seminary (F)

616 N. Highland Avenue, Pittsburgh PA 15206-2596
County: Allegheny FICE Identification: 003356
Unit ID: 215424
Telephone: (412) 362-5610 Carnegie Class: Spec-4-yr-Faith
FAX Number: N/A Calendar System: Semester
URL: www.pts.edu
Established: 1794 Annual Graduate Tuition & Fees: N/A
Enrollment: 209 Coed
Affiliation or Control: Presbyterian Church (U.S.A.) IRS Status: 501(c)3
Highest Offering: Doctorate; No Undergraduates
Accreditation: M, THEOL

01 President .... Dr. Asa LEE
05 Int Dean of Faculty/VP Acad Affairs .... Dr. Leanna FULLER
111 VP Seminary Advancement .... Mr. Charles FISCHER, III
32 Assoc Dean of Students & Formation .... Rev. Ayana TETER
10 Vice Pres Finance & Administration .... Mr. Thomas HINDS
06 Registrar .... Ms. Anne B. MALONE
08 Director of the Library .... Ms. Michelle SPOMER
78 Assoc Dean Acad Pgms/Field Educ .... Dr. Barbara BLODGETT
29 Director of Alumni/ae Services .... Rev. Carolyn CRANSTON
73 Int Dir Doctor of Ministry Program .... Dr. Denise THORPE
51 Director Continuing Education .... Dr. Helen BLIER
37 Associate Director of Financial Aid .... Mr. Ryan JENSEMA
84 Sr Dir of Enrollment Services .... Ms. Tracy RIGGLE YOUNG
04 Exec Asst to President/Sec to BOD .... Rev. Andrew GREENHOW
13 Director of Information Technology .... Mr. David MIDDLETON
15 Human Resources Manager .... Ms. Kathleen GREEN
18 Facilities Director .... Mr. Tom FULTON
30 Director of Development .... Mr. Dominick OLIVER
26 Sr Director of Communications .... Ms. Melissa LOGAN

Point Park University (G)

201 Wood Street, Pittsburgh PA 15222-1984
County: Allegheny FICE Identification: 003357
Unit ID: 215442
Telephone: (412) 391-4100 Carnegie Class: Masters/L
FAX Number: (412) 392-3998 Calendar System: Semester
URL: www.pointpark.edu
Established: 1960 Annual Undergrad Tuition & Fees: $34,200
Enrollment: 3,591 Coed
Affiliation or Control: Independent Non-Profit IRS Status: 501(c)3
Highest Offering: Doctorate
Accreditation: M, CLPSY, DANCE, IACBE

01 President .... Dr. Don GREEN
05 Provost .... Dr. Michael SOTO
20 Associate Provost .... Dr. Jonas PRIDA
10 Sr VP Finance and Operations .... Ms. Bridget MANCOSH
43 Sr VP and General Counsel .... Vacant
26 VP of External Affairs .... Ms. Mariann K. GEYER
84 VP Enrollment Management .... Ms. Trudy WILLIAMS
30 Asst VP Development/Alumni Rels ...... Ms. Stephanie ADAMCZYK
32 VP of Student Affairs .... Mr. Keith PAYLO
15 VP of Human Resources .... Ms. Lisa STEFANKO
18 Vice President of Operations .... Mr. Christopher J. HILL
19 AVP Public Safety/Chief Police .... Mr. Jeffrey D. BESONG
09 Assoc VP Institutional Research ...... Mr. Christopher E. CHONCEK
21 AVP of Finance .... Mr. Jim HARDT
20 Asst VP Academic Affairs .... Mr. Nelson CHIPMAN
13 Asst Vice Pres Info Technology .... Mr. Tim WILSON
50 Dean Rowand School of Business .... Dr. Steve TANZILLI
53 Dean Sch of Education .... Dr. Darlene MARNICH
79 Chair Psychology .... Dr. Matthew ALLEN
54 Chair Natural Science/Engr Tech .... Dr. Gregg JOHNSON
88 Chair Criminal Justice/Intell Stds .... Mr. Michael BOTTA
88 Chair Business Management .... Mr. Patrick MULVIHILL
88 Chair Accounting/Econ/Finance/IT .... Ms. Margaret GILFILLAN
88 Chair Theatre .... Ms. April DARAS
88 Chair Dance .... Mr. Garfield LEMONIUS
88 Interim Chair Cinema .... Mr. Garfield LEMONIUS
88 Chair Literary Arts .... Dr. Sarah PERRIER
60 Dean School of Communication .... Dr. Raymond ANCKNEY
88 Chair Sport Art Entertain Mgmt .... Mr. Bob DERDA
83 Chair Humanities/Social Science .... Dr. Channa NEWMAN
88 Chair Community Engagement .... Dr. Heather STARR FIEDLER
06 University Registrar .... Mr. Scott SPENCER
08 Director/Librarian/Academic Svcs .... Ms. Liz EVANS
27 Mng Dir Marketing/Public Relations .... Mr. Louis CORSARO
39 Director of Campus Life .... Ms. Janet D. EVANS
07 Director of Admissions .... Ms. Joell MINFORD
41 Director of Athletics .... Mr. John ASHAOLU
88 Dir Conference & Event Services .... Ms. Christina MORTON
38 Director of Counseling Services .... Dr. Kurt KUMLER
106 AVP Online Education/E-learning .... Mr. Nelson CHIPMAN
29 Director Alumni Relations .... Vacant
37 Director Student Financial Aid .... Mr. George SANTUCCI
44 Director Annual Fund Pgms/Indiv Giv .... Vacant
88 Dir Center for Media Innovation .... Mr. Andrew CONTE
28 AVP of Title IX & Diversity .... Ms. Vanessa LOVE

Reading Area Community College (H)

PO Box 1706, Reading PA 19603-1706
County: Berks FICE Identification: 010388
Unit ID: 215585
Telephone: (610) 372-4721 Carnegie Class: Assoc/MT-VT-Mix Trad/Non
FAX Number: (610) 372-4264 Calendar System: Semester
URL: www.racc.edu
Established: 1971 Annual Undergrad Tuition & Fees (In-District): $9,990
Enrollment: 3,924 Coed
Affiliation or Control: State/Local IRS Status: 501(c)3
Highest Offering: Associate Degree
Accreditation: M, ADNUR, COARC, MLTAD, PNUR

01 President .... Dr. Susan D. LOONEY
05 SVP Academic Affairs/Provost .... Ms. Cynthia SEAMAN
10 Sr VP Fin & Admin Svcs/Treasurer .... Mr. Kenneth DEARSTYNE
111 VP Col Advance/Exec Dir Foundation ...... Mr. Anthony DEMARCO
32 Dean of Student Affairs .... Ms. Maria MITCHELL
21 VP Fiscal Svcs/Controller .... Ms. Dolores PETERSON
15 VP of Human Resources .... Ms. Dolores PETERSON
84 Dean of Enrollment Management .... Ms. Kay LITMAN
09 Dir Assessment/Research/Planning .... Mr. David SWEELEY
81 Assoc Dean STEM .... Ms. Patricia MEJABI
62 Assoc Dean Library Svcs/Lrng Res ...... Ms. Mary Ellen HECKMAN
50 Assoc Dean of Business Division .... Ms. Linda BELL
79 Assoc Dean Comm/Arts & Humanities .... Mr. Brian SCHELL
83 Assoc Dean Soc Sci/Human Svc/Fnd St .... Dr. Robin ECKERT
103 Exec Dir Workforce Dev/Cmty Educ .... Ms. Bonnie SPAYD
26 Director Marketing/Communications .... Mr. David HESSEN
13 Director Information Technology .... Mr. Anderson FORREST
37 Director Financial Aid/Registrar ..... Mr. Benjamin ROSENBERGER
96 Director of Purchasing .... Ms. Cindy URICK
18 Director of Facilities/Safety .... Mr. Alberto OTHUON
04 Exec Admin Asst to the President .... Ms. Sandra STRAUSE
20 Dean of Instruction .... Mr. Kevin COOTS
07 Dir Admiss & Enrollment Svcs .... Ms. Kathy CUNNINGHAM
35 Coordinator of Student Life .... Ms. Jamica ANDREWS
76 Assoc Dean of Health Prof .... Dr. Stacia VISGARDA

Reconstructionist Rabbinical College (I)

1299 Church Road, Wyncote PA 19095-1898
County: Montgomery FICE Identification: 022734
Unit ID: 215619
Telephone: (215) 576-0800 Carnegie Class: Spec-4-yr-Faith
FAX Number: (215) 576-6143 Calendar System: Semester
URL: www.rrc.edu
Established: 1968 Annual Graduate Tuition & Fees: N/A
Enrollment: 43 Coed
Affiliation or Control: Jewish IRS Status: 501(c)3
Highest Offering: Doctorate; No Undergraduates
Accreditation: M

01 President .... Rabbi Deborah WAXMAN
05 Vice Pres Academic Affairs .... Dr. Elsie STERN
03 Executive Vice President .... Rabbi Amber POWERS
26 Asst Vice Pres Communications .... Mr. Robert BERSHAD
11 Director of Operations .... Mr. Robert CHAVEZ
08 Library Director .... Rabbi Alan LAPAYOVER
15 Director of Human Resources .... Ms. Cheryl TYSON

Reformed Episcopal Seminary (J)

826 Second Avenue, Blue Bell PA 19422-1257
County: Montgomery Identification: 667050
Unit ID: 216348
Telephone: (610) 292-9852 Carnegie Class: Spec-4-yr-Faith
FAX Number: (610) 292-9853 Calendar System: Quarter
URL: www.reseminary.edu

Established: 1887 Annual Graduate Tuition & Fees: N/A
Enrollment: 18 Coed
Affiliation or Control: Reformed Episcopal Church IRS Status: 501(c)3
Highest Offering: Master's; No Undergraduates
Accreditation: THEOL

01 President and Dean ....Rev Dr. Jonathan S. RICHES
05 Associate Dean of Faculty ....Rev Dr. Derek COOPER
07 Associate Dean of Admissions & Aid ....Dr. Robert ARNER
13 Dir Information Technology/Web Dev ....Rev. Vic BROBERG
18 Assoc Dean of Facilities/Finance ....Rev. Shawn D. RILEY
32 Chief Student Affairs/Life Officer ....Mr. John MAZZAMUTO

Reformed Presbyterian Theological Seminary (A)

7418 Penn Avenue, Pittsburgh PA 15208-2594
County: Allegheny FICE Identification: 003358
Unit ID: 215628
Telephone: (412) 731-6000 Carnegie Class: Spec-4-yr-Faith
FAX Number: N/A Calendar System: Quarter
URL: www.rpts.edu
Established: 1810 Annual Graduate Tuition & Fees: N/A
Enrollment: N/A Coed
Affiliation or Control: Reformed Presbyterian Church IRS Status: 501(c)3
Highest Offering: Doctorate; No Undergraduates
Accreditation: THEOL

01 President ....Dr. Barry J. YORK
08 Head Librarian ....Mr. Jordan FEAGLEY
10 Treasurer ....Mr. James MCFARLAND
06 Registrar/Dir Admiss & Stdnt Svcs ....Mr. Edwin BLACKWOOD
37 Director of Financial Aid ....Mrs. Sharon SAMPSON
111 Dir of Development & Inst Advance ....Mr. Mark SAMPSON
18 Director of Support Services ....Mr. Joshua NYE

Robert Morris University (B)

6001 University Boulevard,
Moon Township PA 15108-1189
County: Allegheny FICE Identification: 003359
Unit ID: 215655
Telephone: (412) 397-6400 Carnegie Class: DU-Mod
FAX Number: N/A Calendar System: Semester
URL: www.rmu.edu
Established: 1921 Annual Undergrad Tuition & Fees: $32,130
Enrollment: 4,134 Coed
Affiliation or Control: Independent Non-Profit IRS Status: 501(c)3
Highest Offering: Doctorate
Accreditation: M, CAEP, HSA, MPCAC, NMT, NURSE

01 President ....Dr. Christopher B. HOWARD
10 SVP Business Affairs/Treasurer ....Mr. Jeffrey A. LISTWAK
05 Provost & Sr VP Academic Affairs ....Dr. Mary Ann A. RAFOTH
43 General Counsel & VP Legal Affairs ....Ms. Renee T. CAVALOVITCH
103 SVP Corporate Rels & Strategic Init ....Dr. Derya A. JACOBS
84 VP Enrollment Management ....Dr. Kevin HEARN
32 Vice President for Student Life ....Mr. John A. MICHALENKO
30 Vice President Development ....Mr. Matthew B. MILLET
18 Vice Pres for Facilities ....Mr. Perry F. ROOFNER
26 Vice Pres Public Rels/Marketing ....Mr. Jonathan E. POTTS
100 VP Planning & Admin/Chief of Staff ....Dr. David R. MAJKA
41 VP & Director of Athletics ....Mr. Chris A. KING
50 Dean School of Business ....Dr. Michelle L. PATRICK
54 Dean School of Engr/Math/Science ....Dr. Maria V. KALEVITCH
79 Dean Sch Informatics/Humanities/SS ....Dr. Amjad ALI
66 Dean School of Nursing/Educ ....Dr. Mark M. MEYERS
88 Dir Univ/Athletic Sponsorship ....Mr. Matt F. O'BRIEN
84 Assoc VP Enrollment Management ....Ms. Kellie L. LAURENZI
31 AVP Cmty Engage/Leadership Devel ....Ms. Peggy M. OUTON
46 Assoc Provost Research/Graduate ....Dr. Sushil ACHARYA
35 Assistant Dean of Students ....Mrs. Maureen H. KEEFER
08 Director University Library ....Dr. Timothy M. SCHLAK
21 Chief Acctg/Financial Planning Ofcr ....Ms. Melissa A. MICCO
06 University Registrar ....Ms. Daniell C. MATTHEWS
19 Chief of Police ....Mr. Jeff JAMES
36 Senior Director Career Center ....Mr. David J. AUSMAN
39 Director Residence Life ....Mrs. Anne L. LAHODA
28 Chief Diversity/Inclusion Officer ....Dr. Anthony G. ROBINS
27 Sr Dir Marketing & Public Relations ....Mr. Brian J. EDWARDS
37 Sr Director Financial Aid ....Ms. Stephanie N. HENDERSHOT
44 Director Alumni Engagement ....Ms. Jennifer C. YOUNG
04 Exec Assistant to the President ....Ms. Valerie M. MURRAY
101 Board Liaison & Asst Secretary ....Ms. Jill M. KRIEGER
13 Chief Information Technology Ofcr ....Mr. Phillip G. MILLER
15 Chief Human Resources Officer ....Ms. Lisa H. HERNANDEZ

Rosedale Technical College (C)

215 Beecham Drive, Suite 2, Pittsburgh PA 15205-9791
County: Allegheny FICE Identification: 012050
Unit ID: 215682
Telephone: (412) 521-6200 Carnegie Class: Spec 2-yr-Tech
FAX Number: (412) 521-2520 Calendar System: Semester
URL: www.rosedaletech.org
Established: 1949 Annual Undergrad Tuition & Fees: $15,125
Enrollment: 385 Coed
Affiliation or Control: Independent Non-Profit IRS Status: 501(c)3
Highest Offering: Associate Degree
Accreditation: ACCSC

01 President ....Dennis F. WILKE
05 Director of Education ....Kara CHAN
30 VP College Development/Comm ....Debbie BIER
84 Dir Student Enrollment & Outreach ....Kim BELL

Rosemont College (D)

1400 Montgomery Avenue, Rosemont PA 19010-1699
County: Montgomery FICE Identification: 003360
Unit ID: 215691
Telephone: (610) 527-0200 Carnegie Class: Masters/M
FAX Number: (610) 527-0341 Calendar System: Semester
URL: www.rosemont.edu
Established: 1921 Annual Undergrad Tuition & Fees: $20,650
Enrollment: 777 Coed
Affiliation or Control: Roman Catholic IRS Status: 501(c)3
Highest Offering: Master's
Accreditation: M, CACREP

01 President ....Dr. Jayson BOYERS
05 Provost/VP Academic/Student Affairs ....Dr. Mika NASH
10 VP for Finance & Administration ....Mr. Marty MEHRINGER
30 Vice Pres College Relations ....Vacant
32 Dean Student Success & Engagement ....Dr. Karen GEIGER
84 VP of Enrollment & Marketing ....Mrs. Meghan HALEY
110 Asst VP of Development ....Ms. Mary REINETTE ANDREWS
08 Exec Director of Library & Learning ....Mr. Brice PETERSON
58 Dean Schools Graduate/Prof Studies ....Mrs. Jennifer BARRY
20 Academic Dean Undergrad College ....Mrs. Paulette HUTCHINSON
07 Dir Enrollment Information Systems ....Ms. Diana CLAVIN
29 Director of Alumni Relations ....Mr. Joseph DARRAH
26 Managing Director of Communications ....Ms. Kathleen SMYSER
41 Director of Athletics ....Mr. Joseph PAVLOW
15 Senior Director Human Resources ....Ms. Raeann BILLEY
42 Director of Campus Ministry ....Vacant
18 Director of Operations ....Mr. Robert HUGHES
38 Director of Counseling Cntr ....Vacant
39 Director of Residence Life ....Mr. Malek STEWART
19 Director of Public Safety ....Mr. Matthew BAKER
21 Controller ....Ms. Faith BYRNE
37 Director of Financial Aid ....Ms. Sharna PATTERSON
06 Registrar ....Ms. Maureen MALONE
100 Chief of Staff/VP Diversity & Belon ....Dr. Yoli ALOVOR

Saint Charles Borromeo Seminary (E)

100 E Wynnewood Road, Wynnewood PA 19096-3099
County: Montgomery FICE Identification: 003364
Unit ID: 216047
Telephone: (610) 667-3394 Carnegie Class: Spec-4-yr-Faith
FAX Number: (610) 667-7635 Calendar System: Semester
URL: www.scs.edu
Established: 1832 Annual Undergrad Tuition & Fees: $22,570
Enrollment: 180 Male
Affiliation or Control: Roman Catholic IRS Status: 501(c)3
Highest Offering: Master's
Accreditation: M, THEOL

01 Rector & President ....M.Rev. Timothy C. SENIOR
05 Vice President for Academic Affairs ....Rev. Robert A. PESARCHICK
03 Vice Rector ....Rev. Patrick BRADY
10 Chief Financial Officer ....Mr. Mark MCLAUGHLIN
108 VP Info Services & Assessment ....Mrs. Cait KOKOLUS
33 Dean of Men Theology ....Rev. Brian KANE
33 Dean of Men College ....Rev. George SZPARAGOWSKI
08 Director of Library Services ....Mr. James HUMBLE
06 Registrar ....Mr. Todd CHIARAVALLOTI
42 Dir Spiritual Formation Theology ....Fr. Herb SPERGER
42 Dir Spiritual Formation College ....Fr. Dennis CARBONARO
88 Director Pastoral/Apostolic Form ....Rev. George SZPARAGOWSKI
73 Dean School of Theological Studies ....Msgr. Michael MAGEE
21 Director of Financial Services ....Ms. Barbara COADY
37 Director Student Financial Aid ....Ms. Nora DOWNEY
29 Director Alumni Affairs ....Ms. Aileen KAIN

Saint Francis University (F)

PO Box 600, Loretto PA 15940-0600
County: Cambria FICE Identification: 003366
Unit ID: 215743
Telephone: (814) 472-3000 Carnegie Class: Masters/L
FAX Number: (814) 472-3003 Calendar System: Semester
URL: www.francis.edu
Established: 1847 Annual Undergrad Tuition & Fees: $39,278
Enrollment: 2,769 Coed
Affiliation or Control: Roman Catholic IRS Status: 501(c)3
Highest Offering: Doctorate
Accreditation: M, ARCPA, EXSC, IACBE, NURSE, OT, PTA, SW

01 President ....Rev. Malachi VAN TASSELL, TOR
05 Vice President for Academic Affairs ....Dr. Karan POWELL
10 Vice President for Finance ....Mr. Jeffrey SAVINO
32 Vice Pres for Student Development ....Dr. Frank MONTECALVO
42 Director of Mission Integration ....Fr. Matthew SIMONS, TOR
111 Vice President for Advancement ....Mr. Robert CRUSCIEL
84 Vice Pres for Enrollment Management ....Vacant
86 Asst VP Govt Rels/Grants/Found ....Mr. Robert YOUNG
08 Dean of Library Services ....Ms. Sandra A. BALOUGH
97 Dean of General Education ....Dr. Jessica CAMMARATA
06 Registrar ....Mr. Jacob TAYLOR
09 Director of Institutional Research ....Ms. Kate DEATER
37 Financial Aid Director ....Mr. Shane HIMES
26 VP for Communications & Marketing ....Ms. Erin MCCLOSKEY
30 Director of Development ....Ms. Marie B. MELUSKY
38 Director of Counseling Center ....Ms. Laura CONTORCHICK
13 Director Computer Services ....Mr. Jason NAIRN
29 Director of Alumni Relations ....Mr. Eric HORELL
51 Dean Francis Worldwide ....Dr. Trisha MCFADDEN
18 Director of Physical Plant ....Mr. David WILLIAMS
21 Controller ....Mr. Thomas R. FRITZ
41 Director of Athletics ....Mr. James DOWNER
88 Dir Small Business Devel Center ....Mr. Jeff BOLDIZAR
19 University Police ....Capt. Eric ALLEN
39 Director of Residence Life ....Mr. Donald MILES
42 Director of Campus Ministry ....Rev. Stephen WARUSZEWSKI
121 Dean of Student Academic Success ....Dr. Renee BERNARD
124 Dir of Student Engagement ....Ms. Kristen CORCORAN
15 Director of Human Resources ....Ms. Marian BENDER
28 Director of Multicultural Affairs ....Ms. Lynne BANKS
96 Director of Purchasing ....Mr. Michael KUTCHMAN
20 Associate Provost ....Dr. Peter R. SKONER
40 Manager of Bookstore ....Ms. Barbara SHINGLE
04 Admin Assistant to the President ....Ms. Vickie SOYKA
07 Director of Admissions ....Dr. Bobby ANDERSON
104 Director Study Abroad ....Vacant

Saint Joseph's University (G)

5600 City Avenue, Philadelphia PA 19131-1376
County: Philadelphia FICE Identification: 003367
Unit ID: 215770
Telephone: (610) 660-1000 Carnegie Class: Masters/L
FAX Number: (610) 660-1201 Calendar System: Semester
URL: www.sju.edu
Established: 1851 Annual Undergrad Tuition & Fees: $47,940
Enrollment: 6,779 Coed
Affiliation or Control: Roman Catholic IRS Status: 501(c)3
Highest Offering: Doctorate
Accreditation: M

01 President ....Dr. Mark C. REED
05 Provost ....Dr. Cheryl A. MCCONNELL
10 VP Financial Affairs ....Mr. David R. BEAUPRE
26 VP University Relations ....Mr. Joseph P. KENDER
88 Executive Director of Mission ....Rev. Daniel R. JOYCE, SJ
49 Dean College of Arts & Sciences ....Vacant
50 Dean Haub School of Business ....Dr. Joseph A. DIANGELO, JR.
32 VP Student Life ....Dr. Cary M. ANDERSON
41 VP Director of Athletics ....Ms. Jill R. BODENSTEINER
84 VP Enrollment Management ....Ms. Karen PELLEGRINO
27 Chief Marketing/Communications Ofcr ....Ms. Elizabeth K. WALSH
18 AVP Administrative Services ....Mr. Timothy MCGURIMAN
43 General Counsel ....Ms. Tracey PACHMAN
100 AVP Chief of Staff ....Ms. Sarah F. QUINN
84 AVP Enrollment Management ....Mr. Robert J. MCBRIDE
13 Chief Information Officer ....Mr. Francis J. DISANTI
04 Admin Assistant to the President ....Ms. Jennifer L. FALCON
06 Registrar ....Vacant
07 Director of Admissions ....Ms. Maureen MATHIS
08 Chief Library Officer ....Ms. Anne Z. KRAKOW
09 Director of Institutional Research ....Mr. James F. GRASELL
101 Secretary of the Institution/Board ....Ms. Sarah F. QUINN
104 Director Study Abroad ....Mr. Thomas KESARIS
15 Chief Human Resources Officer ....Ms. Zenobia HARGUST
19 Director Security/Safety ....Mr. Arthur G. GROVER
28 Director of Diversity ....Dr. Nicole R. STOKES
37 Director Student Financial Aid ....Ms. Elizabeth A. RIHL LEWINSKY
38 Director Student Counseling ....Dr. Gregory K. NICHOLLS
44 Director Annual Giving ....Mr. Michael A. RATH
86 Director Government Relations ....Mr. Wadell RIDLEY
96 Director of Purchasing ....Ms. Deborah T. TAVERA
102 Director Foundation/Corporate Rels ....Ms. Janet Y. SCHULZE
53 Dean Health Studies/Education ....Dr. Angela R. MCDONALD

St. Tikhon's Orthodox Theological Seminary (H)

PO Box 130, South Canaan PA 18459-0130
County: Wayne FICE Identification: 039193
Telephone: (570) 561-1818 Carnegie Class: Not Classified
FAX Number: N/A Calendar System: Semester
URL: www.stots.edu
Established: 1938 Annual Undergrad Tuition & Fees: N/A
Enrollment: N/A Coed
Affiliation or Control: Other IRS Status: 501(c)3
Highest Offering: First Professional Degree
Accreditation: THEOL

01 President ....Metr. Tikhon MOLLARD
03 Rector/CEO ....Abp. Michael DAHULICH
05 Seminary Dean/COO ....V.Rev. John PARKER
10 Chief Financial Officer ....Ms. Janet A. VANDUYN
04 Administrative Asst to Dean/COO ....Ms. Marina HITCHCOCK
08 Librarian ....Vacant
06 Registrar/Assoc Dean Academic Affs ....Dr. Paul J. WITEK
30 Dir Office of Mission Development ....Dr. David FOX
32 Director Student Life ....Fr. Ignatius GAUVAIN

Saint Vincent College (I)

300 Fraser Purchase Road, Latrobe PA 15650-2690
County: Westmoreland FICE Identification: 003368
Unit ID: 215798
Telephone: (724) 805-2500 Carnegie Class: Bac-A&S
FAX Number: (724) 805-2019 Calendar System: Semester
URL: www.stvincent.edu

Established: 1846 Annual Undergrad Tuition & Fees: $37,604
Enrollment: 1,634 Coed
Affiliation or Control: Roman Catholic IRS Status: 501(c)3
Highest Offering: Doctorate
Accreditation: M, ACBSP, ANEST

01 President Fr. Paul TAYLOR, OSB
05 VP Academic Affairs Dr. John SMETANKA
10 VP/Chief Finance/Admin Officer Mr. Richard WILLIAMS
111 VP Institutional Advancement Mr. David HOLLENBAUGH
32 VP Student Affairs Ms. Mary COLLINS
07 Dean of Admissions Ms. Heather KABALA
13 Chief Information Officer Mr. Peter E. MAHONEY
50 Dean McKenna Sch Bus/Econ/Govt Dr. Gary QUINLIVAN
81 Dean Science/Math & Computing Dr. Stephen M. JODIS
49 Dean Arts/Humanities/Social Science Dr. Margaret WATKINS
06 Registrar Ms. Celine R. BRUDNOK
08 Librarian Bro. David KELLY, OSB
30 Sr Director of Devel/Alumni Affairs Mr. Ben BECZE
36 Director Career Services Ms. Courtney BAUM
15 Director of Human Resources Ms. Judith MAHER
42 Director of Campus Ministry Rev. Killian LOCH, OSB
23 Director Wellness Center Ms. Gretchen FLOCK
19 Director Public Safety Ms. Stephanie FAGO
41 Athletic Director Rev. Myron KIRSCH, OSB
35 Dean of Students Mr. Robert BAUM
96 Director of Purchasing Mr. Terry NOEL
18 Director of Facility Management Mr. Douglas EPPLEY
40 Manager Book Center Rev. Anthony GROSSI, OSB
58 Coord of Graduate Studies Ms. Amanda GUNTHER
04 Executive Asst to President Ms. Lisa POOLE
104 Director Study Abroad Ms. Sara HART
37 Director Student Financial Aid Ms. Mary GAZAL
102 Dir Foundation/Govt/Corporate Rels Ms. Christine FOSCHIA
43 Dir Legal Services/General Counsel Mr. Bruce ANTKOWIAK
108 Director Assessment & IR Ms. Julia CAVALLO
26 Sr Dir Marketing/Communications Mr. Michael HUSTAVA
39 Asst Dir Res Life/Multicult Stdnts Mr. Ishmael SOLOMON

Saint Vincent Seminary (A)

300 Fraser Purchase Road, Latrobe PA 15650-2690
County: Westmoreland Identification: 666018
Unit ID: 215813
Telephone: (724) 805-2592 Carnegie Class: Spec-4-yr-Faith
FAX Number: (724) 532-5052 Calendar System: Semester
URL: www.saintvincentseminary.edu
Established: 1846 Annual Undergrad Tuition & Fees: N/A
Enrollment: 54 Coed
Affiliation or Control: Roman Catholic IRS Status: 501(c)3
Highest Offering: Master's
Accreditation: THEOL

01 Rector V.Rev. Edward M. MAZICH, OSB
00 Chancellor Rt Rev. Martin BARTEL, OSB
88 Director of Spiritual Formation Rev. Boniface N. HICKS, OSB
05 Academic Dean Rev. Patrick T. CRONAUER, OSB
03 Vice-Rector Rev. John-Mary TOMPKINS, OSB
42 Director of Liturgy Rev. Cyprian G. CONSTANTINE, OSB
88 Director of Pastoral Formation Rev. Jude BRADY
32 Dean of Students Rev. Emmanuel O. AFUNUGO
38 Dir of Pre-Theologian Formation Dr. Lawrence SUTTON
04 Administrative Asst to President Ms. Lisa POOLE
06 Registrar Ms. Celine BRUDNOK
07 Dean of Admissions Ms. Heather KABALA
08 Director of Libraries Br. David KELLY, OSB
09 Director of Institutional Research Vacant
10 Vice Pres Finance/Administration Vacant
101 Secretary of the Institution/Board Rev. Jeffrey S. NYARDY, OSB
26 Sr Director Marketing/Communication Mr. Mike HUSTAVA
13 Chief Info Technology Officer (CIO) Mr. Justin FABIN
15 Director Personnel Services Mrs. Judith MAHER
18 Chief Facilities/Physical Plant Mr. Douglas EPPLEY
19 Director Security/Safety Sgt. Stephanie FAGO
22 Dir Affirmative Action/EEO Miss Eileen FLINN
25 Chief Contracts/Grants Admin Ms. Christine L. FOSCHIA
26 Assoc Dir Marketing & Communication Vacant
29 Sr Dir Development & Alumni Rels Mr. Ben BECZE
30 Chief Development/Advancement Mr. Shannon JORDAN
37 Director Student Financial Aid Ms. Mary GAZAL
41 Athletic Director Rev. Myron KIRSCH, OSB
43 Dir Legal Services/General Counsel Mr. Bruce ANTKOWIAK
44 Director Annual or Planned Giving Mr. David HOLLENBAUGH
96 Director of Purchasing Mr. Terry NOEL
108 Director Institutional Assessment Mr. Joshua W. SHRUM
26 Dir of PR - Archabbey & Seminary Ms. Kim METZGAR
104 Director International Education Ms. Sara HART
106 Director Application Services Mr. Roberto WISNESCK
36 Director Student Placement Ms. Courtney BAUM
39 Asst Director Resident Life Mr. Colin MCLAUGHLIN
45 Chief Institutional Planning Office Mrs. Gina NALEVANKO
50 Dean of School of Business Dr. Gary M. QUINLIVAN
49 Dean Arts/Humanities & Social Sci Vacant
86 Assistant to President/Mission Rev. Thomas HART, OSB
117 Dir Technical/Cybersecurity Svcs Vacant
91 User Services Manager Mr. Joshua SEEVERS

Salus University (B)

8360 Old York Road, Elkins Park PA 19027-1516
County: Philadelphia FICE Identification: 003311
Unit ID: 214564
Telephone: (215) 780-1400 Carnegie Class: Spec-4-yr-Other Health
FAX Number: (215) 780-1325 Calendar System: Quarter
URL: www.salus.edu
Established: 1919 Annual Undergrad Tuition & Fees: N/A
Enrollment: 1,280 Coed
Affiliation or Control: Independent Non-Profit IRS Status: 501(c)3
Highest Offering: Doctorate
Accreditation: M, ARCPA, AUD, OPT, OPTR, OT, SP

01 President Dr. Michael H. MITTLEMAN
05 Vice President Faculty Affairs Dr. Barry ECKERT
10 Vice Pres Finance/Business Affairs Mr. Donald KATES
17 Vice Pres Clinical Services Dr. John GAAL
45 Vice Pres Institutional Planning Vacant
32 Dean Student Affairs Dr. James CALDWELL
09 Asst Dir Research Admin Mr. Nicholaus JONES
06 Registrar Ms. Shannon BOSS
13 Chief Information Officer Ms. Regina SCRIVEN
38 Director Personal/Prof Development Dr. James CALDWELL
37 Assoc Dean Student Financial Affs Ms. Jamie SCHLANG
18 Director Physical Plant Mr. Richard ECHEVARRI
30 Director of Development Ms. Jackie PATTERSON
26 Director Publications/Communication Ms. Alexis ABATE
29 Director Alumni Relations/Giving Ms. Olivia SWEGER
51 Coord Continuing/Post-Graduate Educ Mrs. Melissa VITEK
40 Bookstore Manager Mr. Joe NOCE
24 Director Instructional Media Mr. Glenn ROEDEL
36 Dir Student Placement/Student Affs Mr. Ryan HOLLISTER
84 Director Enrollment Management Dr. Jim CALDWELL
88 Exec Dir Inst Visually Impaired Dr. Brooke KRUEMMLING
08 Head Librarian Ms. Marietta DOOLEY
19 Director of Security Mr. Carlos RODRIGUEZ
15 Dir Human Res/Affirm Action/Facil Ms. Maura KEENAN
96 Director of Purchasing Ms. Lydia FRIEL
28 Director of Diversity Dr. Juliana WILLIAMS

Seton Hill University (C)

1 Seton Hill Drive, Greensburg PA 15601-1599
County: Westmoreland FICE Identification: 003362
Unit ID: 215947
Telephone: (724) 834-2200 Carnegie Class: Masters/M
FAX Number: N/A Calendar System: Semester
URL: www.setonhill.edu
Established: 1883 Annual Undergrad Tuition & Fees: $37,946
Enrollment: 1,935 Coed
Affiliation or Control: Roman Catholic IRS Status: 501(c)3
Highest Offering: Doctorate
Accreditation: M, ARCPA, DENT, DIETC, EXSC, IACBE, MFCD, MUS, PTA, SW

01 President Dr. Mary FINGER
88 VP Mission Sr. Maureen O'BRIEN, SC
05 Provost Sr. Susan YOCHUM, SC
10 Vice Pres Finance & Business Ms. Jennifer LUNDY
111 Vice Pres Institutional Advancement Ms. Molly ROBB SHIMKO
13 Chief Information Officer Ms. Melissa ALSING
84 Vice Pres Enrollment Management Mr. Brett FRESHOUR
21 Controller Mr. Brent JACKSON
32 Vice President for Student Affairs Dr. Rosalie CARPENTER
07 Director Undergraduate Admissions Ms. Amanda GODULA
08 Director of Library Mr. David STANLEY
29 Director of Alumni Relations Ms. Ashley ZWIERZELEWSKI
37 Director of Financial Aid Ms. Tracey DE BAEZ SNYDER
36 Director of Career Development Ms. Renee STAREK
15 Asst VP Human Resources Mrs. Darlene SAUERS
18 Director Facilities Mr. Cale GEARY
41 Executive Athletic Director Mr. Chris SNYDER
42 Director Campus Ministry Mr. Tony KRZMARZICK
06 Registrar Ms. Constance BECKEL
38 Director Student Counseling Ms. Teresa BASSI-COOK
09 Director of Institutional Research Dr. Jason DRAPER
26 Chief Public Relations Officer Ms. Jennifer REEGER
96 Director of Purchasing Mr. Charles O'NEILL
19 Director Public Safety/Police Chief Ms. Michele PROCTOR
22 Dir Affirmative Action/EEO Ms. Darlene SAUERS
25 Dir Grants & Government Support Ms. Cynthia FERRARI
39 Director Student Housing Mr. Cory CAMPBELL
04 Exec Asst to the President/Provost Ms. Jennifer ZEMBA
100 Chief of Staff Ms. Carol BILLMAN
43 General Counsel Ms. Imogene CATHEY
28 Director of Diversity Dr. Adriel HILTON

South Hills School of Business and Technology (D)

508 58th Street, Altoona PA 16602
Telephone: (814) 944-6134 Identification: 770772
Accreditation: ACCSC, CAHIIM, MAAB

South Hills School of Business and Technology (E)

480 Waupelani Drive, State College PA 16801-4516
County: Centre FICE Identification: 013263
Unit ID: 216083
Telephone: (814) 234-7755 Carnegie Class: Assoc/HT-High Trad
FAX Number: (814) 234-0926 Calendar System: Quarter
URL: www.southhills.edu
Established: 1970 Annual Undergrad Tuition & Fees: $18,475
Enrollment: 307 Coed
Affiliation or Control: Proprietary IRS Status: Proprietary
Highest Offering: Associate Degree
Accreditation: ACCSC, CAHIIM, DMS, MAAB

00 Owner Mrs. Maralyn MAZZA
01 President Mr. S. Paul MAZZA, III
11 Campus Director Mr. Mark MAGGS
05 Academic Affairs Officer Ms. Ingrid THOMPSON
07 Director of Admissions/Marketing Mr. Glenn SLATER
37 Director Student Financial Aid Mr. LeRoy SPICER
20 Director of Education/Reg Affairs Ms. Natalie LOMBARDO-BEAVER

Susquehanna University (F)

514 University Avenue, Selinsgrove PA 17870-1025
County: Snyder FICE Identification: 003369
Unit ID: 216278
Telephone: (570) 374-0101 Carnegie Class: Bac-A&S
FAX Number: (570) 372-4040 Calendar System: Semester
URL: www.susqu.edu
Established: 1858 Annual Undergrad Tuition & Fees: $51,140
Enrollment: 2,241 Coed
Affiliation or Control: Evangelical Lutheran Church In America
IRS Status: 501(c)3
Highest Offering: Master's
Accreditation: M, MUS

01 President Dr. Jonathan GREEN
100 VP & Chief of Staff Vacant
05 Provost/Dean of Faculty Dr. Dave RAMSARAN
10 Executive VP for Finance & Admin Mr. Michael COYNE
111 Vice President for Advancement Ms. Melissa KOMORA
84 VP for Enrollment & Student Fin Svc Mr. Delorean J. MENIFEE
32 VP Student Engagement & Success Dr. Susan LANTZ
20 Assoc Provost/Dean A&S Dr. Valerie G. MARTIN
50 Dean Weis School of Business Dr. Matthew ROUSU
26 VP for Marketing & Communications Mr. Aaron MARTIN
112 Asst VP Adv/Major & Planned Giving Ms. Kim ANDRETTA
04 Senior Admin Asst to the President Ms. Sharon POPE
38 Dean Health & Wellness Dr. Stacey PEARSON-WHARTON
89 Director of First Year Experience Ms. Samantha PROFFITT
22 Asst Dean Student Div & Inclusion Ms. Dena SALERNO
07 Director of Admission Mr. Philip BETZ
08 Director of the Library Mr. Robert SIECZKIEWICZ
37 Director of Student Financial Svcs Mr. Justin RUMMEL
06 Registrar Ms. Alison A. RICHARD
42 University Chaplain Rev. Scott M. KERSHNER
13 Chief Information Officer Ms. Jennifer SERVIDO
41 Director of Athletics Mr. Sharief HASHIM
18 Director of Facilities Management Mr. Chris C. BAILEY
36 Asst Provost/Dir Career Development Ms. Michaeline SHUMAN
88 Director of Event Management Ms. Michelle HARMAN
29 Asst VP Alumni/Parent & Donor Ms. Becky DEITRICK
108 Asst Prov of Inst Effectiveness Ms. Danielle BROWN
25 Grants Coordinator Mr. Malcolm DERK
104 Dean of Global Programs Dr. Scott MANNING
15 VP of Human Resources Ms. Jennifer BUCHER
19 Director Public Safety Mr. Angelo MARTIN
92 Director of Honors Program Dr. Marcos KRIEGER
28 Chief Inclusion/Diversity Officer Mr. Michael DIXON

Swarthmore College (G)

500 College Avenue, Swarthmore PA 19081-1390
County: Delaware FICE Identification: 003370
Unit ID: 216287
Telephone: (610) 328-8000 Carnegie Class: Bac-A&S
FAX Number: (610) 328-8000 Calendar System: Semester
URL: www.swarthmore.edu
Established: 1864 Annual Undergrad Tuition & Fees: $54,456
Enrollment: 1,437 Coed
Affiliation or Control: Independent Non-Profit IRS Status: 501(c)3
Highest Offering: Master's
Accreditation: M

01 President Valerie A. SMITH
05 Provost & Dean of the Faculty Sarah WILLIE LEBRETON
10 Vice President Finance & Admin Gregory N. BROWN
111 Vice President for Advancement Elizabeth BOLUCH WOOD
15 Int Vice Pres for Human Resources Catherine GEDDIS
26 VP Communications Andy HIRSCH
07 Vice Pres & Dean of Admissions Jim BOCK
18 Assoc VP Sustainable Fac Op/Cap Pln Andrew FEICK
21 Asst Vice Pres Finance & Controller Alice TURBIVILLE
32 Vice President for Student Affairs James TERHUNE
28 Asst Dean of Diversity/Inclusion Imaani EL-BURKI
06 Registrar Kristen SMITH
08 College Librarian Peggy SEIDEN
108 Asst VP Institutional Effect/Asses Robin H. SHORES
29 Director Alumni & Parent Engagement Lisa SHAFER
37 Director of Financial Aid Varo L. DUFFINS
36 Senior Assoc Dir Career Services Erin MASSEY
19 Director of Public Safety Michael HILL
43 General Counsel Sharmaine LAMAR
23 Director Worth Health Center Casey ANDERSON
38 Director Psychological Services David RAMIREZ
41 Director Physical Educ/Athletics Brad KOCH
13 Chief Info Technology Officer Joel COOPER
35 Director Student Engagement Rachel HEAD
104 Director Off-Campus Study Pat MARTIN
39 Director of Residential Communities Estrellita LONGORIA
105 Web Developer Les LEACH
22 Dir Equal Opportunity & Engagement Vacant
96 Sr Manager Strategic Sourcing Chris KANE
102 Director Institutional Relations David FOREMAN

Talmudical Yeshiva of Philadelphia (A)

6063 Drexel Road, Philadelphia PA 19131-1296
County: Philadelphia　FICE Identification: 012523
Unit ID: 216311
Telephone: (215) 477-1000　Carnegie Class: Spec-4-yr-Faith
FAX Number: (215) 477-5065　Calendar System: Semester
Established: 1953　Annual Undergrad Tuition & Fees: $9,725
Enrollment: 132　Male
Affiliation or Control: Independent Non-Profit　IRS Status: 501(c)3
Highest Offering: First Talmudic Degree
Accreditation: RABN

01 Chief Executive Officer (President) .... Mr. Alexander TAUB
05 Dean .... Rabbi Shmuel KAMENETSKY
05 Dean .... Rabbi Yehuda SVEI
05 Dean .... Rabbi Sholom KAMENETSKY

Temple University (B)

1801 N Broad Street, Philadelphia PA 19122
County: Philadelphia　FICE Identification: 003371
Unit ID: 216339
Telephone: (215) 204-7405　Carnegie Class: DU-Highest
FAX Number: (215) 204-5600　Calendar System: Semester
URL: www.temple.edu
Established: 1884　Annual Undergrad Tuition & Fees (In-State): $16,970
Enrollment: 37,236　Coed
Affiliation or Control: State Related　IRS Status: 501(c)3
Highest Offering: Doctorate
Accreditation: M, #ARCPA, ART, CAATE, CAHIIM, CAPRT, CARTE, CLPSY, DANCE, DENT, @DIETC, IPSY, JOUR, LAW, LSAR, MED, MUS, NURSE, OT, PCSAS, PH, PHAR, PLNG, POD, PTA, SCPSY, SP, SW, THEA

01 President .... Dr. Jason WINGARD
03 VP for Public Affairs .... Mr. William T. BERGMAN, JR.
05 Exec VP and Provost .... Ms. JoAnne A. EPPS
11 Exec VP & COO .... Mr. Kevin G. CLARK
43 VP & University Counsel .... Mr. Michael B. GEBHARDT
32 VP for Student Affairs .... Dr. Theresa A. POWELL
13 VP Computer/CIO .... Ms. Cindy LEAVITT
17 President/CEO Health Sys/Hospitals .... Mr. Michael A. YOUNG
26 Sr Vice Provost Strategic Comm .... Dr. Elizabeth LEEBRON TUTELMAN
10 VP/CFO & Treasurer .... Mr. Kenneth H. KAISER
85 VP International Affairs .... Dr. Hai-Lung DAI
35 Assoc VP/Dean of Students .... Dr. Stephanie IVES
111 VP Institutional Advancement .... Mr. James F. CAWLEY
46 VP for Research Administration .... Dr. Michele M. MASUCCI
18 VP Planning & Capital Projects .... Mr. Gennaro J. LEVA
21 Sr Assoc VP Finance .... Mr. William J. WILKINSON
109 Assoc VP Business Services .... Mr. Michael D. SCALES
15 Assoc VP Human Resources .... Ms. Sharon I. BOYLE
21 Assoc VP/Controller .... Mr. David MARINO
22 Sr Advisor Equity/Diver/Inclusion .... Ms. Valerie I. HARRISON
21 Asst VP Fin/Admin & Treasurer .... Ms. Kathryn P. D'ANGELO
20 Vice Provost for Faculty Affairs .... Dr. Kevin J. DELANEY
20 Vice Provost Undergrad Studies .... Dr. Daniel BERMAN
108 Vice Provost Assessment .... Dr. Jodi LEVINE LAUFGRABEN
08 Dean for University Libraries .... Mr. Joseph P. LUCIA
06 Registrar .... Mr. Bhavesh BAMBHROLIA
41 Interim Director of Athletics .... Mr. Francis J. DUNPHY
38 Int Dir Tuttleman Counseling Svcs .... Dr. Daniel DENGEL
36 Director Career Services .... Ms. Shannon CONKLIN
88 Chief Compliance Officer .... Mr. Alejandro J. DIAZ
09 Director IR/Assessment .... Ms. Gina L. CALZAFERRI
104 Director Educ Abroad & Overseas .... Ms. Maureen GORDON
23 Sr Admin Student & Employee Health .... Dr. Mark DENYS
37 Director Student Financial Svcs .... Ms. Emilie VANTRIESTE
97 Vice Provost University College .... Dr. Vicki Lewis MCGARVEY
96 Director Purchasing .... Ms. Donna L. SCHWEIBENZ
113 Dir Financial Accounting/Bursar .... Mr. Conrad MUTH
20 Assoc Vice Provost Undergrad .... Ms. Michele O'CONNOR
12 Director TU Center City .... Mr. William PARSHALL
84 Vice Provost Enroll Mgmt .... Mr. Shawn L. ABBOTT
40 Bookstore General Manager .... Mr. James HANLEY
49 Dean College of Liberal Arts .... Dr. Richard DEEG
53 Dean Col of Education & Human Dev .... Dr. Greg ANDERSON
61 Dean Beasley School of Law .... Mr. Gregory M. MANDEL
64 Dean Boyer College of Music .... Dr. Robert T. STROKER
57 Dean Tyler School of Art .... Ms. Susan CAHAN
50 Dean College of Business & Mgmt .... Dr. Ronald ANDERSON
52 Dean Kornberg School of Dentistry .... Dr. Amid ISMAIL
63 Int Dean Lewis Katz Sch of Medicine .... Dr. Amy J. GOLDBERG
67 Dean School of Pharmacy .... Dr. Jayanth PANYAM
54 Dean College of Engineering .... Dr. Keya SADEGHIPOUR
88 Dean School of Podiatric Medicine .... Dr. John A. MATTIACCI
72 Dean College of Science & Tech .... Dr. Michael KLEIN
60 Dean Klein College of Media & Comm .... Mr. David BOARDMAN
69 Dean College of Public Health .... Dr. Laura SIMINOFF
88 Dean Sch Sport/Tourism/Hosp Mgmt .... Dr. Ronald ANDERSON
12 Dean Temple Japan Campus .... Mr. Matthew WILSON
12 Dean Temple Rome .... Dr. Emilia ZANKINA
07 Director of Admissions .... Ms. Karin W. MORMANDO
101 VP & Secretary of Board of Trustees .... Ms. Anne K. NADOL
19 Executive Director Public Safety .... Mr. Charles LEONE

Thaddeus Stevens College of Technology (C)

750 E King Street, Lancaster PA 17602-3198
County: Lancaster　FICE Identification: 007912
Unit ID: 216296
Telephone: (717) 299-7731　Carnegie Class: Assoc/HVT-High Trad
FAX Number: (717) 299-7748　Calendar System: Semester
URL: www.stevenscollege.edu
Established: 1905　Annual Undergrad Tuition & Fees (In-State): $8,450
Enrollment: 1,227　Coed
Affiliation or Control: State　IRS Status: 501(c)3
Highest Offering: Associate Degree
Accreditation: M

01 President .... Mr. Pedro RIVERA
03 Vice President/Spec Asst to Pres .... Dr. Timothy BIANCHI
05 Dean of Academic Affairs .... Mr. Michael DEGROFT
10 Vice President Finance and Admin .... Mrs. Betty TOMPOS
32 Director of Student Services .... Dr. Christopher METZLER
84 Dean of Enrollment Services .... Ms. Melissa WISNIEWSKI
08 Learning Resources Center Director .... Ms. Jennifer LANDIS
108 Director Assessment/Accountability .... Ms. Cheryl LUTZ
15 Human Resource Specialist .... Ms. Heather BURKY
26 Director of Marketing .... Ms. Ann VALUCH
86 Exec Dir Government Affairs .... Mr. Alex MUNRO
41 Dir Student Svcs/Athletic Director .... Dr. Christopher METZLER
30 Director of Development .... Mr. Warren TAYLOR
36 Director of Career Services .... Ms. Laurie GROVE
38 Coordinator of Student Counseling .... Ms. Debra SCHUCH
39 Director Residence Life/Registrar .... Mr. Jason KUNTZ
18 Facilities Maintenance Manager .... Mr. Darryl NUNN, JR.
13 Director of Information Technology .... Gregory SEITZ
37 Director of Financial Aid .... Ms. Emily SMOKER
06 Registrar .... Stacy SCOTT

† Qualified individuals are eligible for full scholarships based on family/financial status.

Thiel College (D)

75 College Avenue, Greenville PA 16125-2181
County: Mercer　FICE Identification: 003376
Unit ID: 216357
Telephone: (724) 589-2000　Carnegie Class: Bac-Diverse
FAX Number: (724) 589-2850　Calendar System: Semester
URL: www.thiel.edu
Established: 1866　Annual Undergrad Tuition & Fees: $33,520
Enrollment: 768　Coed
Affiliation or Control: Evangelical Lutheran Church In America
IRS Status: 501(c)3
Highest Offering: Master's
Accreditation: M, #ARCPA, @SP

01 President .... Dr. Susan TRAVERSO
05 VP Academic Affairs/Dean of College .... Dr. Elizabeth FROMBGEN
111 Vice Pres for College Advancement .... Ms. Roberta LEONARD
10 VP Finance & Administration .... Ms. Amy ARBOGAST
13 Director IT Services .... Mr. Homer BLOOM
04 Executive Asst to President .... Mrs. Amy TACZANOWSKY
32 VP of Student Life .... Mr. Michael MCKINNEY
84 VP Enrollment Management .... Mrs. Ashley ZULLO
20 Assoc Academic Dean .... Dr. Greg BUTCHER
26 Exec Dir Communications/Marketing .... Mr. Richard ORR
41 Director of Athletics .... Ms. Amy SCHAFER
112 Dir of Special & Planned Giving .... Mr. Mark BATT
29 Director of Alumni Relations .... Mr. David HUMMEL
18 Director of Facilities .... Mr. Andrew M. HOUPT
08 Director Library .... Ms. Tressa A. SNYDER
15 Director Human Resources .... Mrs. Jennifer CLARK
36 Director of Career Development .... Ms. Liza SCHAEF
19 Chief of Police/Dir Public Safety .... Mr. Dennis BISH
06 Registrar .... Ms. Denise UREY
42 Campus Pastor .... Rev. Brian T. RIDDLE
07 Director of Admissions .... Mrs. Sonya L. LAPIKAS
37 Exec Director Financial Aid .... Ms. Cynthia H. FARRELL
28 Assoc Dean for Diversity .... Mr. Anthony E. JONES
38 Director Counseling Center .... Ms. Melanie R. BROADWATER

Thomas Jefferson University (E)

925 Chestnut Street, Suite #110, Philadelphia PA 19107
County: Philadelphia　FICE Identification: 012393
Unit ID: 216366
Telephone: (215) 955-6000　Carnegie Class: DU-Higher
FAX Number: (215) 955-1122　Calendar System: Quarter
URL: www.jefferson.edu
Established: 1824　Annual Undergrad Tuition & Fees: $41,866
Enrollment: 8,286　Coed
Affiliation or Control: Independent Non-Profit　IRS Status: 501(c)3
Highest Offering: Doctorate
Accreditation: M, ACBSP, ANEST, ARCPA, ART, CAATE, CAMPEP, CIDA, CYTO, DENT, @DIETC, DMS, EMT, LSAR, MED, MFCD, MIDWF, MT, NURSE, OT, OTA, PAST, PERF, PH, PHAR, PTA, RAD, RADDOS, RADMAG, RTT, @SP

01 President/CEO Jefferson Health .... Dr. Stephen K. KLASKO
11 EVP & Chief Operating Officer .... Ms. Kathleen GALLAGHER
100 EVP/Chief of Staff .... Mr. John EKARIUS
05 Provost/EVP Academic Affairs .... Dr. Mark L. TYKOCINSKI
26 EVP Univ Marketing/Relations .... Mr. Charles LEWIS
10 Exec VP/Chief Financial Officer .... Mr. Peter L. DEANGELIS, JR.
111 EVP Institutional Advancement .... Dr. Elizabeth DALE
43 EVP & Chief Legal Counsel .... Ms. Cristina G. CAVALIERI
46 Assoc Provost Clinical Research .... Dr. David WHELLAN
18 Sr Vice Pres for Facilities Mgmt .... Mr. Clayton MITCHELL
15 EVP/Chief Human Resources Ofcr .... Mr. Clayton FITZHUGH
28 EVP/Chief Diversity/Inclusion Ofcr .... Ms. Lisette MARTINEZ
58 Dean Jeff College of Life Sciences .... Dr. Gerald GRUNWALD
63 Dean Sidney Kimmel Medical College .... Dr. Mark L. TYKOCINSKI
66 Dean Jeff Col of Nursing .... Dr. Marie MARINO
67 Dean Jefferson College of Pharmacy .... Dr. Rebecca FINLEY
76 Dean Jeff Col Health Professions .... Dr. Michael DRYER
69 Interim Dean Jeff Sch of Pop Health .... Dr. Willie OGLESBY
32 Dean of Student & Admissions SKMC .... Dr. Clara A. CALLAHAN
07 Director of Admissions .... Ms. Erin FINN
06 University Registrar .... Mr. Kris PELUSZAK
29 Exec Director of Alumni Assoc SKMC .... Ms. Cristina GESO
08 University Librarian .... Mr. Anthony FRISBY
23 Medical Director Univ Health Svcs .... Dr. Ellen M. O'CONNOR
24 Director Medical Media Services .... Mr. Pejman MAKARECHI
35 Assoc VP Student Affairs .... Ms. Jennifer FOGERTY
39 Manager Housing/Residence Life .... Ms. Laurie YUNKE
37 Univ Director Student Financial Aid .... Ms. Susan MCFADDEN
40 Director Bookstore .... Mr. Travis HARLEY
13 Chief Information Officer .... Mr. Nassar NIZAMI
19 Director of Security .... Mr. Joseph BYHAM
85 Dir International Exchange Services .... Ms. Janice M. BOGEN
07 Dir Admission/Recruitment/Grad Stds .... Mr. Marc STEARNS
22 Assoc Dean Diversity/Minority Affs .... Dr. Bernard LOPEZ
96 Director of Purchasing .... Mr. Robert C. BURKHOLDER
35 Associate Provost Student Affairs .... Dr. Charles A. POHL
04 Executive Associate to President .... Ms. Grace L. HARDESKI
09 Interim Dir of Inst Research .... Dr. Raelynn COOTER
101 Secretary of the Institution/Board .... Ms. Michele R. DOUGHERTY
102 Dir Foundation/Corporate Relations .... Ms. Molly GERBER
103 Dir Workforce/Career Development .... Ms. Jennifer M. GRONSKY
105 Director Web Services .... Ms. Chris MCNAMEE-SMITH
25 Dir Grants/Research Admin .... Mr. Timothy SCHAILEY
36 Director Student Placement .... Ms. Jennifer GRONSKY
38 Director Student Counseling .... Dr. Deanna NOBLEZA
44 Director Annual or Planned Giving .... Ms. Lisa REPKO
45 Chief Institutional Planning .... Vacant
84 Director Enrollment Management .... Ms. Erin M. FINN
86 Director Government Relations .... Mr. Hugh J. LAVERY
90 Director Academic Computing .... Mr. Michael DEVENNEY
104 Director Study Abroad .... Ms. Madeleine WILCOX
106 Dean Online Education/E-learning .... Dr. Anthony FRISBY
41 Athletic Director .... Mr. Thomas SHIRLEY
50 Dean of Business Administration .... Dr. Philip RUSSEL
53 Dean School of Education .... Dr. Matt D. BAKER
54 Dean School of Engineering .... Dr. Ron KANDER
79 Dean Col of Humanities and Science .... Dr. Barbara KIMMELMAN
48 Dean Architecture/Built Environment .... Dr. Barbara KLINKHAMMER

Triangle Tech (F)

191 Performance Road, Sunbury PA 17801
Telephone: (570) 988-0700　Identification: 770586
Accreditation: ACCSC

Triangle Tech, Bethlehem (G)

3184 Airport Road, Bethlehem PA 18017
Telephone: (610) 266-2910　Identification: 770587
Accreditation: ACCSC

Triangle Tech, DuBois (H)

225 Tannery Row Rd, Falls Creek PA 15840
County: Clearfield　FICE Identification: 021744
Unit ID: 216454
Telephone: (814) 371-2090　Carnegie Class: Assoc/HVT-High Trad
FAX Number: (814) 371-9227　Calendar System: Semester
URL: www.triangle-tech.edu
Established: 1982　Annual Undergrad Tuition & Fees: $17,800
Enrollment: 132　Coed
Affiliation or Control: Proprietary　IRS Status: Proprietary
Highest Offering: Associate Degree
Accreditation: ACCSC

01 Director .... Mr. Jarred HETRICK
05 Academic Affairs Advisor .... Mrs. Joan HOCKMAN
07 Admiss/Recruiting/Training Coord .... Mrs. Joy BURKE
36 Career Advisor .... Ms. Erica HAND
37 Financial Aid Administrator .... Ms. Michelle L. JASHINSKI

Triangle Tech, Greensburg (I)

222 E Pittsburgh Street, Suite A, Greensburg PA 15601-3304
County: Westmoreland　FICE Identification: 021290
Unit ID: 216445
Telephone: (724) 832-1050　Carnegie Class: Spec 2-yr-Tech
FAX Number: (724) 834-0325　Calendar System: Semester
URL: www.triangle-tech.edu
Established: 1944　Annual Undergrad Tuition & Fees: $17,758
Enrollment: 127　Coed
Affiliation or Control: Proprietary　IRS Status: Proprietary
Highest Offering: Associate Degree
Accreditation: ACCSC

00 Chairman/CEO .... James R. AGRAS

01 President ... Timothy J. MCMAHON
05 Exec Dir of Compliance & Education ... Deborah G. HEPBURN
12 Director of Branch Campus/CEO ... John GOLOFSKI

Triangle Tech, Pittsburgh (A)

1940 Perrysville Avenue, Pittsburgh PA 15214-3897
County: Allegheny FICE Identification: 007839
Unit ID: 216436
Telephone: (412) 359-1000 Carnegie Class: Assoc/HVT-Mix Trad/Non
FAX Number: (412) 359-1012 Calendar System: Semester
URL: www.triangle-tech.edu
Established: 1944 Annual Undergrad Tuition & Fees: $17,792
Enrollment: 109 Coed
Affiliation or Control: Proprietary IRS Status: Proprietary
Highest Offering: Associate Degree
Accreditation: ACCSC

00 Chairman/Chief Executive Officer ... James R. AGRAS
01 President ... Timothy J. MCMAHON
15 Vice President of Human Resources ... Sofia A. JANIS
12 School Director/Title IX Coord ... Christopher LUND
05 Exec Dir of Compliance & Education ... Deborah G. HEPBURN
07 Executive Director of Admissions ... Terry KUCIC
37 Exec Dir of Financial Aid ... Catherine A. WAXTER

Trinity Episcopal School for Ministry (B)

311 11th Street, Ambridge PA 15003-2397
County: Beaver FICE Identification: 022993
Unit ID: 216463
Telephone: (724) 266-3838 Carnegie Class: Spec-4-yr-Faith
FAX Number: (724) 266-4617 Calendar System: Semester
URL: www.tsm.edu
Established: 1976 Annual Graduate Tuition & Fees: N/A
Enrollment: 160 Coed
Affiliation or Control: Protestant Episcopal IRS Status: 501(c)3
Highest Offering: Doctorate; No Undergraduates
Accreditation: THEOL

01 Dean/President ... Rev. Henry L. THOMPSON
05 Academic Dean ... Dr. Erika MOORE
32 Dean of Students/Director of Chapel ... Mr. Geoffrey MACKEY
07 Director of Admissions/Recruitment ... Mrs. Janessa FISK
11 Dean of Administration/Registrar ... Mrs. Stacey WILLIARD
30 Director of Development ... Vacant
26 Director of Communications ... Vacant
15 Human Resources Administrator ... Mrs. Elaine LUCCI
13 Information Technology Manager ... Mr. Steve SIMS
08 Chief Library Officer ... Mrs. Susanah HANSON
106 Director of Online Education ... Mr. Russ WARREN
18 Director of Facilities ... Mr. Justin FISK
29 Director Alumni Affairs ... Mr. Jack WALSH
10 Director of Accounting ... Mr. John MCCOY
04 Admin Assistant to the President ... Ms. Allyson MARTIN
36 Director Student Placement ... Rev. Karen STEVENSON
44 Director Annual Giving ... Ms. Carrie SHREWSBURY

United Career Institute (C)

PO Box 278 1015 Mount Braddock Road,
Mount Braddock PA 15465-0278
Telephone: (724) 437-4600 Identification: 666035
Accreditation: ABHES

† Branch campus of West Virginia Junior College, Morgantown, WV.

United Lutheran Seminary (D)

61 Seminary Ridge, Gettysburg PA 17325-1795
County: Adams FICE Identification: 003291
Unit ID: 213631
Telephone: (717) 338-3000 Carnegie Class: Spec-4-yr-Faith
FAX Number: N/A Calendar System: 4/1/4
URL: www.unitedlutheranseminary.edu
Established: 1826 Annual Graduate Tuition & Fees: N/A
Enrollment: 390 Coed
Affiliation or Control: Evangelical Lutheran Church In America
IRS Status: 501(c)3
Highest Offering: Doctorate; No Undergraduates
Accreditation: M, THEOL

01 President ... Dr. R. Guy ERWIN
05 Dean /VP Student Svcs ... Dr. J. Jayakiran SEBASTIAN
111 Interim VP Advancement ... Mr. Conor BROOKS
10 Chief Financial Officer/CFO ... Mr. Buff CARLSON
26 Dir Strategic Marketing & Comm ... Ms. Linda FIORE
08 Library Director and Archivist ... Mr. Evan E. BOYD
37 Director of Financial Aid ... Mr. Tyrone GADSON
06 Registrar ... Ms. Julie RITTER
13 Director of IT Systems/Ed Tech ... Mr. Donald L. REDMAN
28 Dir of Diversity/Equity/Inclusion ... Vacant

The University of the Arts (E)

320 S Broad Street, Philadelphia PA 19102-4944
County: Philadelphia FICE Identification: 003350
Unit ID: 215105
Telephone: (215) 717-6030 Carnegie Class: Spec-4-yr-Arts
FAX Number: (215) 717-6045 Calendar System: Semester
URL: www.uarts.edu
Established: 1876 Annual Undergrad Tuition & Fees: $46,680
Enrollment: 1,530 Coed
Affiliation or Control: Independent Non-Profit IRS Status: 501(c)3
Highest Offering: Doctorate
Accreditation: M, MUS

01 President ... Mr. David YAGER
05 Vice President for Academic Affairs ... Ms. Carol GRANEY
04 Admin Assistant to the President ... Ms. Melanie ROMAY
10 Vice Pres Finance/Administration ... Mr. Stephen LIGHTCAP
13 Vice Pres Technology & Info Svcs ... Vacant
32 VP Enroll Mgmt & Student Affairs ... Mr. Rick LONGO
111 Vice Pres Advancement ... Mr. Andrew PACK
06 Registrar ... Mr. Jeffrey KISLER
04 Senior Administrative Assistant ... Ms. Carley JOHNSON
28 Title IX Coord & Diversity Admin ... Ms. Lexi MORRISON
07 AVP of Admissions ... Ms. Heeseung LEE
15 AVP for Human Resources ... Ms. Christine SCHAEFER
26 AVP for Enrollment Marketing ... Ms. Maria RAHA
37 AVP for Student Financial Aid ... Ms. Mariann CARDONICK
09 Dir of Inst Rsrch & Effectiveness ... Dr. Deborah DUFFY

University of Pennsylvania (F)

1 College Hall, Room 100, Philadelphia PA 19104-6830
County: Philadelphia FICE Identification: 003378
Unit ID: 215062
Telephone: (215) 898-5000 Carnegie Class: DU-Highest
FAX Number: (215) 898-5756 Calendar System: Semester
URL: www.upenn.edu
Established: 1740 Annual Undergrad Tuition & Fees: $60,042
Enrollment: 26,552 Coed
Affiliation or Control: Independent Non-Profit IRS Status: 501(c)3
Highest Offering: Doctorate
Accreditation: M, ANEST, CAMPEP, CEA, CLPSY, DENT, IPSY, LAW, LSAR, MED, MIDWF, NURSE, PAST, PCSAS, PH, PLNG, SW, VET

01 President ... Dr. Amy GUTMANN
03 Executive Vice President ... Mr. Craig CARNAROLI
05 Provost ... Dr. Wendell E. PRITCHETT
20 Vice Provost for Education ... Dr. Karen DETLEFSEN
06 Registrar ... Ms. Margaret KIP
07 Dean of Admissions ... Ms. Whitney SOULE
32 Vice Provost University Life ... Dr. Mamta ACCAPADI
10 Vice Pres Finance & Treasurer ... Ms. MaryFrances MCCOURT
18 Vice Pres Facil/Real Est Svcs ... Ms. Anne PAPAGEORGE
17 CEO Univ of PA Health System ... Mr. Kevin B. MAHONEY
08 Vice Provost/Dir of Libraries ... Ms. Constantia CONSTANTINOU
13 Vice Pres Info Technology/CIO ... Mr. Thomas H. MURPHY
100 SVP & Chief of Staff ... Mr. Gregory S. ROST
28 SVP Inst Affs/Chief Diversity Ofcr ... Ms. Joann MITCHELL
30 SVP Development/Alumni Relations ... Mr. John H. ZELLER
15 Vice Pres Human Resources ... Dr. John J. HEUER
86 Vice Pres Govt & Cmty Affairs ... Mr. Jeffrey COOPER
19 Vice President Public Safety ... Ms. Maureen RUSH
26 Vice Pres for Univ Communications ... Mr. Stephen J. MACCARTHY
21 Vice Pres Business Services ... Ms. Marie D. WITT
114 Vice Pres Budget Mgmt Analysis ... Mr. Trevor C. LEWIS
43 Senior Vice Pres/General Counsel ... Ms. Wendy S. WHITE
101 VP & University Secretary ... Ms. Medha NARVEKAR
31 VP Social Equity & Community ... Rev. Charles L. HOWARD
09 VP Inst Rsrch/Sr Adv to Pres ... Dr. Stacey J. LOPEZ
20 Deputy Provost ... Dr. Beth A. WINKELSTEIN
20 Vice Provost Faculty Affairs ... Dr. Laura PERNA
29 Assoc VP Alumni Relations ... Mr. Fredrick H. WAMPLER
46 Sr Vice Provost for Research ... Dr. Dawn A. BONNELL
88 Assoc Vice Pres Rsrch Svcs ... Ms. Elizabeth D. PELOSO
116 VP Audit/Compliance & Privacy ... Mr. Gregory J. PELLICANO
31 Assoc VP/Dir Ctr Cmty Partnerships ... Dr. Ira HARKAVY
28 Assoc Vice Prov Equity & Access ... Rev. William GIPSON
21 Comptroller ... Mr. Russell DI LEO
63 Exec Vice Pres/Dean Sch of Medicine ... Dr. J. L. JAMESON
49 Dean School Arts & Sciences ... Dr. Steven J. FLUHARTY
54 Dean School of Engr/Applied Science ... Dr. Vijay KUMAR
66 Dean School of Nursing ... Dr. Antonia VILLARRUEL
50 Dean Wharton School ... Dr. Erika H. JAMES
60 Dean Annenberg Sch Communications ... Dr. John L. JACKSON, JR.
52 Dean School of Dental Medicine ... Dr. Mark S. WOLFF
48 Dean Weitzman School of Design ... Dr. Frederick STEINER
53 Dean Graduate School Education ... Dr. Pam GROSSMAN
61 Dean School of Law ... Dr. Theodore W. RUGER
70 Dean School Social Policy/Practice ... Dr. Sara BACHMAN
74 Dean School of Veterinary Medicine ... Dr. Andrew HOFFMAN
107 Vice Dean Liberal & Prof Studies ... Ms. Nora E. LEWIS
85 Dir Intl Student & Scholar Svcs ... Dr. Rodolfo R. ALTAMIRANO
36 Exec Dir of Career Services ... Dr. Barbara HEWITT
37 Dir Student Financial Aid ... Ms. Elaine P. VARAS
35 Assoc Vice Prov for Student Affairs ... Ms. Tamara KING
38 Dir Counseling/Psych Services ... Vacant
102 Exec Dir Corp & Found Rels ... Dr. Diana B. ALTEGOER
28 Exec Dir Affirm Action & Equal Opp ... Mr. Sam B. STARKS
23 Sr Dir Student Health Services ... Dr. Robin OLIVER-VERONESI
57 Exec Art Dir Annenberg Ctr Per Arts ... Mr. Christopher A. GRUITS
88 Exec Dir Morris Arboretum ... Mr. William CULLINA
88 Dir Institute of Contemporary Art ... Ms. Zoe RYAN
88 Dir Museum of Archeology/Anthrplgy ... Mr. Christopher WOODS
41 Dir Intercollegiate Athletics ... Ms. Alanna SHANAHAN
14 IT Director ... Mr. James F. JOHNSON
91 IT Exec Dir Admin Info Tech ... Ms. Jeanne F. CURTIS
39 Exec Dir Col Houses & Acad Svcs ... Ms. Lisa LEWIS
104 Director Study Abroad ... Mr. Nigel COSSAR
106 Exec Director Online Learning Init ... Dr. Rebecca STEIN
04 Executive Asst to President ... Ms. Jodi SARKISIAN
105 Dir Web Strategy & Visual Comm ... Mr. Steven MINICOLA
44 Exec Dir Gift Plng/Assoc Gen Couns ... Ms. Marcie L. MERZ
96 Director of Purchasing ... Mr. Mark MILLS

University of Phoenix Philadelphia Campus (G)

30 South 17th Street, Philadelphia PA 19103-4001
Telephone: (267) 234-2000 Identification: 770933
Accreditation: &HLC

† No longer accepting campus-based students.

University of Pittsburgh (H)

4200 Fifth Avenue, Pittsburgh PA 15260-3583
County: Allegheny FICE Identification: 003379
Unit ID: 215293
Telephone: (412) 624-4141 Carnegie Class: DU-Highest
FAX Number: N/A Calendar System: Semester
URL: www.pitt.edu
Established: 1787 Annual Undergrad Tuition & Fees (In-State): $19,679
Enrollment: 32,277 Coed
Affiliation or Control: State Related IRS Status: 501(c)3
Highest Offering: Doctorate
Accreditation: M, ANEST, ARCPA, ATECH, AUD, CAATE, CACREP, CAHIIM, CAMPEP, CEA, CLPSY, DENT, DH, DIETC, EMT, HSA, HT, IPSY, LAW, LIB, MED, @MIDWF, NURSE, OPE, OT, PCSAS, PH, PHAR, PTA, SP, SPAA, SW, THEA

01 Chancellor and Chief Exec Officer ... Dr. Patrick GALLAGHER
05 Sr Vice Chancellor & Provost ... Dr. Ann E. CUDD
63 Sr VC Health Sci/Dean Sch of Med ... Dr. Anantha SHEKHAR
101 Sr VC Engagement/Secy BOT ... Vacant
10 Senior Vice Chancellor and CFO ... Mr. Hari SASTRY
21 Controller ... Mr. Thurman D. WINGROVE
88 Treasurer ... Mr. Paul LAWRENCE
115 Acting Chief Investment Officer ... Mr. Paul LAWRENCE
46 Sr Vice Chancellor for Research ... Dr. Rob A. RUTENBAR
111 SVC Philanthropic & Alumn Engage ... Ms. Kristin DAVITT
29 Vice Chancellor Alumni Relations ... Ms. Nancy MERRIT
43 Sr Vice Chanc & Chief Legal Officer ... Ms. Geovette E. WASHINGTON
26 Vice Chanc for Communications ... Ms. Ellen L. MORAN
100 Chief of Staff ... Mr. Kevin WASHO
11 Sr VC Business & Operations ... Mr. David N. DEJONG
86 Vice Chanc Community & Govt Rels ... Mr. Paul A. SUPOWITZ
15 Vice Chanc Human Resources ... Vacant
20 Vice Provost Undergraduate Studies ... Dr. Joseph J. MCCARTHY
58 Vice Provost Graduate Studies ... Dr. Amanda J. GODLEY
88 Vice Prov Faculty Diversity & Dev ... Mr. John M. WALLACE
88 Vice Provost Faculty Affairs ... Ms. Lu-in WANG
88 Vice Provost for Budget & Analytics ... Mr. Stephen R. WISNIEWSKI
21 Assoc VC Planning Design & Real Est ... Ms. Mary Beth MCGREW
102 VC Corporate & Foundation Relations ... Mr. Thomas P. CRAWFORD
109 VC Business Services ... Mr. Matthew STERNE
88 Director Sustainability ... Ms. Aurora SHARRARD
11 Director Administration ... Ms. Laura W. ZULLO
19 Assoc VC Public Safety & Emer Mgmt ... Mr. Ted P. FRITZ
18 Assoc VC Facilities Mgmt ... Mr. Scott C. BERNOTAS
16 Asst VC Consulting Services ... Mr. Mark D. BURDSALL
27 University Spokesperson ... Mr. Kevin ZWICK
06 University Registrar ... Mr. Jonathan C. HELM
41 Director of Athletics ... Ms. Heather R. LYKE
07 Chief Enrollment Officer ... Mr. Marc L. HARDING
32 Vice Provost Student Affairs ... Mr. Kenyon R. BONNER
35 Dean of Students ... Dr. Carla PANZELLA
49 Dean Deitrich Sch Arts & Sci/CGS ... Dr. Kathleen M. BLEE
92 Dean Honors College ... Dr. Nicola FOOTE
50 Dean Jos M Katz Gr Sch Bus ... Dr. Arjang A. ASSAD
53 Dean School of Education ... Dr. Valerie KINLOCH
54 Dean Swanson School of Engineering ... Mr. James R. MARTIN, II
61 Dean School of Law ... Ms. Amy J. WILDERMUTH
80 Dean Grad Sch Public/Intl Affs ... Dr. Carissa SLOTTERBACK
70 Dean School of Social Work ... Ms. Elizabeth M. FARMER
62 Dean School of Computing and Inform ... Mr. Bruce CHILDERS
52 Dean School of Dental Medicine ... Dr. Bernard J. COSTELLO
66 Dean School of Nursing ... Dr. Jacqueline DUNBAR-JACOB
67 Dean School of Pharmacy ... Dr. Patricia D. KROBOTH
69 Dean Grad School Public Health ... Dr. Maureen LICHTVELD
76 Dean Sch of Health & Rehabilitation ... Dr. Anthony DELITTO
12 President Johnstown Campus ... Dr. Jem M. SPECTAR
12 President Greensburg Campus ... Dr. Robert G. GREGERSON
12 Pres Bradford & Titusville ... Dr. Catherine KOVEROLA
104 Vice Provost Global Affairs ... Dr. Ariel ARMONY
40 Director University Stores ... Ms. Monica D. RATTIGAN
24 Dir Univ Ctr for Teach & Learning ... Ms. Cynthia GOLDEN
13 Chief Info Officer and Vice Chanc ... Mr. Mark HENDERSON
09 Int Director Institutional Research ... Mr. Rob G. RODGERS
116 Director Internal Audit ... Mr. John P. ELLIOTT
36 Assoc Dean & Dir Career Dev ... Ms. Cheryl S. FINLAY
39 Assoc Dean and Dir Residence Life ... Mr. Steven L. ANDERSON
88 Director Student Conduct ... Mrs. Barbara D. RUPRECHT
35 Assoc Dean & Dir Student Life ... Ms. Linda WILLIAMS-MOORE
08 Dir Univ Library System ... Ms. Kornelia TANCHEVA
19 Chief University Police ... Mr. James K. LOFTUS
23 Executive Director Wellness Center ... Ms. Marian S. VANEK
96 Manager Purchasing Services ... Mr. Thomas E. YOUNGS, JR.
04 Exec Asst to the Chancellor ... Ms. Alison WATESKA
106 Dir Online Programs ... Mr. Stephen M. BUTLER
37 Director Financial Aid ... Dr. Randall MCCREADY

38 Director Counseling Center ....Mr. Jay E. DARR
28 VC Diversity & Inclusion ....Dr. Clyde WILSON PICKETT
88 Director University Press ....Mr. Peter KRACHT
88 Int Dir Univ Ctr Soc & Urban Res ....Mr. Scott R. BEACH
88 Dir Ctr for Philosophy of Science ....Mr. Edouard MACHERY
88 Dir Learning Research & Dev Center ....Mr. Charles A. PERFETTI

University of Pittsburgh at Bradford (A)

300 Campus Drive, Bradford PA 16701-2812
Telephone: (814) 362-7500 FICE Identification: 003380
Accreditation: &M, ADNUR, CAATE, NUR

† Regional accreditation is carried under the parent institution in Pittsburgh, PA.

University of Pittsburgh at Greensburg (B)

150 Finoli Drive, Greensburg PA 15601-5898
Telephone: (724) 837-7040 FICE Identification: 003381
Accreditation: &M

† Regional accreditation is carried under the parent institution in Pittsburgh, PA.

University of Pittsburgh at Johnstown (C)

450 Schoolhouse Road, Johnstown PA 15904-2990
Telephone: (814) 269-7000 FICE Identification: 003382
Accreditation: &M, COARC

† Regional accreditation is carried under the parent institution in Pittsburgh, PA.

University of Pittsburgh at Titusville (D)

504 E Main, Titusville PA 16354-2097
Telephone: (814) 827-4400 FICE Identification: 003383
Accreditation: &M

† Regional accreditation is carried under the parent institution in Pittsburgh, PA.

University of the Sciences in Philadelphia (E)

600 S 43rd Street, Philadelphia PA 19104-4495
County: Philadelphia FICE Identification: 003353
Unit ID: 215132
Telephone: (215) 596-8800 Carnegie Class: Spec-4-yr-Other Health
FAX Number: (215) 895-1100 Calendar System: Semester
URL: www.usciences.edu
Established: 1821 Annual Undergrad Tuition & Fees: $27,500
Enrollment: 2,375 Coed
Affiliation or Control: Independent Non-Profit IRS Status: 501(c)3
Highest Offering: Doctorate
Accreditation: M, ACBSP, #ARCPA, OT, PHAR, PTA

01 Interim President ....Dr. Valerie P. WEIL
05 Provost/VP Academic Affairs ....Ms. Jill BAREN
106 VP USciences Online ....Mr. Ron KISHEN
111 VP Institutional Advancement ....Mr. Robert RUDD
10 Int Chief Financial/Operating Ofcr ....Ms. Brigid K. ISACKMAN
102 Dir of Corporate/Foundation Rels ....Ms. Madalina VERES
13 Associate VP & CIO ....Dr. Mark NESTOR
110 AVP Institutional Advancement ....Ms. Kim BARKHAMER
14 Exec Dir Information Technology ....Mr. John MASCIANTONIO
37 Director of Financial Aid ....Ms. Pamela RAMANATHAN
06 Registrar ....Ms. Therese ANDERSON
29 Director of Alumni Relations ....Mr. Casey J. RYAN
32 VP Student Affairs/Dean of Students ....Mr. Ross RADISH
49 Int Dean Misher Col Arts/Sciences ....Dr. Vojislava POPHRISTIC
76 Dean Samson Col of Health Sciences ....Dr. Sinclair SMITH
15 Director Human Resources ....Ms. Ruth ROBERTS
19 Director Public Safety/Security ....Mr. Michael LAPOTASKY
41 Director of Athletics ....Dr. Mark CASERIO
21 Controller/Asst VP Finance ....Ms. Brigid K. ISACKMAN
96 Director Purchasing/Auxiliary Svcs ....Mr. Vincent HORN
20 Associate Provost Academic Affairs ....Dr. John CONNORS
04 Executive Asst to President ....Ms. Beth PILIPZECK
90 Exec Director Academic Technology ....Dr. Rodney B. MURRAY
07 Executive Director of Admissions ....Mr. Augustine DISTEFANO, JR.

The University of Scranton (F)

800 Linden St, Scranton PA 18510-4622
County: Lackawanna FICE Identification: 003384
Unit ID: 215929
Telephone: (570) 941-7400 Carnegie Class: Masters/L
FAX Number: (570) 941-6369 Calendar System: Semester
URL: www.scranton.edu
Established: 1888 Annual Undergrad Tuition & Fees: $47,084
Enrollment: 4,957 Coed
Affiliation or Control: Roman Catholic IRS Status: 501(c)3
Highest Offering: Doctorate
Accreditation: M, ANEST, CACREP, CSHSE, EXSC, HSA, NURSE, OT, PTA

01 President ....Rev. Joseph G. MARINA, SJ
05 Sr VP Academic Affairs & Provost ....Dr. Jeff GINGERICH
10 Sr VP Finance & Administration ..Mr. Edward J. STEINMETZ, JR.
111 VP for University Advancement ....Mr. Thomas MACKINNON
84 VP Enroll Mgmt/External Affairs ....Mr. Gerald C. ZABOSKI
114 Asst VP Budget/Financial Planning ....Mr. Patrick R. DONOHUE
13 CIO ....Dr. Susan G. BOWEN
15 Assoc Vice Pres Human Resources ....Ms. Patricia L. TETREAULT
42 Exec Dir of the Jesuit Center ....Rev. Patrick ROGERS, SJ
43 General Counsel ....Mr. Robert B. FARRELL
49 Dean Arts & Sciences ....Dr. Michelle MALDONADO
50 Dean Kania School of Management ....Dr. Sam BELDONA
107 Dean Panuska Col of Prof Studies ....Dr. Debra A. PELLEGRINO
08 Int Dean of Library/Info Fluency ....Ms. Jean LENVILLE
51 Asst Dir for OL/Off-Campus Programs ....Dr. Lisa M. LOBASSO
32 Vice President for Student Life ....Dr. Robert W. DAVIS, JR.
20 Assoc Provost Academic Affs ....Dr. David MARX
07 Assoc VP Admiss & Undergrad Enroll ....Mr. Joseph M. ROBACK
37 Assoc VP Financial Aid & Enrollment ....Ms. Mary Kay ASTON
18 Assoc VP Facilities Operations ....Mr. James L. CAFFREY
29 Exec Dir Alumni/Donor Engagement ....Ms. Ashley ALT
06 Registrar ....Ms. Julie FERGUSON
36 Director of Career Services ....Ms. Chris WHITNEY
28 Exec Dir of Equity/Diversity Office ....Ms. Elizabeth GARCIA
38 Director of Counseling Center ....Mr. Thomas P. SMITH
96 Director of Purchasing ....Mr. Mark CRUCIANI
04 Admin Assistant to the President ....Ms. Maribeth A. SMITH
101 Secretary of the Institution/Board ....Mrs. Tara M. SEELY
104 Assoc Director Global Education ....Ms. Kara BISHOP
108 Director Institutional Assessment ....Dr. Mary Jane K. DIMATTIO
19 Director Security/Safety ....Mr. Donald J. BERGMANN
41 Athletic Director ....Mr. David L. MARTIN
09 Director of Institutional Research ....Dr. Tabbi MILLER-SCANDLE
39 Dir Resident Life/Student Housing ....Mr. Bradley TROY
44 Director Annual Giving ....Ms. Ashley ALT

University of Valley Forge (G)

1401 Charlestown Road, Phoenixville PA 19460-2373
County: Chester FICE Identification: 003306
Unit ID: 216542
Telephone: (610) 935-0450 Carnegie Class: Bac-Diverse
FAX Number: (610) 935-9353 Calendar System: Semester
URL: www.valleyforge.edu
Established: 1939 Annual Undergrad Tuition & Fees: $22,606
Enrollment: 557 Coed
Affiliation or Control: Assemblies Of God Church IRS Status: 501(c)3
Highest Offering: Master's
Accreditation: M, SW

01 President ....Rev. David J. KIM
32 VP of Student Life ....Rev. Jennifer D. GALE
05 VP of Academic Affairs ....Dr. Jerome N. DOUGLAS
09 VP of Institutional Effectiveness ....Dr. Todd G. GUEVIN
43 University Counsel ....Rev. Shahan G. TEBERIAN
10 VP of Finance ....Mr. Frank J. VIOLA, JR.
13 Director of Information Technology ....Mr. Paul VAN RIJN
21 Controller ....Mr. Valen P. CIANCI
18 Director of Facilities Operations ....Ms. Mindy S. ROWE
07 Exec Dir of Marketing & Admis ....Mr. Zack KASSEBAUM
30 VP of Development ....Rev. Steven R. DEFRAIN
41 Director of Athletics ....Ms. Gretchen L. LEVAN
37 Director of Financial Aid ....Vacant
19 Director of Security ....Mr. John T. YOUNT
15 Director Human Resources ....Mrs. Veronica A. BIRD
96 Director of Purchasing ....Vacant
08 Librarian/Dir Storms Research Ctr ....Ms. Melanie R. OESTREICH
121 Director of Student Success ....Ms. Claire EILER
11 Director of Operations ....Mrs. Julia G. PATTON
26 Director of Marketing ....Vacant
06 Registrar ....Mr. Chris J. ADDICKS
23 Director of Health Services ....Mrs. Lauren E. BORN
39 Housing Coordinator ....Ms. Angel R. PARISOT
04 Administrative Asst to President ....Ms. Milan A. JACKSON

Ursinus College (H)

PO Box 1000, 601 East Main Street, Collegeville PA 19426-1000
County: Montgomery FICE Identification: 003385
Unit ID: 216524
Telephone: (610) 409-3000 Carnegie Class: Bac-A&S
FAX Number: (610) 489-0627 Calendar System: Semester
URL: www.ursinus.edu
Established: 1869 Annual Undergrad Tuition & Fees: $55,210
Enrollment: 1,493 Coed
Affiliation or Control: Independent Non-Profit IRS Status: 501(c)3
Highest Offering: Baccalaureate
Accreditation: M

01 Interim President ....Ms. Jil LEAUBER MARSTELLER
05 Vice Pres Academic Affairs/Dean ....Dr. Mark SCHNEIDER
10 Vice Pres Finance & Administration ....Ms. Annette PARKER
111 Senior Vice Pres for Advancement ....Ms. Jill A. MARSTELLER
43 Vice Pres and General Counsel ....Mr. Robert CLOTHIER
84 Vice President/Dean for Enrollment ....Ms. Shannon ZOTTOLA
32 VP for College & Comm Engagement ....Dr. Heather LOBBAN-VIRAVONG
21 Assoc Vice President Finance/Admin ....Ms. Mary CORRELL
111 Assoc Vice Pres Advancement ....Ms. Ava WILLIS-BARKSDALE
15 Assoc Vice Pres Human Resources ....Ms. Kelley WILLIAMS
13 Chief Info Technology Officer (CIO) ....Mr. Gene SPENCER
112 Exec Director of Planned Giving ....Mr. Mark P. GADSON
08 Manager Library Operations ....Ms. Maureen DAMIANO
36 Director of Career & Post-Grad Dev ....Ms. Sharon HANSEN
18 Director of Facilities ....Mr. Steve GEHRINGER
41 Director of Athletics ....Mrs. Laura MOLIKEN
26 Chief Communications Officer ....Mr. Thomas YENCHO
37 Director Student Financial Services ....Mrs. Ellen CURCIO
06 Registrar ....Ms. Barbara A. BORIS
29 Exec Director of Alumni Relations ....Ms. Pamela PANARELLA
09 Director of Institutional Research ....Vacant
28 Dir of Institute for Incl & Equity ....Ms. Ashley HENDERSON
07 Director of Admission ....Ms. Diane GREENWOOD

Valley Forge Military College (I)

1001 Eagle Road, Wayne PA 19087-3695
County: Delaware FICE Identification: 003386
Unit ID: 216551
Telephone: (610) 989-1200 Carnegie Class: Assoc/HT-High Trad
FAX Number: (610) 975-9642 Calendar System: Semester
URL: www.vfmac.edu
Established: 1935 Annual Undergrad Tuition & Fees: $30,975
Enrollment: 110 Coed
Affiliation or Control: Independent Non-Profit IRS Status: 501(c)3
Highest Offering: Associate Degree
Accreditation: M

00 Chairman of the Board ....Mr. John ENGLISH
01 President/CEO ....Col. Stu HELGESON
03 Commandant of Cadets ....Col. Julian J. RIVERA
05 Dean of Academics ....Dr. Robert F. SMITH
32 Dean of Student Services ....Dr. Jesse PHILLIPS
10 Director of Finance and Operations ....Mr. D. Eric SAUL
06 Registrar ....Dr. Robert F. SMITH
07 Dir Admissions/Financial Aid ....Dr. Jesse PHILLIPS
13 Director Information Technology ....Mr. Michael G. BROCK
18 Director of Facilities ....Mr. George ELSE
23 Director of Health Services ....Ms. Debbie HAMMER
08 Director of Library Services ....Ms. Dana KERRIGAN
15 Director of Human Resources ....Ms. Lauren GUARDINO
26 Chief Public Relations/Marketing ....Ms. Mary HELLER
111 Dir of Institutional Advancement ....Ms. Kathleen ELSMORE
29 Director Alumni Relations ....Mr. Tom GOLDBLUM
09 Director of Institutional Research ....Ms. Deepa RAMAKRISHNAN

Vet Tech Institute (J)

125 Seventh Street, Pittsburgh PA 15222-3400
County: Allegheny FICE Identification: 008568
Unit ID: 213914
Telephone: (412) 391-7021 Carnegie Class: Spec 2-yr-Health
FAX Number: (412) 232-4348 Calendar System: Semester
URL: www.vti.edu
Established: 1958 Annual Undergrad Tuition & Fees: $15,140
Enrollment: 292 Coed
Affiliation or Control: Proprietary IRS Status: Proprietary
Highest Offering: Associate Degree
Accreditation: ACCSC

01 Director ....Ms. Jackie FLYNN
05 Director of Education ....Ms. Lynn SLACK
32 Director of Student Services ....Ms. Deborah SPOZARSKI

Villanova University (K)

800 Lancaster Avenue, Villanova PA 19085-1699
County: Delaware FICE Identification: 003388
Unit ID: 216597
Telephone: (610) 519-4500 Carnegie Class: DU-Higher
FAX Number: (610) 519-5000 Calendar System: Semester
URL: www.villanova.edu
Established: 1842 Annual Undergrad Tuition & Fees: $57,460
Enrollment: 11,032 Coed
Affiliation or Control: Roman Catholic IRS Status: 501(c)3
Highest Offering: Doctorate
Accreditation: M, ANEST, CACREP, LAW, NURSE, SPAA

01 President ....RevDr. Peter M. DONOHUE, OSA
43 Vice President & General Counsel ....Mr. E. Michael ZUBEY, JR.
05 Provost ....Dr. Patrick G. MAGGITTI
111 Sr Vice Pres University Advancement ....Mr. Michael O'NEILL
03 Exec Vice President ....Mr. Kenneth G. VALOSKY
13 Chief Information Officer ....Ms. Kelly DONEY
32 Vice President for Student Life ....Rev. Kathy J. BYRNES
26 Vice Pres University Communication ....Ms. Ann DIEBOLD
42 Vice Pres for Mission & Ministry ....Rev. Kevin DEPRINZIO, OSA
10 Vice President for Finance ....Mr. Neil J. HORGAN
20 Vice Provost for Academics ....Dr. Craig WHEELAND
41 Vice Pres/Director of Athletics ....Mr. Mark JACKSON
35 Assoc Vice Pres for Student Life ....Ms. Kathleen J. BYRNES
15 AVP Human Res/Affirm Action Ofcr ....Mr. Raymond DUFFY
109 Assoc Vice Pres for Auxiliary Svcs ....Mr. Anthony ALFANO
29 Assoc Vice Pres Alumni Relations ....Mr. George R. KOLB
46 Assoc Vice Provost for Research ....Dr. Amanda GRANNAS
28 Assoc Vice Prov Diversity/Inclusion ....Dr. Teresa A. NANCE
84 Dean Enrollment Management ....Mr. J. Leon WASHINGTON
09 Exec Dir Planning/Inst Research ....Dr. James F. TRAINER
18 Vice Pres Facilities Management ....Mr. Robert MORRO
07 Director University Admission ....Mr. Michael M. GAYNOR
08 Librarian & Dir of Falvey Library ....Ms. Millicent GASKELL
35 Asst Vice Pres & Dean of Students ....Mr. Tom DEMARCO
49 Dean Liberal Arts & Sciences ....Dr. Adele LINDENMEYR
50 Dean Villanova Sch of Business ....Dr. Joyce RUSSELL
58 Dean Graduate Studies LA&S ....Dr. Emory WOODARD
61 Dean Widger School of Law ....Mr. Mark ALEXANDER
66 Dean of Nursing ....Dr. Donna HAVENS

54 Dean of Engineering .... Dr. Michele MARCOLONGO
88 Dir Ctr Worship/Spirituality .... Ms. Linda JACZYNSKI
88 Dir Ctr Service/Social Justice .... Ms. Kate GIANCATARINO
88 Dir Ctr Grad Pastoral Ministry Educ .... Dr. John P. EDWARDS
107 Dean Col of Professional Studies .... Dr. Christine PALUS
85 Dir Intl Students & Human Services .... Mr. Stephen T. MCWILLIAMS
37 Director Financial Assistance .... Ms. Amanda CONSTABLE
19 Director of Public Safety .... Mr. David TEDJESKE
36 Executive Director Career Services .... Mr. Kevin GRUBB
92 Director of the Honors Program .... Dr. Anna MORELAND
38 Director of Univ Counseling Center .... Dr. Joan G. WHITNEY
94 Dir Gender & Women's Studies .... Dr. Shauna M. MACDONALD
39 Director for Housing Services .... Ms. Marie SCHAUDER
96 Director of Procurement .... Mr. John R. DURHAM
27 Director of Media Relations .... Mr. Jonathan GUST
23 Director Student Health Center .... Dr. Mary MCGONIGLE
23 Medical Director Student Health Ctr .... Dr. Brian BULLOCK
06 Registrar .... Ms. Pamela BRAXTON
88 University Compliance Officer .... Ms. Leyda L. BENITEZ
100 Executive Assistant to President .... Ms. Erin BUCKLEY
106 Exec Dir Online Programs .... Ms. Kristy IRWIN
53 AVP Teaching/Learning .... Dr. Matthew KERBEL
86 AVP Government Relations .... Mr. Chris KOVOLSKI

Walnut Hill College (A)

4207 Walnut Street, Philadelphia PA 19104-3518
County: Philadelphia FICE Identification: 021928
Unit ID: 215637
Telephone: (215) 222-4200 Carnegie Class: Spec-4-yr-Other
FAX Number: (215) 222-4219 Calendar System: Other
URL: www.walnuthillcollege.edu
Established: 1974 Annual Undergrad Tuition & Fees: $23,550
Enrollment: 159 Coed
Affiliation or Control: Proprietary IRS Status: Proprietary
Highest Offering: Baccalaureate
Accreditation: ACCSC

01 President .... Mr. Daniel LIBERATOSCIOLI
03 Executive Vice President .... Mr. Karl D. BECKER
05 Chief Academic Officer .... Mr. David MORROW
11 Vice President Administrative Svcs .. Ms. Peggy LIBERATOSCIOLI
10 Vice President of Operations .... Mr. Dennis LIBERATI
88 Director of Culinary Arts .... Chef Todd BRALEY
20 Assoc Dean Teaching/Learning .... Dr. Joshua SEERY
07 Director of Admissions .... Mr. Karl BECKER
21 Controller .... Mr. Chris MOLZ
32 Dir Student/Community Engagement .... Ms. Meghan BLOOME
37 Director Financial Aid .... Ms. Peggy LIBERATOSCIOLI
26 Director of Marketing .... Ms. Valery SNISARENKO

Washington & Jefferson College (B)

60 S Lincoln Street, Washington PA 15301-4801
County: Washington FICE Identification: 003389
Unit ID: 216667
Telephone: (724) 503-1001 Carnegie Class: Bac-A&S
FAX Number: (724) 223-6534 Calendar System: 4/1/4
URL: www.washjeff.edu
Established: 1781 Annual Undergrad Tuition & Fees: $50,169
Enrollment: 1,167 Coed
Affiliation or Control: Independent Non-Profit IRS Status: 501(c)3
Highest Offering: Master's
Accreditation: M

01 President .... Dr. John KNAPP
05 VP Academic Affairs/Dean of College .... Dr. Jeffrey FRICK
10 CFO/VP Business/Finance .... Mr. Jim IRWIN
30 VP Development/Alumni Relations .... Dr. Carolyn CAMPBELL-GOLDEN
84 VP for Enrollment .... Ms. Nicole FOCARETO
21 Assoc VP for Business & Finance .... Mr. Thomas SZEJKO
32 VP Student Life/Dean of Students .... Ms. Eva CHATTERJEE-SUTTON
20 Associate Dean for Academic Affairs .... Dr. Dana SHILLER
20 Associate Dean for Academic Affairs .... Dr. Steven MALINAK
18 Director of Facilities .... Mr. Tim LUCAS
26 VP Marketing/Communications .... Ms. Kelly KIMBERLAND
06 Registrar .... Ms. Kara CLARK
29 Asst VP Alumni Engagement .... Ms. Kerri LACOCK
07 Dean of Admission .... Mr. Robert ADKINS
37 Director of Financial Aid .... Ms. Bethany BOWMAN
13 Dir of Information/Technology Svcs .... Vacant
15 Director Human Resources .... Ms. Sharon KOLESAR
19 Interim Dir Campus & Public Safety .... Mr. John ROCHE
36 Assoc Dean/Dir of Career Pathways .... Ms. Vivienne FELIX
40 Bookstore Manager .... Ms. Cynthia BRICELAND
41 Director of Athletics .... Mr. Scott MCGUINNESS
08 Director of Library Services .... Ms. Ronalee CIOCCO
102 Foundation & Corp Relations Officer .... Vacant
91 Director for Admin Computing .... Mr. Michael A. TIMKO
104 Director of Study Abroad .... Ms. Sara KOCHUBA
108 Dir of Institutional Effectiveness .... Ms. Theresa FORD
121 Director of Academic Advising .... Mr. Richard BARBER
88 Director Conferences and Events .... Ms. Maureen VALENTINE
38 Director of Counseling Services .... Ms. Shelly LEAR
39 Director of Residence Life .... Mr. Justin SWANK
88 Ethics & Compliance Officer .... Vacant

Waynesburg University (C)

51 W College Street, Waynesburg PA 15370-1222
County: Greene FICE Identification: 003391
Unit ID: 216694
Telephone: (724) 627-8191 Carnegie Class: Masters/M
FAX Number: N/A Calendar System: Semester
URL: www.waynesburg.edu
Established: 1849 Annual Undergrad Tuition & Fees: $26,500
Enrollment: 1,576 Coed
Affiliation or Control: Presbyterian Church (U.S.A.) IRS Status: 501(c)3
Highest Offering: Doctorate
Accreditation: M, #CAATE, CACREP, IACBE, NURSE

00 Chancellor .... Dr. Timothy R. THYREEN
01 President .... Mr. Doug LEE
05 Provost .... Dr. Dana BAER
10 Chief Financial Officer .... Mrs. Laura COSS
32 Int Dean of Students .... Ms. Patricia BRISTOR
06 Registrar .... Mrs. Vicki WILSON
41 Athletic Director .... Mr. Adam JACK
13 VP Information Technology Services .... Mr. William DUMIRE
08 Director Eberly Library .... Mr. Rea REDD
26 Communication Specialist .... Ms. Ashley WISE
36 Career Development Specialist .... Ms. Sarah BELL
38 Student Counselor .... Mrs. Jane S. OWEN
21 Business Ofc Supervisor/Controller .... Mrs. Laura COSS
23 Director of Student Health Services .... Ms. Sherry PARSONS
15 Director Human Resources .... Mr. Tom HELMICK
37 Director Student Financial Aid .... Mr. Matthew STOKAN

Westminster College (D)

319 South Market Street, New Wilmington PA 16172-0001
County: Lawrence FICE Identification: 003392
Unit ID: 216807
Telephone: (724) 946-8761 Carnegie Class: Bac-A&S
FAX Number: (724) 946-7132 Calendar System: Semester
URL: www.westminster.edu
Established: 1852 Annual Undergrad Tuition & Fees: $37,675
Enrollment: 1,228 Coed
Affiliation or Control: Presbyterian Church (U.S.A.) IRS Status: 501(c)3
Highest Offering: Master's
Accreditation: M, MUS, NURSE

01 President .... Dr. Kathy B. RICHARDSON
05 Vice Pres Academic Affairs .... Dr. Jamie G. MCMINN
111 VP Institutional Advancement .... Dr. Jean M. HALE
10 Vice Pres Finance/Mgmt Services .... Mr. Kenneth J. ROMIG
84 Vice President for Enrollment .... Dr. Karen H. SCHEDIN
32 VP Student Affs/Dean Student Affs .... Ms. Gina M. VANCE
42 College Chaplain .... Rev. James R. MOHR
35 Assoc Dean of Student Affairs .... Ms. Candace C. OKELLO
13 CIO .... Ms. Erin T. SMITH
37 Director Student Financial Aid .... Ms. Cheryl GERBER
06 Registrar .... Mr. Scott D. WIGNALL
36 Director of Professional Dev Center .... Ms. Jennifer A. HOUGH
29 Sr Director of Alumni Engagement ... Ms. Kara H. MONTGOMERY
58 Director of Graduate School .... Vacant
41 Athletic Director .... Mr. Jason A. LENER
18 Director of Physical Plant .... Mr. Jason R. JANUSZIEWICZ
21 Business Manager .... Ms. Janet M. SMITH
19 Interim Director of Public Safety .... Ms. Bonnie J. MARS
23 Director of the Wellness Center .... Ms. Melissa M. BARON
40 Bookstore Manager .... Ms. Kay A. GALANSKI
15 Director of Human Resources .... Ms. Kimberlee K. CHRISTOFFERSON
38 Counselor .... Ms. Sarah M. GELLMAN

Westminster Theological Seminary (E)

2960 Church Road, Glenside PA 19038
County: Montgomery FICE Identification: 003393
Unit ID: 216816
Telephone: (215) 887-5511 Carnegie Class: Spec-4-yr-Faith
FAX Number: (215) 887-5404 Calendar System: Semester
URL: www.wts.edu
Established: 1929 Annual Graduate Tuition & Fees: N/A
Enrollment: 854 Coed
Affiliation or Control: Independent Non-Profit IRS Status: 501(c)3
Highest Offering: Doctorate; No Undergraduates
Accreditation: M, THEOL

01 President .... Dr. Peter A. LILLBACK
05 Academic Dean .... Dr. David B. GARNER
43 General Counsel .... Mr. James M. SWEET
32 VP for Campus Life/Dean of Students .... Rev. Steven J. CARTER
111 Vice Pres Advancement .... Mr. Jerry TIMMIS
11 Vice President of Operations .... Mr. Chun LAI
106 Dean of Online Learning .... Dr. Iain DUGUID
07 Admissions Coord & Fin Aid Officer .... Mrs. Cyndi MYERS
84 Director of Enrollment .... Mr. Jonathan M. BRACK
08 Director of Library Services ... Mr. Alexander (Sandy) FINLAYSON
73 Dean of Pastoral Theology .... Dr. John CURRIE
13 Associate Director of Technology .... Mr. Sam IM
18 Physical Plant Manager .... Mr. Richard W. MAIENSHEIN
04 Executive Asst to President .... Ms. Lisa CASTOR
29 Director Alumni Affairs .... Dr. David FILSON
06 Registrar .... Ms. Jaclyn GOBER
10 Director of Finance .... Ms. Pau Ping SZE TO

Westmoreland County Community College (F)

145 Pavilion Lane, Youngwood PA 15697-1895
County: Westmoreland FICE Identification: 010176
Unit ID: 216825
Telephone: (724) 925-4000 Carnegie Class: Assoc/HVT-Mix Trad/Non
FAX Number: (724) 925-1150 Calendar System: Semester
URL: www.westmoreland.edu
Established: 1970 Annual Undergrad Tuition & Fees (In-District): $9,732
Enrollment: 4,369 Coed
Affiliation or Control: Local IRS Status: 501(c)3
Highest Offering: Associate Degree
Accreditation: M, ACFEI, ADNUR, DA, DH, DMS, MAC

01 President .... Dr. Tuesday STANLEY
05 Vice Pres Acad Affs/Stdnt Svcs .... Dr. Kristy BISHOP
11 Vice Pres Administrative Services .... Mr. Gregory ROSE
103 VP Workforce & Cmty Devel/Cont Educ .... Vacant
25 Director of Grants .... Ms. Debra J. WILLIAMS
15 Director Human Resources .... Ms. Lauren M. FARRELL
106 Dean Dist Educ/Learning Resources .... Ms. Annette BOYER
50 Dean Business/Math/Science/Engineer .... Ms. Cynthia PROCTOR
76 Dean Health Professions/Nursing .... Ms. Sue SNYDER
72 Dean Technology .... Dr. Byron KOHUT
79 Dean Public Svc/Human/Soc Science .... Dr. Andrew BARNETTE
84 Vice Pres Enrollment Mgmt .... Dr. Sydney BEELER
102 Exec Director Education Foundation .... Ms. Debra D. WOODS
37 Director Financial Aid .... Ms. Janet DAVIDSON
18 Director Facilities .... Mr. Stephen MARKIEWICZ
13 Director Information Technology .... Mr. Steve BUDNY
26 Exec Dir Marketing/ Communications .... Ms. Janet K. CORRINNE-HARVEY
07 Director Admissions/Registrar .... Vacant
41 Director Student Life/Athletics .... Vacant
45 Dean Planning/Assessment & IE .... Ms. Lindsay HERROD
96 Director of Purchasing .... Ms. Jill BUDNY

Widener University (G)

One University Place, Chester PA 19013-5792
County: Delaware FICE Identification: 003313
Unit ID: 216852
Telephone: (610) 499-4000 Carnegie Class: DU-Mod
FAX Number: N/A Calendar System: Semester
URL: www.widener.edu
Established: 1821 Annual Undergrad Tuition & Fees: $48,575
Enrollment: 6,150 Coed
Affiliation or Control: Independent Non-Profit IRS Status: 501(c)3
Highest Offering: Doctorate
Accreditation: M, CLPSY, HSA, IFSY, LAW, NURSE, PTA, @SP, SW

01 President .... Dr. Julie E. WOLLMAN
05 Provost .... Dr. Andrew A. WORKMAN
10 Vice Pres Administration/Finance .... Ms. Linda K. GILBERT
111 Vice Pres University Advancement .... Ms. Theresa TRAVIS
13 VP Library & Info Systems .... Mr. Eric BEHRENS
84 VP for Enrollment Services .... Mr. Joseph E. HOWARD
21 Associate VP & Controller .... Mr. William LOCKARD, III
15 Assoc VP for Human Resources .... Ms. Keesha CHAVIS
20 Vice Provost Academic Affairs .... Dr. Kimberly C. O'HALLORAN
121 Associate Provost Student Success .. Dr. Geraldine A. BLOEMKER
32 Dean of Students .... Dr. John P. DOWNEY
54 Dean School of Engineering .... Dr. Fred A. AKL
49 Dean College Arts & Sciences .... Dr. David E. LEAMAN
50 Dean School of Business Admin .... Dr. Anthony WHEELER
66 Dean School of Nursing .... Dr. Anne M. KROUSE
76 Dean Col Health/Human Services .... Dr. Robin L. DOLE
113 Bursar .... Ms. Diana BARRACLOUGH
08 Director Wolfgram Library .... Ms. Deborah G. MORLEY
06 Director of Records/Registration .... Ms. Kristen CHANDO
09 Dir of Inst Res & Effectiveness .... Dr. Stephen W. THORPE
36 Placement Director .... Ms. Janet R. LONG
41 Director of Athletics .... Mr. Jack L. SHAFER
85 Director International Student Svcs .... Ms. Kandy TURNER
19 Executive Director of Campus Safety .... Mr. Anthony PLURETTI
40 Manager Campus Bookstore .... Vacant
91 Assoc VP Digital Transformation .... Mrs. Linda TAYLOR
88 Director Technical Resources .... Mr. Perry M. DRAYFAHL
96 Director of Purchasing .... Ms. Michelle SHELTON
121 Dir Student Success/Retention .... Mr. Timothy J. CAIRY
92 Dir Honors Program in General Educ .... Dr. Mark S. GRAYBILL
94 Director of Women's Studies .... Dr. Annalisa CASTALDO
86 Director Government Relations .... Vacant
100 Chief of Staff .... Dr. Kathryn J. HERSCHEDE
26 Director of Communications .... Ms. Mary ALLEN
39 Assoc Dean of Students .... Ms. Catherine A. FEMINELLA
07 Exec Director of Admissions .... Ms. Courtney KELLY
105 Director of Digital Communications .... Ms. Bridget HILFERTY
28 Chief Diversity Officer .... Ms. Micki DAVIS
37 Director Student Financial Aid .... Ms. Paula LEHRBERGER
18 Chief Facilities/Physical Plant Ofc .... Mr. Kevin M. KANE

† See Delaware listing of Widener University School of Law.

Widener University Commonwealth Law School (H)

3800 Vartan Way, PO Box 69380,
Harrisburg PA 17106-9380
Telephone: (717) 541-3900 Identification: 667244
Accreditation: &M, LAW

† Branch campus of Widener University, Chester, PA.

Wilkes University (A)

84 W South Street, Wilkes-Barre PA 18766-0001
County: Luzerne FICE Identification: 003394
Unit ID: 216931
Telephone: (570) 408-5000 Carnegie Class: DU-Mod
FAX Number: (570) 408-2934 Calendar System: Semester
URL: www.wilkes.edu
Established: 1933 Annual Undergrad Tuition & Fees: $38,752
Enrollment: 4,781 Coed
Affiliation or Control: Independent Non-Profit IRS Status: 501(c)3
Highest Offering: Doctorate
Accreditation: M, ACBSP, CEA, NURSE, PHAR

01 President .... Dr. Greg CANT
05 Provost & Sr Vice President .... Dr. David WARD
10 Vice Pres Finance & General Counsel ... Mr. Loren D. PRESCOTT
84 VP for Enrollment Mgmt & Marketing .... Ms. Kishan ZUBER
32 Vice President Student Affairs .... Dr. Paul S. ADAMS
30 Chief Development Officer .... Mrs. Margaret A. STEELE
21 Controller .... Ms. Jessica SWINGLE
20 Associate Provost for Academics .... Dr. Jonathan D. FERENCE
15 AVP/Human Resource Officer .... Mr. Joseph HOUSENICK
35 Dean of Students .... Mr. Mark R. ALLEN
54 Int Dean of Science & Engineering .... Dr. Prahlad N. MURTHY
49 Dean College Arts & Humanities .... Dr. Paul RIGGS
67 Dean Nesbitt School of Pharmacy .... Dr. Scott STOLTE
53 Dean School of Education .... Dr. Rhonda RABBITT
50 Dean Sidhu School of Business .... Dr. Abel ADEKOLA
62 Dean Library/Information Tech .... Mr. John STACHACZ
88 Special Assistant to President .... Mr. Michael WOOD
66 Dean Passan School of Nursing .... Dr. Deborah A. ZBEGNER
09 Exec Director Info/Analysis/Plng .... Mr. Brian BOGERT
29 Director of Alumni Affairs .... Ms. Leigh Ann JACOBSON
41 Director of Athletics .... Ms. Addy MALATESTA
23 Director Health Services .... Ms. Diane E. O'BRIEN
36 Director Career Services .... Mrs. Carol A. BOSACK-KOSEK
39 Director Residence Life .... Mr. Raymond FEDORA
58 Director Graduate Teacher Education .... Ms. Grace SURDOVEL
06 Registrar .... Mrs. Susan A. HRITZAK
37 Executive Director of Financial Aid .... Ms. Jane F. DESSOYE
26 Executive Director of Marketing ... Ms. Kimberly BOWER SPENCE
18 Director Facilities Services .... Mr. Charles CARY
07 Exec Dir Undergraduate Enrollment .... Mr. Christopher MAYERSKI
28 Exec Director of Diversity .... Ms. Georgia COSTALAS
96 Dir Procurement & Financial Svcs .... Ms. Alicia BOND
25 Director of Sponsored Programs .... Ms. Amanda MODROVSKY
27 Director of Communications .... Ms. Gabrielle D'AMICO
04 Executive Assistant to President .... Ms. Bridget GIUNTA
19 Director Security/Safety .... Mr. Christopher J. JAGOE

Williamson College of the Trades (B)

106 S New Middletown Road, Media PA 19063-5299
County: Delaware FICE Identification: 041238
Unit ID: 216940
Telephone: (610) 566-1776 Carnegie Class: Not Classified
FAX Number: (610) 566-6502 Calendar System: Semester
URL: www.williamson.edu
Established: 1888 Annual Undergrad Tuition & Fees: $28,320
Enrollment: 249 Male
Affiliation or Control: Independent Non-Profit IRS Status: 501(c)3
Highest Offering: Associate Degree
Accreditation: @M, ACCSC

01 President .... Mr. Michael J. ROUNDS
03 Executive Vice President .... Dr. Todd M. ZACHARY
05 Chief Academic Officer .... Dr. Michelle H. WILLIAMS
10 Chief Financial Officer .... Ms. Nancy M. CATANIA
111 VP Institutional Advancement .... Ms. Arlene A. SNYDER
11 VP of Operations .... Mr. Corey A. JACKSON
108 VP Research and Assessment .... Mr. Thomas E. WISNESKI
32 Dean of Students .... Mr. Thomas J. MOFFITT
84 VP Enrollment Management .... Mr. Jason C. MERILLAT
41 Athletic Director .... Mr. Dale H. PLUMMER
38 Chaplain/Counselor .... Rev. Mark A. SPECHT
06 Registrar .... Ms. Stephanie C. BOON
04 Executive Assistant/President .... Ms. Joan E. BERRY
36 Director Student Placement .... Mrs. Margret T. KINGHAM
39 Director Residence Life .... Mr. John J. TULLY
20 Associate CAO .... Ms. Olivia MARTINEZ

Wilson College (C)

1015 Philadelphia Avenue, Chambersburg PA 17201-1285
County: Franklin FICE Identification: 003396
Unit ID: 217013
Telephone: (717) 264-4141 Carnegie Class: Masters/S
FAX Number: (717) 264-1578 Calendar System: 4/1/4
URL: www.wilson.edu
Established: 1869 Annual Undergrad Tuition & Fees: $26,090
Enrollment: 1,535 Coed
Affiliation or Control: Presbyterian Church (U.S.A.) IRS Status: 501(c)3
Highest Offering: Master's
Accreditation: M

01 President .... Dr. Wesley R. FUGATE
05 VP for Academic Affairs/Dean of Fac .... Dr. Elissa HEIL
111 VP for Institutional Advancement .... Dr. Angela ZIMMANN
10 VP for Finance & Administration .... Mr. Brian ECKER
84 VP for Enrollment Management .... Mr. William SOMMERS
32 VP for Student Dev/Dean of Students ... Dr. Mary Beth WILLIAMS
100 Chief of Staff .... Ms. Melissa J. IMES
06 Registrar .... Ms. Jean B. HOOVER
37 Dean of Financial Aid .... Ms. Linda D. BRITTAIN
09 Director of Institutional Effective .... Ms. Cynthia M. EMORY
18 Director of Physical Plant .... Mr. Jason WARRENFELTZ
26 VP of Marketing & Communications . Ms. Cassandra H. LATIMER
40 College Store Coordinator .... Ms. Robin HERRING
41 Director of Athletics .... Ms. Tina HILL
88 Director of Conferences .... Ms. Kelsey YOUNG
29 Director of Alumnae Programs .... Ms. Marybeth FAMULARE
15 Director of Human Resources .... Vacant
121 Assoc Dean of Academic Advising .... Dr. Deborah AUSTIN
21 Assoc VP for Finance/Admin .... Ms. Lori A. TOSTEN
36 Director of Career Development .... Ms. Linda A. BOECKMAN
38 Director of Counseling .... Ms. Angela BAKER
88 Dir of Single Parent Scholars Pgm .... Ms. Katherine KOUGH
37 Coordinator of Financial Aid .... Ms. Christine KNOUSE
28 Coordinator of Diversity .... Vacant
42 Chaplain .... Rev. Derek WADLINGTON
39 Director of Residence Life .... Mr. Ryan COLL
102 Dir of Strategic Relationship Dev .... Ms. Dianna HEIM
07 Director of Admissions .... Mr. Michael MONTANA
30 Director of Development .... Ms. Denise MCDOWELL
13 Chief Info Technology Officer .... Dr. Amy DIEHL

Won Institute of Graduate Studies (D)

137 S Easton Road, Glenside PA 19038
County: Montgomery FICE Identification: 039493
Unit ID: 442064
Telephone: (215) 884-8942 Carnegie Class: Spec-4-yr-Other Health
FAX Number: (215) 884-9002 Calendar System: Trimester
URL: www.woninstitute.edu
Established: 2002 Annual Graduate Tuition & Fees: N/A
Enrollment: 124 Coed
Affiliation or Control: Independent Non-Profit IRS Status: 501(c)3
Highest Offering: Doctorate; No Undergraduates
Accreditation: M, ACUP

01 President .... Dr. Bokin KIM
11 Chief Administrative Officer .... Ms. Colleen O'CONNELL
10 Chief Financial Officer .... Ms. Maria PERRY
05 Chief Academic Officer .... Dr. Gerry O'SULLIVAN
06 Registrar .... Mr. Max FINKEL
08 Librarian .... Vacant
85 International Student Advisor .... Dr. Hojin PARK
13 Chief Info Technology Officer .... Ms. Elizabeth REED
04 Admin Assistant to the President .... Mr. Frederick RANALLO-HIGGINS
18 Chief Facilities/Phys Plant Ofcr .... Mr. Youngbin KIM

Yeshiva Beth Moshe (E)

930 Hickory Street, Scranton PA 18505-2196
County: Lackawanna FICE Identification: 013134
Unit ID: 217040
Telephone: (570) 346-1747 Carnegie Class: Spec-4-yr-Faith
FAX Number: (570) 346-2251 Calendar System: Semester
Established: 1965 Annual Undergrad Tuition & Fees: $9,800
Enrollment: 42 Male
Affiliation or Control: Independent Non-Profit IRS Status: 501(c)3
Highest Offering: Second Talmudic Degree
Accreditation: RABN

01 Chief Executive Officer .... Rabbi Yaakov SCHNAIDMAN
03 Executive Director .... Rabbi Avrohom PRESSMAN

York College of Pennsylvania (F)

441 Country Club Road, York PA 17403-3651
County: York FICE Identification: 003399
Unit ID: 217059
Telephone: (717) 846-7788 Carnegie Class: Masters/S
FAX Number: (717) 849-1607 Calendar System: Semester
URL: www.ycp.edu
Established: 1787 Annual Undergrad Tuition & Fees: $21,700
Enrollment: 4,039 Coed
Affiliation or Control: Independent Non-Profit IRS Status: 501(c)3
Highest Offering: Doctorate
Accreditation: M, ACBSP, ANEST, CAPRT, COARC, COSMA, MUS, NURSE

01 President .... Dr. Pamela J. GUNTER-SMITH
05 Provost & Dean Academic Affairs .... Dr. Laura NIESEN DE ABRUNA
10 VP Finance & Campus Operations .... Mr. Anthony DECOCINIS
20 Assoc Dean Academic Affairs .... Dr. Carl SEAQUIST
121 Associate Provost .... Dr. Joshua LANDAU
32 Dean of Student Affairs .... Mr. Joseph F. MERKLE
35 Dean Stdnt Development/Campus Life .... Dr. Richard SATTERLEE
18 Dean of Campus Operations .... Dr. Kenneth M. MARTIN
111 VP of Development .... Mr. Troy MILLER
50 Associate Dean Business .... Dr. James NORRIE
41 Asst Dean Athletics & Recreation .... Mr. Paul SAIKIA
84 Vice Pres Enrollment Management .... Dr. Danny GREEN
26 Chief Communication & Mktg Officer ... Ms. Mary E. DOLHEIMER
07 Director of Admissions .... Mr. Michael THORP
06 Registrar .... Mr. William R. BENTON, JR.
08 Librarian .... Mr. Jim KAPOUN
37 Director of Financial Aid .... Mr. Eric DINSMORE
13 CIO .... Dr. Ilya YAKOVLEV
29 Director Alumni Relations .... Mrs. Kristin SCHAB
36 Asst Dean Career Development .... Ms. Beverly A. EVANS
06 Assistant Registrar .... Mr. Matthew ROSS
19 Director of Public Safety .... Mr. Edward C. BRUDER
39 Director of Residence Life .... Mr. Robbie BACON
15 Director Human Resources .... Mrs. Vicki L. STEWART
38 Director Counseling Services .... Mr. Darrell WILT
91 Dir Administrative Computer Center .... Vacant
23 Director Health Services .... Mrs. Amy DOWNS
40 Director Bookstore .... Mrs. Lynn P. FERRO
88 Director Campus & Special Events .... Ms. Sherry HEFLIN
102 Dir Corporate/Foundation/Govt Rels .... Mr. Jeffrey VERMEULEN
27 College Editor .... Mrs. Gail HUGANIR
42 Coordinator Religious Activities .... Mrs. Louise WORLEY
31 Dean Ctr for Community Engagement .... Dr. Dominic F. DELLICARPINI
09 Director of Institutional Research .... Dr. Sarah GALLIMORE
24 Dir Center for Teaching & Learning .... Vacant
04 Sr Executive Asst to President .... Mrs. Cynthia E. REISINGER

YTI Career Institute (G)

2900 Fairway Drive, Altoona PA 16602
County: Blair FICE Identification: 030819
Unit ID: 375939
Telephone: (814) 944-5643 Carnegie Class: Assoc/HVT-High Trad
FAX Number: (959) 282-5093 Calendar System: Quarter
URL: www.yti.edu
Established: 2006 Annual Undergrad Tuition & Fees: N/A
Enrollment: 59 Coed
Affiliation or Control: Proprietary IRS Status: Proprietary
Highest Offering: Associate Degree
Accreditation: ACCSC, #COARC

02 Campus Dir of Operations/Education .... Mr. Carl KENYON

† Effective February 12, 2018, Altoona Campus has ceased recruiting new students

YTI Career Institute / Lancaster (H)

3050 Hempland Road, Lancaster PA 17601
Telephone: (717) 295-1100 Identification: 770588
Accreditation: ACCSC, CAHIIM

YTI Career Institute (I)

1405 Williams Road, York PA 17402-9017
County: York FICE Identification: 021274
Unit ID: 217077
Telephone: (717) 757-1100 Carnegie Class: Assoc/HVT-High Trad
FAX Number: (717) 757-4964 Calendar System: Quarter
URL: https://yti.edu
Established: 1967 Annual Undergrad Tuition & Fees: N/A
Enrollment: 708 Coed
Affiliation or Control: Proprietary IRS Status: Proprietary
Highest Offering: Associate Degree
Accreditation: ACCSC, ACFEI

00 President and CEO .... Mr. James BOLOGA
02 Campus Dir Operations/Education .... Dr. Thomas BANKS
05 VP Academics .... Ms. Vicki KANE
07 Asst Dir of Admissions .... Ms. Angie JONES
06 Registrar .... Ms. JoElle HEINBAUGH

RHODE ISLAND

Brown University (J)

One Prospect Street, Providence RI 02912
County: Providence FICE Identification: 003401
Unit ID: 217156
Telephone: (401) 863-1000 Carnegie Class: DU-Highest
FAX Number: (401) 863-3700 Calendar System: Semester
URL: www.brown.edu
Established: 1764 Annual Undergrad Tuition & Fees: $60,696
Enrollment: 9,948 Coed
Affiliation or Control: Independent Non-Profit IRS Status: 501(c)3
Highest Offering: Doctorate
Accreditation: EH, CAMPEP, IPSY, MED, PDPSY, PH

01 President .... Christina H. PAXSON
05 Provost .... Richard LOCKE
45 Exec VP Planning & Policy .... Russell CAREY
11 Exec VP Finance/Administration .... Barbara CHERNOW
111 Senior VP for Advancement .... Sergio GONZALEZ
26 VP Communications .... Cass CLIATT
28 VP Institutional Equity & Diversity .... Vacant
32 VP Campus Life & Student Services .... Eric ESTES
43 VP & General Counsel .... Eileen GOLDGEIER
69 Dean School of Public Health .... Ashish JHA
100 Chief of Staff/Asst to President .... Marguerite JOUTZ
15 VP Human Resources .... Vacant
58 Dean of Graduate School .... Andrew G. CAMPBELL
115 VP & Chief Investment Officer .... Jane DIETZE
63 Dean of Medicine/Biological Science .... Jack ELIAS
54 Dean of Engineering .... Lawrence LARSON
20 Dean of the Faculty .... Kevin MCLAUGHLIN
46 VP for Research .... Jill PIPHER
13 Chief Digital & Information Officer .... William THIRSK
10 VP Finance/Chief Financial Officer .... Michael WHITE
20 Dean of the College .... Rashid ZIA
09 Director of Institutional Research .... Katharine BARNES

23 Assoc VP Health & Wellness .... Vanessa BRITTO
86 Asst VP Govt & Community Relations .... Albert DAHLBERG
20 Deputy Provost for Academic Affairs .... Elizabeth DOHERTY
06 University Registrar .... Robert FITZGERALD
18 VP for Facilities Management .... Michael GUGLIELMO, JR.
41 Director of Athletics .... Grace CALHOUN
38 Dir Counseling & Psychological Svcs .... Vacant
08 University Librarian .... Joseph MEISEL
19 Exec Dir & Chief of Public Safety .... Vacant
07 Dean of Admission .... Logan POWELL
80 Interim Dir Master Public Affairs .... Shankar PRASAD
29 Vice President Alumni Relations .... Andrew SHAINDLIN
88 VP for Strategic Initiatives .... Vacant
21 Assoc VP & University Controller .... Charlene SWEENEY
37 Dean of Financial Aid .... James TILTON
107 Dean School Professional Studies .... Leah VANWEY

Bryant University (A)

1150 Douglas Pike, Smithfield RI 02917-1291
County: Providence FICE Identification: 003402
Unit ID: 217165
Telephone: (401) 232-6000 Carnegie Class: Masters/M
FAX Number: (401) 232-6319 Calendar System: Semester
URL: www.bryant.edu
Established: 1863 Annual Undergrad Tuition & Fees: $46,863
Enrollment: 3,674 Coed
Affiliation or Control: Independent Non-Profit IRS Status: 501(c)3
Highest Offering: Beyond Master's But Less Than Doctorate
Accreditation: EH, ARCPA

00 Chairman Board of Trustees .... Mr. David BEIRNE
01 President .... Dr. Ross GITTELL
05 Interim Provost .... Dr. Wendy SAMTER
32 VP Student Affairs/Dean of Students .... Dr. Inge-Lise AMEER
82 VP International Affairs .... Dr. Hong YANG
10 VP Business Affairs .... Mr. Barry F. MORRISON
111 VP University Advancement .... Mr. David WEGRZYN
13 VP Information Services/CIO .... Mr. Chuck LOCURTO
84 VP Enrollment Management .... Ms. Michelle CLOUTIER
26 AVP Communications/Marketing .... Ms. Elizabeth O'NEIL
15 AVP Human Resources .... Mr. Timothy PAIGE
22 AVP Diversity/Equity & Inclusion .... Dr. Kevin MARTINS
18 Assoc VP Facilities Opers .... Mr. Andrew DEMELIA
21 Assoc VP Business & Controller .... Mr. Farokh BHADA
20 Associate Provost .... Dr. Wendy SAMTER
45 Exec Dir Inst Effect & Strategy .... Dr. Edinaldo TEBALDI
49 Dean College of Arts & Sciences .... Dr. Veronica MCCOMB
50 Dean College of Business .... Dr. Madan ANNAVARJULA
51 Interim Dir Exec Development Center .... Ms. Tracy QUARELLA
88 Exec Dir Hassenfeld Institute .... Mr. Gary SASSE
88 Dir RI Export Assistance Center .... Mr. Mark MURPHY
121 Asst Dean for Student Success .... Dr. Laurie L. HAZARD
20 Dir Faculty Dev and Innovation .... Dr. Edward KAIRISS
06 Interim Registrar .... Ms. Laura HAYWARD
28 Asst VP Student Engagement .... Dr. Mailee KUE
35 Asst VP for Student Affairs .... Mr. John DENIO
36 Dir Career Services .... Dr. Kevin GAW
38 Dir Counseling/Rel/Spiritual Life .... Dr. Noelle HARRIS
19 Dir Public Safety .... Mr. Stephen BANNON
88 Dir Capital Projects .... Mr. Thomas MANN
88 Asst Dir Women's Center .... Ms. Kelly BOUTIN
37 Dir Financial Aid .... Mr. John B. CANNING
88 Dir Conference Services .... Ms. Nicole BEAUREGARD
30 Exec Dir Development .... Mr. Edward MAGRO
29 Dir Alumni Relations .... Ms. Robin T. WARDE
90 Dir Acad Computing & Media Svcs .... Mr. Phillip LOMBARDI
91 Dir Admin Systems .... Ms. Christine BIGWOOD
14 Dir Campus Technology .... Mr. David GANNON
16 Assoc Dir Human Resources .... Ms. Catherine CURRIE
41 Dir Athletics .... Mr. Bill SMITH
09 Dir Inst Effect & Strategy .... Mr. Robert JONES
88 Exec Dir US-China Institute .... Dr. Hong YANG
105 Chief Library Officer .... Ms. Laura KOHL
104 Director Study Abroad .... Ms. Cindi LEWIS
102 Dir Foundation/Corporate Relations .... Ms. Robin RICHARDSON
96 Asst Dir Purchasing & Aux Svc .... Ms. Paula DOYLE
40 Manager Bookstore .... Mr. Stanley STOWIK

College Unbound (B)

325 Public Street, Providence RI 02905
County: Providence Identification: 667355
Telephone: (401) 752-2640 Carnegie Class: Not Classified
FAX Number: N/A Calendar System: Semester
URL: www.collegeunbound.edu
Established: 2009 Annual Undergrad Tuition & Fees: N/A
Enrollment: N/A Coed
Affiliation or Control: Independent Non-Profit IRS Status: 501(c)3
Highest Offering: Baccalaureate
Accreditation: EH

01 President .... Dennis LITTKY
05 VP Academic Affairs/Provost .... Adam BUSH
03 Executive Vice President .... Robert CAROTHERS
04 Exec Assistant to the President .... Tara HAGOPIAN

Community College of Rhode Island (C)

400 East Avenue, Warwick RI 02886-1807
County: Kent FICE Identification: 003408
Unit ID: 217475
Telephone: (401) 825-1000 Carnegie Class: Assoc/MT-VT-High Trad
FAX Number: (401) 825-2166 Calendar System: Semester
URL: www.ccri.edu
Established: 1964 Annual Undergrad Tuition & Fees (In-State): $4,806
Enrollment: 13,684 Coed
Affiliation or Control: State IRS Status: 501(c)3
Highest Offering: Associate Degree
Accreditation: EH, ACBSP, ADNUR, ART, COARC, COMTA, DA, DH, DMS, HT, MLTAD, MUS, NAEYC, OTA, PNUR, PTAA, RAD

01 President .... Dr. Meghan HUGHES
05 Vice President for Academic Affairs .... Dr. Rosemary COSTIGAN
10 Vice President Finance/Strategy .... Ms. Kristen ALBRITTON
32 VP Stdnt Affs & Chf Outcomes Ofcr .... Ms. Sara ENRIGHT
111 AVP Institutional Advancement/ Col .... Mr. Robert (Bobby) G. GONDOLA, JR.
18 Interim Director of Physical Plant .... Mr. David A. SNOW
79 Interim Dean, Arts/Humanities/SoSc .... Mr. John COLE
76 Dean Health & Rehab Service .... Dr. Suzanne M. CARR
50 Interim Dean Bus/Sci/Tech & Math .... Ms. Barbara NAUMAN
103 Vice President of Workforce Develop .... Vacant
08 Dean of Library & Academic Innovati .... Mr. George K. HART
35 Dean of Students .... Mr. Michael J. CUNNINGHAM, II
21 Controller .... Mr. David J. RAWLINSON
35 Assoc Dean Student Life/Svc Lrng .... Dr. Rebecca H. YOUNT
15 Director of Human Resources .... Ms. Sybil F. BAILEY
13 Director Information Technology .... Ms. Pamela J. CHRISTMAN
19 Chief of Police .... Mr. Sean COLLINS
26 Director Marketing & Communications .... Ms. Amy P. KEMPE
41 Interim Director of Athletics .... Mr. Kevin S. SALISBURY
09 Interim Dir Inst Research/Planning .... Mr. Phillip S. GORDON
113 Bursar .... Vacant
88 Director Access to Opportunity .... Ms. Tracy KARASINSKI
109 Auxiliary Svcs Business Director .... Dr. Raymond N. KARASEK, III
22 Dir AA/EEO/Div/Incl/Title IX Coord .... Vacant
96 Director of Purchasing .... Ms. Lisa M. CONSIDINE-FONTES
36 Coordinator Career Services .... Ms. Camille NUMRICH
37 Director of Financial Aid .... Ms. Kelly A. MORRISSEY
04 Assistant to the President .... Ms. Deborah M. ZIELINSKI
06 Registrar .... Ms. Cathy L. PICARD-TESSIER
07 Director of Admissions .... Ms. Teresa M. KLESS
11 AVP for Administration .... Ms. Alix R. OGDEN
14 Director of Operations (IS) .... Mr. William R. FERLAND
38 Dean Student Dev/Assessment .... Mr. Robert D. CIPOLLA
43 Dir Legal Services/General Counsel .... Mr. Ronald A. CAVALLARO

Johnson & Wales University (D)

8 Abbott Park Place, Providence RI 02903-3703
County: Providence FICE Identification: 003404
Unit ID: 217235
Telephone: (401) 598-1000 Carnegie Class: Masters/L
FAX Number: (401) 598-2880 Calendar System: Semester
URL: https://www.jwu.edu/
Established: 1914 Annual Undergrad Tuition & Fees: $34,736
Enrollment: 5,676 Coed
Affiliation or Control: Independent Non-Profit IRS Status: 501(c)3
Highest Offering: Doctorate
Accreditation: EH, #ARCPA, DIETD

00 Chancellor .... Ms. Mim L. RUNEY
02 President Providence Campus .... Ms. Marie BERNARDO-SOUSA
05 Provost .... Mr. Kyle MCINNIS
84 VP of Enrollment Management .... Mr. Akhil GUPTA
86 VP Comm & Government Relations .... Ms. Lisa PELOSI
45 VP of Strategic Plng & Research .... Dr. W. Neal FOGG
13 VP of Information Technology .... Mr. Dave SOUZA
26 VP of Strategic Communications .... Mr. Michael RAIA
20 Vice Provost Academic Affairs .... Dr. Richard WISCOTT
08 Dean of Libraries .... Ms. Rosita HOPPER
76 Dean College of Health & Wellness .... Ms. Laura GALLIGAN
49 Dean College of Arts & Sciences .... Mr. Michael R. FEIN
50 Dean College of Business .... Ms. Mary MEIXELL
106 Dean College of Online Education .... Mr. David R. CARTWRIGHT
88 Assoc Dean Col of Culinary Arts .... Dr. Susan MARSHALL
54 Dean College of Engr & Design .... Mr. Frank TWEEDIE
88 Dean Col of Food Innov & Tech .... Mr. Jason EVANS
88 Interim Dean Col Hospitality Mgmt .... Ms. Jennifer GALIPEAU
106 VP Col Online Education .... Ms. Cindy PARKER
111 VP of Advancement & Univ Relations .... Ms. Maureen DUMAS
10 Vice Chancellor of Finance & Admin .... Mr. Joseph J. GREENE
21 Vice President of Finance .... Ms. Danielle SANTAMARIA
27 Director University Marketing .... Mr. Joe MAGENNIS
109 Vice President of Auxiliary Service .... Mr. Michael DOWNING
114 University Budget Director .... Ms. Eileen T. HASKINS
21 Director of Accounting Services .... Ms. Laurie O'KEEFE
116 Dir of Financial Plng & Analysis .... Ms. Michele VON HEIN
121 Dir of Academic Success Center .... Ms. Wendy ALEMAN
15 Vice President of Human Resources .... Ms. Diane D'AMBRA
16 Director of Human Resources .... Ms. Rebecca TONDREAU
118 Director of Benefits .... Ms. Christine OLIVER
09 Director Inst Research & Analysis .... Ms. Kristen SULLIVAN
29 Dir of Alumni Relations .... Ms. Lori ZABATTA
43 Vice President & General Counsel .... Ms. Luba SHUR
19 Exec Dir of Campus Safety/Security .... Mr. LeRoy ROSE, JR.
18 VP of Facilities Management .... Mr. Jason WITHAM
119 Director of Information Security .... Mr. Nicholas TELLA
32 VP of Stdnt Affairs/Dean of Stdnts .... Vacant
38 Assoc Dean Counsel/Health/Wellness .... Mr. Joseph BARRESI, JR.
35 Assoc Dean of Students .... Ms. Mel GRAF
35 Assoc Dean for Student Services .... Mr. Dameian SLOCUM
101 University Secretary .... Ms. Emily GILCREAST
07 Director of Admissions .... Ms. Amy OCONNELL
88 Dir of Enrollment Planning .... Ms. Teresa MAUK
06 University Registrar .... Ms. Tammy HARRIGAN
37 VP Stdnt Academic & Financial Svcs .... Ms. Lynn ROBINSON
39 Director of Residential Life .... Mr. Nev KRAGULJEVIC
36 Dean Experiential Educ/Career Svcs .... Ms. Sheri YOUNG
85 Dir International Student Services .... Mr. Wesley ROY
104 Asst Director of Study Abroad .... Ms. Amy EWEN
44 Director Annual Giving .... Vacant
96 Dir of Culinary Purchasing & Ops .... Mr. Erik GOELLNER

New England Institute of Technology (E)

One New England Tech Blvd., East Greenwich RI 02818
County: Kent FICE Identification: 007845
Unit ID: 217305
Telephone: (800) 736-7744 Carnegie Class: Bac/Assoc-Mixed
FAX Number: (401) 886-0859 Calendar System: Quarter
URL: www.neit.edu
Established: 1940 Annual Undergrad Tuition & Fees: $31,827
Enrollment: 2,031 Coed
Affiliation or Control: Independent Non-Profit IRS Status: 501(c)3
Highest Offering: Doctorate
Accreditation: EH, ADNUR, COARC, MLTAD, NUR, OT, OTA, PTAA, SURGT

01 President .... Mr. Richard I. GOUSE
03 Executive Vice President .... Mr. Scott FREUND
05 Senior Vice President and Provost .... Dr. Douglas H. SHERMAN
10 Sr VP Financial Affs & Endowment .... Ms. Cheryl C. CONNORS
32 Vice Pres Student Support Services .... Ms. Catherine B. KENNEDY
21 VP of Finance & Business Admin .... Mr. Kenneth JALBERT
103 VP Corporate Educ & Training .... Mr. Steven H. KITCHIN
20 Associate Provost .... Dr. Henry YOUNG
84 VP of Enrollment Mgt & Marketing .... Mr. Tim REARDON
37 Director Financial Aid .... Ms. Anna KELLY
08 Director Library .... Ms. Sharon CHARETTE
36 Director of Career Services .... Ms. Patricia BLAKEMORE
109 Director Auxiliary Services .... Mr. Patrick TRACEY
06 Registrar .... Ms. Sarah BOSWORTH
35 Director of Student Support Service .... Ms. Lee PEEBLES
13 Chief Info Technology Officer (CIO) .... Mr. Jacques LAFLAMME
19 Director Security/Safety .... Ms. Pamela MOFFATT-LIMOGES
43 Dir Legal Services/General Counsel .... Mr. Philip PARSONS
96 Director of Purchasing .... Mr. William MENARD
39 Director Student Housing .... Ms. Danielly JAMOUS

Providence College (F)

1 Cunningham Square, Providence RI 02918-0001
County: Providence FICE Identification: 003406
Unit ID: 217402
Telephone: (401) 865-1000 Carnegie Class: Masters/L
FAX Number: (401) 865-2057 Calendar System: Semester
URL: www.providence.edu
Established: 1917 Annual Undergrad Tuition & Fees: $54,388
Enrollment: 4,821 Coed
Affiliation or Control: Roman Catholic IRS Status: 501(c)3
Highest Offering: Master's
Accreditation: EH, SW

01 President .... Rev. Kenneth SICARD, OP
03 Executive Vice President/ Treasurer .... Ms. Ann MANCHESTER-MOLAK
04 Asst to Pres & Exec Vice President .... Vacant
05 Sr VP Academic Affairs/Provost .... Dr. Sean F. REID
10 Sr VP for Finance & Business/CFO .... Mr. John M. SWEENEY
30 Sr VP for Institutional Advancement .... Mr. Gregory T. WALDRON
32 Vice Pres Student Affairs .... Vacant
43 Vice President/General Counsel .... Mr. Christopher NERONHA
42 Vice Pres for Mission & Ministry .... Rev. James CUDDY, OP
21 Assoc VP for Finance/Asst Treasurer .... Ms. Jacqueline M. WHITE
35 Assoc VP for Student Affairs .... Dr. Steven A. SEARS
20 Assoc VP for Academic Affairs .... Dr. Brian J. BARTOLINI
41 Assoc VP for Athletics/Athletic Dir .... Mr. Robert G. DRISCOLL
15 Assoc Vice Pres for Human Resources .... Ms. Kathleen M. ALVINO
28 Assoc VP/Chief Diversity Officer .... Vacant
26 Assoc VP Public Affairs/Cmty Rels .... Mr. Steven J. MAURANO
20 Asst Vice Pres for Academic Affairs .... Mr. Charles J. HABERLE
21 Asst Vice Pres for Business Svcs .... Vacant
29 Asst Vice Pres for Alumni Relations .... Mr. Robert FERREIRA
44 Asst Vice Pres for Development .... Ms. Andrea B. KEEFE
45 Asst VP Capital Projects & Fac Plng .... Mr. Mark F. RAPOZA
58 Dean of Undergrad & Grad Studies .... Vacant
49 Dean School of Arts & Sciences .... Dr. Sheila A. LIOTTA
107 Dean School of Professional Studies .... Vacant
07 Assoc VP Admissions/Financial Aid .... Mr. Raul A. FONTS
50 Dean School of Business .... Dr. Sylvia MAXFIELD
51 Actg Dean Sch Continuing Education .... Ms. Carmen AGUILAR
35 AVP Stdnt Affs/Asst Dean of Stdnts .... Ms. Tiffany D. GAFFNEY
06 Registrar .... Ms. Yvonne D. ARRUDA
104 Dean of Global Education .... Vacant
35 Director of Student Activities .... Ms. Sharon L. HAY
84 Associate Dean of Enrollment Svcs .... Ms. Lucille A. CALORE
37 Exec Director of Financial Aid .... Ms. Sandra J. OLIVEIRA
19 Exec Director Safety & Security .... Vacant
88 Asst VP Integrated Learning & Admin .... Ms. Patricia A. GOFF
18 Exec Director of Physical Plant .... Mr. Andrew J. SULLIVAN
08 Director of Library .... Dr. Donald R. BAILEY
09 Director of Institutional Research .... Ms. Melanie R. SULLIVAN
90 Dir Enterprise Infrastructure & Ops .... Mr. Carmine R. PISCOPO
92 Director Liberal Arts Honors .... Dr. Stephen J. LYNCH
96 Exec Director of Business Services .... Mr. Gene R. ROBBINS
88 Exec Dir Academic Svcs/Writing Ctr .... Mr. Bryan D. MARINELLI

38 VP Student Development & Compliance ...Dr. James F. CAMPBELL
13 Chief Information Officer/CIO ...Mr. Paul V. FONTAINE
102 Dir Foundation/Corporate Relations ...Ms. Marilyn E. DESCHENES
105 Director Web Services ...Mr. Daniel C. DEMMONS
108 Director Institutional Assessment ...Ms. Cathy A. GAGNE

Rhode Island College (A)

600 Mount Pleasant Avenue, Providence RI 02908-1991
County: Providence FICE Identification: 003407
Unit ID: 217420
Telephone: (401) 456-8000 Carnegie Class: Masters/L
FAX Number: (401) 456-8379 Calendar System: Semester
URL: www.ric.edu
Established: 1854 Annual Undergrad Tuition & Fees (In-State): $10,260
Enrollment: 7,072 Coed
Affiliation or Control: State IRS Status: 501(c)3
Highest Offering: Doctorate
Accreditation: EH, ANEST, ART, CACREP, IACBE, MUS, NURSE, SW

01 President ...Dr. Frank A. SANCHEZ
05 Provost/VP Academic Affairs ...Dr. Helen TATE
10 VP Administration/Finance ...Mr. Stephen NEDDER
32 Int VP for Student Success ...Dr. Ducha HANG
111 VP College Advance & Ext Rels ...Ms. Kimberly C. DUMPSON
45 Exec Dir Strategic Initiative ...Mr. Clark M. GREENE
107 Assoc VP Prof Studies & Cont Educ ...Ms. Jenifer GIROUX
28 Assoc VP Comm/Equity & Diversity ...Ms. Anna M. CANO-MORALES
102 Executive Director RIC Foundation ...Mr. Edwin R. PACHECO
20 Vice Prov Undergraduate Affairs ...Dr. Holly L. SHADOIAN
35 Asst VP Stdnt Success/Dean of Stdnt ...Dr. Tamika WORDLOW-WILLIAMS
13 Asst VP Information Services/CIO ...Mr. Jon BARTELSON
84 Dean of Enrollment Management ...Mr. James TWEED
11 Asst VP Administration ...Mr. Jeffrey L. MARTIN
58 Int Dean of Graduate Studies ...Dr. Leslie SCHUSTER
49 Dean Faculty Arts & Sciences ...Dr. Earl L. SIMSON
53 Dean Sch Education & Human Dev ...Dr. Jeannine DINGUS-EASON
50 Int Dean School of Business ...Dr. Alema KARIM
66 Dean School of Nursing ...Dr. Carolynn MASTERS
70 Int Dean School of Social Work ...Dr. Jayashree NIMMAGADDA
15 Director of Human Resources ...Ms. Maggie SULLIVAN
22 Dir Institutional Equity ...Ms. Margaret A. LYNCH GADALETA
19 Director of Security & Safety ...Mr. James MENDONCA
09 Dir Inst Research & Planning ...Dr. Christopher P. HOURIGAN
114 Director of Budget & Fin Plng ...Mr. Robert EATON
18 Director Facilities & Operations ...Mr. James M. JERUE
18 Director Capital Projects ...Mr. Kevin J. FITTA
96 Director of Purchasing ...Ms. Jessica L. SILVA
08 Director of the Library ...Ms. Carissa DELIZIO
07 Director of Admissions ...Mr. Jason S. ANTHONY
121 Director of Academic Advising ...Mr. Christopher DACOSTA
06 Director of Records ...Ms. Tamecka C. HARDMON
37 Int Director Student Financial Aid ...Ms. Nancy A. BESSETTE
41 Dir of Athletics ...Mr. Donald E. TENCHER
90 Director User Support Services ...Mr. David E. TOMS
91 Director Management Info Sys ...Dr. Bin YU
119 Director of Information Security ...Mr. Henk E. SONDER
39 Director Res Life/Housing ...Ms. Darcy DUBOIS
36 Director Career Dev Center ...Ms. Demetria MORAN
23 Int Dir College Health Services ...Ms. Christie RISHWORTH
38 Int Director Counseling Center ...Dr. Ryan PORELL
29 Director Alumni Affairs ...Ms. Suzanna ALBA
104 Director of Study Abroad ...Ms. Gersende CHANFRAU
28 Director of Unity Center ...Ms. Pegah RAHMANIAN
113 Bursar ...Ms. Charlene L. SZCZEPANEK
105 Director Web Services ...Ms. Karen M. RUBINO
26 Dir of College Comm & Marketing ...Vacant

Rhode Island School of Design (B)

2 College Street, Providence RI 02903-2784
County: Providence FICE Identification: 003409
Unit ID: 217493
Telephone: (401) 454-6100 Carnegie Class: Spec-4-yr-Arts
FAX Number: (401) 454-6320 Calendar System: 4/1/4
URL: www.risd.edu
Established: 1877 Annual Undergrad Tuition & Fees: $54,890
Enrollment: 2,227 Coed
Affiliation or Control: Independent Non-Profit IRS Status: 501(c)3
Highest Offering: Master's
Accreditation: EH, LSAR

01 Interim President ...Mr. David PROULX
100 Chief of Staff and Communications ...Ms. Taylor SCOTT
05 Provost ...Dr. Kent KLEINMAN
10 Sr VP Finance and Administration ...Mr. Dave PROULX
84 VP Enrollment & Student Affairs ...Mr. Jamie O'HARA
88 Interim Director RISD Museum of Art ...Ms. Sarah GANZ BLYTHE
111 VP Institutional Engagement ...Mr. O'Neil OUTAR
26 Chief Marketing/Communcation Ofcr ...Ms. Kerci M. STROUD
20 Vice Provost ...Dr. Dan CAVICCHI
28 Assoc Prov Social Equity/Inclusion ...Mr. Matthew SHENODA
20 Assoc Prov Rsrch/Strtgic Prtnrships ...Ms. Sarah CUNNINGHAM
15 VP Human Resources ...Ms. Candace BAER
18 VP Campus Services ...Mr. Jack SILVA
43 General Counsel ...Ms. Renee BYAS
32 Assoc VP Student Affairs ...Ms. Barbara LOMONACO
20 Dean of Faculty ...Dr. Patricia BARBEITO
48 Dean Architecture & Design ...Ms. Scheri FULTINEER
57 Dean of Fine Arts ...Mr. Brooks HAGAN
88 Dean Experimental/Foundation Stds ...Ms. Joanne STRYKER
49 Dean of Liberal Arts ...Dr. Damian WHITE
08 Dean of Libraries ...Ms. Margot NISHIMURA
37 Asst VP for Enrollment Services ...Mr. Anthony GALLONIO
13 CIO ...Mr. Rick MICKOOL
06 Registrar ...Ms. Alison SHERMAN

Roger Williams University (C)

One Old Ferry Road, Bristol RI 02809-2921
County: Bristol FICE Identification: 003410
Unit ID: 217518
Telephone: (401) 253-1040 Carnegie Class: Masters/M
FAX Number: N/A Calendar System: Semester
URL: www.rwu.edu
Established: 1956 Annual Undergrad Tuition & Fees: $38,274
Enrollment: 4,702 Coed
Affiliation or Control: Independent Non-Profit IRS Status: 501(c)3
Highest Offering: First Professional Degree
Accreditation: EH, CONST, LAW

01 President ...Dr. Ioannis MIAOULIS
05 Provost ...Dr. Margaret EVERETT
10 Interim EVP Finance/Administration ...Mr. Marc LEONETTI
84 Chief of Staff/VP Marketing ...Mr. Brian WILLIAMS
21 Int VP for Accounting/Treasury Mgmt ...Ms. Nicole TURNER
32 Vice President for Student Life ...Mr. John J. KING
111 VP Institutional Advancement ...Ms. Amy BERKELEY
28 Vice President/Chief Diversity Ofcr ...Dr. Stephanie AKUNVABEY
08 Dean University Library ...Ms. Betsy P. LEARNED
26 Assoc VP Enrollment Mgmt/Marketing ...Ms. Tracy M. DACOSTA
84 VP & Dean Enrollment Mgmt ...Ms. Amy TIBERIO
15 Asst Vice Pres of Human Resources ...Mr. Thomas MCDONOUGH
09 AVP for Institutional Research ...Ms. Jennifer DUNSEATH
51 Dean of University College ...Ms. Gena BIANCO
27 AVP of Marketing/Communications ...Ms. Lynne MELLO
110 AVP of Institutional Advancement ...Ms. Christine PARKER
28 Dir Inst Diversity/Equity/Inclusion ...Ms. Zolla QUEZADA
61 Dean RWU School of Law ...Mr. Gregory BOWMAN
48 Dean Sch Arch/Art & Hist Preserv ...Mr. Stephen E. WHITE
50 Dean Gabelli School of Business ...Dr. Susan MCTIERNAN
54 Dean Sch Engrng/Comput/Constr Mgmt ...Dr. Robert GRIFFIN
88 Dean School of Justice Studies ...Dr. Eric BRONSON
123 Director Graduate Admissions ...Mr. Marcus HANSCOM
49 Dean Sch Social/Natural Sciences ...Dr. Benjamin GREENSTEIN
13 Chief Information Officer ...Mr. Daryl FORD
07 Assoc Dean of Undergrad Admissions ...Ms. Amanda MARSILI
37 Director Student Financial Aid ...Ms. Diane USHER
96 Director of Purchasing ...Ms. Kathy KANTERMAN
88 Director of Special Events ...Ms. Heidi DAGWAN
06 Registrar ...Mr. Daniel O'DRISCOLL
19 Director of Public Safety ...Mr. Steven MELARAGNO
41 Director of Athletics ...Ms. Kristen JACOBS
18 Asst VP Facilities/Capitol Projects ...Mr. William SEYMOUR
38 Dir Counseling/Student Devel ...Mr. Christopher BAILEY
23 Director Health Services ...Ms. Anne M. MITCHELL
39 Int Dir of Residence Life/Housing ...Ms. Katie RIBEIRO
88 Director of Prospect Research ...Ms. Nancy L. RAMOS
22 Title IX Coord/Associate Dean ...Ms. Jennifer STANLEY
40 Manager Bookstore ...Vacant

Salve Regina University (D)

100 Ochre Point Avenue, Newport RI 02840-4192
County: Newport FICE Identification: 003411
Unit ID: 217536
Telephone: (401) 847-6650 Carnegie Class: Masters/L
FAX Number: (401) 341-2925 Calendar System: Semester
URL: www.salve.edu
Established: 1947 Annual Undergrad Tuition & Fees: $42,920
Enrollment: 2,771 Coed
Affiliation or Control: Roman Catholic IRS Status: 501(c)3
Highest Offering: Doctorate
Accreditation: EH, ART, CACREP, IACBE, NURSE, SW

00 Chair of the Board of Trustees ...Ms. Cheryl MROZOWSKI
01 President ...Dr. Kelli ARMSTRONG
05 Vice Pres Academic Affairs/Provost ...Dr. Nancy SCHREIBER
32 Vice President Student Affairs ...Vacant
111 VP University Relations ...Mr. Michael L. SEMENZA
10 Vice President Administration & CFO ...Mr. William B. HALL
84 Vice Pres Enrollment Management ...Mr. James R. FOWLER
45 Vice Pres Strategic Initiatives ...Dr. James LUDES
88 Vice Pres for Mission Integration ...Dr. Theresa LADRIGAN-WHELPLEY
26 Assoc Vice Pres/Chief Comm Officer ...Ms. Kristine HENDRICKSON
21 Assoc Vice Pres Finance/ Controller ...Mr. Michael N. GRANDCHAMP
13 Assoc VP Info Technology/CIO ...Mr. Irving BRUCKSTEIN
20 Associate Provost ...Dr. Donna M. COOK
18 Asst VP for Facilities Management ...Mr. Eric MILNER
28 Asst VP Diversity and Retention ...Dr. Sami NASSIM
110 Asst VP for Advancement ...Ms. Katherine HOROSCHAK
112 Asst VP Development /Planned Giving ...Ms. Sandra ANTHOINE
07 Dean of Undergraduate Admissions ...Ms. Colleen EMERSON
44 Sr Director of Annual Giving Pgm ...Ms. Victoria DUCLOS-BARRETT
14 Sr Dir of Enterprise Applications ...Ms. Christine DUMONT
15 Director Human Resources ...Ms. Nancy ESCHER
41 Athletic Director ...Ms. Jody MOORADIAN
09 Dir Inst Research/Effectiveness ...Ms. Annemarie BARTLETT
32 Assoc VP/Dean of Students ...Ms. Kathleen FARLEY
06 Registrar ...Ms. Alissa BERTRAM
37 Director of Financial Aid ...Ms. Anne MCDERMOTT
29 Director Alumni & Parent Pgms ...Dr. Gerry WILLIS
08 Director of Library Services ...Ms. Dawn EMSELLEM
39 Director of Residence Life ...Mr. Jim MOURNIGHAN
90 Director Academic Computing ...Mr. Brian A. MCDONNELL
19 Director of Security/Safety ...Mr. Michael CARUOLO
40 Director of Bookstore ...Mr. Michael LEDDY
23 Director Health Services ...Ms. Elizabeth GALVIN
36 Director of Career Development ...Mr. Michael WISNEWSKI
96 Director of Purchasing ...Ms. Patrice COLEMAN
104 Director of International Programs ...Ms. Erin FITZGERALD
38 Dir of Student Counseling Services ...Ms. Meghan M. DECARVALHO
30 Chief Advancement Officer ...Ms. MaeLynn PATTEN
31 Dir Community Engagement/Service ...Ms. Kelly POWERS
112 Director of Major Gifts ...Ms. Katherine BREZINA
35 Associate Dean of Students ...Ms. Jennifer JENSEN
124 Director of Student Engagement ...Vacant
04 Admin Assistant to the President ...Ms. Janice VIOLANTE

University of Rhode Island (E)

45 Upper College Road, Kingston RI 02881
County: Washington FICE Identification: 003414
Unit ID: 217484
Telephone: (401) 874-1000 Carnegie Class: DU-Higher
FAX Number: (401) 874-7149 Calendar System: Semester
URL: www.uri.edu
Established: 1892 Annual Undergrad Tuition & Fees (In-State): $15,004
Enrollment: 17,649 Coed
Affiliation or Control: State IRS Status: 501(c)3
Highest Offering: Doctorate
Accreditation: EH, CAMPEP, CLPSY, CYTO, DIETD, DIETI, EXSC, LIB, LSAR, MFCD, MUS, NURSE, PHAR, PTA, SCPSY, SP

01 President ...Dr. Marc PARLANGE
100 Chief of Staff ...Ms. Michelle CURRERI
05 Int Provost/VP Academic Affairs ...Ms. Laura BEAUVAIS
46 Vice Pres Research/Economic Devel ...Dr. Peter SNYDER
10 Vice Pres for Admin & Finance ...Ms. Abigail RIDER
88 Assoc VP Res/Int Prop Mgmt/Comm ...Mr. Michael KATZ
88 Dir Univ Res External Relations ...Ms. Melissa MCCARTHY
88 Dir Research Development ...Ms. Karen MARKIN
46 Assoc VP Research Admin ...Dr. Theodore A. MYATT
29 Exec Dir Alumni Relations/Secy Assn ...Ms. Michele NOTA
26 Int Exec Dir Ext Relations/Comm ...Ms. Linda A. ACCIARDO
114 Dir Budget & Financial Planning ...Ms. Linda BARRETT
21 Controller ...Vacant
15 Asst Vice Pres Human Resource Admin ...Ms. Anne Marie COLEMAN
16 Director Personnel Services ...Ms. Laura KENERSON
19 Director Public Safety ...Mr. Stephen N. BAKER
12 Dir W.A. Jones Campus ...Ms. Maria DISANO
88 Assoc Dean Business Administration ...Dr. Shaw CHEN
88 Dir Capital Projects ...Mr. Paul DEPACE
88 Dir Planning & Real Estate Dev ...Mr. Ryan CARILLO
88 Dir Property & Support Svc ...Mrs. Vicki DUBE
96 Director Purchasing & Univ Stores ...Ms. Tracey ANGELL
28 AVP/Chief Diversity Officer ...Ms. Mary Grace ALMANDREZ
43 General Counsel ...Ms. Alyssa BOSS
32 Vice President Student Affairs ...Ms. Kathy M. COLLINS
109 Dir Dining Services ...Mr. Pierre ST-GERMAIN
41 Director of Athletics ...Mr. Thorr D. BJORN
103 Dir Career and Experiential Edu ...Ms. Kim STACK
38 Int Director Counseling Center ...Dr. Cory CLARK
88 Dir Recreational Services ...Ms. Jodi HAWKINS
35 Dean of Students ...Mr. Daniel GRANEY
88 Dir Special Pgms/Talent Devel ...Mr. Gerald WILLIAMS
88 Int Mgr Conf & Spec Pgm ...Ms. Sheri DAVIS
35 Asst VP Student Affs & Dir HRL ...Mr. Frankie MINOR
39 Assoc Dir Housing & Res Life ...Dr. Jeffrey PLOUFFE
23 Director Health Services ...Ms. Ellen REYNOLDS
40 Administrator Bookstore ...Mr. Paul WHITNEY
88 Spec Asst to the Prov for Acad Plng ...Ms. Ann M. MORRISSEY
88 Vice Prov Acad Finance/Personnel ...Dr. Matthew H. BODAH
84 AVP Enrollment Mgmt/Stdnt Success ...Mr. Dean LIBUTTI
07 Dean of Admissions ...Ms. Cynthia L. BONN
06 Dir Enrollment Services/Registrar ...Dr. Carnell JONES, JR.
20 Vice Provost for Acad & Fac Init ...Dr. Anne VEEGER
13 Int Chief Information Officer ...Mr. Karlis KAUGARS
90 Dir Media & Technology Services ...Mr. David S. PORTER
91 Dir University Computing Systems ...Ms. Donna BELDEN
51 Dean Col Educ & Prof Studies ...Dr. Anthony ROLLE
49 Dean of Arts & Sciences ...Dr. Jeanette E. RILEY
50 Dean Business Administration ...Dr. Maling EBRAHIMPOUR
54 Dean of Engineering ...Dr. Raymond M. WRIGHT
89 Dean Univ Col & Spec Acad Pgms ...Dr. Jayne E. RICHMOND
58 Dean of Graduate School ...Dr. Nasser H. ZAWIA
66 Dean of Nursing ...Dr. Barbara E. WOLFE
67 Dean of Pharmacy ...Dr. Paul LARRAT
69 Dean Col of Health Sciences ...Dr. Gary LIGUORI
53 Director School of Education ...Dr. David BYRD
88 Dean Grad School Oceanography ...Dr. Bruce CORLISS
88 Dean of Environment & Life Sciences ...Dr. John KIRBY
08 Dean University Libraries ...Mr. Karim B. BOUGHIDA
22 Director Affirm Act/Equal Oppty/Div ...Ms. Roxanne GOMES
37 Assoc Dir Enrol Svcs/Fin Aid ...Mr. Kenneth S. FERUS
92 Director Honors Program ...Dr. Lynne DERBYSHIRE
102 President URI Foundation ...Ms. Elizabeth O'ROURKE
85 Vice Provost for Global Initiatives ...Ms. Gifty AKO-ADOUNVO
106 Dir Learning/Assessment & Online ...Dr. Diane GOLDSMITH

94 Dir Gender and Women Studies .... Dr. Rosaria PISA
105 Manager Web Services .... Ms. Lisa CHEN
111 Sr Dir Advancement Services .... Mr. Scott BURDICK
44 Dir of Annual & Parent Giving .... Mr. John GARCIA

University of Rhode Island Feinstein Providence Campus (A)

80 Washington Street, Providence RI 02903
Telephone: (401) 277-5000 Identification: 770118
Accreditation: &EH

University of Rhode Island Narragansett Bay Campus (B)

215 South Ferry Road, Narragansett RI 02882-1197
Telephone: (401) 874-6222 Identification: 770129
Accreditation: &EH

SOUTH CAROLINA

Aiken Technical College (C)

PO Drawer 696, Aiken SC 29802-0696
County: Aiken FICE Identification: 010056
Unit ID: 217615
Telephone: (803) 508-7263 Carnegie Class: Assoc/MT-VT-High Trad
FAX Number: N/A Calendar System: Semester
URL: www.atc.edu
Established: 1972 Annual Undergrad Tuition & Fees (In-District): $5,306
Enrollment: 1,925 Coed
Affiliation or Control: State/Local IRS Status: 501(c)3
Highest Offering: Associate Degree
Accreditation: SC, ACBSP, ADNUR, DA, MAC, NAEYC, PNUR, RAD, SURGT

01 President .... Dr. Forest E. MAHAN
04 Executive Assistant to President .... Ms. Jill UHLER
05 VP Academic & Student Affairs .... Dr. Vinson BURDETTE
111 VP Advancement/Inst Effectiveness .... Ms. Mechelle ENGLISH
76 Dean of Health Sciences .... Dr. Brian LOGAN
51 Dean of Continuing Education .... Dr. Steve SIMMONS
97 Dean of General Education .... Fr. Frederick ROGERS
10 Vice Pres Administrative Services .... Mr. Andy JORDAN
37 Director of Financial Aid .... Ms. Erynn BLACK
13 Director of Info Systems Mgmt .... Mr. Walter BUSBEE
15 Director of Human Resources .... Ms. Sylvia BYRD
21 Controller .... Ms. Betsy CLINE
96 Director of Purchasing .... Vacant
18 Director Facilities & Operations .... Mr. Kevin MCCARTHY
84 Director of Enrollment Services .... Mrs. Dawn BUTTS
38 Director Counseling/Disabilities .... Mr. Rich WELDON
26 Director Marketing & PR .... Ms. Nikasha DICKS
30 Director Foundation & Alumni .... Dr. Elizabeth LACLAIR

Allen University (D)

1530 Harden Street, Columbia SC 29204-1085
County: Richland FICE Identification: 003417
Unit ID: 217624
Telephone: (803) 376-5700 Carnegie Class: Bac-A&S
FAX Number: N/A Calendar System: Semester
URL: www.allenuniversity.edu
Established: 1870 Annual Undergrad Tuition & Fees: $13,340
Enrollment: 705 Coed
Affiliation or Control: African Methodist Episcopal IRS Status: 501(c)3
Highest Offering: Master's
Accreditation: SC

01 President .... Dr. Ernest MCNEALEY
05 VP Academic Affairs .... Dr. Toni MUHAMMAD
81 Dean Mathematics/Natural Sciences .... Vacant
79 Dean Arts and Humanities .... Dr. Kevin TRUMPETER
73 Dean D.G. Theological Seminary ..Dr. Jamal-Dominique HOPKINS
50 Dean Business/Soc Sci & Education .... Vacant
32 VP Student Affairs .... Dr. John Michael HARPE
10 VP Fiscal Affairs .... Ms. Ruby FIELDING
111 VP Institutional Advancement .... Mr. Dub TAYLOR
30 AVP Inst Advance/Dir Development .... Mr. Ti BARNES
26 Dir Marketing & Communications .... Ms. Anika V. COBB
15 Chief Human Resources Officer .... Ms. Andraea HERRIN
41 Athletic Director .... Mr. Theodore KEATON
09 Director Institutional Research .... Vacant
08 Director of Library Services .... Ms. Carol BOWERS
90 Director of IT Services .... Mr. Samuel PASCHAL
36 Director Counseling/Placement .... Dr. Flavia ELDEMIRE
39 Director Residential Life & Health .... Ms. Oveta GLOVER
35 Director of Student Activities .... Ms. Lisa REEVES
19 Chief of Police .... Chief Kelvin DAVIS
84 Dean Enrollment Mgmt/Registrar .... Ms. Marilyn DEBERRY
07 Director of Admissions .... Mrs. Heather TURNER
37 Director of Financial Aid .... Ms. Lola KENNEDY
21 Asst VP Fiscal Affairs/Comptroller .... Mr. John SAMPSON
113 Bursar .... Ms. Sharon DAVIS
18 Director of Operations .... Mr. Robert RILEY
29 Director of Alumni Affairs .... Vacant
25 Director of Sponsored Programs .... Ms. Sunya YOUNG
88 Director of Bands .... Mr. Eddie ELLIS
04 Executive Assistant .... Ms. Violet HARRISON

American College of the Building Arts (E)

649 Meeting St, Charleston SC 29403
County: Charleston FICE Identification: 042830
Unit ID: 485698
Telephone: (843) 577-5245 Carnegie Class: Not Classified
FAX Number: (843) 764-9832 Calendar System: Semester
URL: acba.edu
Established: 2004 Annual Undergrad Tuition & Fees: $20,572
Enrollment: 93 Coed
Affiliation or Control: Independent Non-Profit IRS Status: 501(c)3
Highest Offering: Baccalaureate
Accreditation: ACCSC

01 President .... Lt.Gen. Colby M. BROADWATER, III
05 Chief Academic Officer .... Dr. A. Wade RAZZI
10 Chief Financial Officer .... Mr. Chad H. URBAN

Anderson University (F)

316 Boulevard, Anderson SC 29621-4035
County: Anderson FICE Identification: 003418
Unit ID: 217633
Telephone: (864) 231-2000 Carnegie Class: Masters/M
FAX Number: (864) 231-2004 Calendar System: Semester
URL: www.andersonuniversity.edu
Established: 1911 Annual Undergrad Tuition & Fees: $29,980
Enrollment: 3,848 Coed
Affiliation or Control: Other IRS Status: 501(c)3
Highest Offering: Doctorate
Accreditation: SC, ACBSP, ART, CAEPN, MUS, NURSE, @PTA, THEA

01 President .... Dr. Evans P. WHITAKER
20 Provost .... Dr. Ryan NEAL
11 Sr VP Administration & Brand .... Mr. David RASHED
30 SVP Development/Pres Affairs .... Mr. James LANDRITH
32 Sr VP Student Development .... Dr. James FEREIRA
13 Chief Information Officer .... Mr. Ron OPPATT
10 VP Finance/Chief Financial Officer .... Ms. Kristie COLE
28 VP Diversity and Inclusion .... Dr. James NOBLE
41 VP Athletics .... Mr. Bert EPTING
42 VP Church Rel/Sr Campus Pastor .... Mr. Mayson EASTERLING
42 VP Christian Life/Campus Min .... Vacant
84 VP Enrollment Management .... Ms. Pam ROSS
106 VP Tech/Online Learning/Innovation .... Dr. Benjamin DEATON
26 AVP Marketing & Communications .... Mr. James DUGUID
27 Exec Dir Public Relations .... Mr. Andrew BECKNER
20 Asst Provost .... Mr. Nathan COX
29 AVP for Alumni/Parent Relations .... Mr. Jason RUTLAND
73 Dean COCS & Clamp Div Sch .... Mr. James DUDUIT
66 Dean School of Nursing .... Vacant
49 Dean College of Arts/Sciences .... Dr. Wayne COX
57 Dean SC School of the Arts .... Dr. David LARSON
88 Dean School Int Design .... Ms. Anne MARTIN
50 Dean College of Business .... Mr. Steven NAIL
76 Dean College of Health Professions .... Dr. Donald PEACE
82 Dean School Pub Svc/Admin .... Dr. Clarence WILLIAMSON
53 Dean College of Education .... Dr. Mark BUTLER
88 Assoc Dean College of Business .... Dr. Evie MAXEY
121 Dean Student Success .... Dr. Dianne KING
06 University Registrar .... Mrs. Elizabeth CRANFORD
35 Dean Student Life .... Mr. Jonathan GROPP
35 Dean Student Development .... Ms. Robyn SANDERSON
100 Chief of Staff .... Mr. John DON
88 Exec Dir Conf Svcs/Univ Events .... Mrs. Jody BRYANT
07 Dir Admission .... Mr. William MONTS
08 Dir Thrift Library .... Mr. Neal MILLWOOD
09 Dir External Reporting .... Mr. Daryl A. IVERSON
15 Dir Human Resources .... Mrs. Amy PORPILIA
18 Dir Facilities .... Mr. Charles DICKERSON
19 Dir Campus Safety .... Mr. Edward AMAN
21 Controller .... Mrs. Victoria PIERCE
88 Dir Sports Med/Asst Dir Ath .... Mr. William DUVALL
23 Dir Health Services/Nurse .... Mrs. Debbie TAYLOR
35 Dir Student Activities .... Ms. Brenna MORRIS
36 Dir Career Services .... Mrs. Rebecca DHANARINE
37 Dir Financial Aid & Scholarships .... Mr. Mike SAPIENZA
38 Dir Counseling .... Ms. Erin MAURER
104 Dir International Programs .... Dr. Ann-Margaret THEMISTOCLEOUS
04 Exec Assistant to the President .... Mrs. Alana DEAN PRICE

Benedict College (G)

1600 Harden Street, Columbia SC 29204-1086
County: Richland FICE Identification: 003420
Unit ID: 217721
Telephone: (803) 253-5000 Carnegie Class: Bac-Diverse
FAX Number: (803) 253-5059 Calendar System: Semester
URL: www.benedict.edu
Established: 1870 Annual Undergrad Tuition & Fees: $17,200
Enrollment: 1,731 Coed
Affiliation or Control: Independent Non-Profit IRS Status: 501(c)3
Highest Offering: Master's
Accreditation: SC, ACBSP, ART, CAEPN, SW

01 President .... Dr. Roslyn C. ARTIS
05 Vice Pres for Academic Affairs .... Dr. Janeen WITTY
100 Chief of Staff .... Dr. Ceeon D. SMITH
10 Vice President Business/Finance .... Mr. Chris THOMPSON

108 Assoc VP for Academic Assessment .... Dr. Kimberly HAYNES STEPHENS
32 Vice President Student Affairs .... Mr. Gary E. KNIGHT
111 Vice Pres Institutional Advancement ..... Mrs. Leandra H. BURGESS
20 Assoc Vice Pres Academic Affairs .... Dr. George A. DEVLIN
21 Asst VP for Business & Finance .... Ms. Jackie BROWN
26 Asst VP for Comm & Marketing .... Ms. Kymm HUNTER
07 Director of Admissions .... Ms. Keisha MONTGOMERY
29 Assistant VP for Alumni Relations .... Mrs. Ada A. BELTON
13 System Administrator .... Mr. Darren CLINTON
84 VP for Enrollment Management .... Dr. Emmanuel LALANDE
15 Interim Director of Human Resources .... Ms. Elaine BROWN
06 Registrar/Director Student Records .... Mrs. Wanda A. SCOTT-KINNEY
41 Athletics Director .... Mr. Willie WASHINGTON
38 Exec Dir Career Pathways Initiative .... Ms. Tondaleya JACKSON
42 Campus Minister .... RevDr. Lillie A. BURGESS
19 Director Campus Safety .... Mr. Kevin PORTEE
36 Career Development Coordinator .... Ms. Sonya JOHNSON
37 Director Financial Aid .... Ms. Monique RICKENBAKER
19 Director Physical Plant .... Mr. Todd FOSTER
08 Director of Library .... Mrs. Darlene ZINNERMAN-BETHEA
09 Research Coordinator .... Dr. Dawn MILLS CAMPBELL
88 Assessment Coordinator .... Dr. Chasisity SPRINGS
25 Coordinator Title III .... Ms. Deborah MCKENZIE
49 Dean Sch Human/Arts/Soc Sci .... Vacant
50 Dean School of Bus/Econ .... Dr. Tracy DUNN
53 Interim Dean Educ/Health Human Svcs ...... Dr. Tracy MIDDLETON
72 Dean Sch Science/Tech/Engrng/Math .... Dr. Fouzi ARAMMASH
92 Dean School of Honors .... Dr. Warren ROBINSON
57 Chair Communications and Arts .... Ms. Gina MOORE
50 Chair Business Admin/Mgmt/Mktg .... Mr. Melvin MILLER
59 Chair Education and Family Studies .... Dr. Tracy MIDDLETON
70 Chair Social Work .... Dr. John MILLER
81 Chair Bio/Chem/Environment Hlth Sci .... Dr. Larry LOWE
68 Chair Health/Physical Ed/Recreation .... Dr. Paula SHELBY
54 Chair Comp Science/Physics/Engr .... Dr. Fouzi H. ARAMMASH
88 Int Chair Economics/Finance/Acctg .... Dr. Victor OYINBO

Bob Jones University (H)

1700 Wade Hampton Boulevard, Greenville SC 29614-0001
County: Greenville FICE Identification: 003421
Unit ID: 217749
Telephone: (864) 242-5100 Carnegie Class: Masters/S
FAX Number: (864) 235-6661 Calendar System: Semester
URL: www.bju.edu
Established: 1927 Annual Undergrad Tuition & Fees: $20,890
Enrollment: 3,029 Coed
Affiliation or Control: Independent Non-Profit IRS Status: 501(c)3
Highest Offering: Doctorate
Accreditation: SC, NURSE, TRACS

00 Chancellor .... Dr. Bob JONES, III
01 President .... Dr. Stephen D. PETTIT
05 Exec Vice Pres for Academic Affairs .... Dr. Gary M. WEIER
111 VP Advancement & Alumni Relations ..... Mr. John D. MATTHEWS
26 Chief Communication Officer .... Ms. Carol A. KEIRSTEAD
11 Vice Provost for Academic Admin .... Dr. David A. FISHER
45 Vice Provost Strategic Initiatives .... Dr. Beverly CORMICAN
10 VP for Business and Finance .... Mr. Steve DICKINSON
32 VP Student Develop & Discipleship .... Dr. Alan T. BENSON
84 Chief Enrollment Officer .... Dr. Bobby WOOD
15 Chief Human Resources Officer .... Mr. Kevin L. TAYLOR
13 Chief Information Officer .... Mr. Marvin P. REEM
49 Dean College of Arts and Science .... Dr. Renae WENTWORTH
73 Dean School of Religion .... Dr. Kevin OBERLIN
73 Dean BJU Seminary .... Dr. Neal CUSHMAN
57 Dean Sch Fine Arts & Communication ..... Dr. Darren P. LAWSON
53 Dean School of Education .... Dr. Brian A. CARRUTHERS
50 Dean School of Business .... Mr. Mike BUITER
76 Dean School of Health Professions .... Dr. Jessica MINOR
06 Registrar .... Dr. Daniel SMITH
35 Director of Student Life .... Mr. Jonathan G. DAULTON
34 Women's Director of Student Life .... Ms. Deneen LAWSON
07 Director of Admission .... Rev. Stephen L. BRADLEY
88 Director of Ministry Training .... Dr. Nathan G. CROCKETT
41 Athletic Director .... Dr. Neal RING
37 Director of Financial Aid .... Mrs. Susan YOUNG
08 Dean of Libraries .... Vacant
09 Sr Dir Planning/Rsrch/Assessment .... Rev. Phil GERARD
100 Chief of Staff .... Mr. Randy PAGE

Central Carolina Technical College (I)

506 N Guignard Drive, Sumter SC 29150-2499
County: Sumter FICE Identification: 003995
Unit ID: 218858
Telephone: (803) 778-1961 Carnegie Class: Assoc/MT-VT-High Trad
FAX Number: (803) 778-7880 Calendar System: Semester
URL: www.cctech.edu
Established: 1962 Annual Undergrad Tuition & Fees (In-State): $6,594
Enrollment: 2,885 Coed
Affiliation or Control: State IRS Status: 501(c)3
Highest Offering: Associate Degree
Accreditation: SC, ADNUR, CSHSE, MAC, NAEYC, SURGT

01 President .... Dr. Kevin POLLOCK
05 Vice President for Academic Affairs .... Dr. Jeffery THOMAS
10 Vice President for Business Affairs .... Ms. Terry L. BOOTH
32 Vice President for Student Affairs .... Ms. Lisa BRACKEN

111 Vice Pres Institutional Advancement ....Ms. Misty HATFIELD
04 Assistant to the President ....Ms. Diana REARDON
51 Dean Cont Educ/Workforce Devel ....Ms. Elizabeth WILLIAMS
08 Dean of Learning Resources ....Ms. Nancy BISHOP
26 Director Public Relations ....Ms. Catherine FRYE
15 Director Human Resources ....Mrs. Ronalda S. STOVER
13 Director Information Systems ....Mr. Brian DAVIS
06 Registrar ....Ms. Jennifer SZUPKA
07 Dir Recruitment & Admissions ....Ms. A. Sierra NEAL
37 Director Student Financial Aid ....Mr. Ken BERNARD
09 Dir Research/Institutional Effect ....Mr. Bryan MAY
121 Dir Stdnt Support Svcs/TRIO ....Ms. Gwendolyn PARKER
54 Dean of Industrial and Engineering ....Mr. Bert HANCOCK
76 Dean of Health Sciences ....Ms. Mary Jo ARDIS
97 Dean of General Education ....Mr. Jason TISDEL

Charleston School of Law (A)

81 Mary Street, PO Box 535, Charleston SC 29402
County: Charleston FICE Identification: 040963
Unit ID: 451510
Telephone: (843) 329-1000 Carnegie Class: Spec-4-yr-Law
FAX Number: (843) 720-7899 Calendar System: Semester
URL: www.charlestonlaw.edu
Established: 2003 Annual Graduate Tuition & Fees: N/A
Enrollment: 558 Coed
Affiliation or Control: Proprietary IRS Status: Proprietary
Highest Offering: First Professional Degree; No Undergraduates
Accreditation: LAW

01 President ....Mr. J. Edward BELL, III
05 Dean & Provost ....Mr. Larry CUNNINGHAM
20 Associate Dean Academic Affairs ....Mrs. Margaret M. LAWTON
07 Assoc Dean Admission/Financial Aid ....Ms. Jacqueline B. BELL
32 Assoc Dean of Students ....Mr. Brett BARKER
13 Assoc Dean of Info Services ....Ms. Lisa SMITH-BUTLER
36 Asst Dean Career Services ....Mr. Mark S. MOORE
10 Chief Financial Officer ....Ms. Wende WOOD
06 Registrar ....Ms. Emma BAKER
15 Director Human Resources ....Ms. Shera L. SILVIS
08 Director of Library ....Ms. Katie BROWN

Charleston Southern University (B)

PO Box 118087, Charleston SC 29423-8087
County: Charleston FICE Identification: 003419
Unit ID: 217688
Telephone: (843) 863-7000 Carnegie Class: Masters/M
FAX Number: (843) 863-8074 Calendar System: Semester
URL: www.csuniv.edu
Established: 1964 Annual Undergrad Tuition & Fees: $28,100
Enrollment: 3,350 Coed
Affiliation or Control: Southern Baptist IRS Status: 501(c)3
Highest Offering: Doctorate
Accreditation: SC, #ARCPA, CAATE, CAEPN, IACBE, MUS, NUR

01 President ....Dr. Dondi E. COSTIN
46 Vice Pres for Strategic Planning ....Dr. Michael BRYANT
05 Vice President Academic Affairs ....Dr. Jacqueline FISH
10 VP for Business Affairs ....Mr. Luke BLACKMON
04 Exec Assistant to the President ....Mrs. Faye WOOD
07 Director of Admissions ....Mrs. Kimberly FORD
84 Vice Pres Enrollment Management ....Dr. Tony TURNER
30 Vice Pres Development ....Mr. David BAGGS
20 Asst VP for Academic Affairs ....Dr. Scott YARBROUGH
32 VP for Student Affs/Dean of Stdnts ....Mr. Clark CARTER
13 Chief Information Officer ....Mr. Shannon PHILLIPS
08 Director of the Library ....Mr. Eric KISTLER
06 Registrar ....Mrs. Amanda BARON
21 Controller ....Mrs. Janelle FOX
26 Director of Integrated Marketing ....Mr. Richard ESPOSITO
09 Dir of Institutional Effectiveness ....Mr. Jeffrey BABETZ
58 Dir of Graduate Business Program ....Dr. Maxwell ROLLINS
41 Athletic Director ....Mr. Jeff BARBER
42 Asst Dean Campus Ministries ....Mr. Jon DAVIS
19 Director of Security ....Mr. John WILSON
90 Director of Computer Science ....Dr. Sean HAYES
18 Director of Facility Services ....Mr. Nick CIMORELLI
07 Director of Enrollment Services ....Mr. Nick BALLENGER
15 Director of Human Resources ....Mrs. Lindsey WALKE
36 Assistant Dean for Career Center ....Dr. Nina GRANT
38 Director of Student Counseling ....Mrs. Kimberly PERKINS
96 Director of Purchasing ....Mrs. Lisa OROZCO
37 Director Student Financial Aid ....Mrs. Teri KARGES
39 Assistant Dean of Residence Life ....Ms. Casey BOLDUC
50 Dean College of Business ....Dr. David PALMER
83 Dean Humanities/Social Sciences ....Dr. John KUYKENDALL
81 Dean Science & Mathematics ....Dr. Todd ASHBY
66 Dean of Nursing/Health Sciences ....Dr. Andreea MEIER
53 Dean College of Education ....Dr. Julie FERNANDEZ
104 Director International Programs ....Mrs. Stephanie LEVAN
108 Director Institutional Assessment ....Mr. Jeff BABETZ
106 Assoc VP for CSU Online ....Dr. Marc EMBLER
28 Director of Diversity ....Rev. Tim GRANT
29 Director Alumni Affairs ....Mr. Hunter MIZELL

The Citadel, The Military College of South Carolina (C)

171 Moultrie Street, Charleston SC 29409-0001
County: Charleston FICE Identification: 003423
Unit ID: 217864
Telephone: (843) 225-3294 Carnegie Class: Masters/L
FAX Number: (843) 953-5287 Calendar System: Semester
URL: www.citadel.edu
Established: 1842 Annual Undergrad Tuition & Fees (In-State): $12,620
Enrollment: 3,740 Coed
Affiliation or Control: State IRS Status: 501(c)3
Highest Offering: Beyond Master's But Less Than Doctorate
Accreditation: SC, CACREP, CAEPN, MPCAC, NURSE

01 President ....Gen. Glenn M. WALTERS, RET.
00 Chairman of the Board ....Col. Dylan W. GOLF
05 Provost/Dean ....BGen. Sally SELDEN
11 Senior Vice Pres for Operations ....Col. Thomas G. PHILIPKOSKY
10 Vice President of Finance ....Col. Charles CANSLER
32 Commandant of Cadets ....Capt. Eugene PALUSO
26 Vice President for Comm & Marketing ....Vacant
41 Dir Intercollegiate Athletics ....Mr. Mike CAPACCIO
102 Chief Exec Officer of Foundation ....Dr. Jay DOWD
04 Executive Assistant to President ....Cdr. William LIND
18 Vice Pres Facilities/Engineering ....Cdr. Jeffrey LAMBERSON
43 General Counsel ....Mr. Mark C. BRANDENBURG
20 Assoc Provost Academic Affairs ....Col. Kevin BOWER
108 Dir Accreditation and Assessment ....Dr. Karin ROOF
07 Director of Admissions ....Vacant
06 Registrar ....Maj. Lisa M. BLAKE
113 Treasurer ....Ms. Lindsey M. NETTLES
29 Exec Dir Alumni Affairs ....Mr. Tom MCALISTER
08 Director of Library ....Mr. Aaron WIMER
13 Chief Information Officer ....Maj. Kyle HERRON
109 Asst VP Auxiliary Services ....Maj. Kevin REID
37 Director Financial Aid/ Scholarships ....LtCol. Henry M. FULLER, JR.
15 Chief Human Resources Officer ....Maj. Leah S. SCHONFELD
36 Director of Career Services ....Ms. Page TISDALE
38 Director of Citadel Counseling Ctr ....Dr. Suzanne BUFANO
84 Assoc Provost for Enrollment Mgmt ....Dr. Kelly BRENNAN
09 Director of Institutional Research ....Ms. Lisa L. PACE
19 Director of Public Safety ....Chief Michael TURNER
23 College Physician ....Dr. Carey M. CAPELL
40 Director of the Cadet Store ....Ms. Linda MATTINGLY
42 Chaplain/Dir Religious Activities ....Mr. Aaron MEADOWS
92 Director Honors Program ....Dr. Deirdre RAGAN
86 Director Govt & Community Affairs ....Col. Cardon B. CRAWFORD
96 Director of Purchasing ....Vacant
22 Dir Affirmative Action/Equal Oppty ....Dr. Shawn EDWARDS
50 Dean of the School of Business ....Col. Michael WEEKS
53 Dean of the School of Education ....Col. Evan T. ORTLIEB
54 Dean of the School of Engineering ....Col. Ronald W. WELCH
81 Dean School of Science/Math ....Col. Darin T. ZIMMERMAN
79 Dean Sch Humanities/Social Sciences ....Col. Brian M. JONES
101 Spec Asst to President/Brd Matters ....Ms. Lori HEDSTROM
93 Director Multicultural Affairs ....LtCol. Robert P. PICKERING
16 Deputy Director of Human Resources ....Mr. Wesley S. SAMS
114 Chief Budget Administrator ....Maj. Michael S. KEENEY
121 Director of Student Success ....LtCol. Robert P. PICKERING
116 Audit Officer ....Mr. Gary MALLOY
28 Asst Provost for Diversity ....Vacant
21 Controller ....Vacant
105 College Web Designer ....Mr. Morgan SPENCER
119 IT Security Manager ....Mr. Justin CONSOLVO
58 Asst Dean of Graduate College ....Vacant
44 Sr Director of Legacy Giving ....Mr. Bill YAEGER
112 VP Legacy/Annual Reunion Giving ....Mr. Jonathan KRESKEN
27 Director of Marketing ....Ms. Kara KLEIN
104 Director Study Abroad ....Maj. Zane SEGLE
120 Director Teaching Innovation ....Dr. Diana CHESHIRE

Claflin University (D)

400 Magnolia Street, Orangeburg SC 29115-4477
County: Orangeburg FICE Identification: 003424
Unit ID: 217873
Telephone: (800) 922-1276 Carnegie Class: Bac-Diverse
FAX Number: (803) 531-2860 Calendar System: Semester
URL: www.claflin.edu
Established: 1869 Annual Undergrad Tuition & Fees: $17,046
Enrollment: 2,048 Coed
Affiliation or Control: United Methodist IRS Status: 501(c)3
Highest Offering: Master's
Accreditation: SC, ACBSP, CAEP, MUS, NURSE

01 President ....Dr. Dwaun J. WARMACK
05 Provost/Chief Academic Officer ....Dr. Karl S. WRIGHT
10 Vice President for Fiscal Affairs ....Mrs. Tijuana R. HUDSON
111 Int VP Institutional Advancement ....Mr. Marcus H. BURGESS
32 Vice Pres Student Devel & Services ....Dr. Leroy A. DURANT
45 VP Plng/Assessment/Information Svcs ....Dr. Zia HASAN
20 Int Vice Provost Academic Programs ....Dr. Verlie A. TISDALE
26 AVP Communications & Marketing ....Mr. George W. JOHNSON
108 AVP Institutional Effectiveness ....Dr. Bridget P. DEWEES
15 Assoc Vice Pres Human Resources ....Ms. Shirley A. BIGGS
39 Exec Dir Housing & Residence Life ....Mr. Dillon BECKFORD
07 Director of Admissions ....Mr. Michael ZEIGLER
79 Dean Sch Humanities & Soc Science ....Dr. Isaiah R. MCGEE
50 Dean School of Business ....Dr. Nicholas HILL
53 Dean School of Education ....Dr. Anthony PITTMAN
81 Dean Sch Natural Sciences & Math ....Dr. Verlie A. TISDALE
13 Assoc VP Information Tech Svcs ....Mr. James E. BRENN
51 Exec Dir Prof/Continuing Studies ....Vacant
08 Library Director ....Mrs. Marilyn GIBBS DRAYTON
37 Director of Financial Aid ....Ms. Terria C. WILLIAMS
36 Director of Career Development ....Mrs. Carolyn R. SNELL
41 Athletic Director ....Mr. Robert O'NEAL
06 Registrar ....Mrs. Tanika L. BEARD
29 Director Alumni Affairs/Annual Fund ....Mrs. Zelda LEE

19 Int Exec Director of Public Safety ....Mr. Melvin WILLIAMS
46 Asst Vice Provost for Research ....Vacant
04 Executive Admin Asst to President ....Ms. Melvenia WILLIAMS
09 Director of Institutional Research ....Vacant
84 Int Vice Pres Enrollment Management ....Mr. Reynolda BROWN

Clemson University (E)

201 Sikes Hall, Clemson SC 29634-0001
County: Pickens FICE Identification: 003425
Unit ID: 217882
Telephone: (864) 656-3311 Carnegie Class: DU-Highest
FAX Number: (864) 656-4040 Calendar System: Semester
URL: www.clemson.edu
Established: 1889 Annual Undergrad Tuition & Fees (In-State): $15,558
Enrollment: 26,406 Coed
Affiliation or Control: State IRS Status: 501(c)3
Highest Offering: Doctorate
Accreditation: SC, ART, CACREP, CAEPN, CAPRT, CARTE, CONST, CVT, DIETD, IPSY, LSAR, NURSE, PH, PLNG

01 President ....Dr. James P. CLEMENTS
05 Provost ....Dr. Robert H. JONES
43 General Counsel/Sec to Board ....Mr. W.C. (Chip) HOOD
10 Exec VP for Finance & Operations ....Mr. Anthony E. WAGNER
32 VP Student Affairs ....Dr. Chris MILLER
86 VP Governmental Affairs ....Ms. Angela LEIDINGER
111 Vice President for Advancement ....Mr. A. Neill CAMERON, JR.
86 Vice Pres Public Services ....Dr. George R. ASKEW
46 Vice President for Research ....Dr. Tanju KARANFIL
103 Vice Pres for Economic Development ....Dr. John M. BALLATO
13 Int Vice Pres & Chief Info Officer ....Mr. Brian VOSS
85 Vice Provost for International Affs ....Ms. Sharon NAGY
100 Chief of Staff ....Mr. Max ALLEN
29 VP Development/Alumni Relations ....Mr. Brian J. O'ROURKE
18 AVP/Chief Facilities Officer ....Mr. Todd BARNETTE
35 Sr Assoc Dean of Students ....Ms. Kimberly M. POOLE
20 Assoc Provost Faculty Development ....Ms. Amy L. LAWTON-RAUH
22 AVP Access & Equity ....Mr. Lewis J. KNIGHTON, JR.
26 AVP Strategic Comm/Univ Relations ....Mr. Joseph P. GALBRAITH
28 Chief Inclusion/Equity Officer ....Mr. Lee A. GILL
08 Dean of Libraries ....Mr. Christopher N. COX
84 AVP Enrollment Management ....Mr. David KUSKOWSKI
06 Registrar ....Mrs. Debra SPARACINO
37 Director of Financial Aid ....Mrs. Elizabeth MILAM
36 Exec Director of Career Center ....Mr. O'Neil BURTON
38 Interim Director of Counseling ....Dr. Birma GAINOR
47 Dean Col Agric/Forestry/Life Sci ....Dr. Keith L. BELLI
58 Dean Graduate School/Vice Provost ....Dr. John M. LOPES
48 Dean Col Arch/Arts/Humanities ....Dr. Nicholas VAZSONYI
54 Dean Col Engr/Sciences ....Dr. Anand GRAMOPADHYE
83 Dean Col of Behavioral/Social Sci ....Dr. Leslie HOSSFELD
50 Dean College of Business ....Ms. Wendy YORK
53 Dean College of Education ....Dr. George J. PETERSON
81 Dean of Science ....Dr. Cynthia YOUNG
09 Director Institutional Research ....Dr. Juan XU
39 Executive Director of Housing ....Ms. Kathy B. HOBGOOD
41 Director of Athletics ....Mr. Dan RADAKOVICH
112 AVP of Estate & Planned Giving ....Ms. Jovanna J. KING
23 Director Student Health Services ....Mr. George W. CLAY
15 Human Resources Director ....Mr. Joseph J. BYRNE
91 Exec Dir Enterprise Applications ....Mr. Barrett KENDJORIA
25 Director Sponsored Programs ....Ms. Sheila T. LISCHWE
19 AVP Public Safety/Police Chief ....Chief Greg MULLEN
96 Director of Purchasing ....Mr. Michael NEBESKY
04 Exec Assistant to the President ....Ms. Donna Jean (DJ) LAWS
88 Exec Dir Teaching Effect/Innovation ....Ms. Taimi OLSEN
121 Director of Academic Success Center ....Ms. Susan WHORTON
104 Director Study Abroad ....Ms. Johnsie L. STANCIL
07 Director of Admissions ....Vacant

Clinton College (F)

1029 Crawford Road, Rock Hill SC 29730-5152
County: York FICE Identification: 004923
Unit ID: 217891
Telephone: (803) 327-7402 Carnegie Class: Bac/Assoc-Mixed
FAX Number: (803) 327-3261 Calendar System: Semester
URL: www.clintoncollege.edu
Established: 1894 Annual Undergrad Tuition & Fees: $10,020
Enrollment: 119 Coed
Affiliation or Control: African Methodist Episcopal Zion Church
IRS Status: 501(c)3
Highest Offering: Baccalaureate
Accreditation: TRACS

01 President ....Dr. Lester A. MCCORN
04 Exec Assistant to the President ....Ms. Cheryl J. MCCULLOUGH
05 VP Academic Affairs/Dean ....Dr. Alvin MCLAMB
111 VP Institutional Advancement ....Mr. Adrian SCOTT
32 VP for Student Affairs ....Dr. Angelyne BROWN
10 VP for Business & Finance ....Ms. Archinya INGRAM
06 Registrar ....Ms. Laveria WYNN
37 Financial Aid ....Ms. Pamela WHITE
08 Director Library Services ....Ms. Nina ISHOKIR
41 Athletic Director ....Mr. Alfonzo DUNCAN
18 Superintendent Buildings/Grounds ....Mr. Donnie INGRAM
07 Director of Admissions ....Mr. Sedrick SINGLETARY
35 Director Student Support Services ....Ms. Judith COWAN

Coastal Carolina University (A)

PO Box 261954, Conway SC 29528-6054
County: Horry FICE Identification: 003451
Unit ID: 218724
Telephone: (843) 347-3161 Carnegie Class: Masters/L
FAX Number: (843) 349-2990 Calendar System: Semester
URL: www.coastal.edu
Established: 1954 Annual Undergrad Tuition & Fees (In-State): $11,640
Enrollment: 10,118 Coed
Affiliation or Control: State IRS Status: 501(c)3
Highest Offering: Doctorate
Accreditation: SC, ART, CAEP, MUS, NUR, PH, THEA

01 President Dr. Michael T. BENSON
05 Provost and EVP Academic Affairs Dr. Daniel J. ENNIS
10 Vice President Finance/CFO Mr. David FROST
30 Interim Vice Pres Philanthropy Mr. Bryan STEROS
32 VP Student Affairs/Enroll Mgmt Dr. James SOLAZZO
26 Vice Pres Univ Communications Vacant
41 Vice Pres of Athletics Mr. Matthew L. HOGUE
50 Int Dean Business Administration Dr. Erika E. SMALL
53 Dean of Education Dr. Edward JADALLAH
79 Dean of Humanities & Fine Arts Dr. Claudia BORNHOLDT
81 Dean of Science Dr. Michael H. ROBERTS
97 Dean of University College Dr. Sara HOTTINGER
13 Interim VP Information Tech Svcs Mr. Fadi BAROODY
29 Int VP Advancement/Alumni Relations Ms. Diane F. SANDERS
108 Assoc Provost Strategy & Devel Dr. Holley TANKERSLEY
20 Asc Prov Curriculum/Stdnt Progress Dr. James SOLAZZO
58 Interim Dean Graduate Studies Dr. Robert F. YOUNG
104 Assoc Provost Global Initiatives Dr. Darla J. DOMKE-DAMONTE
09 Exec Dir of Planning and Research Ms. Christine L. MEE
06 Interim University Registrar Ms. Stacy A. WYETH
19 Director Public Safety Mr. David ROPER
21 Controller Mr. Gregory T. THOMPSON
28 VP for Diversity/Equity & Inclusion Dr. Atiya STOKES-BROWN
39 Sr Director of Housing Ms. Kathy A. DALEY
37 Associate Director of Client Svcs Ms. Samantha HICKS
37 Associate Director of Operations Ms. Sarah WEAVER
92 Director Honors Program Dr. Louis E. KEINER
36 Director Career Services Dr. Verne W. WALKER
96 Dir Procurement/Business Services Mr. Dean P. HUDSON
18 Director of Facilities Planning Mr. T. Rein MUNGO
27 Assoc VP for Univ Communications Ms. Martha S. HUNN
07 Assoc Provost Admiss & Merit Awards Ms. Amanda E. CRADDOCK
22 Assoc VP Human Resources/EEO Ms. Kimberly B. SHERFESEE
43 Sr VP/University Counsel Mr. Carlos JOHNSON
08 University Librarian Dr. Melvin D. DAVIS
100 Chief of Staff/VP Exec Initiatives Mr. Travis E. OVERTON

Coker University (B)

300 E College Avenue, Hartsville SC 29550-3797
County: Darlington FICE Identification: 003427
Unit ID: 217907
Telephone: (843) 383-8000 Carnegie Class: Masters/S
FAX Number: (843) 383-8319 Calendar System: Semester
URL: www.coker.edu
Established: 1908 Annual Undergrad Tuition & Fees: $31,524
Enrollment: 1,087 Coed
Affiliation or Control: Independent Non-Profit IRS Status: 501(c)3
Highest Offering: Master's
Accreditation: SC, ART, DANCE, MUS

01 President Dr. Natalie HARDER
05 Provost & Dean of Faculty Dr. Susan HENDERSON
28 Dir of Diversity/Interfaith/Inclus Ms. Darlene SMALL
13 Director of IT Dr. Cathy CUPPETT
41 VP Athletics & Athletic Facilities Dr. Lynn GRIFFIN
108 VP of Institutional Effectiveness Dr. Kathryn FLAHERTY
111 Interim VP for Advancement Mr. Grady JONES
10 VP for Finance & Administration Mr. Dan BURYJ
32 VP for Student Services Mr. Tyson BEALE
35 AVP for Resource Development Ms. Brianna DOUGLAS
09 Dir of Institutional Research Ms. Lynn RAWLS
21 Chief Financial Officer Ms. Robin A. PERDUE
37 Director of Student Financial Svcs Vacant
29 Director of Alumni Engagement Mr. Evan VAUGHN
08 Director of the Library Mr. Todd RIX
19 Director of Campus Safety Mr. Michael WILLIAMSON
04 Executive Asst to President Ms. Heather NORMENT
15 Director of Human Resources Ms. Ella MARSHALL
39 Dir Resident Life/Student Housing Mr. Cole HEATHERLY
53 Dean of Education Dr. Karen CARPENTER
06 Registrar Ms. Shannon FLOWERS

College of Charleston (C)

66 George Street, Charleston SC 29424-0100
County: Charleston FICE Identification: 003428
Unit ID: 217819
Telephone: (843) 805-5507 Carnegie Class: Masters/L
FAX Number: (843) 953-5811 Calendar System: Semester
URL: www.cofc.edu
Established: 1770 Annual Undergrad Tuition & Fees (In-State): $12,978
Enrollment: 10,384 Coed
Affiliation or Control: State IRS Status: 501(c)3
Highest Offering: Master's
Accreditation: SC, CAEP, MUS, SPAA, THEA

01 President Dr. Andrew T. HSU
05 Provost & Exec Vice Pres Dr. Suzanne AUSTIN
100 Chief of Staff Mr. Paul D. PATRICK
101 Vice Pres Col Events/Exec Sec BOT Ms. Elizabeth W. KASSEBAUM
04 Exec Admin to the President Ms. Michelle MCGREW
10 EVP for Business Affairs Mr. John LOONAN
18 VP for Facilities Management Mr. John P. MORRIS
26 VP Marketing/Enrollment Plng Ms. Amy TAKAYAMA-PEREZ
111 Exec VP Institutional Advancement Mr. Chris TOBIN
32 Exec Vice President Student Affairs Ms. Alicia D. CAUDILL
35 Dean of Students Dr. Jeri O. CABOT
43 General Counsel Legal Affairs Ms. Angela B. MULHOLLAND
19 Chief of Police/Dir Public Safety Chief Robert S. REESE
20 Associate Provost Dr. Deanna M. CAVENY
20 Associate Vice Pres Dr. Lynne E. FORD
104 Assoc Provost International Educ Dr. Andrew M. SOBIESUO
13 Senior VP/Chief Information Officer Mr. Mark STAPLES
21 Dir of Financial Services Ms. Debye B. ALDERMAN
109 Dir Business & Auxiliary Services Ms. Amy K. ORR
96 Chief Procurement Officer Ms. Wendy E. WILLIAMS
30 Vice President Development Ms. Cathryn A. MAHON
15 VP of Human Resources Mr. Edward POPE
22 Dir Equal Opportunity Programs Ms. Kimberly A. GERTNER
84 Vice Pres Enrollment Planning Mr. Jimmie A. FOSTER
09 Director of Institutional Research Ms. Michelle L. SMITH
28 Associate VP Diversity Dr. Renard HARRIS
89 Asst VP New Student Programs Ms. Melinda MILEY
06 Registrar Ms. Mary C. BERGSTROM
21 Treasurer Mr. David G. KATZ
58 Interim Dean of the Graduate School Dr. Godfrey GIBBISON
57 Dean School of the Arts Ms. Valerie B. MORRIS
50 Dean School of Business Dr. Alan T. SHAO
53 Dean School of Education Dr. Frances C. WELCH
79 Dean School of Languages Dr. Timothy JOHNSON
81 Interim Dean School Science & Math Dr. Sebastian VAN DELDEN
83 Interim Dean Sch of Human/Soc Sci Dr. Gibbs KNOTTS
107 Dean College Professional Studies Dr. Godfrey GIBBISON
62 Dean of Libraries Dr. John WHITE
51 Director CCEPD Dr. Alice M. HAMILTON
92 Int Dean Honors College Dr. Elizabeth MEYER-BERNSTEIN
41 Director Athletics Mr. Matt ROBERTS
25 Director Research and Grants Ms. Susan A. RIVALEAU
37 Interim Dir Fin Asst/Vet Affairs Mr. Robert N. KERSEY
07 Exec Dir of Admissions Ms. Suzette STILLE
29 Vice President Alumni Affairs Ms. Ann PRYOR
121 Dir Center for Academic Advising Ms. Karen HAUSCHILD
88 Dir Center for Student Learning Ms. Melinda L. COLEMAN
108 AVP Inst Effectiveness Dr. Divya BHATI
22 Dir Ctr for Disabilities Services Ms. Deborah F. MIHAL
35 Dir Student Life & Stern Center Ms. Christine WORKMAN
36 Director Career Services Mr. Jim ALLISON, JR.
38 Dir Counseling & Substance Abuse Ms. Leslie F. ARMENIOX
23 Director Health Services Ms. Bridget MCLERNON-SYKES
39 Director Residence Life Ms. Melantha ARDREY
88 Dir Environmental Health and Safety Mr. Randy L. BEAVER
88 Director of ECDC Ms. Katie HOUSER
35 AVP Student Affairs/Dir HSLC Mr. K. Michael DUNCAN
18 Director of Sustainability Mr. P. Brian FISHER
31 Exec Dir Cmty Rels/Ombudsperson Ms. Evelyn H. NADEL
20 Dir Undergrad Academic Services Ms. Michelle G. FUTRELL

Columbia College (D)

1301 Columbia College Drive, Columbia SC 29203-5998
County: Richland FICE Identification: 003430
Unit ID: 217934
Telephone: (803) 786-3012 Carnegie Class: Masters/S
FAX Number: (803) 786-3752 Calendar System: Semester
URL: www.columbiasc.edu
Established: 1854 Annual Undergrad Tuition & Fees: $20,690
Enrollment: 1,218 Coed
Affiliation or Control: United Methodist IRS Status: 501(c)3
Highest Offering: Master's
Accreditation: SC, CAEPN, DANCE, NURSE, SW

01 President Dr. William T. BOGART
05 Provost Dr. Madeleine SCHEP
10 Vice President for Finance Ms. Wilma ALLEN
111 VP for Advancement Mr. Francis G. SCHODOWSKI
32 VP for Student Affairs Ms. LaNae R. BUDDEN
29 Exec Director of Alumnae Relations Ms. Julie KING
09 Director Institutional Research Dr. Scott A. SMITH
08 Director of Library Ms. Jane TUTTLE
19 Chief of Police Mr. Windell HARRIS
37 Director of Financial Aid Mr. Justin PICHEY
36 Director of Ctr for Career Coaching Mr. Nigel SMITH
13 Dir of Info Technology Services Vacant
18 Director of Facilities Management Ms. Gaby HICKMAN
26 Director of Public Relations Vacant
41 Director of Athletics Ms. Debra WARDLAW
40 Director Bookstore Ms. Cory CORP
38 Director Counseling Services Ms. Mimi MERIWETHER
04 Executive Assistant to President Ms. Joye G. HIPP
84 Director of Enrollment Management Mr. Vinnie MALONEY
92 Director Honors Program/Faculty Dev Dr. Marlee MARSH
06 Registrar Ms. Sharon HOFFMAN
15 Chief Human Resources Officer Ms. Beverly JAMES
28 Director of Diversity Ms. Melissia BRANNEN
39 Director Residence Life Ms. Shade' HOLMES
44 Director Annual Giving Ms. Hope WATSON

Columbia International University (E)

7435 Monticello Road, Columbia SC 29203
County: Richland FICE Identification: 003429
Unit ID: 217925
Telephone: (803) 754-4100 Carnegie Class: Masters/S
FAX Number: (803) 786-4209 Calendar System: Semester
URL: www.ciu.edu
Established: 1923 Annual Undergrad Tuition & Fees: $24,650
Enrollment: 2,098 Coed
Affiliation or Control: Independent Non-Profit IRS Status: 501(c)3
Highest Offering: Doctorate
Accreditation: SC, BI, CACREP, THEOL

01 President Dr. Mark A. SMITH
00 Chancellor Dr. Bill H. JONES
05 Senior Vice President/Provost Dr. Jim LANPHER
111 VP of Institutional Advancement Mrs. Diane MULL
32 VP Student Svcs & Online Studies Dr. Rick CHRISTMAN
73 Dean Seminary & School of Ministry Dr. David CROTEAU
49 Dean College of Arts & Sciences Dr. Jim LANPHER
53 Dean College of Education Dr. Connie MITCHELL
104 Dean College Intercultural Studies Dr. Edward SMITHER
50 Dean Sch of Business & Prof Studies Dr. Scott ADAMS
09 Dir Institutional Research/Assessmt Dr. Roxianne SNODGRASS
101 Assoc Provost Online Studies Dr. Brian SIMMONS
08 Director of Library Mrs. Cynthia SNELL
06 University Registrar Dr. Jennifer BOOTH
15 Director Human Resources Mr. Donald E. JONES
32 Dean of Students Mr. Rick SWIFT
13 VP Information Technology Mrs. Michele BRANCH-FRAPPIER
18 Director Physical Plant Mr. Phil MILLER
10 Chief Financial Officer Mr. Rob HARTMAN
37 Director Financial Aid Mrs. Patty HIX
04 Executive Asst to President Mrs. Debbie GERMANY
19 Director Security/Safety Mr. Scott DEAL
41 Athletic Director Mr. Darren RICHIE
106 Dean of Online Education/E-learning Dr. Kevin JONES

Converse College (F)

580 E Main, Spartanburg SC 29302-0006
County: Spartanburg FICE Identification: 003431
Unit ID: 217961
Telephone: (864) 596-9000 Carnegie Class: Masters/S
FAX Number: (864) 596-9158 Calendar System: 4/1/4
URL: www.converse.edu
Established: 1889 Annual Undergrad Tuition & Fees: $20,500
Enrollment: 1,377 Coed
Affiliation or Control: Independent Non-Profit IRS Status: 501(c)3
Highest Offering: Doctorate
Accreditation: SC, ART, CIDA, MFCD, MUS

01 Interim President Dr. Boone J. HOPKINS
05 Interim Provost Dr. Lienne F. MEDFORD
10 Vice Pres for Finance and Business Ms. Dianne CROCKER
11 VP Operations and Strategic Plng Ms. Kristin LACEY
111 Interim VP for Philanthropy Mr. Mike KENNEDY
79 Dean Humanities/Sciences/Business Dr. Erin TEMPLETON
57 Dean School of the Arts Dr. Christopher VANEMAN
53 Dean of Education/Grad Studies Dr. Lienne MEDFORD
32 Dean of Students Ms. Rhonda MINGO
08 Librarian Mr. Wade WOODWARD
37 Director of Financial Planning Mr. James KELLAM
06 Registrar Vacant
15 Human Resources Director Dr. Claire GREGG
13 Chief Information Officer Mr. Zach CORBITT
26 Director of Media/Communications Ms. Holly DUNCAN
04 Exec Assistant to the President Mrs. Pamela GREENWAY
38 Director of Counseling Services Ms. Bethany GARR
09 Director Institutional Research Vacant
84 Vice Pres of Enrollment Management Ms. Jamie GRANT
18 Chief Facilities/Physical Plant Mr. Gladden SMOKE
29 Director Alumni Affairs Ms. Jessica EGGIMAN

Denmark Technical College (G)

PO Box 327, Denmark SC 29042-0327
County: Bamberg FICE Identification: 005363
Unit ID: 217989
Telephone: (803) 793-5176 Carnegie Class: Assoc/HVT-Mix Trad/Non
FAX Number: (803) 793-5942 Calendar System: Semester
URL: www.denmarktech.edu
Established: 1948 Annual Undergrad Tuition & Fees (In-State): $5,648
Enrollment: 491 Coed
Affiliation or Control: State IRS Status: 501(c)3
Highest Offering: Associate Degree
Accreditation: SC, ACBSP, NAEYC

01 President Dr. Willie L. TODD, JR.
03 Executive Vice President Dr. A. Clifton MYLES
05 VP for Academic Affairs/CAO Ms. Tia WRIGHT-RICHARDS
32 VP for Student Affairs Dr. Lamar J. WHITE
10 VP for Fiscal Affairs/CFO Mr. Clarence BONNETTE
35 Dean of Students Dr. Samuel HINTON
111 VP Institutional Advancement Dr. Sasha JOHNSON-COLEMAN
08 Dean of Learning Resources Ctr Ms. Carolyn FORTSON
13 Director of Information Technology Dr. Sid EMORY
19 Chief of Public Safety Mr. Rodney BONDS
15 Director of Human Resources Mr. Thomas MAYER
36 Dir Career Plng/PLC/Student Success Ms. Leslie HOLMAN-BROOKS

37 Director of Financial Aid .... Ms. Vanessa CHILDS
49 Dean of Arts & Sciences .... Ms. Rosaland KENNER
66 Dean of Nursing .... Ms. Karen MYERS
50 Dean Business/Computer/Related Tech .... Dr. Danny SWILLEY
84 Director of Admissions & Recruitmnt .... Dr. Stacey ROBERSON
103 Dean/Industrial Related Technology .... Dr. Hadi HAMID
39 Director of Residence Life .... Mr. Patrick SCIPIO
06 Registrar .... Ms. Renee SPELLS
88 Special Assistant to the President .... Mr. Kenneth CRAWFORD
41 Athletic Director .... Mr. Andre PAYNE
09 Statistical/Research Analyst .... Ms. Diane V. JACKSON
26 Chief Public Relations Officer .... Ms. Amy ROPER

ECPI University-Charleston (A)

7410 Northside Drive, Ste 100,
North Charleston SC 29420
Telephone: (843) 606-5902 Identification: 770955
Accreditation: &SC, MAAB

† Branch campus of ECPI University, Virginia Beach, VA

ECPI University-Columbia (B)

250 Berryhill Road, Ste 300, Columbia SC 29210-6467
Telephone: (803) 772-3333 Identification: 770956
Accreditation: &SC, MAAB

† Branch campus of ECPI University, Virginia Beach, VA

ECPI University-Greenville (C)

1001 Keys Drive, Ste 100, Greenville SC 29615
Telephone: (864) 288-2828 Identification: 770954
Accreditation: &SC, MAAB

† Branch campus of ECPI University, Virginia Beach, VA

Edward Via College of Osteopathic Medicine-Carolinas Campus (D)

350 Howard Street, Sparntanburg SC 29303
Telephone: (864) 327-9800 Identification: 770941
Accreditation: &OSTEO

† Branch campus of Edward Via College of Osteopathic Medicine, Blacksburg, VA.

Erskine College (E)

PO Box 338, 2 Washington Street,
Due West SC 29639-0338
County: Abbeville FICE Identification: 003432
Unit ID: 217998
Telephone: (864) 379-2131 Carnegie Class: Bac-Diverse
FAX Number: (864) 379-2167 Calendar System: Semester
URL: www.erskine.edu
Established: 1837 Annual Undergrad Tuition & Fees: $36,510
Enrollment: 943 Coed
Affiliation or Control: Other IRS Status: 501(c)3
Highest Offering: Doctorate
Accreditation: SC, CAEP, THEOL

01 Interim President .... Dr. J. T. HELLAMS
10 VP for Finance & Operations .... Mr. Christian HABEGER
111 VP for Advancement .... Mr. J. Paul BELL
41 Vice President for Athletics .... Mr. Mark L. PEELER
32 VP for Student Success .... Dr. Wendi SANTEE
29 Vice Pres of Alumni Affairs .... Mr. Paul BELL
05 Dean of College .... Mr. Shane BRADLEY
05 Dean of Seminary .... Mr. Seth NELSON
08 Assoc Dean of Library & Inst Effect .... Mr. John F. KENNERLY, JR.
06 Registrar .... Mrs. Tracy M. SPIRES
26 Director of Marketing .... Ms. Brianne HOLMES
37 Director of Student Financial Aid .... Mrs. Amanda TAYLOR
13 Director of Information Technology .... Mrs. Stephanie HUDSON
09 Director of Institutional Research .... Mr. Buck F. BROWN, JR.
42 Interim Chaplain .... Mr. Joshua CHILES
21 Accounting Manager .... Mrs. Kelly MCALHANEY
15 Director Human Resources .... Ms. Kathy ROLLINS
19 Chief of Erskine Police .... Mr. Matthew BUSBY
04 Administrative Asst to President .... Mrs. Polly JONES
07 Director of Admissions .... Ms. Kasey MCNAIR
27 Director Communications/Media Rels .... Mrs. Joyce GUYETTE
84 Dean of Enrollment .... Dr. Tim REES
18 Chief Facilities/Physical Plant .... Mr. Michael LEWIS

Florence - Darlington Technical College (F)

PO Box 100548, Florence SC 29502-0548
County: Florence FICE Identification: 003990
Unit ID: 218025
Telephone: (843) 661-8324 Carnegie Class: Assoc/HVT-High Trad
FAX Number: (843) 661-8011 Calendar System: Semester
URL: www.fdtc.edu
Established: 1964 Annual Undergrad Tuition & Fees (In-District): $5,030
Enrollment: 3,315 Coed
Affiliation or Control: State/Local IRS Status: 501(c)3
Highest Offering: Associate Degree
Accreditation: SC, ADNUR, CAHIIM, COARC, CSHSE, DA, DH, MLTAD, RAD, SURGT

01 Interim President .... Mr. Edward E. BETHEA
05 Vice President Academic Affairs .... Dr. Marc DAVID
10 Vice Pres Business Affairs .... Vacant
111 Director Institutional Advancement .... Ms. Lauren DORTON
26 Int VP Institutional Marketing .... Mr. Tyron JONES
12 VP of the SiMT .... Mr. Mark ROTH
76 Assoc VP Allied Health .... Dr. Dan AVERETTE
15 Assoc VP Internal Relations/EEO .... Mr. Terry DINGLE
09 Director Institutional Research .... Mr. Gary ANCHETA
06 Registrar .... Ms. Genell GAUSE
37 Director Financial Aid .... Ms. Monica STARR
96 Director of Purchasing .... Ms. Toni RICHARDSON
07 Director of Admissions .... Ms. Paula MCLAUGHLIN
18 Director of Facilities .... Mr. Christopher TAYLOR
04 Exec Assistant to the President .... Ms. Kimberley LUTZ

Francis Marion University (G)

PO Box 100547, Florence SC 29501-0547
County: Florence FICE Identification: 009226
Unit ID: 218061
Telephone: (843) 661-1362 Carnegie Class: Masters/S
FAX Number: (843) 661-1202 Calendar System: Semester
URL: www.fmarion.edu
Established: 1970 Annual Undergrad Tuition & Fees (In-State): $11,160
Enrollment: 4,148 Coed
Affiliation or Control: State IRS Status: Exempt
Highest Offering: Doctorate
Accreditation: SC, ART, CAEP, MPCAC, NURSE, @SP, THEA

01 President .... Dr. Luther F. CARTER
05 Provost/Dean Col of Liberal Arts .... Dr. Peter D. KING
10 Vice President Business Affairs .... Vacant
11 Vice Pre Administration/Planning .... Dr. Charlene WAGES
30 Vice President Devel/Exec Dir .... Mr. Darryl BRIDGES
26 VP University Communications .... Mr. Tucker MITCHELL
32 Vice President for Student Affairs .... Vacant
41 Athletic Director .... Mr. Murray G. HARTZLER
20 Assoc Provost For Academic Affairs .... Dr. Christopher KENNEDY
84 Assoc Provost of Enrollment Mgmt .... Dr. Alissa WARTERS
121 Assoc Provost for Advising .... Dr. Jennifer KUNKA
21 Asst Vice Pres for Accounting .... Mrs. Cathy SWARTZ
21 Asst Vice Pres Financial Services .... Mr. Thomas WELCH
50 Dean School of Business .... Dr. Hari K. RAJAGOPALAN
53 Dean School of Education .... Dr. Tracy MEETZE-HOLCOMBE
76 Dean School of Health Sciences .... Vacant
08 Dean of the Library .... Mrs. Joyce M. DURANT
37 Financial Assistance Director .... Ms. Kimberly M. ELLISOR
06 Registrar .... Vacant
38 Director Counseling and Testing .... Dr. Rebecca L. LAWSON
18 Director of Facilities Management .... Mr. Ralph U. DAVIS
36 Director Career Development .... Dr. Ronald E. MILLER, JR.
07 Director of Admissions .... Vacant
35 Asst Dean of Students .... Ms. R. Daphne CARTER
29 Director of Alumni Affairs .... Vacant
96 Director of Purchasing .... Mr. Paul MACDONALD
92 Director of Honors Program .... Dr. Jon W. TUTTLE
13 Chief Information Officer .... Mr. John DIXON
04 Administrative Asst to President .... Mrs. Kim DAVIS
105 Director of Multimedia Services .... Mr. Larry B. FALCK
19 Chief of Campus Police .... Mr. Donald R. TARBELL
39 Director Student Housing .... Mrs. Cheryl R. TUTTLE
96 AVP of Purchasing/Contractual Svcs .... Mr. Eric GARRIS

Furman University (H)

3300 Poinsett Highway, Greenville SC 29613-0001
County: Greenville FICE Identification: 003434
Unit ID: 218070
Telephone: (864) 294-2000 Carnegie Class: Bac-A&S
FAX Number: (864) 294-3001 Calendar System: Semester
URL: www.furman.edu
Established: 1826 Annual Undergrad Tuition & Fees: $52,092
Enrollment: 2,567 Coed
Affiliation or Control: Independent Non-Profit IRS Status: 501(c)3
Highest Offering: Master's
Accreditation: SC, CAEPN, MUS

01 President .... Dr. Elizabeth DAVIS
05 VP Academic Affairs & Provost .... Dr. Ken PETERSON
10 VP for Finance & Administration .... Ms. Susan MADDUX
07 Vice President for Enrollment .... Dr. Michael HENDRICKS
32 Vice President for Student Life .... Ms. Connie L. CARSON
30 Vice President for Development .... Ms. Heidi H. MCCRORY
26 VP University Communications .... Mr. Tom EVELYN
20 Associate Academic Dean .... Dr. Beth PONTARI
100 Chief of Staff .... Ms. Elizabeth SEMAN
06 University Registrar .... Ms. Kendra WOODSON
58 Director Graduate Studies .... Dr. Troy M. TERRY
08 Director Libraries .... Dr. Caroline MILLS
19 Chief of Police .... Mr. John MILBY
108 Asst Vice President Assessment .... Dr. David EUBANKS
37 Assoc Vice Pres of Financial Aid .... Vacant
29 Director of Alumni Association .... Ms. Allsion FOY
07 Assoc Vice President of Admissions .... Mr. Brad POCHARD
44 Director of Annual Giving .... Ms. Gloria GOOSBY
112 Director of Planned & Major Gifts .... Mr. John KEMP
25 Grants Administrator .... Ms. Judith J. ROMANO
94 Dir Women's/Gender/Sexuality Study .... Dr. Gretchen BRAUN
15 Asst VP Human Resources/AAO .... Ms. Sharen BEAULIEU

13 Chief Information Officer .... Mr. David STEINOUR
36 Director Career Services .... Dr. John D. BARKER
109 Auxiliary Services Director .... Mr. Tony MCGUIRT
18 Asst VP for Facilities Services .... Mr. Jeff P. REDDERSON
51 Director Continuing Education .... Vacant
41 Director of Athletics .... Mr. Jason DONNELLY
46 Director UG Research .... Dr. Erik CHING
88 Director CTL .... Dr. Min-Ken LIAO
17 Director Student Health Services .... Dr. Ann KNOWLES
38 Director Counseling Center .... Dr. Thomas BAEZ
39 Director University Housing .... Mr. Ronald C. THOMPSON
88 Director Accessibility Resources .... Ms. Judy BAGLEY
42 Chaplain .... Dr. Vaughn CROWETIPTON
40 Director Bookstore .... Ms. Crystal JARROUGE
04 Executive Asst to President .... Ms. Cindy ALEXANDER
114 Assoc VP Finance Budget Director .... Ms. Amy BLACKWELL
96 Director of Purchasing .... Ms. Jannie CHOICE
35 Director Student Activities .... Ms. Jessica BERKEY
104 Director Study Abroad .... Ms. Nancy GEORGIEV
43 Dir Legal Services/General Counsel .... Ms. Meredith GREEN
28 Director of Diversity .... Dr. Michael E. JENNINGS
09 Director of Institutional Research .... Dr. David A. EUBANKS

Greenville Technical College (I)

PO Box 5616, Greenville SC 29606-5616
County: Greenville FICE Identification: 003991
Unit ID: 218113
Telephone: (864) 250-8000 Carnegie Class: Assoc/MT-VT-High Trad
FAX Number: N/A Calendar System: Semester
URL: www.gvltec.edu
Established: 1962 Annual Undergrad Tuition & Fees (In-State): $5,186
Enrollment: 10,536 Coed
Affiliation or Control: State IRS Status: 501(c)3
Highest Offering: Baccalaureate
Accreditation: SC, ACBSP, ACFEI, ADNUR, CAHIIM, COARC, DA, DH, DMS, EMT, MAC, MLTAD, NAEYC, OTA, PTAA, RAD, SURGT

01 President .... Dr. Keith MILLER
05 Int VP Learning/Workforce Devel .... Dr. Larry MILLER
10 Vice President Finance .... Mrs. Jacqueline DIMAGGIO
32 Vice President Student Services .... Dr. Matteel KNOWLES
111 VP Advancement .... Ms. Ann WRIGHT
103 AVP Econ Dev/Corp Training .... Mrs. Jennifer MOOREFIELD
45 VP Institutional Effectiveness .... Mrs. Lauren SIMER
04 Administrative Asst to President .... Ms. Rita SNYDER
06 Registrar .... Mrs. Gloria CARDEN
84 Dean Enrollment Services .... Ms. Tanisha LATIMER
15 VP Human Resources .... Ms. Susan M. JONES
18 Director Facilities .... Mr. Scott WILBANKS
19 Chief of Police .... Mr. Terence BROOKS
25 Director Research and Grants .... Ms. Elizabeth VARGA
26 Director Marketing/Communications .... Mr. Joshua FRIESEN
28 AVP Executive Affairs .... Ms. Wendy WALDEN
37 Director Financial Aid .... Mr. Marty CARNEY
50 Dean School of Business & Comp Tech .... Ms. Michelle E. BYRD
13 Chief Information Officer .... Vacant
86 Director Government Relations .... Mr. Eric BEDINGFIELD
21 AVP Finance .... Ms. Lisa MANGIONE
09 Director of Institutional Research .... Dr. Larry MILLER
104 Director of Global Education .... Ms. Karen KOTIW
108 Director Accreditation & Assessment .... Vacant
96 Procurement Manager .... Ms. Kristal DOHERTY
08 Chief Library Officer .... Ms. Stephanie BROKER
100 Chief of Staff .... Ms. Julie A. EDDY

Horry-Georgetown Technical College (J)

2050 Highway 501 E, Conway SC 29526-9521
County: Horry FICE Identification: 004925
Unit ID: 218140
Telephone: (843) 347-3186 Carnegie Class: Assoc/MT-VT-High Trad
FAX Number: (843) 347-4207 Calendar System: Semester
URL: www.hgtc.edu
Established: 1966 Annual Undergrad Tuition & Fees (In-District): $5,356
Enrollment: 6,409 Coed
Affiliation or Control: State/Local IRS Status: 501(c)3
Highest Offering: Associate Degree
Accreditation: SC, ACFEI, ADNUR, #COARC, DA, DH, DMS, EMT, PNUR, PTAA, RAD, SURGT

01 President .... Dr. Marilyn J. FORE
05 Executive VP for Academics .... Dr. Jennifer WILBANKS
10 VP Business Affairs/Administration .... Mr. Harold HAWLEY
13 VP for Technology Solutions .... Mr. John DOVE
103 VP Wrkfc Dev/Prov GS/Georgetwn Camp .... Mr. Gregory MITCHELL
84 Registrar .... Mrs. Heather HOPPE
32 VP for Student Affairs .... Dr. Melissa BATTEN
20 AVP for Accreditation/Inst Support .... Dr. Becky BOONE
49 AVP Acad Affs Arts and Sciences .... Dr. Candace HOWELL
66 AVP Acad Affs Health Sci/Per Svc .... Mrs. Ann DANIELS
15 VP Human Res/Employee Rels .... Mrs. Jacquelyne SNYDER
08 Director of Library Services .... Mr. Richard MONIZ
21 AVP/Controller .... Ms. Ellen BLACK
84 AVP Student Enrollment Services .... Ms. Cynthia JOHNSTON
18 Superintendent Buildings & Grounds .... Mr. Kevin BROWN
37 Dir of Financial Aid/Veterans Affs .... Ms. Susan THOMPSON
36 Career Resource Ctr Coordinator .... Vacant
09 VP Inst Effectiveness & Dev .... Ms. Lori HEAFNER
96 Procurement Manager .... Ms. Dianna CECALA
105 Web Services Coordinator .... Mr. Kevin ENGELMAN

19 Director Security/Safety .... Mr. Barry MARSH
106 Exec Dir Acad Svcs/Prof Dev .... Mr. Daniel HOPPE
26 Director of Public Relations .... Ms. Nicole HYMAN
27 Director of Marketing .... Ms. Lari ROPER

Lander University (A)

320 Stanley Avenue, Greenwood SC 29649-2099
County: Greenwood FICE Identification: 003435
Unit ID: 218229
Telephone: (864) 388-8000 Carnegie Class: Bac-Diverse
FAX Number: (864) 388-8890 Calendar System: Semester
URL: www.lander.edu
Established: 1872 Annual Undergrad Tuition & Fees (In-State): $11,700
Enrollment: 3,513 Coed
Affiliation or Control: State IRS Status: 501(c)3
Highest Offering: Master's
Accreditation: SC, ART, CAEP, MACTE, MUS, NURSE

01 President .... Dr. Richard E. COSENTINO
05 Provost/Vice Pres Academic Affairs .... Dr. Scott JONES
10 Vice Pres Business/Administration .... Dr. Stacie BOWIE
32 Vice President for Student Affairs .... Mr. Boyd YARBROUGH
111 Vice President for Univ Advancement .... Mr. Mike WORLEY
100 Chief of Staff/VP Strategic Init .... Mr. Adam TAYLOR
84 VP for Enrollment & Access Mgmt .... Mr. Todd GAMBILL
08 Librarian .... Ms. Lisa WIECKI
38 Director Counseling .... Ms. Kim SHANNON
41 Director of Athletics .... Mr. Brian REESE
15 Director Human Resources .... Ms. London THOMAS
19 Director University Police .... Mr. Greg ALLEN
26 AVP Univ Relations/Publications .... Mrs. Megan PRICE
37 Director of Financial Aid .... Ms. Michelle LODATO
36 Director of Career Services .... Mrs. Amanda MORGAN
21 Controller .... Mr. Tom COVAR
40 Dir Bookstore/Procurement/Print Svc .... Mr. Scott PILGRIM
13 Chief Info & Technology Officer .... Mr. Abdallah P. HADDAD
07 Director of Admissions .... Mrs. Jennifer M. MATHIS
18 Director Physical Plant/Engr Svcs .... Mr. Jeff S. BEAVER
06 Registrar .... Ms. Kelly PROCTOR
29 Assist Director Alumni Relations .... Ms. Debbie DILL
09 Director of Institutional Research .... Mr. Mac KIRKPATRICK

Limestone University (B)

1115 College Drive, Gaffney SC 29340-3799
County: Cherokee FICE Identification: 003436
Unit ID: 218238
Telephone: (864) 489-7151 Carnegie Class: Bac-Diverse
FAX Number: (864) 487-8706 Calendar System: Semester
URL: www.limestone.edu
Established: 1845 Annual Undergrad Tuition & Fees: $26,300
Enrollment: 1,943 Coed
Affiliation or Control: Independent Non-Profit IRS Status: 501(c)3
Highest Offering: Master's
Accreditation: SC, ACBSP, CAATE, CAEPN, MUS, NURSE, SW

01 President .... Dr. Darrell PARKER
05 Provost .... Dr. Monica BALOGA
10 VP Finance/Operations & Admin .... Mr. Reggie BROWNING
111 VP Institutional Advancement .... Ms. Kelly T. CURTIS
84 Vice President Enrollment Services . Mr. Christopher N. PHENICIE
13 Chief Information Officer .... Mr. Terry MCKINNY
41 Vice Pres Intercollegiate Athletics .... Mr. Michael H. CERINO
53 Dean Education & Health Professions .... Dr. Shelly MEYERS
32 Assoc Provost of Student Success .... Mrs. Stacey W. MASON
04 Executive Asst to the President .... Mrs. Brandi P. HARTMAN
35 Dir of Recruitment & Student Svcs .... Mr. Kip ALTMAN
06 Registrar .... Ms. Pennie D. HUGHES
37 Director Financial Aid .... Ms. Summer NANCE
08 Director Library .... Ms. Lizah ISMAIL
26 Vice Pres Communications/Marketing .... Mr. Charles W. WYATT
36 Dir Center for Professional Dev .... Ms. Lindsay BATHOLOMEW
18 Director Physical Plant .... Mr. Hayden HUTCHINGS
92 Director Academic Honors Program .... Dr. Jonathan SARNOFF
70 Director & Chair of Social Work .... Mr. Henry HIOTT
19 Chief Campus Security .... Mr. William J. PETTY
21 Controller .... Vacant
23 Campus Nurse .... Mrs. Sandy B. GREEN
121 Director Academic Advising .... Ms. Pennie D. HUGHES
30 Assoc VP for Development .... Ms. Candace R. WATERS
109 Director Food Services .... Mr. Joe FIELDS
42 College Chaplain .... Dr. Tom LEGRAND
53 Dir of Teacher Education .... Dr. Jimmie HALE
28 Director of Equity & Inclusion .... Ms. Selena S. BLAIR
15 Dir Human Resources/AAEEO Officer .... Ms. Janie CORRY
123 Dir Grad Studies/Admiss & Enroll .... Ms. Adair HUDSON
88 Sr Assoc Athletics Dir Compliance .... Mr. Dennis L. BLOOMER
07 Director Admissions/Recruiting .... Mr. John BLALOCK
40 Campus Store Manager .... Mrs. Patti H. MCCRAW
38 College Counselor .... Mrs. Mary B. CAMPBELL
50 Dean Business .... Dr. Paul R. LEFRANCOIS
49 Dean Liberal Arts & Sciences .... Dr. Brian F. AMELING
57 Chair Dept Visual & Performing Arts .... Dr. Gena E. POOVEY
58 Dean of Graduate Education .... Dr. Betsy A. WITT
22 Dir Affirm Action/Equal Opportunity .... Ms. Janie CORRY
39 Director Residential Life & Housing .... Ms. Jessica D. GOINS
09 Dir Inst Research & Effectiveness .... Mr. Andrew ENGLISH
101 Secretary of the Institution/Board .... Mrs. Brandi P. HARTMAN
28 Director of Diversity .... Ms. Selena BLAIR

Medical University of South Carolina (C)

179 Ashley Avenue, Charleston SC 29425
County: Charleston FICE Identification: 003438
Unit ID: 218335
Telephone: (843) 792-2300 Carnegie Class: Spec-4-yr-Med
FAX Number: N/A Calendar System: Semester
URL: www.musc.edu
Established: 1824 Annual Undergrad Tuition & Fees (In-State): N/A
Enrollment: 3,083 Coed
Affiliation or Control: State IRS Status: Exempt
Highest Offering: Doctorate
Accreditation: SC, ANEST, ARCPA, CAHIIM, CAMPEP, DENT, DIETI, HSA, IPSY, MED, NURSE, OT, PERF, PHAR, PTA, @SP

01 President .... Dr. David J. COLE
05 EVP Academic Affairs & Provost .... Dr. Lisa SALADIN
63 Dean College of Medicine .... Dr. Raymond DUBOIS
10 Int Exec Vice Pres Finance & Admin .... Mr. Stewart MIXON
30 VP Institutional Advancement .... Ms. Kate AZIZI
12 CEO MUSC Charleston Division .... Dr. David ZAAS
13 MUSC Information Solutions .... Mr. Mark MCMATH
20 Assoc Prov Educ Innov/Student Life .... Dr. Gigi SMITH
46 VP Research .... Dr. Lori MCMAHON
108 Assoc Prov Educ Plng/Effectiveness .... Dr. Suzanne THOMAS
52 Dean of Dental Medicine .... Dr. Sarandeep HUJA
76 Dean of Health Professions .... Dr. Zoher F. KAPASI
58 Dean of Graduate Studies .... Dr. Paula TRAKTMAN
66 Dean of Nursing .... Dr. Linda WEGLICKI
67 Dean of Pharmacy .... Dr. Philip D. HALL
08 Director of Libraries .... Ms. Shannon JONES
84 Director Enrollment Management .... Ms. Melissa FREELAND
23 Director Student Wellness Programs .... Mr. Kevin SMUNIEWSKI
43 General Counsel .... Ms. Annette R. DRACHMAN
26 Chief Communication & Marketing Ofc .... Ms. Sheila CHAMPLIN
22 Dir Equity/EEO/Accessibility Svcs .... Ms. Stephanie T. PRICE
07 Director of Admissions .... Ms. Lyla HUDSON
18 Chief Facilities Ofcr/Physical Plnt .... Mr. Brad TAYLOR
06 Registrar .... Mr. Patrick CASSANO
15 Director University Human Resources .... Ms. Susan H. CARULLO
38 Dir Counseling/Psych Services CAPS .... Dr. Alice Q. LIBET
29 Director Alumni Affairs .... Ms. Linda COX
37 Director Student Financial Aid .... Ms. Tami WYNDHAM-COOKE
96 Director of Purchasing .... Ms. Velma STAMP

† Tuition varies by degree program.

Midlands Technical College (D)

PO Box 2408, Columbia SC 29202-2408
County: Lexington, Richland, Fairfiel FICE Identification: 003993
Unit ID: 218353
Telephone: (803) 738-8324 Carnegie Class: Assoc/MT-VT-High Trad
FAX Number: (803) 738-7784 Calendar System: Semester
URL: www.midlandstech.edu
Established: 1974 Annual Undergrad Tuition & Fees (In-District): $5,916
Enrollment: 8,794 Coed
Affiliation or Control: State/Local IRS Status: 501(c)3
Highest Offering: Associate Degree
Accreditation: SC, ACBSP, ADNUR, COARC, CSHSE, DA, DH, MAC, MLTAD, NAEYC, NMT, PNUR, PTAA, RAD, SURGT

01 President .... Dr. Ronald RHAMES
03 Provost .... Dr. Barrie KIRK
05 Vice Provost Academics .... Dr. Diane CARR
51 Vice Provost Corp & Continuing Ed .... Ms. Amy SCULLY
10 Vice President for Business Affairs .... Ms. Debbie WALKER
32 Vice Pres Student Development Svcs .... Dr. Mary HOLLOWAY
30 VP for Institutional Support .... Ms. Starnell BATES
26 Asst Vice President for Marketing .... Ms. Stefanie GOEBELER
43 General Counsel .... Mr. Joseph BIAS
102 Associate VP for Philanthropy .... Ms. Nancy MCKINNEY
06 Registrar .... Ms. Carla KAISER
13 Director Information Resource Mgmt .... Mr. Tony HOUGH
37 Director of Student Financial Aid .... Ms. Angela WILLIAMS
84 AVP Enrollment Management Services .... Ms. Sylvia LITTLEJOHN
26 Director of Public Information .... Mr. Kevin FLOYD
15 Human Resource Director .... Ms. Faye GOWANS
07 Director of Admissions .... Mr. Derrah CASSIDY
124 Director of Student Retention .... Mr. Shickre SABBAGHA
04 Executive Asst to the President .... Ms. Kim BOATWRIGHT
08 Chief Library Officer .... Ms. Florence MAYS
09 Dir of Assessment/Research & Plng .... Mr. Kevin BRAY
106 Director of Distance Learning .... Ms. Mary Helen HENDRIX
108 Asst Dir Assessment/Research & Plng .... Mr. Chris LOWNES
18 Chief Facilities/Physical Plant Ofc .... Ms. Teresa COOK
19 Director Security/Safety .... Mr. Myron CHAMBLISS
25 Chief Contract/Grants Administrator .... Ms. Alice APPLEBY
29 Director Alumni Affairs .... Mr. Allen SHARPE
96 Director of Purchasing .... Ms. Latitia TREZEVANT
121 Director Academic & Career Advising .... Mr. Andrew NEWTON

Miller-Motte Technical College (E)

2451 Highway 501, Conway SC 29526
Telephone: (843) 614-3638 Identification: 770778
Accreditation: ACCSC, MAC

† Branch campus of Platt College, Tulsa, OK.

Miller-Motte Technical College (F)

8085 Rivers Avenue, Suite E, Charleston SC 29418
Telephone: (843) 574-0101 Identification: 666256
Accreditation: ACCSC

† Branch campus of Platt College, Tulsa, OK.

Morris College (G)

100 W College Street, Sumter SC 29150-3599
County: Sumter FICE Identification: 003439
Unit ID: 218399
Telephone: (803) 934-3200 Carnegie Class: Bac-Diverse
FAX Number: (803) 773-3687 Calendar System: Semester
URL: www.morris.edu
Established: 1908 Annual Undergrad Tuition & Fees: $14,980
Enrollment: 395 Coed
Affiliation or Control: Baptist IRS Status: 501(c)3
Highest Offering: Baccalaureate
Accreditation: SC, ACBSP, CAEP

00 Chairman of the Board .... Dr. Kenny ROSE
01 President .... Dr. Leroy STAGGERS
05 Interim Academic Dean .... Dr. Jacob BUTLER
10 Director of Business Affairs .... Mr. Robert EAVES
45 Dir Planning/Govt Relations/IT .... Ms. Dorothy S. CHEAGLE
32 Dean Student Affairs .... Dr. Juana DAVIS-FREEMAN
15 Dir Human Resources .... Mrs. Abby LAWSON
111 Dir Inst Advancement/Church Rels .... Dr. Gloria SEABROOK-WRIGHT
42 College Minister .... Dr. Charles M. PEE
84 Int Dir Enrollment Mgmt & Records .... Dr. Christopher HALL
37 Director of Financial Aid .... Ms. Sul BLACK
06 Registrar .... Ms. Gloria SCRIVEN
108 Director of Assessment .... Dr. Lewis P. GRAHAM, JR.
13 Director MIS/Computer Center .... Mr. Monterrio JONES
21 Chief Accountant .... Mrs. Bernice IRBY
29 Director Alumni Affairs .... Vacant
26 Director Public Relations .... Vacant
24 Director Learning Resources Ctr .... Ms. Janet S. CLAYTON
08 Head Librarian .... Ms. Margaret N. MUKOOZA
36 Director Career Services .... Vacant
38 Director Counseling .... Ms. Quanda D. SIMS
39 Director Residential Life .... Mrs. Tonia T. WASHINGTON
41 Director of Athletics .... Mr. Clarence M. HOUCK
23 Director of Health Services .... Ms. Felicia HEYWARD
40 Bookstore Manager .... Ms. Jeanette MOSES-HOLMES
19 Coordinator Campus Safety Services .... Ms. Lucille W. WILLIAMS
18 Chief Facilities/Physical Plant Off .... Vacant
19 Director of Security/Safety .... Ms. Carlotta STACKHOUSE
81 Chairperson Mathematics/Science .... Dr. Radman ALI
50 Chairperson Business Admin .... Dr. Kevin RICHARDSON
53 Chairperson Education .... Dr. Carol M. MCCLAIN
83 Chairperson Rel/Human/Social Sci .... Ms. Karen HEBERT
97 Chairperson General Studies .... Dr. Evelyn COHENS

Newberry College (H)

2100 College, Newberry SC 29108-2126
County: Newberry FICE Identification: 003440
Unit ID: 218414
Telephone: (800) 845-4955 Carnegie Class: Bac-Diverse
FAX Number: (803) 321-5627 Calendar System: Semester
URL: www.newberry.edu
Established: 1856 Annual Undergrad Tuition & Fees: $28,150
Enrollment: 1,256 Coed
Affiliation or Control: Evangelical Lutheran Church In America
IRS Status: 501(c)3
Highest Offering: Master's
Accreditation: SC, CAEP, MUS, NURSE

01 President .... Dr. Maurice W. SCHERRENS
05 VP for Academic Affairs .... Dr. Sid PARRISH
10 VP for Administrative Affairs & CFO .... Mr. David SAYERS
111 VP for Institutional Advancement .... Ms. Lori Ann SUMMERS
20 Assoc VP Academic Affairs .... Dr. Timothy G. ELSTON
84 Dean of Enrollment Management .... Vacant
32 Dean of Student Affairs .... Dr. Sandra ROUSE
41 Director of Athletics .... Mr. Ralph PATTERSON
15 Director of Human Resources .... Mrs. Nikki BROOKS
06 Registrar .... Ms. Whitney MERINAR
29 Assoc Dir of Alumni Relations .... Vacant
08 Librarian .... Mr. Austin REID
18 Assoc Director of Facilities .... Mr. Bobby LONG
42 Chaplain .... Vacant
21 Director of Accounting .... Ms. Landee BUZHARDT
38 Dir Health & Counseling Services .... Mrs. Martha DORRELL
37 Assoc Dir of Financial Aid .... Mrs. Danielle BELL
26 Director of Marketing & PR .... Mr. Russell RIVERS
19 Director Security/Safety .... Mr. Paul WHITMAN
37 Director of Financial Aid .... Vacant
100 Chief of Staff .... Ms. Bobbie SIDES

North Greenville University (I)

PO Box 1892, Tigerville SC 29688-1892
County: Greenville FICE Identification: 003441
Unit ID: 218441
Telephone: (864) 977-7000 Carnegie Class: Masters/S
FAX Number: (864) 977-7021 Calendar System: Semester
URL: www.ngu.edu
Established: 1892 Annual Undergrad Tuition & Fees: $22,050
Enrollment: 2,280 Coed

Affiliation or Control: Southern Baptist IRS Status: 501(c)3
Highest Offering: Doctorate
Accreditation: SC, #ARCPA, CAEP, COSMA, MUS

01 President/CEO .... Dr. Gene C. FANT, JR.
04 Admin Assistant for President .... Ms. Angie WATSON
03 Executive Vice President .... Mr. Rich GRIMM
05 Provost & Dean of Univ Faculty .... Dr. Nathan FINN
32 Vice President Student Services .... Ms. Rachael RUSSIAKY
20 Assoc Provost for Undergrad Studies .... Dr. Linwood HAGIN
10 Senior Vice President for Finance .... Mr. Michael STOWELL
07 Senior Director of NGU Central .... Ms. Keli SEWELL
111 Vice President for Advancement .... Mr. Marty O'GWYNN
42 Senior Campus Pastor .... Dr. Steve CROUSE
102 Director of Dev & Foundation Giving .... Dr. Phil GARDNER
13 VP Information Technology Services .... Mr. Tim HUGGINS
109 Senior AVP Tigerville Operations .... Mr. Billy WATSON
108 Asst Provost Instruct & Assessment .... Dr. Jan FOSTER
06 Registrar .... Ms. Pam FARMER
18 VP Campus Enhancement Service .... Mr. Mick DANIEL
41 Athletic Director .... Ms. Jan MCDONALD
08 Director of Hester Library .... Ms. Carla MCMAHAN
19 Director Campus Safety & Security .... Mr. Tony EIGNER
88 Assoc Prov for Acad Engagement .... Dr. Tawana SCOTT
35 VP Campus Ministries/Student Engage .... Mr. Jody JENNINGS
26 Director of Communications .... Mr. LaVerne B. HOWELL
107 Dir Leadership/Prof Development .... Ms. Jill RAYBURN
15 Director of Personnel Services .... Mrs. Michelle L. SABOU
16 Human Resource Manager .... Mrs. Beth HOUCK
40 Bookstore Manager .... Mrs. Cindy COWAN
38 Personal Counselor Men .... Mr. Steve BIELBY
38 Personal Counselor Women .... Miss Sara BLACK
36 Director of Career Planning .... Mr. Stuart FLOYD
23 Director Health Services .... Mrs. Helen NEELY
102 Dir of Dev & Corporate Relations .... Mr. Jason ROSS
14 Asst VP Information Tech Services .... Mr. Paul GARRETT
37 Director Financial Aid .... Mrs. Cindi PATTERSON
53 Dean Education .... Dr. Constance WRIGHT
79 Dean Humanities & Sciences .... Dr. H. Paul THOMPSON
57 Dean Communication & Fine Arts .... Dr. Web DRAKE
73 Dean Christian Studies .... Dr. Walter JOHNSON
50 Dean Business & Entrepreneurship .... Dr. John DUNCAN
106 Director of the eLearning Center .... Dr. Lena MASLENNIKOVA
35 Assoc VP for Student Engagement .... Dr. Jared THOMAS
12 Asst VP of Greer Campus Operations .... Mr. Justin PITTS
29 AVP Advancement & Alumni Engagement . Mr. Lamont SULLIVAN
31 Sr Dir of Church & Cmty Engagement .... Dr. Tony BEAM

Northeastern Technical College (A)

1201 Chesterfield Hwy, Cheraw SC 29520
County: Chesterfield FICE Identification: 007602
Unit ID: 217837
Telephone: (843) 921-6900 Carnegie Class: Assoc/HVT-Mix Trad/Non
FAX Number: (843) 537-6148 Calendar System: Semester
URL: www.netc.edu
Established: 1969 Annual Undergrad Tuition & Fees (In-State): $5,186
Enrollment: 1,465 Coed
Affiliation or Control: State IRS Status: 501(c)3
Highest Offering: Associate Degree
Accreditation: SC

01 President .... Dr. Kyle WAGNER
05 Vice President of Instruction .... Dr. Edwin DELGADO
10 Director of Finance .... Mr. Robert CHARLES
111 Asst VP for Inst Advancement .... Ms. Erin FANN
15 Director for Human Resources .... Mrs. Christi MEGGS
06 Registrar .... Ms. Anne JONES
26 Coordinator for Public Relations .... Vacant
84 Dean of Student Engagement .... Mr. Darin COLEMAN
08 Head Librarian .... Mr. Ronnie STAFFORD
09 Director of Institutional Research .... Vacant
04 Executive Assistant .... Ms. Sharekka BRIDGES
101 Secretary of the Board .... Ms. Lib NORTON
13 Information Technology Manager .... Mr. Josh BRITT
32 Dean of Students .... Ms. Danielle PACE
37 Director Student Financial Aid .... Ms. Sheryll MARSHALL

Orangeburg-Calhoun Technical College (B)

3250 Saint Matthews Road, Orangeburg SC 29118-8299
County: Orangeburg FICE Identification: 006815
Unit ID: 218487
Telephone: (803) 536-0311 Carnegie Class: Assoc/HVT-Mix Trad/Non
FAX Number: (803) 535-1388 Calendar System: Semester
URL: www.octech.edu
Established: 1966 Annual Undergrad Tuition & Fees (In-State): $5,714
Enrollment: 2,257 Coed
Affiliation or Control: State IRS Status: 501(c)3
Highest Offering: Associate Degree
Accreditation: SC, ACBSP, ADNUR, MAC, NAEYC, PNUR, PTAA, RAD

01 President .... Dr. Walt TOBIN
05 Vice Pres Academic Affairs .... Mrs. Donna ELMORE
10 Vice President Business Affairs .... Mr. Kim HUFF
32 Vice President of Student Services .... Dr. Sandra S. DAVIS
11 Dean of Administration .... Mr. Mike HAMMOND
36 Training/Econ Development Director .... Mrs. Sandra MOORE
06 Registrar .... Ms. Amy OTT
46 Dean Planning/Research/Development .... Ms. Faith MCCURRY
13 Director Information Technology .... Mr. John MCCASKILL

08 Dean Learning Resource Ctr/Library .... Mr. Haley HALL
18 Physical Plant Director .... Mr. James S. BRYANT, III
37 Director Student Financial Aid .... Ms. Connie WILLIAMS
07 Director of Admissions .... Vacant
19 Chief of Safety/Security .... Vacant
09 Dir Acad Support/Inst Effectiveness .... Mr. Cleveland WILSON
15 Human Resource Director .... Ms. Marie HOWELL
96 Procurement Manager .... Mrs. Scarlet GEDDINGS
84 Director of Enrollment .... Ms. Tracy DIBBLE

Piedmont Technical College (C)

620 N. Emerald Road, Greenwood SC 29646
County: Greenwood FICE Identification: 003992
Unit ID: 218520
Telephone: (864) 941-8324 Carnegie Class: Assoc/HVT-High Trad
FAX Number: (864) 941-8555 Calendar System: Semester
URL: www.ptc.edu
Established: 1966 Annual Undergrad Tuition & Fees (In-District): $5,315
Enrollment: 4,712 Coed
Affiliation or Control: State/Local IRS Status: 501(c)3
Highest Offering: Associate Degree
Accreditation: SC, ADNUR, COARC, CVT, FUSER, MAC, OTA, RAD, SURGT

01 President .... Dr. Hope E. RIVERS
10 VP Business & Finance .... Ms. K. Paige CHILDS
05 VP Academic Affairs .... Dr. Keli FEWOX
32 VP Student Affairs/Communications .... Mr. Joshua BLACK
102 Asst VP Development/PTC Foundation .... Ms. Fran K. WILEY
51 Assoc VP Econ Dev & Cont Educ .... Mr. Rusty DENNING
108 Assoc VP Assessment & Compliance .... Dr. Donna FOSTER
15 Assoc VP Human Resources .... Ms. Alesia BROWN
13 Asst VP Information Tech .... Mr. Joel GRIFFIN
49 Dean Arts & Science .... Dr. Lisa MARTIN
76 Dean Health Care .... Ms. Tara GONCE
54 Dean Engr/Industrial Technology .... Mr. Alvie COES
106 Dean Curriculum/Online Learning .... Ms. Karla GILLIAM
35 Dean of Student Services .... Ms. Tamatha SELLS
07 Dean of Admissions .... Ms. Renae FRAZIER
26 Director Marketing/PR .... Mr. Russell MARTIN
88 Director Genesis Initiatives .... Mr. Steve B. COLEMAN
18 Director Facilities Management .... Vacant
08 Head Librarian .... Ms. Meredith DANIEL
19 Director Campus Police/Security .... Mr. Jeffrey CRISP
37 Director of Financial Aid .... Ms. Missy PERRY
06 Registrar .... Ms. Jalissa ALGER
21 Controller .... Ms. Wendy HUGHES
21 Sr Accountant .... Ms. Crystal PITTMAN
04 Exec Asst to the President .... Ms. Sally M. COOKE
25 Chief Contract and Grants Administr .... Ms. Caroline CHAPPELL
96 Director of Purchasing .... Mr. Brian MCKENNA

Presbyterian College (D)

503 S Broad Street, Clinton SC 29325-2865
County: Laurens FICE Identification: 003445
Unit ID: 218539
Telephone: (864) 833-2820 Carnegie Class: Bac-A&S
FAX Number: (864) 833-8481 Calendar System: Semester
URL: www.presby.edu
Established: 1880 Annual Undergrad Tuition & Fees: $40,260
Enrollment: 1,309 Coed
Affiliation or Control: Presbyterian Church (U.S.A.) IRS Status: 501(c)3
Highest Offering: Doctorate
Accreditation: SC, #ARCPA, CAEPN, PHAR

01 President .... Mr. Robert E. STATON
04 Executive Asst to the President .... Mrs. Jenny G. BOGAN
05 Provost .... Dr. Donald R. RABER, II
84 Dean of Enrollment Management .... Mr. Brian J. FORTMAN
07 Director of Admissions .... Mr. Mark O. FOX, II
20 Dean of Academic Programs .... Dr. J. Alicia ASKEW
37 VP for Enrollment & Financial Aid .. Mrs. Suzanne M. PETRUSCH
09 Director of Institutional Research .... Dr. Norman B. BRYAN, JR.
08 Director of Thomason Library .... Vacant
24 Director of Media Services .... Mr. Douglas J. WALLACE
104 Director of International Programs .... Mr. Viet X. HA
85 Asst Dir of International Programs .... Ms. Adriana K. SMITH
06 Registrar & Director of Records .... Mrs. Vicky W. WILSON
67 Dean School of Pharmacy .... Dr. Kurt A. WARGO
07 Dir of Admissions Pharmacy School .... Ms. Katherine J. KANE
10 VP Finance/Administration .... Mr. Jeff P. SCACCIA
21 Controller .... Ms. Dawn W. DURHAM
18 Exec Director of Campus Services .... Mr. Michael D. CRISP
37 Director of Financial Aid .... Mr. Brian J. FORTMAN
13 Director of Information Technology .... Mr. H. William ROACH
90 Academic Computing Services Coord .... Dr. Robert W. HOWILER
91 Desktop Support/Aux Systems Sr Tech .... Ms. Nellie R. SHELTON
109 Manager of Auxiliary Services .... Mr. Jason T. KOENIG
32 VP for Campus Life/Dean of Students .... Dr. Joy S. SMITH
39 Assoc Dean Students/Residence Life .... Mr. Andrew T. PETERSON
36 Assoc Dean Students/Career Dev .... Ms. Kimberly A. LANE
42 Director of Campus Ministries .. Ms. Rachel E. PARSONS-WELLS
19 Director of Safety & Risk Mgmt .... Mr. Lawrence P. MULHALL
38 Director Counseling Services .... Ms. Susan C. GENTRY-WRIGHT
111 VP for Advancement .... Ms. Jacki BERKSHIRE
88 Asst Athletic Dir for Development .... Mr. Harold E. NICHOLS, JR.
29 Director Alumni Relations .... Ms. Leni N. PATTERSON
41 Director of Athletics .... Mr. Rob L. ACUNTO
15 VP of Human Resources .... Ms. Barbara H. FAYAD

Professional Golfers Career College (E)

4454 Bluffton Pk Crescent, Ste 200, Bluffton SC 29910
Telephone: (843) 757-9611 Identification: 770779
Accreditation: CNCE

† Branch campus of Professional Golfers Career College, Temecula, CA

Sherman College of Chiropractic (F)

PO Box 1452, Spartanburg SC 29304-1452
County: Spartanburg FICE Identification: 020637
Unit ID: 218751
Telephone: (864) 578-8770 Carnegie Class: Spec-4-yr-Other Health
FAX Number: (864) 599-4860 Calendar System: Quarter
URL: www.sherman.edu
Established: 1973 Annual Graduate Tuition & Fees: N/A
Enrollment: 423 Coed
Affiliation or Control: Independent Non-Profit IRS Status: 501(c)3
Highest Offering: Doctorate; No Undergraduates
Accreditation: SC, CHIRO

01 President .... Dr. Edwin CORDERO
03 Exec Asst to President/Sr VP .... Ms. Roberta THOMAS-WOOD
11 Senior Vice President .... Dr. Neil COHEN
05 Provost .... Dr. Robert IRWIN
20 Vice Pres of Academic Affairs .... Dr. Joseph DONOFRIO
10 COO/Chief Financial Officer .... Mrs. Karen CANUP
32 Vice Pres for Student Affairs .... Mrs. LaShanda HUTTO-HARRIS
84 Assoc VP for Enrollment Services .... Ms. Kendra STRANGE
111 Assoc VP for Inst Advancement .... Dr. Jillian FARRELL
21 Assoc VP for Finance .... Mr. David BEDFORD
45 AVP for Institutional Effectivenes .... Mrs. Crissy LEWIS
06 Registrar .... Ms. Melody SABIN
08 Director of Learning Resouces .... Mrs. Chandra PLACER
37 Director of Financial Aid .... Mr. Chris ROBERSON
26 Sr Director for Marketing & Comm .... Mrs. Karen RHODES
88 Director for Scholarly Activity .... Dr. Christopher KENT
88 Dir for Teaching & Learning .... Dr. Billie HARRINGTON
15 Director Personnel Services .... Mrs. Mandy SMITH

South Carolina State University (G)

300 College Street, NE, Orangeburg SC 29117-0001
County: Orangeburg FICE Identification: 003446
Unit ID: 218733
Telephone: (803) 536-7000 Carnegie Class: Masters/S
FAX Number: (803) 533-3622 Calendar System: Semester
URL: www.scsu.edu
Established: 1896 Annual Undergrad Tuition & Fees (In-State): $11,060
Enrollment: 2,339 Coed
Affiliation or Control: State IRS Status: 501(c)3
Highest Offering: Doctorate
Accreditation: SC, AAFCS, ART, CACREP, CAEP, CAEPN, DIETD, MUS, SP, SW

01 Acting President .... Mr. Alexander CONYERS
100 Chief of Staff .... Ms. Shondra F. ABRAHAM
05 Provost .... Dr. Learie B. LUKE
03 VP Strategic Alliances/Initiatives .... Mr. Alexander CONYERS
10 Vice Pres for Finance/Mgmt .... Mrs. Teare BREWINGTON
32 Vice Pres for Student Affairs ...... Dr. Tamara JEFFRIES-JACKSON
88 VP/Executive Dir 1890 Programs .... Dr. Louis D. WHITESIDES
43 General Counsel .... Vacant
20 Acting Associate Provost .... Dr. William H. WHITAKER
111 VP Inst Advancement/External Rels .... Ms. Sonja A. BELLAMY-BENNETT
46 Assoc Provost/Sponsored Program .... Mr. Elbert R. MALONE
07 Director of Admissions .... Ms. Stacey SOWELL
81 Dean Col Sci/Math/Engineering Tech . Dr. Stanley N. IHEKWEAZU
53 Actg Dean Col Educ/Human & Soc Sci .... Dr. Janice B. OWENS
58 Dean Col of Graduate Studies .... Dr. Frederick M G. EVANS
50 Dean School of Business .... Dr. Barbara L. ADAMS
54 Dean of Engineering .... Dr. Stanley N. IHEKWEAZU
08 Acting Dean Library Services .... Dr. Ruth A. HODGES
124 Manager Student Success Retention .... Dr. Diane S. BRUCE
06 Acting Registrar .... Ms. Felicia L. MCMILLAN
13 Director UCITS .... Mr. Travis T. JOHNSON
37 Director of Financial Aid .... Ms. Tangar YOUNG
38 Director Counseling/Student Dev .... Dr. Cherilyn Y. TAYLOR-MINNIEFIELD
26 Director of Marketing .... Ms. Kay E. SNIDER
36 Director of Career Placement .... Mr. Joseph THOMAS
15 Director Human Resource Mgmt .... Mr. Ronald S. YORK
41 Director Athletics .... Mr. Stacy L. DANLEY
18 Director of Facilities Mgmt .... Mr. Ken DAVIS
96 Director Procurement Services .... Ms. Jessica FAVOR
39 Director of Residential Life .... Ms. Cammy GRATE
19 Chief of Campus Police .... Mr. Joseph B. NELSON
92 Dean Honors College .... Dr. Harriet A. ROLAND
88 Director Sports Information .... Mr. Kendrick D. LEWIS
25 Dir Grants & Contract .... Ms. Gwendolyn F. MITCHELL
22 Director of Title III .... Ms. Gloria D. PYLES
28 Director of Multicultural Affairs .... Ms. Carolyn G. FREE
88 Station Manager WSSB-FM .... Mr. Carlito D. A'SEE
88 Director of Compliance .... Ms. Theresa LAURENTE
101 Secretary/Board of Trustees .... Ms. Eartha J. MOSLEY
104 Dir International/National Exchange .... Ms. Dominique ROLLE
105 Web Services .... Mr. Jason BARR
29 Director Alumni Relations .... Mr. Davion L. PETTY
108 Dir of Institutional Effectiveness .... Ms. Valerie GOODWIN
88 Director IP Stanback Museum/Planet .... Dr. Frank C. MARTIN
106 Exe Dir Teach/Learning/Ext Studies .... Dr. Diane M. BURNETTE
09 Director Institutional Research .... Mrs. Cammie S. BERRY

84 Director Enrollment Management ....Ms. Betty R. BOATWRIGHT
27 Public Information Officer ....Mr. Samuel WATSON
102 Exec Dir Development/AVP Inst Adv ....Dr. Gwynth NELSON

South University Columbia Campus (A)

9 Science Court, Columbia SC 29203-6400
Telephone: (803) 799-9082 FICE Identification: 004922
Accreditation: &SC, ACBSP, CACREP, MAC, NURSE, OTA, PTAA

† Regional accreditation is carried under the parent institution in Savannah, GA.

Southeastern College (B)

1628 Browning Rd, Columbia SC 29210
County: Richland FICE Identification: 037464
Unit ID: 444866
Telephone: (803) 798-8800 Carnegie Class: Not Classified
FAX Number: (803) 798-0003 Calendar System: Semester
URL: www.southeasterninstitute.edu
Established: 1997 Annual Undergrad Tuition & Fees: N/A
Enrollment: 193 Coed
Affiliation or Control: Proprietary IRS Status: Proprietary
Highest Offering: Associate Degree
Accreditation: ACCSC, MAAB

Southeastern College (C)

2431 Aviation Ave., Ste 703, North Charleston SC 29406
County: Charleston FICE Identification: 035554
Unit ID: 443261
Telephone: (843) 747-1279 Carnegie Class: Not Classified
FAX Number: (843) 747-7159 Calendar System: Semester
URL: www.southeasterninstitute.edu
Established: 1997 Annual Undergrad Tuition & Fees: N/A
Enrollment: N/A Coed
Affiliation or Control: Proprietary IRS Status: Proprietary
Highest Offering: Associate Degree
Accreditation: ACCSC, MAAB

Southern Wesleyan University (D)

907 Wesleyan Drive, PO Box 1020,
Central SC 29630-1020
County: Pickens FICE Identification: 003422
Unit ID: 217776
Telephone: (864) 644-5556 Carnegie Class: Masters/L
FAX Number: N/A Calendar System: Semester
URL: www.swu.edu
Established: 1906 Annual Undergrad Tuition & Fees: $25,676
Enrollment: 1,345 Coed
Affiliation or Control: Wesleyan Church IRS Status: 501(c)3
Highest Offering: Doctorate
Accreditation: SC, CAEPN, MUS, NURSE

01 Interim President ....Dr. Bill S. CROTHERS
05 Provost ....Dr. April WHITE PUGH
10 Chief Financial Officer ....Mr. Ken WHITENER
32 Vice President for Student Life ....Dr. Chris CONFER
111 Vice President for Advancement ....Mr. Scott DRURY
45 Director of Institutional Planning ....Mrs. Lisa CORBIN
49 Dean College of Arts & Sciences ....Dr. Randolph JOHNSON
41 Athletic Director ....Mrs. Julia REININGA
50 Dean of the School of Business ....Dr. Stephen PREACHER
53 Dean of the School of Education ....Dr. Sandra MCLENDON
37 Director of Financial Aid ....Mrs. Tasha MORGAN
15 Director of Human Resources ....Mrs. Dana L. FROST
08 Director of Library Services ....Mrs. Shannon BROOKS
06 Interim Registrar ....Ms. Regina BOLDING
29 Alumni Director ....Mr. Heath MULLIKIN
38 Director Student Counseling ....Ms. Monica PEREZ
124 Director of Retention ....Mr. Brice BICKEL
07 Director of Admissions ....Mr. David SLABAUGH
19 Director Security/Safety ....Mr. Brad BOWEN
39 Director of Residence Life ....Mr. Jason TEGAN
36 Director of Career Services ....Mrs. Ellen PATE
42 AVP Spiritual Life/Univ Chaplain ....Rev. Ken DILL
04 Administrative Asst to President ....Ms. Amy JARRETT

Spartanburg Community College (E)

107 Community College Drive, Spartanburg SC 29303
County: Spartanburg FICE Identification: 003994
Unit ID: 218830
Telephone: (864) 592-4600 Carnegie Class: Assoc/MT-VT-Mix Trad/Non
FAX Number: (864) 592-4642 Calendar System: Semester
URL: www.sccsc.edu
Established: 1963 Annual Undergrad Tuition & Fees (In-State): $6,030
Enrollment: 4,108 Coed
Affiliation or Control: State IRS Status: 501(c)3
Highest Offering: Associate Degree
Accreditation: SC, ACFEI, ADNUR, COARC, DA, EMT, MAC, MLTAD, NAEYC, RAD, SURGT

01 President ....Dr. G. Michael MIKOTA
05 Sr Vice President Academic Affairs ....Dr. Cheryl COX
03 Vice President Strategic Innovation ....Dr. Stacey L. OBI
10 Vice Pres for Business Affairs ....Mr. Ray SWITZER
111 Exec Dir Advancement/SCC Foundation ....Mrs. Bea W. SMITH
32 Vice President for Student Affairs ....Mr. Ron JACKSON
84 Assc Vice Pres Enroll Mgt/Retention ....Mrs. Lynn F. DALE
20 Assoc Vice Pres of Instruction ....Mrs. Kem HARVEY
88 Vice Pres for Economic Development ....Mr. Michael P. FORRESTER
12 Executive Director Cherokee Campus ....Ms. Amanda PAINTER
12 Exec Director Tyger River Campus ....Mrs. Rhonda JOHNS
12 Exec Director Downtown Campus ....Ms. Witney FISHER
12 Director County Campus ....Mr. Issac MCKISSICK
108 AVP Eval/Accreditation/Plng ....Dr. Jay JACKSON
88 Dean of CCE ....Ms. Rhonda JOHNS
08 Dean of Learning Resources ....Mr. Mark ROSEVEARE
76 Dean Health & Human Services ....Dr. Benita YOWE
49 Dean of Arts & Sciences ....Ms. Jenny WILLIAMS
07 Director Recruiting/Admissions Svcs ....Ms. Quiana REED
15 Assoc Vice Pres of Human Resources ....Vacant
13 Director Information Technologies ....Mr. Peter C. GALLEN
09 Director of Institutional Research ....Dr. Amanda ADAMS
26 Director Marketing/Public Relations ....Mrs. Cheri ANDERSON-HUCKS
29 Alumni Relations Coordinator ....Ms. Charm LOWE
38 Director Advising/Early Alert Svcs ....Mr. Michael HARVEY
14 Director Computer Center ....Mr. David AUGHINBAUGH
18 Director Campus Operations ....Mr. Winston ANDERSON
19 Director Security/Safety ....Mr. Richard POWERS
06 Registrar ....Ms. Celia N. BAUSS
96 Director Procurement ....Mr. Michael D. CLARDY
21 Director of Finance ....Ms. Melissa P. HUGHES
37 Director of Financial Aid ....Mr. Jeffery BOYLE
106 Dir Online Education/E-learning ....Mr. Neil GRIFFIN
25 Director of Contracts & Grants ....Ms. Caroline SEXTON
72 Dean of Technologies ....Mr. Jeff HUNT
04 Administrative Asst to President ....Mrs. Donna WALKER
36 Director Student Placement ....Ms. Jennifer LITTLE
90 Director Academic Computing ....Mr. Roy SMITH
103 Director Workforce Development ....Mrs. Latokia TRIGG

Spartanburg Methodist College (F)

1000 Powell Mill Road, Spartanburg SC 29301-5899
County: Spartanburg FICE Identification: 003447
Unit ID: 218821
Telephone: (864) 587-4000 Carnegie Class: Assoc/HT-High Trad
FAX Number: (864) 587-4355 Calendar System: Semester
URL: www.smcsc.edu
Established: 1911 Annual Undergrad Tuition & Fees: $17,540
Enrollment: 1,051 Coed
Affiliation or Control: United Methodist IRS Status: 501(c)3
Highest Offering: Baccalaureate
Accreditation: SC

01 President ....Mr. W. Scott COCHRAN
05 Exec VP Acad Affairs/Student Dev ....Mr. Kris NEELY
10 Executive VP for Business Affairs ....Mr. Eric MCDONALD
111 Vice Pres Institutional Advancement ..... Mrs. Jennifer DILLENGER
84 Vice Pres Enrollment Management ....Mr. Ben MAXWELL
26 Vice President for Marketing ....Mrs. Lisa WARE
32 VP for Student Development ....Ms. Courtney SHELTON
13 Vice Pres for Operations Info Tech ....Mr. Trey ARRINGTON
09 VP for Analytics & Improvement ....Mr. Jason WOMICK
11 Dean of Admin & Family Services ....Mr. DeAndre HOWARD
06 Registrar ....Ms. Jill R. JOHNSON
08 Library Director ....Ms. Lori HETRICK
04 Admin Assistant to the President ....Vacant
44 Director of Planned Giving ....Mr. Don TATE
37 Director of Financial Aid ....Mr. Kyle WADE
38 Director of Student Counseling .... Ms. Alesia LOWE-JENKINS
42 Chaplain/Director Church Relations ....Rev. Tim DRUM
41 Director of Athletics ....Ms. Megan AIELLO
18 Director Facilities Management ....Mr. Marty WOODS
29 Director of Alumni Relations ....Mrs. Leah L. PRUITT
15 Exec Director of Human Resources ....Mrs. Jenny R. DUNN
19 Chief of Campus Safety ....Mr. Chris CARTER
39 Director Student Housing ....Mr. Kendrick REED
108 Director Institutional Assessment ....Ms. Jessica HARWOOD
07 Executive Director of Admissions ....Ms. Julie LANFORD

Technical College of the Lowcountry (G)

921 S Ribaut Road, PO Box 1288,
Beaufort SC 29901-1288
County: Beaufort FICE Identification: 009910
Unit ID: 217712
Telephone: (843) 525-8211 Carnegie Class: Assoc/HVT-High Trad
FAX Number: (843) 525-8330 Calendar System: Semester
URL: www.tcl.edu
Established: 1969 Annual Undergrad Tuition & Fees (In-State): $5,740
Enrollment: 2,119 Coed
Affiliation or Control: State IRS Status: 501(c)3
Highest Offering: Associate Degree
Accreditation: SC, ADNUR, COMTA, PNUR, PTAA, RAD, SURGT

01 President ....Dr. Richard J. GOUGH
11 Vice Pres Administrative Services ....Ms. Janis HOFFMAN
05 Vice President for Academic Affairs ....Ms. Nancy WEBER
32 Vice President for Student Affairs ....Ms. Nancy WEBER
35 AVP for Student Affairs ....Mr. Rodney ADAMS
09 Director for Research/Planning ....Ms. Camille MYERS
15 Human Resources Director ....Ms. Sharon O'NEAL
20 Director for Learning Resources ....Ms. Sasha BISHOP
50 Div Dean Business Technologies ....Ms. Shunda WARE
49 Div Dean Arts & Sciences ....Dr. Fredrick COOPER
76 Dean Health Sciences ....Dr. Glenn LEVICKI
13 Director of Information Technology ....Mr. Hayes WISER
37 Director Financial Aid ....Ms. Georgeann WILLIAMS
111 VP for Inst Advancement ....Ms. Mary Lee CARNS
26 AVP for Public Relations ....Ms. Leigh COPELAND
109 Director for Auxiliary Services ....Ms. Louise RENNIX
18 Director of Facility Management ....Mr. Larry BECKLER
96 Procurement Manager ....Ms. Randee JOHNSON
06 Registrar ....Ms. Jillian KIRKLAND
103 Director for Workforce Solutions ....Ms. Melanie GALLION
04 Administrative Asst to President ....Ms. Ann CULLEN

Tri-County Technical College (H)

PO Box 587, Pendleton SC 29670-0587
County: Anderson FICE Identification: 004926
Unit ID: 218885
Telephone: (864) 646-8361 Carnegie Class: Assoc/MT-VT-High Trad
FAX Number: (864) 646-1889 Calendar System: Semester
URL: www.tctc.edu
Established: 1962 Annual Undergrad Tuition & Fees (In-District): $5,792
Enrollment: 5,582 Coed
Affiliation or Control: State/Local IRS Status: 501(c)3
Highest Offering: Associate Degree
Accreditation: SC, ACBSP, ADNUR, DA, MAC, MLTAD, NAEYC, PNUR, SURGT

01 President ....Dr. Galen DEHAY
10 Vice Pres Business Affairs ....Ms. Cara HAMILTON
111 VP Inst Advancement/Business Rels ....Mr. Grayson KELLY
15 Asst VP Human Resources ....Mrs. Marcie LEAKE
32 Asst VP Student Support/Engagement ....Ms. Linda JAMEISON
51 Dean of Continuing Education ....Mr. Rick COTHRAN
124 AVP College Transitions ....Ms. Jenni CREAMER
35 Dean of Student Development ....Mr. Mark DOUGHERTY
49 Dean Arts & Sciences Division ....Mr. Tom LAWRENCE
72 Dean Engineering Technology Div ....Ms. Amanda ELMORE
50 Dean Business/Human Services Div ....Mrs. Jacquelyn BLAKLEY
76 Dean Health Education Division ....Mr. Ahmad CHAUDHRY
37 Student Financial Aid Director ....Ms. Melanie GILLESPIE
13 CIO/Information Technology Dir .... Mr. Luke VANWINGERDEN
26 Dir Public Relations/Communication .... Mrs. Karen POTTER
30 Director of Development ....Mrs. Courtney WHITE
07 Director of Admissions ....Ms. Tiffiny BLACKWELL
06 Registrar ....Mr. Scott HARVEY
09 Director of Institutional Research ....Mr. Chris MARINO
18 Chief Facilities/Physical Plant ....Mr. Ken KOPERA
21 Director of Fiscal Affairs ....Ms. Tracy WACTOR
96 Director of Purchasing ....Mr. Matthew WHITTEN
38 Director of Student Life/Counseling .... Ms. Croslena JOHNSON
04 Admin Assistant to the President ....Ms. Kathleen C. BRAND
100 Chief of Staff ....Mr. Dan COOPER
36 Student Placement ....Mr. Edward Adam PAIGE
84 Enrollment Management ....Mr. Adam GHILONI

Trident Technical College (I)

PO Box 118067, Charleston SC 29423-8067
County: Charleston FICE Identification: 004920
Unit ID: 218894
Telephone: (843) 574-6111 Carnegie Class: Assoc/MT-VT-High Trad
FAX Number: N/A Calendar System: Semester
URL: www.tridenttech.edu
Established: 1964 Annual Undergrad Tuition & Fees (In-District): $5,143
Enrollment: 11,650 Coed
Affiliation or Control: State/Local IRS Status: 501(c)3
Highest Offering: Associate Degree
Accreditation: SC, ACBSP, ACFEI, ADNUR, CAHIIM, COARC, CSHSE, DA, DH, EMT, MAC, MLTAD, NAEYC, OTA, PNUR, PTAA, RAD

01 President ....Dr. Mary THORNLEY
10 Sr Vice President Business Affairs ....Mr. Scott POELKER
05 Vice President Education ....Dr. Cathy ALMQUIST
32 Vice President Student Services ....Dr. Patrice DAVIS
111 Vice President Advancement ....Ms. Meg HOWLE
13 Vice Pres Information Technology ....Mr. M.G MITCHUM
45 Assoc VP Planning/Accreditation .... Mr. James "Dub" GREEN
20 Asst Vice Pres Instruction ....Mr. David HARRIS
20 Asst VP Academic Programs ....Dr. Tim BROWN
35 Asst VP for Student Development ....Ms. Pam BROWN
15 Associate VP Human Resources ....Ms. DeVetta HUGHES
96 Dir Procurement/Risk Management ....Ms. Carol BELCHER
109 Dir Auxiliary Enterprises/Bookstore ....Ms. Jloundia PINCKNEY
18 Director Facilities ....Mr. Eric HAMILTON
21 Director Finance ....Ms. Gamellia DAVIS
26 Director Marketing ....Ms. Tina AHLEMANN
27 Director Public Info ....Mr. David HANSEN
88 Assistant VP Community Partnerships ....Ms. Melissa STOWASSER
30 Vice President Development ....Ms. Lisa PICCOLO
119 Information Security Officer ....Mr. Joseph GIBSON
124 Dean of Student Engagement ....Mr. Brian ALMQUIST
81 Dean Science & Mathematics ....Dr. Shakitha BARNER
79 Dean Humanities & Social Sciences ....Ms. Michelle CAYA
50 Dean Business Technology ....Dr. Laurie BOEDING
106 Asst VP Educ Tech/Online College ....Ms. Connie JOLLY
54 Dean Engineering & Construction ....Mr. Tim FULFORD
76 Dean Health Sciences ....Ms. Krista HARRINGTON
57 Dean Film Media and Visual Arts ....Mr. Glenn SEALE
88 Dean Manufacturing & Maintenance ....Mr. Robert ELLIOTT
88 Dean Culinary Inst of Charleston ....Mr. Mike SABOE
66 Dean Nursing ....Ms. Nancy HILBURN

75 Dean Aeronautical Studies .... Dr. Barry FRANCO
12 Dean Berkeley Campus .... Dr. Karen WRIGHTEN
12 Dean Mount Pleasant Campus .... Dr. Darren FELTY
12 Dean Palmer Campus .... Dr. Amy HUDOCK
19 Director Public Safety .... Mr. Mario EVANS
06 Registrar .... Mr. Evan REICH
07 Director of Admissions .... Mr. Tim MARTIN
09 Director of Institutional Research .... Ms. Samantha RICHARDS
37 Director Student Financial Aid .... Ms. Sarah DOWD
04 Executive Asst to President .... Ms. Helen SUGHRUE

University of South Carolina Columbia (A)

Columbia SC 29208-0001
County: Richland FICE Identification: 003448
Unit ID: 218663
Telephone: (803) 777-7000 Carnegie Class: DU-Highest
FAX Number: (803) 777-0101 Calendar System: Semester
URL: www.sc.edu
Established: 1801 Annual Undergrad Tuition & Fees (In-State): $12,688
Enrollment: 35,470 Coed
Affiliation or Control: State IRS Status: 501(c)3
Highest Offering: Doctorate
Accreditation: SC, ANEST, ARCPA, ART, CAATE, CACREP, CAEP, CAHIIM, CEA, CLPSY, DANCE, HSA, IPSY, JOUR, LAW, LIB, MED, MUS, NURSE, PH, PHAR, PTA, SCPSY, SP, SPAA, SW, THEA

01 Interim President .... Dr. Harris PASTIDES
100 Chief of Staff .... Col. Mark BIEGER, RET.
13 Vice President for IT & CIO .... Mr. Doug FOSTER
10 University Treasurer .... Mr. Patrick LARDNER
116 Exec Dir of Audit & Advisory Svcs .... Ms. Pam DORAN
05 Interim Provost .... Dr. Stephen CUTLER
20 Vice Prov/Dean Undergrad Studies .... Dr. Sandra KELLY
11 Exec VP for Administration & CFO .... Mr. Edward I. WALTON
32 Dean of Students/Title IX Dir .... Mr. Marc SHOOK
15 Vice President Human Resources .... Ms. Caroline AGARDY
30 Vice President for Development .... Ms. Monica DELISA
46 Interim Vice President for Research .... Dr. Julius FRIDRIKSSON
26 Director of Public Relations .... Mr. Jeff STENSLAND
101 Univ Secretary & Sec to Board .... Mr. Cantey HEATH
58 Vice Prov & Dean Grad School .... Dr. Cheryl ADDY
85 Vice Provost & Dir Global Carolina .... Dr. Sandra J. KELLY
84 Asst V Prov Enrl Mgmt & Dean UG Adm .... Mr. Scott VERZYL
63 Exec Dean School of Medicine .... Dr. Les HALL
08 Dean of University Libraries .... Dr. Tom MCNALLY
43 Gen Counsel & Exec Dir Compliance .... Mr. Walter H. PARHAM
09 Exec Dir Inst Rsch/Assess/Analytics .... Ms. Sabrina ANDREWS
18 VP for Facilities & Transportation .... Mr. Derrick E. HUGGINS
19 AVP Law Enforce & Chief of Police .... Mr. Christopher L. WUCHENICH
37 Dir Student Fin Aid & Scholarship .... Mr. Joey DERRICK
36 Director Career Center .... Ms. Helen POWERS
06 University Registrar .... Mr. Aaron C. MARTERER
22 Interim Director Equal Oppty Pgms .... Dr. Carl R. WELLS
88 NCAA Compliance Coord .... Mr. Christopher ROGERS
07 Director of Admissions .... Dr. Mary WAGNER
39 Exec Director of Student Housing .... Ms. April BARNES
23 Interim VP of Health & Chief Ofcr .... Dr. Jason STACY
41 Athletic Director .... Mr. Ray TANNER
45 Exec Dir Strategic Initiatives/Dev .... Mr. Jerry T. BREWER
27 Director News & Internal Relations .... Mr. Wesley T. HICKMAN
96 Director of Purchasing .... Mrs. Venis MANIGO
29 Exec Director Alumni Association .... Mr. Jack CLAYPOOLE
88 VP for System Planning .... Dr. Mary Anne FITZPATRICK
12 Chancellor Palmetto College .... Dr. Susan ELKINS
88 Interim Dean Hosp/Retail/Sport HMgt .... Mr. Matt BROWN
50 Dean Moore School of Business .... Dr. Peter J. BREWS
53 Interim Dean College of Education .... Dr. Thomas E. HODGES
54 Dean Col Engineering & Computing ...... Dr. Hossein HAJ-HARIRI
69 Dean Arnold School of Public Health .. Dr. G. Thomas CHANDLER
60 Dean Col of Info & Communications ..... Mr. Charles BIERBAUER
61 Dean School of Law .... Mr. William C. HUBBARD
88 Sr Assoc Dean School of Medicine .... Dr. Caughman TAYLOR
63 Dean Greenville School of Medicine .... Dr. Jerry R. YOUKEY
67 Dean College of Pharmacy .... Dr. Stephen J. CUTLER
49 Dean Col of Arts & Sciences .... Dr. Lacy FORD
64 Dean School of Music .... Dr. Tayloe HARDING
92 Dean SC Honors College .... Dr. Steve LYNN
66 Dean College of Nursing .... Dr. Jeannette ANDREWS
70 Dean College of Social Work .... Dr. Sarah GEHLERT
92 Dir Fellowships & Scholar Programs .... Ms. Novella BESKID
88 Interim Director for Academic Pgms .... Dr. Trena HOUP
88 Executive Director USC Connect .... Dr. Irma J. VANSCOY
28 VP of Diversity/Equity & Inclusion .... Mr. Julian R. WILLIAMS
86 Director Govt & Community Relations .... Ms. Shirley D. MILLS
103 Director of Economic Engagement .... Mr. William B. KIRKLAND
86 Director of State Govt Relations .... Mr. Derrick MEGGIE

University of South Carolina Aiken (B)

471 University Parkway, Aiken SC 29801-6399
County: Aiken FICE Identification: 003449
Unit ID: 218645
Telephone: (803) 648-6851 Carnegie Class: Bac-Diverse
FAX Number: (803) 641-3362 Calendar System: Semester
URL: www.usca.edu
Established: 1961 Annual Undergrad Tuition & Fees (In-State): $10,760
Enrollment: 3,944 Coed
Affiliation or Control: State IRS Status: 501(c)3
Highest Offering: Master's
Accreditation: SC, CAEP, MPCAC, MUS, NURSE

01 Chancellor .... Dr. Sandra JORDAN
111 Vice Chanc Advance & External Rels .... Ms. Mary DRISCOLL
05 Provost & EVC of Academic Affairs .... Dr. Daren TIMMONS
32 Vice Chanc Student Affairs .... Mr. Ahmed SAMAHA
13 Vice Chancellor Information Tech .... Mr. Ernest PRINGLE
10 VC for Admin and Finance/CFO .... Mr. Cam REAGIN
20 Asst Vice Chanc Academic Affairs .... Dr. Tim LINTNER
84 Assoc Vice Chanc Enrollment Mgmt .... Mr. Daniel J. ROBB
50 Int Dean School of Business Admin .... Dr. Sanela PORCA
53 Dean of the School of Education .... Dr. Judy BECK
66 Dean of the School of Nursing .... Dr. Thayer MCGAHEE
09 Dir Inst Effect/Research/Compliance .... Ms. Nicole SPENSLEY
08 Library Director .... Rodney LIPPARD
25 Director Sponsored Research .... Dr. Bill PIRKLE
40 Purchasing Manager .... Ms. Heidi DIFRANCO
109 Exc Dir Campus Auxil & Support Svcs .... Mr. Jeff JENIK
88 Director Children's Center .... Ms. Lynn WILLIAMS
12 Exec Dir of Etherredge Center .... Mr. Jack BENJAMIN
21 Controller .... Mr. Kevin CRAWFORD
15 Director of Human Resources .... Ms. Carla HAYES
88 Dir Campus Recreation & Wellness .... Ms. Mila PADGETT
07 Director of Admissions .... Mr. Andrew HENDRIX
36 Director of Career Services .... Mr. Corey FERALDI
37 Director Financial Aid .... Mr. Tony CARTER
06 Registrar .... Mr. Brock GILLIAM
14 Director of Client Services .... Mr. Chris SPIRES
41 Director of Athletics .... Mr. Jim HERLIHY
38 Director Counseling & Disabilities .... Ms. Cynthia B. GELINAS
39 Assoc Director of Housing .... Ms. Hope SMITH-DUNBAR
19 Chief of Police .... Mr. Jason ZIKE
29 Dir Alumni Rels/Cmty Partnerships .... Mr. Randy DUCKETT
112 Director of Major Gifts .... Ms. Robin CALLICOTT
26 Dir Marketing & Community Relations .... Mr. James RABY
88 Director Instructional Services .... Mr. Keith PIERCE

University of South Carolina Beaufort (C)

1 University Boulevard, Bluffton SC 29909-6085
County: Beaufort FICE Identification: 003450
Unit ID: 218654
Telephone: (843) 208-8000 Carnegie Class: Bac-A&S
FAX Number: (843) 208-8299 Calendar System: Semester
URL: www.uscb.edu
Established: 1959 Annual Undergrad Tuition & Fees (In-State): $10,730
Enrollment: 2,006 Coed
Affiliation or Control: State IRS Status: 501(c)3
Highest Offering: Baccalaureate
Accreditation: SC, CAEPN, CSHSE, NURSE

01 Chancellor .... Dr. Al M. PANU
05 Provost & Exec VC for Acad Affairs .... Dr. Eric SKIPPER
111 Vice Chanc Advancement & Ext Rels .... Dr. Anna PONDER
84 Vice Chanc for Enrollment Mgmt .... Mr. Mack PALMOUR
10 Vice Chanc Finance/IT .... Ms. Beth G. PATRICK
32 Vice Chanc Student Development .... Dr. Angela D. SIMMONS
41 Athletic Director .... Mr. Quin MONAHAN
13 Chief Information Officer .... Vacant
20 Assoc Vice Chanc for Acad Affairs .... Dr. Martha MORIARTY
35 Asst Vice Chanc Student Development .... Ms. Deonne YEAGER
08 Librarian .... Ms. Melanie HANES-RAMOS
15 Director of Human Resources .... Dr. Sue GOLABEK
37 Director of Financial Aid .... Ms. Patricia GREENE
09 Dir Inst Effectiveness/Research .... Mr. Brian MALLORY
18 Director of Facilities .... Mr. Mike PARROTT
36 Director of Career Services .... Ms. Allison REYNOLDS
06 Registrar .... Mr. Gary SUTTON
88 Director of Student Life .... Mr. Joshua LOCKHART
88 Director of Military Program .... Mr. Michael WEISS
114 Budget Director .... Ms. Mary CORDRAY

University of South Carolina Lancaster (D)

PO Box 889, Lancaster SC 29721-0889
Telephone: (803) 313-7000 FICE Identification: 003453
Accreditation: &SC, ACBSP, PNUR

† Regional accreditation is carried under University of South Carolina - Columbia.

University of South Carolina Salkehatchie (E)

PO Box 617, Allendale SC 29810-0617
County: Allendale FICE Identification: 003454
Unit ID: 218681
Telephone: (803) 584-3446 Carnegie Class: Assoc/HT-Mix Trad/Non
FAX Number: (803) 584-5038 Calendar System: Semester
URL: uscsalkehatchie.sc.edu
Established: 1965 Annual Undergrad Tuition & Fees (In-State): $7,558
Enrollment: 878 Coed
Affiliation or Control: State IRS Status: 501(c)3
Highest Offering: Associate Degree
Accreditation: &SC

01 Dean .... Dr. Chris NESMITH
32 Asc Dean Student Svcs/Dir Athletics .... Ms. Jane T. BREWER
05 Assoc Dean for Acad & Stdnt Affs .... Mr. C Bryan LOVE
08 Head Librarian .... Mr. Daniel JOHNSON
11 Director of Finance .... Ms. Jessica ALL
37 Director Financial Aid .... Ms. Julie HADWIN
18 Dir Facilities/Safety/HR Director .... Dr. William A. SANDIFER
40 Business Office/Bookstore Manager .... Mr. Lamar HEWETT
07 Director of Admissions/Registrar .... Ms. Carmen BROWN
30 Chief Development .... Dr. Ann C. CARMICHAEL
84 Exec Director Enrollment Mgmt Svcs .... Mr. Tony JACKSON
88 Director Leadership Institute .... Mr. Greg FENNESSY
88 Sports Information Director .... Mr. Trent KINARD
15 Human Resource Manager .... Ms. Lisa BONNETTE

† Regional accreditation is carried under University of South Carolina - Columbia.

University of South Carolina School of Medicine Greenville (F)

607 Grove Road, Greenville SC 29605
County: Greenville Identification: 667114
Telephone: (864) 455-7992 Carnegie Class: Not Classified
FAX Number: (864) 455-8404 Calendar System: Semester
URL: greenvillemed.sc.edu
Established: 2010 Annual Graduate Tuition & Fees: N/A
Enrollment: N/A Coed
Affiliation or Control: State IRS Status: 501(c)3
Highest Offering: Doctorate; No Undergraduates
Accreditation: MED

01 Dean .... Dr. Marjorie JENKINS
05 Associate Dean for Faculty Affairs .... Dr. Paul V. CATALANA
20 Asst Dean Academic Affairs .... Dr. April BUCHANAN
10 Assoc Dean Finance & Business Opers .... Eboni L. MARTEZ
30 Sr Director of Development .... Susan WARD
13 Director of IT and Facilities .... Vacant
15 Director of HR and Faculty Affairs .... Vacant
37 Sr Asst Dir Financial Aid .... Casey WILEY
07 Assistant Dean of Admissions .... Dr. Julie M. LINTON

University of South Carolina Sumter (G)

200 Miller Road, Sumter SC 29150-2498
County: Sumter FICE Identification: 003426
Unit ID: 218690
Telephone: (803) 775-8727 Carnegie Class: Assoc/HT-High Non
FAX Number: (803) 775-2180 Calendar System: Semester
URL: www.uscsumter.edu
Established: 1966 Annual Undergrad Tuition & Fees (In-State): $7,558
Enrollment: 1,387 Coed
Affiliation or Control: State IRS Status: 501(c)3
Highest Offering: Associate Degree
Accreditation: &SC

01 Regional Campus Dean .... Mr. Michael SONNTAG
05 Exec Assoc Dean Acad/Stdnt Affairs .... Mr. Eric REISENAUER
32 Dir of Student Life and eSports ... Mr. Kristopher E. WEISSMANN
09 Institutional Research Analyst .... Mr. Chuck W. WRIGHT
08 Head Librarian .... Ms. Sharon H. CHAPMAN
07 Director of Admissions Services .... Mr. Keith E. BRITTON
51 Dir of Educational Partnerships .... Ms. Lara K. RICHARDSON
26 Dir of Marketing/Public Relations .... Ms. Alethia HUMMEL
40 Bookstore Manager .... Ms. Julie MCCOY
15 Human Resources Officer .... Ms. Marchetta L. WILLIAMS
88 Program Dir Opportunity Scholars .... Ms. Lisa ROSDAIL
87 Director Shaw AFB Programs .... Mr. Rick BOYD
41 Athletic Director .... Ms. Adrienne CATALDO
13 Director of Info Technology .... Mr. Brian SMITH
37 Dir of Fin Aid & Veterans Affairs .... Ms. Lisa JEFFORDS
06 Registrar .... Ms. Sandra RHYNE

† Regional accreditation is carried under University of South Carolina - Columbia.

University of South Carolina Union (H)

PO Drawer 729, Union SC 29379-0729
County: Union FICE Identification: 004927
Unit ID: 218706
Telephone: (864) 429-8728 Carnegie Class: Assoc/HT-High Non
FAX Number: (864) 427-3682 Calendar System: Semester
URL: uscunion.sc.edu
Established: 1965 Annual Undergrad Tuition & Fees (In-State): $7,558
Enrollment: 1,071 Coed
Affiliation or Control: State IRS Status: 501(c)3
Highest Offering: Associate Degree
Accreditation: &SC

01 Interim Campus Dean .... Dr. Randy LOWELL
05 Associate Dean Acad Affairs .... Vacant
84 Enrollment Director .... Mr. Bradley GREER
37 Director Financial Aid .... Mr. Bobby HOLCOMBE
15 Human Resource Manager .... Ms. Susan P. JETT
40 Bookstore Manager .... Ms. Tanja BLACK
13 Director of Information Technology .... Mr. Jeremy BLACK
30 Director of Marketing & Development .... Ms. Annie SMITH
08 Library Manager .... Ms. Sharon L. RUPP
121 Coord Academic Success Center .... Vacant
10 Director of Budget and Business Ops .... Ms. Michele LEE
12 USC Laurens Location Director .... Mr. Matt DEAN
19 Health and Safety/Security Director .... Mr. Tony GREGORY
18 Maintenance Director .... Mr. Donald LAWSON
06 Registrar .... Mr. Blake WILSON

† Regional accreditation is carried under University of South Carolina - Columbia.

University of South Carolina Upstate (A)

800 University Way, Spartanburg SC 29303-4996
County: Spartanburg FICE Identification: 006951
Unit ID: 218742
Telephone: (864) 503-5000 Carnegie Class: Bac-Diverse
FAX Number: (864) 503-5375 Calendar System: Semester
URL: www.uscupstate.edu
Established: 1967 Annual Undergrad Tuition & Fees (In-State): $11,583
Enrollment: 6,038 Coed
Affiliation or Control: State IRS Status: 501(c)3
Highest Offering: Master's
Accreditation: SC, ART, CAEP, CAHIIM, NURSE

Code	Title	Name
01	Chancellor	Mr. Bennie HARRIS
05	Prov/Sr Vice Chanc Academic Affairs	Dr. David SCHECTER
13	Chief Information Officer	Mr. Adam LONG
10	Vice Chanc for Finance and Admin	Ms. Sheryl TURNER-WATTS
111	Int VC Advance/Upstate Foundation	Ms. Kim JOLLEY
12	Dir Acad Engagement Greenville Ctr	Dr. Judith PRINCE
20	Assoc VC Academic Affairs	Dr. Warren CARSON
32	VC Student Affs/Dean of Students	Dr. Britton KATZ
06	Registrar	Ms. Mary David FOX
84	Vice Chanc Enrollment Services	Ms. Donette STEWART
38	Director Counseling Services	Dr. Elizabeth JODOIN
28	Chief Diversity Officer	Mr. Alphonso ATKINS, JR.
08	Dean Library	Ms. Frieda M. DAVISON
37	Director Financial Aid	Ms. Bonnie C. CARSON
49	Dean Arts & Sciences	Dr. Dirk SCHLINGMANN
50	Dean Johnson Col Business & Econ	Dr. Frank RUDISILL
53	Interim Dean Education	Dr. Charles LOVE
66	Dean Nursing	Dr. Katharine GIBB
58	Director Graduate Education	Dr. Tina HERZBERG
29	Director of Alumni Relations	Mr. Joshua JONES
102	Director Dev & Found Scholarships	Vacant
40	Director Bookstore	Mr. Jerry CARROLL
41	Athletic Director	Mr. Daniel FEIG
18	Director Custodial Services	Mr. Paul SCHMIDT
19	Dir Public Safety & Chief of Police	Mr. Klay PETERSON
35	Asst Dean/Director Student Life	Ms. Khrystal SMITH
39	Dir Housing Residential Life	Ms. Julie MCMAHON
23	Director Health Services	Ms. Mary BUCHER
26	Exec Dir Univ Boards & Public Affs	Mr. John F. PERRY
09	Director of Planning and Research	Ms. Sammara EVANS
88	Dir for Fitness and Campus Rec	Mr. Mark RITTER
22	Dir Disability Services	Ms. Wendy WOODSBY
51	Dir Continuing Education	Dr. Faruk TANYEL
114	Budget Manager	Ms. Vintress BROWN
22	Dir Equal Opp & Employee Relations	Ms. Sharon WOODS
104	Dir Intl Studies & Language Svcs	Dr. Deryle HOPE
25	Dir Sponsored Awards	Ms. Elaine MARSHALL
106	Dir Distance Education	Dr. David MCCURRY
92	Director Honors Program	Dr. Cathy CANINO
88	Dir Ctr Teaching Excellence	Dr. June CARTER
108	Dir Inst Effectiveness & Compliance	Dr. Kimberly WALKER

Voorhees College (B)

PO Box 678, Denmark SC 29042-0678
County: Bamberg FICE Identification: 003455
Unit ID: 218919
Telephone: (803) 780-1234 Carnegie Class: Bac-Diverse
FAX Number: (803) 780-1015 Calendar System: Semester
URL: www.voorhees.edu
Established: 1897 Annual Undergrad Tuition & Fees: $12,630
Enrollment: 368 Coed
Affiliation or Control: Protestant Episcopal IRS Status: 501(c)3
Highest Offering: Baccalaureate
Accreditation: SC, ACBSP

Code	Title	Name
01	President	Dr. Ronnie HOPKINS
05	Int Provost/VP Academic Affairs	Dr. Damara HIGHTOWER-MITCHELL
10	VP Fiscal/Business Affairs	Mrs. V. Diane O'BERRY
111	VP Inst Advancement & Development	Dr. Prince BROWN
32	Vice President Student Affairs	Ms. Charlene JOHNSON
84	VP Enrollment Management	Ms. Phyllis THOMPSON
13	Interim Chief Technology Officer	Mr. John STEWART
100	Interim Chief of Staff	Ms. Karen COUNTZ
06	Registrar	Ms. Felicia MASON-GARNER
32	Dean of Students	Mr. Adrian WEST
37	Director of Financial Aid	Mr. Augusta KITCHEN
35	Director Student Support Services	Ms. Lynda JEFFERSON
08	Director of Library Services	Mr. Herman MASON, JR.
18	Int Director Facilities Management	Mr. George ELMORE
29	Director Alumni Affairs/ Development	Ms. Stephanie RIVERS-KLUTTZ
88	Spec Asst to Pres Innov/Spec Init	Mr. Kimoni HICKMAN
31	Director Community Relations	Mr. Willie JEFFERSON
19	Director of Campus Safety/Security	Mr. Shawn HALE
23	Director of Health Services	Ms. Suzanne WILLIAMS
41	Director of Athletics	Ms. Charlene JOHNSON
07	Director of Admissions/Recruitment	Mr. Ricky SYNDAB
15	Director of Human Resources	Mrs. Constance COLTER-BRABHAM
39	Director Housing & Residential Life	Ms. Allison CLARK
40	Campus Store Clerk	Mr. Travis FREDRICK

Williamsburg Technical College (C)

601 Martin Luther King, Jr. Avenue,
Kingstree SC 29556-4103
County: Williamsburg FICE Identification: 009322
Unit ID: 218955
Telephone: (843) 355-4110 Carnegie Class: Assoc/MT-VT-High Non
FAX Number: (843) 355-4296 Calendar System: Semester
URL: www.wiltech.edu
Established: 1969 Annual Undergrad Tuition & Fees (In-District): $4,800
Enrollment: 635 Coed
Affiliation or Control: State/Local IRS Status: 501(c)3
Highest Offering: Associate Degree
Accreditation: SC, NAEYC

Code	Title	Name
01	President	Dr. Patricia A. LEE
10	VP Administration & Finance	Ms. Melissa A. COKER
05	VP for Academic/Student Affairs	Dr. Clifton R. ELLIOTT
09	Director of Planning and Research	Ms. Veronica G. JACKSON
18	Assoc VP for Facilities Management	Mr. Tyrone THOMAS
32	Assoc VP for Student Affairs	Dr. Alexis W. DUBOSE
20	Assoc VP for Academic Affairs	Dr. Gayle TREMBLE
103	Dir of Workforce Dev/Cont Education	Vacant
08	Library Director	Dr. Brandolyn LOVE
37	Director of Financial Aid	Mrs. Jean BOOS
13	Director MIS	Mr. Strong ROBERT
07	Director of Admissions/Advisement	Ms. Cheryl DUBOSE
26	Director of Public Relations	Ms. Rebecca BRADFORD
21	Comptroller	Ms. Suzanna PUSHIA
15	Human Resources Manager	Mrs. Jennifer STRONG
40	Bookstore Manager/Purchasing Agent	Mrs. Monica ELLIOTT

Winthrop University (D)

Oakland Avenue, Rock Hill SC 29733-0001
County: York FICE Identification: 003456
Unit ID: 218964
Telephone: (803) 323-2211 Carnegie Class: Masters/L
FAX Number: (803) 323-3001 Calendar System: Semester
URL: www.winthrop.edu
Established: 1886 Annual Undergrad Tuition & Fees (In-State): $15,836
Enrollment: 5,576 Coed
Affiliation or Control: State IRS Status: 501(c)3
Highest Offering: Beyond Master's But Less Than Doctorate
Accreditation: SC, ART, #CAATE, CACREP, CAEP, CIDA, COSMA, DANCE, DIETD, DIETI, EXSC, JOUR, MUS, SW, THEA

Code	Title	Name
01	Interim President	Dr. George W. HYND
05	Provost/Exec VP Academic Affairs	Dr. Adrienne MCCORMICK
10	Vice Pres Finance & Business/CFO	Mr. Justin T. OATES
111	Int VP/Institutional Advancement	Dr. Jack DEROCHI
32	Vice President for Student Affairs	Ms. Sheila BURKHALTER
84	VP Enrollment Management/Marketing	Mr. Joseph MILLER
100	VP/Chief of Staff	Dr. Kimberly A. FAUST
19	Assistant Chief Campus Police	Mr. Charles S. YEARTA
20	Vice Prov Acad Quality/Innovation	Dr. Meg WEBBER
88	Asst VP Curriculum/Program Support	Mr. Tim DRUEKE
13	Asst VP Computing/Information Tech	Mr. Patrice BRUNEAU
21	Assistant VP Finance	Mr. Jeremy C. WHITAKER
18	Associate VP Facilities Management	Mr. James J. GRIGG
15	VP Human Res/Empl Div & Wellness	Ms. Lisa COWART
26	Assoc VP Univ Comm/Marketing	Ms. Ellen M. WILDER-BYRD
58	Dean Graduate School	Dr. Jack DEROCHI
49	Dean College Arts & Science	Dr. Takita SUMTER
50	Dean College Business Admin	Dr. P.N SAKSENA
53	Dean College of Education	Dr. Jennie RAKESTRAW
64	Dean College Visual/Performing Arts	Dr. Jeffrey BELLANTONI
08	Dean Library Services	Ms. Kaetrena D. KENDRICK
97	Dean University College	Dr. Jamie COOPER
35	Interim Dean of Students	Mr. Anthony K. DAVIS
41	Interim Athletic Director	Mr. Hank HARRAWOOD
06	Registrar	Ms. Gina G. JONES
07	Director Admissions Ops & Systems	Mr. David ROLLINGS
37	Director of Financial Aid	Ms. Michelle HARE
39	Interim Director Residence Life	Mr. Howard SEIDLER
36	Director of Career Development/Svcs	Vacant
96	Senior Procurement Officer	Ms. Melissa O. MIMS
53	Director Teaching/Learning Ctr	Vacant
23	Director Health/Counseling Services	Ms. Jackie CONCODORA
85	Director International Center	Dr. Leigh POOLE
29	Exec Dir Alumni Rels/Annual Giving	Ms. Lori TUTTLE
110	Advancement Services Manager	Ms. Katherine LANGER
105	Director Web Development	Mr. James U. RAY
106	Director of Online Learning	Dr. Kimarie WHETSTONE
104	Study Abroad Coordinator	Ms. Chelsi COLLETON
108	Exec Dir Inst Effective/Dir Assess	Dr. Noreen GAUBATZ
28	Assoc VP HR & Director of Diversity	Ms. Zantrell Y. JONES
04	Assistant to the President	Ms. Tammie C. PHILLIPS
102	Dir Foundation/Corporate Relations	Ms. Robin EMBRY
09	Director Institutional Research	Ms. Steffaney B. COHEN

Wofford College (E)

429 N Church Street, Spartanburg SC 29303-3663
County: Spartanburg FICE Identification: 003457
Unit ID: 218973
Telephone: (864) 597-4000 Carnegie Class: Bac-A&S
FAX Number: (864) 597-4018 Calendar System: 4/1/4
URL: www.wofford.edu
Established: 1854 Annual Undergrad Tuition & Fees: $47,650
Enrollment: 1,764 Coed
Affiliation or Control: United Methodist IRS Status: 501(c)3
Highest Offering: Baccalaureate
Accreditation: SC

Code	Title	Name
01	President	Dr. Nayef H. SAMHAT
10	Chief Financial Officer	Mr. Christopher L. GARDNER
05	Interim Provost	Dr. Timothy J. SCHMITZ
111	Int Sr Vice Pres for Advancement	Mr. Calhoun L. KENNEDY
11	Sr Vice Pres for Administration	Mr. David M. BEACHAM
32	VP for Student Affairs/Dean Stdnts	Ms. Roberta HURLEY
13	CIO/Assoc VP Information Services	Dr. Baz ABOUDENEIN
84	Vice President for Enrollment	Mr. Brand R. STILLE
18	Assoc VP Facilities/Cap Projects	Mr. Jason H. BURR
21	Assoc VP for Finance and Controller	Mr. Chris L. GARDNER
37	AVP Enrollment/Dir Financial Aid	Ms. Carolyn B. SPARKS
08	Dean of Library	Ms. Elizabeth ROBERTS
82	Dean of International Programs	Ms. Amy E. LANCASTER
23	Assoc Dean Students/Dir Health Svcs	Ms. Beth D. WALLACE
20	Associate Academic Officer	Dr. Dan B. MATHEWSON
04	Exec Admin Asst to President	Ms. Tonya K. BRYSON
41	Director of Athletics	Mr. Richard A. JOHNSON
06	College Registrar	Ms. Jennifer R. ALLISON
42	Chaplain	Rev.Dr. Ronald R. ROBINSON
26	Dir for Marketing/Communications	Ms. Crystal CRAWFORD
15	Director of Human Resources	Ms. Chee J. LEE
07	Director of Admissions	Ms. Megan TYLER
09	Director of Institutional Research	Mr. Raymond H. RUFF, III
101	Secretary to the Board of Trustees	Mr. David M. BEACHAM
108	Dir Institutional Effectiveness	Dr. Ben J. BRYAN
38	Director Student Counseling	Ms. Perry V. HENSON
19	Director Campus Safety	Col. James R. HALL
28	Dir Diversity/Inclusion/Title IX	Mr. Matthew K. HAMMETT
29	Director Alumni & Parents	Mr. Thomas M. HENSON, JR.
36	Exec Dir The Space Career Center	Mr. P. Curtis MCPHAIL
39	Asst Dean of Students for Res Life	Mr. Brian J. LEMERE
44	Director Gift Planning	Ms. Lisa H. DE FREITAS
96	Director Business Srvs/Risk Mgmt	Mr. Daniel P. DEETER
22	Chief Equity Officer	Dr. Dwain C. PRUITT

York Technical College (F)

452 S Anderson Road, Rock Hill SC 29730-3395
County: York FICE Identification: 003996
Unit ID: 218991
Telephone: (803) 327-8000 Carnegie Class: Assoc/MT-VT-High Trad
FAX Number: (803) 327-8059 Calendar System: Semester
URL: www.yorktech.edu
Established: 1964 Annual Undergrad Tuition & Fees (In-State): $5,395
Enrollment: 4,178 Coed
Affiliation or Control: State IRS Status: 501(c)3
Highest Offering: Associate Degree
Accreditation: SC, ACBSP, ADNUR, DA, DH, MLTAD, NAEYC, PNUR, RAD, SURGT

Code	Title	Name
01	President	Dr. Greg F. RUTHERFORD
05	EVP Academic/Student Affairs	Dr. Stacey MOORE
10	VP Business Services	Vacant
111	Vice President for Advancement	Ms. Melanie E. JONES
50	Assoc VP Business/Computer/AA/AS	Vacant
76	Assoc VP Health & Human Services	Ms. Phoebe COQUEREL
54	Assoc Dean Industry/Engineer Tech	Mr. Michael MCCLAIN
103	Asst VP Economic/Workforce Dev	Ms. Sonia YOUNG
15	Asst Vice Pres of Human Resources	Ms. Edwina ROSEBORO-BARNES
08	Head Librarian	Ms. Esther BURGESS
35	Dean for Student Engagement	Mr. James ROBSON
09	Director of Institutional Research	Dr. Mary Beth SCHWARTZ
37	Director Compliance/Financial Aid	Vacant
13	Information Services Director	Mr. Richard PARTRIDGE
19	Chief Campus Security	Mr. Bryan L. MCDOUGALD
18	Facilities Management Director	Mr. Robert L. BROWN
06	Registrar	Vacant
26	Director of Strategic Communication	Vacant
07	Director Admissions	Ms. Lydia HALL

SOUTH DAKOTA

Augustana University (G)

2001 S Summit, Sioux Falls SD 57197-0001
County: Minnehaha FICE Identification: 003458
Unit ID: 219000
Telephone: (605) 274-0770 Carnegie Class: Masters/S
FAX Number: (605) 274-5299 Calendar System: 4/1/4
URL: www.augie.edu
Established: 1860 Annual Undergrad Tuition & Fees: $35,884
Enrollment: 2,019 Coed
Affiliation or Control: Evangelical Lutheran Church In America
IRS Status: 501(c)3
Highest Offering: Doctorate
Accreditation: HLC, CAATE, MUS, NURSE

Code	Title	Name
01	President	Ms. Stephanie HERSETH SANDLIN
05	Sr VP Academic Affairs/Provost	Dr. Colin IRVINE
100	Chief of Staff	Ms. Pamela MILLER
10	Vice Pres Finance/Administration	Mr. Shannan NELSON
111	Vice President for Advancement	Dr. Pamela HOMAN
15	Vice President of Human Resources	Ms. Deanna VERSTEEG
21	Assoc Vice President/Controller	Ms. Carol SPILLUM
18	Assoc VP for University Services	Mr. Rick TUPPER
32	Dean of Students	Mr. Mark BLACKBURN
13	Director of IT	Mr. Daniel D. DRENKOW
37	Director of Financial Aid	Ms. Tresse EVENSON
08	Director of Library	Ms. Ronelle THOMPSON

84 Asst Vice President for Enrollment ... Mr. Adam HEINITZ
30 Asst VP for Development ... Mr. Jon MAMMENGA
41 Athletic Director ... Mr. Josh MORTON
06 Registrar/Asst Dean of Instr Pgm ... Ms. Joni KRUEGER
121 Asst Vice Provost Student Success ... Ms. Billie STREUFERT
22 Accessibility/Acad Support Service ... Ms. Susan BIES
104 Director of Intl Pgm/Enrollment ... Mr. Ben IVERSON
20 Asst Vice Provost Acad Excellence ... Mr. Jay KAHL
28 Chief Diversity Officer ... Ms. Willette CAPERS
29 Sr Director Alumni Engagement ... Mr. Joel GACKLE
04 Exec Assistant to the President ... Ms. Teresa OTTO
53 Dean of Education ... Dr. Laurie DAILY
64 Dean of School of Music ... Dr. Peter FOLLIARD

Dakota Wesleyan University (A)

1200 W University, Mitchell SD 57301-4398
County: Davison FICE Identification: 003461
Unit ID: 219091
Telephone: (605) 995-2600 Carnegie Class: Bac-Diverse
FAX Number: (605) 995-2699 Calendar System: Semester
URL: www.dwu.edu
Established: 1885 Annual Undergrad Tuition & Fees: $29,770
Enrollment: 933 Coed
Affiliation or Control: United Methodist IRS Status: 501(c)3
Highest Offering: Master's
Accreditation: HLC, CAATE, IACBE, NURSE

01 Interim President/CFO ... Ms. Theresa KRIESE
05 Provost ... Dr. Joseph ROIDT
07 VP Admissions/Mktg/Communications ... Ms. Fredel THOMAS
111 VP for Institutional Advancement ... Ms. Kitty ALLEN
26 Dir of Marketing & Communications ... Ms. Jan LARSON
06 Registrar ... Mr. Stuart KEENAN
88 Dir Kelley Ctr for Entrepreneurship ... Ms. Rhonda POLE
88 Executive Director McGovern Center ... Dr. Joel ALLEN
08 Public Services Librarian ... Ms. Alexis BECKER
29 Director of Alumni Relations ... Mr. Jory HANSEN
37 Director of Financial Aid ... Ms. Mary ALEXANDER
15 Director of Human Resources ... Ms. Janet HAYEN
42 Campus Pastor ... Rev. Eric VAN METER
41 Director of Athletics ... Mr. Jon HART
18 Director of Physical Plant ... Mr. Louis SCHOENFELDER
32 Director of Student Life ... Mr. John KIPPES
80 Dean Col Ldrshp & Pub Service ... Dr. Anne KELLY
20 Associate Provost ... Dr. Derek DRIEDGER
88 Assoc Provost Program Development ... Dr. Alisha VINCENT
79 Dean College Arts & Humanities ... Dr. Vince REDDER
76 Dean Col Health/Fitness & Science ... Dr. Bethany MELROE LEHRMAN
04 Exec Admin Asst to Pres/Provost ... Ms. Emily GEORGE
50 Chair of Business ... Ms. Christine MAUSZYCKI
53 Chair of Education ... Dr. Ashley DIGMANN
13 Chief Info Technology Officer (CIO) ... Mr. Travis WALZ
50 Director of Business Grad Program ... Dr. Diana GOLDAMMER
53 Coord of Master of Arts in Educ ... Ms. Melissa WEBER
88 Dir of Master of Athletic Training ... Dr. Dan WAGNER
66 Administrative Chair of Nursing ... Dr. Stacy EDEN
39 Dir Resident Life/Student Housing ... Mr. Dustin WHEELER

Institute of Lutheran Theology (B)

PO Box 833, Brookings SD 57006
County: Brookings Identification: 667318
Telephone: (605) 692-9337 Carnegie Class: Not Classified
FAX Number: N/A Calendar System: Semester
URL: www.ilt.edu
Established: 2009 Annual Undergrad Tuition & Fees: N/A
Enrollment: N/A Coed
Affiliation or Control: Independent Non-Profit IRS Status: 501(c)3
Highest Offering: Doctorate
Accreditation: BI

01 President ... Dr. Dennis BIELFELDT
03 Executive Vice President ... Mr. Leon MILES
84 Director of Enrollment Services ... Mr. Joel WILLIAMS
10 Director of Business Services ... Ms. Kelli ANAWSKI
08 Librarian ... Rev. David PATTERSON

John Witherspoon College (C)

4024 Sheridan Lake Road, Rapid City SD 57702
County: Pennington Identification: 667246
Telephone: (605) 342-0317 Carnegie Class: Not Classified
FAX Number: N/A Calendar System: Semester
URL: www.jwc.edu
Established: 2004 Annual Undergrad Tuition & Fees: N/A
Enrollment: N/A Coed
Affiliation or Control: Independent Non-Profit IRS Status: 501(c)3
Highest Offering: Baccalaureate
Accreditation: TRACS

01 President ... Dr. Ronald J. LEWIS
05 Chief Academic Officer ... Mr. Edwin C. EGBERT
00 Chairman of the Board ... Dr. Donald E. OLIVER
10 Chief Financial Officer ... Mrs. Carol B. HARRIS
08 Director of Learning Resources ... Mrs. Megan R. FERGUSON
88 Coordinator of Learning Resources ... Ms. Michelle C. PORTER
06 Registrar ... Mrs. Pamela S. RIDER
07 Director of Admissions ... Mrs. Rebecca E. PONTIOUS
125 President Emeritus/Chancellor ... Dr. C. Richard WELLS

Lake Area Technical College (D)

1201 Arrow Avenue, PO Box 730,
Watertown SD 57201-2869
County: Codington FICE Identification: 005309
Unit ID: 219143
Telephone: (605) 882-5284 Carnegie Class: Assoc/HVT-High Trad
FAX Number: (605) 882-6299 Calendar System: Semester
URL: www.lakeareatech.edu
Established: 1965 Annual Undergrad Tuition & Fees (In-District): $6,862
Enrollment: 2,217 Coed
Affiliation or Control: Local IRS Status: Exempt
Highest Offering: Associate Degree
Accreditation: HLC, DA, EMT, MAC, MLTAD, OTA, PNUR, PTAA

01 President ... Mr. Michael D. CARTNEY
03 Executive Vice President ... Ms. Diane STILES
32 Director of Student Services ... Ms. LuAnn STRAIT
84 Director of Enrollment ... Mr. Eric SCHULTZ
37 Director of Financial Aid ... Ms. Marlene SEEKLANDER
05 Dean of Academics ... Mr. Mike BUTTS
13 Director of Information Technology ... Ms. Christi CHANEY
30 Foundation Director ... Ms. Tracy HLAVACEK
108 Assessment Coordinator ... Ms. Gina GRANT
103 Director of Corporate Education ... Mr. Steven HAUCK
88 Director of Outreach ... Mr. Shane SWENSON
25 Grant Writer ... Vacant
08 Librarian ... Ms. Nicki YACKLEY-FRANKEN
38 Counselor ... Ms. Jessi WHETSEL
121 Student Support & Equity Coord ... Ms. Stephanie JOHNSON
40 Assistant Bookstore Manager ... Mr. Darrin CHRISTENSEN

Mitchell Technical College (E)

1800 E Spruce, Mitchell SD 57301-2002
County: Davison FICE Identification: 008284
Unit ID: 219189
Telephone: (605) 995-3025 Carnegie Class: Assoc/HVT-High Trad
FAX Number: (605) 995-3083 Calendar System: Semester
URL: www.mitchelltech.edu
Established: 1968 Annual Undergrad Tuition & Fees (In-District): $7,359
Enrollment: 1,162 Coed
Affiliation or Control: State/Local IRS Status: 501(c)3
Highest Offering: Associate Degree
Accreditation: HLC, ACFEI, MAC, MLTAD, RAD, RTT

01 President ... Mr. Mark WILSON
11 Vice President of Operations ... Mr. John HEEMSTRA
05 Vice President for Academics ... Dr. Carol GRODE-HANKS
84 Vice Pres for Enrollment Services ... Mr. Clayton DEUTER
13 Dean of Technology Systems ... Mr. David BOOS
10 Dean of Financial Operations ... Mr. Jared HOFER
121 Dean of Student Success ... Mr. Scott FOSSUM
09 Accred & Inst Effectiveness Dir ... Ms. Marla SMITH
18 Buildings & Grounds Director ... Mr. John SIEVERDING
36 Career Svcs & Advising Dir ... Ms. Janet GREENWAY
06 Registrar ... Ms. Jill GREENWAY
37 Director Student Financial Aid ... Ms. Morgan HUBER
105 Marketing Director ... Mr. Bob KOBERNUSZ
07 Director of Admissions ... Ms. Jenna REIS
30 Director of Development ... Vacant

Mount Marty University (F)

1105 W 8th, Yankton SD 57078-3724
County: Yankton FICE Identification: 003465
Unit ID: 219198
Telephone: (605) 668-1545 Carnegie Class: Masters/S
FAX Number: N/A Calendar System: Semester
URL: www.mtmc.edu
Established: 1936 Annual Undergrad Tuition & Fees: $29,136
Enrollment: 1,167 Coed
Affiliation or Control: Roman Catholic IRS Status: 501(c)3
Highest Offering: Doctorate
Accreditation: HLC, ANEST, NURSE

01 President ... Dr. Marcus LONG
101 Assistant to the President ... Ms. Joanna MUELLER
05 Vice President for Academic Affairs ... Dr. William MILLER
10 VP for Finance & Administration ... Ms. Tabitha LIKNESS
111 VP for Mission & Advancement ... Ms. Barb REZAC
32 VP for Student Success ... Dr. Katie HARRELL
18 Vice President for Operations ... Mr. Chad ALTWINE
09 Director of Inst Effectiveness ... Ms. Kristen WELKER
66 Dean of Nursing & Health Sciences ... Dr. Kathy MAGORIAN
42 Director of Campus Ministry ... Mr. Jordan FOOS
12 Director of Watertown Location ... Ms. Kim BELLUM
37 Director Student Financial Aid ... Mr. Ken KOCER
06 Registrar ... Ms. Jonna SUPURGECI
13 Chief Information Officer ... Mr. Christian HUNHOFF
08 Director of Library ... Ms. Sandra BROWN
40 Dir Bookstore/Central Scheduling ... Mr. Max MORRIS
36 Dir Career Planning ... Ms. Keley SMITH-KELLER
41 VP for Strategy & Athletic Director ... Mr. Chris KASSIN
15 Director of Human Resources ... Ms. Julie DATHER
26 Exec Dir of Marketing & Comm ... Ms. Kelsey FREIDEL NELSON
44 Director of Annual/Planned Giving ... Ms. Shannon VIERECK
29 Director Alumni Relations ... Ms. Ashley GULLIKSON
84 Interim Dean of Enrollment ... Dr. Katie HARRELL
39 Dir of Res Life/Campus Security ... Mr. Nicholas HEMSCHEMEYER
04 Admin Assistant to the President ... Ms. Joanna MUELLER

National American University (G)

5301 Mt. Rushmore Road, Rapid City SD 57701-8932
County: Pennington FICE Identification: 004057
Unit ID: 219204
Telephone: (605) 721-5200 Carnegie Class: Bac-Diverse
FAX Number: (605) 721-5241 Calendar System: Quarter
URL: www.national.edu
Established: 1941 Annual Undergrad Tuition & Fees: $14,985
Enrollment: 1,440 Coed
Affiliation or Control: Proprietary IRS Status: Proprietary
Highest Offering: Doctorate
Accreditation: HLC, CAHIIM, IACBE

01 Chief Executive Officer/President ... Dr. Ronald SHAPE
05 Provost & Chief Academic Officer ... Dr. Cindy MATHENA
10 Chief Financial Officer ... Mr. Thomas BICKART
11 COO ... Mr. Mark MENDOZA
37 Director Financial Aid ... Ms. Cheryl BULLINGER
08 Librarian ... Ms. Marsha STACEY
15 Director of Human Resources ... Mr. Gordon BROOKS

Oglala Lakota College (H)

Box 490, Kyle SD 57752-0490
County: Oglala Lakota FICE Identification: 014659
Unit ID: 219277
Telephone: (605) 455-6000 Carnegie Class: Tribal
FAX Number: (605) 455-2787 Calendar System: Semester
URL: www.olc.edu
Established: 1971 Annual Undergrad Tuition & Fees: $2,684
Enrollment: 1,251 Coed
Affiliation or Control: Tribal Control IRS Status: 501(c)3
Highest Offering: Master's
Accreditation: HLC, SW

01 President ... Mr. Thomas H. SHORTBULL
05 Vice President for Instruction ... Dr. Dawn FRANK
10 Vice President for Business ... Ms. Julie JOHNSON
06 Registrar ... Ms. Leslie MESTETH
08 Director Learning Resources ... Ms. Sharon JANIS
15 Personnel Director ... Ms. Faith RICHARDS
37 Financial Aid Director ... Ms. Cheryce GULLIKSON
84 Director Enrollment Management ... Mr. Don GIAGO
07 Director of Admissions ... Ms. Leslie MESTETH
09 Director of Institutional Research ... Ms. Susanne AUER
29 Director Alumni Relations ... Ms. Marilyn POURIER
89 Director of Freshman Studies ... Ms. Susanne AUER
13 MIS Director ... Mr. Cliff DELONG
32 Director Student Affairs ... Mr. Don GIAGO
30 Inst Development Coordinator ... Ms. Marilyn POURIER
51 Community/Cont Education Coord ... Ms. Kateri MONTILEAUX
88 Applied Science Department Chair ... Ms. Ellen WHITE THUNDER
81 Math & Science Department Chair ... Ms. Karla WITT
49 Art & History Department Chair ... Ms. Kim BETTELYOUN
53 Education Department Chair ... Ms. Shannon AMIOTTE
66 Nursing Department Chair ... Ms. Michelle BRUNS
83 Social Work Department Chair ... Ms. Monique APPLE
88 LAKOTA Studies Department Chair ... Ms. Karen LONE HILL
18 Chief Facilities/Physical Plant ... Mr. Tony WARD

Presentation College (I)

1500 N Main Street, Aberdeen SD 57401-1280
County: Brown FICE Identification: 003467
Unit ID: 219295
Telephone: (605) 225-1634 Carnegie Class: Spec-4-yr-Other Health
FAX Number: (605) 229-8330 Calendar System: Semester
URL: www.presentation.edu
Established: 1951 Annual Undergrad Tuition & Fees: $21,375
Enrollment: 625 Coed
Affiliation or Control: Roman Catholic IRS Status: 501(c)3
Highest Offering: Master's
Accreditation: HLC, CAATE, IACBE, NURSE, RAD

01 President ... Dr. Paula LANGTEAU
05 Vice Pres for Academics ... Vacant
10 Vice Pres for Finance ... Dr. Daisy HALVORSON
84 Vice Pres for SAEM ... Dr. Marcus GARSTECKI
111 Vice President for Advancement ... Mr. Matthew BLAIR
06 Registrar ... Vacant
37 Director Student Financial Aid ... Ms. Amber BROCKEL
108 Assessment Coordinator ... Dr. Nancy VANDER HOEK
15 Director of Human Resources ... Dr. Jason PETTIGREW
04 Administrative Asst to President ... Ms. Stacy BAUER
26 Dir of Marketing/Public Relations ... Mr. Andy HANSEN
07 Director of Admissions ... Ms. India KLIPFEL
09 Director of Institutional Research ... Vacant
29 Director Alumni Relations ... Vacant
39 Director Student Housing ... Mr. DJ MOUNGA
41 Athletic Director ... Mr. Daniel GARRETT

Sinte Gleska University (J)

PO Box 105, Mission SD 57555-0105
County: Todd FICE Identification: 021437
Unit ID: 219374
Telephone: (605) 856-5880 Carnegie Class: Tribal
FAX Number: (605) 856-5401 Calendar System: Semester
URL: www.sintegleska.edu
Established: 1970 Annual Undergrad Tuition & Fees: $3,154
Enrollment: 438 Coed
Affiliation or Control: Independent Non-Profit IRS Status: 501(c)3

Highest Offering: Master's
Accreditation: HLC

01 President ... Mr. Lionel BORDEAUX
05 Provost/COO ... Mr. Phil BAIRD
32 Vice Pres Student Services ... Ms. Debra BORDEAUX
20 Vice Pres Academic Affairs ... Ms. Cheryl MEDEARIS
11 Vice Pres Administration ... Ms. Cheryl WHIRLWIND SOLDIER
10 CFO/VP Finance ... Ms. Ieshia POIGNEE
06 Registrar ... Mr. Jack HERMAN
08 Int Library Director ... Ms. Diana DILLON
37 Director Financial Aid/Admissions ... Mr. Midas GUNHAMMER
55 Director Adult Education ... Mr. Sherman MARSHALL, II
15 Director Human Resources ... Ms. Brenda FARMER

Sioux Falls Seminary (A)

2100 S Summit Avenue, Sioux Falls SD 57105-2729
County: Minnehaha FICE Identification: 004056
Unit ID: 219240
Telephone: (605) 336-6588 Carnegie Class: Spec-4-yr-Faith
FAX Number: (605) 335-9090 Calendar System: 4/1/4
URL: www.sfseminary.edu
Established: 1858 Annual Undergrad Tuition & Fees: $3,600
Enrollment: 508 Coed
Affiliation or Control: North American Baptist IRS Status: 501(c)3
Highest Offering: Doctorate
Accreditation: HLC, THEOL

01 President ... Mr. Gregory J. HENSON
05 Chief Academic Officer & Dean ... Dr. Larry W. CALDWELL
10 CFO and VP of Operations ... Mr. Nathan M. HELLING
26 Chief Creative Ofcr/VP Proj Design ... Ms. Shanda L. STRICHERZ
84 Office Manager/Enrollment Advisor ... Ms. LaNeil R. BARTELL
88 Dir of Luther House of Study ... Dr. Chris M. CROGHAN
88 Dir of Wesley House of Study ... Dr. Steve A. TREFZ

Sisseton-Wahpeton College (B)

PO Box 689, Sisseton SD 57262-0689
County: Roberts FICE Identification: 022773
Unit ID: 219408
Telephone: (605) 698-3966 Carnegie Class: Tribal
FAX Number: (605) 698-3132 Calendar System: Semester
URL: https://www.swcollege.edu/
Established: 1979 Annual Undergrad Tuition & Fees (In-District): $4,510
Enrollment: 125 Coed
Affiliation or Control: Local IRS Status: 501(c)3
Highest Offering: Associate Degree
Accreditation: HLC

01 President ... Dr. Lane AZURE
05 Vice President of Academic Affairs ... Dr. Jeanette GRAVDAHL
10 Comptroller ... Ms. Rhonda LABATTE
37 Financial Aid Director ... Mr. Sylvan FLUTE
07 Admissions Director ... Mrs. Darlene REDDAY
66 Director Nursing ... Ms. Nola RAGAN
32 Student Services Director ... Mr. Vince OWEN
13 Director Information Technology ... Mr. Derrick LAWRENCE
18 Facilities Manager ... Mr. Russell EBERHARDT
06 Registrar ... Ms. Darlene REDDAY
09 Director Institutional Research ... Mr. Scott MORGAN

*South Dakota State Board of Regents System Office (C)

306 E Capitol Avenue, Suite 200, Pierre SD 57501-2545
County: Hughes FICE Identification: 033438
Telephone: (605) 773-3455 Carnegie Class: N/A
FAX Number: (605) 773-5320
URL: www.sdbor.edu

01 Executive Director & CEO ... Dr. Brian MAHER
00 Board President ... Mr. John BASTIAN
10 System VP Finance & Administration ... Ms. Heather FORNEY
05 System VP Academic Affairs ... Dr. Janice MINDER
43 General Counsel ... Mr. Nathan LUKKES
15 System Director of Human Resources ... Ms. Kayla BASTIAN
26 System Director of Communications ... Dr. Janelle TOMAN
09 System Dir Institutional Research ... Vacant
13 System CIO ... Mr. David HANSEN
20 System Assoc VP of Academic Affairs ... Dr. Rebecca HOEY
116 System Internal Auditor ... Ms. Shelly ANDERSON

*The University of South Dakota (D)

414 E Clark, Vermillion SD 57069-2390
County: Clay FICE Identification: 003474
Unit ID: 219471
Telephone: (605) 677-5011 Carnegie Class: DU-Higher
FAX Number: (605) 677-5073 Calendar System: Semester
URL: www.usd.edu
Established: 1862 Annual Undergrad Tuition & Fees (In-State): $9,332
Enrollment: 9,459 Coed
Affiliation or Control: State IRS Status: 501(c)3
Highest Offering: Doctorate
Accreditation: HLC, ARCPA, ART, AUD, CACREP, #CAEP, CLPSY, DH, EMT, JOUR, LAW, MED, MUS, NURSE, OT, PH, PTA, SP, SPAA, SW, THEA

02 President ... Ms. Sheila K. GESTRING
05 Provost/VP Academic Affairs ... Dr. Kurt HACKEMER
17 VP Health Affairs/Dean Med School ... Dr. Timothy RIDGWAY
10 Vice Pres Administration/Finance ... Ms. JoAnn KUNKEL
46 VP Research/Sponsored Programs ... Dr. Daniel ENGEBRETSON
26 VP Marketing/Enroll Svcs/Univ Rels ... Mr. Scott POHLSON
32 VP Student Svcs & Dean of Students ... Dr. Kimberly GRIEVE
15 Chief Human Resources Officer ... Mr. Warren TOLLEY
13 Chief Information Officer ... Ms. Cheryl TIAHRT
102 President/CEO Univ Foundation ... Mr. Steve BROWN
28 Int Associate VP of Diversity ... Mr. Travis LETELLIER
18 Asst VP Facilities Management ... Mr. Brian LIMOGES
09 AVP Inst Research/Plng/Assessment ... Mr. Daniel PALMER
20 Assoc Provost ... Dr. Lisa BONNEAU
12 Exec Dir University Ctr Sioux Falls ... Vacant
100 Chief of Staff ... Ms. Laura MCNAUGHTON
43 General Counsel ... Mr. AJ FRANKEN
96 Director of Auxiliary Services ... Mr. Darby GANSCHOW
08 Dean of Libraries ... Mr. Daniel R. DAILY
36 Dir Ctr for Academic & Career Plng ... Mr. Steve WARD
37 Director of Financial Aid ... Ms. Lindsay MILLER
41 Director Athletics ... Mr. David HERBSTER
19 Dir University Police Department ... Mr. Bryant JACKSON
06 Registrar ... Ms. Jennifer M. THOMPSON
84 Dean of Enrollment ... Mr. Mark PETTY
49 Int Dean College Arts & Sciences ... Dr. John DUDLEY
50 Dean School of Business ... Dr. Venky VENKATACHALAM
53 Dean School of Education ... Dr. Amy SCHWEINLE
57 Dean College Fine Arts ... Dr. Bruce KELLEY
61 Dean School of Law ... Mr. Neil FULTON
58 Dean Graduate School ... Dr. Beth FREEBURG
76 Dean School of Health Sciences ... Dr. Haifa ABOUSAMRA
04 Assistant to the President ... Ms. Niki SMIDT
22 Director EEO/Chief Title IX Officer ... Ms. Jean MERKLE

*Black Hills State University (E)

1200 University Street #9500, Spearfish SD 57799-9500
County: Lawrence FICE Identification: 003459
Unit ID: 219046
Telephone: (605) 642-6111 Carnegie Class: Masters/S
FAX Number: (605) 642-6763 Calendar System: Semester
URL: www.bhsu.edu
Established: 1883 Annual Undergrad Tuition & Fees (In-State): $8,672
Enrollment: 3,608 Coed
Affiliation or Control: State IRS Status: 501(c)3
Highest Offering: Master's
Accreditation: HLC, CAEP, CAEPN, MUS

02 President ... Dr. Laurie NICHOLS
05 Provost/Vice Pres Academic Affairs ... Dr. Priscilla ROMKEMA
10 Vice President Finance/Admin ... Ms. Kathy J. JOHNSON
111 Vice Pres University Advancement ... Mr. Steve L. MEEKER
84 VP for Enrollment Management ... Dr. John ALLRED
26 Int Sr Director of Marketing ... Ms. Julie OLSON
13 Data Processing Supervisor ... Ms. Roxy SCHMIT
37 Director Student Financial Aid ... Ms. Gail JOHNSON
38 Director Counseling Center ... Ms. Sarah HEWITT
22 Title IX Coordinator ... Dr. Michael L. ISAACSON
32 Dean of Students ... Dr. Jane KLUG
15 Director of Human Resources ... Ms. Melissa HART
06 Registrar ... Ms. April M. MEEKER
07 Director of Admissions ... Mr. Joe RAINBOTH
21 Director of Business Services ... Mr. Terry MILLER
18 Director Facilities/Physical Plant ... Mr. Randy CULVER
29 Director Alumni Relations ... Mr. Tom WHEATON
09 Director of Institutional Research ... Mr. Rich LOOSE
08 Director Library Operations ... Mr. Scott AHOLA
104 Director International Studies ... Ms. Kaitlin PALMER
30 Director of Development ... Ms. Shauna JUNEK
19 Director Security/Safety ... Mr. Philip PESHECK
40 Director University Bookstore ... Mr. Michael JASTORFF
41 Director of Athletics ... Mr. Padriac MCMEEL
14 Director Network & Computer Svcs ... Mr. Fred NELSON
49 Dean College of Liberal Arts ... Dr. Amy FUQUA
50 Dean Col of Business & Natural Sci ... Dr. Gregory FARLEY
53 Int Dean Col of Educ/Behavioral Sci ... Dr. Betsy SILVA
04 Administrative Asst to President ... Ms. Lindsey JAKOBSEN
25 Chief Contracts/Grants Admin ... Ms. Sharon HEMMINGSON

*Dakota State University (F)

820 N Washington Avenue, Madison SD 57042-1799
County: Lake FICE Identification: 003463
Unit ID: 219082
Telephone: (888) 378-9988 Carnegie Class: Masters/S
FAX Number: N/A Calendar System: Semester
URL: www.dsu.edu
Established: 1881 Annual Undergrad Tuition & Fees (In-State): $9,536
Enrollment: 3,186 Coed
Affiliation or Control: State IRS Status: 501(c)3
Highest Offering: Doctorate
Accreditation: HLC, ACBSP, CAEP, CAHIIM, COARC

02 President ... Dr. José -Marie GRIFFITHS
04 Senior Secretary President's Ofc ... Ms. Megan BOUSQUET
05 Provost & VP Academic Affairs ... Dr. Richard HANSON
10 Vice Pres for Business & Admin Svcs ... Mr. Stacy L. KRUSEMARK
32 Int Vice Pres Student Affairs ... Ms. Amy CRISSINGER
13 CIO ... Mr. David MILLER
15 Vice Pres Human Resources/Title IX ... Ms. Angi KAPPENMAN
41 Director of Athletics ... Mr. Jeff L. DITTMAN
26 Dir Communications & Marketing ... Ms. Kelli KOEPSELL
49 Dean Col of Arts and Sciences ... Dr. David KENLEY
50 Dean Col Business/Info Systems ... Dr. Dorine BENNETT
77 Dean Beacom College ... Dr. Pat ENGEBRETSON
53 Interim Dean College of Education ... Dr. Mark HAWKES
58 Dean of Graduate Studies ... Dr. Mark HAWKES
46 VP for Research ... Dr. Ashley PODHRADSKY
108 Director of Assessment ... Dr. Jeanette MCGREEVY
09 Dir Institutional Research ... Ms. Laura CROSS
08 Director of Library ... Ms. Jan Brue ENRIGHT
106 Director Online Education ... Ms. Sarah RASMUSSEN
25 Director of Sponsored Programs ... Dr. Pete HOESING
06 Registrar ... Ms. Kathryn CALLIES
21 Controller ... Ms. Amy L. DOCKENDORF
18 Director Facilities Management ... Mr. Corey BRASKAMP
25 Director of Budget & Grants Admin ... Ms. Sara HARE
36 Director Career Services ... Ms. Deb ROACH
84 Assoc VP of Enrollment/Marketing ... Ms. Amy S. CRISSINGER
35 Asst Dean for Student Affairs ... Vacant
121 Director Student Success ... Ms. Kristen UILK
40 Int Director of Bookstore ... Ms. Donna FAWBUSH
28 Coordinator Diversity & Inclusion ... Vacant
37 Director Financial Aid ... Ms. Denise R. GRAYSON
07 Asst Director of Admissions ... Ms. Amber SCHMIDT
104 Dir International Programs ... Ms. Nicole CLAUSSEN
14 Chief Tech Officer ... Mr. Brent VAN AARTSEN
91 Dir Admin Computing Services ... Mrs. Stephanie BAATZ
119 Security Engineer ... Mr. Ben CABLE
24 Manager of Multimedia Services ... Mr. Tyler STEELE
111 VP for Institutional Advancement ... Mr. Jon SCHEMMEL
30 Development Officer ... Ms. Jill RUHD
38 Dir Student Counseling ... Ms. Nicole BOWEN
39 Interim Dir of Residence Life ... Ms. Wendi CARLSON-KENLEY

*Northern State University (G)

1200 S Jay Street, Aberdeen SD 57401-7198
County: Brown FICE Identification: 003466
Unit ID: 219259
Telephone: (605) 626-3011 Carnegie Class: Masters/S
FAX Number: (605) 626-3022 Calendar System: Semester
URL: www.northern.edu
Established: 1901 Annual Undergrad Tuition & Fees (In-State): $8,750
Enrollment: 3,431 Coed
Affiliation or Control: State IRS Status: 501(c)3
Highest Offering: Master's
Accreditation: HLC, ACBSP, ART, CACREP, CAEPN, MUS

02 President ... Dr. Neal SCHNOOR
05 Provost/VP Academic Affairs ... Dr. Michael WANOUS
10 VP Finance/Administration ... Mrs. Veronica PAULSON
84 VP Enroll Mgmt/Comm/Mktg ... Mr. Justin FRAASE
20 Associate VP Academic Affairs ... Dr. Erin FOUBERG
13 VP Information Technologies/CIO ... Dr. Debbi BUMPOUS
102 President/CEO Foundation ... Mr. Zack FLAKUS
06 Registrar ... Mrs. Peggy HALLSTROM
08 Director Library ... Mr. Robert RUSSELL
38 Director Counseling Center ... Ms. Heather ALDENTALER
09 Dir Inst Research/Assessment ... Dr. Brenda MAMMENGA
37 Director Financial Aid ... Ms. Becky PRIBYL
39 Director Residence Life ... Mr. Martin SABOLO
21 Controller ... Ms. Kay FREDRICK
88 Assistant Controller ... Mr. David KNIGGE
15 Director Human Resources ... Ms. Susan BOSTIAN
18 Director Facilities Management ... Mr. Monte MEHLHOFF
49 Dean College Arts & Science ... Dr. Alyssa KIESOW
88 Assoc Dean College Arts & Sciences ... Dr. Ellizabeth HALLER
107 Dean College Professional Studies ... Dr. Douglas OHMER
53 Assoc Dean School of Education ... Dr. Cheryl WOLD
50 Assoc Dean School of Business ... Dr. Sara SCHMIDT
57 Dean School of Fine Arts ... Dr. Kenneth BOULTON
58 Director Graduate Studies ... Dr. Erin FOUBERG
41 Director Athletics ... Mr. Joshua MOON
96 Purchasing Agent ... Ms. Crystal JOSEPH
92 Director Honors Program ... Dr. Kristi BOCKORNY
85 Director International Programs ... Ms. Dominika BLUM
04 Executive Admin Asst to President ... Ms. Lisa GROTE
104 Coordinator Study Abroad ... Ms. Dominika BLUM
106 Director Online Education ... Mr. Ronald BROWNIE
124 Executive Director Student Success ... Vacant
36 Director Student Placement ... Ms. Margaret PENCE
30 Sr VP Development ... Vacant
110 Director Development ... Ms. Kelli FRITZ
29 Coordinator Alumni Operations ... Ms. Lauren BITTNER
32 Dean of Students ... Mr. Sean BLACKBURN
07 Director Admissions ... Mr. Layton COOPER
88 Dir Student Involvement/Leadership ... Ms. Megan FREWALDT
88 Director Student Rights & Resp ... Ms. Krista BAU

*South Dakota School of Mines and Technology (H)

501 E Saint Joseph, Rapid City SD 57701-3995
County: Pennington FICE Identification: 003470
Unit ID: 219347
Telephone: (605) 394-2511 Carnegie Class: Spec-4-yr-Eng
FAX Number: (605) 394-3388 Calendar System: Semester
URL: www.sdsmt.edu
Established: 1885 Annual Undergrad Tuition & Fees (In-State): $11,020
Enrollment: 2,475 Coed
Affiliation or Control: State IRS Status: 501(c)3
Highest Offering: Doctorate
Accreditation: HLC

02 President ..... Dr. James RANKIN
05 Provost/VP Academic Affairs ..... Dr. Lance ROBERTS
10 Vice Pres Finance/Admin/Controller ..... Dr. Bill SPINDLE
46 Vice President of Research ..... Dr. Ralph DAVIS
32 VP Student Affs/Dean of Students ..... Dr. Patricia G. MAHON
15 Vice President Human Resources ..... Ms. Kelsey O'NEILL
20 Associate Provost Academic Affairs ..... Dr. Kathryn E. ALLEY
88 Assoc Provost Acad Administration ..... Ms. Molly MOORE
96 Director of Business Services ..... Ms. Barbara MUSTARD
26 Dir of Marketing & Communications . Ms. Ann M. BRENTLINGER
29 Interim Dir of Alumni Association ..... Mr. Shane LEE
13 Director of Information Tech Svcs ..... Mr. Bryan J. SCHUMACHER
08 Director of Devereaux Library ..... Ms. Patricia M. ANDERSEN
36 Assistant VP for Student Dev ..... Vacant
37 Director of Financial Aid ..... Mr. David W. MARTIN
41 Director of Athletics ..... Mr. Joel LUEKEN
102 President SDSM&T Foundation ..... Ms. Sharon CHONTOS
18 Director of Facilities & Risk Mgmt ..... Ms. Jerilyn C. ROBERTS
39 Asst Dean of Students/Dir of Res ..... Vacant
85 Director Ivanhoe International Ctr ..... Ms. Susan R. AADLAND
58 Dean of Graduate Education ..... Dr. Maribeth H. PRICE
38 Director Counseling/ADA Svcs ..... Mr. Duane KAVANAUGH
06 Registrar ..... Ms. Diana EASTMAN
40 Director of University Bookstore ..... Mr. Marlin L. KINZER
35 Dir of Student Act/Leadership Ctr ..... Mr. Cory L. HEADLEY
28 Director of Multicultural Affairs ..... Mr. Jesse HERRERA

*South Dakota State University (A)

Campanile Avenue, Brookings SD 57007-2298
County: Brookings | FICE Identification: 003471
Unit ID: 219356
Telephone: (605) 688-4151 | Carnegie Class: DU-Higher
FAX Number: (605) 688-5822 | Calendar System: Semester
URL: www.sdstate.edu
Established: 1881 | Annual Undergrad Tuition & Fees (In-State): $9,200
Enrollment: 11,405 | Coed
Affiliation or Control: State | IRS Status: 501(c)3
Highest Offering: Doctorate
Accreditation: HLC, AAB, ART, CAATE, CACREP, #CAEP, CAEPN, CIDA, DIETD, DIETI, EXSC, JOUR, LSAR, MT, MUS, NURSE, PH, PHAR, THEA

01 President ..... Dr. Barry H. DUNN
05 Provost/Vice Pres Acad Affairs ..... Dr. Dennis HEDGE
32 Vice President Student Affairs ..... Dr. Michaela WILLIS
46 VP for Research/Economic Dev ..... Dr. Daniel SCHOLL
13 VP for Technology and Safety ..... Mr. David OVERBY
10 Vice Pres Finance & Budget ..... Mr. Michael HOLBECK
20 Vice Pres for Academic Affs ..... Dr. Donald MARSHALL
88 Asst VP AA Intl Affairs/Outreach ..... Dr. Jon STAUFF
15 Vice Pres Human Resources ..... Ms. Tracy GREENE
100 Chief of Staff ..... Ms. Karyn WEBER
08 Dean of the Library ..... Dr. Kristi TORNQUIST
07 Director of Admissions ..... Mr. Shawn HELMBOLT
06 Registrar ..... Ms. Joyce KEPFORD
38 Dir of Student Health & Counseling ..... Ms. Tammy LUNDAY
37 Financial Aid Director ..... Ms. Beth VOLLAN
102 President & CEO of Foundation ..... Mr. Steve ERPENBACH
29 President & CEO Alumni Association ..... Ms. Andi FOUBERG
19 Chief Security/Safety ..... Mr. Tim HEATON
39 Director of Residential Life ..... Ms. Rebecca PETERSON
40 Director of Bookstore/Aux Ops ..... Mr. Derek PETERSON
41 Director of Athletics ..... Mr. Justin SELL
28 Dir of Diver/Equity/Inclus/Access ..... Ms. Kas WILLIAMS
56 Director of Extension ..... Dr. Karla TRAUTMAN
26 Dir Marketing & Communications ..... Mr. Michael LOCKREM
96 Purchasing Director ..... Vacant
43 General Counsel ..... Dr. Tracy GREENE
25 Director of Grants/Contracts ..... Ms. Jill O'NEIL
24 Dir Instructional Design Services ..... Dr. Shouhong ZHANG
85 Dir International Students/Scholars ..... Mr. Greg WYMER
47 Dean Col of Agric/Food/Environ Sci ..... Dr. John KILLEFER
49 Dean Col of Arts/Hum & SS ..... Dr. Lynn SARGEANT
54 Dean of Engineering ..... Dr. Bruce BERDANIER
53 Dean Education & Human Science ..... Dr. Paul BARNES
66 Dean of Nursing ..... Dr. Mary Anne KROGH
67 Dean of Pharmacy ..... Dr. Dan HANSEN
58 Vice Provost for Graduate Educatio ..... Vacant
92 Dean Honors College ..... Dr. Rebecca BOTT
81 Dean Col of Natural Science ..... Dr. Charlene WOLF-HALL
09 Coordinator Institutional Research ..... Ms. Jennifer VANDER WAL
104 Director Study Abroad ..... Ms. Sally GILLMAN
108 AVP Inst Research & Assessment ..... Dr. Jana HANSON
22 Title IX Coord/EEO ..... Ms. Michelle JOHNSON

Southeast Technical College (B)

2320 N Career Avenue, Sioux Falls SD 57107-1302
County: Minnehaha | FICE Identification: 007764
Unit ID: 219426
Telephone: (605) 367-7624 | Carnegie Class: Assoc/HVT-High Trad
FAX Number: (605) 367-8305 | Calendar System: Semester
URL: www.southeasttech.edu
Established: 1968 | Annual Undergrad Tuition & Fees (In-District): $7,470
Enrollment: 2,330 | Coed
Affiliation or Control: Local | IRS Status: 501(c)3
Highest Offering: Associate Degree
Accreditation: HLC, ADNUR, CVT, DMS, MAC, NDT, SURGT

01 President ..... Mr. Robert J. GRIGGS
05 Vice President of Academics ..... Mr. Benjamin VALDEZ
10 Vice President Finance & Operations ..... Mr. Richard KLUIN
84 VP for Enrollment Management ..... Ms. Megan FISCHER
06 Director Student Success/Registrar ..... Ms. Kristie VORTHERMS
13 Chief Information Officer ..... Mr. Erik VANLAECKEN
15 Human Resources Director ..... Ms. Kathy STRUCK
20 Dean of Curriculum/Instruction ..... Dr. Craig PETERS
20 Dean of Curriculum/Instruction ..... Ms. Kristin POSSEHL
26 Marketing/Communications Coord ..... Ms. Jennifer LAMBLEY
37 Financial Aid Director ..... Mr. Micah HANSEN
102 Foundation Director ..... Mr. Stephen WILLIAMSON
113 Director of Student Accounts ..... Mr. James WESTCOTT
38 Student Personal Counselor ..... Ms. Nicole MCMILLIN
04 Admin Assistant to the President ..... Ms. Vicki OSWALD
07 Director of Admissions ..... Ms. Mandy FREY
39 Director of Housing ..... Mr. Andy VANZANTEN

University of Sioux Falls (C)

1101 W 22nd Street, Sioux Falls SD 57105-1699
County: Minnehaha | FICE Identification: 003469
Unit ID: 219383
Telephone: (605) 331-5000 | Carnegie Class: Masters/M
FAX Number: (605) 331-6615 | Calendar System: 4/1/4
URL: www.usiouxfalls.edu
Established: 1883 | Annual Undergrad Tuition & Fees: $19,520
Enrollment: 1,628 | Coed
Affiliation or Control: American Baptist | IRS Status: 501(c)3
Highest Offering: Doctorate
Accreditation: HLC, CAEP, IACBE, NURSE, SW

01 President ..... Dr. Brett BRADFIELD
100 Dir Presidential and Bd Operations ..... Ms. Karen BANGASSER
05 VP for Academic Affairs ..... Ms. Joy LIND
50 Chair School of Business ..... Mr. Bradley VAN KALSBEEK
53 Chair School of Education ..... Ms. Michelle HANSON
57 Chair Visual & Performing Arts ..... Mr. Jonathan NEIDERHISER
65 Chair of Natural Sciences ..... Dr. William SOEFFING
79 Chair of Humanities ..... Ms. Jenny BANGSUND
83 Chair of Social Sciences ..... Ms. Beth O'TOOLE
66 Director School of Nursing ..... Ms. Jessica CHERENEGAR
88 Director of Degree Comp Program ..... Ms. LuAnn GROSSMAN
06 Registrar ..... Ms. Anna HECKENLAIBLE
10 VP for Business and Finance ..... Mr. Rick GILBERTSON
21 Senior Accountant ..... Ms. Staci ATTEMA
111 VP for Institutional Advancement ..... Mr. Todd KNUTSON
112 VP for Principal Gifts ..... Mr. Jon HIATT
30 Dir of Institutional Advancement ..... Ms. Julie IVERSON
26 Dir of Marketing and Communications ..... Ms. Sarah STRASBURG
84 VP for Enrollment Management ..... Ms. Aimee VANDER FEEN
07 Director of Admissions ..... Mr. Ben WEINS
37 Director of Financial Aid ..... Ms. Karrie MORGAN
15 VP of Human Resources ..... Ms. Julie GEDNALSKE
09 AVP of Institutional Research ..... Dr. Jason DOUMA
39 Director of Student Life & Housing ..... Mr. Andrew PORTEOUS
88 Doctoral Program Director ..... Dr. Bruce BLUMER
42 Dean of the Chapel ..... Rev. Dennis L. THUM
38 University Counselor ..... Ms. Michelle DEHOOGH-KLIEWER
104 Director of International Education ..... Mr. Randy NELSON
13 VP Info Technology and CIO ..... Mr. William BARTELL
91 Dir Administrative Applications ..... Mr. Rob HARRINGTON
106 Director of Online Education ..... Ms. Tara JOHANNESON
08 Librarian ..... Ms. Annie STERNBURG
41 Director of Athletics ..... Ms. Pam GOHL
18 Director of Facilities ..... Mr. Brad FLAYTON
19 Director of Campus Safety ..... Mr. Kevin GREBIN
40 Dir of Cougar Central Bookstore ..... Ms. Jennifer KNUTSON

Western Dakota Technical College (D)

800 Mickelson Drive, Rapid City SD 57703-4018
County: Pennington | FICE Identification: 010170
Unit ID: 219480
Telephone: (605) 394-4034 | Carnegie Class: Assoc/HVT-Mix Trad/Non
FAX Number: (605) 394-1789 | Calendar System: Semester
URL: www.wdt.edu
Established: 1968 | Annual Undergrad Tuition & Fees (In-District): $8,274
Enrollment: 1,324 | Coed
Affiliation or Control: Local | IRS Status: 501(c)3
Highest Offering: Associate Degree
Accreditation: HLC, EMT, MLTAD, SURGT

01 President ..... Dr. Ann BOLMAN
05 VP for Teaching and Learning ..... Ms. Tiffany HOWE
10 VP for Finance and Operations ..... Ms. Christine GOLDSMITH
108 VP for Institutional Effectiveness ..... Ms. Kelly OEHLERKING
15 Director of Human Resources ..... Ms. Jade HOLLISTER
07 Admissions & Financial Aid Director ..... Ms. Jill ELDER
06 Director Student Success/Registrar ..... Ms. Debbie TOMS
18 Director of Facilities ..... Mr. Bob GRIMSRUD
26 Director Strategic Communications ..... Ms. Pam STILLMAN-ROKUSEK
111 Director Industry Relations/Grants ..... Ms. Chandra CALVERT
04 Executive Assistant to President ..... Ms. Kathi MAXSON
09 Reporting & Analysis Director ..... Vacant
102 Foundation Director ..... Ms. Danita SIMONS
13 Director of Information Systems ..... Mr. Matthew GREENE

TENNESSEE

All Saints Bible College (E)

930 Mason Street, Memphis TN 38126
County: Shelby | Identification: 667014
Telephone: (901) 322-0120 | Carnegie Class: Not Classified
FAX Number: (901) 947-3504 | Calendar System: Semester
URL: www.allsaintsonline.info
Established: 2002 | Annual Undergrad Tuition & Fees: N/A
Enrollment: N/A | Coed
Affiliation or Control: Church of God in Christ | IRS Status: 501(c)3
Highest Offering: Baccalaureate
Accreditation: @BI

00 Chancellor ..... Bishop Charles E. BLAKE
01 President ..... Dr. Joseph E. FISHER

American Baptist College (F)

1800 Baptist World Center Drive, Nashville TN 37207
County: Davidson | FICE Identification: 010460
Unit ID: 219505
Telephone: (615) 256-1463 | Carnegie Class: Spec-4-yr-Faith
FAX Number: (615) 226-7855 | Calendar System: Semester
URL: www.abcnash.edu
Established: 1924 | Annual Undergrad Tuition & Fees: $12,474
Enrollment: 55 | Coed
Affiliation or Control: Baptist | IRS Status: 501(c)3
Highest Offering: Baccalaureate
Accreditation: BI

01 President ..... Dr. Forrest E. HARRIS, SR.
05 Provost/Vice Pres Academic Affairs ..... Dr. LaShante WALKER
10 EVP Admin/Finance/Legal Affairs ..... Atty. Richard JACKSON
32 Vice Pres Campus Life ..... Mr. Martin ESPINOSA
06 Registrar/Student Records ..... Ms. Pamela TABOR
21 Controller ..... Ms. Brooke BELL
08 Director Library Services ..... Ms. Nicole WHITE
04 Executive Assistant to President ..... Ms. Mary CARPENTER
25 Dir Proposal/Grant Research Devel ..... Dr. Regina PRUDE
07 Dir Admissions/Public Relations ..... Vacant

Aquinas College (G)

4210 Harding Pike, Nashville TN 37205-2005
County: Davidson | FICE Identification: 003477
Unit ID: 219578
Telephone: (615) 297-7545 | Carnegie Class: Spec-4-yr-Other Health
FAX Number: N/A | Calendar System: Semester
URL: www.aquinascollege.edu
Established: 1961 | Annual Undergrad Tuition & Fees: N/A
Enrollment: N/A | Coed
Affiliation or Control: Roman Catholic | IRS Status: 501(c)3
Highest Offering: Master's
Accreditation: SC

01 President ..... Sr. Cecilia Anne WARNER, OP
05 Provost and Vice Pres for Academics ..... Sr. Mary Edith HUMPHRIES, OP
32 Director of Student Activities ..... Vacant
20 Associate Provost ..... Dr. William SMART
26 Dir of Communications/Marketing ..... Vacant
07 Dir of Admiss & Registrar ..... Sr. Gianna JUNKER, OP
08 Librarian ..... Sr. Mary Esther POTTS, OP
53 Dean School of Education ..... Sr. Mary Grace WATSON, OP
21 Business Manager ..... Mrs. Monica WARREN
09 Director of Institutional Research ..... Dr. William SMART
18 Chief of Facilities/Physical Plant ..... Mr. John WALL
121 Director of Student Learning Svcs ..... Vacant
88 Director of Catechetics ..... Mr. Jason GALE
88 Dir Center for Catholic Education ..... Sr. Elizabeth Anne ALLEN, OP
19 Director Security/Safety ..... Mr. Andrew ATWOOD
04 Executive Asst to President ..... Ms. Kathleen L. DILLINER
101 Secretary of the Institution/Board ..... Sr. John Mary FLEMING, OP
13 Chief Info Technology Officer (CIO) ..... Mrs. Joyce WALL
15 Chief Human Resources Officer ..... Ms. Anne TARWATER
37 Director Student Financial Aid ..... Mrs. Cynthia PIANA

Austin Peay State University (H)

601 College Street, Clarksville TN 37044-0002
County: Montgomery | FICE Identification: 003478
Unit ID: 219602
Telephone: (931) 221-7011 | Carnegie Class: Masters/L
FAX Number: (931) 221-7475 | Calendar System: Semester
URL: www.apsu.edu
Established: 1927 | Annual Undergrad Tuition & Fees (In-State): $8,303
Enrollment: 10,272 | Coed
Affiliation or Control: State | IRS Status: 501(c)3
Highest Offering: Doctorate
Accreditation: SC, ART, CACREP, CAEPN, MT, MUS, NURSE, RAD, RTT, SW

02 President ..... Dr. Michael LICARI
05 Provost/VP Academic Affairs ..... Dr. Maria CRONLEY
10 Vice President for Finance & Admin ..... Mr. Mitch ROBINSON
43 VP Legal Affairs & Org Strategy ..... Ms. Dannelle WHITESIDE
32 VP for Student Affairs ..... Dr. Eric NORMAN
21 Assoc VP for Finance ..... Mr. Benjamin HARMON
20 Vice Provost/Assoc VP Acad Affairs ..... Dr. Lynne CROSBY
121 Vice Prov for Student Achievement ..... Dr. Nancy KING SANDERS
111 Vice Pres Univ Advancement ..... Mr. Kristopher PHILLIPS
86 Chief Cmty/Govt Relations/Board Sec ..... Dr. Carol D. CLARK
26 Exec Dir Marketing/Public Rels ..... Mr. Bill PERSINGER
12 Exec Dir APSU Fort Campbell ..... Dr. Kristine NAKUTIS
29 Director of Alumni Relations ..... Ms. Nicole PETERSON
114 Director Budgets ..... Ms. Sonja STEWART
08 Director Library ..... Mr. Joe WEBER
13 Assoc VP & Chief Info Officer ..... Dr. David SANCHEZ

09 Dir Decision Support/Inst Effective .... Dr. Andrew LUNA
07 Director of Admissions .... Ms. Amy CORLEW
06 Registrar .... Vacant
18 Director of Plant Administration .... Mr. Thomas HUTCHINS
45 Dir University Design/Construction .... Mr. Marc BRUNNER
41 Athletic Director .... Mr. Gerald HARRISON
88 Athletics Communication Manager .... Mr. Cody BUSH
37 Director of Student Financial Aid .... Ms. Donna PRICE
121 AVP Student Success/Strategic Init .... Dr. Loretta GRIFFY
38 Dir of Student Counseling Services .... Dr. Jeff RUTTER
35 Assoc Vice Pres & Dean of Students ..... Mr. Gregory SINGLETON
88 Dir African Amer Cultural Ctr .... Mr. Harold WALLACE
15 Exec Director Human Resources .... Ms. Sheraine GILLIAM-HOLMES
16 Director of Human Resources .... Ms. Fonda FIELDS
19 Assistant VP for Public Safety .... Mr. Michael KASITZ
39 Asst Vice President Student Affairs .... Mr. F. Joe MILLS
116 Director Internal Audit .... Mr. Blayne CLEMENTS
25 Dir Research & Sponsored Pgms .... Mr. Timothy ATKINSON
96 Director of Purchasing .... Ms. Judy BLAIN
22 Dir Equal Opportunity/Affirm Action .... Ms. Sheila M. BRYANT
36 Director of Career Services .... Vacant
49 Dean College Arts & Letters .... Mr. Barry JONES
81 Dean College STEM .... Dr. Karen MEISCH
83 Dean Col Behav Health Science .... Dr. Tucker BROWN
58 Assoc Provost/Dean Col Grad Stds .... Dr. Chad BROOKS
56 Exec Dir Extend/Intl Educ .... Dr. Tim HUDSON
106 Director of Distance Education .... Ms. Lady MORAN
104 Dir Study Abroad/Intl Exchange .... Dr. Marissa CHANDLER
50 Dean College of Business .... Dr. Mickey HEPNER
53 Dean College of Education .... Dr. Prentice CHANDLER
28 Chief Diversity Officer/Title IX .... Ms. LaNeeca WILLIAMS
04 Executive Asst to the President .... Ms. Lenora PARKS
101 Secretary of the Institution/Board .... Mrs. Carol CLARK
44 Director Annual Giving .... Ms. Rebekah BISHOP

Baptist Health Sciences University (A)

1003 Monroe Avenue, Memphis TN 38104-3199

County: Shelby | FICE Identification: 034403 | Unit ID: 219639
Telephone: (901) 575-2268 | Carnegie Class: Spec-4-yr-Other Health
FAX Number: (901) 572-2497 | Calendar System: Trimester
URL: https://www.baptistu.edu/
Established: 1994 | Annual Undergrad Tuition & Fees: $12,572
Enrollment: 890 | Coed
Affiliation or Control: Independent Non-Profit | IRS Status: 501(c)3
Highest Offering: Doctorate
Accreditation: SC, COARC, DMS, MT, NDT, NMT, NURSE, RAD, RTT

01 President .... Dr. Betty Sue MCGARVEY
04 Administrative Asst to President .... Ms. Dina BACHOR
05 Provost/VP Academic Affairs .... Dr. Barry SCHULTZ
84 VP Enrollment Mgmt & Student Affs .... Dr. Tammy FOWLER
10 Vice President Financial & Business .... Ms. Leanne SMITH
11 Vice President Admin Svcs/HR .... Dr. Adonna CALDWELL
97 Dean General Educ & Health Studies .... Dr. Michelle MCDONALD
66 Dean Nursing .... Dr. Anne M. PLUMB
76 Dean Allied Health .... Vacant
32 Dean Student Services .... Ms. Nancy REED
06 Registrar .... Mrs. Erica CHANDLER
07 Director of Admissions .... Vacant
09 Dir Institutional Effectiveness/Pln .... Dr. Cameron A. CONN
29 Director Alumni Relations/Marketing .... Ms. Megan M. BURSI
35 Director Student Services & Housing .... Mr. Jeremy WILKES
37 Director Financial Aid .... Ms. Joanna DARDEN

Belmont University (B)

1900 Belmont Boulevard, Nashville TN 37212-3757

County: Davidson | FICE Identification: 003479 | Unit ID: 219709
Telephone: (615) 460-6000 | Carnegie Class: DU-Mod
FAX Number: (615) 460-6446 | Calendar System: Semester
URL: www.belmont.edu
Established: 1890 | Annual Undergrad Tuition & Fees: $37,030
Enrollment: 8,204 | Coed
Affiliation or Control: Non-denominational | IRS Status: 501(c)3
Highest Offering: Doctorate
Accreditation: SC, ART, CACREP, CAEPN, CIDA, LAW, MUS, NURSE, OT, PHAR, PTA, SW, THEA

01 President .... Dr. Gregory JONES
05 Provost .... Dr. Thomas D. BURNS
100 Vice President/Chief of Staff .... Dr. Susan H. WEST
43 Vice Pres for Admin & Univ Counsel .... Dr. Jason ROGERS
108 VP for Institutional Effectiveness .... Dr. Paula GILL
30 VP Development/External Relations .... Dr. Perry MOULDS
10 Vice President Finance & Operations .... Mr. Steven T. LASLEY
42 VP Spiritual Development .... Dr. Todd LAKE
26 VP Marketing & Public Relations .... Mr. John CARNEY
13 Assoc VP/Chief Information Officer .... Mr. William INGRAM
32 Dean of Students .... Dr. Tamika WILLIAMS
20 Vice Provost for Academic Affairs .... Dr. Phil JOHNSTON
84 Assoc Prov/Dean Enroll Svcs/Admiss .... Dr. Chris GAGE
35 Associate Dean of Students .... Dr. Anthony DONOVAN
09 Assoc Prov Assessment/Inst Research .... Ms. Patricia WHITE
88 Assoc Provost ISGE/Global Educ .... Dr. Mimi BARNARD
50 Dean College of Business .... Dr. Sarah FISHER GARDIAL
57 Dean College Visual/Performing Arts .... Dr. Stephen EAVES
88 Dean College of Ent & Music Bus .... Mr. Doug HOWARD
49 Dean Col of Lib Arts & Soc Sci .... Dr. Bryce SULLIVAN
81 Dean Col of Sciences & Mathematics .... Dr. Thomas SPENCE
76 Dean Col Health Sciences/Nursing .... Dr. Cathy TAYLOR
73 Dean of Col Theol & Christian Min .... Dr. Darrell GWALTNEY
61 Dean College of Law .... Dr. Alberto GONZALES
67 Dean College of Pharmacy .... Dr. David GREGORY
53 Dean of Education .... Vacant
06 University Registrar .... Mr. Steven REED
35 Asst Dean of Student Support Svcs .... Ms. Angie BRYANT
39 Assistant Dean of Student Housing .... Mr. Anthony DONOVAN
15 Sr Director of Human Resources .... Mrs. Leslie A. LENSER
37 Director of Financial Aid .... Mr. Charles HARPER
29 Assoc Director of Alumni Relations .... Ms. Julie THOMAS
18 Director of Facilities Management .... Mr. Robert CHAVEZ
19 Chief of Campus Security .... Mr. Pat CUNNINGHAM
90 Director Technology Services .... Mr. Randall REYNOLDS
08 Director of Library Services .... Ms. Sue MASZAROS
41 Athletics Director .... Mr. Scott CORLEY
40 Manager Bookstore .... Mrs. Catherine MURPHY
36 Dir Career & Professional Develop .... Ms. Mary Claire DISMUKES
38 Director Student Counseling .... Ms. Katherine CONZALES
104 Director of Global Education .... Ms. Thandi DINANI
07 Director of Admissions .... Ms. Brooke GRANNIN
96 Director of Diversity .... Dr. Susan WEST

Bethel University (C)

325 Cherry Avenue, McKenzie TN 38201-1705

County: Carroll | FICE Identification: 003480 | Unit ID: 219718
Telephone: (731) 352-4000 | Carnegie Class: Masters/L
FAX Number: (731) 352-4069 | Calendar System: Semester
URL: www.bethelu.edu
Established: 1842 | Annual Undergrad Tuition & Fees: $17,010
Enrollment: 4,001 | Coed
Affiliation or Control: Cumberland Presbyterian | IRS Status: 501(c)3
Highest Offering: Master's
Accreditation: #SC, ARCPA, NURSE

01 President .... Dr. Walter BUTLER
05 Chief Academic Officer .... Dr. Phyllis CAMPBELL
49 VP College of Arts and Sciences .... Ms. Cindy MALLARD
107 VP College of Professional Studies .... Mrs. Kimberly MARTIN
76 VP College of Health Sciences .... Dr. Joe HAMES
10 VP of Finance .... Mr. David HUSS
30 Vice President for Development .... Vacant
06 University Registrar .... Ms. Deborah NOBLE
07 Director Admissions/Recruitment .... Mrs. Tina HODGES
26 VP Strategic Initiatives .... Ms. Michelle MITCHELL
89 Director of College Orientation .... Mrs. Sandy LOUDEN
42 Senior Chaplain .... Rev. Anne HAMES
08 Library Director .... Ms. Jill WHITFILL
15 Human Resource Director .... Ms. Carolyn DOTSON
41 Athletic Director .... Mr. Dale KELLEY
09 Dir of Institutional Effectiveness .... Ms. Lisa TYLER
29 Director Alumni Relations .... Mrs. Myra CARLOCK
18 Chief Facilities/Physical Plant .... Mr. Randy TANAKA
04 Administrative Asst to President .... Ms. Vicky WILLIAMS
105 Director Web Services .... Mr. Jon MITCHELL
13 Chief Info Technology Officer (CIO) .... Mr. Jimmy BOMAR
19 Director Security/Safety .... Mr. Daniel THOMAS
39 Director Student Housing .... Ms. Peggy CARTER

Bryan College (D)

721 Bryan Drive, Dayton TN 37321-6275

County: Rhea | FICE Identification: 003536 | Unit ID: 219790
Telephone: (423) 775-2041 | Carnegie Class: Masters/S
FAX Number: (423) 775-7330 | Calendar System: Semester
URL: www.bryan.edu
Established: 1930 | Annual Undergrad Tuition & Fees: $17,050
Enrollment: 1,412 | Coed
Affiliation or Control: Independent Non-Profit | IRS Status: 501(c)3
Highest Offering: Master's
Accreditation: SC, IACBE

01 President .... Dr. Douglas F. MANN
04 Exec Assistant to the President .... Ms. Margaret A. LEGG
05 Provost/VP of Academics .... Dr. David CALLAND
10 SVP of Business Operations/Finance .... Mr. Tim J. HOSTETLER
111 Vice Pres of Advancement/Athletics .... Mr. David HOLCOMB
32 VP Student Services/Ministries .... Vacant
58 Dean Sch of Adult & Graduate Stds .... Dr. Adina SCRUGGS
54 Dean School of Engineering .... Vacant
35 Dean of Students .... Mr. Bruce A. MORGAN
37 Director of Financial Aid .... Mr. David L. HAGGARD
13 Director of Information Technology .... Mr. James SULLIVAN
06 Registrar .... Ms. Janet M. PIATT
08 Director of Library Services .... Dr. Gary N. FITSIMMONS
15 Director Personnel Services .... Mrs. Angie C. PRICE
41 Athletic Director .... Mr. Mike KEEN
18 Director of Physical Plant .... Mr. David A. MORGAN
29 Director of Alumni Affairs .... Mrs. Paulakay HALL
07 Exec Director of Admissions .... Mr. Andrew SMITH
88 Accreditation Liaison .... Mr. Samuel J. YOUNGS

Carson-Newman University (E)

1646 Russell Avenue, PO Box 557, Jefferson City TN 37760-2204

County: Jefferson | FICE Identification: 003481 | Unit ID: 219806
Telephone: (865) 471-2000 | Carnegie Class: DU-Mod
FAX Number: (865) 471-3502 | Calendar System: Semester
URL: www.cn.edu
Established: 1851 | Annual Undergrad Tuition & Fees: $29,500
Enrollment: 2,911 | Coed
Affiliation or Control: Southern Baptist | IRS Status: 501(c)3
Highest Offering: Doctorate
Accreditation: SC, AAFCS, ART, CACREP, CAEP, DIETD, MUS, NURSE

01 President .... Mr. Charles FOWLER
05 Provost .... Dr. Jeremy BUCKNER
111 Vice President University Relations .... Mr. Kevin TRIPLETT
32 Vice President Student Affairs .... Ms. Gloria WALKER
35 Asst Vice Pres of Student Affairs .... Mrs. Shelley BALL
08 Dean of Library Services .... Mr. Bruce KOCOUR
26 Exec Dir University Relations .... Mr. Charles KEY
37 Director Financial Aid .... Mrs. Danette SEALE
38 Director Counseling Services .... Mrs. Jennifer CATLETT
13 Chief Information Officer .... Mr. David TUELL
18 Chief Facilities/Physical Plant .... Mr. Ondes WEBSTER
84 Acting Vice Pres Enrollment Mgmt .... Mrs. Danette SEALE
92 Director of Honors Program .... Dr. Andrew SMITH
10 Chief Business Officer .... Mrs. Elaine SMITH
41 Athletic Director .... Mr. Matthew POPE
85 Dean of Global Education .... Vacant
06 Registrar .... Mrs. Sheryl GRAY
04 Executive Assistant to President .... Mrs. Libby MILLER

Chattanooga College (F)

5600 Brainerd Road #B-38, Chattanooga TN 37411

County: Hamilton | FICE Identification: 022042 | Unit ID: 220118
Telephone: (423) 305-7783 | Carnegie Class: Spec 2-yr-Health
FAX Number: (423) 624-1575 | Calendar System: Quarter
URL: www.chattanoogacollege.edu
Established: 1968 | Annual Undergrad Tuition & Fees: $10,690
Enrollment: 252 | Coed
Affiliation or Control: Proprietary | IRS Status: Proprietary
Highest Offering: Associate Degree
Accreditation: ACCSC

01 President .... Mr. William G. FAOUR
03 Vice President .... Mr. Toney C. MCFADDEN
05 Director of Education .... Ms. Karen WORLEY
37 Director Financial Aid .... Ms. Beth GASS

Christian Brothers University (G)

650 East Parkway South, Memphis TN 38104-5581

County: Shelby | FICE Identification: 003482 | Unit ID: 219833
Telephone: (901) 321-3000 | Carnegie Class: Masters/L
FAX Number: (901) 321-3494 | Calendar System: Semester
URL: www.cbu.edu
Established: 1871 | Annual Undergrad Tuition & Fees: $34,880
Enrollment: 1,918 | Coed
Affiliation or Control: Roman Catholic | IRS Status: 501(c)3
Highest Offering: Master's
Accreditation: SC, ARCPA, CAEPN, NURSE

01 President .... Mr. John T. SHANNON, JR.
10 CFO & VP Administration .... Mr. Ronald BRANDON
05 VP Academics .... Dr. Paul HAUGHT
111 VP Advancement .... Mr. Mark BILLINGSLEY
84 VP Enrollment Mgmt .... Dr. Brian DALTON
32 VP Student Devel & Campus Life .... Ms. Beth GERL
13 VP ITS/Chief Info Officer .... Mr. Brett DOTY
26 VP Communications & Marketing .... Dr. Leslie GRAFF
88 VP Mission & Identity .... Br. Patrick CONWAY
28 VP Diversity/Equity & Inclusion .... Dr. Mary MCCONNER
11 VP Operations & Facilities .... Vacant
41 Director of Athletics .... Mr. Brian SUMMERS
100 Chief of Staff .... Ms. Susan ELLIOTT
88 Dir Cen Enterpreneurship & Innov .... Mr. Bryan BARRINGER
20 Assoc VP Acad & Strat Initiatives .... Dr. Jack HARGETT
85 Assoc VP Intl Initiatives .... Dr. Daniel S. HARPER
49 Dean School of Arts .... Dr. Benjamin R. JORDAN
50 Dean School of Business .... Dr. Lydia ROSENCRANTS
54 Dean School of Engineering .... Dr. Faris MALHAS
81 Dean School of Science .... Dr. James MCGUFFEE
55 Dean College Adult Prof Studies .... Dr. Divya CHOUDHARY
121 Dean Student Success .... Vacant
15 Assoc VP Human Resources .... Ms. Theresa JACQUES
21 Controller .... Ms. Lisa LUCAS
102 AVP Corp & Foundation Relations .. Ms. Kathleen TERRY-SHARP
110 Associate VP for Donor Relations .... Dr. Anne KENWORTHY
35 Associate VP for Student Life .... Dr. Timothy DOYLE
06 Registrar .... Mr. Scott SUMMERS
36 Director Career Services .... Ms. Amy WARE
31 Director Center Community Engage .... Dr. Leslie MCABEE
106 Director Center Digital Instruction .... Dr. Dale HALE
92 Director Honors Program .... Ms. Connie BECK
09 Dir Inst Research/Effectiveness .... Ms. Melissa S. ANDREWS
08 Director of Plough Library .... Ms. Kay CUNNINGHAM
18 Director Physical Plant .... Mr. Bill HECHT
29 Director Alumni Relations .... Ms. Torie MARION
44 Director Annual Giving .... Ms. Jennie DICKERSON
07 Director of Admissions .... Ms. Raquel SAULSBERRY
37 Director Student Financial Aid .... Ms. Elizabeth ROMAGNI
42 Director Campus Ministry .... Mr. Joseph PRESTON
19 Director Campus Police & Safety .... Mr. John D. LOTRIONTE
38 Director Counseling Center .... Ms. Beverly WORD
23 Director Health Resources .... Ms. Heather HARRINGTON

39 Director Residence Life .... Mr. Alton WADE
53 Dir Undergrad & Graduate Education .... Dr. Rosetta MAYFIELD-BURFORD
66 Director of Nursing .... Dr. Jennifer HITT-MAYO
96 Dir Procurement & Contract Services .... Ms. Susan BANNING
123 Director Graduate Admissions .... Ms. Erica MITCHELL
04 Executive Administrative Coord .... Ms. Chastity BLAIR
89 Coord 1st & 2nd Year Experience .... Vacant
40 Director Bookstore .... Ms. Melissa ROGERS

Concorde Career College (A)

5100 Poplar Avenue, Suite 132, Memphis TN 38137-0132
County: Shelby | FICE Identification: 021571 | Unit ID: 219903
Telephone: (901) 761-9494 | Carnegie Class: Spec 2-yr-Health
FAX Number: (901) 761-3293 | Calendar System: Semester
URL: https://www.concorde.edu/campus/memphis-tennessee
Established: 1967 | Annual Undergrad Tuition & Fees: N/A
Enrollment: 1,367 | Coed
Affiliation or Control: Proprietary | IRS Status: Proprietary
Highest Offering: Associate Degree
Accreditation: **COE**, CAHIIM, COARC, DH, MLTAD, OTA, POLYT, PTAA, RAD

01 Campus President .... Mr. Tommy STEWART
05 Academic Dean .... Ms. Michelle GOLDEN

The Crown College of the Bible (B)

2307 W. Beaver Creek Drive, Powell TN 37849
County: Knox | Identification: 667141
Telephone: (865) 938-8186 | Carnegie Class: Not Classified
FAX Number: (865) 938-8188 | Calendar System: Semester
URL: thecrowncollege.edu
Established: 1991 | Annual Undergrad Tuition & Fees: N/A
Enrollment: N/A | Coed
Affiliation or Control: Baptist | IRS Status: 501(c)3
Highest Offering: Master's
Accreditation: **TRACS**

01 Founder & President .... Dr. Clarence SEXTON
03 Executive Vice President .... Mr. James ZENKER
05 Vice President of Academics .... Mr. Tim TOMLINSON
11 Vice President of Operations .... Mr. M. Shannon SEXTON
10 Vice President of Finance .... Dr. Charles PRESCOTT
75 Vice President Trades .... Dr. Janice GILLIAM

Cumberland University (C)

1 Cumberland Square, Lebanon TN 37087-3554
County: Wilson | FICE Identification: 003485 | Unit ID: 219949
Telephone: (615) 444-2562 | Carnegie Class: Masters/M
FAX Number: (615) 444-2569 | Calendar System: Semester
URL: www.cumberland.edu
Established: 1842 | Annual Undergrad Tuition & Fees: $25,386
Enrollment: 2,704 | Coed
Affiliation or Control: Independent Non-Profit | IRS Status: 501(c)3
Highest Offering: Master's
Accreditation: **SC**, ACBSP, CAATE, NURSE

01 President .... Dr. Paul STUMB, IV
05 Provost/Vice Pres Academic Affairs .... Dr. William MCKEE
10 Vice President of Finance .... Ms. Judy G. JORDAN
111 Vice President of Advancement .... Ms. Courtney WHEELER
32 AVP/Dean of Students .... Ms. Stephanie DAVIS
66 Dean Nursing and Health Sciences .... Dr. Mary GRIFFITH
100 Executive Coordinator to President .... Ms. Leslie STEELE
08 Director Library Services .... Ms. Bettina WARKENTIN
84 Exec Director Enrollment Services .... Dr. Eddie LOVIN
41 Director of Athletics .... Mr. Ron PAVAN
06 Registrar .... Ms. Tammi PAVAN
15 Director of Human Resources .... Ms. Tammy MARSHALL
13 Director of Information Technology .... Mr. Jerry ENGLAND
09 Director of Institutional Research .... Mr. Larry F. VAUGHAN
26 Exec Dir Communications/Marketing .... Ms. Caitlin VAUGHN
36 Dir of Career Services/Internships .... Ms. N. Leann BLEVINS
37 Director Student Financial Aid .... Ms. Beatrice LACHANCE
39 Director Student Housing .... Vacant
50 Dean Labry School of Business .... Dr. Chris FULLER
53 Dean of Humanities/Education & Art .... Dr. Eric CUMMINGS
27 Exec Dir Public Relations .... Mr. William "Rusty" RICHARDSON
39 Exec Director of Housing & Services .... Mr. Steve GIORDANO
108 Director Institutional Assessment .... Dr. Laurie DISHMAN
19 Director Security/Safety .... Mr. Mike THORNHILL

Daymar College (D)

2691 Trenton Road, Clarksville TN 37040-6718
Telephone: (931) 552-7600 | Identification: 666492
Accreditation: **ACCSC**, PTAA

† Branch campus of Daymar College, Nashville, TN.

Daymar College (E)

415 Golden Bear Court, Murfreesboro TN 37128-5508
Telephone: (615) 217-9347 | Identification: 666392
Accreditation: **ACCSC**

† Branch campus of Daymar College, Nashville, TN.

Daymar College (F)

560 Royal Parkway, Nashville TN 37214
County: Davidson | FICE Identification: 004934 | Unit ID: 220002
Telephone: (615) 361-7555 | Carnegie Class: Bac/Assoc-Mixed
FAX Number: (615) 367-2736 | Calendar System: Quarter
URL: www.daymarcollege.edu
Established: 1884 | Annual Undergrad Tuition & Fees: $20,724
Enrollment: 204 | Coed
Affiliation or Control: Proprietary | IRS Status: Proprietary
Highest Offering: Baccalaureate
Accreditation: **ACCSC**

01 Interim Campus President .... Ms. Laurna TAYLOR
11 Assoc VC Campus Operations .... Ms. Laurna TAYLOR

East Tennessee State University (G)

1276 Gilbreath Drive, Johnson City TN 37614-1700
County: Washington | FICE Identification: 003487 | Unit ID: 220075
Telephone: (423) 439-1000 | Carnegie Class: DU-Higher
FAX Number: (423) 439-5770 | Calendar System: Semester
URL: www.etsu.edu
Established: 1911 | Annual Undergrad Tuition & Fees (In-State): $9,259
Enrollment: 13,713 | Coed
Affiliation or Control: State | IRS Status: 501(c)3
Highest Offering: Doctorate
Accreditation: **SC**, ART, AUD, CACREP, CAEPN, CIDA, CLPSY, COARC, CSHSE, DH, DIETD, DIETI, MED, MUS, NAEYC, NURSE, PH, PHAR, PTA, RAD, SP, SW, THEA

02 President .... Dr. Brian E. NOLAND
00 Chairman Board of Trustees .... Mr. Scott M. NISWONGER
100 Chief of Staff .... Dr. Adam S. GREEN
11 Chief Operating Officer .... Mr. Jeremy B. ROSS
10 Chief Financial Officer .... Dr. B.J KING
05 Sr VP for Academics/Provost .... Dr. Kimberly MCCORKLE
17 Vice President Clinical Affairs .... Dr. William A. BLOCK
111 VP University Advancement .... Ms. Pamela S. RITTER
32 VP for Student Life and Enrollment .... Dr. Joe H. SHERLIN
41 Director of Athletics .... Mr. Scott N. CARTER
28 VP of Equity and Inclusion .... Dr. Keith V. JOHNSON
116 Director of Internal Audit .... Ms. Rebecca B. LEWIS
43 University Counsel .... Dr. Mark A. FULKS
26 Chief Marketing/Communications Ofcr .... Ms. Jessica VODDEN
124 Assoc VP Student Engagement .... Dr. Jeffery S. HOWARD
84 Asst VP Student Life & Enrollment .... Dr. Sam MAYHEW
07 Director of Admissions .... Ms. Heather A. LEVESQUE
35 Dean of Students .... Dr. T. Michelle BYRD
51 Dean Cont Studies & Acad Outreach .... Vacant
20 Exec Vice Prov Academics & Health .... Dr. David LINVILLE
46 Int VProv Research/Sponsored Pgms .... Mr. Nick HAGEMEILER
88 Int Assoc Vice Provost for Faculty .... Dr. Amy D. JOHNSON
88 Int Assc Vice Prov Acad Initiatives .... Dr. William F. FLORA
35 Assoc VP Student Life & Engagement .... Dr. William G. KIRKWOOD
18 Assoc VP for Facilities Management .... Ms. Laura BAILEY
13 CIO/Sr Vice Provost for ITS .... Dr. Karen D. KING
88 Assoc VP Administrative Services .... Dr. Katherine M. KELLEY
112 Exec Director for Planned Giving .... Mr. Robert A. LANGE
29 Exec Director Alumni Association .... Ms. Whitney GOETZ
86 Assoc VP for Comm & Gov Relations .... Ms. Bridget R. BAIRD
49 Dean College Arts & Science .... Dr. Gordon K. ANDERSON
50 Dean College of Business/Technology .... Dr. Dennis R. DEPEW
76 Dean College of Clin/Rehab Sci .... Dr. Donald A. SAMPLES
53 Interim Dean College of Education .... Dr. Janna L. SCARBOROUGH
92 Dean Honors College .... Dr. Christopher J. KELLER
63 Dean College of Medicine .... Dr. William A. BLOCK
67 Dean College of Pharmacy .... Dr. Debbie C. BYRD
66 Interim Dean College of Nursing .... Dr. Kathryn WILHOIT
69 Dean College of Public Health .... Dr. Randolph F. WYKOFF
58 Dean School of Graduate Studies .... Dr. Sharon J. MCGEE
08 Dean of Libraries .... Mr. David P. ATKINS
06 University Registrar .... Dr. Thomas N. DONOHOE
36 Director University Career Services .... Vacant
38 Director Counseling Center .... Dr. Dan L. JONES
37 Director of Financial Aid .... Ms. Catherine A. MORGAN
88 Director University Honors Program .... Dr. Karen R. KORNWEIBEL
39 Director Student Housing .... Dr. Bonnie L. BURCHETT
85 Dir International Programs/Services .... Dr. Maria D. COSTA
93 Multicultural Director .... Ms. Laura C. TERRY
19 Police Chief/Public Safety .... Mr. Cesar GARCIA
25 Director of Sponsored Programs .... Ms. Wendy ECKERT
94 Director of Women's Studies .... Dr. Phyllis A. THOMPSON
105 Web Manager .... Ms. Michaele D. LAWS
15 Asst Vice Pres Human Resources .... Ms. Lori ERICKSON
108 Dir Institutional Effectiveness .... Dr. Cheri CLAVIER
45 Assoc VP/Chief Planning Officer .... Dr. Michael B. HOFF

Fisk University (H)

1000 17th Avenue N, Nashville TN 37208-3051
County: Davidson | FICE Identification: 003490 | Unit ID: 220181
Telephone: (615) 329-8500 | Carnegie Class: Bac-A&S
FAX Number: N/A | Calendar System: Semester
URL: www.fisk.edu
Established: 1866 | Annual Undergrad Tuition & Fees: $22,132
Enrollment: 911 | Coed
Affiliation or Control: Independent Non-Profit | IRS Status: 501(c)3
Highest Offering: Master's
Accreditation: **SC**, #ACBSP, MUS

01 President .... Dr. Vann R. NEWKIRK, SR.
03 Executive Vice President .... Dr. Jens FREDERIKSEN
05 Provost and VP of Academic Affairs .... Dr. John JONES
10 Vice President for Finance and CFO .... Mr. Norm E. JONES
88 Exec Director of Special Projects .... Dr. Kenneth E. JONES
04 Exec Assistant to the President .... Mrs. Sherri B. RUCKER
88 Special Asst to the President .... Dr. Jason R. CURRY
20 Sr Vice Prov Faculty Initiatives .... Dr. Arnold BURGER
13 Chief Information Officer .... Mr. Suresh B. MURUGAN
32 Associate Provost Student Affairs .... Dr. Natara GARVIN
108 Executive Director of Assessment .... Dr. Tdka M. KILIMANJARO
14 Director of Information Technology .... Mr. Brian GARNER
37 Director of Financial Aid .... Ms. Amber J. WHITE
06 Registrar .... Mr. James DENNIS
08 Director of Library Services .... Mr. Brandon OWENS, SR.
81 Dean/Chair Math & Comp Sci .... Dr. Cathy MARTIN
106 Assoc Vice Prov Online Initiative .... Dr. Shirley BROWN
41 Dir of Athletics & Intramural Pgms .... Dr. Larry GLOVER
25 Dir Sponsored Research & Programs .... Dr. Sajid HUSSAIN
111 Assoc VP Inst Advancement .... Ms. Sheila SMITH
96 Director of Purchasing .... Mr. David COBB
19 Chief/Director of Campus Safety .... Mr. Mickey WEST
84 AVP Enroll Mgmt & Career Plng .... Ms. Latreace WELLS
15 Director of Human Resources .... Vacant
105 Web Administrator .... Vacant
39 Residence Life Director .... Dr. Christopher DUKE
43 Dir Legal Services/General Counsel .... Ms. Stacey GARRETT-KOJU
26 Director Marketing & Communication .... Ms. Madeline GUINEE
124 Director of AESP .... Ms. Lisa B. DIXON
50 Chair of Business Admin .... Dr. Nicholas UMONTUEN

Fortis Institute (I)

1025 Highway 111, Cookeville TN 38501-4305
County: Putnam | FICE Identification: 023263 | Unit ID: 418870
Telephone: (931) 526-3660 | Carnegie Class: Spec 2-yr-Health
FAX Number: (931) 372-2603 | Calendar System: Quarter
URL: www.fortis.edu/cookeville-tennessee.php
Established: 1970 | Annual Undergrad Tuition & Fees: N/A
Enrollment: N/A | Coed
Affiliation or Control: Proprietary | IRS Status: Proprietary
Highest Offering: Associate Degree
Accreditation: **ACCSC**, MLTAD, RAD, SURGT

01 Campus President .... Mr. James WILLIAMSON
06 Registrar .... Ms. Wendy BANDY
07 Director of Admissions .... Mr. David HANEY
10 Chief Business Officer .... Ms. Melissa LEWIS
36 Director Career Services .... Ms. Cindy GARRISON
37 Director Financial Aid .... Ms. Lisa WALLING

Fortis Institute-Nashville (J)

3354 Perimeter Hill Drive Suite 200, Nashville TN 37211
Telephone: (615) 320-5917 | Identification: 770509
Accreditation: **ABHES**, CVT, MLTAD, RAD, SURGT, SURTEC

† Branch campus of Fortis Institute, Baton Rouge, LA.

Freed-Hardeman University (K)

158 E Main, Henderson TN 38340-2398
County: Chester | FICE Identification: 003492 | Unit ID: 220215
Telephone: (731) 989-6000 | Carnegie Class: Masters/S
FAX Number: (731) 989-6023 | Calendar System: Semester
URL: www.fhu.edu
Established: 1869 | Annual Undergrad Tuition & Fees: $22,950
Enrollment: 2,188 | Coed
Affiliation or Control: Churches Of Christ | IRS Status: 501(c)3
Highest Offering: Doctorate
Accreditation: **SC**, ACBSP, CACREP, CAEP, NURSE, SW, THEOL

01 President .... Mr. David R. SHANNON
04 Executive Assistant to President .... Mrs. Donna STEELE
05 Provost and VP Academics .... Dr. Charles VIRES
10 Acting Chief Financial Officer .... Mrs. Courtney INSELL
111 VP for Community Engagement .... Mr. Dave CLOUSE
32 ActingVP Student Services .... Mr. Tony ALLEN
110 Associate VP for Advancement .... Mr. Kyle LAMB
84 Associate VP Enrollment Management .... Mr. Joseph ASKEW
115 Chief Investment Officer .... Mr. Jay SATTERFIELD
41 Director of Athletics .... Mr. Michael MCCUTCHEN
31 Associate VP Community Engagement .... Mr. Ryan MALECHA
07 Director of Admissions .... Mrs. Kaylan STEWART
29 Director of Alumni Engagement .... Mr. Chris RAMEY
35 Dean of Students .... Mr. Stuart VARNER
06 Registrar .... Mrs. Susan KIMPEL
37 Director Student Financial Services .... Mrs. Summer JUDD
08 Library Director .... Mr. Wade OSBURN
70 Director of Social Work Program .... Dr. Nadine MCNEAL
24 A-V Supervisor .... Mrs. Gail NASH
21 Controller .... Mr. Ethan DARETY
108 Dir Institutional Effectiveness .... Mr. A.B WHITE
09 Director of Institutional Research .... Mr. Micah SMITH
18 Director of Facilities and Grounds .... Mr. Shannon SEWELL
73 Dean College of Biblical Studies .... Dr. Mark A. BLACKWELDER
50 Dean College of Business .... Dr. Jason BRASHIER
53 Dean College of Educ & Behav Sci .... Dr. Sharen CYPRESS
49 Dean College of Arts & Sciences .... Dr. LeAnn SELF-DAVIS

92 Dean of Honors College ... Dr. Jenny JOHNSON
96 Purchasing Coordinator ... Mrs. Mallory WHITE
40 University Book Store Manager ... Mrs. Katie THURMAN
19 Director of Campus Safety/Security ... Mr. Stewart BRACKIN
88 Dir of Emerging/Innovation & QEP ... Mr. Jared GOTT
13 Chief Information Technology Ofcr ... Mr. Greg MAPLES
30 Assistant VP of Development ... Mr. David NEWBERRY
38 Director of Univ Counseling Center ... Mr. Jonathan HARRISON
39 Dir Resident Life/Student Housing ... Mrs. Lona BOLTON

Harding School of Theology (A)

1000 Cherry Road, Memphis TN 38117-5499
Telephone: (901) 761-1350 FICE Identification: 004081
Accreditation: &HLC, THEOL

† Regional accreditation is carried under Harding University, Searcy, AR.

Huntington University of Health Sciences (B)

118 Legacy View Way, Knoxville TN 37918
County: Knox Identification: 666971
Unit ID: 488068
Telephone: (865) 524-8079 Carnegie Class: Bac-A&S
FAX Number: (865) 524-8339 Calendar System: Semester
URL: www.huhs.edu
Established: 1985 Annual Undergrad Tuition & Fees: $6,610
Enrollment: 147 Coed
Affiliation or Control: Proprietary IRS Status: Proprietary
Highest Offering: Doctorate
Accreditation: DEAC

01 Chief Executive Officer/President ... Dr. Art PRESSER
05 Provost ... Mr. Gene BRUNO
10 Chief Financial Officer ... Mr. Robert SCHMAEFF
11 Director of Administration ... Ms. Amy STEWART
20 Assoc Director of Academic Affairs ... Vacant
07 Director of Admissions ... Mr. Gregory SCOTT
21 Director of Finance ... Vacant
37 Director of Financial Aid ... Ms. Heather MORRISON-MONGER
06 Registrar ... Ms. Amy STEWART
08 Head Librarian ... Ms. Pam WREN
58 Dean of Graduate Studies ... Mr. Chris NUTTING

The Institute for G.O.D. (C)

401 Center Street, Old Hickory TN 37188
County: Davidson Identification: 667419
Telephone: (615) 879-2022 Carnegie Class: Not Classified
FAX Number: N/A Calendar System: Semester
URL: instituteforgod.org
Established: 2004 Annual Undergrad Tuition & Fees: N/A
Enrollment: N/A Coed
Affiliation or Control: Independent Non-Profit IRS Status: 501(c)3
Highest Offering: Master's
Accreditation: @BI

01 Founder & President ... Gregg GARNER

John A. Gupton College (D)

1616 Church Street, Nashville TN 37203-2920
County: Davidson FICE Identification: 008859
Unit ID: 220464
Telephone: (615) 327-3927 Carnegie Class: Spec 2-yr-A&S
FAX Number: (615) 321-4518 Calendar System: Semester
URL: www.guptoncollege.edu
Established: 1946 Annual Undergrad Tuition & Fees: $11,583
Enrollment: 167 Coed
Affiliation or Control: Independent Non-Profit IRS Status: 501(c)3
Highest Offering: Associate Degree
Accreditation: SC, FUSER

01 President ... Mr. B. Steven SPANN
08 Dir Educational Support/Librarian ... Mr. William P. BRUCE
06 Registrar ... Ms. Lisa MOFFITT

Johnson University (E)

7900 Johnson Drive, Knoxville TN 37998-0001
County: Knox FICE Identification: 003495
Unit ID: 220473
Telephone: (865) 573-4517 Carnegie Class: Spec-4-yr-Faith
FAX Number: (865) 251-2337 Calendar System: Semester
URL: www.johnsonu.edu
Established: 1893 Annual Undergrad Tuition & Fees: $18,290
Enrollment: 1,039 Coed
Affiliation or Control: Christian Churches And Churches of Christ
IRS Status: 501(c)3
Highest Offering: Doctorate
Accreditation: SC, BI, CACREP

01 President ... Dr. Thomas SMITH
05 Provost ... Dr. Greg LINTON
111 VP for Advancement ... Richard CLARK
32 VP for Student Services ... David LEGG
10 VP for Finance ... Cindy BARNARD
11 VP for Administration ... Cliff MCCARTNEY
125 President Emeritus ... Dr. Gary WEEDMAN
49 Dean Arts & Sciences ... Dr. Gary STRATTON
60 Dean Communication & Creative Arts ... Dr. Matthew BROADDUS
73 Dean Congregational Ministry ... Dr. Daniel OVERDORF
82 Dean Intercultural Studies ... Dr. Linda WHITMER
83 Dean Social & Behavioral Sciences ... Dr. Sean RIDGE
53 Dean Templar School of Education ... Dr. Roy MILLER
42 Dean of the Chapel ... Dr. Bill WOLF
20 Director of Program Administration ... Joy WINGFIELD
13 Director of IT ... Glenn FEASTER
41 Athletic Director ... Brandon PERRY
07 Director of Admissions ... Lisa TARWATER
20 Assoc Provost for Online Education ... Dr. John KETCHEN
15 Director Human Resources ... Beverly DARNELL
18 Director of Facilities Services ... Ben LUTZ, JR.
08 Library Director ... Carrie Beth LOWE
09 Director of IE & Accreditation ... Emili WILLIAMS
37 Director of Financial Aid ... Rocky CHRISTENSEN
06 Registrar ... Andrew FRAZIER
121 Director of Academic Support ... Kelly ESTES
35 Assoc Dean of Students ... Deborah LANE

King University (F)

1350 King College Road, Bristol TN 37620-2699
County: Sullivan FICE Identification: 003496
Unit ID: 220516
Telephone: (423) 968-4861 Carnegie Class: Masters/L
FAX Number: (423) 968-4456 Calendar System: Other
URL: www.king.edu
Established: 1867 Annual Undergrad Tuition & Fees: $31,840
Enrollment: 1,746 Coed
Affiliation or Control: Presbyterian Church (U.S.A.) IRS Status: 501(c)3
Highest Offering: Doctorate
Accreditation: SC, NURSE, SW

01 President ... Mr. Alexander W. WHITAKER, IV
05 Provost ... Dr. Matthew ROBERTS
10 Vice President for Admin & Finance ... Mr. James P. DONAHUE
32 Vice President for Student Affairs ... Dr. Robert A. LITTLETON
84 Vice Pres of Enrollment Mgmt ... Dr. Jon HARR
111 Vice President for Advancement ... Mr. Brent DAVISON
100 Chief of Staff ... Vacant
08 Dean of Library Services ... Dr. Matt PELTIER
04 Executive Assistant to President ... Ms. Holly L. STEVENS
06 Registrar/Dir Regist & Records ... Mrs. Jessica SWINEY
110 Associate Director of Development ... Mr. Logan JENNINGS
42 Chaplain ... Dr. Brian ALDERMAN
21 Director of Business Operations ... Mr. Thomas R. LARSON
41 Athletic Director ... Mr. J. David HICKS
38 Director of Counseling ... Ms. Heather C. BRADDOCK
88 Sports Information Director ... Mr. Travis L. CHELL
40 Bookstore Manager ... Ms. Susan D. MARSHALL
37 Director Student Financial Aid ... Ms. Lauren PIZZO
18 Chief Facilities/Physical Plant ... Mr. Todd THOMAS
92 Director of Honors Program ... Dr. Craig STREETMAN
27 Assoc Director of Communication ... Mr. Greg EVANS
36 Director of Career Services ... Ms. Finley GREEN
29 Director Alumni & Cmty Engagement ... Mrs. Jenna M. CHRISTIE
13 Chief Information Officer ... Mr. Joel ROBERTSON
19 Director Safety & Security ... Mr. Benny BERRY
39 Dir Resident Life/Student Housing ... Mr. Chase ARNDT

Lane College (G)

545 Lane Avenue, Jackson TN 38301-4598
County: Madison FICE Identification: 003499
Unit ID: 220598
Telephone: (731) 426-7500 Carnegie Class: Bac-A&S
FAX Number: (731) 427-3987 Calendar System: Semester
URL: www.lanecollege.edu
Established: 1882 Annual Undergrad Tuition & Fees: $11,790
Enrollment: 1,095 Coed
Affiliation or Control: Christian Methodist Episcopal IRS Status: 501(c)3
Highest Offering: Baccalaureate
Accreditation: SC

01 President ... Dr. Logan C. HAMPTON
11 Exec Vice Pres Administration ... Ms. Sherrill B. SCOTT
32 Vice President Student Affairs ... Mr. Darryl MCGEE
13 Assoc VP Information Technology ... Mr. Earnest L. MITCHELL, III
100 Chief of Staff/VP Inst Advancement ... Ms. Darlette C. SAMUELS
42 Head Chaplain ... Dr. Freeman MCKINDRA
09 Director of Financial Aid ... Ms. Regina ANDERSON
08 Librarian ... Ms. Lan WANG
06 Registrar ... Mr. Terry W. BLACKMON
20 Director Academic Assessment ... Vacant
19 Director of Safety/Security ... Mr. Steaven JOY
29 Director Alumni Relations ... Ms. Braylin LASTER
27 Chief Information Officer ... Vacant
86 Dir Gov Relations/Sr Adv to Pres ... Mr. Richard DONNELL, SR.
102 Director of Annual Fund ... Ms. Lisa PEOPLES

Lee University (H)

1120 N Ocoee St, Cleveland TN 37320-3450
County: Bradley FICE Identification: 003500
Unit ID: 220613
Telephone: (423) 614-8000 Carnegie Class: Masters/M
FAX Number: (423) 614-8083 Calendar System: Semester
URL: www.leeuniversity.edu
Established: 1918 Annual Undergrad Tuition & Fees: $19,540
Enrollment: 5,204 Coed
Affiliation or Control: Church Of God IRS Status: 501(c)3
Highest Offering: Doctorate
Accreditation: SC, ACBSP, CAATE, CAEP, CAEPN, MFCD, MUS, NURSE

01 President ... Dr. Mark L. WALKER
04 Executive Assistant to President ... Mrs. Andrea CAMPBELL-BROWN
10 Vice President Business & Finance ... Mr. Chris CONINE
05 Vice President for Academic Affairs ... Dr. Deborah MURRAY
84 Assistant VP for Enrollment ... Dr. Shane GRIFFITH
32 VP for Student Development ... Dr. Mike HAYES
26 VP for University Relations ... Dr. Brad MOFFETT
13 VP for Enrollment & Marketing ... Dr. Jayson VANHOOK
11 VP for Operations ... Mr. Cole STRONG
20 Asst VP Academic Affairs ... Dr. Jean ELEDGE
21 Comptroller/Dir Accounting Services ... Mr. Duane PACE
37 Director of Financial Aid ... Mrs. Marian DILL
35 Dean of Students ... Vacant
15 Director of Human Resources ... Mrs. Amy BALLARD
14 Director of IT Operations ... Mr. Chris GOLDEN
14 Director of IT Systems ... Mr. Nate TUCKER
29 Director of Alumni Relations ... Ms. Susan ASHCRAFT
39 Director of Residential Life ... Mr. Jarad RUSSELL
06 University Registrar ... Mrs. Erin LOONEY
113 Director Student Financial Services ... Ms. Kristy HARNER
08 Director Library Services ... Dr. Louis MORGAN
42 Director of Campus Ministries ... Dr. Rob FULTZ
25 Director of Grants/Foundation ... Mrs. Vanessa HAMMOND
19 Director of Campus Safety ... Mr. Matt BRINKMAN
23 Director of Health Services ... Ms. Rachel COFFEY
27 Director of Public Relations ... Mr. Brian CONN
73 Dean School of Religion ... Dr. Terry CROSS
49 Dean College of Arts & Sciences ... Dr. Matthew MELTON
53 Dean College of Education ... Dr. William ESTES
64 Dean School of Music ... Dr. William GREEN
66 Dean School of Nursing ... Dr. Sara CAMPBELL
51 Exec Dir of Div of Adult Learning ... Dr. Joshua BLACK
50 Dean School of Business ... Dr. Dewayne THOMPSON
123 Director of Graduate Enrollment ... Vacant
38 Director of Counseling Center ... Dr. David QUAGLIANA
18 Dir Physical Plant/Building Svcs ... Mr. Larry BERRY
41 Athletic Director ... Mr. Larry CARPENTER
104 Director of Global Perspectives ... Mrs. Angeline MCMULLIN
36 Dir Center of Calling and Career ... Dr. Sheila CORNEA
07 Director of Admissions ... Mr. Darren ECHOLS
09 Director of Institutional Research ... Mrs. Shannon ROWLAND

LeMoyne-Owen College (I)

807 Walker Avenue, Memphis TN 38126-6595
County: Shelby FICE Identification: 003501
Unit ID: 220604
Telephone: (901) 435-1477 Carnegie Class: Bac-Diverse
FAX Number: (901) 435-1699 Calendar System: Semester
URL: www.loc.edu
Established: 1862 Annual Undergrad Tuition & Fees: $12,076
Enrollment: 654 Coed
Affiliation or Control: Multiple Protestant Denominations
IRS Status: 501(c)3
Highest Offering: Baccalaureate
Accreditation: SC, ACBSP, CAEPN

01 President ... Dr. Vernell BENNETT-FAIRS
05 Provost/VP Academic Affairs ... Dr. Lisa LANG
10 VP Finance and Administration ... Dr. Curtis CREAG
32 Dean of Students ... Ms. Jean SAULSBERRY
111 VP Institutional Advancement ... Vacant
13 VP Information Technology ... Mr. Charles G. ELLIOTT
84 Exec Dir Strategic Enrollment Mgmt ... Vacant
15 Exec Dir Human Resources ... Ms. Shanta BROOKS
22 Director Title III Administration ... Mrs. Angela A. WOOTEN
08 Librarian ... Ms. Stacey SMITH
37 Director Student Financial Services ... Vacant
06 Registrar ... Ms. Mona WASHINGTON
100 Chief of Staff ... Vacant
29 Director of Alumni Relations ... Dr. June CHINN-JOINTER
09 Director Institutional Research ... Mr. Reoungeneria MCFARLAND
92 Director Du Bois Honors Program ... Mr. Dorsey PATTERSON
50 Chair Business/Economic Development ... Dr. Katherine CAUSEY
53 Chair Education Division ... Dr. Ralph CALHOUN
57 Chair Div Fine Arts & Humanities ... Dr. Linda WHITE
65 Chair Div Natural & Math Science ... Dr. Sherry PAINTER
83 Chair Div Social & Behavioral Sci ... Mr. Michael ROBINSON
38 Director Student Counseling ... Mrs. Shalunda ASKEW-ELLIOTT
26 Exec Dir Communications ... Vacant
41 Director of Athletics ... Mr. William ANDERSON
11 Director Administrative Services ... Mr. Jesse CHATMAN
07 Director of Admissions ... Mrs. Wendy HARRIS
04 Administrative Asst to President ... Ms. Velma GRAY
18 Chief Facilities/Physical Plant ... Mr. Anthony COWAN

Lincoln College of Technology Nashville (J)

1524 Gallatin Avenue, Nashville TN 37206-3298
County: Davidson FICE Identification: 007440
Unit ID: 221148
Telephone: (615) 226-3990 Carnegie Class: Spec 2-yr-Tech
FAX Number: (615) 262-8466 Calendar System: Other
URL: www.lincolncollegeoftechnology.com
Established: 1919 Annual Undergrad Tuition & Fees: N/A
Enrollment: 1,638 Coed
Affiliation or Control: Proprietary IRS Status: Proprietary
Highest Offering: Associate Degree
Accreditation: ACCSC

01 President ... Mr. Jim COAKLEY
05 Academic Dean ... Ms. Jackie RODDY
07 Director of Admissions ... Mr. Lawrence HAWKINS
37 Director of Financial Aid ... Mr Chris BIDDLE
36 Director of Career Services ... Ms. Sandra JORDAN

Lincoln Memorial University (A)

6965 Cumberland Gap Parkway,
Harrogate TN 37752-1901

County: Claiborne FICE Identification: 003502
Unit ID: 220631
Telephone: (423) 869-3611 Carnegie Class: DU-Mod
FAX Number: (423) 869-6250 Calendar System: Semester
URL: https://www.lmunet.edu/
Established: 1897 Annual Undergrad Tuition & Fees: $23,490
Enrollment: 4,885 Coed
Affiliation or Control: Independent Non-Profit IRS Status: 501(c)3
Highest Offering: Doctorate
Accreditation: SC, ACBSP, ADNUR, ANEST, ARCPA, CACREP, CAEP, LAW, MT, NUR, OSTEO, PTA, SW, VET

01 President ... Dr. E. Clayton HESS
111 VP University Advancement ... Ms. Cynthia L. WHITT
05 Executive VP Academic Affairs ... Dr. Jay STUBBLEFIELD
10 Exec VP Finance & Administration ... Ms. Christy GRAHAM
35 Assoc Dean Stdnts LMU-DCOM Knox ... Dr. Justina HYFANTIS
35 Assistant Dean of Students LMU-DCOM ... Dr. Kali WEAVER
61 VP/Dean School of Law ... Mr. Matthew LYON
11 Executive VP for Administration ... Dr. Jody GOINS
74 Dean College of Veterinary Med ... Dr. Stacy ANDERSON
63 Dean/CAO College of Osteopathic Med ... Dr. Christopher LOYKE
76 Dean Allied Health Sciences ... Dr. Elizabeth THOMPSON
89 Asst Dean Students/Dir 1st Yr Exp ... Ms. Elise SYOEN
53 Interim Dean of School of Education ... Dr. Teresa BICKNELL
81 Dean of Mathematics & Sciences ... Dr. Adam ROLLINS
66 Dean School of Nursing ... Dr. Tammy DEAN
50 Dean School of Business ... Dr. James MAXWELL
04 Exec Assistant to the President ... Mrs. Janet SMITH
37 Exec Dir Student Financial Services ... Ms. Tammy TOMFOHRDE
46 AVP Planning/Inst Effectiveness ... Dr. Kala PERKINS-HOLTSCLAW
108 Director of Assessment ... Dr. Carlton LARSEN
41 Athletic Director ... Mr. Jasher COX
18 Director Infrastructure Management ... Mr. David LAWS
15 Chief Human Resources Officer ... Ms. Amy EADS
96 Director Purchasing ... Ms. Aprile MASON
06 Registrar ... Ms. Helen BAILEY
42 University Chaplain ... Vacant
43 General Counsel ... Mr. Ryan BROWN
13 Chief Information Officer ... Mr. Jason MCCONNELL
26 Sr Dir Marketing/Public Relations ... Mrs. Katherine M. REAGAN
29 Sr Director Alumni Services ... Ms. Sheliah COSBY
40 Bookstore Manager (Barnes & Noble) ... Mr. Grey JANEWAY
49 Dean of Arts/Humanities/Social Sci ... Dr. Martin SELLERS
88 Special Assistant to the President ... Mr. Tommy THOMAS
63 VP/Dean School of Medical Sciences ... Dr. Mark MORAN
22 Title IX Coord/Ofc Inst Compliance ... Ms. Kelly HAWK
84 Executive Director for Enrollment ... Ms. Lindsay HAYWOOD
08 Director of the Library ... Ms. Rhonda ARMSTRONG
103 Director of Career Services ... Mr. Roger HOLTSCLAW
19 Chief of Campus Police & Security ... Mr. Patrick VAUGHT
25 Exec Director of Grants and Sponsor ... Ms. Carolyn GULLEY
28 Director for Inclusion & Diversity ... Ms. Wanda ELDAHAN
32 Assoc Dean of Student Affairs CVM ... Dr. Bess PIERCE
38 Director Mental Health Counseling ... Dr. Jason KISHPAUGH
44 Asst Dir of Alumni & Annual Giving ... Mr. Jared ZANET

Lipscomb University (B)

One University Park Dr., Nashville TN 37204-3951

County: Davidson FICE Identification: 003486
Unit ID: 219976
Telephone: (615) 966-1000 Carnegie Class: DU-Mod
FAX Number: (615) 966-1798 Calendar System: Semester
URL: www.lipscomb.edu
Established: 1891 Annual Undergrad Tuition & Fees: $34,744
Enrollment: 4,884 Coed
Affiliation or Control: Churches Of Christ IRS Status: 501(c)3
Highest Offering: Doctorate
Accreditation: SC, ACBSP, #ARCPA, CACREP, CAEP, DIETD, DIETI, MFCD, MUS, NUR, PHAR, SW, THEOL

01 President ... Dr. Candice MCQUEEN
05 Provost ... Dr. W. Craig BLEDSOE
45 SVP for Strategy ... Dr. Susan C. GALBREATH
10 Senior VP Finance & Technology ... Mr. Jeffrey BAUGHN
111 SVP Advancement ... Dr. John LOWRY
32 SVP Enroll Mgmt/Student Engagement ... Dr. Matt PADEN
43 General Counsel ... Dr. David WILSON
23 Director of Health and Wellness ... Dr. Kevin EIDSON
26 VP Marketing ... Mr. Dave BRUNO
21 VP Finance ... Mr. Darrell DUNCAN
15 VP Human Resources ... Ms. Christy HOOPER
13 VP Information Technology ... Mr. Brett HINSON
41 Director of Athletics ... Mr. Philip HUTCHESON
27 VP University Relations ... Mr. Walt LEAVER
84 VP Enrollment Management ... Mr. Byron LEWIS
42 VP Church Services ... Dr. Scott SAGER
35 VP of Student Life ... Vacant
22 Spec Counsel for Diversity/Inclus ... Dr. William L. TURNER
20 Vice Provost for Academic Affairs ... Dr. Randy BOULDIN
17 Vice Provost of Health Affairs ... Dr. Quincy BYRDSONG
28 Assoc Prov Diversity & Inclusion ... Dr. Norma BURGESS
88 Vice Provost for Inst Effectiveness ... Dr. Elaine GRIFFIN
20 Associate Provost Academic Support ... Mr. Steve PREWITT
108 Assoc Provost Inst Effectiveness ... Dr. Catherine TERRY
06 Registrar ... Ms. Angel BEBOUT
73 Dean College of Bible & Ministry ... Dr. C. Leonard ALLEN
53 Dean Col of Education ... Dr. Trace HEBERT
49 Dean Col of Liberal Arts & Sciences ... Dr. David HOLMES
67 Dean College of Pharmacy ... Dr. Tom CAMPBELL
66 Executive Director Nursing ... Dr. Chelsia HARRIS
50 Dean College of Business ... Dr. Ray ELDRIDGE
54 Dean College of Engineering ... Mr. David ELROD
57 Dean Shinn Col Ent & Arts ... Mr. Mike FERNANDEZ
80 Dean Col Leadership & Public Svc ... Dr. Steve JOINER
77 Dean School of Computing/Technology .. Dr. Steve NORDSTROM
106 Int Exec Dir Col of Prof Studies ... Mr. Ted MEYER
08 Director of Library Services ... Ms. Julie HARSTON
88 Asst Dean Intercultural Development ... Mr. Prentice ASHFORD
73 Assoc Dean Hazelip Sch of Theology ... Dr. Frank GUERTIN
88 Dean Vocation/Spiritual Formation ... Mr. Deron SMITH
88 Director Academic Finance ... Ms. Carol LUSK
88 Found Dir Inst for Sustain Practice ... Mr. Dodd GALBREATH
88 Dir Inst for Law Justice & Society ... Ms. Kimberly MCCALL
88 Dir Inst for Civic Leadership ... Ms. Sara OESER
103 Director of Career Development Ctr ... Dr. Monica WENTWORTH
83 Chair Grad Studies in Psychology ... Dr. Shanna RAY
09 Director of Institutional Research ... Mr. Matt REHBEIN
38 Director Counseling Center ... Ms. Andrea MILLS
88 Dir Inst for Christian Spirituality ... Dr. Kris MILLER
19 ED of Campus Security & Safety ... Mr. Kyle DICKERSON
86 Director Community & Govt Relations ... Ms. Amanda MARTIN
07 Asst VP of Undergrad Admissions ... Mr. Johnathan AKIN
39 Dean of Housing and Residence Life ... Ms. Laurie SAIN
37 Assoc VP Student Financial Services ... Mr. Ron ANDERSON
44 Asst VP Annual Giving & Advanc Svcs ... Vacant
18 Director Campus Constr & Facilities ... Mr. Mike ENGELMAN
104 Director Global Learning ... Ms. Rebecca ZANOLINI
04 Admin Assistant to the President ... Ms. Leslie LANDISS

Maryville College (C)

502 E Lamar Alexander Parkway,
Maryville TN 37804-5907

County: Blount FICE Identification: 003505
Unit ID: 220710
Telephone: (865) 981-8000 Carnegie Class: Bac-Diverse
FAX Number: (865) 981-8010 Calendar System: Semester
URL: www.maryvillecollege.edu
Established: 1819 Annual Undergrad Tuition & Fees: $36,292
Enrollment: 1,072 Coed
Affiliation or Control: Independent Non-Profit IRS Status: 501(c)3
Highest Offering: Master's
Accreditation: SC, MUS

01 President ... Dr. Bryan F. COKER
04 Assistant to President ... Ms. Suzette DONOVAN
00 Chairman of the Board ... Dr. Cole PIPER
05 Vice Pres & Dean of College ... Dr. Dan KLINGENSMITH
10 VP of Finance & Administration ... Mr. Jeffery S. INGLE
32 Vice President & Dean of Students ... Dr. Melanie V. TUCKER
111 VP for Institutional Advancement ... Ms. Suzy BOOKER
07 VP for Admissions & Financial Aid ... Ms. Alayne BOWMAN
26 Exec Dir for Mktg & Communications ... Ms. Karen ELDRIDGE
45 Exec Director Strategic Initiatives ... Ms. Christy MCDONALD SLAVICK
20 Associate Dean & Director of IR ... Dr. Jerilyn SWANN
121 Asst Dean of Academic Success ... Ms. Jan TAYLOR
06 Registrar ... Ms. Kathi WILSON
21 Controller ... Ms. Kelly LEONARD
35 Assistant Dean of Students ... Ms. Kristin GOURLEY
104 Director of International Education ... Ms. Kirsten SHEPPARD
13 Director of Information Technology ... Mr. John BERRY
121 Director Academic Support Center ... Ms. Kim D. OCHSENBEIN
36 Director of the Career Center ... Ms. Sarah TAYLOR-YEAPLE
37 Director of Financial Aid ... Ms. Erin JOHNSON
41 Athletic Director ... Ms. Sara QUATROCKY
08 Director of the Library ... Ms. Angela QUICK
18 Director of Physical Plant ... Mr. Reggie DAILEY
42 Campus Minister ... Rev. Anne MCKEE
15 Director of Human Resources ... Ms. Keni LANAGAN
38 Director of Counseling ... Ms. Claudia WERNER
30 Director of Development ... Mr. Eric BELLAH
29 Director of Alumni Affairs ... Ms. Angie HARRIS
112 Director of Major Gifts ... Ms. Diana CANACARIS
28 Director of Multicultural Affairs ... Mr. Larry ERVIN
40 Bookstore Manager ... Mr. Ryan LILLY
88 Gen Mgr Clayton Center for the Arts ... Mr. Blake SMITH
19 Director of Safety & Security ... Mr. John MCMURTRIE
39 Asst Director Housing Operations ... Ms. Raeann REIHL
44 Director Annual Giving ... Ms. Meghan FAGG
09 Director of Institutional Research ... Dr. Jerilyn SWANN

Meharry Medical College (D)

1005 Dr. D. B. Todd Jr. Boulevard,
Nashville TN 37208-3501

County: Davidson FICE Identification: 003506
Unit ID: 220792
Telephone: (615) 327-6111 Carnegie Class: Spec-4-yr-Med
FAX Number: (615) 327-6540 Calendar System: Semester
URL: www.mmc.edu
Established: 1876 Annual Graduate Tuition & Fees: N/A
Enrollment: 944 Coed
Affiliation or Control: Independent Non-Profit IRS Status: 501(c)3
Highest Offering: Doctorate; No Undergraduates
Accreditation: SC, DENT, MED, PH

01 President/Chief Executive Ofcr ... Dr. James E.K HILDRETH, SR.
05 Exec Vice Dean School ... Vacant
03 EVP for Administration ... Dr. Peter E. MILLET
63 Int Dean School of Medicine ... Dr. Digna FORBES
11 Sr Vice Pres for BOT Relations ... Dr. Saletta HOLLOWAY
26 VP Marketing/Communications ... Vacant
10 Sr Vice President Finance/CFO ... Mrs. LaMel BANDY-NEAL
32 Sr Vice Pres Student Affairs ... Dr. A. Dexter SAMUELS
58 Int Dean School of Graduate Studies ... Dr. Evangeline MOTLEY JOHNSON
20 Int VP Faculty Affairs ... Dr. Allysceaeioun BRITT
13 CIO/Ellucian Contract ... Mr. Dennis GENDRON
15 Assoc Vice Pres Human Resources ... Mr. Mark SMITH
21 Assoc Vice Pres Financial Systems ... Mr. Larry HOLDEN
111 SVP Institutional Advancement ... Mr. Patrick H. JOHNSON
25 Asst Controller Grants/Contracts ... Ms. Zulfat A. SUARA
43 SVP/General Counsel/Corp Sec ... Mrs. Ivanetta DAVIS-SAMUELS
46 SVP Research/Innovation ... Dr. Anil SHANKER
51 Director Lifelong Learning ... Dr. Allyson FLEMING
76 Dean Allied Health Professions ... Vacant
52 SVP & Dean School of Dentistry ... Dr. Cherae FARMER-DIXON
81 SVP/Dean Sch App Computational Sci ... Dr. Fortune MHLANGA
29 Executive Director Alumni Affairs ... Dr. Henry MOSES
07 Dir Admissions & Recruitment ... Ms. April E. CURRY-ROBERTS
08 Director of Library ... Vacant
19 Int Dir Campus Safety & Security ... Mr. Dontez HUSKEY
37 Director Student Financial Aid ... Ms. Barbara THARPE
09 Director Institutional Research ... Dr. Chau-Kuang CHEN
100 Chief of Staff/Dir Title III Adm ... Mrs. Sandra ANDERSON-WILLIAMS
18 Director Facilities ... Mr. Lewis ETHRIDGE
38 Director Counseling Center ... Ms. Sharda D. MISHRA
06 Registrar ... Ms. Miacia PORTER
04 Executive Assistant to the Pres ... Ms. Kimberly STEVENSON

Memphis Theological Seminary (E)

168 East Parkway S at Union, Memphis TN 38104-4395

County: Shelby FICE Identification: 010529
Unit ID: 220871
Telephone: (901) 458-8232 Carnegie Class: Spec-4-yr-Faith
FAX Number: (901) 452-4051 Calendar System: Semester
URL: www.memphisseminary.edu
Established: 1852 Annual Graduate Tuition & Fees: N/A
Enrollment: 183 Coed
Affiliation or Control: Cumberland Presbyterian IRS Status: 501(c)3
Highest Offering: Doctorate; No Undergraduates
Accreditation: SC, THEOL

01 President ... Dr. Jody HILL
05 Vice President Academic Affs & Dean ... Dr. Peter GATHJE
10 Vice President of Operations/CFO ... Cassandra F. PRICE-PERRY
84 VP Enrollment Services & IE ... Dr. Gail ROBINSON
08 Director of Library Services ... Ed HUGHES
32 Exec Director of Student Services ... Dr. Barry L. ANDERSON
06 Dir Acad Rec/Regist & Accreditation ... Dr. Gail D. ROBINSON
07 Dir of Admission/Financial Aid ... Fekecia GUNN
36 Director Student Placement ... Barry ANDERSON
90 Director Academic Computing ... Chris SMITH

Meridian Institute of Surgical Assisting (F)

1507 County Hospital Road, Nashville TN 37218

County: Davidson FICE Identification: 041650
Unit ID: 461324
Telephone: (877) 954-1500 Carnegie Class: Spec 2-yr-Health
FAX Number: (615) 746-6765 Calendar System: Semester
URL: www.meridian-institute.edu
Established: 1999 Annual Undergrad Tuition & Fees: N/A
Enrollment: 816 Coed
Affiliation or Control: Proprietary IRS Status: Proprietary
Highest Offering: Associate Degree
Accreditation: ABHES, SURGA, SURTEC

01 President ... Mr. Dennis STOVER
05 Dean of Academic Affairs ... Mr. Roy G. ZACHARIAS
10 CFO ... Ms. April WEST

Mid-America Baptist Theological Seminary (G)

2095 Appling Road, Cordova TN 38016-4911

County: Shelby FICE Identification: 029172
Telephone: (901) 751-8453 Carnegie Class: Not Classified
FAX Number: (901) 751-8454 Calendar System: Semester
URL: www.mabts.edu
Established: 1972 Annual Undergrad Tuition & Fees: N/A
Enrollment: N/A Coed
Affiliation or Control: Independent Non-Profit IRS Status: 501(c)3
Highest Offering: Doctorate
Accreditation: SC

01 President ... Dr. Michael R. SPRADLIN
03 Exec Vice Pres/Dean of the College ... Dr. Bradley THOMPSON
05 Vice Pres/Dean of the Seminary ... Dr. Lee BRAND, JR.
10 Vice Pres for Finance & Operations ... Mr. Randy REDD

111 VP of Institutional Advancement ... Mr. Nathan COLE
12 Director NE Branch ... Dr. Michael HAGGARD
06 Registrar ... Mrs. Rose MINK
08 Director of Library Services ... Mr. Terrence BROWN
04 Admin Assistant to the President ... Ms. Cary Beth DUFFEL

Mid-South Christian College (A)

PO Box 181056, Memphis TN 38181
County: Shelby Identification: 667046
Unit ID: 481225
Telephone: (901) 375-4400 Carnegie Class: Spec-4-yr-Faith
FAX Number: N/A Calendar System: Semester
URL: www.midsouthchristian.edu
Established: 1959 Annual Undergrad Tuition & Fees: $9,215
Enrollment: 22 Coed
Affiliation or Control: Independent Non-Profit IRS Status: 501(c)3
Highest Offering: Baccalaureate
Accreditation: BI

01 President ... Mr. Larry GRIFFIN
05 Academic Dean ... Dr. Robert GRIFFIN
04 Executive Assistant ... Mrs. Jane GIBSON
06 Registrar ... Mr. Keith GRAHAM
08 Head Librarian ... Mrs. Judi HOMAN
10 Business Manager ... Mrs. Renae MASK
32 Director of Student Services ... Mr. John BLIFFEN

Middle Tennessee School of Anesthesia (B)

315 Hospital Drive, Madison TN 37115
County: Davidson FICE Identification: 007783
Unit ID: 220996
Telephone: (615) 868-6503 Carnegie Class: Spec-4-yr-Other Health
FAX Number: (615) 868-9885 Calendar System: Quarter
URL: www.mtsa.edu
Established: 1950 Annual Graduate Tuition & Fees: N/A
Enrollment: 229 Coed
Affiliation or Control: Independent Non-Profit IRS Status: 501(c)3
Highest Offering: Doctorate; No Undergraduates
Accreditation: SC, ANEST

01 President ... Dr. Christopher P. HULIN
05 Dean/VP Academics ... Dr. Mana OVERSTREET
10 VP for Finance & Administration ... Jon RONNING
111 VP for Advancement & Alumni ... James B. CLOSSER
20 Program Administrator ... Dr. Rusty GENTRY
09 Dir of Inst Effectiveness & LR ... Dr. Amy C. GIDEON
07 Coord Admissions/Recruitment ... Pam NIMMO
13 Director Information Technology ... Aaron HASTINGS
37 Director Financial Aid ... Jennifer SPEER
06 Registrar ... Jessica CREASON

Middle Tennessee State University (C)

1301 E Main Street, Murfreesboro TN 37132-0001
County: Rutherford FICE Identification: 003510
Unit ID: 220978
Telephone: (615) 898-2300 Carnegie Class: DU-Mod
FAX Number: N/A Calendar System: Semester
URL: www.mtsu.edu
Established: 1911 Annual Undergrad Tuition & Fees (In-State): $9,070
Enrollment: 22,080 Coed
Affiliation or Control: State IRS Status: 501(c)3
Highest Offering: Doctorate
Accreditation: SC, AAB, AAFCS, ART, CAATE, CACREP, CAEPN, CAPRT, CIDA, DIETD, JOUR, MUS, NAIT, NURSE, SW, THEA

02 President ... Dr. Sidney A. MCPHEE
05 University Provost ... Dr. Mark E. BYRNES
10 VP Business & Finance ... Mr. Alan R. THOMAS
111 VP University Advancement ... Mr. William J. BALES
32 VP Student Affairs ... Dr. Debra K. SELLS
13 VP Info Tech/Chief Info Officer ... Mr. Bruce PETRYSHAK
26 VP Marketing/Communications ... Mr. Andrew J. OPPMANN
58 Vice Prov Research/Dean Grad Stds ... Dr. David L. BUTLER
121 Vice Prov Student Success ... Dr. Richard D. SLUDER
43 Univ Counsel & Board Secretary ... Mr. James C. FLOYD
100 Exec Asst to Pres & Chief of Staff ... Ms. Kimberly S. EDGAR
22 Asst to Pres for Equity/Compliance ... Ms. Christy SIGLER
20 Vice Provost Faculty Affairs ... Dr. Cheryl B. TORSNEY
20 Assoc Prov Academic Resources ... Ms. Rebecca COLE
45 Assoc Prov Strategic Planning ... Dr. Mary S. HOFFSCHWELLE
07 Assoc Vice Prov Enrollment Svcs ... Dr. Laurie B. WITHEROW
14 Assoc Vice Pres Info Technology ... Mr. Tom WALLACE
21 Assoc Vice Pres Business Office ... Ms. Kathy THURMAN
35 Assoc Vice Pres/Dean Student Life ... Ms. Sarah SUDAK
15 Asst Vice Pres Human Resource Svcs ... Ms. Kathy I. MUSSELMAN
18 Asst Vice Pres Facilities Services ... Mr. Joe WHITEFIELD
11 Asst Vice Pres Admin/Business Svcs ... Ms. Kimberly WILLIAMS
91 Senior Associate VP for ITD ... Mrs. Lisa C. ROGERS
90 Asst Vice Pres Acad & Instruct Tech ... Dr. Albert C. WHITTENBERG
81 Dean Col Basic/Applied Sciences ... Dr. Paul G. VAN PATTEN
83 Dean College Behavioral & Hlth Sci ... Dr. Harold D. WHITESIDE
60 Dean College of Media/Entertainment ... Ms. Beverly KEEL
50 Dean College of Business ... Dr. David J. URBAN
53 Dean College of Education ... Dr. Frederick P. VANOSDALL
49 Dean College of Liberal Arts ... Dr. Leah T. LYONS
92 Dean University Honors College ... Dr. John R. VILE
08 Dean University Library ... Ms. Kathleen SCHMAND
106 Chief Online Learning Officer ... Dr. Trey MARTINDALE
09 Asst Vice Provost for IEPR ... Mr. Chris BREWER
36 Dir Career & Development Center ... Ms. Beka CROCKET
88 Assoc Vice Prov Student Success ... Mr. Vincent L. WINDROW
37 Dir of Financial Aid & Scholarship ... Mr. Stephen F. WHITE
25 Dir Research & Sponsored Programs ... Dr. Dawn M. MCCORMACK
29 Director Alumni Relations ... Ms. Ginger C. FREEMAN
40 General Manager Bookstore ... Ms. Natalie KAROUSATOS
24 Dir Center for Educational Media ... Dr. Laura B. CLARK
38 Director Counseling Services ... Dr. Mary Kaye G. ANDERSON
30 Director Development Office ... Ms. Patricia BRANAM
84 Dir Enrollment Technical Systems ... Ms. Teresa W. THOMAS
27 Director News & Media Relations ... Mr. Jimmy W. HART
41 Director of Athletics ... Mr. Chris J. MASSARO
23 Director of Student Health Services ... Mr. Richard L. CHAPMAN
06 Registrar ... Ms. Susan FIELDHOUSE
19 Chief of Police/Dir Public Safety ... Mr. Kevin H. WILLIAMS
39 Dir Resident Life/Student Housing ... Ms. Michelle SAFEWRIGHT
96 Executive Director of Procurement ... Mr. Shirman THOMAS
104 Director Education Abroad ... Ms. Melissa C. MILLER
85 Vice Provost International Affairs ... Dr. Robert SUMMERS
44 Director Annual Giving ... Ms. Kristen KEENE

Miller-Motte Technical College (D)

6397 Lee Highway, Suite 100, Chattanooga TN 37421
Telephone: (423) 414-3247 Identification: 770781
Accreditation: ACCSC, SURGT

† Branch campus of Platt College, Tulsa, OK.

Milligan University (E)

PO Box 500, Milligan TN 37682
County: Carter FICE Identification: 003511
Unit ID: 486901
Telephone: (423) 461-8700 Carnegie Class: Masters/M
FAX Number: (423) 461-8755 Calendar System: Semester
URL: www.milligan.edu
Established: 1866 Annual Undergrad Tuition & Fees: $35,600
Enrollment: 1,338 Coed
Affiliation or Control: Independent Non-Profit IRS Status: 501(c)3
Highest Offering: Doctorate
Accreditation: SC, ACBSP, #ARCPA, CACREP, CAEPN, NURSE, OT, THEOL

01 President ... Dr. William B. GREER
05 Vice Pres Academic Affairs/Dean ... Dr. Garland YOUNG
32 Dean of Students ... Mr. Tony JONES
111 Vice Pres Institutional Advancement ... Mrs. Rhajon SMITH
84 Vice Pres Enrollment Management ... Dr. Lee HARRISON
10 Vice Pres Business & Finance ... Mrs. Jacqui STEADMAN
06 Registrar ... Mrs. Stacy DAHLMAN
07 Director of Admissions ... Mr. Marty RILEY
08 Director of Library Services ... Mr. Gary DAUGHT
35 Director of Student Activities ... Mrs. Brealle DAVIS
29 Director of Alumni Rels/Development ... Ms. Theresa GARBE
15 Director Human Resources ... Ms. Leslie BEAN
09 Director of Institutional Research ... Ms. Brenda BOURN
37 Director of Financial Aid ... Mr. Gus MORGAN
88 Director of Church Relations ... Mr. Kit DOTSON
36 Director Student Placement ... Ms. Beth ANDERSON
18 Service Manager Facilities ... Mr. Ken BROYLES
28 Director Multicultural Engagement ... Ms. Gwen ELLIS
26 Director of Marketing ... Ms. Chandrea SHELL
19 Director Property & Risk Management ... Mr. Brent NIPPER
90 Director of Information Technology ... Mrs. Amanda BRISTOL
04 Admin Assistant to the President ... Ms. Kathy BARNES
38 Director Student Counseling ... Dr. Rebecca SAPP
41 Director of Athletics ... Mr. Christian POPE

New College Franklin (F)

136 3rd Ave South, PO Box 1575, Franklin TN 37064
County: Williamson Identification: 667390
Telephone: (615) 815-8360 Carnegie Class: Not Classified
FAX Number: N/A Calendar System: Semester
URL: www.newcollegefranklin.org
Established: 2006 Annual Undergrad Tuition & Fees: N/A
Enrollment: N/A Coed
Affiliation or Control: Independent Non-Profit IRS Status: 501(c)3
Highest Offering: Baccalaureate
Accreditation: TRACS

01 President ... Gregory WILBUR
05 Dean of Academics ... Brandon SPUN
32 Dean of Students ... Tammy MCCOY

North Central Institute (G)

168 Jack Miller Boulevard, Clarksville TN 37042-4810
County: Montgomery FICE Identification: 030791
Unit ID: 418889
Telephone: (931) 431-9700 Carnegie Class: Spec 2-yr-Tech
FAX Number: (931) 431-9771 Calendar System: Semester
URL: www.nci.edu
Established: 1988 Annual Undergrad Tuition & Fees: N/A
Enrollment: 62 Coed
Affiliation or Control: Proprietary IRS Status: Proprietary
Highest Offering: Associate Degree
Accreditation: COE

01 President ... Tamela K. TALIENTO
06 Registrar ... Michelle HARTSON
07 Dean of Admissions ... Dale WOOD
37 Director of Financial Aid ... Michelle HARTSON
13 Director of Information Technology ... Leo JORDAN
10 Comptroller ... Patricia BELL

Nossi College of Art (H)

590 Creative Way, Nashville TN 37115
County: Davidson FICE Identification: 025782
Unit ID: 368452
Telephone: (615) 514-2787 Carnegie Class: Spec-4-yr-Arts
FAX Number: (615) 514-2788 Calendar System: Trimester
URL: www.nossi.edu
Established: 1973 Annual Undergrad Tuition & Fees: $19,150
Enrollment: 289 Coed
Affiliation or Control: Proprietary IRS Status: Proprietary
Highest Offering: Baccalaureate
Accreditation: ACCSC

01 President ... Ms. Nossi VATANDOOST
03 Executive Vice President ... Mr. Cyrus VATANDOOST
05 Vice President for Academic Affairs ... Dr. Byron EDWARDS
07 Admissions Director ... Mrs. Mitzi HATFIELD
06 Registrar ... Mrs. Mindy GILBERT
08 Head Librarian ... Mrs. Kolleen LONGMIRE
26 Chief Public Relations/Marketing ... Mrs. Libby LUFF
10 Business Office Manager ... Mrs. Rachel DEWAAL
36 Director Student Placement ... Mr. Barry HOWARD

Omega Graduate School (I)

500 Oxford Drive, Dayton TN 37321-6736
County: Rhea FICE Identification: 038403
Unit ID: 461120
Telephone: (423) 775-6596 Carnegie Class: Spec-4-yr-Other
FAX Number: (423) 775-6599 Calendar System: Semester
URL: www.ogs.edu
Established: 1981 Annual Graduate Tuition & Fees: N/A
Enrollment: 77 Coed
Affiliation or Control: Independent Non-Profit IRS Status: 501(c)3
Highest Offering: Doctorate; No Undergraduates
Accreditation: TRACS

01 President ... Dr. Joshua REICHARD
00 Chancellor ... Dr. David ANDERSON
05 Dean of Faculty ... Dr. Cathie HUGHES
11 Vice President of Administration ... Vacant
32 Chief Student Success Officer ... Dr. Curtis MCCLANE
108 Director of Assessment ... Dr. Joshua REICHARD
10 Chief Finance & Operations Officer ... Ms. Sharlene DANIEL
29 Director Alumni Relations ... Vacant
62 Director of Library Science ... Dr. David WARD
06 Registrar ... Mr. Richard GAMBLE
08 Librarian ... Ms. Sarah LAMBERT
26 Dir Public Relations/Marketing ... Vacant

Pentecostal Theological Seminary (J)

900 Walker Street, NE, Cleveland TN 37311
County: Bradley FICE Identification: 021883
Unit ID: 219842
Telephone: (423) 478-1131 Carnegie Class: Spec-4-yr-Faith
FAX Number: (423) 478-7711 Calendar System: 4/1/4
URL: www.ptseminary.edu
Established: 1975 Annual Graduate Tuition & Fees: N/A
Enrollment: 442 Coed
Affiliation or Control: Church Of God IRS Status: 501(c)3
Highest Offering: Doctorate; No Undergraduates
Accreditation: SC, THEOL

01 President ... Dr. Michael L. BAKER
05 Dean of Faculty/VP for Academics ... Dr. David S. HAN
108 VP for Inst Effect/Accreditation ... Dr. Oliver L. MCMAHAN
10 Director of Finance ... Mr. Caleb PEACOCK
04 Exec Assistant to the President ... Mrs. Connie MERCER
06 Director of Acad Records/Registrar ... Ms. Anita F. BLEVINS
15 Director of Human Resources ... Mrs. Joylita W. TERPSTRA
18 Dir of Facilities/Support Services ... Mr. Phillip WOOD
32 Sr Dir of Student Svcs & Cmty Life ... Dr. Welton WRISTON
37 Director of Financial Aid ... Mrs. Robin SLUDER
07 Director of Admissions ... Mr. Lee SEALS
106 Director Online Learning ... Dr. Robert BLACKABY
29 Director of Alumni Relations ... Mrs. Sharon BAKER
13 Director of Information Technology ... Mr. Ken L. SMITH
36 Director Student Placement ... Dr. Daniel D. TOMBERLIN

Remington College (K)

2710 Nonconnah Boulevard, Memphis TN 38132-2110
Telephone: (901) 345-1000 Identification: 666062
Accreditation: ACCSC

† Branch campus of Remington College, Mobile, AL.

Remington College (L)

441 Donelson Pike, Suite 150, Nashville TN 37214-3558
Telephone: (615) 889-5520 Identification: 666307
Accreditation: ACCSC, DH

† Branch campus of Remington College, Mobile, AL.

Rhodes College (A)

2000 North Parkway, Memphis TN 38112-1690
County: Shelby FICE Identification: 003519
Unit ID: 221351
Telephone: (901) 843-3000 Carnegie Class: Bac-A&S
FAX Number: N/A Calendar System: Semester
URL: www.rhodes.edu
Established: 1848 Annual Undergrad Tuition & Fees: $50,910
Enrollment: 1,875 Coed
Affiliation or Control: Presbyterian Church (U.S.A.) IRS Status: 501(c)3
Highest Offering: Master's
Accreditation: SC, MUS

01 Interim President .... Mr. Carroll STEVENS
100 Exec Assistant to the President .... Ms. Melody H. RICHEY
05 Provost .... Dr. Kathy BASSARD
32 VP for Student Life .... Dr. Meghan HARTE WEYANT
10 VP for Finance & Business Affairs .... Mr. Kyle WEBB
30 Vice President for Development .... Ms. Jennifer G. WADE
84 Vice Pres Enrollment/Communications .... Mr. Carey THOMPSON
45 Vice Pres of Strategic Initiatives .... Dr. Sherry TURNER
13 Chief Information Officer .... Mr. Jose RODRIGUEZ
35 Dean of Students .... Dr. Alicia GOLSTON
121 Assoc Dean of Students/Acad Support .... Dr. Jamia STOKES
20 Associate Provost .... Dr. Tim HUEBNER
06 Registrar .... Ms. Amanda MAXSON
37 Director of Financial Aid .... Mr. Michael MORGAN
08 Director of Info Services .... Ms. Darlene D. BROOKS
29 Director of Alumni Relations .... Ms. Tracy PATTERSON
15 Director of Human Resources .... Ms. Claire R. SHAPIRO
14 Director of Info Services .... Mr. Richard TRENTHEM
19 Director of Campus Safety .... Mr. Ike SLOAS
41 Director of Athletics .... Mr. Jim DUNCAN
36 Director of Career Services .... Ms. Sandra G. TRACY
38 Director of Counseling Services .... Ms. Pam DETRIE
18 Director of Physical Plant .... Mr. Brian E. FOSHEE
26 Director of Communications .... Mr. Dylan SANDIFER
09 Director of Institutional Research .... Ms. Jill TRIPLETT ELLIS
07 Director of Admission .... Ms. Megan STARLING
108 Director of Assessment .... Mr. Brian BRASKICH
31 Director of Community Relations .... Ms. Kerri CAMPBELL
44 Director of Annual Giving .... Ms. Jessi WILSON
110 Senior Director of Development .... Ms. Amanda TAMBURRINO
112 Director of Golden Lynx Program .... Dr. Nichole SOULE
21 Senior Associate Comptroller .... Ms. Wanda JONES
25 Director of Grants .... Ms. Lydia SPENCER
04 Exec Admin Asst to the President .... Ms. Kristen H. HUNT
39 Director Resident Life .... Ms. Aretha MILLIGAN

Richmont Graduate University (B)

1815 McCallie Avenue, Chattanooga TN 37404
County: Hamilton FICE Identification: 033554
Unit ID: 441104
Telephone: (423) 266-4574 Carnegie Class: Spec-4-yr-Other Health
FAX Number: (423) 265-7375 Calendar System: Semester
URL: www.richmont.edu
Established: 1933 Annual Graduate Tuition & Fees: N/A
Enrollment: 296 Coed
Affiliation or Control: Independent Non-Profit IRS Status: 501(c)3
Highest Offering: Master's; No Undergraduates
Accreditation: SC, CACREP

01 President .... Dr. Timothy QUINNAN
05 Acting Provost .... Dr. Josh RICE
10 VP of Finance .... Mr. Tim MCPHERSON
13 VP of Information Technology .... Mr. Darwin BLANDON
11 VP of Administration .... Ms. Roxanne SHELLABARGER
88 VP of Integration .... Dr. Dan SARTOR
32 Dean of Students .... Dr. Amanda BLACKBURN
73 Dean School of Ministry .... Dr. Josh RICE
88 Dean School of Counseling .... Dr. Stephen BRADSHAW
88 Asst Dean of Clinical Affairs .... Ms. Jama WHITE
100 Chief of Staff .... Mr. Philip BURNS
08 Director of Libraries .... Mr. Ron BUNGER
09 Director of Institutional Research .... Dr. Mary PLISCO
108 Dir Institutional Effectiveness .... Mr. Peter BRINDLEY
18 Facilities & IT Manager .... Mr. Neil ANDERSON
26 Director of Communications .... Ms. Talia ASHLEY
29 Director Alumni Relations .... Ms. Martha BUSBY
30 Director of Development .... Ms. Amy ESTES
37 Director of Financial Aid .... Ms. Laura LILLARD
07 AVP Enrollment Mgmt .... Mr. Tyson FANT

SAE Institute Nashville (C)

7 Music Circle North, Nashville TN 37203
County: Davidson FICE Identification: 038303
Unit ID: 446525
Telephone: (615) 244-5848 Carnegie Class: Spec 2-yr-Tech
FAX Number: (615) 244-3192 Calendar System: Other
URL: nashville.sae.edu
Established: 1976 Annual Undergrad Tuition & Fees: $33,199
Enrollment: 211 Coed
Affiliation or Control: Proprietary IRS Status: Proprietary
Highest Offering: Baccalaureate
Accreditation: ACCSC

01 Campus Director .... Shannon MEGGERT
05 Director of Education .... Ryan GRIFFIN
06 Registrar .... Robin GARCIA
07 Director of Admissions .... Gail MUSSER
10 Chief Financial/Business Officer .... Luis MATA
11 Chief of Operations/Administration .... Jake ELSEN
36 Director Student Placement .... David ANDRIS
37 Director Student Financial Aid .... Shelly PICINICH
53 Dean of Education .... Gabriel JONES
84 Director Enrollment Management .... Sarah SIZEMORE

Sewanee: The University of the South (D)

735 University Avenue, Sewanee TN 37383-1000
County: Franklin FICE Identification: 003534
Unit ID: 221519
Telephone: (931) 598-1000 Carnegie Class: Bac-A&S
FAX Number: (931) 598-1145 Calendar System: Semester
URL: www.sewanee.edu
Established: 1857 Annual Undergrad Tuition & Fees: $47,980
Enrollment: 1,800 Coed
Affiliation or Control: Protestant Episcopal IRS Status: 501(c)3
Highest Offering: Doctorate
Accreditation: SC, THEOL

01 Vice Chancellor & President .... Dr. Reuben E. BRIGETY, II
05 Senior Vice President and Provost .... Dr. Nancy BERNER
111 Vice President for Univ Relations .... Mr. Jay FISHER
88 Special Asst to VC for SI .... Ms. Karen PROCTOR
13 Assoc Provost Info Tech/Librarian .... Dr. Vicki G. SELLS
49 Vice Provost/Dean of College .... Dr. Terry L. PAPILLON
73 VP/Dean of the School of Theology .... Rev. James TURRELL
32 AProv Stdnt Life/Dean of Students .... Ms. Erica HOWARD
09 Asst Prov Academic Svcs/Inst Rsrch .... Dr. Paul G. WILEY
07 Assoc Prov/Dean of Admiss & Fin Aid .... Mr. Alan RAMIREZ
37 Assoc Dean Student Financial Aid .... Ms. Beth CRAGAR
20 Associate Dean for Academic Affairs .... Dr. Alex M. BRUCE
26 Assoc VP Marketing/Communications .... Mr. Parker OLIVER
15 Director of Human Resources .... Ms. Mary WILSON
41 Director of Athletics .... Mr. Mark F. WEBB
29 Director of Alumni Relations .... Ms. Susan S. ASKEW
36 Director of Career Services .... Ms. Kim D. HEITZENRATER
38 Director of Wellness Center .... Ms. Karen THARP
93 Dir of Multicultural Student Affs .... Ms. Rachel FREDERICKS
18 AVP Facilities Planning/Operations .... Ms. Karen SINGER
43 University Legal Counsel .... Ms. Marquitte STARKEY
19 Vice President for Public Safety .... Mr. Chip SCHANE
10 VP for Finance and Treasurer .... Dr. Douglass WILLIAMS
23 Director of Univ Health Services .... Ms. Karen THARP
24 Director of Media Services .... Mr. Michael OSTROWSKI
42 University Chaplain .... Rev. Peter W. GRAY
28 Assoc Dean Faculty Dev & Inclusion .... Dr. Betsy SANDLIN
45 VP for Planning/Strat Initiatives .... Dr. Scott WILSON
04 Admin Assistant to the President .... Ms. Rene WORLEY
39 Dir Resident Life/Student Housing .... Mr. Bobby SILK
44 Director Sewanee Fund .... Ms. Whitney FRANKLIN

South College (E)

3904 Lonas Drive, Knoxville TN 37909-3323
County: Knox FICE Identification: 004938
Unit ID: 220552
Telephone: (865) 251-1800 Carnegie Class: Spec-4-yr-Other Health
FAX Number: (865) 584-7335 Calendar System: Quarter
URL: www.south.edu
Established: 1882 Annual Undergrad Tuition & Fees: $16,975
Enrollment: 5,171 Coed
Affiliation or Control: Proprietary IRS Status: Proprietary
Highest Offering: Doctorate
Accreditation: SC, ARCPA, DMS, IACBE, MAC, NMT, NURSE, OTA, PHAR, PTA, PTAA, RAD

01 Chancellor .... Mr. Stephen A. SOUTH
111 VC Inst Advancement & Effectiveness .... Dr. Kim B. HALL
10 Chief Operating/Financial Officer .... Mr. Brad ADAMS
05 Chief Academic Officer .... Dr. Jay STUBBLEFIELD
106 Vice Chanc Online Operations .... Dr. Amy HILBELINK
12 Campus President Atlanta .... Mr. Joshua HUFFAKER
12 Campus President Nashville .... Mr. Nick SOUTH
12 Campus President Asheville .... Dr. Lisa SATTERFIELD
15 VP Talent & HR .... Mr. Randall CARR
88 VP Financial Aid .... Dr. Carol COLVIN
11 Director of Administrative Support .... Mr. Ron HALL
84 VP Enrollment Management .... Ms. Carrie MAJOR
20 VP Student Success/Acad Dean Lonas .... Dr. A.J CHASE
37 Sr Director of Financial Aid .... Mr. Larry BROADWATER
13 Director Instructional Technology .... Mr. Jason PIETROPAULO
08 Head Librarian .... Ms. Anya MCKINNEY
06 Inst Registrar .... Ms. Kristi MORGAN
36 Career Services Coordinator .... Mr. Ben LANDERS

Southern Adventist University (F)

4881 Taylor Cir, Collegedale TN 37315
County: Hamilton FICE Identification: 003518
Unit ID: 221661
Telephone: (423) 236-2000 Carnegie Class: Masters/M
FAX Number: (423) 236-1777 Calendar System: Semester
URL: www.southern.edu
Established: 1892 Annual Undergrad Tuition & Fees: $22,930
Enrollment: 2,730 Coed
Affiliation or Control: Seventh-day Adventist IRS Status: 501(c)3
Highest Offering: Doctorate
Accreditation: SC, ADNUR, CACREP, CAEP, IACBE, MUS, NUR, PTAA, SW

01 President .... Dr. Ken SHAW
05 Sr Vice Pres Academic Admin .... Dr. Robert YOUNG
10 Sr Vice Pres Financial Admin .... Mr. Tom VERRILL
32 Vice Pres Student Development .... Dr. Dennis NEGRÓN
111 Vice Pres Advancement .... Vacant
84 Vice Pres Enrollment Management .... Mr. Jason MERRYMAN
26 Vice Pres Marketing/University Rels .... Ms. Ingrid SKANTZ
20 Assoc VP Academic Admin .... Dr. Dionne FELIX
21 Assoc VP Financial Admin .... Mr. Marty HAMILTON
13 Assoc VP Information Systems .... Mr. Gary SEWELL
15 Assoc VP Human Resources .... Mrs. Brenda FLORES-LOPEZ
39 Dean of Students/Dir Residence Life .... Dr. Lisa HALL
50 Dean School of Business/Mgmt .... Dr. Stephanie SHEEHAN
53 Dean School of Education/Psych .... Dr. Tammie OVERSTREET
57 Dean School of Visual Art/Design .... Mr. Randy CRAVEN
60 Dean School of Journalism/Comm .... Dr. Rachel WILLIAMS-SMITH
64 Dean School of Music .... Dr. Peter COOPER
66 Dean School of Nursing .... Dr. Holly GADD
68 Dean Sch of Phys Ed/Health/Wellness .... Dr. Robert BENGE
73 Dean School of Religion .... Dr. Greg KING
77 Dean School of Computing .... Dr. Rick HALTERMAN
70 Dean Social Work/Family Studies .... Dr. Laura RACOVITA
72 Chair Technology .... Mr. Dale WALTERS
88 Chair Phys Therapist Asst Program .... Dr. Chris STEWART
81 Chair Mathematics .... Dr. Kevin BROWN
76 Chair Biology/Allied Health .... Dr. Keith SNYDER
88 Chair Chemistry .... Dr. Brent HAMSTRA
79 Chair English .... Dr. Keely TARY
82 Chair History & Political Studies .... Dr. Lisa DILLER
54 Chair Physics/Engineering .... Dr. Ken CAVINESS
18 Assoc Director Plant Services .... Mr. Bill CRUTTENDEN
35 Director Student Life/Activities .... Ms. Kari SHULTZ
37 Director Student Finance .... Mrs. Paula WALTERS
09 Director Inst Research/Planning .... Dr. Chris HANSEN
45 Director Strategic Initiatives .... Mrs. Barb EDENS
07 Director of Admissions .... Mr. Rick ANDERSON
08 Director of Libraries .... Mrs. Deyse BRAVO
06 Director Records & Advisement .... Ms. Karon POWELL
29 Director Alumni Relations .... Ms. Evonne CROOK
38 Director Student Success Center .... Dr. Jim WAMPLER
04 Administrative Asst to President .... Mrs. Joylynn SCOTT
28 Director of Diversity .... Mrs. Stephanie GUSTER

Southern College of Optometry (G)

1245 Madison Avenue, Memphis TN 38104-2222
County: Shelby FICE Identification: 003517
Unit ID: 221670
Telephone: (901) 722-3200 Carnegie Class: Spec-4-yr-Other Health
FAX Number: (901) 722-3279 Calendar System: Trimester
URL: www.sco.edu
Established: 1932 Annual Graduate Tuition & Fees: N/A
Enrollment: 538 Coed
Affiliation or Control: Independent Non-Profit IRS Status: 501(c)3
Highest Offering: Doctorate; No Undergraduates
Accreditation: SC, OPT, OPTR

01 President .... Dr. Lewis REICH
04 Executive Admin Assistant to Pres .... Ms. Sandra S. STEPHENS
101 Secretary to the Institution/Board .... Ms. Sandra STEPHENS
05 VP for Academic Affairs .... Dr. John B. CAMPBELL
09 Director of Institutional Research .... Dr. Michael CHRISTENSEN
108 Director Institutional Assessment .... Ms. Pamela MOSS
51 Dir of Continuing Education .... Ms. Kate BUCKO
20 Chair Optometric Education .... Dr. Lindsay ELKINS
121 Dir of Academic Support Services .... Dr. Carrie LEBOWITZ
17 Vice Pres for Clinical Programs .... Dr. James E. VENABLE
23 Director of Clinic Operations .... Mr. Gary SNUFFIN
84 Vice President for Student Services .... Mr. Joseph H. HAUSER
123 Dir of Admissions/Enrollment Svcs .... Mr. Michael N. ROBERTSON
88 Director of Student Recruitment .... Ms. Sunnie EWING
93 Coord of Minority Recruitment .... Dr. Jannette D. PEPPER
40 Campus Store Manager .... Ms. Denise HENSON
37 Director of Financial Aid .... Ms. Cindy GARNER
10 Vice President for Finance & Admin .... Mr. David L. WEST
21 Controller .... Ms. Carolyn WARREN
19 Manager of Security/Safety .... Mr. Don HENSON
18 Physical Plant Manager .... Mr. Trey ADAMS
13 Exec Dir of Information Services .... Mr. Dean SWICK
08 Director of Library .... Ms. Leslie HOLLAND
15 Executive Director Human Resources .... Ms. Tracy LINDOW
111 Vice President for Inst Advancement .... Mr. George C. MILLER
26 Dir of Strategic Communication/Mktg .... Mr. Jim HOLLIFIELD
29 Director of Alumni & Spec Events .... Ms. Beth FISHER
30 Senior Dir of Development .... Ms. Cecily FREEMAN
36 Director of Hayes Center .... Dr. Lisa WADE

*Tennessee Board of Regents Office (H)

1 Bridgestone Park, Nashville TN 37214
County: Davidson FICE Identification: 029031
Unit ID: 409379
Telephone: (615) 366-4400 Carnegie Class: N/A
FAX Number: N/A
URL: www.tbr.edu

01 Chancellor .... Dr. Flora TYDINGS
03 Exec Vice Chanc Policy & Strategy .... Dr. Russ DEATON
111 Vice Chanc External Affairs .... Dr. Kimberly MCCORMICK
10 Vice Chanc Business & Finance .... Mr. Danny GIBBS
43 General Counsel .... Mr. Brian LAPPS

108 VC Organizational Effectiveness .... Dr. Wendy J. THOMPSON
05 Vice Chancellor Academic Affairs .... Dr. Allana HAMILTON
32 Vice Chanc Student Success .... Dr. Heidi LEMING
13 Chief Information Officer .... Mr. Stephen VIEIRA
15 Asst Vice Chanc for Human Resources .... Ms. April PRESTON
26 Communications Director .... Mr. Rick LOCKER

*Chattanooga State Community College (A)

4501 Amnicola Highway, Chattanooga TN 37406-1097
County: Hamilton FICE Identification: 003998
Unit ID: 219824
Telephone: (423) 697-4400 Carnegie Class: Assoc/MT-VT-High Trad
FAX Number: N/A Calendar System: Semester
URL: www.chattanoogastate.edu
Established: 1965 Annual Undergrad Tuition & Fees (In-State): $4,063
Enrollment: 7,452 Coed
Affiliation or Control: State IRS Status: 501(c)3
Highest Offering: Associate Degree
Accreditation: SC, ACBSP, ADNUR, CAHIIM, COARC, DA, DH, DMS, EMT, MAC, NAEYC, NMT, PTAA, RAD, RTT, SURGT

02 President .... Dr. Rebecca ASHFORD
05 Vice Pres Academic Affairs .... Ms. Beth NORTON
10 Exec Vice Pres Business & Finance .... Ms. Tammy SWENSON
32 Int Vice Pres Student Affairs .... Ms. Amanda BENNETT
72 Exec VP Technical College .... Dr. James BARROTT
13 Vice Pres Information Technology .... Dr. Gardner LONG
111 Vice President College Adv & PR .... Ms. Nancy PATTERSON
21 Asst Vice Pres Business & Finance .... Ms. Susan JOSEPH
84 Asst Vice Pres Enrollment Services .... Mr. Brad MCCORMICK
45 Exec Director Inst Eff/Rsrch/Plng .... Dr. Traci WILLIAMS
18 Executive Director Plant Operations .... Mr. Guy DAVIS
20 Asst VP Academic Resources .... Ms. Judy LOWE
09 Director Institutional Research .... Ms. Bonnie RIGGS
26 Director Marketing .... Ms. Jennifer COOPER
37 Director Student Financial Aid .... Mr. Reed ALLISON
07 Dir of Admissions/Col Registrar .... Ms. Donna BETTIS
28 Director Multicultural Services .... Ms. Mary KNAFF
88 Dean Acad Assessment/Accred/Compl .... Mr. John HAWORTH
08 Dean Library Services .... Ms. Susan JENNINGS
76 Dean Allied Health & Nursing .... Dr. Mark KNUTSEN
79 Dean Humanities & Fine Arts .... Mr. Darrin HASSEVOORT
83 AVP Acad Affs/Dean Soc/Behav Sci .... Dr. Mosunmola GEORGE-TAYLOR
81 Interim Dean Math & Sciences .... Dr. Karen EASTMAN
50 Dean Business .... Mr. Barry JENNISON
35 Dean Student Engag/Support Svcs .... Ms. Sandy RUTTER
75 Dean Technical College .... Vacant
54 Dean Engineering & Info Technology .... Dr. Tremaine POWELL
88 Dir Welcome Center/Recruiting .... Ms. Kisha CALDWELL
15 Exec Dir HR/Affirm Action/Title I .... Mr. Brian EVANS
103 Director Economic & Workforce Dev .... Mr. Bo DRAKE
19 Interim Chief Security/Safety .... Mr. Donald COLEMAN
36 Director Student Placement .... Ms. Stephanie HOLLIS
124 Dir Educ Outreach Program/Retention .... Ms. Michelle KILGORE
110 Director College Advancement .... Ms. Tamberly SAWYERS
96 Director of Purchasing .... Ms. Kristie FARRIS

*Cleveland State Community College (B)

PO Box 3570, Cleveland TN 37320-3570
County: Bradley FICE Identification: 003999
Unit ID: 219879
Telephone: (423) 472-7141 Carnegie Class: Assoc/HT-Mix Trad/Non
FAX Number: (423) 478-6255 Calendar System: Semester
URL: www.clevelandstatecc.edu
Established: 1967 Annual Undergrad Tuition & Fees (In-State): $4,338
Enrollment: 3,074 Coed
Affiliation or Control: State IRS Status: 501(c)3
Highest Offering: Associate Degree
Accreditation: SC, ACBSP, ADNUR, EMT, MAC, NAEYC, NAIT

02 President .... Dr. William SEYMOUR
05 VP for Academic Affairs .... Dr. Barsha PICKELL
32 VP for Student Services .... Dr. Michael STOKES
10 VP of Finance & Chief Op Officer .... Mrs. Alisha FOX
103 VP Workforce & Economic Dev .... Dr. Patricia WEAVER
111 Exec Dir of Advancement & Planning .... Dr. John SQUIRES
28 Asst to the Pres for Equity/Incl .... Mr. Willie THOMAS
50 Dean of Business & Healthcare .... Ms. Susan WEBB-CURTIS
92 Dean of Honors College & Acad Enh .... Dr. Victoria BRYAN
79 Dean of Arts/Hum/Social Sci/Ed .... Dr. Ryan THOMPSON
81 Dean of STEM & Advanced Technology .... Mrs. Karen WYRICK
66 Director of Nursing .... Mrs. Nancy THOMAS
15 Director of Human Resources .... Mrs. Kellie FRANK
13 Director of Information Technology .... Mr. Chris MOWERY
103 Dir Workforce Development .... Ms. Heather BROWN
07 Director of Admissions .... Mrs. Cate GREEN
08 Director of the Library .... Ms. Gina CASH
19 Chief of Campus Police .... Mrs. Jennifer BLEDSOE
38 Dir of Counseling & Career Services .... Mr. Mark WILSON
41 Athletic Director .... Mr. Mike POLICASTRO
37 Director of Financial Aid .... Mrs. Jamie HAMBY
26 Director of Communications .... Ms. Holly TROTTER-VINCENT
29 Director of Development/ Alum .... Mrs. Cindy DAWSON
06 Registrar .... Mrs. Gail GREENWOOD

*Columbia State Community College (C)

1665 Hampshire Pike, Columbia TN 38401-5653
County: Maury FICE Identification: 003483
Unit ID: 219888
Telephone: (931) 540-2722 Carnegie Class: Assoc/HT-High Trad
FAX Number: (931) 540-2535 Calendar System: Semester
URL: www.columbiastate.edu
Established: 1966 Annual Undergrad Tuition & Fees (In-State): $4,582
Enrollment: 5,931 Coed
Affiliation or Control: State IRS Status: 501(c)3
Highest Offering: Associate Degree
Accreditation: SC, ACBSP, ADNUR, COARC, EMT, MLTAD, NAIT, RAD

02 President .... Dr. Janet F. SMITH
05 VP for Academic Affairs .... Ms. Joni LENIG
10 VP for Finance & Administration .... Ms. Elaine CURTIS
111 VP for Advancement .... Ms. Bethany LAY
20 Assoc VP Faculty/Curric & Programs .... Vacant
32 VP for Student Affairs .... Ms. Ruth Ann HOLT
13 Assoc VP for Info Technology .... Dr. Emily SICIENSKY
21 Assoc VP for Business Services .... Mr. Keith ISBELL
26 Director of Communications .... Ms. Amy SPEARS-BOYD
28 Asst to Pres for Access & Diversity .... Dr. Christa S. MARTIN
06 Director Records .... Vacant
15 Director Human Resources .... Ms. Laura JENT
08 Director Library .... Ms. Anne SCOTT
45 AVP Strat Plng/Effect/Retention .... Ms. Tammy BORREN
37 Director Financial Aid .... Mr. Roderick JOHNSON
41 Director Athletics .... Mr. Johnny LITTRELL
18 Director Facility Services & Safety .... Dr. Tim HALLMARK
12 VP for Williamson Campus & Ext Svcs .... Dr. Dearl LAMPLEY
96 Coordinator Purchasing .... Mr. Jon ARNOLD
84 Chief Enrollment Svcs Officer .... Ms. Jill RILEY
103 Dir Workforce/Career Development .... Vacant
104 Director Study Abroad .... Mr. Wes DULANEY
106 Dir Academic Engagement/Innovation ... Ms. Marla CARTWRIGHT
108 Director Institutional Assessment .... Mr. Harry DJUNAIDI
19 Director Security/Safety .... Mr. Randy CARROLL
04 Exec Assistant to the President .... Ms. Cheryl CASNER
07 Director of Admissions .... Ms. Jill RILEY
25 Development Officer/Grants Admin .... Mr. Patrick MCELHINEY
29 Director Alumni Affairs .... Ms. Molly COCHRAN
44 Director Annual Giving .... Mr. Chris HENSON

*Dyersburg State Community College (D)

1510 Lake Road, Dyersburg TN 38024-2450
County: Dyer FICE Identification: 006835
Unit ID: 220057
Telephone: (731) 286-3200 Carnegie Class: Assoc/HT-Mix Trad/Non
FAX Number: (731) 286-3333 Calendar System: Semester
URL: www.dscc.edu
Established: 1967 Annual Undergrad Tuition & Fees (In-State): $4,338
Enrollment: 2,650 Coed
Affiliation or Control: State IRS Status: 501(c)3
Highest Offering: Associate Degree
Accreditation: SC, ACBSP, ADNUR, CAHIIM, EMT, NAEYC

02 President .... Dr. Karen A. BOWYER
05 Vice President for the College .... Dr. Jan REID-BUNCH
10 Vice President Finance/Admin Svcs .... Dr. Sharon BURNETT
111 VP Inst Advancement/Cont Education .... Dr. Amanda WALKER
13 Vice President of Technology .... Mr. Josh DUGGIN
32 VP/Dean of Student Services .... Ms. Larenda FULTZ
08 Dean of Learning Resources Center .... Ms. Susan CHARLEY
37 Director of Financial Aid .... Mrs. Kacee HARDY
09 Director of Institutional Research .... Ms. Mary RICKS
15 Director of Human Resources .... Vacant
103 Exec Director of Workforce Services .... Ms. Connie STEWART
29 Director of Alumni Relations .... Ms. Amy FINCH
121 Academic/Career Counselor .... Ms. Sherry BAKER
41 Director of Athletics .... Mr. David ANDERSON
18 Director of Physical Plant .... Mr. Kent JETTON
07 Director of Admissions & Records .... Vacant
26 Director of Public Information .... Ms. Amy FINCH
96 Director of Administrative Services .... Ms. Beth MULLINS
21 Business & Student Fin Svcs Manager .... Ms. Donna MEALER
49 Dean of Arts & Sciences .... Mr. James BARHAM
72 Dean of Business/Tech/Allied Health .... Ms. Julie FRAZIER
66 Dean of Nursing .... Ms. Amy JOHNSON
04 Administrative Asst to President .... Ms. Edith CARLTON

*Jackson State Community College (E)

2046 North Parkway, Jackson TN 38301-3797
County: Madison FICE Identification: 004937
Unit ID: 220400
Telephone: (731) 424-3520 Carnegie Class: Assoc/HT-Mix Trad/Non
FAX Number: (731) 425-2647 Calendar System: Semester
URL: www.jscc.edu
Established: 1965 Annual Undergrad Tuition & Fees (In-State): $4,324
Enrollment: 4,203 Coed
Affiliation or Control: State IRS Status: 501(c)3
Highest Offering: Associate Degree
Accreditation: SC, ACBSP, ADNUR, #COARC, EMT, MLTAD, NAIT, OTA, PTAA, RAD

02 President .... Dr. George PIMENTEL
05 Interim VP of Academic Affairs .... Dr. Tom PIGG
10 Vice Pres of Finance & Admin Affs .... Mr. Tim DELLINGER
30 Director of Development .... Ms. Lindsey TRITT
32 Interim VP of Student Services .... Ms. Robin MAREK
116 Internal Auditor .... Ms. Chrystal PITTMAN
15 Dir Human Resources/Affirm Action .... Ms. Amy WEST
09 Dir Inst Research & Accountability .... Mr. Don MYERS
13 Director of Information Technology .... Ms. Dana NAILS
21 Director of Business Services .... Mr. Adina KERFOOT
18 Director of Physical Plant .... Mr. Preston TURNER
96 Director of Purchasing .... Mr. Robert D. HEMRICK
12 Director Lexington Campus .... Ms. Sandy STANFILL
12 Director Savannah Campus .... Mrs. Meda FALLS
12 Director Humboldt Campus .... Ms. Lisa ROJAS
26 Director of PR and Marketing .... Mr. John MCCOMMON
37 Director Student Financial Aid .... Mr. John BRANDT
07 Director of Admissions and Records .... Ms. Robin MAREK
08 Head Librarian .... Mr. Scott COHEN
19 Director Security/Safety .... Mr. Shane YOUNG
41 Athletic Director .... Mr. Steve CORNELISON
04 Admin Assistant to the President .... Ms. Heather FREEMAN
22 Dir Affirmative Action/Equal Opp .... Ms. Amy WEST
103 Director Workforce Development .... Ms. Kimberly JOHNSON
106 Dean of Online Education/E-learning .... Dr. Patrick DAVIS, SR.

*Motlow State Community College (F)

PO Box 8500, Lynchburg TN 37352-8500
County: Moore FICE Identification: 006836
Unit ID: 221096
Telephone: (931) 393-1500 Carnegie Class: Assoc/HT-High Trad
FAX Number: (931) 393-1681 Calendar System: Semester
URL: www.mscc.edu
Established: 1969 Annual Undergrad Tuition & Fees (In-State): $4,330
Enrollment: 6,616 Coed
Affiliation or Control: State IRS Status: 501(c)3
Highest Offering: Associate Degree
Accreditation: SC, ACBSP, ADNUR, EMT, MLTAD, NAIT

02 President .... Dr. Michael TORRENCE
05 Sp Asst to Pres/Chief Academic Ofcr .... Dr. Greg SEDRICK
103 EVP Workforce and Cmty Development .... Dr. Tony MILLICAN
10 Vice Pres for Finance & Admin .... Ms. Hilda TUNSTILL
26 VP External Affairs .... Ms. Terri BRYSON
13 Chief Information Officer .... Mr. Carlos PADILLA
32 Interim AVP for Student Success .... Dr. Sydney MCPHEE
72 Interim Dean Career & Tech Programs .... Mr. Larry FLATT
35 Int Dean of Students .... Ms. Debra SMITH
66 Dean of Nursing and Allied Health .... Ms. Amy HOLDER
12 Asst Dean of McMinnville Campus .... Ms. Misty MAZZIE
12 Dean of Moore County Campus .... Vacant
12 Asst Dean Fayetteville Campus .... Ms. Lisa SANDERS
12 Dean of Smyrna Campus .... Dr. Gregory KILLOUGH
18 Director of Facilities .... Mr. Brian GAFFORD
31 Exec Dir of Community Relations .... Ms. Brenda CANNON
08 Director of Libraries .... Ms. Sharon EDWARDS
102 Asst Dir of the Foundation .... Ms. Sharon BATEMAN
37 Exec Dir of Financial Aid .... Mr. Joe MYERS, JR.
38 Director of Disability & Testing .... Ms. Belinda CHAMPION
07 Director of Admissions & Records .... Ms. Mae SANDERS
19 Director of Public Safety .... Mr. Ray HIGGINBOTHAM
41 Dean of Athletics .... Vacant
91 Director Admin Computing .... Vacant
84 Director of Recruitment .... Vacant
15 Executive Dir of Human Resources .... Mr. Brian ROWE
21 Director of Fiscal Services .... Ms. Sandy SCHAFFER
121 Int Director of Student Success .... Mr. Kyle MACON
04 Executive Administrator .... Mrs. Alissa ROEBUCK
55 Director of Adult Initiatives .... Ms. Allison BARTON
27 Dir of Communications & Media Rels .... Vacant
90 Dean of Academic Technology .... Mr. Terry DURHAM
14 Director of Tech Operations .... Mr. Jeffery SHORT
88 Director of TN Promise .... Mr. Jonathan GRAHAM
108 Director of Quality Assurance .... Dr. Meagan MCMANUS
25 Director of Grants .... Ms. Tammy O'DELL
28 Compliance Officer .... Ms. Barbara SCALES
96 Purchasing and Contract Coordinator .... Ms. Kristin LUKE

*Nashville State Community College (G)

120 White Bridge Road, Nashville TN 37209-4515
County: Davidson FICE Identification: 008145
Unit ID: 221184
Telephone: (615) 353-3333 Carnegie Class: Assoc/HT-High Trad
FAX Number: (615) 353-3713 Calendar System: Semester
URL: www.nscc.edu
Established: 1969 Annual Undergrad Tuition & Fees (In-State): $4,294
Enrollment: 7,064 Coed
Affiliation or Control: State IRS Status: 501(c)3
Highest Offering: Associate Degree
Accreditation: SC, ACBSP, ACFEI, ADNUR, NAEYC, NAIT, OTA, SURGT

02 President .... Dr. Shanna L. JACKSON
10 VP Finance & Administration .... Ms. Mary M. CROSS
05 VP Academic Affairs & Workforce Dev .... Dr. Carol ROTHSTEIN
103 VP Economic & Community Dev .... Ms. Ginger HAUSSER
45 Assoc VP Planning/Research .... Mr. Charles CLARK
30 Exec Dir of Development .... Ms. Lauren P. BELL
32 VP Student Affairs & Enroll .... Dr. Carol J. MARTIN-OSORIO
20 Assoc VP Academic Affairs .... Dr. Sarah ROBERTS
116 Internal Auditor .... Mr. Henry HO

12 Director Clarksville Campus ... Ms. Kathleen AKERS
06 Int Dir of Records & Registration ... Mr. Kevin THOMAS
84 Interim Chief Enrollment Officer ... Ms. Laura P. MORAN
13 Director Technology Services ... Mr. Paul A. KAMINSKY
19 Director of Safety and Security ... Mr. Derrek G. SHEUCRAFT
37 Director of Financial Aid ... Ms. Jennifer D. BYRD
15 Director of Human Resources ... Ms. Jill FERRAND
18 Executive Director of Operations ... Mr. Christopher SAUNDERS
26 AVP Communications & Marketing ... Mr. Tom HAYDEN
106 Director of Online Learning ... Ms. Heather RIPPETOE
83 Dean of Social and Life Sciences ... Dr. Julie E. WILLIAMS
81 Dean Science/Tech/Eng/Math (STEM) ... Dr. Jennifer KNAPP
79 Dean English/Humanities & Arts ... Dr. Patricia J. ARMSTRONG
62 Dean Lrng Resources & Online Learn ... Dr. Faye M. JONES
50 Dean Business/Mgmt & Hospitality ... Ms. Karen L. STEVENSON
96 Director of Purchasing ... Mr. Mark HODGES
76 Director of Healthcare Professions ... Dr. Cynthia G. WALLER
22 Compliance & Diversity Officer ... Ms. Mia SNEED

*Northeast State Community College (A)

PO Box 246, 2425 Highway 75, Blountville TN 37617-0246
County: Sullivan — FICE Identification: 005378
Unit ID: 221908
Telephone: (423) 323-3191 — Carnegie Class: Assoc/MT-VT-High Trad
FAX Number: (423) 279-7636 — Calendar System: Semester
URL: www.northeaststate.edu
Established: 1965 — Annual Undergrad Tuition & Fees (In-State): $4,326
Enrollment: 5,397 — Coed
Affiliation or Control: State — IRS Status: 501(c)3
Highest Offering: Associate Degree
Accreditation: SC, ACBSP, ADNUR, CVT, DA, EMT, MLTAD, NAEYC, NAIT, SURGT

02 President ... Dr. Bethany BULLOCK
100 Chief of Staff ... Dr. Stephanie BARHAM
05 Int Vice Pres Academic Affairs ... Dr. Connie MARSHALL
11 Vice Pres Administration ... Ms. Linda CALVERT
32 Vice President Student Success ... Dr. Susan GRAYBEAL
103 VP Economic & Workforce Development ... Dr. Sam ROWELL
10 Vice Pres Finance/Info Tech ... Mr. Chad BAILEY
56 Asst VP Multi-Campus Programs ... Dr. Pashia HOGAN
111 Chief Advancement Officer ... Ms. Megan ALMAROAD
06 Registrar ... Ms. Deidra CLOSE
15 Director Human Resources ... Ms. Megan JONES
31 Director Community Relations ... Mr. Robert CARPENTER
26 Director of Marketing ... Ms. Amanda ADAMS
45 Director Planning & Assessment ... Mr. John GRUBB
08 Dean Library ... Mr. Christopher DEMAS
79 Dean Humanities ... Mr. William WILSON
81 Dean Mathematics ... Ms. Malissa TRENT
76 Dean Health Professions ... Ms. Connie MARSHALL
72 Interim Dean Technologies ... Ms. Donna FARRELL
83 Dean Behavior/Social Sciences ... Dr. Xiaoping WANG
81 Dean Science Division ... Mr. Chris HITECHEW
50 Dean Business Technologies ... Mr. Danny L. LAWSON
66 Director of Nursing ... Dr. Johanna NEUBRANDER
35 Dean of Students ... Ms. Jennifer STARLING
88 Veterans Affairs Specialist ... Mr. John ADCOX
18 Director of Plant Operations ... Mr. Pete MILLER
37 Director of Financial Aid ... Ms. Mary CHAMBLISS
96 Purchasing Coordinator ... Ms. Bernice HAGAMAN

*Pellissippi State Community College (B)

PO Box 22990, Knoxville TN 37933-0990
County: Knox — FICE Identification: 012693
Unit ID: 221643
Telephone: (865) 694-6400 — Carnegie Class: Assoc/HT-Mix Trad/Non
FAX Number: (865) 539-7240 — Calendar System: Semester
URL: www.pstcc.edu
Established: 1974 — Annual Undergrad Tuition & Fees (In-State): $4,318
Enrollment: 9,334 — Coed
Affiliation or Control: State — IRS Status: 501(c)3
Highest Offering: Associate Degree
Accreditation: SC, ACBSP, ACFEI, ADNUR, NAEYC, NAIT

02 President ... Dr. L. Anthony WISE, JR.
05 VP of Academic Affairs ... Dr. Kellie TOON
13 Vice President Information Services ... Ms. Audrey J. WILLIAMS
10 Vice President Business & Finance ... Mr. Ronald L. KESTERSON
21 Asst VP Business Services ... Ms. Renee MOORE
102 Exec Director of Foundation ... Ms. Aneisa L. ROLEN
32 Vice President of Student Affairs ... Dr. Rushton W. JOHNSON, JR.
103 Exec Dir Business/Workforce Dev ... Ms. Teri T. BRAHAMS
12 Campus Dean Blount County Programs ... Ms. Priscilla DUENKEL
12 Campus Dean Strawberry Pl Program ... Dr. Mike NORTH
12 Campus Dean Magnolia Ave Programs ... Vacant
12 Campus Dean Division Street Program ... Ms. Esther L. DYER
35 Dean of Students/Asst VP Stdnt Affs ... Mr. Travis C. LOVEDAY
88 Manager Student Transitions ... Mr. Barry SHUMPERT
35 Asst VP of Student Services ... Vacant
88 Manager Accounts Payable ... Ms. Debra CLARK
20 Asst VP of AA University Parallel ... Dr. Angela HUGHES
20 Asst VP AA Career & Technical Pgm ... Ms. Judy GOSCH
84 Asst VP Enrollment Services ... Ms. Leigh A. TOUZEAU
22 Exec Director Equity & Compliance ... Ms. Annazette HOUSTON
35 Dir of Student Engagement & Leaders ... Mr. Matt SPRAKER
36 Director of Placement ... Ms. Cynthia ATCHLEY
28 Director of Disability Services ... Ms. Ann E. SATKOWIAK
26 Director Marketing & Communications ... Ms. Julia H. WOOD
07 Dir of Admiss & Records/Registrar ... Ms. Melanie M. PARADISE
08 Director of Library Services ... Dr. Mary Ellen SPENCER
24 Dir Educ Technology Svcs ... Ms. Kristy M. CONGER
37 Director of Financial Aid ... Mr. Dick W. SMELSER
108 Dir Inst Effective/Assessment/Plng ... Ms. Nancy A. RAMSEY
88 Asst Director Inst Effectiveness ... Ms. Olga EBERT-HOLBERG
18 Director of Facilities ... Ms. Regina MCNEW
19 Chief of Police ... Mr. Terry M. CROWE, JR.
114 Director Budget & Payroll ... Ms. Nancy DONAHUE
96 Director of Purchasing ... Mr. John S. CLARK
15 Interim Director Human Resources ... Ms. Elizabeth (Liz) ROSS
16 Int Director Talent Management/HR ... Mr. Alan RAMOS
25 Director Grant Development ... Ms. Danette JOHNSON
104 Exec Dir TnCIS/International Educ ... Ms. Tracey BRADLEY
112 Director Major Gift Development ... Ms. Marilyn RODDY
44 Dir Annual Giving & Scholarships ... Mr. David L. HARRELL
29 Director Alumni & Donor Engagement ... Ms. Britney SINK
91 Dir Applications Programming Sup ... Mr. James (Dean) COPPLE
105 Dir of Network & Technical Services ... Mr. Larry BATES
28 Director of Access & Diversity ... Ms. Gayle E. WOOD
88 Director of Academic Testing ... Ms. Joan NEWMAN
88 Dir of Student Care & Advocacy ... Dr. Drema BOWERS
121 Director of Advising ... Ms. Rachael C. CRAGLE
88 Dir Academic Support Programs ... Ms. Jan T. SHARP
113 Bursar ... Ms. Mandy BENTZ
116 Director of Internal Audit ... Ms. Suzanne WALKER
88 Interim Director of PACE ... Mr. Bramdon WALTERS
89 Dir Student Transition/Persistence ... Ms. Rebecca MILAM
88 Director TRIO Student Support Svcs ... Ms. Venetia C. WILLLIAMS
88 Director Veteran Services ... Vacant
88 Director of Sales/Bus & Cmty Svcs ... Mr. Tim WILSON
88 Dir of Solution Mgmt/Bus & Cmty Svc ... Mr. Todd EVANS

*Roane State Community College (C)

276 Patton Lane, Harriman TN 37748-5011
County: Roane — FICE Identification: 009914
Unit ID: 221397
Telephone: (865) 354-3000 — Carnegie Class: Assoc/HT-High Trad
FAX Number: (865) 882-4585 — Calendar System: Semester
URL: www.roanestate.edu
Established: 1971 — Annual Undergrad Tuition & Fees (In-State): $4,552
Enrollment: 5,172 — Coed
Affiliation or Control: State — IRS Status: 501(c)3
Highest Offering: Associate Degree
Accreditation: SC, ACBSP, ADNUR, CAHIIM, COARC, COMTA, DH, EMT, NAEYC, OPD, OTA, POLYT, PTAA, RAD, SURGT

02 President ... Dr. Chris WHALEY
05 Vice Pres for Student Learning/CAO ... Dr. Diane WARD
10 Vice Pres Business & Finance ... Ms. Marsha MATHEWS
103 VP Workforce Devel/Cmty Outreach ... Ms. Teresa S. DUNCAN
84 VP Stdnt Svcs/Enroll Mgt/Innovation ... Dr. Jamie STRINGER
12 Int Dir of Oak Ridge Branch Campus ... Mrs. Teresa S. DUNCAN
32 Dean of Students ... Dr. Lisa STEFFENSEN
108 VP Inst Effect/Plng/Stdnt Success ... Ms. Karen L. BRUNNER
21 Director of Financial Services ... Ms. Michelle PATTERSON
17 Dean of Health Sciences ... Dr. Patricia JENKINS
13 Computer Information Officer ... Ms. Keri PHILLIPS
09 Director Institutional Research ... Mr. Jeffrey J. TINLEY
22 Coordinator Affirmative Action ... Mr. Odell FEARN
08 Interim Dir of Library Services ... Ms. Laura VAUGHN
18 Director Physical Plant & Expo Ctr ... Mr. Stan R. STARKEY
29 Director Alumni Relations ... Mr. Scott K. NIERMANN
96 Director of Purchasing & Contracts ... Ms. Dana WEST
36 Workforce Placement & Job Placement ... Ms. Kim HARRIS
04 Assistant to President ... Ms. Sherry JACKSON
19 Director Safety/Chief of Police ... Mr. William KAIN
88 Special Assistant to President ... Ms. Tamsin MILLER
41 Interim Athletic Director ... Mr. Alan HOLT
104 Int Dir of International Education ... Mr. Charlie COBB
79 Interim Dean Humanities ... Dr. Geol GREENLEE
83 Int Dean Social/Behavioral Sciences ... Mr. Daniel C. HYDER
81 Interim Dean Math & Science ... Mr. Bruce CANTRELL
20 Int Dean of Student Academic Svcs ... Ms. Amy KEELING
121 Director of Student Success ... Ms. Kathryn R. BAKER
116 Director of Internal Audit ... Ms. Cynthia CORTESIO
119 Director IT Computing ... Mr. Peter SOUZA
88 Interim Dir Academic Advising ... Ms. Susan PEARSON
118 Manager Employee Benefits ... Ms. Joyce MARSALIS
06 Registrar ... Ms. Jessica HUNSAKER
102 Executive Director Foundation ... Mr. Scott K. NIERMANN
106 Dir Online Education/E-learning ... Dr. Susan R. SUTTON
15 Director Human Resources ... Mr. Odell FEARN
26 Dir Marketing & Public Relations ... Ms. Sarah SELF
37 Director Student Financial Aid ... Ms. Robin TOWNSON
38 Dir Student Counseling/Disability ... Ms. Tracey WATSON
91 Director Administrative Computing ... Mr. Chris PANKRATZ
88 Dir Acad Pgm Initiatives & Grants ... Dr. Shelley ESQUIVEL

*Southwest Tennessee Community College (D)

PO Box 780, Memphis TN 38101-0780
County: Shelby — FICE Identification: 010439
Unit ID: 221485
Telephone: (901) 333-5000 — Carnegie Class: Assoc/HT-High Trad
FAX Number: (901) 333-4645 — Calendar System: Semester
URL: www.southwest.tn.edu
Established: 2000 — Annual Undergrad Tuition & Fees (In-State): $4,343
Enrollment: 7,371 — Coed
Affiliation or Control: State — IRS Status: 501(c)3
Highest Offering: Associate Degree
Accreditation: SC, ACBSP, ACFEI, ADNUR, EMT, MLTAD, NAEYC, PTAA, RAD

02 President ... Dr. Tracy D. HALL
05 Vice President of Academic Affairs ... Vacant
86 Exec Dir Govt Rels/Dir Athletics ... Mr. Sherman D. GREER
111 Vice Pres Institutional Advancement ... Vacant
10 Chief Financial Officer ... Mrs. Jeannette SMITH
32 Vice Pres Student Affairs ... Mrs. Jacqueline A. FAULKNER
84 Assoc VP of Enrollment Services ... Ms. Shanita L. BROWN
103 Assoc Vice Pres of Workforce Dev ... Ms. Anita BRACKIN
26 Exec Director of Comm & Marketing ... Ms. Daphne J. THOMAS
13 Exec Dir Information Systems (CIO) ... Mr. Michael D. BOYD
18 Director Physical Plant ... Mr. Jonathan A. WELDON
19 Director Public Safety ... Mrs. Lezley A. WEBB
04 Exec Admin Assistant to President ... Ms. Mary CANO
15 Assoc VP Human Resources ... Ms. Iliana RICELLI
50 Dean of Business & Technology ... Mr. Robin COLE

*Volunteer State Community College (E)

1480 Nashville Pike, Gallatin TN 37066-3188
County: Sumner — FICE Identification: 009912
Unit ID: 222053
Telephone: (615) 452-8600 — Carnegie Class: Assoc/HT-High Trad
FAX Number: (615) 230-3577 — Calendar System: Semester
URL: www.volstate.edu
Established: 1970 — Annual Undergrad Tuition & Fees (In-State): $4,312
Enrollment: 8,832 — Coed
Affiliation or Control: State — IRS Status: 501(c)3
Highest Offering: Associate Degree
Accreditation: SC, ACBSP, CAHIIM, COARC, DA, DMS, EMT, MLTAD, POLYT, PTAA, RAD

02 President ... Dr. Orinthia MONTAGUE
05 Vice President Academic Affairs ... Dr. Jenniffer BREZINA
10 Vice President Business & Finance ... Ms. Beth CARPENTER
32 Vice President Student Services ... Dr. Emily SHORT
30 Vice Pres for Resource Development ... Ms. Karen MITCHELL
45 Vice Pres Inst Planning/Research ... Ms. Colette CATANIA
20 Asst VP of Academic Affairs ... Dr. Tom EKMAN
21 Asst Vice Pres Business & Finance ... Ms. Renee AUSTIN
51 Asst VP for Economic & Cmty Devel ... Mrs. Hilary B. MARABETI
76 Dean of Health ... Ms. Kim CHRISTMON
79 Dean Humanities ... Dr. Erin MANN
83 Dean Social Science/Education ... Mr. James BROWN
81 Dean Math & Science ... Dr. Everett Shane TALBOTT
50 Dean of Business ... Dr. Andy WHITE
15 Dir Personnel/Affirm Act/Human Res ... Ms. Lori CUTRELL
08 Director Library Services ... Ms. Rebecca FRANK
07 Dir Admissions & College Registrar ... Mr. Tim AMYX
13 Director Information Technology ... Mr. Kevin BLANKENSHIP
37 Director Student Financial Aid ... Ms. Donna H. DUNAWAY
26 Director Public Relations ... Mrs. Tami WALLACE
18 Senior Director Physical Plant ... Mr. William NEWMAN
19 Chief Security & Safety ... Ms. Angela LAWSON
41 Director of Athletics ... Mr. Bobby HUDSON
121 Dean of Academic Support ... Ms. Rhonda GREGORY
88 Special Adult Programs/ADA Director ... Ms. Leslie SMITH
09 Director of Institutional Research ... Mrs. Ann Marie CALDERON
96 Director Purchasing ... Ms. Molly ROWDEN
124 Director Retention Support Services ... Ms. Heather HARPER
36 Admin of Work-Based Learning ... Dr. Rick PARRENT
38 Director Counseling & Testing ... Mr. Terry BUBB
28 Manager of Diversity & Inclusion ... Mr. Jeff KING
88 Dir Health Sciences Ctr of Emphasis ... Ms. Terri CRUTCHER
06 Registrar ... Mr. Tim AMYX
04 Executive Administrative Associate ... Ms. Karen WALLER
102 Foundation Development Officer ... Ms. Alison MUNCY
35 Mgr of Student Engagement & Support ... Ms. Heather HARPER

*Walters State Community College (F)

500 S Davy Crockett Parkway, Morristown TN 37813-6899
County: Hamblen — FICE Identification: 008863
Unit ID: 222062
Telephone: (423) 585-2600 — Carnegie Class: Assoc/HT-High Trad
FAX Number: (423) 585-6853 — Calendar System: Semester
URL: www.ws.edu
Established: 1969 — Annual Undergrad Tuition & Fees (In-State): $4,328
Enrollment: 5,742 — Coed
Affiliation or Control: State — IRS Status: 501(c)3
Highest Offering: Associate Degree
Accreditation: SC, ACBSP, ACFEI, ADNUR, CAHIIM, COARC, EMT, NAEYC, NAIT, OTA, PTAA, SURGT

02 President ... Dr. Anthony R. MIKSA
04 Exec Director to the President ... Ms. Leann LONG
05 Vice President Academic Affairs ... Dr. Donna SEAGLE
10 Vice President Business Affairs ... Dr. Mark HURST
32 Vice President Student Affairs ... Ms. Angi SMITH
111 Asst Vice Pres College Advancement ... Mr. Chris CATES
45 VP for Planning/Research/Assessment ... Vacant
20 VP for Educational Outreach ... Dr. John LAPRISE
35 Asst Vice Pres Student Affairs ... Vacant
18 Asst Vice Pres Facilities Mgmt ... Vacant
21 Asst Vice Pres Business Affairs ... Ms. Heather CARRIER
08 Dean of Library ... Dr. Jamie POSEY
103 Dean of Workforce Training ... Vacant
19 Dean of Public Safety Division ... Mr. Chad BRYANT
17 Dean Health Programs ... Ms. Marty K. RUCKER
12 Dean Greenville/Greene Co Center ... Mr. Mark WILLS

12 Dean Sevier County Campus .... Dr. Jama SUTTON
83 Dean of Behavioral/Social Sciences .... Vacant
50 Dean of Business .... Vacant
79 Interim Dean of Humanities .... Mr. Rob PRATT
81 Dean of Mathematics .... Mr. John C. KNIGHT
65 Dean of Natural Science .... Dr. Matthew SMITH
75 Dean of Technical Education .... Mr. Thomas R. SEWELL
06 Dean Student Info System/Records .... Ms. Linda MASON
37 Director of Financial Aid .... Ms. Laura RODRIGUEZ
38 Exec Director Counseling/Testing .... Dr. Andy HALL
15 Exec Director of Human Resources .... Mr. Jarvis JENNINGS
26 Vice President Public Information .... Mr. James B. PECTOL
13 Chief Information Officer .... Mr. Stephen ANNIS
41 Director of Athletics .... Mr. Derek CREECH
07 Director of Admissions .... Ms. Avery SWINSON
19 Chief of Campus Police .... Vacant
89 Director Freshmen Studies .... Vacant
36 Director Student Placement .... Dr. Andy HALL
92 Director Honors Program .... Mr. David ATKINS
96 Asst Director of Purchasing .... Ms. Renee JARNIGAN
105 Director of Network Services .... Mr. Bill R. MOREFIELD
84 Director Enrollment Development .... Ms. Avery SWINSON
93 Coord Minority Student Recruit .... Ms. Roxanne BOWEN
108 Exec Dir of Planning & Assessment .... Dr. Deanna GARMAN

Tennessee State University (A)

3500 John A Merritt Boulevard, Nashville TN 37209-1561
County: Davidson FICE Identification: 003522
Unit ID: 221838
Telephone: (615) 963-5000 Carnegie Class: DU-Higher
FAX Number: (615) 963-7412 Calendar System: Semester
URL: www.tnstate.edu
Established: 1912 Annual Undergrad Tuition & Fees (In-State): $9,012
Enrollment: 7,615 Coed
Affiliation or Control: State IRS Status: 501(c)3
Highest Offering: Doctorate
Accreditation: SC, AAFCS, ART, CAEP, CAHIIM, CEA, COARC, COPSY, DH, DIETD, MUS, NAIT, NUR, OT, PH, PTA, SP, SPAA, SW

02 President .... Dr. Glenda GLOVER
05 Int Provost/VP Academic Affairs .... Dr. Michael HARRIS
04 Senior Office Assistant .... Ms. Zanetta GOOCH
10 VP Business & Finance .... Mr. Douglas ALLEN
11 VP Administrative Affairs .... Vacant
32 Vice Pres Student Affairs .... Vacant
111 Dir Institutional Advancement .... Vacant
41 Athletic Director .... Mr. Michael ALLEN
43 University Legal Counsel .... Mr. Laurence PENDLETON
84 VP Enrollment Management .... Dr. John CADE
20 Assoc VP Academic Affairs .... Dr. Patricia CROOK
51 AVP Extended Education Center .... Dr. Evelyn NETTLES
15 Assoc VP Human Resources .... Ms. Linda C. SPEARS
21 Assoc VP Financial Services .... Mr. Bradley WHITE
37 Asst VP Financial Aid .... Ms. Amy B. WOOD
26 Asst VP Public Rels/Communication .... Ms. Kelli SHARPE
09 Exec Director Inst Effectiveness .... Ms. Charlise ANDERSON
18 AVP Facilities Management .... Mr. Viron LYNCH
22 Director Equity & Inclusion .... Ms. Razel JONES
06 Registrar .... Mrs. Thelria HARDAWAY
19 AVP/Chief of Police .... Mr. Gregory RIBINSON
08 Int Exec Director Libraries .... Ms. Glenda ALVIN
49 Int Dean College of Liberal Arts .... Dr. Samantha MORGAN-CURTIS
50 Dean College of Business .... Dr. Millicent LOWNES-JACKSON
53 Int Dean College of Education .... Dr. Heraldo RICHARDS
54 Dean College of Engr/Tech/Comp Sci .... Dr. S. Keith HARGROVE
47 Dean Agriculture/Human/Natural Sci .... Dr. Carter CATLIN
76 Dean College of Health Sciences .... Dr. Ronald BARREDO

Tennessee Technological University (B)

1 William L. Jones Drive, Cookeville TN 38505
County: Putnam FICE Identification: 003523
Unit ID: 221847
Telephone: (931) 372-3101 Carnegie Class: DU-Higher
FAX Number: (931) 372-3898 Calendar System: Semester
URL: www.tntech.edu
Established: 1915 Annual Undergrad Tuition & Fees (In-State): $9,636
Enrollment: 10,177 Coed
Affiliation or Control: State IRS Status: 501(c)3
Highest Offering: Doctorate
Accreditation: SC, AAFCS, ART, CACREP, CAEP, CAEPN, @DIETC, DIETD, MUS, NURSE

02 President .... Dr. Philip B. OLDHAM
05 Provost/Vice President .... Dr. Lori M. BRUCE
10 Vice Pres Planning & Finance .... Dr. Claire STINSON
84 VP of Enrollment Management .... Dr. Brandon JOHNSON
32 Vice President of Student Affairs .... Dr. Cythnia POLK- JOHNSON
28 Chief Diversity Officer .... Dr. Robert OWENS
46 VP Research/Econ Development .... Dr. Jennifer TAYLOR
86 Chief Government Affairs Officer .... Dr. Terry SALTSMAN
100 Chief of Staff/Board Secretary .... Mr. Lee WRAY
88 Assoc VP for Research .... Dr. Francis O. OTUONYE
111 Vice President Univ Advancement .... Dr. Kevin BRASWELL
41 Director of Athletics .... Mr. Mark WILSON
26 Chief Communication Officer .... Ms. Karen LYKINS
43 Director University Counsel .... Mr. Troy PERDUE
20 Sr Assoc VP Academic Affairs .... Dr. Mark STEPHENS
20 Assoc Provost/Vice Pres Acad Affs .... Dr. Xiaoming (Sharon) HUO
13 Chief Information Officer .... Mr. Matt SMITH
37 Dir Financial Aid & Veteran Affairs .... Ms. Mary MCCASKEY
45 Director of Strategic Planning .... Mr. Dewayne WRIGHT
15 Assoc VP Human Resources .... Mr. Kevin VEDDER
88 Compliance Ofcr/Clery Coordinator .... Mr. Greg HOLT
19 Director of University Police .... Mr. Tony NELSON
39 Director of Housing .... Mr. Joshua EDMONDS
18 Assoc VP Physical Plant .... Mr. Chuck ROBERTS
38 Interim Director Counseling Center .... Ms. Christina MICK
23 Director of Health Svcs .... Ms. Leigh A. RAY
36 Director Career Development .... Mr. Russ COUGHENOUR
85 Director International Education .... Mr. Charles WILKERSON
06 Registrar .... Ms. Brandi FLETCHER
92 Director Honors Program .... Dr. Rita BARNES
96 Interim Director of Purchasing .... Ms. Donna WALLIS
21 Associate VP Business .... Ms. Emily WHEELER
29 Dir Alumni Engagement & Annual Giv .... Mr. Brandon BOYD
116 Director of Internal Audit .... Ms. Deanna METTS
07 Director of Admissions .... Dr. Stephen KELLER
19 Dir Capital Project Administration .... Mr. James COBB
49 Interim Dean of Arts & Sciences .... Dr. Jeff ROBERTS
54 Dean of Engineering .... Dr. Joseph SLATER
47 Dean Agric & Human Ecology .... Dr. Darron SMITH
50 Dean of Business Admin .... Dr. Thomas PAYNE
53 Dean College of Education .... Dr. Lisa ZAGUMNY
57 Dean of College of Fine Arts .... Dr. Jennifer SHANK
66 Dean School of Nursing .... Dr. Kim HANNA
88 Dean Interdisciplinary Studies .... Dr. Mike GOTCHER
08 Dean Library & Learning Asst .... Dr. Doug BATES
58 Assoc Dean of Graduate Studies .... Dr. Alice CAMUTI
04 Executive Asst to President .... Ms. Diane SMITH
105 Director Web Services .... Mr. Cody BRYANT
108 Int Dir Inst Assess/Rsrch/Effective .... Dr. Kevin HARRIS
90 Director Academic Computing .... Mr. Will HOFFERT
91 Dir Enterprise Application System .... Ms. Lisa MAAS
110 Exec Dir of Univ Advancement .... Mr. John W. SMITH
104 Director Study Abroad .... Ms. Amy MILLER

Tennessee Wesleyan University (C)

204 East College St., Athens TN 37303
County: McMinn FICE Identification: 003525
Unit ID: 221731
Telephone: (423) 745-7504 Carnegie Class: Bac-Diverse
FAX Number: (423) 744-9968 Calendar System: Semester
URL: www.tnwesleyan.edu
Established: 1857 Annual Undergrad Tuition & Fees: $25,850
Enrollment: 1,116 Coed
Affiliation or Control: United Methodist IRS Status: 501(c)3
Highest Offering: Master's
Accreditation: SC, DH, NURSE, OT, SW

01 President .... Dr. Harley KNOWLES
05 Vice President for Academic Affairs .... Dr. Grant WILLHITE
10 Vice Pres Financial/Business Affs .... Mrs. Gail HARRIS
32 Vice President for Student Life .... Dr. Scott MASHBURN
111 VP of Advancement/Alumni Affairs .... Mr. Blake MCCASLIN
37 Assoc VP Financial Aid .... Mrs. Lacey WEESE
108 VP for Inst Effectiveness .... Dr. Stephanie SMALLEN
07 Asst VP of Admissions .... Vacant
04 Executive Assistant to President .... Mrs. Gail ROGERS
08 Dir of Library & Info Svcs .... Ms. Julie ADAMS
06 Registrar .... Mrs. Julie MCCASLIN
41 Athletic Director .... Mr. Donny MAYFIELD
15 Human Resources Director .... Mr. Kyle FULBRIGHT
18 Chief of Facilities/Physical Plant .... Mr. Danny DUCKETT
26 Asst VP Marketing/Communications .... Ms. Katherine DAVIS
13 Assoc VP of Information Tech/CIO .... Mr. Brandon LAMBDIN

Trevecca Nazarene University (D)

333 Murfreesboro Road, Nashville TN 37210-2877
County: Davidson FICE Identification: 003526
Unit ID: 221892
Telephone: (615) 248-1200 Carnegie Class: DU-Mod
FAX Number: (615) 248-7728 Calendar System: Semester
URL: www.trevecca.edu
Established: 1901 Annual Undergrad Tuition & Fees: $26,898
Enrollment: 3,968 Coed
Affiliation or Control: Church Of The Nazarene IRS Status: 501(c)3
Highest Offering: Doctorate
Accreditation: SC, ARCPA, CACREP, CAEPN, MUS, NURSE, SW

01 President .... Dr. Dan BOONE
04 Assistant to the President .... Ms. Anne TWINING
05 Provost & Senior Vice President .... Dr. Tom MIDDENDORF
26 Vice President External Relations .... Mrs. Peggy J. COONING
20 Assoc VP/Dean of Sch of Business .... Dr. Jim HIATT
86 Assoc VP Accred/State Authorization .... Dr. Jonathan BARTLING
27 Assoc Vice Pres Marketing & Comm .... Ms. Mollie YODER
32 Assoc VP/Dean of Student Dev .... Ms. Jessica DYKES
84 VP Enrollment & Marketing .... Ms. Holly WHITBY
73 Dean School of Theol/Christian Min .... Dr. Timothy M. GREEN
88 Assoc Dn Acad Integrity/Innovation .... Dr. Heidi VENTURA
35 Assoc Dean Student Community Life .... Ms. Megan MCGHEE
39 Asc Dean Students Residential Life .... Mrs. Ronda LILIENTHAL
53 Dean of the School of Education .... Dr. Suzann HARRIS
49 Dean of School of Arts & Science .... Dr. Lena WELCH
64 Dean School of Music & Worship Arts .... Dr. David DIEHL
13 Chief Information Officer/ITS .... Dr. John EBERLE
06 Registrar .... Ms. Katrina CHAPMAN
19 Director of Security .... Mr. Greg DAWSON
07 Exec Director of Admissions .... Ms. Melinda MILLER
41 Athletic Director .... Mr. Mark ELLIOTT
121 Assoc Dean of Student Success .... Ms. Michelle GAERTNER
38 Director Counseling Services .... Dr. Sara HOPKINS
85 Dir Global Engagement .... Mr. Michael NEWLAND
106 Dean of Online Lrng & Support Svcs .... Ms. LaMetrius DANIELS
21 Director of Financial Services .... Mr. Chuck SEAMAN
37 Dir of Student Financial Services .... Ms. Kylie PRUITT
15 Director Human Resources .... Mr. Steve SEXTON
76 Director Physician Asst Pgm .... Mr. Bret REEVES
29 Director Alumni/Church Engagement .... Dr. Michael JOHNSON
30 Director of Development Operations .... Ms. Christy GRANT
88 Mgr of Communications .... Mr. Brian BENNETT
124 Coordinator of Assessment/Retention .... Mr. Jeffrey SWINK

Tusculum University (E)

60 Shiloh Road, Greeneville TN 37745-9997
County: Greene FICE Identification: 003527
Unit ID: 221953
Telephone: (423) 636-7300 Carnegie Class: Masters/M
FAX Number: (423) 638-7166 Calendar System: Semester
URL: https://home.tusculum.edu/
Established: 1794 Annual Undergrad Tuition & Fees: $25,500
Enrollment: 1,664 Coed
Affiliation or Control: Presbyterian Church (U.S.A.) IRS Status: 501(c)3
Highest Offering: Master's
Accreditation: SC, ACBSP, NURSE

01 President .... Dr. Scott HUMMEL
05 Provost & VP Academic Affairs .... Dr. Tricia HUNSADER
10 Vice Pres/Chief Financial Officer .... Ms. Benita BARE
84 VP Enrollment Mgmt & Financial Aid .... Dr. Ramona WILLIAMS
41 VP Athletics & Univ Initiatives .... Mr. Doug JONES
35 AVP/Dean Student Affairs/Retention .... Dr. Lisa JOHNSON
111 Assoc VP Inst Advancement .... Ms. Kimberly KIDWELL
06 Registrar .... Ms. Sheryl BURNETTE
21 Controller .... Ms. Tammy CHILDS
15 Chief Human Resource Officer .... Vacant
08 Library Director .... Mrs. Kathy HIPPS
37 Director of Financial Aid .... Ms. Ashley EDENS
26 Director of Communications .... Mr. Jim WOZNIAK
13 Director of Information Systems .... Mr. Chris SUMMEY
18 Director Facilities Management .... Mr. Chad GRINDSTAFF
92 Director of Honors Program .... Vacant
40 Bookstore Manager .... Vacant
19 Director of Campus Safety .... Mr. Jonathan GRESHAM
49 Dean Col of Civic & Liberal Arts .... Mr. Wayne THOMAS
50 Dean College of Business .... Dr. Jacob FAIT
53 Dean College of Education .... Dr. Miriam STRODER
66 Dean of School of Nursing .... Vacant
09 Dir of Inst Research/Effectiveness .... Ms. Christy COLE

Union University (F)

1050 Union University Drive, Jackson TN 38305-3697
County: Madison FICE Identification: 003528
Unit ID: 221971
Telephone: (731) 668-1818 Carnegie Class: DU-Mod
FAX Number: (731) 661-5175 Calendar System: 4/1/4
URL: www.uu.edu
Established: 1823 Annual Undergrad Tuition & Fees: $34,630
Enrollment: 3,071 Coed
Affiliation or Control: Southern Baptist IRS Status: 501(c)3
Highest Offering: Doctorate
Accreditation: SC, ANEST, ART, CAATE, CAEP, MUS, NURSE, PHAR, SW

01 President .... Dr. Samuel (Dub) W. OLIVER
05 Provost/VP Academic Affairs .... Dr. John T. NETLAND
10 VP for Business Affairs .... Dr. Rick TAPHORN
111 Vice Pres Institutional Advancement .... Mrs. Catherine KWASIGROH
84 Vice Pres Enrollment Management .... Mr. Dan GRIFFIN
32 VP Student Life/Dean of Students .... Dr. Bryan CARRIER
42 Vice Pres for University Ministries .... Dr. Todd BRADY
108 Asst Provost Accred & Research .... Dr. Michele ATKINS
04 Exec Assistant to the President .... Mrs. Sheryl WREN
21 Assoc Vice Pres Business Svcs .... Mr. Robert SIMPSON
08 Director of the Library Services .... Ms. Melissa MOORE
26 Assoc VP University Communications .... Mr. Tim ELLSWORTH
13 Assoc VP Information Technology .... Mr. James AVERY
15 AVP Human Resources/Business Ofc .... Dr. John CARBONELL
07 Asst VP for Undergraduate Admiss .... Mr. Robbie GRAVES
37 Director Student Financial Planning .... Mr. Derek MOORE
49 Dean College Arts & Sciences .... Dr. Hunter BAKER
50 Dean School of Business .... Dr. Jason GARRETT
66 Dean School of Nursing .... Dr. Kelly HARDEN
53 Dean College of Education .... Dr. John FOUBERT
73 Dean Sch of Theology & Missions .... Dr. Ray VANNESTE
67 Dean School of Pharmacy .... Dr. Sheila MITCHELL
91 Assoc Dir Information Technology .... Miss Karen MCWHERTER
36 Dir Vocation Ctr/Life Call/Career .... Mr. Alex HUGUENARD
14 Director of Data Management .... Mr. David PORTER
06 Registrar .... Mrs. Susan HOPPER
19 Director of Security/Safety .... Mr. Yancey PETTIGREW
41 Director of Athletics .... Mr. Tommy SADLER
18 Chief Facilities/Physical Plant .... Mr. Stephen HOPPER
70 Dean School of Social Work .... Mrs. Mary Anne POE
51 Dean School Adult & Prof Studies .... Dr. Beverly ABSHER

The University of Memphis (G)

Southern Avenue, Memphis TN 38152
County: Shelby FICE Identification: 003509
Unit ID: 220862
Telephone: (901) 678-2000 Carnegie Class: DU-Higher

FAX Number: N/A　Calendar System: Semester
URL: www.memphis.edu
Established: 1912　Annual Undergrad Tuition & Fees (In-State): $9,912
Enrollment: 22,205　Coed
Affiliation or Control: State　IRS Status: 501(c)3
Highest Offering: Doctorate
Accreditation: SC, ART, AUD, CACREP, CAEPN, CIDA, CLPSY, COPSY, DIETD, DIETI, HSA, IPSY, JOUR, LAW, MUS, NURSE, PH, PLNG, SCPSY, SP, SPAA, SW, THEA

02 President .... Dr. M. David RUDD
05 Provost .... Dr. Tom NENON
20 Vice Provost Academic Innovation .... Dr. Richard IRWIN
10 EVP & Chief Financial Officer .... Mr. Raaj KURAPATI
45 Chief University Planning Officer .... Mr. Tony POTEET
18 VP Physical Plant .... Mr. Ron BROOKS
19 Chief of Police .... Mr. Derek MYERS
116 Chief Audit Executive .... Ms. Vicki DEATON
111 Vice Pres Advancement .... Ms. Joanna CURTIS
32 Vice Pres Student Academic Success .. Dr. Karen WEDDLE-WEST
35 Asst VP Student Aff/Dev .... Vacant
26 EVP External Relations .... Ms. Tammy HEDGES
46 Exec VP Research & Innovation .... Dr. Jasbir DHALIWAL
41 Director of Athletics .... Mr. Laird VEATCH
43 University Counsel .... Ms. Melanie MURRY
22 Dir of Institutional Equity .... Ms. Tiffany COX
13 CIO/Vice Provost for Info Tech .... Dr. Robert JACKSON
84 Vice Provost Enrollment Services .... Dr. Darla KEEL
58 Dean Graduate School .... Dr. Robin POSTON
21 Asst Vice Pres Business & Finance .... Vacant
15 Asst Vice Pres Human Resources .... Ms. Maria ALAM
08 Assoc Dean U of M Libraries .... Mr. John EVANS
09 Director Institutional Research .... Ms. Bridgette DECENT
36 Director Career & Employment Svcs .... Ms. Alisha D. ROSE
06 Registrar .... Ms. Darla KEEL
37 Executive Director of Student Aid .... Dr. Rob KNISS
96 Executive Director Procurement Svcs .... Mr. Nick PAPPAS
29 Director of Alumni Relations .... Ms. Kristie GOLDSMITH
92 Director University Honors Program .... Dr. Melinda L. JONES
07 Assistant Vice Provost Admissions .... Dr. Eric STOKES
28 Director of Diversity Initiatives .... Dr. Karen WEDDLE-WEST
60 Dean Comm Sciences/Disorders .....Dr. Linda D. JARMULOWICZ
49 Dean of Arts & Sciences .... Dr. Abby PARRILL-BAKER
50 Interim Dean Business & Economics .... Dr. Chuck PIERCE
53 Dean of Education .... Dr. Kandi HILL-CLARKE
54 Dean of Engineering .... Dr. Richard J. SWEIGARD
89 Dean University College .... Dr. Richard IRWIN
57 Dean Communication & Fine Arts .... Dr. Anne HOGAN
61 Dean School of Law .... Ms. Kate SCHAFFZIN
66 Interim Dean College of Nursing .... Dr. Larry SLATER
69 Int Dean School of Public Health .... Dr. Marian LEVY
76 Dean College of Health Studies .... Dr. Richard J. BLOOMER
104 Director Study Abroad .... Ms. Rebecca DYCK-LAUMANN
108 Director Institutional Assessment .... Dr. Colton COCKRUM
38 Director Student Counseling .... Dr. Jane CLEMENT
112 Director of Planned Giving .... Ms. Wesley LARUE
102 Dir Foundation/Corporate Relations ......Ms. Kimberly GRANTHAM
106 Exe Dean Global/Academic Innovation .... Dr. Richard L. IRWIN
44 Director of Annual Giving .... Vacant
86 Director Government Relations .... Mr. Ted TOWNSEND
39 Interim Director of Residence Life .... Ms. Amanda VIRAG
04 Admin Assistant to the President .... Ms. LaTondra ARNETT
100 Chief of Staff .... Ms. Stephanie BEASLEY
105 Director Web Services/Digital .... Ms. Holly SNYDER
101 Secretary of the Institution/Board .... Ms. Melanie MURRY

*University of Tennessee System Office (A)

800 Andy Holt Tower, Knoxville TN 37996-0180
County: Knox　FICE Identification: 008051
Telephone: (865) 974-1000　Carnegie Class: N/A
FAX Number: (865) 974-3753
URL: www.tennessee.edu

01 President .... Mr. Randy BOYD
10 Sr Vice President/CFO .... Mr. David L. MILLER
05 VP Academic Affairs/Student Success .... Dr. Linda C. MARTIN
30 CEO Fndn/VP Development/Alumni Affs .... Mr. Kerry WITCHER
86 VP for Government Rels/Advocacy .... Ms. Carey WHITWORTH
45 VP Research/Outreach/Economic Dev .... Dr. Stacey PATTERSON
43 General Counsel/Secretary .... Mr. C. Ryan STINNETT
15 Chief Human Resources Officer .... Mr. Brian DICKENS
86 Vice Pres Institute for Public Svc .... Dr. Herb BYRD
26 VP Communications/Marketing .... Ms. Tiffany CARPENTER
13 Chief Information Officer .... Mr. Ramon PADILLA, JR.
21 Exec Dir Auditing/Consulting Svcs .... Mr. Brian DANIELS
29 Asst VP UTN Alumni Affairs .... Mr. Kerry WITCHER

*University of Tennessee, Knoxville (B)

1331 Circle Park, Knoxville TN 37996
County: Knox　FICE Identification: 003530
Unit ID: 221759
Telephone: (865) 974-1000　Carnegie Class: DU-Highest
FAX Number: (865) 974-1182　Calendar System: Semester
URL: www.utk.edu
Established: 1794　Annual Undergrad Tuition & Fees (In-State): $13,264
Enrollment: 30,559　Coed
Affiliation or Control: State　IRS Status: 501(c)3
Highest Offering: Doctorate
Accreditation: SC, ANEST, ART, CACREP, CAEP, CAMPEP, CAPRT, CIDA, CLPSY, COPSY, DENT, DIETC, DIETD, DIETI, IPSY, JOUR, LAW, LIB, LSAR, MT, MUS, NURSE, PAST, PH, RAD, SCPSY, SW, THEA, VET

02 Chancellor .... Dr. Donde PLOWMAN
100 Chancellor's Executive Assistant .... Ms. Susan ENGLAND
100 Chief of Staff .... Mr. Matthew SCOGGINS
05 Provost/Senior Vice Chancellor .... Dr. John ZOMCHICK
32 Vice Chancellor for Student Life .... Dr. Frank CUEVAS
46 Vice Chancellor for Research .... Dr. Deborah CRAWFORD
10 Senior VC Finance & Administration .... Mr. Chris CIMINO
28 VC for Diversity & Engagement .... Mr. Tyvi SMALL
26 Vice Chancellor for Communications .... Mrs. Tisha BENTON
30 Vice Chancellor for Development .... Mr. Chip BRYANT
20 Vice Provost for Faculty Affairs .... Dr. Diane KELLY
20 Vice Provost for Academic Affairs .... Dr. RJ HINDE
58 Vice Provost/Dean Graduate School .... Dr. Dixie THOMPSON
121 Vice Provost Student Success .... Dr. Amber WILLIAMS
35 AVC Student Life/Dean of Students .... Dr. Shea K. HOUZE
84 Vice Provost Enrollment Svcs .... Ms. Kari ALLDREDGE
18 Interim Assoc VC Facilities Svcs .... Mr. Terry LEDFORD
41 Vice Chancellor/Dir Athletics .... Dr. Daniel WHITE
22 Int Assoc VC Equity & Diversity .... Ms. Katrice MORGAN
37 Director of Financial Aid .... Mr. Jeffrey G. GERKIN
09 Dir Inst Research/Assessment .... Ms. Denise GARDNER
38 Director of Student Counseling .... Dr. Paul MCANEAR
06 Interim Registrar .... Mr. Jeff GERKIN
47 Dean Herbert College of Agriculture .... Dr. Caula BEYL
48 Dean of Architecture and Design .... Dr. Jason YOUNG
50 Dean Haslam College of Business .... Dr. Steve MANGUM
60 Dean Communication/Information .... Dr. Joe MAZER
53 Dean Educ/Health/Human Sciences .... Dr. Ellen MCINTYRE
54 Dean Tickle College of Engineering .... Dr. Matthew MENCH
61 Interim Dean of Law .... Prof. Doug BLAZE
49 Dean of Arts & Sciences .... Dr. Theresa LEE
66 Dean of Nursing .... Dr. Victoria NIEDERHAUSER
70 Dean of Social Work .... Dr. Lori MESSINGER
74 Dean of Veterinary Medicine .... Dr. James P. THOMPSON
12 Chancellor of UTIA .... Dr. Tim L. CROSS
08 Dean of Libraries .... Dr. Steve SMITH
12 Interim Executive Director of UTSI .... Dr. James SIMONTON
07 Director of Undergrad Admissions .... Mr. Fabrizio D'ALOISIO
13 Associate VC & CIO .... Mr. Joel REEVES
29 Associate VC of Alumni Affairs .... Mr. Duane WILES
104 Vice Provost Global Engagement .... Dr. Gretchen NEISLER
15 Assoc Vice Chancellor HR .... Dr. Mary LUCAL
19 Assoc Vice Chancellor Public Safety .... Mr. Troy LANE
36 Exec Dir Career Development .... Ms. Stephanie KIT

*University of Tennessee at Chattanooga (C)

615 McCallie Avenue, Chattanooga TN 37403-2504
County: Hamilton　FICE Identification: 003529
Unit ID: 221740
Telephone: (423) 425-4111　Carnegie Class: DU-Mod
FAX Number: (423) 425-2200　Calendar System: Semester
URL: www.utc.edu
Established: 1886　Annual Undergrad Tuition & Fees (In-State): $9,656
Enrollment: 11,728　Coed
Affiliation or Control: State　IRS Status: 501(c)3
Highest Offering: Doctorate
Accreditation: SC, ANEST, ART, CAATE, CACREP, CAEP, CIDA, @DIETC, JOUR, MUS, NURSE, OT, PTA, SPAA, SW, THEA

02 Chancellor .... Dr. Steven R. ANGLE
05 Provost & Sr VC Academic Affs .... Dr. Jerold HALE
20 Vice Prov for Academic Affairs .... Dr. Matt MATTHEWS
111 Interim VC University Advancement .... Mr. Lofton STUART
10 Vice Chanc Finance/Administration .... Mr. Tyler FORREST
46 Vice Chancellor for Research .... Dr. Joanne ROMAGNI
32 Vice Chanc Student Development .... Vacant
21 Assoc Vice Chanc Business/Fin Affs .. Ms. Vanasia Conley PARKS
26 Vice Chanc Comm & Mktg .... Mr. George HEDDLESTON
41 Vice Chanc & AD .... Mr. Mark WHARTON
26 Asst VC University Relations .... Ms. Gina STAFFORD
18 Asst VC Operations/Fac Plng & Mgt .... Mr. Tom M. ELLIS
13 VC for Communications and CIO .... Ms. Vicki FARNSWORTH
100 Chief of Staff .... Mr. David STEELE
08 Dean of UTC Library .... Ms. Theresa LIEDTKA
35 Assoc Dean of Student Life .... Mr. Jim HICKS
84 VC Enroll Mgmt/Student Success .... Dr. Yancy FREEMAN
06 Director Records & Registrar .... Mr. Joel WELLS
13 Manager Client Solutions/IT .... Vacant
09 Dir of Planning/Eval/Inst Research .... Ms. Eva LEWIS
36 Asst Dir Placement/Stdnt Employment .... Mrs. Donna COOPER
15 Asst Vice Chanc Human Resources .... Ms. Laure POU
38 Executive Director of Counseling .... Dr. Elizabeth O'BRIEN
37 Director of Financial Aid .... Ms. Jennifer BUCKLES
58 Dean of the Graduate School .... Dr. Joanne ROMAGNI
49 Dean of Arts & Sciences .... Dr. Pamela RIGGS-GELASCO
50 Dean of Business Administration .... Dr. Robert DOOLEY
53 Dean of Health/Educ/Prof Studies .... Dr. Valerie RUTLEDGE
54 Dean Engineering/Comp Science .... Dr. Daniel PACK
66 Director of Nursing .... Dr. Christine SMITH
22 Director of Equity & Inclusion .... Ms. Rosite DELGADO
25 Director of Sponsored Programs .... Ms. Meredith PERRY
29 Int Asst Vice Chanc Alumni Affairs .... Ms. Andrea LYONS
96 Procurement/Contracts (Purchasing) .... Mr. Ken GUTHRIE
19 Chief of Police .... Mr. Robert RATCHFORD
39 Director Student Housing .... Ms. Valara SAMPLE
92 Dean Honors College .... Dr. Linda FROST
88 Coordinator of Civic Engagement .... Ms. Jill N. WOODRUFF
104 Exec Director International Program .... Mr. Takeo SUZUKI
43 Dir Legal Services/General Counsel .... Mr. Yousef A. HAMADEH
04 Admin Assistant to the Chancellor .... Ms. Teresa F. MCKINNEY
28 Vice Chanc Diversity/Engagement .... Ms. Stacy G. LIGHTFOOT

*University of Tennessee at Martin (D)

554 University Street, Martin TN 38238-0001
County: Weakley　FICE Identification: 003531
Unit ID: 221768
Telephone: (731) 881-7000　Carnegie Class: Masters/S
FAX Number: (731) 881-7019　Calendar System: Semester
URL: www.utm.edu
Established: 1900　Annual Undergrad Tuition & Fees (In-State): $9,748
Enrollment: 7,117　Coed
Affiliation or Control: State　IRS Status: 501(c)3
Highest Offering: Master's
Accreditation: SC, AAFCS, CAEP, DIETD, DIETI, MUS, NUR, SW

02 Chancellor .... Dr. Keith S. CARVER, JR.
05 Provost & SVC for Academic Affairs .... Dr. Philip A. CAVALIER
10 Sr Vice Chanc for Finance & Admin .... Ms. Petra R. MCPHEARSON
32 Vice Chanc for Student Affairs .... Dr. John A. LEWTER
111 Vice Chancellor Univ Advancement .... Dr. Charles T. DEAL
20 Assoc Provost for Academic Affs .... Dr. Victoria S. SENG
13 Chief Information Officer .... Ms. Amy C. BELEW
28 Chief Diversity & Inclusion Officer .... Dr. Mark MCCLOUD
114 Dir Budget & Mgmt Report .... Ms. Carol WILLIAMS
35 Asst Vice Chanc for Student Affairs .... Mr. John C. ABEL
30 Assoc VC Devel & Planned Giving .....Ms. Jeanna C. SWAFFORD
04 Senior Advisor to the Chancellor .... Ms. Edie B. GIBSON
29 Asst Vice Chanc Alumni Relations .... Ms. Jacqueline JOHNSON
06 Dir of Acad Records & Registrar .... Ms. Martha BARNETT
28 Equity & Diversity Ofcr AA/EEO .... Mr. Joe T. HENDERSON
15 Director of Human Resources .... Mr. Michael WASHINGTON
09 Director Institutional Research .... Dr. Rion MCDONALD
41 VC & Dir Intercollegiate Athletics .... Mr. Kurt MCGUFFIN
08 Dean of Library .... Dr. Erik NORDBERG
18 Int Dir of Physical Plant Opers .... Mr. Brad BURKETT
19 Dir of Public Safety .... Mr. Monte BELEW
96 Purchasing Agent .... Ms. Lori A. DONAVANT
23 Dir Student Health & Counseling Svc .... Ms. Shannon DEAL
39 Asst VC Student/Residential Life .... Ms. Gina MCCLURE
26 VC Communications & Marketing .... Mr. Robert (Bud) D. GRIMES
47 Dean Col Agri & App Sciences .... Dr. Todd A. WINTERS
50 Dean Col Business & Global Affs .... Dr. Ahmad TOOTOONCHI
53 Dean Col Educ/Health/Behav Sci .... Ms. Cynthia L. WEST
79 Dean Col Humanities/Fine Arts .... Dr. Lynn M. ALEXANDER
54 Dean Col Engr & Natural Sci .... Dr. Shadow ROBINSON
58 Int Dean of Graduate Studies .... Dr. Joey MEHLHORN
105 Director Web Services .... Mr. Brian C. INGRAM
25 Int Exec Dir Res Outreach/Econ Dev .... Dr. Victoria SENG
84 Exec Dir Enr Svcs/Stdnt Engagement ... Dr. James D. MANTOOTH
07 Director of Admissions .... Ms. Destin TUCKER
37 Dir Financial Aid/Scholarship .... Ms. Jana COX
93 Asst Dir Multicultural Affairs .... Mr. Anthony PREWITT

*The University of Tennessee Southern (E)

433 W Madison Street, Pulaski TN 38478-2799
County: Giles　FICE Identification: 003504
Unit ID: 220701
Telephone: (931) 363-9800　Carnegie Class: Bac-Diverse
FAX Number: (931) 363-9818　Calendar System: Semester
URL: www.utsouthern.edu
Established: 1870　Annual Undergrad Tuition & Fees (In-State): $25,850
Enrollment: 812　Coed
Affiliation or Control: State　IRS Status: 170(c)1
Highest Offering: Master's
Accreditation: SC, NURSE

01 Chancellor .... Dr. Mark D. LA BRANCHE
04 Exec Assistant to the Chancellor .... Mrs. Kim W. HARRISON
05 Provost & VC of Academic Affairs .... Dr. Judy B. CHEATHAM
10 VC for Finance & Administration .... Mr. Robby SHELTON
32 Assoc VC for Student Affairs .... Dr. Daniel N. MCMASTERS
84 Assoc VC of Enrollment Management .... Mr. Tyler COX
111 Ast VC for Advancement Services .... Mrs. Edna G. LUNA
21 Asst VC of Finance .... Ms. Rhonda CLINARD
41 Athletic Director .... Mrs. Brandie PAUL
15 Chief Human Resources Officer .... Mr. James R. HLUBB
13 Chief Information Officer .... Mr. Cedrick NKULU
26 Chief Marketing & Comm Officer .... Mrs. Abby C. STANTON
06 Registrar & Director of IR .... Dr. Chris MATTINGLY
37 Director of Financial Aid .... Mrs. Emma HLUBB
19 Director of Safety & Security .... Mrs. Josie B. TREVARTHEN
105 Director of Publications & Website .... Mrs. Susan CARLISLE
36 Director of Career Services .... Mrs. Julie SHELTON
40 Director of Bookstore .... Mrs. Margaret W. JACKSON
29 Alumni Affairs Director .... Mrs. Laura K. MCMASTERS
18 Facilities Director .... Mr. Rich BRICKER
08 Librarian .... Mr. Richard MADDEN

*University of Tennessee Health Science Center (F)

875 Monroe Avenue, Memphis TN 38163
Telephone: (901) 448-5500　FICE Identification: 006725
Accreditation: SC, ANEST, ARCPA, AUD, CAHIIM, CYTO, DENT, DH, HT, IPSY, MED, @MIDWF, MT, NURSE, OT, PHAR, PTA, SP

Vanderbilt University (A)

2201 West End Avenue, Nashville TN 37235
County: Davidson FICE Identification: 003535
Unit ID: 221999
Telephone: (615) 322-7311 Carnegie Class: DU-Highest
FAX Number: (615) 343-7765 Calendar System: Semester
URL: www.vanderbilt.edu
Established: 1873 Annual Undergrad Tuition & Fees: $54,158
Enrollment: 13,537 Coed
Affiliation or Control: Independent Non-Profit IRS Status: 501(c)3
Highest Offering: Doctorate
Accreditation: SC, AUD, CACREP, CAEP, CAMPEP, CLPSY, DENT, DIETI, DMS, IPSY, LAW, MED, MIDWF, MT, MUS, NDT, NMT, NURSE, #PAST, PCSAS, PERF, PH, SP, THEOL

01 Chancellor .... Dr. Daniel DIERMEIER
05 Provost/Vice Chanc Academic Affairs .... Dr. Susan R. WENTE
125 Chancellor Emeritus .... Dr. Nicholas ZEPPOS
63 Dean School of Medicine .... Dr. Jeffrey R. BALSER
10 Vice Chancellor Finance/CFO .... Mr. Brett SWEET
11 Vice Chanc Administration .... Mr. Eric KOPSTAIN
30 Int Vice Chanc Dev/Alumni Relations .... Mr. John M. LUTZ
46 Vice Provost for Research .... Dr. Padma RAGHAVAN
115 Vice Chanc for Investments .... Mr. Anders W. HALL
28 VC Equity/Diversity/Inclusion .... Dr. Andre L. CHURCHWELL
15 Chief Human Resources Ofcr .... Ms. Barbara CARROLL
41 Vice Chanc/Dir Athletics .... Dr. Candice STOREY LEE
112 Dir Trust and Estate Admin .... Ms. Susan HART
26 Vice Chancellor for Communications .... Mr. Steve ERTEL
13 Vice Chancellor Information Tech .... Mr. John M. LUTZ
86 Vice Chanc Govt/Cmty Relations .... Mr. Nathan GREEN
43 Vice Chancellor/General Counsel .... Ms. Ruby Z. SHELLAWAY
09 Asst Provost/Exec Dir Inst Research .... Ms. Olivia KEW-FICKUS
20 Vice Provost Learning & Res Affairs .... Ms. Cynthia J. CYRUS
58 Int Dean of the Graduate School .... Dr. Bunmi OLATUNJI
08 University Librarian .... Dr. Valerie HOTCHKISS
27 Dean of Student Publications/Comm .... Mr. F. Clark WILLIAMS
21 Asst V Chanc for Finance/Controller .... Ms. Dalana ROBERTSON
06 Registrar .... Mr. Bart P. QUINET
84 Vice Provost Univ Enrollment Affs .... Dr. Douglas CHRISTIANSEN
07 Dir Undergraduate Admissions .... Mr. John GAINES
37 Director Student Financial Aid .... Mr. Brent B. TENER
38 Director Univ Counseling Center .... Dr. Todd WEINMAN
36 Exec Dir Career Center .... Dr. Katharine S. BROOKS
25 Director Sponsored Programs .... Mr. Andrew BUDELL
32 Dean of Students .... Mr. Mark BANDAS
106 Assoc Provost for Educ Tech & Dev .... Dr. John M. SLOOP
49 Dean College of Arts & Science .... Dr. John G. GEER
54 Dean School of Engineering .... Dr. Philippe M. FAUCHET
66 Dean School of Nursing .... Dr. Linda NORMAN
53 Dean Education & Human Development .... Dr. Camilla P. BENBOW
64 Dean Blair School of Music .... Dr. Lorenzo CANDELARIA
73 Dean of the Divinity School .... Dr. Emilie M. TOWNES
61 Dean of the School of Law .... Dr. Chris GUTHRIE
50 Dean Owen Grad School of Mgmt .... Dr. M. Eric JOHNSON
45 Vice Prov Strategic Initiatives .... Vacant
20 Vice Prov Acad Affairs/Dean of Fac .... Dr. Vanessa BEASLEY
20 Vice Prov for Faculty Affairs .... Dr. Tracey GEORGE
42 University Chaplain .... Rev. Gretchen PERSON
19 AVC/Chief of Public Safety .... Mr. August J. WASHINGTON
22 Dir EO/AA & Disability Svcs .... Ms. Anita JENIOUS
88 Dir Sport Operations/Asst Vice Chan .... Mr. Brockton WILLIAMS
39 Sr Director Housing Operations .... Mr. James S. KRAMKA
44 Asst Vice Chancellor Annual Giving .... Mr. Kyle D. MCGOWAN
88 Asst Vice Chanc Federal Relations .... Ms. Christina D. WEST

Visible Music College (B)

200 Madison Avenue, Memphis TN 38103
County: Shelby FICE Identification: 039823
Unit ID: 449764
Telephone: (901) 381-3939 Carnegie Class: Spec-4-yr-Arts
FAX Number: (901) 377-0544 Calendar System: Semester
URL: www.visible.edu
Established: 2000 Annual Undergrad Tuition & Fees: $20,000
Enrollment: 209 Coed
Affiliation or Control: Independent Non-Profit IRS Status: 501(c)3
Highest Offering: Master's
Accreditation: TRACS

01 President .... Dr. Ken STEORTS
05 Vice President of Academics .... Dr. Cameron HARVEY
111 Vice President of Advancement .... Geordy WELLS
10 Vice President of Business .... Ben RAWLEY
32 Vice President of Students .... JD WILSON
06 Registrar .... Sunethra GUY
37 Financial Aid Manager .... Tonya WILLIAMS
15 Human Resources Coordinator .... Toni MELTON
18 Operations/IT Manager .... Heath BENSON
84 Enrollment Manager .... LaToya CHAVERS

Welch College (C)

1045 Bison Trail, Gallatin TN 37066
County: Sumner FICE Identification: 030018
Unit ID: 220206
Telephone: (615) 675-5255 Carnegie Class: Bac-Diverse
FAX Number: (615) 296-0400 Calendar System: Semester
URL: www.welch.edu
Established: 1942 Annual Undergrad Tuition & Fees: $19,582
Enrollment: 358 Coed
Affiliation or Control: Free Will Baptist IRS Status: 501(c)3
Highest Offering: Master's
Accreditation: SC, BI

01 President .... Dr. Matt PINSON
05 Provost .... Dr. Matthew J. MCAFFEE
45 Vice Pres for Strategic Initiatives .... Dr. P. Greg KETTEMAN
10 Vice President Financial Affairs .... Mr. Craig MAHLER
32 VP Student Svcs/Dean of Students .... Dr. Jon FORLINES
111 Vice Pres Institutional Advancement .... Mr. David WILLIFORD
108 Vice Pres for Inst Effectiveness .... Dr. Kevin HESTER
20 Vice Provost for Academic Admin .... Mr. Matthew BRACEY
34 Dean of Women .... Mrs. Susan FORLINES
55 Dean of Enriched Adult Studies .... Mr. William SLATER
08 Librarian .... Mrs. Christa THORNSBURY
09 Director of Institutional Research .... Mr. Wayne SPRUILL
84 Dir of Enrollment Services .... Mr. Daniel WEBSTER
26 Chief Public Relations/Marketing .... Mr. Josh OWENS
106 Dir of Online and Adult Studies .... Mr. William SLATER
44 Director of the Welch Fund .... Mr. Tim OWEN
18 Director of Plant Operations .... Mr. DeWayne WHITE
41 Athletic Director .... Mr. Greg FAWBUSH
37 Student Financial Aid Coordinator .... Mrs. Angie EDGMON
06 Registrar .... Mrs. Anna MCAFFEE
04 Exec Assistant to the President .... Ms. Martha FLETCHER

William Moore College of Technology (D)

1200 Poplar Avenue, Memphis TN 38104
County: Shelby FICE Identification: 011553
Unit ID: 222105
Telephone: (901) 726-1977 Carnegie Class: Spec 2-yr-Tech
FAX Number: (901) 726-1978 Calendar System: Trimester
URL: www.mooretech.edu
Established: 1909 Annual Undergrad Tuition & Fees: $8,848
Enrollment: 378 Coed
Affiliation or Control: Independent Non-Profit IRS Status: 501(c)3
Highest Offering: Associate Degree
Accreditation: COE

01 President .... Mr. Skip REDMOND
05 CAO/VP of Student Services .... Ms. Andrea BAIRD

Williamson College (E)

274 Mallory Station Road, Franklin TN 37067
County: Williamson FICE Identification: 035135
Unit ID: 443340
Telephone: (615) 771-7821 Carnegie Class: Spec-4-yr-Bus
FAX Number: (615) 771-7810 Calendar System: Other
URL: www.williamsoncc.edu
Established: 1996 Annual Undergrad Tuition & Fees: $14,350
Enrollment: 68 Coed
Affiliation or Control: Non-denominational IRS Status: 501(c)3
Highest Offering: Master's
Accreditation: BI

01 President .... Dr. Ed SMITH
05 Dir of Academic & Student Affairs .... Dr. Bryan THOMAS
11 Vice President for Operations .... Ms. Susan MAYS
32 Director of Student Services .... Ms. Robyn WOLLAS
06 Registrar/Dir Instl Effectiveness .... Ms. Karen HUDSON
37 Dir Financial Aid/Veteran Affairs .... Ms. Cristina MAJORS
07 Admissions Department Manager .... Ms. Laura FLOWERS
26 Dir Marketing & Advancement .... Ms. Courtney STAFFORD

TEXAS

Abilene Christian University (F)

ACU Box 29100, Abilene TX 79699-9100
County: Taylor FICE Identification: 003537
Unit ID: 222178
Telephone: (325) 674-2000 Carnegie Class: Masters/L
FAX Number: (325) 674-2202 Calendar System: Semester
URL: www.acu.edu
Established: 1906 Annual Undergrad Tuition & Fees: $37,800
Enrollment: 5,291 Coed
Affiliation or Control: Churches Of Christ IRS Status: 501(c)3
Highest Offering: Doctorate
Accreditation: SC, AAQEP, CAATE, CIDA, DIETD, DIETI, JOUR, MFCD, MUS, NURSE, OT, SP, SW, THEOL

01 President .... Dr. Phil SCHUBERT
100 Senior Advisor to the President .... Ms. Suzanne ALLMON
05 Provost .... Dr. Robert RHODES
111 VP for Advancement .... Mr. Jim ORR
84 VP for Enrollment & Student Life .... Mrs. Tamara LONG
12 VP/Administrative Ofcr ACU Dallas .... Dr. Stephen JOHNSON
115 Chief Investment Ofcr/Pres ACIMCO .... Mr. Jack W. RICH
43 Vice President & General Counsel .... Mr. Slade SULLIVAN
00 Chancellor .... Dr. Royce MONEY
102 ACU Foundation President .... Vacant
20 Vice Provost .... Dr. Susan LEWIS
84 Asst VP Enrollment Dallas .... Ms. Jessica MANNING
49 Dean College of Arts & Sciences .... Dr. Greg STRAUGHN
73 Dean College of Biblical Studies .... Dr. Ken R. CUKROWSKI
50 Dean College of Business Admin .... Dr. Brad CRISP
53 Dean College of Educ & Human Svcs .... Dr. Jennifer SHEWMAKER
92 Dean Honors College .... Dr. Jason MORRIS
58 Dean Graduate & Professional Stds .... Dr. Joey COPE
66 Dean School of Nursing .... Dr. Marcia STRAUGHN
08 Dean Library/Educational Technology .... Mr. James WISER
104 Director of the Ctr Intl Educ .... Dr. Stephen SHEWMAKER
32 Dean of Students .... Mr. Mark LEWIS
36 Director Career Center .... Mrs. Jill FORTSON
06 Registrar/Dir of Academic Dev .... Dr. Eric GUMM
11 Senior VP of Operations .... Mr. Kevin CAMPBELL
26 SVP for Marketing/Strategic Comm .... Mrs. Linda BONNIN
39 Dir Residence Life/Stdnt Advocacy .... Ms. Shannon KACZMAREK
38 Director Univ Counseling Center .... Mr. Tyson ALEXANDER
18 Associate VP of Operations .... Mr. Corey RUFF
24 Exec Dir Teaching & Learning .... Dr. Laura CARROLL
29 Asst VP Alumni & Univ Relations .... Mr. Craig FISHER
19 Chief of Police .... Mr. Jason ELLIS
112 Dir Endowment Strategy/Sr Adv Ofcr .... Mr. Don GARRETT
41 Director of Athletics .... Mr. Allen WARD
15 Chief HR Officer/Title IX Coord .... Mrs. Wendy JONES
88 Director of Faculty Development .... Dr. Cliff BARBARICK
09 Asst Provost for Inst Effectiveness .... Dr. Chris RILEY
96 Director of Purchasing/Procurement .... Ms. Sandy HALL
101 Secretary to the Board of Trustees .... Mr. Slade SULLIVAN
04 Exec Assistant Office of President .... Mrs. Stephanie A. WOODLEE
46 Dir Research/Sponsored Programs .... Dr. Megan ROTH
07 Director of Enrollment Operations .... Mr. Garrett SUBLETTE
22 Title IX Deputy Coordinator .... Mrs. Sherita NICKERSON
28 Chief Diversity Officer .... Vacant
13 Chief Information Technology Ofcr .... Mr. Jon BRUNER
37 Director Student Financial Services .... Mr. Thomas RATLIFF

*Alamo Community College District Central Office (G)

2222 North Alamo Street, San Antonio TX 78215
County: Bexar FICE Identification: 003607
Unit ID: 222497
Telephone: (210) 485-0020 Carnegie Class: N/A
FAX Number: (210) 486-9166
URL: www.alamo.edu

01 Chancellor .... Dr. Mike FLORES
05 Vice Chanc for Academic Success .... Dr. George RAILEY, JR.
11 Vice Chanc for Finance & Admin .... Dr. Diane E. SNYDER
32 Vice Chancellor for Student Success .... Dr. Adelina SILVA
103 Vice Chanc Economic/Workforce Devel .... Mr. Robert MCKINLEY
13 VC Plng/Performance/Info Systems .... Dr. Thomas CLEARY
15 Assoc Vice Chanc Human Resources .... Ms. Linda BOYER-OWENS
18 Assoc Vice Chanc Facilities .... Vacant
10 Assoc VC Finance & Fiscal Services .... Ms. Pamela ANSBOURY
04 Exec Assistant to the Chancellor .... Vacant
111 Int Exec Director Inst Advancement .... Dr. Marie KANE
116 Director of Internal Audit .... Mr. Bill WULLENJOHN
96 Director Acquisitions & Admin Svcs .... Mr. Gary O'BAR
19 Chief Department of Public Safety .... Vacant
21 Comptroller .... Vacant
12 President Northwest Vista College .... Dr. Ric BASER
12 President San Antonio College .... Dr. Robert VELA
12 President St Philip's College .... Dr. Adena WILLIAMS LOSTON
12 President Palo Alto College .... Dr. Robert GARZA
12 Pres Northeast Lakeview College .... Dr. Veronica GARCIA
37 Director Student Financial Aid .... Mr. Harold WHITIS
43 Dir Legal Services/General Counsel .... Mr. Ross LAUGHEAD
09 Dist Dir Inst Rsch/Effect/Planning .... Mr. Velda VILLARREAL

*Northeast Lakeview College (H)

1201 Kitty Hawk Road, Universal City TX 78148
County: Bexar Identification: 667278
Unit ID: 488730
Telephone: (210) 486-5000 Carnegie Class: Assoc/HT-Mix Trad/Non
FAX Number: N/A Calendar System: Semester
URL: www.alamo.edu/nlc
Established: 2007 Annual Undergrad Tuition & Fees (In-District): $6,592
Enrollment: 6,657 Coed
Affiliation or Control: Local IRS Status: 501(c)3
Highest Offering: Associate Degree
Accreditation: SC

02 President .... Dr. Veronica GARCIA
05 Vice Pres Academic Success .... Dr. Laura BOYER
32 Vice Pres Student Success .... Dr. Tangila DOVE

*Northwest Vista College (I)

3535 N Ellison Drive, San Antonio TX 78251-4217
County: Bexar FICE Identification: 033723
Unit ID: 420398
Telephone: (210) 486-4000 Carnegie Class: Assoc/HT-High Non
FAX Number: (210) 486-9105 Calendar System: Semester
URL: www.alamo.edu/nvc
Established: 1995 Annual Undergrad Tuition & Fees (In-District): $6,592
Enrollment: 18,542 Coed
Affiliation or Control: Local IRS Status: 501(c)3
Highest Offering: Associate Degree
Accreditation: SC

02 President .... Dr. Ric N. BASER
11 Vice President for College Services .... Mrs. Erin L. SHERMAN
05 Vice President for Academic Success .... Dr. Daniel POWELL
32 Vice President for Student Success .... Mrs. Deborah GAITAN
04 Executive Assistant to President .... Vacant
08 Director Learning Resources Center .... Mrs. Norma VELEZ-VENDRELL

38 Dean for Student Success .... Mrs. Jennifer COMEDY-HOLMES
26 Dir of Marketing & Strategic Comm .... Mrs. Renata SERAFIN
13 Director Info/Communications Tech .... Mr. Felix SALINAS
37 Associate Director of Financial Aid .... Mrs. Rosalinda ENCINA
113 Assistant Bursar .... Mrs. Patricia SANCHEZ
15 Sr Human Resources Generalist .... Mrs. Stacey L. BLUM
45 Director of Resources & College Dev .... Ms. Judy V. CAMARGO
18 Superintendent NVC .... Vacant
88 Dean for Academic Success/Support .... Mr. Patrick FONTENOT
20 Dean for Academic Success .... Dr. Russell FROHARDT
09 Director of Institutional Research .... Dr. Eliza HERNANDEZ
84 Director of Enrollment Management .... Dr. Yolanda REYES-GUEVARA
07 Associate Director of Admissions .... Mrs. Yvonne GUERRA
121 Dean for Student Success-Academic .... Mrs. Robin LUND

*Palo Alto College (A)

1400 W Villaret Boulevard, San Antonio TX 78224-2499

County: Bexar | FICE Identification: 023413 | Unit ID: 246354
Telephone: (210) 486-3000 | Carnegie Class: Assoc/HT-High Non
FAX Number: (210) 921-5005 | Calendar System: Semester
URL: www.alamo.edu
Established: 1985 | Annual Undergrad Tuition & Fees (In-District): $6,592
Enrollment: 11,193 | Coed
Affiliation or Control: Local | IRS Status: 501(c)3
Highest Offering: Associate Degree
Accreditation: SC

02 President .... Dr. Robert GARZA
05 Vice President for Academic Success .... Ms. Elizabeth TANNER
10 Vice Pres of College Services .... Ms. Katherine DOSS
32 Vice President for Student Success .... Mr. Gilberto BECERRA
49 Dean Academic Success .... Mr. Patrick LEE
50 Dean Academic Success .... Dr. Raymond PFANG
08 Dean of Learning Resources .... Ms. Tina MESA
35 Dean of Student Success .... Ms. Monica AYALA-JIMENEZ
26 Director of Public Relations .... Mr. Jerry ARELLANO
113 Bursar .... Mr. Edward SANCHEZ
37 Assc Dir Student Financial Services .... Ms. Shirley LEIJA
41 Athletic Director .... Mr. Edward J. MORENO
18 Facilities Superintendnt/Phys Plant .... Mr. Sergio RIVERA
29 Coordinator Alumni Relations .... Ms. Priscilla AGUILAR
09 Dir Inst Rsrch/Plng/Effectiveness .... Ms. Caroline HARING
25 Director of Advancement & Grants .... Mr. Gaston CANTU
04 Administrative Asst to President .... Ms. Connie MARTINEZ
13 Chief Info Technology Director .... Mr. Nicolas BLAKENEY
84 Director Enrollment Management .... Ms. Elizabeth AGUILAR-VILLARREAL

*St. Philip's College (B)

1801 Martin Luther King, San Antonio TX 78203-2098

County: Bexar | FICE Identification: 003608 | Unit ID: 227854
Telephone: (210) 486-2000 | Carnegie Class: Assoc/HVT-High Non
FAX Number: N/A | Calendar System: Semester
URL: www.alamo.edu/spc/
Established: 1898 | Annual Undergrad Tuition & Fees (In-District): $6,592
Enrollment: 12,696 | Coed
Affiliation or Control: Local | IRS Status: 501(c)3
Highest Offering: Associate Degree
Accreditation: SC, ACFEI, CAHIIM, COARC, CVT, DMS, HT, MLTAD, NAEYC, OTA, PTAA, RAD, SURGT

02 President .... Dr. Adena LOSTON WILLIAMS
05 Vice Pres of Academic Success .... Dr. Randall DAWSON
32 Int Vice Pres of Student Success .... Dr. Paul MACHEN
11 Int Vice Pres for College Svcs .... Dr. Vanessa ANDERSON
35 Int Dean for Student Success .... Ms. Destiny HARPER-LANE
84 Dean Student Success/Enroll Mgmt .... Ms. Christina CORTEZ
75 Dean Acad Success Appl Sci/Tech-SW .... Mr. Christopher BEARDSALL
75 Dean Acad Success Appl Sci/Tech-MLK .... Ms. Edith OROZCO
49 Dean for Acad Success Arts & Sci .... Mr. George JOHNSON
76 Dean for Acad Success Health Sci .... Ms. Jessica COOPER
37 Asst Director of Financial Aid .... Ms. Grace ZAPATA
45 Dir Planning/Research/Effectiveness .... Vacant
113 Assistant Bursar .... Ms. Sophia GONZALEZ
26 Director of Public Relations .... Ms. Adrian JACKSON
72 Director Instructional Technology .... Mr. John ORONA
18 Chief Facilities/Physical Plant .... Vacant
111 Director Institutional Advancement ... Dr. Sharon CROCKETT-BELL
114 Campus Budget Officer .... Mr. Jorge FLORES
106 Int Dean for Acad Success/Acad Svcs .... Dr. Diane GAVIN
25 Acad Pgm Dir/Title III/Grants Mgmt .... Dr. Tomeka WILSON
46 Director of Strategic Initiatives .... Mr. Jeffrey FRENCH
04 Executive Asst to President .... Ms. Marsha HALL

*San Antonio College (C)

1819 N Main, San Antonio TX 78212-4299

County: Bexar | FICE Identification: 009163 | Unit ID: 227924
Telephone: (210) 486-0000 | Carnegie Class: Assoc/HT-High Non
FAX Number: N/A | Calendar System: Semester
URL: www.alamo.edu/sac
Established: 1925 | Annual Undergrad Tuition & Fees (In-District): $6,592
Enrollment: 19,231 | Coed
Affiliation or Control: Local | IRS Status: 501(c)3
Highest Offering: Baccalaureate
Accreditation: SC, ADNUR, CEA, DA, EMT, FUSER, MAC, NAEYC

02 President .... Dr. Robert H. VELA
32 Interim VP of Student Success .... Dr. Tiffany COX HERNANDEZ
11 Vice President of College Services .... Dr. Stella LOVATO
05 Interim VP of Academic Success .... Dr. Stella LOVATO
35 Interim Dean of Student Success .... Ms. Christina HORTON
72 Int Dean Acad Success Prof/Tech .... Dr. Jonathan LEE
106 Dean of Academic Success Online DC .... Dr. Sobia KHAN
49 Dean of Academic Success Art & Sci .... Dr. Conrad KRUEGER
88 Dean of Performance Excellence .... Dr. Francisco SOLIS
35 Dean of Student Success .... Dr. Maria DE LOS REYES
26 Director of Public Relations .... Mr. Ken SLAVIN
08 Director of Library Services .... Mr. LeBlanc LEE
84 Director of Enrollment Management .... Ms. Amy C. PENA
06 Dir of Student Success/Registrar .... Mr. J. Martin ORTEGA
85 Coordinator International Students .... Ms. Patrice BALLARD

Alvin Community College (D)

3110 Mustang Road, Alvin TX 77511-4898

County: Brazoria | FICE Identification: 003539 | Unit ID: 222567
Telephone: (281) 756-3500 | Carnegie Class: Assoc/MT-VT-High Non
FAX Number: (281) 756-3854 | Calendar System: Semester
URL: www.alvincollege.edu
Established: 1948 | Annual Undergrad Tuition & Fees (In-District): $2,834
Enrollment: 5,737 | Coed
Affiliation or Control: Local | IRS Status: 501(c)3
Highest Offering: Associate Degree
Accreditation: SC, ADNUR, COARC, DMS, EMT, NDT, POLYT

01 President .... Dr. Robert J. EXLEY
05 Vice President Instruction .... Dr. Cynthia GRIFFITH
10 VP Administrative Services .... Mr. Karl STAGER
32 VP Student Services .... Dr. Jade BORNE
49 Dean of Arts & Sciences .... Mr. John MATULA
76 Dean Legal and Health Sciences .... Dr. Stacy EBERT
51 Dean Continued Educ/Wkforce Devel .... Vacant
97 Dean General Educ/Academic Support .... Dr. Nadezhda (Nadia) NAZARENKO
88 Dean Prof/Tech/Human Performance .... Mr. Jeffrey PARKS
06 Registrar .... Ms. Irene M. ROBINSON
08 Director Library Services .... Vacant
21 Director Fiscal Affairs/Controller .... Ms. Beth NELSON
13 Exec Dir Information Technology .... Mr. Kelly KLIMPT
37 Director Student Financial Aid .... Ms. Gabriela LEON
15 VP Human Resources .... Vacant
18 Director Physical Plant .... Ms. Hameedah MAJEED
29 Director Alumni Relations .... Ms. Wendy DEL BELLO
07 Dean Student Support Services .... Dr. Akilah MARTIN
09 Exec Dir of Inst Effective/Research .... Dr. Pamelyn SHEFMAN
30 VP Development & Outreach .... Ms. Wendy DEL BELLO
26 Chief Public Relations Officer .... Ms. Wendy DEL BELLO
88 Assistant Director Fiscal Affairs .... Ms. Laurel JOSEPH
35 Coordinator Student Activities .... Ms. Querencia JOSHUA
04 Sr Exec Asst to President/Board Mgr .... Ms. Tammy GIFFROW
19 Chief of Police .... Mr. Ronald PHILLIPS
96 Director of Purchasing .... Mr. Alan PHILLIPS

Amarillo College (E)

PO Box 447, Amarillo TX 79178-0001

County: Potter | FICE Identification: 003540 | Unit ID: 222576
Telephone: (806) 371-5000 | Carnegie Class: Assoc/MT-VT-High Trad
FAX Number: (806) 371-5370 | Calendar System: Semester
URL: www.actx.edu
Established: 1929 | Annual Undergrad Tuition & Fees (In-District): $3,168
Enrollment: 9,079 | Coed
Affiliation or Control: State/Local | IRS Status: 501(c)3
Highest Offering: Associate Degree
Accreditation: SC, ADNUR, COARC, DA, DH, EMT, MLTAD, MUS, NMT, OTA, PTAA, RAD, RTT, SURGT

01 President .... Dr. Russell D. LOWERY-HART
43 EVP/General Counsel .... Mr. Mark D. WHITE
05 VP of Academic Affairs .... Dr. Tamara T. CLUNIS
10 VP of Business Affairs .... Mr. Chris SHARP
26 VP Communications & Marketing .... Mr. Kevin J. BALL
84 VP of Enrollment Management .... Mr. Bob C. AUSTIN
32 VP of Student Affairs .... Ms. Denese SKINNER
15 VP for Human Resources .... Ms. Cheryl JONES
20 Assoc VP Academic Affairs .... Mr. Frank E. SOBEY
78 AVP Innovation & Work-Based Lrng .... Ms. Reagan HALES
88 Associate VP Academic Services .... Ms. Becky K. BURTON
103 Exec Director Workforce Development .... Ms. Toni B. GRAY
76 Dean of Health Sciences .... Mrs. Kimberly A. CROWLEY
18 Manager Physical Plant .... Mr. Jim BACA
37 Director Financial Aid .... Vacant
08 Director AC Library Network .... Ms. Emily R. GILBERT
06 Registrar/Dir of Admissions .Ms. Kristin D. MCDONALD-WILLEY
19 Chief of Police .... Mr. Scott ACKER
102 COO AC Foundation .... Mrs. Tracy D. DOUGHERTY
09 Exec Dir Decision Analytics & IR .. Mr. Collin C. WITHERSPOON
121 Director of Advising .... Mr. Ernesto F. OLMOS
88 Director Amarillo Museum of Art .... Mrs. Kim B. MAHAN
88 Director Criminal Justice Program .... Mr. Eric C. WALLACE
96 Director of Purchasing/Records Ret .... Ms. Kimberly L. CARLILE
81 Dean of STEM .... Ms. Edythe L. CARTER
72 Dean of Technical Education .... Dr. Linda MUNOZ
49 Dean of Liberal Arts .... Ms. Rebecca EASTON
46 Vice Pres Strategic Initiatives .... Ms. Cara J. CROWLEY
13 Chief Information Officer .... Mr. Shane E. HEPLER
04 Administrative Asst to President .... Ms. Joy D. BRENNEMAN
106 Dir Online Education/E-learning .... Vacant
108 Director Inst Effectiveness .... Ms. Tina M. BABB
35 Director of Student Life .... Ms. Amber HAMILTON
28 Director of Outreach Services .... Ms. Cassie MONTGOMERY
12 Dean of Campus Ops Moore County .... Ms. Renee VINCENT
12 Dean of Campus Ops Hereford .... Mr. Daniel ESQUIVEL
112 Major Gifts Officer .... Ms. B. Peyton BIVINS

Amberton University (F)

1700 Eastgate Drive, Garland TX 75041

County: Dallas | FICE Identification: 022594 | Unit ID: 222628
Telephone: (972) 279-6511 | Carnegie Class: Masters/L
FAX Number: (972) 279-9773 | Calendar System: Semester
URL: www.amberton.edu
Established: 1971 | Annual Undergrad Tuition & Fees: N/A
Enrollment: 1,103 | Coed
Affiliation or Control: Independent Non-Profit | IRS Status: 501(c)3
Highest Offering: Master's
Accreditation: SC

01 President .... Dr. Melinda REAGAN
05 Academic Dean .... Dr. Blair STEPHENSON
111 Dean Univ Advance/VP Strategic Svcs .... Dr. Jo Lynn LOYD
10 Chief Business Officer .... Mr. Brent BRADSHAW
06 Registrar .... Ms. Hannah GRAY
32 Dean for Student Services .... Vacant
84 Director for Recruiting .... Vacant
08 Head Librarian .... Ms. Jody PENDLETON

American College of Acupuncture and Oriental Medicine (G)

9100 Park West Drive, Houston TX 77063-4104

County: Harris | FICE Identification: 031533 | Unit ID: 429085
Telephone: (713) 780-9777 | Carnegie Class: Spec-4-yr-Other Health
FAX Number: (713) 781-5781 | Calendar System: Trimester
URL: www.acaom.edu
Established: 1991 | Annual Graduate Tuition & Fees: N/A
Enrollment: 123 | Coed
Affiliation or Control: Proprietary | IRS Status: Proprietary
Highest Offering: Doctorate; No Undergraduates
Accreditation: SC, ACUP

01 President .... Dr. John Paul LIANG
11 Vice President of Operations .... Ms. Angel GUINARA
05 Dean of Academic Affairs .... Dr. Wen HUANG
20 Dean of Clinical Training .... Dr. Baisong ZHONG
06 Registrar .... Ms. Vicki ROSMANN
09 Dir Inst Research/Effectiveness .... Mr. Michael Dale STAFFORD
37 Financial Aid Ofcr/Inst Compliance .... Ms. Theresa LIGON

American InterContinental University - Houston (H)

9999 Richmond Avenue, Houston TX 77042-4516

Telephone: (832) 201-3600 | Identification: 666335
Accreditation: &HLC, ACBSP

† Regional accreditation is carried under the parent institution in Schaumburg, IL.

Ana G. Mendez University Dallas Campus (I)

3010 N. Stemmons Fwy, Dallas TX 75247

Telephone: (469) 341-7300 | Identification: 770947
Accreditation: &M

† Branch campus of Universidad Ana G. Mendez, Rio Piedras, PR

Angelina College (J)

PO Box 1768, Lufkin TX 75902-1768

County: Angelina | FICE Identification: 006661 | Unit ID: 222822
Telephone: (936) 639-1301 | Carnegie Class: Assoc/HVT-Mix Trad/Non
FAX Number: (936) 639-4299 | Calendar System: Semester
URL: www.angelina.edu
Established: 1966 | Annual Undergrad Tuition & Fees (In-District): $4,380
Enrollment: 4,195 | Coed
Affiliation or Control: State/Local | IRS Status: 501(c)3
Highest Offering: Associate Degree
Accreditation: SC, COARC, DMS, EMT, RAD, SURGT

01 President .... Dr. Michael SIMON
05 Vice Pres Academic Affairs .... Dr. Cynthia CASPARIS
10 Vice President Business Services .... Mr. Chris SULLIVAN
31 Dean of Community Services .... Mr. Tim DITORO
111 Exec Dir Inst Advancement .... Mrs. Dana SMITHHART
84 Exec Dir Marketing & Enrollment .... Mrs. Krista BROWN
13 Sr Dir Information Technology .... Mr. Kenneth STREET
15 Sr Director Human Resources .... Mrs. Tifini WHIDDON
18 Chief Facilities/Physical Plant .... Mr. Steve CAPPS
21 Controller .... Mrs. Melissa GOINS
37 Dir Student Financial Aid .... Mr. Glen GOFORTH

AOMA Graduate School of Integrative Medicine (A)

4701 West Gate Boulevard, Austin TX 78745
County: Travis FICE Identification: 031564
Unit ID: 429094
Telephone: (512) 454-1188 Carnegie Class: Spec-4-yr-Other Health
FAX Number: (512) 454-7001 Calendar System: Quarter
URL: www.aoma.edu
Established: 1993 Annual Graduate Tuition & Fees: N/A
Enrollment: 135 Coed
Affiliation or Control: Proprietary IRS Status: Proprietary
Highest Offering: Doctorate; No Undergraduates
Accreditation: SC, ACUP

01 President .... Dr. Mary FARIA
05 Vice President of Faculty .... Dr. Qianzhi (Jamie) WU
20 VP of Academics .... Dr. Beth HOWLETT
32 Sr Dir Student Services & Diversity .... Dr. Dami TOKOYA
10 Acting CFO .... Ms. Linda FONTAINE
17 Sr Dir Doctoral Pgm/Clinical Excel .... Dr. Violet SONG
11 Sr Director of Operations .... Ms. Stephanee OWENBY
08 Head Librarian .... Ms. Rita TERRELL
07 Dir or Admissions & Marketing .... Mr. Brian BECKER
06 Registrar .... Ms. Ashley LOYD
58 Dean of Academics .... Dr. Yuxin HE
88 Dir Clinical Doctorate and IE .... Dr. Diane STANLEY
88 Director Acupuncture .... Dr. Yuxing LIU
106 Sr Dir Masters Pgm & Distance Educ .... Dr. Phil GARRISION
88 Dir International Academic Research .... Dr. Jing FAN
37 Director Student Financial Aid .... Ms. Estella PROCTOR
81 Director of Biomedical Sciences .... Dr. Randi SAVAGE
88 Director of Clinical Readiness .... Ms. Reagan TAYLOR

Arlington Baptist University (B)

3001 W Division, Arlington TX 76012-3497
County: Tarrant FICE Identification: 020814
Unit ID: 222877
Telephone: (817) 461-8741 Carnegie Class: Spec-4-yr-Faith
FAX Number: (817) 274-1138 Calendar System: Semester
URL: www.ABU.edu
Established: 1939 Annual Undergrad Tuition & Fees: $15,050
Enrollment: 160 Coed
Affiliation or Control: Baptist IRS Status: 501(c)3
Highest Offering: Master's
Accreditation: BI

01 President .... Dr. Clifton MCDANIEL
05 Vice Pres Academic Affairs .... Ms. Janie TAYLOR
32 Dean of Students .... Vacant
10 Business Manager/Dir Financial Aid .... Mr. David INGRAM
06 Registrar .... Mrs. Kristi HUGHES
08 Head Librarian .... Ms. Amy SCHAEFFER
18 Director Physical Plant .... Mr. Wes HRABAL
40 Director Bookstore .... Mrs. Vickie BRYANT
111 Director Institutional Advancement .... Vacant
41 Athletic Director .... Vacant
106 Dir Online Education/E-learning .... Vacant
37 Director Student Financial Aid .... Mr. John ROCHA
13 Chief Info Technology Officer (CIO) .... Vacant

The Art Institute of Austin (C)

101 W. Louis Henna Blvd, Ste 100, Austin TX 78728
Telephone: (512) 691-1707 Identification: 770973
Accreditation: &SC, CIDA

Art Institute of Dallas (D)

8080 Park Lane, Suite 100, Dallas TX 75231-5993
Telephone: (214) 692-8080 FICE Identification: 025396
Accreditation: &SC, CIDA

† Regional accreditation is carried under the parent institution, Miami International University, Miami, FL.

The Art Institute of Houston (E)

4140 Southwest Freeway, Houston TX 77027
County: Harris FICE Identification: 021171
Unit ID: 222938
Telephone: (713) 623-2040 Carnegie Class: Spec-4-yr-Arts
FAX Number: (713) 966-2700 Calendar System: Quarter
URL: www.aih.aii.edu
Established: 1978 Annual Undergrad Tuition & Fees: $19,354
Enrollment: 511 Coed
Affiliation or Control: Proprietary IRS Status: Proprietary
Highest Offering: Baccalaureate
Accreditation: SC, CIDA

01 President .... Harvey M. GIBLIN
05 Dean of Academic Affairs .... Eric WATSON
32 Vice President of Student Affairs .... LaToya WILLIAMS
07 Dean of Admissions .... Pierre LAFAILLE
37 Financial Aid Director .... Cory TYBERENDT
06 Registrar .... Cynthia HOOPER
04 Executive Assistant to President .... Tanya LITTLE-PALMER

The Art Institute of San Antonio (F)

10000 IH-10 W, Ste 200, San Antonio TX 78230
Telephone: (210) 338-7320 Identification: 770974
Accreditation: &SC, CIDA

Auguste Escoffier School of Culinary Arts (G)

6020-B Dilliard Circle, Austin TX 78752-4438
County: Travis FICE Identification: 037276
Unit ID: 444556
Telephone: (512) 451-5743 Carnegie Class: Spec 2-yr-A&S
FAX Number: (512) 467-9120 Calendar System: Quarter
URL: www.escoffier.edu
Established: 1997 Annual Undergrad Tuition & Fees: N/A
Enrollment: 610 Coed
Affiliation or Control: Proprietary IRS Status: Proprietary
Highest Offering: Associate Degree
Accreditation: COE, ACFEI

01 Campus President .... Mr. Marcus MCMELLON
07 Director of Admissions .... Mr. David NORRIS
37 Director Student Financial Aid .... Ms. Theresa BARGAS
36 Director of Career Services .... Ms. Ann DERRICK
10 Director Business Operations .... Ms. Mary REARDON

Austin College (H)

900 N Grand Avenue, Sherman TX 75090-4400
County: Grayson FICE Identification: 003543
Unit ID: 222983
Telephone: (903) 813-2000 Carnegie Class: Bac-A&S
FAX Number: (903) 813-3199 Calendar System: 4/1/4
URL: www.austincollege.edu
Established: 1849 Annual Undergrad Tuition & Fees: $42,590
Enrollment: 1,302 Coed
Affiliation or Control: Presbyterian Church (U.S.A.) IRS Status: 501(c)3
Highest Offering: Master's
Accreditation: SC

01 President .... Mr. Steven P. O'DAY
05 VP Acad Aff & Dean of the Faculty .... Dr. Beth GILL
32 VP Stdnt Affs/Chief Incl & Div Ofcr .... Mr. Carllos LASSITER
111 Vice President for Institutional Ad .... Ms. Gillian LOCKE
10 Vice President for Business Affairs .... Ms. Heidi B. ELLIS
84 Vice President for Inst Enrollment .... Ms. Baylee L. KOWERT
21 Assoc VP Business Affairs .... Ms. Karen JOHNSON
110 Sr Assoc VP Inst Advancement .... Ms. Suzanne CROUCH
29 Exec Dir Inst Events/Alumni Engmt .... Ms. Kate SHELLEY
37 AVP Enrollmt/Exec Dir Financial Aid .... Ms. Laurie COULTER
07 AVP Enrollment/Dean of Admission .... Vacant
42 Chaplain/Dir of Church Relations .... Dr. John D. WILLIAMS
35 Dean of Students .... Mr. Michael DEEN
06 Exec Dir Inst Research/Registrar .... Dr. Eugenia HARRIS
08 College Librarian/Library Director .... Ms. Barbara CORNELIUS
79 Dean of Humanities .... Dr. Greg KINZER
81 Dean of Sciences .... Dr. Michael HIGGS
83 Dean of Social Sciences .... Dr. Lisa M. BROWN
15 Director of Human Resources .... Ms. Melanie OELFKE
36 Director Career Services .... Ms. Margie A. NORMAN
13 Director IT .... Mr. Garrett HUBBARD
53 Chair of Education Dept .... Dr. Sandy PHILIPOSE
104 International Education Coordinator .... Ms. Cheryl MARCELO
26 Chief Mktg & Communications Ofcr .... Dr. Lynn Z. WOMBLE
19 Chief of Police .... Ms. Kelly KENNEMER
40 Manager of Campus Bookstore .... Ms. Kelly JACKSON
27 Director of Communications .... Ms. Vickie S. KIRBY
18 Exec Director of Facilities .... Mr. David TURK
96 Purchasing & Accounts Payable Acct .... Ms. Kathy ABATE
102 Dir Corp/Foundation/Gov Relations .... Ms. Lisa EMERY
41 Director of Athletics .... Mr. David NORMAN
101 Asst to Pres/Asst Sec of Board .... Ms. Genna BETHEL
38 Director of Counseling Services .... Ms. Teresa MOORE
39 Director of Residence Life .... Mr. Patrick MILLER
09 Director of Institutional Research .... Mr. Amon SEAGULL

Austin Community College District (I)

5930 Middle Fiskville Road, Austin TX 78752-4390
County: Travis FICE Identification: 012015
Unit ID: 222992
Telephone: (512) 223-7598 Carnegie Class: Assoc/MT-VT-Mix Trad/Non
FAX Number: (512) 223-7638 Calendar System: Semester
URL: www.austincc.edu
Established: 1972 Annual Undergrad Tuition & Fees (In-District): $10,830
Enrollment: 39,896 Coed
Affiliation or Control: State/Local IRS Status: 501(c)3
Highest Offering: Baccalaureate
Accreditation: SC, ACBSP, ACFEI, ADNUR, CAHIIM, DH, DMS, EMT, MLTAD, NAEYC, NUR, OTA, PNUR, PTAA, RAD, SURGT

01 Chancellor .... Dr. Richard M. RHODES
03 Provost/Exec Vice Pres .... Dr. Charles COOK
10 EVP Finance & Administration .... Mr. Neil W. VICKERS
11 EVP Campus Operation & Public Affs .. Dr. Molly Beth MALCOLM
05 VP Instruction .... Mr. Michael T. MIDGLEY
32 VP Student Affairs .... Dr. Shasta BUCHANAN
15 VP Human Resources .... Ms. Geraldine TUCKER
09 VP Effectiveness & Accountability .... Dr. Jenna O. CULLINANE HEGE
21 VP Business Services .... Ms. Angela HODGE
13 VP Information Technology .... Mr. Imad CONSTANTINI
45 VP Inst Planning/Develop & Eval .... Dr. Mary E. HARRIS
18 Int VP Facilities & Construction .... Mr. Aziz HUSSAINI
26 VP Communications & Marketing .... Ms. Brette E. LEA
06 Registrar .... Ms. Glynis MILLER
07 Executive Director of Admissions .... Ms. Linda TERRY
08 Dean Library Services .... Dr. Julie TODARO
19 Chief of Police .... Mr. Lynn DIXON
37 Executive Director Financial Aid .... Mr. Jason BRISENO
96 Director Procure to Pay .... Mr. Robert HALL
29 Director Alumni Relations .... Ms. Mary Ann CICALA
04 Special Assistant to the Chancellor .... Ms. Pamela SUTTON
28 Director of Diversity .... Mr. Larry DAVIS
30 Director of Development .... Ms. Amy BAWCOM

Austin Presbyterian Theological Seminary (J)

100 E 27th Street, Austin TX 78705-5797
County: Travis FICE Identification: 003544
Unit ID: 223001
Telephone: (512) 472-6736 Carnegie Class: Spec-4-yr-Faith
FAX Number: (512) 479-0738 Calendar System: Semester
URL: www.austinseminary.edu
Established: 1902 Annual Graduate Tuition & Fees: N/A
Enrollment: 181 Coed
Affiliation or Control: Presbyterian Church (U.S.A.) IRS Status: 501(c)3
Highest Offering: Doctorate; No Undergraduates
Accreditation: SC, THEOL

01 President .... Rev. Theodore J. WARDLAW
05 Academic Dean .... Dr. David H. JENSEN
10 Vice Pres Finance/Administration .... Ms. Heather ZDANCEWICZ
111 Vice Pres Institutional Advancement .... Ms. Donna SCOTT
32 Dean of Students .... Rev. Sarah GAVENTA
84 Vice Pres for Enrollment Management .... Rev. Jorge D. HERRERA
51 VP Education Beyond the Walls .... Ms. Melissa WIGINTON
08 Director of the Stitt Library .... Dr. Timothy LINCOLN
06 Asst Dean Academic Affs/Registrar .... Ms. Mary WALL
26 Director of Communications .... Ms. Randal WHITTINGTON
100 Chief of Staff/President's Office .... Ms. Mona SANTANDREA
13 Senior Director of Info Technology .... Ms. Julie NEWTON
37 Director of Financial Aid .... Mr. William WEST
18 Chief Facilities/Physical Plant .... Mr. John EVERETT
30 Director of Development .... Rev. Alan KRUMMENACHER
110 Director of Advancement Services .... Mr. JR BARDEN
29 Director Alumni & Church Relations .... Mr. Gary MATHEWS

Bakke Graduate University (K)

8515 Greenville Ave, S206, Dallas TX 75243-7039
County: Dallas FICE Identification: 031108
Unit ID: 420705
Telephone: (214) 329-4447 Carnegie Class: Spec-4-yr-Faith
FAX Number: (214) 347-9367 Calendar System: Semester
URL: www.bgu.edu
Established: 1990 Annual Graduate Tuition & Fees: N/A
Enrollment: 159 Coed
Affiliation or Control: Independent Non-Profit IRS Status: 501(c)3
Highest Offering: Doctorate; No Undergraduates
Accreditation: TRACS

01 President .... Dr. Brad SMITH
05 Academic Dean .... Dr. Bryan MCCABE
10 Chief Operations/Financial Ofcr .... Ms. Carolyn COCHRAN
06 Registrar .... Ms. Judi MELTON
07 Director of Admissions .... Ms. Kafi CARRASCO
08 Head Librarian .... Ms. Jennifer ROMAN
106 Dir Online Education/E-learning .... Ms. Nathalia BURROWS
37 Director Student Financial Aid .... Ms. Carolyn COCHRAN
09 Dir Institutional Effectiveness .... Dr. Judi MELTON

Baptist Health System School of Health Professions (L)

8400 Datapoint Drive, San Antonio TX 78229
County: Bexar FICE Identification: 006606
Unit ID: 223083
Telephone: (210) 297-9636 Carnegie Class: Spec-4-yr-Other Health
FAX Number: (210) 297-0075 Calendar System: Semester
URL: www.bshp.edu
Established: 1903 Annual Undergrad Tuition & Fees: N/A
Enrollment: 567 Coed
Affiliation or Control: Proprietary IRS Status: Proprietary
Highest Offering: Master's
Accreditation: ABHES, ADNUR, NUR, RAD, SURGT, SURTEC

01 President and Dean .... Dr. Bill DREES
04 Administrative Asst to President .... Diane TYLER
08 Director of Library .... Karen HOLT
10 Director of Finance .... Priti LAXMI
37 Director of Student Financial Aid .... Patrick REYNA
13 Director of Information Systems .... Nancy ORTIZ
06 Registrar .... Allison MCDANIEL

† Tuition varies by degree program.

Baptist Hospitals of Southeast Texas School of Radiologic Technology (A)

3030 Fannin Ste A, Beaumont TX 77704

County: Jefferson Identification: 667153
Telephone: (409) 212-5724 Carnegie Class: Not Classified
FAX Number: N/A Calendar System: Semester
URL: https://www.bhset.net/our-services/school-of-radiologic-tech
Established: 1952 Annual Undergrad Tuition & Fees: N/A
Enrollment: N/A Coed
Affiliation or Control: Independent Non-Profit IRS Status: 501(c)3
Highest Offering: Associate Degree
Accreditation: **ABHES**, RAD

01 Program Director ... Deborah SMITH
11 Chief of Administration ... Justin DOSS

Baptist Missionary Association Theological Seminary (B)

P.O. Box 670/1530 East Pine Street, Jacksonville TX 75766-5407

County: Cherokee FICE Identification: 023312
Unit ID: 223117
Telephone: (903) 586-2501 Carnegie Class: Spec-4-yr-Faith
FAX Number: (903) 586-0378 Calendar System: Semester
URL: www.bmats.edu
Established: 1957 Annual Undergrad Tuition & Fees: $6,900
Enrollment: 110 Coed
Affiliation or Control: Baptist IRS Status: 501(c)3
Highest Offering: Master's
Accreditation: **SC**, THEOL

01 President ... Dr. Charley HOLMES
05 Dean/Registrar ... Dr. Philip ATTEBERY
04 Assistant to the President ... Keri SOUTHERN
32 Director of Student Services ... Dr. Ronnie J. JOHNSON
08 Library Director ... Jacob GUCKER
10 Chief Business Officer ... Chris PROCTOR

Baptist University of the Americas (C)

2418 W. Ansley Blvd., Bldg #3, San Antonio TX 78224-1336

County: Bexar FICE Identification: 037333
Unit ID: 444398
Telephone: (210) 924-4338 Carnegie Class: Spec-4-yr-Faith
FAX Number: (210) 924-0888 Calendar System: Semester
URL: www.bua.edu
Established: 1947 Annual Undergrad Tuition & Fees: $6,480
Enrollment: 117 Coed
Affiliation or Control: Baptist IRS Status: 501(c)3
Highest Offering: Baccalaureate
Accreditation: **BI**

01 President/CEO ... Dr. Abraham JAQUEZ
100 Chief of Staff ... Dr. Gabriel CORTES
05 Dean Academic Affairs ... Dr. Sam GARCIA
10 Director for Admin and Finance ... Mr. Kevin RODRIGUEZ
37 Director of Financial Aid ... Mrs. Araceli ACOSTA
06 Registrar ... Ms. Maria DIAZ

Baylor College of Medicine (D)

One Baylor Plaza, Houston TX 77030-3411

County: Harris FICE Identification: 004949
Unit ID: 223223
Telephone: (713) 798-4951 Carnegie Class: Spec-4-yr-Med
FAX Number: (713) 798-3692 Calendar System: Quarter
URL: www.bcm.edu
Established: 1900 Annual Graduate Tuition & Fees: N/A
Enrollment: 1,607 Coed
Affiliation or Control: Independent Non-Profit IRS Status: 501(c)3
Highest Offering: Doctorate; No Undergraduates
Accreditation: **SC**, ANEST, ARCPA, IPSY, MED, OPE

00 Chancellor ... Dr. Bert O'MALLEY
01 President and CEO ... Dr. Paul KLOTMAN
05 Provost/SVP Acad & Faculty Affairs ... Dr. Alicia MONROE
17 EVP/Dean of Clinical Affairs ... Dr. James MCDEAVITT
10 Sr VP/Chief Business Officer ... Mrs. Kimberly C. DAVID
111 Vice Pres Inst Advancement ... Ms. Stephanie YOUNG
43 Sr Vice Pres/General Counsel ... Mr. Robert F. CORRIGAN, JR.
26 VP Communications/Cmty Outreach ... Ms. Lori WILLIAMS
15 Vice President Human Resources ... Mr. Dane FRIEND
46 Sr Vice President/Dean Research ... Dr. Adam KUSPA
13 VP Information Technology ... Mr. Lee LEIBER
86 Vice Pres Government Relations ... Mr. Herb BUTRUM
88 Dean Natl Sch Tropical Medicine ... Dr. Peter J. HOTEZ
21 VP Finance/CFO ... Ms. Julie NICKELL
63 Dean School of Medicine ... Dr. Jennifer CHRISTNER
58 Dean Graduate Sch Biomed Sciences ... Dr. Carolyn SMITH
76 Dean School of Health Professions ... Dr. Robert MCLAUGHLIN
51 Sr Assoc Dean Cont Medical Educ ... Dr. C. Michael FORDIS, JR.
07 Assoc Dean for Admissions ... Dr. Karen JOHNSON
28 Assoc Dean Diversity/Equity/Admiss ... Dr. Jesus G. VALLEJO
32 Assoc Dean of Student Affairs ... Dr. Joseph KASS
35 Assistant Dean Student Affairs ... Dr. Andrea G. STOLAR
21 Controller ... Mr. Douglas R. SPADE
20 Assoc Provost Academic Affairs ... Ms. Lily SHIH
37 Director Student Financial Planning ... Ms. Hilda DELEON
88 Exec Director Environmental Safety ... Mr. Paul MURACA
75 Director Occupational Medicine ... Dr. James E. KELAHER
29 Director Alumni Affairs ... Mr. Alexander M. HOPKINS
96 Director Supply Chain Management ... Mr. Miguel MACHADO
06 Registrar ... Ms. Latoya R. WHITAKER
88 Asst Dean Graduate Medical Educ ... Dr. Nana E. COLEMAN
20 Associate Dean Curriculum ... Dr. Nadia ISMAIL
20 Associate Provost Faculty Affairs ... Dr. William THOMSON
09 Assoc Provost Fac Dev/Inst Research ... Dr. Nancy MORENO
28 Assoc Prov Inst Diversity/Stdnt Svc ... Dr. Toi HARRIS
04 Admin Assistant to the President ... Ms. Julie WOLKEN
100 Chief of Staff ... Ms. Lorie TABAK
101 Exec Dir Inst Gov/Board Rels ... Ms. Carolyn COCANOUGHER

Baylor University (E)

One Bear Place #97096, Waco TX 76798-7096

County: McLennan FICE Identification: 003545
Unit ID: 223232
Telephone: (254) 710-3555 Carnegie Class: DU-Higher
FAX Number: (254) 710-3557 Calendar System: Semester
URL: www.baylor.edu
Established: 1845 Annual Undergrad Tuition & Fees: $49,246
Enrollment: 19,297 Coed
Affiliation or Control: Baptist IRS Status: 501(c)3
Highest Offering: Doctorate
Accreditation: **SC**, CAATE, CIDA, CLPSY, DIETD, DIETI, HSA, IPSY, JOUR, LAW, MIDWF, MUS, NURSE, PH, PTA, SP, SW, THEA, THEOL

01 President ... Dr. Linda A. LIVINGSTONE
05 Provost ... Dr. Nancy W. BRICKHOUSE
100 Chief of Staff to the President ... Ms. Tiffany HOGUE
10 Chief Business Officer ... Mr. Brett DALTON
117 Senior Director of Risk Management ... Mr. Paul FOX
111 VP for Advancement ... Mr. David ROSSELLI
32 Vice President Student Life ... Dr. Kevin P. JACKSON
26 VP Marketing & Comm/CMO ... Mr. Jason D. COOK
29 Assoc Vice Pres Alumni Engagement ... Ms. Amy ARMSTRONG
43 Gen Counsel/CLO & Corp Sec ... Mr. Christopher W. HOLMES
41 VP & Director of Athletics ... Mr. Mack RHOADES, IV
09 Director Inst Research/Testing ... Dr. Kathleen MORLEY
21 VP of Financial Operations ... Mrs. Susan D. ANZ
114 AVP of Budget & Planning ... Mr. Brian S. DENMAN
18 Asst VP for Facilities & Planning ... Mr. Don BAGBY
15 VP & Chief Human Resource Officer ... Mrs. Cheryl GOCHIS
13 VP Information Tech/Deputy CIO ... Mr. Jon ALLEN
08 Dean of Libraries ... Mr. Jeffry ARCHER
35 Vice Pres of Student Life ... Mr. Kevin P. JACKSON
06 Interim Registrar ... Mr. Gabe OLSZEWSKI
90 AVP Library/Academic Technology ... Mr. David BURNS
108 Dir of Inst Planning & Assessment ... Dr. J. Ben COX
97 Vice Provost Undergrad Education ... Dr. Wesley NULL
20 Vice Prov/Academic Affs & Policy ... Dr. James BENNIGHOFF
46 Vice Provost Research ... Dr. Kevin CHAMBLISS
84 Assoc VP of Enrollment Mgmt ... Ms. Jennifer CARRON
115 Chief Investment Officer ... Mr. David MOREHEAD
19 Chief of Police ... Mr. John KOLINEK, III
93 Dir Multicultural Affairs ... Mrs. Pearlie BEVERLY
121 Assoc Dir Stdnt Success Initiative ... Ms. Amber THOMPSON
23 Medical Director Health Center ... Dr. Sharon STERN
51 Assoc Director of Professional Educ ... Ms. Jenna KINKEADE
25 Asst Vice Prov Rsrch/Dir Spons Pgm ... Ms. Lisa H. MCKETHAN
38 Exec Director Counseling Svcs ... Dr. James G. MARSH
40 Director Baylor Bookstore ... Ms. Larissa RUPLEY
86 Director Governmental Relations ... Ms. Rochonda FARMER-NEAL
96 Director of Procurement Services ... Mr. Richard WRIGHT
49 Dean College of Arts/Sciences ... Dr. Lee C. NORDT
50 Dean School of Business ... Dr. Terry S. MANESS
53 Dean School of Education ... Dr. Shanna HAGAN-BURKE
61 Dean School of Law ... Mr. Bradley TOBEN
64 Dean School of Music ... Dr. Gary MORTENSON
66 Dean School of Nursing ... Dr. Linda PLANK
58 Vice Provost & Dean Graduate School ... Dr. Larry LYON
73 Dean Truett Theological Sem ... Dr. Todd D. STILL
54 Dean Engineering & Computer Science ... Dr. Dennis L. O'NEAL
92 Dean Honors College ... Dr. Douglas V. HENRY
85 Vice Provost for Global Engagement ... Dr. Jeffrey S. HAMILTON
35 Dean Student Development ... Dr. Elizabeth PALACIOS
89 Director of New Student Programs ... Dr. Nathan SHELBURNE
42 University Chaplain ... Dr. Burt BURLESON
88 Assoc Dean Student Conduct Admin ... Ms. Bethany J. MCCRAW
37 Sr Dir of Student Financial Aid ... Ms. Lisa MARTIN
88 Assoc VP Public Safety & Security ... Mr. Mark CHILDERS
04 Exec Assistant to the President ... Ms. Mia CASEY
101 Board Professional ... Ms. Kristy ORR
104 Director Study Abroad ... Mr. Bo WHITE
22 Affirmative Action & Equal Opp Mgr ... Ms. Shirl BROWN
39 Director Campus Living & Learning ... Ms. Tiffany P. LOWE
44 Director Leadership/Annual Giving ... Mr. Stephen SULLIVAN
07 Sr Director Undergrad Admissions ... Mr. Ross VANDYKE

B.H. Carroll Theological Institute (F)

6500 N Belt Line Road, Suite 100, Irving TX 75063-6056

County: Tarrant Identification: 667089
Telephone: (972) 580-7600 Carnegie Class: Not Classified
FAX Number: (972) 756-0600 Calendar System: Semester
URL: www.bhcarroll.edu
Established: 2004 Annual Graduate Tuition & Fees: N/A
Enrollment: N/A Coed
Affiliation or Control: Southern Baptist IRS Status: 501(c)3
Highest Offering: Doctorate; No Undergraduates
Accreditation: **BI**, THEOL

01 President ... Dr. C. Gene WILKES
10 CFO/Director Business Affairs ... Ms. Debra HOLDER
07 Director of Admissions ... Ms. Michelle MARTIN
13 Director Information Technology ... Mr. Carl HEATH
30 Director of Development ... Mr. Stacey WHITT

The Bible Seminary (G)

2655 South Mason Rd, Katy TX 77450

County: Harris Identification: 667371
Telephone: (281) 646-1109 Carnegie Class: Not Classified
FAX Number: (281) 646-1110 Calendar System: Semester
URL: thebibleseminary.edu
Established: 2010 Annual Undergrad Tuition & Fees: N/A
Enrollment: N/A Coed
Affiliation or Control: Non-denominational IRS Status: 501(c)3
Highest Offering: Master's
Accreditation: **TRACS**

01 President ... Dr. K. Lynn LEWIS
05 Provost ... Dr. Scott STRIPLING
10 Vice Pres Finance & Administration ... Mr. Rick MCCALIP
06 Registrar ... Mrs. Carousel PIETERSE
08 Librarian ... Mrs. Janice HAMRIC
26 Communications Director ... Mr. Blake QUIMBY
21 Business Manager ... Mrs. Yamile SOTO
58 Dean of Graduate Programs ... Dr. Douglas PETROVICH
30 Director of Development ... Mrs. Angela MCCLINTON

Blinn College (H)

902 College Avenue, Brenham TX 77833-4098

County: Washington FICE Identification: 003549
Unit ID: 223427
Telephone: (979) 830-4000 Carnegie Class: Assoc/HT-High Trad
FAX Number: (979) 830-4030 Calendar System: Semester
URL: www.blinn.edu
Established: 1883 Annual Undergrad Tuition & Fees (In-District): $5,700
Enrollment: 18,220 Coed
Affiliation or Control: State/Local IRS Status: 501(c)3
Highest Offering: Associate Degree
Accreditation: **SC**, ADNUR, CAHIIM, DH, EMT, PTAA, RAD, SURGT

01 Chancellor ... Dr. Mary HENSLEY
03 Exec Vice Chancellor ... Mr. Leighton SCHUBERT
101 Special Asst to BOT/Chancellor ... Ms. Laurie CLARK
05 Vice Chancellor Academic Affairs ... Dr. Marcelo BUSSIKI
17 VC Health Sci/Tech Ed & Cmty Pgms . Mr. Jon (Jay) ANDERSON
32 Vice Chancellor Student Svcs ... Dr. Becky MCBRIDE
19 Chief College Police Department ... Mr. John CHANCELLOR
10 Vice Chanc Business/Finance/CFO ... Mr. Richard CERVANTES
15 Vice Chanc Human Resources ... Ms. Marie KIRBY
12 Executive Dean Brenham Campus ... Dr. John TURNER
12 Executive Dean Bryan Campus ... Dr. Jimmy BYRD
12 Executive Dean RELLIS Campus ... Mr. Chris MARRS
18 Asst VC Facilities/Planning/Constr ... Mr. Richard O'MALLEY
84 Dir Enrollment Management ... Ms. Elaine ABSHIRE
21 Asst VC Business & Finance ... Ms. Vicki WARD
09 Dir Inst Research/Effectiveness ... Mr. George GUARJARDO
88 Student Conduct Coord/Title IX Inv ... Ms. Sigrid WOODS
102 Exec Dir Foundation/Alumni Rel ... Ms. Susan MYERS
12 Exec Dean Schulenburg Campus ... Dr. Rebecca GARLICK
12 Exec Dean Sealy Campus ... Ms. Lisa CATON
13 Dir Administrative Computing Svcs ... Ms. Christine WIED
37 Dean Financial Aid/Scholarships ... Mr. Brent WILLIFORD
41 Athletic Dir/Mens Head Bsktbl Coach ... Mr. Scott SCHUMACHER
75 Dean Technology & Community Ed ... Ms. Karla FLANAGAN
96 Director Purchasing/Transportation ... Mr. Ross SCHROEDER
114 Director Budgets & Insurance ... Ms. Kristina BECKENDORF
103 Director Small Business Dev Center ... Mr. Matthew WEHRING
06 Registrar ... Ms. Kristi URBAN
26 Dir Comm/Media Relations/Marketing ... Mr. Rich BRAY
35 Dir Student Leadership/Activities ... Mr. Peter RIVERA
39 Dir Housing & Student Life ... Mr. Ryan MILLER
109 Dir Food Services ... Mr. James HARVILL
04 Exec Assistant to the Chancellor ... Ms. Sharon JOHNSTON
121 Exec Dir Academic Success ... Ms. Joyce LANGENEGGER
54 Academic Dean ECT ... Mr. Max HIBBS
81 Acad Dean Natural & Phys Science ... Dr. Elmer GODNEY
79 Acad Dean Humanities ... Dr. Patricia WESTERGAARD
50 Acad Dean Business & Mathematics ... Dr. Charles M. SMITH
83 Acad Dean Social Sciences ... Mr. Brandon FRANKE
57 Acad Dean Visual/Perf Arts & Kin ... Ms. Deborah VAVRA
106 Dean Distance Learning ... Dr. Mark WORKMAN
90 Dean Acad Tech Services ... Mr. Michael WELCH
76 Dean Health Sciences ... Ms. Michelle TRUBENSTEIN
28 Dean Title IX/Inst Divers/Equity ... Dr. Bennie GRAVES
38 Dir Disability Svcs & Counseling ... Ms. Samantha JOHNSON

Brazosport College (I)

500 College Drive, Lake Jackson TX 77566-3199

County: Brazoria FICE Identification: 007287
Unit ID: 223506
Telephone: (979) 230-3000 Carnegie Class: Bac/Assoc-Mixed
FAX Number: (979) 230-3443 Calendar System: Semester
URL: www.brazosport.edu
Established: 1968 Annual Undergrad Tuition & Fees (In-District): $3,304
Enrollment: 3,852 Coed
Affiliation or Control: Local IRS Status: 501(c)3
Highest Offering: Baccalaureate

Accreditation: SC, EMT

01 President .... Dr. Millicent M. VALEK
05 VP Academic & Student Affairs .... Dr. Shelley DIVINEY
103 VP Industry & Community Resources .... Ms. Anne BARTLETT
111 VP College Advancement .... Ms. Tracee WATTS
15 VP Human Resources .... Mr. Marshall CAMPBELL
10 VP Financial Services & CFO .... Ms. Lisa TEMPLER
32 Dean of Student Services .... Ms. Jo GREATHOUSE
20 Dean of Instruction .... Mr. Jeffrey DETRICK
45 Dean Plng/Inst Effectiv/Research .... Vacant
07 Director Admissions/Registrar .... Mr. Jerry MARTINEZ
38 Director Counseling and Testing .... Mr. Arnold RAMIREZ
26 Director Marketing & Communications . Ms. Lauren MCCORMICK
13 Director Information Technology .... Mr. Ron PARKER
37 Director of Financial Aid .... Mr. Daniel YARRITU
08 Director Library & Learning Service .... Vacant
18 Director Facility Services .... Mr. John DITTO
88 Director Small Business Dev Center .... Ms. Jennifer FINNEY
31 Director Community Education .... Ms. Deborah EWING
88 Director Children's Center .... Ms. Christine WEBSTER
109 Director Business Services .... Ms. Ginger WOOSTER
116 Internal Auditor .... Ms. Evelyn CRUZ
09 Dir Planning/Inst Effectiv/Research .... Ms. Cindy ULLRICH
04 Admin Assistant to the President .... Ms. Kasie GUTHRIE
19 Director Security/Safety .... Mr. Chad LEVERITT
88 Dean School & College Partnerships .... Ms. Priscilla SANCHEZ

Brite Divinity School (A)

2925 Princeton Street, Fort Worth TX 76129-0001
County: Tarrant Identification: 666228
Unit ID: 450304
Telephone: (817) 257-7575 Carnegie Class: Spec-4-yr-Faith
FAX Number: (817) 257-6932 Calendar System: Semester
URL: www.brite.tcu.edu
Established: 1873 Annual Graduate Tuition & Fees: N/A
Enrollment: 142 Coed
Affiliation or Control: Independent Non-Profit IRS Status: 501(c)3
Highest Offering: Doctorate; No Undergraduates
Accreditation: SC, THEOL

01 President & Chief Executive Officer .... Dr. D. Newell WILLIAMS
05 Exec Vice President/Dean .... Dr. Michael MILLER
10 Vice President Business/Finance .... Ms. Michele G. SMITH
07 Assistant Dean of Admissions .... Rev. Monique CRAIN SPELLS

Carrington College - Mesquite (B)

3733 West Emporium Circle, Mesquite TX 75150
Telephone: (972) 682-2800 Identification: 770967
Accreditation: &WJ

† Branch campus of Carrington College - Sacramento, Sacramento, CA

Center for Advanced Legal Studies (C)

800 W Sam Houston Pkwy, S Suite 100,
Houston TX 77042
County: Harris FICE Identification: 026047
Unit ID: 379782
Telephone: (713) 529-2778 Carnegie Class: Spec 2-yr-Other
FAX Number: (855) 422-4466 Calendar System: Other
URL: www.paralegal.edu
Established: 1987 Annual Undergrad Tuition & Fees: N/A
Enrollment: 243 Coed
Affiliation or Control: Proprietary IRS Status: Proprietary
Highest Offering: Associate Degree
Accreditation: ACCSC, COE

01 School Director/Co-Founder .... Mr. Doyle HAPPE
05 Dean .... Mr. Thomas SWANSON
07 Director of Admissions .... Mr. James SCHEFFER

Central Texas College (D)

PO Box 1800, Killeen TX 76540-9990
County: Bell FICE Identification: 004003
Unit ID: 223816
Telephone: (254) 526-7161 Carnegie Class: Assoc/HT-High Non
FAX Number: N/A Calendar System: Semester
URL: www.ctcd.edu
Established: 1965 Annual Undergrad Tuition & Fees (In-District): $3,540
Enrollment: 10,173 Coed
Affiliation or Control: Local IRS Status: 501(c)3
Highest Offering: Associate Degree
Accreditation: SC, ADNUR, EMT, HT, MLTAD

01 Chancellor .... Mr. Jim YEONOPOLUS
103 Dep Chanc Inst Workforce Initiative .... Dr. Tina ADY
10 Deputy Chanc Finance & Admin .... Dr. Michele CARTER
05 Deputy Chanc Acad & Student Success .... Dr. Robin GARRETT
12 Dean Fort Hood .... Ms. Jacqueline HAIRE
20 Dean of Instruction .... Ms. Janice ANDERSON
32 Dean Student Services .... Dr. Johnelle WELSH
08 Dean Library Services .... Ms. Lori PURSER
84 Associate Dean Enrollment Services .... Ms. Eva HUTCHENS
06 Associate Dean Admiss/Regist/Records .... Mr. Stephen O'DONOVAN
21 Assoc Dep Chanc Financial Mgmt .... Mr. Bob LIBERTY
15 Assoc Dep Chanc Human Res Mgmt .... Ms. Holly JORDAN
106 Dean Distance Educ/Curriculum Devel .... Ms. Sharon DAVIS
18 Assoc Dep Chanc Facilities & Const .... Mr. Mark HARMSEN
30 Director College Development .... Ms. Marcine CHAMBERS
09 Dir Institutional Effectiveness .... Dr. Jennifer CAMERON
13 Assoc Dep Chanc Info Technology .... Mr. Cliff GAINES
07 Director Admissions/Recruitment .... Ms. Amy WILLIAMS
88 Director Testing .... Mr. Victor GATES
85 Director International Student Svcs .... Ms. Rebecca LOPEZ
22 Director Disability Support Svcs .... Dr. Christy SHANK
88 Director Substance Abuse Resource . Dr. Gerald MAHONE-LEIWS
36 Director Career Services .... Ms. Keisha HOLMAN
26 Director Marketing & Outreach .... Ms. Barbara MERLO
88 QA Liaison/C&I Campus Ops .... Ms. Diana CASTILLO
19 Chief Police/Security Services .... Chief Joseph BARRAGAN
40 Manager Bookstore .... Ms. Regina MARTINEZ-WOODRUFF
37 Assoc Dean Fin Aid/Veteran Svcs .... Ms. Annabelle SMITH
96 Assoc Dep Chanc Business Services .... Mr. Ted GONZALEZ
04 Administrative Asst to President .... Ms. Debra HAVENS
43 Dir Legal Services/General Counsel .... Ms. Deborah SHIBLEY
86 Director Government Relations .... Mr. Rudy SANDOVAL
25 Chief Contract/Grants Administrator .... Vacant
105 Web & Digital Media Manager .... Ms. Erica BURTON
28 Director of Diversity .... Dr. Michele CARTER

Chamberlain University-Houston (E)

11025 Equity Drive, Houston TX 77041
Telephone: (713) 277-9800 Identification: 770500
Accreditation: &HLC, NURSE

† Branch campus of Chamberlain University-Addison, Addison, IL

Chamberlain University-Irving (F)

4800 Regent Boulevard, Irving TX 75063
Telephone: (469) 706-6705 Identification: 770853
Accreditation: &HLC, NURSE

† Branch campus of Chamberlain University-Addison, Addison, IL

Chamberlain University-Pearland (G)

12000 Shadow Creek Pkwy, Pearland TX 77584
Telephone: (832) 664-7000 Identification: 770934
Accreditation: &HLC, NURSE

† Branch campus of Chamberlain College of Nursing-Addison, Addison, IL.

Christ Mission College (H)

10822 FM 1560, San Antonio TX 78254
County: Bexar Identification: 667320
Telephone: (210) 688-3101 Carnegie Class: Not Classified
FAX Number: N/A Calendar System: Semester
URL: www.cmctx.org
Established: 1926 Annual Undergrad Tuition & Fees: N/A
Enrollment: N/A Coed
Affiliation or Control: Independent Non-Profit IRS Status: 501(c)3
Highest Offering: Baccalaureate
Accreditation: BI

01 President .... Dr. Monte MADSEN
05 VP of Academics .... Rev. Alicia CARRASCO
32 VP of Student Services .... Rev. Reva MADSEN
10 Sr Director of Finance .... Ms. Evelyn ARIAS
84 Enrollment Manager/Registrar .... Mr. Samuel HERNANDEZ

Cisco College (I)

101 College Heights, Cisco TX 76437-1900
County: Eastland FICE Identification: 003553
Unit ID: 223898
Telephone: (254) 442-5000 Carnegie Class: Assoc/MT-VT-High Trad
FAX Number: (254) 442-5100 Calendar System: Semester
URL: www.cisco.edu
Established: 1940 Annual Undergrad Tuition & Fees (In-State): $4,860
Enrollment: 3,256 Coed
Affiliation or Control: State IRS Status: 501(c)3
Highest Offering: Associate Degree
Accreditation: SC, COARC, MAC, SURGT

01 President .... Dr. Thad ANGLIN
05 Provost/Chief Instruction Officer .... Dr. Carol DUPREE
32 Vice President for Student Services .... Dr. Jerry DODSON
10 Dean of Business Svcs/CFO .... Ms. Audra TAYLOR
13 Exec Dir of Information Technology .... Dr. Tim MURPHY
30 Director of Development .... Ms. Martha MONTGOMERY
37 Director of Financial Aid .... Ms. Linda SELLERS
15 Director of Human Resources .... Vacant
08 Director of Library Services .... Ms. Donna CLARK
19 Director Campus Safety .... Mr. Roger TIGHE
07 Dir of Enrollment Svcs/Registrara .... Ms. Shirley DOVE
04 Executive Asst to President .... Ms. Sydni RABB
103 Dean Workforce/Economic Development .... Mr. Link HARRIS
106 Dir Online Education/E-learning .... Ms. Sheron CATON
35 Dean of Student Services .... Mr. Bryan COTTRELL
96 Director of Purchasing .... Ms. Beverly MASSEY

Clarendon College (J)

PO Box 968, Clarendon TX 79226-0968
County: Donley FICE Identification: 003554
Unit ID: 223922
Telephone: (806) 874-3571 Carnegie Class: Assoc/HVT-Mix Trad/Non
FAX Number: (806) 874-3201 Calendar System: Semester
URL: www.clarendoncollege.edu
Established: 1898 Annual Undergrad Tuition & Fees (In-District): $4,290
Enrollment: 1,334 Coed
Affiliation or Control: State/Local IRS Status: 501(c)3
Highest Offering: Associate Degree
Accreditation: SC

01 President .... Mr. Tex BUCKHAULTS
13 Vice Pres of Information Technology .... Mr. Will THOMPSON
05 Vice President of Academic Affairs .... Mr. Brad VANDEN BOOGAARD
10 Comptroller .... Ms. Kae HEWETT
04 Assistant to the President .... Mrs. Cindy LAMBERT
41 Athletic Director .... Mr. Mark JAMES
32 Director of Student Life .... Mr. Tadd ANDREWS
84 Assoc Dean of Enrollment Services .... Mrs. Janean REISH
37 Director of Financial Aid .... Mrs. Amanda SMITH
06 Registrar .... Mrs. Brandi HAVENS
08 Librarian .... Ms. Pamela REED
81 Division Chair Science/Health .... Mrs. Scarlet ESTLACK
49 Division Chair Liberal Arts .... Mrs. Kim JEFFREY
47 Division Chair Agriculture .... Mr. Johnny TREICHEL
76 Division Chair Allied Health .... Mrs. Jamie MEARS
75 Dean of CTE .... Mr. Mike DAVIS

Coastal Bend College (K)

3800 Charco Road, Beeville TX 78102-2197
County: Bee FICE Identification: 003546
Unit ID: 223320
Telephone: (361) 358-2838 Carnegie Class: Assoc/HVT-High Non
FAX Number: (361) 354-2333 Calendar System: Semester
URL: www.coastalbend.edu
Established: 1965 Annual Undergrad Tuition & Fees (In-District): $4,493
Enrollment: 4,105 Coed
Affiliation or Control: State/Local IRS Status: 501(c)3
Highest Offering: Associate Degree
Accreditation: SC, DH, RAD

01 President .... Dr. Justin HOGGARD
05 Provost/CAO .... Dr. Patricia REHAK
97 Dean of Transfer & General Studies .... Mr. Mark SECORD
32 Dean Student Svcs & Accessibility .... Ms. Kayla DEVORA-JONES
07 Director of Admissions/Registrar .... Ms. Candy FULLER
26 Director of Marketing & PR .... Mr. Bernard SAENZ
37 Director of Financial Aid .... Ms. Nora MORALES
12 Director of Alice Campus .... Vacant
12 Director of Kingsville Campus .... Mr. Keenan WOODS
10 Accounting Director/CFO .... Vacant
08 Director Library Services .... Ms. Sarah MILNARICH
15 Int Director Human Resources .... Ms. Dixie LYTLE
13 Director of IT/CIO .... Mr. Amador RAMIREZ
18 Director of Physical Plant .... Mr. Jacinto (JC) COLMENERO
04 Executive Asst to President .... Ms. Anna GARCIA
103 Dean of Career & Technical Educ .... Mr. Jarod BLEIBDREY
09 Dir of Institutional Effectiveness .... Dr. Patricia REHAK
102 Exec Dir CBC Foundation .... Ms. Madeline MADDEN
19 Director Security/Safety .... Dr. Kevin BEHR
41 Athletic Director .... Mr. Paul CANTRELL
76 Assistant Dean of Allied Health .... Ms. Loana HERNANDEZ
88 Director of Dual Enrollment .... Ms. Susie GAITAN

College of Biblical Studies-Houston (L)

7000 Regency Square Boulevard, Houston TX 77036-3298
County: Harris FICE Identification: 034224
Unit ID: 388520
Telephone: (713) 785-5995 Carnegie Class: Spec-4-yr-Faith
FAX Number: (713) 785-5998 Calendar System: Semester
URL: www.cbshouston.edu
Established: 1976 Annual Undergrad Tuition & Fees: $6,801
Enrollment: 431 Coed
Affiliation or Control: Independent Non-Profit IRS Status: 501(c)3
Highest Offering: Baccalaureate
Accreditation: SC, BI

01 President .... Dr. Bill BLOCKER
04 Executive Assistant .... Mrs. Vicki PATTERSON
05 Provost .... Dr. Joseph D. PARLE
11 VP Administration/COO .... Mr. Paul KEITH
88 Vice President of Discipleship .... Dr. J. Paul NYQUIST
10 Vice Pres/Chief Financial Officer .... Mr. Benjamin CHELLADURAI
84 VP Enrollment/Student Success .... Vacant
26 Exec Dir Communications/PR .... Ms. Melinda MERILLAT
106 Dean Distance Educ Operations .... Mr. Shane BOOTHE
09 Dean Institutional Effectiveness .... Dr. Joel BADAL
18 Dir Real Estate Operations .... Mr. Terry BRYAN
15 Director of Human Resources .... Mr. Paul KEITH
06 Registrar .... Ms. Twyla GILLS
08 Director of Library Services .... Mr. Artis LOVELADY, III
32 Dean of Students .... Ms. Luzmar COBOS
20 Assoc Dean Faculty and Curr Dev .... Dr. Brittany BURNETTE
37 Senior Financial Aid Officer .... Vacant
111 Assoc VP Advancement .... Ms. Chelsea WHITE
88 Exec Director Grace Relations .... Dr. Charles WARE

College of Biomedical Equipment Technology (A)

11550 IH 10 West Suite 190, San Antonio TX 78230
County: Bexar Identification: 667323
Telephone: (210) 233-1102 Carnegie Class: Not Classified
FAX Number: N/A Calendar System: Other
URL: www.cbet.edu
Established: 2010 Annual Undergrad Tuition & Fees: N/A
Enrollment: N/A Coed
Affiliation or Control: Proprietary IRS Status: Proprietary
Highest Offering: Associate Degree
Accreditation: CNCE

01 President .... Dr. Richard (Monty) GONZALES
05 Director of Education .... Mr. Scott MCKNIGHT

The College of Health Care Professions (B)

6330 East Highway 290, Suite 180, Austin TX 78723
County: Travis FICE Identification: 034263
Unit ID: 437635
Telephone: (512) 617-5700 Carnegie Class: Spec 2-yr-Health
FAX Number: (512) 892-6643 Calendar System: Other
URL: www.chcp.edu
Established: 1988 Annual Undergrad Tuition & Fees: N/A
Enrollment: 666 Coed
Affiliation or Control: Proprietary IRS Status: Proprietary
Highest Offering: Associate Degree
Accreditation: ABHES, DMS, SURTEC

01 President .... Ms. Sara RAMBIKUR
05 Director of Education .... Mr. George DAIY
07 Director of Admissions .... Ms. Kelly DEMARS

The College of Health Care Professions (C)

240 Northwest Mall Boulevard, Houston TX 77092
County: Harris FICE Identification: 031281
Unit ID: 392257
Telephone: (713) 425-3100 Carnegie Class: Spec-4-yr-Other Health
FAX Number: (713) 425-3192 Calendar System: Other
URL: www.chcp.edu
Established: 1988 Annual Undergrad Tuition & Fees: N/A
Enrollment: 2,811 Coed
Affiliation or Control: Proprietary IRS Status: Proprietary
Highest Offering: Baccalaureate
Accreditation: ABHES, SURGT, SURTEC

01 Campus President .... Mr. Lee JONES
05 Director of Education .... Mr. Khawar AIZAZ

The College of Health Care Professions-Dallas (D)

8585 N Stemmons Freeway, Ste N-300, Dallas TX 75247
Telephone: (214) 420-3400 Identification: 770531
Accreditation: ABHES

The College of Health Care Professions-Fort Worth (E)

4248 North Freeway, Fort Worth TX 76137
Telephone: (817) 632-5900 Identification: 770532
Accreditation: ABHES, DMS

The College of Health Care Professions-McAllen (F)

1917 Nolana Avenue, Ste 100, McAllen TX 78504
Telephone: (956) 800-1500 Identification: 770963
Accreditation: ABHES

The College of Health Care Professions-San Antonio (G)

4738 Northwest Loop 410, San Antonio TX 78229
Telephone: (210) 298-3600 Identification: 770964
Accreditation: ABHES, SURTEC

College of the Mainland (H)

1200 Amburn Road, Texas City TX 77591-2499
County: Galveston FICE Identification: 007096
Unit ID: 226408
Telephone: (409) 938-1211 Carnegie Class: Assoc/HVT-Mix Trad/Non
FAX Number: (409) 933-8010 Calendar System: Semester
URL: www.com.edu
Established: 1966 Annual Undergrad Tuition & Fees (In-District): $2,973
Enrollment: 4,335 Coed
Affiliation or Control: Local IRS Status: 501(c)3
Highest Offering: Associate Degree
Accreditation: SC, ADNUR, CAHIIM, EMT, #MAC

01 President .... Dr. Warren NICHOLS
05 Vice President for Instruction .... Dr. Jerry FLIGER
10 Vice President for Fiscal Affairs .... Dr. Clen BURTON
32 Vice President for Student Services .... Dr. Vicki STANFIELD
35 AVP Student Success/Dean of Stdnts .... Ms. Kris KIMBARK
07 Dir Admissions & Registrar .... Mr. Tomas GARCIA
18 Assoc VP Facility Services .... Mr. Charles KING
08 Director Library Services .... Ms. Kathryn PARK
102 Director of Foundation .... Dr. Lisa WATSON
28 Director of Institutional Equity .... Vacant
96 Director of Purchasing .... Ms. Sonja BLINKA
09 Research Specialist .... Ms. Lauren HARPER
04 Admin Assistant to the President .... Ms. Michelle GERAMI

Collin College (I)

3452 Spur 399, McKinney TX 75069
County: Collin FICE Identification: 023614
Unit ID: 247834
Telephone: (972) 758-3805 Carnegie Class: Assoc/HT-Mix Trad/Non
FAX Number: (972) 758-3807 Calendar System: Semester
URL: www.collin.edu
Established: 1985 Annual Undergrad Tuition & Fees (In-District): $3,004
Enrollment: 35,390 Coed
Affiliation or Control: State/Local IRS Status: 501(c)3
Highest Offering: Baccalaureate
Accreditation: SC, ACFEI, ADNUR, CAHIIM, COARC, DH, EMT, NAEYC, POLYT, SURGA, SURGT

01 District President .... Dr. H. Neil MATKIN
04 Exec Asst to Pres/Board Secy .... Ms. Kristy HORKMAN
100 Chief of Staff .... Ms. Kimberly K. DAVISON
03 Executive VP .... Dr. Sherry L. SCHUMANN
11 Sr VP Campus Operations .... Dr. Abe JOHNSON
10 Chief Financial Officer .... Ms. Melissa IRBY
26 VP External Relations .... Mr. Steve M. MATTHEWS
13 Chief Innovation Officer (IT) .... Mr. Michael DICKSON
15 Chief Human Resources Officer .... Mr. Floyd W. NICKERSON
43 General Counsel .... Ms. Monica A. VELAZQUEZ
111 VP Advancement .... Ms. Lisa R. VASQUEZ
18 VP Facilities & Construction .... Mr. Chris EYLE
116 Director Internal Audit .... Mr. Ali SUBHANI
19 Chief of Police .... Mr. D. Scott JENKINS
05 VP Academic Affairs .... Dr. Jon H. HARDESTY
20 Assoc Provost Instruction .... Dr. L. Cameron NEAL
12 VP/Provost-Frisco .... Mr. Craig C. LEVERETTE
12 Executive Dean-Celina .... Ms. Brenda C. CARTER
12 VP/Provost-McKinney .... Dr. Mark SMITH
12 Executive Dean-Farmersville .... Dr. Diana L. HOPES
12 VP/Provost-Plano .... Dr. Mary E. BARNES-TILLEY
12 VP/Provost-Allen Tech .... Dr. Bill L. KING
12 VP/Provost-Wylie .... Dr. Mary S. MCRAE
106 Exec Dean Virtual Campus .... Dr. Sarah K. LEE
121 Chief Student Success Officer .... Dr. Jay CORWIN
09 VP Institutional Research .... Dr. Thomas K. MARTIN
21 Assoc VP Financial Svcs & Rprtng .... Ms. Barbara A. JOHNSTON
21 Assoc VP/Controller .... Ms. Julie M. BRADLEY
32 VP Student & Enrollment Services .... Dr. Albert TEZENO
88 Assoc VP P-12 Partnerships .... Mr. Raul J. MARTINEZ
39 Dir Student Housing Operations .... Ms. Angela MCGILL
35 Assoc VP Student & Enrollment Svcs .... Dr. Alicia L. HUPPE
14 Assoc VP/Chief Info Officer (IT) .... Vacant
76 Dean Health Sci/Emergency Svcs .... Ms. Michelle L. MILLEN
66 Dean Nursing .... Dr. Jane L. LEACH
103 Dean Workforce Educ-Frisco .... Dr. Brenden D. MESCH
97 Dean Academic Affairs-Frisco .... Dr. Dawn J. RICHARDSON
97 Dean Academic Affairs-McKinney .... Dr. Garry W. EVANS
79 Dean Comm & Humanities-Plano .... Dr. Meredith L. WANG
57 Dean Fine Arts & Educ-Plano .... Dr. Lupita M. TINNEN
81 Dean Math & Sciences-Plano .... Dr. Kristen L. STREATER
97 Dean Academic Affairs-Allen Tech .... Dr. Amy T. GAINER
103 Dean Workforce Educ-Allen Tech .... Mr. Michael COFFMAN
20 Dean Academic & Workforce-Wylie .... Ms. Daphne H. BABCOCK
55 Dean Evening & Weekend College .... Ms. Gaye M. COOKSEY
51 Exec Dean Cont Ed & Corp College .... Ms. Karen M. MUSA
51 COO Corporate College .... Dr. Roger H. WIDMER
106 Dean Strategic Initiatives .... Mr. Mark S. GARCIA
06 Dean Admissions/District Registrar .... Mr. Todd E. FIELDS
35 District Dean of Students .... Mr. Terrence P. BRENNAN
84 Dean Student & Enrol Svcs-Frisco .... Ms. De'Aira M. HOLLOWAY
84 Dean Student & Enrol Svcs-McKinney .... Mr. James N. BARKO
84 Dean Student & Enrol Svcs-Plano .... Mr. Kirk D. LEE
84 Dean Student & Enrol Svcs-Wylie .... Mr. Doug G. WILLIS
08 Exec Dir Library-Frisco .... Ms. Vidya KRISHNASWAMY
08 Exec Dir Library-McKinney .... Ms. Faye M. DAVIS
08 Exec Dir Library-Plano .... Ms. Linda A. KYPRIOS
08 Exec Dir Library-Wylie .... Ms. Nichole N. BOONE
37 Dir Financial Aid & Vet Affairs .... Mr. Alan D. PIXLEY
41 Director Athletics .... Dr. Albert TEZENO
96 Director Purchasing .... Ms. Cynthia L. WHITE
25 Dir Workforce & Econ Dev (Grants) .. Ms. Natalie G. GREENWELL

Commonwealth Institute of Funeral Service (J)

415 Barren Springs Drive, Houston TX 77090-5913
County: Harris FICE Identification: 003556
Unit ID: 366261
Telephone: (281) 873-0262 Carnegie Class: Spec 2-yr-A&S
FAX Number: (281) 873-5232 Calendar System: Quarter
URL: www.commonwealth.edu
Established: 1936 Annual Undergrad Tuition & Fees: $13,363
Enrollment: 256 Coed
Affiliation or Control: Independent Non-Profit IRS Status: 501(c)3
Highest Offering: Associate Degree
Accreditation: FUSER

01 President .... Mr. Cody LOPASKY
05 Dean of Academics .... Mr. James ROBINSON
32 Dean of Students .... Mr. Christopher LAYTON
37 Director Student Financial Aid .... Ms. Marlene PERRY
06 Registrar .... Ms. Patricia MORENO
08 Head Librarian .... Ms. Melissa DAVIS

Concorde Career College (K)

12606 Greenville Avenue, Suite 130, Dallas TX 75243
Telephone: (469) 221-3400 Identification: 770593
Accreditation: ACCSC, COARC, DH, PTAA, #SURGT

† Branch campus of Concorde Career College, Aurora, CO

Concorde Career College (L)

4803 NW Loop 410, Suite 200, San Antonio TX 78229
Telephone: (210) 428-2000 Identification: 770594
Accreditation: ACCSC, COARC, DH, PTAA, SURGT

† Branch campus of Concorde Career College, Kansas City, MO

Concorde Career Institute (M)

3015 West I-20, Grand Prairie TX 75052
County: Tarrant FICE Identification: 035423
Unit ID: 441742
Telephone: (469) 348-2500 Carnegie Class: Spec 2-yr-Health
FAX Number: (469) 348-2580 Calendar System: Semester
URL: https://www.concorde.edu/campus/grand-prairie-texas
Established: 1991 Annual Undergrad Tuition & Fees: N/A
Enrollment: 862 Coed
Affiliation or Control: Proprietary IRS Status: Proprietary
Highest Offering: Associate Degree
Accreditation: ACCSC, DH, NDT, POLYT, SURGT

01 Campus President .... Mr. Mike LOVEJOY

Concordia University Texas (N)

11400 Concordia University Drive, Austin TX 78726
County: Travis FICE Identification: 003557
Unit ID: 224004
Telephone: (512) 313-3000 Carnegie Class: Masters/L
FAX Number: (512) 313-3999 Calendar System: Semester
URL: www.concordia.edu
Established: 1926 Annual Undergrad Tuition & Fees: $33,800
Enrollment: 2,257 Coed
Affiliation or Control: Lutheran Church - Missouri Synod
IRS Status: 501(c)3
Highest Offering: Doctorate
Accreditation: SC, IACBE, NURSE

01 President/CEO .... Dr. Donald CHRISTIAN
04 Executive Asst to Pres/CEO .... Ms. Dana KORNFUEHRER
05 Provost & Executive VP .... Dr. Kristi KIRK
26 Sr VP External Affairs .... Ms. Beth ATHERTON
10 Chief Financial Officer .... Dr. Lynette GILLIS
45 Sr VP Planning & Quality .... Dr. Shane SOKOLL
84 VP of Enrollment Management .... Ms. Lara BAILIFF
11 VP of Administration .... Mr. Dan GREGORY
20 VP of Academic Operations .... Dr. KC POSPISIL
41 VP of Athletics .... Ms. Ronda SEAGRAVES
32 VP of Student Affairs .... Ms. Jennielle STROTHER
106 Assoc VP Digital Operations .... Dr. Alex HERRON
42 Campus Pastor .... Rev. Steve FICK
21 Controller .... Mr. Sairam PATHI
88 Dean of Teaching & Learning .... Dr. Sara SHIPPEY
66 Dean College of Nursing .... Dr. Jason SHUFFITT
79 Dir School of Humanities .... Dr. Ann SCHWARTZ
30 Director of Philanthropy .... Ms. Amanda KEETER
06 Dir Student Info Systems & Records .... Mr. Ricky ALLEN
15 Director Human Resources .... Mr. Sairam PATHI
37 Director Student Financial Services .... Mr. Russell JEFFREY
121 Director Student Success Center .... Ms. Ruth COOPER
36 Dir Vocation & Prof Development .... Ms. Randa SCOTT
35 Dean of Students .... Ms. Martha COMPTON
08 Director of Library Services .... Ms. Mikail MCINTOSH-DOTY
58 Director MBA Graduate Program .... Dr. Elise BRAZIER
19 Chief of Police .... Mr. Manuel JIMENEZ
29 Dir Donor & Alumni Relations .... Mr. Jeff FROSCH
102 Dir Found/Corp & Govt Relations .... Ms. Meghann BOLTON
112 Director of Major Gifts .... Ms. Tiffany JOHNSON
09 Dir Inst Research & Effectiveness .... Dr. Trey BUCHANAN
96 Director Support Services .... Mr. Eric SILBER
105 Web Administrator .... Mr. Bryan GILBERT

Criswell College (O)

4010 Gaston Avenue, Dallas TX 75246-1537
County: Dallas FICE Identification: 041218
Unit ID: 475608
Telephone: (214) 821-5433 Carnegie Class: Spec-4-yr-Faith
FAX Number: (214) 370-0497 Calendar System: Semester
URL: www.criswell.edu
Established: 1970 Annual Undergrad Tuition & Fees: $12,624
Enrollment: 209 Coed
Affiliation or Control: Independent Non-Profit IRS Status: 501(c)3
Highest Offering: Master's
Accreditation: SC

01 President Dr. Barry CREAMER
05 VP of Academic Affairs Dr. Christopher GRAHAM
10 VP of Finance Kevin STILLEY
32 VP of Student Affairs Russell MARRIOTT
111 VP of Advancement Dr. Joseph WOODDELL
04 Exec Assistant to President Daisy REYNOLDS
88 Admin Assistant to Chief of Staff Judy FOWLER
06 Registrar Dr. Matthew HARRISON
07 Director of Admissions Kyle HAMBY
08 Director of Library Services Vacant
100 Chief of Staff Winston HOTTMAN
13 Senior Director of Information Tech Dr. Scott SHIFFER
15 Director of Human Resources Martha BATTS
19 Chief of Police & Sr Dir Phys Plant Brad CORDER
26 Director of Communications Kendall LYONS
30 Director of Development Sharon MAXWELL
37 Director of Financial Aid Jimmy CRISWELL
09 Dir Acad Programmng & Inst Research Dr. David HIONIDES

Culinary Institute LeNotre (A)

7070 Allensby Street, Houston TX 77022-4322
County: Harris FICE Identification: 037233
Unit ID: 444565
Telephone: (713) 692-0077 Carnegie Class: Spec 2-yr-A&S
FAX Number: (713) 692-7399 Calendar System: Other
URL: www.culinaryinstitute.edu
Established: 1998 Annual Undergrad Tuition & Fees: $17,782
Enrollment: 382 Coed
Affiliation or Control: Proprietary IRS Status: Proprietary
Highest Offering: Associate Degree
Accreditation: ACCSC, ACFEI

05 VP of Operations/Campus Director Dr. Arturo CERVANTES

Culinary Institute of America San Antonio (B)

312 Pearl Parkway, Bldg 3,Ste 2102,
San Antonio TX 78215
Telephone: (210) 554-6400 Identification: 770131
Accreditation: &M

† Branch campus of The Culinary Institute of America, Hyde Park, NY

Dallas Baptist University (C)

3000 Mountain Creek Parkway, Dallas TX 75211-9299
County: Dallas FICE Identification: 003560
Unit ID: 224226
Telephone: (214) 333-7100 Carnegie Class: DU-Mod
FAX Number: (214) 333-5447 Calendar System: 4/1/4
URL: www.dbu.edu
Established: 1898 Annual Undergrad Tuition & Fees: $31,940
Enrollment: 4,247 Coed
Affiliation or Control: Baptist IRS Status: 501(c)3
Highest Offering: Doctorate
Accreditation: SC, ACBSP, CAEP, CEA, MUS

01 President Dr. Adam WRIGHT
02 Chancellor Dr. Gary COOK
100 Chief of Staff Mr. Dan GIBSON
10 Vice Pres for Financial Affairs Dr. Matt MURRAH
11 VP of Administration and Enrollment Mr. Jonathan TEAT
26 Vice President for Communications Dr. Blake KILLINGSWORTH
32 Vice President for Student Affairs Dr. Jay HARLEY
111 Vice President for Advancement Mr. Ryan HEFTON
85 Vice Pres for International Affairs Mr. Randy BYERS
13 VP for IT & Dean Online Education Dr. Matt WINN
27 Assistant VP for Communications Dr. Layna EVANS
88 Sr Advisor to Pres for Acad Affs Dr. Denny DOWD
05 Provost Dr. Norma HEDIN
20 Associate Provost Mrs. Deemie NAUGLE
20 Assistant Provost Dr. Mark HALE
108 Acad Dean/Accreditation Liaison Dr. Gail LINAM
06 Registrar Ms. Linda RONEY
35 Dean of Students Mrs. Tempress ASAGBA
84 Associate VP for Enrollment Mr. Jason WILLIAMS
07 Associate VP for UG Enrollment Dr. John BORUM
07 Director of UG Admissions Ms. Erin SMITH
58 Dean Cook School of Leadership Dr. Jack GOODYEAR
107 Dean Global Studies/Pre-Prof Pgms Dr. David COOK
50 Dean College of Business Dr. Jeff JOHNSON
81 Dean College Natural Science & Math Dr. Dionisio FLEITAS
53 Dean College of Education Dr. DeAnna JENKINS
57 Dean College of Fine Arts Dr. Wes MOORE
73 Dean College of Christian Faith Dr. Wayne DAVIS
79 Dean Col Humanities/Social Sciences Dr. Rob SULLIVAN
114 Asst VP for Financial Affairs Mr. Danny HASSETT
21 Controller Mrs. Mendi MCMAHAN
37 Director of Financial Aid Mrs. Shermain REED
113 Dir of Student Account Services Ms. Joy BONDURANT
105 Director of Web Services Mrs. Anu CHIVUKULA
29 Director of Alumni Affairs Mrs. Kathryn ROBNETT
08 Director of the Library Mr. Scott JEFFRIES
15 Director of Human Resources Mrs. Tamy ROGERS
43 General Counsel Ms. Christa POWERS
88 Director of Immigration Mr. Aaron PARISH
85 Director of Intl Student Services Mrs. Susie CASSEL
41 Director of Athletics Mr. Connor SMITH
35 Director of Student Life Mr. Wayne BRIGGS
121 Director of Student Success Mrs. Molly TAYLOR
36 Director of Career Development Mrs. Leoni MICHAEL
38 Dir Counseling & Spiritual Care Dr. Jordan DAVIS
39 Director of University Housing Ms. Allyson MILLER
24 Director of Media Services Mr. Rob LEWIS
19 Chief of Police Mr. Chris HAVENS
19 Director of Campus Security Mr. Donald KABETZKE
40 Manager Bookstore Vacant

Dallas Christian College (D)

2700 Christian Parkway, Dallas TX 75234-7299
County: Dallas FICE Identification: 006941
Unit ID: 224244
Telephone: (972) 241-3371 Carnegie Class: Spec-4-yr-Faith
FAX Number: (972) 241-8021 Calendar System: 4/1/4
URL: www.dallas.edu
Established: 1950 Annual Undergrad Tuition & Fees: $19,086
Enrollment: 246 Coed
Affiliation or Control: Christian Churches And Churches of Christ
IRS Status: 501(c)3
Highest Offering: Baccalaureate
Accreditation: BI

01 President Dr. Brian D. SMITH
05 VP for Academic Affairs Dr. John DERRY
84 VP for Enrollment Management Mr. Ken FAFFLER
111 VP for Institutional Advancement Mr. Mark WORLEY
10 VP of Finance & Operations Ms. Andrea SHORT
108 Dir Institutional Effectiveness Mr. Bruce LONG
06 Registrar Mrs. Crystal LAIDACKER
37 Dir of Student Financial Svcs Ms. Breanda WILLIAMS
18 Director of Facilities Mr. David LAGUNEZ
04 Exec Admin Assistant to the Pres Ms. Annette ESCLAVON

*Dallas College (E)

1601 South Lamar Street, Dallas TX 75215
County: Dallas FICE Identification: 009331
Unit ID: 224253
Telephone: (214) 378-1601 Carnegie Class: N/A
FAX Number: (214) 378-1810
URL: www.dcccd.edu

01 Chancellor Dr. Joe D. MAY
86 EVC Public/Govt Affairs Dr. Justin LONON
05 District Provost Dr. Shawnda FLOYD
111 Vice Chanc Advancement/Dev Dr. Iris A. FREEMON
43 District General Counsel Mr. Robert WENDLAND
86 Chief Legislative Counsel Mr. Isaac FAZ
45 Chief Strategy Officer Ms. Mary BRUMBACH
10 Chief Financial Officer Mr. John ROBERTSON
13 Chief Innovation Officer (CIO) Mr. Tim MARSHALL
101 Board Relations Executive Mrs. Perla MOLINA
102 Chief Advancement Ofcr/Dir of Fndn Dr. Pyeper WILKINS

*Dallas College, Brookhaven Campus (F)

3939 Valley View, Dallas TX 75244-4997
County: Dallas FICE Identification: 021002
Unit ID: 223524
Telephone: (972) 860-4700 Carnegie Class: Assoc/MT-VT-High Non
FAX Number: (972) 860-4897 Calendar System: Semester
URL: www.brookhavencollege.edu
Established: 1978 Annual Undergrad Tuition & Fees (In-District): N/A
Enrollment: N/A Coed
Affiliation or Control: State/Local IRS Status: 501(c)3
Highest Offering: Baccalaureate
Accreditation: &SC, ADNUR, ART, EMT, NAEYC, RAD

02 President Dr. Linda BRADDY
32 Vice Pres Student Dev/Enroll Mgmt Mr. Oscar LOPEZ
100 Chief of Staff Ms. Lori HIGGINS
103 Assoc VP Workforce/Continuing Educ Mr. Vernon L. HAWKINS
30 Assoc Vice Pres Development Ms. Marilyn K. LYNCH
50 Exec Dean Business Studies Dr. Giraud POLITE
45 Exec Dean Educational Resources Ms. Sarah FERGUSON
57 Exec Dean Fine Arts/Physical Educ Ms. Megan ABAJIAN
81 Exec Dean Science/Math Mr. Benjamin PEACOCK
76 Vice Provost of Health Sciences Dr. Juanita FLINT
13 Director Information Technology Mr. Michael DEASON
83 Exec Dean Social Sci/Distance Lrng Mr. Sam GOVEA
26 Executive Dean Communications Mrs. Kendra VAGLIENTI
38 Sr Exec Dean Guidance & Counseling Ms. Brenda DALTON
27 Dir Marketing/Public Information Ms. Meridith MCLARTY
06 Registrar Ms. Thoa Hoang VO
88 Sr Manager Intramural Sports Mr. Kevin HURST
21 Director of Business Operations Ms. Willadean MARTIN
36 Administrator of Placement Ms. Dominica MCCARTHY
18 Sr Director Physical Plant Mr. Garry HODGES
15 Chief Human Resources Officer Ms. Sherri ENRIGHT
35 Admin Office of Student Life Mr. Brian BORSKI
19 Commander of College Police Mr. Mark LOPEZ
88 Director of Sustainability Mr. Brandon MORTON

*Dallas College, Cedar Valley Campus (G)

3030 N Dallas Avenue, Lancaster TX 75134-3799
County: Dallas FICE Identification: 003561
Unit ID: 223773
Telephone: (972) 860-8201 Carnegie Class: Assoc/MT-VT-High Non
FAX Number: (972) 682-7075 Calendar System: Semester
URL: www.cedarvalleycollege.edu
Established: 1974 Annual Undergrad Tuition & Fees (In-District): N/A
Enrollment: N/A Coed
Affiliation or Control: State/Local IRS Status: 501(c)3
Highest Offering: Baccalaureate
Accreditation: &SC

02 President Dr. Joseph SEABROOKS
05 Provost Dr. Shawnda NAVARRO FLOYD
32 VP Student Services/Enrollment Mgmt Dr. Lisa COPPRUE
10 Vice Pres Business/Admin Services Mr. Huan LUONG
81 Exec Dean Science/Tech/Engr/Math Mr. Eddy RAWLINSON
50 Exec Dean of Business/Technology Dr. Ruben JOHNSON
49 VProv Creative Arts/Design Dr. Solomon CROSS
51 Assoc Dean Open Enroll/Cont Educ Mr. Raymond RIVERA
88 Dir Sustainability/Advance Projects Dr. Maria BOCCALANDRO
35 Dean Student Support Services Ms. Grenna ROLLINGS
84 Sr Exec Dean Enrollment Mgmt Ms. Jarlene DECAY
08 Director Library Services Ms. Vidya KRISHNASWAMY
09 Dir Plng/Rsrch/Inst Effectiveness Ms. Nicole HAAN
18 Director Facilities Management Mrs. Cindy A. ROGERS
26 Chief Marketing Officer Mr. Nevin GRINNELL
15 Exec Director of Human Resources Mr. Warren DAVIS
13 Director Information Technology Mr. Michael WHITE
111 Exec Director of Advancement Ms. Patricia DAVIS
21 Assoc Director of Business Office Mr. Jim JONES

*Dallas College, Eastfield Campus (H)

3737 Motley Drive, Mesquite TX 75150-2099
County: Dallas FICE Identification: 008510
Unit ID: 224572
Telephone: (972) 860-7100 Carnegie Class: Assoc/HT-High Non
FAX Number: (972) 860-8373 Calendar System: Semester
URL: www.eastfieldcollege.edu
Established: 1970 Annual Undergrad Tuition & Fees (In-District): N/A
Enrollment: N/A Coed
Affiliation or Control: State/Local IRS Status: 170(c)1
Highest Offering: Baccalaureate
Accreditation: &SC

02 President Dr. Eddie TEALER
05 Exec VP Academic Affairs Vacant
10 VP Business Services Mr. Jose C. RODRIGUEZ
45 Vice President Planning & Research Vacant
15 Senior Director Human Resources Mr. Andre JOHNSON
32 Assoc VP Student Svcs Admin Dr. Jose DELA CRUZ
111 AVP Advancement & Communication Ms. Sharon L. COOK
20 Assoc VP Academic Affairs Ms. Rachel B. WOLF
84 Exec Dean Access and Enrollment Dr. Patty R. YOUNG
12 Exec Dir Pleasant Grove Campus Dr. Javier E. OLGUIN
103 Senior Director Workforce Planning Ms. Tiffanie DOUGLAS
08 Executive Dean Library Ms. Karla J. GREER
72 Executive Dean of Career Tech Ms. Johnnie O. BELLAMY
81 Executive Dean STEM Dr. Jess P. KELLY
83 Exec Dean Social Sciences Ms. DeShaunta STEWART
57 Exec Dean Arts and Communications Ms. Courtney CARTER-HARBOUR
21 Exec Admin of Financial Affairs Ms. Heidi M. BASSETT
18 Director Facilities Management Mr. Michael BRANTLEY
28 Dir Ctr Equity/Inclusion/Diversity Ms. Ashmi PATEL
124 Dean Ofc Stdnt Engagement/Retention Ms. Tania WITTGENFELD
46 Dean Resource Development Dr. Tricia THOMAS-ANDERSON
51 Exec Dean Continuing Education Ms. Alisa JONES
26 Director of Marketing Ms. Donielle R. JOHNSON
106 Dean Inst Support & Distance Educ Mr. Abuzafar M. BASHET
88 Assoc Dean Educational Resources Ms. Lucinda A. GONZALES

*Dallas College, El Centro Campus (I)

801 Main Street, Dallas TX 75202-3604
County: Dallas FICE Identification: 004453
Unit ID: 224615
Telephone: (214) 860-2000 Carnegie Class: Assoc/HVT-High Non
FAX Number: (214) 860-2335 Calendar System: Semester
URL: www.elcentrocollege.edu
Established: 1966 Annual Undergrad Tuition & Fees (In-District): $4,050
Enrollment: 74,781 Coed
Affiliation or Control: State/Local IRS Status: 501(c)3
Highest Offering: Baccalaureate
Accreditation: &SC, ACFEI, ADNUR, COARC, CVT, DH, DMS, EMT, MAC, MLTAD, PNUR, RAD, SURGT

02 President Dr. Jose ADAMES
05 Exec VP Academic Affairs Dr. Greg MORRIS
32 VP Student Svcs & Enrollment Ms. Karen STILLS
10 VP Business Services Ms. Lenora REECE
30 Manager of Development Vacant
76 Int Exec Dean Health Sciences Dr. Greg MORRIS
97 Exec Dean Academic Transfer Dr. Anthony MANSUETO
81 Exec Dean STEM Ms. Beth STALL
50 Exec Dean Business/Design/Pub Svc Dr. Sherry JONES
103 Dean of Instruct/CE/Workforce Educ Ms. Elizabeth GUERRA
106 Dean Instruct Innov/Acad Support Ms. Karla DAMRON
108 Int Dean Curriculum/Assessment Ms. Joselyn GONZALEZ
09 Assoc Dir Inst Effectiveness Ms. Nicosha PORTER
35 Dean Student Support Services Dr. Tracy JOHNSON
121 Dean Student Success Dr. Cornelius JOHNSON
89 Director College Programs Mr. Patrick VASQUEZ
08 Asst Dean Library Dr. Norman HOWDEN
84 Assoc Dean Enroll Services Ms. Rebecca J. GARZA
12 Exec Director West Campus Ms. Kathy ACOSTA
15 Exec Dir Human Resources Dr. Alfredo SANJUAN

19 College Police Captain .... Mr. James SMITH
26 Dir Marketing/Communications .... Ms. Priscilla A. STALEY
18 Col Director Facilities Services .... Mr. Jeremy MCCLELLAND
21 Dir Business Operations .... Ms. Keisha FARRINGTON
37 Dir Student Financial Aid .... Ms. Pam A. LUCAS
13 Sr Director Information Technology .... Mr. Michael C. JOHNSON
85 Dir Col Pgms/International Center .... Mr. Robert G. REYES
36 Pgm Svcs Coord Career Services .... Ms. Christol JOHNSON
38 Licensed Psychologist .... Mr. David THOMPSON
23 Senior Manager Health Center .... Ms. LaJoyya JOHNSON
04 Executive Asst to President .... Ms. Ida KELLER
40 Manager Bookstore .... Ms. Venus MCGUIRE

*Dallas College, Mountain View Campus (A)

4849 W Illinois Avenue, Dallas TX 75211-6599
County: Dallas FICE Identification: 008503
Unit ID: 226930
Telephone: (214) 860-8680 Carnegie Class: Assoc/HT-High Non
FAX Number: (214) 860-8521 Calendar System: Semester
URL: www.mountainviewcollege.edu
Established: 1970 Annual Undergrad Tuition & Fees (In-District): N/A
Enrollment: N/A Coed
Affiliation or Control: State/Local IRS Status: 501(c)3
Highest Offering: Baccalaureate
Accreditation: &SC, ADNUR, OTA

01 College President .... Dr. Beatriz JOSEPH
05 Vice President of Instruction .... Vacant
32 VP Student Svcs/Enrollment Mgmt .... Dr. Leonard GARRETT
10 Int Vice Pres of Business Services .... Dr. Elsy CARRANZA
84 Exec Dean Student Support Svcs .... Mr. Matthew SANCHEZ
90 Exec Dean Curriculum & Instruction .... Dr. Karen VALENCIA
06 Assoc Dean Lrng Sppt Svcs/Registrar .... Ms. Glenda GARRETT
18 Director Facilities Management .... Vacant
09 Dir of Planning/Research & IE .... Ms. Iva BERGERON
88 Administrator of Special Programs .... Ms. Cathy EDWARDS
103 Exec Dean of Workforce/Cont Educ .... Ms. Pat WEBB
26 Director Public Info/Marketing .... Ms. Jill LAIN
15 Exec Director Human Resources .... Mr. Warren DAVIS
36 Director Career Development .... Ms. Regina GARNER
45 Dean Resource Development .... Mr. Garth CLAYTON
04 Administrative Asst to President .... Mr. Michael ARREDONDO
08 Dir Library Services .... Ms. Jean BAKER
41 Athletic Director .... Mr. Manuel MANTRANA

*Dallas College, North Lake Campus (B)

5001 N MacArthur Boulevard, Irving TX 75038-3899
County: Dallas FICE Identification: 020774
Unit ID: 227191
Telephone: (972) 273-3000 Carnegie Class: Assoc/HT-High Non
FAX Number: (972) 273-3014 Calendar System: Semester
URL: www.dcccd.edu
Established: 1977 Annual Undergrad Tuition & Fees (In-District): N/A
Enrollment: N/A Coed
Affiliation or Control: State/Local IRS Status: 501(c)3
Highest Offering: Baccalaureate
Accreditation: &SC, CONST

02 President .... Dr. Christa SLEJKO
05 Vice Pres Academic Affairs/Provost .... Dr. Shawnda FLOYD
10 Vice Pres Business Services .... Vacant
32 VP Stdnt Success/Enrollment Mgmt .... Dr. Marisa PIERCE
84 Dean of Enrollment Mgmt/Stdnt Svcs .... Ms. Anabel JUAREZ
07 Dean Admissions/Registrar .... Ms. Francyenne MAYNARD
26 Director Marketing & Public Info .... Ms. Gina FEDERER
12 Exec Dean North & South Campus .... Mr. Arthur JAMES
12 Exec Dean West Campus .... Dr. Paul KELEMEN
09 Exec Dir Institutional Research .... Dr. Karen MONGO
18 Director Facilities Services .... Mr. John WATSON
19 Director Campus Police .... Mr. Randy REED
111 Dean of Advancement .... Dr. Kristine MASSEY
15 Exec Director Human Resources .... Vacant
21 Director Business Operations .... Ms. Elsy CARRANZA
35 Asst Dir Stdnt Pgms/Resources/Life .... Ms. Beth NIKOPOULOS
103 Exec Dean Workforce Dev/CE .... Mr. Tim SAMUELS
49 Executive Dean Liberal Arts .... Dr. Kenneth CHAPMAN
81 Exec Dean Math/Science .... Dr. Matthew DEMPSEY
50 Exec Dean Arts/Bus/Sports Sci Tech .... Dr. David EVANS
04 Administrative Asst to President .... Ms. Kari ANDREWS
41 Athletic Director .... Mr. Greg SOMMERS

*Dallas College, Richland Campus (C)

12800 Abrams Road, Dallas TX 75243-2199
County: Dallas FICE Identification: 008504
Unit ID: 227766
Telephone: (972) 238-6100 Carnegie Class: Assoc/HT-High Non
FAX Number: (972) 238-6957 Calendar System: Semester
URL: www.rlc.dcccd.edu
Established: 1972 Annual Undergrad Tuition & Fees (In-District): N/A
Enrollment: N/A Coed
Affiliation or Control: State/Local IRS Status: 501(c)3
Highest Offering: Baccalaureate
Accreditation: &SC, MAC

02 President .... Dr. Kathryn K. EGGLESTON
04 Dean/Exec Assistant to President .... Ms. Janet C. JAMES

Dallas Institute of Funeral Service (D)

3909 S Buckner Boulevard, Dallas TX 75227-4314
County: Dallas FICE Identification: 010761
Unit ID: 224271
Telephone: (214) 388-5466 Carnegie Class: Spec 2-yr-A&S
FAX Number: (214) 388-0316 Calendar System: Quarter
URL: www.dallasinstitute.edu
Established: 1945 Annual Undergrad Tuition & Fees: $12,790
Enrollment: 364 Coed
Affiliation or Control: Independent Non-Profit IRS Status: 501(c)3
Highest Offering: Associate Degree
Accreditation: FUSER

01 President .... Mr. Wayne CAVENDER
76 College Dean .... Ms. Erin WILSON
06 Registrar/Office Manager .... Ms. Tammy LEONARD
07 Director of Admissions .... Ms. Jan PERKINS
37 Director Financial Aid .... Ms. LaSonya BRYANT

Dallas International University (E)

7500 W Camp Wisdom Road, Dallas TX 75236-5629
County: Dallas FICE Identification: 038513
Telephone: (972) 708-7340 Carnegie Class: Not Classified
FAX Number: (972) 708-7292 Calendar System: Other
URL: www.diu.edu
Established: 1999 Annual Undergrad Tuition & Fees: N/A
Enrollment: N/A Coed
Affiliation or Control: Independent Non-Profit IRS Status: 501(c)3
Highest Offering: Doctorate
Accreditation: SC

01 President .... Dr. Doug TIFFIN
11 Vice President of Operations .... Mr. Jeff MINARD
15 Chief Human Resources Officer .... Mrs. Jodi EGAN
10 Vice President of Finance .... Mr. Rod JENKINS
32 Dean of Students .... Mrs. Meg TRIHUS
05 Dean of Academic Affairs .... Dr. Scott BERTHIAUME
42 Chaplain .... Mrs. Christine HARLAN
101 Secretary to the Board of Trustees .... Mr. Tad OLDENBURGER
30 Director of Development .... Vacant
04 Special Asst to President .... Ms. Valerie RHODES
09 Director of Inst Research/Svcs .... Mr. Richard LYNCH
21 Business Manager .... Mr. Paul SETTER
96 Lead Accountant .... Mr. Dan WALTON
35 Assistant Dean of Students .... Mr. Stephen PETERSON
20 Academic Dean Assistant .... Mr. Dan BOERGER
08 Library Director .... Ms. Brenda FLOWERS
84 Int Director of Recruiting .... Mr. John OH
07 Director of Admissions .... Mr. Stephen NASH
104 International Student Coordinator .... Mrs. Maggie JOHNSON
06 Registrar .... Mrs. Lynne LAMIMAN
37 Financial Aid Administrator .... Mr. Ken PRETTOL
29 Alumni Relations Coordinator .... Ms. Debbie MANTER
13 Director of Information Services .... Mr. Matt LONG
24 Director of Media Services .... Mr. Bill HARRIS
44 Development Assistant .... Mrs. Tricia REIMAN
26 Director of External Relationships .... Mr. John OH
125 President Emeritus .... Dr. David ROSS

† (f.k.a. Graduate Institute of Applied Linguistics)

Dallas Theological Seminary (F)

3909 Swiss Avenue, Dallas TX 75204-6493
County: Dallas FICE Identification: 003562
Unit ID: 224305
Telephone: (214) 887-5000 Carnegie Class: Spec-4-yr-Faith
FAX Number: (214) 887-5532 Calendar System: Semester
URL: www.dts.edu
Established: 1924 Annual Graduate Tuition & Fees: N/A
Enrollment: 2,447 Coed
Affiliation or Control: Independent Non-Profit IRS Status: 501(c)3
Highest Offering: Doctorate; No Undergraduates
Accreditation: SC, THEOL

01 President .... Dr. Mark M. YARBROUGH
05 Vice President for Education .... Dr. George HILLMAN
10 VP for Business & Finance .... Mr. Dale C. LARSON
32 Dean of Student Life .... Rev. Herman BAXTER
111 Vice President for Advancement .... Ms. Kimberly B. TILL
11 Vice President Campus Operations .... Mr. Robert F. RIGGS
26 Exec Dir of Mktg and Communications .... Mr. Kraig MCNUTT
102 Exec Dir Dallas Seminary Found .... Mr. Scott TALBOT
20 Academic Dean/Dean of Acad Admin .... Dr. James H. THAMES
12 Dean of DTS Houston .... Vacant
12 Dean DTS Washington DC .... Dr. Rodney ORR
58 Director of PhD Studies .... Dr. Vic A. ANDERSON
58 Director of DMin Studies .... Dr. D. Scott BARFOOT
09 Dir Inst Research & Effectiveness .... Vacant
06 Registrar .... Ms. Sabrina HOPSON
88 Exec Dir of Leadership Center .... Dr. Bill HENDRICKS
88 Exec Dir of Cultural Engagement .... Dr. Darrell L. BOCK
07 Director of Admissions .... Mr. Luke BRYANT
08 Library Director .... Mr. Marvin T. HUNN, II
84 VP for Enrollment Svcs & Educ Tech .... Dr. John DYER
29 Director of Alumni Services .... Dr. Greg A. HATTEBERG
36 Director of Placement .... Dr. Paul E. PETTIT
42 Campus Pastor .... Dr. Joe M. ALLEN, JR.
35 Assistant Dean of Students .... Ms. Rebecca JOWERS
35 Assistant Dean of Students .... Dr. Terrance S. WOODSON

88 Associate Dean of Academic Admin .... Mr. Nate MCKANNA
13 Director of Information Technology .... Mr. Kevin COX
19 Chief of Campus Police .... Mr. John S. BLOOM
10 VP for Global Ministries .... Dr. Michael ORTIZ
39 Manager of Housing .... Ms. Sarah CHAPELL
106 Director Online Education .... Mr. Martin MCKEE
88 Director of Chinese Studies .... Dr. Samuel CHIA
88 Director of DTS en Espanol .... Dr. Gerardo ALFARO
38 Director of Counseling Services .... Dr. Kelly CHEATHAM
21 Controller .... Ms. Sonja FLORES
40 Director of Book Center .... Ms. Rachelle CERDA
85 Dir for Intl Stdnt Svcs/Disability .... Mr. Voltaire CACAL
04 Administrative Asst to President .... Ms. Michelle B. SCHIWIETZ
15 Director Human Resources .... Mr. Wes WADA
88 Dir of Maintenance Operations .... Mr. Brian GERBERICH
18 Director of Facilities Coord .... Mr. Glenn MONRO
88 Campus Operations Administrator .... Mrs. Dee LITTLEJOHN
110 Executive Dir for Advancement .... Vacant
112 Director of Donor Management .... Mr. Jacob BECK
101 Admin Coord for Board Mtgs .... Ms. Margaret TOLLIVER
37 Director Student Financial Aid .... Mrs. Jennifer MCCORMACK
96 Director of Purchasing .... Ms. Lisa REEVES
108 Director Institutional Assessment .... Vacant

Del Mar College (G)

101 Baldwin Blvd., Corpus Christi TX 78404-3897
County: Nueces FICE Identification: 003563
Unit ID: 224350
Telephone: (361) 698-1200 Carnegie Class: Assoc/HVT-High Trad
FAX Number: (361) 698-1559 Calendar System: Semester
URL: www.delmar.edu
Established: 1935 Annual Undergrad Tuition & Fees (In-District): $4,820
Enrollment: 10,678 Coed
Affiliation or Control: Local IRS Status: 501(c)3
Highest Offering: Associate Degree
Accreditation: SC, ACFEI, ADNUR, ART, CAHIIM, COARC, DA, DH, DMS, EMT, MLTAD, MUS, NAEYC, OTA, PTAA, RAD, SURGT, THEA

01 President & CEO .... Dr. Mark ESCAMILLA
43 General Counsel .... Mr. Augustin RIVERA, JR.
03 Exec Vice Pres/Chief Operating Ofcr .... Ms. Lenora KEAS
05 VP & Chief Academic Officer .... Dr. Jonda HALCOMB
10 VP & Chief Financial Officer .... Mr. Raul GARCIA
13 Vice Pres/Chief Information Ofcr .... Mr. August ALFONSO
11 VP Administration & Human Resources . Ms. Tammy MCDONALD
32 Vice President for Student Affairs .... Ms. Patricia BENAVIDES-DOMINGUEZ
18 VP/Chief Physical Facilities Ofcr .... Mr. John STRYBOS
108 AVP Planning & Inst Effectiveness .... Dr. Kristina WILSON
35 AVP for Student Affairs .... Ms. Cheryl SANDERS
86 Exec Dir Govt & Board Relations .... Dr. Natalie VILLARREAL
19 Chief of Security .... Ms. Lauren WHITE
26 Exec Dir Communication & Marketing .... Ms. Lorette WILLIAMS
30 Exec Director of Development .... Ms. Mary MCQUEEN
103 Director Strategic Initiatives .... Ms. Kiwana DENSON
84 Dean Student Outreach/Enroll Svcs .... Ms. Graciela MARTINEZ
124 Dean Student Engagement & Retention .... Ms. Cheryl SANDERS
49 Dean Division Arts & Sciences .... Dr. Cynthia BRIDGES
50 Dean Business/Educ/Health Sciences .... Ms. Jennifer SRAMEK
88 Dean Industry & Public Service .... Mr. Davis MERRELL
51 Dean CE & Off Campus Programs .... Dr. Leonard RIVERA
103 Dean Workforce Pgms/Corporate Svcs .... Mr. Daniel KORUS
08 Dean of Learning Resources .... Mr. Cody GREGG
21 Comptroller/Revenue Budget Admin .... Mr. John J. JOHNSON
114 Dir Accounting/Budget Officer .... Dr. Cathy WEST
96 Director of Purchasing/Business Svc .... Mr. David DAVILA
88 Dir Environmental/Health/Safety .... Mr. Jack TWEDDLE
37 Director of Financial Aid .... Mr. Joseph RUIZ
06 Registrar .... Ms. Elizabeth ADAMSON
35 Dir Student Leadership/Campus Life .... Ms. Beverly CAGE
09 Director of Institutional Research .... Mr. Sushil PALLEMONI
15 Director of Human Resources .... Mr. Jerry W. HENRY
117 Director of Risk Management .... Ms. Jessica ALANIZ
88 Director of Payroll .... Ms. Katrina GARCIA
14 Deputy Chief Information Officer .... Ms. Jessica MONTALVO-CUMMINGS
119 Information Security Officer .... Mr. Gregory PALMER
30 Director of Development .... Mr. Matthew BUSBY
108 Dir Accreditation & Assessment .... Ms. Sydney SAUMBY

East Texas Baptist University (H)

One Tiger Drive, Marshall TX 75670-1498
County: Harrison FICE Identification: 003564
Unit ID: 224527
Telephone: (903) 935-7963 Carnegie Class: Bac-Diverse
FAX Number: (903) 938-7798 Calendar System: Semester
URL: www.etbu.edu
Established: 1912 Annual Undergrad Tuition & Fees: $27,640
Enrollment: 1,714 Coed
Affiliation or Control: Baptist IRS Status: 501(c)3
Highest Offering: Master's
Accreditation: SC, MT, MUS, NURSE

01 President .... Dr. J. Blair BLACKBURN
05 Provost & Vice Pres Acad Affairs .... Dr. Thomas SANDERS
10 Vice Pres Financial Affairs .... Mr. Lee FERGUSON
111 Vice Pres University Advancement .... Dr. Scott BRYANT
41 Vice Pres Student Engage/Athletics .... Mr. Ryan ERWIN
26 Vice Pres Strat Initiatives & Comm .... Mrs. Becky DAVIS
84 Vice President for Enrollment .... Mr. Jeremy JOHNSTON

20 Assoc Provost for Academic Affairs Vacant
21 Assoc Vice Pres for Financial Affs Mrs. Tara BACHTEL
32 Assoc Vice Pres Student Engagement Vacant
11 Asst Vice Pres for Univ Operations Mr. Chris CRAWFORD
55 Asst Provost/Dir of Adult Ed & Grad Mr. Vince BLANKENSHIP
09 Dean Acad Services & Inst Research Dr. Marty WARREN
107 Dean School of Professional Studies Dr. Joseph BROWN
53 Dean School of Education Dr. Amber DAUB
88 Dean School of Christian Studies Vacant
83 Dean Sch of Natural/Social Sci Dr. Laurie SMITH
50 Dean School of Business Dr. Barry EVANS
79 Dean School of Humanities Dr. Sandy HOOVER
57 Dean School of Comm & Perf Arts Dr. Justin HODGES
106 Dean of Online Education Dr. Colleen HALUPA
66 Dean School of Nursing Dr. Rebekah GRIGSBY
13 Director of Inst Technology Mr. Barry HALE
08 Dean of Library Services Mrs. Elizabeth PONDER
37 Director of Financial Aid Mrs. Linda SLAWSON
88 Director Baptist Student Ministry Mr. David GRIFFIN
40 Bookstore Manager Mr. Jamie DOWDY
18 Director of Physical Operations Mr. Stephen RATCLIFF
85 Dir Great Commission Ctr/Global Ed Dr. Lisa SEELEY
121 Director of Academic Success Dr. Donovan FREDRICKSEN
19 Director of Security & Compliance Mr. Larry NORTHCUTT
58 Director of Graduate Programs Vacant
39 Director of Residence Life Mrs. Desirae' BRADLEY
35 Director of Student Activities Ms. Laura COURSEY
06 University Registrar Mr. Troy WHITE
42 Dean of Spiritual Life Dr. Scott STEVENS
29 Dir Alumni Relations/Advance Comm Ms. Emily CLARK
04 Assistant to the President Mrs. Janet BRECKENRIDGE

El Paso Community College (A)

P.O. Box 20500, El Paso TX 79998
County: El Paso FICE Identification: 010387
Unit ID: 224642
Telephone: (915) 831-2000 Carnegie Class: Assoc/HT-High Trad
FAX Number: N/A Calendar System: Semester
URL: www.epcc.edu
Established: 1969 Annual Undergrad Tuition & Fees (In-District): $3,274
Enrollment: 26,034 Coed
Affiliation or Control: Local IRS Status: 501(c)3
Highest Offering: Associate Degree
Accreditation: **SC**, ADNUR, CAHIIM, COARC, DA, DH, DMS, EMT, MAC, MLTAD, PTAA, RAD, SURGT

01 President Dr. William SERRATA
05 Vice Pres Instruction & WF Educ Dr. Steven SMITH
11 Vice Pres Financial and Admin Ops Ms. Josette SHAUGHNESSY
13 Vice Pres Information Tech/CIO Dr. Jenny GIRON
32 Vice Pres Student & Enroll Svcs Dr. Kenneth GONZALEZ
108 Vice Pres Rsrch/Accred & Planning Dr. Julie PENLEY
114 AVP Budget and Financial Svcs Mr. Fernando FLORES
26 AVP External Rels/Comm and Dev Ms. Keri L. MOE
20 AVP Instruction & Student Success Dr. Paula MITCHELL
103 Int AVP Workforce and CE Dr. Carlos C. AMAYA
12 Campus Dean Mission del Paso Mr. Joshua I. VILLALOBOS
12 Int Campus Dean RG Dr. Souraya HAJJAR
66 Dean Nursing RG Ms. Paula G. MEAGHER
76 Dean Hlth Career/TechEd/Math/Sci RG Dr. Souraya HAJJAR
12 Int Campus Dean TM Mr. Ernest R. WEBB, II
81 Dean Math/Sci/Career Tech Educ TM Mr. Ernest R. WEBB, II
12 Campus Dean Valle Verde Ms. Susana RODARTE
49 Dean Arch/Arts/Math/Science VV Dr. Carlos C. AMAYA
57 Dean Comm/Performing Arts VV Mr. Blayne J. PRIMOZICH
53 Dean Education/Career/Tech VV Dr. Myshie M. PAGEL
88 Dean ATC VV Dr. Olga L. VALERIO
12 Campus Dean Instructional Pgms NW Dr. Lydia TENA
88 Dean Dual Credit & Early Col Ms. Maria Antonieta BADILLO
15 Exec Dir Human Resources Dr. Andrew M. PENA
14 Exec Dir Net Sys & Support Svcs Mr. Marco A. FERNANDEZ
14 Exec Dir IT Soft A Analytics Mr. Abraham A. HUBAIL
37 Exec Dir Student Financial Aid Ms. Ines LOPEZ
18 Exec Director Physical Plant Mr. Richard L. LOBATO
07 Exec Director Admissions/ Registrar Dr. Cassandra M. LACHICA-CHAVEZ
102 Exec Dir Resource Dev/Foundation Dr. Dolores GROSS
41 Athletic Director Mr. Felix HINOJOSA
25 Int Dir Grants Mgmt & Dev Mr. Robert T. ELLIOTT
45 Dir Institutional Effectiveness Dr. James Ron STROUD
84 Dir Recruitment Services Vacant
88 Dir WF Strategic Initiatives Dr. Carmen AGUILERA-GOERNER
88 Dir Contract Opportunity Center Mr. Pablo ARMENDARIZ
23 Dir CE Health Ms. Cheryl L. STILES
88 Dir Small Business Dev Center Mr. Joseph C. FERGUSON
27 Int Dir Marketing/Cmty Rels Mr. James HEINEY
90 Dir Acad Computing Media Svc Vacant
109 Dir Auxiliary Services Mr. Juan S. FLORES
45 Dir Institutional Planning Ms. Christina C. FRESCAS
88 Dir College Accred Compliance Ms. Mary Beth HAAN
88 Dir Curriculum Instruction Dev Ms. Yvette V. HUERTA
56 Dir Community Education Program Mr. Andres MURO
55 Dir Senior Adult Programs Ms. Mary A. YANEZ
88 Dir Quality Enhancement Plan Assess Dr. Ondrea M. QUIROS
35 Dir Stdnt Ldrshp Campus Life Ms. Arvis C. JONES
36 Dir Career & Transfer Services Ms. Carla CARDOZA
88 Dir CE Bus Tech Ed Per Ms. Leticia GUERRA
96 Dir Purchasing & Contract Mgmt Mr. Ruben C. GALLARDO
09 Director Institutional Research Dr. Carol KAY
28 Dir Diversity & Inclusion Programs Ms. Olga CHAVEZ
16 Dir Human Resources Development Mr. Alex HERNANDEZ
114 Director Budget Ms. Laura TELLEZ
22 Dir Ctr for Students w/Disabilities Ms. Maria LOPEZ
103 Director Workforce Development Ms. Luz E. TABOADA
121 Director Student Success Ms. Lucia M. RODRIGUEZ
88 Dir Law Enforcement Trng Academy Mr. Barry J. BOGLE
88 Dir Student Learning Outcomes Ms. Rebekah A. BELL
88 Project Dir Stemgrow Artic Program Dr. Mozella GARCIA
19 Chief of Police Mr. Jose L. RAMIREZ
21 Comptroller Ms. Ana ZUNIGA
118 Assoc Dir Employee Benefits Ms. Victoria VIGGERS
04 Exec Asst to the President & BOT Ms. Pamela PAYNE

Fortis College (B)

1201 West Oaks Mall, Houston TX 77082
County: Harris FICE Identification: 034244
Unit ID: 392415
Telephone: (713) 266-6594 Carnegie Class: Spec 2-yr-Health
FAX Number: (713) 782-5873 Calendar System: Quarter
URL: https://www.fortis.edu/campuses/texas/houston-north.html
Established: Annual Undergrad Tuition & Fees: N/A
Enrollment: 394 Coed
Affiliation or Control: Proprietary IRS Status: Proprietary
Highest Offering: Associate Degree
Accreditation: **ACCSC**, SURGT

01 Campus President Justin POND
05 Director of Education Lee Ann HIETT

Frank Phillips College (C)

PO Box 5118, Borger TX 79008-5118
County: Hutchinson FICE Identification: 003568
Unit ID: 224891
Telephone: (806) 457-4200 Carnegie Class: Assoc/HT-High Non
FAX Number: (806) 457-4224 Calendar System: Semester
URL: www.fpctx.edu
Established: 1948 Annual Undergrad Tuition & Fees (In-District): $4,118
Enrollment: 1,575 Coed
Affiliation or Control: Local IRS Status: 501(c)3
Highest Offering: Associate Degree
Accreditation: **SC**

01 President Dr. Glendon FORGERY
05 Vice President of Academic Affairs Dr. Shannon CARROLL
103 Dean of Career & Technical Educ Ms. Taryn FRALEY
12 Dean of Allen Campus Ms. Amber JONES
12 Dean of Rahll Campus Ms. Ilene WALTON
10 Chief Financial Officer Ms. Teri LANGWELL
111 Director Advancement Ms. Jackie BRAND
26 Director of Marketing Ms. Arielle PRITCHETT
38 Director Student Counseling/Testing Ms. Becky GREEN
07 Director Admissions & Records Ms. Michele STEVENS
08 Director of the Library Mr. Jason PRICE
37 Dir Student Financial Services Ms. Beverly FIELDS
18 Director Physical Plant Ms. Regina HANEY

Galen College of Nursing (D)

7411 John Smith Drive, Suite 1400,
San Antonio TX 78229
Telephone: (210) 733-3056 Identification: 770538
Accreditation: **&SC**, ADNUR, NURSE

† Branch campus of Galen College of Nursing, Louisville, KY

Galveston College (E)

4015 Avenue Q, Galveston TX 77550-7496
County: Galveston FICE Identification: 004972
Unit ID: 224961
Telephone: (409) 944-4242 Carnegie Class: Assoc/MT-VT-Mix Trad/Non
FAX Number: (409) 944-1500 Calendar System: Semester
URL: www.gc.edu
Established: 1966 Annual Undergrad Tuition & Fees (In-District): $2,950
Enrollment: 2,060 Coed
Affiliation or Control: State/Local IRS Status: 501(c)3
Highest Offering: Baccalaureate
Accreditation: **SC**, ADNUR, DMS, EMT, NMT, RAD, RTT, SURGT

01 President Dr. Myles SHELTON
05 Vice President of Instruction Dr. Cissy MATTHEWS
11 VP for Admin/Student Services Dr. Van PATTERSON
32 Associate VP of Student Services Mr. Ron C. CRUMEDY
75 Dean of Tech & Prof Education Ms. Vera LEWIS-JASPER
30 Dir of Development/GC Foundation Ms. Kelly MERRY
10 Comptroller/CFO Mr. M. Jeff ENGBROCK
13 Director of Info Technology Mr. Jason SMITH
26 Director of Public Affairs Ms. Carol LANGSTON
15 Dir Human Resources/Risk Management Dr. Mary Jan LANTZ
41 Athletic Director/Head Coach Ms. Christa WALLACE
07 Director Admissions/Registrar Mr. Scott BRANUM
66 Director of Nursing Ms. Donna CARLIN
09 Director Inst Effectiveness/Rsrch Ms. Carmen ALLEN
18 Director of Facilities Mr. Jorge OTERO
08 Dir of Library/Learning Resources Ms. Telishia MICKENS
37 Director of Financial Aid Ms. Meghann NASH
04 Executive Assistant Ms. Carla D. BIGGERS

Grace School of Theology (F)

3705 College Park Drive, The Woodlands TX 77384
County: Montgomery Identification: 667100
Unit ID: 481401
Telephone: (877) 476-8674 Carnegie Class: Spec-4-yr-Faith
FAX Number: (877) 735-2867 Calendar System: Semester
URL: www.gsot.edu
Established: 2002 Annual Undergrad Tuition & Fees: $6,480
Enrollment: 590 Coed
Affiliation or Control: Independent Non-Profit IRS Status: 501(c)3
Highest Offering: Doctorate
Accreditation: **THEOL**, TRACS

01 President Dr. Dave ANDERSON
43 Exec Vice President/General Counsel Mr. Tom KRUPPSTADT
05 Provost/Chief Student Svcs Ofcr Mr. Mark HAYWOOD
111 Vice Pres Advancement/COO Mr. Daniel LABRY
32 Dean of Students Mr. Willie GAINES

Grayson College (G)

6101 Grayson Drive, Denison TX 75020-8299
County: Grayson FICE Identification: 003570
Unit ID: 225070
Telephone: (903) 465-6030 Carnegie Class: Assoc/MT-VT-Mix Trad/Non
FAX Number: (903) 463-5284 Calendar System: Semester
URL: www.grayson.edu
Established: 1963 Annual Undergrad Tuition & Fees (In-District): $3,872
Enrollment: 4,066 Coed
Affiliation or Control: State/Local IRS Status: 501(c)3
Highest Offering: Baccalaureate
Accreditation: **SC**, ACFEI, ADNUR, DA, EMT, MLTAD, NAEYC, NUR

01 President Dr. Jeremy P. MCMILLEN
05 Vice President of Instruction Dr. Dava WASHBURN
32 Vice President of Student Affairs Vacant
10 Vice President for Business Svcs Mr. Giles BROWN
13 VP for Information Technology Mr. Gary PAIKOWSKI
04 Assistant to the President Vacant
102 Exec Dir Grayson College Foundation Mr. Randy TRUXAL
07 Director of Admissions/Registrar Ms. Brandi FURR
37 Director of Financial Aid Ms. Amanda HOWELL
14 Director of Network Services Mr. Mike BROWN
19 Director Public Safety Mr. Roger KISLOSKI
26 Director Marketing & Communications Ms. Rhea BERMEL
21 Director of Fiscal Services Mr. Danny HYATT
41 Director of Athletics Mr. Mike MCBRAYER
40 Bookstore Manager Ms. Helen BERGMAN
08 Director of Library Mrs. Lisa HEBERT
09 Dean of Planning/Inst Effectiveness Dr. Debbie SMARR
103 Exec Dir Ctr for Workforce Learning Mrs. Djuna FORRESTER
15 Director Human Resources Office Mrs. Robyn VOIGHT
35 Dir Student Life & Development Ms. Shantee SIEBUHR
20 Dean of Academic Studies Dr. Chase MACHEN
12 Dean of South Campus Mrs. Logan MAXWELL
101 Secretary of the Institution/Board Mrs. Elaine BOTKA
104 International Student Advisor Mr. Bradley MCCLENNY
18 Director of Maintenance Mr. Matt CORDER
25 Chief Grants Administrator Mrs. Janis THOMPSON
30 Director of Development Mrs. Kathy HENDRICK
38 Dir Student Counseling/Social Svcs Mrs. Barbara MALONE

Hallmark University (H)

10401 IH-10 W, San Antonio TX 78230-1737
County: Bexar FICE Identification: 010509
Unit ID: 225201
Telephone: (210) 690-9000 Carnegie Class: Bac/Assoc-Mixed
FAX Number: (210) 697-8225 Calendar System: Semester
URL: www.hallmarkuniversity.edu
Established: 1969 Annual Undergrad Tuition & Fees: N/A
Enrollment: 987 Coed
Affiliation or Control: Independent Non-Profit IRS Status: 501(c)3
Highest Offering: Master's
Accreditation: **ACCSC**

01 President/CEO Mr. Joseph B. FISHER
45 Sr VP of Institutional Strategy Mr. Taylor MERCIER
10 VP of Financial Affairs Ms. Roxanne DARTY
84 VP Enrollment & Support Services Dr. Samuel (Lee) BEAUMONT
05 University Provost Dr. Michael PHILLIPS
111 Vice President of Philanthropy Ms. Marion LEE

Hardin-Simmons University (I)

2200 Hickory, Abilene TX 79698-0001
County: Taylor FICE Identification: 003571
Unit ID: 225247
Telephone: (325) 670-1000 Carnegie Class: Masters/M
FAX Number: (325) 670-1267 Calendar System: Semester
URL: www.hsutx.edu
Established: 1891 Annual Undergrad Tuition & Fees: $31,364
Enrollment: 2,128 Coed
Affiliation or Control: Baptist IRS Status: 501(c)3
Highest Offering: Doctorate
Accreditation: **SC**, ACBSP, #ARCPA, #CAATE, CACREP, MUS, NURSE, PTA, @SP, SW, THEOL

01 President Mr. Eric I. BRUNTMYER
05 Provost & Chief Academic Officer Dr. Christopher L. MCNAIR
10 Vice President for Finance Dr. Jodie MCGAUGHEY
30 VP for Institutional Advancement Mr. Mike HAMMACK
84 VP for Enrollment Management Mrs. Vicki HOUSE
32 Vice President for Student Life Mrs. Stacey MARTIN
49 Dean College of Liberal Arts Dr. Stephen COOK

50 Dean Kelley College of Business ... Dr. Robert TUCKER
76 Dean College of Health Professions ... Dr. Janelle O'CONNELL
66 Dean School of Nursing ... Dr. Donalyn ALEXANDER
64 Assoc Dean School of Music ... Dr. Jeffrey COTTRELL
73 Assoc Dean Logsdon Sch of Theology ... Dr. Larry MCGRAW
53 Assoc Dean Irvin Sch of Education ... Dr. Renee COLLINS
13 Assoc Vice Pres Technical Services ... Mr. Travis P. SEEKINS
21 Asst VP for Finance and Controller ... Ms. Mary Beth KOUBA
38 Assoc VP Academic Advising/Retent ... Mrs. Gracie CARROLL
08 University Librarian ... Ms. Elizabeth NORMAN
06 Registrar ... Mrs. Kacey HIGGINS
29 Assoc VP for Alumni Engagement ... Ms. Heather HADLOCK
42 Chaplain ... Dr. Travis CRAVER
39 Director of Residence Life ... Vacant
15 Director of Human Resources ... Ms. Tera GIBSON
27 Dir of Univ Marketing ... Ms. Nikki SLATER
37 Dir Student Fin Aid & Scholarships ... Ms. Monica SMART
18 Facilities Services Director ... Mr. Tim MCCARRY
41 Athletic Director ... Mr. John M. NEESE
85 Director of International Studies ... Dr. Allan J. LANDWER

Hill College (A)

112 Lamar Drive, Hillsboro TX 76645-2711
County: Hill FICE Identification: 003573
Unit ID: 225371
Telephone: (254) 659-7500 Carnegie Class: Assoc/MT-VT-High Non
FAX Number: (254) 582-7591 Calendar System: Semester
URL: www.hillcollege.edu
Established: 1923 Annual Undergrad Tuition & Fees (In-District): $2,982
Enrollment: 4,038 Coed
Affiliation or Control: Local IRS Status: 501(c)3
Highest Offering: Associate Degree
Accreditation: SC, CVT, EMT

01 President ... Dr. Pamela BOEHM
04 Executive Asst to the President ... Ms. Vonnie MORPHEW
05 Vice President Instruction ... Dr. Kerry SCHINDLER
25 Vice President External Affairs ... Ms. Jessyca BROWN
10 Vice Pres Administrative Services ... Mr. Billy D. CURBO
32 Vice President Student Services ... Ms. Lizza TRENKLE
13 Vice Pres Information Technology ... Mrs. Jessie WHITE
21 Dean Financial Services ... Mrs. Debbie GERIK
08 Librarian - Hill Campus ... Ms. Eve BOWEN
08 Library Services Director ... Mr. Kevin HENARD
15 Director Human Resources ... Mrs. Jamie JASKA
12 Exec Dir JCC/Dean of Students ... Mr. Craig BALCH
41 Athletic Director ... Mr. Paul BROWN
26 Coord Ext Affairs/Cmty Rels/Events ... Ms. Ashley TELLO
09 Dir of Institutional Effectiveness ... Ms. Sherry DAVIS
37 Director of Financial Aid ... Ms. Kathleen PUSTEJOVSKY
18 Director Physical Plant ... Vacant
30 Director Development ... Vacant

Houston Baptist University (B)

7502 Fondren Road, Houston TX 77074-3298
County: Harris FICE Identification: 003576
Unit ID: 225399
Telephone: (281) 649-3000 Carnegie Class: Masters/L
FAX Number: (281) 649-3012 Calendar System: Semester
URL: www.hbu.edu
Established: 1960 Annual Undergrad Tuition & Fees: $34,500
Enrollment: 3,963 Coed
Affiliation or Control: Southern Baptist IRS Status: 501(c)3
Highest Offering: Doctorate
Accreditation: SC, NUR, NURSE

01 President ... Dr. Robert SLOAN
05 Provost/VP Acad Affairs ... Dr. Stan NAPPER
10 CFO/COO ... Ms. Sandra MOONEY
111 VP Advancement & Univ Relations ... Mrs. Sharon SAUNDERS
84 VP Enrollment Management ... Dr. James STEEN
26 VP Innovation & Strategic Mktg ... Dr. Jerome JOHNSTON
112 VP Major Gifts ... Mr. Charles BACARISSE
20 Associate Provost ... Ms. Ritamarie TAUER
20 Associate Provost ... Dr. Jeffrey GREEN
18 Assoc VP Facilities & Campus Opers ... Mr. John HOLMES
114 Assist VP Planning & Budget ... Mr. Michael DEI
79 Dean College of Arts & Humanities ... Dr. Jodey HINZE
50 Interim Dean Dunham Col of Business ... Dr. Greggory KEIFFER
81 Dean Col of Science & Engineering ... Dr. Katie EVANS
92 Director Honors College ... Dr. Gary HARTENBURG
53 Dean College of Education & Beh Sci ... Dr. Kristie CERLING
57 Dean College of Arts & Humanities ... Dr. Jodey HINZE
66 Inter Dean Sch Nur & Allied Hlth ... Dr. Carol LAVENDER
41 Athletic Director ... Mr. Steve MONIACI
06 Director of Academic Records ... Mr. Jean TARRATS RIVERA
08 Director of Libraries ... Mr. Dean RILEY
42 Assoc University Minister ... Mr. Saleim KAHLEH
21 Assoc VP Financial Operations ... Ms. Loree WATSON
39 Interim Director Residence Life ... Mr. Giovanni ARELLANO
13 Chief Information Officer (IT) ... Ms. Rosa BEAUGENE
09 Dir Inst Research & Effectiveness ... Mr. Todd COCKRELL
32 Assistant Provost ... Mr. Ed BORGES
88 SACS Liaison ... Ms. Ritamarie TAUER
04 Admin Asst to the President ... Ms. Karen FRANCIES
15 Director of Human Resources ... Ms. Jill STRUTTON
36 Dir of Career & Calling ... Mr. Aaron SWARTS
37 Sr Dir Financial Aid & Scholarships . Ms. Marisela MALDONADO
96 Cost Control Analyst ... Ms. Jody WILDING
07 Director of Admissions ... Mr. Clint STRICKLAND
106 Assoc Provost E-Learning & Cont Edu ... Dr. Paulita BROOKER
108 Director Assessment & Compliance ... Ms. Lisa COVINGTON
19 Director Security/Safety ... Chief John KARSHNER
29 Asst VP Univ Relations/Events ... Ms. Candace DESROSIERS
30 Development Officer ... Ms. Sarah DENNIS
43 General Counsel ... Mr. Tyler BOYD
44 Director Annual Giving ... Ms. Page HERNANDEZ
90 Academic Technology Support Manager ... Ms. Tia CASTER
91 Dir Enterprise Applications/ITS ... Ms. Linda PEREZ
73 Dean School Christian Thought ... Dr. Philip TALLON
101 Board Liaison ... Mrs. Sharon SAUNDERS
105 Asst VP Recruitment Marketing ... Mr. Cary DELMARK
38 Director Student Counseling ... Dr. Diane LAMBERSON

Houston Community College (C)

3100 Main Street, Houston TX 77002
County: Harris FICE Identification: 010633
Unit ID: 225423
Telephone: (713) 718-2000 Carnegie Class: Assoc/HT-High Trad
FAX Number: N/A Calendar System: Semester
URL: www.hccs.edu
Established: 1971 Annual Undergrad Tuition & Fees (In-State): $4,344
Enrollment: 48,329 Coed
Affiliation or Control: State IRS Status: 501(c)3
Highest Offering: Associate Degree
Accreditation: SC, ACBSP, ACFEI, ART, CAHIIM, COARC, DA, DH, DMS, EMT, HT, MAC, MLTAD, NAEYC, NMT, OTA, PTAA, RAD, SURGT

01 Chancellor ... Dr. Cesar MALDONADO
04 Sr Exec Assistant to the Chancellor ... Ms. Keiana BLAKE
10 Int Sr VC Finance & Admin/CFO ... Mr. Marshall B. HEINS
43 General Counsel ... Mr. E. Ashley SMITH
05 VC Instructional Services/CAO ... Dr. Norma PEREZ
32 VC Student Services ... Dr. Shantay GRAYS
13 Chief Information Officer ... Ms. Fheryl J. PRESTAGE
45 VC Plng & Inst Effect/Chf of Staff ... Dr. Kurt EWEN
20 AVC Instructional Services ... Dr. Jerome DRAIN
21 AVC Finance & Accounting ... Ms. Devi BALA
88 AVC College Readiness ... Dr. Catherine O'BRIEN
20 AVC Curriculum & Learning ... Mr. Miguel RAMOS
84 AVC Enrollment Management ... Ms. Indra PELAEZ
35 AVC Student Engagement/Success ... Dr. Debbie HAMILTON
18 Chief Facilities Officer ... Mr. Marshall B. HEINS
15 Chief Human Resources Officer ... Ms. Janet MAY
22 Director EEO/Compliance ... Mr. David CROSS
114 Exec Director Budget & Treasury Ops ... Dr. Karla BENDER
26 VC Public Info/Comm & Ext Affairs ... Mr. Remmele YOUNG
66 Dean Nursing ... Vacant
07 Director of Admissions & Registrar ... Ms. Mary LEMBURG
09 AVC Research Analytics & Support ... Dr. Andrea BURRIDGE
102 Executive Director Foundation ... Ms. Karen SCHMIDT
12 President Northeast College ... Dr. Monique UMPHREY
103 VC Workforce Ed/Pres Southwest Col ... Dr. Madeline BURILLO-HOPKINS
12 President Central College ... Dr. Muddassir SIDDIQI
12 Int President Southeast College ... Mr. Matias GARZA
12 President Northwest College ... Dr. Zachary HODGES
12 President Coleman College ... Dr. Phillip NICOTERA
106 President Online College ... Dr. Margaret FORD FISHER
96 Exec Dir Procurement Operations ... Mr. Joseph GAVIN
113 Director Student Financial Svcs ... Ms. Paula STAPLETON
37 Exec Director Student Financial Aid ... Ms. JoEllen PRICE
116 Director Internal Auditing ... Mr. Terrance CORRINGAN
50 COE Dean Business/Logistics ... Ms. Connie PORTER
60 Dean English/Communications ... Ms. Amy TAN
46 COE Dean Arch/Design/Construction ... Mr. Kris ASPER
59 COE Dean Consumer Arts & Sci ... Ms. Suzette BRIMMER
72 COE Dean Digital & Info Tech ... Mr. Jim LIVESEY
65 Dean Earth/Life/Natural Science ... Dr. Tosha BARCLAY
54 COE Dean Engineering ... Mr. John VASSELLI
88 COE Dean Global Energy ... Mr. Mehmet ARGIN
76 COE Dean Health Science ... Mr. Jeff GRICAR
49 Dean Liberal Arts & Humanities ... Mr. Theodore HANLEY
88 COE Dean Advanced Manufacturing ... Mr. Jim LIVESEY
88 COE Dean Material Science ... Mr. Urbina ALBERTO
81 Dean Mathematics ... Mr. Timor SEVER
88 COE Dean Public Safety ... Mr. Alvin COLLINS
83 Dean Social & Behavioral Science ... Mr. Fabian VEGA
57 COE Dean Visual & Performing Arts ... Ms. Colleen REILLY
88 COE Dean Automotive Technology ... Mr. David VOGEL
106 Dean Online College/Instruct Tech ... Vacant
88 Exec Director Accounting ... Ms. Frederica WATSON
08 Exec Director Library Resources ... Mr. Michael STAFFORD
101 Director Board Services ... Ms. Sharon WRIGHT
121 AVC Special Programs/ Success ... Ms. Chassity HOLLIMAN-DOUGLAS
28 DEI Officer ... Dr. Donna DAVIS

Houston Graduate School of Theology (D)

4300-C West Bellfort, Houston TX 77035
County: Harris FICE Identification: 023202
Unit ID: 246345
Telephone: (713) 942-9505 Carnegie Class: Spec-4-yr-Faith
FAX Number: (713) 942-9506 Calendar System: Semester
URL: www.hgst.edu
Established: 1983 Annual Graduate Tuition & Fees: N/A
Enrollment: 131 Coed
Affiliation or Control: Independent Non-Profit IRS Status: 501(c)3
Highest Offering: Doctorate; No Undergraduates
Accreditation: THEOL

01 President ... Dr. Becky L. TOWNE
04 Executive Assistant ... Dr. Rita H. JENKINS
37 Financial Aid Officer ... Ms. Linda LONG

Houston International College-Cardiotech Ultrasound School (E)

12135 Bissonnet, Ste E, Houston TX 77099
County: Harris FICE Identification: 041385
Unit ID: 458034
Telephone: (281) 495-0078 Carnegie Class: Spec 2-yr-Health
FAX Number: (281) 495-5618 Calendar System: Semester
URL: www.cardiotech.org
Established: 2003 Annual Undergrad Tuition & Fees: $11,868
Enrollment: 73 Coed
Affiliation or Control: Proprietary IRS Status: Proprietary
Highest Offering: Associate Degree
Accreditation: ABHES

01 CEO/Director ... Ms. Joan DOUGLAS
05 Director of Education ... Dr. Yasser SHERKAWY

Howard College (F)

1001 Birdwell Lane, Big Spring TX 79720-3799
County: Howard FICE Identification: 003574
Unit ID: 225520
Telephone: (432) 264-5000 Carnegie Class: Assoc/HT-High Non
FAX Number: (432) 264-5082 Calendar System: Semester
URL: www.howardcollege.edu
Established: 1945 Annual Undergrad Tuition & Fees (In-District): $3,980
Enrollment: 3,674 Coed
Affiliation or Control: State/Local IRS Status: 501(c)3
Highest Offering: Associate Degree
Accreditation: SC, ADNUR, COARC, DH, EMT, RAD, SURGT

01 President ... Dr. Cheryl T. SPARKS
03 Executive Vice President ... Dr. Amy BURCHETT
10 Chief Business Ofcr/Internal Audit ... Mr. Steve SMITH
18 Chief Ops/Safety/Security Officer ... Mr. Fabian SERRANO
10 Chief Fiscal Officer/Controller ... Ms. Brenda CLAXTON
08 Dean of Libraries/County Librarian ... Ms. Mavour BRASWELL
13 Chief Tech/System/Data Sec Ofcr ... Mr. Eric HANSEN
106 Dir eLearning Svcs/PASS Ctr Coord ... Ms. Kym CLARK
37 Dean Financial Aid ... Mrs. Candice MALDONADO
26 Director Information/Marketing ... Ms. Cindy SMITH
88 Special Projects Officer ... Mr. Terry HANSEN
15 Chief Human Resources Officer ... Ms. Rhonda KERNICK
12 Executive Dean SWCD ... Mr. Danny CAMPBELL
12 Executive Dean San Angelo ... Ms. Pam CALLAN
06 District Registrar ... Mrs. TaNeal RICHARDSON
21 Director Student Accounting ... Ms. Laura FITZPATRICK
30 Director Institutional Advancement ... Mrs. Julie BAILEY
76 Dean Health Professions ... Ms. Luci GABEHART
09 Research and Reporting Officer ... Ms. Rebecca VILLANUEVA
21 Director Financial Accounting ... Ms. Jeannie CARROLL
108 Director Institutional Assessment ... Mr. Bryan STOKES
121 Director Student Support ... Ms. Tara LISLE
41 Athletic Director ... Mr. Mike YEATER
04 Executive Asst to the President ... Ms. Emma GARCIA

Howard Payne University (G)

1000 Fisk Street, Brownwood TX 76801-2715
County: Brown FICE Identification: 003575
Unit ID: 225548
Telephone: (325) 649-8020 Carnegie Class: Bac-Diverse
FAX Number: (325) 649-8975 Calendar System: Semester
URL: www.hputx.edu
Established: 1889 Annual Undergrad Tuition & Fees: $29,198
Enrollment: 1,060 Coed
Affiliation or Control: Baptist IRS Status: 501(c)3
Highest Offering: Master's
Accreditation: SC, #CAATE, MUS, SW

01 President ... Dr. Cory HINES
05 Vice President for Academic Affairs ... Dr. Donnie AUVENSHINE
10 VP for Finance & Admin/CFO ... Mr. Mike RODGERS
30 Vice President for Development ... Dr. Dale MEINECKE
84 AVP for Enrollment Management ... Dr. Ben MARTIN
18 Director of Facilities ... Mr. Roger DEWELL
13 AVP for Info Tech Svcs/CIO ... Dr. Jodi GOODE
06 AVP of Univ Records/Dean of Gen Ed ... Dr. Wendy MCNEELEY
37 Director Financial Aid ... Mrs. Karen LAQUEY
07 Director of Admission ... Mrs. P.J GRAMLING
26 AVP for University Communications ... Mr. Kyle C. MIZE
20 AVP for Academic Affairs ... Dr. Celeste CHURCH
41 Director of Athletics ... Mr. Hunter SIMS
91 Database Administrator ... Mr. Tyler CHRISTIANSEN
90 Dir of Net & Infrastructure Svcs ... Mr. Russell EZZELL
29 AVP for Alumni Relations ... Dr. Kalie LOWRIE
04 Special Assistant to President ... Mrs. Laura BENOIT
38 University Counselor ... Mrs. Kimberly THOMAS
08 Director Walker Memorial Library ... Mrs. Deborah DILL
81 Dean School of Science & Math ... Dr. Gerry CLARKSON
50 Dean of the School of Business ... Dr. Brad LEMLER
53 Dean of the School of Education ... Dr. Kylah CLARK-GOFF
64 Dean School of Music & Fine Arts ... Dr. Richard FIESE
73 Dean School of Christian Studies ... Dr. Gary GRAMLING
79 Dean School of Humanities ... Dr. Millard KIMERY
104 Dir Intl Study & Academic Travel ... Dr. Jennifer MCNIECE

19 Chief of Police .... Lt. Bob PACATTE
110 Director of Development .... Mrs. Shannon SIMS

Huston-Tillotson University (A)

900 Chicon Street, Austin TX 78702-2795

County: Travis — FICE Identification: 003577
Unit ID: 225575
Telephone: (512) 505-3000 — Carnegie Class: Bac-Diverse
FAX Number: (512) 505-3190 — Calendar System: Semester
URL: www.htu.edu
Established: 1875 — Annual Undergrad Tuition & Fees: $14,703
Enrollment: 1,058 — Coed
Affiliation or Control: Multiple Protestant Denominations
IRS Status: 501(c)3
Highest Offering: Master's
Accreditation: SC, ACBSP

01 President & CEO .... Dr. Colette PIERCE BURNETTE
04 Executive Assistant to President .... Ms. Demetria BARKSDALE
11 VP/COO/Clerk to Board .... Mr. Wayne KNOX
10 VP for Administration & Finance .... Ms. Katrina MONTGOMERY
111 Vice Pres Institutional Advancement .... Ms. Nakeenya S. WILSON
05 Provost/VP Academic Affairs .... Dr. Archibald W. VANDERPUYE
20 Associate Provost .... Dr. Beverly L. DOWNING
32 Dean of Student Affairs .... Dr. Ericka JONES
84 Dean of Enrollment Management .... Mr. Johannis JOB
15 Director of Human Resources .... Ms. Quinika QUALLS
08 Director of Library and Media Svcs .... Ms. Danielle MCGHEE
36 Director Career & Grad Development .... Mr. Steven HATCHETT
41 Director of Athletics .... Dr. Monique CARROLL
06 Director Records and Registration .... Mr. Maurice OSBORNE
13 Int Director Information Technology .... Mr. Malcolm HARAWAY
26 Director of Public Relations .... Mr. Duane LEWIS
18 Director of Facilities Operations .... Mr. Elbert GORDON
30 Civic Engagement/Community Outreach .... Ms. Linda Y. JACKSON
29 Director of Alumni Affairs .... Mr. Gilbert CUTKELVIN
35 Coordinator of Campus Life .... Ms. Sarah GAINES
88 Dir of Ctr for Academic Excellence .... Ms. Jenifer MILES
38 Dir Counseling & Consultation Ctr .... Ms. Eboni HAMILTON
42 University Chaplain .... Rev. Donald E. BREWINGTON
07 Director of Recruitment/Admission .... Ms. Asia HANEY
49 Dean College of Arts & Sciences .... Dr. Michael HIRSCH
50 Dean School of Business/Technology .... Dr. Rohan THOMPSON
37 Asst Director of Financial Aid .... Mr. Ambrose PRICE
22 Coord Counseling/Disability Svcs .... Ms. Sarah GAINES
09 Director of Institutional Research .... Mr. Marcus JACKSON
19 Director Campus Safety .... Mr. Leslie YORK

Interactive College of Technology (B)

213 West Southmore, Ste 101, Pasadena TX 77502

County: Harris — FICE Identification: 023313
Unit ID: 440776
Telephone: (713) 920-1120 — Carnegie Class: Spec 2-yr-Other
FAX Number: (713) 477-0348 — Calendar System: Semester
URL: https://www.ict.edu/campuses/tx/pasadena/
Established: — Annual Undergrad Tuition & Fees: $9,890
Enrollment: 45 — Coed
Affiliation or Control: Proprietary — IRS Status: Proprietary
Highest Offering: Associate Degree
Accreditation: COE

01 Campus Director .... Mr. Greg WEAVER

Jacksonville College (C)

105 B. J. Albritton Drive, Jacksonville TX 75766-4759

County: Cherokee — FICE Identification: 003579
Unit ID: 225876
Telephone: (903) 586-2518 — Carnegie Class: Assoc/HT-High Non
FAX Number: (903) 586-0743 — Calendar System: Semester
URL: www.jacksonville-college.edu
Established: 1899 — Annual Undergrad Tuition & Fees: $8,000
Enrollment: 482 — Coed
Affiliation or Control: Baptist — IRS Status: 501(c)3
Highest Offering: Associate Degree
Accreditation: SC

01 President .... Dr. Mike SMITH
05 VP Academic Affairs/Academic Dean .... Mrs. Marolyn WELCH
32 Dean of Students .... Mr. Jonathan BECKER
10 Business Manager .... Ms. Jennifer HUGHES
41 Athletic Director .... Mr. Ken HAMILTON
06 Registrar .... Ms. Jodye JAY
08 Director of Library Services .... Vacant
07 Director of Admissions .... Mr. Will CUMBEE
18 Director of Maintenance .... Mr. Martin MCRAE
26 Director Public Relations .... Dr. Jan MODISETTE
29 Director of Alumni Relations .... Mr. Randy DECKER
37 Director of Financial Aid .... Mr. Paul GALYEAN
39 Director of Housing .... Mr. David WHITE
19 Chief of Security .... Mr. Micael MORSE
13 Chief Info Officer/Dir Distance Edu .... Mr. Michael CREECH
15 Director Human Resources .... Ms. Esmeralda REYES
35 Director of Student Life .... Mrs. Mirtha ECKLES
38 Director Student Counseling .... Ms. Amber SANCHEZ
84 Director Enrollment Management .... Mr. Will CUMBEE
96 Director of Purchasing .... Ms. Esmeralda REYES

Jarvis Christian College (D)

Highway 80 E., PR 7631, Hawkins TX 75765-1470

County: Wood — FICE Identification: 003637
Unit ID: 225885
Telephone: (903) 730-4890 — Carnegie Class: Bac-Diverse
FAX Number: (903) 769-4842 — Calendar System: Semester
URL: www.jarvis.edu
Established: 1912 — Annual Undergrad Tuition & Fees: $11,720
Enrollment: 719 — Coed
Affiliation or Control: Christian Church (Disciples Of Christ)
IRS Status: 501(c)3
Highest Offering: Baccalaureate
Accreditation: SC, ACBSP, SW

01 President .... Dr. Lester C. NEWMAN
05 Provost/Vice Pres Academic Affairs .... Dr. Glenell PRUITT
10 Vice Pres Administration & Finance .... Ms. Paula LOVE
111 VP Institutional Advancement/Devel .... Dr. Kenoye EKE
32 Acting Vice Pres Student Services .... Mr. Cory GIPSON
09 Dir Inst Research & Effectiveness .... Vacant
13 Director Information Technology .... Mr. Christopher WATSON
06 Registrar .... Ms. Laura LANDER
39 Director Student Facilities/Housing .... Ms. Courtney GRAY
84 Exec Director Enrollment Management .... Vacant
26 Director of Communications .... Vacant
100 Chief of Staff/Director Title III .... Mrs. Cynthia STANCIL
08 Head Librarian .... Mr. Rodney ATKINS
38 Director Career Services .... Mr. Chestley TALLEY
37 Director of Financial Aid .... Ms. Cecelia JONES
41 Athletic Director .... Mr. Bobby LADNER
42 Chaplain/Director of Religious Life .... Mr. Sedaric DINKENS
15 Director Human Resources .... Ms. Danielle DELINT
18 Chief Facilities/Physical Plant .... Mr. Willie SANDIFER
04 Admin Assistant to the President .... Vacant
19 Director Security/Safety .... Mr. Dean RIVARD
28 Coordinator of Diversity .... Mrs. Linda HERNANDEZ
29 Executive Director Alumni Affairs .... Mr. William HAMPTON
50 Dean of Business .... Dr. Benson KARIUKI
53 Dean of Education .... Dr. DeMesia STARLING
51 Dean Adult & Continuing Education .... Dr. Dorothy LANGLEY
96 Purchasing Clerk .... Ms. Cheryl JACKSON

KD Conservatory College of Film and Dramatic Arts (E)

2600 N Stemmons Fwy, Suite 117, Dallas TX 75207-2111

County: Dallas — FICE Identification: 023182
Unit ID: 225991
Telephone: (214) 638-0484 — Carnegie Class: Spec 2-yr-A&S
FAX Number: (214) 630-5140 — Calendar System: Semester
URL: www.kdstudio.com
Established: 1979 — Annual Undergrad Tuition & Fees: $17,187
Enrollment: 71 — Coed
Affiliation or Control: Proprietary — IRS Status: Proprietary
Highest Offering: Associate Degree
Accreditation: THEA

01 President/CEO .... Ms. Kathy TYNER
05 Director/CAO .... Mr. Michael SCHRAEDER
64 Program Chair - MT .... Mr. Michael SERRECCHIA
88 Program Chair - Film Program .... Mr. Robert CASTALDO
11 Head of Operations .... Ms. Becky HARRIS
32 Head of Student Services .... Ms. Jennifer LAUGHLIN
37 Student Financial Aid .... Ms. Rikki WASHINGTON
08 Chief Library Officer .... Ms. Judith HEAD

Kilgore College (F)

1100 Broadway, Kilgore TX 75662-3299

County: Gregg — FICE Identification: 003580
Unit ID: 226019
Telephone: (903) 984-8531 — Carnegie Class: Assoc/HVT-High Trad
FAX Number: (903) 983-8600 — Calendar System: Semester
URL: www.kilgore.edu
Established: 1935 — Annual Undergrad Tuition & Fees (In-District): $4,056
Enrollment: 5,100 — Coed
Affiliation or Control: Local — IRS Status: 501(c)3
Highest Offering: Associate Degree
Accreditation: SC, ADNUR, EMT, PTAA

01 President .... Dr. Brenda S. KAYS
05 Vice President of Instruction .... Dr. Michael H. TURPIN
32 EVP & Chief Student Affairs Ofcr .... Dr. Mike JENKINS
09 Vice Pres Institutional Planning .... Mrs. Staci MARTIN
57 Div Dean Liberal & Fine Arts .... Mrs. Becky JOHNSON
81 Div Dean Science/Math/Health Sci .... Dr. Sandra CARROLL
80 Div Dean Public Services/Technology .... Mr. D'Wayne SHAW
50 Div Dean Business/Info Tech .... Mr. Richard CRUTCHER
78 Dir of Adult Vocational Education .... Ms. Martha WOODRUFF
06 Registrar .... Mr. Dennis CLIBORN
15 Director of Human Resources .... Mr. Tony JOHNSON
13 Director of Information Technology .... Mr. John COLVILLE
08 Director Library .... Ms. Susan BLACK
40 Manager of Bookstore .... Mr. Kenton BEAL
19 Chief of Police .... Chief Heath CARIKER
84 Dir of Marketing & Enrollment Mgmt .... Mr. Manny ALMANZA
04 Assistant to the President .... Mrs. Nancy LAW
30 Chief Development Officer .... Mr. Michael HAGELOH
37 Financial Aid Officer .... Mr. Reggie BRAZZLE
85 Admissions/International Specialist .... Ms. Chrissy PATTERSON
26 Asst Dir of Marketing & Public Info .... Mr. Chris CRADDOCK
09 Coord of Institutional Research .... Ms. Natalie BRYANT
38 Coordinator of Counseling .... Mrs. Pam GATTON
39 Coordinator of Residential Life .... Mrs. Ashley MASON
07 Director of Admissions .... Mr. Dennis CLIBORN
84 Dean of Enrollment Management .... Mr. Chris GORE
106 Distance Learning Specialist .... Mr. William STOWE
18 Chief Facilities/Physical Plant .... Mr. Jeff WILLIAMS
41 Athletic Director .... Mr. Jimmy RIEVES
10 Chief Financial/Business Officer .... Ms. Dawn JONES
101 Secretary of the Institution/Board .... Mrs. Nancy LAW
102 Dir of Fndn/Community Relations .... Mrs. Merlyn HOLMES

The King's University (G)

2121 E. Southlake Boulevard, South Lake TX 76092-6507

County: Tarrant — FICE Identification: 035163
Unit ID: 439701
Telephone: (817) 722-1700 — Carnegie Class: Spec-4-yr-Faith
FAX Number: N/A — Calendar System: Semester
URL: tku.edu/
Established: 1997 — Annual Undergrad Tuition & Fees: $15,450
Enrollment: 666 — Coed
Affiliation or Control: Interdenominational — IRS Status: 501(c)3
Highest Offering: Doctorate
Accreditation: BI, THEOL, TRACS

01 President .... Dr. Jon CHASTEEN
05 Provost/CAO .... Dr. David COLE
10 Vice Pres Business Admin/CFO .... Ms. Ashley GREEN
84 VP Enrollment Mgmt/Student Dev .... Dr. Rhonda DAVIS
20 Exec Dean Academic Affairs .... Dr. Robb BREWER
32 Chief Student Affairs/Life Officer .... Ms. Julie COLE
21 Director of Finance .... Ms. Pauline MOTTS
15 Director Human Resources .... Ms. Gloria WILLIAMS
121 Director Student Success .... Ms. Alicka CULLISON
07 Director of Admissions .... Ms. Angela PRUIS
06 Registrar .... Ms. Megan GRONDIN
37 Director Student Financial Services .... Ms. Jessica STEED
08 Director of Library Services .... Mr. Tracey R. LANE
111 Exec Director of Advancement .... Mr. Bryan CHAMBERS
13 Director Information Technology .... Mr. Matt WILSON
113 Assoc Dir Student Accounts .... Ms. LeAnne DOOLITTLE
108 Assoc Dir of Inst Assessment .... Mr. Allen GUTIERREZ
102 Dir Foundation/Corporate Relations .... Mr. Lee S. MIMMS
26 Dir of Marketing/Communications .... Mr. Michael KEITH
18 Director Buildings/Operations .... Mr. David REYES
106 Distance Education Coordinator .... Ms. Stephanye STRIDER

Laredo College (H)

West End Washington Street, Laredo TX 78040-4395

County: Webb — FICE Identification: 003582
Unit ID: 226134
Telephone: (956) 722-0521 — Carnegie Class: Assoc/MT-VT-High Trad
FAX Number: (956) 721-5381 — Calendar System: Semester
URL: www.laredo.edu
Established: 1946 — Annual Undergrad Tuition & Fees (In-District): $4,480
Enrollment: 9,292 — Coed
Affiliation or Control: Local — IRS Status: 501(c)3
Highest Offering: Baccalaureate
Accreditation: SC, ADNUR, EMT, OTA, PTAA, RAD

01 President .... Dr. Ricardo SOLIS
05 Provost/VP of Academic Affairs .... Dr. Marisela RODRIGUEZ
84 VP of Student Success & Enrollment .... Dr. Federico SOLIS
25 VP for Resource Dev & Ext Affairs .... Dr. Nora R. GARZA
10 VP of Finance .... Mr. Cesar VELA
117 VP of Compliance & Risk Mgmt .... Dr. David ARREAZOLA
103 Dean of Workforce Educ .... Mr. Heriberto HERNANDEZ
76 Dean of Health Sciences .... Dr. Dianna MILLER
51 Dean of Community Education .... Ms. Sandra CORTEZ
49 Dean of Arts & Sciences .... Dr. Horacio SALINAS

Lee College (I)

511 S Whiting, PO Box 818, Baytown TX 77522-0818

County: Harris — FICE Identification: 003583
Unit ID: 226204
Telephone: (281) 427-5611 — Carnegie Class: Assoc/HVT-High Trad
FAX Number: (281) 425-6555 — Calendar System: Semester
URL: www.lee.edu
Established: 1934 — Annual Undergrad Tuition & Fees (In-District): $3,762
Enrollment: 7,487 — Coed
Affiliation or Control: State/Local — IRS Status: 501(c)3
Highest Offering: Associate Degree
Accreditation: SC, ADNUR, CAHIIM

01 President .... Dr. Lynda VILLANUEVA
100 Chief of Staff/Dir Strategic Opers .... Ms. Leslie D. GALLAGHER
03 VP PIER/Chief Learning Officer .... Dr. Douglas WALCERZ
32 VP Student Affairs .... Dr. Donnetta SUCHON
103 VP Workforce/Community Development .... Dr. Angela ORIANO
05 Interim VP Instruction .... Dr. Douglas WALCERZ
10 VP Finance & Administration .... Ms. Annette FERGUSON
12 AVP Huntsville Center .... Ms. Donna P. ZUNIGA
13 Chief Information Officer .... Dr. Carolyn A. LIGHTFOOT
84 Exec Dir Enrollment Svcs/Registrar .... Mr. Scott BENNETT
102 ED Foundation/Resource Development .... Vacant
108 Exec Dir Assessment & Accreditation .... Dr. Brandon COMBS
124 ED Retention/Transition/Diversity .... Dr. Victoria MARRON
18 Exec Dir Facilities .... Mr. Terry ROYE

38 Director Advising & Counseling .... Dr. Marissa MORENO
86 Government Relations Liaison ....Ms. Leslie D. GALLAGHER
25 Director Grants Management ....Ms. Laurie OEHLER
07 Director Admissions/Asst Registrar ....Dr. Carl HUSBAND
101 Board Liaison ....Ms. Leslie D. GALLAGHER
37 Director Financial Aid .... Mr. Felipe LEAL
96 Director Purchasing ....Mr. Mike SPARKES
26 Director Marketing & Public Affairs ....Vacant
15 Director Human Resources ....Ms. Amanda SUMMERS
04 Admin Assistant President's Office ....Vacant

LeTourneau University (A)

PO Box 7001, 2100 S Mobberly Ave,
Longview TX 75607-7001
County: Gregg FICE Identification: 003584
Unit ID: 226231
Telephone: (903) 233-3000 Carnegie Class: Masters/M
FAX Number: (903) 233-3101 Calendar System: Semester
URL: www.letu.edu
Established: 1946 Annual Undergrad Tuition & Fees: $32,490
Enrollment: 3,122 Coed
Affiliation or Control: Independent Non-Profit IRS Status: 501(c)3
Highest Offering: Master's
Accreditation: SC, NURSE

01 President .... Dr. Steven D. MASON
05 Int Provost/VP for Academic Affairs ...... Dr. Benjamin CALDWELL
30 VP for Development/Alumni Relations ....Dr. Terry ZEITLOW
10 VP Finance/Administration .... Mr. Mike HOOD
32 VP Student Affairs/Dean of Students ....Dr. Kristy MORGAN
84 VP Residential Enrollment Services ....Mr. Carl ARNOLD
26 VP Marketing & Communications ....Mr. Don EGLE
85 VP Global Initiatives Office ....Mr. Alan CLIPPERTON
20 Assoc Prov for Academic Admin .... Dr. Benjamin CALDWELL
88 VP for Global Operations ....Vacant
18 Asst VP of Facilities Services .... Mr. Chris CHAPMAN
53 Dean School of Education ....Dr. Larry FRAZIER
50 Dean School of Business ....Dr. Van GRAHAM
54 Dean Sch Engineering & Engr Tech ....Dr. Steve STARRETT
49 Dean School of Arts & Sciences ....Dr. Larry FRAZIER
88 Dean School of Aeronautical Science .... Mr. Fred L. RITCHEY
35 Dean of Students ....Mr. Steve CONN
08 Director Learning Resource Center ....Ms. Shelby WARE
41 Director of Athletics .... Ms. Terri DEIKE
25 Director Office of Sponsored Pgms .... Mr. Paul R. BOGGS
13 Chief Information Officer ....Mr. Ken JOHNSON
15 Director of Human Resources ....Mrs. Phyllis TURNER
23 Director Health Services ....Ms. Julie MOORE
19 Chief of Police .... Mr. Michael SCHULTZ
36 Director of Career Services .... Dr. Rachel OLSHINE FRASIER
06 University Registrar ....Dr. Texas RUEGG
84 Director of Enrollment Services ....Ms. Kristine SLATE
29 Director of Alumni & Parent Rels ....Vacant
27 Director of University Relations ....Ms. Janet RAGLAND
27 Director Marketing & Communication ...... Ms. Kate GRONEWALD
21 Controller ....Ms. Vikki KEILERS
09 AVP for Accreditation & QA ....Dr. Karl PAYTON
88 Executive Dir Ctr for Faith & Work ....Mr. Bill PEEL
04 Administrative Asst to President ....Mrs. Denise BAILEY
106 Assoc VP for Global Student Success .... Mr. Carlton MITCHELL
37 Director Student Financial Aid .... Ms. Tracy WATKINS
38 Director Center for Counseling .... Mrs. Treva BARHAM
73 Dean School of Theology & Vocation ....Dr. Kelly LIEBENGOOD
66 Dean School of Nursing .... Dr. Kimberly QUIETT
101 Secretary of the Institution/Board .... Mr. Bud MCGUIRE
105 Director Web Services .... Mr. Mark ROEDEL
39 Director Student Housing ....Mr. Tony ZAPPASODI

Lincoln College of Technology (B)

2915 Alouette Drive, Grand Prairie TX 75052
County: Tarrant FICE Identification: 008353
Unit ID: 226277
Telephone: (972) 660-5701 Carnegie Class: Spec 2-yr-Tech
FAX Number: (972) 660-6148 Calendar System: Other
URL: www.lincolntech.com
Established: Annual Undergrad Tuition & Fees: N/A
Enrollment: 1,455 Coed
Affiliation or Control: Proprietary IRS Status: Proprietary
Highest Offering: Associate Degree
Accreditation: ACCSC

01 Campus President .... Mr. Mike COULING

Lone Star College System (C)

5000 Research Forest Drive,
The Woodlands TX 77381-4356
County: Harris FICE Identification: 011145
Unit ID: 227182
Telephone: (832) 813-6500 Carnegie Class: Assoc/HT-Mix Trad/Non
FAX Number: N/A Calendar System: Semester
URL: www.lonestar.edu
Established: 1972 Annual Undergrad Tuition & Fees (In-District): $4,680
Enrollment: 70,109 Coed
Affiliation or Control: State/Local IRS Status: 501(c)3
Highest Offering: Baccalaureate
Accreditation: SC, ADNUR, CAHIIM, COARC, DH, DMS, EMT, MAC, MUS, OTA, PTAA, RAD, SURGT

01 Chancellor ....Dr. Stephen HEAD
04 Executive Assistant to Chancellor ....Ms. Fatima BARNETT
100 Chief of Staff/Board Liaison .... Ms. Deseree PROBASCO
12 President of LSC-CyFair .... Dr. Seelpa KESHVALA
12 President of LSC-Houston North ....Dr. Quentin WRIGHT
12 President of LSC-Kingwood ....Dr. Melissa GONZALEZ
12 President of LSC-Montgomery ....Dr. Rebecca RILEY
12 President of LSC-North Harris ....Dr. Archie BLANSON
12 President of LSC-Tomball ....Dr. Lee Ann NUTT
12 President of LSC-University Park ....Dr. Shah ARDALAN
11 Chief Operating Officer/Gen Counsel .... Mr. Mario CASTILLO
13 Vice Chanc College Services/CIO ....Mr. Link ALANDER
119 Information Security Officer ....Mr. William DERWOSTYP
10 Chief Financial Officer .... Ms. Jennifer MOTT
88 VC/Special Assistant to Chancellor ....Dr. Gerald NAPOLES
05 Vice Chancellor Academic Success .... Dr. Dwight SMITH, III
37 Senior Assoc VC Financial Aid ....Vacant
103 Senior AVC External/Employer Rels ....Ms. Linda HEAD
21 Senior Assoc VC Administrative Svcs .... Ms. Bridgett JOHNSON
20 Senior Assoc VC Academic Affairs ....Dr. Valerie JONES
15 Senior Assoc VC Human Resources ....Ms. Margaret KERSTENS
19 Senior Assoc VC & Chief of Police ....Mr. Paul WILLINGHAM
120 Senior Assoc VC LSC Online ....Vacant
28 Chief Diversity Officer .... Ms. Carlecia WRIGHT
92 AVC Honors & International Educ ....Vacant
09 Assoc VC Analytics & Inst Reporting ....Vacant
114 Associate VC Budget & Treasury ....Vacant
105 Assoc VC Enterprise Applications .... Mr. Longin GOGU
88 AVC Governance/Audit & Compliance ... Ms. Sandra GREGERSON
109 Associate VC Supply Management .... Ms. Kathie GRIFFIS
32 Associate VC Student Services .... Mr. Garth HOWARD
14 Associate VC Campus Services .... Mr. Earl JUELG
21 AVC Fin Reporting & Ops/Controller .... Ms. Valerie KOT
18 Assoc VC Facilities & Construction .... Ms. Denise NEU
121 AVC Student Success & Completion ....Ms. Jamie POSEY
26 Exec Dir Communication Services .... Mr. Jed YOUNG
105 Executive Director Digital Services .... Mr. John KING
96 Executive Director Procurement .... Ms. Cynthia BRIGHT
116 Exec Dir Audit & Consulting Svcs ... Ms. Leticia CHARBONNEAU
88 Exec Dir Organizational/Prof Dev .... Dr. Alicia FRIDAY
06 Exec Dir Records/Enroll & Registrar .... Ms. Connie GARRICK
120 Exec Dir Online Instruct Dev/Supp ....Dr. Robert GREENE
07 Exec Dir Admissions/Prosp Students .... Dr. Laura ISDELL
102 Executive Director LSC Foundation ....Ms. Nicole ROBINSON GAUTHIER
25 Int Exec Dir Resource Dev/Grants ....Ms. Cynthia DRUMMOND
108 Exec Dir Strategic Plng/Assessment ....Dr. Christopher TKACH
08 Director Library Technical Services ....Ms. Carol STEINMETZ

Lubbock Christian University (D)

5601 19th Street, Lubbock TX 79407-2099
County: Lubbock FICE Identification: 003586
Unit ID: 226383
Telephone: (806) 796-8800 Carnegie Class: Masters/M
FAX Number: (806) 720-7255 Calendar System: Semester
URL: www.lcu.edu
Established: 1957 Annual Undergrad Tuition & Fees: $24,260
Enrollment: 1,664 Coed
Affiliation or Control: Churches Of Christ IRS Status: 501(c)3
Highest Offering: Master's
Accreditation: SC, ACBSP, NUR, SW, @THEOL

01 President ....Dr. Scott MCDOWELL
05 Provost & Chief Academic Officer .... Dr. Foy MILLS
10 VP/Chief Financial Officer ....Mr. Andy BURCHAM
111 Vice Pres University Advancement ..... Mr. Raymond RICHARDSON
21 Controller .... Mr. Brandon GOEN
13 Vice President for Technology .... Dr. Karl MAHAN
26 Sr Vice Pres University Relations .... Mr. John KING
27 VP of University Relations .... Mr. Warren MCNEILL
32 Vice Pres Student Life ....Mr. Randal DEMENT
84 Vice Pres Enrollment Management .... Ms. Lisa SHACKLETT
102 President University Foundation ....Mr. Bill BUNDY
107 Dean Col of Professional Studies .... Dr. Toby ROGERS
49 Dean Col Liberal Arts/Educ/Honors .... Dr. Stacy PATTY
73 Dean College of Biblical Studies .... Dr. Jeff CARY
50 Dean School of Business .... Mr. Matt BUMSTEAD
09 VP for Institutional Effectiveness ....Ms. Yvonne HARWOOD
41 Athletic Director ....Mr. Scott LARSON
06 Registrar ....Ms. Sonja DIXON
37 Director of Financial Assistance ....Mrs. Amy HARDESTY
35 Dean of Students .... Mr. Josh STEPHENS
08 Director of Library Services ....Mrs. Amanda GUTHRIE
18 Director of Campus Facilities ....Mr. Kyle TURNER
38 Director Student Counseling ....Mr. John MAPLES
23 Director of Medical Clinic .... Dr. Jeff SMITH
14 Sr Director of Technology Services ....Mr. Robert SMITH
22 Disability Services Coordinator ....Ms. Larinda CREEL
39 Director of Residential Life ....Mrs. Sunny PARK
07 Director Undergraduate Admissions ....Dr. Jody REDING
15 Human Resources Director/AVP .... Mrs. Brenda LOWE
19 Dir Public Safety/Chief Police .... Mr. Michael SMITH
40 Bookstore Manager ....Vacant
104 Director Global Campus .... Mrs. Heather HOWELL
53 Dean School of Education .... Dr. David BOYER
04 Admin Assistant to the President ....Ms. Rhonda SHOOTER

McLennan Community College (E)

1400 College Drive, Waco TX 76708-1498
County: McLennan FICE Identification: 003590
Unit ID: 226578
Telephone: (254) 299-8000 Carnegie Class: Assoc/HT-Mix Trad/Non
FAX Number: (254) 299-8654 Calendar System: Semester
URL: www.mclennan.edu
Established: 1965 Annual Undergrad Tuition & Fees (In-District): $4,200
Enrollment: 7,742 Coed
Affiliation or Control: State/Local IRS Status: 501(c)3
Highest Offering: Associate Degree
Accreditation: SC, ADNUR, CAHIIM, COARC, EMT, MAC, MLTAD, OTA, PTAA, RAD, SURGT

01 President ....Dr. Johnette MCKOWN
10 Vice Pres Finance & Administration .... Dr. Stephen BENSON
05 Vice President Instruction .... Dr. Fred HILLS
22 Equal Employment Opportunity Ofcr .... Mr. Al POLLARD
32 Vice President Student Success .... Dr. Drew CANHAM
09 Vice Pres Research/Effectiveness ....Dr. Phil RHODES
102 Exec Director MCC Foundation ....Ms. Kim PATTERSON
96 Director Purchasing & Auxil Svcs ....Ms. Jodi TINDELL
37 Director Financial Aid .... Mr. James KUBACAK
26 Director Marketing & Communication ....Ms. Lisa ELLIOTT
41 Director Athletics ....Mrs. Shawn TROCHIM
06 Director Records & Registration ....Mr. Herman V. TUCKER
07 Director Admissions & Recruitment ....Mrs. Karen CLARK
08 Director Library Services .... Mr. Daniel MARTINSEN
15 Director Human Resources ....Ms. Missy KITTNER
18 Director Physical Plant ....Mrs. Dianne E. FEYERHERM
21 Director Financial Services .... Mr. Grayson MEEK
76 Dean Health Professions .... Ms. Glynnis GAINES
49 Dean Arts & Sciences ....Dr. Chad EGGLESTON
51 Dean Continuing Education ....Dr. Frank GRAVES

McMurry University (F)

1400 Sayles Boulevard, Abilene TX 79697
County: Taylor FICE Identification: 003591
Unit ID: 226587
Telephone: (325) 793-3800 Carnegie Class: Bac-Diverse
FAX Number: (325) 793-4805 Calendar System: Semester
URL: www.mcm.edu
Established: 1923 Annual Undergrad Tuition & Fees: $28,830
Enrollment: 1,094 Coed
Affiliation or Control: United Methodist IRS Status: 501(c)3
Highest Offering: Master's
Accreditation: SC, NURSE

01 President .... Dr. Sandra HARPER
05 Vice Pres Academic Affairs .... Dr. Matt DRAUD
10 Vice Pres Finance & Administration ....Mrs. Lisa L. WILLIAMS
111 Vice Pres Institutional Advancement .... Mr. Mike HUTCHISON
26 Vice Pres Marketing/Communication ....Ms. Robin DANIELS
84 VP/Director Enrollment Management ....Mr. Grant GREENWOOD
105 Webmaster ....Mr. Abraham SALAZAR
13 Director of Administrative Systems ....Vacant
14 Director of Customer Services ....Vacant
06 Registrar .... Mrs. Carolyn A. CALVERT
08 Director Jay-Rollins Library ....Ms. Terry YOUNG
32 Dean of Students & Campus Life ....Mr. Allen WITHERS
66 Dean School of Nursing .... Dr. Donalyn ALEXANDER
35 Director of Student Activities ....Ms. Erica MEDINA
37 Director of Financial Aid ....Mr. Tim SECHRIST
21 Controller .... Ms. Tina SCHUELLER
15 Director of Human Resources ....Ms. Lecia HUGHES
108 Dir of Institutional Effectiveness ....Dr. Jori SECHRIST
09 Director of Institutional Research ....Ms. Terry NIXON
29 Director Alumni Relations ....Vacant
36 Director Counseling & Career Svcs ....Vacant
41 Director of Athletics .... Dr. Sam FERGUSON
42 Dir of Religious Life/Univ Chaplain ....Rev. Marty CASHBURLESS
19 Director of Campus Security ....Mr. Mark R. ODOM
23 Director of Health Services .... Ms. Brenda JOHNSON
39 Director of Residence Life .... Ms. Courtney GODDING
102 Executive Director Donor Relations .... Ms. Nancy SMITH
92 Director Honors Program .... Dr. Philip LE MASTERS
106 Director of Online Education ....Dr. Alicia WYATT
04 Executive Asst to President ....Ms. Renee SCOTT
50 Dean School of Business ....Dr. Paul MASON
18 Dir Facilities & Campus Projects .... Mr. Carl SCOTT
44 Director Annual Giving .... Ms. Ashlee BRADFORD

MediaTech Institute (G)

13300 Branch View Lane, Dallas TX 75234
County: Dallas FICE Identification: 041298
Unit ID: 455336
Telephone: (972) 869-1122 Carnegie Class: Not Classified
FAX Number: N/A Calendar System: Other
URL: mediatech.edu
Established: 1999 Annual Undergrad Tuition & Fees: N/A
Enrollment: 217 Coed
Affiliation or Control: Proprietary IRS Status: Proprietary
Highest Offering: Associate Degree
Accreditation: ACCSC

01 President ....Joel DEPUE
11 Campus Director .... Rhonda EVANS

Messenger College (H)

2705 Brown Trail Ste 408, Bedford TX 76021
County: Tarrant FICE Identification: 030926
Unit ID: 417752
Telephone: (817) 554-5950 Carnegie Class: Spec-4-yr-Faith
FAX Number: (817) 391-4003 Calendar System: Semester
URL: www.messengercollege.edu
Established: 1987 Annual Undergrad Tuition & Fees: $9,180
Enrollment: 33 Coed

Affiliation or Control: Pentecostal Church of God IRS Status: 501(c)3
Highest Offering: Baccalaureate
Accreditation: TRACS

01 President Rev. Randall K. LAWRENCE
05 VP of Academic Affairs Dr. Candace RAYBURN
08 Head Librarian Mary THOMASON
10 VP of Business Affairs Angela HEPPNER
32 VP of Student Development Fiona PARKER
37 Dir Student Financial Aid/Registrar Carolyn R. DOWD

MIAT College of Technology (A)

533 Northpark Central Drive, Houston TX 77073
Telephone: (713) 401-3399 Identification: 770972
Accreditation: ACCSC

† Branch campus of MIAT College of Technology, Canton, MI

Midland College (B)

3600 N Garfield, Midland TX 79705-6397
County: Midland FICE Identification: 009797
Unit ID: 226806
Telephone: (432) 685-4500 Carnegie Class: Bac/Assoc-Assoc Dom
FAX Number: (432) 685-4714 Calendar System: Semester
URL: www.midland.edu
Established: 1969 Annual Undergrad Tuition & Fees (In-District): $4,350
Enrollment: 4,737 Coed
Affiliation or Control: Local IRS Status: 501(c)3
Highest Offering: Baccalaureate
Accreditation: SC, CAHIIM, COARC, DMS, EMT

01 President Dr. Steve THOMAS
05 Vice President Instructional Svcs Dr. Damon KENNEDY
88 Special Advisor to President Dr. Deana SAVAGE
10 Vice Pres Administrative Services Mr. Rick BENDER
32 Vice President Student Services Mrs. Julia VICKERY
13 Vice Pres Info Tech/Facilities Mr. Shawn SHREVES
101 Exec Asst to President/Board Mrs. Leslie SHOEMAKER
51 Dean Adult & Continuing Educ Mr. Dale BEIKIRCH
57 Dean Engl/Humanities/FA/Comm Dr. William FEELER
72 Dean of Applied Technology Mr. Curt PERVIER
76 Dean of Health Sciences Ms. Carmen EDWARDS
81 Dean of Math/Natural Sciences Dr. Miranda POAGE
103 Associate VP of Workforce Educ Dr. Jennifer MYERS
111 Exec Dir Inst Advancement/MC Found Ms. Rebecca BELL
06 Registrar Mrs. Crystal VELASQUEZ
08 Head Librarian Mr. Howard MARKS
15 Director of Human Resources/Payroll Mrs. Natasha MORGAN
18 Executive Director Facilities Mr. Joseph BUTTS
19 Chief of Police Mr. Richard MCKEE
35 Dean of Student Life Mrs. Wendy KANE
41 Athletic Director Mr. Forrest ALLEN
09 Dir Institutional Effect/Planning Mrs. Heather CHAVEZ
37 Director Student Financial Aid Ms. Yolanda RAMOS
96 Director Purchasing Ms. Barbara FENNELL
84 Dean of Enrollment Management Vacant
30 Director Devel & Alumni Relations Vacant
26 Director Marketing & Communication Ms. Jaclynn TORRES
108 Dir Institutional Effectiveness Mrs. Kathryn ZIMMERHANZEL
20 Assoc VP of Instruction Mr. Michael DIXON
39 Dir Resident Life/Student Housing Mr. Ty SOLIZ

Midwestern State University (C)

3410 Taft Boulevard, Wichita Falls TX 76308-2095
County: Wichita FICE Identification: 003592
Unit ID: 226833
Telephone: (940) 397-4000 Carnegie Class: Masters/L
FAX Number: (940) 397-4042 Calendar System: Semester
URL: www.msutexas.edu
Established: 1922 Annual Undergrad Tuition & Fees (In-State): $9,796
Enrollment: 5,860 Coed
Affiliation or Control: State IRS Status: 501(c)3
Highest Offering: Doctorate
Accreditation: SC, ART, #CAATE, CACREP, CAEP, CAEPN, COARC, DH, MPCAC, MUS, NURSE, RAD, SW, THEA

01 Interim President Dr. James JOHNSTON
05 Interim Provost/VP Academic Affairs Dr. Martin CAMACHO
10 VP Business Affairs & Finance Dr. Beth REISSENWEBER
111 VP Univ Advancement & Student Affs Mr. Anthony VIDMAR
32 VP Student Affairs Dr. Keith LAMB
84 VP Enrollment Management Mr. Fred DIETZ
18 Assoc VP Facilities Services Mr. Kyle OWEN
35 Assoc VP Student Affairs Mr. Matthew PARK
13 Chief Information Officer Mr. Paul CHAPPELL
06 Registrar Ms. Darla INGLISH
08 University Librarian Ms. Cortny BATES
37 Interim Director of Financial Aid Ms. Michelle WELLS
38 Director of Counseling Center Dr. Pam MIDGETT
51 Director of Extended Education Dr. Pamela MORGAN DAVIS
07 Director of Admissions Ms. Gayonne BEAVERS
19 Chief of University Police Mr. Patrick COGGINS
26 Director Public Info/Marketing Ms. Julie GAYNOR
112 Dir Donor Services and Scholarships Ms. Laura PETERSON
36 Director Career Management Center Mr. Dirk WELCH
41 Director of Athletics Mr. Kyle WILLIAMS
15 Director of Human Resources Ms. Dawn FISHER
09 Director of Planning/Assessment Ms. Eboneigh HARRIS
21 Controller Mr. Chris STOVALL
23 Director Vinson Health Center Dr. Keith WILLIAMSON
20 Associate VP Academic Affairs Dr. Kristen GARRISON
50 Dean College Business Admin Dr. Jeff STAMBAUGH
53 Interim Dean College of Education Dr. Leann CURRY
57 Interim Dean College of Fine Arts Dr. James SERNOE
76 Dean Col Health Sci/Human Svcs Dr. Jeffrey KILLION
79 Dean College Humanities/Social Sci Dr. Samuel E. WATSON, III
81 Dean College of Science/Math & Engr Dr. Margaret BROWN MARSDEN
86 Director Board & Govt Relations Ms. Deborah L. BARROW
29 Liaison Alumni Engagement Ms. Leslee PONDER
121 Director of Academic Success Center Ms. Ashley HURST
105 Webmaster Mr. Jonathan SHIREY
96 Director of Purchasing Ms. Tracy NICHOLS
22 Dir Disability Support Services Ms. Debra HIGGINBOTHAM
39 Director Housing & Residence Life Ms. Kristi SCHULTE
30 Director University Development Mr. Steve SHIPP
104 Director Global Education Office Dr. Michael MILLS
88 Assoc Dir of Career Mgmt & Testing Ms. Lynn DUCIOAME
114 Director Budget & Management Ms. Valarie MAXWELL
88 Dir Museum of Art at MSU Texas Ms. Tracee ROBERTSON
88 Director Student Support Services Ms. Lisa ESTRADA-HAMBY
88 Campus Postal Supervisor Mr. Jon LANE
92 Coordinator Honors Program Dr. Steve GARRISON
43 Dir Legal Services/General Counsel Mr. Barry MACHA
28 Dir Eqty/Inclusion/Multi-Cult Affs Dr. Syreeta GREENE

Navarro College (D)

3200 W Seventh Avenue, Corsicana TX 75110-4899
County: Navarro FICE Identification: 003593
Unit ID: 227146
Telephone: (903) 874-6501 Carnegie Class: Assoc/MT-VT-High Trad
FAX Number: (903) 874-4636 Calendar System: Semester
URL: www.navarrocollege.edu
Established: 1946 Annual Undergrad Tuition & Fees (In-District): $4,508
Enrollment: 7,139 Coed
Affiliation or Control: Local IRS Status: 501(c)3
Highest Offering: Associate Degree
Accreditation: SC, ADNUR, EMT, MLTAD, OTA, PTAA

01 District President Dr. Kevin G. FEGAN
05 Vice Pres Academic Affairs Dr. Carol HANES
84 VP Enroll Mgmt/Inst Effect Ms. Sina RUIZ
10 Vice President Finance & Admin Ms. Teresa THOMAS
15 VP Human Resources Ms. Marcy BALLEW
111 VP Oper/Institutional Advancement Dr. Harold HOUSLEY
32 Vice President Student Services Ms. Maryann HAILEY
26 Director of Mktg/Public Relations Ms. Stacie SIPES
41 Athletic Director Mr. Michael LANDERS
20 Executive Dean of Acad Studies Dr. Jeanetta GROCE
103 Exec Dir Wrkfc/Career & Tech Educ Dr. Tara PETERS
106 Dean of Online Instruction Mr. Matthew MILLER
88 Dean of Midlothian Campus/Dual Cred Ms. Jeanette UNDERWOOD
76 Dean Waxahachie Campus/Health Prof Mr. Guy FEATHERSTON
12 Asst Dean of Mexia Campus Ms. Christina MIMS
51 Dean Wrkfrc Dev & Cont Educ Ms. Leslie HAYES
08 Dean of Libraries Mr. Tim KEVIL
07 Dir of Admissions/Registrar Ms. Tammy ADAMS
18 Exec Director of Facilities Mr. Todd HARRISON
13 Director of IT Mr. Barry SULLIVAN
37 Director Student Financial Aid Ms. Kristal NICHOLSON
39 Director of Residence Life Ms. Marisol ARENIVAS
104 Director of International Programs Ms. Elizabeth PILLANS
20 Dean Academic Studies Dr. Richard PHILLIPS
04 Exec Asst to District President Ms. Leslie SMITH

North American University (E)

11929 W. Airport Boulevard, Houston TX 77477
County: Fort Bend FICE Identification: 041795
Unit ID: 461795
Telephone: (832) 230-5555 Carnegie Class: Masters/M
FAX Number: N/A Calendar System: Semester
URL: www.na.edu
Established: 2010 Annual Undergrad Tuition & Fees: $9,900
Enrollment: 785 Coed
Affiliation or Control: Non-denominational IRS Status: 501(c)3
Highest Offering: Master's
Accreditation: ACCSC

01 President Dr. Serif A. TEKALAN
05 Provost/Vice Pres Academic Affairs Dr. Faruk TABAN
11 VP Administrative Affairs Dr. Kudbettin AKSOY
04 Administrative Asst to President Jill SELTZER
06 Registrar Edra EDWARDS
07 Senior Admissions Officer Anthony SORIANO
08 Head Librarian Gary CHAUFFEE
106 Dir Online Education/E-learning Mustafa MALDAR
13 Chief Info Technology Officer (CIO) Khudoyor S. ORTIKOV
32 Dean Student Affairs/Student Life Vacant
37 Assoc Dir Student Financial Aid Tia SIMON
10 Chief Financial Ofcr/Dir Bus Affs Dovran OVEZOV

North Central Texas College (F)

1525 W. California Street, Gainesville TX 76240-4699
County: Cooke FICE Identification: 003558
Unit ID: 224110
Telephone: (940) 668-7731 Carnegie Class: Assoc/MT-VT-High Trad
FAX Number: (940) 668-6049 Calendar System: Semester
URL: www.nctc.edu
Established: 1924 Annual Undergrad Tuition & Fees (In-District): $4,560
Enrollment: 8,352 Coed
Affiliation or Control: State/Local IRS Status: 501(c)3
Highest Offering: Associate Degree
Accreditation: SC, ADNUR, EMT, SURGT

01 Chancellor Dr. G. Brent WALLACE
05 Vice Chanc Instruct Svcs/Provost Dr. Bruce KING
32 Vice Chanc Student Services Ms. Melinda CARROLL
10 Vice Chanc Fiscal Affairs Dr. Van MILLER
11 Vice Chanc Administrative Affairs Mr. Robbie BAUGH
30 Vice Chanc External Affairs Ms. Debbie SHARP
28 VC Equity/Diversity/Inclusion Dr. Bonita VINSON
108 Assoc VC Strategic Planning/IR Mr. David BROWN
13 AVC Information Technology/CIO Ms. Denise CASON
08 Dean of Libraries Ms. Diane ROETHER
15 Director Human Resources Ms. Kay SCHROEDER
37 Director Financial Aid Ms. Ashley TATUM
06 Registrar/Sr Director of Admissions Ms. Jennifer BEAL
38 Sr Director Advising/Counseling Ms. Tracey FLENIKEN
26 Sr Dir Marketing/Public Relations Ms. Ski SULLIVAN
41 Athletic Director Mr. Van HEDRICK
35 Director of Student Life Ms. Daisy GARCIA
76 Dean of Instruction Health Science Mr. Brandon HERNANDEZ
81 Dean Instruct Science/Teacher Ed Ms. Sara FLUSCHE
88 Dean of Instruction Dual Credit Dr. Larry GILBERT
49 Dean of Instruction Flower Mound Mrs. Sara ALFORD
19 Police Chief Ms. Nicole SHAW
35 Dean of Student Affairs Dr. Roxanne DEL RIO
12 Dir of Denton County Campuses Ms. Jessica DEROCHE
12 Director of Flower Mound Campus Ms. Jessica DEROCHE
12 Director of Bowie Campus Dr. Jose DASILVA
12 Director of Graham Campus Ms. Kim BIRDWELL

Northeast Texas Community College (G)

PO Box 1307, Mount Pleasant TX 75456-1307
County: Titus FICE Identification: 023154
Unit ID: 227225
Telephone: (903) 434-8100 Carnegie Class: Assoc/MT-VT-High Non
FAX Number: (903) 434-4402 Calendar System: Semester
URL: www.ntcc.edu
Established: 1984 Annual Undergrad Tuition & Fees (In-District): $5,009
Enrollment: 2,758 Coed
Affiliation or Control: Local IRS Status: 501(c)3
Highest Offering: Associate Degree
Accreditation: SC, EMT, FUSER, MAC, MLTAD, PTAA

01 President Dr. Ron CLINTON
04 Executive Asst to the President Ms. Shemetric T. WILLIAMS
05 Vice Pres for Instruction Dr. Kevin ROSE
11 Vice Pres Administrative Services Mr. Jeffrey CHAMBERS
111 Executive Vice Pres Advancement Dr. Jonathan W. MCCULLOUGH
32 VP for Student & Outreach Services Dr. Josh STEWART
37 Dean Enroll/Dir Student Fin Assist Ms. Kim IRVIN
76 Dean of Health Sciences Dr. Marta URDANETA
56 Associate Dean of Outreach Services Ms. Melody HENRY
18 Director of Plant Services Mr. Tom RAMLER
08 Director Learning Commons Mr. Ron BOWDEN
13 Director of Computer Services Mr. Sebastian BARRON
26 Director Marketing/Public Relations Ms. Jodi PACK
06 Registrar Ms. Betsy GOODING
15 Director Human Resources Ms. Amy ADKINS
10 Controller Ms. Brandi M. CAVE
09 Dir Institutional Effectiveness Vacant
07 Admissions Coordinator Mr. Nick JACKSON
36 Career Development/Advisor Ms. Lynda WATSON
84 Dean of Enrollment Management Ms. Kim IRVIN
28 Director of Diversity Vacant
30 Director of Development Ms. Nita MAY
121 Advising Team Lead Ms. Katherine BELEW

Oblate School of Theology (H)

285 Oblate Drive, San Antonio TX 78216-6693
County: Bexar FICE Identification: 003595
Unit ID: 227289
Telephone: (210) 341-1366 Carnegie Class: Spec-4-yr-Faith
FAX Number: (210) 341-4519 Calendar System: Semester
URL: www.ost.edu
Established: 1903 Annual Graduate Tuition & Fees: N/A
Enrollment: 179 Coed
Affiliation or Control: Roman Catholic IRS Status: 501(c)3
Highest Offering: Doctorate; No Undergraduates
Accreditation: PAST, THEOL

01 President Dr. Scott WOODWARD
05 Vice Pres Academic Affairs/Dean Rev. Ken HANNON
10 Vice Pres Finance Mr. Rene ESPINOSA
111 Vice Pres Institutional Advancement Vacant
20 Associate Dean Sr. Linda GIBLER
51 Director of Continuing Education Mrs. Victoria LUNA
88 Director Oblate Renewal Center Mrs. K.T COCKERELL
18 Director of Physical Plant Mr. Edward BERRIGAN
08 Director of the Library Ms. Maria GARCIA
06 Registrar & Director of Admissions Mrs. Brenda REYNA
88 Director Theological Field Edu Mrs. Bonnie ABADIE
88 Director Ministry to Ministers Pgm Rev. James MYERS
88 Director DMin Program Rev. Wayne CAVALIER
88 Director PhD Program Rev. John MARKEY
26 Director Marketing/Communications Mr. John MARDEN

Odessa College (A)

201 W University Boulevard, Odessa TX 79764-7127
County: Ector FICE Identification: 003596
Unit ID: 227304
Telephone: (432) 335-6400 Carnegie Class: Assoc/MT-VT-Mix Trad/Non
FAX Number: (432) 335-6860 Calendar System: Semester
URL: www.odessa.edu
Established: 1946 Annual Undergrad Tuition & Fees (In-District): $3,504
Enrollment: 7,019 Coed
Affiliation or Control: Local IRS Status: 501(c)3
Highest Offering: Baccalaureate
Accreditation: SC, ADNUR, EMT, MUS, PTAA, RAD, SURGT

01 President .... Dr. Gregory D. WILLIAMS
05 Vice President for Instruction .... Dr. Tramaine ANDERSON
20 Assoc VP Instruction/Operations .... Ms. Karen DOUGHTY
20 Assoc VP Instruction/Efficacy .... Dr. Janice HICKS
32 VP Student Svcs/Enrollment Mgmt .... Ms. Kimberly MCKAY
13 Vice Pres Information Technology .... Vacant
09 VP for Institutional Effectiveness .... Vacant
100 Chief of Staff .... Mr. Robert RIVAS
11 Vice President for Administration .... Mr. Ken ZARTNER
10 Chief Financial Officer .... Ms. Brandy HAM
49 Dean Liberal Arts & Educ w/STEM .... Mr. Pervis EVANS
81 Sr Dean School of STEM .... Vacant
50 Dean Business & Industry w/STEM .... Mr. Jeremy SANCHEZ
76 Int Dean Health Sciences w/STEM .... Ms. Nicole HAYS
111 VP Advance/Business & Govt Rels .... Ms. Jacqui GORE
84 Exec Director Enrollment Services .... Mr. Timothy CLARK
88 VP for Academic Partnerships .... Dr. Jonathan FUENTES
06 Registrar .... Ms. Cara HOGAN
41 Director Intercollegiate Athletics .... Mr. Wayne BAKER
37 Director Student Financial Svcs .... Ms. Daisy GARCIA
18 Director Facilities & Construction .... Mr. Bryan HEIFNER
26 Exec Director of Marketing .... Mr. Frank RICH
96 Dir of Purchasing/Business Services .... Ms. Cindy CURNUTT
04 Exec Assistant to the President .... Ms. Ashley WARREN

Our Lady of the Lake University (B)

411 SW 24th Street, San Antonio TX 78207-4689
County: Bexar FICE Identification: 003598
Unit ID: 227331
Telephone: (210) 434-6711 Carnegie Class: DU-Mod
FAX Number: (210) 431-3928 Calendar System: Semester
URL: www.ollusa.edu
Established: 1895 Annual Undergrad Tuition & Fees: $29,926
Enrollment: 2,771 Coed
Affiliation or Control: Roman Catholic IRS Status: 501(c)3
Highest Offering: Doctorate
Accreditation: SC, ACBSP, COPSY, MFCD, SP, SW

01 President .... Dr. Diane MELBY
10 Vice President Finance & Facilities .... Mr. Anthony TURRIETTA
05 Provost/Vice Pres Academic Affairs .... Dr. Lourdes ALVAREZ
11 Vice President Administration .... Ms. Rosalinda GARCIA
111 Vice President of Inst Advancement .... Ms. Georgina SCHMAHL
13 Vice Pres of Mission and Ministry .... Ms. Gloria URRABAZO
32 Vice President of Student Affairs .... Dr. George A. WILLIAMS, JR.
13 Chief Technology Officer .... Mr. Curtis L. SPEARS
26 Chief Communication Officer .... Ms. Anne GOMEZ
84 Chief Enrollment Officer .... Mr. Nelson DELGADO
09 Director of Institutional Research .... Mr. Humberto ESPINOZA-MOLINA
14 Director of Infrastructure Services .... Mr. Jeffrey ALLEN
37 Director of Financial Aid .... Ms. Esmarelda FLORES
18 Director Facilities Management .... Mr. Darrell R. GLASSCOCK
15 Director Human Resources .... Mr. Phillip VARGAS
19 Chief of Police/Dir Campus Safety .... Mr. Ramon ZERTUCHE
06 Registrar .... Ms. Betty GALVAN
42 University Chaplain .... Fr. Kevin FAUSZ
39 Director Residence Life .... Ms. Victor G. SALAZAR
36 Director Career Counsel/Placement .... Mr. Andres JAIME
23 Director of Health Services .... Ms. Julie KNEUPPER
41 Athletic Director .... Mr. Donald (Shane) HURLEY
44 Director Advancement Services .... Mr. Douglas SEAMAN
29 Dir Alumni/Family Relations .... Ms. Debora PEREZ
08 Director of the Library .... Ms. Maria CABANISS
04 Executive Asst to the President .... Ms. Ida PEREZ

Panola College (C)

1109 West Panola Street, Carthage TX 75633-2397
County: Panola FICE Identification: 003600
Unit ID: 227386
Telephone: (903) 693-2000 Carnegie Class: Assoc/MT-VT-Mix Trad/Non
FAX Number: (903) 693-1167 Calendar System: Semester
URL: www.panola.edu
Established: 1947 Annual Undergrad Tuition & Fees (In-District): $3,576
Enrollment: 2,513 Coed
Affiliation or Control: Local IRS Status: 501(c)3
Highest Offering: Associate Degree
Accreditation: SC, ADNUR, CAHIIM, EMT, MLTAD, OTA

01 President .... Dr. Gregory S. POWELL
05 Vice President of Instruction .... Dr. Billy W. ADAMS
32 Vice President of Student Services .... Mr. Don CLINTON
10 Vice President of Fiscal Services .... Mr. Alan HOWARD
49 Dean of Arts/Sciences/Technology .... Mrs. Natalie OSWALT
106 Dean of Distance/Digital Learning .... Mrs. Teresa BROOKS
76 Dean of Health Sciences .... Mrs. Kelly REED-HIRSCH
15 Director of Human Resources .... Mr. Jeremy DORMAN
07 Director of Admissions/Registrar .... Mr. Chris WOOD
111 Dir Institutional Advancement .... Mrs. Jessica PACE
08 Director of Library .... Mrs. Cristie FERGUSON
103 Dir of Workforce & Economic Devel .... Mrs. Whitney MCBEE
09 Director of Institutional Research .... Mrs. Tryphena WALKER
12 Director of Shelby County Operation .... Mrs. Cancee LESTER
12 Director of Marshall Operations .... Mrs. Laura WOOD
13 Director of IT Service .... Mr. Allen WEST
19 Campus Police Chief .... Mr. Jeff JONES
37 Director Student Financial Aid .... Mrs. Denise WELCH
18 Dir of Facilities/Physical Plant .... Mr. Alan MOON
04 Admin Assistant to the President .... Ms. Mary CHANCE
30 Director of Development .... Mrs. Jessica PACE

Paris Junior College (D)

2400 Clarksville Street, Paris TX 75460-6298
County: Lamar FICE Identification: 003601
Unit ID: 227401
Telephone: (903) 785-7661 Carnegie Class: Assoc/MT-VT-High Non
FAX Number: (903) 782-0370 Calendar System: Semester
URL: www.parisjc.edu
Established: 1924 Annual Undergrad Tuition & Fees (In-District): $3,960
Enrollment: 4,421 Coed
Affiliation or Control: State/Local IRS Status: 501(c)3
Highest Offering: Associate Degree
Accreditation: SC, ADNUR, EMT, RAD, SURGT

01 President .... Dr. Pamela D. ANGLIN
05 Vice President of Academic Instruct .... Mr. Bryan RENFRO
103 Vice President Workforce Education .... Mr. John SPRADLING
32 VP Student Access/Success .... Mrs. Sheila REECE
60 Dean Communications/Arts .... Vacant
76 Dean Health Occupations .... Dr. Greg FERENCHAK
06 Registrar .... Mrs. Amie CATO
10 Controller .... Mr. Cody HELM
37 Director Student Financial Aid .... Mrs. Kimberly HERRON
09 Director Institutional Research .... Dr. Jacque MESSINGER
111 Director Institutional Advancement .... Mrs. Baleigh MCCOIN
35 Director Student Life .... Mr. Kenneth WEBB
13 Director Information Technology .... Mr. Eddie MAHAR
26 Chief Public Relations Officer .... Ms. Margaret RUFF
18 Manager Plant Operations .... Mr. Jon EUBANKS
15 Director Personnel Services .... Mrs. Melanie HATCHER

Parker University (E)

2540 Walnut Hill Lane, Dallas TX 75229-5609
County: Dallas FICE Identification: 023053
Unit ID: 243823
Telephone: (972) 438-6932 Carnegie Class: Spec-4-yr-Other Health
FAX Number: (214) 902-2496 Calendar System: Trimester
URL: www.parker.edu
Established: 1982 Annual Undergrad Tuition & Fees: $15,672
Enrollment: 1,697 Coed
Affiliation or Control: Independent Non-Profit IRS Status: 501(c)3
Highest Offering: Doctorate
Accreditation: SC, CAHIIM, CHIRO, COMTA, DMS, OTA

01 President .... Dr. William E. MORGAN
05 Provost .... Dr. Jayne MOSCHELLA
63 Vice Pres College of Chiropractic .... Dr. Patrick BODNAR
15 VP/Chief Human Resources Officer .... Sandra SEPEDA MCLEAN
20 Associate Provost Academics .... Dr. Dana J. LAWRENCE
10 Vice Pres Finance .... Vacant

Paul Quinn College (F)

3837 Simpson Stuart Road, Dallas TX 75241-4398
County: Dallas FICE Identification: 003602
Unit ID: 227429
Telephone: (214) 376-1000 Carnegie Class: Bac-Diverse
FAX Number: (214) 379-5559 Calendar System: Semester
URL: www.pqc.edu
Established: 1872 Annual Undergrad Tuition & Fees: $9,992
Enrollment: 468 Coed
Affiliation or Control: African Methodist Episcopal IRS Status: 501(c)3
Highest Offering: Baccalaureate
Accreditation: TRACS

01 President .... Dr. Michael J. SORRELL
05 Vice Pres Academic Affairs .... Dr. Chris DOWDY
10 Chief Financial Officer .... Mr. Bruce BRINSON
11 Chief Administrative Officer .... Dr. Kizuwanda GRANT
100 Chief of Staff .... Ms. Paola ESMIEU
06 Registrar .... Ms. Marquita MITCHELL
08 Director Library Services .... Ms. Clarice MEDLEY-WEEKS
13 Director of Technology .... Vacant
41 Athletic Director .... Mr. James (Zip) SUMMERS
26 Director External Affairs .... Ms. Kelsel THOMPSON
37 Director of Financial Aid .... Ms. Natalie GONZALEZ
35 Dir Student Support Services .... Ms. Theran HERNANDEZ
18 Facilities Manager .... Mr. Nahydiel MOLINA
30 Corporate External Affairs .... Mr. Maurice WEST
23 Campus Nurse .... Ms. Glenda DAVIS
84 Dir of Recruiting/Enrollment Mgmt .... Vacant

Peloton College (G)

8150 N. Central Expy, M-2240, Dallas TX 75206
County: Dallas FICE Identification: 041687
Unit ID: 459514
Telephone: (214) 777-6433 Carnegie Class: Not Classified
FAX Number: (214) 777-6477 Calendar System: Quarter
URL: pelotoncollege.edu
Established: 2005 Annual Undergrad Tuition & Fees: N/A
Enrollment: 131 Coed
Affiliation or Control: Proprietary IRS Status: Proprietary
Highest Offering: Associate Degree
Accreditation: COE

01 Campus President .... Michelle O. ANDERSON
05 VP of Academic Operations .... David PRICE
07 District Director of Admissions .... Suzann MCDOWELL

Pima Medical Institute-El Paso (H)

6926 Gateway Blvd., E., El Paso TX 79915
Telephone: (915) 633-1133 Identification: 770962
Accreditation: ABHES, DMS, OTA, RAD

† Branch campus of Pima Medical Institute-Tucson, Tucson, AZ

Pima Medical Institute-Houston (I)

11125 Equity Drive, Suite 100, Houston TX 77041
Telephone: (713) 778-0778 Identification: 770510
Accreditation: ABHES, COARC, DH, DMS, OTA, PTAA, RAD

† Branch campus of Pima Medical Institute-Tucson, Tucson, AZ

Quest College (J)

5430 Fredericksburg Road, Ste 310,
San Antonio TX 78229
County: Bexar FICE Identification: 034003
Unit ID: 439507
Telephone: (210) 366-2701 Carnegie Class: Not Classified
FAX Number: (210) 366-0738 Calendar System: Semester
URL: www.questcollege.edu
Established: 1995 Annual Undergrad Tuition & Fees: N/A
Enrollment: 359 Coed
Affiliation or Control: Proprietary IRS Status: Proprietary
Highest Offering: Associate Degree
Accreditation: COE

00 President/CEO .... Ms. Jeanne MARTIN
01 School Director .... Ms. Christine URDIALEZ
06 Registrar .... Mrs. Veronica PEREZ
07 Director of Admissions .... Mrs. Denise SOSA
37 Director Student Financial Aid .... Ms. Sandy CLAUSS
05 Dean of Education .... Mrs. Veronica PAZ

Ranger College (K)

1240 College Circle, Ranger TX 76470-3298
County: Eastland FICE Identification: 003603
Unit ID: 227687
Telephone: (254) 647-3234 Carnegie Class: Assoc/HT-High Trad
FAX Number: (254) 647-1656 Calendar System: Semester
URL: www.rangercollege.edu
Established: 1926 Annual Undergrad Tuition & Fees (In-District): $4,510
Enrollment: 2,200 Coed
Affiliation or Control: Local IRS Status: 501(c)3
Highest Offering: Associate Degree
Accreditation: SC

01 President .... Dr. William J. CAMPION
12 Vice President Brown County .... Dr. Gordon WARREN
05 Vice President of Instruction .... Mrs. Dayna PROCHASKA
10 Vice President Business Service/CFO .... Mrs. Gaylyn MENDOZA
103 Vice President Workforce Devel .... Mr. Dixon BAILEY
32 Vice President of Student Services .... Mr. Derrick WORRELS
108 Vice President of Accreditation .... Mr. Matt CARDIN
09 Director of Institutional Research .... Mr. John SLAUGHTER
84 Dean of Enrollment Management .... Mr. Robert CULVERHOUSE
18 Director of Physical Plant .... Mr. Chuck LEMASTER
37 Director of Financial Aid .... Mr. Don HILTON
38 Director of Counseling .... Mr. Gabe LEWIS
15 Human Resources .... Mr. Brad KELLER
113 Bursar .... Ms. Evonne CHERRY
41 Athletic Director .... Mr. Stan FEASTER
40 Director Bookstore .... Miss Cindy STRINGER
08 Director of Library Services .... Vacant
04 Admin Assistant to the President .... Mrs. Lindy L. MATTHEWS
13 Information Technology Admin .... Mr. Glenn PAUL

Redeemed Christian Bible College and Seminary (L)

4320 Highway 380 Business, Greenville TX 75401
County: Hunt Identification: 667391
Telephone: (903) 303-7853 Carnegie Class: Not Classified
FAX Number: N/A Calendar System: Trimester
URL: www.rccgnaseminary.org
Established: 2012 Annual Undergrad Tuition & Fees: N/A
Enrollment: N/A Coed
Affiliation or Control: Independent Non-Profit IRS Status: 501(c)3
Highest Offering: Doctorate
Accreditation: @TRACS

01 President .... Oluwasayo AJIBOYE

Regional Christian University (A)

510 E. Van Week Street, Edinburg TX 78541
County: Hidalgo — Identification: 667394
Telephone: (956) 867-8721 — Carnegie Class: Not Classified
FAX Number: (956) 378-9644 — Calendar System: Semester
URL: regionalchristianuniversity.org
Established: 1998 — Annual Undergrad Tuition & Fees: N/A
Enrollment: N/A — Coed
Affiliation or Control: Non-denominational — IRS Status: 501(c)3
Highest Offering: Baccalaureate
Accreditation: @BI

01 President ... Dr. David J. HOYTE

Remington College-Dallas Campus (B)

1800 Eastgate Drive, Garland TX 75041-5513
County: Dallas — FICE Identification: 030265
Unit ID: 223463
Telephone: (972) 686-7878 — Carnegie Class: Bac/Assoc-Mixed
FAX Number: (972) 686-5116 — Calendar System: Quarter
URL: www.remingtoncollege.edu
Established: 1987 — Annual Undergrad Tuition & Fees: $16,075
Enrollment: 628 — Coed
Affiliation or Control: Independent Non-Profit — IRS Status: 501(c)3
Highest Offering: Baccalaureate
Accreditation: ACCSC

01 Director of Campus Administration ... Diana MCWILLIAMS
05 Campus Dean ... Lyvier LEFFLER
07 Director of Admissions ... Andrea WADY
36 Director of Career Services ... Christi KOEHLER
06 Registrar ... Michael BELL

Remington College-Fort Worth Campus (C)

5555 Rufe Snow Drive, Suite 150,
North Richland Hills TX 76180
Telephone: (817) 451-0017 — Identification: 666063
Accreditation: ACCSC

Remington College-Houston Southeast Campus (D)

20985 Interstate 45 South, Webster TX 77598
Telephone: (281) 554-1700 — Identification: 770601
Accreditation: ACCSC

Remington College-North Houston Campus (E)

11310 Greens Crossing, Suite 300, Houston TX 77067
Telephone: (281) 885-4450 — Identification: 770600
Accreditation: ACCSC

Rice University (F)

PO Box 1892, Houston TX 77251-1892
County: Harris — FICE Identification: 003604
Unit ID: 227757
Telephone: (713) 348-0000 — Carnegie Class: DU-Highest
FAX Number: N/A — Calendar System: Semester
URL: www.rice.edu
Established: 1891 — Annual Undergrad Tuition & Fees: $51,107
Enrollment: 7,643 — Coed
Affiliation or Control: Independent Non-Profit — IRS Status: 501(c)3
Highest Offering: Doctorate
Accreditation: SC

01 President ... Mr. David W. LEEBRON
101 Deputy Sec to Board of Trustees ... Ms. Cynthia L. WILSON
05 Provost & Dean ... Dr. Reginald DESROCHES
11 Vice President Administration ... Dr. Kevin KIRBY
10 Vice President Finance ... Ms. Kathy COLLINS
30 Vice Pres Development/Alumni Rels ... Ms. Kathi D. WARREN
115 Vice Pres Investments/Treasurer ... Ms. Allison THACKER
84 Vice President for Enrollment ... Ms. Yvonne DASILVA
26 Vice President for Public Affairs ... Ms. Linda THRANE
13 Vice President IT ... Ms. Klara JELINKOVA
46 Vice Provost Research ... Dr. Yousif SHAMOO
20 Vice Provost for Academic Affairs ... Dr. Fred HIGGS
08 Vice Provost/University Librarian ... Ms. Sara LOWMAN
45 Vice Pres Strategic Initiatives ... Dr. Caroline LEVANDER
15 Associate Vice Pres Human Resources ... Ms. Joan NELSON
91 Assoc Vice Pres for Admin Systems ... Vacant
43 VP & General Counsel ... Mr. Richard A. ZANSITIS
06 Registrar ... Mr. David TENNEY
29 Asst VP for Alumni Relations ... Vacant
37 Director Student Financial Services ... Ms. Anne E. WALKER
25 AVP Sponsored Proj/Res Compliance ... Ms. Krystal TOUPS
41 Director of Athletics ... Dr. Joseph KARLGAARD
85 Assoc Vice Provost Intl Education ... Dr. Adria BAKER
39 Assoc Vice Pres Housing & Dining ... Mr. Mark DITMAN
23 Director Student Health Services ... Dr. Jessica MCKELVEY
09 Assoc VP Institutional Research ... Dr. John M. CORNWELL
21 University Controller ... Mr. Bradley FRALIC
116 Director of Internal Audit ... Ms. Janet COVINGTON
19 Chief of Campus Police ... Mr. Clemente RODRIGUEZ
22 Director of Affirmative Action ... Dr. Richard BAKER
27 Dir of News & Media Relations ... Mr. Doug MILLER
21 Director Administrative Services ... Mr. Eugen RADULESCU
28 Director of Diversity ... Dr. Roland B. SMITH
38 Director of Student Counseling ... Dr. Timothy K. BAUMGARTNER
36 Dir Center for Career Development ... Ms. Nicole VAN DEN HEUVEL
96 Director of Procurement ... Vacant
79 Dean of School of Humanities ... Dr. Kathleen CANNING
58 Dean Graduate/Postdoctoral Stds ... Dr. Seiichi MATSUDA
97 Dean of Undergraduate Education ... Dr. Bridget GORMAN
48 Interim Dean of Architecture ... Dr. John CASBARIAN
64 Dean of Shepherd School of Music ... Dr. Robert YEKOVICH
54 Int Dean Brown School Engineering ... Dr. Rob GRIFFIN
50 Dean JH Jones Graduate Sch Business ... Dr. Peter RODRIGUEZ
83 Interim Dean of Social Sciences ... Dr. Susan MCINTOSH
81 Dean of Wiess Sch Natural Science ... Dr. Peter ROSSKY
51 Dean Glasscock Sch Continuing Stds ... Dr. Robert BRUCE
22 Director of Compliance ... Mr. Ken LIDDLE
18 Chief Facilities/Physical Plant ... Ms. Kathy JONES
04 Admin Assistant to the President ... Ms. Hope GATLIFF
102 Dir Foundation/Corporate Relations ... Ms. Katie CERVENKA
86 Director Government Relations ... Mr. Nathan L. COOK

Rio Grande Bible Institute (G)

4300 South US Highway 281, Edinburg TX 78539-9650
County: Hidalgo — Identification: 666395
Unit ID: 475185
Telephone: (956) 380-8100 — Carnegie Class: Spec-4-yr-Faith
FAX Number: (956) 380-8256 — Calendar System: Semester
URL: www.riogrande.edu
Established: 1946 — Annual Undergrad Tuition & Fees: N/A
Enrollment: N/A — Coed
Affiliation or Control: Independent Non-Profit — IRS Status: 501(c)3
Highest Offering: Baccalaureate
Accreditation: BI

01 President ... Dr. Lawrence B. WINDLE
04 Admin Assistant to President ... Mr. Eduardo CALLEJA
05 Vice Pres of Academic Division ... Dr. Julio VARELA
26 Vice Pres Ministerial Advancement ... Mr. Bob ALLEN
06 Registrar ... Mr. Keith SWARTZBAUGH

Rio Grande Valley College (H)

5419 N. Cage Blvd, Pharr TX 78577
County: Hidalgo — FICE Identification: 041930
Unit ID: 476726
Telephone: (956) 781-6806 — Carnegie Class: Not Classified
FAX Number: (956) 781-6807 — Calendar System: Semester
URL: www.rgvcollege.edu
Established: 2008 — Annual Undergrad Tuition & Fees: N/A
Enrollment: 614 — Coed
Affiliation or Control: Proprietary — IRS Status: Proprietary
Highest Offering: Associate Degree
Accreditation: ABHES

01 CEO/School Director ... Dr. Annabelle RODRIGUEZ

St. Edward's University (I)

3001 S Congress Avenue, Austin TX 78704-6489
County: Travis — FICE Identification: 003621
Unit ID: 227845
Telephone: (512) 448-8400 — Carnegie Class: Masters/L
FAX Number: (512) 448-8492 — Calendar System: Semester
URL: www.stedwards.edu
Established: 1885 — Annual Undergrad Tuition & Fees: $49,076
Enrollment: 3,591 — Coed
Affiliation or Control: Independent Non-Profit — IRS Status: 501(c)3
Highest Offering: Doctorate
Accreditation: SC, CACREP, SW

00 Board Chair ... Mr. Steve D. SHADOWEN
01 President ... Dr. Montserrat FUENTES
05 Interim Provost ... Dr. Marianne WARD-PERADOZA
10 Vice Pres for Finance & Admin ... Dr. Kimberly KVAAL
13 Vice President Information Tech ... Mr. David E. WALDRON
45 VP Inst Effectiveness & Planning ... Vacant
111 Vice President for Advancement ... Mr. Joe DEMEDEIROS
84 Vice Pres for Enrollment Management ... Ms. Tracy L. MANIER
32 Vice President for Student Affairs ... Dr. Lisa L. KIRKPATRICK
26 Vice Pres Marketing & Communication ... Ms. Christie CAMPBELL
42 Director of Campus Ministry ... Fr. Peter J. WALSH
100 Chief of Staff/Sustainability Coord ... Vacant
20 Assoc VP Academic Affairs ... Dr. Glenda BALLARD
124 Assoc VP Student Success ... Dr. Nicole G. TREVINO
58 Dir Graduate/Professional Studies ... Dr. Ellen C. MELTON
83 Dean Behavioral & Social Sciences ... Dr. Catherine E. CAMPBELL
50 Interim Dean Munday Sch of Business ... Dr. Louise E. SINGLE
79 Dean School of Arts & Humanities ... Dr. Sharon D. NELL
81 Dean School of Natural Sciences ... Dr. Jonathan HODGE
21 Assoc VP for Finance ... Ms. Kelli L. GREEN
11 Assoc VP Operations ... Mr. James H. MORRIS
15 Assoc VP Human Resources ... Dr. Melissa G. ESQUEDA
91 Assoc VP Digital Effectiveness ... Ms. Angela M. SVOBODA
120 Assoc VP Digital Learning ... Ms. Rebecca F. DAVIS
14 Assoc VP IT Resource Mgmt ... Mr. Danny LORENTY
30 Assoc VP for Development ... Mr. Gregory PERRIN
35 Assoc VP Student Affairs ... Mr. Thomas B. SULLIVAN
41 Associate VP Athletics ... Ms. Debora W. TAYLOR
86 Dir Govt & Community Relations ... Ms. Liz JOHNSON
06 Registrar ... Mr. Patrick W. FIELDS
35 Dean of Students/Title IX Deputy ... Mr. Steven J. PINKENBURG
07 Dean of Admissions ... Mr. Drew NICHOLS
08 Interim Director Library ... Mr. Robert C. GIBBS
109 Assoc VP for Business Services ... Ms. Rebekah DESAI
37 Sr Director Student Financial Aid ... Ms. Jennifer M. BECK
27 Director of Communications ... Ms. Gwendollyn SCHULER
88 Director Master Planning ... Mr. Steve D. RAMIREZ
113 Director of Student Accounts ... Mr. Peter J. BEILHARZ
114 Dir Budget & Resource Planning ... Ms. Lisa P. GRANTHAM
18 Director of Facilities Operations ... Mr. Bobby BULLARD
19 Chief/Director of Police Services ... Mr. Homer J. HUERTA
16 Director of Human Resources ... Ms. Jennifer CHARLES
97 Director of General Education ... Vacant
121 Dir Academic Counseling & Support ... Ms. Kendall P. SWANSON
36 Dir Career & Prof Development ... Mr. Jason B. DELAROSA
123 Dir Graduate and Transfer Admission ... Mr. David C. BRALOWER
85 Dir International Student Services ... Ms. Kathy JACKSON
104 Director of Study Abroad ... Vacant
119 Senior Cyber Security Analyst ... Mr. Brant C. CHRISTIANSEN
39 Director for Housing Operations ... Vacant
38 Dir Health & Counseling Center ... Vacant
89 Dir Student Activities/Transitions ... Mr. Carey J. MAYES
88 Assoc VP Faculty DEI ... Dr. Monique JIMENEZ-HERRERA
28 Director of Diversity & Inclusion ... Ms. Erica A. ZAMORA
110 Director of Development ... Ms. Anne E. WESTDYKE
102 Director Foundation Relations ... Ms. Jessica D. WILSON
44 Director Constituent Relations ... Ms. Sarah B. DICKENS
108 Director Institutional Assessment ... Dr. Jocelyn SHADFORTH
09 Director of Institutional Research ... Ms. Danica D. FRAMPTON
92 Director of Honors Program ... Dr. Emma WOELK
29 Assoc Dir Development & Alumni Ops ... Ms. Karin DICKS
96 Assistant Procurement Manager ... Mr. Tony ACEVEDO
04 Admin Assistant to President ... Ms. Lorraine M. PAGAN
40 Campus Stores Manager ... Ms. Veronica LARA

St. Mary's University (J)

One Camino Santa Maria, San Antonio TX 78228-8572
County: Bexar — FICE Identification: 003623
Unit ID: 228149
Telephone: (210) 436-3011 — Carnegie Class: Masters/L
FAX Number: (210) 436-3500 — Calendar System: Semester
URL: www.stmarytx.edu
Established: 1852 — Annual Undergrad Tuition & Fees: $33,720
Enrollment: 3,458 — Coed
Affiliation or Control: Roman Catholic — IRS Status: 501(c)3
Highest Offering: Doctorate
Accreditation: SC, CACREP, LAW, MFCD, MUS

01 President ... Mr. Thomas M. MENGLER
05 Int Provost/VP Academic Affairs ... Dr. William (Bill) BUHRMAN
10 Vice Pres for Admin & Finance ... Mr. Aaron HANNA
84 Vice Provost/Enrollment Management ... Dr. Rosalind ALDERMAN
32 Vice Prov Stdnt Dev/Dean of Stdnts ... Mr. Timothy (Tim) BESSLER
111 Vice Pres for Univ Advancement ... Mr. Joel LAUER
88 Vice President Mission ... Rev. John THOMPSON, SM
50 Dean Bill Greehey Sch of Business ... Dr. Rowena ORTIZ-WALTERS
79 Int Dean Humanities/Social Science ... Dr. Leona PALLANSCH
54 Int Dean Science/Engineering/Tech ... Dr. Ian MARTINES
61 Dean of Law ... Ms. Patricia ROBERTS
39 Director Residence Life ... Mr. James VILLARREAL
100 Chief of Staff/Office of President ... Ms. Dianne L. PIPES
06 Registrar ... Ms. Christina VILLANUEVA
07 Director Undergraduate Admission ... Vacant
08 Int Exec Dir Louis J Blume Library ... Dr. Felicia CRUZ
37 Dir Financial Aid/Enrollment Ops ... Ms. Marivel OJEDA
38 Assoc Dir Student Counseling Ctr ... Ms. Deidra COLEMAN
90 Exec Dir Academic Tech Svcs ... Mr. Jeff SCHOMBURG
15 Exec Dir Human Res/Title IX Coord ... Ms. Janet GUADARRAMA
13 Vice Pres Information Services ... Mr. Curtis WHITE
119 Dir Ntwrk/Security Admin Info Svcs ... Mr. Robert STOOKSBERRY
14 Director Systems Support Services ... Mr. Frank NIEWIERSKI
42 Exec Director University Ministry ... Vacant
29 Executive Director Alumni Relations ... Mr. Peter HANSEN
21 Director of Accounting Operations ... Vacant
26 Senior Director Communications ... Ms. Jennifer LLOYD

*San Jacinto College District (K)

4624 Fairmont Parkway, Pasadena TX 77504-3323
County: Harris — FICE Identification: 029137
Telephone: (281) 998-6150 — Carnegie Class: N/A
FAX Number: N/A
URL: www.sanjac.edu

01 Chancellor ... Dr. Brenda HELLYER
03 Deputy Chancellor and President ... Dr. Laurel WILLIAMSON
05 Chief Academic Officer ... Mr. Van WIGGINTON
10 Vice Chancellor Fiscal Affairs ... Mrs. Teri ZAMORA
15 Vice Chanc Human Resources ... Mrs. Sandra RAMIREZ
13 CIO ... Mr. Rob STANICIC
26 Vice Chanc Marketing/Govt Rels ... Mrs. Teri CRAWFORD
45 Vice Chanc Strategic Initiatives ... Dr. Allatia HARRIS
84 Dean Enroll Mgmt/College Registrar ... Mr. Kevin MCKISSON
09 Director of Research ... Mr. George GONZALEZ
37 Dean Financial Aid Services ... Mr. Robert MERINO
96 Director Contracts & Purchasing ... Ms. Ann KOKX-TEMPLET
04 Administrative Asst to President ... Ms. Mandi REILAND
19 Manager SHERM ... Mrs. Susana GONZALEZ
25 Director Grants Management ... Mrs. Tomoko OLSON
29 Director Alumni Relations ... Ms. Ruth KEENAN
32 Chief Student Affairs/Student Life ... Ms. Joanna ZIMMERMANN
43 Dir Legal Services/General Counsel ... Ms. Clare IANNELLI
06 College Registrar ... Mr. Kevin MCKISSON

*San Jacinto College Central (A)

8060 Spencer Highway, Pasadena TX 77505-5903
County: Harris FICE Identification: 003609
Unit ID: 227979
Telephone: (281) 998-6150 Carnegie Class: Assoc/MT-VT-Mix Trad/Non
FAX Number: N/A Calendar System: Semester
URL: www.sanjac.edu
Established: 1960 Annual Undergrad Tuition & Fees (In-District): $3,240
Enrollment: 31,110 Coed
Affiliation or Control: Local IRS Status: 501(c)3
Highest Offering: Baccalaureate
Accreditation: &SC, ADNUR, COARC, DMS, MLTAD, NAEYC, RAD, SURGT

02 Deputy Chancellor and President .... Dr. Laurel WILLIAMSON
05 Provost .... Mr. Van A. WIGGINTON
32 Associate VC Student Services .... Ms. Joanna ZIMMERMANN
72 Assoc VC/SVP Ctr Petro/Energy/Tech .... Mr. James GRIFFIN
88 Director CPET Resources Contractor .... Ms. Clarissa BELBAS
88 Director Petrochemical Technology .... Mr. Thomas STANG
06 Col Registrar/Dean of Records Mgmt ..... Mr. Kevin R. MCKISSON
50 Dean Business & Technology .... Dr. James RAGAISIS
49 Dean of Liberal Arts .... Dr. DeRhonda MCWAINE
76 Dean Health and Health Sciences .... Dr. Rhonda BELL
11 Dean of Administration .... Mr. Scott R. GERNANDER
35 Dean Student Development .... Ms. Deborah SMITH
88 Dean of Student Support Services .... Ms. Tanesha ANTOINE
84 Dean of Enrollment Services .... Mr. Jose DEJESUSGIL
37 Dean Financial Aid Services .... Mr. Robert MERINO
43 Dean Compliance & Judicial Affairs .... Ms. Clare IANNELLI
92 Director Honors Program .... Dr. Eddie WELLER
08 Director Library .... Ms. Karen BLANKENSHIP
109 Director Campus Services .... Mr. Christopher CRUMLEY
121 Director Student Success Center .... Ms. Dawn SHEDD
88 Dir Educ Planning/Couns/Completion .... Ms. Melinda THOMAS
88 Dual Credit Director .... Ms. Priscilla CULVER

† Regional accreditation is carried under the parent institution (district office) in Pasadena, TX.

*San Jacinto College North (B)

5800 Uvalde Road, Houston TX 77049-4599
County: Harris Identification: 666747
Unit ID: 22797901
Telephone: (281) 998-6150 Carnegie Class: Not Classified
FAX Number: (281) 459-7125 Calendar System: Semester
URL: www.sanjac.edu
Established: 1974 Annual Undergrad Tuition & Fees (In-District): N/A
Enrollment: N/A Coed
Affiliation or Control: Local IRS Status: 501(c)3
Highest Offering: Baccalaureate
Accreditation: &SC, ACFEI, CAHIIM, EMT, MAC

02 Deputy Chancellor and President .... Dr. Laurel WILLIAMSON
05 Provost .... Dr. William RAFFETTO
32 Associate VC Student Services .... Ms. Joanna ZIMMERMAN
07 College Registrar/Dean of Enroll .... Mr. Kevin MCKISSON
11 Dean Administration .... Ms. Minelia IZAGUIRRE
76 Dean Natural and Health Sciences .... Dr. Teddy FARIAS
50 Dean Business and Technology .... Ms. Heather RHODES
43 Dean Comp & Judicial Affairs .... Ms. Clare IANNELLI
62 Director Library .... Ms. Lyn GARNER
49 Dean Liberal Arts .... Mr. Shawn SILMAN
41 Athletic Director .... Mr. Tom ARRINGTON
92 Director Honors Program .... Dr. Eddie WELLER
88 Dual Credit Director .... Dr. Anne DICKENS
55 Director Evening/Weekend Services .... Mr. Don SPIES
121 Director Student Success Center .... Ms. Erika HERNANDEZ
37 Dean Financial Aid Services .... Mr. Robert MERINO
32 Dean Student Development .... Ms. Deborah SMITH
88 Dir Educational Planning & Counsel .... Ms. Sonia TOWNSEND

† Regional accreditation is carried under the parent institution (district office) in Pasadena, TX.

*San Jacinto College South (C)

13735 Beamer Road, Houston TX 77089-6099
County: Harris Identification: 666748
Unit ID: 22797902
Telephone: (281) 484-1900 Carnegie Class: Not Classified
FAX Number: (281) 922-3401 Calendar System: Semester
URL: www.sanjac.edu
Established: 1979 Annual Undergrad Tuition & Fees (In-District): N/A
Enrollment: N/A Coed
Affiliation or Control: Local IRS Status: 501(c)3
Highest Offering: Baccalaureate
Accreditation: &SC, ADNUR, OTA, PTAA

02 Deputy Chancellor and President .... Dr. Laurel WILLIAMSON
05 Provost .... Dr. Aaron KNIGHT
32 Associate VC Student Services .... Ms. Joanna ZIMMERMANN
49 Dean of Liberal Arts & College Prep .... Dr. Kimberly DELAURO
50 Dean Business & Technology .... Mr. Kevin MORRIS
76 Dean Health and Natural Sciences .... Ms. Rhonda BILL
11 Dean Administration .... Mr. Joseph HEBERT
84 Dean Enrollment Services .... Mr. Kevin MCKISSON
43 Dean Comp & Judicial Affairs .... Ms. Clare IANNELLI
92 Director Honors Program .... Dr. Eddie WELLER
55 Director Evening Division .... Mr. Ross KELSEY
08 Director Library .... Mr. Richard MCKAY
41 Director Athletics .... Ms. Kelly SAENZ
88 Dual Credit Director .... Ms. Kristen ROSS
35 Dean Student Development .... Ms. Debbie SMITH
88 Director Education Planning .... Ms. Tanesha ANTOINE
121 Director Student Success Center .... Ms. Diana SHOKRALLA
37 Dean Financial Aid Services .... Mr. Robert MERINO

† Regional accreditation is carried under the parent institution (district office) in Pasadena, TX.

School of Automotive Machinists & Technology (D)

1911 Antoine Drive, Houston TX 77055
County: Harris FICE Identification: 030323
Unit ID: 377218
Telephone: (713) 683-3817 Carnegie Class: Spec 2-yr-Tech
FAX Number: (713) 683-7077 Calendar System: Semester
URL: www.samtech.edu
Established: 1985 Annual Undergrad Tuition & Fees: N/A
Enrollment: 152 Coed
Affiliation or Control: Proprietary IRS Status: Proprietary
Highest Offering: Associate Degree
Accreditation: ACCSC

01 President/Dir of Education .... Judson MASSINGILL
11 CEO/Sch Exec Director/Administrator .... Linda MASSINGILL
37 Financial Aid Director .... Susie FAERMAN

Schreiner University (E)

2100 Memorial Boulevard, Kerrville TX 78028-5611
County: Kerr FICE Identification: 003610
Unit ID: 228042
Telephone: (830) 896-5411 Carnegie Class: Bac-Diverse
FAX Number: (830) 896-3232 Calendar System: Semester
URL: www.schreiner.edu
Established: 1923 Annual Undergrad Tuition & Fees: $31,938
Enrollment: 1,244 Coed
Affiliation or Control: Presbyterian Church (U.S.A.) IRS Status: 501(c)3
Highest Offering: Master's
Accreditation: SC, NURSE

01 President .... Dr. Charlie MCCORMICK
05 Provost/Vice Pres Academic Affairs .... Dr. Travis FRAMPTON
10 Vice Pres Planning & Finance .... Dr. Lucien COSTLEY
84 VP Stdnt Recruit/Ext Rels/Mktg/Comm .... Mr. Mark TUSCHAK
13 Vice Pres Infrastructure .... Mr. Rex QUICK
30 Director of Development .... Ms. Marta DIFFEN
07 Director of Admissions .... Ms. Danielle JENSCHKE
37 Director of Financial Aid .... Ms. Judy CUELLAR
06 Assistant Provost & Registrar .... Ms. Darlene BANNISTER
121 Dean Acad Support/Student Outcomes .... Dr. William WOODS
20 Dean of Faculty .... Dr. William DAVIS
21 Controller .... Ms. Elizabeth OEHLER
42 Campus Minister .... Vacant
32 Dean of Students .... Dr. Charlie HUEBER
27 University Relations Specialist .... Mr. Toby APPLETON
41 Athletic Director .... Mr. Bill RALEIGH
15 Director of Human Resource Services .... Vacant
18 Director Campus Operations .... Mr. Ed WINGARD
29 Alumni Relations Officer .... Mr. Micah WRASE
38 Director Student Counseling .... Ms. Kimberly J. WOODS
36 Director Advising & Career Devel .... Ms. Wendy BLAETTNER
04 Exec Assistant to the President .... Ms. Deborah SCOTT
08 Director Library .... Ms. Lisa MCCORMICK
19 Chief of Security .... Mr. Ken JACOBS
39 Director Residence Life .... Ms. Rachel CAVE
102 Foundation Relations Officer .... Mr. Roy BARTELS
104 Coordinator Multicultural Programs .... Mr. Thomas WOODS

Seminary of the Southwest (F)

501 E. 32nd St., Austin TX 78705
County: Travis FICE Identification: 003566
Unit ID: 224712
Telephone: (512) 472-4133 Carnegie Class: Spec-4-yr-Faith
FAX Number: (512) 472-3098 Calendar System: 4/1/4
URL: www.ssw.edu
Established: 1952 Annual Graduate Tuition & Fees: N/A
Enrollment: 135 Coed
Affiliation or Control: Protestant Episcopal IRS Status: 501(c)3
Highest Offering: Master's; No Undergraduates
Accreditation: SC, CACREP, THEOL

01 Dean & President .... V.Rev. Cynthia B. KITTREDGE
05 Academic Dean .... Dr. Scott BADER-SAYE
03 Executive Vice President .... Mr. Fred CLEMENT
111 VP of Institutional Advancement ...... Mr. Charley SCARBOROUGH
07 Director of Admissions .... Rev. Hope BENKO
26 VP of Communications .... Mr. Eric SCOTT
10 Controller .... Ms. Susan VERSLUYS
06 Registrar/Director of Assessment .... Ms. Madelyn SNODGRASS
08 Director of the Booher Library .... Ms. Alison POAGE
18 Director of Facilities Management .... Mr. Tigh WALTERS
13 Director Information Technology .... Mr. Erik MORROW
100 Chief of Staff to Dean/President .... Ms. Lesley WILDER
30 Director of Development .... Ms. Donna EMERY
88 Director Loise Henderson Wessendorf .... Ms. Gena MINNIX
31 Dean of Community Life ...... Rev. Dan JOSLYN-SIEMIATKOSKI

South Plains College (G)

1401 College Avenue, Levelland TX 79336-6595
County: Hockley FICE Identification: 003611
Unit ID: 228158
Telephone: (806) 894-9611 Carnegie Class: Assoc/MT-VT-Mix Trad/Non
FAX Number: N/A Calendar System: Semester
URL: www.southplainscollege.edu
Established: 1957 Annual Undergrad Tuition & Fees (In-State): $3,892
Enrollment: 8,880 Coed
Affiliation or Control: State IRS Status: 501(c)3
Highest Offering: Associate Degree
Accreditation: SC, ADNUR, COARC, EMT, PTAA, SURGT

01 President .... Dr. Robin SATTERWHITE
05 Vice President Academic Affairs .... Dr. Ryan GIBBS
10 Vice Pres Business Affairs .... Ms. Teresa GREEN
32 Vice President of Student Affairs .... Dr. Stan DEMERRITT
111 Vice Pres Institutional Advancement .... Mr. Stephen S. JOHN
49 Dean of Arts & Sciences .... Mr. Alan WORLEY
76 Dean of Health Occupations .... Mr. Jerry FINLEY
75 Dean of Technical Education .... Mr. Robbie M. BLAIR
51 Dean Continuing & Distance Educ .... Mr. Ryan FITZGERALD
11 Dean Administrative Services .... Mr. Ronnie WATKINS
07 Dean of Admissions & Records .... Ms. Kathryn PEREZ
12 Dean of Reese Center .... Ms. Kara MARTINEZ
09 Assoc Dean of Research & Reports .... Vacant
26 Assoc Dean of College Relations .... Mr. Dane DEWBRE
13 Assoc Dean Information Technology .... Mr. James HOWELL
103 Assoc Dean Workforce Development .... Vacant
35 Assoc Dean of Students .... Mr. Shane HILL
121 Director of Advising and Testing .... Mrs. Lola HERNANDEZ
37 Director of Financial Aid .... Ms. Susan NAZWORTH
08 Director of Libraries .... Mr. Mark GOTTSCHALK
30 Director of Development .... Ms. Julie GERSTENBERGER
15 Director of Human Resources .... Mrs. Jeri Ann DEWBRE
41 Director of Athletics .... Mr. Roger REDING
06 Registrar .... Mr. Andrew RUIZ
18 Director of Physical Plant .... Mr. Cary MARROW
40 Bookstore Manager .... Mr. Roger SHULL
28 Diversity Coord/Career Counselor ..... Ms. Maria LOPEZ-STRONG

South Texas College (H)

3201 W Pecan, McAllen TX 78501
County: Hidalgo FICE Identification: 031034
Unit ID: 409315
Telephone: (956) 872-5051 Carnegie Class: Bac/Assoc-Assoc Dom
FAX Number: (956) 971-3739 Calendar System: Semester
URL: www.southtexascollege.edu
Established: 1993 Annual Undergrad Tuition & Fees (In-District): $4,530
Enrollment: 28,233 Coed
Affiliation or Control: State/Local IRS Status: 501(c)3
Highest Offering: Baccalaureate
Accreditation: SC, ACBSP, ADNUR, CAHIIM, COARC, EMT, OTA, PTAA

01 President .... Mr. Ricardo J. SOLIS
05 Int Vice Pres Academic Affs/CAO .... Dr. Anahid PETROSIAN
10 VP Finance/Administrative Svcs .... Ms. Maria G. ELIZONDO
32 VP Student Affairs/Enroll Mgmt .... Mr. Matthew HEBBARD
88 VP Information Svcs/Planning .... Vacant
111 Vice Pres Institutional Advancement .... Vacant
103 Assoc Dean for Industry & Economy .... Mr. Carlos MARGO
49 Dean Liberal Arts .... Dr. Christopher NELSON
50 Dean Business/Technology .... Vacant
76 Int Dean Nursing/Allied Health .... Mr. Jayson VALERIO
81 Dean Math/Science/BA Programs .... Dr. Ali ESMAEILI
37 Director Student Financial Svcs .... Mr. Juan M. GALVAN
21 Comptroller .... Ms. Myriam LOPEZ
15 Director Human Resources .... Ms. Laura REQUENA
88 Special Assistant to the President .... Mr. Juan Carlos AGUIRRE
96 Director Purchasing .... Ms. Rebecca CAVAZOS
09 Dir Research/Analytical Svcs .... Mr. Serkan CELTEK
121 Dean Student Support Svcs .... Mr. Pablo HERNANDEZ, JR.
18 Director Operations/Maintenance .... Mr. George MCCALEB
18 Director Facilities Plng/Construct .... Mr. Ricardo DE LA GARZA
25 Grants/Contracts Compliance Officer .... Ms. Samantha URIEGAS
12 Campus Administrator Starr Cty .... Dr. Arthuro MONTIEL
12 Campus Administrator Mid-Valley .... Mr. Daniel MONTEZ
16 Employee Relations Officer .... Ms. Jim NAVARRO
106 Dean Distance Learning .... Ms. Rachel SALE
26 Director Public Rels/Marketing .... Vacant
23 Dir of Student Activity/Wellness .... Mr. Elibariki NGUMA
06 Director Student Records/Registrar .... Ms. Cynthia BLANCO
20 Asst to VP Instructional Svcs .... Vacant
19 Director Regional Center for PSE .... Mr. Jose MOROLES
13 Chief Information Officer .... Ms. Alicia GOMEZ
08 Dean Library/Learning Support Svcs .... Mr. Jesus CAMPOS
88 Dir Centers for Lrng Excellence .... Ms. Lynell WILLIAMS
88 Dean Dual Credit Programs .... Dr. Rebecca DE LEON
90 Dir Info Commons Open Labs .... Dr. Lelia SALINAS
35 Dean Student Affairs .... Mr. Pablo HERNANDEZ, JR.
119 Chief Information Security Officer .... Mr. Victor GONZALEZ

South Texas College of Law Houston (I)

1303 San Jacinto Street, Houston TX 77002-7000
County: Harris FICE Identification: 004977
Unit ID: 228194
Telephone: (713) 659-8040 Carnegie Class: Spec-4-yr-Law
FAX Number: (713) 646-2909 Calendar System: Semester
URL: www.stcl.edu
Established: 1923 Annual Graduate Tuition & Fees: N/A

Enrollment: 999 Coed
Affiliation or Control: Independent Non-Profit IRS Status: 501(c)3
Highest Offering: First Professional Degree; No Undergraduates
Accreditation: LAW

01 President and Dean ... Mr. Michael F. BARRY
111 VP Advancement/Alumni Engagement ... Ms. Darcy DOUGLAS
32 Vice President Student Services ... Ms. Mandi GIBSON
05 Vice Pres & Assoc Dean Academics ... Ms. Cherie O. TAYLOR
04 Sr Exec Assistant to President/Dean ... Ms. Jennifer M. HUDSON
10 CFO ... Vacant
20 Vice Pres & Assoc Dean Faculty ... Mr. Ted FIELD
08 Director Library Services ... Ms. Colleen MANNING
88 Senior Director of Advocacy ... Mr. Robert GALLOWAY
78 VP & Assoc Dean Experiential Lrng ... Ms. Catherine G. BURNETT
13 Vice President Technology ... Mr. Randy MARAK
28 VP of Diversity/Equity & Inclusion ... Prof. Shelby MOORE
15 COO & General Counsel ... Mr. Steve ALDERMAN
26 Director Marketing/Communications ... Vacant
35 Assistant Dean Student Affairs ... Ms. Gena L. SINGLETON
36 Sr Director of Career Resources ... Ms. Nazleen JIWANI
07 Assistant Dean for Admissions ... Ms. Alicia CRAMER
21 Controller ... Ms. Kim GOODWIN
19 Director Security ... Mr. Kent BRAZELTON
24 Sr Director Instruct Technology ... Mr. Terry SMITH
14 Sr Director Information Services ... Mr. George MILZ
44 Dir Annual Giv & Alumni Engagement ... Ms. Kia WISSMILLER
102 Dir of Foundations & Corp Relations ... Ms. Julie BLAIR
18 Chief Facilities/Physical Plant ... Mr. William HILL
96 Sr Dir Purchasing & Office Services ... Ms. Dorrie RUSHING
26 Director of Public Relations ... Ms. Claire CATON
101 Secretary of the Institution/Board ... Ms. Jennifer M. HUDSON
104 Asst Dean Inst Compl & Intl Pgms ... Ms. Wanda MORROW
108 Director Institutional Assessment ... Ms. Francesca BONADUCE DE NIGRIS
121 Asst Dean Academic Success ... Ms. Lisa YARROW
15 Director of Human Resources ... Ms. Lauren DEVORE

South University-Austin (A)

1220 W. Louis Henna Boulevard, Round Rock TX 78681
Telephone: (512) 516-8800 Identification: 770917
Accreditation: &SC, ACBSP, NURSE, PTAA

† Branch campus of South University, Savannah, GA

Southern Bible Institute and College (B)

PO Box 763609, Dallas TX 75376
County: Dallas Identification: 667365
Telephone: (972) 224-5481 Carnegie Class: Not Classified
FAX Number: (972) 224-9517 Calendar System: Semester
URL: www.southernbible.org
Established: Annual Undergrad Tuition & Fees: N/A
Enrollment: N/A Coed
Affiliation or Control: Non-denominational IRS Status: 501(c)3
Highest Offering: Baccalaureate
Accreditation: @BI

01 President ... Dr. Martin E. HAWKINS
05 EVP & Chief Academic Officer ... Rev. Terrance FORD

Southern Careers Institute (C)

1701 W. Ben White Blvd, Ste 100, Austin TX 78704
County: Travis FICE Identification: 030353
Unit ID: 226903
Telephone: (512) 432-1400 Carnegie Class: Not Classified
FAX Number: (512) 432-1401 Calendar System: Other
URL: scitexas.edu
Established: 1960 Annual Undergrad Tuition & Fees: N/A
Enrollment: 987 Coed
Affiliation or Control: Proprietary IRS Status: Proprietary
Highest Offering: Associate Degree
Accreditation: COE

01 Campus Director ... David PALMER

Southern Methodist University (D)

6425 Boaz Lane, Dallas TX 75205-0100
County: Dallas FICE Identification: 003613
Unit ID: 228246
Telephone: (214) 768-2000 Carnegie Class: DU-Higher
FAX Number: (214) 768-1001 Calendar System: Semester
URL: www.smu.edu
Established: 1911 Annual Undergrad Tuition & Fees: $58,540
Enrollment: 12,373 Coed
Affiliation or Control: Independent Non-Profit IRS Status: 501(c)3
Highest Offering: Doctorate
Accreditation: SC, ART, CACREP, CLPSY, DANCE, LAW, MUS, THEA, THEOL

01 President ... Dr. R. Gerald TURNER
11 VP Executive Affairs ... Dr. Harold W. STANLEY
05 Provost/VP Academic Affairs ... Dr. Elizabeth G. LOBOA
10 VP Business & Finance/Treasurer ... Ms. Chris C. REGIS
30 VP Devel & External Affairs ... Mr. Brad E. CHEVES
43 Gen Counsel/VP Leg Affs/Govt Rels ... Mr. Paul J. WARD
32 VP Student Affairs ... Dr. Kenechukwu (K.C.) MMEJE
41 Director of Athletics ... Mr. Richard L. HART
115 Chief Investment Officer ... Mr. Rakesh DAHIYA
13 Chief Information Officer ... Dr. Michael H. HITES
20 Assoc Provost for Faculty Success ... Dr. Paige WARE
20 Assoc Prov Curric Innov/Policy ... Dr. Peter K. MOORE
121 Assoc Provost Stdnt Acad Success ... Dr. Sheri KUNOVICH
108 Assoc Prov Inst Plng/Effectiveness ... Dr. Patricia ALVEY
51 Int Assoc Provost Continuing Educ ... Dr. Michael J. ROBERTSON
58 Assoc Provost Rsrch/Dean Grad Stds ... Dr. James E. QUICK
84 Assoc VP Enroll Management ... Mr. Wes K. WAGGONER
15 Assoc VP/Chief Human Res Officer ... Ms. Sheri STARKEY
117 Assoc VP/Chief Risk Officer ... Mr. Warren RICKS
114 Assoc VP Budgets ... Mr. Ernie BARRY
35 Assoc VP & Dean of Students ... Dr. Melinda SUTTON NOSS
109 Assoc VP of Campus Services ... Ms. Alison TWEEDY
18 Assoc VP Facilities Plng/Management ... Mr. Michael S. MOLINA
100 Asst Provost/Chief of Staff ... Mr. Daniel P. EADY
49 Dean Dedman College ... Dr. Thomas DIPIERO
50 Dean Cox School of Business ... Dr. Matthew B. MYERS
54 Dean Lyle School of Engr ... Dr. Marc CHRISTENSEN
57 Dean Meadows Sch of the Arts ... Dr. Sam HOLLAND
53 Dean Sch of Educ/Human Dev ... Dr. Stephanie L. KNIGHT
61 Dean Dedman School of Law ... Ms. Jennifer M. COLLINS
73 Dean Perkins School of Theology ... Dr. Craig C. HILL
08 Dean of SMU Libraries ... Ms. Holly JEFFCOAT
07 Dean of Undergraduate Admissions ... Ms. Elena D. HICKS
26 Asst VP for Public Affairs ... Ms. Regina MOLDOVAN
112 Asst VP for Principal & Major Gifts ... Mr. Blake DAVIS
19 Chief of Police ... Mr. Jim L. WALTERS
06 Exec Dir Enroll Services/Registrar ... Mr. Robert L. LOTHRINGER
113 University Bursar ... Mr. Albert JABOUR
42 Chaplain/Minister to the University ... Rev. Lisa GARVIN
37 Exec Director Financial Aid ... Mr. Marc PETERSON
12 Executive Director SMU-in-Taos ... Dr. Michael ADLER
27 Exec Dir of Creative Marketing ... Ms. Emily HUGHES ARMOUR
88 Exec Dir Program Services/Donor Rel ... Ms. Dana AYRES
44 Exec Dir Annual Giving/Alumni Rel ... Ms. Astria SMITH
23 Assoc Dean of Health Services ... Dr. Randy P. JONES
04 EA to Pres/Exec Dir Inst Acc/Eqty ... Ms. Samantha THOMAS
119 Chief Security Officer ... Mr. George FINNEY
116 Chief of Compliance/Audit Services ... Mr. Dexter E. BURGER
58 Asst Dean of Graduate Studies ... Dr. Alan ITKIN
104 Director Study Abroad ... Ms. Christie PEARSON
96 Director of Procurement ... Ms. Shannon BROWN
25 Director of Sponsored Projects ... Ms. Ruth V. LOZANO
38 Director of Counseling Services ... Dr. Cathey SOUTTER
102 Dir Corp & Foundation Relations ... Mr. Rob STRAUSS
29 Dir Alumni Relations/Engagement ... Ms. Mary Margaret RANGEL
91 Exec Dir of Application Support ... Mr. Curt HERRIDGE
90 Exec Dir of Academic Technology ... Mr. Jason WARNER
09 Director of Institutional Research ... Dr. Michael D. TUMEO
39 Asst VP/Dean Res Life/Stdnt Housing ... Ms. Melinda CARLSON

Southern Reformed College and Seminary (E)

26111 Beckendorff Rd, Katy TX 77493
County: Harris Identification: 667364
Telephone: (713) 467-4501 Carnegie Class: Not Classified
FAX Number: N/A Calendar System: Semester
URL: srsem.net
Established: Annual Undergrad Tuition & Fees: N/A
Enrollment: N/A Coed
Affiliation or Control: Independent Non-Profit IRS Status: 501(c)3
Highest Offering: Master's
Accreditation: @BI

01 President/CEO ... Dr. James A. LEE
32 Vice President for Student Affairs ... Dr. Steve W. HALL
05 Academic Dean ... Sungho KIM
10 Chief Financial Officer ... Ileen YIM

Southwest School of Art (F)

300 Augusta Street, San Antonio TX 78205
County: Bexar Identification: 667407
Telephone: (210) 200-8200 Carnegie Class: Not Classified
FAX Number: (210) 224-9337 Calendar System: Semester
URL: www.swschool.org
Established: 1965 Annual Undergrad Tuition & Fees: N/A
Enrollment: N/A Coed
Affiliation or Control: Independent Non-Profit IRS Status: 501(c)3
Highest Offering: Baccalaureate
Accreditation: ART

01 President ... Paula OWENS

Southwest Texas Junior College (G)

2401 Garner Field Road, Uvalde TX 78801-6221
County: Uvalde FICE Identification: 003614
Unit ID: 228316
Telephone: (830) 278-4401 Carnegie Class: Assoc/HT-Mix Trad/Non
FAX Number: (830) 591-7354 Calendar System: Semester
URL: www.swtjc.edu
Established: 1946 Annual Undergrad Tuition & Fees (In-District): $4,062
Enrollment: 6,480 Coed
Affiliation or Control: Local IRS Status: 501(c)3
Highest Offering: Associate Degree
Accreditation: SC

01 President ... Dr. Hector GONZALES
11 Vice President Administrative Svcs ... Mr. Derek SANDOVAL
32 Vice President Student Services ... Mrs. Margot MATA
10 Vice President Finance ... Dr. Anne TARSKI
05 Vice President Academic Services ... Dr. Mark UNDERWOOD
12 Vice President Del Rio ... Mrs. Connie BUCHANAN
12 Vice President Eagle Pass ... Mr. Gilbert S. BERMEA
103 Dean of Workforce Education ... Mr. Juan (Johnny) C. GUZMAN
49 Dean of College of Liberal Arts ... Dr. Cheryl L. SANCHEZ
121 Director of Academic Advising ... Vacant
37 Director of Financial Aid ... Ms. Yvette HERNANDEZ
13 Co-Director of Information Tech ... Ms. Denise ODEN
13 Co-Director of Information Tech ... Mr. Frankie PANNELL
18 Physical Plant Director ... Mr. Kirk M. PALERMO
35 Director Student Success ... Dr. Randa SCHELL
15 Human Resources Coordinator ... Mr. Oscar S. GARCIA
09 Director of Institutional Research ... Dr. Renee ZIMMERMAN
06 Registrar ... Mr. Steve MARTINEZ
08 Head Librarian ... Ms. Brenda CANTU
19 Director Security/Safety ... Mr. Jimmy CALLIHAM
96 Purchasing Manager ... Vacant

Southwest University at El Paso (H)

1414 Geronimo Drive, El Paso TX 79925
County: El Paso FICE Identification: 041317
Unit ID: 451556
Telephone: (915) 778-4001 Carnegie Class: Bac/Assoc-Mixed
FAX Number: (915) 778-1575 Calendar System: Other
URL: www.southwestuniversity.edu
Established: 2001 Annual Undergrad Tuition & Fees: $16,000
Enrollment: 1,558 Coed
Affiliation or Control: Proprietary IRS Status: Proprietary
Highest Offering: Baccalaureate
Accreditation: ABHES, IACBE, NURSE, #RAD

02 President ... Mr. Ben ARRIOLA, JR.
11 Vice President/School Director ... Ms. Marisol GUTIERREZ
05 Vice Pres/Academic Dean ... Mr. Jeremy BURCIAGA

Southwestern Adventist University (I)

100 W Hillcrest Street, Keene TX 76059-0567
County: Johnson FICE Identification: 003619
Unit ID: 228468
Telephone: (817) 645-3921 Carnegie Class: Bac-Diverse
FAX Number: (817) 202-6744 Calendar System: Semester
URL: www.swau.edu
Established: 1893 Annual Undergrad Tuition & Fees: $22,836
Enrollment: 754 Coed
Affiliation or Control: Seventh-day Adventist IRS Status: 501(c)3
Highest Offering: Master's
Accreditation: SC, IACBE, NURSE

01 President ... Mrs. Ana PATTERSON
05 VP for Academic Administration ... Dr. Donna BERKNER
10 VP for Financial Administration ... Mr. Joel WALLACE
84 VP for Enrollment ... Ms. Rahneeka HAZELTON
32 VP for Student Services ... Mr. James THE
111 VP for Advancement ... Mr. Tony REYES
42 VP for Spiritual Development ... Mr. Russ LAUGHLIN
20 Asst VP for Academic Admin ... Dr. Marcel SARGEANT
37 Asst VP for Student Finance ... Mr. Duane VALENCIA
21 Asst VP Financial Administration ... Mr. Greg A. WICKLUND
06 Registrar ... Mr. Jason KOWARSCH
08 Librarian ... Ms. Cristina M. THOMSEN
34 Dean of Women ... Mrs. Janelle D. WILLIAMS
33 Dean of Men ... Mr. William IVERSON
13 Dir Information Technology Svcs ... Mr. E. Charles LEWIS
18 Plant Engineer ... Mr. Ken HANSON
26 Director of Marketing ... Mr. Timothy KOSAKA
30 Director for Development ... Mrs. Mirasari LAM
29 Alumni/Communications Officer ... Mrs. Susan GRADY
38 Director of Counseling & Testing ... Dr. Keila SANTOS-CRESPO
22 Director of Disability Services ... Dr. Marcel SARGEANT
121 Dir Ctr for Acad Success/Advising ... Mrs. Renata OCAMPO
89 Project Director for HSI ... Mr. Austen POWELL
07 Director of Admissions ... Ms. Rahneeka HAZELTON
15 Director of Human Resources ... Ms. Genelle ROGERS
19 Assoc Director of Security ... Mr. Matthew AGEE
25 Grant Writer ... Dr. Tom BUNCH
41 Athletic Director ... Mr. Tyler WOOLDRIDGE
50 Chair Business Dept ... Dr. Aaron MOSES
53 Chair Education Dept ... Dr. Cheryl THE
04 Special Assistant to the President ... Vacant

Southwestern Assemblies of God University (J)

1200 Sycamore, Waxahachie TX 75165-2397
County: Ellis FICE Identification: 003616
Unit ID: 228325
Telephone: (972) 937-4010 Carnegie Class: Masters/S
FAX Number: (972) 923-0488 Calendar System: Semester
URL: www.sagu.edu
Established: 1927 Annual Undergrad Tuition & Fees: $19,834
Enrollment: 1,985 Coed
Affiliation or Control: Assemblies Of God Church IRS Status: 501(c)3
Highest Offering: Doctorate
Accreditation: SC, IACBE, SW

01 President ... Dr. Kermit S. BRIDGES
05 Vice President for Academics ... Dr. Paul BROOKS

32 Vice President for Student Develop ... Rev. Terry PHIPPS
10 Vice Pres for Business & Finance ... Dr. Fred GORE
111 Vice President for Univ Advancement ... Rev. Rick BOWLES
20 Dean of Academic Services ... Rev. Donny LUTRICK
58 Dean of Graduate Studies ... Dr. Dennis ROBINSON
73 Dean Col Bible & Church Ministries ... Dr. Michael CLARENSAU
50 Dean Col of Business & Education ... Dr. Sue TAYLOR
09 VP Inst Effectiveness/Dn Col Music ... Dr. Kim JAMES
106 Dean for Dist Educ & Ext Sites ... Rev. Joseph HARTMAN
06 Registrar ... Ms. Shelly MCMULLIN
35 Dean of Students ... Rev. Lance MECHE
88 Director of Learning Centers ... Mr. Nolan JONES
13 Sr Dir Information Technology ... Mr. Kirk PASCHALL
29 Director of Alumni Relations ... Vacant
08 Director of Learning Resources ... Ms. Radonna HOLMES
14 Director of Campus Software ... Mr. Mark WALKER
21 Dir of Business Services ... Ms. Katie WHITE
88 Senior Director of Accounting ... Ms. Alicia HAMILTON
37 Sr Director of Financial Aid ... Mr. Jeff FRANCIS
19 Director of Security ... Mr. Ron CRANE
07 Assistant Dean of Admissions ... Mr. Joshua MARTIN
24 Director of Media Services ... Mr. John COOKMAN
88 Director of Accounts Receivable ... Ms. Candace LUTRICK
36 Director of Career Development ... Ms. Beverly ROBINSON
41 Athletic Director ... Dr. Jesse GODDING
26 Director of University Marketing ... Rev. Rick BOWLES
15 Director of Human Resources ... Mrs. Ruth ROBERTS
88 Director of Admissions Info Systems ... Mr. Jarrod PACE
04 Executive Asst to President ... Ms. Patricia BROOKS
108 Director Institutional Assessment ... Rev. Jerry ROBERTS

Southwestern Baptist Theological Seminary (A)

PO Box 22370, Fort Worth TX 76122
County: Tarrant — FICE Identification: 003617
Unit ID: 494603
Telephone: (817) 923-1921 — Carnegie Class: Not Classified
FAX Number: (817) 921-8766 — Calendar System: Semester
URL: www.swbts.edu
Established: 1908 — Annual Undergrad Tuition & Fees: $8,980
Enrollment: N/A — Coed
Affiliation or Control: Southern Baptist — IRS Status: 501(c)3
Highest Offering: Doctorate
Accreditation: SC, MUS, THEOL

01 President ... Dr. Adam W. GREENWAY
05 Provost & VP for Academic Admin ... Dr. David S. DOCKERY
10 VP for Business Administration ... Mr. Clark LOGAN
111 VP for Institutional Advancement ... Dr. Ed UPTON
26 VP for Strategic Initiatives ... Mr. Colby T. ADAMS
20 Assoc Provost for Academic Svcs ... Dr. Travis H. TRAWICK
73 Dean School of Theology ... Dr. Jeffrey BINGHAM
53 Dean Sch of Educational Ministries ... Dr. Michael S. WILDER
64 Dean School of Church Music/Worship ... Dr. Joseph R. CRIDER
88 Dean School of Evangelism/Missions ... Dr. John D. MASSEY
12 Dean Texas Baptist College ... Dr. Benjamin M. SKAUG
32 Dean of Students ... Dr. Charles CARPENTER
34 Dean of Women ... Dr. Terri H. STOVALL

Southwestern Christian College (B)

Box 10, Terrell TX 75160-9002
County: Kaufman — FICE Identification: 003618
Unit ID: 228486
Telephone: (972) 524-3341 — Carnegie Class: Bac/Assoc-Mixed
FAX Number: (972) 563-7133 — Calendar System: Semester
URL: www.swcc.edu
Established: 1949 — Annual Undergrad Tuition & Fees: $8,132
Enrollment: 84 — Coed
Affiliation or Control: Churches Of Christ — IRS Status: 501(c)3
Highest Offering: Baccalaureate
Accreditation: #SC

01 President/CEO ... Dr. Ervin SEAMSTER, JR.
30 Vice President for Inst Expansion ... Dr. James MAXWELL
05 Chief Academic Officer ... Dr. Deborah HODRIDGE
10 Vice President Fiscal Affairs ... Mr. Douglas HOWIE
26 Vice President Public Relations ... Vacant
09 VP of Inst Research/Comptroller ... Ms. Joyce CATHEY
08 Librarian ... Ms. Shirley HUDSON
32 Interim Dean of Students ... Mr. Matthew L. TERRY, SR.
07 Director Admissions/Retention ... Mr. Shane MUSHONGA
37 Director of Financial Aid ... Mr. Eric KING
121 Director of Student Success ... Ms. Kecia BAKER
04 Admin Assistant to the President ... Dr. Stevie ROBERTS
06 Registrar ... Dr. Lisa JACKSON
19 Chief of Police ... Mr. Matthew L. TERRY, SR.
29 President Alumni Affairs ... Ms. Vernesha CATHEY
41 Athletic Director ... Mr. Bruce JOHNSON

Southwestern University (C)

1001 E University Avenue, Georgetown TX 78626-6144
County: Williamson — FICE Identification: 003620
Unit ID: 228343
Telephone: (512) 863-6511 — Carnegie Class: Bac-A&S
FAX Number: (512) 863-5788 — Calendar System: Semester
URL: www.southwestern.edu
Established: 1840 — Annual Undergrad Tuition & Fees: $45,120
Enrollment: 1,506 — Coed
Affiliation or Control: United Methodist — IRS Status: 501(c)3
Highest Offering: Baccalaureate
Accreditation: SC, MUS

01 President ... Dr. Laura TROMBLEY
42 University Chaplain ... Vacant
04 Exec Asst for Pres/Board Liaison ... Ms. Patricia WITT
05 Dean of Faculty ... Dr. Alisa GAUNDER
32 Vice President for Student Life ... Ms. Jaime WOODY
13 Assoc VP Information Technology ... Mr. Todd WATSON
10 VP for Finance and Administration ... Mr. Craig ERWIN
30 Vice Pres for University Relations ... Mr. Paul SECORD
20 Assoc VP for Academic Affairs ... Ms. Julie A. COWLEY
26 VP Integrated Communications/CMO ... Ms. Scarlett MOSS
15 Assoc VP for Human Resources ... Ms. Elma F. BENAVIDES
35 Dean of Students ... Ms. Shelley STORY
29 Assoc VP for Alumni & Parents ... Ms. Megan FRISQUE
44 Director of Annual Giving ... Mr. Wesley CLARK
41 Assoc VP Intercollegiate Athletics ... Dr. Glenn SCHWAB
21 Assoc VP Finance Acct/Controller ... Ms. Brenda THOMPSON
19 Chief of Police ... Mr. Brad DUNN
84 Dean of Enrollment Services ... Ms. Christine BOWMAN
36 Dir Ctr Career & Prof Development ... Mr. Daniel OROZCO
121 Dir of Academic Success ... Mr. David SEILER
88 Dir Paideia Program/Assoc Professor ... Dr. Sergio COSTOLA
85 Director Intercultural Learning ... Ms. Monya LEMERY
09 Dir Inst Research & Effectiveness ... Ms. Natasha WILLIAMS
28 Asst Dean Multicultural Affairs ... Ms. Terri JOHNSON
31 Sr Dir Community Engaged Learning ... Dr. Sarah BRACKMANN
08 Dir of Library Resources ... Ms. Amy ANDERSON
84 VP Recruitment & Enrollment ... Mr. Tom F. DELAHUNT
91 Director Administrative Computing ... Ms. Jennifer O'DANIEL
102 Senior Dir of Foundation Relations ... Ms. Sonya ROBINSON
105 Webmaster ... Mr. Ed HILLIS
18 Assoc VP Facilities Management ... Mr. Rick MARTINEZ
39 Director of Residence Life ... Ms. Lisa DELA CRUZ

Stark College & Seminary (D)

7000 Ocean Drive, Corpus Christi TX 78412
County: Nueces — Identification: 667345
Telephone: (361) 991-9403 — Carnegie Class: Not Classified
FAX Number: N/A — Calendar System: Semester
URL: www.stark.edu
Established: 1947 — Annual Undergrad Tuition & Fees: N/A
Enrollment: N/A — Coed
Affiliation or Control: Independent Non-Profit — IRS Status: 501(c)3
Highest Offering: Master's
Accreditation: BI

01 President ... Dr. Anthony CELELLI
05 Provost ... Dr. Jena DUNN
10 Chief Financial/ Business Officer ... Dr. Chris STAPPER
32 Chief Student Affairs/Life Officer ... Tina VILLARREAL COOPER

Stephen F. Austin State University (E)

1936 North St., Nacogdoches TX 75962
County: Nacogdoches — FICE Identification: 003624
Unit ID: 228431
Telephone: (936) 468-3401 — Carnegie Class: DU-Mod
FAX Number: N/A — Calendar System: Semester
URL: www.sfasu.edu
Established: 1923 — Annual Undergrad Tuition & Fees (In-State): $10,600
Enrollment: 12,620 — Coed
Affiliation or Control: State — IRS Status: 501(c)3
Highest Offering: Doctorate
Accreditation: SC, AAFCS, ART, #CAATE, CACREP, CAEPN, CIDA, DIETD, DIETI, IPSY, MUS, NUR, SP, SW, THEA

01 President ... Dr. Scott GORDON
05 Provost/EVP Academic Affairs ... Dr. Lorenzo SMITH
10 Int VP Finance/Administration ... Ms. Judith KRUWELL
32 VP for University Affairs ... Dr. Brandon FRYE
111 Vice Pres University Advancement ... Ms. Jill STILL
29 Exec Director Alumni ... Mr. Craig A. TURNAGE
20 Assoc Provost Academic Affairs ... Dr. Marc GUIDRY
84 Exec Dir of Enrollment Mgmt ... Ms. Erma BRECHT
26 Exec Dir Univ Mktg Comm ... Dr. Shirley LUNA
43 General Counsel ... Mr. Damon DERRICK
06 Registrar ... Mr. Mickey DIEZ
09 Director Institutional Research ... Ms. Karyn HALL
08 Library Director ... Mr. Jonathan HELMKE
39 Director of Residence Life ... Mr. Winston BAKER
18 Director of Physical Plant ... Mr. Ron WATSON
37 Director of Financial Aid ... Ms. Rachele GARRETT
22 Director Affirmative Action ... Vacant
13 Chief Information Officer ... Mr. Anthony ESPINOZA
15 Interim Director of Human Resources ... Mr. John WYATT
19 Chief of University Police ... Mr. John FIELDS
23 Director Health Services ... Dr. Janice LEDET
41 Director of Athletics ... Mr. Ryan IVEY
35 Assistant Dean for Student Affairs ... Dr. Hollie GAMMEL-SMITH
38 Director of Counseling ... Ms. Jill MILEM
96 Director of Procurement ... Ms. Kay JOHNSON
46 Dir Research/Sponsored Programs ... Vacant
58 Dean Research & Graduate Studies ... Dr. Pauline SAMPSON
49 Dean College Liberal/Applied Arts ... Dr. Brian MURPHY
47 Dean College Forestry/Agriculture ... Dr. Hans M. WILLIAMS
53 Dean of College of Education ... Dr. Judy A. ABBOTT
57 Dean College Fine Arts ... Dr. A.C. (Buddy) HIMES
50 Dean College of Business ... Dr. Timothy BISPING
81 Dean College Sciences & Math ... Dr. Kimberly M. CHILDS
04 Asst to the President ... Ms. Joann BLACK
101 Coordinator of Board Affairs ... Ms. April SMITH
30 Exec Director of Development ... Dr. Trey TURNER
104 Director International Programs ... Ms. Heather CATTON
105 Asst Director Web Services ... Mr. Jason L. JOHNSTONE
106 Int Dir Ctr for Teaching & Learning ... Ms. Megan WEATHERLY
108 Dir Institutional Effectiveness ... Mr. John CALAHAN
28 Asst Dn Equity/Diversity/ Inclusion ... Dr. Michara DELANEY-FIELDS
07 Associate Director of Admissions ... Mr. Kevin L. DAVIS

Tarrant County College District (F)

300 Trinity Campus Circle, Fort Worth TX 76102-6599
County: Tarrant — FICE Identification: 003626
Unit ID: 228547
Telephone: (817) 515-5100 — Carnegie Class: Assoc/HT-Mix Trad/Non
FAX Number: (817) 515-5350 — Calendar System: Semester
URL: www.tccd.edu
Established: 1965 — Annual Undergrad Tuition & Fees (In-District): $3,402
Enrollment: 43,000 — Coed
Affiliation or Control: State/Local — IRS Status: 501(c)3
Highest Offering: Associate Degree
Accreditation: SC, ACFEI, ADNUR, CAHIIM, COARC, CONST, DH, DIETT, DMS, EMT, NMT, PTAA, RAD, SURGT

01 Chancellor ... Dr. Eugene V. GIOVANNINI
11 Chief Operating Officer ... Ms. Susan ALANIS
13 Chief Technology Officer ... Mr. Robert PACHECO
05 Exec Vice Chancellor & Provost ... Dr. Elva C. LEBLANC
103 EVP Corp Solutions/Economic Dev ... Ms. Shannon BRYANT
26 VC Communications/External Affairs ... Mr. Reginald GATES
20 VP Academic Affairs SO ... Dr. Shannon YDOYAGA
20 VP Academic Affairs NE ... Dr. Ritu RAJU
20 VP Academic Affairs NW ... Dr. Judith GALLAGHER
20 VP Academic Affairs SE ... Dr. Zena JACKSON
20 VP Academic Affairs TR ... Dr. Thomas MILLS
20 VP Academic Affairs TCC Connect ... Dr. Shelley PEARSON
32 VP Student Dev Services NE ... Dr. Mayra OLIVARES-URUETA
32 VP Student Dev Services SE ... Dr. Michael DUPONT
32 VP Student Dev Services SO ... Vacant
32 VP Student Dev Services TR ... Dr. Julie AMON
32 VP Student Dev Services NW ... Dr. Jan CLAYTON
12 President South Campus ... Dr. Daniel LUFKIN
12 President Northwest Campus ... Dr. Zarina BLANKENBAKER
12 President Northeast Campus ... Dr. Kenya AYERS
12 President Southeast Campus ... Dr. William COPPOLA
12 President Trinity River Campus ... Dr. Stephen S. MADISON
12 President TCC Connect Campus ... Dr. Carlos MORALES
84 Assoc Vice Chanc Enrol/Acad Support ... Mr. David XIMENEZ
15 Exec Director of Human Resources ... Ms. Gloria MADDOX-POWELL
25 District Exec Dir Grants Dev/Compl ... Ms. Kim MOSS-LINNEAR
21 Assoc Vice Chancellor Finance ... Mrs. Nancy H. CHANG
20 Assoc VChanc Acad Affs/Stdnt Dev ... Vacant
111 Executive Vice Pres of Advancement ... Dr. Kristen BENNETT
09 Exec Dir Inst Intell & Research ... Vacant
27 Exec Dir Comm/PR/Marketing ... Ms. Suzanne GROVES
18 Exec Dir Real Estate/Facilities ... Mr. Okang HEMMINGS
19 Chief of Police ... Mr. Shaun WILLIAMS
20 Dist Reg & Dir Academic Supp Svcs ... Mr. John D. SPENCER
08 Director Library Services NE ... Mr. Mark DOLIVE
08 Director Library Services SO ... Ms. Laura MCKINNON
08 Director Library Services NW ... Mr. Alex POTEMKIN
08 Director Library Services SE ... Ms. Jotisa KLEMM
08 Director Library Services TR ... Ms. Susan SMITH
06 Registrar South Campus ... Ms. Vanessa WALKER
06 Registrar Northeast Campus ... Vacant
06 Registrar Northwest Campus ... Ms. Christy KLEMIUK
06 Registrar Southeast Campus ... Mr. Kenne EVANS
06 Registrar Trinity Campus ... Mr. Vikas RAJPUROHIT
38 Director of Counseling SO ... Ms. Ticily MEDLEY
38 Director of Counseling NE ... Dr. Condoa PARRENT
38 Director of Counseling NW ... Ms. Robin WASHINGTON-WHITE
38 Director of Counseling SE ... Ms. Renetta WRIGHT
38 Director of Counseling TR ... Dr. Deidra TURNER
37 District Director Financial Aid ... Ms. Samantha STALNAKER
37 Director of Financial Aid SO ... Ms. JoLynn H. SPROLE
37 Director of Financial Aid NE ... Ms. Mary BLEDSOE
37 Director of Financial Aid NW ... Ms. Trina SMITH-PATTERSON
37 Director of Financial Aid SE ... Ms. Elizabeth LANDWERMEYER
37 Director of Financial Aid TR ... Mr. William MCMULLEN
35 Dir Student Development Svcs NE ... Mr. Victor BALLESTEROS
35 Dir Student Development Svcs SO ... Vacant
35 Dir Student Development Svcs NW ... Dr. Vesta M. MARTINEZ
35 Dir Student Development Svcs SE ... Mr. Douglas C. PEAK
35 Dir Student Development Svcs TR ... Mr. Carter BEDFORD
109 Director of Business Services ... Mrs. Kathy M. CRUSTO-WAY
96 Exec Dir of Procurement ... Mr. Michael (Mike) HERNDON
18 Exec Dir Inst Strategic Development ... Ms. Margaret K. LUTTON
07 Dist Dir of Admiss & Records ... Ms. Rebecca (Becki) GRIFFITH
28 Chief Diversity/Equity/Inclus Ofcr ... Dr. Eric CASTILLO
43 Associate General Counsel ... Ms. Carol BRACKEN
100 Chief of Staff ... Dr. Kelley MILLS

Temple College (G)

2600 S First Street, Temple TX 76504-7435
County: Bell — FICE Identification: 003627
Unit ID: 228608
Telephone: (254) 298-8282 — Carnegie Class: Assoc/MT-VT-High Trad
FAX Number: (254) 298-8266 — Calendar System: Semester
URL: www.templejc.edu
Established: 1926 — Annual Undergrad Tuition & Fees (In-District): $4,512
Enrollment: 4,940 — Coed
Affiliation or Control: Local — IRS Status: 501(c)3

Highest Offering: Associate Degree
Accreditation: SC, ADNUR, COARC, DH, DMS, EMT, SURGT

01 President ....Dr. Christina PONCE
05 Vice Pres Academic Affairs ....Dr. Susan GUZMAN-TREVINO
10 Vice Pres Administrative Svcs/CFO ....Mr. Brandon BOZON
30 Vice President Development ....Dr. Evelyn WAIWAIOLE
103 Vice Pres Workforce Development ....Ms. Dede GRIFFITH
21 AVP of Finance ....Ms. Susan ALLAMON
15 Assoc VP Resource Management ....Vacant
106 Dir Web Applications & System ....Ms. Lindsay WILLIAMS
84 Div Dir Student & Enrollment Svcs ....Mrs. Carey ROSE
08 Div Director of Learning Resources ....Ms. Carrie CRUCE
38 Director Student Advising ....Ms. Mandy HART
04 Assistant to the President & Board ....Mrs. Judith DOHNALIK
37 Director of Financial Aid ....Ms. Mary DANIEL
26 Director Marketing/Public Relations ....Ms. Ellen DAVIS
18 Dir Facilities/Physical Plant ....Mr. Jeremy ALLAMON
96 Director of Purchasing ....Mr. Brian SUPAK
32 Director Student Life ....Mrs. Ruth BRIDGES
06 Registrar ....Mrs. Toni CUELLAR
41 Athletic Director ....Mr. Craig MCMURTRY
19 Chief of Police ....Mr. Michael MARKUM
13 Dir Information Technology Svcs ....Mr. Shawn DACH

Texarkana College (A)

2500 N Robison Road, Texarkana TX 75599
County: Bowie
FICE Identification: 003628
Unit ID: 228699
Telephone: (903) 823-3456
Carnegie Class: Assoc/HVT-High Non
FAX Number: (903) 823-3451
Calendar System: Semester
URL: www.texarkanacollege.edu
Established: 1927
Annual Undergrad Tuition & Fees (In-District): $3,820
Enrollment: 3,810
Coed
Affiliation or Control: Local
IRS Status: 501(c)3
Highest Offering: Associate Degree
Accreditation: SC, ADNUR, EMT

01 President ....Dr. Jason SMITH
05 Vice President of Instruction ....Dr. Donna MCDANIEL
10 Chief Finance Officer ....Mrs. Kim JONES
32 Dean of Students ....Mr. Robert JONES
13 Chief Info Technology Officer ....Mr. Mike DUMDEI
30 Director Foundation/Development ....Mrs. Katie ANDRUS
09 Director Inst Rsrch & Effectiveness ....Mrs. Phyllis DEESE
18 Director Facilities Services ....Mr. Rick BOYETTE
26 Director Inst Adv/Public Relations ....Mrs. Suzy IRWIN
88 Director KTXK Radio ....Mr. Steve MITCHELL
15 Director Human Resources ....Mrs. Phyllis DEESE
103 Dean Workforce & Cont Education ....Mr. Brandon WASHINGTON
81 Dean STEM ....Dr. Catherine HOWARD
76 Dean Health Sciences ....Mrs. Courtney SHOALMIRE
49 Dean Liberal & Performing Arts ....Mrs. Mary E. YOUNG
50 Dean Business & Social Sciences ....Dr. John Dixon BOYLES
08 Director Library/Student Support ....Dr. Tonja MACKEY
84 Enrollment Management/Registrar ....Mr. Brandon HIGGINS
07 Director of Admissions ....Mr. Lee WILLIAMS
37 Director Student Financial Aid ....Mrs. Susan JOHNSTON
04 Presidential Events Coordinator ....Mrs. Mindy PRESTON

*The Texas A & M University System Office (B)

301 Tarrow Street, 7th Floor, College Station TX 77840
County: Brazos
FICE Identification: 003629
Unit ID: 228732
Telephone: (979) 458-6000
Carnegie Class: N/A
FAX Number: (979) 458-6044
URL: www.tamus.edu

01 Chancellor ....Mr. John SHARP
05 Vice Chanc for Academic Affairs ....Dr. James HALLMARK
10 Deputy Chancellor & CFO ....Mr. Billy HAMILTON
26 Vice Chanc for Marketing & Comm ....Mr. Laylan COPELIN
116 Chief Auditor ....Ms. Charlie HRNCIR
108 Vice Chanc Strategic Initiatives ....Mr. Greg HARTMAN
43 General Counsel ....Mr. Ray BONILLA
46 Vice Chancellor for Research ....Dr. Jon MOGFORD
21 Vice Chanc for Business Affairs ....Mr. Phillip RAY
13 Chief Information Officer ....Mr. Mark STONE
115 Chief Investment Ofcr/Treasurer ....Ms. Maria ROBINSON
86 Vice Chanc for Govt Relations ....Ms. Jenny JONES
88 Vice Chanc for Dis & Emerg Svc ....Chief Nim KIDD
100 Exec Assistant to the Chancellor ....Ms. Stephanie BJUNE
12 Director RELLIS Campus ....Mr. Kellly TEMPLIN

*Prairie View A & M University (C)

P.O. Box 519 Mail Stop 1337, Prairie View TX 77446-0519
County: Waller
FICE Identification: 003630
Unit ID: 227526
Telephone: (936) 261-3311
Carnegie Class: Masters/L
FAX Number: (936) 261-2115
Calendar System: Semester
URL: www.pvamu.edu
Established: 1876
Annual Undergrad Tuition & Fees (In-State): $11,099
Enrollment: 9,248
Coed
Affiliation or Control: State
IRS Status: 501(c)3
Highest Offering: Doctorate
Accreditation: SC, DIETD, DIETI, MUS, NUR, NURSE, SW

02 President ....Dr. Ruth J. SIMMONS
05 Provost/Sr VP Academic Affairs ....Dr. James M. PALMER
20 Assoc Prov/VP Acad Affairs ....Vacant
10 Sr Vice Pres Business Affairs/CFO ....Ms. Cynthia CARTER-HORN
32 AVP Student Affairs/Dean Students ....Mr. Steve RANSOM
46 VP Research/Innov/Spons Pgms ....Dr. Magesh RAJAN
41 Director of Athletics ....Mr. Donald R. REED
11 Vice President for Administration ....Vacant
30 Vice Pres of Development ....Vacant
100 Chief of Staff ....Vacant
84 Vice Pres Enroll Mgt/Accred Liaison ....Dr. Sarina WILLIS
21 Asst VP for Financial Accounting ....Ms. Dianne EVANS
92 Director of Honors Program ....Dr. Quincy MOORE
109 Asst VP Auxiliary Enterprises ....Vacant
09 AVP Institutional Research ....Mr. Dean WILLIAMSON
07 Director of Admissions ....Vacant
15 Director of Human Resources ....Ms. Cheryl GREENE
63 Director Undergrad Med Acad ....Dr. Dennis E. DANIELS
13 Chief Information Officer ....Mr. Tony MOORE
58 Interim Dean Graduate Studies ....Dr. Tyrone TANNER
50 Dean College of Business ....Dr. Munir QUDDUS
47 Dean Col Agriculture/Human Sciences ....Dr. Gerard D'SOUZA
66 Dean College of Nursing ....Dr. Betty ADAMS
49 Dean Col of Arts/Sciences ....Dr. Doris J. GILBERT
48 Dean School of Architecture ....Dr. Ikhlas SABOUNI
83 Int Dean Col of Juv Justice/Psych ....Dr. Camille GIBSON
53 Dean College of Education ....Dr. Michael L. MCFRAZIER
54 Dean College of Engineering ....Dr. Pamela OBIOMON
21 Director of Treasury Services ....Ms. Equilla JACKSON
56 Administrator Coop Extension ....Dr. Carolyn J. WILLIAMS
19 AVP Public Safety/Chief of Police ....Dr. Keith JEMISON
29 Director Alumni Affairs ....Mr. Billy DAVIS
06 Registrar ....Ms. Tina MONTGOMERY
85 Exec Director Intl Programs ....Dr. Godlove FONJWENG
88 Sr Intl Student Advisor II ....Mrs. Evelyn J. MCGINTY
96 Exec Dir Proc & Disburse Svcs ....Ms. A. Marie JOHNSON
04 Executive Assistant ....Ms. Delphia ESTERS
08 Director Library Services ....Dr. Musa OLAKA
104 Director Study Abroad ....Vacant
22 Director Affirm Action/Equal Opp ....Ms. Renee WILLIAMS
25 Director Contracts & Grants ....Dr. Theresa BAILEY
26 Exec Director Marketing & Comm ....Ms. Candace JOHNSON
37 Director Student Financial Aid ....Dr. Joy THOMAS
38 Director Student Counseling ....Dr. Bernadine DUNCAN
39 Dir Resident Life/ Student Housing ....Vacant
44 Director Annual Giving ....Ms. LaShonda WILLIAMS

*Tarleton State University (D)

1333 W Washington, Box T-0001,
Stephenville TX 76402-0001
County: Erath
FICE Identification: 003631
Unit ID: 228529
Telephone: (254) 968-9000
Carnegie Class: Masters/L
FAX Number: (254) 968-9920
Calendar System: Semester
URL: www.tarleton.edu
Established: 1899
Annual Undergrad Tuition & Fees (In-State): $8,276
Enrollment: 14,016
Coed
Affiliation or Control: State
IRS Status: 501(c)3
Highest Offering: Doctorate
Accreditation: SC, ACBSP, CAATE, CACREP, DIETD, DMOLS, HT, MLTAD, MT, MUS, NURSE, SW

02 President ....Dr. James HURLEY
100 Chief of Staff/VP University Rels ....Ms. Amanda K. TOLLETT
05 Provost/Exec VPAA ....Dr. Karen MURRAY
111 Vice Pres Inst Advancement ....Dr. Gabriel CAGWIN
10 VP Finance/Administration ....Ms. Lori BEATY
32 VP Student Affairs ....Dr. Kelli C. STYRON
84 VP Enrollment Mgmt ....Dr. Javier GARZA
12 VP External Ops/Dean Fort Worth ....Dr. Kim MCCUISTION
46 VP Research/Innovation & Econ Dev ....Dr. Rupa IYER
20 Assoc VP Academic Administration ....Dr. Jordan BARKLEY
20 Assoc Provost & Dean of Faculty ....Dr. Aimee SHOUSE
36 Director of Career Services ....Ms. Alana HEFNER
18 AVP Campus Operations ....Mr. David MARTIN
35 Exec Director Student Services ....Ms. Donna STROHMEYER
30 Asst VP Development ....Ms. Jennifer COLLEY
76 Dean Col Health Sci/Human Svcs ....Dr. Sally LEWIS
81 Dean College Science & Technology ....Dr. Michael HUGGINS
50 Dean College of Business ....Dr. Chris SHAO
47 Dean Col Agricultural/Natural Res ....Dr. Steve DAMRON
53 Dean College of Education ....Dr. Kim RYNEARSON
49 Dean College Liberal/Fine Arts ....Dr. Eric MORROW
58 Dean Col Graduate Studies & Global ....Dr. Credence BAKER
07 Director Undergraduate Admissions ....Ms. Cynthia HESS
22 Dir Student Disability Services ....Dr. Laura GORDEY
08 Dean of University Libraries ....Dr. Katherine QUINNELL
92 Exec Dir of Honors College ....Dr. Craig CLIFFORD
37 Director Student Financial Aid ....Ms. Kathy PURVIS
13 CIO/Exec Dir Information Tech Svcs ....Ms. Rebecca GRAY
15 Director of Employee Services ....Ms. Eva LOPEZ
35 Asst VP for Student Affairs ....Dr. Lora HEVIE-MASON
26 Asst VP Marketing & Communications ....Ms. Cecilia JACOBS
41 Athletic Director ....Mr. Lonn REISMAN
23 Director Student Health Center ....Ms. Bridgette BEDNARZ
38 Director Student Counseling ....Dr. Brenda FAULKNER
19 University Police Chief ....Mr. Matt WELCH
124 Exec Dir of Student Engagement ....Mr. Darrell BROWN
44 Asst VP Advancement & Ext Relations ....Ms. Sabra GUERRA
28 Dir Diversity/Inclusion & Intl Pgm ....Mr. Tiburcio LINCE
06 Assoc Registrar ....Mr. David SUTTON
96 Director Procurements and Contracts ....Mr. Thad TURMAN
40 Manager Campus Bookstore ....Mr. Cliff HOY
105 Director of Web Services ....Mr. Johnny THOMPSON
04 Administrative Asst to President ....Ms. Tauna BERTSCH
29 Director Alumni Relations ....Ms. Jessica EVANS
117 AVP Univ Compliance ....Mr. Kent STYRON
39 Dir Resident Life/Student Housing ....Ms. Shelly BROWN
54 Assoc Dean Engineering ....Dr. Denise MARTINEZ

*Texas A & M International University (E)

5201 University Boulevard, Laredo TX 78041-1900
County: Webb
FICE Identification: 009651
Unit ID: 226152
Telephone: (956) 326-2001
Carnegie Class: Masters/L
FAX Number: (956) 326-2348
Calendar System: Semester
URL: www.tamiu.edu
Established: 1969
Annual Undergrad Tuition & Fees (In-State): $7,683
Enrollment: 8,525
Coed
Affiliation or Control: State
IRS Status: 501(c)3
Highest Offering: Doctorate
Accreditation: SC, MPCAC, NUR, SPAA

02 President ....Dr. Pablo ARENAZ
05 Provost ....Dr. Thomas R. MITCHELL
10 Vice Pres Finance & Administration ....Mr. Juan J. CASTILLO, JR.
111 Vice Pres Institutional Advancement ....Ms. Rosanne PALACIOS
32 Vice Pres for Student Success ....Dr. Minita RAMIREZ
11 AVP for Finance & Administration ....Mr. Fred JUAREZ, III
88 Dir of Compliance ....Mrs. Lorissa M. CORTEZ
13 Assoc VP Information Technology/CIO ....Mr. Miguel MUNOA
20 Associate Provost ....Dr. Stephen M. DUFFY
49 Dean College Arts & Sciences ....Dr. Claudia E. SAN MIGUEL
50 Dean AR Sanchez Jr Sch of Business ....Dr. Steve R. SEARS
66 Dean School of Nursing ....Dr. Marivic TORREGOSA
08 Dir Sue & Radcliffe Killam Library ....Mr. Benjamin S. RAWLINS
07 Director Admissions ....Mrs. Rosie A. DICKINSON
06 Associate VP/Univ Registrar ....Mr. Juan G. GARCIA, JR.
15 Director of Human Resources ....Ms. Jan ASPELUND
26 Director Public Rels Mktg/Info Svcs ....Mr. Steve K. HARMON
37 Director Financial Aid ....Mrs. Laura M. ELIZONDO
41 Director of Athletics ....Mr. Gilbert G. ZIMMERMANN
18 Director Physical Plant ....Mr. Roberto A. GARZA
29 Assistant Director Alumni Relations ....Ms. Jackelyne K. BRISENO
36 Director Career Services ....Ms. Yelitza M. HOWARD
39 Director of Residence Life/Housing ....Mr. Manuel VELA, III
38 Dir Student Couns/Disability Svcs ....Dr. Guillermo E. GONZALEZ, JR.
96 Dir Purchasing & Support Services ....Ms. Ann E. GUTIERREZ
92 Assoc Prof Director Honors Pgm ....Dr. Deborah L. BLACKWELL
21 Comptroller ....Ms. Elena M. MARTINEZ
35 Associate VP Student Success ....Ms. Gina D. GONZALEZ
123 Dir Grad Admissions/ Recruitment ....Mr. Guillermo F. GONZALEZ, JR.
108 Assoc VP Institutional Assessment ....Dr. David E. ALLEN
97 Dean of University College ....Dr. Barbara S. HONG
09 Director of Institutional Research ....Mr. Sheng Chien R. LEE

*Texas A & M University (F)

1246 TAMU, College Station TX 77843-1246
County: Brazos
FICE Identification: 003632
Unit ID: 228723
Telephone: (979) 845-2217
Carnegie Class: DU-Highest
FAX Number: (979) 845-5027
Calendar System: Semester
URL: www.tamu.edu
Established: 1876
Annual Undergrad Tuition & Fees (In-State): $12,783
Enrollment: 70,418
Coed
Affiliation or Control: State
IRS Status: 501(c)3
Highest Offering: Doctorate
Accreditation: SC, CAATE, CLPSY, CONST, COPSY, DENT, DH, DIETD, DIETI, FEPAC, HSA, IPSY, LAW, LSAR, MED, NURSE, PH, PLNG, SCPSY, SPAA, VET

02 President ....Dr. M. Katherine BANKS
05 Int Provost/Exec Vice President ....Dr. Mark H. WEICHOLD
17 VP Health Science Center ....Dr. Jon E. MOGFORD
10 Chief Financial Officer ....Mr. John CRAWFORD
11 SVP and Chief Operating Officer ....Mr. Greg HARTMAN
26 VP Marketing/Communications ....Ms. Marilyn MARTELL
13 Interim Vice President IT ....Mr. Edwin PIERSON
15 VP HR & Org Effectiveness ....Dr. Jeff RISINGER
32 Interim VP Student Affairs ....Gen. Joe E. RAMIREZ, JR.
46 Interim VP Research ....Dr. Jack G. BALDAUF
86 VP Government Relations ....Mr. Norman R. GARZA, JR.
103 Dean/VP Innovation/Econ Development ....Dr. Andrew P. MORRISS
88 VP Brand & Business Dev ....Mr. R. Shane HINCKLEY
12 VP/COO TAMU Galveston Campus ....Col. Michael E. FOSSUM
28 Interim VP/Assoc Prov Diversity ....Dr. Annie MCGOWAN
20 Interim Vice Prov Faculty Affairs ....Dr. Patrick LOUCHOUARN
84 VP Enrollment & Acad Svcs ....Mr. Joseph P. PETTIBON, II
43 Deputy General Counsel ....Mr. Brooks MOORE
47 Dean Agriculture & Life Science ....Dr. Patrick J. STOVER
48 Dean Architecture ....Dr. Jorge A. VANEGAS
50 Interim Dean Business ....Dr. R. Duane IRELAND
52 Interim Dean Dentistry ....Dr. Lynne OPPERMAN
53 Dean Education & Human Development ....Dr. Joyce M. ALEXANDER
54 Interim Dean Engineering ....Dr. John E. HURTADO
65 Dean Geosciences ....Dr. Debbie J. THOMAS
80 Dean Govt & Public Service ....Gen. Mark A. WELSH, III
61 Dean Law ....Mr. Robert B. AHDIEH
49 Interim Dean Liberal Arts ....Dr. Steven M. OBERHELMAN
63 Dean Medicine ....Dr. Amy L. WAER

66 Dean Nursing .... Dr. Nancy FAHRENWALD
67 Dean Pharmacy .... Dr. Indra K. REDDY
69 Dean Public Health .... Dr. Shawn G. GIBBS
81 Dean Science .... Dr. Valen E. JOHNSON
74 Dean Vet Med & Biomed Sci .... Dr. John R. AUGUST
08 Interim Dean/Director Libraries .... Ms. Julie MOSBO BALLESTRO
88 Dir Inst Biosciences & Tech .... Dr. Kenneth S. RAMOS
12 Dean & COO TAMU Qatar Campus .... Dr. Cesar O. MALAVE
20 Dean of Faculties/Assoc Prov .... Dr. Blanca M. LUPIANI
20 Assoc Prov Undergrad Studies .... Dr. Ann L. KENIMER
107 Assoc Prov Grad/Prof Studies .... Dr. Karen BUTLER-PURRY
07 Assoc VP Enrollment Services .... Dr. Lisa BLAZER
37 Asst VP Scholarships & Fin Aid .... Ms. Delisa F. FALKS
35 Assoc VP Student Affairs .... Dr. Victoria E. DOBIYANSKI
06 Registrar .... Ms. Venesa A. HEIDICK
36 Exec Dir Career Center .... Ms. Samantha WILSON
23 Director Student Health Center .... Dr. Martha C. DANNENBAUM
38 Exec Dir Student Counseling Svcs .... Dr. Mary Ann COVEY
39 Exec Dir Residence Life/Housing .... Ms. Chareny L. RYDL
92 Assistant Provost Honors Programs .... Dr. Sumana DATTA
104 Executive Director Education Abroad .... Dr. Holly HUDSON
09 Interim Dir Data & Research Svcs .... Ms. Margot H. GOFF
102 President Texas A&M Foundation .... Mr. Tyson VOELKEL
29 Pres Assoc of Former Students .... Mr. Porter GARNER
19 Chief University Police .... Mr. J. Mike JOHNSON
41 Athletic Director .... Mr. Ross BJORK
106 Asst Prov Academic Innovation .... Dr. Jocelyn WIDMER
121 Assoc Prov Acad Affs/Stdnt Success .... Dr. Timothy P. SCOTT
18 Chf Facilities/Physical Plant Ofcr .... Ms. S. Jane SCHNEIDER
21 Asst VP Finance/Strategic Sourcing .... Mr. Dean K. ENDLER

*Texas A&M University-Central Texas (A)

1001 Leadership Place, Killeen TX 76549
County: Bell Identification: 667086
Unit ID: 483036
Telephone: (245) 519-5400 Carnegie Class: Masters/M
FAX Number: (245) 519-5482 Calendar System: Semester
URL: www.tamuct.edu
Established: 1999 Annual Undergrad Tuition & Fees (In-State): $6,483
Enrollment: 2,339 Coed
Affiliation or Control: State IRS Status: 501(c)3
Highest Offering: Master's
Accreditation: SC, ACBSP, CACREP, NURSE, SW

02 President .... Dr. Marc A. NIGLIAZZO
46 VP for Research and Economic Dev .... Dr. Russell PORTER
04 Administrative Asst to President .... Ms. Vicky FERGUSON
05 Chief Academic Officer .... Dr. Peg GRAY-VICKREY
07 Director Recruitment & Admissions .... Mr. Joshua SMITH
08 Dean of the University Library .... Ms. Bridgit MCCAFFERTY
09 Dir Inst Research/Assessment .... Mr. Paul TURCOTTE
10 Interim VP for Finance & Admin .... Mr. Todd LUTZ
13 Interim AVP IT/CIO .... Ms. Gail WALLIN
15 Director Human Resources .... Ms. Tina FLOREZ-NEVAREZ
22 Chief Compliance Officer .... Ms. Deserie MENSCH
111 Chief Comm & Advancement Officer .... Dr. Karen CLOS
32 Dean of Student Affairs .... Dr. Brandon GRIGGS
36 Dir Career/Professional Development ... Ms. Michelle BOLLINGER
37 Dir Student Financial Assistance .... Ms. Irene MONTALVO
50 Dean of Business Administration .... Dr. Faiza KHOJA
53 Dean of Education/Human Development .... Dr. Jeff KIRK
49 Dean of Arts & Sciences .... Dr. Jerry JONES
06 Registrar .... Ms. Hannah MCDONALD
106 Dir Online Education/E-learning .... Dr. Richard SCHILKE
19 Acting Chief of Police .... Mr. Andrew FLORES
28 Chief Diversity Officer .... Dr. Sanfrena BRITT
84 AVP for Enrollment Management .... Mr. Clifton JONES
96 Director of Purchasing .... Mr. Johnathan FUSELIER
38 Director Student Counseling .... Dr. Carmelia AMUNA
90 Director Academic Computing .... Dr. Richard SCHILKE

*Texas A & M University - Commerce (B)

PO Box 3011, Commerce TX 75429-3011
County: Hunt FICE Identification: 003565
Unit ID: 224554
Telephone: (903) 886-5000 Carnegie Class: DU-Mod
FAX Number: (903) 886-5888 Calendar System: Semester
URL: www.tamuc.edu
Established: 1889 Annual Undergrad Tuition & Fees (In-State): $9,820
Enrollment: 12,249 Coed
Affiliation or Control: State IRS Status: 501(c)3
Highest Offering: Doctorate
Accreditation: SC, ART, CACREP, MUS, NURSE, SW

02 President & CEO .... Dr. Mark J. RUDIN
125 President Emeritus .... Dr. Ray M. KECK, III
125 President Emeritus .... Dr. Keith MCFARLAND
05 Provost & VP Academic Affairs .... Dr. John HUMPHREYS
10 VP Finance & Administration .... Ms. Tina LIVINGSTON
111 Int VP Div of Philanthropy/Engage .... Ms. Amber COUNTIS
46 VP Research & Economic Development .... Ms. Cece GASSNER
100 Chief of Staff .... Ms. Linda KING
88 Chief Ethics & Compliance Officer .... Ms. Katelyn SEVERANCE
41 Athletic Director .... Mr. Tim MCMURRAY
26 Exec Director Marketing & Comm .... Mr. Michael JOHNSON
20 Assoc Provost Academic Foundations .... Dr. Ricky DOBBS
21 AVP Finance & Admin/Comptroller .... Ms. Sarah BAKER
114 Budget Director .... Ms. Arlana MARTIN
113 Bursar & Director Student Accounts .... Mr. Charles ROBNETT
06 Registrar .... Ms. Paige BUSSELL
88 Assistant Comptroller .... Mr. Brad HALL
08 Dean of Libraries .... Ms. Lanee DUNLAP
13 Chief Information Officer .... Mr. Jeremy GAMEZ
37 Dir Financial Aid & Scholarships .... Ms. Renee WALKER
58 Dean Graduate School .... Dr. Jennifer SCHROEDER
53 Dean Education & Human Services .... Dr. Kimberly MCLEOD
79 Dean Humanities/Social Sci & Art .... Dr. William KURACINA
54 Dean Science & Engineering .... Dr. Brent DONHAM
50 Dean Business .... Dr. Mario HAYEK
47 Dean Agric & Natural Resources .... Dr. Randy HARP
92 Dean Honors College .... Dr. Ray GREEN
106 Dean College of Innovation & Design .... Dr. Yvonne VILLANUEVA-RUSSELL
09 Exec Dir Inst Effective & Research .... Dr. Dan SU
07 Director of Undergrad Admissions .... Mr. Jody TODHUNTER
88 Director of Academic Testing .... Dr. Hattie POWELL
32 Int VP Stdnt Success/Dean of Stdnts .... Ms. Judy SACKFIELD
35 Assoc Dean Campus Life/Student Dev .... Mr. Steve HIRST
29 Director of Alumni Relations .... Mr. Derryle PEACE
19 Chief of Police .... Mr. Bryan VAUGHN
56 Program Dir Extended University .... Ms. Araceli HILL
12 Director Metroplex Center .... Mr. Russell BLANCHETT
12 Director Navarro Partnership .... Ms. Virginia MONK
38 Director Counseling Center .... Dr. Nick PATRAS
39 Dir Residential Living & Learning .... Mr. Michael STARK
117 Dir of Campus Operations & Safety .... Mr. Ethan D. PREAS
23 Director Student Health Center ... Ms. Maxine MENDOZA-WELCH
85 Director International Programs .... Ms. Pri RISAL
96 Chief Procurement Ofcr & HUB Coord .... Mr. Travis BALL
105 Web Application Developer .... Mr. Rick BARR
120 LMS Coordinator .... Mr. Brett MURREY
15 Chief Human Resources Officer .... Dr. Edward W. ROMERO
16 Assoc Director Human Resources .... Ms. Tammi THOMPSON
118 Sr Employee Benefits Rep .... Ms. Cindy TODHUNTER
18 Exec Dir Facilities Support Svcs .... Mr. Tony BRANDT
22 Civil Rights/Title IX Administrator .... Mr. Michael HILL
30 Director of Philanthropy .... Ms. April CARL
44 Director Annual Programs .... Mr. Justin FERRELL
110 Restricted Funds & Exec Gifts Admin .... Ms. Brenda MORRIS
109 Auxiliary Services Manager .... Ms. Jennifer PERRY
84 VP Enrollment Management .... Ms. Nechell BONDS
36 Director Career Development .... Ms. Lacey HENDERSON
89 Dir New Students & Family Program .... Ms. Kristen NEELEY
28 Exec Dir LATINX Outreach & Engage .... Dr. Fred FUENTES
122 Director Fraternity & Sorority Life .... Ms. Amanda HORNE

*Texas A & M University - Corpus Christi (C)

6300 Ocean Drive, Corpus Christi TX 78412
County: Nueces FICE Identification: 011161
Unit ID: 224147
Telephone: (361) 825-7245 Carnegie Class: DU-Higher
FAX Number: (361) 825-5810 Calendar System: Semester
URL: www.tamucc.edu
Established: 1947 Annual Undergrad Tuition & Fees (In-State): $9,553
Enrollment: 10,820 Coed
Affiliation or Control: State IRS Status: 501(c)3
Highest Offering: Doctorate
Accreditation: SC, CAATE, CACREP, MT, MUS, NURSE

02 President/CEO .... Dr. Kelly M. MILLER
05 Provost & VP for Acad Affairs .... Dr. Clarenda PHILLIPS
10 Exec VP for Finance/Admin .... Ms. Jaclyn MAHLMANN
111 VP Institutional Advancement .... Ms. Jaime NODARSE BARRERA
32 VP Student Engagement & Success .... Dr. Bill KIBLER
46 VP for Research & Innovation .... Dr. Ahmed MAHDY
20 Assoc Provost .... Dr. Amy ALDRIDGE SANFORD
88 Project Manager IV .... Ms. Claire SNYDER
13 Sr Assoc VP for Technology/CIO .... Mr. Edward EVANS
84 VP Enrollment Management .... Mr. Andy BENOIT
35 Assoc VP Student Engagement .... Ms. Ann DEGAISH
08 Dean of University Libraries .... Dr. Catherine RUDOWSKY
09 Exec Dir Institutional Research ..... Ms. Erin MULLIGAN-NGUYEN
26 Director of Marketing .... Ms. Ashley LARRABEE
30 Asst VP Development .... Ms. Kimberly BECERRA
20 Asst VP for Academic Affairs .... Vacant
07 Exec Director of Admissions .... Mr. Oscar REYNA
37 Director of Financial Assistance .... Ms. Jeannie GAGE
31 Director Community Outreach .... Mr. Joseph MILLER
15 Director of Human Resources .... Ms. Debra CORTINAS
36 Director Career Services .... Dr. Leslie MILLS
38 Exec Director Student Engagement .... Dr. Amanda DRUM
22 Dir Equal Opportunity Employee .... Mr. Sam RAMIREZ
11 Exec Dir Administrative Services .... Ms. Judy HARRAL
96 Dir Procurement & Disbursements .... Mr. Will HOBART
113 Bursar .... Ms. Christina HOLZHEUSER
58 Dean College of Grad Studies .... Dr. Karen MCCALEB
49 Dean College of Liberal Arts .... Dr. Shawnrece CAMPBELL
50 Dean College of Business .... Dr. Brian TIETJE
53 Dean College of Education .... Dr. David SCOTT
54 Dean College of Science & Engr .... Dr. Frank PEZOLD
66 Dean College of Nursing/Health Sci .... Dr. Hassan AZIZ
04 Exec Assistant to the President .... Ms. Erin LONGORIA
19 Director Environ Health & Safety .... Mr. Roy COONS
25 Manager Contracts .... Ms. Deborah ZENTMIRE
29 Exec Director of Alumni Relations .... Mr. Russell WAGNER
39 Manager Housing Business Operations .... Ms. Stephanie BOX
41 Athletic Director .... Mr. Jonathan PALUMBO

*Texas A & M University - Kingsville (D)

700 University Boulevard, Kingsville TX 78363-8202
County: Kleberg FICE Identification: 003639
Unit ID: 228705
Telephone: (361) 593-2111 Carnegie Class: DU-Higher
FAX Number: (361) 593-3107 Calendar System: Semester
URL: www.tamuk.edu
Established: 1925 Annual Undergrad Tuition & Fees (In-State): $9,779
Enrollment: 6,932 Coed
Affiliation or Control: State IRS Status: 501(c)3
Highest Offering: Doctorate
Accreditation: SC, CACREP, DIETD, DIETI, MUS, NAIT, PHAR, SP, SW

02 President .... Dr. Mark A. HUSSEY
100 Chief of Staff II .... Vacant
43 Director of Risk & Compliance .... Vacant
05 Provost & Vice President .... Dr. Lou REINISCH
10 VP Finance/Chief Financial Officer .... Mr. Jacob FLOURNOY
111 VP Institutional Advancement .... Mr. Bradley WALKER
21 Exec Dir Financial Svcs/Controller .... Ms. Joanne CASTRO
117 Exec Director Risk Management .... Dr. Shane CREEL
36 Director of Academic Success .... Ms. Christina RODRIGUEZ-GONZALEZ
109 Dir of Prop Mgmt & Auxil Services .... Mr. Crispin TREVINO
88 Director of Recreational Sports .... Mr. Ian BROWN
84 VP Enroll Services/ Student Affair .... Dr. Rito SILVA
13 Chief Information Officer ...... Mr. Madhavkrishna SANKHAVARAM
119 Chief Information Security Officer .... Mr. Lonnie NAGEL
91 Dir Enterprise Applications .... Vacant
35 Assistant VP Student Affairs .... Ms. Kirsten COMPARY
20 Associate VP Academic Affairs .... Dr. Jaya S. GOSWAMI
85 Dir International Student Services .... Mr. Peter LI
58 VP Research & Grad Studeis .... Dr. Allen RASMUSSEN
22 Associate VP Student Access .... Dr. Maria MARTINEZ
47 Dean College Agriculture .... Dr. Shad NELSON
49 Dean Arts & Sciences .... Dr. Dolores GUERRERO
50 Dean Business Administration .... Dr. Natalya DELCOURE
53 Dean College of Education .... Dr. Steve BAIN
54 Interm Dean Engineering .... Dr. Robert DIERSING
121 Assoc VP for Student Success .... Dr. Shannon BAKER
26 Director Marketing & Communications .... Ms. Adriana GARZA
08 Library Director .... Mr. Bruce R. SCHUENAMAN
09 Institutional Research Director .... Ms. Miao ZHUANG
88 Interm Exec Director Citrus Center .... Dr. Mamoudou SETAMOU
88 Director King Ranch Institute .... Dr. Clay P. MATHIS
88 Exec Dir Wildlife Research CKWRI .... Dr. David HEWITT
06 Registrar .... Ms. Mildred SLAUGHTER
07 Exec Director of Admissions .... Vacant
41 Exec Dir Athletics & Campus Rec .... Mr. Stephen ROACH
106 Dir Distance Learning & Instr Tech .... Mr. Rolando GARZA
110 Advancement Services Director .... Ms. Lori RUSSEK
23 Director Student Health Services .... Ms. Jo Elda CASTILLO-ALANIZ
88 Director John E Conner Museum .... Vacant
15 Chief Human Resources Officer .... Mr. Henry BURGOS
18 Exec Director Physical Plant .... Mr. Andy GONZALEZ
96 Assoc VP Support Services .... Vacant
39 Exec Director Residence Life .... Mr. Tom MARTIN
88 Exec Dir Disburs/Trvl/Prop Mgmt .... Ms. Maricela CISNEROS
35 Director Student Activities .... Ms. Erin MCCLURE
19 Chief of Police .... Mr. Felipe GARZA
37 Director Student Financial Aid .... Mr. Raul CAVAZOS
04 Sr Exec Asst to President .... Ms. Margarita M. GALVAN

*Texas A & M University-San Antonio (E)

One University Way, San Antonio TX 78224
County: Bexar Identification: 666689
Unit ID: 459949
Telephone: (210) 784-1000 Carnegie Class: Masters/L
FAX Number: (210) 784-6219 Calendar System: Semester
URL: www.tamusa.edu
Established: 2009 Annual Undergrad Tuition & Fees (In-District): $8,901
Enrollment: 6,759 Coed
Affiliation or Control: State/Local IRS Status: 501(c)3
Highest Offering: Master's
Accreditation: SC

02 President .... Dr. Cynthia TENIENTE-MATSON
05 Provost/VP Academic Affairs .... Dr. Michael O'BRIEN
10 VP Business Affairs & CFO .... Ms. Kathryn FUNK-BAXTER
111 VP for University Advancement .... Dr. Jeanette DEDIEMAR
84 VP for Enrollment Management .... Dr. Brandy MCLELLAND
121 VP Student Success/Engagement ...... Dr. Mari FUENTES-MARTIN
09 AVP of Institutional Effectiveness .... Ms. Jane MIMS
50 Dean College of Business .... Dr. Rohan CHRISTIE-DAVID
49 Dean College of Arts & Sciences .... Dr. Debra FEAKES
53 Dean College of Education & Devel .... Dr. Carl SHEPERIS
100 Chief of Staff/Dir Pres Operation .... Ms. Jessica LOUDERMILK
29 Director Alumni Affairs .... Dr. Mary Kay COOPER
26 Dir of Marketing/Communications .... Ms. Adriana CONTRERAS
13 Chief Information Officer .... Mr. William GRIFFENBERG
07 Director of Admissions .... Vacant
37 Dir of Financial Aid & Scholarships .... Mr. Phillip RODGERS
06 Registrar .... Ms. Rachel MONTEJANO
15 Chief Human Resources Officer .... Ms. Martha GONZALEZ
18 Director of Facilities .... Ms. Mary WALKER
38 Director of Counseling .... Dr. Mary BUZZETTA
96 Dir Procurement/Auxiliary Services .... Mr. Christopher SCOTT
41 Dir of Intercollegiate Athletics .... Mr. Darnell SMITH

*Texas A & M University - Texarkana (A)

7101 University Avenue, Texarkana TX 75503
County: Bowie FICE Identification: 031703
Unit ID: 224545
Telephone: (903) 223-3000 Carnegie Class: Masters/M
FAX Number: (903) 832-8890 Calendar System: Semester
URL: www.tamut.edu
Established: 1971 Annual Undergrad Tuition & Fees (In-State): $7,764
Enrollment: 2,171 Coed
Affiliation or Control: State IRS Status: 501(c)3
Highest Offering: Doctorate
Accreditation: SC, CACREP, NURSE

02 President ..... Dr. Emily CUTRER
05 Provost/Vice Pres Academic Affairs ..... Dr. Melinda ARNOLD
10 Chief Financial Officer ..... Mr. Jeff HINTON
111 Assoc VP University Advancement ..... Mrs. LeAnne WRIGHT
84 VP Student Engagement/Enrol/Success ..... Ms. Kathy WILLIAMS
100 Chief of Staff to the President ..... Ms. Vicki MELDE
13 Chief Information Officer ..... Vacant
32 Assistant VP of Student Affairs ..... Mr. Carl GREIG
121 Asst Vice Pres for Student Success ... Mrs. Elizabeth PATTERSON
20 Assoc Provost/SACSCOC Liaison ..... Vacant
49 Dean Col Arts & Sciences/Education ..... Dr. Delbert DOUGHTY
50 Dean Col of Bus/Engineering/Tech ..... Dr. Gary STADING
114 Director of Budgets ..... Mrs. Ramona GREEN
113 Bursar ..... Ms. Joni MILLICAN
37 Dir Financial Aid & Veteran Svcs ..... Mr. Michael FULLER
15 Director Human Resources & EEO ..... Ms. Charlotte BANKS
08 Library Director ..... Mrs. Teri STOVER
19 Police Chief/Director Security ..... Mr. Alex SERRANO
96 Director Purchasing ..... Mrs. Cynthia HENDERSON
07 Asst VP of Admissions/Recruiting ..... Mr. Toney FAVORS
26 Director Communications ..... Mr. John BUNCH
104 Director of International Studies ..... Dr. Jennifer DAVIS
41 Director of Athletics ..... Mr. Michael GALVAN
04 Executive Assistant to President ..... Mrs. Sarah NEWMAN
06 Registrar ..... Mrs. Jana BOATRIGHT
38 Director Student Counseling ..... Vacant
29 Alumni Relations Coordinator ..... Mr. Mark MISSILDINE

*West Texas A & M University (B)

2501 4th Ave., Canyon TX 79016
County: Randall FICE Identification: 003665
Unit ID: 229814
Telephone: (806) 651-0000 Carnegie Class: Masters/L
FAX Number: (806) 651-2126 Calendar System: Semester
URL: www.wtamu.edu
Established: 1910 Annual Undergrad Tuition & Fees (In-State): $8,456
Enrollment: 10,036 Coed
Affiliation or Control: State IRS Status: 501(c)3
Highest Offering: Doctorate
Accreditation: SC, MUS, NURSE, SP, SW, THEA

02 President ..... Dr. Walter V. WENDLER
05 Executive Vice President/Provost ..... Dr. Neil W. TERRY
10 Vice Pres for Business & Finance ..... Mr. Randy RIKEL
32 Vice Pres Student Enroll Eng & Succ ..... Mr. Michael J. KNOX
111 VP Philanthropy & Ext Relations ..... Dr. Todd W. RASBERRY
28 Chief Diversity/Inclusion Officer ..... Ms. Angela ALLEN
100 Chief of Staff/Asst VP Strat Comm ..... Ms. Tracee POST
06 Registrar ..... Ms. Diane BRICE
07 Director of Admissions ..... Mr. Jeff S. BAYLOR
08 Dir Information/Library Resources ..... Ms. Shawna J. KENNEDY-WITTHAR
36 Dir Career Planning/Placement ..... Ms. Kim MULLER
37 Director Student Financial Aid ..... Ms. Marian K. GIESECKE
56 Director of Extended Studies ..... Ms. Andrea PORTER
23 Director Medical Service ..... Dr. Jim GIBBS
19 Police Chief ..... Chief Shawn G. BURNS
26 AVP Marketing and Communications ..... Ms. Kelly POLDEN
29 Executive Dir of Alumni Relations ..... Mr. Ronnie L. HALL
38 Director Counseling Services ..... Ms. Dayna SCHERTLER
41 Director of Athletics ..... Mr. Michael MCBROOM
09 AVP Inst Research & Effectiveness ..... Mr. Jarvis D. HAMPTON
13 VP for Information Technology/CIO ..... Mr. James D. WEBB
96 Director of Purchasing ..... Ms. Elaine K. CHEW
40 Manager Bookstore ..... Mr. Terry S. NEPPER
15 Director of Human Resources ..... Ms. Nancy HAMPTON
47 Dean Col Agri/Natural Sciences ..... Dr. Kevin POND
50 Dean College of Business ..... Dr. Amjad A. ABDULLAT
53 Dean Col Education/Social Sciences ... Dr. Eddie W. HENDERSON
57 Dean College Fine Arts/Humanities ..... Dr. Jessica MALLARD
54 Dean College of Engineering ..... Dr. Emily HUNT
46 VP for Research & Compliance ..... Dr. Angela SPAULDING
66 Dean College of Nursing/Health Sci ..... Dr. Dirk NELSON
104 Director Study Abroad ..... Ms. Carolina GALLOWAY

*Texas A & M University at Galveston (C)

PO Box 1675, Galveston TX 77553-1675
Telephone: (409) 740-4414 FICE Identification: 010298
Accreditation: &SC

† Regional accreditation is carried under the parent institution Texas A & M University, College Station, TX.

Texas Baptist Institute and Seminary (D)

1300 Longview Drive, Henderson TX 75652
County: Rusk Identification: 667363
Telephone: (903) 657-6543 Carnegie Class: Not Classified
FAX Number: N/A Calendar System: Semester
URL: tbi.edu
Established: 1948 Annual Undergrad Tuition & Fees: N/A
Enrollment: N/A Coed
Affiliation or Control: Independent Non-Profit IRS Status: 501(c)3
Highest Offering: Doctorate
Accreditation: @BI

01 President ..... Dr. Ray O. BROOKS
05 Academic Dean/CEO ..... Dr. Steve BUTLER
111 Vice Pres Advancement ..... Robert WALLACE
06 Registrar ..... Jimmy JONES

Texas Chiropractic College (E)

5912 Spencer Highway, Pasadena TX 77505-1699
County: Harris FICE Identification: 003635
Unit ID: 228866
Telephone: (281) 487-1170 Carnegie Class: Spec-4-yr-Other Health
FAX Number: (281) 487-2009 Calendar System: Trimester
URL: www.txchiro.edu
Established: 1908 Annual Undergrad Tuition & Fees: N/A
Enrollment: 250 Coed
Affiliation or Control: Independent Non-Profit IRS Status: 501(c)3
Highest Offering: Doctorate
Accreditation: SC, CHIRO

01 President ..... Dr. Stephen FOSTER
10 Controller ..... Mr. David MASKELL
11 Executive Vice President ..... Dr. Sandra HUGHES
84 Assoc VP of Enrollment Management ..... Ms. Monique LEWIS
121 Student Success Program Coord ..... Ms. Emily PYRON
100 Chief of Staff ..... Dr. Kent GRAY
06 Registrar ..... Ms. Sarah TROTMAN
15 Director of Human Resources ..... Mrs. Sue ARNOLD
26 Graphic Designer & Communications ..... Ms. Alysa CAMPOS
08 Director of Library Services ..... Ms. Carol WEBB
37 Director of Financial Aid ..... Mr. Arthur GOUDEAU
07 Director of Admissions ..... Ms. Ericka GARDUZA
101 Exec Admin Asst/Board Liaison ..... Mrs. Marian MOORE

Texas Christian University (F)

2800 S University Drive, Fort Worth TX 76129-2800
County: Tarrant FICE Identification: 003636
Unit ID: 228875
Telephone: (817) 257-7000 Carnegie Class: DU-Higher
FAX Number: N/A Calendar System: Semester
URL: www.tcu.edu
Established: 1873 Annual Undergrad Tuition & Fees: $51,660
Enrollment: 11,379 Coed
Affiliation or Control: Christian Church (Disciples Of Christ)
IRS Status: 501(c)3
Highest Offering: Doctorate
Accreditation: SC, ANEST, ART, CAATE, CIDA, DANCE, DIETC, DIETD, JOUR, #MED, MUS, NURSE, SP, SW

01 Chancellor ..... Dr. Victor J. BOSCHINI, JR.
05 Provost/Vice Chanc Academic Affairs ..... Dr. Teresa ABI-NADER DAHLBERG
10 Vice Chanc Finance & Administration ..... Mr. Brian G. GUTIERREZ
111 Vice Chanc University Advancement . Mr. Donald J. WHELAN, JR.
32 Vice Chancellor Student Affairs ..... Dr. Kathryn CAVINS-TULL
26 Vice Chanc Mktg & Communication ..... Ms. Tracy SYLER-JONES
15 Vice Chancellor Human Resources ..... Ms. Yohna CHAMBERS
20 Vice Provost for Academic Affairs ..... Dr. Susan M. WEEKS
41 Director Athletics ..... Mr. Jeremiah DONATI
115 Chief Investment Officer ..... Mr. Jim HILLE
13 Chief Technology Officer ..... Mr. Bryan LUCAS
88 Chief University Compliance Officer ..... Ms. Andrea NORDMANN
100 Chief of Staff/Sec of the Board ..... Ms. Jean MRASEK
86 Government Affairs Officer ..... Dr. Lauren NIXON
29 Assoc Vice Chanc Alumni Relations ..... Ms. Amanda STALLINGS
110 Assoc Vice Chanc Advancement Ops ..... Mr. Travis SOYER
35 Assoc VC/Dean Student Development ..... Vacant
35 Assoc Vice Chanc/Dean Campus Life ..... Dr. Michael RUSSEL
21 Assoc VC & Controller ..... Ms. Cheryl KENNON
16 Asst VC for Human Resources ..... Ms. Rachelle BLACKWELL
18 Assoc Vice Chanc for Facilities ..... Mr. Todd S. WALDVOGEL
44 Assoc VC Donor Relations ..... Ms. Julie WHITT
28 Int Sr Advisor/Chief Inclusion Ofcr . Ms. Aisha TORREY-SAWYER
30 Assoc VC University Development ..... Mr. David NOLAN
88 Asst VC School & College Dev ..... Mr. Adam BAGGS
09 Assoc Provost Research/Dean Grad ..... Dr. Floyd L. WORMLEY, JR.
20 Assoc Provost Academic Plng/Budget ..... Ms. Megan M. SOYER
94 Dean School of Interdisc Stds ..... Vacant
108 Director Inst Effectiveness ..... Dr. David ALLEN
49 Dean AddRan College of Liberal Arts ..... Dr. Sonja S. WATSON
50 Dean Neeley School of Business ..... Mr. Daniel W. PULLIN
60 Dn Bob Schieffer Col Communication ..... Dr. Kristie BUNTON
53 Dean College of Education ..... Dr. Frank HERNANDEZ
57 Dean College of Fine Arts ..... Dr. Richard GIPSON
66 Dean Harris College of Nursing ..... Dr. Christopher WATTS
54 Dean Col of Science & Engineering ..... Dr. Michael KRUGER
63 Dean School of Medicine ..... Dr. Stuart FLYNN
92 Int Dean John V Roach Honors Col ..... Dr. Ron PITCOCK
08 Dean of the Library ..... Ms. Tracy HULL
07 Dean of Admission ..... Mr. Heath A. EINSTEIN
06 Registrar ..... Ms. Mary KINCANNON
19 Chief TCU Police ..... Mr. Steve G. MCGEE
42 Minister to the University ..... Rev. Angela KAUFMAN
110 Assoc VC Strategy/Advance Admin ..... Ms. Michelle CLARK
106 Int Dir Ctr for Instr/Innov & Eng ..... Ms. Joanna SCHMIDT
104 Dir Ctr Intl Studies/Study Abroad ..... Dr. Sandra CALLAGHAN
25 Director Contract Administration ..... Mr. Matthew WALLIS
16 Director Employee Relations ..... Ms. Kristen TAYLOR
51 Int Director Extended Education ..... Ms. Julie LOVETT
07 Director of Undergraduate Admission ..... Ms. Mandy CASTRO
88 Assoc Director Transfer Admission ..... Ms. April YANDELL
23 Director Health Services ..... Dr. Jane TORGERSON
09 Director Institutional Research ..... Dr. Cathan COGHLAN
24 Director Instructional Services ..... Vacant
85 Director International Student Svcs ..... Mr. John L. SINGLETON
38 Director Mental Health Services ..... Dr. Eric WOOD
96 Asst Dir/Purchasing Agent ..... Mr. Roger D. FULLER
39 Director Housing & Residential Life ..... Mr. Craig ALLEN
37 Dir Scholarships & Financial Aid ..... Ms. Victoria CHEN
105 Dir Website Social Media Management ..... Mr. Corey REED
25 Director Sponsored Programs ..... Ms. LeAnn FORSBERG
36 Exec Dir Career Services ..... Mr. Mike CALDWELL
102 Sr Dir Corporate/Found Relations ..... Mr. Jason BYRNE
19 Asst Vice Chan Public Safety ..... Mr. Adrian ANDREWS
93 Int Asst VC Multicult/Intl Impact ..... Dr. Trung NGUYEN
43 General Counsel ..... Mr. Lee TYNER
84 Assoc Provost of Enrollment Manage ..... Mr. Mike SCOTT
22 Director of Institutional Equity ..... Ms. Sharon GOODING

Texas College (G)

2404 N Grand Avenue, Tyler TX 75702-1962
County: Smith FICE Identification: 003638
Unit ID: 228884
Telephone: (903) 593-8311 Carnegie Class: Bac-Diverse
FAX Number: (903) 593-0588 Calendar System: Semester
URL: www.texascollege.edu
Established: 1894 Annual Undergrad Tuition & Fees: $10,000
Enrollment: 764 Coed
Affiliation or Control: Christian Methodist Episcopal IRS Status: 501(c)3
Highest Offering: Baccalaureate
Accreditation: SC

01 President ..... Dr. Dwight FENNELL
05 Vice President Academic Affairs ..... Dr. Jan DUNCAN
10 Vice Pres Business & Finance ..... Ms. Millicent RICKENBACKER
32 Vice Pres Student Affairs ..... Dr. Cynthia MARSHALL BIGGINS
84 Dean Enrollment Mgmt & Registrar ..... Mr. John ROBERTS
30 Development Officer ..... Vacant
42 Dean of Chapel/Campus Ministry ..... Dr. Jamie CAPERS
09 Dir Inst Research/ Effectiveness ..... Dr. Cynthia MARSHALL-BIGGINS
08 Director of Library Services ..... Mrs. Linda SIMMONS-HENRY
13 Acting Dir Information Technology ..... Mr. Yaw LABANG
15 Director Human Resources ..... Ms. Lois BOWIE
41 Athletic Director ..... Mr. Greg ELLIS
37 Director Financial Aid ..... Mrs. Shadana MINGO
18 Director Physical Plant ..... Mr. Anthony PARKER
19 Director Security/Safety ..... Mr. Derrick BROWN
26 Chief Marketing & Communications ..... Mr. Jake MARTIN
04 Exec Asst to the President ..... Mrs. Angelia FENNELL
07 Director of Admissions/Registrar ..... Mr. John ROBERTS

Texas Health and Science University (H)

4005 Menchaca Road, Austin TX 78704-6737
County: Travis FICE Identification: 031795
Unit ID: 430704
Telephone: (512) 444-8082 Carnegie Class: Spec-4-yr-Other Health
FAX Number: (512) 444-6345 Calendar System: Trimester
URL: www.thsu.edu
Established: 1990 Annual Undergrad Tuition & Fees: N/A
Enrollment: 104 Coed
Affiliation or Control: Proprietary IRS Status: Proprietary
Highest Offering: Master's; No Lower Division
Accreditation: ACICS, ACUP

01 President ..... Dr. Louis AGNESE
85 VP of International Affairs ..... Mr. Wen Huei CHEN
58 VP/MBA Director ..... Dr. Shu-Chiang LIN
05 Academic Dean/Biomed Dir Austin ..... Dr. Maoyi CAI
108 Assessment Dir ..... Ms. Martha CALLIHAM
37 Financial Aid/Intl Student Advisor ..... Mr. Antonio HOLLOWAY
08 Administrative Coordinator ..... Mrs. Iris GONG
06 Registrar/Administrator ..... Ms. Alexis SANFTNER
20 Academic Dean/Clinic Director SA ..... Dr. Roberto GUERRERO
08 Librarian SA Campus ..... Mrs. Heidi HOECKER
88 Clinic Director Austin Campus ..... Dr. Hai Tao CAO
88 Director of Herbal Department ..... Ms. Allison YU
88 Director of Acupuncture Austin ..... Dr. Sung Wook HONG
07 Director of Admissions ..... Dr. Naomi GARCIA
10 Accountant ..... Zhen SUN

† Granted candidacy at the Doctorate level by ACAOM.

Texas Lutheran University (A)

1000 W Court Street, Seguin TX 78155-5999
County: Guadalupe　FICE Identification: 003641
Unit ID: 228981
Telephone: (830) 372-8000　Carnegie Class: Bac-Diverse
FAX Number: (830) 372-8001　Calendar System: Semester
URL: www.tlu.edu
Established: 1891　Annual Undergrad Tuition & Fees: $31,850
Enrollment: 1,499　Coed
Affiliation or Control: Evangelical Lutheran Church In America
IRS Status: 501(c)3
Highest Offering: Master's
Accreditation: SC, ACBSP, CAATE, MUS, NURSE

01 President .... Dr. Debbie COTTRELL
05 VP for Academic Affairs .... Dr. Sarah FERGUSON
10 Vice President Finance .... Ms. Edie RICHARDSON
84 VP for Enrollment and Marketing .... Ms. Sarah STORY
30 VP for Development/Alumni Relations .... Ms. Renee REHFELD
32 VP/Dean of Student Life & Learning .... Dr. Gourjoine WADE
13 VP for Administration & CIO .... Mr. William SENTER
06 Director of Records & Registration .... Mr. Glenn YOCKEY
08 Library Director .... Dr. Daniel FLORES
113 Dir of Student Financial Services .... Ms. Cathleen WRIGHT
42 Campus Pastor .... Vacant
38 Director Counseling & Disabilities .... Dr. Marlene MORIARITY
07 Director of Admissions .... Ms. ALecia MCCAIN
15 Director of Human Resources .... Ms. Toi TURNER
41 Director of Athletics .... Mr. Bill MILLER
09 Director of Institutional Research .... Vacant
04 Exec Assistant to the President .... Ms. Susan RINN
102 Dir Foundation/Corporate Relations .... Ms. Jena MCKINZIE
104 Director Study Abroad .... Ms. Charla BAILEY
26 Director of Marketing .... Ms. Ashlie FORD
108 Director of Academic Assessment .... Dr. Michael CZUCHRY
18 Chief Facilities/Physical Plant .... Mr. Kirk HERBOLD
19 University Police Chief .... Chief Irene GARCIA
29 Director Alumni Relations .... Ms. Taylor CARLETON
39 Director of Residence Life .... Mr. Tim WESTMORELAND
22 Dir Affirm Action/EEO/Diversity .... Ms. Toi TURNER
43 Dir Legal Services/General Counsel .... Mr. James FROST
28 Chair Diversity Committee .... Dr. Chris BOLLINGER
50 Chair Business & Econ Department .... Dr. Fernando GARZA
53 Chair Education Department .... Dr. Jeannette JONES
36 Director Student Placement .... Dr. Bernadette BUCHANAN
37 Director Student Financial Aid .... Ms. Erika MILLER
90 Director Academic Computing .... Dr. Rodrick SHAO

Texas Southern University (B)

3100 Cleburne Street, Houston TX 77004-4584
County: Harris　FICE Identification: 003642
Unit ID: 229063
Telephone: (713) 313-7011　Carnegie Class: DU-Higher
FAX Number: (713) 313-1092　Calendar System: Semester
URL: www.tsu.edu
Established: 1927　Annual Undergrad Tuition & Fees (In-State): $9,173
Enrollment: 7,015　Coed
Affiliation or Control: State　IRS Status: 170(c)1
Highest Offering: Doctorate
Accreditation: SC, CAEPN, CAHIIM, COARC, DIETD, LAW, MT, NAIT, PHAR, PLNG, SPAA, SW

01 President .... Dr. Lesia L. CRUMPTON-YOUNG
05 Acting Provost/VP Academic Affairs .... Dr. Lillian B. POATS
10 EVP Administration/Finance & CFO .... Mr. Kenneth HUEWITT
111 VP Advancement/Communication .... Ms. Melinda SPAULDING
13 VP Info Tech/Chief Information Ofcr .... Mr. Mario BERRY
100 Chief of Staff .... Ms. Heidi SMITH
43 General Counsel .... Mr. Hao LE
41 VP Intercollegiate Athletics .... Mr. Kevin GRANGER
32 VP Student Affairs .... Dr. Teresa MCKINNEY
09 Int Assoc Provost/Assoc VP Research .... Dr. Adebayo O. OYEKAN
88 Dir Title III/Ofc of Sponsored Proj .... Ms. Demetria JOHNSON-WEEKS
15 Sr Assoc VP of Human Resources .... Ms. Yolanda EDMOND
26 Assoc VP of Communications .... Mr. Steve SCHEFFLER
84 Assoc VP Enrollment Management .... Mr. Wendell WILLIAMS
08 Exec Director Libraries/Museums .... Dr. Janice L. PEYTON
50 Int Dean School of Business .... Dr. John H. WILLIAMS
51 Int Dir Office of Cont Education .... Dr. Melanie LAWSON
53 Dean College of Education .... Dr. Lillian B. POATS
80 Dean School of Public Affairs .... Dr. Theophilus HERRINGTON
61 Acting Dean School of Law .... Dr. Gary L. BLEDSOE
67 Int Dean Col Pharmacy & Health Sci .... Dr. Shirlette MILTON
19 Chief of Police .... Chief Mary YOUNG
39 Director of Student Housing .... Ms. Yvette BARKER
92 Dean Freeman Honors College .. Dr. Dianne JEMISON-POLLARD
18 Exec Dir Facilities & Maintenance .... Mr. Bertran HARRISON
58 Dean Graduate School .... Dr. Gregory H. MADDOX
21 Exec Dir of Business Svcs .... Mr. Charles E. HENRY
124 Dir Acad Ret Svcs Spec Asst/Provost .... Ms. Lori A. LABRIE
108 Exec Dir Inst Assess/Plng/Effect .... Dr. Raijanel CROCKEM
29 Asst VP Alumni Rels/Spec Events .... Ms. Connie L. COCHRAN
90 Senior Academic Technology Officer .... Mr. Darnell JOSEPH
88 Associate Director of QEP Office .... Dr. Arbolina L. JENNINGS
106 Dir Online Education/E-learning .... Vacant
86 Director of Governmental Relations .... Mr. Dominique CALHOUN
04 Exec Admin Asst to President .... Ms. Regina WILLIAMS

Texas Southmost College (C)

80 Fort Brown, Brownsville TX 78520-4993
County: Cameron　FICE Identification: 003643
Unit ID: 227377
Telephone: (956) 295-3600　Carnegie Class: Assoc/MT-VT-High Non
FAX Number: (956) 295-3384　Calendar System: Semester
URL: www.tsc.edu
Established: 1926　Annual Undergrad Tuition & Fees (In-District): $3,748
Enrollment: 8,777　Coed
Affiliation or Control: State/Local　IRS Status: 501(c)3
Highest Offering: Associate Degree
Accreditation: SC, COARC, DMS, EMT, MLTAD

01 President .... Dr. Jesus R. RODRIGUEZ
05 Vice President of Instruction .... Dr. Joanna KILE
10 Vice Pres of Finance/Administration .... Dr. Gisela FIGUEROA
111 Vice Pres of Inst Advancement .... Vacant
20 Assoc VP of Instruction/Acad Svcs .... Dr. Angelica M. FUENTES
81 Dean of STEM .... Dr. Murad ABUSALIM
79 Dean of Humanities .... Dr. Brian MCCORMACK
76 Dean of Health Professions .... Dr. David PEARSE
07 Exec Dir of Admissions & Records .... Ms. Vanessa VASQUEZ
09 Exec Director of IR & Compliance .... Mr. Oscar O. HERNANDEZ
106 Dir Educ Technology & Online Lrng .... Vacant
13 Vice President of Information Tech .... Mr. Luis VILLARREAL
15 Exec Director of Human Resources .... Vacant
25 Coord Sponsored Pgms/Grants Ctr .... Dr. Leonor HERNANDEZ
32 Exec Director of Student Life .... Mr. Armando PONCE
36 Coord Career & Employ Svcs .... Mr. Rene VALDEZ
37 Director Student Financial Aid .... Ms. Pamela JONES
96 Coordinator of Purchasing .... Ms. Patricia SALDIVAR

Texas State Technical College Waco (D)

3801 Campus Drive, Waco TX 76705-1695
County: McLennan　FICE Identification: 003634
Unit ID: 487320
Telephone: (254) 867-4891　Carnegie Class: Assoc/HVT-Mix Trad/Non
FAX Number: (254) 867-3973　Calendar System: Semester
URL: www.tstc.edu
Established: 1965　Annual Undergrad Tuition & Fees (In-State): $6,169
Enrollment: 10,654　Coed
Affiliation or Control: State　IRS Status: 501(c)3
Highest Offering: Associate Degree
Accreditation: SC, CAHIIM, DH, EMT, SURGT

01 Chancellor/CEO .... Mr. Mike REESER
05 VC/Chief Academic Officer .... Mr. Jeff KILGORE
86 SVC/Chief Govt Affairs Officer .... Mr. Roger MILLER
10 VC/Chief Financial Officer .... Mr. Jonathan HOEKSTRA
100 EVC/Chief of Staff to Chancellor .... Mrs. Gail LAWRENCE
32 VC/Chief Student Services Officer .... Mr. Rick HERRERA
43 VC/Chief Legal Officer .... Mr. Ray RUSHING
88 VC/Chief Policy Officer .... Mr. Michael A. BETTERSWORTH
12 Provost Fort Bend County .... Mr. Randall WOOTEN
12 Provost Harlingen .... Ms. Cledia HERNANDEZ
12 Provost Marshall .... Mr. Barton DAY
12 Provost West Texas .... Mr. Rick DENBOW
12 Provost North Texas .... Mr. Marcus BALCH
20 Provost Wako .... Mr. Edgar PADILLA
04 Exec Assistant to the Chancellor .... Ms. Jennifer TINDELL
06 Registrar .... Ms. Maria ARREDONDO
15 Associate VC Human Resources .... Ms. Pamela MAYFIELD
18 Chief Facilities/Physical Plant Ofc .... Mr. Ray FRIED
102 CEO TSTC Foundation .... Ms. Beth WOOTEN
19 Police & Safety Commissioner .... Mr. Aurelio TORRES
36 Exec Director Student Placement .... Ms. Kacey DARNELL
37 Director Student Financial Aid .... Ms. Jackie ADLER
96 Senior Exec Director of Purchasing .... Ms. Melinda BOYKIN
84 Director Enrollment Management .... Ms. Christine STUART-CARRUTHERS

*The Texas State University System (E)

601 Colorado Street, Austin TX 78701-2904
County: Travis　FICE Identification: 033442
Telephone: (512) 463-1808　Carnegie Class: N/A
FAX Number: N/A
URL: www.tsus.edu

01 Chancellor .... Brian MCCALL
05 Vice Chanc Academic & Health Affs .... John HAYEK
43 Vice Chanc & General Counsel .... Nelly HERRERA
10 Vice Chancellor and CFO .... Daniel HARPER
86 Vice Chanc Government Relations .... Sean CUNNINGHAM
26 Vice Chancellor Marketing & Comm .... Mike WINTEMUTE
116 Chief Audit Executive .... Carole M. FOX
11 Director of Administration .... Laura TIBBITTS

*Lamar Institute of Technology (F)

PO Box 10043, Beaumont TX 77710-0043
County: Jefferson　FICE Identification: 036273
Unit ID: 441760
Telephone: (409) 880-8321　Carnegie Class: Assoc/HVT-High Trad
FAX Number: (409) 813-1844　Calendar System: Semester
URL: www.lit.edu
Established: 1995　Annual Undergrad Tuition & Fees (In-State): $3,602
Enrollment: 4,417　Coed
Affiliation or Control: State　IRS Status: 501(c)3
Highest Offering: Associate Degree
Accreditation: SC, CAHIIM, COARC, DH, DMS, EMT, RAD

02 President .... Dr. Lonnie HOWARD
05 Executive Vice President/Provost .... Dr. Kerry MIX
10 Chief Business and Financial Office .... Mr. Rudolfo GONZALES
15 Director of Human Resources .... Ms. Beth KNAPE
45 Vice Pres Strategic Initiatives .... Vacant
103 AVP Strategic & Workforce Init .... Ms. Miranda PHILLIPS
32 AVP Student and Academic Success .... Dr. Angela HILL
37 Director of Financial Aid .... Ms. Linda KORNS
13 Director Information Technology .... Mr. Samuel DOCKENS
30 Exec Dir Devel/Dir LIT Foundation .... Ms. Amanda CLAYTON
26 Dir Marketing & Communication .... Mr. Chris ELLIOTT
11 Director of Administration .... Ms. Amber CLARK
21 Senior Accounting Associate .... Ms. Dawna WHITMIRE
04 Exec Assistant to the President .... Vacant

*Lamar University (G)

PO Box 10001, Beaumont TX 77710-0009
County: Jefferson　FICE Identification: 003581
Unit ID: 226091
Telephone: (409) 880-7011　Carnegie Class: DU-Mod
FAX Number: (409) 880-8404　Calendar System: Semester
URL: www.lamar.edu
Established: 1923　Annual Undergrad Tuition & Fees (In-State): $8,591
Enrollment: 16,637　Coed
Affiliation or Control: State　IRS Status: 501(c)3
Highest Offering: Doctorate
Accreditation: SC, AAQEP, ACFEI, ART, AUD, CAEPN, CONST, DIETD, DIETI, MUS, NUR, SP, SW

02 President .... Dr. Jaime R. TAYLOR
05 Provost/VP Academic Affairs .... Dr. Brenda S. NICHOLS
10 Vice Pres Finance/Operations .... Mr. Jeremy ALLTOP
111 Vice Pres University Advancement .... Mr. Juan ZABALA
13 VP of Information Managment .... Dr. Arne ALMQUIST
20 Associate Provost .... Dr. Daniel BROWN
15 Asst VP Human Resources/Talent Mgmt .... Mr. Anthony SANCHEZ
18 Director of Facilities Mgmt .... Mr. David MARTIN
21 Assoc Vice Pres Finance/Controller .... Ms. Jamie LARSON
58 Dean of Graduate Studies .... Dr. Jerry LIN
49 Dean College Arts & Sciences .... Dr. Lynn MAURER
50 Dean College of Business .... Dr. Dan FRENCH
53 Dean College of Educ & Human Devel .... Dr. Robert SPINA
54 Dean College of Engineering .... Dr. Brian CRAIG
57 Dean College of Fine Arts & Comm .... Dr. Derina HOLTZHAUSEN
08 Dean Mary and John Gray Library .... Dr. Arne ALMQUIST
06 Registrar .... Mr. David SHORT, JR.
56 Assoc Provost of Distance Learning .... Dr. Poonam KUMAR
09 Director Institutional Research .... Dr. Gregory MARSH
23 Director Health Services .... Ms. Shawn GRAY
19 Chief University Police .... Mr. Hector FLORES
26 Director of Public Affairs .... Vacant
29 Director Alumni Relations .... Ms. Shannon FIGUEROA
37 Exec Director Student Financial Aid .... Ms. Carly BROUSSARD
96 Director of Purchasing/Pymt Svcs .... Ms. Amberr MELO
07 Director of Admissions .... Vacant
04 Dir of Opers President's Office .... Ms. Amy M. TROHA
41 Athletic Director .... Mr. Marco BORN

*Lamar State College Orange (H)

410 Front Street, Orange TX 77630-5802
County: Orange　FICE Identification: 023582
Unit ID: 226107
Telephone: (409) 883-7750　Carnegie Class: Assoc/HVT-Mix Trad/Non
FAX Number: (409) 882-3374　Calendar System: Semester
URL: www.lsco.edu
Established: 1969　Annual Undergrad Tuition & Fees (In-State): $3,192
Enrollment: 2,382　Coed
Affiliation or Control: State　IRS Status: 501(c)3
Highest Offering: Associate Degree
Accreditation: SC

02 President .... Dr. Thomas A. JOHNSON
05 Executive VP/Provost .... Dr. Wendy ELMORE
10 CFO .... Mrs. Mary WICKLAND
32 Dean of Student Services .... Mr. Brian HULL
08 Director of Library Services .... Ms. Samantha SMITH
06 Registrar .... Mrs. Becky J. MCANELLEY
37 Director Student Financial Aid .... Ms. Diana KINTO
15 Human Resources Director .... Ms. Lora RIVES
18 Director of Physical Plant .... Mr. Charles MITCHELL
13 Director of Enterprise Applications .... Ms. Lisa SEDTAL
09 Coordinator Institutional Research .... Mr. Nathan CAMPOS
25 Contracts/Grants Administrator .... Mrs. Mary WICKLAND
72 Dean of Technical Studies .... Ms. Kristin WALKER
20 Dean of Academic Studies .... Dr. Suzonne CROCKETT
96 Director of Purchasing .... Ms. Alexandra QUAVE
04 Executiv Assistant to the President .... Ms. Stephanie JONES
19 Director Safety & Security .... Mr. Joseph HARGRAVE
26 Director of Public Relations/Devel .... Ms. Emily MELLEN

*Lamar State College-Port Arthur (I)

1500 Procter Street, Port Arthur TX 77640-6604
County: Jefferson　FICE Identification: 023485
Unit ID: 226116
Telephone: (409) 983-4921　Carnegie Class: Assoc/HVT-High Trad
FAX Number: (409) 984-6032　Calendar System: Semester
URL: www.lamarpa.edu
Established: 1909　Annual Undergrad Tuition & Fees (In-State): $4,331
Enrollment: 2,485　Coed

Affiliation or Control: State IRS Status: 501(c)3
Highest Offering: Associate Degree
Accreditation: SC, SURGT

02 President .... Dr. Betty REYNARD
05 Vice President Academic Affairs .... Dr. Pamela MILLSAP
10 Vice President Finance & Operations .... Ms. Mary WICKLAND
32 Dean of Student Services .... Dr. Tessie BRADFORD
04 Exec Assistant to the President .... Mrs. Judy HOFFPAUIR
08 Dean Library Services .... Ms. Helena GAWU
06 Registrar .... Ms. Robin HUMPHREY
37 Director Financial Aid .... Ms. Sharon THIBODEAUX
45 Director Inst Effectiveness .... Mr. James M. KNOWLES
18 Director of Physical Plant .... Mr. Reed RICHARD
26 Public Information Officer .... Mr. Gerry DICKERT
56 Dir External Learning Experiences .... Mr. Wayne WELLS
13 Dir Information Technology Services .... Mr. Samir GHORAYEB
15 Director Human Resources .... Ms. Tammy RILEY
09 Director of Institutional Research .... Mrs. Petra UZORUO
103 VP Workforce/Continuing Educ .... Dr. Ben STAFFORD
72 Dean Technical Programs .... Dr. Melissa ARMENTOR
97 Dept Head Gen Ed & Developmental .... Dr. Michelle DAVIS
50 Dept Head Business & Technology .... Mrs. Sheila GUILLOT
39 Director Student Housing .... Dr. Tessie BRADFORD
41 Athletic Director .... Mr. Scott STREET
96 Director of Purchasing/Contracts .... Mrs. Maria GARCIA
76 Dept Head Allied Health .... Ms. Shirley MACNEILL
64 Dept Head Commercial Music .... Mr. Richard VANDEWALKER
84 Director Enrollment Services .... Mr. David MORALES

*Sam Houston State University (A)

1905 University Avenue, Huntsville TX 77340
County: Walker FICE Identification: 003606
Unit ID: 227881
Telephone: (936) 294-1111 Carnegie Class: DU-Mod
FAX Number: (936) 294-1465 Calendar System: Semester
URL: www.shsu.edu
Established: 1879 Annual Undergrad Tuition & Fees (In-State): $8,736
Enrollment: 21,912 Coed
Affiliation or Control: State IRS Status: Exempt
Highest Offering: Doctorate
Accreditation: SC, ART, CACREP, CAEPN, CIDA, CLPSY, DIETD, DIETI, FEPAC, IPSY, MUS, NURSE, @OSTEO, THEA

02 President .... Ms. Alisa WHITE
05 Chief Academic Officer & Provost .... Dr. Richard EGLSAER
10 CFO & Senior VP for Operations .... Dr. Carlos HERNANDEZ
111 VP for University Advancement .... Mr. Frank HOLMES
84 VP for Enrollment Management .... Dr. Heather THIELEMANN
32 VP for Student Affairs .... Mr. Frank PARKER
13 VP for Information Technology .... Mr. Mark ADAMS
41 Athletic Director .... Mr. Bobby WILLIAMS
100 Chief of Staff .... Ms. Kathy GILCREASE
20 Vice Provost .... Dr. Chris MAYNARD
61 Dean of Criminal Justice .... Dr. Phillip LYONS
57 Dean of Arts & Media .... Dr. Ronald SHIELDS
83 Dean of Humanities/Social Sciences .... Vacant
81 Dean of Sciences & Engineering Tech .... Dr. John PASCARELLA
50 Dean of Business Administration .... Dr. Mitchell MUEHSAM
53 Dean of Education .... Dr. Stacey EDMONSON
63 Dean of Osteopathic Medicine .... Dr. Charles HENLEY
76 Dean of Health Sciences .... Dr. Rodney RUNYAN
58 Dean Graduate Studies .... Dr. Ken HENDRICKSON
106 Assoc VP Distance Learning .... Dr. William ANGROVE
18 VP Facilities Operations/Management .... Mr. Juan NUNEZ
21 Assoc VP Finance & Operations .... Ms. Sylvia RAPPE
21 Assoc VP Finance & Operations .... Ms. Lenora CHAPMAN
15 Asst VP for HR & Diversity .... Ms. Rhonda BEASSIE
109 Asst VP Auxiliary Services .... Dr. Kristy VIENNE
26 Assoc VP Marketing & Comm .... Ms. Kris KASKEL-RUIZ
30 Assoc VP for Development .... Ms. Thelma MOONEY
29 Assoc VP Alumni Relations .... Mr. Charlie VIENNE
110 Director Advancement Services .... Ms. Patricia LEWIS
88 Museum Director .... Mr. Mac WOODWARD
06 AVP Enrollment Management/Registrar .... Ms. Teresa RINGO
88 Assoc VP Enrollment Management .... Ms. Leah MULLIGAN
88 Assoc VP Enrollment Management .... Ms. Ann THEODORI
09 Asst VP Institutional Effectiveness .... Ms. Donna ARTHO
88 Dir of Operations/Enrollment Mgmt .... Mr. Clint LOCKWOOD
35 Assoc VP Student Affairs/Rec Sports .... Dr. Keith JENKINS
38 AVP Stdnt Affairs/Couns/Health Svcs .... Dr. Drew MILLER
35 Dean of Students .... Mr. John YARABECK
19 Exec Dir Public Safety Services .... Mr. Kevin MORRIS
39 Exec Dir Residence Life .... Ms. Joellen TIPTON
35 Director of Student Activities .... Mr. Brandon COOPER
88 Dir of Leadership Initiatives .... Ms. Meredith CONREY
14 AVP Infrastructure/Support Svcs .... Mr. Michael DEWEY
105 Assoc VP Enterprise Services .... Vacant
90 Assoc VP Client Services .... Mr. Terry BLAYLOCK
88 Director IT Project Management .... Mr. Kevin HAMMEL
119 Director Information Security .... Mr. Steven FREY
88 Director IT Business Services .... Ms. Deborah MCKERALL
28 Dir Equity/Inclusion & Title IX .... Ms. Jeanine BIAS
43 Associate General Counsel .... Ms. Sandra HORNE

*Sul Ross State University (B)

PO Box C-100, Alpine TX 79832-0001
County: Brewster FICE Identification: 003625
Unit ID: 228501
Telephone: (432) 837-8011 Carnegie Class: Masters/L
FAX Number: (432) 837-8334 Calendar System: Semester
URL: www.sulross.edu
Established: 1917 Annual Undergrad Tuition & Fees (In-State): $8,777
Enrollment: 2,345 Coed
Affiliation or Control: State IRS Status: 501(c)3
Highest Offering: Master's
Accreditation: SC, NURSE

02 President .... Dr. Pete P. GALLEGO
05 Exec Vice President/Provost .... Vacant
10 Vice Pres Budget & Finance .... Mr. Jim GOODMAN
84 Vice Pres Enrollment Management .... Dr. Matt MOORE
100 Chief of Staff .... Mr. Michael PACHECO
30 Asst Vice Pres Development .... Vacant
12 Dean of Academic Affairs RGC .... Ms. Patricia NICOSIA
11 Asst VP of Administration .... Vacant
09 AVP Institutional Effectiveness .... Dr. Jeanne QVARNSTROM
06 University Registrar .... Ms. Pamela S. PIPES
08 Dean Library & Info Technology .... Ms. Betsy EVANS
32 Dean of Students .... Ms. Brandy SNYDER
92 Dir Honors Prog/Acad Ctr Excellence .... Dr. Kathy STEIN
26 Director Communications .... Mr. Dean WILKINSON
37 Dir Financial Assistance .... Mr. Michael CORBETT
49 Dean Arts & Science .... Dr. Jay DOWNING
107 Dean Education & Professional Stds .... Dr. Barbara TUCKER
47 Dean Agricult/Natural Resource Sci .... Dr. Bonnie WARNOCK
15 Director of Human Resources .... Mrs. Karlin DEVOLL
18 Asst Director of Physical Plant .... Mr. Victor ROMERO
19 Director Dept of Public Safety .... Mr. Kent DUNEGAN
21 Director of Accounting/Finance .... Ms. Corina RAMIREZ
39 Asst Director Residential Living .... Mr. Jose POLIO
41 Athletics Director .... Ms. Amanda WORKMAN
38 Director of Counseling Center .... Ms. Rebecca-Greathouse WREN
13 Chief Information Officer .... Mr. David W. GIBSON
96 Director of Purchasing .... Vacant
88 Dir Center for Big Bend Studies .... Mr. Bryon SCHROEDER
29 Dir of Alumni Relations .... Ms. Kathy MORENO
88 Director of Upward Bound .... Ms. Barbara VEGA
88 Director of University Archives .... Ms. Melleta BELL
88 Law Enforcement Academy Coord .... Ms. Melissa FIERRO
07 Asst Dir Admissions & Recruiting .... Ms. Dafne WESTERLINK
88 Mail Service Supervisor .... Ms. Leticia GONZALES
116 Director Office of Internal Audit .... Mr. Scott A. CUPP
36 Dir of Career Services Testing .... Mr. Rocio AGUARDO
04 Admin Assistant to the President .... Ms. Marina CAVAZOS
103 Director Workforce Development .... Ms. Elizabeth PENA
104 Director Study Abroad .... Dr. Mary ELIZABETH TOMPSON
105 Director Web Services .... Mr. Al BRAUTIGAM
25 Chief Contract and Grants Administr .... Dr. Eric T. FUNASAKI
28 Director of Diversity .... Ms. April AULTMAN-BECKER
50 Dean of Business .... Mr. Edison MOURA

*Texas State University (C)

601 University Drive, San Marcos TX 78666-4615
County: Hays FICE Identification: 003615
Unit ID: 228459
Telephone: (512) 245-2111 Carnegie Class: DU-Higher
FAX Number: (512) 245-3040 Calendar System: Semester
URL: www.txstate.edu
Established: 1899 Annual Undergrad Tuition & Fees (In-State): $10,855
Enrollment: 37,812 Coed
Affiliation or Control: State IRS Status: 170(c)1
Highest Offering: Doctorate
Accreditation: SC, CAATE, CACREP, CAEPT, CAHIIM, CAPRT, CIDA, COARC, CONST, DIETD, DIETI, HSA, IPSY, JOUR, MT, MUS, NAIT, NURSE, PTA, RTT, SP, SPAA, SW

02 President .... Dr. Denise M. TRAUTH
05 Provost/Vice Pres Academic Affairs .... Dr. Gene BOURGEOIS
11 VP University Administration .... Dr. Lisa LLOYD
32 VP Student Affairs .... Dr. Cynthia HERNANDEZ
10 Vice Pres Finance/Support Services .... Mr. Eric ALGOE
111 Vice Pres University Advancement .... Dr. Barbara BREIER
13 Vice Pres Information Technology .... Mr. Kenneth PIERCE
88 Dean College of Applied Arts .... Dr. T. Jaime CHAHIN
50 Dean McCoy Col of Business Admin .... Dr. Sanjay RAMCHANDER
57 Dean College Fine Arts & Comm .... Dr. John FLEMING
53 Dean College of Education .... Dr. Michael O'MALLEY
76 Dean College Health Professions .... Dr. Ruth B. WELBORN
79 Dean College Liberal Arts .... Dr. Mary BRENNAN
81 Dean College of Science & Engr .... Dr. Christine HAILEY
58 Dean The Graduate College .... Dr. Andrea GOLATO
97 Dean Univ Col & Dir PACE Center .... Dr. Mary Ellen CAVITT
92 Dean Honors College .... Dr. Heather GALLOWAY
20 Assoc Vice Pres Academic Affairs .... Dr. Vedaraman SRIRAMAN
15 Asst VP for Human Resources .... Ms. Carole E. CLERIE
20 Associate Provost .... Dr. Debbie M. THORNE
18 Associate VP of Facilities .... Mr. Thomas F. SHEWAN
46 Assoc VP Research & Dir of Fed Rels .... Vacant
35 Assoc VP Student Affairs .... Vacant
108 Assoc VP for Inst Effectiveness .... Dr. Beth E. WUEST
21 Assoc VP Financial Services .... Mr. Darryl BORGONAH
84 Assoc VP Enroll Mgmt/Marketing .... Mr. Gary T. RAY
08 Associate VP University Library .... Ms. Joan L. HEATH
20 Assistant VP for Academic Services .... Dr. Mary Ellen CAVITT
26 Asst VP for UA Communications .... Ms. Sandra PANTLIK
38 Director Counseling Center .... Dr. Lynne REEDER
07 AVP Enroll Mgmt/Dir Undergrad Admis .... Vacant
93 Asst VP IIE/Student Initiatives .... Dr. Sherri BENN
110 Assoc VP University Advancement .... Dr. Dan PERRY
115 Asst VP UA Business Operations .... Mr. Cesquinn CURTIS
88 Assoc VP Finance/Support Svcs Plng .... Ms. Nancy NUSBAUM
14 Assoc VP for Technology Resources .... Mr. Mark HUGHES
90 Assoc VP Technology Innovation .... Dr. Carlos SOLIS
106 Asst VP Distance & Extended Learn .... Mr. Dana WILLETT
06 Interim University Registrar .... Ms. Martha FRAIRE-CUELLAR
91 Director Enterprise Systems .... Mr. Martin MILLS
37 Director of Fin Aid & Scholarships .... Dr. Christopher MURR
36 Director Career Services .... Mr. Ray ROGERS
41 Director of Athletics .... Dr. Lawrence B. TEIS
29 Interim Director of Alumni Affairs .... Mr. Cesquinn CURTIS
27 Director Univ News Services .... Mr. Jayme L. BLASCHKE
19 Interim Chief of Police .... Mr. James DIXON
23 Asst VP/Dir Student Health Ctr .... Dr. Emilio CARRANCO
39 Int Director Housing/Residence Life .... Mr. Kyle ESTES
40 Manager University Bookstore .... Mr. John ROOT
28 Asst VP IIE/Fac & Staff Initiative .... Dr. Stella SILVA
96 Director Purchasing .... Mr. Dan ALDEN
88 Asst VP University Marketing .... Mr. Elias L. MARTINEZ
116 Director of Audit & Analysis .... Mr. Steve R. MCGEE
88 Interim Director Campus Recreation .... Dr. Jen BECK
88 Director LBJ Student Center .... Mr. Jack RAHMANN
108 Student Affs Assessment & Planning .... Dr. Jen BECK
88 Director Disability Services .... Mr. Gavin STEIGER
104 Asst VP/Dir International Affairs .... Ms. Rosario DAVIS
88 Director Learning Spaces .... Mr. Brian SHANKS
119 Chief Information Security Officer .... Mr. Daniel C. OWEN
90 Assoc VP IT Assistance Center .... Mr. Benjamin ROGERS
22 Asst VP Compliance/Chief Compl Ofcr .... Mr. Bobby MASON
88 Dir Student Affairs Technology .... Mr. Kevin MCCARTY

*Texas Tech University System (D)

1508 Knoxville Ave, Lubbock TX 79409-2013
County: Lubbock Identification: 667242
Telephone: (806) 742-0012 Carnegie Class: N/A
FAX Number: N/A
URL: www.texastech.edu

01 Chancellor .... Dr. Tedd L. MITCHELL
10 Vice Chancellor & CFO .... Mr. Gary BARNES
111 Vice Chancellor Inst Advancement .... Mr. Patrick KRAMER
86 Vice Chanc Government Relations .... Ms. Martha BROWN
18 Vice Chanc Facil Plng/Construction .... Mr. Billy BREEDLOVE
43 Vice Chancellor & General Counsel .... Mr. Eric D. BENTLEY
116 Vice Chancellor Audit .... Mrs. Kim TURNER

*Angelo State University (E)

2601 West Avenue N, San Angelo TX 76909-0001
County: Tom Green FICE Identification: 003541
Unit ID: 222831
Telephone: (325) 942-2555 Carnegie Class: Masters/L
FAX Number: N/A Calendar System: Semester
URL: www.angelo.edu
Established: 1928 Annual Undergrad Tuition & Fees (In-State): $7,907
Enrollment: 10,775 Coed
Affiliation or Control: State IRS Status: 501(c)3
Highest Offering: Doctorate
Accreditation: SC, ACBSP, CAEP, MUS, NURSE, PTA, SW

02 President .... Mr. Ronnie D. HAWKINS, JR.
05 Provost/Vice Pres Academic Affairs .... Dr. Donald R. TOPLIFF
111 VP for External Affairs .... Ms. Jamie AKIN
10 VP for Finance & Admin .... Ms. Angelina WRIGHT
32 VP for Student Affairs .... Dr. Javier FLORES
58 Dean Col of Grad Studies & Research .... Dr. Micheal SALISBURY
54 Dean of College of Sci & Engr .... Dr. Paul SWETS
50 Interim Dean College of Business .... Dr. Andrew TIGER
53 Dean College of Education .... Dr. Scarlet CLOUSE
66 Dean College Health & Human Service .... Dr. Leslie MAYRAND
79 Dean College of Arts & Humanities .... Dr. John KLINGEMANN
06 Director of Registrar Services .... Ms. Rosalinda CASTRO
89 Dean Freshman College .... Dr. John WEGNER
108 Exec Director of Accountability .... Ms. Brandy HAWKINS
08 Exec Director of Library Services .... Mr. Chris MATZ
36 Director Career Development .... Ms. Julie J. RUTHENBECK
15 Director of Human Resources .... Mr. Kurtis R. NEAL
37 Director of Student Financial Aid .... Mr. Charles E. KERESTLY
26 Int Dir of Communications & Mktg .... Ms. Brittney MILLER
29 Director Development & Alumni Svcs .... Ms. Kimberly ADAMS
35 Exec Director of Student Affairs .... Dr. Bradley PETTY
18 Director of Facilities Management .... Mr. Jay HALBERT
39 Dir of Housing & Residential Pgm .... Ms. Tracy W. BAKER
40 Manager Bookstore .... Ms. Michaela REYNOLDS
41 Athletic Director .... Mr. James REID
19 Chief of University Police .... Mr. James E. ADAMS
13 Assoc VP Information Technology/CIO .... Mr. Douglas FOX
21 Director of Business Services .... Ms. Jessica MANNING
96 Exec Director Materials Management .... Ms. Lanell NICHOLS
92 Director of Honors Program .... Dr. Shirley EOFF
04 Executive Asst to the President .... Ms. Adelina C. MORALES
104 Director of International Studies .... Ms. Meghan PACE
07 Director of Admissions .... Ms. Sharla ADAM
38 Director of Counseling Services .... Mr. Mark REHM
84 Director Enrollment Management .... Mr. Jeffrey SEFCIK
43 Sr Exec Asst to Pres/Gen Counsel .... Mr. Joe MUNOZ
28 Chief of Diversity & Inclusion .... Dr. Flor MADERO
30 Director of Development .... Mrs. Jennifer LOVE

† Affiliated with Texas Tech University in Lubbock, TX

*Texas Tech University (F)

2500 Broadway, Lubbock TX 79409
County: Lubbock FICE Identification: 003644
Unit ID: 229115
Telephone: (806) 742-2121 Carnegie Class: DU-Highest
FAX Number: (806) 742-2138 Calendar System: Semester

URL: www.ttu.edu
Established: 1923 Annual Undergrad Tuition & Fees (In-State): $11,600
Enrollment: 40,322 Coed
Affiliation or Control: State IRS Status: 170(c)1
Highest Offering: Doctorate
Accreditation: SC, ARCPA, ART, CACREP, CAEPN, CIDA, CLPSY, COPSY, DANCE, DIETD, DIETI, IPSY, LAW, LSAR, MFCD, MIDWF, MUS, SPAA, SW, THEA, #VET

00 Chancellor .... Dr. Tedd L. MITCHELL
02 President .... Dr. Lawrence SCHOVANEC
101 Sec Board Regents/Ex Asst to Chanc ..... Ms. Christina MARTINEZ
05 Provost and Senior Vice President .... Dr. Ron HENDRICK
10 Chief Operating Ofcr/SVP Admin/Fin .... Ms. Noel SLOAN
26 Chief Marketing & Comm Officer .... Mr. Matthew DEWEY
111 Vice Chanc Inst Advancement .... Mr. Patrick KRAMER
86 Vice Chancellor Govt Relations .... Ms. Martha BROWN
43 Vice Chanc & General Counsel .... Mr. Eric D. BENTLEY
18 VC Facilities Planning Construction .... Mr. Billy BREEDLOVE
20 Sr Vice Provost Academic Affairs .... Dr. Rob STEWART
100 President's Chief of Staff .... Ms. Grace HERNANDEZ
29 EVP & CEO Texas Tech Alumni Assoc .... Mr. Curt LANGFORD
46 Vice President for Research .... Dr. Joseph HEPPERT
28 Vice Pres Institutional Diversity .... Dr. Carol A. SUMNER
84 VP Enrollment Management .... Mrs. Jamie HANSARD
20 Vice Provost Academic Affairs .... Ms. Genevieve DURHAM DECESARO
21 Chief Accounting Ofcr & Controller .... Mr. Eric FISHER
82 Vice Provost International Affairs .... Dr. Sukant MISRA
08 Dean of Libraries .... Ms. Earnstein DUKES
60 Dean Media & Communications .... Dr. David PERLMUTTER
32 Asst Dean of Students .... Ms. Denise TIJERINA
37 Exec Director Financial Aid .... Ms. Shannon VENEZIA
13 Chief Information Officer .... Mr. Sam SEGRAN
06 Registrar .... Ms. Bobbie BROWN
07 Executive Director of Admissions .... Mr. Jason HALE
27 Managing Dir Commun & Marketing .... Vacant
04 Executive Asst to President .... Mrs. Mikki ROSS
88 Assoc VProvost for Outreach/Engage .... Mr. John OPPERMAN
44 Managing Director Annual Giving .... Vacant
23 Managing Dir Student Health Svcs .... Ms. Juli MCCAULEY
39 Managing Dir Student Housing .... Mr. Sean DUGGAN
36 Director Career Center .... Mr. Jay KILLOUGH
15 Assistant VP of Human Resources .... Mrs. Jodie BILLINGSLEY
22 Asst Vice Chanc Admin/Mng Dir EEO ..... Ms. Charlotte BINGHAM
38 Director Student Counseling .... Dr. Richard LENOX
41 Director of Athletics .... Mr. Kirby HOCUTT
47 Dean Agricultural Sci/Natural Res .... Dr. Cindy AKERS
49 Dean of Arts & Sciences .... Vacant
48 Interim Dean of Architecture .... Dr. Urs Peter (Upe) FLUECKIGER
50 Dean Business Administration .... Dr. Margaret L. WILLIAMSON
53 Dean of Education .... Dr. Jesse PEREZ MENDEZ
54 Dean of Engineering .... Dr. Albert SACCO, JR.
88 Dean of Human Sciences .... Dr. Tim DODD
61 Dean School of Law .... Dr. Jack NOWLIN
58 Dean of Graduate School .... Dr. Mark SHERIDAN
92 Interim Dean Honors College .... Dr. Aliza WONG
57 Int Dean Visual & Performing Arts .... Mrs. Genevieve DURHAM-DECESARO
19 Chief of Police .... Mr. Kyle K. BONATH
09 Managing Dir Institutional Research .... Dr. Valcik NICOLAS
96 Chief Procurement Officer .... Ms. Jennifer ADLING

*Texas Tech University Health Sciences Center (A)

3601 4th Street Mailstop 6258, Lubbock TX 79430-0001
County: Lubbock FICE Identification: 010674
Unit ID: 229337
Telephone: (806) 743-2900 Carnegie Class: Spec-4-yr-Med
FAX Number: N/A Calendar System: Semester
URL: www.ttuhsc.edu
Established: 1969 Annual Undergrad Tuition & Fees (In-State): N/A
Enrollment: 5,274 Coed
Affiliation or Control: State IRS Status: 501(c)3
Highest Offering: Doctorate
Accreditation: SC, AUD, CAATE, CACREP, DMOLS, MED, MT, NURSE, OT, PH, PHAR, PTA, SP

02 President .... Dr. Lori RICE-SPEARMAN
10 Exec VP for Finance & Operations .... Ms. Penny HARKEY
05 Provost/Chief Academic Officer .... Dr. Darrin D'AGOSTINO
26 Vice Pres External Relations .... Ms. Ashley HAMM
17 Exec Vice Pres Rural/Community Hlth .. Dr. Billy U. PHILIPS, JR.
46 Int Sr Vice President for Research .... Dr. Min KANG
13 Vice Pres Info Tech/Chief Info Ofcr .... Mr. Vince FELL
86 Sr Director Governmental Relations .... Mr. Smiley GARCIA
88 Vice President of Health Policy .... Dr. Cynthia JUMPER
28 Director of Diversity & Inclusion .... Ms. Doris HEREFORD
100 Chief of Staff .... Mr. Coleman JOHNSON
43 Managing Attorney .... Ms. Vicki DORRIS
15 Chief People Officer .... Mr. Steven SOSLAND
108 Vice Prov Effective/Accreditation .... Dr. Kari DICKSON
32 Asst Provost for Student Affairs .... Dr. Erin JUSTNYA
22 Vice Pres Inst Compliance .... Dr. Sonya CASTRO-QUIRINO
18 Vice Pres Facilities/Safety Svcs .... Dr. Harry SLIFE, JR.
63 Dean Medical Sch/EVP Clinical Affs .... Dr. Steven L. BERK
58 Dean Grad Sch Biomed Sciences .... Dr. Brandt L. SCHNEIDER
66 Dean of Nursing School .... Dr. Michael L. EVANS
76 Dean School Health Professions .... Dr. Dawndra SECHRIST
67 Dean of Pharmacy School .... Dr. Quentin R. SMITH
63 Reg Dean Medicine Amarillo Campus .... Dr. Richard JORDAN
63 Int Reg Dean Medicine Odessa Campus .... Dr. Timothy BENTON
66 Reg Dean Nursing Abilene .... Ms. Pearl E. MERRITT
66 Reg Dean Nursing Odessa Campus .... Dr. Sharon CANNON
76 Reg Dean Health Profession Amarillo .... Dr. Joan POTTER
76 Reg Dean Health Professions Odessa .... Dr. Deborah YORK-EDWARDS
67 Reg Dean Pharmacy Abilene .... Dr. Sara BROUSE
67 Reg Dean Pharmacy Amarillo .... Dr. Thomas THEKKUMKARA
67 Reg Dean Pharmacy Dallas .... Dr. Steven PASS
67 Reg Dean Pharmacy Lubbock .... Dr. Charles E. SEIFERT
06 Registrar .... Ms. Amanda MCSWEEN
08 Exec Director of HSC Libraries .... Dr. Richard NOLLAN
21 Managing Dir Accounting Services .... Ms. Melody OLIPHINT
22 Director of Equal Employment .... Ms. Charlotte BINGHAM
25 Director of Sponsored Programs .... Ms. Erin WOODS
37 Director of Financial Aid .... Mr. Marcus WILSON
96 Managing Dir of Procurement Service .... Mr. John G. HAYNES
09 Chief Analyst Inst Research .... Mr. Kevin MCINTYRE
29 Alumni Relations Manager .... Ms. Clarissa SANCHEZ
88 Sr Director Office of Global Health ...... Ms. Michelle ENSMINGER

*Texas Tech University Health Sciences Center at El Paso (B)

5001 El Paso Drive, El Paso TX 79905
County: El Paso Identification: 667243
Telephone: (915) 215-4300 Carnegie Class: Not Classified
FAX Number: N/A Calendar System: Semester
URL: www.elpaso.ttuhsc.edu
Established: 2013 Annual Undergrad Tuition & Fees (In-State): N/A
Enrollment: N/A Coed
Affiliation or Control: State IRS Status: 170(c)1
Highest Offering: Doctorate
Accreditation: SC, DENT, MED, NURSE

01 President .... Dr. Richard LANGE
05 Vice Pres for Academic Affairs .... Dr. Richard BROWER
111 Vice Pres for Inst Advancement .... Dr. Andrea TAWNEY
10 Vice Pres Finance & Administration .... Vacant
11 Vice President for Operations .... Vacant
26 Vice Pres Outreach/Cmty Engagement .... Dr. Jose Manuel DE LA ROSA
13 Assoc VP Information Technology .... Mr. Jerry RODRIGUEZ
32 Asst VP Student Services .... Dr. Robin DANKOVICH
63 Dean School of Medicine .... Dr. Richard LANGE
66 Dean School of Nursing .... Dr. Stephanie WOODS
81 Dean Graduate School of Biomedical .... Dr. Rajkumar LAKSHMANASWAMY
52 Dean School of Dental Medicine .... Dr. Richard BLACK
04 Assistant to President .... Ms. Vanessa SOLIS
06 Registrar .... Ms. Diana ANDRADE
15 Chief Human Resources Officer .... Ms. Jennifer ERICKSON
18 Chief Facilities/Physical Plant Ofc .... Mr. Al FLORES

Texas Wesleyan University (C)

1201 Wesleyan, Fort Worth TX 76105-1536
County: Tarrant FICE Identification: 003645
Unit ID: 229160
Telephone: (817) 531-4444 Carnegie Class: DU-Mod
FAX Number: (817) 531-4425 Calendar System: Semester
URL: www.txwes.edu
Established: 1890 Annual Undergrad Tuition & Fees: $33,408
Enrollment: 2,197 Coed
Affiliation or Control: United Methodist IRS Status: 501(c)3
Highest Offering: Doctorate
Accreditation: SC, ANEST, CAATE, MFCD, MUS, NURSE

01 President .... Mr. Frederick G. SLABACH
05 Provost/Sr Vice President .... Dr. Hector QUINTANILLA
10 VP Finance & Administration .... Mrs. Donna NANCE
100 Chief of Staff and General Counsel .... Ms. Patti GEARHART TURNER
32 VP Student Affairs/Dean of Students .... Dr. Dennis HALL
111 VP University Advancement .... Ms. Jerri SCHOOLEY
26 Assoc VP Marketing/ Communications .... Ms. Shannon LAMBERSON
15 AVP of Human Resources .... Dr. Angela DAMPEER
20 Assoc Provost Academic Affairs .... Dr. Steven DANIELL
20 Associate Provost .... Dr. Helena BUSSELL
41 Athletic Director .... Mr. Ricky DOTSON
53 Dean School of Education .... Dr. Carlos MARTINEZ
50 Dean of School of Business .... Dr. Sameer VAIDYA
49 Dean School of Arts & Sciences .... Dr. Ricardo RODRIGUEZ
39 Asst Dn Stdnts/Dir Residence Life .... Ms. Jill GERLOFF
06 Registrar .... Mr. Sloan WHITE
21 Controller .... Ms. Jacqueline RUTLEDGE
07 Assoc Vice Pres Enrollment .... Ms. Djuana YOUNG
42 Chaplain .... Dr. Gladys CHILDS
38 Director of Counseling .... Dr. Linda METCALF
96 Director of Purchasing .... Ms. Deborah CAVITT
36 Director Career Services/Counselor .... Dr. Gary STOUT
18 Exec Dir of Facil/Opers/Emerg Svcs .... Mr. Brian FRANKS
04 Executive Assistant to the Pres .... Mrs. Sherry SANDLES
09 Director Institutional Research .... Mr. Sean M. BRIGADIER
19 Director Campus Safety/Security .... Mr. Chris BECKRICH

Texas Woman's University (D)

304 Administration Dr, Denton TX 76204
County: Denton FICE Identification: 003646
Unit ID: 229179
Telephone: (940) 898-2000 Carnegie Class: DU-Mod
FAX Number: (940) 898-3198 Calendar System: Semester
URL: www.twu.edu
Established: 1901 Annual Undergrad Tuition & Fees (In-State): $8,255
Enrollment: 16,433 Coed
Affiliation or Control: State IRS Status: 501(c)3
Highest Offering: Doctorate
Accreditation: SC, ACBSP, CACREP, COPSY, DANCE, DH, DIETD, DIETI, HSA, IPSY, LIB, MFCD, MUS, NURSE, OT, PTA, SCPSY, SP, SW

01 Chancellor & President .... Dr. Carine FEYTEN
05 Provost/Exec VP Acad Affairs .... Dr. Carolyn KAPINUS
10 VP Finance/Administration .... Mr. Jason TOMLINSON
32 VP Student Life .... Dr. Monica MENDEZ-GRANT
111 VP University Advancement .... Dr. Kimberly RUSSELL
84 Interim VP Enrollment Services .... Dr. Monica MENDEZ-GRANT
20 Executive Vice Provost .... Dr. Jennifer MARTIN
88 VP Undergrad Studies/Acad Partnersh .... Dr. Barbara LERNER
09 Vice Prov Inst Research/Improvement .... Dr. Mark S. HAMNER
15 Sr Assoc VP Human Resources .... Mr. Lewis BENAVIDES
13 Deputy CIO .... Ms. Cori TREVINO
58 Dean Graduate School .... Dr. Holly HANSEN-THOMAS
49 Dean College Arts & Sciences .... Dr. Abigail TILTON
50 Dean College of Business .... Dr. Rama YELKUR
66 Dean College Nursing .... Dr. Rosalie MAINOUS
69 Dean College Health Sciences .... Dr. Christopher T. RAY
107 Dean College Prof Education .... Dr. Lisa HUFFMAN
46 Vice Provost Research/Innovation .... Dr. Holly HANSEN-THOMAS
121 Assistant Provost Student Success .... Dr. Joshua ADAMS
08 Dean of Libraries .... Ms. Suzanne SEARS
06 Registrar .... Ms. Jenna LEE
18 Associate VP Facilities .... Mr. Robert RAMIREZ
26 Assoc VP Marketing/Communication .... Ms. Cindy POLLARD
21 Associate VP Finance .... Ms. Rana ASKINS
21 Assistant VP Controller .... Ms. Melanie RAMIREZ
113 Bursar .... Mr. Glen RAY
19 Executive Dir of Public Safety .... Mr. Samuel GARRISON
41 Athletic Director .... Ms. Sandee MOTT
23 Dir Operations Student Health Svcs .... Ms. Tanisha FREEMAN
39 Director University Housing .... Ms. Jill ECKARDT
29 Exec Dir Alumni Engagement .... Ms. Jasmine CARTER
37 Exec Dir Student Financial Aid .... Ms. Lacey THOMPSON
04 Executive Asst to Chancellor/Pres .... Ms. Lorie HUSLIG
100 Chief of Staff .... Mr. Christopher JOHNSON
104 Director Study Abroad .... Dr. Annie PHILLIPS
106 Dir Teach & Learn w/Technology .... Dr. Lynda MURPHY
108 Dir Academic Assessment .... Dr. Gray SCOTT
07 Director of Admissions .... Ms. Nikki YOUNG
86 Dir Governmental/Legislative Affs .... Mr. Kevin CRUSER
43 General Counsel .... Ms. Katherine GREEN

Trinity University (E)

One Trinity Place, San Antonio TX 78212-7200
County: Bexar FICE Identification: 003647
Unit ID: 229267
Telephone: (210) 999-7011 Carnegie Class: Masters/S
FAX Number: (210) 999-7696 Calendar System: Semester
URL: www.trinity.edu
Established: 1869 Annual Undergrad Tuition & Fees: $46,456
Enrollment: 2,677 Coed
Affiliation or Control: Independent Non-Profit IRS Status: 501(c)3
Highest Offering: Master's
Accreditation: SC, HSA

01 President .... Dr. Danny ANDERSON
05 Vice Pres Academic Affairs .... Dr. Megan MUSTAIN
10 VP Finance and Administration .... Mr. Gary LOGAN
111 VP Alumni Relations & Development .... Mr. Michael BACON
13 VP Info Resources .... Vacant
84 VP Enrollment/Student Retention .... Mr. Eric MALOOF
32 Vice Pres Student Life .... Dr. Sheryl R. TYNES
20 Assoc VP Faculty Recruitment & Dev .... Dr. Duane COLTHARP
114 Assoc VP Budget & Research .... Dr. Jennifer HENDERSON
21 Assoc VP for Finance .... Ms. Diana HEEREN
35 AVP Student Affs/Dean of Students .... Dr. Demitrius BROWN
09 Assoc VP/Dir Institutional Research .... Ms. Kara LARKAN
109 Sr Dir Conf/Spec Pgms/Aux Svcs .... Mr. Bruce BRAVO
37 Dir Student Financial Aid .... Ms. Christina PIKLA
19 Asst VP Public Safety/Ent Risk Mgmt .... Mr. Paul CHAPA
15 Assistant VP Human Resources .... Mr. James HERTEL
06 Registrar .... Mr. Alfred RODRIGUEZ
07 Dean Enrollment Operations .... Ms. Valerie SCHWEERS
38 Sr Director Counseling/Health Svcs .... Dr. Marcy YOUNGDAHL
35 Director Student Involvement .... Ms. Jamie THOMPSON
36 Director of Career Services .... Ms. Katie RAMIREZ
13 Sr Dir Technology Operations .... Mr. David PERSALES
44 Sr Director of Annual Giving Pgms .... Ms. Kathy MCNEILL
29 Senior Director of Alumni Relations .... Mr. Ryan FINNELLY
04 Exec Assistant to the President .... Ms. Claire SMITH
18 Sr Director Facility Services .... Mr. James BAKER
42 Chaplain .... Rev. Alex SERNA-WALLENDER
96 Director of Purchasing .... Vacant
28 Director Diversity .... Ms. Jamie THOMPSON
41 Athletic Director .... Mr. Bob KING

Trinity Valley Community College (F)

100 Cardinal Drive, Athens TX 75751-2734
County: Henderson FICE Identification: 003572
Unit ID: 225308
Telephone: (903) 677-8822 Carnegie Class: Assoc/MT-VT-High Non
FAX Number: (903) 675-6316 Calendar System: Semester
URL: www.tvcc.edu
Established: 1946 Annual Undergrad Tuition & Fees (In-District): $4,920
Enrollment: 5,600 Coed

Affiliation or Control: State/Local IRS Status: 501(c)3
Highest Offering: Associate Degree
Accreditation: SC, ADNUR, EMT, SURGT

01 President Dr. Jerry KING
05 Vice President for Instruction Ms. Kristin SPIZZIRRI
32 Vice President Student Services Dr. Philip PARNELL
13 VP of Information Technology Mr. Brett DANIEL
10 Vice Pres Administrative Services Mr. David HOPKINS
20 Assoc VP Instruction Academic Educ Mrs. Erica RICHARDSON
103 Associate VP of Workforce Education Ms. Kelley TOWNSEND
106 AVP of Instructional Innov/Support Ms. Holley COLLIER
12 Assoc VP of TDCJ Programs Dr. Sam HURLEY
84 AVP of Enrollment Management Ms. Tammy DENNEY
18 Asst VP of Facilities Management Mr. David GRAEM
76 Provost Health Occupations Dr. Helen REID
12 Provost Kaufman County Campus Dr. Algia ALLEN
12 Provost Anderson County Campus Dr. Jeff WATSON
102 Executive Director of Foundation Ms. Emily HEGLUND
09 Dir Strategic Plng/Effect/Accred Mr. Spencer WAGLEY
21 Dir of Acct Services & Controller Ms. Stephanie GOLEM
08 Director Learning Resource Center Ms. Karla BRYAN
07 Dir of Admissions/Registrar Ms. Caroline WHITAKER
26 Director Marketing/Communications Ms. Marlo BITTER
28 Dir Student Engagement & Diversity Ms. Audrey HAWKINS
37 Dir Student Fin Aid/Veteran Svcs Ms. Tonya RICHARDSON-DEAN
41 Athletic Director Mr. Eddie KITE
19 Director of Campus Police Mr. Stewart NEWBY
40 Bookstore Manager Mrs. Beth Ann KIDD
39 Director of Housing/Judicial Ofc Mr. Harold JONES
51 Dir Adult/Continuing Education Ms. Chris HICKS
15 Director of Human Resources Ms. Janene DOTTS
96 Purchasing/Contracts/Ins Coord Ms. Lawanna SEWALT
04 Executive Asst to the President Ms. Norma SHERAM
25 Sr Accountant/Grants Ms. Delana NEWMAN
36 Director of Student Pathways Ms. Janet GREEN
88 Director of Dual Credit Ms. Mary Helen KELM
18 Dir Transportation & Logistics Mr. Leon HANSON

Tyler Junior College (A)

PO Box 9020, Tyler TX 75711-9020
County: Smith FICE Identification: 003648
Unit ID: 229355
Telephone: (903) 510-2200 Carnegie Class: Bac/Assoc-Assoc Dom
FAX Number: (903) 510-2632 Calendar System: Semester
URL: www.tjc.edu
Established: 1926 Annual Undergrad Tuition & Fees (In-District): $4,762
Enrollment: 11,749 Coed
Affiliation or Control: State/Local IRS Status: 170(c)1
Highest Offering: Baccalaureate
Accreditation: SC, CAHIIM, COARC, #COARCP, DA, DH, DMS, EMT, MLTAD, OTA, PTAA, RAD, SURGT

01 President/Chief Executive Officer Dr. Juan E. MEJIA
05 VP Acad & Stdnt Affairs/Provost Ms. Deana SHEPPARD
11 VP Operations/COO Ms. Kimberly LESSNER
10 VP Finance & Admin Affairs/CFO Ms. Sarah E. VAN CLEEF
111 VP Inst Advance/Exec Dir Foundation Mr. D. Mitch ANDREWS
15 Exec Dir Human Resources Mr. S. Kevin FOWLER
04 Exec Asst to President Ms. Debra HOLCOMB
101 Spec Asst President/Board Ms. Ellen MATTHEWS
13 Chief Information Officer Vacant
103 Assoc Vice Prov Acad & Wrkfc Affs Mr. Terry PETERMAN
32 Assoc Vice Prov Student Affairs Dr. Timothy S. DRAIN
81 Dean Engineering Math and Sciences Dr. J. Cliff BOUCHER
66 Dean Nursing/Health Science Ms. Elizabeth OLIVIA
79 Dean Humanities/Comm/Fine Arts Mr. Jim RICHEY
107 Dean Professional Tech Programs Ms. Lorretta SWAN
51 Dean Continuing Studies Mr. Brent WALLACE
35 Dean of Students Ms. Tampa J. NANNEN
88 Exec Dir Business Services Ms. Carol HUTSON
21 Controller Mr. Hunter THROCKMORTON
108 Dir Institutional Effectiveness Dr. Belinda PRIHODA
22 Dir Employee Relations/Title IX Mr. Andrew CANTEY
16 Director HR Services/Operations Vacant
18 Dir Facilities & Construction Mr. Mark GARTMAN
119 Director Information Security Ms. Kaytee HASSELL
19 Director Campus Police Mr. Michael SEALE
39 Director Residential Life Mr. Steven LOGAN
96 Director Campus Services Ms. Dana BALLARD
110 Dir Advancement Oper/Scholarships Mr. Bill WONG
41 Director Intercollegiate Athletics Mr. Kevin VEST
07 Director Admissions Mrs. Claire MIZELL
06 Director Acad Records/Registrar Ms. Britt SABOTA
121 Director Academic Advising/Testing Mr. Chris FONTAINE
37 Director Financial Aid Ms. Devon WIGGINS
106 Director Distance Education Mr. Ken CRAVER
08 Director Learning Resource Center Mrs. Maggie RUELLE
92 Director Honors Program Mr. David FUNK
35 Director Student Life Mrs. Lauren TYLER
29 Director Alumni Relations Ms. Susan FARRINGTON
27 Dir Public Affairs Media Relations Mrs. Rebecca SANDERS
88 Director SBDC Mr. Donald W. PROUDFOOT
44 Director Annual Giving Mr. Paul PREWITT
112 Director Major Gifts Ms. Barabara GREENBAUER
118 Manager Benefits Compensation Ms. DeVonne CAGLE
38 Counselor Learning Specialist Mrs. Tracey WILLIAMS
36 Specialist Career Planning Ms. Sherry FULLER

University of Dallas (B)

1845 E Northgate Drive, Irving TX 75062-4736
County: Dallas FICE Identification: 003651
Unit ID: 224323
Telephone: (972) 721-5000 Carnegie Class: Masters/L
FAX Number: (972) 721-5017 Calendar System: Semester
URL: www.udallas.edu
Established: 1956 Annual Undergrad Tuition & Fees: $45,160
Enrollment: 2,489 Coed
Affiliation or Control: Roman Catholic IRS Status: 501(c)3
Highest Offering: Doctorate
Accreditation: SC

01 President Dr. Jonathan J. SANFORD
04 Special Asst to the President Mr. Benjamin GIBBS
84 Assistant VP Enrollment Mrs. Elizabeth GRIFFIN-SMITH
10 Vice President for Finance and CFO Mr. Robert WATLING
05 Interim Provost Dr. Tammy LEONARD
111 Vice President for Advancement Mrs. Kristine MUNOZ-VETTER
43 VP for Board and Legal Services Mrs. Heather A. LACHENAUER
13 Chief Information Officer Mrs. Ruchi SHETH
32 Dean of Students Ms. Julia L. CARRANO
50 Dean College of Business Dr. Brett LANDRY
49 Interim Dean of Constantin College Dr. David A. ANDREWS
58 Dean Grad School of Liberal Arts Dr. Joshua S. PARENS
08 Dean of Libraries and Research Ms. Cherie L. HOHERTZ
06 Registrar Ms. Marisa DARBY
19 Police Chief Mr. Russell GREENE
13 Director Information Technology Mr. Richard HAYTER
14 Director of IT User Support Service Mr. Sabyasachi SANYAL
41 Director of Athletics Mr. Richard STROCKBINE
42 Assoc Director of Campus Ministry Vacant
15 Director Human Resources Dr. Mary FLECK
09 Dir of Institutional Effectiveness Vacant
26 VP Marketing & Communications Ms. Clare VENEGAS
96 Manager of Purchasing Mr. Ron CARVALHO
104 Director for Rome & Summer Programs Mrs. Becky DAVIES
23 Physician & Dir of Health Center Dr. Lora RODRIGUEZ
36 Director of Career Services Ms. Amy YOUNG
37 Director Financial Aid Vacant
07 Director of Undergraduate Admission Mr. Michael J. PROBUS
123 Director of Graduate Admissions Ms. Breanna COLLINS
35 Director Student Activities Ms. Marissa C. BROWN
39 Director Housing Operations Mrs. Betty PERRETTA
29 Director Alumni Relations Ms. Julie A. ABELL
100 Chief of Staff Mr. Ryan D. REEDY
22 Director Civil Rights & Title IX Ms. Luciana E. HAMPILOS
38 Director Counseling Center Mr. Johnathan M. SUMPTER
90 Director IS Apps & Security Mr. Blake E. PALMER
91 Director Information Systems Mr. Ryan M. HALLER

*University of Houston System (C)

4302 University Dr., 212 E. Cullen,
Houston TX 77204-2018
County: Harris FICE Identification: 011721
Unit ID: 229407
Telephone: (713) 743-1000 Carnegie Class: N/A
FAX Number: N/A
URL: www.uhsa.uh.edu

01 Chancellor Dr. Renu KHATOR
05 Sr VC for Academic Affairs/Provost Dr. Paula M. SHORT
10 Sr VC Administration/Finance Mr. Raymond BARTLETT
43 Vice Chancellor/General Counsel Ms. Dona H. CORNELL
32 Vice Chanc Student Affs/Enrol Mgmt Dr. Richard WALKER
111 VC University Advancement Ms. Eloise D. BRICE
86 Vice Chanc Govt Relations Mr. Jason S. SMITH
26 Vice Chanc Marketing/Comm/Media Ms. Lisa K. HOLDEMAN
21 Assoc Vice Chancellor Finance Mr. Karin LIVINGSTON
11 Assoc VC Administration Dr. Emily MESSA
13 Assoc VC Information Technology/CIO Dr. Dennis FOUTY
100 Chief of Staff Mr. Michael JOHNSON
116 Director Internal Auditing Mr. Phillip HURD
88 Treasurer Ms. Roberta (Robbi) PURYEAR
15 Assoc VC Human Resources Mr. Gaston REINOSO
04 Sr Exec Admin Asst to the Chanc Ms. Carmen HERNANDEZ

*University of Houston (D)

4302 University Dr., 212 E. Cullen,
Houston TX 77204-2018
County: Harris FICE Identification: 003652
Unit ID: 225511
Telephone: (713) 743-1000 Carnegie Class: DU-Highest
FAX Number: N/A Calendar System: Semester
URL: www.uh.edu
Established: 1927 Annual Undergrad Tuition & Fees (In-State): $9,457
Enrollment: 47,090 Coed
Affiliation or Control: State IRS Status: Exempt
Highest Offering: Doctorate
Accreditation: SC, AAFCS, CAATE, CAEP, CEA, CLPSY, CONST, COPSY, DIETD, DIETI, IPSY, LAW, #MED, MUS, NAIT, NURSE, OPT, OPTR, PHAR, SCPSY, SP, SW

02 President Dr. Renu KHATOR
88 Chief Energy Officer Dr. Ramanan KRISHNAMOORTI
41 VP Intercollegiate Athletics Mr. Chris PEZMAN
31 VP for Community Rels & Inst Access Dr. Elwyn C. LEE
100 Chief of Staff Mr. Mike JOHNSON
20 Vice Provost & Dean UG Stdnts Dr. Teri E. LONGACRE
58 Vice Provost & Dean Grad School Dr. Sarah LARSEN
21 Assoc Provost Finance & Admin Dr. Sabrina HASSUMANI
88 Assoc Prov Educ Innov & Tech Dr. Jeff MORGAN
88 Assoc Provost Fac Dev/Affairs Dr. Mark CLARKE
21 Associate VC/VP Finance Mr. Karin LIVINGSTON
05 SVP Academic Affairs/Provost Dr. Paula M. SHORT
11 Assoc VC/VP Administration Dr. Emily MESSA
35 Assoc VC/VP Student Affairs Dr. Daniel MAXWELL
35 Assoc VP Stdnt Affs/Dean of Stdnts Dr. Donell YOUNG
29 Assoc VP Alumni Association Mr. Mike PEDE
13 Assoc VP Information Tech/CIO Dr. Dennis FOUTY
15 Assoc VP Human Resources Mr. Gaston REINOSO
22 Asst VC/VP Equal Opportunity Ms. Toni J. BENOIT
19 Asst VC/VP Public Safety/Security Ms. Kelly BOYSEN
91 Asst VP Enterprise Sys Adm Mr. Keith MARTIN
10 Sr Vice Pres Administration/Finance Mr. Raymond BARTLETT
39 Asst VP Res Life/Student Housing Mr. Don YACKLEY
63 Dean Col Medicine/VP Medical Affs Dr. Stephen J. SPANN
48 Dean College of Architecture Ms. Patricia Belton OLIVER
57 Dean McGovern College of the Arts Dr. Andrew DAVIS
50 Dean Bauer Col Business Admin Mr. Paul A. PAVLOU
49 Int Dean Col Liberal Arts/Soc Sci Dr. Daniel P. O'CONNOR
53 Dean College of Education Dr. Robert MCPHERSON
54 Dean Cullen College of Engineering Dr. Joseph W. TEDESCO
92 Dean Honors College Dr. William MONROE
88 Dean Hilton Col Htl/Restaurant Mgt Dr. Dennis REYNOLDS
43 VP Legal Affairs & Gen Counsel Ms. Dona H. CORNELL
61 Dean UH Law Center Mr. Leonard M. BAYNES
81 Dean Col Natural Sci & Math Dr. Dan WELLS
66 Dean School of Nursing Dr. Kathryn M. TART
88 Dean College of Optometry Dr. Michael D. TWA
85 Asst Director Global Initiatives Ms. Corissa WANDMACHER
80 Dean Hobby School of Public Affairs Dr. Jim GRANATO
08 Dean University Libraries Ms. Athena JACKSON
67 Dean College of Pharmacy Dr. Lamar PRITCHARD
70 Dean Graduate Col of Social Work Dr. Alan DETLAFF
72 Dean College of Technology Dr. Anthony P. AMBLER
46 VP Research/Tech Transfer Dr. Amr ELNASHAI
101 Exec Administrator to Board Ms. Germaine MATHISEN
27 Executive Director Media Relations Mr. Mike S. ROSEN
37 Exec Dir Scholarships & Fin Aid Ms. Briget JANS
07 Executive Director of Admissions Mr. Mardell MAXWELL
25 Exec Dir Contract and Grants Ms. Beverly RYMER
04 Sr Exec Assistant to the President Ms. Carmen HERNANDEZ
06 University Registrar Mr. Scott SAWYER
96 Director of Purchasing Mr. Robert ADKINS
111 VP University Advancement Ms. Eloise D. BRICE
32 VP Student Affairs/Enrollment Svcs Dr. Richard WALKER
86 VP Govt & Community Relations Mr. Jason S. SMITH
26 VP for Mktg/Communications Ms. Lisa K. HOLDEMAN

*University of Houston - Clear Lake (E)

2700 Bay Area Boulevard, Houston TX 77058
County: Harris FICE Identification: 011711
Unit ID: 225414
Telephone: (281) 283-7600 Carnegie Class: Masters/L
FAX Number: (281) 283-2219 Calendar System: Semester
URL: www.uhcl.edu
Established: 1971 Annual Undergrad Tuition & Fees (In-State): $7,504
Enrollment: 9,053 Coed
Affiliation or Control: State IRS Status: 501(c)3
Highest Offering: Doctorate
Accreditation: SC, ABAI, IPSY, MFCD, NUR, PSPSY, SW

02 President Dr. Ira K. BLAKE
05 Sr Vice Pres for Acad Affairs Dr. Steven BERBERICH
10 VP Administration & Finance Mr. Mark DENNEY
04 Executive Asst to the President Ms. Berenice WEBSTER
20 Assoc VP Academic Affairs Dr. Kathryn MATTHEW
111 VP University Advancement Mr. Joseph L. STALEY
32 Vice President of Student Affairs Dr. Aaron J. HART
21 Interim Associate Vice Pres Finance Ms. Krista BUCKMINSTER
121 Assoc VP Stdnt Success Initiatives Dr. Timothy RICHARDSON
84 VP Strategic Enrollment Mgmt Dr. Lee YOUNG
50 Dean College Business Dr. Edward WALLER
79 Dean College Human Sci/Humanities Dr. Glenn SANFORD
35 Dean of Students Mr. David A. RACHITA
28 Dir Student Diversity/Equity & Incl Ms. Aliya BEAVERS
88 Exec Dir Strategic Partnerships Mr. Dwayne BUSBY
85 Asst VP Global Lrng/Strat/SIO Dr. Gigi DO
45 Int Exec Dir Planning & Assessment Ms. Miriam QUMSIEH
15 Executive Director Human Resources Dr. William B. MCGONAGLE
13 Asst VP Info Technology and CIO Dr. LeeBrian E. GASKINS
96 Exec Dir of Procurement & Payables Ms. Debra CARPENTER
25 Exec Dir Sponsored Programs Dr. Nancy DEVINO
37 Exec Director Financial Aid Ms. Holly NOLAN
88 Exec Dir Environment Inst Houston Dr. George GUILLEN
51 Exec Dir Cont Educ/Dist & OC Educ Ms. Lisa GABRIEL
26 Assoc VP Marketing & Communications Vacant
29 Exec Dir University Advancement Ms. Elbby ANTONY
36 Ex Dir Counseling/Hlth/Career Svcs Dr. Cindy COOK
12 Dir Campus Opers/UHCL Pearland Dr. Kathy DUPREE
23 Dir Student Health Services Ms. Regina PICKETT
07 Exec Director of Admissions Ms. Kara HADLEY-SHAKYA
06 Registrar Mr. Bryan HEARD
08 Exec Director Library Dr. Vivienne MCCLENDON
09 Assoc Dir Institutional Research Ms. Miriam QUMSIEH
105 Director Web & Multimedia Services Mr. Ed PUCKETT
18 Assoc VP Facilities Mgmt Vacant
19 Exec Dir Public Safety Chief Russell L. MILLER
22 Univ Compliance/Diversity Officer Dr. Scott RICHARDSON

39 Dir Resident Life/Student Housing .... Mr. Matthew PERRY
53 Dean of Education .... Dr. Joan PEDRO
54 Dean of Science & Engineering .... Dr. Miguel A. GONZALEZ
90 Director Academic Computing Labs .... Ms. Sana ZEIDAN
30 Senior Development Officer .... Mr. Richard J. ZALESAK

*University of Houston - Downtown (A)

One Main Street, Houston TX 77002-1014
County: Harris FICE Identification: 003612
Unit ID: 225432
Telephone: (713) 221-8001 Carnegie Class: Masters/L
FAX Number: (713) 221-8075 Calendar System: Semester
URL: www.uhd.edu
Established: 1974 Annual Undergrad Tuition & Fees (In-State): $7,222
Enrollment: 15,239 Coed
Affiliation or Control: State IRS Status: Exempt
Highest Offering: Master's
Accreditation: SC, NURSE, SW

02 President .... Dr. Loren J. BLANCHARD
04 Executive Assoc to President .... Ms. Vanessa PIGEON
22 Title IX/Equity & Diversity Ofcr .... Ms. Erika HARRISON
05 Interim Sr VP/Provost .... Dr. James C. UZMAN
84 VP Enrollment Management .... Dr. Daniel VILLANUEVA
20 Assoc VP Academic Affairs .... Dr. Sheila LLOYD
88 AVP Programming & Curriculum .... Dr. Michelle MOOSALLY
50 Dean Davies College of Business .... Dr. Charles E. GENGLER
80 Dean College of Public Service .... Dr. Jonathan SCHWARTZ
72 Interim Dean Col Sciences & Tech .... Dr. Ermelinda DELAVINA
49 Dean University College .... Dr. T. Scott MARZILLI
79 Dean Humanities & Social Science .... Dr. Wendy BURNS-ARDOLINO
08 Executive Director WI Dykes Library .... Ms. Pat ENSOR
106 Exec Dir Off Campus/OL Coordinator .... Mr. Louis D. EVANS, III
46 Assoc VP Faculty Rsrch & Spons Pgm .... Dr. Jerry JOHNSON
108 Exec Dir Assessment & Accred .... Dr. Lea CAMPBELL
09 Exec Dir Data Analytics/Inst Rsrch .... Dr. Nazly DYER
88 Exec Director of Scholars Academy .... Dr. Mary Jo PARKER
88 Dir Teaching & Learning Excel .... Dr. Gregory DEMENT
124 Dir Gator Success Center .... Dr. Jemma SYLVESTER-CAESAR
88 Director of Advising Services .... Ms. Reyna ROMERO
88 Director of Academic Support Center .... Dr. Isidro GRAU
88 Exec Dir Academic Admin & Ops .... Ms. Chris RODNEY
88 Exec Dir Academic & Student Affs .... Ms. Lucy BOWEN
92 Director Honors Program .... Dr. Mari NICHOLSON-PREUSS
88 Dir Applied Business/Technology Ctr .... Mr. G. V. KRISHNAN
88 Dir Criminal Justice Center .... Mr. Steven BRACKEN
88 Dir Ctr Public Svc & Com Res .... Mr. Steven VILLANO
117 Dir Insurance & Risk Management Ctr .... Ms. Priscilla OEHLERT
36 Dir Davies COB Career Dev Center .... Mr. Brett HOBBY
38 Dir Student & Advising Services .... Mr. Ben ROBLES
88 Dir DCOB Admin & Operations .... Ms. Berna MCELYEA
88 Dir of Retail Mgmt Center .... Mr. Tracy DAVIS
10 Interim VP Administration & Finance .... Ms. Karin LIVINGSTON
111 VP Advancement & External Rels .... Ms. Johanna WOLFE
13 Assoc VP Information Technology .... Mr. Hossein SHAHROKHI
91 Director Enterprise Systems .... Mr. Kong YIN
88 Dir Technology Learning Services .... Mr. John LANE
14 Director Technical Services .... Ms. Grace DAVILA
88 Dir IT Infrastructure & Comm Svcs .... Mr. Miguel RUIZ
90 Exec Dir Information Technology .... Mr. Said FATTOUH
88 Dir IT Business Services .... Ms. Jacqueline SMITH
88 Dir IT Project Management Office .... Ms. Kimberly SOLOMON
88 Dir User Support Services .... Ms. Cheryl ROBERTSON
88 Dir University Business Services .... Ms. Mary TORRES
11 Dir Admin Ops & Compliance .... Ms. Stefany RECORDS
105 Dir Web & Digital Marketing .... Ms. Laura WAITS
114 Interim AVP Business Affairs .... Ms. Theresa MENELEY
18 Asst VP Facilities Management .... Mr. Timothy RYCHLEC
88 Dir MEP .... Mr. Kris ZIMMERMAN
19 Ex Dir Public Safety/Chf of Police .... Mr. Michael BENFORD
88 Dir Environmental Health & Safety .... Mr. Edward ARIAS
113 Interim Dir Student Financials .... Ms. Krystal LEBLANC
15 VP Employment Svcs & Operations .... Ms. Ivonne MONTALBANO
118 Dir Benefits & Compensation .... Ms. Erica MORALES
16 Director Payroll & Records .... Ms. April FRANK
06 University Registrar .... Mr. Ovidio GALVAN
88 Director Student Activities .... Mr. Tremaine KWASIKPUI
28 Dir Ctr Stdnt Diversity/Eqty/Incl .... Dr. John HUDSON
07 Exec Dir Enrollment Management .... Ms. Ceshia LOVE
37 Director Financial Aid .... Ms. LaTasha GOUDEAU
41 Director Sports & Fitness .... Mr. Richard SEBASTIANI
36 Dir Career Development Center .... Ms. Katherine KNAPP
28 Int Dir Counseling/Disability Svcs .... Dr. Hope PAMPLIN
88 Director Veterans Services .... Mr. Antonio GUERRA
88 Director Testing Services .... Mr. Robert ALONZO
88 Dir Campus Solution Services .... Ms. Rocio BEIZA
88 Exec Dir Student Comm & Trans Pgm .... Ms. Jenna TABAKMAN
88 Dir Student Life .... Mr. Eugene BERNARD
88 Director Talent Search .... Mr. Brian FLORES
88 Director Upward Bound .... Ms. Dawanna LEWIS
26 Exec Dir of University Relations .... Ms. Elisa OLSEN
102 Director Advancement .... Mr. Jacob LIPP
29 Director Events & Alumni Relations .... Dr. Liza ALONZO
27 Director Communications .... Mr. P. Michael EMERY
27 Director Marketing .... Ms. Toye SIMMONS
121 Dir Academic Advising Center .... Dr. John INDIATSI

*University of Houston - Victoria (B)

3007 N Ben Wilson St., Victoria TX 77901-4450
County: Victoria FICE Identification: 013231
Unit ID: 225502
Telephone: (361) 570-4848 Carnegie Class: Masters/L
FAX Number: (361) 580-5534 Calendar System: Semester
URL: www.uhv.edu
Established: 1973 Annual Undergrad Tuition & Fees (In-State): $7,313
Enrollment: 4,922 Coed
Affiliation or Control: State IRS Status: 501(c)3
Highest Offering: Master's
Accreditation: SC, CACREP, NURSE

02 President .... Dr. Robert K. GLENN
10 Vice Pres Administration & Finance .... Mr. Wayne B. BERAN
05 Provost/VP Acad Affairs .... Dr. Chance M. GLENN, SR.
32 Vice President Student Affairs .... Dr. Jay LAMBERT
84 VP for Enrollment Management .... Dr. Jose CANTU
49 Dean Arts & Sciences .... Dr. Kyoko AMANO
50 Dean Business Admin .... Dr. Ken COLWELL
53 Int Dean Educ & Human Development .... Dr. Rachel MARTINEZ
111 VP Advancement & External Relations .... Mr. Jesse D. PISORS
08 Director of Library .... Ms. Karen LOCHER
09 Dir Inst Research/Effectiveness .... Dr. Sharon M. BAILEY
10 Director Business Services .... Mr. Tim MICHALSKI
13 Sr Dir of Instructional Technology .... Mr. Randy FAULK
22 Sr Director Equal Opportunity .... Ms. Rebecca LAKE
15 Dir Human Res/Deputy EO/Title IX .... Ms. Laura L. SMITH
88 Dir Small Business Development Ctr .... Ms. Lindsay YOUNG
06 Registrar .... Ms. Angela BIGBY
37 Director Financial Aid .... Ms. Lashon WILLIAMS
36 Director Career Services .... Ms. Amy HATMAKER
18 Director Facilities .... Mr. John BURKE
21 Sr Director Finance .... Ms. Erin GOODWIN
41 Director Athletics .... Mr. Ashley WALYUCHOW
26 Director Marketing & Communications .... Ms. Paula COBLER
38 Counseling Center .... Vacant
35 Dir Student Svcs & Judicial Affs .... Dr. Michael WILKINSON
114 Director of Budget .... Ms. Karen SANDERS
39 Director Residence Life & Univ Comm .... Mr. Brandon W. LEE
88 Director Capital Projects .... Mr. Matt ALEXANDER
04 Executive Adm Asst to President .... Ms. Kathy WALTON
25 Dir Grants & Contracts .... Ms. Angela HARTMANN
102 Sr Dir Corp/Foundation Relations .... Ms. Courtney M. SIDES
29 Dir Alumni/Annual Giving .... Vacant
20 Assoc Prov Academic Affairs .... Dr. Beverly TOMEK
85 Director International Programs .... Ms. Ludmi HERATH
88 Sr Dir Enroll Mgmt/External Rels .... Ms. Karla DECUIR
07 Director Admissions/Recruitment .... Mr. Billy LAGAL
19 Campus Security & Safety .... Mr. Travis GUNDELACH
35 Director Student Services .... Ms. Hilary KOFRON

University of the Incarnate Word (C)

4301 Broadway, San Antonio TX 78209-6397
County: Bexar FICE Identification: 003578
Unit ID: 225627
Telephone: (210) 829-6000 Carnegie Class: DU-Mod
FAX Number: (210) 829-1220 Calendar System: Semester
URL: www.uiw.edu
Established: 1881 Annual Undergrad Tuition & Fees: $32,286
Enrollment: 7,917 Coed
Affiliation or Control: Roman Catholic IRS Status: 501(c)3
Highest Offering: Doctorate
Accreditation: SC, ACBSP, CAATE, CIDA, DIETD, DIETI, HSA, MUS, NMT, NURSE, OPT, OPTR, OSTEO, PHAR, PTA, THEA

01 President .... Dr. Thomas M. EVANS
05 Provost/Chief Academic Officer . Dr. Barbara ARANDA-NARANJO
03 Vice President Mission and Ministry .... Sr. Walter MAHER
20 Vice Provost .... Dr. Glenn E. JAMES
04 Admin Asst to the President .... Ms. Melissa C. MOLINA
43 VP Legal Affairs/General Counsel .... Ms. Cynthia S. ESCAMILLA
30 VP Development/Univ Relations ... Mr. Christopher M. GALLEGOS
88 Vice Pres International Affairs .... Mr. Marcos FRAGOSO
10 Vice Pres Administrative Svcs/CFO .... Dr. Darrell HAYDON
42 University Chaplain .... Vacant
28 AVP Mission & Ministry/DEI .... Dr. Arturo E. CHAVEZ
88 AVP Cap Planning/Facilities Mgmt .... Dr. Rafael HOYLE
13 AVP Information Resources/CIO .... Mr. Neil SCHROEDER
15 AVP for Human Resources .... Ms. Annette THOMPSON
84 AVP Enrollment/Academic Innovation .... Dr. Osman OZTURGUT
46 Assoc Provost Research/Grad Studies .... Dr. Ana WANDLESS-HAGENDORF
20 Assoc Provost UG/Graduate Educ .... Dr. Kevin VICHALES
17 Assoc Prov for Health Professions .... Dr. Caroline GOULET
06 Registrar .... Ms. Marisol M. SCHEER
50 Dean H-E-B Sch Business & Admin .... Dr. Jeannie J. SCOTT
79 Dean Humanities/Arts & Social Sci .... Dr. Lydia M. ANDRADE
66 Dean Nursing & Health Professions .... Dr. Holly CASSELLS
81 Dean Math/Science/Engineering .... Dr. Carlos GARCIA
60 Dean Interactive Media & Design .... Dr. Sharon WELKEY
53 Dean Dreeben School of Education .... Dr. Denise STAUDT
88 Dean School of Optometry .... Dr. Timothy WINGERT
67 Dean Feik School of Pharmacy .... Dr. David MAIZE
29 Dean of Alumni/Parent Relations .... Dr. Lisa MCNARY
88 Dean School Physical Therapy .... Vacant
63 Dean School of Osteopathic Medicine .... Dr. Robyn PHILLIPS-MADSON
32 Dean of Campus Life .... Dr. Christopher A. SUMMERLIN
107 Dean School of Professional Studies .... Mr. Jonathan LOVEJOY
58 Director of Graduate Studies .... Dr. Trinidad MACIAS
26 Director of Comm/Marketing .... Ms. Margaret L. GARCIA
38 Director of Counseling .... Dr. Christie MELONSON
121 Director of Academic Advising .... Ms. Kedra GRANT-BRINKLEY
37 Director of Financial Aid .... Vacant
39 Director of Residence Life .... Ms. Diane SANCHEZ
08 Dean of Library Services .... Ms. Tracey MENDOZA
88 Director of Campus Ministry .... Ms. Elisabeth VILLARREAL
96 Director of Procurement .... Vacant
18 Director Facilities Mgmt .... Mr. Philip W. LOPES, JR.
41 Director of Athletics .... Mr. Richard P. DURAN
24 Director Instructional Technology .... Ms. Kathy BOTTARO
14 Dir Infrastructure/Opers/Security .... Mr. Brian J. ANDERSON
07 Director of Admissions .... Ms. Jessica DELAROSA
112 Dir of Major Gifts/Planned Giving .... Mr. Alex CASTANEDA
89 Director of First Year Engagement .... Dr. Raul ZENDEJAS
85 Dir Intl Students/Scholar Svcs .... Mr. Jose F. MARTINEZ, JR.
35 Director of Campus Engagement .... Vacant
09 Director of Institutional Research .... Dr. Andrew T. PAGEL
36 Director of Career Services .... Ms. Jessica L. WILSON
105 Director Web & Mobile Operations .... Mr. Nicholas A. GARCIA
102 Dir Foundation/Corporate Relations .... Mr. Jon GILLESPIE
16 Director of Human Resources .... Ms. Shannon A. ROOT
110 Director of Individual Giving .... Ms. Ana P. BRIBIESCA HOFF
23 Medical Director Health Svcs .... Dr. David E. GARZA
114 Budget Manager .... Ms. Amy M. DEATLEY
104 Study Abroad Coordinator .... Ms. Brooke PAYNTER
117 AVP for Public Safety .... Dr. Nathan JOHNSON
21 AVP for Finance/Comptroller .... Ms. Elisa GONZALES
19 University Police Chief .... Ms. Jessica A. SERBANTES
44 Annual Giving Officer .... Ms. Brittany SHARNSKY
108 Assoc Provost Inst Effectiveness .... Dr. David B. STEIN
20 Assoc Provost Academic Support .... Ms. Sandra MCMAKIN

University of Mary Hardin-Baylor (D)

900 College Street, Belton TX 76513-2578
County: Bell FICE Identification: 003588
Unit ID: 226471
Telephone: (254) 295-8642 Carnegie Class: Masters/L
FAX Number: (254) 295-4535 Calendar System: Semester
URL: www.umhb.edu
Established: 1845 Annual Undergrad Tuition & Fees: $30,750
Enrollment: 3,876 Coed
Affiliation or Control: Southern Baptist IRS Status: 501(c)3
Highest Offering: Doctorate
Accreditation: SC, ACBSP, #ARCPA, ART, CACREP, MUS, NURSE, PTA, SW

01 President/CEO .... Dr. Randy G. O'REAR
03 Sr Vice Pres Admin/COO .... Dr. Steve THEODORE
05 Provost/Sr VP Academic Affs .... Dr. John VASSAR
108 Assoc Prov for Institutional Effect .... Dr. Emily PREVOST
45 VP Campus Planning & Support .... Mr. Marvin EE
111 Vice Pres for Advancement .... Dr. Rebecca O'BANION
32 Vice Pres for Student Life .... Dr. Brandon SKAGGS
41 Vice Pres Athletics .... Mr. Mickey KERR
10 Vice Pres Business/Finance/CFO .... Mrs. Jennifer RAMM
15 Vice Pres Human Resources .... Mrs. Susan OWENS
13 Vice Pres Info Tech .... Mr. Greg BRANDENBURG
84 Vice Pres Enrollment Mgmt .... Dr. Gary LAMM
21 Controller .... Mrs. Charla KAHLIG
50 Dean McLane College of Business .... Dr. Ken SMITH
79 Dean of Humanities & Sciences .... Dr. Stephen BALDRIDGE
66 Dean of Nursing .... Dr. Michele HACKNEY
53 Dean of Education .... Dr. Joan BERRY
76 Executive Dean Health Sciences .... Dr. Colin WILBORN
88 Dean of Christian Studies .... Dr. Tim CRAWFORD
57 Dean Visual/Performing Arts .... Dr. Kathryn FOUSE
35 Dean of Students .... Dr. Michael BURNS
39 Director of Residence Life .... Dr. Kyle SMITH
04 Special Asst to President .... Mrs. Candace WILLIAMS
06 Registrar .... Mrs. Elizabeth WEBB
88 Director Strategic Engagement .... Ms. Melissa WILLIAMS
07 Director of Admissions & Recruiting .... Dr. Brent BURKS
08 Interim Director Learning Resources .... Ms. Teresa BUCK
09 Director Institutional Research .... Ms. Jen JONES
37 Director Financial Aid .... Mr. Ron BROWN
92 Director Honors Program .... Dr. David HOLCOMB
19 Director Campus Police .... Mr. Gary SARGENT
96 Purchasing Manager .... Mrs. Jennifer WEBB
29 Director Alumni Relations .... Mr. Jeff SUTTON
42 University Chaplain .... Mr. Jason PALMER
36 Director Career Services .... Mr. Don OWENS
38 Int Director Couns Testing & Health .... Dr. Brandon SKAGGS
85 Dir International Student Services .... Mrs. Elizabeth TANAKA
110 Senior Director of Development .... Mr. Michael BALL
40 Bookstore Manager .... Ms. Debbie COTTRELL
104 Director Study Abroad .... Dr. Michelle REINA

University of North Texas (E)

1155 Union Circle #311277, Denton TX 76203-5013
County: Denton FICE Identification: 003594
Unit ID: 227216
Telephone: (940) 565-2000 Carnegie Class: DU-Highest
FAX Number: (940) 565-7600 Calendar System: Semester
URL: www.unt.edu
Established: 1890 Annual Undergrad Tuition & Fees (In-State): $11,090
Enrollment: 40,953 Coed
Affiliation or Control: State IRS Status: 501(c)3
Highest Offering: Doctorate
Accreditation: SC, ABAI, ART, AUD, CACREP, CAEP, CEA, CIDA, CLPSY, COPSY, FEPAC, JOUR, LIB, MUS, SP, SPAA, SW

01 President .... Dr. Neal SMATRESK
00 Chancellor .... Ms. Lesa ROE
05 Provost/Vice Pres Academic Affairs .... Dr. Jennifer COWLEY
10 VP Finance/Administration .... Mr. Clayton GIBSON
46 VP Research/Innovation .... Dr. Mark MCLELLAN

32 Vice President Student Affairs ... Dr. Elizabeth WITH
43 Vice Chancellor/General Counsel ... Mr. Alan STUCKY
26 VP Brand Strategy/Communications ... Mr. Jim BERSCHEIDT
30 Associate VP for Development ... Ms. Eileen P. MORAN
84 VP for Enrollment ... Mr. Shannon M. GOODMAN
13 Assoc VP for Univ Info Svcs ... Vacant
20 Vice Provost for Academic Affairs ... Dr. Michael MCPHERSON
20 Vice Provost for Academic Resources .. Ms. Jennifer STEVENSON
20 Vice Provost Faculty Success ... Dr. Holly HUTCHINS
100 VP for Planning/Chief of Staff ... Dr. Debbie ROHWER
41 VP & Director of Athletics ... Mr. Wren BAKER
35 Asst VP and Dean of Students ... Dr. Maureen MCGUINNESS
13 Chief Information Officer ... Mr. Chris MCCOY
114 Budget Director ... Vacant
121 Exec Dir Lrng Technologies ... Dr. Patrick PLUSCHT
28 VP Institutional Equity & Diversity ... Dr. Joanne WOODARD
31 Vice Prov Academic Partnerships ... Ms. Brenda KIHL
18 Assoc Vice President for Facilities ... Vacant
08 Dean of Libraries ... Ms. Diane BRUXVOORT
37 Exec Dir Fin Aid/Univ Admissions ... Ms. Zelma DELEON
49 Dean College of Liberal Arts & Sci ... Dr. Tamara BROWN
81 Dean College of Science ... Dr. Pamela PADILLA
50 Dean College Business ... Dr. Marilyn WILEY
53 Dean College of Education ... Dr. Randy BOMER
57 Dean College of CVAD ... Ms. Karen HUTZEL
69 Dean Health & Public Service ... Dr. Nicole DASH
64 Dean College of Music ... Dr. John W. RICHMOND
59 Dean Col of Merch/Hosp & Tourism ... Dr. Jana HAWLEY
77 Dean College of Information ... Dr. KINSHUK
58 Dean Toulouse Grad School ... Dr. Victor PRYBUTOK
92 Dean of TAMS/Honors College ... Dr. Glenisson DE OLIVEIRA
60 Dean Mayborn Sch of Journalism ... Dr. Andrea MILLER
54 Dean College of Engineering ... Dr. Hanchen HUANG
88 Dean New College at Frisco ... Dr. Wesley RANDALL
90 Director Acad Computing/User Svcs .... Dr. Philip C. BACZEWSKI
09 Director Institutional Research ... Dr. Mary BARTON
108 Associate Vice President DAIR ... Dr. Jason F. SIMON
88 Director of Accreditation ... Ms. Elizabeth VOGT
51 Director Lifelong Learning ... Dr. Stephanie REINKE
06 AVP Enrollment & Registrar ... Ms. Shari SCHWARTZ
15 Chief Human Capital Officer ..... Ms. Sheraine GILLIAM-HOLMES
36 Exec Dir Career & Leadership ... Mr. Dan NAEGELI
19 Director/Chief of Police ... Mr. Ed REYNOLDS
39 Exec Director Housing ... Ms. Gina VANACORE
85 Vice Provost & Dean Intl Affairs ... Dr. Pia WOOD
23 Exec Dir Stdnt Health/Wellness ... Dr. Herschel VOORHEES
111 Vice President for Advancement ... Dr. David WOLF
04 Executive Asst to President ... Ms. Louise DUNN
101 Secretary of the Institution/Board ... Dr. Rosemary R. HAGGETT
104 Director Study Abroad ... Ms. Amy SHENBERGER
88 VP Digital Strategy/Innovation ... Dr. Adam FEIN
88 Chief Compliance Officer ... Mr. Clay SIMMONS
22 AVP/Director Equal Opportunity ... Ms. Eve BELL
25 Director Pre-Awards/Contracts ... Vacant
29 Exec Director Alumni Relations ... Mr. Rob MCINTURF
38 AVP Student Counseling/Testing ... Vacant
86 Director Government Relations ... Mr. Jack MORTON

University of North Texas at Dallas (A)

7300 University Hills Blvd, Dallas TX 75241
County: Dallas — Identification: 667124
Unit ID: 484905
Telephone: (972) 780-3600 — Carnegie Class: Masters/M
FAX Number: (972) 780-3606 — Calendar System: Semester
URL: www.untdallas.edu
Established: 2001 — Annual Undergrad Tuition & Fees (In-State): $8,143
Enrollment: 4,164 — Coed
Affiliation or Control: State — IRS Status: 501(c)3
Highest Offering: Doctorate
Accreditation: SC, CACREP, #LAW

01 President ... Robert MONG
10 Exec Vice Pres Administration & CFO ... Arthur BRADFORD
05 Provost/EVP Academic Affairs ... Dr. Betty STEWART
49 Dean of Liberal Arts & Sciences ... Dr. Orlando PEREZ
88 Dean of Human Services ... Dr. Constance LACY
04 Exec Assistant to the President ... Angie CASTILLO
06 Registrar ... John CAPOCCI
07 Director of Admissions ... Luis FRANCO
08 Chief Library Officer ... Brenda ROBERTSON
09 Director of Institutional Research ... Brody DU
106 Director Distance Learning ... Desmond MORRIS
13 Chief Information Technology Ofcr ... Kevin ROCHA
15 Chief Human Resources Officer ... Wanda BOYD
18 Chief Facilities/Physical Plant Ofc ... Wayne MCINNIS
19 Director Security/Safety ... Chris SHAW
26 Chief Public Relations Officer ... Yolanda FRANKLIN
29 Director Alumni Affairs ... Derrick MORGAN
32 Dean of Students ... Vacant
36 Director Student Placement ... Arthur LUMZY
37 Director Student Financial Aid ... Garrick HILDEBRAND
38 Director Student Counseling ... Dr. Shanda RILEY
39 Dir Resident Life/Student Housing ... Daniel (Dee) GOINES
41 Athletic Director ... Jack ALLDAY
50 Dean of Business ... Dr. Karen SHUMWAY
84 Director Enrollment Management ... Stephanie HOLLEY

University of North Texas Health Science Center at Fort Worth (B)

3500 Camp Bowie Boulevard, Fort Worth TX 76107-2699
County: Tarrant — FICE Identification: 009768
Unit ID: 228909
Telephone: (817) 735-2000 — Carnegie Class: Spec-4-yr-Med
FAX Number: N/A — Calendar System: Semester
URL: www.unthsc.edu
Established: 1966 — Annual Graduate Tuition & Fees: N/A
Enrollment: 2,329 — Coed
Affiliation or Control: State — IRS Status: 501(c)3
Highest Offering: Doctorate; No Undergraduates
Accreditation: SC, ARCPA, HSA, #MED, OSTEO, PH, PHAR, PTA

01 President ... Dr. Michael R. WILLIAMS
10 EVP for Finance and Operations ... Mr. Gregory R. ANDERSON
05 Provost/Exec VP Academic Affairs ... Dr. Charles TAYLOR
86 Vice President Governmental Affairs ... Mr. Dan JENSEN
63 Dean Texas Col of Osteopathic Med ... Dr. Frank FILIPETTO
46 VP Research ... Dr. Brian GLADUE
58 Dean Grad Sch Biomed Sciences ... Dr. Michael MATHIS
76 Dean School of Health Professions ... Dr. J. Glenn FORISTER
69 Dean of School of Public Health ... Dr. Dennis THOMBS
37 Director Student Financial Aid ... Mr. Joseph SANCHEZ
32 Sr Vice Provost Student Affairs ... Ms. Trisha VANDUSER
19 Chief of Police ... Mr. Cliff JAYNES
111 SVP Inst Advancement/Communication ... Ms. Lacey LAPOINTE
45 VP of Culture and Experience ... Ms. Jeanie FOSTER
21 Vice President Finance & Planning ... Mr. Chuck FOX
26 AVP Marketing/Communications ... Ms. Laken RAPIER
15 Exec Director Human Resources ... Ms. Janine WATKINS
06 Dir Enrollment & Records ... Mrs. Elizabeth MEDDERS
08 Director of Lewis Library ... Mr. Daniel BURGARD
88 SVP/Chief Integrity Officer ... Mrs. Desiree RAMIREZ
100 Chief of Staff ... Mr. James MEINTJES

University of Phoenix Dallas Campus (C)

12400 Coit Road, Dallas TX 75251-2004
Telephone: (972) 385-1055 — Identification: 770227
Accreditation: &HLC, ACBSP

† Branch campus of University of Phoenix, Phoenix, AZ-No longer enrolling new students

University of Phoenix Houston Campus (D)

11451 Katy Freeway, Houston TX 77079-2004
Telephone: (713) 465-9966 — Identification: 770229
Accreditation: &HLC, ACBSP

† Branch campus of University of Phoenix, Phoenix, AZ

University of Phoenix San Antonio Campus (E)

8200 IH-10 West, Suite 1000, San Antonio TX 78230-3876
Telephone: (210) 524-2100 — Identification: 770231
Accreditation: &HLC

† Branch campus of University of Phoenix, Phoenix, AZ

University of St. Augustine for Health Sciences (F)

5401 La Crosse Ave, Austin TX 78739
Telephone: (512) 394-9766 — Identification: 770940
Accreditation: &WC, OT, PTA, @SP

† Branch campus of University of St. Augustine for Health Sciences, San Marcos, CA.

University of St. Thomas (G)

3800 Montrose Boulevard, Houston TX 77006-4696
County: Harris — FICE Identification: 003654
Unit ID: 227863
Telephone: (713) 522-7911 — Carnegie Class: Masters/L
FAX Number: (713) 525-2125 — Calendar System: Semester
URL: www.stthom.edu
Established: 1947 — Annual Undergrad Tuition & Fees: $31,560
Enrollment: 3,692 — Coed
Affiliation or Control: Roman Catholic — IRS Status: 501(c)3
Highest Offering: Doctorate
Accreditation: SC, CACREP, NURSE, THEOL

01 President ... Dr. Richard LUDWICK
04 Special Assistant to the President ... Ms. Cindy VIAUD
04 Exec Assistant to the President ... Ms. Anne LAMBERT
05 Vice Pres Academic Affairs ... Dr. Chris P. EVANS
10 Vice President for Finance ... Mr. Spencer CONROY
30 Chief Development Officer ... Ms. Dawn KOENNING
32 Vice Pres Student Engagement ... Mr. Arthur ORTIZ
13 Chief Information Officer ... Mr. Roger PARKS
84 Vice Pres Enrollment Management ... Mr. Arthur ORTIZ
26 VP Marketing/University Engagement ... Mr. Jeff OLSEN
15 Assoc VP of Human Resources ... Mr. Randy GRAHAM
35 Asst VP Student Affs/Dean Students ... Mr. David HAO
66 Dean School of Nursing ... Dr. Poldi TSCHIRCH
49 Dean Arts & Sciences ... Dr. George A. HARNE
73 Dean School of Theology ... Rev. Paul LOCKEY
50 Dean Cameron School of Business ... Dr. Mario ENZLER
53 Interim Dean School of Education ... Dr. Ana-Lisa GONZALEZ
08 Dean of Libraries ... Mr. James PICCININNI
37 Dean of Scholarships/Financial Aid ... Ms. Lynda MCKENDREE
58 Dir Center for Thomistic Studies ... Dr. Brian CARL
82 Director Center for Intl Studies ... Dr. Richard SINDELAR
88 Director Center for Irish Studies ... Ms. Lori GALLAGHER
88 Director Center for Faith & Culture ... Fr. Binh QUACH
06 Registrar ... Mr. Nathan DUGAT
90 Director of Technical Svcs ... Mr. Al DESHOTEL
91 Director of Application Svcs ... Ms. Kelly KLITZ
38 Exec Dir Counseling & Disability ... Vacant
42 Director of Campus Ministry ... Ms. Nicole LABADIE
39 Director Residence Life ... Ms. Ana Alicia LOPEZ
88 Asst Dir of Recreational Sports ... Mr. Scott LATHAM
18 Asst VP Facilities Operations ... Mr. Edgar MOCTEZUMA
21 Controller ... Mr. Keith SCHEFFLER
113 Bursar ... Mr. Richard SHUMAN
88 Director of Veteran Services ... Ms. Trisha RUIZ
27 Director of Communications ... Ms. Sandra SOLIZ
108 Dir Assessment/Inst Effectiveness ... Dr. Dominic AQUILA
19 Chief of Police ... Mr. H. E JENKINS
41 Athletic Director ... Mr. Todd SMITH
104 Director Study Abroad ... Dr. Ulyses BALDERAS
29 Director Alumni Relations ... Ms. Amy YOUNGBLOOD
88 Asst VP of Program Marketing ... Mr. Chris ZEGLIN

*The University of Texas System Administration (H)

210 West 7th Street, Austin TX 78701-2982
County: Travis — FICE Identification: 003655
Unit ID: 229090
Telephone: (512) 499-4201 — Carnegie Class: N/A
FAX Number: (512) 499-4215
URL: www.utsystem.edu

01 Chancellor ... Mr. James B. MILLIKEN
88 Sr Adv to the Chanc/Chief T&I Ofcr . Ms. Julie GOONEWARDENE
100 Chief of Staff Office of Chanc ... Mr. Art MARTINEZ
05 Exec VC Academic Affairs ... Dr. Archie L. HOLMES, JR.
17 Exec VC Health Affairs ... Dr. John M. ZERWAS
88 Sr Vice Chanc for Health Affairs ... Ms. Amy SHAW THOMAS
88 VC Health Affairs & Chief Med Ofcr ... Dr. David L. LAKEY
10 Exec Vice Chanc Business Affairs ... Dr. Scott C. KELLEY
43 Vice Chanc & General Counsel ... Mr. Dan SHARPHORN
86 Vice Chanc for Govt Relations ... Ms. Stacey NAPIER
26 Vice Chanc for Ext Rels/Comm & Adv ... Dr. Randa S. SAFADY
45 Assoc VC Inst Rsrch & Analysis ... Dr. David R. TROUTMAN
18 Asst VC for Capital Projects ... Mr. Stephen HARRIS
13 Assoc VC & Chief Info Officer ... Mr. David R. CRAIN
21 Assoc VC & Controller ... Ms. Veronica HINOJOSA-SEGURA
27 Director of Media Relations ... Ms. Karen E. ADLER
88 Executive Director of Real Estate ... Mr. Geoffrey RICHARDS
111 AVC for Advancement Services ... Ms. Andria BRANNON
19 Director of Police ... Mr. Michael J. HEIDINGSFIELD
04 Administrative Asst to Chancellor ... Ms. Katherine IANNESSA
88 Ex Dir of Syswide Cmpl & Ethics Ofr ... Mr. Jason KING
117 Chief Compliance & Risk Officer ... Mr. Phillip B. DENDY
119 Chief Info Security Officer ... Ms. Helen MOHRMANN

*The University of Texas at Arlington (I)

701 S Nedderman Drive, Arlington TX 76013
County: Tarrant — FICE Identification: 003656
Unit ID: 228769
Telephone: (817) 272-2101 — Carnegie Class: DU-Highest
FAX Number: (817) 272-5656 — Calendar System: Semester
URL: www.uta.edu
Established: 1895 — Annual Undergrad Tuition & Fees (In-State): $11,378
Enrollment: 48,072 — Coed
Affiliation or Control: State — IRS Status: 170(c)1
Highest Offering: Doctorate
Accreditation: SC, AAQEP, ART, CAATE, CAEPN, CEA, CIDA, LSAR, MUS, NURSE, PLNG, SPAA, SW

02 Interim President ... Dr. Teik LIM
05 Interim Provost & VP Acad Affairs ... Dr. Pranesh ASWATH
10 Chief Financial Officer and VP ... Ms. Kelly DAVIS
32 VP Student Affairs ... Ms. Lisa NAGY
46 Interim Vice President Research ... Dr. Jim GROVER
13 Chief Information Officer ... Mr. Jeffery NEYLAND
11 Vice Pres Admin & Campus Operations ... Mr. John D. HALL
15 Vice President for Human Resources ... Ms. Jean HOOD
84 VP for Enrollment Management ... Dr. Troy JOHNSON
111 VP for Institutional Advancement ... Vacant
45 Asst V Provost Inst Eff/Report ... Dr. Rebecca LEWIS
16 Asst Vice Pres Human Resources ... Ms. Eunice M. CURRIE
18 Int Asst VP Campus Opers/Facilities ... Mr. Don LANGE
121 Assoc V Prov Div of Stdnt Success ... Dr. Ashley PURGASON
100 Chief of Staff and Assoc VP ... Ms. Salma ADEM
58 Assoc Dean of Graduate Studies ... Mr. Raymond L. JACKSON
48 Dean College Arch/Urban/Pub Affairs ... Dr. Adrian PARR
50 Dean College of Business ... Mr. Harry DOMBROSKI
54 Dean of Engineering ... Dr. Peter CROUCH
49 Dean of Liberal Arts ... Dr. Elisabeth CAWTHON
66 Dean of Nursing ... Dr. Elizabeth MERWIN
81 Dean of Science ... Dr. Morteza KHALEDI
70 Dean School of Social Work ... Dr. Scott RYAN
53 Dean College of Education ... Dr. Teresa TABER DOUGHTY
92 Interim Dean Honors College ... Dr. Tim HENRY
08 Dean of Libraries ... Dr. Rebecca BICHEL
12 Exec Dir of UTA Ft Worth Center ... Vacant
37 Director of Financial Aid ... Dr. Karen KRAUSE
23 Director Student Health Center ... Ms. Angela MIDDLETON
22 Director Equal Opportunity Services ... Mr. Eddie FREEMAN
41 Athletic Director ... Mr. Jim BAKER
19 Dir Environmental Health Safety ... Ms. Leah HOY
85 Executive Director Intl Education ... Mr. Jay HORN
28 Director Multicultural Outreach ... Mr. Casey GONZALES

93 Director Multicultural Affairs .... Ms. Melanie JOHNSON
86 VP Government Relations .... Mr. Jeff JETER
43 Dir Legal Services/General Counsel .... Mr. Shelby BOSEMAN
96 Director of Purchasing .... Ms. Julia CORNWELL
29 Exec Dir for Alumni & Donor Rels .... Ms. Julie BARFIELD
04 Executive Assoc to President .... Ms. Elsa CORRAL

*University of Texas at Austin (A)

110 Inner Campus Drive, Austin TX 78705
County: Travis FICE Identification: 003658
Unit ID: 228778
Telephone: (512) 471-3434 Carnegie Class: DU-Highest
FAX Number: N/A Calendar System: Semester
URL: www.utexas.edu
Established: 1883 Annual Undergrad Tuition & Fees (In-State): $11,448
Enrollment: 50,476 Coed
Affiliation or Control: State IRS Status: 170(c)1
Highest Offering: Doctorate
Accreditation: SC, ART, AUD, CAATE, CEA, CIDA, CLPSY, COPSY, DANCE, DIETC, DIETD, IPSY, JOUR, LAW, LIB, LSAR, MED, MUS, NURSE, PCSAS, PHAR, PLNG, SCPSY, SP, SPAA, SW

02 President .... Dr. Jay C. HARTZELL
05 Int Exec Vice President & Provost .... Dr. Dan T. JAFFE
10 SVP & Chief Financial Officer .... Mr. Darrell BAZZELL
28 VP for Diversity & Cmty Engagement .... Dr. LaToya SMITH
11 Associate Vice President .... Dr. Marla MARTINEZ
46 Vice President for Research .... Dr. Alison T. PRESTON
63 Vice President for Medical Affairs .... Dr. S. Claiborne JOHNSTON
30 Vice Pres for Development .... Mr. Scott A. RABENOLD
32 VP Stdnt Affairs & Dean of Students .... Dr. Soncia REAGINS-LILLY
41 Vice President & Athletics Director .... Mr. Chris M. DEL CONTE
26 VP/Chief Marketing/Communications .... Ms. Emily REAGAN
43 Vice President Legal Affairs .... Mr. James E. DAVIS
21 Exec Dir of Finance and Admin .... Ms. Mary C. LINDHOLM
88 Deputy to the President .... Ms. Nancy BRAZZIL
04 Administrative Manager .... Ms. Christine SOBEY
88 Sr Vice Prov Resource Management .... Dr. Larry SINGELL
20 Sr Vice Prov for Faculty Affairs .... Dr. Tasha BERETVAS
85 Sr Vice Prov for Global Engagement .... Ms. Sonia FEIGENBAUM
84 Int Vice Prov for Enrollment Mgmt .... Ms. Carolyn K. CONNERAT
58 SVP for Acad Affs/Dean Grad School .... Dr. Mark SMITH
88 Chief of Staff to Exec VP/Prov .... Ms. Rosemaria MARTINELLI
16 VP Advocacy & Dispute Resolution .... Dr. Janet M. DUKERICH
25 Asst VP Res/Dir Sponsored Projects .... Ms. Renee K. GONZALES
08 Vice Provost/Director UT Libraries .... Dr. Lorraine J. HARICOMBE
20 Vice Provost Undergrad Acad Affs .... Dr. David E. PLATT
88 Vice Provost for Diversity .... Dr. Edmund T. GORDON
104 Dir of Intl Student & Scholar Svcs .... Ms. Margaret Y. LUEVANO
88 Assoc VP Strat Acad Initiatives .... Dr. Linda N. DICKENS
100 Director of Admin for President .... Mrs. Monica HORVAT
86 Deputy to Pres for Strategy & Polic .... Ms. Andrea SHERIDAN
114 Budget Office Director .... Mr. John MCGEADY
105 Web and Mobile Applications Manager .... Ms. Tracy H. BROWN
07 Asst Vice Prov for Enrollment Svcs .... Mr. Mark SIMPSON
18 Associate VP Utilities/Energy Mgmt .... Mr. Juan ONTIVEROS
15 Associate VP Human Resources .... Ms. Adrienne HOWARTH-MOORE
09 Exec Dir Inst Research & Reporting .... Dr. Shiva JAGANATHAN
37 Exec Dir Office of Financial Aid .... Ms. Diane C. TODD SPRAGUE
39 Director Housing & Food Service .... Mr. Rene RODRIGUEZ
100 Chief of Staff & Exec Sr Assoc AD .... Ms. Christine A. PLONSKY
19 Asst VP Campus Sec/Chief of Police .... Mr. David CARTER
48 Dean of School of Architecture .... Dr. Michelle ADDINGTON
50 Dean of School of Business .... Ms. Lillian MILLS
60 Dean of College of Communication .... Dr. Jay M. BERNHARDT
53 Dean of College of Education .... Dr. Charles MARTINEZ
54 Dean of School of Engineering .... Dr. Sharon L. WOOD
57 Dean of College of Fine Arts .... Dr. Douglas J. DEMPSTER
62 Dean of School of Information .... Dr. Eric T. MEYER
65 Dean of School of Geosciences .... Ms. Claudia I. MORA
61 Dean of School of Law .... Dr. Ward FARNSWORTH
49 Dean of College of Liberal Arts .... Dr. Ann STEVENS
81 Int Dean College of Natural Science .... Dr. David A. VANDEN BOUT
66 Dean of School of Nursing .... Dr. Alexa M. STUIFBERGEN
67 Dean of College of Pharmacy .... Dr. Samuel POLOYAC
80 Int Dean School of Public Affairs .... Dr. David W. SPRINGER
70 Dean of School of Social Work .... Dr. Luis H. ZAYAS
97 Dean of School of Undergrad Studies .... Dr. Brent L. IVERSON
26 Director of Communications .... Mr. Joey WILLIAMS
88 Executive Director for Univ Unions .... Mr. Mulugeta FEREDE
27 Director/Editor-in-Chief .... Mr. Robert DEVENS

*The University of Texas at Dallas (B)

800 West Campbell Road, Richardson TX 75080
County: Collin FICE Identification: 009741
Unit ID: 228787
Telephone: (972) 883-2111 Carnegie Class: DU-Highest
FAX Number: (972) 883-2237 Calendar System: Semester
URL: www.utdallas.edu
Established: 1969 Annual Undergrad Tuition & Fees (In-State): $13,992
Enrollment: 28,669 Coed
Affiliation or Control: State IRS Status: 501(c)3
Highest Offering: Doctorate
Accreditation: SC, ACAE, AUD, IPSY, SP, SPAA

02 President .... Dr. Richard BENSON
100 Vice President and Chief of Staff .... Mr. Rafael O. MARTIN
05 VP Academic Affairs and Provost .... Dr. Inga MUSSELMAN
10 Vice President for Business Affairs .... Dr. Calvin D. JAMISON
32 Vice President Student Affairs .... Dr. Gene FITCH
46 VP for Research .... Dr. Joseph J. PANCRAZIO
30 Vice President for Development .... Dr. Kyle EDGINGTON
13 VP Info Technology and CIO .... Mr. Frank FEAGANS
28 Vice President of Diversity .... Dr. Yvette E. PEARSON
114 Asst VP and Chief Budget Officer .... Mr. Orkun TOROS
21 VP Finance & Controller .... Mr. Terry PANKRATZ
26 VP Public Affairs .... Ms. Amanda O. ROCKOW
45 Exec Director Strategic Planning .... Dr. Lawrence J. REDLINGER
35 Assoc VP/Dean of Students .... Dr. Amanda SMITH
58 Dean Graduate Studies .... Dr. Juan E. GONZALEZ
53 Dean Undergraduate Education .... Dr. Jessica C. MURPHY
79 Int Dean School Arts & Humanities .... Dr. Nils ROEMER
50 Dean School of Management .... Dr. Hasan PIRKUL
81 Dean Sch Natural Science/Math .... Dr. David HYNDMAN
82 Dean Sch Econ/Political Science .... Dr. Jennifer HOLMES
76 Dean Sch Behavioral/Brain Science .... Dr. Steven L. SMALL
97 Dean School General Studies .... Dr. George W. FAIR
54 Dean EJ Sch of Engr/Computer Sci .... Dr. Stephanie G. ADAMS
57 Dean Sch Arts/Tech & Emerg Media .... Dr. Anne BALSAMO
92 Dean Honors College .... Dr. Edward HARPHAM
08 Dean of Libraries .... Dr. Ellen SAFLEY
06 Registrar .... Ms. Jennifer MCDOWELL
12 Exec Director of Callier Center .... Dr. Angela SHOUP
18 Assoc VP Facilities Management .... Mr. Doug TOMLINSON
15 Assoc VP Human Resources .... Ms. Colleen DUTTON
96 Asst VP Operations (Purchasing) .... Dr. Brian BERNOUSSI
19 Chief of Police .... Mr. Larry ZACHARIAS
36 Director Career Services .... Ms. Keri BURNS
38 Assoc Dean Student Counseling .... Ms. Laura SMITH
116 Institutional Chief Audit Executive .... Ms. Toni STEPHENS
41 Director Intercollegiate Athletics .... Mr. Bill PETITT
78 Assoc Dir Co-operative Education .... Mr. Michael J. CHOATE
90 Assoc VP/Chief Tech Officer .... Mr. Brian DOURTY
29 Senior Director of Alumni Relations .... Ms. Jill ARREDONDO
04 Executive Associate to President .... Ms. Kimberly GOODFRIEND
105 Director Web Services .... Mr. Joe WILSON
106 Asst Provost Learning Tech .... Mr. Darren CRONE
39 Asst VP Residential Life .... Mr. Ryan WHITE
104 Asst Director International Pgms .... Ms. Andrea DIAZ
37 Director Student Financial Aid .... Ms. Beth TOLAN
43 University Attorney .... Mr. Timothy SHAW
84 Sr Director Enrollment Management .... Mr. Michael SEELIGSON

*University of Texas at El Paso (C)

500 W University Avenue, El Paso TX 79968-8900
County: El Paso FICE Identification: 003661
Unit ID: 228796
Telephone: (915) 747-5000 Carnegie Class: DU-Highest
FAX Number: (915) 747-5111 Calendar System: Semester
URL: www.utep.edu
Established: 1914 Annual Undergrad Tuition & Fees (In-State): $9,450
Enrollment: 24,879 Coed
Affiliation or Control: State IRS Status: 501(c)3
Highest Offering: Doctorate
Accreditation: SC, CACREP, MT, MUS, NURSE, OT, PH, PHAR, PTA, SP, SPAA, SW

02 President .... Dr. Heather WILSON
05 Provost/VP Academic Affairs .... Dr. John WIEBE
100 Vice President & Chief of Staff .... Ms. Andrea CORTINAS
10 VP Business Affairs .... Mr. Mark MCGURK
111 Vice President Inst Advancement .... Mr. Jake LOGAN
46 Vice President for Research .... Dr. Roberto OSEGUEDA
13 VP Information Resources .... Mr. Luis HERNANDEZ
32 Vice President Student Affairs .... Dr. Gary EDENS
58 Dean of Graduate School .... Dr. Stephen L. CRITES
50 Dean of Business Administration .... Dr. James E. PAYNE
53 Dean of Education .... Dr. Clifton TANABE
54 Interim Dean of Engineering .... Dr. Patricia NAVA
49 Dean of Liberal Arts .... Dr. Denis O'HEARN
76 Interim Dean of Health Sciences .... Dr. William ROBERTSON
67 Founding Dean School of Pharmacy .... Dr. Jose O. RIVERA
81 Dean of Science .... Dr. Robert KIRKEN
66 Dean of School of Nursing .... Dr. Leslie H. ROBBINS
106 Dean Extended Univ/Online Educ .... Ms. Beth L. BRUNK-CHAVEZ
18 Assoc VP Business Affs/Facilities .... Mr. Greg L. MCNICOL
08 Assoc Vice President Library .... Mr. Robert L. STAKES
26 Asst Vice Pres University Relations .... Mr. Beto LOPEZ
15 Assoc VP Human Resources .... Ms. Sandy VASQUEZ
29 Asst VP Alumni Relations .... Ms. Maribel VILLALVA
84 Asst VP Enrollment Services .... Dr. Amanda VASQUEZ
19 Chief Campus Police .... Mr. Clifton WALSH
37 Asst VP for Financial Services .... Dr. Heidi GRANGER
23 Admin Dir of Student Health Center .... Ms. Leticia PAEZ
36 Director of Career Services .... Ms. Betsy CASTRO-DUARTE
35 Associate VP/Dean of Students .... Dr. Catherine M. MCCORRY-ANDALIS
45 Assoc VP for Planning .... Dr. Roy MATHEW
39 Executive Dir of Housing Services .... Mr. Raymond GORDON
40 Manager of University Bookstore .... Mr. Matt CULBERSON
41 Athletics Director .... Mr. Jim SENTER
38 Director Counseling Services .... Ms. Brian SNEED
96 Assoc VP Purchasing/General Svcs .... Dr. Diane N. DEHOYOS
27 Director Communications .... Ms. Jenn CRAWFORD
04 Exec Assistant to the President .... Ms. Patti MARTINEZ
43 Chief Legal Officer .... Ms. Priscilla CASTILLO
116 Chief Audit Executive .... Ms. Lori N. WERTZ
88 Dir/Chief Compliance & Ethics Ofcr .... Ms. Mary SOLIS
88 Title IX Coordinator .... Mr. Gabriel RAMIREZ

*The University of Texas Rio Grande Valley (D)

1201 W University Drive, Edinburg TX 78539-2999
County: Hidalgo FICE Identification: 003599
Unit ID: 227368
Telephone: (888) 882-8201 Carnegie Class: DU-Higher
FAX Number: (956) 665-2150 Calendar System: Semester
URL: www.utrgv.edu
Established: 2015 Annual Undergrad Tuition & Fees (In-State): $8,917
Enrollment: 32,441 Coed
Affiliation or Control: State IRS Status: 501(c)3
Highest Offering: Doctorate
Accreditation: SC, ARCPA, CACREP, CAEPN, @DIETC, #MED, MT, MUS, NURSE, OT, SP, SW, THEA

02 President .... Dr. Guy BAILEY
03 Deputy President .... Dr. Janna ARNEY
05 Interim Provost .... Dr. Janna ARNEY
10 EVP for Finance and Administration .... Mr. Rick ANDERSON
46 EVP Research/Graduate Studies .... Dr. Parwinder GREWAL
111 EVP for Institutional Advancement .... Dr. Kelly NASSOUR
86 VP for Government/Cmty Relations .... Ms. Veronica GONZALES
32 Assoc Provost for Student Success .... Dr. Jonikka CHARLTON
84 Sr VP for Strategic Enrollment .... Dr. Maggie HINOJOSA
20 AVP Faculty Affairs .... Dr. Shawn SALADIN
21 Sr Assoc VP Finance & Planning .... Mr. Michael MUELLER
11 VP for Admin Support Services .... Mr. Doug ARNEY
18 Assoc VP for Facilities Planning .... Ms. Marta SALINAS-HOVAR
110 VP for Institutional Advancement .... Ms. Tracie A. ASHLOCK
88 Assoc VP for Governmental Relations .... Mr. Richard P. SANCHEZ
26 Assoc VP for University Marketing .... Mr. Patrick GONZALES
109 Assoc VP for Campus Auxiliary Svcs .... Ms. Letty BENAVIDES
31 Assoc VP for Community Engagement .... Vacant
09 AVP Strategic Analysis and Inst Res .... Ms. Susan BROWN
108 AVP Inst Accred/Pgm Dev & Analysis .... Dr. Christine SHUPALA
88 Assoc VP Acad Inst Excellence .... Dr. Laura SAENZ
53 Dean College of Educ & P-16 .... Dr. Alma RODRIGUEZ
50 Dean Business Entrepreneurship .... Dr. Lance NAIL
81 Dean College of Sciences .... Dr. Vivian INCERA
54 Dean College Engr/Comp Sci .... Dr. Ala QUBBAJ
76 Dean College of Health Professions .... Dr. Michael LEHKER
49 Dean College of Fine Arts .... Dr. Steven BLOCK
83 Dean College of Liberal Arts .... Dr. Walter DIAZ
63 Dean School of Medicine .... Dr. Michael B. HOCKER
66 Dean School of Nursing .... Dr. Sharon RADZYMINSKI
43 Chief Legal Officer .... Ms. Karen ADAMS
15 Chief Human Resources Officer .... Mr. Mike JAMES
06 University Registrar .... Ms. Sofia MONTES
22 Chief Compliance Officer .... Ms. Samantha ALLEN
13 Chief Information Officer .... Dr. Jeffrey GRAHAM
119 Chief Info Security Officer .... Dr. Kevin CROUSE
29 Exec Dir of Alumni Relations .... Mrs. Marisa CAMPIRANO
41 VP and Director of Athletics .... Mr. Chasse CONQUE
114 Dir for Budget & Ops RGSNPD .... Ms. Rosalinda SALAZAR
04 Assistant to the President .... Ms. Maria CONDE
08 Dean of Libraries .... Mr. Paul SHARPE
37 Director of Financial Aid .... Mr. Elias OZUNA
92 Dean Honors College .... Dr. Mark ANDERSEN
88 Interim Exec Dir B3 Institute .... Dr. Dania LOPEZ GARCIA
88 Chief Operating Officer SOM HA .... Ms. Sofia HERNANDEZ
116 Chief Audit Executive .... Mr. Eloy R. ALANIZ, JR.
19 Chief Police .... Mr. Adan CRUZ
28 Chief Equity & Diversity Officer .... Ms. Florence NOCAR
88 Dir Victim Advocacy & Violence .... Dr. Cynthia JONES
07 Dir of Undergraduate Admissions .... Ms. Marybel VILLASENOR
104 Director of International Programs .... Mr. Alan EARHART
30 Director of Development .... Mr. John GARZA
39 Dir Resident Life/Student Housing .... Mr. Sergio MARTINEZ
44 Director of Planned Giving .... Ms. Serena PUTEGNAT
96 Chief Procurement Officer .... Mr. Alex VALDEZ

*The University of Texas at San Antonio (E)

One UTSA Circle, San Antonio TX 78249-0169
County: Bexar FICE Identification: 010115
Unit ID: 229027
Telephone: (210) 458-4011 Carnegie Class: DU-Higher
FAX Number: (210) 458-4187 Calendar System: Semester
URL: www.utsa.edu
Established: 1969 Annual Undergrad Tuition & Fees (In-State): $8,566
Enrollment: 34,742 Coed
Affiliation or Control: State IRS Status: 501(c)3
Highest Offering: Doctorate
Accreditation: SC, ART, CACREP, CEA, CIDA, CONST, DIETC, MUS, NAEYC, SPAA, SW

02 President .... Dr. Taylor EIGHMY
05 Provost/Vice Pres Academic Affs .... Dr. Kimberly ANDREWS ESPY
10 SVP Business Affairs/CFO .... Ms. Veronica SALAZAR MENDEZ
46 VP for Research/Econ Development .... Dr. Bernard ARULANANDAM
32 SVP Student Affs/Dean of Students .... Ms. LT ROBINSON
26 Int VP for University Relations .... Mr. Rod MCSHERRY
20 AVP/AV Provost Inst Initiatives .... Dr. Howard GRIMES
13 VP Information Mgmt/Technology .... Ms. Kendra KETCHUM
30 Vice Pres Development/Alumni Rels .... Mr. Karl MILLER-LUGO
28 Vice President Inclusive Excellence .... Dr. Myron ANDERSON
09 AVP Acad Compl/Inst Effectiveness .... Mr. Steve L. WILKERSON
12 Vice Provost for Downtown Campus .... Dr. Jesse T. ZAPATA
100 Chief of Staff .... Mr. Carlos MARTINEZ

20 Int Vice Prov/Dean Univ College .... Dr. Heather J. SHIPLEY
21 Associate VP Financial Affairs .... Ms. Sheri HARDISON
27 AVP Comm & Special Projects Officer .... Ms. Anne C. PETERS
08 Dean of Libraries .... Dr. Dean D. HENDRIX
92 Dean of Honors College .... Dr. Sean KELLY
58 Int Vice Prov/Dean Graduate School .... Dr. Can SAYGIN
50 Dean College of Business .... Dr. Wm Gerard (Gerry) Y. SANDERS
57 Dean College of Liberal & Fine Arts .... Mr. Martin CAMACHO
54 Dean College of Engineering .... Dr. Joann BROWNING
83 Interim Dean College of Sciences .... Dr. Howard GRIMES
48 Dean School of Architecture .... Prof. John MURPHY
53 Int Dean Col Educ/Human Development .... Dr. Juliet LANGMAN
80 Dean College of Public Policy .... Dr. Lynne SITTIG COSSMAN
19 AVP Public Safety/Chief of Police .... Mr. Gerald LEWIS
41 VP ICA and Athletics Director .... Dr. Lisa D. CAMPOS
43 Interim Chief Legal Officer .... Mr. John P. DANNER
117 Dir Inst Compliance & Risk Services .... Mr. James R. WEAVER
116 Chief Audit Executive .... Paul A. TYLER
27 AVP Communications/Marketing .... Mr. Joe IZBRAND
86 AVP Government Relations & Policy .. Mr. Albert A. CARRISALEZ
04 Exec Assistant Office of President .... Ms. Yvonne DE LEON
07 Director of Admissions .... Ms. Beverly WOODSON DAY
88 Asst VP Strategic Initiatives .... Ms. Elvira E. LEAL
105 Associate Director of Web/Portal .... Mr. Shashi B. PINHEIRO
106 Director of Online Learning .... Ms. Marcela V. RAMIREZ
108 Assistant Vice Provost Assessment .... Dr. Kasey NEECE-FIELDER
18 Int Senior AVP for Business Affairs .... Mr. David J. RIKER
25 Dir Grants/Contracts/Financial Svcs .... Mr. Daniel ANZAK
28 Associate Provost .... Col. Lisa C. FIRMIN, RET.
37 Director of Student Financial Aid .... Ms. Diana S. MARTINEZ
38 Director Counseling Services .... Dr. Melissa HERNANDEZ
39 Director Student Housing/Residence .... Mr. Daniel L. GOCKLEY
15 Asst VP Operations/Talent Mgmt .... Ms. Rebecca ANDERSON
90 Director of Academic Computing .... Mr. John P. SOUDAH
96 Director Business Contracts .... Mr. Robert L. DICKENS

*University of Texas at Tyler (A)

3900 University Boulevard, Tyler TX 75799-6699
County: Smith FICE Identification: 011163
Unit ID: 228802
Telephone: (903) 566-7000 Carnegie Class: DU-Mod
FAX Number: (903) 566-7068 Calendar System: Semester
URL: www.uttyler.edu
Established: 1971 Annual Undergrad Tuition & Fees (In-State): $9,146
Enrollment: 9,781 Coed
Affiliation or Control: State IRS Status: 501(c)3
Highest Offering: Doctorate
Accreditation: SC, CACREP, IPSY, MUS, NAIT, NURSE, OT, PHAR

02 President .... Dr. Kirk A. CALHOUN
05 Provost/VP Academic Affairs .... Dr. Amir MIRMIRAN
111 Vice President Univ Advancement .... Vacant
32 Vice Pres for Student Success .... Ms. Ona TOLLIVER
13 Vice President & CIO IT .... Dr. Sherri WHATLEY
20 Vice Provost AA/Grad Studies .... Dr. Steven IDELL
46 Assoc Provost Research/Scholarship .... Dr. Kouider MOKHTARI
10 VP for Budget and CFO .... Dr. Kimberly LAIRD
15 Director of Human Resources .... Ms. Gracy BUENTELLO
86 AVP Gov & Community Relations .... Dr. Laura JACKSON
84 Assoc VP for Enrollment Management .... Mr. David BARRON
108 Asst Vice Pres for Assessment/IE .... Dr. Lou Ann BERMAN
49 Dean College of Arts & Sciences .... Dr. Neil GRAY
50 Dean College Business & Technology .... Dr. Krist SWIMBERGHE
53 Dean College Educ & Psych .... Dr. Wesley HICKEY
54 Dean College of Engineering .... Dr. Javier KYPUROS
66 Dean College Nursing & Health Sci .... Dr. Barbara HAAS
67 Dean College of Pharmacy .... Dr. Lane BRUNNER
08 Exec Director of the Library .... Ms. Rebecca MCKAY JOHNSON
21 Director of Financial Services .... Ms. Cindy TROYER
18 VP for Operations/Strategic Init .... Mr. Jerry STUFF
29 Exec Dir Career Success & Alumni .... Dr. Rosemary COOPER
26 Exec Dir Marketing & Communication .... Ms. Beverley GOLDEN
121 Associate Dean of Student Success .... Ms. Kim HARVEY-LIVINGSTON
39 Assoc Dean of Students .... Dr. Jennifer WATERS
06 Registrar .... Ms. Gisele ABRON
09 Director Institutional Analysis .... Ms. Cindy STRAWN
19 Chief University Police .... Mr. Mike W. MEDDERS
04 Executive Asst to President .... Ms. Janet ROBERTSON
07 Asst Director of Admissions .... Ms. Whitney RAINS
37 Director of Student Financial Aid .... Vacant
43 Chief Legal Officer .... Mr. Michael DONLEY
106 Assoc Provost UG Adm & On-line Educ .... Dr. Colleen SWAIN
41 Athletic Director .... Dr. Howard PATTERSON
44 Director of Annual Giving .... Mr. Daniel ONDERKO

*The University of Texas Health Science Center at Houston (UTHealth) (B)

PO Box 20036, Houston TX 77225-0036
County: Harris FICE Identification: 004951
Unit ID: 229300
Telephone: (713) 500-4472 Carnegie Class: Spec-4-yr-Med
FAX Number: (713) 500-3026 Calendar System: Semester
URL: www.uth.edu
Established: 1972 Annual Undergrad Tuition & Fees (In-State): N/A
Enrollment: 5,608 Coed
Affiliation or Control: State IRS Status: 501(c)3
Highest Offering: Doctorate
Accreditation: SC, ANEST, CAHIIM, CAMPEP, DENT, DH, DIETI, HSA, IPSY, MED, NURSE, PERF, PH

02 President .... Dr. Giuseppe N. COLASURDO
11 Exec VP & COO .... Mr. T. Kevin DILLON
05 Exec VP & Chief Academic Officer ... Dr. Michael R. BLACKBURN
28 EVP Student Affairs & Diversity .... Dr. Latonya J. LOVE
03 Senior VP & COO UT Physicians .... Mr. Andrew CASAS
63 Dean McGovern Medical School .... Dr. Richard J. ANDRASSY
69 Dean School of Public Health .... Dr. Eric BOERWINKLE
52 Dean School of Dentistry .... Dr. John A. VALENZA
58 Dean Grad Sch Biomedical Sciences ..... Dr. Michael BLACKBURN
58 Dean Grad Sch Biomedical Sciences .... Dr. Michelle C. BARTON
66 Dean Cizik School of Nursing .... Dr. Diane M. SANTA MARIA
88 Dean Sch of Biomed Informatics .... Dr. Jiajie W. ZHANG
117 VP Enterprise Risk Mgmt/Compliance .... Ms. Karen K. SPILLAR
10 Sr VP Finance & Business Svcs & CFO .... Mr. Michael TRAMONTE
46 Vice Dn Rsrch/Dir Molecular Med .... Dr. John HANCOCK
30 Vice Pres Development .... Mr. Kevin J. FOYLE
15 VP/Chief Human Resources Officer .... Mr. Eric FERNETTE
43 VP/Chief Legal Officer .... Mr. Melissa K. PIFKO
86 VP Govt Relations .... Mr. Scott FORBES
88 VP Research & Technology .... Dr. Bruce D. BUTLER
109 VP Auxiliary Enterprises .... Mr. Charles A. FIGARI
13 VP/Chief Information Officer .... Mr. Amar YOUSIF
18 VP Facilities Planning & Engr .... Mr. Wes STEWART
90 Asst VP Academic Technology .... Dr. William A. WEEMS
116 Asst VP & Chief Audit Officer .... Mr. Daniel SHERMAN
09 Asst VP Institutional Research .... Ms. Deanne HERNANDEZ
06 Registrar .... Mr. Robert JENKINS
19 Assoc VP/Chief of Police .... Mr. William ADCOX
40 Executive Director HCPC .... Dr. Jair C. SOARES
41 Director Recreation/Intramural Pgms .... Ms. Pauline M. HABETZ
85 Director International Affairs .... Ms. Rose Mary VALENCIA
39 Director University Housing .... Ms. Peree E. GRIFFIN
26 Assistant VP Public Affairs .... Ms. Meredith RAINE
37 Director Student Financial Svcs ... Ms. Heather BECKLES-BRIGHT
25 Assoc VP Sponsored Projects Admin ...... Ms. Kathleen KREIDLER
14 Exec Director & Chief Tech Ofcr .... Mr. Kevin B. GRANHOLD
88 Director Educational Tech Nursing .... Ms. Linda L. CRAYS
88 Director Interactive Video Medical .... Dr. Stephen J. FATH
100 Chief of Staff Office of the Pres .... Ms. Rose HOCHNER
105 Executive Director Univ Web Svcs .... Ms. Jennifer L. CANUP
22 AVP Diversity & Equal Opportunity .... Ms. Deana K. MOYLAN

*University of Texas Health Science Center at San Antonio (C)

7703 Floyd Curl Drive, San Antonio TX 78229-3900
County: Bexar FICE Identification: 003659
Unit ID: 228644
Telephone: (210) 567-7000 Carnegie Class: Spec-4-yr-Med
FAX Number: N/A Calendar System: Other
URL: www.uthscsa.edu
Established: 1959 Annual Undergrad Tuition & Fees (In-State): N/A
Enrollment: 3,478 Coed
Affiliation or Control: State IRS Status: 501(c)3
Highest Offering: Doctorate
Accreditation: SC, ARCPA, CAMPEP, COARC, DENT, DH, EMT, HT, IPSY, MED, MT, NURSE, OT, PTA, RADDOS, @SP

02 President .... Dr. William L. HENRICH
03 Sr Exec Vice President & COO .... Mrs. Andrea MARKS
11 Exec VP for Facility Planning/Admin .... Mr. James D. KAZEN
10 Vice President & CFO .... Mrs. Ginny GOMEZ-LEON
05 VP Acad/Fac & Student Affairs .... Dr. Jacqueline L. MOK
13 Vice Pres & Chief Information Ofcr .... Mr. Yeman COLLIER
46 Vice President for Research .... Dr. Andrea GIUFFRIDA
86 VP for Governmental Relations .... Mr. Armando DIAZ
111 VP Inst Advancement/Chief Dev Ofcr ... Ms. Deborah H. MORRILL
26 VP & Chief Marketing/Comm Officer .... Ms. Heather ADKINS
15 Vice Pres of Human Resources .... Mrs. Amy TAWNEY
100 VP & Chief of Staff .... Ms. Mary G. DELAY
21 Asst Vice Pres for Business Affairs .... Mr. Gerard E. LONG
09 Asst VP Research .... Dr. Mark J. NIJLAND
43 Chief Legal Officer .... Mr. Jack C. PARK
63 Dean School of Medicine .... Dr. Robert HROMAS
52 Dean School of Dentistry .... Dr. Peter M. LOOMER
58 Dean Graduate Biomed Science .... Dr. David WEISS
76 Dean School Health Professions .... Dr. David C. SHELLEDY
66 Dean School of Nursing .... Dr. Eileen T. BRESLIN
32 Director for Student Life .... Ms. Le Keisha JOHNSON
06 Registrar .... Dr. Blanca GUERRA
08 Senior Director of Libraries .... Mr. Owen H. ELLARD
19 Chief of Police .... Mr. Michael PARKS
88 Exec Dir Acad/Fac/Stdnt Ombudspers .... Dr. Bonnie L. BLANKMEYER
37 Dir Veterans Svcs & Financial Aid .... Ms. Ellen NYSTROM
38 Director of Student Counseling .... Dr. Mia VEVE
96 Sr Dir Supply Chain Management .... Mr. Eric R. WALLS
07 Director of Admissions & Intl Pgm .... Mr. Henry CANTU
102 Dir Corp & Foundation Relations .... Ms. Leslie M. PAYNE
112 Senior Director Planned Giving .... Vacant

*The University of Texas MD Anderson Cancer Center (D)

1515 Holcombe Boulevard, Houston TX 77030-4000
County: Harris FICE Identification: 025554
Unit ID: 416801
Telephone: (713) 792-6161 Carnegie Class: Spec-4-yr-Other Health
FAX Number: N/A Calendar System: Semester
URL: www.mdanderson.org
Established: 1941 Annual Undergrad Tuition & Fees (In-District): N/A
Enrollment: 358 Coed
Affiliation or Control: State/Local IRS Status: 501(c)3
Highest Offering: Doctorate
Accreditation: SC, CAMPEP, CGTECH, CYTO, DENT, DMOLS, HT, MT, PAST, RAD, RADDOS, RADMAG, RTT

02 President .... Dr. Peter PISTERS
05 Provost & Executive Vice Presiden .... Dr. Ethan DMITROVSKY
10 Sr Vice President/CFO .... Mr. Ben MELSON
17 Chief Medical Officer .... Dr. Stephen HAHN

*The University of Texas Medical Branch (E)

301 University Boulevard, Galveston TX 77555-0129
County: Galveston FICE Identification: 004952
Unit ID: 228653
Telephone: (409) 772-1011 Carnegie Class: Spec-4-yr-Med
FAX Number: N/A Calendar System: Semester
URL: www.utmb.edu
Established: 1891 Annual Undergrad Tuition & Fees (In-State): N/A
Enrollment: 3,458 Coed
Affiliation or Control: State IRS Status: 170(c)1
Highest Offering: Doctorate
Accreditation: SC, ARCPA, BBT, COARC, DENT, DIETI, MED, MT, NURSE, OT, PH, PTA

02 Interim President .... Dr. Ben G. RAIMER
05 EVP/Provost/Dean Sch of Med .... Dr. Charles P. MOUTON
23 EVP & CEO Health System .... Dr. Tim HARLIN
10 EVP & Chief Financial Officer .... Ms. Cheryl SADRO
88 VP & Chief Physician Executive .... Dr. Rex M. MCCALLUM
17 Chief Medical Officer .... Dr. Gulshan SHARMA
66 Sr VP & Dean of Nursing .... Dr. Deborah J. JONES
76 SVP & Dean Sch Health Professions .... Dr. David A. BROWN
58 Interim Dean Grad Sch Biomed Sci ...... Dr. Giulio TAGLIALATELA
15 VP and Chief HR Officer .... Dr. Vivian D. KARDOW
13 Interim VP Information Svcs & CIO .... Mr. George GADDIE
21 VP Finance Academic Enterprise .... Mr. Gabe HERNANDEZ
18 VP Business Ops & Facilities .... Mr. Steven B. LEBLANC
11 VP/Chief Admin Officer AE .... Mr. Loren SKINNER
21 Assoc VP Finance CMC .... Mr. David M. CONNAUGHTON
45 EVP Bus Dev & Chief Strategy Ofcr .... Ms. Rebecca KORENEK
43 Sr VP General Counsel .... Ms. Carolee KING
32 Assoc Dean Student Affairs/Adm SON .... Dr. Diana PRESSLEY
25 Dir Grants & Contracts Acctg .... Ms. Claudia J. DELGADO
08 Assoc VP Academic Res/Library .... Ms. Patricia A. CIEJKA
09 Assoc VP Inst Effectiveness .... Dr. John C. MCKEE
27 Assoc VP Public Affairs .... Ms. Mary G. HAVARD
21 AVP Financial Capital Planning .... Mr. Matthew FURLONG
114 VP Health System Finance .... Mr. David GRUENER
114 VP Finance Institution Support .... Ms. Lynn MCGINLEY
116 VP Audit Services .... Ms. Foy DESOLYN
30 VP Chief Development Officer .... Ms. Betsy B. CLARDY
88 VP & Chief Compliance Officer .... Mr. Tobin R. BOENIG
06 AVP Univ Student Svcs & Registrar .... Mr. William S. BOEH
19 VP & Chief of University Police .... Mr. Kenith ADCOX
96 VP Supply Chain Management .... Mr. Christopher TOOMES
38 Director Student Wellness Services ... Dr. Olawunmi A. AKINPELU
100 Interim Chief of Staff .... Ms. Beth STUM
16 Assoc VP HR Opers & Employee Health .... Ms. Philesha EVANS
105 Director Digital Communications .... Mr. Eduardo VALDES
108 Asst Director Inst Effectiveness .... Mr. Jason FRY
37 Director Student Financial Service .... Ms. Ann HALE
88 Field House Facilities Ops Manager .... Ms. Leslie BLACKETER
53 VP Education IE & HEC .... Dr. Janet H. SOUTHERLAND
28 Diversity & Inclusion Consultant .... Ms. Leah JACOBS
44 Sr Dir Alumni Rels & Annual Giving .... Ms. Rena LIDSTONE
86 Asst VP Government Relations .... Mr. Frederick Ryan MICKS

*University of Texas Permian Basin (F)

4901 E University Boulevard, Odessa TX 79762-0001
County: Ector FICE Identification: 009930
Unit ID: 229018
Telephone: (432) 552-2020 Carnegie Class: Masters/L
FAX Number: (432) 552-2374 Calendar System: Semester
URL: www.utpb.edu
Established: 1969 Annual Undergrad Tuition & Fees (In-State): $4,837
Enrollment: 5,530 Coed
Affiliation or Control: State IRS Status: 501(c)3
Highest Offering: Master's
Accreditation: SC, ART, CAEPN, MUS, NURSE, SW

02 President .... Dr. Sandra WOODLEY
05 Provost/Vice Pres Academic Affairs .... Dr. Dan HEIMMERMANN
32 VP Student Affairs & Leadership .... Dr. Rebecca SPURLOCK
111 Vice President of Advancement .... Mr. Wendell SNODGRASS
13 VP Information Technology/Analytics .... Mr. Bradley SHOOK
49 Dean College of Arts & Science .... Dr. Scott MCKAY
50 Dean School of Business .... Dr. Steven BEACH
53 Dean College of Education .... Dr. Larry DANIEL
66 Dean College of Nursing .... Dr. Donna BEUK
54 Dean College of Engineering .... Dr. George NNANNA
07 Director Admissions .... Mr. Scott SMILEY
06 Registrar .... Mr. Joe SANDERS
18 Chief Facilities/Physical Plant .... Mr. David WAYLAND
36 Director Career Services .... Ms. Maribea MERRITT
29 Director of Special Projects JBS .... Mr. Jeff MEYERS
39 Director Student Housing .... Ms. Chermae PEEL
10 Chief Financial/Business Officer .... Mr. Cesar VALENZUELA

15 Director of Human Resources .... Mr. Ron APPLING
96 Director of Purchasing .... Ms. Elsa MONTALVO
35 Associate Student Affairs Officer .... Mr. Corey BENSON
04 Executive Assistant to President .... Ms. Delma LAY
41 Athletic Director .... Mr. Scott FARMER
08 Chief Library Officer .... Dr. Sophia KAANE
37 Director Student Financial Aid .... Mr. Scott LAPINSKI
84 Director Enrollment Management .... Ms. PJ WOOLSTON
100 Chief of Staff/Exec Dir of Comm .... Ms. Tatum HUBBARD
21 Assoc Financial/Business Officer .... Ms. Felecia BURNS
114 Chief Budget Administrator .... Ms. Griselda MEDINA
102 Director Foundation/Corporate Rels .... Ms. Marisol CHRIESMAN
104 Director Study Abroad .... Ms. Lorinda TERCERO
106 Director of Online Learning .... Ms. Katrieva JONES-MONROE
19 Chief of Police .... Mr. Tom HAIN
44 Director Annual Giving .... Ms. Danielle DAVILA
86 Director Government Relations .... Ms. Paige COOPER

*University of Texas Southwestern Medical Center (A)

5323 Harry Hines Boulevard, Dallas TX 75390-9002
County: Dallas
FICE Identification: 010019
Unit ID: 228635
Telephone: (214) 648-3111
Carnegie Class: Spec-4-yr-Med
FAX Number: N/A
Calendar System: Semester
URL: www.utsouthwestern.edu
Established: 1943
Annual Undergrad Tuition & Fees (In-State): N/A
Enrollment: 2,299
Coed
Affiliation or Control: State
IRS Status: 501(c)3
Highest Offering: Doctorate
Accreditation: SC, ARCPA, CAMPEP, CLPSY, DIETC, IPSY, MED, OPE, PAST, PTA, RTT

02 President .... Dr. Daniel K. PODOLSKY
100 Chief of Staff .... Ms. Courtney ROTTMAN
05 EVP Acad Affs/Provost/Dean Med Sch .... Dr. W. P. Andrew LEE
20 Vice Provost/Sr Assoc Dean Educ .... Dr. Charles M. GINSBURG
20 Vice Provost/Sr Assoc Dean Faculty .... Dr. Dwain L. THIELE
46 Vice Provost/Dean of Basic Research .... Dr. David W. RUSSELL
03 Exec VP Health System Affairs .... Dr. John WARNER
10 Exec Vice Pres Business Affairs .... Mr. Arnim DONTES
111 Exec VP Institutional Advancement .... Dr. Marc A. NIVET
23 Vice President Clinical Operations .... Dr. John D. RUTHERFORD
88 VP & Chief Quality Officer .... Dr. William DANIEL
17 VP Clin Pgm & Facility Development .... Ms. Becky MCCULLEY
21 Vice President Financial Affairs .... Mr. Michael SERBER
86 Vice Pres Govt Affairs & Policy .... Ms. Angelica MARIN-HILL
15 Vice President Human Resources .... Ms. Janelle BROWNE
88 VP Institutional Compliance .... Ms. Natalie A. RAMELLO
116 Vice President Internal Audit .... Ms. Valla F. WILSON
43 Vice President Legal Affairs .... Ms. Leah A. HURLEY
30 Vice President Development .... Ms. Amanda BILLINGS
102 Vice Pres Community and Corp Rels .... Mr. Ruben E. ESQUIVEL
13 Vice Pres Information Resources .... Mr. Russell POOLE
18 Vice President Facilities Mgmt .... Mr. Juan M. GUERRA, JR.
20 Vice Pres Academic Affairs/COO .... Mr. Cameron SLOCUM
88 Vice Pres/COO Medical Group .... Dr. Christopher MADDEN
58 Dean Grad School Biomedical Science .... Dr. Andrew ZINN
76 Dean School of Health Professions .... Dr. Jon WILLIAMSON
28 Assoc Dean Faculty Diversity & Dev .... Dr. Byron L. CRYER
88 Assoc Dean Global Health .... Dr. Fiemu E. NWARIAKU
63 Assoc Dean Grad Medical Education .... Dr. Larissa VELEZ
63 Assoc Dean Undergrad Medical Educ .... Dr. Robert REGE
32 Assoc Dean Student Affairs .... Dr. Angela MIHALIC
88 Assoc Dean Credentialing Ed Outcome .... Dr. James M. WAGNER
32 Assoc Dean Student Affairs .... Dr. Blake BARKER
93 Assoc Dean Student Diversity & Incl .... Dr. Shawna NESBITT
06 Registrar .... Mr. Adam ABERCROMBIE
07 Dir of Admissions & Recruitment .... Ms. Leah SCHOUTEN-KRESSER
37 Director Student Financial Aid .... Ms. Melet LEAFGREEN

Veritas College International Graduate School (B)

708 W. Summit Avenue, San Antonio TX 78212
County: Bexar
Identification: 667395
Telephone: (210) 446-6719
Carnegie Class: Not Classified
FAX Number: N/A
Calendar System: Semester
URL: www.veritascollege.org
Established: 2001
Annual Undergrad Tuition & Fees: N/A
Enrollment: N/A
Coed
Affiliation or Control: Independent Non-Profit
IRS Status: 501(c)3
Highest Offering: Doctorate
Accreditation: @BI

01 President .... RevDr. Bennie WOLVAARDT

Vernon College (C)

4400 College Drive, Vernon TX 76384-4092
County: Wilbarger
FICE Identification: 010060
Unit ID: 229504
Telephone: (940) 552-6291
Carnegie Class: Assoc/MT-VT-High Non
FAX Number: (940) 553-3902
Calendar System: Semester
URL: www.vernoncollege.edu
Established: 1970
Annual Undergrad Tuition & Fees (In-District): $4,520
Enrollment: 2,773
Coed
Affiliation or Control: State/Local
IRS Status: 501(c)3
Highest Offering: Associate Degree
Accreditation: SC, SURGT

01 President .... Dr. Dusty R. JOHNSTON
04 Admin Secretary to the President .... Ms. Mary KING
05 Vice Pres of Instructional Services .... Dr. Elizabeth CRANDALL
10 Vice Pres Administrative Services .... Mrs. Mindi FLYNN
32 Vice President of Student Services .... Vacant
103 Dean of Instructional Services .... Ms. Shana DRURY
111 Dir Inst Advance/VC Foundation .... Ms. Michelle ALEXANDER
88 Director of Quality Enhancement .... Dr. Donnie KIRK
09 Dir of Institutional Effectiveness .... Mrs. Betsy HARKEY
37 Director Financial Aid .... Mrs. Melissa J. ELLIOTT
08 Director of Library Services .... Ms. Marion GRONA
18 Director Physical Plant .... Mr. Lyle BONNER
15 Director of Human Resources .... Mrs. Jackie POLK
39 Director of Housing .... Mr. Jesse DOMINQUEZ
35 Dean of Student Services .... Mrs. Kristin HARRIS
84 Dir of Enrollment Mgmt & Registrar .... Mrs. Amanda RAINES
66 Dir Associate Degree in Nursing .... Dr. Mary RIVARD
19 Director of Campus Police .... Mr. Kevin HOLLAND

Vet Tech Institute of Houston (D)

4669 Southwest Freeway, Suite 100, Houston TX 77027
County: Harris
FICE Identification: 021448
Unit ID: 223472
Telephone: (713) 629-8940
Carnegie Class: Spec 2-yr-Health
FAX Number: (713) 629-0059
Calendar System: Semester
URL: www.vettechinstitute.edu/houston
Established: 2007
Annual Undergrad Tuition & Fees: $15,020
Enrollment: 202
Coed
Affiliation or Control: Proprietary
IRS Status: Proprietary
Highest Offering: Associate Degree
Accreditation: ACCSC

01 Director/Chief Academic Officer .... Mr. Elbert HAMILTON, JR.

Victoria College (E)

2200 E Red River, Victoria TX 77901-4494
County: Victoria
FICE Identification: 003662
Unit ID: 229540
Telephone: (361) 573-3291
Carnegie Class: Assoc/MT-VT-High Trad
FAX Number: (361) 572-3850
Calendar System: Semester
URL: www.victoriacollege.edu
Established: 1925
Annual Undergrad Tuition & Fees (In-District): $3,744
Enrollment: 3,274
Coed
Affiliation or Control: Local
IRS Status: 501(c)3
Highest Offering: Associate Degree
Accreditation: SC, ADNUR, COARC, EMT, PTAA

01 President .... Dr. Jennifer KENT
05 Vice President of Instruction .... Ms. Cindy BUCHHOLZ
10 Vice Pres Administrative Svcs .... Mr. Keith BLUNDELL
32 Dean of Student Services .... Dr. Edrel STONEHAM
111 VP College Advance/External Affairs .... Vacant
09 Dir Inst Effect/Research/Assess .... Mr. Matt WILEY
07 Registrar .... Ms. Madelyne TOLLIVER
18 Director Physical Plant .... Mr. Marty DECKARD
37 Director Financial Aid .... Ms. Kim OBSTA
15 Director Human Resources .... Ms. Terri KURTZ
26 Dir Marketing & Communications .... Mr. Darin KAZMIR
38 Director Advising/Counseling .... Mr. Robert CUBRIEL, III
96 Director of Purchasing .... Ms. Lydia HUBER
21 Director of Finance .... Ms. Tracey BERGSTROM
35 Director of Student Life .... Ms. Elaine EVERETT-HENSLEY
13 Director Technology Services .... Mr. Andy FARRIOR
04 Exec Admin Asst to President .... Ms. Mary Ann RODRIGUEZ
102 Exec Dir of College Advance & Found .... Ms. Amy MUNDY

Vista College (F)

6101 Montana Avenue, El Paso TX 79925-2021
County: El Paso
FICE Identification: 025720
Unit ID: 365204
Telephone: (915) 779-8031
Carnegie Class: Assoc/HVT-High Trad
FAX Number: (915) 779-8097
Calendar System: Semester
URL: www.vistacollege.edu
Established: 1987
Annual Undergrad Tuition & Fees: $15,825
Enrollment: 2,945
Coed
Affiliation or Control: Proprietary
IRS Status: Proprietary
Highest Offering: Associate Degree
Accreditation: COE

01 Campus Director .... Mr. Antonio RICO
06 Registrar .... Ms. Valerie PARKS
07 Assoc Director of Admissions .... Ms. Cindy HUERTA
37 Director Student Financial Aid .... Ms. Adrianna DURAN
63 Program Director Allied Health .... Ms. Juana CERVANTES
36 Director of Career Services .... Ms. Maribel CARRASCO

Vista College-Online (G)

300 N. Coit Road, Suite 650, Richardson TX 75080
County: Davis
FICE Identification: 025728
Unit ID: 377342
Telephone: (972) 707-8600
Carnegie Class: Bac/Assoc-Mixed
FAX Number: (972) 707-8575
Calendar System: Other
URL: www.vistacollege.edu/online/
Established:
Annual Undergrad Tuition & Fees: $15,943
Enrollment: 574
Coed
Affiliation or Control: Proprietary
IRS Status: Proprietary
Highest Offering: Baccalaureate
Accreditation: #ACCSC

01 Campus Director .... Mr. Greg GOSSETT
05 Director of Academic Operations .... Ms. Ann LARSON

Wade College (H)

1950 Stemmons Fwy, Ste 4080, LB 562, Dallas TX 75207
County: Dallas
FICE Identification: 010130
Unit ID: 226879
Telephone: (214) 637-3530
Carnegie Class: Bac/Assoc-Mixed
FAX Number: (214) 637-0827
Calendar System: Trimester
URL: www.wadecollege.edu
Established: 1962
Annual Undergrad Tuition & Fees: $14,955
Enrollment: 180
Coed
Affiliation or Control: Proprietary
IRS Status: Proprietary
Highest Offering: Baccalaureate
Accreditation: SC, CIDA

01 President .... Dr. Harry DAVROS
03 Executive Vice President .... Mr. John CONTE
05 Dean of Academic Affairs .... Ms. Elizabeth JOHNSTON
37 Director Compliance & Finance .... Ms. Lisa HOOVER
07 Director of Admissions .... Mr. James SCHROEDER
36 Director of Career Services .... Mrs. Jennifer MAGEE
08 Director Learning Resources .... Mrs. April LUYCKX

Wayland Baptist University (I)

1900 West Seventh Street, Plainview TX 79072-6998
County: Hale
FICE Identification: 003663
Unit ID: 229780
Telephone: (806) 291-1000
Carnegie Class: Masters/L
FAX Number: (806) 291-1975
Calendar System: Semester
URL: www.wbu.edu
Established: 1908
Annual Undergrad Tuition & Fees: $21,304
Enrollment: 4,062
Coed
Affiliation or Control: Southern Baptist
IRS Status: 501(c)3
Highest Offering: Doctorate
Accreditation: SC, MUS, NUR

01 President .... Dr. Bobby L. HALL
05 Vice Pres of Academic Affairs .... Dr. Cindy M. MCCLENAGAN
32 Sr VP of Operations & Student Life .... Dr. D. Claude LUSK
20 Vice Pres of External Campuses .... Dr. David BISHOP
111 Exec Dir of Inst Advancement .... Mr. Mike MELCHER
10 Chief Financial Officer .... Mrs. Lezlie HUKILL
84 Vice President of Enrollment Mgmt .... Dr. Daniel BROWN
26 Exec Dir of Marketing .... Mr. Gary VAUGHN
12 Exec Dir/Campus Dean Albuquerque .... Dr. Tom FISHER
12 Exec Dir/Campus Dean Wichita Falls .... Dr. Jerry FAUGHT
12 Exec Dir/Campus Dean Amarillo .... Dr. J. B BOREN
12 Exec Dir/Campus Dean Anchorage .... Dr. Eric ASH
12 Exec Dir/Campus Dean Fairbanks .... Vacant
12 Exec Dir/Campus Dean Hawaii .... Dr. Henrique REGINA
12 Int Exec Dir/Campus Dean Lubbock .... Dr. Judy JARRATT
12 Exec Dir/Campus Dean San Antonio .... Dr. James ANTENEN
12 Exec Dir/Camp Dn Phnx/Sierra Vista .... Dr. Andrew MARQUEZ
83 Acad Dean School Behav & Soc Sci .... Dr. Peter BOWEN
50 Academic Dean School of Business .... Dr. Kelly WARREN
53 Academic Dean School of Education .... Dr. Sarah HARTMAN
79 Acad Dean Sch of Lang & Lit .... Dr. Kimberlee MENDOZA
81 Academic Dean School Math/Sciences .... Dr. Adam REINHART
64 Acad Dean The Sch of Creative Arts .... Dr. Ann B. STUTES
66 Academic Dean School of Nursing .... Dr. Diane FRAZOR
73 Academic Dean Sch Christian Studies .... Dr. Stephen STOOKEY
06 University Registrar .... Mrs. Julie BOWEN
35 Exec Dir Student Services .... Mr. Shawn THOMAS
41 Dir of Intercollegiate Athletics .... Mr. Bill WEIDNER
07 Director of Admissions .... Mrs. Debbie STENNETT
29 Director Alumni Relations .... Mrs. Teresa YOUNG
42 Dir Denominational Rel/Mission Ctr .... Mr. Donnie BROWN
44 Director of Core Mission Fund .... Mr. Gary ZACHER
30 Dir of Donor Relations/Stewardship .... Mrs. Amber MCCLOUD
37 Executive Director of Financial Aid .... Mrs. Christi MILLER
58 Director of Graduate Studies .... Ms. Amanda STANTON
15 Exec Director of Human Resources .... Mr. Rafael AGUILERA
13 Chief Information Officer .... Mrs. Katrina SMITH
09 Dir Inst Research/Effectiveness .... Dr. Gregg GREER
08 Director of Libraries .... Ms. Sally QUIROZ
88 Exec Director Property Management .... Mr. Trevor MORRIS
27 Director of Communications .... Mr. Jonathan PETTY
23 Director of Health Services .... Mrs. Coralyn DILLARD
39 Coordinator of Student Housing .... Mr. Glynn BOYDSTON
38 Dir Counseling/Career/Disability .... Mrs. Brandy HEADS
40 Director of University Store .... Mr. Brad HENDERSON
106 Director of WBUonline .... Dr. Trish RITSCHEL-TRIFILO
88 Dir BAS/BCM & Assoc Registrar .... Mrs. Caitlin BAKER
19 WBU Chief of Police .... Vacant
18 Chief Facilities/Physical Plant .... Mr. David MURPHREE
04 Exec Asst to President .... Mrs. Cynthia TREVINO
110 Director of Advancement Services .... Mrs. Amber SMITH
112 Senior Major Gift Officer .... Mr. Mike MELCHER
88 Dir of Multi Tutorial Services .... Dr. Brent LYNN
92 Director of Honors Program .... Dr. D. Niler PYEATT
121 Director of Student Success .... Dr. Rosemary PEGGRAM
88 Director of Museums .... Ms. Melissa GONZALEZ

Weatherford College (J)

225 College Park Drive, Weatherford TX 76086-5699
County: Parker
FICE Identification: 003664
Unit ID: 229799
Telephone: (817) 594-5471
Carnegie Class: Assoc/MT-VT-High Trad
FAX Number: (817) 598-6210
Calendar System: Semester

URL: www.wc.edu
Established: 1869 Annual Undergrad Tuition & Fees (In-District): $5,130
Enrollment: 5,480 Coed
Affiliation or Control: Local IRS Status: 501(c)3
Highest Offering: Baccalaureate
Accreditation: SC, ADNUR, COARC, DMS, EMT, NUR, OTA, PTAA, RAD

01 President .... Dr. Tod Allen FARMER
04 Exec Asst to the President .... Mrs. Theresa R. HUTCHISON
10 Exec Vice Pres Finance/Admin Affs .... Dr. Andra R. CANTRELL
05 VP of Instruction & Student Svcs .... Mr. Michael ENDY
111 Vice Pres Institutional Advancement .... Mr. Brent BAKER
76 Dean of Health & Human Sciences .... Ms. Katherine BOSWELL
20 Dean Educational/Instructional Sppt .... Ms. Rhonda TORRES
32 Executive Dean of Student Services .... Mr. Adam FINLEY
103 Dean Workforce/Economic Devel .... Mrs. Janetta KRUSE
26 Dir Communications/Public Relations .... Mrs. Crystal WOERLY
57 Dean of Fine Arts/Education .... Mr. Duane DURRETT
09 Exec Dir Inst Research .... Mr. John JONES
35 Assoc Dean Student Development .... Mr. Doug JEFFERSON
124 Dir Student Engage & Outreach Advis .... Mr. John TURNTINE
109 Director Food Services .... Ms. Erin DAVIDSON
37 Director of Financial Aid .... Mr. Donnie PURVIS
21 Controller .... Mrs. Lisa SIMONS
15 Director Human Resources .... Mrs. Ralinda STONE
07 Director of Admissions .... Mrs. Mika FOREMAN
13 Exec Director Info Technology .... Mrs. Priscilla PARSONS
08 Director of Learning Resources Ctr .... Mrs. Valorie STARR
18 Director of Facilities .... Ms. Rhonda SWAN
96 Director of Purchasing .... Mrs. Jeanie HOBBS
19 Chief of Campus Police .... Mr. Anthony BIGONGIARI
88 Director Upward Bound .... Mr. Jeff KHALDEN
29 Director Alumni Relations .... Mr. Brent BAKER
53 Director of Teacher Education .... Mrs. Shannon STOKER
06 Registrar .... Vacant
88 Director of Testing .... Ms. Gwen CRABTREE
121 Assoc Dean Student Success .... Ms. Kay LANDRUM
88 Dir Spec Populations/Pathways Spec .... Mrs. Dawn KAHLDEN
39 Director Student Housing .... Miss Faith STIFFLER
41 Athletic Director .... Mr. Bob MCKINLEY
102 Director Foundation .... Mr. Bob GLENN
105 Director Creative/Graphic Svcs .... Mrs. Katie EDWARDS
106 Director E-learning .... Dr. Sarah LOCK
43 General Counsel .... Mr. Dan CURLEE
25 Director Grants/Compliance & Accred .... Mrs. Stephenie FIELDS

West Coast University (A)

8435 N Stemmons Freeway, Dallas TX 75247-3900
Telephone: (214) 453-4533 Identification: 770485
Accreditation: &WC, #ARCPA

† Branch campus of West Coast University, North Hollywood, CA

Western Technical College (B)

9624 Plaza Circle, El Paso TX 79927-2105
County: El Paso FICE Identification: 020983
Unit ID: 224679
Telephone: (915) 532-3737 Carnegie Class: Spec 2-yr-Tech
FAX Number: (915) 532-6946 Calendar System: Other
URL: www.westerntech.edu
Established: 1969 Annual Undergrad Tuition & Fees: N/A
Enrollment: 1,324 Coed
Affiliation or Control: Proprietary IRS Status: Proprietary
Highest Offering: Associate Degree
Accreditation: ACCSC, MAC, PTAA

01 Chief Executive Officer .... Mr. Brad KUYKENDALL
11 Chief Operating Officer .... Ms. Mary CANO
07 Director of Admissions .... Mr. Marco MARTINEZ
05 Academic Dean .... Mr. Javier ZAVALA
10 Accounting Controller .... Ms. Laura PLUMMER
37 Student Financial Services Director .... Ms. Danielle PICCHI
36 Director Career Services .... Ms. Helen GARCIA
13 Information Technology Manager .... Mr. Eric PLASENCIO
18 Facilities Maintenance Director .... Mr. Jose PEREZ

Western Technical College (C)

9451 Diana Drive, El Paso TX 79924-6936
Telephone: (915) 566-9621 Identification: 666103
Accreditation: ACCSC

Western Texas College (D)

6200 College Avenue, Snyder TX 79549-6189
County: Scurry FICE Identification: 009549
Unit ID: 229832
Telephone: (325) 573-8511 Carnegie Class: Assoc/HT-High Non
FAX Number: (325) 573-9321 Calendar System: Semester
URL: www.wtc.edu
Established: 1969 Annual Undergrad Tuition & Fees (In-District): $4,200
Enrollment: 1,442 Coed
Affiliation or Control: State/Local IRS Status: 501(c)3
Highest Offering: Associate Degree
Accreditation: SC

01 President .... Dr. Barbara R. BEEBE
04 Assistant to the President .... Ms. Melanie SCHWERTNER
10 Chief Financial Officer .... Ms. Patricia CLAXTON
09 Dean Inst Research & Effectiveness .... Mr. Britt CANADA
05 Dean of Instructional Affairs .... Ms. Stephanie DUCHENEAUX
32 Dean of Student Services .... Mr. Ralph RAMON
72 Dean of Technology/Info Security .... Ms. Emily POWELL
103 Dean Workforce Development .... Mr. Shawn FONNVILLE
41 Athletic Director .... Ms. Tammy DAVIS
06 Registrar .... Ms. Donna MORRIS
37 Director Financial Aid .... Ms. Tevian SIDES
21 Controller .... Ms. Marjann MORROW
15 Director of Human Resources .... Mr. Brad KELLER
85 Dir International Student Services .... Ms. Nicole COOPER
96 Director of Purchasing & Compliance .... Mr. Mitch CALHOUN

Wharton County Junior College (E)

911 Boling Highway, Wharton TX 77488-3298
County: Wharton FICE Identification: 003668
Unit ID: 229841
Telephone: (979) 532-4560 Carnegie Class: Assoc/MT-VT-High Trad
FAX Number: (979) 532-6526 Calendar System: Semester
URL: www.wcjc.edu
Established: 1946 Annual Undergrad Tuition & Fees (In-District): $3,624
Enrollment: 6,099 Coed
Affiliation or Control: Local IRS Status: 501(c)3
Highest Offering: Associate Degree
Accreditation: SC, CAHIIM, CSHSE, DH, EMT, NAEYC, PTAA, RAD

01 President .... Ms. Betty A. MCCROHAN
05 Vice President of Instruction .... Ms. Leigh Ann COLLINS
11 Vice President Administrative Svcs .... Mr. Bryce KOCIAN
13 Vice President of Technology .... Ms. Pamela YOUNGBLOOD
09 VP of Planning/Inst Effectiveness .... Dr. Amanda ALLEN
21 Dean of Financial & Business Svcs .... Mr. Gus WESSELS
26 Director of Marketing & Comm .... Ms. Zina CARTER
06 Registrar/Director of Admissions .... Ms. Terri BARNES
37 Director of Financial Aid .... Ms. Leslie KOLOJACO
08 Director Library Info/Tech Services .... Ms. Kwei HSU
18 Director of Facilities Management .... Mr. Mike FEYEN
15 Director of Human Resources .... Ms. Judy JONES
96 Director of Purchasing .... Mr. Philip WUTHRICH
101 Secretary of the Institution/Board .... Mrs. Deanna FEYEN
19 Director Security/Safety .... Mr. Danny TERRONEZ
41 Athletic Director .... Mr. Keith CASE

Wiley College (F)

711 Wiley Avenue, Marshall TX 75670-5199
County: Harrison FICE Identification: 003669
Unit ID: 229887
Telephone: (903) 927-3300 Carnegie Class: Bac-Diverse
FAX Number: (903) 938-8100 Calendar System: Semester
URL: www.wileyc.edu
Established: 1873 Annual Undergrad Tuition & Fees: $13,500
Enrollment: 615 Coed
Affiliation or Control: United Methodist IRS Status: 501(c)3
Highest Offering: Baccalaureate
Accreditation: SC, ACBSP

01 President and CEO .... Dr. Herman J. FELTON, JR.
10 Sr VP for Business & Finance .... Mr. George STIELL
05 VP for Academic Affairs .... Dr. Howard O. GIBSON
32 Int VP Student Affairs/Enrollment .... Mr. Jonas VANDERBILT
32 Int VP Student Affairs & Enrollment .... Dr. Rae LUNDY
111 Sr VP Institutional Advancement .... Dr. W. Anthony NEAL
11 Chief Operating Officer/VP Admin .... Dr. Tashia BRADLEY
13 Chief Information Officer .... Mr. Darren ASHLEY
21 Controller .... Ms. Melissa BOGUE
53 Dean School of Educ & Sciences .... Dr. Sophia MARSHALL-CHAPMAN
42 Dean of Chapel .... Rev. Cecil DUFFIE
04 Special Asst to Pres/Dir of T3 .... Mrs. Cassandra M. JOHNSON
50 Dean Sch of Business & Social Sci .... Dr. Stephanie COX
26 Asst VP of Mktg/Communications .... Ms. Maya BROWN
08 Director of Library Services .... Dr. Martha Lopez COLEMAN
06 Registrar .... Mrs. Gloria MITCHELL
84 Exec Director Enrollment Mgmt .... Mr. Shaquille DILLION
15 Chief Human Resource Officer .... Mrs. Krystal MOODY
37 Director of Financial Aid .... Mrs. Corliss COOPER
09 Exec Dir Office Institutional Rsrch .... Dr. Jerelyn DUNCAN
11 Director Administrative Svcs .... Mr. O. Ivan WHITE
23 Director of Health Services .... Ms. Pamela BRADLEY
41 AVP of Athletics & Strategic Retent .... Mr. Bruce PEIFER
96 Purchasing Manager .... Mr. Johnny JOHNSON
35 Director of Student Activities .... Ms. Darby SMITH
101 Secretary of the Institution/Board .... Mrs. Cassandra M. JOHNSON
106 Distance/Online Educ .... Vacant
19 Director of Public Safety .... Mr. Howard SYLVE
39 Director of Residence Life .... Mr. Howard FISHER
43 Dir Legal Services/General Counsel .... Vacant
29 Executive Director of Alumni Affs .... Mr. Charles CORNISH
90 Director Academic Computing .... Ms. Tamisha CULBERSON
04 Executive Asst to the President .... Mrs. Cassandra JOHNSON
23 Associate VP Student Health .... Dr. Rae LUNDY
07 Director of Admissions .... Mr. Shaquille DILLION
108 Director Institutional Assessment .... Dr. Jerelyn DUNCAN
18 Chf Facilities/Physical Plant Ofcr .... Mr. O. I. WHITE
36 Director Student Placement .... Mr. Jeremy HODGE
38 Director Student Counseling .... Dr. Rae LUNDY
91 Director Administrative Computing .... Ms. Tamisha CULBERSON

UTAH

Ameritech College of Healthcare (G)

12257 Business Park Dr, Ste 100, Draper UT 84020
County: Salt Lake FICE Identification: 022708
Unit ID: 447263
Telephone: (801) 618-0438 Carnegie Class: Spec-4-yr-Other Health
FAX Number: (801) 816-1456 Calendar System: Semester
URL: www.ameritech.edu
Established: 1979 Annual Undergrad Tuition & Fees: $12,544
Enrollment: 1,429 Coed
Affiliation or Control: Proprietary IRS Status: Proprietary
Highest Offering: Master's
Accreditation: @NW, ABHES, ADNUR, NURSE

01 President .... Sherry JONES
12 Campus Director .... Mike MANGELSON
10 VP of Finance .... Ashley JONES LEE
26 VP of Brand/Marketing & Strategy .... Joshua KNOTTS
15 VP Culture/People & Dir Human Res .... Ann JOHNSON
05 Associate Provost & CAO .... Dr. Ray RODRIGUEZ
32 Asst Provost Student Affairs .... Michelle RICHARDS
45 Asst Provost Inst Effectiveness .... Dr. Rebecca COLLINS
108 Asst Prov Curriculum & Assessment .... Melanie THOMPSON
07 Director of Admissions .... April FULLER
100 Chief of Staff .... Heather BAILEY
116 Chief Compliance Officer .... Colleen RUSSO
37 Sr Director of Financial Aid .... Dean RILING
32 Director of Student Services .... Wendy WINDER
20 Director Ctr Teaching & Learning .... Nicolette WATKINS
88 Director Clinical/Simulation & Lab .... Joshua RAY
88 Accreditation Liaison Officer .... Dr. Larry BANKS

Brigham Young University (H)

701 E. University Parkway, Provo UT 84602-0002
County: Utah FICE Identification: 003670
Unit ID: 230038
Telephone: (801) 422-4000 Carnegie Class: DU-Higher
FAX Number: N/A Calendar System: Semester
URL: www.byu.edu
Established: 1875 Annual Undergrad Tuition & Fees: $5,970
Enrollment: 36,461 Coed
Affiliation or Control: Latter-day Saints IRS Status: 501(c)3
Highest Offering: Doctorate
Accreditation: NW, ART, CAATE, CAEP, CAEPT, CAPRT, CLPSY, COPSY, DANCE, DIETD, DIETI, IPSY, JOUR, LAW, MFCD, MT, MUS, NURSE, PH, SP, SPAA, SW, THEA

01 President .... Mr. Kevin J. WORTHEN
05 Academic Vice President .... Dr. C. Shane REESE
111 Advancement Vice President .... Mr. Keith VORKINK
13 VP of Finance & Administration .... Mr. Steven J. HAFEN
88 International Vice President .... Dr. Renata FORSTE
32 Student Life Vice President .... Mrs. Julie FRANKLIN
13 VP Information Tech & CIO .... Mr. Tracy W. FLINDERS
43 Asst to President/General Counsel .... Mr. Steven M. SANDBERG
45 Asst to Pres Planning/Assessment .... Dr. Rosemary THACKERAY
26 Asst to Pres Univ Communications .... Mrs. Carri P. JENKINS
20 Assoc Academic VP Faculty Dev .... Dr. Laura BRIDGEWATER
20 Assoc Academic VP Faculty Rels .... Dr. Brad L. NEIGER
20 Assoc Acad VP Undergraduate Stds .... Dr. John R. ROSENBERG
46 Assoc Acad VP Research/Grad Stds .... Dr. Larry L. HOWELL
35 Assoc Student Life Vice Pres/Dean .... Dr. Sarah WESTERBERG
18 Asst Admin VP Physical Facilities .... Mr. Ole M. SMITH
15 Asst Admin VP Human Resource Svcs .... Mr. David TUELLER
35 Asst Admin VP/Stdnt Auxiliary Svc .... Mr. Carr KRUEGER
29 Managing Dir Alumni/Ext Rels .... Mr. Mike ROBERTS
30 Managing Dir LDS Philanthropies .... Dr. Tanise CHUNG-HOON
84 Exec Dir Enrollment Services .... Mr. Christian FAULCONER
37 Director Financial Aid/Scholarships .... Mr. Stephen E. HILL
97 Dean Undergraduate Education .... Dr. Susan RUGH
08 University Librarian .... Mr. Richard ANDERSON
58 Dean Graduate Studies .... Dr. Adam WOOLLEY
51 Dean Continuing Education .... Dr. Lee GLINES
47 Dean Life Sciences .... Dr. James P. PORTER
54 Dean Engineering & Technology .... Dr. Michael A. JENSEN
83 Dean Family Home & Social Science .... Dr. Laura PADILLA-WALKER
57 Dean Fine Arts & Communications .... Dr. Edward E. ADAMS
79 Dean Humanities .... Dr. J. Scott MILLER
61 Dean Law School .... Dr. D. Gordon SMITH
50 Dean Marriott School Management .... Dr. Brigitte MADRIAN
53 Dean McKay School of Education .... Dr. Rich OSGUTHORPE
81 Dean Physical & Math Science .... Dr. Grant JENSEN
66 Dean Nursing .... Dr. Jane H. LASSETTER
73 Dean Religious Education .... Dr. Scott ESPLIN
38 Director Counseling & Career Ctr .... Dr. Kara CATTANI
09 Dir Institutional Assess/Analysis .... Dr. Danny R. OLSEN
06 University Registrar .... Mr. Barry ALLRED
07 Director Admission Services .... Ms. Lori GARDINER
96 Director of Purchasing .... Mr. W. Timothy HILL
22 Dir University Accessibility Center .... Dr. Gerilynn VORKINK
19 Managing Dir/Chief Univ Police .... Mr. James C. AUTRY
39 Director Student Housing .... Mr. Paul BARTON
41 Athletic Director .... Mr. Tom HOLMOE
88 Director BYU Broadcasting .... Mr. Jeff SIMPSON
88 University Treasurer .... Mr. David W. PAUL
14 Assistant VP Technology .... Mr. Scott H. HUNT
119 Chief Information Security Officer .... Mr. John PAYNE
28 Asst to Pres for Stdnt Succ & Incl .... Dr. Vernon L. HEPERI
43 Deputy General Counsel .... Mr. Christian A. FOX

Bottega University (A)

50 W. Broadway, Suite 300, Salt Lake City UT 84101
County: Salt Lake FICE Identification: 041292
Telephone: (801) 883-8336 Carnegie Class: Not Classified
FAX Number: (801) 855-5922 Calendar System: Trimester
URL: https://bottega.edu/
Established: 1994 Annual Undergrad Tuition & Fees: N/A
Enrollment: N/A Coed
Affiliation or Control: Proprietary IRS Status: Proprietary
Highest Offering: Master's
Accreditation: DEAC

01 President/Provost ....Dr. Mary Beth FINN
20 Academic Dean ....Dr. Troy ROLAND
26 Marketing Director ....Vacant
06 Registrar ....Ms. Megan BRENNAN
10 Accounting Director ....Ms. Connie TEAGUE

Broadview College (B)

1902 W 7800 S, West Jordan UT 84088-4021
County: Salt Lake FICE Identification: 011166
Unit ID: 230056
Telephone: (801) 542-7600 Carnegie Class: Bac/Assoc-Mixed
FAX Number: (801) 542-7601 Calendar System: Quarter
URL: www.broadview.edu
Established: 1971 Annual Undergrad Tuition & Fees: $17,712
Enrollment: 268 Coed
Affiliation or Control: Proprietary IRS Status: Proprietary
Highest Offering: Master's
Accreditation: ACICS

01 President ....Mr. Terry MYHRE
05 Campus Admin/Dean of Education ....Ms. Crystal DEWEERD

Eagle Gate College (C)

915 North 400 West, Layton UT 84041
Telephone: (801) 546-7500 Identification: 770812
Accreditation: ABHES

Eagle Gate College (D)

5588 S Green Street, Suite 150, Murray UT 84123-6965
County: Salt Lake FICE Identification: 021785
Unit ID: 230366
Telephone: (801) 333-8100 Carnegie Class: Bac/Assoc-Mixed
FAX Number: (801) 263-6520 Calendar System: Other
URL: www.eaglegatecollege.edu
Established: 1979 Annual Undergrad Tuition & Fees: $14,900
Enrollment: 271 Coed
Affiliation or Control: Proprietary IRS Status: Proprietary
Highest Offering: Master's
Accreditation: ABHES, NURSE

01 Campus Director ....Nicole KOCH

Ensign College (E)

95 North 300 West, Salt Lake City UT 84101-3500
County: Salt Lake FICE Identification: 003672
Unit ID: 230418
Telephone: (801) 524-8100 Carnegie Class: Assoc/MT-VT-High Trad
FAX Number: (801) 524-1900 Calendar System: Semester
URL: www.ldsbc.edu
Established: 1886 Annual Undergrad Tuition & Fees: $3,550
Enrollment: 1,829 Coed
Affiliation or Control: Latter-day Saints IRS Status: 501(c)3
Highest Offering: Associate Degree
Accreditation: NW, MAC

01 President ....Dr. Bruce C. KUSCH
04 Executive Admin Asst ....Ms. Kristen WILLIAMS
05 Vice Pres of Academics ....Mr. Tim SLOAN
32 Vice Pres Student Services ....Dr. Guy M. HOLLINGSWORTH
11 Vice Pres of Administration ....Mr. Mark A. RICHARDS
13 Chief Information Officer ....Ms. Christina BAUM
10 Director Financial Svcs/Controller ....Mr. Chris REITZ
106 Managing Dir Online Programs ....Mr. Alan YOUNG
20 Dir Curriculum/Academic Programs ....Ms. Cathy T. CAREY
84 Dir Enrollment Management/Admission ....Ms. Maren LYTHGOE
15 Director of Human Resources ....Mr. Brady J. KIMBER
26 Manager of Public Affairs ....Mr. C. Royce HINTON
36 Director of Career Services ....Mr. Rob BAGLEY
06 Registrar ....Ms. Kelsey TAN
08 Dir of Library/Info Resources ....Vacant
37 Student Financial Services Manager ....Ms. Melanie CONOVER
40 Bookstore Manager ....Mr. Kent CHRISTENSEN
09 Director of Institutional Research ....Tracey ANDERSON

Fortis College (F)

3949 South 700 East, Suite 150, Salt Lake City UT 84107
Telephone: (801) 713-0915 Identification: 666762
Accreditation: ACCSC, ADNUR, DH

† Tuition varies by degree program.

Midwives College of Utah (G)

1174 E Graystone Way Suite 2,
Salt Lake City UT 84106-2671
County: Salt Lake City Identification: 666281
Unit ID: 480985
Telephone: (866) 680-2756 Carnegie Class: Spec-4-yr-Other Health
FAX Number: (866) 207-2024 Calendar System: Semester
URL: www.midwifery.edu
Established: 1980 Annual Undergrad Tuition & Fees: $7,635
Enrollment: 238 Coed
Affiliation or Control: Independent Non-Profit IRS Status: 501(c)3
Highest Offering: Master's
Accreditation: MEAC

01 President ....Ms. Kristi RIDD-YOUNG
05 Academic Dean ....Ms. Megan KOONTZ
06 Registrar ....Ms. Laura PARK
07 Admissions ....Ms. Allyson JUNEAU-BUTLER
13 Chief Info Technology Officer ....Mr. Alan BELLOWS
37 Financial Aid Director ....Ms. Whitney MESYEF
58 Graduate Dean ....Ms. Megan KOONTZ
26 Marketing Director ....Ms. Masha MESYEF
35 Director of Student Services ....Ms. Cheryl FURER
32 Dir Student Life/Equity & Access ....Ms. Tamara TAIT
113 Bursar ....Ms. Darliegh WEBB
30 Director of Development/Fundraising ....Ms. Masha MESYEF

Neumont University (H)

143 South Main, Salt Lake City UT 84111
County: Salt Lake FICE Identification: 010098
Unit ID: 445692
Telephone: (801) 302-2800 Carnegie Class: Spec-4-yr-Other Tech
FAX Number: (801) 302-2811 Calendar System: Quarter
URL: www.neumont.edu
Established: 2003 Annual Undergrad Tuition & Fees: $25,440
Enrollment: 529 Coed
Affiliation or Control: Proprietary IRS Status: Proprietary
Highest Offering: Baccalaureate
Accreditation: @NW, ACCSC

01 President/Campus Director Utah ....Aaron REED
05 VP Academic Operations ....Tim CLARK
10 VP/Chief Financial Officer ....Andrew FULLER
32 Director of Student Affairs ....Janet HEAD-PARRISH
06 Registrar ....Alice NGUYEN
37 Director Financial Aid ....Kasie HADLEY

Nightingale College (I)

175 South Main Street, Suite 400,
Salt Lake City UT 84405
County: Salt Lake FICE Identification: 038383
Unit ID: 444787
Telephone: (801) 689-2160 Carnegie Class: Spec-4-yr-Other Health
FAX Number: (801) 689-3114 Calendar System: Semester
URL: www.nightingale.edu
Established: 2010 Annual Undergrad Tuition & Fees: N/A
Enrollment: 1,337 Coed
Affiliation or Control: Proprietary IRS Status: Proprietary
Highest Offering: Master's
Accreditation: @NW, ABHES, NURSE

01 President/CEO ....Mr. Mikhail SHNEYDER
10 Vice Pres Operations/Controller ....Mr. Thomas REAMS
26 VP Partnerships & Business Devel ....Mr. Jonathan TANNER
06 Registrar ....Ms. Jannette ANDERSON
84 Sr Director of Enrollment ....Ms. Jeana REECE
37 Int Director Student Financial Aid ....Ms. Noemi MCCORMICK

Provo College (J)

1450 W 820 N, Provo UT 84601-1305
County: Utah FICE Identification: 023608
Unit ID: 380438
Telephone: (801) 818-8900 Carnegie Class: Bac/Assoc-Mixed
FAX Number: (801) 375-9728 Calendar System: Other
URL: www.provocollege.edu
Established: 1984 Annual Undergrad Tuition & Fees: $15,219
Enrollment: 579 Coed
Affiliation or Control: Proprietary IRS Status: Proprietary
Highest Offering: Master's
Accreditation: ABHES, NURSE, PTAA

01 Campus Director ....Ms. Kristen WHITTAKER
66 Academic Dean Nursing ....Mrs. Somerset WARNER
88 Program Director PTA ....Dr. Suzanne REESE
10 Business Office Coordinator ....Mr. Jose GUTIERREZ
37 Asst Dir of Financial Aid ....Ms. Haley GONZALES
06 Registrar ....Ms. Brieanna MADSON
32 Dir Student Services/Placement ....Ms. Christine ANDERSON

Rocky Mountain University of Health Professions (K)

122 East 1700 South, Building 3, Provo UT 84606-7379
County: Utah FICE Identification: 041932
Unit ID: 475495
Telephone: (801) 375-5125 Carnegie Class: Spec-4-yr-Other Health
FAX Number: (801) 375-2125 Calendar System: Trimester
URL: www.rm.edu
Established: 1998 Annual Graduate Tuition & Fees: N/A
Enrollment: 1,193 Coed
Affiliation or Control: Proprietary IRS Status: Proprietary
Highest Offering: Doctorate; No Undergraduates
Accreditation: NW, ARCPA, NURSE, PTA, @SP

01 President/CEO ....Dr. Richard P. NIELSEN
05 Exec VP Academic Affairs/Provost ....Dr. Mark HORACEK
10 Exec VP Finance/CFO ....Mr. Jeff B. BATE
45 EVP Strategy & Engagement ....Dr. Sandra L. PENNINGTON
13 VP of Technology/Chief Info Officer ....Mr. David PAYNE
84 AVP Enrollment Management ....Mr. Bryce GREENBERG
20 AVP Academic Administration ....Mr. Richard PETERSON
46 Director ORSP ....Dr. Robert PETTITT
51 Director Continuing Education ....Vacant
32 AVP Student Affairs ....Ms. Lori SISK
100 VP Operations/Chief of Staff ....Dr. Cameron K. MARTIN

University of Phoenix Utah Campus (L)

5373 South Green Street, Salt Lake City UT 84123-4642
Telephone: (801) 263-1444 Identification: 770232
Accreditation: &HLC, CAEPN

† No longer accepting campus-based students.

The Utah College of Dental Hygiene at Careers Unlimited (M)

1176 S 1480 West, Orem UT 84058-4905
County: Utah FICE Identification: 034633
Unit ID: 448239
Telephone: (801) 426-8234 Carnegie Class: Spec-4-yr-Other Health
FAX Number: (801) 224-5437 Calendar System: Other
URL: www.ucdh.edu
Established: 2006 Annual Undergrad Tuition & Fees: N/A
Enrollment: 119 Coed
Affiliation or Control: Proprietary IRS Status: Proprietary
Highest Offering: Baccalaureate
Accreditation: ACCSC, DH

01 College President ....Mr. Brent MOLEN
10 College VP/CFO/Director Compliance ....Ms. Krista MCCLURE
00 Director Emeritus/CEO ....Mr. Kenneth MOLEN
07 Director of Admissions ....Ms. Kaydrie TOLBERT
08 Chief Library Officer ....Ms. Lindsay LAURDSEN

*Utah System of Higher Education (N)

The Gateway, 60 S 400 W, Salt Lake City UT 84101-1284
County: Salt Lake FICE Identification: 009339
Telephone: (801) 321-7101 Carnegie Class: N/A
FAX Number: (801) 321-7199
URL: www.ushe.edu

01 Exec Ofcr/Int Comm of Higher Educ ....Dr. David WOOLSTENHULME
05 Assoc Comm Academic Education ....Dr. Julie HARTLEY
103 Assoc Comm Access ....Ms. Melanie HEATH
32 Chief Student Affairs Officer ....Mr. Spencer JENKINS
10 Chief Financial Officer ....Dr. Richard AMON
37 Exec Director Student Financial Aid ....Mr. David A. FEITZ
88 UESP Executive Director ....Ms. Lynne WARD

*The University of Utah (O)

201 South 1460 East, Salt Lake City UT 84112-1107
County: Salt Lake FICE Identification: 003675
Unit ID: 230764
Telephone: (801) 581-7200 Carnegie Class: DU-Highest
FAX Number: (801) 581-3007 Calendar System: Semester
URL: www.utah.edu
Established: 1850 Annual Undergrad Tuition & Fees (In-State): $8,615
Enrollment: 33,081 Coed
Affiliation or Control: State IRS Status: 501(c)3
Highest Offering: Doctorate
Accreditation: NW, ARCPA, AUD, CAATE, CAEP, CAMPEP, CAPRT, CEA, CLPSY, COPSY, DANCE, DENT, DIETC, HSA, IPSY, LAW, MED, MIDWF, MPCAC, MT, MUS, NDT, NMT, NURSE, OT, PH, PHAR, PLNG, PTA, SCPSY, SP, SPAA, SW

02 Interim President ....Dr. Michael L. GOOD
100 Chief of Staff/Secretary to Univ ....Ms. Laura SNOW
05 Sr Vice Pres Academic Affairs ....Dr. Daniel A. REED
43 General Counsel & Vice President ....Ms. Phyllis J. VETTER
32 Vice President Student Affairs ....Dr. Lori K. MCDONALD
111 Vice Pres Institutional Advancement ....Ms. Heidi D. WOODBURY
86 Vice President Government Relations ....Mr. Jason P. PERRY
22 VP Equity/Diversity & Inclusion ....Dr. Mary Ann VILLARREAL
10 CFO & VP Admin Svcs Main Campus ....Ms. Cathy ANDERSON
46 Vice President Research ....Dr. Andrew S. WEYRICH
04 Exec Asst to the President ....Ms. Brynn FRONK
04 Exec Asst to the President ....Ms. Bonnie WIESE
13 Chief Information Officer ....Dr. Stephen H. HESS
21 Chief Business Strategy Officer ....Ms. Patricia A. ROSS
85 Chief Global Officer ....Dr. Brian GIBSON
16 Chief Human Resources Officer ....Mr. Jeff C. HERRING
26 Chief Mktg & Communications Officer ....Mr. William J. WARREN
117 Interim Chief Safety Officer ....Mr. Keith SQUIRES
124 Chief Sustainability Officer ....Ms. Kerry CASE
20 Sr AVP AA & Dean Undergrad Studies ....Dr. Thomas C. HAGOOD
84 Sr Assoc VP for Enrollment Mgmt ....Mr. Steve ROBINSON

18 Chief Design & Construction Officer .... Ms. Robin BURR
88 Associate Vice President Research .... Dr. Diane E. PATAKI
20 Assoc VP Acad Affairs/Faculty .... Dr. Sarah PROJANSKY
35 AVP Student Affs/Bus/Auxil Svcs .... Dr. Jerry L. BASFORD
109 Assoc VP Admin Svc/Auxiliary Svc .... Dr. Gordon N. WILSON
48 Dean Architecture & Planning .... Dr. Keith D. MOORE
50 Dean David Eccles Sch of Business .... Dr. Taylor R. RANDALL
52 Dean School of Dentistry .... Dr. Wyatt R. HUME
53 Dean College of Education .... Dr. Nancy SONGER
54 Dean College of Engineering .... Dr. Richard B. BROWN
57 Dean Col of Fine Arts/AVP the Arts .... Dr. John W. SCHEIB
68 Dean College of Health .... Dr. David H. PERRIN
92 Dean Honors College .... Dr. Sylvia D. TORTI
79 Dean College of Humanities .... Dr. Stuart K. CULVER
61 Dean S J Quinney College of Law .... Ms. Elizabeth KRONK-WARNER
65 Dean Coll of Mines & Earth Science .... Dr. Darryl P. BUTT
63 Dean Sch Med/SVP Health Sciences .... Dr. Michael L. GOOD
66 Dean College of Nursing .... Dr. Marla DE JONG
67 Dean College of Pharmacy .... Dr. Randall T. PETERSON
81 Dean College of Science .... Dr. Peter TRAPA
88 Dean School Social/Cultural Transf ...... Dr. Kathryn B. STOCKTON
83 Dean Col Social/Behav Science .... Dr. Cynthia BERG
70 Dean College of Social Work .... Dr. Martell L. TEASLEY
35 Dean of Students .... Mr. Jason RAMIREZ
06 University Registrar .... Mr. Timothy J. EBNER
17 CEO Univ Hospitals & Clinics .... Vacant
96 Director Procurement .... Mr. Glendon G. MITCHELL
94 Chair Gender Studies .... Dr. Susie S. PORTER
77 Director School of Computing .... Mr. Ross T. WHITAKER
106 AVP/Dean Online & Cont Educ .. Dr. Deborah KEYEK-FRANSSEN
88 Dir Dental Clinic/Gen Residence .... Dr. Craig PROCTOR
07 Director Admissions .... Dr. John MARFIELD
29 Int Chief Alumni Relations Officer .... Ms. Linda DUNN
112 Director Planned Giving .... Ms. Jessica NELSON
37 Exec Dir Financial Aid/Scholarships .... Dr. Anthony JONES
08 Dean MLIB/University Librarian .... Ms. Alberta D. COMER
08 Dir Eccles Health Sciences Library ..... Ms. Catherine B. SOEHNER
08 Dir S J Quinney Col of Law Library .... Ms. Melissa BERNSTEIN
36 Director of Career Services .... Mr. Stan D. INMAN
38 Director Counseling Center .... Dr. Lauren WEITZMAN
39 Director Housing & Res Education .... Ms. Barbara REMSBURG
39 Director Univ Student Apartments .... Ms. Jennifer G. REED
88 Exec Dir Nat History Museum of Utah .... Dr. Jason CRYAN
19 Acting Chief of Police .... Mr. Jason HINOJOSA
40 Director Campus Bookstore .... Mr. Daniel L. ARCHER
85 Director Intl Student/Scholar Svcs .... Ms. Chelsea WELLS
25 Dir Office of Sponsored Projects .... Mr. Brent K. BROWN
31 Dir Univ Neighborhood Partners . Ms. Jennifer A. MAYOR-GLENN
09 Director Institutional Analysis .... Dr. Michael D. MARTINEAU
41 Athletics Director .... Mr. Mark M. HARLAN
104 Exec Director Learning Abroad .... Dr. Sabine C. KLAHR
44 Interim Director Annual Giving .... Ms. Rachel ROBERTSON

*Southern Utah University (A)

351 W University Blvd, Cedar City UT 84720-2470
County: Iron FICE Identification: 003678
Unit ID: 230603
Telephone: (435) 586-7700 Carnegie Class: Masters/L
FAX Number: (435) 586-5475 Calendar System: Semester
URL: www.suu.edu
Established: 1897 Annual Undergrad Tuition & Fees (In-State): $6,770
Enrollment: 12,582 Coed
Affiliation or Control: State IRS Status: 501(c)3
Highest Offering: Master's
Accreditation: NW, ART, CAATE, CAEP, DANCE, IPSY, MUS, NURSE, SPAA, THEA

02 Interim President .... Ms. Mindy BENSON
05 Provost/Vice Prov Academic Affairs .... Dr. Jon ANDERSON
10 Vice Pres of Finance & Admin .... Mr. Marvin DODGE
32 Vice Pres for Student Affairs .... Mr. Jared TIPPETS
111 Vice Pres Advance/Enrollment Mgmt .... Mr. Stuart JONES
58 Assoc Provost .... Dr. James SAGE
29 Vice Pres Alumni/Community Rels .... Mr. Ron CARDON
28 Chief Diversity Officer .... Ms. Daneka SOUBERBIELLE
35 Asst VP/Dean Student Affairs .... Mr. Eric KIRBY
84 AVP Enroll Mgt Graduate/Online Pgm .... Mr. Steven MEREDITH
18 AVP of Facilities Management .... Mr. Tiger FUNK
26 Exec Dir Marketing Communication .... Ms. Nikki KOONTZ
08 Exec Director of Library .... Mr. Matt NICKERSON
114 Director of Budget and Planning .... Ms. Mary Jo ANDERSON
06 Registrar .... Vacant
15 Director Human Resources .... Mr. David T. MCGUIRE
37 Director of Financial Aid .... Mr. David HUGHES
41 Athletic Director .... Ms. Debbie CORUM
43 General Counsel .... Ms. Maureen REDEKER
79 Dean Col Humanities/Soc Sci .... Ms. Jean BOREEN
50 Dean School of Business .... Ms. Mary PEARSON
53 Dean College of Education .... Dr. Shawn L. CHRISTIANSEN
54 Int Dean College of Engineering .... Dr. James BRANDT
76 Int Dean College of Health Sciences .... Dr. Camille THOMAS
81 Dean College of Science .... Dr. Frank HALL
57 Dean College Performing/Visual Arts .... Mrs. Shauna MENDINI
96 Director of Purchasing .... Mr. Bradley BROWN
09 Exec Dir Inst Research/Assessment .... Mr. Christian REINER
38 Director Student Counseling .... Dr. Curtis HILL
04 Exec Assistant to the President .... Ms. Bailey BOWTHORPE
13 Chief Information Technology Office .... Mr. Matt ZUFELT
86 Director Government Relations .... Ms. Donna LAW
19 Chief of Police .... Mr. Rick BROWN
45 Chief Institutional Planning Ofcr .... Dr. Steve MEREDITH

103 Exec Director Regional Services .... Mr. Stephen LISONBEE
104 Director Study Abroad .... Dr. Kurt HARRIS
105 Director Web Services .... Ms. Jill WHITAKER
25 Chief Contract and Grants Administr .... Ms. Sylvia BRADSHAW
36 Director Career Services .... Mr. Brandon STREET
39 Dir Resident Life/Student Housing .... Mr. Christopher RALPHS

*Dixie State University (B)

225 S University Avenue, Saint George UT 84770-3876
County: Washington FICE Identification: 003671
Unit ID: 230171
Telephone: (435) 652-7500 Carnegie Class: Bac/Assoc-Mixed
FAX Number: (435) 656-4001 Calendar System: Semester
URL: www.dixie.edu
Established: 1911 Annual Undergrad Tuition & Fees (In-State): $5,662
Enrollment: 12,043 Coed
Affiliation or Control: State IRS Status: 501(c)3
Highest Offering: Master's
Accreditation: NW, ACBSP, ADNUR, CAEPT, COARC, DH, EMT, MT, MUS, NUR, PTAA, RAD, SURGT

02 President .... Dr. Richard B. WILLIAMS
11 Vice Pres Administrative Services .... Mr. Paul MORRIS
05 Provost/VP Academic Affairs .... Dr. Michael LACOURSE
32 Vice Pres Student Affairs .... Mr. Del BEATTY
111 Vice Pres Advancement .... Mr. Brad LAST
86 Asst to Pres for Govt/Comm Rels .... Mr. Henrie WALTON
79 Dean College Humanities/Social Sci .... Dr. Stephen LEE
66 Dean College Health Sciences .... Dr. Eliezer BERMUDEZ
50 Dean College of Business .... Dr. Kyle WELLS
81 Dean College Science & Technology .... Dr. Eric PEDERSEN
53 Dean College Education .... Dr. Brenda SABEY
51 Assoc Prov Cmty Global Outreach .... Dr. Nancy HAUCK
35 Dean of Students .... Mr. Del BEATTY
13 Chief Information Officer .... Mr. Mark WALTON
10 AVP Admin Svcs Spec Proj .... Vacant
15 Exec Director of Human Resources .... Mr. Travis ROSENBERG
18 Exec Dir Facilities Management .... Ms. Sherry RUESCH
08 Dean of Library & Learning Svcs .... Ms. Kelly PETERSEN-FAIRCHILD
109 Executive Director Auxiliaries .... Mr. Seth GUBLER
37 Exec Director Financial Aid .... Mr. J. D ROBERTSON
84 Assoc Prov Enrollment Mgmt .... Ms. Darlene DILLEY
06 Registrar .... Ms. Julie STENDER
121 Director of College Advisement .... Ms. Katie ARMSTRONG
26 VP of Mktg & Communication .... Dr. Jordan SHARP
18 Director Facilities Services .... Mr. Jack FREEMAN
19 Dir Public Safety/Chief of Police .... Mr. Blair BARFUSS
41 Exec Director of Athletics .... Dr. Jason BOOTHE
39 Director Housing & Residential Life .... Mr. Seth GUBLER
09 Interim Exec Dir Inst Effectiveness .... Dr. Matt NICKODEMUS
04 Assistant to the President .... Ms. Theresa BONDAD
35 Dir Student Involvement & Ldrshp .... Mr. Luke KEROUAC
96 Director of Purchasing .... Ms. Jackie FREEMAN
29 Director of Alumni Relations .... Mr. John BOWLER
36 Exec Director of Career Services .... Ms. Ali THREET
105 Director of Network Services .... Mr. Allen FOX
25 Director of Payroll & Grants .... Ms. Krystal THOMPSON
28 Assoc VP for Campus Diversity .... Dr. Tasha TOY
43 General Counsel .... Ms. Becky BROADBENT
91 Director Administrative Computing .... Mr. James MILLER
100 Chief of Staff .... Mr. Courtney WHITE
104 Director of Global Education .... Dr. Michael CARTMILL
108 Director of Assessment .... Vacant
07 Director of Admissions .... Mr. Jay SORENSEN
106 Exec Director of DSU Online .... Mr. Ryan HOBBS
20 Assoc Provost Acad & Budget Plng .... Dr. Pamela CANTRELL
21 Exec Dir Business Services .... Mr. Scott JENSEN
30 Director of Development .... Mr. Ken BEAZER
38 Director of Booth Wellness Center .... Dr. Garyn GULBRANSON
121 Sr Assoc Prov for Acad Success .... Dr. Sarah VANDERMARK

*Utah State University (C)

1400 Old Main Hill, Logan UT 84322-0001
County: Cache FICE Identification: 003677
Unit ID: 230728
Telephone: (435) 797-1000 Carnegie Class: DU-Higher
FAX Number: (435) 797-3880 Calendar System: Semester
URL: www.usu.edu
Established: 1888 Annual Undergrad Tuition & Fees (In-State): $8,764
Enrollment: 27,691 Coed
Affiliation or Control: State IRS Status: 501(c)3
Highest Offering: Doctorate
Accreditation: NW, AAQEP, ART, AUD, CACREP, CEA, CIDA, DIETC, DIETD, DIETI, IPSY, LSAR, MFCD, MUS, NUR, PSPSY, SCPSY, SP, SW, THEA

02 President .... Dr. Noelle E. COCKETT
05 Executive VP & Provost .... Dr. Frank GALEY
43 Vice President Legal Affairs .... Ms. Mica MCKINNEY
10 Vice President Business & Finance .... Mr. Dave COWLEY
32 Vice President Student Services .... Mr. James MORALES
20 VP for Academic/Instructional Svcs .... Dr. Robert WAGNER
26 VP of Marketing & Communications .... Mr. William M. PLATE
56 VP Extension & Dean Agriculture .... Dr. Kenneth L. WHITE
86 VP Government Relations .... Mr. Neil N. ABERCROMBIE
46 Vice President Research .... Dr. Lisa BERREAU
12 VP Statewide Campuses .... Dr. Laurens H. SMITH
58 Vice Provost of Graduate Stds .... Dr. Richard CUTLER
13 CIO/Assoc VP Information Technology .... Dr. Eric HAWLEY
18 Associate VP for Facilities .... Mr. Ben BERRETT

20 Assistant Vice President AIS .... Mr. John MORTENSEN
47 Dean of Agriculture .... Dr. Kenneth L. WHITE
57 Dean of Arts .... Dr. Rachel NARDO
50 Dean of Business .... Mr. Douglas D. ANDERSON
53 Dean of Education .... Dr. Alan SMITH
54 Dean of Engineering .... Dr. Jagath J. KALUARACHCHI
79 Dean Humanities/Social Science .... Dr. Joseph WARD
65 Dean of Natural Resources .... Dr. Chris LUECKE
81 Dean of Science .... Dr. Maura E. HAGAN
08 Dean Libraries .... Ms. Jeanne DAVIDSON
07 Director of Admissions .... Mr. Jeff SORENSEN
09 Exec Dir Analysis Assessment/Accred .... Mr. Michael TORRENS
22 Exec Director Affirmative Action .... Ms. Alison ADAMS-PERLAC
41 Athletic Director .... Mr. John HARTWELL
25 Exec Director Sponsored Programs .... Mr. Kevin PETERSON
15 Exec Director of Human Resources .... Mr. Doug BULLOCK
19 Exec Director Univ Police Dept .... Mr. Earl MORRIS
06 Registrar .... Mr. Fran HOPKIN
36 Exec Dir Career Services/Coop Educ ...... Ms. Janet B. ANDERSON
37 Director of Financial Aid .... Ms. Heather BRYSON
38 Exec Director Counseling Center .... Mr. Scott DEBERARD
40 Director of Campus Store .... Mr. Jason BROWN
92 Director of Honors .... Dr. Kristine MILLER
96 Director of Purchasing .... Mr. Jeff CROSBIE

*Utah Valley University (D)

800 W University Parkway, Orem UT 84058-5999
County: Utah FICE Identification: 004027
Unit ID: 230737
Telephone: (801) 863-8000 Carnegie Class: Masters/S
FAX Number: (801) 226-5207 Calendar System: Semester
URL: www.uvu.edu
Established: 1941 Annual Undergrad Tuition & Fees (In-State): $5,906
Enrollment: 40,936 Coed
Affiliation or Control: State IRS Status: 501(c)3
Highest Offering: Master's
Accreditation: NW, AAQEP, ACFEI, ADNUR, #ARCPA, CEA, #COARC, DH, EMT, IFSAC, IPSY, MUS, NUR, SW

02 President .... Dr. Astrid TUMINEZ
05 Provost/Sr VP Academic Affairs .... Dr. Wayne VAUGHT
11 VP Administration/Strategic Rels .... Dr. Val L. PETERSON
32 VP Student Affairs .... Dr. Kyle REYES
111 VP Advancement/CEO Foundation .... Mr. Mark H. ARSTEIN
15 VP People & Culture/CHRO .... Ms. Marilyn S. MEYER
45 VP Planning/Budgets & Finance .... Ms. Linda MAKIN
13 VP Digital Transformation/CIO .... Dr. J. Kelly FLANAGAN
100 Chief of Staff/VP Mktg & Comm .... Ms. Kara SCHNECK
28 Chief Inclusion & Diversity Officer .... Dr. Belinda OTUKOLO SALTIBAN
43 General Counsel .... Mr. Clark COLLINGS
10 Assoc VP Finance .... Mr. Jacob ATKIN
20 Assoc Provost Engaged Learning .... Ms. Janet COLVIN
18 Assoc VP Facilities Planning .... Mr. Frank YOUNG
20 Assoc Provost Academic Programs .... Mr. David CONNELLY
26 Assoc VP University Mktg/Comm .... Mr. Henry MOLINA
27 Assoc VP University Relations .... Mr. Stephen L. WHYTE
20 Deputy Provost Academic Admin .... Dr. Kathren BROWN
35 Assoc VP Student Life/Dean Students .... Dr. Alexis PALMER
124 Assoc VP Student Success/Retention .... Ms. Michelle KEARNS
31 Assoc Provost Community Outreach .... Ms. Belkis TORRES-CAPELES
25 Assoc VP Grants & Outreach .... Dr. William NYE
21 Asst VP/Controller Business Svcs .... Mr. Kedric BLACK
88 AVP Academic/Student Digital Svcs .... Ms. Christina BAUM
14 Assoc VP IT/CTO .... Dr. Troy MARTIN
119 Sr Director Product Portfolio .... Mr. Brett MCKEACHNIE
07 Sr Director Admissions .... Mr. Kris COLES
84 Assoc VP Enrollment Management .... Mr. Andrew STONE
54 Dean College Engineering/Technology .... Dr. Saeed MOAVENI
57 Dean School of the Arts .... Dr. Courtney DAVIS
81 Dean College of Science .... Dr. Daniel HORNS
50 Dean School of Business .... Dr. Norman WRIGHT
97 Dean University College .... Dr. Forrest G. WILLIAMS
76 Dean College Health/Public Svcs .... Dr. Cheryl HANEWICZ
53 Dean School of Education .... Dr. Vessela K. ILIEVA
79 Dean Humanities & Social Sciences .... Dr. Steven C. CLARK
37 Director Financial Aid/Scholarship .... Mr. John D. CURL
19 Dir Public Safety/Chief of Police .... Mr. Matthew D. PEDERSEN
112 Director of Gift Planning .... Ms. Cristina PIANEZZOLA
09 Director Institutional Research .... Mr. Timothy STANLEY
41 Assoc VP & Director of Athletics .... Mr. Jared M. SUMSION
24 Director Studios & Broadcast Svcs .... Mr. Will MCKINNON
40 Director Bookstore .... Ms. Louise BRIDGE
06 Registrar .... Ms. LuAnn SMITH
28 Dir Multicultural Student Services .... Ms. Darah M. SNOW
29 Sr Director Alumni Relations .... Ms. Alex C. TOBECK
121 Director Academic Counseling Center .... Mr. Adam BLACK
96 Sr Director of Procurement .... Mr. Ryan LINDSTROM
04 Executive Asst to President .... Ms. Annette LUND
08 Director Library .... Ms. Lesli BAKER
102 Director UVU Foundation .... Ms. Julie S. ANDERSON
36 Director Career Development .... Mr. Michael J. SNAPP
104 Director Study Abroad .... Mr. Baldomero LAGO
105 Director Web Development Services .... Mr. Nathan GERBER
108 Institutional Review Board Chair .... Mr. Cyrill SLEZAK
90 Director Academic IT & Analytics .... Ms. Laura BUSBY
22 Dir Affirmative Action/Equal Oppty .... Ms. Laura CARLSON
30 Assoc VP Development .... Vacant
44 Director Annual Giving .... Ms. Vicky HOPPER
114 Director of Budgets .... Mr. Scott WOOD
113 Bursar .... Mr. David PHILLIPS

116 Director of Internal Audit .... Mr. Peter VANDERHEIDE
118 Director of Benefits/Workforce Svcs .... Ms. Judy MARTINDALE
89 Director First Yr Experience .... Ms. Noemy MEDINA
38 Sr Director Student Health Svcs .... Mr. Bill ERB
86 Sr Director Government Relations .... Mr. Steven ANDERSON

*Weber State University (A)

3850 Dixon Parkway, Ogden UT 84408
County: Weber FICE Identification: 003680
Unit ID: 230782
Telephone: (801) 626-6000 Carnegie Class: Masters/L
FAX Number: (801) 626-7922 Calendar System: Semester
URL: www.weber.edu
Established: 1889 Annual Undergrad Tuition & Fees (In-State): $5,956
Enrollment: 29,596 Coed
Affiliation or Control: State IRS Status: 501(c)3
Highest Offering: Master's
Accreditation: NW, AAQEP, ADNUR, ART, CAATE, CAHIIM, CIDA, COARC, DH, EMT, HSA, MLTAD, MT, MUS, NAEYC, NUR, SW

02 President .... Dr. Brad L. MORTENSEN
05 Provost/VP Academic Affairs .... Dr. Ravi KROVI
10 Vice Pres Administrative Services .... Dr. Norm TARBOX
111 Vice Pres for Univ Advancement .... Dr. Betsy MENNELL
32 Vice Pres Student Affairs .... Dr. Brett PEROZZI
13 VP for Information Technology .... Dr. Bret ELLIS
106 Interim Dean Online/Cont Educ .... Dr. Brian STECKLEIN
28 AVP Diversity/Chief Diversity Ofcr ....Dr. Adrienne G. ANDREWS
21 Asst VP for Financial Services .... Mr. Steven E. NABOR
15 Asst VP for Human Resources .... Dr. Jessica OYLER
88 Asst VP Regional Partnerships .... Ms. Julie SNOWBALL
18 Assoc VP for Facilities Management .... Mr. Mark HALVERSON
84 Asst Prov for Enrollment Services .... Dr. Bruce BOWEN
20 Asst Prov & Dean of Undergraduates ...... Dr. Brenda MARSTELLER-KOWALEWSKI
76 Dean Health Professions .... Dr. Yasmen SIMONIAN
50 Dean Business/Economics .... Dr. Matthew MOURITSEN
53 Dean of Education .... Dr. Kristin HADLEY
83 Dean Social/Behavioral Sciences .... Dr. Julie RICH
79 Dean of Arts & Humanities .... Dr. Deborah UMAN
81 Dean of Science .... Dr. Andrea EASTER-PILCHER
54 Dean Engr/Applied Science & Tech .... Dr. David FERRO
35 Dean of Students .... Dr. Jeffrey J. HURST
06 Registrar .... Mr. Casey D. BULLOCK
19 Director Public Safety .... Mr. Dane LEBLANC
29 Exec Director Alumni Association .... Ms. Nancy COLLINWOOD
38 Dir Counseling & Psycholog Services .... Dr. Dianna K. ABEL
36 Director of Career Services .... Dr. Winn STANGER
37 Director of Financial Aid .... Mr. Jed SPENCER
27 Director of Media Relations .... Mr. John L. KOWALEWSKI
07 Director of Admissions .... Mr. Scott TEICHERT
08 Dean of the Library .... Ms. Wendy HOLLIDAY
22 Dir Equal Opportunity/Affirm Action .... Dr. Laura THOMPSON
41 Dir of Intercollegiate Athletics .... Mr. Tim CROMPTON
40 Bookstore Director .... Mr. Tim ECK
25 Director Sponsored Projects .... Mr. James TAYLOR
85 Director Services Intl Students .... Dr. Mary A. MACHIRA
23 Director Student Health Center .... Dr. Benjamin HEATON
26 Director Public Relations .... Ms. Allison B. HESS
43 University Counsel .... Dr. G. Richard HILL
39 Int Dir Housing & Residence Life ...... Ms. Angelica BETANCOURT
96 Director of Purchasing .... Ms. Nancy E. EMENGER
92 Director of Honors Program .... Dr. Dan BEDFORD
114 Dir of Financial Rep & Investments .... Mr. Wendall RICH
94 Director Women's Center .... Ms. Andrea HERNANDEZ
04 Executive Asst to the President .... Ms. Sherri COX
09 Director of Institutional Research .... Mr. Clayton ANDERSON
104 Director Study Abroad .... Ms. Rebecca SCHWARTZ
108 Dir of Institutional Effectiveness .... Dr. Gail NIKLASON
90 Director Academic Computing .... Ms. Elise WAIKART
45 Director of Strategic Initiatives .... Mr. Steven RICHARDSON
103 Director of Economic Development .... Mr. Guy LETENDRE
105 Director Web Services .... Mr. Peter WAITE
44 Director Annual Giving .... Ms. Nancy COLLINWOOD
86 Exec Director Government Relations .... Mr. Devin WISER
101 Secretary of the Institution/Board .... Ms. Sherri COX

*Snow College (B)

150 College Avenue, Ephraim UT 84627-1299
County: Sanpete FICE Identification: 003679
Unit ID: 230597
Telephone: (435) 283-7000 Carnegie Class: Bac/Assoc-Assoc Dom
FAX Number: (435) 283-6879 Calendar System: Semester
URL: www.snow.edu
Established: 1888 Annual Undergrad Tuition & Fees (In-State): $3,912
Enrollment: 5,800 Coed
Affiliation or Control: State IRS Status: 501(c)3
Highest Offering: Baccalaureate
Accreditation: NW, ACBSP, ADNUR, MUS, PNUR, THEA

02 President .... Dr. Bradley J. COOK
05 Interim Provost .... Dr. Melanie JENKINS
10 VP Finance/Administrative Services .... Mr. Carson HOWELL
32 Vice President Student Success .... Vacant
20 Assoc Provost Academic Affairs .... Ms. Melanie JENKINS
13 Chief Info Technology Officer (CIO) .... Mr. Phil ALLRED
35 Director Student Life/Leadership .... Ms. Michelle BROWN
75 Dean Business & Applied Tech .... Mr. Mike MEDLEY
36 Director of Student Support Svcs .... Mr. Michael ANDERSON
08 Director of Libraries .... Mr. Jon OSTLER
09 Dir Institutional Planning/Research .... Ms. Beckie HERMANSEN
15 Director Human Resources .... Mr. Randy BRABY
18 Director Campus Services Ephraim .... Ms. Leslee COOK
24 Director TTC .... Mr. Chase MITCHELL
39 Director Residential Life .... Ms. Jessica SIEGFRIED
41 Athletic Director .... Mr. Robert NIELSON
06 Registrar .... Mr. Alex SNYDER
84 AVP Enrollment Management .... Ms. Teri CLAWSON
21 Budget Director .... Ms. Sherri HANSEN
26 Marketing/Communications Director .... Mr. John STEVENS
35 Director Student Affairs .... Mr. Mike ANDERSON
37 Director Student Financial Svcs .... Mr. Jack DALENE
38 Dir Student Counseling/Wellness Ctr .... Mr. Allen RIGGS
96 Director of Purchasing .... Mr. Michael JORGENSEN
111 Int Director Advancement .... Mr. Rick WHEELER
27 Director of Campus Relations .... Ms. Heidi STRINGHAM
04 Senior Assistant to President .... Ms. Marci LARSEN

*Salt Lake Community College (C)

4600 S Redwood Road, Salt Lake City UT 84123-3197
County: Salt Lake FICE Identification: 005220
Unit ID: 230746
Telephone: (801) 957-4111 Carnegie Class: Assoc/HT-Mix Trad/Non
FAX Number: (801) 957-4444 Calendar System: Semester
URL: www.slcc.edu
Established: 1948 Annual Undergrad Tuition & Fees (In-State): $3,989
Enrollment: 27,293 Coed
Affiliation or Control: State IRS Status: 501(c)3
Highest Offering: Associate Degree
Accreditation: NW, ACFEI, ADNUR, #COARC, DH, FUSER, OTA, PTAA, RAD, SURGT

02 President .... Dr. Deneece HUFTALIN
05 Provost for Academic Affairs .... Dr. Clifton SANDERS
10 Vice Pres Business Services .... Mr. Jeff WEST
32 VP Student Affairs/Enrollment Mgmt .... Dr. Charles LEPPER
111 Vice Pres Institutional Advancement .... Ms. Alison MCFARLANE
86 VP Govt & Community Relations .... Mr. Tim SHEEHAN
108 VP Institutional Effectiveness .... Mr. Jeffrey AIRD
28 Spec Asst to President & CDO .... Dr. Lea Lani KINIKINI
20 Assoc Provost Learning Advancement .... Dr. David HUBERT
88 Exec Dir Bus Dev Resources .... Ms. Beth COLOSIMO
103 Assoc VP Workforce & Econ Dev .... Mr. Rick BOUILLON
114 Asst VP Budget Svcs/Financial Plng .... Mr. Darren MARSHALL
21 Asst VP/Controller .... Ms. Debra GLENN
18 Assoc VP of Facilities Services .... Mr. Robert ASKERLUND
13 Chief Information/Security Officer .... Mr. Bill ZOUMADAKIS
116 Director Internal Audit .... Mr. Travis LANSING
88 Sr Dir Implementation & Planning .... Ms. Candida DARLING
19 Executive Director Public Safety .... Mr. Shane CRABTREE
41 Director Athletics .... Mr. Kevin M. DUSTIN
35 Dean of Students/Asst Vice Pres .... Dr. Kenneth STONEBROOK
84 Assoc VP Enrollment Management .... Mr. Ryan FARLEY
39 Asst VP Student Services .... Mr. Curt LARSEN
121 Asst VP Student Development .... Dr. Kathryn COQUEMONT
15 Int Asst VP of Human Resources .... Dr. Sara REED
108 Asst VP Strategy and Analysis .... Dr. Lauralea EDWARDS
20 Asst Provost Curriculum & Acad Sys .... Ms. Rachel LEWIS
09 Strategic Analysis/Accred Director .... Dr. Jessie WINITZKY-STEPHENS
30 Exec Dir Development/Foundation .... Ms. Nancy MICHALKO
26 Asst VP Inst Mktg/Communications .... Mr. Michael NAVARRE
31 Director Community Relations .... Ms. Jennifer SELTZER-STITT
43 General Counsel & Risk Management .... Mr. Chris LACOMBE
86 Director Local Govt Relations .... Mr. Scott E. BROWN
25 Director Sponsored Projects .... Ms. Nicole OMER
88 Assoc VP People & Workplace Culture .... Dr. Sara REED
60 Dean Arts/Communication/Media .... Mr. Richard SCOTT
50 Dean School of Business .... Dr. Dennis BROMLEY
72 Dean SAT/Technical Specialties .... Dr. Jennifer SAUNDERS
76 Dean School of Health Sciences .... Dr. Erica WIGHT
79 Dean Humanities/Social Sciences .... Dr. Roderic LAND
81 Dean Science/Math & Engineering .... Dr. Craig CALDWELL
07 Director of Admissions .... Ms. Kate GILDEA-BRODERICK
37 Dir Financial Aid & Scholarships .... Ms. Cristi MILLARD
36 Director of Career Services .... Ms. Ella BUTLER
121 Director Academic Advising .... Ms. Ashley SOKIA
06 Registrar & Academic Records .... Ms. MaryEtta CHASE
117 Director Risk Management .... Vacant
88 Director Special Events .... Ms. Marilee DUNN
96 Director Purchasing & AP .... Mr. Brandon THOMAS
88 Director Testing Services .... Ms. Lakiesha FEHOKO
04 Exec Asst to President & Board Sec .... Ms. Sandra LEHMAN
88 Director Concurrent Enrollment .... Mr. Brandon KOWALLIS
88 Learning Outcomes Assessment Coord .... Dr. Tom ZANE

*Utah State University Eastern (D)

451 E 400 N, Price UT 84501-2699
Telephone: (435) 613-5000 FICE Identification: 003676
Accreditation: &NW, ADNUR, MAAB, PNUR, SURTEC

† Regional accreditation is carried under the parent institution in Logan, UT.

Western Governors University (E)

4001 S 700 E, Suite 700, Salt Lake City UT 84107-2533
County: Salt Lake FICE Identification: 033394
Unit ID: 433387
Telephone: (801) 274-3280 Carnegie Class: Masters/L
FAX Number: (801) 274-3305 Calendar System: Other
URL: www.wgu.edu
Established: 1996 Annual Undergrad Tuition & Fees: $6,670
Enrollment: 147,866 Coed
Affiliation or Control: Independent Non-Profit IRS Status: 501(c)3
Highest Offering: Master's
Accreditation: NW, AAQEP, ACBSP, CAEP, CAEPN, CAHIIM, MAC, NURSE

01 President .... Scott D. PULSIPHER
05 Provost/Chief Academic Officer .... Dr. Marni B. STEIN
30 VP University Development .... Dr. Sarah DEMARK
10 Vice Pres Finance/Administration .... David GROW
09 Vice Pres Quality/Inst Research .... Jason LEVIN
26 Vice President of Marketing .... Carey HILDERBRAND
15 Vice President of Human Resources .... Bonnie PATTEE
37 Vice Pres of Financial Aid .... Bob COLLINS
27 Vice President of Public Relations .... Joan MITCHELL
86 Director Government Relations .... Chris BONNELL
100 Chief of Staff .... Gilbert ROJAS
13 Chief Information Officer .... David MORALES

Westminster College (F)

1840 S 1300 E, Salt Lake City UT 84105-3697
County: Salt Lake FICE Identification: 003681
Unit ID: 230807
Telephone: (801) 484-7651 Carnegie Class: Masters/L
FAX Number: (801) 466-6916 Calendar System: Semester
URL: www.westminstercollege.edu
Established: 1875 Annual Undergrad Tuition & Fees: $37,960
Enrollment: 1,849 Coed
Affiliation or Control: Independent Non-Profit IRS Status: 501(c)3
Highest Offering: Doctorate
Accreditation: NW, AAQEP, ACBSP, ANEST, CACREP, NURSE, PH

01 President .... Dr. Bethami DOBKIN
05 Provost .... Dr. Debbie TAHMASSEBI
10 AVP Finance & Administration .... Ms. Syd TERVORT
111 Vice Pres Institutional Advancement .... Mr. Daniel LEWIS
84 Vice President Enrollment Mgmt .... Ms. Erica JOHNSON
28 Int VP Diversity/Equity/Inclusion .... Dr. Tamara STEVENSON
26 Chief Marketing Officer .... Ms. Sheila YORKIN
49 Dean School of Arts & Sciences .... Dr. Lance NEWMAN
66 Dean School of Nursing/Hlth Science .... Dr. Sheryl STEADMAN
50 Dean School of Business .... Dr. Orn B. BODVARSSON
53 Dean School of Education .... Dr. Melanie AGNEW
32 VP of Student Affairs & DOS .... Vacant
29 Director Alumni Relations .... Ms. Heather STRINGFELLOW
09 Director of Inst Research/Assess .... Ms. Nichole GREENWOOD
13 VP and Chief Information Officer .... Mr. Peter GRECO
43 General Counsel/Chief Risk Officer .... Ms. Kathryn HOLMES
21 Director of Accounting Services .... Ms. Jennifer MEDRANO
15 Director of Human Resources .... Ms. Julie FREESTONE
06 Registrar .... Mr. Michael SANTAROSA
37 Director of Financial Aid .... Mr. Joshua MONTAVON
07 Director Undergraduate Admissions .... Ms. Quincey OTUAFI
18 Director Plant/Facilities .... Mr. Richard A. BROCKMYER
36 Director of Career Resource Center .... Ms. Brianna MIDGLEY
08 Director Giovale Library .... Ms. Emily SWANSON
35 Dean of Students .... Mr. Karnell BLACK
39 Director of Student Involvement .... Mr. Oliver ANDERSON
88 Director of Conference Services .... Mr. Jeff BROWN
19 Director of Campus Safety .... Ms. Bri BUCKLEY
41 Director of Athletics .... Mr. Shay WYATT
42 Director of Spiritual Life .... Ms. Jan SAAED
38 Director of Campus Counseling .... Ms. Trisha JENSEN
92 Dean of Honors College .... Dr. Richard BADENHAUSEN
91 Database Administrator .... Ms. Roksana REZAEI
04 Exec Asst to Pres/Dir Board Rels .... Ms. Emmalee SZWEDKO
22 Title IX Coordinator/EEO Compliance .... Ms. Katherine THOMAS
102 Dir Foundation/Corporate Relations .... Mr. Jeff DRIGGS
86 Director Government Relations .... Ms. Nancy BROWN

VERMONT

Bennington College (G)

One College Drive, Bennington VT 05201-6003
County: Bennington FICE Identification: 003682
Unit ID: 230816
Telephone: (802) 442-5401 Carnegie Class: Bac-A&S
FAX Number: (802) 447-4269 Calendar System: Semester
URL: www.bennington.edu
Established: 1932 Annual Undergrad Tuition & Fees: $58,124
Enrollment: 799 Coed
Affiliation or Control: Independent Non-Profit IRS Status: 501(c)3
Highest Offering: Master's
Accreditation: EH

01 President .... Dr. Isabel ROCHE
05 Acting Provost .... Mr. John BULLOCK
20 Acting Dean of the College .... Ms. Oceana WILSON
10 SVP for Finance & Administration .... Mr. Brian MURPHY
45 AVP for Institutional Initiatives .... Ms. Meredith MCCOY
88 Sr VP for Strategic Partnerships .... Ms. Paige BARTELS
111 VP Institutional Advancement .... Vacant
84 VP for Enrollment .... Mr. Tony CABASCO
28 VP for Inst Inclusion/Equity .... Ms. Delia SAENZ
18 AVP for Facilities Mgmt & Planning .... Mr. Andy SCHLATTER
26 Chief Communications Officer .... Mr. Duncan DOBBELMANN
32 Dean of Students .... Ms. Natalie BASIL
09 Dean of Research/Plng/Assessment .... Mr. Zeke BERNSTEIN
08 Dean of the Library .... Ms. Oceana WILSON
15 Director of Human Resources .... Ms. Heather FALEY
37 Director of Financial Aid .... Ms. Heather CLIFFORD

13 Director of IT .... Mr. Jude HIGDON
04 Senior Exec Asst to the Pres .... Ms. Shannon HOWLETT
19 Director Security/Safety .... Mr. Ken COLLAMORE

Champlain College (A)

163 S Willard Street, Burlington VT 05402-0670
County: Chittenden FICE Identification: 003684
Unit ID: 230852
Telephone: (802) 860-2700 Carnegie Class: Masters/L
FAX Number: (802) 860-2750 Calendar System: Semester
URL: www.champlain.edu
Established: 1956 Annual Undergrad Tuition & Fees: $42,784
Enrollment: 4,137 Coed
Affiliation or Control: Independent Non-Profit IRS Status: 501(c)3
Highest Offering: Master's
Accreditation: EH, ACBSP, ART, SW

01 President .... Vacant
05 Provost and Chief Academic Officer .... Monique TAYLOR
10 Vice President Finance and Planning .... Shelley NAVARI
84 Vice Pres Enrollment .... Robin GRONLUND
13 Vice Pres Technology & CIO .... Diana MATOT
32 Vice President of Student Affairs .... Danelle BERUBE
11 Chief Operating Officer .... Leslie AVERILL
21 Director Finance & Asst Treasurer .... April O'DELL
111 Vice President Advancement .... Sarah ANDRIANO
53 Dean Education/Human Stds Div .... Dr. Laurel BONGIORNO
50 Dean Stiller School of Business .... Vacant
77 Dean Information Tech/Science .... Dr. Scott STEVENS
106 Asst Provost for Online Education .... Dr. Johnna HERRICK-PHELPS
07 Director of Admissions .... Diane SOBOSKI
06 Registrar .... Tara ARNESON
37 Director of Financial Aid .... Gregory DAVIS
100 Director of Operations Pres Office .... Liza GEDULDIG
09 Director of Institutional Research .... Gabrielle SEALY
108 Director Assessment/Curriculum .... Ellen ZEMAN
08 Library Director .... Emily CRIST
38 Director of Counseling Center .... Skip HARRIS
35 Dean of Students .... Susan WARYCK
19 Director of Security & Safety .... Bruce BOVAT
85 Senior Director Intl Education .... Vacant
26 External Relations & Comm Director .... Sandy YUSEN
18 Director of Physical Plant .... Timothy VAN WOERT
23 Medical Director .... Annika HAWKINS-HILKE
88 Senior Dir Learning & Teaching .... Rebecca MILLS
40 Campus Store Manager .... Kevin MCCANN
36 Director Career Collaborative .... Dr. Tanja HINTERSTOISSER
105 Director Web Services .... Brian ANDREWS
25 Chief Contracts/Grants Admin .... Ted WINOKUR
103 Assoc Dir Talent & Engagement .... Sara QUINTANA
44 Director Lead Giving/Donor Rels .... Danielle ALTENBURG

Goddard College (B)

123 Pitkin Road, Plainfield VT 05667-9432
County: Washington FICE Identification: 003686
Unit ID: 230889
Telephone: (800) 468-4888 Carnegie Class: Masters/M
FAX Number: N/A Calendar System: Semester
URL: www.goddard.edu
Established: 1863 Annual Undergrad Tuition & Fees: $18,210
Enrollment: 366 Coed
Affiliation or Control: Independent Non-Profit IRS Status: 501(c)3
Highest Offering: Master's
Accreditation: EH

01 President .... Dr. Dan HOCOY
05 Chief Academic Officer .... Dr. Steven JAMES
10 Chief Financial and Admin Officer .... Ms. Leesa STEWART
30 Director of Development .... Vacant
26 Director of Marketing .... Mr. Joshua AUERBACH
13 Director of ITS .... Mr. John BAKER
07 Director of Admissions .... Ms. Lucy BOURGEAULT
06 Registrar .... Ms. Jillehn WASHBURN
37 Director of Financial Aid .... Ms. Beverly JENE
08 Director of Information Access .... Ms. Eileen GATTI
18 Director of Facilities Operations .... Mr. J.C MYERS
32 Director of Student Services .... Ms. Deborah BLOOM
04 Executive Assistant to President .... Ms. Lisa LARIVEE

Landmark College (C)

19 River Road South, Putney VT 05346
County: Windham FICE Identification: 025326
Unit ID: 247649
Telephone: (802) 387-4767 Carnegie Class: Bac/Assoc-Mixed
FAX Number: (802) 387-6868 Calendar System: Semester
URL: www.landmark.edu
Established: 1985 Annual Undergrad Tuition & Fees: $60,280
Enrollment: 559 Coed
Affiliation or Control: Independent Non-Profit IRS Status: 501(c)3
Highest Offering: Associate Degree
Accreditation: EH

01 President .... Dr. Peter A. EDEN
03 Executive Vice President .... Mr. Jon A. MACCLAREN
05 VP Academic Affairs .... Dr. Gail GIBSON SHEFFIELD
10 Exec VP/Chief Financial Officer .... Mr. Jon MACCLAREN
111 VP Institutional Advancement .... Ms. Cheryl ADOLPH
32 VP Student Affairs/Dean Campus Life .... Mr. Michael LUCIANI
84 VP Enrollment Management .... Mr. Kevin MAYNE
88 VP Educational Research/Innovation .... Ms. Manju BANERJEE
26 VP Marketing & Communications .... Mr. Mark DIPIETRO
04 Assistant to the President .... Ms. Tiffany KERYLOW
13 Dir Information Technology Svcs .... Ms. Tina LAFLAM
36 Director Career Connections .... Ms. Jan COPLAN
18 Director of Facilities .... Mr. Kyle SKROCKI
08 Director Library Services .... Ms. Jennifer LANN
06 Registrar .... Ms. Nichole NIETSCHE
41 Director Athletics .... Ms. Kari POST
37 Director Financial Aid .... Mr. Michael MERTES
38 Director of Counseling/Wellness .... Ms. Jacala MILLS
23 Director of Health Services .... Mr. Jeff HUYETT
15 Director Human Resources .... Ms. Janie JENKINS-EVANS
21 Controller .... Ms. Maureen RYAN HOFFMAN
35 Dean of Students .... Ms. Kelly O'RYAN
07 Director of Admissions .... Ms. Sydney RUFF
19 Director Campus Safety .... Mr. Michael GIANNETTO
29 Associate Director Alumni Affairs .... Ms. Tricia STANLEY
30 Sr Dir Institutional Advancement .... Ms. Carol NARDINO
104 Director International Education .... Ms. Peg ALDEN
106 Director Online Learning .... Ms. Denise JAFFE
40 Assistant Bookstore Manager .... Ms. Kimberly KEMPF

Middlebury Bread Loaf School of English (D)

75 Franklin Street, Middlebury VT 05753
Telephone: (802) 443-5418 Identification: 770119
Accreditation: &EH

† Bread Loaf School of English is a summer graduate program and the enrollment figure is for the summer term.

Middlebury College (E)

Old Chapel, Middlebury VT 05753-6200
County: Addison FICE Identification: 003691
Unit ID: 230959
Telephone: (802) 443-5000 Carnegie Class: Bac-A&S
FAX Number: (802) 443-2071 Calendar System: 4/1/4
URL: www.middlebury.edu
Established: 1800 Annual Undergrad Tuition & Fees: $58,316
Enrollment: 2,669 Coed
Affiliation or Control: Independent Non-Profit IRS Status: 501(c)3
Highest Offering: Doctorate
Accreditation: EH

01 President .... Dr. Laurie L. PATTON
05 Exec VP and Provost .... Dr. Jeff CASON
10 Exec VP Finance & Administration .... Mr. David J. PROVOST
15 VP for Human Resources .... Vacant
111 VP for Advancement .... Ms. Colleen FITZPATRICK
20 VP Academic Affairs/Dean of Faculty .... Dr. Sujata MOORTI
26 VP for Communications & Marketing .... Mr. David J. GIBSON
32 Dean of Students .... Mr. Derek DOUCET
43 General Counsel/Chief of Staff .... Ms. Hannah ROSS
28 Chief Diversity Officer .... Dr. Miguel FERNANDEZ
58 VP Acad Affs/Dean of the Institute .... Dr. Jeffrey DAYTON-JOHNSON
07 Dean of Admissions .... Ms. Nicole CURVIN
104 Dean of International Programs .... Dr. Carlos VELEZ
45 Assoc Provost for Planning .... Mr. LeRoy GRAHAM
08 Dean of the Library .... Mr. Michael D. ROY
37 Assoc VP Student Financial Services .... Ms. Kim DOWNS-BURNS
13 Associate VP/CIO for ITS .... Mr. Vijay MENTA
79 VP for AA/Dean of Language Schs .... Dr. Stephen SNYDER
117 VP Administration/Chief Risk Ofcr .... Mr. Michael D. THOMAS
20 Dean of Curriculum .... Dr. Suzanne GURLAND
09 Dean for Faculty Dev & Research .... Dr. James RALPH
21 Director of Business Services .... Mr. Matt CURRAN
29 Assoc VP Alumni & Parent Programs .... Ms. Margaret STOREY GROVES
17 Exec Director Health & Wellness .... Ms. Barbara MCCALL
23 Chief Health Ofcr/College Physician .... Dr. W. Mark PELUSO
42 Dean of Spiritual/Religious Life .... Mr. Mark ORTEN
41 Director of Athletics .... Mr. Erin QUINN
19 Interim Director Public Safety .... Mr. Daniel V. GAIOTTI
06 Registrar .... Ms. Jennifer THOMPSON
15 Director of Human Resources .... Vacant
40 Bookstore Manager .... Ms. Erin JONES-POPPE
108 Dir Assessment & Inst Rsch .... Ms. Adela LANGROCK
25 Director of Grants & Sponsored Pgm .... Mr. Chuck MASON

† Tuition figure is a comprehensive fees figure.

Norwich University (F)

158 Harmon Drive, Northfield VT 05663-1000
County: Washington FICE Identification: 003692
Unit ID: 230995
Telephone: (802) 485-2000 Carnegie Class: Masters/L
FAX Number: (802) 485-2032 Calendar System: Semester
URL: www.norwich.edu
Established: 1819 Annual Undergrad Tuition & Fees: $42,950
Enrollment: 3,975 Coed
Affiliation or Control: Independent Non-Profit IRS Status: 501(c)3
Highest Offering: Master's
Accreditation: EH, ACBSP, #CAATE, NURSE

01 President .... Col. Mark ANARUMO
05 Interim Provost & Dean of Faculty .... Dr. Stephen FITZHUGH
58 VP & Dean Col of Grad/Cont Studies .... Dr. William CLEMENTS
32 Sr Vice Pres Student Affairs .... Dr. Frank VANECEK
03 Executive Vice President .... Mr. David J. WHALEY
30 VP of Development/Alumni Relations .... Ms. Elizabeth KENNEDY
88 VP Strategic Partnership .... Mr. Phillip SUSMANN
84 VP of Enrollment Management .... Mr. Greg MATTHEWS
26 VP of Communications .... Ms. Kathy MURPHY-MORIARITY
10 VP of Finance .... Mr. Martin HANIFIN
28 VP of Diversity/Equity/Inclusion .... Dr. Julia BERNARD
107 Dean Col of Professional Schools .... Mr. Aron TEMKIN
83 Dean College of Liberal Arts .... Dr. Edward KOHN
81 Dean College of Science/Mathematics .... Dr. Michael MCGINNIS
80 Dean College of National Services .... Col. Joel NEWSOM
29 Assoc VP Alumni Relations .... Ms. Diane SCOLARO
20 Assoc VP Academic Affairs .... Vacant
04 Exec Assistant to President .... Ms. Laura AMELL
35 Interim Dean of Students .... Mr. Greg MCGRATH
08 Interim Head Librarian .... Mr. Greg SAUER
41 Athletic Director .... Mr. Anthony A. MARIANO
18 Director Facilities/Operations .... Mr. Bizhan YAHYAZADEH
37 Director of Student Financial Aid .... Ms. Mel DEFLORIO
38 Dir Student Counseling/Wellness .... Ms. Nicole KROTINGER
07 Director of Admissions .... Mr. Steve WOLF
06 Registrar .... Ms. Cynthia SUTER
102 Dir Foundation/Corporate Relations .... Ms. Lindsay BUDNIK
103 Director Career Development .... Ms. Meghan OLIVER
19 Director Security/Safety .... Mr. Larry ROONEY
15 Director of Human Resources .... Mr. Dana MOSS

Saint Michael's College (G)

One Winooski Park, Colchester VT 05439-0001
County: Chittenden FICE Identification: 003694
Unit ID: 231059
Telephone: (802) 654-2000 Carnegie Class: Bac-A&S
FAX Number: (802) 654-2297 Calendar System: Semester
URL: www.smcvt.edu
Established: 1904 Annual Undergrad Tuition & Fees: $48,175
Enrollment: 1,724 Coed
Affiliation or Control: Roman Catholic IRS Status: 501(c)3
Highest Offering: Master's
Accreditation: EH

01 President .... Dr. D. E. Lorraine M. STERRITT
04 Assistant to the President .... Mrs. Ellen M. DEORSEY
05 VP for Academic Affairs .... Dr. Jeffrey TRUMBOWER
10 Vice President for Finance .... Mr. Robert ROBINSON
32 Vice President for Student Affairs .... Dr. Dawn M. ELLINWOOD
84 Vice Pres Enrollment/Marketing .... Ms. Kristin MCANDREW
111 Vice Pres for Inst Advancement .... Ms. Krystyna DAVENPORT BROWN
42 Director Edmundite Campus Ministry .... Rev. Brian J. CUMMINGS, SSE
07 Director of Admission .... Mr. Michael STEFANOWICZ
41 Director of Athletics .... Mr. Christopher KENNEY
26 Dir Marketing/Communications .... Mr. Alex BERTONI
06 Registrar .... Ms. Marnie OWEN
09 Director of Institutional Research .... Ms. Mary Jane RUSSELL
100 Chief of Staff .... Dr. Jonathan D'AMORE
19 Director Security/Safety .... Vacant
29 Director Alumni Affairs .... Ms. Angela ARMOUR
37 Director Student Financial Services .... Ms. Diane CORBETT
102 Director Foundation/Corporate Rels .... Ms. Angela IRVINE

School for International Training (SIT) (H)

1 Kipling Road, Brattleboro VT 05302-0676
County: Windham FICE Identification: 008860
Unit ID: 231068
Telephone: (802) 257-7751 Carnegie Class: Masters/M
FAX Number: (802) 258-3110 Calendar System: Other
URL: www.sit.edu
Established: 1964 Annual Undergrad Tuition & Fees: N/A
Enrollment: 137 Coed
Affiliation or Control: Independent Non-Profit IRS Status: 501(c)3
Highest Offering: Doctorate
Accreditation: EH

01 President .... Dr. Sophia HOWLETT
05 Academic Dean .... Mr. Said GRAIOUID
05 Academic Dean .... Ms. Aynn SETRIGHT
05 Academic Dean .... Mr. Brian HAMMER
05 Academic Dean .... Ms. Katy DE LA GARZA
10 CFO .... Mr. Kote LOMIDZE
13 Director of IT .... Mr. Roger BOYLE
43 General Counsel .... Ms. Lisa RAE
58 Dean SIT Graduate Institute .... Dr. Kenneth WILLIAMS
19 Dean Stdnt Safety/Health/Well-being .... Dr. Michael ZOLL
07 Assoc Dean of Admissions .... Mr. Eric WIRTH
06 Registrar .... Ms. Ginny NELLIS
04 Executive Asst to SIT President .... Ms. Adelee AUSTIN
108 Dean for Assessment & Learning Supp .... Dr. Kathryn INSKEEP
29 Director of Alumni Engagement .... Ms. Carla LINEBACK
08 Head Librarian .... Mr. Patrick SPURLOCK

Sterling College (I)

PO Box 72, Craftsbury Common VT 05827-0072
County: Orleans FICE Identification: 021435
Unit ID: 231095
Telephone: (802) 586-7711 Carnegie Class: Bac-A&S
FAX Number: (802) 586-2596 Calendar System: Semester
URL: www.sterlingcollege.edu
Established: 1958 Annual Undergrad Tuition & Fees: $39,200

Enrollment: 139 Coed
Affiliation or Control: Independent Non-Profit IRS Status: 501(c)3
Highest Offering: Baccalaureate
Accreditation: EH

01 President .... Mr. Matthew A. DERR
05 Dean of Academics .... Dr. Laura SPENCE
07 Dean of Admission/Financial Aid .... Ms. Moxie MEHEGAN
111 Dean of Advancement and Alumni Rels . Ms. Christina GOODWIN
10 Vice President and COO .... Mr. Peter MERRILL
08 Librarian .... Ms. Petra VOGEL
18 Director of Facilities .... Mr. Kelly JONES
32 Int Dean of Student Life .... Favor ELLIS
06 Asst Dean of Academics & Registrar .... Ms. Laura Lea BERRY
26 Assoc Dean Marketing/Communications .... Ms. Heidi MYERS
37 Director of Financial Aid .... Ms. Barbara STUART

University of Vermont (A)

South Prospect Street, Burlington VT 05405-0160
County: Chittenden FICE Identification: 003696
Unit ID: 231174
Telephone: (802) 656-3131 Carnegie Class: DU-Higher
FAX Number: N/A Calendar System: Semester
URL: www.uvm.edu
Established: 1791 Annual Undergrad Tuition & Fees (In-State): $19,062
Enrollment: 13,292 Coed
Affiliation or Control: State IRS Status: 501(c)3
Highest Offering: Doctorate
Accreditation: EH, CAATE, CACREP, CAEP, CLPSY, DENT, DIETC, DIETD, IPSY, MED, MT, NURSE, PH, PTA, RTT, SP, SPAA, SW

01 President .... Dr. Suresh GARIMELLA
05 Provost and Sr Vice President .... Dr. Patricia A. PRELOCK
10 VP for Finance & Treasurer .... Mr. Richard H. CATE
46 VP for Research .... Dr. Kirk DOMBROWSKI
30 CEO & President The UVM Foundation .... Mr. Jim KELLER
43 VP Legal Affairs & General Counsel .... Ms. Sharon REICH PAULSEN
84 VP Enrollment Management .... Dr. Jay JACOBS
13 Chief Information Officer .... Dr. Simeon ANANOU
88 Vice Provost for Faculty Affairs .... Dr. Jim VIGOREAUX
20 Vice Provost for Academic Affairs .... Dr. Jennifer DICKINSON
32 Interim VP for Student Affairs .... Ms. Erica CALOIERO
28 VP for Diversity/Equity & Inclusion .... Dr. Amer R. AHMED
11 VP for Executive Operations .... Dr. Gary L. DERR
15 Chief Human Resource Officer .... Mr. Jes KRAUS
35 Dean of Students .... Dr. David A. NESTOR
29 Exec Dir Ldrshp/Engmnt/Philanthropy .... Mr. Alan E. RYEA
63 Dean College of Medicine .... Dr. Richard L. PAGE
66 Dean Nursing & Health Sciences .... Dr. Noma ANDERSON
49 Dean Arts & Sciences .... Dr. William A. FALLS
47 Dean Agriculture & Life Sci .... Dr. Leslie V. PARISE
54 Dean Engineering & Math Sciences .... Dr. Linda SCHADLER
53 Int Dean Education & Social Svcs .... Dr. Katharine SHEPHERD
50 Dean Business Administration .... Dr. Sanjay SHARMA
92 Dean Honors College .... Dr. David JENEMANN
65 Dean Environment & Natural Resource ... Dr. Nancy E. MATHEWS
56 Director Extension .... Dr. Roy BECKFORD
58 Dean Graduate College .... Dr. Cynthia J. FOREHAND
51 Dean Continuing & Distance Educ .... Ms. Cynthia L. BELLIVEAU
08 Dean of University Libraries .... Dr. Bryn GEFFERT
06 Registrar .... Ms. Veronika CARTER
09 Director Institutional Research .... Dr. Alexander C. YIN
26 Chief Communications Officer .... Mr. Joel SELIGMAN
14 Assoc Chief Information Officer .... Ms. Julia H. RUSSELL
25 Executive Director Research Admin .... Mr. Brian PRINDLE
114 University Budget Director .... Ms. Shari BERGQUIST
19 Chief of Police Services .... Mr. Timothy BILODEAU
41 Director of Athletics .... Mr. Jeffrey L. SCHULMAN
36 Director Career Services .... Ms. Pamela K. GARDNER
23 Int Dir Ctr for Health & Wellbeing .... Mr. John Paul GROGAN
38 Counsel/Psych Services Program Dir .... Dr. Todd N. WEINMAN
39 Executive Director Residential Life .... Dr. Rafael RODRIGUEZ
40 Director University Bookstore .... Mr. Robert SANTRY
85 Director Intl Education Services .... Ms. Kimberly A. HOWARD
112 VP for Principal Gifts .... Ms. Kathleen KELLEHER
44 Int VP of Development .... Ms. Alli LAMBERT
123 Director Graduate Admissions .... Ms. Kimberly L. HESS
07 Director Undergrad Admissions .... Mr. Moses MURPHY
37 Director Student Financial Services .... Ms. Marie D. JOHNSON
96 Director Purchasing Services .... Ms. Natalie L. GUILLETTE
94 Director Women's Center .... Ms. Melissa MURRAY
24 Access/Media Services Librarian .... Mr. Aaron F. NICHOLS
101 Board of Trustees Coordinator .... Ms. Corinne B. THOMPSON
04 Admin Assistant to the President .... Ms. Janis AUDET-KRANS
102 Int Exec Dir Corporate/Found Rels .... Ms. Lisa TOWNSON
18 Executive Dir of Facilities Mgmt .... Ms. Luce HILLMAN

Vermont College of Fine Arts (B)

36 College Street, Montpelier VT 05602-3145
County: Washington FICE Identification: 003697
Unit ID: 455992
Telephone: (802) 828-8600 Carnegie Class: Spec-4-yr-Other
FAX Number: (802) 828-8649 Calendar System: Semester
URL: www.vcfa.edu
Established: 2008 Annual Graduate Tuition & Fees: N/A
Enrollment: 371 Coed
Affiliation or Control: Independent Non-Profit IRS Status: 501(c)3
Highest Offering: Master's; No Undergraduates
Accreditation: EH, ART

01 President .... Ms. Leslie Colis WARD
05 Academic Dean .... Mr. Matthew MONK
10 VP for Finance & Admin .... Ms. Katie GUSTAFSON
32 VP Student Services .... Mr. David MARKOW
04 Assistant to President .... Ms. Kerry MACDONALD
26 Exec Dir Marketing/Communications .... Mr. Alastair HAYES
06 Registrar .... Ms. Jody MAUNSELL
08 Head Librarian .... Mr. Jim NOLTE
13 Director of IT .... Mr. Peter TIMPONE
18 Dir Facilities/Operations .... Mr. Matthew COYNE
07 Dir Admissions & Financial Aid .... Vacant
29 Director Alumni Affairs .... Ms. Jericho PARMS

† Carnegie Graduate Instructional Program classification is Postbac-A&S

Vermont Law School (C)

164 Chelsea Street, PO Box 96,
South Royalton VT 05068-0096
County: Windsor FICE Identification: 011934
Unit ID: 231147
Telephone: (802) 831-1000 Carnegie Class: Spec-4-yr-Law
FAX Number: (802) 831-1163 Calendar System: Semester
URL: www.vermontlaw.edu
Established: 1972 Annual Graduate Tuition & Fees: N/A
Enrollment: 624 Coed
Affiliation or Control: Independent Non-Profit IRS Status: 501(c)3
Highest Offering: First Professional Degree; No Undergraduates
Accreditation: EH, LAW

01 Interim President and Dean .... Mr. Beth MCCORMACK
05 Vice Dean for Faculty .... Ms. Cynthia LEWIS
32 Vice Dean for Students .... Mr. Joe BRENNAN
10 Vice President for Finance .... Ms. Lorraine ATWOOD
07 Vice President for Enrollment .... Mr. John MILLER
30 Vice President for Development .... Ms. Brooke HERNDON
88 Director Environmental Law Ctr .... Ms. Jennifer RUSHLOW
35 Assoc Dean Student Affs & Diversity .... Ms. Shirley JEFFERSON
20 Assoc Dean for Academic Affs .... Vacant
106 Director of Distance Learning .... Ms. Sarah REITER
15 Human Resources Director .... Ms. Betsy ERWIN
08 Library Director .... Ms. Jane WOLDOW
21 Comptroller .... Ms. Angela CARPENTER
06 Registrar .... Ms. Maureen MORIARTY
37 Director of Financial Aid .... Ms. Mel DEFLORIO
18 Facilities Manager .... Mr. Jeffrey KNUDSEN
26 Director of Communications .... Mr. Justin CAMPFIELD
13 Technology Operations Manager .... Mr. Oscar TREVINO
04 Exec Asst to the President/Dean .... Ms. Susan FOLGER
40 Bookstore Manager .... Ms. Amy MCDOWELL
29 Director of Alumni Affairs .... Ms. Crystal BROWNELL
102 Director Foundation/Corporate Rels .... Mr. David THURLOW
44 Director Annual Giving .... Vacant
36 Director Career Services .... Ms. Abby ARMSTRONG

*Vermont State Colleges Office of the Chancellor (D)

PO Box 7, Montpelier VT 05601
County: Washington FICE Identification: 029162
Unit ID: 231156
Telephone: (802) 224-3000 Carnegie Class: N/A
FAX Number: (802) 224-3035
URL: www.vsc.edu

01 Chancellor .... Ms. Sophie ZDATNY
43 General Counsel .... Ms. Patty TURLEY
10 Chief Financial/OOperating Officer .... Ms. Sharron SCOTT
05 Chief Academic/Tech Officer .... Dr. Yasmine ZIESLER
11 Administrative Director .... Ms. Jennifer PORRIER
86 Dir External/Governmental Affairs .... Ms. Katherine LEVASSEUR
26 Chief Information Officer .... Ms. Kellie CAMPBELL
18 Director of Facilities .... Mr. Richard ETHIER
13 Director of Information Technology .... Mr. Doug EASTMAN
15 Director of Human Resources .... Ms. Katrina MEIGS
88 Director of Payroll/Benefits .... Ms. Tracy SWEET
25 Grants Compliance Officer .... Ms. Betsy WARD

*Castleton University (E)

62 Alumni Drive, Castleton VT 05735-4454
County: Rutland FICE Identification: 003683
Unit ID: 230834
Telephone: (802) 468-5611 Carnegie Class: Bac-Diverse
FAX Number: (802) 468-6470 Calendar System: Semester
URL: www.castleton.edu
Established: 1787 Annual Undergrad Tuition & Fees (In-State): $13,044
Enrollment: 2,211 Coed
Affiliation or Control: State IRS Status: 501(c)3
Highest Offering: Master's
Accreditation: EH, CAATE, NURSE, SW

02 Interim President .... Dr. Jonathan SPIRO
04 Exec Assistant to the President .... Ms. Rita B. GENO
05 Provost .... Dr. Thomas MAUHS-PUGH
20 Associate Academic Dean .... Dr. Gillian GALLE
10 Director of Finance .... Ms. Laura JAKUBOWSKI
32 Dean of Students .... Mr. Dennis PROULX
84 Dean of Enrollment .... Mr. Maurice OUIMET
50 Dean College of Business .... Ms. Cathy KOZLIK
81 Dean College of Health & Science .... Dr. Francesca CATALANO
111 Assoc Dean of Advancement .... Mr. James LAMBERT
15 Director of Human Resources .... Ms. Janet HAZELTON
35 Associate Dean of Students .... Ms. Victoria ANGIS
06 Registrar .... Ms. Lori ARNER
37 Director Student Financial Aid .... Ms. Teresa MCCORMACK
53 Director of Education .... Dr. Richard REARDON
18 Director of Physical Plant .... Mr. Chuck LAVOIE
36 Dir of Career Development .... Ms. Renee BEAUPREWHITE
23 Wellness Center Director .... Ms. Martha COULTER
13 Chief Technology Officer .... Ms. Gayle MALINOWSKI

*Community College of Vermont (F)

PO Box 489, Montpelier VT 05601
County: Washington FICE Identification: 011167
Unit ID: 230861
Telephone: (802) 828-2800 Carnegie Class: Assoc/MT-VT-Mix Trad/Non
FAX Number: (802) 828-2805 Calendar System: Semester
URL: www.ccv.edu
Established: 1970 Annual Undergrad Tuition & Fees (In-State): $6,920
Enrollment: 5,102 Coed
Affiliation or Control: State IRS Status: 501(c)3
Highest Offering: Associate Degree
Accreditation: EH

02 President .... Ms. Joyce M. JUDY
11 Dean of Administration .... Mr. Andrew PALLITO
05 Dean of Academic Services .... Ms. Deborah STEWART
32 Dean of Student Services .... Ms. Heather WEINSTEIN
20 Associate Academic Dean .... Ms. Candace LEWIS
20 Associate Academic Dean .... Ms. Diane HERMANN-ARTIM
35 Associate Dean of Students .... Ms. Angela ALBECK
84 Dean of Enrollment & Cmty Relations .... Ms. Katie MOBLEY
88 Dean of Academic Center Admin .... Ms. Tapp BARNHILL
15 Director Human Resources .... Mr. Robert FINNEGAN
06 Registrar .... Mr. John Paul REES
07 Director of Admissions .... Mr. Adam WARRINGTON
37 Director of Financial Aid .... Mr. Ryan DULUDE
09 Dir Institutional Research/Planning .... Ms. Laura MASSELL
26 Director of Communications .... Ms. Katherine KEZEY
88 Director of Secondary Initiatives .... Ms. Natalie SEARLE
36 Director of Career Training Program .... Vacant
27 Dir of Marketing Operations .... Ms. Danielle BRESETTE
10 Dir of Business Operations .... Ms. Gisele HODGDON
30 Director of Resource Development .... Ms. Aimee STEPHENSON
106 Dir of Online Teaching & Learning .... Ms. Jennifer ALBERICO
13 Director of IT Infrastructure .... Mr. Charles BOMBARD
90 Director of Academic Technology .... Mr. Anthony HARRIS
91 Dir of Administrative Technology .... Ms. Megan TUCKER
20 Associate Academic Dean .... Ms. Nicole STESTON

*Northern Vermont University-Johnson (G)

337 College Hill, Johnson VT 05656
County: Lamoille FICE Identification: 003688
Unit ID: 230913
Telephone: (802) 635-1240 Carnegie Class: Masters/S
FAX Number: (802) 635-1230 Calendar System: Semester
URL: www.northernvermont.edu
Established: 1828 Annual Undergrad Tuition & Fees (In-State): $12,804
Enrollment: 1,999 Coed
Affiliation or Control: State IRS Status: 501(c)3
Highest Offering: Master's
Accreditation: EH

02 Interim President .... Mr. John W. MILLS
05 Provost .... Dr. Nolan T. ATKINS
11 Dean of Administration .... Ms. Sharron R. SCOTT
32 Dean of Students/Student Life .... Mr. Jonathan M. DAVIS
13 Chief Info Technology Officer/CIO .... Mr. Jason RYAN
35 Associate Dean of Students .... Ms. Michele WHITMORE
06 Registrar .... Ms. Miranda FOX
106 Assoc Dean of Distance Education .... Ms. Bobbi Jo CARTER
18 Director of Physical Plant .... Mr. Michael STEVENS
41 Assoc Dean Athletics/Recreation .... Mr. Jamey VENTURA
38 Director of Counseling Services .... Ms. Kate MCCARTHY
30 Univ Development/External Rels Ofcr . Ms. Leah HOLLENBERGER
36 Director of Advising .... Ms. Sara KINERSON
89 Dir First-Year Exp/Student Life .... Ms. Erin ROSSETTI
19 Director of Public Safety .... Mr. Michael PALAGONIA
26 Director Marketing/Communications .... Ms. Sylvia PLUMB
07 Director of Admissions/Enroll Mgmt .... Mr. Patrick ROGERS
79 Chair Humanities .... Dr. David PLAZEK
53 Chair Education .... Dr. Rob SCHULZE
65 Chair Environ/Health Sciences .... Dr. Elizabeth DOLCI
88 Chair Performing Arts .... Mr. Isaac EDDY
57 Chair Fine Arts .... Mr. Ken LESLIE
50 Chair Business Administration .... Mr. William MORISON
60 Chair Writing/Literature .... Dr. Sharon TWIGG
81 Chair Mathematics .... Dr. Julie THEORET
83 Chair Behavioral Sciences .... Dr. Susan GREEN

*Northern Vermont University-Lyndon (H)

1001 College Road, PO Box 919,
Lyndonville VT 05851-0919
Telephone: (802) 626-6200 FICE Identification: 003689
Accreditation: &EH, EXSC

*Vermont Technical College (A)

124 Admin Drive, PO Box 500,
Randolph Center VT 05061-0500
County: Orange FICE Identification: 003698
Unit ID: 231165
Telephone: (802) 728-1000 Carnegie Class: Bac/Assoc-Mixed
FAX Number: (802) 728-1508 Calendar System: Semester
URL: www.vtc.edu
Established: 1866 Annual Undergrad Tuition & Fees (In-State): $16,044
Enrollment: 1,520 Coed
Affiliation or Control: State IRS Status: 501(c)3
Highest Offering: Master's
Accreditation: EH, COARC, DH, EMT

02 President .... Ms. Patricia L. MOULTON
05 Dean of Academic Affairs .... Dr. Ana GAILLAT
32 Dean of Students .... Mr. Jason ENSER
11 Dean of Administration .... Mr. Littleton TYLER
13 Chief Technology Officer .... Ms. Kellie B. CAMPBELL
30 Assoc Dean Inst Advancement .... Vacant
66 Assoc Dean of Nursing .... Ms. Sarah BILLINGS-BERG
07 Asst Dean of Admissions .... Ms. Jessica VAN DEREN
06 Registrar .... Ms. Shelly RUSS
37 Exec Director of Student Services ... Ms. Catherine MCCULLOUGH
19 Director Public Safety .... Mr. Emile FREDETTE
18 Director Facilities .... Mr. Theodore MANAZIR
36 Director Career Development .... Ms. Karry BOOSKA
15 Director of Human Resources .... Ms. Kelly-Rue RISO
26 Dir Marketing/Communications .... Ms. Amanda CHAULK
08 Director of Library .... Mr. James ALLEN

VIRGINIA

Advanced Technology Institute (B)

5700 Southern Boulevard, Virginia Beach VA 23462-2409
County: City of Virginia Beach FICE Identification: 031275
Unit ID: 231411
Telephone: (757) 490-1241 Carnegie Class: Spec 2-yr-Tech
FAX Number: (757) 499-5929 Calendar System: Semester
URL: www.auto.edu
Established: 1993 Annual Undergrad Tuition & Fees: $13,200
Enrollment: 461 Coed
Affiliation or Control: Proprietary IRS Status: Proprietary
Highest Offering: Associate Degree
Accreditation: ACCSC

02 Vice President .... Mr. Andy GLADSTEIN
05 Director of Education .... Ms. Debbie WIGGINS
07 Director of Admissions .... Mr. Mike AMBROSE
32 Director of Student Services .... Mr. Kirk CLAYTON
37 Director Student Financial Aid .... Mr. Chad MARTS
06 Registrar .... Mrs. Shannon VOIGT
20 Director of Training .... Mr. Rob METZGER
36 Director Student Placement .... Mr. Kirk CLAYTON
39 Director Student Housing .... Mr. Kirk MANGHAM

American National University (C)

1813 E Main Street, Salem VA 24153-4598
County: Roanoke FICE Identification: 003726
Unit ID: 232797
Telephone: (540) 986-1800 Carnegie Class: Bac/Assoc-Mixed
FAX Number: (540) 444-4198 Calendar System: Quarter
URL: www.an.edu
Established: 1886 Annual Undergrad Tuition & Fees: $10,772
Enrollment: 931 Coed
Affiliation or Control: Proprietary IRS Status: Proprietary
Highest Offering: Master's
Accreditation: DEAC, CAHIIM, MAC, NURSE

01 President .... Mr. Frank E. LONGAKER
11 Sr Exec VP of Campus Operations .... Mr. Joel MUSGROVE
10 Vice President of Financial Svcs .... Ms. April HOWARD

Appalachian College of Pharmacy (D)

1060 Dragon Road, Oakwood VA 24631
County: Buchanan FICE Identification: 041806
Unit ID: 449922
Telephone: (276) 498-4190 Carnegie Class: Spec-4-yr-Other Health
FAX Number: (276) 498-4193 Calendar System: Semester
URL: https://www.acp.edu/
Established: 2003 Annual Graduate Tuition & Fees: N/A
Enrollment: 180 Coed
Affiliation or Control: Independent Non-Profit IRS Status: 501(c)3
Highest Offering: Doctorate; No Undergraduates
Accreditation: SC, PHAR

01 President .... Mr. Michael G. MCGLOTHLIN
05 Dean .... Dr. Susan L. MAYHEW
10 Chief Financial Officer .... Ms. Holli HARMAN
07 Dir of Admissions/Fin Aid/Registrar .... Ms. Vickie KEENE
103 Dir of Institutional Development .... Mr. Terry KILGORE
32 Dir Student Services/Alumni Affairs .... Mr. Jason MCGLOTHLIN
13 Dir Safety/Information Technology .... Mr. David DEEL
08 Library Director .... Ms. Melissa SPEED

Appalachian School of Law (E)

1169 Edgewater Drive, Grundy VA 24614-2825
County: Buchanan FICE Identification: 035593
Unit ID: 432348
Telephone: (800) 895-7411 Carnegie Class: Spec-4-yr-Law
FAX Number: (276) 935-8261 Calendar System: Semester
URL: www.asl.edu
Established: 1995 Annual Undergrad Tuition & Fees: N/A
Enrollment: 170 Coed
Affiliation or Control: Independent Non-Profit IRS Status: 501(c)3
Highest Offering: First Professional Degree
Accreditation: LAW

01 President and Dean .... Mr. B. Keith FAULKNER
05 Chief Academic Officer .... Mr. Mason HEIDT
04 Executive Asst to the President .... Ms. Ashley A. KELSEY
36 Director of Career Services .... Ms. Lucy MCGEE
13 Director of Information Services .... Mr. Brian PRESLEY
15 Director Cmty Service & Personnel .... Ms. Jina M. SAULS
07 Dean of Admissions .... Ms. Holly CLINE
06 Registrar .... Ms. Beth STANLEY
32 Dean of Students .... Hon. Chadwick S. DOTSON
26 Director of Communications .... Mr. Mark N. KELSEY
09 Director of Institutional Research .... Ms. Rebecca ENGLAND
10 Director of the Business Office .... Ms. Peggy STREET
11 Chief Operating Officer .... Ms. Abigail WESCOTT
08 Int Assoc Director of Library .... Ms. Glenna OWENS
111 Director of Advancement .... Ms. Haley ALLISON
19 Director of Campus Safety .... Mr. Michael KIRKPATRICK

The Art Institute of Virginia Beach (F)

4500 Main Street, Ste 200, Virginia Beach VA 23462
Telephone: (757) 493-6701 Identification: 770977
Accreditation: &SC, ACFEI

† Branch campus of The Art Institute of Atlanta, Atlanta, GA

Ascent College (G)

1705 Todds Lane, Hampton VA 23666
County: Hampton City FICE Identification: 041538
Unit ID: 458113
Telephone: (757) 826-1883 Carnegie Class: Spec-4-yr-Faith
FAX Number: (757) 826-5436 Calendar System: Semester
URL: www.ascent.edu
Established: 2004 Annual Undergrad Tuition & Fees: $8,420
Enrollment: 35 Coed
Affiliation or Control: Assemblies Of God Church IRS Status: 501(c)3
Highest Offering: Baccalaureate
Accreditation: BI

01 President .... Dr. Rob RHODEN
05 Academic Dean/Exec Vice President .... Dr. Ron DEBERRY
32 Student Affairs .... Vacant
06 Registrar/Dir Student Svcs .... Sonji THEE
08 Librarian .... Dr. Ron DEBERRY

Atlantic University (H)

215 67th Street, Virginia Beach VA 23451-8101
County: Virginia Beach Identification: 666653
Telephone: (757) 631-8101 Carnegie Class: Not Classified
FAX Number: (757) 631-8096 Calendar System: Trimester
URL: www.atlanticuniv.edu
Established: 1930 Annual Graduate Tuition & Fees: N/A
Enrollment: N/A Coed
Affiliation or Control: Independent Non-Profit IRS Status: 501(c)3
Highest Offering: Master's; No Undergraduates
Accreditation: DEAC

01 CEO .... Kevin TODESCHI
05 Vice Pres Academic Affairs .... James VAN AUKEN
84 Assoc VP Enrollment Management .... Rachel VINCITORE

Averett University (I)

420 W Main Street, Danville VA 24541-3692
County: Independent City FICE Identification: 003702
Unit ID: 231420
Telephone: (434) 791-5600 Carnegie Class: Bac-Diverse
FAX Number: (434) 791-7181 Calendar System: Semester
URL: www.averett.edu
Established: 1859 Annual Undergrad Tuition & Fees: $36,670
Enrollment: 887 Coed
Affiliation or Control: Independent Non-Profit IRS Status: 501(c)3
Highest Offering: Master's
Accreditation: SC, NURSE

01 President .... Dr. Tiffany M. FRANKS
111 Asst to Pres for External Relations .... Mr. Charles S. HARRIS
05 Vice Pres for Academic Affairs .... Dr. Timothy FULOP
10 Vice President Business & Finance .... Mr. Don AUNGST
30 Vice Pres for Philanthropy .... Ms. Melissa WOHLSTEIN
15 Director of Human Resources .... Mrs. Kathie TUNE
84 Vice Pres Enrollment Management .... Ms. Stacy GATO
37 Director Student Financial Services .... Mr. Carl BRADSHER
21 Controller .... Ms. Lisa STEWART
08 Director of Library .... Ms. Pam MCKIRDY
36 Director of Career Development .... Ms. Angie MCADAMS
06 Registrar .... Mrs. Janet ROBERSON
26 Dir of Marketing/Communications .... Ms. Cassie JONES
29 Director Alumni Relations .... Mr. Dan HAYES
09 Dir Institutional Research/Effect .... Ms. Dana MEHALKO
07 Assoc VP of Admissions .... Mr. Joel NESTER
18 Chief Facilities/Physical Plant .... Mr. Bruce DEVLIN
32 VP of Student Engagement .... Dr. Venita MITCHELL
38 Director of Student Counseling .... Dr. Jennifer WAGSTAFF
04 Exec Assistant to the President .... Ms. Cyndie BASINGER
102 Dir Dev/Corporations & Foundations .... Ms. Emma SELLERS
104 Director Study Abroad .... Dr. Catherine CLARK
13 Chief Information Tech Officer .... Mr. Michael BOEHM
19 Chief of Campus Safety & Security .... Mr. Bruce DEVLIN
41 VP Operations/Athletic Director .... Ms. Meg STEVENS

Bluefield College (J)

3000 College Avenue, Bluefield VA 24605-1799
County: Tazewell FICE Identification: 003703
Unit ID: 231554
Telephone: (276) 326-3682 Carnegie Class: Bac-Diverse
FAX Number: (276) 326-4288 Calendar System: Semester
URL: www.bluefield.edu
Established: 1922 Annual Undergrad Tuition & Fees: $27,570
Enrollment: 965 Coed
Affiliation or Control: Baptist IRS Status: 501(c)3
Highest Offering: Master's
Accreditation: SC, CAEPT, NURSE

01 President .... Dr. David W. OLIVE
04 Assistant to the President .... Mrs. Jordan P. DILLON
05 Provost .... Dr. Marshall FLOWERS
10 VP Finance/Administration .... Mrs. Ruth BLANKENSHIP
111 VP of Advancement/Alumni .... Mr. Josh CLINE
06 Registrar .... Ms. Jennifer LAMB
08 Co-Director of Library Services .... Ms. Paula BEASLEY
08 Co-Director of Library Services .... Mr. Werner LIND
07 VP of Admissions & Student Devel .... Dr. Joshua ARNOLD
110 Associate VP of Advancement .... Mr. Jacob KEY
88 Dean of Registration Services .... Dr. Paul LEMON
09 Dean Inst Effectiveness & Research .... Dr. Lewis BROGDON
37 Director of Financial Aid .... Mrs. Cary WRIGHT
42 Campus Minister .... Mr. Robbie GAINES
41 VP of Intercollegiate Athletics .... Mrs. Tonia WALKER
40 Campus Store Manager .... Mrs. Kelley LAMBERT
18 Director of Maintenance .... Vacant
19 Coordinator of Campus Safety .... Mr. Gary RUTH
28 Coordinator of Care & Belonging .... Mrs. Sherelle MORGAN
15 Human Resources Director .... Mrs. Judy PEDNEAU
13 Chief Info Technology Officer .... Mr. Chip LAMBERT
53 Dean School of Education .... Dr. Tom BREWSTER
07 Director of Admissions .... Mr. Matthew HAMILTON
106 Exec VP of Online Education .... Dr. Patricia NEELY
26 Director Marketing/Public Relations .... Mrs. Rebecca KASEY
39 Dir Resident Life/Student Housing .... Mrs. Jessica SMITH
112 Dir Planned Giving/Major Gifts .... Mr. Vincent KEENE
07 Associate Director of Admissions .... Mr. Scott POLHAMUS
88 Director Center of Worship Arts .... Dr. David PEDDE
88 Director of Spiritual Formation .... Dr. Henry CLARY

Bon Secours Memorial College of Nursing (K)

8550 Magellan Parkway, Ste 1100, Richmond VA 23227
County: Henrico FICE Identification: 010043
Unit ID: 233356
Telephone: (804) 627-5300 Carnegie Class: Spec-4-yr-Other Health
FAX Number: (804) 627-5330 Calendar System: Semester
URL: www.bsmcon.edu
Established: 1961 Annual Undergrad Tuition & Fees: N/A
Enrollment: 456 Coed
Affiliation or Control: Independent Non-Profit IRS Status: 501(c)3
Highest Offering: Baccalaureate
Accreditation: ABHES, NURSE

05 Vice Pres Academic Affairs/Provost .... Dr. Melanie H. GREEN
66 Dean of Nursing .... Dr. Barbara C. SORBELLO
11 Dean of Administration .... Dr. Benji DJEUKENG
32 Dean of Student Services .... Ms. Leslie WINSTON
88 Dean of Clinical Simulation Center .... Ms. Holly PUGH
10 Dean of Finance .... Ms. Amy POZZA
88 Associate Dean of Nursing .... Dr. Chris-Tenna M. PERKINS
32 Associate Dean of Student Services .... Ms. Carrie NEWCOMB
06 Registrar Specialist .... Mr. Shawn RUPPERT
08 Librarian .... Ms. Tina METZGER
29 Director Alumni Relations .... Ms. Jennifer GOINS
36 Director of Student Success .... Ms. Lydia LISNER
37 Director Student Financial Aid .... Ms. Kelley FLORIAN

Bridgewater College (L)

402 E College Street, Bridgewater VA 22812-1599
County: Rockingham FICE Identification: 003704
Unit ID: 231581
Telephone: (540) 828-8000 Carnegie Class: Bac-A&S
FAX Number: (540) 828-5479 Calendar System: Semester
URL: www.bridgewater.edu
Established: 1880 Annual Undergrad Tuition & Fees: $37,720
Enrollment: 1,597 Coed
Affiliation or Control: Church Of The Brethren IRS Status: 501(c)3
Highest Offering: Master's
Accreditation: SC, CAATE, CAEP

01 President ...Dr. David W. BUSHMAN
117 Vice Pres Risk Mgmt/Compliance ... Mr. Roy W. FERGUSON, JR.
05 Provost/EVP for Academic Affairs ...Dr. Leona SEVICK
10 Vice Pres for Finance & Treasurer ...Vacant
111 VP for Institutional Advancement ...Dr. Maureen SILVA
26 Assoc VP Marketing & Communications ...Ms. Abbie PARKHURST
13 AVP for IT & CIO ...Ms. Kristy K. RHEA
84 Vice President for Enrollment Mgmt ...Mr. Michael A. POST
18 Director of Sustainability ...Mr. Teshome H. MOLALENGE
40 Bookstore Manager ...Ms. Sarah LANDIS
20 Associate Dean of Academic Affairs ...Dr. Robert HAMMILL
32 VP for Student Life/Dean of Student ...Dr. Leslie FRERE
36 Director of Career Services ...Ms. Sherry TALBOTT
121 Director of Academic Support Svcs ...Vacant
42 Chaplain ...Rev. Robert R. MILLER
07 Director of Admissions ...Mr. Jarret L. SMITH
37 Director of Financial Aid ...Mr. Scott D. MORRISON
113 Director of Finance & Budget ...Ms. Penny E. REARDON
41 Director of Athletics ...Mr. Curtis L. KENDALL
38 Director of Counseling Services ...Dr. J. N. RITTENHOUSE
29 Dir of Alumni Rels & Annual Giving ...Mr. Colby HORNE
09 Director of Institutional Research ...Ms. Dawn S. DALBOW
15 Director of Human Resources ...Mrs. Kimberly P. HARPER
08 Library Director ...Mr. Andrew L. PEARSON
06 Registrar ...Ms. Cynthia K. HOWDYSHELL
21 Controller ...Mr. Eric BLACK
27 Editor/Dir of Media Relations ...Ms. Jessica E. LUCK
18 Director of Facilities ...Mr. Reggie SLAUGHTER
19 Campus Police Chief ...Mr. Milton S. FRANKLIN
23 Director of Student Health Services ...Ms. Pamela GIPSON
28 Assoc Dean of Stdnts Diversity/Incl ...Dr. Manuela GABRIEL
109 Director of Dining Services ...Ms. Geordon DUNCAN
04 Administrative Asst to President ...Mrs. Elaine C. DELLINGER
39 Director Student Housing ...Mrs. Alexandra C. JOHNSON
104 Director International Education ...Mrs. Anne MARSH
30 Director of Development ...Ms. Meg RINER

Bryant & Stratton College (A)

8141 Hull Street Road, North Chesterfield VA 23235-6411
Telephone: (804) 745-2444 Identification: 666496
Accreditation: &M, ADNUR, MAC, PNUR

† Regional accreditation is carried under the parent institution (corporate office) in Buffalo, NY.

Bryant & Stratton College (B)

301 Centre Pointe Drive, Virginia Beach VA 23462-4417
Telephone: (757) 499-7900 FICE Identification: 010061
Accreditation: &M, ADNUR, MAC

† Regional accreditation is carried under the parent institution (corporate office) in Buffalo, NY.

California University of Management and Sciences Virginia (C)

12801 Fair Lakes Pkwy., Fairfax VA 22033
Telephone: (703) 663-8088 Identification: 666734
Accreditation: ACICS

† Branch campus of California University of Management and Sciences, Anaheim, CA.

Centra College (D)

905 Lakeside Drive, Suite A, Lynchburg VA 24501
County: Independent City FICE Identification: 021758
Unit ID: 232618
Telephone: (434) 200-3070 Carnegie Class: Spec-4-yr-Other Health
FAX Number: (434) 200-5505 Calendar System: Semester
URL: www.centracollege.edu
Established: 2011 Annual Undergrad Tuition & Fees: $12,325
Enrollment: 314 Coed
Affiliation or Control: Independent Non-Profit IRS Status: 501(c)3
Highest Offering: Baccalaureate
Accreditation: ABHES

01 Dean ...Dr. Heather GABLE
66 Academic Director ADN Program ...Dr. Holly PUCKETT
66 Academic Director PN Program ...Dr. Sarah HUFFER
108 Accreditation Specialist ...Ms. Ashley HENRY
32 Director of Student Services ...Ms. Ashley FOSTER

Centura College (E)

932 Ventures Way, Chesapeake VA 23320
Telephone: (757) 549-2121 Identification: 770608
Accreditation: ACCSC

Centura College (F)

616 Denbigh Boulevard, Newport News VA 23608
Telephone: (757) 874-2121 Identification: 770606
Accreditation: ACCSC

Centura College (G)

7020 N Military Highway, Norfolk VA 23518-4202
Telephone: (757) 853-2121 Identification: 770605
Accreditation: ACCSC, DA

Centura College (H)

7914 Midlothian Turnpike, North Chesterfield VA 23235
County: Chesterfield FICE Identification: 031264
Unit ID: 427982
Telephone: (804) 330-0111 Carnegie Class: Spec 2-yr-Health
FAX Number: (804) 330-3809 Calendar System: Semester
URL: www.centuracollege.edu
Established: 1992 Annual Undergrad Tuition & Fees: $16,637
Enrollment: 160 Coed
Affiliation or Control: Proprietary IRS Status: Proprietary
Highest Offering: Associate Degree
Accreditation: ACCSC

01 Campus Executive Director ...Robert JONES, III
05 Director of Education ...Ann TRIBBEY

Centura College (I)

2697 Dean Drive, Suite 100, Virginia Beach VA 23452-7431
County: City of Virginia Beach FICE Identification: 023344
Unit ID: 232016
Telephone: (757) 340-2121 Carnegie Class: Bac/Assoc-Mixed
FAX Number: (757) 340-9704 Calendar System: Semester
URL: www.centuracollege.edu
Established: 1969 Annual Undergrad Tuition & Fees: $16,637
Enrollment: 99 Coed
Affiliation or Control: Proprietary IRS Status: Proprietary
Highest Offering: Baccalaureate
Accreditation: ACCSC

01 Campus Executive Director ...Dennis RYAN
05 Director of Education ...Kristy HAWKINS
06 Registrar ...Crystal PAYNE
10 Bursar ...Sarah TROUT
36 Career Services Coordinator ...Brittney FULBRIGHT
08 Librarian ...Jeffery BARBOUR
07 Director of Admissions ...Malkia LYNCH

Chamberlain University-Tyson's Corner (J)

1951 Kidwell Drive, Vienna VA 22182
Telephone: (703) 416-7300 Identification: 770497
Accreditation: &HLC, NURSE

† Branch campus of Chamberlain University-Addison, Addison, IL

Chester Career College (K)

751 West Hundred Road, Chester VA 23836-2516
County: Chesterfield FICE Identification: 034095
Unit ID: 437769
Telephone: (804) 751-9191 Carnegie Class: Spec 2-yr-Health
FAX Number: (804) 751-2599 Calendar System: Semester
URL: www.chestercareercollege.edu
Established: 1997 Annual Undergrad Tuition & Fees: N/A
Enrollment: 159 Coed
Affiliation or Control: Proprietary IRS Status: Proprietary
Highest Offering: Associate Degree
Accreditation: COE

01 School Director ...Ms. Debbie HARRIS
05 Academic Dean ...Mr. Donte JOHNSON
06 Registrar ...Ms. Annette WHITE
08 Head Librarian ...Ms. Kathy PHILO
36 Director Job Placement ...Mrs. Tamara KNIGHT
37 Director Student Financial Aid ...Ms. Jennifer GLOVER

Christendom College (L)

134 Christendom Drive, Front Royal VA 22630-6534
County: Warren FICE Identification: 036653
Telephone: (540) 636-2900 Carnegie Class: Not Classified
FAX Number: (540) 636-1655 Calendar System: Semester
URL: www.christendom.edu
Established: 1977 Annual Undergrad Tuition & Fees: N/A
Enrollment: N/A Coed
Affiliation or Control: Roman Catholic IRS Status: 501(c)3
Highest Offering: Master's
Accreditation: SC

01 President ...Dr. Timothy T. O'DONNELL
03 Executive Vice President ...Mr. Mark ROHLENA
45 Vice President of Innovation ...Mr. Kenneth FERGUSON
05 Vice President Academic Affairs ...Dr. Gregory TOWNSEND
111 Vice President for Advancement ...Mr. Paul JALSEVAC
11 Vice President of Operations ...Mr. Michael S. FOECKLER
84 VP Enrollment & Student Success ...Mr. Thomas MCFADDEN
32 VP for Student Affairs ...Ms. Amanda GRAF
20 Academic Dean ...Dr. Ben REINHARD
10 Director of Finance ...Mr. Luke FIER
06 Registrar ...Mr. Walter A. JANARO
07 Director of Admissions ...Mr. Sam PHILLIPS
08 Director of Christendom Library ...Mr. Andrew V. ARMSTRONG
37 Financial Aid Officer ...Ms. Alisa L. POLK
29 Dir Alumni/Donor Relations ...Mr. Vince CRISTE
13 Director of Computer Services ...Mr. Douglas S. BRIGGS
88 Registrar/Business Officer NDGS ...Miss Olivia COLVILLE
41 Athletic Director ...Mr. Patrick QUEST
04 Exec Assistant to the President ...Mrs. Brenda SEELBACH

58 Dean of the Graduate School ...Dr. Robert J. MATAVA
26 Director Marketing & Creative Svcs ...Mr. Niall O'DONNELL
44 Director Annual Giving ...Mr. Adam WILSON

Christopher Newport University (M)

1 Avenue of the Arts, Newport News VA 23606-3072
County: Independent City FICE Identification: 003706
Unit ID: 231712
Telephone: (757) 594-7000 Carnegie Class: Masters/S
FAX Number: N/A Calendar System: Semester
URL: www.cnu.edu
Established: 1960 Annual Undergrad Tuition & Fees (In-State): $14,924
Enrollment: 4,868 Coed
Affiliation or Control: State IRS Status: 501(c)3
Highest Offering: Master's
Accreditation: SC, CAEP, MUS, SW, THEA

01 President ...Hon. Paul S. TRIBLE, JR.
100 Chief of Staff ...Mrs. Adelia P. THOMPSON
05 Provost ...Dr. David C. DOUGHTY, JR.
43 University Counsel ...Ms. Maureen MATSEN
111 Vice Pres for Univ Advancement ...Mr. Keith D. ROOTS
10 Chief Financial Officer ...Mrs. Jennifer B. LATOUR
26 Chief Communications Officer ...Mr. James HANCHETT
15 Director of Human Resources ...Ms. Ashleigh ANDREWS
04 Exec Assistant to President/Board ...Mrs. Beverley D. MUELLER
07 Dean of Admission ...Mr. Robert J. LANGE
84 VP for Enroll/Student Success ...Dr. Lisa DUNCAN RAINES
32 Vice President of Student Affairs ...Dr. Kevin M. HUGHES
49 Dean College Arts & Humanities ...Dr. Lori J. UNDERWOOD
83 Dean College of Social Sciences ...Dr. Quentin KIDD
65 Dean College Nat/Behav Science ...Dr. Nicole R. GUAJARDO
50 Dean Luter School of Business ...Dr. George H. EBBS
41 Director of Athletics ...Mr. Kyle S. MCMULLIN
21 University Comptroller ...Mrs. Diane REED
06 AVP Enrollment/University Registrar ...Mrs. Julianna M. WAIT
37 Director of Financial Aid ...Ms. Keely D. HAYNES
39 Asst Director of Housing Admin ...Mr. Andrew H. KOERNERT
09 Director of Institutional Research ...Ms. Donna A. VARNER
13 Chief Information Officer ...Mr. Andrew B. CRAWFORD
114 Asst VP for Finance & Planning ...Ms. Ashleigh ANDREWS
116 Director of University Audit ...Ms. Faith D. BELOTE
108 Director of Assessment & Evaluation ...Mr. Jason C. LYONS
96 Asst Director Procurement Services ...Ms. Shannon BAILEY
08 University Librarian ...Ms. Mary K. SELLEN
19 University Police Chief ...Mr. Daniel WOLOSZYNOWSKI
18 Director of Facilities Management ...Mr. Scott GESELE
27 Exec Dir of University Events ...Mrs. Amie G. DALE
88 Exec Director of the Wason Center ...Mr. Thomas E. KRAMER
29 Sr Director for Alumni Engagement ...Mr. Baxter VENDRICK
22 Director of Title IX and EO ...Ms. Michelle L. MOODY
38 Exec Dir Counseling/Health Services ...Dr. William V. RITCHEY
36 Interim Director Career Planning ...Ms. Sarah HOBGOOD
104 Director of Study Abroad ...Mrs. Amanda K. PIERCE
11 Vice Pres for Admin & Aux Services ...Ms. Christine LEDFORD
28 Chief Diversity Officer ...Mrs. Angela N. SPRANGER

College of William & Mary (N)

PO Box 8795, Williamsburg VA 23187-8795
County: Independent City FICE Identification: 003705
Unit ID: 231624
Telephone: (757) 221-4000 Carnegie Class: DU-Higher
FAX Number: (757) 221-1259 Calendar System: Semester
URL: www.wm.edu
Established: 1693 Annual Undergrad Tuition & Fees (In-State): $23,628
Enrollment: 8,939 Coed
Affiliation or Control: State IRS Status: 501(c)3
Highest Offering: Doctorate
Accreditation: SC, CACREP, CAEP, CAEPN, IPSY, LAW

01 President ...Dr. Katherine A. ROWE
05 Provost/Chief Academic Officer ...Ms. Peggy AGOURIS
11 Chief Operating Officer ...Ms. Amy S. SEBRING
101 Secretary to the Board of Visitors ...Mr. Michael J. FOX
04 Executive Asst to President ...Ms. Cynthia A. BRAUER

Columbia College (O)

8620 Westwood Center Drive, Vienna VA 22182
County: Fairfax FICE Identification: 041273
Unit ID: 455983
Telephone: (703) 206-0508 Carnegie Class: Assoc/HT-High Trad
FAX Number: (703) 206-0488 Calendar System: Other
URL: www.ccdc.edu
Established: 1999 Annual Undergrad Tuition & Fees: N/A
Enrollment: 371 Coed
Affiliation or Control: Proprietary IRS Status: Proprietary
Highest Offering: Associate Degree
Accreditation: COE

01 President/Founder ...Dr. Richard KIM
05 Academic Director ...Dr. Hanna KANG

Culinary Institute of Virginia (P)

2428 Almeda Avenue, Ste 106, Norfolk VA 23513-2448
Telephone: (757) 858-2433 Identification: 770960
Accreditation: &SC

Divine Mercy University (A)

45154 Underwood Ln, Sterling VA 20166
County: Loudoun FICE Identification: 038724
Unit ID: 445869
Telephone: (703) 416-1441 Carnegie Class: Spec-4-yr-Other Health
FAX Number: (703) 416-8588 Calendar System: Semester
URL: www.divinemercy.edu
Established: 1998 Annual Graduate Tuition & Fees: N/A
Enrollment: 392 Coed
Affiliation or Control: Independent Non-Profit IRS Status: 501(c)3
Highest Offering: Doctorate; No Undergraduates
Accreditation: SC, CLPSY

01 President .... Fr. Charles SIKORSKY
10 Chief Financial & Admin Ofcr .... Mr. Rigg MOHLER
05 VP Academic Affairs/Digital Lrng .... Dr. Harvey PAYNE
15 VP HR & Operations .... Mr. Antonio MAZA
84 VP Enrollment and Marketing .... Mr. Tom BROOKS
108 VP Academic & Student Support/IE .... Ms. Laura TUCKER
07 Associate VP Admissions .... Ms. Tambi SPITZ-KILHEFNER
13 IT Manager .... Vacant
08 Director of Library Services .... Mr. Jeffrey ELLIOTT
06 Registrar .... Ms. Catherine ROSASCHI
37 Director of Financial Aid .... Ms. Antoinette WORMLEY
111 Director of Inst Advancement .... Mr. Thomas CRONQUIST
121 Student Success Advisor .... Ms. Merita MCCORMACK
113 Student Accounts Administrator .... Ms. Hermela WOGAYEHU
42 Director of Campus Ministry .... Mr. Tony MACDONNELL
83 MS Counseling Program Director .... Dr. John WEST
83 MS Psychology Program Director .... Dr. Julia KLAUSLI
83 PsyD Program Director .... Dr. Lisa KLEWICKI
73 Exec Dir Spiritual Direction Cert .... Ms. Maria BRACKETT

Eastern Mennonite University (B)

1200 Park Road, Harrisonburg VA 22802-2462
County: Independent City FICE Identification: 003708
Unit ID: 232043
Telephone: (540) 432-4000 Carnegie Class: Masters/M
FAX Number: (540) 432-4444 Calendar System: Semester
URL: www.emu.edu
Established: 1917 Annual Undergrad Tuition & Fees: $39,220
Enrollment: 1,394 Coed
Affiliation or Control: Mennonite Church IRS Status: 501(c)3
Highest Offering: Doctorate
Accreditation: SC, CACREP, CAEP, NURSE, PAST, SW, THEOL

01 President .... Dr. Susan SCHULTZ-HUXMAN
05 Provost .... Dr. Fred L. KNISS
20 Associate Provost .... Dr. Mary K. JENSEN
111 Vice President for Advancement .... Mr. Kirk L. SHISLER
10 Vice President of Finance .... Mr. Timothy W. STUTZMAN
09 VP of Institutional Effectiveness .... Dr. Scott BARGE
84 VP Innovation & Student Recruitment .... Vacant
04 Executive Assistant to President .... Ms. Amy HARTSELL
00 Board Chairperson .... Dr. Manuel A. NUÑEZ
79 Dean Theology/Humanities/Arts .... Dr. Suzanne K. COCKLEY
81 Dean Science/Engr/Art/Nursing .... Dr. Tara KISHBAUGH
83 Dean Social Sciences & Professions .... Dr. David BRUBAKER
32 Dean of Students .... Ms. Shannon DYCUS
06 University Registrar .... Mr. David A. DETROW
07 Director Undergraduate Admissions .... Mr. Matthew RUTH
08 Director of Libraries .... Dr. G. Marcille H. FREDERICK
37 Director of Financial Assistance .... Ms. Michele R. HENSLEY
36 Director Career Services/Testing .... Ms. Kimberly PHILLIPS
29 Director of Alumni/Parent Relations .... Mr. Jeffrey A. SHANK
41 Athletic Director .... Mr. David A. KING
42 Campus Pastor .... Mr. Brian M. BURKHOLDER
18 Director of Physical Plant .... Mr. Ed LEHMAN
15 Director Human Resources .... Ms. Marybeth SHOWALTER
38 Director Student Counseling .... Ms. Allison COLLAZO
28 Director of Diversity .... Dr. Jacqueline FONT-GUZMÁN

Eastern Virginia Career College (C)

10304 Spotsylvania Avenue, Ste. 400,
Fredericksburg VA 22408-8605
County: Spotsylvania FICE Identification: 036543
Unit ID: 441858
Telephone: (540) 373-2200 Carnegie Class: Spec 2-yr-Health
FAX Number: (540) 373-4465 Calendar System: Other
URL: www.evcc.edu
Established: 2000 Annual Undergrad Tuition & Fees: N/A
Enrollment: 190 Coed
Affiliation or Control: Proprietary IRS Status: Proprietary
Highest Offering: Associate Degree
Accreditation: COE, OTA

01 Chief Executive Officer/President .... Ms. Christine CARROLL
03 Executive Vice President .... Ms. Dorie MILFORD
05 Academic Director .... Mr. Cisco ARNOLD
07 Campus Director & Dir of Admissions .... Mr. Abdullah JOHNSON
11 Director of Operations .... Ms. Dana CORNETT
37 Director of Financial Aid .... Mr. Jameson DELOATCH
36 Director of Career Services .... Ms. Cynthia ROTHELL
06 Registrar/Bursar .... Ms. Jessica LEWIS

Eastern Virginia Medical School (D)

Box 1980, Norfolk VA 23501-1980
County: Independent City FICE Identification: 010338
Unit ID: 231970
Telephone: (757) 446-5600 Carnegie Class: Spec-4-yr-Med
FAX Number: (757) 446-5135 Calendar System: Other
URL: www.evms.edu
Established: 1973 Annual Graduate Tuition & Fees: N/A
Enrollment: 1,289 Coed
Affiliation or Control: Independent Non-Profit IRS Status: 501(c)3
Highest Offering: Doctorate; No Undergraduates
Accreditation: SC, ACATE, ARCPA, CLPSY, MED, PA, PH, SURGA

01 Interim President/Provost/Dean .... Dr. Alfred Z. ABUHAMAD
04 Sr Exec Assistant to the President .... Ms. Tracy L. MORTON
116 Director Internal Audit .... Mr. Robert B. WOOD
11 VP and Chief Operating Officer .... Mr. Brant M. COX
17 Vice Pres/Dean Sch of Health Prof .... Dr. Charles D. COMBS
88 Assoc Dean for Health Professions .... Dr. Jeffrey A. JOHNSON
10 Vice Pres Administration/Finance .... Ms. Helen HESELIUS
19 Chief of Police .... Mr. Andrew J. MITCHELL
18 Director Facilities/Physical Plant .... Mr. Doug MARTIN
28 Vice President for Diversity .... Mr. Mekbib L. GEMEDA
88 Vice Provost for Faculty Affairs .... Dr. Elza MYLONA
88 Vice Dean Clinical Affairs .... Dr. L.D BRITT
23 Interim CEO EVMS Medical Group .... Mr. Brant M. COX
05 Vice Dean Academic Affairs .... Dr. Ronald W. FLENNER
43 Vice President and General Counsel .... Ms. Stacy R. PURCELL
58 Vice Dean Grad Medical Education .... Dr. Linda R. ARCHER
09 Vice Dean for Research .... Dr. William J. WASILENKO
88 Asst Dean Hum Sub Protection/IRB .... Dr. Harry J. TILLMAN
50 Assoc Dean Business/Admin Affairs .... Mr. David E. HUBAND
84 Assoc Dean Admissions and Enroll .... Dr. Thomas D. KIMBLE
32 Assoc Dean for Student Affairs .... Dr. Allison P. KNIGHT
88 Assoc Dean Clinical Education .... Dr. Brooke HOOPER
20 Assoc Dean for Academic Affairs ... Dr. Senthil K. RAJASEKARAN
88 Assoc Dean Translational Research .... Dr. John SEMMES
88 Assoc Dean Clinical Research .... Dr. Elias SIRAJ
88 Assoc Dean Clinical Integration .... Dr. Mily KANNARKAT
08 Director of Library Services .... Ms. Kerrie S. SHAW
35 Director of Student Affairs .... Ms. Joann BAUTTI
93 Asst Dean for Diversity .... Ms. Gail C. WILLIAMS
06 Registrar .... Mr. David R. GOLAY
15 Director Human Resources .... Mr. Matthew R. SCHENK
21 Assoc VP for Financial Services .... Ms. Tammy S. CHRISMAN
37 Director Student Financial Aid .... Ms. Deborah R. BROWN
21 Director for Business Management .... Ms. Tammy A. CHRISMAN
96 Director of Materials Management .... Mr. Steven LEE
13 Chief Information Officer .... Mr. Michael J. HERZOG
26 Asst VP Marketing/Communication .... Dr. Vincent A. RHODES
29 Director Alumni Relations .... Ms. Tamara N. POULSON
30 Sr Assoc VP Development and Alumni .Ms. Connie L. MCKENZIE
88 Director of the Brock Institute .... Dr. Cynthia ROMERO
51 Director for Continuing Med Educ .... Ms. Drucie A. PAPAFIL
75 Director Occupational Health .... Ms. Heather SINGLETON
25 Director Sponsored Programs .... Ms. Yolanda F. DEMORY
88 Director Rad Safety Env Health .... Mr. Courtney A. KERR
117 Director Risk Management .... Ms. Donita M. LAMARAND
118 Director Health Analytics .... Dr. Sunita DODANI
88 Director Bus Intel & Analytics .... Mr. Stephen RICHARD

† Member of Virginia Consortium for Professional Psychology.

ECPI University (E)

5555 Greenwich Road, Virginia Beach VA 23462-6554
County: Independent City FICE Identification: 010198
Unit ID: 248934
Telephone: (757) 671-7171 Carnegie Class: Masters/M
FAX Number: (757) 671-8661 Calendar System: Semester
URL: www.ecpi.edu
Established: 1966 Annual Undergrad Tuition & Fees: $16,639
Enrollment: 14,353 Coed
Affiliation or Control: Proprietary IRS Status: Proprietary
Highest Offering: Master's
Accreditation: SC, ACFEI, MAAB, NUR, NURSE

01 President .... Mr. Mark B. DREYFUS
05 Vice President Academic Affairs .... Mr. David SHOOP
32 Vice President Student Development .... Ms. Maryse LEVY

ECPI University-Newport News (F)

1001 Omni Boulevard Suite 200,
Newport News VA 23606-4388
Telephone: (757) 873-2423 FICE Identification: 022472
Accreditation: &SC, CAHIIM, EMT, MAAB, PTAA, RAD

† Regional accreditation is carried under the parent institution, ECPI College of Technology, in Virginia Beach, VA.

ECPI University-Northern Virginia (G)

10021 Balls Ford Road, Ste 100, Manassas VA 20109
Telephone: (703) 330-5300 Identification: 770957
Accreditation: &SC, MAAB, RAD, SURTEC

ECPI University-Richmond/Innsbrook (H)

4305 Cox Road, Glen Allen VA 23060
Telephone: (804) 894-9150 Identification: 770961
Accreditation: &SC

ECPI University-Richmond/Moorefield (I)

800 Moorefield Park Drive, Richmond VA 23236
Telephone: (804) 330-5533 Identification: 770958
Accreditation: &SC, CAHIIM, MAAB

ECPI University-Roanoke (J)

5234 Airport Road, Ste 200, Roanoke VA 24012
Telephone: (540) 563-8000 Identification: 770959
Accreditation: &SC, MAAB

Edward Via College of Osteopathic Medicine (K)

2265 Kraft Drive, Blacksburg VA 24060
County: Montgomery FICE Identification: 037093
Unit ID: 442806
Telephone: (540) 231-4000 Carnegie Class: Spec-4-yr-Med
FAX Number: (540) 231-5252 Calendar System: Semester
URL: www.vcom.edu
Established: 2002 Annual Graduate Tuition & Fees: N/A
Enrollment: 2,123 Coed
Affiliation or Control: Independent Non-Profit IRS Status: 501(c)3
Highest Offering: Doctorate; No Undergraduates
Accreditation: OSTEO

01 President .... Dr. Dixie TOOKE-RAWLINS
05 Provost .... Dr. Dixie TOOKE-RAWLINS
03 Sr Vice President .... Dr. John LUCAS
10 Vice President Finance/CFO .... Mr. Chuck SWAHA
84 Vice Pres Recruitment .... Mr. William KING
26 VP Communication/Marketing ... Ms. Cindy SHEPARD RAWLINS
11 Vice President Operations .... Mr. Bill PRICE
30 VP College Development/Alumni Rel .... Mr. Thim CORVIN
46 Vice Provost for Research .... Dr. Gunnar BROLINSON
12 Dean Carolinas Campus .... Dr. Matthew CANNON
12 Dean Virginia Campus .... Dr. Jan M. WILLCOX
12 Dean Auburn Campus .... Dr. Heath PARKER
12 Dean Louisiana Campus .... Dr. Mark SANDERS
63 Dean MABS .... Dr. Brian W. HILL
100 Sr Exec Director Administration .... Ms. Patty SMITH

Emory & Henry College (L)

PO Box 947, 30461 Garnand Drive,
Emory VA 24327-0947
County: Washington FICE Identification: 003709
Unit ID: 232025
Telephone: (276) 944-4121 Carnegie Class: Bac-A&S
FAX Number: (276) 944-6934 Calendar System: Semester
URL: www.ehc.edu
Established: 1836 Annual Undergrad Tuition & Fees: $35,100
Enrollment: 1,230 Coed
Affiliation or Control: United Methodist IRS Status: 501(c)3
Highest Offering: Doctorate
Accreditation: SC, #ARCPA, CAEPT, OT, PTA

01 President .... Dr. John W. WELLS
43 VP for Admin/General Counsel .... Mr. Mark R. GRAHAM
05 Exec VP/Provost .... Dr. Michael J. PUGLISI
76 SVP/Dean School of Health Sciences .... Dr. Louise FINCHER
10 Chief Financial Officer .... Ms. Angie EDMONDSON
28 VP Diversity/Equity/Inclusion .... Mr. John HOLLOWAY
111 VP for Advancement .... Mr. Gregory C. MCMILLAN
26 VP for Enrollment/External Affairs .... Ms. Jennifer PEARCE
09 AVP Process/Effectiveness .... Mr. Gregory G. STEINER
100 Exec Dir of Strategic Initiatives .... Mr. Ryan BOWYER
41 Director of Athletics .... Ms. Anne CRUTCHFIELD
15 Director Human Resources .... Ms. Tracy PEERY
35 Dean of Students .... Ms. Tracey L. WRIGHT
121 Dean of Student Success .... Mr. Travis PROFFITT
20 Associate Provost .... Dr. Matthew FREDERICK
29 Director of Alumni Affairs .... Ms. Monica S. HOEL
37 Director of Financial Aid .... Ms. Scarlett BLEVINS
06 Registrar .... Ms. Tammy SHEETS
36 Director of Career Center .... Mr. Lee SVETE
38 Director Student Counseling .... Mr. Todd STANLEY
08 Librarian .... Ms. Ruth CASTILLO
18 Director of Facilities .... Mr. Scott E. WILLIAMS
40 Bookstore Manager .... Mr. Terry RICHARDSON
42 Chaplain .... Rev. Sharon WRIGHT
39 Director of Housing .... Ms. Samantha LOPEZ
19 Chief of Campus Police .... Mr. Scott POORE
25 Director for Research/Grants .... Ms. Bonnie BINKLEY
104 Director Study Abroad .... Dr. Celeste GAIA
105 Web Content Manager .... Ms. Rachael WILBUR
44 Director Annual Giving .... Ms. Ronan KING

Fairfax University of America (M)

4401 Village Drive, Fairfax VA 22030
County: Fairfax FICE Identification: 041440
Unit ID: 460376
Telephone: (703) 591-7042 Carnegie Class: Spec-4-yr-Other Tech
FAX Number: (703) 591-7046 Calendar System: Semester
URL: www.fxua.edu
Established: 1998 Annual Undergrad Tuition & Fees: $10,328
Enrollment: 65 Coed
Affiliation or Control: Independent Non-Profit IRS Status: 501(c)3
Highest Offering: Master's
Accreditation: ACICS

01 President .... Dr. Ahmed ALWANI
10 Chief Financial Officer .... Mr. Ron SOMERVELL

05 Executive Dean of Academic Programs ... Dr. NS HASAN
32 Chief Student Experience Officer ... Mr. Bradley DAWSON
108 Dir Institutional Effectiveness ... Dr. Kevin MARTIN
20 Director of Academic Operations ... Ms. Eve WONG
13 Dir of Information Technology ... Mr. Ben SIYUM
11 Director of Business Services ... Mr. Bayarjargal BATTULGA

Faith Bible College (A)

6330 Newtown Road, Suite 211, Norfolk VA 23502
County: Independent City | Identification: 667285
Telephone: (757) 423-2095 | Carnegie Class: Not Classified
FAX Number: (757) 222-1341 | Calendar System: Semester
URL: www.faithbiblecollege.com
Established: 1995 | Annual Undergrad Tuition & Fees: N/A
Enrollment: N/A | Coed
Affiliation or Control: Independent Non-Profit | IRS Status: 501(c)3
Highest Offering: Associate Degree
Accreditation: **BI**

05 Interim Pres/Academic Dean ... Dr. Kevin NEWMAN
26 Director Community/Church Relations ... Capt. Dale PARKER
06 Registrar ... Ms. Dawn MARTIN
10 Business Manager ... Ms. Darla BOLGER

Ferrum College (B)

PO Box 1000, 215 Ferrum Mtn Road,
Ferrum VA 24088-9001
County: Franklin | FICE Identification: 003711
Unit ID: 232089
Telephone: (540) 365-2121 | Carnegie Class: Bac-Diverse
FAX Number: (540) 365-4269 | Calendar System: Semester
URL: www.ferrum.edu
Established: 1913 | Annual Undergrad Tuition & Fees: $36,695
Enrollment: 972 | Coed
Affiliation or Control: United Methodist | IRS Status: 501(c)3
Highest Offering: Master's
Accreditation: **SC**, SW

01 President ... Dr. David L. JOHNS
05 Provost & VP for Academic Affairs ... Dr. Aime SPOSATO
10 VP for Business and Finance ... Ms. Barb D. HATCHER
111 Vice Pres Institutional Advancement ... Mr. Wilson PAINE
84 VP for Enrollment Management ... Mr. James A. PENNIX
32 Dean of Students ... Ms. Nicole LENEZ
42 Dean of Chapel ... Dr. Jan C. NICHOLSON ANGLE
101 Spec Asst to Pres/Liaison to Board ... Ms. Courtney L. BROWN
04 Exec Assistant to President ... Ms. Felicia WOODS
06 Registrar ... Vacant
07 Dean of Admissions ... Mr. Jason D. BYRD
09 Director of Inst Research ... Mrs. Ursa JOHNSON
08 Director Stanley Library ... Dr. Eric RECTOR
37 Director of Financial Aid ... Ms. Heather HOLLANDSWORTH
29 Director Alumni & Family Programs ... Mrs. Tracy S. HOLLEY
26 Director of Public Relations ... Vacant
41 Director of Athletics ... Mr. John SUTYAK
18 Director of Physical Plant ... Mr. Brad BISHOP
35 Dir Student Leadership & Engagement ... Mr. Justin MUSE
13 Dir of Network Services ... Mr. Eugene HACKER
15 Dir of Human Resources ... Mr. Chris CHANDLER
40 Bookstore Manager ... Vacant
19 Chief of Ferrum College Police Dept ... Chief J. F. OWENS
36 Dir of Career Services ... Mrs. Leslie HOLDEN
88 Director of Academic Accessibility ... Ms. Nancy S. BEACH
91 Dir Administrative Computing ... Mr. Shawn SHIRLEY
58 Dir School of Graduate/Online Stds ... Dr. Sandra VIA
49 Dean Sch Arts/Sciences & Business ... Dr. Jason POWELL
83 Dean Sch Health Prof/Social Science ... Dr. Angie DAHL

Fortis College (C)

6300 Center Drive, Building 22, Norfolk VA 23502
County: Independent City | FICE Identification: 023427
Unit ID: 233329
Telephone: (757) 499-5447 | Carnegie Class: Spec 2-yr-Health
FAX Number: N/A | Calendar System: Quarter
URL: www.fortis.edu/campuses
Established: | Annual Undergrad Tuition & Fees: $15,977
Enrollment: 454 | Coed
Affiliation or Control: Proprietary | IRS Status: Proprietary
Highest Offering: Associate Degree
Accreditation: **ABHES**

01 President ... Mr. Matthew ALBANO
05 Dean of Education ... Ms. Theresa TUTTLE

Fortis College (D)

2000 Westmoreland Street, Suite A, Richmond VA 23230
Telephone: (804) 323-1020 | Identification: 770815
Accreditation: **ABHES**, DA, SURGT

George Mason University (E)

4400 University Drive - MSN 3A1, Fairfax VA 22030-4444
County: Fairfax | FICE Identification: 003749
Unit ID: 232186
Telephone: (703) 993-1000 | Carnegie Class: DU-Highest
FAX Number: N/A | Calendar System: Semester
URL: www.gmu.edu
Established: 1957 | Annual Undergrad Tuition & Fees (In-State): $13,014
Enrollment: 38,541 | Coed
Affiliation or Control: State | IRS Status: 501(c)3
Highest Offering: Doctorate
Accreditation: **SC**, ART, CAATE, CAEP, CAEPN, CAHIIM, CAPRT, CEA, CLPSY, EXSC, HSA, IPSY, LAW, MUS, NURSE, PH, SPAA, SW

01 President ... Dr. Gregory WASHINGTON
05 Provost & Executive VP ... Dr. Mark GINSBERG
10 Senior VP of Administration/Finance ... Ms. Carol D. KISSAL
100 VP Strat Initiatives/Chief of Staff ... Mr. Kenneth WALSH
28 Int VP Compliance/Diversity/Ethics ... Dr. Dietra Y. TRENT
84 Vice Pres Enrollment Management ... Mr. David BURGE
18 Vice Pres for Facilities ... Mr. Frank STRIKE
86 VP Government & Community Relations ... Mr. Paul LIBERTY
111 VP Advancement/Alumni Rels/Fndn ... Ms. Trishana BOWDEN
13 VP Information Technology/CIO ... Mr. Kevin BOREK
32 Vice President for University Life ... Ms. Rose PASCARELL
46 Int Vice President for Research ... Ms. Aurali DADE
26 VP Communications & Marketing ... Mr. Paul ALLVIN
15 VP for Human Resources/Payroll ... Mr. Lester L. ARNOLD, SR.
43 University Counsel ... Mr. Brian WALTHER
45 Assoc VP for Business Services ... Mr. Bill DRACOS
21 Vice President for Finance ... Ms. Deb DICKENSON
20 Exec Dir Academic Innovation ... Dr. Charles KREITZER
20 Assoc Prov Acad Initiatives & Svcs ... Dr. Janette MUIR
103 AVP Innovation/Economic Development ... Ms. Paula SORRELL
88 Assoc Prov for Academic Admin ... Ms. Renate H. GUILFORD
88 Assoc Prov for a Sustainable Earth ... Dr. Cody EDWARDS
35 Exec Dir Office Student Involvement ... Ms. Lauren LONG
35 Assoc Vice Pres University Life ... Ms. Pamela L. PATTERSON
06 University Registrar ... Mr. Doug MCKENNA
37 Director Student Financial Aid ... Dr. Sandra TARBOX
36 Exec Dir Univ Career Services ... Ms. Saskia CAMPBELL
08 Dean of Libraries/Univ Librarian ... Mr. John G. ZENELIS
23 Exec Dir Student Health Svcs ... Dr. Lisa PARK
29 Assoc VP Alumni Relations ... Vacant
41 Asst VP/Dir Intercol Athletics ... Mr. Brad EDWARDS
108 Assoc Prov Inst Effectiveness/Plng ... Ms. Gesele DURHAM
19 Chief of Police ... Mr. Carl ROWAN
79 Dean Col Humanities/Social Sciences ... Ms. Ann ARDIS
61 Dean School of Law ... Dr. Henry BUTLER
80 Dean Schar School of Policy & Govt ... Dr. Mark ROZELL
50 Dean School of Business ... Dr. Maury PEIPERL
53 Int Dean Col of Educ & Human Dev ... Dr. Robert BAKER
54 Dean Volgenau School of Engineering ... Dr. Kenneth BALL
66 Dean College of Health & Human Svcs ... Dr. Germaine LOUIS
81 Assoc Dean College of Science ... Mr. Ali ANDALIBI
88 Dean Sch Conflict Analysis & Resol ... Dr. Alpaslan OZERDEM
88 Dean CVPA/Exec Dir HPAC ... Dr. Rick DAVIS
38 Assoc Dean/Chief Mental Health Ofcr ... Dr. Rachel WERNICKE
09 Asst Provost Institutional Research ... Ms. Angela DETLEV
96 Chief Procurement Officer ... Mr. Cliff SHORE
04 Director of Presidential Admin ... Ms. Sharon CULLEN
101 Exec Coord to Board of Visitors ... Ms. Sarah HANBURY
21 Assoc Director Finance & Business ... Ms. Maria FIORE
25 Assoc VP Research Services ... Mr. Mike LASKOFSKI
44 Dir Annual Giving/Ofc Advancement ... Mr. William AYREA
102 Dir Corporate/Foundation Relations ... Ms. Mercedes PRICE
27 Assoc Vice President for Marketing ... Mr. Eric WOODALL
106 Director Digital Learning ... Dr. Faisal MAHMUD
90 Exec Dir Learning Support Svcs ... Ms. Joy TAYLOR
07 Assoc Dean of Admissions ... Mr. Darren TROXLER
88 Director of Strategic Real Estate ... Mr. Steve GOLDIN
114 AVP Strategic Planning & Budgeting ... Ms. Rene STEWART O'NEAL

Hampden-Sydney College (F)

PO Box 128, Hampden-Sydney VA 23943-0667
County: Prince Edward | FICE Identification: 003713
Unit ID: 232256
Telephone: (434) 223-6000 | Carnegie Class: Bac-A&S
FAX Number: N/A | Calendar System: Semester
URL: www.hsc.edu
Established: 1775 | Annual Undergrad Tuition & Fees: $48,110
Enrollment: 881 | Male
Affiliation or Control: Presbyterian Church (U.S.A.) | IRS Status: 501(c)3
Highest Offering: Baccalaureate
Accreditation: **SC**

01 President ... Dr. John L. STIMPERT
05 Dean of the Faculty ... Dr. Walter M. MCDERMOTT
10 VP Business Affairs & Finance ... Mr. P. Kenneth COPELAND, JR.
111 VP for College Advancement ... Ms. Heather L. KRAJEWSKI
84 VP for Enrollment ... Mr. Jeffery S. NORRIS
32 Dean of Students ... Dr. Richard M. PANTELE
121 Director for Academic Success ... Ms. Lisa A. BURNS
41 Director of Athletics ... Mr. Chad E. EISELE
08 Director of the Library & Computing ... Ms. Shaunna E. HUNTER-MCKINNEY
06 Registrar ... Ms. Dawn L. CONGLETON
37 Director of Financial Aid ... Ms. Zita M. BARREE
29 Director of Alumni Relations ... Mr. Cameron MARSHALL
18 Director of Physical Plant ... Mr. Kevin MILLER
36 Dir Career Ed/Vocational Reflection ... Ms. Stephanie N. JOYNES
15 Director of Human Resources ... Ms. Sue V. CARTER
19 Dir Public Safety/Chief of Police ... Mr. T. Mark FOWLER
40 Bookstore Manager ... Ms. Kimberly S. MICHAUX
09 Assoc Dean Inst Effectiveness ... Dr. Christine C. ROSS
26 Director Communications & Marketing ... Mr. Gordon W. NEAL
21 Controller ... Ms. Cheryl HILL
35 Dir of Student Affairs Operations ... Ms. Sandy P. COOKE
28 Dean of Inclusive Excellence ... Mr. John HOLLEMON
25 Grant Administrator ... Ms. Sachiyo DINMORE

104 Dir Global Education & Study Abroad ... Dr. Daniella WIDDOWS
04 Executiv Assistant to the President ... Ms. Angela T. CLARK
38 Director of Counseling Center ... Vacant
07 Director of Admissions ... Mr. Jason FERGUSON

Hampton University (G)

200 William R. Harvey Way, Hampton VA 23668
County: Independent City | FICE Identification: 003714
Unit ID: 232265
Telephone: (757) 727-5000 | Carnegie Class: DU-Higher
FAX Number: (757) 727-5085 | Calendar System: Semester
URL: www.hamptonu.edu
Established: 1868 | Annual Undergrad Tuition & Fees: $29,312
Enrollment: 3,516 | Coed
Affiliation or Control: Independent Non-Profit | IRS Status: 501(c)3
Highest Offering: Doctorate
Accreditation: **SC**, AAB, CACREP, CAEP, CAEPN, IACBE, #JOUR, MUS, NURSE, PTA, SP

01 President ... Dr. William R. HARVEY
05 Chancellor & Provost ... Dr. JoAnn W. HAYSBERT
10 Vice Pres Business Affs/Treasurer ... Mrs. Doretha J. SPELLS
11 Vice Pres for Administrative Svcs ... Dr. Barbara L. INMAN
43 Vice President/General Counsel ... Atty. Faye HARDY-LUCAS
30 Vice Pres for Development ... Mrs. Evelyn GRAHAM
100 Vice President & Chief of Staff ... Dr. Charrita D. QUIMBY
21 Asst VP Business Affs/Comptroller ... Mrs. Denise NICHOLS
20 Asst Provost Academic Affairs ... Dr. Pollie MURPHY
26 Asst VP for Marketing ... Ms. B. DaVida PLUMMER
45 Asst Prov Research & Grantsmanship ... Dr. Michelle PENN-MARSHALL
32 Dean of Students ... Mr. Aleczander WHITFIELD
39 Int Dir of Residential Life/Housing ... Mr. Andrew MORRISON
07 Dean of Admissions ... Mrs. Angela BOYD
06 Registrar ... Mrs. Jorsene COOPER
36 Dir Career Counsel/Planning Ctr ... Mrs. Bessie WILLIS
38 Director Counseling Center ... Dr. Kristie NORWOOD
08 Administrator University Libraries ... Mrs. Tina ROLLINS
29 Director of Alumni Affairs ... Ms. Brint MARTIN
15 Director of Human Resources ... Ms. Rikki THOMAS
37 Financial Aid Officer ... Mr. Martin MILES
27 Director of University Relations ... Mr. Matthew WHITE
09 Director Institutional Research ... Dr. Michelle CLAWSON
42 University Chaplain ... Dr. Debra L. HAGGINS
18 Director Buildings & Grounds ... Mr. Randall HARDY
87 Director of Summer Sessions ... Dr. Pollie MURPHY
19 Chief of Campus Police ... Mr. David GLOVER
86 Director Government Relations ... Mr. Wilbert L. THOMAS
96 Asst Director of Purchasing ... Ms. Debra HARDEN
40 University Bookstore Manager ... Ms. Patricia KNIGHT
53 Dean School of Liberal Arts & Educ . Dr. Linda MALONE-COLON
66 Dean School of Nursing ... Dr. Shevallanie LOTT
50 Interim Dean School of Business ... Dr. Sylvia ROSE
54 Dean Sch of Science/Engineering ... Dr. Joyce SHIRAZI
67 Dean School of Pharmacy ... Dr. Anand IYER
58 Dean the Graduate College ... Dr. Michelle PENN-MARSHALL
60 Dean Scripps Howard Sch Journ/Comm ... Ms. DaVida PLUMMER
81 Int Dean School of Science ... Dr. Isi ERO-TOLLIVER

Hollins University (H)

PO Box 9707, Roanoke VA 24020-1688
County: Roanoke | FICE Identification: 003715
Unit ID: 232308
Telephone: (540) 362-6000 | Carnegie Class: Bac-A&S
FAX Number: (540) 362-6642 | Calendar System: 4/1/4
URL: www.hollins.edu
Established: 1842 | Annual Undergrad Tuition & Fees: $40,110
Enrollment: 795 | Female
Affiliation or Control: Independent Non-Profit | IRS Status: 501(c)3
Highest Offering: Master's
Accreditation: **SC**, CAEPT

01 President ... Dr. Mary D. HINTON
10 Executive VP and COO ... Ms. Kerry EDMONDS
05 Provost ... Dr. Laura MCLARY
111 Vice Pres for External Relations ... Ms. Suzy MINK
84 Vice Pres Enrollment and Marketing ... Ms. Ashley BROWNING
20 Chair of the Faculty ... Ms. Judith CLINE
32 Dean of Students ... Ms. Patty O'TOOLE
58 VP for Graduate Programs ... Dr. Steven E. LAYMON
28 Associate Dean Intercultural Pgms ... Ms. Jeri L. SUAREZ
04 Executive Assistant to President ... Ms. Sheyonn L. BAKER
06 Registrar ... Ms. Patricia BROKKEN
08 Director of the Library ... Mr. Luke VILELLE
15 Director of Human Resources ... Ms. Alicia GODZWA
26 Director of Public Relations ... Mr. Jeff HODGES
29 Director of Alumnae Relations ... Ms. Lauren WALKER
36 Director Career Dev & Life Design ... Ms. Christine HARRIGER
37 Director Financial Aid ... Ms. Mary Jean CORRISS
41 Director of Athletics ... Ms. Myra SIMS
18 Director Plant Operations/Services ... Ms. Mae RAMSEY
104 Director International Programs ... Ms. Ramona R. KIRSCH
13 Chief Info Officer ... Mr. Brad OECHSLIN
19 Director Security/Safety ... Mr. David CARLSON
39 Dir Housing & Residential Life ... Ms. Sarah LIKINS
09 Director of Institutional Research ... Dr. Maliha ZAMAN
28 VP for Diversity ... Dr. Nakeshia WILLIAMS

IGlobal University (A)

8133 Leesburg Pike, #230, Vienna VA 22182
County: Fairfax — Identification: 667105
Unit ID: 483780
Telephone: (703) 941-2020 — Carnegie Class: Spec-4-yr-Bus
FAX Number: (703) 941-2025 — Calendar System: Quarter
URL: www.igu.edu
Established: 2008 — Annual Undergrad Tuition & Fees: $14,000
Enrollment: 254 — Coed
Affiliation or Control: Proprietary — IRS Status: Proprietary
Highest Offering: Master's
Accreditation: ACCSC

01 President & CEO .... Dr. David Y. SOHN
05 Director of Education .... Dr. Zafer PIRIM

Ivy Christian College (B)

9401 Mathy Drive, Suite 380, Fairfax VA 22031
County: Fairfax — Identification: 667213
Telephone: (703) 425-4143 — Carnegie Class: Not Classified
FAX Number: (703) 425-4148 — Calendar System: Quarter
URL: www.ivy.edu
Established: 2006 — Annual Undergrad Tuition & Fees: N/A
Enrollment: N/A — Coed
Affiliation or Control: Independent Non-Profit — IRS Status: 501(c)3
Highest Offering: Baccalaureate
Accreditation: TRACS

01 President .... Dr. David Y. PAK
05 Academic Dean .... Mr. Paul CLAY-ROOLS
11 Chief Operating Officer .... Mr. John YOO
32 Director of Student Affairs .... Mr. Byung KIM
07 Director of Admissions .... Ms. Nicole ARDELEAN
10 Director of Finance & Registrar .... Yoomin KIM
09 Librarian .... Mr. Steven KROMPF

James Madison University (C)

800 S Main Street, Harrisonburg VA 22807-0001
County: Independent City — FICE Identification: 003721
Unit ID: 232423
Telephone: (540) 568-6211 — Carnegie Class: Masters/L
FAX Number: N/A — Calendar System: Semester
URL: www.jmu.edu
Established: 1908 — Annual Undergrad Tuition & Fees (In-State): $12,330
Enrollment: 21,594 — Coed
Affiliation or Control: State — IRS Status: 501(c)3
Highest Offering: Doctorate
Accreditation: SC, ARCPA, ART, AUD, CAATE, CACREP, CAEP, CAEPN, DANCE, DIETD, IPSY, MUS, NURSE, OT, PSPSY, SP, SPAA, SW, THEA

01 President .... Mr. Jonathan R. ALGER
05 Provost/Senior VP Academic Affairs .... Dr. Heather COLTMAN
10 Sr Vice Pres Administration/Finance .... Mr. Charles W. KING
32 VP Student Affairs .... Dr. Timothy M. MILLER
111 Vice Pres University Advancement .... Dr. Nick LANGRIDGE
84 VP Access and Enrollment Mgmt .... Ms. Donna L. HARPER
13 AVP Information Technology .... Vacant
81 Interim Dean College Science/Math .... Dr. Samantha PRINS
49 Dean College Arts/Letters .... Dr. Robert AGUIRRE
76 Dean Col of Health & Behav Studies .... Dr. Sharon LOVELL
50 Dean College of Business .... Dr. Michael BUSING
57 Dean College Visual Performing Arts .... Mr. Ruben GRACIANI
53 Dean College of Education .... Dr. Mark L'ESPERANCE
72 Dean College of Int Science & Engr .... Dr. Robert KOLVOORD
58 Dean Graduate School .... Dr. Linda THOMAS
97 Vice Provost University Programs .... Dr. Linda C. HALPERN
08 Dean Libraries .... Dr. Bethany NOWVISKIE
43 University Counsel .... Mr. Jack KNIGHT
114 Asst Vice Pres Budget Management .... Ms. Diane L. STAMP
07 Dean of Admissions .... Mr. Michael D. WALSH
37 Dir Financial Aid & Scholarships .... Mr. Brad BARNETT
15 Director Human Resources .... Mr. Chuck FLICK
09 Director Institutional Research .... Dr. Christopher D. OREM
41 Director of Athletics .... Mr. Jeffrey T. BOURNE
26 Dir Comm & Univ Spokesperson .... Ms. Mary-Hope VASS
06 University Registrar .... Ms. Michele M. WHITE
19 Interim Chief of Police .... Mr. Kevin LANOUE
22 Dir of EEO .... Dr. Art DEAN
29 Director Alumni Relations .... Ms. Carrie COMBS
110 Sr Dir of Advancement/Marketing .... Mr. David R. TAYLOR
04 Admin Assistant to the President .... Ms. Anita C. WESTFALL
102 CEO JMU Foundation .... Mr. Warren K. COLEMAN
104 Director Study Abroad .... Mr. Dietrich MAUNE
25 Int Dir Sponsored Programs .... Ms. Tamara T. HATCH
39 Director Residence Life .... Mr. Kevin M. MEANEY
44 Director of Annual Giving .... Ms. Gretchen H. ARMENTROUT
86 Director Government Relations .... Ms. Caitlyn READ
96 Director of Procurement .... Ms. Catherine B. WEAVER
100 Executive Advisor to President .... Dr. Mike DAVIS
28 AVP Diversity/Equity & Inclusion .... Dr. Brent LEWIS

The John Leland Center for Theological Studies (D)

1306 N Highland Street, Arlington VA 22201
County: Arlington — Identification: 666340
Telephone: (703) 812-4757 — Carnegie Class: Not Classified
FAX Number: (703) 812-4764 — Calendar System: Other
URL: www.leland.edu
Established: 1998 — Annual Graduate Tuition & Fees: N/A
Enrollment: N/A — Coed
Affiliation or Control: Baptist — IRS Status: 501(c)3
Highest Offering: Master's; No Undergraduates
Accreditation: THEOL

01 President .... Dr. Bill SMITH
05 Academic Dean .... Dr. John LEE
04 Executive Assistant .... Ms. Abbie TOLBERT
08 Librarian .... Ms. Monica LEAK
06 Registrar .... Ms. Belinda BARNETT
84 Director of Enrollment .... Ms. Mindy STEWART
10 Director of Finance .... Mr. Mel HARRIS

Liberty University (E)

1971 University Boulevard, Lynchburg VA 24515
County: Independent City — FICE Identification: 020530
Unit ID: 232557
Telephone: (434) 582-2000 — Carnegie Class: DU-Mod
FAX Number: N/A — Calendar System: Semester
URL: www.liberty.edu
Established: 1971 — Annual Undergrad Tuition & Fees: $21,587
Enrollment: 93,349 — Coed
Affiliation or Control: Other — IRS Status: 501(c)3
Highest Offering: Doctorate
Accreditation: SC, AAB, ACBSP, CAATE, CACREP, CAEPN, COARC, COSMA, EXSC, FEPAC, LAW, MUS, NURSE, OSTEO, SW, THEOL

01 President .... Dr. Jerry PREVO
05 Provost .... Dr. Scott HICKS
106 Provost for Online Programs .... Mr. Shawn D. AKERS
20 Vice Provost .... Dr. Ronald E. HAWKINS
32 Sr Vice President Student Affairs .... Dr. Mark L. HINE
10 Chief Financial Officer .... Dr. Robert L. RITZ
84 Exec VP of Enrollment Mgmt & Mktg .... Mr. Ron KENNEDY
15 Exec VP Human Resources .... Mrs. Laura J. WALLACE
115 Sr VP Finance & Investment Mgmt .... Mr. Don MOON
42 Campus Pastor .... Mr. Jonathan FALWELL
37 VP of Student Financial Services .... Mrs. Ashley REICH
26 Sr VP of University Communications .... Mr. Scott LAMB
27 VP of Marketing .... Ms. Kristin CONRAD
108 AVP for Institutional Effectiveness .... Mr. H. Skip KASTROLL
13 Chief Information Officer .... Mr. John GAUGER
06 University Registrar .... Mr. Jason BYRD
43 General Counsel .... Mr. David M. CORRY
08 Dean Jerry Falwell Library .... Mrs. Angela RICE
80 Dean School of Govt .... Mr. Robert HURT
18 Sr VP Campus Facilities & Transport .... Mr. Charles SPENCE
88 VP of Major Construction .... Mr. Daniel DETER
30 VP of Development .... Mr. Jim NICHOLS
41 Director of Athletics .... Mr. Ian MCCAW
49 Dean College of Arts & Sciences .... Dr. Roger D. SCHULTZ
83 Dean School of Behavioral Sciences .... Dr. Kenyon KNAPP
50 Dean School of Business .... Dr. Dave BRAT
57 Dean School of Comm & the Arts .... Dr. Scott HAYES
97 Dean CASAS .... Dr. Brian YATES
73 Interim Dean School of Divinity .... Dr. Troy TEMPLE
53 Interim Dean School of Education .... Dr. Deanna KEITH
88 VP of Campus Recreation .... Mr. Chris MISIANO
88 VP Designated Off Campus Facilities .... Mr. Scott STARNES
19 Chief of Police LUPD .... Col. Richard HINKLEY
54 Dean School of Engineering .... Dr. Mark HORSTEMEYER
97 Dean College of General Studies .... Dr. Ester WARREN
28 VP for Equity & Inclusion/CDO .... Mr. Greg DOWELL
61 Dean School of Law .... Dr. Keith FAULKNER
88 Dean School of Aeronautics .... Dr. Rick ROOF
88 Dir Center for Teaching Excellence .... Dr. Shawn BIELICKI
58 Admin Dean for Grad Education .... Dr. David CALLAND
76 Dean School of Health Sciences .... Dr. Ralph LINSTRA
63 Dean College of Osteopathic Med .... Dr. Peter BELL
64 Interim Dean School of Music .... Dr. Stephen MULLER
35 Assoc Dean of Students .... Dr. Mark HYDE
66 Dean School of Nursing .... Dr. Shanna AKERS
04 Exec Assistant to the President .... Ms. Amanda STANLEY
07 Director of UG Admissions .... Mr. Chris JONES
29 Sr Alumni Relations Officer .... Mr. Jeremy OWEN
36 Executive Director Career Services .... Mr. Richard DIDDAMS
38 Exec Director Student Counseling .... Mr. Michael KUNZINGER
96 Chief Procurement Administrator .... Mr. Americus GILL
09 Director of Institutional Research .... Ms. Sue MISJUNS

Longwood University (F)

201 High Street, Farmville VA 23909-1801
County: Prince Edward — FICE Identification: 003719
Unit ID: 232566
Telephone: (434) 395-2000 — Carnegie Class: Masters/M
FAX Number: (434) 395-2635 — Calendar System: Semester
URL: www.longwood.edu
Established: 1839 — Annual Undergrad Tuition & Fees (In-State): $13,910
Enrollment: 4,841 — Coed
Affiliation or Control: State — IRS Status: 501(c)3
Highest Offering: Master's
Accreditation: SC, CAATE, CACREP, CAEP, CAEPN, CAPRT, EXSC, MUS, NURSE, SP, SW, THEA

01 President .... Mr. W. Taylor REVELEY, IV
05 Provost/Vice Pres Academic Affairs .... Dr. Larissa SMITH
10 Vice Pres Administration & Finance .... Ms. Louise WALLER
32 Vice President for Student Affairs .... Dr. Tim J. PIERSON
111 VP for Institutional Advancement .... Ms. Courtney HODGES
45 VP for Strategic Operations .... Ms. Victoria KINDON
13 Chief Information Officer .... Ms. Victoria KINDON
84 Assoc VP Enrollment Management .... Dr. Jennifer K. GREEN
26 AVP Marketing/Communications/Engage .... Mr. Dave HOOPER
09 Director Assessment/Inst Research .... Dr. David LEHR
06 Registrar .... Mrs. Susan HINES
07 Asst VP Admissions & Retention .... Dr. Emily HEADY
08 Dean of Library .... Mr. Brent ROBERTS
28 Director Multicultural Affairs .... Mr. Jonathan E. PAGE
38 Director Student Counseling .... Dr. Maureen J. WALLS-MCKAY
121 Assoc Dir Campus Career Engagement .... Ms. Megan MILLER
37 Assoc Director Financial Aid .... Ms. Sharon DRINKARD
15 Assoc VP Human Resources .... Ms. Lisa MOONEY
100 Chief of Staff/Vice President .... Mr. Justin POPE
41 Director of Athletics .... Ms. Michelle MEADOWS

Mary Baldwin University (G)

318 Prospect Street, Staunton VA 24401
County: Augusta — FICE Identification: 003723
Unit ID: 232672
Telephone: (540) 887-7000 — Carnegie Class: DU-Mod
FAX Number: (540) 886-5561 — Calendar System: Other
URL: www.marybaldwin.edu
Established: 1842 — Annual Undergrad Tuition & Fees: $31,110
Enrollment: 2,110 — Coed
Affiliation or Control: Presbyterian Church (U.S.A.) — IRS Status: 501(c)3
Highest Offering: Doctorate
Accreditation: SC, ARCPA, CAEPT, NURSE, OT, PTA, SW

01 President .... Dr. Pamela FOX
05 Interim Provost/Chief Academic Ofcr .... Dr. Tynisha WILLINGHAM
10 VP of Administration/CFO/Treasurer .... Mr. Sean S. SIMPLICIO
84 VP Enrollment Mgmt .... Mr. Matt MUNSEY
111 VP University Advancement .... Mr. Charles E. DAVIS, III
26 Assoc VP of Marketing .... Ms. Beth REABOLD
76 VP MDCHS/Chief Health Officer .... Dr. Deb GREUBEL
32 VP for Student Engagement .... Dr. Ernest E. JEFFRIES
28 Chief Diversity Officer .... Rev. Andrea CORNELL-SCOTT
88 Commandant VWIL/Sr Advisor to Pres .... BGen. Teresa A. DJURIC
09 Institutional Report/Research Coord .... Vacant
13 Dir of Enterprise Systems Mgmt .... Mr. Lee REID
06 Registrar .... Ms. Sheila F. TOLLEY
08 Director of Library .... Ms. Carol CREAGER
49 Dean of College of Arts & Sciences .... Dr. Martha J. WALKER
50 Dean of Col Business & Prof Stds .... Dr. Joseph R. SPRANGEL, JR.
53 Dean of College of Education .... Dr. Rachel POTTER
57 Dean of Visual & Perform Arts .... Dr. Paul MENZER
15 Director of Human Resources .... Ms. Shelly IRVINE
18 AVP of Facilities & Capital Plng .... Vacant
114 Dir of Budgets/Business Operation .... Vacant
29 Exec Director of Alumni Engagement .... Ms. Adrienne L. TEAGUE
36 Director Career to Career Center .... Ms. Nell DESMOND
37 AVP Enroll Mgmt/Dir Financial Aid .... Ms. Megan SPETH
04 Executive Presidential Assistant .... Ms. Sharon S. BOSSERMAN
41 Athletic Director .... Mr. Thomas P. BYRNES
19 Director Security/Safety .... Mr. Thomas L. BYERLY

Marymount University (H)

2807 N Glebe Road, Arlington VA 22207
County: Arlington — FICE Identification: 003724
Unit ID: 232706
Telephone: (703) 522-5600 — Carnegie Class: Masters/L
FAX Number: (703) 284-1637 — Calendar System: Semester
URL: www.marymount.edu
Established: 1950 — Annual Undergrad Tuition & Fees: $34,540
Enrollment: 3,294 — Coed
Affiliation or Control: Roman Catholic — IRS Status: 501(c)3
Highest Offering: Doctorate
Accreditation: SC, ACBSP, CACREP, CAEP, CIDA, HSA, NURSE, PTA

00 Chair Board of Trustees .... Dr. Edward BERSOFF
01 President .... Dr. Irma BECERRA
125 President Emeritus .... Dr. Matthew SHANK
05 Provost & Senior VP Acad Affairs .... Dr. Hesham EL-REWINI
10 Vice Pres Financial Affairs .... Mr. Barry HARTE
26 Interim Vice Pres Marketing & Comm .... Dr. Irma BECERRA
32 VP Enroll Mgmt/Student Affairs .... Dr. William BISSET
111 Interim Vice Pres Univ Advancement .... Mr. Dennis SLON
20 Vice Provost Academic Affairs .... Dr. Stephanie ELLIS FOSTER
09 AVP Planning & Inst Effectiveness .... Ms. Ann BOUDINOT
84 Assoc VP Enrollment Management .... Mr. Troy COGBURN
124 Int Assoc VP Student Engagement .... Dr. William BISSET
46 Assoc Vice Pres of Research .... Dr. Rita WONG
106 Assoc Prov Online Ed & Strat Init .... Dr. Jason CRAIG
13 Chief Information Officer .... Mr. Carl WHITMAN
15 CHRO & Asst VP Human Resources .... Ms. Kendra GILLESPIE
113 Bursar .... Ms. Karen WHITE
19 Asst VP Campus Safety & Security .... Vacant
21 Asst VP Fin Affairs & Controller .... Ms. Robin WHITFIELD
23 Asst VP Student Health & Well-Being .... Dr. Laura FINKELSTEIN
39 Asst VP Student Living .... Mrs. Susan BOYD
45 Asst VP Strategic Initiatives .... Vacant
109 Asst VP Campus Planning & Mgmt .... Mr. Upendra MALANI
121 Asst VP Student Success .... Dr. Michelle STEINER
88 Asst Vice Provost .... Dr. Louis FRISENDA
06 University Registrar .... Ms. Meghan ARIAS
08 University Librarian .... Ms. Alison GREGORY
50 Dean Col Bus/Innov/Leadership/Tech .... Mr. Jonathan ABERMAN
76 Dean College of Health & Education .... Dr. Kenneth HARWOOD
49 Dean College of Science/Humanities .... Dr. Marnel NILES GOINS
58 Int Assoc Dean Grad & Prof Studies .... Dr. Jason CRAIG

04 Executive Asst to President Mr. Joseph GREENE
104 Exec Director Center Global Studies Mr. Victor BETANCOURT SANTIAGO
07 Director Admissions Ms. Melissa WARD
14 Director IT Support Services Mr. Oscar VENTURA-MENDOZA
16 Director Talent Management Ms. Natalie DRISTAS
18 Interim Director Physical Plant Mr. Upendra MALANI
25 Dir Office of Sponsored Programs Mr. Philip HELIG
30 Director Prospect Management Ms. Michelle RYDER
31 Director Saints Center for Service Dr. Kelly DALTON
36 Director Career Services Mr. Joe GEBBIE
37 Director Financial Aid Ms. Keia BROWN
38 Director Student Counseling Ms. Allana TAYLOR
41 Director Athletics Ms. Jill MCCABE
42 Univ Chaplain & Dir Campus Ministry Fr. Gabriel MUTERU
85 Dir International Student Services Ms. Liliana VEDIA
91 Int Dir Admin Information Systems Mr. Carl WHITMAN
92 Director Honors Program Dr. Stacy LOPRESTI-GOODMAN
96 Dir Procurement & Payment Services Mrs. La'Sandra LOCKETT
114 Director Budget & Risk Management Ms. Pamela RYPKEMA
118 Director Total Rewards Mrs. Paula POLSON
119 Director Infrastructure & Security Mr. David LUTES
120 Dir Fac Dev Teaching & Instr Design Dr. Joseph PROVENZANO
88 Director Enrollment Support Ms. Jackie BIBLER
88 Director Student Access Services Mr. Sven JONES
88 Int Dir Stdnt Conduct/Conflict Res Dr. William BISSET
88 Director Student Health Services Ms. Jennifer GAGNON
88 Dir Wellness Educ/Interven/Preven Ms. Karina GUZMAN
40 Manager Marymount Univ Bookstore Mr. Troy KELLY
105 Webmaster Mr. Jaime GAONA

Norfolk State University (A)

700 Park Avenue, Norfolk VA 23504-8000
County: Independent City FICE Identification: 003765
Unit ID: 232937
Telephone: (757) 823-8600 Carnegie Class: Masters/M
FAX Number: (757) 823-2067 Calendar System: Semester
URL: www.nsu.edu
Established: 1935 Annual Undergrad Tuition & Fees (In-State): $9,622
Enrollment: 5,457 Coed
Affiliation or Control: State IRS Status: 501(c)3
Highest Offering: Doctorate
Accreditation: SC, CAEPN, CLPSY, DIETD, JOUR, KIN, MUS, NAIT, NUR, SW

01 President Dr. Javaune M. ADAMS-GASTON
101 Executive Advisor to Pres & BOV Mr. Ericke S. CAGE
05 Provost/Vice Pres Academic Affs Dr. DoVeanna FULTON
10 Vice Pres Finance and Admin Dr. Gerald E. HUNTER
111 Vice Pres Univ Advancement Mr. Clifford PORTER
32 Vice Pres Student Affairs Dr. Leonard E. BROWN
11 Vice Pres Operations Dr. Justin L. MOSES
21 AVP/University Controller Mrs. Karla J. AMAYA GORDON
43 University Counsel Ms. Pamela F. BOSTON
84 AVP Enrollment Management Dr. Juan M. ALEXANDER
38 Director of Counseling Dr. Vanessa C. JENKINS
06 Registrar Mr. Michael CARPENTER
08 Dean Library Services Vacant
37 Director of Financial Aid Dr. Melissa BARNES
88 AVP Operations Ms. Alisha BAZEMORE
15 AVP/Chief HR Officer Dr. Karen H. PRUDEN
29 Dir Alumni Relations/Annual Giving Ms. Michelle D. HILL
49 Dean College of Liberal Arts Dr. Cassandra L. NEWBY-ALEXANDER
50 Dean School of Business Mr. Glenn R. CARRINGTON
81 Dean Science/Engr/Technology Dr. Michael KEEVE
70 Dean of Social Work Dr. Elizabeth DUNGEE-ANDERSON
92 Interim Dean Honors College Dr. Khadijah O. MILLER
58 Dean of Graduate Studies & Research Dr. George E. MILLER, III
86 Legislative Liaison Mr. Robert L. TURNER
26 AVP Communications & Marketing Ms. Stevalynn R. ADAMS
09 Dir Institutional Research Mr. Ephraim BENNETT
39 Exec Dir Housing & Residence Life Dr. Faith M. FITZGERALD
41 Athletics Director Ms. Melody WEBB
18 Assoc Vice Pres Facilities Mgmt Mr. Anton KASHIRI
85 Dir Intl & Disability Services Dr. Beverly HARRIS
35 Dean of Students Ms. Michelle D. MARABLE
35 Assoc Vice Pres for Student Affairs Mrs. Julia WINGARD
13 Chief Information Technology Office Ms. Sandra MONROE-DAVIS
19 Chief of Police Mr. Vincent MOORE
28 Exec Dir Inst Equity & EEO Mr. James ROBINSON
96 Director Procurement Svcs Ms. Ruby SPICER
100 Chief of Staff Ms. Tanya WHITE

† Member of Virginia Consortium for Professional Psychology.

Old Dominion University (B)

5115 Hampton Boulevard, Norfolk VA 23529-0001
County: Independent City FICE Identification: 003728
Unit ID: 232982
Telephone: (757) 683-3000 Carnegie Class: DU-Higher
FAX Number: (757) 683-4505 Calendar System: Semester
URL: www.odu.edu
Established: 1930 Annual Undergrad Tuition & Fees (In-State): $10,800
Enrollment: 24,286 Coed
Affiliation or Control: State IRS Status: 501(c)3
Highest Offering: Doctorate
Accreditation: SC, ANEST, CAATE, CACREP, CAEP, CAPRT, CLPSY, CSHSE, CYTO, DH, EXSC, MT, MUS, NMT, NURSE, PH, #PTA, SP, SPAA

01 President Dr. Brian O. HEMPHILL
05 Provost/VP Academic Affairs Dr. Austin O. AGHO
10 Interim VP Admin & Finance Mr. Todd K. JOHNSON
46 Vice President for Research Dr. Morris W. FOSTER
15 Vice Pres for Human Resources Ms. September C. SANDERLIN
111 Vice Pres University Advancement Mr. Alonzo C. BRANDON
32 VP Student Engage/Enroll Svcs Dr. Donald M. STANSBERRY
100 Chief of Staff/VP Strategic Opers Ms. Ashley L. SCHUMAKER
88 Vice Prov Faculty Affs/Strat Init Dr. Katherine W. HAWKINS
88 Vice Prov Academic Programs Dr. Brian K. PAYNE
20 Assoc Vice Pres Academic Affairs Ms. Nina GONSER
88 Asst VP Regional/Higher Educ Ctrs Ms. Renee E. OLANDER
56 Assoc VP Distance Learning Mr. Andrew R. CASIELLO
84 Assoc Vice Pres Enrollment Mgmt Ms. Jane H. DANE
44 Assoc Vice Pres for Advancement Mr. Daniel J. GENARD
121 Assoc VP Student Engagement Dr. Johnny W. YOUNG
109 Interim Asst VP Auxiliary Services Ms. Shannon M. HURT
21 Asst VP Finance/Univ Controller Ms. Mary C. DENEEN
13 Assoc Vice Pres University Svcs/ CIO Mr. James R. WATERFIELD
31 Asst Vice Pres Community Engagement Ms. Karen F. MEIER
20 Asst VP Undergraduate Studies Ms. Judith M. BOWMAN
29 Assoc Vice Pres of Alumni Rels Ms. Joy L. JEFFERSON
26 AVP Strategic Comm/Marketing Ms. Giovanna M. GENARD
58 Vice Prov/Dean The Graduate School Dr. Robert WOJTOWICZ
49 Interim Dean College Arts & Letters Dr. Jonathan LEIB
81 Dean College of Sciences Dr. Gail DODGE
76 Dean College Health Sciences Dr. Bonnie VAN LUNEN
50 Dean Strome College of Business Dr. Jeff F. TANNER
53 Int Dean Darden Coll of Education Dr. Tammi F. DICE
54 Int Dean College Engineering/Tech Dr. Khan IFTEKHARUDDIN
92 Dean Honors College Dr. David D. METZGER
20 Exec Dir Ctr High Impact Practices Ms. Lisa MAYES
93 Exec Dir of Intercultural Relations Ms. Lesa C. CLARK
43 Asst Atty Gen/Assoc Univ Counsel Mr. Allen T. WILSON
85 Senior International Officer Dr. Paul CURRANT
08 Interim University Librarian Mr. Stuart FRAZER
06 University Registrar Mr. Humberto PORTELLEZ
07 Asst VP Enroll/Exec Dir Admissions Dr. J. Christopher FLEMING
41 Director of Athletics Dr. C. Wood SELIG
37 Director Student Financial Aid Ms. Vera E. RIDDICK
31 Director of Community Relations Ms. Cecelia T. TUCKER
88 Director Military Affairs Mr. Robert E. CLARK
38 Interim Director Counseling Svcs Dr. Angela M. HOLLEY
23 Director Student Health Services Dr. Darylnet LYTTLE
85 Deputy Dir International Programs Ms. Kasie REYES
88 Assoc VP for Learning - SEES Dr. Bridget K. WEIKEL
18 Asst VP for Facilities Management Mr. Michael J. BRADY
19 AVP for Public Safety/Chief Police Ms. Rhonda L. HARRIS
28 Dir Inst Equity/Diversity/EO/AA Ms. Ariana WRIGHT
96 Director of Procurement Services Ms. Etta A. HENRY
94 Dir Women & Gender Equity Center Ms. La Wanza LETT-BREWINGTON
16 Asst VP for Human Resources Ms. JaRenae WHITEHEAD
40 University Bookstore Manager Ms. Rhyannon POTTER
04 Special Asst to the President Ms. Velvet L. GRANT
86 Asst to Pres Governmental Relations Ms. Annie K. GIBSON
36 Interim Dir Career Development Svcs Ms. Alice L. JONES
88 Exec Dir Student Eng & Trad Fam Pgm Ms. Catherine PEDERSEN
09 Director of Institutional Research Dr. Alona SMOLOVA
101 Univ Policy Mgr/Sec Bd of Visitors Ms. Donna W. MEEKS
103 Int AVP Institute Innov & Entr Ms. Nancy GRDEN
104 Deputy Director Study Abroad Mr. Michael DEAN
108 Dir Inst Effectiveness & Assessment Mr. David SHIRLEY

† Member of Virginia Consortium for Professional Psychology.

Patrick Henry College (C)

Ten Patrick Henry Circle, Purcellville VA 20132
County: Loudoun FICE Identification: 039513
Unit ID: 451927
Telephone: (540) 338-1776 Carnegie Class: Bac-A&S
FAX Number: (540) 441-8709 Calendar System: Semester
URL: www.phc.edu
Established: 2000 Annual Undergrad Tuition & Fees: $28,400
Enrollment: 340 Coed
Affiliation or Control: Independent Non-Profit IRS Status: 501(c)3
Highest Offering: Baccalaureate
Accreditation: @SC, TRACS

01 President Mr. Jack HAYE
125 Chancellor Emeritus Dr. Michael P. FARRIS
03 Executive Vice President Mr. Howard SCHMIDT
10 VP for Administration & Finance Mr. Daryl WOLKING
09 VP for Institutional Effectiveness Mr. Rodney J. SHOWALTER
111 Vice President for Advancement Mr. Tom ZIEMNICK
05 Dean of Academic Affairs Dr. Mark MITCHELL
32 Dean of Student Affairs Ms. Sandra K. CORBITT
08 Director of the Library Ms. Sara E. PENSGARD
07 Director of Student Recruitment Mr. Stephen PIERCE
26 Director of Communications Mr. Stephen C. ALLEN

Radford University (D)

801 East Main Street, Radford VA 24142
County: Radford City FICE Identification: 003732
Unit ID: 233277
Telephone: (540) 831-5000 Carnegie Class: Masters/L
FAX Number: N/A Calendar System: Semester
URL: www.radford.edu
Established: 1910 Annual Undergrad Tuition & Fees (In-State): $11,416
Enrollment: 10,695 Coed
Affiliation or Control: State IRS Status: 170(c)1
Highest Offering: Doctorate
Accreditation: SC, ARCPA, ART, CAATE, CACREP, CAEP, CAPRT, CIDA, COARC, COPSY, DANCE, DIETD, EMT, MT, MUS, NURSE, OT, OTA, PTA, PTAA, SP, SURGT, SW, THEA

01 Interim President Dr. Lyn LEPRE
05 Interim Provost/VP Academic Affairs Dr. J. Orion ROGERS
10 VP Finance and Administration/CFO Mr. Chad REED
32 VP Student Affairs Dr. Susan TRAGESER
111 VP for Advancement & Univ Relations Ms. Wendy LOWERY
84 VP Enrollment Mgmt Mr. Craig CORNELL
50 Dean Davis Col Business & Econ Dr. Joy BHADURY
53 Dean Col Education & Human Dev Dr. Tamara WALLACE
76 Dean Waldron Col Health/Human Svcs Dr. Kenneth COX
79 Dean Col Humanities/Behav Sci Dr. Matthew SMITH
81 Int Dean Artis College Sci & Tech Dr. Art CARTER
57 Dean Col Visual & Performing Arts Ms. Margaret DEVANEY
58 Dean Graduate Studies/Research Dr. Benjamin D. CALDWELL
66 Dean School of Nursing Dr. Johnnie Sue WIJEWARDANE
07 Dean of Admissions Mr. Anthony GRAHAM
08 Interim Dean of the Library Dr. Benjamin D. CALDWELL
06 Registrar Mr. Matthew BRUNNER
37 Director of Financial Aid Ms. Allison PRATT
29 Executive Dir of Alumni Relations Ms. Laura TURK
41 Director Intercollegiate Athletics Mr. Robert LINEBURG
15 Asst VP for Human Resources Mr. Amel CUSKOVIC
35 AVP Student Affs/Dean of Student Ms. Angela MITCHELL
19 Chief of Police Dr. Eric PLUMMER
09 Director of Institutional Research Dr. Eric LOVIK
101 Secretary to the Board of Visitors Ms. Karen CASTEELE
100 Interim Chief of Staff Dr. Angela M. JOYNER
102 Dir Foundation/Corporate Relations Mr. Benjamin HILL
28 Director of Institutional Equity Dr. Andrea ZUSCHIN
44 Director Annual Giving Ms. Carolyn CLAYTON
86 Exec Director of Govt Relations Ms. Lisa GHIDOTTI
96 Exec Director of Strategic Sourcing Ms. Kimberly DULANEY
104 Asst Prov Ctr Global Educ & Engage Mr. Ismael J. BETANCOURT VELEZ
108 Director Academic Assessment Dr. Sandra BAKER
11 Exec Director of Administration Ms. Heather MIANO
18 Asst VP for Facilities Management Mr. Jorge COARTNEY
25 Dir Sponsored Programs/Grants Mr. Thomas CRUISE
110 Assoc VP for Advancement Mr. Tom LILLARD
36 Dir Center for Career & Talent Dev Mr. Jason CLAYTON
38 Director Student Counseling Service Mr. Brian LUSK
39 Dir Housing & Residential Life Dr. Anthony WHITE
13 Assoc VP for Info Technology & CIO Mr. Ed OAKES

Randolph College (E)

2500 Rivermont Avenue, Lynchburg VA 24503-1555
County: Independent City FICE Identification: 003734
Unit ID: 233301
Telephone: (434) 947-8000 Carnegie Class: Bac-A&S
FAX Number: (434) 947-8139 Calendar System: Semester
URL: www.randolphcollege.edu
Established: 1891 Annual Undergrad Tuition & Fees: $25,610
Enrollment: 566 Coed
Affiliation or Control: Independent Non-Profit IRS Status: 501(c)3
Highest Offering: Master's
Accreditation: SC, CAEP

01 President Dr. Bradley W. BATEMAN
05 VP Academic Affs & Dean of College Dr. Carl A. GIRELLI
111 Vice Pres Institutional Advancement Ms. Farah MARKS
10 Vice Pres Finance & Administration Vacant
32 Dean of Students Mr. Christopher LEMASTERS
07 Dean of Admissions Mr. Travis CARTER
100 Special Assistant to the President Mr. Steve WILLIS
20 Associate Dean of the College Ms. Bunny GOODJOHN
29 Director Alumnae & Alumni Pgm Ms. Phebe WESCOTT
09 Dir IR/Planning & Assessment Dr. John F. KEENER
15 Director Human Resources Ms. Sharon SAUNDERS
18 Chief Facilities/Physical Plant Mr. John LEARY
21 Director of Finance Mr. Jonathan TYREE
38 Director Student Counseling Ms. Jennifer BONDURANT
08 Librarian Ms. Lisa BROUGHMAN
06 Registrar Ms. Jeanette RORK
37 Dir Student Financial Services Vacant
36 Director of Career Development Ms. Maegan FALLEN
13 Director of Information Technology Mr. Victor GOSNELL
04 Administrative Asst to President Ms. Cindy LYONS
19 Director Security/Safety Mr. Kris IRWIN
41 Athletic Director Mr. Anthony BERICH
26 Chief Public Relations/Marketing Ms. Brenda EDSON

Randolph-Macon College (F)

114 College Ave, Ashland, Ashland VA 23005
County: Hanover FICE Identification: 003733
Unit ID: 233295
Telephone: (804) 752-7200 Carnegie Class: Bac-A&S
FAX Number: (804) 752-7231 Calendar System: Other
URL: www.rmc.edu
Established: 1830 Annual Undergrad Tuition & Fees: $43,940
Enrollment: 1,554 Coed
Affiliation or Control: United Methodist IRS Status: 501(c)3
Highest Offering: Master's
Accreditation: SC, CAEP

01 President Mr. Robert R. LINDGREN
05 Provost/VP for Academic Affairs Dr. Alisa J. ROSENTHAL
10 Vice Pres of Admin & Finance Mr. Paul DAVIES
111 Vice Pres for College Advancement Ms. Diane M. LOWDER

84 Vice Pres for Enroll/Admiss/Fin Aid .... Dr. David L. LESESNE
32 Vice President for Student Affairs .... Dr. Grant L. AZDELL
04 Executive Assistant to the Pres .... Mr. Tim BULLIS
07 Director of Admissions .... Ms. Erin SLATER
29 Exec Director Alumni Relations .... Ms. Alice D. LYNCH
26 Assoc VP Marketing/Communications .... Ms. Beth CAMPBELL
37 Director of Financial Aid .... Mrs. Julie HICKMAN-GODOY
13 CIO and ITS Director .... Mr. Kirk BAUMBACH
06 Registrar .... Mrs. Alana DAVIS
38 Director of Counseling Services .... Dr. Beth SCHUBERT
09 Director of Institutional Research .... Dr. Katherine D. WALKER
18 Dir of Operations & Physical Plant .... Mr. John HERRON
42 Chaplain .... Rev. Kendra S. GRIMES
19 Director of Campus Safety .... Mr. Maurice J. KIELY
41 Athletic Director .... Mr. Jeffrey S. BURNS
15 Director Human Resources .... Mrs. Sharon S. JACKSON
21 Controller .... Ms. Barbara A. DAUBERMAN
20 Associate Dean of the College .... Dr. Lauren C. BELL
36 Director of Professional Develop .... Ms. Catherine A. ROLLMAN
35 Asst Dean of Students .... Mr. James D. MCGHEE, JR.
40 Bookstore Manager .... Mrs. Barclay F. DUPRIEST
114 Director of Budget/Financial Analys .... Ms. Missy STANLEY
08 Head Librarian .... Ms. Nancy K. FALCIANI-WHITE
102 Dir Foundation/Corporate Relations .... Mr. Robert H. PATTERSON
104 Director Study Abroad .... Ms. Mayumi NAKAMURA
28 Director of Diversity .... Ms. Alicia C. ELMS
39 Director Student Housing .... Ms. Sara WEINSTEIN
44 Dir Annual Giving & Alumni Rel .... Mr. Richard M. GOLEMBESKI
101 Asst Secretary of the Board .... Ms. Emily P. HARRISON

Reformed Theological Seminary (A)

8227 Old Courthouse Rd, Suite 300, Vienna VA 22182
Telephone: (703) 448-3393 Identification: 666079
Accreditation: &SC, THEOL

† Regional accreditation is carried under the parent institution in Jackson, MS.

Regent University (B)

1000 Regent University Drive,
Virginia Beach VA 23464-9800
County: Independent City FICE Identification: 030913
Unit ID: 231651
Telephone: (757) 352-4127 Carnegie Class: DU-Mod
FAX Number: (757) 352-4381 Calendar System: Semester
URL: www.regent.edu
Established: 1977 Annual Undergrad Tuition & Fees: $18,720
Enrollment: 10,483 Coed
Affiliation or Control: Independent Non-Profit IRS Status: 501(c)3
Highest Offering: Doctorate
Accreditation: SC, ACBSP, CACREP, CAEPT, CLPSY, LAW, NURSE, THEOL

01 Chancellor & CEO .... Dr. M.G. (Pat) ROBERTSON
05 Executive VP for Academic Affairs .... Dr. William L. HATHAWAY
32 Executive VP for Student Life .... Dr. Joseph UMIDI
43 Senior VP & General Counsel .... Mr. Louis A. ISAKOFF
111 Vice President for Advancement .... Mr. Chris LAMBERT
26 VP Enrollment/Mktg & Public Rels .... Ms. Claire FOSTER
10 VP for Business Administration .... Mr. Steve BRUCE
15 VP for Human Resources & Admin .... Mrs. Martha J. SMITH
20 Associate VP for Academic Affairs .... Vacant
61 Dean School of Law .... Hon. Mark MARTIN
49 Dean College of Arts & Sciences .... Dr. Joshua MCMULLEN
08 Dean University Library .... Dr. Esther GILLIE
50 Dean School of Business/Leadership .... Dr. Doris GOMEZ
80 Dean Robertson Sch of Government .... Hon. Michele BACHMANN
53 Dean School of Education .... Dr. Kurt KREASSIG
83 Dean Psychology & Counseling .... Dr. Anna S. ORD
73 Dean School of Divinity .... Dr. Corne BEKKER
06 Registrar .... Dr. Elizabeth BAYLESS
84 Associate VP of Enrollment Mgmt .... Mr. Chris GRAHAM
35 Director of Student Activities .... Ms. Amber STEELE
106 Director of CTL .... Vacant
37 Director of Financial Aid .... Ms. Rachael MOSER
09 Director of Institutional Research .... Dr. Amanda WYNN
18 Dir of Facilities/Engineering .... Mr. Kim HEGWER
29 Dir of Alumni Rels/Annual Giving .... Ms. Andrea TATUM
42 Director of Campus Ministries .... Mr. Mark LAWRENCE
108 Director of Assessment .... Dr. Ryan MURNANE
123 Sr Dir Military & Veterans Affairs .... Vacant
39 Assoc VP for Student Life .... Mr. Adam WILLIAMS
96 Director of Purchasing .... Mrs. Pauline CARRAWAY
04 Assistant to the Chancellor .... Ms. Laurie Ann FINN
13 Assoc Vice Pres of Info Technology .... Mr. Jonathan HARRELL
41 Athletic Director .... Dr. Samuel BOTTA

Richard Bland College (C)

11301 Johnson Road,
South Prince George VA 23805-7100
County: South Prince George FICE Identification: 003707
Unit ID: 233338
Telephone: (804) 862-6100 Carnegie Class: Assoc/HT-High Trad
FAX Number: (804) 862-6207 Calendar System: Semester
URL: www.rbc.edu
Established: 1960 Annual Undergrad Tuition & Fees (In-State): $8,100
Enrollment: 2,218 Coed
Affiliation or Control: State IRS Status: 501(c)3
Highest Offering: Associate Degree
Accreditation: SC

01 President .... Dr. Debbie L. SYDOW
05 Provost .... Dr. Maria DEZENBERG
10 Chief Business Officer .... Mr. Paul EDWARDS
100 Chief of Staff .... Ms. Lashrecse AIRD
18 Director Capital Assets/Operations .... Mr. Eric KONDZIELAWA
13 Chief Innovation & Strategy Officer .... Dr. Kenneth LATESSA
04 Executive Assistant to President .... Ms. Lisa L. POND
30 Chief Development Officer .... Dr. James T. HART
86 Director of Government Relations .... Ms. Joanne WILLIAMS
15 Director of Human Resources .... Ms. Cassandra STANDBERRY
19 Chief Campus Safety/Police .... Mr. Jeffrey BROWN
43 College Counsel .... Ms. Ramona TAYLOR
41 Director Athletics & Recreation .... Mr. Scott NEWTON
121 Director of Student Success .... Ms. Celia BROCKWAY
106 Director of Online Education .... Ms. Stacey SOKOL
37 Director of Financial Aid .... Ms. Lisa JOHNSON
06 Director of Records & Registration .... Vacant
07 Director of Admissions .... Mr. Ryan CHISHOLM
38 Dir of Counseling/Student Support .... Dr. Evanda WATTS-MARTINEZ
26 Asst Director Communications .... Mr. Robin J. DEUTSCH
21 Controller .... Ms. Melissa MAHONEY
113 Bursar .... Ms. Melissa MAHONEY
96 Procurement Manager .... Ms. Layne WARREN
119 Information Security Officer .... Ms. Deborah JAMES
14 Manager Projects & Telecom .... Mr. George JELLERSON
14 Technology Support Manager .... Mr. Bryan ROETHEL
16 HR Specialist .... Ms. Alice JABBOUR
08 Head Librarian .... Ms. Carly BASKERVILLE
88 Director of Account & Finance .... Mr. Mark JACOBSON
88 Business Manager .... Mr. Preston BOUSMAN

Riverside College of Health Careers (D)

316 Main Street, Newport News VA 23601
County: Independent City FICE Identification: 021400
Unit ID: 233408
Telephone: (757) 240-2200 Carnegie Class: Spec 2-yr-Health
FAX Number: (757) 240-2225 Calendar System: Semester
URL: www.riverside.edu
Established: 1916 Annual Undergrad Tuition & Fees: $17,610
Enrollment: 303 Coed
Affiliation or Control: Independent Non-Profit IRS Status: 501(c)3
Highest Offering: Associate Degree
Accreditation: ABHES, ADNUR, PNUR, PTAA, RAD, SURGT, SURTEC

01 Campus Admin/System Dir Education .... Robin M. NELHUEBEL
05 Director Academic Affairs .... Terri DEL CORSO
06 Registrar .... Lori ARNDER
08 Head Librarian .... Cassandra MOORE
10 Director of Campus Resources .... Michael HAMILTON
07 Senior Recruitment Coordinator .... Cynthia REDDINGTON
37 Dir Financial Aid/Student Svcs .... Saleem CHAUDHRY

Roanoke College (E)

221 College Lane, Salem VA 24153-3747
County: Independent City FICE Identification: 003736
Unit ID: 233426
Telephone: (540) 375-2500 Carnegie Class: Bac-A&S
FAX Number: (540) 375-2205 Calendar System: Semester
URL: www.roanoke.edu
Established: 1842 Annual Undergrad Tuition & Fees: $47,020
Enrollment: 1,920 Coed
Affiliation or Control: Evangelical Lutheran Church In America
IRS Status: 501(c)3
Highest Offering: Baccalaureate
Accreditation: SC, ACBSP, CAEPT

01 President .... Mr. Michael C. MAXEY
05 Interim VP Academic/Student Affairs .... Dr. Rich A. GRANT
84 VP of Enroll Svcs/Dean Adm/Fin Aid .... Dr. Brenda P. POGGENDORF
10 Vice President Business Affairs .... Mr. David MOWEN
30 Vice President Resource Development .... Mr. Aaron L. FETROW
32 Dean of Students .... Dr. Brian T. CHISOM
26 Exec Dir/Marketing Communications .... Ms. Melanie W. TOLAN
13 Chief Information Officer .... Mr. Mark D. POORE
09 Dir Institutional Research .... Dr. Jack K. STEEHLER
20 Assoc Dean Academic Affairs .... Dr. Gail A. STEEHLER
06 Assoc Dean Acad Affairs/Registrar .... Ms. Leah L. RUSSELL
07 Director of Recruitment .... Mr. Courtney PENN
39 Director of Residence Life/Housing .... Mr. Jimmy R. WHITED
92 Director of Honors Programs .... Dr. Chad T. MORRIS
08 Director of the Library .... Ms. Elizabeth MCCLENNEY
24 Media Technology Director .... Vacant
31 Dir of Community Programs .... Ms. Tanya RIDPATH
26 Director of Public Relations .... Ms. Teresa T. GEREAUX
29 Dir of Alumni/Family Relations .... Mrs. Sally WALKER
114 Director of Finance & Budget .... Mr. Adam NEAL
91 Database Director .... Ms. Mitzi B. STEELE
15 Director Human Resources .... Mrs. Kathy MARTIN
40 Bookstore Coordinator/Buyer .... Ms. Melissa B. RUTLEDGE
19 Director Campus Safety .... Mr. Thomas A. RAMBO
23 Dir Student Health/Counseling Svcs .... Ms. Sandra W. MCGHEE
41 Athletic Director .... Mr. M. Scott ALLISON
42 Chaplain/Dean of the Chapel .... Rev. Christopher M. BOWEN
104 Director of International Education .... Ms. Carmen E. BOGGS PARKER
28 Director of Multicultural Affairs .... Ms. Natasha SAUNDERS
04 Executive Assistant to President .... Mrs. Whitney C. ALDRIDGE

37 Director of Financial Aid .... Mr. Thomas S. BLAIR, JR.
45 Director of Institutional Planning .... Dr. Ryan OTTO

Sentara College of Health Sciences (F)

1441 Crossways Boulevard, Ste 105,
Chesapeake VA 23320
County: Chesapeake City FICE Identification: 031065
Unit ID: 232885
Telephone: (757) 388-2900 Carnegie Class: Spec-4-yr-Other Health
FAX Number: (757) 222-7694 Calendar System: Semester
URL: www.sentara.edu
Established: 1892 Annual Undergrad Tuition & Fees: N/A
Enrollment: 341 Coed
Affiliation or Control: Independent Non-Profit IRS Status: 501(c)3
Highest Offering: Master's
Accreditation: ABHES, CVT, NURSE, SURGT, SURTEC

01 Executive Director & Dean .... Dr. Angela TAYLOR
05 Dean Academic Affairs .... Dr. Cynthia BANKS
09 Dean Inst Effectiveness/Dist Lrng .... Ms. Metta ALSOBROOK
10 Assoc Dean Administration & Finance .... Mr. Christopher NELSON
84 Asst Dean Enrollment Management .... Mr. Joseph HOWE
06 Registrar .... Ms. Jennie POND
37 Financial Aid Advisor .... Ms. Mary Ann RIVERA
07 Admissions Recruiter .... Mr. Kevin LAWRENCE

Shenandoah University (G)

1460 University Drive, Winchester VA 22601-5195
County: Independent City FICE Identification: 003737
Unit ID: 233541
Telephone: (540) 665-4500 Carnegie Class: DU-Mod
FAX Number: N/A Calendar System: Semester
URL: www.su.edu
Established: 1875 Annual Undergrad Tuition & Fees: $33,900
Enrollment: 4,174 Coed
Affiliation or Control: United Methodist IRS Status: 501(c)3
Highest Offering: Doctorate
Accreditation: SC, ARCPA, CAATE, CAEP, CAEPT, MIDWF, NURSE, OT, PHAR, PTA

01 President .... Dr. Tracy FITZSIMMONS
05 Provost .... Dr. Adrienne G. BLOSS
10 Vice Pres Administration & Finance .... Mr. Robert L. KEASLER
32 Vice President for Student Life .... Vacant
111 Senior VP for Advancement .... Mr. Mitchell L. MOORE
84 VP for Student Success .... Dr. Yolanda BARBIER GIBSON
35 Dean of Students .... Dr. Sue O'DRISCOLL
26 Director of Media Relations .... Vacant
49 Dean of College of Arts & Sciences .... Dr. Jeffrey COKER
50 Dean of Byrd School of Business .... Dr. Astrid SHEIL
64 Dean of Shenandoah Conservatory .... Dr. Michael J. STEPNIAK
67 Dean of Dunn School of Pharmacy .... Dr. Robert DICENZO
07 Exec of Recruitment & Admissions .... Mr. Andy WOODALL
124 Dir of Student Engagement .... Mr. Matt LEVY
08 Director of Library Services .... Vacant
06 Registrar .... Ms. Emily HOLLINS
21 Asst VP Admin & Finance/Controller .... Ms. Courtney JARRETT
37 Student Financial Services Dir .... Dr. Karen H. BUCHER
36 Director of Career/Prof Development .... Ms. Jennifer A. SPATARO-WILSON
18 Director of Physical Plant .... Mr. Barry SCHNOOR
23 Interim Director of Wellness Center .... Mrs. Lisa DARSCH
15 Assoc Director of Human Resources .... Ms. Kim MCDONALD
41 Athletic Director .... Dr. Bridget LYONS
91 Database & System Administrator .... Mr. Seth BURKE
13 Director of Institutional Computing .... Mr. Quaiser ABSAR
66 Dean Custer School of Nursing .... Dr. Andra HANLON
88 Director Div of Athletic Training .... Dr. Rose A. SCHMIEG
76 Dir Div of Occupational Therapy .... Dr. Cathy SHANHOLTZ
76 Dir Div of Physical Therapy .... Dr. Sheri ALLEN
112 Director of Planned Gifts .... Vacant
19 Director of Public Safety .... Mr. Ricky FRYE
102 Dir of Grant Supp & Foundation Rels .... Ms. Marguerite LANDENBURGER
109 Director Auxiliary Services .... Ms. Pamela B. BURKE
88 Dir Div of Physician Asst Studies .... Dr. Anthony MILLER
20 Director Learning Services .... Ms. Holli PHILLIPS
42 Dean of Spiritual Life .... Rev Dr. Justin ALLEN
09 Director Institutional Research .... Mr. Howard BALLENTINE
40 Bookstore Manager .... Ms. Kimberly OTYENOH
96 Purchasing/Accounts Payable Manager .... Ms. Susan LANDIS
24 Coordinator Media Services .... Ms. Rebecca LAYNE
38 Director of Counseling Center .... Vacant
04 Executive Asst to President .... Ms. Kim KECKLEY
101 Exec Secretary of the BOT .... Ms. Laura CLAWSON
53 Assoc Provost School of Education .... Dr. Jill LINDSEY
104 Director International Programs .... Dr. Bethany GALIPEAU-KONATE
44 Director of Annual Giving .... Ms. Aimee NUWAR
43 AVP & General Counsel .... Mr. Philip EVANS
28 Asst Dean Student Dev/Leadership .... Ms. Margaret MCCAMPBELL LIEN
29 Executive Director Alumni Affairs .... Ms. Emily BURNER

South University (H)

2151 Old Brick Road, Glen Allen VA 23060
Telephone: (888) 422-5076 Identification: 770919
Accreditation: &SC, ACBSP, ARCPA, CACREP, NURSE, OTA, PTAA

† Branch campus of South University, Savannah, GA

South University (A)

301 Bendix Road, Suite 100, Virginia Beach VA 23452
Telephone: (877) 206-1845 Identification: 770920
Accreditation: &SC, ACBSP, CACREP, NURSE, OTA, PTAA

† Branch campus of South University, Savannah, GA

Southern Virginia University (B)

1 University Hill Drive, Buena Vista VA 24416-3097
County: Rockbridge FICE Identification: 003738
Unit ID: 233611
Telephone: (540) 261-8400 Carnegie Class: Bac-A&S
FAX Number: (540) 266-3859 Calendar System: Semester
URL: www.svu.edu
Established: 1867 Annual Undergrad Tuition & Fees: $17,696
Enrollment: 1,140 Coed
Affiliation or Control: Independent Non-Profit IRS Status: 501(c)3
Highest Offering: Baccalaureate
Accreditation: SC

01 President .... Dr. Reed N. WILCOX
100 Executive VP/Chief of Staff .... Mr. Brett GARCIA
05 VP of Academics/Provost .... Dr. James LAMBERT
10 Chief Financial officer .... Mr. Tyson COOPER
111 VP Institutional Advancement .... Dr. Jon WALLIN
84 VP Enrollment & Marketing .... Mr. Christopher PENDLETON
32 Dean of Students .... Mr. William BRADDY
46 VP Educational Research & Dev .... Dr. Karen M. WALKER
11 VP of Operations .... Mr. Chris PACKER
04 Administrative Asst to President .... Mrs. Kristie GIBBONS
06 University Registrar .... Ms. Whitney M. LARSEN
08 Director of Library Services .... Mrs. Stephanie K. HARDY
20 Associate Provost .... Dr. Samuel HIRT
57 Division Chair Fine & Perf Arts .... Dr. Eric HANSON
79 Division Chair Humanities .... Dr. Jan-Erik JONES
81 Div Chair Science & Mathematics .... Dr. Roger JOHNSON
83 Div Chair Social & Behavioral Sci ..... Dr. Iana KONSTANTINOVA
83 Div Chair Business/Family Dev/Psych .... Dr. Jeffrey BATIS
53 Director of Teacher Education .... Ms. Kimberly KEARNEY
37 Director of Financial Aid .... Mr. Aaron CARLSON
15 Human Resources Manager .... Mr. Adam WHIPPLE
88 Title IX .... Ms. Stephanie HARDY
96 Senior Accountant .... Mr. Trenton DESPAIN
41 Athletic Director .... Ms. Deidra DRYDEN
38 Director of Student Support .... Vacant
85 Foreign Students PDSO .... Ms. Whitney M. LARSEN
19 Director Security/Safety .... Mr. Zachary ELLIOTT
109 Director of Food Services .... Mr. Joseph WHETSTONE
18 Asst Dir Facilities/Physical Plant .... Mr. Byron PORTER
101 Secretary of the Institution/Board .... Mr. Hugh REDD
13 Chief Information Technology Office .... Dr. Jeffrey SWIFT
50 Program Coordinator Business .... Dr. W. Todd BROTHERSON
07 Director of Admissions .... Ms. Madison HUGIE
09 Director of Institutional Research .... Dr. Jonathan WALLIN
39 Dir Resident Life/Student Housing .... Ms. April HARRIS

Southside College of Health Sciences (C)

430 Clairmont Court, Suite 200,
Colonial Heights VA 23834
County: Independent City FICE Identification: 012744
Unit ID: 233082
Telephone: (804) 765-5800 Carnegie Class: Spec 2-yr-Health
FAX Number: (804) 765-5944 Calendar System: Semester
URL: https://www.schs.edu/
Established: 1895 Annual Undergrad Tuition & Fees: $15,813
Enrollment: 115 Coed
Affiliation or Control: Proprietary IRS Status: Proprietary
Highest Offering: Associate Degree
Accreditation: ABHES, ADNUR, DMS, RAD

03 Vice President .... Mrs. Cynthia SWINEFORD

Sovah School of Health Professions (D)

142 South Main Street, Danville VA 24541
County: Independent City FICE Identification: 021116
Unit ID: 232724
Telephone: (434) 799-2271 Carnegie Class: Spec 2-yr-Health
FAX Number: (434) 799-3718 Calendar System: Semester
URL: www.danvilleregional.com
Established: 1898 Annual Undergrad Tuition & Fees: N/A
Enrollment: 13 Coed
Affiliation or Control: Proprietary IRS Status: Proprietary
Highest Offering: Associate Degree
Accreditation: ABHES, RAD

01 Dean .... R. Alan LARSON

Standard Healthcare Services College of Nursing (E)

7704 Leesburg Pike, Suite 1000, Falls Church VA 22043
County: Fairfax Identification: 667129
Unit ID: 483814
Telephone: (703) 891-1787 Carnegie Class: Spec 2-yr-Health
FAX Number: (703) 891-1789 Calendar System: Other
URL: www.standardcollege.edu
Established: 2004 Annual Undergrad Tuition & Fees: N/A
Enrollment: 441 Coed
Affiliation or Control: Proprietary IRS Status: Proprietary
Highest Offering: Associate Degree
Accreditation: ABHES

01 Executive Director .... Ms. Isibor J. NOSEGBE
03 Deputy Executive Director .... Mrs. Heather ETTUS
06 Registrar .... Ms. Lisley M. ANCO
05 Director of Education .... Mr. Sakpa S. AMARA
32 Dean of Student Services .... Mrs. Sondra BROWN
37 Financial Aid .... Mr. Petros YOSIEF
07 Admissions .... Ms. Cara GLASER
10 Business Office .... Mrs. Brenda GARCES

Stratford University (F)

7777 Leesburg Pike, Suite 1LN, Falls Church VA 22043
County: Fairfax FICE Identification: 025412
Unit ID: 438498
Telephone: (703) 810-3852 Carnegie Class: Masters/L
FAX Number: N/A Calendar System: Quarter
URL: www.stratford.edu
Established: 1976 Annual Undergrad Tuition & Fees: $15,135
Enrollment: 1,947 Coed
Affiliation or Control: Proprietary IRS Status: Proprietary
Highest Offering: Master's
Accreditation: ACICS, NURSE

01 Campus President .... Dr. Roblyn LEWTER
07 Director of Admissions .... Ms. Nadia OUKHEIRA BAKER
05 VP Faculty and Academic Affairs .... Dr. Dutchie REID
88 VP International Programs .... Mr. Feroze KHAN
26 EVP Marketing .... Ms. Mary Ann SHURTZ
10 Controller .... Mr. John RUMFORD

† University administration building is located at 3201 Jermantown Rd, Ste 500 Fairfax, VA 22030.

Stratford University Alexandria Campus (G)

2900 Eisenhower Avenue, Alexandria VA 22314
Telephone: (571) 777-0130 Identification: 770856
Accreditation: ACICS, ACFEI

Stratford University Woodbridge Campus (H)

14349 Gideon Drive, Woodbridge VA 22192
Telephone: (703) 810-3254 Identification: 770817
Accreditation: ACICS, ACFEI

Sweet Briar College (I)

134 Chapel Road, Sweet Briar VA 24595-9998
County: Amherst FICE Identification: 003742
Unit ID: 233718
Telephone: (434) 381-6100 Carnegie Class: Bac-A&S
FAX Number: (434) 381-6173 Calendar System: Semester
URL: www.sbc.edu
Established: 1901 Annual Undergrad Tuition & Fees: $22,700
Enrollment: 362 Female
Affiliation or Control: Independent Non-Profit IRS Status: 501(c)3
Highest Offering: Master's
Accreditation: SC

01 President .... Dr. Meredith WOO
11 VP Finance/Operations & Auxiliary .... Mr. Luther T. GRIFFITH
04 Exec Asst Office of the President .... Ms. Kim MURRAY
30 Vice Pres Alumnae Relations/Devel ... Ms. Mary Pope M. HUTSON
84 Vice Pres Enrollment Management .... Mr. Aaron BASKO
09 Dir of Institutional Effectiveness .... Ms. Kim SINHA
05 Dean of Academic Affairs .... Dr. Teresa GARRETT
13 Dir of Technology Services .... Mr. Hooshang FOROUDASTAN
41 Athletics Director .... Ms. Jodi CANFIELD
32 Dean of Student Life .... Mr. Kerry GREENSTEIN
15 Sr Human Resource Mgr .... Ms. Nickcole MAYNARD-ERRAMI
18 Director Physical Plant .... Mr. Rich MEYER
19 Director of Campus Safety .... Mr. Brian MARKER
37 Director Financial Aid .... Ms. Wanda SPRADLEY
40 Book Shop Manager .... Ms. Dottie BOONE
96 Purchasing Manager .... Ms. Karen L. THORP
88 Director of Hospitality .... Ms. Cathy MAYS
36 Director Career Services .... Ms. Barbara WATTS
26 Sr Director of Communications .... Ms. Amy OSTROTH
27 Dir of Media Rels/Content Strategy .... Ms. Dana POLESKI
06 Registrar .... Mr. Jay FLYNN
07 Director of Admissions Operations .... Ms. Melanie CAMPBELL
25 Chief Contracts/Grants Admin .... Ms. Kathleen PLACIDI
29 Director Alumnae Relations .... Ms. Claire GRIFFITH
21 Assistant VP & Controller .... Ms. Jenni SAUER

Union Presbyterian Seminary (J)

3401 Brook Road, Richmond VA 23227-4597
County: Independent City FICE Identification: 003743
Unit ID: 233842
Telephone: (804) 355-0671 Carnegie Class: Spec-4-yr-Faith
FAX Number: (804) 355-3919 Calendar System: Semester
URL: www.upsem.edu
Established: 1812 Annual Graduate Tuition & Fees: N/A
Enrollment: 169 Coed
Affiliation or Control: Presbyterian Church (U.S.A.) IRS Status: 501(c)3
Highest Offering: Doctorate; No Undergraduates
Accreditation: SC, THEOL

01 President .... Dr. Brian K. BLOUNT
10 Vice Pres Finance & Administration ... Mr. Michael B. CASHWELL
30 Vice President Advancement .... Mr. Richard WONG
32 Dean of Students .... Ms. Michelle WALKER
05 Dean Union Presby Sem/Academics ... Dr. Kenneth J. MCFAYDEN
12 Dean Union Presby Sem (Charlotte) .... Dr. Richard N. BOYCE
07 Director of Admissions .... Ms. Lisa L. MCLENNAN
06 Registrar .... Mr. J. Stanley HARGRAVES
08 Seminary Librarian .... Dr. Christopher RICHARDSON
13 Director Technology Services .... Mr. John R. WILSON
36 Director Student Services .... Ms. Susan BLANCHARD
37 Director of Financial Aid .... Ms. Michelle WALKER

University of Fairfax (K)

1813 E. Main Street, Salem VA 24153
County: Independent City Identification: 667094
Telephone: (888) 980-9151 Carnegie Class: Not Classified
FAX Number: N/A Calendar System: Other
URL: www.ufairfax.edu
Established: 2002 Annual Undergrad Tuition & Fees: N/A
Enrollment: N/A Coed
Affiliation or Control: Other IRS Status: Proprietary
Highest Offering: Doctorate
Accreditation: DEAC

01 President .... Mr. Frank LONGAKER
05 Dean/Chief Academic Officer .... Dr. Rick LIVINGOOD
11 Vice President Operations .... Mr. Joel MUSGROVE
26 VP Marketing & Communications .... Mr. Chuck STEENBURGH

† Tuition is $895 per semester credit.

University of Lynchburg (L)

1501 Lakeside Drive, Lynchburg VA 24501-3199
County: Independent City FICE Identification: 003720
Unit ID: 232609
Telephone: (434) 544-8100 Carnegie Class: Masters/M
FAX Number: (434) 544-8539 Calendar System: Semester
URL: www.lynchburg.edu
Established: 1903 Annual Undergrad Tuition & Fees: $41,880
Enrollment: 2,692 Coed
Affiliation or Control: Christian Church (Disciples Of Christ)
IRS Status: 501(c)3
Highest Offering: Doctorate
Accreditation: SC, ACBSP, ARCPA, CAATE, CACREP, EXSC, MUS, NURSE, PTA

01 President .... Dr. Alison MORRISON-SHETLAR
05 Provost & VP for Academic Affs .... Dr. Allison JABLONSKI
10 Vice President Business & Finance .... Mr. Steve BRIGHT
111 Vice President Advancement .... Dr. J. Michael BONNETTE
84 Vice Pres Enrollment Management .... Mrs. Rita DETWILER
32 VP & Dean of Student Development .... Vacant
45 VP Inst Planning/Effectiveness .... Dr. Debbie DRISCOLL
26 VP Communications & Marketing .... Mr. Mike JONES
50 Dean College of Business .... Dr. Nancy HUBBARD
53 Dean Col of Educ/Ldrship Stds/Couns .... Dr. Roger JONES
20 Assoc Provost .... Dr. Charles WALTON
49 Assoc Dean LC Arts & Sciences .... Dr. Oeida HATCHER
81 Assoc Dean School of Sciences .... Vacant
76 Dean College of Health Sciences .... Dr. Rusty SMITH
06 Registrar/Academic/Student Info .... Mrs. Susan KENNON
08 Director of the Library .... Mrs. Jennifer HORTON
37 Director of Financial Aid .... Ms. Elayne PELOQUIN
07 Director of Admissions .... Ms. Sharon WALTERS-BOWER
102 Assoc Dir of Grants Management .... Ms. Jennifer WILLIAMS
13 Director Information and Technology .... Mrs. Jackie ALMOND
15 Human Resource Director .... Ms. Linda HALL
19 Director Security/Safety .... Vacant
28 Diversity and Inclusion Officer .... Dr. Robert CANIDA
29 Director Alumni Relations .... Ms. Heather GARNETT
39 Director Residence Life .... Ms. Kristen COOPER
41 Athletic Director .... Mr. Jon WATERS
96 Purchasing and Logistics Coord .... Mrs. Cynthia PONTON
04 Exec Assistant to the President .... Mrs. Debra WYLAND
09 Director of Institutional Research .... Dr. Aurelia KOLLASCH

University of Management & Technology (M)

1901 Fort Myer Drive, Suite 700, Arlington VA 22209-1609
County: Arlington FICE Identification: 041103
Unit ID: 437097
Telephone: (703) 516-0035 Carnegie Class: DU-Mod
FAX Number: (703) 516-0985 Calendar System: Semester
URL: www.umtweb.edu
Established: 1998 Annual Undergrad Tuition & Fees: $9,450
Enrollment: 295 Coed
Affiliation or Control: Proprietary IRS Status: Proprietary
Highest Offering: Doctorate
Accreditation: DEAC

01 President .... Dr. Yanping CHEN
05 Academic Dean .... Dr. J. Davidson FRAME

University of Mary Washington (N)

1301 College Avenue, Fredericksburg VA 22401-5300
County: Independent City FICE Identification: 003746
Unit ID: 232681

Telephone: (540) 654-1000 Carnegie Class: Masters/M
FAX Number: (540) 654-1073 Calendar System: Semester
URL: www.umw.edu
Established: 1908 Annual Undergrad Tuition & Fees (In-State): $13,845
Enrollment: 4,293 Coed
Affiliation or Control: State IRS Status: 501(c)3
Highest Offering: Master's
Accreditation: SC, CAEP, NURSE

01 President ... Dr. Troy PAINO
05 Interim Provost ... Dr. Timothy O'DONNELL
100 Chief of Staff ... Dr. Jeffrey MCCLURKEN
10 VP for Admin & Finance ... Mr. Paul MESSPLAY
32 Vice President Student Affairs ... Dr. Juliette LANDPHAIR
111 Vice Pres for Advance & Univ Rels ... Ms. Lisa BOWLING
102 CEO of UMW Foundation ... Mr. Jeffrey W. ROUNTREE
13 Chief Information Officer ... Mr. Hall CHESHIRE
88 Exec Dir Ctr Economic Development ... Mr. Brian J. BAKER
22 VP Equity & Access/Chief Div Ofcr ... Vacant
15 Executive Director Human Resources ... Ms. Beth WILLIAMS
105 Director of Digital Communication ... Dr. Anand RAO
21 Director of Business Svcs ... Ms. Kathy SANDOR
20 Assoc Provost for Academic Affairs ... Vacant
84 Vice Pres for Enrollment Mgmt ... Ms. Kimberley BUSTER-WILLIAMS
110 Assoc VP Univ Advance/Alumni Rel ... Mr. Kenneth L. STEEN
53 Dean of College of Education ... Dr. Peter KELLY
50 Interim Dean College of Business ... Mr. Ken MACHANDE
49 Dean College of Arts & Sciences ... Dr. Keith MELLINGER
35 Assoc VP & Dean of Student Life ... Mr. Cedric B. RUCKER
37 Director of Financial Aid ... Mr. Timothy SAULNIER
09 Director of Institutional Research ... Mr. Mathew C. WILKERSON
116 Director of Internal Audit ... Mr. Davis MCCRORY
39 Asst Dean for Res Life & Housing ... Mr. David FLEMING
06 Registrar ... Ms. Rita DUNSTON
41 Athletic Director ... Mr. Patrick CATULLO
08 University Librarian ... Ms. Rosemary ARNESON
88 Director of Publications ... Ms. Neva S. TRENIS
88 Director of Dodd Auditorium ... Mr. Doug NOBLE
121 Assoc Provost Academic Engagement ... Vacant
19 Chief of Police ... Mr. Michael W. HALL
29 Exec Director Alumni Relations ... Mr. Mark THADEN
107 Ex Dir Continuing/Professional Stds ... Ms. Kimberly YOUNG
38 Director of Talley Center ... Mr. Tevya ZUKOR
28 Director of Disability Resources ... Ms. Jessica MACHADO
23 University Physician/Health Center ... Ms. Nancy WANG
96 Director of Procurement Services ... Ms. Melva KISHPAUGH
09 Assoc Provost for Inst Analysis/Eff ... Dr. Debra SCHLEEF
26 Assoc VP University Relations ... Ms. Anna B. BILLINGSLEY
27 Asst Dir Media & Public Relations ... Ms. Lisa MARVASHTI
27 Director of University Marketing ... Mr. Malcolm HOLMES
88 Director of Design Services ... Ms. AJ NEWELL
04 Executive Office Manager ... Ms. Paula ZERO
101 Clerk of Board of Visitors ... Dr. Jeff MCCLURKEN
104 Dir Ctr for International Education ... Dr. Jose SAINZ
30 Director of Development ... Vacant
44 Director Annual Giving ... Vacant

University of North America (A)

12750 Fair Lakes Circle, Fairfax VA 22033
County: Fairfax Identification: 667241
Telephone: (571) 633-9651 Carnegie Class: Not Classified
FAX Number: (703) 890-3372 Calendar System: Semester
URL: www.uona.edu
Established: Annual Undergrad Tuition & Fees: N/A
Enrollment: N/A Coed
Affiliation or Control: Independent Non-Profit IRS Status: 501(c)3
Highest Offering: Master's
Accreditation: ACICS

00 CEO ... Marty MARTIN
01 President ... Jill MARTIN
05 VP of Academic Affairs ... Peter WEST
20 VP of Educational Operations ... Jason KOO
37 Director Financial Affairs ... Vacant

University of the Potomac (B)

7799 Leesburg Pike, Suite 200, Falls Church VA 22043
Telephone: (202) 521-1290 Identification: 666178
Accreditation: &M

† Regional accreditation is carried under the parent institution in Washington, DC.

University of Richmond (C)

28 Westhampton Way, Richmond VA 23173-1903
County: Independent City FICE Identification: 003744
Unit ID: 233374
Telephone: (804) 289-8000 Carnegie Class: Bac-A&S
FAX Number: (804) 287-6540 Calendar System: Semester
URL: www.richmond.edu
Established: 1830 Annual Undergrad Tuition & Fees: $56,860
Enrollment: 4,056 Coordinate
Affiliation or Control: Independent Non-Profit IRS Status: 501(c)3
Highest Offering: Doctorate
Accreditation: SC, CAEPT, LAW

01 President ... Dr. Ronald A. CRUTCHER
05 Executive VP & Provost ... Dr. Jeffrey LEGRO
10 EVP & COO Business & Finance ... Mr. David B. HALE
32 Vice President Student Affairs ... Dr. Stephen D. BISESE
111 Vice President Advancement ... Ms. Martha CALLAGHAN
13 VP & Chief Information Officer ... Mr. Keith J. MCINTOSH
84 Vice Pres Enrollment Management ... Dr. Stephanie DUPAUL
45 Vice President Planning & Policy ... Dr. Lori G. SCHUYLER
101 VP & Secretary Board of Trustees ... Dr. Ann Lloyd BREEDEN
04 Assistant to President ... Ms. Ashleigh BROCK
88 President & CIO Spider Mgmt Company ... Mr. William MCLEAN
88 CEO Spider Mgmt Company ... Mr. Rob BLANDFORD
15 Senior Assoc VP Human Resources ... Mr. Carl K. SORENSEN
18 AVP for Facilities & Univ Architect ... Mr. Andrew S. MCBRIDE
29 Asst VP Alumni & Career Services ... Ms. Denise D. SMITH
102 Asst VP Foundation/Corp/Govt Rels ... Ms. Michelle E. WAMSLEY
42 University Chaplain ... Rev. Craig T. KOCHER
07 Assoc VP and Dean of Admissions ... Mr. Gil VILLANUEVA
08 University Librarian ... Mr. Kevin BUTTERFIELD
09 Dir Institutional Effectiveness ... Ms. Melanie JENKINS
06 University Registrar ... Ms. Kristen BALL
37 AVP & Director ... Mr. William B. BRYAN
36 Dir Career Development Center ... Ms. Leslie W. STEVENSON
38 Director of CAPS ... Dr. Peter O. LEVINESS
96 Director Strategic Sourcing ... Ms. Jean C. HINES
35 Assoc VP Student Development ... Dr. Tina Q. CADE
41 Director of Athletics ... Mr. John HARDT
104 Director Study Abroad ... Ms. Michele D. COX
105 Director Web Services ... Mr. Eric F. PALMER
33 Dean of Richmond College ... Dr. Joseph R. BOEHMAN
34 Dean Westhampton College ... Dr. Mia R. GENONI
49 Interim Dean School Arts & Sciences ... Dr. Dan PALAZZOLO
50 Dean School of Business ... Dr. Mickey QUIÑONES
61 Dean School of Law ... Dr. Wendy C. PERDUE
51 Dean School Continuing Studies ... Dr. Jamelle WILSON
88 Dean Jepson School Leader Stds ... Dr. Sandra J. PEART
19 Assc VP Public Sfty/Chief of Police ... Mr. David M. MCCOY
23 Director Health Center ... Dr. Lynne P. DEANE
26 Asst VP for Communications ... Mr. John M. BARRY
40 Manager University Bookstore ... Ms. Liz ST. JOHN
28 Dir of Inst Equity & Inclusion ... Dr. Glyn HUGHES
39 Director Student Housing ... Mr. Patrick B. BENNER
43 VP & General Counsel ... Ms. Shannon E. SINCLAIR
91 Dir Enterprise Application ... Mr. Lee PARKER, III
44 Director Annual Giving ... Ms. Kim LEBAR

University of Virginia (D)

1827 University Avenue, Charlottesville VA 22904
County: Independent City FICE Identification: 003745
Unit ID: 234076
Telephone: (434) 924-0311 Carnegie Class: DU-Highest
FAX Number: (434) 924-0938 Calendar System: Semester
URL: www.virginia.edu
Established: 1819 Annual Undergrad Tuition & Fees (In-State): $18,960
Enrollment: 25,628 Coed
Affiliation or Control: State IRS Status: 501(c)3
Highest Offering: Doctorate
Accreditation: SC, CAATE, CACREP, CAEP, CAEPT, CAMPEP, CLPSY, DENT, DIETI, IPSY, LAW, LSAR, MED, NURSE, PAST, PCSAS, PH, PLNG, PSPSY, SP

01 President ... Mr. James E. RYAN
00 Rector ... Mr. Whittington W. CLEMENT
101 Special Asst & Secretary/BOV ... Ms. Susan G. HARRIS
05 Exec Vice President & Provost ... Ms. M. Elizabeth MAGILL
03 Exec Vice Pres/Chief Operating Ofcr ... Ms. Jennifer (J.J.) WAGNER DAVIS
43 University Counsel ... Mr. Timothy J. HEAPHY
116 Chief Audit Executive ... Ms. Carolyn SAINT
100 Asst VP & Chief of Staff ... Ms. Margaret S. GRUNDY
22 Assoc VP Equal Opp Pgms/Civ Rights ... Ms. Emily SPRINGSTON
17 Exec Vice Pres for Health Affairs ... Dr. K. Craig KENT
23 CEO Medical Center ... Ms. Wendy M. HORTON
88 Health System CFO ... Mr. Douglas E. LISCHKE
111 Sr Vice Pres for Advancement ... Vacant
10 Vice President for Finance ... Ms. Melody BIANCHETTO
115 Chief Investment Officer ... Mr. Robert DURDEN
88 Exec Director The Jefferson Trust ... Mr. Brent PERCIVAL
32 VP/Chief Student Affairs Officer ... Ms. Robyn HADLEY
35 Associate VP/Dean of Students ... Mr. Allen W. GROVES
36 Assoc VP Career & Prof Development ... Mr. Everette FORTNER
93 Dean African-American Affairs ... Dr. Maurice APPREY
23 Exec Director Student Health ... Dr. Christopher HOLSTEGE
39 Exec Dir Housing & Residence Life ... Ms. Gay PEREZ
35 Assoc VP for Student Affairs ... Ms. Susan M. DAVIS
35 Assoc VP for Student Affairs ... Ms. Elisa HOLQUIST
40 Assistant Director of UVa Bookstore ... Mr. Roy CADOFF
46 Vice Pres for Research ... Mr. Melur RAMASUBRAMANIAN
25 Sr AVP/Dir Academic Rsrch Comp ... Mr. David J. HUDSON
28 VP Diversity/Equity/Incl/Cmty Prtnr ... Mr. Kevin G. MCDONALD
41 Dir Intercollegiate Athletic Pgms ... Ms. Carla WILLIAMS
88 Director/CEO Miller Center ... William J. ANTHOLIS
15 Int VP/Chief Human Resources Ofcr ... Mr. John KOSKY
26 VP Communication/Chief Mktg Officer ... Mr. David W. MARTEL
12 Chancellor UVA's College at Wise ... Ms. Donna P. HENRY
11 Sr VP Operations/State Govt Rels ... Ms. Colette SHEEHY
21 Assoc VP Business Operations ... Mr. Richard A. KOVATCH
88 Architect for the University ... Ms. Alice J. RAUCHER
88 University Building Official ... Mr. Ben HAYS
18 Assoc VP & Chief Facilities Officer ... Mr. Donald E. SUNDGREN
37 Asst VP Student Financial Svcs ... Mr. Stephen A. KIMATA
96 Dir of Procurement/Diversity Svcs ... Ms. Jenn GLASSMAN
13 Vice Pres & Chief Information Ofcr ... Ms. Virginia H. EVANS
20 Vice Prov for Academic Affairs ... Vacant
84 Vice Provost for Enrollment ... Mr. Stephen FARMER
20 Vice Prov Academic Initiatives ... Ms. Megan BARNETT
45 Vice Provost Planning ... Mr. Adam DANIEL
108 Assoc Prov Institutional Research ... Ms. Christina MORELL
20 Vice Prov Faculty Affairs ... Ms. Manté BRANDT-PEARCE
88 Vice Prov for Administration ... Ms. Anda L. WEBB
57 Vice Prov for the Arts ... Mr. Jody K. KIELBASA
88 Vice Prov for Acad Outreach ... Mr. Louis NELSON
90 Vice Provost Academic Technology ... Mr. Ronald R. HUTCHINS
85 Vice Provost for Global Affairs ... Mr. Stephen D. MULL
06 Assoc Vice Provost and Registrar ... Ms. Laura HAWTHORNE
07 Dean of Admission ... Mr. Gregory W. ROBERTS
61 Dean School of Law ... Ms. Risa L. GOLUBOFF
49 Dean School of Arts & Sciences ... Mr. Ian B. BAUCOM
63 Dean School of Medicine ... Dr. David S. WILKES
66 Dean School of Nursing ... Dr. Pam CIPRIANO
54 Dean Schl Engr/Applied Science ... Ms. Jennifer L. WEST
48 Dean School of Architecture ... Ms. Ila BERMAN
50 Dean School of Commerce ... Ms. Nicole T. JENKINS
80 Dean Sch Leadership/Public Policy ... Mr. Ian H. SOLOMON
53 Dean School of Education ... Mr. Robert C. PIANTA
50 Dean Grad School Business Admin ... Mr. Scott C. BEARDSLEY
51 Dean Cont/Professional Studies ... Mr. Alejandro HERNANDEZ
88 Director Applied Research Inst ... Ms. Joan M. BIENVENUE
88 Director Center for Politics ... Mr. Larry J. SABATO
77 Dean School of Data Science ... Mr. Philip E. BOURNE
88 Exec Dir Biocomplexity Inst ... Mr. Christopher L. BARRETT
08 Univ Librarian/Dean of Libraries ... Mr. John M. UNSWORTH
104 Dir Intl Studies/Summer/Sp Acad Pgm ... Mr. Dudley J. DOANE
19 Associate VP Safety/Chief of Police ... Mr. Timothy LONGO
94 Dir Study in Women Gender Sexuality ... Ms. Charlotte PATTERSON
102 Director Foundation/Corporate Rels ... Ms. Katie SHEVLIN
38 Dir Counseling & Psych Services ... Dr. Nicole RUZEK
86 Exec Dir State Govt Rels/SA to Pres ... Vacant

The University of Virginia's College at Wise (E)

One College Avenue, Wise VA 24293-4412
County: Wise FICE Identification: 003747
Unit ID: 233897
Telephone: (276) 328-0100 Carnegie Class: Bac-A&S
FAX Number: (276) 376-1012 Calendar System: Semester
URL: www.uvawise.edu
Established: 1954 Annual Undergrad Tuition & Fees (In-State): $10,836
Enrollment: 1,905 Coed
Affiliation or Control: State IRS Status: 501(c)3
Highest Offering: Baccalaureate
Accreditation: SC, CAEP, MUS, NURSE

01 Chancellor ... Dr. Donna P. HENRY
05 Provost/Vice Chanc for Acad Affairs ... Dr. Trisha FOLDS-BENNETT
111 VC Advancement/Alumni Engagement ... Ms. Valerie S. LAWSON
10 Vice Chanc Finance/Operations ... Mr. Joe KISER
84 Vice Chancellor Enrollment Mgmt ... Mr. Chris DEARTH
20 Academic Dean ... Dr. Mark CLARK
32 Vice Chancellor for Student Affairs ... Ms. Gail ZIMMERMAN
21 Comptroller ... Mrs. Kristy ROBERTSON
13 Assoc Prov for Information Svcs/CIO ... Dr. P. Scott BEVINS
06 Registrar ... Ms. Narda PORTER
15 Director of Human Resources ... Ms. Stephanie D. PERRY
29 Director of Alumni Relations ... Vacant
37 Director of Financial Aid ... Ms. Rebecca HUFFMAN
35 Asst Dir of Student Activities ... Ms. Mikaela LOGAN
36 Dir of Discovery & Planning ... Ms. Neva BRYAN
38 Personal Counselor/Health Services ... Ms. Sara SCHILL
19 Interim Campus Police Chief ... Mr. Beau BOGGS
12 Site Director UVA-Wise Programs ... Ms. Courtney L. CONNER-STRINGER
27 Director of Marketing ... Ms. Genna WELSH KASUN
24 Director of Media Services ... Ms. Rosa BOTT
40 Bookstore Manager ... Vacant
39 Director of Residence Life ... Mr. Robbie CHULICK
108 Director Institutional Assessment ... Mr. David KLOCEK
100 Chief of Staff ... Ms. Huda ADEN
28 AVC Diversity/Equity/Inclusion ... Ms. Tabitha SMITH

Virginia Beach Theological Seminary (F)

2221 Centerville Turnpike, Virginia Beach VA 23464-6847
County: Virginia Beach FICE Identification: 039663
Unit ID: 449834
Telephone: (757) 479-3706 Carnegie Class: Spec-4-yr-Faith
FAX Number: N/A Calendar System: Semester
URL: www.vbts.edu
Established: 1995 Annual Graduate Tuition & Fees: N/A
Enrollment: 35 Coed
Affiliation or Control: Baptist IRS Status: 501(c)3
Highest Offering: Doctorate; No Undergraduates
Accreditation: TRACS

01 President ... Dr. Daniel K. DAVEY
05 Chief Academic Officer ... Dr. Eric J. LEHNER
07 Director of Admissions/Registrar ... Mr. Edward R. ESTES, IV
10 Financial Officer ... Capt. Tony A. BRAZAS
08 Head Librarian ... Dr. Michael H. WINDSOR

Virginia Bible College (G)

1006 Williamstown Dr, Dumfries VA 22026
County: Prince William Identification: 667327
Telephone: (703) 445-9056 Carnegie Class: Not Classified

FAX Number: (703) 445-9057 Calendar System: Quarter
URL: vabiblecollege.edu
Established: 2011 Annual Undergrad Tuition & Fees: N/A
Enrollment: N/A Coed
Affiliation or Control: Independent Non-Profit IRS Status: 501(c)3
Highest Offering: Doctorate
Accreditation: TRACS

01 President .... Dr. Derek GRIER
05 VP of Academic & Student Affs .... Dr. Shennell JANUARY
58 Director of Graduate Studies .... Dr. James BOWERS
06 Registrar .... Ms. Monique MAXWELL
08 Librarian .... Ms. Donna MCDONALD

Virginia Christian University (A)

14012-F Sullyfield Circle, Chantilly VA 20151
County: Fairfax Identification: 667352
Telephone: (703) 629-1281 Carnegie Class: Not Classified
FAX Number: (703) 657-0690 Calendar System: Semester
URL: vacu.edu/
Established: 2005 Annual Undergrad Tuition & Fees: N/A
Enrollment: N/A Coed
Affiliation or Control: Presbyterian Church In America IRS Status: 501(c)3
Highest Offering: Master's
Accreditation: BI

01 President .... Dr. Thomas RHEE
05 Academic Dean & Dir Graduate Pgm .... Dr. Sunik HWANG
15 Vice Pres & Dir Human Resources .... Dr. Joshua PARK
32 Dean of Students .... Dr. Hyejoo LEE
10 Director of Finance .... Mr. Dae C. KIM
06 Director of Registration .... Ms. Sooyoung YIM
13 Director of Technology .... Mr. Junwhan KIM

Virginia Commonwealth University (B)

901 W Franklin Street, Box 842527,
Richmond VA 23284-2527
County: Independent City FICE Identification: 003735
Unit ID: 234030
Telephone: (804) 828-0100 Carnegie Class: DU-Highest
FAX Number: N/A Calendar System: Semester
URL: www.vcu.edu
Established: 1838 Annual Undergrad Tuition & Fees (In-State): $14,710
Enrollment: 29,070 Coed
Affiliation or Control: State IRS Status: 501(c)3
Highest Offering: Doctorate
Accreditation: SC, ANEST, ART, CACREP, CAEPN, CAMPEP, CEA, CIDA, CLPSY, COPSY, DANCE, DENT, DH, DIETI, DMS, EMT, FEPAC, HSA, IPSY, JOUR, MED, MT, MUS, NMT, NURSE, OT, PAST, PDPSY, PH, PHAR, PLNG, PTA, RAD, RTT, SPAA, SW, THEA

01 President/Pres & Chair VCU Hlth Sys .... Dr. Michael RAO
05 Provost & VP for Academic Affairs .... Dr. Gail HACKETT
17 VP Health Sci/CEO VCU Hlth Sys .... Dr. Arthur KELLERMANN
10 SVP & Chief Financial Officer .... Ms. Karol GRAY
46 VP for Research & Innovation .... Dr. Srirama P. RAO
111 VP Development/Alumni Relations .... Mr. Jason DAVENPORT
86 Exec Dir Govt Rels & Health Policy .... Ms. Karah L. GUNTHER
32 Sr Vice Prov Student Affairs .... Dr. Charles J. KLINK
88 Vice Prov for Life Sciences .... Dr. Robert M. TOMBES
09 Asst VProv Inst Rsrch & Decision Su .... Ms. Monal PATEL
84 VProv Strategic Enrollment Mgmt .... Dr. Tomika LEGRANDE
13 Chief Information Officer Tech Svcs .... Mr. Alexander L. HENSON
18 Assoc VP Facilities Management .... Mr. Richard F. SLIWOSKI
88 AVP Strategic Enrollment Svcs .... Mr. Norman F. BEDFORD
15 Asst Vice Pres for Human Resources .... Ms. Cathleen C. BURKE
08 Int Dean Libraries/Univ Librarian .... Ms. Teresa L. KNOTT
43 University Counsel .... Mr. Mike F. MELIS
41 Vice Pres & Director of Athletics .... Mr. Edward K. MCLAUGHLIN
21 Asst Vice Pres of Business Services .... Ms. Diane L. REYNOLDS
39 Asst VP/Exec Dir Res Life/Housing .... Mr. Curtis ERWIN
06 Univ Registrar & Dir Records/Regis .... Mr. Bernard C. HAMM
37 Executive Director of Financial Aid .... Mr. Evan UDOWITCH
38 Exec Dir of Counseling Services .... Dr. Jihad N. AZIZ
36 Sr Associate Dir Career Advising .... Ms. Haley SIMS
35 Assoc Vice Prov/Dean Student Affs .... Dr. Reuban B. RODRIGUEZ
29 Assistant VP Alumni Relations .... Ms. Elizabeth BASS
88 Exec Dir Global Education Office .... Dr. Jill BLONDIN
88 Dir Ctr for Environmental Studies .... Dr. Rodney J. DYER
25 Sr Assoc VP Rsrch Admin/Compliance .... Ms. Susan E. ROBB
19 Asst Vice Pres Public Safety .... Mr. John A. VENUTI
31 Exec Dir Community Engagement .... Ms. Heidi A. CRAPOL
92 Dean Honors College .... Dr. Scott BREUNINGER
67 Dean of Pharmacy .... Dr. Joseph T. DIPIRO
66 Dean of School of Nursing .... Dr. Jean GIDDENS
63 Dean of School of Medicine .... Dr. Peter F. BUCKLEY
53 Dean School of Education .... Dr. Andrew P. DAIRE
52 Dean of Dentistry .... Dr. David C. SARRETT
50 Dean School of Business .... Mr. Ed GRIER
79 Dean Humanities & Sciences .... Dr. Jennifer MALAT
57 Dean School of Arts .... Dr. Carmenita HIGGINBOTHAM
70 Dean School of Social Work .... Dr. Beth ANGELL
76 Dean College Health Professions .... Dr. Susan PARISH
58 Dean Graduate School .... Dr. Daniel C. BULLARD
54 Dean of School of Engineering .... Dr. Barbara D. BOYAN
96 Director Procurement Svcs .... Mr. John MCHUGH
26 Vice President University Relations .... Mr. Grant J. HESTON
104 Director Education Abroad .... Ms. Stephanie DAVENPORT TIGNOR
45 Sr Exec for Special Projects .... Dr. Kevin ALLISON
106 Executive Director Online @VCU .... Dr. Mandara SAVAGE
90 Director Academic Technologies .... Ms. Colleen BISHOP
108 Dir Academic Integrity & Assessment .... Dr. Scott F. OATES
22 VP Inclusive Excellence .... Dr. Aashir NASIM
105 Deputy Dir Application Services .... Mr. James B. YUCHA
30 Sr Assoc VP for Development .... Mr. Magnus H. JOHNSSON
44 Executive Director Annual Giving .... Mr. Michael P. ANDREWS

*Virginia Community College System Office (C)

300 Arboretum Place, Suite 200, Richmond VA 23236
County: Independent City FICE Identification: 008904
Telephone: (804) 819-4901 Carnegie Class: N/A
FAX Number: N/A
URL: www.vccs.edu

01 Chancellor .... Dr. Glenn DUBOIS
05 Sr Vice Chanc Acad/Workforce Pgms .... Dr. Sharon MORRISSEY
10 Sr Vice Chanc Admin/Finance/Tech .... Dr. Craig HERNDON
13 Chief Information Officer .... Dr. Michael RUSSELL
111 Vice Chanc Institutional Advance .... Dr. Jennifer SAGER GENTRY
15 Assoc Vice Chanc Human Resource Svc .... Ms. Malinda CARTER
18 Assoc Vice Chanc/Facility Mgmt .... Mr. Bert JONES
43 General Counsel .... Ms. Greer SAUNDERS
116 Int Director of Internal Audit .... Ms. Mary BARNETT
21 Controller .... Mr. Randall ELLIS
04 Exec Assistant to the Chancellor .... Ms. Rose Marie OWEN

*Blue Ridge Community College (D)

PO Box 80, Weyers Cave VA 24486-0080
County: Augusta FICE Identification: 006819
Unit ID: 231536
Telephone: (540) 234-9261 Carnegie Class: Assoc/HT-Mix Trad/Non
FAX Number: (540) 234-8189 Calendar System: Semester
URL: www.brcc.edu
Established: 1967 Annual Undergrad Tuition & Fees (In-State): $5,364
Enrollment: 3,462 Coed
Affiliation or Control: State IRS Status: 501(c)3
Highest Offering: Associate Degree
Accreditation: SC, ADNUR

02 President .... Dr. John A. DOWNEY
05 Vice Pres Instruction/Student Svcs .... Dr. Robert YOUNG
10 VP Finance/Administration .... Ms. Cynthia PAGE
15 Director of Human Resources .... Mr. Tim NICELY
30 Exec Dir Development/Foundation .... Ms. Amy L. KIGER
20 Dean of Academic Affairs .... Ms. Marlena JARBOE
20 Dean of Academic Affairs .... Dr. David URSO
51 Dean Continuing Educ/Workforce Dev .... Dr. Kevin B. RATLIFF
32 Dean Student Svcs/Acad Compliance .... Ms. Velma BRYANT
08 Head Librarian .... Ms. Dawn WALTON
26 Chief Public Relations Officer .... Ms. Bridget BAYLOR
06 Registrar/Admissions .... Ms. Lisa ADKINS
21 Director of Finance & Facilities .... Ms. Franki HAMPTON
09 Director Institutional Research .... Dr. Susan E. CROSBY
37 Financial Aid Coordinator .... Ms. Megan HARTLESS
36 Career Services/Recruitment Coord .... Ms. Carmel MURPHY-NORRIS

*Central Virginia Community College (E)

3506 Wards Road, Lynchburg VA 24502-2498
County: Independent City FICE Identification: 004988
Unit ID: 231697
Telephone: (434) 832-7600 Carnegie Class: Assoc/HT-High Non
FAX Number: (434) 386-4700 Calendar System: Semester
URL: www.centralvirginia.edu
Established: 1966 Annual Undergrad Tuition & Fees (In-State): $4,838
Enrollment: 3,370 Coed
Affiliation or Control: State IRS Status: 501(c)3
Highest Offering: Associate Degree
Accreditation: SC, COARC, EMT, MLTAD, RAD

02 President .... Dr. John CAPPS
05 Int VP Student & Academic Services .... Dr. Kris OGDEN
10 Vice President Finance & Admin Svcs .... Mr. Lewis BRYANT, III
111 VP Inst Advancement/Exec Dir Fndn .... Mr. Christopher BRYANT
13 Vice Pres of Information Technology .... Mr. David LIGHTFOOT
45 Dean Inst Effectiveness/Planning .... Dr. Cynthia DEUTSCH
32 Dean of Student Services .... Ms. Patricia SAFFIOTI
09 Director of Strategic Initiatives .... Mr. William SANDIDGE
26 Dir Advancement/Public Relations .... Mr. Kenneth BUNCH
06 College Registrar .... Ms. Karen ALEXANDER
84 Dean of Enrollment Management .... Mr. Michael FARRIS
15 Human Resource Director .... Mr. Randall FRANKLIN
56 Distance Education Supervisor .... Mr. Ed MCGEE
08 Coordinator of Library Services .... Mr. Michael T. FEIN
75 AVP Professional & Career Studies .... Dr. Jason FERGUSON
49 AVP of Arts & Sciences .... Dr. Cynthia WALLIN
04 General Administration Coordinator .... Ms. Dianne SYKES

*Dabney S. Lancaster Community College (F)

1000 Dabney Drive, Clifton Forge VA 24422-1000
County: Alleghany FICE Identification: 004996
Unit ID: 231873
Telephone: (540) 863-2820 Carnegie Class: Assoc/HT-High Non
FAX Number: (540) 863-2915 Calendar System: Semester
URL: www.dslcc.edu
Established: 1962 Annual Undergrad Tuition & Fees (In-State): $4,710
Enrollment: 1,075 Coed
Affiliation or Control: State IRS Status: 501(c)3
Highest Offering: Associate Degree
Accreditation: SC, ADNUR

02 President .... Dr. John J. RAINONE
05 Vice President of Academic Affairs .... Dr. Benjamin WORTH
10 Vice Pres Financial/Admin Svcs .... Mrs. Angela GRAHAM
51 VP Continuing Educ/Workforce Svcs .... Mr. Gary S. KEENER
09 AVP of Institutional Effectiveness .... Dr. Matthew MCGRAW
32 Director of Student Services .... Mr. Joseph HAGY
111 Director of Inst Advancement .... Ms. Rachael G. THOMPSON
08 Director of Learning Resources .... Ms. Nova WRIGHT
13 Technical Services Manager .... Mr. Wayne RAUENZAHN
15 Director of Human Resources .... Ms. April TOLLEY
18 Buildings & Grounds Supervisor .... Mr. Steven N. RICHARDS
21 Business Manager .... Ms. Deidre WOLFE
07 Admissions Officer .... Ms. Suzanne OSTLING
37 Coord of Student Financial Aid .... Mrs. Coty LANFORD
30 Marketing & Development Coordinator .... Ms. Jodi BURGESS
04 Executive Asst to President .... Ms. Phyllis BARTLEY
06 Records Clerk .... Miss Rebecca STOVER

*Danville Community College (G)

1008 S Main Street, Danville VA 24541-4088
County: Independent City FICE Identification: 003758
Unit ID: 231882
Telephone: (434) 797-2222 Carnegie Class: Assoc/MT-VT-High Non
FAX Number: (434) 797-8514 Calendar System: Semester
URL: www.danville.edu
Established: 1967 Annual Undergrad Tuition & Fees (In-State): $4,725
Enrollment: 2,411 Coed
Affiliation or Control: State IRS Status: 501(c)3
Highest Offering: Associate Degree
Accreditation: SC, NAEYC

02 President .... Dr. Muriel MICKLES
05 VP Academic Affs/Student Services .... Dr. Cornelius H. JOHNSON
10 Vice Pres Financial/Admin Services .... Mr. Charles TOOTHMAN
30 Vice President of Development .... Mr. Shannon HAIR
103 Vice President of Workforce Service .... Dr. Brian JACKSON
09 Dir of Plng/Effectiveness/Research .... Mr. Cory POTTER
07 Coordinator of Admissions .... Ms. Cathy PULLLIAM
38 Coordinator of Counseling .... Mr. Howard GRAVES
26 Public Relations/Marketing Manager .... Ms. Faith O'NEIL
04 Exec Assistant to the President .... Ms. Connie P. WANN
08 Chief Library Officer .... Mr. Christopher FORD
15 Chief Human Resources Officer .... Mr. Bruce COTTRILL
37 Director Student Financial Aid .... Ms. Angela TURNER

*Eastern Shore Community College (H)

29316 Lankford Highway, Melfa VA 23410-9755
County: Accomack FICE Identification: 003748
Unit ID: 232052
Telephone: (757) 789-1789 Carnegie Class: Assoc/MT-VT-Mix Trad/Non
FAX Number: N/A Calendar System: Semester
URL: www.es.vccs.edu
Established: 1971 Annual Undergrad Tuition & Fees (In-State): $4,800
Enrollment: 677 Coed
Affiliation or Control: State IRS Status: 501(c)3
Highest Offering: Associate Degree
Accreditation: SC

02 President .... Dr. James M. SHAEFFER
05 VP of Acad/Workforce/Student Prgms .... Dr. Patrick TOMPKINS
11 Assoc VP Administration .... Ms. Eve BELOTE
32 Coordinator of Student Services .... Mrs. Cheryll MILLS
09 Director of Institutional Research .... Ms. Judith GRIER
26 Marketing and Development Officer .... Mr. William LECATO
37 Financial Aid Coordinator .... Ms. Carole READ
15 Human Resource Officer .... Ms. Beth LUNDE
04 Admin Assistant to the President .... Ms. Bette CORNELL
19 Chief of Police .... Mr. David BRANCH
30 Director of Development .... Ms. Patricia KELLAM
06 Registrar .... Vacant
103 Business Dev & Workforce Officer .... Mr. Scott HALL
13 Chief Info Technology Officer .... Mr. Mike SMITH

*Germanna Community College (I)

2130 Germanna Highway, Locust Grove VA 22508-2102
County: Orange FICE Identification: 008660
Unit ID: 232195
Telephone: (540) 423-9030 Carnegie Class: Assoc/HT-Mix Trad/Non
FAX Number: (540) 727-3207 Calendar System: Semester
URL: www.germanna.edu
Established: 1970 Annual Undergrad Tuition & Fees (In-State): $4,140
Enrollment: 7,679 Coed
Affiliation or Control: State IRS Status: 501(c)3
Highest Offering: Associate Degree
Accreditation: SC, ADNUR, DA, PTAA

02 President .... Dr. Janet GULLICKSON
04 Exec Assistant to the President .... Ms. Lorraine PENDLETON
05 VP Academic Affairs & Workforce Dev .... Dr. Shashuna GRAY
10 VP Finance & Administrative Svcs .... Dr. John DAVIS
32 Dean of Student Services .... Ms. Pam FREDERICK
45 Director Planning/Research/Effectiv .... Mr. David DEMEDICIS
08 Head Librarian .... Ms. Tamara REMHOF

06 Registrar .... Ms. Cheri MAEA
72 Dean Professional & Technical Study .... Ms. Denise TALLEY
106 Dean Distance Educ & Lrng Resources .... Dr. Yanyan YONG
66 Dean of Nursing & Health Technology .... Dr. Patti LISK
15 Associate VP of Human Resources .... Mrs. Laurie BOURNE
18 Director of Facilities .... Mr. Garland FENWICK
26 Director of Marketing .... Mr. William BERRY
49 Dean of Arts & Sciences .... Vacant
103 AVP of Workforce Prof Development .... Ms. Martha O'KEEFE
19 Chief of Police .... Mr. Craig BRANCH
37 Director Student Financial Aid .... Mr. Aaron WHITACRE

*J. Sargeant Reynolds Community College (A)

PO Box 85622, Richmond VA 23285-5622
County: Henrico FICE Identification: 003759
Unit ID: 232414
Telephone: (804) 371-3000 Carnegie Class: Assoc/MT-VT-Mix Trad/Non
FAX Number: (804) 371-3650 Calendar System: Semester
URL: www.reynolds.edu
Established: 1972 Annual Undergrad Tuition & Fees (In-State): $4,998
Enrollment: 7,759 Coed
Affiliation or Control: State IRS Status: 501(c)3
Highest Offering: Associate Degree
Accreditation: SC, ACFEI, ADNUR, COARC, DA, EMT, MLTAD, OPD

02 President .... Dr. Paula P. PANDO
05 Vice President Academic Affairs .... Vacant
111 Vice President Advancement .... Mrs. Elizabeth S. LITTLEFIELD
103 VP Comm Col Workforce Alliance .... Mr. Wesley SMITH
10 VP Finance and Administration .... Ms. Amelia M. BRADSHAW
32 VP Student Affairs/Title IX Coord .... Vacant
84 VP Enroll Mgmt/Student Success .... Dr. Terricita E. SASS
45 Assoc VP Strat Plng/Inst Effective .... Dr. Timothy MERRILL
50 Dean School of Business .... Mr. David J. BARRISH
76 Dean School of Nursing/Allied Hlth .... Dr. Patricia P. LAWSON
81 Dean School of Math Sci Engineering .. Mr. Raymond A. BURTON
20 Asst VP Academic Affairs .... Dr. Lori DWYER
15 Assoc VP HR/Equal Emp Oppty Ofcr .... Ms. Corliss B. WOODSON
37 Director of Financial Aid .... Ms. Sherika CHARITY
07 Director of Admissions & Records .... Mrs. Karen M. PETTIS-WALDEN
27 Director Communications .... Mr. Joseph SHILLING
26 Director of Marketing .... Ms. Kelly A. SMITH
08 Director of Info/Library Services .... Ms. Hong WU
18 Director Facilities Mgmt/Planning .... Vacant
30 Director of Development .... Ms. Marianne S. MCGHEE
88 Director of Middle College .... Ms. Mary Jo WASHKO
06 Registrar .... Ms. Angela ROSS
19 Chief of Police .... Mr. Paul L. RONCA
04 Admin Assistant to the President .... Ms. Ann M. BUSHEY
106 Dean of Online Learning .... Dr. Danielle R. LEEK

*John Tyler Community College (B)

13101 Jefferson Davis Highway, Chester VA 23831-5316
County: Chesterfield FICE Identification: 004004
Unit ID: 232450
Telephone: (804) 796-4000 Carnegie Class: Assoc/HT-High Non
FAX Number: (804) 796-4163 Calendar System: Semester
URL: www.jtcc.edu
Established: 1965 Annual Undergrad Tuition & Fees (In-State): $4,800
Enrollment: 9,440 Coed
Affiliation or Control: State IRS Status: 501(c)3
Highest Offering: Associate Degree
Accreditation: SC, ADNUR, EMT, FUSER

02 President .... Dr. Edward (Ted) E. RASPILLER
04 Admin Assistant to the President .... Ms. Kara ARMSTRONG
05 VP Learning & Student Success .... Dr. William FIEGE
10 VP Administration .... Ms. Susan GRINNAN
111 VP Institutional Advancement .... Ms. Rachel BIUNDO
103 VP Workforce Dev/Credential Attain .... Ms. Elizabeth CREAMER
21 Assoc VP of Financial Services .... Ms. Natolyn QUASH
35 Dean of Students .... Ms. Sandra KIRKLAND
20 Assoc VP of Learning .... Dr. Johanna WEISS
20 Assoc VP Academics .... Dr. Mikell BROWN
09 Dir Institutional Effectiveness .... Dr. Keri-Beth PETTENGILL
08 Dir of Library Services .... Ms. Suzanne SHERRY
37 Interim Director Financial Aid .... Ms. Linda SMITH
19 Asst Dir College Safety & Security .... Ms. Tanya BROWN
26 Public Relations Manager .... Ms. Holly WALKER
121 Assoc Dean of Advising .... Ms. Altrice SMITH
19 Dir Facilities Operations & Safety .... Mr. Chip KRAMER
06 Dir Admissions & Records/Registrar .... Mr. Leigh BAXTER

*Lord Fairfax Community College (C)

173 Skirmisher Lane, Middletown VA 22645-1745
County: Frederick FICE Identification: 008659
Unit ID: 232575
Telephone: (540) 868-7000 Carnegie Class: Assoc/HT-High Non
FAX Number: (540) 868-7100 Calendar System: Semester
URL: www.lfcc.edu
Established: 1970 Annual Undergrad Tuition & Fees (In-State): $4,739
Enrollment: 6,337 Coed
Affiliation or Control: State IRS Status: 501(c)3
Highest Offering: Associate Degree
Accreditation: SC, ADNUR, CAHIIM, EMT, SURGT

02 President .... Dr. Kim BLOSSER
12 Provost Fauquier Campus .... Dr. Christopher COUTTS
05 AVP Academic & Student Affairs .... Dr. Caroline WOOD
103 VP of Workforce & Prof Development .... Ms. Jeanian CLARK
111 Exec Dir of Inst Advance/Educ Fdn .... Ms. Liv HEGGOY
09 Dir Planning/Inst Effectiveness .... Dr. John MILAM
50 Dean Business/Technology/Education .... Ms. Brenda BYARD
81 Dean Science/Eng/Math & Health .... Dr. Ia GOMEZ
83 Dean Hum/Social Sciences/Stdnt Dev .... Dr. James GILLISPIE
32 Dean of Students .... Ms. Amber FOLTZ
20 Dean Fauquier Campus .... Dr. Carolline WOOD
24 Director Learning Resources Center .... Mr. David R. GRAY
37 Director of Financial Aid .... Mr. Steven WILSON
08 Librarian .... Ms. Kerry KILPATRICK
25 Grants Manager .... Dr. Melissa DEDOMENICO-PAYNE
26 Dir Marketing & Outreach .... Ms. Brandy BOIES
21 Director Budget/Finance .... Mr. Barry ORNDORFF
84 Dean of Enrollment Svcs/Title IX .... Dr. Mia S. DEZURA
06 Registrar .... Ms. Tina Marie ANDERSON
15 AVP Human Resources .... Ms. JoAnn ELLWOOD
88 Dir Marketing/Business/Ind Trng .... Mr. Guy E. CURTIS, III
20 Associate Dean of Instruction .... Ms. Heather BURTON
88 Director Small Business Dev Center .... Ms. Christine KRIZ

*Mountain Empire Community College (D)

3441 Mountain Empire Road,
Big Stone Gap VA 24219-4634
County: Wise FICE Identification: 009629
Unit ID: 232788
Telephone: (276) 523-2400 Carnegie Class: Assoc/MT-VT-High Non
FAX Number: (276) 523-8297 Calendar System: Semester
URL: www.mecc.edu
Established: 1972 Annual Undergrad Tuition & Fees (In-State): $4,710
Enrollment: 2,253 Coed
Affiliation or Control: State IRS Status: 501(c)3
Highest Offering: Associate Degree
Accreditation: SC, ADNUR, CAHIIM, COARC

02 President .... Dr. Kristen WESTOVER
05 VP Academic & Workforce Solutions .... Vacant
10 Vice Pres Finance & Admin Services .... Mr. Ron VICARS
111 Vice Pres Institutional Advancement .... Dr. Amy GREEAR
32 Dean of Student Services .... Ms. Lelia BRADSHAW
07 Dean Admission/Financial Aid .... Ms. Kristy HALL
08 Director of Library Services .... Dr. Michael GILLEY
76 Dean of Health Sciences .... Ms. Kim DORTON
13 Dir Ctr Computing & Info Technology .... Mr. Ritchie DEEL
15 Director Personnel Services .... Ms. Valerie LEE
18 Chief Facilities/Physical Plant .... Mr. Preston LAYNE
49 Dean Arts & Sciences .... Vacant
72 Dean of Industrial Tech/Health Sci .... Vacant
26 Chief Public Relations Officer .... Ms. Amy GREEAR
19 Chief of Police .... Mr. Grayson COTHRAN
04 Admin Assistant to the President .... Ms. Peggy GIBSON

*New River Community College (E)

5251 College Drive, Dublin VA 24084
County: Pulaski FICE Identification: 005223
Unit ID: 232867
Telephone: (540) 674-3600 Carnegie Class: Assoc/HT-High Non
FAX Number: (540) 674-3642 Calendar System: Semester
URL: www.nr.edu
Established: 1969 Annual Undergrad Tuition & Fees (In-State): $4,697
Enrollment: 4,137 Coed
Affiliation or Control: State IRS Status: 501(c)3
Highest Offering: Associate Degree
Accreditation: SC

02 President .... Dr. Patricia B. HUBER
05 VP for Instruction/Student Services .... Dr. Peter T. ANDERSON
10 Vice Pres for Finance & Technology ... Mr. John L. VAN HEMERT
30 VP for WD and External Relations .... Dr. Mark C. ROWH
09 Dir Inst Effectiveness/Research .... Dr. Frederick M. STREFF
102 Executive Director of Foundation .... Ms. Angie E. COVEY
49 Dean of Arts & Sciences .... Ms. Sarah TOLBERT-HURYSZ
50 Dean of Business & Technologies .... Ms. Debra BOND
32 Dean of Student Services .... Dr. Deborah KENNEDY
15 Dir Human Resources & Business Oper .... Ms. Melissa P. ANDERSON
06 Registrar .... Mrs. Tammy SMITH
37 Financial Aid Manager .... Mrs. Shauna CROSSCUP
88 Emergency Coordination Officer .... Mr. Joseph WILLIAMS
96 Inventory and Purchasing Technician .... Ms. Monica W. CARDEN
106 Director Online Learning .... Mrs. Linda C. CLAUSSEN
08 Coordinator of Library Services .... Mrs. Sandra B. SMITH
07 Coord Admissions/Records/Stdnt Svcs .... Mrs. Tammy SMITH
18 Chief Facilities/Physical Plant .... Mr. Ronald NICHOLS
88 Coordinator of WorkKeys Center .... Mr. Ross MATNEY
88 Enrollment Coordinator .... Mrs. Lori MITCHELL
26 Public Relations Specialist .... Mrs. Jill ROSS
22 Coord Ctr for Disability Services .... Ms. Lucy J. HOWLETT
84 Enroll Mgr & Transfer Svcs Coord .... Ms. Alison WESTON
04 Administrative Asst to President .... Mrs. Kathy T. RIDPATH

*Northern Virginia Community College (F)

4001 Wakefield Chapel Road, Annandale VA 22003-3796
County: Fairfax FICE Identification: 003727
Unit ID: 232946
Telephone: (703) 323-3000 Carnegie Class: Assoc/HT-Mix Trad/Non
FAX Number: (703) 323-3767 Calendar System: Semester
URL: www.nvcc.edu
Established: 1965 Annual Undergrad Tuition & Fees (In-State): $5,610
Enrollment: 52,873 Coed
Affiliation or Control: State IRS Status: 501(c)3
Highest Offering: Associate Degree
Accreditation: SC, ADNUR, CAHIIM, COARC, DA, DH, DMS, EMT, MLTAD, NAEYC, OTA, PTAA

02 President .... Dr. Anne M. KRESS
13 VP of IET & College Computing .... Dr. Chad KNIGHTS
103 VP for Workforce & Strat Partnershp .... Mr. Steve PARTRIDGE
05 VP of Academic Affairs & CAO .... Dr. Eun-Woo CHANG
32 Vice President Student Services .... Dr. Syedur RAHMAN
84 Assoc VP Stdnt Svcs & Enroll Mgmt .... Vacant
12 Provost Alexandria Campus .... Dr. Annette HAGGRAY
12 Provost Loudoun Campus .... Dr. Julie LEIDIG
12 Provost Manassas Campus .... Dr. Molly LYNCH
102 Exec Dir NVCC Education Foundation .... Vacant
25 Director of Grants .... Dr. Syedur RAHMAN
15 AVP of Human Resources .... Ms. Charlotte M. CALOBRISI
37 Dir Stdnt Financial Aid/Support Svc .... Ms. Joan A. ZANDERS
21 Associate VP for Administration .... Mr. Cory THOMPSON
18 Director of Facilities .... Mr. Steven PATTERSON
19 Director Security/Safety .... Chief Daniel DUSSEAU
88 Office Manager .... Ms. Corinne C. HURST
09 Director of Institutional Research .... Mr. Steve PARTRIDGE

*Patrick Henry Community College (G)

645 Patriot Avenue, Martinsville VA 24112
County: Henry FICE Identification: 003751
Unit ID: 233019
Telephone: (276) 638-8777 Carnegie Class: Assoc/HT-Mix Trad/Non
FAX Number: (276) 656-0320 Calendar System: Semester
URL: www.patrickhenry.edu
Established: 1962 Annual Undergrad Tuition & Fees (In-State): $4,720
Enrollment: 2,050 Coed
Affiliation or Control: State IRS Status: 501(c)3
Highest Offering: Associate Degree
Accreditation: SC, ADNUR, EMT, @PTAA

02 President .... Dr. Greg HODGES
05 Int VP Academic/Student Devel Svcs .... Mr. Terry YOUNG
10 VP Finance & Admin Services .... Mr. John HANBURY
103 VP Workforce/Economic/Community Dev .... Mrs. Rhonda HODGES
30 Director of Development .... Mrs. Tiffani UNDERWOOD
121 Dean Academic Success/Col Transfer .... Mr. Terry YOUNG
81 Dean STEM/Health/Applied Programs .... Dr. Colin FERGUSON
66 Coordinator Nursing/Allied Health .... Ms. Amy WEBSTER
13 Dean of Technology .... Mr. David DEAL
15 Director of Human Resources .... Ms. Belinda STOCKTON
84 Dean Student Success/Enroll Svcs .... Vacant
07 Coord Admiss & Accelerated Lrng .... Ms. Meghan EGGLESTON
26 Public Relations & Mktg Mgr .... Mr. Randy FERGUSON
06 Registrar .... Ms. Jessica CARTER
37 Financial Aid/Veterans Admin .... Mrs. Cindy KELLER
08 Coord Library Services .... Ms. Marcia SEATON-MARTIN
25 Chief Contracts/Grants Admin .... Ms. Sarah B. MORRISON
41 Athletic Director .... Mr. Brian HENDERSON
09 Director Institutional Research .... Dr. Christopher WIKSTROM
18 Chief Facilities/Physical Plant .... Ms. Roberta WRIGHT
19 Director Security/Safety .... Mr. Gary DOVE
96 Director of Purchasing .... Ms. Lori CONNER
04 Administrative Asst to President .... Ms. Sue-Ann EHMANN

*Paul D. Camp Community College (H)

100 N College Drive, Franklin VA 23851-0737
County: Independent City FICE Identification: 009159
Unit ID: 233037
Telephone: (757) 569-6700 Carnegie Class: Assoc/HT-High Non
FAX Number: (757) 569-6795 Calendar System: Semester
URL: www.pdc.edu
Established: 1970 Annual Undergrad Tuition & Fees (In-State): $4,730
Enrollment: 1,237 Coed
Affiliation or Control: State IRS Status: 501(c)3
Highest Offering: Associate Degree
Accreditation: SC, ADNUR

02 Interim President .... Dr. Corey L. MCCRAY
05 VP Academic/Student Development .... Dr. Tara ATKINS-BRADY
11 Operations Manager .... Mr. Phillip BRADSHAW
111 Dir Institutional Advancement .... Mr. Jeff ZEIGLER
32 Dean Student Services .... Ms. Trina JONES
20 Dean of Academic Programs .... Dr. Justin OLIVER
08 Coordinator of Library Services .... Ms. Cirrus GUNDLACH
20 Academic Director-Smithfield .... Dr. Antoinette JOHNSON
103 Dir of Workforce Development .... Dr. Angela LAWHORNE
09 Coord Inst Research/Assessment .... Ms. Damay J. BULLOCK
15 Human Resources Manager .... Mrs. Rachel BEALE
37 Financial Aid Coordinator .... Dr. Teresa HARRISON
04 Assistant to the President .... Ms. Cathy CUTCHINS
06 Registrar .... Mrs. Chris RICKS
41 Athletic Director .... Dr. Justin OLIVER

*Piedmont Virginia Community College (I)

501 College Drive, Charlottesville VA 22902-7589
County: Independent City FICE Identification: 009928
Unit ID: 233116

Telephone: (434) 977-5200 Carnegie Class: Assoc/HT-High Non
FAX Number: (434) 296-8395 Calendar System: Semester
URL: www.pvcc.edu
Established: 1972 Annual Undergrad Tuition & Fees (In-State): $4,790
Enrollment: 4,864 Coed
Affiliation or Control: State IRS Status: 501(c)3
Highest Offering: Associate Degree
Accreditation: SC, ADNUR, DMS, EMT, RAD, SURGT

02 President ... Dr. Frank FRIEDMAN
05 VP Instruction/Student Svcs ... Dr. John DONNELLY
10 Vice President Finance/Admin Svcs ... Dr. Benjamin COPELAND
111 Vice Pres Advancement/Development ... Mr. Harry STILLERMAN
79 Dean Humanities/Fine Arts/Soc Sci ... Dr. Leonda KENISTON
32 Dean of Student Svcs/Admissions ... Dr. Andrew RENSHAW
76 Dean Health & Life Sciences ... Ms. Nicole WINKLER
103 Dean Workforce Services ... Dr. Christy HAWKINS
13 Chief Information Officer ... Mr. Tom RUGGERI
09 Dir Inst Research/Planning/Effect ... Ms. Brittany RESMANN
06 Registrar ... Ms. Allyson REA
96 Business Manager ... Ms. Tracy CERSLEY
18 Facilities Manager ... Mr. Kim MCMANUS
15 Human Resources Director ... Ms. Angela NICHOLAS
26 Marketing/Media Relations Director ... Ms. Susian BROOKS
88 Outreach Manager ... Ms. Denise MCCLANAHAN
08 Director Library Services ... Ms. Crystal NEWELL
37 Director Financial Aid ... Ms. Rachel HAILEY
121 Director Advising & Transfer ... Mr. Kemper STEELE
19 Director Security/Safety ... Mr. Dwayne BOYLES
25 Mgr Grants Development & Admin ... Ms. Caitilin MOHR

*Rappahannock Community College (A)

12745 College Drive, Glenns VA 23149-0287
County: Gloucester FICE Identification: 009160
Unit ID: 233310
Telephone: (804) 758-6700 Carnegie Class: Assoc/HT-High Non
FAX Number: (804) 758-3852 Calendar System: Semester
URL: www.rappahannock.edu
Established: 1970 Annual Undergrad Tuition & Fees (In-State): $4,820
Enrollment: 2,629 Coed
Affiliation or Control: State IRS Status: 501(c)3
Highest Offering: Associate Degree
Accreditation: SC, ADNUR, EMT

02 President ... Dr. Shannon KENNEDY
10 Vice Pres Finance/Admin Services ... Ms. Tara WALKER
05 Interim VP of Learning ... Dr. Eric BARNA
49 Dean of Arts & Sciences ... Dr. Marty BROOKS
32 Dean Student Development ... Dr. Dave KEEL
111 VP of College Advancement ... Ms. Sarah POPE
108 Dean Research/Effectiveness/Plng ... Dr. Glenda D. HAYNIE
37 Lead Financial Aid Tech ... Mrs. Mary TOMEK
15 Director Human Resources ... Mrs. Caroline W. STELTER
18 Facilities/Physical Plant Super ... Mr. Richard LEWTER
06 Student Records/Information Coord ... Ms. Felicia B. PACKETT
08 Learning Resources Coordinator ... Mr. Steve ROANE
13 Chief Information Technology Ofcr ... Dr. Jeff HAYMAN

*Southside Virginia Community College (B)

109 Campus Drive, Alberta VA 23821-2930
County: Brunswick FICE Identification: 008661
Unit ID: 233639
Telephone: (434) 949-1000 Carnegie Class: Assoc/HT-High Non
FAX Number: (434) 949-7863 Calendar System: Semester
URL: www.southside.edu
Established: 1970 Annual Undergrad Tuition & Fees (In-State): $4,695
Enrollment: 3,123 Coed
Affiliation or Control: State IRS Status: 501(c)3
Highest Offering: Associate Degree
Accreditation: SC, ADNUR, EMT

02 President ... Dr. Quentin R. JOHNSON
05 VP Academics & Workforce ... Dr. Keith HARKINS
10 VP Finance & Administration ... Mrs. Shannon V. FEINMAN
84 VP Enrollment Mgmt & Stdnt Success ... Dr. Daryl MINUS
111 Director Institutional Advancement ... Mrs. Mary Jane ELKINS
09 Dir Institutional Effectiveness ... Ms. Robin DANIEL
26 Director of Communications ... Mr. Jamie JONES
13 Chief Information Officer ... Mr. Chad WOLLENBERG
15 Human Resources Manager ... Ms. Bethany W. HARRIS
66 Dean of Nursing/Health Technology ... Dr. Michelle K. EDMONDS
79 Dean of Humanities/Social Sciences ... Dr. Dixie DALTON
75 Dean of Career & Occup Technology ... Dr. Chad PATTON
08 College Librarian ... Ms. Marika PETERSON
37 Director of Financial Aid ... Mrs. Sally THARRINGTON
28 Director of Diversity ... Vacant
18 Buildings/Grounds Supt Christanna ... Mr. Roger WRAY
18 Buildings/Grounds Superintendent ... Mr. Eddie BENNETT
21 Business Manager ... Mrs. Toni LAMBERT
04 Exec Assistant to the President ... Ms. Angela JACKSON

*Southwest Virginia Community College (C)

Box SVCC, Richlands VA 24641-1101
County: Tazewell FICE Identification: 007260
Unit ID: 233648
Telephone: (276) 964-2555 Carnegie Class: Assoc/MT-VT-Mix Trad/Non
FAX Number: (276) 964-9307 Calendar System: Semester
URL: www.sw.edu
Established: 1967 Annual Undergrad Tuition & Fees (In-State): $4,703
Enrollment: 2,295 Coed
Affiliation or Control: State IRS Status: 501(c)3
Highest Offering: Associate Degree
Accreditation: SC, ADNUR, EMT, OTA, RAD

02 President ... Dr. Tommy F. WRIGHT
05 VP Acad & Student Services ... Dr. Robert BRANDON
10 Vice Pres Finance/Admin Svcs ... Mr. Chris LEWIS
111 VP Institutional Advancement ... Mrs. Susan L. LOWE
15 AVP Human Resources Officer ... Ms. Kimberly STEINER
13 Chief Info Technology Officer (CIO) ... Mr. Charles MUSICK
79 Dean Humanities/Soc Science ... Dr. Brian WRIGHT
81 Dean Math/Natural Sci/Health Tech ... Dr. Clint PINION
50 Dean Business/Engr & Indust Tech ... Mr. James DYE
103 Dean Workforce/Continuing Education ... Mr. Randall ROSE
32 Dean Student Success ... Mrs. Dyan E. LESTER
11 Dir Administrative Services ... Mrs. Gwendalyn STONE
09 Institutional Research Officer ... Mrs. Cathy L. SMITH-COX
102 Exec Dir Foundation/Development ... Ms. Susan LOWE
19 Campus Police Chief ... Mr. Justin MCCULLEY
21 Business Manager ... Mr. Michael BALES
18 Physical Plant Superintendent ... Mr. Tony MCGHEE
26 Dir of Strategic Communications ... Mr. John DEZEMBER
106 Director Distance Learning ... Ms. Barbie RATLIFF
25 Grants Administrator ... Ms. Phyllis ROBERTS
105 Director Web Services ... Ms. Teresa PRUETT
41 Athletic Director ... Mr. Jason VENCILL
37 Financial Aid Manager ... Mrs. Donna PRICE
08 Coordinator of Library Services ... Dr. Teresa A. YEAROUT

*Thomas Nelson Community College (D)

99 Thomas Nelson Drive, Hampton VA 23666
County: Independent City FICE Identification: 006871
Unit ID: 233754
Telephone: (757) 825-2700 Carnegie Class: Assoc/MT-VT-Mix Trad/Non
FAX Number: (757) 825-2763 Calendar System: Semester
URL: www.tncc.edu
Established: 1967 Annual Undergrad Tuition & Fees (In-State): $4,806
Enrollment: 6,256 Coed
Affiliation or Control: State IRS Status: 501(c)3
Highest Offering: Associate Degree
Accreditation: SC, ADNUR, DH, NAEYC

02 President ... Dr. Towuanna PORTER BRANNON
05 Interim VP Academic Affairs ... Dr. Lonnie J. SCHAFFER
32 Vice President for Student Affairs ... Dr. Kris RARIG
10 Vice President for Admin/Finance ... Mr. Steven R. CARPENTER
111 Vice Pres Institutional Advancement ... Ms. Cynthia CALLAWAY
15 Assistant VP Human Resources ... Vacant
121 Director of Advising ... Dr. Jeannette HOLLINS
37 Dir Financial Aid/Veteran Affairs ... Mr. Marc T. VERNON
18 Mgr Facilities/Plng/Capital Outlay ... Mr. Mark KRAMER
30 Director of Development ... Ms. Tracy ASHLEY
09 Dir Inst Research and Effectiveness ... Mr. Steven FELKER

*Tidewater Community College (E)

121 College Place, Norfolk VA 23510
County: Independent City FICE Identification: 003712
Unit ID: 233772
Telephone: (757) 822-1122 Carnegie Class: Assoc/HVT-High Trad
FAX Number: (757) 822-1055 Calendar System: Semester
URL: www.tcc.edu
Established: 1968 Annual Undergrad Tuition & Fees (In-State): $5,561
Enrollment: 16,769 Coed
Affiliation or Control: State IRS Status: 501(c)3
Highest Offering: Associate Degree
Accreditation: SC, ACFEI, ADNUR, CAHIIM, COARC, DMS, EMT, FUSER, MLTAD, NAEYC, OTA, PTAA, RAD

02 President ... Dr. Marcia CONSTON
05 VP Academic Affairs & CAO ... Dr. Michelle W. WOODHOUSE
10 VP Administration & CFO ... Ms. Heather H. HARDIMAN
26 VP Marketing & Communication ... Vacant
102 Exec Dir Ed Fndn/Dir Govt Cmty Rels ... Vacant
13 VP Info Systems/Inst Effectiveness ... Mr. Curtis K. AASEN
103 VP for Workforce Solutions ... Ms. Tamara S. WILLIAMS
32 VP Student Affairs ... Dr. Karen CAMPBELL
12 Dean Stdnt Supp Svcs/Norfolk Dean ... Mr. Emanuel CHESTNUT
12 Dean of Retention/Portsmouth Dean ... Ms. Dana M. HATHORN
12 Int Dean Stdnt Life & Cond/Ches Dn ... Dr. Kelly T. GILLERLAIN
12 Dean Advising/VB Dean ... Dr. Kia HARDY
88 Special Asst to VP Academic Affairs ... Dr. Michael D. SUMMERS
15 Associate VP Human Resources/EEO ... Ms. Beth LUNDE
11 Chief Admin Officer Educ Foundation ... Ms. Susan M. JAMES
20 AVP Academics ... Dr. Kellie C. SOREY
120 AVP Distance Learning ... Mr. John MOREA
08 AVP for Libraries ... Mr. Steve E. LITHERLAND
88 Pathway Dean Maritime/Skilled Trade ... Mr. Thomas B. STOUT
84 Interim Dean Enrollment Mgmt ... Mr. Kevin MCCARTHY
79 Pathway Dean Arts & Humanities ... Dr. Kerry S. RAGNO
50 Pathway Dean Business/Comp Sci/ IT ... Ms. Nancy N. PRATHER-JOHNSON
54 Pathway Dean Engr/Science/Math ... Dr. Peter T. AGBAKPE
83 Pathway Dean Soc Sciences/Education ... Dr. Jenefer D. SNYDER
66 Discipline Dean School Nursing ... Ms. Rita T. BOUCHARD
81 Discipline Dn Eng/Eng Tech/Phys Sci ... Mr. David A. EKKER
76 Interim Pathway Dean Health Prof ... Ms. Jennifer FERGUSON
81 Interim Discipline Dean of Science ... Dr. Siabhon HARRIS
107 Pathway Dean Pub/Prof Svcs ... Mr. Joseph J. FAIRCHILD
79 Discipline Dean Arts/Humanities ... Ms. Marcanne ANDERSEN
88 Pathway Dean Manufacturing/Transp ... Dr. Beno RUBIN
14 Director of Information Technology ... Mr. Ken BALLARD
06 College Registrar ... Dr. Nicole WILSON
18 Director of Facilities ... Mr. Albert THOMPSON
19 Director of Public Safety ... Mr. Michael C. POWELL
88 Exec Dir Ctr Military Vet Educ ... Vacant
88 Associate VP Prof Dev Solutions ... Ms. Lisa L. PETERSON
88 Exec Dir Roper Performing Arts Ctr ... Mr. Paul H. LASAKOW
96 Dir Materiel Mgmt Procurement Svcs ... Mr. Thom HUTCHINS
37 Dir Central Financial Aid ... Mr. Justin CRISTELLO
109 Director Auxiliary Services ... Vacant
45 Dir of Planning & Accountability ... Dr. Kimberly M. BOVEE
25 Director Grants/Sponsored Programs ... Ms. Laverne ELLERBE
88 Dir Stdnt Resources/Empowerment Ctr ... Dr. Jeanne B. NATALI
04 Exec Asst to President ... Ms. Latesha D. JOHNSON

*Virginia Highlands Community College (F)

PO Box 828, Abingdon VA 24212-0828
County: Washington FICE Identification: 007099
Unit ID: 233903
Telephone: (276) 739-2400 Carnegie Class: Assoc/HT-Mix Trad/Non
FAX Number: (276) 739-2590 Calendar System: Semester
URL: www.vhcc.edu
Established: 1967 Annual Undergrad Tuition & Fees (In-State): $4,710
Enrollment: 2,086 Coed
Affiliation or Control: State IRS Status: 501(c)3
Highest Offering: Associate Degree
Accreditation: SC, ADNUR

02 President ... Dr. Adam HUTCHISON
05 VP Instruction & Student Svcs ... Dr. Stacy THOMAS
10 VP Financial/Administrative Svcs ... Ms. Christine FIELDS
111 VP Institutional Advancement ... Ms. Laura PENNINGTON
49 Dean of Arts & Sciences Div ... Ms. Barbara MANUEL
107 Dean Professional/Tech Studies Div ... Dr. Beth PAGE
09 Dir of Institutional Rsrch/Effectiv ... Mr. Robert E. MAY
66 Interim Coordinator of Nursing ... Dr. Elizabeth WRIGHT
103 Dean of Workforce Development ... Mr. Robert PHILLIPS
106 Dir Learning Resources/Online Lrng ... Mr. Ken FAIRBANKS
08 Coordinator of Library Services ... Ms. Sarah Beth WHITE
121 Academic Counselor ... Mr. Michael MCBRIDE
37 Financial Aid Coordinator ... Ms. Donna PRICE
07 Coordinator of Admissions & Records ... Ms. Paige KELLY
15 Human Resource Manager ... Ms. Laura MCCLELLAN
26 Coord Public Relations & Marketing ... Ms. Kellie CROWE
88 Director of EXCEL ... Ms. Karen CHEERS
21 Finance Manager ... Ms. Mary SNEAD
13 IT Coordinator ... Mr. Glen JOHNSON
18 Buildings & Grounds Superintendent ... Mr. Ernest L. NUNLEY
19 Campus Police Chief ... Mr. Kevin WIDENER

*Virginia Western Community College (G)

3093 Colonial Avenue SW, Roanoke VA 24015-4705
County: Independent City FICE Identification: 003760
Unit ID: 233949
Telephone: (540) 857-8922 Carnegie Class: Assoc/MT-VT-High Non
FAX Number: (540) 857-6526 Calendar System: Semester
URL: www.virginiawestern.edu
Established: 1966 Annual Undergrad Tuition & Fees (In-State): $5,355
Enrollment: 5,738 Coed
Affiliation or Control: State IRS Status: 501(c)3
Highest Offering: Associate Degree
Accreditation: SC, ACBSP, ACFEI, ADNUR, DH, MLTAD, RAD, RTT

02 President ... Dr. Robert H. SANDEL
10 Vice Pres of Finance/Admin Services ... Ms. Lisa RIDPATH
05 Vice Pres Academic/Student Affs ... Dr. Elizabeth WILMER
111 Vice Pres Institutional Advancement ... Ms. Marilyn HERBERT-ASHTON
103 Vice Pres Workforce Development Svc ... Dr. Milan HAYWARD
45 AVP of Institutional Effectiveness ... Dr. Jolene HAMM
49 Dean Liberal Arts/Social Sciences ... Ms. Amy ANGUIANO
76 Dean Health Professions ... Ms. Martha SULLIVAN
81 Dean Science/Tech/Engineering/Math ... Ms. Amy WHITE
50 Dean Business/Trades/Technology ... Ms. Yvonne CAMPBELL
24 Dean Learning Resources ... Mr. Christopher PORTER
32 Dean of Student Services ... Ms. Lori BAKER
09 Director Institutional Research ... Ms. Carol ROWLETT
18 Director of Facilities Planning ... Mr. Kevin G. WITTER
26 Director Marketing/Strategic Comm ... Mr. Josh MEYER
06 Registrar ... Ms. Karin COLE
19 Campus Police Chief ... Mr. Craig HARRIS
37 Coord Financial Aid/Veterans Affs ... Mr. David BROD
103 Workforce Operations Supervisor ... Vacant
13 Dir Information Educ Technology ... Vacant
15 Assoc VP of Human Resources ... Ms. Jennifer PITTMAN
21 Business Manager ... Mrs. Fredona AARON
84 Coordinator for Enrollment Services ... Ms. Brooke FERGUSON
08 Coordinator of the Library ... Vacant
36 Coordinator Career Services ... Ms. Shonny COOKE
25 Coord Grants Dev & Special Projects ... Ms. Marilyn J. HERBERT-ASHTON
30 Coordinator of Development ... Ms. Carole TARRANT
04 Admin Assistant to the President ... Ms. Amy BALZER

*Wytheville Community College (A)

1000 E Main Street, Wytheville VA 24382-3308
County: Wythe FICE Identification: 003761
Unit ID: 234377
Telephone: (276) 223-4700 Carnegie Class: Assoc/HT-High Non
FAX Number: (276) 223-4778 Calendar System: Semester
URL: www.wcc.vccs.edu
Established: 1963 Annual Undergrad Tuition & Fees (In-State): $4,725
Enrollment: 2,244 Coed
Affiliation or Control: State IRS Status: 501(c)3
Highest Offering: Associate Degree
Accreditation: SC, ADNUR, DH, MLTAD, PTAA

02 President ... Dr. Dean E. SPRINKLE
05 VP Academics/Inst Advancement . Dr. Rhonda K. CATRON-WOOD
10 Vice Pres Finance & Admin Services ... Vacant
103 VP Workforce Dev/Occup Programs ... Mr. Perry HUGHES
88 Dean of Transfer & Educ Partnership ... Ms. Susan EVANS
76 Interim Dean Health & Med Services ... Dr. Rita PHILLIPS
32 Dean of Student Services ... Ms. Renee THOMAS
13 Director of Technology/CIO ... Mr. Shawn MCREYNOLDS
09 Director of Inst Effectiveness ... Ms. Christine COLE
15 Director of Human Resources ... Ms. Malinda EVERSOLE
26 Public Relations & Marketing Spec ... Mr. Kenneth AKERS
08 Coordinator of Library Services ... Mr. George E. MATTIS, JR.
96 Procurement Officer ... Vacant
106 Dir Distance/Distributive Learning ... Vacant
37 Coordinator Financial Aid ... Ms. Mary Beth GALLAGHER
04 Administrative Asst to President ... Ms. Denita BURNETT
29 Development Svcs/Alumni Coordinator ... Vacant
18 Chief Facilities/Physical Plant Ofc ... Vacant
19 Director Security/Safety ... Mr. Steve BURNETTE
108 Director Institutional Assessment ... Vacant
07 Coordinator of Admissions/Records ... Ms. April MULLINS

Virginia Military Institute (B)

319 Letcher Avenue, Lexington VA 24450-0304
County: Independent City FICE Identification: 003753
Unit ID: 234085
Telephone: (540) 464-7230 Carnegie Class: Bac-A&S
FAX Number: N/A Calendar System: Semester
URL: www.vmi.edu
Established: 1839 Annual Undergrad Tuition & Fees (In-State): $19,210
Enrollment: 1,698 Coed
Affiliation or Control: State IRS Status: 501(c)3
Highest Offering: Baccalaureate
Accreditation: SC

01 Superintendent ... MG. Cedric T. WINS
05 Deputy Super/Dean of the Faculty ... BGen. Robert W. MORESCHI
10 Deputy Superintendent Finance/Admin ... Col. Dallas B. CLARK
32 Commandant of Cadets ... Col. Adrian t. BOGART, III
100 Interim Chief of Staff ... Col. Jeffrey R. BOOBAR
04 Exec Asst to the Superintendent ... LtCol. Sean P. HARRINGTON
21 Assoc Business Exec/Treasurer ... Col. Jeffrey L. LAWHORNE
07 Director of Admissions ... Col. Vernon L. BEITZEL
88 Exec Director Museum Programs ... Col. Keith E. GIBSON
37 Director of Financial Aid ... LtCol. David G. SIGLER
35 Deputy Commandant ... Col. Gary M. LEVENSON
36 Director of Career Services ... LtCol. Ammand SHEIKH
41 Director Intercollegiate Athletics ... Mr. David L. DILES
26 Director Communications & Marketing ... Col. William J. WYATT
29 COO Alumni Association ... Mr. Thomas A. BRASHEARS
102 Exec VP VMI Foundation/Fund Raising ... Mr. Warren J. BRYAN
102 COO VMI Foundation/Keydet Club ... Mr. Meade B. KING
06 Registrar ... Col. Janet M. BATTAGLIA
15 Director Human Resources ... LtCol. Ellie L. KANIA
18 Director Physical Plant ... LtCol. Michelle P. CARUTHERS
09 Director Institutional Research ... LtCol. Lee L. RAKES
109 Director Auxiliary Services ... LtCol. Howard L. CLARK
40 Manager Bookstore ... Mr. Dalton BRILEY
42 Institute Chaplain ... Col. Robert E. PHILLIPS, SR.
17 Institute Physician ... Dr. David L. COPELAND
88 Director of Athletic Communications ... Mr. Wade H. BRANNER
08 Head Librarian ... Vacant
38 Director of Cadet Counseling ... LtCol. Sarah L. JONES
13 Director Information Technology ... Col. Wesley L. ROBINSON
96 Director of Purchasing ... Maj. Kathy H. TOMLIN
30 CEO Alumni Agencies ... Cmdr. Steve M. MACONI
19 Chief VMI Police ... Chief Michael L. MARSHALL
28 Chief Diversity Officer ... LtCol. Jamica N. LOVE
44 Director Annual & Reunion Giving ... Ms. Patti COOK

† Tuition includes required room and board and quartermaster charges.

Virginia Polytechnic Institute and State University (C)

Blacksburg VA 24061-0202
County: Montgomery FICE Identification: 003754
Unit ID: 233921
Telephone: (540) 231-6000 Carnegie Class: DU-Highest
FAX Number: (540) 231-9263 Calendar System: Semester
URL: www.vt.edu
Established: 1872 Annual Undergrad Tuition & Fees (In-State): $13,749
Enrollment: 37,024 Coed
Affiliation or Control: State IRS Status: 501(c)3
Highest Offering: Doctorate
Accreditation: SC, ART, CACREP, CAEP, CAEPN, CEA, CIDA, CLPSY, CONST, DIETC, DIETD, DIETI, IPSY, LSAR, MED, MFCD, MUS, PCSAS, PH, PLNG, SPAA, THEA, VET

01 President ... Timothy D. SANDS
05 Exec Vice President & Provost ... Cyril R. CLARKE
10 SVP/Chief Business Ofcr ... Dwayne PINKNEY
13 Vice Pres Information Tech & CIO ... Scott F. MIDKIFF
32 Vice President Student Affairs ... Frank X. SHUSHOK, JR.
111 Vice Pres for Advancement ... Charles D. PHLEGAR
29 Assoc Vice Pres Alumni Relations ... Deborah A. DAY
28 VP Strat Affairs/Vice Prov Incl Div ... Menah PRATT-CLARKE
46 VP Research & Innovation ... Dan SUI
20 Exec Vice Provost ... G. Don TAYLOR, JR.
20 Vice Prov for Undergrad Acad Affs ... Rachel L. HOLLOWAY
58 Vice President and Dean Grad Educ ... Aimee SURPRENANT
56 VP Outreach/International Affs ... Guru GHOSH
15 Vice Pres for Human Resources ... Bryan GAREY
88 Vice Pres of Strategic Affairs ... Lisa WILKES
07 AV Prov Enrol Mgt/Dir UG Admiss ... Juan P. ESPINOZA
35 Dean of Students ... Byron A. HUGHES, JR.
108 AV Prov Analyt/Inst Effectiveness ... R. Thulasi KUMAR
43 University Counsel ... Kay K. HEIDBREDER
84 Vice Prov for Enroll & Degree Mgmt ... Luisa HAVENS
37 AVP Enroll Mgmt/Student Fin Aid ... Elizabeth ARMSTRONG
20 Vice Provost Faculty Affairs ... Jack FINNEY
88 Vice Provost Academic Resource Mgmt ... Jeff EARLEY
23 Director Schiffert Health Center ... Kanitta CHAROENSIRI
18 VP Campus Planning/Infastructure ... Christopher KIWUS
109 AVP Housing/Dining/Student Centers ... Ted FAULKNER
100 AVP/Chief of Staff ... Frances KEENE
41 Athletic Director ... Whit BABCOCK
26 Sr Assoc Vice Pres Univ Relations ... Tracy VOSBURGH
38 Exec Dir Mental Health Initiative ... Chris FLYNN
40 Exec Dir Virginia Tech Services ... Donald J. WILLIAMS
08 Dean of University Libraries ... Tyler WALTERS
47 Dean of Agriculture/Life Sciences ... Alan GRANT
48 Int Dean Arch/Urban Studies ... Rosemary BLIESZNER
81 Int Dean College of Science ... Ronald FRICKER
50 Dean of Business ... Robert T. SUMICHRAST
54 Dean of Engineering ... Julia ROSS
79 Dean Liberal Arts & Human Sciences ... Laura BELMONTE
74 Dean of Veterinary Medicine ... Daniel GIVENS
65 Dean of Natural Resources & Environ ... Paul M. WINISTORFER
96 Director of Procurement ... Mary HELMICK
63 Dean of VTC School of Medicine ... Lee LEARMAN
91 Assoc Vice Pres for Enterprise Sys ... Deborah M. FULTON
88 VP for Strategic Alliances ... Steven H. MCKNIGHT
12 VP/Exec Dir Innovation Campus ... Lance R. COLLINS
102 CEO Virginia Tech Foundation ... Elizabeth MCCLANAHAN
04 Special Asst to President ... Lisa WILKES
06 Assoc Vice Prov and Univ Registrar ... Rick SPARKS
101 VP for Policy and Gov/Sec to BOV ... Kim O'ROURKE
104 Director Global Education Office ... Theresa C. JOHANSSON
105 Director Web Communications ... John JACKSON
106 Exec Dir Tech-enhanced Learning ... Dale PIKE
88 Asst Provost Regional Accreditation ... Kristen BUSH
19 Chief of Police/Dir of Security ... Mac BABB
22 Assoc VP Equity and Accessibility ... Kelly OAKS
25 Director of Contracts ... Daniel COCKRUM
44 Director Annual or Planned Giving ... Ann LEHMAN
86 VP Government & Community Relations ... Chris YIANILOS
76 VP for Health Sciences and Tech ... Michael J. FRIEDLANDER
88 Director of Inst Effectiveness ... Bethanny BODO
39 Dir Resident Life/Student Housing ... Sean GRUBE

Virginia State University (D)

One Hayden Drive,
Virginia State University VA 23806-0001
County: Chesterfield FICE Identification: 003764
Unit ID: 234155
Telephone: (804) 524-5000 Carnegie Class: Masters/M
FAX Number: (804) 524-6506 Calendar System: Semester
URL: www.vsu.edu
Established: 1882 Annual Undergrad Tuition & Fees (In-State): $9,154
Enrollment: 4,020 Coed
Affiliation or Control: State IRS Status: 501(c)3
Highest Offering: Doctorate
Accreditation: SC, ART, CAEP, DIETD, DIETI, MUS, SW

01 President ... Dr. Makola M. ABDULLAH
10 Vice President for Finance ... Mr. Kevin DAVENPORT
05 Provost/VP for Academic Affairs ... Dr. Donald PALM
32 VP for Student Success & Engagement ... Vacant
111 VP for Institutional Advancement ... Ms. Tonya S. HALL
100 Chief of Staff ... Mr. Hubert D. HARRIS
20 Vice Provost ... Vacant
21 Assoc Vice President for Finance ... Ms. Sheila MCNAIR
50 Dean Reginald F Lewis Col Business . Dr. Emmanuel OMOJOKUN
54 Dean College of Engineering & Tech ... Dr. Dawit HAILE
79 Dean Col of Humanities & Soc Sci ... Dr. Andrew KANU
47 Dean College of Agriculture ... Dr. Marion R. MCKINNEY
58 Dean Graduate Studies ... Vacant
76 Dean College of Natural Health Sci ... Dr. Lenneal J. HENDERSON
53 Dean College of Education ... Dr. Willis W. WALTER
06 Registrar ... Ms. Nedra W. JONES
09 Director Inst Planning/Assessment ... Dr. Tia A. MINNIS
37 Director of Financial Aid ... Mrs. Myra PHILLIPS
19 Chief of Police and Public Safety ... Mr. David BRAGG
18 Director of Facilities ... Mr. Gilbert HANZLIK
07 Director for Enrollment Services ... Mr. Rodney HALL
26 Director for Communication . Ms. Gwen WILLIAMS DANDRIDGE
15 HR Director ... Mrs. Tanya SIMMONS
39 Director Residence Facilities ... Mr. Derrick L. PETERSON
36 Director Career Services ... Mr. Joseph LYONS
40 Bookstore Manager ... Mr. Kevin POWELL
92 Director Honors Program ... Mr. Daniel M. ROBERTS
41 Athletic Director ... Mrs. Peggy DAVIS
42 Minister ... Rev. Jasmyn GRAHAM
29 Director of Alumni Relations ... Ms. Charmica D. EPPS
13 Deputy Chief Information Officer ... Vacant
23 Director of Student Health Services ... Ms. Danika CLEMMONS
25 Contract Manager ... Ms. Linda SCOTT
87 Director Summer School Session ... Dr. Vykuntapathi THOTA
96 Director of Purchasing ... Mr. Ryan FEREBEE
38 Director University Counseling ... Dr. Cynthia S. ELLISON
04 Executive Assistant to President ... Mrs. Danette JOHNSON
101 Special Asst to President & Board ... Dr. Annie REDD
43 General Counsel ... Vacant

Virginia Theological Seminary (E)

3737 Seminary Road, Alexandria VA 22304-5201
County: Independent City FICE Identification: 003731
Unit ID: 233259
Telephone: (703) 370-6600 Carnegie Class: Not Classified
FAX Number: N/A Calendar System: Semester
URL: www.vts.edu
Established: 1823 Annual Graduate Tuition & Fees: N/A
Enrollment: N/A Coed
Affiliation or Control: Protestant Episcopal IRS Status: 501(c)3
Highest Offering: Doctorate; No Undergraduates
Accreditation: THEOL

01 Dean and President ... Rev. Ian S. MARKHAM
05 VP of Academic Affairs ... Rev. Melody D. KNOWLES
111 VP of Institutional Advancement ... Mrs. Linda DIENNO
10 VP for Finance and Operations ... Ms. Jacqueline BALLOU
32 Assoc Dean of Students ... Rev. Ruthanna HOOKE
21 Director of Finance/Accounting ... Mr. Terrell WHITAKER
06 Registrar/Exec Dir Enrollment Mgmt ... Dr. Gail-Selina HEWITT-CLARKE
08 Head Librarian ... Dr. Mitzi J. BUDDE
26 Director of Communications ... Mr. Curtis PRATHER
07 Director of Admissions ... Mr. Derek GRETEN-HARRISON
04 Exec Assistant to the President ... Ms. Taryn HABBERLEY
102 Director Foundation/Corporate Rels ... Vacant
18 Chief Facilities/Physical Plnt Ofcr ... Mr. John ERBE
38 Director Student Counseling ... Mr. Derek GRETEN-HARRISON

Virginia Union University (F)

1500 N Lombardy Street, Richmond VA 23220-1784
County: Independent City FICE Identification: 003766
Unit ID: 234164
Telephone: (804) 257-5600 Carnegie Class: Bac-A&S
FAX Number: (804) 257-5818 Calendar System: Semester
URL: www.vuu.edu
Established: 1865 Annual Undergrad Tuition & Fees: $13,530
Enrollment: 1,516 Coed
Affiliation or Control: Baptist IRS Status: 501(c)3
Highest Offering: Doctorate
Accreditation: SC, ACBSP, CAEP, SW, THEOL

01 President ... Dr. Hakim J. LUCAS
03 Executive Vice President ... Dr. Allia CARTER
05 Senior VP/Provost ... Dr. Terrell STRAYHORN
10 Sr VP/Chief Financial Ofcr ... Mr. Gregory LEWIS
32 VP Student Affairs ... Dr. Allia L. CARTER
111 VP Institutional Advancement ... Mr. Ralph DICKERSON
41 VP Intercollegiate Athletics ... Mr. Joseph TAYLOR
102 Sr VP Corporate & External Rels ... Mr. Maurice W. CAMPBELL
84 AVP Enrollment Management ... Ms. Keisha POPE
26 AVP Executive Communications ... Ms. Pam H. COX
20 Associate Provost ... Dr. Lisa T. MOON
53 Int Dean Evelyn R Syphax Sch Educ ... Dr. Alphonso LARAY SEALEY
49 Dean Arts & Sciences ... Dr. Ted L. RITTER
50 Dean Sydny Lewis Sch of Business ... Dr. Robin DAVIS
100 Chief of Staff ... Vacant
07 Director of Admissions ... Ms. Toyarna Y. THOMAS
103 Director Workforce Development ... Ms. Felicia COSBY
73 Dean School of Theology ... Dr. Gregory HOWARD
25 Director Sponsored Pgm/Title III ... Dr. Linda JACKSON
15 Director Human Resources ... Ms. Kendra MAYERS
06 Registrar ... Ms. Erica JACKSON
38 Director Counseling ... Dr. Shanita BROWN
29 Director of Alumni Relations ... Mr. Dominique FOWLER
08 Library Director ... Ms. Pamela B. FOREMAN
37 Director Financial Aid ... Ms. Keisha L. POPE
13 Director Bus Intel & Technology ... Ms. Doreen O. DIXON
42 University Pastor ... Rev. Angelo V. CHATMON
19 Chief University Police ... Ms. Meshia THOMAS
21 Comptroller ... Ms. Robin JEFFERSON
40 Bookstore Manager ... Ms. Terri WYATT
35 Dean of Students ... Mr. Brock MAYERS
31 Coordinator Student & Community Eng ... Vacant
18 Director Facilities Management ... Mr. Freddie ROBINSON
96 Director of Purchasing ... Ms. Beverly R. SMITH
04 Executive Asst to President ... Ms. Renee W. JOLLEY
104 Dir Ctr for International Studies ... Vacant
106 Dir Life-long Learning/Exce Ed ... Vacant
108 Director Institutional Assessment ... Dr. Lisa T. MOON
44 AVP Institutional Giving ... Vacant
101 Secretary of the Institution/Board ... Ms. Renee W. JOLLEY
105 Director Web Services ... Vacant

Virginia University of Integrative Medicine (A)

9401 Mathy Drive, Fairfax VA 22031
County: Fairfax Identification: 667208
Unit ID: 490106
Telephone: (703) 323-5690 Carnegie Class: Spec-4-yr-Other Health
FAX Number: (703) 323-5692 Calendar System: Quarter
URL: https://vuim.edu/
Established: Annual Undergrad Tuition & Fees: N/A
Enrollment: 362 Coed
Affiliation or Control: Independent Non-Profit IRS Status: 501(c)3
Highest Offering: Doctorate
Accreditation: ACUP

01 President ... Dr. Lixing LAO
05 Academic Dean ... Jeffrey MILLISON
11 COO ... John YOO
26 Chief Marketing Officer ... Byung KIM
06 Registrar ... Ji BAEK

Virginia University of Lynchburg (B)

2058 Garfield Avenue, Lynchburg VA 24501-6417
County: Independent City FICE Identification: 003762
Unit ID: 234137
Telephone: (434) 528-5276 Carnegie Class: Bac-A&S
FAX Number: (434) 528-4257 Calendar System: Semester
URL: www.vul.edu
Established: 1886 Annual Undergrad Tuition & Fees: $8,600
Enrollment: 244 Coed
Affiliation or Control: Independent Non-Profit IRS Status: 501(c)3
Highest Offering: Doctorate
Accreditation: TRACS

01 President ... Dr. Kathy C. FRANKLIN
05 Vice President of Academic Affairs ... Vacant
10 Vice President of Finance ... Ms. Sheila SCOTT
32 Director of Student Affairs ... Dr. Philip CAMPBELL
11 Chief Operating Officer ... Mr. Treney TWEEDY
06 Head Registrar ... Mr. Robbie ADAMS
84 Director of Admissions ... Ms. Angelique CARTER
18 Dir of Facilities/Maintenance ... Mr. Vern DEBILZAN
106 Director of Online Learning ... Ms. Katrina V. FRANKLIN
19 Director Security/Safety ... Mr. Robert CABLER, JR.
37 Director of Financial Aid ... Ms. Romena MORGAN
04 Special Assistant to the COO ... Mr. Ryan MICKLES
08 Head Librarian ... Mr. Tony SMITH
13 Director of IT/IE ... Vacant

Virginia Wesleyan University (C)

5817 Wesleyan Drive, Virginia Beach VA 23455
County: Independent City FICE Identification: 003767
Unit ID: 234173
Telephone: (757) 455-3200 Carnegie Class: Bac-A&S
FAX Number: (757) 461-4944 Calendar System: 4/1/4
URL: www.vwu.edu
Established: 1961 Annual Undergrad Tuition & Fees: $36,910
Enrollment: 1,347 Coed
Affiliation or Control: United Methodist IRS Status: 501(c)3
Highest Offering: Master's
Accreditation: SC, CAPRT, SW

01 President ... Dr. Scott D. MILLER
111 VP for Advance/Special Asst to Pres ... Ms. Kimberley HAMMER
11 VP for Campus Life & Oper Mgmt ... Dr. Keith E. MOORE
05 Vice President for Academic Affairs ... Dr. Maynard SCHAUS
10 Vice President for Finance ... Mr. James E. COOPER
84 Vice President for Enrollment ... Ms. Heather M. CAMPBELL
101 Exec Asst to President/Board Sec ... Ms. Kelly CORDOVA
04 Admin Asst to President ... Ms. Anja SERBY-WILKENS
41 Exec Dir Intercollegiate Athletics ... Ms. Andrea HOOVER-ERBIG
21 Assoc VP for Finance ... Ms. Sylvia SCHELLY
35 Assoc VP Campus Life & Oper Mgmt ... Mr. Jason SEWARD
110 Assoc Vice Pres for Advancement ... Ms. Lori HARRIS
20 Assoc VP for Academic Affairs ... Dr. Susan LARKIN
112 Asst VP for Advancement ... Ms. Sharon LADERBERG
20 Asst VP for Academic Affairs ... Dr. Loren L. MARQUEZ
26 Chief Marketing Officer ... Ms. Stephanie SMAGLO
13 Chief Information Officer ... Mr. Gregory SKINNER
92 Dean Batten Honors College ... Dr. Travis MALONE
56 Dean of VWU Global Campus ... Dr. Deirdre GONSALVES-JACKSON
79 Dean Sch Arts & Humanities ... Dr. Steven EMMANUEL
81 Dean Sch Math & Natural Sciences ... Dr. Victor TOWNSEND
83 Dean Sch of Social Science ... Dr. Leslie CAUGHELL
107 Dean of Professional Studies ... Dr. Ben DOBRIN
37 Director of Financial Aid ... Ms. Teresa L. RHYNE
96 Purchasing Manager ... Ms. Regina BARLETTA
28 Chief Diversity Officer ... Dr. Brian KURISKY
36 Dir of Career Development ... Ms. Jessica HARRINGTON
19 Director of Security ... Mr. Victor DORSEY
18 Director of Facilities Mgmt ... Mr. David PETERSON
42 Chaplain ... Rev. Kotosha GRIFFIN
38 Director of Counseling Services ... Mr. Bill BROWN
39 Director of Residence Life ... Mr. David STUEBING
27 Content & Media Manager ... Ms. Laynee H. TIMLIN
122 Director of Student Activities ... Ms. Sarah GUZZO
40 Sribner University Store Mgr ... Ms. Kim S. BROWN
88 Dir of Supp Svcs/VWU Global Campus ... Ms. Marion HIBBLER
08 Library Director ... Mrs. Susan ERICKSON
15 Director of Human Resources ... Ms. Karla R. RASMUSSEN
06 Registrar ... Ms. Regina COTTER
09 Director of Institutional Research ... Mr. Shane BOYD
104 Director of Study Away ... Ms. Amanda REINIG
119 Info Security Ofcr/Network Admin ... Ms. Marcia WILLIAMS
78 Exec Dir of Experiential Learning ... Ms. Amy RUSH
44 Asst Dir Annual Giving/Alumni Rels ... Vacant
88 Dir of Innov Teaching/Engaged Lrng ... Dr. Denise WILKINSON
07 Director for Transfer Enrollment ... Ms. Nadine WHITE-SHOOK
88 Dir for Enrollment Batten Honors ... Ms. Brooke NOVKOVIC
102 Dir of Corp & Parent Relations ... Ms. Brandi CALICA
88 Dir of Enrollment VWU Global Campus ... Mr. Larry BELCHER

Washington and Lee University (D)

204 W Washington Street, Lexington VA 24450-2116
County: Independent City FICE Identification: 003768
Unit ID: 234207
Telephone: (540) 458-8400 Carnegie Class: Bac-A&S
FAX Number: N/A Calendar System: Other
URL: www.wlu.edu
Established: 1749 Annual Undergrad Tuition & Fees: $57,285
Enrollment: 2,183 Coed
Affiliation or Control: Independent Non-Profit IRS Status: 501(c)3
Highest Offering: Doctorate
Accreditation: SC, CAEP, JOUR, LAW

01 President ... Dr. William C. DUDLEY
05 Provost ... Dr. Lena HILL
20 Associate Provost ... Dr. Paul YOUNGMAN
10 Vice Pres for Finance and Admin ... Mr. Steven G. MCALLISTER
111 Vice Pres University Advancement ... Mr. Thomas W. JENNINGS
32 VP Student Affs & Dean of Students ... Ms. Sidney S. EVANS
101 Sr Asst to Pres/Sec of University ... Mr. James D. FARRAR, JR.
43 General Counsel ... Ms. Maria FEELEY
49 Dean of the College ... Dr. Chawne KIMBER
50 Dean of the Williams School ... Dr. Robert D. STRAUGHAN
61 Dean of the Law School ... Ms. Michelle DRUMBL
26 Chief Communications Officer ... Ms. Jessica WILLETT
35 Dean of Student Life ... Mr. David M. LEONARD
35 Assoc Dean of Students ... Ms. Tammi R. SIMPSON
30 Exec Dir for University Development ... Ms. Susan W. CUNNINGHAM
41 Director of Athletics ... Ms. Janine M. HATHORN
89 Associate Dean of Students ... Mr. Jason L. RODOCKER
07 Dean of Admissions/Financial Aid ... Ms. Sally STONE RICHMOND
09 Exec Director of Strategic Analysis ... Mr. Bryan PRICE
06 University Registrar ... Dr. Jamie D. KIPFER
08 University Librarian ... Dr. K.T VAUGHAN
85 Director International Education ... Dr. Mark E. RUSH
29 Exec Director of Alumni Affairs ... Mr. Waller T. DUDLEY
15 Exec Director of Human Resources ... Ms. Mary E. MAIN
37 Director of Financial Aid ... Mr. James D. KASTER
18 Exec Dir of University Facilities ... Mr. Tom KALASKY
21 Controller ... Ms. Celia KOVAC
13 Chief Technology Officer ... Mr. David SAACKE
24 Senior Academic Technologist ... Mr. Brandon R. BUCY
36 Dean of Career and Prof Devel ... Mr. John A. JENSEN
23 Director Student Health/Counseling ... Dr. Jane T. HORTON
88 Director of Dining Services ... Ms. Jennifer HICKEY
109 Director of Administrative Services ... Mr. K. C SCHAEFER
04 Admin Assistant to the President ... Ms. Andrea VELASQUEZ
19 Director of Public Safety ... Mr. Ethan KIPNES
28 Dean Diversity/Inclusion/Stdnt Eng ... Ms. Tamara FUTRELL
44 Director Annual Giving ... Ms. Missy WITHEROW
53 Director of Teacher Education ... Dr. Haley SIGLER

Washington Theological Seminary (E)

7700 Little River Turnpike, Ste 205, Annandale VA 22003
County: Fairfax Identification: 667424
Telephone: (703) 712-7073 Carnegie Class: Not Classified
FAX Number: N/A Calendar System: Semester
URL: www.wtsva.org
Established: 1983 Annual Undergrad Tuition & Fees: N/A
Enrollment: N/A Coed
Affiliation or Control: Presbyterian Church In America IRS Status: 501(c)3
Highest Offering: Doctorate
Accreditation: @TRACS

01 President ... Ouk Sup LEE

Washington University of Virginia (F)

4300 Evergreen Lane, Annandale VA 22003
County: Fairfax Identification: 666234
Telephone: (703) 333-5904 Carnegie Class: Not Classified
FAX Number: (703) 333-5906 Calendar System: Semester
URL: www.wuv.edu
Established: 1982 Annual Undergrad Tuition & Fees: N/A
Enrollment: N/A Coed
Affiliation or Control: Non-denominational IRS Status: 501(c)3
Highest Offering: Doctorate
Accreditation: THEOL, TRACS, IACBE

01 President ... Dr. Peter M. CHANG
03 Executive Vice President ... Mrs. Joyce Gunhee PARK
07 Dean of Enrollment ... Mr. David Y. LEE
08 Head Librarian ... Mr. Robert ROSE, JR.
50 Dean School of Business ... Mr. Won Eog KIM
06 Registrar ... Ms. Sunmin AN
38 Dean Student Counseling ... Dr. Young C. YOO

Wave Leadership College (G)

1000 North Great Neck Road, Virginia Beach VA 23454
County: Independent City Identification: 667210
Unit ID: 486594
Telephone: (757) 401-6125 Carnegie Class: Spec 2-yr-Other
FAX Number: (757) 496-6697 Calendar System: Semester
URL: www.wavecollege.com
Established: 2000 Annual Undergrad Tuition & Fees: $8,390
Enrollment: 41 Coed
Affiliation or Control: Independent Non-Profit IRS Status: 501(c)3
Highest Offering: Associate Degree
Accreditation: BI

01 President ... Steve KELLY
03 Executive Vice President ... Sarah HUMMEL
05 Academic Dean ... Jimada ROBINSON
32 Dean of Students ... Vacant
06 Registrar ... Claudette WHITE
08 Librarian ... Sasha MATTHEWS
37 Business & Financial Aid Coord ... Amy STEFFEL
85 International Student Liaison ... Vacant
07 Director of Admissions ... Leslie JONES
108 Institutional Effectiveness ... Sid VENTURA
10 Chief Financial/Business Officer ... Rachel HOEL

WASHINGTON

Bastyr University (H)

14500 Juanita Drive NE, Kenmore WA 98028-4966
County: King FICE Identification: 022425
Unit ID: 235547
Telephone: (425) 602-3000 Carnegie Class: Spec-4-yr-Other Health
FAX Number: (425) 823-6222 Calendar System: Quarter
URL: www.bastyr.edu
Established: 1978 Annual Undergrad Tuition & Fees: N/A
Enrollment: 904 Coed
Affiliation or Control: Independent Non-Profit IRS Status: 501(c)3
Highest Offering: Doctorate
Accreditation: NW, ACUP, DIETD, DIETI, MEAC, NATUR

01 President ... Dr. Devin BYRD
05 Senior Vice President/Provost ... Dr. Dave RULE
111 Vice Pres Advancement/Enroll Svcs ... Dr. Jeanne GALLOWAY
10 AVP Budget & Finance/CFO ... Mr. Ray OEN
32 Vice President of Student Affairs ... Ms. Susan L. WEIDER

Bates Technical College (I)

1101 S Yakima Avenue, Tacoma WA 98405-4895
County: Pierce FICE Identification: 005306
Unit ID: 235671
Telephone: (253) 680-7000 Carnegie Class: Assoc/HVT-High Non
FAX Number: (253) 680-7101 Calendar System: Quarter
URL: www.batestech.edu
Established: 1940 Annual Undergrad Tuition & Fees (In-State): $6,628
Enrollment: 3,369 Coed
Affiliation or Control: State IRS Status: 501(c)3
Highest Offering: Associate Degree
Accreditation: NW, ACBSP, ACFEI, DA, DT, MAC, NAEYC, OTA

01 President ... Dr. Lin ZHOU
05 Vice President of Instruction ... Mr. Johnny HU
04 Exec Asst to the President ... Ms. Karey BRYSON
32 Vice President of Student Services ... Mr. Steve ASHPOLE
15 Exec Dir of Human Resources ... Ms. Christina NELSON
11 Vice President Admin Services ... Mr. Nicholas LUTES
18 Exec Dir Facilities/Operations ... Mr. Chuck DAVIS
96 Director of General Services ... Mr. Nephtalin DRUMMER
37 Financial Aid Director ... Ms. Kimberly UPHOLD
13 Chief Information Officer ... Ms. Agnes FIGUEROA
84 Dir of Enrollment Mgt/Admission ... Vacant
19 Director Security/Safety ... Mr. Dee NELONS
08 Head Librarian ... Mr. Mike WOOD
102 Director of Foundation ... Ms. LeAnn DREIER

Bellevue College (J)

3000 Landerholm Circle, SE, Bellevue WA 98007-6484
County: King FICE Identification: 003769
Unit ID: 234669
Telephone: (425) 564-1000 Carnegie Class: Bac/Assoc-Assoc Dom
FAX Number: (425) 564-4065 Calendar System: Quarter
URL: www.bellevuecollege.edu
Established: 1965 Annual Undergrad Tuition & Fees (In-State): $3,958
Enrollment: 12,286 Coed
Affiliation or Control: State IRS Status: 501(c)3
Highest Offering: Baccalaureate
Accreditation: NW, CIDA, #DMS, NDT, NMT, NURSE, RADDOS, RTT

01 Interim President ... Gary LOCKE
32 Assoc VP Student Affairs ... Dr. Brenda IVELISSE
04 Exec Asst to the President ... Dr. Alicia KEATING POLSON
05 Provost ... Dr. Kristen JONES
28 VP Diversity/Equity & Inclusion ... Dr. Consuelo GRIER
11 VP Administrative Services ... Dennis CURRAN
15 VP Human Resources ... Vacant
111 Int VP Institutional Advancement ... Rebecca CHAWGO
13 VP Information Technology ... Rodger HARRISON
20 Assoc VP Academic Affairs ... Dr. Rob VIENS

Bellingham Technical College (A)

3028 Lindebergh Avenue, Bellingham WA 98225-1599
County: Whatcom FICE Identification: 004999
Unit ID: 234696
Telephone: (360) 752-7000 Carnegie Class: Bac/Assoc-Assoc Dom
FAX Number: (360) 676-2798 Calendar System: Quarter
URL: www.btc.edu
Established: 1957 Annual Undergrad Tuition & Fees (In-District): $3,915
Enrollment: 1,848 Coed
Affiliation or Control: State/Local IRS Status: 501(c)3
Highest Offering: Baccalaureate
Accreditation: NW, ACFEI, ADNUR, DH, SURGT

01 Interim President .... Mr. Walter HUDSICK
04 Exec Assistant to the President .... Ms. Ronda LAUGHLIN
05 Interim VP of Academic Affairs .... Dr. Heidi YPMA
32 Vice President of Student Services .... Ms. Michele WALTZ
11 VP of Administrative Services .... Ms. Chad STITELER
72 Dean of Prof Technical Education .... Ms. Heidi YPMA
72 Dean of Prof Technical Education .... Mr. Ray KUBISTA
102 Director Foundation .... Mr. Dean FULTON
15 Int Exec Director Human Resources .... Ms. Tami WILLETT
37 Exec Dir Stdnt Financial Resources .... Ms. Chantel MCMAHAN
07 Director Registration/Enrollment .... Ms. Joan KAMMERZELL
13 Dir Computer/Info Support Svcs .... Mr. Curtis PERERA
08 Director Library Svcs & eLearning .... Ms. Dawn HAWLEY
18 Chief Facilities/Physical Plant .... Mr. David JUNGKUNTZ
26 Director Marketing/Communications .. Ms. Marni SALING MAYER
36 Exec Dir Student Entry & Advising .... Mr. Matthew SANTOS
45 Exec Dir of Inst Planning & Advance .... Ms. RaeLyn AXLUND MCBRIDE
19 Director Security/Safety .... Mr. Al JENSEN
38 Interim Student Counselor .... Ms. Nyssa HOWELL

Big Bend Community College (B)

7662 Chanute Street NE, Moses Lake WA 98837-3299
County: Grant FICE Identification: 003770
Unit ID: 234711
Telephone: (509) 793-2222 Carnegie Class: Assoc/HT-High Trad
FAX Number: (509) 762-6329 Calendar System: Quarter
URL: www.bigbend.edu
Established: 1962 Annual Undergrad Tuition & Fees (In-State): $4,484
Enrollment: 1,892 Coed
Affiliation or Control: State IRS Status: 501(c)3
Highest Offering: Associate Degree
Accreditation: NW, ADNUR

01 President .... Dr. Sara THOMPSON TWEEDY
10 Vice Pres Administrative Services .... Ms. Linda SCHOONMAKER
05 VP Learning & Student Success .... Dr. Bryce HUMPHERYS
15 VP of Human Resources & Labor .... Mrs. Kim GARZA
103 Dean Workforce Education .... Ms. Daneen BERRY-GUERIN
88 Dean of Transitional Studies .... Vacant
32 Dean of Student Services .... Mr. Andre GUZMAN
49 Dean of Arts & Sciences .... Ms. Kathleen DUVALL
53 Dean Educ/Health/Language Skills .... Vacant
35 Director of Student Programs .... Ms. Kim JACKSON
37 Director of Financial Aid .... Ms. Rita RAMIREZ
06 Registrar .... Ms. Starr BERNHARDT
08 Director of Library Resources .... Mr. Tim FUHRMAN
41 Director of Athletics .... Mr. Mark POTH
102 Dir Inst Advancement/Exec Dir Found .... Mrs. LeAnne PARTON
26 Director of Communications .... Mr. Matt KILLEBREW
21 Exec Director of Business Services .... Ms. Charlene RIOS
40 Director of Bookstore .... Mrs. Caren COURTRIGHT
96 Director of Purchasing .... Mr. Joe AUVIL
39 Residence Hall Coordinator .... Mr. Luis ALVARADO
09 Dean of Institutional Research .... Ms. Valerie PARTON
13 Director of IT .... Vacant
19 Director Security/Safety .... Mr. Kyle FOREMAN
04 Executive Asst to President .... Ms. Melinda DOURTE
18 Chief Facilities/Physical Plant .... Ms. Charlene RIOS

Carrington College - Spokane (C)

10102 E Knox Avenue, Suite 200, Spokane WA 99206
Telephone: (509) 462-3722 Identification: 666385
Accreditation: &WJ, MAAB, #RAD

† Regional accreditation is carried under the parent institution in Sacramento, CA.

Cascadia College (D)

18345 Campus Way, NE, Bothell WA 98011-8205
County: King FICE Identification: 034835
Unit ID: 439190
Telephone: (425) 352-8000 Carnegie Class: Bac/Assoc-Assoc Dom
FAX Number: (425) 352-8313 Calendar System: Quarter
URL: www.cascadia.edu
Established: 2000 Annual Undergrad Tuition & Fees (In-District): $4,226
Enrollment: 2,597 Coed
Affiliation or Control: State/Local IRS Status: Exempt
Highest Offering: Baccalaureate
Accreditation: NW

01 President .... Dr. Eric MURRAY
101 Exec Asst to the President .... Lily ALLEN-RICHTER
11 VP for Administrative Services/HR .... Martin LOGAN
05 VP for Student Learning & Success .... Dr. Kerry LEVETT
111 VP for External Rels & Planning .... Meagan WALKER
20 Dean of Student Learning-Prof Tech .... Dr. Erik TINGELSTAD
20 Dean Student Lrng-Transfer/Gen Ed .... Kristina YOUNG
32 Dean of Student Success Services .... Erin BLAKENEY
20 Dean of Student Learning-Trans Stds .... Lyn EISENHOUR
10 Interim Director of Finance .... Yan LI
13 Dir of Information Services .... Laura HEDAL
18 Dir of Facilities/Capital Projects .... Kimberlee CLARK
45 Dir Institutional Effectiveness .... Dr. Michael HORN
84 Dir Enrollment Services .... Shawn MILLER
37 Dir Student Financial Services .... Deann HOLLIDAY
121 Dir Student Adv & Support Services .... Gordon DUTRISAC
35 Dir of Student Life .... Becky RIOPEL
85 Dir of International Programs .... Yukari ZEDNICK
102 Dir of Cascadia College Foundation .... Mark COLLINS
88 Dir Organization/Professional Devel .... Samantha BROWN
28 Int Exec Dir of Equity/Inclusion .... Chari DAVENPORT
26 Manager Outreach & Marketing .... Sara GOMEZ-TAYLOR
118 Manager of Payroll .... Melissa STONER
16 Human Resources Generalist .... Haley GREEN
16 Human Resources Generalist .... Elizabeth ENGLUND

Central Washington University (E)

400 E University Way, Ellensburg WA 98926-7501
County: Kittitas FICE Identification: 003771
Unit ID: 234827
Telephone: (509) 963-2111 Carnegie Class: Masters/L
FAX Number: (509) 963-3206 Calendar System: Quarter
URL: www.cwu.edu
Established: 1890 Annual Undergrad Tuition & Fees (In-State): $8,444
Enrollment: 11,174 Coed
Affiliation or Control: State IRS Status: 501(c)3
Highest Offering: Master's
Accreditation: NW, CACREP, CONST, DIETD, DIETI, EMT, IPSY, MUS

01 President .... Dr. Jim WOHLPSART
05 Provost/VP Academic & Student Life .... Dr. Michelle DENBESTE
10 VP Business & Financial Affairs .... Mr. Joel KLUCKING
100 Chief of Staff .... Ms. Linda SCHACTLER
20 Assoc Provost UG/Faculty Affairs .... Dr. Gail MACKIN
56 Assoc Provost Ext Learn & Outreach .... Dr. Ediz KAYKAYOGLU
84 Vice Pres Enrollment Management .... Mr. Josh HIBBARD
32 Dean of Student Success .... Dr. Gregg HEINSELMAN
11 VP of Operations .... Mr. Andreas BOHMAN
58 Dean Graduate Studies/Research .... Dr. Kevin ARCHER
49 Dean College of Arts/Humanities .... Dr. Jill HERNANDEZ
50 Dean College of Business .... Mr. Jeffrey L. STINSON
53 Dean College of Educ/Prof Studies .... Dr. Heidi HENSCHEL PELLETT
83 Dean College of the Sciences .... Dr. Tim ENGLUND
08 Dean of Library Services .... Dr. Rebecca LUBAS
111 Vice Pres University Advancement .... Mr. Rick PARADIS
26 Vice Pres of Public Affairs .... Ms. Kremiere JACKSON
28 Vice Pres of Diversity .... Dr. Delores CLEARY
13 AVP/Chief Information Officer .... Ms. Virginia TOMLINSON

Centralia College (F)

600 Centralia College Boulevard,
Centralia WA 98531-4035
County: Lewis FICE Identification: 003772
Unit ID: 234845
Telephone: (360) 736-9391 Carnegie Class: Bac/Assoc-Assoc Dom
FAX Number: (360) 330-7108 Calendar System: Quarter
URL: www.centralia.edu
Established: 1925 Annual Undergrad Tuition & Fees (In-State): $4,652
Enrollment: 2,314 Coed
Affiliation or Control: State IRS Status: 501(c)3
Highest Offering: Baccalaureate
Accreditation: NW

01 President .... Dr. Robert MOHRBACHER
05 Vice President Instruction .... Dr. Joyce HAMMER
32 Vice President of Students .... Mr. Robert COX
10 Vice Pres Finance/Administration .... Ms. Leslie FOUNTAIN WILLIAMS
15 VP Human Resources/Legal Affairs .... Ms. Erica HOLMES
103 Dean Workforce Education .... Mr. Jake FAY
08 Dean of Library Services/E-Learning .... Vacant
88 Dean of Academic Transfer Programs .... Mr. Christian BRUHN
09 Director of Institutional Research .... Ms. Gwen NUSS
88 Dir WorkFirst & Worker Retraining .... Ms. Margret FRIEDLEY
84 Director of Enrollment Services .... Ms. Kimberly INGRAM
37 Director of Financial Aid .... Ms. Tracy DAHL
13 Director Information Technology .... Mr. Samuel SMALL
41 Director of Sports Programs .... Mr. Bob PETERS
29 Director Alumni Relations .... Ms. Christine FOSSETT
96 Director of Purchasing .... Ms. Amanda WITT
26 Dir College Relations & Events .... Ms. Amanda HAINES
40 Bookstore Manager .... Ms. Tammy STRODEMIER
97 Program Coordinator .... Vacant

Charter College (G)

17200 SE Mill Plain Blvd, Suite 100, Vancouver WA 98683
County: Clark FICE Identification: 025769
Unit ID: 102845
Telephone: (360) 448-2000 Carnegie Class: Not Classified
FAX Number: N/A Calendar System: Quarter
URL: www.chartercollege.edu
Established: 2010 Annual Undergrad Tuition & Fees: N/A
Enrollment: 2,120 Coed
Affiliation or Control: Proprietary IRS Status: Proprietary
Highest Offering: Baccalaureate
Accreditation: ABHES

02 Campus President .... Heather ALLEN

City University of Seattle (H)

521 Wall Street, Suite 100, Seattle WA 98121
County: King FICE Identification: 013022
Unit ID: 234915
Telephone: (206) 239-4500 Carnegie Class: Masters/L
FAX Number: (206) 239-4802 Calendar System: Quarter
URL: www.cityu.edu
Established: 1973 Annual Undergrad Tuition & Fees: N/A
Enrollment: 2,052 Coed
Affiliation or Control: Independent Non-Profit IRS Status: 501(c)3
Highest Offering: Doctorate
Accreditation: NW, ACBSP, CACREP

01 Interim President .... Mr. Chris BRYAN
05 Provost .... Dr. Scott CARNZ
04 Exec Asst Office of the President .... Ms. Nandi MOONFLOWER
32 Vice President Student Services .... Dr. Melissa E. MECHAM
26 VP Marketing & Enrollment .... Mr. Jason ELLIOTT
10 Chief Financial Officer .... Mr. Christopher BRYAN
13 Director of Information Technology .... Mr. Kevin H. BROWN
15 Director of Human Resources .... Ms. Janet O'LEARY
20 Dean/EVP Academic Affairs .... Ms. Mary MARA
50 Dean Sch of Business & Management .... Mr. Scott CARNZ
72 Dean Sch of Technology & Computing .... Dr. Sam CHUNG
53 Dean Sch of Education & Leadership .... Dr. Vicki BUTLER
83 Dean Sch of Health & Social Science .... Dr. Pat RUSSELL
84 Director of Enrollment & Advising .... Ms. Teresa D'AMBROSIO
27 AVP Strategic Partnerships .... Ms. Kathy COX
85 Asst Provost International Educ .. Mr. Antonio ESQUEDA FLORES
08 Director Library Services .... Mr. Matthew LECHNER
37 Dir Student Financial Svcs .... Ms. Darcy KELLER
29 Alumni Relations Manager .... Mr. Alex WEBSTER
18 Facilities Manager .... Mr. Troy CRABREE
06 Registrar .... Ms. Melissa MECHAM

Clark College (I)

1933 Fort Vancouver Way, Vancouver WA 98663-3598
County: Clark FICE Identification: 003773
Unit ID: 234933
Telephone: (360) 992-2000 Carnegie Class: Bac/Assoc-Assoc Dom
FAX Number: (360) 992-2871 Calendar System: Quarter
URL: www.clark.edu
Established: 1933 Annual Undergrad Tuition & Fees (In-State): $3,957
Enrollment: 7,665 Coed
Affiliation or Control: State IRS Status: 501(c)3
Highest Offering: Baccalaureate
Accreditation: NW, ADNUR, DH, MAC

01 President .... Dr. Karin EDWARDS
05 Interim VP of Instruction .... Dr. Genevieve HOWARD
32 Interim VP of Student Affairs .... Dr. Michele CRUSE
11 Executive VP of Operations .... Ms. Galina BURLEY
15 Assoc Vice Pres of Human Resources .... Mr. Brad AVAKIAN
84 Dir of Enrollment/Registrar .... Ms. Mirranda SAARI
75 Dir of WF Professional Tech Ed .... Mr. Kevin THOMAS
79 Dean Engl/Comm/Hum/Basic Educ .... Mr. Jim WILKINS-LUTON
76 Interim Dean Wkforce/Tech/Prof Educ .... Ms. Armetta BURNEY
83 Dean Social Sciences/Fine Arts .... Mr. Miles JACKSON
52 Dean of Business & Health Sciences .... Ms. Brenda WALSTEAD
04 Exec Assistant to the President .... Ms. Stephanie WELDY
41 Director of Athletics .... Ms. Laura LEMASTERS
16 Associate Director Human Resources .... Vacant
08 Dir of Library Services .... Mr. Michael BROWN
18 Dir of Facility Services .... Mr. Tim PETTA
26 Chief Communications Officer .... Vacant
36 Assoc Director Career Services .... Ms. Cath KEANE
37 Interim Director of Financial Aid .... Ms. Glendi GADDIS
10 Director of Business Services .... Ms. Sabra SAND
35 Dir Stdnt Life/Multicult Stdnt Affs .... Ms. Sarah GRUHLER
121 Director of Advising Center .... Mr. John MADUTA
25 Director of Grant Development .... Ms. Julie ROBERTSON
28 VP Diversity/Equity/Inclusion .... Ms. Rashida WILLARD
19 Director of Security & Safety .... Mr. Michael SEE
85 International Recruitment Manager .... Ms. Csendi HOPP
40 Bookstore Manager .... Ms. Monica KNOWLES
96 Purchasing Manager .... Ms. Lisa HASART
102 Foundation CEO .... Ms. Lisa GIBERT
105 Information Technology Specialist .... Mr. Chris CONCANNON
29 Director Alumni Relations .... Ms. Vivian MANNING
13 Chief Information Technology Office .... Ms. Valerie MORENO

Clover Park Technical College (J)

4500 Steilacoom Boulevard, SW,
Lakewood WA 98499-4004
County: Pierce FICE Identification: 005752
Unit ID: 234951
Telephone: (253) 589-5800 Carnegie Class: Bac/Assoc-Assoc Dom
FAX Number: (253) 589-5851 Calendar System: Quarter
URL: www.cptc.edu
Established: 1942 Annual Undergrad Tuition & Fees (In-State): $5,740
Enrollment: 3,591 Coed
Affiliation or Control: State IRS Status: 501(c)3
Highest Offering: Baccalaureate
Accreditation: NW, DA, HT, MAC, MLTAD, SURGT

01 President .... Dr. Joyce LOVEDAY
04 Executive Assistant .... Cherie STEELE
05 Vice President Instruction .... Dr. Thomas BROXSON
10 Int Vice Pres Finance & Admin .... Lisa WOLCOTT
10 Int Vice Pres Finance & Admin .... Lisa BEACH
32 VP Student Success .... Scott LATIOLAIS
108 Assoc VP Inst Effectiveness .... Samantha DANA
15 Human Resources Director .... Kirk WALKER
16 Asst Dir Human Resources .... Teresa IEVERS
103 Dean of Workforce Development .... Cristeen CROUCHET
13 Dir Information Technology .... Pamela JETER
37 Director Financial Aid .... Celva BOON
18 Asst Director Facilities Services .... Chris RIDLER
18 Manager Capital Projects .... Wesley PRATER
88 Dean Pre-College Pathways .... Jenna POLLOCK
84 Dir Enrollment Services/Dean .... Cynthia MOWRY
114 Dir Budget & Finance .... Lisa WOLCOTT
121 Dean Student Success .... Dean KELLY
35 Director Student Life .... Jessica WALLACK
11 Exec Director of Operations .... Lisa BEACH
96 Purchasing & Supply Specialist .... Kimberly BILLS
26 Dir Marketing/Communication .... Jenn ADRIEN
40 Bookstore Coordinator .... Kariena MELLOR
06 Registrar .... Tracey SONGAO
88 Dean Division B .... Dr. Claire KORSCHINOWSKI
88 Dean Division C .... Michelle HILLESLAND
88 Dean Division A .... Dr. Chris CHEN MAHONEY
88 Dean Instruction .... Brandon ROGERS
28 Assoc VP Equity/Diversity/Inclusion .... Vacant
105 Web Content Manager .... Jeanna DUFOUR
28 Mgr Student Diversity Programs .... Yuko CHARTRAW
102 Exec Director Foundation .... Janet HOLM
66 Dean Nursing Programs .... Vacant

Columbia Basin College (A)

2600 N 20th Avenue, Pasco WA 99301-3397
County: Franklin FICE Identification: 003774
Unit ID: 234979
Telephone: (509) 547-0511 Carnegie Class: Bac/Assoc-Mixed
FAX Number: (509) 546-0404 Calendar System: Quarter
URL: www.columbiabasin.edu
Established: 1955 Annual Undergrad Tuition & Fees (In-State): $5,755
Enrollment: 6,745 Coed
Affiliation or Control: State IRS Status: 170(c)1
Highest Offering: Baccalaureate
Accreditation: NW, ADNUR, DH, EMT, MAC, NURSE, SURGT

01 President .... Dr. Rebekah WOODS
05 Vice President Instruction .... Dr. Michael LEE
10 Vice Pres Administrative Services .... Mr. Eduardo RODRIGUEZ
32 Vice President of Student Services .... Ms. Cheryl HOLDEN
15 VP Human Resources/Legal Affairs .... Ms. Camilla GLATT
13 Asst VP Infrastructure Services .... Mr. Brian DEXTER
26 Asst VP for Comm & External Affairs .... Mr. Jay FRANK
09 Dean for Organizational Learning .... Dr. Jason ENGLE
49 Dean Arts & Humanities .... Mr. Bill MCKAY
08 Assoc Dean Library/Instruct Svcs .... Ms. Keri LOBDELL
102 Executive Director/CEO Foundation .... Ms. Erin FISHBURN
40 Bookstore Director .... Ms. Debra BRUCE
18 Director of Plant Operations .... Vacant
41 Athletic Director .... Mr. Scott ROGERS
26 Marketing/Communications Director .... Ms. Anna TENSMEYER
35 Director of Student Activities .... Ms. Alice SCHLEGEL
37 Director Student Financial Aid .... Mr. Ben BEUS
114 Director for Budget/Purchasing .... Mr. Brian ANDERSON
06 Associate Registrar .... Ms. Janet GARZA
04 Executive Asst to the President .... Ms. Ronda RODGERS
84 Asst VP Enrollment Svcs & Registrar .... Ms. Kelsey MYERS
39 Director Resident Life .... Mr. Dan QUOCK
50 Int Dean Business .... Ms. Soo PARK
83 Dean for Social Sciences/Education .... Ms. Monica HANSEN
81 Dean for Math & Sciences .... Mr. Roderick TAYLOR
76 Dean of Health Sciences .... Mr. Doug HUGHES
75 Dean for Career & Technical Educ .... Mr. Jesus MOTA
97 Dean for Transitional Studies .... Ms. Daphne LARIOS
108 Dean for Accreditation & Assessment .... Ms. Melissa MCBURNEY
124 Assoc Dean for Student Retention .... Mr. Lane SCHUMACHER
19 Director Security/Safety .... Vacant

*Community Colleges of Spokane District 17 (B)

501 N Riverpoint Boulevard, MS 1009,
Spokane WA 99217-6000
County: Spokane FICE Identification: 010784
Telephone: (509) 434-5107 Carnegie Class: N/A
FAX Number: (509) 434-5120
URL: www.ccs.spokane.edu

01 Chancellor .... Dr. Christine JOHNSON
12 Pres Spokane Community College .... Dr. Kevin BROCKBANK
12 Pres Spokane Falls Cmty College .... Dr. Kimberlee MESSINA
05 Provost .... Ms. Valerie SENATORE
20 Vice Pres Instruction .... Ms. Jenni MARTIN
10 Chief Financial Officer .... Ms. Lisa HJALTALIN
11 Chief Administration Officer .... Mr. Greg L. STEVENS
26 Public Information Officer .... Ms. Carolyn CASEY
41 Dist Director of Athletics PE/Rec .... Mr. Jim FITZGERALD
102 Executive Director CCS Foundation .... Ms. Heather BEEBE STEVENS
18 District Director of Facilities .... Mr. John GILLETTE
103 Exec Dir Ctr Wkforce/Cont Ed .... Mr. Nolan GRUVER
106 Asst Prov E-lrng/Educ Innovation .... Mr. Patrick MCEACHERN

*Spokane Community College (C)

North 1810 Greene Street, Spokane WA 99217-5499
County: Spokane FICE Identification: 003793
Unit ID: 236692
Telephone: (509) 533-7000 Carnegie Class: Bac/Assoc-Assoc Dom
FAX Number: N/A Calendar System: Quarter
URL: www.scc.spokane.edu
Established: 1963 Annual Undergrad Tuition & Fees (In-State): $3,727
Enrollment: 7,081 Coed
Affiliation or Control: State IRS Status: 501(c)3
Highest Offering: Baccalaureate
Accreditation: NW, ACFEI, ADNUR, CAHIIM, COARC, CVT, DA, DMS, MAC, RAD, SURGT

00 District Chancellor .... Dr. Christine JOHNSON
02 President .... Dr. Kevin BROCKBANK
05 VP of Instruction .... Ms. Jenni MARTIN
32 Vice President of Student Services .... Dr. Glen COSBY
121 Director Student Success & Outreach .... Dr. Lori HUNT
07 Director Admissions & Registration .... Ms. Chantel BLACK
35 Associate Dean Student Development .... Mr. Connan CAMPBELL
51 Dean Adult Basic Education .... Dr. Sherri FUJITA
49 Dean Arts & Sciences .... Ms. Gwendolyn JAMES
50 Dean Business/Hospitality/Info Tech .... Mr. Jeff BROWN
88 Assoc Dean Corrections Education .... Mr. Kevin HOUSE
56 Dean Extended Learning .... Ms. Jaclyn JACOT
76 Dean Health & Environmental Science .... Dr. J.L HENRIKSEN
66 Associate Dean of Nursing .... Dr. Cheri OSLER
75 Dean for Technical Education .... Mr. Dave COX
41 Director Athletics .... Mr. Jim FITZGERALD
09 Sr Dir Inst Effectiveness/Planning .... Mr. Roy CALIGAN
88 Assistant Dean PACE Services .... Ms. Stephanie CHILDRESS
06 Registrar .... Ms. Chantel BLACK
37 Director Financial Aid .... Ms. Tammy ZIBELL
10 Chief Financial Officer .... Ms. Lisa HJALTALIN
11 Chief Administration Officer .... Mr. Greg STEVENS
26 Chief Public Information Officer .... Ms. Carolyn CASEY
102 District Devel Ofcr/Foundation .... Ms. Heather BEEBE-STEVENS
20 District Provost .... Dr. Valerie SENATORE
38 Student Counseling Department Chair .... Ms. Rebecca GOSS
96 District Director of Purchasing .... Ms. Nanette SPEAR
04 Executive Asst to President .... Ms. Gaylene MACRAE
13 Chief Info Technology Officer (CIO) .... Mr. Rick SPARKS

*Spokane Falls Community College (D)

3410 W Whistalks Way, Spokane WA 99224-5288
County: Spokane FICE Identification: 009544
Unit ID: 236708
Telephone: (509) 533-3500 Carnegie Class: Bac/Assoc-Assoc Dom
FAX Number: (509) 533-3237 Calendar System: Quarter
URL: www.spokanefalls.edu
Established: 1967 Annual Undergrad Tuition & Fees (In-State): $3,727
Enrollment: 4,189 Coed
Affiliation or Control: State IRS Status: Exempt
Highest Offering: Baccalaureate
Accreditation: NW, OTA, PTAA

02 President .... Dr. Kimberlee MESSINA
04 Exec Asst to the President .... Ms. Jan CARPENTER
05 Vice President of Learning .... Mr. Jim BRADY
32 Vice President of Student Affairs .... Mr. Keith SAYLES
81 Dean Computing/Math/Science .... Dr. Sarah MARTIN
83 Dean Soc Sci/Acct/Econ/Hum Svcs .... Ms. Elodie GOODMAN
79 Dean Humanities .... Dr. Linda BEANE-BOOSE
57 Dean Visual & Performing Arts .... Dr. Bonnie GLANTZ
50 Dean Bus/Prof Stds/Workforce .... Dr. Christopher PELCHAT
121 Dean Student Support Services .... Ms. Cynthia VIGIL
84 Dir Recruit/New Stdnt Entry Center .... Ms. Leslie DAWSON
38 Counseling Department Chair .... Ms. Shawna SHELTON
37 Director of Financial Aid .... Ms. Alex BAILEY
07 Director of Admissions/Registrar .... Ms. Mindy HASENKAMP
41 Athletic Director .... Mr. James FITZGERALD
19 Director of District Security .... Mr. Ken DEMELLO
09 Dir Inst Effectiveness/Research .... Ms. Sally JACKSON
15 Chief Human Resources Officer .... Mr. Greg STEVENS
10 Chief Business Officer .... Ms. Lisa HJALTALIN
13 Chief Info Technology Officer (CIO) .... Mr. Rick SPARKS
102 Exec Director CCS Foundation .... Ms. Heather BEEBE-STEVENS
85 Dean for Global Education .... Ms. Hadda ESTRADA
106 District Director of e-Learning .... Mr. Patrick MCEACHERN
103 Chief Workforce Development Officer .... Mr. Nolan GRUVER
26 Public Information Officer .... Ms. Carolyn CASEY
18 Director of Facilities .... Mr. John GILLETTE
96 Procurement Manager .... Mr. Jim SCOTT

Cornish College of the Arts (E)

1000 Lenora Street, Seattle WA 98121-2707
County: King FICE Identification: 012315
Unit ID: 235024
Telephone: (206) 726-5151 Carnegie Class: Spec-4-yr-Arts
FAX Number: (206) 720-1011 Calendar System: Semester
URL: www.cornish.edu
Established: 1914 Annual Undergrad Tuition & Fees: $34,200
Enrollment: 482 Coed
Affiliation or Control: Independent Non-Profit IRS Status: 501(c)3
Highest Offering: Baccalaureate
Accreditation: NW, ART

01 President .... Dr. Raymond TYMAS-JONES
05 Provost & VP Academic Affairs .... William R. SEIGH
111 VP Institutional Advancement .... Anne DERIEUX
10 VP of Finance & CFO .... Debbie TREEN
84 VP of Enrollment & Marketing .... Vacant
18 VP of Operations .... Brandon BIRD
32 Dean of Student Life .... Dr. Brittany HENDERSON
06 Dean of Academic Services/Registrar .... Adrienne M. BOLYARD
15 Director of Human Resources .... Roy BROWN, III
13 Director of Information Technology .... Jon GRAEF
100 Chief of Staff .... Rick SMITH
21 Controller .... Tina CHAMBERLAIN
08 Director of Library Services .... Bridget NOWLIN
07 Director of Admissions .... Sharron STARLING
26 Dir of Marketing & Communications .... Vacant
38 Director Student Counseling .... Lori KOSHORK
37 Director of Financial Aid .... Sara DRUMMOND
19 Manager Security & Safety .... Dean DEGRAW
30 Director of Development .... Pat BAKO
09 Director of Institutional Research .... Margaret KIRCHNER
43 General Counsel/Title IX Coord .... Tiffany DAVIS

DigiPen Institute of Technology (F)

9931 Willows Road, NE, Redmond WA 98052
County: King FICE Identification: 037243
Unit ID: 443410
Telephone: (425) 558-0299 Carnegie Class: Bac-Diverse
FAX Number: (425) 558-0378 Calendar System: Semester
URL: www.digipen.edu
Established: 1988 Annual Undergrad Tuition & Fees: $33,900
Enrollment: 1,120 Coed
Affiliation or Control: Proprietary IRS Status: Proprietary
Highest Offering: Master's
Accreditation: ACCSC

01 President .... Mr. Claude COMAIR
111 Sr VP External Affairs .... Ms. Angela KUGLER
11 COO - International .... Mr. Chris COMAIR
32 Dean of Students .... Mr. Marshall TRAVERSE
07 Director of Admissions .... Ms. Emily KIRBY

Eastern Washington University (G)

526 5th Street, Cheney WA 99004-1619
County: Spokane FICE Identification: 003775
Unit ID: 235097
Telephone: (509) 359-6200 Carnegie Class: Masters/L
FAX Number: (509) 359-6927 Calendar System: Quarter
URL: www.ewu.edu
Established: 1882 Annual Undergrad Tuition & Fees (In-State): $7,733
Enrollment: 12,349 Coed
Affiliation or Control: State IRS Status: 501(c)3
Highest Offering: Doctorate
Accreditation: NW, CAATE, CACREP, CAPRT, DH, MUS, OT, PH, PLNG, PTA, SP, SPAA, SW

01 Interim President .... Dr. David MAY
05 Provost/VP for Academic Affairs .... Dr. Brian LEVIN-STANKEVICH
10 Vice President for Business/Finance .... Ms. Mary VOVES
32 VP for Student Affairs .... Dr. Robert R. SAUDERS
111 Vice President of Advancement .... Ms. Barbara RICHEY
13 VP Info Technology/CIO .... Mr. Brad CHRIST
28 VP Diversity/Equity/Inclusion .... Ms. Shari J. CLARKE
20 Int Vice Prov Academic Admin .... Dr. Brian DONAHUE
88 AVP Academic Planning .... Mr. Mark BALDWIN
78 Dean of University College .... Ms. Lynn BRIGGS
88 Associate Dean University College .... Mr. Brian DAVENPORT
08 Dean of Libraries .... Dr. Justin OTTO
41 AVP/Director of Athletics .... Ms. Lynn HICKEY
21 Assoc VP Finance/Chief Fin Officer .... Ms. Toni HABEGGER
18 Assoc Vice Pres for Facilities .... Mr. Shawn KING
84 Assoc VP Enrollment Management .... Dr. Jens LARSON
07 Assoc Dir of Admissions Operation .... Mr. Boubacar BOUARÉ
36 Asst VP Student Svcs/Dir Career Dev .... Ms. Virginia (Gini) HINCH
15 AVP of Human Resources .... Ms. Deborah DANNER
26 Asst VP Marketing/Communications .... Mr. Lance KISSLER
101 Exec Assistant to the President/BOT .... Ms. Chandalin BENNETT
100 Chief of Staff .... Ms. Sara SEXTON-JOHNSON
92 Spec Asst to Provost for Honors .... Dr. Naomi YAVNEH KLOS
85 Dir Global Outreach/Intl RCRT .... Mr. Michael REID
37 Dir of Financial Aid & Scholarships .... Mr. Bruce DEFRATES
40 Bookstore Director .... Ms. Devon TINKER
51 Dir of Continuing Education & RS .... Ms. Brenda BLAZEKOVIC
06 Associate Registrar .... Ms. Debra FOCKLER
29 AVP of Philanthropy .... Ms. Lisa POPLAWSKI LEWIS
39 Int Director Housing/Residence Life .... Ms. Debra STAFFORD
38 Director Counseling & Psych Svcs .... Dr. Robert QUACKENBUSH
19 Director Public Safety/Chief Police .... Chief Timothy L. WALTERS
27 Director of Media Relations .... Mr. David MEANY
22 Director Equal Opportunity .... Mr. Ray RECTOR
50 Dean Business & Public Admin .... Dr. Ahmad TOOTOONCHI
79 Int Dean College Arts/Letters/Edu .... Dr. Florian PREISIG
83 Dean Col Soc/Behav Sci/Soc Work .... Dr. Jonathan ANDERSON
81 Dean Col Science/Technology/Math .... Dr. David BOWMAN
66 Dean Health Science & Public Health .... Dr. Laureen O'HANLON
35 Int Assoc VP/Dean of Student Life .... Dr. Samantha (Sam) ARMSTRONG ASH
09 Director Institutional Research .... Vacant
44 Assistant Director of Annual Giving .... Vacant
104 Int Exec Dir of Global Initiatives .... Ms. Megan ABBEY
25 Exec Dir Grants & Research Dev .... Ms. Charlene ALSPACH

Edmonds Community College (A)

20000 68th Avenue W, Lynnwood WA 98036-5999
County: Snohomish FICE Identification: 005001
Unit ID: 235103
Telephone: (425) 640-1459 Carnegie Class: Bac/Assoc-Assoc Dom
FAX Number: (425) 771-3366 Calendar System: Quarter
URL: www.edcc.edu
Established: 1967 Annual Undergrad Tuition & Fees (In-State): $4,107
Enrollment: 6,545 Coed
Affiliation or Control: State IRS Status: 501(c)3
Highest Offering: Baccalaureate
Accreditation: NW, CONST

01 President .... Dr. Amit B. SINGH
05 Int Vice President Instruction .... Ms. Kim CHAPMAN
10 Int VP Finance & Operations .... Mr. Jim MULIK
15 VP Human Resources/Operations .... Ms. Mushka ROHANI
32 Vice President Student Services .... Ms. Christina CASTORENA
84 Assoc Dean Student Enroll/Fin Aid .... Ms. Christina RUSS
35 Dean Student Life/Development .... Mr. Jorge DE LA TORRE
04 Exec Asst to Pres Plng/Operations .... Ms. Kristen NYQUIST
124 Dean Student Success/Retention .... Dr. Steve WOODARD
102 Exec Director College Foundation .... Mr. Brad THOMAS
121 Director Advising .... Ms. Olla IBRAHIM
25 Exec Director Grants & Research .... Ms. Cat CAROTHERS
103 Dir Workforce Development/Training .... Mr. Lance GROB
26 Dir Marketing/Public Information .... Ms. Marisa PIERCE
13 Director Information Technology .... Ms. Eva SMITH
18 Dir Facilities/Planning/Operations .... Ms. Stephanie TEACHMAN
41 Athletic Director .... Mr. Spencer STARK
85 Exec Dir International Student Svcs .... Ms. Lisa THOMPSON
09 Institutional Researcher .... Ms. Wenlan JING
28 VP Equity & Inclusion .... Dr. Yvonne TERRELL-POWELL
108 Inst Effectiveness/Grants Liaison .... Mr. James MULIK
96 Director of Finance .... Ms. Heather LYONS
21 Director of Accounting .... Ms. Geni TEAGUE
37 Director Financial Aid .... Ms. Michelle THORSEN
38 Dir Counseling & Resource Center .... Ms. Jessica BURWELL
39 Housing Dir/Housing for Students .... Mr. Luke BOTZHEIM
50 Dean Business Division .... Mr. Andrew WILLIAMS
29 Dir of Development/Alumni Relations .... Ms. Lisa CARROLL
36 Director Entry Services .... Mr. Mark DIVIRGILIO

Everett Community College (B)

2000 Tower Street, Everett WA 98201-1390
County: Snohomish FICE Identification: 003776
Unit ID: 235149
Telephone: (425) 388-9100 Carnegie Class: Assoc/HT-High Non
FAX Number: (425) 388-9129 Calendar System: Quarter
URL: www.everettcc.edu
Established: 1941 Annual Undergrad Tuition & Fees (In-State): $3,972
Enrollment: 7,580 Coed
Affiliation or Control: State IRS Status: 501(c)3
Highest Offering: Associate Degree
Accreditation: NW, ADNUR, MAC

01 President .... Dr. Daria WILLIS
04 Sr Exec Asst to President .... Ms. Jeri POURCHOT
04 Exec Asst to President .... Ms. Rita BELVILL
05 VP of Instruction .... Ms. Cathy LEAKER
32 Interim VP of Student Services .... Ms. Laurie FRANKLIN
10 Vice President of Finance .... Ms. Shelby BURKE
26 Vice Pres of College Services .... Mr. Patrick SISNEROS
28 AVP of Diversity & Equity .... Dr. Phyllis ESPOSITO
88 Vice Pres of Corporate Training .... Mr. John BONNER
15 Vice Pres Human Resources .... Mr. Joseph WHALEN
60 Dean Communication/Social Sciences .... Mr. Eugene MCAVOY
32 Int Dean of Student Development .... Ms. Jennifer RHODES
81 Dean of Math & Science .... Ms. Joyce BELCHER
62 Dean of Arts & Learning Resources .... Ms. Lynnae DEEKEN
76 Dean Health Sciences/Public Safety .... Mr. Timmothy LOVITT
53 Dean of Basic & Adult Education .... Ms. Katie JENSEN
51 Director Continuing Education .... Ms. Kristen MCCONAHA
84 Dean Enrollment/Student Finan Svcs .... Ms. Laurie FRANKLIN
50 Dean of Business & Applied Tech .... Mr. William STUFLICK
19 Dir of Campus Safety & Security .... Mr. Charles MACKLIN
09 Director Institutional Research .... Mr. Neal PARKER
86 Exec Dir Govt/Community Relations .... Dr. John OLSON
41 Director of Athletics .... Mr. Garet STUDER
40 Director of Bookstore .... Ms. Rachael WATSON
22 Dir Center for Disability Services .... Mr. Eric TREKELL
06 Registrar .... Mr. Karl RITTER SMITH
104 Assoc Vice Pres Intl Studies .... Mr. Visakan GANESON
13 Chief Information Technology Office .... Mr. Tim RAGER

The Evergreen State College (C)

2700 Evergreen Parkway, NW, Olympia WA 98505-0005
County: Thurston FICE Identification: 008155
Unit ID: 235167
Telephone: (360) 867-6000 Carnegie Class: Masters/S
FAX Number: N/A Calendar System: Quarter
URL: www.evergreen.edu
Established: 1967 Annual Undergrad Tuition & Fees (In-State): $8,325
Enrollment: 2,281 Coed
Affiliation or Control: State IRS Status: 501(c)3
Highest Offering: Master's
Accreditation: NW

01 President .... Dr. John CARMICHAEL
05 Provost/VP for Student & Acad Life .... Dr. David MCAVITY
111 Vice President College Advancement .... Ms. Abby KELSO
26 AVP Marketing & Communications .... Ms. Farra HAYES
28 VP Incl Excellence & Stdnt Success .... Dr. Therese SALIBA
88 VP Tribal Relations/Art & Culture .... Ms. Kara BRIGGS
84 Chief Enrollment Officer .... Mr. Eric PEDERSEN
15 Assoc Vice Pres for Human Resources .... Ms. Laurel UZNANSKI
10 Assoc Vice Pres for Finance .... Mr. Dave KOHLER
08 Dean of Library Services .... Mr. Greg MULLINS
121 Dir of Academic and Career Advising .... Dr. Allen THOMPSON
101 Executive Assoc/Secretary to BOT .... Ms. Susan HARRIS
22 Affirm Action/Equal Opp Officer .... Ms. Lorie MASTIN
13 Assoc VP Computing/Communications .... Mr. Antonio ALFONSO
37 Assoc Director of Financial Aid .... Mr. Colby MORELLI
06 Registrar .... Ms. Lori KLATT
09 Director of Institutional Research .... Vacant
11 Assoc VP for Operations .... Mr. William WARD
41 Assoc Dean Wellness/Rec/Athletics .... Ms. Elizabeth MCHUGH
96 Purchasing and Contracts Manager .... Mr. Brant EDDY
07 Director of Admissions .... Mr. Wade ARAVE
88 Director of Sustainability .... Mr. Scott MORGAN
04 Admin Assistant to the President .... Vacant
39 Dir Resident and Dining Services .... Ms. Sharon GOODMAN
86 Director Government Relations .... Mr. Jeremy MOHN

Faith International University (D)

3504 N Pearl Street, Tacoma WA 98407-2607
County: Pierce FICE Identification: 036894
Unit ID: 443049
Telephone: (253) 752-2020 Carnegie Class: Spec-4-yr-Faith
FAX Number: (253) 759-1790 Calendar System: Quarter
URL: www.faithseminary.edu
Established: 1969 Annual Undergrad Tuition & Fees: $11,250
Enrollment: 318 Coed
Affiliation or Control: Interdenominational IRS Status: 501(c)3
Highest Offering: Doctorate
Accreditation: TRACS

01 President .... Dr. Michael J. ADAMS
05 Vice Pres Academic Affs/Provost .... Dr. H. Wayne HOUSE
104 Executive VP/International Affairs .... Dr. Kyu H. LEE
11 Executive VP/COO .... Dr. John WHEELER
88 Admin Dean Korean Division .... Miae LEE
10 Chief Financial Officer .... Dr. Don BELL
07 Director of Admissions .... Karen BURNWORTH
08 Director Library Services .... Dr. Timothy HYUN
04 Exec Administrative Assistant .... Kimberly ADAMS
06 Registrar .... Dr. Andrew CAYANAN
09 Director of Institutional Research .... Mary VELONI
15 Chief Human Resources Officer .... Alexis DONNELLY
26 Chief PR/Marketing/Communications .... Kim WHEELER
37 Director Student Financial Aid .... Laura GUNNARSON

Gather 4 Him Bible College (E)

3021 West Clearwater Avenue, Kennewick WA 99336
County: Benton Identification: 667359
Telephone: (509) 420-4545 Carnegie Class: Not Classified
FAX Number: N/A Calendar System: Semester
URL: college-gather4him.net
Established: 2008 Annual Undergrad Tuition & Fees: N/A
Enrollment: N/A Coed
Affiliation or Control: Independent Non-Profit IRS Status: 501(c)3
Highest Offering: Associate Degree
Accreditation: TRACS

01 President .... Robert B. NASH
05 Dean of Academic Affairs .... Dr. Darrell PULS
06 Registrar .... Kelli TEMPLETON
07 Dir Admissions/Student Life .... Robbie FIOCCHI

Gonzaga University (F)

502 East Boone Avenue, Spokane WA 99258-0102
County: Spokane FICE Identification: 003778
Unit ID: 235316
Telephone: (509) 328-4220 Carnegie Class: DU-Mod
FAX Number: (509) 313-5718 Calendar System: Semester
URL: www.gonzaga.edu
Established: 1887 Annual Undergrad Tuition & Fees: $46,920
Enrollment: 7,295 Coed
Affiliation or Control: Roman Catholic IRS Status: 501(c)3
Highest Offering: Doctorate
Accreditation: NW, ANEST, CACREP, CEA, LAW, MUS, NURSE

01 President .... Dr. Thayne M. MCCULLOH
05 Provost .... Dr. Deena GONZALEZ
100 Chief of Staff .... Dr. Charlita SHELTON
88 Senior Advisor to the President .... Mr. John SKLUT
111 VP for University Advancement .... Mr. Joe POSS
42 VP for Mission Integration .... Ms. Michelle WHEATLEY
32 Vice Prov Student Affairs .... Dr. Kent PORTERFIELD
10 Chief Financial Officer .... Mr. Joe SMITH
45 Chief Strategy Officer .... Mr. Chuck MURPHY
43 General Counsel .... Ms. Maureen MCGUIRE
41 Director of Athletics .... Mr. Chris L. STANDIFORD
28 Chief Diversity Officer .... Dr. Robin KELLEY
04 Executive Asst to President .... Ms. Julia BJORDAHL
101 Secretary to the Board .... Ms. Maureen MCGUIRE
100 Faculty Advisor to the President .... Dr. Ellen M. MACCARONE
17 Director UW-GU Health Partnership .... Mr. John SKLUT
20 Assc Prov Educational Effectiveness .... Dr. Ron LARGE
84 Assoc Prov Enrollment Management .... Ms. Julie A. MCCULLOH
06 Assoc Provost/Registrar .... Dr. Jolanta A. WEBER
93 Assoc VP for Cultural Initiatives .... Dr. Raymond REYES
08 Dean of Library Services .... Dr. Paul J. BRACKE
49 Dean of Arts & Sciences .... Dr. Annmarie CANO
53 Dean of Education .... Dr. Yoli GALLARDO
50 Dean of Business .... Dr. Kenneth ANDERSON
54 Dean Engineering & Applied Sciences .... Dr. Karlene HOO
61 Dean of Law .... Dr. Jacob ROOKSBY
66 Dean of Nursing/Human Phys .... Vacant
88 Dean of Leadership Studies .... Dr. Rosey HUNTER
12 Dean Gonzaga-In-Florence .... Dr. Jason HOUSTON
106 Director of Virtual Campus .... Vacant
108 Faculty Director of Assessment .... Dr. Patrick T. MCCORMICK
110 Asst VP Ops & Fundraising .... Ms. Stephanie ROCKWELL
112 Senior Director Planned Giving .... Ms. Judy ROGERS
88 Senior Director Donor Relations .... Ms. Laura GATEWOOD
27 Director of Community and PR .... Ms. Mary Joan HAHN
29 Director of Engagement & Alumni .... Ms. Kara HERTZ
26 AVP for Marketing/Communications .... Mr. Dave SONNTAG
21 Controller .... Ms. Deena PRESNELL
96 Director Purchasing .... Vacant
15 Assoc VP for Human Resources .... Mr. Thomas CHESTER
22 Asst Director Equity & Inclusion .... Ms. Chris PURVIANCE
09 Director of Institutional Research .... Dr. Maxwell KWENDA
13 Chief Information Officer .... Mr. Borre ULRICHSEN
19 Director Security/Safety .... Ms. Becky WILKEY
18 Director Plant Services .... Mr. Ken SAMMONS
07 Director of Undergraduate Admission .... Ms. Erin HAYS
36 Asst VP Career/Prof Development .... Mr. Ray ANGLE
39 Director Student Housing .... Mr. Dennis COLESTOCK
88 Asst VP Student Well Being/Healthy .... Vacant
37 Dean of Student Finance Services .... Mr. James WHITE
35 Dean of Student Engagement .... Mr. Matt LAMSMA
38 Director of Counseling Services .... Dr. Fernando ORITZ
92 Director Honors Program .... Dr. Linda TREDENNICK
36 Director Career Education .... Mr. Jonathan BYERS
104 Dir Center for Global Engagement .. Ms. Liliya AMBARTSUMYAN
88 Sr Publications Ed & Content Strat .... Ms. Kathryn VANSKIKE
86 Liaison for External & Govt Affairs .... Mr. John SKLUT

Grays Harbor College (G)

1620 Edward P. Smith Drive, Aberdeen WA 98520-7500
County: Grays Harbor FICE Identification: 003779
Unit ID: 235334
Telephone: (360) 532-9020 Carnegie Class: Bac/Assoc-Assoc Dom
FAX Number: (360) 538-4299 Calendar System: Quarter
URL: www.ghc.edu
Established: 1930 Annual Undergrad Tuition & Fees (In-District): $4,296
Enrollment: 1,553 Coed
Affiliation or Control: State/Local IRS Status: 501(c)3
Highest Offering: Baccalaureate
Accreditation: NW, ADNUR

01 Interim President .... Dr. Ed BREWSTER
04 Senior Admin Assistant to President .... Ms. Sandra ZELASKO
05 Vice President for Instruction .... Ms. Nicole LACROIX
10 VP Administrative Svcs .... Mr. Kwabena J. BOAKYE
32 Vice Pres for Student Services .... Mr. Cal ERWIN-SVOBODA
13 Chief Exec Information Technology .... Mr. Derek EDENS
75 Dean Vocational Instruction .... Dr. Lucas RUCKS
35 Assoc Dean for Student Services .... Vacant
08 Assoc Dn Library/Media Svcs/e-Lrng .... Ms. Susan SCHREINER
07 Assoc Dean of Admissions .... Vacant
15 Chief Human Resources Officer .... Mr. Darin JONES
37 Asst Dean Financial Aid .... Ms. Stacey SAVINO
18 Dir Campus Operations/Sfty/Security .... Vacant
38 Director of Counseling .... Vacant
102 Exec Dir GHC Foundation .... Ms. Lisa SMITH
26 Director Public Relations .... Vacant
09 Chief Inst Effect/Col Relations .... Ms. Kristy ANDERSON
06 Dir Enroll Srvs/Assoc Registrar .... Vacant
41 Athletic Director .... Mr. William RIDER
106 Dir Online Education/E-Learning .... Vacant

Great Northern University (H)

611 E. Indiana Avenue, Spokane WA 99207
County: Spokane Identification: 667409
Telephone: (509) 248-7100 Carnegie Class: Not Classified
FAX Number: N/A Calendar System: Semester
URL: greatnorthernu.org
Established: 2018 Annual Undergrad Tuition & Fees: N/A
Enrollment: N/A Coed
Affiliation or Control: Independent Non-Profit IRS Status: 501(c)3
Highest Offering: Baccalaureate
Accreditation: @TRACS

01 President .... Dr. Wendy LIDDELL

Green River College (I)

12401 SE 320th Street, Auburn WA 98092-3699
County: King FICE Identification: 003780
Unit ID: 235343
Telephone: (253) 288-3340 Carnegie Class: Bac/Assoc-Assoc Dom
FAX Number: N/A Calendar System: Quarter
URL: www.greenriver.edu
Established: 1965 Annual Undergrad Tuition & Fees (In-State): $4,233
Enrollment: 7,493 Coed
Affiliation or Control: State IRS Status: 501(c)3
Highest Offering: Baccalaureate

Accreditation: NW, OTA, PTAA

01 President — Dr. Suzanne JOHNSON
05 Vice President of Instruction — Dr. Rolita EZEONU
13 Exec Dir of Information Technology — Camella MORGAN
10 Vice President of Business Affairs — Shirley BEAN
15 Senior Director of Human Resources — Mark BRUNKE
32 Vice President of Student Services — Dr. Deborah CASEY POWELL
56 VP Intl Programs/Extended Learning — Wendy STEWART
49 Dean Fine Arts & Social Science — Christie GILLILAND
79 Dean English/Humanities — Jamie FITZGERALD
84 Dean of Enrollment & Completion — David LARSEN
06 Director of Enrollment Services — Jenny WHEELER
37 Director of Financial Aid — Teresa BUCHMANN
111 VP of College Advancement — George FRASIER
21 Director of Budget — Janee SOMMERFELD
18 Capital Projects Officer — Robert OLSON
26 Senior Director College Relations — Philip DENMAN
12 Dean for Branch Campuses & A&P Dev — Tsai-En CHENG
09 Dir Institutional Effectiveness — Fia ELIASSON-CREEK
28 Dir Diversity/Equity & Inclusion — Marwa ALMUSAWI
19 Director of Campus Safety — Derek RONNFELDT
41 Director Athletics — Shannon PERCELL
04 Executive Assistant to President — Suzanne MCCUDDEN
103 Director Workforce Education — Cathy ALSTON

Heritage University (A)

3240 Fort Road, Toppenish WA 98948-9599
County: Yakima FICE Identification: 003777
Unit ID: 235422
Telephone: (509) 865-8600 Carnegie Class: Masters/L
FAX Number: (509) 865-7976 Calendar System: Semester
URL: www.heritage.edu
Established: 1982 Annual Undergrad Tuition & Fees: $18,332
Enrollment: 999 Coed
Affiliation or Control: Independent Non-Profit IRS Status: 501(c)3
Highest Offering: Master's
Accreditation: NW, MT, NURSE, SW

01 President — Dr. Andrew C. SUND
05 Provost/VP Academic Affairs — Dr. Kazuhiro SONODA
32 VP Student Affairs & Enrollment — Dr. Melissa HILL
10 Chief Financial Officer — Vacant
111 VP Advancement/Marketing/Comm — Mr. David WISE
13 Director Information Technology — Mr. Aaron KRANTZ
84 Assoc VP Enrollment Management — Vacant
53 Dean of Education & Psychology — Mr. Ken BERGEVIN
49 Dean Arts & Sciences — Dr. Kazuhiro SONODA
35 Director of Student Life/Engagement — Mr. Isaias GUERRERO
06 Assoc Registrar — Mr. Pablo CONTRERAS
18 Director Physical Plant/Maintenance — Mr. Jeff BEEHLER
37 Int Director of Financial Aid — Ms. Dianne FERNANDEZ
08 Library Dir/Reference Librarian — Mr. Daniel LIESTMAN
07 Director of Admissions — Mr. Gabriel PINON
26 Communications Officer — Ms. Bonnie HUGHES
09 Inst Research Administrator — Vacant
15 Director Human Resources — Ms. Anita FLORES
21 Controller — Mr. Jeffrey PHELPS
04 Exec Manager President's Office — Ms. Betty J. SAMPSON
103 Director Workforce Development — Mr. Martin VALADEZ
19 Director Security/Safety — Mr. Joseph LAREZ

Highline College (B)

PO Box 98000, 2400 S 240th Street,
Des Moines WA 98198-9800
County: King FICE Identification: 003781
Unit ID: 235431
Telephone: (206) 878-3710 Carnegie Class: Bac/Assoc-Assoc Dom
FAX Number: (206) 870-3779 Calendar System: Quarter
URL: www.highline.edu
Established: 1961 Annual Undergrad Tuition & Fees (In-State): $4,231
Enrollment: 5,829 Coed
Affiliation or Control: State IRS Status: 501(c)3
Highest Offering: Baccalaureate
Accreditation: NW, ADNUR, COARC, MAC, NAEYC

01 President — Dr. John MOSBY
05 Vice Pres for Academic Affairs — Dr. Emily LARDNER
11 Vice Pres Administrative Services — Mr. Michael PHAM
32 Vice Pres for Student Services — Mr. Aaron READER
111 Vice Pres for Inst Advancement — Mr. Josh GERSTMAN
13 Executive Director of ITS and CIO — Mr. Tim WRYE
15 Executive Dir of Human Resources — Ms. Summer KORST
100 Director Office of the President — Ms. Danielle SLOTA
103 Dean of Workforce — Dr. Paulette LOPEZ
88 Associate Dean for BAS & Workforce — Dr. Tanya POWERS
37 Dean for Student Support & Funding — Mr. Ay SAECHAO
22 Assoc Dean for Access/Inclusive Ed — Ms. Jennifer SANDLER
84 Dean for Advising & Enrollment Svcs — Ms. Jennifer SCANLON
35 Associate Dean for Student Life — Ms. Iesha VALENCIA
88 Associate Dean for Student Funding — Mr. Loyal ALLEN, JR
51 Dean for Extended Learning — Ms. Gabrielle BACHMEIER
20 Interim Dean for Instruction/Trans — Ms. Reagan COPELAND
88 Dean College & Career Readiness — Mr. Justin DAMPEER

Lake Washington Institute of Technology (C)

11605 132nd Avenue NE, Kirkland WA 98034-8506
County: King FICE Identification: 005373
Unit ID: 235699
Telephone: (425) 739-8100 Carnegie Class: Bac/Assoc-Assoc Dom
FAX Number: (425) 739-8299 Calendar System: Quarter
URL: www.lwtech.edu
Established: 1949 Annual Undergrad Tuition & Fees (In-State): $4,510
Enrollment: 3,319 Coed
Affiliation or Control: State IRS Status: 170(c)1
Highest Offering: Baccalaureate
Accreditation: NW, ACFEI, ADNUR, DH, FUSER, MAC, OTA, PTAA

01 President — Dr. Amy MORRISON
88 Spec Asst to President — Vacant
04 Sr Exec Asst to President and Board — Ms. Elsa GOSSETT
32 VP Student Services — Dr. Ruby HAYDEN
05 VP of Instruction — Dr. Suzanne AMES
10 VP Administrative Services — Mr. Bruce RIVELAND
53 Dean of Instruction — Ms. Vicki CHEW
76 Dean of Instruction — Dr. Aparna SEN
72 Dean of Instruction — Mr. Michael RICHMOND
72 Dean of Instruction — Mr. Mike POTTER
106 Dean of Instruction — Ms. Sally HEILSTEDT
88 Dean High School Programs — Mr. Tuan DANG
104 Dean of Instruction International — Dr. David RECTOR
30 Exec Director Development — Ms. Elisabeth SORENSEN
15 VP Human Resources — Ms. Meena PARK
09 Director Research & Grants — Ms. Cathy COPELAND
26 Exec Director Comm/Marketing — Ms. Leslie SHATTUCK
13 Chief Information Officer — Mr. Chris MCLAIN
28 Exec Director of EDI — Mr. Robert BRITTEN
88 Assoc Dean Funeral Service Educ — Ms. Lisa MEEHAN
66 Associate Dean Nursing Program — Ms. Lauren CLINE
88 Director TRiO Projects — Mr. Tien DO
08 Librarian — Mr. Greg BEM
76 Director PTA Program — Ms. Andrea WESTMAN
18 Director Facilities & Operations — Mr. Casey HUEBNER
37 Director Financial Aid — Ms. Kimberly GEER
84 Director Enrollment Services — Ms. Larisa AKSELRUD
103 Director Workforce Development — Ms. Demetra BIROS
21 Director of Financial Services — Mr. Xieng LIM
93 Director Student Programs — Ms. Sheila WALTON
96 Manager Purchasing Service — Mr. Isaac ROBINSON
105 Website/Digital Content Specialist — Ms. Alisa SHTROMBERG
40 Manager Bookstore — Mr. Russ MERKOW
19 Director Security/Safety — Mr. Anthony BOWERS
35 Director Student Development — Ms. Katie PEACOCK

Lower Columbia College (D)

1600 Maple Street PO Box 3010,
Longview WA 98632-0310
County: Cowlitz FICE Identification: 003782
Unit ID: 235750
Telephone: (360) 442-2311 Carnegie Class: Assoc/MT-VT-High Non
FAX Number: (360) 442-2109 Calendar System: Quarter
URL: www.lowercolumbia.edu
Established: 1934 Annual Undergrad Tuition & Fees (In-State): $4,068
Enrollment: 2,325 Coed
Affiliation or Control: State IRS Status: 170(c)1
Highest Offering: Baccalaureate
Accreditation: NW, ADNUR, MAC

01 President — Mr. Christopher C. BAILEY
05 Vice President of Instruction — Ms. Kristen FINNEL
11 Vice President Administrative Svcs — Mr. Nolan WHEELER
32 Vice President of Student Services — Ms. Sue ORCHARD
103 Dean Workforce/Continuing Educ — Ms. Tamra GILCHRIST
76 Executive Dean Allied Health/Nurse — Ms. Karen JOINER
09 VP of Effectiveness & Col Relations — Ms. Wendy HALL
18 Director of Campus Services — Mr. Richard HAMILTON
102 VP Foundation/HR/Legal Affairs — Ms. Kendra SPRAGUE
41 Athletic Director — Mr. Kirc J. ROLAND
21 Finance Director — Ms. Desiree GAMBLE
37 Financial Aid Director — Ms. Marisa GEIER
08 Int Associate Dean Resource Svcs — Ms. Lindsay KEEVY
13 Director of Information Technology — Mr. Brandon RAY
40 Director of Bookstore — Ms. Alyssa MILANO-HIGHTOWER
96 Purchasing Manager — Ms. Claudia SLABU
04 Executive Assistant — Ms. Bryanna E. SMITH
106 Dir Online Education/E-learning — Ms. Sarah GRIFFITH
19 Director Security/Safety — Mr. Jason ARROWSMITH
102 Foundation Specialist — Mr. Jamie NELSON

Northwest College of Art & Design (NCAD) (E)

1126 Pacific Avenue, Suite 101, Tacoma WA 98402
County: Pierce FICE Identification: 026021
Unit ID: 377546
Telephone: (253) 272-1126 Carnegie Class: Spec-4-yr-Arts
FAX Number: (253) 572-9058 Calendar System: Semester
URL: www.ncad.edu
Established: 1982 Annual Undergrad Tuition & Fees: $18,100
Enrollment: 101 Coed
Affiliation or Control: Proprietary IRS Status: Proprietary
Highest Offering: Baccalaureate
Accreditation: ACCSC

01 President — Craig FREEMAN
05 Director of Education — Susan OGILVIE
11 Director of Operations — Kim PERIGARD
06 Registrar — Ashley JONES
13 IT Admin — Skye CARLSON
07 Admissions Director — Dan ROTHROCK
37 Financial Aid — Julie PERIGARD
08 Head Librarian — Dan ROTHROCK

Northwest Indian College (F)

2522 Kwina Road, Bellingham WA 98226-9217
County: Whatcom FICE Identification: 021800
Unit ID: 380377
Telephone: (360) 676-2772 Carnegie Class: Tribal
FAX Number: (360) 738-0136 Calendar System: Quarter
URL: www.nwic.edu
Established: 1973 Annual Undergrad Tuition & Fees: $6,787
Enrollment: 555 Coed
Affiliation or Control: Other IRS Status: 501(c)3
Highest Offering: Baccalaureate
Accreditation: NW

01 President — Dr. Justin GUILLORY
10 Chief Financial Officer — Ms. Billie KINLEY
30 Vice Pres Campus Development — Mr. David OREIRO
25 Sponsored Programs Coordinator — Ms. Debbie MELE MAI
04 Exec Assistant to the President — Ms. Frances SELLARS
05 Dean of Academics — Ms. Destiny PETROSKE
32 Dean of Students — Ms. Victoria RETASKET
88 Pgm Coord 2-yr Programs of Study — Mr. Rudy VENDIOLA
37 Financial Aid & Admissions Director — Ms. Shayna NISHIYAMA
13 IS Director — Mr. Cameron REVARD
08 Library Director — Ms. Valerie MCBETH
06 Registrar — Ms. Patricia CUEVA
108 Dir of Institutional Effectiveness — Ms. Carmen BLAND
15 Director Human Resources — Ms. Darcilynn BOB
18 Director of Facilities Maintenance — Mr. Jon DAVIS
19 Security Manager — Ms. Lavonne BALLEW
102 Director of NWIC Foundation — Vacant
78 Director of Cooperative Extension — Vacant
88 Director Coast Salish Institute — Ms. Sharon KINLEY
41 Athletic Director — Mr. Michael SCHJANG
96 Purchasing Manager — Mr. Charlie ROBERTS
26 Chief Public Relations/Marketing — Ms. Barbara LEWIS
103 Director Workforce Development — Mr. Robert DECOTEAU
23 Director NWICCH — Dr. William FREEMAN
88 Director Tribal Voc Rehab Institute — Ms. Laura MAUDSLEY
88 Director Salish Sea Research Center — Ms. Melissa PEACOCK
39 Director Resident Life Center — Mr. Keith TOM
09 Director of Institutional Research — Mrs. Carmen BLAND

Northwest School of Wooden Boatbuilding (G)

42 N Water Street, Port Hadlock WA 98339-8706
County: Jefferson FICE Identification: 041550
Unit ID: 458140
Telephone: (360) 385-4948 Carnegie Class: Spec 2-yr-Tech
FAX Number: (360) 385-5089 Calendar System: Other
URL: www.nwswb.edu
Established: 1981 Annual Undergrad Tuition & Fees: $16,050
Enrollment: 27 Coed
Affiliation or Control: Independent Non-Profit IRS Status: 501(c)3
Highest Offering: Associate Degree
Accreditation: ACCSC

01 Executive Director — Ms. Betsy DAVIS
07 Admissions and Student Services — Ms. Heidi BLEHM

Northwest University (H)

PO Box 579, Kirkland WA 98083-0579
County: King FICE Identification: 003783
Unit ID: 236133
Telephone: (425) 822-8266 Carnegie Class: Masters/M
FAX Number: (425) 889-5224 Calendar System: Semester
URL: www.northwestu.edu
Established: 1934 Annual Undergrad Tuition & Fees: $33,980
Enrollment: 1,184 Coed
Affiliation or Control: Assemblies Of God Church IRS Status: 501(c)3
Highest Offering: Doctorate
Accreditation: NW, ACBSP, COPSY, NURSE

01 President — Dr. Joseph CASTLEBERRY
05 Provost — Dr. Jim HEUGEL
10 Chief Financial Officer — Mr. John JORDAN
111 Senior VP of Advancement — Mr. Ken CORNELL
108 VP of Institutional Effectiveness — Mrs. Vickie REKOW
06 Registrar — Mrs. Sandy HENDRICKSON
84 Sr Dir for Enrollment Management — Mr. Andy HALL
41 Athletic Director — Mr. Gary MCINTOSH
08 Library Director — Mr. Adam EPP
38 Director of Wellness Center — Ms. Denise JOHNSON
29 Director of Alumni Relations — Mr. Cole HASTIE
15 Director of Human Resources — Ms. Amanda BOWMAN
121 Director Academic Success/Advising — Mrs. Traci GRANT
32 Associate Provost — Dr. Rick ENGSTROM
26 Director of Marketing — Mr. John VICORY
04 Administrative Asst to President — Ms. Megan SCOTT
50 Dean College of Business — Dr. Rowlanda CAWTHON
53 Dean College of Education — Dr. Molly QUICK
28 Director of Multicultural Life — Mr. Blake SMALL
30 Executive Director of Development — Mr. Justin KAWABORI

Olympic College (I)

1600 Chester Avenue, Bremerton WA 98337-1699
County: Kitsap FICE Identification: 003784
Unit ID: 236188
Telephone: (360) 792-6050 Carnegie Class: Bac/Assoc-Assoc Dom
FAX Number: (360) 475-7151 Calendar System: Quarter

URL: www.olympic.edu
Established: 1946 Annual Undergrad Tuition & Fees (In-State): $3,971
Enrollment: 5,357 Coed
Affiliation or Control: State IRS Status: 501(c)3
Highest Offering: Baccalaureate
Accreditation: NW, ACFEI, ADNUR, MAC, NURSE, PTAA

01 President .... Dr. Martin CAVALLUZZI
05 Int Vice President for Instruction .... Dr. Martin COCKROFT
11 Vice Pres Administrative Services .... Mr. Ronald ELLISON
32 Vice President for Student Services .... Dr. Brendon TAGA
22 Vice President Equity & Inclusion .... Ms. Cheryl NUÑEZ
15 Vice President of Human Resources .... Dr. E. Lee FELDER
100 Chief of Staff .... Mr. Adam MORRIS
37 Director Student Financial Services .... Ms. Heidi TOWNSEND
26 Director of Communications .... Mr. Shawn DEVINE
84 Dean of Enrollment Services .... Dr. Jennifer GLASIER
18 Mgr Capital Projects .... Ms. Ariel BIRTLEY
10 CFO/Director of Business Services .... Ms. Karen WIKLE
13 CIO/Exec Dir Technical Services .... Ms. Evelyn HERNANDEZ
96 Procurement Officer .... Ms. Diana LAKE
36 Director Career Center .... Ms. Teresa MCDERMOTT
09 Exec Director Inst Effectiveness .... Dr. Allison PHAYRE
28 Supervisor Multicult/Student Pgms .... Ms. Jodie COLLINS
103 Dean Workforce Development .... Ms. Amy HATFIELD
08 Dean Library/Lrng Resources/eLrng .... Ms. Erica COE
50 Dean Business & Technology .... Dr. Norma WHITACRE
81 Dean Math/Engineer/Sci/Health .... Mr. John VAUGHAN
79 Dean Humanities/Social Science .... Dr. Rebecca SEAMAN
19 Director of Campus Safety .... Mr. Stephen DAVIS
25 Director of College Grant Devel .... Ms. Sarah BROWNGOETZ
29 Exec Dir of Foundation/Alumni Assn .... Mr. Trevor ROSS
41 Director of Athletics .... Mr. Barry JANUSCH

Pacific Lutheran University (A)

12180 Park Avenue S., Tacoma WA 98447-0003
County: Pierce FICE Identification: 003785
Unit ID: 236230
Telephone: (253) 531-6900 Carnegie Class: Masters/M
FAX Number: (253) 535-8320 Calendar System: 4/1/4
URL: www.plu.edu
Established: 1890 Annual Undergrad Tuition & Fees: $46,850
Enrollment: 2,907 Coed
Affiliation or Control: Evangelical Lutheran Church In America
IRS Status: 501(c)3
Highest Offering: Doctorate
Accreditation: NW, MFCD, MUS, NURSE, SW

01 President .... Mr. Allan BELTON
101 Director of Admin & Sec to Board .... Ms. Vicky L. WINTERS
04 Asst to the President .... Ms. Julie L. MIX
05 Provost .... Dr. Joanna GREGSON
20 Assoc Provost Undergrad Programs .... Dr. Jan P. LEWIS
51 Assoc Provost for Grad & Cont Educ .... Dr. Geoffrey E. FOY
88 Dean of Inclusive Excellence .... Dr. Jennifer A. SMITH
11 Chief Operating Officer .... Ms. Teri P. PHILLIPS
111 Vice Pres for Univ Relations .... Mr. Daniel J. LEE
32 Vice Pres for Student Life .... Dr. Joanna C. ROYCE-DAVIS
84 Dean for Enrollment Management .... Mr. Michael T. FRECHETTE
121 Exec Dir Ctr for Student Success .... Ms. Kris H. PLAEHN
07 Director of Admissions .... Ms. Melody A. FERGUSON
26 Assoc VP Marketing & Comm .... Ms. Lace M. SMITH
10 Assoc VP for Finance .... Mr. Patrick D. GEHRING
42 University Pastor .... Rev. Jen L. RUDE
57 Dean School of Arts & Communication .... Dr. Cameron D. BENNETT
50 Dean School of Business .... Dr. Mark R. MULDER
53 Dean School of Educ & Kinesiology .... Dr. Karen E. MCCONNELL
66 Dean School of Nursing .... Dr. Barbara HABERMANN
79 Dean Humanities .... Dr. Kevin J. O'BRIEN
81 Dean Natural Sciences .... Dr. Ann J. AUMAN
83 Dean Social Sciences .... Dr. Michelle L. CEYNAR
35 Dean of Students .... Dr. Eva R. FREY
88 Exec Dir Wang Ctr for Global Educ .... Dr. Tamara R. WILLIAMS
41 Director of Athletics & Recreation .... Mr. Michael P. SNYDER
06 Registrar .... Ms. Kelly G. POTH
39 Assoc VP for Campus Life .... Mr. Tom A. HUELSBECK
18 Assoc VP for Facilities Management .... Mr. Ray K. ORR
19 Director of Campus Safety & Info .... Ms. Tara SIMMELINK
36 Director Career Learning & Engage .... Mr. Kevin D. ANDREW
23 Director Health Services .... Ms. Elizabeth A. HOOPER
15 Director Human Resources .... Ms. Gretchen M. HOWELL
90 Dir of Enterprise Systems & Comm .... Mr. David P. ALLEN
13 Chief Information Officer .... Ms. Ardys E. CURTIS
40 Director of Retail Services .... Mr. Josh C. GIRNUS
09 Assoc Dean Institutional Research .... Mr. Kevin A. BERG
102 Exec Director Sponsored Programs .... Ms. Erica S. LUETH
44 Director Annual Giving .... Ms. Andrea N. MICHELBACH
22 Dir Affirmative Action/EEO .... Ms. Teri P. PHILLIPS
28 Asst VP Diversity/Justice/Sustain .... Ms. Angie Z. HAMBRICK
29 Director Alumni Relations .... Ms. Jessica L. PAGEL
38 Interim Director Counseling Center .... Dr. Joanna C. ROYCE-DAVIS
08 Director of the Library .... Ms. Fran R. LANE RASMUS

Pacific Northwest University of Health Sciences (B)

111 University Parkway, Suite 202, Yakima WA 98901
County: Yakima FICE Identification: 041305
Unit ID: 455406
Telephone: (509) 452-5100 Carnegie Class: Spec-4-yr-Med
FAX Number: (509) 452-5101 Calendar System: Semester
URL: www.pnwu.edu
Established: 2005 Annual Graduate Tuition & Fees: N/A
Enrollment: 573 Coed
Affiliation or Control: Independent Non-Profit IRS Status: 501(c)3
Highest Offering: Doctorate; No Undergraduates
Accreditation: NW, OSTEO

01 President .... Dr. Michael J. LAWLER
05 Provost .... Dr. Edward BILSKY
10 Chief Financial Officer .... Ms. Ann HITTLE
11 Chief Operations Officer .... Mr. Frank D. ALVAREZ
30 Chief Development Officer .... Ms. Michele ERICKSON
63 Dean Col of Osteopathic Medicine .... Dr. Thomas SCANDALIS
08 Head Librarian .... Ms. Anita CLEARY
13 Chief Info Technology Officer (CIO) .... Mr. Jameson WATKINS
15 Chief Human Resources Officer .... Ms. Erin MURPHY
18 Chief Facilities/Physical Plant .... Mr. Brent PERRIN
26 Chief Communications Officer .... Mr. Dean O'DRISCOLL
29 Director Alumni Relations .... Ms. Chanda ANDERSON
37 Director Student Financial Aid .... Ms. Laura PENDLETON
45 Chief Institutional Planning .... Ms. Angie GIRARD
04 Administrative Asst to President .... Ms. Vikki GORE
84 Asst Prov Enrollment Mgmt/Registrar .... Ms. LeAnn HUNTER
108 Dir Institutional Effectiveness .... Ms. Lori FULTON
32 Dean Student Affairs .... Dr. Stephen LAIRD
96 Asst Dir Procurement/Asset Mgmt .... Ms. Barbara ANDERSON
25 Chief Contract/Grants Administrator .... Ms. Anita QUINTANA
28 Director of Diversity .... Dr. Mirna RAMOS-DIAZ

Peninsula College (C)

1502 East Lauridsen Boulevard, Port Angeles WA 98362-6698
County: Clallam FICE Identification: 003786
Unit ID: 236258
Telephone: (360) 452-9277 Carnegie Class: Bac/Assoc-Assoc Dom
FAX Number: (360) 457-8100 Calendar System: Quarter
URL: www.pencol.edu
Established: 1961 Annual Undergrad Tuition & Fees (In-District): $4,218
Enrollment: 1,727 Coed
Affiliation or Control: State/Local IRS Status: 501(c)3
Highest Offering: Baccalaureate
Accreditation: NW, MAC

01 President .... Dr. Luke ROBINS
05 Vice President Instruction .... Dr. Steven THOMAS
10 Vice Pres Finance/Administration .... Ms. Carie EDMISTON
32 Vice President Student Services .... Mr. Jack HULS
35 Assoc Dean of Student Success .... Ms. Cathy ENGLE
41 Assoc Dean Athletics/Student Prgms .... Mr. Rick ROSS
13 Director Information Technology .... Ms. Emma JANSSEN
04 Executive Asst to the President .... Ms. Kelly GRIFFITH
26 Public Information Officer .... Ms. Kari DESSER
15 Director of Human Resources .... Ms. Krista FRANCIS
85 Dir Intl Stdnt Pgm/Stdnt Recruit .. Ms. Sophia ILIAKIS-DOHERTY
102 Director College Foundation .... Mr. Paul PITKIN
09 Director of Institutional Research .... Ms. Terye SENDERHAUF
18 Director Physical Plant .... Vacant
40 Bookstore Manager .... Mrs. Camilla RICO

Perry Technical Institute (D)

2011 W. Washington Avenue, Yakima WA 98903
County: Yakima FICE Identification: 009387
Unit ID: 236212
Telephone: (509) 453-0374 Carnegie Class: Spec 2-yr-Other
FAX Number: (509) 453-0375 Calendar System: Quarter
URL: www.perrytech.edu
Established: 1939 Annual Undergrad Tuition & Fees: N/A
Enrollment: 881 Coed
Affiliation or Control: Independent Non-Profit IRS Status: 501(c)3
Highest Offering: Associate Degree
Accreditation: ACCSC

01 President .... Christine COTE
88 Executive Assistant for Foundation .... Maddie SELLS
05 Dean of Education .... Nathan HULL
06 Registrar .... Jill COPE
07 Director of Admissions & Marketing .... Nicole TRAMMELL
10 VP of Finance & Administration .... Cathy STERBENZ
102 Foundation Director .... Tressa SHOCKLEY
13 Director of Information Technology .... Josh PHILLIPS
15 Director of Human Resources .... Carol HELMS
19 Director of Facilities & Safety .... Kaila LOCKBEAM
84 Asst Director of Admissions & CS .... Raul LUNA
37 Director of Financial Aid .... Mayra FERNANDEZ
20 Associate Dean of Education .... Jason LAMIQUIZ
20 Associate Dean of Education .... Garet GASSELING
96 Director of Purchasing & Auxil Svcs .... Maria PULIDO

Pierce College District (E)

1601 39th Avenue SE, Puyallup WA 98374
County: Pierce FICE Identification: 005000
Unit ID: 439145
Telephone: (253) 964-6500 Carnegie Class: Assoc/HT-Mix Trad/Non
FAX Number: N/A Calendar System: Quarter
URL: www.pierce.ctc.edu
Established: 1967 Annual Undergrad Tuition & Fees (In-State): N/A
Enrollment: N/A Coed
Affiliation or Control: State IRS Status: 501(c)3
Highest Offering: Baccalaureate
Accreditation: NW, ADNUR, DH

01 District Chancellor .... Dr. Michele JOHNSON
12 President Pierce College Puyallup .... Dr. Darrell L. CAIN
12 President Fort Steilacoom .... Dr. Julie WHITE
05 VP Learning/Student Success-PY .... Dr. Matthew CAMPBELL
05 VP Learning/Student Success-FS .... Dr. Ilder LOPEZ
111 VP Strategic Advancement .... Mr. Mike WARK
15 VP for Human Resources .... Ms. Holly GORSKI
103 VP Workforce/Economic/Prof Devel .... Ms. Jo Ann BARIA
13 Chief Information Officer .... Mr. Mike STOCKE
84 Dean Enroll Svcs/Fin Aid/Registrar .... Ms. Anne WHITE
08 Dean Libraries & Learning Resources .... Ms. Christie FLYNN
32 Dean of Student Success .... Ms. Agnes STEWARD
26 Dir Marketing and Communications .... Mr. Brian BENEDETTI
35 Dir Student Programs-Ft Steilacoom .... Mr. Cameron COX
41 Director District Athletics .... Mr. Duncan STEVENSON
35 Dir of Student Life-Puyallup .... Vacant
85 Exec Dir of International Education .... Ms. Myung PARK
19 Campus Safety Sergeant-Supervisor .... Mr. Robert ROCKEY
21 Director Fiscal Services .... Ms. Sylvia JAMES
37 District Director Financial Aid .... Ms. Trinity HUTTNER
84 Director Enrollment Services-Puy .... Ms. Els DEMING
96 Procurement Officer .... Vacant
30 Exec Director of Foundation .... Ms. Robin ECHTLE
09 Director Institutional Research .... Mr. Erik GIMNESS
49 Dean Arts & Humanities .... Dr. Holly SMITH
88 Dean Transitional Education .... Ms. Lori GRIFFIN
76 Dean Health & Technology .... Mr. Ronald MAY
81 Dean Natural Sciences .... Mr. Eddie PERRY
83 Dean Business/Social Sciences .... Dr. Allison SIEVING
04 Exec Assistant to the President .... Ms. Christine BOITER
101 Sr Exec Assistant to Board .... Ms. Marie HARRIS
28 VP for Equity/Innovation/Engagement .... Mr. Charlie PARKER
105 Director Web Services .... Ms. Gayle RAMBEAU
18 Chief Facilities/Campus Safety Dir .... Mr. Jeff SCHNEIDER

Pima Medical Institute-Renton (F)

555 South Renton Village Place, Renton WA 98057
Telephone: (425) 228-9600 Identification: 770517
Accreditation: ABHES, COARC, OTA

† Branch campus of Pima Medical Institute-Tucson, Tucson, AZ

Pima Medical Institute-Seattle (G)

9709 3rd Avenue NE, Suite 400, Seattle WA 98115-2052
Telephone: (206) 322-6100 Identification: 666172
Accreditation: ABHES, DH, PTAA, RAD

† Branch campus of Pima Medical Institute-Tucson, Tucson, AZ

Renton Technical College (H)

3000 NE Fourth Street, Renton WA 98056-4123
County: King FICE Identification: 010434
Unit ID: 236382
Telephone: (425) 235-2352 Carnegie Class: Bac/Assoc-Assoc Dom
FAX Number: (425) 235-7832 Calendar System: Quarter
URL: www.rtc.edu
Established: 1942 Annual Undergrad Tuition & Fees (In-State): $5,671
Enrollment: 3,214 Coed
Affiliation or Control: State IRS Status: 501(c)3
Highest Offering: Baccalaureate
Accreditation: NW, ACFEI, DA, MAC, SURGT

01 President .... Dr. Kevin D. MCCARTHY
10 VP Finance/Administration .... Mr. Jacob JACKSON
05 Vice President Instruction .... Ms. Stephanie DELANEY
32 VP Student Services .... Ms. Jessica GILMORE ENGLISH
15 Vice President Human Resources .... Ms. Lesley HOGAN
97 Dean Basic Studies .... Ms. Sofia MARSHAK
76 Dean Allied Health .... Mr. Christopher CARTER
66 Dean Nursing .... Ms. Yasmin ALI
103 Executive Dean Workforce/Econ Dev .... Vacant
50 Dean Bus/Educ/Hum Svcs/Gen Educ .... Ms. Sarah WAKEFIELD
102 Foundation Executive Director .... Ms. Carrie SHAW
13 Exec Director College Technology .... Mr. Jason MAYER
84 Dir Enrollment Services/Registrar .... Ms. Morenika JACOBS
111 Exec Dir Institutional Advancement .... Vacant
08 Assoc Dean of Library .... Ms. Jessica KOSHI-LUM
21 Budget/Accounting/Fin Svcs Dir .... Mr. Hui TONG
37 Director Financial Aid .... Ms. Rahel WELDU
18 Facilities & Grounds Svcs Director .... Mr. Mark DANIELS
19 Safety & Security Manager .... Mr. Matthew VIELBIG
88 Dean Culinary Arts .... Mr. Doug MEDBURY
26 Exec Dir College Relations/Mktg .... Ms. Katherine HANSEN
35 Director Student Programs .... Vacant
06 Registration Coordinator .... Ms. Ly CHANG
121 Dean Student Success .... Mr. Anthony COVINGTON
04 Executive Asst to President .... Ms. Di BEERS
88 Capital Projects/Space Planning Dir .... Mr. Barry BAKER
09 Director of Institutional Research .... Mr. Jichul KIM
96 Purchasing Agent .... Mr. Kawika WAIAMAU-ARIOTA

Saint Martin's University (I)

5000 Abbey Way, SE, Lacey WA 98503-7500
County: Thurston FICE Identification: 003794
Unit ID: 236452
Telephone: (360) 491-4700 Carnegie Class: Masters/M
FAX Number: (360) 459-4124 Calendar System: Semester
URL: www.stmartin.edu
Established: 1895 Annual Undergrad Tuition & Fees: $39,940
Enrollment: 1,638 Coed
Affiliation or Control: Roman Catholic IRS Status: 501(c)3

Highest Offering: Master's
Accreditation: NW, ACBSP, NURSE, SW

00 Chancellor .... Abbot Marion NGUYEN
01 President .... Dr. Roy F. HEYNDERICKX
05 Provost/Vice Pres Academic Affairs .... Dr. Kate BOYLE
10 Vice President of Finance/CFO .... Ms. Sara SAAVEDRA
111 Vice Pres Inst Advancement .... Ms. Cecelia LOVELESS
26 VP of Marketing/Communications .... Ms. Genevieve CHAN
13 Associate Vice President/CIO .... Mr. Greg DAVIS
15 Associate VP of Human Resources .... Ms. Cynthia JOHNSON
49 Dean College of Arts & Sciences .... Dr. Jeff CRANE
53 Dean of Education .... Dr. Celeste TRIMBLE
50 Dean of Business .... Vacant
54 Dean of Engineering .... Dr. David OLWELL
32 Dean of Students .... Ms. Melanie RICHARDSON
84 Dean Enrollment Management .. Ms. Pamela HOLSINGER-FUCHS
104 Associate Dean Intl Programs .... Dr. Roger DOUGLAS
21 Controller .... Ms. Burcu BRYAN
37 Director Financial Aid .... Ms. Julie ANDERSON
29 Alumni Engagement Manager .... Ms. Kim NELSON
06 Assistant Registrar .... Ms. Ronda VANDERGIFF
18 Director Facilities Management .... Mr. Philip CHEEK
110 Asst Vice Pres Inst Advancement .... Ms. Katie WOJKE
36 Assoc Dean Students/Dir Career Dev .... Ms. Ann ADAMS
41 Athletic Director .... Mr. Bob GRISHAM
11 Assoc Dean Administration .... Mr. Cruz ARROYO
08 Dean of Library & Learning Resource .... Ms. Amy STEWART-MAILHIOT
42 Director Campus Ministry .... Ms. Colleen DUNNE
39 Assoc Dean of Students/Dir Housing .... Mr. Justin STERN
38 Dir Office of Counseling & Wellness .... Ms. Michelle GORDON
09 Director Institutional Grants/Rsrch .... Ms. Erin HOILAND
04 Sr Exec Assistant to the President .... Ms. Brenda LUND
108 Dir of Assessment & Accreditation .... Ms. Sheila STEINER
19 Int Director Public Safety .... Mr. Howard THRONSON

*Seattle Colleges (A)

1500 Harvard Avenue, Seattle WA 98122-3803
County: King FICE Identification: 010106
Telephone: (206) 934-4100 Carnegie Class: N/A
FAX Number: (206) 934-3883
URL: www.seattlecolleges.edu

01 Chancellor .... Dr. Shouan PAN
05 VC Academic & Student Success .... Dr. Kurt BUTTLEMAN
13 Chief Information Officer .... Dr. Cindy RICHE
10 VC of Finance & Operations .... Dr. Choi HALLADAY
26 Assoc VC Comms & Strat Initiatives .... Dr. Earnest PHILLIPS
111 VC of Advancement .... Ms. Kerry HOWELL
12 President South Seattle College .... Dr. Rosie RIMANDO-CHAREUNSAP
12 Int President North Seattle College .... Dr. Chemene CRAWFORD
12 President Seattle Central College .... Dr. Sheila EDWARDS LANGE
103 Assoc VC of Workforce Education .... Dr. Malcolm GROTHE
15 Int VC of Human Resources .... Ms. Jennifer DIXON

*North Seattle College (B)

9600 College Way North, Seattle WA 98103-3599
County: King FICE Identification: 009704
Unit ID: 236072
Telephone: (206) 934-3600 Carnegie Class: Bac/Assoc-Assoc Dom
FAX Number: (206) 934-3606 Calendar System: Quarter
URL: www.northseattle.edu
Established: 1970 Annual Undergrad Tuition & Fees (In-State): $4,123
Enrollment: 5,240 Coed
Affiliation or Control: State IRS Status: 170(c)1
Highest Offering: Baccalaureate
Accreditation: NW

02 President .... Dr. Chemene CRAWFORD
05 Vice President for Instruction .... Mr. Peter LORTZ
32 Interim VP for Student Services .... Ms. Toni CASTRO
11 Interim VP Administrative Services .... Mr. Gregory HINTON
36 Exec Dean Career/Workforce Educ .... Dr. John LEDERER
79 Dean Art/Humanities/Social Sciences .... Mr. Brian PALMER
81 Dean Math & Science .... Dr. Vashti BRYANT
103 Dean Workforce Instruction .... Mr. Aaron KORNGIEBEL
08 Dean Library & Media Services .... Dr. Aryana BATES
121 Dean Student Success Svcs .... Ms. Alice MELLING
88 Dean Basic/Transitional Stds .... Mr. Curtis BONNEY
111 Executive Director of Advancement .... Ms. Traci RUSSELL
26 Int Dir Marketing/Communications .... Ms. Sonja RENNER
84 Dean Enrollment Svcs/Registrar .... Ms. Kathy RHODES
51 Director Continuing Education .... Ms. Christy ISAACSON
37 Director Financial Aid Services .... Ms. Brianne SANCHEZ
35 Dean of Student Life .... Dr. Mari ACOB-NASH
103 Director Workforce Retraining .... Ms. Jeanette MILLER
09 Exec Dir Inst Effectiveness .... Dr. Stephanie DYKES
15 Human Resources Director .... Mr. Joshua R. ERNST
18 Dir Facilities & Plant Operations .... Vacant
38 Counselor .... Dr. Lydia MINATOYA
13 Chief Info Technology Officer .... Dr. Cindy RICHE
19 Campus Safety and Security Director .... Mr. Patrick "Fitz" FITZPATRICK
28 Assoc VP Equity/Diversity/Inclusion .... Mr. D'Andre FISHER
07 Admissions/Residency Specialist .... Mr. Fleetwood L. WILSON
04 Executive Asst to President .... Ms. Toni STANKOVIC
114 Interim Dir Budget & Business Ops .... Mr. Soroush MALEKI
25 Director of Grants .... Ms. Ann RICHARDSON
23 Interim Director Wellness Center .... Ms. Lorraine ODOM

*Seattle Central College (C)

1701 Broadway, Seattle WA 98122-2400
County: King FICE Identification: 003787
Unit ID: 236513
Telephone: (206) 934-3800 Carnegie Class: Bac/Assoc-Assoc Dom
FAX Number: (206) 934-4390 Calendar System: Quarter
URL: seattlecentral.edu
Established: 1966 Annual Undergrad Tuition & Fees (In-State): $4,053
Enrollment: 5,763 Coed
Affiliation or Control: State IRS Status: 170(c)1
Highest Offering: Baccalaureate
Accreditation: NW, ACFEI, ADNUR, COARC, DH, MAC, SURGT

02 Acting President .... Dr. Yoshiko HARDEN
05 Int EVP of Instruction/Fin & Plng .... Dr. Wendy ROCKHILL
11 Interim VP Administrative Services .... Mr. Lincoln FERRIS
32 Int Vice President Student Services .... Ms. Kao LEZHEO
103 Executive Dean Workforce Educ .... Mr. Chris SULLIVAN
37 Director of Financial Aid .... Mr. Kyle DARLING
102 Exec Dir Ofc of Strat Partnership .... Ms. Jessica NOROUZI
26 Director of Communications .... Mr. Roberto BONACCORSO
08 Dean of Library Svcs/E-learn .... Ms. Lynn KANNE
09 Interim Dir Institutional Research .... Dr. Jenni BRANSTAD
49 Dean Basic & Transitional Studies .... Dr. Saovra EAR
76 Executive Dean of Allied Health .... Dr. Barry ROBINSON
81 Dean of STEM .... Dr. Wendy ROCKHILL
83 Dean Arts/Humanities/Soc Sciences .... Dr. Jaime CARDENAS, JR.
07 Dir of International Admissions .... Mr. David ROSEBERRY
35 Dean Student Development .... Mr. Ricardo LEYVA-PUEBLA
13 IT Client Services Manager .... Ms. Maria ALES
12 Associate Dean Maritime Academy .... Mr. Dale BATEMAN
12 Assoc Dean Seattle Culinary Academy .... Ms. Katherine KEHRLI
19 Director of Safety and Security .... Mr. Darryl JOHNSON
18 Int Dir Facilities/Plant Operations .... Ms. Sam LUNSFORD
04 Executive Assistant to President .... Ms. Erin LEWIS
10 Director of Business Operations .... Ms. Becca CHEN
15 Director Human Resources .... Mr. Scott RIXON
28 AVP Diversity/Equity & Inclusion .... Dr. Valerie HUNT
20 Director of Instruction Operation .... Ms. Marilyn MCCAMEY
66 Dean of Nursing .... Ms. Vicky HERTIG
106 Director of E-learning .... Mr. Kevin BOWERSOX-JOHNSON
31 Assoc Dir of Community Rels/Events .... Ms. Emily THURSTON
107 Assoc Dean of Wood Technology Centr .... Mr. Robert WATT
41 Athletic Director .... Mr. Jared BLITZ
06 Dean Enrollment Services/Registrar .... Ms. Diane COLEMAN

*South Seattle College (D)

6000 16th Avenue, SW, Seattle WA 98106-1499
County: King FICE Identification: 009706
Unit ID: 236504
Telephone: (206) 934-5300 Carnegie Class: Bac/Assoc-Assoc Dom
FAX Number: (206) 934-5393 Calendar System: Quarter
URL: www.southseattle.edu
Established: 1969 Annual Undergrad Tuition & Fees (In-State): $4,214
Enrollment: 5,324 Coed
Affiliation or Control: State IRS Status: 501(c)3
Highest Offering: Baccalaureate
Accreditation: NW

02 President .... Dr. Rosie RIMANDO-CHAREUNSAP
05 Vice Pres Instruction .... Dr. Sayumi IREY
10 Vice Pres Finance/Admin Services .... Ms. Julienne DEGEYTER
32 Vice President Student Services .... Mr. Joe BARRIENTOS
45 Dean Instructional Resources .... Ms. Mary Jo WHITE
12 Exec Dean of Georgetown Campus .... Ms. Maureen SHADAIR
97 Dean Basic & Transitional Studies .... Mr. John BOWERS
20 Interim Dean of Academic Programs .... Mr. Johnny HU
35 Dean Student Life .... Mr. Daniel JOHNSON
103 Exec Dean Prof/Tech/Workforce Educ .... Ms. Veronica WADE
72 Dean Multi-Trades/Info Tech/Bus .... Vacant
84 Dean Enrollment Services .... Ms. Joyce ALLEN
20 Assoc Dean Academic Programs .... Vacant
06 Assistant Registrar .... Ms. Linda MARTIN
104 Exec Dir Ctr for Intl Education .... Ms. Kathie KWILINSKI
51 Director Continuing Education .... Ms. Luisa MOTTEN
30 Director Foundation .... Vacant
103 Dir Workforce Dev/Employment Svcs .... Ms. Stephanie GUY
37 Dir Student Financial Assistance .... Ms. Corinne SOLTIS
26 Director Communications/Marketing .... Mr. Ty SWENSON
15 Director Human Resources .... Mr. Tim COLLINS
108 Exec Director Inst Effectiveness .... Mr. Greg DEMPSEY
13 Director Business Operation .... Vacant
18 Dir Facilities & Plant Operations .... Vacant
28 AVP Equity/Diversity/Inclusion .... Dr. Betsy HASEGAWA
19 Director Safety/Security .... Mr. James E. LEWIS
40 Manager Bookstore .... Vacant
04 Exec Asst to the President .... Ms. Wendy NAGASAWA

Seattle Film Institute (E)

3210 16th Avenue W., Seattle WA 98119
County: King FICE Identification: 042580
Unit ID: 488448
Telephone: (206) 568-4387 Carnegie Class: Spec-4-yr-Arts
FAX Number: (206) 299-3285 Calendar System: Quarter
URL: www.sfi.edu
Established: 1994 Annual Undergrad Tuition & Fees: $30,240
Enrollment: 96 Coed
Affiliation or Control: Proprietary IRS Status: Proprietary
Highest Offering: Master's
Accreditation: ACCSC

01 President .... David J. SHULMAN

Seattle Institute of East Asian Medicine (F)

226 South Orcas Street, Seattle WA 98108
County: King FICE Identification: 032803
Unit ID: 439914
Telephone: (206) 517-4541 Carnegie Class: Spec-4-yr-Other Health
FAX Number: (206) 299-3538 Calendar System: Trimester
URL: www.sieam.edu
Established: 1994 Annual Graduate Tuition & Fees: N/A
Enrollment: 31 Coed
Affiliation or Control: Independent Non-Profit IRS Status: 501(c)3
Highest Offering: Doctorate; No Undergraduates
Accreditation: ACUP

01 President .... Craig MITCHELL
05 Academic Dean .... Katherine TAROMINA
07 Dir Admissions/Student Services .... Iris CUTLER
08 Chief Library Officer .... Chris FLANAGAN
10 Chief Financial/Business Officer .... Peter MELINCIANU

Seattle Pacific University (G)

3307 Third Avenue W, Seattle WA 98119-1997
County: King FICE Identification: 003788
Unit ID: 236577
Telephone: (206) 281-2111 Carnegie Class: DU-Mod
FAX Number: (206) 281-2115 Calendar System: Quarter
URL: www.spu.edu
Established: 1891 Annual Undergrad Tuition & Fees: $47,244
Enrollment: 3,601 Coed
Affiliation or Control: Free Methodist IRS Status: 501(c)3
Highest Offering: Doctorate
Accreditation: NW, CACREP, CLPSY, DIETD, DIETI, MFCD, MUS, NURSE, THEOL

01 President .... Dr. Daniel J. MARTIN
05 Provost .... Dr. Laura C. HARTLEY
10 Sr VP for Finance & Administration .... Mr. Craig G. KISPERT
32 Vice Provost Student Formation .... Dr. Jeffrey C. JORDAN
111 VP for Advancement .... Mrs. Louise S. FURROW
84 VP for Enrollment Mgmt & Mktg .... Mr. Nate MOUTTET
28 Vice Provost Inclusive Excellence .... Dr. Sandra MAYO
42 University Chaplain .... Rev. Lisa ISHIHARA
20 Vice Provost Academic Affairs .... Dr. Cynthia J. PRICE
58 Assoc Provost Grad & Prof Programs .... Dr. Margaret BROWN
49 Assoc Provost Arts & Sciences .... Vacant
18 Asst VP Facility Management .... Mr. David B. CHURCH
43 Asst VP Risk Mgmt & Univ Counsel .... Mr. Nick GLANCY
21 Asst VP for Financial Affairs .... Ms. Cherry GILBERT
13 Asst VP Information Technology .... Mr. Micah SCHAAFSMA
37 Asst VP UG Enrollment Oper & SFS .... Mr. Jordan L. GRANT
50 Dean School of Business/Govt/Econ .... Dr. Ross STEWART
53 Dean School of Education .... Dr. Nyaradzo MVUDUDU
76 Int Dean School of Health Sciences .... Dr. Antwinett LEE
81 Int Co-Dean CAS Sciences Div .... Dr. Derek WOOD
81 Int Co-Dean CAS Sciences Div .... Dr. Sandra HARTJE
79 Interim Dean CAS Arts & Humanities .... Dr. Rebekah RICE
59 Dean School of Psych/Fam & Cmty .... Dr. Katy TANGENBERG
73 Dean School of Theology .... Dr. Douglas M. STRONG
35 Dean of Students for Cmty Life .... Mr. Chuck STRAWN
35 Assoc VP Student Life .... Dr. Jacqui S. SMITH-BATES
08 University Librarian .... Mr. Michael PAULUS
38 Director Student Counseling Center . Ms. Sharon BARR-JEFFREY
07 Sr Dir Recruitment and Admissions .... Mr. Jobe S. KORB-NICE
07 Director Undergraduate Admissions .... Ms. Ineliz SOTO FULLER
09 Interim Dir Institutional Research .... Ms. Tammy LEE
06 University Registrar .... Mrs. Kenda GATLIN
26 Sr Dir Univ Comm & Marketing .... Mrs. Alison ESTEP
27 News & Media Relations Manager .... Mrs. Tracy C. NORLEN
109 Director of University Services .... Ms. Alexis CRUIKSHANK
19 Director of Safety & Security .... Mr. Mark REID
110 Director of Advancement .... Ms. Maribeth MARTIN LOPIT
29 Director of Alumni/Parent Relations .... Ms. Amanda STUBBERT
41 Athletic Director .... Mr. Jackson STAVA
15 Director of Human Resources .... Mr. Gary E. WOMELSDUFF
39 Director of Residence Life .... Mr. Gabe JACOBSEN
88 Director Student Programs .... Ms. Whitney BROETJE
88 Director of Multi-Ethnic Programs .... Ms. Serena MANZO
104 Director of Global Engagement .... Ms. Caroline MAURER
04 Executive Asst to President .... Mrs. Ruth JACOBSEN

The Seattle School of Theology and Psychology (H)

2501 Elliot Avenue, Seattle WA 98121-1177
County: King FICE Identification: 034664
Unit ID: 441131
Telephone: (206) 876-6100 Carnegie Class: Spec-4-yr-Other Health
FAX Number: (206) 876-6195 Calendar System: Trimester
URL: www.theseattleschool.edu
Established: 2001 Annual Graduate Tuition & Fees: N/A
Enrollment: 266 Coed
Affiliation or Control: Independent Non-Profit IRS Status: 501(c)3
Highest Offering: Master's; No Undergraduates
Accreditation: NW, THEOL

01 Acting President & Provost .... Dr. J. Derek MCNEIL
05 Assoc Dean for Teaching/Learning .. Dr. Misty Anne WINZENREID
10 Chief Financial Officer .... Mr. Mike ANDERSON
32 VP Students & Alumni/Dn of Students .... Mr. Paul STEINKE

111 VP of Advancement .... Dr. Jim EHRMAN
08 Dir Library Svcs/Inst Assessment .... Ms. Cheryl GOODWIN
06 Dir Academic Services/Registrar .... Ms. Kristen HOUSTON
110 Director of Advancement .... Mr. Andrew GREENE
13 Director Computer & Info Services .... Ms. Grace LA TORRA
15 Director of Human Resources .... Ms. Kartha HEINZ

Seattle University (A)

901 12th Avenue, Seattle WA 98122-1090

County: King FICE Identification: 003790

Unit ID: 236595

Telephone: (206) 296-6000 Carnegie Class: DU-Mod

FAX Number: N/A Calendar System: Quarter

URL: www.seattleu.edu

Established: 1891 Annual Undergrad Tuition & Fees: $48,390

Enrollment: 7,050 Coed

Affiliation or Control: Roman Catholic IRS Status: 501(c)3

Highest Offering: Doctorate

Accreditation: NW, CACREP, DMS, LAW, MFCD, MIDWF, NURSE, SPAA, SW, THEOL

01 President .... Mr. Eduardo M. PENALVER
05 Provost .... Dr. Shane MARTIN
20 Vice Provost/VP Planning .... Dr. Robert DULLEA
11 Executive Vice President Admin .... Dr. Timothy LEARY
10 VP/Chief Financial Officer .... Mr. Wilson GARONE
43 Vice Pres and University Counsel .... Ms. Mary S. PETERSEN
111 VP University Advancement .... Mr. Michael PODLIN
32 VP Student Development .... Mr. Alvin STURDIVANT
88 Vice President Mission & Ministry .... Rev. Peter ELY, SJ
108 Assoc VP for Inst Effectiveness .... Dr. Robert DUNIWAY
84 Int Vice President for Enrollment .... Ms. Melore NIELSEN
26 Vice President for Communications .... Mr. Scott MCCLELLAN
28 Chief Diversity Officer .... Ms. Natasha MARTIN
15 VP Human Resources .... Ms. Michelle CLEMENTS
31 Executive Director Cmty Engagement .... Mr. Kent KOTH
49 Dean of Arts & Sciences .... Dr. David POWERS
50 Dean of Business & Economics .... Dr. Joseph M. PHILLIPS
53 Dean of Education .... Dr. Deanna SANDS
66 Dean of Nursing .... Dr. Kristen SWANSON
54 Dean of Science & Engineering .... Dr. Michael QUINN
61 Dean of Law .... Ms. Annette C. CLARK
73 Dean of Theology & Ministry .... Dr. Mark MARKULY
51 Dean Schl New & Continuing Studies . Dr. Rick FEHRENBACHER
08 University Librarian .... Ms. Sara WATSTEIN
20 Assoc Provost Academic Achievement ..... Dr. Charles LAWRENCE
87 Director Summer Programs .... Dr. Eva LASPROGATA
20 Assoc Provost Global Engagement .... Dr. Russell POWELL
123 Graduate Admissions .... Ms. Janet SHANDLEY
13 Chief Information Officer .... Mr. Chris VAN LIEW
21 Assoc VP of Finance .... Mr. Andrew O'BOYLE
18 Assoc VP Facilities Administration .... Mr. Robert SCHWARTZ
29 Asst VP Alumni Relations .... Ms. Susan VOSPER
14 Executive Director .... Mr. Dennis GENDRON
112 Sr Director of Planned Giving .... Ms. Sarah FINNEY
44 Director of Annual Giving .... Ms. Cathy REILLY
102 Dir of Foundation & Corporate Rels .... Ms. Jane SPALDING
06 University Registrar .... Ms. Joyce ALLEN
07 Dean of Admissions .... Ms. Melore NIELSEN
09 Director of Institutional Research .... Dr. Irina VOLOSHIN
42 Director Campus Ministry .... Ms. Tammy LIDDELL
37 Director Student Financial Services .... Mr. Jeff SCOFIELD
41 Director of Athletics .... Mr. Bill HOGAN
19 Executive Director of Public Safety .... Mr. Timothy MARRON
35 AVP/Dean of Students .... Dr. James WILLETTE
85 Director International Student Ctr .... Mr. Ryan GREENE
104 Director Education Abroad .... Ms. Gina LOPARDO
36 Executive Director Career Services .... Ms. Hilary FLANAGAN
38 Director Counseling Center .... Dr. Kimberly CALUZA
93 Director of Multicultural Affairs .... Ms. Tiffany GRAY
39 Dir Housing & Resid Life .... Ms. Kathleen BAKER
25 Director Research & Sponsored Proj .... Dr. Nalini IYER
96 Director of Purchasing .... Ms. Marie PETERSON
23 Director Student Health Center .... Ms. Maura O'CONNOR
04 Executive Secretary to President .... Ms. Liz PILATI
100 Assistant to the President .... Ms. Kathy YBARRA
105 Web Communications Manager .... Mr. Jason BEARD
22 Dir Professional Dev/EEO .... Ms. Helaina SOREY
86 Director of External Affairs .... Mr. Solynn MCCURDY
27 Associate Chief Information Officer .... Mr. Travis NATION

Shoreline Community College (B)

16101 Greenwood Avenue N, Shoreline WA 98133-5696

County: King FICE Identification: 003791

Unit ID: 236610

Telephone: (206) 546-4101 Carnegie Class: Assoc/MT-VT-High Non

FAX Number: (206) 546-4630 Calendar System: Quarter

URL: www.shoreline.edu

Established: 1964 Annual Undergrad Tuition & Fees (In-State): $4,076

Enrollment: 5,382 Coed

Affiliation or Control: State IRS Status: 170(c)1

Highest Offering: Associate Degree

Accreditation: NW, ADNUR, CAHIIM, DH, MLTAD

01 Acting President .... Phillip KING
05 Acting VP Student Learning .... Guy HAMILTON
111 Acting Assoc VP Advancement .... Diana DOTTER
20 Assoc VP Acad Ops & Lrng Resources . Ann GARNSEY-HARTER
32 Assoc VP Stdnt Svcs & Intl Educ .... Samira PARDANANI
26 Exec Dir Communication/Marketing .... Martha LYNN
15 Exec Dir Human Resources .... Veronica ZURA
114 Director Budget .... Cliff FREDERICKSON
04 Exec Asst to the President .... Lori YONEMITSU
18 Director Facilities .... Pete BABINGTON
19 Acting Dir Safety & Security .... Gregory CRANSON
66 Dean Health Occupations & Nursing .... Mary BURROUGHS
84 Dir Enrollment Svcs & Fin Aid .... Frank FRIAS
09 Exec Dir Inst Assessment/Data Mgmt .... Bayta MARING
08 Assoc Dean Library & Lrng Resources .... Dawn LOWE-WINCENTSEN
103 Acting Exec Dean STEM & Workforce .... Crystal HESS
79 Exec Dean Humanities .... Nancy DICK
50 Exec Dean Business/Comm/Soc Sci .... Lucas RUCKS
41 Dir Athletics & Intramurals .... Steve ESKRIDGE
105 Assoc Director Web Strategy .... Adam STAFFA
106 Acting Director eLearning .... Amy ROVNER
13 Acting Dir Technology Support Svcs .... Gavin SMITH
21 Director of Financial Services .... Alyshia JOSLEYN
35 Dir Stdnt Ldrshp/Residential Life .... Sundi MUSNICKI
88 Director-Guided Pathways .... Brigid NULTY
121 Dean Access & Advising .... Lisa MALIK
88 Dean Student Support & Success .... Derek LEVY
88 Associate Dean Transitional Studies .... Jonathan MOLINARO

Skagit Valley College (C)

2405 College Way, Mount Vernon WA 98273-5899

County: Skagit FICE Identification: 003792

Unit ID: 236638

Telephone: (360) 416-7600 Carnegie Class: Bac/Assoc-Assoc Dom

FAX Number: (360) 416-7890 Calendar System: Quarter

URL: www.skagit.edu

Established: 1926 Annual Undergrad Tuition & Fees (In-State): $4,000

Enrollment: 4,227 Coed

Affiliation or Control: State IRS Status: 501(c)3

Highest Offering: Baccalaureate

Accreditation: NW, ACFEI, ADNUR, MAC

01 President .... Dr. Thomas KEEGAN
05 Vice President for Instruction .... Dr. Kenneth LAWSON
10 Vice Pres Administrative Services .... Mr. Ed JARAMILLO
12 Vice President of Whidbey Campus .... Dr. Laura CAILLOUX
15 Assoc Vice Pres of Human Resources .... Ms. Carolyn TUCKER
13 Dir of Information Technology .... Mr. Andy HEISER
103 Dean Workforce Education .... Mr. Darren GREENO
20 Exec Dean for Instruction .... Dr. Gabriel MAST
84 Assoc Dean Enrollment Services .... Ms. Sinead PLAGGE
36 Dir BAS Student Srvs & Wellness .... Ms. Sandy JORDON
32 Director of Student Life .... Mr. Brian MURPHY
37 Director of Financial Aid .... Ms. Crystal ALLISON
18 Director of Facilities & Operations .... Mr. Dave SCOTT
26 Chief Public Information Officer .... Ms. Arden AINLEY
104 Director of International Programs .... Ms. Christa SCHULZ
40 Bookstore Manager .... Ms. Kim HALL
41 Athletic Director .... Mr. Mitch FREEMAN
09 Director of Institutional Research .... Vacant

South Puget Sound Community College (D)

2011 Mottman Road, SW, Olympia WA 98512-6292

County: Thurston FICE Identification: 005372

Unit ID: 236656

Telephone: (360) 596-5200 Carnegie Class: Assoc/HT-Mix Trad/Non

FAX Number: (360) 664-0780 Calendar System: Quarter

URL: www.spscc.edu

Established: 1962 Annual Undergrad Tuition & Fees (In-State): $4,695

Enrollment: 4,665 Coed

Affiliation or Control: State IRS Status: 501(c)3

Highest Offering: Associate Degree

Accreditation: NW, ACFEI, DA, MAC

01 President .... Dr. Timothy STOKES
04 Special Assistant to the President .... Ms. Diana TOLEDO
05 Vice President for Instruction .... Dr. Michelle ANDREAS
32 Vice President for Student Services .... Dr. David PELKEY
10 Vice Pres for Finance & Operations .... Dr. Tysha TOLEFREE
84 Dean of Enrollment Services .... Ms. Valerie ROBERTSON
18 Director of Facilities .... Mr. Marty MATTES
26 Exec Community Relations Officer .... Ms. Kelly GREEN
35 Dean Student Engagement/Retention .... Ms. Jennifer MANLEY
37 Dean of Student Financial Services .... Ms. Johanna DWYER
15 Chief Human Resources Officer .... Ms. Samantha DOTSON
102 Exec Director of College Foundation .... Ms. Tanya MOTE
28 Executive Diversity Officer .... Mr. Parfait BASSALE
09 Director of Institutional Research .... Ms. Jennifer TUIA
06 Director of Enrollment/Registrar .... Ms. Jennifer FENN
121 Dean of Academic Success Programs .... Ms. Amy KELLY
19 Director of Safety & Security .... Vacant
13 Executive Information Officer .... Mr. Rip HEMINWAY
81 Dean of Natural/Applied Sciences .... Mr. Bryan POWELL
72 Dean of Applied Technology .... Dr. Jason SELWITZ
79 Dean of Humanities/Communication .... Dr. Melissa MEADE
83 Dean of Social Sciences & Business .... Dr. Valerie SUNDBY-THORP
96 Procurement & Supply Specialist-4 .... Ms. Vida SHERRARD-HANNON

Tacoma Community College (E)

6501 S 19th Street, Tacoma WA 98466-6100

County: Pierce FICE Identification: 003796

Unit ID: 236753

Telephone: (253) 566-5000 Carnegie Class: Bac/Assoc-Assoc Dom

FAX Number: N/A Calendar System: Quarter

URL: www.tacomacc.edu

Established: 1965 Annual Undergrad Tuition & Fees (In-State): $4,560

Enrollment: 5,823 Coed

Affiliation or Control: State IRS Status: 501(c)3

Highest Offering: Baccalaureate

Accreditation: NW, ADNUR, CAHIIM, COARC, DMS, EMT, RAD

01 President .... Dr. Ivan L. HARRELL, II
05 Provost/VP for Academic Affairs .... Dr. Marissa SCHLESINGER
11 Vice Pres Administrative Services .. Mr. Patty MCCRAY-ROBERTS
32 Vice Pres Student Services .... Mr. Karl SMITH
111 Vice Pres for College Advancement .... Mr. Bill RYBERG
28 VP Equity/Diversity/Inclusion .... Dr. Roderick MORRISON
15 Exec Director of Human Resources .... Mr. Stephen SMITH
88 Dir Conduct/Compliance .... Ms. Dolores HAUGEN
84 Dean for Enrollment & Student Suc .... Mr. Patrick BROWN
124 Dean of Retention & Student Success ...... Ms. Jennifer FOUNTAIN
10 Director Financial Services .... Ms. Sharon SCHRODER
18 Director Facilities/CapitalProjects .... Mr. Lon WHITAKER
35 Director of Student Engagement .... Ms. Sonja MORGAN
37 Director Student Financial Aid .... Ms. Kim MATISON
04 Executive Asst Pres Office .... Ms. Karyssa MATHISON
09 Director of Institutional Research .... Ms. Kelley SADLER
41 Athletic Director .... Mr. Jason PRENEVOST
13 Director Information Technology .... Mr. Clay KRAUSS
106 Dir Online Education/E-learning .... Mr. Dale COLEMAN
19 Director Security/Safety .... Mr. Will HOWARD
26 Director Public Relations/Marketing .... Ms. Tamyra HOWSER
104 Director International Student Svcs .... Mr. James NEWMAN
88 Special Assistant to President .... Mr. Joseph COLON

University of Phoenix Western Washington Campus (F)

7100 Fort Dent Way, Suite 100, Tukwila WA 98188-8553

Telephone: (425) 572-1600 Identification: 770234

Accreditation: &HLC

† No longer accepting campus-based students.

University of Puget Sound (G)

1500 N Warner St., Tacoma WA 98416-0002

County: Pierce FICE Identification: 003797

Unit ID: 236328

Telephone: (253) 879-3100 Carnegie Class: Bac-A&S

FAX Number: (253) 879-3500 Calendar System: Semester

URL: www.pugetsound.edu

Established: 1888 Annual Undergrad Tuition & Fees: $52,775

Enrollment: 2,130 Coed

Affiliation or Control: Independent Non-Profit IRS Status: 501(c)3

Highest Offering: Doctorate

Accreditation: NW, IPSY, MUS, OT, PTA

01 President .... Dr. Isiaah CRAWFORD
05 Provost .... Dr. Laura BEHLING
10 Executive Vice President/CFO .... Ms. Sherry B. MONDOU
43 VP & University Counsel/Board Sec . Ms. Joanna C. CLEVELAND
100 VP Communications/Chief of Staff .... Ms. Gayle MCINTOSH
30 Vice President University Relations .... Mr. David BEERS
84 Vice President Enrollment .... Dr. Matthew BOYCE
32 Interim VP Student Affairs .... Ms. Sarah COMSTOCK
04 Executive Asst to President .... Ms. Lori MAGARO
21 AVP Financial Planning & Analysis .... Ms. Janet S. HALLMAN
109 Dir Ofc Pres/Com Liaison Officer ..... Ms. Mary Elizabeth COLLINS
28 VP Inst Equity/Diversity .... Dr. Lorna HERNANDEZ JARVIS
20 Associate Academic Dean .... Dr. Julie CHRISTOPH
58 Dean of Faculty & Grad Studies .... Dr. Sunil KUKREJA
20 Assoc Acad Dean Exp Lrng ...... Dr. Nick KONTOGEORGOPOULO
53 Dean School of Education .... Dr. Amy RYKEN
50 Dir School of Business/Leadership .... Dr. Lynnette CLAIRE
64 Director School of Music .... Dr. Tracy DOYLE
88 Dir School of Occupational Therapy .... Dr. Yvonne SWINTH
88 Dir School of Physical Therapy .... Dr. Danny MCMILLIAN
108 Assoc Prov IR/Plng/Stdnt Svcs .... Ms. Ellen PETERS
08 Director Collins Memorial Library .... Ms. Jane CARLIN
41 Dir of Intercollegiate Athletics .... Ms. Amy E. HACKETT
18 Assoc Vice Pres Facilities Services .... Mr. Bob KIEF
13 Chief Information Officer .... Mr. Jeremy L. CUCCO
114 Assoc VP Finance .... Ms. Justine JULIANI
15 Assoc Vice Pres Human Resources .... Vacant
29 Assoc VP Constituent Relations .... Ms. Allison CANNADY-SMITH
113 Assoc VP for Student Financial Svcs ..... Ms. Maggie A. MITTUCH
42 University Chaplain .... Mr. Dave WRIGHT
39 Associate Dean of Students .... Ms. Debbie CHEE
38 Dir Counseling/Health/Wellness Svcs .... Dr. Kelly K. BROWN
44 Director Annual Giving .... Ms. Abbie LACSINA
102 Director Foundation/Corporate Rels .... Ms. Jane KENYON
26 Assoc VP Communications .... Ms. Katie BAROSKY
06 Registrar .... Mr. Michael PASTORE
121 Dir Academic Advising .... Mr. Landon WADE
36 Director Career Services .... Ms. Alana HENTGES
37 Director Student Financial Aid .... Mr. Bryan M. GOULD
19 Director of Security .... Mr. Todd BADHAM
90 Deputy CIO/Client Supp/Ed Tech .... Mr. Matthew LINK
122 Dir Student Involvement .... Mr. Moe STEPHENS
104 Director International Programs .... Mr. Roy ROBINSON
118 Total Rewards Manager .... Ms. Kenni SIMONS
40 Logger Store Director .... Ms. Kristi DOPP
105 Web Specialist .... Ms. Barbara WEIST
96 Procurement Manager .... Ms. Linda GREEN

University of Washington (A)

1400 NE Campus Parkway, Seattle WA 98195-0001

County: King FICE Identification: 003798
Unit ID: 236948
Telephone: (206) 543-2100 Carnegie Class: DU-Highest
FAX Number: (206) 543-9285 Calendar System: Quarter
URL: www.washington.edu
Established: 1861 Annual Undergrad Tuition & Fees (In-State): $11,745
Enrollment: 48,149 Coed
Affiliation or Control: State IRS Status: 501(c)3
Highest Offering: Doctorate
Accreditation: NW, ARCPA, CAHIIM, CAMPEP, CLPSY, CONST, DENT, DIETC, EMT, HSA, IPSY, JOUR, LAW, LIB, LSAR, MED, MIDWF, MT, NURSE, OPE, OT, PAST, PCSAS, PDPSY, PH, PHAR, PLNG, PTA, SCPSY, SP, SPAA, SW

01 President ... Dr. Ana Mari CAUCE
05 Provost/Exec Vice Pres ... Dr. Mark RICHARDS
12 Chancellor Bothell Campus ... Dr. Kristin ESTERBERG
12 Chancellor Tacoma Campus ... Dr. Sheila EDWARDS LANGE
28 VP Minority Affs/Vice Prov Div ... Dr. Rickey HALL
17 Exec VP Med Affs/CEO UW Med/Dean ... Dr. Paul G. RAMSEY
15 Vice President Human Resources ... Ms. Mindy KORNBERG
13 Vice President for UW IT ... Mr. Aaron POWELL
30 Senior VP for Advancement ... Ms. Mary GRESCH
21 Vice President for Finance ... Mr. Brian MCCARTAN
26 VP for Comm & Chief Marketing Ofcr ... Vacant
30 Vice President for Development ... Mr. Dan PETERSON
46 Vice Provost Research ... Dr. Mari OSTENDORF
51 Vice Provost UW Continuum College ... Dr. Rovy BRANON
45 Vice Provost Planning & Budgeting ... Ms. Sarah NORRIS HALL
20 Vice Prov/Dean Undergrad Acad Affs ... Dr. Ed TAYLOR
32 Vice President for Student Life ... Mr. Denzil SUITE
88 Vice Provost for Academic Personnel ... Dr. Cheryl A. CAMERON
86 Director Federal Relations ... Ms. Sarah CASTRO
43 Division Chief Attorney General ... Mr. David M. KERWIN
06 University Registrar ... Ms. Helen GARRETT
29 VP Alumni & Stakeholder Engagement ... Mr. Paul RUCKER
17 Chief Operating Ofcr UW Medical Ctr ... Mr. Geoff P. AUSTIN
37 Asst VP Enroll/Exec Dir Fin Aid ... Ms. Kay LEWIS
09 AVP Analytics/Inst Research ... Ms. Erin GUTHRIE
36 Executive Director Career Center ... Ms. Briana RANDALL
14 CFO/UW Information Technology ... Mr. Bill FERRIS
18 Assoc VP Capital Planning Devel ... Vacant
92 Director Honors Program ... Dr. Victoria LAWSON
41 Director Athletics ... Ms. Jennifer COHEN
08 Dean of Libraries ... Mr. Simon NEAME
96 Executive Dir Procurement Services ... Mr. Mark CONLEY
58 Dean Graduate School ... Dr. Joy WILLIAMSON-LOTT
49 Dean Arts & Sciences ... Dr. Dianne HARRIS
47 Dean Col of Built Environments ... Ms. Renee CHENG
22 EOAA Compliance Manager ... Mr. Brian LACOUR
50 Dean Business School ... Dr. Frank HODGE
54 Dean of Engineering ... Dr. Nancy ALLBRITTON
61 Dean Law School ... Mr. Mario L. BARNES
70 Dean Social Work ... Dr. Edwina UEHARA
52 Dean Dentistry ... Dr. Gary T. CHIODO
63 Dean Medicine ... Dr. Paul G. RAMSEY
66 Dean Nursing ... Dr. Azita EMAMI
67 Dean Pharmacy ... Dr. Sean SULLIVAN
69 Dean School of Public Health ... Dr. Hilary GODWIN
53 Dean College of Education ... Dr. Mia TUAN
80 Dean School of Public Affairs ... Dr. Jodi SANDFORT
88 Dean Information School ... Dr. Anind DEY
88 Interim Dean Col of Environment ... Dr. Dennis HAERTMANN
04 Executive Asst to President ... Ms. Stephanie COURT
07 Director of Admissions ... Mr. Paul SEEGERT
104 Director Study Abroad ... Mr. Wolfram LATSCH
108 Director Educational Assessment ... Mr. Sean GEHRKE
19 Interim Chief of Police ... Mr. Randall WEST
38 Director Student Counseling ... Dr. Natacha F. KUNE
39 Asst Vice Pres of Student Life ... Ms. Pam SCHREIBER
101 Secretary to the Board of Regents ... Mr. Tyler LANGE
102 AVP Corporate & Foundation Rels ... Ms. Joanna GLICKLER
44 Sr Director Annual Philanthropy ... Ms. Jennifer MACCORMACK
100 Chief of Staff ... Ms. Margaret SHEPHERD

Walla Walla Community College (B)

500 Tausick Way, Walla Walla WA 99362-9267

County: Walla Walla FICE Identification: 005006
Unit ID: 236887
Telephone: (509) 522-2500 Carnegie Class: Assoc/HVT-High Non
FAX Number: (509) 527-4480 Calendar System: Quarter
URL: www.wwcc.edu
Established: 1967 Annual Undergrad Tuition & Fees (In-State): $4,818
Enrollment: 2,940 Coed
Affiliation or Control: State IRS Status: 170(c)1
Highest Offering: Baccalaureate
Accreditation: NW, ADNUR

01 President ... Dr. Chad HICKOX
05 Vice President of Instruction ... Dr. Jess CLARK
76 Dean of Health Sciences Education ... Ms. Kathleen ADAMSKI
37 Financial Aid Director ... Ms. Maisee PERALEZ
08 Director of Library Services ... Ms. Jacquelyn RAY
12 Dean Clarkston Campus ... Dr. Chad MILTENBERGER
41 Athletic Director ... Mr. Jeffrey E. REINLAND
15 Vice President of Human Resources ... Mrs. Sharon M. HARTFORD
18 Dir Facility Svcs/Capital Projects ... Mr. Shane LOPER
106 Director of eLearning ... Ms. Lisa CHAMBERLIN
20 Dean of Transitional Studies ... Ms. Susan PEARSON
40 Bookstore Manager ... Ms. Alecia ANGELL
56 Director of Extended Learning ... Ms. Jodi WORDEN
26 Exec Dir Communications/Marketing ... Vacant
06 Registrar ... Ms. Erika BOCKMANN
09 Exc Dir Institutional Effectiveness ... Dr. Nicholas VELLUZZI
103 Dean Workforce Education ... Mr. Jerry ANHORN, JR.
13 Director Technology Svcs ... Mr. Kevin COMBS

Walla Walla University (C)

204 S College Avenue, College Place WA 99324-1198

County: Walla Walla FICE Identification: 003799
Unit ID: 236896
Telephone: (509) 527-2615 Carnegie Class: Masters/S
FAX Number: (509) 527-2397 Calendar System: Quarter
URL: www.wallawalla.edu
Established: 1892 Annual Undergrad Tuition & Fees: $29,931
Enrollment: 1,737 Coed
Affiliation or Control: Seventh-day Adventist IRS Status: 501(c)3
Highest Offering: Master's
Accreditation: NW, ACBSP, NURSE, SW

01 President ... Dr. John MCVAY
05 VP Academic Administration ... Dr. Volker HENNING
10 VP Financial Administration ... Mr. Steve ROSE
32 VP Student Life ... Dr. Doug TILSTRA
111 VP Univ Relations/Advancement ... Ms. Jodi WAGNER
28 Asst to President for Diversity ... Dr. Pedrito MAYNARD-REID
04 Executive Asst Office of President ... Ms. Deirdre BENWELL
20 Assoc VP Academic Administration ... Dr. Scott LIGMAN
21 Assoc VP Financial Administration ... Mr. Ken VYHMEISTER
58 Assoc VP Graduate Studies ... Dr. Pam CRESS
84 Assoc VP of Marketing & Enrollment ... Mr. Trevor CONGLETON
110 Assoc VP of Alumni & Advancement ... Mr. Troy PATZER
35 Asst VP Stdnt Life/Dean of Students ... Mr. David IWASA
08 Director of Libraries ... Ms. Carolyn GASKELL
06 Registrar ... Ms. Carolyn DENNEY
42 Chaplain ... Mr. Albert HANDAL
29 Director of Parent/Alumni Relations ... Mrs. Claudia SANTELLANO
13 Director Information Technology ... Mr. Scott MCFADDEN
37 Assoc Director Financial Aid ... Ms. Nancy CALDERA
15 Director Human Resources ... Ms. Erika SANDERSON
18 Director of Facility Services ... Mr. George BENNETT
26 Director Marketing/Public Relations ... Mr. Aaron NAKAMURA
07 Director of Admissions ... Mr. Dale MILAM
36 Director Career Development Center ... Vacant
38 Director Counseling/Testing ... Ms. Michelle NADEN
09 Director of Institutional Research ... Vacant
41 Interim Athletic Director ... Mr. Paul STARKEBAUM
19 Campus Security Director ... Ms. Courtney BRYANT
44 Director Gift Planning ... Ms. Dorita TESSIER
66 Dean of School of Nursing ... Dr. Lucille KRULL
73 Dean of School of Theology ... Dr. Carl COSAERT
54 Dean of School of Engineering ... Dr. Brian ROTH
50 Dean of Business ... Dr. Bruce TOEWS
53 Dean of Education & Psychology ... Dr. Debbie MUTHERSBAUGH
70 Dean of Social Work & Sociology ... Dr. Darold BIGGER

Washington State University (D)

PO Box 645910, Pullman WA 99164-5910

County: Whitman FICE Identification: 003800
Unit ID: 236939
Telephone: (509) 335-3564 Carnegie Class: DU-Highest
FAX Number: N/A Calendar System: Semester
URL: www.wsu.edu
Established: 1890 Annual Undergrad Tuition & Fees (In-District): $12,170
Enrollment: 31,159 Coed
Affiliation or Control: State/Local IRS Status: 501(c)3
Highest Offering: Doctorate
Accreditation: NW, CAATE, CEA, CIDA, CLPSY, CONST, COPSY, DIETC, IPSY, LSAR, MUS, NURSE, PHAR, SP, SPAA, VET

01 President ... Dr. Kirk SCHULZ
05 Provost/Exec Vice President ... Dr. Elizabeth CHILTON
10 VP Finance/Administration ... Ms. Stacy PEARSON
111 VP Advancement/CEO WSU Foundation ... Ms. Lisa CALVERT
106 VP Academic Outreach/Innovation ... Dr. David CILLAY
32 VP Student Affairs ... Dr. Mary Jo GONZALES
13 VP Information Tech & CIO ... Mr. Sasi PILLAY
46 Vice President Research ... Dr. Christopher KEANE
86 VP External Affs/Government Rels ... Ms. Colleen KERR
26 Vice Pres Marketing/Communication ... Mr. Phil WEILER
20 Vice Provost for Faculty Affairs ... Vacant
12 Chancellor WSU Everett ... Dr. Paul PITRE
12 Chancellor WSU Spokane ... Dr. Daryll DEWALD
12 Chancellor WSU Tri-Cities ... Dr. Sandra HAYNES
12 Chancellor WSU Vancouver ... Dr. Mel NETZHAMMER
15 VP/Chief Human Resources Ofcr ... Ms. Theresa ELLIOT-CHESLEK
37 Interim AVP Financial Services ... Ms. Joy SCOUREY
117 Chief Compliance/Risk Officer ... Ms. Sharyl KAMMERZELL
35 AVP Student Affs/Dean of Students ... Ms. Jill CREIGHTON
43 Div Chief State Attorney Gen Office ... Ms. Danielle HESS
58 Dean of the Graduate School ... Dr. Lisa GLOSS
47 Int Dean Agric/Human Natl Res Sci ... Dr. Richard KOENIG
50 Dean Carson College of Business ... Dr. Chip HUNTER
53 Dean College of Education ... Dr. Michael TREVISAN
54 Dean Engineering & Architecture ... Dr. Mary REZAK
66 Dean College of Nursing ... Dr. Mary KOITHAN
67 Dean College of Pharmacy ... Dr. Mark LEID
60 Dean College of Communication ... Dr. Bruce PINKLETON
49 Dean College of Arts & Sciences ... Dr. Todd BUTLER
74 Dean College of Veterinary Medicine ... Dr. Dori BORJESSON
92 Dean Honors College ... Dr. M. Grant NORTON
114 Assoc VP & Chief Budget Officer ... Vacant
18 Assoc VP Facilities Services ... Ms. Olivia YANG
89 Vice Prov for Academic Engagement ... Dr. Mary F. WACK
08 Dean Libraries ... Mr. Joseph STARRATT
06 University Registrar ... Mr. Matthew ZIMMERMAN
07 Interim Director Admissions ... Ms. Nancy WEHRUNG
09 Assoc Dir Institutional Research ... Ms. Fran HERMANSTON
41 Director WSU Athletics ... Mr. Patrick CHUN
116 Director Internal Audit ... Ms. Heather LOPEZ
04 Administrative Asst to President ... Mrs. Ginger DRUFFEL

Washington State University-Spokane (E)

412 East Spokane Falls Blvd, Spokane WA 99207-9600

Telephone: (509) 358-7500 Identification: 770948
Accreditation: &NW, EXSC, MED

Washington State University-Tri Cities (F)

2710 Crimson Way, Richland WA 99354-1671

Telephone: (509) 372-7000 Identification: 770949
Accreditation: &NW

Washington State University-Vancouver (G)

14204 NE Salmon Creek Ave, Vancouver WA 98686-9600

Telephone: (360) 549-9788 Identification: 770950
Accreditation: &NW

Wenatchee Valley College (H)

1300 Fifth Street, Wenatchee WA 98801-1799

County: Chelan FICE Identification: 003801
Unit ID: 236975
Telephone: (509) 682-6800 Carnegie Class: Bac/Assoc-Assoc Dom
FAX Number: (509) 682-6541 Calendar System: Quarter
URL: www.wvc.edu
Established: 1939 Annual Undergrad Tuition & Fees (In-State): $4,320
Enrollment: 3,090 Coed
Affiliation or Control: State IRS Status: 501(c)3
Highest Offering: Baccalaureate
Accreditation: NW, ADNUR, MAC, MLTAD, NURSE, RAD

01 President ... Mr. James RICHARDSON
04 Exec Assistant to President ... Mrs. Maria INIGUEZ
05 Vice President of Instruction ... Dr. Tod TREAT
11 VP of Administrative Services ... Mr. Brett RILEY
32 VP of Student Services & Enrollment ... Dr. Chio FLORES
49 Dean Lib Arts/Sciences/Basic Skills ... Ms. Holly BRINGHAM
103 Dean Workforce & Continuing Educ ... Mr. Joey WALTER
66 Director of Nursing Program ... Ms. Kristen HOSEY
15 Exec Director Human Resources ... Ms. Reagan BELLAMY
35 Associate Dean of Student Services ... Mr. Kevin BERG
18 Director of Facilities & Operations ... Mr. Rich PETERS
06 Dir of Enrollment Svcs/Registrar ... Mr. Jonathan BARNETT
08 Dir Libraries/Learning Technologies ... Ms. Jeannie HENKLE
10 Director of Fiscal Services ... Ms. Janice FREDSON
26 Exec Dir of Communication Rels ... Ms. Libby SIEBENS
27 Web Marketing/Graphic Design Spec ... Mr. Nick WINTERS
09 Exec Director of Inst Effectiveness ... Mr. Ty JONES
19 Safety/Security & Emergency Mgr ... Ms. Maria AGNEW
28 Asst Dean Campus Life/Equity/Inclus ... Ms. Erin TOFTE-NORDVIK
102 Exec Director of WVC Foundation ... Ms. Rachel EVEY

Western Washington University (I)

516 High Street, Bellingham WA 98225-5950

County: Whatcom FICE Identification: 003802
Unit ID: 237011
Telephone: (360) 650-3000 Carnegie Class: Masters/L
FAX Number: (360) 650-3022 Calendar System: Quarter
URL: www.wwu.edu
Established: 1893 Annual Undergrad Tuition & Fees (In-State): $8,508
Enrollment: 15,197 Coed
Affiliation or Control: State IRS Status: 501(c)3
Highest Offering: Doctorate
Accreditation: NW, ART, @AUD, CACREP, CAPRT, MUS, NURSE, PH, PLNG, SP

01 President ... Dr. Sabah RANDHAWA
05 Vice Pres Academic Affairs/Provost ... Dr. Brent CARBAJAL
10 Vice Pres Business/Financial Affs ... Mr. Richard D. VAN DEN HUL
84 VP Enrollment/Student Services ... Dr. Melynda HUSKEY
26 Vice Pres for University Relations ... Mrs. Donna GIBBS
111 Vice Pres University Advancement ... Ms. Kim O'NEILL
13 Vice Prov Info/Chief Info Officer ... Dr. Chuck LANHAM
58 Vice Prov Rsch/Dean Grad Sch ... Dr. David PATRICK
20 Vice Prov Undergraduate Education ... Dr. Jack HERRING
51 Vice Prov Outreach Continuing Educ ... Dr. Robert SQUIRES
35 Dean of Students ... Vacant
15 Asst VP for Human Resources ... Ms. Chyerl WOLFE-LEE
06 Registrar ... Vacant
07 Director of Admissions ... Mr. Cezar MESQUITA
36 Director Career Services Center ... Ms. Effie EISSES
37 Director Financial Aid ... Ms. Clara CAPRON
29 Executive Director Alumni Relations ... Ms. Deborah DEWEES
27 Director University Communications ... Mr. Paul COCKE
08 Dean of Libraries ... Dr. Mark GREENBERG
39 Director University Residences ... Mr. Leonard JONES
100 Chief of Staff/Secretary BOT ... Dr. Paul DUNN

09 Director of Institutional Research ... Dr. Ming ZHANG
18 Director of Facilities Management ... Mr. John A. FURMAN
19 Director of Public Safety ... Mr. Darin RASMUSSEN
41 Athletic Director ... Mr. Steven CARD
92 Director of Honors Program ... Dr. Scott LINNEMAN
96 Director of Business Services ... Mr. Pete HEILGEIST
79 Dean College of Humanities/Soc Sci ... Dr. Paqui PAREDES
72 Dean College of Science/Technology ... Dr. Brad JOHNSON
50 Dean College Business & Econ ... Dr. Scott YOUNG
65 Dean Huxley Col of the Environment . Dr. Steven HOLLENHORST
57 Dean College of Fine & Perf ... Dr. Christopher SPICER
53 Dean Woodring College of Education ... Dr. Bruce LARSON
12 Dean Fairhaven College ... Dr. John BOWER
04 Sr Executive Assistant to President ... Ms. Barbara A. SANDOVAL
104 Director Intl Student/Scholar Svcs ... Mr. Richard BRUCE
25 Contracts Assistant ... Ms. Andrea RODGER
38 Director Counseling Center ... Ms. Sarah GODOY
43 AAG/Chief Legal Advisor ... Ms. Kerena HIGGINS
86 Director Government Relations ... Ms. Becca KENNA-SCHENK
108 Dir Institutional Effectiveness ... Dr. John KRIEG

Whatcom Community College (A)

237 W Kellogg Road, Bellingham WA 98226-8003
County: Whatcom FICE Identification: 010364
Unit ID: 237039
Telephone: (360) 383-3000 Carnegie Class: Bac/Assoc-Assoc Dom
FAX Number: (360) 383-4000 Calendar System: Quarter
URL: www.whatcom.edu
Established: 1970 Annual Undergrad Tuition & Fees (In-State): $4,764
Enrollment: 2,719 Coed
Affiliation or Control: State IRS Status: 501(c)3
Highest Offering: Baccalaureate
Accreditation: NW, ADNUR, MAC, PTAA

01 President ... Dr. Kathi HIYANE-BROWN
05 VP for Instruction ... Mr. Ed HARRI
11 VP for Administrative Services ... Mr. Nate LANGSTRAAT
32 VP for Student Services ... Dr. Luca LEWIS
20 Dean for Instruction ... Ms. Carla GELWICKS
08 Library Director ... Mr. Howard FULLER
10 Director for Business & Finance ... Mr. Matt CONNELLY
06 Registrar ... Mr. Michael SINGLETARY
37 Director of Financial Aid ... Mr. David KLAFFKE
85 Director of International Programs ... Mr. Kelly KESTER
40 Bookstore Manager ... Mr. Jon SPORES
18 Senior Facilities Director ... Mr. Brian KEELEY
04 Special Assistant to the President ... Ms. Rafeeka KLOKE
15 Executive Director Human Resources ... Ms. Becky RAWLINGS
09 Director for Assessment and IR ... Dr. Anne Marie KARLBERG

Whitman College (B)

345 Boyer Avenue, Walla Walla WA 99362-2083
County: Walla Walla FICE Identification: 003803
Unit ID: 237057
Telephone: (509) 527-5411 Carnegie Class: Bac-A&S
FAX Number: (509) 527-5859 Calendar System: Semester
URL: www.whitman.edu
Established: 1882 Annual Undergrad Tuition & Fees: $50,408
Enrollment: 1,360 Coed
Affiliation or Control: Independent Non-Profit IRS Status: 501(c)3
Highest Offering: Baccalaureate
Accreditation: NW

01 President ... Dr. Kathleen MURRAY
05 Provost/Dean of Faculty ... Dr. Alzada TIPTON
30 Vice President for Development ... Mr. Steven SETCHELL
10 Treasurer/Chief Financial Officer ... Mr. Peter W. HARVEY
32 VP Student Affs/Dean Students ... Mr. Kazi JOSHUA
20 Associate Dean Faculty Development ... Dr. Helen KIM
07 Director of Admission ... Mr. Adam MILLER
13 Chief Information Officer ... Mr. Dan M. TERRIO
18 Director of the Physical Plant ... Mr. Tony ICHSAN
08 Director of Penrose Library ... Mrs. Dalia L. CORKRUM
91 Director of Enterprise Technology ... Mr. Michael OSTERMAN
09 Director of Institutional Research ... Dr. Neal J. CHRISTOPHERSON
20 Assoc Dean Academic Affairs ... Dr. Kendra J. GOLDEN
35 Associate Dean of Students ... Ms. Barbara A. MAXWELL
26 VP Enrollment & Communications ... Dr. Joshua JENSEN
38 Counseling Center Director ... Dr. Rae CHRESFIELD
39 Director Residence Life & Housing ... Ms. Nancy J. TAVELLI
29 Director Alumni Relations ... Ms. Nancy L. MITCHELL
104 Director of Off-Campus Studies ... Ms. Susan H. HOLME
15 Director Human Resources ... Ms. Telara MCCULLOUGH
06 Registrar ... Ms. Stacey J. GIUSTI
19 Director of Security ... Mr. Steve DAVIS
23 Director Health Services ... Ms. Claudia L. NESS
36 Director for Career Development ... Ms. Kim ROLFE
37 Director of Financial Aid Services ... Ms. Marilyn K. PONTI
41 Athletic Director ... Ms. Kim CHANDLER
42 Coordinator of Spiritual Life ... Mr. Adam M. KIRTLEY
44 Director of Annual Giving ... Ms. Lara MEYER
26 Senior Director of Communications ... Ms. Gina OHNSTAD
124 Dir of the Student Engagement Ctr ... Mr. Noah LEAVITT
28 VP for Diversity & Inclusion ... Vacant
90 Director of Academic Technology ... Mr. David SPRUNGER

Whitworth University (C)

300 W Hawthorne Road, Spokane WA 99251-0001
County: Spokane FICE Identification: 003804
Unit ID: 237066
Telephone: (509) 777-1000 Carnegie Class: Masters/M
FAX Number: (509) 777-4763 Calendar System: 4/1/4
URL: www.whitworth.edu
Established: 1890 Annual Undergrad Tuition & Fees: $46,250
Enrollment: 2,756 Coed
Affiliation or Control: Presbyterian IRS Status: 501(c)3
Highest Offering: Master's
Accreditation: NW, CAATE, MFCD, MPCAC, MUS

01 Interim President ... Dr. Scott MCQUILKIN
05 Provost & Executive Vice President ... Dr. Gregor THUSWALDNER
04 Exec Asst to President/Board Secy ... Ms. Ruth PELLS
10 VP Finance & Administration ... Mr. Larry PROBUS
32 VP for Student Life/Title IX ... Ms. Rhosetta RHODES
84 VP Admissions & Financial Aid ... Mr. Greg ORWIG
111 Int VP Institutional Advancement ... Ms. Stacey SMITH
15 Interim Chief Human Resources Ofcr ... Ms. Ariane OGLESBEE
21 Assoc VP Finance & Administration ... Ms. Luz MERKEL
13 Chief Information Officer ... Mr. Kenneth BROWN
42 Dean Spiritual Life ... Dr. Forrest BUCKNER
41 Director of Athletics ... Mr. Timothy DEMANT
28 Chief Diversity Officer ... Ms. Roberta WILBURN
20 Associate Provost ... Dr. Brooke KIENER
110 Sr Assoc VP Inst Advancement ... Ms. Stacey SMITH
88 Assoc VP Institutional Advancement ... Mr. Tad WISENOR
123 Dean Cont Studies/Grad Admiss ... Dr. Randy MICHAELIS
55 Assoc Dean Evening Business Pgm ... Ms. Christie ANDERSON
108 Dir of Assessment/Accreditation ... Dr. Deanna OJENNUS
25 Dir Sponsored Program/Grants ... Ms. Melinda STOOPS
88 Int Dir Office of Church Engagement ... Rev. Mindy SMITH
53 Dean School of Education ... Dr. Ronald JACOBSON
50 Dean School of Business ... Dr. Timothy WILKINSON
49 Dean College of Arts & Sciences ... Dr. Noelle WIERSMA
06 Registrar ... Mr. Jose ORTIZ
88 Assoc Dean Grad Studies in Educ ... Vacant
90 Dir Instructional Resources ... Mr. Kenneth PECKA
88 Assoc Dean Com Standards/Compliance ... Mr. Timothy CALDWELL
29 Dir Alumni/Parent Relations ... Mr. Dale HAMMOND
07 Director of Admissions ... Ms. Lara RAMSAY
18 Assoc VP of Facilities Services ... Mr. Christopher EICHORST
23 Director of Student Health Svcs ... Ms. Amy CUTLER
37 Director of Financial Aid ... Ms. Traci STENSLAND
93 Asst Dean Student DEI ... Mr. Shawn WASHINGTON
39 Asst Dean Student Life ... Vacant
68 Director of Athletic Training ... Dr. Cynthia WRIGHT
26 Assoc VP Marketing & Communications ... Ms. Nancy HINES
38 Director Student Counseling Ctr ... Ms. Molly DEWALT
09 Director of Institutional Research ... Ms. Wendy OLSON
08 Dir Library/Assoc Dean Special Pgms ... Dr. Amanda CLARK
88 Interim Director MIT ... Dr. Ronald JACOBSON
19 Director Security Services ... Mr. LeRoy MCCALL
73 Dir Grad Studies in Theology ... Dr. Jeremy WYNNE
104 Dir of International Education Ctr ... Mr. Nick MCKINNEY
88 Dir US Cultural Studies ... Dr. Stacy KEOGH GEORGE
50 Dir Grad Studies Business ... Ms. Sinead VOORHEES
88 Dir Teacher Certification ... Dr. Stacy HILL
36 Director Career Services ... Ms. Tiffany RIDDLE
88 Director University Events ... Ms. Michelle DRENNEN

Yakima Valley College (D)

PO Box 22520, S 16th Ave & Nob Hill,
Yakima WA 98907-2520
County: Yakima FICE Identification: 003805
Unit ID: 237109
Telephone: (509) 574-4600 Carnegie Class: Bac/Assoc-Assoc Dom
FAX Number: (509) 574-6860 Calendar System: Quarter
URL: www.yvcc.edu
Established: 1928 Annual Undergrad Tuition & Fees (In-State): $4,770
Enrollment: 3,954 Coed
Affiliation or Control: State IRS Status: 170(c)1
Highest Offering: Baccalaureate
Accreditation: NW, ADNUR, DH, MAC, RAD, SURGT

01 President ... Dr. Linda KAMINSKI
05 Vice Pres Instruction/Student Svcs ... Dr. Jennifer ERNST
10 Vice Pres Administrative Services ... Dr. Teresa RICH
12 Dean Grandview Campus ... Mr. Marc COOMER
75 Dean College Career Readiness ... Mr. Marc COOMER
13 Director Tech Services ... Mr. Dilbar CHHOKAR
32 Dean Student Services ... Ms. Leslie BLACKABY
49 Dean Arts & Sciences ... Ms. Kerrie CAVANESS
103 Dean Workforce Education ... Ms. Skye FIELD
08 Library Director ... Ms. Leslie POTTER-HENDERSON
37 Director Student Financial Aid ... Mr. Oscar VERDUZCO
06 Registrar/Director of Admissions ... Ms. Lorena ALVARADO-VALDOVINOS
108 Dir Institutional Effectiveness ... Ms. Sheila DELQUADRI
26 Community Relations Coordinator ... Mr. Dustin WUNDERLICH
15 Executive Director Human Resources ... Mr. Steven SLONIKER
18 Director Facilities/Physical Plant ... Mr. Jeff MORROW
21 Director Accounting Services ... Ms. Angela ANTHONY
35 Student Life Coordinator ... Ms. Laura YOLO
04 Executive Asst to President ... Ms. Megan JENSEN
41 Athletic Director ... Mr. Ray FUNK

WEST VIRGINIA

Alderson Broaddus University (E)

101 College Hill Drive, Philippi WV 26416-4600
County: Barbour FICE Identification: 003806
Unit ID: 237118
Telephone: (800) 263-1549 Carnegie Class: Bac-Diverse
FAX Number: (304) 457-6239 Calendar System: Semester
URL: www.ab.edu
Established: 1871 Annual Undergrad Tuition & Fees: $29,220
Enrollment: 863 Coed
Affiliation or Control: American Baptist IRS Status: 501(c)3
Highest Offering: Master's
Accreditation: HLC, ARCPA, NUR

01 President ... Dr. James (Tim) BARRY
05 Provost/Executive Vice President ... Dr. Andrea BUCKLEW
11 Vice Pres for Administration ... Mr. Bruce A. BLANKENSHIP
03 Executive Vice Pres Administration ... Dr. Eric M. SHOR
10 Vice Pres for Finance/CFO ... Mr. Jeff A. ROGERS
32 Dean of Students ... Mr. David A. FALLETA
20 Associate Provost ... Dr. Andrea J. BUCKLEW
56 Asst Provost Extended Learning ... Dr. James M. OWSTON
111 AVP for Inst Advancement/Dir Alumni ... Mr. Joshua D. ALLEN
84 AVP Enrollment Mgmt ... Ms. Jennifer HAWKINBERRY
63 Dean College of Medical Science ... Dr. Thomas F. MOORE
53 Dean College of Education ... Dr. Erin R. BRUMBAUGH
79 Dean Col of Humanities & Soc Sci ... Mrs. Kari M. SISK
81 Dean Col Health/Science/Tech/Math ... Dr. Michael J. BOEHKE
06 Registrar ... Dr. Saundra E. HOXIE
08 Director of Library Services ... Mr. David E. HOXIE
41 Athletic Director ... Mrs. Carrie BODKINS
42 Chaplain ... Dr. Carl W. GITTINGS
121 Dir Academic Ctr for Educ Success ... Dr. Amy MASON
21 Controller ... Mr. Chad A. MAYLE
29 Director of Alumni Relations ... Mr. Joshua D. ALLEN
44 Director of Annual Fund ... Ms. Sandra O. FRAME
40 Director of Campus Services ... Mr. Ed BURDA
35 Associate Dean Students ... Ms. Teresa D. VANALSBURG
38 Director of Counseling Services ... Mr. Chad HOSTETLER
37 Director of Financial Aid ... Ms. Lora R. BRYANT
18 Director of Facilities ... Mr. Lawrence J. TALLMAN
46 Dir of Information and Research ... Ms. Julia M. MORRIS
13 Director of Information Technology ... Ms. Carol WEAVER
26 Director of Mktg/Communications ... Ms. Dionne T. ALLEN
19 Director Security/Safety ... Mr. Matthew SISK
04 Exec Asst to Pres/Sec to the Board ... Mrs. Karla R. HIVELY
105 Web Content Editor ... Vacant
09 Director of Institutional Research ... Dr. Bob S. BUCKINGHAM
15 Director of Human Resources ... Ms. Jennifer R. PHILLIPS
39 Director of Housing/Residence Life ... Mr. Kevin MARSHBURN
30 Dir Development & Corp Relations ... Mr. Chris N. RANDOLPH
27 Assoc Dir Mktg/Communications ... Ms. Leah M. KNICELY
27 Creative Director ... Ms. Sheree D. WENTZ
36 Director of Career Services ... Ms. Kellie J. MCMILLEN
124 Dir of Retention & Student Success ... Ms. Jennifer C. HAWKINBERRY

American Public University System (F)

111 W Congress Street, Charles Town WV 25414-1621
County: Jefferson FICE Identification: 035393
Unit ID: 449339
Telephone: (304) 724-3700 Carnegie Class: Masters/L
FAX Number: (304) 724-3780 Calendar System: Other
URL: www.apus.edu
Established: 1991 Annual Undergrad Tuition & Fees: $7,360
Enrollment: 50,047 Coed
Affiliation or Control: Proprietary IRS Status: Proprietary
Highest Offering: Doctorate
Accreditation: HLC, ACBSP, CAHIIM, IFSAC, NURSE, PH

01 President ... Dr. Wade DYKE
10 EVP/Chief Financial Officer ... Mr. Richard SUNDERLAND, JR.
05 Provost ... Dr. Vernon SMITH
20 Assoc Prov Academic & Faculty Svcs ... Dr. Michael COTTAM
11 SVP/Chief Operating Officer ... Mr. Bob GAY
21 Vice President Finance ... Ms. Claudine STUBBLEFIELD
43 VP/University Counsel ... Ms. J.J HERBERT
26 Sr VP/Chief Marketing Officer ... Ms. Beth LAGUARDIA COOPER
15 Sr VP Human Resources/Cmty Affairs ... Ms. Amy PANZARELLA
88 Sr VP Special Projects ... Mr. Peter GIBBONS
13 Exec VP/Chief Technology Officer ... Mr. Patrik DYBERG
37 VP Financial Aid & Compliance ... Mr. Keith WELLINGS
121 VP Student Support ... Mr. J.B TANNER
21 Sr VP/Controller ... Ms. Melissa FREY
32 Asst Provost Student & Alumni Affs ... Ms. Caroline SIMPSON
06 Asst Provost/Registrar ... Ms. Michelle NEWMAN
53 Dean Academic Svcs/Sch of Education ... Dr. Conrad LOTZE
124 Dean Faculty & Student Success ... Dr. Grady BATCHELOR
90 VP Academic & Instructional Tech ... Ms. Karen V. SRBA
88 Sr VP/Chief Innovation Officer ... Ms. Amy BEVILACQUA
82 Dean Security & Global Studies ... Dr. Mark T. RICCARDI
76 Dean Health Sciences ... Dr. Brian FREELAND
81 Interim Dean STEM ... Dr. Daniel WELSCH
79 Dean Arts & Humanities ... Dr. Grace GLASS
50 Dean Business ... Dr. Marie HARPER

Appalachian Bible College (G)

161 College Drive, Mount Hope WV 25880
County: Raleigh FICE Identification: 007544
Unit ID: 237136
Telephone: (304) 877-6428 Carnegie Class: Spec-4-yr-Faith
FAX Number: N/A Calendar System: Semester
URL: abc.edu
Established: 1950 Annual Undergrad Tuition & Fees: $15,536
Enrollment: 225 Coed
Affiliation or Control: Independent Non-Profit IRS Status: 501(c)3

Highest Offering: Master's
Accreditation: HLC, BI, CAEP

01 President .... Dr. Daniel L. ANDERSON
05 Vice President for Academics .... Mr. Tim ROWE
10 Vice President for Business .... Vacant
30 Vice President for Development .... Vacant
32 Vice President for Student Services .... Rev. David E. CHILDS
42 Vice Pres for Extension Ministries .... Mr. David J. HOLLOWAY
33 Dean of Men .... Mr. Kevin GULLION
34 Dean of Women .... Mrs. Linda J. CHILDS
06 Registrar .... Mr. Tim ROWE
07 Director of Admissions .... Mr. Benjamin CALE
08 Librarian .... Mr. David W. DUNKERTON
37 Director of Financial Aid .... Mrs. Laura MARTIN
04 Admin Assistant to the President .... Miss Megan MULLINS
26 Director of Public Relations .... Miss Karisa A. CLARK

Bethany College (A)

31 E. Campus Drive, Bethany WV 26032-3002
County: Brooke FICE Identification: 003808
Unit ID: 237181
Telephone: (304) 829-7000 Carnegie Class: Bac-A&S
FAX Number: (304) 829-7700 Calendar System: 4/1/4
URL: www.bethanywv.edu
Established: 1840 Annual Undergrad Tuition & Fees: $30,840
Enrollment: 576 Coed
Affiliation or Control: Christian Church (Disciples Of Christ)
IRS Status: 501(c)3
Highest Offering: Master's
Accreditation: HLC, SW

01 President .... Dr. Tamara N. RODENBERG
05 Provost/Vice Pres Academic Affairs .... Dr. Joseph LANE
10 Vice President for Finance .... Mr. Dennis MCMASTER
111 Vice President for Advancement .... Mrs. Lori WEAVER
04 Asst to the President .... Ms. Amy VANHORN
20 Associate Provost .... Dr. Lisa REILLY
32 Vice President & Dean of Students .... Mr. Gerald STEBBINS
37 Director of Financial Aid .... Mrs. Laura DOTY
41 Director of Athletics & Recreation .... Mr. Mike WORRELL
09 Dir Institutional Research/Records .... Vacant
88 Director of McCann Learning Center .... Ms. Heather TAYLOR
124 Dir Student Engag/Responsibility .... Ms. Khali BLANKENSHIP
89 Director First Year Experience .... Dr. Scott BROTHERS
104 Director of International Programs .... Dr. Harald MENZ
36 Director of Career Services .... Ms. Amy VANHORN
23 Director of the Byrd Health Center .... Ms. Amy CUPP
26 Communications Manager .... Ms. Emily LUKE
29 Director of Alumni Engagement .... Mr. Rhone THRASH
30 Director of Advancement Services .... Ms. Shirley KEMP
88 Director of Sports Information .... Ms. Erikka SANSOM
18 Director of Physical Plant .... Mr. Jay EISENHAUER
19 Int Director of Safety & Security .... Ms. Sara DENT
15 Director of Human Resources .... Ms. Kathy BURD
39 Assistant Dean of Student Life .... Mr. Samuel GOODGE
42 Chaplain .... Vacant
08 Director of the Libraries .... Mrs. Heather MAY-RICCIUTI
06 Registrar .... Ms. Stephanie GORDON
84 Vice Pres of Enrollment Management .... Mrs. Karen HUNT
109 Director of Dining Services .... Mr. John SHAFFER
40 Manager of the Bookstore .... Mr. Dean GEORGE
38 College Counselor .... Mrs. Terri RAWSON
07 Director of Admissions .... Ms. Laura DOTY
28 Director of Diversity .... Vacant
102 Director Foundation/Corporate Rels .... Ms. Liz SHORT
105 Director Web Services .... Mr. Edward STOUGH
25 Chief Contract and Grants Administr .... Dr. Julie WILSON
44 Director Annual Giving .... Ms. Rebecca PAULS
96 Purchase Order Processor .... Ms. Michelle BOWER

Catholic Distance University (B)

300 S. George St, Charles Town WV 25414
County: Jefferson FICE Identification: 041242
Unit ID: 475398
Telephone: (304) 724-5000 Carnegie Class: Spec-4-yr-Faith
FAX Number: (304) 724-5017 Calendar System: Other
URL: www.cdu.edu
Established: 1983 Annual Undergrad Tuition & Fees: $8,405
Enrollment: 180 Coed
Affiliation or Control: Independent Non-Profit IRS Status: 501(c)3
Highest Offering: Master's
Accreditation: @HLC, DEAC, THEOL

01 President .... Dr. Marianne E. MOUNT
05 Academic Dean .... Dr. Peter BROWN
88 Dean of Catechetical Programs .... Sr. Mary Margaret SCHLATHER
06 Registrar .... Mrs. Theresa SNIDER
51 Continuing Education Support .... Mrs. Kathleen WOODDELL
26 Director of Communications .... Vacant
07 Director of Admissions .... Mrs. Carol CIULLO
37 Financial Aid Officer .... Mrs. Amy SHOUSE
13 Acting Director of Technology .... Mrs. Carol DALEY
111 Director Institutional Advancement .... Mrs. Annie HAGER
04 Admin Assistant to the President .... Ms. Mary Kate WHITE
08 Librarian .... Sr. Rebecca ABEL
10 Chief Financial/Business Officer .... Mrs. Angela RUDOLPH

Davis & Elkins College (C)

100 Campus Drive, Elkins WV 26241-3996
County: Randolph FICE Identification: 003811
Unit ID: 237358
Telephone: (304) 637-1900 Carnegie Class: Bac-Diverse
FAX Number: (304) 637-1413 Calendar System: Semester
URL: www.dewv.edu
Established: 1904 Annual Undergrad Tuition & Fees: $29,960
Enrollment: 738 Coed
Affiliation or Control: Presbyterian Church (U.S.A.) IRS Status: 501(c)3
Highest Offering: Baccalaureate
Accreditation: HLC, ADNUR, CAEP, IACBE, THEA

01 President .... Mr. Chris A. WOOD
03 Executive Vice President .... Dr. Rosemary M. THOMAS
05 Provost/Vice Pres Academic Affairs .... Dr. Robert J. PHILLIPS
111 Vice President for Inst Advancement .... Mr. Scott D. GODDARD
10 VP for Business & Administration .... Mr. Robert O. HARDMAN, II
15 Director Human Resources .... Ms. Jane COREY
06 Registrar .... Dr. Stephanie C. HAYNES
18 Director of Physical Plant .... Mr. Ryan LABROZZI
37 Director Financial Planning .... Mr. Matthew A. SUMMERS
08 Director Booth Library .... Ms. Mary Jo DEJOICE
42 Chaplain .... Rev. Laura K. BREKKE WAGONER
41 Director of Athletics .... Mr. Patrick SNIVELY
19 Director of Public Safety .... Mr. Michael JORDON
04 Executive Asst to the President .... Ms. Beth KING
13 Chief Information Officer .... Mr. Daniel Scott TERRY
29 Dir Alumni Engagement/Support .... Ms. Wendy MORGAN
110 Sr Dir Institutional Advancement .... Ms. Cathy NOSEL
26 Communications & Marketing Coord .... Ms. Linda HOWELL SKIDMORE
07 Dir of Student Recruitment/Success .... Ms. Angie SCOTT
22 Dir Affirm Action/Equal Opportunity .... Ms. Jane COREY
38 Dir Student Counseling/Wellness .... Ms. Margaret F. FALLETTA

Future Generations University (D)

400 Road Less Traveled, Franklin WV 26807-9201
County: Pendleton Identification: 666714
Unit ID: 481030
Telephone: (304) 358-2000 Carnegie Class: Spec-4-yr-Other
FAX Number: (304) 358-3008 Calendar System: Semester
URL: www.future.edu
Established: 2003 Annual Graduate Tuition & Fees: N/A
Enrollment: 41 Coed
Affiliation or Control: Independent Non-Profit IRS Status: 501(c)3
Highest Offering: Master's; No Undergraduates
Accreditation: HLC

01 President .... Dr. Daniel TAYLOR
11 Chief Operating Officer .... Stephanie HARTMAN
05 Chief Academic Officer .... Kelli FLEMING
06 Registrar .... Chris ROPER

Huntington Junior College (E)

900 Fifth Avenue, Huntington WV 25701-2004
County: Cabell FICE Identification: 009047
Unit ID: 237437
Telephone: (304) 697-7550 Carnegie Class: Spec 2-yr-Health
FAX Number: (304) 697-7554 Calendar System: Quarter
URL: www.huntingtonjuniorcollege.edu
Established: 1936 Annual Undergrad Tuition & Fees: $9,600
Enrollment: 212 Coed
Affiliation or Control: Proprietary IRS Status: Proprietary
Highest Offering: Associate Degree
Accreditation: HLC, MAC

01 President .... Carolyn A. SMITH
11 Director .... Lake TACKETT
05 Academic Affairs Director .... Linda J. WEST
10 Chief Fiscal Officer .... Sharon SNODDY
106 Director Online Learning .... Jason ANGUS

Martinsburg College (F)

341 Aikens Center, Martinsburg WV 25404
County: Berkeley Identification: 667035
Unit ID: 487977
Telephone: (304) 945-0656 Carnegie Class: Assoc/HVT-High Non
FAX Number: (866) 703-6611 Calendar System: Other
URL: www.martinsburgcollege.edu
Established: 1980 Annual Undergrad Tuition & Fees: N/A
Enrollment: 1,691 Coed
Affiliation or Control: Proprietary IRS Status: Proprietary
Highest Offering: Associate Degree
Accreditation: DEAC

01 President .... Paul VIBOCH
05 Vice Pres Academic Affairs .... Rita CLAYPOLE
07 Vice Pres of Admissions .... Laurie MAURO
10 Vice Pres of Administration .... Stella GARLICK

Mountain State College (G)

1508 Spring Street, Parkersburg WV 26101
County: Wood FICE Identification: 005008
Unit ID: 237598
Telephone: (304) 485-5487 Carnegie Class: Assoc/HVT-High Trad
FAX Number: (304) 485-3524 Calendar System: Quarter
URL: www.msc.edu
Established: 1888 Annual Undergrad Tuition & Fees: $8,215
Enrollment: 23 Coed
Affiliation or Control: Proprietary IRS Status: Proprietary
Highest Offering: Associate Degree
Accreditation: ACCSC

01 President .... Mrs. Judith SUTTON
11 Chief Operations Officer .... Mr. Kevin MERRITT
06 Registrar .... Ms. Pam RUSSELL
08 Librarian .... Mr. Roger MCCUNE
37 Dir Student Financial Svcs .... Ms. Faye WAGONER

Ohio Valley University (H)

1 Campus View Drive, Vienna WV 26105-8000
County: Wood FICE Identification: 003819
Unit ID: 237640
Telephone: (304) 865-6000 Carnegie Class: Bac-Diverse
FAX Number: (304) 865-6001 Calendar System: Semester
URL: www.ovu.edu
Established: 1958 Annual Undergrad Tuition & Fees: $22,550
Enrollment: 273 Coed
Affiliation or Control: Churches Of Christ IRS Status: 501(c)3
Highest Offering: Master's
Accreditation: #HLC, CAEP, IACBE

01 President .... Mr. Michael ROSS
05 Vice President of Academic Affairs .... Dr. Wes CRUM
113 Bursar .... Mr. Justin BOYCE
111 Exec Director University Relations .... Mr. Ryan BROOKS
18 Director of Campus Operations .... Vacant
32 Dean of Student Life .... Vacant
08 Library Director .... Ms. Sonya HESCHT
06 Registrar .... Mr. Eric MILLER
07 Director of Admissions .... Mrs. Sarah MILLER
26 Director of Marketing .... Vacant
19 Director Security/Safety .... Mr. Shawn COLLINS
37 Financial Aid Manager .... Ms. Brooke STANLEY
53 Dean College of Education .... Mrs. Kim WILE
50 Dean College of Business .... Dr. Joy JONES
49 Dean College of Arts & Sciences .... Dr. Wes CRUM
41 Athletic Director .... Vacant
29 Director of Alumni .... Mrs. Natalie BRADLEY
39 Dir Resident Life/Student Housing .... Vacant

Salem University (I)

223 W Main Street, Box 500, Salem WV 26426-0500
County: Harrison FICE Identification: 003820
Unit ID: 237783
Telephone: (304) 326-1109 Carnegie Class: Masters/S
FAX Number: (304) 326-1306 Calendar System: Semester
URL: www.salemu.edu
Established: 1888 Annual Undergrad Tuition & Fees: $16,900
Enrollment: 1,008 Coed
Affiliation or Control: Proprietary IRS Status: Proprietary
Highest Offering: Doctorate
Accreditation: HLC, ACBSP, CAEPN

01 CEO/President .... Mr. Danny D. FINUF
05 Provost .... Dr. Karen FERGUSON
04 Executive Asst to President .... Mrs. Barbara L. MCCLAIN
108 CITO/Accreditation Officer .... Dr. Cecil E. KIRKLAND
37 Dir Financial Aid & Compliance .... Vacant
13 Director of Information Technology .... Mr. Ibrahim GIRGIS
10 Chief Financial Officer .... Mr. Dan NELANT
21 Controller .... Ms. Virginia RICHARDS
18 Facilities Director & Business Mgr .... Mrs. Stephanie ROBERTS
06 Registrar .... Ms. Pamela GOFF
50 Dean of Business .... Dr. Marc D. GETTY
53 Dean of Educ & Inst Effectiveness .... Dr. Renee AITKEN
66 Director of Nursing Education .... Dr. Stephanie HOLADAY
08 Dean of Library Services .... Dr. Phyllis D. FREEDMAN
32 Dean of Student Affairs .... Dr. Dennis MCNABOE
19 Director of Campus Security .... Mr. Joseph E. SHAVER
41 Director of Athletics .... Mr. Steve POTTS
29 Director Alumni Relations .... Ms. Carolyn BACON
39 Director Student Housing .... Mr. Mark A. NESMITH

University of Charleston (J)

2300 Maccorkle Avenue, SE, Charleston WV 25304-1099
County: Kanawha FICE Identification: 003818
Unit ID: 237312
Telephone: (304) 357-4800 Carnegie Class: DU-Mod
FAX Number: (304) 357-4715 Calendar System: Semester
URL: https://www.ucwv.edu/
Established: 1888 Annual Undergrad Tuition & Fees: $32,200
Enrollment: 2,967 Coed
Affiliation or Control: Independent Non-Profit IRS Status: 501(c)3
Highest Offering: Doctorate
Accreditation: HLC, ADNUR, ARCPA, CAEP, NUR, OTA, PHAR, RAD

01 President .... Dr. Martin S. ROTH
10 EVP of Administration & CFO .... Mrs. Cleta M. HARLESS
11 EVP of Cont/Professional Educ & COO .... Dr. Jerry FORSTER
30 Vice Pres for Development .... Ms. Gail CARTER
05 EVP/Provost & Dean of Faculty .... Dr. Kim SPIEZIO
84 EVP of Enrollment Management .... Dr. Beth WOLFE
32 VP & Dean of Students .... Ms. Virginia MOORE
88 Chief Innovation Executive .... Mr. David RAMSBURG
06 Registrar .... Ms. Carol SPRADLING
26 VP Marketing & Communications .... Mr. David TRAUBE
29 Director of Alumni Relations .... Ms. Christina CARR
21 Controller .... Ms. Terri UNDERHILL
13 Chief Information Officer .... Mr. Scott TERRY

08 Director of Library Services .... Mr. John ADKINS
85 Director International Student Pgms .... Ms. Violetta PETROSYAN
37 Director Financial Aid .... Ms. Christie TOMCZYK
35 Dir of Student Involvement .... Ms. Skyler HUNT
40 Bookstore Manager .... Mr. Glenn JOHNSON
18 Director of Facilities Services .... Mr. Gary BOYD
41 VP & Athletic Director .... Dr. Bren STEVENS
09 Director of Institutional Research .... Ms. Lisa DAWKINS
50 Dean Graduate School of Business .... Dr. Scott BELLAMY
67 Dean School of Pharmacy .... Dr. Scott WESTON
49 Dean School of Arts & Sciences .... Dr. Tracy BRADLEY
76 Dean School of Health Sciences .... Dr. Mindy SMITH
04 Administrative Asst to President .... Ms. Susan LEFEW
15 Director Human Resources .... Ms. Janice GWINN
19 Director Security/Safety .... Mr. Eric SMITH
38 Director Student Counseling .... Dr. Rance BERRY
44 Director of Annual Fund .... Ms. Catherine ECKLEY

Valley College - Martinsburg Campus (A)

287 Aikens Center, Martinsburg WV 25404-6203
County: Berkeley — FICE Identification: 026094
Unit ID: 377661
Telephone: (304) 263-0979 — Carnegie Class: Spec 2-yr-Health
FAX Number: (304) 263-2413 — Calendar System: Other
URL: www.valley.edu
Established: 1983 — Annual Undergrad Tuition & Fees: N/A
Enrollment: 628 — Coed
Affiliation or Control: Proprietary — IRS Status: Proprietary
Highest Offering: Baccalaureate
Accreditation: ACCSC

01 Campus Director .... Ms. Marianela ALBERTO
05 Dir Academic Affairs-Campus Pgms .... Ms. Judy BAUSERMAN
106 Dir Academic Affairs-Online Pgms .... Ms. Shelly SMITH

*West Virginia Council for Community & Technical College Education (B)

1018 Kanawha Boulevard E, Suite 700,
Charleston WV 25301-2800
County: Kanawha — Identification: 666993
Telephone: (304) 558-0265 — Carnegie Class: N/A
FAX Number: (304) 558-1646
URL: www.wvctcs.org

01 Chancellor .... Sarah A. TUCKER

*Blue Ridge Community and Technical College (C)

13650 Apple Harvest Drive, Martinsburg WV 25403
County: Berkeley — FICE Identification: 039573
Unit ID: 446774
Telephone: (304) 260-4380 — Carnegie Class: Assoc/HT-High Non
FAX Number: (304) 260-1788 — Calendar System: Semester
URL: www.blueridgectc.edu
Established: 1974 — Annual Undergrad Tuition & Fees (In-State): $4,128
Enrollment: 3,912 — Coed
Affiliation or Control: State — IRS Status: 501(c)3
Highest Offering: Associate Degree
Accreditation: HLC, ADNUR, CAHIIM, EMT, PTAA

02 President .... Dr. Peter G. CHECKOVICH
05 Vice President of Instruction .... Ms. Laura BUSEY
103 VP Engineer/Workforce Development .... Dr. Ann M. SHIPWAY
10 Chief Finance Officer .... Dr. Randall MILLER
84 VP of Enrollment Management .... Ms. Leslie C. SEE
11 VP of Administration .... Vacant
13 Vice President of IT .... Mr. Michael BYERS
06 Registrar .... Dr. Angelic M. CUMMINGS
121 Director of Access & Success .... Ms. Brenda NEAL
37 Director of Financial Aid .... Ms. Anna CRAWFORD
18 Director of Facilities .... Mr. Larry BICKETT

*BridgeValley Community & Technical College (D)

2001 Union Carbide Drive, South Charleston WV 25303
County: Kanawha — FICE Identification: 040386
Unit ID: 484932
Telephone: (304) 205-6600 — Carnegie Class: Assoc/HVT-High Trad
FAX Number: N/A — Calendar System: Semester
URL: www.bridgevalley.edu
Established: 2014 — Annual Undergrad Tuition & Fees (In-District): $5,142
Enrollment: 1,662 — Coed
Affiliation or Control: State/Local — IRS Status: Exempt
Highest Offering: Associate Degree
Accreditation: HLC, ACBSP, ADNUR, COARC, DH, DMS, MLTAD

02 President .... Dr. Casey SACKS
05 VP of Academic Affairs .... Ms. Suzette BREEDEN
32 VP Student Affairs .... Dr. Todd JONES
103 VP Workforce .... Dr. Laura MCCULLOUGH
11 VP of Operations .... Mr. Jason STARK
10 Chief Financial Officer .... Ms. Cathy AQUINO
96 Chief Procurement Officer .... Mr. John POWELL
97 Dean of General Education .... Ms. Kristi ELLENBERG
20 Assoc VP Academic Affairs .... Vacant
84 Assoc VP of Enrollment Services .... Mr. Roy SIMMONS
35 Assoc VP of Student Engagement .... Mr. James MCDOUGLE
06 Registrar .... Mr. Jordan ATHA
15 Chief HR/Communications Ofcr .... Vacant
111 Exec Director of Inst Advancement .... Ms. Alicia SYNER
31 Director of Outreach .... Ms. Michelle WICKS
04 Exec Secretary to the President .... Ms. Amy MOORE
08 Director of Library Services .... Ms. Kaitlyn CALVERT
09 Chief Banner Officer .... Mr. James FAUVER
19 Chief of Police .... Mr. Bazra FAKHIR
88 Dean Workforce Development .... Ms. Heather RAINES
50 Dean Business/Legal/Human Svcs .... Ms. Kelly GROSE
76 Dean Allied Health/Nursing .... Mr. Kent WILSON
72 Dean Comp/Manufacture/Engr Tech .... Mr. Norm MORTENSEN
07 Director of Admissions .... Mr. Thomas CONNER, III
37 Director of Financial Aid .... Ms. Mary BLIZZARD
36 Director of Student Placement .... Ms. Judy WHIPKEY
38 Director of Counseling Services .... Ms. Carla BLANKENBUEHLER
18 Chf Facilities/Physical Plant Ofcr .... Mr. George BOSSIE

*Eastern West Virginia Community and Technical College (E)

316 Eastern Drive, Moorefield WV 26836-1155
County: Hardy — FICE Identification: 041190
Unit ID: 438708
Telephone: (304) 434-8000 — Carnegie Class: Assoc/HT-High Non
FAX Number: (304) 434-7000 — Calendar System: Semester
URL: www.easternwv.edu
Established: 1999 — Annual Undergrad Tuition & Fees (In-State): $3,888
Enrollment: 374 — Coed
Affiliation or Control: State — IRS Status: Exempt
Highest Offering: Associate Degree
Accreditation: HLC, ADNUR

02 President .... Dr. Charles TERRELL
11 Exec Dean for Administrative Svcs .... Mr. John GALATIC
05 Dean for Teaching & Learning .... Mr. Curtis HAKALA
32 Dean of Student Access & Success .... Ms. Monica WILSON
04 President's Office Administrator .... Mr. Michael O'LEARY
13 Chief Information Technology Office .... Mr. Ronald HAMILTON
15 Human Resources Assistant III .... M. Jaennae SNYDER

*Mountwest Community and Technical College (F)

One Mountwest Way, Huntington WV 25701
County: Cabell — FICE Identification: 040414
Unit ID: 444954
Telephone: (304) 710-3140 — Carnegie Class: Assoc/HVT-Mix Trad/Non
FAX Number: (000) 000-0000 — Calendar System: Semester
URL: www.mctc.edu
Established: 1975 — Annual Undergrad Tuition & Fees (In-District): $4,464
Enrollment: 1,292 — Coed
Affiliation or Control: State/Local — IRS Status: 501(c)3
Highest Offering: Associate Degree
Accreditation: HLC, ACBSP, CAHIIM, EMT, MAC, PTAA

02 President .... Dr. Josh BAKER
05 Vice President of Academic Affairs .... Mr. Michael MCCOMAS
10 Vice President of Finance/CFO .... Mr. Derek ADKINS
15 VP of Student Services & HR .... Ms. Mesha SHAMBLIN

*New River Community and Technical College (G)

280 University Drive, Beaver WV 25813
County: Raleigh — FICE Identification: 039603
Unit ID: 447582
Telephone: (304) 929-5450 — Carnegie Class: Assoc/HVT-Mix Trad/Non
FAX Number: (304) 929-5478 — Calendar System: Semester
URL: www.newriver.edu
Established: 2003 — Annual Undergrad Tuition & Fees (In-State): $4,372
Enrollment: 1,053 — Coed
Affiliation or Control: State — IRS Status: 501(c)3
Highest Offering: Associate Degree
Accreditation: HLC, EMT, MLTAD, @PTAA

02 President .... Dr. Bonny COPENHAVER
04 Exec Secretary to the President .... Ms. Lori A. MIDKIFF
05 Vice Pres Academic/Student Affairs .... Vacant
13 VP Information Technology Services .... Dr. David J. AYERSMAN
32 Dean of Student Services .... Mr. Pete HOEMAN
15 Director Human Resources .... Ms. Stephanie ADKINS
26 Director of Communications .... Ms. Jenni CANTERBURY
12 Campus Director/Community Outreach .... Mr. Robert QUEEN
12 Campus Director/Community Outreach .... Mr. Roger D. GRIFFITH
06 Registrar .... Ms. Janelle SCHOFIELD
08 Staff Librarian .... Mr. Robert H. COSTON
37 Director of Financial Aid .... Ms. Patricia HARMON
96 Director of Purchasing .... Ms. Twana JACKSON
10 Int VP of Finance/Administration .... Mr. Gerald SHIELDS
18 Director of Physical Plant .... Mr. Robert RUNION
84 Director of Enrollment Services .... Ms. Tracy L. EVANS
103 Interim Dean of Workforce/Tech .... Mr. Brian SAMPSON
88 Dean of Transfer/Pre-Profession Pgm .... Ms. Wendy PATRIQUIN

*Pierpont Community & Technical College (H)

500 Galliher Drive, Fairmont WV 26554
County: Marion — FICE Identification: 040385
Unit ID: 443492
Telephone: (304) 367-4692 — Carnegie Class: Assoc/HVT-Mix Trad/Non
FAX Number: (304) 367-4881 — Calendar System: Semester
URL: www.pierpont.edu
Established: 1974 — Annual Undergrad Tuition & Fees (In-State): $4,986
Enrollment: 1,613 — Coed
Affiliation or Control: State — IRS Status: 501(c)3
Highest Offering: Associate Degree
Accreditation: HLC, ACFEI, CAHIIM, #COARC, @DIETT, EMT, MLTAD, NAIT, PTAA

01 President .... Dr. Johnny M. MOORE
04 Exec Assistant to the President .... Mrs. Cyndee K. SENSIBAUGH
05 Provost/VP for Academic Affairs .... Mr. Michael P. WAIDE
10 VP for Finance and Administration .... Mr. Dale R. BRADLEY
111 VP for Organization and Development .... Mr. Stephen E. LEACH
32 VP Student Services .... Mrs. Lyla D. GRANDSTAFF
50 Dean Sch of Bus/Aviation/Tech .... Dr. Kari COFFINDAFFER
76 Dean School of Health Sciences .... Vacant
97 Dean School Gen Educ/Business Dev .... Mr. David BEIGHLEY
13 Exec Dir InfoTech/Elearning .... Ms. Robin STRADER
07 Director of Admissions .... Mr. John DAVIS
101 Secretary of the Institution/Board .... Mrs. Cyndee K. SENSIBAUGH
37 Director Student Financial Aid .... Mrs. Ashley TENNANT

*Southern West Virginia Community and Technical College (I)

P. O. Box 2900, Mount Gay WV 25637-2900
County: Logan — FICE Identification: 003816
Unit ID: 237817
Telephone: (304) 792-7098 — Carnegie Class: Assoc/MT-VT-High Trad
FAX Number: (304) 792-7046 — Calendar System: Semester
URL: www.southernwv.edu
Established: 1971 — Annual Undergrad Tuition & Fees (In-State): $4,084
Enrollment: 1,474 — Coed
Affiliation or Control: State — IRS Status: 501(c)3
Highest Offering: Associate Degree
Accreditation: HLC, ADNUR, COARC, EMT, MLTAD, RAD, SURGT

00 Board of Governors Chair .... Dr. Lisa J. HADDOX-HESTON
02 President .... Dr. Pamela L. ALDERMAN
10 Chief Finance Officer .... Mr. Samuel M. LITTERAL
05 VP for Academic Affairs .... Dr. Tracey A. HUMAN
32 Exec Dir Student Services .... Dr. Charles A. LOPEZ
103 Exec Dir Econ & Workforce Dev .... Mr. Allyn S. BARKER
13 Chief Information Officer .... Mr. Tom COOK
111 Exec Dir Institutional Advance/Mktg .... Ms. Rita G. ROBERSON
07 Dir Admissions/Student Life .... Mr. Darrell TAYLOR
15 Human Resources Director .... Mr. James D. KENNEDY
18 Dir of Facilities/Campus Operations .... Mr. Joe LINVILLE
04 Exec Asst to President & BOG .... Ms. Emma L. BAISDEN
09 Dir Institutional Research .... Mr. Charles SCOTT
12 Director Wyoming Campus Operations .... Mr. David LORD
12 Dir Williamson Campus Operations .... Vacant
124 Dir of Advising & Retention .... Mr. Timothy D. OOTEN
06 Registrar .... Ms. Teri WELLS
37 Dir Student Financial Assistance .... Ms. Stella ESTEPP
08 Director of Libraries .... Ms. Kimberly L. MAYNARD
108 Dir Accreditation & Assessment .... Mr. Thomas MORRIS
22 Dir Affirmative Action/EEO .... Mr. James D. KENNEDY

*West Virginia Northern Community College (J)

1704 Market Street, Wheeling WV 26003-3643
County: Ohio — FICE Identification: 009054
Unit ID: 238014
Telephone: (304) 233-5900 — Carnegie Class: Assoc/HVT-High Non
FAX Number: (304) 232-4651 — Calendar System: Semester
URL: www.wvncc.edu
Established: 1972 — Annual Undergrad Tuition & Fees (In-State): $4,317
Enrollment: 1,253 — Coed
Affiliation or Control: State — IRS Status: 501(c)3
Highest Offering: Associate Degree
Accreditation: HLC, ACFEI, ADNUR, CAHIIM, MAC, RAD, SURGT

02 President .... Dr. Daniel MOSSER
05 Provost .... Dr. Jill LOVELESS
10 CFO & VP Administrative Services .... Vacant
32 Vice President Student Services .... Mrs. Janet FIKE
09 VP of Institutional Research .... Dr. Pam SHARMA
26 Director of Marketing & PR .... Mr. David BARNHARDT
18 Director of Facilities .... Ms. Trish MARKER
15 Director of Human Resources .... Mr. Robert BRAK
103 VP of Economic & Workforce Dev .... Dr. Phil KLEIN
102 Director of the Foundation .... Ms. Rana SPURLOCK
04 Executive Asst to President .... Ms. Stephanie KAPPEL

*_New River Community and Technical College Greenbrier Valley Campus_ (K)

653 Church Street, Lewisburg WV 24901-1303
Telephone: (304) 647-6560 — Identification: 770468
Accreditation: &HLC

*** New River Community and Technical College Mercer County Campus** (A)
1001 Mercer Street, Princeton WV 24740-8230
Telephone: (304) 425-5858 Identification: 770469
Accreditation: &HLC

*** New River Community and Technical College Nicholas County Campus** (B)
6101 Webster Road, Summersville WV 26651
Telephone: (304) 872-1236 Identification: 770470
Accreditation: &HLC

*** Southern West Virginia Community and Technical College-Boone/Lincoln Campus** (C)
3505 Daniel Boone Parkway, Suite A,
Foster WV 25081-8126
Telephone: (304) 369-2952 Identification: 770471
Accreditation: &HLC

*** Southern West Virginia Community and Technical College-Williamson Campus** (D)
1601 Armory Drive, Williamson WV 25661
Telephone: (304) 235-6046 Identification: 770473
Accreditation: &HLC, COARC

*** Southern West Virginia Community and Technical College-Wyoming/McDowell Campus** (E)
128 College Drive, Saulsville WV 25876
Telephone: (304) 294-8346 Identification: 770472
Accreditation: &HLC

*** West Virginia Northern Community College** (F)
141 Main Street, New Martinsville WV 26155
Telephone: (304) 455-4684 Identification: 770474
Accreditation: &HLC

*** West Virginia Northern Community College** (G)
150 Park Avenue, Weirton WV 26062
Telephone: (304) 723-2210 Identification: 770475
Accreditation: &HLC

* West Virginia Higher Education Policy Commission (H)
1018 Kanawha Boulevard E, Ste 700,
Charleston WV 25301-2887
County: Kanawha FICE Identification: 033440
Telephone: (304) 558-2101 Carnegie Class: N/A
FAX Number: (304) 558-5719
URL: www.wvhepc.edu

01 Chancellor .... Dr. Sarah TUCKER
88 Chancellor WV Cmty/Tech Col System .... Dr. Sarah TUCKER
46 Senior Director Science Research .... Dr. Julie SERAFIN
05 Vice Chancellor for Academic Affs .... Dr. Corley DENNISON
10 Vice Chancellor for Finance .... Dr. Edward MAGEE
15 Vice Chancellor for Human Resources ..... Ms. Trish HUMPHRIES
32 Senior Director of Student Services .... Ms. Elizabeth MANUEL
26 Senior Director of Communications .... Ms. Jessica TICE
43 General Counsel .... Ms. Kristin BOGGS
11 Exec Vice Chancellor Administration .... Mr. Matt TURNER
45 Senior Director Policy & Planning .... Dr. Chris TREADWAY
37 Senior Director of Financial Aid .... Mr. Brian WEINGART
88 Director Administrative Services .... Ms. Cindy L. ANDERSON

* Bluefield State College (I)
219 Rock Street, Bluefield WV 24701-2198
County: Mercer FICE Identification: 003809
Unit ID: 237215
Telephone: (304) 327-4000 Carnegie Class: Bac-Diverse
FAX Number: (304) 325-7747 Calendar System: Semester
URL: www.bluefieldstate.edu
Established: 1895 Annual Undergrad Tuition & Fees (In-State): $7,680
Enrollment: 1,243 Coed
Affiliation or Control: State IRS Status: 501(c)3
Highest Offering: Baccalaureate
Accreditation: HLC, ACBSP, ADNUR, CAEP, CAEPN, NURSE, RAD

02 President .... Dr. Robin CAPEHART
03 Executive Vice President .... Mr. Brent BENJAMIN
05 VP of Academic Affairs/Provost .... Dr. Ted LEWIS
10 Chief Financial Officer .... Mr. J. Ronald HYPES
32 Dean of Students .... Mr. Ronald SHIDEMANTLE
27 VP of Media Relations .... Mr. Jim NELSON
06 Registrar .... Vacant
08 Director Library Services .... Mr. David MCMILLAN
13 Chief Technology Officer .... Mr. John SPENCER, JR.
26 VP of Marketing .... Mr. Ansel PONDER
15 VP of Human Resources .... Ms. Jonette AUGHENBAUGH
19 Director Public Safety .... Vacant
38 Director of Counseling .... Dr. Cravor JONES
29 Director Alumni Affairs .... Ms. Deirdre GUYTON
40 Manager Bookstore .... Ms. Susan PLUMLEY
41 Athletic Director .... Mr. Derrick PRICE
50 Interim Dean School of Business .... Mrs. Karen GROGAN
54 Dean of STEM .... Vacant
53 Dean of Educ/Humanities/Social Sci .... Dr. Shelia SARGENT-MARTIN
66 Dean School Nursing/Allied Health .... Ms. Angela LAMBERT
66 ADN Program Director .... Ms. Sandra WYNN
66 BSN Program Director .... Ms. Carol COFER
88 Program Dir of Radiologic Tech .... Ms. Melissa HAYE
96 Director of Purchasing .... Mr. Paul RUTHERFORD
04 Exec Secretary to the President .... Ms. Jeanne MORICLE
100 Chief of Staff .... Mr. Keith OLSON
18 Director of Physical Plant .... Vacant
104 Director Study Abroad .... Dr. Sudhakar R. JAMKHANDI
108 Director Institutional Assessment .... Dr. Sarita A. RHONEMUS
84 Director Enrollment Management .... Vacant

* Concord University (J)
PO Box 1000, Athens WV 24712-1000
County: Mercer FICE Identification: 003810
Unit ID: 237330
Telephone: (304) 384-3115 Carnegie Class: Masters/M
FAX Number: (304) 384-9044 Calendar System: Semester
URL: www.concord.edu
Established: 1872 Annual Undergrad Tuition & Fees (In-State): $8,385
Enrollment: 1,807 Coed
Affiliation or Control: State IRS Status: 501(c)3
Highest Offering: Master's
Accreditation: HLC, ACBSP, CAATE, CAEP, SW

02 President & CEO .... Dr. Kendra BOGGESS
05 VP & Academic Dean .... Dr. Edward HUFFSTETLER
111 VP for Advancement .... Mrs. Alicia BESENYEI
20 Associate Dean .... Dr. Kathy LIPTAK
32 VP Student Affairs .... Dr. Sarah BEASLEY
10 VP for Business & Finance .... Mr. John GALATIC
15 VP of Operations .... Mr. Daniel FITZPATRICK
13 Chief Info Technology Officer .... Mr. Cayce WILL
06 Registrar .... Mrs. Susie LUSK
08 Director of the Library .... Ms. Elizabeth CHANDLER
37 Director of Student Financial Aid .... Mrs. Tammy BROWN
29 Director Alumni & Donor Relations .... Ms. Sarah TURNER
88 Director Bonner Scholars Program .... Mrs. Kathy BALL
18 Director Physical Plant .... Mr. Gerry VON VILLE
19 Director of Public Safety .... Chief Mark STELLA
36 Director of Career Services .... Mr. Phil LEWIS
40 Bookstore Manager .... Mrs. Sheila CONNER
41 Athletic Director .... Mr. Kevin GARRETT
21 Financial Reporting Officer .... Ms. Elizabeth J. CAHILL-MUSICK
24 Ctr for Academic Technologies .... Mr. Steve MEADOWS
25 Director of Grants and Contracts .... Mrs. Melanie FARMER
12 Director of the Beckley Center .... Dr. Susan WILLIAMS
96 Contract Specialist & Business Mgr .... Ms. Andrea WEBB
121 Director of Student Success .... Dr. Sheila WOMACK
101 Exec Asst to President/BOG Liaison .... Mrs. Lora WOOLWINE
88 Program Coordinator Advancement .... Ms. Amy PITZER
110 Manager of University Advancement .... Mr. Blake FARMER
39 Asst Dean & Dir Student Housing .... Mr. Bill FRALEY
35 Asst Dean of Students .... Mr. Andrew SULGIT
04 Exec Asst to Pres Comm Liaison .... Mrs. Lindsey BYARS

* Fairmont State University (K)
1201 Locust Avenue, Fairmont WV 26554-2470
County: Marion FICE Identification: 003812
Unit ID: 237367
Telephone: (304) 367-4000 Carnegie Class: Masters/S
FAX Number: (304) 367-4789 Calendar System: Semester
URL: www.fairmontstate.edu
Established: 1865 Annual Undergrad Tuition & Fees (In-State): $7,738
Enrollment: 3,848 Coed
Affiliation or Control: State IRS Status: 501(c)3
Highest Offering: Master's
Accreditation: HLC, ACBSP, ADNUR, CAEP, NURSE

02 President FSU .... Dr. Mirta M. MARTIN
05 Provost/VP Academic Affairs .... Dr. Dianna PHILLIPS
10 Vice Pres Finance & Administration ..Ms. Christa KWIATKOWSKI
32 Vice Pres Student Success .... Mr. Kenneth FETTIG
15 VP Human/Legal Affs & Gen Counsel .... Dr. Jacqueline SIKORA
13 VP IT & Chief Info Technology (CIO) .... Dr. Joy A. HATCH
26 VP Univ Relations & Marketing .... Mrs. Lyndsey DUGAN
108 VP Inst Effectiveness & Strat Ops .... Ms. Merri S. INCITTI
18 Asst Vice Pres for Facilities .... Vacant
06 Registrar .... Mrs. Lori SCHOONMAKER
20 Executive Director Academic Program .... Dr. Susan ROSS
49 Dean College of Liberal Arts .... Dr. Christopher KAST
72 Dean College of Science/Tech .... Dr. Steven E. ROOF
50 Dean College of Business & Aviation .... Dr. Timothy R. OXLEY
53 Dean College Educ/Hlth/Hum Perf .... Dr. Amanda METCALF
57 Dean School of Fine Arts .... Vacant
66 Dean College of Nursing .... Dr. Laura H. CLAYTON
14 Deputy CIO .... Mr. Colton GRIFFIN
91 Manager IT Strategic Operations .... Mr. George HERRICK
09 Director Institutional Research .... Mr. Jacob R. ABRAMS
124 Dir Student Retention Initiatives .... Mr. Corey HUNT
41 Director of Athletics .... Mr. Greg BAMBERGER
19 Chief of Police & Dir Emerg Mgmt .... Mr. Matthew SWAIN
38 Dir of Counseling .... Ms. Andrea M. PAMMER
37 Exec Dir Student Support Services .... Ms. Tresa WEIMER
39 Exec Dir Res/Stdnt Life .... Ms. Alicia KALKA
08 Interim Director Library Services .... Ms. Sharon MAZURE
96 Director of Procurement .... Ms. Monica J. COCHRAN
36 Exec Dir Academic & Career Success .... Dr. John DEVAULT
23 Director of Student Health Services .... Ms. Chelsie COLLINS
25 Director of Planning and Grants .... Mrs. Amantha L. COLE
90 Sr Director Banner Administration .... Dr. Senta CHMIEL
119 Chief Technology Officer .... Mr. Jon DODDS
07 Sr Director of Recruitment .... Mr. Chris SHARPS
100 Chief of Staff .... Mrs. Serena SCULLY
104 Director Study Abroad .... Vacant
43 University General Counsel .... Mrs. Jacqueline L. SIKORA

* Glenville State College (L)
200 High Street, Glenville WV 26351-1292
County: Gilmer FICE Identification: 003813
Unit ID: 237385
Telephone: (304) 462-7361 Carnegie Class: Bac-Diverse
FAX Number: (304) 462-7610 Calendar System: Semester
URL: www.glenville.edu
Established: 1872 Annual Undergrad Tuition & Fees (In-State): $7,886
Enrollment: 1,583 Coed
Affiliation or Control: State IRS Status: 501(c)3
Highest Offering: Baccalaureate
Accreditation: HLC, CAEP, CAEPN

02 President .... Dr. Mark A. MANCHIN
05 Provost/Vice Pres Academic Affairs .... Dr. Gary MORRIS
10 Chief Financial Officer .... Mr. Bert JEDAMSKI
41 Athletic Director .... Mr. Jesse SKILES
84 VP for Enrollment & Student Affairs .... Dr. Jason YEAGER
111 Vice President for Advancement .... Mr. David E. HUTCHISON
11 VP for Administration .... Ms. Rita HELMICK
04 Executive Assistant to President .... Ms. Teresa G. STERNS
53 Dean of Education .... Dr. Jeff C. HUNTER
15 Human Resources Director .... Ms. Tegan MCENTIRE
37 Director of Financial Aid .... Ms. Stephany HARPER
18 Exective Director of Facilities .... Mr. Tom RATCLIFF
39 Director of Residence Life .... Mr. J. Trae SPRAGUE
08 Director of Library .... Mr. Jason L. GUM
21 Controller .... Ms. Caren JENKINS
96 Director of Purchasing .... Ms. Joyce E. RIDDLE
29 Dir of Alumni Affairs/Annual Giving .... Mr. Conner FERGUSON
06 Registrar .... Ms. Ann M. REED
13 Director of Information Technology .... Mr. Jason PHARES
38 Professional Counselor .... Mr. Timothy J. UNDERWOOD
19 Associate Director of Public Safety .... Mr. Ronald K. TAYLOR
20 Assoc VP for Academic Affairs .... Dr. Mari CLEMENTS
07 Director of Admissions .... Ms. Chelsea STICKELMAN

* Marshall University (M)
1 John Marshall Drive, Huntington WV 25755-0001
County: Cabell FICE Identification: 003815
Unit ID: 237525
Telephone: (304) 696-3170 Carnegie Class: DU-Higher
FAX Number: (304) 696-6565 Calendar System: Semester
URL: www.marshall.edu
Established: 1837 Annual Undergrad Tuition & Fees (In-State): $8,512
Enrollment: 11,958 Coed
Affiliation or Control: State IRS Status: 501(c)3
Highest Offering: Doctorate
Accreditation: HLC, ADNUR, ANEST, #ARCPA, CAATE, CACREP, CAEP, CAHIIM, CLPSY, COARC, DIETD, DIETI, DMS, FEPAC, JOUR, MED, MLTAD, MT, MUS, NUR, PH, PHAR, PTA, SP, SW

02 President .... Dr. Jerome A. GILBERT
04 Admin Assistant to the President .... Ms. Cora PYLES
05 Provost/Sr VP Academic Affairs .... Dr. Jaime TAYLOR
03 Sr VP Exec Affairs & Gen Counsel .... Mr. F. Layton COTTRILL
10 Chief Financial Officer .... Mr. Mark ROBINSON
26 Senior VP Communication/Marketing ..... Ms. Virginia R. PAINTER
09 Sr VP Inst Rsrch/IT & Interim CIO ...... Mr. Michael J. MCGUFFEY
102 CEO MU Foundation Inc .... Dr. Ron AREA
11 Sr VP for Administration .... Ms. Brandi D. JACOBS
32 VP Student Affairs .... Dr. Maurice COOLEY
46 VP Research .... Mr. John MAHER
30 Vice President Development .... Mr. Lance WEST
20 Assoc VP Academic Affairs .... Dr. Sherri SMITH
108 Assoc VP Assessment .... Dr. Mary Beth REYNOLDS
28 Assoc VP Intercultural Affairs .... Vacant
08 Asst VP Libraries & Online Learning .... Dr. Monica BROOKS
14 Chief Technology Officer .... Mr. Allen TAYLOR
119 Chief Information Security Officer .... Mr. Jon CUTLER
07 Dean of Admissions .... Dr. Tammy JOHNSON
37 Dir Student Financial Aid .... Dr. Beverly BOGGS
15 Director Human Resource Services .... Mr. Bruce B. FELDER
16 Associate Human Resources Officer .... Ms. Mary CHAPMAN
06 Registrar .... Dr. Sonja G. CANTRELL
113 Bursar .... Mr. Barry BECKETT
63 Dean of Medicine .... Dr. Joseph I. SHAPIRO
53 Dean College of Education .... Dr. Teresa EAGLE
49 Dean College Liberal Arts .... Dr. Robert BOOKWALTER
50 Dean College of Business .... Dr. Avinandan MUKHERJEE
57 Interim Dean College Arts & Media .... Dr. Wendell DOBBS
67 Dean School of Pharmacy .... Dr. Gayle A. BRAZEAU
66 Dean College of Health Prof .... Dr. Michael PREWITT
54 Dean Col of Engr/Comp Sci .... Dr. David DAMPIER
81 Dean College of Science .... Dr. Charles SOMERVILLE

92 Dean Honors College ... Dr. Nicola LOCASCIO
41 Director of Athletics ... Mr. Mike HAMRICK
29 Executive Director Alumni Relations ... Mr. Matthew D. HAYES
39 Director Residence Services ... Ms. Mistie BIBBEE
36 Director Career Services ... Ms. Cristina C. MCDAVID
19 Director of Public Safety ... Mr. James E. TERRY
22 Director Equity Programs ... Ms. Debra HART
96 Director of Purchasing ... Ms. Angela WHITE NEGLEY
18 Director Physical Plant ... Mr. Travis BAILEY
114 Budget Director ... Ms. Katrina ESKINS
43 Assoc General Counsel ... Ms. Jendonnae HOUDYSCHELL
86 Asst to Pres for External Liaison ... Mr. William BURDETTE

*Shepherd University (A)

PO Box 5000, Shepherdstown WV 25443-5000
County: Jefferson — FICE Identification: 003822
Unit ID: 237792
Telephone: (304) 876-5000 — Carnegie Class: Bac-A&S
FAX Number: (304) 876-3101 — Calendar System: Semester
URL: www.shepherd.edu
Established: 1871 — Annual Undergrad Tuition & Fees (In-State): $7,784
Enrollment: 3,159 — Coed
Affiliation or Control: State — IRS Status: 501(c)3
Highest Offering: Doctorate
Accreditation: HLC, ART, CAEP, CAPRT, IACBE, MUS, NURSE, SW

02 President ... Dr. Mary HENDRIX
05 Interim Provost ... Dr. Ben MARTZ
10 Vice President Finance ... Ms. Pam STEVENS
32 Vice President for Student Affairs ... Ms. Holly FRYE
84 Vice President for Enrollment Mgmt ... Dr. Kelly HART
43 General Counsel ... Mr. K. Alan PERDUE
11 Assoc VP Campus Services ... Mr. Jack SHAW
81 Dean College of STEM ... Dr. Robert WARBURTON
79 Dean Col Arts/Humanities/Social Sci ... Dr. Robert TUDOR
50 Dean College of Business ... Dr. Ben MARTZ
66 Dean Col of Nursing/Educ/Health ... Dr. Sharon MAILEY
58 Dean School of Grad/Prof Studies ... Dr. Richie STEVENS
26 Exec Director Univ Communications ... Ms. Dana COSTA
09 Director Institutional Research ... Ms. Sara MAENE
39 Director Residence Life ... Dr. Elizabeth SECHLER
15 Director Human Resources ... Dr. Marie DEWALT
13 Director Info Technology Services ... Mr. Joey DAGG
06 Registrar ... Ms. Tracy SEFFERS
07 Director of Admissions ... Ms. Kristen LORENZ
37 Director of Financial Aid ... Ms. Joyce CABRAL
19 Interim Univ Police Chief ... Ms. Lori MARAUGHA
53 Director Teacher Education ... Dr. Jennifer PENLAND
18 Physical Plant Manager ... Ms. Shelley SHAFFER
41 Vice President for Athletics ... Mr. Chauncey WINBUSH
96 Director of Procurement Services ... Ms. Debra LANGFORD
38 Director of Counseling ... Ms. Shanan SPENCER
29 Director of Alumni Affairs ... Ms. Katie GORDON
92 Director Honors Program ... Dr. Mark CANTRELL
30 Executive Director of Development ... Ms. Sherri JANELLE
104 Director International Affairs ... Dr. Lois JARMAN
25 Dir of Office of Sponsored Programs ... Ms. Madge MORNINGSTAR
08 Interim Co-Dean Library/CTL ... Dr. Amy DEWITT
08 Interim Co-Dean Library/CTL ... Dr. Christy WENGER
04 Executive Asst to the President ... Mrs. Sonya SHOLLEY
44 Director of Annual Giving ... Ms. Christine MEYER
102 EVP Shepherd University Foundation ... Ms. Monica LINGENFELTER
105 Dr Marketing & Digital Strategies ... Vacant
22 Dir Social Equity/Inclus/Title IX ... Ms. Annie LEWIN
28 AVP Diversity/Equity/Inclusion ... Dr. Chiquita HOWARD-BOSTIC

*West Liberty University (B)

208 University Drive, West Liberty WV 26074
County: Ohio — FICE Identification: 003823
Unit ID: 237932
Telephone: (304) 336-5000 — Carnegie Class: Masters/S
FAX Number: (304) 336-8403 — Calendar System: Semester
URL: www.westliberty.edu
Established: 1837 — Annual Undergrad Tuition & Fees (In-State): $8,150
Enrollment: 2,481 — Coed
Affiliation or Control: State — IRS Status: 501(c)3
Highest Offering: Master's
Accreditation: HLC, ARCPA, #CAATE, CAEP, DH, IACBE, MT, MUS, NURSE, SW

02 President ... Dr. W. Franklin EVANS
05 Interim Provost ... Dr. Bonnie SUDERMAN
32 VP of Student Svcs & Enrollment Mgt ... Mr. Scott A. COOK
10 Executive Vice President & CFO ... Ms. Lori HUDSON
81 Dean College of Sciences ... Dr. Karen KETTLER
49 Dean College Liberal/Creative Arts ... Dr. Cecelia KONCHAR-FARR
53 Dean College of Education ... Dr. Catherine MONTEROSO
66 Director of Nursing Programs ... Dr. Rose M. KUTLENIOS
50 Dean College of Business ... Dr. Ann SAURBIER
39 Exec Dir Housing & Student Life ... Ms. Marcella T. SNYDER
15 Chief Human Resources Officer ... Ms. Diana L. HARTO
13 Chief Information Officer ... Mr. Joseph RODELLA
09 Dir of University Effectiveness ... Vacant
41 Director of Athletics ... Mr. Lynn ULLOM
07 Exec Dir Admissions & Recruitment ... Ms. Brenda M. KING
51 Director of Cont Educ/Special Pgm ... Vacant
08 Director of Library ... Vacant
29 Executive Director of Alumni ... Mr. Ron A. WITT
37 Director Financial Aid ... Mrs. Katie R. COOPER
111 VP of External Affairs ... Mr. Jason W. KOEGLER

109 Director of Auxiliary Services ... Vacant
38 Director of Counseling ... Mr. Christopher A. MCPHERSON
92 Director of the Honors Program ... Dr. Shannon D. HALICKI
88 Director Dental Hygiene Programs ... Ms. Stephanie MEREDITH
88 Dir Clinical Lab Science Program ... Dr. Lisa JORDAN
23 Director of Health Services ... Ms. Cheryl C. BENNINGTON
88 Dir Physician Assistant Program ... Dr. William A. CHILDERS, JR.
85 Coord International Student Rec ... Ms. Mihaela SZABO
26 Executive Director of Marketing ... Ms. Tammi SECRIST
101 Secretary of the Institution/Board ... Ms. Mary A. EDWARDS
105 Web Master ... Mr. Thomas ESTLACK
106 Dir Online Education/E-learning ... Ms. Lucy KEFAUVER
18 Director of Physical Plant ... Mr. Joe MILLS
19 Chief of Police/Dir Public Safety ... Mr. Ronald E. FOX
96 Director of Purchasing ... Mr. Patrick KELLY
06 Registrar ... Ms. Stephanie M. NORTH
102 Executive Director Foundation ... Ms. Angela ZAMBITO-HILL
04 Admin Assistant to the President ... Ms. Mary Ann EDWARDS
25 Chief Contract & Grants Admin ... Ms. Laura MUSILLI
104 Director Study Abroad ... Dr. Felipe E. ROJAS
43 Dir Legal Services (General Counsel ... Ms. Stephanie HOOPER
28 Dir of Diversity/Strategic Init ... Mr. Shemrico STANLEY

*West Virginia School of Osteopathic Medicine (C)

400 Lee Street North, Lewisburg WV 24901-1196
County: Greenbrier — FICE Identification: 011245
Unit ID: 237880
Telephone: (304) 645-6270 — Carnegie Class: Spec-4-yr-Med
FAX Number: (304) 645-4859 — Calendar System: Semester
URL: www.wvsom.edu
Established: 1972 — Annual Graduate Tuition & Fees: N/A
Enrollment: 800 — Coed
Affiliation or Control: State — IRS Status: 501(c)3
Highest Offering: First Professional Degree; No Undergraduates
Accreditation: HLC, OSTEO

01 President ... Dr. James W. NEMITZ
05 Vice Pres Academic Affairs & Dean ... Dr. Linda BOYD
10 Vice Pres Finance & Facilities ... Larry WARE
11 Vice Pres for Administration ... Dr. Edward BRIDGES
43 Vice Pres Legal/Govt Affairs ... Jeffrey SHAWVER
15 Vice Pres of Human Resources ... Leslie BICKSLER
26 Vice Pres Marketing & Communication ... Vacant
103 VP Community Engagement & Devel ... Dr. Drema MACE
58 Assoc Dean Graduate Medical Educ ... Dr. Victoria SHUMAN
20 Assoc Dean Preclinical Education ... Dr. Roy RUSS
20 Assoc Dean Research & Spons Pgms ... Dr. Jandy HANNA
108 Assoc Dean Assessment/Educ Devel ... Dr. Machelle LINSENMEYER
20 Asst Dean Osteopathic Medical Educ ... Dr. Robert FOSTER
32 Assistant Dean Student Affairs ... Dr. Rebecca MORROW
13 Chief Technology Officer ... Kimberly RANSOM
16 Director of Human Resources ... Tiffany BURNS
06 Registrar ... Jennifer SEAMS
37 Director Financial Aid ... Lisa SPENCER
30 Development Dir/WVSOM Foundation ... Vacant
29 Director of Alumni Relations ... Shannon WARREN
07 Director of Admissions ... Ronnie COLLINS
96 Director of Contracts ... Betty BAKER
08 Director of Library ... Mary ESSIG
24 Director of Media Services ... Michael FOWLER
18 Director of Physical Plant ... William ALDER
35 Director of Student Life ... Belinda EVANS
09 Coordinator Institutional Research ... Lance RIDPATH
40 Business Manager/Bookstore ... Cindi KNIGHT
21 Director of Finance ... Stella DODRILL

*West Virginia State University (D)

PO Box 1000, Institute WV 25112-1000
County: Kanawha — FICE Identification: 003826
Unit ID: 237899
Telephone: (304) 766-3000 — Carnegie Class: Bac-Diverse
FAX Number: (304) 720-2075 — Calendar System: Semester
URL: www.wvstateu.edu
Established: 1891 — Annual Undergrad Tuition & Fees (In-State): $8,437
Enrollment: 3,638 — Coed
Affiliation or Control: State — IRS Status: 501(c)3
Highest Offering: Master's
Accreditation: HLC, ACBSP, CAEPN, SW

02 Acting President ... Mr. Ericke S. CAGE
10 VP for Business and Finance ... Ms. Christina DALTON
05 Int Provost/VP for Academic Affairs ... Dr. J. Paige CARNEY
84 VP Enroll Mgmt/Student Affairs ... Vacant
111 VP for University Advancement ... Ms. Patricia J. SCHUMANN
20 Assoc Prov/AVP Academic Affairs ... Vacant
100 VP/Chief of Staff ... Mr. Ericke S. CAGE
46 VP for Research & Public Service ... Dr. Jose TOLEDO
79 Dean Col of Arts & Humanities ... Dr. Robert WALLACE
81 Dean Col of Natural Sci/Math ... Dr. Naveed ZAMAN
107 Dean Col of Prof Studies ... Dr. J. Paige CARNEY
50 Dean Col of Business/Social Science ... Vacant
26 Assistant VP of Comm & Marketing ... Mr. Jack BAILEY
13 Director of Information Technology ... Mr. Alan SKIDMORE
18 Int Director Physical Facilities ... Mr. Dayton WILSON
06 Director Records & Registration ... Vacant
19 Director of Public Safety ... Vacant
15 Asst VP Human Resource ... Vacant
08 Director of Drain-Jordan Library ... Dr. Willette STINSON

37 Int Dir Student Financial Asst ... Ms. Gwen BAUSLEY
29 Director of Alumni Relations ... Ms. Belinda FULLER
36 Dir of Career Services & Coop Educ ... Vacant
07 Director of Admissions ... Vacant
89 Coordinator of New Student Programs ... Vacant
96 Director of Purchasing ... Vacant
106 Dir of Center for Online Learning ... Dr. Thomas KIDDIE
41 Athletic Director ... Vacant
39 Dir of Housing and Residence Life ... Mr. Derrien WILLIAMS
04 Exec Assistant to the President ... Ms. Crystal WALKER
32 AVP Student Affairs/Student Life ... Mr. Joe ODEN, JR.
86 Director Government Relations ... Vacant

*West Virginia University (E)

1500 University Avenue, PO Box 6201, Morgantown WV 26506
County: Monongalia — FICE Identification: 003827
Unit ID: 238032
Telephone: (304) 293-0111 — Carnegie Class: DU-Highest
FAX Number: (304) 293-5883 — Calendar System: Semester
URL: www.wvu.edu
Established: 1867 — Annual Undergrad Tuition & Fees (In-State): $8,976
Enrollment: 26,269 — Coed
Affiliation or Control: State — IRS Status: 501(c)3
Highest Offering: Doctorate
Accreditation: HLC, ABAI, ANEST, #ARCPA, ART, AUD, CAATE, CACREP, CAEP, CEA, CLPSY, COPSY, DENT, DH, DIETD, DIETI, DMS, FEPAC, HT, IPSY, JOUR, LAW, LSAR, MED, MT, MUS, NMT, NURSE, OT, PA, PAST, PH, PHAR, PTA, RAD, RADMAG, RTT, SP, SPAA, SW, THEA

02 President/Chief Exec Officer ... Mr. E. Gordon GEE
05 Provost & VP Acad Affairs ... Ms. Maryanne REED
10 VP & CFO ... Ms. Paula CONGELIO
26 Vice Pres for University Relations ... Ms. Sharon L. MARTIN
17 Vice Pres/Exec Dean Health Science ... Dr. Clay B. MARSH
32 Vice President Student Affairs ... Vacant
46 Vice President for Research ... Mr. Fred L. KING
102 President & CEO WVU Found ... Ms. Cindi ROTH
15 VP for Talent & Culture ... Mr. Cris DEBORD
20 Vice Provost Academic Affairs ... Dr. Paul KREIDER
20 Assoc Provost Academic Personnel ... Dr. Presha NEIDERMEYER
88 Director Research & Rural Health ... Ms. Sandra Y. POPE
100 Senior Advisor to President ... Mr. John J. COLE
22 Sr Advsr to Pres Diversity/Cmty OR ... Mr. David M. FRYSON
88 Exec Officer for Policy Development ... Dr. Jennifer L. FISHER
45 VP Strategic Initiatives ... Mr. Rob ALSOP
28 VP Diversity Equity & Inclusion ... Ms. Meshea L. POORE
29 VP Alumni Rels/CEO Alumni Assn ... Mr. Sean FRISBEE
21 Assoc Vice Pres for Finance ... Ms. Anjali HALABE
56 Int Dean & Director Extension Svcs ... Dr. Jorge ATILES
13 Assoc Provost IT/CIO ... Ms. Barbara E. DAWSON
18 Sr Assoc VP Facilities & Svcs ... Mr. Jamie F. KOSIK
35 Assoc Vice Pres Student Affairs ... Mr. Michael A. ELLINGTON
76 Asst VP Hlth Sci & Tech Academy ... Ms. Ann L. CHESTER
84 Assoc VP Enroll Mgmt Svcs ... Mr. Stephen LEE
88 Assoc VP Strategic Initiatives ... Ms. Elizabeth P. REYNOLDS
88 Int Director Corporate Relations ... Mr. Jack THOMPSON
25 Asst VP Office of Research Admin ... Mr. Alan B. MARTIN
09 Director of Institutional Research ... Ms. Donielle R. MAUST
39 Director Res Life/Dean of Students ... Ms. Trish CENDANA
41 Dir & Assoc VP Intercoll Athletics ... Mr. Shane LYONS
23 Director of Public Health ... Dr. Cecil R. POLLARD
37 Asst VP Financial Aid ... Ms. Sandra K. OERLY-BENNETT
06 University Registrar ... Ms. Aimee D. PFEIFER
08 Dean of Library Services ... Ms. Karen DIAZ
38 Asst VP Student Wellness ... Vacant
19 Chief of Police/Univ Police Dept ... Capt. W. P. CHEDESTER
109 Sr Assoc VP Auxiliary Services ... Mr. Edward T. SVEHLIK
85 VP Global Strategies ... Dr. Amber BRUGNOLI
69 Assoc VP & Dean Public Health ... Dr. Jeffrey COBEN
50 Dean & VP Business & Economics ... Dr. Javier REYES
49 Dean of Arts & Sciences ... Dr. Gregory DUNAWAY
57 Dean College of Creative Arts ... Dr. Keith JACKSON
53 Interim Dean Educ & Human Resources ... Dr. Tracy L. MORRIS
61 Dean of Law ... Dr. Amelia RINEHART
63 Executive Dean & VP of Medicine ... Dr. Clay B. MARSH
52 Dean of Dentistry ... Dr. Stephen PACHUTA
54 Dean of Engr/Mineral Resources ... Dr. Pedro MAGO
47 Dean of Davis Agric & Forestry ... Dr. Darrell DONAHUE
67 Dean of Pharmacy ... Dr. William P. PETROS
60 Dean of College of Media ... Dr. Diana MARTINELLI
68 Interim Dean Physical Education ... Dr. Jack WATSON
66 Dean of Nursing ... Dr. Tara HULSEY
92 Dean of Honors College ... Mr. Kenneth P. BLEMINGS
106 Dean Online Programs ... Vacant
36 Director Career Services ... Mr. David L. DURHAM
20 Assoc Provost Intl Acad Affairs ... Dr. David STEWART
20 Campus Provost-WVUIT ... Dr. Joan NEFF
58 Assoc Provost Grad Acad Affairs ... Dr. Richard THOMAS
35 Assoc VP & Dean of Students ... Mr. G. Corey FARRIS
105 Director Web Services ... Ms. Cathy ORNDORFF
88 Asst VP Entrepreneurship & Innov ... Ms. Carrie WHITE
116 Director Internal Audit ... Mr. Bryan D. SHAVER

*West Virginia University at Parkersburg (F)

300 Campus Drive, Parkersburg WV 26104-8647
County: Wood — FICE Identification: 003828
Unit ID: 237686
Telephone: (304) 424-8000 — Carnegie Class: Bac/Assoc-Mixed
FAX Number: (304) 424-8315 — Calendar System: Semester
URL: www.wvup.edu

Established: 1961 Annual Undergrad Tuition & Fees (In-State): $3,890
Enrollment: 2,624 Coed
Affiliation or Control: State IRS Status: 501(c)3
Highest Offering: Baccalaureate
Accreditation: HLC, ACBSP, ADNUR, CAEP, NUR, SURGT

02 President .... Dr. Christopher GILMER
18 VP Facilities/Internal Affairs .... Mr. Brady WHIPKEY
05 Provost/Vice PresAcademic Affairs .... Dr. Chad CRUMBAKER
10 Vice Pres Finance/Administration .... Ms. Alice HARRIS
84 Exec VP Enrollment Management .... Dr. Steven SMITH
111 Exec VP Institutional Advancement .... Dr. Torie JACKSON
13 Chief Information Officer .... Mr. Doug ANTHONY
103 Exec Dir Workforce/Economic Develop .... Ms. Michele WILSON
22 Exec Dir Equity/Inclus/Compliance .... Mrs. Debbie RICHARDS
20 Dean for Academic Affairs .... Dr. Cynthia GISSY
32 Exec Dir Student Support Services .... Mr. Kurt KLETTNER
110 Exec Dir Institutional Advancement .... Ms. Senta GOUDY
15 Director Human Resources .... Mr. Scott POE
09 Dean Institutional Research .... Mr. Jeremy STARKEY
06 Registrar/Dir Center Student Svcs .... Mrs. Leslie SIMS
37 Director of Financial Aid .... Mrs. Heather SKIDMORE
21 Exec Dir of CPO .... Ms. Jeannine RATLIFFE
08 Director of Library .... Mr. Stephen HUPP
29 Exec Dir Alumni Relations .... Ms. Nancy BREMAR
50 Chair Business/Economics/Math Div .... Mr. Jeff HOLLAND
53 Chair Education .... Dr. David LANCASTER
81 Chair STEM Division .... Dr. Jared GUMP

West Virginia Junior College (A)

5514 Big Tyler Road Suite 200, Cross Lanes WV 25313
County: Kanawha FICE Identification: 010573
Unit ID: 237987
Telephone: (304) 769-0011 Carnegie Class: Assoc/HVT-High Trad
FAX Number: (304) 769-0013 Calendar System: Quarter
URL: www.wvjc.edu
Established: 1892 Annual Undergrad Tuition & Fees: $14,335
Enrollment: 218 Coed
Affiliation or Control: Proprietary IRS Status: Proprietary
Highest Offering: Associate Degree
Accreditation: ABHES

01 Campus President .... Ms. Michelle MILES
05 Academic Dean .... Ms. Katie HARVEY
06 Registrar .... Ms. Jennifer BIRD
36 Director Student Placement .... Ms. Selena RAMEY
37 Director Student Financial Aid .... Ms. Christina HAYSLETT

West Virginia Junior College (B)

148 Willey Street, Morgantown WV 26505-5596
County: Monongalia FICE Identification: 005007
Unit ID: 237996
Telephone: (304) 296-8282 Carnegie Class: Assoc/HVT-High Trad
FAX Number: (304) 581-6990 Calendar System: Quarter
URL: www.wvjc.edu
Established: 1922 Annual Undergrad Tuition & Fees: $13,950
Enrollment: 622 Coed
Affiliation or Control: Proprietary IRS Status: Proprietary
Highest Offering: Associate Degree
Accreditation: ABHES

01 President .... Ms. Samantha ESPOSITO
05 Academic Dean .... Ms. Rachael SALVUCCI
37 Financial Aid Director .... Ms. Patricia CALLEN

West Virginia Junior College-Bridgeport (C)

176 Thompson Drive, Bridgeport WV 26330
Telephone: (304) 842-4007 Identification: 770823
Accreditation: ABHES

West Virginia Wesleyan College (D)

59 College Avenue, Buckhannon WV 26201-2699
County: Upshur FICE Identification: 003830
Unit ID: 237969
Telephone: (304) 473-8000 Carnegie Class: Masters/S
FAX Number: N/A Calendar System: Semester
URL: www.wvwc.edu
Established: 1890 Annual Undergrad Tuition & Fees: $32,252
Enrollment: 1,066 Coed
Affiliation or Control: United Methodist IRS Status: 501(c)3
Highest Offering: Doctorate
Accreditation: HLC, CAATE, CAEP, MUS, NURSE

01 President .... Dr. Joel THIERSTEIN
05 Dean of Faculty/Chief Academic Ofcr .... Dr. James MOORE
84 VP Enrollment Mgmt & Admissions .... Mr. John WALTZ
111 VP Advancement .... Mr. Robert SKINNER
10 Chief Financial Officer .... Dr. Scott MCKINNEY
42 Dean of the Chapel .... Rev. Lauren WEAVER
102 Director Foundation/Govt Relations .... Ms. Nicki BENTLEY-COLTHART
11 Director of Administrative Services .... Mr. Robert KIMBLE
37 Director Financial Aid .... Ms. Susan GEORGE
29 Assoc VP Adv & Alumni Relations .... Mr. William ARMISTEAD
08 Director of Library Services .... Mr. Brett MILLER
36 Director Academic & Career Services .... Ms. Tammy FREDERICK
39 Director Campus Life & Housing .... Ms. Alisa LIVELY
09 Director of Institutional Research .... Ms. Tammy CRITES
15 Director of Human Resources .... Ms. Vickie CROWDER
18 Director of the Physical Plant .... Mr. Vaughn HARTLEY
30 Director Advancement Operations .... Ms. Rose Ellen LOUDIN
88 Director of Learning Center .... Dr. Shawn KUBA
06 Registrar .... Ms. Tammy FREDERICK
41 Director of Athletics .... Mr. Randall TENNEY
10 Controller .... Mr. Randall CRITES
40 Retail Store Manager .... Ms. Jennifer FLETCHER
92 Director Honors Program .... Ms. Jordana LAFANTASIE
93 Director Multicultural Programs .... Mr. Robert QUARLES
112 Planned Giving Coordinator .... Rev. David PETERS
38 Director of Counseling Services .... Ms. Lori THOMPSON
31 Asst Dir of Community Engagement .... Ms. Jessica VINCENT
13 Director of Computing Services .... Mr. Neil ROTH
04 Administrative Asst to President .... Ms. Deborah K. MULLENS
19 Director of Security .... Mr. David PARKS
43 Dir Legal Services/General Counsel .... Mr. David W. MCCAULEY
101 Secretary of the Institution/Board .... Ms. Deborah K. MULLENS
104 Director Study Abroad .... Dr. Tamara BAILEY

Wheeling University (E)

316 Washington Avenue, Wheeling WV 26003-6295
County: Ohio FICE Identification: 003831
Unit ID: 238078
Telephone: (304) 243-2000 Carnegie Class: Masters/M
FAX Number: (304) 243-2243 Calendar System: Semester
URL: www.wheeling.edu
Established: 1954 Annual Undergrad Tuition & Fees: $29,290
Enrollment: 857 Coed
Affiliation or Control: Roman Catholic IRS Status: 501(c)3
Highest Offering: Doctorate
Accreditation: #HLC, ACBSP, CAATE, NURSE, PTA

01 President .... Ms. Ginny FAVEDE
05 Int VP for Academic Affairs .... Ms. Jackie MCGLADE
32 VP for Student Services .... Mr. Andrew LEWIS
84 Vice Pres of Enrollment Management .... Mr. Justin SCHWARZ
13 Acting Dir Information Technology .... Mr. Ron MAGERS
37 Interim Director Financial Aid .... Ms. Dawn LANGDON
06 Acting Registrar .... Mr. John L'ECUYER
08 Librarian .... Vacant
42 Director of Campus Ministry .... Dr. I. Hadi SASMITA, SJ
41 Athletic Director .... Mr. Patrick SNIVELY
18 Director of Facilities .... Mr. Michael CONNER
04 Executive Asst to President .... Ms. Melissa ROSE
106 Dir Online Education/E-learning .... Mr. D. Jason FRITZMAN
19 Director Public Safety .... Mr. Larry PALMER
29 Director Alumni Relations .... Vacant
38 Director of Counseling Center .... Ms. Tina TORDELLA

WISCONSIN

Alverno College (F)

3400 S 43rd Street, Box 343922,
Milwaukee WI 53234-3922
County: Milwaukee FICE Identification: 003832
Unit ID: 238193
Telephone: (414) 382-6000 Carnegie Class: Masters/M
FAX Number: (414) 382-6066 Calendar System: Semester
URL: www.alverno.edu
Established: 1887 Annual Undergrad Tuition & Fees: $30,658
Enrollment: 1,876 Female
Affiliation or Control: Independent Non-Profit IRS Status: 501(c)3
Highest Offering: Doctorate
Accreditation: HLC, MUS, NURSE, SW

01 President .... Dr. Andrea J. LEE, IHM
100 Vice Pres and Chief of Staff .... Ms. Jill DESMOND
10 Vice Pres Finance/Administration .... Ms. Katie DILLOW
05 Vice Pres for Academic Affairs .... Dr. Joseph FOY
111 Vice President for Advancement .... Vacant
84 VP for Enrollment & Student Success .... Ms. Kate LUNDEEN
32 Interim Dean Student Dev/ Success .... Dr. Heidi ANDERSON-ISAACSON
07 Director of Admissions .... Ms. Janet STIKEL
20 Assoc Vice Pres .... Sr. Marlene NEISES
06 Registrar .... Ms. Lori SZARZYNSKI
08 Director Library .... Mr. Larry DUERR
36 Director Career Studio .... Vacant
13 Chief Information Officer .... Mr. John JERIES
37 Director of Financial Aid .... Ms. Amy CHRISTEN
30 Director of Development .... Ms. Kim MUENCH
29 Alumni Engagement Manager .... Ms. Moira FLOOD
121 Director Academic Advising .... Ms. Kate TISCH
15 Director Human Resources .... Ms. Magda HOFFMAN
41 Director of Athletics .... Ms. Katari KEY
42 Campus Minister .... Rev. Lisa CATHELYN
96 Purchasing Coordinator .... Ms. Anne MCCARRON
66 Dean School of Nursing .... Dr. Laurie KUNKEL-JORDAN
107 Dean of Professional/Grad Studies .... Dr. Jodi EASTBERG
49 Dean School of Arts & Sciences .... Dr. Kevin CASEY
51 Dean School of Adult Learning .... Ms. Meghan WALSH
04 Exec Assistant to the President .... Ms. Anna ARENS
18 Director Plant Operations .... Mr. John MARKS
19 Director Security/Safety .... Mr. Jason PILARSKI

Bellin College, Inc. (G)

3201 Eaton Road, Green Bay WI 54311
County: Brown FICE Identification: 006639
Unit ID: 238324
Telephone: (920) 433-6699 Carnegie Class: Spec-4-yr-Other Health
FAX Number: (920) 433-1923 Calendar System: Semester
URL: www.bellincollege.edu
Established: 1909 Annual Undergrad Tuition & Fees: $21,685
Enrollment: 626 Coed
Affiliation or Control: Independent Non-Profit IRS Status: 501(c)3
Highest Offering: Doctorate
Accreditation: HLC, DMS, NURSE, RAD

01 President & CEO of the College .... Dr. Connie J. BOERST
10 VP of Business & Finance .... Mrs. Ginger B. KRUMMEN SCHRAVEN
66 Dean of Nursing .... Dr. Mary K. ROLLOFF
76 Dean of Allied Health Sciences .... Dr. Mark A. BAKE
32 Dean of Student Services .... Dr. Nancy M. BURRUSS
07 VP of Admissions and Marketing .... Mr. Matt G. RENTMEESTER
13 Director of Technology .... Mr. Travis A. SMITH
06 Registrar .... Mr. Russell J. LEARY
37 Director Financial Aid .... Mrs. Lena C. GOODMAN
04 Executive Assistant to President .... Mrs. Jamie L. ARBEITER
08 Head Librarian .... Ms. Cindy M. REINL
111 VP of Advancement .... Mr. Thomas J. SHEFCHIK

Beloit College (H)

700 College Street, Beloit WI 53511-5595
County: Rock FICE Identification: 003835
Unit ID: 238333
Telephone: (608) 363-2000 Carnegie Class: Bac-A&S
FAX Number: (608) 363-2717 Calendar System: Semester
URL: www.beloit.edu
Established: 1846 Annual Undergrad Tuition & Fees: $53,348
Enrollment: 978 Coed
Affiliation or Control: Independent Non-Profit IRS Status: 501(c)3
Highest Offering: Baccalaureate
Accreditation: HLC

01 President .... Dr. Scott BIERMAN
05 Provost .... Dr. Eric BOYNTON
100 Chief of Staff .... Mr. Daniel J. SCHOOFF
45 VP Budget & Planning .... Ms. Stacie SCOTT
111 VP Development & Alumni Relations .... Ms. Amy WILSON
15 VP Human Resources and Operations .... Ms. Lori RHEAD
84 VP Enrollment .... Ms. Leslie DAVIDSON
32 Dean Equity/Cmty/Student Success .... Mr. Cecil YOUNGBLOOD
13 Chief Information Officer .... Dr. Pam MCQUESTEN
26 Chief Comm & Integ Mktg Officer .... Ms. Elizabeth CONLISK
108 Dir Strategic Research & Assessment .... Ms. Ellie ANDERYRNE
09 Dir Inst Research/Assmt/Planning .... Vacant
06 Registrar .... Ms. Mary BOROS-KAZAI
07 Director of Intl Admissions .... Ms. Erin GUTH
18 Director of Facilities .... Mr. Robert OEHLER
39 Director Resident Life/Conferences .... Mr. Ryan SCHAMP
36 Director of Career Development .... Ms. Jessica FOX-WILSON
37 Director of Financial Aid .... Ms. Deb DEW
41 Athletic Director .... Mr. Dave DEGEORGE

Cardinal Stritch University (I)

6801 N Yates Road, Milwaukee WI 53217-3985
County: Milwaukee FICE Identification: 003837
Unit ID: 238430
Telephone: (414) 410-4000 Carnegie Class: DU-Mod
FAX Number: (414) 410-4239 Calendar System: Semester
URL: www.stritch.edu
Established: 1937 Annual Undergrad Tuition & Fees: $33,770
Enrollment: 1,646 Coed
Affiliation or Control: Roman Catholic IRS Status: 501(c)3
Highest Offering: Doctorate
Accreditation: HLC, ACBSP, NUR, NURSE

01 President .... Dr. Daniel J. SCHOLZ
04 Exec Assistant to the President .... Ms. Yani RODRIGUEZ
05 Vice Pres Academic Affairs .... Dr. Daniel J. SCHOLZ
111 Vice Pres Institutional Advancement .... Mr. Marc C. BARBEAU
10 VP Finance/Administration .... Mr. Thomas J. CONGDON
84 VP Enrollment Management .... Ms. Tracy A. FISCHER
123 Vice President Graduate Enrollment .... Vacant
32 Vice Pres Student Affairs .... Ms. Donney MORONEY
21 Interim Chief Financial Officer .... Mr. Mel L. AUSTIN
42 Director University Ministry .... Mr. Gino GRIVETTI
41 Director of Athletics .... Mr. Danny KUKLINSKI
13 Director Infrastructure Support .... Mr. Steven W. TRACY
66 Int Dean College Nursing/Health Sci .... Dr. Crystal-Rae EVANS
50 Dean College of Business & Mgmt .... Dr. Janette M. BRAVERMAN
53 Dean College of Education & Ldrship .... Dr. Carroll E. BRONSON
49 Dean College of Arts & Sciences .... Vacant
35 Dean of Students .... Ms. Donney MORONEY
15 Director of Human Resources/Payroll .... Ms. Jackie L. SUKOWATY
06 University Registrar .... Ms. Christine GLYNN
37 Dir of Financial Aid .... Mr. Mark W. QUISTORF
20 Director of Academic Affairs .... Vacant
36 Asst Dir Internships/Career Engage .... Mr. Tom E. KIPP
38 Dir for Counseling/Mental Wellness .... Ms. Mary Beth WISNIEWSKI
104 Director International Education .... Ms. Sarah R. SWEENEY
108 Dir of Institutional Effectiveness .... Mr. William L. MARCOU

91 Director of Enterprise Systems ....Ms. Susan L. INGLES
08 Director of University Library ....Ms. Dyan E. BARBEAU
102 Asst Dir Corporate/Foundation Rels ...Ms. Ritamarie WISKOWSKI
26 Sr Dir University Communications ....Ms. Kathleen M. HOHL
18 Director of Facilities ....Mr. Donald PAJEWSKI
19 Director of Security ....Mr. Andrew DE RUBERTIS

Carroll University (A)

100 N East Avenue, Waukesha WI 53186-5593
County: Waukesha FICE Identification: 003838
Unit ID: 238458
Telephone: (262) 547-1211 Carnegie Class: Masters/S
FAX Number: (262) 524-7646 Calendar System: Semester
URL: www.carrollu.edu
Established: 1846 Annual Undergrad Tuition & Fees: $34,010
Enrollment: 3,451 Coed
Affiliation or Control: Presbyterian Church (U.S.A.) IRS Status: 501(c)3
Highest Offering: Doctorate
Accreditation: HLC, ARCPA, CAATE, MUS, NURSE, OT, PTA

01 President ....Dr. Cindy GNADINGER
05 Provost/Vice Pres Academic Affairs ....Dr. Mark BLEGEN
10 Vice Pres Finance/Administration ....Ms. Dana STUART
84 Vice President for Enrollment ....Mr. Teege METTILLE
111 Vice President for Advancement ....Ms. Victoria DOWLING
32 Vice President Student Affairs ....Dr. Theresa BARRY
26 Vice Pres Marketing & Communication ....Ms. Tiffany WYNN
13 Chief Technology Officer ....Vacant
06 Registrar ....Ms. Ann HANDFORD
21 Assoc VP Finance & Administration ....Ms. Deidre ERWIN
37 Assoc VP Enroll/Dir Fin Aid ....Ms. Dawn M. SCOTT
15 Director of Human Resources ....Ms. Kelly PEARSE
08 Library Director ....Mr. Joe HARDENBROOK
41 Athletic Director ....Mr. Mike SCHULIST
107 Dir of Non-Trad Adult/Prof Studies ....Ms. Lynn NOVAK
28 Assoc Dean Multicult Affairs . Ms. Vanessa PEREZ-TOPCZEWSKI
29 Sr Director Alumni Engagement ....Ms. Dolores M. BROWN
109 Sr Director Auxiliary & Gen Svcs ....Vacant
07 Director of Trad & Intl Admissions ....Ms. Annie J. ASCHENBRENNER
18 Facilities Director ....Mr. Tom HEFFERNAN
38 Director Student Counseling ....Ms. Angie R. BRANNAN
04 Exec Assistant to the President ....Ms. Gina M. EHLER
123 Director Graduate Admissions ....Ms. Cindy HOLAHAN
121 Director of Student Success ....Mr. Jeff MCNAMARA
19 Director Security/Safety ....Mr. Mike BAGIN
22 Director of Compliance ....Ms. Suzanne LIDTKE
43 Director of Legal Services ....Ms. Cat JORGENS
50 Dean School of Business ....Dr. Hamid AKBARI
49 Dean College of Arts & Sciences ....Dr. Kareem MOHAMMAD
76 Dean Health Sciences ....Dr. Thomas PAHNKE
09 Director of Institutional Research ....Mr. Joshua MITCHELL
25 Sr Director of Sponsored Projects ....Vacant

Carthage College (B)

2001 Alford Park Drive, Kenosha WI 53140-1994
County: Kenosha FICE Identification: 003839
Unit ID: 238476
Telephone: (262) 551-8500 Carnegie Class: Bac-Diverse
FAX Number: (262) 551-6208 Calendar System: 4/1/4
URL: www.carthage.edu
Established: 1847 Annual Undergrad Tuition & Fees: $31,500
Enrollment: 2,763 Coed
Affiliation or Control: Evangelical Lutheran Church In America
IRS Status: 501(c)3
Highest Offering: Master's
Accreditation: HLC, CAATE, MUS, NURSE, SW

01 President/Chief Executive Officer ....Dr. John R. SWALLOW
04 Special Assistant to the President ....Ms. Dana KROLL
05 Provost/Chief Operating Officer ....Dr. David TIMMERMAN
10 AVP Finance & Administration/CFO ....Mr. Vince CEJA
111 VP for Institutional Advancement ....Dr. Thomas KLINE
26 Assoc VP Marketing/Communications ....Ms. Elizabeth YOUNG
84 VP for Enrollment ....Mr. Nick MULVEY
32 VP Student Affairs/Dean of Students ....Dr. Kimberlie GOLDSBERRY
108 VP Institutional Effectiveness ....Dr. Abigail HANNA
41 Interim Athletic Director ....Mr. Nathan STEWART
42 Campus Pastor ....Ms. Kara BAYLOR
06 Registrar ....Mr. Brandon PORTER
104 Director Study Abroad ....Dr. Erik KULKE
15 Director of Human Resources ....Ms. Marianne MARSHALL
19 Director of Public Safety ....Vacant
37 Director of Financial Aid ....Mr. Jeff TEAGUE

College of Menominee Nation (C)

PO Box 1179, Keshena WI 54135-1179
County: Menominee FICE Identification: 031251
Unit ID: 413617
Telephone: (800) 567-2344 Carnegie Class: Tribal
FAX Number: (715) 799-1336 Calendar System: Semester
URL: www.menominee.edu
Established: 1992 Annual Undergrad Tuition & Fees: $6,200
Enrollment: 173 Coed
Affiliation or Control: Tribal Control IRS Status: 501(c)3
Highest Offering: Baccalaureate
Accreditation: HLC

01 Interim President ....Mr. Christopher M. CALDWELL
05 Chief Academic Officer ....Ms. Geraldine SANAPAW
10 Interim Chief Financial Officer ....Mr. George OTRADOVEC
51 Dean of Continuing Education ....Mr. Brian KOWALKOWSKI
124 Director of Retention ....Mr. Norman SHAWANOKASIC
100 Chief of Staff ....Ms. Melinda COOK
09 Director Institutional Research ....Ms. Geraldine SANAPAW
13 IT Director ....Mr. Edward BOWKER
15 Human Resources Generalist ....Ms. Sarah LYONS
06 Registrar/Bursar ....Ms. Geraldine SANAPAW
37 Financial Aid Mgr ....Mr. Austin RETZLAFF
07 Admissions/Enrollment Manager ....Mr. Luis ORTIZ
78 Director of Vocational Rehab ....Ms. Myrna WARRINGTON
08 Director of Library Services ....Ms. Maria ESCALANTE
96 Director of Purchasing ....Ms. Darla ASENBRENER

College of Menominee Nation Oneida Campus (D)

2733 S Ridge Road, Green Bay WI 54304
Telephone: (920) 965-0070 Identification: 770424
Accreditation: &HLC

Concordia University Wisconsin (E)

12800 N Lake Shore Drive, Mequon WI 53097-2402
County: Ozaukee FICE Identification: 003842
Unit ID: 238616
Telephone: (262) 243-5700 Carnegie Class: DU-Mod
FAX Number: (262) 243-4351 Calendar System: 4/1/4
URL: www.cuw.edu
Established: 1881 Annual Undergrad Tuition & Fees: $31,182
Enrollment: 5,492 Coed
Affiliation or Control: Lutheran Church - Missouri Synod
IRS Status: 501(c)3
Highest Offering: Doctorate
Accreditation: HLC, ARCPA, CAATE, DMS, IACBE, MAC, NURSE, OT, PHAR, PTA, @SP, SW

01 Interim President ....Dr. William R. CARIO
11 Executive VP & Chief Oper Ofcr ....Mr. Allen J. PROCHNOW
05 Interim Provost/Chief Accred Ofcr ....Dr. Leah M. DVORAK
111 Senior VP of Advancement ....Rev Dr. Roy PETERSON
102 VP of Foundation ....Mr. Dean D. RENNICKE
13 VP of Information Technology ....Mr. Thomas G. PHILLIP
32 VP of Student Life ....Dr. Steven P. TAYLOR
20 Vice Provost of Faculty Affairs ....Dr. Leah M. DVORAK
84 Vice Provost of Student Enrollment ....Dr. Michael D. UDEN
121 Asst VP Academics/Student Success ....Dr. Elizabeth A. POLZIN
07 Asst Vice President Admissions ....Mr. Robert J. NOWAK
27 Asst VP Strategic Communications ....Ms. Lisa LILJEGREN
85 Asst VP International Affairs ....Mr. Brian D. CURRY
42 Campus Pastor ....Rev. Steven N. SMITH
42 Campus Pastor ....Rev. Randall S. DUNCAN
88 Chair Faculty Senate ....Mr. Jordan P. BECK
49 Dean School Arts/Sciences ....Dr. Steven R. MONTREAL
50 Dean School of Business ....Dr. Daniel S. SEM
53 Dean School of Education ....Dr. James A. PINGEL
76 Dean School of Health Professions ....Dr. Linda M. SAMUEL
66 Interim Dean School of Nursing ....Dr. Diane AMES
67 Dean School of Pharmacy ....Dr. Erik JORVIG
35 Dean of Students ....Dr. Steven W. GERNER
06 Registrar ....Ms. Michele HOFFMAN
29 Director of Alumni Relations ....Mr. Gregory P. WITTO
41 Director of Athletics ....Dr. Rob M. BARNHILL
19 Director Campus Safety ....Mr. Michael STOLTE
38 Director of Counseling ....Mr. David T. ENTERS
36 Director of Career Engagement ....Mr. Tyler R. LANDERS
37 Director of Financial Aid ....Mr. Kevin P. SHERIDAN
15 Asst VP Human Resources ....Ms. Kimberly R. MASENTHIN
09 Director of Institutional Research ....Dr. Tamara R. FERRY
24 Director Instructional Technology ....Mr. Sean B. YOUNG
08 Director of Library Services ....Mr. Christian R. HIMSEL
39 Director of Residence Life ....Ms. Beckie KRUSE
88 Exec Director Cont & Dist Ed ....Ms. Sarah A. PECOR
18 Superintendent Buildings & Grounds ....Mr. Stephen V. HIBBARD
40 Bookstore Manager ....Ms. Kia LOR

Edgewood College (F)

1000 Edgewood College Drive, Madison WI 53711-1997
County: Dane FICE Identification: 003848
Unit ID: 238661
Telephone: (608) 663-4861 Carnegie Class: DU-Mod
FAX Number: (608) 663-3291 Calendar System: Semester
URL: www.edgewood.edu
Established: 1927 Annual Undergrad Tuition & Fees: $31,700
Enrollment: 2,007 Coed
Affiliation or Control: Roman Catholic IRS Status: 501(c)3
Highest Offering: Doctorate
Accreditation: HLC, ACBSP, MFCD, NURSE

01 President ....Dr. Andrew P. MANION
05 VP Academic Affairs/Academic Dean ....Dr. Angela SALAS
28 VP Mission/Values & Inclusion ....Dr. John LEONARD
32 VP for Student Development ....Dr. Heather HARBACH
10 VP Business & Finance ....Mr. Michael GUNS
84 Interim VP Enrollment Mgmt ....Ms. Kari GRIBBLE
111 VP Inst Advancement ....Ms. Katie VESPERMAN
100 Chief of Staff ....Mr. Edward TAYLOR
28 AVP Diversity/Equity/Inclusion ....Mr. Tony GARCIA
37 AVP Enrollment Mgmt/Financial Aid ....Ms. Kari GRIBBLE
88 Senior Advisor to the President ....Dr. Willie LARKIN
49 Dean Liberal Arts/Educ/Sciences ....Dr. Amy SCHIEBEL
66 Dean Nursing/Bus/Health Sci ....Dr. Margaret NOREUIL
50 Assoc Dean Bus/Comms/Innovation ....Dr. Victoria PALMISANO
53 Assoc Dean Education ....Dr. Julie LUECKE
108 Director Inst Effectiveness ....Dr. Edward J. KEELEY
104 Director Study Abroad/Intl Students ....Dr. Sara LIANG
18 Director Facility Operations ....Ms. Susan VANDERSANDEN
41 Director Athletics ....Mr. Al BRISACK
13 Director Information Technology ....Mr. Patrick GUMIENY
19 Director Transportation/Security ....Mr. Michael METCALF
26 Exec Dir Marketing/Strategic Comm ....Ms. Amy PIKALEK
06 Registrar ....Ms. Michelle KELLEY
21 Controller ....Ms. Jane WILHELM
39 Director Student Life ....Ms. Claire MAND
08 Library Director ....Dr. Nathan DOWD
15 Director Human Resources ....Ms. Arhelia DALLA COSTA BEHM
07 Director Undergrad Admissions ....Ms. Tess FERZOCO
27 Chief Communications Officer ....Mr. Edward TAYLOR
36 Director Career Development ....Vacant
29 Alumni Relations Director ....Ms. Abby BJERKE
38 Director Personal Counseling Svcs .. Dr. Megan COBB-SHEEHAN
23 Director Health Services ....Ms. Suzanne WALLACE

George Williams College of Aurora University (G)

350 Constance Boulevard, Williams Bay WI 53191
Telephone: (262) 245-5564 Identification: 770066
Accreditation: &HLC

† Branch campus of Aurora University, Aurora, IL

Herzing University (H)

5218 E Terrace Drive, Madison WI 53718-8340
County: Dane FICE Identification: 009621
Unit ID: 240392
Telephone: (608) 249-6611 Carnegie Class: Masters/M
FAX Number: (608) 249-8593 Calendar System: Semester
URL: www.herzing.edu
Established: 1965 Annual Undergrad Tuition & Fees: $14,200
Enrollment: 2,392 Coed
Affiliation or Control: Independent Non-Profit IRS Status: 501(c)3
Highest Offering: Master's
Accreditation: HLC, IACBE, NURSE

00 President ....Ms. Renee HERZING
01 Regional President Madison Campus ....Dr. Jeff HILL
10 CFO & Vice President of Finance ....Mr. Robert HERZOG
05 Academic Dean ....Dr. Tracee ISENSEE
37 Educational Funding Manager ....Mr. Clayton GROTH
32 Dir of Student Services/Registrar ....Ms. Amy HERFEL
07 Director of Admissions ....Ms. Danielle OEST
36 Career Development Coach ....Ms. Chris SZOLYGA

Herzing University Brookfield Campus (I)

15895 W Bluemound Rd, Brookfield WI 53005
Telephone: (262) 649-1710 Identification: 770429
Accreditation: &HLC, NURSE, PTAA

Herzing University Kenosha Campus (J)

5800 7th Avenue, Kenosha WI 53140
Telephone: (262) 671-0675 Identification: 770430
Accreditation: &HLC, NURSE

Herzing University Online (K)

W140N8917 Lilly Road, Menomonee Falls WI 53051
Telephone: (866) 508-0748 Identification: 770431
Accreditation: &HLC, CAHIIM

Lac Courte Oreilles Ojibwe College (L)

13466 W Trepania Road, Hayward WI 54843-2181
County: Sawyer FICE Identification: 025322
Unit ID: 260372
Telephone: (715) 634-4790 Carnegie Class: Tribal
FAX Number: (715) 634-5049 Calendar System: Semester
URL: www.lco.edu
Established: 1982 Annual Undergrad Tuition & Fees: $4,590
Enrollment: 278 Coed
Affiliation or Control: Tribal Control IRS Status: 501(c)3
Highest Offering: Baccalaureate
Accreditation: HLC

01 President ....Dr. Russell SWAGGER
10 Chief Financial Officer ....Ms. Lydia DENASHA
05 Provost ....Ms. Lisa MUNIVE
32 Dean of Students & Cmty Engagement ....Ms. Amber MARLOW
11 Chief Operating Officer ....Mr. Mark MONTANO
35 Dean of Continuous Improvement ....Dr. Odawa WHITE
111 Dir Inst Advancement/ Development ....Ms. Jessica WAGNER-SCHULTZ
37 Director of Financial Aid ....Ms. Kimberly PAULSON
13 Information Technology Systems Admn ....Mr. Tristan STEVENS
15 Director of Human Resources ....Ms. Tamara THIMM
07 Admissions Recruiter ....Vacant
08 Chief Library Officer ....Ms. Caryl PFAFF
20 Dean of Academic Affairs ....Ms. Stephanie ST GERMAINE

100 Chief of Staff .... Ms. Karen BREIT
41 Athletic Director .... Mr. Tristan STEVENS
43 General Counsel .... Mr. James SCHLENDER
06 Registrar .... Vacant

Lakeland University (A)

W3718 South Dr, Plymouth WI 53073
County: Sheboygan FICE Identification: 003854
Unit ID: 238980
Telephone: (920) 565-1000 Carnegie Class: Masters/L
FAX Number: (920) 565-1060 Calendar System: Semester
URL: www.lakeland.edu
Established: 1862 Annual Undergrad Tuition & Fees: $30,777
Enrollment: 2,753 Coed
Affiliation or Control: United Church Of Christ IRS Status: 501(c)3
Highest Offering: Master's
Accreditation: HLC

01 President .... Dr. Beth M. BORGEN
04 Assistant to the President .... Mr. Stuart J. SCHMIDT
125 Former President/President Emeritus .... Dr. David R. BLACK
101 Liaison to the Board of Trustees .... Mr. Stuart J. SCHMIDT
00 Board Chairperson .... Mr. Jeffrey SPENCE
05 Vice President of Academic Affairs .... Dr. Joshua P. KUTNEY
12 Vice President Lakeland U Japan .... Dr. Brian T. FRINK
10 Vice President Finance & Operation .... Ms. Amy M. WIRTZ
32 Vice President Campus Life .... Mr. David R. SIMON
15 Vice President Human Resources .... Dr. James JONES
41 Director of Athletics .... Dr. April A. ARVAN
108 Chief Innovation Officer .... Dr. Michael P. DUNLAP
84 Vice President Enrollment Mgmt .... Mr. Sam G. POULLETTE
20 Dean Academic Support Services .... Dr. Margaret L. ALBRINCK
55 Dean William R. Kellett School .... Dr. Rachel J. WARE-CARLTON
79 Dean Humanities & Fine Arts .... Rev. Karl A. KUHN
50 Dean Schilcutt School .... Dr. Paul PICKHARDT
26 Director of External Relations .... Mr. David D. GALLIANETTI
27 Director of Marketing .... Mr. Michael P. LACKOVIC
111 Assoc Vice President Advancement .... Mr. Tylor S. LOEST
78 Assoc Vice President Co-Op/Career . Ms. Jessica N. LAMBRECHT
21 Controller .... Ms. Kathy NEITZEL
37 Sr Dir of Financial Aid & Ed Fund .... Ms. Patty L. TAYLOR
09 Director Institutional Research .... Dr. Paul M. WHITE
06 Registrar .... Ms. Amanda J. HRUSKA
39 Director Residence Life .... Mr. Mark T. EDMOND
38 Director Health & Counseling .... Ms. Alex LIOSATOS
42 Chaplain/Ethicist in Residence .... Rev. Julie A. MAVITY-MADDALENA
08 Director Library Services .... Ms. Ann PENKE
29 Director Alumni Rels/Annual Giving .... Ms. Andrea M. SCHMITZ
102 Dir Corporation & Foundation Rels .... Vacant
114 Financial Analyst .... Mr. Chris J. GROTEGUT
113 Bursar .... Ms. Jalesa C. FREESE
19 Director Campus Security .... Mr. Christopher J. RINGEL
13 Director Technology Services .... Mr. Charles M. GRUBISIC
106 Director Online Learning .... Ms. Florence E. SIEBERT
120 Director Instructional Design .... Mr. Andrew R. DAMP
123 Sr Director Graduate Recruitment .... Ms. Jane A. BOUCHE
04 Sr Advisor International Affairs .... Dr. Stephen SIM

Lawrence University (B)

711 E. Boldt Way, Appleton WI 54911
County: Outagamie FICE Identification: 003856
Unit ID: 239017
Telephone: (920) 832-7000 Carnegie Class: Bac-A&S
FAX Number: (920) 832-6978 Calendar System: Other
URL: www.lawrence.edu
Established: 1847 Annual Undergrad Tuition & Fees: $50,958
Enrollment: 1,430 Coed
Affiliation or Control: Independent Non-Profit IRS Status: 501(c)3
Highest Offering: Baccalaureate
Accreditation: HLC, MUS

01 President .... Ms. Laurie CARTER
04 Executive Asst to the President .... Ms. Alice BOECKERS
05 Provost and Dean of the Faculty .... Ms. Catherine KODAT
10 VP Finance & Administration .... Ms. Mary Alma NOONAN
30 VP Development/Alumni Rels .... Mr. Calvin D. HUSMANN
32 VP for Student Life .... Mr. Christopher D. CARD
29 VP Alumni/Constituency Engagement .... Mr. Mark D. BRESEMAN
28 VP for Diversity & Inclusion .... Vacant
26 Assoc Vice Pres Communications .... Ms. Megan J. SCOTT
44 Campaign Dir/Principal Gifts Ofcr .... Mr. Lucas A. BROWN
110 Assoc Vice Pres Development .... Ms. Stacy J. MARA
21 Controller .... Ms. Amy PRICE
64 Dean Conservatory of Music .... Mr. Brian G. PERTL
36 Dean of Career Services .... Mr. Mike K. O'CONNOR
121 Dean of Academic Success .... Ms. Monita M. GRAY
20 Associate Dean of the Faculty .... Dr. Peter A. BLITSTEIN
28 Asst Dean Students Multicul Affs .... Ms. Brittany M. BELL
09 Director of Research Administration .... Ms. Kristin L. MCKINLEY
84 Vice Pres Enrollment/ Communications .... Mr. Kenneth L. ANSELMENT
37 Director of Financial Aid .... Mr. Ryan L. GEBLER
06 Registrar .... Ms. Angi LONG
08 Librarian .... Mr. Peter J. GILBERT
41 Athletic Director .... Ms. Kim TATRO
13 Director Information Tech Svcs .... Mr. Steven M. ARMSTRONG
15 Assoc Director of Human Resources .... Ms. Tina L. HARRIG
38 Assoc Dean Stdnts Health/Wellness .... Mr. Rich L. JAZDZEWSKI

Maranatha Baptist University (C)

745 West Main Street, Watertown WI 53094-7600
County: Jefferson FICE Identification: 023172
Unit ID: 239071
Telephone: (920) 261-9300 Carnegie Class: Bac-Diverse
FAX Number: (920) 261-9109 Calendar System: Semester
URL: www.mbu.edu
Established: 1968 Annual Undergrad Tuition & Fees: $17,650
Enrollment: 916 Coed
Affiliation or Control: Independent Non-Profit IRS Status: 501(c)3
Highest Offering: Doctorate
Accreditation: HLC, NURSE

00 Chief Executive Officer .... Dr. Matthew DAVIS
01 President .... Dr. Martin MARRIOTT
05 Vice President for Academic Affairs .... Dr. William LICHT
111 Vice President for Inst Advancement .... Dr. Jim H. HARRISON
10 Vice President for Business Affairs .... Mr. Donald DONOVAN
32 Dean of Students .... Dr. Andrew GOODWILL
06 Registrar .... Mr. Mark HANSON
07 Director of Admissions .... Mr. Peter WRIGHT
30 Director of Development .... Mr. Steve BOARD
09 Director of Institutional Research .... Mr. Jonathan COLEMAN
15 Director Personnel Services .... Mr. Eric HASSENPLUG
26 Chief Public Relations Officer .... Mr. Jonathan SHEELEY
41 Athletic Director .... Mr. Robert THOMPSON
08 Librarian .... Mr. James BRAUGHLER
35 Director Student Affairs .... Mr. Luke DEWALD
29 Director Alumni Relations .... Mr. Peter WRIGHT
37 Director Student Financial Aid .... Mr. Matthew UPLINGER
13 Chief Info Technology Officer .... Mr. Scott RILEY
19 Director Security/Safety .... Mr. Timothy JOHNS
106 Dir Online Education/E-learning .... Mrs. Dana DAVIS
18 Chief Facilities/Physical Plant .... Mr. Jared CHESLEY
50 Dean School of Business .... Dr. Tracy FOSTER
53 Dean School of Education .... Dr. Robert LAZZELL

Marian University (D)

45 S National Avenue, Fond Du Lac WI 54935-4699
County: Fond Du Lac FICE Identification: 003861
Unit ID: 239080
Telephone: (920) 923-7600 Carnegie Class: Masters/M
FAX Number: (920) 923-7154 Calendar System: Semester
URL: www.marianuniversity.edu
Established: 1936 Annual Undergrad Tuition & Fees: $28,560
Enrollment: 1,593 Coed
Affiliation or Control: Roman Catholic IRS Status: 501(c)3
Highest Offering: Doctorate
Accreditation: HLC, NURSE, RAD, SW

01 President .... Dr. Michelle E. MAJEWSKI
05 VP Academic Affairs .... Dr. Ken R. MULLIKEN
10 VP Business & Finance .... Mr. David W. WONG
32 Int VP Student Life/Dir Athletics .... Mr. Jason BARTELT
111 Interim Sr VP Advancement & Alumni .... Ms. Kathleen CANDEE
26 Senior VP for University Relations .... Dr. George E. KOONCE, JR.
101 Secretary of the Corporation .... Ms. Carey C. GARDIN
04 Executive Assistant to President .... Ms. Susan L. CAMPBELL
21 Controller .... Ms. Dawn M. GUELL
107 Dean College of the Professions .... Vacant
49 Dean College Arts/Sciences/Letters .... Vacant
18 Operations Manager/Facilities .... Mr. Todd BUSS
90 Assoc VP Academic Administration .... Ms. Lynda K. SCHULTZ
114 Asst VP Budget/Systems/Analytics .... Mr. Thomas P. RICHTER
35 Assistant Dean of Students .... Ms. Pamela C. WARREN
37 Director of Financial Aid .... Ms. Wendy A. HILVO
42 Director of Campus Ministry .... Sr. Edie A. CREWS, CSA
27 Asst VP Marketing & Communication .... Ms. Lisa L. KIDD
84 Asst VP & Dean of Enrollment .... Ms. Shannon S. LALUZERNE
15 Director of Human Resources .... Ms. Sabrina J. JOHNSON
41 Director of Athletics .... Mr. Jason BARTELT
23 Director of Health Services .... Ms. Jodi S. SCHRAUTH
36 Director of Career Services .... Vacant
109 Chef/Manager .... Mr. Bill ROBBINS
40 Director of Spirit Store .... Mr. Charles W. RUFFING
38 Director of Counseling .... Ms. Robyn A. WILLIAMS
92 Director Honors Program .... Dr. Michael T. GARVEY
39 Director of Residence Life .... Ms. Severa KRUEGER
104 Director of Study Abroad .... Dr. Matthew P. SZROMBA
19 Lead Security Supervisor .... Mr. Christopher M. GURECKI
121 Dean of Student Success .... Ms. Jennifer K. FARVOUR
89 Director of First Year Studies .... Ms. Juliet V. LOCKWOOD
06 Interim Registrar .... Ms. Bianca Y. BIRSCHBACH

Marquette University (E)

PO Box 1881, Milwaukee WI 53201-1881
County: Milwaukee FICE Identification: 003863
Unit ID: 239105
Telephone: (414) 288-7700 Carnegie Class: DU-Higher
FAX Number: (414) 288-3300 Calendar System: Semester
URL: www.marquette.edu
Established: 1881 Annual Undergrad Tuition & Fees: $45,666
Enrollment: 11,550 Coed
Affiliation or Control: Roman Catholic IRS Status: 501(c)3
Highest Offering: Doctorate
Accreditation: HLC, ANEST, ARCPA, CAATE, CACREP, CLPSY, COPSY, DENT, LAW, MIDWF, MT, NURSE, PTA, SP, THEA

01 President .... Dr. Michael R. LOVELL
05 Provost/EVP Academic Affairs .... Dr. Kimo AH YUN
10 Sr Vice President/COO .... Mr. Joel POGODZINSKI
15 Vice President Human Resources .... Ms. Claudia PAETSCH
32 Vice President Student Affairs .... Dr. Xavier A. COLE
09 Vice Pres Research and Innovation .... Dr. Jeanne M. HOSSENLOPP
42 Vice Pres Mission & Ministry .... Rev. James VOISS, S.J.
20 Senior Vice Prov Faculty Affairs .... Dr. Gary MEYER
26 VP Univ Relations/Gen Counsel .... Mr. Paul JONES
41 Vice Pres and Director of Athletics .... Mr. Bill SCHOLL
111 Vice Pres University Advancement .... Mr. Tim MCMAHON
28 Vice Pres Inclusive Excellence .... Dr. William WELBURN
21 Vice President Finance .... Mr. Ian GONZALEZ
20 Vice Provost Academic Affairs .... Dr. John J. SU
84 Vice Pres Enrollment Management .... Dr. John BAWOROWSKY
06 University Registrar .... Mr. Seth ZLOTOCHA
07 Dean of Undergrad Admissions .... Mr. Brian TROYER
60 Dean of Communication .... Dr. Sarah FELDNER
76 Dean of Health Sciences .... Dr. William CULLINAN
61 Dean of the Law School .... Mr. Joseph D. KEARNEY
52 Dean of Dentistry .... Dr. William K. LOBB
49 Dean Arts & Sciences/Education .... Dr. Heidi BOSTIC
54 Dean of Engineering .... Dr. Kristina ROPELLA
50 Acting Dean of Business Admin .... Mr. Tim HANLEY
08 Dean of Libraries .... Ms. Janice WELBURN
101 Sr Advisor to Pres/Corp Secretary .... Mr. Steven W. FRIEDER
66 Dean of Nursing .... Dr. Janet WESSEL KREJCI
58 VProv Grad/Prof Stds/Dn of Grad Sch .... Dr. Douglas WOODS
13 Chief Information Officer .... Ms. Laurie PANELLA
35 Dean of Students .... Dr. Stephanie QUADE
30 Senior Philanthropic Advisor .... Mr. Timothy RIPPINGER
21 Director Finance .... Ms. Tari BLAZEI
45 VP Planning/Facilities Mgmt .... Ms. Lora STRIGENS
25 Exec Dir Research & Sponsored Prog .... Ms. Katherine DURBEN
23 Exec Dir University Medical Clinic .... Mrs. Keli WOLLMER
36 Dir Career Services Center .... Ms. Courtney HANSON
38 Interim Dir Counseling Center .... Ms. Brenda LENZ
18 Asst Dir Facilities Services .... Mr. Christopher BARTOLONE
37 Assoc VProv Fin Aid/Enrollment Svcs .... Ms. Susan M. TEERINK
40 Sr Dir Merchandising/Licensing .... Mr. James K. GRAEBERT
29 Sr Engagement Director .... Mr. Daniel DEWEERDT
19 Chief of Police .... Ms. Edith HUDSON
96 Director of Purchasing .... Ms. Jenny ALEXANDER
04 Executive Asst to President .... Mrs. Stacy ROMANT
39 Director Residence Life .... Ms. Mary JANZ

Medical College of Wisconsin (F)

PO Box 26509, Milwaukee WI 53226-0509
County: Milwaukee FICE Identification: 024535
Unit ID: 239169
Telephone: (414) 955-8296 Carnegie Class: Spec-4-yr-Med
FAX Number: (414) 955-6560 Calendar System: Other
URL: www.mcw.edu
Established: 1893 Annual Graduate Tuition & Fees: N/A
Enrollment: 1,506 Coed
Affiliation or Control: Independent Non-Profit IRS Status: 501(c)3
Highest Offering: Doctorate; No Undergraduates
Accreditation: HLC, AA, CAMPEP, IPSY, MED, PDPSY, PH, PHAR

01 President & CEO .... Dr. John R. RAYMOND, SR.
05 Provost/Exec VP/Dean .... Dr. Joseph E. KERSCHNER
04 Executive Asst to President .... Ms. Paula HABERLEIN
88 Sr VP Strategic Acad Partnerships .... Dr. Cheryl A. MAURANA
10 Exec VP/COO/Finance .... Mr. Christopher P. KOPS
81 Dean Grad Sch Biomedical Science .... Dr. Ravi P. MISRA
30 Vice Pres of Development .... Mr. Mitchell BECKMAN
15 VP & Chief People Officer .... Ms. Adrienne MITCHELL
86 VP Government & Community Relations .... Ms. Kathryn A. KUHN
117 VP Corporate Compliance/Risk Mgmt .... Mr. Daniel WICKEHAM
26 SVP Univ Engagement/Strategic Plan .... Ms. Mara LORD
13 VP Information Services/CIO .... Mr. David C. HOTCHKISS
27 Assoc VP Communications .... Ms. Mary REINKE
20 Assoc Provost/Sr Assoc Dean .... Dr. William J. HUESTON
20 Associate Provost Faculty Affairs .... Dr. Christina RUNGE
31 Asst VP Engagement .... Mr. James PECK
28 VP Inclusion & Diversity .... Dr. C. Greer JORDAN
32 Assoc Dean Student Div & Inclusion .... Dr. Malika SIKER
58 Sr Assoc Dean Graduate Med Educ .... Dr. Kenneth B. SIMONS
88 Assoc Dean Neuroscience Rsrch Ctr .... Dr. Cecilia J. HILLARD
20 Associate Dean Curriculum .... Dr. Travis P. WEBB
114 Assoc Director Budget .... Ms. Lisa SCHEELE
13 Director Application Development .... Ms. Rebecca L. MORRISON
08 Director Medical Libraries .... Ms. Ellen N. SAYED
07 Dir Medical School Admissions .... Ms. Alexis MEYER
06 Registrar .... Ms. Kerry J. GROSSE
18 VP Facilities & Operations .... Mr. Jeffrey BORNEMANN
37 Director Student Financial Services .... Ms. Kristin J. STUHR-MOOTZ
25 Director Grants & Contracts .... Ms. April HAVERTY
29 Exec Director Alumni Relations .... Ms. Angela NELSON
96 Dir Purchasing & Payables .... Ms. Joan AGUADO WARE
40 Manager of Bookstore .... Ms. Cathy GRANFIELD
19 Director Public Safety .... Mr. David C. FELLER
43 Sr VP General Counsel .... Mr. John NEWSOME
10 Chief Financial Officer .... Mr. Barclay FERGUSON
67 Dean School of Pharmacy .... Dr. George MACKINNON
88 Managed Care Contract Mgr .... Mr. Jeffrey WOJNOWSKI
46 Assoc Provost for Research .... Dr. Ann NATTINGER
21 Assoc VP Financial Plng & Analysis .... Mr. Kevin EIDE
101 Liaison to Board of Trustees .... Ms. Kristin NIEMIEC
44 Director Non-Major Giving .... Ms. Elsa KNYSAK

Midwest College of Oriental Medicine (A)

6232 Bankers Road, Racine WI 53403-9747
County: Racine FICE Identification: 030612
Unit ID: 383020
Telephone: (800) 593-2320 Carnegie Class: Spec-4-yr-Other Health
FAX Number: (262) 554-7475 Calendar System: Quarter
URL: www.acupuncture.edu
Established: 1979 Annual Undergrad Tuition & Fees: N/A
Enrollment: 62 Coed
Affiliation or Control: Proprietary IRS Status: Proprietary
Highest Offering: Master's; No Lower Division
Accreditation: ACUP

01 President Dr. William J. DUNBAR
05 Director of Academics Dr. Robert CHELNICK
12 Evanston Campus Director Dr. Kristine L. LA POINT
37 Director of Financial Aid Ms. Elizabeth M. HOJAN
07 Admissions Coord/Transfer Credit Ms. Liz WARKENTIN
06 Records Officer/Registrar Ms. Amy L. BENISH
08 Librarian Mr. John BALLARINI
32 Dean of Students Ms. Olga GAJDOSIK
09 Research Director Vacant
85 Dean of Foreign Students Dr. Kris LA POINT
108 Clinic Tracking/Inst Evaluation Ms. Deirdre M. DUNBAR
91 Information Systems Mr. William H. LEHMAN
26 Marketing/Student Affairs Mr. Chris A. KRAJNIAK
88 Office Manager Ms. Stephanie M. PITTMAN

Milwaukee Career College (B)

3077 North Maryfair Road, Suite 300,
Milwaukee WI 53222
County: Milwaukee FICE Identification: 041174
Unit ID: 449861
Telephone: (800) 754-1009 Carnegie Class: Spec 2-yr-Health
FAX Number: (414) 727-9557 Calendar System: Other
URL: www.mkecc.edu
Established: 2002 Annual Undergrad Tuition & Fees: N/A
Enrollment: 231 Coed
Affiliation or Control: Proprietary IRS Status: Proprietary
Highest Offering: Associate Degree
Accreditation: ABHES, SURTEC

01 President Jack TAKAHASHI

Milwaukee Institute of Art & Design (C)

273 E Erie Street, Milwaukee WI 53202-6003
County: Milwaukee FICE Identification: 020771
Unit ID: 239309
Telephone: (414) 847-3200 Carnegie Class: Spec-4-yr-Arts
FAX Number: (414) 291-8077 Calendar System: Semester
URL: www.miad.edu
Established: 1974 Annual Undergrad Tuition & Fees: $39,560
Enrollment: 925 Coed
Affiliation or Control: Independent Non-Profit IRS Status: 501(c)3
Highest Offering: Baccalaureate
Accreditation: HLC, ART

01 President Mr. Jeff MORIN
05 VP of Academic Affairs Vacant
84 VP for Enrollment Management Mr. Mark FETHERSTON
04 Executive Assistant to President Ms. Rachel FOSTER
08 Director of Library Services Ms. Cynthia LYNCH
10 VP for Financial Affairs Ms. Brenda JONES
111 Vice Pres for Institutional Advance Ms. Tracy MILKOWSKI
39 Director of Residential Living Ms. Marianne DI ULIO
32 Dean of Students Vacant
37 Executive Director of Financial Aid Ms. Carol MASSE
07 Director of Admissions Ms. Molly NOYES
88 Asst Dir of Transfer Admissions Mr. Matthew SOTHAN
08 Asst Director of Library Services Ms. Nancy SIKER
36 Exec Dir of Advising & Career Svcs Mr. Duane P. SEIDENSTICKER
51 Dir Pre-College & Continuing Educ Mr. Corbett TOOMSEN
19 Director Security/Safety Mr. Keith A. KOTOWICZ
06 Registrar Ms. Jean WEIMER
38 Director of Advising Vacant
15 Director of Human Resources Mr. Dustin HOOT
20 Director of Academic Operations Ms. Marie COUTURE
18 Director of Building & Grounds Mr. Michael A. GOETZ
13 Director of Technology Mr. Matt OGDEN
88 Director of Emerging Technology Mr. Ben DEMBROSKI
88 Exec Director of Innovation Center Mr. Drew MAXWELL
35 Assoc Dean of Students Ms. Jennifer CRANDALL
21 Director of Accounting Ms. Kelly BERES
26 Director of Communication Ms. Dana MCCULLOUGH
28 Director of Equity & Inclusion Mr. Richard ANDERSON-MARTINEZ
29 Alumni Engagement Coordinator Vacant
44 Devel Database & Donor Svcs Mgr Ms. Anne KIRSCHMANN

Milwaukee School of Engineering (D)

1025 N Broadway, Milwaukee WI 53202-3109
County: Milwaukee FICE Identification: 003868
Unit ID: 239318
Telephone: (414) 277-7300 Carnegie Class: Masters/M
FAX Number: (414) 277-7454 Calendar System: Quarter
URL: www.msoe.edu
Established: 1903 Annual Undergrad Tuition & Fees: $43,575
Enrollment: 2,673 Coed
Affiliation or Control: Independent Non-Profit IRS Status: 501(c)3
Highest Offering: Master's
Accreditation: HLC, NURSE, PERF

01 President Dr. John WALZ
05 Executive Vice President Academics Dr. Eric BAUMGARTNER
10 Vice President of Finance and CFO Ms. Dawn THIBEDEAU
111 VP of University Advancement Mr. Jeff SNOW
18 VP of Campus Infrastructure Dr. Steve WILLIAMS
32 VP of Student Services/Enroll Mgmt Dr. Timothy VALLEY
88 Dean of Applied Research Mr. Sheku KAMARA
48 Chair Architectural Engr Dept Dr. Christopher RAEBEL
54 Chair Electrical Engr/CPU Sci Dept Dr. Sheila ROSS
79 Chair Humanities Department Dr. Alicia DOMACK
81 Chair Physics/Chemistry/Mathematics Dr. Matey KALTCHEV
66 Chair Nursing Department Dr. Carol SABEL
06 Registrar Ms. Mary F. NIELSEN
13 Senior Director of IT Mr. Rick THOMAS
26 VP Marketing & Community Engagement Mr. Sebastian THACHENKARY
27 Sr Dir Comm/Media Relations Ms. JoEllen BURDUE
15 Director of Human Resources Ms. Rebecca PLOECKELMAN
30 Senior Director of Development Mr. Greg CASEY
41 Director Athletics Mr. Brian MILLER
08 Director of Library & Info Services Mr. Gary S. SHIMEK
29 Director Alumni Affairs Ms. Cathy VAREBROOK
07 Dean of Admissions Mr. Paul BORENS
36 Director of Career Services Ms. Julie WAY
40 Bookstore Manager Mr. David P. ABRAHAMSON
04 Executive Admin to the President Ms. Kellyann M. REUTER
20 Assoc VP Academic Success Dr. Jill MEYER
19 Director of Public Safety Mr. Billy FYFE
37 Director of Financial Aid Ms. Stephanie MEALY
38 Director Counseling Services Ms. Colleen CHRISTANSEN
39 Director Residence Life Ms. Elizabeth ALBRECHT
44 Director Annual Giving Ms. Jessica TEDAMRONGWANISH

Mount Mary University (E)

2900 N Menomonee River Parkway,
Milwaukee WI 53222-4597
County: Milwaukee FICE Identification: 003869
Unit ID: 239390
Telephone: (414) 930-3000 Carnegie Class: Masters/M
FAX Number: (414) 930-3712 Calendar System: Semester
URL: www.mtmary.edu
Established: 1913 Annual Undergrad Tuition & Fees: $32,790
Enrollment: 1,200 Female
Affiliation or Control: Roman Catholic IRS Status: 501(c)3
Highest Offering: Doctorate
Accreditation: HLC, CACREP, CIDA, DIETC, DIETI, NURSE, OT, SW

01 President Dr. Christine PHARR
10 VP Finance & Admin Services Mr. Robert O'KEEFE
05 VP Academic Affairs Dr. Karen FRIEDLEN
84 Vice Pres Enrollment Services Mr. David WEGENER
30 Vice Pres Development Ms. Pamela OWENS
88 Vice President Mission/ Identity Sr. Joan PENZENSTADLER, SSND
32 Vice Pres Student Affairs Ms. Keri ALIOTO
28 VP Diversity/Equity/Inclusion Ms. Julie LANDRY
50 Dean School Business/Arts & Design Mr. Robert SCHWARTZ
81 Dean School Nat & Health Sci/Educ Dr. Cheryl BAILEY
79 Dean Sch Hum/Social Sci/Interdisc Dr. Wendy WEAVER
121 Dean Student Success Ms. Beth FELCH
58 Dean of Graduate Education Vacant
21 Sr Dir of Business Ofc/Controller Ms. Nicole LANDRY
06 Registrar Ms. Rachel FISCHER
110 Senior Development Officer Ms. Lisa BREITSPRECKER
26 Dir of Marketing & Communications Ms. Kathy VAN ZEELAND
29 Director of Alumnae Relations Vacant
123 Director of Graduate Admission Mr. Kirk HELLER DE MESSER
07 Director of Undergraduate Admission Mr. James WISEMAN
09 Director of Inst Research Ms. LeeAnn PERKINS
08 Director of Library Mr. Daniel VINSON
13 Senior Director of IT Vacant
37 Director Financial Aid Ms. Angela SARNI
39 Dir Student Engagement/Resid Living Ms. Julie SCHNEITER
36 Dir of Advising/Career Development Vacant
104 Director of International Studies Ms. Nan METZGER
15 Senior Director of Human Resources Ms. April FORRAY
41 Athletic Director Ms. Natalie BALLETO
42 Director of Campus Ministry Ms. Theresa UTSCHIG
18 Director of Buildings & Grounds Mr. Gary KOENEN
19 Director of Public Safety Mr. Dan BRAUER
40 Mgr Barnes & Noble Bookstore Mr. Timothy STERNKE
04 Executive Assistant to President Ms. Mary EGGERT
102 Exec Dir Corp Rels/Foundation/WLI Ms. Anne KAHL

Nashotah House (F)

2777 Mission Road, Nashotah WI 53058-9793
County: Waukesha FICE Identification: 003874
Unit ID: 239424
Telephone: (262) 646-6500 Carnegie Class: Spec-4-yr-Faith
FAX Number: (262) 646-6504 Calendar System: Semester
URL: www.nashotah.edu
Established: 1842 Annual Graduate Tuition & Fees: N/A
Enrollment: 106 Coed
Affiliation or Control: Protestant Episcopal IRS Status: 501(c)3
Highest Offering: Doctorate; No Undergraduates
Accreditation: THEOL

01 President/Dean Dr. Garwood P. ANDERSON
11 Senior Director of Operations Rev. Jason TERHUNE
05 Provost Dr. Garwood P. ANDERSON
111 Exec VP Institutional Advancement Mr. Labin L. DUKE
13 Director Information Systems Mr. Matt BILLS
30 Senior Development Officer Mr. Jim WATKINS
09 Asst Dean Institutional Research Rev. Esther KRAMER
32 Senior Director of Students Rev. Jason TERHUNE
101 Secretary of the Board of Trustees Rev. R. Brien KOEHLER
06 Registrar Ms. Carolee PUCHTER
07 Director of Admissions Ms. Kristen OLVER
08 Dir Francis Donaldson Library Dr. David G. SHERWOOD
26 Director Marketing/Communications Ms. Lisa SWAN
42 Director of Church Relations Ms. Carolyn BARTKUS
18 Director B&G/Maintenance Mr. Ricco MEDINA

Northland College (G)

1411 Ellis Avenue, Ashland WI 54806-3999
County: Ashland FICE Identification: 003875
Unit ID: 239512
Telephone: (715) 682-1699 Carnegie Class: Bac-Diverse
FAX Number: (715) 682-1308 Calendar System: Other
URL: www.northland.edu
Established: 1892 Annual Undergrad Tuition & Fees: $38,596
Enrollment: 570 Coed
Affiliation or Control: United Church Of Christ IRS Status: 501(c)3
Highest Offering: Baccalaureate
Accreditation: HLC

01 President Dr. Karl SOLIBAKKE
100 Chief of Staff Ms. Dawn RIVARD
11 Chief Operating Officer Vacant
20 Dean of Academic Affairs Dr. Alan BREW
32 Dean of Students Ms. Melissa HARVEY
07 Dean of Admissions Mr. Ryan COCKERILL
111 Director of Advancement Ms. Mary ASBACH
26 Director of Advancement & Marketing Ms. Mary O'BRIEN
29 Director of Alumni Relations Ms. Jackie MOORE
41 Director Intercollegiate Athletics Mr. Seamus GREGORY
13 Exec Director Information Svcs Tech Mr. Todd PYDO
15 Exec Director Human Resources Ms. Sherri VENERO
08 Library Director Ms. Julia WAGGONER
39 Director of Residential Life Ms. Tiffany KOESHALL
25 Director of Grants/Sponsored Awards Ms. Lisa WILLIAMSON
37 Director of Financial Aid Ms. Kelly DUNN
38 Campus Counselor Mr. Scott JOHNSON
23 Health Services Manager Ms. Jennifer NEWAGO
21 Chief Business Officer Ms. Sherri VENERO
28 Diversity and Inclusion Coordinator Ms. Ruth DE JESUS
06 Registrar Ms. Michelle BITZER
18 Director of Operations Mr. Paul WEBB
19 Campus Safety Director Mr. Dawayne LAMPSON
04 Admin Assistant to the President Ms. Heather M. KINNUNEN

Ottawa University Brookfield, WI (H)

245 South Executive Drive, Ste 340, Brookfield WI 53005
Telephone: (262) 879-0200 Identification: 666084
Accreditation: &HLC

† Regional accreditation is carried under the parent institution in Ottawa, KS.

Rasmussen University - Green Bay (I)

904 South Taylor Street, Building 1, Green Bay WI 54303
Telephone: (920) 593-8400 Identification: 667063
Accreditation: &HLC, ADNUR, CAHIIM, MAAB, MLTAD

† Regional accreditation is carried under the parent institution in Saint Cloud, MN. The tuition figure is an average, actual tuition may vary.

Ripon College (J)

300 West Seward Street, PO Box 248,
Ripon WI 54971-0248
County: Fond du Lac FICE Identification: 003884
Unit ID: 239628
Telephone: (920) 748-8115 Carnegie Class: Bac-A&S
FAX Number: (920) 748-7243 Calendar System: Semester
URL: www.ripon.edu
Established: 1851 Annual Undergrad Tuition & Fees: $47,123
Enrollment: 816 Coed
Affiliation or Control: Independent Non-Profit IRS Status: 501(c)3
Highest Offering: Baccalaureate
Accreditation: HLC

01 President Zachariah P. MESSITTE
05 Vice Pres/Dean of Faculty John E. SISKO
111 VP for Advancement Shawn F. KARSTEN
10 Vice President for Finance Andrea N. YOUNG
32 Vice President/Dean of Students Christopher M. OGLE
84 Vice President for Enrollment Jennifer L. MACHACEK
06 Assoc Dean of Faculty/Registrar Michele A. WITTLER
36 Dir of Career/Prof Development Mary HATLEN
21 Associate VP for Finance Lori A. SCHULZE
08 Access Services Librarian Karlyn M. SCHUMACHER
35 Dir Student Activities/Orientation Sara VANSTEENBERGEN
121 Director Student Support Svcs Daniel J. KRHIN
39 Director of Residence Life Mark B. NICKLAUS

27 Dir of Creative & Social Media .... Richard T. DAMM
13 Sr Dir of Information Technology .... Brian DISTERHAFT
18 Director Physical Plant .... Brian SKAMRA
41 Director of Athletics .... Ryan KANE
29 Dir Constituent Engagement .... Amy L. GERRETSEN
15 Director of Human Resource .... Paula STETTBACHER
38 Director of Counseling Services .... Cynthia S. VIERTEL
37 Director Financial Aid .... Linda KINZIGER
28 Dir of Multicultural Affairs .... Maria MENDOZA-BAUTISTA
44 Director Annual Giving .... Kelly A. NIELSEN
90 Director Academic Computing .... Andrew P. DESCH
91 Director Administrative Computing .... Gary S. RODMAN
100 Chief of Staff .... Kara K. JANKOWSKI

Sacred Heart Seminary and School of Theology (A)

7335 S Highway 100, P.O. Box 429,
Hales Corners WI 53130-0429
County: Milwaukee FICE Identification: 020780
Unit ID: 239637
Telephone: (414) 425-8300 Carnegie Class: Spec-4-yr-Faith
FAX Number: (414) 529-6999 Calendar System: Semester
URL: www.shsst.edu
Established: 1933 Annual Graduate Tuition & Fees: N/A
Enrollment: 98 Coed
Affiliation or Control: Roman Catholic IRS Status: 501(c)3
Highest Offering: Master's; No Undergraduates
Accreditation: HLC, THEOL

01 President-Rector .... V. Rev. Raúl L. GOMEZ-RUIZ, SDS
10 VP Finance & Business Svcs .... Mr. Christopher LAMBERT
05 VP Intellectual Formation/CAO .... Dr. Patrick J. RUSSELL
42 Vice Rector/VP Formation Programs .... Rev. Vien NGUYEN, SCJ
111 VP for Institutional Advancement .... Ms. Monica MISEY
88 VP Intercultural Prep for Ministry .... Ms. Kelly KORNACKI
26 VP Marketing & Communications .... Vacant
08 Director Library & Acad Supp Svcs .... Ms. Jennifer BARTHOLOMEW
88 Director Liturgy and Music/Organist .... Dr. Benjamin STONE
88 Director Lux Center .... Ms. Bonnie SHAFRIN
07 Director of Admissions .... Dr. Jeremy BLACKWOOD
18 Director Plant Operations .... Mr. Michael J. ERATO
88 Director Hispanic Min Prep Program .... Rev. José GONZÁLEZ
88 Director Faculty Council .... Dr. Steven SHIPPEE
06 Registrar/Acting Academic Dean .... Ms. Julie O'CONNOR
13 Information Systems Coordinator .... Ms. Mary GRIEGER
88 Design Project Manager .... Ms. Ruth MARKWORTH
04 Executive Asst to President-Rector .... Ms. Brittany HAGER MCNEELY
108 Accreditation Spec & Title IX Coord .... Dr. Robert GOTCHER

Saint Norbert College (B)

100 Grant Street, De Pere WI 54115-2099
County: Brown FICE Identification: 003892
Unit ID: 239716
Telephone: (920) 403-3181 Carnegie Class: Bac-A&S
FAX Number: (920) 403-4008 Calendar System: Semester
URL: www.snc.edu
Established: 1898 Annual Undergrad Tuition & Fees: $40,885
Enrollment: 1,939 Coed
Affiliation or Control: Roman Catholic IRS Status: 501(c)3
Highest Offering: Master's
Accreditation: HLC

01 President .... Dr. Brian BRUESS
05 Vice Pres Academic Affairs/Provost .... Dr. Jennifer BONDS-RAACKE
10 Vice President Business & Finance .... Ms. Autumn ANFANG
111 Vice Pres Institutional Advancement .... Mr. Jon ENSLIN
32 Vice Pres Student Affairs .... Mr. Joe WEBB
84 Vice Pres Enrollment Mgmt/Comm .... Mr. Edward LAMM
13 Vice Pres Info Tech & CIO .... Mr. Marc BELANGER
110 Assoc Vice Pres Inst Advancement .... Ms. Lia KAMPMAN
09 Dir Institutional Effectiveness .... Ms. Carolyn UHL
20 Dean Faculty Affairs & Development .... Dr. Lisa VANWORMER
36 Director Career Services .... Ms. Mary Ellen OLSON
38 Dir Counseling/Career Programs .... Mr. Bruce ROBERTSON
07 Exec Director of Admissions .... Mr. Mark SELIN
29 Director Alumni & Parent Relations .... Mr. William FALK
21 Director of Finance .... Ms. Elizabeth MILLER
37 Director of Financial Aid .... Ms. Jessica RAFELD
26 Dir Communications/Marketing .... Ms. Nina ROUSE
08 Director of Library .... Dr. Kristin D. VOGEL
15 Asst Vice Pres Human Resources .... Ms. Heather BUTTERFIELD
41 Director Physical Educ/Athletics .... Mr. Cam FULLER
06 Registrar .... Ms. Lauren GAECKE
104 Assoc Academic Dir Global Affairs .... Mr. Dan STOLL
28 Dir Multicultural Student Services .... Ms. Bridgit MARTIN
18 Director Facilities/Physical Plant .... Mr. Patrick WRENN
40 Manager Bookstore Operations .... Mr. Ryan SILER
04 Executive Asst to President .... Ms. Jamie MCGUIRE
102 Dir Foundation/Corporate Relations .... Ms. Amy KUNDINGER
100 Chief of Staff .... Ms. Julie MASSEY
19 Director Security/Safety .... Mr. Eric DUNNING
39 Director Student Housing .... Mr. Michael PECKHAM
44 Director Annual Giving .... Ms. Monica MCCLURE
50 Dean of Business .... Mr. Dan HEISER

*University of Wisconsin System (C)

1220 Linden Dr, 1720 Van Hise Hall,
Madison WI 53706-1559
County: Dane FICE Identification: 003894
Unit ID: 240435
Telephone: (608) 262-2321 Carnegie Class: N/A
FAX Number: (608) 262-3985
URL: www.wisconsin.edu

01 Int President .... Tommy G. THOMPSON
100 Chief of Staff .... Dean STEINBERG
05 VP Academic/Student Affairs .... Anny MORROBEL-SOSA
11 Int VP Administration .... James LANGDON
10 VP Finance .... Sean NELSON
30 Int VP University Relations .... Scott NEITZEL
15 Int Assoc VP HR & CHRO .... Dan CHANEN
117 Assoc VP Administrative Services .... Ruth ANDERSON
116 Assoc VP Cap Planning & Budget .... Alexandria ROE
119 Assoc VP Info Security .... Kathy MAYER
120 Assoc VP Learning/Info Tech .... Steven HOPPER
88 Int Exec Dir Shared Services .... Stacey ROLSTON
121 Associate VP Student Success .... Christine NAVIA
20 AVP Acad Pgms/Faculty Advancement .... Carleen VANDE ZANDE
56 Sr AVP & Exec Dir Extended Campus .... Aaron BROWER
09 Assoc VP Policy and Research .... Ben PASSMORE
21 Sr Assoc VP Financial Admin .... Julie GORDON
114 Asst VP Budget/Planning .... Renee STEPHENSON
88 Director Trust Funds .... Douglas HOERR
88 Exec Dir Business & Entrepreneur .... Mark LANGE
26 Exec Dir Public & Community Affairs .... Jack JABLONSKI
27 Dir of Strategic Communications .... Heather LAROI
86 AVP Government Relations .... Jeff BUHRANDT
43 General Counsel .... Quinn WILLIAMS
28 System Sr EDI Officer .... Warren ANDERSON
101 ED & Corp Sec to Board of Regents .... Jessica LATHROP
04 Sr Exec Assistant to the President .... Nicole SMENT

*University of Wisconsin-Madison (D)

500 Lincoln Drive, Madison WI 53706-1380
County: Dane FICE Identification: 003895
Unit ID: 240444
Telephone: (608) 262-1234 Carnegie Class: DU-Highest
FAX Number: (608) 262-0123 Calendar System: Semester
URL: www.wisc.edu
Established: 1848 Annual Undergrad Tuition & Fees (In-State): $10,742
Enrollment: 44,640 Coed
Affiliation or Control: State IRS Status: 501(c)3
Highest Offering: Doctorate
Accreditation: HLC, ARCPA, ART, AUD, CAATE, CACREP, CAMPEP, CIDA, CLPSY, COPSY, DANCE, DIETC, DIETD, DMS, IPSY, LAW, LIB, LSAR, MED, MUS, NURSE, OT, PCSAS, PH, PHAR, PLNG, PTA, SCPSY, SP, SW, VET

02 Chancellor .... Dr. Rebecca BLANK
05 Provost Academic Affairs .... Dr. Karl SCHOLZ
46 Vice Chanc Research/Graduate Educ .... Dr. Steven ACKERMAN
11 Int Vice Chancellor Administration .... Mr. Robert CRAMER
100 Chancellor's Chief of Staff .... Mr. Matt MAYRL
26 Vice Chanc University Relations .... Mr. Charles HOSLET
32 Vice Chanc Student Affairs .... Dr. Lori REESOR
84 Vice Provost Enrollment Management .... Mr. Derek KINDLE
13 CIO/Vice Prov Info Technology .... Ms. Lois BROOKS
18 Int Assoc VC Facilities Plng/Mgmt .... Mr. Robert CRAMER
28 Int Vice Provost Diversity/Climate .... Dr. Cheryl GITTENS
20 Vice Provost Faculty/Staff Pgms .... Dr. Beth MEYERAND
20 Vice Provost Teaching/Learning .... Dr. John ZUMBRUNNEN
10 Assoc Vice Chanc Finance/Admin .... Mr. David MURPHY
21 Asst Vice Chanc Business Svcs .... Mr. Dan LANGER
35 Chief of Staff/Student Affairs .... Mr. Argyle WADE
58 Dean Graduate School .... Dr. William J. KARPUS
49 Dean College Letters & Science .... Dr. Eric WILCOTS
63 Dean Medicine and Public Health .... Dr. Robert N. GOLDEN
53 Dean School of Education .... Dr. Diana HESS
50 Dean School of Business .... Dr. Vallabh SAMBAMURTHY
67 Dean School of Pharmacy .... Dr. Steven M. SWANSON
54 Dean of College of Engineering .... Dr. Ian ROBERTSON
47 Dean of Agricultural/Life Sciences .... Dr. Kathryn VANDENBOSCH
66 Dean of School of Nursing .... Dr. Linda SCOTT
59 Dean of Human Ecology .... Dr. Soyeon SHIM
74 Dean of Veterinary Medicine .... Dr. Mark D. MARKEL
61 Dean of the Law School .... Dr. Daniel TOKAJI
82 Dean International Studies .... Dr. Guido PODESTÁ
43 Director of Admin Legal Services .... Mr. Raymond P. TAFFORA
88 Dean Nelson Inst Environmental Stds .... Dr. Paul ROBBINS
41 Director Intercollegiate Athletics .... Mr. Christopher MCINTOSH
88 Director of Physical Plant .... Mr. Jay BIESZKE
88 Director of the Arboretum .... Dr. Karen OBERHAUSER
88 Director State Lab of Hygiene .... Dr. James SCHAUER
88 Director of Wisconsin Union .... Mr. Mark C. GUTHIER
07 Director of Admissions .... Mr. Andre PHILLIPS
08 Director of Libraries .... Ms. Lisa CARTER
27 Director University Communications .... Mr. John LUCAS
102 President UW Foundation .... Dr. Michael M. KNETTER
37 Director Student Financial Aid .... Ms. Helen FAITH
38 Director Mental Health Services .... Dr. Sarah NOLAN
15 Chief Human Resources .... Mr. Mark WALTERS
39 Director of University Housing .... Dr. Jeffrey NOVAK
51 Dean Continuing Studies .... Dr. Jeffrey RUSSELL
19 Chief of University Police .... Ms. Kristen ROMAN
88 Director of Archives .... Ms. Katie NASH
23 Director University Health Svcs .... Dr. Jake BAGGOTT
88 Director of Space Management .... Mr. Brent LLOYD
17 CEO Hospital & Clinics .... Dr. Alan KAPLAN
109 Dir Auxiliary Operations Analysis .... Ms. Donna HALLERAN
06 Registrar .... Mr. Scott OWCZAREK
88 Secretary of the Faculty .... Ms. Heather DANIELS
88 Secretary of Academic Staff .... Mr. Jake SMITH
88 Director of Recreational Sports .... Mr. Aaron HOBSON
85 Dir International Student Svcs .... Ms. Samantha MCCABE
22 Dir Office of Equity & Diversity .... Mr. Luis A. PINERO
96 Director of Purchasing .... Ms. Lori VOSS
09 Dir Inst Rsrch/Acad Plng/Analysis .... Dr. Jocelyn L. MILNER
88 Sr Special Asst to Provost .... Dr. Eden INOWAY-RONNIE
86 Sr Special Asst to Chanc Fed Rels .... Mr. Michael LENN

*University of Wisconsin-Eau Claire (E)

105 Garfield Avenue, PO Box 4004,
Eau Claire WI 54702-4004
County: Eau Claire FICE Identification: 003917
Unit ID: 240268
Telephone: (715) 836-2637 Carnegie Class: Masters/M
FAX Number: (715) 836-2902 Calendar System: Semester
URL: www.uwec.edu
Established: 1916 Annual Undergrad Tuition & Fees (In-State): $8,870
Enrollment: 11,017 Coed
Affiliation or Control: State IRS Status: 501(c)3
Highest Offering: Doctorate
Accreditation: HLC, CAATE, JOUR, MUS, NURSE, SP, SW

02 Chancellor .... Dr. James C. SCHMIDT
05 Prov/Vice Chanc Academic Affairs .... Dr. Patricia A. KLEINE
100 Sr Special Asst to the Chancellor .... Ms. Mary Jane BRUKARDT
84 Vice Chanc Enrollment Management .... Vacant
10 Vice Chanc Finance/Administration .... Ms. Grace CRICKETTE
28 VC Div/Equity/Inclusion/Stdnt Affs .... Dr. Olga DIAZ
46 Asst VC Research/Sponsored Pgm .... Dr. Karen G. HAVHOLM
20 Assoc Vice Chanc Academic Affairs .... Vacant
20 Assoc Vice Chanc Academic Affairs .... Dr. Michael J. CARNEY
26 Executive Director Mktg & Planning .... Ms. Mary Jane BRUKARDT
22 Director of Affirmative Action .... Ms. Teresa E. O'HALLORAN
102 Exec Dir of Foundation .... Ms. Kimera K. WAY
32 Dean of Students .... Dr. LaRue PIERCE
08 Director of Libraries .... Dr. Jill S. MARKGRAF
18 Director of Facilities .... Mr. Troy TERHARK
13 Chief Information Officer .... Mr. Chip P. ECKARDT
14 Dir Learning & Technology Services .... Mr. Craig A. MEY
15 Director of Human Resources .... Mr. David J. MILLER
37 Director of Financial Aid .... Ms. Nicole S. ANDREWS
38 Director of Counseling .... Dr. Riley C. MCGRATH
06 Registrar .... Ms. Kimberly B. O'KELLY
36 Assoc Director Career Services .... Ms. Staci L. HEIDTKE
23 Director of Student Health Services .... Ms. Laura G. CHELLMAN
39 Director of Housing & Res Life .... Mr. J. Quincy CHAPMAN
41 Director of Athletics .... Mr. Daniel J. SCHUMACHER
51 Director Continuing Education .... Mr. Durwin LONG
85 Interim Lead Intl Education .... Ms. Colleen C. MARCHWICK
102 Director Corporate Relations .... Vacant
92 Director of Honors Program .... Dr. Heather FIELDING
26 Director University Relations .... Ms. Paula GILBECK
27 Director of Integrated Marketing .... Ms. Rebecca J. DIENGER
30 Chief Development/Alumni Relations .... Ms. Kimera K. WAY
09 Institutional Planner .... Mr. Andrew J. NELSON
108 Director of Assessment .... Dr. Mary F. HOFFMAN
49 Interim Dean Col of Arts & Sciences .... Dr. Rodd D. FREITAG
66 Dean Col of Nursing/Health Sciences .... Dr. Linda K. YOUNG
53 Dean Col Education/Human Sciences .... Dr. Carmen K. MANNING
50 Interim Dean College of Business .... Dr. Timothy S. VAUGHAN
04 Interim Exec Asst to Chancellor .... Ms. Corrynn MAHNKE

*University of Wisconsin-Green Bay (F)

2420 Nicolet Drive, Green Bay WI 54311-7001
County: Brown FICE Identification: 003899
Unit ID: 240277
Telephone: (920) 465-2000 Carnegie Class: Masters/M
FAX Number: (920) 465-2032 Calendar System: Semester
URL: www.uwgb.edu
Established: 1965 Annual Undergrad Tuition & Fees (In-State): $7,873
Enrollment: 8,954 Coed
Affiliation or Control: State IRS Status: 501(c)3
Highest Offering: Doctorate
Accreditation: HLC, ART, CAATE, CAHIIM, DIETD, DIETI, MUS, NURSE, SW

02 Chancellor .... Dr. Michael ALEXANDER
05 Int Provost/Vice Chanc Acad Affs .... Dr. Kathleen BURNS
12 CEO UW Manitowoc .... Mr. Jamie SCHRAMM
12 CEO UW Marinette .... Ms. Cindy BAILEY
12 CEO UW Sheboygan .... Mr. Jamie SCHRAMM
10 SVC Inst Strategy/Chf Business Ofcr .... Ms. Sheryl VAN GRUENSVEN
111 Vice Chanc University Advancement .... Mr. Tony WERNER
41 Athletic Director .... Mr. Josh MOON
32 Vice Chanc for Student Affairs .... Dr. Corey KING
20 Int Assoc Provost for Acad Affairs .... Dr. Courtney SHERMAN
53 Dean Health/Education/Social Well .... Dr. Susan GALLAGHER-LEPAK
50 Dean Cofrin School of Business .... Dr. Mathew DORNBUSH
49 Dean of Arts/Humanities .... Dr. Chuck RYBAK
81 Dean of Science/Engr & Tech .... Dr. John KATERS
07 Exec Director of Admissions .... Ms. Rachele BAKIC
15 Asst VC Policy & Compliance .... Mr. Christopher PAQUET
35 Asst Vice Chanc for Student Affairs .... Ms. Gail SIMS-AUBERT
35 Dean of Students .... Mr. Mark OLKOWSKI

18 Dir Facilities Management/Planning ....Mr. Paul PINKSTON
19 Director of Public Safety ....Chief David JONES
21 Controller ....Ms. SuAnn DETAMPEL
84 Asst Vice Chanc Enrollment Services ....Ms. Jennifer JONES
46 Director of Institute for Research ....Mr. Bojan LJUBENKO
37 Director Financial Aid ....Mr. James P. ROHAN
39 Director of Residence Life ....Ms. Gail SIMS-AUBERT
24 Director Media Svcs/Telecomm ....Vacant
23 Director Health Services ....Ms. Amy HENNIGES
100 Chief of Staff ....Mr. Ben JONIAUX
26 Director University Communications ....Ms. Janet BONKOWSKI
36 Director Career Services ...... Ms. Linda G. PEACOCK-LANDRUM
29 Director Alumni Relations ....Ms. Kari MOODY
35 Director Student Life ....Ms. Katherine LESPERANCE
06 Registrar ....Mr. Daniel VANDE YACHT
04 Administrative Asst to President ....Ms. Mary Kate ONTANEDA
104 Director Study Abroad ....Mr. Brent BLAHNIK
28 Diversity Director ....Ms. Mai LO LEE
30 Director of Development ....Mr. Jacob DEPAS
13 Asst Vice Chancellor for IT ....Ms. Wendy WOODWARD
102 Director Foundation ....Mr. Anthony WERNER
51 Asst Vice Chanc Continuing Educ ....Ms. Joy RUZEK
54 Dean of Engineering ....Dr. John KATERS
86 Director Government Relations ....Mr. Ben JONIAUX
96 Procurement Specialist ....Mr. Tory ORTSCHEID

*University of Wisconsin-La Crosse (A)

1725 State Street, La Crosse WI 54601-3788

County: La Crosse FICE Identification: 003919
Unit ID: 240329
Telephone: (608) 785-8000 Carnegie Class: Masters/L
FAX Number: (608) 785-8492 Calendar System: Semester
URL: www.uwlax.edu
Established: 1909 Annual Undergrad Tuition & Fees (In-State): $9,160
Enrollment: 10,531 Coed
Affiliation or Control: State IRS Status: 501(c)3
Highest Offering: Doctorate
Accreditation: HLC, ANEST, ARCPA, CAATE, CAPRT, MUS, NMT, OT, PH, PTA, RADDOS, RTT

02 Chancellor ....Dr. Joe GOW
05 Provost/Vice Chanc Acad Affairs ....Dr. Betsy MORGAN
111 Vice Chancellor Advancement ....Mr. Greg REICHERT
10 Vice Chancellor Admin & Finance ....Dr. Bob HETZEL
50 Dean of Business Administration ....Dr. Taggert BROOKS
53 Dean School of Education ....Dr. Marcie WYCOFF-HORN
79 Dean of Liberal Studies ....Dr. Karl KUNKEL
81 Dean Science/Health ....Dr. Mark SANDHEINRICH
32 Vice Chancellor & Dean of Students ....Dr. Vitaliano FIGUEROA
13 Chief Information Officer ....Mr. James JORSTAD
58 Dean of Graduate & Extended Lrng ....Dr. Meredith THOMSEN
08 Director of Library ....Mr. John JAX
85 Dir International Education & Engag ....Ms. Karolyn BALD
07 Director ES/Admissions ....Mr. Corey SJOQUIST
37 Director ES/Financial Aid ....Ms. Louise L. JANKE
38 Director Counseling/Testing ....Ms. Gretchen REINDERS
36 Director of Career Services ....Ms. Becky VIANDEN
41 Athletic Director ....Ms. Kim BLUM
26 Director News and Marketing ....Mr. Brad R. QUARBERG
29 Director Alumni Relations ....Ms. Janie M. MORGAN
23 Dir Student Health Center ....Dr. Abigail DEYO
09 Director Institutional Research ....Ms. Natalie SOLVERSON
28 Vice Chancellor Diversity/Inclusion ....Ms. Barbara E. STEWART
22 Director Affirmative Action ....Ms. Dina ZAVALA
106 Dir CATL ....Ms. Kristin KOEPKE
39 Director Residence Life ....Ms. Jenni BRUNDAGE
06 Registrar ....Ms. Jan VON RUDEN
15 Chief Human Resources Officer ....Mr. John ACARDO

*University of Wisconsin-Milwaukee (B)

PO Box 413, Milwaukee WI 53201-0413

County: Milwaukee FICE Identification: 003896
Unit ID: 240453
Telephone: (414) 229-1122 Carnegie Class: DU-Highest
FAX Number: (414) 229-6329 Calendar System: Semester
URL: www.uwm.edu
Established: 1885 Annual Undergrad Tuition & Fees (In-State): $9,254
Enrollment: 24,565 Coed
Affiliation or Control: State IRS Status: 501(c)3
Highest Offering: Doctorate
Accreditation: HLC, ART, ATECH, #CAATE, CEA, CLPSY, COPSY, DANCE, DMS, HSA, LIB, MPCAC, MT, MUS, NURSE, OT, PH, PLNG, PTA, RAD, SCPSY, SP, SW

02 Chancellor ....Dr. Mark A. MONE
05 Provost/Vice Chanc Academic Affairs ....Dr. Johannes BRITZ
10 Vice Chanc Finance & Admin Affs ....Ms. Robin L. VAN HARPEN
26 Vice Chanc Univ Relations & Comm ....Vacant
46 Vice Provost of Research ....Dr. Mark T. HARRIS
30 Vice Chanc Development & Alumni Rel ....Dr. Patricia A. BORGER
88 Int VC Global Inclusion/Engagement ....Dr. Chia VANG
20 Assoc Vice Chanc Academic Affairs ....Dr. Devarajan VENUGOPALAN
20 Assoc Vice Chanc Academic Affairs ....Dr. Phyllis KING
84 Associate VC for Enrollment Mgmt ....Ms. Kay EILERS
13 Assoc Vice Chanc/CIO ....Dr. Robert J. BECK
18 Assoc VC Facilities Planning/Mgmt .....Ms. Melissa SPADANUDA
102 President UWM Foundation ....Mr. David H. GILBERT
76 Dean College Health Sciences ....Dr. Timothy BEHRENS
48 Interim Dean Arch & Urban Planning ....Dr. Nancy FRANK
50 Dean School of Business ....Dr. Kaushal CHARI
53 Acting Dean School of Education ....Dr. Tina FREIBURGER
54 Dean College Engr & Applied Science ....Dr. Brett PETERS
57 Interim Dean Peck School of Arts ....Mr. Kevin HARTMAN
65 Int Dean Sch of Freshwater Science ....Dr. Mark HARRIS
69 Acting Dean School Public Health ....Dr. Amy HARLEY
58 Interim Dean Graduate School ....Mr. Jason PUSKAR
49 Dean College of Letters & Science ....Dr. Scott GRONERT
62 Interim Dean School Info Studies ....Dr. Mark HARRIS
66 Dean of College of Nursing ....Dr. Kim LITWACK
70 Dean School Social Welfare ....Dr. Tina FREIBURGER
51 Provost's Deputy for Continuing Ed ....Dr. Nancy NELSON
32 Dean of Students ....Mr. Adam JUSSEL
22 Dir Equity/Diversity Services .... Mr. Jamie CIMPL-WIEMER
08 Associate Vice Provost of Libraries ....Dr. Michael DOYLEN
43 Dir Legal Affairs ....Ms. Joely B. URDAN
06 Registrar .... Ms. Kristin HILDEBRANDT
15 Assoc Vice Chanc Human Resources .... Mr. Timothy DANIELSON
19 Chief of University Police ....Mr. Brian SWITALA
25 Dir Office Sponsored Research ....Ms. Kate MOLLEN
23 Dir Health Center ....Dr. Julia BONNER
108 Dir Assess/Institutional Research ....Dr. Jonathan HANES
37 Director Financial Aid ....Mr. Timothy OPGENORTH
35 Senior Student Affairs Officer ....Ms. Kelly HAAG
41 Athletic Director ....Ms. Amanda BRAUN
88 Dir Restaurant Operations ....Mr. Scott HOFFLAND
36 Dir Career Planning & Resources ....Ms. Jean SALZER
27 Sr Dir Integrated Mktg & Comm ....Ms. Michelle JOHNSON
21 Assoc Vice Chanc Business & Finance ....Mr. Drew KNAB
29 Director Alumni/Advancement & Ops ....Ms. Amy TATE
96 Director of Procurement ....Mr. Tom SCRIVENER
114 Dir Budget & Planning ....Ms. Cindy KLUGE
105 Dir Web & Mobile Services ....Mr. Mark JACOBSON
106 Executive Director UWM Online ....Ms. Laura PEDRICK
112 Dir of Gift Planning & Agreements ....Ms. Gretchen MILLER
97 Dean College of General Studies ....Dr. Simon BRONNER
04 Admin Assistant to the Chancellor .. Ms. Christine ADAMS-MATT
07 Interim Director of Admissions ....Ms. Kay EILERS
09 Director of Institutional Research ....Dr. Jonathan HANES
100 Chief of Staff ....Ms. Suzanne WESLOW
104 Director Study Abroad ....Ms. Sharon GOSZ
39 Director University Housing ....Ms. Arcetta KNAUTZ
44 Director Annual Giving ....Mr. Thomas BJORNSTAD

*University of Wisconsin Oshkosh (C)

800 Algoma Boulevard, Oshkosh WI 54901

County: Winnebago FICE Identification: 003920
Unit ID: 240365
Telephone: (920) 424-1234 Carnegie Class: Masters/L
FAX Number: (920) 424-7317 Calendar System: Semester
URL: www.uwosh.edu
Established: 1871 Annual Undergrad Tuition & Fees (In-State): $7,717
Enrollment: 15,314 Coed
Affiliation or Control: State IRS Status: 501(c)3
Highest Offering: Doctorate
Accreditation: HLC, ANEST, CAATE, CACREP, CSHSE, IFSAC, JOUR, MUS, NURSE, SW

02 Chancellor ....Dr. Andrew J. LEAVITT
03 Vice Chancellor ....Dr. John KOKER
05 Provost & VC Academic Affairs ....Ms. Carmen FAYMONVILLE
20 Asst Vice Chanc Acad Support .... Dr. Sylvia CAREY-BUTLER
121 AVC Curric Affs/Stdnt Acad Achvmt ....Dr. Charles HILL
32 Vice Chancellor Student Affairs ....Vacant
10 Vice Chanc Finance/Administration ....Dr. James FLETCHER
21 Associate Vice Chanc Admin Svcs ....Ms. Lori M. WORM
06 Registrar ....Ms. Lisa M. DANIELSON
22 Affirmative Action Officer ....Vacant
09 Director of Institutional Research .... Mr. Michael W. WATSON
38 Director of Counseling Center ....Dr. Sandy COX
13 CIO Director Info Technology ....Mr. Mark CLEMENTS
50 Dean Business ....Dr. Barbara L. RAU
66 Dean Nursing ....Dr. Judith WESTPHAL
53 Dean Education & Human Svcs ....Dr. Linda HALING
49 Interim Dean Letters & Sciences .... Dr. Colleen MCDERMOTT
102 Pres Univ of Wisc Oshkosh Foundatn ....Vacant
29 Director of Alumni Association ....Ms. Christine M. GANTNER
37 Director of Financial Aid ....Mr. Kim DONAT
26 Int Exec Dir Marketing/Comms ....Ms. Peggy BREISTER
35 Dean of Students ....Dr. Art MUNIN
58 Director Graduate Studies .... Mr. Gregory WYPISZYNSKI
07 Director of Admissions ....Mr. Paul GEDLINSKE
15 AVC Human Resources/Int Dir EO/AA ....Ms. Shawna KUETHER
18 Facilities/Physical Plant Director ....Mr. Brian KRUEGER
36 Director of Career Services .... Ms. Jaime PAGE-STADLER
92 Director University Honors Program .... Dr. Laurence CARLIN
08 Interim Director Library ....Ms. Sarah NEISES
04 Administrative Asst to President ....Ms. Suzette THIBADEAU
104 Director Study Abroad ....Ms. Jennifer GRAFF
41 Athletic Director ....Mr. Darryl SIMS
90 Director Academic Computing ....Ms. Laura KNAAPEN

*University of Wisconsin-Parkside (D)

900 Wood Road, Box 2000, Kenosha WI 53141-2000

County: Kenosha FICE Identification: 005015
Unit ID: 240374
Telephone: (262) 595-2345 Carnegie Class: Bac-A&S
FAX Number: (262) 595-2202 Calendar System: Semester
URL: www.uwp.edu
Established: 1968 Annual Undergrad Tuition & Fees (In-State): $7,444
Enrollment: 4,452 Coed
Affiliation or Control: State IRS Status: 501(c)3
Highest Offering: Master's
Accreditation: HLC, CAHIIM, MT

02 Chancellor ....Deborah L. FORD
05 Provost/Vice Chancellor ....Robert DUCOFFE
111 Asst Chanc Univ Rels/Advancement ....Willie JUDE, II
20 Vice Provost Academic Affairs ....Gary WOOD
32 Vice Provost Student Affs & Enroll ....Tammy MCGUCKIN
10 Vice Pres Finance/Administration ....Scott MENKE
28 University Diversity & Inclusion ....Tyler LENZ-FISHER
35 Dean of Students ....Steve WALLNER
50 Dean Col of Bus Econ & Comput ....Dirk BALDWIN
49 Dean College of Arts & Humanities ....Lesley WALKER
81 Dean College of Nat & Hlth Sciences ....Emmanual OTU
83 Dean Social Sci & Prof Studies ....Peggy JAMES
51 Dir Continuing Educ & Cmty Engage ....Debra KARP
08 Director of the Library ....Anna STADICK
13 Chief Information Officer .... Jordania LEON-JORDAN
35 Asst Dean of Students ....Damian EVANS
21 Dir Business Services/Controller ....Ann IVERSON
15 Asst Vice Chanc Human Resources ....Sheronda GLASS
19 Dir Campus Police/Public Safety ....James HELLER
37 Director Financial Aid ....Kristina KLEMENS
44 Annual Fund/Stewardship Coordinator ....Linnea BOOHER
06 Registrar ....Rhonda KIMMEL
36 Dir of Advising/Career Center .... Neil BAUMGARTNER
18 Director Facilities Management ....John BRUCH
94 Director of Women's Studies ....Linda CRAFTON
38 Dir Health/Counseling/Disability ....Renee KIRBY
40 Manager Bookstore ....Kim FLANNERY
07 Interim Director of Admissions ....Richard BARTH
04 Administrative Asst to Chancellor ....Karen GRABHER
104 Admin Program Manager Intl Educ ....Elaine PHILIPPA
39 Asst Director Residence Life ....Jenna SWARTZ
41 Athletic Director ....Andrew GAVIN
105 Director Web Services ....Kimberly SEKAS
26 Chief Public Relations/Marketing ....Vacant

*University of Wisconsin-Platteville (E)

1 University Plaza, Platteville WI 53818-3099

County: Grant FICE Identification: 003921
Unit ID: 240462
Telephone: (608) 342-1491 Carnegie Class: Masters/L
FAX Number: (608) 342-1232 Calendar System: Semester
URL: www.uwplatt.edu
Established: 1866 Annual Undergrad Tuition & Fees (In-State): $7,873
Enrollment: 7,547 Coed
Affiliation or Control: State IRS Status: 501(c)3
Highest Offering: Master's
Accreditation: HLC, MUS, NAIT

02 Chancellor ....Mr. Dennis J. SHIELDS
05 Provost/Vice Chanc Acad Affairs ....Dr. Tammy EVETOVICH
111 Vice Chanc University Relations ....Ms. Rose M. SMYRSKI
10 Vice Chanc Admin Services ....Ms. Paige SMITH
30 Asst Vice Chanc Dev/Alum Engagement ....Mr. Josh BOOTS
06 Registrar ....Mr. David S. KIECKHAFER
84 Vice Chanc Enroll/Student Support ...Ms. Angela M. UDELHOFEN
37 Asst Director of Financial Aid ....Mr. Brian BIRD
38 Director Student Counseling ....Ms. Deirdre L. DALSING
26 Chief Communications Officer ....Mr. Paul J. ERICKSON
41 Director Intercollegiate Athletics ....Dr. Kristina M. NAVARRO
39 Director of Residence Life ....Mrs. Linda A. MULROY-BOWDEN
15 Director Human Resources/AA/EED ....Ms. Sarah VOSBERG
19 Director Security/Safety ....Chief Joseph M. HALLMAN
08 Head Librarian ....Mr. Todd ROLL
18 Engineer/Facilities Management .... Mrs. Katrina M. HECIMOVIC
18 Facilities/Building Maintenance ....Mr. John D. NIEHAUS
36 Director of Career Center ....Mr. Trapper MITCHELL
51 Director Continuing Education ....Ms. Kerie WEDIGE
20 Int Assoc VC for Academic Affairs .... Dr. Melissa E. GORMLEY
54 Int Dean Col of Engr/Math/Science ....Dr. Philip J. PARKER
49 Int Dean Col of Lib Arts/Educ ....Dr. Kory G. WEIN
47 Dean Business Life Sci/Agric ....Dr. Wayne C. WEBER
100 Chief Staff/Asst Chanc Div/Inclus ....Ms. Angela M. MILLER
13 Chief Information Officer ....Mr. Tony HAYES
21 Comptroller ....Ms. Cathy J. RIEDL-FARREY
35 Dean of Students ....Ms. Kate DEMERSE
07 Director Admissions ....Ms. Heidi TUESCHER-GILLE
23 Admin Director Student Health Svcs .... Ms. Rachel HERMAN
121 Director Student Support Services .... Ms. Laura A. FRANKLIN
104 Director International Programs ....Ms. Kari M. HILL
124 Director Retention/Acad Support ....Ms. Karen MCLEER
20 Asst Prov Grad Pgms/Assess/Dist ....Dr. Carolyn KELLER
25 Director Research & Sponsored Pgm ....Mr. William C. HOYER

*University of Wisconsin-River Falls (F)

410 S Third Street, River Falls WI 54022-5013

County: Pierce FICE Identification: 003923
Unit ID: 240471
Telephone: (715) 425-3911 Carnegie Class: Masters/M
FAX Number: (715) 425-4487 Calendar System: Semester
URL: www.uwrf.edu
Established: 1874 Annual Undergrad Tuition & Fees (In-State): $8,063
Enrollment: 5,855 Coed
Affiliation or Control: State IRS Status: 501(c)3
Highest Offering: Beyond Master's But Less Than Doctorate
Accreditation: HLC, CACREP, MACTE, MUS, SP, SW

02 Chancellor ....Dr. Maria GALLO

05 Vice Chancellor & Provost .... Dr. David TRAVIS
10 Vice Chancellor Business/Finance .... Ms. Elizabeth FRUEH
111 Asst Chancellor Advancement .... Mr. Richard FOY
20 Associate Provost .... Dr. Wesley CHAPIN
32 Asst Chancellor for Student Success .... Dr. Jamie ZAMJAHN
21 Controller .... Ms. Jody NICHOLS
47 Dean Agricult/Food/Environ Sci .... Dr. Dale GALLENBERG
53 Interim Dean Educ/Prof Studies .... Dr. Ogden ROGERS
49 Dean of Arts & Sciences .... Dr. Dean YOHNK
50 Interim Dean Business & Economics .... Dr. Marina ONKEN
13 Chief Information Officer .... Mr. Joseph KMIECH
15 Human Resources Director .... Ms. Michelle DROST
18 Exec Dir Facilities Management .... Mr. Alan SYMICEK
22 Director Integrity & Compliance .... Ms. Jennifer LARIMORE
06 Registrar .... Mrs. Kelly BROWNING
07 Executive Director of Admissions .... Mrs. Sarah NELSON
46 Director Grants & Research .... Ms. Molly VAN WAGNER
08 Director of Library .... Ms. Maureen OLLE-LAJOIE
41 Athletic Director .... Mrs. Crystal LANNING
37 Director Financial Assistance .... Mr. Robert BODE
45 Facilities Planner .... Mr. Joe WOLF
19 Director of Protective Services .... Mr. Karl FLEURY
96 Director of Purchasing Services .... Ms. Brandee DRINKEN
121 Dir Student Success Center .... Mr. Ian STROUD
29 Director Alumni Relations .... Mr. Pedro RENTA
92 Director Honors Program .... Dr. Kathleen HUNZER
38 Director Stdnt Counseling & Health .... Ms. Debra JANIS
51 Director Continuing Education .... Mr. Randy ZIMMERMANN
92 McNair Scholars Director .... Dr. Sierra HOWRY
26 Director Communications & Marketing .... Ms. Dina FASSINO
39 Director of Residence Life .... Ms. Karla THOENNES
40 Manager Bookstore .... Ms. Julie EKLUND
04 Executive Assistant to Chancellor .... Ms. Jenna LINDSETH
100 Chief of Staff .... Ms. Beth SCHOMMER

*University of Wisconsin-Stevens Point (A)

2100 Main Street, Stevens Point WI 54481-3871
County: Portage FICE Identification: 003924
Unit ID: 240480
Telephone: (715) 346-0123 Carnegie Class: Masters/S
FAX Number: (715) 346-4841 Calendar System: Semester
URL: https://www.uwsp.edu/Pages/default.aspx
Established: 1894 Annual Undergrad Tuition & Fees (In-State): $8,300
Enrollment: 8,302 Coed
Affiliation or Control: State IRS Status: 501(c)3
Highest Offering: Doctorate
Accreditation: HLC, ART, AUD, CAATE, CAHIIM, CIDA, DANCE, DIETD, MT, MUS, NURSE, SP, SW, THEA

02 Chancellor .... Dr. Thomas GIBSON
05 Provost & Vice Chancellor .... Dr. Greg SUMMERS
10 Chief Financial Officer .... Ms. Pratima GANDHI
32 Vice Chancellor Student Affairs .... Dr. Al THOMPSON
20 AVC for Tech/Learning/Acad Pgms .... Dr. Todd HUSPENI
100 Chief of Staff .... Dr. Robert MANZKE
15 AVC Person/Bdgt/Grants/Summer Pgms .... Dr. Katie JORE
51 Exec Dir UWSP Continuing Education .... Vacant
21 Controller .... Ms. Christina RICKERT
07 Director Admissions .... Vacant
37 Director of Financial Aid .... Ms. Mandy SLOWINSKI
19 Director Safety & Loss Control .... Vacant
111 Vice Chanc Univ Advancement .... Mr. Chris RICHARDS
29 Director of Alumni Affairs .... Ms. Laura GEHRMAN ROTTIER
26 Dir Univ Relations/Communications .... Ms. Lana POOLE
38 Director Counseling Center .... Dr. Stacey GERKEN
13 Dir of Information Technology .... Mr. Peter ZUGE
22 Director Equity/Affirmative Action .... Dr. Eric ROESLER
08 Director University Library .... Ms. Mindy KING
06 Interim Registrar .... Ms. Anne ECKENROD
18 Chief Facilities/Physical Plant .... Mr. Paul HASLER
36 Associate Director Career Services .... Ms. Sue KISSINGER
96 Purchasing Manager .... Ms. Heidi WALLNER
57 Dean Col Fine Arts/Commun .... Dr. Valerie CISLER
49 Dean Col of Letters & Sciences .... Dr. Joshua HAGEN
65 Dean Col of Natural Resources .... Dr. Brian SLOSS
107 Dean Col of Professional Studies .... Dr. Marty LOY
35 Director Student Affairs .... Dr. Al THOMPSON
04 Administrative Asst to President .... Ms. Sara BRANDL-REEVES
104 Director Study Abroad .... Mr. Brad VANDENELZEN
41 Athletic Director .... Mr. Brad DUCKWORTH
50 Dean of Business .... Dr. Kevin NEUMAN
86 Director Government Relations .... Dr. Robert MANZKE
39 Director Student Housing .... Mr. Brian FAUST
09 Director of Institutional Research .... Dr. Katie JORE
84 Director Enrollment Management .... Ms. Lana POOLE

*University of Wisconsin-Stout (B)

712 South Broadway, Menomonie WI 54751-0790
County: Dunn FICE Identification: 003915
Unit ID: 240417
Telephone: (715) 232-1122 Carnegie Class: Masters/L
FAX Number: N/A Calendar System: 4/1/4
URL: www.uwstout.edu
Established: 1891 Annual Undergrad Tuition & Fees (In-State): $9,488
Enrollment: 7,970 Coed
Affiliation or Control: State IRS Status: 501(c)3
Highest Offering: Beyond Master's But Less Than Doctorate
Accreditation: HLC, ACBSP, ART, CACREP, CAEP, CEA, CIDA, CONST, DIETD, DIETI, MFCD

02 Chancellor .... Dr. Katherine P. FRANK
05 Interim Provost & Vice Chancellor .... Dr. Glendali RODRIGUEZ
100 Chief of Staff .... Ms. Kristi KRIMPELBEIN
20 Associate Vice Chancellor .... Dr. Amanda BARNETT
10 Int Vice Chanc Business/Fin/Admin .... Ms. Kim SCHULTE-SHOBERG
111 Vice Chanc Univ Advance/Alumni Rel .... Mr. Willie JOHNSON
84 VChanc Enrollment/Strat Initiative .... Ms. Laura KING
45 Asst Chanc Plng/Assess/Rsrch/Qlty .... Dr. Meridith WENTZ
53 Interim Dean CEHHS .... Dr. Maria ALM
49 Interim Dean CACHSS .... Dr. Robert ZEIDEL
81 Interim Dean CSTEMM .... Dr. Gindy NEIDERMYER
32 Dean of Students .... Ms. Sandi SCOTT
15 Co-Interim Director of HR .... Ms. Erin DUNBAR
15 Co-Interim Director of HR .... Ms. Jo JOHNSON
26 Interim Chief Mktg/Comm Officer .... Mr. Gary SCHUSTER
06 Registrar .... Mr. Josh LIND
28 Assoc Dean Diversity/Equity/Inclus .... Ms. Dominique VARGAS
36 Director Career Services .... Mr. Bryan BARTS
08 Interim Library Director .... Ms. Kate KRAMSCHUSTER
37 Director Financial Aid .... Ms. Beth BOISEN
13 Asst Chanc for Learning & IT/CIO .... Ms. Suzanne TRAXLER
38 Interim Director Counseling Center .... Dr. Chasidy FAITH
23 Director Student Health Services .... Vacant
44 Development Program Specialist .... Ms. Jennifer RUDIGER
85 Director International Educ .... Mr. Scott PIERSON
18 Director Facilities Management .... Mr. Justin UTPADEL
96 Director Purchasing .... Mr. Carley KUKUK
39 Interim Dir University Housing .... Mr. Adam LUDWIG
41 Athletic Director .... Mr. Duey NAATZ
117 Pgm Mgr/Dir of Safety & Risk Mgmt .... Mr. Jim UHLIR
19 Chief of Police/Director of Parking .... Mr. Jason SPETZ
106 Assoc Director Stout Online .... Dr. Amy GULLIXSON
07 Director of Admissions .... Mr. Joel HELMS
35 Asst Director Student Life & Svcs .... Mr. Andrew CLEVELAND
114 Budget Director .... Mr. Curtis WIELAND

*University of Wisconsin-Superior (C)

Belknap and Catlin, PO Box 2000, Superior WI 54880-4500
County: Douglas FICE Identification: 003925
Unit ID: 240426
Telephone: (715) 394-8101 Carnegie Class: Bac-A&S
FAX Number: (715) 394-8454 Calendar System: Semester
URL: www.uwsuper.edu
Established: 1893 Annual Undergrad Tuition & Fees (In-State): $8,140
Enrollment: 2,560 Coed
Affiliation or Control: State IRS Status: 501(c)3
Highest Offering: Beyond Master's But Less Than Doctorate
Accreditation: HLC, MUS, SW

02 Chancellor .... Dr. Renee WACHTER
05 Int Provost/Vice Chanc Acad Affairs .... Dr. Maria CUZZO
111 Vice Chanc University Advancement .... Ms. Jeanne E. THOMPSON
10 Vice Chanc Administration/Finance .... Mr. Jeff KAHLER
26 Dir Communications/Government Rels .... Ms. Jordan MILAN
41 Athletic Director .... Mr. Nick BURSIK
32 Assoc Vice Chanc of Student Affairs .... Mr. Harry ANDERSON
15 Director Human Resources .... Mr. Cory KEMPF
22 Dir of Equity/Diversity/Inclusion .... Ms. Kat WERCHOUSKI
06 Registrar .... Ms. Janie CAMPBELL
07 Exec Dir of Admissions .... Mr. Jeremy NERE
21 Controller .... Mr. Robert B. WAKSDAHL
37 Interim Director Financial Aid .... Ms. Chelsie PARRISH
51 Dir Continuing Educ/Summer College .... Ms. Kathryn GUIMOND
08 Director CLIC & Library .... Dr. Jamie WHITE-FARNHAM
40 Director Bookstore .... Mr. Vaughn N. RUSSOM
29 Director of Alumni Relations .... Ms. Heather THOMPSON
121 Asst Dir Academic Advising .... Ms. Kristen JASPERSON
18 Director Facilities Management .... Mr. Dustin JOHNSON
04 Executive Assistant to Chancellor .... Ms. Debbie SEGUIN
88 Executive Assistant to Provost .... Ms. Amy MISSINNE
09 Dir Inst Research & Spons Pgms .... Ms. Emily NEUMANN
19 Dir Public Safety/Parking Svc .... Mr. Joseph EICKMAN
39 Director Residence Life .... Mr. Ryan KREUSER
13 Chief Informational Officer .... Mr. David WAGNER
20 Dean of Academic Affairs .... Mr. Nick DANZ
88 Director International Admissions .... Mr. Mark MACLEAN
38 Director Counseling Services .... Mr. Randy BARKER

*University of Wisconsin-Whitewater (D)

800 W Main Street, Whitewater WI 53190-1790
County: Walworth FICE Identification: 003926
Unit ID: 240189
Telephone: (262) 472-1918 Carnegie Class: Masters/L
FAX Number: (262) 472-1518 Calendar System: Semester
URL: www.uww.edu
Established: 1868 Annual Undergrad Tuition & Fees (In-State): $7,735
Enrollment: 11,989 Coed
Affiliation or Control: State IRS Status: 501(c)3
Highest Offering: Doctorate
Accreditation: HLC, ART, CACREP, IPSY, MUS, SP, SW, THEA

02 Interim Chancellor .... Mr. James HENDERSON
05 Prov/Vice Chanc Academic Affs .... Dr. John CHENOWETH
32 Vice Chancellor Student Affairs .... Dr. Artanya WESLEY
111 Vice Chanc Univ Advancement .... Vacant
11 Vice Chanc Administrative Affs .... Ms. Taryn CAROTHERS
100 Chief of Staff/Exec Asst to Chanc .... Mrs. Kari HEIDENREICH
20 Assoc VC Academic Affairs .... Ms. Kristin PLESSEL
13 Asst Vice Chanc Information Tech .... Dr. Elena POKOT
84 Assoc Vice Chanc Enroll/Retention .... Mr. Matt ASCHENBRENER
09 Chief of Inst Research/Planning .... Ms. Lynsey SCHWABROW
37 Director of Financial Aid .... Mr. William TRIPPETT
26 AVC University Relations .... Ms. Katharine KUZNACIC
36 Dir of Career & Leadership Dev .... Mr. Ron BUCHHOLZ
15 Chief Human Resources Officer .... Ms. Janelle CROWLEY
85 Dir Center for Global Education .... Ms. Candace A. CHENOWETH
102 CFO Foundation .... Ms. Debbie PETRASEK
18 Director Facility Planning/Mgmt .... Ms. Tami MCCULLOUGH
28 AVC Diversity/Equity/Inclusion .... Dr. Kenny YARBROUGH
92 Director of Honors Program .... Dr. Elizabeth KIM
57 Dean Arts/Communication .... Dr. Eileen M. HAYES
50 Dean of Business & Economics .... Vacant
53 Int Dean Education/Prof Studies .... Dr. Robin FOX
49 Dean Letters & Sciences .... Dr. Franklin GOZA
58 Dean Grad Stds/Continuing Educ .... Dr. Seth MEISEL
41 Athletic Director .... Mr. Ryan CALLAHAN

*University of Wisconsin-Platteville Baraboo Sauk County (E)

1006 Connie Road, Baraboo WI 53913
Telephone: (608) 355-5200 Identification: 770450
Accreditation: &HLC

*University of Wisconsin-Eau Claire - Barron County (F)

1800 College Drive, Rice Lake WI 54868
Telephone: (715) 788-6244 Identification: 770457
Accreditation: &HLC

*University of Wisconsin Oshkosh, Fond du Lac Campus (G)

400 University Drive, Fond du Lac WI 54935
Telephone: (920) 929-1100 Identification: 770451
Accreditation: &HLC

*University of Wisconsin Oshkosh, Fox Cities (H)

1478 Midway Road, Menasha WI 54952
Telephone: (920) 832-2600 Identification: 770456
Accreditation: &HLC

*University of Wisconsin-Stevens Point at Marshfield (I)

2000 West 5th Street, Marshfield WI 54449
Telephone: (715) 389-6530 Identification: 770455
Accreditation: &HLC

*University of Wisconsin-Platteville Richland (J)

1200 Highway 14 West, Richland Center WI 53581-1316
Telephone: (608) 647-6186 Identification: 770458
Accreditation: &HLC

*University of Wisconsin-Stevens Point at Wausau (K)

518 South 7th Avenue, Wausau WI 54401
Telephone: (715) 261-6100 Identification: 770461
Accreditation: &HLC

*University of Wisconsin-Milwaukee at Washington County (L)

400 University Drive, West Bend WI 53095
Telephone: (262) 335-5200 Identification: 770462
Accreditation: &HLC

*University of Wisconsin-Milwaukee at Waukesha (M)

1500 N University Drive, Waukesha WI 53188-2799
Telephone: (262) 521-5200 Identification: 770460
Accreditation: &HLC

*University of Wisconsin-Whitewater at Rock County (N)

2909 Kellogg Avenue, Janesville WI 53546
Telephone: (608) 758-6565 Identification: 770452
Accreditation: &HLC

Viterbo University (O)

900 Viterbo Court, La Crosse WI 54601-8802
County: La Crosse FICE Identification: 003911
Unit ID: 240107
Telephone: (608) 796-3000 Carnegie Class: Masters/L
FAX Number: (608) 796-3050 Calendar System: Semester
URL: www.viterbo.edu
Established: 1890 Annual Undergrad Tuition & Fees: $29,350
Enrollment: 2,516 Coed
Affiliation or Control: Roman Catholic IRS Status: 501(c)3
Highest Offering: Doctorate

Accreditation: HLC, ACBSP, CACREP, DIETC, DIETI, MUS, NURSE, SW

01 President ... Mr. Rick TRIETLEY
05 Vice Pres Academics ... Dr. Sara COOK
32 EVP Student Success ... Vacant
84 VP Enrollment Management ... Dr. Michelle KRONFELD
10 Sr VP Administration/Finance ... Mr. Todd M. ERICSON
111 VP Advancement ... Mr. Jim SALMO
21 Assistant Vice President Finance ... Ms. Kristen SANBORN
42 University Chaplain ... Fr. Conrad A. TARGONSKI
66 Chief Nursing Officer ... Vacant
54 Dean Engr/Letters/Sciences ... Vacant
20 Asst VP Academic Affairs ... Dr. Timothy SCHORR
57 Conservatory Director ... Vacant
50 Dean Business/Ldrship/Ethics ... Dr. Tonya WAGNER
58 Dean Graduate/Prof/Adult Education ... Vacant
88 Director of Ethics in Leadership ... Dr. Richard L. KYTE
06 Registrar ... Ms. Kori SALASKI
08 Director of Library ... Ms. Kim OLSON-KOPP
13 Director Instruct/Info Technology ... Ms. Sarah BEARBOWER
41 Athletic Director ... Mr. Barry J. FRIED
37 Director of Financial Aid ... Ms. Terry W. NORMAN
26 Director of Marketing ... Ms. Audra NOE
29 Director Alumni Relations ... Ms. Kathleen A. DUERWACHTER
36 Director Career Planning/Placement . Ms. Beth D. DOLDER-ZIEKE
15 Director of Human Resources ... Ms. Amy SEXAUER
09 Dir Assessment/Inst Research ... Ms. Naomi R. STENNES-SPIDAHL
18 Director Physical Plant ... Mr. Eugene M. MCCURDY
38 Dir Counseling/Student Development ... Ms. LeeAnn VAN VREEDE
39 Director of Residence Life ... Ms. Margy KROGMAN
53 Director Grad Studies in Education ... Ms. Jeanette ARMSTRONG
19 Director Campus Safety ... Mr. Adam MALIN
07 Asst Director of Admissions ... Ms. Caitlin LOCY
04 Executive Admin Asst to President ... Ms. Sheila SEVERSON

Wisconsin Lutheran College (A)

8800 W Bluemound Road, Milwaukee WI 53226-4699

County: Milwaukee — FICE Identification: 021366 — Unit ID: 240338
Telephone: (414) 443-8800 — Carnegie Class: Bac-Diverse
FAX Number: (414) 443-8514 — Calendar System: Semester
URL: www.wlc.edu
Established: 1973 — Annual Undergrad Tuition & Fees: $31,754
Enrollment: 1,166 — Coed
Affiliation or Control: Independent Non-Profit — IRS Status: 501(c)3
Highest Offering: Master's
Accreditation: HLC, NURSE

01 President ... Dr. Daniel W. JOHNSON
05 Provost & VP of Academic Affairs ... Dr. John D. KOLANDER
32 Vice President Student Life ... Mr. Ryan OERTEL
10 Vice Pres Finance & Administration ... Mr. Gary SCHMID
26 Exec Dir Marketing & Communication ... Vacant
30 Vice Pres Development ... Mr. Richard MANNISTO
15 Exec Director of Human Resources ... Mr. Jon FLANAGAN
21 Asst Vice Pres Finance ... Mrs. Diane HOEHNKE
07 Vice President of Enrollment ... Mr. Lucas FAUST
06 Registrar ... Mr. Brett VALERIO
08 Director of Library Services ... Vacant
37 Director Student Financial Aid ... Mrs. Linda L. LOEFFEL
42 Campus Pastor ... Rev. Wayne SHEVEY
53 Director Teacher Education ... Prof. James HOLMAN
39 Director Residential Life/Housing ... Mr. Adam VOLBRECHT
41 Athletic Director ... Mr. Edward NOON
88 Director of Arts Programming ... Mrs. Loni BOYDL
13 Director of Information Technology ... Mr. John MEYER
29 Director of Alumni Relations ... Mrs. Lisa LEFFEL
88 Research Analyst ... Mr. Robert JUNE
18 Chief Facilities/Physical Plant ... Mr. Gary SCHMID
24 Media Services Coordinator ... Mr. Tim SNYDER
04 Exec Assistant to the President ... Mrs. Barb MATTEK
09 Director of Institutional Research ... Mr. Rob HAHN
19 Director Security/Safety ... Mr. Dan SMITH
49 Dean College of Arts & Sciences ... Dr. Jarrod ERBE
107 Dean College Professional Studies ... Mr. David BRIGHTSMAN
76 Dean College of Health Sciences ... Dr. Robert BALZA, JR.

Wisconsin School of Professional Psychology (B)

9120 W Hampton Avenue #212,
Milwaukee WI 53225-4960

County: Milwaukee — FICE Identification: 022713 — Unit ID: 240213
Telephone: (414) 464-9777 — Carnegie Class: Spec-4-yr-Other Health
FAX Number: (414) 358-5590 — Calendar System: Semester
URL: www.wspp.edu
Established: 1979 — Annual Graduate Tuition & Fees: N/A
Enrollment: 80 — Coed
Affiliation or Control: Independent Non-Profit — IRS Status: 501(c)3
Highest Offering: Doctorate; No Undergraduates
Accreditation: HLC, CLPSY

01 President ... Dr. Kathleen M. RUSCH
05 Dean ... Dr. Kristin A. JUERGENS
04 Assistant to the President ... Ms. Veronica V. EGERSON
17 Director Clinical Training ... Dr. Jamal R. CUNNINGHAM
08 Head Librarian ... Ms. Rebecca DOUGHERTY
37 Director Student Financial Aid ... Mr. Erik MOZOLIK
88 Practica/Internship Director ... Dr. Susan DVORAK

*Wisconsin Technical College System (C)

PO Box 7874, Madison WI 53707-7874

County: Dane — Identification: 666185
Telephone: (608) 266-1207 — Carnegie Class: N/A
FAX Number: (608) 266-1285
URL: www.wtcsystem.edu

01 President ... Dr. Morna K. FOY
03 Executive Vice President ... Mr. James ZYLSTRA
05 Provost/Vice President ... Dr. Colleen MCCABE
26 Dir Strategic Advancement ... Mr. Conor SMYTH
04 Executive Staff Assistant ... Ms. Julie DRAKE

*Blackhawk Technical College (D)

PO Box 5009, Janesville WI 53547-5009

County: Rock — FICE Identification: 005390 — Unit ID: 238397
Telephone: (608) 758-6900 — Carnegie Class: Assoc/HVT-High Trad
FAX Number: (608) 757-7740 — Calendar System: Semester
URL: www.blackhawk.edu
Established: 1912 — Annual Undergrad Tuition & Fees (In-District): $4,505
Enrollment: 2,232 — Coed
Affiliation or Control: State/Local — IRS Status: 501(c)3
Highest Offering: Associate Degree
Accreditation: HLC, ACFEI, ADNUR, CSHSE, DA, DMS, MAC, MLTAD, PTAA, RAD, SURGT

02 President ... Dr. Tracy P. PIERNER
05 Vice President Academic Affairs ... Dr. Karen R. SCHMITT
10 Vice Pres Finance & College Opers ... Ms. Renea L. RANGUETTE
15 Exec Director/Chief HR Officer ... Ms. Kathleen BROSKE
09 Exec Dir Institutional Research ... Dr. Jon TYSSE
32 Exec Dir Student Services ... Mr. Anthony LANDOWSKI
04 Asst to President/District Board ... Ms. Julie M. BARREAU
13 Director IT Services ... Mr. Mitch MILLER
26 Exec Dir Marketing & Communications ... Vacant
97 Dean General Education ... Dr. Helen PROEBER
88 Learning Support Manager ... Mr. Darian SNOW
76 Dean Health Sciences/Public Safety ... Ms. Moira LAFAYETTE
19 Manager of Campus Safety & Security ... Mr. Brad K. SMITH
88 EMS Fire Service & Paramedic Coord ... Mr. Robert BALSAMO
72 Dean Advanced Mfg/Transport/Tech ... Mr. Greg PHILLIPS
50 Dean Business ... Dr. Helen PROEBER
21 Controller ... Mr. Gerri DOWNING
25 Grants Administration ... Ms. Amy E. ANDERSON
37 Financial Aid Manager ... Mr. Craig SCHULTZ
06 Registrar ... Ms. Lissa LANTTA
18 Facilities Director ... Mr. Steve KORMANAK
96 Purchasing Administrator ... Vacant
08 Dir Teaching & Learning Resources ... Ms. Lynn NEITZEL
102 Dir Foundation & Advancement ... Ms. Lisa HURDA
103 Director Workforce & Community Dev ... Mr. Mark BOROWICZ

*Chippewa Valley Technical College (E)

620 W Clairemont Avenue, Eau Claire WI 54701-6162

County: Eau Claire — FICE Identification: 005304 — Unit ID: 240116
Telephone: (715) 833-6200 — Carnegie Class: Assoc/HVT-High Non
FAX Number: (715) 833-6470 — Calendar System: Semester
URL: www.cvtc.edu
Established: 1912 — Annual Undergrad Tuition & Fees (In-District): $4,505
Enrollment: 7,367 — Coed
Affiliation or Control: Local — IRS Status: 501(c)3
Highest Offering: Associate Degree
Accreditation: HLC, ACBSP, ACFEI, ADNUR, CAHIIM, COARC, DH, DMS, EMT, MAC, MLTAD, NAEYC, PTAA, RAD, SURGT

02 President ... Dr. Sunem BEATON-GARCIA
05 Provost ... Julie FURST-BOWE
32 Vice President Student Services ... Margo A. KEYS
10 Vice President Finance & Facilities ... Kirk L. MOIST
13 Vice President IT/CIO ... Tom J. LANGE
15 Exec Dir of HR & Risk Management ... Tam BURGAU
26 Exec Dir Mktg/Com/Recruit & CE/WS ... Joni GEROUX
111 Exec Dir Institutional Advancement ... Karen KOHLER
50 Exec Dean Bus/Arts/Science & Acad ... Lynette LIVINGSTON
23 Exec Dean Health/Emergency Svcs/RF ... Shelly OLSON
75 Dean of Appr/Eng/Mfg/IT ... Jeff SULLIVAN
47 Dean Agric/Energy & Transportation ... Adam WEHLING
66 Dean of Nursing ... Gina BLOCZYNSKI
20 Dean Academic/Development Services ... Holly HASSEMER
20 Director of Curriculum & Prof Devel ... Rachelle PHAKITTHONG
108 Dir of College Effectiveness ... Shana SCHMIDT
18 Director of Facilities ... Rod BAGLEY
21 Director of Finance & Budgeting ... Sara J. NICK
84 Director of Enrollment Services ... Jennifer ANDEREGG
88 Dir Advisement/Title IX Coordinator ... Natalyn M. MARLAIRE
119 Network & Infrastructure Manager ... Nate RUNGE
12 Bus Dev/Menomonie Campus Manager ... Daniel LYTLE
12 Bus Dev/Chip Falls Campus Manager ... Angela ECKMAN
88 Recruitment & Bus Dev Manager ... Kendra WEBER
06 Registrar ... Jessica SCHWARTZ
37 Director Financial Aid ... Claire RODER
105 Marketing & Digital Exp Manager ... Sara PERTZ
88 Director K-12 Initiatives ... Kristel TAVARE
19 Public Safety Manager ... Mark PROVOST

35 Director of Student Central ... Laura ERICSON
35 Director of Student Life ... Alisa S. SCHLEY
96 Purchasing Coordinator ... Jody SCHNEIDER
28 Diversity Manager ... Mitch BARONI
88 Assistant Registrar ... Kristin CREVISTON
88 Criminal Justice Director ... Eric ANDERSON
88 Asst Dir Curriculum & Prof Dev ... Stephanie VOBORNIK
04 Executive Asst to President & Board ... Lauren SULLIVAN

*Fox Valley Technical College (F)

1825 N Bluemound Drive, Appleton WI 54914-1643

County: Outagamie — FICE Identification: 009744 — Unit ID: 238722
Telephone: (920) 735-5600 — Carnegie Class: Assoc/HVT-High Non
FAX Number: (920) 735-2582 — Calendar System: Semester
URL: www.fvtc.edu
Established: 1967 — Annual Undergrad Tuition & Fees (In-District): $4,677
Enrollment: 11,711 — Coed
Affiliation or Control: State/Local — IRS Status: 501(c)3
Highest Offering: Associate Degree
Accreditation: HLC, ACFEI, ADNUR, CAHIIM, DA, DH, EMT, MAC, MLTAD, NDT, OTA, PNUR

02 President/CEO ... Dr. Susan A. MAY
05 Executive VP/CAO ... Dr. Chris MATHENY
32 Associate VP Student Services ... Ms. Elizabeth BURNS
15 VP Human Resources/CHRO ... Ms. Rebecca SCHULTZ
10 VP Financial Svcs & Facilities/CFO ... Ms. Amy VAN STRATEN
13 VP Information Tech/CIO ... Mr. Troy KOHL
97 Dean General Studies ... Dr. Jennifer LANTER
47 Dean Mfg/Construction & Agric ... Mr. Steve STRAUB
102 Exec Dir FVTC Foundation/Cmty Rels . Ms. Rebecca BOULANGER
12 Associate VP Regional Campuses ... Ms. Deb HEATH
37 Director Student Financial Svcs ... Ms. Stacy DORAN
06 Registrar ... Ms. Shannon GERKE-CORRIGAN
26 Director College Marketing ... Ms. Barb DREGER
118 Director Compensation & Benefits ... Ms. Heather ZWEIGER
88 Director Venture Center ... Ms. Amy PIETSCH
108 Dean of Service & Academic Planning ... Dr. Kim OLSON
28 Exec Dir Diversity/Equity/Inclusion ... Mr. Rayon BROWN

*Gateway Technical College (G)

3520 30th Avenue, Kenosha WI 53144-1690

County: Kenosha — FICE Identification: 005389 — Unit ID: 238759
Telephone: (262) 564-2200 — Carnegie Class: Assoc/HVT-High Non
FAX Number: (262) 564-2201 — Calendar System: Semester
URL: www.gtc.edu
Established: 1911 — Annual Undergrad Tuition & Fees (In-District): $4,621
Enrollment: 7,839 — Coed
Affiliation or Control: State/Local — IRS Status: 501(c)3
Highest Offering: Associate Degree
Accreditation: HLC, ACBSP, ADNUR, CAHIIM, CSHSE, DA, EMT, MAC, PTAA, SURGT

*Lakeshore Technical College (H)

1290 North Avenue, Cleveland WI 53015-1414

County: Manitowoc — FICE Identification: 009194 — Unit ID: 239008
Telephone: (920) 693-1000 — Carnegie Class: Assoc/HVT-High Non
FAX Number: (920) 693-8078 — Calendar System: Semester
URL: www.gotoltc.edu
Established: 1912 — Annual Undergrad Tuition & Fees (In-District): $4,417
Enrollment: 2,420 — Coed
Affiliation or Control: State/Local — IRS Status: 501(c)3
Highest Offering: Associate Degree
Accreditation: HLC, ACFEI, ADNUR, CAHIIM, EMT, MAAB, PNUR, RAD

02 President ... Dr. Paul CARLSEN
04 Executive Assistant ... Ms. Heidi SOODSMA
05 Vice President of Instruction ... Mr. James LEMEROND
32 Vice President of Student Success ... Ms. Polly ABTS
11 Vice President of Administration ... Ms. Brenda RIESTERER
45 Vice Pres of Strategy/Outreach ... Ms. Tanya WASMER
111 Vice President of Advancement ... Ms. Kristin LIPHART
15 Executive Dir of Human Resources ... Ms. Shikara BEAUDOIN
26 Executive Director of Marketing ... Ms. Kolina STIEBER
10 Chief Financial Officer ... Ms. Molly O'CONNELL
47 Dean of Manuf/Agric/Engineering ... Ms. Sheila SCHETTER
50 Dean Business & Technology ... Mr. Doug HAMM
103 Dean of Workforce Development ... Mr. Jeff GRUNEWALD
97 Dean General & Pre-College Educ ... Ms. Meredith SAUER
76 Dean of Health & Human Services ... Ms. Michelle ZAUTNER
19 Dean of Public Safety & Energy ... Mr. Ryan SKABROUD
66 Assoc Dean of Nursing/Nursing Asst ... Ms. Lori HERTEL
06 Registrar & Student Conduct Officer ... Vacant
37 Financial Aid Manager ... Mr. Anthony ABNEY
13 Director of Technology Information ... Mr. Peter COOK
35 Exec Dir Pgm Couns/Stdnt Resources ... Ms. Foua HANG
18 Director of Facilities ... Mr. Jason EBERT
08 Director of Teaching & Learning Ctr ... Ms. Kelly CARPENTER
07 Exec Dir Admissions & HS Rels ... Mr. Dave HERMANN
88 Dual Credit Manager ... Vacant
22 Advisor/Accommodations Service ... Ms. Julie DEZEEUW
88 Testing Services Manager ... Ms. Susan KINNESTON
88 Business/Mfg Assessment Svcs Mgr ... Mr. William PERSINGER
25 Grant & Research Specialist ... Ms. Shauna NISCHIK
121 Academic Advisor/Counselor ... Vacant

09 Quality/Continuous Improvement Mgr ....Ms. Cheryl TERP
28 Access Equity & Inclusion Manager ....Ms. Nicole YANG

*Madison Area Technical College (A)

1701 Wright Street, Madison WI 53704-2599
County: Dane FICE Identification: 004007
Unit ID: 238263
Telephone: (608) 246-6100 Carnegie Class: Bac/Assoc-Assoc Dom
FAX Number: (608) 246-6880 Calendar System: Semester
URL: www.madisoncollege.edu
Established: 1912 Annual Undergrad Tuition & Fees (In-District): $4,530
Enrollment: 13,057 Coed
Affiliation or Control: State/Local IRS Status: 501(c)3
Highest Offering: Associate Degree
Accreditation: HLC, ACFEI, ADNUR, COARC, CSHSE, DH, EMT, MAC, MLTAD, OPTT, OTA, RAD, SURGT

02 President ....Dr. Jack E. DANIELS, III
04 Exec Asst to the President ....Ms. Kristin ROLLING
05 Provost/EVP Academic Affairs ....Dr. Turina BAKKEN
32 Vice President Student Affairs ....Vacant
26 Dir Communications/Strat Marketing ....Mr. Cary R. HEYER
45 VP Institutional Learning/Effect ....Dr. Timothy L. CASPER
10 EVP Finance/Administration ....Mr. Mark THOMAS
15 VP Human Resources ....Ms. Rosemary BUSCHHAUS
13 Chief Information Officer ....Mr. Shawn BELLING
103 Dean Workforce Education ....Ms. Schauna RASMUSSEN
88 Dean Academic Advancement ....Mr. Christopher P. VANDALL
54 Asst VP of Academic Operations ....Ms. Denise REIMER
49 Dean Arts & Sciences ....Dr. Todd H. STEBBINS
50 Dean Business & Applied Arts ....Ms. Erin KOHL
76 Dean Health Education ....Dr. Kendricks HOOKER
88 Asst VP Strategic Prtnrshp Innov .....Mr. Bryan M. WOODHOUSE
81 Dir of STEM Center ....Mr. Kevin MIRUS
35 Asst VP/Dean of Students & SDS ....Dr. Geraldo G. VILACRUZ
88 Asst VP Strat Academic Initiative ....Dr. Shawna M. CARTER
35 Director Student Life ....Ms. Renee M. ALFANO
12 Asst VP Regional Campuses ....Mr. James FALCO
20 Dean of Faculty ....Ms. Sarah FRITZ
36 Dir College & Career Transitions ....Ms. Juanita COMEAU
06 Registrar ....Mr. Bill W. DOUGHERTY
08 Director Library Services ....Ms. Julie C. GORES
41 Athletic Director ....Mr. Stephen C. HAUSER
114 AVP Budget & Management ....Ms. Sylvia RAMIREZ
22 Dir Disability Res and Testing ....Mr. Scott RITTER
21 CFO/Controller ....Ms. Laurie M. GRIGG
25 Director Grants & Special Projects ....Ms. Emily J. SANDERS
18 Director Facilities Services ....Mr. Michael M. STARK
102 Chief Exec Officer Foundation ....Ms. Tammy THAYER
09 Dir Inst Research & Effectiveness ....Mr. Ali R. ZARRINNAM
12 Dean Goodman South ....Ms. Valentina AHEDO
88 Assistant Controller ....Ms. Dorothy CONDUAH
37 Director Financial Aid ....Mr. Keyimani ALFORD
28 VP Equity/Diversity/Cmty Relations ....Ms. Lucia NUNEZ
19 Director Public Safety ....Mr. John FLANNERY

*Mid-State Technical College (B)

500 32nd Street N, Wisconsin Rapids WI 54494-5599
County: Wood FICE Identification: 005380
Unit ID: 239220
Telephone: (715) 422-5300 Carnegie Class: Assoc/HVT-Mix Trad/Non
FAX Number: (715) 422-5345 Calendar System: Semester
URL: www.mstc.edu
Established: 1967 Annual Undergrad Tuition & Fees (In-District): $4,451
Enrollment: 2,648 Coed
Affiliation or Control: State/Local IRS Status: 501(c)3
Highest Offering: Associate Degree
Accreditation: HLC, ADNUR, CAHIIM, COARC, EMT, MAC, SURGT

02 President ....Dr. Shelly MONDEIK
05 Vice President Academics ....Dr. Deb STENCIL
32 Vice Pres Student Svcs/Enroll Mgmt ....Dr. Mandy LANG
10 Vice President Finance/Facilities ....Mr. Greg BRUCKBAUER
15 Vice President HR & Org Dev ....Dr. Karen BRZEZINSKI
103 Vice President Workforce & Pub Rels ....Dr. Bobbi DAMROW
97 Dean Gen Educ & Learning Resource .....Ms. Amber STANCHER
50 Dean Business & Technology ....Dr. Missy SKURZEWSKI-SERVANT
65 Dean Trans/Agric/Nat Res & Constr ....Mr. Ryan KAWSKI
76 Dean Health/Protective & Human Svcs ....Dr. Colleen KANE
12 Dean Stevens Point Campus ....Mr. Ben NUSZ
12 Dean Marshfield Campus ....Dr. Alex LENDVED
35 Dean Student Support ....Ms. Christina LORGE-GROVER
26 Director Marketing & Communication ..Mr. John Eric HOFFMANN
102 Director Foundation and Alumni ....Ms. Jill STECKBAUER
18 Director Facilities/Procurement ....Mr. Craig WAGNER
06 Registrar ....Ms. Jennifer CONWELL
04 Executive Administrative Assistant ....Ms. Angela SUSA
37 Manager Financial Aid ....Ms. Shelly WEICHELT

*Milwaukee Area Technical College (C)

700 W State Street, Milwaukee WI 53233-1443
County: Milwaukee FICE Identification: 003866
Unit ID: 239248
Telephone: (414) 297-6600 Carnegie Class: Assoc/HVT-High Trad
FAX Number: (414) 297-7990 Calendar System: Semester
URL: www.matc.edu
Established: 1912 Annual Undergrad Tuition & Fees (In-District): $4,730
Enrollment: 12,618 Coed
Affiliation or Control: Local IRS Status: 501(c)3
Highest Offering: Associate Degree
Accreditation: HLC, ACFEI, ADNUR, AT, CAHIIM, COARC, CVT, DH, DIETT, EMT, FUSER, MAC, MLTAD, NAEYC, OTA, PNUR, PTAA, RAD, SURGT

02 President ....Dr. Vicki J. MARTIN
05 VP Learning ....Dr. Mohammad DAKWAR
84 Int VP of Enrollment Management ....Dr. Sarah ADAMS
10 Vice President of Finance ....Mr. Jeffrey HOLLOW
43 Vice President & Legal Counsel ....Ms. Janice FALKENBERG
13 Interim Chief Information Officer ....Mr. David ROWE
23 Dean Health Occupation ....Dr. Kelly DRIES
12 Campus Exec Dir West Allis Campus ...Dr. Richard BUSALACCHI
24 VP/General Manager Milwaukee PBS ....Mr. Bohdan ZACHARY
35 VP of Retention & Completion ....Dr. Jeff JANZ
08 Dean of Student Experience ....Mr. Equan BURROWS
37 Director Financial Aid ....Ms. Christine ZOLLICOFFER
90 Director Technical Services ....Mr. Michael GAVIN
21 Controller ....Ms. Eva KUETHER
19 Lieutenant Public Safety ....Lt. Karina TAYLOR
06 Int Dean Enrollment Svcs/Registrar ....Dr. Nicole TANNER
09 Dir Ofc of Institutional Research ....Dr. Yan WANG
84 Manager Recruitment ....Ms. Sophia WILLIAMS
29 Vice Pres Coll Advancement/Ext Comm ....Ms. Laura BRAY
108 VP Institutional Effectiveness ....Dr. Christine MANION
38 Director Student Resource Center ....Mr. Walter LANIER
26 Coord Design Center/Mktg & Comm ....Ms. Kathryn KAESERMANN
96 Procurement Manager ....Ms. Laura MOORE
41 Coordinator Athletics ....Mr. Randy CASEY
28 Chief Diversity/Equity/Inclus Ofcr ....Ms. Eva MARTINEZ-POWLESS
121 Exec Vice President Student Success ....Dr. Naydeen GONZALEZ-DE JESUS
15 Vice Pres Ofc Human Resource Svcs ....Ms. Elle BONDS

*Moraine Park Technical College (D)

235 N National Avenue, Fond Du Lac WI 54936-1940
County: Fond Du Lac FICE Identification: 009256
Unit ID: 239372
Telephone: (920) 922-8611 Carnegie Class: Assoc/HVT-High Non
FAX Number: (920) 929-2471 Calendar System: Semester
URL: www.morainepark.edu
Established: 1967 Annual Undergrad Tuition & Fees (In-District): $4,505
Enrollment: 2,654 Coed
Affiliation or Control: State/Local IRS Status: 501(c)3
Highest Offering: Associate Degree
Accreditation: HLC, ADNUR, CAHIIM, COARC, EMT, MAC, MLTAD, RAD, SURGT

02 President ....Bonnie BAERWALD
05 Vice President Academic Affairs ....James R. EDEN
10 VP Finance and Administration ....Carrie KASUBASKI
32 Vice President Student Services ....James BARRETT
13 Chief Information Officer ....Jerry RICHARDS
20 Dean of Applied Technology & Trades ....Fred RICE
23 Dean of Health & Human Services ....Barb JASCR
97 Dean of General Education ....Lane HOLTE
103 Dean Economic & Workforce Devel ....JoAnn HALL
12 Dean of the West Bend Campus ....Peter J. RETTLER
35 Dean of Students ....Scott LIEBURN
111 Director of College Advancement ....Dana BOURLAND
26 Dir Marketing/Communications ....Mandy POTTS
09 Director of Inst Effectiveness ....Laura WAURIO
21 Director of Finance ....Tara WENDT
08 Library Services Coordinator ....Hans BAIERL
18 Facilities Operation Manager ....Benjamin HILL
96 Purchasing Manager ....Timothy KEENAN
19 Security Manager ....John FAEH
04 Admin Assistant to the President ....Jaclyn JELINEK

*Nicolet Area Technical College (E)

5364 College Drive, PO Box 518,
Rhinelander WI 54501-0518
County: Oneida FICE Identification: 005384
Unit ID: 239442
Telephone: (715) 365-4493 Carnegie Class: Assoc/HVT-High Non
FAX Number: (715) 365-4445 Calendar System: Trimester
URL: www.nicoletcollege.edu
Established: 1967 Annual Undergrad Tuition & Fees (In-State): $4,505
Enrollment: 1,236 Coed
Affiliation or Control: State IRS Status: 501(c)3
Highest Offering: Associate Degree
Accreditation: HLC, ADNUR, MAC

02 President ....Ms. Kate FERREL
05 Executive VP Acad & Student Affs ....Vacant
10 VP for Finance/Administration ....Mr. John VAN DE LOO
15 Director of Human Resources ....Vacant
13 CIO ....Mr. Greg MILJEVICH
66 Dean of Health Occupations ....Ms. Candy DAILEY
103 Exec Dir Economic/Community Dev ....Ms. Sandy BISHOP
49 Dean of Univ Transfer/Liberal Arts ......Ms. Laura WIND-NORTON
88 Dean of Trade/Industry/Apprentice ....Mr. Jeff LABS
19 Assoc Dean/Dir Pub Safety/Security ....Mr. Jason GOELDNER
18 Director of Facilities ....Mr. Pete VANNEY
37 Financial Aid Manager ....Mr. Patrick BURNS
102 Foundation Executive Director ....Ms. Heather SCHALLOCK
108 Dir Inst Effectiveness/Staff Dev ....Ms. Kelly HAVERKAMPF
45 Dir Instructional Effectiveness ......Ms. Penny MERTZ KUCKKAHN
06 Registrar ....Mr. Joseph HAFERMAN
04 Exec Asst to President/Board ....Ms. Anne E. WIEDMAIER
08 Manager of Library Services ....Ms. Nora CRAVEN
28 Diversity and Tribal Outreach Coord ....Ms. Susan CRAZY THUNDER

*Northcentral Technical College (F)

1000 W Campus Drive, Wausau WI 54401-1880
County: Marathon FICE Identification: 005387
Unit ID: 239460
Telephone: (715) 675-3331 Carnegie Class: Assoc/HVT-High Non
FAX Number: (715) 675-9776 Calendar System: Semester
URL: www.ntc.edu
Established: 1912 Annual Undergrad Tuition & Fees (In-District): $3,673
Enrollment: 5,939 Coed
Affiliation or Control: Local IRS Status: 501(c)3
Highest Offering: Associate Degree
Accreditation: HLC, #ACBSP, ADNUR, DH, EMT, MAC, MLTAD, RAD, SURGT

02 President ....Dr. Lori A. WEYERS
03 Executive Vice President ....Dr. Jeannie M. WORDEN
05 VP for Learning ....Dr. Darren ACKLEY
10 VP of Finance & General Counsel ....Ms. Roxanne LUTGEN
111 VP College Advancement ....Dr. Vicki JEPPESEN
13 Chief Information Officer ....Dr. Chet A. STREBE
15 AVP of Human Resources ....Ms. Cher VINK
18 AVP of Facilities Management ....Mr. Rob ELLIOTT
26 AVP Mktg/PR & Leg Advoc ....Mrs. Katrina FELCH
107 Exec Dean of Academic Excellence .... Dr. Emily STUCKENBRUCK
88 Dean College Adv/Spec Proj ....Dr. Vicky PIETZ
50 Dean Business and Virtual College ...... Ms. Brandy BREUCKMAN
76 Dean of Health Sciences ....Ms. Marlene ROBERTS
22 Employment Coord/Affirm Action Ofcr ....Ms. Cindy THELEN
36 Dir Accred & Career Pathways ....Dr. Bonnie OSNESS
32 Director of Student Development ....Mr. Shawn P. SULLIVAN
19 Director of Security ....Mr. Jordan SCHULT
06 Registrar ....Mr. Nick BLANCHETTE
84 Dean of College Enrollment ....Dr. Sarah DILLON
121 Dean of Student Success ....Dr. Shannon LIVINGSTON
103 Dean Workforce Training/Prof Devel ....Dr. Brad GAST
04 Executive Asst to President ....Mrs. Nikki KOPP
09 Dean Acad and College Effectiveness ....Dr. Angela M. SERVI
37 Director Student Financial Aid ....Mr. Jeff CICHON
47 Dean Agricultural Sciences ....Dr. Greg CISEWSKI
97 Dean of General Studies ....Ms. Brooke SCHINDLER
54 Dean Engineering/Adv Manufacturing .... Mr. Iain CAMERON
44 Director Annual Giving ....Ms. Sheila ROSSMILLER
106 Dean of Flexible Learning ....Mr. Jon DEGROOT

*Northeast Wisconsin Technical College (G)

PO Box 19042, 2740 W Mason Street,
Green Bay WI 54307-9042
County: Brown FICE Identification: 005301
Unit ID: 239488
Telephone: (920) 498-5444 Carnegie Class: Assoc/HVT-Mix Trad/Non
FAX Number: (920) 498-6260 Calendar System: Semester
URL: www.nwtc.edu
Established: 1913 Annual Undergrad Tuition & Fees (In-District): $4,659
Enrollment: 10,763 Coed
Affiliation or Control: State/Local IRS Status: 501(c)3
Highest Offering: Associate Degree
Accreditation: HLC, ACBSP, ADNUR, CAHIIM, COARC, DA, DH, DMS, EMT, MAC, MLTAD, PNUR, PTAA, RAD, SURGT

02 President ....Dr. H. Jeffrey RAFN
05 Vice President of Learning ....Dr. Kathryn ROGALSKI
32 Vice President of Student Services ....Dr. Colleen SIMPSON
111 Vice Pres of College Advancement ....Vacant
15 Vice President of Human Resources ....Ms. Lisa MAAS
13 Chief Information Officer ....Mr. Daniel MINCHEFF
10 VP Business & Finance ....Dr. Robert MATHEWS
12 Dean Regional Learning ....Ms. Jan SCOVILLE
50 Dean College of Business ....Mr. Michael VANDER HEIDEN
76 Dean Health Science ....Mr. Scott ANDERSON
72 Dean Trades & Engr Technologies ....Dr. Amy KOX
97 Dean General Education .... Ms. Michaeline SCHMIT
19 Dean Public Safety .... Ms. Cynthia ESTRUP
20 Dean Learning Solutions ....Ms. Anne KAMPS
103 Int Dean Corp Training/Economic Dev ....Ms. Meridith JAEGER
121 Dean of Student Success ....Vacant
07 Dean Enrollment Services/Registrar ....Mr. Mark FRANKS
37 Financial Aid Director ....Ms. Stephanie FEUCHT
102 Foundation Director ....Ms. Crystal HARRISON
40 Director Bookstore ....Mr. Patrick SORELLE
26 Public Relations/Comm Specialist ....Ms. Tara CRIBB
18 Director of Facilities ....Mr. Chet LAMERS
08 Manager Library Services ....Ms. Kim LAPLANTE
104 Mgr Student Involvement/Intl Pgm ....Ms. Megan POPKEY
04 Administrative Asst to President ....Ms. Janel KARBAN
09 Institutional Researcher ....Mr. Jeff GREBINOSKI
105 Director Web Services ....Ms. Erica PLAZA
28 Director of Diversity ....Mr. Mohammed BEY
19 Director Security/Safety ....Mr. Philip SCHAEFER

*Northwood Technical College (H)

1900 College Drive, Rice Lake WI 54868
County: Barron FICE Identification: 011824
Unit ID: 240198
Telephone: (715) 234-7082 Carnegie Class: Assoc/HVT-Mix Trad/Non
FAX Number: (715) 234-1241 Calendar System: Semester
URL: www.northwoodtech.edu
Established: 1968 Annual Undergrad Tuition & Fees (In-State): $4,917
Enrollment: 2,818 Coed
Affiliation or Control: State IRS Status: Exempt
Highest Offering: Associate Degree

Accreditation: HLC, ADNUR, CAHIIM, DA, OTA

02 President ... Dr. John WILL
10 VP Admin Svcs/CFO/RL Campus Admin ... Mr. Steven DECKER
05 Vice President Academic Affairs ... Dr. Aliesha R. CROWE
32 VP Student Affs/Ashland Campus Adm ... Dr. Steve BITZER
103 Dean Workforce/Cmty Development ... Ms. Bambi PATTERMAN
09 VP Inst Effective/Richmond Camp Adm ... Ms. Susan YOHNK LOCKWOOD
13 Sr Director Technology Services ... Mr. Bill HODGE
37 Director Financial Aid ... Mr. Terry KLEIN
06 Registrar ... Mr. Shane EVENSON
84 Director of Enrollment Services ... Ms. Laura SULLIVAN
26 AVP Mktg/Comms/Superior Campus Adm ... Ms. Jena VOGTMAN
15 Director Human Resources ... Ms. Amanda GOHDE

*Southwest Wisconsin Technical College (A)

1800 Bronson Boulevard, Fennimore WI 53809-9778
County: Grant FICE Identification: 007669
Unit ID: 239910
Telephone: (608) 822-3262 Carnegie Class: Assoc/HVT-High Non
FAX Number: (608) 822-6019 Calendar System: Semester
URL: www.swtc.edu
Established: 1967 Annual Undergrad Tuition & Fees (In-District): $4,500
Enrollment: 2,581 Coed
Affiliation or Control: State/Local IRS Status: Exempt
Highest Offering: Associate Degree
Accreditation: HLC, ADNUR, CAHIIM, MAC, MEAC, MLTAD, PTAA

02 President ... Dr. Jason S. WOOD
10 VP for Administrative Services ... Mr. Caleb WHITE
05 Chief Academic Officer ... Dr. Kathleen E. GARRITY
47 Dean of Industry/Trades/Agriculture ... Dr. Derek DACHELET
32 Chief Student Services Officer ... Ms. Holly CLENDENEN
15 Chief Human Resources Officer ... Ms. Krista WEBER
108 Manager of College Effectiveness ... Ms. Mandy HENKEL
102 Director of Foundation ... Ms. Kim SCHMELZ
13 Director of IT Services ... Mr. Heath AHNEN
101 Executive Services Director ... Ms. Karen M. CAMPBELL
18 Director of Facilities ... Mr. Dan IMHOFF
37 Financial Aid Manager ... Ms. Corabeth HALVORSON
19 Director of Public Safety ... Ms. Kris WUBBEN
20 Innovative/Alternative Learning Dir ... Ms. Kim MAIER
21 Controller ... Ms. Kelly KELLY
88 Director of Pre-College Programs ... Ms. Julie PLUEMER
06 Registrar ... Ms. Danielle SEIPPEL
109 Dining Services Manager ... Mr. Rex SMITH
76 Dean of Health Occupations/Service ... Ms. Cynde LARSEN

*Waukesha County Technical College (B)

800 Main Street, Pewaukee WI 53072-4696
County: Waukesha FICE Identification: 005294
Unit ID: 240125
Telephone: (262) 691-5566 Carnegie Class: Assoc/HVT-High Non
FAX Number: (262) 691-5593 Calendar System: Semester
URL: www.wctc.edu
Established: 1923 Annual Undergrad Tuition & Fees (In-District): $4,588
Enrollment: 6,952 Coed
Affiliation or Control: State/Local IRS Status: 501(c)3
Highest Offering: Associate Degree
Accreditation: HLC, ACFEI, ADNUR, CAHIIM, DH, EMT, MAC, NAEYC, SURGT

02 President ... Dr. Richard G. BARNHOUSE
05 Provost ... Dr. Ann KRAUSE-HANSON
20 VP Learning ... Dr. Bradley PIAZZA
32 VP Student Services ... Ms. Angela FRAZIER
10 VP Finance ... Dr. Jane KITTEL
15 VP Human Resource Svcs ... Mr. David BROWN
13 Chief Information Officer ... Mr. Rodney NOBLES
102 Dir Foundation/Corporate Relations ... Ms. Ellen PHILLIPS
50 Dean Business Occupations ... Mr. Jon KOCH
38 Dean Support/Couns/Advs & Access ... Dr. Christopher DAOOD
75 Dean Industrial Occupations ... Mr. Michael SHIELS
88 Dean Service Occupations ... Dr. Greg WEST
97 Dean Acad Foundation & General Stds ... Ms. Bethany LEONARD
76 Dean Health Occupations ... Ms. Michele NELSON
26 Director PR/Marketing & Outreach ... Mr. Andrew PALEN
18 Director Facilities Services ... Mr. Jeffrey LEVERENZ
06 Registrar ... Ms. Rachel BURLING
36 Mgr Career Development Services ... Ms. Debra WEBER
51 Dir Corporate Training Ctr ... Mr. James DRAEGER
28 Chief Officer Diversity ... Ms. Sherry SIMMONS
07 Mgr Admissions/Testing Svcs ... Ms. Kathleen KAZDA
88 Director Academic Excellence ... Dr. Randall COOROUGH
09 Director of Institutional Research ... Dr. Viktor BRENNER
37 Manager Financial Aid ... Mr. Justin KEHRING
35 Coordinator Student Life ... Mr. Jonathan N. PEDRAZA
08 Director of Library Services ... Ms. Amy MANION
19 Environ Health & Safety Supervisor ... Mr. Bruce NEUMANN
27 Specialist Public Relations ... Ms. Michelle NELSON
96 Purchasing Specialist ... Ms. Victoria NASH
04 Admin Assistant to the President ... Ms. Kristan GOCHENAUER

*Western Technical College (C)

400 N Seventh Street, La Crosse WI 54601-3368
County: La Crosse FICE Identification: 003840
Unit ID: 240170
Telephone: (608) 785-9200 Carnegie Class: Assoc/HVT-High Trad
FAX Number: (608) 785-9205 Calendar System: Trimester
URL: www.westerntc.edu
Established: 1912 Annual Undergrad Tuition & Fees (In-District): $4,500
Enrollment: 4,240 Coed
Affiliation or Control: State/Local IRS Status: 501(c)3
Highest Offering: Associate Degree
Accreditation: HLC, ADNUR, CAHIIM, COARC, DA, EMT, MAC, MLTAD, OTA, PTAA, RAD, SURGT

02 President ... Dr. Roger STANFORD
10 Vice President Finance/Operations ... Mr. Wade HACKBARTH
05 Vice President of Academic Affairs ... Ms. Kathleen LINAKER
32 VP Student Service & Engagement ... Ms. Amy THORNTON
12 Director of Regional Workforce Dev ... Ms. Patti BALACEK
102 Executive Director Foundation ... Mr. Michael SWENSON
37 Financial Aid Manager ... Ms. Jerolyn R. GRANDALL
21 Controller ... Ms. Christina HEIT
103 Director of Business/Industry Svcs ... Ms. Angie MARTIN
07 Director of Enrollment Services ... Ms. Debra HETHER
36 Director Advising & Career Service ... Ms. Barb KELSEY
38 Director of Counseling & Case Mgmt ... Ms. Ann BRANDAU-HYNEK
06 Registrar/Stdnt Info System Coord ... Ms. Sandy PETERSON
35 Dean of Students ... Ms. Shelley MCNEELY
72 Dean Integrated Technology ... Mr. Josh GAMER
76 Dean Health & Public Safety ... Mr. Kevin DEAN
97 Dean General Education ... Mr. John GILLETTE
50 Dean Business Education ... Mr. Gary BROWN
13 Director Information Technology ... Ms. Joan PIERCE
26 Director Marketing & Communications ... Ms. Julie LEMON
29 Manager Alumni Relations ... Ms. Stephanie KNUTSON
40 Manager Campus Shop ... Mr. David R. WIGNES
15 Director Human Resources ... Mr. John HEATH
09 Exec Dir Planning & Org Excellence ... Ms. Tracy DRYDEN

*Chippewa Valley Technical College-Gateway (D)

2320 Alpine Road, Eau Claire WI 54703
Telephone: (715) 874-4600 Identification: 770420
Accreditation: &HLC

*Chippewa Valley Technical College River Falls Campus (E)

500 South Wasson Lane, River Falls WI 54722
Telephone: (715) 425-3301 Identification: 770423
Accreditation: &HLC

*Chippewa Valley Technical College-West (F)

4000 Campus Road, Eau Claire WI 54703
Telephone: (715) 852-1394 Identification: 770421
Accreditation: &HLC

*Madison Area Technical College Commercial Avenue Education Center (G)

2125 Commercial Avenue, Madison WI 53704
Telephone: (608) 246-6100 Identification: 770436
Accreditation: &HLC

*Madison Area Technical College Downtown Education Center (H)

1701 Wright Street, Madison WI 53704
Telephone: (608) 246-6100 Identification: 770437
Accreditation: &HLC

*Madison Area Technical College Portage (I)

330 West Collins Street, Portage WI 53901
Telephone: (608) 745-3100 Identification: 770438
Accreditation: &HLC

*Madison Area Technical College Fort Atkinson (J)

827 Banker Road, Fort Atkinson WI 53538
Telephone: (920) 568-7200 Identification: 770435
Accreditation: &HLC

*Madison Area Technical College Reedsburg (K)

300 Alexander Avenue, Reedsburg WI 53959
Telephone: (608) 524-7800 Identification: 770439
Accreditation: &HLC

*Madison Area Technical College Watertown (L)

1300 West Main Street, Watertown WI 53098
Telephone: (920) 206-8000 Identification: 770440
Accreditation: &HLC

*Moraine Park Technical College (M)

700 Gould Street, Beaver Dam WI 53916
Telephone: (920) 887-1428 Identification: 770446
Accreditation: &HLC

*Moraine Park Technical College (N)

2151 North Main Street, West Bend WI 53090
Telephone: (262) 335-5713 Identification: 770447
Accreditation: &HLC

*Northeast Wisconsin Technical College-Marinette Campus (O)

1601 University Drive, Marinette WI 54143
Telephone: (715) 735-9361 Identification: 770448
Accreditation: &HLC

*Northeast Wisconsin Technical College-Sturgeon Bay Campus (P)

229 N 14th Avenue, Sturgeon Bay WI 54235
Telephone: (920) 746-4900 Identification: 770449
Accreditation: &HLC

*Northwood Technical College-Ashland Campus (Q)

2100 Beaser Avenue, Ashland WI 54806
Telephone: (715) 682-8040 Identification: 770463
Accreditation: &HLC

*Northwood Technical College-New Richmond Campus (R)

1019 S Knowles Avenue, New Richmond WI 54017
Telephone: (715) 246-6561 Identification: 770464
Accreditation: &HLC, MAC

*Northwood Technical College-Superior Campus (S)

600 North 21st Street, Superior WI 54880
Telephone: (715) 394-6677 Identification: 770466
Accreditation: &HLC, MAC

Wright Graduate University for the Realization of Human Potential (T)

N7698 County Highway H, Elkhorn WI 53121
County: Walworth Identification: 667224
Unit ID: 486460
Telephone: (262) 742-4444 Carnegie Class: Spec-4-yr-Other
FAX Number: (262) 721-0752 Calendar System: Quarter
URL: www.wrightgrad.edu
Established: 2006 Annual Graduate Tuition & Fees: N/A
Enrollment: 30 Coed
Affiliation or Control: Independent Non-Profit IRS Status: 501(c)3
Highest Offering: Doctorate; No Undergraduates
Accreditation: DEAC, IACBE

00 Chief Executive Officer ... Dr. Bob WRIGHT
01 Chancellor/Dir Career Svcs/CFO ... Dr. Michael ZWELL
05 Chief Academic Officer ... Dr. Judith WRIGHT
12 Campus Director ... Ms. Kate HOLMQUEST

WYOMING

Casper College (U)

125 College Drive, Casper WY 82601-2458
County: Natrona FICE Identification: 003928
Unit ID: 240505
Telephone: (307) 268-2110 Carnegie Class: Assoc/MT-VT-Mix Trad/Non
FAX Number: (307) 268-2682 Calendar System: Semester
URL: www.caspercollege.edu
Established: 1945 Annual Undergrad Tuition & Fees (In-District): $3,882
Enrollment: 3,551 Coed
Affiliation or Control: Local IRS Status: 501(c)3
Highest Offering: Associate Degree
Accreditation: HLC, ACBSP, ADNUR, ART, COARC, DANCE, EMT, MLTAD, MUS, NAEYC, OTA, RAD, THEA

01 President ... Dr. Darren D. DIVINE
05 Vice President Academic Affairs ... Dr. Brandon KOSINE
32 Vice President Student Services ... Ms. Kim BYRD
10 Vice Pres Administrative Services ... Ms. Lynnde COLLING
15 Director Human Resources ... Ms. Rhonda FRANZEN
07 Director Admissions/Student Success ... Ms. Leanne LOYA
26 Director of Public Relations ... Mr. Chris LORENZEN
18 Director Physical Plant ... Mr. Eric RULOFSON
38 Director Student Counseling ... Ms. Erin FORD
08 Director of the Library ... Ms. Katrina BROWN
13 Director Information Technology ... Mr. Kent BROOKS
121 Director of Student Success Service ... Ms. Leanne LOYA
39 Director of Housing ... Mr. Corey PEACOCK
41 Athletic Director ... Mr. Paul MARBEL
19 Director Campus Security ... Mr. John BECKER
102 Exec Director Foundation ... Ms. Denise BRESSLER
09 Institutional Researcher ... Mr. Michael DEAL
37 Director of Student Financial Aid ... Mrs. Shannon ESKAM
21 Dir Financial Services/Controller ... Ms. Robyn LANDEN
96 Purchasing Coordinator ... Mr. Shane PULLIAM

06 Registrar .... Ms. Linda NICHOLS
29 Director Alumni Relations .... Vacant
04 Executive Asst to President .... Ms. Tina SILVA
108 Director Institutional Assessment .... Dr. Michael BROOKS
25 Grant Coordinator .... Ms. Katie MCMILLAN

Central Wyoming College (A)

2660 Peck Avenue, Riverton WY 82501-1520
County: Fremont FICE Identification: 007289
Unit ID: 240514
Telephone: (307) 855-2000 Carnegie Class: Assoc/MT-VT-High Non
FAX Number: (307) 855-2095 Calendar System: Semester
URL: www.cwc.edu
Established: 1966 Annual Undergrad Tuition & Fees (In-District): $4,500
Enrollment: 1,755 Coed
Affiliation or Control: Local IRS Status: 501(c)3
Highest Offering: Associate Degree
Accreditation: HLC, ADNUR

01 President .... Dr. Brad TYNDALL
04 Exec Asst to the President/Board .... Ms. Linda BENDER
05 Vice Pres Academic Affairs .... Dr. Katherine WELLS
10 Vice Pres Admin Svcs/CFO .... Mr. Willie NOSEEP
32 Vice Pres Student Affairs .... Dr. Cory DALY
13 Chief Information Officer .... Mr. John WOOD
18 Chief Facilities/Physical Plant .... Mr. Wayne ROBINSON
08 Director of Library Services .... Ms. Kristy HARDTKE
26 Director of Marketing .... Ms. Lori RIDGWAY
15 Dir for Human Resources .... Mr. Scott MILLER
21 Finance Officer .... Ms. Lindy PASKETT
19 Director of Campus Safety/Security .... Mr. Chuck CARR
103 Dean Business/Technical & Workforce .... Ms. Lynne MCAULIFFE
35 Dean of Students .... Mr. Steve BARLOW
06 Registrar .... Ms. Connie NYBERG
49 Dean for Arts & Sciences .... Dr. Mark NORDEEN
102 Exec Director CWC Foundation .... Ms. Beth MONTEIRO
09 Director of Institutional Research .... Ms. Louisa HUNKERSTORM

Eastern Wyoming College (B)

3200 W C Street, Torrington WY 82240-1699
County: Goshen FICE Identification: 003929
Unit ID: 240596
Telephone: (307) 532-8200 Carnegie Class: Assoc/MT-VT-High Non
FAX Number: (307) 532-8229 Calendar System: Semester
URL: ewc.wy.edu/
Established: 1948 Annual Undergrad Tuition & Fees (In-District): $4,110
Enrollment: 1,430 Coed
Affiliation or Control: State/Local IRS Status: 501(c)3
Highest Offering: Associate Degree
Accreditation: HLC

01 President .... Dr. Lesley TRAVERS
04 Exec Asst to President/Board .... Ms. Sally WATSON
05 VP for Academic Services .... Mr. Roger HUMPHREY
10 VP for Admin Services .... Mr. Kwin WILKES
32 VP for Student Services .... Vacant
12 VP for Douglas Campus .... Dr. Margaret FARLEY
30 Dir of Institutional Development .... Mr. John HANSEN
08 Director of Library Services .... Mrs. Casey DEBUS
41 Director of College Athletics .... Mr. Tom ANDERSEN
26 Director of College Relations .... Ms. Tami AFDAHL
18 Director of Physical Plant .... Mr. Keith JARVIS
39 Director of Residence Life .... Mr. Jim RORABAUGH
37 Director of Financial Aid .... Ms. Susan STEPHENSON
15 Director Human Resources .... Ms. Holly LARA
21 Business Office Director .... Ms. Karen PARRIOTT
06 Registrar .... Ms. Sue SCHMIDT
13 Chief Information Tech Officer .... Mr. Tyler VASKO

Eastern Wyoming College-Douglas Campus (C)

800 South Wind River Drive, Douglas WY 82633
Telephone: (307) 624-7000 Identification: 770476
Accreditation: &HLC, ADNUR

Gillette College (D)

300 West Sinclair, Gillette WY 82718
Telephone: (307) 681-6000 Identification: 770478
Accreditation: &HLC

Laramie County Community College (E)

1400 E College Drive, Cheyenne WY 82007-3299
County: Laramie FICE Identification: 009259
Unit ID: 240620
Telephone: (307) 778-5222 Carnegie Class: Assoc/HVT-High Non
FAX Number: (307) 778-1399 Calendar System: Semester
URL: www.lccc.wy.edu
Established: 1968 Annual Undergrad Tuition & Fees (In-District): $4,432
Enrollment: 3,838 Coed
Affiliation or Control: State/Local IRS Status: 501(c)3
Highest Offering: Baccalaureate
Accreditation: HLC, ADNUR, CAHIIM, DH, DMS, EMT, PTAA, RAD, SURGT

01 President .... Dr. Joe SCHAFFER
05 Vice Pres Academic Affairs .... Dr. Kari BROWN-HERBST
10 Vice Pres of Administration/Finance .... Mr. Rick JOHNSON
32 Vice President of Student Services .... Dr. Melissa STUTZ
13 Chief Technology Officer .... Mr. Chad MARLEY
15 Executive Director Human Resources .... Ms. Tammy MAAS
111 Assoc VP Institutional Advancement .... Ms. Lisa TRIMBLE
12 Int Assoc VP Albany County Campus .... Dr. Clark HARRIS
45 Assc VP Institutional Effectiveness .... Dr. Kim BENDER
08 Assoc Dean Library/Learning Commons .... Vacant
37 Director of Financial Aid .... Ms. Brandi PAYNE CERVERA
18 Director of Physical Plant .... Mr. Bill ZINK
21 Comptroller .... Ms. Nola ROCHA
29 Dir Alumni Affairs/Event Plans .... Vacant
09 Director of Institutional Research .... Dr. Mark PERKINS
07 Dir of Admissions and Welcome Ctr .... Ms. Sarah HANNES
06 Registrar .... Ms. Stacy MAESTAS
49 Int Dean Sch of Arts & Humanities .... Dr. Jonathan CARRIER
50 Dean School of BATS .... Dr. Jill KOSLOSKY
76 Dean Sch of Health Sci & Wellness .... Ms. Starla MASON
81 Dean School Math & Science .... Mr. Bryan WILSON
103 Dean Sch of Outreach/Workforce Dev .... Ms. Maryellen TAST
19 Risk Manager Director Campus Safety .... Mr. Jesse BLAIR
41 Int Exec Dir Athletics & Exercise .... Dr. Cynthia HENNING
04 Executive Asst to President .... Ms. Vicki BOREING
26 Manager Strategic Communications .... Mr. Troy RUMPF
39 Director Residential Living .... Ms. Diana WILSON

Laramie County Community College Albany County Campus (F)

1125 Boulder Drive, Laramie WY 82070
Telephone: (307) 721-5138 Identification: 770477
Accreditation: &HLC

Northern Wyoming Community College District (G)

1 Whitney Way, Sheridan WY 82801-1500
County: Sheridan FICE Identification: 003930
Unit ID: 240666
Telephone: (307) 675-0505 Carnegie Class: Assoc/HVT-High Non
FAX Number: (307) 675-0684 Calendar System: Semester
URL: www.sheridan.edu
Established: 1948 Annual Undergrad Tuition & Fees (In-District): $4,290
Enrollment: 3,741 Coed
Affiliation or Control: Local IRS Status: 501(c)3
Highest Offering: Associate Degree
Accreditation: HLC, ADNUR, DH

01 President .... Dr. Walter TRIBLEY
05 VP Academic Affairs .... Dr. Estella CASTILLO-GARRISON
10 VP Admin & Finance/CFO .... Ms. Cheryl A. HEATH
12 VP Gillette College/CEO .... Ms. Janell OBERLANDER
32 VP Student Affairs .... Ms. Jenn CROUSE
75 Dean Career/Technical Education .... Mr. Jed JENSEN
15 Asst VP for Human Resources .... Ms. Jennifer MCARTHUR
26 VP Strategic Comm/Public Info Ofcr .... Ms. Wendy M. SMITH
37 Director Financial Aid Services .... Ms. Heidi BALSTER
13 AVP for Info Tech Svcs/CIO .... Mr. Brady R. FACKRELL
09 AVP for Institutional Research .... Mr. Jason BROWNING
21 Director of Finance/Controller .... Ms. Gina KIDNEIGH
07 Executive Director of Admissions .... Mr. Joe B. MUELLER
39 Director Housing/Residential Educ .... Ms. Larissa B. BONNET
88 Director Veteran Services-Sheridan .... Mr. Tyler JENSEN
88 Director Veteran Services-Gillette .... Mr. Loren GROVES
18 AVP Facilities Management .... Mr. Kent A. ANDERSEN
18 Director Gillette Facilities .... Mr. Mark N. ANDERSEN
08 Librarian .... Ms. Katrina M. BROWN
19 Police Chief .... Mr. Jason VELA
41 Athletic Director .... Vacant
100 Executive Office Manager .... Ms. Jana CLEMENTS
20 Assoc Academic Officer-Sheridan .... Ms. Martha DAVEY
20 Assoc Academic Officer-Gillette .... Dr. Matt EWERS
29 Alumni Relations .... Ms. Bobbi MITZEL
102 Dir Foundation/Corp Rels-Sheridan .... Ms. Jen CROUSE
102 Dir Foundation/Corp Rels-Gillette .... Ms. Heidi GROSS
38 Dir Student Svc/Counselor Gillette .... Ms. Susan SERGE
38 Coord Counseling ADA Svcs-Sheridan .... Ms. Amy BROWNING
84 Director Enrollment Management .... Mr. Micah OLSEN

Northwest College (H)

231 W 6th St, Powell WY 82435
County: Park FICE Identification: 003931
Unit ID: 240657
Telephone: (307) 754-6000 Carnegie Class: Assoc/MT-VT-Mix Trad/Non
FAX Number: (307) 754-6245 Calendar System: Semester
URL: www.nwc.edu
Established: 1946 Annual Undergrad Tuition & Fees (In-District): $4,330
Enrollment: 1,438 Coed
Affiliation or Control: State/Local IRS Status: 501(c)3
Highest Offering: Baccalaureate
Accreditation: HLC, ADNUR, ART, MUS

01 Interim President .... Ms. Lisa WATSON
05 Vice Pres Academic Affairs .... Dr. Gerald GIRAUD
11 Vice Pres Admin Services/Finance .... Ms. Lisa WATSON
102 Executive Director NWC Foundation .... Ms. Shelby WETZEL
08 Library Director .... Ms. Nancy MILLER
10 Finance Director .... Mr. Brad BOWEN
15 Human Resources Director .... Ms. Jill ANDERSON
13 Computing Services Director .... Mr. Casey DEARCORN
18 Interim Facilities Director .... Mr. Dennis QUILLEN
84 Enrollment Services Director .... Mr. West HERNANDEZ
37 Financial Aid/Scholarships Director .... Mr. Shaman QUINN
39 Interim Residence Life Director .... Mr. Lee BLACKMORE
04 Exec Secretary to President & Board .... Ms. Keli BORDERS
07 Admissions Coordinator .... Ms. Kendle JEFFS
09 Institutional Research Manager .... Ms. Lisa SMITH
26 Communications & Marketing Director .... Ms. Carey MILLER
19 Campus Security Coordinator .... Mr. Lee BLACKMORE
41 Athletic Director .... Mr. Brian ERICKSON

University of Wyoming (I)

1000 E University Avenue, Dept 3434,
Laramie WY 82071-3434
County: Albany FICE Identification: 003932
Unit ID: 240727
Telephone: (307) 766-1121 Carnegie Class: DU-Higher
FAX Number: (307) 766-2271 Calendar System: Semester
URL: www.uwyo.edu
Established: 1886 Annual Undergrad Tuition & Fees (In-State): $5,791
Enrollment: 11,829 Coed
Affiliation or Control: State IRS Status: 501(c)3
Highest Offering: Doctorate
Accreditation: HLC, CACREP, CAEPN, CLPSY, DIETD, LAW, MT, MUS, NURSE, PHAR, SP, SW

01 President .... Mr. Edward SEIDEL
05 Provost/VP Academic Affairs .... Dr. Kevin CARMAN
10 SVP Finance & Administration .... Dr. Neil THEOBALD
31 Interim Vice Pres Community Affairs .... Mr. Chris BOSWELL
46 Vice Pres Research & Economic Dev .... Dr. Edmund SYNAKOWSKI
32 Vice President Student Affairs .... Ms. Kim CHESTNUT
13 Vice President Information Tech .... Mr. Robert R. AYLWARD
111 Vice Pres Institutional Advancement .... Mr. W. Ben BLALOCK, III
43 Vice President & General Counsel .... Ms. Tara EVANS
20 Vice Provost Academic Personnel .... Dr. Tami BENHAM-DEAL
20 AVP Undergrad Academic Affairs .... Dr. Steven BARRETT
84 Associate VP Enrollment Management .... Mr. Kyle MOORE
21 AVP Budget and Inst Planning .... Mr. David JEWELL
35 AVP/Dean of Students/Dir Fin Aid .... Dr. Nycole COURTNEY
110 Assoc VP Institutional Advancement .... Mr. John D. STARK
26 Assoc VP Communication/Marketing .... Mr. Chad BALDWIN
41 Director Intercollegiate Athletics .... Mr. Tom BURMAN
47 Dean of Agriculture/Natural Res .... Dr. Barbara RASCO
49 Dean of Arts & Sciences .... Dr. Danny DOLE
50 Dean of Business .... Dr. David SPROTT
53 Int Dean of Education .... Dr. Leslie RUSH
54 Interim Dean of Engineering .... Dr. Cameron WRIGHT
76 Dean of Health Sciences .... Dr. David JONES
61 Dean of Law .... Dr. Klint ALEXANDER
12 Assoc Dean/Director UW at Casper .... Dr. Jeff EDGENS
08 Dean of Libraries .... Dr. Ivan GAETZ
65 Dean Sch Environ/Nat Resources .... Dr. John KOPROWSKI
07 Director of Admissions .... Ms. Shelley DODD
36 Director Advising/Career Services .... Ms. Evelyn J. CHYTKA
29 Exec Director Alumni Affairs .... Mr. Keener FRY
88 Director American Heritage Center .... Ms. Bridgit BURKE
88 Exec Dir School of Energy Resources .... Ms. Holly KRUTKA
88 Director Art Museum .... Ms. Marianne WARDLE
88 Director Campus Recreation .... Mr. Patrick MORAN
15 Int Assoc VP Human Resources .... Ms. Deborah MARUTZKY
18 Assoc Vice President UW Operations .... Mr. John R. DAVIS
92 Dean Honors College .... Mr. Peter PAROLIN
86 Director of Govt Relations .... Ms. Meredith ASAY
39 Exec Dir Res Life/Dining/Stdnt Un .... Mr. Eric WEBB
37 Int Director Student Financial Aid .... Ms. Carrie GOSE
06 Registrar .... Ms. Kwanna KING
23 Director Student Health Clinic .... Dr. Richelle KEINATH
19 Chief University Police Dept .... Mr. Mike SAMP
38 Director Counseling Center .... Dr. Toi GEIL

Western Wyoming Community College (J)

2500 College Drive, Rock Springs WY 82901
County: Sweetwater FICE Identification: 003933
Unit ID: 240693
Telephone: (307) 382-1600 Carnegie Class: Assoc/HT-High Non
FAX Number: (307) 382-1636 Calendar System: Semester
URL: www.westernwyoming.edu
Established: 1959 Annual Undergrad Tuition & Fees (In-District): $3,456
Enrollment: 2,776 Coed
Affiliation or Control: State/Local IRS Status: 501(c)3
Highest Offering: Baccalaureate
Accreditation: HLC, ADNUR

01 President .... Dr. Kim K. DALE
05 VP for Student Learning .... Dr. Clifford WITTSTRUCK, III
11 VP for Administrative Services .... Mr. Burt REYNOLDS
15 Assoc VP of Human Resources .... Ms. Joy ADAMS
10 Assoc VP of Finance .... Ms. Debbie BAKER
07 Director of Admissions .... Vacant
06 Registrar .... Mr. Stuart MOORE
37 Director of Financial Aid .... Vacant
08 Director of Library Services .... Ms. Janice GROVER-ROOSA
18 Assoc VP of Physical Resources .... Vacant
32 Dean of Students .... Mr. Dustin CONOVER
40 Bookstore Manager .... Ms. Natalie LANE
41 Athletic Director .... Dr. Lu SWEET
92 Director of Honors Program .... Vacant
09 Assoc VP of Inst Effectiveness .... Mr. Mark REMBACZ
26 Coord of Marketing/Public Info .... Ms. Kimberly REMBACZ
30 Dir Community College Relations .... Mr. David TATE

22 Dir Student Counseling/Disability .... Ms. Amy GALLEY
96 Director of Purchasing .... Ms. Tammy REGISTER
04 Executive Asst to President .... Ms. Kandy FRINK
19 Protective Services Supervisor .... Mr. Mark PADILLA
13 Director of Information Technology .... Mr. Derek ROBINSON
20 Dean of Academics .... Vacant
103 Director Outreach & Workforce Devel .... Ms. Kasey DAMORI

Wyoming Catholic College (A)

306 Main Street, Lander WY 82520
County: Fremont Identification: 667227
Telephone: (307) 332-2930 Carnegie Class: Not Classified
FAX Number: (307) 332-2918 Calendar System: Semester
URL: www.wyomingcatholic.edu
Established: 2005 Annual Undergrad Tuition & Fees: N/A
Enrollment: N/A Coed
Affiliation or Control: Roman Catholic IRS Status: 501(c)3
Highest Offering: Baccalaureate
Accreditation: HLC

01 President .... Dr. Glen ARBERY
03 Executive Vice President .... Mr. Jonathan TONKOWICH
05 Interim Academic Dean .... Mr. Kyle WASHUT
10 Chief Financial Officer .... Vacant
111 Vice Pres Advancement .... Mr. Joseph SUSANKA
06 Registrar .... Ms. Jennifer WESTMAN
32 Director of Student Services .... Ms. Hillary HALSMER
07 Director of Admissions .... Mr. Jonathan RENSCH

WyoTech (B)

1889 Venture Drive, Laramie WY 82070
County: Albany FICE Identification: 009157
Unit ID: 240718
Telephone: (307) 742-3776 Carnegie Class: Spec 2-yr-Tech
FAX Number: (307) 755-2484 Calendar System: Other
URL: www.wyotech.edu
Established: 1966 Annual Undergrad Tuition & Fees: N/A
Enrollment: 585 Coed
Affiliation or Control: Proprietary IRS Status: Proprietary
Highest Offering: Associate Degree
Accreditation: ACCSC

01 President .... Mr. Jim MATHIS
11 Vice President of Operation .... Mr. Kyle MORRIS
05 Director of Education .... Mr. Guy JACKSON
20 Training Coordinator .... Mr. Shawn NUNLEY
37 Director of Student Finance .... Ms. Alyson MOYER
07 Vice President of Admissions .... Mr. Steve MEYER
06 Registrar .... Ms. Revalee WEERHEIM
36 Director of Career Services .... Mr. Greg TAYLOR
39 Manager of Student Housing .... Mr. Gabe LUCERO
18 Director of Facilities .... Mr. David KUHN

US SERVICE SCHOOLS

Air Force Institute of Technology (C)

2950 Hobson Way, Wright Patterson AFB OH 45433-7765
County: Greene FICE Identification: 003009
Unit ID: 200697
Telephone: (937) 255-6565 Carnegie Class: DU-Higher
FAX Number: (937) 656-7600 Calendar System: Quarter
URL: www.afit.edu
Established: 1919 Annual Graduate Tuition & Fees: N/A
Enrollment: 1,129 Coed
Affiliation or Control: Federal IRS Status: Exempt
Highest Offering: Doctorate; No Undergraduates
Accreditation: HLC

01 Chancellor .... Dr. Walter F. JONES
05 Chief Academic Officer .... Dr. Heidi R. RIES
54 Dean Graduate School of Engr & Mgt .... Dr. Adedeji B. BADIRU
46 Interim Dean for Research .... Dr. Darryl K. AHNER
10 Chief Financial Officer .... Ms. Shelly A. POND
09 Director Institutional Research .... Dr. Nancy J. ROSZELL
07 Director Admissions/Registrar .... Ms. Kathleen K. BURDEN
32 Dean of Students .... Col. Jason R. ANDERSON
20 Associate Dean for Academic Affairs .... Dr. Paul J. WOLF
13 Dir Communications & Information .... Major Darold FROEMMING
08 Director D'Azzo Research Library .... Dr. Ellis BETECK
15 Director Personnel Services .... Ms. Leanne HEAGLE
18 Chief Facilities/Physical Plant .... Mr. Anthony KING
29 Manager Alumni Affairs .... Ms. Kathleen E. SCOTT
85 Director of Intl Student Affairs .... Vacant
40 Bookstore Supervisor .... Mr. Joseph SCOTT
106 Dir Online Education/E-learning .... Mr. John A. REISNER

Air University (D)

55 LeMay Plaza South, Maxwell AFB AL 36112-6335
County: Montgomery FICE Identification: 001001
Telephone: (334) 953-5613 Carnegie Class: Spec-4-yr-Other
FAX Number: (334) 953-2749 Calendar System: Other
URL: www.airuniversity.af.mil
Established: 1946 Annual Undergrad Tuition & Fees: N/A
Enrollment: N/A Coed
Affiliation or Control: Federal IRS Status: Exempt
Highest Offering: Doctorate
Accreditation: SC

01 Commander and President .... LtGen. James B. HECKER
03 Vice Commander .... MajGen. William G. HOLT, II
05 Chief Academic Officer .... Dr. Mark J. CONVERSINO
32 Vice Chancellor Student Affairs .... Vacant
06 Registrar .... Dr. Mehmed ALI

† Parent institution of Community College of the Air Force, School of Advanced Air and Space Studies, and the Air Force Institute of Technology

Community College of the Air Force (E)

100 South Turner Blvd,
Maxwell AFB, Gunter Annex AL 36114-3011
Telephone: (334) 649-5000 FICE Identification: 012308
Accreditation: &SC

† Regional accreditation is carried under the parent institution, Air University, Maxwell AFB, AL.

Defense Language Institute (F)

1759 Lewis Road, Monterey CA 93944
County: Monterey FICE Identification: 001195
Unit ID: 428222
Telephone: (831) 242-5291 Carnegie Class: Spec 2-yr-Other
FAX Number: (831) 242-6495 Calendar System: Other
URL: www.dliflc.edu
Established: 1941 Annual Undergrad Tuition & Fees: N/A
Enrollment: N/A Coed
Affiliation or Control: Federal IRS Status: Exempt
Highest Offering: Associate Degree
Accreditation: WJ

01 Commandant .... Col. Gary M. HAUSMAN
03 Assistant Commandant .... Col. Stephanie R. KELLEY
05 Provost .... Dr. Robert SAVUKINAS
20 Associate Provost .... Dr. Hiam KANBAR
100 Chief of Staff .... Mr. Steven COLLINS
32 Dean of Students .... Maj. Miranda HERNANDEZ

† Associate Arts in Foreign Language authorized by US Congress in December 2001 and approved by ACCJC/WASC in June 2002.

59th Dental Training Squadron (G)

Bldg 3352, JBSA, Lackland AFB TX 78236
Telephone: (210) 292-8850 Identification: 770122
Accreditation: &M

† Branch campus of Uniformed Services University of the Health Sciences, Bethesda, MD

Joint Forces Staff College (H)

7800 Hampton Boulevard, Norfolk VA 23511-1702
Telephone: (757) 443-6124 Identification: 770121
Accreditation: &M

† Branch campus of National Defense University, Washington, DC

The Judge Advocate General's Legal Center & School (I)

600 Massie Road, Charlottesville VA 22903-1781
County: Albemarle Identification: 666974
Telephone: (434) 971-3300 Carnegie Class: Spec-4-yr-Other
FAX Number: (434) 971-3338 Calendar System: Quarter
URL: www.jagcnet.army.mil/tjaglcs
Established: 1951 Annual Graduate Tuition & Fees: N/A
Enrollment: N/A Coed
Affiliation or Control: Federal IRS Status: Exempt
Highest Offering: Master's; No Undergraduates
Accreditation: LAW

01 Commander/Commandant .... BGEN. Joseph B. BERGER
05 Dean .... COL. Sean T. MCGARRY
20 Associate Dean of Academics ...... Mr. Maurice A. LESCAULT, JR.
32 Associate Dean of Students .... LTC. Temi ANDERSON

Marine Corps University (J)

2076 South Street, Quantico VA 22134-5068
County: Prince William Identification: 666745
Telephone: (703) 784-2105 Carnegie Class: Spec-4-yr-Other
FAX Number: (703) 784-1271 Calendar System: Semester
URL: www.usmcu.edu
Established: 1989 Annual Graduate Tuition & Fees: N/A
Enrollment: N/A Coed
Affiliation or Control: Federal IRS Status: Exempt
Highest Offering: Master's; No Undergraduates
Accreditation: SC

01 President .... BGen. Walker M. FIELD
05 Vice President for Academic Affairs .... Dr. Rebecca J. JOHNSON
11 VP for Operations & Planning .... Mr. Jay HATTON
10 VP Business Affairs .... Mr. Keil GENTRY
100 Chief of Staff .... Col. Paul M. MELCHIOR

National Defense University (K)

Fort Lesley J. McNair, Washington DC 20319-5066
FICE Identification: 031893
Unit ID: 423494
Telephone: (202) 685-3924 Carnegie Class: Spec-4-yr-Other
FAX Number: (202) 685-3920 Calendar System: Semester
URL: www.ndu.edu
Established: 1976 Annual Graduate Tuition & Fees: N/A
Enrollment: N/A Coed
Affiliation or Control: Federal IRS Status: Exempt
Highest Offering: Master's; No Undergraduates
Accreditation: M

01 President .... LGen. Michael T. PLEHN
03 Senior Vice President .... Amb. John HOOVER
05 Provost/Vice Pres Academic Affairs .... Dr. John W. YAEGER
11 Chief Operating Officer .... Mr. Robert C. KANE
43 General Counsel .... Ms. Mollie MURPHY
46 Sr Dir Research/Strategic Support .... Dr. Laura J. JUNOR
88 Vice Chanc/Actg Chancellor CISA .... Amb. Michael J. DODMAN
88 Commandant ES .... BGen. Joy L. CURRIERA
88 Commandant NWC .... BGen. Jeffrey HURLBERT
88 Acting Chancellor/Dean of Fac CIC .... Dr. Cassandra C. LEWIS
88 Commandant JFSC .... MGen. Lewis G. IRWIN
107 Deputy Director CAPSTONE .... Mr. Gerard M. MAUER, JR.
20 Deputy Vice Pres Academic Affairs .... Dr. Brian R. SHAW
32 Director of OIRPA .... Dr. B.J MILLER
06 University Registrar .... Mr. Larry JOHNSON
42 Chaplain .... COL. Ken WILLIAMS
26 Director of Strategic Communication .... Mr. Mark PHILLIPS
13 Chief Information Officer .... Ms. Diane E. WEBBER
105 Web/Social Media Manager .... Ms. Jennifer RUSSELL
10 Director Resource Management .... Ms. Ellen B. ROMINES
25 Director Contracting .... Ms. Kathryn GONZALES
23 Director Health Fitness .... Mr. Tony SPINOSA
15 Director Human Resources .... Ms. Leigh Ann MASSEY
08 Director Libraries .... Mr. David GANSZ
85 Dir International Student Mgmt Ofc .... Ms. Makila JAMES
18 Chief Facilities/Physical Plant .... Dr. Thomas J. KARNOWSKI
19 Director Security .... Mr. Tony BROWN
102 President/CEO NDU Foundation .... Mr. James SCHMELING

National Intelligence University (L)

7400 Pentagon, Washington DC 20301
Identification: 666393
Telephone: (301) 243-2118 Carnegie Class: Not Classified
FAX Number: N/A Calendar System: Quarter
URL: www.ni-u.edu
Established: 1962 Annual Undergrad Tuition & Fees: N/A
Enrollment: N/A Coed
Affiliation or Control: Federal IRS Status: Exempt
Highest Offering: Master's
Accreditation: M

01 President .... Dr. J. Scott CAMERON
100 Exec VP Ops & Chief of Staff .... Col. Michael E. SENN
05 Exec VP & Provost .... Dr. Terrence C. MARKIN
09 VP Research .... Mr. Manolis PRINIOTAKIS
88 Executive Asst to Provost .... Mr. Jeffrey D. KIRKWOOD
46 Dir Ctr for Strategic Intel Rsrch .... Dr. Robert SMITH
108 Dir Institutional Effectiveness .... Ms. Ellen ROSENTHAL
10 VP Finance & Administration .... Mr. Stephen J. KERDA
19 Security Officer .... Ms. Thelma FLAMER
06 Registrar/Dir Enrollment Services .... Mr. Eric H. STUPAR
08 Director Library Services .... Ms. Elizabeth E. VENTURA
58 Dean College Strategic Intel .... Dr. Frederick HAMMERSEN
12 Director NSA Campus .... Dr. Irene ZOPPI RODRIGUEZ
12 Director NGA Campus .... Dr. Mayur GOSAI
12 Director Reserve Monthly Pgm .... Lt Col. Andre LOBO
12 Director European Academic Ctr .... Mr. Kevin TALIAFERRO
12 Director Southern Academic Ctr .... Mr. Christopher MARSHALL
12 Director Quantico Academic Ctr .... Mr. William DAVIDSON
58 Dean School of Science & Tech Intel .... Dr. Brian HOLMES
26 VP Engagement .... Mr. Timothy LATTA
29 Dir Outreach & Alumni Affairs .... Mr. Thomas VAN WAGNER

Naval Postgraduate School (M)

1 University Circle, Room M10, Monterey CA 93943-5100
County: Monterey FICE Identification: 001310
Unit ID: 119678
Telephone: (831) 656-2441 Carnegie Class: Masters/L
FAX Number: (831) 656-2921 Calendar System: Quarter
URL: www.nps.edu
Established: 1909 Annual Undergrad Tuition & Fees: N/A
Enrollment: 2,866 Coed
Affiliation or Control: Federal IRS Status: Exempt
Highest Offering: Doctorate
Accreditation: WC, SPAA

01 President .... VAdm. Ann Elisabeth RONDEAU, RET.
05 Provost/Academic Dean .... Dr. Scott GARTNER
100 Chief of Staff .... CAPT. Philip E. OLD
20 Vice Provost for Academic Affairs .... Dr. Michael FREEMAN
46 Dean of Research .... Dr. Jeffrey D. PADUAN
54 Dean Grad Sch Engr/Applied Sci .... Dr. Clyde SCANDRETT
58 Dean Sch of Intl/Defense Studies .... Dr. James C. MOLTZ
50 Dean Grad Sch Defense Management .... Dr. Kieth F. SNIDER
72 Dean Grad Sch Oper & Info Sciences .... Dr. Robert DELL
32 Dean of Students .... LCDR. Chris SHUTT
11 Chief Operations Officer .... Vacant
10 Comptroller .... Mr. John WARD
13 Director Information Technology .... Mr. Scott BISCHOFF
08 University Librarian .... Mr. Thomas ROSKO
06 Registrar .... Ms. Jessica BAWDON
15 Director Human Resources .... Ms. Jennifer AMORIN

56 Director of CED3 ....Mr. Dennis LESTER
07 Director of Admissions ....Ms. Sue DOOLEY
88 Director of Programs ....CDR. Douglas JONES
04 Admin Assistant to the President ....Mr. Michael WEATHERFORD

Naval War College (A)

686 Cushing Road, Newport RI 02841-1207

County: Newport FICE Identification: 003413
Telephone: (401) 841-3089 Carnegie Class: Not Classified
FAX Number: (401) 841-1297 Calendar System: Trimester
URL: www.usnwc.edu
Established: 1884 Annual Graduate Tuition & Fees: N/A
Enrollment: N/A Coed
Affiliation or Control: Federal IRS Status: Exempt
Highest Offering: Master's; No Undergraduates
Accreditation: EH

01 President ....RADM. Shoshana CHATFIELD
04 Exec Assistant to the President ....LCDR. Jorge VARGAS
05 Interim Provost ....Dr. Jay HICKEY
20 Deputy Provost ....Mr. Richard R. MENARD
20 Associate Provost ....Dr. Tom GIBBONS
100 Vice Pres/Chief of Staff ....CAPT. Joseph C. GIRARD
20 Dean of Academic Affairs ....Dr. Phil HAUN
88 Int Dean Center for Warfare Studies ....Dr. Peter A. DUTTON
32 Dean of Students ....CAPT. Cindy DIETERLY
08 Director H.E. Eccles Library ....Dr. Allen C. BENSON
106 Dean College of Distance Education ....Prof. Leonard Walter WILDEMANN
06 Registrar ....CAPT. Cindy DIETERLY
46 Chairman Strategy & Policy ....Prof. David STONE
88 Chairman National Security Affairs ....Prof. Derek REVERON
88 Chairman Joint Military Operations . CAPT. Edmund HERNANDEZ
10 Chief Business Officer ....Mr. Robert SAMPSON
108 Dir Institutional Effectiveness ....Dr. Edward GILLEN
15 Director Military Personnel Svcs ....Vacant
15 Civilian Human Resources Officer ....Ms. Charlene HANSON
18 Chief Facilities/Physical Plant ....Mr. Shawn BOGDAN
26 Chief Public Relations Officer ....CDR. Gary ROSS
13 Chief Information Officer ....Mr. Joseph PANGBORN
19 Director of Security ....Mr. James HULL
29 Director Alumni Affairs ....Prof. Julia GAGE
104 Dean International Programs ....Prof. Thomas MANGOLD
88 Director of Events ....Ms. Karen SELLERS
88 Dean Maritime Operational Warfare ....Prof. Michael WHITE
88 Dean Leadership and Ethics ....Prof. Peg KLEIN

School of Advanced Air and Space Studies (B)

125 Chennault Circle, Maxwell AFB AL 36112-6424

Telephone: (334) 953-5155 Identification: 666746
Accreditation: &SC

† Regional accreditation is carried under the parent institution, Air University, Maxwell AFB, AL.

Uniformed Services University of the Health Sciences (C)

4301 Jones Bridge Road, Bethesda MD 20814-4799

County: Montgomery FICE Identification: 021610
Unit ID: 164137
Telephone: (301) 295-3013 Carnegie Class: Spec-4-yr-Med
FAX Number: (301) 295-3431 Calendar System: Quarter
URL: www.usuhs.edu
Established: 1972 Annual Undergrad Tuition & Fees: N/A
Enrollment: N/A Coed
Affiliation or Control: Federal IRS Status: Exempt
Highest Offering: Doctorate
Accreditation: M, ANEST, CLPSY, DENT, HSA, MED, NURSE, PH

01 Acting University President ....Dr. William M. ROBERTS
05 SVP University Programs South ....Dr. Thomas TRAVIS
05 SVP University Programs West ....Dr. William ROBERTS
10 Vice Pres Finance & Admin ....Mr. Walter TINLING
26 Vice Pres External Affairs ....Dr. Jeffrey LONGACRE
46 Vice President for Research ....Vacant
04 Exec Assistant to the President ....Ms. Lorraine BREEN
21 AVP Resource Management ....Ms. Antoinette WHITMEYER
100 Chief of Staff ....Mr. Robert J. THOMPSON
63 Dean School of Medicine ....Dr. Eric ELSTER
66 Dean Graduate School of Nursing ....Dr. Carol ROMANO
76 Dean School Allied Health Sci ....Dr. Lula PELAYO
52 Dean Postgraduate Dental School ....COL. Drew FALLIS
52 Executive Dean Postgrad Dental ....Dr. Thomas R. SCHNEID
58 Assoc Dean Graduate Education ....Dr. Saibal DEY
07 Assoc Dean Admiss & Recruiting SOM ....CDR. Robert LIOTTA
88 Assoc Dean Graduate Medical Educ ....CAPT. Jerri CURTIS
32 Assoc Dean Student Affairs ....COL. Pamela WILLIAMS
20 Assoc Dean for Curriculum ....Dr. Arnyce POCK
88 Sr Assoc Dean for Faculty ....Dr. Jessica SERVEY
88 Assoc Dean for Medical Education ....COL. Catherine WITKOP
88 Assistant Dean Academic Support ....Vacant
88 Associate Dean Clinical Services ....COL. Ashley MARANICH
20 Sr Assoc Dean Academic Affairs ....Dr. Brian REAMY
13 Chief Information Officer ....Mr. Timothy RAPP
43 General Counsel ....Mr. Mark PETERSON
46 Director AFRRI ....COL. Mohammed NAEEM
15 Director Civilian Human Res ....Mr. Darryl BROWN
08 Director University Librarian ....Ms. Alison ROLLINS
18 Director of Facilities ....Ms. Florence RICHARDSON
96 Director of Contracting ....Mr. Stephen DAVIS
29 Director Alumni Relations ....Ms. Sharon HOLLAND
19 Director Security/Safety ....Mr. Christopher MOTTLER
06 AVP Records/Registrar ....Dr. Wendy LISHEN
108 Director Institutional Assessment ....Mr. Stephen HENSKE

United States Air Force Academy (D)

2304 Cadet Drive,, USAF Academy CO 80840-5002

County: El Paso FICE Identification: 001369
Unit ID: 128328
Telephone: (800) 443-9266 Carnegie Class: Bac-A&S
FAX Number: N/A Calendar System: Semester
URL: www.usafa.af.mil
Established: 1954 Annual Undergrad Tuition & Fees: N/A
Enrollment: 4,307 Coed
Affiliation or Control: Federal IRS Status: Exempt
Highest Offering: Baccalaureate
Accreditation: HLC, DENT

01 Superintendent ....LtGen. Richard M. CLARK
05 Chief Acad Officer/Dean of Faculty ....BGen. Linell A. LETENDRE
101 Vice Superintendent ....Col. Otis C. JONES
100 Chief of Staff/Vice COM Cadets ....Ms. Gail B. COLVIN
09 Director of Institutional Research ....Col. John M. GARVER
10 Chief Financial Officer ....Lt Col. Christopher D. CARROLL
37 Director Student Financial Aid ... Lt Col. Christopher D. CARROLL
103 Dir Workforce/Career Development ....Dr. Steven K. JONES
104 Director Study Abroad ....Lt Col. Christopher S. KEAN
11 Command Chief ....CMSgt. Sarah SPARKS
13 Chief Technology Officer (CTO) ....Mr. Martin K. SCHLACTER
15 Director Personnel Services ....Mr. Dale A. HOGUE
18 Chief Facilities/Physical Plant .... Mr. Carlos R. CRUZ-GONZALEZ
19 Director Security/Safety ....Lt Col. Joseph R. VIGUERIA
22 Dir Affirmative Action/EO ....Vacant
26 Chief Public Affairs ....Lt Col. Tracy A. BUNKO
28 Director of Diversity ....Ms. Yvonne ROLAND
29 Director Alumni Relations ....Ms. Nicole J. COX
30 Chief Development/Advancement ....Dr. Tom R. MABRY
32 Chief Student Affairs/Student Life ....Vacant
36 Director Student Placement ....Ms. Laura A. ANGELES
39 Director Student Housing ....Mr. Dean S. MILLS
41 Exec Director of Athletic Programs ....Ms. Jennifer A. BLOCK
41 Athletic Director ....Mr. Nathan A. PINE
43 Dir Legal Services/General Counsel ....Col. Thomas A. ROGERS
45 Chief Institutional Planning ....Col. Tyler P. FRANDER
50 Head Dept of Management ....Col. Troy R. HARTING
54 Pgm Head Environmental Engineering ....Col. Joel A. SLOAN
08 Head Librarian ....Mrs. Diana G. KLARE
84 Director Enrollment Management ....Col. Arthur W. PRIMAS, JR.
90 Director Academic Computing ....Mr. Eugene K. KAUPPILA
91 Director Administrative Computing ....Mr. Jason L. GUTIERREZ
96 Director of Purchasing ....Mr. James A. ANDERSON
06 Registrar ....Dr. Hal TAYLOR
07 Director of Admissions ....Col. Arthur PRIMAS, JR.
105 Director Web Services ....Mr. Andrew P. HAMILTON
108 Director Institutional Assessment ....Lt Col. Jennifer M. RUSSELL
44 Director Annual Giving ....Lt Col. Carla J. HUNSTAD
86 Director Government Relations ....Ms. Sara PLATT-MOSER
102 Dir Foundation/Corporate Rels ....Mr. Michael PETERSON
25 Chief Contract Grants Administrator ....Mr. James A. ANDERSON
27 Chief Information Officer ....Col. Harold T. HOANG
27 Director Strategic Communications ....Ms. Kimberly TEBRUGGE

United States Army Command and General Staff College (E)

100 Stimson Avenue, Fort Leavenworth KS 66027

County: Leavenworth FICE Identification: 001947
Unit ID: 156055
Telephone: (913) 684-3097 Carnegie Class: Spec-4-yr-Other
FAX Number: (913) 684-2906 Calendar System: Trimester
URL: https://usacac.army.mil/organizations/cace/cgsc
Established: 1881 Annual Graduate Tuition & Fees: N/A
Enrollment: N/A Coed
Affiliation or Control: Federal IRS Status: Exempt
Highest Offering: Master's; No Undergraduates
Accreditation: HLC

01 Commandant ....LTG. Michael D. LUNDY
04 Deputy Commandant ....BG. Stephen MARANIAN
05 Dean of Academics ....Dr. James MARTIN
20 Deputy Director ....Mr. Dirk M. HUTCHINSON
58 Director Graduate Degree Programs ....Dr. Robert BAUMANN
08 Director of Library ....Mrs. Beata MOORE
32 Director CGSS School ....Col. Christopher J. CARDONI
06 Registrar ....Dr. Thomas E. CREVISTON

United States Army War College (F)

122 Forbes Avenue, Carlisle PA 17013-5050

County: Cumberland Identification: 666235
Telephone: (717) 245-4711 Carnegie Class: Spec-4-yr-Other
FAX Number: (717) 245-4721 Calendar System: Other
URL: www.carlisle.army.mil
Established: 1901 Annual Graduate Tuition & Fees: N/A
Enrollment: N/A Coed
Affiliation or Control: Federal IRS Status: Exempt
Highest Offering: Master's; No Undergraduates
Accreditation: M

01 Commandant ....MG. Stephen J. MARANIAN
05 Provost ....Dr. Jim G. BRECKENRIDGE
100 Chief of Staff ....Col. Lance D. OSKEY

United States Coast Guard Academy (G)

31 Mohegan Avenue, New London CT 06320

County: New London FICE Identification: 001415
Unit ID: 130624
Telephone: (860) 444-8444 Carnegie Class: Bac-Diverse
FAX Number: (860) 444-8288 Calendar System: Semester
URL: www.cga.edu
Established: 1876 Annual Undergrad Tuition & Fees: N/A
Enrollment: 1,056 Coed
Affiliation or Control: Federal IRS Status: Exempt
Highest Offering: Baccalaureate
Accreditation: EH

01 Superintendent ....RADM. William G. KELLY
03 Assistant Superintendent ....CAPT. Richard J. WESTER
45 Planning Officer ....CDR. John J. CHRISTENSEN
05 Dean of Academics ....Dr. Kurt J. COLELLA
20 Senior Associate Dean ....CAPT. Russell E. BOWMAN
45 Director of Academic Resources ....Dr. Eric J. PAGE
07 Director of Admissions ....CAPT. Michael C. FREDIE
32 Commandant of Cadets ....CAPT. Arthur L. RAY
06 Registrar ....Vacant
08 Librarian ....Ms. Lucia MAZIAR
10 Comptroller ....CDR. Micheal FRIEND
26 Communication Director ....Mr. David M. SANTOS
09 Institutional Research ....Dr. Leonard M. GIAMBRA
13 Head of Information Services ....CDR. Christopher M. ARMSTRONG
16 Personnel Management Specialist ....Ms. Julie A. KELLY
15 Chief Personnel/Administration ....CAPT. William SMITH
18 Chief Facilities Engineer ....CDR. Cesar ACOSTA
22 Civil Rights Officer ....Mr. Roy P. ZIEGENGEIST
23 Clinic Director ....CAPT. Esan SIMON
38 Chief Cadet Counselor ....Dr. Daria PAPALIA
40 Bookstore Manager ....Ms. Lauri KERP
41 Director of Athletics ....Dr. Dan C. ROSE
42 Command Chaplain ....CAPT. Ryan R. RUPE
43 Staff Legal Officer ....CDR. Aaron J. CASAVANT
85 International Cadet Advisor ....Dr. Kassim M. TARHINI
28 Instructor Inclusion and Diversity ....Dr. Aram DEKOVEN

United States Merchant Marine Academy (H)

300 Steamboat Road, Kings Point NY 11024-1634

County: Nassau FICE Identification: 002892
Unit ID: 197027
Telephone: (516) 773-5000 Carnegie Class: Bac-Diverse
FAX Number: (516) 773-5582 Calendar System: Trimester
URL: www.usmma.edu
Established: 1943 Annual Undergrad Tuition & Fees: $1,095
Enrollment: 1,045 Coed
Affiliation or Control: Federal IRS Status: Exempt
Highest Offering: Master's
Accreditation: M

01 Superintendent ....RADM. Jack BUONO
03 Deputy Superintendent ....RDML. Susan L. DUNLAP
05 Academic Dean & Provost ....Dr. John R. BALLARD
32 Commandant of Midshipmen ....Vacant
20 Assistant Academic Dean ....Ms. Dianne TAHA
18 Asst Supt for Facilities ....CAPT. Theodore DOGONNIUCK
26 Director Office of External Affairs ....Mr. George RHYNEDANCE
07 Director of Admissions ....CDR. Michael BEDRYK
06 Registrar ....Ms. Lisa JERRY
13 Director Computer/Information Mgmt ....Vacant
15 Director Human Resources ....Vacant
10 Chief Financial Officer ....Mr. David SOCOLOF
29 Director Alumni Relations ....Mr. Jim TOBIN
36 Dir of Prof Develop/Career Services ....CAPT. Gene ALBERT
37 Director Student Financial Aid ....Mr. Joseph BECKER
96 Director of Purchasing ....Mr. Max DIAH
09 Director of Institutional Research ....Ms. Lori TOWNSEND
41 Athletic Director ....Ms. Maureen WHITE
108 Director Institutional Assessment ....Ms. Lori TOWNSEND
43 Dir Legal Services/General Counsel ....Ms. Ilene KREITZER
11 Chief of Administration ....Mr. John DEMERS
19 Director Security/Safety ....Mr. Jeffrey THOMAS
22 Director Affirmative Action/EEO ....Mr. Marvin WILLIAMS
04 Admin Assistant to the President ....Ms. Cynthia FLYNN
08 Chief Library Officer ....Ms. Donna SELVAGGIO

United States Military Academy (I)

646 Swift Rd., West Point NY 10996-5000

County: Orange FICE Identification: 002893
Unit ID: 197036
Telephone: (845) 938-4041 Carnegie Class: Bac-A&S
FAX Number: (845) 938-3021 Calendar System: Semester
URL: www.westpoint.edu
Established: 1802 Annual Undergrad Tuition & Fees: N/A
Enrollment: 4,536 Coed
Affiliation or Control: Federal IRS Status: Exempt
Highest Offering: Baccalaureate
Accreditation: M

01 Superintendent/President ... LTG. Darryl A. WILLIAMS
32 Commandant of Cadets ... BG. Mark QUANDER
05 Dean of Academic Board ... BG. Shane REEVES
41 Director Intercollegiate Athletics ... Mr. Mike BUDDIE
100 Chief of Staff ... COL. Mark WEATHERS
88 Garrison Commander ... COL. Evangeline ROSEL
07 Director of Admissions ... COL. Deborah MCDONALD
20 Vice Dean Academic Affairs ... Dr. Susan CARTER
06 Associate Dean for Registrar ... Dr. Jim DALTON
46 Associate Dean for Research ... Dr. Ken WICKISER
88 Dir Center for Teaching Excellence ... Dr. Mark EVANS
121 Dir Ctr for Enhanced Performance ... COL. Darcy SCHNACK
08 USMA Library ... Mr. Christopher BARTH
38 Dir Center for Personal Development ... LTC. Michell GRIFFITH
88 Director of Cadet Activities ... COL. Tom HANSBARGER
13 Chief Information Officer ... COL. Edward TEAGUE
15 Chief Strength Management ... COL. Jennifer HICKS-MCGOWAN
26 Public Affairs Officer ... LTC. Beth SMITH
10 Director of Resource Management ... Ms. Melissa CARDONA
108 Dir Institutional Effectiveness ... Dr. Gerald KOBYLSKI
09 Director Institutional Research ... LTC. Brian NOVOSELICH
18 Director of Public Works ... Mr. William KILLOUGH
28 Chief Diversity Officer ... Vacant

United States Naval Academy (A)

121 Blake Road, Annapolis MD 21402-5000
County: Anne Arundel FICE Identification: 030430
Unit ID: 164155
Telephone: (410) 293-1000 Carnegie Class: Bac-A&S
FAX Number: (410) 293-3734 Calendar System: Semester
URL: www.usna.edu
Established: 1845 Annual Undergrad Tuition & Fees: N/A
Enrollment: 4,594 Coed
Affiliation or Control: Federal IRS Status: Exempt
Highest Offering: Baccalaureate
Accreditation: M

01 Superintendent ... VADM. Sean S. BUCK
32 Commandant of Midshipmen ... Col. James P. MCDONOUGH
05 Academic Dean & Provost ... Dr. Andrew T. PHILLIPS
20 Vice Academic Dean ... Dr. Daniel W. O'SULLIVAN
07 Dean of Admissions ... Mr. Bruce J. LATTA
10 Associate Dean for Finances ... Mr. Peter A. NARDI
20 Assoc Provost for Academic Affairs ... Dr. Samarra FIREBAUGH
08 Assoc Dean Information Svcs/Library ... Mr. James RETTIG
21 CFO/Deputy for Finance ... Mr. Joseph RUBINO
100 Chief of Staff/Deputy Super ... CAPT. James BATES
11 CO Naval Support Activity Annapolis ... CAPT. Homer DENIUS
06 Registrar ... Dr. Christopher A. DAVIS
26 Public Affairs Officer ... CDR. Alana GARAS
29 Senior Director of Engagement ... Mr. Craig WASHINGTON
21 Comptroller ... Mr. Todd W. HAUGE
13 Chief Information Officer ... Mr. Louis J. GIANNOTTI
88 Director Academic Center ... Dr. Bruce J. BUKOWSKI
09 Director Institutional Research ... Mr. Robert J. BRENNAN
18 Public Works Officer ... CAPT. Thomas B. MCLEMORE
41 Athletic Director ... Mr. Chet GLADCHUK
42 Command Chaplain ... CAPT. Richard BONNETTE
30 Director Officer Development ... Maj. David EMISON
15 Director Human Resources ... Mr. William COFFIN
28 Director of Diversity ... CAPT. Herbert E. LACY

AMERICAN SAMOA

American Samoa Community College (B)

PO Box 2609, Pago Pago AS 96799-2609
County: American Samoa FICE Identification: 010010
Unit ID: 240736
Telephone: (684) 699-9155 Carnegie Class: Bac/Assoc-Assoc Dom
FAX Number: (684) 699-6259 Calendar System: Semester
URL: www.amsamoa.edu
Established: 1970 Annual Undergrad Tuition & Fees (In-State): $3,950
Enrollment: 1,081 Coed
Affiliation or Control: State IRS Status: 501(c)3
Highest Offering: Baccalaureate
Accreditation: WJ

01 President ... Dr. Rosevonne M. PATO
05 VP of Academic Affairs ... Mrs. Letupu MOANANU
88 Director of Samoan Studies Inst ... Mrs. Okenaisa FAUOLO-MANILA
88 Director of Land Grant/ACNR ... Mr. Ropeti ARETA
11 VP of Admin/Finance & Spec Advisor ... Dr. Lina SCANLON
108 Executive Director of IE ... Mr. Sony J. LEOMITI
88 Director of UCEDD ... Ms. Tafaimamao TUPUOLA
51 Director of Adult Education-LEL ... Ms. Tauvela FALE
88 Director of Small Business Dev ... Mr. Jason BETHAM
20 Dean of Academic Affairs ... Dr. Siamaua ROPETI
53 Teacher Educ Program Director ... Ms. Shirley DE LA ROSA
66 Nursing Program Director ... Ms. Lele V. AH MU
72 Trade and Tech Program Director ... Mr. Frederick R. SUISALA
32 Dean of Student Services ... Dr. Emilia LE'I
38 Program Director of Counseling ... Ms. Annie PANAMA
06 Registrar/Records Officer ... Mrs. Sifagatogo TUITASI
08 Program Director of Library Svcs ... Mr. Elvis ZODIACAL
37 Financial Aid Officer ... Mr. Peteru K. LAM YUEN
07 Admission Officer ... Mrs. Elizabeth LEUMA
10 Financial Officer ... Ms. Emey SILAFAU-TOA
13 Chief Information Officer ... Mr. Donald NELSON
18 Physical Facilities Maint Officer ... Mr. Lokeni LOKENI
15 Human Resources Officer ... Mrs. Sereima ASIFOA
96 Procurement Officer ... Mrs. Jessie SU'ESU'E
40 Bookstore Mgr/Dir Research Found ... Mrs. Alofia AFALAVA
04 Executive Secretary ... Mrs. Violina HUDSON
101 Board Secretary ... Mrs. Tiare TUPUA
19 Chief Security Officer ... Vacant

FEDERATED STATES OF MICRONESIA

College of Micronesia-FSM (C)

PO Box 159 Kolonia, Pohnpei FM 96941-0159
FICE Identification: 010343
Unit ID: 243638
Telephone: (691) 320-2480 Carnegie Class: Assoc/HT-High Trad
FAX Number: (691) 320-2479 Calendar System: Semester
URL: www.comfsm.fm
Established: 1963 Annual Undergrad Tuition & Fees (In-State): $4,750
Enrollment: 1,861 Coed
Affiliation or Control: State IRS Status: 501(c)3
Highest Offering: Associate Degree
Accreditation: WJ

01 Interim President/CEO ... Mrs. Karen SIMION
05 Vice Pres for Instructional Affairs ... Mrs. Karen SIMION
84 Vice Pres Enroll Mgmt/Student Svcs ... Mr. Joey ODUCADO
11 Vice President Admin Services ... Mr. Joseph HABUCHMAI
12 Dean Chuuk Campus ... Mr. Kind KANTO
12 Dean Kosrae Campus ... Mr. Nena MIKE
12 Dean Yap Campus/VP Instruct Affs ... Ms. Lourdes ROBOMAN
10 Comptroller ... Mrs. Roselle TOGONON
15 Director Human Resources ... Ms. Rencelly NELSON
20 Dean of Academic Programs ... Mrs. Maria DISON
08 Director Learning Resource Center ... Mrs. Jennifer HELEISAR
75 Dir Career & Technical Education ... Mr. Grilly JACK
18 Director Physical Plant/Maintenance ... Mr. Francisco MENDIOLA
06 Registrar ... Mr. Doman DAOAS
21 Business Officer Manager ... Ms. Ritchie VALENCIA
37 Director of Financial Aid ... Mr. Faustino YAROFAISUG
38 Lead Counselor ... Ms. Penselyn SAM
13 Director Information Technology ... Mr. Shaun SULIOL
19 Supervisor Security/Safety ... Mr. Terry MARCUS

GUAM

Guam Community College (D)

PO Box 23069, Barrigada GU 96921-3069
County: Guam FICE Identification: 015361
Unit ID: 240745
Telephone: (671) 735-5531 Carnegie Class: Assoc/MT-VT-High Trad
FAX Number: (671) 734-5238 Calendar System: Semester
URL: www.guamcc.edu
Established: 1977 Annual Undergrad Tuition & Fees (In-District): $3,414
Enrollment: 1,716 Coed
Affiliation or Control: State/Local IRS Status: 501(c)3
Highest Offering: Associate Degree
Accreditation: WJ, ACFEI

01 President ... Dr. Mary Y. OKADA
05 Vice President Academic Affairs ... Dr. Virginia C. TUDELA
32 Dean Technology & Student Services ... Dr. Michael L. CHAN
26 Asst Dir Communications & Promo ... Mr. John DELA ROSA
04 Private Secretary ... Ms. Esther A. MUNA
101 Admin Secretary II BOT-Pres Ofc ... Ms. Bertha M. GUERRERO
07 Coordinator Admissions/Registration ... Ms. Tina M. QUINATA
45 Asst Dir Planning & Development ... Ms. Doris U. PEREZ
88 Assoc Dean Trade & Prof Svcs ... Ms. Pilar WILLIAMS
35 Assoc Dean Tech & Student Svcs ... Mr. Ronald G. HARTZ
15 Chief Human Resources Ofcr ... Ms. Apolline SAN NICOLAS
18 Facilities Engineer Administrator ... Vacant
08 Librarian ... Ms. Christine B. MATSON
20 Admin Ofcr VP's Ofc-Academic Affs ... Ms. Ana Mari C. ATOIGUE
09 Asst Director AIER ... Ms. Marlena O. MONTAGUE
55 Pgm Spc Adult Basic Educ ... Ms. Ava M. GARCIA
88 Pgm Spc TRIO Programs ... Ms. Fermina A. SABLAN
35 Pgm Spc Ctr Student Involvement ... Ms. Latisha Ann N. LEON GUERRERO
23 LPN Health Services Center ... Ms. Eva Marie L. MUI
37 Coordinator Student Financial Aid ... Ms. Esther A. RIOS
88 Program Spec Dean's Ofc TSS ... Dr. Julie ULLOA-HEATH
29 Pgm Specialist Alum & Fundraising ... Ms. Bonnie Mae M. DATUIN
96 Supply Management Administrator ... Ms. Joleen M. EVANGELISTA
13 Chief Info Tech Officer MIS ... Mr. Francisco C. CAMACHO
51 Pgm Spc Continuing Educ ... Vacant
40 Bookstore Manager ... Mr. Daniel T. OKADA
88 Pgm Spc Night Administrator ... Mr. Huan HOSEI
39 Pgm Spc Accommodative Svcs ... Mr. John F. PAYNE
88 Sustainability/Project Coordinator ... Mr. Francisco E. PALACIOS

Pacific Islands University (E)

172 Kinney's Road, Mangilao GU 96913
County: Guam FICE Identification: 034383
Unit ID: 439862
Telephone: (671) 734-1812 Carnegie Class: Bac-Diverse
FAX Number: (671) 734-1813 Calendar System: Semester
URL: www.piu.edu
Established: 1976 Annual Undergrad Tuition & Fees: $6,110
Enrollment: 273 Coed
Affiliation or Control: Independent Non-Profit IRS Status: 501(c)3
Highest Offering: Master's
Accreditation: TRACS

01 President/CEO ... Rev. Howard MERRELL
10 VP Finance/Administration ... Vacant
05 Vice President Academic Affairs ... Vacant
49 Liberal Studies Chair ... Mrs. Dorothy HOUDE
73 Biblical Studies Chair ... Mr. Iotaka CHORAM
32 Vice President Student Development ... Mr. Alex TAVAREZ
21 Operations Director/Bookkeeper ... Ms. Celia ATOIGUE
04 Admin Assistant to the President ... Ms. Kathy MERRELL
08 Library Director ... Mr. Paul DRAKE
15 Human Resource Director ... Mr. Joshua COMBS
84 Int Enrollment Mgmt Dir/Registrar ... Mr. Joshua COMBS
37 Financial Aid Officer ... Mr. Delight SUDA

University of Guam (F)

UOG Station, Mangilao GU 96923-1800
County: Guam FICE Identification: 003935
Unit ID: 240754
Telephone: (671) 735-2990 Carnegie Class: Masters/M
FAX Number: (671) 734-2296 Calendar System: Semester
URL: www.uog.edu
Established: 1952 Annual Undergrad Tuition & Fees (In-State): $5,846
Enrollment: 3,449 Coed
Affiliation or Control: State IRS Status: 501(c)3
Highest Offering: Master's
Accreditation: WC, AAQEP, IACBE, NUR, SW

01 President ... Dr. Thomas W. KRISE
05 Senior VP & Provost ... Dr. Anita B. ENRIQUEZ
10 Vice Pres Administration & Finance ... Mr. Randall V. WIEGAND
46 Director Research & Sponsored Pgm ... Dr. Rachael T. LEON GUERRERO
43 University General Counsel ... Mr. Anthony R. CAMACHO
13 Int Chief Information Officer ... Mr. Manuel B. HECHANOVA, JR.
22 Acting Director EEO & Title IX/ADA ... Mr. Larry GAMBOA
100 Int Chief of Staff & Board Liaison ... Mr. David S. OKADA
26 Chief Mktg & Comm Officer ... Mr. Jonas D. MACAPINLAC
45 Acting Chief Planning Officer ... Mr. James HOLLYER
29 Director Alumni Affairs ... Mr. Norman ANALISTA
102 Exec Director Endowment Foundation ... Ms. Katrina PEREZ
108 Vice Provost Inst Effectiveness ... Ms. Deborah D. LEON GUERRERO
20 Vice Provost Academic Excellence ... Dr. Troy MCVEY
49 Dean Col of Lib Arts & Social Sci ... Dr. James D. SELLMANN
47 Dean Col of Natural & Applied Sci ... Dr. Lee S. YUDIN
50 Dean Sch Business & Pub Admin ... Dr. Annette T. SANTOS
53 Dean School of Education ... Dr. Alicia AGUON
76 Dean School of Health ... Dr. Margaret HATTORI-UCHIMA
54 Interim Dean School of Engineering ... Dr. Shahram KHOSROWPANAH
84 Dean Enroll Mgmt & Student Svcs ... Dr. Lawrence F. CAMACHO
06 Registrar ... Ms. Remy B. CRISTOBAL
37 Financial Aid Director ... Mr. Mark A. DUARTE
32 Student Life Officer ... Vacant
88 Interim Director Guam CEDDERS ... Ms. June DE LEON
08 Dean University Libraries ... Dr. Monique STORIE
88 Dir Micronesia Area Res Center ... Dr. Carlos MADRID
88 Interim Director Marine Laboratory ... Dr. Laurie RAYMUNDO
88 Dir Water Env Rsrch Inst Wstrn Pac ... Dr. John JENSON
88 Dir Ctr for Island Sustainability ... Dr. Austin SHELTON
104 Dir Global Learning & Engagement ... Mr. Carlos TAITANO
15 Actg Chief Human Resources Officer ... Mr. Joseph B. GUMATAOTAO
18 Int Chief Plant/Facility Officer ... Mr. David S. OKADA
41 Field House/Athletics Director ... Mr. Doug PALMER
19 Safety Administrator ... Mr. Alfred GARRIDO
40 Director Bookstore & Auxiliary Svcs ... Ms. Ann S A. LEON GUERRERO
21 Interim Comptroller ... Ms. Abigail MARTIN
39 Int Director of Residence Halls ... Mr. Mark MENDIOLA

MARSHALL ISLANDS

College of the Marshall Islands (G)

PO Box 1258, Majuro MH 96960-1258
County: Marshalls FICE Identification: 030224
Unit ID: 376695
Telephone: (692) 625-3394 Carnegie Class: Assoc/HT-High Trad
FAX Number: (692) 625-7203 Calendar System: Semester
URL: www.cmi.edu
Established: 1989 Annual Undergrad Tuition & Fees (In-State): $4,900
Enrollment: 1,162 Coed
Affiliation or Control: State IRS Status: 501(c)3
Highest Offering: Associate Degree
Accreditation: WJ

01 President ... Dr. Irene J. TAAFAKI
05 Vice Pres Academic/Student Affairs ... Dr. Elizabeth SWITAJ
10 Vice Pres Business & Admin Affairs ... Mr. Stevenson KOTTON
88 Vice President for Land Grant ... Mr. Stanley LORENNIJ
20 Dean of Academic Affairs ... Ms. Vasemaca SAVU
32 Dean of Student Success ... Vacant
06 Registrar ... Ms. Monica GORDON

07 Director of Admissions & Records .... Ms. Jomi CAPELLE
08 Director of Library .... Ms. Verenaisi BAVADRA
15 Human Resources Director .... Ms. Agnes KOTOISUVA
18 Director Physical Plant .... Mr. Linus KEBOS
13 Director Information & Technology .... Mr. Bonifacio SANCHEZ
88 Director Nuclear Institute .... Ms. Mary L. SILK
37 Financial Aid Director .... Ms. Sali ANDRIKE
49 Chair Liberal Arts .... Ms. Oyinada OGUNMOKUN
03 Executive Vice President .... Mr. William REIHER
50 Chair Business & IT .... Ms. Meitaka KENDALL-LEKKA
66 Chair Nursing .... Ms. Florence L. PETER
19 Director Security/Safety .... Mr. David DEBRUM
38 Director of Counseling .... Ms. Demiana NAUSI KUMORU
09 Dir Inst Research/Assessment .... Ms. Cheryl T. VILA
04 Admin Assistant to the President .... Ms. Takbar ISHIGURO
101 Executive Officer .... Ms. Kelly Luce SEBASTIAN
105 Director Web Services .... Mr. John A. VILLAFANIA

NORTHERN MARIANAS

Northern Marianas College (A)

PO Box 501250, Saipan MP 96950-1250

FICE Identification: 030330
Unit ID: 240790

Telephone: (670) 234-5498 Carnegie Class: Bac/Assoc-Mixed
FAX Number: (670) 234-1270 Calendar System: Semester
URL: www.marianas.edu
Established: 1976 Annual Undergrad Tuition & Fees (In-District): $4,038
Enrollment: 1,255 Coed
Affiliation or Control: State/Local IRS Status: Exempt
Highest Offering: Baccalaureate
Accreditation: WC

01 President .... Dr. Galvin DELEON GUERRERO
05 Dean of Academic Programs/Services .... Dr. Randy YATES
10 Chief Financial Officer .... Mr. David ATTAO
04 Executive Secretary to President .... Ms. Becky SABLAN
20 Dean Learning & Student Success .... Ms. Charlotte CEPEDA
13 Dir Information Technology .... Mr. Adrian ATALIG
09 Dir Institutional Effectiveness .... Dr. Wesley WILSON
18 Director of Facilities .... Mr. Vincent MERFALEN
53 Director School of Education .... Mr. Roland MERAR
51 Director of Adult Basic Education .... Ms. Lorraine C. MAUI
37 Director of Financial Aid .... Ms. Daisy MANGLONA-PROPST
96 Procurement Manager .... Ms. Anita C. CAMACHO
106 Director of Distance Learning .... Mr. William HUNTER
06 Registrar .... Ms. Marji TAROPE
101 Executive Secretary to the Board .... Ms. Helen B. CAMACHO
84 Director Enrollment Services .... Mr. Manny CASTRO

PALAU

Palau Community College (B)

PO Box 9, Koror PW 96940-0009
County: Koror FICE Identification: 011009
Unit ID: 243647

Telephone: (680) 488-2470 Carnegie Class: Assoc/HT-High Trad
FAX Number: (680) 488-2447 Calendar System: Semester
URL: www.palau.edu
Established: 1969 Annual Undergrad Tuition & Fees: $3,610
Enrollment: 553 Coed
Affiliation or Control: Federal IRS Status: Exempt
Highest Offering: Associate Degree
Accreditation: WJ

01 President .... Dr. Patrick U. TELLEI
05 Vice President Education & Training .... Vacant
11 Vice Pres Administration & Finance .... Mr. Jay OLEGERIIL
46 Vice Pres Cooperative Rsrch/Exten . Dr. Christopher U. KITALONG
04 Exec Assistant to the President .... Mr. Todd NGIRAMENGIOR
32 Dean of Students/Dir Student Life .... Ms. Hilda N. REKLAI
20 Dean of Academic Affairs .... Ms. Deikola OLIKONG
51 Dean of Continuing Education .... Mr. Jefferson THOMAS
30 Director of Development .... Mr. Tchuzie TADAO
37 Director of Financial Aid .... Ms. Isumechraard K. NGIRAIRIKL
07 Director of Admissions and Records .... Ms. Lesley B. ADACHI
15 Director of Human Resources .... Ms. Marie A. ANDERSON
18 Director of Physical Plant .... Mr. Clement KAZUMA
13 Director of Computer Systems .... Mr. Bruce RIMIRCH
10 Director of Finance .... Ms. Uroi N. SALII
08 Interim Director Library Services .... Ms. Pioria ASITO

PUERTO RICO

American University of Puerto Rico (C)

Box 2037, Bayamon PR 00960-2037
County: Bayamon FICE Identification: 011941
Unit ID: 241100

Telephone: (787) 620-2040 Carnegie Class: Bac-Diverse
FAX Number: (787) 785-7377 Calendar System: Other
URL: www.aupr.edu
Established: 1963 Annual Undergrad Tuition & Fees: $6,555
Enrollment: 294 Coed
Affiliation or Control: Independent Non-Profit IRS Status: 501(c)3
Highest Offering: Master's
Accreditation: M

01 President .... Mr. Juan C. NAZARIO TORRES
03 Executive Vice President .... Mr. Jaime GONZALEZ
05 Vice President Acad/Student Affairs .... Dr. Jose RAMIREZ-FIGUEROA
10 Vice Pres Finance & Admin Affairs .... Mrs. Magda A. CANCEL-PEREZ
32 Dean Student Affairs .... Prof. Claribel RODRIGUEZ-VARGAS
06 Registrar .... Prof. Alex ROBLES MARRERO
07 Admissions Officer .... Ms. Keren LLANOS
08 Learning Resources Center Director .... Vacant
37 Coordinator Financial Aid .... Mrs. Nelly DUARTE
21 Director Accounting .... Mrs. Jeanette AVILES-FERRAN
38 Director Guidance Counseling .... Mrs. Luz S. HERNANDEZ
24 Director Educational Media .... Ms. Carol SANTIAGO
41 Athletic Director .... Mr. Manfredo VEGA
15 Director Human Resources .... Mr. Jorge ESCALERA MUÑOZ
12 Director Manati Campus .... Prof. Milagros RIVERA-OTERO
09 Dir Research/Institutional Planning .... Vacant
18 Chief Facilities/Physical Plant .... Mr. Efrain LUGO
36 Director of Student Placement .... Vacant
96 Coordinator of Purchasing .... Ms. Jacqueline HERNÁNDEZ
92 Director of Honors Program .... Prof. Claribel RODRIGUEZ
30 Chief Development .... Mr. Jaime GONZALEZ
20 Associate Academic Officer .... Prof. Zahira GARCIA
13 Director Computer Center .... Mr. Eric CHAPARRO
53 Dept Chair School of Education .... Dr. Jose RAMIREZ
50 Dept Chair Business Admin/Sec Sci .... Vacant
49 Department Chair Arts & Sciences .... Vacant
100 Chief of Staff .... Ms. Rosabel VAZQUEZ
102 Dir Foundation/Corporate Relations .... Dr. Adela VAZQUEZ
105 Director Web Services .... Vacant
19 Director Security/Safety .... Ms. Rosabel VAZQUEZ
45 Chief Institutional Planning .... Prof. Bolivar RAMIREZ-CARLO, III
04 Administrative Asst to President .... Mrs. Carmen ARROYO

Atenas College (D)

Paseo de las Atenas #101, Manati PR 00674

FICE Identification: 035443
Unit ID: 440651

Telephone: (787) 884-3838 Carnegie Class: Spec-4-yr-Other Health
FAX Number: (787) 854-4530 Calendar System: Semester
URL: www.atenascollege.edu
Established: 1996 Annual Undergrad Tuition & Fees: $7,370
Enrollment: 558 Coed
Affiliation or Control: Independent Non-Profit IRS Status: 501(c)3
Highest Offering: Baccalaureate
Accreditation: M, ADNUR, NURSE, #PTAA

01 President .... Dra. Maria L. HERNANDEZ NUNEZ
05 VP Academic Affairs .... Prof. Widalys GONZALEZ
32 VP of Student Affairs .... Dr. José M. DONATE
45 VP Inst Planning & Development .... Mrs. Ingrid Y. COLON
10 VP Finance & Administrative Affairs ..... Mrs. Astrid Y. MELENDEZ
20 Associate VP of Academic Affairs .... Dra. Cenia K. ROMANO
21 Assoc VP of Finance & Admin Affs .... Mrs. Zulay SOTO
37 Financial Aid Administrator .... Mr. Manuel RAMIREZ

Atlantic University College (E)

PO Box 3918, Guaynabo PR 00970
County: Guaynabo FICE Identification: 025054
Unit ID: 241216

Telephone: (787) 720-1022 Carnegie Class: Spec-4-yr-Other Tech
FAX Number: (787) 720-1092 Calendar System: Quarter
URL: www.atlanticu.edu
Established: 1983 Annual Undergrad Tuition & Fees: $7,500
Enrollment: 1,584 Coed
Affiliation or Control: Independent Non-Profit IRS Status: 501(c)3
Highest Offering: Master's
Accreditation: ACCSC, ACICS

01 President .... Dr. Teresa DE DIOS UNANUE
13 Exec Vice Pres/Dean Technology/ Mktg .... Prof. Heri MARTINEZ DE DIOS
05 Academic Dean .... Prof. Maria VILLALONGA
10 Asst Dean of Administration .... Ms. Viviana SANTIAGO
06 Registrar .... Ms. Edna I. GUTIERREZ
38 Dir Student Counseling/ Placement .... Prof. Maria C. LOPEZ-CEPERO RAMOS
37 Director Financial Aid .... Mrs. Janice RIVERA
08 Head Librarian .... Ms. Awilda MORAN
07 Director of Admissions .... Mr. Joel MONTERO
21 Director Business Office .... Mrs. María del C MONTESINO
15 Officer of Human Resources .... Ms. Viviana SANTIAGO

Caribbean University (F)

Box 493, Bayamon PR 00960-0493
County: Bayamon FICE Identification: 012525
Unit ID: 241377

Telephone: (787) 780-0070 Carnegie Class: Masters/S
FAX Number: N/A Calendar System: Semester
URL: www.caribbean.edu
Established: 1969 Annual Undergrad Tuition & Fees: $5,496
Enrollment: 987 Coed
Affiliation or Control: Independent Non-Profit IRS Status: 501(c)3
Highest Offering: Doctorate
Accreditation: M

01 President/CEO .... Dr. Ana E. CUCURELLA-ADORNO
03 Executive Director .... Mr. Victor T. ADORNO
45 VP of Planning and Development .... Mrs. Lillian MATOS
11 VP Administration Affairs .... Mr. Hector GARCIA
32 Dean of Student Affairs .... Mr. Alex CLAUDIO
15 Int Director Human Resources .... Dr. Rebecca QUINTANA
37 Coordinator Student Financial Aid .... Mrs. Lorell NUÑEZ
06 Registrar .... Ms. Rosalie MORALES
08 Librarian/Director Audio-Visual .... Mrs. Cynthia MIRANDA
12 Director of Carolina Campus .... Dr. Reinaldo DEL VALLE
12 Director of Ponce Campus .... Dr. Rafael NEGRON
12 Director Vega Baja Campus .... Prof. Rafael MARRERO
26 Director of Marketing/Admissions .... Prof. Gricelie TORRES
58 Academic Dean Graduate Programs .... Dr. Zoraida ALONSO
49 Director Department of Liberal Arts .... Prof. Arelis NEVAREZ
50 Coordinator Dept Business Admin .... Prof. Carmen RODRIGUEZ
76 Director Dept Allied Sciences .... Dr. Ricardo MELGAREJO
54 Director Department Engineering/IT .... Dr. Hermes CALDERON
66 Coordinator Department of Nursing .... Prof. Noemi SANTOS
53 Dir Dept Education/Liberal Arts .... Prof. Arelis NEVAREZ
18 Chief Facilities/Physical Plant .... Mr. Ibrahim MESTRES
38 Director Counseling Center (CIOSE) .... Lic. Maria PEREZ
41 Athletic Director .... Mr. Xavier PIZARRO
22 Director of Compliance/Student Svcs .... Mrs. Elena GARCIA
12 Director of Bayamon Campus .... Prof. Alex CLAUDIO
04 Admin Assistant to the President .... Ms. Judith ROMAN
10 Chief Financial/Business Officer .... Mr. Edwin C. LOZADA
19 Director Security/Safety .... Ms. Ana SANCHEZ

Carlos Albizu University (G)

Box 9023711, San Juan PR 00902-3711
County: San Juan FICE Identification: 010724
Unit ID: 241331

Telephone: (787) 725-6500 Carnegie Class: Spec-4-yr-Other Health
FAX Number: (787) 721-7187 Calendar System: Semester
URL: www.albizu.edu
Established: 1966 Annual Undergrad Tuition & Fees: $7,434
Enrollment: 2,344 Coed
Affiliation or Control: Independent Non-Profit IRS Status: 501(c)3
Highest Offering: Doctorate
Accreditation: M, CLPSY, IPSY, SP

01 President .... Dr. Jose PONS MADERA
00 Chair Board of Trustees ..... Mrs. Maria FELICIANO DE LA CRUZ
03 Chancellor .... Dr. Julio SANTANA MARINO
05 Provost/Dean of Academic Affairs .... Dr. José A. PEREZ - SANTIAGO
10 Chief Financial Officer .... Ms. Angel ORTIZ GARCIA
32 Dean of Student Services .... Ms. Carmen RIVERA
84 Dean of Enrollment Management .... Ms. Rosa BELVIS LOPEZ
07 Interim Director of Admissions .... Mrs. Kareline SANTIAGO TORRES
21 Director of Finance .... Mr. Hector PENA
09 Dir of Planning/Inst Research .. Mr. Yoel A. VELAZQUEZ-OLIVER
46 Director Research/Training Program .... Dr. Lymaries PADILLA
51 Director Continuing Education .... Ms. Luaida OYOLA
37 Director Financial Aid .... Mrs. Doris QUERO-MENDEZ
08 Director Library .... Ms. Yolanda ROSARIO-ROSARIO
06 Registrar .... Ms. Maria de Lourdes RIVERA-NIEVES
88 Dir Industrial/Org Psych Program .... Dr. Ramón RODRÍGUEZ MONTALBAN
13 Director Information Systems .... Mr. Juan RIVERA RIVERA
88 Administrator Community Svcs Clinic .... Mr. Epifanio RIVERA
88 Director Community Services Clinic .... Dr. Vanessa RIVERA
88 Dir PhD Clinical Psychology Program .... Mr. Marcos REYES
15 Human Resources Director .... Ms. Carmen M. ACEVEDO RIOS
30 Director Development .... Vacant
97 Director Bachelor's Program .... Dr. Arlene VELEZ
38 President Student Counseling .... Mr. Jose A. GARCIA
11 Director Administration .... Mr. Epifanio RIVERA
108 Dir Assessment and Accreditation .... Mr. Rafael MELENDEZ
58 Director of Graduate Education .... Dr. Luaida OYOLA
04 Admin Assistant to the President .... Ms. Vanessa RAMOS
100 Chief of Staff .... Dr. Angel ORTIZ

CEM College (H)

Calle Degetau #25, Bayamon PR 00961
Telephone: (787) 780-8900 Identification: 770590
Accreditation: ACCSC

CEM College (I)

Calle Dr. Vidal #8 y #53, Humacao PR 00791
Telephone: (787) 852-5505 Identification: 770589
Accreditation: ACCSC

CEM College (J)

Calle Cristy #56, Mayaguez PR 00680
Telephone: (787) 986-7440 Identification: 770591
Accreditation: ACCSC

CEM College (K)

Ext San Agustin,Calle 13 #1206, San Juan PR 00926
County: San Juan FICE Identification: 021891
Unit ID: 241517

Telephone: (787) 765-4210 Carnegie Class: Spec-4-yr-Other Health
FAX Number: (787) 765-4277 Calendar System: Semester
URL: www.cemcollege.edu
Established: 1980 Annual Undergrad Tuition & Fees: $8,616
Enrollment: 277 Coed

Affiliation or Control: Independent Non-Profit IRS Status: 501(c)3
Highest Offering: Baccalaureate
Accreditation: ACCSC

02 Campus Director ....Mr. Hector M. DAVILA RIVERA

Center for Advanced Studies On Puerto Rico and the Caribbean (A)

PO Box 902-3970, Old San Juan PR 00902-3970
County: San Juan FICE Identification: 021660
Unit ID: 241793
Telephone: (787) 723-4481 Carnegie Class: Spec-4-yr-Other
FAX Number: (787) 723-1023 Calendar System: Semester
URL: www.ceaprc.edu
Established: 1976 Annual Graduate Tuition & Fees: N/A
Enrollment: 507 Coed
Affiliation or Control: Independent Non-Profit IRS Status: 501(c)3
Highest Offering: Doctorate; No Undergraduates
Accreditation: M

01 Chancellor ....Vacant
05 Dean of Academic Affairs ....Dr. Wanda I. MARRERO
06 Registrar ....Mrs. Mayra I. RAMIREZ
08 Head Librarian ....Mr. Francis J. MOJICA
11 Administration Dean ....Ms. Clarissa SANTIAGO-TORO
32 Students Affairs Dean ....Mrs. Lydia M. RIVERA
37 Financial Aid Director ....Mr. Jose F. PEREZ-RODRIGUEZ
07 Admissions Director ....Vacant
38 Director Student Counseling ....Mrs. Carmen B. ORTIZ

Colegio de Cinematografia, Artes y Television (B)

51 Calle Dr. Santiago Veve, Bayamon PR 00961
County: Bayamon FICE Identification: 031576
Unit ID: 430935
Telephone: (787) 779-2500 Carnegie Class: Assoc/MT-VT-High Trad
FAX Number: (787) 995-2525 Calendar System: Semester
URL: www.ccatpuertorico.com
Established: 1993 Annual Undergrad Tuition & Fees: $6,660
Enrollment: 619 Coed
Affiliation or Control: Proprietary IRS Status: Proprietary
Highest Offering: Associate Degree
Accreditation: ACCSC

01 President ....Ms. Carola GARCIA
05 Director of Academics ....Mr. Harry VAZQUEZ
32 Dean of Student Affairs ....Ms. Diana CASTILLO

Colegio Universitario de San Juan (C)

180 Jose R. Oliver Avenue, San Juan PR 00918
County: San Juan FICE Identification: 010567
Unit ID: 241720
Telephone: (787) 480-2400 Carnegie Class: Bac-Diverse
FAX Number: (787) 250-7395 Calendar System: Semester
URL: www.cunisanjuan.edu
Established: 1972 Annual Undergrad Tuition & Fees (In-District): $2,340
Enrollment: 840 Coed
Affiliation or Control: Local IRS Status: 501(c)3
Highest Offering: Baccalaureate
Accreditation: M, ADNUR, NURSE

01 Interim Chancellor ....Dr. Ana A. MARCHENA-SEGURA
45 Dir Planning/Inst Research/Ext Revs ....Dr. Haydee M. ZAYAS-HERNANDEZ
05 Interim Dean Academic Affairs ..Prof. Annelis RIVERA-MARQUEZ
32 Dean Student Affairs ....Dr. Melvin VEGA-GONZALEZ
11 Interim Dean Administrative Affairs .....Prof. Relon ACOSTA-TORO
51 Dir Continuing Educ/Extension Pgm ....Mrs. Paola PERALTA-DE LA CRUZ
37 Manager Student Financial Aid .... Mrs. Kennia I. SANTOS-PEREZ
08 Head Librarian ....Mrs. Sheila VERA-MORALES
06 Registrar ....Mrs. Evelyn GUZMAN-LOPEZ
38 Counselor ....Mrs. Mara MALAVE-LASSO
36 Placement Officer ....Prof. Waleska Y. ROSA-NUNEZ
13 Administrator Info Systems/ Telecomm ....Mr. Zacarias POUERIET-DE LA CRUZ
72 Dir Science & Technology Dept ....Prof. Marcus DROZ-RAMOS
76 Dir Health Related Science Dept ....Prof. Elizabeth ROSARIO-RODRIGUEZ
50 Dir Business Administration Dept ....Prof. Nilda E. RODRIGUEZ-MOLINA
97 Manager General Education Dept ....Prof. Carmen J. RODRIGUEZ-VINCENTY
88 Dir Behavioral Related Profess Dept ....Prof. Maria T. PEREZ-CASANOVA
04 Chancellor Assistant ....Prof. Myrna CORTES-HUERTAS
15 Chief Human Resources Officer ....Ms. Isabel LOZADA-CRUZ

Columbia Central University (D)

PO Box 9120, Caguas PR 00726-9120
County: Caguas FICE Identification: 008902
Unit ID: 241304
Telephone: (787) 704-1020 Carnegie Class: Spec-4-yr-Other Health
FAX Number: N/A Calendar System: Semester
URL: www.columbiacentral.edu
Established: 1966 Annual Undergrad Tuition & Fees: $7,180
Enrollment: 798 Coed
Affiliation or Control: Proprietary IRS Status: Proprietary
Highest Offering: Master's
Accreditation: M, NUR

01 President & CEO ....Mr. Jose CORDOVA
05 VP Academic Affairs ....Mrs. Betsy VIDAL
20 Assoc VP of Curricular Development ....Ms. Maria CRUZ
45 VP of Planning and Assessment ....Mrs. Daritza MULERO
10 VP Finance and Administration ....Mrs. Magda CANCEL
32 VP Student Affairs ....Mrs. Brendaliz ZAYAS
26 VP Marketing and Admissions ....Mrs. Josie ARROYO
07 Institutional Admissions Director ....Ms. Zaida LOZADA
12 Chancellor of Caguas Campus ....Mrs. Wilda VELEZ
12 Chancellor of Yauco Branch ....Dr. Jannette MENDEZ
12 Chancellor of Bayam=n Branch ....Mr. Fernando GONZALEZ
12 Chancellor of Carolina Branch ....Mrs. Bethzaida PIÑERO
06 Registrar - Caguas Branch ....Mrs. Iris LOPEZ
06 Registrar - Carolina Branch ....Ms. Enid LOPEZ
06 Registrar - Bayamon Branch ....Ms. Jeannette TORRES
06 Registrar - Yauco Branch ....Mrs. Awilda PASTOR
38 Student Counselor Caguas Branch ....Mrs. Iris SANTIAGO
38 Student Counselor - Carolina Branch ....Mr. David BAEZ
38 Student Counselor Bayamon Branch ....Ms. Zuleika COTTO
124 Retention Officer Caguas ....Mrs. Sandra SANTIAGO
124 Retention Officer Bayamon ....Ms. Vanessa OJEDA
36 Student Placement Officer - Caguas ....Mrs. Wanda DEL VALLE
36 Student Placement Officer Carolina ....Ms. Boamari MENDEZ
36 Student Placement Officer Bayamon ....Ms. Keimily MELENDEZ
36 Student Placement Officer Yauco ....Mr. Salvador IRIZARRY
113 Treasury Officer Caguas ....Ms. Ineabelle CINTRON
113 Treasury Officer Caguas ....Mrs. Ana MERCED
113 Treasury Officer Carolina ....Ms. Karelie SUAZO
113 Treasury Officer Bayamon ....Ms. Wanda ESTREMERA
113 Treasury Officer Yauco ....Ms. Yolanda NIEVES
15 Director Human Resources ....Mrs. Norelis RODRIGUEZ
18 Facilities & Purchases Director ....Mrs. Milagros CARTAGENA
13 IT Director ....Mr. Efrain GUADALUPE
37 Financial Aid Institutional Dir ....Mrs. Gloria MIRABAL

Columbia Centro Universitario (E)

Box 3062, Yauco PR 00698-3062
Telephone: (787) 856-0845 Identification: 666036
Accreditation: &M

† Regional accreditation is carried under the parent institution in Caguas, PR.

Conservatory of Music of Puerto Rico (F)

951 Ponce de Leon Ave. Miramar, Santurce PR 00907
County: San Juan FICE Identification: 010819
Unit ID: 241766
Telephone: (787) 751-0160 Carnegie Class: Spec-4-yr-Arts
FAX Number: (787) 766-1216 Calendar System: Semester
URL: www.cmpr.edu
Established: 1959 Annual Undergrad Tuition & Fees (In-State): $3,370
Enrollment: 370 Coed
Affiliation or Control: State IRS Status: 501(c)3
Highest Offering: Master's
Accreditation: M, MUS

01 Chancellor ....Dr. Manuel CALZADA
05 Dean of Academic/Student Affairs ....Mr. Ariel GUZMAN
20 Assoc Dean of Academic/Student Affs ....Mr. Ernesto V. RAMOS
10 Dean of Finance/Administration ....Ms. Gloryber LABOY
37 Director Financial Aid ....Mr. Luis R. DIAZ
88 Director of Preparatory School ....Mr. Orlando MALDONADO
07 Admission Coordinator ....Mrs. Ana Marta ARRAIZA
08 Librarian ....Mrs. Maria del Carmen MALDONADO
15 Human Resources Director ....Ms. Alba DAVILA
38 Counselor ....Mrs. Indira L. BHAJAN
06 Registrar ....Mrs. Waleska MARTINEZ RIVERA
09 Director of Institutional Research ....Mrs. Eutimia SANTIAGO
18 Chief Facilities/Physical Plant ....Mr. Jose MATOS
13 Information Systems Coordinator ....Mr. Javier CRUZ SANCHEZ

Dewey University (G)

PO Box 19538, San Juan PR 00910-1538
County: San Juan FICE Identification: 031121
Unit ID: 431309
Telephone: (787) 710-8999 Carnegie Class: Not Classified
FAX Number: N/A Calendar System: Trimester
URL: www.dewey.edu
Established: 1992 Annual Undergrad Tuition & Fees: N/A
Enrollment: N/A Coed
Affiliation or Control: Independent Non-Profit IRS Status: 501(c)3
Highest Offering: Master's
Accreditation: ABHES

01 President/CEO ....Mr. Carlos A. QUINONES
03 Executive Vice President ....Ms. Yelitza FELICIANO
15 Chief Human Resources Officer ....Ms. Glenis VELEZ
19 Director Security/Safety ....Ms. Esthefany DE LA CRUZ
07 Director of Admissions ....Ms. Yesenia MACHUCA
105 Director Web Services ....Ms. Yosanalis TORRES
106 Director Online Education ....Vacant
37 Director Student Financial Aid ....Ms. Mayra VILANOVA
10 Chief Financial/Business Officer ....Mr. Jaime MARTIR

Dewey University-Carolina (H)

Carr. #3, Km. 11, Lote 7, Carolina PR 00987
Telephone: (787) 769-1515 Identification: 770776
Accreditation: ABHES

Dewey University-Juana Diaz (I)

Rd 149, KM 55.9 Lomas Industrial PK, Juana Diaz PR 00795
Telephone: (787) 260-1023 Identification: 770774
Accreditation: ABHES

Dewey University-Manati (J)

Rd 604,Km 49.1 Tierra Nueva Salient, Manati PR 00674
Telephone: (789) 854-3800 Identification: 770807
Accreditation: ABHES

EDP University of Puerto Rico (K)

PO Box 192303, San Juan PR 00919-2303
County: San Juan FICE Identification: 021651
Unit ID: 243832
Telephone: (787) 765-3560 Carnegie Class: Masters/S
FAX Number: (787) 777-0025 Calendar System: Semester
URL: www.edpuniversity.edu
Established: 1968 Annual Undergrad Tuition & Fees: $6,200
Enrollment: 1,349 Coed
Affiliation or Control: Independent Non-Profit IRS Status: 501(c)3
Highest Offering: Master's
Accreditation: M, ADNUR

01 President ....Mrs. Gladys T. NIEVES
05 Exec Vice President/Provost ....Dr. Marilyn PASTRANA
20 Dean of Academic Affairs ....Prof. María RIVERA
10 Vice President of Finance ....Mr. Luis RIVERA
111 AVP for Strategic Advancement ....Prof. Mayra RIVERA
108 AVP Institutional Compliance ....Dr. Alberto LOPEZ
13 AVP Administration and Technology ....Eng. Luis FUSTER
85 AVP Educational Innovation ....Prof. Sandra ARROYO
21 AVP for Financial Affairs ....Mrs. Marie Luz PASTRANA
09 AVP Assessment & Research ....Prof. Nydia RIVERA
14 Technology Affairs Dean ....Dr. Ramon MALLOL
06 Registrar ....Mrs. Marien DE JESÚS
08 Librarian ....Mrs. Igrí ENRIQUEZ
32 Dean of Student Affairs ....Prof. Alba FERRER
37 Director of Financial Aid ....Mr. Yaitzaenid GONZALEZ
07 Director of Admissions ....Mrs. Dendy VILA
15 Director Human Resources ....Mr. Héctor VAZQUEZ
36 Director Student Placement ....Ms. Tamara MORALES

EDP University of Puerto Rico (L)

PO Box 1674, 49 Betances Street, San Sebastian PR 00685-1674
Telephone: (787) 896-2252 Identification: 666488
Accreditation: &M

† Regional accreditation is carried under the parent institution in San Juan, PR.

Escuela de Artes Plasticas de Puerto Rico (M)

PO Box 9021112, San Juan PR 00902-1112
County: San Juan FICE Identification: 025694
Unit ID: 241951
Telephone: (787) 725-8120 Carnegie Class: Spec-4-yr-Arts
FAX Number: N/A Calendar System: Semester
URL: www.eap.edu
Established: 1966 Annual Undergrad Tuition & Fees (In-State): $3,942
Enrollment: 405 Coed
Affiliation or Control: State IRS Status: 501(c)3
Highest Offering: Baccalaureate
Accreditation: M, ART

01 Chancellor ....Dra. Ileana MUNOZ LANDRON
11 Dean of Administration .Prof. Maria del Carmen SANTOS RODRIGUEZ
05 Dean Academic Affairs ......Prof. Luis J. BRIGANTTY GONZALEZ
06 Registrar ....Ms. Ileana MALDONADO
07 Officer of Admissions ....Vacant
13 Chief Information Technology ....Ms. Limaris SOTO AQUINO
37 Director Student Financial Aid ..Mr. Victor M. MELENDEZ ORTIZ
45 Director of Planning & Budget ....Mr. Carlos E. RIVERA
09 Institutional Research ....Dr. Shirley A. TAVARES
10 Chief Financial Officer ....Mr. Omar FALU MENDEZ
18 Coord Facilities/Physical Plant ....Mr. Edwin ALICEA
56 Coordinator Extension Program ....Prof. Gabriel MELENDEZ
38 Counselor Student Life/ Counseling ....Ms. Natalia E. PERDOMO RAMIREZ
88 Coordinator Cultural Activities ... Mr. Adrian O. RIVERA NEGRON
105 Director Web Services ....Mr. Celso E. PORTELA IRIGOYEN
08 Library Director ....Ms. Estrella VAZQUEZ
20 Asst Dean Acad/Student Affairs ....Vacant
15 Director Human Resources ....Vacant
57 Director Art Education ....Dra. Griselle SOTO VELEZ
97 Director General Studies ....Dr. Maria VAZQUEZ
88 Director Fashion Design ....Prof. Ana COLORADO
88 Director Industrial Design ....Prof. Vladimir GARCIA

88 Director Digital Art & Design .... Prof. Mauricio CONEJO
88 Director Painting .... Prof. Linda SANCHEZ PINTOR
88 Director Sculpture .... Prof. Linda SANCHEZ PINTOR
88 Director Printmaking .... Prof. Haydee LANDING

Evangelical Seminary of Puerto Rico (A)

Ponce De Leon Avenue 776, San Juan PR 00925-9907
County: San Juan FICE Identification: 006823
Unit ID: 243498
Telephone: (787) 763-6700 Carnegie Class: Spec-4-yr-Faith
FAX Number: N/A Calendar System: Semester
URL: www.se-pr.edu
Established: 1919 Annual Undergrad Tuition & Fees: N/A
Enrollment: 155 Coed
Affiliation or Control: Interdenominational IRS Status: 501(c)3
Highest Offering: Doctorate
Accreditation: M, THEOL

01 President .... Dr. Juan R. MEJIAS-ORTIZ
05 Actg Dean Academic & Student Affs . Dr. Agustina LUVIS-NUÑEZ
10 Financial Director .... Mr. Raul F. SANTIAGO-RIVERA
18 Director of General Services .... Ms. Myrna E. PEREZ-LOPEZ
06 Registrar .... Mrs. Keina TRONCOSO-FERNANDEZ
08 Head Librarian .... Mrs. Milka VIGO-VERESTIN
37 Student Financial Aid Officer ...... Ms. Damaris MERCADO-LÓPEZ
04 Administrative Asst to President .... Vacant
13 Chief Info Technology Officer ... Mr. Jesus RODRIGUEZ-CORTES
108 Director Institutional Assessment .... Dr. Juan R. MEJIAS-ORTIZ
16 Human Resources Officer .... Mrs. Janet SANTIAGO-LÓPEZ

Huertas College (B)

PO Box 8429, Caguas PR 00726-8429
County: Caguas FICE Identification: 022608
Unit ID: 242112
Telephone: (787) 746-1400 Carnegie Class: Spec-4-yr-Other Health
FAX Number: (787) 747-0170 Calendar System: Semester
URL: www.huertas.edu
Established: 1945 Annual Undergrad Tuition & Fees: $7,165
Enrollment: 488 Coed
Affiliation or Control: Proprietary IRS Status: Proprietary
Highest Offering: Baccalaureate
Accreditation: M, CAHIIM, OTA, #PTAA

01 President .... Dr. Isaac ESQUILIN
05 Vice Pres Academic/Student Affairs .... Maribel CONTRERAS
32 Dean of Student Success .... Yolanda ROSARIO
06 Registrar .... Krishna MARQUEZ
08 Head Librarian .... Viones ACEVEDOS
38 Director Student Counseling .... Mayra FLORES
07 Director of Admissions .... Juan ORENGA
36 Director Student Placement .... Veronica RUIZ
37 Director Financial Aid .... Wanda ORTIZ

Humacao Community College (C)

PO Box 9139, Humacao PR 00792-9139
County: Humacao FICE Identification: 023406
Unit ID: 242121
Telephone: (787) 852-1430 Carnegie Class: Bac/Assoc-Mixed
FAX Number: (787) 850-1577 Calendar System: Trimester
URL: www.hccpr.edu
Established: 1978 Annual Undergrad Tuition & Fees: $5,742
Enrollment: 301 Coed
Affiliation or Control: Independent Non-Profit IRS Status: 501(c)3
Highest Offering: Baccalaureate
Accreditation: ACCSC, ACICS

01 President .... Lic. Jorge E. MOJICA
03 Executive Vice President .... Prof. Aida E. RODRIGUEZ
81 STEM Project Director .... Mr. Jaime RIVERA
37 Director Student Financial Aid .... Mrs. Milagros CRUZ
36 Student Placement Officer .... Mrs. Veronica RUIZ
36 Student Placement Officer .... Mrs. Nilkaliz DEL VALLE
07 Director Admissions .... Vacant
06 Registrar .... Mr. Israel LOPEZ
08 Head Librarian .... Mrs. Lourdes ELIZA
10 Treasury Officer (Finance) .... Mrs. Disaliany CARRERO
38 Student Counselor .... Mrs. Maria DELGADO
11 Chief College Administrator .... Mrs. Marianne BERRIOS
04 Admin Asst to Pres/Dir Personnel .... Mrs. Maricelly FANTAUZZI

ICPR Junior College (D)

558 Munoz Rivera Avenue, Hato Rey PR 00919-0304
County: San Juan FICE Identification: 011940
Unit ID: 243841
Telephone: (787) 753-6000 Carnegie Class: Spec 2-yr-Health
FAX Number: (787) 622-3416 Calendar System: Semester
URL: www.icprjc.edu
Established: 1946 Annual Undergrad Tuition & Fees: $7,010
Enrollment: 431 Coed
Affiliation or Control: Proprietary IRS Status: Proprietary
Highest Offering: Associate Degree
Accreditation: M

01 President/Chief Executive Officer .... Dr. Olga RIVERA
12 Hato Rey Campus Director .... Mrs. Awilda FONTANEZ
05 Academic Affairs Dean .... Mrs. Elsa RODRIGUEZ
07 Dir Admissions/Marketing Hato Rey .... Mrs. Laysa FUENTES
07 Dir Admissions/Marketing Mayaguez . Mrs. Lorraine CONTRERAS
07 Dir Admissions/Marketing Arecibo .... Mr. Carlos CONCEPCIÓN
07 Dir Admissions/Marketing Manati .... Mrs. Mariela CRUZ
10 Chief Financial Officer .... Mrs. Arelis DIAZ
37 Financial Aid Director .... Ms. Palmira ARROYO
12 Mayaguez Campus Director .... Dr. Sylvia RAMIREZ
12 Arecibo Campus Director .... Mrs. Magdalena VEGA
12 Manati Campus Director .... Mr. Henberto RODRIGUEZ
06 Registrar Mayaguez .... Mrs. Olga NEGRON
06 Registrar Arecibo .... Mrs. Yaritza SANTIAGO
06 Registrar Manati .... Mrs. Vanessa TRINIDAD
26 Enrollment & Advertising Manager .... Mrs. Vimarie ASENCIO
13 Chief Information Officer .... Mr. Nelson MEJIAS
08 Learning Res Librarian Hato Rey .... Mr. Angel FIGUEROA
08 Lrng Resources Librarian Mayaguez .... Vacant
08 Lrng Resources Librarian Arecibo .... Mrs. Irma JIMENEZ
08 Learning Resources Librarian .... Mr. Martin ROSADO
38 Professional Counselor Mayaguez .. Mrs. Maraynette CARABALLO
38 Professional Counselor Arecibo .... Mrs. Delva PEREZ
38 Professional Counselor Manati .... Mrs. Josephin BORRERO
38 Professional Counselor Hato Rey .... Vacant
15 Human Resources Director .... Mrs. Daisy CASTRO
43 Institutional Compliance Director .... Mrs. Lizzette VARGAS
56 Bayamon Extension Assoc Director .... Mrs. Awilda FONTÁNEZ
20 Academic Coordinator Mayaguez .... Mrs. Erudina ROSAS
20 Academic Coordinator Arecibo .... Mrs. Edith RAMOS
20 Academic Coordinator Manati .... Mrs. Maribel TORRES
20 Academic Coordinator Hato Rey .... Mrs. Catalina FELICIANO

ICPR Junior College-Arecibo Campus (E)

20 Ave San Patricio, Arecibo PR 00614
Telephone: (787) 878-6000 Identification: 770166
Accreditation: &M

ICPR Junior College-Manati Branch Campus (F)

PO Box 49, Manati PR 00674-0049
Telephone: (787) 884-6000 Identification: 770168
Accreditation: &M

ICPR Junior College-Mayaguez Campus (G)

PO Box 1108, Mayaguez PR 00681-9913
Telephone: (787) 832-6000 Identification: 770167
Accreditation: &M

Instituto de Banca y Comercio (H)

709 Ferrocarril Street, Ponce PR 00717
Telephone: (787) 840-6119 Identification: 770773
Accreditation: &M, ACFEI

Instituto de Banca y Comercio (I)

61 Ponce de Leon Ave, San Juan PR 00917
Telephone: (787) 754-7120 Identification: 667107
Accreditation: &M, ACFEI

*Inter American University of Puerto Rico Central Office (J)

GPO Box 363255, San Juan PR 00936-3255
County: San Juan FICE Identification: 008242
Unit ID: 242671
Telephone: (787) 766-1912 Carnegie Class: N/A
FAX Number: (787) 751-3375
URL: www.inter.edu

01 President .... Mr. Manuel J. FERNOS
05 VP Academic & Student Affairs .... Mrs. Jacqueline ALVAREZ
10 VP Financial Affairs/Services .... Mrs. Olga LUNA
42 Vice President Religious Affairs .... Rev. Norberto DOMINGUEZ
20 Associate VP Academic Affairs .... Vacant
21 Assoc VP Financial Affairs/Services .... Mrs. Marlene MANGUAL
32 Associate Vice Pres Student Affairs .... Dr. Patricia ALVAREZ
21 Assoc VP Accounting/Finance .... Mr. Orlando GONZALEZ
100 Exec Dir to Pres/Chief of Staff .... Mr. Dominique A. GILORMINI-DE GRACIA
26 Exec Dir Public Rels/Communications .... Mrs. Zaima NEGRON
84 Dir Inst Promo/Student Recruitment .... Mr. Antonio PANTOJA
09 Exec Director Inst Research .... Dr. Isaac SANTIAGO
13 Exec Dir Information/Telecom .... Mrs. Jossie SALGUERO
43 Exec Director Legal Services .... Mrs. Lorraine JUARBE
43 Exec Director Federal Legal Svcs .... Mr. Vladimir ROMAN
15 Exec Director Human Resources .... Mrs. Maggie COLON
30 Exec Director Devel/Alumni Affairs . Dr. Nelida RIVERA-CLAUDIO

*Inter American University of Puerto Rico Aguadilla Campus (K)

Box 20000, Aguadilla PR 00605-9001
County: Aguadilla FICE Identification: 003939
Unit ID: 242626
Telephone: (787) 891-0925 Carnegie Class: Masters/S
FAX Number: (787) 882-3020 Calendar System: Other
URL: aguadilla.inter.edu
Established: 1957 Annual Undergrad Tuition & Fees: $5,974
Enrollment: 3,517 Coed
Affiliation or Control: Independent Non-Profit IRS Status: 501(c)3
Highest Offering: Master's
Accreditation: M, ADNUR, CAEPT, NUR, SW

02 Chancellor .... Dr. Elie AGESILAS
05 Dean of Academic Affairs .... Dr. Evelyn CASTILLO
20 Associate Dean of Academic Affairs .... Dr. Zenaida SANJURJO
10 Dean of Administrative Affairs .... Mr. Israel AYALA
21 Asst Dean Administrative Affairs .... Mr. Irvin CANALES
32 Dean of Student Affairs .... Mrs. Nararly CLAUDIO
35 Asst Dean Student Affairs .... Mrs. Nayda SOTO
84 Enrollment Manager .... Prof. Myriam MARCIAL
30 Development and Alumni Director .... Mrs. Dolores SEPULVEDA
08 Library Director .... Mrs. Lizzie COLÓN
13 Director Information and Technology .... Mr. Asdrubal JIMENEZ
07 Admissions Director .... Mrs. Doris PEREZ
06 Registrar .... Mrs. Maria PEREZ
37 Financial Aid Director .... Mrs. Gloria CORTÉS
113 Bursar .... Mr. Hancy MUNIZ
15 Human Resources Director .... Mr. Jose R. AREIZAGA
96 Purchasing Officer .... Mrs. Lissette REILLO
121 Student Support Services Director .... Mrs. Ivonne ACEVEDO
81 Sciences and Technology Director .... Prof. Alfredo RIVERA
53 Education & Hum Studies Director .... Prof. Michelle RIVERA
50 Economic & Adm Sciences Director .... Prof. Raul MENDOZA
83 Social Sciences & Behavior Director .... Prof. Janice LORENZO
42 Chaplain .... Mr. Jaime B. GALVAN
88 Director of Upward Bound Program .... Ms. Mayra ROZADA
92 Honor Program Educational Director .... Ms. Yamilette PROSPER
18 Building Maintenance Director .... Mr. Jose CABAN
38 Counseling Office Director .... Ms. Dary ACEVEDO
41 Sports Director .... Ms. Yolanda PAGAN
19 Univ Security Guard Supervisor .... Mr. Efrain RAMOS
120 Distance Education Director .... Prof. Bernabe SOTO
88 Director Upward Bound Math/Sciences .... Mrs. Geidy ACEVEDO
76 Health Sciences Director .... Dr. Lourdes OLAVARRIA
58 Graduate Studies Director .... Dr. Aris ROMAN

*Inter American University of Puerto Rico Arecibo Campus (L)

PO Box 4050, Arecibo PR 00614-4050
County: Arecibo FICE Identification: 005026
Unit ID: 242635
Telephone: (787) 878-5475 Carnegie Class: Masters/M
FAX Number: (787) 880-1624 Calendar System: Semester
URL: www.arecibo.inter.edu
Established: 1957 Annual Undergrad Tuition & Fees: $5,986
Enrollment: 3,359 Coed
Affiliation or Control: Independent Non-Profit IRS Status: 501(c)3
Highest Offering: Master's
Accreditation: M, ANEST, CAEP, NUR, SW

02 Chancellor .... Dr. Rafael RAMIREZ-RIVERA
05 Dean of Academic Affairs .... Dr. Karen WOOLCOCK
11 Dean of Administrative Affairs .... Dr. Grisel CASTELLANOS
32 Dean of Student Affairs .... Mrs. Ilvis AGUIRRE
20 Assoc Dean of Academic Affairs .... Dr. Wanda I. BALSEIRO
08 Educational Resources Center Dir .... Mrs. Sara ABREU
113 Bursar .... Mr. Victor MALDONADO
37 Student Financial Aid Director .... Mr. Angel MENDEZ
06 Registrar .... Mrs. Carmen RODRIGUEZ
07 Director of Admissions .... Mrs. Brenda ROMÁN
04 Executive Assistant to Chancellor .... Mrs. Enid ARBELO
56 Distance Learning Director .... Prof. Ebigaly OLIVER
45 Planning Director .... Mrs. Enid ARBELO
42 Religious Life Director .... Mr. Amilcar SOTO
15 Personnel Director .... Mrs. Ada VELEZ
41 Athletic Department .... Ms. Ileana MORALES
50 Dir Econ/Admin Sciences Dept .... Dr. Alexander ROSADO
51 Continuing Education Director .... Dr. Inia ROSADO
53 Director of Education Department .... Dr. Auris MARTINEZ
66 Director of Nursing Department .... Dr. Frances CORTES
79 Dir of Humanities Department .... Dr. Angel TRINIDAD
81 Director of Sciences & Tech Dept .... Dr. Lizbeth ROMERO
83 Director of Social Sciences Dept .... Dr. Lourdes CARRION
30 Development Director .... Vacant
38 Director Student Counseling .... Ms. Abigail TORRES
13 Director of Computing Center .... Mr. Jose SEGARRA
58 Director Graduate Program in Educ .... Dra. Ramonita DIAZ
18 Chief Facilities/Physical Plant .... Vacant
84 Director Enrollment Management .... Mrs. Carmen MONTALVO
88 Dir Graduate Program Anesthesia .... Prof. Ivan MOLINA
96 Purchasing Officer .... Mrs. Iris GONZALEZ
92 Coordinator Honor Program .... Ms. Vilmaris VAZQUEZ
108 Director Institutional Assessment .... Dr. Pedro RIVERA
26 Director of Marketing .... Mr. Juan RODRIGUEZ

*Inter American University of Puerto Rico Barranquitas Campus (M)

PO Box 517, Barranquitas PR 00794-0517
County: Barranquitas FICE Identification: 005027
Unit ID: 242644
Telephone: (787) 857-3600 Carnegie Class: Bac-Diverse
FAX Number: (787) 857-2244 Calendar System: Semester
URL: www.br.inter.edu
Established: 1957 Annual Undergrad Tuition & Fees: $5,974
Enrollment: 1,303 Coed
Affiliation or Control: Independent Non-Profit IRS Status: 501(c)3
Highest Offering: Doctorate
Accreditation: M, NURSE

02 Chancellor .... Dr. Juan A. NEGRON-BERRIOS

05 Dean Academic Affairs ....Dra. Filomena CINTRON-SERRANO
11 Dean Administrative Affairs ....Mr. Victor SANTIAGO-ROSADO
32 Dean Student Affairs/Athletic Dir ....Mrs. Aramilda CARTAGENA-SANTIAGO
15 Director Human Resources .... Mr. Jonathan ORTIZ-MORALES
113 Bursar Director ....Mr. Cristian J. RIOS-COLON
06 Registrar .... Mrs. Sandra M. MORALES-RODRIGUEZ
07 Director Admissions/Financial Aid ...Mrs. Ana I. COLON-ALONSO
81 Dir Natural Sciences/ Technology .... Mrs. Maria M. MELENDEZ-ORTEGA
76 Dir Health Department .... Dra. Damaris COLON-RIVERA
38 Director Upward Bound Program .... Mrs. Saraliz GONZALEZ-MELENDEZ
51 Director Continuing Education .... Dra. Rosa C. RODRIGUEZ-MORALES
88 Evaluation and Monitoring Officer ....Mrs. Carmen C. ROSADO-BERRIOS
29 Coord Alumni Relations .... Mrs. Aixa SERRANO-FEBO
88 CAI-TC Director .... Mrs. Eleane ROSADO-LOPEZ
42 Chaplain ....Mr. Arnaldo L. CINTRON-MIRANDA

*Inter American University of Puerto Rico Bayamon Campus (A)

500 Dr. John Will Harris Road, Bayamon PR 00957-6257

County: Bayamon FICE Identification: 005028
Unit ID: 242705
Telephone: (787) 279-1912 Carnegie Class: Bac-Diverse
FAX Number: (787) 279-2205 Calendar System: Semester
URL: bayamon.inter.edu
Established: 1912 Annual Undergrad Tuition & Fees: $6,012
Enrollment: 4,123 Coed
Affiliation or Control: Independent Non-Profit IRS Status: 501(c)3
Highest Offering: Master's
Accreditation: M, AAB, ACBSP, NURSE, OPTR

02 Acting Chancellor .... Dr. Carlos J. OLIVARES
04 Assistant to Chancellor .... Dr. Rafael R. CANALES
30 Chief Development ....Mr. Jaime COLON
05 Chief Academic Officer ....Dr. Anthony RIVERA
20 Associate Academic Officer ....Dra. Nydia I. FELICIANO
20 Associate Academic Officer ....Dr. Rafael SALGADO
08 Head Librarian ....Mrs. Sandra ROSA
85 Director of International Relations .... Mrs. Maritza ZAMBRANA
88 Interim Dean School of Aeronautics ......Dr. Jonathan VELAZQUEZ
54 Dean School of Engineering ....Dr. Javier QUINTANA
54 Director Electrical Engr Dept ....Vacant
54 Director Industrial Engr Dept ....Prof. Catherine AGUILAR
54 Director Mechanical Engr Dept ....Dr. Otoniel DIAZ
81 Director Mathematics/Sciences ....Dra. Rosamil REY
50 Dir Business Administration Dept ....Prof. Edward VICENTE
60 Director Communications Dept ....Vacant
77 Director Computer Sciences Dept ....Prof. Jose A. RODRIGUEZ
76 Director of Health Science ....Prof. Jose M. CRUZ
79 Director Humanities/Language Dept ....Dra. Gisela CARRERAS
75 Director Tech Institute ....Mrs. Liza FREYTES
32 Interim Chief Students Life Officer ....Mrs. Grace GOMEZ
38 Director Student Counseling ....Vacant
41 Athletic Director ....Mr. Reynaldo ROLON
10 Chief Financial/Business Officer ....Mr. Serafin RIVERA
96 Purchasing Officer ....Mrs. Gladys ARROYO
18 Chief Facilities/Physical Plant ....Eng. Jose A. FUENTES
15 Human Resources Director .... Mrs. Wilma FIGUEROA
84 Director Enrollment Services ....Miss Ivette NIEVES
35 Director of Students Services ....Mrs. Aurelis BAEZ
06 Registrar ....Mrs. Suhail BRUNET
13 Director Information Technology ....Mr. Edwin RIVERA
42 Director of Chaplaincy Office ....Rvda. Carmen I. PEREZ
106 Dir Online Education/E-learning .... Dra. Vanesa SANTIAGO
39 Housing Administrator ....Vacant
108 Coordinator of Institutional Assess ....Dr. Eduardo PEREZ
113 Director Bursar Office ....Sr. Eduardo BERRIOS
26 Chief Pub Rels/Marketing/Comm Ofcr ....Sr. David LOPEZ

*Inter American University of Puerto Rico Fajardo Campus (B)

Call Box 70003, Fajardo PR 00738-7003

County: Fajardo FICE Identification: 022828
Unit ID: 242680
Telephone: (787) 863-2390 Carnegie Class: Masters/S
FAX Number: (787) 860-3470 Calendar System: Semester
URL: fajardo.inter.edu
Established: 1960 Annual Undergrad Tuition & Fees: $6,012
Enrollment: 1,609 Coed
Affiliation or Control: Independent Non-Profit IRS Status: 501(c)3
Highest Offering: Master's
Accreditation: M, CAEP, SW

02 Chancellor ....Dr. Paula SAGARDIA OLIVERA
05 Dean Academic Affairs ....Dr. Marielis E. RIVERA RUIZ
11 Dean Administrative Affairs .. Mrs. Monica GONZALEZ PACHECO
32 Dean for Student Affairs ....Mrs. Francheska E. DE JESUS CEBALLOS
06 Registrar .... Mrs. Arlene PARRILLA
07 Director of Admissions ....Mrs. Ada CARABALLO
37 Director Student Financial Aid ....Mrs. Marilyn MARTINEZ
08 Librarian ....Ms. Angie COLON
15 Director of Personnel Office ....Mr. Angel J. RUIZ
09 Planning Director ....Ms. Hilda L. ORTIZ
41 Athletic Director ....Vacant
18 Physical Plant Supervisor .... Mr. Eliezer GARCIA

42 Chaplain/Director Campus Ministry ....Vacant
50 Chairperson Business Department .... Prof. Wilfredo DEL VALLE
53 Chairperson Educ & Social Sci Dept ....Dr. Porfirio MONTES
79 Chairperson Humanities Dept .... Dr. Yolanda LOPEZ-MEDERO
81 Chairperson Math/Science Dept ....Dr. Millie GONZALEZ
84 Director Enrollment Management ....Mrs. Glenda DIAZ

*Inter American University of Puerto Rico Guayama Campus (C)

Call Box 10004, Guayama PR 00785

County: Guayama FICE Identification: 022827
Unit ID: 242699
Telephone: (787) 864-2222 Carnegie Class: Bac-Diverse
FAX Number: (787) 866-5006 Calendar System: Semester
URL: www.guayama.inter.edu
Established: 1958 Annual Undergrad Tuition & Fees: $5,974
Enrollment: 1,687 Coed
Affiliation or Control: Independent Non-Profit IRS Status: 501(c)3
Highest Offering: Master's
Accreditation: M, NURSE

02 President .... Mr. Manuel J. FERNOS
00 Chancellor ....Dr. Angela DE JESUS-ALICEA
06 Registrar .... Mr. Luis A. SOTO
08 Librarian ....Mrs. Edny SANTIAGO
113 Bursar .... Ms. Teresa MANAUTOU
05 Dean of Academic Affairs ....Mrs. Elia COLON
11 Dean of Administration ....Mr. Jose ROMERO
32 Dean of Students .... Dr. Rosa J. MARTINEZ
07 Director Admissions ....Mrs. Laura FERRER
37 Director Financial Aid ....Vacant
29 Director Alumni Relations ....Dr. Jose ROMERO
51 Director Continuing Education ....Mrs. Leida VELAZQUEZ
15 Human Resources Officer ....Mrs. Maria MARES
42 Chaplain Director ....Rvdo. Ismael VAZQUEZ
84 Director Enrollment Management ....Mrs. Eileen RIVERA
96 Director of Purchasing ....Mr. Rinaldo ROBLES
31 Dir of Community & New Student Rels ....Mrs. Luz ORTIZ
23 Director Health Services ....Mrs. Arcilia RIVERA
66 Director Nursing Program ....Dr. Marisol VELAZQUEZ
55 Dir Adult Higher Education Program ....Vacant
50 Dir Dept Business Admin/Econ Sci ....Prof. Juan L. TORRES
53 Dir Dept Education/Soc Sci/Hum Std ....Vacant
81 Dir Dept Natural & Applied Science .... Prof. Aida W. MIRANDA
09 Director of Institutional Research .... Dr. Isaac SANTIAGO

*Inter American University of Puerto Rico / Metropolitan Campus (D)

PO Box 191293, San Juan PR 00919-1293

County: San Juan FICE Identification: 003940
Unit ID: 242653
Telephone: (787) 250-1912 Carnegie Class: DU-Mod
FAX Number: (787) 250-0742 Calendar System: Semester
URL: www.metro.inter.edu
Established: 1962 Annual Undergrad Tuition & Fees: $8,655
Enrollment: 6,826 Coed
Affiliation or Control: Independent Non-Profit IRS Status: 501(c)3
Highest Offering: Doctorate
Accreditation: M, ADNUR, #CAEP, MT, NUR, @SP, SW

02 Chancellor ....Prof. Marilina L. WAYLAND
05 Dean of Studies ....Prof. Migdalia TEXIDOR
32 Dean of Students ....Dr. Carmen OQUENDO
11 Dean of Faculty Cs Economics & Adm .... Prof. Fredrick VEGA
53 Dean of Education & Behavioral Sci .... Dr. Carmen COLLAZO
83 Director School of Psychology .... Dr. Jaime SANTIAGO
79 Dean Faculty of Humanities .... Dr. Oscar CRUZ
66 Director of Nursing ....Dr. Maria J. COLÓN
72 Director of Medical Technology .... Dr. Ida A. MEJIAS
81 Dean Faculty of Science & Tech ....Dr. Yogani GOVENDER
06 Registrar .... Ms. Lisette RIVERA
84 Enrollment Management ....Mr. Luis E. RUIZ
20 Associate Dean of Studies ....Ms. Liliam GAYA
08 Dir of Ctr for Access Info ....Ms. Maria de Lourdes RESTO
15 Human Resources Officer .... Mrs. Darlin TORRES
37 Director of Financial Aid ....Ms. Lillian CONCEPCION
18 Dir Conservation & General Services ....Vacant
38 Dir Stdnt Placement/Guidance/Couns ....Ms. Beatriz RIVERA
83 Director School of Social Work .... Dr. Jose CASTRO
53 Director School of Education .... Dr. Carlos CORTÉS
85 Coord International Rels Office .... Dr. Ramon AYALA
73 Dir School of Theology .... Dr. Angel VELEZ
88 Dir School of Criminal Justice ....Prof. Luis SOTO
13 Director Informatic/Telecomm Center ....Mr. Eduardo ORTIZ
36 Director Student Placement ....Mrs. Adabel-Vanessa COLON
07 Dir of Recruit & Admission Office .... Mr. Reinaldo ROBLES
30 Development & Fund Raising ....Mrs. Evelyn VEGA
96 Purchasing Officer ....Mrs. Patricia GONZALEZ
92 Coordinator of Honors Program .... Prof. Mariusz JACKO
113 Bursar .... Ms. Carmen RIVERA
106 Dir Online Education/E-learning .... Mr. Jairo PULIDO
19 Director Security/Safety ....Mr. George RIVERA
41 Athletic Director ....Mr. Jesus CORA

*Inter American University of Puerto Rico Ponce Campus (E)

104 Turpo Industrial Park Road, #1, Mercedita PR 00715-1602

County: Ponce FICE Identification: 005029
Unit ID: 242662
Telephone: (787) 284-1912 Carnegie Class: Masters/S
FAX Number: (787) 841-0103 Calendar System: Semester
URL: ponce.inter.edu
Established: 1962 Annual Undergrad Tuition & Fees: $5,986
Enrollment: 3,910 Coed
Affiliation or Control: Independent Non-Profit IRS Status: 501(c)3
Highest Offering: Doctorate
Accreditation: M, #CAEP, NURSE, PTAA

02 Chancellor .... Dr. Vilma E. COLON
05 Dean of Academic Affairs .... Dr. Victor FELIBERTY
32 Dean of Students ....Mrs. Ana M. VILLANUEVA
10 Financial Officer ....Vacant
08 Director Education Resource Center ....Mrs. Maria SILVESTRINI
35 Director Student Services .... Mrs. Miriam MARTINEZ
113 Bursar ....Mr. Brian HERNANDEZ
06 Registrar ....Mrs. Maria del C PEREZ
30 Director of Development ....Mrs. Hilda V. STELLA
07 Director of Admissions ....Mr. Franco L. DIAZ
15 Human Resource Director ....Vacant
19 Supervisor of University Guard ....Mr. Reinaldo ROSADO
37 Director Student Financial Aid ....Ms. Karen CAQUIAS
41 Athletic Director ....Mr. Raul HERNANDEZ
58 Director of Graduate Programs .... Dr. Delma SANTIAGO
50 Director Business & Administration .... Mrs. Vivien MATTEI
79 Act Dir Humanistics/Pedagogical Std ....Dr. Jose CORDOVES
81 Director Mathematics/Sciences ....Dr. Hector W. COLON
83 Dir Social/Behavioral Science .... Ms. Lidis L. JUSINO
38 Dir Univ Integration Services Ofc .... Mr. Hector MARTINEZ
13 Director Computer Center ....Mr. Antonio RAMOS
26 Public Relations Officer ....Vacant
04 Chief Executive Assistant ....Mrs. Yinaira SANTIAGO
27 Dir Marketing & Student Promotion ....Vacant
106 Director Distance Education Program ....Dra. Alma RIOS
45 Director of Evaluation & Planning ....Vacant
18 Chief Facilities/Physical Plant ....Vacant
36 Director Student Placement .... Mr. Hector MARTINEZ
84 Enrollment Manager ....Mrs. Miriam MARTINEZ
42 Chaplain ....Rev. Lucy ROSARIO
51 Adult Education Director ....Mrs. Marilyn OLIVERAS
20 Assoc Dean Acad Affs/Distance Educ .....Dr. Omayra CARABALLO
11 Dean Administrative Affairs .... Mr. Julio MUNOZ
96 Purchasing Officer ....Mrs. Vivian ARMSTRONG

*Inter American University of Puerto Rico San German Campus (F)

PO Box 5100, San German PR 00683-9801

County: San German FICE Identification: 003938
Unit ID: 242617
Telephone: (787) 264-1912 Carnegie Class: DU-Mod
FAX Number: (787) 264-4448 Calendar System: Semester
URL: www.intersg.edu
Established: 1912 Annual Undergrad Tuition & Fees: $6,012
Enrollment: 3,710 Coed
Affiliation or Control: Independent Non-Profit IRS Status: 501(c)3
Highest Offering: Doctorate
Accreditation: M, #CAEP, IACBE, MT, NURSE, RAD

02 Chancellor ....Prof. Agnes MOJICA
05 Acting Dean of Academic Affairs .... Prof. Vilma MARTINEZ
11 Dean of Administration .... Mrs. Frances CARABALLO
32 Dean of Students .... Mr. Raúl MEDINA
20 Associate Dean of Academic Affairs .... Prof. Vilma MARTÍNEZ
109 Auxiliary Dean of Administration .... Mrs. Marisol GONZÁLEZ
35 Associate Dean of Students .... Mrs. Idalmy RAMOS
15 Director of Human Resources ....Mrs. Evelyn TORRES
18 Acting Director Physical Plant .... Mr. José BERRÍOS
37 Director Financial Aid .... Mrs. Brunilda FERRER
06 Acting Registrar ....Mrs. Rosa VELEZ
07 Director of Admissions ....Mrs. Mildred CAMACHO
08 Director of Library .... Mrs. Mayra RODRÍGUEZ
38 Director Student Counseling .... Mrs. Daisy PEREZ
09 Dir Planning/Assessment/Development .... Dr. Caroline AYALA
19 Director of Security ....Mr. Francisco BARBOSA
13 Director of Computer Center .... Mr. Rogelio TORO-ZAPATA
41 Athletic Director ....Prof. Francisco ACEVEDO
39 Director of Men Student Housing .... Mrs. Erlinda VEGA
39 Director of Women Student Housing .... Mrs. Erlinda VEGA
42 Dir Chaplaincy/Spiritual Well-being .... Rev. Pablo CARABALLO
04 Special Assistant of the Chancellor .... Mrs. Tary GARCÍA
04 Special Assistant of the Chancellor ..Mrs. Janine HADERTHAUER
51 Acting Director Continuing Educ .... Prof. Vilma MARTÍNEZ
58 Director Graduate Programs .... Dr. Carlos IRIZARRY
109 Manager of Food Services .... Mr. Orlando MOLINA
17 Health Services Officer .... Mrs. Neisha TORRES
30 Chief Development Officer .... Mrs. Tary GARCÍA
96 Director of Purchasing .... Mr. Israel CRUZ
113 Director Bursar's Office ....Mr. Carlos SEGARRA
53 Director of Education .... Dr. Nancy COLÓN
83 Dir Social Sciences & Liberal Arts .... Dr. Kenneth DILORENZO
50 Director of Entrepreneurial & Mgmt .... Dr. Ailin PADILLA
88 Director of Biology & Environmental ....Prof. Iris SEDA
72 Director of Technical Studies ....Prof. Mildred ORTIZ

64 Director o Fine Arts/Music .... Dr. Gary MORALES
76 Director of Health Sciences .... Dr. Héctor MERCADO
92 Director of Honor Program ....Mrs. Sulmarie MORALES
26 Acting Coord External Resources .... Dr. Ramón FERNÁNDEZ
106 Dir Online Education/E-learning ....Prof. Luis ZORNOSA
57 Director of Fine Arts/Arts ....Dr. María GARCIA

*Inter American University of Puerto Rico School of Law (A)

PO Box 70351, San Juan PR 00936-8351
County: San Juan Identification: 666813
Unit ID: 242723
Telephone: (787) 751-1912 Carnegie Class: Spec-4-yr-Law
FAX Number: (787) 751-2975 Calendar System: Semester
URL: www.derecho.inter.edu
Established: 1961 Annual Graduate Tuition & Fees: N/A
Enrollment: 712 Coed
Affiliation or Control: Independent Non-Profit IRS Status: 501(c)3
Highest Offering: First Professional Degree; No Undergraduates
Accreditation: M, LAW

02 President ....Mr. Manuel J. FERNOS
61 Dean ....Dr. Julio E. FONTANET-MALDONADO
05 Dean for Academic Affairs ....Dr. Yanira REYES-GIL
32 Dean of Students .... Dr. Iris M. CAMACHO-MELENDEZ
11 Dean of Administration ...Mr. Juan C. HERNÁNDEZ-FERNÁNDEZ
06 Registrar ....Mrs. Sonia I. MONTALVO-COLÓN
08 Head Librarian ....Mr. Hector R. SANCHEZ-FERNANDEZ
88 Director of Legal Aid Clinic .. Mr. Rafael E. RODRÍGUEZ-RIVERA
37 Director of Financial Aid ....Mr. Ricardo CRESPO NEVAREZ
07 Director of Admissions ....Mrs. Angela TORRES
18 Chief Facilities/Physical Plant ....Mr. Jose A. RIVERA
113 Director of Bursar Office ....Mrs. Ileana PIÑERO
88 Exec Asst Planning/Eval/Devel Ofc .... Mrs. Edith C. PABON-RODRIGUEZ
121 Dir of Academic Support Program .. Mrs. Patricia OTÓN-OLIVIERI
88 Master Program Coordinator ....Dr. Luis E. ROMERO-NIEVES
04 Executive Asst to President .... Mr. Dominique GILORMINI
13 Chief Info Technology Officer ....Ms. Olga I. CRUZ-PABÓN
15 Director Personnel Services ....Mrs. Milagros AMALBERT
19 Director Security/Safety ....Mr. Victor RODRIGUEZ-CRUZ
30 Dir Development/Alumni Rels ....Mrs. Sheila GOMEZ
36 Director Student Placement/Counsel ....Mrs. Lin COLLAZO
51 Assoc Dean Acad Affs/Grad Pgm/ CLE ....Mr. Cesar ALVARADO-TORRES
35 Associate Dean for Student Affairs .... Mrs. Lin COLLAZO-CARRO
38 Counselor/Title IX Coord ....Ms. Yarelis PEREZ-RODRIGUEZ

*Inter American University of Puerto Rico School of Optometry (B)

500 John Will Harris Road, Bayamon PR 00957-6257
County: Bayamon Identification: 666601
Unit ID: 404222
Telephone: (787) 765-1915 Carnegie Class: Spec-4-yr-Other Health
FAX Number: (787) 767-3920 Calendar System: Semester
URL: www.optonet.inter.edu
Established: 1981 Annual Graduate Tuition & Fees: N/A
Enrollment: 214 Coed
Affiliation or Control: Independent Non-Profit IRS Status: 501(c)3
Highest Offering: First Professional Degree; No Undergraduates
Accreditation: M, OPT

02 Dean ....Dr. Andres PAGAN
05 Dean for Academic Affairs ....Dr. Angel F. ROMERO
11 Dean of Administration ....Mr. Francisco RIVERA
32 Dean of Student Affairs ....Dr. Iris R. CABELLO
42 Director Religious Life ....Rev. Julio R. VARGAS
30 Director Development ....Ms. Gladys MALAVE
17 Dean of Clinical Affairs ....Dr. Damaris PAGAN
08 Library Director ....Ms. Wilma MARRERO
15 Director Human Resources ....Mrs. Janice A. MARTINEZ
37 Financial Aid Officer ....Mrs. Raquel ROJAS
04 Executive Assistant of the Dean ....Mrs. Jackeline MEJIAS
06 Registrar ....Mrs. Luz OCASIO
26 Director Marketing/Promotion ....Mrs. Jaqueline PABON
07 Director of Admissions .... Mrs. Sirimarie MARTINEZ

Mech-Tech College (C)

PO Box 6118, Caguas PR 00726
County: Caguas FICE Identification: 030255
Unit ID: 414461
Telephone: (787) 744-1060 Carnegie Class: Assoc/HVT-High Trad
FAX Number: (787) 744-1035 Calendar System: Quarter
URL: www.mechtech.edu
Established: 1984 Annual Undergrad Tuition & Fees: $9,618
Enrollment: 1,947 Coed
Affiliation or Control: Proprietary IRS Status: Proprietary
Highest Offering: Associate Degree
Accreditation: CNCE

01 President ....Mr. Edwin J. COLON COSME

National University College (D)

PMB452, PO Box 144035, Arecibo PR 00614-4035
Telephone: (787) 879-5044 Identification: 666489
Accreditation: &M

National University College (E)

P.O. Box 2036, Bayamon PR 00960
County: Puerto Rico FICE Identification: 022606
Unit ID: 242972
Telephone: (787) 780-5134 Carnegie Class: Spec-4-yr-Other Health
FAX Number: (787) 786-9093 Calendar System: Trimester
URL: www.nuc.edu
Established: 1982 Annual Undergrad Tuition & Fees: $6,675
Enrollment: 25,999 Coed
Affiliation or Control: Proprietary IRS Status: Proprietary
Highest Offering: Master's
Accreditation: M, ADNUR, CAEP, NUR, PTAA

00 President .... Mr. Michael BANNETT
01 Campus Chancellor ....Mr. Wigdalys NEGRON-COLON
05 Dean Academic Affairs ....Dr. Waleska MUNIZ-MUNOZ
32 Director Student Affairs ....Vacant
113 Bursar ....Mr. Juan ORTIZ-BELTRAN
37 Director Financial Aid ....Ms. Zorymar GONZALEZ-ZAMBRANA
06 Registrar ....Ms. Glorimar RODRIGUEZ-ANDUJAR

National University College (F)

190 Ave Gautier Benítez, Caguas PR 00725
Telephone: (787) 653-4733 Identification: 770928
Accreditation: &M

† Branch campus of National University College, Bayamon, PR.

National University College Ponce Campus (G)

PO Box 801243, Coto Laurel PR 00780-1243
Telephone: (787) 840-4474 Identification: 770169
Accreditation: &M

National University College Rio Grande Campus (H)

PO Box 3064, Rio Grande PR 00745
Telephone: (787) 809-5100 Identification: 770170
Accreditation: &M

Ponce Health Sciences University (I)

PO Box 7004, Ponce PR 00732-7004
County: Ponce FICE Identification: 024824
Unit ID: 243081
Telephone: (787) 840-2575 Carnegie Class: DU-Higher
FAX Number: (787) 840-9756 Calendar System: Semester
URL: www.psm.edu
Established: 1977 Annual Undergrad Tuition & Fees: N/A
Enrollment: 699 Coed
Affiliation or Control: Independent Non-Profit IRS Status: 501(c)3
Highest Offering: Doctorate
Accreditation: M, CLPSY, IPSY, MED, PH

01 President/CEO .... Dr. David LENIHAN
05 Provost/VP Academic Affairs ....Dr. Jose TORRES-RUIZ
32 Vice Pres Student Affairs ....Dr. Elisandra RODRIGUEZ
15 Vice President of Human Resources ....Mrs. Susan G. HEMMER
45 VP of Strategic Planning ....Mr. Israel A. RUIZ
10 Chief Financial Officer ....Mr. Carlos ROJAS
04 Admin Assistant to the President ....Ms. Quetsy M. ROBLES
08 Chief Library Officer ....Mrs. Carmen MALAVET
06 Registrar ....Mrs. Ivette OLIVERAS
37 Director of Financila Aid ....Mr. Adam L. COLVIN
07 Director of Admissions ....Mrs. Emsley VAZQUEZ
106 Director of Educ Tech & Online Lrng .... Mr. Carlos SELLAS
13 Information Technology Officer .... Ms. Damaris TORRES
19 Director Security/Safety ....Mrs. Miriam PEREZ
38 Student Counseling .... Mr. Jose A. SOTO-FRANCESCHINI
96 Director of Purchasing ....Mr. Jose GONZALEZ

The Pontifical Catholic University of Puerto Rico (J)

2250 Blvd. Luis A. Ferre, Suite 564,
Ponce PR 00717-9997
County: Ponce FICE Identification: 003936
Unit ID: 241410
Telephone: (787) 841-2000 Carnegie Class: DU-Mod
FAX Number: (787) 651-2034 Calendar System: Semester
URL: www.pucpr.edu
Established: 1948 Annual Undergrad Tuition & Fees: $5,510
Enrollment: 6,614 Coed
Affiliation or Control: Roman Catholic IRS Status: 501(c)3
Highest Offering: Doctorate
Accreditation: M, CACREP, CAEPT, LAW, NUR, SW

00 Chancellor ....M.Rev. Ruben A. GONZALEZ MEDINA, CMF
01 President ....Dr. Jorge I. VELEZ AROCHO
04 Executive Assistant to President .... Lic. Liza RIESTRA
05 Vice President Academic Affairs .... Dr. Leandro COLON ALICEA
10 Vice President of Finance .... Lic. Jose A. FRONTERA AGENJO
32 Vice President for Student Affs ....Prof. Myriam D. LOPEZ
20 Assoc Vice Pres Academic Affairs .....Prof. Maria MUNIZ GARCIA
35 Assoc Vice Pres Student Affairs ....Vacant
09 Vice Pres Inst Rsrch/Dev/Planning .... Dr. Felix CORTES
12 Rector Arecibo Branch .... Dr. Edwin HERNANDEZ
12 Rector Mayaguez Branch .... Dr. Olga HERNÁNDEZ
06 Registrar ....Prof. Ivan DAVILA
07 Interim Director of Admissions ....Prof. Carmen Z. TORRES
08 Director of the Library ....Prof. Magda VARGAS
37 Director of Student Aid ....Mrs. Maria NOLASCO
36 Director of Placement Services ....Mr. Enrique ARROYO
13 Director Computer Center ....Mr. Moises CABRERA
24 Director Educational Technology .... Dr. Edgar RODRIGUEZ
79 Dean of Arts & Humanities ...Rev. Juan Luis NEGRON DELGADO
81 Dean of Sciences ....Dra. Alma L. SANTIAGO
61 Dean of the School of Law ....Lic. Fernando MORENO ORAMA
50 Dean Business Administration .... Dr. David ZAYAS
53 Dean of Education ....Prof. Ana I. BAEZ
58 Dean Col of Behav Sci/Cmty Affs ....Dra. Ilia ROSARIO-NIEVES
48 Dean School of Architecture .... Mr. Luis V. BADILLO-LOZANO
51 Coord Continuing Education Inst ....Mrs. Karen G. MORALES
27 Communications ....Mrs. Jalibeth RODRIGUEZ
29 Alumni Relations Officer .... Mrs. Maria S. MASCARO
15 Director Human Resources ....Mr. Wilfredo CORNIER
40 Director Bookstore .... Mrs. Ashley VELEZ
41 Athletic Director ....Mr. Ramon HERNANDEZ
42 Chaplain ....Rev. Victor M. HERNANDEZ
109 Director Auxiliary Enterprises ....Lic. Waddy MERCADO
26 Director Public Relations ....Vacant
38 Director Student Counseling ....Dr. Arvin BAEZ
18 Physical Plant/Safety & Security ....Mr. Julio PALMER
113 Treasurer Bursar's Office ....Mr. Juan E. ROMAN
96 Director of Purchasing .... Sra. Hilda TORRES COLON
88 Director of Biotechnology .... Hna. Nancy ARROYO
88 Accreditation Liaison Officer ....Dra. Maritza RIVERA MORET
30 Infrastructure Director ....Ing. Armando RODRIGUEZ
84 Coord Institutional Recruitment .... Sr. Rene MARRERO
89 Director of Freshmen .... Dra. Elizabeth MARTINEZ
106 Dir Online Education/E-learning .... Dra. Ivette TORRES
19 Director Security/Safety ....Mr. Julio PALMER
43 Dir Legal Services/General Counsel .... Lic. Carolyn COSTAS
86 Director Government Relations ....Vacant
100 Chief of Staff .... Lic. Liza RIESTRA
108 Director Institutional Assessment .... Prof. Mishelle RIVERA
39 Director Student Housing ....Vacant
39 Director Student Housing .Hna. Gloria N. CARABALLO TURRELL
102 Dir Foundation/Corporate Relations ....Sra. Gladys M. DIAZ
104 Director Study Abroad ....Sr. Joel VELEZ
105 Webmaster II ....Mr. Francisco SUAREZ
88 Director of Compliance ....Lic. Waddy MERCADO

Pontifical Catholic University of Puerto Rico-Arecibo Campus (K)

Box 144045, Arecibo PR 00614-4045
Telephone: (787) 881-1212 Identification: 666603
Accreditation: &M

† Regional accreditation is carried under the parent institution in Ponce, PR.

Pontifical Catholic University of Puerto Rico-Mayaguez Campus (L)

Box 1326, Mayaguez PR 00681-1326
Telephone: (787) 834-5151 Identification: 666605
Accreditation: &M

† Branch campus of The Pontifical Catholic University of Puerto Rico, Ponce, PR.

Puerto Rico School of Nurse Anesthetists (M)

656 Ponce de Leon Avenue, Floor 1, Hato Rey PR 00918
County: San Juan Identification: 667341
Telephone: (787) 998-8997 Carnegie Class: Not Classified
FAX Number: (787) 998-8998 Calendar System: Semester
URL: www.eeapr.org
Established: Annual Undergrad Tuition & Fees: N/A
Enrollment: N/A Coed
Affiliation or Control: Proprietary IRS Status: Proprietary
Highest Offering: Doctorate
Accreditation: M

01 President ....Dr. Carlos J. BORRERO-RIOS
05 Dean of Academic Affs & Accred .... Dr. Noraida DOMINGUEZ-FLORES
10 Chief Financial Officer ....Denisse RIVERA-MELENDEZ
37 Director Student Financial Aid .. Mariely VAZQUEZ-SOTOMAYOR
07 Director of Admissions .... Keina TRONCOSO-FERNANDEZ
66 Dean of Nursing ....Joseline LOPEZ-LEBRON
88 Director Master Science in Nursing ....Dr. Karen MORA-HERAS
08 Chief Library Officer .... Dr. Noraida DOMINGUEZ-FLORES
113 Bursar Officer .... Ariana BAEZ-ZABALA

San Juan Bautista School of Medicine (N)

PO Box 4968, Carretera 172, Caguas PR 00726-4968
County: San Juan FICE Identification: 031773
Unit ID: 430670
Telephone: (787) 743-3038 Carnegie Class: Spec-4-yr-Med
FAX Number: (787) 746-3093 Calendar System: Semester
URL: www.sanjuanbautista.edu
Established: 1978 Annual Undergrad Tuition & Fees: $9,192
Enrollment: 344 Coed
Affiliation or Control: Proprietary IRS Status: Proprietary

Highest Offering: First Professional Degree
Accreditation: M, #ARCPA, MED, NURSE

01 President/Dean ... Dr. Yocasta BRUGAL-MENA
11 Dean of Administration/HR ... Mr. Carlos F. ABREU
05 Chief Academic Officer ... Dr. Irving MALDONADO-RIVERA
06 Registrar ... Mrs. Nildalee MELENDEZ
08 Head Librarian ... Mr. Carlos ALTAMIRANO
10 Chief Business Officer ... Mr. Juan C. CASTRO
32 Chief Student Affairs/Student Life ... Dr. Yolanda MIRANDA
37 Director Student Financial Aid ... Miss Beatriz DE LEON
07 Director of Admissions ... Ms. Jaymi SANCHEZ
13 Chief Info Technology Officer (CIO) ... Mr. Jorge TORRES
38 Director Student Counseling ... Ms. Ilsa CENTENO

Seminario Teologico de Puerto Rico (A)

Urb Roosevelt 458 Jose Canals #301,
San Juan PR 00918
Telephone: (787) 274-1142 Identification: 770142
Accreditation: &M

† Branch campus of Nyack College, Nyack, NY

Trinity College of Puerto Rico (B)

PO Box 7313, Ponce PR 00732
FICE Identification: 031159
Unit ID: 431929
Telephone: (787) 848-5739 Carnegie Class: Spec 2-yr-Health
FAX Number: (787) 284-2537 Calendar System: Semester
URL: www.trinitypr.edu
Established: 1969 Annual Undergrad Tuition & Fees: $7,678
Enrollment: 45 Coed
Affiliation or Control: Independent Non-Profit IRS Status: 501(c)3
Highest Offering: Associate Degree
Accreditation: COE

01 Executive Director ... Maria DEL PILAR BONNIN OROZCO
05 Academic Dean ... Elizabeth PEREZ TOLEDO
10 Director of Finance Office ... Margarita PEREZ DE JESUS
06 Registrar ... Ana COLON SOTO
37 Director Student Financial Aid ... Isamari MEDINA MONTES

Universal Technology College of Puerto Rico (C)

111 Comercio Street, Aguadilla PR 00603
County: Aguadilla FICE Identification: 030297
Unit ID: 376385
Telephone: (787) 882-2065 Carnegie Class: Spec-4-yr-Other Health
FAX Number: (787) 891-2370 Calendar System: Semester
URL: www.unitecpr.edu
Established: 1987 Annual Undergrad Tuition & Fees: N/A
Enrollment: 108 Coed
Affiliation or Control: Independent Non-Profit IRS Status: 501(c)3
Highest Offering: Baccalaureate
Accreditation: ABHES

01 Chief Executive Officer ... Mrs. Keila LOPEZ
04 Executive Secretary ... Mrs. Marilyn GONZALEZ
05 Chief Academic Officer ... Vacant
06 Registrar ... Ms. Maria ALVAREZ
08 Director of Library ... Ms. Airlyn VAZQUEZ
10 Accountant ... Ms. Nancy MORALES
12 Director of Branch Campus ... Ms. Nelida CARDONA
13 Director Computer Center ... Mr. Zain CORDERO
15 Director Human Resources ... Ms. Yesenia NATAL
18 Chief Facilities/Physical Plant ... Mr. Danily NIEVES
32 Director Student Affairs ... Vacant
36 Student Placement Officer ... Ms. Evelyn TORRES
45 Director Planning & Development ... Mrs. Evelyn TORRES
37 Director Student Financial Aid ... Mr. Samuel HERNANDEZ
38 Director Student Counsel ... Mrs. Dalia SANTIAGO
96 Purchasing Officer ... Mrs. Dolores MITJANS
23 Healthcare Services ... Mr. Silverio JIMENEZ
07 Coordinator of Admissions ... Mrs. Teresita RIVERA
50 Dir General Studies/Business Admin ... Mrs. Sandra GONZALEZ
72 Director of Industrial Technology ... Mr. Eduardo FIGUEROA

Universidad Adventista de las Antillas (D)

Box 118, Mayaguez PR 00681-0118
County: Mayaguez FICE Identification: 005019
Unit ID: 241191
Telephone: (787) 834-9595 Carnegie Class: Bac-Diverse
FAX Number: (787) 834-9597 Calendar System: Semester
URL: www.uaa.edu
Established: 1961 Annual Undergrad Tuition & Fees: $7,250
Enrollment: 1,056 Coed
Affiliation or Control: Seventh-day Adventist IRS Status: 501(c)3
Highest Offering: Master's
Accreditation: M, ANEST, #COARC, NURSE

01 President ... Dr. Obed JIMENEZ
05 Vice President Academic Affairs ... Dr. Zima E. SANTIAGO
10 Vice President Financial Affairs ... Mr. Misael JIMENEZ
32 Vice President for Students Affairs ... Mr. Jaime LOPEZ
20 Associate VP Academic Affairs ... Mrs. Yolanda PEREZ
21 Associate Financial Vice President ... Mrs. Madeline CRUZ
113 Director Student Finance Office ... Mrs. Gisselle RIVERA
66 Dean of the School of Nursing ... Dr. Evelyn ALVAREZ
66 Director School of Nursing ... Mrs. Sylvia CARMENATTY
53 Dean of the School of Education ... Dr. Maritza LAMBOY
50 Director of Business Administration ... Dr. David L. RAMOS
81 Director Mathematics/Sciences/
Comp ... Mrs. Alicia MORADILLOS-DELGADO
73 Dir Theology/Music Department ... Dr. Efren PAGAN IRIZARRY
06 Registrar ... Mrs. Ana D. TORRES
07 Director of Admissions ... Mrs. Yolanda FERRER
37 Director of Student Financial Aid ... Mrs. Awilda MATOS
26 Dir Public Relations & Promotion ... Miss Lorell VARELA
108 Dir of Institutional Effectiveness ... Dr. Digna WILLIAMS
13 Director ITS ... Mr. Heber VAZQUEZ
08 Librarian ... Mrs. Aixa VEGA
38 Counselor ... Mrs. Ivelisse PEREZ
88 Environmental Services Director ... Mr. Legna VARELA
18 Chief Facilities/Physical Plant ... Mr. Abel RODRIGUEZ
33 Dean of Men ... Mr. Hector MONTILLA

*Universidad Ana G. Mendez (E)

Apartado 21345, Rio Piedras PR 00928-1341
County: San Juan FICE Identification: 029078
Unit ID: 242060
Telephone: (787) 751-0178 Carnegie Class: N/A
FAX Number: (787) 766-1706
URL: www.uagm.edu

01 President ... Mr. Jose F. MENDEZ
05 Vice President for Academic Affairs ... Dr. Claribette RODRÍGUEZ
10 Vice Pres Financial Affairs ... Mr. Carmelo TORRES
32 VP Student Affairs ... Dr. Mayra CRUZ
45 Vice President Planning & Research ... Mr. Jorge CRESPO
11 Executive & Operations Vice Pres ... Mr. Ricardo RODRIGUEZ
15 Vice President Human Resources ... Dr. Victoria DE JESUS
88 Acting Vice Pres International Affs ... Dr. Rafael NADAL
13 Chief Information Officer ... Vacant
26 Associate Vice Pres for Public Rels ... Ms. Maria MARTINEZ
04 Exec Assistant to President ... Ms. Lydia I. MASSARI
06 Registrar ... Ms. Elisa QUILES
07 Director of Admissions ... Ms. Ramonita FUENTES

*Universidad Ana G. Mendez Carolina Campus (F)

Carr #190 Ave. Principal Sabana, Carolina PR 00983-2010
County: San Juan FICE Identification: 003941
Unit ID: 243346
Telephone: (787) 257-7373 Carnegie Class: Masters/L
FAX Number: (787) 776-1220 Calendar System: Semester
URL: https://carolina.uagm.edu/
Established: 1949 Annual Undergrad Tuition & Fees: $5,820
Enrollment: 7,892 Coed
Affiliation or Control: Independent Non-Profit IRS Status: 501(c)3
Highest Offering: Master's
Accreditation: M, ACBSP, ACFEI, ADNUR, CAEPT, NUR, SW

00 President ... Mr. José F. MENDEZ
02 Chancellor ... Dr. Félix R. HUERTAS GONZÁLEZ
05 Vice Chancellor Academic Affairs ... Dr. Evelyza CRESPO
32 Vice Chancellor Student Affairs ... Dr. María G. VEAZ
84 Assoc VC Enrollment Management ... Mrs. Magda E. OSTOLAZA
15 Vice Pres Human Resources ... Dr. Victoria DE JESÚS
88 Dean Intl Sch Hosp/Culinary Arts ... Mrs. Terestella GONZÁLEZ
107 Dean Professional Studies ... Mrs. Mildred Y. RIVERA
06 Registrar ... Mrs. Elisa QUILES
08 Director of Library ... Mrs. Elsa MARIANI
26 Director Public Relations ... Mrs. Ivonne D. ARROYO
83 Dean of Social and Human Sciences ... Dr. Evelyza CRESPO
50 Dean of Business Administration ... Dr. José E. BERRÍOS
72 Dean of Science and Technology ... Dr. Marielis E. RIVERA
76 Dean of Health Science ... Dr. Vanessa ORTIZ
19 Director Security/Safety ... Mr. José E. MACHUCA

*Universidad Ana G. Mendez Cupey Campus (G)

PO Box 21150, San Juan PR 00928-1150
County: San Juan FICE Identification: 025875
Unit ID: 241739
Telephone: (787) 766-1717 Carnegie Class: Masters/L
FAX Number: (787) 759-7663 Calendar System: Semester
URL: https://cupey.uagm.edu/
Established: 1980 Annual Undergrad Tuition & Fees: $5,820
Enrollment: 8,893 Coed
Affiliation or Control: Independent Non-Profit IRS Status: 501(c)3
Highest Offering: Doctorate
Accreditation: M, ACBSP, ADNUR, CAEPT, NUR, SW

00 UAGM President ... Mr. José F. MENDEZ
02 Chancellor ... Dr. Angel A. TOLEDO
05 Vice Chancellor Academic Affairs ... Dr. Jose E. BERRIOS
10 Vice President of Financial Affairs ... Mr. Carmelo TORRES
108 Asst Vice Chanc Inst Assessment ... Dr. Carmen M. LUNA
30 Asst VC Inst Development/Alumni ... Ms. Belissa AQUINO
32 Vice Chanc for Student Affairs ... Dr. Glenda BERMUDEZ
85 Executive Director Intl Affairs ... Dr. Zaida VEGA
26 Vice Chanc External Resources ... Vacant
88 Assoc Vice Chanc Accred/Licensing ... Dr. Giselle TAPIA
11 Assoc Vice Chanc for Admin Affairs ... Vacant
15 Asst Vice Pres for Human Resources ... Mrs. Camile PEREZ
13 Director Information Resources ... Mr. Rafael I. GARCÍA
84 Int Assc Vice Chanc Student Recruit ... Mrs. Elizabeth CANCEL
114 Director Pres Analysis & Budget ... Mrs. Aixa ALDARONDO
45 Asst Vice President of Planning ... Dr. Mariela COLLAZO
124 Assoc Vice Chanc Retention/Devel ... Mrs. Awilda PEREZ
83 Actg Dean Soc Science/Human &
Comm ... Dr. Roxanna DOMENECH
50 Dean of Business ... Dr. Belinda JUNQUERA
53 Dean of Education ... Dr. José R. CINTRON
76 Actg Dean of Health Sciences ... Dr. Kiebelle GONZALEZ
81 Dean of Science/Technology & Envir ... Dr. Karen GONZALEZ
65 Assoc Dean of Environmental Affairs ... Dr. María C. ORTIZ
107 Assoc Dean of Professional Studies ... Vacant
60 Assoc Dean of Communications ... Mrs. Sugelenia COTTO
79 Assoc Dean of Humanities ... Dr. Roxanna D. DOMENECH
75 Dean of Technical Studies ... Mrs. Laura E. APONTE
51 Exec Director Continuing Education ... Dr. Luis A. MARRERO
88 Assoc Dean of Education ... Dr. Janet RUÍZ
08 Head Librarian ... Mrs. Balbina J. ROJAS
18 Manager Operations & Facilities ... Eng. Carmencita TORRES
66 Director of Nursing ... Dr. Yanilda RODRIGUEZ
26 Director Public Relations ... Ms. Yvonne GUADALUPE
06 Registrar ... Mrs. Beatriz NIEVES
12 Additional Location Dir Bayamon ... Mr. Glenda BERMUDEZ
12 Additional Location Dir Aguadilla ... Mr. Luis A. RUIZ
12 Additional Location Dir Jayuya ... Dr. Irma del Pilar CRUZ
07 Admissions Director ... Ms. Yadira RIVERA LUGO
41 Athletic Director ... Mr. Edgar I. DIAZ
19 Director Security/Safety ... Mr. José E. MACHUCA
36 Director Student Placement ... Mrs. Lourdes E. MEDINA
37 Director Student Financial Aid ... Mr. Julio A. RODRÍGUEZ
38 Assoc Vice Chanc Student Wellness ... Mrs. Arelis VILLANUEVA

*Universidad Ana G. Mendez Gurabo Campus (H)

Estacion Universidad, Box 3030, Gurabo PR 00778-3030
County: Gurabo FICE Identification: 011719
Unit ID: 243601
Telephone: (787) 743-7979 Carnegie Class: DU-Mod
FAX Number: (787) 744-5394 Calendar System: Semester
URL: https://gurabo.uagm.edu/
Established: 1972 Annual Undergrad Tuition & Fees: $5,820
Enrollment: 13,553 Coed
Affiliation or Control: Independent Non-Profit IRS Status: 501(c)3
Highest Offering: Doctorate
Accreditation: M, CAEP, COPSY, DIETC, IPSY, JOUR, LSAR, MT, NATUR, NURSE, #SP, SW

02 Chancellor ... Dr. David MENDEZ
11 Actg Vice Chancellor Admin Affairs ... Ms. Mari G. GONZALEZ
05 Vice Chancellor ... Dra. Nydia BOU
32 Vice Chancellor of Student Affairs ... Dra. Brunilda APONTE
08 Vice Chancellor Information Res ... Dr. Sarai LASTRA
92 Internship & Honors Program Coord ... Ms. Wanda I. GONZÁLEZ
88 Asst Vice Chanc Eval & Development ... Ms. Lizbeth RIVERA
21 Director of Admin Affairs ... Mrs. Belinda ROSA
53 Dean Education ... Dra. Elaine GUADALUPEZ
50 Dean Business and Entrepreneurship ... Dr. Juan Carlos SOSA
54 Dean Engineering ... Dr. Rolando GARCIA
81 Dean Natural Science & Technology ... Dr. Teresa LIPSETT
83 Dean Social Sciences/
Communications ... Dra. Maria del C. SANTOS
48 Dean Architecture/Design ... Ms. Aurorisa MATEO
76 Acting Dean Health Sciences ... Dra. Nydia BOU
72 Dean Technical Studies ... Ms. Maria E. FLORES
107 Dean Professional Stds & Cont Educ ... Ms. Mildred Y. RIVERA
58 Associate Dean of Graduate Studies ... Dr. Sharon CANTRELL
06 Registrar ... Mrs. Zoraida ORTIZ
97 Dean of Liberal Arts & Gen Studies ... Mr. Felix R. HUERTAS
26 Director of Marketing ... Vacant
37 Director Office of Financial Aid ... Mrs. Carmen J. RIVERA
26 Director Public Relations ... Ms. Iris SERRANO
18 Chief Facilities/Physical Plant ... Ms. Mayra RODRIGUEZ
29 Coordinator Alumni Relations ... Mr. Wilfredo HILLS
30 Chief Development Officer ... Mr. Rene S. RONDA
96 Director of Purchasing ... Ms. Norma C. DONEZ
07 Director of Admissions ... Mrs. Diriee Y. RODRIGUEZ
45 Aux Vice President of Planning ... Ms. Mari G. GONZALEZ
15 Aux Vice President Human Resources ... Mrs. Iris BERRIOS
36 Assoc Vice Chanc Student Placement ... Ms. Carmen PULLIZA
84 Asst Vice Chanc Enrollment Mgmt ... Ms. Maria V. FIGUEROA
114 Aux Vice President of Budget ... Ms. Camille LAMBOY
38 Assoc Vice Chanc Student Counseling ... Ms. Samaris COLLAZO
106 Dir Online Education/E-learning ... Mr. Israel RODRIGUEZ
108 Asst Vice Chanc Assessment ... Mr. Ernesto ESPINOZA
41 Athletic Director ... Mr. Felix A. CARRASQUILLO

*Universidad Ana G. Mendez Online Campus (I)

PO Box 21345, San Juan PR 00928-1345
County: San Juan Identification: 667292
Telephone: (787) 288-1118 Carnegie Class: Not Classified
FAX Number: (787) 288-1141 Calendar System: Semester
URL: agmonline.suagm.edu
Established: 2011 Annual Undergrad Tuition & Fees: N/A
Enrollment: N/A Coed
Affiliation or Control: Independent Non-Profit IRS Status: 501(c)3
Highest Offering: Doctorate
Accreditation: M

02 Chancellor .... Dr. Gino Q. NATALICCHIO
11 Vice Chancellor Administrative Affs .... Ms. Nilsa RODRÍGUEZ-MARTORELL
10 Vice Chancellor .... Dr. Jose E. MALDONADO-ROJAS
06 Registrar .... Ms. Jessie PEREZ
07 Director of Admissions .... Ms. Marilys RIVERA
05 Director of Faculty .... Ms. Denisse COLON
108 Director of Assessment & Research .... Ms. Dennise RIVERA
32 Vice Chancellor of Student Affairs .... Mr. Jose D. MARTINEZ
37 Director Student Financial Aid .... Mr. Raul HOMS
38 Director Student Counseling .... Ms. Sharon CORREA

Universidad Central de Bayamon (A)

PO Box 1725, Bayamon PR 00960-1725

County: Bayamon　FICE Identification: 005022
Unit ID: 241225
Telephone: (787) 786-3030　Carnegie Class: Masters/S
FAX Number: (787) 740-2200　Calendar System: Semester
URL: www.ucb.edu.pr
Established: 1961　Annual Undergrad Tuition & Fees: $5,462
Enrollment: 1,146　Coed
Affiliation or Control: Roman Catholic　IRS Status: 501(c)3
Highest Offering: Master's
Accreditation: M, NURSE, SW, THEOL

01 President .... Dr. Carmen J. CIVIDANES-LAGO
100 President Assistant .... Mr. Angel VALENTIN
05 Academic Dean .... Dr. Maritza DEL VALLE
10 Dean Admin/Finance .... Vacant
32 Dean of Students .... Mrs. Niza ZAYAS
49 Dir Col Liberal Arts/Humanities/Ed .... Br. Jose M. SANTIAGO
50 Dir Business Development & Tech .... Dr. Nidia COLON
15 Director of Human Resources .... Dr. Julitza ARROYO
07 Director of Admissions .... Mrs. Wanda APONTE
37 Director Student Financial Aid .... Mrs. Elaine NUÑEZ
38 Dir Guidance/Counseling Center Int .... Mr. Cesar LOPEZ
35 Coord Center Learning Stre (CFAEE) .... Mrs. Myrna PEREZ
13 Director of Information System .... Mr. Jose RODRÍGUEZ
18 Director Physical Facilities .... Mrs. Enid RIVERA
96 Purchase Officer .... Mrs. Jessica OJEDA
09 Institutional Research Officer .... Mrs. Luz M. PALACIOS
20 Associate Academic Dean .... Dr. Ángel L. AVILÉS
81 Dir College Sciences/Health Prof .... Dr. Pedro ROBLES
04 Administrative Asst to President .... Mrs. Yazmin RAMOS
105 Director Web Services .... Mr. Jose RODRÍGUEZ
106 Dir Online Education/E-learning .... Mr. Jorge L. DIAZ
108 Director Institutional Assessment .... Mrs. Vivian A. PADILLA
41 Athletic Director .... Mr. Juan A. FIGUEROA
08 Chief Library Officer .... Ms. Yanit DELGADO
84 Director Enrollment Management .... Dr. Kendra ORTÍZ

Universidad Central Del Caribe (B)

PO Box 60327, Bayamon PR 00960-6032

County: Bayamon　FICE Identification: 021633
Unit ID: 243568
Telephone: (787) 798-3001　Carnegie Class: Spec-4-yr-Med
FAX Number: (787) 798-6836　Calendar System: Semester
URL: www.uccaribe.edu
Established: 1976　Annual Undergrad Tuition & Fees: $8,387
Enrollment: 547　Coed
Affiliation or Control: Independent Non-Profit　IRS Status: 501(c)3
Highest Offering: Doctorate
Accreditation: M, CHIRO, MED

01 President .... Dr. Waleska CRESPO-RIVERA
10 VP of Finances and Operations .... Mr. Ariel DAVILA
05 Dean for Academic Affairs .... Dr. Nereida DIAZ-RODRIGUEZ
20 Asst Dean of Curriculum Development .... Dr. Alvaro PEREZ
76 Dean Health Sciences & Tech .... Vacant
88 Interim Director Med Imaging Tech .... Prof. Elaine RUIZ
11 Dean Administrative Affairs .... Ms. Emilia SOTO
32 Dean Student Affairs .... Dr. Omar PEREZ
35 Asst Dean Student Affairs .... Dr. Jose L. OLIVER
63 Dean of Medicine .... Dr. Jose A. CAPRILES
88 Associate Dean of Medicine .... Mrs. Zilka RIOS
06 Registrar .... Ms. Nilda MONTANEZ-LOPEZ
07 Director of Admissions .... Ms. Irma L. CORDERO
37 Director Student Financial Aid .... Mr. Edwin SANCHEZ
21 Director of Finances .... Mrs. Iris J. FONT
08 Librarian .... Ms. Mildred RIVERA
51 Director of Continuing Medical Educ .... Dr. Frances GARCIA
38 Counselor .... Mrs. Lileana BRUNO
46 Assoc Dean Research & Grad Studies .... Vacant
20 Assoc Dean Clinical & Fac Affairs .... Dr. Harry MERCADO
30 Dean of Inst Devel & Strategic Plng .... Ms. Mildred RIVERA-MARRERO
13 Chief Information Technology Office .... Dr. Legier ROJAS

Universidad Pentecostal Mizpa (C)

RR16 Box 4800, San Juan PR 00926

County: San Juan　FICE Identification: 031983
Unit ID: 441690
Telephone: (787) 720-4476　Carnegie Class: Spec-4-yr-Faith
FAX Number: N/A　Calendar System: Semester
URL: www.mizpa.edu
Established: 1937　Annual Undergrad Tuition & Fees: $4,220
Enrollment: 165　Coed
Affiliation or Control: Pentecostal Church of God　IRS Status: 501(c)3
Highest Offering: Master's
Accreditation: BI

01 President .... Mrs. Naury Y. SANCHEZ CINTRON
05 Dean of Academic Affairs .... Mrs. Joan JIMENEZ MARRERO
10 Dean Administration/Finance .... Mrs. Maureen DE LEON MULLERT
32 Dean of Student Affairs .... Mr. Jorge A. BURGOS CARRION
42 Chaplain/Director Campus Ministry .... Mr. Harry MUNOZ COLON
35 Associate Student/Affairs Life .... Mrs. Daulan NIEVES GARCIA
06 Registrar .... Mr. Leonardo MELENDEZ LEON
08 Librarian .... Mrs. Melanie RODRIGUEZ MARTINEZ
37 Student Financial Aid Officer .... Mrs. Myriam JUARBE REY
26 Chief Public Relations Officer .... Mr. Rafael LABOY FUSTER
113 Bursar .... Mr. Geserie CRUZADO ROSADO
04 Administrative Asst to President .... Miss Jaydee A. GUZMAN QUILES

Universidad Politecnica de Puerto Rico (D)

Ponce de Leon 377, Box 192017,
San Juan PR 00919-2017

County: San Juan　FICE Identification: 021000
Unit ID: 243577
Telephone: (787) 622-8000　Carnegie Class: Spec-4-yr-Eng
FAX Number: (787) 754-8268　Calendar System: Trimester
URL: www.pupr.edu
Established: 1966　Annual Undergrad Tuition & Fees: $8,640
Enrollment: 4,367　Coed
Affiliation or Control: Independent Non-Profit　IRS Status: 501(c)3
Highest Offering: Doctorate
Accreditation: M, #LSAR

01 President .... Dr. Ernesto VAZQUEZ-BARQUET
03 Executive Vice President .... Eng. Ernesto VAZQUEZ-MARTINEZ
84 Vice Pres Enrollment Management .... Mr. Carlos PEREZ
05 Chief Academic Officer .... Dr. Miguel A. RIESTRA
06 Registrar .... Mrs. Mayra I. LOPEZ
07 Director Admissions .... Mrs. Teresa CARDONA
08 Head Librarian .... Mrs. Digna DELGADO
37 Director Financial Aid .... Mr. Sergio VILLOLDO
15 Director Personnel Services .... Ms. Ana CASTELLANO
18 Chief Facilities/Physical Plant .... Mr. Herminio ROMERO
29 Alumni Relations .... Ms. Glenda M. COLON-RAMOS
32 Director Student Affairs .... Mr. Carlos PEREZ
36 Director Student Placement .... Mrs. Angie ESCALANTE
38 Director Student Counseling .... Ms. Sheila VAZQUEZ
96 Director of Purchasing .... Mr. Ramon RIVERA
19 Director Security/Safety .... Mr. Miguel ALBARRAN
41 Athletic Director .... Mr. Roberto MEDINA-ORTIZ
50 Dean of Business .... Dr. Enrique MUNOZ-GIL
49 Dean of Arts and Science/Education .... Dr. Catalina VICENS
54 Dean of Engineering .... Dr. Carlos J. GONZALEZ
106 Dir Online Education/E-learning .... Dr. Cuauhtemoc GODOY
108 Director Institutional Assessment .... Dr. Miguel A. RIESTRA-FERNANDEZ
91 Director Administrative Computing .... Mr. Pedro PEREZ-DORTA
09 Director of Institutional Research .... Dr. Miguel A. RIESTRA
101 Secretary of the Institution/Board .... Arch. Ricardo RICARDO LEFRANC-MORALES
13 Chief Information Tech Officer .... Mr. Pedro PEREZ
39 Dir Resident Life/Student Housing .... Mr. William KORBER

Universidad Teologica Del Caribe (E)

PO Box 901, Saint Just PR 00978-0901

County: Trujillo Alto　FICE Identification: 023355
Unit ID: 241614
Telephone: (787) 761-0640　Carnegie Class: Spec-4-yr-Faith
FAX Number: (787) 748-9220　Calendar System: Semester
URL: www.utcpr.edu
Established: 1956　Annual Undergrad Tuition & Fees: $6,366
Enrollment: 433　Coed
Affiliation or Control: Church Of God　IRS Status: 501(c)3
Highest Offering: Master's
Accreditation: BI

01 President .... Francisco ORTIZ
05 Academic Dean .... Carmen AYALA
06 Registrar .... Awilda MORALES
10 Administration Dean .... Frankie NEGRON
32 Students Dean .... Wilfredo ADORNO
37 Financial Aid Director .... Claudia RODRIGUEZ
08 Librarian .... Graciela TORRES
45 Planning & Development Officer .... Ana CEPERO
106 Online Program Coordinator .... Raul MCCLIN
58 Graduate School Coordinator .... Samuel CARABALLO
12 North-Central (Dorado) Campus Coord .... Richard D'COSTA
04 Administrative Asst to the Pres .... Waleska VEGA
07 Admissions Officer .... Avianny PAULINO

*University of Puerto Rico-Central Administration (F)

Flamboy n st 1187 Jardin Bot nico S,
San Juan PR 00926-1117

County: San Juan　FICE Identification: 003942
Unit ID: 243160
Telephone: (787) 250-0000　Carnegie Class: N/A
FAX Number: (787) 759-6917
URL: www.upr.edu

01 President .... Dr. Jorge HADDOCK-ACEVEDO
03 Executive Director .... Lcda. Soniemi RODRIGUEZ DAVILA
05 Executive Vice President .... Dr. Ubaldo M. CORDOVA-FIGUEROA
108 Vice Pres for Acred & Assessment .... Dr. Jennifer ALICEA-CASTILLO
32 Vice Pres - Student Affairs .... Dr. Jose PERDOMO
46 Vice Pres for Research & Technology .... Mrs. Carmen BACHIER
88 Director of Institutional Planning .... Dr. Félix LOPEZ-ROMÁN
88 Director of Intellectual Property .... Eng. Yahveh COMAS-TORRES
88 Director Compliance/Integrity .... Mr. Carlos RODRIGUEZ-RIVERA
88 Dir Innovation/Entreprenurship .... Dr. Jose L. AYALA
12 Chancellor UPR-Rio Piedras Campus .... Dr. Luis A. FERRAO-DELGADO
12 Chanc UPR-Mayaguez Campus .... Dr. Agustin RULLAN TORO
12 Acting Chanc UPR-Medical Sci Campus .... Dr. Wanda MALDONADO
12 Chancellor UPR-Cayey Campus .... Dr. Glorivee ROSARIO-PEREZ
12 Chancellor UPR-Humacao Campus .... Dr. Aida RODRIGUEZ-ROIG
12 Chancellor UPR-Bayamon Campus .... Dr. Miguel VELEZ-RUBIO
12 Chancellor UPR-Ponce Campus .... Dr. Tessie CRUZ-RIVERA
12 Acting Chanc UPR-Carolina Campus .... Dr. Jose I. MEZA PEREIRA
12 Chancellor UPR-Utuado Campus .... Dr. Luis TAPIA-MALDONADO
12 Chancellor UPR-Aguadilla Campus .... Dr. Sonia RIVERA GONZÁLEZ
12 Chancellor UPR-Arecibo Campus .... Dr. Carlos A. ANDÚJAR-ROJAS
30 Dir Devel & Alumni Affairs Office .... Mrs. Margarita MENDEZ ESCUDERO
10 Director Finance Office .... Mr. Antonio TEJERA-ROCAFORT
15 Acting Dir Human Resources Office .... Mr. Nelson RIVERA-VILLANUEVA
11 Director Administrative Service .... Mrs. Myriam MARTINEZ FIGUEROA
13 Dir Information Systems Ofc .... Mr. Jose PABÓN PAGÁN
37 Director Student Financial Aid .... Vacant
43 Acting Director Legal Affairs Ofc .... Lcda. Soniemi RODRÍGUEZ-DÁVILA
88 Acting Dir Botanical Garden .... Mr. Carlos R. DIAZ-PÉREZ
26 Acting Dir Press & Communications .... Ms. Joan M. HERNÁNDEZ-MARRERO
101 Exec Sec University Board .... Dr. Ana E. FALCON EMANUELLI
114 Acting Director Budget Office .... Dr. Osvaldo GUZMÁN LÓPEZ
18 Actg Dir Phys Dev/Infrastrcture Ofc .... Arch. Jennifer LUGO CARDONA
04 Admin Assistant to the President .... Mrs. Adaliz PEREZ COLÓN
07 Director of Admissions .... Mrs. Ivonne CALDERÓN GARCÍA
102 Director Foundation/Corporate Rels .... Arch. Wilma L. SANTIAGO GABRIELINI
105 Director Web Services .... Mr. José MUÑOZ ALVAREZ
106 Dean of Online Education/E-learning .... Lcda. Lisa M. NIEVES OSLÁN
19 Director Security/Safety .... Mrs. Lillyvette CARRAU MARTY
45 Chief Institutional Planning Office .... Mrs. Rosa TORRES-MOLINA
88 Director of Academic Planning .... Dr. Eunice PEREZ-MEDINA
96 Director of Purchasing .... Mr. Nelson QUIÑONES SANTIAGO
09 Director of Institutional Research .... Mrs. Rosa H. TORRES-MOLINA

*University of Puerto Rico-Aguadilla (G)

PO Box 6150, Aguadilla PR 00604-6150

County: Aguadilla　FICE Identification: 012123
Unit ID: 243106
Telephone: (787) 890-2681　Carnegie Class: Bac-Diverse
FAX Number: (787) 891-3455　Calendar System: Semester
URL: www.uprag.edu
Established: 1972　Annual Undergrad Tuition & Fees (In-State): $4,768
Enrollment: 2,444　Coed
Affiliation or Control: State　IRS Status: 501(c)3
Highest Offering: Baccalaureate
Accreditation: M, ACBSP, #CAEP

02 Chancellor .... Dr. Sonia RIVERA-GONZALEZ
05 Dean Academic Affairs .... Dr. Walleska DE JESUS BONILLA
11 Dean Administrative Affairs .... Mrs. Veronica LOPEZ-PADUA
32 Dean Student Affairs .... Dr. Sharon RIVERA-RUIZ
06 Registrar .... Mrs. Wanda FELICIANO-MÉNDEZ
07 Admissions Officer .... Mrs. Melba SERRANO
08 Head Librarian .... Prof. Elsa MATOS
13 Director of Computer Center .... Mr. Carlos JIMENEZ
15 Director of Personnel .... Mrs. Luz A. HERNANDEZ
19 Director of Security/Safety .... Mr. Edwin VAZQUEZ MEDINA
37 Director Student Financial Aid .... Mrs. Marta A. SOTO
51 Director Continuing Education .... Sr. Birilo SANTIAGO-VELÁZQUEZ
38 Director Student Counseling .... Dr. Gilberto HERRERA
45 Dir Planning/Inst Research Office .... Mr. Gerardo JAVARIZ
18 Chief Facilities/Physical Plant .... Mrs. Marjorie MORALES-MATIAS
29 Director Alumni Relations .... Mrs. Jeannette AQUINO
96 Purchasing Supervisor .... Mrs. Widylia MEDINA

*University of Puerto Rico at Arecibo (H)

Call Box 4010, Arecibo PR 00614-4010

County: Arecibo　FICE Identification: 007228
Unit ID: 243115
Telephone: (787) 815-0000　Carnegie Class: Bac-Diverse
FAX Number: (787) 880-2245　Calendar System: Semester
URL: www.upra.edu
Established: 1967　Annual Undergrad Tuition & Fees (In-State): $4,178
Enrollment: 3,414　Coed
Affiliation or Control: State　IRS Status: 501(c)3

Highest Offering: Baccalaureate
Accreditation: M, ACBSP, ADNUR, CAEPN, JOUR, NUR

02 Chancellor ... Dr. Carlos A. ADNÚJUAR ROJAS
05 Int Dean for Academic Affairs ... Dr. Weyna QUINONES
11 Dean of Administrative Affairs ... Dr. Inocencio RODRÍGUEZ
32 Dean of Student Affairs ... Dr. Yeidi ALTIERI
10 Director of Finances ... Mr. Jesus VALDERRAMA
09 Dir Planning/Institutional Research ... Dr. Geissa TORRES
06 Registrar ... Mrs. Yaritza CRUZ
07 Director of Admissions ... Mrs. Magaly MENDEZ
08 Head Librarian ... Prof. Víctor MALDONADO
15 Director Human Resources ... Mrs. Rosaura QUINTANA
38 Director Student Counseling ... Prof. Celia MEDINA
04 Assistant to the Chancellor ... Dr. José SOTO
37 Director Student Financial Aid ... Ms. Daliana FRESSE
41 Athletic Director ... Mr. Alexieyi RIVERA
13 Computing & Information Management ... Prof. Luis COLON
20 Assoc Dean of Academic Affairs ... Dra. Elizabeth CORTÉS
92 Director Honors Program ... Dra. Vanessa MORA

*University of Puerto Rico at Bayamon (A)

Carr. 174, Industrial Minillas 170,
Bayamon PR 00959-1919
County: Bayamon FICE Identification: 010975
Unit ID: 243133
Telephone: (787) 993-0000 Carnegie Class: Bac-Diverse
FAX Number: (787) 993-8900 Calendar System: Semester
URL: www.uprb.edu
Established: 1971 Annual Undergrad Tuition & Fees (In-State): $4,198
Enrollment: 3,592 Coed
Affiliation or Control: State IRS Status: 501(c)3
Highest Offering: Baccalaureate
Accreditation: M, ACBSP, CAEPN

02 Chancellor ... Dr. Miguel VELEZ-RUBIO
05 Dean Academic Affairs ... Dr. Jorge ROVIRA-ALVAREZ
32 Dean Student Affairs ... Dr. Lenis TORRES-BERRIOS
06 Registrar ... Ms. Elizabeth ORTIZ-VARGAS
07 Director Admissions ... Ms. Minerva HERNÁNDEZ-BERNIER
08 Director Learning Resources ... Dr. Raúl PAGÁN-FALCÓN
11 Dean Administrative Affairs ... Mr. Luis MUÑOZ-ALVARADO
15 Director Human Resources . Ms. Carina FIGUEROA-RODRÍGUEZ
35 Director Student Activities ... Mrs. Maribelle PERGOLA-RIVERA
37 Director Student Financial Aid ... Mr. Marcos DE JESÚS
38 Director Student Counseling .. Dr. Irma J. SANTIAGO-SANTIAGO
81 Director Biology ... Dr. Darinel ORTIZ-PADILLAT
50 Director Business Administration ... Dr. Janet CABRERA-RIVERA
09 Director Planning & Inst Research ... Mr. Javier ZAVALA-QUIÑONES
53 Director Education ... Dr. José A. CRESPO-REYES
54 Director Engineering ... Prof. Jorge VELAR-PRIETO
68 Director Physical Education ... Prof. Carlos MARICHAL-LUGO
79 Director Humanities ... Dr. Luis PABÓN-BATLLE
83 Director Social Sciences ... Dr. Elizabeth CRESPO-KEBLER
77 Director Computer Science ... Dr. Nelliud TORRES-BATISTA
75 Director Secretarial Sciences ... Dr. Peggy SANTIAGO-LÓPEZ
72 Director Electronics ... Prof. Samuel LUGO-VÉLEZ
23 Director Health Services ... Dr. Kimberly RIVERA-SANTIAGO
96 Director Purchasing ... Ms. Allison M. BRACHE-MELLO
88 Director Special Services ... Ms. Shelciy COLLAZO-CASTRO
81 Director Physics ... Dr. Javier AVALOS-SÁNCHEZ
88 Director English ... Prof. Carmen SKERRETT-LLANOS
88 Director Spanish ... Dr. Raúl GUADALUPE-DE JESÚS
81 Director Mathematics ... Prof. Angel MORERA-GONZÁLEZ
88 Director Chemistry ... Dr. Marisol CORDERO-RIVERA
18 Coord Facilities/Physical Plant ... Mr. Carlos CLAUDIO-VILLAFAÑE
114 Director Budget ... Mr. Rafael L. GIERBOLINI-SANTIAGO
10 Director Finance ... Ms. Mayra NAVARRO-FIGUEROA
13 Director Information Systems . Ms. Barbara LANDRAU-ESPINOSA
105 Director Web Services ... Mr. Orlando ORENGO-ORTEGA
19 Director Security/Safety ... Mr. Victor RODRÍGUEZ-FIGUEROA
41 Athletic Director ... Mr. Gerardo BATISTA-SANTIAGO
43 Dir Legal Services/General Counsel ... Mr. Angel MARRERO-HERNÁNDEZ

*University of Puerto Rico-Carolina (B)

PO Box 4800, Carolina PR 00984-4800
County: San Juan FICE Identification: 030160
Unit ID: 243142
Telephone: (787) 257-0000 Carnegie Class: Bac-Diverse
FAX Number: (787) 750-7940 Calendar System: Quarter
URL: www.uprc.edu
Established: 1974 Annual Undergrad Tuition & Fees (In-State): $6,252
Enrollment: 2,580 Coed
Affiliation or Control: State IRS Status: 501(c)3
Highest Offering: Baccalaureate
Accreditation: M, ACBSP

02 Chancellor ... Dr. Jose I. MEZA
05 Int Dean of Academic Affairs ... Dr. Rafael MENDEZ
11 Int Dean Administrative Affairs ... Mr. Gregory BERMUDEZ
32 Int Dean Student Affairs ... Ms. Myrna SANCHEZ
06 Registrar ... Mrs. Ana Y. RIVERA
15 Human Resources Director ... Mrs. Sheila D. SABAT
09 Director of Planning/Inst Research ... Dra. Cristina MARTINEZ
08 Director Learning Resources Center ... Prof. Stanley PORTELA
51 Director Continuing Education ... Prof. Miguel PERÉZ
07 Admissions Director ... Mrs. Celia MENDEZ
13 Director Information Systems ... Mr. Juan CRUZ
37 Financial Aid Director ... Mr. Rafael RUIZ
22 Affirmative Action Officer ... Vacant
48 Director Graphic Arts/Advertising ... Prof. Orlando TORRES
50 Director Banking/Finance/Insurance ... Dr. George OTERO
81 Director Natural Sciences ... Dra. Karilys GONZALEZ
88 Director Secretarial Sciences ... Prof. Josefina RODRIGUEZ
83 Director Social Sciences ... Dr. Kathia WALKERS
68 Director Physical Education ... Prof. Walbert MARCANO
88 Director Auto Tech/Mech Engineering ... Dr. Jose MEZA
79 Director Humanities ... Dr. Bianca APONTE
88 Director Spanish ... Dra. Zulma PENCHI
88 Director English ... Prof. Wanda RODRIGUEZ
88 Dean Hotel Administration School ... Prof. Miguel E. PEREZ
23 Director Health Care ... Dr. Zaida DIAZ
18 Supt Operations & Maintenance ... Mr. Herman MUNIZ
41 Athletic Director ... Mr. Arcadio OCASIO
10 Director of Finance ... Mr. Victor GONZALEZ

*University of Puerto Rico at Cayey (C)

PO BOX 372230, Cayey PR 00737-2230
County: Cayey FICE Identification: 007206
Unit ID: 243151
Telephone: (787) 738-2161 Carnegie Class: Bac-A&S
FAX Number: N/A Calendar System: Semester
URL: www.cayey.upr.edu
Established: 1967 Annual Undergrad Tuition & Fees (In-State): $4,208
Enrollment: 2,984 Coed
Affiliation or Control: State IRS Status: 501(c)3
Highest Offering: Baccalaureate
Accreditation: M, ACBSP, CAEP

02 Chancellor ... Dr. Glorivee ROSARIO PEREZ
05 Acting Dean of Academic Affairs ... Prof. Irmannette TORRES-LUGO
11 Actg Dean of Administration Affairs ... Prof. Isamel QUILES
32 Acting Dean of Student Affairs ... Mr. Jesus MARTINEZ
08 Director Library ... Prof. Angel RIOS
06 Registrar ... Mrs. Daisy RAMOS
15 Director Human Resources ... Mrs. Enerida RODRIGUEZ
56 Head Extension Division ... Dr. Aurora GONZALEZ
37 Director Student Financial Aid ... Mrs. Pedro AYALA
38 Director Student Counseling ... Dr. Lino HERNANDEZ
13 Director Computer Center ... Mrs. Minerva DIAZ
45 Director Planning ... Mr. Gabriel APONTE
07 Director Admissions ... Mrs. Elsandra RIVERA
18 Director Facilities/Physical Plant ... Mr. Luis ARROYO
23 Director Health Services ... Dr. Idellisse BALBES
19 Director Security/Safety ... Mr. Luis LOPEZ
92 Director Honor Program ... Dr. Olga COLON
41 Director Athletic Program ... Mr. Ismael RAMOS
96 Director Purchasing ... Mrs. Maria CORTES
43 Director Legal Services ... Ms. Sheila DIAZ
88 Student Ombudsman ... Prof. Efrain COLON
53 Education ... Dr. Gabriel ROMAN
79 Humanities ... Dr. Walter MUCHER
83 Social Sciences ... Dr. Rosana GRAFALS
88 Hispanic Studies ... Dr. Jose PEREZ
88 English ... Dr. Nelly VAZQUEZ
81 Chemistry ... Dr. Wilfredo RESTO
65 Natural Science ... Dr. Maria DE JESUS
88 Biology ... Dr. Edwin VAZQUEZ
94 Women's Studies ... Dr. Lizandra TORRES
10 Chief Business Officer ... Ms. Glorimar ORTIZ
114 Director Budgeting ... Mrs. Maria SANTIAGO
81 Mathematics/Physics ... Dr. Jose ALONSO
50 Business Administration ... Dr. Vilma RIVERA
88 RISE Program ... Dr. Vibha BANSAL
88 Interdisciplinary Research Inst ... Ms. Vionex MARTI
88 Museum ... Mr. Jonathan BERRIOS
100 Chief of Staff ... Prof. Gladys RAMOS
101 Secretary of the Institution/Board ... Ms. Katherine VAZQUEZ
26 Chief PR/Marketing/Communications Ofcr ... Mr. Angel HOYOS
104 Director Study Abroad ... Ms. Elsandra RIVERA
105 Director Web Services ... Vacant
28 Director of Cultural Activities ... Mr. Eleric RIVERA
88 Dir of Preschool Development ... Dr. Carmen BERRIOS
108 Dir Institutional Assessment/Rsrch ... Dr. Xiomara SANTIAGO
22 Dir Affirm Action/Equal Opportunity ... Mrs. Kiara DE JESUS

*University of Puerto Rico-Humacao (D)

Call Box 860, Humacao PR 00792
County: Humacao FICE Identification: 003943
Unit ID: 243179
Telephone: (787) 850-0000 Carnegie Class: Bac-Diverse
FAX Number: (787) 852-4638 Calendar System: Semester
URL: www.uprh.edu
Established: 1962 Annual Undergrad Tuition & Fees (In-State): $4,208
Enrollment: 3,106 Coed
Affiliation or Control: State IRS Status: 501(c)3
Highest Offering: Baccalaureate
Accreditation: M, ACBSP, JOUR, NUR, #PTAA, SW

02 Chancellor ... Dr. Aida I. RODRIGUEZ ROIG
05 Dean of Academic Affairs ... Dr. Hector L. AYALA
11 Dean Administrative Affairs ... Mrs. Mariolga ROTGER
04 Assistant to the Chancellor ... Dr. Gelitza FALERO
04 Assistant to the Chancellor ... Dr. Maria L. CANDELARIA
32 Dean of Student Affairs ... Dr. Ivelisse BLASINI
20 Associate Dean Academic Affairs ... Dr. Deborah E. NIEVES
45 Director Planning Office ... Prof. Ivette IRIZARRY
06 Registrar ... Mrs. Carmen B. RODRIGUEZ
07 Director of Admissions ... Mrs. Carmen RIVERA
08 Director of the Library ... Prof. Evelyn RODRIGUEZ
13 Director System Info Ofc ... Mr. Hiram ORTIZ
15 Director Human Resources ... Mrs. Elsa SANTOS
10 Director of Finance ... Mrs. Ines SANCHEZ
37 Director Financial Aid ... Mr. Hector REYES
38 Director Counseling Office ... Dr. Magaly RODRIGUEZ
51 Dir Continuing Education/Extension ... Dr. Lilliam MORALES
23 Director Health Services ... Vacant
18 Chief Facilities/Physical Plant ... Mrs. Sandra CARRADERO
19 Director Security/Transit ... Mr. Julio VELAZQUEZ
41 Athletic Activities Director ... Mr. Elmer WILLIAMS
114 Director of Budget Office ... Mrs. Daisy RIVERA
108 Office of Institutional Assessment ... Dr. Mildred CUADRADO
101 Sec of Academic Senate/Adm Board ... Prof. Amelia MALDONADO
26 Press Relations ... Ms. Ingrid VAZQUEZ
50 Director Business Administration ... Prof. Aida KALIL
88 Director of Biology Dept ... Dr. Melissa COLON
88 Director of Chemistry Dept ... Dr. Tania MALAVE
60 Director of Communication Dept ... Dr. Hector PINERO
53 Director of Education Dept ... Dr. Ramon D. GARCIA BARRIOS
88 Director of English Dept ... Dr. Nilsa L. LUGO
79 Director of Humanities Dept ... Prof. Luis P. SANCHEZ LONGO
81 Director of Mathematics Dept ... Prof. Barbara I. SANTIAGO
66 Director of Nursing Dept ... Dr. Alejandro BORRERO
88 Director Occup Therapy Dept ... Prof. Madeline ORTIZ
88 Dir Office System Admin Dept ... Prof. Ivelisse REYES
76 Director Physical Therapy Dept ... Prof. Eneida SILVA
88 Director Physics & Elect Dept ... Dr. Rogerio FURLAN
83 Director Social Science Dept ... Dr. Luis R. RODRIGUEZ
70 Director of Social Work Dept ... Prof. Vanessa SANCHEZ
88 Director of Spanish Dept ... Dr. Jeandelize GONZALEZ
88 Graphics Art Supervisor ... Mr. Carlos LAZU
22 Dir Affirmative Action/EEO ... Mrs. Mariolga ROTGER
46 Dir Subsidized Research & Programs ... Dr. Daniel RODRIGUEZ HOWELL
88 Director Day Care Center ... Mrs. Maggaly POMALAZA
88 Student Support Service Director ... Prof. Olga L. BERRIOS
88 Upward Bound Director ... Mrs. Myriam CINTRON
88 Director of ExTgesis Journal ... Dr. Carlos R. GOMEZ
46 Assoc Dean Research & Tech .. Dr. Daniel RODRIGUEZ HOWELL
21 Director of Accounting Office ... Mrs. Wanda FLORES

*University of Puerto Rico-Mayaguez Campus (E)

Call Box 9000, Mayaguez PR 00681-9000
County: Mayaguez FICE Identification: 003944
Unit ID: 243197
Telephone: (787) 832-4040 Carnegie Class: Masters/L
FAX Number: (787) 834-3031 Calendar System: Semester
URL: www.uprm.edu
Established: 1911 Annual Undergrad Tuition & Fees (In-State): $4,168
Enrollment: 12,825 Coed
Affiliation or Control: State IRS Status: 501(c)3
Highest Offering: Doctorate
Accreditation: M, ACBSP, CAEP, NUR

02 Chancellor ... Dr. Agustin RULLAN TORO
05 Dean of Academic Affairs ... Dr. Betsy MORALES
11 Dean of Administration ... Dr. Omar I. MOLINA BAS
32 Dean of Students ... Dr. Jonathan MUNOZ BARRETO
49 Dean of Arts & Sciences ... Dr. Fernando GILBES SANTAELLA
54 Dean of Engineering ... Dr. Bienvenido VELEZ RIVERA
47 Dean Agricultural Sciences ... Dr. Raul E. MACCHIAVELLI
50 Dean Business Administration ... Dr. Maria AMADOR DUMOIS

*University of Puerto Rico-Medical Sciences Campus (F)

PO Box 365067, San Juan PR 00936-5067
County: San Juan FICE Identification: 024600
Unit ID: 243203
Telephone: (787) 758-2525 Carnegie Class: Spec-4-yr-Med
FAX Number: (787) 758-2556 Calendar System: Other
URL: www.rcm.upr.edu
Established: 1950 Annual Undergrad Tuition & Fees (In-State): N/A
Enrollment: 2,218 Coed
Affiliation or Control: State IRS Status: 501(c)3
Highest Offering: Doctorate
Accreditation: M, ANEST, AUD, CAHIIM, CYTO, DA, DENT, DIETI, HSA, MED, MT, NMT, NURSE, OT, PH, PHAR, PTA, #RAD, SP

02 Chancellor ... Dr. Segundo RODRIGUEZ
05 Dean Academic Affairs ... Dr. Jose HAWAYEK
32 Dean Students Affairs ... Dr. Maria M. HERNANDEZ
11 Dean of Administration ... Mr. Manuel COLON
63 Dean School of Medicine ... Dr. Agustin RODRIGUEZ
52 Dean School of Dental Medicine ... Dr. Jose MATOS
69 Dean Grad School Public Health ... Dr. Dharma VAZQUEZ
67 Dean School of Pharmacy ... Dr. Wanda MALDONADO
76 Dean School of Health Professions ... Dr. Barbara SEGARRA
66 Dean School of Nursing ... Dr. Suane SANCHEZ
100 Chief of Staff ... Dr. Ramon F. GONZALEZ
20 Associate Academic Officer ... Dr. Jose CAPRILES
13 Ctr Informatics/Technology Director ... Mr. Francisco PEREZ
43 Director Legal Services ... Ms. Cristina PARES
26 Chief Information Officer ... Ms. Vivian VAZQUEZ

06 Registrar ... Mr. Abelardo MARTINEZ
08 Library Director ... Dr. Carmen M. SANTOS
09 Director Inst & Academic Research ... Dr. Wanda BARRETO
24 Director Educational Media ... Vacant
35 Assoc Dean Student Affairs ... Dr. Blanca AMOROS
07 Director of Admissions ... Mrs. Maribel ORTIZ
38 Director of Student Counseling ... Prof. Blanca AMOROS
37 Director of Student Financial Aid ... Mrs. Yolanda RIVERA
10 Chief Financial Officer ... Ms. Yolanda QUINONES
15 Director Personnel Services ... Mr. Manuel CARDONA
18 Chief Facilities/Physical Plant ... Mr. Julio A. COLLAZO
96 Director of Purchasing ... Mr. Miguel BOBE
19 Director Security Office ... Mr. William FIGUEROA
108 Director Institutional Assessment ... Dr. Jose CAPRILES
25 Chief Contracts/Grants Admin ... Ms. Lysette BARRERAS

*University of Puerto Rico at Ponce (A)

PO Box 7186, Ponce PR 00732-7186
County: Ponce FICE Identification: 009652
Unit ID: 243212
Telephone: (787) 844-8181 Carnegie Class: Bac-A&S
FAX Number: N/A Calendar System: Semester
URL: www.uprp.edu
Established: 1970 Annual Undergrad Tuition & Fees (In-State): $4,198
Enrollment: 2,382 Coed
Affiliation or Control: State IRS Status: 501(c)3
Highest Offering: Baccalaureate
Accreditation: M, ACBSP, CAEP, #PTAA

02 Chancellor ... Dr. Tessie H. CRUZ RIVERA
04 Assistant to the Chancellor ... Prof. Carmen A. BRACERO
05 Interim Dean Academic Affairs ... Dr. Federico IRIZARRY
11 Dean Administrative Affairs ... Mr. Isaac COLON
32 Dean Student Affairs ... Prof. Carlos H. PAGAN
20 Associate Academic Dean ... Dr. Joahana RAMOS
45 Dir Inst Research/Planning Officer ... Dr. Diana LOPEZ
08 Director Library ... Prof. Jose OLIVERAS
06 Registrar ... Mrs. Marya Z. SANTIAGO
38 Director of Student Counseling ... Dr. Efrain RIOS
07 Director of Admissions ... Mrs. Emily MATOS
37 Director of Financial Aid ... Mrs. Vanessa VELEZ
15 Director of Personnel Services ... Dr. Ericka RODRIGUEZ
13 Director of Computer Center ... Mrs. Damarys HERNANDEZ
18 Chief Facilities/Physical Plant ... Mr. Alberto GARCIA
40 Director Bookstore ... Vacant
41 Athletic Director ... Mr. Anibal MONTES
23 Director Health Services ... Dr. Yiselle LOPEZ
29 Director Alumni Relations ... Mrs. Joanne E. VALLS
30 Chief Development ... Vacant
19 Director of Security/Traffic ... Mr. German PIMENTEL
88 Coordinator Security/Safety ... Mrs. Celia GONZALEZ
22 Coordinator Affirmative Action ... Dr. Yesenia QUINONES
10 Chief Financial/Business Officer ... Mr. Arturo ALMODOVAR
43 Director Legal Services ... Mr. Gaddiel MORALES
90 Director Academic Computing ... Mr. Edward GRACIA
96 Director of Purchasing ... Mr. Richard GUZMAN

*University of Puerto Rico-Rio Piedras Campus (B)

10 Ave Universidad, Ste 1001, San Juan PR 00925-2530
County: San Juan FICE Identification: 007108
Unit ID: 243221
Telephone: (787) 763-7099 Carnegie Class: DU-Higher
FAX Number: (787) 764-8799 Calendar System: Semester
URL: www.uprrp.edu
Established: 1903 Annual Undergrad Tuition & Fees (In-State): $4,198
Enrollment: 13,892 Coed
Affiliation or Control: State IRS Status: 501(c)3
Highest Offering: Doctorate
Accreditation: M, ACBSP, CACREP, CAEP, CLPSY, DIETD, JOUR, LAW, LIB, PLNG, SPAA, SW

02 Chancellor ... Dr. Luis A. FERRAO DELGADO
05 Dean Academic Affairs ... Prof. Leticia FERNÁNDEZ MORAL
11 Dean of Administration ... Mrs. Aurora M. SOTOGRAS SALDANA
32 Dean of Students ... Dr. Gloria DÍAZ URBINA
20 Associate Dean Academic Affairs ... Dr. Clarisa CRUZ LUGO
50 Dean Business Administration ... Dr. Myrna LOPEZ DE PINTO
48 Dean of Architecture ... Arq. Mayra JIMÉNEZ MONTANO
81 Dean of Natural Sciences ... Dr. Néstor CARBALLEIRA
83 Dean of Social Sciences ... Dr. Angélica VARELA LLAVONA
61 Dean of Law ... Dr. Vivian NEPTUNE RIVERA
97 Dean of General Studies ... Dr. Carlos SANCHEZ ZAMBRANA
79 Dean of Humanities ... Dr. Agnes BOSCH IRIZARRY
58 Dean Graduate Studies/Research ... Dr. Carlos I. GONZÁLEZ VARGAS
53 Dean of Education ... Dr. Mayra CHARRIEZ CORDERO
35 Asst Dean Student Affairs ... Dr. Marilu PEREZ HERNÁNDEZ
38 Director of Student Counseling ... Dr. María JIMÉNEZ CHAFEY
30 Dean Aux Devel & Alumni Relations ... Mrs. Sandra SANCHEZ GONZÁLEZ
06 Registrar ... Mr. Juan M. APONTE HERNÁNDEZ
08 Director of Library System ... Dr. Noraida DOMÍNGUEZ FLORES
15 Director of Human Resources ... Ms. Nydza IRIZARRY ALGARÍN
07 Director of Admissions ... Dr. Jessica A. MORALES TORRES
13 Director of Computer Center ... Mrs. Zulyn RODRÍGUEZ REYES
62 Director Grad Sch Library/Info Sci ... Dr. Noraida DOMÍNGUEZ FLORES
60 Director School of Communication ... Dr. Haydee SEIJO MALDONADO
58 Dir Graduate Sch of Planning ... Dr. Norma PEÑA RIVERA
51 Dir Continuing Educ/Extension ... Dr. Josué HERNÁNDEZ ÁLVAREZ
09 Director of Institutional Research ... Dr. Isabel MONTANEZ
18 Chief Planning/Physical Devel Ofc .. Mr. Ramón BAYÓN TORRES
26 Chief Public Relations Officer ... Mr. Mario ALEGRE
37 Director of Student Financial Aid ... Mr. Anibal ALVALLE
96 Director of Purchasing ... Mrs. Anaisa LOPEZ CEDRÉS
19 Director Security/Safety ... Mr. Victor ROSARIO DELGADO
10 Chief Financial/Business Officer ... Mr. Basilio RIVERA
102 Director Foundation/Corporate Rels ... Dr. Carmen RUIZ DE FIISCHLER
105 Director Web Services ... Mr. Jose V. CAMACHO LÓPEZ
22 Director Affirm Action/Equal Opp ... Mrs. Gabriela MEDINA
28 Director of Diversity ... Ms. Edith GONZÁLEZ MILLÁN
29 Director Alumni Affairs ... Arq. Luis IRIZARRY RAMÍREZ
39 Dir Resident Life/Student Housing ... Arq. Darwin J. MARRERO CARRER
41 Athletic Director ... Mr. Freddy RAMOS
43 Director Legal Services ... Ms. Lourdes C. RODRÍGUEZ PÉREZ

*University of Puerto Rico at Utuado (C)

PO Box 2500, Utuado PR 00641-2500
County: Utuado FICE Identification: 029384
Unit ID: 243188
Telephone: (787) 894-2828 Carnegie Class: Bac/Assoc-Mixed
FAX Number: (787) 894-1081 Calendar System: Semester
URL: www.uprutuado.edu
Established: 1979 Annual Undergrad Tuition & Fees (In-State): $4,168
Enrollment: 554 Coed
Affiliation or Control: State IRS Status: 501(c)3
Highest Offering: Baccalaureate
Accreditation: M, ACBSP

02 Chancellor ... Dr. Luis A. TAPIA MALDONADO
05 Academic Dean ... Dr. Ana M. ARCE
10 Chief Business Officer ... Dr. Luis E. ORTIZ
32 Chief Student Life Officer ... Dr. Jessica ROMERO
08 Library Director ... Prof. Catalina SOTO
09 Director Institutional Research ... Dr. Javier LUGO
06 Registrar ... Mrs. Lilliam Y. MALDONADO
07 Director of Admission ... Mrs. Maria V. ROBLES
15 Director Human Resources ... Mrs. Zoila GONZALEZ
38 Director Student Counseling ... Dr. Victor M. HERNANDEZ
37 Director Student Financial Aid ... Mrs. Eltie PEREZ
13 Director Information Systems ... Mr. Juan MARTINEZ
19 Director Security/Safety ... Vacant
41 Director of Athletics ... Vacant
47 Director of Agriculture ... Prof. Luis E. DIAZ
50 Dir Office Systems/Business Admin ... Dr. Frank RIVAS
96 Director of Purchasing ... Ms. Luz E. MARTINEZ
51 Director Continuing Education ... Mrs. Livette REYES
65 Director Natural Sciences ... Vacant
79 Director Humanities/Spanish/English ... Dr. Deyka OTERO

University of the Sacred Heart (D)

PO Box 12383, San Juan PR 00914-8505
County: San Juan FICE Identification: 003937
Unit ID: 243443
Telephone: (787) 728-1515 Carnegie Class: Masters/M
FAX Number: (787) 728-1692 Calendar System: Semester
URL: www.sagrado.edu
Established: 1935 Annual Undergrad Tuition & Fees: $6,000
Enrollment: 4,501 Coed
Affiliation or Control: Roman Catholic IRS Status: 501(c)3
Highest Offering: Master's
Accreditation: M, CAEPN, NURSE, SW

01 President ... Gilberto MARXUACH-TORROS
04 Admin Assistant to the President ... Gloriana YDRACH
05 Provost ... María T. MARTÍNEZ
06 Registrar ... Eigna DE JESÚS
07 Director of Admissions ... Katherine CASTILLO
10 Chief Financial/Business Officer ... Rosana LOPEZ
13 Chief Info Technology Officer (CIO) ... Luis GOTELLI
15 Chief Human Resources Officer ... Marilyn FIGUEROA
32 Chief Student Affairs Officer ... Sara TOLOSA
37 Director Student Financial Aid ... Luis VELEZ
39 Dir Resident Life/Student Housing ... Carlos MOLL
41 Athletic Director ... Maria E. BATISTA
43 Director Legal Services ... Camelia FERNÁNDEZ
50 Dean of Business ... Javier HERNÁNDEZ

VIRGIN ISLANDS

University of the Virgin Islands (E)

#2 John Brewers Bay, Saint Thomas VI 00802-9990
FICE Identification: 003946
Unit ID: 243665
Telephone: (340) 776-9200 Carnegie Class: Bac-Diverse
FAX Number: (340) 693-1005 Calendar System: Semester
URL: www.uvi.edu
Established: 1962 Annual Undergrad Tuition & Fees (In-State): $5,235
Enrollment: 1,838 Coed
Affiliation or Control: State IRS Status: 501(c)3
Highest Offering: Doctorate
Accreditation: M, ACBSP, CAEPN, NUR, @SW

01 President ... Dr. David HALL
88 VP Business Development/Innovation ... Dr. Haldane DAVIES
04 Director of Presidential Operations ... Ms. Una DYER
101 Board Liaison ... Ms. Gail T. STEELE
05 Provost/VP of Academic Affairs ... Dr. Camille A. MCKAYLE
46 Interim Vice Provost/ECC/RPS ... Dr. Frank MILLS
53 Dean School of Education ... Dr. Karen H. BROWN
81 Int Dean College of Science/Math ... Dr. Michele PETERSON
50 Dean School of Business ... Dr. Kendra L. HARRIS
49 Dean Col Liberal Arts/Social Sci ... Dr. Kimarie ENGERMAN
66 Dean School of Nursing ... Ms. Beverley A. LANSIQUOT
104 Assoc Provost Grad/Global Acad Affs . Dr. James S. MADDIRALA
84 VP Access/Enroll Services ... Mr. David WUINEE
07 Coordinator Enrollment Services ... Ms. Charmaine I. SMITH
06 Registrar ... Ms. Monifa J. POTTER
37 Director of Financial Aid ... Ms. Cheryl A. ROBERTS
32 Dean of Students-STT Campus ... Ms. Verna J. RIVERS
36 Director Counseling/Career Services ... Ms. Patricia TOWAL
111 VP Institutional Advancement ... Mr. Mitchell NEAVES
44 Director of Annual Giving ... Vacant
30 Capital Campaign Manager ... Mr. Jose Raul CARRILLO
10 VP Administration & Finance ... Ms. Shirley L. LAKE-KING
21 Acting Controller ... Ms. Stacey CHADOS
15 Director of HR/Org Development ... Mr. Charles Ronald MEEK
19 Chief Campus Police/Security ... Mr. Theodore E. GLASFORD
18 Director of Physical Plant ... Mr. Charles MARTIN
13 VP Info Services/Inst Assessment ... Ms. Sharlene J. HARRIS
08 Library Manager ... Mrs. Celia P. PRINCE-RICHARD
32 Dean of Students-STC Campus .. Ms. Hedda T. FINCH-SIMPSON

University of the Virgin Islands-St. Croix (F)

RR1, Box 10,000, Kingshill VI 00850-9781
Telephone: (340) 778-1620 Identification: 770173
Accreditation: &M

Index of Key Administrators

A

AABERG, Audun 701-654-1000 32 A
AABERGE, Nancy 406-874-6161 263 H aabergen@milescc.edu
AADLAND, Susan, R 605-394-6884 416 H susan.aadland@sdsmt.edu
AALDERINK, Leah 616-732-1079 223 E leah.aalderink@davenport.edu
AAMODT, Jennifer 701-777-3000 345 B jennifer.aamodt@und.edu
AAMOT, Chris 505-984-6114 202 A chris.aamot@sjc.edu
AANENSON, Erin 507-389-7342 241 C erin.aanenson@southcentral.edu
AARON, Belinda 303-797-5711 77 I belinda.aaron@arapahoe.edu
AARON, Charlene, S 217-525-5628 149 C charlene.aaron@sjcs.edu
AARON, Cheryl 617-989-4159 219 F aaronc@wit.edu
AARON, Fredona 540-857-6053 475 G faaron@virginiawestern.edu
AARON, Kathy 478-275-6589 123 I
AASEN, Curtis, K 757-822-1070 475 E caasen@tcc.edu
ABADIE, Bonnie 210-341-1366 440 H babadie@ost.edu
ABADINSKY, Alisa 301-405-9001 202 H aabadins@umd.edu
ABAJIAN, Megan 972-860-4731 434 F mabajian@dcccd.edu
ABALOS, Victor 213-615-7270 36 E vabalos@thechicagoschool.edu
ABASOLO, Guillermo 619-216-6614 66 A gabasolo@swccd.edu
ABATE, Alexis 215-780-1284 398 B aabate@salus.edu
ABATE, Kathy 903-813-2431 430 H kabate@austincollege.edu
ABAUNZA, George 845-569-3203 307 D george.abaunza@msmc.edu
ABBA, Crystal 775-784-4901 270 J cabba@nshe.nevada.edu
ABBAS, Loni 319-352-8634 170 J loni.abbas@wartburg.edu
ABBASSI, Pouria 310-825-8011 69 E pabbassi@asucla.ucla.edu
ABBATE, Anthony 505-820-6868 288 F abbate@acupuncturecollege.edu
ABBATE, Salavatore 707-864-7000 64 H salvatore.abbate@solano.edu
ABBATE, Skya 505-820-6868 288 F skya@acupuncturecollege.edu
ABBEY, Craig, W 716-645-2791 316 C cwabbey@buffalo.edu
ABBEY, Megan 509-359-4858 479 G mabbey@ewu.edu
ABBOTT, Amy 850-478-8496 105 G info@pcci.edu
ABBOTT, Cameron 916-660-7110 64 D cabbott@sierracollege.edu
ABBOTT, Catherine 760-862-1324 38 E cabbott@collegeofthedesert.edu
ABBOTT, Charlene, R 337-475-5977 192 E cabbott@mcneese.edu
ABBOTT, Jill, M 218-299-3654 235 H jabbott@cord.edu
ABBOTT, Jim 405-208-5301 367 E jabbott@okcu.edu
ABBOTT, Judy, A 936-468-2901 445 E abbottj@sfasu.edu
ABBOTT, Larry 606-451-6671 182 G larry.abbott@kctcs.edu
ABBOTT, Linda 727-864-7840 98 J abbottlt@eckerd.edu
ABBOTT, Paula 308-254-7404 270 C abbottp@wncc.edu
ABBOTT, Rachel 229-931-2145 120 D rachel.abbott@gsw.edu
ABBOTT, Shawn, L 215-204-4133 399 B shawn.abbott@temple.edu
ABBOUSHI, Fahmi 937-376-6398 349 J fabboushi@centralstate.edu
ABBY, Dean 617-332-3666 220 C dean_abby@williamjames.edu
ABD EL-FATAH, Samir Shahat 208-885-7208 132 F samir@uidaho.edu
ABD-EL-KHALICK, Fouad 919-966-1356 342 C fouad@unc.edu
ABDALLAH, Chaouki 404-894-8885 119 E ctabdallah@gatech.edu
ABDEL, Maria 305-474-6950 107 F mabdel@stu.edu
ABDELKARIM, Shehadeh 216-987-4899 351 E shehadeh.abdelkarim@tri-c.edu
ABDELMAGEED, Ahmed 860-231-5451 90 A aabdelmageed@usj.edu
ABDELRAHMAN, Mohamed 719-549-2090 80 B mohamed.abdelrahman@csupueblo.edu
ABDOW, David 781-239-6015 206 B dabdow@babson.edu
ABDULLAH, Jamar 610-359-5310 382 A jabdullah@follett.com
ABDULLAH, Makola, M 804-524-5070 476 D president@vsu.edu
ABDULLAH, Shakeer 678-466-5433 117 D shakeerabdullah@clayton.edu
ABDULLAT, Amjad, A 806-651-2528 448 B aabdullat@wtamu.edu
ABDY, Joseph 563-588-8000 166 C jabdy@emmaus.edu
ABE, Christopher 805-437-3616 30 C christopher.abe@csuci.edu
ABE, Jennifer 310-338-7598 51 A jennifer.abe@lmu.edu
ABEAR, Lichele 631-687-5158 314 A labear@sjcny.edu
ABEBE, Daniel 773-702-7857 151 E dabebe@uchicago.edu
ABECASSIS, Michael 520-626-0998 16 D mabecassis@arizona.edu
ABEL, Charles 734-457-6007 228 C cabel@monroeccc.edu
ABEL, Dianna, K 801-626-6406 461 A diannaabel@weber.edu
ABEL, John, C 731-881-7526 427 D jabel@utm.edu
ABEL, Kevin 251-380-3024 6 H kabel@shc.edu
ABEL, Marc 847-578-3236 148 F marc.abel@rosalindfranklin.edu
ABEL, Rebecca 304-724-5000 487 B rabel@cdu.edu
ABEL, JR., Robert 213-252-5100 23 K rabeljr@alu.edu
ABEL, Sean 805-922-6966 24 I sean.abel@hancockcollege.edu
ABEL, Susan 513-745-3334 364 G abel@xavier.edu
ABELA, Andrew, V 202-319-5290 92 A abela@cua.edu
ABELL, Anthony 727-376-6911 112 G anthony.abell@trinitycollege.edu
ABELL, Carol 320-363-5511 243 B abell@csbsju.edu
ABELL, Debbie 618-453-5751 150 B kohley@siu.edu
ABELL, Donna 270-686-4575 182 F donna.abell@kctcs.edu
ABELL, Jane 760-366-5280 40 E jabell@cmccd.edu
ABELL, Jason 612-455-3420 234 E jason.abell@bcsmn.edu
ABELL, Julie, A 972-721-5000 452 B jabell@udallas.edu
ABELL, Russ 718-636-3684 311 F rabell@pratt.edu
ABELL, Stacey 319-208-5015 170 D sabell@scciowa.edu
ABELL, Tracey 503-244-0726 371 E traceyabell@achs.edu
ABELMANN, Ruth, E 603-862-2268 274 F ruth.abelmann@unh.edu
ABELS, Arnold 816-235-1218 261 B abelsa@umkc.edu
ABELS, Dianne 309-796-5394 133 G abelsd@bhc.edu
ABELSON, Clifford 978-681-0800 216 C abelson@mslaw.edu
ABERCROMBIE, Adam 214-648-3606 457 A adam.abercrombie@utsouthwestern.edu
ABERCROMBIE, Ai Co 508-854-4354 215 F aabercrombie@qcc.mass.edu
ABERCROMBIE, Barbara 918-631-2616 371 C barbara-abercrombie@utulsa.edu
ABERCROMBIE, Neil, N 435-797-0258 460 C neil.abercrombie@usu.edu
ABERLE-CANNATA, Denise 208-562-3218 131 E denisecannata@cwi.edu
ABERMAN, Jonathan 703-284-5910 468 H jonathan.aberman@marymount.edu
ABERNATHY, Allison 704-922-6486 334 G abernathy.allison@gaston.edu
ABERNATHY, Cammy 352-392-6000 111 A caber@ufl.edu
ABERNATHY, JaNan 870-733-6830 17 F jmabernathy@asumidsouth.edu
ABERNATHY, Jeff 989-463-7146 221 B abernathyj@alma.edu
ABERNATHY, Kat 719-549-2256 80 B kat.abernathy@csupueblo.edu
ABERNATHY, Robert 970-339-6363 77 H robert.abernathy@aims.edu
ABERNETHY, Alexis 626-584-5205 43 B aabernet@fuller.edu
ABESAMIS, Naomi 714-992-7096 54 C nabesamis@fullcoll.edu
ABEYIE, Nana 212-650-6899 293 D nana@ccny.cuny.edu
ABEYTA, Amy 205-226-4922 4 F arbicker@bsc.edu
ABEZETIAN, Garrick 708-456-0300 151 D garrickabezetian@triton.edu
ABI-NADER DAHLBERG, Teresa 817-257-4343 448 F t.dahlberg@tcu.edu
ABLESER, Judith 248-370-2455 229 I ableser@oakland.edu
ABNER, Patrice 904-256-7571 102 H pabner@ju.edu
ABNEY, Anthony 920-693-1838 498 H anthony.abney@gotoltc.edu
ABO, Joel, C 386-312-4063 107 C joelabo@sjrstate.edu
ABORDONADO, Valentina 808-543-1143 128 G vabordonado@hpu.edu
ABORDONADO, Valentina 808-544-1143 128 G vabordonado@hpu.edu
ABORN, Kerrie 617-333-2294 208 G kaborn0315@curry.edu
ABOTSI, Zolicia 646-312-2211 292 L zolicia.abotsi@baruch.cuny.edu
ABOU-EL-KHEIR, Jasmine 773-896-2400 134 L yasmine.abou-el-kheir@ctschicago.edu
ABOUDENEIN, Baz 864-597-4000 414 E baz@wofford.edu
ABOUELENEIN, Baz 800-955-2527 174 C baz@grantham.edu
ABOUFADEL, Edward 616-331-2400 224 G aboufade@gvsu.edu
ABOUFADEL, Kathy 616-451-3511 223 E kaboufadel@davenport.edu
ABOUFARES, Moe 909-580-9661 34 D
ABOUSAMRA, Haifa 605-658-6500 416 D haifa.abousamra@usd.edu
ABOWD, Gregory 617-373-5847 217 I
ABPLANALP, John (Mike) 570-484-2525 394 E jabplana@lockhaven.edu
ABRAHAM, Angela 617-266-2030 217 D abrahama@neco.edu
ABRAHAM, Angeles 310-287-4399 49 H abrahaa@wlac.edu
ABRAHAM, Diane 909-706-3548 75 I dabraham@westernu.edu
ABRAHAM, Doug 303-724-2000 84 D doug.abraham@ucdenver.edu
ABRAHAM, Faustina 417-625-9389 256 F abraham-f@mssu.edu
ABRAHAM, Jyoti 918-688-2444 365 C abrahamj@bacone.edu
ABRAHAM, Margaret 516-463-5400 301 G margaret.abraham@hofstra.edu
ABRAHAM, Martin 309-298-1066 153 A ma-abraham@wiu.edu
ABRAHAM, Raymond 318-678-6000 187 H rabraham@bpcc.edu
ABRAHAM, Renjy 503-255-0332 374 C renjyabraham@multnomah.edu
ABRAHAM, Shondra, F 803-536-7013 411 G sabraham@scsu.edu
ABRAHAM, Susan 510-849-8209 55 G sabraham@psr.edu
ABRAHAM, Thea 314-392-2231 256 E abrahamt@mobap.edu
ABRAHAM, Tracie, A 225-771-3590 191 B tracie_abraham@subr.edu
ABRAHAM, Tracie, A 225-771-3590 191 A tracie_abraham@subr.edu
ABRAHAMSON, April 701-228-5437 346 B april.abrahamson@dakotacollege.edu
ABRAHAMSON, David, P 414-277-7173 494 D abrahams@msoe.edu
ABRAJANO, Barbara 312-939-0111 137 D babrajano@eastwest.edu
ABRAJANO, Marisa, A 858-534-7201 70 C mabrajano@ucsd.edu
ABRAM, Bobbi 626-585-7054 56 D blabram@pasadena.edu
ABRAMOVITZ, Todd 443-412-2291 199 D tabramovitz@harford.edu
ABRAMOVSKY, Aviva 716-645-2052 316 C law-deans@buffalo.edu
ABRAMS, Andrea, C 859-238-5267 180 B andrea.abrams@centre.edu
ABRAMS, Chris 419-448-2062 353 E cabrams@heidelberg.edu
ABRAMS, Elizabeth 831-459-2246 71 A esabrams@ucsc.edu
ABRAMS, Jacob, R 304-367-4798 489 K jabrams1@fairmontstate.edu
ABRAMS, Jhanay 203-576-2433 89 C jabrams@bridgeport.edu
ABRAMS, Kerry 919-613-7001 328 F abrams@law.duke.edu
ABRAMS, Laura 718-997-5541 295 B laura.abrams@qc.cuny.edu
ABRAMS KONIG, Aliza 646-592-4486 326 D aabrams@yu.edu
ABRAMSON, Alexis, R 603-646-2238 273 D alexis.r.abramson@dartmouth.edu
ABRAMSON, Diane 207-741-5568 195 H dabramson@smccme.edu
ABRAMSON, Henry 718-252-7800 322 F henry.abramson@touro.edu
ABRAMSON, Henry 718-252-7800 322 G henry.abramson@touro.edu
ABRAMSON, Jared 202-994-1000 92 D jabramson@gwu.edu

ABRAMSON, Nancy .... 212-678-8036 303 D
naabramson@jtsa.edu
ABREGANO, Laurie .... 808-675-3487 128 D
laurie.abregano@byuh.edu
ABREGO, Joshua .... 209-476-7840.. 67 E
jabrego@clc.edu
ABRESCY, Chris .... 209-228-2586.. 70 A
cabrescy@ucmerced.edu
ABREU, Carlos, F .... 787-743-3038 509 N
cabreu@sanjuanbautista.edu
ABREU, Katie .... 410-334-2904 205 D
kabreu@worwic.edu
ABREU, Melina .... 407-708-2729 108 D
abreum@seminolestate.edu
ABREU, Sara .... 787-878-5475 507 L
sabreu@arecibo.inter.edu
ABREU-HERNANDEZ,
Viviana .... 508-854-4380 215 F
vabreu@qcc.mass.edu
ABREU-HORBOSTEL,
Esmilda .... 718-862-7352 304 M
eabreuhornbostel01@manhattan.edu
ABREU-HORNBOSTEL,
Esmilda .... 718-862-8000 304 M
eabreuhornbostel01@manhattan.edu
ABROMAITIS, James ..... 203-773-8578.. 85 D
jabromaitis@albertus.edu
ABRON, Gisele .... 903-566-7057 456 A
gabron@uttyler.edu
ABSAR, Quaiser .... 540-665-4937 470 G
qabsar@su.edu
ABSHER, Beverly .... 731-661-5363 426 F
babsher@uu.edu
ABSHIRE, Aimee .... 337-482-5519 193 B
aimee.abshire@louisiana.edu
ABSHIRE, Allen .... 606-218-5940 186 B
allenabshire@upike.edu
ABSHIRE, Elaine .... 979-209-7547 431 H
eabshire@blinn.edu
ABSHIRE, Martha Ann .. 225-490-1685 187 B
martha.abshire@franu.edu
ABSTON, Byron .... 205-391-2388.... 3 E
babston@sheltonstate.edu
ABSTON, Kara .... 501-279-4332.. 19 C
kabston@harding.edu
ABTS, Polly .... 920-693-1221 498 H
polly.abts@gotoltc.edu
ABUHAMAD, Alfred, Z .. 757-446-5800 466 D
abuhamaz@evms.edu
ABUSALIM, Murad .... 956-295-3568 449 C
murad.abusalim@tsc.edu
ABUSHABAN, Sahar ...... 619-644-7575.. 44 C
sahar.abushaban@gcccd.edu
ABUTIN, Albert .... 714-992-7076.. 54 C
aabutin@fullcoll.edu
ACAMPORA, Christa, D 404-712-1238 118 E
christa.d.acampora@emory.edu
ACARDO, John .... 608-785-8697 496 A
jacardo@uwlax.edu
ACCAPADI, Mamta .... 215-898-6081 400 F
accapadi@upenn.edu
ACCARDI, Christen .... 585-785-1231 299 F
christen.accardi@flcc.edu
ACCARDI, Jon .... 315-279-5690 303 G
jaccardi@keuka.edu
ACCIARDO, Linda, A ..... 401-874-2116 405 E
lindaa@uri.edu
ACEBO, Andres .... 201-200-2440 279 D
aacebo@njcu.edu
ACEVEDO, Beatriz .... 212-924-5900 321 F
bursar@swedishinstitute.edu
ACEVEDO, Dary .... 787-891-0925 507 K
dacevedo@aguadilla.inter.edu
ACEVEDO, Francisco ..... 787-892-5700 508 F
facevedo@intersg.edu
ACEVEDO, Geidy .... 787-891-0925 507 K
geacevedo@aguadilla.inter.edu
ACEVEDO, Ivonne .... 787-891-0925 507 K
iacevedo@aguadilla.inter.edu
ACEVEDO, Mauricio ...... 818-702-1421.. 56 G
mauricio.acevedo@pepperdine.edu
ACEVEDO, Tanya .... 305-237-8888 104 E
ACEVEDO, Tony .... 512-428-1319 442 I
tonya@stedwards.edu
ACEVEDO RIOS,
Carmen, M .... 787-725-6500 505 G
cacevedo@albizu.edu
ACEVEDOS, Viones .... 787-746-1400 507 B
ACEVES, Salvador, D .... 303-458-4144.. 83 E
saceves@regis.edu
ACEY, Stacy .... 770-228-7372 125 H
stacy.acey@sctech.edu
ACHAN, Jennifer .... 661-395-4482.. 46 L
jennifer.achan@bakersfieldcollege.edu

ACHARYA, Mukul .... 908-737-3358 278 E
macharya@kean.edu
ACHARYA, Raj .... 812-856-1079 156 G
dean@soic.indiana.edu
ACHARYA, Suresh .... 269-749-7666 229 J
sacharya@olivetcollege.edu
ACHARYA, Sushil .... 412-397-6227 397 B
acharya@rmu.edu
ACHENBACH, USMS,
Gerard .... 231-995-1203 229 A
gachenbach@nmc.edu
ACHESON, Carol .... 503-253-3443 374 G
cacheson@ocom.edu
ACHEY, Becky .... 610-921-7663 377 G
bachey@albright.edu
ACHIPA, Joshua .... 405-491-6351 369 H
jachipa@snu.edu
ACHIVARE-HILL,
Rachael .... 918-595-7941 370 C
rachael.achivarehill@tulsacc.edu
ACHS, Carol .... 480-461-7742.. 13 D
carol.achs@mesacc.edu
ACHTERMAN, Douglas .. 408-848-4809.. 43 E
dachterman@gavilan.edu
ACIERNO, Lou .... 212-752-1530 304 A
lou.acierno@limcollege.edu
ACKER, Janet .... 207-326-2220 196 A
janet.acker@mma.edu
ACKER, Lorraine .... 585-395-2772 317 E
ldacker@brockport.edu
ACKER, Scott .... 806-371-5160 429 E
s0311868@actx.edu
ACKER, Shelia .... 248-341-2121 229 C
smacker@oaklandcc.edu
ACKERLEY, Roseanne ... 513-487-3234 301 B
rackerley@huc.edu
ACKERLY, David, D .... 510-642-7171.. 69 A
dackerly@berkeley.edu
ACKERMAN, Ari .... 305-944-0035 104 I
ACKERMAN, Debbie ...... 217-735-7213 142 H
dackerman@lincolncollege.edu
ACKERMAN, Denise ...... 845-758-7526 290 I
ackerman@bard.edu
ACKERMAN, James .... 417-447-2646 257 G
ackermaj@otc.edu
ACKERMAN, Kathy .... 828-395-1522 335 D
kackerman@isothermal.edu
ACKERMAN, Steven ...... 973-328-5550 276 J
sackerman@ccm.edu
ACKERMAN, Steven ...... 608-262-1044 495 D
saackerm@wisc.edu
ACKERMAN, Tom .... 352-271-2905 108 A
thomas.ackerman@sfcollege.edu
ACKERMAN-BEHR, Glen 906-932-4231 224 D
glena@gogebic.edu
ACKLEH, Azmy .... 337-482-6986 193 B
azmy.ackleh@louisiana.edu
ACKLEY, Darren .... 715-675-3331 499 F
ackley@ntc.edu
ACKLEY, Denise .... 815-965-8616 148 C
ACKLEY, Jared .... 601-318-6102 249 H
jackley@wmcarey.edu
ACKMAN, Elizabeth, R .. 315-684-6043 321 A
ackmaner@morrisville.edu
ACKMAN, Robin .... 217-786-2762 143 B
robin.ackman@llcc.edu
ACOB-NASH, Mari .... 206-934-3643 483 B
maria.acob-nash@seattlecolleges.edu
ACOLASTE, Ras .... 703-878-2800.. 93 H
ACOSTA, Araceli .... 210-924-4338 431 C
araceli.acosta@bua.edu
ACOSTA, Cesar .... 860-701-6727 503 G
steven.c.acosta@uscg.mil
ACOSTA, Claudia .... 619-482-6359.. 66 A
cacosta@swccd.edu
ACOSTA, Daniel .... 650-949-7514.. 42 G
acostadaniel@fhda.edu
ACOSTA, Esmeralda, M . 623-845-3012.. 13 C
esmeralda.acosta@gccaz.edu
ACOSTA, Kathy .... 214-860-1464 434 I
kacosta@dcccd.edu
ACOSTA, Kirsten .... 760-245-4271.. 74 D
kirsten.acosta@vvc.edu
ACOSTA, Pilar .... 407-708-2432 108 D
acostap@seminolestate.edu
ACOSTA, Sara .... 708-524-6288 137 C
sacosta@dom.edu
ACOSTA-TORO, Relon ... 787-480-2463 506 C
reacosta@sanjuan.pr
ACQUAAH, George .... 301-860-3610 204 A
gacquaah@bowiestae.edu
ACQUAH, Ken .... 718-518-4369 294 B
kacquah@hostos.cuny.edu

ACREE, Cheryl .... 229-333-2126 128 B
cheryl.acree@wiregrass.edu
ACUFF, Keith .... 660-596-7301 259 M
kacuff@sfccmo.edu
ACUNA, Angela .... 408-498-5133.. 73 B
aacuna@cogswell.edu
ACUNTO, Rob, L .... 864-833-8242 411 D
rlacunto@presby.edu
ADACHI, Lesley, B .... 680-488-2471 505 B
lesleyadachi@palau.edu
ADADE, Anthony .... 508-929-8714 213 G
aadade@worcester.edu
ADADEVOH, Vidal .... 205-929-1603.... 6 B
vadadevoh@miles.edu
ADAIR, Adam .... 870-512-7801.. 18 A
adam_adair@asun.edu
ADAIR, Charles .... 934-420-2198 320 F
charles.adair@farmingdale.edu
ADAIR, Kathy .... 906-248-3354 221 M
kadair@bmcc.edu
ADAIR, Matt .... 580-327-8418 367 A
wmadair@nwosu.edu
ADAIR, Matthew .... 952-829-2459 234 B
matt.adair@bethfel.org
ADAIR, Suzanne, C ...... 814-863-0471 391 G
sca917@psu.edu
ADAM, Sharla .... 325-942-2041 450 E
sharla.adam@angelo.edu
ADAM, Terri .... 207-974-4691 195 E
tadam@emcc.edu
ADAM, Wendy .... 413-597-2353 220 D
ga1@williams.edu
ADAMCHAK, Andrea ...... 765-658-4440 154 J
andreaadamchak@depauw.edu
ADAMCZYK, Julie, L ...... 989-837-4436 229 B
adamczyk@northwood.edu
ADAMCZYK, Stephanie . 412-392-4205 396 G
sadamczyk@pointpark.edu
ADAME, Belinda .... 847-628-2468 141 C
belinda.adame@judsonu.edu
ADAMES, Jose .... 214-860-2010 434 I
jose.adames@dcccd.edu
ADAMIEC, Larissa .... 630-829-6000 133 E
ADAMO, Clare .... 860-632-3009.. 88 C
cadamo@holyapostles.edu
ADAMO, Paul, J .... 607-436-2535 316 F
paul.adamo@oneonta.edu
ADAMS, Adam .... 712-722-6006 165 I
adam.adams@dordt.edu
ADAMS, Alex .... 559-489-2225.. 67 B
alex.adams@fresnocitycollege.edu
ADAMS, Alexandra .... 816-501-2400 250 F
alexandra.adams@avila.edu
ADAMS, Amanda .... 864-592-4276 412 E
adams@sccsc.edu
ADAMS, Amanda .... 423-354-5143 425 A
acadams@northeaststate.edu
ADAMS, Amy .... 740-389-4636 355 F
acamsa@mtc.edu
ADAMS, Angela .... 317-543-3235 159 L
ADAMS, Ann .... 312-491-2869 146 E
a-adams@northwestern.edu
ADAMS, Ann .... 360-486-8842 482 I
aadams@stmartin.edu
ADAMS, Ann Clay .... 404-687-4524 117 G
adamsa@ctsnet.edu
ADAMS, Barbara, L .... 803-536-8980 411 G
badams@scsu.edu
ADAMS, Betty .... 713-797-7000 446 C
bradams@pvamu.edu
ADAMS, Billy, W .... 903-693-2028 441 C
badams@panola.edu
ADAMS, Brad .... 865-251-1800 423 E
badams@south.edu
ADAMS, Brenda .... 501-450-1226.. 19 E
adams@hendrix.edu
ADAMS, Brett, C .... 443-352-4250 202 E
bcadams@stevenson.edu
ADAMS, Brian .... 225-771-2520 191 B
brian_adams@subr.edu
ADAMS, Bruce .... 504-286-5432 191 C
badams@suno.edu
ADAMS, Bryan .... 617-353-3635 207 E
bsadams@bu.edu
ADAMS, Carey .... 812-866-7005 155 G
adamsc@hanover.edu
ADAMS, Carol .... 678-717-2233 127 A
carol.adams@ung.edu
ADAMS, Caroline .... 805-893-3285.. 70 E
caroline.adams@ucsb.edu
ADAMS, Caroline .... 601-426-6346 249 A
cadams@southeasternbaptist.edu

ADAMS, Charles, H .... 813-974-3087 111 C
chadams@honors.usf.edu
ADAMS, Chris .... 573-840-9666 260 E
cadams@trcc.edu
ADAMS, Chris .... 503-251-5767 377 B
chadams@uws.edu
ADAMS, Colby, T .... 817-921-8714 445 A
cadams@swbts.edu
ADAMS, Dave .... 218-299-4000 235 H
ADAMS, David .... 620-331-4100 174 H
dadams@indycc.edu
ADAMS, David, J .... 513-556-5511 361 J
davidj.adams@uc.edu
ADAMS, Dean .... 270-384-8036 183 G
adamsd@lindsey.edu
ADAMS, Denise .... 530-895-2329.. 27 C
adamsde@butte.edu
ADAMS, Doug .... 217-443-8832 136 G
dadams@dacc.edu
ADAMS, Ed .... 870-633-4480.. 19 A
eadams@eacc.edu
ADAMS, Edward .... 646-312-1190 292 L
edward.adams@baruch.cuny.edu
ADAMS, Edward, E .... 801-422-8611 458 H
ed_adams@byu.edu
ADAMS, Grantley .... 860-738-6333.. 87 C
gadams@nwcc.edu
ADAMS, James .... 850-474-2080 111 F
jadams1@uwf.edu
ADAMS, James, E .... 325-942-2071 450 E
james.adams@angelo.edu
ADAMS, Jamie .... 609-984-1105 284 C
jadams@tesu.edu
ADAMS, Janieth .... 601-979-0928 246 F
janieth.f.wilson_adams@jsums.edu
ADAMS, Jann .... 404-639-0999 123 D
jann.adams@morehouse.edu
ADAMS, Jason .... 303-762-6936.. 80 I
jason.adams@denverseminary.edu
ADAMS, Jeff .... 479-788-7221.. 21 G
jeff.adams@uafs.edu
ADAMS, Jeffrey, M .... 336-841-4581 329 F
jeadams@highpoint.edu
ADAMS, Jennie .... 714-564-6433.. 58 F
adams_jennie@sac.edu
ADAMS, Jennifer .... 334-844-7326.... 4 D
jennifer.adams@auburn.edu
ADAMS, Jennifer .... 334-347-2623.... 2 A
jadams@escc.edu
ADAMS, Jennifer .... 925-473-7302.. 40 D
jadams@losmedanos.edu
ADAMS, Jennifer .... 315-792-7810 321 B
jennifer.adams@sunypoly.edu
ADAMS, Jennifer .... 517-796-8482 225 E
adamsjennifes@jccmi.edu
ADAMS, Jennifer .... 614-236-6170 349 B
jadams@capital.edu
ADAMS, Jessica .... 314-256-8801 250 D
adams@ai.edu
ADAMS, Joetta .... 870-743-3000.. 20 B
jadams@northark.edu
ADAMS, John, E .... 828-262-6432 340 I
adamsje2@appstate.edu
ADAMS, Johnnie .... 310-434-4302.. 63 C
adams_johnnie@smc.edu
ADAMS, Jordan .... 918-540-6211 366 F
jordan.m.adams@neo.edu
ADAMS, Josh .... 707-524-1731.. 63 D
jadams2@santarosa.edu
ADAMS, Joshua .... 707-524-1731.. 63 D
jadams2@santarosa.edu
ADAMS, Joshua .... 940-898-3755 451 D
jadams15@twu.edu
ADAMS, Joy .... 307-382-1832 501 J
jadams@westernwyoming.edu
ADAMS, Julie .... 423-746-5251 426 C
jadams@tnwesleyan.edu
ADAMS, Julius, G .... 716-645-1971 316 C
jgadams2@buffalo.edu
ADAMS, Karen .... 956-296-1416 455 D
karen.adams@utrgv.edu
ADAMS, Karen .... 812-856-5596 156 G
kadams@iu.edu
ADAMS, Karen, H .... 812-856-5596 156 F
kadams@iu.edu
ADAMS, Kari .... 620-276-9638 174 B
kari.adams@gcccks.edu
ADAMS, Kate .... 518-244-4594 313 A
adamsk2@sage.edu
ADAMS, Kathryn, F .... 717-337-6660 384 D
kadams@gettysburg.edu
ADAMS, Kelly, L .... 315-792-3047 324 B
kadams@utica.edu

ADAMS, Kenneth 718-482-5050 294 F presidentadams@lagcc.cuny.edu
ADAMS, Kent 620-450-2140 177 B kenta@prattcc.edu
ADAMS, Kimberly 325-942-2122 450 E kimberly.adams@angelo.edu
ADAMS, Kimberly 253-752-2020 480 D kimadams@faithseminary.edu
ADAMS, Kris 620-331-4100 174 H kadams@indycc.edu
ADAMS, L.A 914-323-5168 305 B la.adams@mville.edu
ADAMS, Landon 417-667-8181 252 B ladams@cottey.edu
ADAMS, Larry 606-368-2101 178 G larryadams@alc.edu
ADAMS, Lita 413-748-3641 218 I ladams@springfield.edu
ADAMS, Lynne, I 301-546-0500 201 E adamsil@pgcc.edu
ADAMS, Mark 936-294-1158 450 A ucs_mca@shsu.edu
ADAMS, Michael 910-893-1686 327 D adams@campbell.edu
ADAMS, Michael, J 888-777-7675 480 D mjadams@faithseminary.edu
ADAMS, Michelle 773-291-6211 135 E madams@ccc.edu
ADAMS, Natalie 918-495-6150 368 F nadams@oru.edu
ADAMS, Nathan 413-545-1043 211 G nadams@admin.umass.edu
ADAMS, Neale, J 515-574-1284 167 A adams_n@iowacentral.edu
ADAMS, Nikole 510-430-2229 52 E nhilgeman@mills.edu
ADAMS, Paul 785-628-5866 173 H padams@fhsu.edu
ADAMS, Paul, S 570-408-4114 403 A paul.adams@wilkes.edu
ADAMS, Phillip, D 504-520-5279 193 E pdadams@xula.edu
ADAMS, Rebecca 252-940-6321 332 C rebecca.adams@beaufortccc.edu
ADAMS, Robbie 434-528-5276 477 B
ADAMS, Robert 617-585-0200 207 A robert.adams@the-bac.edu
ADAMS, Robin 202-885-1000 91 F radams@american.edu
ADAMS, Rodney 843-525-8219 412 G radams@tcl.edu
ADAMS, Saketha 478-553-2080 123 H sadams@oftc.edu
ADAMS, Sally Ann 479-575-4140 21 F sally@uark.edu
ADAMS, Sandra 912-260-4416 125 D sandra.adams@sgsc.edu
ADAMS, Sarah 414-297-6595 499 C adamss4@matc.edu
ADAMS, Scott 803-754-4100 408 E
ADAMS, Shane 816-423-4703 166 E smadams@graceland.edu
ADAMS, Shawn 404-225-4005 115 H sadams@atlantatech.edu
ADAMS, Stephanie, G 972-883-2974 455 B stephanie.adams@utdallas.edu
ADAMS, Stevalynn, R 757-823-8373 469 A sadams@nsu.edu
ADAMS, Suzanna 413-572-5790 213 F scadams@westfield.ma.edu
ADAMS, Tammy 903-875-7348 440 D tammy.adams@navarrocollege.edu
ADAMS, Terri 202-806-7040 92 F tadams-fuller@howard.edu
ADAMS, Tina 912-478-7068 120 C tadams@georgiasouthern.edu
ADAMS, Tina 828-339-4269 338 B t_adams@southwesterncc.edu
ADAMS, Todd 303-871-2000 84 E
ADAMS, Tomarra 502-585-9911 184 H tadams@spalding.edu
ADAMS, Trey 901-722-3304 423 G tadams@sco.edu
ADAMS, Vic 606-589-3001 183 A vic.adams@kctcs.edu
ADAMS, Yelizaveta 914-606-6589 325 A yelizaveta.adams@sunywcc.edu
ADAMS-CURTIS, Leah 309-672-5513 144 C ladamscurtis@methodistcol.edu
ADAMS-GASTON, Javaune, M 757-823-8670 469 A president@nsu.edu
ADAMS INGRAM, Hannah 317-738-8140 155 D hadamsingram@franklincollege.edu
ADAMS-KALLOCH, Jenna 458-210-8294 376 H jadamsk@uoregon.edu
ADAMS-MATT, Christine 414-229-5673 496 B adamsmat@uwm.edu
ADAMS-PERLAC, Alison 435-797-1266 460 C alison.adams-perlac@usu.edu
ADAMS SOMERLOT, Lisa 678-839-6428 127 C ladams@westga.edu
ADAMSKI, Kathleen 509-527-4240 485 B kathleen.adamski@wwcc.edu
ADAMSON, Alyssa 657-278-2194 31 C aadamson@fullerton.edu
ADAMSON, Bonnie, J 910-630-7307 331 E adamson@methodist.edu
ADAMSON, Craig 215-416-3723 386 B craigadamson@iirp.edu
ADAMSON, Elizabeth 361-698-1297 435 G eadamson@delmar.edu
ADAMSON, Kenet 828-398-7650 332 B kenetmadamson@abtech.edu
ADAMSON, Richard 320-363-3164 243 B radamson@csbsju.edu
ADAMSON, Robin 620-252-7003 173 A adamson.robin@coffeyville.edu
ADAMSON, Steve 602-386-4103 10 F steve.adamson@arizonachristian.edu
ADAMSON, Wendy 218-855-8062 237 G wendy.adamson@clcmn.edu
ADANU, Sesime 973-720-3115 284 J adanus@wpunj.edu
ADCOCK, Jeffrey 970-330-8008 77 H
ADCOX, John 423-354-2528 425 A jmadcox@northeaststate.edu
ADCOX, Kathy, S 252-451-8274 336 E ksadcox665@nashcc.edu
ADCOX, Kenith 409-772-0650 456 E keadcox@utmb.edu
ADCOX, William 713-792-2275 456 B william.adcox@uth.tmc.edu
ADDANTE, Shylah 518-244-2008 313 A addans@sage.edu
ADDICKS, Chris, J 610-917-1423 401 G cjaddicks@valleyforge.edu
ADDINGTON, Eric, J 218-299-3887 235 H eaddingt@cord.edu
ADDINGTON, Gary 719-384-6859 82 D gary.addington@ojc.edu
ADDINGTON, Michelle 512-471-1922 455 A addington@austin.utexas.edu
ADDINGTON, Nicole 440-775-5302 357 G nicole.addington@oberlin.edu
ADDINGTON, Nicole 216-687-3613 350 J n.addington@csuohio.edu
ADDIS, Edwin 717-947-6213 392 V esaddis@pacollege.edu
ADDISON, Andrea 716-829-7737 298 E addison@dyc.edu
ADDISON, Brenton 985-867-2232 190 K baddison@sjasc.edu
ADDISON, Jennifer 910-775-4606 343 B jennifer.addison@uncp.edu
ADDISON, Lynn 912-583-3285 116 E laddison@bpc.edu
ADDISON, Marcia 330-494-6170 360 K maddison@starkstate.edu
ADDISON, Steve 501-450-3199 23 H saddison@uca.edu
ADDISON, Tarsha 510-780-4500 47 K taddison@lifewest.edu
ADDISON, Trip 912-478-5253 120 C taddison@georgiasouthern.edu
ADDLEMAN, John 651-638-6287 234 D j-addleman@bethel.edu
ADDUCI, Sherri 561-683-1400 94 F
ADDY, Cathryn 603-427-7601 272 J
ADDY, Cheryl 803-777-2808 413 A caddy@mailbox.sc.edu
ADEBAYO, Emma 309-794-7834 133 C emmaadebayo@augustana.edu
ADEDOKUN, Catherine 703-746-8708 93 G
ADEKOLA, Abel 570-408-4701 403 A abel.adekola@wilkes.edu
ADELS, Christen, S 724-847-6658 384 C csadels@geneva.edu
ADEM, Salma 817-272-2101 454 I adem@uta.edu
ADEN, Huda 276-376-3452 472 E haden@uvawise.edu
ADEN, Mike 618-664-6820 138 F mike.aden@greenville.edu
ADEN-FOX, Nancy 402-472-4344 269 J naden1@unl.edu
ADENSANYA, Ineda 503-370-6213 377 F ipadesanya@willamette.edu
ADERELE, Megan, D 305-626-3734 100 D megan.aderele@fmuniv.edu
ADERO, Chad 301-846-2531 198 I cadero@frederick.edu
ADESNIK, Ryan 650-723-2300 66 E
ADGER FULLER, Montrese 678-359-5739 120 F montreseaf@gordonstate.edu
ADISHIAN-ASTONE, Deborah 559-278-2083 31 B debbiea@csufresno.edu
ADKINS, Adele 937-328-3857 350 G adkinsa@clarkstate.edu
ADKINS, Alfred 314-539-5266 259 A aadkins2@stlcc.edu
ADKINS, Amy 903-434-8121 440 G aadkins@ntcc.edu
ADKINS, Bryan 816-271-4417 257 A badkins1@missouriwestern.edu
ADKINS, Chris 919-496-2521 330 I
ADKINS, Christy 270-821-2250 182 D
ADKINS, Derek 304-710-3484 488 F adkinss@mctc.edu
ADKINS, Heather 210-567-2041 456 C adkinsh3@uthscsa.edu
ADKINS, Jason 865-288-6000 93 H
ADKINS, John 304-357-4779 487 J johnadkins@ucwv.edu
ADKINS, Joni 660-562-1803 257 E jadkins@nwmissouri.edu
ADKINS, Kay 870-368-2300 20 E kay.adkins@ozarka.edu
ADKINS, Kenneth, R 734-487-8460 223 K kadkins5@emich.edu
ADKINS, Lisa 828-694-1709 332 E l_adkins@blueridge.edu
ADKINS, Lisa 540-453-2217 473 D adkinsl@brcc.edu
ADKINS, Marc 419-251-1512 355 G marc.adkins@mercycollege.edu
ADKINS, Maria 617-243-2402 211 B madkins@lasell.edu
ADKINS, Mark 317-338-3879 161 B
ADKINS, Robert 713-743-7488 452 D rsadkins@central.uh.edu
ADKINS, Robert 724-503-1001 402 B radkins@washjeff.edu
ADKINS, Roger 765-983-1890 155 A adkinro@earlham.edu
ADKINS, Scott 760-773-2504 38 E rsadkins@collegeofthedesert.edu
ADKINS, Sheldon 405-425-5250 367 C sheldon.adkins@oc.edu
ADKINS, Stephanie 304-929-6717 488 G sadkins@newriver.edu
ADKINSON, Patrick 334-556-2447 2 C padkinson@wallace.edu
ADLER, Andrew 502-863-8405 180 H andrew_adler@georgetowncollege.edu
ADLER, Brian 610-758-3375 388 E bla212@lehigh.edu
ADLER, Brian, D 580-774-3063 370 A brian.adler@swosu.edu
ADLER, E. Scott 303-492-6659 84 B esadler@colorado.edu
ADLER, Jackie 254-867-3620 449 D jackie.adler@tstc.edu
ADLER, Karen, E 512-499-4360 454 H kadler@utsystem.edu
ADLER, Kate 212-343-1234 306 G kadler@mcny.edu
ADLER, Michael 214-768-1864 444 D madler@smu.edu
ADLER, Niall 408-855-5127 75 D niall.adler@missioncollege.edu
ADLER, Shmuel 773-463-7738 150 J sadler@telshe.edu
ADLER, Sy 503-725-5172 375 E adlers@pdx.edu
ADLER, Wendy 508-541-1542 209 A wadler@dean.edu
ADLIN, Eli 718-645-0536 306 J
ADLING, Jennifer 806-742-3844 450 F jennifer.adling@ttu.edu
ADMON, Hadass 626-264-8880 71 F
ADNER, Heather, M 315-386-7616 320 B adnerh@canton.edu
ADNEY, Chris 918-444-2500 366 G adneyc@nsuok.edu
ADNÚJUAR ROJAS, Carlos, A 787-815-0000 511 H rectoria.arecibo@upr.edu
ADOLF, Darci 541-867-8527 374 F darci.adolf@oregoncoast.edu
ADOLPH, Cheryl 718-982-2224 293 E cheryl.adolph@csi.cuny.edu
ADOLPH, Cheryl 802-387-4767 462 C
ADONIZIO, Tanja 570-504-9614 384 B tadonizio@som.geisinger.edu
ADORNETTO, Kate 218-855-8129 237 G kate.adornetto@clcmn.edu
ADORNO, Victor, T 787-780-0070 505 F vadorno@caribbean.edu
ADORNO, Wilfredo 787-761-0640 511 E decanoestudiantes@utcpr.edu
ADOYO, Priscilla 626-448-0023 46 G academicdean@itsla.edu
ADRIAN, Janet 913-360-7117 171 J jadrian@benedictine.edu
ADRIAN, Loretta, P 714-241-6152 37 J ladrian@coastline.edu
ADRIANCE, Anne 212-229-5600 308 A adrianca@newschool.edu
ADRIANZEN, Manuel 718-429-6600 324 D manuel.adrianzen@vaughn.edu
ADRIEN, Jenn 253-589-5619 478 J jenn.adrien@cptc.edu
ADSIT, Jason, N 845-569-3202 307 D jason.adsit@msmc.edu
ADSON, Aaron 918-360-2731 365 C adsona@bacone.edu
ADU-MIREKU, Samuel 910-672-1042 341 C sadu-mireku@uncfsu.edu
ADUKAITIS, Megan 610-796-8225 378 C megan.adukaitis@alvernia.edu
ADY, Tina 254-526-1402 432 D martina.ady@ctcd.edu
ADYA, Monica 856-225-6082 281 G monica.adya@rutgers.edu
AEFSKY, Fern 352-588-7276 107 D fern.aefsky@saintleo.edu
AERTS, Kenneth 575-835-5593 286 K kenneth.aerts@nmt.edu
AESCHLIMANN, Rodney, L 775-784-1113 271 E rod@unr.edu
AFALAVA, Alofia 684-699-9155 504 B a.afalava@amsamoa.edu
AFDAHL, Tami 307-532-8206 501 B tami.afdahl@ewc.wy.edu
AFFUL, Kwamina 212-752-1530 304 A kafful@limcollege.edu
AFFUSO, Paul 626-264-8880 71 F
AFOLAYAN, LaTanya, D 336-750-2184 344 A afolayanld@wssu.edu
AFRANK, Kim 402-465-2418 268 G kafrank@nebrwesleyan.edu
AFSHAR, Fara 631-451-4765 321 D afsharf@sunysuffolk.edu
AFUNUGO, Emmanuel, O 724-805-2473 398 A emmanuel.afunugo@stvincent.edu
AGAH, Arvin 785-864-3881 177 J agah@ku.edu
AGAN, Jeffrey 706-295-6974 120 A jagan@gntc.edu
AGARD, LaTonya 919-267-1640 330 B
AGARDY, Caroline 803-777-7550 413 A agardy@mailbox.sc.edu
AGARWAL, Neelam 650-949-7102 42 I agarwalneelam@foothill.edu
AGARWAL, Pallavi 918-610-0027 365 I pagarwal@communitycarecollege.edu
AGASHE, Vaidehi 518-629-8168 302 C v.agashe@hvcc.edu
AGATON, Bernadette, M 213-252-5100 23 K bagaton@alu.edu
AGATONE, Kristin 646-650-5529 388 E kra216@lehigh.edu
AGBAKPE, Peter, T 757-822-5185 475 E pagbakpe@tcc.edu
AGBARAJI, Casmir 505-387-7371 286 I cagbaraji@navajotech.edu
AGBENYIGA, DeBrenna LaFa 508-565-1311 219 A dagbenyiga@stonehill.edu
AGBOATWALA, Sohail 334-670-3201 7 C agboat@troy.edu

AGDASI, Sam .... 909-274-4750.. 52 J
sagdasi@mtsac.edu
AGEE, Ann .... 408-808-2033.. 34 A
AGEE, Deborah, G .... 530-752-2396.. 69 B
dgagee@ucdavis.edu
AGEE, Donna .... 919-444-2042 366 G
ageedm@nsuok.edu
AGEE, Doug, A .... 636-584-6714 253 B
doug.agee@eastcentral.edu
AGEE, Jarralynne .... 205-929-1530.... 6 B
jagee@miles.edu
AGEE, Matthew .... 817-202-6788 444 I
matthewagee@swau.edu
AGEE, Patty, A .... 660-263-3900 251 D
pattyagee@cccb.edu
AGEGNEHU, Yohannes . 651-450-3526 238 E
yagegnehu@inverhills.edu
AGENOR, Germil .... 561-929-3405 108 E
germil@sfbc.edu
AGESILAS, Elie .... 787-891-0925 507 K
eagesila@aguadilla.inter.edu
AGGARWAL, Reena .... 202-687-3784.. 92 E
aggarwal@georgetown.edu
AGHA, Farooq .... 919-516-4129 339 I
fmagha@st-aug.edu
AGHAEI, Oxana .... 559-243-7511.. 66 H
oxana.aghaei@scccd.edu
AGHO, Austin, O .... 757-683-3079 469 B
aagho@odu.edu
AGID, Shana .... 212-229-8950 308 A
agids@newschool.edu
AGIDIUS, Erin .... 208-885-4285 132 F
erina@uidaho.edu
AGJMURATI, Nick .... 212-592-2002 315 C
nagjmurati@sva.edu
AGLAN, Heshmat .... 334-727-8355.... 7 D
aglan@tuskegee.edu
AGLAN, JR., Heshmat .. 334-727-8011.... 7 D
AGLER, Brian .... 937-327-6458 364 D
aglerb1@wittenberg.edu
AGLIETTI, Annette .... 954-322-1612.. 99 F
AGNE, Anissa .... 904-620-2698 111 B
anissa.agne@unf.edu
AGNESE, Louis .... 512-444-8082 448 H
agnese@thsu.edu
AGNEW, Andrea .... 251-662-5363.... 1 E
aagnew@bishop.edu
AGNEW, Ina .... 918-293-4761 368 B
ina.agnew@okstate.edu
AGNEW, Maria .... 509-682-6659 485 H
magnew@wvc.edu
AGNEW, Melanie .... 801-832-2474 461 F
magnew@westminstercollege.edu
AGO, Emmanuel 718-862-7996 304M
emmanuel.ago@manhattan.edu
AGOONS, Akwai .... 678-466-4000 117 D
akwaiagoons@clayton.edu
AGOSTA, Frank .... 212-592-2620 315 C
fagosta@sva.edu
AGOSTINI, Stephen .... 919-962-3795 342 C
steve.agostini@unc.edu
AGOURIS, Peggy .... 757-221-1693 465 N
AGOVINO, Vikki .... 970-247-7100.. 80 J
vmagovino@fortlewis.edu
AGRAS, James, R .... 412-359-1000 399 I
jagras@triangle-tech.edu
AGRAS, James, R .... 412-359-1000 400 A
jagras@triangle-tech.edu
AGRAWAL, C. Mauli .... 816-235-1101 261 B
chancellor@umkc.edu
AGRAWAL, Devendra ..... 909-469-7040.. 75 I
dagrawal@westernu.edu
AGRE-KIPPENHAN,
Susan .... 503-883-2409 373 F
sagreki@linfield.edu
AGRELA, Ramona .... 949-824-5962.. 69 D
ragrela@uci.edu
AGUADO WARE, Joan .. 414-955-8227 493 F
jaguado@mcw.edu
AGUARDO, Rocio .... 432-837-8178 450 B
maria.aguado@sulross.edu
AGUAYO, Mary .... 909-448-4970.. 71 C
maguayo@laverne.edu
AGUERO-TROTTER,
Dianne .... 973-761-9500 283 C
AGUILAR, Carmen .... 401-865-2816 404 F
caguilar@providence.edu
AGUILAR, Catherine .... 787-279-1912 508 A
caguilar@bayamon.inter.edu
AGUILAR, Cheryl, M ..... 909-607-1232.. 37 D
cheryl.aguilar@cmc.edu
AGUILAR, Elmer .... 559-925-3127.. 75 B
elmeraguilar@whccd.edu
AGUILAR, Gary .... 916-484-8354.. 50 G
aguilag@arc.losrios.edu
AGUILAR, Jose, A .... 951-827-3878.. 70 B
jose.aguilar@ucr.edu
AGUILAR, Nathaly .... 408-864-8705.. 42 H
aguilarnathaly@fhda.edu
AGUILAR, Priscilla .... 210-486-3964 429 A
plopez136@alamo.edu
AGUILAR-VILLARREAL,
Elizabeth .... 210-486-3711 429 A
eaguilar-villarr@alamo.edu
AGUILERA, Mary .... 503-375-7113 372 H
maguilera@corban.edu
AGUILERA, Rafael .... 806-291-3451 457 I
aguilerar@wbu.edu
AGUILERA-GOERNER,
Carmen .... 915-831-7784 436 A
cagui205@epcc.edu
AGUILERA LAWRENSON,
Lisa .... 209-954-5018.. 61 G
lisa.lawrenson@deltacollege.edu
AGUINALDO, Nicole ...... 408-741-2164.. 75 D
nicole.aguinaldo@missioncollege.edu
AGUIRRE, Ilvis .... 787-878-5475 507 L
iaguirre@arecibo.inter.edu
AGUIRRE, Juan Carlos . 956-872-6782 443 H
jcaguirre@southtexascollege.edu
AGUIRRE, Katherine ...... 631-451-4022 321 C
aguirrk@sunysuffolk.edu
AGUIRRE, Katherine ...... 631-451-4022 321 D
aguirrk@sunysuffolk.edu
AGUIRRE, Maria .... 928-317-6180.. 11 A
maria.aguirre@azwestern.edu
AGUIRRE, Raymund .... 657-278-2515.. 31 C
raaguirre@fullerton.edu
AGUIRRE, Robert .... 540-568-7044 468 C
aguirrrd@jmu.edu
AGUIRRE, Tomas, A ..... 607-746-4440 320 D
aguirrta@delhi.edu
AGUON, Alicia .... 671-735-2444 504 F
aliciaaguon@triton.uog.edu
AGWUNOBI, Andrew ..... 860-486-2337.. 89 D
president@uconn.edu
AGWUNOBI, Andrew ..... 860-679-2594.. 89 D
agwunobi@uchc.edu
AH MU, Lele, V .... 684-699-1586 504 B
leleahmu@ymail.com
AH YUN, Kimo .... 414-288-8033 493 E
james.ahyun@marquette.edu
AHA, Christian .... 856-225-6140 281 G
christian.aha@camden.rutgers.edu
AHAD, Badia, S .... 773-274-3000 143 C
bahad@luc.edu
AHDIEH, Robert, B .... 817-212-3838 446 F
dean@law.tamu.edu
AHEARN, Mary Colleen 815-836-5471 142 F
cahearn@lewisu.edu
AHEDO, Valentina .... 608-246-6461 499 A
vahedo@madisoncollege.edu
AHERN, Catherine .... 585-785-1273 299 F
catherine.ahern@flcc.edu
AHERN, Joseph, F .... 845-758-7178 290 I
ahern@bard.edu
AHERN, Kathleen .... 718-390-3100 324 F
AHERN, Kathleen .... 203-285-2092.. 86 E
kahern@gatewayct.edu
AHERN, Martin .... 617-984-1635 218 C
mahern@quincycollege.edu
AHERN, Rob .... 614-236-7115 349 B
rahern@capital.edu
AHERON, Michelle .... 910-898-9610 336 D
aheronm@montgomery.edu
AHI, Sibel .... 610-568-1473 378 C
sibel.ahi@alvernia.edu
AHLBERG, Tim .... 630-617-3309 137 G
ahlbergt@elmhurst.edu
AHLEMANN, Tina .... 843-574-6142 412 I
tina.ahlemann@tridenttech.edu
AHLFELDT,
Stephanie, L .... 218-299-3001 235 H
ahlfeldt@cord.edu
AHLQUIST, Judy .... 916-660-7602.. 64 D
jahlquist@sierracollege.edu
AHLSCHWEDE, Karri ..... 402-465-2375 268 G
studenthealth@nebrwesleyan.edu
AHLUWALIA, Sanjam .... 928-523-8709.. 14 H
sanjam.ahluwalia@nau.edu
AHMAD, Catherine .... 609-497-7804 280 C
AHMAD, Shahzad .... 320-308-4287 240 I
shah@stcloudstate.edu
AHMED, Adil .... 510-466-7200.. 56 H
AHMED, Amel .... 413-545-4135 211 G
aahmed@umass.edu
AHMED, Amer, R .... 802-656-8426 463 A
amer.ahmed@uvm.edu
AHMED, Furquan .... 313-943-4000 232 E
fahmed1@wcccd.edu
AHMED, Furquan .... 313-496-2674 232 E
fahmed1@wcccd.edu
AHMED, Haseeb .... 810-762-7969 226 B
hahmed@kettering.edu
AHMED, Ijaz .... 734-384-4103 228 C
iahmed@monroeccc.edu
AHMED, Juzar .... 812-465-7160 162 C
juzar@usi.edu
AHMED, M. Monir .... 909-537-3132.. 32 E
mahmed@csusb.edu
AHMED, Michael .... 904-632-3153 101 B
michael.ahmed@fscj.edu
AHMED, Sadia .... 505-747-5016 287 H
sadia.ahmed@nnmc.edu
AHMED, Shahid .... 215-392-2938 396 A
AHMED, Shariq .... 562-985-8115.. 31 D
shariq.ahmed@csulb.edu
AHMEDNA, Mohamed ... 336-285-4794 341 D
ahmedna@ncat.edu
AHMIDOUCH, Abdellah 336-334-7567 341 D
abdellah@ncat.edu
AHN, Anne .... 714-533-1495.. 64 I
anneahn@southbaylo.edu
AHN, David .... 718-270-5118 294 G
dahn@mec.cuny.edu
AHN, Diane .... 916-577-2200.. 76 D
dahn@jessup.edu
AHN, Hongjun .... 714-533-3946.. 34 C
finance@calums.edu
AHN, Hongjun .... 714-533-3946.. 34 C
registrar@calums.edu
AHN, Mary .... 508-856-3837 212 C
mary.ahn@umassmed.edu
AHNEN, Heath .... 608-822-2327 500 A
hahnen@swtc.edu
AHNER, Darryl, K .... 937-255-3636 502 C
darryl.ahner@afit.edu
AHOLA, Scott .... 605-642-6359 416 E
scott.ahola@bhsu.edu
AHORRIO, Beatriz .... 212-694-1000 291 J
bahorrio@boricuacollege.edu
AHRENS, Emily .... 218-285-2203 240 E
emily.ahrens@rainyriver.edu
AHRENS, Rebecca .... 417-873-7523 252 G
bahrens@drury.edu
AHUJA, Sima Saran ...... 845-575-3000 305 D
AHUJA, Sunil .... 740-351-3472 360 F
sahuja@shawnee.edu
AIELLO, Frank .... 517-371-5140 233 C
aiellof@cooley.edu
AIELLO, Karen, M .... 973-655-4212 279 B
aiellok@montclair.edu
AIELLO, Megan .... 864-587-4008 412 F
aiellom@smcsc.edu
AIELLO, Ryan, A .... 971-722-7390 375 D
ryan.aiello@pcc.edu
AIGOTTI, Claire .... 317-940-9900 154 C
caigotti@butler.edu
AIKEN, Adel, G .... 724-847-5002 384 C
aaiken@geneva.edu
AIKEN, Donn .... 518-464-8765 299 C
daiken@excelsior.edu
AIKEN, Irene .... 910-521-6271 343 B
irene.aiken@uncp.edu
AIKEN, Jane .... 336-758-5000 344 C
AIKEN, Ryan .... 413-775-1309 214 E
aikenr@gcc.mass.edu
AIKENS, Jane .... 641-472-1260 168 C
jaikens@miu.edu
AIKENS, Laura, M .... 616-331-6000 224 G
laura.aikens@gvsu.edu
AIKONS, Latisha .... 773-371-5470 134 D
laikons@ctu.edu
AILSTER, Felicia .... 404-297-9522 120 B
AILSTOCK, M. Stephen . 410-777-2230 197 G
smailstock@aacc.edu
AIME, Marty .... 225-214-1953 187 B
morton.aime@franu.edu
AIMONE, Chris .... 812-877-8498 160 F
aimone@rose-hulman.edu
AINA, Wendy .... 678-916-2674 115 I
waina@johnmarshall.edu
AINBINDER, Meredith ... 617-824-8908 209 C
meredith_ainbinder@emerson.edu
AINLEY, Arden .... 360-416-7716 484 C
arden.ainley@skagit.edu
AINSLEIGH, Susan .... 413-565-1000 206 D
sainsleigh@baypath.edu
AINSLEY, Sharon .... 908-852-1400 276 G
sharon.ainsley@centenaryuniversity.edu
AINSLIE, Andrew 585-275-3316 323M
andrew.ainslie@simon.rochester.edu
AINSWORTH, Emma, L . 662-685-4771 245 C
eainsworth@bmc.edu
AINSWORTH, Troy .... 928-428-8225.. 12 F
troy.ainsworth@eac.edu
AIONA, Barbara .... 712-749-2637 164 C
aionab@bvu.edu
AIRD, Jeffrey .... 801-957-4090 461 C
jeffrey.aird@slcc.edu
AIRD, Lashrecse .... 804-862-6100 470 C
laird@rbc.edu
AIROZO, Paul .... 508-830-5051 213 D
pairozo@maritime.edu
AISTRUP, Joseph .... 334-844-4026.... 4 D
jaa0025@auburn.edu
AITKEN, Derek .... 510-885-3877.. 31 A
derek.aitken@csueastbay.edu
AITKEN, Meghan .... 973-290-4427 282 I
maitken@steu.edu
AITKEN, Renee .... 304-326-1109 487 I
renee.aitken@salemu.edu
AITSON-ROESSLER,
Mechelle .... 405-733-7308 369 E
maitson-roessler@rose.edu
AIVARS, Paul .... 269-467-9945 224 C
paivars@glenoaks.edu
AIZAZ, Khawar .... 713-425-3100 433 C
AJE, John .... 609-984-1130 284 C
jaje@tesu.edu
AJIBADE, Victoria .... 718-270-3058 317 B
victora.ajibade@downstate.edu
AJIBOYE, Oluwasayo .... 903-303-7853 441 L
AKAKPO, Koffi, C .... 859-246-6501 181 F
koffi.akakpo@kctcs.edu
AKAU, Sherri .... 808-932-7407 129 D
akau714@hawaii.edu
AKBARI, Hamid .... 262-547-1211 492 A
hakbari@carrollu.edu
AKCHIN, Lisa, G .... 410-455-2889 203 B
akchin@umbc.edu
AKENS, Cathy .... 336-334-5099 343 A
caakens@uncg.edu
AKERS, Adam .... 316-284-5261 172 B
akersa@bethelks.edu
AKERS, Brandy .... 800-686-1883 222 G
bakers@cleary.edu
AKERS, Cindy .... 806-742-2808 450 F
cindy.akers@ttu.edu
AKERS, Daniel .... 951-552-8579.. 27 G
dakers@calbaptist.edu
AKERS, Kathleen .... 931-472-3453 424 G
kathleen.akers@nscc.edu
AKERS, Kenneth .... 276-223-4118 476 A
kakers@wcc.vccs.edu
AKERS, Larry .... 850-973-9477 104 L
akersl@nfc.edu
AKERS, Mary Anne .... 443-885-3225 201 A
maryanne.akers@morgan.edu
AKERS, Matthew, P .... 330-972-4933 361 H
akers1@uakron.edu
AKERS, Shanna .... 434-592-3618 468 E
sakers@liberty.edu
AKERS, Shawn, D .... 434-592-5451 468 E
sdakers@liberty.edu
AKERS, Tina .... 209-954-5039.. 61 G
tina.akers@deltacollege.edu
AKEY, Lynn .... 507-389-2419 239 D
lynn.akey@mnsu.edu
AKHATAR, Sumaira .... 510-356-4760.. 77 F
AKHTAR, Shama .... 410-337-6062 199 B
shama.akhtar@goucher.edu
AKIN, Christopher, L .... 813-974-0898 111 C
cakin@usf.edu
AKIN, Daniel, L .... 919-761-2222 340 D
dakin@sebts.edu
AKIN, Jacob, J .... 507-933-7510 236 A
jakin@gustavus.edu
AKIN, Jamie .... 325-942-2116 450 E
jamie.akin@angelo.edu
AKIN, Johnathan .... 615-966-6150 421 B
johnathan.akin@lipscomb.edu
AKIN, Paul .... 502-897-4043 184 G
pakin@sbts.edu
AKIN, Renea .... 270-534-3461 183 B
renea.akin@kctcs.edu
AKINCI, Fevzi .... 412-396-5303 383 A
akincif@duq.edu
AKINJIDE, Kofi .... 831-477-3548.. 27 D

AKINLEYE, Johnson, O . 919-530-6104 341 E
johnson.akinleye@nccu.edu
AKINOLA, Ayodele .... 775-673-7617 271 C
aakinola@tmcc.edu
AKINPELU,
Olawunmi, A .... 409-747-9508 456 E
oaakinpe@utmb.edu
AKINPELUMI,
Kaneisha, B .... 504-520-5442 193 E
kakinpel@xula.edu
AKINS, Erick .... 850-599-3527 109 I
erick.akins@famu.edu
AKINS, Meagan .... 870-612-2144.. 22 H
meagan.akins@uaccb.edu
AKINS, Mike .... 904-596-2464 112 F
makins@tbc.edu
AKINS, Ralitsa .... 515-271-1400 165 G
AKINSANYA,
Oluwafemi .... 718-289-5154 293 B
oluwafemi.akinsanya@bcc.cuny.edu
AKL, Fred, A .... 610-499-4036 402 G
faakl@widener.edu
AKO-ADOUNVO, Gifty ... 401-874-2018 405 E
gako-adounvo@uri.edu
AKOB, Joe .... 570-422-3291 394 A
jakob@esu.edu
AKOH, Harry .... 404-756-4000 115 G
AKOMA, Kachi .... 718-262-2000 295 E
oakoma@york.cuny.edu
AKRIDGE, Jay .... 765-494-7420 160 B
akridge@purdue.edu
AKRIDGE, Travis .... 912-538-3125 125 G
takridge@southeasterntech.edu
AKRIGHT, Jan .... 217-228-5520 133 J
akrightj@brcn.edu
AKSELRUD, Larisa .... 425-739-8515 481 C
larisa.akselrud@lwtech.edu
AKSOY, Kudbettin .... 832-230-5555 440 E
AKSU, Mert .... 313-994-6620 231 E
aksumn@udmercy.edu
AKUNVABEY, Stephanie 401-254-3079 405 C
sakunvabey@rwu.edu
AL-ADAYLEH, Katie .... 303-369-5151.. 82 I
katie.al-adayleh@plattcolorado.edu
AL-AMIN, John .... 415-239-3000.. 36 K
jalamin@ccsf.edu
AL-ASSAF, Yousef .... 585-475-2411 312 F
ymacad@rit.edu
AL-MASRI, Ghada .... 510-659-6187.. 54 J
galmasri@ohlone.edu
ALAI, Meghan .... 732-906-2622 278 G
malai@middlesexcc.edu
ALAIMO, Joseph .... 215-646-7300 385 A
alaimo.j@gmercyu.edu
ALAM, Maria .... 901-678-2867 426 G
malam@memphis.edu
ALAM, Mohammad .... 212-220-1297 293 A
malam@bmcc.cuny.edu
ALAMAT, Natalie .... 303-751-8700.. 78 D
alamat@belrea.edu
ALAMO, Carlos .... 845-437-5601 324 C
ALAMO, JR., Manual .... 909-370-4800.. 29 F
ALAN, Mark .... 478-387-4900 119 F
malan@gmc.edu
ALANDER, Link .... 832-813-6832 439 C
link.s.alander@lonestar.edu
ALANIS, Jennifer .... 909-607-3470.. 44 H
j_alanis@hmc.edu
ALANIS, Susan .... 817-515-5203 445 F
susan.alanis@tccd.edu
ALANIZ, JR., Eloy, R .... 956-665-7944 455 D
eloy.alaniz@utrgv.edu
ALANIZ, Jessica .... 361-698-2214 435 G
jaalaniz@delmar.edu
ALAO, Solomon .... 443-885-3359 201 A
solomon.alao@morgan.edu
ALAPPAT, Bindhu .... 773-298-3000 149 D
ALARCON, Leah .... 805-678-5195.. 74 A
lalarcon@vcccd.edu
ALASIO, Claire .... 732-571-3463 279 A
calasio@monmouth.edu
ALAVALAPATI,
Janaki, R .... 334-844-1007.... 4 D
jra0024@auburn.edu
ALAVI, Maryam .... 404-894-2600 119 E
maryam.alavi@scheller.gatech.edu
ALBA, Suzanna .... 401-456-8086 405 A
salba@ric.edu
ALBANESE, Linda .... 516-323-4025 306 M
lalbanese@molloy.edu
ALBANESE, Marc .... 610-282-1100 382 C
marc.albanese@desales.edu
ALBANO, John .... 209-386-6777.. 52 A
albano.j@mccd.edu
ALBANO, Matthew .... 757-499-5447 467 C
ALBANO, Mike .... 207-725-3000 194 C
malbano@bowdoin.edu
ALBANO, Ralph .... 202-319-5218.. 92 A
albano@cua.edu
ALBANO, Steve, D .... 609-984-1100 284 C
salbano@tesu.edu
ALBARRAN, Agustin ...... 619-644-7161.. 44 E
agustin.albarran@gcccd.edu
ALBARRAN, Charo .... 707-256-7105.. 53 E
calbarran@napavalley.edu
ALBARRAN, Miguel .... 787-622-8000 511 D
malbarran@pupr.edu
ALBAUM, Lauren .... 863-680-4390 100 H
lalbaum@flsouthern.edu
ALBAWANEH,
Mahmoud .... 562-985-5462.. 31 D
mahmoud.albawaneh@csulb.edu
ALBECK, Angela .... 802-654-0505 463 F
ara06040@ccv.vsc.edu
ALBEE, Amy .... 352-435-6331 103 U
albeelea@lssc.edu
ALBENESE, David .... 857-701-1254 215 G
dalbenese@rcc.mass.edu
ALBER, Ivan .... 909-607-0119.. 37 F
ivan_alber@kgi.edu
ALBERICO, Jennifer .... 802-254-6370 463 F
jaa05100@ccv.vsc.edu
ALBERS, Timothy .... 612-238-4516 243 C
talbers@smumn.edu
ALBERT, Gene .... 516-773-5000 503 H
albertg@usmma.edu
ALBERT, Juline .... 712-274-6400 171 B
juline.albert@witcc.edu
ALBERT, Marianne .... 724-222-5330 391 F
malbert@penncommercial.edu
ALBERT, Neil .... 315-228-7408 296 E
nalbert@colgate.edu
ALBERT, OP, Peg .... 517-264-7000 230 H
palbert@sienaheights.edu
ALBERT, Rita .... 561-237-7231 103 W
ralbert@lynn.edu
ALBERT, Scott .... 724-738-4342 395 C
scott.albert@sru.edu
ALBERT, Sharon .... 831-755-6960.. 44 G
salbert@hartnell.edu
ALBERT, Wendy .... 717-867-6302 388 C
walbert@lvc.edu
ALBERT-KNOPP,
Heather .... 207-801-5640 194 E
halbert-knopp@coa.edu
ALBERT LINK, Cindy .... 617-747-3096 206 H
clink@berklee.edu
ALBERTA, Vince .... 702-895-5165 271 D
vince.alberta@unlv.edu
ALBERTIN, Erica .... 574-535-7417 155 E
ealbertin@goshen.edu
ALBERTINI, Velmarie .... 561-868-3891 105 D
albertiv@palmbeachstate.edu
ALBERTO, Christian ...... 212-938-5673 319 E
calberto@sunyopt.edu
ALBERTO, Marianela ..... 304-263-0979 488 A
ALBERTO, Paul, A .... 404-413-8100 120 E
palberto@gsu.edu
ALBERTO, Urbina .... 713-718-6839 437 C
alberto.urbina@hccs.edu
ALBERTS, J.J .... 508-541-1664 209 A
jalberts@dean.edu
ALBERTS, Kristin .... 904-256-7180 102 H
kalbert@ju.edu
ALBERTS, Trev .... 402-554-2305 270 A
talberts@unomaha.edu
ALBERTSON, Elizabeth .. 563-589-0274 171 A
lalbertson@wartburgseminary.edu
ALBERTSON, Hattie .... 701-228-5454 346 B
hattie.c.albertson@dakotacollege.edu
ALBERTSON, Terri .... 610-896-1702 385 I
talbertso1@haverford.edu
ALBERTSON, Trevor, D . 530-251-8820.. 47 F
talbertson@lassencollege.edu
ALBIERI, Guilherme ...... 212-938-5500 319 E
galbieri@sunyopt.edu
ALBIERI, Guilherme ...... 212-938-5508 319 E
galbieri@sunyopt.edu
ALBITZ, Becky .... 845-575-3000 305 D
rebecca.albitz@marist.edu
ALBO-LOPEZ, Nicole ...... 310-233-4031.. 49 B
albolonm@lahc.edu
ALBON, Darrell, J .... 740-368-3070 359 G
djalbon@owu.edu
ALBRECHT, Elizabeth .... 414-277-7265 494 D
ALBRECHT, Jana .... 309-438-2157 140 D
jlalbre2@ilstu.edu
ALBRECHT, Janet .... 973-684-6136 280 A
jalbrecht@pccc.edu
ALBRECHT, John .... 775-673-7300 271 A
jalbrecht@dri.edu
ALBRECHT, Marisa .... 317-788-3398 161 H
albrechtm@uindy.edu
ALBRIGHT, Geri .... 205-929-6315.... 2 H
galbright@lawsonstate.edu
ALBRIGHT, Mike .... 845-341-4728 310 G
mike.albright@sunyorange.edu
ALBRIGHT, Richard, C .. 773-508-3899 143 C
ralbright@luc.edu
ALBRIGHT, Scott .... 785-242-5200 176 I
scott.albright@ottawa.edu
ALBRIGHT, Thomas ...... 601-979-2580 246 F
thomas.e.albright@jsums.edu
ALBRIGHT-JURS, Lisa ... 704-922-2256 334 G
jurs.lisa@gaston.edu
ALBRINCK, Margaret, L 920-565-1000 493 A
albrinckm@lakeland.edu
ALBRITTON, Darrin ...... 919-267-1640 330 B
ALBRITTON, Kristen ...... 401-825-2194 404 C
kbalbritton@ccri.edu
ALBURCHER, Ronald ..... 650-723-2300.. 66 E
ALBURN, Amelia .... 508-999-8658 212 A
amelia.alburn@umassd.edu
ALBURY, Gary .... 510-464-3257.. 57 B
galbury@peralta.edu
ALBURY, Jennifer .... 301-576-0105 205 A
jalbury@wau.edu
ALBURY, Wayne .... 402-872-2350 268 E
walbury@peru.edu
ALCAINO, Ricardo .... 805-893-4504.. 70 E
ricardo.alcaino@oeosh.ucsb.edu
ALCALA-BURKHARDT,
Celena .... 310-287-4290.. 49 H
alcalac@wlac.edu
ALCANTARA, Ryan .... 310-377-5501.. 51 C
ralcantara@marymountcalifornia.edu
ALCARAZ, Christine .... 559-934-2111.. 74 N
christinealcaraz@whccd.edu
ALCIDE, Tom .... 443-412-2489 199 D
talcide@harford.edu
ALCIDONIS, Sendy .... 610-436-2122 395 D
salcidonis@wcupa.edu
ALCINDOR, Frantz, L .... 212-217-3000 299 D
frantz_alcindor@fitnyc.edu
ALCOCER, Amy .... 252-335-0821 333 G
amy_alcocer68@albemarle.edu
ALCOCER, David .... 510-987-9112.. 68 L
david.alcocer@ucop.edu
ALCOCK, Sherry, B .... 563-387-1862 168 B
alcock@luther.edu
ALCON, Arnaa .... 508-531-6131 212 D
aalcon@bridgew.edu
ALCORN, Jill .... 916-660-7160.. 64 D
jalcorn1@sierracollege.edu
ALDAMA, Ben .... 479-986-6934.. 20 C
baldama@nwacc.edu
ALDAMA, Julie .... 562-907-4286.. 76 B
jaldama@whittier.edu
ALDANA, Maylen .... 337-482-6471 193 B
maylenaldana@louisiana.edu
ALDARONDO, Aixa .... 787-766-1717 510 G
aialdarondo@uagm.edu
ALDAVA, Jesse .... 310-342-5206.. 73 F
ALDAVA, Lawrence .... 310-665-6855.. 55 C
laldava@otis.edu
ALDAY, Inaki .... 504-865-5000 191 F
ALDEN, Bernadette .... 413-662-5203 213 C
bernadette.alden@mcla.edu
ALDEN, Dan .... 512-245-2521 450 C
d_a29@txstate.edu
ALDEN, Kathy .... 770-533-6949 122 B
kalden@laniertech.edu
ALDEN, Peg .... 802-387-6821 462 C
palden@landmark.edu
ALDEN-RIVERS,
Bethany .... 636-949-4737 254 H
balden-rivers@lindenwood.edu
ALDENTALER, Heather ... 605-626-2371 416 G
heather.aldentaler@northern.edu
ALDER, William .... 304-647-6203 490 C
walder@osteo.wvsom.edu
ALDERFER, Gregg .... 215-368-5000 390 A
helpdesk@missio.edu
ALDERMAN, Brian .... 423-652-4708 420 F
bjalderman@king.edu
ALDERMAN, Debye, B ... 843-953-7458 408 C
aldermanda@cofc.edu
ALDERMAN,
Norman (Mike), M ..... 863-667-5129 108 K
nmalderman@seu.edu
ALDERMAN, Pamela, L . 304-896-7439 488 I
pamela.alderman@southernwv.edu
ALDERMAN, Rosalind ... 210-436-3995 442 J
ralderman@stmarytx.edu
ALDERMAN, Steve .... 713-646-1812 443 I
salderman@stcl.edu
ALDES, Heidi .... 612-659-6775 239 A
heidi.aldes@minneapolis.edu
ALDOUS, Mary .... 518-743-2275 320 A
aldousm@sunyacc.edu
ALDRICH, Adrian, M ..... 630-637-5201 145 F
amaldrich@noctrl.edu
ALDRICH, B.J .... 907-474-7043.. 10 A
bjaldrich@alaska.edu
ALDRICH, Christine .... 310-900-1600.. 39 F
caldrich@elcamino.edu
ALDRICH, Kimberly, J .. 269-337-7302 225 F
kim.aldrich@kzoo.edu
ALDRICH, Michael .... 808-675-3851 128 D
michael.aldrich@byuh.edu
ALDRIDGE, Evan .... 405-912-9007 368 J
ealdridge@ru.edu
ALDRIDGE, Mary .... 516-877-3843 289 I
aldridge@adelphi.edu
ALDRIDGE, Tristam .... 912-443-4107 125 B
taldridge@savannahtech.edu
ALDRIDGE, Whitney, C . 540-375-2201 470 E
aldridge@roanoke.edu
ALDRIDGE SANFORD,
Amy .... 361-825-2852 447 C
amy.aldridge.sanford@tamucc.edu
ALEGRE, Mario .... 787-764-0000 513 B
mario.alegre@upr.edu
ALEJANDRE, Monica ..... 909-537-5644.. 32 E
malejandre@csusb.edu
ALEMAN, Nicolle .... 541-552-7246 376 B
alemann@sou.edu
ALEMAN, Wendy .... 401-598-1309 404 D
wendy.aleman@jwu.edu
ALEONG, Natasha .... 786-331-1000 104 H
naleong@maufl.edu
ALES, Maria .... 206-934-5446 483 C
maria.ales@seattlecolleges.edu
ALES, Reynaldo .... 305-821-3333 100 E
rales@fnu.edu
ALESSANDRELLO,
Thomas .... 201-291-1111 291 E
tom@berkeleycollege.edu
ALESSANDRELLO,
Thomas .... 201-291-1111 275 I
tom@berkeleycollege.edu
ALESSANDRO, Lisa .... 216-584-2459 360 B
ALEWINE, J. Alan .... 618-537-6524 144 A
jaalewine@mckendree.edu
ALEX-ASSENSOH,
Yvette, M .... 541-346-9170 376 H
yalex@uoregon.edu
ALEXANDER, Adrian, W 918-631-2356 371 C
adrian-alexander@utulsa.edu
ALEXANDER, Akeem ..... 256-551-3130.... 2 E
akeem.alexander@drakestate.edu
ALEXANDER, Amber ..... 217-773-4441 142 C
aalexander@lakelandcollege.edu
ALEXANDER, Andrea .... 408-223-6796.. 62 G
andrea.alexander@evc.edu
ALEXANDER, Beth, A .... 317-940-6378 154 C
balexand@butler.edu
ALEXANDER, Bishop ..... 256-765-4201.... 8 E
jmalexander@una.edu
ALEXANDER, Bruce .... 315-786-2364 303 C
balexander@sunyjefferson.edu
ALEXANDER, Bryant, K . 310-338-7430.. 51 A
bryantkeithalexander@lmu.edu
ALEXANDER, Candi ...... 559-453-3448.. 43 A
candi.alexander@fresno.edu
ALEXANDER, Carol .... 701-349-5776 346 I
carolalexander@trinitybiblecollege.edu
ALEXANDER, Charlene .. 541-737-5936 375 A
ALEXANDER, Charlene .. 541-737-0123 375 A
ALEXANDER, Chaz .... 907-563-7575.... 9 E
chaz.alexander@alaskacareercollege.edu
ALEXANDER, Chris, D .. 717-358-3912 383 I
christine.alexander@fandm.edu
ALEXANDER, Cindy .... 864-294-3324 409 H
cindy.alexander@furman.edu
ALEXANDER, Dannie ..... 269-488-4298 225 G
dalexander@kvcc.edu
ALEXANDER, David .... 919-546-8351 340 B
david.alexander@shawu.edu

ALEXANDER, Debra ...... 989-328-1276 228 D
debraj@montcalm.edu
ALEXANDER, Donalyn ... 325-670-1198 436 I
donalyn.alexander@hsutx.edu
ALEXANDER, Donalyn ... 325-670-1198 439 F
donalyn.alexander@phssn.edu
ALEXANDER, Gary .... 617-731-3500 210 G
ALEXANDER, Gary .... 617-850-1322 210 G
galexander@hchc.edu
ALEXANDER, Ginny ...... 904-646-2205 101 B
ginny.alexander@fscj.edu
ALEXANDER, Herbert .... 585-594-6818 312 E
alexander_herbert@roberts.edu
ALEXANDER, Herman ... 504-526-4745 190 E
hermana@nationsu.edu
ALEXANDER, Jeffery ..... 805-546-3138.. 40 F
jeffery_alexander@cuesta.edu
ALEXANDER, Jeffrey ..... 775-673-7090 271 C
jalexander@tmcc.edu
ALEXANDER, Jennifer ... 352-588-8298 107 D
jennifer.alexander@saintleo.edu
ALEXANDER, Jenny ...... 414-288-7362 493 E
jenny.alexander@marquette.edu
ALEXANDER, Jessica .... 734-487-6570 223 K
jalexande1@emich.edu
ALEXANDER, John .... 205-391-2343.... 3 E
jalexander@sheltonstate.edu
ALEXANDER, Joyce, M . 979-862-6649 446 F
joycemalexander@tamu.edu
ALEXANDER, Juan, M .. 757-823-8396 469 A
jmalexander@nsu.edu
ALEXANDER, Karen .... 434-832-7623 473 E
alexanderk2@centralvirginia.edu
ALEXANDER, Katie .... 734-432-5837 227 C
ksalexander@madonna.edu
ALEXANDER, Keith .... 928-428-8279.. 12 F
keith.alexander@eac.edu
ALEXANDER, Kerri .... 504-520-7359 193 E
kalexa12@xula.edu
ALEXANDER, Kevin .... 970-943-0120.. 85 C
ALEXANDER, Kevin, L .. 714-449-7450.. 51 B
kalexander@ketchum.edu
ALEXANDER, Kimberly .. 845-758-7516 290 I
kalexand@bard.edu
ALEXANDER, Klint .... 307-766-6416 501 I
klint.alexander@uwyo.edu
ALEXANDER, Laura .... 719-255-3696.. 84 C
lalexand@uccs.edu
ALEXANDER,
Laurence, B .... 870-575-8535.. 22 D
alexanderl@uapb.edu
ALEXANDER, Linda .... 913-782-3529 176 C
lalexand@mnu.edu
ALEXANDER, Lisa .... 315-464-4700 317 C
alexandl@upstate.edu
ALEXANDER, Lorraine ... 229-430-6624 114 I
lalexander@albanytech.edu
ALEXANDER, Lynn, M .. 731-881-7490 427 D
lalexand@utm.edu
ALEXANDER, Mark .... 610-519-7005 401 K
alexander@law.villanova.edu
ALEXANDER, Mary .... 605-995-2656 415 A
mary.alexander@dwu.edu
ALEXANDER, Matt .... 361-570-4823 453 B
alexanderm@uhv.edu
ALEXANDER, Michael ... 805-678-5580.. 74 A
malexander@vcccd.edu
ALEXANDER, Michael ... 920-465-2207 495 F
alexandm@uwgb.edu
ALEXANDER,
Michael, B .... 617-243-2221 211 B
malexander@lasell.edu
ALEXANDER, Michelle .. 940-552-6291 457 C
malexander@vernoncollege.edu
ALEXANDER, Missy ...... 203-837-8400.. 86 B
alexanderm@wcsu.edu
ALEXANDER, Nathan ..... 501-374-6305.. 20 G
nathan.alexander@shortercollege.edu
ALEXANDER, Paige, E .. 404-420-5100 118 E
paige.eve.alexander@emory.edu
ALEXANDER, Paul .... 508-362-2131 214 D
palexander@capecod.edu
ALEXANDER, Paul .... 701-349-5444 346 I
paulalexander@trinitybiblecollege.edu
ALEXANDER, Paul, H .... 714-879-3901.. 45 G
palexander@hiu.edu
ALEXANDER, Pearl .... 404-894-0300 119 E
pearl.alexander@ohr.gatech.edu
ALEXANDER,
Raquel, M .... 570-577-1753 379 C
raquel.alexander@bucknell.edu
ALEXANDER, Rebecca ... 770-962-7580 121 E
ralexander@gwinnetttech.edu
ALEXANDER, Ross, C .... 256-765-5950.... 8 E
ralexander3@una.edu
ALEXANDER, Sanquita .. 334-291-4996.... 1 H
sanquita.alexander@cv.edu
ALEXANDER, Scott .... 207-786-6000 194 A
salexan2@bates.edu
ALEXANDER, Seth .... 617-253-4900 216 B
ALEXANDER, State, W .. 704-216-6067 330 H
salexan@livingstone.edu
ALEXANDER, Stephanie 740-245-7366 363 A
alexandr@rio.edu
ALEXANDER, Taylor ...... 606-326-2432 181 D
ALEXANDER, Thomas ... 978-542-6000 213 E
thomas.alexander@salemstate.edu
ALEXANDER, Tim .... 205-665-6155.... 8 D
talexand@montevallo.edu
ALEXANDER, Tyson ...... 325-674-2878 428 F
tma08a@acu.edu
ALEXANDER-HERRIOTT,
Vicki .... 641-472-1161 168 C
dof@miu.edu
ALEXANDER-HUNT,
Shirley .... 617-521-2000 218 G
ALEXANDER-WALLACE,
Linda .... 718-518-4432 294 B
lalexander@hostos.cuny.edu
ALEXANDRE, Michele ... 727-562-7858 112 A
malexandre@law.stetson.edu
ALEXIS STEPHENS,
Grace .... 312-922-1884 143 G
chancellor@maccormac.edu
ALEXO, JR., Kenneth .... 973-596-8293 279 E
kenneth.alexo@njit.edu
ALEXO, Michael .... 302-831-2129.. 91 C
malexo@udel.edu
ALEY, Danielle .... 828-395-1633 335 D
daley@isothermal.edu
ALFANO, Anthony .... 610-519-7730 401 K
anthony.alfano@villanova.edu
ALFANO, Cindy .... 309-268-8019 138 H
cindy.alfano@heartland.edu
ALFANO, Michael .... 203-365-7621.. 89 A
alfanom3@sacredheart.edu
ALFANO, Renee, M .... 608-243-4539 499 A
ralfano@madisoncollege.edu
ALFANO, Tara .... 914-594-2726 309 B
tara_alfano@nymc.edu
ALFARO, Carolina .... 209-667-3982.. 33 B
calfaro@csustan.edu
ALFARO, Christina .... 619-594-1354.. 33 D
calfaro@sdsu.edu
ALFARO, Gerardo .... 214-887-5206 435 F
galfaro@dts.edu
ALFARO, Richard .... 408-855-5145.. 75 D
richard.alfaro@missioncollege.edu
ALFERNESS, Rod .... 805-893-3141.. 70 E
alferness@engineering.ucsb.edu
ALFIE, Dario .... 305-642-4104 106 D
ALFIE, Rebeca .... 305-642-4104 106 D
ALFONSO, Antonio .... 360-867-6238 480 C
alfonsoa@evergreen.edu
ALFONSO, August .... 361-698-1300 435 G
aalfonso@delmar.edu
ALFONSO, Daniel .... 954-262-8835 105 A
djalfonso@nova.edu
ALFORD, Andrew .... 601-276-3704 249 B
aalford@smcc.edu
ALFORD, Brian .... 212-678-8195 322 C
ba2361@tc.columbia.edu
ALFORD, Cynthia .... 336-838-6111 339 B
clalford287@wilkescc.edu
ALFORD, Julie .... 419-447-6442 361 D
ALFORD, Keith .... 315-443-4110 321 G
kalford@syr.edu
ALFORD, Keith, A .... 716-645-1267 316 C
sw-dean@buffalo.edu
ALFORD, Keri .... 334-386-7179.... 5 C
kalford@faulkner.edu
ALFORD, Keyimani .... 608-246-6320 499 A
klalford@madisoncollege.edu
ALFORD, Rodney .... 256-890-4733.... 1 F
rodney.alford@calhoun.edu
ALFORD, Sara .... 972-899-8414 440 F
salford@nctc.edu
ALFORD, Stephanie .... 410-337-6431 199 B
stephanie.alford@goucher.edu
ALFORQUE, Patrick .... 312-341-2277 148 E
palforque@roosevelt.edu
ALFRED, Reina .... 718-270-2611 317 B
reina.alfred@downstate.edu
ALFRED, Tangelia .... 323-241-5333.. 49 E
alfredtm@lasc.edu
ALFULTIS, Michael, A ... 718-409-7271 320 G
ALGARIN, Richard, J .... 845-569-3598 307 D
richard.algarin@msmc.edu
ALGATE, Jill .... 800-280-0307 153 E
jill.algate@ace.edu
ALGER, Jalissa .... 864-941-8364 411 C
alger.j@ptc.edu
ALGER, Jonathan, R ...... 540-568-6868 468 C
president@jmu.edu
ALGIER, Anne-Marie ..... 585-275-4085 323 M
anne-marie.algier@rochester.edu
ALGOE, Eric .... 512-245-2244 450 C
e_a231@txstate.edu
ALI, Adel .... 320-308-3110 240 I
alai@stcloudstate.edu
ALI, Amjad .... 412-397-6461 397 B
alia@rmu.edu
ALI, Asim .... 334-844-8728.... 4 D
aliasim@auburn.edu
ALI, Cheryl .... 609-497-7757 280 C
cheryl.ali@ptsem.edu
ALI, Khaliff .... 386-267-0565.. 98 C
director@daytonacollege.edu
ALI, Mahmood .... 641-472-1126 168 C
housing@miu.edu
ALI, Mansoor .... 401-225-2321 200 D
mali01@mica.edu
ALI, Mehmed .... 334-953-4827 502 D
ALI, Mohammad .... 937-376-6191 349 J
mali@centralstate.edu
ALI, Neena .... 571-553-3601.. 92 D
neena20147@gwu.edu
ALI, Omar .... 336-334-5538 343 A
ohali@uncg.edu
ALI, Radman .... 803-934-3284 410 G
rali@morris.edu
ALI, Rita .... 309-694-5561 139 B
rali@icc.edu
ALI, Yasmin .... 718-951-5000 293 C
yali@brooklyn.cuny.edu
ALI, Yasmin .... 425-235-5728 482 H
yali@rtc.edu
ALIBERTI, Fred .... 518-629-7210 302 C
f.aliberti@hvcc.edu
ALICANDRO, Jean .... 860-832-1664.. 85 G
alicandro@ccsu.edu
ALICEA, Edwin .... 787-725-8120 506 M
ealicea@eap.edu
ALICEA, Victor, G .... 212-694-1000 291 J
valicea@boricuacollege.edu
ALICEA-CASTILLO,
Jennifer .... 787-250-0000 511 F
jennifer.alicea@upr.edu
ALICEA-MALDONADO,
Rafael .... 585-345-6820 300 F
ralicea-maldonado@genesee.edu
ALIMBOYOGUEN,
Maribel .... 847-376-7053 146 G
malimboyoguen@oakton.edu
ALIMO, Craig .... 707-256-7364.. 53 E
calmio@napavalley.edu
ALIOTO, Keri .... 414-930-3525 494 E
aliotok@mtmary.edu
ALIPOE Dovi .... 601-877-6543 245 A
alipoe@alcorn.edu
ALIVISATOS, Paul .... 773-702-8001 151 E
ALIVISATOS, Paul .... 510-643-7371.. 69 A
paul.alivisatos@berkeley.edu
ALIX, Jeff .... 419-289-5093 347 J
jalix@ashland.edu
ALJOE, Jaria .... 203-576-4183.. 89 C
jaljoe@bridgeport.edu
ALKIRE, Amy .... 612-330-1188 234 A
alkirea@augsburg.edu
ALL, Jessica .... 803-812-7398 413 E
allj@mailbox.sc.edu
ALLAHBACHAYO,
Salima .... 626-852-6439.. 36 J
sallahbachayo@citruscollege.edu
ALLAIN, Kimberly .... 909-869-5152.. 30 A
kgallain@cpp.edu
ALLAIRE, André .... 212-229-5662 308 A
allairea@newschool.edu
ALLAMON, Jeremy .... 254-298-8692 445 G
jeremy.allamon@templejc.edu
ALLAMON, Susan .... 254-298-8452 445 G
susan.allamon@templejc.edu
ALLAN, Kevin .... 845-451-1460 297 G
kevin.allan@culinary.edu
ALLAR, Holly .... 909-537-3680.. 32 E
holly.allar@csusb.edu
ALLARD, Cathy .... 406-756-3803 263 E
callarc@fvcc.edu
ALLARD, Dei .... 662-325-3555 247 F
da1112@msstate.edu
ALLARD, Ingrid, M .... 518-262-5919 289 L
allardi@amc.edu
ALLARD, Lee .... 716-566-7879 298 A
lallard@daemen.edu
ALLBRITTEN, Jeffery ...... 239-489-9211 101 A
president@fsw.edu
ALLBRITTON, Nancy ...... 206-543-1829 485 A
nlallbr@uw.edu
ALLCOCK, Melissa .... 270-534-3090 183 B
melissa.allcock@kctcs.edu
ALLCORN, Terry, A .... 417-268-6003 250 G
tallcorn@gobbc.edu
ALLCORN, Terry, L .... 606-474-3258 181 B
tallcorn@kcu.edu
ALLDAY, Jack .... 972-780-3600 454 A
jack.allday@untdallas.edu
ALLDREDGE, Annita .... 415-749-4560.. 61 C
aalldredge@sfai.edu
ALLDREDGE, Brian .... 415-514-0421.. 70 D
brian.alldredge@ucsf.edu
ALLDREDGE, Kari .... 865-974-1350 427 B
kalldre1@utk.edu
ALLEE, Amanda .... 719-255-3838.. 84 C
aallee@uccs.edu
ALLEE, Kelly .... 217-234-5215 142 C
kallee@lakeland.cc.il.us
ALLEE, Rodney .... 317-632-5553 159 I
rallee@lincolntech.edu
ALLEGRETTA, Kerri .... 516-403-5392 324 G
kallegretta@webb.edu
ALLEGRETTO,
Stephen, A .... 203-582-7962.. 88 G
stephen.allegretto@quinnipiac.edu
ALLEMAN, Michael .... 337-550-1308 189 G
malleman@lsue.edu
ALLEMAN-BEYERS,
Natalie .... 913-468-8500 174 I
nalleman@jccc.edu
ALLEN, Alex .... 812-237-2584 156 D
alex.allen@indstate.edu
ALLEN, Algia .... 972-563-9573 451 F
aallen@tvcc.edu
ALLEN, Aliquippa .... 205-652-3687.... 9 B
aallen@uwa.edu
ALLEN, Amanda .... 979-532-6468 458 E
allena@wcjc.edu
ALLEN, Andre .... 309-672-5513 144 C
aallen@methdistcol.edu
ALLEN, Andrew .... 619-260-4816.. 72 I
andrewt@sandiego.edu
ALLEN, Andrew .... 651-290-6463 242 L
andrew.allen@mitchellhamline.edu
ALLEN, Angela .... 806-651-8482 448 B
aallen@wtamu.edu
ALLEN, Anita .... 478-825-6304 118 F
anita.allen@fvsu.edu
ALLEN, Anna .... 858-513-9240.. 68 K
anna.allen@ashford.edu
ALLEN, Anna, M .... 215-951-1374 387 A
aallen@lasalle.edu
ALLEN, Annmarie .... 207-602-2339 197 E
aallen17@une.edu
ALLEN, Anthony .... 718-933-6700 307 A
aallen@monroecollege.edu
ALLEN, Anthony, W .... 573-629-3252 253 J
anthony.allen@hlg.edu
ALLEN, Aswad .... 760-750-4407.. 33 A
aswadallen@csusm.edu
ALLEN, Augusta .... 610-341-5870 383 B
aallen6@eastern.edu
ALLEN, Bob .... 702-567-1920 270 I
ALLEN, Bob .... 956-380-8125 442 G
ballen@riogrande.edu
ALLEN, Brenda .... 303-315-2104.. 84 D
brenda.j.allen@ucdenver.edu
ALLEN, Brenda, A .... 484-365-7400 388 H
ballen@lincoln.edu
ALLEN, Brian .... 815-939-5255 147 A
ballen@olivet.edu
ALLEN, Brian .... 256-352-8057.... 3 I
brian.allen@wallacestate.edu
ALLEN, Brian .... 919-546-8417 340 B
brian.allen@shawu.edu
ALLEN, Brian, D .... 815-939-5255 147 A
ballen@olivet.edu
ALLEN, C. Leonard .... 615-966-6064 421 B
leonard.allen@lipscomb.edu
ALLEN, Caitlin .... 607-436-2844 316 F
caitlin.allen@oneonta.edu
ALLEN, Calhoun .... 318-869-5120 186 F
callen@centenary.edu
ALLEN, Carmen .... 409-944-1208 436 E
callen@gc.edu

ALM, Deborah .... 413-748-3216 218 I
dalm@springfield.edu
ALM, Maria .... 715-232-2687 497 B
almm@uwstout.edu
ALMAN, Shelly .... 704-922-6406 334 G
alman.shelly@gaston.edu
ALMANDREZ,
Mary Grace .... 401-874-7077 405 E
mgalmandrez@uri.edu
ALMANZA, Khiera .... 620-432-0381 176 D
kalmanza@neosho.edu
ALMANZA, Manny .... 903-983-8218 438 F
malmanza@kilgore.edu
ALMANZAR, Karoline .... 909-469-5318.. 75 I
kalmanzar@westernu.edu
ALMAROAD, Megan ...... 423-323-3191 425 A
ALMASI-BUSH, Ann ...... 630-844-4578 133 D
aalmasi@aurora.edu
ALMEDA, Delilah .... 305-237-2951 104 E
dalmeda1@mdc.edu
ALMEIDA, Mark .... 510-885-4376.. 31 A
mark.almeida@csueastbay.edu
ALMEIDA, Paul, A .... 202-687-3883.. 92 E
almeidap@georgetown.edu
ALMENDAREZ, Elena .... 412-536-1053 386 H
elena.almendarez@laroche.edu
ALMOAYYED, Jasmine .. 319-398-5525 167 J
jasmine.almoayyed@kirkwood.edu
ALMODOVAR, Arturo .... 787-844-8181 513 A
arturo.almodovar@upr.edu
ALMON, Robert, C .... 212-346-1200 311 A
ralmon@pace.edu
ALMOND, Jackie .... 434-544-8457 471 L
almond.j@lynchburg.edu
ALMOND, James, S ...... 765-494-9706 160 B
jsalmond@purdue.edu
ALMONTE, Loreto .... 305-821-3333 100 E
lalmonte@fnu.edu
ALMORADIE, Joel .... 718-522-9073 290 E
jalmoradie@asa.edu
ALMQUIST, Arne .... 409-880-8118 449 G
arne.almquist@lamar.edu
ALMQUIST, Brian .... 843-574-6011 412 I
brian.almquist@tridenttech.edu
ALMQUIST, Cathy .... 843-574-6057 412 I
cathy.almquist@tridenttech.edu
ALMQUIST, Steve .... 251-380-2262.... 6 H
provost@shc.edu
ALMUSAWI, Marwa .... 253-833-9111 480 I
malmusawi@greenriver.edu
ALMY, Marilynn .... 912-525-5000 124 I
malmy@scad.edu
ALNAJJAR, Hisham .... 860-768-4846.. 89 G
alnajjar@hartford.edu
ALNUTT, Mark, M .... 716-645-6811 316 C
ub-athleticdirector@buffalo.edu
ALO, Richard .... 850-412-5978 109 I
richard.alo@famu.edu
ALOISIO, Simone .... 707-826-5086.. 33 C
simone.aloisio@humboldt.edu
ALONSO, Carlos, J .... 212-854-6935 297 C
ca2201@columbia.edu
ALONSO, Jose .... 787-738-2161 512 C
jose.alonso@upr.edu
ALONSO, Zoraida .... 787-780-0070 505 F
zalonso@caribbean.edu
ALONZO, Jessica .... 602-275-7133.. 15 M
ALONZO, Joseph .... 714-628-5040.. 58 G
alonzo_joseph@sccollege.edu
ALONZO, Liza .... 713-221-8682 453 A
alonzol@uhd.edu
ALONZO, Mia .... 909-607-9192.. 37 B
mia.alonzo@claremont.edu
ALONZO, Robert .... 713-221-8977 453 A
alonzor@uhd.edu
ALOVOR, Yoli .... 610-527-0200 397 D
yolanda.alovor@rosemont.edu
ALOYO, JR., Victor .... 609-688-1941 280 C
victor.aloyo@ptsem.edu
ALP, Nesli .... 812-237-3166 156 D
nesli.alp@indstate.edu
ALPERN, Robert, J .... 203-785-4672.. 90 C
robert.alpern@yale.edu
ALPI, Kristine .... 503-494-0455 374 H
alpi@ohsu.edu
ALPIN, Jolie .... 760-366-5210.. 40 E
jalpin@cmccd.edu
ALRAMAHI, Sameer ...... 330-972-5767 361 H
salramahi1@uakron.edu
ALREFAE, Omar .... 660-831-4000 256 I
ALSHEIMER, Michael .... 315-792-7210 321 B
michael.alsheimer@sunypoly.edu
ALSING, Melissa .... 724-830-1850 398 C
malsing@setonhill.edu
ALSIP, Morgan .... 405-692-3244 366 D
ALSOBROOK, Metta ...... 757-388-5733 470 F
malsobrook@sentara.edu
ALSOBROOKS, Scott ..... 662-476-5050 246 B
salsobrooks@eastms.edu
ALSOP, Rob .... 304-293-5841 490 E
rob.alsop@mail.wvu.edu
ALSOP, Robert .... 641-585-8130 170 I
alsopb@waldorf.edu
ALSPACH, Charlene ...... 509-359-2479 479 G
calspach@ewu.edu
ALSTER, Samuel .... 732-765-9126 285 C
ALSTER, Shimon .... 732-765-9126 285 C
ALSTON, Cathy .... 253-833-9111 480 I
calston@greenriver.edu
ALSTON, Dawn .... 404-270-5077 126 B
dalston@spelman.edu
ALSTON, Ellen .... 501-450-1263.. 19 E
alston@hendrix.edu
ALSTON, Kay .... 270-789-5360 180 A
klalston@campbellsville.edu
ALSTON, Kenyon .... 205-366-8980.... 7 A
kalston@stillman.edu
ALSTON, Micah, N .... 714-879-3901.. 45 G
mnalston@hiu.edu
ALSTON, Sharon .... 202-885-6053.. 91 F
salston@american.edu
ALSTON, Susan .... 860-512-2903.. 86 G
salston@manchestercc.edu
ALSTON, Vickie .... 479-979-1303.. 23 I
valston@ozarks.edu
ALSTON FORBES,
Lakesha .... 252-328-6804 341 A
alstonl@ecu.edu
ALSTON-PINCKNEY,
Elizabeth .... 704-216-6100 330 H
ealston-pinckney@livingstone.edu
ALSUP, Margaret .... 870-307-7474.. 19 I
margaret.alsup@lyon.edu
ALT, Ashley .... 570-941-6497 401 F
ashley.alt@scranton.edu
ALT, Ashley .... 570-941-6497 401 F
ALT, Susan .... 406-994-3344 264 C
salt@montana.edu
ALT, Tamara .... 319-398-4509 167 J
tamara.alt@kirkwood.edu
ALTAMIRANO, Carlos ... 787-743-3038 509 N
caltamirano@sanjuanbautista.edu
ALTAMIRANO,
Rodolfo, R .... 215-573-6332 400 F
rudiea@pobox.upenn.edu
ALTARRIBA, Jeanette .... 518-442-5004 316 A
jaltarriba@albany.edu
ALTAYLI, Benek .... 719-255-3257.. 84 C
zaltayli@uccs.edu
ALTEGOER, Diana, B ..... 215-898-8493 400 F
altegoer@upenn.edu
ALTEMOSE, Jane .... 610-758-4637 388 E
jca209@lehigh.edu
ALTENBURG, Danielle ... 802-865-8473 462 A
daltenburg@champlain.edu
ALTERIO, Christopher ... 315-279-5483 303 G
calterio1@keuka.edu
ALTHAUS, Jon .... 217-234-5225 142 C
jalthaus@lakeland.cc.il.us
ALTIER, Jeffrey, P .... 386-822-8100 112 A
jaltier@stetson.edu
ALTIER, Matthew .... 504-568-3712 189 H
matthewaltier@lsuhsc.edu
ALTIERE, Ralph .... 303-724-2887.. 84 D
ralph.altiere@ucdenver.edu
ALTIERI, Anthony .... 561-237-7275 103 W
aaltieri@lynn.edu
ALTIERI, Yeidi .... 787-815-0000 511 H
yeidi.altieri@upr.edu
ALTIKULAC, John .... 770-426-2644 122 C
jaltikulac@life.edu
ALTMAN, Carolyn .... 912-486-1149 120 C
caltman@georgiasouthern.edu
ALTMAN, Don .... 480-219-6008 250 A
daltman@atsu.edu
ALTMAN, J.J .... 912-871-1648 123 J
jaltman@ogeecheetech.edu
ALTMAN, Joanne, D ..... 336-841-9613 329 F
jaltman0@highpoint.edu
ALTMAN, Kip .... 864-488-4012 410 B
caltman@limestone.edu
ALTMAN, Miranda .... 410-778-7261 205 B
maltman2@washcoll.edu
ALTMAN, Stacie .... 303-273-3056.. 79 J
saltman@mines.edu
ALTMAN-COSGROVE,
Megan .... 716-286-8314 309 H
mcosgrove@niagara.edu
ALTMANN, Barbara, K .. 717-358-3971 383 I
president@fandm.edu
ALTOBELLO, Maria, R ... 603-647-3530 273 E
altobellom@franklinpierce.edu
ALTONGY-MAGEE,
Kristy .... 508-373-5726 216 D
kristy.altongy-magee@mcphs.edu
ALTSHULER, Gina .... 215-335-0800 388 G
galtshuler@lincolntech.edu
ALTUSKY,
Sh omo Avidgor .... 718-868-2300 291 C
ALTWINE, Chad .... 605-668-1502 415 F
chad.altwine@mountmarty.edu
ALVA, Sylvia, A .... 909-869-4382.. 30 A
saalva@cpp.edu
ALVALLE, Anibal .... 787-764-0000 513 B
anibal.alvalle@upr.edu
ALVARADO, Christian ... 949-582-4340.. 65 D
calvarado@saddleback.edu
ALVARADO, George ...... 559-443-8627.. 67 B
george.alvarado@fresnocitycollege.edu
ALVARADO, Jose Luis .. 323-343-3800.. 31 E
alvarado@calstatela.edu
ALVARADO, Jose Luis .. 212-636-6470 300 C
alvarado@fordham.edu
ALVARADO, Luis .... 509-793-2291 478 B
luisa@bigbend.edu
ALVARADO, Miguel ...... 617-422-7423 217 F
malvarado@nesl.edu
ALVARADO, Nelly .... 310-900-1600.. 39 F
nalvarado@compton.edu
ALVARADO, Norman ...... 718-779-1430 311 E
nalvarado@plazacollege.edu
ALVARADO-TORRES,
Cesar .... 787-751-1912 509 A
calvarado@juris.inter.edu
ALVARADO-VALDOVINOS,
Lorena .... 509-574-4702 486 D
lalvarado-valdovinos@yvcc.edu
ALVAREZ, Alex .... 323-466-6663.. 43 H
ALVAREZ, Alvin .... 415-338-6480.. 33 E
aalvarez@sfsu.edu
ALVAREZ, Ana .... 305-284-3584 113 C
aalvarez@miami.edu
ALVAREZ, Arlene .... 909-558-4567.. 48 E
sm8026@bncollege.com
ALVAREZ, Brian .... 516-364-0808 308 D
balvarez@nycollege.edu
ALVAREZ, Celso .... 718-429-6600 324 D
celsc.alvarez@vaughn.edu
ALVAREZ, Cristina .... 909-537-5669.. 32 E
cristina.alvarez@csusb.edu
ALVAREZ, Ed .... 951-571-6186.. 59 B
ed.alvarez@mvc.edu
ALVAREZ, Eduardo .... 352-371-2833.. 98 G
academicdean@dragonrises.edu
ALVAREZ, Evelyn .... 787-834-9595 510 D
ealvarez@uaa.edu
ALVAREZ, Frank, D .... 509-452-5100 482 B
falvarez@pnwu.edu
ALVAREZ, Ivonne .... 619-388-2689.. 60 J
ialvarez@sdccd.edu
ALVAREZ, Jacqueline .... 413-542-2354 205 G
jalvarez@amherst.edu
ALVAREZ, Jacqueline .... 787-763-5845 507 J
jalvarez@inter.edu
ALVAREZ, Jon .... 617-253-1727 216 B
ALVAREZ, Linda .... 507-389-2986 239 D
linda.alvarez@mnsu.edu
ALVAREZ, Lourdes .... 210-431-4187 441 B
lalvarez@ollusa.edu
ALVAREZ, Lucy .... 408-846-4964.. 43 E
lalvarez@gavilan.edu
ALVAREZ, Maria .... 787-882-2065 510 C
malvarez@unitecpr.edu
ALVAREZ, Maria, L .... 305-899-3085.. 96 A
malvarez@barry.edu
ALVAREZ, Maryan .... 650-325-5621.. 59 J
ALVAREZ, Patricia .... 787-766-1912 507 J
palvarez@inter.edu
ALVAREZ, Rebecca .... 408-741-2072.. 75 D
rebecca.alvarez@westvalley.edu
ALVAREZ, Richard .... 718-997-5929 295 B
richard.alvarez@qc.cuny.edu
ALVAREZ, Rory .... 503-399-2594 372 B
rory.alvarez@chemeketa.edu
ALVAREZ, Ruby .... 407-582-1548 113 I
ralvarez15@valenciacollege.edu
ALVAREZ, Timothy .... 719-384-6871.. 82 D
timothy.alvarez@ojc.edu
ALVAREZ-ORTIZ,
Genette .... 516-572-7775 307 E
genette.ortiz@ncc.edu
ALVAREZ-ROBINSON,
Sonia .... 404-385-3306 119 E
sonia@consulting.gatech.edu
ALVERO, Alicia .... 718-997-5903 295 B
alicia.alvero@qc.cuny.edu
ALVERSON, Amelia, J ... 212-851-7929 297 C
amelia.alverson@columbia.edu
ALVES, Daniel .... 203-672-6654.. 85 D
dalves@albertus.edu
ALVES, Eddie .... 541-881-5590 376 F
ealves@tvcc.cc
ALVES, Melisa .... 978-665-3150 212 E
malves8@fitchburgstate.edu
ALVEY, Patricia .... 214-768-4519 444 D
palvey@smu.edu
ALVIN, Glenda .... 615-963-5000 426 A
ALVINO, Kathleen, M .... 401-865-2430 404 F
kalvino@providence.edu
ALVIS, Robert .... 812-357-6543 161 A
ralvis@saintmeinrad.edu
ALVITI, Eileen .... 617-747-2375 206 H
hroperations@berklee.edu
ALWANI, Ahmed .... 703-591-7042 466 M
aalwani@fxua.edu
ALWAY, Tom .... 231-843-5967 233 A
talway@westshore.edu
AMACK, April .... 970-542-3187.. 81 N
april.amack@morgancc.edu
AMADI, Emmanual .... 662-254-3363 248 B
amadi@mvsu.edu
AMADOR, Lui .... 562-860-2451.. 35 H
lamador@cerritos.edu
AMADOR, Steve .... 209-588-5142.. 76 K
amadors@yosemite.edu
AMADOR, Tristen .... 303-458-4174.. 83 E
tamador@regis.edu
AMADOR DUMOIS,
Maria .... 787-833-8918 512 E
decano.adem@upr.edu
AMALBERT, Milagros .... 787-751-1912 509 A
mamalber@juris.inter.edu
AMALFITANO, Andrea ... 517-355-9616 227 F
amalfit1@msu.edu
AMAN, Edward .... 864-231-2000 406 F
eaman@andersonuniversity.edu
AMAN, Rick .... 208-535-5366 131 B
rick.aman@cei.edu
AMANO, Kyoko .... 361-570-4848 453 B
AMAR, Angela .... 702-895-3360 271 D
angela.amar@unlv.edu
AMAR, Salomon .... 914-594-4900 309 B
AMAR, Salomon .... 914-594-3036 322 F
salomon_amar@nymc.edu
AMAR, Salomon .... 914-594-3036 322 G
salomon_amar@nymc.edu
AMAR, Vikram .... 217-333-0931 152 B
amar@illinois.edu
AMARA, Sakpa, S .... 703-891-1787 471 E
samara@standardcollege.edu
AMARI, Jonathan .... 781-768-7019 218 D
AMAROK, Barbara .... 907-443-8402.. 10 A
bjamarok@alaska.edu
AMARONE, Ben .... 203-787-8635.. 85 D
bamarone@albertus.edu
AMASON, Allen .... 912-478-2622 120 C
aamason@georgiasouthern.edu
AMATO, Christina .... 937-512-3703 360 G
christina.amato@sinclair.edu
AMATO, Christopher ..... 863-298-6876 106 A
AMATO, John .... 515-271-2849 165 J
john.amato@drake.edu
AMATO, Leslie .... 530-541-4660.. 47 E
amato@ltcc.edu
AMATO, Paula, A .... 603-428-2461 273 G
pamato@nec.edu
AMATO YAZZOLINO,
Gina .... 503-943-8000 377 A
AMATRUDO, Susan ...... 508-999-8233 212 A
samatrudo@umassd.edu
AMATUCCI, Kelly .... 772-462-7674 102 F
kamatucc@irsc.edu
AMAVIZCA, Gabriela ..... 520-417-4708.. 11 M
amavizcag@cochise.edu
AMAYA, Carlos, C .... 915-831-2164 436 A
camaya3@epcc.edu
AMAYA, Mercedes .... 305-237-0388 104 E
mamaya@mdc.edu
AMAYA GORDON,
Karla, J .... 757-823-8275 469 A
kjagordon@nsu.edu

ANDERSON, Cheryl .... 503-517-1206 377 C
clanderson@warnerpacific.edu
ANDERSON, Chris .... 507-537-6272 241 D
chris.anderson@smsu.edu
ANDERSON, Chris .... 704-527-9909 210 C
canderson3@gcts.edu
ANDERSON, Chris .... 704-527-9909 210 C
canderson3@gordonconwell.edu
ANDERSON, Christie ..... 509-777-4218 486 C
canderson@whitworth.edu
ANDERSON, Christine ... 801-818-8900 459 J
christine.anderson@provocollege.edu
ANDERSON, Cindy, L ... 304-558-4016 489 H
cindy.anderson@wvhepc.edu
ANDERSON, Clayton ..... 801-626-6465 461 A
canderson@weber.edu
ANDERSON, Cliff .... 763-433-1100 237 D
clifford.anderson@anokaramsey.edu
ANDERSON, Clifford ..... 763-433-1100 237 E
clifford.anderson@anokaramsey.edu
ANDERSON, Corey .... 701-845-7216 345 G
corey.anderson@vcsu.edu
ANDERSON, Corey .... 541-684-7354 371 I
canderson@bushnell.edu
ANDERSON, Cynthia ..... 708-974-5347 145 A
anderson@morainevalley.edu
ANDERSON, Cynthia ..... 828-398-7161 332 B
cynthiaianderson@abtech.edu
ANDERSON, Daisy .... 717-796-1800 389 H
anderson@messiah.edu
ANDERSON, Daniel, G .. 541-278-5743 371 H
daanderson@bluecc.edu
ANDERSON, Daniel, J ... 336-278-7410 328 J
andersd@elon.edu
ANDERSON, Daniel, L .. 304-877-6428 486 G
president@abc.edu
ANDERSON, Danielle ..... 989-328-1217 228 D
daniellea@montcalm.edu
ANDERSON, Danny .... 210-999-8401 451 E
tupresident@trinity.edu
ANDERSON, Daphne ..... 312-949-7000 139 D
danderson@ico.edu
ANDERSON, Darrel .... 913-971-3294 176 C
dwanderson@mnu.edu
ANDERSON, Daryl .... 718-779-1430 311 E
danderson1@mail.plazacollege.edu
ANDERSON, Dave .... 877-476-8674 436 F
ANDERSON, David .... 616-234-3638 224 F
danderso@grcc.edu
ANDERSON, David .... 423-775-6596 422 I
ANDERSON, David .... 731-286-3259 424 D
dbanderson@dscc.edu
ANDERSON, David, R ... 507-786-3000 243 D
anderson@stolaf.edu
ANDERSON, Deanna ..... 601-266-5020 249 F
deedee.anderson@usm.edu
ANDERSON,
Deborah, L .... 815-224-0406 140 E
deborah_anderson@ivcc.edu
ANDERSON, Delia, C .... 617-732-2910 216 D
delia.anderson@mcphs.edu
ANDERSON, Diane, K ... 269-387-2152 233 B
diane.anderson@wmich.edu
ANDERSON, Diann .... 256-372-8094.... 1 A
diann.anderson@aamu.edu
ANDERSON, Donald ...... 785-242-5200 176 I
donald.anderson@ottawa.edu
ANDERSON, Donna .... 406-243-2288 263 K
ANDERSON, Dorothy .... 505-277-5824 288 J
unmvphr@unm.edu
ANDERSON,
Douglas, D .... 435-797-2376 460 C
douglas.anderson@usu.edu
ANDERSON, Duane .... 406-756-3384 263 E
danderson@fvcc.edu
ANDERSON, Elizabeth ... 609-586-4800 278 F
andersoe@mccc.edu
ANDERSON, Elizabeth ... 706-295-6846 120 A
eanderson@gntc.edu
ANDERSON, Emily .... 773-481-8830 135 G
efitzmaurice@ccc.edu
ANDERSON, Emily .... 575-439-3806 287 D
emilyt@nmsu.edu
ANDERSON, Eric .... 712-707-7132 169 D
eric.anderson@nwciowa.edu
ANDERSON, Eric .... 715-855-7512 498 E
eanderson72@cvtc.edu
ANDERSON, Eric, R ...... 614-236-6606 349 B
eanderson@capital.edu
ANDERSON, Erin .... 575-492-2676 287 A
eanderson@nmjc.edu
ANDERSON, Eugene ..... 315-443-9601 321 G
genea@syr.edu
ANDERSON, Faith .... 912-443-5776 125 B
fanderson@savannahtech.edu
ANDERSON,
Garwood, P .... 262-646-6523 494 F
ganderson@nashotah.edu
ANDERSON,
Garwood, P .... 262-646-6500 494 F
ganderson@nashotah.edu
ANDERSON, Gary, C ..... 612-624-3908 243 F
ander018@umn.edu
ANDERSON, Genna .... 612-659-6000 239 A
genna.anderson@minneapolis.edu
ANDERSON, Glenn .... 318-342-1600 193 C
ganderson@ulm.edu
ANDERSON, Gordon, K 423-439-5671 419 G
andersgk@etsu.edu
ANDERSON, Grace .... 208-792-2465 132 A
glanderson@lcsc.edu
ANDERSON, Greg .... 215-204-8017 399 B
gregory.anderson@temple.edu
ANDERSON, Gregory .... 951-222-8804.. 59 D
ANDERSON, Gregory .... 951-222-8804.. 59 A
gregory.anderson@rcc.edu
ANDERSON, Gregory .... 601-979-2144 246 F
gregory.l.anderson@jsums.edu
ANDERSON, Gregory, R 817-735-7600 454 B
gregory.anderson@unthsc.edu
ANDERSON, Harry .... 715-394-8241 497 C
handerso@uwsuper.edu
ANDERSON, Heidi, M ... 410-651-6101 203 D
hmanderson@umes.edu
ANDERSON, Holly .... 541-885-1389 374 I
holly.anderson@oit.edu
ANDERSON, JR.,
Horace, E .... 914-422-4407 311 A
ANDERSON, Ian .... 207-699-5033 195 A
ianderson@meca.edu
ANDERSON, Jacqui .... 620-343-4600 173 G
janderson@fhtc.edu
ANDERSON, James .... 508-999-8042 212 A
jim.anderson@umassd.edu
ANDERSON, James .... 202-462-2101.. 93 A
janderson@iwp.edu
ANDERSON, James, A .. 719-333-2074 503 D
james.anderson.72@us.af.mil
ANDERSON, James, A .. 800-443-9266 503 D
james.anderson.72@us.af.mil
ANDERSON, James, D .. 217-333-7404 152 B
janders@illinois.edu
ANDERSON, James, T .. 973-655-7022 279 B
andersonja@montclair.edu
ANDERSON, Janet, B .... 435-797-5557 460 C
janet.anderson@usu.edu
ANDERSON, Janice .... 254-526-1116 432 D
janice.anderson@ctcd.edu
ANDERSON, Jannette .... 801-689-2160 459 I
janderson@nightingale.edu
ANDERSON, Jason, R ... 937-255-3636 502 C
jason.anderson@afit.edu
ANDERSON, Jeanette .... 626-571-8811.. 73 E
jeanettea@uwest.edu
ANDERSON, Jeff .... 808-245-8384 130 B
jeffa@hawaii.edu
ANDERSON, Jeffrey, J .. 847-574-5210 142 B
janderson@lfgsm.edu
ANDERSON, Jennifer .... 785-539-3571 176 A
janderson@mccks.edu
ANDERSON, Jennifer .... 203-254-4000.. 87 I
janderson@fairfield.edu
ANDERSON, Jennifer .... 334-229-4950.... 4 A
janderson@alasu.edu
ANDERSON, Jennifer .... 614-287-5581 351 C
jander02@cscc.edu
ANDERSON, Jennifer .... 503-594-6222 372 C
jennifer.anderson@clackamas.edu
ANDERSON, Jeremy ...... 606-337-1533 180 C
jeremy.anderson@ccbbc.edu
ANDERSON, Jeremy ...... 218-751-8670 242 O
jeremyanderson@oakhills.edu
ANDERSON, Jerry .... 515-271-3985 165 J
jerry.anderson@drake.edu
ANDERSON, Jill .... 307-754-6401 501 H
jill.anderson@nwc.edu
ANDERSON, Jill .... 717-393-0654 387 G
ANDERSON, Jill, C .... 610-625-7910 390 F
andersonj@moravian.edu
ANDERSON, Jillian .... 508-929-8072 213 G
jillian.anderson@worcester.edu
ANDERSON, Joanna ...... 660-596-7223 259 M
janderson@sfccmo.edu
ANDERSON, Jody .... 706-778-8500 124 D
jandersonl@piedmont.edu
ANDERSON, John .... 970-824-1110.. 79 H
john.anderson@cncc.edu
ANDERSON, Jon .... 435-586-7700 460 A
jonanderson@suu.edu
ANDERSON, Jon (Jay) .. 979-209-7296 431 H
jay.anderson@blinn.edu
ANDERSON, Jonathan ... 509-359-6081 479 G
janderson@ewu.edu
ANDERSON, Jordan ...... 770-534-6126 116 D
janderson6@brenau.edu
ANDERSON, Joshua ...... 602-429-4432.. 15 A
janderson@ps.edu
ANDERSON, JP .... 585-594-6832 310 C
anderson_jp@roberts.edu
ANDERSON, Julie .... 507-457-5122 241 F
julie.anderson@winona.edu
ANDERSON, Julie .... 507-222-4321 234 G
janderso@carleton.edu
ANDERSON, Julie .... 309-556-3780 140 F
janders3@iwu.edu
ANDERSON, Julie .... 360-486-8868 482 I
janderson@stmartin.edu
ANDERSON, Julie, S ..... 801-863-5378 460 D
julie.anderson@uvu.edu
ANDERSON, Justin .... 603-646-3661 273 D
justin.anderson@dartmouth.edu
ANDERSON, Kathy .... 501-370-5306.. 20 F
kanderson@philander.edu
ANDERSON, Kay .... 478-445-6286 119 B
kay.anderson@gcsu.edu
ANDERSON, Kelsi .... 402-481-8602 265 K
kelsi.anderson@bryanhealthcollege.edu
ANDERSON, Kenneth ..... 509-313-3404 480 F
anderson@gonzaga.edu
ANDERSON, Kent .... 701-483-2214 345 C
kent.w.anderson@dickinsonstate.edu
ANDERSON, Kevin .... 617-747-2359 206 H
physicalplant@berklee.edu
ANDERSON, Kevin .... 251-380-3006.... 6 H
jkanderson@shc.edu
ANDERSON, Kevin .... 239-432-6706 101 A
kevin.anderson@fsw.edu
ANDERSON, Kevin, L .... 563-589-0211 171 A
kanderson@wartburgseminary.edu
ANDERSON, Kim .... 800-561-2606 388 H
kanderson@lincoln.edu
ANDERSON, Kimberly ... 602-285-7466.. 13 F
kimberly.anderson@phoenixcollege.edu
ANDERSON, Kirk, D ...... 309-794-7203 133 C
kirkanderson@augustana.edu
ANDERSON, Kristina ..... 334-222-6591.... 2 I
kanderson@lbwcc.edu
ANDERSON, Kristine ..... 231-777-0447 228 G
kristine.anderson@muskegoncc.edu
ANDERSON, Kristy .... 360-538-4151 480 G
kanderso@ghc.edu
ANDERSON, OFM,
Lawrence .... 518-783-2332 315 E
landerson@siena.edu
ANDERSON, Layne .... 218-477-2447 239 E
layne.anderson@mnstate.edu
ANDERSON, Leif, B ...... 612-330-1497 234 A
andersol@augsburg.edu
ANDERSON, Leslie .... 870-733-6732.. 17 F
landerson@asumidsouth.edu
ANDERSON, Leslie .... 408-498-5100.. 73 B
landerson@cogswell.edu
ANDERSON, Leslie .... 888-488-4968.. 46 F
landeson@itu.edu
ANDERSON, Linda .... 256-726-7095.... 6 C
landerson@oakwood.edu
ANDERSON, Lisa .... 718-270-5000 294 G
lisa@mec.cuny.edu
ANDERSON, Liz .... 479-619-4176.. 20 C
eanderson14@nwacc.edu
ANDERSON, Lois .... 301-387-3042 199 A
lois.anderson@garrettcollege.edu
ANDERSON, Lori .... 828-227-7271 343 E
landerson@wcu.edu
ANDERSON, Maria .... 708-656-8000 145 C
maria.anderson@morton.edu
ANDERSON, Maria .... 973-655-5225 279 B
andersonmar@montclair.edu
ANDERSON, Marianne .. 410-386-8000 198 D
manderson@carrollcc.edu
ANDERSON, Marie .... 909-469-5485.. 75 I
manderson@westernu.edu
ANDERSON, Marie, A ... 680-488-2470 505 B
mariea@palau.edu
ANDERSON, Mark .... 970-351-1890.. 84 F
ANDERSON, Mark .... 908-709-7010 284 D
mark.anderson2@ucc.edu
ANDERSON, Mark, D .... 937-775-3570 364 E
mark.anderson@wright.edu
ANDERSON, Marlene .... 701-224-5578 346 A
marlene.anderson@bismarckstate.edu
ANDERSON, Mary Jo .... 435-865-8491 460 A
andersonm@suu.edu
ANDERSON,
Mary Kaye, G .... 615-898-2670 422 C
marykaye.anderson@mtsu.edu
ANDERSON, Melinda, F 318-619-2916 189 F
manderson@lsua.edu
ANDERSON,
Melinda, R .... 252-335-3187 341 B
mranderson@ecsu.edu
ANDERSON, Melissa ..... 785-833-4512 175 E
melissa.anderson@kwu.edu
ANDERSON, Melissa ..... 330-263-2082 351 A
melanderson@wooster.edu
ANDERSON, Melissa, L 336-841-9220 329 F
manderson@highpoint.edu
ANDERSON, Melissa, P 540-674-3635 474 E
manderson@nr.edu
ANDERSON, Michael .... 435-283-7000 461 B
michael.anderson@snow.edu
ANDERSON, Michael .... 318-345-9261 188 D
michaelanderson19@ladelta.edu
ANDERSON,
Michelle, J .... 718-951-5671 293 C
bcpresident@brooklyn.cuny.edu
ANDERSON,
Michelle, O .... 214-777-6433 441 G
ANDERSON, Mike .... 503-255-0332 374 C
mikeanderson@multnomah.edu
ANDERSON, Mike .... 435-283-7393 461 B
mike.anderson@snow.edu
ANDERSON, Mike .... 206-876-6107 483 H
manderson@theseattleschool.edu
ANDERSON, Myron .... 210-458-4011 455 E
ANDERSON,
N. Douglas .... 740-376-4536 355 E
doug.anderson@marietta.edu
ANDERSON, Natalie ...... 585-475-2638 312 F
nzadar@rit.edu
ANDERSON, Nathan ...... 520-795-0787.. 10 I
ANDERSON, Neal .... 303-963-3463.. 78 H
nanderson@ccu.edu
ANDERSON, Neil .... 423-648-2673 423 B
nanderson@richmont.edu
ANDERSON, Nick .... 651-290-6358 242 L
nick.anderson@mitchellhamline.edu
ANDERSON, Nickoel ..... 218-733-5990 238 G
nickoel.anderson@lsc.edu
ANDERSON, Nina .... 732-571-7551 279 A
nanderso@monmouth.edu
ANDERSON, Noma .... 901-490-2989 463 A
noma.anderson@uvm.edu
ANDERSON, Oliver .... 801-832-2242 461 F
oanderson@westminstercollege.edu
ANDERSON, Patricia ..... 775-327-2354 271 A
pat.anderson@gbcnv.edu
ANDERSON, Paula .... 641-784-5148 166 E
pkanders@graceland.edu
ANDERSON, Pauline ..... 850-729-6485 104 M
ander113@nwfsc.edu
ANDERSON, Per, M ...... 218-299-3932 235 H
anderson@cord.edu
ANDERSON, Peter .... 216-987-3538 351 E
peter.anderson@tri-c.edu
ANDERSON, Peter, T .... 540-674-3631 474 E
ptanderson@nr.edu
ANDERSON, Randy .... 513-618-1925 350 E
randerson@ccms.edu
ANDERSON, Rayelle ...... 208-769-5978 132 D
rayelle_anderson@nic.edu
ANDERSON, Raymond .. 480-965-9911.. 10 J
ray.anderson@asu.edu
ANDERSON, Rebecca .... 210-458-4132 455 E
rebecca.anderson@utsa.edu
ANDERSON, Regina ...... 731-426-7536 420 G
rkanderson@lanecollege.edu
ANDERSON, Richard ...... 801-422-4301 458 H
rick_anderson@byu.edu
ANDERSON, Richard, C 386-312-4265 107 C
richardanderson@sjrstate.edu
ANDERSON, Rick .... 956-665-2121 455 D
rick.anderson@utrgv.edu
ANDERSON, Rick .... 423-236-2843 423 F
randerson@southern.edu
ANDERSON,
Roberta (Bobbie) .... 651-793-1931 238 I
roberta.anderson@metrostate.edu
ANDERSON, Ron .... 651-201-1498 237 B
ron.anderson@minnstate.edu

ANG, Felix .... 831-459-2973.. 71 A
felix@ucsc.edu
ANGE, Nate .... 919-365-7711 340 E
ANGEL, Andrea, L .... 812-237-6155 156 D
andrea.angel@indstate.edu
ANGEL, Leigh .... 828-694-1729 332 E
ANGELES, Laura, A .... 719-333-1042 503 D
laura.angeles@usafa.edu
ANGELIS, Peter .... 310-825-4941.. 69 E
pangelis@ha.ucla.edu
ANGELL, Alecia .... 509-527-3683 485 B
alecia.angell@wwcc.edu
ANGELL, Beth .... 804-827-1030 473 B
keangell@vcu.edu
ANGELL, Tracey .... 401-874-2326 405 E
tracey@uri.edu
ANGELO, Caroline .... 404-225-4545 115 H
cangelo@atlantatech.edu
ANGELO, Lisa .... 215-968-8048 379 D
lisa.angelo@bucks.edu
ANGELONI, Lisa .... 609-771-3080 276 I
angeloni@tcnj.edu
ANGELOS, Peter .... 218-879-0839 238 B
peter.angelos@fdltcc.edu
ANGEMI, Karen .... 909-621-8384.. 44 H
karen_angemi@hmc.edu
ANGEMI, Karen .... 909-621-8384.. 44 H
kangemi@hmc.edu
ANGENY, Karen .... 610-861-5460 391 C
kangeny@northampton.edu
ANGER, Paul .... 928-428-8334.. 12 F
paul.anger@eac.edu
ANGIOLETTI, Lindsey .... 516-572-9634 307 E
lindsey.angioletti@ncc.edu
ANGION, Stanford .... 334-872-2533.... 6 F
ANGIS, Victoria .... 802-468-1231 463 E
victoria.angis@castleton.edu
ANGLE, Jay Scott .... 352-392-1971 111 A
jangle@ufl.edu
ANGLE, Ray .... 509-313-4100 480 F
angle@gonzaga.edu
ANGLE, Steven, R .... 423-425-4141 427 C
steven-angle@utc.edu
ANGLESIO, Marco .... 610-861-4585 391 C
manglesio@northampton.edu
ANGLIM, Sean .... 315-568-3092 310 B
sanglim@nycc.edu
ANGLIN, Pamela, D ...... 903-785-7661 441 D
panglin@parisjc.edu
ANGLIN, Regina .... 910-678-8527 334 E
anglinr@faytechcc.edu
ANGLIN, Roland .... 216-687-5269 350 J
r.anglin@csuohio.edu
ANGLIN, Thad .... 254-442-5111 432 I
thad.anglin@cisco.edu
ANGLIONGTO,
Maryanne .... 636-481-3318 254 C
manglion@jeffco.edu
ANGLO, Annabelle .... 949-794-9090.. 66 D
ANGOLA HARPER,
Tameka .... 334-727-8421.... 7 D
tharper@tuskegee.edu
ANGRIST, Michele, P .... 518-388-6234 323 J
angristm@union.edu
ANGROVE, William .... 936-294-2774 450 A
wla002@shsu.edu
ANGRY, Rose .... 719-502-4106.. 82 E
rose.angryl@ppcc.edu
ANGSMAN, Rhonda ...... 317-921-4479 158 E
rangsman@ivytech.edu
ANGST, JR., Arthur, H .. 516-876-3094 318 C
angsta@oldwestbury.edu
ANGUIANO, Amy .... 540-857-7254 475 G
aanguiano@virginiawestern.edu
ANGULO, Gaby .... 908-497-4363 284 D
marieanne.angulo@ucc.edu
ANGULO, Michael .... 609-626-6072 283 E
michael.angulo@stockton.edu
ANGUS, Jason .... 304-697-7550 487 E
ANHORN, JR., Jerry ...... 509-527-4299 485 B
jerry.anhorn@wwcc.edu
ANICETTI, Rachel .... 925-473-7446.. 40 D
ranicetti@losmedanos.edu
ANICH, SVD, Kenneth ... 563-876-3353 165 H
kanich@dwci.edu
ANID, Nada .... 212-261-1572 308 I
nanid@nyit.edu
ANISFELD, Sharon, C ... 617-559-8773 210 F
sanisfeld@hebrewcollege.edu
ANISKOVICH, William ... 203-773-8550.. 85 D
waaniskovich@albertus.edu
ANKE, Sharla, M .... 724-287-8711 379 E
sharla.anke@bc3.edu
ANKENY, Carrie .... 630-829-6028 133 E
croberts@ben.edu
ANKER, Laura, M .... 516-876-3460 318 C
ankerl@oldwestbury.edu
ANKERBERG, Erik .... 708-209-3278 136 E
erik.ankerberg@cuchicago.edu
ANKERSON, Katherine .. 402-472-9216 269 J
kankerson1@unl.edu
ANNABLE, Ross .... 716-614-6407 309 G
rannable@niagaracc.suny.edu
ANNAN, Vidal .... 908-737-4866 278 E
vannan@kean.edu
ANNARELLI, James, J ... 727-864-8243.. 98 J
annarejj@eckerd.edu
ANNAVARJULA, Madan 401-232-6227 404 A
mannavar@bryant.edu
ANNEAR, Patricia, T ..... 724-287-8711 379 E
patricia.annear@bc3.edu
ANNETT, JR., Bruce, J .. 248-204-2206 227 A
bannett@ltu.edu
ANNETTE, Harold .... 218-322-2353 238 F
harold.annette@itascacc.edu
ANNINO, Lou .... 203-932-7153.. 89 H
lannino@newhaven.edu
ANNIS, Stephen .... 423-318-2736 425 F
stephen.annis@ws.edu
ANNUNZIATA,
Margaret, H .... 828-395-1300 335 D
mannunziata@isothermal.edu
ANSARI, Sami .... 978-542-7015 213 E
sami.ansari@salemstate.edu
ANSBOURY, Pamela ...... 210-485-0307 428 G
pansboury@alamo.edu
ANSBRO, Dawn .... 845-341-4337 310 G
dawn.ansbro@sunyorange.edu
ANSCHUTZ, Mendi .... 785-738-9090 176 F
manschutz@ncktc.edu
ANSEL, Ryan .... 313-664-7470 222 H
ransel@collegeforcreativestudies.edu
ANSELMENT,
Kenneth, L .... 920-832-6992 493 B
ken.anselment@lawrence.edu
ANSELMO, Peter .... 575-835-5438 286 K
peter.anselmo@nmt.edu
ANSEVIN-ALLEN, Scott .. 603-899-4151 273 E
ansevis@franklinpierce.edu
ANSLEY, Kelly .... 706-880-8311 122 A
kansley@lagrange.edu
ANSTOETTER, Don .... 314-792-6120 254 F
anstoetter@kenrick.edu
ANT, Susan .... 952-358-8906 239 G
susan.ant@normandale.edu
ANTELMAN, Kristin .... 805-893-3256.. 70 E
kantelman@ucsb.edu
ANTENEN, James .... 210-826-7595 457 I
antenenj@wbu.edu
ANTER, David .... 805-378-1415.. 73 J
danter@vcccd.edu
ANTHOINE, Sandra .... 401-341-2102 405 D
sandra.anthoine@salve.edu
ANTHOLIS, William, J .. 434-924-6061 472 D
wja8yh@virginia.edu
ANTHONY, Angela .... 509-574-4651 486 D
aanthony@yvcc.edu
ANTHONY, Cynthia, T .. 205-929-6300.... 2 H
canthony@lawsonstate.edu
ANTHONY, David .... 315-464-8047 317 C
anthonyd@upstate.edu
ANTHONY, Doug .... 304-424-8280 490 F
doug.anthony@wvup.edu
ANTHONY, Jason, S ..... 401-456-8234 405 A
janthony@ric.edu
ANTHONY, Kathy .... 610-526-6045 385 D
kanthony@harcum.edu
ANTHONY, Linda .... 866-492-5336 244 F
linda.anthony@laureate.net
ANTHONY, Marra .... 301-546-4180 201 E
marratj@pgcc.edu
ANTHONY, Michael, D . 708-709-3501 147 D
manthony@prairiestate.edu
ANTHONY, Ryan .... 704-290-5870 337 I
ranthony@spcc.edu
ANTHWAL, Sunny .... 845-398-4061 314 G
sunny@stac.edu
ANTIGUA, Diony .... 786-391-1167.. 95 G
ANTIGUA, Jose .... 786-391-1167.. 95 G
ANTKOWIAK, Bruce .... 724-805-2940 398 A
bruce.antkowiak@stvincent.edu
ANTKOWIAK, Bruce ...... 724-805-2940 397 I
bruce.antkowiak@stvincent.edu
ANTLE, Austin .... 518-458-5435 296 G
antlea@strose.edu
ANTMAN, Karen, H .... 617-358-9600 207 E
kha4@bu.edu
ANTOINE, Kevin .... 215-968-8093 379 D
kevin.antoine@bucks.edu
ANTOINE, Linda .... 225-771-4580 191 A
linda_antoine@subr.edu
ANTOINE, Linda, B .... 225-771-4587 191 B
linda_antoine@subr.edu
ANTOINE, Tanesha .... 281-922-3453 443 C
tanesha.antoine@sjcd.edu
ANTOINE, Tanesha .... 281-922-3453 443 A
tanesha.antoine@sjcd.edu
ANTON, Vanessa .... 918-444-3701 366 G
anton@nsuok.edu
ANTONAKAKIS, Helen ... 856-227-7200 276 E
hantonakakis@camdencc.edu
ANTONE, Blaine .... 520-383-0075.. 16 A
bantone@tocc.edu
ANTONELLI, Fred .... 585-582-8201 298 F
fredantonelli@elim.edu
ANTONELLO, Michael ... 561-237-7960 103 W
mantonello@lynn.edu
ANTONIKOWSKI,
Angela .... 518-262-5848 289 L
antonia@amc.edu
ANTONIO, Edward .... 218-299-3894 235 H
eantonio@cord.edu
ANTONISHEN, Ashley ... 231-348-6600 228 H
aantonishen@ncmich.edu
ANTONOVICS, Kate .... 858-246-5340.. 70 C
seventhprovost@ucsd.edu
ANTONOWICZ, Joseph . 908-737-3150 278 E
jantonow@kean.edu
ANTONUCCI, Carl .... 860-832-2099.. 85 G
antonucci@ccsu.edu
ANTONUCCI-DURGAN,
Dana .... 631-451-4539 321 D
antonud@sunysuffolk.edu
ANTONY, Elbby .... 281-283-2016 452 E
antonye@uhcl.edu
ANTROBUS, Barbara ..... 859-858-2285 179 C
ANTROP-GONZÁLEZ,
René .... 845-257-2800 316 E
antropgr@newpaltz.edu
ANTRUM, Curtis .... 203-857-7090.. 87 D
ANTUNES, Nancy .... 781-891-2686 206 G
nantunes@bentley.edu
ANTURKAR, Anjali, N ... 734-764-5132 231 H
anturkar@umich.edu
ANUMBA, Chimay .... 352-392-4836 111 A
anumba@ufl.edu
ANUNDSON, Brock .... 907-474-7780.. 10 A
bsanundson@alaska.edu
ANVINSON, Kimberly .... 701-231-7761 345 F
kimberley.anvinson@ndsu.edu
ANYANWU,
Fitzpatrick, U .... 337-421-6905 188 J
fitzpatrick.anyanwu@sowela.edu
ANZ, Susan, D .... 254-710-3731 431 E
susan_anz@baylor.edu
ANZAK, Daniel .... 210-458-5905 455 E
daniel.anzak@utsa.edu
ANZALDUA, Ricardo ...... 212-237-8316 294 D
ranzaldua@jjay.cuny.edu
ANZALONE, Alessandro 772-462-5604 102 F
aanzalone@irsc.edu
ANZALONE, Nancy .... 619-297-9700.. 68 A
ANZALOTTA, Jaime .... 305-237-3336 104 E
janzalot@mdc.edu
ANZINGER, John .... 240-629-7858 198 I
janzinger@frederick.edu
ANZUONI, Rebecca .... 617-373-7780 217 I
AOUN, Joseph, E .... 617-373-2101 217 I
AOYAMA, Yuko .... 508-793-7676 208 C
yaoyama@clarku.edu
APANEL, Stephen, J ..... 570-577-1195 379 C
stephen.apanel@bucknell.edu
APANOVICH, Val .... 570-674-6749 390 B
vapanovich@misericordia.edu
APARICIO, Sally .... 520-515-8757.. 11 M
aparicios@cochise.edu
APAW, David .... 410-225-2464 200 D
dapaw@mica.edu
APEKEY, Stella .... 202-687-0100.. 92 E
APEL, Scott .... 562-985-1658.. 31 D
scott.apel@csulb.edu
APEN, Lynette .... 408-270-6448.. 62 G
lynette.apen@evc.edu
APFELBAUM, Randy ...... 646-592-4227 326 D
randy.apfelbaum@yu.edu
APFELTHALER, Gerhard . 805-493-3352.. 29 C
apfeltha@callutheran.edu
APGAR, Travis .... 518-276-6266 312 C
apgart@rpi.edu
APICELLA, Paul .... 215-895-1403 382 F
pwa29@drexel.edu
APICERNO, Amy .... 727-864-8058.. 98 J
apiceral@eckerd.edu
APIGO, Mary-Jo .... 310-287-4110.. 49 H
apigomj@wlac.edu
APODACA, John .... 505-428-1630 288 E
john.apodaca1@sfcc.edu
APODACA, Phillip, C .... 719-389-6613.. 78 I
papodaca@coloradocollege.edu
APOLLO, Richard, M ..... 516-463-5405 301 G
richard.apollo@hofstra.edu
APOLLONIO, Heather .... 914-674-7394 306 C
hapollonio@mercy.edu
APONTE, Bianca .... 787-257-0000 512 B
bianca.aponte1@upr.edu
APONTE, Brunilda .... 787-743-7979 510 H
baponte@suagm.edu
APONTE, Gabriel .... 787-738-2161 512 C
gabriel.aponte2@upr.edu
APONTE, Laura, E .... 787-766-1717 510 G
um_laponte@uagm.edu
APONTE, Madelene .... 845-574-4492 312 H
maponte@sunyrockland.edu
APONTE, Wanda .... 787-786-3030 511 A
waponte@ucb.edu.pr
APONTE HERNÁNDEZ,
Juan, M .... 787-764-0000 513 B
juan.aponte6@upr.edu
APOSTOLAKIS, Vy .... 504-568-6518 189 H
vpham@lsuhsc.edu
APOSTOLAKOS,
Michael, J .... 585-275-4786 323 M
michael_apostolakos@urmc.rochester.edu
APPEANING,
V. Alexander .... 225-771-2705 191 A
appeaning@sus.edu
APPEANING,
Vladimir, A .... 225-771-2705 191 B
appeaning@sus.edu
APPEL, Elizabeth, H ...... 410-777-7383 197 G
ehappel@aacc.edu
APPEL, Heidi .... 419-530-6031 363 B
heidi.appel@utoledo.edu
APPEL, Kellie .... 678-547-6397 122 E
appel_k@mercer.edu
APPEL, Shari, A .... 330-471-8116 355 D
sappel@malone.edu
APPEL, Steve .... 575-492-2187 289 F
sappel@usw.edu
APPELGET, Kristin .... 609-258-3018 280 D
appelget@princeton.edu
APPELT, Uschi .... 812-866-7221 155 G
appelt@hanover.edu
APPIAH-PADI,
Stephen, K .... 570-577-3796 379 C
s.appiahpadi@bucknell.edu
APPLE, Monique .... 605-455-6055 415 H
mapple@olc.edu
APPLE, Ryan .... 517-321-0242 225 A
rapple@glcc.edu
APPLEBAUM, Melanie ... 314-505-7117 252 A
applebaumm@csl.edu
APPLEBY, Alice .... 803-822-3588 410 D
applebya@midlandstech.edu
APPLEBY, Karen .... 208-282-2171 131 G
karenappleby@isu.edu
APPLEBY, Leigh .... 860-723-0617.. 85 F
APPLEBY, Scott .... 574-631-6972 162 A
rappleby@nd.edu
APPLEGATE, John, S .... 812-855-9198 156 G
jsapple@iu.edu
APPLEGATE, John, S .... 812-855-9011 156 F
provost@iu.edu
APPLEMAN, Boomer ..... 505-566-3318 288 D
applemanb@sanjuancollege.edu
APPLETON, Abigail .... 352-588-6720 107 D
abigail.appleton@saintleo.edu
APPLETON, Amber .... 503-253-3443 374 G
amber.appleton@ocom.edu
APPLETON, Toby .... 830-792-7462 443 E
tappleton@schreiner.edu
APPLIN, Mary Beth .... 601-857-3380 246 C
mary.applin@hindscc.edu
APPLING, Michele .... 229-500-2939 114 H
michelle.appling@asurams.edu
APPLING, Ron .... 432-552-2750 456 F
appling_r@utpb.edu
APPREY, Augustine .... 717-290-8747 387 G
aapprey@lancasterseminary.edu

APPREY, Maurice ... 434-924-7923 472 D
ma9h@virginia.edu
AQUILA, Dominic ... 713-525-6999 454 G
aquilad@stthom.edu
AQUILA, Jennifer, K ... 610-799-1120 388 D
jaquila@lccc.edu
AQUILA, Scott, W ... 610-799-1550 388 D
saquila@lccc.edu
AQUINO, Belissa ... 787-766-1717 510 G
beaquino@suagm.edu
AQUINO, Cathy ... 304-734-6611 488 D
cathy.aquino@bridgevalley.edu
AQUINO, Jeannette ... 787-890-2681 511 G
jeanette.aquino@upr.edu
ARABIE, Claire ... 337-482-1502 193 B
claire@louisiana.edu
ARACENA, Dan ... 212-678-8231 322 C
da2352@tc.columbia.edu
ARADINE, Bethany ... 585-345-6812 300 F
baaradine@genesee.edu
ARAGON, Beverly ... 575-769-4001 285 O
beverly.aragon@clovis.edu
ARAGON, Marinita ... 620-227-9261 173 D
maragon@dc3.edu
ARAGON, Paul ... 575-769-4167 285 O
paul.aragon@clovis.edu
ARAGON, Ruben ... 505-454-3332 286 J
rubenaragon@nmhu.edu
ARAGON, Tammy ... 480-858-9100.. 15 Q
t.aragon@scnm.edu
ARAGON-JOYCE, Karla .. 602-383-8228.. 16 C
karagon@uat.edu
ARAIMO, Angelo, G ... 718-390-3412 324 F
aaraimo@wagner.edu
ARAKAWA, Bonnie ... 808-689-2539 129 F
bonniea@hawaii.edu
ARAMBULA, Erika ... 308-367-5247 270 B
earambula@unl.edu
ARAMMASH, Fouzi ... 803-705-4311 406 G
fouzi.arammash@benedict.edu
ARAMMASH, Fouzi, H .. 803-705-4311 406 G
fouzi.arammash@benedict.edu
ARANA, Jason ... 408-498-5100.. 73 B
ARANDA, David ... 863-680-6236 100 H
daranda@flsouthern.edu
ARANDA, Jeff ... 518-381-1279 315 B
arandaj@sunysccc.edu
ARANDA-NARANJO,
Barbara ... 210-829-3943 453 C
naranjo@uiwtx.edu
ARANEO, Mary Lou ... 631-451-4611 321 C
araneom@sunysuffolk.edu
ARANGO, Alexis ... 305-760-7500 103 V
ARANT, Alicia ... 406-243-5710 263 K
alicia.arant@umontana.edu
ARANT, Mark ... 660-543-4030 260 G
arant@ucmo.edu
ARAQUE, Teresa, M ... 239-513-1122 102 D
taraque@hodges.edu
ARASIMOWICZ, George 620-341-5171 173 F
garasimo@emporia.edu
ARASIMOWICZ, George 937-376-6453 349 J
garasimowicz@centralstate.edu
ARATA, Raquel ... 916-484-8364.. 50 G
aratar@arc.losrios.edu
ARAVE, Wade ... 360-867-6176 480 C
aravew@evergreen.edu
ARAYA, George ... 530-422-7927.. 74 G
garaya@weimar.edu
ARAYA, Temesgen ... 413-597-2121 220 D
ARBALLO, Madelyn ... 909-274-4220.. 52 J
marballo@mtsac.edu
ARBEITER, Jamie, L ... 920-433-6665 491 G
jamie.arbeiter@bellincollege.edu
ARBELO, Enid ... 787-878-5475 507 L
earbelo@arecibo.inter.edu
ARBERY, Glen ... 307-332-2930 502 A
garbery@wyomingcatholic.edu
ARBIDE, Donna ... 202-994-1058.. 92 D
arbide@gwu.edu
ARBOGAST, Amy ... 724-589-2102 399 D
aarbogast@thiel.edu
ARBONEAUX, Annette ... 225-216-8268 187 G
arboneauxa@mybrcc.edu
ARBUCKLE, Joanne ... 212-217-4000 299 D
joanne_arbuckle@fitnyc.edu
ARBUTHNOT, Beth ... 706-864-1440 127 A
beth.arbuthnot@ung.edu
ARCARIO, Paul ... 718-482-5400 294 F
arcariop@lagcc.cuny.edu
ARCE, Ana, M ... 787-894-2828 513 C
ana.arce1@upr.edu
ARCE, Elsa, M ... 412-365-1282 380 G
arce@chatham.edu
ARCE, Katherine ... 310-338-2881.. 51 A
katherine.arce@lmu.edu
ARCE, Linda ... 617-243-2113 211 B
larce@lasell.edu
ARCE, Wendy ... 510-649-2400.. 44 B
ARCELUS, Victor, J ... 860-439-2834.. 87 H
victor.arcelus@conncoll.edu
ARCENEAUX, Ashley ... 225-578-0971 189 E
ash@lsu.edu
ARCENEAUX,
John Claude ... 337-482-1000 193 B
ARCH, Xan ... 503-943-7310 377 A
arch@up.edu
ARCHAGA, Teresea ... 925-473-7552.. 40 D
tarchaga@losmedanos.edu
ARCHAMBAULT, Karen .. 856-222-9311 281 C
karchambault@rcbc.edu
ARCHBOLD, David, J ... 248-370-3358 229 I
archbold@oakland.edu
ARCHER, Daniel, L ... 801-581-7028 459 O
dan.archer@utah.edu
ARCHER, Elizabeth ... 619-876-4250.. 68 H
earcher@usuniversity.edu
ARCHER, Jeffry ... 254-710-3555 431 E
jeffry_archer@baylor.edu
ARCHER, Keith, A ... 641-269-9700 166 G
archerke@grinnell.edu
ARCHER, Kevin ... 509-963-3101 478 E
kevin.archer@cwu.edu
ARCHER, Linda, R ... 757-446-6190 466 D
archerlr@evms.edu
ARCHER, Lynden, A ... 607-255-9679 297 F
laa25@cornell.edu
ARCHER, Lynn ... 412-536-1182 386 H
lynn.archer@laroche.edu
ARCHER, Marsi ... 417-625-9565 256 F
archer-m@mssu.edu
ARCHER, Rebecca ... 321-674-7571 100 C
rarcher@fit.edu
ARCHER, Ron ... 714-879-3901.. 45 G
rarcher@hiu.edu
ARCHER-RIERSON,
Abby ... 620-242-0439 176 B
archera@mcpherson.edu
ARCHIBALD, Jeffrey, D . 310-287-4374.. 49 H
ARCHIE, Tracey ... 716-851-1118 299 B
archie@ecc.edu
ARCHINAL, Ginette ... 336-278-7228 328 J
garchinal@elon.edu
ARCHULETTA, Justin ... 907-745-3201.... 9 C
ARCIA, Gloria ... 479-979-1431.. 23 I
garcia@ozarks.edu
ARCIERI, Michelle, C ... 202-994-5729.. 92 D
michelle@gwu.edu
ARCUINO, Cathy Lee ... 910-521-6000 343 B
cathylee.arcuino@uncp.edu
ARCURI, Cody ... 718-817-4339 300 C
carcuri@fordham.edu
ARD, Bri ... 251-460-6085.... 9 A
bard@southalabama.edu
ARDAGNA, Wendy ... 215-951-1049 387 A
ardagnaw1@lasalle.edu
ARDALAN, Shah ... 281-290-2777 439 C
shah.ardalan@lonestar.edu
ARDARY, Darlene ... 570-484-3427 394 E
dardary@lockhaven.edu
ARDELEAN, Nicole ... 703-425-4143 468 B
ARDEN, Warwick, A ... 919-515-2195 342 A
warwick_arden@ncsu.edu
ARDIS, Ann ... 703-993-8715 467 E
aardis@gmu.edu
ARDIS, Mary Jo ... 803-778-7825 406 I
ardismj@cctech.edu
ARDNT, Peter, C ... 312-947-0001 148 G
peter_c_ardnt@rush.edu
ARDOVINI, Joanne ... 212-343-1234 306 G
jardovini@mcny.edu
ARDREY, Melantha ... 843-953-3257 408 C
ardreym@cofc.edu
AREA, Ron ... 304-696-2826 489M
area@marshall.edu
AREIZAGA, Jose, R ... 787-891-0925 507 K
jareizag@aguadilla.inter.edu
AREL, Jennifer ... 860-632-3070.. 88 C
jarel@holyapostles.edu
ARELLANO, Carmen ... 773-878-7193 149 A
ARELLANO, Giovanni ... 281-649-3641 437 B
arellanoga@hbu.edu
ARELLANO, Jerry ... 210-486-3884 429 A
jarellano59@alamo.edu
ARENA, Amanda ... 217-234-5475 142 C
ARENA, Maryanne ... 585-345-6802 300 F
mcarena@genesee.edu
ARENARE, Debra ... 516-367-6890 296 C
ARENAS, Ruben ... 323-265-8641.. 48 J
arenasrj@elac.edu
ARENAZ, Pablo ... 956-326-2320 446 E
president@tamiu.edu
AREND, Matthew ... 517-629-0521 221 A
marend@albion.edu
ARENDT, Thomas, K ... 562-902-3355.. 65 I
tomarendt@scuhs.edu
ARENIVAS, Marisol ... 903-875-7540 440 D
marisol.arenivas@navarrocollege.edu
ARENS, Anna ... 414-382-6064 491 F
anna.arens@alverno.edu
ARENS, Dave ... 712-279-1715 164 B
dave.arens@briarcliff.edu
ARENS, Timothy, E ... 312-329-4191 144 I
timothy.arens@moody.edu
ARENSDORF, Jill ... 785-628-4241 173 H
jrarensdorf@fhsu.edu
ARENSMEYER, Lauri, D 208-496-1010 130 I
arensmeyerl@byui.edu
ARENTSEN, Marc ... 508-541-1608 209 A
marentsen@dean.edu
ARES, Samantha ... 973-803-5000 280 B
sares@pillar.edu
ARETA, Ropeti ... 684-699-1575 504 B
a.areta@amsamoa.edu
AREVALO, Aurora ... 323-731-2383.. 55 H
AREY, George, A ... 617-552-3060 207 C
george.arey@bc.edu
AREY, Jason ... 207-216-4399 195 J
yjarey@yccc.edu
ARGIN, Mehmet ... 713-718-5251 437 C
mehmet.argin@hccs.edu
ARGIRI, Elizabeth ... 586-445-7306 227 B
argiril@macomb.edu
ARGO, Jennifer ... 256-782-5769.... 6 A
jlargo@jsu.edu
ARGO, Mike, A ... 870-235-4083.. 21 C
maargo@saumag.edu
ARGO, Scott ... 912-279-5775 117 F
ARGOUDELIS, Patricia .. 847-543-2316 136 A
pargoudelis@clcillinois.edu
ARGOV, Sharon ... 305-760-7500 103 V
ARGUELLES, Adrianna ... 718-939-5100 304 C
aarguelles@libi.edu
ARHIN, Afua ... 910-672-1106 341 C
aarhin@uncfsu.edu
ARIA, Dawn, J ... 518-580-5490 315 F
daria@skidmore.edu
ARIA, Iyob ... 323-860-0789.. 50 B
ARIANO, Patricia ... 630-829-6003 133 E
pariano@ben.edu
ARIAS, Edward ... 713-221-8040 453 A
ariase@uhd.edu
ARIAS, Evelyn ... 210-688-3101 432 H
ARIAS, Meghan ... 703-284-1520 468 H
meghan.arias@marymount.edu
ARICK, Bruce, E ... 317-940-9481 154 C
barick@butler.edu
ARIDA, Lisa, A ... 716-839-8218 298 A
larida@daemen.edu
ARIES, Nancy ... 646-660-6700 292 L
nancy.aries@baruch.cuny.edu
ARIOLA-SUKISAKI,
Kainoa ... 808-932-7445 129 D
kariola@hawaii.edu
ARIOLA-SUKISAKI,
Kainoa ... 808-932-7776 129 D
kariola@hawaii.edu
ARIOVICH, Laura ... 301-546-0741 201 E
ariovilx@pgcc.edu
ARISPE, Iancarlo ... 305-223-4561 107 B
ARISTIGUETA, Maria, P 302-831-4570.. 91 C
mariaa@udel.edu
ARISTIZABAL,
Humberto, X ... 410-543-6426 204 D
hxarisitzabal@salisbury.edu
ARITHSON, Andryn ... 303-871-6814.. 84 E
andryn.arithson@du.edu
ARIZA, Diane, M ... 203-392-8377.. 86 A
arizad1@southernct.edu
ARLEDGE, Cora ... 740-689-4453 356 E
carledge@mccn.edu
ARLINGTON, David, L .. 716-851-1987 299 B
arlington@ecc.edu
ARLITSCH, Kenning ... 406-994-6978 264 C
kenning.arlitsch@montana.edu
ARMACOST, Andrew ... 701-777-2121 345 B
andrew.armacost@und.edu
ARMAN, Beth ... 925-969-2240.. 40 C
barman@dvc.edu
ARMBRISTER,
Clarence (Clay), D ... 704-378-1000 330 D
ARMBRUSTER, Anne ... 217-786-2478 143 B
anne.armbruster@llcc.edu
ARMBRUSTER, Shirley .. 559-278-5292.. 31 B
shirleya@csufresno.edu
ARMENDARIZ, Pablo ... 915-831-7747 436 A
parmend1@epcc.edu
ARMENDARIZ, Rosa ... 925-929-2233.. 40 C
rarmendariz@dvc.edu
ARMENIOX, Leslie, F ... 843-953-5640 408 C
armenioxlf@cofc.edu
ARMENTOR, Melissa ... 409-984-6239 449 I
armentormf@lamarpa.edu
ARMENTROUT,
Gretchen, H ... 540-568-8902 468 C
housergh@jmu.edu
ARMENTROUT, Janie ... 951-343-4210.. 27 G
jarmentrout@calbaptist.edu
ARMER, Linda ... 573-729-7071 259 I
larmer@sbuniv.edu
ARMIJO, Danny ... 575-624-8250 287 B
darmijo@nmmi.edu
ARMINI, Michael, A ... 617-373-5718 217 I
ARMINIAK, Anthony ... 734-374-3227 232 E
aarmini1@wcccd.edu
ARMINIAK, Anthony ... 734-699-7008 232 E
aarmini1@wcccd.edu
ARMISTEAD, Katya ... 805-893-8912.. 70 E
katya.armistead@sa.ucsb.edu
ARMISTEAD, Lisa ... 404-413-2000 120 E
ARMISTEAD, William ... 304-473-8509 491 D
armistead_w@wvwc.edu
ARMONY, Ariel ... 412-648-7374 400 H
armony@pitt.edu
ARMOUR, Angela ... 802-654-2000 462 G
aarmour@smcvt.edu
ARMOUR, Lisa ... 352-381-3642 108 A
lisa.armour@sfcollege.edu
ARMSTEAD, Derrick ... 252-862-1200 337 C
dlarmstead@roanokechowan.edu
ARMSTEAD, Paula ... 510-748-5255.. 57 A
parmstead@peralta.edu
ARMSTONG-ENGLISH,
Rebecca ... 504-816-4325 186 I
rarmstrong@dillard.edu
ARMSTRONG, Abby ... 802-831-1208 463 C
aarmstrong@vermontlaw.edu
ARMSTRONG, Amy ... 254-710-2561 431 E
amy_c_armstrong@baylor.edu
ARMSTRONG, Amy ... 918-465-1777 366 A
aarmstrong@eosc.edu
ARMSTRONG,
Andrew, V ... 540-551-9157 465 L
andrew.armstrong@christendom.edu
ARMSTRONG, Cammie . 575-492-2514 287 A
carmstrong@nmjc.edu
ARMSTRONG,
Christopher, M ... 860-701-6194 503 G
christopher.m.armstrong@uscg.mil
ARMSTRONG, David, A . 305-628-6663 107 F
darmstrong@stu.edu
ARMSTRONG, David, M 816-501-2423 250 F
david.armstrong@avila.edu
ARMSTRONG, Dayle ... 909-469-5322.. 75 I
darmstrong@westernu.edu
ARMSTRONG, Elizabeth 540-231-7197 476 C
beth1@vt.edu
ARMSTRONG, Franca ... 315-334-7701 306 K
farmstrong@mvcc.edu
ARMSTRONG, Franklin .. 775-831-1314 272 D
farmstrong@sierranevada.edu
ARMSTRONG, Gary ... 816-415-7651 262 F
armstrongg@william.jewell.edu
ARMSTRONG, Greg ... 630-620-2175 146 C
grarmstrong@seminary.edu
ARMSTRONG, Jeanette .. 608-796-3395 497 O
jearmstrong@viterbo.edu
ARMSTRONG,
Jeffrey, D ... 805-756-1111.. 29 I
presidentsoffice@calpoly.edu
ARMSTRONG, Jennifer .. 800-747-2687 144 H
jmarmstrong@monmouthcollege.edu
ARMSTRONG, Jennifer .. 909-607-9100.. 63 F
jarmstro@scrippscollege.edu
ARMSTRONG, Jerry ... 303-373-2008.. 83 G
jarmstrong@rvu.edu
ARMSTRONG, Joanne ... 714-628-5030.. 58 G
armstrong_joanne@sccollege.edu
ARMSTRONG, Jon ... 785-628-4091 173 H
jdarmstrong@fhsu.edu

ARMSTRONG, Kara .... 804-594-1578 474 B
karmstrong@jtcc.edu
ARMSTRONG, Karla ...... 620-276-9577 174 B
karla.armstrong@gcccks.edu
ARMSTRONG, Katie ...... 435-652-7975 460 B
karmstrong@dixie.edu
ARMSTRONG, Keith ...... 719-590-6758.. 80 D
karmstrong@coloradotech.edu
ARMSTRONG, Kelli .... 401-341-2337 405 D
kelli.armstrong@salve.edu
ARMSTRONG, Kevin ...... 402-375-7510 268 F
kearmst1@wsc.edu
ARMSTRONG, Kim .... 501-332-0231.. 18 B
karmstrong@asutr.edu
ARMSTRONG, Kim .... 309-694-5599 139 B
kim.armstrong@icc.edu
ARMSTRONG, LaTonya . 773-291-6613 135 E
tarmstrong11@ccc.edu
ARMSTRONG, Lori .... 618-634-3313 149 G
loria@shawneecc.edu
ARMSTRONG, Lori, B ... 410-704-3570 204 E
larmstrong@towson.edu
ARMSTRONG,
Mary Beth .... 205-665-6015.... 8 D
armstrom@montevallo.edu
ARMSTRONG, Myeshia . 323-265-8690.. 48 J
armstrmd@elac.edu
ARMSTRONG, Neal, R ... 520-621-3513.. 16 D
nra@arizona.edu
ARMSTRONG,
Patricia, J .... 615-353-3758 424 G
patricia.armstrong@nscc.edu
ARMSTRONG, Rhonda .. 423-869-6436 421 A
rhonda.armstrong@lmunet.edu
ARMSTRONG, Shirley ... 334-291-4964.... 1 H
shirley.armstrong@cv.edu
ARMSTRONG,
Steven, M .... 920-832-6769 493 B
steven.m.armstrong@lawrence.edu
ARMSTRONG, Susan ..... 207-768-9400 197 C
ARMSTRONG, Susan ..... 937-393-3431 360 H
slarmstrong1@sscc.edu
ARMSTRONG, Tamara ... 916-568-3021.. 50 F
armstrt@losrios.edu
ARMSTRONG, Taylor ..... 601-857-3632 246 C
taylor.armstrong@hindscc.edu
ARMSTRONG, Vivian .... 787-284-1912 508 E
varmstro@ponce.inter.edu
ARMSTRONG, Wesley ... 828-262-2190 340 I
armstrongwr@appstate.edu
ARMSTRONG ASH,
Samantha (Sam) .... 509-359-7852 479 G
sarmstrong@ewu.edu
ARNADE, Peter .... 808-956-6460 129 E
parnade@hawaii.edu
ARNDER, Lori .... 757-240-2200 470 D
lori.arnder@rivhs.com
ARNDT, Chase .... 423-652-4341 420 F
chasevarndt@king.edu
ARNDT, Cheryl .... 484-664-3163 390 H
cherylarndt@muhlenberg.edu
ARNDT, Justin .... 406-994-4647 264 C
justin.arndt@montana.edu
ARNDT, Serenna .... 217-234-5253 142 C
ARNDT, Wayne .... 732-987-2237 278 A
warndt@georgian.edu
ARNER, Joe .... 352-588-7426 107 D
joseph.arner@saintleo.edu
ARNER, Katelynn .... 910-410-1761 337 B
kdarner@richmondcc.edu
ARNER, Lori .... 802-468-1211 463 E
lori.arner@castleton.edu
ARNER, Robert .... 610-292-9852 396 J
robert.arner@reseminary.edu
ARNER, Timothy .... 641-269-4529 166 G
arnertim@grinnell.edu
ARNESON, Dean .... 912-201-6123 125 F
darneson@southuniversity.edu
ARNESON, Eric .... 470-578-6000 121 M
ARNESON, Rosemary .... 540-654-1147 471 N
rarneso3@umw.edu
ARNESON, Stephen .... 707-664-2848.. 34 B
ARNESON, Tara .... 802-865-5702 462 A
tarneson@champlain.edu
ARNETT, Carrie .... 510-879-9270.. 60 C
carnett@samuelmerritt.edu
ARNETT, David, J .... 978-478-3400 218 A
darnett@northpoint.edu
ARNETT, Donna .... 859-218-2247 185 F
donna.arnett@uky.edu
ARNETT, Jennifer .... 415-476-4998.. 70 D
jennifer.arnett@ucsf.edu
ARNETT, Katy, E .... 240-895-4451 202 B
kearnett@smcm.edu
ARNETT, LaTondra .... 901-678-2234 426 G
larnett@memphis.edu
ARNETT, Nathan .... 618-985-3741 140 H
nathanarnett@jalc.edu
ARNETTE, Drew .... 502-413-8801 185 A
darnette@sullivan.edu
ARNEY, Doug .... 956-882-7145 455 D
doug.arney@utrgv.edu
ARNEY, Janna .... 956-882-8833 455 D
janna.arney@utrgv.edu
ARNEY, Karl .... 215-455-2300 378 F
ARNHOLT, JoAnn .... 848-932-7692 282 A
arnholt@echo.rutgers.edu
ARNITZ, Deborah .... 602-429-4927.. 15 A
darnitz@ps.edu
ARNN, Larry .... 517-607-2301 225 C
larnn@hillsdale.edu
ARNO, Marlene .... 716-851-1431 299 B
arno@ecc.edu
ARNOLD, Alicia .... 402-481-8752 265 K
alicia.arnold@bryanhealthcollege.edu
ARNOLD, Amelia .... 317-977-7778 259 F
amelia.arnold@slu.edu
ARNOLD, Angela .... 952-358-9045 239 G
angela.arnold@normandale.edu
ARNOLD, Audrey .... 505-277-2511 288 J
aaronld5@unm.edu
ARNOLD, Bill .... 989-463-7111 221 B
arnoldwh@alma.edu
ARNOLD, Brian .... 575-492-2104 289 F
barnold@usw.edu
ARNOLD, Brian .... 704-406-4732 329 A
barnold@gardner-webb.edu
ARNOLD, Brian .... 602-850-8000.. 15 A
ARNOLD, Carl .... 903-233-4310 439 A
carlarnold@letu.edu
ARNOLD, Cisco .... 540-373-2200 466 C
carnold@evcc.edu
ARNOLD, Claire .... 404-962-3024 127 D
claire.arnold@usg.edu
ARNOLD, Clinton, E ...... 562-903-4816.. 27 A
clinton.arnold@biola.edu
ARNOLD, David .... 575-492-2124 289 F
darnold@usw.edu
ARNOLD, David .... 570-945-8310 386 F
dave.arnold@keystone.edu
ARNOLD, Eli .... 404-364-8885 123 K
earnold@oglethorpe.edu
ARNOLD, Elizabeth .... 570-484-2293 394 E
earnold@lockhaven.edu
ARNOLD, Jeff .... 270-852-3300 183 E
jeff.arnold@kwc.edu
ARNOLD, Jill .... 573-629-3103 253 J
jarnold@hlg.edu
ARNOLD, Jon .... 714-895-8183.. 38 A
jarnold@gwc.cccd.edu
ARNOLD, Jon .... 931-540-2538 424 C
jarnold15@columbiastate.edu
ARNOLD, Joseph, E .... 202-885-8649.. 94 D
jearnold@wesleyseminary.edu
ARNOLD, Joshua .... 246-326-4206 464 J
jarnold@bluefield.edu
ARNOLD, Josi .... 308-367-5200 270 B
jarnold7@unl.edu
ARNOLD, Julie .... 419-448-2953 353 E
jarnold3@heidelberg.edu
ARNOLD, Kathy, R .... 651-962-6510 244 E
arno2932@stthomas.edu
ARNOLD, Kenneth, L ..... 707-256-7777.. 53 E
karnold@napavalley.edu
ARNOLD, SR.,
Lester, L .... 703-993-2602 467 E
llarnold@gmu.edu
ARNOLD, Lisa .... 319-352-8238 170 J
lisa.arnold@wartburg.edu
ARNOLD, Melinda .... 903-223-3004 448 A
marnold@tamut.edu
ARNOLD, Paloma .... 805-965-0581.. 63 A
ARNOLD, Richard .... 617-243-2217 211 B
rarnold@lasell.edu
ARNOLD, Rodney .... 870-743-3000.. 20 B
rarnold@northark.edu
ARNOLD, Shirley, E ...... 828-641-0762 327 B
arnoldse@brevard.edu
ARNOLD, Stephen .... 316-978-5600 178 D
stephen.arnold@wichita.edu
ARNOLD, Sue .... 281-998-6003 448 E
sarnold@txchiro.edu
ARNOLD, Susan .... 610-647-4400 385 L
sarnold@immaculata.edu
ARNOLD, Tai .... 518-587-2100 320 E
ARNOLD, Tai .... 518-587-2100 320 E
tai arnold@esc.edu
ARNOLD, Timothy .... 716-338-1125 303 A
timothyarnold@mail.sunyjcc.edu
ARNOLD, Tracy .... 704-406-2361 329 A
ARNOLD, III, W. Ellis .. 501-450-1351.. 19 E
arnold@hendrix.edu
ARNOULD, Karen, A ..... 810-762-3344 232 A
karnould@umich.edu
ARNQUIST, Lynn .... 320-762-4464 237 C
lynn.arnquist@alextech.edu
ARNST, Scott .... 810-762-3123 232 A
sarnst@umich.edu
ARNUSH, Michael, F .... 518-580-5462 315 F
marnush@skidmore.edu
AROCHA, Karen .... 305-443-9170 107 A
karocha@sabercollege.edu
AROCHO, Ashley .... 212-650-6460 293 D
aarocho@ccny.cuny.edu
AROMANDO, Drew, C .. 609-896-5367 281 B
aromando@rider.edu
ARON, Bill .... 510-845-5373.. 29 B
ARON-SMITH, Lashun ... 317-543-3235 159 L
ARONIN, Heidi, J .... 718-270-1025 317 B
heidi.aronin@downstate.edu
ARONSON, Ann .... 612-624-1755 243 F
aronson@umn.edu
ARONSON, Hans-Erik .... 516-367-6890 296 C
ARONSON, Krista, M .... 207-786-6280 194 A
karonson@bates.edu
ARONSON, Stacey .... 320-589-6250 244 B
aronsosp@morris.umn.edu
ARONSTEIN, A-J .... 212-854-7758 291 A
aaronste@barnard.edu
ARORA, Deepa .... 478-934-6588 122 F
deepa.arora@mga.edu
ARORA SINGH, Alka ...... 623-845-3968.. 13 C
alka.arora.singh@gccaz.edu
AROSKAR, Rajarshi .... 518-454-2122 296 G
aroskarr@strose.edu
AROZ, Susan, D .... 480-732-7075.. 12 O
sue.aroz@cgc.edu
ARP, Robert .... 707-654-1037.. 32 A
rarp@csum.edu
ARQUETTE, Toby .... 630-844-5614 133 D
tarquett@aurora.edu
ARRAIZA, Ana Marta .... 787-751-0160 506 F
aarraiza@cmpr.pr.gov
ARRASTIA, Anna .... 502-897-4121 184 G
aarrastia@sbts.edu
ARREAZOLA, David .... 956-764-5950 438 H
darreazola@laredo.edu
ARREDONDO, Jill .... 972-883-5380 455 B
jill.arredondo@utdallas.edu
ARREDONDO, Maria ..... 965-364-4322 449 D
paula.arredondo@tstc.edu
ARREDONDO, Michael .. 214-860-8639 435 A
marredondo@dcccd.edu
ARREDONDO SAMSON,
Marisol .... 714-628-7339.. 36 B
arredond@chapman.edu
ARRELLANO, Carmen .... 773-878-3728 149 A
ARRIAZA, Cecilia .... 714-992-7087.. 54 C
carriaza@fullcoll.edu
ARRIETA, Cynthia .... 626-914-8597.. 36 J
carrieta@citruscollege.edu
ARRINGTON, Jeffrey ...... 334-386-7105.... 5 C
jarrington@faulkner.edu
ARRINGTON,
Manuel, A .... 301-546-0635 201 E
arringma@pgcc.edu
ARRINGTON, Pam .... 330-966-5460 360 K
parrington@starkstate.edu
ARRINGTON,
Stephanie, K .... 765-285-8304 153 H
skarrington@bsu.edu
ARRINGTON, Tom .... 281-459-7613 443 B
tom.arrington@sjcd.edu
ARRINGTON, Trey .... 864-587-4396 412 F
arringtont@smcsc.edu
ARRIOLA, JR., Ben .... 915-778-4001 444 H
ARRIOLA, Susan .... 559-442-8237.. 67 B
susan.arriola@fresnocitycollege.edu
ARROWOOD, Roarke ...... 828-835-4305 338 E
rarrowood@tricountycc.edu
ARROWSMITH, Jason ... 360-442-2270 481 D
jarrowsmith@lowercolumbia.edu
ARROYO, Carmen .... 787-620-2040 505 C
carroyo@aupr.edu
ARROYO, Cheryl .... 219-989-2977 160 D
cheryla@pnw.edu
ARROYO, Cruz .... 253-964-4688 482 I
carroyo@stmartin.edu
ARROYO, Enrique .... 787-841-2000 509 J
earroyo@pucpr.edu
ARROYO, Erica .... 305-284-1724 113 C
earroyo@miami.edu
ARROYO, Gladys .... 787-279-1912 508 A
garroyo@bayamon.inter.edu
ARROYO, Ivonne, D ...... 787-257-7323 510 F
ARROYO, Josie .... 787-704-1020 506 D
jarroyo@columbiacentral.edu
ARROYO, Julitza .... 787-786-3030 511 A
jarroyo@ucb.edu.pr
ARROYO, Luis .... 787-738-2161 512 C
luis.arroyo20@upr.edu
ARROYO, Nancy .... 787-841-2000 509 J
nancy_arroyo@pucpr.edu
ARROYO, Palmira .... 787-753-6335 507 D
parroyo@icprjc.edu
ARROYO, Patti .... 303-404-5111.. 81 A
patti.arroyo@frontrange.edu
ARROYO, Rina .... 386-822-7773 112 A
rarroyo@stetson.edu
ARROYO, Sandra .... 787-765-3560 506 K
sandraarroyo@edpuniversity.edu
ARRUDA, Yvonne, D ..... 401-865-2480 404 F
yarruda@providence.edu
ARRUTI, Duane .... 505-277-8125 288 J
darruti@unm.edu
ARSENAULT, Randi .... 207-859-4000 194 D
ARSTEIN, Mark, H .... 801-863-5189 460 D
mark.arstein@uvu.edu
ARTALE, Maureen, P ..... 607-436-3216 316 F
maureen.artale@oneonta.edu
ARTAMENKO, Dan .... 620-417-1550 177 F
dan.artamenko@sccc.edu
ARTAZ, Nancy .... 316-295-5514 174 A
artaz@friends.edu
ARTEAGA, Elizabeth ...... 714-628-5051.. 58 G
arteaga_elizabeth@sccollege.edu
ARTEAGA, Tom .... 213-477-2512.. 52 I
tarteaga@msmu.edu
ARTER, Neil .... 405-425-5906 367 C
neil.arter@oc.edu
ARTHO, Donna .... 936-294-3101 450 A
artho@shsu.edu
ARTHUR, Candis .... 859-985-3192 179 I
arthurc@berea.edu
ARTHUR, Chandra .... 216-987-4659 351 E
chandra.arthur@tri-c.edu
ARTHUR, Christon .... 269-471-3404 221 D
christon@andrews.edu
ARTHUR, David .... 617-746-1990 210 H
david.arthur@hult.edu
ARTHUR, Kaycee .... 850-729-6089 104 M
arthur2@nwfsc.edu
ARTHUR, Mark .... 405-789-7661 369 I
mark.arthur@swcu.edu
ARTHUR, Scott .... 303-724-8469.. 84 D
scott.arthur@ucdenver.edu
ARTHUR, Virginia .... 651-793-1900 238 I
ginny.arthur@metrostate.edu
ARTIGUES, Jay .... 985-549-2395 193 A
jay.artigues@selu.edu
ARTIM, Chris .... 219-473-4314 154 D
cartim@ccsj.edu
ARTIS, Christine .... 718-933-6700 307 A
cartis@monroecollege.edu
ARTIS, Lori .... 618-468-3000 142 E
lartis@lc.edu
ARTIS, Roslyn, C .... 803-705-4681 406 G
roslyn.artis@benedict.edu
ARTLEY, James .... 904-516-8745.. 99 Q
jartley@fcsl.edu
ARTZ, Liz .... 937-327-7820 364 D
artze@wittenberg.edu
ARTZE VEGA, Isis .... 407-582-3055 113 I
iartzevega@valenciacollege.edu
ARUCK, Janette .... 585-785-1298 299 F
janette.aruck@flcc.edu
ARULANANDAM,
Bernard .... 210-458-6859 455 E
bernard.arulanandam@utsa.edu
ARUM, Richard .... 949-824-8026.. 69 D
richard.arum@uci.edu
ARUSH, Ilan .... 661-824-2977.. 53 H
iarush@ntps.edu
ARVAN, April, A .... 920-565-1000 493 A
arvanaa@lakeland.edu
ARVAY, Anna .... 570-504-9695 384 B
aarvay@som.geisinger.edu
ARVIDSON, Susie .... 620-223-2700 173 I
susiea@fortscott.edu
ARVIN, Lorraine .... 503-517-7625 375 G
arvinl@reed.edu

ATKINS, David, P .... 423-439-4337 419 G
atkinsdp@etsu.edu
ATKINS, Deb .... 763-424-0993 240 A
datkins@nhcc.edu
ATKINS, Elizabeth .... 856-225-2521 281 G
atkins1@camden.rutgers.edu
ATKINS, Elizabeth, A ..... 856-225-2521 281 G
atkins1@camden.rutgers.edu
ATKINS, Garry, L .... 205-726-2763.... 6 E
glatkins@samford.edu
ATKINS, Lisa .... 618-235-2700 150 E
lisa.atkins@swic.edu
ATKINS, Michael .... 301-860-4362 204 A
matkins@bowiestate.edu
ATKINS, Michele .... 731-661-5465 426 F
matkins@uu.edu
ATKINS, Nolan, T .... 802-626-6406 463 G
nolan.atkins@northernvermont.edu
ATKINS, Paula .... 318-797-5116 190 A
paula.atkins@lsus.edu
ATKINS, Regina .... 812-237-2510 156 D
regina.atkins@indstate.edu
ATKINS, Rodney .... 903-730-4890 438 D
ratkins@jarvis.edu
ATKINS, Victoria .... 610-399-2097 393 F
vatkins@cheyney.edu
ATKINS-BRADY, Tara .... 757-569-6713 474 H
tatkins-brady@pdc.edu
ATKINSON, Charles ...... 606-218-5194 186 B
charlesatkinson@upike.edu
ATKINSON, Denese .... 606-886-3863 181 E
denese.atkinson@kctcs.edu
ATKINSON, Eva, G .... 270-686-4282 179 J
eva.atkinson@brescia.edu
ATKINSON, Judith .... 856-415-2115 281 D
jatkinson@rcsj.edu
ATKINSON, Juli .... 918-495-7650 368 F
juatkinson@oru.edu
ATKINSON, Rose .... 406-768-6317 263 F
ratkinson@fpcc.edu
ATKINSON, Sander .... 601-484-8707 247 A
satkinso@meridiancc.edu
ATKINSON, Sheri .... 530-752-8787.. 69 B
slatkinson@ucdavis.edu
ATKINSON, Simon .... 785-864-7298 177 J
satkinson@ku.edu
ATKINSON, Susan .... 870-245-5581.. 20 D
atkinsons@obu.edu
ATKINSON, Timothy ...... 931-221-7011 417 H
atkinsont@apsu.edu
ATKINSON, Vicki .... 847-925-6346 138 G
vatkinso@harpercollege.edu
ATKINSON-WILLOUGHBY,
Brenda .... 202-687-5677.. 92 E
ba3@georgetown.edu
ATLAN, Stephanie .... 213-613-2200.. 65 E
ATOIGUE, Ana Mari, C . 671-735-5527 504 D
anamari.atoigue@guamcc.edu
ATOIGUE, Celia .... 671-734-1812 504 E
catoigue@piu.edu
ATTALLA, Mohamed ...... 646-664-9100 292 K
ATTAO, David .... 670-237-6887 505 A
david.attao@marianas.edu
ATTEBERY, Jani .... 520-494-5364.. 11 K
jani.attebery@centralaz.edu
ATTEBERY, Philip .... 903-586-2501 431 B
philip.attebery@bmats.edu
ATTEMA, Staci .... 605-331-6814 417 C
staci.attema@usiouxfalls.edu
ATTIPOE, Sherika .... 256-306-2560.... 1 F
sherika.attipoe@calhoun.edu
ATTORD, DeNeen .... 813-663-0100.. 93 H
ATWATER, Caryn .... 336-272-7102 329 C
caryn.atwater@greensboro.edu
ATWATER, Harry, A .... 626-395-4100.. 28 J
haa@its.caltech.edu
ATWATER, Ken .... 813-253-7050 102 B
katwater@hccfl.edu
ATWELL, Patrick .... 573-288-6424 252 F
patwell@culver.edu
ATWOOD, Andrew .... 615-297-7545 417 G
atwooda@aquinascollege.edu
ATWOOD, Lorraine .... 802-831-1204 463 C
latwood@vermontlaw.edu
ATWOOD, Peter .... 617-585-0200 207 A
peter.atwood@the-bac.edu
ATWOOD, Steve .... 573-840-9708 260 E
satwood@trcc.edu
ATZERT, Andy .... 516-877-3424 289 I
aatzert@adelphi.edu
AU, Gerard .... 909-537-5100.. 32 E
gau@csusb.edu
AU, Mark .... 808-956-6423 129 E
mgsau@hawaii.edu
AU, Peggy .... 510-628-8038.. 48 C
peggyau@lincolnuca.edu
AU, Valerie .... 508-999-8826 212 A
valerie.au@umassd.edu
AU-MULLANEY,
Rebecca .... 212-659-3601 303 H
rau@tkc.edu
AUBE, Maureen .... 207-755-5235 195 D
maube@cmcc.edu
AUBIN, Mary Ann .... 314-792-6302 254 F
aubin@kenrick.edu
AUBREY, Karen .... 706-880-8235 122 A
kaubrey@lagrange.edu
AUBRY, Ann .... 309-556-3874 140 F
aaubry@iwu.edu
AUBRY, Dawn, M .... 248-370-3228 229 I
dmaubry@oakland.edu
AUBRY, Nadine .... 617-627-3310 219 C
nadine.aubry@tufts.edu
AUCHINCLOSS, Robin ... 718-960-8000 294 A
AUCOIN, Brent .... 765-448-1986 155 B
AUCOIN, Martin, C .... 704-461-6258 326 L
martinaucoin@bac.edu
AUD, Peggy, R .... 240-895-3060 202 B
praud@smcm.edu
AUDANT, Babette .... 718-518-4241 294 B
baudant@hostos.cuny.edu
AUDAS, JP .... 405-224-3140 371 B
jpaudas@usao.edu
AUDET, Shirley .... 860-465-5337.. 85 H
audets@easternct.edu
AUDET, Suzanne .... 508-999-8076 212 A
saudet@umassd.edu
AUDET-KRANS, Janis .... 802-656-7878 463 A
janis.audet-krans@uvm.edu
AUDETTE, Bert .... 207-974-4682 195 E
baudette@emcc.edu
AUDETTE, Jordan .... 316-295-5658 174 A
jordan_audette@friends.edu
AUDUSSEAU, Loic .... 310-660-3593.. 41 E
laudusseau@elcamino.edu
AUDYATIS, Todd .... 508-531-2608 212 D
taudyatis@bridgew.edu
AUER, Matthew, R .... 706-542-2059 126 G
matthew.auer@uga.edu
AUER, Susanne .... 605-455-6049 415 H
sauer@olc.edu
AUER, Susanne .... 605-455-6097 415 H
sauer@olc.edu
AUERBACH, Joshua ...... 802-322-1619 462 B
joshua.auerbach@goddard.edu
AUERNHEIMER, Brent ... 559-278-4373.. 31 B
brent_auernheimer@csufresno.edu
AUGENSTEIN, Amee ...... 317-813-2320 158 C
aaugenstein@ibcindianapolis.edu
AUGENSTEIN, Heather ... 928-428-8333.. 12 F
heather.augenstein@eac.edu
AUGENSTEIN, Mike .... 740-386-4138 355 F
augensteinm@mtc.edu
AUGESTINE-COLLINS,
Sandy .... 518-244-2274 313 A
augsts@sage.edu
AUGHENBAUGH,
Barbara .... 410-837-5719 204 F
baughenbaugh@ubalt.edu
AUGHENBAUGH,
Jonette .... 304-327-4049 489 I
jaughenbaugh@bluefieldstate.edu
AUGHENBAUGH, Lisa ... 410-386-8494 198 D
laughenbaugh@carrollcc.edu
AUGHINBAUGH, David . 864-592-4482 412 E
aughinbaughd@sccsc.edu
AUGOSTINI,
Christopher .... 404-712-6018 118 E
christopher.l.augostini@emory.edu
AUGUST, James .... 805-437-2099.. 30 C
jim.august@csuci.edu
AUGUST, John, R .... 979-845-5053 446 F
j-august@tamu.edu
AUGUST, Michele .... 620-241-0723 172 J
michele.august@centralchristian.edu
AUGUSTINE, Gina .... 740-264-5591 352 B
gaugustine@egcc.edu
AUGUSTINE, Jacqueline 760-245-4271.. 74 D
jacqueline.augustine@vvc.edu
AUGUSTINE, Lailani ..... 570-674-6248 390 B
laugustine@misericordia.edu
AUGUSTINE, TJ .... 312-413-1454 151 G
aaugustn@uic.edu
AUGUSTINE-PLAISANCE,
Lu-Ann .... 718-409-7302 320 G
laugustine@sunymaritime.edu
AUKAI-PAIA, Lori .... 808-735-4785 128 E
lori.aukai-paia@chaminade.edu
AULGUR, Jeff .... 479-964-0583.. 18 C
jaulgur@atu.edu
AULICINO, Christy, L ... 727-816-3443 105 F
aulicic@phsc.edu
AULL, JR., Zeke .... 251-460-6609.... 9 A
zaull@southalabama.edu
AULT, Jill .... 530-242-7689.. 64 C
jault@shastacollege.edu
AULT, Kathy .... 308-635-6350 270 C
aultk@wncc.edu
AULTMAN-BECKER,
April .... 432-837-8121 450 B
axa15ee@sulross.edu
AUMAN, Ann, J .... 253-535-8485 482 A
aumanaj@plu.edu
AUMAN, Timothy, L ..... 336-758-5210 344 C
aumantl@wfu.edu
AUNAI, Samasoni .... 559-934-2222.. 75 A
samaunai@whccd.edu
AUNE, Dave .... 763-433-1306 237 D
david.aune@anokaramsey.edu
AUNE, Krystyna .... 808-956-7541 129 E
krystyna@hawaii.edu
AUNE, Mark .... 724-938-4535 393 E
aune@calu.edu
AUNE, Richard, S .... 507-933-7676 236 A
raune@gustavus.edu
AUNE, Tami .... 507-933-6113 236 A
taune@gustavus.edu
AUNGST, Don .... 434-791-5651 464 I
daungst@averett.edu
AUPPERLE, Jared .... 302-831-2171.. 91 C
jaup@udel.edu
AUPPERLE, Jeff .... 765-998-4553 161 C
jeffry_aupperle@taylor.edu
AURICCHIO, Laura .... 212-636-6300 300 C
lauricchio@fordham.edu
AURIGEMMA, Maureen . 845-758-6822 290 I
AURINGER, Melissa ...... 303-458-3510.. 83 E
mauringer@regis.edu
AURITI, Brian .... 239-410-4147 327 A
bauriti@bennett.edu
AURO, Fadi .... 314-792-6119 254 F
auro@kenrick.edu
AURORA, Teri .... 770-533-6918 122 B
taurora@laniertech.edu
AUSBAND, Avrohom ..... 718-601-3523 326 C
AUSBORN, Dawn .... 910-630-7610 331 E
dausborn@methodist.edu
AUSBURY, Brad .... 417-862-9533 253 F
bausbury@globaluniversity.edu
AUSBURY, D. Bradley ... 417-862-9533 253 F
bausbury@globaluniversity.edu
AUSEL, Jill .... 412-365-1244 380 G
jausel@chatham.edu
AUSMAN, David, J .... 412-397-5424 397 B
ausman@rmu.edu
AUSTAD, Janica .... 651-450-3521 238 E
jaustad@inverhills.edu
AUSTEIN, Chad, K .... 646-592-4237 326 D
chad.austein@yu.edu
AUSTER, Julie .... 646-592-4335 326 D
julie.auster@yu.edu
AUSTERMAN,
Hannah, M .... 765-494-4600 160 B
AUSTIN, Adelee .... 802-258-3359 462 H
adelee.austin@worldlearning.org
AUSTIN, Alton .... 352-854-2322.. 97 N
austina@cf.edu
AUSTIN, Amber .... 502-863-7008 180 H
amber_austin@georgetowncollege.edu
AUSTIN, Ann, E .... 517-355-1734 227 F
aaustin@msu.edu
AUSTIN, Anne .... 870-612-2058.. 22 H
anne.austin@uaccb.edu
AUSTIN, April .... 404-270-5153 126 B
aprila@spelman.edu
AUSTIN, Bob .... 318-473-6571 189 F
raustin@lsua.edu
AUSTIN, Bob, C .... 806-371-5024 429 E
rcaustin@actx.edu
AUSTIN, Christine .... 479-880-4282.. 18 C
caustin@atu.edu
AUSTIN, Christopher ..... 225-578-2841 189 E
ccaustin@lsu.edu
AUSTIN, Dale, F .... 616-395-7950 225 D
austin@hope.edu
AUSTIN, Deborah .... 717-261-4381 403 C
daustin@wilson.edu
AUSTIN, Geoff, P .... 206-598-8318 485 A
graustin@uw.edu
AUSTIN, Jane .... 570-288-8400 383 G
janea@fortisinstitute.edu
AUSTIN, Jonathan .... 502-897-4121 184 G
jaustin@sbts.edu
AUSTIN, Kristin .... 610-436-1725 395 D
kaustin@wcupa.edu
AUSTIN, L. Bruce .... 847-214-7366 137 F
baustin@elgin.edu
AUSTIN, Laurie .... 718-960-8706 294 A
laurie.austin@lehman.cuny.edu
AUSTIN, Marcia, M .... 727-816-3264 105 F
austinm@phsc.edu
AUSTIN, Mel, L .... 414-410-4002 491 I
mlaustin@stritch.edu
AUSTIN, Michael .... 812-488-1178 161 G
ma352@evansville.edu
AUSTIN, Renee .... 615-230-3587 425 E
renee.austin@volstate.edu
AUSTIN, Sheila .... 334-244-3425.... 4 E
saustin1@aum.edu
AUSTIN, Susan .... 212-229-8950 308 A
austins@newschool.edu
AUSTIN, Suzanne .... 843-805-5507 408 C
AUSTIN, Tiffany .... 201-559-3620 277 J
austint@felician.edu
AUSTIN, Tracey, M .... 603-526-3886 272 H
taustin@colby-sawyer.edu
AUSTIN, William .... 908-689-7618 284 H
will@warren.edu
AUSTIN-KETCH, Tammy 315-464-3900 317 C
austinkt@upstate.edu
AUTERO, Esa .... 954-545-4500 108 E
academics@sfbc.edu
AUTHIER, Adam .... 734-462-4400 230 G
aauthier@schoolcraft.edu
AUTIO, Wesley .... 413-545-2963 211 G
autio@umass.edu
AUTREY, Krista, M .... 724-847-6636 384 C
kmautrey@geneva.edu
AUTRY, Dean .... 270-686-4464 182 F
dean.autry@kctcs.edu
AUTRY, James, C .... 801-422-3928 458 H
autry@byu.edu
AUVENSHINE, Donnie ... 325-649-8002 437 G
dauvenshine@hputx.edu
AUVIL, Joe .... 509-793-2016 478 B
joea@bigbend.edu
AUXENTIOS, Bishop ..... 530-467-3544.. 60 A
rector@spots.edu
AVAKIAN, Brad .... 360-992-2986 478 I
bavakian@clark.edu
AVAKIAN, Satenik .... 510-925-4282.. 25 K
savakian@aua.am
AVALONE, Valarie, L ..... 585-292-3021 307 B
vavalone@monroecc.edu
AVALOS, Jesse .... 617-236-8827 209 G
javalos@fisher.edu
AVALOS, Juan .... 949-582-4566.. 65 D
javalos@saddleback.edu
AVALOS, Marlena .... 773-252-6464 146 F
marlena.avalos@oakpoint.edu
AVALOS, Natalie .... 818-767-0888.. 76 E
natalie.avalos@woodbury.edu
AVALOS, Natalie .... 818-252-5107.. 76 E
natalie.avalos@woodbury.edu
AVALOS, Robert .... 323-343-3060.. 31 E
robert.avalos@calstatela.edu
AVALOS-SÁNCHEZ,
Javier .... 787-993-8863 512 A
javier.avalos@upr.edu
AVANT, Robin .... 203-332-5984.. 86 F
ravant@housatonic.edu
AVANT, Toni, D .... 662-915-7174 249 D
tavant@olemiss.edu
AVEDESIAN, Starr .... 714-628-4862.. 58 G
avedesian_starr@sccollege.edu
AVEGALIO, Daniel .... 660-596-7393 259 M
davegalio@sfccmo.edu
AVELINO, Melanie .... 336-633-0256 337 A
mlavelino@randolph.edu
AVELLA, Christine .... 619-574-5803.. 42 J
cavella@fst.edu
AVENDANO, John .... 904-632-5032 101 B
john.avendano@fscj.edu
AVENIA, Bradford .... 303-273-3548.. 79 J
bavenia@mines.edu
AVENT, Jenna .... 336-272-7102 329 C
jenna.avent@greensboro.edu
AVENT, Randy, K .... 863-583-9050 110 B
AVENT, Sherri, M .... 336-334-7973 341 D
avent@ncat.edu
AVERETTE, Dan .... 843-661-8161 409 F
dan.averette@fdtc.edu

AVERILL, Gary 916-306-1628 67 F gaverill@sum.edu
AVERILL, Leslie 802-865-5715 462 A laverill@champlain.edu
AVERY, Alycia 603-626-9490 274 C a.avery@snhu.edu
AVERY, Cynthia 619-260-4588 72 I cynthiaavery@sandiego.edu
AVERY, Diane 661-362-3640 38 D diane.avery@canyons.edu
AVERY, Hannah 606-693-5000 183 C havery@kmbc.edu
AVERY, James 731-661-5329 426 F javery@uu.edu
AVERY, Kathy 918-293-4988 368 B kathy.avery@okstate.edu
AVERY, Kristine 207-893-7755 196 C kavery@sjcme.edu
AVERY, Lisa 541-917-4200 373 G averyl@linnbenton.edu
AVERY, Martin, D 315-386-7222 320 B averym@canton.edu
AVERY, Michael 219-473-4323 154 D mavery@ccsj.edu
AVERY, Paula 310-303-7213 51 C pavery@marymountcalifornia.edu
AVERY, Rebecca 610-896-1230 385 I ravery@haverford.edu
AVERY, Sherri, M 781-736-3706 208 A savery@brandeis.edu
AVETISYAN, Lucy 310-206-6771 69 E lucyavetisyan@ucla.edu
AVILÉS, Ángel, L 787-786-3030 511 A aaviles@ucb.edu.pr
AVILA, Alyssa 657-278-2998 31 C alavila@fullerton.edu
AVILA, Esmerelda 954-378-2400 93 H
AVILA, Holly 405-422-6283 369 A holly.avila@redlandscc.edu
AVILA, Jason 562-938-4313 48 F javila@lbcc.edu
AVILA, Jennifer 626-571-8811 73 E jennifera@uwest.edu
AVILA, Kelly 209-384-6000 52 A kelly.avila@mccd.edu
AVILA, Mitch 805-437-8400 30 C
AVILA, Pedro 707-524-1647 63 D pavila@santarosa.edu
AVILA, Sumer 559-651-2500 61 H
AVILA, Susan 510-594-3661 28 B savila@cca.edu
AVILES, Gladys, M 248-204-4123 227 A gaviles@ltu.edu
AVILES, Jose 225-578-2111 189 D
AVILES, Jose 225-578-1175 189 E javiles1@lsu.edu
AVILES-FERRAN, Jeanette 787-620-2040 505 C javiles@aupr.edu
AVIOLA, Joseph, P 302-295-1165 91 E joseph.p.aviola@wilmu.edu
AVIS ROGERS, Julie 617-824-8036 209 C julie_avisrogers@emerson.edu
AVISSAR, Roni 305-421-4000 113 C avissar@miami.edu
AVITIA, Amber 559-935-3221 75 B amberavitia@whccd.edu
AW, Fanta 202-885-3357 91 F fanta@american.edu
AWADALLAH, Baha 773-602-5068 135 D bawadallah@ccc.edu
AWAI-WILLIAMS, Anika 734-487-2202 223 K aawaiwil@emich.edu
AWAKUNI, Gene 808-983-4100 128 H
AWAN, Seher 323-241-5276 49 E awans@lasc.edu
AWAYA, Kevin 808-237-5140 128 F
AWE, Jacqueline 912-358-3114 125 A awej@savannahstate.edu
AWES-FREEMAN, Jennifer 651-255-6140 243 E jawes-freeman@unitedseminary.edu
AWONIYI, Beatrice 352-395-5513 108 A bea.awoniyi@sfcollege.edu
AWOPETU, Lawrence 870-575-8649 22 D awopetul@uapb.edu
AWUAH, Agatha 315-498-2500 310 F awuaha@sunyocc.edu
AWUAH, Emmanuel 320-308-5030 241 A emmanuel.awuah@sctcc.edu
AWWAD, Elise 630-515-3105 137 A eawwad@devry.edu
AXLUND MCBRIDE, RaeLyn 360-752-8344 478 A raelyn.axlund.mcbride@btc.edu
AXON, Diane 910-221-2224 331 B daxon@manna.edu
AXTELL, Denise 530-242-7771 64 C daxtell@shastacollege.edu
AXTELL, Richard, D 859-238-5342 180 B rick.axtell@centre.edu
AXVIG, Samantha 218-299-4562 235 H axvig@cord.edu
AYABE, John 530-226-4152 64 E jayabe@simpsonu.edu
AYAD, Nada 212-353-4302 297 E nada.ayad@cooper.edu
AYALA, Aurora 619-482-6320 66 A aayala@swccd.edu
AYALA, Carmen 787-761-0640 511 E decanaacademica@utcpr.edu
AYALA, Caroline 787-264-1912 508 F caroline_ayala@intersg.edu
AYALA, Hector, L 787-850-9303 512 D hector.ayala5@upr.edu
AYALA, Israel 787-891-0925 507 K iayala@aguadilla.inter.edu
AYALA, Javier 619-644-7158 44 E javier.ayala@gcccd.edu
AYALA, Jose, L 787-250-0000 511 F jose.ayala5@upr.edu
AYALA, Mary 575-562-2421 286 B mary.ayala@enmu.edu
AYALA, Oliva 818-364-7795 49 C sancheo@lamission.edu
AYALA, Pedro 787-738-2161 512 C pedro.ayala1@upr.edu
AYALA, Ramon 787-250-1912 508 D rayala@intermetro.edu
AYALA, Sharon 619-849-2988 57 J sharonayala@pointloma.edu
AYALA, Shawn 617-588-1352 206 F sayala@bfit.edu
AYALA-AUSTIN, Eliazer 408-288-3137 62 H eliazer.ayala-austin@sjcc.edu
AYALA-JIMENEZ, Monica 210-486-3338 429 A mayala5@alamo.edu
AYAR, Christina 586-445-7302 227 B ayarc84@macomb.edu
AYARS, Daniel 937-328-6040 350 G ayarsd@clarkstate.edu
AYARS, Matthew, I 601-366-8880 249 G miayars@wbs.edu
AYCOCK, Allan 706-542-9902 126 G aaycock@uga.edu
AYCOCK, Greg 951-739-7802 59 C greg.aycock@norcocollege.edu
AYCOCK, Jim 662-246-6331 247 D jaycock@msdelta.edu
AYCOCK, Larry 909-389-3663 60 E laycock@sbccd.cc.ca.us
AYER, Dorothy, R 805-437-8517 30 C dorothy.ayer@csuci.edu
AYERS, Ann 303-871-6801 84 E ann.ayers@du.edu
AYERS, Benjamin, C 706-542-8100 126 G busdean@uga.edu
AYERS, James, P 716-880-2179 305 G james.p.ayers@medaille.edu
AYERS, Julia 470-578-6033 121 M jayers30@kennesaw.edu
AYERS, Kenya 817-515-6200 445 F kenya.ayers@tccd.edu
AYERS, Lee 541-552-6505 376 B ayersl@sou.edu
AYERS, Mary 662-562-3438 248 D
AYERS, Megan 252-328-6105 341 A ayersm@ecu.edu
AYERS, Michael 718-758-8127 293 C mrayers@brooklyn.cuny.edu
AYERS, Sheli 209-954-5139 61 G sayers@deltacollege.edu
AYERS, Susan 978-232-2066 209 E sayers@endicott.edu
AYERS, Tom 810-762-9787 226 B tayers@kettering.edu
AYERSMAN, David, J 304-256-0281 488 G dayersman@newriver.edu
AYEVA, Maawiya 323-731-2383 55 H
AYKROID, David 847-543-2259 136 A daykroid@clcillinois.edu
AYLESBURY, Charles, T 626-568-8850 48 H tom@lacm.edu
AYLETT, Ashley 870-584-1125 22 F aaylett@cccua.edu
AYLWARD, Denise 570-422-3203 394 A
AYLWARD, Paige 785-309-3100 177 E paige.johnson@salinatech.edu
AYLWARD, Robert, R 307-766-4860 501 I raylward@uwyo.edu
AYNES, Danny 541-917-4999 373 G aynesd@linnbenton.edu
AYON, Carlos 714-992-7033 54 C cayon@fullcoll.edu
AYON, Maria 928-505-3300 14 F mayon@mohave.edu
AYOUBI, Amjad 504-865-5107 191 F aamjad@tulane.edu
AYOUCH, Karen 315-866-0300 301 D ayouchka@herkimer.edu
AYRAVAINEN, Eija 212-772-4878 294 C eija.ayravainen@hunter.cuny.edu
AYREA, William 703-993-8614 467 E wayrea@gmu.edu
AYRES, Amy 405-208-7910 367 E aayres@okcu.edu
AYRES, Christina, M 573-202-6959 253 B christina.ayres@eastcentral.edu
AYRES, Dana 214-768-2841 444 D dwayres@smu.edu
AYRES, Deb 636-949-4405 254 H dayres@lindenwood.edu
AYRES, Jessica 650-433-3824 55 L jayres@paloaltou.edu
AZAMA, Anthony, J 314-935-5000 262 A anthony.j.azama@wustl.edu
AZAR, Eve 908-835-2335 284 H azar@warren.edu
AZDELL, Grant, L 804-752-7266 469 F gazdell@rmc.edu
AZEVEDO, Steve 480-461-7974 13 D steve.azevedo@mesacc.edu
AZHIKANNICKAL, Elizabeth 740-386-4134 355 F azhikannickale@mtc.edu
AZIZ, Hassan 361-825-2649 447 C hassan.aziz@tamucc.edu
AZIZ, Jihad, N 804-828-6200 473 B jnaziz@vcu.edu
AZIZI, Kate 843-792-4281 410 C azizi@musc.edu
AZKOUL, Emilie 616-222-1447 223 C emilie.azkoul@cornerstone.edu
AZURE, Beverly 914-633-2625 302 E bazure@iona.edu
AZURE, Lane 605-698-3966 416 B lazure@swcollege.edu
AZURE, Lisa 701-255-3285 347 A lazure@uttc.edu
AZURE, Tracy 701-477-7809 346 J tazure@tm.edu
AZZAM-GOMEZ, Shady 631-451-4920 321 C azzamgs@sunysuffolk.edu
AZZARA, Thomas 934-420-2599 320 F azzaratf@farmingdale.edu
AZZARELLO, Tony 419-227-3141 362 F amazzare@unoh.edu
AZZI, Amanda, R 607-871-2325 290 B ruscitto@alfred.edu
AZZU, Heather 336-734-7273 334 F hazzu@forsythtech.edu
A'SEE, Carlito, D 803-536-7485 411 G cdasee@scsu.edu

B

BAACH, Laurence, A 212-217-3400 299 D laurence_baach@fitnyc.edu
BAACK, Cathryn 614-781-1085 352 F cbaack@felbrycollege.edu
BAAR, Tricia 501-337-5000 18 B tbaar@asutr.edu
BAARMAND, Fanak 321-674-8885 100 C fbaarman@fit.edu
BAART, Aaron 712-722-6079 165 I aaron.baart@dordt.edu
BAARTMAN, Randy 712-324-5061 169 C rbaartman@nwicc.edu
BAAS, Beth 712-722-6990 165 I beth.baas@dordt.edu
BAAS, John 712-722-6020 165 I john.baas@dordt.edu
BAAS, Mark 507-431-2202 240 G mark.baas@riverland.edu
BAASKE, Kevin 323-343-4004 31 E kbaaske@calstatela.edu
BAATZ, Stephanie 605-256-5675 416 F stephanie.baatz@dsu.edu
BABAKER, Jessica 352-335-2332 94 E
BABALIS, Eva 718-779-1430 311 E ebabalis@plazacollege.edu
BABANI, Henry 305-442-9223 104 G hbabani@mru.edu
BABASOLOUKIAN, Alin 212-217-4000 299 D alin_babasoloukian@fitnyc.edu
BABB, Billy 636-229-7900 261 F bbabb@upci.org
BABB, Brian 386-506-4457 98 D brian.babb@daytonastate.edu
BABB, Brian, T 386-506-4457 98 D brian.babb@daytonastate.edu
BABB, Genie 518-564-2000 318 E
BABB, Mac 540-231-5123 476 C wmb1@vt.edu
BABB, Michael 614-287-2473 351 C mbabb6@cscc.edu
BABB, Stephanie 559-325-5242 67 A stephanie.babb@cloviscollege.edu
BABB, Tina, M 806-371-5420 429 E tmbabb@actx.edu
BABBITT, Terry 505-277-2626 288 J tbabbitt@unm.edu
BABCOCK, Daphne, H 972-378-8835 433 I dbabcock@collin.edu
BABCOCK, Ed 309-694-5337 139 B ebabcock@icc.edu
BABCOCK, Jamie, T 607-871-2460 290 B babcock@alfred.edu
BABCOCK, Rob 402-461-7344 267 C rbabcock@hastings.edu
BABCOCK, Whit 540-231-3977 476 C hokiead@vt.edu
BABEL, Rebecca 815-753-1395 146 B rbabel@niu.edu
BABENCHUK, Iaroslava 631-451-4409 321 C babenci@sunysuffolk.edu
BABER, Jared 567-661-7227 359 I jared_baber@owens.edu
BABER, III, Jimmie 734-677-5359 232 D jbaberiii@wccnet.edu
BABER, Kathleen 336-334-3147 343 A kababer@uncg.edu
BABER, Thomas 919-573-5350 340 C tbaber@shepherds.edu
BABETZ, Jeff 843-863-7921 407 B jbabetz@csuniv.edu
BABETZ, Jeffrey 843-863-7921 407 B jbabetz@csuniv.edu
BABIC, Djuradj 323-260-8120 48 J babicd@elac.edu
BABIN, Lisa 318-675-8769 189 I lisa.babin@lsuhs.edu
BABINGTON, Lynn 808-735-4741 128 E president@chaminade.edu
BABINGTON, Pete 206-546-4514 484 B pbabington@shoreline.edu
BABOWICZ, Debra, P 315-684-6078 321 A babowidp@morrisville.edu
BABU KONDUBHATLA, Deena 844-872-8680 73 A
BABUSZCZAK, Keith 919-866-5817 338 G kbabuszczak@waketech.edu
BACA, Amy 575-538-6169 289 G amy.baca@wnmu.edu
BACA, Brad 970-943-2186 85 C bbaca@western.edu
BACA, Clair 909-667-4481 37 G cbaca@claremontlincoln.edu
BACA, Diana 505-428-1267 288 E diana.baca@sfcc.edu
BACA, Jim 806-345-5561 429 E j0512060@actx.edu
BACA, Julie 970-943-2061 85 C jfeier@western.edu
BACA, Lori 505-747-2186 287 H lbaca@nnmc.edu
BACA, Max 505-454-3272 286 J mbaca@nmhu.edu
BACA, Sylvia 505-426-2048 286 J sbaca@nmhu.edu
BACARISSE, Charles 281-649-3428 437 B cbacarisse@hbu.edu
BACCAM, Stephanie 712-722-6014 165 I stephanie.baccam@dordt.edu
BACCAR, Cindy 503-725-5533 375 E baccarc@pdx.edu
BACCARY, Annie 303-541-1321 84 A annie.baccary@cu.edu

BACCHETTA, Aldo 816-802-3334 254 D abacchetta@kcai.edu

BACCILE, Peter 734-973-3300 232 D pbaccile@wccnet.edu

BACCOUS, Alesheia 919-833-3003 340 B alesheia.baccous@shawu.edu

BACH, Alex 913-234-0610 172 K alex.bach@cleveland.edu

BACH, Larry, C 612-343-4703 242 M lcbach@northcentral.edu

BACHAND, Donald, J 989-964-4041 230 E dbachand@svsu.edu

BACHAS, Leonidas, G 305-284-4117 113 C bachas@miami.edu

BACHHER, Jagdeep, S 510-987-0260 68 L jagdeep.baccher@ucop.edu

BACHIER, Carmen 787-250-0000 511 F carmen.bachier1@upr.edu

BACHLE, Lori 402-552-6127 266 E bachle@clarksoncollege.edu

BACHMAN, Katie 760-384-6150 46 M katie.bachman@cerrocoso.edu

BACHMAN, Rob 303-762-6970 80 I rob.bachman@denverseminary.edu

BACHMAN, Sara 215-898-5511 400 F sbachman@upenn.edu

BACHMANN, Kirk 303-494-7988 78 B

BACHMANN, Michele 757-352-4127 470 B

BACHMEIER, Gabrielle 206-878-3710 481 B gbachmeier@highline.edu

BACHMEIER, Jim 231-591-2164 224 A jimbachmeier@ferris.edu

BACHMEIER, Mark 828-262-6483 340 I bachmeiermd@appstate.edu

BACHOR, Dina 901-572-2585 418 A dina.bachor@baptistu.edu

BACHRACH, Gavriel 847-982-2500 138 I bachrach@htc.edu

BACHRACH, Steven 732-571-3421 279 A sbachrac@monmouth.edu

BACHRI, Abdel 870-235-4290 21 C agbachri@saumag.edu

BACHTEL, Tara 903-923-2119 435 H tbachtel@etbu.edu

BACIGALUPI, Michael 606-218-5510 186 B mbacigalupi@upike.edu

BACIK, Valerie 814-871-5571 384 A bacik001@gannon.edu

BACK, Tony 606-487-3302 181 I tony.back@kctcs.edu

BACKELS, Kelsey, K 717-871-7821 395 A kelsey.backels@millersville.edu

BACKER, Joni 402-375-7200 268 F jobacke1@wsc.edu

BACKES, Karen 320-363-5933 235 F kbackes@csbsju.edu

BACKHAUS, Kristin 845-257-2930 316 E backhauk@newpaltz.edu

BACKLIN, William 785-833-4511 175 E bill.backlin@kwu.edu

BACKMAN, Andrea 202-419-0400 93 H

BACKOFEN, Susan 229-226-1621 126 C sbackofen@thomasu.edu

BACKUS, Amy 216-368-2866 349 D amy.backus@case.edu

BACKUS, Bruce, D 314-935-9882 262 A backusb@wustl.edu

BACKUS, Karlyn 585-345-6850 300 F kmbackus@genesee.edu

BACKUS, Robert, H 607-746-4677 320 D backusrh@delhi.edu

BACON, Amy 417-447-2660 257 G bacona@otc.edu

BACON, Carolyn 304-326-1242 487 I carolyn.bacon@salemu.edu

BACON, Gus 406-395-4875 265 G gbacon@stonechild.edu

BACON, Jen 610-436-0045 395 D jbacon@wcupa.edu

BACON, John 541-888-7001 376 C john.bacon@socc.edu

BACON, John 252-493-7229 336 H jbacon@email.pittcc.edu

BACON, Karen 646-592-4150 326 D kbacon@yu.edu

BACON, Michael 210-999-7320 451 E mbacon@trinity.edu

BACON, Pamela 320-363-5401 235 F pbacon@csbsju.edu

BACON, Pamela 320-363-5167 243 B pbacon@csbsju.edu

BACON, Robbie 717-815-6818 403 F rbacon2@ycp.edu

BACON, Scott 904-256-7543 102 H sbacon@ju.edu

BACON, Scott, A 317-381-6028 162 F sbacon@vinu.edu

BACON, Tiffany 954-486-7728 113 B tbacon@uftl.edu

BACOTE, Jenia 478-471-2700 122 F jenia.bacote@mga.edu

BACOTE-CHARLES, Terri, K 301-546-0409 201 E bacotetk@pgcc.edu

BACOW, Lawrence, S 617-495-1502 210 E president@harvard.edu

BACZEWSKI, Philip, C 940-565-3886 453 E baczewski@unt.edu

BADAKHSH, Diane 912-478-5555 120 C dbadakhsh@georgiasouthern.edu

BADAL, Amy, A 570-577-1601 379 C amy.badal@bucknell.edu

BADAL, Joel 832-252-4615 432 L joel.badal@cbshouston.edu

BADALYAN, Anna 323-953-4000 49 A badalya@lacitycollege.edu

BADAR, Bryan 330-490-7417 363 E bbadar@walsh.edu

BADASZEWSKI, Philip 716-878-3000 317 F badaszpd@buffalostate.edu

BADE, Michael 415-502-6460 70 D michael.bade@ucsf.edu

BADE, Robert, E 727-816-3413 105 F badeb@phsc.edu

BADEAU, Melissa 607-871-2698 290 B badeau@alfred.edu

BADEAUX, Margo 985-448-4518 192 F margo.badeaux@nicholls.edu

BADEN, Cory 407-646-2264 106 L cbaden@rollins.edu

BADENES, José 310-338-7684 51 A jose.badenes@lmu.edu

BADENHAUSEN, Richard 801-832-2460 461 F rbadenhausen@westminstercollege.edu

BADER, Greg 740-587-0810 352 A

BADER, Irv 718-820-4877 322 G irv.bader@touro.edu

BADER, Irv 718-820-4877 322 F irv.bader@touro.edu

BADER, Jerad 740-474-8896 358 A jbader@ohiochristian.edu

BADER, Melissa 951-372-7062 59 C melissa.bader@norcocollege.edu

BADER-SAYE, Scott 512-472-4133 443 F scott.bader-saye@ssw.edu

BADGER, Michelle 508-830-5045 213 D mbadger@maritime.edu

BADHAM, Todd 253-879-3313 484 G tbadham@pugetsound.edu

BADIA, Janet 260-481-6895 160 C badiaj@pfw.edu

BADILLO, Adriana 657-287-8280 31 C abadillo@fullerton.edu

BADILLO, Maria Antonieta 919-831-6755 436 A mbadill4@epcc.edu

BADILLO-LOZANO, Luis, V 787-841-2000 509 J luis_badillo@pucpr.edu

BADIRU, Adedeji, B 937-255-3025 502 C adedeji.badiru@afit.edu

BADMAN, Jodie 574-239-8404 156 A jbadman@hcc-nd.edu

BADOVINAC, Amanda 406-496-4828 265 A abadovinac@mtech.edu

BADOVINAC, Michele 209-468-9141 67 I mbadovinac@sjcoe.net

BADOWSKA, Eva 718-817-4400 300 C badowska@fordham.edu

BADOWSKI, Ryan 415-442-7833 43 I rbadowski@ggu.edu

BADZEK, Laurie, A 814-863-9734 391 G lzb340@psu.edu

BAEK, Ji 703-323-5690 477 A registrar@vuim.edu

BAEK, Kyunghee 310-739-0132 40 H

BAEK, Seongyul 714-525-0088 43 J

BAER, Candace 401-454-6426 405 B cbaer@risd.edu

BAER, Christopher 240-500-2341 199 C wcbaer@hagerstowncc.edu

BAER, Dana 724-852-3295 402 C dbaer@waynesburg.edu

BAER, Lori 816-802-3448 254 D lbaer@kcai.edu

BAERWALD, Bonnie 920-929-2127 499 D bbaerwald@morainepark.edu

BAEZ, Ana, I 787-841-2000 509 J abaez@pucpr.edu

BAEZ, Arvin 787-841-2000 509 J arvin_baez@pucpr.edu

BAEZ, Aurelis 787-279-1912 508 A abaez@bayamon.inter.edu

BAEZ, David 787-701-5100 506 D dbaez@columbiacentral.edu

BAEZ, Jeanette, G 909-869-4088 30 A jgbaez@cpp.edu

BAEZ, Juan 310-233-4427 49 B baezrj@lahc.edu

BAEZ, Lorenley 212-229-5459 308 A baezl@newschool.edu

BAEZ, Thomas 864-294-3031 409 H thomas.baez@furman.edu

BAEZ MILAN, Tony 724-653-2183 382 E tbaez@dec.edu

BAEZ-ZABALA, Ariana 787-998-8997 509 M abaez@eeapr.org

BAEZA, Marco 714-438-4707 37 I mbaeza2@cccd.edu

BAEZA-ORTEGO, Gilda 575-538-6358 289 G ortegog@wnmu.edu

BAFFA, Joe 714-556-3610 73 H joe.baffa@vanguard.edu

BAGANHA, Margarida 508-531-2877 212 D m1baganha@bridgew.edu

BAGBY, Don 254-710-8400 431 E don_bagby@baylor.edu

BAGBY, Sara 606-693-5000 183 C srichardson@kmbc.edu

BAGBY, Tammy, A 610-399-2534 393 F tbagby@cheyney.edu

BAGDAZIAN, Robert, A 805-525-4417 67 K rbagdazian@thomasaquinas.edu

BAGG, Eva 760-252-2411 26 G ebagg@barstow.edu

BAGG, Mary Beth 317-788-3262 161 H bagg@uindy.edu

BAGGETT, Ryan 859-622-8261 180 E ryan.baggett@eku.edu

BAGGOT, Joseph 507-222-4075 234 G jbaggot@carleton.edu

BAGGOTT, Jake 608-262-1885 495 D jake.baggott@wisc.edu

BAGGS, Adam 817-257-6814 448 F a.baggs@tcu.edu

BAGGS, David 843-863-7513 407 B dbaggs@csuniv.edu

BAGGSON, Gulizar 479-619-2203 20 C gbaggson@nwacc.edu

BAGILEO, Nick, J 202-526-3799 93 E nbagileo@johnpaulii.edu

BAGIN, Mike 262-547-1211 492 A mbagin@carrollu.edu

BAGLEY, Angela 252-862-1316 337 C abagley@roanokechowan.edu

BAGLEY, Elizabeth 404-471-6339 114 G ebagley@agnesscott.edu

BAGLEY, Judy 864-294-2320 409 H judy.bagley@furman.edu

BAGLEY, Michael 530-741-5564 77 E mbagley@yccd.edu

BAGLEY, Michelle, M 971-722-4497 375 D michelle.bagley@pcc.edu

BAGLEY, Rob 801-524-1952 459 E robbagley@ldsbc.edu

BAGLEY, Rod 715-833-6480 498 E rbagley1@cvtc.edu

BAGLEY, Shawn 330-823-2280 362 E bagleysp@mountunion.edu

BAGLINI, Shane 610-799-1718 388 D sbaglini@lccc.edu

BAGLIVO, Mary 212-346-1200 311 A

BAGNALL, James 928-428-8414 12 F jim.bagnall@eac.edu

BAGNELL, William 252-328-6858 341 A bagnellw@ecu.edu

BAGNOLI, Joseph, P 641-269-3600 166 G bagnolij@grinnell.edu

BAGSTAD, Kristi 563-588-6314 164 E kristi.bagstad@clarke.edu

BAGWELL, Christopher 228-896-2500 247 E christopher.bagwell@mgccc.edu

BAGWELL, Dana 814-871-7238 384 A bagwell002@gannon.edu

BAGWELL, Jack 252-335-0821 333 G

BAH, Ibrahim 919-546-8565 340 B ibrahim.bah@shawu.edu

BAHAM, Tracey 662-325-6941 247 F tbaham@oire.msstate.edu

BAHAMONDE, Rafael, E 317-274-2344 157 D rbahamon@iupui.edu

BAHAN, Liz 415-420-8094 58 H lbahan@reachinst.org

BAHAN, Rebecca 314-977-2500 259 F rebecca.bahan@slu.edu

BAHARANYI, Ntam 334-727-8659 7 D nbaharanyi@tuskegee.edu

BAHLS, Steven, C 309-794-7208 133 C stevenbahls@augustana.edu

BAHR, Brett 218-755-2599 237 F brett.bahr@bemidjistate.edu

BAHR, Deb 319-399-8877 164 F dbahr@coe.edu

BAHR, Jon 517-750-1200 231 C jonathan.bahr@arbor.edu

BAHREMAND, Manijeh 610-399-2260 393 F mbahremand@cheyney.edu

BAI, Kang 815-836-5640 142 F kbai@lewisu.edu

BAI, Lynn 516-739-1545 308 F admissions@nyctcm.edu

BAI, Monica, S 928-523-6514 14 H monica.bai@nau.edu

BAI, Shuming 337-475-5514 192 E sbai@mcneese.edu

BAI, Yifeng 973-748-9000 276 A yifeng_bai@bloomfield.edu

BAIA, Larissa 603-366-5215 272 K lbaia@ccsnh.edu

BAIARDI, Janet 313-993-1208 231 E baiardjm@udmercy.edu

BAICKER, Katherine 773-702-0711 151 E kbaicker@uchicago.edu

BAIDA, Ana 470-578-6555 121 M abaida@kennesaw.edu

BAIDOO, Christopher, E 619-239-0391 34 G cbaidoo@cwsl.edu

BAIER, Henry, D 734-764-3402 231 H hbaier@umich.edu

BAIER, Valerie, A 570-326-3761 392 W vbaier@pct.edu

BAIERL, Hans 920-924-3112 499 D hbaierl@morainepark.edu

BAIK, Sang 213-763-7007 49 F baiks@lattc.edu

BAILARD, Rhiannon 415-851-8858 69 C bailardrhiannon@uchastings.edu

BAILER, Joseph 910-678-8585 334 E bailerj@faytechcc.edu

BAILEY, Albert 937-502-3750 363 G a_bailey@wilberforce.edu

BAILEY, Alex 509-533-3402 479 D alexandra.bailey@sfcc.spokane.edu

BAILEY, Alison 309-438-2947 140 D baileya@ilstu.edu

BAILEY, Andrew 563-387-1507 168 B bailan01@luther.edu

BAILEY, Angela, W 252-335-3513 341 B awbailey@ecsu.edu

BAILEY, Anthony 213-740-2852 73 D arbailey@usc.edu

BAILEY, Aprille 828-652-0629 336 B

BAILEY, Barbara 773-252-5311 146 F barbara.bailey@oakpoint.edu

BAILEY, Brad 228-497-7627 247 E brad.bailey@mgccc.edu

BAILEY, Brian 312-567-6937 140 A bbailey4@iit.edu

BAILEY, Cassy 785-594-8484 171 F cassy.bailey@bakeru.edu

BAILEY, Chad 423-323-3191 425 A

BAILEY, Charla 830-372-8098 449 A cbailey@tlu.edu

BAILEY, Cheryl 414-930-3111 494 E baileyc@mtmary.edu

BAILEY, Chris, C 570-372-4149 398 F baileycj@susqu.edu

BAILEY, Christine 315-268-6578 295 F cbailey@clarkson.edu

BAILEY, Christopher 401-254-3124 405 C cjbailey@rwu.edu

BAILEY, Christopher, C 360-442-2101 481 D cbailey@lowercolumbia.edu

BAILEY, Cindy 715-735-4312 495 F baileyc@uwgb.edu

BAILEY, Clint 252-328-2606 341 A baileyrc@ecu.edu

BAILEY, David, C 574-631-1097 162 A bailey.77@nd.edu

BAILEY, Denice .... 503-594-3002 372 C
denice.bailey@clackamas.edu
BAILEY, Denise .... 714-628-4816.. 58 G
bailey_denise@sccollege.edu
BAILEY, Denise .... 903-233-3100 439 A
denisebailey@letu.edu
BAILEY, Dennis, A .... 850-644-8136 110 C
dbailey@fsu.edu
BAILEY, JR., Dexter, F . 626-395-6307.. 28 J
dbailey@caltech.edu
BAILEY, Dixon .... 254-647-3234 441 K
dbailey@rangercollege.edu
BAILEY, Donald, R .... 401-865-1188 404 F
drbailey@providence.edu
BAILEY, Ed .... 231-995-1215 229 A
ebailey@nmc.edu
BAILEY, Gary .... 616-538-2330 224 E
gbailey@gracechristian.edu
BAILEY, Guy .... 956-665-9102 455 D
president@utrgv.edu
BAILEY, Heather .... 801-618-0438 458 G
hbailey@ameritech.edu
BAILEY, Helen .... 423-869-6434 421 A
helen.bailey@lmunet.edu
BAILEY, Jack .... 304-766-4109 490 D
jbaile19@wvstateu.edu
BAILEY, Jalynda .... 918-293-5266 368 B
jalynda@okstate.edu
BAILEY, Jeff .... 870-972-3077.. 17 E
jbailey@astate.edu
BAILEY, Jessica, H .... 601-984-6300 249 E
jhbailey@umc.edu
BAILEY, Jessika .... 580-559-5252 365 K
jbailey@ecok.edu
BAILEY, Jodi .... 201-200-3507 279 D
jbailey2@njcu.edu
BAILEY, Jodi .... 704-637-4292 327 I
jsbailey21@catawba.edu
BAILEY, Joseph, A .... 585-345-6900 300 F
jabailey@genesee.edu
BAILEY, Julie .... 404-687-4593 117 G
baileyj@ctsnet.edu
BAILEY, Julie .... 432-264-5051 437 F
jbailey@howardcollege.edu
BAILEY, Kelly .... 724-738-4223 395 C
kelly.bailey@sru.edu
BAILEY, Kevin .... 704-687-0350 342 D
baileyk@uncc.edu
BAILEY, Kevin, S .... 573-882-1639 261 A
baileyks@missouri.edu
BAILEY, Kimberly .... 252-398-6526 328 C
ksbailey@chowan.edu
BAILEY, Laura .... 423-439-1000 419 G
BAILEY, Lena .... 517-371-5140 233 C
baileyl@cooley.edu
BAILEY, Lisa .... 909-652-6532.. 35 L
lisa.bailey@chaffey.edu
BAILEY, Mara .... 515-961-1684 170 B
mara.bailey@simpson.edu
BAILEY, Mark .... 205-853-1200.... 2 G
mjbailey@jeffersonstate.edu
BAILEY, Mary .... 620-331-8332 174 H
mbailey@indycc.edu
BAILEY, Mary Kaye .... 702-651-7437 270 K
marykaye.bailey@csn.edu
BAILEY, Michael .... 352-588-8464 107 D
michael.bailey@saintleo.edu
BAILEY, Michael, A .... 202-687-6021.. 92 E
baileyma@georgetown.edu
BAILEY, Mike .... 620-417-1044 177 F
mike.bailey@sccc.edu
BAILEY, Mitchell, A ...... 650-574-6510.. 62 I
baileym@smccd.edu
BAILEY, Monique .... 606-337-3196 180 C
BAILEY, Patrick .... 818-677-4452.. 32 C
patrick.bailey@csun.edu
BAILEY, Paul .... 256-352-8359.... 3 I
paul.bailey@wallacestate.edu
BAILEY, Peter, A .... 302-295-1191.. 91 E
peter.a.bailey@wilmu.edu
BAILEY, Phillip .... 501-450-3262.. 23 H
phillipb@uca.edu
BAILEY, JR., Richard, J 505-747-2147 287 H
rick.bailey@nnmc.edu
BAILEY, JR., Richard, J 505-747-2140 287 H
rick.bailey@nnmc.edu
BAILEY, Rita .... 470-578-2364 121 M
rbaile62@kennesaw.edu
BAILEY, Robyn .... 847-635-1428 146 G
rbailey@oakton.edu
BAILEY, Shannon .... 757-594-7553 465 M
shannon.bailey@cnu.edu
BAILEY, Sharon, M .... 361-570-4236 453 B
baileysm@uhv.edu
BAILEY, Shaun .... 559-934-2254.. 75 A
shaunbailey@whccd.edu
BAILEY, Sybil, F .... 401-825-2311 404 C
sfbailey@ccri.edu
BAILEY, Tamara .... 304-473-8424 491 D
bailey_t@wvwc.edu
BAILEY, Tammy .... 252-789-0253 335 H
tammy.bailey@martincc.edu
BAILEY, Theresa .... 936-261-1570 446 C
tlbailey@pvamu.edu
BAILEY, Thomas, R .... 212-678-3131 322 C
tb3@tc.columbia.edu
BAILEY, Tonya .... 517-483-1116 226 H
bailet20@lcc.edu
BAILEY, Travis .... 304-696-3032 489 M
bailey53@marshall.edu
BAILEY FISCHER,
Valerie .... 413-597-2483 220 D
vb7@williams.edu
BAILEY-JONES, Jenny ... 662-472-9174 246 D
jbailey@holmescc.edu
BAILEY MURPHY,
Krista .... 215-248-7142 381 A
murphyk@chc.edu
BAILIE, John, W .... 267-246-5891 386 B
johnbailie@iirp.edu
BAILIFF, Lara .... 512-313-4705 433 N
lara.bailiff@concordia.edu
BAILLARGEON, Betty ...... 860-215-9207.. 87 F
bbaillargeon@threerivers.edu
BAILO, Carole Anne ..... 480-212-1704.. 15 O
caroleanne@sessions.edu
BAILY, Jessica .... 914-674-7611 306 C
jbaily@mercy.edu
BAIMA, Thomas, A .... 847-970-4866 152 I
tbaima@usml.edu
BAIN, Abbey .... 318-427-4468 189 F
abbey@lsua.edu
BAIN, Ann .... 501-916-3204.. 22 A
abbain@ualr.edu
BAIN, Brandi .... 520-494-5577.. 11 K
brandi.bain@centralaz.edu
BAIN, Joe .... 785-628-4233 173 H
jbbain@fhsu.edu
BAIN, Steve .... 361-593-2802 447 D
steve.bain@tamuk.edu
BAIN-SELBO, Eric .... 765-455-9280 157 B
ebainsel@iu.edu
BAINE, Brad .... 870-248-4000.. 18 F
brad.baine@blackrivertech.edu
BAINTER, Bradley .... 309-298-1808 153 A
bl-bainter@wiu.edu
BAIR, Ava .... 719-336-1574.. 81 K
ava.bair@lamarcc.edu
BAIR, Matthew, S .... 260-422-5561 156 E
msbair@indianatech.edu
BAIR, Ryan .... 309-677-2697 134 A
rbair@fsmail.bradley.edu
BAIRD, Andrea .... 901-726-1977 428 D
abaird@mooretech.edu
BAIRD, Anthony, M ...... 315-792-3310 324 B
ambaird@utica.edu
BAIRD, Bridget, R .... 423-439-8222 419 G
bairdb@etsu.edu
BAIRD, David .... 860-685-2119.. 90 B
dbaird@wesleyan.edu
BAIRD, Denise .... 651-690-6720 243 A
dmbaird417@stkate.edu
BAIRD, Phil .... 605-586-5880 415 J
phil.baird@sintegleska.edu
BAIRD, Rebecca .... 973-720-2713 284 J
bairdr3@wpunj.edu
BAIRD, Sara Lynn .... 256-765-4288.... 8 E
sbaird@una.edu
BAIRD, Stephanie .... 405-425-5205 367 C
stephanie.baird@oc.edu
BAIRD, Susan .... 662-243-2682 246 B
sbaird@eastms.edu
BAIRD, Thomas, A .... 734-647-6030 231 H
baird@umich.edu
BAIRD, Timothy, R .... 724-847-6490 384 C
trbaird@geneva.edu
BAIRD-JAMES, Allison .. 310-794-8686.. 69 E
abaird-james@finance.ucla.edu
BAIRSTOW-ALLEN,
Deirdre .... 212-229-5150 308 A
bairstod@newschool.edu
BAISDEN, Emma, L ...... 304-896-7402 488 I
emma.baisden@southernwv.edu
BAISEY, Michael .... 301-624-2892 198 I
mbaisey@frederick.edu
BAJANDAS, Ivette .... 305-629-2929 107 H
ibajandas@sanignaciouniversity.edu
BAJOR, William .... 570-422-3588 394 A
wbajor@esu.edu
BAJRAMI, Diana .... 510-748-2301.. 57 A
dbajrami@peralta.edu
BAJWA, Sreekala .... 406-994-5154 264 C
sreekala.bajwa@montana.edu
BAK, Doug .... 719-846-5513.. 83 L
doug.bak@trinidadstate.edu
BAKAMITSOS, Yiorgos .. 386-822-7432 112 A
bakamitsos@stetson.edu
BAKANE, Samir .... 973-655-7773 279 B
bakanes@montclair.edu
BAKAR, Senem .... 202-885-3352.. 91 F
bakar@american.edu
BAKARI, R. Sentwali ..... 516-877-3151 289 I
sbakari@adelphi.edu
BAKE, Mark, A .... 920-433-6626 491 G
mark.bake@bellincollege.edu
BAKEMEIER, Emily, P ... 203-432-9492.. 90 C
emily.bakemeier@yale.edu
BAKER, Adria .... 713-348-6095 442 F
abaker@rice.edu
BAKER, Aja .... 701-255-3285 347 A
abaker@uttc.edu
BAKER, Alvin .... 606-326-2422 181 D
alvin.baker@kctcs.edu
BAKER, Amy .... 573-288-6493 252 F
abaker@culver.edu
BAKER, Andrew, R .... 301-447-5295 201 B
baker@msmary.edu
BAKER, Angela .... 717-264-2630 403 C
angela.baker@wilson.edu
BAKER, Barry .... 425-235-5839 482 H
bbaker@rtc.edu
BAKER, Betty .... 304-793-6873 490 C
bbaker@osteo.wvsom.edu
BAKER, Bonnie .... 928-523-0090.. 14 H
bonnie.baker@nau.edu
BAKER, Brad .... 610-459-0905 391 A
bakerb@neumann.edu
BAKER, Brent .... 765-641-4138 153 G
bababer@anderson.edu
BAKER, Brent .... 817-598-6275 457 J
bbaker@wc.edu
BAKER, Brian .... 812-749-1212 159 O
bbaker@oak.edu
BAKER, Brian .... 336-278-7453 328 J
bbaker7@elon.edu
BAKER, Brian, J .... 540-654-1302 471 N
bbaker@umw.edu
BAKER, Bryan .... 740-454-2501 365 B
bbaker@zanestate.edu
BAKER, Byron .... 501-205-8939.. 18 H
bbaker@cbc.edu
BAKER, Caitlin .... 806-291-3575 457 I
bakerc@wbu.edu
BAKER, Carey .... 870-235-4042.. 21 C
clbaker@saumag.edu
BAKER, Caroline .... 410-455-8171 203 B
cbaker@umbc.edu
BAKER, Cindy .... 863-669-2898 106 A
cbaker@polk.edu
BAKER, Credence .... 254-968-9420 446 D
cbaker@tarleton.edu
BAKER, Cynthia .... 909-607-9224.. 37 C
cynthia.baker@cgu.edu
BAKER, Dan .... 217-424-3757 144 G
drbaker@millikin.edu
BAKER, David, A .... 541-737-3871 375 A
david.baker@oregonstate.edu
BAKER, Deb .... 603-206-8152 272 L
dbaker@ccsnh.edu
BAKER, Debbie .... 307-382-1611 501 J
dbaker@westernwyoming.edu
BAKER, Deborah .... 413-565-1000 206 D
dbaker@baypath.edu
BAKER, Debra .... 662-246-6301 247 D
dbaker@msdelta.edu
BAKER, Derrick .... 217-351-2524 147 C
dbaker@parkland.edu
BAKER, Diane .... 269-927-6287 226 F
baker@lakemichigancollege.edu
BAKER, Donna .... 816-584-6847 258 C
donna.baker@park.edu
BAKER, Dylan .... 301-405-5632 202 H
dbaker@umd.edu
BAKER, Elissa .... 518-629-8196 302 C
e.baker@hvcc.edu
BAKER, Elizabeth .... 252-222-6216 333 A
bakere@carteret.edu
BAKER, Elizabeth, A ...... 312-942-2702 148 G
elizabeth_baker@rush.edu
BAKER, Emily .... 909-748-8047.. 72 F
emily_baker@redlands.edu
BAKER, Emma .... 843-329-1000 407 A
BAKER, Frankie .... 513-569-1453 350 F
frankie.baker@cincinnatistate.edu
BAKER, Gail, F .... 619-260-4553.. 72 I
provost@sandiego.edu
BAKER, Gary .... 941-752-5431 109 G
bakerg@scf.edu
BAKER, Gisella .... 319-296-4465 166 H
gisella.baker@hawkeyecollege.edu
BAKER, Hilary .... 818-677-7750.. 32 C
hilary.baker@csun.edu
BAKER, Hunter .... 731-661-5519 426 F
hbaker@uu.edu
BAKER, James .... 210-999-8076 451 E
jbaker5@trinity.edu
BAKER, James, P .... 417-836-8501 256 G
jbaker@missouristate.edu
BAKER, Jean .... 214-860-8885 435 A
jeanbaker@dcccd.edu
BAKER, Jeff .... 760-773-2500.. 38 E
jebaker@collegeofthedesert.edu
BAKER, Jeff .... 859-371-9393 179 G
jbaker@beckfield.edu
BAKER, Jeffrey, A .... 704-687-8457 342 D
jbaker88@uncc.edu
BAKER, Jennifer .... 410-516-7490 199 G
jbaker94@jhu.edu
BAKER, Jeremy .... 618-650-3839 150 C
jbaker@siue.edu
BAKER, Jerry .... 229-391-4782 114 F
jbaker@abac.edu
BAKER, Jim .... 817-272-2261 454 I
jimbaker@uta.edu
BAKER, Jimmy .... 513-562-8762 347 I
jbaker@artacademy.edu
BAKER, Jimmy, H .... 334-293-4524.... 1 C
jimmy.baker@accs.edu
BAKER, John .... 802-490-5159 462 B
john.baker@goddard.edu
BAKER, John, T .... 508-856-5538 212 C
john.baker@umassmed.edu
BAKER, Johnny .... 256-549-8357.... 2 B
jbaker@gadsdenstate.edu
BAKER, Josh .... 304-710-3355 488 F
bakerj@mctc.edu
BAKER, Joshua, C .... 630-515-7277 144 F
jbaker@midwestern.edu
BAKER, Judith, G .... 585-389-2824 307 F
jbaker51@naz.edu
BAKER, Julie .... 567-429-3535 359 I
julie_baker5@owens.edu
BAKER, Karen .... 570-702-8908 386 D
kbaker@johnson.edu
BAKER, Kathleen .... 206-296-6305 484 A
bakerkat@seattleu.edu
BAKER, Kathryn, R .... 865-354-3000 425 C
bakerkr@roanestate.edu
BAKER, Kecia .... 972-524-3341 445 B
kecia.baker@swcc.edu
BAKER, Ken .... 412-918-3086 125 F
kbaker@southuniversity.edu
BAKER, Kevin .... 662-227-2222 246 D
kbaker@holmescc.edu
BAKER, Leigh .... 386-822-8900 112 A
labaker@stetson.edu
BAKER, Lesli .... 801-863-8286 460 D
lbaker@uvu.edu
BAKER, Libba .... 205-652-3878.... 9 B
lbaker@uwa.edu
BAKER, Linda .... 610-799-1584 388 D
lbaker4@lccc.edu
BAKER, Lisa .... 989-686-9826 223 J
lisabaker@delta.edu
BAKER, Lisa .... 252-246-1310 339 C
lbaker@wilsoncc.edu
BAKER, Lori .... 540-857-6348 475 G
lbaker@virginiawestern.edu
BAKER, Luanne .... 205-247-8147.... 7 A
lbaker@stillman.edu
BAKER, Margaret, W ..... 415-422-2959.. 72 J
mwbaker@usfca.edu
BAKER, Matt .... 660-562-1219 257 E
mcbaker@nwmissouri.edu
BAKER, Matt, D .... 215-951-6803 399 E
bakerm@philau.edu
BAKER, Matthew .... 610-527-0200 397 D
matthew.baker@rosemont.edu
BAKER, Melinda .... 859-246-6819 181 F
melinda.baker@kctcs.edu

BAKER, Michael .... 765-641-4237 153 G
mtbaker@anderson.edu
BAKER, Michael .... 814-886-6368 390 G
mbaker@mtaloy.edu
BAKER, Michael, F .... 508-856-3040 212 C
michael.baker@umassmed.edu
BAKER, Michael, L .... 423-478-7702 422 J
mbaker@ptseminary.edu
BAKER, Mickey .... 334-556-2485.... 2 C
mbaker@wallace.edu
BAKER, Mike .... 859-442-4188 181 H
mike.baker@kctcs.edu
BAKER, Nancy .... 704-636-6882 330 A
nbaker@hoodseminary.edu
BAKER, Natalie .... 404-880-6879 117 C
nbaker@cau.edu
BAKER, Nelson .... 404-894-8920 119 E
nelson.baker@pe.gatech.edu
BAKER, Nick .... 989-275-5000 226 D
nick.baker@kirtland.edu
BAKER, Nikki, M .... 336-334-4225 343 A
nmwilson@uncg.edu
BAKER, Ric .... 203-931-2905.. 89 H
rbaker@newhaven.edu
BAKER, Richard .... 812-249-9188 198 C
rebaker@captechu.edu
BAKER, Richard .... 601-643-8302 245 F
richard.baker@colin.edu
BAKER, Richard .... 713-348-4350 442 F
BAKER, Rick .... 828-689-1215 331 C
rbaker@mhu.edu
BAKER, Robert .... 703-993-2004 467 E
rbaker2@gmu.edu
BAKER, Robert, T .... 336-758-5224 344 C
bakerrt@wfu.edu
BAKER, Robin, E .... 503-554-2101 373 A
rbaker@georgefox.edu
BAKER, Ross .... 618-664-7115 138 F
ross.baker@greenville.edu
BAKER, Russell, D .... 317-921-4313 158 D
rbaker80@ivytech.edu
BAKER, Ruth, E .... 410-334-2825 205 D
rbaker@worwic.edu
BAKER, Sandra .... 540-831-5783 469 D
sbaker10@radford.edu
BAKER, Sarah .... 910-672-1918 341 C
sdbaker@uncfsu.edu
BAKER, Sarah .... 903-886-5045 447 B
sarah.baker@tamuc.edu
BAKER, Scott .... 828-339-4249 338 B
scottb@southwesterncc.edu
BAKER, Seth .... 312-850-7038 135 H
sbaker71@ccc.edu
BAKER, Shannon .... 361-593-3290 447 D
shannon.baker@tamuk.edu
BAKER, Sharon .... 423-478-7898 422 J
sbaker@ptseminary.edu
BAKER, Shawn .... 314-340-5095 254 A
bakers@hssu.edu
BAKER, Shawn .... 402-354-7230 268 B
shawn.baker@methodistcollege.edu
BAKER, Sherry .... 731-286-3242 424 D
baker@dscc.edu
BAKER, Sheyonn, L .... 540-362-6287 467 H
bakersl@hollins.edu
BAKER, Stephen, N .... 401-874-2109 405 E
snbaker@uri.edu
BAKER, Steve .... 805-565-7156.. 76 A
stbaker@westmont.edu
BAKER, Steven .... 301-387-3791 199 A
steven.baker@garrettcollege.edu
BAKER, Thomas, N .... 315-267-2900 319 A
bakertn@potsdam.edu
BAKER, Todd .... 208-467-8365 132 E
toddbaker@nnu.edu
BAKER, Tracy, W .... 325-942-2035 450 E
tracy.baker@angelo.edu
BAKER, Uchenna .... 201-692-2000 277 I
BAKER, Valparisa .... 863-292-3602 106 A
vbaker@polk.edu
BAKER, Wanda .... 314-838-8858 261 F
assessment@ugst.edu
BAKER, Wayne .... 432-335-6574 441 A
wbaker@odessa.edu
BAKER, Wendy .... 518-562-4195 296 A
wendy.baker@clinton.edu
BAKER, Winston .... 936-468-2601 445 E
bakerwa@sfasu.edu
BAKER, Wren .... 940-565-2789 453 E
wren.baker@unt.edu
BAKER, Yvonne .... 513-569-4942 350 F
BAKER, Zeb .... 513-529-3398 356 A
zeb.baker@miamioh.edu

BAKER-BARNES, Kiki .... 504-816-4752 186 I
kbarnes@dillard.edu
BAKER-DEMARAY,
Twyla .... 701-627-4738 346 F
tbaker@nhsc.edu
BAKER-FLOWERS,
Kimberly .... 510-885-2809.. 31 A
kimberly.bakerflowers@csueastbay.edu
BAKER-WATSON, Stevie 765-658-6075 154 J
steviebaker-watson@depauw.edu
BAKEWELL-SACHS,
Susan .... 503-494-7445 374 H
sondeansoffice@ohsu.edu
BAKHIT, Kathy .... 661-362-5042.. 38 D
kathy.bakhit@canyons.edu
BAKHIT, Norman .... 574-372-5100 155 F
bakhitn@grace.edu
BAKIC, Rachele .... 920-465-2111 495 F
bakicr@uwgb.edu
BAKK, Kelly .... 218-749-7765 238 H
k.bakk@mesabirange.edu
BAKKE, Lisa .... 702-651-4211 270 K
lisa.bakke@csn.edu
BAKKE, Sarah .... 845-437-7751 324 C
BAKKEN, Jeffrey .... 309-677-3997 134 A
jbakken@bradley.edu
BAKKEN, Jim .... 205-934-3887.... 8 A
jimb@uab.edu
BAKKEN, John .... 919-866-5319 338 G
jrbakken@waketech.edu
BAKKEN, Phillip .... 402-472-7554 269 H
pbakken@nebraska.edu
BAKKEN, Turina .... 608-246-6516 499 A
bakken@madisoncollege.edu
BAKKEN, Virgil .... 218-755-3370 237 F
virgil.bakken@bemidjistate.edu
BAKKER, Theresa .... 907-474-6218.. 10 A
uaf-alumni@alaska.edu
BAKO, Pat .... 206-726-5052 479 E
pbako@cornish.edu
BAKOWSKI, Tracy .... 410-287-1923 198 E
tbakowski@cecil.edu
BAKOYEMA, Bryn .... 334-229-4100.... 4 A
bbakoyema@alasu.edu
BAKSH-JARRETT, Gail ... 718-482-5116 294 F
gailbj@lagcc.cuny.edu
BAKSI, Christine .... 717-245-1916 382 D
baksic@dickinson.edu
BAKST, M, S .... 248-968-3360 233 F
BAKST, Y .... 248-968-3360 233 F
BAKTHAKUMAR, Davi ... 954-545-4500 108 E
dbakthakumar@sfbc.edu
BAKULA, Timothy, L ..... 319-273-2722 164 A
tim.bakula@uni.edu
BALA, Devi .... 713-718-8430 437 C
devi.bala@hccs.edu
BALA, Kavita .... 607-255-1383 297 F
kavitabala@cornell.edu
BALABAN, Mark .... 845-431-8044 298 D
mark.balaban@sunydutchess.edu
BALACEK, Patti .... 608-785-5201 500 C
balacekp@westerntc.edu
BALAKRISHNAN, Raju .. 313-593-5248 231 I
rajub@umich.edu
BALAKRISHNAN,
Venkataramanan .... 216-368-3227 349 D
cse-dean@case.edu
BALANA MOLTER,
Sarah .... 317-955-6319 159 K
sbalanamolter@marian.edu
BALANOFF, Janet .... 407-708-2963 108 D
balanoffj@seminolestate.edu
BALARIN, Alfredo .... 518-629-7348 302 C
a.balarin@hvcc.edu
BALASKI, Keith .... 320-222-5211 240 F
keith.balaski@ridgewater.edu
BALASUBRAMANIAN,
Ramprasad .... 508-999-8827 212 A
r.bala@umassd.edu
BALASUBRAMANIAN,
Sunder .... 573-681-5138 254 G
balasubramanians@lincolnu.edu
BALASZ, Anne .... 419-530-2087 363 B
anne.balasz@utoledo.edu
BALATBAT, Joseph .... 212-924-5900 321 F
jbalatbat@swedishinstitute.edu
BALBACH, Donna .... 812-357-6525 161 A
dbalbach@saintmeinrad.edu
BALBES, Idellisse .... 787-738-2161 512 C
idelisse.balbes@upr.edu
BALCAZAR, Genaro .... 708-524-6562 137 C
gbalcazar@dom.edu
BALCAZAR, Hector .... 323-563-4815.. 36 C
hectorbalcazar@cdrewu.edu

BALCER, Jesse .... 215-248-7046 381 A
balcerj@chc.edu
BALCH, Craig .... 817-760-5504 437 A
cbalch@hillcollege.edu
BALCH, Marcus .... 972-617-4128 449 D
marcus.balch@tstc.edu
BALCH, Robert .... 575-835-5143 286 K
robert.balch@nmt.edu
BALCH-LINDSAY,
Suzanne .... 575-562-2314 286 B
suzanne.balch@enmu.edu
BALCHAK, Sharon .... 216-373-5295 357 F
sbalchak@ndc.edu
BALCOM, David, A .... 410-651-6199 203 D
dabalcom@umes.edu
BALD, Karolyn .... 608-785-8017 496 A
kbald@uwlax.edu
BALDA, Jose .... 201-200-3381 279 D
jbalda@njcu.edu
BALDAUF, Jack, G .... 979-845-8585 446 F
jbaldauf@tamu.edu
BALDERAS, Guillermo .... 702-254-7577 272 A
guillermo.balderas@
northwestcareercollege.edu
BALDERAS, Ulyses .... 713-525-3533 454 G
balderj@stthom.edu
BALDIN, Antoinette .... 419-995-8406 360 C
baldin.a@rhodesstate.edu
BALDINI, Fred .... 510-879-0784.. 60 C
fbaldini@samuelmerritt.edu
BALDONEDO, Claudia .. 718-482-5236 294 F
claudiab@lagcc.cuny.edu
BALDRIDGE, Amber ...... 706-880-8238 122 A
abjohnson@lagrange.edu
BALDRIDGE, Stephen ... 254-295-4732 453 D
sbaldridge@umhb.edu
BALDUCCI, Laureen ...... 408-864-8945.. 42 H
balduccilaureen@deanza.edu
BALDWIN, Ally .... 617-236-8878 209 G
abaldwin@fisher.edu
BALDWIN, Anne, E .... 585-245-5547 318 B
baldwina@geneseo.edu
BALDWIN, Candice .... 301-624-2867 198 I
cbaldwin@fredreick.edu
BALDWIN, Chad .... 307-766-2929 501 I
cbaldwin@uwyo.edu
BALDWIN, Christine, A . 714-850-4800.. 67 H
baldwin@taftu.edu
BALDWIN, Christine, A . 714-850-4800.. 83 K
baldwin@taftu.edu
BALDWIN, Darin .... 334-745-6437.... 3 G
dbaldwin@suscc.edu
BALDWIN, David, N ...... 508-626-4645 213 A
dbaldwin@framingham.edu
BALDWIN, Deborah, J .. 501-320-5780.. 22 A
djbaldwin@ualr.edu
BALDWIN, Diane .... 617-353-4377 207 E
dbaldwin@bu.edu
BALDWIN, Dirk .... 262-595-2379 496 D
baldwin@uwp.edu
BALDWIN, Erin .... 515-294-7971 163 G
baldwine@iastate.edu
BALDWIN, Kate .... 207-602-4828 194 H
kbaldwin@landingschool.edu
BALDWIN, Kate .... 207-602-4858 194 H
kbaldwin@landingschool.edu
BALDWIN, Latosha .... 202-274-6604.. 94 B
latosha.baldwin@udc.edu
BALDWIN, Laura .... 215-572-2909 378 E
baldwinl@arcadia.edu
BALDWIN, Mark .... 509-359-2449 479 G
mbaldwin@ewu.edu
BALDWIN, Melanie, C .. 302-295-1181.. 91 E
melanie.c.baldwin@wilmu.edu
BALDWIN, Melissa .... 303-556-2400.. 84 D
BALDWIN, Michael .... 510-780-4500.. 47 K
mbaldwin@lifewest.edu
BALDWIN, Naomi .... 716-673-3451 316 D
naomi.baldwin@fredonia.edu
BALDWIN, R. Chad .... 636-584-6609 253 B
robert.baldwin@eastcentral.edu
BALDWIN, Sarah, T ...... 859-858-3511 179 D
sarah.baldwin@asbury.edu
BALDWIN, Stan .... 601-925-3321 247 C
sbaldwin@mc.edu
BALDWIN, Terri, M .... 740-588-1210 365 B
tbaldwin2@zanestate.edu
BALDWIN, Tony .... 704-216-6272 330 H
tbaldwin@livingstone.edu
BALDWIN, Tony .... 704-216-6005 330 H
tbaldwin@livingstone.edu
BALDWIN-DIMEO,
Caren, L .... 603-526-3714 272 H
cbaldwin-dimeo@colby-sawyer.edu

BALDWIN-SAYRE,
Carrie .... 503-517-5459 375 G
cbsayre@reed.edu
BALENTINE, Jerry .... 516-686-3999 308 I
jerry.balentine@nyit.edu
BALES, Jennifer .... 913-621-8733 173 E
jennifer@donnelly.edu
BALES, Michael .... 276-964-7323 475 C
michael.bales@sw.edu
BALES, William, J .... 615-898-5014 422 C
joe.bales@mtsu.edu
BALESTRA, Elisa .... 914-813-9242 315 A
ebalestra@sarahlawrence.edu
BALESTRERI, Teresa, A . 314-516-5002 261 C
tkb@umsl.edu
BALFOUR, Stephen, P .. 706-357-0049 126 G
stephen.balfour@uga.edu
BALI, Sunjay .... 412-809-5180 396 E
bali.sunjay@ptcollege.edu
BALIGH, Mohamed .... 518-255-5473 319 C
saeedmg@cobleskill.edu
BALINSKI, Joseph .... 231-439-6347 228 H
jbalinski@ncmich.edu
BALINSKI, Joseph .... 231-348-6600 228 H
jbalinski@ncmich.edu
BALINT, Elizabeth .... 530-541-4660.. 47 E
BALINT, William, S .... 724-357-7854 394 C
wsbalint@iup.edu
BALKANSKY, Andrew .... 618-453-2466 150 B
cola.dean@siu.edu
BALKIN, Timothy, P ..... 716-888-2480 292 F
balkin4@canisius.edu
BALKISSOON, Tony ...... 212-237-8000 294 D
BALL, Christine .... 706-771-4150 115 J
cball@augustatech.edu
BALL, Diane .... 352-588-8417 107 D
diane.ball@saintleo.edu
BALL, Don .... 330-494-6170 360 K
dball@starkstate.edu
BALL, Donald .... 330-494-6170 360 K
dball@starkstate.edu
BALL, Doug .... 620-235-4107 177 A
dbball@pittstate.edu
BALL, Gregory, F .... 301-405-1691 202 H
gball@umd.edu
BALL, James, D .... 410-386-8188 198 D
jball@carrollcc.edu
BALL, Jamie .... 618-650-2333 150 C
jball@siue.edu
BALL, Jason .... 561-297-3440 109 J
jball@fau.edu
BALL, Jennifer .... 315-268-4208 295 F
jball@clarkson.edu
BALL, John .... 504-568-4500 189 H
jball@lsuhsc.edu
BALL, Justin .... 309-677-3850 134 A
jball@fsmail.bradley.edu
BALL, Kathy .... 304-384-6009 489 J
bonner@concord.edu
BALL, Kenneth .... 703-993-1500 467 E
vsdean@gmu.edu
BALL, Kevin .... 330-941-1560 364 H
keball@ysu.edu
BALL, Kevin, A .... 248-364-8673 229 I
kevinball@oakland.edu
BALL, Kevin, J .... 806-371-5225 429 E
k0364101@actx.edu
BALL, Kim .... 704-894-2521 328 E
kiball@davidson.edu
BALL, Kimberly .... 657-278-4968.. 31 C
kball@fullerton.edu
BALL, Kristen .... 804-289-8401 472 C
kball@richmond.edu
BALL, Margaret .... 570-422-3211 394 A
mball@esu.edu
BALL, Margaret, T .... 718-817-3010 300 C
mball@fordham.edu
BALL, Marquez .... 301-736-3631 200 C
marquez.ball@msbbcs.edu
BALL, Mary Alice .... 410-778-7704 205 B
mball2@washcoll.edu
BALL, Michael .... 859-246-6512 181 F
michael.ball@kctcs.edu
BALL, Michael .... 254-295-4688 453 D
mball@umhb.edu
BALL, Michelle .... 740-826-8024 356 H
mball@muskingum.edu
BALL, Shelley .... 865-471-3235 418 E
sball@cn.edu
BALL, Travis .... 903-886-5060 447 B
travis.ball@tamuc.edu
BALL-DAVIS, Marsha .... 860-906-5042.. 86 D
mball-davis@ccc.commnet.edu

BAOUA, Kesha ... 501-450-3824 .. 19 E baoua@hendrix.edu

BAPTISTE, Brian ... 215-951-1425 387 A

BAPTISTE, JoRae ... 808-245-8323 130 B jorae@hawaii.edu

BAR, Rosann ... 732-255-0400 279 F rbar@ocean.edu

BARABE, Becky ... 559-443-8514 .. 67 B becky.barabe@fresnocitycollege.edu

BARABINO, Gilda, A ... 781-292-2301 210 A

BARAGONA, Michelle ... 662-720-7375 248 C mabaragona@nemcc.edu

BARAJAS, Ruben ... 310-303-7293 .. 51 C rbarajas@marymountcalifornia.edu

BARAJAS, Silvia ... 310-287-4369 .. 49 H barajas2@wlac.edu

BARAKAT, Nabeel, M ... 310-233-4351 .. 49 B barakanm@lahc.edu

BARAKEH, Zeina ... 415-351-3571 .. 61 C zbarakeh@sfai.edu

BARALDI, Michael ... 919-209-2051 335 F m_baraldi@johnstoncc.edu

BARAN, Kelley ... 508-531-2492 212 D kelley.baran@bridgew.edu

BARAN, Victoria ... 716-488-3021 302 H victoriabaran@jbc.edu

BARATO, Ruben ... 914-606-6777 325 A ruben.barato@sunywcc.edu

BARATTA, Peter ... 609-626-6080 283 E peter.baratta@stockton.edu

BARBA, Jesse, D ... 413-542-5485 205 G jbarba@amherst.edu

BARBARICK, Cliff ... 325-674-3767 428 F cab11c@acu.edu

BARBATIS, Peter ... 561-868-3142 105 D barbatip@palmbeachstate.edu

BARBAULD, Ryan, J ... 812-888-4313 162 F ryan.barbauld@vinu.edu

BARBEAU, Dyan, E ... 414-410-4118 491 I debarbeau@stritch.edu

BARBEAU, Marc, C ... 414-410-4000 491 I mbarbeau1@stritch.edu

BARBEE, Brent ... 910-410-1809 337 B btbarbee@richmondcc.edu

BARBEE, Danielle ... 856-225-2965 281 G danielle.barbee@camden.rutgers.edu

BARBEE, Holly ... 252-493-7206 336 H hbarbee@email.pittcc.edu

BARBEE, Julianna ... 505-747-2240 287 H jbarbee@nnmc.edu

BARBEE, Kelsey ... 719-384-6824 .. 82 D kelsey.barbee@ojc.edu

BARBEITO, Patricia ... 401-709-6575 405 B pbarbeit@risd.edu

BARBER, Adrianne ... 208-459-5268 131 C abarber@collegeofidaho.edu

BARBER, Billy ... 252-789-0303 335 H billy.barber@martincc.edu

BARBER, Carolyn ... 816-235-6151 261 B barberce@umkc.edu

BARBER, Charles ... 202-994-6503 .. 92 D cbarber@gwu.edu

BARBER, Christina ... 518-454-2142 296 G barberc@strose.edu

BARBER, Cindy ... 870-307-7527 .. 19 I cindy.barber@lyon.edu

BARBER, DiAnna ... 919-739-7021 338 H wcc-bookstore@waynecc.edu

BARBER, Eric ... 402-460-5722 267 E ebarber@marylanning.org

BARBER, Gary ... 740-374-8716 363 F gbarber@wscc.edu

BARBER, Isaac, C ... 260-359-4328 156 C ibarber@huntington.edu

BARBER, Jacques ... 516-877-4800 289 I jbarber@adelphi.edu

BARBER, Jeff ... 843-863-7080 407 B jbarber@csuniv.edu

BARBER, Jennifer ... 916-278-3634 .. 32 D jbarbar@csus.edu

BARBER, Kim ... 252-792-1521 335 H

BARBER, Kimberly ... 850-644-6127 110 C kabarber@admin.fsu.edu

BARBER, Lindsay ... 231-591-2697 224 A lindsaybarber@ferris.edu

BARBER, Lori ... 208-535-5419 131 B lori.barber@cei.edu

BARBER, Luanne ... 870-612-2119 .. 22 H luanne.barber@uaccb.edu

BARBER, Melinda ... 352-435-6351 103 U barberm@lssc.edu

BARBER, Richard ... 724-503-1001 402 B rbarber@washjeff.edu

BARBER, Robbi ... 502-863-7047 180 H robbi_barber@georgetowncollege.edu

BARBER, Sarah ... 315-229-5083 314 D sbarber@stlawu.edu

BARBER, Tracy ... 719-255-7507 .. 84 C tbarber@uccs.edu

BARBER, Trent, J ... 860-512-3283 .. 86 G tbarber@manchestercc.edu

BARBER, Wendi ... 937-395-8520 354 J wendi.barber@ketteringhealth.org

BARBERA, Anthony ... 516-876-3135 318 C barberaa@oldwestbury.edu

BARBERA, Bridget ... 718-960-8000 294 A

BARBERIAN, Wazkein ... 818-988-2300 .. 53 F

BARBERICH, Kim ... 609-896-5000 281 B kbarberich@rider.edu

BARBIER GIBSON, Yolanda ... 540-665-4783 470 G ygibson@su.edu

BARBIERI, Lina ... 610-282-1100 382 C lina.barbieri@desales.edu

BARBONE, Tony ... 626-585-3203 .. 56 D tbarbone@pasadena.edu

BARBOSA, Francisco ... 787-264-1912 508 F fbarbosa@intersg.edu

BARBOSA, Mary Kate ... 207-768-9613 197 C mary.barbosa@maine.edu

BARBOSA, Miguel ... 570-422-3545 394 A mbarbosa@esu.edu

BARBOUR, A. Sandy ... 814-865-1086 391 G asb25@psu.edu

BARBOUR, Anthony ... 704-272-5300 337 I abarbour@spcc.edu

BARBOUR, Channell ... 859-985-3251 179 I barbourc@berea.edu

BARBOUR, Cheryl ... 303-546-3565 .. 82 A cheryl@naropa.edu

BARBOUR, Darrell ... 641-585-8138 170 I darrell.barbour@waldorf.edu

BARBOUR, Denise ... 770-412-5740 125 H denise.barbour@sctech.edu

BARBOUR, Jeffery ... 757-340-2121 465 I librariancvab@centura.edu

BARBOUR, Monica ... 313-993-1951 231 E barbourmm@udmercy.edu

BARBOUR, Suzanne, W 919-962-7791 342 C sbarbour@unc.edu

BARCLAY, Beth ... 563-884-5586 169 F beth.barclay@palmer.edu

BARCLAY, Kent ... 978-232-2282 209 E kbarclay@endicott.edu

BARCLAY, Ryan ... 813-988-5131 .. 99 R barclayr@floridacollege.edu

BARCLAY, Tosha ... 713-718-6140 437 C tosha.barclay@hccs.edu

BARCO, Jessica ... 657-278-5256 .. 31 C jbarco@fullerton.edu

BARCO, Nicole, S ... 989-774-3902 222 E sparl1nl@cmich.edu

BARCUS, Krista ... 660-562-1128 257 E kbarcus@nwmissouri.edu

BARD, JR., Branville ... 410-516-3486 199 G branville.bard@jhu.edu

BARD, Sharon, K ... 704-463-3428 339 E sharon.bard@pfeiffer.edu

BARDEGUEZ, Lemuel ... 405-682-7814 367 D lbardeguez@occc.edu

BARDEN, John ... 203-432-3262 .. 90 C john.barden@yale.edu

BARDEN, JR ... 512-404-4805 430 J jrbarden@austinseminary.edu

BARDNEY, Eileen ... 845-569-3254 307 D eileen.bardney@msmc.edu

BARE, Benita ... 423-636-5096 426 E bbare@tusculum.edu

BAREFIELD, Kevin ... 662-685-4771 245 C kbarefield@bmc.edu

BAREFOOT, Jon ... 317-921-4882 158 D jon.barefoot@ivytech.edu

BAREFOOT, Russell ... 908-526-1200 281 A russell.barefoot@raritanval.edu

BARELMAN, Jason ... 402-375-7327 268 F jabarel1@wsc.edu

BAREN, Jill ... 215-596-8800 401 E

BARENDS, Frans ... 404-894-5000 119 E frans.barends@business.gatech.edu

BARFIELD, Carnelia ... 318-274-6375 192 C barfieldc@gram.edu

BARFIELD, Julie ... 817-272-2584 454 I barfield@uta.edu

BARFIELD, Kem ... 860-215-9210 .. 87 F kbarfield1@threerivers.edu

BARFIELD, Randy ... 215-489-6378 382 B randall.barfield@delval.edu

BARFOOT, D. Scott ... 214-887-5151 435 F sbarfoot@dts.edu

BARFUSS, Blair ... 435-652-7515 460 B blair.barfuss@dixie.edu

BARGA, Brian ... 619-201-8951 .. 65 G brian.barga@socalsem.edu

BARGAR, Robin ... 562-985-4364 .. 31 D robin.bargar@csulb.edu

BARGAS, DeLynn ... 575-562-2175 286 B delynn.bargas@enmu.edu

BARGAS, Theresa ... 512-859-7239 430 G tbargas@escoffier.edu

BARGE, Scott ... 540-432-4304 466 B scott.barge@emu.edu

BARGE-MILES, Linda ... 850-599-3225 109 I linda.bargemiles@famu.edu

BARGER, Debbie, M ... 515-263-6012 166 F dbarger@grandview.edu

BARGER, Eric, C ... 503-943-7507 377 A barger@up.edu

BARGER, Judith ... 678-916-2653 115 I jbarger@johnmarshall.edu

BARGER, Melanie ... 573-592-6050 262 E melanie.barger@westminster-mo.edu

BARGER, Mollie ... 601-928-6264 247 E mollie.barger@mgccc.edu

BARGER, Peter, S ... 630-637-5362 145 F psbarger@noctrl.edu

BARGERHUFF, Eric ... 727-376-6911 112 G eric.bargerhuff@trinitycollege.edu

BARGHOTHI, Jane ... 828-262-2090 340 I janebar@appstate.edu

BARGO, Sarah ... 417-447-7813 257 G bargos@otc.edu

BARHAM, James ... 731-286-3371 424 D jbarham@dscc.edu

BARHAM, Stephanie ... 423-323-0210 425 A srbarham@northeaststate.edu

BARHAM, Treva ... 903-233-3470 439 A trevabarham@letu.edu

BARIA, Jo Ann ... 253-964-6640 482 E jbaria@pierce.ctc.edu

BARIL, Kathleen, T ... 419-772-2180 358 C k-baril@onu.edu

BARILAR, Stephen, J ... 570-577-3333 379 C steve.barilar@bucknell.edu

BARILE, Brandon ... 315-781-3051 301 F barile@hws.edu

BARILOVITS, Karlyn ... 866-492-5336 244 F karlyn.barilovits@mail.waldenu.edu

BARIOLA, Kristi ... 662-246-6376 247 D kbariola@msdelta.edu

BARISH, Robert ... 312-413-0340 151 G rbarish@uic.edu

BARKALOW, Susan ... 252-618-6502 334 D barkalows@edgecombe.edu

BARKAN, Chester ... 516-572-7131 307 E chester.barkan@ncc.edu

BARKE, Brady, L ... 573-651-2227 259 H bbarke@semo.edu

BARKER, Allyn, S ... 304-896-7404 488 I allyn.barker@southernwv.edu

BARKER, Anita, S ... 530-898-6470 .. 30 D abarker@csuchico.edu

BARKER, Blake ... 214-648-2168 457 A blake.barker@utsouthwestern.edu

BARKER, Brett ... 843-377-2149 407 A bbarker@charlestonlaw.edu

BARKER, Brian ... 970-945-8691 .. 78 L

BARKER, Bruce ... 828-227-3100 343 E bbarker@wcu.edu

BARKER, Christopher ... 203-392-6025 .. 86 A barkerc7@southernct.edu

BARKER, Curtis ... 336-841-9372 329 F cbarker@highpoint.edu

BARKER, Eddie ... 606-337-3196 180 C

BARKER, Ellie ... 919-508-2041 344 E erbarker@peace.edu

BARKER, Greg ... 815-753-1000 146 B

BARKER, John, D ... 864-294-2106 409 H john.barker@furman.edu

BARKER, John, F ... 716-286-8220 309 H jfb@niagara.edu

BARKER, Marco ... 402-472-3751 269 J marco.barker@unl.edu

BARKER, MarQuita ... 336-278-7300 328 J mbarker4@elon.edu

BARKER, Michael ... 919-962-4314 342 C michael_barker@unc.edu

BARKER, Neva ... 909-621-8306 .. 63 F neva.barker@scrippscollege.edu

BARKER, Randy ... 715-394-8394 497 C rbarker@uwsuper.edu

BARKER, Ryan ... 315-470-5710 291 I ryanbarker@crouse.org

BARKER, Sandy ... 336-812-7234 125 F sbarker@southuniversity.edu

BARKER, Stephen ... 949-824-8792 .. 69 D barker@uci.edu

BARKER, Tess ... 765-455-9360 157 B tessbark@iu.edu

BARKER, Yvette ... 713-313-7201 449 B yvette.barker@tsu.edu

BARKHAMER, Kim ... 215-596-8800 401 E

BARKIS, Kimberly ... 310-506-6110 .. 56 G kimberly.barkis@pepperdine.edu

BARKLEY, Alexander ... 914-323-3172 305 B alexander.barkley@mville.edu

BARKLEY, Beatrice, L ... 215-368-5000 390 A bbarkley@missio.edu

BARKLEY, Bill ... 866-492-5336 244 F william.barkley@mail.waldenu.edu

BARKLEY, Brian ... 770-836-6830 128 A brian.barkley@westgatech.edu

BARKLEY, Jordan ... 254-968-9103 446 D jbarkley@tarleton.edu

BARKLEY, Lisa, C ... 252-536-6399 335 B lbarkley150@halifaxcc.edu

BARKLEY-GIFFIN, Adrienne ... 618-985-3741 140 H adriennebarkley@jalc.edu

BARKLIND, Amanda ... 651-450-3887 238 E abarklind@inverhills.edu

BARKO, James, N ... 972-881-5847 433 I jbarko@collin.edu

BARKO, Valerie ... 808-245-8336 130 B vabarko@hawaii.edu

BARKOFF, Larry ... 734-677-5413 232 D lbarkoff@wccnet.edu

BARKOWITZ, Daniel, T ... 407-582-1458 113 I dbarkowitz@valenciacollege.edu

BARKSDALE, Demetria ... 512-505-3002 438 A dbarksdale@htu.edu

BARKSDALE, Elizabeth ... 706-295-6592 120 A ebarksdale@gntc.edu

BARKSDALE, Glasetta ... 312-850-7288 135 H gbarksdale@ccc.edu

BARKSDALE, Tina, M ... 302-356-6940 .. 91 E tina.m.barksdale@wilmu.edu

BARKWILL, Joseph ... 516-463-6623 301 G joseph.barkwill@hofstra.edu

BARLAND, Karen ... 410-951-3704 204 B kbarland@coppin.edu

BARLETTA, Regina ... 757-455-3230 477 C rbarletta@vwu.edu

BARLEY, Robert ... 812-237-8439 156 D bob.barley@indstate.edu

BARLEY, Tracy ... 225-771-3740 191 B tracy_barley@subr.edu

BARLEY, Tracy ... 225-771-2304 191 A tracy_barley@subr.edu

BARLEY, Tracy ... 225-771-2304 191 B tracy_barley@subr.edu

BARLOK, Tracy ... 508-793-3776 208 D tbarlok@holycross.edu

BARLOW, Angela ... 501-450-3124 .. 23 H abarlow5@uca.edu

BARLOW, Charlene ... 859-344-3348 185 B barlowc@thomasmore.edu

BARLOW, Christopher ... 405-744-7665 367 G christopher.barlow@okstate.edu

BARLOW, Elizabeth, A ... 603-646-1247 273 D elizabeth.a.barlow@dartmouth.edu

BARLOW, Felicia, R ... 336-633-0244 337 A frbarlow@randolph.edu

BARLOW, Justin ... 678-839-5000 127 C jbarlow@westga.edu

BARLOW, Matthew ... 413-775-1000 214 E

BARLOW, Michael ... 270-706-8614 181 G mbarlow0002@kctcs.edu

BARLOW, Rachael ... 860-685-2423 .. 90 B rbarlow02@wesleyan.edu

BARLOW, Sarah ... 225-216-8361 187 G barlows@mybrcc.edu

BARLOW, Steve ... 307-855-2029 501 A sbarlow@cwc.edu

BARLOW-KELLEY, Jill ... 207-801-5633 194 E jbk@coa.edu

BARMAN, Emily ... 773-508-3396 143 C ebarman@luc.edu

BARMANN, Terry ... 303-797-5738 .. 77 I terry.barmann@arapahoe.edu

BARNA, Eric ... 804-333-6771 475 A ebarna@rappahannock.edu

BARRETT, Dustin .... 912-650-6250 125 F
dbarrett@southuniversity.edu
BARRETT, Gary .... 910-323-5614 327 F
gbarrett@ccbs.edu
BARRETT, James .... 920-924-6431 499 D
jbarrett8@morainepark.edu
BARRETT, James, F ...... 330-325-6274 357 D
jbarrett@neomed.edu
BARRETT, Joan .... 417-447-6914 257 G
barrettj@otc.edu
BARRETT, Laura .... 845-257-3520 316 E
barrettl@newpaltz.edu
BARRETT, Lawrence ...... 386-752-1822 100 B
lawrence.barrett@fgc.edu
BARRETT, Leah .... 402-844-7055 268 H
lbarrett@northeast.edu
BARRETT, Linda .... 401-874-2509 405 E
lindab@uri.edu
BARRETT, Mary, C .... 607-735-1790 298 H
mbarrett@elmira.edu
BARRETT, Michael .... 616-432-3412 230 A
michael.barrett@prts.edu
BARRETT, Michele .... 812-237-7829 156 D
michele.barrett@indstate.edu
BARRETT, Pam, J .... 770-534-6176 116 D
pbarrett@brenau.edu
BARRETT, Pamela .... 505-438-8884 288 F
pamela@acupuncturecollege.edu
BARRETT, Richard .... 319-363-1323 168 F
rbarrett@mtmercy.edu
BARRETT, Sarah .... 518-244-2441 313 A
barres2@sage.edu
BARRETT, Scott .... 310-243-3787.. 30 E
sbarrett@csudh.edu
BARRETT, Steve .... 507-389-2015 239 D
steve.barrett@mnsu.edu
BARRETT, Steven .... 307-766-4286 501 I
BARRETT, Tracy .... 704-922-6309 334 G
barrett.tracy@gaston.edu
BARRETT, Zunilka .... 617-287-7050 211 F
zbarrett@umassp.edu
BARRETTA, Jacqueline .. 503-370-6004 377 F
jbarretta@willamette.edu
BARRETTE, Catherine .... 313-577-1615 232 K
c.barrette@wayne.edu
BARRETTO, Kelly .... 919-807-7100 331 L
BARRICELLI, Franca ...... 978-665-3627 212 E
fbarrice@fitchburgstate.edu
BARRICK, Bradley .... 405-733-7961 369 E
bbarrick@rose.edu
BARRIENTOS, Joe .... 206-934-6788 483 D
joe.barrientos@seattlecolleges.edu
BARRIER, Jeremy .... 256-766-6610.... 5 E
jbarrier@hcu.edu
BARRINEAU, Annette .... 904-381-3724 101 B
annette.barrineau@fscj.edu
BARRINGER, Bryan .... 901-321-4409 418 G
bbarring@cbu.edu
BARRINGER, Judy .... 212-659-7215 303 H
jbarringer@tkc.edu
BARRINGER, Susan, J .. 336-217-7221 329 C
susan.barringer@greensboro.edu
BARRINGER, Tony .... 239-590-7849 109 K
tbarring@fgcu.edu
BARRINGHAUS, Jill ...... 660-248-6977 251 E
jbarring@centralmethodist.edu
BARRINGTON, Beverly .. 850-599-8316 109 I
beverly.barrington@famu.edu
BARRIO, Brian .... 410-455-2207 203 B
bbarrio@umbc.edu
BARRIO-SOTILLO,
Ramona .... 818-240-1000.. 43 G
rbarrio@glendale.edu
BARRIOS, Kristin .... 626-568-8850.. 48 H
kristin@lacm.edu
BARRIOS, Sharon, A ..... 530-898-4473.. 30 D
sbarrios@csuchico.edu
BARRIS, Brad .... 706-236-2272 116 B
bbarris@berry.edu
BARRISH, David, J .... 804-523-5934 474 A
dbarrish@reynolds.edu
BARRON, Caulyne .... 602-648-5750.. 12 E
cbarron@dunlap-stone.edu
BARRON, David .... 903-566-7051 456 A
dbarron@uttyler.edu
BARRON, Dori .... 828-448-3170 339 A
dbarron@wpcc.edu
BARRON, Eric, J .... 814-865-7611 391 G
president@psu.edu
BARRON, Jose .... 575-624-8263 287 B
barron@nmmi.edu
BARRON, Lee .... 314-275-3510 147 E
lee.barron@principia.edu
BARRON, Matthew .... 906-217-4054 222 A
barronm@baycollege.edu
BARRON, Nicole .... 312-341-2114 148 E
nbarron03@roosevelt.edu
BARRON, Sebastian ...... 903-434-8260 440 G
sbarron@ntcc.edu
BARRON, Travis .... 229-500-4004 114 H
travis.barron@asurams.edu
BARROS, Ben .... 419-530-7877 363 B
ben.barros@utoledo.edu
BARROSO, Laura .... 805-652-5500.. 73 I
BARROTT, James .... 423-697-3211 424 A
jim.barrott@chattanoogastate.edu
BARROW, Carla .... 229-225-5077 126 A
cbarrow@southernregional.edu
BARROW, Danny .... 225-578-1175 189 E
dbarrow1@lsu.edu
BARROW, Deborah, L ... 940-397-4212 440 C
debbie.barrow@msutexas.edu
BARROW, Geoff .... 706-583-2544 115 F
gbarrow@athenstech.edu
BARROW, Laurie .... 717-901-5143 385 H
lbarrow@harrisburgu.edu
BARROW, Terry .... 620-792-9318 171 I
barrowt@bartonccc.edu
BARROWS, India .... 603-428-2293 273 G
ibarrows@nec.edu
BARROWS, James .... 520-515-5339.. 11 M
barrowsj@cochise.edu
BARROWS, Jamie .... 251-981-3771.... 5 A
james.barrows@columbiasouthern.edu
BARROWS, Karen, A ..... 585-475-2396 312 F
kab7050@rit.edu
BARROWS, Karen, A ..... 585-475-2396 312 F
karen.barrows@rit.edu
BARROWS, Kimberly ..... 406-353-2607 262 H
kbarrows@ancollege.edu
BARROWS, Robert .... 617-228-2241 214 C
rbarrows@bhcc.mass.edu
BARRY, Ben .... 212-229-5600 308 A
barryb@newschool.edu
BARRY, Bernard .... 913-621-8765 173 E
bbarry@donnelly.edu
BARRY, Carol .... 225-578-1480 189 E
carolbarry@lsu.edu
BARRY, Catherine .... 603-578-8900 272 M
cbarry@ccsnh.edu
BARRY, Chris .... 217-786-2410 143 B
chris.barry@llcc.edu
BARRY, Christy .... 229-931-2053 120 D
christy.barry@gsw.edu
BARRY, Danyell .... 478-827-3232 118 F
barnesd@fvsu.edu
BARRY, Ernie .... 214-768-2004 444 D
ebarry@smu.edu
BARRY, Heather .... 631-687-5109 314 A
hbarry@sjcny.edu
BARRY, James (Tim) ..... 304-457-6317 486 E
barryjt@ab.edu
BARRY, Jeannette .... 402-375-7466 268 F
jebarry1@wsc.edu
BARRY, Jennifer .... 610-527-0200 397 D
jennifer.barry@rosemont.edu
BARRY, Jessica .... 937-294-0592 356 D
jessica.barry@themodern.edu
BARRY, John, M .... 804-289-8778 472 C
jbarry2@richmond.edu
BARRY, Kevin, A .... 213-477-2875.. 52 I
kbarry@msmu.edu
BARRY, Kevin, G .... 302-295-1170.. 91 E
kevin.g.barry@wilmu.edu
BARRY, Lisa .... 508-856-6507 212 C
lisa.barry@umassmed.edu
BARRY, Liz, M .... 734-764-6270 231 H
lizbarry@umich.edu
BARRY, Maria .... 202-885-2121.. 91 F
mariab@american.edu
BARRY, Michael, F .... 713-646-1819 443 I
mbarry@stcl.edu
BARRY, Richard .... 610-526-6532 379 B
rbarry@brynmawr.edu
BARRY, Taylor .... 828-898-3368 330 E
barryt@lmc.edu
BARRY, Theresa .... 262-524-7334 492 A
tbarry@carrollu.edu
BARSOM, Michelle .... 770-836-4712 128 A
michelle.barsom@westgatech.edu
BARSTAD, Joel, I .... 412-312-8383 379 F
housefather@bcs.edu
BARTA, Gary .... 319-335-9435 163 H
gary-barta@uiowa.edu
BARTA, Lou .... 217-641-4215 141 A
lbarta@jwcc.edu
BARTEE, Robert .... 402-559-4203 269 K
bbartee@unmc.edu
BARTEK, Jennifer, J ...... 724-738-2339 395 C
jennifer.bartek@sru.edu
BARTEL, Charles, R ...... 412-396-1090 383 A
bartelc@duq.edu
BARTEL, Mae .... 918-223-1363 368 B
mbartel@osugiving.com
BARTEL, OSB, Martin ... 724-805-2146 398 A
martin.bartel@stvincent.edu
BARTELL, LaNeil, R .... 605-336-6588 416 A
lbartell@sfseminary.edu
BARTELL, William .... 605-331-6703 417 C
bill.bartell@usiouxfalls.edu
BARTELS, Michael .... 563-387-1352 168 B
bartmi03@luther.edu
BARTELS, Paige .... 802-440-4300 461 G
pbartels@bennington.edu
BARTELS, Roy .... 830-792-7213 443 E
rbartels@schreiner.edu
BARTELS, Suzanne, M .. 336-316-2046 329 D
bartelssm@guilford.edu
BARTELSON, Jon .... 401-456-8200 405 A
jbartelson@ric.edu
BARTELT, Jason .... 920-923-8090 493 D
jbartelt@marianuniversity.edu
BARTFIELD, Joel .... 518-262-7302 289 L
bartfij@amc.edu
BARTGES, Ellyn .... 320-308-5123 240 I
elbartges@stcloudstate.edu
BARTH, Christopher ...... 845-938-3833 503 I
christopher.barth@westpoint.edu
BARTH, Doug .... 785-594-4526 171 F
doug.barth@bakeru.edu
BARTH, Michael .... 406-496-4233 265 A
mbarth@mtech.edu
BARTH, Richard .... 262-595-2495 496 D
barthr@uwp.edu
BARTH, Rick .... 256-233-8176.... 4 C
rick.barth@athens.edu
BARTH, Sean .... 407-708-4570 108 D
barths@seminolestate.edu
BARTHA, Jaimee .... 847-628-2514 141 C
jbartha@judsonu.edu
BARTHEL, Jamie .... 763-422-6082 237 D
jbarthel@anokatech.edu
BARTHELEMY, Diana ..... 773-577-8100 136 F
dberthelemy@coynecollege.edu
BARTHELMAS, Rick .... 518-244-2200 313 A
barthf@sage.edu
BARTHOLOMEW, Diane 660-831-4146 256 I
bartholomewd@moval.edu
BARTHOLOMEW,
Jennifer .... 414-425-8300 495 A
jbartholomew@shsst.edu
BARTHOLOMEW,
Melody .... 810-762-0453 228 F
melody.bartholomew@mcc.edu
BARTHOLOMEW-FEIS,
Dixee .... 712-749-1803 164 C
bartholomew@bvu.edu
BARTINDALE, Becky ..... 650-949-6107.. 42 G
bartindalebecky@fhda.edu
BARTINE, Hunt .... 610-526-6012 385 D
hbartine@harcum.edu
BARTKOWSKI, Frances . 973-353-5444 282 B
franb@newark.rutgers.edu
BARTKOWSKI, Reggie ... 850-478-8496 105 G
rbartkowski@pcci.edu
BARTKUS, Carolyn .... 262-422-1686 494 F
cbartkus@nashotah.edu
BARTL, Noelle .... 575-562-2412 286 B
noelle.bartl@enmu.edu
BARTLE, John, R .... 402-554-3989 270 A
jbartle@unomaha.edu
BARTLETT, Abby .... 913-360-7400 171 J
abartlett@benedictine.edu
BARTLETT, Andy .... 218-755-2746 237 F
andy.bartlett@bemidjistate.edu
BARTLETT, Anne .... 973-290-4418 282 I
abartlett@steu.edu
BARTLETT, Anne .... 979-230-3202 431 I
anne.bartlett@brazosport.edu
BARTLETT, Annemarie ... 401-847-6650 405 D
annemarie.bartlett@salve.edu
BARTLETT, Julia .... 651-846-1314 241 B
julia.bartlett@saintpaul.edu
BARTLETT, Raymond ..... 832-842-5550 452 C
rbartlett@uh.edu
BARTLETT, Raymond ..... 832-842-5530 452 D
rbartlett@uh.edu
BARTLETT, Stacey .... 530-242-7730.. 64 C
sbartlett@shastacollege.edu
BARTLETT, Stacy .... 706-385-1100 124 E
stacy.bartlett@point.edu
BARTLEY, Mary, E .... 515-961-1511 170 B
mimi.bartley@simpson.edu
BARTLEY, Phyllis .... 540-863-2824 473 F
pbartley@dslcc.edu
BARTLING, Jonathan ..... 615-248-1258 426 D
jdbartling@trevecca.edu
BARTLING, Kelly, H ...... 308-865-8455 269 I
bartlingkh@unk.edu
BARTLOW, Jon, A .... 620-235-4761 177 A
jbartlow@pittstate.edu
BARTO, Christopher, E . 212-752-1530 304 A
cbarto@limcollege.edu
BARTO, Daniel .... 727-341-3051 107 E
barto.daniel@spcollege.edu
BARTOLD, Milissa .... 312-949-7440 139 D
mbartold@ico.edu
BARTOLINI, Brian, J ..... 401-865-1554 404 F
bbartoli@providence.edu
BARTOLOMEI, Chris, J . 716-645-2227 316 C
cbartolo@buffalo.edu
BARTOLOMEO, Jamin ... 240-567-1993 200 G
jamin.bartolomeo@montgomerycollege.edu
BARTOLOMEO, Joseph . 413-545-2554 211 G
jbartolo@uww.umass.edu
BARTOLONE,
Christopher .... 414-288-6103 493 E
christopher.bartolone@marquette.edu
BARTON, Allison .... 615-220-7826 424 F
abarton@mscc.edu
BARTON, Andrea, M ..... 503-943-8715 377 A
barton@up.edu
BARTON, April .... 412-396-6280 383 A
ambarton@duq.edu
BARTON,
Charles (Lennie) .... 919-760-8375 331 D
bartonl@meredith.edu
BARTON, Jennifer, K .... 520-626-0314.. 16 D
barton@arizona.edu
BARTON, Mary .... 940-565-2085 453 E
mary.barton@unt.edu
BARTON, Michael .... 256-782-5277.... 6 A
msbarton@jsu.edu
BARTON, Michelle .... 760-744-1150.. 56 B
mbarton@palomar.edu
BARTON, Michelle, C .... 713-834-6268 456 B
michelle.barton@uth.tmc.edu
BARTON, Oscar .... 443-885-3073 201 A
oscar.barton@morgan.edu
BARTON, Patricia .... 510-136-1220.. 45 E
barton@hnu.edu
BARTON, Paul .... 801-422-2738 458 H
paul_barton@byu.edu
BARTON, Sara .... 310-506-4275.. 56 G
sara.barton@pepperdine.edu
BARTON, Scott .... 717-477-1375 395 B
swbarton@ship.edu
BARTON II, Barkley ...... 706-542-2112 126 G
barkley.barton@uga.edu
BARTOVICS, Laura .... 718-482-5073 294 F
lbartovics@lagcc.cuny.edu
BARTOW, Patricia .... 619-216-6795.. 66 A
pbartow@swccd.edu
BARTROM, Floyd .... 617-745-3719 209 B
floyd.bartrom@enc.edu
BARTRUG, Reba .... 740-374-8716 363 F
rbartrug@wscc.edu
BARTS, Bryan .... 715-232-1469 497 B
bartsb@uwstout.edu
BARTSCH, Melissa .... 859-622-1303 180 E
melissa.bartsch@eku.edu
BARTUNEK, Tami .... 913-288-7166 175 B
tbartunek@kckcc.edu
BARTUSIK, LisaMarie ... 850-484-2007 105 H
lbartusik@pensacolastate.edu
BARUA, Susamma .... 657-278-3362.. 31 C
sbarua@fullerton.edu
BARWICK, Ruth .... 202-319-5100.. 92 A
barwick@cua.edu
BARZACCHINI, Mike ..... 847-925-6510 138 G
mbarzacc@harpercollege.edu
BASALA, Nissim .... 732-370-1560 275 G
BASCH, Hersch .... 718-438-1002 306 D
BASCOM, Shawn .... 208-282-5304 131 G
bascshaw@isu.edu
BASCOMB, Cheryl, A .... 603-646-2258 273 D
cheryl.a.bascomb@dartmouth.edu
BASEL, Barbara .... 609-586-4800 278 F
baselb@mccc.edu
BASER, Ric .... 210-486-4908 428 G
rbaser@alamo.edu

BAUCOM, Eva 704-233-8633 344 F
e.baucom@wingate.edu

BAUCOM, Ian, B 434-924-4611 472 D
ibb4n@virginia.edu

BAUCUM, Natasha 601-928-6281 247 E
natasha.baucum@mgccc.edu

BAUDOIN, Jessica 337-521-8988 188 I
jessica.baudoin@solacc.edu

BAUDOUX, Brandy 352-245-4119 112 E
brandy.barnett@taylorcollege.edu

BAUDRY YOUNG,
Rebecca 513-529-3438 356 A
baudryrm@miamioh.edu

BAUER, Amanda 661-763-7853.. 67 G
abauer@taftcollege.edu

BAUER, Amie 785-227-3380 172 A
baueral@bethanylb.edu

BAUER, Angela, C 336-841-9501 329 F
abauer@highpoint.edu

BAUER, Blanca 337-482-6306 193 B
blanca.bauer@louisiana.edu

BAUER, C. Jon 636-584-6501 253 B
jon.bauer@eastcentral.edu

BAUER, Christine 208-426-5903 130 H
christinebauer@boisestate.edu

BAUER, Cortney, A 402-280-3533 266 H
cortneybauer@creighton.edu

BAUER, Dan 724-738-2773 395 C
dan.bauer@sru.edu

BAUER, Daniel, C 314-446-8308 260 H
daniel.bauer@stlcop.edu

BAUER, David 859-858-3581 179 C

BAUER, Denise 845-451-1345 297 G
denise.bauer@culinary.edu

BAUER, Dennis 479-308-2282.. 17 A
dennis.bauer@acheedu.org

BAUER, James 863-680-4186 100 H
jbauer@flsouthern.edu

BAUER, Jason, K 515-263-2887 166 F
jbauer@grandview.edu

BAUER, Jeffrey 740-351-3208 360 F
jbauer@shawnee.edu

BAUER, Jeffrey, C 513-732-5209 362 B
jeff.bauer@uc.edu

BAUER, Jeremy 203-596-8359.. 88 F
jebauer@post.edu

BAUER, Joanna 909-667-4411.. 37 G

BAUER, Joy 918-540-6720 366 F
joyb@neo.edu

BAUER, Kara 619-594-0489.. 33 D
kbauer@sdsu.edu

BAUER, Karen 918-495-7371 368 F
kbauer@oru.edu

BAUER, Kelli 620-252-7180 173 A
bauer.kelli@coffeyville.edu

BAUER, Marc 308-865-8332 269 I
bauermd@unk.edu

BAUER, Mark, D 507-354-8221 236 J
bauermd@mlc-wels.edu

BAUER, Mary 718-405-3233 296 F
mary.bauer@mountsaintvincent.edu

BAUER, Matt 919-735-5151 338 H
mattb@waynecc.edu

BAUER, Nancy 617-627-4230 219 C
nancy.bauer@tufts.edu

BAUER, Sarah 657-278-2929.. 31 C
sarahbauer@fullerton.edu

BAUER, Stacy 605-229-8405 415 I
stacy.bauer@presentation.edu

BAUER, Susan 646-592-4090 326 D
susan.bauer@yu.edu

BAUER, Tawana 662-243-1923 246 B
tbauer@eastms.edu

BAUER, Tom 650-358-6782.. 62 I
bauert@smccd.edu

BAUER, Warren, K 515-574-1120 167 A
bauer@iowacentral.edu

BAUGH, Anita, G 320-308-5936 241 A
abaugh@sctcc.edu

BAUGH, Frank 601-318-6772 249 H
frank.baugh@wmcarey.edu

BAUGH, Robbie 940-668-3338 440 F
rbaugh@nctc.edu

BAUGH, Stephanie 478-757-5209 127 F
sbaugh@wesleyancollege.edu

BAUGHMAN, Leslie 305-428-5700 104 F

BAUGHMAN, Linda, M . 651-962-6053 244 E
lmbaughman@stthomas.edu

BAUGHMAN, Matthew .. 618-453-2341 150 B
baughman@siu.edu

BAUGHMAN, Philip 515-271-1340 165 G
philip.baughman@dmu.edu

BAUGHMAN, Sara 828-669-8012 331 K
sara.baughman@montreat.edu

BAUGHMAN, Terry 314-838-8858 261 F

BAUGHN, Jeffrey 615-966-7650 421 B
jeff.baughn@lipscomb.edu

BAUGOUS, Amanda 309-794-7340 133 C
amandabaugous@augustana.edu

BAUGUESS, Seth 937-912-0622 364 E
seth.bauguess@wright.edu

BAUISTA, Annabelle 859-344-3572 185 B
bauista@thomasmore.edu

BAUM, Benjamin 410-626-2522 202 A
benjamin.baum@sjc.edu

BAUM, Christina 801-863-8405 460 D
christina.baum@uvu.edu

BAUM, Christina 801-524-8195 459 E
christinabaum@ldsbc.edu

BAUM, Courtney 724-805-2253 397 I
courtney.baum@email.stvincent.edu

BAUM, Courtney 724-805-2253 398 A
courtney.baum@stvincent.edu

BAUM, Cynthia 609-984-1100 284 C

BAUM, Dan, B 410-777-2011 197 G
dbbaum@aacc.edu

BAUM, Lucy 404-378-8821 117 G

BAUM, Richard 212-998-2345 309 F

BAUM, Robert 724-805-2590 397 I
bob.baum@stvincent.edu

BAUMAN, Joel 412-396-5002 383 A
baumanj@duq.edu

BAUMAN, Michael 312-935-4242 140 G
mbauman@icsw.edu

BAUMAN, Sandra 406-447-6928 264 B
sandra.bauman@helenacollege.edu

BAUMAN POWER,
Angie 319-895-4818 164 G
abaumanpower@cornellcollege.edu

BAUMANN, Diana 785-623-6150 176 F
dbaumann@ncktc.edu

BAUMANN, Erick 708-524-5054 137 C
ebauman@dom.edu

BAUMANN, Lawra 513-569-1759 350 F
lawra.baumann@cincinnatistate.edu

BAUMANN, Melissa, J . 513-745-3837 364 G
baumannm@xavier.edu

BAUMANN, Robert 913-684-2741 503 E
robert.baumann@leavenworth.army.mil

BAUMBACH, Kirk 804-752-7263 469 F
kirkbaumbach@rmc.edu

BAUMBERGER, Jessica . 217-206-8384 152 A
jbaum02s@uis.edu

BAUMEISTER, Barbara .. 405-736-0208 369 E
bbaumeister@rose.edu

BAUMER, Brian 718-990-3292 313 G
baumerb@stjohns.edu

BAUMET, Robert 315-279-5328 303 G
rbaumet@keuka.edu

BAUMGARD, Heath 651-423-8298 238 A
heath.baumgard@dctc.edu

BAUMGARDNER,
Brice, D 573-629-3280 253 J
bbaumgardner@hlg.edu

BAUMGARDNER,
Deidra 317-738-8189 155 D
dbaumgardner@franklincollege.edu

BAUMGARDNER, Doug . 574-372-5100 155 F
doug.baumgardner@grace.edu

BAUMGART, Reilly 618-262-8641 139 I
baumgartr@iecc.edu

BAUMGARTNER, Aileen 914-241-3500 305 E
abaumgartner@mmm.edu

BAUMGARTNER,
Danielle 815-921-4849 148 B
d.baumgartner@rockvalleycollege.edu

BAUMGARTNER, Eric .... 414-277-7190 494 D

BAUMGARTNER, Erin .... 503-838-8348 377 D
baumgare@wou.edu

BAUMGARTNER,
Gretchen 530-283-0202.. 42 A
gbaumgartner@frc.edu

BAUMGARTNER, Holly .. 800-541-6682 105 A

BAUMGARTNER,
Holly, L 419-772-2130 358 C
h-baumgartner@onu.edu

BAUMGARTNER, Neil .... 262-595-2151 496 D
baumgarn@uwp.edu

BAUMGARTNER, Renee . 408-554-5344.. 63 B
rbaumgartner@scu.edu

BAUMGARTNER,
Timothy, K 713-348-4867 442 F
timothy.k.baumgartner@rice.edu

BAUMHOVER, Lynne 563-589-0300 171 A
lbaumhover@wartburgseminary.edu

BAUMUNK, Jeffrey 310-660-3593.. 41 E
jbaumunk@elcamino.edu

BAUN, Dan 507-537-6978 241 D
dan.baun@smsu.edu

BAUN, Jeff 610-436-2705 395 D
jbaun@wcupa.edu

BAUR, Cheryl 570-740-0368 389 A
cbaur@luzerne.edu

BAURAIN, Thomas 816-311-0110 251 B
thomas.baurain@calvary.edu

BAUSANO, Darren 906-487-7396 224 B
jason.sullivan@finlandia.edu

BAUSERMAN, Judy 304-263-0979 488 A

BAUSINGER, Patricia, E 570-321-4049 389 B
baus@lycoming.edu

BAUSLEY, Gwen 304-766-4366 490 D
gbausley@wvstateu.edu

BAUSS, Celia, N 864-592-4754 412 E
baussc@sccsc.edu

BAUTE, Aaron 765-446-1154 158 D
abaute@ivytech.edu

BAUTE, Brian 704-229-2070 339 F
bauteb@queens.edu

BAUTISTA, Adrian 518-580-5352 315 F

BAUTISTA, Maria 808-734-9519 129 H
mariab@hawaii.edu

BAUTTI, Joann 757-446-5244 466 D
bauttij@evms.edu

BAVA, Brian 208-459-5271 131 C
bbava@collegeofidaho.edu

BAVADRA, Verenaisi 692-625-3394 504 G

BAVER, Debra 610-921-7256 377 G
dbaver@albright.edu

BAVERMAN, David 309-298-1414 153 A

BAVISI, Lata 505-922-2889 286 D
lata@eccu.edu

BAVISI, Sanjay 505-922-2889 286 D

BAWA, Opinder 415-422-2787.. 72 J
osbawa@usfca.edu

BAWCOM, Amy 512-223-7619 430 I
amy.bawcom@austincc.edu

BAWCUM, Audrey 334-699-2266.... 1 B
ambawcum@acom.edu

BAWDON, Jessica 831-656-1062 502 M
jessica.bawdon@nps.edu

BAWOROWSKY, John ... 414-288-4976 493 E
john.baworowsky@marquette.edu

BAX, Conny 231-843-5710 233 A
cbax@westshore.edu

BAX, John 573-681-5860 254 G
baxj2@lincolnu.edu

BAXTER, Agnes 919-546-8212 340 B
abaxter@shawu.edu

BAXTER, Aimee, F 318-257-2641 192 D
abaxter@latech.edu

BAXTER, Herman 214-887-5000 435 F

BAXTER, Hilary 617-327-6777 220 C
hilary_baxter@williamjames.edu

BAXTER, Jamie 513-745-2800 364 G
baxterj1@xavier.edu

BAXTER, Kathleen 951-372-8080.. 45 D

BAXTER, Kean 301-891-4139 205 A
kbaxter@wau.edu

BAXTER, Keith 580-745-2250 369 G
kbaxter@se.edu

BAXTER, Leigh 804-706-5214 474 B
lbaxter@jtcc.edu

BAXTER, Melissa 315-568-3271 310 B
mbaxter@nycc.edu

BAXTER, Susanna 706-880-8230 122 A
sbaxter@lagrange.edu

BAYÓN TORRES,
Ramón 787-764-0000 513 B
ramon.bayon@upr.edu

BAY, Kelly 309-467-6431 138 A
kbay@eureka.edu

BAY, Willow, C 213-740-6180.. 73 D
wbay@usc.edu

BAYARDELLE, Eddy 718-289-5185 293 B
eddy.bayardelle@bcc.cuny.edu

BAYER, Amy 305-395-1121.. 98 E
amy@dolphins.org

BAYER, Deborah 989-358-7458 221 C
bayerd@alpenacc.edu

BAYLES, Kenneth 402-559-4945 269 K
kbayles@unmc.edu

BAYLESS, Elizabeth 757-352-5152 470 B
ebayless@regent.edu

BAYLESS, Laura 978-665-3215 212 E
lbayless@fitchburgstate.edu

BAYLISS-CARR, Sandy .. 252-638-4755 334 A
bayliss-carrs@cravencc.edu

BAYLOR, Bridget 540-453-2358 473 D
baylorb@brcc.edu

BAYLOR, Jeff, S 806-651-2020 448 B
jbaylor@wtamu.edu

BAYLOR, Kara 262-551-5812 492 B
kbaylor@carthage.edu

BAYNE, Deann 402-481-8718 265 K
deann.bayne@bryanhealthcollege.edu

BAYNES, Leonard, M .... 713-743-2478 452 D
lbaynes@central.uh.edu

BAYOUMI, Magdy, A .... 337-482-6147 193 B
mab@louisiana.edu

BAYS, Lindsay 620-341-5221 173 F
lbays@emporia.edu

BAYTO, Tammy 478-274-7852 123 I
tbayto@oftc.edu

BAYUS, Jenelle 330-569-5287 353 G
bayusj1@hiram.edu

BAZAN, Yamilet 951-785-2100.. 47 C
ybazan@lasierra.edu

BAZANT, Robert, S 724-222-5330 391 F
rbazant@penncommercial.edu

BAZARSKY, Debbie 717-396-7833 392 U
dbazarsky@pcad.edu

BAZEMORE, Alisha 757-823-2406 469 A
albazemore@nsu.edu

BAZEMORE, Dennis 910-893-1540 327 D
bazemored@campbell.edu

BAZEMORE,
Qiana Anngel 336-744-0900 327 E
qiana.bazemore@carolina.edu

BAZIL, Ted 914-961-8313 314 H
ted@svots.edu

BAZILE, Samantha 845-398-4102 314 G
sbazile@stac.edu

BAZILE, Stanley 718-960-8242 294 A
stanley.bazile@lehman.cuny.edu

BAZIN, Angela 860-465-0147.. 85 H
bazina@easternct.edu

BAZZEL, Matthew 706-419-1126 118 A
matthew.bazzel@covenant.edu

BAZZEL, Mitchell 256-233-8161.... 4 C
mitchell.bazzel@athens.edu

BAZZELL, Darrell 512-471-1422 455 A
bazzell@austin.utexas.edu

BEA, David 520-206-4519.. 15 B
dbea@pima.edu

BEACH, Adam, R 765-285-1300 153 H
arbeach@bsu.edu

BEACH, David 913-288-7284 175 B
dbeach@kckcc.edu

BEACH, Justin 406-377-9410 263 D
jbeach@dawson.edu

BEACH, Lisa 253-589-5603 478 J
lisa.beach@cptc.edu

BEACH, Michael 913-288-7645 175 B
mbeach@kckcc.edu

BEACH, Nancy, S 540-365-4529 467 B
nbeach@ferrum.edu

BEACH, Natalie 503-399-5105 372 B
natalie.beach@chemeketa.edu

BEACH, Scott, R 412-624-4141 400 H
scottb@pitt.edu

BEACH, Steven 432-552-2170 456 F
beach_s@utpb.edu

BEACH, Vincent 641-585-8133 170 I
vince.beach@waldorf.edu

BEACH, Wendy 906-635-2213 226 G
wbeach1@lssu.edu

BEACHAM, David, M .... 864-597-4206 414 E
beachamdm@wofford.edu

BEACHAM, Ralph 620-724-0390 173 I
ralphb@fortscott.edu

BEACHE, Vidda, P 240-500-2357 199 C
vpbeache@hagerstowncc.edu

BEACHLER, Kelly 941-309-4022 106 J
kbeachle@ringling.edu

BEACHY, Jeff 408-554-5360.. 63 B
jdbeachy@scu.edu

BEADLES, Cindy 800-747-2687 144 H
cbeadles@monmouthcollege.edu

BEADLES, Mary 706-245-7226 118 D
mbeadles@ec.edu

BEAGHAN, John, W 248-370-2445 229 I
beaghan@oakland.edu

BEAGLE, Donald 704-461-6740 326 L
donaldbeagle@bac.edu

BEAGLE, Mike 541-552-6127 376 B
beaglem@sou.edu

BEAHM, John, A 617-873-0430 208 B
john.beahm@cambridgecollege.edu

BEAKMAN, Andrew, W . 315-792-3111 324 B
awbeakma@utica.edu

BECK, Ronda .... 517-371-5140 233 C
beckr@cooley.edu
BECK, Stacie .... 480-423-6520.. 13 H
stacie.beck@scottsdalecc.edu
BECK, Teresa .... 616-331-2735 224 G
beckt@gvsu.edu
BECK, Zach .... 937-512-4603 360 G
zachary.beck@sinclair.edu
BECKA, Nathan .... 510-594-3787.. 28 B
n.becka@cca.edu
BECKA, Roberta .... 310-973-3134.. 41 E
rbecka@elcamino.edu
BECKEL, Constance .... 724-838-4219 398 C
beckel@setonhill.edu
BECKEMEYER, Wendy ... 319-895-4173 164 G
wbeckemeyer@cornellcollege.edu
BECKENDORF, Kristina . 979-830-4122 431 H
kbeckendorf@blinn.edu
BECKER, Alex .... 870-460-1022.. 22 C
beckera@uamont.edu
BECKER, Alexis .... 605-995-2617 415 A
alexis.becker@dwu.edu
BECKER, Amy .... 612-874-3799 237 A
amy_naughton@mcad.edu
BECKER, Brian .... 512-492-3017 430 A
bbecker@aoma.edu
BECKER, Carol .... 212-854-9847 297 C
cbecker@columbia.edu
BECKER, Christopher .... 626-300-5444.. 57 F
cbecker@plattcollege.edu
BECKER, Dennis, M ...... 303-871-3897.. 84 E
dbecker@du.edu
BECKER, Gerrie .... 505-224-4551 285 N
gbecker1@cnm.edu
BECKER, Jim .... 812-855-4884 156 F
jambecke@iu.edu
BECKER, Joe .... 503-768-7971 373 E
jbecker@lclark.edu
BECKER, John .... 307-268-2672 500 U
j.becker@caspercollege.edu
BECKER, Jonathan .... 845-758-7378 290 I
jbecker@bard.edu
BECKER, Jonathan .... 903-586-2518 438 C
jbecker@jacksonville-college.edu
BECKER, Joseph .... 516-773-5000 503 H
beckerj@usmma.edu
BECKER, Karl .... 267-295-2311 402 A
kbecker@walnuthillcollege.edu
BECKER, Karl, D .... 267-295-2307 402 A
kbecker@walnuthillcollege.edu
BECKER, Kate .... 505-272-2111 288 J
katebecker@salud.unm.edu
BECKER, Keri .... 616-331-8800 224 G
beckeker@gvsu.edu
BECKER, Laura .... 805-922-6966.. 24 I
laura.becker@hancockcollege.edu
BECKER, Laurel .... 970-943-7004.. 85 C
lbecker@western.edu
BECKER, Lois .... 312-341-3615 148 E
lbecker05@roosevelt.edu
BECKER, Mark, P .... 404-413-1300 120 E
mbecker@gsu.edu
BECKER, Maureen .... 718-262-2000 295 E
mbecker@york.cuny.edu
BECKER, Maureen .... 718-262-5310 295 E
mbecker@york.cuny.edu
BECKER, Pete, D .... 708-209-3092 136 E
pete.becker@cuchicago.edu
BECKER, Sara, M .... 856-225-6409 281 G
sara.becker@rutgers.edu
BECKER, Sheila, R .... 844-642-2338 169 A
beckers@nicc.edu
BECKER, Tawney .... 719-587-8305.. 77 G
tbecker@adams.edu
BECKER, Theresa .... 760-921-5444.. 56 A
theresa.becker@paloverde.edu
BECKER-LUTZ, Jill .... 303-797-5882.. 77 I
jill.becker-lutz@arapahoe.edu
BECKETT, Barry .... 304-696-2207 489 M
beckett@marshall.edu
BECKETT, Karen, J .... 305-284-5749 113 C
kbeckett@miami.edu
BECKFORD, Dillon .... 803-535-5301 407 D
dbeckford@claflin.edu
BECKFORD, Roy .... 802-656-3131 463 A
fitzroy.beckford@uvm.edu
BECKHAM, Vanessa .... 863-680-6285 100 H
vbeckham@flsouthern.edu
BECKHORN, Nisha .... 916-484-8376.. 50 G
beckhon@arc.losrios.edu
BECKHORN, Roy .... 916-568-3190.. 50 F
beckhor@losrios.edu

BECKLER, Larry .... 843-525-8282 412 G
lbeckler@tcl.edu
BECKLES-BRIGHT,
Heather .... 713-500-3871 456 B
heather.m.beckles@uth.tmc.edu
BECKLEY, Clark .... 913-234-0609 172 K
clark.beckley@cleveland.edu
BECKLEY, Jodie .... 734-462-4400 230 G
jbeckley@schoolcraft.edu
BECKMAN, Amy .... 620-242-0400 176 B
beckmana@mcpherson.edu
BECKMAN, John, H ...... 212-998-6848 309 F
john.beckman@nyu.edu
BECKMAN, Mitchell ...... 414-955-4871 493 F
mrbeckman@mcw.edu
BECKMAN, Seth .... 765-285-5495 153 H
svbeckman@bsu.edu
BECKNELL, James .... 606-546-1233 185 D
james.becknell@unionky.edu
BECKNER, Andrew .... 864-231-2000 406 F
abeckner@andersonuniversity.edu
BECKNER, Christine ...... 718-368-5051 294 E
cbeckner@kbcc.cuny.edu
BECKNER, Scott .... 319-335-5026 163 H
scott-beckner@uiowa.edu
BECKRICH, Chris .... 817-531-4251 451 C
cabeckrich@txwes.edu
BECKS, Crystal .... 661-654-3012.. 30 B
cbecks@csub.edu
BECKSTROM, Amy, D ... 303-492-6494.. 84 B
amy.beckstrom@colorado.edu
BECKSTROM, Brian .... 319-352-8217 170 J
brian.beckstrom@wartburg.edu
BECKSTROM, Ron .... 218-755-2743 237 F
ronald.beckstrom@bemidjistate.edu
BECKWITH, Melissa ...... 317-940-9900 154 C
mbeckwit@butler.edu
BECKWITH, Rachel .... 413-559-5765 210 D
rbeckwith@hampshire.edu
BECSEY, Jim .... 906-635-2639 226 G
jbecsey@lssu.edu
BECTON, Bret .... 601-266-4659 249 F
bret.becton@usm.edu
BECZE, Ben .... 724-805-2457 398 A
ben.becze@stvincent.edu
BECZE, Ben .... 724-805-2457 397 I
ben.becze@stvincent.edu
BEDA, Cheri .... 308-398-7437 266 A
cheribeda@cccneb.edu
BEDARD, Brooke .... 413-265-2314 208 E
bedardb@elms.edu
BEDDARD, Wesley .... 252-789-0222 335 H
wb07479@martincc.edu
BEDELL, Duane .... 906-248-3354 221 M
BEDELL, Honey .... 563-336-3302 165 K
hbedell@eicc.edu
BEDELL, Michael, D ...... 773-442-6150 146 A
m-bedell@neiu.edu
BEDELL, Todd .... 603-271-6484 273 A
tbedell@ccsnh.edu
BEDETTE, Kathryn .... 470-578-6000 121 M
BEDFORD, Allen .... 218-755-2015 237 F
allen.bedford@bemidjistate.edu
BEDFORD, April .... 718-951-5214 293 C
abedford@brooklyn.cuny.edu
BEDFORD, Carter .... 817-515-1193 445 F
carter.bedford@tccd.edu
BEDFORD, Dan .... 801-626-8091 461 A
dbedford@weber.edu
BEDFORD, David .... 864-578-8770 411 F
dbedford@sherman.edu
BEDFORD, Grant .... 209-946-2537.. 71 E
gbedford@pacific.edu
BEDFORD, John .... 405-208-5322 367 E
jbedford@okcu.edu
BEDFORD, Michelle .... 770-412-4005 125 H
michelle.bedford@sctech.edu
BEDFORD, Norm .... 702-774-8000 271 D
norm.bedford@unlv.edu
BEDFORD, Norman, F .. 804-828-3618 473 B
bedfordn@vcu.edu
BEDI, Param, S .... 570-577-1557 379 C
param.bedi@bucknell.edu
BEDIENT, Sonya .... 971-722-4520 375 D
sonya.bedient@pcc.edu
BEDILLION, Char .... 336-316-2410 329 D
cbedillion@guilford.edu
BEDINGFIELD, Eric .... 864-250-8700 409 I
eric.bedingfield@gvltec.edu
BEDNARZ, Bridgette ..... 254-968-9271 446 D
bednarz@tarleton.edu
BEDNARZ, Jeffrey .... 413-205-3208 205 F
jeffrey.bednarz@aic.edu

BEDNEY, Elynda, A .... 269-471-6040 221 D
bedney@andrews.edu
BEDOLLA, Juan .... 559-638-0300.. 67 D
juan.bedolla@reedleycollege.edu
BEDOYA, Eduardo .... 231-777-0332 228 G
eduardo.bedoya@muskegoncc.edu
BEDRYK, Michael .... 516-726-5644 503 H
bedrykm@usmma.edu
BEDSOLE, C. Blake .... 479-968-0343.. 18 C
bbedsole@atu.edu
BEDTKE, James .... 507-457-1458 243 C
jbedtke@smumn.edu
BEDWELL, Deborah, A .. 812-888-7777 162 F
dbedwell@vinu.edu
BEE, Richard .... 562-944-0351.. 27 A
richard.e.bee@biola.edu
BEEBE, Barbara, R .... 325-574-6501 458 D
bbeebe@wtc.edu
BEEBE, Craig .... 970-943-2314.. 85 C
cbeebe@western.edu
BEEBE, Gayle, D .... 805-565-6024.. 76 A
president@westmont.edu
BEEBE, Jennifer .... 716-338-1404 303 A
jenniferbeebe@mail.sunyjcc.edu
BEEBE, Norman .... 413-775-1333 214 E
beebe@gcc.mass.edu
BEEBE STEVENS,
Heather .... 509-434-5123 479 B
h.beebe-stevens@ccs.spokan.edu
BEEBE-STEVENS,
Heather .... 509-434-5123 479 C
heather.beebe-stevens@ccs.spokane.edu
BEEBE-STEVENS,
Heather .... 509-434-5125 479 D
heather.beebe-stevens@ccs.spokane.edu
BEEBY, James .... 603-358-2112 274 H
james.beeby@keene.edu
BEECH, Amanda .... 661-255-1050.. 28 G
abeech@calarts.edu
BEECHER, Brian .... 616-234-3869 224 F
brianbeecher@grcc.edu
BEECHER, Shan, L .... 515-574-1985 167 A
beecher@iowacentral.edu
BEEHLER, Jeff .... 509-865-0446 481 A
beehler_j@heritage.edu
BEEK, Ashtyn .... 641-844-5715 167 G
ashtyn.beek@iavalley.edu
BEEKE, Joel, R .... 616-432-3403 230 A
joel.beeke@prts.edu
BEEKE, Jonathon .... 616-432-3408 230 A
jonathon.beeke@prts.edu
BEEKEY, Mark .... 203-371-7783.. 89 A
beekeym@sacredheart.edu
BEELEN, Joan .... 616-957-6027 222 B
jrb44@calvinseminary.edu
BEELER, Jeremy .... 908-835-2301 284 H
jbeeler@warren.edu
BEELER, Sydney .... 724-925-4050 402 F
beelers@westmoreland.edu
BEEMAN, Greg .... 646-378-6100 310 D
greg.beeman@nyack.edu
BEEMAN, Meredith .... 252-249-1851 336 F
mbeeman@pamlicocc.edu
BEEMER, Matthew .... 904-596-2473 112 F
mbeemer@tbc.edu
BEEN, Nicole .... 918-781-7321 365 C
beenn@bacone.edu
BEERS, David .... 253-879-3902 484 G
dbeers@pugetsound.edu
BEERS, Di .... 425-235-2426 482 H
dbeers@rtc.edu
BEERS, Maggie .... 415-338-3613.. 33 E
mbeers@sfsu.edu
BEERS, Stephen, T .... 479-524-7252.. 19 H
sbeers@jbu.edu
BEESE, Cheryl .... 918-895-9401 368 I
cheryl.beese@plattcollege.org
BEESLEY, Wendy .... 845-688-1980 323 H
beesleyw@sunyulster.edu
BEESON, Duane, L .... 712-707-7116 169 D
beeson@nwciowa.edu
BEEZLEY, Erin .... 970-247-7429.. 80 J
ebeezley@fortlewis.edu
BEGANY, James .... 502-852-5555 186 A
jim.begany@louisville.edu
BEGARLY, Brandon, J ... 718-960-8357 294 A
brandon.begarly@lehman.cuny.edu
BEGAY, Janice .... 785-749-8419 174 D
janice.begay@bie.edu
BEGAY, Karen, F .... 520-621-0964.. 16 D
kfbegay@arizona.edu

BEGAY, Melissa .... 575-835-5120 286 K
melissa.begay@nmt.edu
BEGAYE, Nolan, S .... 928-724-6857.. 12 D
nsbegaye@dinecollege.edu
BEGG, Melissa .... 212-851-2289 297 C
mdb3@columbia.edu
BEGGS, Beth .... 828-898-2417 330 E
beggsb@lmc.edu
BEGGS, Gail .... 251-405-7021.... 1 E
gbeggs@bishop.edu
BEGIN, Gene, P .... 508-286-3223 220 B
begin_gene@wheatoncollege.edu
BEGIN, Russell .... 207-453-5123 195 F
rbegin@kvcc.me.edu
BEGLEY, John, B .... 270-384-8505 183 G
begleyj@lindsey.edu
BEGLEY, Mary Ann .... 352-854-2322.. 97 N
begleym@cf.edu
BEGLEY, Shannon .... 215-670-9072 391 E
svbegley@peirce.edu
BEGOR, Alison .... 859-233-8520 185 C
abegor@transy.edu
BEHAN, Kate .... 859-371-9393 179 G
BEHAN KRAUS,
Carolyn, A .... 203-672-5323.. 85 D
cbehan@albertus.edu
BEHAUNEK, Luke .... 515-961-1562 170 B
luke.behaunek@simpson.edu
BEHEN, Joseph .... 312-499-4272 149 F
jbehen@saic.edu
BEHL, Josh, J .... 218-477-4654 239 E
joshua.behl@mnstate.edu
BEHLING, Laura .... 253-879-3205 484 G
provost@pugetsound.edu
BEHMAND, Mojgan ...... 415-458-3759.. 41 C
BEHNEN, Bob .... 660-626-2395 250 A
bbehnen@atsu.edu
BEHNEY, Melissa .... 860-343-5833.. 87 A
mbehney@mxcc.edu
BEHNKE, Wade, P .... 207-859-5504 194 D
wade.behnke@colby.edu
BEHR, Andrea .... 937-433-3410 352 G
abehr@fortiscollege.edu
BEHR, Eileen, W .... 215-571-3548 382 F
eileen.w.behr@drexel.edu
BEHR, Fred, C .... 507-786-3636 243 D
behr@stolaf.edu
BEHR, Julie .... 706-778-8500 124 D
jbehr@piedmont.edu
BEHR, Kevin .... 361-354-2338 432 K
kevind@coastalbend.edu
BEHRE, William .... 724-738-2000 395 C
william.behre@sru.edu
BEHRENDT, Todd .... 315-792-5616 306 K
tbehrendt@mvcc.edu
BEHRENS, Eric .... 610-499-1036 402 G
ebehrens@widener.edu
BEHRENS, Kim .... 559-791-2322.. 47 A
kbehrens@portervillecollege.edu
BEHRENS, Michael .... 217-351-2433 147 C
mbehrens@parkland.edu
BEHRENS, Scott .... 734-384-4224 228 C
sbehrens@monroeccc.edu
BEHRENS, Timothy .... 414-229-5663 496 B
behrens5@uwm.edu
BEHRS, David .... 312-893-7145 137 H
dbehrs@erikson.edu
BEIDLEMAN, David, C .. 717-361-1493 383 C
beidlemand@etown.edu
BEIER, Nancy, A .... 410-777-2834 197 G
nabeier@aacc.edu
BEIGHLEY, David .... 304-367-4726 488 H
david.beighley@pierpont.edu
BEIKIRCH, Dale .... 432-685-5539 440 B
dbeikirch@midland.edu
BEIL, Cheryl .... 202-994-6712.. 92 D
cbeil@gwu.edu
BEILHARZ, Peter, J .... 512-448-8521 442 I
peterb@stedwards.edu
BEILOCK, Sian, L .... 212-854-2021 291 A
beilock@barnard.edu
BEIMER, Connie .... 505-277-5808 288 J
cbeimer@unm.edu
BEIRNE, David .... 401-232-6000 404 A
BEISE, Elizabeth, J .... 301-405-6836 202 H
beise@umd.edu
BEISECKER, Mark .... 805-893-4071.. 70 E
mark.beisecker@bookstore.ucsb.edu
BEISEL, Catherine .... 440-375-7223 354 K
cbeisel@lec.edu
BEISSNER, Katherine ..... 315-464-6560 317 C
beissnek@upstate.edu

BEISWANGER, Chris ..... 719-255-3088.. 84 C cbeiswan@uccs.edu
BEITEL, Leland, R .... 443-334-2064 202 E lbeitel@stevenson.edu
BEITING, Sarah .... 641-585-8671 170 I sarah.beiting@waldorf.edu
BEITLER, Sidney .... 561-868-3484 105 D beitlers@palmbeachstate.edu
BEITZEL, Vernon, L .... 540-464-7211 476 B beitzelvl@vmi.edu
BEIZA, Rocio .... 713-221-8562 453 A beizar@uhd.edu
BEJAR, Elizabeth .... 305-348-2151 110 A elizabeth.bejar@fiu.edu
BEJARANO, Hope .... 602-384-2555.. 11 F hope.bejarano@bryanuniversity.edu
BEJARANO, Ricky, A .... 505-747-5050 287 H ricky.bejarano@nnmc.edu
BEJUNE, Matthew .... 508-929-8511 213 G mbejune@worcester.edu
BEKCHIAN, Arina .... 510-925-4282.. 25 K abekchya@aua.am
BEKISZ, Peter .... 315-279-5262 303 G pbekisz@keuka.edu
BEKKER, Corne .... 757-352-4716 470 B clbekker@regent.edu
BELANGER, Annie .... 616-331-2621 224 G belange1@gvsu.edu
BELANGER, OFM, Brian, C .... 518-783-5047 315 E bbelanger@siena.edu
BELANGER, David, J ..... 413-585-2530 218 H dbelange@smith.edu
BELANGER, Lisa .... 207-780-5411 197 D lisa.belanger@maine.edu
BELANGER, Marc .... 920-403-3181 495 B marc.d.belanger@snc.edu
BELBAS, Clarissa .... 281-476-1894 443 A clarissa.belbas@sjcd.edu
BELCASTRO, Richard ..... 678-331-4459 122 C richard.belcastro@life.edu
BELCHER, Carol .... 843-574-6230 412 I carol.belcher@tridenttech.edu
BELCHER, Chris .... 208-792-2166 132 A cpbelcher@lcsc.edu
BELCHER, Chris .... 417-865-2815 250 E belcherc@evangel.edu
BELCHER, Chris .... 417-865-2815 253 D belcherc@evangel.edu
BELCHER, Dana .... 580-559-5564 365 K dbelcher@ecok.edu
BELCHER, Joyce .... 425-388-9399 480 B jbelcher@everettcc.edu
BELCHER, Larry .... 757-455-3292 477 C lbelcher@vwu.edu
BELCHER, Lawrence ...... 317-788-2397 161 H belcherl@uindy.edu
BELD, Jo, M .... 507-786-3632 243 D beld@stolaf.edu
BELDEN, Donna .... 401-874-7049 405 E
BELDEN, Doug .... 651-290-6360 242 L doug.belden@mitchellhamline.edu
BELDEN, Eric .... 330-490-7337 363 E ebelden@walsh.edu
BELDING, Orhan, K ...... 503-357-6151 375 C
BELDONA, Sam .... 570-941-4049 401 F sam.beldona@scranton.edu
BELETE, Yared .... 303-797-5092.. 77 I yared.belete@arapahoe.edu
BELEW, Amy, C .... 731-881-7901 427 D abelew@utm.edu
BELEW, Katherine .... 903-434-8264 440 G kbelew@ntcc.edu
BELEW, Monte .... 731-881-7775 427 D mbelew3@utm.edu
BELFIELD, Kevin, D .... 973-596-3676 279 E kevin.d.belfield@njit.edu
BELFIELD, Sherri .... 704-378-1032 330 D sbelfield@jcsu.edu
BELFIORE, Cathy .... 419-448-2262 353 E cbelfior@heidelberg.edu
BELFIORE, Michael .... 914-606-7895 325 A michael.belfiore@sunywcc.edu
BELICS, Patrick .... 312-621-9650 145 D pbelics@nl.edu
BELIN, Jacki .... 908-526-1200 281 A jacki.belin@raritanval.edu
BELINER, Janice .... 413-565-1000 206 D jberliner@baypath.edu
BELISLE, Andria .... 320-308-3117 240 I aebelisle@stcloudstate.edu
BELISLE, William, R ...... 504-284-5539 191 C wbelisle@suno.edu
BELK, Peter .... 913-469-8500 174 I pbelk@jccc.edu
BELKNAP, Peggy .... 928-536-6231.. 14 J peggy.belknap@npc.edu
BELKO, Dawn .... 763-424-0817 240 A dbelko@nhcc.edu
BELL, Aimee, B .... 330-569-5279 353 G bella1@hiram.edu
BELL, Alecia .... 404-756-8919 123 E ambell@msm.edu
BELL, Angel, M .... 563-588-7130 168 A angel.bell@loras.edu
BELL, Angela .... 404-962-3069 127 D angela.bell@usg.edu
BELL, Barbara .... 216-987-4851 351 E barbara.bell@tri-c.edu
BELL, Brett .... 619-388-7815.. 61 A bbell@sdccd.edu
BELL, Brigitte .... 815-740-3447 152 H bbell@stfrancis.edu
BELL, Brittany, M .... 920-832-7030 493 B brittany.m.bell@lawrence.edu
BELL, Brooke .... 615-687-6906 417 F bbell@abcnash.edu
BELL, Caroline .... 513-562-6267 347 I caroline.bell@artacademy.edu
BELL, Christopher .... 207-768-9511 197 C chris@maine.edu
BELL, Christopher .... 617-984-1798 218 C cbell@quincycollege.edu
BELL, Cindy .... 406-657-2363 264 D cindy.bell@msubillings.edu
BELL, Cynthia, M .... 330-941-3101 364 H cmbell02@ysu.edu
BELL, Dana .... 580-745-2132 369 G dbell@se.edu
BELL, Danielle .... 803-321-5128 410 H danielle.bell@newberry.edu
BELL, Darrell .... 585-389-2411 307 F dbell3@naz.edu
BELL, David .... 646-565-6000 322 F david.bell@touro.edu
BELL, David .... 646-565-6000 322 G david.bell@touro.edu
BELL, Dean, P .... 312-322-1791 150 F dbell@spertus.edu
BELL, Denise .... 508-793-2397 208 D dbell@holycross.edu
BELL, Denise .... 850-973-9481 104 L belld@nfc.edu
BELL, Don .... 888-777-7675 480 D dbell@faithseminary.edu
BELL, Elma .... 205-929-6313.... 2 H ebell@lawsonstate.edu
BELL, Erick .... 925-424-1275.. 35 K ebell@laspositascollege.edu
BELL, Eve .... 940-565-2759 453 E eve.bell@unt.edu
BELL, Gregory, J .... 570-321-4395 389 B bell@lycoming.edu
BELL, Harold .... 404-270-5269 126 B hbell@spelman.edu
BELL, III, J. Edward ..... 843-377-2426 407 A ebell@charlestonlaw.edu
BELL, J. Paul .... 864-379-8772 409 E paul.bell@erskine.edu
BELL, Jacqueline, B ...... 843-377-1327 407 A jbell@charlestonlaw.edu
BELL, James .... 918-444-2468 366 G bell02@nsuok.edu
BELL, James, L .... 580-327-8590 367 A jlbell@nwosu.edu
BELL, Jeff .... 507-537-6251 241 D jeff.bell@smsu.edu
BELL, Kati .... 415-482-2483.. 41 C kathrina.bell@dominican.edu
BELL, Katrina .... 973-328-5064 276 J kbell@ccm.edu
BELL, Kelli .... 563-425-5274 170 H bellk59@uiu.edu
BELL, Kim .... 412-521-6200 397 C kim.bell@rosedaletech.org
BELL, Lauren, C .... 804-752-7268 469 F lbell@rmc.edu
BELL, Lauren, P .... 615-353-3604 424 G lauren.bell@nscc.edu
BELL, Leslie, T .... 910-521-6760 343 B leslie.bell@uncp.edu
BELL, Linda .... 610-372-4721 396 H lbell@racc.edu
BELL, Linda .... 212-854-2708 291 A labell@barnard.edu
BELL, Lisa, G .... 859-246-6564 181 F lisag.bell@kctcs.edu
BELL, Marty .... 515-961-1678 170 B marty.bell@simpson.edu
BELL, Marylin .... 410-857-2755 200 F mlbell@mcdaniel.edu
BELL, Melanie .... 919-735-5151 338 H mjbell@waynecc.edu
BELL, Melleta .... 432-837-8388 450 B mbell@sulross.edu
BELL, Michael .... 972-686-7878 442 B
BELL, Nicole .... 256-551-3129.... 2 E nicole.bell@drakestate.edu
BELL, Patrice .... 504-520-7558 193 E pbellmer@xula.edu
BELL, Patricia .... 931-431-9700 422 G pbell@nci.edu
BELL, Paul .... 864-379-8881 409 E paul.bell@erskine.edu
BELL, Peter .... 434-592-7296 468 E pabell2@liberty.edu
BELL, Rebecca .... 432-685-4556 440 B rbell@midland.edu
BELL, Rebekah, A .... 915-831-5834 436 A rbell13@epcc.edu
BELL, Rhonda .... 281-476-1858 443 A rhonda.bell@sjcd.edu
BELL, Richette .... 310-900-1600.. 39 F rbell@elcamino.edu
BELL, Robin .... 229-931-2352 125 E rbell@southgatech.edu
BELL, Sara .... 913-758-6104 178 B
BELL, Sarah .... 724-852-7790 402 C sbell@waynesburg.edu
BELL, Sheree .... 636-481-3119 254 C sbell6@jeffco.edu
BELL, Stephen, T .... 610-558-5549 391 A bells@neumann.edu
BELL, Steven .... 410-626-2502 202 A skbell@sjc.edu
BELL, Stuart, R .... 205-348-5100.... 7 G president@ua.edu
BELL, Tom, J .... 828-641-0436 327 B bellt@brevard.edu
BELL, Wylie .... 910-410-1826 337 B wdbell@richmondcc.edu
BELL ADAMS, Sandra ... 718-262-2363 295 E sadams@york.cuny.edu
BELL-JORDAN, Katrina .. 773-442-5711 146 A k-bell1@neiu.edu
BELL-ROBINSON, Vicka 513-529-1809 356 A
BELLA, Andres .... 510-763-7787.. 24 C abella@acchs.edu
BELLACERO, Cynthia ..... 252-737-3614 341 A bellacero18@ecu.edu
BELLAH, Eric .... 865-981-8225 421 C eric.bellah@maryvillecollege.edu
BELLALTA, Maria .... 617-585-0200 207 A maria.bellalta@the-bac.edu
BELLAM, Gayle .... 260-481-6105 160 C bellamg@pfw.edu
BELLAMKONDA, Ravi, V .... 404-727-6055 118 E ravi@emory.edu
BELLAMY, Antoinette, P 910-630-7257 331 E abellamy@methodist.edu
BELLAMY, James .... 419-267-1267 357 E jbellamy@northweststate.edu
BELLAMY, Johnnie, O ... 972-860-7619 434 H johnniebellamy@dcccd.edu
BELLAMY, Reagan .... 509-682-6445 485 H rbellamy@wvc.edu
BELLAMY, Sandra .... 212-694-1000 291 J sbellamy@boricuacollege.edu
BELLAMY, Scott .... 304-357-6696 487 J scottbellamy@ucwv.edu
BELLAMY-BENNETT, Sonja, A .... 803-813-1147 411 G sbennet5@scsu.edu
BELLANCA, Rose, B ...... 734-973-3491 232 D rbellanca@wccnet.edu
BELLANGER, Angela ..... 218-477-2211 239 E angela.bellanger@mnstate.edu
BELLANI, Rajesh .... 740-587-6281 352 A bellanir@denison.edu
BELLANTONI, Charles ... 207-509-7280 196 E cbellantoni@unity.edu
BELLANTONI, Jeffrey ..... 803-323-2323 414 D bellantonij@winthrop.edu
BELLAVIA, Rand .... 716-829-7616 298 E bellavia@dyc.edu
BELLE ISLE, Denell .... 651-213-4678 236 C
BELLEFEUILLE, Barbara, K .... 574-807-7210 154 B barb.bellefeuille@betheluniversity.edu
BELLEMER, Jess .... 828-898-8770 330 E bellemerj@lmc.edu
BELLEN, Katherine .... 815-455-8764 143 I kbellen@mchenry.edu
BELLEW, Kevin, M .... 859-858-3511 179 D kevin.bellew@asbury.edu
BELLI, Keith, L .... 864-656-3013 407 E kbelli@clemson.edu
BELLICK, II, Morris, A .. 904-632-3244 101 B morris.a.bellick@fscj.edu
BELLIN, Derek, C .... 303-735-5449.. 84 B derek.bellin@colorado.edu
BELLINA, Amy .... 732-571-3586 279 A abellina@monmouth.edu
BELLING, Karen .... 630-752-5021 153 C karen.belling@wheaton.edu
BELLING, Shawn .... 608-243-4180 499 A sbelling@madisoncollege.edu
BELLINGER, Andrew ..... 315-792-7141 321 B abellinger@sunypoly.edu
BELLINGER, Patricia ..... 617-495-6495 210 E patricia_bellinger@harvard.edu
BELLINGS, Andy .... 563-588-6420 164 E andy.bellings@clarke.edu
BELLINI, Michel .... 217-265-5297 152 B bellini@illinois.edu
BELLINO, Maria .... 480-517-8220.. 13 G maria.bellino@riosalado.edu
BELLIVEAU, Brian .... 303-753-6046.. 83 F bbelliveau@rmcad.edu
BELLIVEAU, Cynthia, L . 802-656-3890 463 A cynthia.belliveau@uvm.edu
BELLO, Diane .... 631-632-6179 317 A diane.bello@stonybrook.edu
BELLO-DECASTRO, Leigh .... 973-877-3483 277 G bellodecastro@essex.edu
BELLOMY, Chasley .... 256-228-6001.... 3 B bellomyc@nacc.edu
BELLOT, Dario .... 610-526-6614 385 D dbellot@harcum.edu
BELLOW, Kathleen, D ... 504-520-7691 193 E ibcs@xula.edu
BELLOWS, Alan .... 801-649-5230 459 G technicalsupport@midwifery.edu
BELLOWS, Charlene ...... 508-793-2514 208 D cbellows@holycross.edu
BELLOWS, Laurie .... 402-472-3755 269 J lbellows1@unl.edu
BELLUCCI, Anthony, D .. 973-378-2655 283 C anthony.bellucci@shu.edu
BELLUCCI, Debbie .... 413-755-4334 216 A dbellucci@stcc.edu
BELLUCCI, Keith .... 617-732-2145 216 D keith.bellucci@mcphs.edu
BELLUM, Kim .... 605-886-6777 415 F kimberly.bellum@mountmarty.edu
BELMAN, David .... 925-473-7423.. 40 D dbelman@losmedanos.edu
BELMAR, Ricardo .... 305-607-6123 105 A belmar@nova.edu
BELMODIS, Cassie .... 503-399-5159 372 B cassie.belmodis@chemeketa.edu
BELMONT, Amanda .... 701-349-5416 346 I amandabelmont@trinitybiblecollege.edu
BELMONT, Heather .... 772-462-7215 102 F hbelmont@irsc.edu
BELMONTE, Laura .... 540-231-6779 476 C belmonte@vt.edu
BELOBRAJDIC, Scott ..... 618-650-2298 150 C sbelobr@siue.edu
BELOTE, Eve .... 757-789-1767 473 H ebelote@es.vccs.edu
BELOTE, Faith, D .... 757-594-7618 465 M faith.belote@cnu.edu
BELOVICH, Joanne .... 216-687-3502 350 J j.belovich@csuohio.edu
BELOW, Debbie .... 573-986-6888 259 H dbelow@semo.edu
BELSER, Nakia .... 205-929-1569.... 6 B
BELSHER, Judy, K .... 602-243-8200.. 14 A judy.belsher@southmountaincc.edu
BELSKY, Marianne .... 202-651-5031.. 92 C marianne.belsky@gallaudet.edu
BELT, Jennifer .... 479-788-7007.. 21 G jennifer.belt@uafs.edu
BELT, Mazel .... 603-456-2656 273 H mbelt@magdalen.edu
BELTER, Joe .... 541-888-7800 376 C joseph.belter@socc.edu

BELTON, Ada, A .... 803-705-4327 406 G
ada.belton@benedict.edu
BELTON, Allan .... 253-535-7101 482 A
allan.belton@plu.edu
BELTON, Ray .... 225-771-4680 191 B
ray_belton@sus.edu
BELTON, Ray, L .... 225-771-4680 191 A
ray_belton@sus.edu
BELTON, Tammie .... 216-791-5000 350 I
tamatha.belton@cim.edu
BELTRAN, Adrian .... 559-730-3885.. 39 B
adrianb@cos.edu
BELTRAN, Delia .... 714-966-8500.. 74 C
dbeltran@ves.edu
BELTRAN, Dulce .... 305-348-7347 110 A
dulce.beltran@fiu.edu
BELTRAN, Jake .... 847-970-4961 152 I
jbeltran@usml.edu
BELTRAN, Philip .... 408-554-4161.. 63 B
pjbeltran@scu.edu
BELTRAN, Renz .... 808-954-4934 128 F
rbeltran@hmi.edu
BELTZ, Marah .... 386-481-2928.. 96 D
beltzm@cookman.edu
BELVILL, Rita .... 425-388-9202 480 B
rbelvill@everettcc.edu
BELVINS, Walter .... 510-723-6648.. 35 J
wbelvins@clpccd.org
BELVIS LOPEZ, Rosa .... 787-725-6500 505 G
rbelvis@albizu.edu
BEM, Greg .... 425-739-8100 481 C
greg.bem@lwtech.edu
BEMBRY, Deborah .... 229-500-2141 114 H
deborah.bembry@asurams.edu
BEMIS, Scot, R .... 603-646-3768 273 D
scot.r.bemis@dartmouth.edu
BENABESS, Najiba .... 217-424-6285 144 G
nbenabess@millikin.edu
BENABESS, Najibu .... 217-424-6285 144 G
nbenabess@millikin.edu
BENANDER, Mark .... 413-565-1000 206 D
mbenander@baypath.edu
BENASUTTI, Regina .... 215-489-4440 382 B
regina.ball@delval.edu
BENAVIDES, Dominique 510-748-5264.. 57 A
dbenavides@peralta.edu
BENAVIDES, Elma, F ..... 512-863-1441 445 C
benavide@southwestern.edu
BENAVIDES, Letty .... 956-665-2255 455 D
letty.benavides@utrgv.edu
BENAVIDES, Lewis .... 940-898-3555 451 D
lbenavides@twu.edu
BENAVIDES-DOMINGUEZ,
Patricia .... 361-698-2250 435 G
studentaffairs@delmar.edu
BENBOW, Camilla, P ..... 615-322-8407 428 A
camilla.benbow@vanderbilt.edu
BENBROOK, Tabitha ..... 918-335-6854 368 E
tbenbrook@okwu.edu
BENDAPUDI, Neeli .... 502-852-5417 186 A
neeli@louisville.edu
BENDARSH, Joe .... 646-592-4615 326 D
joe.bednarsh@yu.edu
BENDELE, Jennifer .... 419-227-3141 362 F
jennifer@unoh.edu
BENDER, Christina .... 267-341-3017 385 J
cbender@holyfamily.edu
BENDER, David, L .... 989-837-4374 229 B
bender@northwood.edu
BENDER, Donna .... 504-314-2148 191 F
dbender@tulane.edu
BENDER, Jennie, M ...... 606-474-3226 181 B
jbender@kcu.edu
BENDER, Jim .... 651-635-2378 234 D
j-bender@bethel.edu
BENDER, Karla .... 713-718-8247 437 C
karla.bender@hccs.edu
BENDER, Kim .... 307-778-4337 501 E
kbender@lccc.wy.edu
BENDER, Linda .... 307-855-2102 501 A
lbender@cwc.edu
BENDER, Loren, J .... 407-582-3408 113 I
lbender2@valenciacollege.edu
BENDER, Marian .... 814-472-3931 397 F
mbender@francis.edu
BENDER, Melinda .... 717-477-1123 395 B
mkbend@ship.edu
BENDER, Michael .... 845-207-0330 290 F
BENDER, Rick .... 432-685-4529 440 B
rbender@midland.edu
BENDER, Starr, S .... 407-303-5765.. 95 B
starr.bender@ahu.edu
BENDER, IV,
Thomas, B .... 504-866-7426 190 G
library@nds.edu
BENDER, Virginia .... 201-761-6024 283 A
vbender@saintpeters.edu
BENDER, Yaakov .... 718-868-2300 291 C
BENDER SHETLER, Jan . 574-535-7108 155 E
jans@goshen.edu
BENDERS, Alison .... 408-554-4064.. 63 B
ambenders@scu.edu
BENDES, Caren .... 313-993-3354 231 E
bendescm@udmercy.edu
BENDEZU PALOMINO,
Cyndi .... 661-259-7800.. 38 D
cyndi.palomino@canyons.edu
BENDL, Colleen .... 740-593-1630 358 K
bendl@ohio.edu
BENEDETTI, Brian .... 253-864-3235 482 E
bbenedetti@pierce.ctc.edu
BENEDICT, Barbara .... 719-549-3039.. 82 J
barbara.benedict@pueblocc.edu
BENEDICT, David .... 860-486-2725.. 89 D
david.benedict@uconn.edu
BENEDICT, JR.,
Gregory .... 908-709-7520 284 D
gregory.benedict@ucc.edu
BENEDICT, Jody, C .... 585-385-8322 313 F
jbenedict@sjfc.edu
BENEDICT, Sherri, J ...... 315-655-7245 292 H
sjbenedict@cazenovia.edu
BENEDICT-JONES,
Michelle .... 607-255-5056 297 F
mbenedict-jones@cornell.edu
BENEFIEL, Lori .... 541-383-7572 372 A
lbenefiel@cocc.edu
BENEFIEL, Patricia .... 619-574-6909.. 55 E
pbenefiel@pacificcollege.edu
BENEFIEL, Ron .... 619-849-2613.. 57 J
ronbenefiel@pointloma.edu
BENEFIELD, Lenore .... 239-590-7048 109 K
lbenefie@fgcu.edu
BENEKE, Thomas, J ...... 515-574-1050 167 A
beneke@iowacentral.edu
BENET, Micol, A .... 415-485-9502.. 39 A
mabenet@marin.edu
BENET, Suzeanne .... 616-331-2400 224 G
benets@gvsu.edu
BENEVENTO, Erin .... 410-386-4821 200 F
ebenevento@mcdaniel.edu
BENFANTI, William, J .... 716-878-5557 317 F
benfanwj@buffalostate.edu
BENFER, Pamela, A ...... 570-577-1561 379 C
pam.benfer@bucknell.edu
BENFORD, Jeffrey .... 925-473-7425.. 40 D
jbenford@losmedanos.edu
BENFORD, Michael .... 713-221-8129 453 A
benfordm@uhd.edu
BENGE, Robert .... 423-236-2855 423 F
rcbenge@southern.edu
BENGEL, Kristi .... 513-244-4624 356 F
kristi.bengel@msj.edu
BENHAM, Maenette ...... 808-689-2770 129 F
mbenham@hawaii.edu
BENHAM, Rebekah .... 503-375-7093 372 H
rbenham@corban.edu
BENHAM-DEAL, Tami ... 307-766-4286 501 I
benham@uwyo.edu
BENINGHOVE, Linda ..... 201-216-5412 283 D
linda.beninghove@stevens.edu
BENISH, Amy, L .... 262-554-2010 494 A
BENITEZ, Hubert .... 816-501-1100 258 I
hubert.benitez@rockhurst.edu
BENITEZ, Leyda, L .... 610-519-3976 401 K
leyda.benitez@villanova.edu
BENITEZ, JR., Michael . 303-615-2063.. 81 M
mbenite4@msudenver.edu
BENITIZ, Yvette .... 575-527-7552 287 F
ybenitiz@nmsu.edu
BENJAMIN, Brent .... 304-327-4014 489 I
bbenjamin@bluefieldstate.edu
BENJAMIN, Daneida ...... 954-486-7728 113 B
dbenjamin@uftl.edu
BENJAMIN, Eric, M ...... 240-567-5048 200 G
eric.benjamin@montgomerycollege.edu
BENJAMIN, Jack .... 803-641-3327 413 B
jackb@usca.edu
BENJAMIN, Jodi .... 402-941-6102 267 L
benjamin@midlandu.edu
BENJAMIN, Kathi .... 508-289-2705 220 E
kbenjamin@whoi.edu
BENJAMIN, Robert .... 617-745-3595 209 B
robert.j.benjamin@enc.edu
BENJAMIN, Valerie, C .. 585-385-7247 313 F
vbenjamin@sjfc.edu
BENKE, Jack .... 573-592-6231 262 E
jack.benke@westminster-mo.edu
BENKE, Jack .... 573-642-3361 262 E
BENKERT, Ramona .... 313-577-4138 232 K
ramonabenkert@wayne.edu
BENKESER, Kristina ...... 724-738-2052 395 C
kristina.benkeser@sru.edu
BENKO, Hope .... 512-472-4133 443 F
hope.benko@ssw.edu
BENKO, Jared .... 912-478-5047 120 C
benko@georgiasouthern.edu
BENKO, Richard, A .... 724-287-8711 379 E
richard.benko@bc3.edu
BENLOLO, Henri .... 352-854-2322.. 97 N
benloloh@cf.edu
BENMAMOUN, Abbas ... 919-684-4997 328 F
elabbas.benmamoun@duke.edu
BENN, Delores .... 704-403-3502 327 C
delores.benn@atriumhealth.org
BENN, Sherri .... 512-245-2278 450 C
sb17@txstate.edu
BENN MARSHALL,
Karen .... 256-726-8044.... 6 C
kmarshall@oakwood.edu
BENNANI, Wissem .... 650-306-3100.. 62 J
BENNE, Jennifer .... 573-681-5125 254 G
bennej@lincolnu.edu
BENNEIAN, Teresa .... 717-290-8748 387 G
tbenneian@lancasterseminary.edu
BENNER, Brent, W .... 813-253-6211 113 H
bbenner@ut.edu
BENNER, Patrick .... 707-965-6242.. 55 I
pbenner@puc.edu
BENNER, Patrick, B ...... 804-289-8930 472 C
pbenner@richmond.edu
BENNER, Tracy .... 614-823-1580 359 H
tbenner@otterbein.edu
BENNETT, Amanda .... 423-697-4400 424 A
BENNETT, Amber .... 906-487-2538 228 A
ambennet@mtu.edu
BENNETT, Amy .... 317-955-6768 159 K
abennett@marian.edu
BENNETT, Anthony, T ... 910-672-1314 341 C
abennett@uncfsu.edu
BENNETT, Breely .... 816-802-3420 254 D
bbennett@kcai.edu
BENNETT, Brian .... 615-248-7782 426 D
bmbennett2@trevecca.edu
BENNETT, Cameron, D . 253-535-7150 482 A
bennetcd@plu.edu
BENNETT, Candida .... 719-255-3868.. 84 C
candida.bennett@uccs.edu
BENNETT, Carol .... 330-941-3001 364 H
clbennett04@ysu.edu
BENNETT, Carolyn .... 516-876-3203 318 C
bennettc@oldwestbury.edu
BENNETT, Chandalin ..... 509-359-6362 479 G
cmbennett@ewu.edu
BENNETT, Curtis .... 562-985-5559.. 31 D
curtis.bennett@csulb.edu
BENNETT, Daniel .... 828-669-8012 331 K
dbennett@montreat.edu
BENNETT, David, A .... 606-474-3256 181 B
dbennett@kcu.edu
BENNETT, David, P .... 202-806-6100.. 92 F
BENNETT, Dorine .... 605-256-5137 416 F
dorine.bennett@dsu.edu
BENNETT, Douglas .... 714-432-5126.. 38 B
dbennett@occ.cccd.edu
BENNETT, Eddie .... 434-736-2055 475 B
eddie.bennett@southside.edu
BENNETT, Elbert .... 870-575-8504.. 22 D
bennette@uapb.edu
BENNETT, Elizabeth, C .. 949-824-7982.. 69 D
bennette@uci.edu
BENNETT, Elizabeth, P .. 717-290-8713 387 G
ebennett@lancasterseminary.edu
BENNETT, Elizabeth, P .. 717-396-7833 392 U
ebennet@pcad.edu
BENNETT, Ephraim .... 757-823-8214 469 A
ejbennett@nsu.edu
BENNETT, Erika .... 314-505-7286 252 A
bennette@csl.edu
BENNETT, Gary .... 919-668-3420 328 F
gary.bennett@duke.edu
BENNETT, Gene .... 870-780-1201.. 17 B
gbennett@smail.anc.edu
BENNETT, George .... 509-527-2092 485 C
george.bennett@wallawalla.edu
BENNETT, Heather .... 309-796-5301 133 G
bennetth@bhc.edu
BENNETT, Holly, L .... 561-868-3279 105 D
bennetth@palmbeachstate.edu
BENNETT, Jabbar, R ..... 517-353-3924 227 F
jrb1619@msu.edu
BENNETT, James .... 913-288-7259 175 B
jbennett@kckcc.edu
BENNETT, Janice, G ...... 563-588-8000 166 C
jbennett@emmaus.edu
BENNETT, Jeffrey, L ...... 570-321-4031 389 B
bennett@lycoming.edu
BENNETT, Jen .... 918-631-2276 371 C
jsb8472@utulsa.edu
BENNETT, Jeremy .... 580-559-5256 365 K
jbennett@ecok.edu
BENNETT, JoAnn .... 937-327-6185 364 D
jbennett@wittenberg.edu
BENNETT, Kari, A .... 518-783-2368 315 E
kbennett@siena.edu
BENNETT, Kevin .... 904-256-7585 102 H
kbennet1@ju.edu
BENNETT, Kim .... 260-665-4438 161 E
bennettk@trine.edu
BENNETT, Kristen .... 817-515-5377 445 F
kristen.bennett@tccd.edu
BENNETT, Lori .... 559-325-5200.. 67 A
BENNETT, Marcus .... 231-995-1401 229 A
mbennett@nmc.edu
BENNETT, Mark .... 909-607-8740.. 37 F
mark_bennett@kgi.edu
BENNETT, Matt .... 517-338-3014 222 G
mbennett@cleary.edu
BENNETT, Matthew .... 202-885-1000.. 91 F
mattbennett@american.edu
BENNETT, Maybelle, T .. 202-806-4771.. 92 F
maybelle.bennett@howard.edu
BENNETT, Michael, J .... 727-341-3012 107 E
bennett.michael@spcollege.edu
BENNETT, Nicole .... 610-436-3557 395 D
nbennett@wcupa.edu
BENNETT, Patricia .... 601-925-7100 247 C
pbennett@mc.edu
BENNETT, Patrick .... 623-245-4600.. 16 B
pabennett@uti.edu
BENNETT, Patrick .... 614-947-6836 352 J
patrick.bennett@franklin.edu
BENNETT, Patrick .... 614-947-6636 352 J
patrick.bennett@franklin.edu
BENNETT, Rex .... 765-998-5389 161 C
rex_bennett@taylor.edu
BENNETT, Rodney, D .... 601-266-5001 249 F
president@usm.edu
BENNETT, Sari, M .... 603-862-4285 274 F
sari.bennett@unh.edu
BENNETT, Scott .... 904-620-2002 111 B
sbennett@unf.edu
BENNETT, Scott .... 281-425-6396 438 I
sbennett@lee.edu
BENNETT, Shannon .... 336-285-2433 341 D
spbennett@ncat.edu
BENNETT, Stacey .... 740-593-2626 358 K
sbennett@ohio.edu
BENNETT, Steve .... 315-443-5725 321 G
sbenne04@syr.edu
BENNETT, Sutton .... 510-987-9134.. 68 L
sutton.bennett@ucop.edu
BENNETT, Tameika .... 718-429-6600 324 D
tameika.bennett@vaughn.edu
BENNETT, Tina .... 678-839-6443 127 C
tbennett@westga.edu
BENNETT, Tracy .... 951-571-6100.. 59 B
BENNETT, Valerie .... 309-677-3961 134 A
vbennett@bradley.edu
BENNETT-FAIRS,
Vernell .... 901-435-1676 420 I
BENNETT-SMITH, Laura 573-681-5099 254 G
bennett-smith@lincolnu.edu
BENNIE, Kevin .... 740-474-8896 358 A
kbennie@ohiochristian.edu
BENNIGHOFF, James ..... 254-710-3601 431 E
james_bennighoff@baylor.edu
BENNINGS, Adrien .... 269-965-3931 225 H
benningsa@kellogg.edu
BENNINGTON, Brad ...... 217-581-3511 137 E
bbennington@eiu.edu
BENNINGTON,
Cheryl, C .... 304-336-8049 490 B
cbennington@westliberty.edu
BENNION, Paul .... 208-459-5841 131 C
pbennion@collegeofidaho.edu
BENNISON, Steve .... 812-941-2450 157 F
sbenniso@iu.edu
BENOIT, Andy .... 361-825-5785 447 C
andy.benoit@tamucc.edu
BENOIT, Anthony .... 617-588-1324 206 F
abenoit@bfit.edu

BERGMAN, Helen .... 903-463-8698 436 G
bergmanh@grayson.edu
BERGMAN, Joe .... 309-694-5367 139 B
joe.bergman@icc.edu
BERGMAN, Matthew ..... 217-228-5432 147 F
bergmma@quincy.edu
BERGMAN, Rebecca, M 507-933-7538 236 A
president@gustavus.edu
BERGMAN, JR.,
William, T .... 215-204-7405 399 B
william.bergman@temple.edu
BERGMANN, Donald, J . 570-941-7400 401 F
donald.bergmann@scranton.edu
BERGMANN, Leah .... 785-738-9062 176 F
lbergmann@ncktc.edu
BERGMANN, Michelle ... 541-440-4620 376 G
michelle.bergmann@umpqua.edu
BERGMANN, Ronald ..... 718-960-8421 294 A
ronald.bergmann@lehman.cuny.edu
BERGMANN, Tom .... 847-947-5516 145 D
tbergmann@nl.edu
BERGQUIST, David .... 951-827-2228.. 70 B
david.bergquist@ucr.edu
BERGQUIST, Shari .... 802-656-3427 463 A
shari.bergquist@uvm.edu
BERGREN, Rebecca, A .. 717-337-6866 384 D
rbergren@gettysburg.edu
BERGRUD, Erik .... 816-584-6412 258 C
erik.bergrud@park.edu
BERGS, Thomas .... 651-846-1322 241 B
thomas.bergs@saintpaul.edu
BERGSMA, Brad .... 785-890-3641 176 H
brad.bergsma@nwktc.edu
BERGSTROM, Amy .... 218-723-6067 235 G
abergstrom@css.edu
BERGSTROM, Mary, C .. 843-953-0193 408 C
bergstromm@cofc.edu
BERGSTROM, Tracey ..... 361-582-2565 457 E
tracey.bergstrom@victoriacollege.edu
BERHIE, Girmay .... 601-979-6386 246 F
girmay.berhie@jsums.edu
BERHORST, Ben .... 573-897-5000 260 A
BERHORST, Todd .... 323-860-1199.. 53 D
toddb@mi.edu
BERHOW, Justin .... 661-654-2522.. 30 B
jberhow@csub.edu
BERICH, Anthony .... 434-947-8537 469 E
aberich@randolphcollege.edu
BERIGAN, Jennifer .... 513-936-1734 362 A
jennifer.berigan@uc.edu
BERK, Steven, L .... 806-743-3000 451 A
steven.berk@ttuhsc.edu
BERKE, Deborah .... 203-436-8057.. 90 C
deborah.berke@yale.edu
BERKELEY, Amy .... 401-254-3302 405 C
aberkeley@rwu.edu
BERKENPAS, Barb .... 507-537-6215 241 D
barb.berkenpas@smsu.edu
BERKEY, Jessica .... 864-294-2267 409 H
jessica.berkey@furman.edu
BERKEY, Jonathan .... 704-894-2529 328 E
joberkey@davidson.edu
BERKHEIMER, Eric, J .... 410-677-6553 204 D
ejberkheimer@salisbury.edu
BERKHEIMER, Karen ...... 410-334-2915 205 D
kberkheimer@worwic.edu
BERKINSHAW,
Stewart, M .... 405-325-1271 370 K
sberkinshaw@ou.edu
BERKLAS, Jennifer, L .... 909-607-7976.. 63 F
jberklas@scrippscollege.edu
BERKLE, Paul .... 941-752-5000 109 G
BERKLEY, Shelley .... 702-777-1776.. 68 B
shelley.berkley@tun.touro.edu
BERKNER, Donna .... 817-202-6214 444 I
dberkner@swau.edu
BERKNER, Paul, D .... 207-859-4460 194 D
paul.berkner@colby.edu
BERKOWITZ, Bobbie ..... 212-305-3582 297 C
bb2509@columbia.edu
BERKSHIRE, Jacki .... 864-833-8006 411 D
jberkshire@presby.edu
BERKSHIRE, Sarah .... 270-706-8836 181 G
sarah.berkshire@kctcs.edu
BERKUN, Mike .... 718-409-4841 320 G
BERLEY, Susan, A .... 828-448-6125 339 A
sberley@wpcc.edu
BERLIN, Linda .... 231-995-1533 229 A
lberlin@nmc.edu
BERLINER, Donna .... 630-942-2475 135 I
berliner@cod.edu
BERLO, Josh .... 218-726-8168 243 G
jpberlo@d.umn.edu

BERMAN, Ari .... 212-960-5300 326 D
president@yu.edu
BERMAN, Bruce .... 714-895-8315.. 38 A
bberman@gwc.cccd.edu
BERMAN, Daniel .... 215-204-2044 399 B
daniel.berman@temple.edu
BERMAN, Ila .... 434-924-7019 472 D
ilb8r@virginia.edu
BERMAN, Joel .... 954-262-2130 105 A
jb@nsu.nova.edu
BERMAN, Larry, S .... 404-413-5570 120 E
larryberman@gsu.edu
BERMAN, Lou Ann .... 903-566-7052 456 A
lberman@uttyler.edu
BERMAN, Marc .... 619-961-4271.. 68 A
mberman@tjsl.edu
BERMAN, Mark, A .... 518-782-6957 315 E
mberman@siena.edu
BERMAN, Paula .... 617-277-3915 207 D
bermanp@bgsp.edu
BERMEA, Gilbert, S ...... 830-758-4111 444 G
gbermea@swtjc.edu
BERMEL, John .... 507-222-4427 234 G
jbermel@carleton.edu
BERMEL, Rhea .... 903-463-8628 436 G
bermelr@grayson.edu
BERMUDEZ, Eliezer .... 453-879-4817 460 B
eliezer.bermudez@dixie.edu
BERMUDEZ, Glenda ...... 787-766-1717 510 G
glbermudez@uagm.edu
BERMUDEZ, Gregory .... 787-257-0000 512 B
BERMUDEZ, Luis .... 773-838-7544 135 F
lbermudez6@ccc.edu
BERNA, Laurie .... 603-578-8900 272 M
BERNABE, Arnaldo .... 718-518-6888 294 B
abernabe@hostos.cuny.edu
BERNAL,
Eduardo (Eddie) .... 626-571-8811.. 73 E
BERNAL, Jesse, M .... 616-331-3296 224 G
bernalje@gvsu.edu
BERNAL, Omar .... 708-237-5050 146 D
obernal@nc.edu
BERNAL-OLSON,
Patricia .... 937-229-4211 362 C
pbernalolson1@udayton.edu
BERNARD, Barbara .... 781-239-2629 214 G
bbernard@massbay.edu
BERNARD, Eugene .... 713-221-8679 453 A
bernarde@uhd.edu
BERNARD, Gregory .... 203-392-6501.. 86 A
bernardg2@southernct.edu
BERNARD, Hans .... 503-412-3715 376 H
hbernard@uoregon.edu
BERNARD, Julia .... 802-485-2000 462 F
jbernar3@norwich.edu
BERNARD, Kacey .... 610-341-1459 383 B
kbernard@eastern.edu
BERNARD, Ken .... 803-778-6668 406 I
bernardkd@cctech.edu
BERNARD, Kyle .... 518-580-5820 315 F
kbernar1@skidmore.edu
BERNARD, Michelle ...... 706-379-3111 128 C
mmbernard@yhc.edu
BERNARD, Pamela .... 919-684-3955 328 F
pam.bernard@duke.edu
BERNARD, Renee .... 814-472-2766 397 F
rbernard@francis.edu
BERNARD-AMOS,
Marion .... 484-365-7224 388 H
mba@lincoln.edu
BERNARDINI, Paola ...... 305-223-4561 107 B
pbernardini@sjvcs.edu
BERNARDIS, Tim .... 406-638-3113 263 G
tim@lbhc.edu
BERNARDO, Antonio ..... 310-825-4321.. 69 E
a.bernardo@anderson.ucla.edu
BERNARDO, Lisa, M ...... 209-667-3094.. 33 B
lbernardo@csustan.edu
BERNARDO-SOUSA,
Marie .... 401-598-1754 404 D
marie.bernardo-sousa@jwu.edu
BERNAT, Carol .... 716-926-8963 301 E
cbernat@hilbert.edu
BERNATZ, Richard .... 563-387-2000 168 B
bernatzr@luther.edu
BERNAUER, Edmund ...... 808-521-2288 129 A
dean@orientalmedicine.edu
BERNAUER, Jeanne ...... 808-521-2288 129 A
BERNDT, Michael .... 651-450-3641 238 E
michael.berndt@minnstate.edu
BERNDT, Michael, D ..... 651-423-8000 238 A
michael.berndt@minnstate.edu

BERNE, Jennifer, I .... 248-341-2051 229 C
jiberne@oaklandcc.edu
BERNER, JR.,
Howard, E .... 314-275-3514 147 E
howard.berner@principia.edu
BERNER, Jason .... 510-215-4131.. 40 B
jberner@contracosta.edu
BERNER, Nancy .... 931-598-1172 423 D
nberner@sewanee.edu
BERNET, Kristin .... 610-892-1500 393 B
BERNHARD, Anne .... 860-439-2030.. 87 H
aeber@conncoll.edu
BERNHARD, Margaret ... 980-224-8467 217 I
BERNHARD, Robert, J .. 574-631-3902 162 A
bernhard.9@nd.edu
BERNHARD, William ..... 217-333-6677 152 B
bernhard@illinois.edu
BERNHARDSON,
Bonnie .... 218-879-0828 238 B
bonnie@fdltcc.edu
BERNHARDSON, Mark .. 218-879-0703 238 B
mbernhar@fdltcc.edu
BERNHARDT, Jay, M .... 512-471-8100 455 A
moody.dean@austin.utexas.edu
BERNHARDT, Starr .... 509-793-2065 478 B
starrb@bigbend.edu
BERNHARDT, Thomas ... 804-763-6300.. 93 H
BERNHEIM, Michelle .... 562-902-3343.. 65 I
michellebernheim@scuhs.edu
BERNIER, Brandon .... 970-491-1833.. 79 N
brandon.bernier@colostate.edu
BERNIER, Carrie .... 203-857-7270.. 87 D
cbernier@norwalk.edu
BERNIER, Jose .... 386-822-7045 112 A
jbernier@stetson.edu
BERNOI, Verna, A .... 443-518-4773 199 F
vbernoi@howardcc.edu
BERNOT, C. Tina .... 270-809-3250 184 D
cbernot@murraystate.edu
BERNOTAS, Scott, C ..... 412-624-9510 400 H
bernotas@pitt.edu
BERNOTAS, Vivian .... 701-671-2221 346 D
vivian.bernotas@ndscs.edu
BERNOTSKY,
R. Lorraine .... 610-436-6977 395 D
lbernotsky@wcupa.edu
BERNOUSSI, Brian .... 972-883-2676 455 B
brian_bernoussi10@utdallas.edu
BERNSTEIN, Alan .... 229-333-5860 127 E
abernste@valdosta.edu
BERNSTEIN, Andy .... 203-582-7882.. 88 G
andy.bernstein@qu.edu
BERNSTEIN, David .... 845-406-4308 325 F
BERNSTEIN, Melissa ..... 801-581-3386 459 O
melissa.bernstein@law.utah.edu
BERNSTEIN, Pamela ...... 603-880-8308 274 D
pbernstein@thomasmorecollege.edu
BERNSTEIN, Robin .... 402-557-7300 265 J
robin.bernstein@bellevue.edu
BERNSTEIN, Zeke .... 802-440-4594 461 G
zbernstein@bennington.edu
BERNSTEIN CHARGIN,
Jan .... 408-852-2826.. 43 E
alumni@gavilan.edu
BERNSTEIN-CHARGIN,
Jan .... 408-848-4724.. 43 E
jbchargin@gavilan.edu
BEROWSKI, Alfred .... 315-866-0300 301 D
berowskfj@herkimer.edu
BERQUAM, Lori .... 480-461-7300.. 13 D
BERQUE, David .... 765-658-4735 154 J
vpaa@depauw.edu
BERQUIST, Gina .... 503-255-0332 374 C
ginab@multnomah.edu
BERREAU, Lisa .... 435-797-3509 460 C
lisa.berreau@usu.edu
BERRETT, Ben .... 435-797-1957 460 C
ben.berrett@usu.edu
BERRIEN, Joel .... 712-749-2379 164 C
berrienj@bvu.edu
BERRIEN, Tara .... 443-885-3359 201 A
tara.berrien@morgan.edu
BERRIGAN, Edward .... 210-341-1366 440 H
eberrigan@ost.edu
BERRIOS, Anthony .... 305-821-3333 100 E
aberrios@fnu.edu
BERRIOS, Carmen .... 787-738-2161 512 C
carmen.berrios@upr.edu
BERRIOS, Eduardo .... 787-603-1515 508 A
eberrios@bayamon.inter.edu
BERRIOS, Eric .... 814-864-6666 384 F
ericb@glit.edu

BERRIOS, Iris .... 787-743-7979 510 H
ac_irberrios@suagm.edu
BERRIOS, Jonathan .... 787-738-2161 512 C
jonathan.berrios@upr.edu
BERRIOS, Jose, E .... 787-766-1717 510 G
BERRIOS, Marianne ...... 787-852-1430 507 C
mberrios@hccpr.edu
BERRIOS, Olga, L .... 787-850-9340 512 D
olga.berrios@upr.edu
BERRIOS, William .... 212-592-2043 315 C
wberrios@sva.edu
BERRY, Abby .... 315-655-7292 292 H
alberry@cazenovia.edu
BERRY, Alex .... 217-786-4912 143 B
alex.berry@llcc.edu
BERRY, Anna .... 413-775-1868 214 E
BERRY, Anthony, T .... 860-297-2177.. 89 B
anthony.berry@trincoll.edu
BERRY, Benny .... 423-652-4333 420 F
blberry@king.edu
BERRY, Brian .... 870-777-5722.. 22 I
brian.berry@uaht.edu
BERRY, Cammie, S .... 803-536-8961 411 G
cberry@scsu.edu
BERRY, Carolynn .... 336-750-2110 344 A
berryc@wssu.edu
BERRY, Chad .... 859-985-3730 179 I
berry@berea.edu
BERRY, Clay .... 870-508-6124.. 17 G
cberry@asumh.edu
BERRY, Doug .... 602-787-7668.. 13 E
doug.berry@paradisevalley.edu
BERRY, Elizabeth, D ..... 607-746-4573 320 D
berryee@delhi.edu
BERRY, Emily .... 513-529-9625 356 A
emily.berry@miamioh.edu
BERRY, Gwennette, C ... 319-273-2820 164 A
gwenne.berry@uni.edu
BERRY, Joan .... 254-295-4010 453 D
joan.berry@umhb.edu
BERRY, Joan, E .... 610-566-1776 403 B
jberry@williamson.edu
BERRY, John .... 740-364-9510 349 F
berry.19@cotc.edu
BERRY, John .... 865-981-8145 421 C
john.berry@maryvillecollege.edu
BERRY, Joshua .... 203-582-8695.. 88 G
joshua.berry@quinnipiac.edu
BERRY, Keith .... 813-253-7714 102 B
kberry@hccfl.edu
BERRY, Larry .... 423-614-8086 420 H
lberry@leeuniversity.edu
BERRY, Laura .... 870-743-3000.. 20 B
lberry@northark.edu
BERRY, Laura Lea .... 802-586-7711 462 I
lberry@sterlingcollege.edu
BERRY, Linda, C .... 708-209-3209 136 E
linda.berry@cuchicago.edu
BERRY, Mario .... 713-313-7011 449 B
BERRY, Michael .... 724-222-5330 391 F
BERRY, Rance .... 304-357-4862 487 J
ranceberry@ucwv.edu
BERRY, Ronald .... 352-294-7439 111 A
rberry@ufl.edu
BERRY, Ronald, L .... 318-342-1010 193 C
rberry@ulm.edu
BERRY, Steve .... 530-541-4660.. 47 E
sberry@ltcc.edu
BERRY, Steve .... 530-541-4660.. 47 E
BERRY, Steve .... 919-365-7711 340 E
BERRY, Steven .... 410-386-8145 198 D
sberry@carrollcc.edu
BERRY, Theodorea .... 407-823-2373 110 E
theodorea.berry@ucf.edu
BERRY, Tina .... 520-494-5972.. 11 K
tina.berry@centralaz.edu
BERRY, Trey .... 870-235-4001.. 21 C
tcberry@saumag.edu
BERRY, William .... 540-423-9069 473 I
wberry@germanna.edu
BERRY, Yvonne .... 630-617-3012 137 G
yvonne.berry@elmhurst.edu
BERRY-GUERIN,
Daneen .... 509-793-2053 478 B
daneenb@bigbend.edu
BERRY-HUNG, Rima ...... 313-593-5190 231 I
rberry@umich.edu
BERRYHILL, Kelly, M .... 989-774-2849 222 E
berry1km@cmich.edu
BERRYMAN, Cynthia ..... 708-237-5050 146 D
cberryman@nc.edu
BERRYMAN, Jennifer .... 508-856-2900 212 C
jennifer.berryman@umassmed.edu

BIBB-SANDERS, Angelia .... 323-860-0789.. 50 B
BIBBEE, Mistie .... 304-696-3152 489 M
bibbeem@marshall.edu
BIBBENS, Matthew, G ... 909-607-8966.. 37 D
matthew.bibbens@cmc.edu
BIBBO, Chris, J .... 727-816-3261 105 F
bibboc@phsc.edu
BIBLE, Brice, J .... 716-645-7979 316 C
bible@buffalo.edu
BIBLE, Robert .... 918-549-2800 365 H
rbible@cmn.edu
BIBLER, Jackie .... 703-284-6484 468 H
jbibler@marymount.edu
BIBLER, Nicole .... 913-758-6123 178 B
nicole.bibler@stmary.edu
BIBO, JR., Tim .... 410-704-4685 204 E
tbibo@towson.edu
BICAK, Charles, J .... 308-865-8209 269 I
bicakc@unk.edu
BICE, Patricia .... 914-251-6360 319 B
patricia.bice@purchase.edu
BICHEL, Rebecca .... 817-272-1413 454 I
rbichel@uta.edu
BICHELMEYER, Barbara . 785-864-4904 177 J
bichelmeyer@ku.edu
BICKART, Thomas .... 605-394-4800 415 G
BICKEL, Brice .... 864-644-5133 412 D
bdbickel@swu.edu
BICKERTON, Molly .... 912-871-1600 123 J
mbickerton@ogeecheetech.edu
BICKETT, Brian .... 847-970-4861 152 I
bbickett@usml.edu
BICKETT, Larry .... 304-260-4380 488 C
lbickett@blueridgectc.edu
BICKFORD, Deborah, J . 937-229-5360 362 C
dbickford1@udayton.edu
BICKING, Michael .... 610-341-1720 383 B
michael.bicking@eastern.edu
BICKLEY, Craig .... 724-357-4874 394 C
cbickley@iup.edu
BICKNELL, Brian .... 603-206-8002 272 L
bbicknell@ccsnh.edu
BICKNELL, Patricia .... 215-951-1430 387 A
bicknell@lasalle.edu
BICKNELL, Teresa .... 865-531-4108 421 A
teresa.bicknell@lmunet.edu
BICKNELL-HOLMES, Tracy .... 208-426-1234 130 H
tracybicknell-holmes@boisestate.edu
BICKSLER, Leslie .... 304-647-6279 490 C
lbicksler@osteo.wvsom.edu
BIDDINGER, Mark .... 618-664-7100 138 F
mark.biddinger@greenville.edu
BIDDINGS-MURO, Regina .... 805-493-3828.. 29 C
rbiddingsmuro@callutheran.edu
BIDDLE, Chris .... 615-226-3990 420 J
cbiddle@lincolntech.edu
BIDDLE, Elizabeth, A .... 570-326-3761 392 W
ebiddle@pct.edu
BIDLE, Kelly .... 609-895-5418 281 B
kbidle@rider.edu
BIDWELL, Mary .... 860-253-3118.. 86 C
mbidwell@asnuntuck.edu
BIEBER, Ann, D .... 610-799-1581 388 D
abieber@lccc.edu
BIEBER, Harold .... 678-916-2690 115 I
hbieber@johnmarshall.edu
BIEBER, Joshua .... 785-227-3380 172 A
bieberjb@bethanylb.edu
BIEBUYCK, Bill .... 563-588-6405 164 E
bill.biebuyck@clarke.edu
BIECHLER, Laura .... 508-531-1341 212 D
lbiechler@bridgew.edu
BIEDERMANN, Heather . 507-389-7223 241 C
heather.biedermann@southcentral.edu
BIEDERMANN, Scott ..... 209-946-2166.. 71 E
sbiedermann@pacific.edu
BIEDERMANN, Scott ..... 209-946-2011.. 71 E
BIEGEL, Peter .... 561-868-3532 105 D
biegelp@palmbeachstate.edu
BIEGENZAHN, Nathan ... 919-497-3250 330 I
nbiegenzahn@louisburg.edu
BIEGER, RET., Mark ...... 803-777-7000 413 A
mbieger@mailbox.sc.edu
BIEHL, Peter .... 831-459-0111.. 71 A
BIEHN, Christopher, M 585-385-5251 313 F
mbiehn@sjfc.edu
BIEK, David .... 478-757-2544 122 F
david.biek@mga.edu
BIEL, Kirsten .... 317-917-5988 158 D
kbiel@ivytech.edu
BIEL, Michael, J .... 219-989-2510 160 D
bielm@pnw.edu
BIELAT SOLTOW, Keely 585-245-5566 318 B
ksoltow@geneseo.edu
BIELAWSKI, Bill .... 312-329-8047 144 I
bill.bielawski@moody.edu
BIELBY, Steve .... 864-977-0249 410 I
steve.bielby@ngu.edu
BIELFELDT, Dennis .... 605-692-9337 415 B
president@ilt.edu
BIELICKI, Shawn .... 434-582-3035 468 E
smbielicki@liberty.edu
BIELITZ, Colleen, Q ...... 203-392-5459.. 86 A
bielitzc1@southernct.edu
BIELSTEIN, Jennifer ...... 415-439-2366.. 25 E
jbielstein@act-sf.org
BIENVENUE, Joan, M ... 434-243-2233 472 D
jmb7ug@virginia.edu
BIENVENUE, Scott .... 603-578-8900 272 M
sbienvenue@ccsnh.edu
BIENZ, Richard, A .... 260-399-7700 162 B
rbienz@sf.edu
BIER, Debbie .... 412-521-6200 397 C
debbie.bier@rosedaletech.org
BIERBAUER, Charles ..... 803-777-4105 413 A
bierbauer@sc.edu
BIERBAUM, Joseph ...... 203-287-3031.. 88 E
BIERIG, Samuel .... 816-414-3731 256 C
sbierig@mbts.edu
BIERLE, Brad .... 763-544-9501 235 L
BIERLE, Sarah .... 763-544-9501 235 L
sarah.bierle@flbc.edu
BIERMAN, Cindy .... 909-607-3305.. 37 C
cindy.bierman@cgu.edu
BIERMAN, Derek .... 402-826-8333 267 A
derek.bierman@doane.edu
BIERMAN, Luke .... 336-279-9201 328 J
lbierman@elon.edu
BIERMAN, Matt .... 309-556-3021 140 F
mbierman@iwu.edu
BIERMAN, Scott .... 402-557-7245 265 J
scott.bierman@bellevue.edu
BIERMAN, Scott .... 608-363-2201 491 H
biermans@beloit.edu
BIERMANN, Mark, L ..... 217-854-3231 133 I
BIERMANN, Matt .... 989-275-5000 226 D
matt.biermann@kirtland.edu
BIERNBAUM, John .... 309-298-3320 153 A
j-biernbaum@wiu.edu
BIERSCHBACH, Richard 313-577-3933 232 K
rbierschbach@wayne.edu
BIES, Susan .... 605-274-5503 414 G
susan.bies@augie.edu
BIESCHKE, Kathleen ...... 814-863-7494 391 G
kxb11@psu.edu
BIESECKER, James .... 717-337-6700 384 D
jbieseck@gettysburg.edu
BIESTY, Cathy .... 518-243-4471 291 D
biestyc@ellismedicine.org
BIESZKE, Jay .... 608-262-1234 495 D
jay.bieszke@wisc.edu
BIETELCHIES, Wade ...... 517-265-5161 220 G
wbietelchies@adrian.edu
BIG SPRING, Anita ...... 406-275-4974 265 F
anita_bigspring@skc.edu
BIGALK, Roberta .... 970-542-3113.. 81 N
roberta.bigalk@morgancc.edu
BIGARD, Heather .... 352-365-3525 103 U
bigardh@lssc.edu
BIGBEE, Leah, M .... 205-853-1200.... 2 G
leah.bigbee@jeffersonstate.edu
BIGBY, Angela .... 361-570-4121 453 B
bigbya@uhv.edu
BIGDELI JAHED, Fariba 502-597-6604 183 D
fariba.bigdelijahed@kysu.edu
BIGELOW, Shannon ...... 317-632-5553 159 I
sbigelow@lincolntech.edu
BIGG, Dort .... 954-763-9840.. 95 J
executivedirector@atom.edu
BIGGANE, Michael, J .... 716-851-1416 299 B
biggane@ecc.edu
BIGGER, Darold .... 509-527-2389 485 C
darold.bigger@wallawalla.edu
BIGGER, Kimberly .... 870-248-4000.. 18 F
kim.bigger@blackrivertech.edu
BIGGERS, Carla, D .... 409-944-1200 436 E
cbiggers@gc.edu
BIGGERSTAFF, Elizabeth .... 704-233-8368 344 F
erogers@wingate.edu
BIGGIN, Margot .... 617-627-3287 219 C
margot.biggin@tufts.edu
BIGGS, Aaron, A .... 405-325-4861 370 K
abiggs@ou.edu
BIGGS, Jessie, N .... 260-422-5561 156 E
nbiggs@indianatech.edu
BIGGS, Michelle .... 985-549-2150 193 A
michelle.biggs@selu.edu
BIGGS, Patsy .... 501-420-1201.. 16 L
patsy.biggs@arkansasbaptist.edu
BIGGS, Shirley, A .... 803-535-5268 407 D
sbiggs@claflin.edu
BIGGS, Vicki .... 314-505-7266 252 A
biggsv@csl.edu
BIGGS GARBUIO, Judi . 202-319-5619.. 92 A
judibg@cua.edu
BIGHAM, Bill .... 937-775-2350 364 E
bill.bigham@wright.edu
BIGHAM-STEPHENS, Dana .... 850-729-6469 104 M
stephed@nwfsc.edu
BIGONGIARI, Anthony .. 817-599-6320 457 J
abigongiari@wc.edu
BIGWOOD, Christine .... 401-232-6348 404 A
cbigwood@bryant.edu
BILACH, Bernadett .... 480-994-9244.. 15 R
bernadettb@swiha.edu
BILAL, Waheedah .... 573-681-5505 254 G
bilald@lincolnu.edu
BILBRUCK, Tom .... 661-362-3235.. 38 D
tom.bilbruck@canyons.edu
BILEN-GREEN, Canan .... 701-231-7040 345 F
canan.bilen.green@ndsu.edu
BILES, Brad .... 816-584-6888 258 C
brad.biles@park.edu
BILGER, Audrey .... 503-777-7500 375 G
abilger@reed.edu
BILGER, Bonnie .... 760-366-5285.. 40 E
bbilger@cmccd.edu
BILGER, Cindy, L .... 570-577-1631 379 C
cbilger@bucknell.edu
BILKER, Mitch .... 215-248-7084 381 A
bilkerm@chc.edu
BILL, Rhonda .... 281-484-1900 443 C
BILL, Tim .... 309-268-8129 138 H
tim.bill@heartland.edu
BILLEAUDEAU, Kim, A .. 337-262-5300 193 B
kimberlyb@louisiana.edu
BILLECI, Celesta .... 805-893-3437.. 70 E
celesta.billeci@sa.ucsb.edu
BILLEN, Isabelle .... 405-733-7580 369 E
ibillen@rose.edu
BILLET, Bill .... 805-969-3626.. 55 J
bbillet@pacifica.edu
BILLETTA, Michael .... 610-718-1844 390 C
mbilletta@mc3.edu
BILLEY, Raeann .... 610-527-0200 397 D
raeann.billey@rosemont.edu
BILLEY, Terry .... 580-928-5533 370 A
terry.billey@swosu.edu
BILLHARTZ, Scott, L ..... 618-537-6869 144 A
slbillhartz@mckendree.edu
BILLIE, Marie .... 650-574-6161.. 62 K
BILLINGS, Amanda .... 214-648-2344 457 A
amanda.billings@utsouthwestern.edu
BILLINGS, James .... 866-776-0331.. 54 D
jbillings@ncu.edu
BILLINGS, Lora .... 973-655-5108 279 B
billingsl@montclair.edu
BILLINGS, Maria .... 201-216-9901 277 B
maria.billings@eicollege.edu
BILLINGS, Mindi .... 866-294-3974 154 H
BILLINGS, Molly .... 402-280-4722 266 H
mollybillings@creighton.edu
BILLINGS, Patricia .... 413-552-2248 214 F
pbillings@hcc.edu
BILLINGS, Stephanie, L 828-262-2366 340 I
billingssl@appstate.edu
BILLINGS-BERG, Sarah . 802-728-1586 464 A
sberg@vtc.edu
BILLINGSLEY, Anna, B .. 540-654-1686 471 N
abilling@umw.edu
BILLINGSLEY, Jennifer .. 217-234-5253 142 C
jbillingsley@lakelandcollege.edu
BILLINGSLEY, Jodie .... 806-742-2020 450 F
jodie.billingsley@ttu.edu
BILLINGSLEY, Joel .... 251-460-6697.... 9 A
lewis@southalabama.edu
BILLINGSLEY, Linda ...... 318-487-7630 187 E
linda.billingsley@lacollege.edu
BILLINGSLEY, Mark ...... 901-321-3278 418 G
mark.billingsley@cbu.edu
BILLINGSLEY, Sarah ..... 916-278-7737.. 32 D
BILLINGSLEY, Scott ...... 910-521-6224 343 B
scott.billingsley@uncp.edu
BILLINGTON, Dave .... 517-607-2451 225 C
dbillington@hillsdale.edu
BILLITIER, Rick .... 585-594-7777 312 E
billitier_rick@roberts.edu
BILLMAN, Carol .... 724-838-4204 398 C
billman@setonhill.edu
BILLMAN, Tyler .... 618-252-5400 149 I
tyler.billman@sic.edu
BILLOCK, Gary .... 303-722-5724.. 81 L
gbillock@lincolntech.edu
BILLS, Andy .... 336-841-4538 329 F
abills@highpoint.edu
BILLS, Kimberly .... 253-589-5846 478 J
kimberly.bills@cptc.edu
BILLS, Marsha .... 563-387-1042 168 B
billma02@luther.edu
BILLS, Matt .... 262-646-6513 494 F
mbills@nashotah.edu
BILLS-WINDT, Caryn, A 312-413-8145 151 G
cabw@uic.edu
BILLUPS, Kyle .... 408-848-4901.. 43 E
kbillups@gavilan.edu
BILLY, Amanda .... 904-256-7161 102 H
abilly1@ju.edu
BILLY, Cameron .... 406-395-4875 265 G
cbilly@stonechild.edu
BILODEAU, Leta .... 207-859-1201 196 D
bilodeaul@thomas.edu
BILODEAU, Timothy ...... 802-316-0078 463 A
timothy.bilodeau@uvm.edu
BILOKONSKY, George ... 740-374-8716 363 F
gbilokonsky@wscc.edu
BILOTTA, Barbara, J ..... 716-880-2265 305 G
barbara.bilotta@medaille.edu
BILSKY, Edward .... 509-452-5100 482 B
ebilsky@pnwu.edu
BILYEU, Bethany .... 217-206-7122 152 A
bilyeu.bethany@uis.edu
BIMER, Tammy, C .... 734-763-9954 231 H
tammyc@umich.edu
BIMONTE, Maria .... 561-237-7173 103 W
mbimonte@lynn.edu
BINARD, Kris .... 309-694-5323 139 B
kris.binard@icc.edu
BINDER, Kirsten .... 417-447-2651 257 G
binderk@otc.edu
BINDER, Maureen .... 407-823-2771 110 E
maureen.binder@ucf.edu
BINDER, Ron .... 319-399-8204 164 F
rbinder@coe.edu
BINESH, Behzad .... 714-744-7099.. 36 B
binesh@chapman.edu
BINFORD, Sarah .... 620-450-2112 177 B
sarahb@prattcc.edu
BING, Andrea .... 415-565-4733.. 69 C
wellesan@uchastings.edu
BING, Sarah .... 870-743-3000.. 20 B
sbing@northark.edu
BINGAMON, Cindy .... 314-837-6777 258 K
cbingamon@stlchristian.edu
BINGEMAN, Jeff .... 717-396-7833 392 U
jbingeman@pcad.edu
BINGHAM, Charlotte ..... 806-742-3627 451 A
charlotte.bingham@ttu.edu
BINGHAM, Charlotte ..... 806-742-3627 450 F
charlotte.bingham@ttu.edu
BINGHAM, Jeffrey .... 817-921-8613 445 A
jbingham@swbts.edu
BINGHAM, Tom .... 808-956-7166 129 E
bingham@hawaii.edu
BINGHAM, Vicki, L .... 662-846-4268 245 G
vbingham@deltastate.edu
BINK, Cynthia .... 718-260-5030 295 A
cbink@citytech.cuny.edu
BINKERD, James .... 707-638-5935.. 68 B
james.binkerd@tu.edu
BINKLEY, Bonnie .... 276-944-6921 466 L
bbinkley@ehc.edu
BINNEY, Craig .... 508-565-1107 219 A
cbinney@stonehill.edu
BINNEY, Diane, M .... 626-395-6651.. 28 J
dbinney@caltech.edu
BINNICKER, Paul .... 816-423-4710 166 E
binnicke@graceland.edu
BINSFELD, Doug .... 563-425-5284 170 H
binsfeldd08@uiu.edu
BINSTOCK, Jonathan ..... 585-276-8902 323 M
jbinstock@mag.rochester.edu
BINUYA, Catherine .... 404-527-5732 121 L
cbinuya@itc.edu
BIONDO, Drew .... 631-451-4776 321 C
biondodr@sunysuffolk.edu

BIRCH, Andrea, C .... 770-718-5325 116 D
abirch@brenau.edu
BIRCH, Jenna .... 610-436-2813 395 D
jbirch@wcupa.edu
BIRCH, Laura, A .... 217-420-6661 144 G
lbirch@millikin.edu
BIRCH, Sara .... 269-467-9945 224 C
sbirch@glenoaks.edu
BIRCHARD, Michael ...... 651-290-6416 242 L
michael.birchard@mitchellhamline.edu
BIRCHFIELD, Todd .... 678-466-4377 117 D
toddbirchfield@clayton.edu
BIRCHWOOD, Rachel .... 845-451-1459 297 G
rachel.birchwood@culinary.edu
BIRCHWOOD, Rachel .... 845-452-9600 297 G
rachel.birchwood@culinary.edu
BIRCK, Ken .... 513-231-2223 348 B
kwbirck@athenaeum.edu
BIRCKBICHLER,
Carrie, J .... 724-738-2150 395 C
carrie.birckbichler@sru.edu
BIRD, Barb .... 765-998-4571 161 C
brbird@taylor.edu
BIRD, Brandon .... 206-315-5024 479 E
bbird@cornish.edu
BIRD, Brian .... 608-342-7584 496 E
birdbr@uwplatt.edu
BIRD, Christopher .... 740-264-5591 352 B
cbird@egcc.edu
BIRD, David .... 785-242-5200 176 I
david.bird@ottawa.edu
BIRD, Jamie .... 909-370-4800.. 29 F
BIRD, Janelle .... 707-468-3012.. 51 F
jbird@mendocino.edu
BIRD, Jennifer .... 304-769-0011 491 A
jbird@wvjc.edu
BIRD, Jill .... 315-279-5726 303 G
jbird1@keuka.edu
BIRD, Karla .... 406-338-5441 263 A
BIRD, Lee, E .... 405-744-5328 367 G
lee.bird@okstate.edu
BIRD, Su Ann .... 229-931-2110 125 E
sbird@southgatech.edu
BIRD, Veronica, A .... 610-917-1422 401 G
rabird@valleyforge.edu
BIRDSELL, Rebecca .... 217-245-3035 139 C
becky.birdsell@ic.edu
BIRDSONG, Jeff .... 918-540-6348 366 F
jbirdsong@neo.edu
BIRDWELL, Cindy, A .... 517-264-7194 230 H
cbirdwell@sienaheights.edu
BIRDWELL, Kim .... 940-521-0720 440 F
kbirdwell@nctc.edu
BIRELINE, David .... 740-474-8896 358 A
dbireline@ohiochristian.edu
BIRENBAUM, Hylah ...... 828-627-4544 335 C
BIRGE, James .... 413-662-5201 213 C
james.birge@mcla.edu
BIRGE, Susan, N .... 203-254-4000.. 87 I
sbirge@fairfield.edu
BIRINGER, Bobbi .... 309-672-5513 144 C
bbiringer@methodistcol.edu
BIRKAM, Sally .... 231-773-9131 228 G
BIRKEL, Michelle .... 402-323-3411 269 C
mbirkel@southeast.edu
BIRKES, R. Dennis .... 724-287-8711 379 E
dennis.birkes@bc3.edu
BIRKLAND, Amy .... 320-222-5977 240 F
BIRKNER, Linda .... 479-968-0300.. 18 C
lbirkner@atu.edu
BIRKNER, Linda .... 479-964-0543.. 18 C
lbirkner@atu.edu
BIRMAN, Julio .... 410-334-2966 205 D
jbirman@worwic.edu
BIRNBAUM, Jeremiah ... 415-824-7000.. 61 E
BIRNEY, Vanessa .... 740-264-5591 352 B
vbirney@egcc.edu
BIRNIE, Christine, R ..... 585-385-7202 313 F
cbirnie@sjfc.edu
BIRON, Louise .... 518-255-5623 319 C
bironl@cobleskill.edu
BIROS, Demetra .... 425-739-8315 481 C
demetra.biros@lwtech.edu
BIRSCHBACH,
Bianca, Y .... 920-923-7619 493 D
bybirschbach76@marianuniversity.edu
BIRTLEY, Ariel .... 360-475-7814 481 I
abirtley@olympic.edu
BIRX, Donald, L .... 603-535-2210 275 A
dlbirx@plymouth.edu
BISANTZ, Ann, M .... 716-645-8989 316 C
bisantz@buffalo.edu
BISBEE, Karin .... 717-796-5220 389 H
kbisbee@messiah.edu
BISBEE, Nina .... 610-526-7935 379 B
nbisbee@brynmawr.edu
BISBEE, Yolanda .... 208-885-2468 132 F
yobiz@uidaho.edu
BISCEGLIE, Kara .... 504-280-6990 190 B
kmbisceg@uno.edu
BISCHOFF, Richard, W . 216-368-5445 349 D
richard.bischoff@case.edu
BISCHOFF, Scott .... 831-656-1998 502 M
scott.bischoff@nps.edu
BISCOE, Belinda, P .... 405-325-0473 370 K
bpbiscoe@ou.edu
BISESE, Stephen, D ...... 804-289-8615 472 C
sbisese@richmond.edu
BISH, Courtney, D .... 315-386-7120 320 B
bish@canton.edu
BISH, Dennis .... 724-589-2186 399 D
dbish@thiel.edu
BISH, Gregory .... 585-567-9524 302 B
greg.bish@houghton.edu
BISH, Kevin .... 859-858-2272 179 C
BISHKO, David .... 907-474-7700.. 10 A
dbishko@alaska.edu
BISHKO, David .... 907-796-6100.. 10 B
ua-hr@alaska.edu
BISHKO, David .... 907-450-8200.... 9 I
dbishko@alaska.edu
BISHOP, Ben .... 208-376-7731 130 G
bbishop@boisebible.edu
BISHOP, Brad .... 540-365-4250 467 B
bradbishop@ferrum.edu
BISHOP, Brandan .... 616-222-1954 223 C
brandan.bishop@cornerstone.edu
BISHOP, Carl .... 704-290-5281 337 I
cbishop@spcc.edu
BISHOP, Carol, M .... 607-746-4582 320 D
bishopcm@delhi.edu
BISHOP, Catherine .... 612-330-1117 234 A
bishopc@augsburg.edu
BISHOP, Chad .... 406-243-5521 263 K
chad.bishop@umontana.edu
BISHOP, Chanel .... 773-907-4724 135 C
cbishop13@ccc.edu
BISHOP, Colleen .... 804-828-9914 473 B
cbishop4@vcu.edu
BISHOP, David .... 806-291-3417 457 I
bishopd@wbu.edu
BISHOP, Donald, C ...... 574-631-7505 162 A
dbishop1@nd.edu
BISHOP, Eric .... 510-659-6200.. 54 J
ebishop@ohlone.edu
BISHOP, Janet .... 909-621-8026.. 37 B
janet.bishop@claremont.edu
BISHOP, Janet .... 909-621-8924.. 37 C
janetbishop@claremont.edu
BISHOP, Jeff .... 770-720-5966 124 G
wjb@reinhardt.edu
BISHOP, Jesse .... 706-368-7776 119 D
jebishop@highlands.edu
BISHOP, Joseph .... 616-554-5687 223 E
joseph.bishop@davenport.edu
BISHOP, Kara .... 570-941-7400 401 F
kara.bishop@scranton.edu
BISHOP, Kaylee .... 405-789-7661 369 I
kaylee.bishop@swcu.edu
BISHOP, Kelley .... 301-314-7236 202 H
kbishop1@umd.edu
BISHOP, Kim .... 641-782-1413 170 F
kbishop@swcciowa.edu
BISHOP, Kristy .... 724-925-4212 402 F
bishopkr@westmoreland.edu
BISHOP, Laura .... 561-803-2012 105 C
laura_bishop@pba.edu
BISHOP, Mary Kay .... 585-389-2012 307 F
mbishop2@naz.edu
BISHOP, Melanie .... 314-392-2323 256 E
melanie.bishop@mobap.edu
BISHOP, Mike .... 951-552-8759.. 27 G
mbishop@calbaptist.edu
BISHOP, Nancy .... 803-778-6638 406 I
bishopnw@cctech.edu
BISHOP, Penny .... 207-581-1865 196 G
BISHOP, Rebekah .... 931-221-1277 417 H
bishopr@apsu.edu
BISHOP, Richard .... 209-476-7840.. 67 E
rbishop@clc.edu
BISHOP, Robert, H .... 813-974-3864 111 C
robertbishop@usf.edu
BISHOP, Sandy .... 715-365-4564 499 E
sbishop@nicoletcollege.edu
BISHOP, Sasha .... 843-470-8396 412 G
sbishop@tcl.edu
BISHOP, Steve .... 601-276-3701 249 B
bishop@smcc.edu
BISHOP, Valerie .... 601-484-8642 247 A
vbishop@meridiancc.edu
BISHOP, William .... 916-278-7469.. 32 D
william.bishop@csus.edu
BISHOP -SAMUELS,
Kellei .... 334-724-4777.... 7 D
ksamuels@tuskegee.edu
BISHOP BENTLEY,
Ember .... 478-471-2700 122 F
BISHOP-CLARK,
Catherine, U .... 513-529-6721 356 A
bishopcu@miamioh.edu
BISIGNANO, Chris .... 914-251-6530 319 B
chris.bisignanoi@purchase.edu
BISKUPIAK, Walter, H .. 406-447-5521 263 B
dbiskupi@carroll.edu
BISPING, Timothy .... 936-468-3101 445 E
bispingto@sfasu.edu
BISSELL, Monika .... 207-795-2846 195 B
bisselmo@mchp.edu
BISSELL, Sally .... 419-783-2366 351 K
sbissell@defiance.edu
BISSEN, Randi .... 712-325-3428 167 I
rbissen@iwcc.edu
BISSET, Matthew, S ...... 727-864-8482.. 98 J
bissetms@eckerd.edu
BISSET, William .... 703-284-1646 468 H
william.bisset@marymount.edu
BISSINGER, Mary .... 805-482-2755.. 59 G
mbissinger@stjohnsem.edu
BISSONETTE, David .... 218-855-8178 237 G
david.bissonette@clcmn.edu
BISSONETTE, Matt .... 507-280-3152 240 H
matt.bissonette@rctc.edu
BISSONNETTE, Ali .... 530-541-4660.. 47 E
BISSONNETTE, Mignon . 954-262-7239 105 A
mbissonnet@nova.edu
BISSOONDIAL, Laxmi ... 508-929-8543 213 G
lbissoondial@worcester.edu
BISWAS, Harun .... 678-466-4240 117 D
harunbiswas@clayton.edu
BITNER, Scott .... 410-706-3822 203 A
sbitner@umaryland.edu
BITNER, Teddy .... 816-322-0110 251 B
teddy.bitner@calvary.edu
BITSOI, LeManuel .... 970-247-7222.. 80 J
lbitsoi@fortlewis.edu
BITTEL, Jill .... 412-809-5250 396 E
bittel.jill@ptcollege.edu
BITTER, Marlo .... 903-675-6327 451 F
marlo.bitter@tvcc.edu
BITTER, Michael .... 808-932-7095 129 D
bitter@hawaii.edu
BITTERBAUM, Erik, J .... 607-753-2201 318 A
erik.bitterbaum@cortland.edu
BITTERMAN, Kevin .... 336-770-1442 343 D
bittermank@uncsa.edu
BITTINGER, Dale .... 410-455-2278 203 B
bittinger@umbc.edu
BITTINGER, Sara Beth .. 301-687-3130 204 C
sbittinger@frostburg.edu
BITTLE, Tyler .... 501-882-8960.. 17 D
tdbittle@asub.edu
BITTNER, Lauren .... 605-626-2550 416 G
lauren.bittner@northern.edu
BITTON, Yoram .... 513-824-2261 301 B
ybitton@huc.edu
BITTORF, David, C .... 240-500-2266 199 C
dcbittorf@hagerstowncc.edu
BITZER, Michelle .... 715-682-1484 494 G
mbitzer@northland.edu
BITZER, Steve .... 715-685-3034 499 H
steve.bitzer@northwoodtech.edu
BIUNDO, Rachel .... 804-594-1479 474 B
rbiundo@jtcc.edu
BIVINS, B. Peyton .... 806-371-5324 429 E
bpbivins@actx.edu
BIVINS, Chip .... 205-348-9449.... 7 F
cbivins@uasystem.edu
BIVINS, Christy .... 706-754-7772 123 G
cbivins@northgatech.edu
BIVINS, Dallas .... 480-941-1993.. 43 D
dallasbivins@gs.edu
BIXBY, David, E .... 626-815-5334.. 26 F
dbixby@apu.edu
BIXBY, Gary .... 610-436-3200 395 D
gbixby@wcupa.edu
BIXEL, Patricia .... 207-941-7104 194 F
bixelp@husson.edu
BIXLER, Kirk, J .... 317-738-8803 155 D
kbixler@franklincollege.edu
BIXLER, Luke .... 909-388-6900.. 60 D
BIXLER, Sharon, G .... 859-858-3511 179 D
sharon.bixler@asbury.edu
BIZOT, Kenny .... 601-925-3819 247 C
kbizot@mc.edu
BIZOUKAS, Tim .... 630-466-7900 152 K
tbizoukas@waubonsee.edu
BIZZARRO, Deana .... 518-458-5373 296 G
bizzarrd@strose.edu
BJELLA, Traci, A .... 407-582-1016 113 I
tthornton12@valenciacollege.edu
BJELLAND, David .... 320-762-4407 237 C
davidb@alextech.edu
BJERKE, Abby .... 608-663-2309 492 F
abjerke@edgewood.edu
BJERKLIE, J. R .... 607-431-4997 301 A
bjerkliej@hartwick.edu
BJERKLIE, Joseph .... 607-431-4997 301 A
bjerkliej@hartwick.edu
BJERKLIE-BARRY, Jane . 603-641-7371 274 A
jberkliebarry@anselm.edu
BJOKNE, Daniel, H .... 515-964-0601 166 D
bjokned@faith.edu
BJORDAHL, Julia .... 509-313-6102 480 F
bjordahl@gonzaga.edu
BJORGAN, Heather .... 309-796-5340 133 G
bjorganh@bhc.edu
BJORK, Johanna .... 208-792-2395 132 A
jcbjork@lcsc.edu
BJORK, Ross .... 979-845-5129 446 F
feedback@athletics.tamu.edu
BJORKLUND, Robert, B 651-638-6396 234 D
robert-bjorklund@bethel.edu
BJORKLUND, Tarah ...... 651-846-1415 241 B
tarah.bjorklund@saintpaul.edu
BJORKMAN, Karen .... 419-530-2729 363 B
karen.bjorkman@utoledo.edu
BJORN, Thorr, D .... 401-874-5245 405 E
tbjorn@uri.edu
BJORNSEN, Lee .... 740-392-6868 356 G
lee.bjornsen@mvnu.edu
BJORNSTAD,
Christopher, S .... 770-394-8300 115 C
BJORNSTAD, Thomas ... 414-229-3298 496 B
bjornsta@uwm.edu
BJUNE, Stephanie .... 979-458-6000 446 B
sbjune@tamus.edu
BLACHE, Corinne .... 225-771-4680 191 B
corinne_blache@sus.edu
BLACHE, Corinne .... 225-771-4680 191 A
corinne_blache@sus.edu
BLACHFORD, Charles ... 215-368-5000 390 A
cblachford@missio.edu
BLACK, Adam .... 801-863-6378 460 D
blackad@uvu.edu
BLACK, Adrian .... 410-617-2000 200 B
abblack@loyola.edu
BLACK, Andrew .... 808-956-8310 129 E
ablack22@hawaii.edu
BLACK, Ann .... 505-428-1811 288 E
ann.black@sfcc.edu
BLACK, April .... 405-789-7661 369 I
april.black@swcu.edu
BLACK, Bernadette .... 619-644-7100.. 44 E
bernadette.black@gcccd.edu
BLACK, Carrie .... 813-988-5131.. 99 R
blackc@floridacollege.edu
BLACK, Chantel .... 509-533-7067 479 C
chantel.black@scc.spokane.edu
BLACK, Charles .... 218-322-2451 238 F
charles.black@itascacc.edu
BLACK, Connie .... 208-562-3252 131 E
connieblack@cwi.edu
BLACK, David, R .... 920-565-1101 493 A
blackdr@lakeland.edu
BLACK, Diane .... 251-442-2209.... 8 C
dblack@umobile.edu
BLACK, Downey .... 318-345-9297 188 D
harryblack@ladelta.edu
BLACK, Ellen .... 843-349-5211 409 J
ellen.black@hgtc.edu
BLACK, Eric .... 540-828-5487 464 L
eblack@bridgewater.edu
BLACK, Erynn .... 803-508-7337 406 C
blacke@atc.edu
BLACK, Gary .... 440-826-2900 348 D
gblack@bw.edu
BLACK, Heather .... 412-365-2776 380 G
hblack@chatham.edu
BLACK, Janet, M .... 303-963-3357.. 78 H
jblack@ccu.edu

BLACK, Jared .... 602-489-5300.. 10 F jared.black@arizonachristian.edu
BLACK, Jason .... 205-726-3673.... 6 E jjblack@samford.edu
BLACK, Jeffrey, S .... 215-702-4347 380 A jblack@cairn.edu
BLACK, Jeremy .... 864-424-8081 413 H jdblack@mailbox.sc.edu
BLACK, Jessica .... 205-726-2487.... 6 E jblack@samford.edu
BLACK, Joann .... 936-468-2201 445 E blackjoann@sfasu.edu
BLACK, John .... 248-689-8282 232 C jblack@walshcollege.edu
BLACK, John Paul .... 252-527-6223 335 G jpblack73@lenoircc.edu
BLACK, Joshua .... 864-941-8542 411 C black.j@ptc.edu
BLACK, Joshua .... 423-614-8370 420 H jblack@leeuniversity.edu
BLACK, Karnell .... 801-832-2231 461 F kblack@westminstercollege.edu
BLACK, Katherine .... 860-768-4103.. 89 G kablack@hartford.edu
BLACK, Kedric .... 801-863-8536 460 D kedric.black@uvu.edu
BLACK, Kevin .... 717-531-4803 391 G kpb4@psu.edu
BLACK, Kim .... 970-351-1102.. 84 F kim.black@unco.edu
BLACK, Laura .... 505-566-3837 288 D blackl@sanjuancollege.edu
BLACK, Lendley, C .... 218-726-7106 243 G chan@d.umn.edu
BLACK, Linda .... 970-351-1638.. 84 F linda.black@unco.edu
BLACK, Linda .... 207-288-5015 194 E
BLACK, Lynda, K .... 336-838-6148 339 B lkblack932@wilkescc.edu
BLACK, Mary .... 217-424-6220 144 G mblack@millikin.edu
BLACK, Matthew .... 606-337-3196 180 C
BLACK, Michael, M .... 229-245-6517 127 E mmblack@valdosta.edu
BLACK, Richard .... 915-215-4320 451 B richard.black@ttuhsc.edu
BLACK, Rochelle, A .... 248-370-3658 229 I black@oakland.edu
BLACK, Sara .... 864-977-2094 410 I sara.black@ngu.edu
BLACK, Shaun, C .... 315-445-4569 303 I blacksc@lemoyne.edu
BLACK, Sul .... 803-934-3419 410 G sulblack@morris.edu
BLACK, Susan .... 903-983-8236 438 F sblack@kilgore.edu
BLACK, Tanja .... 864-424-8080 413 H trblack@mailbox.sc.edu
BLACK, Tyrone .... 860-913-2043.. 88 A
BLACK HUDGINS, Carri 386-506-3000.. 98 D
BLACK-PATEL, Jennifer . 706-419-1136 118 A jennifer.blackpatel@covenant.edu
BLACKABY, Leslie .... 509-574-6806 486 D lblackaby@yvcc.edu
BLACKABY, Robert .... 423-478-7723 422 J rblackaby@ptseminary.edu
BLACKBURN, Amanda .. 404-835-6114 423 B ablackburn@richmont.edu
BLACKBURN, Amber .... 336-838-6419 339 B alblackburn893@wilkescc.edu
BLACKBURN, Brenda .... 828-694-1773 332 E bc_blackburn@blueridge.edu
BLACKBURN, Brian .... 919-658-7889 340 G bblackburn@umo.edu
BLACKBURN, Fred .... 619-201-8780.. 60 G fred.blackburn@sdcc.edu
BLACKBURN, J. Blair .... 903-923-2222 435 H bblackburn@etbu.edu
BLACKBURN, Jan .... 706-437-6811 115 J jan.blackburn@augustatech.edu
BLACKBURN, Jessamine .... 217-786-3441 143 B jessie.blackburn@llcc.edu
BLACKBURN, JR .... 614-292-2424 358 D blackburn.23@osu.edu
BLACKBURN, Kellye .... 318-274-3350 192 C blackburnk@gram.edu
BLACKBURN, Kristi .... 323-241-5218.. 49 E blackbkv@lasc.edu
BLACKBURN, Lisa .... 606-218-5296 186 B lisablackburn@upike.edu
BLACKBURN, Mark .... 605-274-4124 414 G mark.blackburn@augie.edu
BLACKBURN, Michael ... 713-500-6087 456 B michael.r.blackburn@uth.tmc.edu
BLACKBURN, Michael, R .... 713-500-3019 456 B michael.r.blackburn@uth.tmc.edu
BLACKBURN, Sean .... 605-626-3007 416 G sean.blackburn@northern.edu
BLACKBURN-SMITH, Jefferson .... 614-823-1031 359 H jblackburnsmith@otterbein.edu
BLACKETER, Leslie .... 409-772-1304 456 E lmblacke@utmb.edu
BLACKFORD, Ben .... 660-562-1282 257 E blkfrd@nwmissouri.edu
BLACKFORD, Devin, K .. 260-422-5561 156 E dkblackford@indianatech.edu
BLACKHURST, Anne .... 218-477-2243 239 E anne.blackhurst@mnstate.edu
BLACKIE, Crisanne .... 207-581-1359 196 G cblackie@maine.edu
BLACKLANCE, Charles .. 218-855-8119 237 G charles.blacklance@clcmn.edu
BLACKLAW, Stuart .... 412-237-8182 381 D sblacklaw@ccac.edu
BLACKMAN, Bret .... 402-554-2227 270 A bblackman@unomaha.edu
BLACKMAN, Bret, R .... 402-554-2227 269 H bblackman@nebraska.edu
BLACKMAN, Cheryl, H .. 301-860-3257 204 A cblackman@bowiestate.edu
BLACKMER, Jennifer ..... 765-285-2783 153 H jsblackmer@bsu.edu
BLACKMON, Bruce .... 704-687-7010 342 D ablackm8@uncc.edu
BLACKMON, Chianti ..... 301-846-2531 198 I cblackmon@frederick.edu
BLACKMON, Jamie .... 256-352-8461.... 3 I jamie.blackmon@wallacestate.edu
BLACKMON, Luke .... 843-863-8004 407 B lblackmon@csuniv.edu
BLACKMON, Paul .... 334-420-4461.... 3 H pblackmon@trenholmstate.edu
BLACKMON, Terry, W ... 731-426-7601 420 G tblackmon@lanecollege.edu
BLACKMORE, Lee .... 307-754-6067 501 H lee.blackmore@nwc.edu
BLACKSHER DIABATE, Dafina .... 484-365-7785 388 H ddiabate@lincoln.edu
BLACKSMITH, Lourdes .. 847-214-7273 137 F lblacksmith@elgin.edu
BLACKSON, Ginny .... 503-883-2517 373 F gblackson@linfield.edu
BLACKSTON, Misty .... 912-650-6233 125 F mblackston@southuniversity.edu
BLACKSTONE, Barbara .. 207-768-9415 197 C barbara.blackstone@maine.edu
BLACKWELDER, Mark, A .... 731-989-6624 419 K mblackwelder@fhu.edu
BLACKWELDER, Megan . 847-467-1730 146 E megan.blackwelder@northwestern.edu
BLACKWELL, Amy .... 864-294-3496 409 H amy.blackwell@furman.edu
BLACKWELL, Barbara .... 314-275-3521 147 E barbara.blackwell@principia.edu
BLACKWELL, Deborah, L .... 956-326-2628 446 E dblackwell@tamiu.edu
BLACKWELL, Jody .... 405-912-9463 368 J jblackwell@ru.edu
BLACKWELL, Jody, B .... 336-322-2185 336 G jody.blackwell@piedmontcc.edu
BLACKWELL, Joe .... 405-789-7661 369 I joe.blackwell@swcu.edu
BLACKWELL, Joshua .... 763-488-0236 240 A joshua.blackwell@nhcc.edu
BLACKWELL, Rachelle ... 817-257-5920 448 F r.blackwell@tcu.edu
BLACKWELL, Tiffiny .... 864-646-1492 412 H tblackw7@tctc.edu
BLACKWOOD, David ..... 575-392-6561 289 F
BLACKWOOD, Edwin .... 412-731-6000 397 A eblackwood@rpts.edu
BLACKWOOD, Houston . 256-306-2664.... 1 F houston.blackwood@calhoun.edu
BLACKWOOD, James .... 706-880-8050 122 A jblackwood@lagrange.edu
BLACKWOOD, Jeremy .. 414-425-8300 495 A jblackwood@shsst.edu
BLAD, Cory .... 718-862-7345 304 M cory.blad@manhattan.edu
BLADE, Michael .... 541-463-5566 373 D bladem@lanecc.edu
BLAETTNER, Wendy .... 830-792-7212 443 E careerdevelopment@schreiner.edu
BLAGUSZEWSKI, Edward, F .... 413-545-0444 211 G edblag@admin.umass.edu
BLAHNIK, Brent .... 920-465-2190 495 F blahnikb@uwgb.edu
BLAHNIK, Hannah, K .... 651-628-3332 244 D hkblahnik@unwsp.edu
BLAHNIK, Jeffrey, J .... 405-325-2151 370 K jblahnik@ou.edu
BLAICH, Charles, F .... 765-361-6311 163 B blaichc@wabash.edu
BLAIN, Judy .... 931-221-7691 417 H blainj@apsu.edu
BLAIR, Alan .... 413-572-5582 213 F alan@westfield.ma.edu
BLAIR, Anissa .... 404-627-2681 116 C anissa.blair@beulah.edu
BLAIR, Anthony, L .... 717-866-5775 383 F ablair@evangelical.edu
BLAIR, Audrey, D .... 563-333-6364 169 G blairaudreyd@sau.edu
BLAIR, Austin .... 309-624-8980 149 B
BLAIR, Brian .... 202-885-2842.. 91 F bblair@american.edu
BLAIR, Brian .... 267-502-2407 379 A brian.blair@brynathyn.edu
BLAIR, Caroline .... 616-234-4164 224 F carolineblair@grcc.edu
BLAIR, Chastity .... 901-321-3552 418 G cblair3@cbu.edu
BLAIR, Cinnamon .... 505-277-1806 288 J cblair@unm.edu
BLAIR, Daniel .... 978-556-3820 215 E dblair@necc.mass.edu
BLAIR, Darren .... 815-939-5265 147 A dblair1@olivet.edu
BLAIR, Douglas .... 574-239-8380 156 A dblair@hcc-nd.edu
BLAIR, Eric .... 816-415-5217 262 F blaire@william.jewell.edu
BLAIR, Jeff .... 614-251-4735 358 B blairj@ohiodominican.edu
BLAIR, Jesse .... 307-778-1340 501 E jblair@lccc.wy.edu
BLAIR, Jim .... 925-969-2025.. 40 C jblair@dvc.edu
BLAIR, John Paul .... 270-745-6520 186 C jp.blair@wku.edu
BLAIR, Julie .... 713-646-1793 443 I jblair@stcl.edu
BLAIR, Kathryn .... 207-453-5000 195 F kblair@kvcc.me.edu
BLAIR, Kristine .... 412-396-6388 383 A blairk2@duq.edu
BLAIR, Matthew .... 605-225-1634 415 I matthew.blair@presentation.edu
BLAIR, Neil, B .... 913-253-5090 177 D neil.blair@spst.edu
BLAIR, Patti .... 805-652-5502.. 73 I pblair@vcccd.edu
BLAIR, Paul, G .... 574-372-5100 155 F blairp@grace.edu
BLAIR, Robbie, M .... 806-716-2336 443 G rblair@southplainscollege.edu
BLAIR, Sara, B .... 734-764-9290 231 H sbblair@umich.edu
BLAIR, Scott .... 610-282-1100 382 C scott.blair@desales.edu
BLAIR, Selena .... 864-488-4394 410 B ssblair@limestone.edu
BLAIR, Selena, S .... 864-488-4394 410 B ssblair@limestone.edu
BLAIR, Shelly .... 714-241-6251.. 37 J sblair12@coastline.edu
BLAIR, Thomas, A .... 770-216-2960 121 I tab@ict.edu
BLAIR, JR., Thomas, S 540-375-2235 470 E blair@roanoke.edu
BLAIR, Wray .... 419-289-5118 347 J wblair@ashland.edu
BLAIR, Zulema .... 718-270-6127 294 G zblair@mec.cuny.edu
BLAISDELL, John .... 845-575-3000 305 D john.blaisdell@marist.edu
BLAISDELL, Stephanie .. 845-257-3260 316 E blaisdes@newpaltz.edu
BLAISE, Butterfly, L .... 518-564-3002 318 E bblai001@plattsburgh.edu
BLAKE, Charles, E .... 901-322-0120 417 E
BLAKE, Christopher .... 478-471-2712 122 F christopher.blake@mga.edu
BLAKE, Christopher, T .. 631-451-4283 321 D blakec@sunysuffolk.edu
BLAKE, Corey .... 251-626-3303.... 7 E cblake@ussa.edu
BLAKE, Dave .... 619-239-0391.. 34 G dblake@cwsl.edu
BLAKE, David .... 912-525-5000 124 I dblake@scad.edu
BLAKE, Donnesha .... 989-463-7463 221 B blakeda@alma.edu
BLAKE, Ira, K .... 281-283-2004 452 E president@uhcl.edu
BLAKE, Karen .... 203-575-8269.. 87 B kblake@nv.edu
BLAKE, Keiana .... 713-718-5059 437 C keiana.blake@hccs.edu
BLAKE, Lawrence .... 651-962-6561 244 E blak0035@stthomas.edu
BLAKE, Lindsey .... 970-675-3275.. 79 H lindsey.blake@cncc.edu
BLAKE, Lisa, M .... 843-953-6964 407 C lisa.blake@citadel.edu
BLAKE, Melody, A .... 478-757-5229 127 F mblake@wesleyancollege.edu
BLAKE, Monique .... 954-201-6455.. 96 F mblake@broward.edu
BLAKE, Richard .... 610-861-1409 390 F blaker@moravian.edu
BLAKE, Scott .... 906-487-7242 224 B scott.blake@finlandia.edu
BLAKE, Susan .... 828-327-7000 333 B skillian@cvcc.edu
BLAKELY, Christopher .. 239-590-7900 109 K cblakely@fgcu.edu
BLAKELY, Colette .... 541-969-3088 374 A colette.blakely@mtangel.edu
BLAKELY, Craig, H .... 502-852-3297 186 A crag.blakely@louisville.edu
BLAKELY, Dedria, A .... 573-334-6825 259 G dblakely@sehcollege.edu
BLAKEMAN, Donald, L . 502-863-8091 180 H don_blakeman@georgetowncollege.edu
BLAKEMORE, Jerry, D .. 336-334-3067 343 A j_blakem@uncg.edu
BLAKEMORE, Molly .... 707-476-4254.. 58 I molly-blakemore@redwoods.edu
BLAKEMORE, Patricia ... 401-739-5000 404 E pblakemore@neit.edu
BLAKENEY, Erin .... 425-352-8534 478 D eblakeney@cascadia.edu
BLAKENEY, Nicolas .... 210-486-3777 429 A nblakeney@alamo.edu
BLAKES, Cara .... 205-226-4727.... 4 F clblakes@bsc.edu
BLAKESLEE, Amber .... 707-826-5702.. 33 C amber.blakeslee@humboldt.edu
BLAKEY, Linda .... 734-973-3536 232 D lblakey@wccnet.edu
BLAKLEY, Jacquelyn ..... 864-646-1305 412 H jblakle1@tctc.edu
BLAKLEY, Linda .... 312-362-7734 136 H lblakley@depaul.edu
BLALARK, Frank .... 919-684-2813 328 F registrar@duke.edu
BLALOCK, John .... 864-488-4615 410 B jblalock@limestone.edu
BLALOCK, III, W. Ben .. 307-766-3948 501 I bblalock@uwyo.edu
BLAMEY, Katrin .... 610-282-1100 382 C katrin.blamey@desales.edu
BLANC, Doug .... 607-729-1581 298 B dblanc@davisny.edu
BLANCERO, Donna Maria .... 781-891-2357 206 G dblancero@bentley.edu
BLANCHARD, Gina, A ... 740-392-6868 356 G gina.blanchard@mvnu.edu
BLANCHARD, Gordon ... 847-578-3232 148 F gordon.blanchard@rosalindfranklin.edu
BLANCHARD, Jack .... 301-405-8438 202 H jblancha@umd.edu
BLANCHARD, Jeffrey ..... 201-559-6170 277 J blanchardj@felician.edu
BLANCHARD, Jon, A ... 207-768-2795 195 G jblanch@nmcc.edu
BLANCHARD, Joyce .... 207-621-3403 196 H joyceb@maine.edu
BLANCHARD, Kristen, A .... 302-622-8000.. 90 D kblanchard@dcad.edu
BLANCHARD, Kym .... 815-921-4015 148 B k.blanchard@rockvalleycollege.edu
BLANCHARD, Lloyd .... 860-486-0930.. 89 D lloyd.blanchard@uconn.edu

BLOOM, Homer .... 724-589-2040 399 D
hbloom@thiel.edu
BLOOM, Joel, S .... 973-596-3102 279 E
joel.s.bloom@njit.edu
BLOOM, John, S .... 214-887-5591 435 F
jbloom@dts.edu
BLOOM, Ronald .... 914-606-6912 325 A
ronald.bloom@sunywcc.edu
BLOOM, Sue .... 814-393-2045 393 G
sbloom@clarion.edu
BLOOM, Tara .... 315-279-5465 303 G
tbloom@keuka.edu
BLOOM, Vicki .... 574-520-4448 157 E
vdbloom@iusb.edu
BLOOM, William .... 760-384-6221.. 46 M
william.bloom@cerrocoso.edu
BLOOM, Yvonne .... 314-539-5150 259 A
ybloom1@stlcc.edu
BLOOMBERG, Laura ...... 612-625-0608 243 F
bloom004@umn.edu
BLOOMBERG, Laura, J . 216-687-3588 350 J
laura.bloomberg@csuohio.edu
BLOOMBERG, Steven .... 870-543-5907.. 21 B
sbloomberg@seark.edu
BLOOME, Meghan .... 267-295-2376 402 A
mbloome@walnuthillcollege.edu
BLOOMER, Dennis, L ... 864-488-4561 410 B
dbloomer@limestone.edu
BLOOMER, Richard, J ... 901-678-4316 426 G
rbloomer@memphis.edu
BLOOMER, Sherm .... 541-737-0123 375 A
BLOOMFIELD, Stewart .. 212-938-5540 319 E
sbloomfield@sunyopt.edu
BLOSHINSKI, John .... 570-422-3631 394 A
jbloshinski@esu.edu
BLOSS, Adrienne, G ...... 540-665-4525 470 G
abloss@su.edu
BLOSS, Kim, K .... 870-235-4057.. 21 C
kkbloss@saumag.edu
BLOSS, Kim, K .... 870-235-4055.. 21 C
kkbloss@saumag.edu
BLOSSER, Joseph, D .... 336-841-9337 329 F
jblosser@highpoint.edu
BLOSSER, Kim .... 540-868-7101 474 C
kblosser@lfcc.edu
BLOUCH, Christine ...... 309-677-2395 134 A
blouch@fsmail.bradley.edu
BLOUGH, Alisaa .... 805-437-8916.. 30 C
alissa.blough@csuci.edu
BLOUIN, Bob, A .... 919-962-2198 342 C
bob_blouin@unc.edu
BLOUIN, Mike .... 770-962-7580 121 E
mblouin@gwinnetttech.edu
BLOUNT, Amanda .... 863-680-6221 100 H
ablount@flsouthern.edu
BLOUNT, Brian, K .... 804-278-4200 471 J
bblount@upsem.edu
BLOUNT, Lori .... 610-558-5630 391 A
blountl@neumann.edu
BLOUNT, Nicole .... 513-556-3233 361 J
nicole.blount@uc.edu
BLOUNT, Pamela .... 850-412-5072 109 I
pamela.blount@famu.edu
BLOUNT-FENNEY, Alice 201-200-3094 279 D
ablountfenny@njcu.edu
BLOWERS, Amanda .... 315-781-3309 301 F
blowers@hws.edu
BLOWERS, Kelsy .... 218-683-8543 240 B
kelsy.blowers@northlandcollege.edu
BLOYE, Alex .... 231-995-2929 229 A
abloye@nmc.edu
BLUE, Bob .... 318-869-5127 186 F
vpfa@centenary.edu
BLUE, Janeal .... 805-922-6966.. 24 I
janeal.blue@hancockcollege.edu
BLUE, Jean .... 910-695-3739 337 H
bluej@sandhills.edu
BLUE, Joe .... 270-824-1828 182 D
joe.blue@kctcs.edu
BLUE, Kevin .... 530-752-4557.. 69 B
athleticsdirector@ucdavis.edu
BLUE, Paula, B .... 585-340-9648 296 D
pblue@crcds.edu
BLUE, Shella .... 847-578-8807 148 F
shella.blue@rosalindfranklin.edu
BLUEBAUGH, Wade ...... 301-687-3175 204 C
ewadebluebaugh@frostburg.edu
BLUEHORSE, Byron ...... 907-474-5439.. 10 A
bdbluehorse@alaska.edu
BLUM, Aron .... 718-522-6646 325 I
BLUM, Dominika .... 605-626-7802 416 G
dominika.blum@northern.edu
BLUM, Eric .... 909-554-3814.. 54 H
BLUM, Janice .... 317-274-1020 157 D
jblum@iupui.edu
BLUM, Janice, S .... 317-278-1715 157 D
jblum@iupui.edu
BLUM, Jonathan .... 712-274-5408 168 E
blumj@morningside.edu
BLUM, Kim .... 608-785-8616 496 A
kblum@uwlax.edu
BLUM, Stacey, L .... 210-486-4111 428 I
sblum6@alamo.edu
BLUM, Susan .... 631-444-8250 317 A
susan.blum@stonybrook.edu
BLUM, Thomas .... 914-395-2203 315 A
tblum@sarahlawrence.edu
BLUM, Thomas, L .... 914-395-2203 315 A
tblum@sarahlawrence.edu
BLUM, Victoria .... 312-322-1700 150 F
BLUM MALLEY,
Suzanne .... 910-630-7005 331 E
smalley@methodist.edu
BLUMBERG, Elizabeth ... 781-239-2762 214 G
eblumberg@massbay.edu
BLUMBERG, James, J ... 309-556-3066 140 F
jblumber@iwu.edu
BLUME, Travis .... 906-217-4116 222 A
travis.blume@baycollege.edu
BLUMENFELD, Lee .... 858-646-3100.. 62 M
lblumenfeld@sbpdiscovery.org
BLUMENSTEIN, Robert ... 610-282-1100 382 C
robert.blumenstein@desales.edu
BLUMENTHAL, Chava ... 212-678-8072 303 D
chblumenthal@jtsa.edu
BLUMENTHAL, Eric .... 971-722-2913 375 D
eric.blumenthal2@pcc.edu
BLUMENTHAL, Jeff .... 989-358-7231 221 C
blumenthalj@alpenacc.edu
BLUMENTRITT, Timothy 470-578-2075 121 M
tblument@kennesaw.edu
BLUMER, Bruce .... 605-331-6648 417 C
bruce.blumer@usiouxfalls.edu
BLUML, Joel .... 785-670-2100 178 C
joe.bluml@washburn.edu
BLUMMER, Brian .... 219-864-2400 159 N
BLUNDELL, Keith .... 361-582-2535 457 E
keith.blundell@victoriacollege.edu
BLUNK, Shelly, R .... 515-574-1901 167 A
blunk@iowacentral.edu
BLUNT, Shelly, B .... 812-465-1617 162 C
sblunt@usi.edu
BLUTH, Ellen .... 563-336-3331 165 K
ebluth@eicc.edu
BLUTREICH, Peter .... 912-478-5406 120 C
pblutreich@georgiasouthern.edu
BLY, Scott .... 323-856-7643.. 25 G
sbly@afi.com
BLYTHE, Gretchen .... 816-604-2631 255 F
gretchen.blythe@mcckc.edu
BLYTHE, Janett .... 270-534-3079 183 B
janett.blythe@kctcs.edu
BLYTHE, Keith .... 336-734-7212 334 F
kblythe@forsythtech.edu
BOADA, Maria, F .... 845-431-8966 298 D
maria.boada@sunydutchess.edu
BOAKYE, Augustine, A . 973-877-4462 277 G
aboakye@essex.edu
BOAKYE, Kwabena, J .... 360-532-9020 480 G
BOARD, Afarah .... 909-554-3814.. 54 H
BOARD, Steve .... 920-206-2325 493 C
steven.board@mbu.edu
BOARDER, Matthew ...... 610-796-8243 378 C
matthew.boarder@alvernia.edu
BOARDMAN, David .... 215-204-4822 399 B
david.boardman@temple.edu
BOAST, Gary .... 814-262-6483 393 A
gboast@pennhighlands.edu
BOATENG, Henry .... 716-829-8349 298 E
boatengh@dyc.edu
BOATRIGHT, Bryan .... 330-823-6596 362 E
boatribr@mountunion.edu
BOATRIGHT, Christine .. 386-752-1822 100 B
christine.boatright@fgc.edu
BOATRIGHT, Darron ...... 316-978-5498 178 D
dboatright@goshockers.com
BOATRIGHT, Jana .... 903-223-3047 448 A
jboatright@tamut.edu
BOATRIGHT, Jill .... 504-865-3864 190 C
boatrigh@loyno.edu
BOATWRIGHT, Betty, R . 803-536-8556 411 G
bboatwright@scsu.edu
BOATWRIGHT, Kim .... 803-738-7601 410 D
boatwrightk@midlandstech.edu
BOB, Darcilynn .... 360-676-2772 481 F
dbob@nwic.edu
BOBADILLA, Leobardo .. 305-237-2598 104 E
lbobadi1@mdc.edu
BOBART, David .... 410-837-4331 204 F
dbobart@ubalt.edu
BOBBIN, Michael .... 904-256-7055 102 H
mbobbin@ju.edu
BOBBIN, Steffi .... 617-559-8640 210 F
sbobbin@hebrewcollege.edu
BOBBIT, Lindy .... 410-337-6000 199 B
lindy.bobbit@goucher.edu
BOBBITT, Donald, R ..... 501-686-2505.. 21 E
dbobbitt@uasys.edu
BOBBOUINE, Art .... 570-342-8000 383 H
abobbouine@fortisinstitute.edu
BOBE, Miguel .... 787-758-2525 512 F
miguel.bobe2@upr.edu
BOBEA, Jenny .... 201-360-4381 278 C
jbobea@hccc.edu
BOBEN, Jen .... 218-262-7363 238 D
jenniferboben@hibbing.edu
BOBICK, Aaron, F .... 314-935-6350 262 A
afb@wustl.edu
BOBINCHOCK, Edward .. 412-536-1209 386 H
edward.bobinchock@laroche.edu
BOBINSKI, Mary Anne .. 404-712-8815 118 E
mary.anne.bobinski@emory.edu
BOBLEY, Laurie .... 212-463-0400 322 G
laurie.bobley@touro.edu
BOBO, David .... 205-853-1200.... 2 G
dbobo@jeffersonstate.edu
BOBO, Kristen .... 205-391-2211.... 3 E
kbobo@sheltonstate.edu
BOBOC, Marius .... 216-687-4700 350 J
m.boboc@csuohio.edu
BOBROWSKI, Paul .... 970-351-2764.. 84 F
paul.bobrowski@unco.edu
BOCANEGRA, Melanie .. 818-677-2969.. 32 C
elizabeth.t.adams@csun.edu
BOCCACINO, Samantha 585-785-1459 299 F
samantha.boccacino@flcc.edu
BOCCALANDRO, Maria . 972-860-2973 434 G
mboccalandro@dcccd.edu
BOCCARDI, Megan .... 217-228-5432 147 F
boccame@quincy.edu
BOCCHICCHIO, Rebecca 916-660-7502.. 64 D
rbocchicchio@sierracollege.edu
BOCK, Darrell, L .... 214-887-5251 435 F
dbock@dts.edu
BOCK, Jim .... 610-328-8529 398 G
jbock1@swarthmore.edu
BOCK, Wendy .... 309-796-5180 133 G
bockw@bhc.edu
BOCKMANN, Erika .... 509-527-4282 485 B
erika.bockmann@wwcc.edu
BOCKORNY, Kristi .... 605-626-3001 416 G
kristi.bockorny@northern.edu
BOCKSTEIN, Mindy .... 212-393-6340 294 D
mbockstein@jjay.cuny.edu
BOCZER, Amy .... 203-254-4000.. 87 I
aboczer@fairfield.edu
BODAH, Matthew, H ..... 401-874-2497 405 E
mbodah@uri.edu
BODDEN, Lisha .... 212-517-0618 305 E
lbodden@mmm.edu
BODDIE, Angelette .... 716-884-9120 292 B
acboddie@bryantstratton.edu
BODDIE-FORBES,
Rasheda .... 662-325-2033 247 F
rboddie-forbes@saffairs.msstate.edu
BODDIE-LAVAN,
Jeanine .... 229-333-5709 127 E
jyboddielavan@valdosta.edu
BODE, Lori .... 314-434-4044 252 C
lori.bode@covenantseminary.edu
BODE, Robert .... 715-425-3141 496 F
robert.bode@uwrf.edu
BODEEN, Rob .... 657-278-2339.. 31 C
rbodeen@fullerton.edu
BODEN, Alison .... 609-258-6244 280 D
aboden@princeton.edu
BODEN, Stacia .... 316-978-6792 178 D
stacia.boden@wichita.edu
BODENSCHATZ,
Matthew .... 814-262-6456 393 A
mbodenschatz@pennhighlands.edu
BODENSTEINER, Jill, R . 610-660-1707 397 G
jbodenst@sju.edu
BODIE, Matthew .... 727-791-2415 107 E
bodie.matthew@spcollege.edu
BODIFORD, Glenn .... 216-881-1700 358 J
gbodiford@ohiotech.edu
BODIFORD, John .... 229-500-2926 114 H
john.bodiford@asurams.edu
BODIMER, Jeffrey .... 207-947-4591 194 B
jbodimer@bealcollege.edu
BODIN, Joy .... 218-855-8058 237 G
joy.bodin@clcmn.edu
BODKINS, Carrie .... 304-457-6347 486 E
bodkinscl@ab.edu
BODMER, Brad, R .... 518-783-2315 315 E
bbodmer@siena.edu
BODNAR, Jennifer .... 504-520-7503 193 E
jbodnar@xula.edu
BODNAR, Molly .... 719-389-6351.. 78 I
molly.bodnar@coloradocollege.edu
BODNAR, Patrick .... 972-438-6932 441 E
pbodnar@parker.edu
BODNAR, Seth .... 406-243-2311 263 K
seth.bodnar@umontana.edu
BODO, Bethanny .... 540-231-6003 476 C
bbodo@vt.edu
BODONI, June .... 978-867-4217 210 B
june.bodoni@gordon.edu
BODOR, Jim .... 619-201-8700.. 60 G
jim.bodor@sdcc.edu
BODOR, Jim .... 619-201-8725.. 60 G
jim.bodor@sdcc.edu
BODREY, Kari .... 229-931-2700 125 E
kbodrey@southgatech.edu
BODUR, Niyazi .... 607-777-3621 316 B
nbodur@binghamton.edu
BODVARSSON, Orn .... 503-370-6868 377 F
obodvarsson@willamette.edu
BODVARSSON, Orn, B .. 801-832-2601 461 F
obodvarsson@westminstercollege.edu
BOE, Chris .... 704-463-1360 339 E
christopher.boe@pfeiffer.edu
BOE, Cindy .... 320-589-6065 244 B
cindyboe@morris.umn.edu
BOE, Jennifer .... 816-802-3436 254 D
jboe@kcai.edu
BOE, Ken .... 504-568-6130 189 H
kboe@lsuhsc.edu
BOECK, Mark .... 515-294-8959 163 G
mboeck@foundation.iastate.edu
BOECKENSTEDT, Jon .... 541-737-0123 375 A
BOECKERS, Alice .... 920-832-6525 493 B
alice.o.boeckers@lawrence.edu
BOECKMAN, Linda, A ... 717-262-2616 403 C
linda.boeckman@wilson.edu
BOEDEKER, Katrina, P .. 260-399-7700 162 B
kboedeker@sf.edu
BOEDER, John, C .... 507-354-8221 236 J
boederjc@mlc-wels.edu
BOEDING, Laurie .... 843-574-6172 412 I
laurie.boeding@tridenttech.edu
BOEGEL, Thomas .... 415-239-3322.. 36 K
tboegel@ccsf.edu
BOEH, William, S .... 409-772-9803 456 E
wsboeh@utmb.edu
BOEHKE, Michael, J ..... 304-457-6300 486 E
boehkemj@ab.edu
BOEHLEIN, Sandi .... 314-918-2691 253 C
sboehlein@eden.edu
BOEHLER, Susan .... 217-735-7227 142 H
sboehler@lincolncollege.edu
BOEHM, Beth .... 502-852-5110 186 A
beth.boehm@louisville.edu
BOEHM, Michael .... 402-472-2871 269 J
mboehm3@unl.edu
BOEHM, Michael .... 434-791-7273 464 I
mboehm@averett.edu
BOEHM, Michael, J ...... 402-472-2871 269 H
mboehm3@unl.edu
BOEHM, Pamela .... 254-659-7501 437 A
pboehm@hillcollege.edu
BOEHMAN, Joseph, R .. 804-289-8061 472 C
jboehman@richmond.edu
BOEHME, David, L .... 815-835-6353 149 E
steven.w.allert@svcc.edu
BOEHME, Laura .... 541-383-7219 372 A
lboehme@cocc.edu
BOEHMER, Ann .... 636-584-6679 253 B
ann.boehmer@eastcentral.edu
BOEHMER, Brian .... 740-364-9535 349 F
boehmer.23@osu.edu
BOEHMER, Jennifer ...... 541-917-4214 373 G
boehmj@linnbenton.edu
BOEHMER, Nick .... 660-831-4228 256 I
boehmern@moval.edu
BOEHMLER, Brook, S ... 641-422-4212 168 G
boehmbro@niacc.edu
BOEHNE, Cheryl .... 618-545-3486 141 E
cboehne@kaskaskia.edu
BOEKE, Joseph .... 208-426-1000 130 H

BOMELEY, Bruce .... 203-332-5034.. 86 F
bbomely@housatonic.edu
BOMER, Randy .... 940-565-2231 453 E
randy.bomer@unt.edu
BOMMER, Sharon .... 937-328-6038 350 G
bommers@clarkstate.edu
BOMOTTI, Gerry .... 951-827-7310.. 70 B
gerry.bomotti@ucr.edu
BONA, Dennis .... 218-793-2465 240 B
dennis.bona@northlandcollege.edu
BONACCORSO, Roberto 206-934-5487 483 C
roberto.bonaccorso@seattlecolleges.edu
BONACOSSA, Pietro ...... 305-389-7256.. 96 A
pbonacossa@barry.edu
BONADIE, Heidi .... 909-599-5433.. 48 A
hbonadie@lifepacific.edu
BONADUCE DE NIGRIS, Francesca .... 713-646-1811 443 I
fbonaducedenigris@stcl.edu
BONAGURA, Thom .... 712-749-2271 164 C
bonagura@bvu.edu
BONAHUE, Edward .... 631-451-4112 321 C
bonahue@sunysuffolk.edu
BONAMICI, Andrew ...... 973-408-3322 277 A
abonamici@drew.edu
BONANNO, Joseph, A .. 812-855-4440 156 G
jbonanno@indiana.edu
BONAPARTE, Donna ..... 781-239-6434 206 B
dbonaparte@babson.edu
BONATH, Kyle, K .... 806-742-3931 450 F
kyle.k.bonath@ttu.edu
BONATO, Frederick .... 201-761-6020 283 A
fbonato@saintpeters.edu
BONAVIA, Jan .... 708-709-7844 147 D
jbonavia@prairiestate.edu
BONCHI, Joseph .... 973-596-3002 279 E
joseph.bonchi@njit.edu
BOND, Alicia .... 570-408-6024 403 A
alicia.bond@wilkes.edu
BOND, Bradley .... 815-753-9403 146 B
bbond@niu.edu
BOND, Christopher .... 207-509-7179 196 E
cbond@unity.edu
BOND, Dawn .... 413-545-2100 211 G
dbond@umass.edu
BOND, Deanna .... 614-236-6011 349 B
BOND, Debra .... 540-674-3607 474 E
dbond@nr.edu
BOND, Enoch, D .... 252-335-3224 341 B
edbond@ecsu.edu
BOND, Erin .... 212-431-2199 309 A
erin.bond@nyls.edu
BOND, Helen .... 202-806-0870.. 92 F
hbond@howard.edu
BOND, Lynette .... 413-662-5106 213 C
lynette.bond@mcla.edu
BOND, Meredith, R .... 216-687-5580 350 J
m.bond40@csuohio.edu
BOND, Michelle .... 334-386-7275.... 5 C
mbond@faulkner.edu
BOND, Millie .... 610-526-7805 379 B
mbond@brynmawr.edu
BOND, Terrance .... 309-268-8238 138 H
terrance.bond@heartland.edu
BOND, Travis .... 573-592-4560 262 G
travis.bond@williamwoods.edu
BOND-MAUPIN, Lisa .... 707-826-4491.. 33 C
lisa.bond-maupin@humboldt.edu
BONDAD, Theresa .... 435-652-7502 460 B
theresa.bondad@dixie.edu
BONDEROFF, Mary .... 315-684-6981 321 A
bonderm@morrisville.edu
BONDI, Nathanael .... 303-273-3537.. 79 J
nbondi@mines.edu
BONDS, Elle .... 414-297-6422 499 C
bonds12@matc.edu
BONDS, Jess .... 209-478-0800.. 45 I
jbonds@humphreys.edu
BONDS, Nechell .... 903-886-5101 447 B
nechell.bonds@tamuc.edu
BONDS, Nell .... 870-743-3000.. 20 B
nbonds@northark.edu
BONDS, Rodney .... 803-793-5170 408 G
bondsr@denmarktech.edu
BONDS, Thomas .... 662-862-8130 246 E
tabonds@iccms.edu
BONDS-RAACKE, Jennifer .... 920-403-3001 495 B
jennifer.bonds-raacke@snc.edu
BONDURANT, Jennifer .. 434-947-4113 469 E
jbondurant@randolphcollege.edu
BONDURANT, Joy .... 214-333-5104 434 C
joyb@dbu.edu
BONDY, Jeff .... 406-994-2661 264 C
jbondy@montana.edu
BONDY, Kaylyn .... 701-224-5638 346 A
kaylyn.bondy@bismarckstate.edu
BONE, Jennifer .... 618-235-2700 150 E
jennifer.bone@swic.edu
BONE, Rodney .... 256-228-6001.... 3 B
bonejr@nacc.edu
BONEBRIGHT, Terri ...... 501-450-1273.. 19 E
bonebright@hendrix.edu
BONERI, Jacqueline ...... 954-776-4476 103 B
jboneri@keiseruniversity.edu
BONES, Whit .... 816-802-3532 254 D
wbones@kcai.edu
BONEWALD, Karen, I .... 603-526-3748 272 H
kbonewald@colby-sawyer.edu
BONFANTI, Phil .... 601-928-8402 247 E
phil.bonfanti@mgccc.edu
BONGARTZ, Michael ..... 816-235-1515 261 B
bongartzm@umkc.edu
BONGIORNO, Laurel ..... 802-651-5978 462 A
bongiorno@champlain.edu
BONGIOVANNI, Lynne .. 718-405-3753 296 F
lynne.bongiovanni@mountsaintvincent.edu
BONI, Bethyn .... 315-568-3252 310 B
bboni@nycc.edu
BONIADI, Ani .... 818-252-5224.. 76 E
ani.boniadi@woodbury.edu
BONIECKI, Kurt, A .... 501-450-3126.. 23 H
kurtb@uca.edu
BONIFAS, Angela .... 309-298-2010 153 A
aj-bonifas@wiu.edu
BONIFER, Duane .... 309-457-2321 144 H
dbonifer@monmouthcollege.edu
BONIFIELD, Susan .... 404-727-9252 118 E
susan.bonifield@emory.edu
BONIFORTI, Chris, G 561-237-7163 103W
cboniforti@lynn.edu
BONILLA, Angelita .... 973-353-1037 282 B
bonillan@newark.rutgers.edu
BONILLA, Anie .... 954-492-5353.. 97 G
abonilla@citycollege.edu
BONILLA, David .... 406-771-4425 264 F
dbonilla@gfcmsu.edu
BONILLA, Kathleen .... 559-489-2221.. 67 B
kathy.bonilla@fresnocitycollege.edu
BONILLA, Mary Kay ...... 406-771-5123 264 F
mbonilla@gfcmsu.edu
BONILLA, Matthew .... 212-463-0400 322 F
matthew.bonilla3@touro.edu
BONILLA, Matthew, F ... 212-463-0400 322 G
matthew.bonilla@touro.edu
BONILLA, Ray .... 979-458-6128 446 B
rbonilla@tamus.edu
BONIN, Keith .... 336-758-5000 344 C
BONITATIBUS, Alexandra .... 518-587-2100 320 E
BONK, Sharon, B .... 617-588-1356 206 F
sbonk@bfit.edu
BONKOWSKI, Janet ...... 920-465-2527 495 F
bonkowsj@uwgb.edu
BONLARRON, Rachael, E .... 561-868-3140 105 D
bonlarr@palmbeachstate.edu
BONN, Cynthia, L .... 401-874-7100 405 E
cynthia_bonn@uri.edu
BONNEAU, Lisa .... 605-658-3853 416 D
lisa.bonneau@usd.edu
BONNEE, Peter .... 504-286-5258 191 C
pbonnee@suno.edu
BONNEKESSEN, Barbara, E .... 217-581-2922 137 E
bbonnekessen@eiu.edu
BONNELL, Chris .... 801-274-3280 461 E
chris.bonnell@wgu.edu
BONNELL, Dawn, A ...... 215-898-7236 400 F
vpr@pobox.upenn.edu
BONNER, Carol .... 937-512-4463 360 G
carol.bonner@sinclair.edu
BONNER, Connie, C ..... 260-359-4006 156 C
cbonner@huntington.edu
BONNER, Davita .... 386-481-2143.. 96 D
bonnerd@cookman.edu
BONNER, John .... 425-276-9520 480 B
jbonner@everettcc.edu
BONNER, Julia .... 414-229-5684 496 B
jbonner@uwm.edu
BONNER, Kenyon, R ...... 412-648-1006 400 H
krb114@pitt.edu
BONNER, Lisa .... 212-229-5600 308 A
bonner@newschool.edu
BONNER, Lyle .... 940-552-6291 457 C
lbonner@vernoncollege.edu
BONNER, Mason .... 205-366-8814.... 7 A
mbonner@stillman.edu
BONNER, Tiffany .... 909-537-5211.. 32 E
tiffany.bonner@csusb.edu
BONNER, Tommy .... 507-222-4199 234 G
tbonner@carleton.edu
BONNES, Catherine .... 269-337-7228 225 F
catherine.bonnes@kzoo.edu
BONNET, Larissa, B ...... 307-675-0511 501 G
lbonnet@sheridan.edu
BONNETTE, Clarence .... 803-793-5264 408 G
bonnettec@denmarktech.edu
BONNETTE, J. Michael . 434-544-8907 471 L
bonnette@lynchburg.edu
BONNETTE, Lisa .... 843-782-8612 413 E
lisarj@mailbox.sc.edu
BONNETTE, Richard ...... 410-293-1104 504 A
bonnette@usna.edu
BONNEVILLE, Janice ..... 309-438-5507 140 D
jbonnev@ilstu.edu
BONNEY, Curtis .... 206-934-4551 483 B
curtis.bonney@seattlecolleges.edu
BONNEY, Emily .... 657-278-2715.. 31 C
ebonney@fullerton.edu
BONNEY, Keith .... 863-669-2843 106 A
kbonney@polk.edu
BONNIN, Linda .... 325-674-2000 428 F
lhb19b@acu.edu
BONNSTETTER, Beth ..... 719-587-7800.. 77 G
bbonstetter@adams.edu
BONONES, Patrick .... 404-471-6396 114 G
pbonones@agnesscott.edu
BONSER, Matthew .... 719-389-6745.. 78 I
mbonser@coloradocollege.edu
BONTATIBUS, Donna .... 860-343-5745.. 87 A
smathis@mxcc.edu
BONTE, Troy, A .... 614-823-1300 359 H
tbonte@otterbein.edu
BONTRAGER, Bonita ..... 406-683-7520 264 A
bonita.bontrager@umwestern.edu
BONTRAGER, Cindy, A . 785-532-6226 175 C
cab@ksu.edu
BONTRAGER, Karen ...... 419-358-3629 348 F
bontragerk@bluffton.edu
BONUCHI, Molly .... 308-635-6112 270 C
bonuchim@wncc.edu
BONVENUTO, Christopher .... 310-434-4508.. 63 C
bonvenuto_chris@smc.edu
BOOBAR, Jeffrey, R ...... 540-464-7104 476 B
boobarjr@vmi.edu
BOOCKER, David, J .... 402-554-2338 270 A
dboocker@unomaha.edu
BOODY, Kathleen .... 732-987-2229 278 A
kboody@georgian.edu
BOODY, Kathleen .... 732-987-2490 278 A
kboody@georgian.edu
BOOG, Melissa, M .... 410-543-6330 204 D
mmboog@salisbury.edu
BOOHER, Adam, D .... 812-888-4225 162 F
abooher@vinu.edu
BOOHER, Linnea .... 262-595-2404 496 D
booher@uwp.edu
BOOHER, Mark .... 805-922-6966.. 24 I
mbooher@pcpa.org
BOOKAS, Olga .... 860-685-2122.. 90 B
obookas@wesleyan.edu
BOOKER, Alicia .... 216-987-3048 351 E
alicia.booker@tri-c.edu
BOOKER, Ansley, A ...... 478-301-2856 122 E
booker_aa@mercer.edu
BOOKER, James, W ...... 301-860-4035 204 A
jbooker@bowiestate.edu
BOOKER, Kevin .... 470-639-0309 123 D
kevin.booker@morehouse.edu
BOOKER, Kevin .... 470-639-0355 123 D
kevin.booker@morehouse.edu
BOOKER, Latoya .... 616-554-5819 223 E
latoya.booker@davenport.edu
BOOKER, Latrice .... 219-980-6547 157 C
lbooker@iun.edu
BOOKER, Lonnie .... 785-833-4360 175 E
lonnie.booker@kwu.edu
BOOKER, Marc .... 205-934-9847.... 8 A
mbooker@uab.edu
BOOKER, Mary .... 302-831-2126.. 91 C
mbooker@udel.edu
BOOKER, Michael .... 636-481-3312 254 C
mbooker@jeffco.edu
BOOKER, Ndala .... 407-303-6413.. 95 B
ndala.booker@ahu.edu
BOOKER, Pamela .... 478-757-2647 122 F
pamela.booker@mga.edu
BOOKER, Steve .... 407-646-2395 106 L
sbooker@rollins.edu
BOOKER, Suzy .... 865-981-8203 421 C
suzy.booker@maryvillecollege.edu
BOOKHART, Nancy .... 706-396-7597 124 B
nbookhart@paine.edu
BOOKOUT, James .... 334-670-3617.... 7 C
jbookout@troy.edu
BOOKOUT, Jeff .... 870-358-8614.. 18 A
jeff_bookout@asun.edu
BOOKS, Sandra .... 530-891-6900.. 27 E
BOOKWALA, Jamila .... 610-330-5070 387 C
bookwalj@lafayette.edu
BOOKWALTER, Robert .. 304-696-2350 489M
bookwalt@marshall.edu
BOOM, Philip .... 563-588-8000 166 C
pboom@emmaus.edu
BOOMER, Brian .... 559-934-2152.. 74 N
brianboomer@whccd.edu
BOOMGAARDEN, Donald, R .... 718-940-5902 314 A
dboomgaarden@sjcny.edu
BOOMS, Carole .... 734-462-4400 230 G
cbooms@schoolcraft.edu
BOON, Celva .... 253-589-5822 478 J
celva.boon@cptc.edu
BOON, Rachel, L .... 515-281-3332 163 F
rachel.boon@iowaregents.edu
BOON, Stephanie, C ..... 610-566-1776 403 B
sboon@williamson.edu
BOONE, Addie .... 601-276-3720 249 B
aboone@smcc.edu
BOONE, Becky .... 843-349-5274 409 J
becky.boone@hgtc.edu
BOONE, Beth .... 352-392-1311 111 A
bboone@ufl.edu
BOONE, Brenda .... 770-426-2808 122 C
brenda.boone@life.edu
BOONE, Christopher, G 480-965-2236.. 10 J
christopher.g.boone@asu.edu
BOONE, Dan .... 615-248-1251 426 D
dboone@trevecca.edu
BOONE, Debbie .... 205-853-1200.... 2 G
dboone@jeffersonstate.edu
BOONE, Dottie .... 434-381-6106 471 I
dboone@sbc.edu
BOONE, John, B .... 919-866-5923 338 G
jbboone@waketech.edu
BOONE, Kyle .... 616-331-2120 224 G
booneky@gvsu.edu
BOONE, Megan .... 606-783-2233 184 C
m.boone@moreheadstate.edu
BOONE, Nichole, N ...... 972-378-8573 433 I
nboone@collin.edu
BOONE, Nicole .... 252-538-4326 335 B
nboone@halifaxcc.edu
BOONE, Rebecca .... 318-357-5621 192 G
booner@nsula.edu
BOONE, Scott .... 678-916-2638 115 I
sboone@johnmarshall.edu
BOONE, Steve, E .... 501-686-7348.. 22 B
seboone@uams.edu
BOONE, Zak .... 541-383-7212 372 A
zboone@cocc.edu
BOONSTRA, Brenda ...... 706-778-8500 124 D
bboonstra@piedmont.edu
BOONTHAVONGKHAM, Bonnie .... 559-325-5205.. 67 A
bonnie.boonthavongkham@cloviscollege.edu
BOOR, Kathryn, J .... 607-255-5820 297 F
kjb4@cornell.edu
BOOROM, Richard .... 303-867-1155.. 83 K
boorom@taft.edu
BOOS, David .... 605-995-3065 415 E
david.boos@mitchelltech.edu
BOOS, Jean .... 843-355-4167 414 C
boosj@wiltech.edu
BOOS, Matt .... 440-684-6021 363 C
mboos@ursuline.edu
BOOSKA, Karry .... 802-728-1320 464 A
kbooska@vtc.edu
BOOSKOS, George .... 609-343-5116 275 D
gbooskos@atlantic.edu
BOOTE, Marlys .... 319-335-2043 163 H
marlys-boote@uiowa.edu
BOOTH, Daria .... 530-898-4054.. 30 D
dbooth3@csuchico.edu
BOOTH, Derrick .... 916-484-8411.. 50 G
boothd@arc.losrios.edu
BOOTH, Diana .... 847-574-5152 142 B
dbooth@lfgsm.edu
BOOTH, Edward, C .... 850-263-3261.. 95 P
ecbooth@baptistcollege.edu

BOSTIC, Peter 310-233-4288 49 B bosticpf@lahc.edu
BOSTICK, William 504-520-5243 193 E wbostick@xula.edu
BOSTON, Denise 866-492-5336 244 F denise.boston@mail.waldenu.edu
BOSTON, Genyne 850-599-3276 109 I genyne.boston@famu.edu
BOSTON, Joanna 212-343-1234 306 G jboston@mcny.edu
BOSTON, Kay 318-678-6000 187 H kboston@bpcc.edu
BOSTON, Ken 308-635-6736 270 C bostonk1@wncc.edu
BOSTON, Melissa 914-798-2734 305 B melissa.boston@mville.edu
BOSTON, Pamela, F 757-823-2293 469 A pfboston@nsu.edu
BOSTON, Pasiley 256-761-8520 7 B pboston@talladega.edu
BOSTON, Troy 641-673-1170 171 C troy.boston@wmpenn.edu
BOSTWICK, Keri 918-335-6291 368 E kbostwick@okwu.edu
BOSWELL, Angela 870-230-5320 19 D boswela@hsu.edu
BOSWELL, Chris 307-766-6934 501 I chris.boswell@uwyo.edu
BOSWELL, Erin 314-529-9333 255 B eboswell@maryville.edu
BOSWELL, Katherine 817-598-6216 457 J kboswell@wc.edu
BOSWELL, Robert 303-735-1332 84 B robert.boswell@colorado.edu
BOSWELL, Samantha 478-471-2430 122 F samantha.boswell@mga.edu
BOSWELL, Talisa 662-252-8000 248 G tboswell@rustcollege.edu
BOSWORTH, Sarah 401-739-5000 404 E sbosworth@neit.edu
BOSWORTH, Theresa 541-278-5957 371 H tbosworth@bluecc.edu
BOTANA, II, Joseph, D 870-307-7589 19 I joseph.botana@lyon.edu
BOTCHAN, Michael, R 510-642-5716 69 A mbotchan@berkeley.edu
BOTENGAN, Tim 760-252-2411 26 G rbotengan@barstow.edu
BOTERO, Cecilia 662-915-5858 249 D cbotero@olemiss.edu
BOTHE, Dan 619-849-2290 57 J danbothe@pointloma.edu
BOTHNER, Peter, G 585-389-2196 307 F pbothne4@naz.edu
BOTHOF, Ken 859-572-6639 184 E bothofk1@nku.edu
BOTKA, Elaine 903-463-8700 436 G botkae@grayson.edu
BOTMAN, Selma 212-960-5217 326 D selma.botman@yu.edu
BOTSTEIN, Leon 845-758-7423 290 I president@bard.edu
BOTT, Jennifer, P 269-387-2378 233 B jennifer.bott@wmich.edu
BOTT, Rebecca 605-688-5268 417 A rebecca.bott@sdstate.edu
BOTT, Rosa 276-328-0312 472 E grb5u@uvawise.edu
BOTTA, Michael 412-392-3833 396 G mfbotta@pointpark.edu
BOTTA, Samuel 757-352-4491 470 B sambott@regent.edu
BOTTARO, Kathy 210-805-2591 453 C bottaro@uiwtx.edu
BOTTELBERGHE, John 303-360-4718 80 E john.bottelberghe@ccaurora.edu
BOTTEM, Lisa 218-683-8544 240 B lisa.bottem@northlandcollege.edu
BOTTI, Romayne 848-932-1991 282 A romayne.botti@rutgers.edu
BOTTINELLI, Stasi 303-751-8700 78 D bottinelli@belrea.edu
BOTTO, Karin 315-445-4155 303 I bottoka@lemoyne.edu
BOTTORFF, Allen 863-297-1081 106 A abottorff@polk.edu
BOTZHEIM, Luke 425-640-1946 480 A luke.botzheim@edcc.edu
BOTZMAN, Thomas, J 330-823-6050 362 E botzmatj@mountunion.edu
BOU, J. Andrew 770-216-2960 121 I abou@ict.edu
BOU, Nydia 787-743-7979 510 H ut_nbou@suagm.edu
BOUARÉ, Boubacar 509-359-6200 479 G
BOUCHARD, Norma 714-997-6826 36 B nbouchard@chapman.edu
BOUCHARD, Rita, T 757-822-2308 475 E rbouchard@tcc.edu
BOUCHE, Jane, A 920-565-1000 493 A boucheja@lakeland.edu
BOUCHER, Gery 252-638-7283 334 A boucherg@cravencc.edu
BOUCHER, Helen 617-628-5000 219 C helen.boucher@tufts.edu
BOUCHER, J. Cliff 903-510-2546 452 A cliff.boucher@tjc.edu
BOUCHER, Jeanne 207-985-7976 194 H jeanne@landingschool.edu
BOUCHER, John 907-450-8389 9 I jbouche1@alaska.edu
BOUCHER, Robert 207-755-5100 195 D rboucher@cmcc.edu
BOUCHER, Susan 315-792-3013 324 B salberi@utica.edu
BOUCHER-JARVIS, Allison 973-720-2123 284 J boucherjarvisa@wpunj.edu
BOUCHER MORRIS, Kelly 212-228-1888 312 B
BOUCHEREAU, Chantal 336-750-3400 344 A bouchereauc@wssu.edu
BOUCHEY, BettyJo 312-261-3505 145 D bbouchey@nl.edu
BOUDINOT, Ann 703-284-3809 468 H ann.boudinot-amin@marymount.edu
BOUDO, Lori 978-542-7404 213 E lori.boudo@salemstate.edu
BOUDOURIS, Jeff 937-512-2537 360 G jeff.boudouris@sinclair.edu
BOUDREAU, Charles 630-466-7900 152 K cboudreau@waubonsee.edu
BOUDREAU, John 860-906-5071 86 D jboudreau@capitalcc.edu
BOUDREAU, Mark 413-775-1311 214 E boudreaum@gcc.mass.edu
BOUDREAU, Nicole 207-834-7500 197 A nicole.boudreau@maine.edu
BOUDREAU, Timothy 516-364-0808 308 D tboudreau@nycollege.edu
BOUDREAU, Vincent, G 212-650-7285 293 D vboudreau@ccny.cuny.edu
BOUDREAUX, Carol 225-752-4233 187 D cboudreaux@iticollege.edu
BOUDREAUX, Gregory 330-494-6170 360 K gboudreaux@starkstate.edu
BOUFAS, Maureen 315-866-0300 301 D boufasmn@herkimer.edu
BOUGHEY, Robin 502-245-6177 184 A
BOUGHIDA, Karim, B 401-874-4602 405 E boughida@uri.edu
BOUGHMAN, Joann 301-445-1992 202 G jboughman@usmd.edu
BOUILLON, Rick 801-957-5158 461 C rick.bouillon@slcc.edu
BOUKHMAN, Anna 718-522-9073 290 E aboukhman@asa.edu
BOULANGER, Brie 316-295-5525 174 A brie_boulanger@friends.edu
BOULANGER, Rebecca 920-735-2407 498 F boulanger@fvtc.edu
BOULDER, James 814-732-1047 394 B jboulder@edinboro.edu
BOULDIN, Randy 615-966-5711 421 B randy.bouldin@lipscomb.edu
BOULDING, William 919-660-7822 328 F bb1@duke.edu
BOULERSOX, Kate 573-875-8700 251 I
BOULES, Raouf 860-231-5803 90 A rboules@usj.edu
BOULGER, Lynn 207-801-5620 194 E lboulger@coa.edu
BOULTER, Brandon 415-257-1334 41 C
BOULTON, April 301-696-3811 199 E boulton@hood.edu
BOULTON, Kenneth 605-626-2497 416 G kenneth.boulton@northern.edu
BOULUKOS, Tracy 561-297-3531 109 J tbouluko@fau.edu
BOUNDS, Roger 928-523-4331 14 H roger.bounds@nau.edu
BOUQUOT, Gregory 860-486-3903 89 D gregory.bouquot@uconn.edu
BOURA, Ahmad 530-898-5830 30 D aboura@csuchico.edu
BOURANIS, Christin 978-921-4242 217 B christin.bouranis@montserrat.edu
BOURDON, Marsha 603-366-5206 272 K mbourdon@ccsnh.edu
BOURG, Chris 617-253-5297 216 B
BOURGEAULT, Lucy 800-468-4888 462 B
BOURGEOIS, Angi 662-325-2202 247 F abourgeois@caad.msstate.edu
BOURGEOIS, Donna 504-865-3523 190 C dhbourg@loyno.edu
BOURGEOIS, Gene 512-245-2205 450 C eb04@txstate.edu
BOURGEOIS, Sheryl 714-997-6523 36 B sbourgeo@chapman.edu
BOURGEOIS, Thomas 662-325-3611 247 F thomasb@saffairs.msstate.edu
BOURGET, Jose 269-471-3211 221 D bourget@andrews.edu
BOURHIS NOLAN, Ellen 845-569-3116 307 D ellen.nolan@msmc.edu
BOURLAND, Dana 920-924-3225 499 D dbourland1@morainepark.edu
BOURLAND HUIZENGA, Annette 563-589-3858 170 G ahuizenga@dbq.edu
BOURLIER, Julie 310-660-3383 41 E jbourlier@elcamino.edu
BOURN, Brenda 423-461-8414 422 E bsbourn@milligan.edu
BOURNE, Anthony 419-448-2316 353 E tbourne1@heidelberg.edu
BOURNE, Brandy 828-251-6639 342 B bbourne@unca.edu
BOURNE, Don, E 208-535-5360 131 B don.bourne@cei.edu
BOURNE, Jeffrey, T 540-568-6164 468 C bournejt@jmu.edu
BOURNE, Laurie 540-423-9055 473 I lbourne@germanna.edu
BOURNE, Philip, E 434-924-6867 472 D peb6a@virginia.edu
BOURQUE, Alicia 504-865-3835 190 C aabourqu@loyno.edu
BOURQUE, Daniel, F 617-552-6067 207 C daniel.bourque@bc.edu
BOURQUE, Kathleen 413-565-1000 206 D kbourque@baypath.edu
BOURQUE, Michael, J 617-552-0343 207 C michael.bourque.2@bc.edu
BOURQUE, Nancy 773-878-2998 149 A
BOURQUIN, Becky 218-322-2324 238 F becky.bourquin@itascacc.edu
BOUSCHER, Jordan 724-847-6556 384 C jdbousch@geneva.edu
BOUSLAUGH, Megan 949-854-8002 39 K
BOUSMAN, Preston 804-862-6100 470 C pbousman@rbc.edu
BOUSQUET, Megan 605-256-5112 416 F megan.bousquet@dsu.edu
BOUSSON, Eduardo 402-465-2222 268 G ebousson@nebrwesleyan.edu
BOUTE, Bradley 480-393-1396 15 R bradb@swiha.edu
BOUTELLE, Ken 866-776-0331 54 D kboutelle@ncu.edu
BOUTIN, Karyn 508-588-9100 215 A kboutin@massasoit.mass.edu
BOUTIN, Kelly 401-232-6855 404 A kboutin1@bryant.edu
BOUVIN, David 850-718-2380 97 E bouvind@chipola.edu
BOUWHUIS, Ryan 928-776-2195 16 J ryan.bouwhuis@yc.edu
BOUYEA, Aaron, M 585-292-2833 307 B abouyea@monroecc.edu
BOUZAS, Maria 973-761-9081 283 C maria.bouzas@shu.edu
BOUZIGARD, Cambria 985-448-4101 192 F cambria.bouzigard@nicholls.edu
BOVA, Keith 716-829-7551 298 E bovak@dyc.edu
BOVAT, Bruce 802-860-2755 462 A bovat@champlain.edu
BOVE, Elena, M 310-338-2885 51 A ebove@lmu.edu
BOVEE, Kimberly, M 757-822-1913 475 E kbovee@tcc.edu
BOVIA, Wendy 860-738-6325 87 C wbovia@nwcc.edu
BOVIA, Wendy 860-773-1420 87 G wbovia@commnet.edu
BOVID, Nicholas 989-686-9234 223 J nicholasbovid@delta.edu
BOVINGDON, Ali 406-449-9166 263 J abovingdon@montana.edu
BOWAB, Lynn 978-681-0800 216 C bowab@mslaw.edu
BOWAN, Carmen 626-316-5312 63 E cbowan@saybrook.edu
BOWAR, Alicia 712-722-6022 165 I alicia.bowar@dordt.edu
BOWDEN, Michael 410-951-6280 204 B mbowden@coppin.edu
BOWDEN, Nathan, E 805-437-3719 30 C nathan.bowden@csuci.edu
BOWDEN, Ron 903-434-8157 440 G rbowden@ntcc.edu
BOWDEN, Steve 207-699-5010 195 A sbowden@meca.edu
BOWDEN, Trishana 703-993-8756 467 E tbowden2@gmu.edu
BOWDEN, Vicky 626-815-2034 26 F vbowden@apu.edu
BOWDEN, Zach 937-766-7901 349 E zbowden@cedarville.edu
BOWDLER, Michelle, D 617-627-3766 219 C michelle.bowdler@tufts.edu
BOWDRE, Paul 812-749-1431 159 O pbowdre@oak.edu
BOWE, Mona 574-284-4587 160 I mbowe@saintmarys.edu
BOWE, Terry 812-535-5284 160 H terry.bowe@smwc.edu
BOWEN, Alyncia 614-947-6226 352 J alyncia.bowen@franklin.edu
BOWEN, Bonnie 616-331-2400 224 G bowenb@gvsu.edu
BOWEN, Brad 864-508-0107 412 D bbowen@swu.edu
BOWEN, Brad 307-754-6404 501 H brad.bowen@nwc.edu
BOWEN, Brendan 678-839-6348 127 C bbowen@westga.edu
BOWEN, Bruce 801-626-6006 461 A babowen@weber.edu
BOWEN, Christopher, M 540-375-2300 470 E bowen@roanoke.edu
BOWEN, Eve 254-659-7500 437 A
BOWEN, Gary, L 919-962-6542 342 C glbowen@email.unc.edu
BOWEN, Heath 845-398-4380 314 G hbowen@stac.edu
BOWEN, Jennifer 330-263-2008 351 A jbowen@wooster.edu
BOWEN, Julie 806-291-3470 457 I bowenj@wbu.edu
BOWEN, Kim, T 517-750-1200 231 C kbowen@arbor.edu
BOWEN, Lance 410-777-2873 197 G ldbowen1@aacc.edu
BOWEN, Laura 704-669-4106 333 E bowen@clevelandcc.edu
BOWEN, Lauren 814-641-3121 386 E bowenl@juniata.edu
BOWEN, Lucy 713-221-8024 453 A bowenl@uhd.edu
BOWEN, Marie 617-287-5150 211 H marie.bowen@umb.edu
BOWEN, Mark 478-445-4467 119 B mark.bowen@gcsu.edu
BOWEN, Nicole 605-256-5121 416 F nicole.bowen@dsu.edu
BOWEN, Patricia, A 606-693-5000 183 C pbowen@kmbc.edu
BOWEN, Peter 806-291-1171 457 I pbowen@wbu.edu
BOWEN, Rachel 610-526-6157 385 D rbowen@harcum.edu
BOWEN, Randyll 716-926-8895 301 E rbowen@hilbert.edu
BOWEN, Robert 603-271-6484 273 A
BOWEN, Robin, E 479-968-0228 18 C rbowen@atu.edu
BOWEN, Roxanne 423-585-6806 425 F roxanne.bowen@ws.edu
BOWEN, Sam 320-222-5206 240 F sam.bowen@ridgewater.edu
BOWEN, Susan, G 570-941-6344 401 F susan.bowen@scranton.edu
BOWEN, Taleisha 336-316-2183 329 D bowentq@guilford.edu
BOWEN, Thomas 334-683-2316 3 A tbowen@marionmilitary.edu

BOWEN, Tom .... 870-972-2100.. 17 E
BOWENS, Laura Lee ..... 201-328-5196 276 J
lbowens@ccm.edu
BOWENS, Pacey .... 870-762-3134.. 17 B
pbowens@smail.anc.edu
BOWENS, Vernita .... 501-975-6050.. 20 F
vbowens@philander.edu
BOWER, David, A .... 812-465-7149 162 C
bower@usi.edu
BOWER, Eric .... 216-791-5000 350 I
eric.bower@cim.edu
BOWER, Jami .... 678-839-6464 127 C
jbower@westga.edu
BOWER, John .... 360-650-7217 485 I
john.bower@wwu.edu
BOWER, Kevin .... 843-953-5155 407 C
bowerk1@citadel.edu
BOWER, Michelle .... 304-829-7214 487 A
mbower@bethanywv.edu
BOWER, Robin .... 727-791-2665 107 E
bower.robin@spcollege.edu
BOWER SPENCE,
Kimberly .... 570-408-4764 403 A
kimberly.bowerspence@wilkes.edu
BOWERS, Anthony .... 425-739-8135 481 C
anthony.bowers@lwtech.edu
BOWERS, Betsy .... 850-474-2210 111 F
bbowers@uwf.edu
BOWERS, Carol .... 803-376-6030 406 D
cbowers@allenuniversity.edu
BOWERS, David, A .... 212-938-5666 319 E
dbowers@sunyopt.edu
BOWERS, Drema .... 865-539-7346 425 B
dbowers@pstcc.edu
BOWERS, James .... 703-445-9056 472 G
BOWERS,
Jerome (J.D.), D .... 573-882-3893 261 A
bowersjd@missouri.edu
BOWERS, John .... 206-934-6869 483 D
john.bowers@seattlecolleges.edu
BOWERS, Kevin .... 618-544-8657 139 G
bowersk@iecc.edu
BOWERS, Kimberly .... 510-436-1218.. 45 E
bowers@hnu.edu
BOWERS, Krista .... 704-991-0297 338 C
kbowers2274@stanly.edu
BOWERS, Kristen .... 315-655-7180 292 H
klbowers@cazenovia.edu
BOWERS, Matt .... 765-361-6455 163 B
bowersm@wabash.edu
BOWERS, Melinda .... 850-863-6557 111 F
mbowers@uwf.edu
BOWERS, Rodney .... 321-674-8080 100 C
rbowers@fit.edu
BOWERS, William .... 315-312-2888 318 D
william.bowers@oswego.edu
BOWERSOCK, Gary .... 303-273-3330.. 79 J
gbowerso@mines.edu
BOWERSOX-JOHNSON,
Kevin .... 206-934-2966 483 C
kevin.bowersox-johnson@
seattlecolleges.edu
BOWES, Kristen .... 914-674-7544 306 C
kbowes@mercy.edu
BOWHAY, Vincent .... 620-331-4100 174 H
vbowhay@indycc.edu
BOWIE, DeWayne .... 337-482-6287 193 B
dkbowie@louisiana.edu
BOWIE, Jalonna .... 913-234-0681 172 K
jalonna.bowie@cleveland.edu
BOWIE, John .... 207-755-5432 195 D
jbowie@cmcc.edu
BOWIE, Lois .... 903-593-8311 448 G
lbowie@texascollege.edu
BOWIE, Matthew .... 505-454-5385 286 F
mbowie@luna.edu
BOWIE, Michelle .... 202-884-9611.. 94 A
bowiem@trinitydc.edu
BOWIE, Pamela .... 870-972-2782.. 17 E
pbowie@astate.edu
BOWIE, Stacie .... 864-388-8305 410 A
sbowie@lander.edu
BOWIE, Thomas .... 303-458-4040.. 83 E
tbowie@regis.edu
BOWKER, Edward .... 800-567-2344 492 C
ebowker@menominee.edu
BOWKER, Mike .... 303-384-2034.. 79 J
mbowker@mines.edu
BOWLER, John .... 435-652-7913 460 B
john.bowler@dixie.edu
BOWLER, Shaun .... 951-827-4302.. 70 B
shaun.bowler@ucr.edu
BOWLES, Brooke .... 205-226-4625.... 4 F
bgbowles@bsc.edu
BOWLES, Diane .... 704-378-1202 330 D
dbowles@jcsu.edu
BOWLES, Donna, J .... 812-941-2204 157 F
dbowles@ius.edu
BOWLES, James, H .... 270-824-8588 182 D
james.bowles@kctcs.edu
BOWLES, Rick .... 972-825-4850 444 J
rbowles@sagu.edu
BOWLES, Robin .... 215-619-7391 390 C
rbowles@mc3.edu
BOWLES, Ryan, A .... 507-786-3965 243 D
bowles@stolaf.edu
BOWLES, Ulisa .... 910-672-1411 341 C
ubowles@uncfsu.edu
BOWLES PALACIOZ,
Crystal .... 918-293-5274 368 B
crystal.bowles@okstate.edu
BOWLIN, Stephanie ...... 909-469-5390.. 75 I
sbowlin@westernu.edu
BOWLING, Damon .... 918-836-6886 370 B
damon.bowling@spartan.edu
BOWLING, Dee .... 252-737-1133 341 A
bowlingde@ecu.edu
BOWLING, Doug .... 513-569-1752 350 F
douglas.bowling@cincinnatistate.edu
BOWLING, Karen, E ...... 904-620-4013 111 B
karen.bowling@unf.edu
BOWLING, Lisa .... 540-654-1372 471 N
lbowling@umw.edu
BOWLUS, Robin .... 419-358-3543 348 F
bowlusr@bluffton.edu
BOWMAN, Alayne .... 865-981-8096 421 C
alayne.bowman@maryvillecollege.edu
BOWMAN, Amanda .... 425-889-7824 481 H
amanda.bowman@northwestu.edu
BOWMAN, Benjamin ..... 574-284-4552 160 I
bbowman@saintmarys.edu
BOWMAN, Bethany .... 724-503-1001 402 B
bbowman@washjeff.edu
BOWMAN, Chad .... 714-895-8966.. 38 A
cbowman@gwc.cccd.edu
BOWMAN, Chris .... 989-275-5000 226 D
chris.bowman@kirtland.edu
BOWMAN, Christine ..... 512-863-1200 445 C
bowmanc@southwestern.edu
BOWMAN, Corey, L ...... 660-543-4114 260 G
bowman@ucmo.edu
BOWMAN, David .... 509-359-6244 479 G
dbowman@ewu.edu
BOWMAN, Elizabeth ..... 805-965-0581.. 63 A
bowmane@sbcc.edu
BOWMAN, F. DuBois ... 734-936-0192 231 H
fdbowman@umich.edu
BOWMAN, Gregory .... 401-254-4509 405 C
gbowman@law.rwu.edu
BOWMAN, Helen, Y ...... 215-895-2803 382 F
helen.y.bowman@drexel.edu
BOWMAN, Jeff .... 740-427-5114 354 I
bowmanj@kenyon.edu
BOWMAN, Jessie .... 541-962-3740 372 I
jbrett@eou.edu
BOWMAN, Jonathan ..... 916-278-6312.. 32 D
bowman@csus.edu
BOWMAN, Judith, M .... 757-683-3260 469 B
jbowman@odu.edu
BOWMAN, Kathy .... 863-583-9050 110 B
BOWMAN, Keith .... 410-455-3400 203 B
kjb@umbc.edu
BOWMAN, Lisa .... 918-495-6888 368 F
lbowman@oru.edu
BOWMAN, Michael .... 510-659-6064.. 54 J
mbowman@ohlone.edu
BOWMAN, Michael .... 503-725-4576 375 E
bowman@pdx.edu
BOWMAN, Pam .... 662-685-4771 245 C
pbowman@bmc.edu
BOWMAN, JR.,
Ronald, L .... 330-972-2157 361 H
rbowman@uakron.edu
BOWMAN, Russell, E ... 860-444-8381 503 G
russell.e.bowman@uscga.edu
BOWMAN, Sharon .... 318-345-9241 188 D
sbowman@ladelta.edu
BOWNE, Andrew .... 913-469-8500 174 I
bownea@jccc.edu
BOWNE, Kristine .... 626-396-2474.. 26 B
kristine.bowne@artcenter.edu
BOWNES, Kim, M .... 603-535-2771 275 A
kbownes@plymouth.edu
BOWNES-JOHNSON,
Beth .... 256-352-8190.... 3 I
beth.johnson@wallacestate.edu
BOWRIN, Anthony .... 973-720-3984 284 J
bowrina@wpunj.edu
BOWSER, Chris .... 573-897-5000 260 A
BOWSER, David .... 919-516-4236 339 I
dbowser@st-aug.edu
BOWSER, Steve .... 404-270-5326 126 B
sbowser@spelman.edu
BOWTHORPE, Bailey ..... 435-586-7702 460 A
baileybowthorpe@suu.edu
BOWYER, Karen, A .... 731-286-3301 424 D
bowyer@dscc.edu
BOWYER, Ryan .... 276-944-6528 466 L
rbowyer@ehc.edu
BOX, Jay .... 859-256-3132 181 C
president@kctcs.edu
BOX, Jennifer .... 541-684-7241 371 I
jbox@bushnell.edu
BOX, Stephanie .... 361-825-6290 447 C
stephanie.box@tamucc.edu
BOX, Tony .... 740-389-4636 355 F
boxt@mtc.edu
BOXDORFER, Bill .... 573-288-6571 252 F
bboxdorfer@culver.edu
BOXILL, David .... 212-817-7706 293 F
dboxill@gc.cuny.edu
BOYAN, Barbara, D ...... 804-828-0190 473 B
bboyan@vcu.edu
BOYCE, Eric .... 828-251-6951 342 B
eboyce@unca.edu
BOYCE, Glenn .... 662-915-7111 249 D
chancellor@olemiss.edu
BOYCE, Jessica .... 704-330-6710 333 D
jessica.boyce@cpcc.edu
BOYCE, Justin .... 304-865-6077 487 H
justin.boyce@ovu.edu
BOYCE, Mary, C .... 212-854-1123 297 C
boyce@columbia.edu
BOYCE, Mary, C .... 212-854-1754 297 C
BOYCE, Matthew .... 253-879-3211 484 G
mpboyce@pugetsound.edu
BOYCE, Richard, N .... 980-636-1700 471 J
rboyce@upsem.edu
BOYD, Ali .... 563-588-6436 164 E
ali.boyd@clarke.edu
BOYD, Angela .... 757-727-5328 467 G
angela.boyd@hamptonu.edu
BOYD, Betsy, A .... 541-346-0946 376 H
eaboyd@uoregon.edu
BOYD, Brandon .... 931-372-6285 426 B
bboyd@tntech.edu
BOYD, Brian .... 407-823-3016 110 E
brian.boyd@ucf.edu
BOYD, Carla, L .... 218-726-8795 243 G
clboyd@d.umn.edu
BOYD, Carla, M .... 217-443-8753 136 G
cboyd@dacc.edu
BOYD, Chantel .... 334-727-8254.... 7 D
cboyd@tuskegee.edu
BOYD, Clarence .... 918-495-7703 368 F
cboyd@oru.edu
BOYD, Cristine .... 330-972-6476 361 H
cboyd@uakron.edu
BOYD, Cynthia .... 770-426-2756 122 C
cboyd@life.edu
BOYD, Cynthia, E .... 312-942-6915 148 G
cynthia_e_boyd@rush.edu
BOYD, Danielle .... 618-634-3298 149 G
danielleb@shawneecc.edu
BOYD, Delaina .... 765-285-2770 153 H
dboyd@bsu.edu
BOYD, JR., Eulas .... 718-780-0395 291 K
eulas.boyd@brooklaw.edu
BOYD, Evan, E .... 215-248-6330 400 D
eboyd@uls.edu
BOYD, Gary .... 304-357-4704 487 J
garyboyd@ucwv.edu
BOYD, Gerald .... 240-629-7840 198 I
gboyd@frederick.edu
BOYD, Jeffery .... 507-285-7215 240 H
jeffery.boyd@rctc.edu
BOYD, Jim .... 218-741-3095 238 H
BOYD, John, C .... 828-766-1270 336 A
jboyd@mayland.edu
BOYD, Justin .... 719-587-7401.. 77 G
jboyd@adams.edu
BOYD, Katie .... 334-844-6875.... 4 D
kbb0035@auburn.edu
BOYD, Kayla .... 781-280-3625 215 B
BOYD, Keishea .... 816-235-1047 261 B
boydkm@umkc.edu
BOYD, Kevin .... 773-702-5305 151 E
kevin.boyd@chicagobooth.edu
BOYD, Kim .... 918-495-7108 368 F
kboyd@oru.edu
BOYD, Laura .... 417-625-9501 256 F
boyd-l@mssu.edu
BOYD, Linda .... 304-647-6363 490 C
lboyd@osteo.wvsom.edu
BOYD, Lonnie .... 620-229-6136 177 G
lonnie.boyd@sckans.edu
BOYD, Lorenzo .... 203-931-2988.. 89 H
lboyd@newhaven.edu
BOYD, Lynn .... 870-972-3079.. 17 E
lyboyd@astate.edu
BOYD, Mary .... 970-945-8691.. 78 L
BOYD, Mary, K .... 706-236-2216 116 B
mboyd@berry.edu
BOYD, Mary Alice .... 704-337-2561 339 F
boydma@queens.edu
BOYD, Michael .... 706-754-7807 123 G
mboyd@northgatech.edu
BOYD, Michael .... 815-802-8110 141 D
president@kcc.edu
BOYD, Michael, D .... 901-333-4318 425 D
mdboyd@southwest.tn.edu
BOYD, Nick .... 530-283-0202.. 42 A
nboyd@frc.edu
BOYD, Rachael .... 402-486-2600 269 F
rachael.boyd@ucollege.edu
BOYD, Randy .... 865-974-2241 427 A
utpresident@tennessee.edu
BOYD, JR., Reginald .... 704-636-6455 330 A
rboyd@hoodseminary.edu
BOYD, Rick .... 803-775-8727 413 G
boydrl@uscsumter.edu
BOYD, Ruth .... 580-774-3177 370 A
ruth.boyd@swosu.edu
BOYD, Shane .... 757-455-3384 477 C
sboyd@vwu.edu
BOYD, Sharon, H .... 910-962-7769 343 C
boyds@uncw.edu
BOYD, Steven .... 212-563-6647 323 I
s.boyd@uts.edu
BOYD, Susan .... 586-445-7408 227 B
boyds@macomb.edu
BOYD, Susan .... 703-284-1609 468 H
susan.boyd@marymount.edu
BOYD, Tarik .... 404-639-0999 123 D
tarik.boyd@morehouse.edu
BOYD, Todd .... 580-772-6611 370 A
todd.boyd@swosu.edu
BOYD, Todd .... 580-774-3782 370 A
todd.boyd@swosu.edu
BOYD, Tyler .... 281-649-3209 437 B
tboyd@hbu.edu
BOYD, Vincent .... 641-844-5716 167 G
vincent.boyd@iavalley.edu
BOYD, Wanda .... 972-780-3600 454 A
wanda.boyd@untdallas.edu
BOYD, William .... 805-565-6043.. 76 A
wboyd@westmont.edu
BOYD, Yuko .... 252-638-7229 334 A
boydy@cravencc.edu
BOYD MCELROY, Diana 816-604-2326 255 F
diana.mcelroy@mcckc.edu
BOYD-PUGH,
Jennifer, N .... 305-899-4057.. 96 A
jpugh@barry.edu
BOYDL, Loni .... 414-443-8702 498 A
loni.boyd@wlc.edu
BOYDSTON, Glynn .... 806-291-3766 457 I
boydstong@wbu.edu
BOYDSTUN, Morris .... 479-394-7622.. 23 C
mboydstun@uarichmountain.edu
BOYER, Annette .... 724-925-4138 402 F
boyera@westmoreland.edu
BOYER, Anthony 850-729-5259 104M
boyera@nwfsc.edu
BOYER, Brian .... 603-428-2375 273 G
bboyer@nec.edu
BOYER, Bruce .... 508-565-1380 219 A
bboyer@stonehill.edu
BOYER, Bruce, E .... 573-875-7251 251 I
beboyer@ccis.edu
BOYER, David .... 806-720-7578 439 D
david.boyer@lcu.edu
BOYER, Jenny .... 904-256-7532 102 H
jboyer1@ju.edu
BOYER, John, W .... 773-702-8576 151 E
jwboyer@uchicago.edu
BOYER, Kim, L .... 518-956-8241 316 A
kboyer3@albany.edu
BOYER, Laura .... 210-486-5000 428 H
BOYER, Mary .... 215-702-4541 380 A
mboyer@cairn.edu
BOYER, Mary Jo .... 610-450-6524 382 A
mboyer@dccc.edu

BOYER, Phara .... 508-270-5311 214 G
pboyer@massbay.edu
BOYER, Sara .... 812-535-5114 160 H
sboyer@smwc.edu
BOYER, Suzanne, L ...... 410-777-2045 197 G
slboyer1@aacc.edu
BOYER-OWENS, Linda .. 210-485-0230 428 G
lboyer-owens@alamo.edu
BOYERS, Jayson .... 610-527-0200 397 D
BOYERS, Pamela .... 402-559-2442 269 K
pamela.boyers@unmc.edu
BOYES, Monica .... 530-895-2936.. 27 C
boyesmo@butte.edu
BOYETT, Chad .... 912-287-5808 117 E
cboyett@coastalpines.edu
BOYETT, Chris .... 270-707-3711 182 B
chris.boyett@kctcs.edu
BOYETT, Patricia .... 504-865-3082 190 C
pbboyett@loyno.edu
BOYETTE, Alan, J .... 336-334-5494 343 A
jaboyett@uncg.edu
BOYETTE, Rick .... 903-823-3274 446 A
ricky.boyette@texarkanacollege.edu
BOYK, Linda .... 610-902-8255 379 G
lb837@cabrini.edu
BOYKIN, Celyn .... 504-280-6225 190 B
ccboykin@uno.edu
BOYKIN, Coretta .... 251-578-1313.... 3 D
cboykin@rstc.edu
BOYKIN, Gregory .... 252-985-5117 339 D
gboykin@ncwc.edu
BOYKIN, Justin .... 251-981-3771.... 5 A
justin.boykin@columbiasouthern.edu
BOYKIN, Melinda .... 254-867-3761 449 D
melinda.boykin@tstc.edu
BOYKIN, Regena .... 601-635-2111 246 A
rboykin@eccc.edu
BOYKIN, Sutonia .... 724-480-3423 381 H
sutonia.boykin@ccbc.edu
BOYKIN, Ted .... 570-585-9327 381 B
tboykin@clarkssummitu.edu
BOYKIN, Tiffany, F .... 410-777-1239 197 G
tfboykin@aacc.edu
BOYLAN, Erin .... 607-753-2516 318 A
erin.boylan@cortland.edu
BOYLAN, Joyce .... 562-977-6041.. 42 K
joyce.boylan@fremont.edu
BOYLAN, Stanley .... 646-565-6412 322 G
stanley.boylan@touro.edu
BOYLAN, Stanley, L ...... 646-565-6412 322 F
stanley.boylan@touro.edu
BOYLE, Allison, J .... 410-576-7644 202 B
aboyle@oag.state.md.us
BOYLE, Ann .... 480-219-6107 250 A
aboyle@atsu.edu
BOYLE, Ann, L .... 610-799-1736 388 D
aboyle@lccc.edu
BOYLE, Antonio .... 302-857-7172.. 90 E
aboyle@desu.edu
BOYLE, Brian .... 251-442-2287.... 8 C
bboyle@umobile.edu
BOYLE, Carol Ann .... 516-877-3775 289 I
boyle@adelphi.edu
BOYLE, Jeffery .... 864-592-4823 412 E
boylej@sccsc.edu
BOYLE, Kate .... 360-438-4310 482 I
kboyle@stmartin.edu
BOYLE, Kevin .... 973-618-3372 276 D
kboyle@caldwell.edu
BOYLE, Nuala .... 585-389-2670 307 F
nboyle5@naz.edu
BOYLE, Robert, J .... 904-620-4663 111 B
rboyle@unf.edu
BOYLE, Roger .... 202-464-6464 462 H
roger.boyle@worldlearning.org
BOYLE, Sharon, I .... 215-926-2200 399 B
sharon.boyle@temple.edu
BOYLE, Thomas, A .... 630-515-6147 144 F
tboyle@midwestern.edu
BOYLE, Tracy .... 267-341-3616 385 J
tboyle2@holyfamily.edu
BOYLES, Bruce .... 704-406-3275 329 A
bboyles@gardner-webb.edu
BOYLES, Dwayne .... 434-961-5488 474 I
dboyles@pvcc.edu
BOYLES, Elinda .... 740-351-3265 360 F
eboyles@shawnee.edu
BOYLES, Erin, I .... 412-578-8774 380 B
eiboyles@carlow.edu
BOYLES, Joel .... 662-562-3451 248 D
jsboyles@northwestms.edu
BOYLES, John Dixon .... 903-823-3192 446 A
johndixon.boyles@texarkanacollege.edu
BOYLES, Shery .... 919-760-8581 331 D
boyless@meredith.edu
BOYMAN, Robert .... 626-529-8033.. 55 F
rboyman@pacificoaks.edu
BOYNTON, Andrew, C .. 617-552-4107 207 C
andy.boynton@bc.edu
BOYNTON,
Christopher, E .... 207-581-1484 196 G
christopher.boynton@maine.edu
BOYNTON, Diane .... 831-646-4097.. 52 G
dboynton@mpc.edu
BOYNTON, Eric .... 608-363-2667 491 H
boyntone@beloit.edu
BOYS, Kevin, S .... 937-393-3431 360 H
kboys@sscc.edu
BOYSEN, Kelly .... 713-743-2841 452 D
krboysen@uh.edu
BOYSUN, Virginia .... 406-377-9404 263 D
vboysun@dawson.edu
BOZARTH, Diane .... 573-288-6473 252 F
dbozarth@culver.edu
BOZARTH, Sandra .... 661-654-3043.. 30 B
sbozarth2@csub.edu
BOZIAN, Charles .... 718-262-5165 295 E
cbozian@york.cuny.edu
BOZINSKI, Glenn .... 570-674-6434 390 B
gbozinski@misericordia.edu
BOZON, Brandon .... 254-298-8606 445 G
bozonb819@templejc.edu
BOZYLINSKY, Garry ...... 860-465-5537.. 85 H
bozylinskyg@easternct.edu
BOZYM, Rebecca .... 412-536-1158 386 H
rebecca.bozym@laroche.edu
BOZZA, Brian .... 239-590-1250 109 K
bbozza@fgcu.edu
BRAATZ, Brady, J .... 913-971-3452 176 C
bbraatz@mnu.edu
BRABBLE, Megan .... 252-985-5299 339 D
mbrabble@ncwc.edu
BRABHAM, Sherry, F .... 212-217-4020 299 D
sherry_brabham@fitnyc.edu
BRABO, Andria .... 970-339-6518.. 77 H
andria.brabo@aims.edu
BRABY, Randy .... 435-283-7058 461 B
randy.braby@snow.edu
BRACCIANO, Susan .... 816-271-4214 257 A
braccian@missouriwestern.edu
BRACCO, Anthony .... 212-237-8613 294 D
abracco@jjay.cuny.edu
BRACERO, Carmen, A ... 787-844-8181 513 A
carmen.bracero@upr.edu
BRACEROS, Amy .... 909-537-3224.. 32 E
abracero@csusb.edu
BRACEY,
Christopher, A .... 202-994-6510.. 92 D
cbracey@gwu.edu
BRACEY,
Christopher, A .... 202-994-6510.. 92 D
cabracey@gwu.edu
BRACEY, David .... 714-772-3330.. 25 M
BRACEY, Matthew .... 615-675-5329 428 C
mbracey@welch.edu
BRACH, Philip .... 704-461-5073 326 L
philipbrach@bac.edu
BRACHE-MELLO,
Allison, M .... 787-993-8886 512 A
allison.brache@upr.edu
BRACK, Jonathan, M .... 215-572-3878 402 E
jbrack@wts.edu
BRACKE, Paul, J .... 509-313-6533 480 F
bracke@gonzaga.edu
BRACKEN, Carol .... 817-515-5137 445 F
carol.bracken@tccd.edu
BRACKEN, Damien, S .... 617-747-2221 206 H
admissions@berklee.edu
BRACKEN, Diane .... 850-484-1175 105 H
dbracken@pensacolastate.edu
BRACKEN, Lisa .... 803-778-6652 406 I
brackenlm@cctech.edu
BRACKEN, Steven .... 713-226-5276 453 A
brackens@uhd.edu
BRACKENRIDGE,
Quentin .... 217-735-7299 142 H
qbrackenridge@lincolncollege.edu
BRACKETT, Geoffrey, L . 845-575-3000 305 D
geoffrey.brackett@marist.edu
BRACKETT, Maria .... 703-416-1441 466 A
mbrackett@divinemercy.edu
BRACKETT, Robert .... 708-563-1577 140 A
rbrackett@iit.edu
BRACKETT, Stacey .... 828-328-7309 330 F
stacey.brackett@lr.edu
BRACKETT, Suzanne ...... 252-985-5102 339 D
sbrackett@ncwc.edu
BRACKIN, Anita .... 901-333-4018 425 D
abrackin@southwest.tn.edu
BRACKIN, Chad .... 225-578-4736 189 D
cmb@lsu.edu
BRACKIN, Stewart .... 731-989-6911 419 K
sbrackin@fhu.edu
BRACKMANN, Sarah ...... 512-863-1987 445 C
brackmas@southwestern.edu
BRACKNELL, Ann .... 205-391-2958.... 3 E
ann.bracknell@sheltonstate.edu
BRACY, Judy .... 504-520-7317 193 E
jbracy@xula.edu
BRACY, Marion .... 504-520-7507 193 E
mbracy@xula.edu
BRACY, JR., Randolph .. 386-481-2115.. 96 D
bracyr@cookman.edu
BRACY KNIGHT, Becca . 310-954-5080.. 27 B
BRADACH, Carmen .... 218-749-7743 238 D
c.bradach@mesabirange.edu
BRADACH, Carmen .... 800-996-6422 238 F
c.bradach@mesabirange.edu
BRADACH, Carmen .... 218-749-7743 238 H
c.bradach@mesabirange.edu
BRADBERRY, Richard ... 443-885-3488 201 A
richard.bradberry@morgan.edu
BRADBURY, Amy .... 850-201-8519 112 C
amy.bradbury@tcc.fl.edu
BRADBURY, Nikki .... 205-665-6044.... 8 D
bradburynp@montevallo.edu
BRADDIX, D'Andre .... 314-516-5205 261 C
braddixd@umsl.edu
BRADDOCK, Glenn .... 518-782-6567 315 E
gbraddock@siena.edu
BRADDOCK, Heather, C 423-652-4742 420 F
hcbraddock@king.edu
BRADDOCK, Reb .... 850-644-0453 110 C
rbraddock@admin.fsu.edu
BRADDY, Linda .... 972-860-4806 434 F
BRADDY, William .... 540-261-8450 471 B
bill.braddy@svu.edu
BRADEN, Jeffery, P .... 919-515-2468 342 A
jeff_braden@ncsu.edu
BRADEN, Kale .... 916-484-8408.. 50 G
bradenk@arc.losrios.edu
BRADFIELD, Brett .... 605-331-6712 417 C
brett.bradfield@usiouxfalls.edu
BRADFIELD, Carol .... 407-303-9585.. 95 B
carol.bradfield@ahu.edu
BRADFIELD, Jennifer, S 440-775-8400 357 G
jennifer.bradfield@oberlin.edu
BRADFIELD, Tanisha ..... 714-432-5509.. 38 B
tbradfield@occ.cccd.edu
BRADFORD, Adam .... 208-282-2490 131 G
adambradford@isu.edu
BRADFORD, Arthur .... 972-780-3600 454 A
arthur.bradford@untdallas.edu
BRADFORD, Ashlee .... 325-793-4984 439 F
bradford.ashlee@mcm.edu
BRADFORD, Brian .... 323-466-6663.. 43 H
BRADFORD, Carmen ...... 501-370-5214.. 20 F
cebradford@philander.edu
BRADFORD, Carol, R .... 614-685-4411 358 D
bradford.885@osu.edu
BRADFORD, Darryl .... 616-432-3418 230 A
darryl.bradfor@prts.edu
BRADFORD, George .... 909-607-8709.. 37 F
george_bradford@kgi.edu
BRADFORD, Kelema, K . 718-289-5100 293 B
kelema.bradford@bcc.cuny.edu
BRADFORD, Kevin .... 606-878-4718 182 G
kevin.bradford@kctcs.edu
BRADFORD, Lawrence .. 323-241-5280.. 49 E
bradfoll@lasc.edu
BRADFORD, Michael ..... 860-486-4037.. 89 D
michael.bradford@uconn.edu
BRADFORD, Michele .... 256-439-6822.... 2 B
mbradford@gadsdenstate.edu
BRADFORD, Paul .... 805-565-6033.. 76 A
pbradford@westmont.edu
BRADFORD, Rebecca .... 843-355-4121 414 C
bradfordr@wiltech.edu
BRADFORD, Tessie .... 409-984-6156 449 I
bradfordts@lamarpa.edu
BRADFORD, Todd .... 706-236-2231 116 B
tbradford@berry.edu
BRADFORD DIAZ,
Morgan .... 641-784-5108 166 E
mjbradfo@graceland.edu
BRADLEY, Akirah .... 303-492-9048.. 84 B
akirah.bradley@colorado.edu
BRADLEY, Angela .... 228-497-7630 247 E
angela.bradley@mgccc.edu
BRADLEY, Anna, S .... 310-825-4321.. 69 E
BRADLEY, Bonita .... 912-358-3159 125 A
bradleyb@savannahstate.edu
BRADLEY, Brandon .... 660-263-3900 251 D
brandonbradley@cccb.edu
BRADLEY, Carla .... 404-894-2575 119 E
carla.bradley@studentlife.gatech.edu
BRADLEY, Cedric .... 228-896-2519 247 E
cedric.bradley@mgccc.edu
BRADLEY, Christian .... 918-293-5440 368 B
christian.bradley@okstate.edu
BRADLEY, Dale, R .... 304-367-4692 488 H
dale.bradley@pierpont.edu
BRADLEY, Dana .... 202-994-8500.. 92 D
dana_bradley@gwu.edu
BRADLEY, Dana .... 443-543-5628 203 B
bradleyd@umbc.edu
BRADLEY, Dennis, J ..... 814-732-1030 394 B
bradley@edinboro.edu
BRADLEY, Desirae' .... 903-923-2321 435 H
desiraeb@etbu.edu
BRADLEY, Donna .... 217-732-7275 142 H
donna.bradley@lincolncollege.edu
BRADLEY, Earlhagi .... 315-229-5311 314 D
ebradley@stlawu.edu
BRADLEY, Elizabeth ...... 845-437-7200 324 C
elbradley@vassar.edu
BRADLEY, Heather .... 229-732-5928 115 B
heatherbradley@andrewcollege.edu
BRADLEY, Jennifer .... 319-398-5537 167 J
jennifer.bradley@kirkwood.edu
BRADLEY, Jennifer .... 808-734-9890 129 H
jbradley@hawaii.edu
BRADLEY, Jon-Pierre .... 630-829-6077 133 E
jbradley@ben.edu
BRADLEY, Joseph .... 410-617-2865 200 B
jbradley@loyola.edu
BRADLEY, Julie, M .... 972-758-3821 433 I
jbradley@collin.edu
BRADLEY, Karen .... 951-552-8913.. 27 G
kbradley@calbaptist.edu
BRADLEY, Kathy .... 717-337-6960 384 D
kbradley@gettysburg.edu
BRADLEY, Katy .... 405-789-6400 369 H
kbradley@snu.edu
BRADLEY, Katy .... 405-491-6336 369 H
kbradley@snu.edu
BRADLEY, Kim, S .... 704-687-5700 342 D
kim.bradley@uncc.edu
BRADLEY, Kirk .... 850-484-1764 105 H
kbradley@pensacolastate.edu
BRADLEY, LaKisha .... 831-646-4261.. 52 G
lbradley@mpc.edu
BRADLEY, Lola .... 252-246-1251 339 C
lbradley@wilsoncc.edu
BRADLEY, Marcy, K .... 607-871-2350 290 B
bradlemk@alfred.edu
BRADLEY, Mark .... 360-882-2200.. 43 D
markbradley@gs.edu
BRADLEY, Mary Jane ... 870-972-3057.. 17 E
mbradley@astate.edu
BRADLEY, Monica .... 603-230-3512 272 I
mbradley@ccsnh.edu
BRADLEY, Natalie .... 304-865-6041 487 H
natalie.bradley@ovu.edu
BRADLEY, Nedra .... 601-484-8674 247 A
nbradley@meridiancc.edu
BRADLEY, Pamela .... 903-927-3260 458 F
pbradley@wileyc.edu
BRADLEY, Patricia .... 410-704-0203 204 E
pbradley@towson.edu
BRADLEY, Rebecca .... 559-453-2021.. 43 A
rebecca.bradley@fresno.edu
BRADLEY, Roger .... 386-267-0565.. 98 C
BRADLEY, Ryan .... 205-348-8327.... 7 G
ryan.bradley@ua.edu
BRADLEY, Ryan .... 503-552-1862 374 D
rbradley@nunm.edu
BRADLEY, Shane .... 864-379-8766 409 E
bradley@erskine.edu
BRADLEY, Shannon .... 575-527-7524 287 F
shanbrad@nmsu.edu
BRADLEY, Stephen, L .... 864-242-5100 406 H
BRADLEY, Susie .... 352-245-4119 112 E
susie.bradley@taylorcollege.edu
BRADLEY, Tashia .... 937-708-5648 363 G
tbradley@wilberforce.edu
BRADLEY, Tashia .... 903-927-3329 458 F
tbradley@wileyc.edu
BRADLEY, Thomas, G ... 502-852-5295 186 A
tgerard.bradley@louisville.edu
BRADLEY, Tina .... 870-508-6130.. 17 G
tbradley@asumh.edu

BRADLEY, Tracey 865-539-7158 425 B tcbradley@pstcc.edu
BRADLEY, Tracy 304-357-4813 487 J tracybradley@ucwv.edu
BRADLEY, Vinson 251-580-2103 1 I vinson.bradley@coastalalabama.edu
BRADLEY-HASTY, Barbara 252-536-3386 335 B bhasty399@halifaxcc.edu
BRADSHAW, Amanda 910-592-8081 337 G jbradshaw@sampsoncc.edu
BRADSHAW, Amelia, M 804-523-5867 474 A abradshaw@reynolds.edu
BRADSHAW, Boyd, A 317-274-3880 157 D bobradsh@iupui.edu
BRADSHAW, Brent 972-279-6511 429 F bbradshaw@amberton.edu
BRADSHAW, Debra 816-268-5472 257 C dlbradshaw@nts.edu
BRADSHAW, Erin 505-224-4415 285 N ebradshaw3@cnm.edu
BRADSHAW, George 909-274-4419 52 J gbradshaw@mtsac.edu
BRADSHAW, Keifer 336-517-1589 327 A kbradshaw@bennett.edu
BRADSHAW, Kimberly 704-991-0206 338 C kbradshaw9661@stanly.edu
BRADSHAW, Lelia 276-523-2400 474 D lbradshaw@mecc.edu
BRADSHAW, Michael 601-477-4161 246 G michael.bradshaw@jcjc.edu
BRADSHAW, Phillip 757-569-6744 474 H pbradshaw@pdc.edu
BRADSHAW, Ryan 617-521-2000 218 G
BRADSHAW, Stephen 404-835-6136 423 B sbradshaw@richmont.edu
BRADSHAW, Sylvia 435-865-8175 460 A sylviabradshaw@suu.edu
BRADSHER, Carl 434-791-5646 464 I carl.bradsher@averett.edu
BRADSHER, Elizabeth 334-291-4979 1 H elizabeth.bradsher@cv.edu
BRADSTREET, Wendy 207-768-2771 195 G wbradstreet@nmcc.edu
BRADT, Jeremy 815-599-3500 139 A jeremy.bradt@highland.edu
BRADTKE, Ronny 651-255-6119 243 E rbradtke@unitedseminary.edu
BRADWAY, Marshall 413-748-3946 218 I mbradway@springfield.edu
BRADWAY, Marshall 413-565-1000 206 D mbradway@baypath.edu
BRADY, Allison 706-886-6831 126 D abrady@tfc.edu
BRADY, Anne Marie 240-895-2103 202 B ambrady@smcm.edu
BRADY, Bridget 805-898-4003 42 D bbrady@fielding.edu
BRADY, Chris 402-891-2991 267 A chris.brady@doane.edu
BRADY, Christian 859-257-1375 185 F cmbr284@uky.edu
BRADY, Christopher, D 815-921-2151 148 B c.brady@rockvalleycollege.edu
BRADY, Douglas 716-375-2455 313 C dbrady@sbu.edu
BRADY, Gerlinde 831-477-5672 27 D gebrady@cabrillo.edu
BRADY, Henry, E 510-642-5116 69 A hbrady@econ.berkeley.edu
BRADY, Jim 509-533-3538 479 D jim.brady@sfcc.spokane.edu
BRADY, Joseph 508-849-3447 205 H jbrady@annamaria.edu
BRADY, Jude 724-805-2612 398 A jude.brady@stvincent.edu
BRADY, Matthew 575-624-8442 287 B mbrady@nmmi.edu
BRADY, Michael, J 757-683-4156 469 B mbrady@odu.edu
BRADY, Patrick 610-785-6520 397 E pbrady@scs.edu
BRADY, Scott 630-942-2219 135 I bradys310@cod.edu
BRADY, Steven, P 812-877-8784 160 F brady1@rose-hulman.edu
BRADY, Teresa 918-465-1761 366 A tbrady@eosc.edu
BRADY, Todd 731-661-6566 426 F tbrady@uu.edu
BRADY, William, D 413-545-6124 211 G wdbrady@umass.edu
BRADY INCE, Robyn 973-353-5213 282 B ri131@newark.rutgers.edu
BRAEUNIG, Ray 856-566-6136 281 F braeunrc@rowan.edu
BRAGG, Chris 208-732-6775 131 D cbragg@csi.edu
BRAGG, David 804-524-5598 476 D dbragg@vsu.edu
BRAGG, Elizabeth 503-760-3131 371 G elizabeth@birthingway.edu
BRAGG, Kayce 662-685-4771 245 C kbragg@bmc.edu
BRAGG, Michele 765-998-5257 161 C mcbragg@taylor.edu
BRAGG CAREY, Amy 316-295-5888 174 A abcarey@friends.edu
BRAGIN, Marc 740-427-5228 354 I braginm@kenyon.edu
BRAHAMS, Teri, T 865-694-6476 425 B tbrahams@pstcc.edu
BRAHM, Gary 949-753-4774 71 D chancellor@brandman.edu
BRAHM, Teresa 563-589-3125 170 G tbrahm@univ.dbq.edu
BRAILER, James 410-516-8070 199 G jbraile1@jhu.edu
BRAINARD, Lisa, C 518-292-1959 313 A brainl@sage.edu
BRAINARD, Nancy 561-803-2116 105 C nancy_brainard@pba.edu
BRAINER, Charles 765-998-5271 161 C chbrainer@taylor.edu
BRAISHER, Mark 541-683-5141 373 B
BRAK, Robert 304-214-8901 488 J rbrak@wvncc.edu
BRAKER-BALKUM, Camile 201-355-1465 277 J brakerc@felician.edu
BRAKKE, Maureen 406-657-2243 264 D maureen.brakke@msubillings.edu
BRAKO, Lois 734-615-8936 231 H lbrako@umich.edu
BRAL, Jean 712-749-2220 164 C bralj@bvu.edu
BRALEY, Todd 267-295-2313 402 A
BRALLEY, Jeffrey 812-749-1455 159 O jbralley@oak.edu
BRALOWER, David, C 512-233-1424 442 I davidcb@stedwards.edu
BRALY, JR., Cliff 336-272-7102 329 C bralyc@greensboro.edu
BRAMAN, Sarah 919-684-2424 328 F sarah.braman@duke.edu
BRAME, Javon 303-797-5759 77 I javon.brame@arapahoe.edu
BRAME, Tracey 616-301-6800 233 C bramet@cooley.edu
BRAMHANDKAR, Alka 607-274-3341 302 G abramhandkar@ithaca.edu
BRAMLETT, Nancy 913-758-4372 178 B nancy.bramlett@stmary.edu
BRAMLETTE, Jeff 706-291-2121 125 C jbramlette@shorter.edu
BRAMMER, Robyn 714-892-7711 38 A rbrammer@gwc.cccd.edu
BRAMUCCI, Robert, S 949-582-4960 65 B rbramucci@socccd.edu
BRAMWELL, Kathleen 973-972-4121 282 A kfb44@rbhs.rutgers.edu
BRANAM, Patricia 615-904-8409 422 C pat.branam@mtsu.edu
BRANCACCIO, Matthew 860-701-5045 88 D brancaccio_m@mitchell.edu
BRANCATO, Katie, M 216-368-7577 349 D katie.brancato@case.edu
BRANCH, Carol 310-846-2554 55 C ananse@otis.edu
BRANCH, Craig 540-891-3007 473 I cbranch@germanna.edu
BRANCH, David 757-789-7990 473 H dbranch@es.vccs.edu
BRANCH, Enobong (Anna) 848-932-4400 282 A enobong.branch@rutgers.edu
BRANCH, Gary 256-395-2211 3 G gbranch@suscc.edu
BRANCH, Rachel, U 904-819-6294 99 E rbranch@flagler.edu
BRANCH-FRAPPIER, Michele 803-754-4100 408 E
BRANCHEAU, Ed 877-559-3621 28 H ebrancheau01@ciat.edu
BRANCHICK, Vivian 323-409-6302 50 A vbranchick1@dhs.lacounty.gov
BRANCHINI, Ann, Z 516-323-3008 306 M office-of-academic-affairs@molloy.edu
BRANCINI, Janine 516-323-3458 306 M jpayton@molloy.edu
BRANCOLINI, Kristine 310-338-4593 51 A kbrancol@lmu.edu
BRAND, Amy 617-253-4078 216 B
BRAND, Beth, G 302-831-3043 91 C bgbrand@udel.edu
BRAND, Frederick 609-984-1588 284 C fbrand@tesu.edu
BRAND, Jackie 806-457-4200 436 C jbrand@fpctx.edu
BRAND, Jonathan 319-895-4324 164 G jbrand@cornellcollege.edu
BRAND, Kathleen, C 864-646-1774 412 H kbrand@tctc.edu
BRAND, JR., Lee 901-751-8453 421 G
BRAND, Todd 606-326-2163 181 D todd.brand@kctcs.edu
BRAND, Tricia 971-722-6111 375 D tricia.brand@pcc.edu
BRANDAU-HYNEK, Ann 608-785-9585 500 C brandauhyneka@westerntc.edu
BRANDAUER, Samantha, C 717-245-8068 382 D brandaus@dickinson.edu
BRANDENBURG, Aurelia 859-985-3173 179 I brandenburga@berea.edu
BRANDENBURG, Greg 254-295-4658 453 D gbrandenburg@umhb.edu
BRANDENBURG, Mark, C 843-953-5252 407 C mark.brandenburg@citadel.edu
BRANDES, David 610-625-7753 390 F brandesd@moravian.edu
BRANDES, Paul 620-278-2173 177 H paul.brandes@sterling.edu
BRANDES, Rand 828-328-7077 330 F rand.brandes@lr.edu
BRANDI, Anne, E 516-572-7205 307 E anne.brandi@ncc.edu
BRANDI, Erica 610-398-5300 388 F ebrandi@lincolntech.edu
BRANDL-REEVES, Sara 715-346-2123 497 A sbrandlr@uwsp.edu
BRANDON, Alonzo, C 757-683-5383 469 B abrandon@odu.edu
BRANDON, Aylin 908-737-3101 278 E abrandon@kean.edu
BRANDON, Carolyn 828-327-7000 333 B cbrandon@cvcc.edu
BRANDON, Deborah 310-243-3789 30 E dbrandon@csudh.edu
BRANDON, Eric 828-328-7301 330 F eric.brandon@lr.edu
BRANDON, Felicia 914-674-7718 306 C fbrandon@mercy.edu
BRANDON, Mark, E 205-348-5117 7 G mbrandon@law.ua.edu
BRANDON, Robert 276-964-7200 475 C robert.brandon@sw.edu
BRANDON, Ronald 901-321-3256 418 G ronald.brandon@cbu.edu
BRANDSTATER, Nate 937-395-8618 354 J nate.brandstater@kc.edu
BRANDT, Alexander 910-521-6573 343 B alexander.brandt@uncp.edu
BRANDT, James 435-586-5454 460 A brandt@suu.edu
BRANDT, John 731-425-2624 424 E jbrandt@jscc.edu
BRANDT, Martin 934-420-2333 320 F martin.brandt@farmingdale.edu
BRANDT, Terry 218-299-4000 235 H
BRANDT, Tony 903-886-5761 447 B
BRANDT-PEARCE, Manté 434-924-1470 472 D mb9q@virginia.edu
BRANDT-RAUF, Paul 215-895-2215 382 F paul.w.brandt-rauf@drexel.edu
BRANDVOLD, Kelli 808-235-7403 130 E kellib@hawaii.edu
BRANDYBURG, Lawrence 251-405-7055 1 E lbrandyburg@bishop.edu
BRANGAITIS, David 845-758-7225 290 I dbrangaitis@bard.edu
BRANGAN MELL, Eileen 508-831-5000 220 F
BRANHAM, Carla 606-889-4827 181 E cbranham0022@kctcs.edu
BRANHAM, Janie 985-549-2000 193 A
BRANHAM, LaTonya 765-658-4141 154 J latonyabranham@depauw.edu
BRANHAM, Rich, A 651-631-5285 244 D rabranham@unwsp.edu
BRANKLE, Steve 479-524-7209 19 H sbrankle@jbu.edu
BRANNAN, Angie, R 262-524-7335 492 A abrannan@carrollu.edu
BRANNAN, Jessica 215-951-1355 387 A brannan@lasalle.edu
BRANNAN, Thomas, I 205-934-0177 8 A tbrannan@uab.edu
BRANNEN, Andrew 908-737-7023 278 E abrannen@kean.edu
BRANNEN, Melissia 803-786-3888 408 D mbrannen@columbiasc.edu
BRANNEN, Tammy 912-443-4797 125 B tbrannen@savannahtech.edu
BRANNER, Wade, H 540-464-7515 476 B brannerwh@vmi.edu
BRANNIGAN, Amber 719-389-6568 78 I abrannigan@coloradocollege.edu
BRANNOCK, Marina 336-838-6142 339 B mwbrannock859@wilkescc.edu
BRANNON, Andria 512-499-4346 454 H abrannon@utsystem.edu
BRANNON, Brett 618-664-6410 138 F brett.brannon@greenville.edu
BRANNON, Jennifer 478-934-3352 122 F jennifer.brannon@mga.edu
BRANNON, Nancy 417-777-5062 250 H nbrannon@texascountytech.edu
BRANON, Mark 256-306-2500 1 F mark.branon@calhoun.edu
BRANON, Rovy 206-685-6313 485 A rbranon@uw.edu
BRANSCOME, Tara 256-331-5438 3 C tbranscome@nwscc.edu
BRANSON, Carol 317-543-3235 159 L
BRANSON, Carol 904-819-6255 99 E cbranson@flagler.edu
BRANSON, Cathy 606-487-3550 181 I cathy.branson@kctcs.edu
BRANSON, Jeff 217-234-5253 142 C jbranson@lakelandcollege.edu
BRANSON, Mark 312-662-4121 132 G mbranson@adler.edu
BRANSON, Nick 847-543-2417 136 A nbranson@clcillinois.edu
BRANSON, Salinda Jo 309-649-6217 150 G jo.branson@src.edu
BRANSTAD, Jenni 206-934-5454 483 C jennifer.branstad@seattlecolleges.edu
BRANT, Todd 405-491-6312 369 H tbrant@snu.edu
BRANTLEY, Allison 205-652-3665 9 B abrantley@uwa.edu
BRANTLEY, Andra 706-379-3111 128 C abrantley@yhc.edu
BRANTLEY, Fiona 912-478-5371 120 C fbrantley@georgiasouthern.edu
BRANTLEY, Linda 978-762-4000 215 D lbrantley@northshore.edu
BRANTLEY, Loretta 870-230-5103 19 D brandll@hsu.edu
BRANTLEY, Michael 972-860-7640 434 H mbrantley@dcccd.edu
BRANTLEY, Will 405-585-5016 367 B will.brantley@okbu.edu
BRANTON-HOUSLEY, Mary 970-204-8121 81 A mary.branton-housley@frontrange.edu
BRANUM, Candise 503-253-3443 374 G cbranum@ocom.edu
BRANUM, Scott 409-944-1216 436 E tbranum@gc.edu
BRASE, Don 503-399-6149 372 B don.brase@chemeketa.edu
BRASE, Terry 559-934-2709 75 A terrybrase@whccd.edu
BRASE, Wendell 949-824-5107 69 D wcbrase@uci.edu
BRASEL, Steve 312-329-4194 144 I steve.brasel@moody.edu
BRASFIELD, Logan 870-633-4480 19 A lbrasfield@eacc.edu
BRASFIELD, Molly, A 601-984-1010 249 E mbrasfield@umc.edu
BRASHEAR, Jenna 270-852-3291 183 E jbrashear@kwc.edu

BRASHEAR, Kurth .... 402-643-7408 266 G
kurth.brashear@cune.edu
BRASHEAR, Pam .... 714-895-8234.. 38 A
pbrashear@gwc.cccd.edu
BRASHEARS, Randolph . 978-934-2384 212 B
randolph_brashears@uml.edu
BRASHEARS,
Thomas, A .... 540-464-7221 476 B
tbrashears@vmiaa.org
BRASHIER, Jason .... 731-989-6571 419 K
jbrashier@fhu.edu
BRASIER, Terry .... 828-398-7146 332 B
terrygbrasier@abtech.edu
BRASKAMP, Corey .... 605-256-5227 416 F
corey.braskamp@dsu.edu
BRASKICH, Brian .... 901-843-2430 423 A
braskichb@rhodes.edu
BRASSIL, Kristoffer, W .. 617-358-7000 207 E
kbrassil@bu.edu
BRASSORD, James, D .. 413-542-2202 205 G
jdbrassord@amherst.edu
BRASTETER, Christina .. 856-256-5173 281 F
brasteter@rowan.edu
BRASURE, III, Ralph ..... 860-515-3873.. 85 E
BRASWELL, Cara .... 251-460-6340.... 9 A
cbraswell@southalabama.edu
BRASWELL, Debbi .... 601-968-5920 245 B
dbraswell@belhaven.edu
BRASWELL, Don .... 318-257-2120 192 D
braswell@latech.edu
BRASWELL, Jody .... 417-690-3376 251 H
braswell@cofo.edu
BRASWELL, Kevin .... 931-372-6092 426 B
kbraswell@tntech.edu
BRASWELL, Macy .... 870-235-4078.. 21 C
macybraswell@saumag.edu
BRASWELL, Macy .... 870-235-4991.. 21 C
macybraswell@saumag.edu
BRASWELL, Mavour ...... 432-264-5025 437 F
mbraswell@howardcollege.edu
BRAT, Dave .... 434-582-7367 468 E
dabrat@liberty.edu
BRATCHER, Emily .... 630-752-5148 153 C
emily.bratcher@wheaton.edu
BRATCHER, James .... 636-922-8238 258 J
BRATHWAITE, Ormond . 216-987-5008 351 E
ormond.brathwaite@tri-c.edu
BRATHWAITE, Renea, C 612-343-4166 242M
rcbrathw@northcentral.edu
BRATSCH, John .... 559-730-3830.. 39 B
johnbr@cos.edu
BRATSCH-PRINCE,
Dawn .... 515-294-6410 163 G
deprince@iastate.edu
BRATTEN, Amy .... 863-667-5238 108 K
anbratten@seu.edu
BRATTON, Kevin .... 248-942-3214 229 C
kmbratto@oaklandcc.edu
BRATTON, Marissa .... 808-544-0249 128 G
mbratton@hpu.edu
BRATTON, Tara .... 501-337-5000.. 18 B
tbratton@asutr.edu
BRATULIN, Paul .... 909-384-8978.. 60 F
pbratulin@sbccd.cc.ca.us
BRAUCKMULLER, Lois .. 352-854-2322.. 97 N
brauckml@cf.edu
BRAUD, Terry .... 985-448-4017 192 F
terry.braud@nicholls.edu
BRAUER, Cynthia, A ..... 757-221-1693 465 N
cabra1@wm.edu
BRAUER, Dan .... 414-930-3121 494 E
brauerd@mtmary.edu
BRAUER, Douglas .... 904-632-5151 101 B
douglas.brauer@fscj.edu
BRAUGHLER, James ..... 920-206-2375 493 C
james.braughler@mbu.edu
BRAULT, Kelly, N .... 248-370-4921 229 I
brault@oakland.edu
BRAUN, Amanda .... 414-229-6599 496 B
abraun25@uwm.edu
BRAUN, Bernie .... 225-578-1295 189 E
bbraun@lsu.edu
BRAUN, Eric .... 740-351-3542 360 F
ebraun@shawnee.edu
BRAUN, Frank .... 440-826-3566 348 D
fbraun@bw.edu
BRAUN, Gregory .... 815-280-2263 141 B
gbraun@jjc.edu
BRAUN, Gretchen .... 864-294-3137 409 H
gretchen.braun@furman.edu
BRAUN, Janice, E .... 510-430-2047.. 52 E
jbraun@mills.edu

BRAUN, Keith, V .... 727-816-3336 105 F
braunk@phsc.edu
BRAUN, Lynn .... 419-783-2548 351 K
lbraun@defiance.edu
BRAUN, Mark, J .... 515-281-6426 163 F
mark.braun@iowaregents.edu
BRAUN, Mary, C .... 319-273-6144 164 A
mary.braun@uni.edu
BRAUN, Raymond .... 419-372-3411 348 G
rwbraun@bgsu.edu
BRAUN, Ronald .... 620-947-3121 177 I
ronb@tabor.edu
BRAUN, Sarah .... 207-834-7602 197 A
sarah.t.braun@maine.edu
BRAUN, Shannon .... 909-607-8170.. 37 F
sbraun@kgi.edu
BRAUNGARD, John ...... 518-629-4507 302 C
j.braungard@hvcc.edu
BRAUNSCHWEIG, Jim ... 712-274-6400 171 B
jim.braunschweig@witcc.edu
BRAUSCH, Anthony, R .. 513-231-2223 348 B
abrausch@athenaeum.edu
BRAUTIGAM, Al .... 432-837-8766 450 B
abrautigam@sulross.edu
BRAVER, Joel .... 845-782-1380 326 G
BRAVERMAN,
Janette, M .... 414-410-4004 491 I
jmbraverman@stritch.edu
BRAVMAN, John, C ...... 570-577-1511 379 C
john.bravman@bucknell.edu
BRAVO, Bruce .... 210-999-7601 451 E
bbravo@trinity.edu
BRAVO, Deyse .... 423-236-2789 423 F
dbravo@southern.edu
BRAVO, Karen, E .... 317-274-2581 157 D
kbravo@iupui.edu
BRAWLEY, Matt .... 269-467-9945 224 C
mbrawley@glenoaks.edu
BRAXTER, Andrew .... 501-279-5126.. 19 C
abraxter@harding.edu
BRAXTON, Asella .... 404-270-5078 126 B
aybraxton@spelman.edu
BRAXTON, Joanne, E .... 631-451-4160 321 C
braxtoj@sunysuffolk.edu
BRAXTON, Pamela .... 610-519-4032 401 K
pamela.braxton@villanova.edu
BRAY, Brian .... 207-859-4730 194 D
brain.bray@colby.edu
BRAY, Carrie .... 916-558-2120.. 50 J
brayc@scc.losrios.edu
BRAY, Corey .... 417-873-7290 252 G
cbray003@drury.edu
BRAY, Crystal .... 405-382-9287 369 F
c.bray@sscok.edu
BRAY, John .... 765-677-1771 158 B
john.bray@indwes.edu
BRAY, Kevin .... 803-822-3586 410 D
brayk@midlandstech.edu
BRAY, Laura .... 414-297-6048 499 C
braylm@matc.edu
BRAY, Lee .... 252-493-7264 336 H
lbray@email.pittcc.edu
BRAY, Paul .... 515-964-0601 166 D
brayp@faith.edu
BRAY, Rich .... 979-209-7285 431 H
richard.bray@blinn.edu
BRAY, Russell .... 616-526-6444 222 C
rtb2@calvin.edu
BRAY, Sean .... 410-617-2838 200 B
sbray@loyola.edu
BRAY, Stefanie .... 319-895-4243 164 G
sbray@cornellcollege.edu
BRAZAS, Tony, A .... 757-479-3706 472 F
tbrazas@vbts.edu
BRAZEAU, Gayle, A 304-696-7302 489M
brazeau@marshall.edu
BRAZELL, Frank .... 910-221-2224 331 B
fbrazell@manna.edu
BRAZELTON, Kent .... 713-646-1889 443 I
kbrazelton@stcl.edu
BRAZIER, Elise .... 512-313-3000 433 N
elise.brazier@concordia.edu
BRAZILL, Derrick .... 718-262-2780 295 E
dbrazill@york.cuny.edu
BRAZZIL, Nancy .... 512-471-1232 455 A
nancy@po.utexas.edu
BRAZZLE, Reggie .... 903-983-8217 438 F
rbrazzle@kilgore.edu
BREARLEY, Don .... 218-262-7309 238 D
donbrearley@hibbing.edu
BREAU, Walter, C .... 413-265-2222 208 E
breauw@elms.edu

BREAULT, Donna .... 419-289-5377 347 J
dbreault@ashland.edu
BREAULT, Susan .... 860-932-4062.. 87 E
sbreault@qvcc.edu
BREAUX, Aminta .... 301-860-3555 204 A
president@bowiestate.edu
BREAUX, Brad .... 337-521-8978 188 I
brad.breaux@solacc.edu
BREAUX, Megan .... 337-482-1394 193 B
mbreaux@louisiana.edu
BREAUX, Paula .... 337-482-6981 193 B
paula.breaux@louisiana.edu
BREAVLT, Donna .... 201-200-2101 279 D
dbreavlt@njcu.edu
BREAZILE, Chad .... 816-279-7000 250 B
chad@abtu.edu
BRECHBILL, Ryan .... 614-823-1520 359 H
rbrechbill@otterbein.edu
BRECHER, Sharon .... 305-534-7050 112 D
sbrecher@talmudicu.edu
BRECHT, Erma .... 936-468-2504 445 E
brechte@sfasu.edu
BRECKENRIDGE, Diane . 323-568-3304.. 36 C
dianebreckenridge@cdrewu.edu
BRECKENRIDGE, James 650-433-3826.. 55 L
jbreckenridge@paloaltou.edu
BRECKENRIDGE, Janet .. 903-923-2222 435 H
jbreckenridge@etbu.edu
BRECKENRIDGE,
Jim, G .... 717-245-4711 503 F
james.g.breckenridge.civ@mail.mil
BRECKHEIMER, Debra ... 310-660-5182.. 41 E
dbreckhe@elcamino.edu
BRECKNER, Laura, S .... 517-750-1200 231 C
lowen@arbor.edu
BRECZINSKI, Christian . 218-755-3883 237 F
christian.breczinski@bemidjistate.edu
BREDEMAN, Blaine .... 573-681-5187 254 G
bredemanb@lincolnu.edu
BREDESON, Janna .... 770-426-2700 122 C
janna.bredeson@life.edu
BREE, Kristin .... 812-357-6610 161 A
kbree@saintmeinrad.edu
BREEDEN, Ann Lloyd .... 804-289-8732 472 C
abreeden@richmond.edu
BREEDEN, Suzette .... 304-205-6614 488 D
BREEDLOVE, Billy .... 806-742-2011 450 D
BREEDLOVE, Billy .... 806-742-2116 450 F
billy.breedlove@ttu.edu
BREEDLOVE, Paul .... 541-880-2239 373 C
breedlove@klamathcc.edu
BREEMS, Jennifer .... 712-722-6043 165 I
jenni.breems@dordt.edu
BREEN, Dennis .... 740-284-5201 352 I
dbreen@franciscan.edu
BREEN, Lorraine .... 301-295-3007 503 C
lorraine.breen@usuhs.edu
BREER, Mary .... 217-234-5401 142 C
mbreer@lakeland.cc.il.us
BREERWOOD, Adam, J . 601-403-1201 248 E
abreerwood@prcc.edu
BREES, Chris .... 641-844-5679 167 G
chris.brees@iavalley.edu
BREESE, Eric .... 312-567-3153 140 A
ebreese@iit.edu
BREESE, Jeffrey, R .... 330-823-2690 362 E
breesejr@mountunion.edu
BREGE, Nicholas .... 989-358-7202 221 C
bregen@alpenacc.edu
BREHENY, Marie .... 413-775-1397 214 E
brehenym@gcc.mass.edu
BREHLER, Elizabeth .... 336-506-4138 332 A
elizabeth.brehler@alamancecc.edu
BREHUN, Megan .... 704-991-0161 338 C
mbrehun6994@stanly.edu
BREIER, Barbara .... 512-245-2396 450 C
blb137@txstate.edu
BREINER, Ozzie .... 610-758-3500 388 E
lb05@lehigh.edu
BREISTER, Peggy .... 920-424-1133 496 C
BREIT, Karen .... 715-634-4790 492 L
kbreit@lco.edu
BREITBACH, William ..... 530-242-7555.. 64 C
wbreitbach@shastacollege.edu
BREITBART, Donna .... 406-447-6954 264 B
donna.breitbart@helenacollege.edu
BREITBARTH,
Jonathan, S .... 651-641-8796 235 I
breitbarth@csp.edu
BREITENBACH, Edward . 231-777-0526 228 G
edward.breitenbach@muskegoncc.edu
BREITFELD, Adrian .... 310-476-9777.. 25 I
adrian.breitfeld@aju.edu

BREITHAUPT, Jeff .... 917-493-4702 305 A
jbreithaupt@msmnyc.edu
BREITHAUPT, Scott .... 706-238-5897 116 B
sbreithaupt@berry.edu
BREITIGAN, Katie .... 585-567-9227 302 B
katie.breitigan@houghton.edu
BREITLER, Alex .... 209-954-5151.. 61 G
alex.breitler@deltacollege.edu
BREITMEYER, Chris ...... 503-338-2425 372 D
cbreitmeyer@clatsopcc.edu
BREITSPRECKER, Lisa ... 414-930-3131 494 E
breitspl@mtmary.edu
BREJA, Lisa .... 641-844-5576 167 E
lisa.breja@iavalley.edu
BREJC, Jessica .... 303-546-5291.. 82 A
jbrejc@naropa.edu
BREKKE, Paul .... 701-858-3485 345 E
paul.brekke@minostateu.edu
BREKKE WAGONER,
Laura, K .... 304-637-1267 487 C
brekkel@dewv.edu
BRELAND, Jennifer, R ... 205-934-3555.... 8 A
jbreland@uab.edu
BRELAND, Moddie .... 914-674-7325 306 C
mbreland@mercy.edu
BREMAR, Nancy .... 304-424-8000 490 F
nancy.bremar@wvup.edu
BREMER, Cris, M .... 559-489-2220.. 67 B
crism.bremer@fresnocitycollege.edu
BREMNER, Ellen .... 860-439-2413.. 87 H
ebremner@conncoll.edu
BREMS, Nora .... 317-738-8864 155 D
nbrems@franklincollege.edu
BRENBERG, Brian .... 212-659-7200 303 H
bbrenberg@tkc.edu
BRENEMAN, Curt .... 518-276-6305 312 C
brenec@rpi.edu
BRENEMAN, Matt .... 714-449-7480.. 51 B
mbrenema@ketchum.edu
BRENES, Omar .... 913-288-7386 175 B
obrenes@kckcc.edu
BRENIZER, Sherri .... 641-784-5051 166 E
brenizer@graceland.edu
BRENN, James, E .... 803-535-5326 407 D
jbrenn@claflin.edu
BRENNAN, Anne .... 847-376-7046 146 G
abrennan@oakton.edu
BRENNAN, Catherine .... 973-596-3124 279 E
catherine.brennan@njit.edu
BRENNAN,
Christopher, P .... 727-864-8122.. 98 J
brennacp@eckerd.edu
BRENNAN, David .... 410-857-2284 200 F
dbrennan@mcdaniel.edu
BRENNAN, Jennifer .... 215-489-2346 382 B
jennifer.brennan@delval.edu
BRENNAN, Joe .... 802-831-1244 463 C
jbrennan@vermontlaw.edu
BRENNAN, Jonathan ...... 518-629-7311 302 C
j.brennan@hvcc.edu
BRENNAN, Joseph, A ... 973-655-3054 279 B
brennanjos@montclair.edu
BRENNAN, Joyce .... 508-678-2811 214 B
joyce.brennan@bristolcc.edu
BRENNAN, Kate .... 856-225-6577 281 G
katecb@camden.rutgers.edu
BRENNAN, Kelly .... 843-953-1642 407 C
kbrenna1@citadel.edu
BRENNAN, Kristin .... 207-725-3000 194 C
BRENNAN, Kwi .... 201-200-3489 279 D
kbrennan@njcu.edu
BRENNAN, Kyle .... 309-438-5626 140 D
ksbren1@ilstu.edu
BRENNAN, Lipa .... 718-438-2727 326 H
rlb@novominsk.com
BRENNAN, Mary .... 512-245-2317 450 C
mb18@txstate.edu
BRENNAN, Megan .... 801-883-8336 459 A
BRENNAN, Michael .... 813-253-7124 102 B
mbrennan@hccfl.edu
BRENNAN, Monica .... 207-453-5129 195 F
mbrennan@kvcc.me.edu
BRENNAN, Robert, J ..... 301-447-7432 201 B
brennan@msmary.edu
BRENNAN, Robert, J ..... 410-293-1482 504 A
rbrennan@usna.edu
BRENNAN, Terence .... 303-753-6046.. 83 F
tbrennan@rmcad.edu
BRENNAN, Terrence, P . 972-881-5734 433 I
tbrennan@collin.edu
BRENNAN, Victoria .... 805-482-2755.. 59 G
vbrennan@stjohnsem.edu

BRIGGS, Susan .... 406-683-7303 264 A
susan.briggs@umwestern.edu
BRIGGS, Tammie .... 334-876-9236.... 2 D
tammie.briggs@wccs.edu
BRIGGS, Thyra .... 909-607-4408.. 44 H
thyra_briggs@hmc.edu
BRIGGS, Wayne .... 214-333-5111 434 C
wayne@dbu.edu
BRIGGS, William .... 406-477-6215 263 C
wbriggs@cdkc.edu
BRIGGS-PICKETT,
Jodi, M .... 508-929-5000 213 G
BRIGHAM, Brooke .... 508-849-3596 205 H
bbrigham@annamaria.edu
BRIGHAM, Doug .... 208-459-5268 131 C
dbrigham@collegeofidaho.edu
BRIGHAM, Jim .... 256-782-5820.... 6 A
jbrigham@jsu.edu
BRIGHAM, Reginald ...... 573-466-4087 253 B
reginald.brigham@eastcentral.edu
BRIGHT, Brett .... 402-323-3400 269 C
BRIGHT, Brett .... 620-665-3579 174 G
brightb@hutchcc.edu
BRIGHT, Cynthia .... 832-813-6568 439 C
cynthia.i.bright@lonestar.edu
BRIGHT, David .... 863-667-5310 108 K
drbright@seu.edu
BRIGHT, George, L .... 252-335-3396 341 B
glbright@ecsu.edu
BRIGHT, Harold .... 480-219-6036 250 A
hbright@atsu.edu
BRIGHT, Harry .... 641-472-1178 168 C
hbright@miu.edu
BRIGHT, Josh .... 951-827-1012.. 70 B
BRIGHT, Kristina .... 573-642-3361 262 E
BRIGHT, Sarah .... 636-481-3218 254 C
sbright@jeffco.edu
BRIGHT, Steve .... 434-544-8208 471 L
bright@lynchburg.edu
BRIGHTON, Robyn, M .. 407-582-3895 113 I
rbrighton1@valenciacollege.edu
BRIGHTSMAN, David .... 414-443-8739 498 A
david.brightsman@wlc.edu
BRIGNONI, Linda, M .... 818-677-2085.. 32 C
linda.brignoni@csun.edu
BRIKER, Olga .... 610-795-6079 385 I
obriker@haverford.edu
BRILEY, Dalton .... 540-464-7637 476 B
dbriley@follett.com
BRILL, Ann, M .... 785-864-4755 177 J
abrill@ku.edu
BRILLEY, Amy .... 217-362-6488 144 G
abrilley@millikin.edu
BRILLHART, David .... 740-366-9319 349 F
brillhart.5@cotc.edu
BRIMBERRY, Ryan .... 812-877-8621 160 F
brimberr@rose-hulman.edu
BRIMHALL, Carrie .... 218-736-1503 239 C
carrie.brimhall@minnesota.edu
BRIMHALL, Joseph .... 503-251-5712 377 B
jebrimhall@uws.edu
BRIMHALL-VARGAS,
Mark .... 781-736-4411 208 A
mbv@brandeis.edu
BRIMLEY, Pamela .... 501-420-1219.. 16 L
pamela.brimley@arkansasbaptist.edu
BRIMMER, Suzette .... 713-718-6158 437 C
suzette.brimmer@hccs.edu
BRIMMER, Zachary .... 518-783-2302 315 E
zbrimmer@siena.edu
BRIMMERMAN, Roger .. 620-242-0435 176 B
BRINDLE, Denise .... 978-665-3454 212 E
dbrindl1@fitchburgstate.edu
BRINDLEY, Peter .... 423-266-4574 423 B
BRINDLEY, Roger, N .... 814-863-4030 391 G
rnb5238@psu.edu
BRINER, Clare .... 708-974-5376 145 A
brinerc@morainevalley.edu
BRINER, Sean .... 760-750-4404.. 33 A
sbriner@csusm.edu
BRINEY, Colleen .... 479-575-5459.. 21 F
cbriney@uark.edu
BRINGER, Michael .... 573-288-6528 252 F
mbringer@culver.edu
BRINGHAM, Holly .... 509-682-6705 485 H
hbringham@wvc.edu
BRINGLEY, Courtney ..... 518-327-6059 311 C
cbringley@paulsmiths.edu
BRINING, Patricia .... 215-968-8091 379 D
patricia.brining@bucks.edu
BRINK, Ben .... 314-246-7150 262 C
benjaminbrink87@webster.edu
BRINK, Benita .... 719-587-7426.. 77 G
babrink@adams.edu
BRINK, Laura .... 617-521-2127 218 G
laura.brink@simmons.edu
BRINK, Stephanie .... 573-823-8594 251 E
sbrink@centralmethodist.edu
BRINK-DRESCHER,
Judith .... 516-323-3925 306 M
jdrescher@molloy.edu
BRINKER, Jessica .... 919-445-4636 342 C
jessica_brinker@unc.edu
BRINKER, JR.,
Thomas, M .... 215-572-4039 378 E
brinkert@arcadia.edu
BRINKLEY, David .... 270-745-6140 186 C
david.brinkley@wku.edu
BRINKLEY, Derek .... 312-369-7493 136 D
dbrinkley@colum.edu
BRINKLEY, Frank .... 336-770-3349 343 D
brinkleyt@uncsa.edu
BRINKLEY, Martin .... 919-962-4417 342 C
martin92@unc.edu
BRINKLEY, Tom .... 336-278-7452 328 J
tbrinkley@elon.edu
BRINKLEY-KENNEDY,
Rhonda .... 513-861-6400 361 F
BRINKMAN, Kevin .... 513-618-1926 350 E
kbrinkman@ccms.edu
BRINKMAN, Matt .... 423-614-8395 420 H
mmbrinkman@leeuniversity.edu
BRINKMANN, Robert .... 815-753-1000 146 B
BRINSON, Bruce .... 214-379-5573 441 F
bbrinson@pqc.edu
BRINSON, Donna .... 770-533-6921 122 B
dbrinson@laniertech.edu
BRINSON, Leigh, T .... 309-341-7130 141 G
ltbrinson@knox.edu
BRINSON, Reginald ...... 404-756-8458 123 E
rwbrinson@msm.edu
BRINSON, Sarah .... 229-500-2173 114 H
sarah.brinson@asurams.edu
BRINSON, Willie, L ...... 919-735-5151 338 H
wlbrinson@waynecc.edu
BRINTON, Peggy .... 412-281-2600 396 B
pbrinton@pci.edu
BRIONES, Eloisa .... 650-574-6161.. 62 K
BRIONES, Eloisa, M ..... 650-738-4227.. 62 L
briones@smccd.edu
BRIONES, Evonne .... 816-472-4852 254 D
ebriones@kcai.edu
BRISACK, Al .... 608-663-3289 492 F
abrisack@edgewood.edu
BRISBON, T. Muriel ...... 610-896-1250 385 I
tbrisbon@haverford.edu
BRISCOE, Chad, C .... 574-372-5100 155 F
chad.briscoe@grace.edu
BRISCOE, Connie .... 407-646-2194 106 L
cbriscoe@rollins.edu
BRISCOE-ALBA, Susana 845-569-3414 307 D
susana.alba@msmc.edu
BRISENO, Jackelyne, K . 956-326-2170 446 E
jackelyne.briseno@tamiu.edu
BRISENO, Jason .... 512-223-7550 430 I
jbrisen2@austincc.edu
BRISKEY, Barbara .... 845-758-6822 290 I
BRISKEY, Marvin .... 614-947-6002 352 J
marv.briskey@franklin.edu
BRISLIN, Shawn, P .... 607-746-4670 320 D
brislisp@delhi.edu
BRISSON, Michelle .... 973-408-3454 277 A
mbrisson@drew.edu
BRISTER, Amelia .... 318-345-9000 188 D
BRISTLE, Shawn .... 928-757-0860.. 14 F
sbristle@mohave.edu
BRISTOL, Amanda .... 423-461-8490 422 E
abristol@milligan.edu
BRISTOL, Caterina .... 334-229-4297.... 4 A
cbristol@alasu.edu
BRISTOL, Lori .... 610-225-5010 383 B
lbristol@eastern.edu
BRISTOR, Patricia .... 724-852-3315 402 C
pbristor@waynesburg.edu
BRISTOW, Aimee .... 573-592-5365 262 E
aimee.bristow@westminster-mo.edu
BRISTOW, Cliff .... 405-912-9037 368 J
cbristow@ru.edu
BRITE, Chris .... 660-944-2863 251 J
cbrite@conception.edu
BRITIGAN, Bradley, E ... 402-599-8878 269 K
bradley.britigan@unmc.edu
BRITT, Allysceaeioun .... 615-327-6457 421 D
abritt@mmc.edu
BRITT, Amber, N .... 601-643-8301 245 F
nikki.britt@colin.edu
BRITT, Denise .... 404-752-1500 123 E
dbritt@msm.edu
BRITT, Eddie .... 601-643-8628 245 F
eddie.britt@colin.edu
BRITT, Frank .... 480-947-6644.. 14 N
frank.britt@pennfoster.edu
BRITT, Frank, F .... 770-729-8400 115 D
BRITT, Jeanette .... 814-824-2247 389 G
jbritt@mercyhurst.edu
BRITT, Josh .... 843-921-6997 411 A
jbritt@netc.edu
BRITT, Kenith .... 317-955-6209 159 K
kbritt@marian.edu
BRITT, Kimberly .... 602-285-7607.. 13 F
kimberly.britt@phoenixcollege.edu
BRITT, L.D .... 757-446-8996 466 D
brittld@evms.edu
BRITT, Sanfrena .... 254-519-5447 447 A
sanfrena.britt@tamuct.edu
BRITT, Shane .... 785-738-9075 176 F
sbritt@ncktc.edu
BRITT, Sharda, D .... 252-862-1307 337 C
sdbritt0117@roanokechowan.edu
BRITT, Tamara .... 718-862-7858 304 M
tamara.britt@manhattan.edu
BRITT, Tammy, T .... 704-233-8111 344 F
tbritt@wingate.edu
BRITT-PETTY, Debra ...... 408-848-4711.. 43 E
dbrittpetty@gavilan.edu
BRITTAIN, Kate .... 732-445-3783 282 A
k.brittain@admissions.rutgers.edu
BRITTAIN, Linda, D ...... 717-264-3787 403 C
lbrittain@wilson.edu
BRITTEN, Robert .... 425-739-8100 481 C
robert.britten@lwtech.edu
BRITTEN, Scott .... 734-973-5981 232 D
csbritten@wccnet.edu
BRITTO, Vanessa .... 401-863-5970 403 J
vanessa_britto@brown.edu
BRITTON, Bill .... 805-756-2190.. 29 I
bibritto@calpoly.edu
BRITTON, Dana, J .... 800-233-4220 389 H
dbritton@messiah.edu
BRITTON, Danielle .... 607-778-5203 317 D
brittondf@sunybroome.edu
BRITTON, JB .... 616-526-6695 222 C
jbritton@calvin.edu
BRITTON, Karen .... 781-239-3101 214 G
kbritton@massbay.edu
BRITTON, Keith, E .... 803-938-3882 413 G
kbritton@uscsumter.edu
BRITTON, Mark .... 419-289-5057 347 J
mbritto3@ashland.edu
BRITTON-SPEARS, Ona . 918-463-2931 365 J
ona.britton-spears@connorsstate.edu
BRITZ, Johannes .... 412-229-4501 496 B
britz@uwm.edu
BRIX, Timothy .... 636-922-8211 258 J
tbrix@stchas.edu
BRIZUELA, Erika .... 310-289-5123.. 74 I
erika.brizuela@wcui.edu
BRNCICH, Lisa .... 815-479-7589 143 I
lbrncich@mchenry.edu
BROADBENT, Becky ...... 435-879-4242 460 B
becky.broadbent@dixie.edu
BROADDUS, Matthew ... 865-573-4517 420 E
mbroaddus@johnsonu.edu
BROADHURST, Gary ..... 315-792-5573 306 K
gbroadhurst@mvcc.edu
BROADIE, II, Paul .... 352-395-5164 108 A
paul.broadie@sfcollege.edu
BROADWATER, Bonnie . 301-387-3050 199 A
bonnie.broadwater@garrettcollege.edu
BROADWATER, III,
Colby, M .... 843-577-5245 406 E
BROADWATER,
Kimberly .... 662-254-3484 248 B
kbroadwater@mvsu.edu
BROADWATER, Larry .... 865-251-1800 423 E
lbroadw@south.edu
BROADWATER,
Melanie, R .... 724-589-2754 399 D
mbroadwater@thiel.edu
BROADWAY, Shane ...... 501-660-1001.. 17 C
sbroadway@asusystem.edu
BROADWELL, Phyllis .... 912-279-5816 117 F
pbroadwell@ccga.edu
BROBERG, Loretta .... 402-878-2380 267 D
loretta.broberg@littlepriest.edu
BROBERG, Sarah .... 828-251-6967 342 B
sbroberg@unca.edu
BROBERG, Vic .... 610-292-9852 396 J
vic.broberg@reseminary.edu
BROCCHINI, Jenna .... 602-383-8228.. 16 C
jbrocchini@uat.edu
BROCIOUS, Heather ...... 973-720-2705 284 J
brocioush@wpunj.edu
BROCK, Ashleigh .... 804-289-8749 472 C
ash.brock@richmond.edu
BROCK, Casson .... 501-337-5000.. 18 B
cbrock@asutr.edu
BROCK, III, Harry, B .... 205-726-4071.... 6 E
bbrock@samford.edu
BROCK, James .... 805-893-4151.. 70 E
BROCK, Jeffrey .... 203-432-2550.. 90 C
BROCK, Jessica .... 479-356-2188.. 18 C
jbrock15@atu.edu
BROCK, Lisa .... 256-840-4185.... 3 F
lisa.brock@snead.edu
BROCK, Marcius .... 507-389-1180 239 D
marcius.brock@mnsu.edu
BROCK, Marty, A .... 662-329-7152 248 A
mabrock@muw.edu
BROCK, Michael, G .... 610-989-1246 401 I
mbrock@vfmac.edu
BROCK, Michele .... 559-737-5441.. 39 B
michelebr@cos.edu
BROCK, Michelle .... 704-290-5357 337 I
mbrock@spcc.edu
BROCKBANK, Kevin ...... 509-533-7042 479 B
kevin.brockbank@scc.spokane.edu
BROCKBANK, Kevin ...... 509-533-7042 479 C
kevin.brockbank@scc.spokane.edu
BROCKEL, Amber .... 605-229-8427 415 I
amber.brockel@presentation.edu
BROCKELBANK, Steve ... 740-826-6109 356 H
stevenb@muskingum.edu
BROCKETT, Lori .... 760-750-4405.. 33 A
brockett@csusm.edu
BROCKGREITENS,
Kathy .... 636-922-8229 258 J
kbrockgreitens@stchas.edu
BROCKHOFF, Jennifer ... 502-585-9911 184 H
jbrockhoff@spalding.edu
BROCKIE, Clarena .... 406-353-2607 262 H
cbrockie@ancollege.edu
BROCKIE, Kim .... 406-353-2607 262 H
kbrockie@ancollege.edu
BROCKIE, Michele .... 406-353-2607 262 H
mbrockie@ancollege.edu
BROCKMAN, Beverly ..... 812-488-2954 161 G
bb318@evansville.edu
BROCKMAN, Diane .... 660-596-7205 259 M
dbrockman@sfccmo.edu
BROCKMAN, Mark .... 513-745-4842 364 G
brockmanm1@xavier.edu
BROCKMAN, Tom .... 614-251-4453 358 B
brockmat2@ohiodominican.edu
BROCKMAN, Tracy .... 614-985-2324 359 L
tbrockman@pcj.edu
BROCKMYER,
Richard, A .... 801-832-2516 461 F
rbrockmyer@westminstercollege.edu
BROCKSMITH, Susan .... 812-888-4588 162 F
BROCKWAY, Celia .... 804-862-6100 470 C
cbrockway@rbc.edu
BROD, David .... 540-857-6675 475 G
dbrod@virginiawestern.edu
BRODA, Joanna .... 212-346-1652 311 A
jbroda@pace.edu
BRODA, Mary .... 517-750-1200 231 C
mary.broda@arbor.edu
BRODERICK, Daniela .... 815-479-7873 143 I
dbroderick@mchenry.edu
BRODERICK, Jo .... 978-921-4242 217 B
jo.broderick@montserrat.edu
BRODERICK, Kimberley 413-755-4490 216 A
kebroderick@stcc.edu
BRODERICK, Mac .... 603-513-1327 274 G
mac.broderick@granite.edu
BRODERICK, Marybeth . 845-848-7824 298 C
marybeth.broderick@dc.edu
BRODERICK, Michael .... 860-515-3885.. 85 E
mbroderick@charteroak.edu
BRODERICK, Shannon .. 413-572-5403 213 F
sbroderick@westfield.ma.edu
BRODERICK, Victor, K .. 217-786-2414 143 B
victor.broderick@llcc.edu
BRODERSEN, Lisa .... 319-226-2034 163 C
lisa.brodersen@allencollege.edu
BRODIGAN,
Rebecca, H .... 207-859-4692 194 D
becky.brodigan@colby.edu

BROWN, Alanka .... 305-237-6034 104 E abrown4@mdc.edu
BROWN, Alesia .... 864-941-8611 411 C brown.a@ptc.edu
BROWN, Alex .... 404-712-8822 118 E alexander.brown@emory.edu
BROWN, Alison .... 256-761-6310.... 7 B akbrown@talladega.edu
BROWN, Allen .... 816-268-5400 257 C
BROWN, Amanda .... 419-207-6301 347 J abrown18@ashland.edu
BROWN, Amy .... 704-463-3037 339 E amy.brown@pfeiffer.edu
BROWN, Amy, L .... 607-746-4584 320 D brownal@delhi.edu
BROWN, Andrea .... 419-517-8893 355 C abrown@lourdes.edu
BROWN, Andrew .... 651-696-6069 236 I dabrown@macalester.edu
BROWN, Angela .... 315-312-4100 318 D angela.brown@oswego.edu
BROWN, Angelyne .... 803-327-7402 407 F abrown@clintoncollege.edu
BROWN, Anita .... 937-319-6164 347 G abrown@antiochcollege.edu
BROWN, Ann .... 919-516-5083 339 I abrown@st-aug.edu
BROWN, Anne .... 704-687-5770 342 D abrow316@uncc.edu
BROWN, Ansel, E .... 919-530-7477 341 E browna@nccu.edu
BROWN, Anthony .... 718-951-5000 293 C anthony.brown@brooklyn.cuny.edu
BROWN, Anthony .... 866-217-9823 187 G
BROWN, Art .... 515-964-6394 165 A acbrown9@dmacc.edu
BROWN, Barbara .... 229-430-3504 114 I bbrown@albanytech.edu
BROWN, Barry .... 406-243-6800 263 K barry.brown@umontana.edu
BROWN, Beverly .... 718-262-2238 295 E bbrown@york.cuny.edu
BROWN, Beverly, D ...... 239-590-1051 109 K bdbrown@fgcu.edu
BROWN, Bill .... 919-760-2367 331 D brownw@meredith.edu
BROWN, Bill .... 757-455-5730 477 C bbrown@vwu.edu
BROWN, Bob .... 707-476-4239.. 58 I bob-brown@redwoods.edu
BROWN, Bobbie .... 806-742-3661 450 F bobbie.brown@ttu.edu
BROWN, Bonita .... 859-572-5172 184 E brownb33@nku.edu
BROWN, Bradley .... 435-586-7871 460 A brown@suu.edu
BROWN, Brandon .... 410-951-3817 204 B brabrown@coppin.edu
BROWN, Brent, K .... 801-581-3003 459 O brent.brown@osp.utah.edu
BROWN, Brian .... 315-364-3207 324 I bbrown@wells.edu
BROWN, Brianna .... 412-365-1262 380 G b.brown@chatham.edu
BROWN, JR., Buck, F .. 864-379-8805 409 E brown@erskine.edu
BROWN, Calvin .... 404-880-6042 117 C cbrown@cau.edu
BROWN, Calvin .... 205-348-5966.... 7 G cbrown@alumni.ua.edu
BROWN, Camille .... 781-280-3200 215 B
BROWN, Candice .... 678-359-5010 120 F candiceb@gordonstate.edu
BROWN, Carl .... 614-947-6080 352 J carl.brown@franklin.edu
BROWN, Carmen .... 662-246-6275 247 D cbrown@msdelta.edu
BROWN, Carmen .... 803-812-7318 413 E cdbrown@mailbox.sc.edu
BROWN, Carolanne ...... 561-803-2050 105 C carolanne_brown@pba.edu
BROWN, Carolus .... 408-498-5100.. 73 B cbrown@cogswell.edu
BROWN, Carolyn .... 229-500-2821 114 H carolyn.brown@asurams.edu
BROWN, Catherine .... 716-614-5950 309 G cbrown@niagaracc.suny.edu
BROWN, Cathy .... 620-241-0723 172 J cathy.brown@centralchristian.edu
BROWN, Chad .... 918-647-1375 365 E cbrown@carlalbert.edu
BROWN, Chad, M .... 740-588-1201 365 B cbrown@zanestate.edu
BROWN, Chelsea .... 301-934-2251 198 G crclute@csmd.edu
BROWN, Chris .... 205-934-1294.... 8 A csbrown@uab.edu
BROWN, Chris .... 845-257-3231 316 E browncl@newpaltz.edu
BROWN, Chris .... 507-389-1713 239 D christopher.brown@mnsu.edu
BROWN, Chris .... 937-433-3410 352 G
BROWN, Christi .... 985-545-1500 188 E
BROWN, Christopher .... 785-864-4904 177 J jcbrown2@ku.edu
BROWN, Christopher .... 949-376-6000.. 47 D cbrown@lcad.edu
BROWN, Cindy .... 417-455-5540 252 E cindybrown@crowder.edu
BROWN, Cinnamon ...... 573-592-5192 262 E cinnamon.brown@westminster-mo.edu
BROWN, Claude, E .... 601-977-6181 249 C cebrown@tougaloo.edu
BROWN, Coleen .... 573-875-8700 251 I
BROWN, Courtney, L .... 540-365-4201 467 B cbrown@ferrum.edu
BROWN, Craig .... 208-562-3412 131 E craigbrown@cwi.edu
BROWN, Curressia .... 662-254-3600 248 B cbrown@mvsu.edu
BROWN, Cynthia .... 706-754-7714 123 G cbrown@northgatech.edu
BROWN, Dale .... 413-552-2420 214 F dbrown@hcc.edu
BROWN, Damon .... 989-463-7151 221 B browndm@alma.edu
BROWN, Daniel .... 409-880-8400 449 G dbrown109@lamar.edu
BROWN, Daniel .... 806-291-3416 457 I dbrown@wbu.edu
BROWN, Danielle .... 570-372-4757 398 F browndd@susqu.edu
BROWN, Darrell .... 254-968-9497 446 D dwbrown@tarleton.edu
BROWN, Darryl .... 301-295-3412 503 C darryl.brown@usuhs.edu
BROWN, David .... 262-691-5346 500 B dbrown@wctc.edu
BROWN, David .... 910-668-3331 440 F dbrown@nctc.edu
BROWN, David .... 270-745-4449 186 C david.brown@wku.edu
BROWN, David .... 256-233-8187.... 4 C david.brown@athens.edu
BROWN, David, A .... 409-772-3001 456 E davibrow@utmb.edu
BROWN, Davin .... 916-558-2142.. 50 J brownd@scc.losrios.edu
BROWN, Deborah .... 202-319-6915.. 92 A browndl@cua.edu
BROWN, Deborah, R .... 757-446-5828 466 D browndr@evms.edu
BROWN, Demetrius ...... 601-974-1225 247 B browndl@millsaps.edu
BROWN, Demitrius .... 210-999-8844 451 E dbrown7@trinity.edu
BROWN, Denelle .... 570-577-2071 379 C denelle.brown@bucknell.edu
BROWN, Derek .... 620-862-5252 171 H
BROWN, Derek .... 303-404-5492.. 81 A derek.brown@frontrange.edu
BROWN, Derrick .... 903-593-8311 448 G dbrown@texascollege.edu
BROWN, Diane, M .... 484-365-7400 388 H dbrown@lincoln.edu
BROWN, Dina .... 603-897-8232 273 I dbrown@rivier.edu
BROWN, Dolores, M .... 262-524-7133 492 A docampo@carrollu.edu
BROWN, Donna .... 951-372-8080.. 45 D
BROWN, Donna .... 479-248-7236.. 19 B dbrown@ecollege.edu
BROWN, Donna .... 701-477-7862 346 J dbrown@tm.edu
BROWN, Donnie .... 806-291-1168 457 I brownd@wbu.edu
BROWN, Douglas .... 508-588-9100 215 A dbrown43@massasoit.mass.edu
BROWN, Douglas, E ..... 515-964-0601 166 D brownd@faith.edu
BROWN, Ed .... 406-657-2044 264 D edward.brown2@msubillings.edu
BROWN, Edward .... 303-615-0060.. 81 M ebrow100@msudenver.edu
BROWN, Elaine .... 803-705-4529 406 G elaine.brown@benedict.edu
BROWN, Elizabeth .... 504-862-8335 191 F beth@tulane.edu
BROWN, Eric .... 207-778-7276 196 I brown.eric@maine.edu
BROWN, Eric .... 530-221-4275.. 64 B ebrown@shasta.edu
BROWN, Erik .... 650-203-4865.. 24 G
BROWN, Erik .... 218-726-8891 243 G etbrown@d.umn.edu
BROWN, Erika .... 404-752-1723 123 E etbrown@msm.edu
BROWN, Erin .... 405-789-7661 369 I erin.brown@swcu.edu
BROWN, Erinn .... 308-345-8112 267 J browne@mpcc.edu
BROWN, Fran .... 248-476-1122 227 E fbrown@msp.edu
BROWN, Gary .... 608-785-9167 500 C browng@westerntc.edu
BROWN, Gary, L .... 252-335-3277 341 B glbrown@ecsu.edu
BROWN, Gary, M .... 919-497-3213 330 I gmbrown@louisburg.edu
BROWN, Geeta, A .... 714-712-7900.. 46 B
BROWN, George, H ...... 828-227-7028 343 E ghbrown@wcu.edu
BROWN, Giles .... 903-463-8620 436 G browng@grayson.edu
BROWN, Glenn .... 973-684-5402 280 A gbrown@pccc.edu
BROWN, Gloria, M .... 252-335-3268 341 B gmbrown@ecsu.edu
BROWN, Gregory, N ..... 610-328-8316 398 G gbrown1@swarthmore.edu
BROWN, Guilbert .... 717-871-4087 395 A guilbert.brown@millersville.edu
BROWN, H. David .... 816-271-4327 257 A browndav@missouriwestern.edu
BROWN, Harold .... 415-452-5163.. 36 K hbrown@ccsf.edu
BROWN, Haywood .... 813-974-4373 111 C haywood@usf.edu
BROWN, Heather .... 916-686-7400.. 29 E
BROWN, Heather .... 423-472-7141 424 B hbrown@clevelandstatecc.edu
BROWN, Howard .... 601-979-3060 246 F howard.brown@jsums.edu
BROWN, Hubert .... 352-392-0466 111 A hub.brown@ufl.edu
BROWN, Ian .... 361-593-3065 447 D ian.brown@tamuk.edu
BROWN, Ivey .... 336-750-2074 344 A browniv@wssu.edu
BROWN, J. Lee .... 910-672-1592 341 C jbrown84@uncfsu.edu
BROWN, J. Steven .... 202-319-4738.. 92 A brownj@cua.edu
BROWN, J.J .... 828-262-2060 340 I brownjj1@appstate.edu
BROWN, Jackie .... 803-705-4971 406 G jackie.brown@benedict.edu
BROWN, James .... 661-824-2977.. 53 H jbrown@ntps.edu
BROWN, James .... 615-230-3787 425 E james.brown@volstate.edu
BROWN, James .... 570-389-4410 393 D jbrown@bloomu.edu
BROWN, James, M .... 570-340-6044 389 D jmbrown@marywood.edu
BROWN, Jamie, C .... 301-447-5586 201 B j.c.brown@msmary.edu
BROWN, Janice .... 301-846-2484 198 I jbrown@frederick.edu
BROWN, Jared .... 417-455-5566 252 E jaredbrown@crowder.edu
BROWN, Jasmin, K ...... 910-630-7035 331 E jabrown@methodist.edu
BROWN, Jason .... 435-797-3322 460 C jason.brown@usu.edu
BROWN, Jeff .... 801-832-2900 461 F jbrown@westminstercollege.edu
BROWN, Jeff .... 509-533-7373 479 C jeff.brown@scc.spokane.edu
BROWN, Jeffery .... 202-885-3165.. 91 F jtbrown@american.edu
BROWN, Jeffrey .... 217-333-2747 152 B brownjr@illinois.edu
BROWN, Jeffrey .... 804-862-6100 470 C jbrown@rbc.edu
BROWN, Jefrey .... 309-298-1544 153 A j-brown2@wiu.edu
BROWN, Jennifer .... 860-465-0781.. 85 H brownje@easternct.edu
BROWN, Jennifer .... 785-738-9085 176 F jbrown@ncktc.edu
BROWN, Jennifer .... 775-327-2079 271 A jennifer.brown@gbcnv.edu
BROWN, Jennifer, G ..... 203-582-8200.. 88 G jennifer.brown@quinnipiac.edu
BROWN, Jeremy .... 951-639-5404.. 53 A jebrown@msjc.edu
BROWN, Jeremy .... 970-248-1962.. 78 J jbrown@coloradomesa.edu
BROWN, Jeremy .... 530-741-6700.. 77 E jbrown2@yccd.edu
BROWN, Jerri .... 928-350-2113.. 15 L jbrown@prescott.edu
BROWN, Jerri .... 928-350-2100.. 15 L
BROWN, Jesse .... 765-998-5379 161 C jesse_brown@taylor.edu
BROWN, Jessyca .... 254-659-7504 437 A jbrown@hillcollege.edu
BROWN, Jill .... 660-562-1642 257 E jillb@nwmissouri.edu
BROWN, JoAnn .... 318-274-6238 192 C brownj@gram.edu
BROWN, John .... 404-270-5227 126 B jbrow109@spelman.edu
BROWN, John .... 614-236-6771 349 B jbrown18@capital.edu
BROWN, John, V .... 919-684-0539 328 F jbrown@duke.edu
BROWN, Jonathan .... 336-249-8186 334 B jonathan_brown@davidsondavie.edu
BROWN, Jordan .... 706-886-6831 126 D jbrown@tfc.edu
BROWN, Joseph .... 910-246-4957 337 H brownjo@sandhills.edu
BROWN, Joseph .... 903-923-2270 435 H jbrown@etbu.edu
BROWN, Josie .... 413-782-1218 220 A josie.brown@wne.edu
BROWN, Joyce .... 443-885-3015 201 A joyce.brown@morgan.edu
BROWN, Joyce, F .... 212-217-4000 299 D joyce_brown@fitnyc.edu
BROWN, Julia .... 662-472-9011 246 D jubrown@holmescc.edu
BROWN, Julie .... 718-625-2200 291 K
BROWN, Justin, C .... 402-472-3484 269 J justin.brown@unl.edu
BROWN, Kali .... 253-492-2061 338 F brownk@vgcc.edu
BROWN, Kanika .... 405-208-5501 367 E kbrown2@okcu.edu
BROWN, Karen .... 815-599-3402 139 A karen.brown@highland.edu
BROWN, Karen, A .... 607-436-2524 316 F karen.brown@oneonta.edu
BROWN, Karen, H .... 340-693-1324 513 E karen.brown@uvi.edu
BROWN, Karen, J .... 603-899-4280 273 E brownkj@franklinpierce.edu
BROWN, Katherine .... 330-490-7509 363 E ktbrown@walsh.edu
BROWN, Kathleen, M ... 574-284-4557 160 I kbrown@saintmarys.edu
BROWN, Kathren .... 801-863-8517 460 D kbrown@uvu.edu
BROWN, Katie .... 303-333-4224.. 78 A registrar@aspen.edu
BROWN, Katie .... 843-377-2432 407 A kbrown@charlestonlaw.edu
BROWN, Katrina .... 307-268-2036 500 U katrina.brown@caspercollege.edu
BROWN, Katrina, M ...... 307-675-0221 501 G kbrown@sheridan.edu
BROWN, Keia .... 703-284-1530 468 H kabrown@marymount.edu
BROWN, Keith .... 443-674-1915 198 E kbrown@cecil.edu
BROWN, Keith .... 440-366-7692 355 B
BROWN, Keith, A .... 205-853-1200.... 2 G kbrown@jeffersonstate.edu
BROWN, Kelli, R .... 828-227-7100 343 E kbrown@wcu.edu
BROWN, Kelly .... 443-482-6575 202 A kelly.brown@sjc.edu
BROWN, Kelly, K .... 253-879-3778 484 G kkbrown@pugetsound.edu
BROWN, Ken .... 620-278-4217 177 H kbrown@sterling.edu
BROWN, Kendra .... 580-774-3785 370 A kendra.brown@swosu.edu
BROWN, Kendrick, T ..... 404-639-0999 123 D kendrick.brown@morehouse.edu

BROWN, Kenneth .... 318-675-3395 189 I kenny.brown@lsuhs.edu

BROWN, Kenneth .... 509-777-4486 486 C kbrown@whitworth.edu

BROWN, Kevin .... 660-263-3900 251 D kevinbrown@cccb.edu

BROWN, Kevin .... 812-866-7061 155 G brownk@hanover.edu

BROWN, Kevin .... 843-349-5398 409 J kevin.brown@hgtc.edu

BROWN, Kevin .... 517-750-1200 231 C kbrown@arbor.edu

BROWN, Kevin .... 423-236-2874 423 F kbrown@southern.edu

BROWN, Kevin, A .... 919-866-5475 338 G kabrown@waketech.edu

BROWN, Kevin, H .... 206-239-4500 478 H

BROWN, Kevin, J .... 859-858-3511 179 D president@asbury.edu

BROWN, Kiara .... 661-255-1050.. 28 G kiara@calarts.edu

BROWN, Kim .... 859-985-3912 179 I brownkim@berea.edu

BROWN, Kim, S .... 757-455-2103 477 C kbrown@vwu.edu

BROWN, Kimbaya .... 601-266-4360 249 F kimbaya.brown@usm.edu

BROWN, Kimberley .... 641-673-1182 171 C kimberley.brown@wmpenn.edu

BROWN, Kimberly .... 515-271-1462 165 G kimberly.brown@dmu.edu

BROWN, Kirby .... 816-584-6308 258 C kirby.brown@park.edu

BROWN, Krista .... 936-633-4780 429 J kbrown@angelina.edu

BROWN, Kristen .... 502-852-4319 186 A kristen.brown@louisville.edu

BROWN, Kristen .... 617-587-5751 217 D brownk@neco.edu

BROWN, Kristen .... 585-594-6408 310 C brown_kristen@roberts.edu

BROWN, Kristen .... 585-594-6201 312 E brown_kristen@roberts.edu

BROWN, Kristen .... 919-546-8434 340 B kristen.brown@shawu.edu

BROWN, Kristine, A .... 609-896-5192 281 B kbrown@rider.edu

BROWN, Kyle .... 716-338-1000 303 A

BROWN, Kyle .... 315-386-7164 320 B brownk@canton.edu

BROWN, Kyle .... 405-945-3252 368 C kyle.j.brown@okstate.edu

BROWN, Kyris .... 205-366-8817.... 7 A kbrown@stillman.edu

BROWN, Lanette .... 404-413-1515 120 E lanettebrown@gsu.edu

BROWN, Laura .... 847-925-6133 138 G lbrown@harpercollege.edu

BROWN, Laura, C .... 863-667-5041 108 K lcbrown@seu.edu

BROWN, Lawrence .... 714-628-2876.. 36 B

BROWN, LeAnn .... 651-213-4092 236 C ltbrown@hazeldenbettyford.edu

BROWN, Leonard, E .... 757-823-8141 469 A lebrown@nsu.edu

BROWN, Leslie .... 717-477-1151 395 B lrbrown@ship.edu

BROWN, Levy .... 252-492-2061 338 F brownl@vgcc.edu

BROWN, Linda, J .... 218-299-4206 235 H linbrown@cord.edu

BROWN, Lindsey .... 208-885-5566 132 F lindseybrown@uidaho.edu

BROWN, Lisa .... 405-682-7896 367 D lbrown@occc.edu

BROWN, Lisa .... 440-366-7559 355 B

BROWN, Lisa, M .... 202-687-6457.. 92 E lbrown@georgetown.edu

BROWN, Lisa, M .... 903-813-2218 430 H lbrown@austincollege.edu

BROWN, Lori, A .... 973-313-6132 283 C lori.brown@shu.edu

BROWN, Lorie .... 973-596-3336 279 E lorie.brown@njit.edu

BROWN, Lourdes .... 310-204-1666.. 58 K

BROWN, Lucas, A .... 920-993-6027 493 B lucas.a.brown@lawrence.edu

BROWN, Lynne .... 212-998-2350 309 F lynne.brown@nyu.edu

BROWN, Madelyn .... 678-359-5011 120 F madelynb@gordonstate.edu

BROWN, Maggie .... 252-222-6140 333 A brownm@carteret.edu

BROWN, Marc .... 310-377-5501.. 51 C mbrown@marymountcalifornia.edu

BROWN, Marcia, W .... 973-353-5541 282 B mwbrown@newark.rutgers.edu

BROWN, Marcus .... 661-654-2713.. 30 B mbrown59@csub.edu

BROWN, Margaret .... 206-281-2174 483 G mbrown@spu.edu

BROWN, Marie .... 470-639-0339 123 D marie.brown@morehouse.edu

BROWN, Marissa, C .... 972-721-5273 452 B mbrown@udallas.edu

BROWN, Martha .... 806-742-2120 450 F martha.brown@ttu.edu

BROWN, Martha .... 806-742-0012 450 D

BROWN, Matt .... 803-777-3720 413 A mtbrown@mailbox.sc.edu

BROWN, Matthew .... 618-650-3187 150 C mattheb@siue.edu

BROWN, Matthew .... 585-271-3657 313 B admissions@stbernards.edu

BROWN, Maya .... 903-927-3300 458 F mbrown@wileyc.edu

BROWN, Melanie, A .... 904-808-7410 107 C melaniebrown@sjrstate.edu

BROWN, Melissa .... 412-809-5100 396 E brown.melissa@ptcollege.edu

BROWN, Melissa, S .... 909-607-0109.. 37 F melissa_brown@kgi.edu

BROWN, Merv, R .... 208-496-2010 130 I brownme@byui.edu

BROWN, Michael .... 256-761-6246.... 7 B mbrown@talladega.edu

BROWN, Michael .... 708-656-8000 145 C michael.brown@morton.edu

BROWN, Michael .... 970-247-7695.. 80 J msbrown@fortlewis.edu

BROWN, Michael .... 510-987-9120.. 68 L michael.brown@ucop.edu

BROWN, Michael .... 360-992-2472 478 I mbrown@clark.edu

BROWN, Michael .... 614-891-3200 357 A

BROWN, Michael .... 937-376-2946 359 K mbrown@payneseminary.edu

BROWN, Michael (Embee) .... 406-683-7145 264 A michael.brown@umwestern.edu

BROWN, Michele .... 847-635-1981 146 G mbrown@oakton.edu

BROWN, Michelle .... 215-641-6323 390 C mbrownnevers@mc3.edu

BROWN, Michelle .... 919-962-9533 342 C michellebrown@unc.edu

BROWN, Michelle .... 706-310-6205 127 A michelle.brown@ung.edu

BROWN, Michelle .... 435-283-7127 461 B michelle.brown@snow.edu

BROWN, Michelle, L .... 203-837-9400.. 86 B brownm@wcsu.edu

BROWN, Mike .... 440-375-7060 354 K mbrown@lec.edu

BROWN, Mike .... 903-463-8772 436 G mbrown@grayson.edu

BROWN, Mikell .... 804-706-5068 474 B mbrown@jtcc.edu

BROWN, Missy .... 618-985-5980 140 H missybrown@jalc.edu

BROWN, Monica .... 530-893-7737.. 27 C brownmo@butte.edu

BROWN, Monica, R .... 240-567-4341 200 G monica.brown@montgomerycollege.edu

BROWN, Morgan .... 310-846-2648.. 55 C mbrown@otis.edu

BROWN, Naima .... 352-395-5648 108 A naima.brown@sfcollege.edu

BROWN, Nancy .... 303-762-6980.. 80 I nancy.brown@denverseminary.edu

BROWN, Nancy .... 801-832-2731 461 F nbrown@westminstercollege.edu

BROWN, Narren .... 507-389-7462 241 C narren.brown@southcentral.edu

BROWN, Natalya .... 541-440-4632 376 G natalya.brown@umpqua.edu

BROWN, Nathan .... 208-535-5349 131 B nathan.brown@cei.edu

BROWN, Nicholas .... 303-410-2407.. 83 J nicholas.brown@spartan.edu

BROWN, Nicole .... 315-445-5497 303 I brownnr@lemoyne.edu

BROWN, Olu .... 617-258-7870 216 B

BROWN, Pam .... 480-994-9244.. 15 R

BROWN, Pam .... 843-574-6246 412 I pam.brown@tridenttech.edu

BROWN, Pamela .... 510-987-9251.. 68 L pamela.brown@ucop.edu

BROWN, Pamela .... 718-260-5560 295 A pbrown@citytech.cuny.edu

BROWN, Patrick .... 217-245-3176 139 C patrick.brown@ic.edu

BROWN, Patrick .... 253-566-6006 484 E pbrown@tacomacc.edu

BROWN, Paul .... 254-659-7860 437 A pbrown@hillcollege.edu

BROWN, Peter .... 304-724-5000 487 B pbrown@cdu.edu

BROWN, Phillip, J .... 410-864-3613 202 C brownpj@stmarys.edu

BROWN, Phillip, M .... 618-650-3415 150 C phbrown@siue.edu

BROWN, Prince .... 803-780-1199 414 B pbrown@voorhees.edu

BROWN, Rachel .... 405-208-5270 367 E rbrown2@okcu.edu

BROWN, Rachel, A .... 202-994-6495.. 92 D rabrown@gwu.edu

BROWN, Rachelle .... 541-956-7001 376 A rbrown@roguecc.edu

BROWN, Ralph .... 303-273-3538.. 79 J rabrown@mines.edu

BROWN, Rana .... 719-384-6988.. 82 D rana.brown@ojc.edu

BROWN, Randy .... 408-848-4847.. 43 E rbrown@gavilan.edu

BROWN, Randy .... 517-884-1119 227 F brownra@uadv.msu.edu

BROWN, Rashayla .... 312-629-6869 149 F maffai@saic.edu

BROWN, Raymond .... 504-520-5439 193 E rbrown@xula.edu

BROWN, Rayon .... 920-735-4820 498 F brown@fvtc.edu

BROWN, Rebecca .... 850-599-3090 109 I rebecca.brown@famu.edu

BROWN, Rebecca .... 601-554-4646 248 E rbrown@prcc.edu

BROWN, Rebecca, L .... 314-935-4947 262 A rebeccabrown@wustl.edu

BROWN, Rebekkah, L .... 484-664-3247 390 H rebekkahbrown@muhlenberg.edu

BROWN, Regena .... 704-687-0030 342 D rybrown1@uncc.edu

BROWN, Reynolda .... 803-535-5569 407 D reybrown@claflin.edu

BROWN, Richard, B .... 801-585-7498 459 O brown@utah.edu

BROWN, Rick .... 435-586-7700 460 A brownr@suu.edu

BROWN, Ricky .... 252-493-7423 336 H rbrown@email.pittcc.edu

BROWN, Ricky .... 810-762-9845 226 B rbrown@kettering.edu

BROWN, Robert .... 570-321-4250 389 B brownr@lycoming.edu

BROWN, Robert .... 251-460-6586.... 9 A rbrown@southalabama.edu

BROWN, Robert .... 410-386-8224 198 D rbrown@carrollcc.edu

BROWN, Robert .... 310-342-5200.. 73 F

BROWN, Robert .... 859-622-1693 180 E bob.brown@eku.edu

BROWN, Robert, A .... 617-353-2200 207 E rabrown@bu.edu

BROWN, Robert, L .... 803-981-7375 414 F rbrown@yorktech.edu

BROWN, Robin .... 256-395-2211.... 3 G rbrown@suscc.edu

BROWN, Robyn, K .... 330-972-6798 361 H rkb@uakron.edu

BROWN, Rod .... 317-921-4384 158 E rsbrown@ivytech.edu

BROWN, Rolanda .... 662-621-4244 245 D rbrown@coahomacc.edu

BROWN, Ron .... 254-295-4517 453 D rbrown@umhb.edu

BROWN, Ronald, T .... 702-895-3693 271 D ronald.brown@unlv.edu

BROWN, Roy .... 217-206-8457 152 A rbrow24@uis.edu

BROWN, III, Roy .... 206-726-5004 479 E rbrown@cornish.edu

BROWN, Russ .... 772-462-6004 102 F rbrown@irsc.edu

BROWN, Ryan .... 415-503-6309.. 61 D rbrown@sfcm.edu

BROWN, Ryan .... 408-561-6172.. 62 F ryan.brown@sjeccd.edu

BROWN, Ryan .... 423-869-6906 421 A ryan.brown@lmunet.edu

BROWN, Saketta .... 428-274-7643 123 I sdbrown@oftc.edu

BROWN, Samantha .... 425-352-8514 478 D sbrown@cascadia.edu

BROWN, Sandra .... 386-481-2510.. 96 D browns@cookman.edu

BROWN, Sandra .... 858-534-3526.. 70 C sandrabrown@ucsd.edu

BROWN, Sandra .... 225-771-2169 191 B sandra_brown@subr.edu

BROWN, Sandra .... 605-668-1555 415 F sbrown@mountmarty.edu

BROWN, Sarah .... 918-647-1471 365 E sbrown@carlalbert.edu

BROWN, Scott .... 712-749-2016 164 C browns@bvu.edu

BROWN, Scott .... 617-451-0010 217 F

BROWN, Scott .... 717-477-1302 395 B sdbrownr@ship.edu

BROWN, Scott, E .... 801-957-2020 461 C scott.e.brown@slcc.edu

BROWN, Shanita .... 804-342-3812 476 F

BROWN, Shanita, L .... 901-333-5325 425 D sbrown@southwest.tn.edu

BROWN, Shannon .... 267-341-3314 385 J sbrown10@holyfamily.edu

BROWN, Shannon .... 828-726-2288 332 G sbrown@cccti.edu

BROWN, Shannon .... 214-768-4909 444 D shannonbrown@smu.edu

BROWN, Shareka .... 336-249-8186 334 B shareka_brown@davidsondavie.edu

BROWN, Sharon .... 252-335-0821 333 G sharon_brown@albemarle.edu

BROWN, Shawn .... 914-606-6434 325 A shawn.brown@sunywcc.edu

BROWN, Sheila .... 937-376-6349 349 J sbrown@centralstate.edu

BROWN, Shelly .... 254-968-9083 446 D sbrown@tarleton.edu

BROWN, Shirl .... 254-710-2000 431 E shirl_johnson@baylor.edu

BROWN, Shirley .... 615-329-8756 419 H sbrown@fisk.edu

BROWN, Shondae .... 256-395-2211.... 3 G sbrown@suscc.edu

BROWN, Simon .... 215-751-8039 381 I sbrown@ccp.edu

BROWN, Siri .... 510-466-7200.. 56 H

BROWN, Sondra .... 703-891-1787 471 E dean@standardcollege.edu

BROWN, Stephanie .... 561-237-7784 103W scbrown@lynn.edu

BROWN, Stephanie .... 954-262-7456 105 A browstep@nova.edu

BROWN, Stephanie .... 440-525-7228 354 L sbrown127@lakelandcc.edu

BROWN, Stephen, G .... 530-221-4275.. 64 B sbrown@shasta.edu

BROWN, Stephen, R .... 478-301-2683 122 E brown_sr@mercer.edu

BROWN, Steve .... 850-474-2405 111 F sbrown4@uwf.edu

BROWN, Steve .... 605-677-6703 416 D steve.brown@usdfoundation.org

BROWN, Steven .... 850-474-3340 111 F sbrown4@uwf.edu

BROWN, Stewart .... 202-274-2303.. 94 C

BROWN, Sue, C .... 309-655-2206 149 B sue.c.brown@osfhealthcare.org

BROWN, Susan .... 956-665-2383 455 D susan.brown@utrgv.edu

BROWN, Susan, M .... 859-233-8225 185 C subrown@transy.edu

BROWN, Suzi .... 601-928-8480 247 E suzana.brown@mgccc.edu

BROWN, Suzie .... 912-260-4320 125 D suzie.brown@sgsc.edu

BROWN, Sylvia .... 252-744-6422 341 A brownsy@ecu.edu

BROWN, T. Rhett .... 704-233-8111 344 F r.brown@wingate.edu

BROWN, Takeshia .... 912-478-5409 120 C fbrown@georgiasouthern.edu

BROWN, Talia .... 641-784-5117 166 E talia.brown@graceland.edu

BROWN, Tamara .... 940-565-2046 453 E tamara.brown@unt.edu

BROWN, Tammy .... 304-384-5358 489 J
tbrown@concord.edu
BROWN, Tanya .... 804-594-1414 474 B
tbrown01@jtcc.edu
BROWN, Tavonda .... 870-743-3000.. 20 B
tbrown@northark.edu
BROWN, Teresa .... 404-297-9522 120 B
BROWN, Teresa .... 507-285-7217 240 H
teresa.brown@rctc.edu
BROWN, Teressa .... 479-401-6021.. 17 A
teressa.brown@acheedu.org
BROWN, Terrance .... 270-745-2344 186 C
terrance.brown@wku.edu
BROWN, Terrence .... 901-751-8453 421 G
tbrown@mabts.edu
BROWN, Terri .... 478-289-2062 118 C
thbrown@ega.edu
BROWN, Theodore .... 256-726-7070.... 6 C
tbrown@oakwood.edu
BROWN, Thomas, W .... 507-933-7005 236 A
brownie@gustavus.edu
BROWN, Tim .... 843-574-6211 412 I
tim.brown@tridenttech.edu
BROWN, Timi .... 909-652-6322.. 35 L
timi.brown@chaffey.edu
BROWN, Timothy .... 704-847-5600 340 F
tbrown@ses.edu
BROWN, Toni .... 919-536-7200 334 C
BROWN, Tony .... 202-685-2207 502 K
browna@ndu.edu
BROWN, Tracy, H .... 512-475-9411 455 A
tbrown@tacc.utexas.edu
BROWN, Travis .... 419-372-6067 348 G
brownst@bgsu.edu
BROWN, Travis .... 503-491-7219 374 B
travis.brown@mhcc.edu
BROWN, Trevor, L .... 614-292-4533 358 D
brown.2296@osu.edu
BROWN, Troy .... 310-342-5256.. 73 F
BROWN, Tucker .... 931-221-7725 417 H
brownt@apsu.edu
BROWN, Veronica .... 334-876-9335.... 2 D
veronica.brown@wccs.edu
BROWN, Vintress .... 864-503-5553 414 A
vbrown@uscupstate.edu
BROWN, Wanda .... 336-750-2446 344 A
brownwa@wssu.edu
BROWN, Wilfred, E .... 805-893-4155.. 70 E
willie.brown@auxiliary.ucsb.edu
BROWN, Will .... 678-466-4115 117 D
willbrown@clayton.edu
BROWN, William .... 301-696-3402 199 E
brownw@hood.edu
BROWN, William .... 719-549-3144.. 82 J
william.brown@pueblocc.edu
BROWN, William .... 775-327-2118 271 A
william.brown@gbcnv.edu
BROWN, William, T ...... 203-285-2000.. 86 E
BROWN, Zachariah, D .. 508-565-1058 219 A
zbrown@stonehill.edu
BROWN, Zakiya .... 573-681-5501 254 G
brownz@lincolnu.edu
BROWN-ALDRIDGE,
Linda .... 708-596-2000 149 H
lbrown@ssc.edu
BROWN-CORNELIUS,
Denise .... 502-272-8270 179 H
dbrowncornelius@bellarmine.edu
BROWN CORNELIUS,
Lisa .... 216-397-4408 353 O
lmbrown@jcu.edu
BROWN-ELIZE, Rashitta 661-722-6300.. 26 A
rbrownelize@avc.edu
BROWN GORDAN,
Loria .... 601-979-2107 246 F
loria.c.brown@jsums.edu
BROWN-HARRIS,
Brandi .... 618-537-6813 144 A
BROWN-HAYWOOD,
Felicia .... 717-871-4473 395 A
felicia.brown-haywood@millersville.edu
BROWN-HERBST, Kari .. 307-778-1103 501 E
kherbst@lccc.wy.edu
BROWN-JOHNSON,
Leah .... 973-748-9000 276 A
leah_brown@bloomfield.edu
BROWN-LAVEIST,
Cynthia .... 443-885-4720 201 A
cynthia.brownlaveist@morgan.edu
BROWN MARSDEN,
Margaret .... 940-397-4253 440 C
margaret.brownmarsden@msutexas.edu

BROWN-MCCLURE,
Fran 'Cee .... 518-388-6116 323 J
brownmcf@union.edu
BROWN-NAGIN,
Tomiko .... 617-495-8602 210 E
tbrownnagin@radcliffe.harvard.edu
BROWN WYATT, Donna 660-626-2790 250 A
dbrown@atsu.edu
BROWN YOUNG,
Danita .... 217-300-1300 152 B
dbyoung@illinois.edu
BROWNAWELL,
Carolyn .... 303-556-2400.. 84 D
carolyn.brownawell@ucdenver.edu
BROWNE, Brian .... 718-990-2762 313 G
browneb@stjohns.edu
BROWNE, Doug .... 620-417-1201 177 F
doug.browne@sccc.edu
BROWNE, Heather .... 417-667-8181 252 B
hbrowne@cottey.edu
BROWNE, Jacob .... 727-864-8846.. 98 J
brownejh@eckerd.edu
BROWNE, Janelle .... 214-648-7101 457 A
janelle.browne@utsouthwestern.edu
BROWNE, Jason .... 504-278-6421 188 G
jbrowne@nunez.edu
BROWNE, Joan, M .... 202-806-7513.. 92 F
jmbrowne@howard.edu
BROWNE, Kathleen .... 740-587-6654 352 A
brownek@denison.edu
BROWNE, Kevin .... 312-413-3471 151 G
kbrowne@uic.edu
BROWNE, Lorraine .... 860-509-9502.. 88 B
lbrowne@hartsem.edu
BROWNE, Patrick .... 503-256-3180 377 B
pbrowne@uws.edu
BROWNE, Robert .... 603-641-7287 274 A
rbrowne@anselm.edu
BROWNE-BOATSWAIN,
Venoreen .... 763-422-6094 237 D
venoreen.browne-boatswain@anokaramsey.edu
BROWNE-BOATSWAIN,
Venoreen .... 763-422-6094 237 E
venoreen.browne-boatswain@anokaramsey.edu
BROWNELL, Crystal ...... 802-831-1339 463 C
cbrownell@vermontlaw.edu
BROWNELL, Jayne, E .... 513-529-4631 356 A
browneje@miamioh.edu
BROWNELL, Jennifer ..... 336-506-4237 332 A
jennifer.brownell@alamancecc.edu
BROWNGOETZ, Sarah ... 360-475-7129 481 I
sbrowngoetz@olympic.edu
BROWNIE, Ronald .... 605-626-2568 416 G
ronald.brownie@northern.edu
BROWNING, Allison ..... 740-474-8896 358 A
abrowning@ohiochristian.edu
BROWNING, Amy .... 307-675-0122 501 G
abrowning@sheridan.edu
BROWNING, Angela ...... 772-462-4703 102 F
abrownin@irsc.edu
BROWNING, Ashley ...... 540-362-6210 467 H
abrowning@hollins.edu
BROWNING, David .... 336-917-5472 340 A
david.browning@salem.edu
BROWNING, David, A ... 252-399-6329 326 K
dabrowning@barton.edu
BROWNING, Eric .... 740-392-6868 356 G
eric.browning@mvnu.edu
BROWNING, Janelle ..... 617-747-2358 206 H
jbrowning@berklee.edu
BROWNING, Jason .... 307-675-0210 501 G
jbrowning@sheridan.edu
BROWNING, Jay .... 215-641-6543 390 C
jbrowning@mc3.edu
BROWNING, Joann .... 210-458-7379 455 E
joann.browning@utsa.edu
BROWNING, Kelly .... 715-425-3342 496 F
kelly.browning@uwrf.edu
BROWNING, Lynn .... 225-768-1724 187 B
lynn.browning@franu.edu
BROWNING, Mark .... 208-562-3508 131 E
markbrowning@cwi.edu
BROWNING, Mark .... 541-278-5950 371 H
mbrowning@bluecc.edu
BROWNING, Peter .... 417-873-7231 252 G
pbrowning@drury.edu
BROWNING, Reggie ...... 864-488-4522 410 B
rbrowning@limestone.edu
BROWNING, Shea .... 828-227-7116 343 E
srbrowning@wcu.edu
BROWNING, Steve .... 870-235-4102.. 21 C
dsbrowning@saumag.edu

BROWNLEE, David, W .. 610-558-5628 391 A
dbrownle@neumann.edu
BROWNLEE, Jamie .... 619-849-6785.. 57 J
jamiebrownlee@pointloma.edu
BROWNLEE,
Mordecai, I .... 303-360-4775.. 80 E
mordecai.brownlee@ccaurora.edu
BROWNLEE, Reb .... 814-262-3842 393 A
rbrownlee@pennhighlands.edu
BROWNLEE, Robert .... 707-527-4964.. 63 D
rbrownlee@santarosa.edu
BROWNLOW, Antonio ... 662-254-3411 248 B
abrownlow@mvsu.edu
BROXSON, Thomas ...... 253-589-5510 478 J
thomas.broxson@cptc.edu
BROYLES, Ken .... 423-461-8734 422 E
kbroyles@milligan.edu
BROYLES, Kevin .... 334-699-2266.... 1 B
krbroyles@acom.edu
BROYLES, Steven .... 626-300-5444.. 57 F
sbroyles@plattcollege.edu
BROYLES, Toni .... 208-885-4700 132 F
tbroyles@uidaho.edu
BROYLES, Wendy .... 334-983-6556.... 7 C
whuckabee@troy.edu
BROZ, Roger .... 612-659-6805 239 A
roger.broz@minneapolis.edu
BRUBACHER, Don .... 517-607-3130 225 C
dbrubacher@hillsdale.edu
BRUBAKER, David .... 585-567-9484 302 B
david.brubaker@houghton.edu
BRUBAKER, David .... 540-432-4000 466 B
dean-ssp@emu.edu
BRUBAKER, Karl .... 620-327-8216 174 E
karl.brubaker@hesston.edu
BRUBAKER, Sam, R ...... 208-496-9817 130 I
brubakers@byui.edu
BRUBAKER, Sara .... 620-242-0413 176 B
brubakes@mcpherson.edu
BRUBAKER-COLE,
Susie .... 650-723-2300.. 66 E
susiebc@stanford.edu
BRUCE, Aaron .... 626-396-2200.. 26 B
aaron.bruce@artcenter.edu
BRUCE, Alex, M .... 931-598-1187 423 D
ambruce@sewanee.edu
BRUCE, Ben .... 706-292-3900 125 C
bbruce@shorter.edu
BRUCE, Bernadette .... 954-262-8856 105 A
bb968@nova.edu
BRUCE, David .... 617-521-2000 218 G
BRUCE, Debra .... 509-542-4604 479 A
dbruce@columbiabasin.edu
BRUCE, Diane, S .... 803-533-3963 411 G
dlary@scsu.edu
BRUCE, Dustin .... 502-897-4555 184 G
dbruce@sbts.edu
BRUCE, Edie .... 386-312-4074 107 C
ediebruce@sjrstate.edu
BRUCE, Gonzalo .... 208-426-2272 130 H
gonzalobruce@boisestate.edu
BRUCE, Josh .... 954-771-0376 103 S
BRUCE, Karen .... 205-879-5588.... 5 C
kbruce@faulkner.edu
BRUCE, Kimberly .... 318-345-9147 188 D
kbruce@ladelta.edu
BRUCE, Lori, M .... 931-372-3224 426 B
lbruce@tntech.edu
BRUCE, Philip .... 518-276-6234 312 C
brucep@rpi.edu
BRUCE, R. Todd .... 216-397-1600 353 O
rbruce@jcu.edu
BRUCE, Richard .... 360-650-6517 485 I
richard.bruce@wwu.edu
BRUCE, Robert .... 713-348-2599 442 F
rgbruce@rice.edu
BRUCE, Steve .... 574-520-4457 157 E
stbruce@iusb.edu
BRUCE, Steve .... 757-352-4429 470 B
stepbru@regent.edu
BRUCE, Susan .... 704-233-8015 344 F
s.bruce@wingate.edu
BRUCE, William, P .... 615-327-3927 420 D
pbruce@guptoncollege.edu
BRUCE-SMITH, Soo Lee 208-792-2378 132 A
slbruce@lcsc.edu
BRUCELAS, Joy .... 510-215-3841.. 40 B
jbrucelas@contracosta.edu
BRUCH, Courtney .... 505-747-2244 287 H
courtney.bruch@nnmc.edu
BRUCH, John .... 262-595-2228 496 D
bruch@uwp.edu

BRUCKBAUER, Greg ..... 715-422-5327 499 B
greg.bruckbauer@mstc.edu
BRUCKI, Mark, J .... 248-204-2310 227 A
mbrucki@ltu.edu
BRUCKLER, Michael, L . 240-895-2045 202 B
mlbruckler@smcm.edu
BRUCKMAN, Steven ...... 415-239-3000.. 36 K
BRUCKSTEIN, Irving ...... 401-847-6650 405 D
irving.bruckstein@salve.edu
BRUDER, Caroline .... 217-424-6383 144 G
cbruder@millikin.edu
BRUDER, Edward, C ..... 717-815-1314 403 F
ebruder@ycp.edu
BRUDER, Eric .... 904-620-2115 111 B
eric.bruder@unf.edu
BRUDER, Remylin .... 248-218-2281 230 B
rbruder@rochesteru.edu
BRUDNICKI, James .... 856-222-9311 281 C
jbrudnic@rcbc.edu
BRUDNOCK, Ben .... 724-938-4725 393 E
brudnock@calu.edu
BRUDNOK, Celine .... 724-805-2720 398 A
celine.brudnok@stvincent.edu
BRUDNOK, Celine, R .... 724-805-2720 397 I
celine.brudnok@email.stvincent.edu
BRUECK, Joshua .... 217-641-4320 141 A
jbrueck@jwcc.edu
BRUEHL, Allen, A .... 508-767-7311 206 A
abruehl@assumption.edu
BRUEHL, Amanda .... 732-247-5241 279 C
BRUESS, Brian .... 920-403-3165 495 B
brian.bruess@snc.edu
BRUFFEY, L. Mark .... 763-417-8250 235 A
mbruffey@centralseminary.edu
BRUGAL-MENA,
Yocasta .... 787-743-3038 509 N
ybrugal@sanjuanbautista.edu
BRUGGEMAN, John, H . 513-487-3269 301 B
jbruggeman@huc.edu
BRUGGEMAN, Michael . 313-664-1440 222 H
mikeb@collegeforcreativestudies.edu
BRUGH, Suzanne .... 814-262-6463 393 A
sbrugh@pennhighlands.edu
BRUGNOLI, Amber .... 304-293-9298 490 E
amber.brugnoli@mail.wvu.edu
BRUHN, Christian .... 360-623-8364 478 F
christian.bruhn@centralia.edu
BRUINGTON, Toni .... 620-331-4100 174 H
bbruington@indycc.edu
BRUINSMA, Paul .... 618-842-3711 139 F
bruinsmap@iecc.edu
BRUKARDT, Mary Jane 715-836-2320 495 E
brukarmj@uwec.edu
BRUKLEY, Reuben .... 313-317-6573 225 B
rjbrukley@hfcc.edu
BRUMAGIN, Ruth .... 570-288-8400 383 G
ruthb@fortisinstitute.edu
BRUMBACH, Mary .... 214-378-1549 434 E
mbrumbach@dcccd.edu
BRUMBAUGH, Erin, R .. 304-457-6272 486 E
brumbaugher@ab.edu
BRUMBAUGH, Pete, S .. 913-971-3275 176 C
pjbrumbaugh@mnu.edu
BRUMBERG, Joshua ..... 212-817-7242 293 F
jbrumberg@gc.cuny.edu
BRUMFIELD, Sean .... 770-229-3269 125 H
sean.brumfield@sctech.edu
BRUMITT, Jane .... 312-629-6184 149 F
jbrumitt@saic.edu
BRUMLEY, Jessica .... 305-284-5314 113 C
jbrumley@miami.edu
BRUMLEY, Larry, D ...... 478-301-5700 122 E
brumley_ld@mercer.edu
BRUMMEL, Joe .... 641-628-7648 164 D
brummelj@central.edu
BRUMMER, James, M .. 651-962-6595 244 E
jbrummer@stthomas.edu
BRUMMUND, Barry .... 520-621-9723.. 16 D
brummund@arizona.edu
BRUNACINI, Kelly .... 585-271-3657 313 B
kelly.brunacini@stbernards.edu.edu
BRUNDAGE, Christina .. 570-348-6247 389 D
brundage.c@marywood.edu
BRUNDAGE, Isaac .... 575-538-6339 289 G
isaac.brundage@wnmu.edu
BRUNDAGE, Jenni .... 608-785-8075 496 A
jbrundage@uwlax.edu
BRUNDAGE, Kelley, L ... 785-532-6254 175 C
kbrundage@ksu.edu
BRUNDAGE, Ken .... 814-871-7551 384 A
brundage001@gannon.edu
BRUNDAGE, Tracy .... 570-945-8500 386 F
tracy.brundage@keystone.edu

BUCHANAN, Barbara .... 336-322-2106 336 G
barbara.buchanan@piedmontcc.edu
BUCHANAN, Bernadette 830-372-6412 449 A
bbuchanan@tlu.edu
BUCHANAN, Candace ... 910-843-5304 331 A
office@nabc.edu
BUCHANAN, Connie ..... 830-703-1555 444 G
cwbuchanan@swtjc.edu
BUCHANAN, Emily, B ... 336-694-8042 336 G
emily.buchanan@piedmontcc.edu
BUCHANAN, James ...... 570-585-9235 381 B
BUCHANAN, Julie .... 575-492-2597 287 A
jbuchanan@nmjc.edu
BUCHANAN, Kelly .... 619-201-8702.. 60 G
kelly.buchanan@sdcc.edu
BUCHANAN, Kent .... 719-587-7622.. 77 G
kbuchanan@adams.edu
BUCHANAN, Lauren, A . 724-346-2073 379 E
lauren.buchanan@bc3.edu
BUCHANAN, Linda, R ... 229-732-5926 115 B
lindabuchanan@andrewcollege.edu
BUCHANAN, Mercedes . 205-226-4979.... 4 F
mdbucha1@bsc.edu
BUCHANAN, Pamela ..... 828-227-7640 343 E
pmbuchanan@wcu.edu
BUCHANAN, Shasta ...... 512-223-7053 430 I
shasta.buchanan@austincc.edu
BUCHANAN, Tony .... 910-843-5304 331 A
tony@buchanan.net
BUCHANAN, Trey .... 512-313-5002 433 N
trey.buchanan@concordia.edu
BUCHANAN MILLER,
Pamela .... 251-442-2360.... 8 C
pbuchanan@umobile.edu
BUCHBAUER, Victoria ... 717-477-1484 395 B
vmbuchbauer@ship.edu
BUCHE, Nathan .... 620-665-3569 174 G
buchen@hutchcc.edu
BUCHELE, Ann .... 541-917-4211 373 G
buchela@linnbenton.edu
BUCHEN, Lucas .... 309-649-6230 150 G
lucas.buchen@src.edu
BUCHER, Denise .... 303-404-5481.. 81 A
denise.bucher@frontrange.edu
BUCHER, Fred .... 706-778-8500 124 D
BUCHER, Jacob .... 708-524-6694 137 C
jbucher@dom.edu
BUCHER, Jennifer .... 570-372-4157 398 F
bucherjennifer@susqu.edu
BUCHER, Karen, H .... 540-665-4621 470 G
kbucher@su.edu
BUCHER, Lisa .... 860-832-2556.. 85 G
bucherl@ccsu.edu
BUCHER, Mary .... 864-503-5197 414 A
mbucher@uscupstate.edu
BUCHHEIT, Rudolph ...... 859-257-1687 185 F
rudolph.buchheit@uky.edu
BUCHHOLZ, Cindy .... 361-582-2587 457 E
cindy.buchholz@victoriacollege.edu
BUCHHOLZ, Meagan .... 314-434-4044 252 C
meagan.buchholz@covenantseminary.edu
BUCHHOLZ, Richard ..... 405-422-6204 369 A
richard.buchholz@redlandscc.edu
BUCHHOLZ, Ron .... 262-472-1498 497 D
buchholr@uww.edu
BUCHKO, Lindsay .... 202-448-7037.. 92 C
lindsay.buchko@gallaudet.edu
BUCHMAN, Ashley .... 870-512-7812.. 18 A
ashley_buchman@asun.edu
BUCHMAN, Lorne, M ... 626-396-2301.. 26 B
president@artcenter.edu
BUCHMANN, Teresa ..... 253-833-9111 480 I
tbuchmann@greenriver.edu
BUCHTERKIRCHEN,
Rebekah .... 503-517-1910 377 E
rbuchterkirchen@westernseminary.edu
BUCHWALD, Adam .... 503-768-7227 373 E
buchwald@lclark.edu
BUCHWALD, Carrie .... 847-574-5164 142 B
cbuchwald@lfgsm.edu
BUCHWALD, Staci .... 541-552-6998 376 B
buchwalds@sou.edu
BUCHWALDER,
Mary, P .... 937-229-3131 362 C
mbuchwalder1@udayton.edu
BUCIOR, Autumn .... 973-275-2259 283 C
autumn.bucior@shu.edu
BUCK, Angela .... 207-760-1128 195 G
nabuck@nmcc.edu
BUCK, Charles .... 208-292-1737 132 F
buck@uidaho.edu
BUCK, Heather .... 570-702-8906 386 D
hbuck@johnson.edu
BUCK, Jason .... 603-428-2241 273 G
jbuck@nec.edu
BUCK, John .... 314-968-6980 262 C
buckjh@webster.edu
BUCK, Joseph, E .... 610-758-4711 388 E
job316@lehigh.edu
BUCK, Katherine .... 973-290-4203 282 I
kbuck@steu.edu
BUCK, Kevan .... 405-208-5498 367 E
kbuck@okcu.edu
BUCK, Laurie .... 217-206-6724 152 A
lbuck01s@uis.edu
BUCK, Leah .... 207-768-2768 195 G
lbuck@nmcc.edu
BUCK, Luther, S .... 301-736-3631 200 C
BUCK, Sean, S .... 410-293-1000 504 A
sbuck@usna.edu
BUCK, Teresa .... 254-295-4640 453 D
tbuck@umhb.edu
BUCKEL, Maria .... 314-889-4533 253 E
mbuckel@fontbonne.edu
BUCKELS, Carol .... 386-738-6686 112 A
cbuckels@stetson.edu
BUCKENMEYER, Janet ... 812-237-2919 156 D
janet.buckenmeyer@indstate.edu
BUCKHAULTS, Tex .... 806-874-3571 432 J
tex.buckhaults@clarendoncollege.edu
BUCKHAULTS,
Tresea, L .... 318-342-5247 193 C
buckhaults@ulm.edu
BUCKINGHAM, Bob, S . 304-457-6588 486 E
buckinghamrs@ab.edu
BUCKINGHAM, Richard 617-573-8605 219 B
rbuckingham@suffolk.edu
BUCKINGHAM, Stacy .... 618-985-3741 140 H
stacybuckingham@jalc.edu
BUCKINGHAM, Stacy .... 618-985-8204 140 H
stacybuckingham@jalc.edu
BUCKLAND, Stephen .... 503-255-0332 374 C
stephenbuckland@multnomah.edu
BUCKLER, C. Adam ...... 317-896-9324 161 F
abuckler@ubca.org
BUCKLER, Christina ...... 845-434-5750 321 E
BUCKLES, Beverly, J ..... 909-558-4528.. 48 E
bbuckles@llu.edu
BUCKLES, Cassie .... 386-752-1822 100 B
cassandra.buckles@fgc.edu
BUCKLES, Dale .... 270-706-8431 181 G
dale.buckles@kctcs.edu
BUCKLES, Jennifer .... 423-425-4677 427 C
jennifer-buckles@utc.edu
BUCKLES, Michael .... 337-475-5192 192 E
mbuckles@mcneese.edu
BUCKLESS, Frank .... 919-515-5560 342 A
buckless@ncsu.edu
BUCKLEW, Andrea .... 800-263-1549 486 E
BUCKLEW, Andrea, J ..... 304-457-6438 486 E
bucklewaj@ab.edu
BUCKLEY, Anne, L .... 858-534-7572.. 70 C
albuckley@ucsd.edu
BUCKLEY, Bri .... 801-832-2529 461 F
bbuckley@westminstercollege.edu
BUCKLEY, Candice .... 404-297-9522 120 B
buckleyc@gptc.edu
BUCKLEY, Cynthia, S .... 405-466-3204 366 C
cynthia.buckley@langston.edu
BUCKLEY, David .... 530-898-6411.. 30 D
dbuckley@csuchico.edu
BUCKLEY, Dawn .... 228-897-3835 247 E
dawn.buckley@mgccc.edu
BUCKLEY, Emily .... 913-621-8731 173 E
ebuckley@donnelly.edu
BUCKLEY, Erin .... 610-519-8881 401 K
erin.buckley@villanova.edu
BUCKLEY, Gerard .... 315-781-3701 301 F
buckley@hws.edu
BUCKLEY, Gerard, J ...... 585-475-6317 312 F
gjbcfo@ntid.rit.edu
BUCKLEY, Jennifer .... 630-844-6155 133 D
jbuckley@aurora.edu
BUCKLEY, Jerry, L .... 559-638-0300.. 67 D
jerry.buckley@reedleycollege.edu
BUCKLEY, John, M .... 302-857-1200.. 91 A
john.buckley@dtcc.edu
BUCKLEY, John, W .... 718-817-4000 300 C
jbuckley@fordham.edu
BUCKLEY, Keith .... 503-352-2180 375 C
buckleyk@pacificu.edu
BUCKLEY, Kelley .... 615-871-2260.. 93 H
BUCKLEY, Linda, J .... 978-556-3224 215 E
lbuckley@necc.mass.edu
BUCKLEY, Neil .... 781-239-3193 214 G
nbuckley@massbay.edu
BUCKLEY, Nicholas .... 580-559-5602 365 K
nicpbuc@ecok.edu
BUCKLEY, Noah .... 541-737-4411 375 A
osuadmit@oregonstate.edu
BUCKLEY, Patricia .... 518-458-5444 296 G
buckleyp@strose.edu
BUCKLEY, Peter, F .... 804-828-9788 473 B
peter.buckley@vcuhealth.org
BUCKLEY, Sally .... 508-286-3857 220 B
buckley_sally@wheatoncollege.edu
BUCKLEY, Tera .... 701-777-4941 345 B
tera.buckley@und.edu
BUCKLEY, Toni .... 413-236-3075 214 A
tbuckley@berkshirecc.edu
BUCKLIN, Carolyn .... 515-643-6744 168 D
cbucklin@mercydesmoines.org
BUCKMAN, Anna .... 270-384-8033 183 G
buckmana@lindsey.edu
BUCKMAN, Michael, R . 724-458-3355 384 G
mrbuckman@gcc.edu
BUCKMINSTER, Krista ... 281-283-2128 452 E
buckminster@uhcl.edu
BUCKNER, Edmund .... 601-877-6137 245 A
ebuckner@alcorn.edu
BUCKNER, Forrest .... 509-777-4506 486 C
fbuckner@whitworth.edu
BUCKNER, Jeremy .... 865-471-3219 418 E
jbuckner@cn.edu
BUCKNER, Melody .... 520-626-9484.. 16 D
mbuckner@arizona.edu
BUCKNER, Nichole .... 828-689-1103 331 C
nbuckner@mhu.edu
BUCKNER, R. Ty .... 336-316-2248 329 D
rbuckner@guilford.edu
BUCKNER, S. Jamila ..... 415-442-7079.. 43 I
BUCKNER, Terry .... 859-246-6397 181 F
terry.buckner@kctcs.edu
BUCKNER INNISS,
Lolita .... 303-492-8047.. 84 B
lawdean@colorado.edu
BUCKO, Kate .... 901-722-3397 423 G
kbucko@sco.edu
BUCKOVICH, John .... 912-525-5000 124 I
jbuckovi@scad.edu
BUCKOVICH, Lucas .... 877-722-3285 124 I
lbuckovi@scad.edu
BUCKRIDGE, Brett .... 610-902-8781 379 G
beb99@cabrini.edu
BUCKSON, Ryan .... 803-750-2500.. 93 H
BUCKWALTER, John ..... 208-426-4062 130 H
johnbuckwalter@boisestate.edu
BUCKWALTER, Kristine . 828-669-8012 331 K
kristine.buckwalter@montreat.edu
BUCY, Brandon, R .... 540-458-8651 477 D
bucyb@wlu.edu
BUCZKOWSKI,
Stephanie .... 716-286-8720 309 H
sbuczkowski@niagara.edu
BUDA, Pawel .... 507-433-0620 240 G
pawel.buda@riverland.edu
BUDDE, Bruce .... 309-694-5477 139 B
bbudde@icc.edu
BUDDE, Jill .... 641-683-5111 166 I
jill.budde@indianhills.edu
BUDDE, Mitzi, J .... 703-370-6600 476 E
BUDDEN, LaNae, R .... 803-786-3856 408 D
lrbriggs@columbiasc.edu
BUDDIE, Mike .... 845-938-3701 503 I
allison.wright@westpoint.edu
BUDELL, Andrew .... 615-343-3896 428 A
andrew.m.budell@vanderbilt.edu
BUDESKI, Brittany .... 406-791-5207 265 H
brittany.budeski@uprovidence.edu
BUDGE, Aaron .... 507-389-5998 239 D
aaron.budge@mnsu.edu
BUDIG, Michelle .... 413-545-5972 211 G
budig@soc.umass.edu
BUDINE, Julie .... 217-228-5432 147 F
hendrju@quincy.edu
BUDNIK, Lindsay .... 802-485-2824 462 F
lbudnik@norwich.edu
BUDNY, Jill .... 724-925-4185 402 F
budnyj@westmoreland.edu
BUDNY, Steve .... 724-925-4085 402 F
budnys@westmoreland.edu
BUDWAY, Joshua .... 480-947-6644.. 14 N
BUDZIAK, Chase .... 815-825-1708 141 F
cbudziak@kish.edu
BUDZILOWICZ, Mary .... 610-902-8352 379 G
mary.m.budzilowicz@cabrini.edu
BUECHELE, Angela, K ... 937-229-2941 362 C
abuechele1@udayton.edu
BUECHELE, Thomas ...... 312-899-7420 149 F
tbuechele@saic.edu
BUECHER, Eileen, C .... 805-756-5726.. 29 I
ebuecher@calpoly.edu
BUEHLER, Charlie .... 612-351-0631 236 E
cbuehler@ipr.edu
BUEHLER, Julie .... 585-245-5601 318 B
buehler@geneseo.edu
BUEHLER, Lesley .... 510-659-6082.. 54 J
lbuehler@ohlone.edu
BUEHRER, Anna .... 309-672-5513 144 C
abuehrer@methodistcol.edu
BUEHRER, Danielle .... 470-578-4426 121 M
dbuehrer@kennesaw.edu
BUEL, Kevin, A .... 646-378-6143 310 D
kevin.buel@nyack.edu
BUELL, Lige .... 606-589-3040 183 A
e.buell@kctcs.edu
BUENTELLO, Gracy .... 903-566-7480 456 A
gbuentello@uttyler.edu
BUETTNER, John .... 443-352-4494 202 E
jbuettner@stevenson.edu
BUETTNER, Rita .... 410-617-2146 200 B
rfbuettner@loyola.edu
BUFANO, Suzanne .... 843-953-6799 407 C
suzanne.bufano@citadel.edu
BUFF, Sam .... 704-825-6260 334 G
buff.sam@gaston.edu
BUFFINGTON, James .... 714-437-9697.. 37 H
BUFFONE, Nancy .... 413-577-1101 211 G
buffone@admin.umass.edu
BUFFUM, Don .... 662-325-2861 247 F
dbuffum@procurement.msstate.edu
BUGADO, Lai Sha .... 808-932-7365 129 D
sdelo@hawaii.edu
BUGAIGHIS, Elizabeth .. 610-332-6272 391 C
ebugaighis@northampton.edu
BUGAIGHIS, Yasmin ..... 610-861-1480 390 F
bugaighisy@moravian.edu
BUGAJSKI, Kenneth, A . 260-399-7700 162 B
kbugajski@sf.edu
BUGAJSKI, OFS,
Trish, J .... 260-399-7700 162 B
tbugajski@sf.edu
BUGG, Gary, D .... 859-238-5535 180 B
gary.bugg@centre.edu
BUGGLIN, Tracy, F .... 740-826-8142 356 H
tbugglin@muskingum.edu
BUGGS, Richard .... 415-575-6116.. 28 I
rbuggs@ciis.edu
BUGLIONE, Suzanne ..... 508-678-2811 214 B
suzanne.buglione@bristolcc.edu
BUGOS, Michelle .... 309-694-5593 139 B
michelle.bugos@icc.edu
BUHAGIAR, Jon .... 412-809-5216 396 E
buhagiar.jon@ptcollege.edu
BUHL, Patrick .... 952-358-8595 239 G
patrick.buhl@normandale.edu
BUHLER, Doug, D .... 517-355-0123 227 F
buhler@msu.edu
BUHLIG, Gretchen, E .... 480-965-5769.. 10 J
gretchen.buhlig@asu.edu
BUHLIG, Lynda .... 775-682-6013 271 E
lbuhlig@unr.edu
BUHR, Brian .... 612-625-7173 243 F
bbuhr@umn.edu
BUHR, Connie .... 319-296-4281 166 H
connie.buhr@hawkeyecollege.edu
BUHR, Heather .... 812-866-7097 155 G
buhr@hanover.edu
BUHRANDT, Jeff .... 608-262-1312 495 C
jbuhrandt@uwsa.edu
BUHRMAN,
William (Bill) .... 210-436-3716 442 J
wbuhrman@stmarytx.edu
BUHRMASTER, John ..... 305-899-3336.. 96 A
jbuhrmaster@barry.edu
BUHROW, William, C ... 503-554-2340 373 A
bbuhrow@georgefox.edu
BUI, Brooke .... 949-451-5336.. 65 C
bbui21@ivc.edu
BUI, Derek .... 714-241-6594.. 37 J
vbui34@coastline.edu
BUIE, Melissa, K .... 601-857-3927 246 C
melissa.buie@hindscc.edu
BUISMAN, Kevin .... 507-389-6111 239 D
kevin.buisman@mnsu.edu
BUITER, Mike .... 864-242-5100 406 H
BUJAK, Jeanette, K .... 704-233-8149 344 F
jbujak@wingate.edu
BUJAK, Valerie .... 816-331-5700 258 D
BUJAKI, Jim .... 989-774-1771 222 E
bujak1jf@cmich.edu

BUKOWSKI, Bruce, J .... 410-293-2934 504 A bukowski@usna.edu
BUKOWSKI, Mark .... 863-784-7104 108 F mark.bukowski@southflorida.edu
BUKOWSKI, Tamzin ...... 320-762-4415 237 C tamzinb@alextech.edu
BULAN, Anita .... 718-951-5000 293 C
BULCOCK, Jennifer .... 610-902-8297 379 G jennifer.bulcock@cabrini.edu
BULEY, Paula Marie ..... 603-897-8202 273 I pbuley@rivier.edu
BULITTA, Sue .... 309-694-5522 139 B sue.bulitta@icc.edu
BULKLEY, Katrina .... 973-655-2063 279 B bulkleyk@montclair.edu
BULL, Bernard .... 402-643-3651 266 G
BULL, Joe .... 937-481-2263 364 A joe.bull@wilminton.edu
BULL, Kam .... 530-895-1352.. 27 C bullka@butte.edu
BULL, Karen .... 336-315-7044 343 A kzbull@uncg.edu
BULL, Karen, Z .... 336-315-7044 343 A kzbull@uncg.edu
BULL, Prince .... 704-406-4402 329 A pbull@gardner-webb.edu
BULLARD, Anthony .... 662-685-4771 245 C abullard@bmc.edu
BULLARD, Bobby .... 512-448-8569 442 I bobbyb@stedwards.edu
BULLARD, Cora .... 910-521-6219 343 B cora.bullard@uncp.edu
BULLARD, Daniel, C ..... 804-828-2233 473 B bullarddc@vcu.edu
BULLARD, Eric .... 310-825-5551.. 69 E ebullard@unex.ucla.edu
BULLARD, Jayne .... 417-269-3473 252 D jayne.bullard@coxcollege.edu
BULLARD, Jessica .... 910-272-3235 337 D jbullard@robeson.edu
BULLARD, Roland .... 504-816-4916 186 I rbullard@dillard.edu
BULLARD, Scott, W ...... 704-463-3030 339 E scott.bullard@pfeiffer.edu
BULLINGER, Cheryl ...... 605-394-4800 415 G
BULLINGHAM, Bree ...... 212-517-0532 305 E bbullingham@mmm.edu
BULLINGTON, Jeffrey .... 719-587-7820.. 77 G jsbullington@adams.edu
BULLINS, Chris .... 419-372-2343 348 G chrishb@bgsu.edu
BULLINS, David .... 704-978-5446 336 C dbullins@mitchellcc.edu
BULLIS, Tim .... 804-752-7315 469 F timbullis@rmc.edu
BULLMASTER-DAY, Marcella .... 212-463-0400 322 G marcella.bullmaster-day@touro.edu
BULLOCK, Ann .... 336-278-5900 328 J abullock9@elon.edu
BULLOCK, Bethany .... 423-279-7633 425 A bhbullock@northeaststate.edu
BULLOCK, Brian .... 610-519-4070 401 K brian.bullock@villanova.edu
BULLOCK, Casey, D ...... 801-626-6750 461 A caseybullock@weber.edu
BULLOCK, Charles .... 949-753-4774.. 71 D
BULLOCK, Damay, J ..... 757-569-6704 474 H dbullock@pdc.edu
BULLOCK, Doug .... 435-797-1812 460 C doug.bullock@usu.edu
BULLOCK, Elizabeth ...... 918-631-2525 371 C elizabeth-bullock@utulsa.edu
BULLOCK, James .... 949-824-7727.. 69 D bullock@uci.edu
BULLOCK, James, R ..... 336-978-0688 344 F j.bullock@wingate.edu
BULLOCK, Jeffrey, F ..... 563-589-3224 170 G jbullock@dbq.edu
BULLOCK, John .... 802-440-4406 461 G jbullock@bennington.edu
BULLOCK, Josh .... 217-234-5222 142 C jbullock@lakeland.cc.il.us
BULLOCK, Kelly .... 602-386-4104.. 10 F kelly.bullock@arizonachristian.edu
BULLOCK, Nathan .... 573-986-6127 259 H nbullock@semo.edu
BULLOCK, Quintin, B .... 412-237-4413 381 D brichardson@ccac.edu
BULLOCK, Thomas .... 912-443-4150 125 B tbullock@savannahtech.edu
BULLUCK, Bruce .... 256-551-5210.... 2 E bruce.bulluck@drakestate.edu
BULLUCK, Travis .... 828-227-7733 343 E tlbulluck@email.wcu.edu
BULLWINKEL, Michelle, L .... 727-816-3212 105 F bullwim@phsc.edu
BULMER, Sandra .... 203-392-6993.. 86 A bulmers1@southernct.edu
BULZONI, Donna, R ..... 570-422-3117 394 A dbulzoni@esu.edu
BUMGARNER, Brittany .. 704-233-8303 344 F b.bumgarner@wingate.edu
BUMGARNER, Jennifer . 252-514-6715 334 A bumgarnerj@cravencc.edu
BUMILLER, Taylor .... 636-327-4645 256 B
BUMPERS, Claude .... 251-665-4139.... 1 E cbumpers@bishop.edu
BUMPERS, Eddie .... 417-328-1500 259 I eddiebumpers@crosswaybc.org
BUMPOUS, Debbi .... 605-626-2283 416 G debbi.bumpous@northern.edu
BUMPS, Heather .... 309-341-7000 141 G hsbumps@knox.edu
BUMPUS, Danielle .... 508-830-5037 213 D dbumpus@maritime.edu
BUMSTEAD, Matt .... 806-720-7380 439 D matt.bumstead@lcu.edu
BUNCE, Heather .... 517-321-0242 225 A hbunce@glcc.edu
BUNCE, Larry .... 419-289-5032 347 J lbunce@ashland.edu
BUNCH, Brandon .... 252-940-6426 332 C brandon.bunch@beaufortccc.edu
BUNCH, Ella .... 252-335-0821 333 G ella_bunch44@albemarle.edu
BUNCH, John .... 903-334-6628 448 A john.bunch@tamut.edu
BUNCH, Kenneth .... 434-832-6691 473 E bunchk@centralvirginia.edu
BUNCH, Kirsten .... 828-694-1804 332 E kirstenb@blueridge.edu
BUNCH, Martha, M .... 336-272-7102 329 C bunchm@greensboro.edu
BUNCH, Tom .... 817-202-6207 444 I buncht@swau.edu
BUNCH, Tony .... 870-236-6901.. 18 J tbunch@crc.edu
BUNCH, Wes .... 828-327-7000 333 B wbunch@cvcc.edu
BUNDICK, Chris .... 504-398-2125 192 A cbundick@uhcno.edu
BUNDY, Alfred .... 973-877-3156 277 G abundy@essex.edu
BUNDY, Bailey .... 859-344-3345 185 B bundyb@thomasmore.edu
BUNDY, Barbara .... 213-624-1200.. 42 B bbundy@fidm.edu
BUNDY, Bill .... 806-720-7126 439 D bill.bundy@lcu.edu
BUNDY, James, A .... 203-432-1505.. 90 C james.bundy@yale.edu
BUNDY, III, O. Richard 814-863-4826 391 G orb100@psu.edu
BUNGAY, Sophia .... 505-438-8884 288 F admissions@acupuncturecollege.edu
BUNGER, Ron .... 404-835-6120 423 B rbunger@richmont.edu
BUNING, Tom .... 808-739-8578 128 E thomas.buning@chaminade.edu
BUNIS, David .... 508-831-4993 220 F dabunis@wpi.edu
BUNJER, Alice .... 515-964-0601 166 D bunjera@faith.edu
BUNJER, Jeff .... 515-964-0601 166 D bunjerj@faith.edu
BUNKELMANN, Jeff ...... 520-494-5365.. 11 K jeffrey.bunkelmann@centralaz.edu
BUNKER, Aaron .... 918-335-6875 368 E abunker@okwu.edu
BUNKER, Larissa .... 208-467-8588 132 E lbunker@nnu.edu
BUNKER, Laurel .... 651-638-6372 234 D l-bunker@bethel.edu
BUNKO, Tracy, A .... 719-333-7731 503 D tracy.bunko@usafa.edu
BUNKOWSKI, Elise .... 775-674-7544 271 C ebunkowski@tmcc.edu
BUNN, Colleen .... 607-431-4504 301 A bunnc@hartwick.edu
BUNN, Doug .... 541-888-1673 376 C doug.bunn@socc.edu
BUNNELL, Bob .... 856-351-2239 283 B bbunell@salemcc.edu
BUNNELL, Stephen, P .. 208-496-3000 130 I bunnells@byui.edu
BUNNELL-RHYNE, Melinda .... 301-369-2543 198 C mabunnell-rhyne@captechu.edu
BUNNING, Matt .... 859-441-4500 181 H matt.bunning@kctcs.edu
BUNT, Stephanie .... 714-556-3610.. 73 H stephanie.bunt@vanguard.edu
BUNTEN, Tricia .... 218-726-6995 243 G tbunten@d.umn.edu
BUNTING, Amy .... 334-699-2266.... 1 B aebunting@southeasthealth.org
BUNTING, Gene .... 336-841-9583 329 F gbunting@highpoint.edu
BUNTING, Taryn .... 618-395-7777 139 H buntingt@iecc.edu
BUNTON, Kristie .... 817-257-6550 448 F k.bunton@tcu.edu
BUNTON, Thomas .... 501-916-3010.. 22 A tebunton@ualr.edu
BUNTON, Tim, M .... 217-443-8780 136 G tbunton@dacc.edu
BUONICONTI, Bridget ... 781-768-7895 218 D bridget.buoniconti@regiscollege.edu
BUONO, Jack .... 516-773-5000 503 H
BUONO, Lisa .... 805-493-3663.. 29 C llbuono@callutheran.edu
BUONOPANE, Gerard .... 973-761-9121 283 C gerard.buonopane@shu.edu
BURAK, Deborah .... 610-861-4137 391 C dburak@northampton.edu
BURBA, Dave .... 530-541-4660.. 47 E burba@ltcc.edu
BURBA, Randy .... 714-997-6763.. 36 B burba@chapman.edu
BURBACK, Michael .... 202-884-9812.. 94 A burbackm@trinitydc.edu
BURBANTE, Gilberto ..... 985-448-4208 192 F gilberto.burbante@nicholls.edu
BURCH, Ann Lee .... 480-219-6061 250 A aburch@atsu.edu
BURCH, Beth .... 503-568-9941 374 G bburch@ocom.edu
BURCH, Chuck, S .... 704-406-4342 329 A cburch@gardner-webb.edu
BURCH, Daphne .... 912-478-5054 120 C dburch@georgiasouthern.edu
BURCH, Stacie .... 410-777-1963 197 G sqburch@aacc.edu
BURCHAM, Andy .... 806-720-7408 439 D andy.burcham@lcu.edu
BURCHAM, Joshua .... 336-734-7714 334 F jburcham@forsythtech.edu
BURCHARD, Eric .... 740-593-1804 358 K burchard@ohio.edu
BURCHARD, Robert ...... 573-875-8700 251 I
BURCHETT, Amy .... 432-264-5063 437 F aburchett@howardcollege.edu
BURCHETT, Bonnie, L ... 423-439-4446 419 G bonnie@etsu.edu
BURCHETT, Jennifer ...... 760-252-2411.. 26 G
BURCHETT, Lance .... 470-578-6033 121 M
BURCHETT, Rachelle ...... 606-788-2863 181 E rachelle.burchett@kctcs.edu
BURCHFIELD, Doug ...... 828-564-5128 335 C ddburchfield@haywood.edu
BURCHINAL, Mitzi, W .. 336-334-4036 343 A mjwilder@uncg.edu
BURCIAGA, Jeremy .... 915-778-4001 444 H
BURCKARDT, Jennifer ... 860-486-2337.. 89 D
BURCKEL, Daryl .... 337-475-5556 192 E dburckel@mcneese.edu
BURCKHALTER, Regina . 406-604-4300 262 I r.burckhalter@apollos.edu
BURD, Gail, D .... 520-621-1856.. 16 D gburd@arizona.edu
BURD, Kathy .... 304-829-7131 487 A kburd@bethanywv.edu
BURD, Randy .... 516-299-2917 304 D randy.burd@liu.edu
BURDA, Ed .... 304-457-6238 486 E burdaep@ab.edu
BURDA, Jeffrey .... 860-768-4482.. 89 G burda@hartford.edu
BURDEN, Chris .... 619-260-4655.. 72 I cburden@sandiego.edu
BURDEN, John .... 502-585-9911 184 H jburden@spalding.edu
BURDEN, Kathleen, K ... 937-255-6234 502 C kathleen.burden@afit.edu
BURDEN, Matthew .... 630-637-5433 145 F mburden@noctrl.edu
BURDEN, Susan .... 660-263-4100 257 B susanburden@macc.edu
BURDETTE, Darcy .... 319-208-5050 170 D dburdette@scciowa.edu
BURDETTE, Vinson .... 803-508-7244 406 C burdettv@atc.edu
BURDETTE, William .... 304-696-6523 489 M burdette@marshall.edu
BURDICK, Alexis .... 805-765-9307.. 62 N alexisburdick@collegesoflaw.edu
BURDICK, Gary .... 269-471-3501 221 D gburdick@andrews.edu
BURDICK, Jonathan .... 607-255-2000 297 F jrb538@cornell.edu
BURDICK, Kirsten, N .... 205-934-4319..... 8 A knburdick@uab.edu
BURDICK, Phillip .... 520-206-4850.. 15 B pburdick@pima.edu
BURDICK, Scott .... 401-874-2383 405 E sburdick@uri.edu
BURDINE, Mike .... 208-459-5663 131 C mburdine@collegeofidaho.edu
BURDSALL, Mark, D ..... 412-624-8038 400 H pauab5@pitt.edu
BURDUE, JoEllen .... 414-277-7117 494 D burdue@msoe.edu
BURFITT, William .... 619-849-2540.. 57 J williamburfitt@pointloma.edu
BURFORD, Amy .... 309-341-5497 134 B aburford@sandburg.edu
BURFORD, Kristina .... 501-450-1362.. 19 E burford@hendrix.edu
BURFORD, Kyla .... 618-252-5400 149 I kyla.burford@sic.edu
BURFORD, Nancy .... 816-501-3618 250 F
BURGARD, Bambi .... 816-802-3455 254 D bburgard@kcai.edu
BURGARD, Daniel .... 817-735-2589 454 B daniel.burgard@unthsc.edu
BURGAU, Tam .... 715-858-1377 498 E tburgau@cvtc.edu
BURGAY, Stephen, P .... 617-353-1168 207 E burgay@bu.edu
BURGE, Danielle .... 251-981-3771.... 5 A danielle.burge@columbiasouthern.edu
BURGE, David .... 703-993-5487 467 E dburge@gmu.edu
BURGE, Gary .... 616-957-6032 222 B gb051@calvinseminary.edu
BURGE, Jennifer, G ...... 309-677-4939 134 A jgruening@bradley.edu
BURGENER, Ricki .... 562-985-7502.. 31 D ricki.burgener@csulb.edu
BURGER, Alissa .... 583-288-6350 252 F aburger@culver.edu
BURGER, Arnold .... 615-329-8516 419 H aburger@fisk.edu
BURGER, Cindy, L .... 717-796-1800 389 H cburger@messiah.edu
BURGER, Crystal .... 870-733-6831.. 17 F ccburger@asumidsouth.edu
BURGER, Dexter, E .... 214-768-4767 444 D dburger@smu.edu
BURGER, Mark .... 417-667-8181 252 B mburger@cottey.edu
BURGER, Rosemary ...... 570-348-6280 389 D burger@marywood.edu
BURGER, Tony .... 734-936-1320 231 H tburger@umich.edu
BURGER, Wes .... 662-325-7552 247 F w.burger@msstate.edu
BURGESS, Aaron .... 323-343-3000.. 31 E
BURGESS, Amanda .... 612-330-1791 234 A burgessa@augsburg.edu
BURGESS, Brandy .... 303-273-3282.. 79 J burgess@mines.edu
BURGESS, Brenda, K .... 580-774-3000 370 A brenda.burgess@swosu.edu
BURGESS, Craig .... 706-507-8800 117 H burgess_craig@columbusstate.edu
BURGESS, Douglas .... 513-556-9900 361 J douglas.burgess@uc.edu
BURGESS, Esther .... 803-981-7075 414 F eburgess@yorktech.edu
BURGESS, Frederick ...... 607-255-2000 297 F
BURGESS, Jodi .... 540-863-2835 473 F jburgess@dslcc.edu
BURGESS, Kimberly ...... 912-279-5770 117 F kburgess@ccga.edu
BURGESS, Leandra, H ... 803-705-4604 406 G leandra.burgess@benedict.edu
BURGESS, Lillie, A .... 803-253-5000 406 G

BURGESS, Linda .... 913-288-7450 175 B
lburgess@kckcc.edu
BURGESS, Marcus, H ... 803-535-5238 407 D
mburgess@claflin.edu
BURGESS, Norma .... 615-966-5062 421 B
norma.burgess@lipscomb.edu
BURGESS, Robert .... 870-512-8617.. 18 A
robert_burgess@asun.edu
BURGESS, Ronald, L ..... 334-844-4650.... 4 D
rlb0029@auburn.edu
BURGESS, Shane, C ..... 520-621-7621.. 16 D
sburgess@cals.arizona.edu
BURGESS, Valerie .... 603-880-8308 274 D
vburgess@thomasmorecollege.edu
BURGGRAFF, Lucy .... 919-573-5350 340 C
lburggraff@shepherds.edu
BURGIN, Jeffrey .... 256-761-6231.... 7 B
jburgin@talladega.edu
BURGIN, Vicki .... 251-442-2238.... 8 C
vburgin@umobile.edu
BURGMAYER, Sharon ... 610-526-5106 379 B
sburmay@brynmawr.edu
BURGNER, Ryan .... 308-635-6798 270 C
burgnerr@wncc.edu
BURGOS, Blanca .... 305-485-7700 113 A
BURGOS, Henry .... 361-593-2258 447 D
henry.burgos@tamuk.edu
BURGOS, Kathy .... 562-860-2451.. 35 H
kburgos@cerritos.edu
BURGOS CARRION,
Jorge, A .... 787-720-4476 511 C
decanatoestudiantes@mizpa.edu
BURGRAFF, Tom .... 970-943-2237.. 85 C
tburgraff@western.edu
BURGUNDER-JOHNSON,
Dominique .... 574-535-7568 155 E
dominiquebj@goshen.edu
BURHANNA, Kenneth ... 330-672-1660 354 A
kburhann@kent.edu
BURIK, Larry .... 909-607-4366.. 37 D
larry.burik@cmc.edu
BURILLO-HOPKINS,
Madeline .... 713-718-7748 437 C
madeline.burillo@hccs.edu
BURINGTON, Stacie ...... 563-425-5899 170 H
buringtons63@uiu.edu
BURK, Ann, M .... 308-432-6311 268 D
aburk@csc.edu
BURKE, Alison .... 610-921-6711 377 G
aburke@albright.edu
BURKE, Andrew .... 575-646-2431 287 C
aburke@nmsu.edu
BURKE, Barbara .... 718-260-5173 295 A
bburke@citytech.cuny.edu
BURKE, Belinda .... 828-771-2000 344 D
bburke@warren-wilson.edu
BURKE, Brenda .... 330-672-6000 354 A
bburke21@kent.edu
BURKE, Brian, W .... 413-545-2204 211 G
bwburke@umass.edu
BURKE, Bridgit .... 307-766-3753 501 I
BURKE, Brigid .... 973-443-8520 277 I
brigid_burke@fdu.edu
BURKE, Cathleen, C ..... 804-828-6549 473 B
ccburke@vcu.edu
BURKE, Christina .... 301-687-4467 204 C
cnburke@frostburg.edu
BURKE, Christy .... 740-376-4708 355 E
christy.burke@marietta.edu
BURKE, Colleen .... 215-572-2785 378 E
burkec@arcadia.edu
BURKE, Courtney .... 518-262-9590 289 L
burkec4@amc.edu
BURKE, Dave .... 617-745-3000 209 B
BURKE, Derek, A .... 252-398-6369 328 C
burked@chowan.edu
BURKE, Gary .... 301-369-2544 198 C
gaburke@captechu.edu
BURKE, Greg .... 318-357-5251 192 G
burkeg@nsula.edu
BURKE, Greg .... 812-749-1288 159 O
gburke@oak.edu
BURKE, Indy .... 203-432-5109.. 90 C
indy.burke@yale.edu
BURKE, James .... 216-397-4484 353 O
burke@jcu.edu
BURKE, Jeanmarie, R ... 315-568-3869 310 B
jburke@nycc.edu
BURKE, Jim .... 601-974-1036 247 B
BURKE, John .... 845-848-4079 298 C
john.burke@dc.edu
BURKE, John .... 361-570-4550 453 B
burkej@uhv.edu

BURKE, John, D .... 617-552-3387 207 C
john.burke.7@bc.edu
BURKE, Jon .... 816-604-6620 255 E
jon.burke@mcckc.edu
BURKE, Jonathan .... 949-376-6000.. 47 D
jburke@lcad.edu
BURKE, Jonathan, L ..... 816-604-6620 255 D
jon.burke@mcckc.edu
BURKE, Joy .... 814-371-2090 399 H
jburke@triangle-tech.edu
BURKE, Judith, M .... 978-656-3116 215 B
BURKE, Kathleen, F ...... 949-582-4840.. 65 B
kburke@socccd.edu
BURKE, Katie .... 860-231-5364.. 90 A
kathrynburke@usj.edu
BURKE, Kelly, J .... 336-334-5375 343 A
kjburke@uncg.edu
BURKE, Keri .... 503-883-2269 373 F
kburke@linfield.edu
BURKE, SJ, Kevin, F .... 303-458-4087.. 83 E
kburke@regis.edu
BURKE, Letitia .... 201-327-8877 277 F
lburke@eastwick.edu
BURKE, Lisa .... 630-617-5197 137 G
lisab@elmhurst.edu
BURKE, Lucy .... 315-859-4999 300 H
lburke@hamilton.edu
BURKE, Marcilynn .... 541-346-3836 376 H
maburke@uoregon.edu
BURKE, Matthew .... 978-665-3313 212 E
mburke4@fitchburgstate.edu
BURKE, Pamela, B .... 540-665-4925 470 G
pburke2@su.edu
BURKE, Patty .... 513-487-1287 361 F
patty.burke@myunion.edu
BURKE, Paula .... 660-831-4105 256 I
burkep@moval.edu
BURKE, Robyn .... 907-852-1838.... 9 H
robyn.burke@ilisagvik.edu
BURKE, Sandra .... 662-252-8000 248 G
sburke@rustcollege.edu
BURKE, Sara, K .... 330-471-8288 355 D
sburke@malone.edu
BURKE, Scott, M .... 404-413-2088 120 E
sburke@gsu.edu
BURKE, Sean .... 563-387-2110 168 B
burke.sean@luther.edu
BURKE, Seth .... 540-665-6257 470 G
sburke@su.edu
BURKE, Shelby .... 425-388-9254 480 B
saburke@everettcc.edu
BURKE, Tammy .... 406-447-6352 264 B
tammy.burke@helenacollege.edu
BURKE, Thomas .... 410-864-3602 202 C
tburke@stmarys.edu
BURKE, Vic .... 229-225-3978 126 A
vburke@southernregional.edu
BURKE, William .... 570-702-8907 386 D
wburke@johnson.edu
BURKE-SULLIVAN,
Eileen, C .... 402-280-3285 266 H
e_burkesullivan@creighton.edu
BURKERT, Amy, L .... 412-268-5865 380 C
ak11@andrew.cmu.edu
BURKES, Kate .... 479-619-4299.. 20 C
kburkes@nwacc.edu
BURKET, Jamie .... 904-256-7542 102 H
jburket@ju.edu
BURKETT, Brad .... 731-881-7641 427 D
bburkett@utm.edu
BURKETT, Kaia .... 510-587-7890.. 57 C
kburkett@peralta.edu
BURKEY, Robert .... 816-604-4062 255 H
robert.burkey@mcckc.edu
BURKHALTER, Sheila .... 803-323-2251 414 D
burkhalters@winthrop.edu
BURKHARD, Englert .... 970-351-2877.. 84 F
englert.burkhard@unco.edu
BURKHARDT, Janet .... 303-871-4757.. 84 E
janet.burkhardt@du.edu
BURKHARDT, Paul .... 928-350-4100.. 15 L
pburkhardt@prescott.edu
BURKHARDT, Ronald .... 856-351-2608 283 B
rburkhardt@salemcc.edu
BURKHART, Bethani, M 330-569-5132 353 G
burkhartbm@hiram.edu
BURKHART, Cindy .... 910-938-6145 333 F
burkhartc@coastalcarolina.edu
BURKHOLDER,
Brian, M .... 540-432-4132 466 B
brian.burkholder@emu.edu
BURKHOLDER, Mary, E 419-783-2360 351 K
mburkholder@defiance.edu

BURKHOLDER,
Robert, C .... 215-503-6249 399 E
robert.burkholder@jefferson.edu
BURKINK, Tim, J .... 308-865-1547 269 I
burkinktj@unk.edu
BURKITT, David .... 419-517-8968 355 C
dburkitt@lourdes.edu
BURKLO, Daniel .... 419-267-1342 357 E
dburklo@northweststate.edu
BURKMAN, Roger .... 502-585-9911 184 H
rburkman@spalding.edu
BURKS, A. Wesley .... 919-966-4161 342 C
wesley.burks@unc.edu
BURKS, Brent .... 254-295-4514 453 D
bburks@umhb.edu
BURKS, Bryan .... 501-279-4312.. 19 C
bburks@harding.edu
BURKS, Cherryl .... 770-229-3409 125 H
cherryl.burks@sctech.edu
BURKS, David .... 501-279-4274.. 19 C
president@harding.edu
BURKS, Eric .... 785-738-9057 176 F
eburks@ncktc.edu
BURKS, Gwenevera, E .. 559-453-2010.. 43 A
gwen.burks@fresno.edu
BURKS, Scott, A .... 502-852-4661 186 A
scott.burks@louisville.edu
BURKWHAT, Louis, E ... 530-226-4979.. 64 E
lburkwhat@simpsonu.edu
BURKY, Heather .... 717-391-6935 399 C
BURLEIGH-JONES,
Bronté .... 717-245-1943 382 D
jonesbro@dickinson.edu
BURLESON, Brooke .... 828-766-1269 336 A
bburleson@mayland.edu
BURLESON, Burt .... 254-710-3517 431 E
burt_burleson@baylor.edu
BURLESON, Rachel .... 603-899-4080 273 E
burlesonr@franklinpierce.edu
BURLESON, Susan, D ... 336-224-4840 334 B
susan_burleson@davidsondavie.edu
BURLEW, Jon .... 606-451-6748 182 G
jon.burlew@kctcs.edu
BURLEW, Lynette .... 318-473-6401 189 F
lburlew@lsua.edu
BURLEY, Diana .... 202-885-1000.. 91 F
dburley@american.edu
BURLEY, Galina .... 360-992-2123 478 I
gburley@clark.edu
BURLEY, Hansel, E .... 505-277-6525 288 J
hburley@unm.edu
BURLING, Rachel .... 262-691-5266 500 B
rburling@wctc.edu
BURLINGAME, Kathy .... 502-410-6200 180 G
kburlingame@galencollege.edu
BURLINGAME, Suzette .. 330-829-8175 362 E
burlinsu@mountunion.edu
BURMA, William, H .... 515-263-2975 166 F
bburma@grandview.edu
BURMAN, Tom .... 307-766-2292 501 I
tburman@uwyo.edu
BURMEISTER, Justin ..... 718-429-6600 324 D
justin.burmeister@vaughn.edu
BURMENKO, Neil .... 510-464-3520.. 57 B
nburmenko@peralta.edu
BURNELL, Hope .... 207-786-8388 194 A
hburnell@bates.edu
BURNER, Emily .... 540-665-3489 470 G
eburner@su.edu
BURNETT, Amber .... 909-599-5433.. 48 A
aburnett@lifepacific.edu
BURNETT, Belinda .... 520-417-4028.. 11 M
burnettb@cochise.edu
BURNETT, Benjamin .... 601-318-6144 249 H
bburnett@wmcarey.edu
BURNETT, Bradley, T .... 405-325-9899 370 K
bburnett@ou.edu
BURNETT, Brian .... 205-934-4011.... 8 A
brianburnett@uab.edu
BURNETT, Catherine, G 713-646-1831 443 I
cburnett@stcl.edu
BURNETT, Denita .... 276-223-4769 476 A
dburnett@wcc.vccs.edu
BURNETT, Edward, T .... 508-286-8214 220 B
burnett_edward@wheatoncollege.edu
BURNETT, Farah .... 718-270-2488 317 B
farah.burnett@downstate.edu
BURNETT, Grace .... 208-882-1566 132 C
registrar@nsa.edu
BURNETT, John .... 724-938-5425 393 E
burnett@calu.edu
BURNETT, Kimberly ...... 205-226-4906.... 4 F
kmburnet@bsc.edu

BURNETT, Lindsay .... 870-972-2586.. 17 E
lburnett@astate.edu
BURNETT, Lonnie .... 251-442-2201.... 8 C
lburnett@umobile.edu
BURNETT, Mary .... 717-477-1279 395 B
meburnett@ship.edu
BURNETT, Myra .... 404-270-5027 126 B
mburnett@spelman.edu
BURNETT, Sharon .... 731-286-3200 424 D
cwhite@dscc.edu
BURNETT, Shirley .... 601-979-2127 246 F
shirley.f.burnett@jsums.edu
BURNETT-HACKBARTH,
Kimberly .... 563-876-3353 165 H
kburnetthackbarth@dwci.edu
BURNETTE, Brittany .... 832-252-0737 432 L
brittany.burnette@cbshouston.edu
BURNETTE, Daarel .... 662-252-8000 248 G
dburnette@rustcollege.edu
BURNETTE, Diane, M .... 803-536-7187 411 G
dburnet1@scsu.edu
BURNETTE, Monica .... 973-761-9147 283 C
monica.burnette@shu.edu
BURNETTE, Sheryl .... 423-636-7300 426 E
sburnette@tusculum.edu
BURNETTE, Steve .... 276-223-4705 476 A
sburnette@wcc.vccs.edu
BURNETTE, Teri .... 706-396-8132 124 B
tburnette@paine.edu
BURNEY, Armetta .... 360-992-2936 478 I
aburney@clark.edu
BURNEY, Christina, M .. 508-565-1325 219 A
cburney@stonehill.edu
BURNEY, David .... 479-524-7427.. 19 H
dburney@jbu.edu
BURNEY, Linda .... 910-879-5519 332 D
lburney@bladencc.edu
BURNEY, Michelle .... 662-227-2304 246 D
mburney@holmescc.edu
BURNEY, Rolanda, C .... 413-545-2211 211 G
rburney@umass.edu
BURNFIELD, Robert .... 954-731-8880.. 97 Q
BURNHAM, Don .... 601-605-3301 246 D
dburnham@holmescc.edu
BURNIP, David, W .... 330-471-8251 355 D
dburnip@malone.edu
BURNLEY, Lawrence, A 937-229-4073 362 C
lburnley1@udayton.edu
BURNLEY, Linda .... 646-888-6639 304 J
burnleyl@sloankettering.edu
BURNOTES, Scott, G ..... 202-994-1000.. 92 D
burnotes@gwu.edu
BURNS, Alana .... 603-629-3467 274 C
a.burns1@snhu.edu
BURNS, Andrew .... 718-862-7958 304 M
aburns01@manhattan.edu
BURNS, Angelina, L .... 302-327-4809.. 91 E
angelina.l.burns@wilmu.edu
BURNS, Barbara .... 478-471-2502 122 F
barbara.burns@mga.edu
BURNS, Cathy .... 918-343-7791 369 B
cburns@rsu.edu
BURNS, Cindy .... 910-678-8564 334 E
griffinw@faytechcc.edu
BURNS, Craig, D .... 617-552-3310 207 C
craig.burns@bc.edu
BURNS, Daniel, P .... 985-867-2225 190 K
acdean@sjasc.edu
BURNS, David .... 254-710-6669 431 E
david_burns@baylor.edu
BURNS, Edward, R .... 718-430-2000 290 A
BURNS, Elizabeth .... 920-735-5795 498 F
burnse@fvtc.edu
BURNS, Ellen .... 386-312-4149 107 C
ellenburns@sjrstate.edu
BURNS, Ellen .... 309-341-5274 134 B
eburns@sandburg.edu
BURNS, Eric .... 479-308-2235.. 17 A
eric.burns@acheedu.org
BURNS, Erick .... 530-741-6838.. 77 E
eburns@yccd.edu
BURNS, Felecia .... 432-552-2712 456 F
burns_f@utpb.edu
BURNS, Gary .... 816-501-4854 258 I
gary.burns@rockhurst.edu
BURNS, J. Joseph .... 617-552-3273 207 C
joe.burns@bc.edu
BURNS, Jack .... 734-384-4249 228 C
jburns@monroeccc.edu
BURNS, IVD, James, P 507-457-1503 243 C
president@smumn.edu
BURNS, James, T .... 215-670-9235 391 E
jtburns@peirce.edu

BUSQUET, Aimee .... 813-253-7432 102 B
abusquet@hccfl.edu
BUSS, Britton .... 405-585-5256 367 B
britton.buss@okbu.edu
BUSS, James .... 859-572-5946 184 E
bussj1@nku.edu
BUSS, Marney .... 508-213-2101 217 H
marney.buss@nichols.edu
BUSS, Todd .... 920-923-8762 493 D
tcbuss45@marianuniversity.edu
BUSSELL, Helena .... 817-531-4405 451 C
hbussell@txwes.edu
BUSSELL, Jeff .... 714-619-6615.. 73 H
jeff.bussell@vanguard.edu
BUSSELL, Paige .... 903-468-3209 447 B
paige.bussell@tamuc.edu
BUSSELL, Rachelle .... 909-558-4544.. 48 E
rbussell@llu.edu
BUSSEY, Brenda .... 508-929-8455 213 G
bbussey@worcester.edu
BUSSEY, Tosha .... 404-225-4596 115 H
tbussey@atlantatech.edu
BUSSIKI, Marcelo .... 979-209-7460 431 H
mbussiki@blinn.edu
BUSTAMANTE,
Alexander .... 510-987-9090.. 68 L
alexander.bustamante@ucop.edu
BUSTAMANTE, JR.,
Tom .... 909-218-3253.. 25 C
tbustamantejr@americancareercollege.edu
BUSTARD, James .... 217-351-2211 147 C
jbustard@parkland.edu
BUSTER, Larissa .... 402-399-2674 266 F
lbuster@csm.edu
BUSTER, Marcella .... 406-657-1043 265 E
marcella.buster@rocky.edu
BUSTER-WILLIAMS,
Kimberley .... 540-654-1618 471 N
kwilli23@umw.edu
BUSTINZA, Reggie .... 815-753-8821 146 B
rbustinza@niu.edu
BUSTOS, Adam .... 505-454-3053 286 J
adambustos@nmhu.edu
BUSTOS, Leon .... 505-454-3366 286 J
leonbustos@nmhu.edu
BUSTOS, Nick .... 760-634-1771.. 28 E
BUTCARIS, Michael .... 203-857-7309.. 87 D
mbutcaris@norwalk.edu
BUTCHER, Claudette ..... 918-293-5256 368 B
claudette.butcher@okstate.edu
BUTCHER, Greg .... 724-589-2031 399 D
gbutcher@thiel.edu
BUTCHER, Matt .... 928-757-0861.. 14 F
mbutcher@mohave.edu
BUTCHER, Melissa .... 712-749-2049 164 C
butcherm@bvu.edu
BUTCHER, Michael .... 912-279-5815 117 F
mbutcher@ccga.edu
BUTCHER, Michelle, C .. 859-858-3511 179 D
michelle.butcher@asbury.edu
BUTCHKO, Thomas .... 570-208-5928 386 G
thomasbutchko@kings.edu
BUTDORFF, Carla .... 419-747-5401 357 B
196mgr@fheg.follett.com
BUTERA, Peter .... 716-286-8060 309 H
pbutera@niagara.edu
BUTERA, Rae-Anne .... 617-521-2000 218 G
BUTERA, Rae-Anne .... 781-292-2321 210 A
rae-anne.butera@olin.edu
BUTERA, Vince .... 847-578-8374 148 F
vince.butera@rosalindfranklin.edu
BUTEYN, Derek .... 712-722-6076 165 I
derek.buteyn@dordt.edu
BUTKOVICH, Michelle ... 248-204-2111 227 A
mbutkovic@ltu.edu
BUTLER, Amy .... 202-885-1000.. 91 F
aebutler@american.edu
BUTLER, Andra .... 606-546-1224 185 D
abutler@unionky.edu
BUTLER, Andrew .... 508-831-6634 220 F
abutler@wpi.edu
BUTLER, Andrew, J .... 205-934-5149.... 8 A
andrewbutler@uab.edu
BUTLER, Barry .... 386-226-6000.. 99 A
butlerb@erau.edu
BUTLER, Blake .... 501-760-4176.. 20 A
blake.butler@np.edu
BUTLER, Brady .... 412-536-1300 386 H
brady.butler@laroche.edu
BUTLER, Bruce, D .... 713-500-3369 456 B
bruce.d.butler@uth.tmc.edu
BUTLER, Bryant .... 601-968-5930 245 B
bbutler@belhaven.edu
BUTLER, Carmen .... 704-406-3980 329 A
cbutler@gardner-webb.edu
BUTLER, Chorissa .... 928-350-2104.. 15 L
BUTLER, Connie .... 402-643-7332 266 G
connie.butler@cune.edu
BUTLER, David, L .... 615-898-2182 422 C
david.butler@mtsu.edu
BUTLER, Deborah .... 541-463-5608 373 D
butlerd@lanecc.edu
BUTLER, Debra .... 662-252-8000 248 G
dbutler@rustcollege.edu
BUTLER, Duan .... 540-374-4300.. 93 H
BUTLER, Ella .... 801-957-4592 461 C
ella.butler@slcc.edu
BUTLER, Fay .... 718-482-5281 294 F
fbutler@lagcc.cuny.edu
BUTLER, Heidi .... 251-380-4000.... 6 H
BUTLER, Henry .... 703-993-8644 467 E
hnbutler@gmu.edu
BUTLER, Isaac .... 314-446-8438 260 H
isaac.butler@stlcop.edu
BUTLER, Jacob .... 803-934-3274 410 G
jbutler@morris.edu
BUTLER, Jay .... 215-702-4401 380 A
jbutler@cairn.edu
BUTLER, John, L .... 773-442-4219 146 A
j-butler1@neiu.edu
BUTLER, S.J., John, T .. 617-552-6855 207 C
john.butler@bc.edu
BUTLER, Kevin .... 702-992-2351 271 B
kevin.butler@nsc.edu
BUTLER, Kim, I .... 515-263-2841 166 F
maintenance@grandview.edu
BUTLER, JR., Lee, H ..... 918-610-6466 368 G
lee.butler@ptstulsa.edu
BUTLER, LeRoy .... 815-836-5923 142 F
butlerle@lewisu.edu
BUTLER, Linc .... 919-843-6298 342 C
linc_butler@unc.edu
BUTLER, Lisa, J .... 478-301-2951 122 E
butler_lj@mercer.edu
BUTLER, Malinda .... 601-877-6141 245 A
mbutler@alcorn.edu
BUTLER, Mark .... 864-231-2000 406 F
mbutler@andersonuniversity.edu
BUTLER, Michael .... 909-469-5534.. 75 I
mbutler@westernu.edu
BUTLER, Rebecca .... 614-287-2180 351 C
rbutler17@cscc.edu
BUTLER, Renee .... 470-578-5414 121 M
rbutle35@kennesaw.edu
BUTLER, Rhett .... 334-833-4474.... 5 G
chaplain@hawks.huntingdon.edu
BUTLER, Robert .... 617-824-8953 209 C
robert_butler@emerson.edu
BUTLER, S. Kent .... 407-823-6479 110 E
skbutler@ucf.edu
BUTLER, Sara .... 760-776-7365.. 38 E
sbutler@collegeofthedesert.edu
BUTLER, Shai .... 413-755-4197 216 A
slbutler@stcc.edu
BUTLER, Stephen, M .... 412-383-3547 400 H
smb285@pitt.edu
BUTLER, Steve .... 903-657-6543 448 D
BUTLER, Tamaka .... 313-577-6606 232 K
tamaka.butler@wayne.edu
BUTLER, Todd .... 509-335-3854 485 D
butlert@wsu.edu
BUTLER, Vicki .... 206-239-4500 478 H
BUTLER, Walter .... 731-352-4000 418 C
butlerw@bethelu.edu
BUTLER-JOHNSON,
Serena .... 202-274-5670.. 94 B
sbutlerjohnson@udc.edu
BUTLER-PURRY, Karen . 979-845-3631 446 F
ogaps@tamu.edu
BUTRUM, Herb .... 713-798-4951 431 D
BUTT, Darryl, P .... 801-581-8767 459 O
darryl.butt@utah.edu
BUTT, Debi, S .... 336-841-9202 329 F
debib@highpoint.edu
BUTT, Ryan .... 815-836-5267 142 F
rbutt@lewisu.edu
BUTT, Steven .... 269-276-3253 233 B
steven.butt@wmich.edu
BUTTAFARRO, JR.,
Thomas .... 716-375-2155 313 C
tbuttafa@sbu.edu
BUTTARS, Ryan, J .... 208-496-2710 130 I
buttarsr@byui.edu
BUTTERFIELD, Heather .. 920-403-3210 495 B
BUTTERFIELD, Kevin ..... 804-289-8456 472 C
kbutterf@richmond.edu
BUTTERFIELD, Robyn .... 781-239-2605 214 G
rbutterfield@massbay.edu
BUTTERFIELD,
Sherri-Ann, P .... 973-353-5541 282 B
sbutter@newark.rutgers.edu
BUTTERFIELD, Valerie ... 616-234-4105 224 F
registrars@grcc.edu
BUTTIMER, Richard, J .. 904-620-5280 111 B
richard.buttimer@unf.edu
BUTTLEMAN, Kurt .... 206-934-4111 483 A
kurt.buttleman@seattlecolleges.edu
BUTTON, Emiley .... 270-384-7442 183 G
buttone@lindsey.edu
BUTTON, Mark .... 402-472-6262 269 J
mbutton2@unl.edu
BUTTRICK, Hilary .... 317-940-8748 154 C
BUTTRY, Tonya .... 573-334-6825 259 G
tbuttry@sehcollege.edu
BUTTS, Cory .... 719-549-3064.. 82 J
cory.butts@pueblocc.edu
BUTTS, Dawn .... 803-508-7332 406 C
buttsd@atc.edu
BUTTS, Gary .... 212-241-8276 302 D
gary.butts@mssm.edu
BUTTS, Jeffrey .... 212-237-8486 294 D
jbutts@jjay.cuny.edu
BUTTS, John .... 252-618-6598 334 D
buttsj@edgecombe.edu
BUTTS, Joseph .... 432-685-4569 440 B
jbutts@midland.edu
BUTTS, Mike .... 605-882-5284 415 D
mike.butts@lakeareatech.edu
BUTTS, Montez .... 970-351-3403.. 84 F
montez.butts@unco.edu
BUTTS, Sue .... 251-981-3771.... 5 A
sue.butts@columbiasouthern.edu
BUTTS, Tracy .... 530-898-5146.. 30 D
tbutts@csuchico.edu
BUTTS-FREEMAN,
Jolene .... 470-453-0428 117 C
jbuttsfreeman@cau.edu
BUTTY, David, C .... 313-496-2526 232 E
dbutty1@wcccd.edu
BUTTZ, William .... 724-357-4844 394 C
wbuttz@iup.edu
BUTWELL, Ann .... 859-985-3924 179 I
butwella@berea.edu
BUTWELL, Justin .... 845-575-3000 305 D
justin.butwell@marist.edu
BUTWIN, Bridget, K ...... 812-237-4141 156 D
bridget.butwin@indstate.edu
BUTZ, Michael .... 216-421-7417 350 H
mcbutz@cia.edu
BUTZER, Hans, W .... 405-325-3505 370 K
butzer@ou.edu
BUVINGER, Nancy .... 562-860-2451.. 35 H
nbuvinger@cerritos.edu
BUWICK, Amy .... 309-298-2453 153 A
aj-buwick@wiu.edu
BUXBAUM, Hannah ...... 812-855-4350 156 F
hbuxbaum@iu.edu
BUXBAUM, Hannah ...... 812-855-8669 156 G
ovpia@iu.edu
BUXTON, Bonnie .... 678-225-7465 395 G
bonnieb@pcom.edu
BUXTON, Jasmine .... 302-857-6300.. 90 E
jbuxton@desu.edu
BUXTON, John, B .... 919-536-7200 334 C
BUYSSE, James .... 909-388-6900.. 60 D
BUZAK, Anne .... 916-323-0853.. 26 C
abuzak@asher.edu
BUZANSKI, Catherine ... 315-279-5646 303 G
cbuzanski@keuka.edu
BUZBEE, Brandon .... 303-871-2702.. 84 E
brandon.buzbee@du.edu
BUZGO, Gabrielle .... 717-871-5626 395 A
gabrielle.buzgo@millersville.edu
BUZHARDT, Landee ...... 803-321-5106 410 H
landee.buzhardt@newberry.edu
BUZZANCA, Cristine ..... 239-280-2511.. 95 M
cristine.buzzanca@avemaria.edu
BUZZARD, Janet .... 918-444-2900 366 G
buzzardj@nsuok.edu
BUZZETTA, Mary .... 210-784-1336 447 E
mary.buzzetta@tamusa.edu
BYAM, Latrice .... 202-806-2705.. 92 F
latrice.byam@howard.edu
BYAM, Stephan, A .... 410-462-7410 198 B
sbyam@bccc.edu
BYARD, Brenda .... 540-868-7208 474 C
bbyard@lfcc.edu
BYARS, Lindsey .... 304-384-5223 489 J
lbyars@concord.edu
BYAS, Renee .... 401-277-4955 405 B
rbyas@risd.edu
BYBEE, Paivi .... 816-501-4832 258 I
paivi.bybee@rockhurst.edu
BYBEE, Tamika .... 443-518-1000 199 F
BYCURA, Samantha ...... 412-809-5144 396 E
bycura.samantha@ptcollege.edu
BYCZEK, Sara .... 313-593-5430 231 I
sbyczek@umich.edu
BYEON, Soon C .... 636-327-4645 256 B
aviation@midwest.edu
BYER, Larry .... 805-969-3626.. 55 J
lbyer@pacifica.edu
BYER, Shanda .... 217-786-2290 143 B
shanda.byer@llcc.edu
BYERLEY, Julie, S .... 919-962-8499 342 C
julie_byerley@med.unc.edu
BYERLY, Alison, R .... 507-222-4000 234 G
BYERLY, Alison, R .... 610-330-5200 387 C
byerlya@lafayette.edu
BYERLY, Thomas, L .... 540-887-7000 468 G
tbyerly@marybaldwin.edu
BYERS, Ashley .... 618-537-6532 144 A
aabyers@mckendree.edu
BYERS, Eric, C .... 240-500-2501 199 C
ecbyers@hagerstowncc.edu
BYERS, Fred .... 970-675-3407.. 79 H
fred.byers@cncc.edu
BYERS, Gary .... 704-355-8894 327 G
gary.byers@atriumhealth.org
BYERS, Jonathan .... 509-313-4667 480 F
byers@gonzaga.edu
BYERS, Martha .... 816-322-0110 251 B
martha.byers@calvary.edu
BYERS, Merrie .... 970-675-3204.. 79 H
merrie.byers@cncc.edu
BYERS, Michael .... 304-260-4380 488 C
mbyers@blueridgectc.edu
BYERS, Michelle, C .... 319-273-2422 164 A
michelle.byers@uni.edu
BYERS, Mike .... 828-227-7321 343 E
mtbyers@wcu.edu
BYERS, Randy .... 214-333-5691 434 C
randy@dbu.edu
BYERS, Rhonda .... 573-341-4241 261 D
byersrf@mst.edu
BYHAM, Joseph .... 215-503-3997 399 E
joseph.byham@jefferson.edu
BYINGTON, Carrie .... 510-987-0700.. 68 L
BYINGTON, Kathleen ..... 631-632-6340 317 A
kathleen.byington@stonybrook.edu
BYINGTON, Scott .... 919-718-7425 333 C
sbyington@cccc.edu
BYLAND, KK .... 800-280-0307 153 E
kk.byland@ace.edu
BYLAND, Tammy .... 785-532-6318 175 C
tbyland@ksu.edu
BYLSMA, Thomas, W .... 616-395-7781 225 D
bylsma@hope.edu
BYNOG, Jennie .... 318-797-5058 190 A
jennie.bynog@lsus.edu
BYNUM, Chris .... 616-949-5300 223 C
chris.bynum@cornerstone.edu
BYNUM, Jo Ellen .... 443-334-2880 205 D
jbynum@worwic.edu
BYNUM, Leroy .... 503-725-3340 375 E
lbynumjr@pdx.edu
BYNUM, Lynn, M .... 502-272-8236 179 H
lbynum@bellarmine.edu
BYRD, Ajani .... 650-949-7777.. 42 I
BYRD, Bonita, E .... 410-651-6088 203 D
bebyrd@umes.edu
BYRD, Cal .... 847-608-5457 137 F
cbyrd@elgin.edu
BYRD, David .... 919-546-8237 340 B
david.byrd@shawu.edu
BYRD, David .... 401-874-5484 405 E
dbyrd@uri.edu
BYRD, Debbie, C .... 423-439-2068 419 G
byrddc1@etsu.edu
BYRD, Devin .... 626-316-5320.. 63 E
dbyrd@saybrook.edu
BYRD, Devin .... 425-602-3000 477 H
BYRD, Donna .... 404-880-8411 117 C
dbyrd@cau.edu
BYRD, Herb .... 865-974-6621 427 A
hbyrdiii@tennessee.edu
BYRD, James .... 918-293-4940 368 B
james.w.byrd@okstate.edu
BYRD, Jason .... 434-592-3539 468 E
registrar@liberty.edu
BYRD, Jason, D .... 540-365-4295 467 B
jbyrd@ferrum.edu

CALAIS, Erica .... 225-342-6950 192 B
erica.calais@ulsystem.edu
CALAIS, Kyle .... 337-482-6367 193 B
kyle.calais@louisiana.edu
CALAMAIO, Caprice ...... 913-234-0733 172 K
caprice.calamaio@cleveland.edu
CALAMETTI, Jeffrey, D .. 251-442-2242.... 8 C
jcalametti@umobile.edu
CALAMIA, James .... 732-255-0400 279 F
jcalamia@ocean.edu
CALANDRA, Viviana ..... 407-303-7894.. 95 B
viviana.calandra@ahu.edu
CALARESE, Mary .... 508-831-5423 220 F
mcalarese@wpi.edu
CALARESO, Joe .... 305-595-9500.. 94 G
admissions@amcollege.edu
CALDARELLO, Beth .... 660-359-3948 257 D
bcaldarello@mail.ncmissouri.edu
CALDBECK, Kellie .... 406-275-4744 265 F
kellie_caldbeck@skc.edu
CALDERÓN GARCÍA,
Ivonne .... 787-250-0000 511 F
ivonne.calderon@upr.edu
CALDER, Kent .... 202-663-5628 199 G
kcalder@jhu.edu
CALDERA, Nancy .... 509-527-2315 485 C
nancy.caldera@wallawalla.edu
CALDERO FIGUEROA,
Ana, J .... 407-582-1431 113 I
acalderofigueroa@valenciacollege.edu
CALDERON, Alfredo, B .. 215-455-1300 378 F
acalderon@aspirapa.org
CALDERON, Amalia .... 661-395-4011.. 46 L
CALDERON, Ann Marie . 615-230-3401 425 E
annmarie.calderon@volstate.edu
CALDERON, Christina ... 760-252-2411.. 26 G
ccalderon@barstow.edu
CALDERON, Hermes ...... 787-780-0070 505 F
hcalderon@caribbean.edu
CALDERON, Janet .... 407-303-6108.. 95 B
janet.calderon@ahu.edu
CALDERON, Laurena ..... 816-501-4287 258 I
laurena.calderon@rockhurst.edu
CALDERON, Maria .... 661-362-5563.. 38 D
maria.calderon@canyons.edu
CALDERON, Nancy, T ... 408-554-4400.. 63 B
ntcalderon@scu.edu
CALDERON, Paula .... 985-549-2217 193 A
paula.calderon@selu.edu
CALDERON, Rosa .... 310-338-8839.. 51 A
rosa.calderon@lmu.edu
CALDERONE, Jackie ...... 508-541-1530 209 A
0558mgr@fheg.follett.com
CALDERONE, Jennifer ... 812-488-2021 161 G
jj130@evansville.edu
CALDERONE, Jill .... 574-631-2622 162 A
jcalder2@nd.edu
CALDERWOOD, Jon ...... 810-406-4825 228 F
jon.calderwood@mcc.edu
CALDWELL, Adonna ...... 901-572-2592 418 A
adonna.caldwell@baptistu.edu
CALDWELL, Agnes .... 419-783-2402 351 K
acaldwell@defiance.edu
CALDWELL, Benjamin ... 903-233-3200 439 A
benjamincaldwell@letu.edu
CALDWELL,
Benjamin, D .... 540-831-5471 469 D
bcaldwell13@radford.edu
CALDWELL,
Benjamin, D .... 540-831-5723 469 D
bcaldwell13@radford.edu
CALDWELL, Brinda, W .. 828-398-7134 332 B
bcaldwell@abtech.edu
CALDWELL, Bryan .... 305-899-3250.. 96 A
bcaldwell@barry.edu
CALDWELL, Chris .... 502-776-1443 184 F
ccaldwell@simmonscollegeky.edu
CALDWELL,
Christopher, M .... 800-567-2344 492 C
CALDWELL, Craig .... 801-957-5180 461 C
craig.caldwell@slcc.edu
CALDWELL, Dallas .... 405-974-2631 370 I
dcaldwell@uco.edu
CALDWELL, Daniel .... 601-318-6101 249 H
dcaldwell@wmcarey.edu
CALDWELL, Donna .... 706-864-1410 127 A
donna.caldwell@ung.edu
CALDWELL, Gail .... 256-726-7024.... 6 C
gcaldwell@oakwood.edu
CALDWELL, Helen .... 704-378-1014 330 D
hcaldwell@jcsu.edu
CALDWELL, James .... 970-675-3236.. 79 H
james.caldwell@cncc.edu
CALDWELL, James .... 215-780-1306 398 B
jcaldwell@salus.edu
CALDWELL, James .... 215-780-1311 398 B
jcaldwell@salus.edu
CALDWELL, Jim .... 215-780-1313 398 B
jcaldwell@salus.edu
CALDWELL, Jodi, K .... 912-478-5541 120 C
jodic@georgiasouthern.edu
CALDWELL, Katrina .... 410-516-7564 199 G
kcaldwell@jhu.edu
CALDWELL, Kisha .... 423-697-3250 424 A
kisha.caldwell@chattanoogastate.edu
CALDWELL, Larry, W .... 605-336-6588 416 A
lcaldwell@sfseminary.edu
CALDWELL, Mike .... 817-257-7523 448 F
m.a.caldwell@tcu.edu
CALDWELL, Nina .... 314-529-9485 255 B
ncaldwell@maryville.edu
CALDWELL, Patrice .... 575-562-2315 286 B
patrice.caldwell@enmu.edu
CALDWELL, Samuel .... 518-956-8112 316 A
sjcaldwell@albany.edu
CALDWELL, Stephanie ... 973-408-3061 277 A
scaldwell@drew.edu
CALDWELL, OSB,
Teresio .... 503-845-3169 374 A
teresio.caldwell@mtangel.edu
CALDWELL, Timothy ..... 509-777-3749 486 C
tcaldwell@whitworth.edu
CALDWELL, Troy .... 740-695-9500 348 E
tcaldwell@belmontcollege.edu
CALDWELL, IV,
William, B .... 478-387-4775 119 F
wcaldwell@gmc.edu
CALDWELL, Yolanda ..... 518-485-3133 296 G
caldwely@strose.edu
CALDWELL-KAN, Sara ... 907-786-4070.... 9 J
CALE, Benjamin .... 304-877-6428 486 G
admissions@abc.edu
CALEB, Peter .... 917-493-4507 305 A
library@msmnyc.edu
CALEFFI-PRICHARD,
Vivi .... 503-365-4723 372 B
vivi.caleffi.prichard@chemeketa.edu
CALFIN, Matthew .... 805-378-1448.. 73 J
mcalfin@vcccd.edu
CALHOUN, Chantae ...... 334-291-4945.... 1 H
chantae.calhoun@cv.edu
CALHOUN, Cheryl .... 352-395-5719 108 A
cheryl.calhoun@sfcollege.edu
CALHOUN, David .... 863-583-9050 110 B
CALHOUN, Dominique .. 713-313-7640 449 B
dominique.calhoun@tsu.edu
CALHOUN, Grace .... 401-863-2972 403 J
grace_calhoun@brown.edu
CALHOUN, Jay .... 603-862-1622 274 F
jay.calhoun@unh.edu
CALHOUN, Kirk, A .... 903-566-7325 456 A
mitziharris@uttyler.edu
CALHOUN, Larry .... 912-538-3101 125 G
lcalhoun@southeasterntech.edu
CALHOUN, Linda .... 270-686-4473 182 F
linda.calhoun@kctcs.edu
CALHOUN, Lozanne ...... 870-850-4826.. 21 B
lcalhoun@seark.edu
CALHOUN, Matthew ...... 601-276-3718 249 B
mattc@smcc.edu
CALHOUN, Mitch .... 325-574-7612 458 D
mcalhoun@wtc.edu
CALHOUN, Paula, M ..... 330-471-8236 355 D
pcalhoun@malone.edu
CALHOUN, Ralph .... 901-435-1276 420 I
ralph_calhoun@loc.edu
CALHOUN, Ric .... 678-359-5018 120 F
ricc@gordonstate.edu
CALHOUN, Rica .... 850-412-5479 109 I
rica.calhoun@famu.edu
CALHOUN, Rochelle ...... 609-258-3056 280 D
rochelle.calhoun@princeton.edu
CALHOUN, Roy .... 229-430-1729 114 I
rcalhoun@albanytech.edu
CALHOUN, Shawn .... 415-422-6167.. 72 J
calhouns@usfca.edu
CALHOUN, JR.,
Thomas .... 662-254-3636 248 B
thomas.calhoun@mvsu.edu
CALHOUN-BROWN,
Allison .... 404-413-2067 120 E
acalhounbrown@gsu.edu
CALHOUN-FRENCH,
Diane .... 502-213-2621 182 C
diane.calhoun-french@kctcs.edu
CALHOUN-FRENCH,
Diane .... 502-213-5333 182 C
diane.calhoun-french@kctcs.edu
CALHOUN-WARD,
Stephanie .... 860-906-5253.. 86 D
scalhoun-ward@capitalcc.edu
CALICA, Brandi .... 757-524-5508 477 C
bmcalica@vwu.edu
CALICA, Corinna .... 415-485-9132.. 39 A
cdyliacco@marin.edu
CALIENES, Chris .... 315-781-4085 301 F
calienes@hws.edu
CALIGAN, Roy .... 509-533-8861 479 C
roy.caligan@scc.spokane.edu
CALIHAN, Heather .... 910-938-6241 333 F
calihanh@coastalcarolina.edu
CALILAN,
James (Kimo) .... 707-864-7264.. 64 H
james.calilan@solano.edu
CALISE, Lisa .... 617-287-7050 211 F
lcalise@umassp.edu
CALISE, Thomasina, L .. 203-857-7003.. 87 D
tcalise@norwalk.edu
CALISSI, Barbara .... 516-323-3035 306 M
bcalissi@molloy.edu
CALKA, Anna .... 973-313-6314 283 C
anna.calka@shu.edu
CALKINS, Kevin .... 863-583-9050 110 B
CALL, Patrick .... 970-339-6657.. 77 H
patrick.call@aims.edu
CALLAGHAN, Carolyn ... 828-227-3068 343 E
ccallaghan@wcu.edu
CALLAGHAN, Connor .... 415-503-6235.. 61 D
ccallaghan@sfcm.edu
CALLAGHAN, James ..... 478-445-4789 119 B
james.callaghan@gcsu.edu
CALLAGHAN, Karen, A .. 305-899-3401.. 96 A
kcallaghan@barry.edu
CALLAGHAN, Martha .... 804-289-8000 472 C
CALLAGHAN, MaryEllen 914-633-2512 302 E
mcallaghan@iona.edu
CALLAGHAN, Sandra .... 817-257-6483 448 F
s.callaghan@tcu.edu
CALLAHAN, Audra .... 508-999-8620 212 A
audra.callahan@umassd.edu
CALLAHAN, Brigid .... 847-947-5409 145 D
bcallahan2@nl.edu
CALLAHAN, Caitlin .... 617-449-7038 219 D
caitlin.callahan@urbancollege.edu
CALLAHAN, Candice ..... 718-779-1499 311 E
cmc2@plazacollege.edu
CALLAHAN, Caroline ..... 718-779-1499 311 E
cmc@plazacollege.edu
CALLAHAN, III,
Charles, E .... 718-779-1499 311 E
cec3@plazacollege.edu
CALLAHAN, IV,
Charles, E .... 718-779-1499 311 E
cec4@plazacollege.edu
CALLAHAN, Christena ... 321-674-8927 100 C
ccallahan@fit.edu
CALLAHAN,
Christopher .... 209-946-2011.. 71 E
CALLAHAN, Clara, A ..... 215-955-6983 399 E
clara.callahan@jefferson.edu
CALLAHAN, JR.,
Jack, F .... 203-432-1185.. 90 C
jack.callahan@yale.edu
CALLAHAN, Janet .... 906-487-2005 228 A
callahan@mtu.edu
CALLAHAN, Larry, A ..... 202-806-6100.. 92 F
CALLAHAN, Margaret .... 215-517-2654 378 E
callahanm@arcadia.edu
CALLAHAN,
Margaret, F .... 708-216-9222 143 C
mcallahan3@luc.edu
CALLAHAN, Mark .... 402-461-5177 267 E
CALLAHAN, Michael ...... 805-289-6344.. 74 B
mcallahan@vcccd.edu
CALLAHAN, Pat .... 215-489-2208 382 B
patrick.callahan@delval.edu
CALLAHAN, Ryan .... 909-607-3183.. 37 C
ryan.callahan@cgu.edu
CALLAHAN, Ryan .... 262-472-4661 497 D
callahanrm19@uww.edu
CALLAHAN, Sean .... 678-872-8542 119 D
scallaha@highlands.edu
CALLAHAN, Tristin .... 256-840-4219.... 3 F
tristin.callahan@snead.edu
CALLAN, Pam .... 325-481-8300 437 F
pcallan@howardcollege.edu
CALLANAN, Cara .... 978-921-4242 217 B
cara.callanan@montserrat.edu
CALLAND, Dana .... 606-759-7141 182 E
dana.calland@kctcs.edu
CALLAND, David .... 434-592-7336 468 E
dcalland@liberty.edu
CALLAND, David .... 423-775-7200 418 D
dcalland2423@bryan.edu
CALLANDRILLO, Traci ... 202-885-1000.. 91 F
callandr@american.edu
CALLAWAY, Cynthia ...... 757-825-2725 475 D
callawayc@tncc.edu
CALLEJA, Eduardo .... 956-380-8183 442 G
psecretary@riogrande.edu
CALLEN, Patricia .... 304-296-8282 491 B
pcallen@wvjc.edu
CALLEY, Addison .... 850-478-8496 105 G
acalley@pcci.edu
CALLICO, Jason .... 504-398-2143 192 A
jcallico@uhcno.edu
CALLICOTT, Robin .... 803-641-3342 413 B
robinc@usca.edu
CALLIER, Theodore .... 504-816-4018 186 I
tcallier@dillard.edu
CALLIES, Kathryn .... 605-256-5143 416 F
kathy.callies@dsu.edu
CALLIES, Mona .... 941-309-4009 106 J
mcallies@ringling.edu
CALLIHAM, Jimmy .... 830-591-7333 444 G
jwcalliham@swtjc.edu
CALLIHAM, Martha .... 512-444-8082 448 H
mcalliham@thsu.edu
CALLINAN, Dennis .... 845-574-4481 312 H
dcallina@sunyrockland.edu
CALLIS, Jennifer .... 785-309-3120 177 E
jennifer.callis@salinatech.edu
CALLISTER, Melanie ...... 507-285-7461 240 H
melanie.callister@rctc.edu
CALLISTO, Anthony .... 315-443-2225 321 G
acallist@syr.edu
CALLOW-WRIGHT,
Katie .... 773-795-3361 151 E
ccallow@uchicago.edu
CALLOWAY, Brad .... 336-841-9841 329 F
scallowa@highpoint.edu
CALLOWAY, Terence ..... 850-599-3256 109 I
terence.calloway@famu.edu
CALOBRISI,
Charlotte, M .... 703-323-3110 474 F
ccalobrisi@nvcc.edu
CALOCA, Luis .... 208-562-3396 131 E
luiscaloca@cwi.edu
CALOIERO, Erica .... 802-656-3858 463 A
erica.caloiero@uvm.edu
CALORE, Lucille, A .... 401-865-1199 404 F
tomasell@providence.edu
CALOVINE, Iris .... 203-932-7297.. 89 H
icalovine@newhaven.edu
CALPIN, Fran .... 570-945-8170 386 F
fran.calpin@keystone.edu
CALTABIANO, Ronald .... 312-362-7256 136 H
rcalt@depaul.edu
CALUS-MCLAIN, Martha 503-352-2764 375 C
martha@pacificu.edu
CALUZA, Kimberly .... 206-296-6090 484 A
caluzak@seattleu.edu
CALVELLI, Louis .... 718-862-7977 304 M
lcalvelli01@manhattan.edu
CALVERLEY, Darla .... 320-629-5118 240 D
darla.calverley@pine.edu
CALVERT, Carolyn, A .... 325-793-3808 439 F
ccalvert@mcm.edu
CALVERT, Chandra .... 605-718-2419 417 D
chandra.calvert@wdt.edu
CALVERT, Christopher ... 513-569-1586 350 F
christopher.calvert@cincinnatistate.edu
CALVERT, Jodi .... 860-215-9220.. 87 F
jcalvert@threerivers.edu
CALVERT, Kaitlyn .... 304-205-6697 488 D
kaitlyn.calvert@bridgevalley.edu
CALVERT, Linda .... 423-323-0222 425 A
lwcalvert@northeaststate.edu
CALVERT, Lisa .... 509-335-3564 485 D
CALVERT, Mike .... 620-672-2700 177 B
michaelc@prattcc.edu
CALVIN, Anitra .... 504-520-7365 193 E
acalvin3@xula.edu
CALVIN, Brent .... 559-730-3745.. 39 B
brentc@cos.edu
CALVIN, Linda .... 317-289-5697 158 D
ldcalvin@ivytech.edu
CALVO, Dean .... 909-621-8211.. 63 F
dcalvo@scrippscollege.edu
CALVO, JR., Miguel, A . 305-899-5413.. 96 A
mcalvo@barry.edu

CALZADA, Manuel .... 787-751-0160 506 F
mcalzada@cmpr.pr.gov
CALZADA, Maria .... 504-865-2011 190 C
calzada@loyno.edu
CALZAFERRI, Gina, L ..... 215-204-8277 399 B
gina.calzaferri@temple.edu
CALZONETTI, Frank, J ... 419-530-6171 363 B
frank.calzonetti@utoledo.edu
CAMACHO, Albert .... 909-384-8242.. 60 F
acamacho@sbccd.cc.ca.us
CAMACHO, Anita, C ...... 670-237-6824 505 A
anita.camacho@marianas.edu
CAMACHO, Anthony, R . 671-735-2978 504 F
arcamacho@triton.uog.edu
CAMACHO, Carie .... 530-257-6181.. 47 F
ccamacho@lassencollege.edu
CAMACHO, Carmen, S .. 805-922-6966.. 24 I
ccamacho@hancockcollege.edu
CAMACHO,
Francisco, C .... 671-734-0540 504 D
francisco.camacho@guamcc.edu
CAMACHO, George .... 518-782-6982 315 E
gcamacho@siena.edu
CAMACHO, Helen, B ..... 670-237-6702 505 A
helen.camacho@marianas.edu
CAMACHO,
Lawrence, F .... 671-735-2292 504 F
lcamacho@triton.uog.edu
CAMACHO, Martin .... 940-397-4000 440 C
martin.camacho@msutexas.edu
CAMACHO, Martin .... 210-458-4011 455 E
CAMACHO, Mildred ...... 787-264-1912 508 F
milcama@intersg.edu
CAMACHO LÓPEZ,
Jose, V .... 787-764-0000 513 B
jose.camacho1@upr.edu
CAMACHO-MELENDEZ,
Iris, M .... 787-751-1912 509 A
icamacho@juris.inter.edu
CAMAHALAN, Faye, M .. 812-941-2136 157 F
fcamahal@ius.edu
CAMANIA VINNETT,
Sarah .... 504-762-3021 188 B
scaman@dcc.edu
CAMARA, Lydia .... 508-588-9100 215 A
lcamara5@massasoit.mass.edu
CAMARDA-WEBB,
Sheleta .... 724-938-5758 393 E
camardawebb@calu.edu
CAMARDELLA,
Christina .... 914-813-9212 315 A
ccamardella@sarahlawrence.edu
CAMARENA, Phame ...... 575-646-2005 287 C
phame@nmsu.edu
CAMARGO, Judy, V ...... 210-486-4951 428 I
jcamargo@alamo.edu
CAMARILLO, Richard .... 805-546-3279.. 40 F
richard_camarillo@cuesta.edu
CAMASSO, Kimberly ..... 617-735-9736 209 D
camassok@emmanuel.edu
CAMBER, Jean .... 303-964-6183.. 83 E
jcamber@regis.edu
CAMBIA, Barbara 561-237-7360 103W
bcambia@lynn.edu
CAMBONE, Joseph .... 978-542-6266 213 E
joseph.cambone@salemstate.edu
CAMBRA, Dena .... 570-585-9358 381 B
dcambra@clarkssummitu.edu
CAMBRA, Ronald .... 808-956-6231 129 E
cambra@hawaii.edu
CAMBRAY, Joseph .... 805-969-3626.. 55 J
jcambray@pacifica.edu
CAMBRE, Charles .... 225-743-8500 188 H
ccambre@rpcc.edu
CAMBRIDGE, Lisa .... 816-654-7000 254 E
CAMBRON, Jerrilyn .... 630-889-6853 145 E
jcambron@nuhs.edu
CAMEJO, Ian .... 417-255-7960 256 H
CAMELIO, Jason .... 617-747-2700 206 H
jcamelio@berklee.edu
CAMELO, Kathleen, M .. 518-564-2187 318 E
camelokm@plattsburgh.edu
CAMERLENGO, Renee ... 412-268-2075 380 C
reneec@andrew.cmu.edu
CAMERON, JR.,
A. Neill .... 864-656-2123 407 E
cameron@clemson.edu
CAMERON,
Aundreia, M .... 323-343-3040.. 31 E
acamero6@calstatela.edu
CAMERON, Charley .... 318-678-6000 187 H
ccameron@bpcc.edu
CAMERON, Cheryl, A .... 206-221-1405 485 A
ccameron@uw.edu
CAMERON, Cori .... 719-549-2456.. 80 B
cori.cameron@csupueblo.edu
CAMERON, Dori .... 575-624-8080 287 B
cameron@nmmi.edu
CAMERON, Iain .... 715-675-3331 499 F
cameron@ntc.edu
CAMERON, J. Scott .... 301-243-2118 502 L
CAMERON, Jaclyn, A .... 323-259-2966.. 54 I
CAMERON, Jennifer ...... 254-526-1264 432 D
jennifer.cameron@ctcd.edu
CAMERON, Kimberly ..... 859-246-6279 181 F
kcameron0004@kctcs.edu
CAMERON, Matthew, R . 305-899-3875.. 96 A
mcameron@barry.edu
CAMERON, Richard, L .. 478-301-5500 122 E
cameron_rl@mercer.edu
CAMERON, Samantha ... 906-248-8429 221M
scameron@bmcc.edu
CAMFIELD, Gregg .... 209-228-4439.. 70 A
CAMILLE, Marc, M .... 203-773-8529.. 85 D
mcamille@albertus.edu
CAMILLE, Michael .... 318-342-3011 193 C
camille@ulm.edu
CAMILLERI, Michael ..... 507-284-9328 235 B
camilleri.michael@mayo.edu
CAMILLO, Thomas, P ... 814-871-7413 384 A
camillo001@gannon.edu
CAMIN, Joyce .... 661-824-2977.. 53 H
jcamin@ntps.edu
CAMMACK, Cindy .... 402-872-2313 268 E
ccammack@peru.edu
CAMMANN, Nicole .... 208-459-5508 131 C
ncammann@collegeofidaho.edu
CAMMARATA, Jessica ... 814-472-3217 397 F
jcammarata@francis.edu
CAMMARATA, Maria ...... 510-430-3322.. 52 E
mcammarata@mills.edu
CAMMARATA, Miki .... 973-720-2179 284 J
cammaratam@wpunj.edu
CAMMARATA, Rita .... 212-217-3820 299 D
rita_cammarata@fitnyc.edu
CAMOU, Fernando .... 623-845-3677.. 13 C
f.camou@gccaz.edu
CAMP, Aarika .... 410-337-6000 199 B
aarika.camp@goucher.edu
CAMP, Billy .... 334-386-7255.... 5 C
bcamp@faulkner.edu
CAMP, Carol .... 251-442-2213.... 8 C
ccamp@umobile.edu
CAMP, Cathryn, L .... 301-546-0412 201 E
campcl@pgcc.edu
CAMP, Clifford .... 734-432-5829 227 C
ccamp@madonna.edu
CAMP, Jon .... 863-680-6278 100 H
jcamp@flsouthern.edu
CAMP, Sarah .... 805-565-7257.. 76 A
scamp@westmont.edu
CAMP, Skip, L .... 239-513-1122 102 D
bcamp@hodges.edu
CAMP, Susan .... 580-581-5952 365 D
susanc@cameron.edu
CAMPA, Jeff .... 816-322-0110 251 B
jeff.campa@calvary.edu
CAMPAGNA, Julia .... 410-532-3172 201 D
jcampagna@ndm.edu
CAMPANA, Karen .... 630-829-6345 133 E
kcampana@ben.edu
CAMPANA, Maryjo .... 570-484-2181 394 E
drt831@lockhaven.edu
CAMPANARO, Jennifer .. 207-699-5023 195 A
jcampanaro@meca.edu
CAMPANARO, Kyle, A ... 315-684-6000 321 A
CAMPANELLI, Kenneth .. 718-482-5502 294 F
kcampanelli@lagcc.cuny.edu
CAMPANINI, Albino, P . 321-674-8434 100 C
bcampanini@fit.edu
CAMPBELL, Alvin .... 479-788-7188.. 21 G
alvin.campbell@uafs.edu
CAMPBELL, Andrea .... 315-279-5217 303 G
acampbell@keuka.edu
CAMPBELL, Andrea .... 814-864-6666 384 F
CAMPBELL, Andrew, G . 401-863-2532 403 J
andrew_campbell@brown.edu
CAMPBELL, Angela .... 610-902-8416 379 G
angela.campbell@cabrini.edu
CAMPBELL, Barbara ...... 606-759-7141 182 E
barbara.campbell@kctcs.edu
CAMPBELL, Beth .... 804-752-7226 469 F
bethcampbell@rmc.edu
CAMPBELL, Betty Lynn . 504-282-4455 190 F
CAMPBELL, Bill .... 412-365-1140 380 G
bcampbell@chatham.edu
CAMPBELL, Bonnie, L ... 815-224-0408 140 E
bonnie_campbell@ivcc.edu
CAMPBELL, Brandon ..... 815-280-6606 141 B
brcampbe@jjc.edu
CAMPBELL, Carson .... 503-838-8141 377 D
campbellcg@wou.edu
CAMPBELL,
Catherine, E .... 512-448-8550 442 I
campbell@stedwards.edu
CAMPBELL, Celia .... 617-627-3313 219 C
celia.campbell@tufts.edu
CAMPBELL, Charles .... 334-386-7528.... 5 C
ccampbell@faulkner.edu
CAMPBELL, Charlie .... 859-985-3674 179 I
campbellc@berea.edu
CAMPBELL, Chris .... 630-515-3000 137 A
CAMPBELL, Christie ...... 512-233-1635 442 I
christie@stedwards.edu
CAMPBELL, Clark .... 562-903-4706.. 27 A
clark.campbell@biola.edu
CAMPBELL, Connan .... 509-533-7081 479 C
connan.campbell@scc.spokane.edu
CAMPBELL, Conway, C . 508-767-7325 206 A
ccampbel@assumption.edu
CAMPBELL, Corey, A .... 315-786-6561 303 C
ccampbell@sunyjefferson.edu
CAMPBELL, Cory .... 724-838-4260 398 C
ccampbell@setonhill.edu
CAMPBELL, Craigon ...... 973-748-9000 276 A
craigon_campbell@bloomfield.edu
CAMPBELL, Curtis .... 404-639-0999 123 D
curtis.campbell@morehouse.edu
CAMPBELL, Dan .... 413-552-2705 214 F
dcampbell@hcc.edu
CAMPBELL, Daniel .... 907-786-1493.... 9 J
drcampbell4@alaska.edu
CAMPBELL, Danny .... 432-264-3752 437 F
dcampbell@howardcollege.edu
CAMPBELL, David .... 904-276-6891 107 C
davidcampbell@sjrstate.edu
CAMPBELL, Deanna .... 760-872-5301.. 46M
dcampbel@cerrocoso.edu
CAMPBELL, Debra .... 231-843-5819 233 A
djcampbell@westshore.edu
CAMPBELL, Donald .... 610-896-1100 385 I
dcampbel@haverford.edu
CAMPBELL, Elizabeth .... 617-358-7355 207 E
eavery@bu.edu
CAMPBELL, Emily .... 225-922-2373 187 F
emilycampbell@lctcs.edu
CAMPBELL, Emily .... 225-743-8500 188 H
ecampbell@rpcc.edu
CAMPBELL, Eric .... 248-218-2080 230 B
ecampbell@rochesteru.edu
CAMPBELL, Erika .... 870-368-2037.. 20 E
erika.campbell@ozarka.edu
CAMPBELL, Fran .... 937-766-7653 349 E
campf@cedarville.edu
CAMPBELL, Gail .... 928-289-6535.. 14 J
gail.campbell@npc.edu
CAMPBELL, Gina .... 610-902-8206 379 G
gc10266@cabrini.edu
CAMPBELL, Heather, M 757-455-3389 477 C
hmcampbell@vwu.edu
CAMPBELL, J. David ..... 256-228-6001.... 3 B
campbelld@nacc.edu
CAMPBELL, James, F .... 401-865-2676 404 F
james.campbell@providence.edu
CAMPBELL, Janell .... 701-224-5431 346 A
janell.i.campbell@bismarckstate.edu
CAMPBELL, Janie .... 715-394-8259 497 C
jcampb41@uwsuper.edu
CAMPBELL, Jason .... 773-291-6100 135 E
CAMPBELL, Jeffrey .... 910-962-3108 343 C
campbelljl@uncw.edu
CAMPBELL, Jenifer .... 212-636-7104 300 C
jecampbell@fordham.edu
CAMPBELL, Jenni, L ..... 321-682-4981 113 I
jcampbell60@valenciacollege.edu
CAMPBELL, Jennifer ...... 260-470-2740 159 J
jahenriksen@manchester.edu
CAMPBELL, Jennifer ...... 918-595-7018 370 C
jennifer.campbell@tulsacc.edu
CAMPBELL,
Jennifer Kelly .... 212-938-5604 319 E
jcampbell@sunyopt.edu
CAMPBELL, Jo .... 805-756-7990.. 29 I
jcampb33@calpoly.edu
CAMPBELL, Joann, N .... 904-620-2002 111 B
jcampbel@unf.edu
CAMPBELL, John, B ...... 901-722-3372 423 G
jbcampbell@sco.edu
CAMPBELL, Jonathan .... 870-230-5098.. 19 D
campbej@hsu.edu
CAMPBELL, Joseph .... 870-680-8725.. 18 A
joe_campbell@asun.edu
CAMPBELL, Joseph .... 856-256-4199 281 F
campbellj@rowan.edu
CAMPBELL, Kai .... 828-251-6470 342 B
kai@unca.edu
CAMPBELL, Karen .... 610-921-7643 377 G
kcampbell@albright.edu
CAMPBELL, Karen .... 757-822-1225 475 E
kcampbell@tcc.edu
CAMPBELL, Karen, M ... 608-822-2300 500 A
kcampbell@swtc.edu
CAMPBELL, Katherine ... 313-664-7428 222 H
kcampbell@collegeforcreativestudies.
edu
CAMPBELL, Keisha .... 443-885-3229 201 A
keisha.campbell@morgan.edu
CAMPBELL, Keisha .... 443-885-3000 201 A
keisha.campbell@morgan.edu
CAMPBELL, Kellie .... 802-224-3000 463 D
CAMPBELL, Kellie, B ..... 802-728-1511 464 A
CAMPBELL, Kelly, D ..... 404-687-4547 117 G
campbellk@ctsnet.edu
CAMPBELL, Keni .... 907-796-6509.. 10 B
klcampbell4@alaska.edu
CAMPBELL, Kerri .... 901-843-3846 423 A
campbellk@rhodes.edu
CAMPBELL, Kevin .... 325-674-6552 428 F
kac96b@acu.edu
CAMPBELL, Kim .... 614-234-5144 356 E
kcampbell@mccn.edu
CAMPBELL, Lauren .... 859-246-6285 181 F
lauren.campbell@kctcs.edu
CAMPBELL, Lauren .... 267-341-3331 385 J
lcampbell@holyfamily.edu
CAMPBELL, Lea .... 713-221-5548 453 A
campbellc@uhd.edu
CAMPBELL, Lenora .... 336-285-3508 341 D
lrcampbell@ncat.edu
CAMPBELL, Lindsey ...... 916-608-6572.. 50 I
campbel@flc.losrios.edu
CAMPBELL, Lisa, M ...... 724-287-8711 379 E
lisa.campbell@bc3.edu
CAMPBELL, Mark .... 212-353-4126 297 E
mark.campbell@cooper.edu
CAMPBELL, Marshall ..... 979-230-3474 431 I
marshall.campbell@brazosport.edu
CAMPBELL, Mary, B ..... 314-935-3617 262 A
marycampbell@wustl.edu
CAMPBELL, Mary, B ..... 864-488-8280 410 B
mcampbell@limestone.edu
CAMPBELL, Mason .... 501-812-2211.. 23 B
mcampbell@uaptc.edu
CAMPBELL, Matthew ..... 334-844-4765.... 4 D
campbmw@auburn.edu
CAMPBELL, Matthew ..... 253-840-8419 482 E
mcampbell@pierce.ctc.edu
CAMPBELL, Maurice, W 804-257-5606 476 F
mwcampbell@vuu.edu
CAMPBELL, Melanie ...... 434-381-6332 471 I
mhcampbell@sbc.edu
CAMPBELL, Michael ...... 760-384-6159.. 46M
michael.campbell@cerrocoso.edu
CAMPBELL, Michael ...... 816-279-7000 250 B
michael.campbell@abtu.edu
CAMPBELL, Michael ...... 216-881-1700 358 J
mcampbell@ohiotech.edu
CAMPBELL, Michael, A . 419-372-2346 348 G
campbem@bgsu.edu
CAMPBELL, Michelle ..... 732-906-2551 278 G
mcampbell@middlesexcc.edu
CAMPBELL, Mitchell ..... 906-217-4012 222 A
mitchell.campbell@baycollege.edu
CAMPBELL, Mitchell, L . 916-558-2426.. 50 J
campbem@scc.losrios.edu
CAMPBELL, Nicole, J .... 405-325-1978 370 K
njudice@ou.edu
CAMPBELL, Patricia ...... 209-946-2424.. 71 E
pcampbell@pacific.edu
CAMPBELL, Patriece ...... 717-871-7506 395 A
patriece.campbell@millersville.edu
CAMPBELL, Peter .... 201-684-7363 280 H
pcampbel@ramapo.edu
CAMPBELL, Philip .... 434-528-5276 477 B
CAMPBELL, Phyllis .... 731-352-4046 418 C
campbellp@bethelu.edu
CAMPBELL, Ralph .... 623-935-8051.. 13 A
ralph.campbell@estrellamountain.edu
CAMPBELL, Randy .... 607-778-5196 317 D
campbellrj@sunybroome.edu

CAMPBELL, Rebecca ..... 575-646-3203 287 C
rjpc@nmsu.edu
CAMPBELL, Rina .... 619-201-8753.. 60 G
rina.campbell@sdcc.edu
CAMPBELL, Robert .... 410-704-4862 204 E
rcampbell@towson.edu
CAMPBELL, Robin .... 336-517-2229 327 A
rcampbell@bennett.edu
CAMPBELL, Robin .... 336-721-2600 340 A
robin.campbell@salem.edu
CAMPBELL, Rosana .... 570-484-2723 394 E
rcampbel@lockhaven.edu
CAMPBELL, Samerah ..... 559-243-7122.. 66 H
samerah.campbell@scccd.edu
CAMPBELL, Sara .... 423-614-8525 420 H
scampbell@leeuniversity.edu
CAMPBELL, Saskia .... 703-993-3738 467 E
scampb22@gmu.edu
CAMPBELL, Scott .... 773-834-3390 151 E
scottcampbell@uchicago.edu
CAMPBELL, Scott, L ...... 740-392-6868 356 G
scott.campbell@mvnu.edu
CAMPBELL, Shannon .... 228-865-4531 249 F
shannon.campbell@usm.edu
CAMPBELL, Sharon .... 919-760-8011 331 D
sharonca@meredith.edu
CAMPBELL, Shawnrece . 361-825-2659 447 C
shawnrece.campbell@tamucc.edu
CAMPBELL,
Shoshanna, M .... 718-780-7501 291 K
shoshanna.campbell@brooklaw.edu
CAMPBELL, Stacy .... 352-245-4119 112 E
CAMPBELL, Stephanie ... 904-470-8114.. 98 L
s.campbell@ewc.edu
CAMPBELL, Stephen, M 216-368-5555 349 D
stephen.campbell@case.edu
CAMPBELL, Susan .... 623-845-3876.. 13 C
susan.j.campbell@gccaz.edu
CAMPBELL, Susan, L ..... 920-923-7617 493 D
slcampbell73@marianuniversity.edu
CAMPBELL, Suzanne ..... 620-417-1403 177 F
suzanne.campbell@sccc.edu
CAMPBELL, Tami .... 660-359-3948 257 D
tcampbell@mail.ncmissouri.edu
CAMPBELL, Terrance ..... 630-752-5490 153 C
terrance.campbell@wheaton.edu
CAMPBELL, Terri .... 303-458-4231.. 83 E
tcampbell007@regis.edu
CAMPBELL, Terri .... 402-399-2419 266 F
tcampbell@csm.edu
CAMPBELL, Timothy, G 859-858-3511 179 D
tim.campbell@asbury.edu
CAMPBELL, Tom .... 615-966-7164 421 B
tom.campbell@lipscomb.edu
CAMPBELL, Toma .... 406-353-2607 262 H
tcampbell@ancollege.edu
CAMPBELL, Yvonne ...... 540-857-6829 475 G
ycampbell@virginiawestern.edu
CAMPBELL-BROWN,
Andrea .... 423-614-8600 420 H
acampbell@leeuniversity.edu
CAMPBELL-GOLDEN,
Carolyn .... 724-503-1001 402 B
ccampbellgolden@washjeff.edu
CAMPBELL JACKSON,
Candace .... 315-443-3494 321 G
candace1@syr.edu
CAMPBELL-KYUREGHYAN,
Naira .... 978-837-5265 216 F
campbellnk@merrimack.edu
CAMPEAU, Tony .... 406-994-5541 264 C
tcampeau@montana.edu
CAMPER, Shannon .... 845-451-1352 297 G
shannon.camper@culinary.edu
CAMPER, Starr .... 704-669-4066 333 E
camper@clevelandcc.edu
CAMPFIELD, Justin .... 802-831-1228 463 C
jcampfield@vermontlaw.edu
CAMPION, Alyssa .... 218-736-1502 239 C
alyssa.campion@minnesota.edu
CAMPION, Setareh .... 701-252-3467 347 B
setareh.campion@uj.edu
CAMPION, William, J .... 254-647-3234 441 K
bcampion@rangercollege.edu
CAMPIRANO, Marisa ...... 956-665-3137 455 D
marisa.campirano01@utrgv.edu
CAMPLESE, Cole .... 617-373-2752 217 I
CAMPO, Carlos .... 419-289-5050 347 J
ccampo@ashland.edu
CAMPO, Jeffrey .... 973-655-7081 279 B
campoj@montclair.edu
CAMPO, Juan, E .... 805-893-3945.. 70 E
jcampo@religion.ucsb.edu
CAMPOS, Alysa .... 281-487-1170 448 E
acampos@txchiro.edu
CAMPOS, Brian .... 805-482-2755.. 59 G
registrar-sjs@stjohnsem.edu
CAMPOS, Cesar .... 312-939-0111 137 D
cesar@eastwest.edu
CAMPOS, Darcie, R .... 708-534-5000 138 E
dcampos@govst.edu
CAMPOS, Diana .... 575-234-9227 287 E
dcampos@nmsu.edu
CAMPOS, Javier .... 559-453-4600.. 43 A
javier.campos@fresno.edu
CAMPOS, Jesus .... 956-872-8330 443 H
jhcampos@southtexascollege.edu
CAMPOS, Lisa, D .... 210-458-8149 455 E
lisa.campos@utsa.edu
CAMPOS, Luis .... 575-646-2101 287 C
campos1@nmsu.edu
CAMPOS, Nathan .... 409-882-3305 449 H
nathan.campos@lsco.edu
CAMPOS, Nicolette .... 910-521-6695 343 B
nicolette.campos@uncp.edu
CAMPOS, Susan .... 708-456-0300 151 D
susancampos@triton.edu
CAMPOS FACCHINATO,
Ana .... 562-947-8755.. 65 I
anafacchinato@scuhs.edu
CAMPS, Manel .... 831-459-2411.. 71 A
mcamps@ucsc.edu
CAMUTI, Alice .... 931-372-6006 426 B
acamuti@tntech.edu
CANAAN, Shirley .... 203-371-7946.. 89 A
canaans@sacredheart.edu
CANACARIS, Diana .... 865-981-8198 421 C
diana.canacaris@maryvillecollege.edu
CANADA, Allison, M ...... 410-334-2918 205 D
acanada@worwic.edu
CANADA, Britt .... 325-574-7671 458 D
bcanada@wtc.edu
CANADA, Jeff, H .... 410-543-6056 204 D
jhcanada@salisbury.edu
CANADA, Mark .... 765-455-9227 157 B
canadam@iuk.edu
CANAL, Marcie .... 213-738-6800.. 66 B
administrativeservices@swlaw.edu
CANALDA, Tabitha .... 239-687-5300.. 95 L
CANALE, Brad .... 906-227-2610 228 I
bcanale@nmu.edu
CANALE, Mary .... 315-312-5558 318 D
mary.canale@oswego.edu
CANALES, Irvin .... 787-891-0925 507 K
icanales@aguadilla.inter.edu
CANALES, Jason .... 413-662-5413 213 C
jason.canales@mcla.edu
CANALES, Leticia .... 805-289-6000.. 74 B
CANALES, Luis .... 309-438-5276 140 D
lacanal@ilstu.edu
CANALES, Rafael, R ...... 787-279-1912 508 A
rrcanales@bayamon.inter.edu
CANAN, Michelle .... 918-293-5494 368 B
michelle.canan@okstate.edu
CANARY, Sharnie .... 845-569-3548 307 D
sharnie.canary@msmc.edu
CANAS, Carlos .... 305-626-3698 100 D
carlos.canas@fmuniv.edu
CANATELLA, Holle .... 570-484-2178 394 E
hcanatel@lockhaven.edu
CANAVAN, Brian .... 617-253-4784 216 B
CANAVAN, Linda, T ...... 781-292-2341 210 A
linda.canavan@olin.edu
CANCEL, Elizabeth .... 787-766-1717 510 G
um_ecancel@uagm.edu
CANCEL, Magda .... 787-704-1020 506 D
mcancel@columbiacentral.edu
CANCEL-PEREZ,
Magda, A .... 787-620-2040 505 C
mcancel@aupr.edu
CANCILLA, Mike .... 256-549-8311.... 2 B
mcancilla@gadsdenstate.edu
CANDA, Angela .... 216-397-1531 353 O
acanda@jcu.edu
CANDANEDO, Jose .... 602-286-8000.. 13 B
CANDEE, Kathleen .... 920-923-8727 493 D
kcandee@marianuniversity.edu
CANDELARIA,
J. Randel .... 336-734-7311 334 F
jcandelaria@forsythtech.edu
CANDELARIA, Lorenzo .. 615-322-7311 428 A
CANDELARIA, Maria, L . 787-850-9375 512 D
maria.candelaria2@upr.edu
CANDIA-BAILEY,
Antoinette .... 413-594-2761 208 E
CANDLER, George, B .... 212-327-7801 312 G
candler@rockefeller.edu
CANDLER, Marietta .... 870-612-2070.. 22 H
marietta.candler@uaccb.edu
CANDLISH, Karen .... 317-955-6190 159 K
kcandlish@marian.edu
CANEIRO-LIVINGSTON,
Graciela .... 402-465-2110 268 G
gcaneiro@nebrwesleyan.edu
CANEPA, Janet, A .... 203-254-4280.. 87 I
jcanepa@fairfield.edu
CANEPI, Karen .... 702-968-2033 272 C
kcanepi@roseman.edu
CANER, Emir .... 706-865-2134 126 E
ecaner@truett.edu
CANFIELD, Barbara .... 607-962-9000 320 C
CANFIELD, Clarke .... 207-741-5575 195 H
ccanfield@smccme.edu
CANFIELD, Jodi .... 434-381-6100 471 I
jcanfield@sbc.edu
CANFIELD, Kathleen ...... 847-925-6437 138 G
kcanfiel@harpercollege.edu
CANFIELD, Kipton .... 309-341-5325 134 B
kcanfield@sandburg.edu
CANFIELD, Susan .... 641-628-7642 164 D
canfields@central.edu
CANGELLARIS,
Andreas, C .... 217-333-6677 152 B
provost@illinois.edu
CANGEMI, Livia .... 212-772-4475 294 C
livia.cangemi@hunter.cuny.edu
CANGIANO, George ...... 781-891-2380 206 G
gcangiano@bentley.edu
CANHAM, Drew .... 254-299-8645 439 E
dcanham@mclennan.edu
CANIA, Sal .... 315-267-2174 319 A
caniasj@potsdam.edu
CANIDA, Robert .... 434-544-8540 471 L
canida_rl@lynchburg.edu
CANIGLIA, Alan, S .... 717-358-3934 383 I
alan.caniglia@fandm.edu
CANINE, Chris .... 402-486-2502 269 F
chris.canine@ucollege.edu
CANINE, Kim .... 402-486-2507 269 F
kim.canine@ucollege.edu
CANINO, Cathy .... 864-503-5657 414 A
ccanino@uscupstate.edu
CANIPE, Steve .... 866-492-5336 244 F
stephen.canipe@mail.waldenu.edu
CANIZALES, Rafael .... 937-395-8837 354 J
rafael.canizales@kc.edu
CANNADA, JR.,
Robert, C .... 601-923-1600 248 F
rcannada@rts.edu
CANNADAY SAULNY,
Helen .... 202-994-6710.. 92 D
saulnyh@gwu.edu
CANNADY, Sharell .... 704-378-3572 330 D
scannady@jcsu.edu
CANNADY-SMITH,
Allison .... 253-879-3450 484 G
acannadysmith@pugetsound.edu
CANNAN, Erin .... 845-758-7454 290 I
cannan@bard.edu
CANNEY, Catherine .... 978-665-3653 212 E
ccanney@fitchburgstate.edu
CANNIFF, James, F .... 617-228-2435 214 C
jfcanniff@bhcc.mass.edu
CANNING, John, B .... 401-232-6020 404 A
jcanning@bryant.edu
CANNING, Kathleen ...... 713-348-4810 442 F
CANNISTRACI, Patti .... 518-268-5131 314 J
patricia.cannistraci@sphp.com
CANNON, Amy .... 270-901-1012 182 H
amy.cannon@kctcs.edu
CANNON, Barbie .... 318-797-5116 190 A
barbie.cannon@lsus.edu
CANNON, Brenda .... 931-393-1548 424 F
bcannon@mscc.edu
CANNON, Chris .... 251-460-6161.... 9 A
ccannon@southalabama.edu
CANNON, D. Glen .... 770-962-7580 121 E
gcannon@gwinnetttech.edu
CANNON, Gordon .... 601-266-5116 249 F
gordon.cannon@usm.edu
CANNON, Gregory .... 973-720-6268 284 J
cannong@wpunj.edu
CANNON, Jason .... 256-840-4150.... 3 F
jason.cannon@snead.edu
CANNON, Jo Ann .... 252-222-6141 333 A
cannonj@carteret.edu
CANNON, Julie .... 386-752-1822 100 B
julie.cannon@fgc.edu
CANNON, Kathleen .... 503-847-2557 377 B
kcannon@uws.edu
CANNON, Matthew .... 864-327-9800 466 K
mcannon@vcom.vt.edu
CANNON, Rebecca .... 225-768-0810 187 B
rebecca.cannon@franu.edu
CANNON, Sharon .... 432-703-5270 451 A
sharon.cannon@ttuhsc.edu
CANNON, Thomas .... 646-592-4327 326 D
thomas.cannon@yu.edu
CANNON SMITH, Betsy 413-542-2031 205 G
ecsmith@amherst.edu
CANO, Annmarie .... 509-313-3883 480 F
cano@gonzaga.edu
CANO, Mary .... 915-566-9621 458 B
mcano@westerntech.edu
CANO, Mary .... 901-333-4462 425 D
mcano1@southwest.tn.edu
CANO-MORALES,
Anna, M .... 401-456-8810 405 A
acanomorales@ric.edu
CANON, Susan .... 507-786-3647 243 D
canon@stolaf.edu
CANOY, Eugenio .... 408-274-7900.. 62 G
eugenio.canoy@evc.edu
CANOY, Robert, W .... 704-406-4395 329 A
rcanoy@gardner-webb.edu
CANSLER, Charles .... 843-953-6982 407 C
ccansler@citadel.edu
CANT, Greg .... 570-408-4000 403 A
greg.cant@wilkes.edu
CANTENS, Bernardo .... 610-861-1589 390 F
cantensb@moravian.edu
CANTER, Bridget .... 270-534-3088 183 B
bridget.canter@kctcs.edu
CANTER, Bridget .... 270-534-3155 183 B
bridget.canter@kctcs.edu
CANTERBURY, Jay .... 419-434-4076 362 D
canterbury@findlay.edu
CANTERBURY, Jenni ...... 304-929-6727 488 G
jcanterbury@newriver.edu
CANTERINO, Patricia ..... 610-647-4400 385 L
pcanterino@immaculata.edu
CANTEY, Andrew .... 903-510-2186 452 A
acan2@tjc.edu
CANTLEY, Adam, D .... 302-831-8939.. 91 C
adamcan@udel.edu
CANTONIS, George, M .. 617-731-3500 210 G
CANTOR, Nancy, E .... 973-353-5541 282 B
nancy.cantor@rutgers.edu
CANTOR, Ronald, G ...... 315-294-9070 292 G
CANTRELL, Andra, R ..... 817-598-6260 457 J
acantrell@wc.edu
CANTRELL, Betsy .... 678-717-3941 127 A
betsy.cantrell@ung.edu
CANTRELL, Bruce .... 865-354-3000 425 C
cantrellbe@roanestate.edu
CANTRELL, Dwayne .... 661-654-2160.. 30 B
dcantrell2@csub.edu
CANTRELL, Hampton ...... 925-631-8097.. 59 I
hnc2@stmarys-ca.edu
CANTRELL, Jill .... 770-533-6903 122 B
cantrell@laniertech.edu
CANTRELL, Mark .... 304-876-5528 490 A
mcantrel@shepherd.edu
CANTRELL, Pamela .... 435-879-4260 460 B
cantrellp@dixie.edu
CANTRELL, Paul .... 361-354-2771 432 K
pcantrell@coastalbend.edu
CANTRELL, Sharon .... 501-907-6670.. 23 B
scantrell@uaptc.edu
CANTRELL, Sharon .... 787-743-7979 510 H
scantrel@suagm.edu
CANTRELL, Sirena .... 601-266-6028 249 F
sirena.cantrell@usm.edu
CANTRELL, Sonja, G 304-696-2258 489M
cantrel1@marshall.edu
CANTRELL, Tiffany .... 334-386-7450..... 5 C
tcantrell@faulkner.edu
CANTRELL, Will .... 906-487-2326 228 A
cantrell@mtu.edu
CANTU, Brenda .... 830-591-7252 444 G
bmcantu@swtjc.edu
CANTU, Gaston .... 210-486-3941 429 A
gcantu@alamo.edu
CANTU, Henry .... 210-567-5807 456 C
cantuh@uthsca.edu
CANTU, Jose .... 361-570-4149 453 B
cantujl1@uhv.edu
CANTU, Laura .... 323-265-8646.. 48 J
cantulb@elac.edu

CARL, April 903-468-8167 447 B april.carl@tamuc.edu
CARL, Ashley 813-253-7158 102 B acarl@hccfl.edu
CARL, Brian 713-522-7911 454 G carlbt@stthom.edu
CARL, Courtney 319-385-6386 167 H courtney.carl@iw.edu
CARL, Denise 859-344-3538 185 B carld@thomasmore.edu
CARL, Diane 570-321-4101 389 B carl@lycoming.edu
CARL, Drew 770-216-2960 121 I
CARL, Heidi, A 765-494-4600 160 B
CARL, Peggy 570-662-4636 394 F pcarl@mansfield.edu
CARL, Rebecca 812-855-9634 156 G rebcarl@iu.edu
CARL, Rebecca 812-855-9634 156 F rebcarl@iu.edu
CARL, Steven, B 508-767-7267 206 A sb.carl@assumption.edu
CARLAND, J. Paul 407-708-2363 108 D carlandp@seminolestate.edu
CARLAND, Tammy Rae 510-594-3649 28 B tcarland@cca.edu
CARLBLOM, Shelia 765-677-2191 158 B sheila.carlblom@indwes.edu
CARLES, Gilberto 574-631-0946 162 A gcarlesb@nd.edu
CARLESSO, Dennis 313-993-3360 231 E carlesdm@udmercy.edu
CARLETON, Dia, M 607-436-2518 316 F dia.carleton@oneonta.edu
CARLETON, Taylor 830-372-8026 449 A tcarleton@tlu.edu
CARLETON, Tori 707-664-2880 34 B
CARLEY, Christelle 318-487-7051 187 E christelle.carley@lacollege.edu
CARLEY, Michael 559-791-2275 47 A mcarley@portervillecollege.edu
CARLILE, Kimberly, L 806-371-5017 429 E k0153833@actx.edu
CARLIN, Donna 409-944-1387 436 E dcarlin@gc.edu
CARLIN, Jane 253-879-3118 484 G jcarlin@pugetsound.edu
CARLIN, Laurence 920-424-7364 496 C carlin@uwosh.edu
CARLIN, Michael 704-687-8485 342 D mike.carlin@uncc.edu
CARLINEO, Renee 607-735-1730 298 H rcarlineo@elmira.edu
CARLINEO, Renee, M 716-878-5561 317 F carlinrm@buffalostate.edu
CARLISLE, Brian, A 706-880-8976 122 A bcarlisl@lagrange.edu
CARLISLE, David, M 323-563-4987 36 C davidcarlisle@cdrewu.edu
CARLISLE, Elizabeth 812-749-1241 159 O lcarlisle@oak.edu
CARLISLE, Nadis 256-372-5555 1 A nadis.carlisle@aamu.edu
CARLISLE, Sandi 320-629-5140 240 D sandi.carlisle@pine.edu
CARLISLE, Susan 931-424-4063 427 E scarlis2@utsouthern.edu
CARLOCK, Myra 731-352-4090 418 C carlockm@bethelu.edu
CARLOS, Raymond 909-384-8253 60 F rcarlos@sbccd.cc.ca.us
CARLOW, Regina 410-704-3288 204 E rcarlow@towson.edu
CARLSEN, Paul 920-693-1123 498 H paul.carlsen@gotoltc.edu
CARLSON, Aaron 540-261-8503 471 B aaron.carlson@svu.edu
CARLSON, Anna 218-755-2737 237 F anna.carlson@bemidjistate.edu
CARLSON, Ashley 406-683-7115 264 A ashley.carlson@umwestern.edu
CARLSON, Beth, L 724-847-6666 384 C bcarlson@geneva.edu
CARLSON, Bob 630-682-6002 140 A carlson@iit.edu
CARLSON, Britt 978-867-4221 210 B britt.carlson@gordon.edu
CARLSON, Brooke 212-217-4300 299 D brooke_carlson@fitnyc.edu
CARLSON, Bryan 951-827-4592 70 B bryan.carlson@ucr.edu
CARLSON, Buff 215-248-6392 400 D bcarlson@uls.edu
CARLSON, Cameron 316-942-4291 176 E carlsonc@newmanu.edu
CARLSON, Caroline 949-376-6000 47 D ccarlson@lcad.edu
CARLSON, Casey 530-893-7544 27 C carlsonca@butte.edu
CARLSON, Catherina 781-891-2989 206 G ccarlson@bentley.edu
CARLSON, Catherine 513-732-5233 362 B carlsoc2@ucmail.uc.edu
CARLSON, Cathy 507-222-4075 234 G ccarlson@carleton.edu
CARLSON, Christopher 978-867-4073 210 B chris.carlson@gordon.edu
CARLSON, Craig 203-857-3344 87 D ccarlson@norwalk.edu
CARLSON, David 540-362-6675 467 H dcarlson@hollins.edu
CARLSON, Deb 402-354-7257 268 B deb.carlson@methodistcollege.edu
CARLSON, Dennis 817-984-0550 93 H
CARLSON, Douglas 415-476-4527 70 D doug.carlson@ucsf.edu
CARLSON, Jeffrey 708-524-6813 137 C jcarlson@dom.edu
CARLSON, Jennifer 517-264-3124 220 G jennycarlson@adrian.edu
CARLSON, Jim 985-545-1500 188 E
CARLSON, Jim 225-743-8500 188 H jcarlson@rpcc.edu
CARLSON, Julie 402-844-7142 268 H juliec@northeast.edu
CARLSON, Karen 413-565-6850 206 D kcarlson@baypath.edu
CARLSON, Kathleen 574-284-4543 160 I kcarlson@saintmarys.edu
CARLSON, Kathleen 773-298-3305 149 D carlson@sxu.edu
CARLSON, Kevin, R 563-333-6070 169 G carlsonkevinr@sau.edu
CARLSON, Kirk 507-933-6362 236 A kcarlson@gustavus.edu
CARLSON, Laina 651-450-3654 238 E lcarlso@inverhills.edu
CARLSON, Laina 651-423-8000 238 A laina.carlson@dctc.edu
CARLSON, Laura 574-631-8052 162 A lcarlson@nd.edu
CARLSON, Laura 801-863-5704 460 D lcarlson@uvu.edu
CARLSON, Leslie 716-375-2143 313 C lcarlson@sbu.edu
CARLSON, Mary 704-669-6000 333 E carlsone141@clevelandcc.edu
CARLSON, Melinda 214-768-2422 444 D mpcarlson@smu.edu
CARLSON, Neil 616-526-6420 222 C nec4@calvin.edu
CARLSON, Nicholas 309-457-2391 144 H
CARLSON, Nicki 218-683-8546 240 B nicki.carlson@northlandcollege.edu
CARLSON, Nicole 763-493-0597 240 A ncarlson@nhcc.edu
CARLSON, Paul 815-802-8652 141 D pcarlson@kcc.edu
CARLSON, Peggy 402-486-2600 269 F peggy.carlson@ucollege.edu
CARLSON, Renee 712-324-5061 169 C rcarlson@nwicc.edu
CARLSON, Ria, M 949-824-7911 69 D ria.carlson@uci.edu
CARLSON, Robert 785-227-3380 172 A carlsonr@bethanylb.edu
CARLSON, Ruth 906-217-4032 222 A ruth.carlson@baycollege.edu
CARLSON, Skye 253-272-1126 481 E scarlson@ncad.edu
CARLSON, Steve 906-217-4080 222 A steve.carlson@baycollege.edu
CARLSON, Steve 937-298-3399 354 J steve.carlson@ketteringhealth.org
CARLSON, Steven 269-782-1305 231 A scarlson01@swmich.edu
CARLSON, Susan 510-987-0728 68 L susan.carlson@ucop.edu
CARLSON-KENLEY, Wendi 605-256-5149 416 F wendi.carlson-kenley@dsu.edu
CARLTON, Christopher 717-477-1481 395 B cocarlton@ship.edu
CARLTON, Edith 731-286-3300 424 D carlton@dscc.edu
CARLTON, Jeremy 541-552-7672 376 B
CARLTON, William 912-279-5892 117 F wcarlton@ccga.edu
CARMAN, James 989-463-7111 221 B
CARMAN, Kevin 307-766-4286 501 I provost@uwyo.edu
CARMAN, Kristi 678-839-5306 127 C kcarman@westga.edu
CARMAN, Robert 562-938-4238 48 F rcarman@lbcc.edu
CARMEL, Julie 508-929-8754 213 G jcarmel@worcester.edu
CARMEN, Kim 318-675-5207 189 I kimberly.carmen@lsuhs.edu
CARMENATTY, Sylvia 787-834-9595 510 D sylviac@uaa.edu
CARMER, Laura 978-468-7111 210 C lcarmer@gcts.edu
CARMICHAEL, Ann, C 803-812-7330 413 E anncar@mailbox.sc.edu
CARMICHAEL, Brenda 620-343-4600 173 G bcarmichael@fhtc.edu
CARMICHAEL, Demetrius, L 309-677-3155 134 A dcarmichael@fsmail.bradley.edu
CARMICHAEL, Jason 678-839-5000 127 C jcarmichael@westga.edu
CARMICHAEL, John 360-867-6100 480 C carmichj@evergreen.edu
CARMICHAEL, Lisandra 912-478-5116 120 C lcarmichael@georgiasouthern.edu
CARMICHAEL, Matthew 541-346-4127 376 H mecarmic@uoregon.edu
CARMICHAEL, Paul 860-343-5787 87 A pcarmichael@mxcc.edu
CARMINE, Kevin 718-319-7965 294 B kcarmine@hostos.cuny.edu
CARMITCHEL, Michelle 913-758-4359 178 B michelle.carmitchel@stmary.edu
CARMODY, Patricia 507-537-6206 241 D patricia.carmody@smsu.edu
CARMONA, Josefina 575-527-7639 287 F jocarmon@nmsu.edu
CARNAHAN, Diane 209-468-9155 67 I dcarnahan@sjcoe.net
CARNAROLI, Craig 215-898-6693 400 F carnarol@upenn.edu
CARNAVAS, Ria 718-390-3131 324 F ria.carnavas@wagner.edu
CARNE, Kim 906-217-4027 222 A carnek@baycollege.edu
CARNES, Gregory, A 256-765-4245 8 E gacarnes@una.edu
CARNES, Kathy, M 252-493-7220 336 H kcarnes@email.pittcc.edu
CARNEVALE, David 714-532-6049 36 B carneva@chapman.edu
CARNEY, Chuck 812-855-1892 156 F ccarney@indiana.edu
CARNEY, Ginger 208-885-6195 132 F gingercarney@uidaho.edu
CARNEY, J. Paige 304-766-3194 490 D pcarney@wvstateu.edu
CARNEY, Jennifer 585-785-1388 299 F jennifer.carney@flcc.edu
CARNEY, John 615-460-6000 418 B john.carney@belmont.edu
CARNEY, Lindsey 229-391-5066 114 F lroberts@abac.edu
CARNEY, Marty 864-250-8166 409 I marty.carney@gvltec.edu
CARNEY, Michael, J 715-836-4353 495 E carneymj@uwec.edu
CARNEY, Michelle 785-864-8975 177 J mmcarney@ku.edu
CARNEY, Paul 316-942-4291 176 E carneyp@newmanu.edu
CARNEY, RSM, Sheila, A 412-578-6424 380 B sacarney@carlow.edu
CARNEY, Susie 620-278-4228 177 H susie.carney@sterling.edu
CARNEY, Timothy 202-319-5619 92 A carneyt@cua.edu
CARNEY-DEBORD, Nan 740-587-6428 352 A carneydebord@denison.edu
CARNEY-HALL, Karla 309-556-3111 140 F dstudent@iwu.edu
CARNIE, Andrew, H 520-621-7815 16 D carnie@arizona.edu
CARNLEY, Lisa 334-222-6591 2 I lcarnley@lbwcc.edu
CARNS, Mary Lee 843-525-5692 412 G mcarns@tcl.edu
CARNZ, Scott 206-239-4500 478 H
CARNZ, Scott 206-239-4500 478 H provost@cityu.edu
CARO, Mary Ellen 215-545-6400 391 E
CAROLAN, Brian, V 203-365-4657 89 A carolanb2@sacredheart.edu
CAROLIN, Robert 760-750-4089 33 A rcarolin@csusm.edu
CAROLIN, Robert 701-777-4202 345 B robert.carolin@und.edu
CAROLINA, Kimberly 860-343-5757 87 A kcarolina@commnet.edu
CAROLINO, Josiane 404-627-2681 116 C josiane.carolino@beulah.edu
CAROLLO, Sandy 212-616-7200 301 C scarollo@helenefuld.edu
CARON, Elizabeth 620-241-0723 172 J elizabeth.caron@centralchristian.edu
CARON, John 518-464-8500 299 C
CARON, Justine 617-879-7906 213 B jmcaron@massart.edu
CARON, Lenn 410-455-3260 203 B carlen@umbc.edu
CARON, Linda 937-775-2225 364 E linda.caron@wright.edu
CARON, Paul 310-506-4621 56 G paul.caron@pepperdine.edu
CARONNA, Gina 815-921-4043 148 B g.caronna@rockvalleycollege.edu
CAROTHERS, Amy 775-784-6620 271 E acarothers@unr.edu
CAROTHERS, Brad 408-274-7900 62 G brad.carothers@evc.edu
CAROTHERS, Cat 425-640-1112 480 A cat.carothers@edcc.edu
CAROTHERS, Robert 401-752-2640 404 B
CAROTHERS, Taryn 262-472-1918 497 D
CAROW, Ken, A 317-274-2481 157 D kcarow@iupui.edu
CARPEN, Katie 716-338-1210 303 A katiecarpen@mail.sunyjcc.edu
CARPENTER, Amanda 805-437-3565 30 C amanda.carpenter@csuci.edu
CARPENTER, Angela 802-831-1209 463 C acarpenter@vermontlaw.edu
CARPENTER, Ariel 909-607-0434 37 C ariel.carpenter@cgu.edu
CARPENTER, B. Stephen 814-865-2591 391 G bsc5@psu.edu
CARPENTER, Barbara 225-771-2016 191 A barbara_carpenter@subr.edu
CARPENTER, Barbara, W 225-771-2613 191 B barbara_carpenter@subr.edu
CARPENTER, Beth 615-230-3560 425 E beth.carpenter@volstate.edu
CARPENTER, Betsy 413-585-2052 218 H ewcarpen@smith.edu
CARPENTER, Carol 616-977-5520 223 C carol.carpenter@cornerstone.edu
CARPENTER, Carol 505-984-6102 202 A carol.carpenter@sjc.edu
CARPENTER, Catherine 213-738-6875 66 B ccarpenter@swlaw.edu
CARPENTER, Charles 817-921-5883 445 A ccarpenter@swbts.edu
CARPENTER, Courtney 410-386-4866 200 F ccarpenter@mcdaniel.edu
CARPENTER, David 913-722-0272 175 A david.carpenter@kansaschristian.edu
CARPENTER, Deanna 620-901-6338 171 D carpenter@allencc.edu
CARPENTER, Deb 765-998-5200 161 C dbcarpenter@taylor.edu
CARPENTER, Debra 281-283-2150 452 E carpenter@uhcl.edu
CARPENTER, Hedy, L 818-677-2138 32 C hcarpenter@csun.edu
CARPENTER, James 417-447-6981 257 G carpentj@otc.edu
CARPENTER, Jan 509-533-3535 479 D jan.carpenter@sfcc.spokane.edu
CARPENTER, Jane 785-670-1526 178 C jane.carpenter@washburn.edu
CARPENTER, Jenna 910-814-4018 327 D carpenter@campbell.edu
CARPENTER, Jennifer 407-303-5727 95 B jennifer.carpenter@ahu.edu
CARPENTER, Jessica 607-735-1812 298 H jcarpenter@elmira.edu
CARPENTER, Karen 843-383-8130 408 B kcarpenter@coker.edu

CARSON, Elizabeth, M .. 815-282-7900 148 I bethcarson@sacn.edu

CARSON, Jacqueline, M .... 585-292-2523 307 B jcarson@monroecc.edu

CARSON, Jeffrey .... 732-235-8629 282 A jeffrey.carson@rutgers.edu

CARSON, Jessica .... 212-237-8717 294 D jcarson@jjay.cuny.edu

CARSON, Nathan .... 918-495-7972 368 F ncarson@oru.edu

CARSON, Rebecca .... 310-506-4558.. 56 G rebecca.carson@pepperdine.edu

CARSON, Scott .... 601-426-6346 249 A scarson@southeasternbaptist.edu

CARSON, Sylvia .... 678-717-2373 127 A sylvia.carson@ung.edu

CARSON, Warren .... 864-503-5634 414 A wcarson@uscupstate.edu

CARSTARPHEN, Minnie . 334-876-9345.... 2 D minnie.carstarphen@wccs.edu

CARSTENS, Joel, B .... 603-862-3671 274 F joel.carstens@unh.edu

CARSTENS, John .... 336-734-7313 334 F jcarstens@forsythtech.edu

CARSTENS, Lisa .... 503-352-3065 375 C carstens@pacificu.edu

CARSTENSEN, Lundie .... 619-201-8705.. 60 G lundie.carstensen@sdcc.edu

CARSWELL, Justin .... 417-690-3446 251 H carswell@cofo.edu

CARSWELL, Pamela .... 386-752-1822 100 B pamela.carswell@fgc.edu

CARTAGENA, Milagros .. 787-704-1020 506 D mcartagena@columbiacentral.edu

CARTAGENA, Shannell .. 508-767-7107 206 A s.cartagena@assumption.edu

CARTAGENA-SANTIAGO, Aramilda .... 787-857-3600 507M aramildacartagena@br.inter.edu

CARTE, Mandy .... 216-368-2595 349 D mmc111@case.edu

CARTEE, Dawn, H .... 478-289-2027 118 C dhcartee@ega.edu

CARTEE, Dawn, H .... 706-542-3451 126 G cartee@uga.edu

CARTER, Abby .... 229-227-3177 126 A acarter@southernregional.edu

CARTER, Allia .... 804-257-5719 476 F alcarter@vuu.edu

CARTER, Allia, L .... 804-924-5507 476 F alcarter@vuu.edu

CARTER, Allison, A .... 906-487-1888 228 A aagranik@mtu.edu

CARTER, Amanda .... 860-701-5061.. 88 D carter_a@mitchell.edu

CARTER, Amber .... 859-442-1712 181 H amber.carter@kctcs.edu

CARTER, Andy .... 701-858-3042 345 E andy.carter@minotstateu.edu

CARTER, Angela, M ...... 336-334-4822 335 A amcarter@gtcc.edu

CARTER, Angelique .... 434-528-5276 477 B

CARTER, Art .... 540-831-5958 469 D aecarter@radford.edu

CARTER, Ashley .... 770-534-6164 116 D acarter@brenau.edu

CARTER, Ben .... 317-916-7825 158 E bcarter145@ivytech.edu

CARTER, Bessie .... 405-945-3211 368 C bessie.carter@okstate.edu

CARTER, Beth .... 910-630-7425 331 E bcarter@methodist.edu

CARTER, Bobbi Jo .... 802-635-1381 463 G bobbijo.carter@northernvermont.edu

CARTER, Brenda, C .... 469-365-1988 433 I bcarter@collin.edu

CARTER, Brett .... 336-334-5514 343 A bacarte2@uncg.edu

CARTER, Brett .... 607-778-5003 317 D carterbd@sunybroome.edu

CARTER, Caroline .... 919-516-4000 339 I

CARTER, Chris .... 864-587-4003 412 F carterc@smcsc.edu

CARTER, Christopher .... 425-235-2352 482 H ccarter@rtc.edu

CARTER, Christopher, C .... 610-758-5802 388 E ccc317@lehigh.edu

CARTER, Christy .... 316-295-8701 174 A christy_carter@friends.edu

CARTER, Cindy .... 641-585-8130 170 I carterc@waldorf.edu

CARTER, Cindy .... 906-217-4107 222 A carterc@baycollege.edu

CARTER, Clark .... 843-863-8008 407 B ccarter@csuniv.edu

CARTER, Clay .... 252-940-6357 332 C clay.carter@beaufortccc.edu

CARTER, Clinton, P .... 919-962-1000 340 H

CARTER, SR., Dameon, R .... 410-951-3906 204 B damecarter@coppin.edu

CARTER, Danita .... 314-918-2625 253 C dcarter@eden.edu

CARTER, Darryl .... 716-878-6522 317 F carterdc@buffalostate.edu

CARTER, David .... 909-607-7692.. 37 F david_carter@kgi.edu

CARTER, David .... 800-785-0585.. 39 D

CARTER, David .... 512-232-6400 455 A david.carter@austin.utexas.edu

CARTER, Dawn .... 910-962-2659 343 C carterdb@uncw.edu

CARTER, Deena .... 909-687-1465.. 43 D deenacarter@gs.edu

CARTER, Derek .... 410-951-3748 204 B dcarter@coppin.edu

CARTER, Diana .... 404-727-4264 118 E diana.carter@emory.edu

CARTER, Dione .... 310-434-4858.. 63 C carter_dione@smc.edu

CARTER, Don .... 928-523-1605.. 14 H don.carter@nau.edu

CARTER, Edythe, L .... 806-335-4228 429 E elcarter@actx.edu

CARTER, Emily, A .... 310-825-2052.. 69 E evc@conet.ucla.edu

CARTER, Evonne .... 252-335-0821 333 G evonne_carter@albemarle.edu

CARTER, FeRita .... 951-222-8837.. 59 D ferita.carter@rcc.edu

CARTER, Gail .... 304-357-4849 487 J gailcarter@ucwv.edu

CARTER, Glenn .... 302-831-3358.. 91 C gcarter@udel.edu

CARTER, Helene, T .... 706-821-8323 124 B hcarter@paine.edu

CARTER, Holly .... 812-488-1040 161 G hc110@evansville.edu

CARTER, Hope .... 601-974-1000 247 B carterhm@millsaps.edu

CARTER, Hugh .... 334-222-6591.... 2 I hcarter@lbwcc.edu

CARTER, Jade .... 405-682-1611 367 D jade.j.carter@occc.edu

CARTER, Jaime .... 912-260-4367 125 D jaime.carter@sgsc.edu

CARTER, Janet .... 912-427-5817 117 E jcarter@coastalpines.edu

CARTER, Jasmine .... 940-898-3869 451 D jcarter21@twu.edu

CARTER, Jason .... 406-994-2891 264 C jcarter@montana.edu

CARTER, Jason .... 216-987-4883 351 E jason.carter@tri-c.edu

CARTER, Jeffrey .... 252-335-0821 333 G jeffrey_carter@albemarle.edu

CARTER, Jeffrey, J .... 919-866-5148 338 G jjcarter@waketech.edu

CARTER, Jeffrey, W .... 800-287-8822 154 A president@bethanyseminary.edu

CARTER, Jennifer .... 318-257-4730 192 D jcarter@latech.edu

CARTER, Jennings .... 618-545-3169 141 E jcarter@kaskaskia.edu

CARTER, Jeremiah .... 808-735-4774 128 E jeremiah.carter@chaminade.edu

CARTER, Jessica .... 276-656-0312 474 G jcarter@patrickhenry.edu

CARTER, Jimmy .... 919-573-5350 340 C jcarter@shepherds.edu

CARTER, John, B .... 413-542-2771 205 G jbcarter@amherst.edu

CARTER, June .... 864-503-5881 414 A junecar@uscupstate.edu

CARTER, Kaira .... 954-486-7728 113 B

CARTER, Kathleen .... 706-778-8500 124 D kcarter@piedmont.edu

CARTER, Keith .... 662-915-6684 249 D jkcarter@olemiss.edu

CARTER, Kim, C .... 859-257-9420 185 F kccarter.1@uky.edu

CARTER, Larance .... 404-880-8074 117 C lcarter@cau.edu

CARTER, Laurie .... 920-832-6525 493 B laurie.carter@lawrence.edu

CARTER, Lawrence, E .... 470-639-0323 123 D lawrence.carter@morehouse.edu

CARTER, Lawrence, L .... 517-321-0242 225 A lcarter@glcc.edu

CARTER, Linda .... 816-604-3081 255 G linda.carter@mcckc.edu

CARTER, Lindsey .... 859-622-3541 180 E lindsey.carter@eku.edu

CARTER, Linnie, S .... 717-780-2321 385 B lscarter@hacc.edu

CARTER, Lisa .... 608-262-1234 495 D lisa.carter@wisc.edu

CARTER, Luther, F .... 843-661-1210 409 G lcarter@fmarion.edu

CARTER, Malika .... 315-470-6866 319 D mcarte06@esf.edu

CARTER, Malinda .... 804-819-4685 473 C mcarter@vccs.edu

CARTER, Matt .... 505-277-3003 288 J mdcarter@unm.edu

CARTER, Melanie .... 202-806-2550.. 92 F melcarter@howard.edu

CARTER, Melodie .... 919-546-8320 340 B melodie.carter@shawu.edu

CARTER, Melondia, R ... 205-726-2278.... 6 E mcarte10@samford.edu

CARTER, Michael .... 213-738-6800.. 66 B administrativeservices@swlaw.edu

CARTER, Michael .... 937-512-3883 360 G michael.carter@sinclair.edu

CARTER, Michele .... 254-526-1331 432 D michele.carter@ctcd.edu

CARTER, Michelle .... 225-578-3202 189 E michellec@lsu.edu

CARTER, Michelle, R ..... 202-806-7540.. 92 F

CARTER, Miranda .... 406-656-9950 265 I mcarter@yellowstonechristian.edu

CARTER, Pam .... 215-751-8737 381 I pcarter@ccp.edu

CARTER, Parris .... 937-502-3649 363 G pcarter@wilberforce.edu

CARTER, Paul .... 863-667-5000 108 K prcarter@seu.edu

CARTER, Peggy .... 731-352-4096 418 C carterp@bethelu.edu

CARTER, Prudence .... 510-643-6644.. 69 A pcarter@berkeley.edu

CARTER, Quamina .... 909-621-8965.. 37 C quamina.carter@cgu.edu

CARTER, R. Daphne ...... 843-661-1188 409 G rcarter@fmarion.edu

CARTER, Regina, W ...... 501-916-5310.. 22 A rswade@ualr.edu

CARTER, Richard .... 251-460-6283.... 9 A rcarter@southalabama.edu

CARTER, Rock .... 562-907-4972.. 76 B rcarter@whittier.edu

CARTER, Ronald, L .... 909-558-4528.. 48 E rcarter@llu.edu

CARTER, Ronald, L .... 909-558-7616.. 48 E rcarter@llu.edu

CARTER, Saundra .... 202-274-5531.. 94 B scarter@udc.edu

CARTER, Scott, N .... 423-439-4343 419 G cartersn@etsu.edu

CARTER, Seth, M .... 785-460-5400 173 B seth.carter@colbycc.edu

CARTER, Shawna, M ...... 608-246-6249 499 A smcarter@madisoncollege.edu

CARTER, Sheila .... 312-369-7187 136 D scarter@colum.edu

CARTER, Sherryl .... 562-860-2451.. 35 H scarter@cerritos.edu

CARTER, Shree .... 714-556-3610.. 73 H vutrustees@vanguard.edu

CARTER, Shree .... 714-556-3610.. 73 H vaschoolcertifyingofficial@vanguard.edu

CARTER, Shree .... 714-556-3610.. 73 H scarter@vanguard.edu

CARTER, Steven, J .... 215-887-5511 402 E scarter@wts.edu

CARTER, Sue .... 831-459-3275.. 71 A sacarter@ucsc.edu

CARTER, Sue, V .... 434-223-6220 467 F svcarter@hsc.edu

CARTER, Susan .... 845-938-4041 503 I susan.carter@westpoint.edu

CARTER, Tasha .... 251-343-8200.... 6 D

CARTER, Ted, E .... 402-472-8636 269 H president@nebraska.edu

CARTER, Thomas, E ...... 315-470-6691 319 D tecarter@esf.edu

CARTER, Tina, P .... 919-866-5419 338 G tcarter@waketech.edu

CARTER, Todd .... 316-322-3201 172 D tcarter@butlercc.edu

CARTER, Tom .... 256-331-5263.... 3 C tom.carter@nwscc.edu

CARTER, Tony .... 803-641-3444 413 B tonyc@usca.edu

CARTER, Tracie .... 334-420-4426.... 3 H tcarter@trenholmstate.edu

CARTER, Travis .... 434-947-8000 469 E

CARTER, Veronika .... 802-656-0589 463 A vlcarter@uvm.edu

CARTER, Zina .... 979-532-6417 458 E zinac@wcjc.edu

CARTER-CONWAY, Joan 443-885-3950 201 A joan.carterconway@morgan.edu

CARTER-FISHER, Andrea .... 910-879-5512 332 D acarterfisher@bladencc.edu

CARTER-HARBOUR, Courtney .... 972-860-7335 434 H courtneycarter@dcccd.edu

CARTER-HORN, Cynthia 936-261-3311 446 C

CARTER-STEVENS, Marilyn .... 718-862-7958 304M marilyn.carter@manhattan.edu

CARTER-TELLISON, Katrina .... 561-237-7412 103W kcartertellison@lynn.edu

CARTIER, Cheryl .... 203-582-8431.. 88 G cheryl.cartier@quinnipiac.edu

CARTIER, Jennifer .... 207-509-7282 196 E jcartier@unity.edu

CARTIER, Jolie, L .... 619-239-0391.. 34 G jcartier@cwsl.edu

CARTIER, Missy, M ...... 559-323-2100.. 61 F mcartier@sjcl.edu

CARTLEDGE, Ernest .... 240-567-7991 200 G ernest.cartledge@montgomerycollege.edu

CARTMILL, Christopher . 716-375-7888 313 C

CARTMILL, Michael .... 435-652-7899 460 B michael.cartmill@dixie.edu

CARTNAL, Ryan .... 805-546-3933.. 40 F rcartnal@cuesta.edu

CARTNEY, Michael, D ... 605-882-5284 415 D cartneym@lakeareatech.edu

CARTOLANO, Joseph ...... 718-631-6231 295 C jcartolano@qcc.cuny.edu

CARTRIGHT, Jonathan ... 573-882-2011 260 I cartrightj@umsystem.edu

CARTWRIGHT, Alexander, N .... 407-823-1823 110 E alexander.cartwright@ucf.edu

CARTWRIGHT, Bill .... 415-422-5417.. 72 J jcartwri@usfca.edu

CARTWRIGHT, David, R 401-598-4826 404 D david.cartwright@jwu.edu

CARTWRIGHT, Marla ..... 931-540-2618 424 C mcartwright1@columbiastate.edu

CARTWRIGHT, Michael, G .... 317-788-3233 161 H mcartwright@uindy.edu

CARTWRIGHT, Natalie ... 610-683-4153 394 D cartwright@kutztown.edu

CARTWRIGHT-COLLINS, Carissa .... 317-921-4717 158 E ccartwright2@ivytech.edu

CARTY, Cheryl .... 478-471-5235 122 F cheryl.carty@mga.edu

CARTY, Karenann .... 718-933-6700 307 A kcarty@monroecollege.edu

CARTY, Raymond, W .... 573-629-3094 253 J rcarty@hlg.edu

CARULLO, Susan, H ..... 843-792-5802 410 C carullos@musc.edu

CARUOLO, Michael .... 401-341-2334 405 D michael.caruolo@salve.edu

CARUSO, Anne-Marie ... 617-989-4174 219 F carusoa@wit.edu

CARUSO, Britni .... 217-814-5440 149 C britni.caruso@sjcs.edu

CARUSO, Janet .... 516-572-7472 307 E janet.caruso@ncc.edu

CARUSO, Kelly .... 318-487-5443 187 J kellycaruso@cltcc.edu

CARUSO, Matthew .... 908-737-5263 278 E mcaruso@kean.edu

CARUSO, Michele, E ..... 985-448-4081 192 F michele.caruso@nicholls.edu

CARUSO, Nicole ... 770-216-2960 121 I nicole@ict.edu
CARUTHERS, Janet ... 573-875-7372 251 I jaocaruthers@ccis.edu
CARUTHERS, Michelle, P ... 540-464-7992 476 B caruthersmp@vmi.edu
CARVAJAL, Lorelei ... 623-845-3729.. 13 C lorelei.carvajal@gccaz.edu
CARVAJAL, Richard ... 229-333-5952 127 E rcarvajal@valdosta.edu
CARVALHO, Andrea ... 831-476-9424.. 42 F scadmin@fivebranches.edu
CARVALHO, Kimberly ... 617-266-2030 217 D carvalho@neco.edu
CARVALHO, Marco ... 321-671-7150 100 C mcarvalho@fit.edu
CARVALHO, Ron ... 972-721-4058 452 B rcarvalho@udallas.edu
CARVALHO, Susan ... 205-348-8280.... 7 G secarvalho@ua.edu
CARVALLOZA, Anthony . 212-327-7161 312 G anthony.carvalloza@rockefeller.edu
CARVAN, Moreen ... 847-578-8787 148 F moreen.carvan@rosalindfranklin.edu
CARVELL, Regina ... 508-286-3408 220 B carvell_regina@wheatoncollege.edu
CARVER, Andrea ... 701-774-4242 346 E andrea.carver@willistonstate.edu
CARVER, Andrew ... 618-453-5774 150 B acarver@siu.edu
CARVER, JR., Curtis, A . 205-975-0250.... 8 A carverc@uab.edu
CARVER, David, S ... 402-559-7276 269 K dcarver@unmc.edu
CARVER, Eric ... 727-341-3664 107 E carver.eric@spcollege.edu
CARVER, Jerelene ... 919-546-8525 340 B jcarver@shawu.edu
CARVER, JR., Keith, S .. 731-881-7500 427 D kcarver@utm.edu
CARVER, Leslie ... 858-534-4004.. 70 C tmcprovost@ucsd.edu
CARVER, Maureen ... 215-641-6565 390 C mcarver@mc3.edu
CARVER, Molly ... 785-227-3380 172 A carvermm@bethanylb.edu
CARY, Alice ... 217-333-1216 152 B
CARY, Charles ... 570-408-4553 403 A charles.cary@wilkes.edu
CARY, Jeff ... 806-720-7667 439 D jeff.cary@lcu.edu
CARY, Kim ... 417-447-6933 257 G caryk@otc.edu
CARY, Stacey ... 309-796-5225 133 G carys@bhc.edu
CARZOLI, Amy ... 815-455-8670 143 I acarzoli@mchenry.edu
CASABLANCA, Sonia, P 321-682-4136 113 I sperez62@valenciacollege.edu
CASADA, Tracy, L ... 606-451-6631 182 G tracy.casada@kctcs.edu
CASAINE, Wil ... 609-771-2602 276 I casainew@tcnj.edu
CASALEGNO, Gina ... 412-268-2075 380 C ginac@andrew.cmu.edu
CASALES, Isel ... 305-821-3333 100 E icasales@fnu.edu
CASALINUOVO-ADAMS, Christine ... 585-292-2215 307 B ccasalinuovo-adams@monroecc.edu
CASAMENTO, Laura ... 315-792-3222 324 B lcasamento@utica.edu
CASANOVA, Carmen, L . 302-356-6897.. 91 E carmen.l.casanova@wilmu.edu
CASARENO, Alexander .. 916-691-7740.. 50 H casarea@crc.losrios.edu
CASARES, Jason, A ... 410-651-7848 203 D jacasares@umes.edu
CASARES, Jeanne ... 585-475-4455 312 F jvccio@rit.edu
CASAS, Alexander ... 305-348-1657 110 A alexander.casas@fiu.edu
CASAS, Andrew ... 832-325-7317 456 B andrew.casas@uth.tmc.edu
CASAS, Tanya ... 215-489-4865 382 B tanya.casas@delval.edu
CASAS HERNANDEZ, Veronica ... 650-949-7200.. 42 I casashernandezveronica@fhda.edu
CASAVANT, Aaron, J ... 860-444-8255 503 G aaron.j.casavant@uscg.mil
CASAZZA, Jacqualyn ... 847-491-4302 146 E jcasazza@northwestern.edu
CASBARIAN, John ... 713-348-0000 442 F jjc@rice.edu
CASCAMO, John ... 805-546-3973.. 40 F john_cascamo@cuesta.edu
CASCARDI, Anthony ... 510-642-5396.. 69 A ajcascardi@berkeley.edu
CASCELLA, Joseph ... 315-801-8253 313 D jcascell@secon.edu
CASCIANO, Tony ... 413-572-5468 213 F tcasciano@westfield.ma.edu
CASCIO, Joseph ... 559-791-2260.. 47 A joseph.cascio@portervillecollege.edu
CASCIONE, Greg ... 248-204-2305 227 A gcascione@ltu.edu
CASCIOTTA, Tony ... 954-201-7520.. 96 F acasciot@broward.edu
CASDORPH, Michael ... 706-721-3364 116 A mcasdorph@augusta.edu
CASE, Beau ... 419-530-4286 363 B beau.case@utoledo.edu
CASE, Chad ... 662-862-8232 246 E cgcase@iccms.edu
CASE, Corrine ... 716-338-1072 303 A corrinecase@mail.sunyjcc.edu
CASE, Daniel ... 601-643-8385 245 F daniel.case@colin.edu
CASE, Danuta ... 585-582-8258 298 F danutacase@elim.edu
CASE, David ... 601-635-2111 246 A dcase@eccc.edu
CASE, John ... 404-752-1500 123 E jcase@msm.edu
CASE, Judd ... 260-982-5271 159 J jacase@manchester.edu
CASE, Karyn ... 860-512-3103.. 86 G kcase@manchestercc.edu
CASE, Keith ... 979-532-6369 458 E casek@wcjc.edu
CASE, Kerry ... 801-585-9352 459 O kerry.case@utah.edu
CASE, Kim ... 765-998-4557 161 C kmcase@taylor.edu
CASE, Mary ... 312-996-2716 151 G marycase@uic.edu
CASE, Michael, A ... 607-587-3535 319 F casema@alfredstate.edu
CASE BARTON, Allison . 805-378-1413.. 73 J abarton@vcccd.edu
CASEBEER, Clarice ... 417-967-5466 260 D
CASEL, Michael ... 610-896-1000 385 I mcasel@haverford.edu
CASERIO, Mark ... 215-596-7432 401 E m.caseri@usciences.edu
CASEWIT, Daoud ... 773-281-4700 133 B
CASEY, Anne, M ... 386-226-6000.. 99 A caseya3@erau.edu
CASEY, Barb ... 518-580-5678 315 F bcasey@skidmore.edu
CASEY, Brian ... 530-754-4105.. 69 B bscasey@ucdavis.edu
CASEY, Brian, W ... 315-228-7444 296 E president@colgate.edu
CASEY, Carolyn ... 509-434-5109 479 B carolyn.casey@ccs.spokane.edu
CASEY, Carolyn ... 509-434-5109 479 D carolyn.casey@ccs.spokane.edu
CASEY, Carolyn ... 509-434-5108 479 C carolyn.casey@ccs.spokane.edu
CASEY, Chris ... 256-782-8128.... 6 A ccasey@jsu.edu
CASEY, Derrick ... 217-735-7290 142 H dcasey@lincolncollege.edu
CASEY, Dwayne ... 662-562-3200 248 D
CASEY, Greg ... 414-277-4510 494 D
CASEY, James ... 239-590-7021 109 K jcasey@fgcu.edu
CASEY, Janet, G ... 518-580-5705 315 F jcasey@skidmore.edu
CASEY, Jason ... 402-472-3821 269 J jcasey10@unl.edu
CASEY, Joanne ... 518-472-5875 289 K jcase@albanylaw.edu
CASEY, Karla ... 617-253-0260 216 B
CASEY, Kathleen ... 607-587-4507 319 F
CASEY, Kevin ... 207-453-5141 195 F kcasey@kvcc.me.edu
CASEY, Kevin ... 414-382-6225 491 F kevin.casey@alverno.edu
CASEY, Kimberly ... 708-209-3003 136 E kimberly.casey@cuchicago.edu
CASEY, Marsha ... 317-955-6465 159 K mcasey@marian.edu
CASEY, Mary ... 781-283-2223 219 E mc4@wellesley.edu
CASEY, Megan ... 570-208-5900 386 G megansellick@kings.edu
CASEY, Meghan ... 914-323-5112 305 B meghan.casey@mville.edu
CASEY, Mia ... 254-710-3555 431 E mia_casey@baylor.edu
CASEY, Michael ... 860-297-2361.. 89 B michael.casey@trincoll.edu
CASEY, Patrick ... 269-965-3931 225 H caseyp@kellogg.edu
CASEY, Paul ... 831-755-6860.. 44 G pcasey@hartnell.edu
CASEY, Peter ... 978-934-2310 212 B peter_casey@uml.edu
CASEY, Randy ... 414-297-7872 499 C caseyr@matc.edu
CASEY, Sandra ... 518-320-1100 315 H
CASEY, Terry ... 256-782-5492.... 6 A tcasey@jsu.edu
CASEY, Warren ... 501-279-4056.. 19 C casey@harding.edu
CASEY-LOVELESS, Tasha ... 405-208-5000 367 E tasha.loveless@okcu.edu
CASEY POWELL, Deborah ... 253-833-9111 480 I dcasey@greenriver.edu
CASEY-ROSE, Cheryl ... 315-229-5512 314 D ccaseyrose@stlawu.edu
CASH, Bradley ... 252-398-6259 328 C bacash0306@chowan.edu
CASH, Erin ... 859-280-1249 183 F ecash@lextheo.edu
CASH, Gina ... 423-472-7141 424 B gcash@clevelandstatecc.edu
CASH, Jared ... 207-780-4770 197 D jared.cash@maine.edu
CASH, Jason ... 616-395-7085 225 D cash@hope.edu
CASH, JR., John ... 904-596-2494 112 F jcashjr@tbc.org
CASH, Regina ... 323-343-4967.. 31 E regina.cash@calstatela.edu
CASH, Tammie, L ... 501-569-8474.. 22 A tlcash@ualr.edu
CASH-DARVELL, Sarah .. 612-330-1019 234 A cashdar@augsburg.edu
CASHBURLESS, Marty ... 325-793-4775 439 F cashburless.marty@mcm.edu
CASHELL, Andrea ... 859-622-4484 180 E andrea.cashell@eku.edu
CASHION, Robert ... 212-998-1212 309 F
CASHMAN, Jesse ... 507-222-5992 234 G jcashman@carleton.edu
CASHMAN, Laurie ... 708-656-8000 145 C laurie.cashman@morton.edu
CASHWELL, Candace ... 252-985-5232 339 D ccashwell@ncwc.edu
CASHWELL, Debbie ... 910-410-1803 337 B dccashwell@richmondcc.edu
CASHWELL, Michael, B . 804-278-4205 471 J mcashwell@upsem.edu
CASIELLO, Andrew, R ... 757-683-3726 469 B acasiell@odu.edu
CASIMIR, Samuel ... 908-709-7087 284 D samuel.casimir@ucc.edu
CASKEY, Amy ... 580-387-7000 366 E acaskey@mscok.edu
CASKEY, Brad ... 205-226-4650.... 4 F bjcaskey@bsc.edu
CASKEY-JAMES, Jacqueline ... 478-825-6174 118 F caskeyj@fvsu.edu
CASLER, Adam ... 518-782-2919 315 E acasler@siena.edu
CASLER, Tess, C ... 315-268-7882 295 F tcasler@clarkson.edu
CASNER, Cheryl ... 931-540-2504 424 C ccasner@columbiastate.edu
CASO, Ann ... 508-626-4043 213 A acaso@framingham.edu
CASON, Craig ... 719-549-2211.. 80 B craig.cason@csupueblo.edu
CASON, Denise ... 940-668-3307 440 F dcason@nctc.edu
CASON, Jeff ... 802-443-5404 462 E cason@middlebury.edu
CASON, Scott ... 785-628-4206 173 H sacason@fhsu.edu
CASPAR, Timothy ... 517-607-2238 225 C tcaspar@hillsdale.edu
CASPARIS, Cynthia ... 936-633-5203 429 J ccasparis@angelina.edu
CASPER, George ... 208-282-3398 131 G caspgeor@isu.edu
CASPER, Monica ... 619-594-5456.. 33 D mjcasper@sdsu.edu
CASPER, Ruth ... 252-398-6269 328 C wommar@chowan.edu
CASPER, Timothy, L ... 608-246-6033 499 A tcasper@madisoncollege.edu
CASS, Jeffrey ... 479-968-0274.. 18 C jcass@atu.edu
CASS, Lori ... 570-662-4873 394 F lcass@mansfield.edu
CASS, Martin ... 386-506-3961.. 98 D martin.cass@daytonastate.edu
CASS, Rose ... 508-830-5080 213 D rcass@maritime.edu
CASSADY, David ... 502-863-8300 179 F david.cassady@bsk.edu
CASSADY, Patrick ... 313-883-8696 230 C cassady.patrick@shms.edu
CASSADY, Sandra, L ... 563-333-6409 169 G cassadysandral@sau.edu
CASSADY, Steve ... 209-384-6000.. 52 A cassady.s@mccd.edu
CASSANO, Patrick ... 843-792-1639 410 C cassanpj@musc.edu
CASSAR, Josephine ... 810-989-5539 230 F jcassar@sc4.edu
CASSARD, Anita ... 303-867-1155.. 83 K cassard@taft.edu
CASSARD, Courtney ... 985-448-4405 192 F courtney.cassard@nicholls.edu
CASSAT, DeAnna ... 636-584-6701 253 B deanna.cassat@eastcentral.edu
CASSEL, Kimberly, R ... 570-326-3761 392 W kcassel@pct.edu
CASSEL, Stephen ... 215-702-4243 380 A scassel@cairn.edu
CASSEL, Susie ... 214-333-6806 434 C susie@dbu.edu
CASSELL, Ryan ... 501-450-1362.. 19 E cassell@hendrix.edu
CASSELLS, Holly ... 210-829-3977 453 C cassells@uiwtx.edu
CASSENS, David ... 314-977-3095 259 F david.cassens@slu.edu
CASSENS, Treisa ... 714-484-7302.. 54 B tcassens@cypresscollege.edu
CASSIDY, Annamarie ... 610-892-1520 393 B acassidy@pit.edu
CASSIDY, Carleen ... 406-496-4249 265 A ccassidy@mtech.edu
CASSIDY, Dale ... 208-795-4266 131 F
CASSIDY, Derrah ... 803-790-7582 410 D cassidyd@midlandstech.edu
CASSIDY, Jane ... 225-578-5513 189 E jcassid@lsu.edu
CASSIDY, Joseph ... 630-942-2316 135 I cassidyj1180@cod.edu
CASSIDY, Joseph, L ... 207-741-5501 195 H jcassidy@smccme.edu
CASSIDY, Kimberly ... 610-526-5156 379 B president@brynmawr.edu
CASSIDY, Lisa ... 714-992-7803.. 51 B lcassidy@ketchum.edu
CASSIDY, Michael ... 312-341-3500 148 E mcassidy@roosevelt.edu
CASSIDY, Paul ... 650-738-7174.. 62 L cassidyp@smccd.edu
CASSIDY, Susan ... 516-323-3601 306 M scassidy@molloy.edu
CASSINELLI, Daniel ... 203-837-8680.. 86 B cassinellid@wcsu.edu
CASSIS, Lisa, A ... 859-257-5294 185 F lcassis@uky.edu
CASSITY, Kathy ... 503-838-8226 377 D cassityk@wou.edu
CASSONI, Jammie ... 567-661-2647 359 I jammie_cassoni@owens.edu
CASTADIO, Paula ... 559-278-6050.. 31 B pcastadio@csufresno.edu
CASTALDO, Annalisa ... 610-499-1112 402 G acastaldo@widener.edu
CASTALDO, Robert ... 214-638-0484 438 E
CASTANEDA, Alex ... 210-829-6071 453 C mcasta1@uiwtx.edu
CASTANEDA-CALLEROS, Russell ... 562-463-7268.. 58 L rcastanedacalleros@riohondo.edu
CASTANO, Beatriz ... 631-451-4435 321 C castanb@sunysuffolk.edu

CASTANO, Vincent .... 910-678-8535 334 E
castanov@faytechcc.edu
CASTANON, Miriam ...... 619-594-6298.. 33 D
castanon@sdsu.edu
CASTANOS, Elba .... 305-266-7678 104 A
e.castanos@miuniversity.edu
CASTANOS, Frank .... 760-245-4271.. 74 D
frank.castanos@vvc.edu
CASTAÑEDA, Monica .... 623-845-3053.. 13 C
monica.castaneda@gccaz.edu
CASTEEL, Matthew .... 918-631-2960 371 C
matthew-casteel@utulsa.edu
CASTEELE, Karen .... 540-831-5426 469 D
bov@radford.edu
CASTELBUONO, Audrey 269-471-6667 221 D
audreyc@andrews.edu
CASTELINO, Paul .... 740-593-1616 358 K
castelin@ohio.edu
CASTELLANO, Ana .... 787-622-8000 511 D
acastellano@pupr.edu
CASTELLANO, Cecilia .... 419-372-7803 348 G
ccast@bgsu.edu
CASTELLANO, Melissa .. 562-903-4883.. 27 A
melissa.c.castellano@biola.edu
CASTELLANOS, Grisel .... 787-878-5475 507 L
gcastellanos@arecibo.inter.edu
CASTELLANOS, Joshua .. 562-938-4343.. 48 F
jcastellanos@lbcc.edu
CASTELLAW, Joel .... 619-644-7155.. 44 E
joel.castellaw@gcccd.edu
CASTELLO, Sergio .... 704-233-8147 344 F
s.castello@wingate.edu
CASTELLOE, Stephen ..... 336-334-4822 335 A
srcastelloe@gtcc.edu
CASTENEDA, Debbie ...... 970-542-3140.. 81 N
debbie.casteneda@morgancc.edu
CASTER, Tia .... 281-649-3289 437 B
tcaster@hbu.edu
CASTERTON, Deanna ..... 563-387-1038 168 B
castde01@luther.edu
CASTETE, Ralynn, F ...... 337-475-5140 192 E
rcastete@mcneese.edu
CASTEÑEDA, Mari .... 413-545-2483 211 G
mari@comm.umass.edu
CASTIGLIONE,
Joseph, R .... 405-325-8208 370 K
jcastiglione@ou.edu
CASTIGLIONE, Thomas . 212-650-8150 293 D
tcastiglione@ccny.cuny.edu
CASTILAW, Timothy ...... 660-543-4113 260 G
castilaw@ucmo.edu
CASTILLA, Rafael .... 201-327-8877 277 F
rcastilla@eastwick.edu
CASTILLA, Sandra .... 518-262-4019 289 L
castils@amc.edu
CASTILLE, Laura .... 575-646-3635 287 C
castille@nmsu.edu
CASTILLO, Angie .... 972-780-3600 454 A
angie.castillo@untdallas.edu
CASTILLO, Carlos .... 305-348-2103 110 A
carlos.castillo8@fiu.edu
CASTILLO, Dale .... 785-309-3108 177 E
dale.castillo@salinatech.edu
CASTILLO, David .... 831-479-6213.. 27 D
dacastil@cabrillo.edu
CASTILLO, David .... 559-934-2166.. 74 N
davidcastillo2@whccd.edu
CASTILLO, Diana .... 787-779-2500 506 B
CASTILLO, Diana .... 254-526-1348 432 D
diana.castillo@ctcd.edu
CASTILLO, Elisa .... 978-542-6410 213 E
elisa.castillo@salemstate.edu
CASTILLO, Eric .... 817-515-1657 445 F
eric.castillo@tccd.edu
CASTILLO, Evelyn .... 787-891-0925 507 K
ecastillo@aguadilla.inter.edu
CASTILLO, Henry .... 718-862-7249 304 M
bookstore@manhattan.edu
CASTILLO, Jay .... 510-436-1648.. 45 E
jcastillo@hnu.edu
CASTILLO, JR., Juan, J . 956-326-2380 446 E
jjcastillo@tamiu.edu
CASTILLO, Katherine ..... 787-728-1515 513 D
katherine.castillo@sagrado.edu
CASTILLO, Keith .... 951-552-8720.. 27 G
kcastillo@calbaptist.edu
CASTILLO, Kelly .... 516-686-7902 308 I
kcasti08@nyit.edu
CASTILLO, Maggie .... 623-935-8839.. 13 A
maggie.castillo@estrellamountain.edu
CASTILLO, Mario .... 832-813-6655 439 C
mario.k.castillo@lonestar.edu
CASTILLO, Mayra .... 410-287-1043 198 E
mcastillo@cecil.edu
CASTILLO, Nicole .... 209-946-2496.. 71 E
ncastillo@pacific.edu
CASTILLO, Pio .... 818-364-7866.. 49 C
castilpg@lamission.edu
CASTILLO, Priscilla .... 915-747-5850 455 C
castillop@utep.edu
CASTILLO, Raul, V .... 818-947-2618.. 49 G
castilrv@lavc.edu
CASTILLO, Richard .... 301-891-4134 205 A
rcastillo@wau.edu
CASTILLO, Roy .... 661-362-3418.. 38 D
roy.castillo@canyons.edu
CASTILLO, Ruth .... 276-944-6754 466 L
rcastillo@ehc.edu
CASTILLO, Salvador ...... 541-737-8083 375 A
salvador.castillo@oregonstate.edu
CASTILLO, Toni .... 405-733-7498 369 E
tcastillo@rose.edu
CASTILLO-ALANIZ,
Jo Elda .... 361-593-2382 447 D
jcastillo-alaniz@tamuk.edu
CASTILLO CLARK,
Evette .... 925-631-4238.. 59 I
ecc4@stmarys-ca.edu
CASTILLO-FRICK, Iliana . 305-237-0294 104 E
ifrick@mdc.edu
CASTILLO-GARRISON,
Estella .... 307-675-0819 501 G
egarrison@sheridan.edu
CASTILLON, Carrie .... 209-478-0800.. 45 I
carrie.castillon@humphreys.edu
CASTLE, Ashley .... 919-301-6500.. 93 H
CASTLE, Carey .... 606-451-6602 182 G
carey.castle@kctcs.edu
CASTLE, Cathy .... 620-947-3121 177 I
CASTLE, Clinton .... 218-683-8600 240 B
clinton.castle@northlandcollege.edu
CASTLE, Lyle .... 208-282-7880 131 G
castlyle@isu.edu
CASTLE, Tom .... 319-363-1323 168 F
tcastle@mtmercy.edu
CASTLEBERRY, Joseph .. 425-889-4202 481 H
joseph.castleberry@northwestu.edu
CASTLEBERRY, Phillip ... 585-475-7721 312 F
pdcdar@rit.edu
CASTLEBURY, Lisa .... 812-357-6515 161 A
lcastlebury@saintmeinrad.edu
CASTLEMAN, Louanna .. 910-678-0141 334 E
castleml@faytechcc.edu
CASTLES, Steve .... 661-253-3071.. 28 G
scastles@calarts.edu
CASTONGUAY, Sharon .. 860-685-3377.. 90 B
scastonguay@wesleyan.edu
CASTOR, Lisa .... 215-887-5511 402 E
lcastor@wts.edu
CASTORENA, Christina .. 425-640-1668 480 A
christina.castorena@edcc.edu
CASTREE, John .... 405-682-1611 367 D
john.w.castree@occc.edu
CASTRIOTTA, Sue .... 603-358-2112 274 H
scastrio@keene.edu
CASTRO, Adam .... 914-674-7548 306 C
acastro@mercy.edu
CASTRO, Cynthia .... 208-885-6307 132 F
cynthiacastro@uidaho.edu
CASTRO, Daisy .... 787-753-6335 507 D
dcastro@icprjc.edu
CASTRO, Evelyn .... 718-804-8805 294 G
ecastro@mec.cuny.edu
CASTRO, Francia, L .... 212-694-1000 291 J
fcastro@boricuacollege.edu
CASTRO, Ida, L .... 570-504-9647 384 B
icastro@som.geisinger.edu
CASTRO, Joanne .... 361-593-3085 447 D
joanne.castro@tamuk.edu
CASTRO, Jose .... 787-250-1912 508 D
jlcastro@intermetro.edu
CASTRO, Joseph, I .... 562-951-4000.. 29 H
csu-chancellor@calstate.edu
CASTRO, Juan, C .... 787-743-3038 509 N
jcastro@sanjuanbautista.edu
CASTRO, Kaye .... 239-687-5343.. 95 L
kcastro@avemarialaw.edu
CASTRO, Mandy .... 817-257-7490 448 F
m.castro@tcu.edu
CASTRO, Manny .... 670-237-6772 505 A
manny.castro@marianas.edu
CASTRO, Maria, V .... 562-860-2451.. 35 H
mvcastro@cerritos.edu
CASTRO, Monaco .... 561-237-7035 103 W
mocastro@lynn.edu
CASTRO, Rosalinda .... 325-942-2043 450 E
rosalinda.castro@angelo.edu
CASTRO, Roz .... 630-953-3681 134 F
rcastro@chamberlain.edu
CASTRO, Sarah .... 202-624-1426 485 A
smcastro@uw.edu
CASTRO, Shirley .... 406-604-4300 262 I
s.castro@apollos.edu
CASTRO, Toni .... 206-934-3669 483 B
toni.castro@seattlecolleges.edu
CASTRO-DUARTE, Betsy 915-747-5640 455 C
bcastro@utep.edu
CASTRO-QUIRINO,
Sonya .... 806-743-3949 451 A
sonya.castro@ttuhsc.edu
CASTRUITA, Javier .... 408-741-2042.. 75 C
javier.castruita@wvm.edu
CASUCCIO, Anthony ...... 716-896-0700 324 E
acasuccio@villa.edu
CATALANA, Paul, V .... 864-455-9808 413 F
paul.catalana@prismahealth.org
CATALANO, Francesca .. 802-468-1214 463 E
francesca.catalano@castleton.edu
CATALANO, Philip .... 315-279-5252 303 G
pcatalano@keuka.edu
CATALANO, Steven .... 718-489-5309 313 E
scatalano@sfc.edu
CATALDI, Amy, E .... 405-208-5446 367 E
acataldi@okcu.edu
CATALDI, Jennifer .... 317-738-8256 155 D
jcataldi@franklincollege.edu
CATALDO, Adrienne ...... 803-938-3906 413 G
cataldo@uscsumter.edu
CATALFAMO, Kevin .... 856-351-2701 283 B
kcatalfamo@salemcc.edu
CATALLOZZI, Lori, A ..... 617-228-2048 214 C
lacatallozzi@bhcc.mass.edu
CATANESE, Matthew ..... 313-664-7496 222 H
mcatanese@collegeforcreativestudies.
edu
CATANIA, Colette .... 615-230-3204 425 E
colette.catania@volstate.edu
CATANIA, Nancy, M ...... 610-566-1776 403 B
ncatania@williamson.edu
CATANZARO, Jim .... 847-735-6137 142 A
catanzaro@lakeforest.edu
CATARUZOLO,
Aleksandra .... 212-220-8011 293 A
acataruzolo@bmcc.cuny.edu
CATCHING,
Christopher, C .... 609-652-4225 283 E
christopher.catching@stockton.edu
CATCHINGS, Robert ...... 202-806-6700.. 92 F
rcatchings@howard.edu
CATE, Fred, H .... 812-856-2096 156 F
fcate@iu.edu
CATE, Fred, H .... 812-856-2096 156 G
vpr@iu.edu
CATE, Patrick .... 603-366-5281 272 K
pcate@ccsnh.edu
CATE, Richard, H .... 802-656-0219 463 A
richard.cate@uvm.edu
CATERINICCHIO,
Madeline .... 732-906-2519 278 G
mcaterinicchio@middlesexcc.edu
CATES, Carl .... 870-972-3973.. 17 E
ccates@astate.edu
CATES, Chris .... 423-585-2618 425 F
chris.cates@ws.edu
CATES, Jared .... 417-255-7233 256 H
jaredcated@missouristate.edu
CATES, Jo .... 312-369-8781 136 D
jcates@colum.edu
CATH, Tom .... 219-464-5005 162 D
tom.cath@valpo.edu
CATHCART, Chris .... 704-330-6647 333 D
chris.cathcart@cpcc.edu
CATHELINE, Jim .... 724-964-8811 391 B
jcatheline@ncstrades.edu
CATHELYN, Lisa .... 414-382-6352 491 F
lisa.cathelyn@alverno.edu
CATHER, Darci .... 217-234-5253 142 C
dcather@lakelandcollege.edu
CATHEY, Edie .... 405-382-9717 369 F
CATHEY, Imogene .... 724-552-4499 398 C
icathey@setonhill.edu
CATHEY, Joyce .... 972-524-3341 445 B
jcath@swcc.edu
CATHEY, Patrice, A .... 716-878-4055 317 F
catheypc@mail.buffalostate.edu
CATHEY, Ron .... 318-257-4336 192 D
rcathey@latech.edu
CATHEY, Vernesha .... 972-524-3341 445 B
swccactivties@mail.com
CATLETT, Darlene .... 570-585-9203 381 B
dcatlett@clarkssummitu.edu
CATLETT, Deborrah, L ... 859-246-6810 181 F
deborrah.catlett@kctcs.edu
CATLETT, Jennifer .... 865-471-3530 418 E
jcatlett@cn.edu
CATLETT, Nick .... 217-443-8864 136 G
ncatlett@dacc.edu
CATLIN, Carter .... 615-963-5319 426 A
ccatlin@tnstate.edu
CATLIN, Michele, E .... 812-221-1714 162 E
michelecatlin@vbc.edu
CATO, Amie .... 903-785-7661 441 D
acato@parisjc.edu
CATO, Jim .... 937-766-7610 349 E
catoj@cedarville.edu
CATO, Michael .... 207-725-3050 194 C
mcato@bowdoin.edu
CATON, Brock, E .... 207-778-7033 196 I
brock.caton@maine.edu
CATON, Claire .... 713-646-1799 443 I
ccaton@stcl.edu
CATON, Lisa .... 979-627-0286 431 H
lisa.caton@blinn.edu
CATON, Rebecca, A .... 630-515-6190 144 F
rcaton@midwestern.edu
CATON, Rhonda .... 479-788-7073.. 21 G
rhonda.caton@uafs.edu
CATON, Sheron .... 325-794-4530 432 I
sheron.caton@cisco.edu
CATONE, Christopher, J 610-921-7581 377 G
ccatone@albright.edu
CATOTA, Claudia .... 661-654-2137.. 30 B
ccatota@csub.edu
CATRON, Arielle .... 717-477-1790 395 B
agcatron@ship.edu
CATRON, Kathleen .... 907-474-7721.. 10 A
kacatron@alaska.edu
CATRON, Susan, D .... 530-754-9158.. 69 B
sdcatron@ucdavis.edu
CATRON-WOOD,
Rhonda, K .... 276-223-4772 476 A
rcatronwood@wcc.vccs.edu
CATT, Helen .... 229-430-3506 114 I
hcatt@albanytech.edu
CATTANI, Jessica .... 213-624-1200.. 42 B
jcattani@fidm.edu
CATTANI, Kara .... 801-422-3035 458 H
kara_cattani@byu.edu
CATTERSON, Anna .... 309-268-8297 138 H
anna.catterson@heartland.edu
CATTOLICA, Carolee ...... 707-256-7161.. 53 E
ccattolica@napavalley.edu
CATTON, Heather .... 936-468-5597 445 E
hcatton@sfasu.edu
CATTOOR, Chad, A .... 314-505-7304 252 A
cattoorc@csl.edu
CATULLO, LeeAnna .... 863-680-4108 100 H
lcatullo@flsouthern.edu
CATULLO, Patrick .... 540-654-2489 471 N
pcatullo@umw.edu
CAUBLE, Christie .... 828-641-0450 327 B
caublecl@brevard.edu
CAUCE, Ana Mari .... 206-543-5010 485 A
pres@uw.edu
CAUDILL, Alicia, D .... 843-953-5522 408 C
caudillad@cofc.edu
CAUDILL, Brenda .... 859-622-6327 180 E
brenda.caudill2@eku.edu
CAUDILL, Helene .... 209-667-3407.. 33 B
hcaudill@csustan.edu
CAUDILL, Sarah .... 859-985-3037 179 I
caudillsar@berea.edu
CAUDLE, Grainger .... 828-689-1127 331 C
gcaudle@mhu.edu
CAUDLE, Mary Anne ..... 252-789-0280 335 H
maryanne.caudle@martincc.edu
CAUDLE, Patricia, M ..... 909-748-8171.. 72 F
pat_caudle@redlands.edu
CAUGHELL, Leslie .... 757-233-8853 477 C
lcaughell@vwu.edu
CAULEY, Cleon .... 302-857-7827.. 90 E
ccauley@desu.edu
CAULEY, Phil .... 828-227-7317 343 E
cauley@wcu.edu
CAULFIELD, Julene .... 914-323-7285 305 B
julene.caulfield@mville.edu
CAULFIELD, Kim .... 267-341-3481 385 J
kcaulfield@holyfamily.edu
CAUSBY, Cory .... 828-227-3142 343 E
causby@wcu.edu
CAUSEY, Bruce .... 256-306-2569.... 1 F
bruce.causey@calhoun.edu

CHADWICK, Becky .... 313-593-5030 231 I
bjch@umich.edu
CHADWICK, Gregory ..... 252-737-7703 341 A
chadwickg@ecu.edu
CHADWICK, Scott .... 314-529-9681 255 B
schadwick@maryville.edu
CHADWICK, Steven .... 607-255-5070 297 F
CHADWICK, Susan .... 610-526-7922 379 B
schadwick@brynmawr.edu
CHAE, Ki Byung .... 910-521-6352 343 B
kibyung.chae@uncp.edu
CHAFFEE, Brandy .... 218-281-8434 244 A
brandy@umn.edu
CHAFFEE, Cynthia .... 312-567-3084 140 A
cchaffee@iit.edu
CHAFFEE, Julie, A .... 508-929-5000 213 G
CHAFFEE, Reta .... 603-513-1350 274 G
reta.chaffee@granite.edu
CHAFFIN, Doug .... 580-327-8645 367 A
dechaffin@nwosu.edu
CHAFFIN, Jason .... 910-362-7275 332 H
jchaffin@cfcc.edu
CHAGOYA, Felix .... 530-541-4660.. 47 E
CHAH, Namy .... 213-325-2760.. 52 C
registrar@meritu.edu
CHAHAL, Monica .... 559-325-5214.. 67 A
monica.chahal@cloviscollege.edu
CHAHAL, Sonia .... 415-565-4788.. 69 C
chahalsonia@uchastings.edu
CHAHIN, T. Jaime .... 512-245-3333 450 C
tc03@txstate.edu
CHAHINO, Michael .... 847-214-7161 137 F
mchahino@elgin.edu
CHAI, Lin .... 407-888-8689 100 A
lchai@fcim.edu
CHAIDEZ, Beatriz, S ...... 408-223-6704.. 62 F
beatriz.chaidez@sjeccd.edu
CHAIMOV, John .... 319-399-8594 164 F
jchaimov@coe.edu
CHAISSON, Rebecca ..... 504-286-5469 191 C
rchaisson@suno.edu
CHAJES, Michael, J ...... 302-831-6756.. 91 C
chajes@udel.edu
CHAKA, Wendi .... 508-999-8711 212 A
wchaka@umassd.edu
CHAKRABARTI,
Amitabha .... 785-532-6900 175 C
amitc@ksu.edu
CHAKRABARTI, Parth .... 508-856-5610 212 C
parth@umassmed.edu
CHAKRABORTY, David .. 781-283-2474 219 E
dchakraborty@wellesley.edu
CHALENBURG, Mike ...... 501-279-4041.. 19 C
chalenburg@harding.edu
CHALEUNPHONH,
Seuth .... 812-941-2319 157 F
schaleun@ius.edu
CHALFONTE, Barb .... 413-545-0941 211 G
bchalfonte@umass.edu
CHALK, Andrew .... 502-776-1443 184 F
achalk@simmonscollegeky.edu
CHALK, Gregg .... 508-541-1668 209 A
gchalk@dean.edu
CHALMERS, John .... 617-451-0010 217 F
CHALMERS, Scott .... 773-256-0685 143 F
schalmer@lstc.edu
CHALOUX, Matthew, P . 561-237-7699 103W
mchaloux@lynn.edu
CHAMARTHI, Raju .... 844-872-8680.. 73 A
CHAMBALA, Bryan .... 607-844-8222 322 D
chambab@tompkinscortland.edu
CHAMBERLAIN, Brad .... 563-387-1627 168 B
brad.chamberlain@luther.edu
CHAMBERLAIN,
Jonathan .... 704-216-3765 337 F
jonathan.chamberlain@rccc.edu
CHAMBERLAIN, Kathy ... 765-998-5222 161 C
kathy_chamberlain@taylor.edu
CHAMBERLAIN, Kendra 619-201-8700.. 60 G
kendra.chamberlain@sdcc.edu
CHAMBERLAIN,
LaShanda .... 228-897-3886 247 E
lashanda.chamberlain@mgccc.edu
CHAMBERLAIN,
MaryEllen .... 518-891-2915 310 A
mchamberlain@nccc.edu
CHAMBERLAIN,
Michelle .... 909-621-8096.. 37 D
CHAMBERLAIN,
Michelle .... 909-621-8111.. 37 D
CHAMBERLAIN, Tina ..... 206-726-5197 479 E
tchamberlain@cornish.edu
CHAMBERLIN, Brian ..... 312-369-8669 136 D
bchamberlin@colum.edu
CHAMBERLIN,
Christopher .... 212-353-4099 297 E
CHAMBERLIN, Lisa .... 509-527-5145 485 B
lisa.chamberlin@wwcc.edu
CHAMBERLIN, Mona ..... 918-631-2656 371 C
mona-chamberlin@utulsa.edu
CHAMBERS, Amy .... 309-341-7200 141 G
adchambers@knox.edu
CHAMBERS, Andy .... 314-392-2201 256 E
andy.chambers@mobap.edu
CHAMBERS, Ben .... 678-664-0525 128 A
ben.chambers@westgatech.edu
CHAMBERS, Bryan .... 817-722-1651 438 G
bryan.chambers@tku.edu
CHAMBERS, Cynthia ...... 562-988-2278.. 25 L
clchambers@auhs.edu
CHAMBERS, Danielle .... 618-235-2700 150 E
CHAMBERS, Eric .... 573-651-2249 259 H
echambers@semo.edu
CHAMBERS,
Franklin, D .... 607-436-2513 316 F
franklin.chambers@oneonta.edu
CHAMBERS, Jamila, J ... 323-259-2500.. 54 I
CHAMBERS, Jason .... 828-835-4297 338 E
jchambers@tricountycc.edu
CHAMBERS, Jeffrey .... 903-434-8106 440 G
jchambers@ntcc.edu
CHAMBERS, Jessica ...... 937-778-8600 352 D
CHAMBERS, John 561-237-7973 103W
jchambers@lynn.edu
CHAMBERS, Karen .... 574-284-4594 160 I
kchambers@saintmarys.edu
CHAMBERS, Kathleen .... 413-796-2080 220 A
kathleen.chambers@wne.edu
CHAMBERS, Kemba ...... 334-420-4216.... 3 H
kchambers@trenholmstate.edu
CHAMBERS, Marcine .... 254-526-1472 432 D
marcine.chambers@ctcd.edu
CHAMBERS, Melody ..... 660-626-2164 250 A
melodychambers@atsu.edu
CHAMBERS, Robert .... 617-879-7000 213 B
CHAMBERS, Robert .... 617-266-1400 206 H
rchambers2@berklee.edu
CHAMBERS, Sarah .... 203-285-2132.. 86 E
sarahchambers@gatewayct.edu
CHAMBERS, Shanna ..... 828-398-7178 332 B
shannarchambers@abtech.edu
CHAMBERS, Yohna .... 817-257-7790 448 F
y.chambers@tcu.edu
CHAMBERS-KLATT,
Elizabeth .... 309-556-3849 140 F
echamber@iwu.edu
CHAMBERS-TAUBE,
Jennifer .... 562-947-8755.. 65 I
jenniferchamberstaube@scuhs.edu
CHAMBLAS, Dimitri .... 661-253-7898.. 28 G
dchamblas@calarts.edu
CHAMBLEE, Marquita ..... 313-577-2200 232 K
mtchamblee@wayne.edu
CHAMBLESS, Greta .... 334-244-3750.... 4 E
gchamble@aum.edu
CHAMBLESS, Kimberly .. 205-391-2298.... 3 E
kim.chambless@sheltonstate.edu
CHAMBLISS, Chandra .... 334-727-8503.... 7 D
cchambliss@tuskegee.edu
CHAMBLISS, Kevin .... 254-710-3763 431 E
kevin_chambliss@baylor.edu
CHAMBLISS, Mary .... 423-323-0233 425 A
mjchambliss@northeaststate.edu
CHAMBLISS, Myron .... 803-738-7173 410 D
chamblissm@midlandstech.edu
CHAMNESS, Kayla .... 661-824-2977.. 53 H
kchamness@ntps.edu
CHAMP, Karli .... 716-338-1046 303 A
karlichamp@mail.sunyjcc.edu
CHAMPA, Kristin .... 317-931-2310 154 G
kchampa@cts.edu
CHAMPAGNE, Gerald .... 734-462-4400 230 G
gchampag@schoolcraft.edu
CHAMPAGNE, Michael .. 225-752-4233 187 D
mchampagne@iticollege.edu
CHAMPION, Belinda ..... 931-393-1765 424 F
bchampion@mscc.edu
CHAMPION, Grace .... 828-898-8828 330 E
championg@lmc.edu
CHAMPION, Laura .... 616-526-6187 222 C
ldc4@calvin.edu
CHAMPION, Marion ...... 760-346-8041.. 38 E
mchampion@collegeofthedesert.edu
CHAMPLIN, Sheila .... 843-792-2691 410 C
champlin@musc.edu
CHAMPOLI, John, F ...... 717-361-3736 383 C
champolij@etown.edu
CHAMRA, Louay, M ...... 248-370-2217 229 I
chamra@oakland.edu
CHAMSAZ, Amir .... 410-706-3802 203 A
achamsaz@umaryland.edu
CHAN, Andy .... 336-758-4662 344 C
achan@wfu.edu
CHAN, Bill .... 614-947-6054 352 J
bill.chan@franklin.edu
CHAN, Caleb, K .... 517-750-1200 231 C
cchan@arbor.edu
CHAN, Claudia .... 718-482-5005 294 F
cichan@lagcc.cuny.edu
CHAN, Emily .... 719-389-6679.. 78 I
echan@coloradocollege.edu
CHAN, Eva .... 718-270-6487 294 G
echan@mec.cuny.edu
CHAN, Genevieve .... 360-438-4332 482 I
gchan@stmartin.edu
CHAN, Gilen .... 718-260-4981 295 A
gchan@citytech.cuny.edu
CHAN, Hokeung, C .... 626-917-9482.. 36 G
cliffc@cesna.edu
CHAN, Juliet .... 510-549-4719.. 66 G
registrar@sksm.edu
CHAN, Kara .... 412-521-6200 397 C
kara.chan@rosedaletech.org
CHAN, Michael, L .... 671-735-5573 504 D
michael.chan@guamcc.edu
CHAN, Paul, H .... 303-871-4646.. 84 E
phchan@du.edu
CHAN, Regina .... 212-517-0501 305 E
rchan@mmm.edu
CHAN, Yau-Gene .... 888-488-4968.. 46 F
CHANCE, Bill .... 207-221-4373 197 E
wchance@une.edu
CHANCE, Chelsey .... 318-797-5364 190 A
chelsea.chance@lsus.edu
CHANCE, Dayne .... 908-709-7089 284 D
chance@ucc.edu
CHANCE, Katie .... 256-551-5214.... 2 E
katie.chance@drakestate.edu
CHANCE, Kenneth, B ..... 216-368-3266 349 D
kenneth.b.chance@case.edu
CHANCE, Mary .... 903-693-1142 441 C
mchance@panola.edu
CHANCE, Terri .... 219-980-6983 157 C
tschance@iun.edu
CHANCE MERCURIUS,
Karen 585-275-1710 323M
karen.mercurius@rochester.edu
CHANCELLOR, Ashley ... 314-838-8858 261 F
achancellor@ugst.edu
CHANCELLOR, Beth .... 573-882-2434 260 I
chancellorb@umsystem.edu
CHANCELLOR, Beth, C .. 573-882-2434 261 A
chancellorb@missouri.edu
CHANCELLOR, John ...... 979-830-4590 431 H
john.chancellor@blinn.edu
CHANCEY, Debra .... 251-442-2332.... 8 C
dchancey@umobile.edu
CHAND, Mihir .... 913-288-7330 175 B
mchand@kckcc.edu
CHANDI, Balbir .... 661-362-5416.. 38 D
balbir.chandi@canyons.edu
CHANDLER, Brandon .... 856-225-6471 281 G
brandonc@scarletmail.rutgers.edu
CHANDLER, Chris .... 540-365-4287 467 B
cchandler@ferrum.edu
CHANDLER, Cullen .... 570-321-4173 389 B
chandler@lycoming.edu
CHANDLER, Debbie .... 318-675-5341 189 I
debbie.chandler@lsuhs.edu
CHANDLER, Derrall .... 619-388-3537.. 60 I
dchandle@sdccd.edu
CHANDLER, Elizabeth .... 304-384-5366 489 J
echandler@concord.edu
CHANDLER, Erica .... 901-572-2452 418 A
erica.chandler@baptistu.edu
CHANDLER, G. Thomas 803-777-5032 413 A
tchandler@sc.edu
CHANDLER, Joe .... 205-226-4667.... 4 F
jchandle@bsc.edu
CHANDLER, Kevin .... 586-445-7244 227 B
chandlerk85@macomb.edu
CHANDLER, Kim .... 509-527-5288 486 B
chandlkc@whitman.edu
CHANDLER, Kimberly .... 502-863-7057 180 H
kimberly_chandler@georgetowncollege.edu
CHANDLER, Kirk .... 336-334-4822 335 A
kdchandler@gtcc.edu
CHANDLER, Kristin .... 318-342-5327 193 C
morris@ulm.edu
CHANDLER, Legail, P ... 314-362-4930 262 A
legail_chandler@wustl.edu
CHANDLER, Lucinda ..... 937-481-2346 364 A
lucinda_chandler@wilmington.edu
CHANDLER, Marissa ..... 931-221-6851 417 H
chandlerm@apsu.edu
CHANDLER, Mary .... 315-445-4300 303 I
richermm@lemoyne.edu
CHANDLER, Morgan ..... 205-853-1200.... 2 G
morgan.chandler@jeffersonstate.edu
CHANDLER, Navarro ..... 541-956-7030 376 A
tchandler@roguecc.edu
CHANDLER, Norma .... 602-787-7073.. 13 E
norma.chandler@paradisevalley.edu
CHANDLER, Prentice ..... 931-221-7511 417 H
chandlerp@apsu.edu
CHANDLER, Rebecca ..... 310-338-2723.. 51 A
rchandler@lmu.edu
CHANDLER, Roger .... 303-963-3341.. 78 H
rchandler@ccu.edu
CHANDLER, Scott .... 208-467-8550 132 E
scottchandler@nnu.edu
CHANDLER, Sean .... 406-353-2607 262 H
schandler@ancollege.edu
CHANDLER, Shelly .... 352-638-9710.. 96 B
schandler@beaconcollege.edu
CHANDLER, Susan .... 607-962-9000 320 C
schandl2@corning-cc.edu
CHANDLER, Todd .... 813-988-5131.. 99 R
chandlert@floridacollege.edu
CHANDLER, Vernita .... 256-469-7333.... 5 H
reg@hbc1.edu
CHANDO, Kristen .... 610-499-4142 402 G
kmchando@widener.edu
CHANDO, Michael .... 856-415-2282 281 D
mchando@rcsj.edu
CHANDRAKASAN,
Anantha .... 617-253-3291 216 B
CHANDRASEKAR,
Edwin .... 847-635-1876 146 G
echandra@oakton.edu
CHANEN, Dan .... 608-890-0291 495 C
dchanen@uwsa.edu
CHANETSA, Bernadette .. 800-477-2254.. 29 G
bchanetsa@calsouthern.edu
CHANEY, Carmela .... 323-856-7698.. 25 G
cchaney@afi.com
CHANEY, Christi .... 605-882-5284 415 D
christi.chaney@lakeareatech.edu
CHANEY, Jayn .... 641-269-3200 166 G
chaneyj@grinnell.edu
CHANEY, Jeff .... 859-281-3690 185 C
jchaney@transy.edu
CHANEY, Kevin .... 740-392-6868 356 G
kevin.chaney@mvnu.edu
CHANEY, Matthew, C .... 937-775-2501 364 E
matthew.chaney@wright.edu
CHANEY, Rob .... 850-201-6085 112 C
rob.chaney@tcc.fl.edu
CHANEY, Susan .... 505-438-8884 288 F
susan@acupuncturecollege.edu
CHANFRAU, Gersende .. 401-456-8392 405 A
gchanfrau@ric.edu
CHANG, Charles .... 312-893-7245 137 H
cchang@erikson.edu
CHANG, Chaw-ye .... 610-436-3043 395 D
cchang@wcupa.edu
CHANG, Christopher ..... 845-687-5096 323 H
changc@sunyulster.edu
CHANG, Dean .... 301-314-8121 202 H
deanc@umd.edu
CHANG, Diane, T .... 510-464-3294.. 57 B
dtchang@peralta.edu
CHANG, Eun-Woo .... 703-323-3087 474 F
echang@nvcc.edu
CHANG, Frank .... 213-740-4623.. 73 D
fjc@usc.edu
CHANG, Garret .... 808-518-4791 129 B
garretchang@pacrim.edu
CHANG, George .... 908-737-3600 278 E
gchang@kean.edu
CHANG, Jimmy .... 727-341-4305 107 E
chang.jimmy@spcollege.edu
CHANG, Jin .... 626-395-2908.. 28 J
jin.chang@caltech.edu
CHANG, John .... 503-594-6186 372 C
john.chang@clackamas.edu
CHANG, Ling Ling .... 516-739-1545 308 F
library@nyctcm.edu
CHANG, Ly .... 425-235-2352 482 H
lchang@rtc.edu

CHAVEZ, Todd .... 813-974-1642 111 C
tchavez@usf.edu
CHAVEZ, Vanessa .... 785-442-6016 174 F
vchavez@highlandcc.edu
CHAVEZ-SILVA, Monica 641-269-3900 166 G
chavezsm@grinnell.edu
CHAVIRA, Melissa .... 575-646-4571 287 C
chavira@nmsu.edu
CHAVIRA, Rejoice .... 909-389-3456.. 60 E
rchavira@craftonhills.edu
CHAVIS, Gordon .... 407-823-3004 110 E
gordon.chavis@ucf.edu
CHAVIS, Keesha .... 610-499-1301 402 G
kchavis@widener.edu
CHAVIS, Kimberly .... 847-925-6507 138 G
kchavis@harpercollege.edu
CHAW, Debbie .... 510-885-3803.. 31 A
debbie.chaw@csueastbay.edu
CHAWANA, John .... 816-604-1160 255 C
john.chawana@mcckc.edu
CHAWGO, Rebecca .... 425-564-3061 477 J
rebecca.chawgo@bellevuecollege.edu
CHAY, Su Chung .... 714-527-0691.. 41 J
CHAYA, Patricia .... 585-343-0055 300 F
pechaya@genesee.edu
CHAYKIN, Rachelle .... 610-892-1528 393 B
rchaykin@pit.edu
CHAZHUR, Bess .... 914-594-2730 309 B
bchazhur@nymc.edu
CHEAGLE, Dorothy, S ... 803-934-3227 410 G
dcheagle@morris.edu
CHEAK, Laura .... 501-686-2901.. 21 E
lcheak@uasys.edu
CHEAL, Sheryl .... 617-732-2880 216 D
sheryl.cheal@mcphs.edu
CHEARO, David .... 508-793-8837 208 C
dchearo@clarku.edu
CHEASTY, Michelle .... 567-200-6829 353 B
michellecheasty@globaltech.edu
CHEATEM, Michelle ...... 410-617-5171 200 B
mlcheatem@loyola.edu
CHEATHAM,
Amberdawn .... 410-777-2653 197 G
acheatham@aacc.edu
CHEATHAM, Judy, B ..... 931-363-9823 427 E
jbcheat@utsouthern.edu
CHEATHAM, Kelly .... 214-887-5370 435 F
kcheatham@dts.edu
CHEATHAM, Laura .... 773-907-4365 135 C
lcheatham2@ccc.edu
CHECA, Lorena .... 760-750-4056.. 33 A
lcheca@csusm.edu
CHECKOVICH, Peter, G . 304-260-4380 488 C
pcheckov@blueridgectc.edu
CHEDESTER, W, P .... 304-293-3136 490 E
CHEE, Debbie .... 253-879-2640 484 G
dchee@pugetsound.edu
CHEEK, Annesa .... 320-308-5017 241 A
annesa.cheek@sctcc.edu
CHEEK, Crystal .... 580-745-2470 369 G
ccheek@se.edu
CHEEK, Philip .... 360-688-2361 482 I
philip.cheek@stmartin.edu
CHEEKS, James .... 714-712-7900.. 46 B
CHEERS, Karen .... 276-739-2561 475 F
kcheers@vhcc.edu
CHEEVER, Rex .... 620-665-3382 174 G
cheeverr@hutchcc.edu
CHEFFER, Sandra .... 479-964-0821.. 18 C
scheffer@atu.edu
CHEIKEN, Danielle .... 415-503-6307.. 61 D
dcheiken@sfcm.edu
CHEIN, Zalman .... 718-774-5050 322 B
CHELBERG, Gene .... 415-405-3728.. 33 E
chelberg@sfsu.edu
CHELL, Travis, L .... 423-652-6368 420 F
tlchell@king.edu
CHELLADURAI,
Benjamin .... 832-252-4616 432 L
benjamin.chelladurai@cbshouston.edu
CHELLMAN, Laura, G .... 715-836-5954 495 E
chellmlg@uwec.edu
CHELNICK, Robert .... 773-975-1295 494 A
CHELONIS, Nicole .... 978-665-3354 212 E
ncheloni@fitchburgstate.edu
CHELSEN, Paul, O .... 630-752-5026 153 C
paul.chelsen@wheaton.edu
CHELSTROM, Gina .... 323-265-3746.. 48 J
chelstg@elac.edu
CHEMBARS, Joanie .... 706-864-1838 127 A
joanie.chembars@ung.edu
CHEMERINSKY, Erwin .... 510-642-6483.. 69 A
echemerinsky@law.berkeley.edu
CHEMISHANOVA,
Marieta .... 973-596-3602 279 E
marieta.p.chemishanova@njit.edu
CHEN, Allan .... 661-255-1050.. 28 G
achen@calarts.edu
CHEN, Becca .... 206-934-5479 483 C
rebecca.chen@seattlecolleges.edu
CHEN, Bill .... 626-571-8811.. 73 E
billchen@uwest.edu
CHEN, Chau-Kuang ...... 615-327-6848 421 D
ckchen@mmc.edu
CHEN, Chunju .... 978-542-2046 213 E
chunju.chen@salemstate.edu
CHEN, Elsa, Y .... 408-551-7055.. 63 B
echen@scu.edu
CHEN, I .... 650-508-3587.. 54 G
ichen@ndnu.edu
CHEN, Jane .... 212-472-1500 309 D
info@nysid.edu
CHEN, Judy .... 718-990-1428 313 G
chenr@stjohns.edu
CHEN, Julie .... 978-934-2226 212 B
julie_chen@uml.edu
CHEN, Letty .... 626-448-0023.. 46 G
CHEN, Liana .... 408-260-0208.. 42 E
accountant@fivebranches.edu
CHEN, Liana .... 408-345-2633.. 42 F
accountant@fivebranches.edu
CHEN, Linda .... 574-520-4183 157 E
lchen@iusb.edu
CHEN, Lisa .... 401-874-4638 405 E
lchen@uri.edu
CHEN, Luke .... 626-289-7719.. 24 H
lchen@amu.edu
CHEN, Meghan .... 909-274-5140.. 52 J
mchen@mtsac.edu
CHEN, Meng .... 660-543-4218 260 G
mchen@ucmo.edu
CHEN, Oliver .... 573-341-4011 261 D
chenhs@mst.edu
CHEN, Shaw .... 401-874-4339 405 E
schen@uri.edu
CHEN, Stephen .... 415-338-7348.. 33 E
stephenchen@sfsu.edu
CHEN, Victoria .... 817-257-5169 448 F
v.chen@tcu.edu
CHEN, Vivian .... 503-821-1266 374 I
vivian.chen@oit.edu
CHEN, Wen Huei .... 512-444-8082 448 H
wchen@thsu.edu
CHEN, Xiangming .... 860-297-5170.. 89 B
xiangming.chen@trincoll.edu
CHEN, Yanping .... 703-516-0035 471 M
yanping.chen@umtweb.edu
CHEN, Yemeng .... 516-739-1545 308 F
president@nyctcm.edu
CHEN, Ze (Wade) .... 812-888-4156 162 F
zchen@vinu.edu
CHEN MAHONEY,
Chris .... 253-589-6004 478 J
chris.mahoney@cptc.edu
CHEN-MENICHINI,
Desiree .... 630-617-3033 137 G
chend@elmhurst.edu
CHENAIL, Ronald, J ...... 954-262-5796 105 A
ron@nova.edu
CHENARD, Susan .... 203-285-2000.. 86 E
CHENEY, Austin, C .... 217-581-3526 137 E
acheney@eiu.edu
CHENEY, John .... 413-542-2331 205 G
jtcheney@amherst.edu
CHENEY, Victor .... 904-819-6213.. 99 E
vcheney@flagler.edu
CHENG, Debbie .... 408-260-0208.. 42 E
daomassociate@fivebranches.edu
CHENG, Emily .... 405-945-3385 368 C
emily.cheng@okstate.edu
CHENG, Judy .... 714-895-8382.. 38 A
jcheng@gwc.cccd.edu
CHENG, Michael .... 305-919-4506 110 A
michael.cheng@fiu.edu
CHENG, Renee .... 206-616-2442 485 A
rycheng@uw.edu
CHENG, Tsai-En .... 253-833-9111 480 I
tcheng@greenriver.edu
CHENG, Weili .... 203-432-1940.. 90 C
weili.cheng@yale.edu
CHENG-LEVINE, Jia-Yi .. 661-362-5806.. 38 D
jia-yi.cheng-levine@canyons.edu
CHENIER, Jessie .... 413-265-2288 208 E
chenierj@elms.edu
CHENKIN, David .... 212-353-4122 297 E
CHENOWETH,
Candace, A .... 262-472-1592 497 D
chenowec@uww.edu
CHENOWETH, Gregg, A 815-939-5221 147 A
gachenoweth@olivet.edu
CHENOWETH, John .... 262-472-1672 497 D
chenowej@uww.edu
CHENTLAND, Elizabeth .. 773-256-0704 143 F
elizabeth.chentland@lstc.edu
CHEOKAS, Gaynor .... 229-931-2090 120 D
gaynor.cheokas@gsw.edu
CHERAGHI, S. Hossein . 413-782-1272 220 A
cheraghi@wne.edu
CHERAMIE, Robin .... 470-578-6425 121 M
rcheram1@kennesaw.edu
CHERENEGAR, Jessica .. 605-331-6671 417 C
jessica.cherenegar@usiouxfalls.edu
CHERETTA, Robson .... 718-405-3200 296 F
cheretta.robson@mountsaintvincent.edu
CHEREWICK, Daniel, P . 248-232-4622 229 C
dpcherew@oaklandcc.edu
CHERLAND, Ryan, M .... 949-824-4521.. 69 D
ryan.cherland@uci.edu
CHERNER, Barbara .... 602-285-7777.. 13 F
CHERNOBILSKY, Ellina . 973-618-3951 276 D
echernobilsky@caldwell.edu
CHERNOW, Barbara ...... 401-863-9400 403 J
barbara_chernow@brown.edu
CHERRIN, Bruce, E .... 505-277-1740 288 J
cherrin@unm.edu
CHERRY, Bennett .... 760-750-4211.. 33 A
bcherry@csusm.edu
CHERRY, Evonne .... 254-267-7042 441 K
echerry@rangercollege.edu
CHERRY, Jennifer .... 252-789-0316 335 H
jennifer.cherry@martincc.edu
CHERRY, Jermaine .... 704-330-1110 330 D
jcherry@jcsu.edu
CHERRY, Jessica .... 617-984-1734 218 C
jcherry@quincycollege.edu
CHERRY, Luke .... 661-362-2603.. 51 D
lcherry@masters.edu
CHERRY, Mark .... 321-433-7031.. 98 I
cherrym@easternflorida.edu
CHERRY, Paul .... 501-205-8805.. 18 H
pcherry@cbc.edu
CHERRY, Shirley .... 870-575-8461.. 22 D
cherrys@uapb.edu
CHERRY, Tonya .... 321-433-7094.. 98 I
cherryt@easternflorida.edu
CHERUBINI, Angela ...... 914-395-2567 315 A
acherubini@sarahlawrence.edu
CHERUVELIL, Kendra, S 517-353-6486 227 F
ksc@msu.edu
CHESBROUGH,
Ronald, D .... 315-655-7128 292 H
rdchesbrough@cazenovia.edu
CHESHIRE, Diana .... 843-953-5163 407 C
diana.cheshire@citadel.edu
CHESHIRE, Grace .... 828-835-4207 338 E
gcheshire@tricountycc.edu
CHESHIRE, Hall .... 540-654-1379 471 N
hcheshir@umw.edu
CHESLEY, Amy .... 402-437-2711 269 C
achesley@southeast.edu
CHESLEY, Colin .... 386-506-3720.. 98 D
colin.chesley@daytonastate.edu
CHESLEY, Jared .... 920-390-2820 493 C
jared.chesley@mbu.edu
CHESLEY, Laurie .... 541-383-7201 372 A
lchesley@cocc.edu
CHESNEY, Linda, H .... 718-262-5119 295 E
chesney@york.cuny.edu
CHESNEY, Mark .... 203-596-4666.. 88 F
mchesney@post.edu
CHESNEY, Robert .... 973-655-6804 279 B
chesneyr@montclair.edu
CHESNEY, Thom, D .... 563-588-6385 164 E
thom.chesney@clarke.edu
CHESNUT, Meghann ..... 606-546-1758 185 D
mchesnut@unionky.edu
CHESNUT, Renae .... 515-271-1814 165 J
renae.chesnut@drake.edu
CHESNUT, Robert, W .... 217-581-8453 137 E
rwchesnut@eiu.edu
CHESTER, Ann, L .... 304-293-1026 490 E
achester@hsc.wvu.edu
CHESTER, Brandi .... 870-248-4000.. 18 F
brandic@blackrivertech.edu
CHESTER, Cathie .... 914-251-5976 319 B
cathie.chester@purchase.edu
CHESTER, Detrenyona ... 904-470-8244.. 98 L
d.chester@ewc.edu
CHESTER, Kate .... 971-722-8233 375 D
kate.chester@pcc.edu
CHESTER, Shellond ...... 504-520-5470 193 E
schester@xula.edu
CHESTER, Steven .... 860-343-5864.. 87 A
schester@mxcc.edu
CHESTER, Thomas .... 509-313-6827 480 F
chester@gonzaga.edu
CHESTER, Timothy, M ... 706-542-3145 126 G
tchester@uga.edu
CHESTNUT, Emanuel ..... 757-822-1421 475 E
echestnut@tcc.edu
CHESTNUT, Kim .... 307-766-5123 501 I
studentaffairs@uwyo.edu
CHESTNUT, Lisa .... 303-797-5746.. 77 I
lisa.chestnut@arapahoe.edu
CHET, Alicia .... 216-584-2390 360 B
CHEU, Susan .... 650-949-6202.. 42 G
cheususan@fhda.edu
CHEUNG, Alvin .... 916-686-8883.. 29 E
CHEUNG, Floyd .... 413-585-2241 218 H
fcheung@smith.edu
CHEUNG-SUN TSANG,
Jacob .... 408-433-2280.. 36 H
CHEVALIER, Charles ...... 531-622-2368 267 G
chchevalier@mccneb.edu
CHEVALIER, David .... 478-289-2370 118 C
dchevalier@ega.edu
CHEVALIER, Jason .... 909-652-6904.. 35 L
jason.chevalier@chaffey.edu
CHEVALIER, JR.,
Joseph .... 404-756-5773 123 E
jchevalier@msm.edu
CHEVALIER, Lizette ...... 618-453-7653 150 B
lizette.chevalier@siu.edu
CHEVERTON, Holly .... 518-783-2341 315 E
hcheverton@siena.edu
CHEVES, Brad, E .... 214-768-2667 444 D
bcheves@smu.edu
CHEW, Elaine, K .... 806-651-2110 448 B
echew@wtamu.edu
CHEW, Kenneth .... 812-237-3939 156 D
kenneth.chew@indstate.edu
CHEW, Vicki .... 425-739-8311 481 C
vicki.chew@lwtech.edu
CHEYNE, Larry .... 503-316-3279 372 B
larry.cheyne@chemeketa.edu
CHEZUM, Kelly, O .... 315-268-4483 295 F
kchezum@clarkson.edu
CHHOKAR, Dilbar .... 507-574-4710 486 D
dchhokar@yvcc.edu
CHI, Robert .... 949-502-6252.. 74 F
CHI-WEI YU, Annie .... 510-666-8248.. 24 D
advising@aimc.edu
CHIA, Israel .... 973-313-6128 283 C
israel.chia@shu.edu
CHIA, Samuel .... 214-887-5121 435 F
schia@dts.edu
CHIANG, Jane .... 714-683-1207.. 26 J
CHIAPA, Ramona .... 559-791-2308.. 47 A
ramona.chiapa@portervillecollege.edu
CHIAPPA, Jonathan .... 603-646-0343 273 D
jonathan.chiappa@dartmouth.edu
CHIAPPETTA, Anthony ... 202-319-5623.. 92 A
chiappetta@cua.edu
CHIAPPETTA, Frank .... 212-431-2894 309 A
frank.chiappetta@nyls.edu
CHIAPPINI, Thomas, A . 330-494-6170 360 K
tchiappini@starkstate.edu
CHIARAVALLOTI,
Nicholas .... 201-360-4009 278 C
nchiaravalloti@hccc.edu
CHIARAVALLOTI, Todd .. 610-785-6235 397 E
tchiaravalloti@scs.edu
CHIARELLI, Linda .... 212-998-1212 309 F
CHIARO, Erin .... 203-479-4520.. 89 H
echiaro@newhaven.edu
CHIASERA, Janelle .... 203-582-5241.. 88 G
janelle.chiasera@quinnipiac.edu
CHIBANGA, Megan .... 505-277-1775 288 J
mcj28@unm.edu
CHICARELLI, Morgan ..... 503-552-1761 374 D
mchicarelli@nunm.edu
CHICAS, Jennifer .... 847-628-2053 141 C
jennifer.chicas2@judsonu.edu
CHICHESTER, Susan, E . 585-245-5577 318 B
sue@geneseo.edu
CHICK, Brian .... 603-206-8158 272 L
bchick@ccsnh.edu
CHICK, Phil .... 513-745-3445 364 G
chickp@xavier.edu
CHICO HURST, Karen .... 518-442-5540 316 A
kchicohurst@albany.edu

CHRISTENSEN, Erik .... 773-256-0696 143 F
erik.christensen@lstc.edu
CHRISTENSEN, Erik .... 863-784-7424 108 F
erik.christensen@southflorida.edu
CHRISTENSEN, Eva .... 727-341-3166 107 E
christensen.eva@spcollege.edu
CHRISTENSEN, John, J . 860-444-8322 503 G
john.j.christensen@uscg.mil
CHRISTENSEN,
Jolene, D .... 507-933-7538 236 A
jolene@gustavus.edu
CHRISTENSEN, Kelly ..... 308-338-4002 266 A
kchristensen@cccneb.edu
CHRISTENSEN, Kent ...... 801-524-8129 459 E
kchristensen@ldsbc.edu
CHRISTENSEN, Laure .... 816-584-6810 258 C
laure.christensen@park.edu
CHRISTENSEN, Marc ..... 214-768-3051 444 D
dean@engr.smu.edu
CHRISTENSEN, Matt ...... 707-256-7565.. 53 E
mchristensen@napavalley.edu
CHRISTENSEN,
Melissa, K .... 603-535-2342 275 A
mkchristensen@plymouth.edu
CHRISTENSEN, Michael 901-722-3326 423 G
mchristensen@sco.edu
CHRISTENSEN, Monica . 917-493-4036 305 A
mchristensen@msmnyc.edu
CHRISTENSEN, Nicole ... 510-879-9278.. 60 C
nchristensen@samuelmerritt.edu
CHRISTENSEN, Rachel .. 212-799-5000 303 E
CHRISTENSEN, Rocky ... 865-573-4517 420 E
rochristensen@johnsonu.edu
CHRISTENSEN, Thayne .. 775-831-1314 272 D
tchristensen@sierranevada.edu
CHRISTENSON, Larry .... 478-445-5160 119 B
larry.christenson@gcsu.edu
CHRISTENSON, Shari ... 218-749-7755 238 H
s.christenson@mesabirange.edu
CHRISTENSON, Yun ...... 510-594-3641.. 28 B
ychristenson@cca.edu
CHRISTENSON-JONES,
Marybeth .... 763-488-2525 238 C
marybeth.christenson-jones@
hennepintech.edu
CHRISTIAENS, Beckie .... 406-756-3808 263 E
rchristiaens@fvcc.edu
CHRISTIAN, Carl .... 718-262-5115 295 E
cchristian@york.cuny.edu
CHRISTIAN, Clayton, T . 406-449-9125 263 J
cchristian@montana.edu
CHRISTIAN, Donal .... 518-629-4523 302 C
d.christian@hvcc.edu
CHRISTIAN, Donald ...... 512-313-3000 433 N
donald.christian@concordia.edu
CHRISTIAN, Donald, P .. 845-257-3288 316 E
president@newpaltz.edu
CHRISTIAN, Elizabeth .... 318-487-7496 187 E
elizabeth.christian@lacollege.edu
CHRISTIAN, Gene .... 503-936-5350 373 A
gchristian@georgefox.edu
CHRISTIAN, Hannah ...... 660-562-1251 257 E
hannahc@nwmissouri.edu
CHRISTIAN, Sonya .... 661-336-5104.. 46 K
chancelloroffice@kccd.edu
CHRISTIAN, Sonya .... 661-395-4211.. 46 L
sonya.christian@bakersfieldcollege.edu
CHRISTIANE, Mueller .... 845-451-1258 297 G
christiane.mueller@culinary.edu
CHRISTIANS,
Sharolyn, J .... 616-526-6101 222 C
chrish@calvin.edu
CHRISTIANSEN,
Brant, C .... 512-448-8555 442 I
brantc@stedwards.edu
CHRISTIANSEN,
Douglas .... 615-322-2111 428 A
douglas.christiansen@vanderbilt.edu
CHRISTIANSEN, Kari ..... 218-855-8060 237 G
kari.christiansen@clcmn.edu
CHRISTIANSEN, Klaus ... 415-485-9449.. 39 A
kchristiansen@marin.edu
CHRISTIANSEN,
Shawn, L .... 435-865-8171 460 A
christiansen@suu.edu
CHRISTIANSEN, Tyler .... 325-649-8036 437 G
tchristiansen@hputx.edu
CHRISTIANSON, Joshua 218-755-2876 237 F
joshua.christianson@bemidjistate.edu
CHRISTIANSON, Kelley . 208-426-1664 130 H
kelleychristianson@boisestate.edu
CHRISTIANSON,
Leslie, W .... 570-961-2492 389 D
lchristianson@marywood.edu

CHRISTIANSON, Lori ..... 480-285-1761.. 12 B
CHRISTIE, Barbara .... 934-420-2115 320 F
christbl@farmingdale.edu
CHRISTIE, Brian .... 301-985-7000 203 E
CHRISTIE, Christina ...... 310-825-0432.. 69 E
tina.christie@ucla.edu
CHRISTIE, Cindy .... 315-279-5368 303 G
cchristie@keuka.edu
CHRISTIE, Jenna, M ...... 423-652-6399 420 F
jmchristie@king.edu
CHRISTIE, Lindsey, M ... 515-574-1034 167 A
christie@iowacentral.edu
CHRISTIE, Marla .... 828-726-2203 332 G
mchristie@cccti.edu
CHRISTIE, Pamela, L ..... 989-837-4212 229 B
christie@northwood.edu
CHRISTIE, Ray, L .... 989-774-7062 222 E
chris2r@cmich.edu
CHRISTIE, Shari .... 301-860-3416 204 A
schristie@bowiestate.edu
CHRISTIE-DAVID,
Rohan .... 210-784-1220 447 E
rohan.christie-david@tamusa.edu
CHRISTISON, Dominic .. 918-293-4987 368 B
dominic.christison@okstate.edu
CHRISTMAN,
Harold (Bud), G .... 828-689-1102 331 C
bchristman@mhu.edu
CHRISTMAN, Pamela, J 401-825-2197 404 C
pjchristman@ccri.edu
CHRISTMAN, Rick .... 803-754-4100 408 E
CHRISTMAN, Van, D ..... 208-496-4610 130 I
christmanv@byui.edu
CHRISTMAN, Vanessa ... 610-526-6594 379 B
vchristma@brynnmawr.edu
CHRISTMAS, Christy ..... 231-843-5834 233 A
cchristmas1@westshore.edu
CHRISTMON, Darryl, E .. 202-687-6400.. 92 E
christed@georgetown.edu
CHRISTMON, Kim .... 615-230-3375 425 E
CHRISTNER, Jennifer .... 713-798-8878 431 D
jennifer.christner@bcm.edu
CHRISTODOULOU,
Christos .... 505-277-6880 288 J
christos@unm.edu
CHRISTOFFERS,
Collette .... 701-788-4782 345 D
c.christoffers@mayvillestate.edu
CHRISTOFFERS,
Pamela, M .... 515-263-6023 166 F
pchristoffers@grandview.edu
CHRISTOFFERSON,
Kimberlee, K .... 724-946-7247 402 D
christkk@westminster.edu
CHRISTOPH, Julie .... 253-879-3207 484 G
jchristoph@pugetsound.edu
CHRISTOPHER, Gary ...... 641-673-1295 171 C
christopherg@wmpenn.edu
CHRISTOPHER, Greg ...... 513-745-3499 364 G
christopherg@xavier.edu
CHRISTOPHER, Henry ... 212-563-6647 323 I
h.christopher@uts.edu
CHRISTOPHER, Jennifer 201-360-4061 278 C
jchristopher@hccc.edu
CHRISTOPHER, John, J 732-571-3598 279 A
jochrist@monmouth.edu
CHRISTOPHER,
Kimberly .... 508-999-8586 212 A
kchristopher@umassd.edu
CHRISTOPHER, Lee, C .. 303-797-5965.. 77 I
lee.christopher@arapahoe.edu
CHRISTOPHER, Robert .. 563-333-6260 169 G
christopherrobert@sau.edu
CHRISTOPHERSON,
Michelle .... 218-281-8369 244 A
mchristo@umn.edu
CHRISTOPHERSON,
Neal, J .... 509-527-5056 486 B
christnj@whitman.edu
CHRISTOPHERSON,
Toni .... 530-741-6785.. 77 E
tchristo@yccd.edu
CHRISTOPOULUS-NUTTING,
Suellen .... 315-568-3115 310 B
CHRISTY, Alan .... 831-459-5031.. 71 A
achristy@ucsc.edu
CHRISTY, Chermele ...... 504-520-5450 193 E
cchrist2@xula.edu
CHRISTY, Dick .... 910-521-6560 343 B
dick.christy@uncp.edu
CHRISTY, Gregory, E .... 712-707-7100 169 D
president@nwciowa.edu
CHRISTY, John, R .... 256-961-7763.... 8 B
john.christy@uah.edu

CHRISTY, Kathleen .... 716-926-8960 301 E
kchristy@hilbert.edu
CHRISTY, William .... 412-396-6020 383 A
christyw458@duq.edu
CHRITE, E. LaBrent .... 781-891-2101 206 G
officeofthepresident@bentley.edu
CHRITE, E. LaBrent .... 386-481-2001.. 96 D
chriteb@cookman.edu
CHRONIS, Christos .... 480-461-7356.. 13 D
christos.chronis@mesacc.edu
CHRONISTER, Eric .... 702-895-3487 271 D
eric.chronister@unlv.edu
CHRONISTER, Krista ..... 541-346-8468 376 H
kmg@uoregon.edu
CHRONISTER, Lynne ..... 251-460-6333.... 9 A
lchronister@southalabama.edu
CHRUSCIEL, Carolyn ..... 815-825-9324 141 F
cchrusciel@kish.edu
CHRUSCIEL, Donald ...... 816-604-1253 255 C
donald.chrusciel@mcckc.edu
CHRYSANTHOU,
Juanita .... 702-651-7374 270 K
juanita.chrysanthou@csn.edu
CHRYSOSTOMOS,
Schemamonk .... 530-467-3544.. 60 A
fc@spots.edu
CHRZANOWSKI,
Damian .... 248-836-1275 231 D
dchrzanowski@sscms.edu
CHRZASTEK, OP, Brian . 202-495-3842.. 93 D
bchrzastek@dhs.edu
CHU, Anita .... 518-276-6287 312 C
chua3@rpi.edu
CHU, Gary .... 617-587-5541 217 D
chug@neco.edu
CHU, Melanie .... 530-541-4660.. 47 E
mchu@ltcc.edu
CHU, Zduy .... 229-333-5920 127 E
zchu@valdosta.edu
CHUA, Nate .... 641-844-5743 167 G
nate.chua@iavalley.edu
CHUBB, Andrew, M ...... 989-964-4144 230 E
achubb@svsu.edu
CHUBBUCK, Kay .... 212-517-3929 315 G
k.chubbuck@sothebysinstitute.com
CHUBINSKAYA,
Susanna .... 312-942-6306 148 G
susanna_chubinskaya@rush.edu
CHUCHIAK, John, F ...... 417-836-5425 256 G
johnchuchiak@missouristate.edu
CHUCKLUCK, Cheryl ..... 785-749-8463 174 D
cheryl.chuckluck@bie.edu
CHUDNICK, Steven .... 732-224-2482 276 B
schudnick@brookdalecc.edu
CHUDY, Erika .... 870-972-2060.. 17 E
echudy@astate.edu
CHUI, Kevin .... 503-352-7377 375 C
chuik@pacificu.edu
CHULICK, Robbie .... 276-328-0114 472 E
rchulick@uvawise.edu
CHULOS, Chris .... 410-704-2129 204 E
cchulos@towson.edu
CHUM, Chungwai .... 510-748-2211.. 57 A
cchum@peralta.edu
CHUN, Marvin .... 203-432-2900.. 90 C
marvin.chun@yale.edu
CHUN, Patrick .... 509-335-3564 485 D
CHUN, Victoria .... 203-432-1414.. 90 C
victoria.chun@yale.edu
CHUN-OYADOMARI,
Tammi .... 808-956-4561 129 G
tammi@hawaii.edu
CHUNG, Jay .... 213-262-3939.. 46 D
CHUNG, Joel .... 714-222-1110.. 27 F
CHUNG, Joy .... 714-222-1110.. 27 F
CHUNG, Lucy .... 847-866-3877 138 D
jaeyeon.chung@garrett.edu
CHUNG, Norm .... 502-897-4209 184 G
nchung@sbts.edu
CHUNG, Peggy .... 718-779-1499 311 E
pchung@plazacollege.edu
CHUNG, Regina .... 212-431-2100 309 A
CHUNG, Sam .... 206-239-4500 478 H
CHUNG, Silvan .... 808-845-9264 130 A
silvan@hawaii.edu
CHUNG, Silvan .... 808-845-9404 130 A
silvan@hawaii.edu
CHUNG, Y. Barry .... 619-594-1424.. 33 D
ybchung@sdsu.edu
CHUNG-HOON, Tanise .. 801-356-5330 130 I
tanise@churchofjesuschrist.org
CHUNG-HOON, Tanise .. 801-356-5333 458 H

CHUPALIO, Brie .... 585-394-3522 299 F
brie.chupalio@flcc.edu
CHUPP, Tim .... 616-988-3658 226 E
tchupp@kuyper.edu
CHURCH, Celeste .... 325-649-8081 437 G
cchurch@hputx.edu
CHURCH, David, B .... 206-281-2602 483 G
dchurch@spu.edu
CHURCH, David, M .... 719-884-5000.. 82 B
dmchurch@nbc.edu
CHURCH, Donna .... 828-726-2210 332 G
dchurch@cccti.edu
CHURCH, Kelly .... 336-838-6175 339 B
kachurch667@wilkescc.edu
CHURCH, Marjorie, R ... 336-841-4692 329 F
mchurch@highpoint.edu
CHURCH, Sarah .... 650-723-2300.. 66 E
CHURCH LEWANDOWSKI,
Tina .... 913-288-7201 175 B
tchurch@kckcc.edu
CHURCHICH, Elizabeth .. 402-280-2703 266 H
elizabethchurchich@creighton.edu
CHURCHILL,
Clifford, W .... 772-546-5534 102 C
cliffchurchill@hsbc.edu
CHURCHILL, David .... 405-682-1611 367 D
dchurchill@occc.edu
CHURCHILL, Sally, J ..... 734-763-5553 231 H
sjc@umich.edu
CHURCHMAN, Jim .... 919-668-2565 328 F
jim.churchman@duke.edu
CHURCHWELL,
Andre, L .... 615-322-7311 428 A
CHUSID, Eileen .... 212-410-8127 308 E
echusid@nycpm.edu
CHUTE, Mary .... 609-292-6201 284 C
mchute@njstatelib.org
CHVIRKO, Meghan .... 212-875-4687 290 H
mchvirko@bankstreet.edu
CHYCINSKI, Jodi .... 616-331-2025 224 G
chycinsj@gvsu.edu
CHYKA, Robert, D .... 716-880-2343 305 G
robert.d.chyka@medaille.edu
CHYTKA, Evelyn, J .... 307-766-2398 501 I
jchytka@uwyo.edu
CHYUN, Deborah, A ..... 860-486-0537.. 89 D
deborah.chyun@uconn.edu
CIACCIO, Dolores .... 934-420-2411 320 F
dolores.ciaccio@farmingdale.edu
CIALLELLA, Sandra .... 619-260-2720.. 72 I
sciallella@sandiego.edu
CIAMBRIELLO,
Christine .... 909-602-2505.. 57 K
christina.ciambriello@pomona.edu
CIANCHETTA, Susan, A . 410-827-5811 198 F
scianchetta@chesapeake.edu
CIANCI, Valen, P .... 610-917-1426 401 G
vpcianci@valleyforge.edu
CICALA, Mary Ann .... 512-223-7109 430 I
mary.cicala@austincc.edu
CICCARELLI, Andrea ...... 812-855-3550 156 G
aciccare@indiana.edu
CICCHELLI, Cindy .... 734-462-4400 230 G
ccicchel@schoolcraft.edu
CICCONE, Lori .... 702-895-5541 271 D
lori.ciccone@unlv.edu
CICH, Keith .... 218-879-0837 238 B
keith.cich@fdltcc.edu
CICHOCKI, Eileen .... 707-468-3068.. 51 F
ecichocki@mendocino.edu
CICHON, Jeff .... 715-675-3331 499 F
cichon@ntc.edu
CICHOSZ, Chris .... 507-453-2741 239 B
ccichosz@southeastmn.edu
CICHOSZ, Christopher .. 507-457-5555 241 F
ccichosz@winona.edu
CICOTTI, Cheryl .... 407-708-2483 108 D
cicottic@seminolestate.edu
CICUTO, Chris .... 818-240-1000.. 43 G
ccicuto@glendale.edu
CIEJKA, Patricia, A .... 409-772-8745 456 E
pciejka@utmb.edu
CIENSKI, John .... 631-451-4000 321 D
cienskj@sunysuffolk.edu
CIEPLY, Kevin .... 239-687-5305.. 95 L
kcieply@avemarialaw.edu
CIESEMIER, Kristin .... 815-280-2862 141 B
kciesemi@jjc.edu
CIESLA, James .... 419-372-8242 348 G
jciesla@bgsu.edu
CIEZ-VOLZ, Kathleen ..... 904-361-6257 101 B
kathleen.ciez.volz@fscj.edu
CIFRA, Jason .... 510-215-3869.. 40 B
jcifra@contracosta.edu

CLARK, John, S .... 865-694-6601 425 B
jclark@pstcc.edu
CLARK, Joy .... 334-244-3539.... 4 E
jclark@aum.edu
CLARK, Joye .... 313-577-2161 232 K
joye.clark@wayne.edu
CLARK, Kara .... 724-503-1001 402 B
kclark@washjeff.edu
CLARK, Karen .... 765-973-8242 157 A
krclark@iue.edu
CLARK, Karen .... 937-529-2201 361 G
kclark@united.edu
CLARK, Karen .... 254-299-8689 439 E
kclark@mclennan.edu
CLARK, Karen, M .... 708-344-4700 143 A
kclark@lincolntech.edu
CLARK, Karisa, A .... 304-877-6428 486 G
publicrelations@abc.edu
CLARK, Kathleen .... 305-809-3188.. 97 O
kathleen.clark2@cfk.edu
CLARK, Kathy .... 630-844-5443 133 D
kclark@aurora.edu
CLARK, Kelly .... 918-595-7000 370 C
kelly.clark@tulsacc.edu
CLARK, Kevin, G .... 215-204-2452 399 B
keviclar@temple.edu
CLARK, Kimberlee .... 425-352-8204 478 D
kclark@cascadia.edu
CLARK, Kristin .... 559-934-2131.. 74 N
kristinclark@whccd.edu
CLARK, Kyle .... 850-644-4242 110 C
kyle@fsu.edu
CLARK, Kym .... 432-264-5144 437 F
kclark@howardcollege.edu
CLARK, L. Nathan, N .... 775-241-4445 270 E
nclark@ccnn4u.com
CLARK, Lanette .... 406-758-6328 263 F
lclark@fpcc.edu
CLARK, Laura .... 870-777-5722.. 22 I
laura.clark@uaht.edu
CLARK, Laura, B .... 615-898-5405 422 C
laura.clark@mtsu.edu
CLARK, Laurie .... 979-830-4336 431 H
laurie.clark@blinn.edu
CLARK, Lawrence, S ..... 318-797-5234 190 A
larry.clark@lsus.edu
CLARK, Len .... 765-983-1687 155 A
lenclark@earlham.edu
CLARK, Lesa, C .... 757-683-4406 469 B
lclark@odu.edu
CLARK, Letitia .... 949-582-4920.. 65 B
lclark31@socccd.edu
CLARK, Linda .... 662-332-8750 247 D
liclark@msdelta.edu
CLARK, Lindsay .... 217-732-3168 142 G
CLARK, Mandi .... 541-885-1087 374 I
mandi.clark@oit.edu
CLARK, Marcy, R .... 413-545-3359 211 G
mroeclark@umass.edu
CLARK, Mark .... 515-964-6213 165 A
maclark@dmacc.edu
CLARK, Mark .... 276-376-4576 472 E
mwc4n@uvawise.edu
CLARK, Marla .... 269-927-8762 226 F
mclark@lakemichigancollege.edu
CLARK, Marta .... 718-289-5113 293 B
marta.clark@bcc.cuny.edu
CLARK, Mary .... 863-297-1009 106 A
mclark@polk.edu
CLARK, Mary .... 501-977-2011.. 23 A
clark@uaccm.edu
CLARK, Mary .... 303-871-2966.. 84 E
mary.clark@du.edu
CLARK, Matt .... 910-892-3189 329 E
mclark@heritagebiblecollege.edu
CLARK, Matthew .... 417-268-1059 250 E
clarkm@evangel.edu
CLARK, OSB, Matthew .. 985-867-2245 190 K
mrclark@sjasc.edu
CLARK, Melinda .... 813-226-4858 107 D
melinda.clark@saintleo.edu
CLARK, Michael .... 570-321-4249 389 B
clark@lycoming.edu
CLARK, Michelle .... 954-262-1384 105 A
miclark@nova.edu
CLARK, Michelle .... 817-257-5262 448 F
m.clark@tcu.edu
CLARK, Michelle, R ...... 626-395-6832.. 28 J
michelle.clark@caltech.edu
CLARK, Nelson .... 256-782-8557.... 6 A
nclark@jsu.edu
CLARK, Nora .... 301-846-2565 198 I
nclark@frederick.edu
CLARK, Pam .... 989-686-9225 223 J
pamelaclark@delta.edu
CLARK, Patricia .... 910-272-3505 337 D
pclark@robeson.edu
CLARK, Patrick, E .... 513-556-2628 361 J
patrick.clark@uc.edu
CLARK, Richard .... 702-895-1469 271 D
richard.clark@unlv.edu
CLARK, Richard .... 404-894-4154 119 E
rick.clark@admission.gatech.edu
CLARK, Richard .... 865-573-4517 420 E
rclark@johnsonu.edu
CLARK, Richard, M .... 800-443-9266 503 D
CLARK, Robert .... 404-880-6623 117 C
rclark@cau.edu
CLARK, Robert, A .... 207-941-7138 194 F
clarkr@husson.edu
CLARK, Robert, E .... 757-683-3018 469 B
reclark@odu.edu
CLARK, Rodney .... 412-809-5301 396 E
clark.rodney@ptcollege.edu
CLARK, Rodney, E .... 316-978-5520 178 D
CLARK, Ryan .... 971-722-7724 375 D
ryan.clark13@pcc.edu
CLARK, Sara .... 419-530-4039 363 B
sara.clark2@utoledo.edu
CLARK, Sarah .... 215-951-1732 387 A
clarks@lasalle.edu
CLARK, Sarah .... 406-657-1007 265 E
sarah.clark@rocky.edu
CLARK, Sarah, E .... 863-667-5463 108 K
seclark@seu.edu
CLARK, Scott, D .... 716-888-8357 292 F
clarks@canisius.edu
CLARK, Sharon .... 607-844-8222 322 D
CLARK, Sherri .... 606-248-2224 183 A
sherril.clark@kctcs.edu
CLARK, Stephanie .... 850-474-2492 111 F
sclark2@uwf.edu
CLARK, Steve .... 541-737-4875 375 A
steve.clark@oregonstate.edu
CLARK, Steven, C .... 801-863-8082 460 D
steven.clark@uvu.edu
CLARK, Susan .... 517-629-0798 221 A
sclark@albion.edu
CLARK, Tammie, L .... 252-451-8372 336 E
tlckark215@nashcc.edu
CLARK, Tammy, L .... 813-258-7522 113 H
tclark@ut.edu
CLARK, Terry .... 618-453-7960 150 B
tclark@business.siu.edu
CLARK, Tim .... 801-302-2800 459 H
tim.clark@neumont.edu
CLARK, Timothy .... 432-335-6848 441 A
tclark@odessa.edu
CLARK, Todd .... 870-972-2947.. 17 E
tclark@astate.edu
CLARK, Todd .... 909-469-5473.. 75 I
tclark@westernu.edu
CLARK, Traci .... 318-345-9185 188 D
traciclark@ladelta.edu
CLARK, Tracie .... 704-330-6022 333 D
tracie.clark@cpcc.edu
CLARK, Treka .... 870-236-6901.. 18 J
tclark@crc.edu
CLARK, Treva .... 717-867-6106 388 C
tclark@lvc.edu
CLARK, Tricia .... 316-394-5227 172 B
tclark@bethelks.edu
CLARK, Victoria .... 618-664-7101 138 F
victoria.clark@greenville.edu
CLARK, Wesley .... 512-863-1227 445 C
clarkw@southwestern.edu
CLARK, Whitney .... 212-659-7200 303 H
whitney_clark@tkc.edu
CLARK, William .... 856-351-2602 283 B
clark@salemcc.edu
CLARK, William (Bill) .... 740-376-4601 355 E
wbc001@marietta.edu
CLARK, Yvette .... 603-645-9623 274 C
y.clark@snhu.edu
CLARK, Zak .... 907-786-1215.... 9 J
CLARK-EVANS, Barbara . 913-288-7504 175 B
bclark@kckcc.edu
CLARK-FAGGS, Diane .... 202-408-2400.. 93 H
CLARK-GOFF, Kylah ...... 325-649-8148 437 G
kclarkgoff@hputx.edu
CLARK-SHAW, Kimberly 410-651-7660 203 D
kclarkshaw@umes.edu
CLARKBERG, Marin, E .. 607-255-9101 297 F
mec30@cornell.edu
CLARKE, Anthony .... 336-334-4822 335 A
CLARKE, Arlene, V .... 404-527-5264 121 L
avclarke@itc.edu
CLARKE, Beth .... 601-974-1062 247 B
CLARKE, Calaundra .... 225-771-2552 191 E
cclarke@sulc.edu
CLARKE, Cara .... 606-759-7141 182 E
cara.clarke@kctcs.edu
CLARKE, Christopher .... 717-477-1476 395 B
cjclarke@ship.edu
CLARKE, Connor .... 716-827-2437 323 G
CLARKE, Courtney .... 216-987-5504 351 E
courtney.clarke@tri-c.edu
CLARKE, Cyril, R .... 540-231-6122 476 C
provost@vt.edu
CLARKE, Debbi .... 919-445-0956 342 C
clarked@email.unc.edu
CLARKE, Edmond .... 570-577-3215 379 C
ed.clarke@bucknell.edu
CLARKE, Ginger .... 606-759-7141 182 E
ginger.clarke@kctcs.edu
CLARKE, Jaime .... 503-594-3220 372 C
jaimec@clackamas.edu
CLARKE, Judith, B .... 631-632-6265 317 A
judith.b.clarke@stonybrook.edu
CLARKE, Karen .... 808-518-4791 129 B
karenclarke@pacrim.edu
CLARKE, Kristen .... 815-226-2840 148 D
kclarke@rockford.edu
CLARKE, Malaine .... 212-621-4101 294 D
maclarke@jjay.cuny.edu
CLARKE, Mark .... 713-743-9854 452 D
mclarke@uh.edu
CLARKE, Megan .... 906-248-8435 221 M
mclarke@bmcc.edu
CLARKE, Rachel, M .... 218-299-4816 235 H
rclarke@cord.edu
CLARKE, Rachelle .... 480-517-8544.. 13 G
rachelle.clark@riosalado.edu
CLARKE, Raymond .... 912-358-4338 125 A
clarker@savannahstate.edu
CLARKE, Shari, J .... 509-359-6200 479 G
CLARKE-ANDERSON,
Shannon .... 718-270-5143 294 G
shannon@mec.cuny.edu
CLARKE EBERT, Helen .. 507-222-4183 234 G
hebert@carleton.edu
CLARKE-GLOVER,
Jazzmine .... 718-390-3280 324 F
j.clarke-glover@wagner.edu
CLARKSON, Gerry .... 325-649-8153 437 G
gclarkson@hputx.edu
CLARO, Aida .... 305-899-3674.. 96 A
aclaro@barry.edu
CLARY, Bruce .... 620-242-0506 176 B
claryb@mcpherson.edu
CLARY, Dean .... 309-649-6316 150 G
dean.clary@src.edu
CLARY, Gail .... 229-931-2318 125 E
gclary@southgatech.edu
CLARY, Henry .... 276-326-4471 464 J
hclary@bluefield.edu
CLARY, Joshua .... 785-442-6132 174 F
jclary@highlandcc.edu
CLARY, Joshua, R .... 270-686-4332 179 J
josh.clary@brescia.edu
CLARY, Shalena .... 607-962-9000 320 C
sclary@corning-cc.edu
CLARY, Stephanie .... 270-686-9550 179 J
stephanie.clary@brescia.edu
CLASBY, Caroline .... 314-889-4509 253 E
cclasby@fontbonne.edu
CLASEMANN-RYAN,
Corey .... 317-917-5707 158 D
cclasemann@ivytech.edu
CLAUDIO, Alex .... 787-780-0070 505 F
aclaudio@caribbean.edu
CLAUDIO, Leshia .... 415-338-1381.. 33 E
leshia@sfsu.edu
CLAUDIO, Nararly .... 787-891-0925 507 K
nclaudio@aguadilla.inter.edu
CLAUDIO-VILLAFAÑE,
Carlos .... 787-993-8896 512 A
carlos.claudio2@upr.edu
CLAUSEN, Beth .... 651-793-1618 238 I
beth.clausen@metrostate.edu
CLAUSEN, Janice .... 661-654-3360.. 30 B
jclausen@csub.edu
CLAUSS, Daniel .... 949-582-4547.. 65 D
dclauss@saddleback.edu
CLAUSS, Karl, W .... 315-228-7489 296 E
kclauss@colgate.edu
CLAUSS, Sandy .... 210-366-2701 441 J
clauss@questcollege.edu
CLAUSSEN, Linda, C ..... 540-674-3614 474 E
lclaussen@nr.edu
CLAUSSEN, Nicole .... 605-256-5744 416 F
nicole.claussen@dsu.edu
CLAVELL, Edward .... 602-489-5300.. 10 F
edward.clavell@arizonachristian.edu
CLAVELLE, Martha .... 619-644-7000.. 44 E
martha.clavelle@gcccd.edu
CLAVER, Jennifer .... 336-744-0900 327 E
cla@outfitters4.com
CLAVERIE, Mark .... 518-587-2100 320 E
mark.claverie@esc.edu
CLAVIER, Cheri .... 423-439-7483 419 G
clavier@etsu.edu
CLAVIER, Sophie .... 415-338-7160.. 33 E
sclavier@sfsu.edu
CLAVIN, Diana .... 610-527-0200 397 D
diana.clavin@rosemont.edu
CLAW, Chandra .... 520-383-8401.. 16 A
CLAWSON, Laura .... 540-665-4505 470 G
lclawson@su.edu
CLAWSON, Michelle ...... 757-727-5474 467 G
michelle.clawson@hamptonu.edu
CLAWSON, Teri .... 435-283-7154 461 B
teri.clawson@snow.edu
CLAWSON, Tom .... 619-684-8777.. 53 K
CLAXTON, Brenda .... 432-264-5160 437 F
bclaxton@howardcollege.edu
CLAXTON, Patricia .... 325-574-7607 458 D
pclaxton@wtc.edu
CLAXTON, Stephanie, L 315-267-2154 319 A
claxtosc@potsdam.edu
CLAY, Aileen .... 603-206-8175 272 L
aclay@ccsnh.edu
CLAY, Angel .... 301-548-5500.. 93 H
CLAY, Antoinette, M ...... 732-255-0400 279 F
aclay@ocean.edu
CLAY, Brian .... 501-370-5336.. 20 F
bclay@philander.edu
CLAY, Claire .... 419-358-3456 348 F
clayc@bluffton.edu
CLAY, Daniel .... 319-335-5380 163 H
daniel-clay@uiowa.edu
CLAY, Doreen .... 818-710-2510.. 49 D
claydj@piercecollege.edu
CLAY, Elonda .... 740-362-3435 355 H
eclay@mtso.edu
CLAY, George, W .... 864-656-0723 407 E
gclay@clemson.edu
CLAY, John, L .... 256-469-7333.... 5 H
president@hbc1.edu
CLAY, Karen .... 662-329-7104 248 A
kgclay@muw.edu
CLAY, Karen .... 541-962-3792 372 I
karen.clay@eou.edu
CLAY, Kristi .... 870-245-5417.. 20 D
clayk@obu.edu
CLAY, Lauren .... 601-484-8618 247 A
lclay1@meridiancc.edu
CLAY, Martyn .... 813-757-2110 102 B
mclay6@hccfl.edu
CLAY, Melanie, N .... 678-839-0627 127 C
melaniec@westga.edu
CLAY, Mercedes .... 419-783-2362 351 K
mclay@defiance.edu
CLAY, Patricia .... 201-360-4351 278 C
pclay@hccc.edu
CLAY, Philip, N .... 508-831-5507 220 F
pclay@wpi.edu
CLAY, Quinton .... 314-889-1478 253 E
qclay@fontbonne.edu
CLAY, Quinton .... 815-753-8305 146 B
qclay@niu.edu
CLAY, Stacey .... 417-625-9521 256 F
clay-s@mssu.edu
CLAY-ROOLS, Paul .... 703-425-4143 468 B
CLAYBAUGH, Tracy, L .. 603-535-2550 275 A
tlclaybaugh@plymouth.edu
CLAYBON, John .... 405-682-1611 367 D
jclaybon@occc.edu
CLAYBORN, Kathy .... 501-450-3134.. 23 H
kathyc@uca.edu
CLAYBROOK, Jennifer ... 662-329-7962 248 A
jlclaybrook@muw.edu
CLAYCOMB, Ann .... 970-491-6211.. 79 N
ann.claycomb@colostate.edu
CLAYCOMB, Carri .... 503-491-6701 374 B
carri.claycomb@mhcc.edu
CLAYPOLE, Rita .... 304-263-6262 487 F
rclaypole@martinsburgcollege.edu
CLAYPOOL, Joe .... 859-323-5445 185 F
joseph.claypool@uky.edu

CLOUTIER, Michelle ...... 401-232-6722 404 A
mcloutier@bryant.edu
CLOUTIER MIHAL,
Christine .... 201-559-6000 277 J
CLOUTIER MIHAL,
Christine .... 201-599-6074 277 J
mihalc@felician.edu
CLOVER, Susan .... 508-588-9100 215 A
sclover@massasoit.mass.edu
CLOVIS, Stephen .... 503-845-3570 374 A
stephen.clovis@mtangel.edu
CLOW, Melanie .... 909-554-3814.. 54 H
CLOW, William .... 309-298-1552 153 A
wt-clow@wiu.edu
CLOWER, Matthew .... 334-808-6313.... 7 C
mclower@troy.edu
CLOWERS, Laurie, C ..... 919-866-5929 338 G
lcclowers@waketech.edu
CLOWERS, Linda .... 562-860-2451.. 35 H
lclowers@cerritos.edu
CLOWNEY-JOHNSON,
Shannon .... 501-370-5276.. 20 F
CLOYD, Angela .... 859-858-3581 179 C
CLOYD, Benjamin .... 662-246-6256 247 D
bcloyd@msdelta.edu
CLOYD, Timothy .... 417-873-7201 252 G
jtcloyd16@drury.edu
CLUETT, Jennifer, A ...... 508-831-5286 220 F
jcluett@wpi.edu
CLUM, Gerald .... 678-331-4366 122 C
gerard.clum@life.edu
CLUM, Randy .... 845-758-7468 290 J
clum@bard.edu
CLUNE, Jay .... 985-448-4003 192 F
jay.clune@nicholls.edu
CLUNE, Michael .... 415-476-0944.. 70 D
michael.clune@ucsf.edu
CLUNIE, Chris .... 704-894-2337 328 E
chclunie@davidson.edu
CLUNIS, Tamara, T .... 806-371-5226 429 E
ttclunis@actx.edu
CLUSKEY, Molly .... 309-677-2450 134 A
mcluskey@fsmail.bradley.edu
CLUSSERATH, Michael .. 770-426-4479 122 C
michael.clusserath@life.edu
CLUTE, Claire .... 610-902-8201 379 G
cc736@cabrini.edu
CLUTTER, Archie .... 402-472-7084 269 J
aclutter2@unl.edu
CLUTTERHAM, Joshua .. 314-773-0083 250 I
jclutterham@brookes.edu
CLYBURN, Adrian .... 573-840-9106 260 E
aclyburn@trcc.edu
CLYDE, Katherine .... 252-493-7262 336 H
kclyde@email.pittcc.edu
CLYDE, JR., William ..... 516-572-0607 307 E
william.clyde@ncc.edu
CLYDESDALE, Timothy .. 609-771-1855 276 I
clydesda@tcnj.edu
CLYNE, Dylan .... 203-596-4500.. 88 F
COACH, Michelle .... 860-253-3002.. 86 C
mcoach@asnuntuck.edu
COACHMAN, Kenneth .... 205-929-1457.... 6 B
kcoachman@miles.edu
COAD, Alex .... 985-493-3304 192 F
alex.coad@nicholls.edu
COADY, Barbara .... 610-785-6201 397 E
bcoady@scs.edu
COAKLEY, James .... 541-737-6024 375 A
COAKLEY, Jim .... 615-226-3990 420 J
jcoakley@lincolntech.edu
COAKLEY, Katrina .... 312-341-3542 148 E
kcoakley01@roosevelt.edu
COAKLEY, Sarah .... 678-872-8015 119 D
stesar@highlands.edu
COALLEY, Justin .... 706-865-2134 126 E
jcoalley@truett.edu
COARTNEY, Jorge .... 540-831-7803 469 D
jcoartne@radford.edu
COATES, Jeff .... 407-882-2326 110 E
jeff.coates@ucf.edu
COATES, Mitchel .... 412-578-8880 380 B
micoates@carlow.edu
COATS, Bruce .... 419-434-4250 364 C
bcoats@winebrenner.edu
COATS, Eddie .... 252-985-5108 339 D
ecoats@ncwc.edu
COATS, Karen .... 601-266-4369 249 F
karen.coats@usm.edu
COATS, Lindsay .... 603-428-2358 273 G
lcoats@nec.edu
COATS, Meagan .... 870-850-3124.. 21 B
mcoats@seark.edu
COAXUM, Julian .... 704-894-2915 328 E
jucoaxum@davidson.edu
COBANE, Craig .... 270-745-2085 186 C
craig.cobane@wku.edu
COBB, Anika, V .... 803-376-5717 406 D
acobb@allenuniversity.edu
COBB, Charles .... 270-706-8566 181 G
charles.cobb@kctcs.edu
COBB, Charles, G .... 404-413-4000 120 E
ccobb13@gsu.edu
COBB, Charlie .... 865-354-3000 425 C
cobbcc@roanestate.edu
COBB, Christopher .... 323-343-3942.. 31 E
ccobb3@calstatela.edu
COBB, David .... 615-329-8848 419 H
dcobb@fisk.edu
COBB, Donna .... 405-974-5298 370 I
dcobb@uco.edu
COBB, James .... 931-372-3524 426 B
jimcobb@tntech.edu
COBB, Jeffrey .... 231-995-1338 229 A
jcobb@nmc.edu
COBB, Katharine .... 646-660-6660 292 L
katharine.cobb@baruch.cuny.edu
COBB, Keith .... 310-900-1600.. 39 F
kcobb@compton.edu
COBB, Kim, S .... 256-549-8236.... 2 B
kcobb@gadsdenstate.edu
COBB, Larry .... 334-229-6802.... 4 A
lcobb@alasu.edu
COBB, Mary .... 318-675-6065 189 I
mcobb@lsuhsc.edu
COBB, Michael .... 910-362-7347 332 H
mcobb203@mail.cfcc.edu
COBB, Michael .... 910-755-7397 332 F
cobbm@brunswickcc.edu
COBB, Nickie .... 502-213-5333 182 C
nicole.cobb@kctcs.edu
COBB, Nol .... 503-589-7743 372 B
nol.cobb@chemeketa.edu
COBB, P. Denise .... 618-650-3779 150 C
pcobb@siue.edu
COBB, Raisha .... 336-750-2092 344 A
cobbr@wssu.edu
COBB, Rebecca .... 626-585-7385.. 56 D
rcobb1@pasadena.edu
COBB, Ron, K .... 770-484-1204 122 D
rob.cobb@lutherrice.edu
COBB, Tim .... 503-370-6280 377 F
tcobb@willamette.edu
COBB, Tommi .... 870-584-1158.. 22 F
tcobb@cccua.edu
COBB, Travis .... 334-699-2266.... 1 B
tcobb@acom.edu
COBB, Velma, L .... 212-463-0400 322 G
velma.cobb@touro.edu
COBB-SHEEHAN,
Megan .... 608-663-4861 492 F
mcobbsheehan@edgewood.edu
COBEN, Jeffrey .... 304-293-2362 490 E
jcoben@hsc.wvu.edu
COBIAN, Oscar .... 805-678-5847.. 74 A
ocobian@vcccd.edu
COBINE, Stewart .... 812-855-7657 156 G
scobine@iu.edu
COBINE, Stewart, T .... 812-855-7657 156 F
scobine@iu.edu
COBLE, Chris .... 501-760-4177.. 20 A
chris.coble@np.edu
COBLE, Keith .... 662-325-3006 247 F
keith.cobl@msstate.edu
COBLE, Kristopher .... 614-947-6728 352 J
kristopher.coble@franklin.edu
COBLER, Paula .... 361-570-4350 453 B
coblerp@uhv.edu
COBOS, Luzmar .... 713-785-5995 432 L
COBURN, Amy .... 505-277-9289 288 J
acoburn@unm.edu
COBURN, Danielle .... 205-853-1200.... 2 G
dcoburn@jeffersonstate.edu
COBURN, David .... 850-644-3347 110 C
dcoburn@fsu.edu
COBURN, Walter .... 575-492-2721 287 A
wcoburn@nmjc.edu
COCANOUGHER,
Carolyn .... 713-798-9091 431 D
cocanoug@bcm.edu
COCCIOLO, Anthony ...... 718-636-3702 311 F
acocciol@pratt.edu
COCCO, Melissa .... 917-493-4584 305 A
mcocco@msmnyc.edu
COCCO DE FILIPPIS,
Daisy .... 718-518-4300 294 B
COCHRAN, B. Barnett ... 740-392-6868 356 G
barney.cochran@mvnu.edu
COCHRAN, Bob .... 503-594-6790 372 C
bobc@clackamas.edu
COCHRAN, Carolyn .... 214-329-4447 430 K
carolyn.cochran@bgu.edu
COCHRAN, Connie, L ... 713-313-7606 449 B
cochrancl@tsu.edu
COCHRAN, Eli .... 415-703-9500.. 28 B
ecochran@cca.edu
COCHRAN, Glenn .... 508-626-4636 213 A
gcochran@framingham.edu
COCHRAN, Jason, A ..... 256-765-5241.... 8 E
jacochran@una.edu
COCHRAN, Jeanne .... 619-849-2513.. 57 J
jeannecochran@pointloma.edu
COCHRAN, Karen .... 407-882-2861 110 E
karen.cochran@ucf.edu
COCHRAN, Keirsh, A .... 260-359-4035 156 C
kcochran@huntington.edu
COCHRAN, Mark, J .... 501-686-2540.. 21 E
mjcochran@uasys.edu
COCHRAN, Matt .... 918-444-3926 366 G
cochranm@nsuok.edu
COCHRAN, Michelle ...... 203-773-8535.. 85 D
mcochran@albertus.edu
COCHRAN, Molly .... 931-540-2554 424 C
mcochran3@columbiastate.edu
COCHRAN, Monica, J ... 304-367-4711 489 K
monica.cochran@fairmontstate.edu
COCHRAN, Ralph .... 614-236-6181 349 B
rcochran@capital.edu
COCHRAN, Raylene .... 850-478-8496 105 G
rcochran@pcci.edu
COCHRAN, Teri .... 918-444-3410 366 G
cochrant@nsuok.edu
COCHRAN, W. Scott ...... 864-587-4236 412 F
COCHRANE, Ashley .... 859-985-3605 179 I
cochranea@berea.edu
COCHRANE, Kelsey .... 303-765-3163.. 81 G
kcochrane@iliff.edu
COCHRANE, Ken, S .... 937-529-2201 361 G
kscochrane@united.edu
COCHRANE, Paul .... 207-228-8598 197 D
paul.cochrane@maine.edu
COCKE, Paul .... 360-650-3350 485 I
paul.cocke@wwu.edu
COCKERELL, K.T .... 210-341-1366 440 H
ktcockerell@ost.edu
COCKERHAM, Dean .... 319-352-8251 170 J
dean.cockerham@wartburg.edu
COCKERHAM, Richard ... 318-678-6000 187 H
rcockerham@bpcc.edu
COCKERILL, Ryan .... 715-682-1336 494 G
rcockerill@northland.edu
COCKETT, Noelle, E .... 435-797-7172 460 C
noelle.cockett@usu.edu
COCKFIELD, Barbara ..... 518-244-4720 313 A
b.cockfield@sage.edu
COCKFIELD, Barbara ..... 518-743-2200 320 A
COCKLEY, Suzanne, K ... 540-432-4984 466 B
dean-thpa@emu.edu
COCKRELL, Grant .... 205-391-2384.... 3 E
gcockrell@sheltonstate.edu
COCKRELL, Jordan .... 251-380-3470.... 6 H
COCKRELL, Phillip .... 419-530-7963 363 B
phillip.cockrell@utoledo.edu
COCKRELL, Phillip, A .... 216-687-2048 350 J
p.cockrell@csuohio.edu
COCKRELL, Todd .... 281-649-3417 437 B
tcockrell@hbu.edu
COCKROFT, Martin .... 360-792-6050 481 I
COCKRUM, Colton .... 901-678-2156 426 G
ccockrum@memphis.edu
COCKRUM, Daniel .... 540-231-8897 476 C
dcockrum@vt.edu
COCKRUM, Larry, L .... 606-539-4201 185 E
presoff@ucumberlands.edu
COCLANIS-LODING,
Chris .... 815-479-8713 143 I
ccoclanis-loding@mchenry.edu
COCO, Karen .... 318-670-9324 191 D
kcoco@susla.edu
COCOZZA, Christopher . 610-282-1100 382 C
christopher.cocozza@desales.edu
COCOZZOLI, Gary, R .... 248-204-3006 227 A
gcocozzol@ltu.edu
CODDINGTON, Andrew . 315-228-6921 296 E
acoddington@colgate.edu
CODERKO, Charles .... 217-206-7375 152 A
ccode2@uis.edu
CODJOE, Henry .... 706-272-4406 118 B
hcodjoe@daltonstate.edu
CODNER, Jackie .... 580-745-2810 369 G
jcodner@se.edu
CODNER, Kolton .... 724-480-3460 381 H
kolton.codner@ccbc.edu
CODNER, Renee .... 619-688-0800.. 39 J
CODY, Ginnie .... 662-476-5728 246 B
mcody@eastms.edu
CODY, Mary Ellen .... 203-285-2296.. 86 E
mcody@gatewayct.edu
CODY, Ukemah, D .... 404-627-2681 116 C
ukemah.cody@beulah.edu
COE, Cheri .... 978-921-4242 217 B
cheri.coe@montserrat.edu
COE, Erica .... 360-475-7263 481 I
ecoe@olympic.edu
COE, Lea .... 229-931-2381 125 E
lcoe@southgatech.edu
COE REGAN,
Jo Ann, R .... 202-319-5454.. 92 A
cua-ncsss@cua.edu
COEHOORN, Joel .... 402-363-5603 270 D
jcoehoorn@york.edu
COELHO, Marty .... 707-476-4358.. 58 I
marty-coelho@redwoods.edu
COES, Alvie .... 864-941-8417 411 C
coes.a@ptc.edu
COFER, Carol .... 304-327-4144 489 I
ccofer@bluefieldstate.edu
COFER, Shayne .... 773-442-5919 146 A
r-shaynecofer@neiu.edu
COFFARO, Joanie .... 732-906-7707 278 G
jcoffaro@middlesexcc.edu
COFFEE, Carol, L .... 260-399-7700 162 B
ccoffee@sf.edu
COFFEY, Amanda, A ...... 717-796-1800 389 H
acoffey@messiah.edu
COFFEY, Brittany .... 812-258-9510 154 E
bcoffey@cariscollege.edu
COFFEY, Elijah .... 270-789-5005 180 A
evcoffey@campbellsville.edu
COFFEY, Jennifer .... 610-436-2848 395 D
jcoffey@wcupa.edu
COFFEY, Paul .... 312-899-5176 149 F
pcoffey@saic.edu
COFFEY, Peter .... 312-362-7144 136 H
pcoffey2@depaul.edu
COFFEY, Rachel .... 423-614-8430 420 H
rcoffey@leeuniversity.edu
COFFEY, Randon .... 417-667-8181 252 B
rcoffey@cottey.edu
COFFEY, Ron, L .... 260-359-4029 156 C
rcoffey@huntington.edu
COFFIN, Gordie .... 402-465-2544 268 G
gcoffin@nebrwesleyan.edu
COFFIN, Lee, A .... 603-646-2604 273 D
lee.a.coffin@dartmouth.edu
COFFIN, William .... 410-293-2809 504 A
coffin@usna.edu
COFFINDAFFER, Kari ..... 304-367-4638 488 H
kari.coffindaffer@pierpont.edu
COFFMAN, Benjamin, S 989-774-3581 222 E
coffm1bs@cmich.edu
COFFMAN, Curt .... 812-888-4373 162 F
ccoffman@vinu.edu
COFFMAN, Louie .... 858-646-3100.. 62 M
lcoffman@sbpdiscovery.org
COFFMAN, Michael .... 972-758-3805 433 I
mcoffman@collin.edu
COFFMAN, Michelle ...... 405-912-9058 368 J
mcoffman@ru.edu
COFFMAN, Renee .... 702-968-2020 272 C
rcoffman@roseman.edu
COFIELD, Bridgette, N .. 412-578-8897 380 B
bncofield@carlow.edu
COFONE, Albin .... 631-451-4335 321 D
cofonea@sunysuffolk.edu
COGBURN, Troy .... 703-284-5906 468 H
troy.cogburn@marymount.edu
COGBURN, Wendy, L ... 205-348-0537.... 7 G
wcogburn@ua.edu
COGER, Robin, N .... 336-285-2640 341 D
rncoger@ncat.edu
COGGESHALL, Ken .... 513-761-2020 350 E
COGGIN, Rod .... 662-720-7306 248 C
rbcoggin@nemcc.edu
COGGINS, Patrick .... 940-397-4239 440 C
patrick.coggins@msutexas.edu
COGHLAN, Cathan .... 817-257-7475 448 F
c.coghlan@tcu.edu
COHEN, Alise .... 845-848-4036 298 C
alise.cohen@dc.edu
COHEN, Avi .... 212-410-8044 308 E
avi.cohen24@touro.edu

COLEMAN, Lynn, C ...... 443-518-4918 199 F
lcoleman@howardcc.edu
COLEMAN, Mark .... 270-384-8040 183 G
colemanm@lindsey.edu
COLEMAN,
Martha Lopez .... 903-972-3275 458 F
mlcoleman@wileyc.edu
COLEMAN, Mary .... 646-313-8000 295 D
mary.coleman@guttman.cuny.edu
COLEMAN, Melinda, L .. 843-953-8180 408 C
colemanm@cofc.edu
COLEMAN, Michael .... 919-866-6226 338 G
mccoleman@waketech.edu
COLEMAN, Michael .... 828-565-4220 335 C
mwcoleman@haywood.edu
COLEMAN, Michelle ...... 410-888-9048 200 E
mcoleman@muih.edu
COLEMAN, Mychal .... 616-331-2215 224 G
colemamy@gvsu.edu
COLEMAN, Nana, E .... 832-826-6230 431 D
necolema@bcm.edu
COLEMAN, Nancy .... 617-495-2930 210 E
dce_dean@fas.harvard.edu
COLEMAN, Patrice .... 401-341-2950 405 D
patrice.coleman@salve.edu
COLEMAN, Rachel, C .... 620-417-1125 177 F
rachel.coleman@sccc.edu
COLEMAN, Robert .... 518-694-7357 289 J
robert.coleman@acphs.edu
COLEMAN, Sandy .... 508-286-3504 220 B
coleman_sandra@wheatoncollege.edu
COLEMAN, Sean .... 406-657-1092 265 E
colemans@rocky.edu
COLEMAN, Sean .... 412-365-1164 380 G
scoleman1@chatham.edu
COLEMAN, Stephanie .... 734-432-5315 227 C
sdcoleman@madonna.edu
COLEMAN, Stephanie .... 252-328-6975 341 A
colemans@ecu.edu
COLEMAN, JR.,
Sterling, J .... 937-328-6023 350 G
colemans@clarkstate.edu
COLEMAN, Steve, B ...... 864-941-8603 411 C
coleman.s@ptc.edu
COLEMAN, Susan .... 503-375-7000 372 H
scoleman@corban.edu
COLEMAN, Tammy .... 870-584-1149.. 22 F
tcoleman@cccua.edu
COLEMAN, Teresa .... 912-538-3103 125 G
tcoleman@southeasterntech.edu
COLEMAN, Tia .... 704-878-3345 336 C
tcoleman@mitchellcc.edu
COLEMAN, Tiffany .... 541-440-7809 376 G
tiffany.coleman@umpqua.edu
COLEMAN, Tonya, R ..... 678-359-5435 120 F
tonya_c@gordonstate.edu
COLEMAN, Tracy .... 251-460-6574.... 9 A
tcoleman@southalabama.edu
COLEMAN, Valorie .... 417-690-2212 251 H
vcoleman@cofo.edu
COLEMAN, Vicki .... 336-285-4185 341 D
vcoleman@ncat.edu
COLEMAN, Warren, K ... 540-568-3187 468 C
colemawk@jmu.edu
COLEMAN, Wendy .... 334-229-4232.... 4 A
wcoleman@alasu.edu
COLEMAN, Wes .... 848-932-2916 282 B
samcolem@finance.rutgers.edu
COLEMAN, Woodie .... 405-682-1611 367 D
rcoleman@occc.edu
COLEMAN-CARTER,
Margaree .... 973-655-7548 279 B
carterm@montclair.edu
COLEMAN-DUNN,
Olivia .... 502-863-8007 180 H
olivia_coleman@georgetowncollege.edu
COLEMAN-FERRELL,
Tunjarnika .... 561-868-3474 105 D
ferrelln@palmbeachstate.edu
COLEMAN-MARTINS,
Shelly .... 316-978-3456 178 D
COLEMER, Dena .... 763-424-0853 240 A
dcolemer@nhcc.edu
COLES, Barbara .... 919-747-0175 338 G
bacoles@waketech.edu
COLES, Hakien .... 215-785-0111 392 S
COLES, Kris .... 801-863-6548 460 D
coleskr@uvu.edu
COLES, Natalie .... 937-708-4023 363 G
ncoles@wilberforce.edu
COLESTOCK, Dennis ...... 509-313-4103 480 F
colestock@gonzaga.edu
COLESTOCK, Kian .... 949-824-4059.. 69 D
kcolestock@uci.edu

COLETTA, Chip .... 617-628-5000 219 C
gerard.coletta@tufts.edu
COLETTI, Jocelyn, J ...... 617-422-7228 217 F
jcoletti@nesl.edu
COLEY, Derrick .... 301-860-4076 204 A
dcoley@bowiestate.edu
COLEY, Donovan .... 334-727-8580.... 7 D
dcoley@tuskegee.edu
COLEY, Jason .... 518-861-2598 305 C
jcoley@mariacollege.edu
COLEY, JR., Norman ..... 308-635-6123 270 C
coleyn@wncc.edu
COLEY, Phylicia .... 518-454-5295 296 G
coleyp@strose.edu
COLEY, Ron .... 657-278-2115.. 31 C
rcoley@fullerton.edu
COLEY, Soraya, M .... 909-869-2290.. 30 A
president@cpp.edu
COLGAN, Ann .... 610-436-3505 395 D
acolgan@wcupa.edu
COLGAN, OSB, Tobias .. 812-357-6304 161 A
tcolgan@saintmeinrad.edu
COLGATE, Beverly .... 805-893-2218.. 70 E
beverly.colgate@ucsb.edu
COLGROVE,
Marianne, M .... 503-777-7792 375 G
mcolgrov@reed.edu
COLIN, Cherie .... 650-574-6161.. 62 K
COLIN, Cherie .... 650-738-4346.. 62 L
colinc@smccd.edu
COLIN, Jennifer .... 616-222-3000 226 E
jcolin@kuyper.edu
COLIP, Mark, C .... 312-949-7700 139 D
mcolip@ico.edu
COLL, James, P .... 601-266-4491 249 F
james.coll@usm.edu
COLL, Jose .... 503-725-4712 375 E
coll@pdx.edu
COLL, Ryan .... 717-262-2612 403 C
ryan.coll@wilson.edu
COLL, Stephen, W .... 212-854-6056 297 C
steve.coll@columbia.edu
COLLAMORE, Ken .... 802-440-4420 461 G
kcollamore@bennington.edu
COLLAROS, Phelosha .... 505-984-6000 288 C
phelosha.collaros@sjc.edu
COLLAROS, Phelosha .... 505-984-6109 288 C
pcollaros@sjc.edu
COLLAZO, Allison .... 540-432-4314 466 B
allison.collazo@emu.edu
COLLAZO, Carmen .... 787-250-1912 508 D
ccollazo@metro.inter.edu
COLLAZO, Julio, A .... 787-758-2525 512 F
julio.collazo@upr.edu
COLLAZO, Lin .... 787-751-1912 509 A
lcollazo@juris.inter.edu
COLLAZO, Luis .... 973-278-5400 291 E
luis-collazo@berkeleycollege.edu
COLLAZO, Luis .... 973-278-5400 275 I
luis_collazo@berkeleycollege.edu
COLLAZO, Mariela .... 787-766-1717 510 G
mcollazo@uagm.edu
COLLAZO, Samaris .... 787-743-7979 510 H
s_collazo@suagm.edu
COLLAZO-CARRO, Lin ... 787-751-1912 509 A
lcollazo@juris.inter.edu
COLLAZO-CASTRO,
Shelciy .... 787-993-8876 512 A
shelciy.collazo@upr.edu
COLLER, Barry, S .... 212-327-7490 312 G
collerb@rockefeller.edu
COLLETON, Chelsi .... 803-323-2376 414 D
colletonc@winthrop.edu
COLLETTA, Louis .... 504-568-3126 189 H
lcolletta@lsuhsc.edu
COLLETTE, Michael .... 765-641-4354 153 G
collette@anderson.edu
COLLETTE, Sherwin .... 240-567-9033 200 G
sherwin.collette@montgomerycollege.edu
COLLEY, Debra .... 716-286-8317 309 H
dcolley@niagara.edu
COLLEY, Jennifer .... 254-968-9769 446 D
jcolley@tarleton.edu
COLLEY, Karen .... 312-413-2548 151 G
karenc@uic.edu
COLLEY, Scott .... 318-473-6490 189 F
scolley@lsua.edu
COLLIE, Richard .... 256-233-8100.... 4 C
richard.collie@athens.edu
COLLIER, Annina .... 918-595-7050 370 C
annina.collier@tulsacc.edu
COLLIER, Barry, S .... 317-940-8421 154 C
bcollier@butler.edu

COLLIER, Bridget .... 773-702-5671 151 E
bcollier@uchicago.edu
COLLIER, Eartha, W .... 405-466-3210 366 C
eartha.collier@langston.edu
COLLIER, Gail .... 405-491-6333 369 H
gcollier@snu.edu
COLLIER, Hemie .... 319-895-4000 164 G
hcollier@cornellcollege.edu
COLLIER, Holley .... 903-677-8822 451 F
holley.collier@tvcc.edu
COLLIER, Isaiah .... 785-670-1723 178 C
isaiah.collier@washburn.edu
COLLIER, Jackie .... 859-985-3110 179 I
collierj@berea.edu
COLLIER, Jay .... 402-375-7325 268 F
jacolli1@wsc.edu
COLLIER, Kristen, L ...... 937-327-7523 364 D
kcollier@wittenberg.edu
COLLIER, Li .... 707-524-1797.. 63 D
lcollier@santarosa.edu
COLLIER, Rhonda .... 334-725-2307.... 7 D
rcollier@tuskegee.edu
COLLIER, Sam .... 859-442-1146 181 H
sam.collier@kctcs.edu
COLLIER, Yeman .... 210-567-7052 456 C
colliery@uthscsa.edu
COLLIGAN, Amanda ...... 617-984-1727 218 C
acolligan@quincycollege.edu
COLLIGNON, Kaitlyn ..... 916-558-2442.. 50 J
colligk@scc.losrios.edu
COLLING, Lynnde .... 307-268-2247 500 U
lcolling@caspercollege.edu
COLLINGS, Clark .... 801-863-8898 460 D
ccollings@uvu.edu
COLLINGWOOD, Marlin 603-535-2475 275 A
mcollingwood@plymouth.edu
COLLINGWOOD, Tracy .. 716-673-3327 316 D
tracy.collingwood@fredonia.edu
COLLINS, Aaron .... 251-981-3771.... 5 A
aaron.collins@columbiasouthern.edu
COLLINS, Alvin .... 713-718-8363 437 C
alvin.collins@hccs.edu
COLLINS, Anthony, G ... 315-268-6444 295 F
president@clarkson.edu
COLLINS, Aristide, J ..... 202-994-6500.. 92 D
aristide@gwu.edu
COLLINS, Arthur .... 978-630-9188 215 C
acollins@mwcc.mass.edu
COLLINS, Ashley .... 703-729-8800.. 93 H
COLLINS, Berkeley .... 202-885-6074.. 94 D
bcollins@wesleyseminary.edu
COLLINS, Bob .... 801-274-3280 461 E
robert.collins@wgu.edu
COLLINS, Breanna .... 972-721-5304 452 B
bcollins@udallas.edu
COLLINS, Bryan .... 256-830-2626.... 5 C
bcollins@faulkner.edu
COLLINS, Candy .... 301-423-3600.. 93 H
COLLINS, Carrie .... 215-871-6154 395 G
carrieco@pcom.edu
COLLINS, Charlie .... 912-871-1632 123 J
cpcollins@ogeecheetech.edu
COLLINS, Chelsea .... 229-928-4116 120 D
chelsea.collins@gsw.edu
COLLINS, Chelsie .... 304-367-4214 489 K
chelsea.collins@fairmontstate.edu
COLLINS, Christine .... 337-421-6969 188 J
christine.collins@sowela.edu
COLLINS,
Christopher, J .... 651-962-5200 244 E
christopher.collins@stthomas.edu
COLLINS, Craig .... 859-323-0301 185 F
craig.collins@email.uky.edu
COLLINS, Dana .... 580-349-1574 367 F
dcollins@opsu.edu
COLLINS, Darron .... 207-801-5601 194 E
dcollins@coa.edu
COLLINS, Dave .... 937-512-5182 360 G
dave.collins@sinclair.edu
COLLINS, David .... 501-279-4291.. 19 C
dcollins@harding.edu
COLLINS, Dawn, M .... 773-508-3802 143 C
dcollins4@luc.edu
COLLINS, Dean, C .... 706-385-1094 124 E
dean.collins@point.edu
COLLINS, Deanne .... 770-533-6924 122 B
dcollins@laniertech.edu
COLLINS, Deborah .... 309-647-7030 142 C
dcollins@lakelandcollege.edu
COLLINS, Debra .... 860-773-1350.. 87 G
dcollins@tunxis.edu
COLLINS, Denise .... 812-237-3087 156 D
denise.collins@indstate.edu

COLLINS, Derrick, K ..... 773-995-3505 134 K
dkcollins@csu.edu
COLLINS, Donald .... 318-473-6427 189 F
dcollins@lsua.edu
COLLINS, Dorothy .... 610-799-1342 388 D
dcollins2@lccc.edu
COLLINS, Elizabeth .... 303-860-5600.. 84 A
elizabeth.collins@cu.edu
COLLINS, Ellen .... 617-323-6662 220 C
ellen_collins@williamjes.edu
COLLINS, Emmanuel ..... 502-852-6281 186 A
emmanuel.collins@louisville.edu
COLLINS, Erin Michelle 909-621-8147.. 57 K
COLLINS, Ernest .... 215-635-7300 384 E
ecollins@gratz.edu
COLLINS, Gary .... 478-301-2970 122 E
collins_g@mercer.edu
COLLINS, Gregory .... 530-251-8889.. 47 F
gcollins@lassencollege.edu
COLLINS, Holly .... 651-523-2800 236 B
COLLINS,
Jacqueline, M .... 410-651-6407 203 D
jmcollins@umes.edu
COLLINS, James .... 508-793-7443 208 C
jcollins@clarku.edu
COLLINS, James .... 916-558-2279.. 50 J
collins@scc.losrios.edu
COLLINS, James, E .... 563-588-7103 168 A
jim.collins@loras.edu
COLLINS, Jennifer .... 504-816-4263 186 I
jcollins@dillard.edu
COLLINS, Jennifer .... 850-599-8347 109 I
jennifer.bowers@famu.edu
COLLINS, Jennifer, M ... 214-768-8999 444 D
jmc@smu.edu
COLLINS, Jim .... 319-385-6280 167 H
jim.collins@iw.edu
COLLINS, Jodie .... 360-475-7682 481 I
jcollins@olympic.edu
COLLINS, John .... 315-228-7714 296 E
jhcollins@colgate.edu
COLLINS, John, D .... 727-816-3310 105 F
collinj@phsc.edu
COLLINS, Joseph .... 763-424-0964 240 A
jcollins@nhcc.edu
COLLINS, Julie .... 816-235-5758 261 B
collinsju@umkc.edu
COLLINS, Kamari .... 410-827-5858 198 F
kcollins@chesapeake.edu
COLLINS, Kathy .... 713-348-5147 442 F
kcollins@rice.edu
COLLINS, Kathy, M .... 401-874-2427 405 E
kmcollins@uri.edu
COLLINS, Ken .... 440-366-7738 355 B
COLLINS, Kimberley ...... 585-292-2105 307 B
kcollins@monroecc.edu
COLLINS, Kris .... 208-426-2484 130 H
kcollin@boisestate.edu
COLLINS, Kristy .... 310-506-4116.. 56 G
kristy.collins@pepperdine.edu
COLLINS, Kyle .... 314-977-5353 259 F
kyle.collins@health.slu.edu
COLLINS, Kyle, T .... 844-642-2338 169 A
collinsky@nicc.edu
COLLINS, Lance, R .... 571-384-4839 476 C
lrcollins@vt.edu
COLLINS, Latrina .... 225-771-4312 191 B
latrina_collinis@subr.edu
COLLINS, Leigh Ann .... 979-532-6520 458 E
lacollins@wcjc.edu
COLLINS, Loleta .... 937-778-8600 352 D
COLLINS, Marianne .... 507-457-5196 241 F
mcollins@winona.edu
COLLINS, Mark .... 425-352-8260 478 D
mcollins@cascadia.edu
COLLINS, Mark, G .... 407-582-2375 113 I
mcollins68@valenciacollege.edu
COLLINS, Mary .... 660-562-1599 257 E
maryc@nwmissouri.edu
COLLINS, Mary .... 724-805-2564 397 I
mary.collins@email.stvincent.edu
COLLINS, Mary, K .... 315-445-4791 303 I
collinsm@lemoyne.edu
COLLINS,
Mary Elizabeth .... 253-879-3237 484 G
lcollins@pugetsound.edu
COLLINS, Matthew .... 989-463-7111 221 B
collinsms@alma.edu
COLLINS, Melanie .... 985-448-4415 192 F
melanie.collins@nicholls.edu
COLLINS, Melanie .... 985-448-4944 192 F
melanie.collins@nicholls.edu

CONFER, Chris 864-644-5142 412 D cconfer@swu.edu
CONFER, Robert, N 260-422-5561 156 E rnconfer@indianatech.edu
CONGDON, Marybeth 203-432-5471 90 C marybeth.congdon@yale.edu
CONGDON, Thomas, J 414-410-4002 491 I tjcongdon@stritch.edu
CONGELIO, Paula 304-293-7304 490 E pacongelio@mail.wvu.edu
CONGER, Amy 734-763-0395 231 H aconger@umich.edu
CONGER, Heather 609-894-9311 281 C hconger@rcbc.edu
CONGER, Kristy, M 865-539-7333 425 B kmconger@pstcc.edu
CONGLETON, Dawn, L 434-223-6203 467 F dcongleton@hsc.edu
CONGLETON, Jonell 973-877-3068 277 G jcongleton@essex.edu
CONGLETON, Randi 412-365-2499 380 G r.congleton@chatham.edu
CONGLETON, Trevor 509-527-2256 485 C trevor.congleton@wallawalla.edu
CONGLETON, Yasemin 859-246-6487 181 F yasemin.congleton@kctcs.edu
CONIGLIO, Michael 706-880-8184 122 A mconiglio@lagrange.edu
CONINE, Chris 423-614-8102 420 H cconine@leeuniversity.edu
CONINE, Darren 978-837-5154 216 F conined@merrimack.edu
CONINE, Frances 318-357-5285 192 G coninef@nsula.edu
CONINE, Richard 518-832-7791 320 A coniner@sunyacc.edu
CONKLIN, Christina 716-488-3023 302 H chrissyconklin@jbc.edu
CONKLIN, Claudia 601-925-3943 247 C cconklin@mc.edu
CONKLIN, David 716-488-3026 302 H davidconklin@jbc.edu
CONKLIN, Kathleen 517-371-5140 233 C conklink@cooley.edu
CONKLIN, Lara, L 217-443-8798 136 G lconklin@dacc.edu
CONKLIN, Peter 603-513-1384 274 G peter.conklin@granite.edu
CONKLIN, Robin 845-574-4484 312 H rconklin@sunyrockland.edu
CONKLIN, Shane, R 413-545-1581 211 G sconklin@admin.umass.edu
CONKLIN, Shannon 609-771-2161 276 I conklins@tcnj.edu
CONKLIN, Shannon 215-204-7981 399 B shannon.conklin@temple.edu
CONKLIN BUESCHEL, Andrea 848-932-7454 282 B andrea.bueschel@rutgers.edu
CONKLIN BUESCHEL, Andrea 848-932-7454 281 G andrea.bueschel@rutgers.edu
CONKLIN BUESCHEL, Andrea 848-932-7454 282 A andrea.bueschel@rutgers.edu
CONLEY, Amanda, K 606-759-7141 182 E amanda.conley@kctcs.edu
CONLEY, Carlotta 847-543-2345 136 A chd340@clcillinois.edu
CONLEY, Cynthia 651-690-6525 243 A caconley@stkate.edu
CONLEY, Dennis 618-395-7777 139 H conleyd@iecc.edu
CONLEY, Fatimah, R 302-831-7361 91 C fconley@udel.edu
CONLEY, Jeremy, D 515-574-1086 167 A conley@iowacentral.edu
CONLEY, Jerome 513-529-2800 356 A conleyj@miamioh.edu
CONLEY, Kelli 256-840-4101 3 F kelli.conley@snead.edu
CONLEY, Laura, H 330-972-5793 361 H lhc1@uakron.edu
CONLEY, Mark 206-543-4211 485 A mconley@uw.edu
CONLEY, Marsha, A 717-866-5775 383 F mconley@evangelical.edu
CONLEY, Tony 870-759-4166 23 J tconley@williamsbu.edu
CONLEY, Valerie 719-255-4119 84 C vconley@uccs.edu
CONLIN, Katryn 651-385-6364 239 B kconlin@southeastmn.edu
CONLIN, Pam 419-372-7678 348 G pconlin@bgsu.edu
CONLISK, Elizabeth 608-363-2625 491 H conliske@beloit.edu
CONLON, Cindy, H 256-765-4293 8 E chconlon@una.edu
CONLON, Jim 609-896-5188 281 B jconlon@rider.edu
CONLON, Maureen 732-255-0400 279 F mconlon@ocean.edu
CONN, Brian 423-614-8621 420 H bconn@leeuniversity.edu
CONN, Cameron, A 901-572-2538 418 A cameron.conn@baptistu.edu
CONN, Jeana Rae 918-343-7707 369 B jconn@rsu.edu
CONN, Megan 603-206-8005 272 L mconn@ccsnh.edu
CONN, Michael 618-395-7777 139 H connm@iecc.edu
CONN, Nerissa 215-455-2300 378 F
CONN, Robert 618-262-8641 139 I connr@iecc.edu
CONN, Steve 903-233-4431 439 A steveconn@letu.edu
CONNAGHAN, Stephen 202-319-5055 92 A connaghan@cua.edu
CONNAUGHTON, David, M 409-747-2606 456 E dmconnau@utmb.edu
CONNEELY, James 706-864-1818 127 A james.conneely@ung.edu
CONNELL, Dan, J 606-783-2612 184 C d.connell@moreheadstate.edu
CONNELL, Gregory 321-674-8095 100 C gconnell@fit.edu
CONNELL, Jack 617-745-3703 209 B jack.connell@enc.edu
CONNELL, Joseph 201-684-7462 280 H jconnell@ramapo.edu
CONNELL, Steven 215-972-2027 392 T sconnell@pafa.edu
CONNELLY, Christian 914-888-5226 306 C cconnelly@mercy.edu
CONNELLY, David 801-863-8642 460 D dconnelly@uvu.edu
CONNELLY, Judy 815-280-2265 141 B jconnell@jjc.edu
CONNELLY, Katherine 212-875-4515 290 H kconnelly@bankstreet.edu
CONNELLY, Krysti, H 618-537-6861 144 A khconnelly@mckendree.edu
CONNELLY, Matt 360-383-3000 486 A
CONNELLY, Maureen, T 888-576-3348 46 I
CONNELLY, Scott 815-772-7218 145 B
CONNELLY, Shannon 406-338-5441 263 A
CONNELLY, Susan 602-275-7133 15 M
CONNELLY GOIDAS, Traci 215-641-6529 390 C tconnellygoidas@mc3.edu
CONNELLY-WEIDA, Cecelia, A 610-799-1630 388 D cconnellyweida@lccc.edu
CONNER, Arabie 785-242-5200 176 I arabie.conner@ottawa.edu
CONNER, Barbara 207-741-5571 195 H bconner@smccme.edu
CONNER, Cassandra 228-702-1829 249 H cconner@wmcarey.edu
CONNER, Dyonne 601-979-2021 246 F 0364mgr@follett.com
CONNER, Jamelle 727-341-3344 107 E conner.jamelle@spcollege.edu
CONNER, Jean 218-726-6202 243 G jconner@d.umn.edu
CONNER, Kristin 707-864-7000 64 H kristin.conner@solano.edu
CONNER, Lori 276-656-0286 474 G lconner@patrickhenry.edu
CONNER, Marc, C 518-580-5700 315 F mconner@skidmore.edu
CONNER, Michael 304-243-2317 491 E mconner@wheeling.edu
CONNER, Sheila 304-384-5385 489 J conners@concord.edu
CONNER, Steven 850-644-2145 110 C sconner@fsu.edu
CONNER, III, Thomas 304-205-6738 488 D thomas.conner@bridgevalley.edu
CONNER, Tracy 815-802-8405 141 D tconner@kcc.edu
CONNER-STRINGER, Courtney, L 276-619-4317 472 E cstringer@uvawise.edu
CONNERAT, Carolyn, K 512-475-9223 455 A connerat@austin.utexas.edu
CONNICK, George 212-757-1190 290 D
CONNIRY, Charles 503-517-1860 377 E cconniry@westernseminary.edu
CONNOLLY, Ann Marie 313-883-8500 230 C connolly.annmarie@shms.edu
CONNOLLY, Barbara 845-569-3202 307 D barbara.connolly@msmc.edu
CONNOLLY, Derry 858-653-6740 46 H dconnolly@jpcatholic.com
CONNOLLY, James 203-332-5090 86 F jconnolly@hcc.commnet.edu
CONNOLLY, Jerry 239-489-9203 101 A jconnolly1@fsw.edu
CONNOLLY, Jon, H 973-300-2120 284 A jconnolly@sussex.edu
CONNOLLY, Justin 256-766-6610 5 E jconnolly@hcu.edu
CONNOLLY, Laura 970-351-2707 84 F laura.connolly@unco.edu
CONNOLLY, Lidy 858-653-6740 46 H lconnolly@jpcatholic.com
CONNOLLY, Mary 314-977-7121 259 F mary.connolly@slu.edu
CONNOLLY, Melissa, A 516-463-4160 301 G melissa.a.connolly@hofstra.edu
CONNOLLY, Michael 320-363-2737 243 B mconnolly@csbsju.edu
CONNOLLY, Michael 320-363-3512 243 B mconnolly@csbsju.edu
CONNOLLY, Robert 404-894-2500 119 E robert.connolly@police.gatech.edu
CONNOLLY, Sandra 910-893-1241 327 D sconnolly@campbell.edu
CONNOLLY, Shawn, M 973-655-5427 279 B connollys@montclair.edu
CONNOLLY, Tara 515-964-6447 165 A tkconnolly@dmacc.edu
CONNOR, Andrea 847-735-5200 142 A conner@lakeforest.edu
CONNOR, Anissa 203-672-6661 85 D aconner@albertus.edu
CONNOR, Cammie 314-340-5089 254 A connorc@hssu.edu
CONNOR, James 510-592-9688 54 F jim.connor@npu.edu
CONNOR, Joanne, M 856-256-4102 281 F connorj@rowan.edu
CONNOR, Kate 773-907-4452 135 C kconnor@ccc.edu
CONNOR, Kevin 501-623-2272 18 I
CONNOR, Lorri, B 704-403-3207 327 C lorri.connor@atriumhealth.org
CONNOR, Pat 812-855-0973 156 G connorp@indiana.edu
CONNOR, Rianne 707-476-4187 58 I rianne-connor@redwoods.edu
CONNOR, Roger 203-837-9301 86 B connorr@wcsu.edu
CONNOR, Terry, D 859-344-3308 185 B connort@thomasmore.edu
CONNORS, Anne-Marie, E 216-523-7221 350 J a.e.connors@csuohio.edu
CONNORS, Brian 516-323-3504 306 M bconnors@molloy.edu
CONNORS, Cheryl, C 401-739-5000 404 E cconnors@neit.edu
CONNORS, Christopher 609-652-4836 283 E chris.connors@stockton.edu
CONNORS, Joan 863-297-1039 106 A jconnors@polk.edu
CONNORS, John 215-596-8973 401 E j.connors@usciences.edu
CONNORS, Natalie 219-989-2600 160 D natalie.connors@pnw.edu
CONNUCK, Wendy 215-489-2921 382 B wendy.connuck@delval.edu
CONOLEY, Jane, C 562-985-4121 31 D csulb-president@csulb.edu
CONOVER, David 419-267-1462 357 E dconover@northweststate.edu
CONOVER, Dustin 307-382-1644 501 J dconover@westernwyoming.edu
CONOVER, Melanie 801-524-1927 459 E conoverm@ldsbc.edu
CONOVER, Phillip 217-228-5432 147 F conoverp@quincy.edu
CONQUE, Chasse 956-665-5301 455 D chasse.conque@utrgv.edu
CONRAD, Ann 216-987-2464 351 E ann.conrad@tri-c.edu
CONRAD, Craig 309-298-2442 153 A ca-conrad1@wiu.edu
CONRAD, Deb 775-445-4236 271 F deb.conrad@wnc.edu
CONRAD, Eric, W 405-325-3917 370 K eric.conrad@ou.edu
CONRAD, Jacqueline 617-873-0621 208 B jacqueline.conrad@cambridgecollege.edu
CONRAD, James, A 509-535-4051 144 I jim.conrad@moody.edu
CONRAD, Jon, B 610-861-1527 390 F conradj@moravian.edu
CONRAD, Karen 518-438-2586 305 C kconrad@mariacollege.edu
CONRAD, Kari, M 570-577-1217 379 C kari.conrad@bucknell.edu
CONRAD, Kelley 231-777-0321 228 G kelley.conrad@muskegoncc.edu
CONRAD, Kristin 434-592-4941 468 E klconrad@liberty.edu
CONRAD, Lara 614-251-4718 358 B conradl@ohiodominican.edu
CONRAD, Rhonda 641-683-5115 166 I rhonda.conrad@indianhills.edu
CONRAD, Scott 760-757-2121 52 F sconrad@miracosta.edu
CONRAD, Sonya 484-664-3126 390 H sonyaconrad@muhlenberg.edu
CONRAD, Suzanna 410-704-2450 204 E sconrad@towson.edu
CONRAD WEISMAN, Sarah 315-312-3557 318 D sarah.weisman@oswego.edu
CONRADSEN, Susan 706-236-5494 116 B sconradsen@berry.edu
CONREY, Meredith 936-294-3602 450 A meredithconrey@shsu.edu
CONROY, Kristen 617-732-1714 209 D conroyk@emmanuel.edu
CONROY, Spencer 713-525-6960 454 G conroysc@stthom.edu
CONSELYEA, Mark, E 614-293-2562 358 D conselyea.1@osu.edu
CONSIDINE-FONTES, Lisa, M 401-825-2444 404 C lfontes@ccri.edu
CONSOLVO, Justin 843-953-5600 407 C consolvoj1@citadel.edu
CONSTABLE, Amanda 610-519-6456 401 K amanda.constable@villanova.edu
CONSTABLE, Peter 217-333-2760 152 B constabl@illinois.edu
CONSTANT, Jason 318-342-1028 193 C bconstant@ulm.edu
CONSTANT, Kristin, P 515-294-3337 163 G constant@iastate.edu
CONSTANTINE, OSB, Cyprian, G 724-805-2332 398 A cyprian.constantine@stvincent.edu
CONSTANTINE, Liane 314-516-6983 261 C constantinel@umsl.edu
CONSTANTINEAU RIES, Tressa 303-273-3005 79 J tries@mines.edu
CONSTANTINI, Imad 512-223-1200 430 I imad.constantini@austincc.edu
CONSTANTINO, John 808-245-8245 130 B johncons@hawaii.edu
CONSTANTINO, Patricia 617-745-3724 209 B patricia.constantino@enc.edu
CONSTANTINO, Rocco 805-965-0581 63 A rfconstantino@sbcc.edu
CONSTANTINOU, Constantia 215-898-7091 400 F cc1@upenn.edu
CONSTON, Marcia 757-822-1122 475 E
CONTARDI, Heather 570-342-8000 383 H hcontardi@fortisinstitute.edu
CONTARINO, Sue 847-925-6200 138 G scontari@harpercollege.edu
CONTE, Andrew 412-392-8055 396 G aconte@pointpark.edu
CONTE, John 214-637-3530 457 H jconte@wadecollege.edu
CONTINETTI, Robert, E 858-534-3131 70 C savcaa@ucsd.edu
CONTOMANOLIS, Laurel 585-275-3166 323 M laurel.contomanolis@rochester.edu

COOPER, Coty .... 405-736-0362 369 E
ccooper@rose.edu
COOPER, Craig .... 714-992-7858.. 51 B
ccooper@ketchum.edu
COOPER, Dan .... 864-646-1762 412 H
dcooper2@tctc.edu
COOPER, Deb .... 616-732-1165 223 E
deb.cooper@davenport.edu
COOPER, Derek .... 610-292-9852 396 J
derek.cooper@reseminary.edu
COOPER, Donna .... 559-442-8218.. 67 B
donna.cooper@fresnocitycollege.edu
COOPER, Donna .... 423-425-4184 427 C
donna-cooper@utc.edu
COOPER, Emmett .... 212-875-4679 290 H
ecooper@bankstreet.edu
COOPER, Erik .... 916-660-7512.. 64 D
ecooper1@sierracollege.edu
COOPER, Frank .... 609-771-2357 276 I
fcooper@tcnj.edu
COOPER, Franklin .... 406-638-3161 263 G
cooperf@lbhc.edu
COOPER, Fredrick .... 843-525-8293 412 G
fcooper@tcl.edu
COOPER, Greg .... 765-455-9463 157 B
gregcoop@iuk.edu
COOPER, Hans, S .... 410-651-6587 203 D
hscooper@umes.edu
COOPER, Ian .... 866-776-0331.. 54 D
icooper@ncu.edu
COOPER, Ian .... 410-287-1625 198 E
mcooper@cecil.edu
COOPER, James .... 619-239-0391.. 34 G
jcooper@cwsl.edu
COOPER, James, E .... 757-455-5707 477 C
jcooper@vwu.edu
COOPER, Jamie .... 803-323-2000 414 D
cooperj@winthrop.edu
COOPER, Jeffrey .... 215-898-1388 400 F
jeffcoop@upenn.edu
COOPER, Jennifer .... 423-697-2437 424 A
COOPER, Jeremy .... 303-466-1714.. 83 J
jeremy.cooper@spartan.edu
COOPER, Jessica .... 210-486-2217 429 B
jshaw36@alamo.edu
COOPER, Joe, J .... 906-487-2622 228 A
jjcooper@mtu.edu
COOPER, Joel .... 610-328-7679 398 G
jcooper2@swarthmore.edu
COOPER, Jorsene .... 757-727-5323 467 G
jorsene.cooper@hamptonu.edu
COOPER, Josh .... 617-327-6777 220 C
josh_cooper@williamjames.edu
COOPER, Joy .... 212-472-1500 309 D
giving@nysid.edu
COOPER, Judi .... 407-708-2138 108 D
cooperja@seminolestate.edu
COOPER, Karen .... 603-897-8508 273 I
kcooper@rivier.edu
COOPER, Karen, S .... 650-723-0198.. 66 E
karen.cooper@stanford.edu
COOPER, Katie, R .... 304-336-8131 490 B
katie.cooper@westliberty.edu
COOPER, Kelly .... 559-934-2231.. 74 N
kellycooper@whccd.edu
COOPER, Kenneth .... 925-424-1013.. 35 K
kcooper@laspositascollege.edu
COOPER, Kevin .... 772-462-7546 102 F
kcooper@irsc.edu
COOPER, Kevin .... 734-384-4128 228 C
kcooper@monroeccc.edu
COOPER, Kristen .... 434-544-8112 471 L
cooper.k@lynchburg.edu
COOPER, Layton .... 605-626-2544 416 G
layton.cooper@northern.edu
COOPER, Lesley .... 815-802-8370 141 D
lcooper@kcc.edu
COOPER, Linda .... 260-665-4124 161 E
cooperl@trine.edu
COOPER, Lisa, A .... 229-931-2921 120 D
lisa.cooper@gsw.edu
COOPER, Major .... 269-927-6284 226 F
mcooper@lakemichigancollege.edu
COOPER, Mark .... 614-251-4576 358 B
cooperm2@ohiodominican.edu
COOPER, Mary Kay .... 210-784-1121 447 E
mary.cooper@tamusa.edu
COOPER, Mary-Beth, A . 413-748-3241 218 I
mbcooper@springfield.edu
COOPER, Matthew .... 609-984-1140 284 C
mcooper@tesu.edu
COOPER, Matthew .... 907-450-8080.... 9 I
mcooper10@alaska.edu
COOPER, Micah .... 937-766-7905 349 E
micahcooper@cedarville.edu
COOPER, Michelle .... 678-916-2675 115 I
mcooper@johnmarshall.edu
COOPER, Mila .... 937-767-0123 347 G
mcooper@antiochcollege.edu
COOPER, Myra .... 828-641-0623 327 B
coopermm@brevard.edu
COOPER, Natalie, F .... 270-824-8599 182 D
natalie.cooper@kctcs.edu
COOPER, Nickie .... 251-981-3771.... 5 A
nickie.cooper@columbiasouthern.edu
COOPER, Nicole .... 325-574-7650 458 D
nicole.cooper@wtc.edu
COOPER, Paige .... 512-568-1422 456 F
cooper_p@utpb.edu
COOPER, Pam .... 479-498-6028.. 18 C
pcooper@atu.edu
COOPER, Paul .... 631-451-4445 321 C
cooperp@sunysuffolk.edu
COOPER, Peter .... 423-236-2165 423 F
cooperp@southern.edu
COOPER, Rick .... 251-981-3771.... 5 A
rick.cooper@columbiasouthern.edu
COOPER, Rosemary .... 903-565-5535 456 A
rcooper@uttyler.edu
COOPER, Ruth .... 512-313-3000 433 N
ruth.cooper@concordia.edu
COOPER, Shannon .... 707-864-7000.. 64 H
shannon.cooper@solano.edu
COOPER, Shelly .... 504-282-4455 190 F
COOPER, Stephanie .... 973-300-2161 284 A
scooper@sussex.edu
COOPER, Stewart, E ...... 219-464-5002 162 D
stewart.cooper@valpo.edu
COOPER, Susan .... 270-706-8564 181 G
scooper0151@kctcs.edu
COOPER, Tammi .... 866-776-0331.. 54 D
tcooper@ncu.edu
COOPER, Tana .... 620-792-9241 171 I
coopert@bartonccc.edu
COOPER, Tara, L .... 606-546-1241 185 D
tcooper@unionky.edu
COOPER, Tiffany .... 202-274-6085.. 94 B
tecooper@udc.edu
COOPER, Tomekia .... 229-430-3605 114 I
tcooper@albanytech.edu
COOPER, Tuesday .... 860-512-2603.. 86 G
tcooper@manchestercc.edu
COOPER, Tyson .... 540-261-8463 471 B
tyson.cooper@svu.edu
COOPER, Valerie .... 860-343-5861.. 87 A
vcooper@mxcc.edu
COOPER, William .... 573-840-9682 260 E
wcooper@trcc.edu
COOPER, Yolanda .... 404-727-6861 118 E
yolanda.cooper@emory.edu
COOPER-GIBSON,
Shawna .... 617-552-4796 207 C
shawna.cooper.gibson@bc.edu
COOPER-JOHNSON,
Chrystal .... 910-672-1073 341 C
ccooper3@uncfsu.edu
COOPER-WHITE,
Pamela .... 212-280-1550 323 K
pcooperwhite@uts.columbia.edu
COOROUGH, Randall .... 262-691-5168 500 B
rcoorough@wctc.edu
COOTER, Raelynn .... 215-503-6595 399 E
raelynn.cooter@jefferson.edu
COOTS, Frank .... 315-859-4144 300 H
fcoots@hamilton.edu
COOTS, Kevin .... 610-372-4721 396 H
kcoots@racc.edu
COP, Kenneth, B .... 732-932-7211 282 A
kcop@aps.rutgers.edu
COPE, Aaron .... 616-538-2330 224 E
acope@gracechristian.edu
COPE, Jill .... 509-453-0374 482 D
jill.cope@perrytech.edu
COPE, Joey .... 325-674-2000 428 F
copej@acu.edu
COPE, Marla .... 913-234-0687 172 K
marla.cope@cleveland.edu
COPE, Michael .... 310-506-4270.. 56 G
mike.cope@pepperdine.edu
COPE, Tara .... 518-782-6987 315 E
tcope@siena.edu
COPELAND, Benjamin ... 434-961-5207 474 I
bcopeland@pvcc.edu
COPELAND, Cathy .... 425-739-8156 481 C
cathy.copeland@lwtech.edu
COPELAND, D. Gayle ..... 559-453-2031.. 43 A
gayle.copeland@fresno.edu
COPELAND, David, L .... 540-464-7218 476 B
copelanddl@vmi.edu
COPELAND, Jackie .... 919-962-2315 342 C
jackie_copeland@unc.edu
COPELAND, Kristopher . 918-595-7224 370 C
kristopher.copeland@tulsacc.edu
COPELAND, Leigh .... 843-525-8231 412 G
lcopeland@tcl.edu
COPELAND, Lena .... 321-433-5631.. 98 I
copelandl@easternflorida.edu
COPELAND, Maura .... 912-478-7481 120 C
mconley@georgiasouthern.edu
COPELAND, Michele ...... 612-659-6248 239 A
michele.copeland@minneapolis.edu
COPELAND, JR.,
P. Kenneth .... 434-223-6216 467 F
kcopeland@hsc.edu
COPELAND, Reagan ...... 206-878-3710 481 B
rcopeland@highline.edu
COPELAND-MORGAN,
Youlonda .... 310-825-2665.. 69 E
ycopeland-morgan@saonet.ucla.edu
COPELIN, Laylan .... 979-458-6425 446 B
lcopelin@tamus.edu
COPENHAVER, Bonny ... 304-929-5472 488 G
bcopenhaver@newriver.edu
COPENHAVER, Diane, L 717-871-4950 395 A
diane.copenhaver@millersville.edu
COPENHAVER, Michael . 619-644-7000.. 44 E
michael.coppenhaver@gcccd.edu
COPENHAVER-JOHNSON,
Jeane .... 604-274-3113 302 G
jcopenhaverjohnson@ithaca.edu
COPLAN, Jan .... 802-387-7175 462 C
jancoplan@landmark.edu
COPLAND, Janet .... 954-771-0376 103 S
jcopland@knoxseminary.edu
COPLAND, Katherine ...... 917-493-4030 305 A
kcopland@msmnyc.edu
COPLEN, Amy .... 503-352-7252 375 C
amy.coplen@pacificu.edu
COPLEY-SPIVEY, Aaron . 773-256-0771 143 F
aaron.copley@lstc.edu
COPLIN, Kimberly, A .... 740-587-6243 352 A
coplin@denison.edu
COPLIN, Louis .... 518-629-7307 302 C
l.coplin@hvcc.edu
COPONITI, Laura, I .... 405-224-3140 371 B
lcoponiti@usao.edu
COPONITI, Mick, D .... 405-224-3140 371 B
mcoponiti@usao.edu
COPONITI, Mike .... 405-224-3140 371 B
mcoponiti@usao.edu
COPP, Crista .... 310-338-1745.. 51 A
crista.copp@lmu.edu
COPPAGE, Chaste .... 405-466-3217 366 C
chaste.coppage@langston.edu
COPPEDGE, Robin .... 580-387-7000 366 E
rcoppedge@mscok.edu
COPPER, Christine .... 419-755-4753 357 B
ccopper@ncstatecollege.edu
COPPER GLENZ, Becky . 978-665-3564 212 E
bcopperg@fitchburgstate.edu
COPPERSMITH, Clifford 410-827-5802 198 F
ccoppersmith@chesapeake.edu
COPPERSMITH, Terri .... 212-353-4136 297 E
terri.coppersmith@cooper.edu
COPPERWHEAT,
Melissa .... 315-792-5499 306 K
mcopperwheat@mvcc.edu
COPPI, Matt .... 520-335-1079.. 11 M
coppi@cochise.edu
COPPINGER, Katherine . 914-674-7238 306 C
kcoppinger@mercy.edu
COPPLA, Colleen .... 973-655-4214 279 B
copplac@montclair.edu
COPPLE, Chad .... 618-437-5321 147 I
copplec@rlc.edu
COPPLE, James (Dean) . 865-694-6536 425 B
jdcopple@pstcc.edu
COPPLE, Ryan .... 760-921-5548.. 56 A
ryan.copple@paloverde.edu
COPPLE, Therese .... 712-279-5433 164 B
therese.copple@briarcliff.edu
COPPOLA, David .... 203-365-4809.. 89 A
coppolad@sacredheart.edu
COPPOLA, John .... 410-617-2345 200 B
jccoppola@loyola.edu
COPPOLA, Sandra .... 973-278-5400 275 I
sec@berkeleycollege.edu
COPPOLA, Sandra, E .... 973-278-5400 291 E
sec@berkeleycollege.edu
COPPOLA, Stephen, A .. 704-687-5965 342 D
scoppola@uncc.edu
COPPOLA, William .... 817-515-3001 445 F
william.coppola@tccd.edu
COPPRUE, Lisa .... 972-860-8147 434 G
lcopprue@dcccd.edu
COQUEMONT, Kathryn .. 801-957-4186 461 C
kathryn.coquemont@slcc.edu
COQUEREL, Phoebe .... 803-327-8000 414 F
CORA, Jesus .... 787-250-1912 508 D
jacora@metro.inter.edu
CORACE-LANGBEEN,
Annaliese .... 734-432-5245 227 C
acoracelangbeen@madonna.edu
CORAGGIO, Jackie .... 212-752-1530 304 A
jackie.coraggio@limcollege.edu
CORBELL, Alicia .... 505-566-4034 288 D
corbella@sanjuancollege.edu
CORBELL, Kristen .... 336-334-4822 335 A
kacorbell@gtcc.edu
CORBETT, Ann .... 207-621-3145 196 H
annie@maine.edu
CORBETT, Diane .... 802-654-2000 462 G
dcorbett@smcvt.edu
CORBETT, Faith .... 718-260-5564 295 A
fcorbett@citytech.cuny.edu
CORBETT, Heather .... 207-753-6930 194 A
hcorbett@bates.edu
CORBETT, Lisa .... 607-431-4162 301 A
corbettl@hartwick.edu
CORBETT, Martin .... 315-781-3656 301 F
corbett@hws.edu
CORBETT, Michael .... 432-837-8056 450 B
mcorbett@sulross.edu
CORBETT, Patricia .... 603-428-2775 273 G
pcorbett@nec.edu
CORBIE-SMITH, Giselle . 919-843-8271 342 C
gcorbie@med.unc.edu
CORBIN, David .... 866-323-0233.. 58 D
CORBIN, Donna .... 781-280-3200 215 B
CORBIN, Edith .... 856-222-9311 281 C
ecorbin@rcbc.edu
CORBIN, Kirsten .... 916-484-8363.. 50 G
corbink@arc.losrios.edu
CORBIN, Lisa .... 864-644-5035 412 D
lcorbin@swu.edu
CORBIN, Mark .... 610-399-2178 393 F
mcorbin@cheyney.edu
CORBIN, Russ .... 315-498-2831 310 F
corbinr@sunyocc.edu
CORBIN, Sue .... 216-373-5429 357 F
scorbin@ndc.edu
CORBITT, Sandra, K ...... 540-338-1776 469 C
slife@phc.edu
CORBITT, Timothy .... 315-229-5392 314 D
tcorbitt@stlawu.edu
CORBITT, Zach .... 864-596-9215 408 F
zach.corbitt@converse.edu
CORBY, John, T .... 330-972-7345 361 H
jcorby@uakron.edu
CORCHADO, Regina ...... 570-208-5900 386 G
reginacorchado@kings.edu
CORCORAN, D.J .... 978-934-3328 212 B
dj_corcoran@uml.edu
CORCORAN, Heather, A 314-935-6525 262 A
hcorcoran@wustl.edu
CORCORAN, Jerry, M ... 815-224-0404 140 E
jerry_corcoran@ivcc.edu
CORCORAN, Kevin, J .... 248-370-2140 229 I
corcoran@oakland.edu
CORCORAN, Kristen ...... 570-740-0429 389 A
CORCORAN, Kristen ...... 814-472-3386 397 F
kcorcoran@francis.edu
CORCORAN, Paul .... 507-389-2267 239 D
paul.corcoran@mnsu.edu
CORCORAN, Thomas .... 315-294-8557 292 G
tcorcoran@cayuga-cc.edu
CORCORAN, Tim .... 619-644-7572.. 44 C
tim.corcoran@gcccd.edu
CORCORAN, William ..... 570-208-5846 386 G
wmcorcor@kings.edu
CORDA HADJAOUI,
Jamie .... 217-234-5253 142 C
jcorda@lakelandcollege.edu
CORDAHL, Susan .... 701-788-4767 345 D
susan.cordahl@mayvillestate.edu
CORDANO,
Roberta (Bobbi) .... 202-651-5005.. 92 C
roberta.cordano@gallaudet.edu
CORDEIRO, Aaron .... 541-485-1780 374 E
aaroncordeiro@newhope.edu
CORDEIRO, Uilani .... 541-485-1780 374 E
uilanicordeiro@newhope.edu
CORDEIRO, Wayne .... 541-485-1780 374 E
waynecordeiro@newhope.edu

CORTES, Dario, A .... 305-442-9223 104 G
CORTES, Felix .... 787-841-2000 509 J
fcortes@pucpr.edu
CORTES, Frances .... 787-878-5475 507 L
fcortes@arecibo.inter.edu
CORTES, Gabriel .... 210-924-4338 431 C
gabriel.cortes@bua.edu
CORTES, Jorge .... 706-446-5732 116 A
jcortes1@augusta.edu
CORTES, Maria .... 787-738-2161 512 C
maria.cortes1@upr.edu
CORTES, Maria, R .... 773-577-8100 136 F
mcortes@coynecollege.edu
CORTES, Stephanie .... 352-854-2322.. 97 N
cortess@cf.edu
CORTES-HUERTAS, Myrna .... 787-480-2372 506 C
mcortes@sanjuan.pr
CORTESIO, Cynthia .... 865-354-3000 425 C
cortesiocl@roanestate.edu
CORTEZ, Alicia .... 408-864-5338.. 42 H
cortezalicia@deanza.edu
CORTEZ, Carrie .... 985-448-7936 188 C
carrie.cortez@fletcher.edu
CORTEZ, Christina .... 210-486-2894 429 B
ccortez109@alamo.edu
CORTEZ, Dorinna .... 808-934-2510 129 I
dorinna@hawaii.edu
CORTEZ, Lori, A .... 815-835-6260 149 E
lori.a.cortez@svcc.edu
CORTEZ, Lorissa, M ..... 956-326-2857 446 E
lorissam.cortez@tamiu.edu
CORTEZ, Ronald .... 949-824-5109.. 69 D
rscortez@uci.edu
CORTEZ, Sandra .... 956-794-4982 438 H
sandra.cortez@laredo.edu
CORTEZ-DIAZ, Marisol . 954-201-7350.. 96 F
CORTINA, Mary .... 516-877-3259 289 I
cortina@adelphi.edu
CORTINAS, Andrea .... 915-747-5555 455 C
acortinas@utep.edu
CORTINAS, Debra .... 361-825-5743 447 C
debra.cortinas@tamucc.edu
CORTNER, Laquetta .... 614-837-4088 363 D
cortnerl@valorcollege.edu
CORUM, Amanda .... 719-549-3163.. 82 J
amanda.corum@pueblocc.edu
CORUM, Debbie .... 435-865-8330 460 A
debbiecorum@suu.edu
CORVIN, Thim .... 540-231-7189 466 K
tcorvin@com.vt.edu
CORVINO, John .... 505-224-4639 285 N
jcorvino@cnm.edu
CORVINO, John .... 313-577-3030 232 K
ae9123@wayne.edu
CORWIN, Jay .... 972-549-6320 433 I
jcorwin@collin.edu
CORWIN, Julie .... 617-266-2030 217 D
corwinj@neco.edu
CORWIN, Rhonda .... 620-665-3500 174 G
corwinr@hutchcc.edu
CORY, Gerald .... 888-488-4968.. 46 F
gcory@itu.edu
COSAERT, Carl .... 509-527-2194 485 C
carl.cosaert@wallawalla.edu
COSBY, Felicia .... 804-257-5616 476 F
fdcosby@vuu.edu
COSBY, Glen .... 509-533-7015 479 C
glen.cosby@scc.spokane.edu
COSBY, Kevin, W .... 502-776-1443 184 F
COSBY, Sheliah .... 423-869-6353 421 A
sheliah.cosby@lmunet.edu
COSBY-GAITHER, Christine .... 502-776-1443 184 F
ccosby@simmonscollegeky.edu
COSBY RONNENBERG, Susan .... 507-457-6900 243 C
scosbyro@smumn.edu
COSCIA, Danielle .... 914-395-2365 315 A
dcoscia@sarahlawrence.edu
COSCIA, Paul .... 336-917-5577 340 A
paul.coscia@salem.edu
COSENTINO, Lauren ...... 310-506-4898.. 56 G
lauren.cosentino@pepperdine.edu
COSENTINO, Richard, E 864-388-8300 410 A
cosentino@lander.edu
COSGRIFF, Lawrence .... 202-462-2101.. 93 A
lcosgriff@iwp.edu
COSGROVE, Ellen .... 518-262-5919 289 L
cosgroe@amc.edu
COSGROVE, John .... 570-662-4586 394 F
jcosgrov@mansfield.edu
COSGROVE, Theresa ..... 707-654-1000.. 32 A
COSIMO, Julie .... 630-829-6037 133 E
jcosimo@ben.edu
COSKRAN, John .... 612-330-1000 234 A
coskranj@augsburg.edu
COSNER BERZIN, Stephanie .... 617-521-2000 218 G
COSPER, Emily .... 504-762-3224 188 B
ecospe@dcc.edu
COSS, Laura .... 724-852-7629 402 C
lcoss@waynesburg.edu
COSS, Reydecel .... 575-562-2108 286 B
reydecel.coss@enmu.edu
COSSAR, Nigel .... 215-898-9073 400 F
ncossar@upenn.edu
COSSE, Ted .... 626-584-5501.. 43 B
ted_cosse@fuller.edu
COSSEY, Jeannie .... 870-972-2030.. 17 E
jcossey@astate.edu
COSSICH, Marc .... 850-474-2022 111 F
mcossich@uwf.edu
COST, Timothy, P .... 904-256-7016 102 H
tcost@ju.edu
COSTA, Dana .... 304-876-5465 490 A
dcosta@shepherd.edu
COSTA, Daniel .... 831-459-2464.. 71 A
costa@ucsc.edu
COSTA, Darin .... 310-233-4450.. 49 B
costadv@lahc.edu
COSTA, Erik .... 860-701-5787.. 88 D
costa_e@mitchell.edu
COSTA, Karen .... 716-829-7640 298 E
costak@dyc.edu
COSTA, Kris .... 559-925-3218.. 75 B
kriscosta@whccd.edu
COSTA, Linda, J .... 848-932-7711 282 A
smeds@gradadm.rutgers.edu
COSTA, Maria, D .... 423-439-7737 419 G
costa@etsu.edu
COSTA, Vic .... 410-778-5080 205 B
vcosta2@washcoll.edu
COSTALAS, Georgia .... 570-408-7854 403 A
georgia.costalas@wilkes.edu
COSTANTINI, Camilla .... 203-332-5222.. 86 F
ccostantini@housatonic.edu
COSTANTINIDIS, Teresa 505-277-7520 288 J
tcostant@unm.edu
COSTANTINO, Tracie ..... 661-255-1050.. 28 G
provost@calarts.edu
COSTANZA, Laina, T ..... 334-387-3878.... 4 B
lainacostanza@amridgeuniversity.edu
COSTANZO, Brian .... 570-961-7841 387 B
costanzob@lackawanna.edu
COSTAS, Carolyn .... 787-841-2000 509 J
ccostas@pucpr.edu
COSTAS, Pamela, G ...... 312-915-6194 143 C
pcostas@luc.edu
COSTE, Mike .... 303-914-6636.. 83 C
mike.coste@rrcc.edu
COSTELLO, Bernard, J ... 412-648-1938 400 H
bjc1@pitt.edu
COSTELLO, Dennis .... 586-445-7318 227 B
costellod@macomb.edu
COSTELLO, Gregory, W . 507-344-7305 234 C
gregory.costello@blc.edu
COSTELLO, Jamie .... 617-879-7703 213 B
jcostello@massart.edu
COSTELLO, Kevin .... 617-327-6777 220 C
kevin_costello@williamjames.edu
COSTELLO, Leon .... 406-994-4226 264 C
lcostello@msubobcats.com
COSTELLO, Richard, J ... 219-989-2539 160 D
rick@pnw.edu
COSTIGAN, Harry .... 610-359-5288 382 A
hcostigan@dccc.edu
COSTIGAN, Rosemary ... 401-825-2142 404 C
rcostigan@ccri.edu
COSTIN, Dondi, E .... 843-863-7502 407 B
dcostin@csuniv.edu
COSTLEY, Lucien .... 830-895-7116 443 E
vpaf@schreiner.edu
COSTNER, Kelly .... 866-492-5336 244 F
kelley.costner@mail.waldenu.edu
COSTOLA, Sergio .... 512-863-1373 445 C
costolas@southwestern.edu
COSTON, Andrew .... 507-933-7575 236 A
acoston@gustavus.edu
COSTON, Linda .... 229-430-2751 114 I
lcoston@albanytech.edu
COSTON, Robert, H .... 304-647-6575 488 G
rcoston@newriver.edu
COSTON, Sophia .... 216-659-7200 303 H
sophia_coston@tkc.edu
COSTON, Todd .... 661-395-4601.. 46 L
tcoston@bakersfieldcollege.edu
COT, Alea .... 504-280-7484 190 B
amcot@uno.edu
COTA, Clarissa .... 702-651-2728 270 K
clarissa.cota@csn.edu
COTA, Marco .... 909-384-8630.. 60 F
mcota@sbccd.cc.ca.us
COTE, Christine .... 509-453-0374 482 D
christine.cote@perrytech.edu
COTE, Christy .... 907-745-3201.... 9 C
ccote@akbible.edu
COTE, Erik .... 617-989-4590 219 F
cotee1@wit.edu
COTE, Matthew .... 907-745-3201.... 9 C
mcote@akbible.edu
COTE, Melissa .... 603-752-1060 273 C
mcote@ccsnh.edu
COTE, Robin .... 617-287-5777 211 H
robin.cote@umb.edu
COTE-BONANNO, Joanne, F .... 973-655-6234 279 B
bonannoj@montclair.edu
COTHAM, Brian .... 559-278-2111.. 31 B
bcotham@csufresno.edu
COTHRAN, Ginger .... 580-387-7112 366 E
gcothran@mscok.edu
COTHRAN, Grayson ...... 276-523-7473 474 D
gcothran@mecc.edu
COTHRAN, Rick .... 864-646-1701 412 H
rcothran@tctc.edu
COTO, Jennifer .... 714-628-4775.. 58 G
coto_jennifer@sccollege.edu
COTRONE, Allan, L .... 651-962-4561 244 E
alcotrone@stthomas.edu
COTSONES, Rena .... 815-753-9503 146 B
rcotsones@niu.edu
COTSONIS, Joachim ...... 617-850-1243 210 G
jcotsonis@hchc.edu
COTTAM, Michael .... 304-724-3700 486 F
mcottam@apus.edu
COTTEN, Brian .... 501-686-5684.. 22 B
cottenbrian@uams.edu
COTTER, Bob .... 513-487-1144 361 F
bob.cotter@myunion.edu
COTTER, Bonnie .... 704-272-5300 337 I
COTTER, George .... 813-974-3340 111 C
gcotter@usf.edu
COTTER, Janel .... 870-508-6133.. 17 G
jcotter@asumh.edu
COTTER, Michael .... 914-594-3675 309 B
michael_cotter@nymc.edu
COTTER, Regina .... 757-455-3352 477 C
rcotter@vwu.edu
COTTET, Sarah .... 914-594-4574 309 B
sarah_cottet@nymc.edu
COTTI, Nadia .... 661-259-7800.. 38 D
nadia.cotti@canyons.edu
COTTINGHAM, Ryan, T . 517-750-1200 231 C
ryanc@arbor.edu
COTTO, Marguerite, C ... 231-995-1775 229 A
mcotto@nmc.edu
COTTO, Sugelenia .... 787-766-1717 510 G
sucotto@uagm.edu
COTTO, Zuleika .... 787-665-7910 506 D
zucotto@columbiacentral.edu
COTTON, III, Charles .... 563-588-6319 164 E
charles.cotton@clarke.edu
COTTON, Gina .... 662-476-5063 246 B
gcotton@eastms.edu
COTTON, Gregory .... 319-895-4454 164 G
gcotton@cornellcollege.edu
COTTON, Michael .... 336-517-2286 327 A
mcotton@bennett.edu
COTTON, Renee .... 601-857-3364 246 C
renee.cotton@hindscc.edu
COTTON, Sabrina .... 256-726-7408.... 6 C
cotton@oakwood.edu
COTTON, Todd .... 205-726-4144.... 6 E
tcotton@samford.edu
COTTON KELLY, Montique .... 860-486-2240.. 89 D
mcottonkelly@foundation.uconn.edu
COTTONE, John .... 607-753-2701 318 A
john.cottone@cortland.edu
COTTONER, Brittany ...... 812-258-9510 154 E
bcottoner@cariscollege.edu
COTTONHAM, Patricia ... 337-482-6266 193 B
patcottonham@louisiana.edu
COTTRELL, Bryan .... 254-442-5173 432 I
bryan.cottrell@cisco.edu
COTTRELL, Danny .... 501-337-5000.. 18 B
dcottrell@asutr.edu
COTTRELL, Debbie .... 830-372-8001 449 A
president@tlu.edu
COTTRELL, Debbie .... 254-295-5059 453 D
dcottrell@umhb.edu
COTTRELL, Jeffrey .... 325-670-1484 436 I
jcottrell@hsutx.edu
COTTRELL, Liesl .... 773-252-5114 146 F
liesl.cottrell@oakpoint.edu
COTTRELL, Terrance, L .. 815-740-5041 152 H
tcottrell@stfrancis.edu
COTTRILL, Bruce .... 434-797-8477 473 G
bruce.cottrill@danville.edu
COTTRILL, F. Layton ..... 304-696-6295 489 M
cottrill@marshall.edu
COTTRILL, Liesl .... 708-209-3053 136 E
liesl.cottrill@cuchicago.edu
COUCH, Charlie .... 970-351-2231.. 84 F
charlie.couch@unco.edu
COUCH, Cheryl .... 402-363-5696 270 D
ccouch@york.edu
COUCH, Laurie, L .... 606-783-2434 184 C
l.couch@moreheadstate.edu
COUCH, Lisa .... 760-384-6230.. 46 M
lcouch@cerrocoso.edu
COUCHEY, Evangeline ... 646-378-6113 310 D
evangeline.couchey@nyack.edu
COUGHENOUR, Russ .... 931-372-6153 426 B
rcoughenour@tntech.edu
COUGHLIN, Cass .... 620-341-5264 173 F
ccoughli@emporia.edu
COUGHLIN, Chris .... 623-845-3205.. 13 C
chris.coughlin@gccaz.edu
COUGHLIN, III, Jay, J .. 443-518-4032 199 F
jcoughlin@howardcc.edu
COUGHLIN, Kevin .... 305-348-2320 110 A
kevin.coughlinjr@fiu.edu
COUGHLIN, Mary Ann .. 413-748-3959 218 I
mcoughlin@springfield.edu
COUGHLIN, Meredith .... 772-462-7304 102 F
mcoughli@irsc.edu
COUGHLIN, Robert, D .. 860-685-2543.. 90 B
rdcoughlin@wesleyan.edu
COUILLARD, Michael .... 719-502-3352.. 82 E
mike.couillard@ppcc.edu
COULE, Phillip, L .... 706-721-1083 116 A
pcoule@augusta.edu
COULING, Mike .... 972-660-5701 439 B
mcouling@lincolntech.com
COULLIETTE, Holly .... 904-808-7441 107 C
hollycoulliette@sjrstate.edu
COULOMBE, Jennifer, B .... 336-734-7957 334 F
jcoulombe@forsythtech.edu
COULON, Richard .... 949-824-6510.. 69 D
rcoulon@uci.edu
COULOUTE, Clifford ...... 718-997-5100 295 B
clifford.couloute@qc.cuny.edu
COULSON, Joseph .... 877-248-6724.. 12 K
jcoulson@hmu.edu
COULSON-CLARK, Margery .... 502-597-6916 183 D
margery.clark@kysu.edu
COULSTON, Susan .... 269-782-1396 231 A
scoulston@swmich.edu
COULTER, Ann .... 641-782-1340 170 F
coulter@swcciowa.edu
COULTER, Cindy .... 828-327-7000 333 B
ccoulter@cvcc.edu
COULTER, Denise .... 609-343-5007 275 D
dcoulter@atlantic.edu
COULTER, Laurie .... 903-813-2900 430 H
lcoulter@austincollege.edu
COULTER, Lisa .... 610-683-4072 394 D
coulter@kutztown.edu
COULTER, Martha .... 802-468-1314 463 E
martha.coulter@castleton.edu
COULTER, Seana .... 443-885-3110 201 A
seana.coulter@morgan.edu
COUNCIL, Juanette .... 910-672-1208 341 C
jcouncil@uncfsu.edu
COUNCIL, Mark .... 910-362-7009 332 H
mcouncil@cfcc.edu
COUNCIL, Timothy .... 909-607-7811.. 37 C
admissions@cgu.edu
COUNLEY, Meagan .... 402-472-3417 269 J
mcounley2@unl.edu
COUNTEE, Jerome .... 559-243-7262.. 66 H
jerome.countee@scccd.edu
COUNTIS, Amber .... 903-468-8198 447 B
amber.countis@tamcu.edu
COUNTS, LaNeta .... 404-471-6483 114 G
lcounts@agnesscott.edu
COUNTS, Richard .... 501-354-2465.. 23 A

COYNE, Michael .... 928-681-0800 216 C
coyne@mslaw.edu
COYNE, Michael .... 978-681-0800 216 C
mcoyne@mslaw.edu
COYNE, Michael .... 570-372-4128 398 F
coyne@susqu.edu
COYNE, Mildred .... 954-201-7811.. 96 F
mcoyne@broward.edu
COYNE, Renee .... 724-738-2028 395 C
renee.coyne@sru.edu
COYNE, Rob .... 317-738-8113 155 D
rcoyne@franklincollege.edu
COZART, Michael .... 251-380-3472.... 6 H
COZBY, Brian .... 256-824-6596.... 8 B
brian.cozby@uah.edu
COZZENS, Christine ...... 404-471-6000 114 G
ccozzens@agnesst.edu
COZZENS, Glenn .... 417-268-6133 250 G
gcozzens@gobbc.edu
COZZOCREA, Rebecca ... 518-736-3622 300 D
rebecca.cozzocrea@fmcc.suny.edu
CRABB, Ann .... 208-467-8593 132 E
atcrabb@nnu.edu
CRABB, Ann .... 208-467-8542 132 E
atcrabb@nnu.edu
CRABB, Jenna, S .... 505-277-2531 288 J
jennas@unm.edu
CRABBE, Heather .... 513-244-4630 356 F
heather.crabbe@msj.edu
CRABBE, Kim .... 518-580-5790 315 F
kcrabbe@skidmore.edu
CRABDREE, Julie .... 573-518-2282 256 D
jcrabdree@mineralarea.edu
CRABILL, Casey .... 315-498-2211 310 F
president@sunyocc.edu
CRABREE, Troy .... 206-239-4500 478 H
CRABTREE, Aaron, T ..... 574-372-5100 155 F
crabtrat@grace.edu
CRABTREE, April .... 415-422-5287.. 72 J
acrabtree@usfca.edu
CRABTREE, Brian .... 678-547-6311 122 E
crabtree_bl@mercer.edu
CRABTREE, Diane .... 503-883-2507 373 F
dcrabtre@linfield.edu
CRABTREE, Ellen .... 208-665-5060 132 D
ellen.crabtree@nic.edu
CRABTREE, Gina, D .... 316-978-3672 178 D
gina.crabtree@wichita.edu
CRABTREE, Gwen .... 817-598-6488 457 J
gcrabtree@wc.edu
CRABTREE, Jenna .... 217-228-5520 133 J
crabtreej@brcn.edu
CRABTREE, Jerry .... 256-233-8222.... 4 C
jerry.crabtree@athens.edu
CRABTREE, Kacy .... 541-440-4682 376 G
kacy.crabtree@umpqua.edu
CRABTREE, Robbin, D ... 310-338-2716.. 51 A
robbin.crabtree@lmu.edu
CRABTREE, Shane .... 801-957-4571 461 C
shane.crabtree@slcc.edu
CRACKENBERG, Peter ... 503-554-2138 373 A
pcrackenberg@georgefox.edu
CRACRAFT, Faith .... 502-863-8000 180 H
faith_cracraft@georgetowncollege.edu
CRADDOCK, Alden .... 314-529-6687 255 B
acraddock@maryville.edu
CRADDOCK, Amanda, E 843-349-2979 408 A
acraddoc@coastal.edu
CRADDOCK, Chris .... 903-983-8181 438 F
ccraddock@kilgore.edu
CRADDOCK, Jackie .... 510-594-3612.. 28 B
jcraddock@cca.edu
CRAFT, Alissa .... 909-469-8820.. 75 I
acraft@westernu.edu
CRAFT, Edwin .... 662-846-4760 245 G
ecraft@deltastate.edu
CRAFT, Jonathan .... 256-216-3310.... 4 C
jonathan.craft@athens.edu
CRAFT, Shonda, M .... 320-308-4894 240 I
smcraft@stcloudstate.edu
CRAFT, Stephen .... 205-665-6540.... 8 D
scraft@montevallo.edu
CRAFT, William, J .... 218-299-3000 235 H
president@cord.edu
CRAFTON, Linda .... 262-595-2341 496 D
crafton@uwp.edu
CRAFTON, Teresa .... 478-274-7833 123 I
tcrafton@oftc.edu
CRAFTS, Deborah .... 978-556-3691 215 E
dcrafts@necc.mass.edu
CRAGAR, Beth .... 931-598-1312 423 D
bcragar@sewanee.edu
CRAGER, Cindy .... 609-626-3658 283 E
cindy.crager@stockton.edu
CRAGG, Michael .... 718-990-6223 313 G
craggm@stjohns.edu
CRAGG, Michael .... 315-781-3740 301 F
cragg@hws.edu
CRAGLE, Rachael, C ..... 865-539-7219 425 B
rccragle@pstcc.edu
CRAHEN, Sherri .... 216-397-4423 353 O
scrahen@jcu.edu
CRAIDER, Holly .... 216-987-2006 351 E
holly.craider@tri-c.edu
CRAIG, Adrienne, M ..... 336-334-5513 343 A
amcraig2@uncg.edu
CRAIG, Barbara .... 269-927-8147 226 F
craig@lakemichigancollege.edu
CRAIG, Brian .... 409-880-8804 449 G
brian.craig@lamar.edu
CRAIG, Calvin .... 704-922-6357 334 G
craig.calvin@gaston.edu
CRAIG, Camilla .... 301-423-3600.. 93 H
CRAIG, Carrick .... 269-387-1900 233 B
carrick.craig@wmich.edu
CRAIG, Christopher, J .. 417-836-5215 256 G
chriscraig@missouristate.edu
CRAIG, Cornell .... 516-463-5102 301 G
cornell.craig@hofstra.edu
CRAIG, Debra .... 520-515-3674.. 11 M
craigd@cochise.edu
CRAIG, Dennis .... 607-436-2500 316 F
dennis.craig@oneonta.edu
CRAIG, Erin .... 616-632-2853 221 E
ebc001@aquinas.edu
CRAIG, James .... 520-206-6916.. 15 B
jcraig7@pima.edu
CRAIG, Jason .... 703-284-5988 468 H
jason.craig@marymount.edu
CRAIG, Jim .... 208-885-6125 132 F
jimcraig@uidaho.edu
CRAIG, John .... 610-436-3133 395 D
jcraig@wcupa.edu
CRAIG, Johnny .... 219-473-4301 154 D
jcraig@ccsj.edu
CRAIG, Johnny .... 407-708-2166 108 D
craigj@seminolestate.edu
CRAIG, Kimberly .... 651-641-8718 235 I
craig@csp.edu
CRAIG, Kris .... 952-358-8150 239 G
kris.craig@normandale.edu
CRAIG, Kristy .... 252-222-6000 333 A
kristyr8434@carteret.edu
CRAIG, Marci .... 330-821-5320 362 E
CRAIG, Marva .... 212-220-8131 293 A
mcraig@bmcc.cuny.edu
CRAIG, Michael .... 816-501-4065 258 I
michael.craig@rockhurst.edu
CRAIG, Myrana .... 478-757-4024 127 F
mcraig@wesleyancollege.edu
CRAIG, Paige .... 708-209-3509 136 E
paige.craig@cuchicago.edu
CRAIG, Sandy .... 618-262-8641 139 I
craigs@iecc.edu
CRAIG, Sarah .... 413-577-4276 211 G
sccraig@umass.edu
CRAIG, William, G .... 732-571-3427 279 A
craig@monmouth.edu
CRAIG-MARIUS, Renee . 559-638-0300.. 67 D
renee.craig-marius@reedleycollege.edu
CRAIGG, Dorende .... 336-315-7800.. 93 H
CRAIGMILES, Janet .... 863-638-7524 114 A
janet.craigmiles@warner.edu
CRAIK, Rebecca, L .... 215-572-2143 378 E
craikr@arcadia.edu
CRAIN, David, R .... 469-284-7366 454 H
dcrain@utsystem.edu
CRAIN, John, L .... 985-549-2280 193 A
jcrain@selu.edu
CRAIN, Lena .... 570-577-2000 379 C
lkc007@bucknell.edu
CRAIN, Rick .... 678-717-3623 127 A
rick.crain@ung.edu
CRAIN, Stacey .... 407-265-8383.. 96 H
CRAIN SPELLS,
Monique .... 817-257-7513 432 A
m.crainspells@tcu.edu
CRAKES, Aileen .... 619-388-2896.. 60 J
acrakes@sdccd.edu
CRAM-RAHLF, Shelly .... 563-288-6011 166 A
scramrahlf@eicc.edu
CRAMB, Alan .... 312-567-3106 140 A
president@iit.edu
CRAMER, Alicia .... 713-646-1808 443 I
acramer@stcl.edu
CRAMER, Gregory, D .... 630-889-6467 145 E
gcramer@nuhs.edu
CRAMER, Joel .... 317-738-8197 155 D
jcramer@franklincollege.edu
CRAMER, Luba .... 330-972-6272 361 H
lcramer@uakron.edu
CRAMER, Renee .... 515-271-3751 165 J
renee.cramer@drake.edu
CRAMER, Robert .... 608-262-3488 495 D
rgcramer@wisc.edu
CRAMER, Tricia, A .... 517-750-1200 231 C
tr700519@arbor.edu
CRAMER, Walter .... 203-837-8547.. 86 B
cramerw@wcsu.edu
CRAMPTON,
Anne-Marie .... 719-336-1520.. 81 K
anne-marie.crampton@lamarcc.edu
CRAMPTON, Donald ...... 508-362-2131 214 D
CRAMPTON, Scott .... 719-336-1681.. 81 K
scott.crampton@lamarcc.edu
CRAMPTON, Troy, D ...... 515-574-1114 167 A
crampton@iowacentral.edu
CRAMSEY, Rachel .... 217-228-5520 133 J
cramseyr@brcn.edu
CRANDALL, Donald, W . 479-524-7150.. 19 H
dcrandal@jbu.edu
CRANDALL, Elizabeth .... 940-552-6291 457 C
lisa.crandall@vernoncollege.edu
CRANDALL, Jackie, K ... 330-569-5975 353 G
noalljk@hiram.edu
CRANDALL, James .... 530-242-7989.. 64 C
jcrandall@shastacollege.edu
CRANDALL, Jennifer ...... 414-847-3344 494 C
jennifercrandall@miad.edu
CRANDALL, Jill .... 607-871-2164 290 B
crandallj@alfred.edu
CRANDALL, Laura .... 315-470-4865 319 D
ldcranda@esf.edu
CRANDALL, Mariella ..... 916-660-7340.. 64 D
mcrandall4@sierracollege.edu
CRANE, Anne .... 316-295-5610 174 A
annec@friends.edu
CRANE, Daniel, R .... 651-631-5100 244 D
drcrane@unwsp.edu
CRANE, David .... 508-531-6145 212 D
dcrane@bridgew.edu
CRANE, Elizabeth .... 315-792-3222 324 B
eacrane@utica.edu
CRANE, Ellen, E .... 989-964-4109 230 E
ecrane@svsu.edu
CRANE, Jeff .... 270-384-8150 183 G
cranej@lindsey.edu
CRANE, Jeff .... 360-438-4564 482 I
jcrane@stmartin.edu
CRANE, Lindsay .... 585-395-5616 317 E
lcrane@brockport.edu
CRANE, Paul .... 810-762-9887 226 B
pcrane@kettering.edu
CRANE, Rob, M .... 913-288-7283 175 B
rcrane@kckcc.edu
CRANE, Ron .... 972-825-4818 444 J
rcrane@sagu.edu
CRANE, Susan, L .... 989-964-4350 230 E
scrane@svsu.edu
CRANFORD, Bill .... 601-925-3283 247 C
cranford@mc.edu
CRANFORD, Elizabeth ... 864-231-2000 406 F
ecranford@andersonuniversity.edu
CRANFORD, Shannon ... 580-628-6229 366 J
shannon.cranford@noc.edu
CRANFORD, Timothy .... 510-879-9223.. 60 C
tcranford@samuelmerritt.edu
CRANHAM, John, B ...... 919-508-2336 344 E
jbcranham@peace.edu
CRANMORE, Jill, A .... 217-443-8756 136 G
jcranmore@dacc.edu
CRANNELL, Annalisa ..... 717-358-4283 383 I
annalisa.crannell@fandm.edu
CRANSON, Gregory .... 206-546-4503 484 B
gcranson@shoreline.edu
CRANSTON, Carolyn ..... 412-924-1375 396 F
ccranston@pts.edu
CRANWELL, Mary .... 732-987-2285 278 A
mcranwell@georgian.edu
CRAPOL, Heidi, A .... 804-828-8824 473 B
hcrapol@vcu.edu
CRAPSER, Bryce .... 860-465-5778.. 85 H
crapserb@easternct.edu
CRAREY, II, Patrick .... 301-891-4481 205 A
pcrarey@wau.edu
CRASTRO-BOLIN, Irene . 914-594-4470 309 B
icrastro@nymc.edu
CRATER, Lucas .... 217-545-9362 150 A
lcrater@siumed.edu
CRATER, Matt .... 805-378-1457.. 73 J
mcrater@vcccd.edu
CRATTY, Frederic, W ..... 203-837-8665.. 86 B
crattyf@wcsu.edu
CRAUN, Elizabeth .... 413-549-4600 210 D
ecpp@hampshire.edu
CRAVEN, Bryan, C .... 850-718-2375.. 97 E
cravenb@chipola.edu
CRAVEN, Christa .... 330-263-2576 351 A
ccraven@wooster.edu
CRAVEN, Deborah .... 303-678-3868.. 81 A
deborah.craven@frontrange.edu
CRAVEN, Heather .... 973-328-5281 276 J
hcraven@ccm.edu
CRAVEN, Katherine .... 781-239-5955 206 B
kcraven@babson.edu
CRAVEN, Kendra .... 402-354-7848 268 B
kendra.craven@methodistcollege.edu
CRAVEN, Nora .... 715-365-4576 499 E
ncraven@nicoletcollege.edu
CRAVEN, Randy .... 423-236-2076 423 F
rlcraven@southern.edu
CRAVENS, Alyssa .... 918-343-7612 369 B
acravens@rsu.edu
CRAVENS, Keith .... 770-859-9779 121 C
CRAVENS, Michael .... 419-824-3620 355 C
mcravens@sistersosf.org
CRAVER, Ken .... 903-510-2591 452 A
kcra@tjc.edu
CRAVER, Robert .... 303-369-5151.. 82 I
robert.craver@plattcolorado.edu
CRAVER, Travis .... 325-670-1856 436 I
travis.craver@hsutx.edu
CRAVER, III, William .... 229-668-3172 395 G
williamcr@pcom.edu
CRAWFORD, Abby .... 863-638-7248 114 A
abby.crawford@warner.edu
CRAWFORD, Adrian .... 318-678-6000 187 H
acrawford@bpcc.edu
CRAWFORD, Andrew ..... 216-987-2053 351 E
andrew.crawford@tri-c.edu
CRAWFORD, Andrew, B 757-594-7663 465 M
andrew.crawford@cnu.edu
CRAWFORD, Ann .... 860-509-9560.. 88 B
acrawford@hartsem.edu
CRAWFORD, Anna .... 304-260-4380 488 C
acrawfor@blueridgectc.edu
CRAWFORD, Arminda ... 614-985-2241 359 L
acrawford@pcj.edu
CRAWFORD, Audrey ..... 205-665-6030.... 8 D
acrawford@montevallo.edu
CRAWFORD, Bill .... 619-201-8700.. 60 G
bill.crawford@sdcc.edu
CRAWFORD, Brittany .... 334-683-2382.... 3 A
bcrawford@marionmilitary.edu
CRAWFORD, Bruce .... 205-929-6312.... 2 H
bcrawford@lawsonstate.edu
CRAWFORD, Bryan .... 719-562-7001.. 82 J
bryan.crawford@pueblocc.edu
CRAWFORD, Cali .... 734-462-4400 230 G
ccrawfor@schoolcraft.edu
CRAWFORD, Cardon, B 843-953-6966 407 C
cardon.crawford@citadel.edu
CRAWFORD, Chemene .. 206-934-3601 483 B
chemene.crawford@seattlecolleges.edu
CRAWFORD, Chemene .. 206-934-3601 483 A
chemene.crawford@seattlecolleges.edu
CRAWFORD, Chris .... 903-923-2225 435 H
chrisc@etbu.edu
CRAWFORD, Chyna, N . 252-335-3113 341 B
cncrawford@ecsu.edu
CRAWFORD, Clinton ..... 718-270-5140 294 G
crawford@mec.cuny.edu
CRAWFORD, Colin .... 415-442-7000.. 43 I
CRAWFORD, Crystal ..... 864-597-4199 414 E
crawfordcr@wofford.edu
CRAWFORD, David .... 773-947-6301 143 H
dcrawford@mccormick.edu
CRAWFORD, David, S ... 202-526-3799.. 93 E
dcrawford@johnpaulii.edu
CRAWFORD, Debbie ..... 970-945-8691.. 78 L
CRAWFORD, Deborah ... 865-974-3053 427 B
dcrawf19@utk.edu
CRAWFORD, Dickie .... 318-257-2445 192 D
crawford@latech.edu
CRAWFORD, Ethan .... 319-296-4204 166 H
ethan.crawford@hawkeyecollege.edu
CRAWFORD, Gina .... 405-208-5900 367 E
gcrawford@okcu.edu
CRAWFORD, Gregory .... 513-529-2345 356 A
president@miamioh.edu

CROCITTO, Peter .... 954-776-4476 103 B
peterc@keiseruniversity.edu
CROCKEM, Raijanel .... 713-313-1066 449 B
crockemr@tsu.edu
CROCKER, Dennis .... 913-722-0272 175 A
CROCKER, Dianne .... 864-596-9028 408 F
dianne.crocker@converse.edu
CROCKER, Harold .... 201-684-7091 280 H
hcrocker@ramapo.edu
CROCKER, Heidi .... 323-731-2383.. 55 H
hcrocker@psuca.edu
CROCKER, Jack .... 575-538-6318 289 G
jack.crocker@wnmu.edu
CROCKER, Jane, S .... 856-415-2250 281 D
jcrocker@rcsj.edu
CROCKER, Jeffery .... 207-602-2303 197 E
jcrocker@une.edu
CROCKER, Kate .... 603-542-7744 273 B
kcrocker@ccsnh.edu
CROCKER, Marjorie .... 706-419-1544 118 A
crocker@covenant.edu
CROCKET, Beka .... 615-898-2501 422 C
beka.crocket@mtsu.edu
CROCKETT, Bennie, R ... 601-318-6116 249 H
crockett@wmcarey.edu
CROCKETT, Nathan, G ... 864-242-5100 406 H
CROCKETT, Suzonne ..... 409-882-3062 449 H
suzonne.crockett@lsco.edu
CROCKETT, William, P .. 410-706-3902 203 A
bcrocket@umaryland.edu
CROCKETT-BELL,
Sharon .... 210-486-2887 429 B
scrockett-bell@alamo.edu
CROCQUET, Marc .... 954-262-8842 105 A
crocquet@nsu.nova.edu
CROFF, Troy .... 503-581-8600 372 H
tcroff@corban.edu
CROFT, Paul .... 908-737-3733 278 E
pcroft@kean.edu
CROFTON,
Stephanie, O .... 336-841-4569 329 F
scrofton@highpoint.edu
CROGHAN, Chris, M .... 605-336-6588 416 A
croghan@augie.edu
CROMARTIE, Anthony ... 973-877-1873 277 G
cromartie@essex.edu
CROMARTIE, Fred .... 251-626-3303.... 7 E
fcromart@ussa.edu
CROMARTIE, Stanley ..... 863-297-1017 106 A
scromartie@polk.edu
CROMER, Elyse .... 765-641-4039 153 G
emcromer@anderson.edu
CROMER, Julie .... 740-593-1711 358 K
jcromer@ohio.edu
CROMPTON, Tim .... 801-626-8078 461 A
tcrompton@weber.edu
CROMWELL, Michelle .... 518-564-2000 318 E
CROMWELL, Susan .... 617-373-2101 217 I
CRONAN, David .... 630-617-3020 137 G
david.cronan@elmhurst.edu
CRONAUER, OSB,
Patrick, T .... 724-805-2324 398 A
patrick.cronauer@stvincent.edu
CRONE, Darren .... 972-883-4826 455 B
darren.crone@utdallas.edu
CRONE, Kimberly .... 860-231-5360.. 90 A
kcrone@usj.edu
CRONE, Paula .... 909-469-5563.. 75 I
pcrone@westernu.edu
CRONIN, Corey .... 978-542-7517 213 E
corey.cronin@salemstate.edu
CRONIN, Elizabeth .... 585-389-2461 307 F
ecronin5@naz.edu
CRONIN, Laura .... 212-229-5662 308 A
croninl@newschool.edu
CRONIN, Mark, W .... 603-641-7250 274 A
mwcronin@anselm.edu
CRONIN, Marta .... 541-506-6103 372 F
mcronin@cgcc.edu
CRONIN, Shawn .... 978-762-4000 215 D
scronin@northshore.edu
CRONIN, Trish .... 508-793-7160 208 C
tcronin@clarku.edu
CRONK, Brian, C .... 716-878-6326 317 F
cronkbc@buffalostate.edu
CRONK, Keith .... 501-279-5700.. 19 C
kcronk@harding.edu
CRONK, Shantel .... 406-265-3594 264 E
shantel.cronk@msun.edu
CRONLEY, Maria .... 931-221-7676 417 H
cronleym@apsu.edu
CRONMILLER, Janelle ... 610-647-4400 385 L
jcronmiller@immaculata.edu

CRONQUIST, Thomas .... 703-416-1441 466 A
tcronquist@divinemercy.edu
CRONRATH, David .... 301-405-6011 202 H
cronrath@umd.edu
CROOK, Chris .... 785-864-9331 177 J
ccrook@ku.edu
CROOK, David .... 646-664-8102 292 K
david.crook@cuny.edu
CROOK, Evonne .... 423-236-2830 423 F
ercrook@southern.edu
CROOK, Patricia .... 615-963-5280 426 A
pcrook@tnstate.edu
CROOK, Rebecca .... 321-674-8099 100 C
bcrook@fit.edu
CROOKENDALE,
Humphrey .... 212-343-1234 306 G
hcrookendale@mcny.edu
CROOKER, Benjamin ..... 718-817-3048 300 C
crooker@fordham.edu
CROOKS, John .... 740-264-5591 352 B
jcrooks@egcc.edu
CROOM, H. Edward ...... 919-658-7745 340 G
hcroom@umo.edu
CROPPER, USMS,
Thomas, A .... 707-654-1011.. 32 A
tacropper@csum.edu
CROSBIE, Jeff .... 435-797-1042 460 C
jeff.crosbie@usu.edu
CROSBY, Anita, L .... 334-387-3877.... 4 B
anitacrosby@amridgeuniversity.edu
CROSBY, Cherie .... 215-885-2360 389 C
ccrosby@manor.edu
CROSBY, Cheryl .... 352-854-2322.. 97 N
crosbyc@cf.edu
CROSBY, Devin .... 561-237-7213 103 W
dcrosby@lynn.edu
CROSBY, Devin .... 530-749-3804.. 77 C
dcrosby@yccd.edu
CROSBY, Gary .... 256-372-8164.... 1 A
gary.crosby@aamu.edu
CROSBY, Gary, B .... 973-290-4475 282 I
gcrobsy@steu.edu
CROSBY, Jean, K .... 765-285-7057 153 H
jkcrosby@bsu.edu
CROSBY, Jesse .... 207-947-4591 194 B
jcrosby@bealcollege.edu
CROSBY, Karen .... 225-771-4845 191 B
karen_crosby@subr.edu
CROSBY, Kim .... 870-307-7275.. 19 I
kim.crosby@lyon.edu
CROSBY, Lynne .... 931-221-6240 417 H
crosbyl@apsu.edu
CROSBY, Mark .... 207-859-5500 194 D
mark.crosby@colby.edu
CROSBY, Michael .... 207-985-7976 194 H
CROSBY, Stephanie .... 805-922-6966.. 24 I
stephanie.crosby@hancockcollege.edu
CROSBY, Susan, E .... 540-453-2363 473 D
crosbys@brcc.edu
CROSBY LEHMANN,
Carl .... 507-786-3894 243 D
lehmann@stolaf.edu
CROSE, Brian .... 407-708-2396 108 D
croseb@seminolestate.edu
CROSE, Sarah .... 563-387-1477 168 B
sarah.crose@luther.edu
CROSLIN, Joey .... 405-208-5075 367 E
jcroslin@okcu.edu
CROSON, Rachel .... 612-626-1616 243 F
CROSS, Berri, V .... 336-334-4822 335 A
bvcross@gtcc.edu
CROSS, Cara, R .... 417-865-2815 250 E
crossca@evangel.edu
CROSS, Charles, E .... 415-422-6522.. 72 J
cross@usfca.edu
CROSS, Cheryl .... 870-512-7827.. 18 A
cheryl_cross@asun.edu
CROSS, Chip .... 828-652-6021 336 B
CROSS, Connie .... 417-865-2815 253 D
crossc@evangel.edu
CROSS, David .... 713-718-8636 437 C
david.cross@hccs.edu
CROSS, Elizabeth, H ...... 252-334-2058 331 F
beth.cross@macuniversity.edu
CROSS, Jeffrey .... 248-476-1122 227 E
jcross@msp.edu
CROSS, Jesse .... 336-334-4822 335 A
jlcross@gtcc.edu
CROSS, Jon .... 937-708-5254 363 G
jcross@wilberforce.edu
CROSS, Kristen .... 870-612-2011.. 22 H
kristen.cross@uaccb.edu

CROSS, Laura .... 605-256-5023 416 F
laura.cross@dsu.edu
CROSS, Mary, M .... 615-353-3301 424 G
mary.cross@nscc.edu
CROSS, Nigel .... 310-544-6424.. 60 B
nigel.cross@usw.salvationarmy.org
CROSS, Penny .... 828-652-6021 336 B
pennyc@mcdowelltech.edu
CROSS, Solomon .... 972-860-8120 434 G
scross@dcccd.edu
CROSS, Stacy .... 310-544-6442.. 60 B
stacy.cross@usw.salvationarmy.org
CROSS, Terry .... 423-614-8140 420 H
tcross@leeuniversity.edu
CROSS, Tim, L .... 865-974-7114 427 B
tlcross@utk.edu
CROSSCUP, Shauna ...... 540-674-3615 474 E
scrosscup@nr.edu
CROSSLAND, Martin ..... 913-971-3514 176 C
mcrossland@mnu.edu
CROSSLIN, Cara .... 205-391-3905.... 3 E
ccrosslin@sheltonstate.edu
CROSSMAN,
Raymond, E .... 312-662-4001 132 G
rec@adler.edu
CROSWELL, Kat, A .... 510-841-1905.. 26 I
CROSWELL, Sky .... 603-897-8514 273 I
CROTEAU, David .... 803-754-4100 408 E
CROTHERS, Bill, S .... 864-644-5011 412 D
president@swu.edu
CROTHERS, Tammy .... 309-467-6309 138 A
tcrothers@eureka.edu
CROTTE, Kirsten .... 614-823-1525 359 H
kcrotte@otterbein.edu
CROTTY, Kaitlyn .... 918-343-7715 369 B
kcrotty@rsu.edu
CROUCH, Alicia .... 859-256-3100 181 C
alicia.crouch@kctcs.edu
CROUCH, Dani .... 541-956-7199 376 A
dcrouch@roguecc.edu
CROUCH, Leon .... 541-552-7672 376 B
CROUCH, Michael, A ..... 205-726-2820.... 6 E
mcrouch@samford.edu
CROUCH, Mike .... 620-343-4600 173 G
mcrouch@fhtc.edu
CROUCH, Peter .... 817-272-2571 454 I
peter.crouch@uta.edu
CROUCH, Robert .... 415-575-6100.. 28 I
rcrouch@ciis.edu
CROUCH, Suzanne .... 903-813-2059 430 H
scrouch@austincollege.edu
CROUCH, Tony .... 620-229-6368 177 G
tony.crouch@sckans.edu
CROUCHET, Cristeen ..... 253-589-5895 478 J
cristeen.crouchet@cptc.edu
CROUGHAN, May .... 530-752-4964.. 69 B
provost@ucdavis.edu
CROUNSE, Cheryl .... 978-542-7591 213 E
cheryl.crounse@salemstate.edu
CROUSE, Jen .... 307-675-0701 501 G
jcrouse@sheridan.edu
CROUSE, Jenn .... 307-675-0701 501 G
jcrouse@sheridan.edu
CROUSE, Kevin .... 956-665-7823 455 D
kevin.crouse@utrgv.edu
CROUSE, Steve .... 864-977-7022 410 I
steve.crouse@ngu.edu
CROUSO, Lena .... 405-491-6304 369 H
lcrouso@snu.edu
CROUSO, Lena .... 405-789-6400 369 H
lcrouso@snu.edu
CROW, Amy .... 937-778-8600 352 D
CROW, Angela .... 479-968-0271.. 18 C
acrow@atu.edu
CROW, Brook .... 314-838-8858 261 F
bcrow@ugst.edu
CROW, Cecily .... 706-236-2293 116 B
ccrow@berry.edu
CROW, Jeff .... 870-245-4258.. 20 D
crowj@obu.edu
CROW, Michael, M .... 480-965-8972.. 10 J
michael.crow@asu.edu
CROW, Scott .... 916-484-8647.. 50 G
crows@arc.losrios.edu
CROW, Steven .... 831-755-6700.. 44 G
CROWDER, Darren .... 417-328-1797 259 I
dcrowder@sbuniv.edu
CROWDER, Jim .... 732-224-1987 276 B
jcrowder@brookdalecc.edu
CROWDER, Sabrina .... 334-229-4156.... 4 A
scrowder@alasu.edu

CROWDER,
Stephanie, B .... 773-896-2400 134 L
sbcrowder@ctschicago.edu
CROWDER, Vickie .... 304-473-8032 491 D
crowder_v@wvwc.edu
CROWE, Aliesha, R .... 715-788-7208 499 H
aliesha.crowe@northwoodtech.edu
CROWE, Beth .... 618-634-3200 149 G
CROWE, Ellen .... 816-604-3108 255 G
ellen.crowe@mcckc.edu
CROWE, Kellie .... 276-739-2456 475 F
kcrowe@vhcc.edu
CROWE, Ken .... 706-864-1499 127 A
ken.crowe@ung.edu
CROWE, Lindsey .... 270-852-3118 183 E
lcrowe@kwc.edu
CROWE, Michael .... 270-745-5429 186 C
michael.crowe@wku.edu
CROWE, Peggy .... 270-745-3159 186 C
peggy.crowe@wku.edu
CROWE, Sarah .... 770-533-7009 122 B
scrowe@laniertech.edu
CROWE, Shad, M .... 315-792-3472 324 B
smcrowe@utica.edu
CROWE, JR., Terry, M .. 865-694-6619 425 B
tmcrowe1@pstcc.edu
CROWE, Thomas .... 847-543-2473 136 A
tcrowe@clcillinois.edu
CROWELL, Anthony .... 212-431-2840 309 A
anthony.crowell@nyls.edu
CROWELL, Heidi .... 603-897-8630 273 I
hcrowell@rivier.edu
CROWELL, Scott .... 507-537-6844 241 D
scott.crowell@smsu.edu
CROWETIPTON, Vaughn 864-294-2138 409 H
vaughn.crowetipton@furman.edu
CROWFOOT, Dara .... 312-996-8586 151 G
CROWL, Ronald .... 330-829-2756 362 E
crowlrl@mountunion.edu
CROWLEY, Cara, J .... 806-345-5518 429 E
cjcrowley@actx.edu
CROWLEY, Janelle .... 262-472-1918 497 D
CROWLEY, Karlyn, A ..... 740-368-3101 359 G
kacrowley@owu.edu
CROWLEY, Kimberly, A . 806-354-6087 429 E
kacrowley@actx.edu
CROWLEY, Merritt .... 508-286-3464 220 B
crowley_merritt@wheatoncollege.edu
CROWLEY, Michael .... 408-554-4300.. 63 B
mcrowley@scu.edu
CROWLEY, Tanya .... 978-665-4789 212 E
tcrowle7@fitchburgstate.edu
CROWLEY, Tim .... 785-628-4241 173 H
tcrowley@fhsu.edu
CROWLEY, Timothy, D .. 207-768-2811 195 G
tcrowley@nmcc.edu
CROWN, Deborah, F ...... 407-646-2405 106 L
dcrown@rollins.edu
CROWSON, Natalie .... 978-626-7111 210 C
ncrowson@gcts.edu
CROWTHER, Kristi .... 336-334-4227 343 A
klcrowth@uncg.edu
CROWTHER, Lori .... 620-792-9216 171 I
crowtherl@bartonccc.edu
CROWTHER, Steven .... 910-221-2224 331 B
scrowther@manna.edu
CROYLE, Kristin .... 315-312-2285 318 D
kristin.croyle@oswego.edu
CROYLE, Randi .... 208-885-5522 132 F
rcroyle@uidaho.edu
CROZIER, Nate .... 305-284-5766 113 C
nac132@miami.edu
CRUCE, Carrie .... 254-298-8425 445 G
carrie.cruce@templejc.edu
CRUCIANI, Mark .... 570-941-4274 401 F
mark.cruciani@scranton.edu
CRUCITTI, Thomas .... 203-837-9090.. 86 B
crucittit@wcsu.edu
CRUDDAS, Shanti .... 408-847-4060.. 52 H
CRUICKSHANK, Cam ..... 704-403-1521 327 C
cameron.cruickshank@atriumhealth.org
CRUICKSHANK, Laura ... 860-486-1656.. 89 D
laura.cruickshank@uconn.edu
CRUIKSHANK, Alexis .... 206-281-2752 483 G
acruikshank@spu.edu
CRUISE, Charmaine, T .. 717-337-6579 384 D
ccruise@gettysburg.edu
CRUISE, Thomas .... 540-831-5479 469 D
tcruise@radford.edu
CRULL, Matthew .... 815-825-2086 141 F
mcrull@kish.edu
CRUM, Claude .... 606-368-6061 178 G
claudecrum@alc.edu

CUMBERLAND, Lyndsay .... 662-329-7295 248 A
ldcumberland@muw.edu
CUMBIE, Donna, L .... 252-222-6161 333 A
cumbied@carteret.edu
CUMENS, Chris .... 270-901-1113 182 H
chris.cumens@kctcs.edu
CUMINGS, Victoria .... 616-538-2330 224 E
vcumings@gracechristian.edu
CUMISKEY, James .... 207-602-4800 194 H
jimcumiskey@landingschool.edu
CUMMING, Carrie .... 269-387-4300 233 B
carrie.cumming@wmich.edu
CUMMING, Tammie ...... 718-951-5864 293 C
tammie.cumming@brooklyn.cuny.edu
CUMMINGS, Alessia ..... 918-836-6886 370 B
CUMMINGS, Alison .... 404-270-5353 126 B
acummin3@spelman.edu
CUMMINGS, Andrea, M 904-470-8220.. 98 L
a.cummings@ewc.edu
CUMMINGS, Andrew ..... 503-845-3505 374 A
andrew.cummings@mtangel.edu
CUMMINGS, Angelic, M .... 304-260-4380 488 C
acumming@blueridgectc.edu
CUMMINGS, SSE, Brian, J .... 802-654-2386 462 G
bcummings@smcvt.edu
CUMMINGS, Brittany ..... 405-491-6365 369 H
bcummings@snu.edu
CUMMINGS, Carmen .... 850-599-3707 109 I
carmen.cummings@famu.edu
CUMMINGS, Chris .... 937-778-8600 352 D
CUMMINGS, Christopher .... 508-588-9100 215 A
cwcummings@massasoit.mass.edu
CUMMINGS, Corlis .... 678-466-5505 117 D
corliscummings@clayton.edu
CUMMINGS, Dana .... 317-738-8235 155 D
dcummings@franklincollege.edu
CUMMINGS, Edie .... 318-869-5191 186 F
ecummings@centenary.edu
CUMMINGS, Eric .... 615-547-1323 419 C
ecummings@cumberland.edu
CUMMINGS, Evangeline 352-294-7158 111 A
ecummings@ufl.edu
CUMMINGS, Glenn, T ... 207-780-4480 197 D
glennc@maine.edu
CUMMINGS, Jan .... 850-718-2201.. 97 E
cummingsj@chipola.edu
CUMMINGS, John .... 518-782-6932 315 E
jcummings@siena.edu
CUMMINGS, Katherine .. 570-740-0420 389 A
CUMMINGS, Keith .... 405-491-6396 369 H
kcummings@snu.edu
CUMMINGS, Kevin, R ... 914-594-4536 309 B
kevin_cummings@nymc.edu
CUMMINGS, Liz .... 910-775-4155 343 B
liz.cummings@uncp.edu
CUMMINGS, JR., McDuffie .... 910-521-6690 343 B
mcduffie.cummings@uncp.edu
CUMMINGS, Robin, G .. 910-521-4471 343 B
chancellor@uncp.edu
CUMMINGS, Simone ..... 314-968-5951 262 C
simonecummings84@webster.edu
CUMMINGS, Terri .... 217-443-8786 136 G
tcummings@dacc.edu
CUMMINGS, Torreya ..... 415-551-9227.. 28 B
tcummings@cca.edu
CUMMINGS, Twyla .... 585-475-5567 312 F
tjcppr@rit.edu
CUMMINGS, Wanda ...... 314-362-6590 253 G
wanda.cummings@barnesjewishcollege.edu
CUMMINGS-DANSON, Gail, L .... 518-580-5730 315 F
gcumming@skidmore.edu
CUMMINGS-DANSON, Gail, L .... 518-580-5370 315 F
gcumming@skidmore.edu
CUMMINS, Bev .... 402-437-2554 269 C
bcummins@southeast.edu
CUMMINS, Jeffrey .... 559-278-3013.. 31 B
jcummins@csufresno.edu
CUMMINS, Kendra .... 918-540-6201 366 F
kendra.cummins@neo.edu
CUMMINS, Michelle ...... 812-888-4573 162 F
mcummins@vinu.edu
CUMMINS, Stephen, B .. 530-898-5917.. 30 D
sbcummins@csuchico.edu
CUMMO, Salvatrice .... 626-585-7693.. 56 D
scummo@pasadena.edu
CUMPSTSON, Jennifer ... 630-942-3570 135 I
cumpstonj@cod.edu
CUNEO, Sean, P .... 814-824-2118 389 G
scuneo@mercyhurst.edu
CUNHA, Carlos .... 478-289-2063 118 C
ccunha@ega.edu
CUNION, Jessica .... 330-823-6051 362 E
cunionjs@mountunion.edu
CUNION, William .... 216-987-2341 351 E
william.cunion@tri-c.edu
CUNNINGHAM, Annie, S .... 765-658-4800 154 J
CUNNINGHAM, Beverly 765-361-6221 163 B
cunningb@wabash.edu
CUNNINGHAM, Chad ... 563-588-8000 166 C
ccunningham@emmaus.edu
CUNNINGHAM, Dana ... 785-628-4424 173 H
dacunningham@fhsu.edu
CUNNINGHAM, Denise, S .... 516-463-6864 301 G
denise.cunningham@hofstra.edu
CUNNINGHAM, Eric ...... 573-875-7649 251 I
ercunningham@ccis.edu
CUNNINGHAM, Gary .... 651-201-1818 237 B
gary.cunningham@minnstate.edu
CUNNINGHAM, Huie, J 601-979-1111 246 F
huie.t.cunningham@jsums.edu
CUNNINGHAM, Jamal, R .... 414-464-9777 498 B
cunningham.jamal@wspp.edu
CUNNINGHAM, James .. 315-279-5228 303 G
jcunning@keuka.edu
CUNNINGHAM, Janet ... 954-771-0376 103 S
CUNNINGHAM, Janet, L .... 580-327-8400 367 A
jlcunningham@nwosu.edu
CUNNINGHAM, Jennifer, L .... 610-758-5799 388 E
jlc516@lehigh.edu
CUNNINGHAM, Jill ...... 209-381-6470.. 52 A
jill.cunningham@mccd.edu
CUNNINGHAM, Jim ...... 660-596-7208 259 M
jcunningham@sfccmo.edu
CUNNINGHAM, John, A .... 513-556-0626 361 J
bearcat.ad@uc.edu
CUNNINGHAM, Joi, M . 248-370-2190 229 I
cunning3@oakland.edu
CUNNINGHAM, Julie .... 580-581-2612 365 D
jucunnin@cameron.edu
CUNNINGHAM, Karla, K .... 317-940-9570 154 C
kcunning@butler.edu
CUNNINGHAM, Kathy ... 610-372-4721 396 H
kcunningham@racc.edu
CUNNINGHAM, Kay ...... 901-321-3430 418 G
kay.cunningham@cbu.edu
CUNNINGHAM, Kevin, A .... 563-884-5898 169 F
kevin.cunningham@palmer.edu
CUNNINGHAM, Kim ...... 951-343-4227.. 27 G
kcunningham@calbaptist.edu
CUNNINGHAM, Kima .... 937-376-6566 349 J
kcunningham@centralstate.edu
CUNNINGHAM, Larry .... 843-329-1000 407 A
CUNNINGHAM, Lawrence (Bubba), R .. 919-962-8200 342 C
bubba.cunningham@unc.edu
CUNNINGHAM, Linda ... 402-559-7394 269 K
lcunningham@unmc.edu
CUNNINGHAM, Mark .... 404-756-4654 115 G
mcunningham@atlm.edu
CUNNINGHAM, Michael .... 504-865-5261 191 F
mcunnin1@tulane.edu
CUNNINGHAM, Michael .... 201-684-7666 280 H
mcunning@ramapo.edu
CUNNINGHAM, II, Michael, J .... 401-333-7121 404 C
mjcunningham2@ccri.edu
CUNNINGHAM, Michael, R .... 858-642-8101.. 53 I
mcunningham@nu.edu
CUNNINGHAM, Nicole .. 508-793-2265 208 D
ncunning@holycross.edu
CUNNINGHAM, Pat .... 615-460-6617 418 B
pat.cunningham@belmont.edu
CUNNINGHAM, Patricia, A .... 205-940-7800.... 5 D
pcunningham@fortisinstitute.edu
CUNNINGHAM, Phillip . 205-366-8979.... 7 A
pcunninghan@stillman.edu
CUNNINGHAM, Rebecca, M .... 734-764-1185 231 H
stroh@umich.edu
CUNNINGHAM, Richardo .... 563-589-3115 170 G
CUNNINGHAM, Sarah ... 314-977-2226 259 F
sarah.cunningham@slu.edu
CUNNINGHAM, Sarah ... 401-454-6100 405 B
scunning@risd.edu
CUNNINGHAM, Sean .... 512-463-4930 449 E
sean.cunningham@tsus.edu
CUNNINGHAM, Stephen .... 607-753-5565 318 A
stephen.cunningham@cortland.edu
CUNNINGHAM, Susan, W .... 540-458-8489 477 D
scunningham@wlu.edu
CUNNINGHAM, Tamara 201-200-3454 279 D
tcunningham@njcu.edu
CUNNINGHAM, Tamara 951-487-3116.. 53 A
tcunningham@msjc.edu
CUNNINGHAM, Todd, D .... 724-357-7872 394 C
todd.cunningham@iup.edu
CUNNINGHAM, William 636-584-6651 253 B
william.cunningham@eastcentral.edu
CUNNINGHAM, William 215-248-7120 381 A
cunninghamw@chc.edu
CUNNINGS, Chris .... 217-424-6244 144 G
ccunnings@millikin.edu
CUP, Jo Beth .... 312-662-4101 132 G
jcup@adler.edu
CUPICH, Blase .... 847-566-6401 152 I
CUPICH, Krista .... 402-280-1823 266 H
kristacupich@creighton.edu
CUPP, Amy .... 304-829-7567 487 A
acupp@bethanywv.edu
CUPP, Craig .... 870-236-6901.. 18 J
CUPP, Jason .... 312-506-4634.. 39 D
jason.cupp@columbiacollege.edu
CUPP, Scott, A .... 432-837-8303 450 B
scott.cupp@sulross.edu
CUPPETT, Cathy .... 843-383-8121 408 B
ccuppett@coker.edu
CUPPLES, Tamara .... 212-217-4069 299 D
tamara_cupples@fitnyc.edu
CURBO, Billy, D .... 254-659-7701 437 A
bdcurbo@hillcollege.edu
CURCHACK, Barb .... 651-450-3739 238 E
bcurchack@inverhills.edu
CURCI, Roberto .... 708-524-6321 137 C
rcurci@dom.edu
CURCIO, Ellen .... 610-409-3600 401 H
ecurcio@ursinus.edu
CURD, Michael .... 877-248-6724.. 12 K
mcurd@hmu.edu
CURETON, Alan, S .... 651-631-5250 244 D
ascureton@unwsp.edu
CURFMAN, Mike .... 218-683-8630 240 B
mike.curfman@northlandcollege.edu
CURIEL, Erika .... 714-997-6736.. 36 B
curiel@chapman.edu
CURKO, Sandy, A .... 718-997-5725 295 B
sandy.curko@qc.cuny.edu
CURL, Bridget .... 309-438-2231 140 D
kbcurl@ilstu.edu
CURL, John, D .... 801-863-6746 460 D
jcurl@uvu.edu
CURLE, Thomas .... 919-508-2366 344 E
tocurle@peace.edu
CURLEE, Dan .... 817-598-6227 457 J
dcurlee@wc.edu
CURLEY, Amy .... 928-757-0801.. 14 F
acurley@mohave.edu
CURLEY, Greg, M .... 814-641-3521 386 E
curleyg@juniata.edu
CURLEY, Jami .... 419-824-3708 355 C
jcurley@lourdes.edu
CURLEY, Lauren .... 781-239-2572 214 G
lcurley@massbay.edu
CURLEY, Rian .... 805-493-3100.. 29 C
rcurley@callutheran.edu
CURLEY, Russell .... 989-686-9339 223 J
russellcurley@delta.edu
CURLEY, Scott .... 815-224-0301 140 E
scott_curley@ivcc.edu
CURNIN, Kevin .... 914-633-2213 302 E
kcurnin@iona.edu
CURNUTT, Cindy .... 432-335-6601 441 A
ccurnutt@odessa.edu
CURNUTT, Deana .... 575-624-8040 287 B
curnutt@nmmi.edu
CURPHEY, Richena .... 805-525-4417.. 67 K
rcurphey@thomasaquinas.edu
CURPHY, Kathleen .... 618-634-3260 149 G
kathleenc@shawneecc.edu
CURRALL, Steven, C ..... 813-974-5437 111 C
president@usf.edu
CURRAN, Dennis .... 425-564-2446 477 J
dennis.curran@bellevuecollege.edu
CURRAN, Jack .... 718-862-7934 304 M
jack.curran@manhattan.edu
CURRAN, James .... 914-594-3723 309 B
jcurran6@nymc.edu
CURRAN, James, W ...... 404-727-8720 118 E
jcurran@sph.emory.edu
CURRAN, Jennifer .... 860-685-2008.. 90 B
jcurran@wesleyan.edu
CURRAN, Joel .... 919-962-2011 342 C
joel.curran@unc.edu
CURRAN, Kathy .... 541-776-9942 375 B
kathy.c@pacificbible.edu
CURRAN, Lizzy, E .... 402-280-2221 266 H
lizzycurran@creighton.edu
CURRAN, Matt .... 802-443-5835 462 E
matthewc@middlebury.edu
CURRAN, Sheri, L .... 309-794-8058 133 C
shericurran@augustana.edu
CURRAN, Terrence .... 904-620-5063 111 B
terrence.curran@unf.edu
CURRAN, SJ, Thomas, B .... 816-501-4250 258 I
thomas.curran@rockhurst.edu
CURRAN-HEADLEY, Marie .... 518-255-5127 319 C
curranmc@cobleskill.edu
CURRANT, Paul .... 757-683-3956 469 B
pcurrant@odu.edu
CURREN, Kerry .... 207-236-8581 196 B
kcurren@mainemedia.edu
CURRENT, Lori, M .... 800-287-8822 154 A
currelo@bethanyseminary.edu
CURRERI, Michelle .... 401-874-4462 405 E
mcurreri@uri.edu
CURRERI-ERMATINGER, Dyana .... 510-430-2392.. 52 E
dcurreri@mills.edu
CURRIE, Catherine .... 401-232-6369 404 A
ccurrie@bryant.edu
CURRIE, Cathleen .... 208-562-2008 131 E
cathleencurrie@cwi.edu
CURRIE, David .... 978-468-7111 210 C
dcurrie@gcts.edu
CURRIE, Deborah .... 413-662-5410 213 C
deborah.currie@mcla.edu
CURRIE, Eunice, M .... 817-272-5554 454 I
currie@uta.edu
CURRIE, Jennifer .... 508-531-2338 212 D
j1currie@bridgew.edu
CURRIE, John .... 215-887-5511 402 E
jcurrie@wts.edu
CURRIE, John, D .... 336-758-5000 344 C
CURRIE, Kathy .... 734-677-5143 232 D
kcurrie@wccnet.edu
CURRIE, Wayne .... 603-222-4282 274 A
wcurrie@anselm.edu
CURRIER, Christine .... 785-248-2562 176 I
christine.currier@ottawa.edu
CURRIER, Michelle .... 315-386-7401 320 B
currierm@canton.edu
CURRIER, Nicole, A ...... 301-546-0560 201 E
curriena@pgcc.edu
CURRIERA, Joy, L .... 202-685-3924 502 K
CURRIN, Bruce, A .... 402-472-3105 269 J
bcurrin1@unl.edu
CURRINGTON, Adrienne .... 530-226-4788.. 64 E
acurrington@simpsonu.edu
CURRIVAN, Megan, D .. 617-322-3568 211 A
megan_currivan@laboure.edu
CURRY, Adora .... 501-812-2771.. 23 B
acurry@uaptc.edu
CURRY, Angela .... 502-852-5777 186 A
angela.curry@louisville.edu
CURRY, Bill .... 601-318-6486 249 H
bcurry@wmcarey.edu
CURRY, Brian, D .... 262-243-5700 492 E
brian.curry@cuw.edu
CURRY, Carolyn, S .... 240-895-4282 202 B
cscurry@smcm.edu
CURRY, Christa .... 513-244-4614 356 F
christa.curry@msj.edu
CURRY, Gina .... 916-278-7461.. 32 D
curryg@skymail.csus.edu
CURRY, James .... 402-844-7063 268 H
jamesc@northeast.edu
CURRY, James .... 718-997-5545 295 B
james.curry@qc.cuny.edu

CURRY, Janel, M .... 716-880-2241 305 G janel.m.curry@medaille.edu
CURRY, Jason, R .... 615-329-8697 419 H jcurry@fisk.edu
CURRY, Judson .... 815-825-9532 141 F jcurry2@kish.edu
CURRY, Kathleen .... 413-265-2412 208 E curryk@elms.edu
CURRY, Keith .... 310-900-1600.. 39 F kcurry@compton.edu
CURRY, Leann .... 940-397-4138 440 C leann.curry@msutexas.edu
CURRY, Marilyn .... 662-252-8000 248 G mcurry@rustcollege.edu
CURRY, Milton, S .... 213-740-2723.. 73 D archdean@usc.edu
CURRY, R. Esther .... 954-492-5353.. 97 G ecurry@citycollege.edu
CURRY, Reva .... 989-686-9298 223 J revacurry@delta.edu
CURRY, Robert .... 646-660-6000 292 L robert.curry@baruch.cuny.edu
CURRY, Robert .... 805-922-6966.. 24 I rcurry@hancockcollege.edu
CURRY, Stanmetrica ...... 256-761-6208.... 7 B scurry@talladega.edu
CURRY, Susan .... 618-514-3110 147 E susan.curry@principia.edu
CURRY, Terri, A .... 712-274-5259 168 E curryte@morningside.edu
CURRY, Theresa .... 413-545-5867 211 G tcurry@umass.edu
CURRY, Tim .... 606-546-1682 185 D tcurry@unionky.edu
CURRY-ROBERTS, April, E .... 615-327-6453 421 D acurry@mmc.edu
CURTIN, Jason, E .... 410-546-6938 204 D jecurtin@salisbury.edu
CURTIN, Katie, M .... 410-548-4773 204 D kmcurtin@salisbury.edu
CURTIN, Shawn, P .... 717-867-6207 388 C curtin@lvc.edu
CURTIN, Valerie .... 406-447-6913 264 B valerie.curtin@helenacollege.edu
CURTIS, Amy .... 207-879-8757 194 G acurtis@idsva.edu
CURTIS, Ardys, E .... 253-535-7149 482 A acurtis@plu.edu
CURTIS, Cesquinn .... 512-245-2396 450 C cmc496@txstate.edu
CURTIS, Dawn .... 334-683-2350.... 3 A dcurtis@marionmilitary.edu
CURTIS, Deborah .... 812-237-4000 156 D president@indstate.edu
CURTIS, Deborah .... 716-286-8711 309 H dcurtis@niagara.edu
CURTIS, Elaine .... 931-540-2534 424 C bcurtis@columbiastate.edu
CURTIS, III, Guy, E ...... 540-868-4079 474 C gcurtis@lfcc.edu
CURTIS, Jacki .... 800-553-4674 156 B jcurtis@horizonuniversity.edu
CURTIS, Jason .... 805-546-3122.. 40 F jason_curtis@cuesta.edu
CURTIS, Jeanne, F .... 215-898-6300 400 F curtis@isc.upenn.edu
CURTIS, Jena .... 607-753-2979 318 A jena.curtis@cortland.edu
CURTIS, Jennifer .... 760-384-6212.. 46 M jennifer.curtis@cerrocoso.edu
CURTIS, Jerri .... 301-295-3638 503 C jerri.curtis@usuhs.edu
CURTIS, Joanna .... 901-678-3951 426 G jecurtis@memphis.edu
CURTIS, Kelly, T .... 864-488-4601 410 B kcurtis@limestone.edu
CURTIS, Matt .... 914-831-0313 297 A mcurtis@cw.edu
CURTIS, Regina .... 413-775-1426 214 E curtis@gcc.mass.edu
CURTIS, Rick .... 406-243-2122 263 K richard.curtis@umontana.edu
CURTIS, Roxie .... 816-802-3437 254 D rcurtis@kcai.edu
CURTIS, Sandra .... 406-243-2611 263 K sandra.curtis@umontana.edu
CURTIS, Shannon .... 508-767-7248 206 A sj.curtis@assumption.edu
CURTIS, Trina .... 828-726-2303 332 G tcurtis@cccti.edu
CURTIS-CHAVEZ, Mark .. 630-942-2800 135 I curtis-chavezm@cod.edu
CURTRIGHT, Jonathan, W .... 573-884-8738 261 A curtrightj@health.missouri.edu
CURVIN, Nicole .... 802-443-3000 462 E deanofadmissions@middlebury.edu
CURZAN, Anne, L .... 734-764-0322 231 H acurzan@umich.edu
CUSACK, Emma .... 949-794-9090.. 66 D ecusack@stanbridge.edu
CUSACK, Jacqueline, L . 973-596-6445 279 E jacqueline.l.cusack@njit.edu
CUSACK, Kristen .... 303-360-4701.. 80 E kristen.cusack@ccaurora.edu
CUSATO, Brian .... 859-238-5218 180 B b.cusato@centre.edu
CUSEO, Vincent .... 323-259-2700.. 54 I vcuseo@oxy.edu
CUSHING, Ryan .... 815-394-5047 148 D rcushing@rockford.edu
CUSHION, Danielle .... 563-425-5765 170 H cushiond46@uiu.edu
CUSHMAN, Neal .... 864-242-5100 406 H
CUSHMAN, Robert .... 585-395-2032 317 E rcushman@brockport.edu
CUSICK, Dianna .... 612-659-6319 239 A dianna.cusick@minneapolis.edu
CUSICK, Sherry .... 563-589-3115 170 G
CUSICK, Timothy .... 561-732-4424 107 G tcusick@svdp.edu
CUSIMANO, Domonic, A .... 443-518-4448 199 F dcusimano@howardcc.edu
CUSIMANO, Theresa ...... 570-577-2000 379 C tmc013@bucknell.edu
CUSKOVIC, Amel .... 540-831-5008 469 D acuskovic@radford.edu
CUSSACK, Missy .... 770-528-4545 117 B
CUSSEN, Susan .... 845-451-1471 297 G susan.cussen@culinary.edu
CUSTARDO, Lisa .... 815-394-3600 148 D lcustardo@rockford.edu
CUSTER, Carole, A .... 515-294-3134 163 G cacuste@iastate.edu
CUSTER, Laura .... 859-344-3314 185 B custerl@thomasmore.edu
CUSTODIA-LORA, Noemi .... 978-738-7401 215 E ncustodialora@necc.mass.edu
CUTCHENS, Melinda ..... 229-333-5952 127 E cutchens@valdosta.edu
CUTCHER, Rachael .... 707-527-4011.. 63 D
CUTCHINS, Cathy .... 757-569-6712 474 H ccutchins@pdc.edu
CUTIETTA, Robert, A ..... 213-740-5389.. 73 D musicdean@thornton.usc.edu
CUTILLO, Michael .... 617-236-5447 209 G mcutillo@fisher.edu
CUTKELVIN, Gilbert .... 512-505-3074 438 A gccutkelvin@htu.edu
CUTLER, Amy .... 509-777-4733 486 C acutler@whitworth.edu
CUTLER, Brooke .... 310-506-4246.. 56 G brooke.cutler@pepperdine.edu
CUTLER, Chris .... 315-268-6745 295 F ccutler@clarkson.edu
CUTLER, Iris .... 206-517-4541 483 F admissions@sieam.edu
CUTLER, Jerry .... 212-229-5671 308 A jerry.cutler@newschool.edu
CUTLER, Jon .... 304-696-3270 489 M jon.cutler@marshall.edu
CUTLER, Nancy .... 408-554-4915.. 63 B ncutler@scu.edu
CUTLER, Richard .... 435-797-3981 460 C richard.cutler@usu.edu
CUTLER, Spencer .... 208-732-6600 131 D scutler@csi.edu
CUTLER, Stephen .... 803-777-0221 413 A sjcutler@cop.sc.edu
CUTLER, Stephen, J ...... 803-777-8310 413 A ashley@sccp.sc.edu
CUTRELL, Lori .... 615-230-4834 425 E lori.cutrell@volstate.edu
CUTRER, Emily .... 903-223-3001 448 A emily.cutrer@tamut.edu
CUTRI, David .... 419-530-6294 363 B david.cutri@utoledo.edu
CUTRIGHT, Bruce .... 402-461-5177 267 E
CUTRIGHT, Robyn, E .... 859-238-5573 180 B robyn.cutright@centre.edu
CUTSINGER, Carmen ..... 618-985-2828 140 H carmencutsinger@jalc.edu
CUTSPEC, John .... 828-251-6868 342 B jcutspec@unca.edu
CUTTER, Cheri, L .... 407-582-1322 113 I ccutter1@valenciacollege.edu
CUTTER, Todd .... 828-328-1741 330 F todd.cutter@lr.edu
CUTTING, J. Cooper ..... 309-438-2922 140 D jccutti@ilstu.edu
CUTTING, Jeff .... 508-286-3785 220 B cutting_jeff@wheatoncollege.edu
CUTTING, Judith .... 831-646-4000.. 52 G jcutting@mpc.edu
CUTTLE-OLIVER, Ellen ... 508-531-2691 212 D e2oliver@bridgew.edu
CUTTS, Keely .... 812-488-2602 161 G kc391@evansville.edu
CUZ, Julio .... 951-571-6380.. 59 B julio.cuz@mvc.edu
CUZZO, Maria .... 715-394-8447 497 C mcuzzo@uwsuper.edu
CUZZOLINA, Brian .... 610-795-6139 385 I bcuzzolina@haverford.edu
CVETIC, Mike .... 412-237-4146 381 D mcvetic@ccac.edu
CVITKOVIC, Viki .... 847-543-6504 136 A vcvitkovic@clcillinois.edu
CWYK, Alysson .... 215-965-4050 390 E acwyk@moore.edu
CYFERS, Melissa .... 781-762-1211 209 F mcyfers@fmc.edu
CYGAN, Brian, L .... 570-326-3761 392 W brian.cygan@pct.edu
CYPHERS, Christopher, J .... 212-592-2550 315 C ccyphers@sva.edu
CYPRESS, Sharen .... 731-989-6074 419 K scypress@fhu.edu
CYR, Jamie .... 315-684-6000 321 A
CYREE, Kendall, B .... 662-915-1103 249 D kbcyree@olemiss.edu
CYRUS, Cynthia, J .... 615-322-4474 428 A cynthia.j.cyrus@vanderbilt.edu
CYRUS, Danielle .... 906-487-2510 228 A dcyrus@mtu.edu
CZAJKA, Darcy .... 518-388-6101 323 J czajkad@union.edu
CZARAPATA, Paul .... 859-256-3100 181 C paul.czarapata@kctcs.edu
CZARDA, Lawrence, D .. 336-217-7221 329 C lczarda@greensboro.edu
CZARNECKI, John .... 607-431-4318 301 A czarneckij@hartwick.edu
CZARTOSKI, Ted .... 419-783-2503 351 K tczartoski@defiance.edu
CZEKANSKI, Kathleen ... 215-951-1432 387 A czekanski@lasalle.edu
CZERNIECKI, Thomas, J .... 856-222-9311 281 C tczerniecki@rcbc.edu
CZERWIEC, Kristofer ...... 402-399-2309 266 F kczerwiec@csm.edu
CZEZULIN, Annalisa ...... 410-337-6046 199 B annalisa.czeczulin@goucher.edu
CZUCHRY, Michael .... 830-372-6047 449 A mczuchry@tlu.edu
CZYZ, Vito .... 716-926-8925 301 E vczyz@hilbert.edu

D

DA CUNHA, Ana .... 617-236-8810 209 G adacunha@fisher.edu
DAAR, Judith .... 859-572-5717 184 E daarj1@nku.edu
DAAR, Karen .... 818-947-2378.. 49 G daarkl@lavc.edu
DAAS, Mahesh .... 617-585-0200 207 A mahesh.daas@the-bac.edu
DABIDAT, Mike Vishol . 212-812-4040 308 G mdabidat@nycda.edu
DABIRIAN, Amir .... 657-278-8500.. 31 C adabirian@fullerton.edu
DABLOW, Joseph .... 502-852-6145 186 A jsdabl01@louisville.edu
DABNEY, Emily, C .... 662-846-4040 245 G edabney@deltastate.edu
DABNEY, Natasha .... 619-961-4256.. 68 A ndabney@tjsl.edu
DABOLL-LAVOIE, Kathleen .... 585-389-2591 307 F kdaboll9@naz.edu
DABROWSKI, Keisha .... 848-932-8576 282 A kd383@echo.rutgers.edu
DACE, Karen, L .... 317-278-3820 157 D kdace@iupui.edu
DACEY, Joe .... 508-565-1804 219 A jdacey@stonehill.edu
DACEY, Susan .... 973-748-9000 276 A susan_dacey@bloomfield.edu
DACH, Shawn .... 254-298-8464 445 G shawn.dach@templejc.edu
DACHELET, Derek .... 608-822-2417 500 A ddachelet@swtc.edu
DACHILLE, Nancy .... 215-248-7048 381 A ndachill@chc.edu
DACOSTA, Christopher .. 401-456-8083 405 A cdacosta@ric.edu
DACOSTA, Romario .... 914-632-5400 307 A rdacosta@monroecollege.edu
DACOSTA, Tracy, M ...... 401-254-3541 405 C tdacosta@rwu.edu
DACRUZ, Becky .... 229-333-5800 127 E bdacruz@valdosta.edu
DACUNHA, Rhiannon, L .... 315-684-6020 321 A dacunhrl@morrisville.edu
DACUS, Kent .... 951-343-4687.. 27 G kdacus@calbaptist.edu
DADABHOY, Khushnur . 805-378-1408.. 73 J kdadabhoy@vcccd.edu
DADABHOY, Zavareh .... 661-395-4204.. 46 L zav.dadabhoy@bakersfieldcollege.edu
DADARRIA, Nikki .... 908-835-9222 284 H ndadarria@warren.edu
DADE, Aurali .... 703-993-1000 467 E
DADEY, Bryan .... 313-593-6422 231 I bdadey@umich.edu
DAFFER, Steve .... 405-733-7424 369 E sdaffer@rose.edu
DAFFRON, Justin .... 504-865-2011 190 C jdaffron@loyno.edu
DAGANAAR, Mark .... 913-469-8500 174 I mdaganaar@jccc.edu
DAGEFOERDE, Diane .... 614-292-9500 358 D dagefoerde.2@osu.edu
DAGES, Stephen .... 330-829-8717 362 E dagesst@mountunion.edu
DAGG, Joey .... 304-876-5395 490 A jdagg@shepherd.edu
DAGHER, Lisa, M .... 773-947-6320 143 H ldagher@mccormick.edu
DAGLEY, Stephen .... 978-867-4552 210 B stephen.dagley@gordon.edu
DAGWAN, Heidi .... 401-254-3154 405 C hdagwan@rwu.edu
DAHER, Dominic .... 415-422-5124.. 72 J dldaher@usfca.edu
DAHIYA, Rakesh .... 214-768-2802 444 D rdahiya@smu.edu
DAHL, Angie .... 540-365-4404 467 B adahl@ferrum.edu
DAHL, Barbara, A .... 219-981-4235 157 C badahl@iun.edu
DAHL, Diane .... 651-638-6327 234 D diane-dahl@bethel.edu
DAHL, Mark .... 503-768-7339 373 E dahl@lclark.edu
DAHL, Tracy .... 360-623-8388 478 F tracy.dahl@centralia.edu
DAHLBERG, Albert .... 401-369-4613 403 J albert_a_dahlberg@brown.edu
DAHLBERG, Margaret ... 701-845-7200 345 G margaret.dahlberg@vcsu.edu
DAHLBERG, Ryan .... 770-537-6012 128 A ryan.dahlberg@westgatech.edu
DAHLE, Tammi .... 205-665-6262..... 8 D dahlet@montevallo.edu
DAHLEN, Anne .... 507-538-4897 235 C
DAHLEN, Chris .... 701-766-4415 344 G
DAHLGREN, Donna, J ... 812-941-2682 157 F ddahlgre@ius.edu
DAHLGREN, Jean .... 302-622-8000.. 90 D president@dcad.edu
DAHLGREN, Jerod, T .... 716-878-5569 317 F dahlgrjt@buffalostate.edu
DAHLMAN, Anne .... 507-389-2900 239 D anne.dahlman@mnsu.edu
DAHLMAN, Hilary .... 651-450-3626 238 E hdahlman@inverhills.edu
DAHLMAN, Stacy .... 423-461-8729 422 E srdahlman@milligan.edu
DAHLOR, Cara .... 816-415-5223 262 F dahlorc@william.jewell.edu
DAHLSTROM, Thomas, A .... 610-341-5898 383 B tdahlstr@eastern.edu

DAHMS, David, W .... 844-642-2338 169 A
dahmsd@nicc.edu

DAHULICH, Michael ..... 570-561-1818 397 H
bishop.michael@stots.edu

DAI, Hai-Lung .... 215-204-9570 399 B
hai-lung.dai@temple.edu

DAI, Kit .... 415-237-6545.. 36 K
kdai@ccsf.edu

DAICHENDT, Jim .... 619-849-2412.. 57 J
jimdaichendt@pointloma.edu

DAIG, Bart .... 989-729-3350 221 F
bdaig01@baker.edu

DAIGLE, Anna .... 504-865-3158 190 C
apdaigle@loyno.edu

DAIGLE, Claire .... 415-351-3573.. 61 C
cdaigle@sfai.edu

DAIGLE, David .... 207-216-4410 195 J
ddaigle@yccc.edu

DAIGLER, David .... 207-629-4017 195 C
ddaigler@mccs.me.edu

DAILEY, Bracken, J ...... 951-827-3427.. 70 B
bracken.dailey@ucr.edu

DAILEY, Brian .... 910-962-3711 343 C
daileyb@uncw.edu

DAILEY, Candy .... 715-365-4539 499 E
csdailey@nicoletcollege.edu

DAILEY, John .... 919-684-6571 328 F
john.dailey@duke.edu

DAILEY, Kyle .... 610-606-4666 380 D
kyle.dailey@cedarcrest.edu

DAILEY, Reggie .... 865-981-8113 421 C
reggie.dailey@maryvillecollege.edu

DAILEY, Shawn .... 740-427-5151 354 I
daileys@kenyon.edu

DAILY, Daniel, R .... 605-658-3369 416 D
dan.daily@usd.edu

DAILY, David .... 479-979-1456.. 23 I
ddaily@ozarks.edu

DAILY, Joseph .... 719-365-1160.. 83 N
joseph.daily@uchealth.org

DAILY, Laurie .... 605-274-5211 414 G
laurie.daily@augie.edu

DAILY, Nathan, B .... 256-766-6610..... 5 E
ndaily@hcu.edu

DAIN, Claudette, E .... 626-914-8886.. 36 J
cdain@citruscollege.edu

DAIN, Merritt .... 662-846-4020 245 G
mdain@deltastate.edu

DAIR, Desmond .... 415-422-2772.. 72 J
ddair@usfca.edu

DAIRE, Andrew, P .... 804-827-2670 473 B
apdaire@vcu.edu

DAIS, Olga .... 646-312-3320 292 L
olga.dais@baruch.cuny.edu

DAISEY, Mary Beth .... 856-225-6044 281 G
daisey@camden.rutgers.edu

DAISY, Jennifer .... 620-432-2808 176 D
jdaisy@neosho.edu

DAISY, Joseph .... 808-245-8210 130 B
jdaisy@hawaii.edu

DAITCH, Jonathan .... 909-469-8522.. 75 I
jdaitch@westernu.edu

DAIY, George .... 512-617-5700 433 B

DAJUSTE, Billy (Malik) . 386-481-2000.. 96 D

DAKE, Michael .... 520-626-5394.. 16 D
mddake@arizona.edu

DAKWAR, Mohammad .. 414-297-8087 499 C
dakwarmm@matc.edu

DALAGER, Jon .... 651-201-1800 237 B

DALAGER, Jon .... 651-659-7140 238 I
jon.dalager@metrostate.edu

DALBOW, Dawn, S .... 540-828-5310 464 L
ddalbow@bridgewater.edu

DALE, Amie, G 757-594-7672 465M
amie.dale@cnu.edu

DALE, Andrew .... 662-562-3319 248 D
adale@northwestms.edu

DALE, Brad .... 520-515-3692.. 11M
daleb@cochise.edu

DALE, Cheryl .... 601-318-6199 249 H
cheryl.dale@wmcarey.edu

DALE, David .... 516-463-6611 301 G
david.dale@hofstra.edu

DALE, Deb 585-275-6030 323M
debora.dale@rochester.edu

DALE, Elizabeth .... 215-503-5138 399 E
elizabeth.dale@jefferson.edu

DALE, Jeffrey .... 770-720-5522 124 G
jdale@reinhardt.edu

DALE, Karen .... 520-335-1883.. 11M
dalek@cochise.edu

DALE, Kim, K .... 307-382-1602 501 J
kdale@westernwyoming.edu

DALE, Kory, J .... 479-524-7116.. 19 H
kdale@jbu.edu

DALE, Lynn, F .... 864-592-4833 412 E
dalel@sccsc.edu

DALE, Marc .... 630-466-7900 152 K
mdale@waubonsee.edu

DALE, Paul .... 602-787-6610.. 13 E
paul.dale@paradisevalley.edu

DALE-CARTER, April ...... 909-384-8922.. 60 F
acarter@sbccd.cc.ca.us

DALEKE, David .... 812-855-6902 156 G
daleked@indiana.edu

DALENBERG, David .... 765-361-6288 163 B
dalenbed@wabash.edu

DALENE, Jack .... 435-283-7130 461 B
jack.dalene@snow.edu

DALES, Sandra .... 910-246-4133 337 H
daless@sandhills.edu

DALEY, Ben .... 619-929-9748.. 45 C
bdaley@hightechhigh.org

DALEY, Caitlin .... 413-782-3111 220 A

DALEY, Carol .... 540-338-2700 487 B
cdaley@cdu.edu

DALEY, Cheryl, R .... 407-708-2010 108 D
daleyc@seminolestate.edu

DALEY, Elizabeth .... 213-821-4035.. 73 D

DALEY, Elizabeth, M ..... 213-740-2804.. 73 D
edaley@cinema.usc.edu

DALEY, George, Q .... 617-432-1501 210 E
george_daley@hms.harvard.edu

DALEY, Karen .... 203-365-4508.. 89 A
daleyk3@sacredheart.edu

DALEY, Karen .... 616-698-7111 223 E
kdaley@davenport.edu

DALEY, Kathy, A .... 843-349-6407 408 A
kdaley@coastal.edu

DALEY, Lauren .... 773-907-4725 135 C
ldaley@ccc.edu

DALEY, Maggie .... 617-746-1990 210 H
maggie.daley@hult.edu

DALEY, Suzanne, L .... 518-564-2080 318 E
daleysl@plattsburgh.edu

DALGLISH, Lucy, A .... 301-405-8806 202 H
dalglish@umd.edu

DALLA COSTA BEHM,
Arhelia .... 608-663-2387 492 F
adallacostabehm@edgewood.edu

DALLAIRE, Matthew, N . 603-535-2215 275 A
mndallaire01@plymouth.edu

DALLAS, Deedra .... 928-774-3890.. 12 L

DALLAS, Marty .... 602-557-1453.. 16 G
martha.dallas@phoenix.edu

DALLIS-COMENTALE,
Diane, M .... 812-855-5679 156 F
ddallis@indiana.edu

DALLMANN, Denise ...... 503-251-2800 377 B
ddallmann@uws.edu

DALLY, Brenda .... 580-581-2230 365 D
brendad@cameron.edu

DALLY, Timothy .... 714-879-3901.. 45 G
thdally@hiu.edu

DALMAGE, Sharon .... 818-710-2523.. 49 D
dalmagsc@piercecollege.edu

DALOLA, Lorie, A .... 252-399-6300 326 K
ldalola@barton.edu

DALONZO, Beth .... 740-392-6868 356 G
beth.dalonzo@mvnu.edu

DALPE, Kyle .... 775-445-4431 271 F
kyle.dalpe@wnc.edu

DALRYMPLE, Jim .... 417-626-1234 257 F
dalrymple.jim@occ.edu

DALRYMPLE, Scott .... 518-327-6223 311 C
sdalrymple@paulsmiths.edu

DALSING, Deirdre, L ..... 608-342-1865 496 E
dalsingd@uwplatt.edu

DALSKE, James .... 760-355-6457.. 45 K
james.dalske@imperial.edu

DALSKE, James .... 707-654-1070.. 32 A
jdalske@csum.edu

DALTO, Joseph .... 561-912-2166.. 99 D
jdalto@evergladesuniversity.edu

DALTON, Brenda .... 972-860-4677 434 F
bdalton@dcccd.edu

DALTON, Brett .... 254-710-3554 431 E
brett_dalton@baylor.edu

DALTON, Brian .... 901-321-3605 418 G
bdalton@cbu.edu

DALTON, Christina .... 304-766-3061 490 D
christina.dalton@wvstateu.edu

DALTON, Cody .... 828-327-7000 333 B
cdalton880@cvcc.edu

DALTON, Dana, L .... 336-272-7102 329 C
dana.dalton@greensboro.edu

DALTON, Diane .... 317-813-2300 158 C

DALTON, Dixie .... 434-736-2085 475 B
dixie.dalton@southside.edu

DALTON, Jaime .... 620-235-4101 177 A
jdalton@pittstate.edu

DALTON, James .... 205-348-4892..... 7 G
jim.dalton@ua.edu

DALTON, Jim .... 845-768-3991 503 I
jim.dalton@westpoint.edu

DALTON, John .... 765-973-8450 157 A
jodalton@iue.edu

DALTON, Judith .... 215-572-4088 378 E
daltonj@arcadia.edu

DALTON, Kelly .... 703-284-5780 468 H
kelly.dalton@marymount.edu

DALTON, Matthew .... 413-545-4475 211 G
matthew.dalton@umass.edu

DALTON, Valerie .... 404-215-2666 123 D
valerie.dalton@morehouse.edu

DALTRY, Rachel .... 610-436-2301 395 D
rdaltry@wcupa.edu

DALY, Adrian .... 213-621-2200.. 38 C

DALY, Arthur .... 740-266-5591 352 B
adaly@egcc.edu

DALY, Cory .... 307-855-2186 501 A
cdaly@cwc.edu

DALY, Dion .... 716-829-8176 298 E
dalyd@dyc.edu

DALY, Erin .... 952-358-8834 239 G
erin.daly@normandale.edu

DALY, Jacqueline .... 908-835-2309 284 H
jdaly@warren.edu

DALY, Jillian .... 209-575-6159.. 77 A
dalyj@mjc.edu

DALY, Jon, C .... 315-655-7225 292 H
jcdaly@cazenovia.edu

DALY, Jonathan, P .... 805-525-4417.. 67 K
jdaly@thomasaquinas.edu

DALY, Kelly .... 714-432-0202.. 38 B
kdaly@occ.cccd.edu

DALY, Kenneth, D .... 845-398-4000 314 G

DALY, Lois, K .... 518-783-2306 315 E
daly@siena.edu

DALY, Mark .... 620-341-6522 173 F
mdaly@emporia.edu

DALY, Maura .... 312-893-7110 137 H
mdaly@erikson.edu

DALY, Melissa .... 856-227-7200 276 E
mdaly@camdencc.edu

DALY, Pamela .... 951-343-3901.. 27 G
pdaly@calbaptist.edu

DALY, Rebecca .... 906-487-7253 224 B
rebecca.daly@finlandia.edu

DALY-EIMER, Anne .... 856-227-7200 276 E
adalyeimer@camdencc.edu

DALZIEL, Murray .... 410-837-4955 204 F
mdalziel@ubalt.edu

DAM, Stacy .... 402-481-8698 265 K
stacy.dam@bryanhealthcollege.edu

DAMAR, Andrea .... 718-409-7200 320 G

DAMARI, David .... 231-591-3706 224 A
daviddamari@ferris.edu

DAMARJIAN, Steve .... 312-850-7140 135 H
sdamarjian@ccc.edu

DAMAS, Tammi, L .... 202-806-4859.. 92 F
tammi.damas@howard.edu

DAMATO, Haylee .... 910-788-6343 338 A
haylee.damato@sccnc.edu

DAMAZO, Dennis, E ...... 724-847-5678 384 C
dedamazo@geneva.edu

DAMES, Christopher ..... 314-516-6473 261 C
cdames@umsl.edu

DAMES, Jeanine .... 203-432-8040.. 90 C
jeanine.dames@yale.edu

DAMIANI, Joel, J .... 716-851-1405 299 B
damiani@ecc.edu

DAMIANI, Susan, M ..... 718-990-7562 313 G
damianis@stjohns.edu

DAMIANO, Ann .... 315-223-2568 324 B
aedamiano@utica.edu

DAMIANO, Fred .... 315-781-3955 301 F
damiano@hws.edu

DAMIANO, Maureen ...... 610-409-3607 401 H
mdamiano@ursinus.edu

DAMICO, Debra, L 718-862-7213 304M
debra.damico@manhattan.edu

DAMM, Christine .... 217-228-5432 147 F
dammch@quincy.edu

DAMM, Richard, T .... 920-748-8322 494 J
dammr@ripon.edu

DAMMERS, Rick .... 856-256-4551 281 F
dammers@rowan.edu

DAMMON, Dave .... 815-825-9538 141 F
ddammon@kish.edu

DAMMON, Robert .... 412-268-3696 380 C
rd19@andrew.cmu.edu

DAMODARAN, Purush .. 815-753-1000 146 B

DAMON, Jud .... 904-819-6252.. 99 E
jdamon@flagler.edu

DAMORI, Kasey .... 307-872-1315 501 J
kdamori@westernwyoming.edu

DAMP, Andrew, R .... 920-565-1000 493 A
dampar@lakeland.edu

DAMPEER, Angela .... 817-531-4403 451 C
adampeer@txwes.edu

DAMPEER, Justin .... 206-592-3301 481 B
jdampeer@highline.edu

DAMPHOUSSE, Kelly .... 870-972-3030.. 17 E
kdamp@astate.edu

DAMPIER, David 304-696-3066 489M
dampierd@marshall.edu

DAMPIER, Paul .... 212-346-1200 311 A

DAMPIER, Paula .... 770-297-5896 116 D
pland@brenau.edu

DAMRAUER, Robert ...... 303-315-2131.. 84 D
robert.damrauer@ucdenver.edu

DAMRON, Barbara .... 505-277-2498 288 J
bdamron@salud.unm.edu

DAMRON, Donald, M ... 606-474-3151 181 B
dmdamron@kcu.edu

DAMRON, Karla .... 214-860-2473 434 I
kdamron@dcccd.edu

DAMRON, Nancy .... 913-971-3393 176 C
nldamron@mnu.edu

DAMRON, Steve .... 254-968-9227 446 D
sdamron@tarleton.edu

DAMROW, Bobbi .... 715-422-5421 499 B
bobbi.damrow@mstc.edu

DAMS, Scott .... 610-861-1601 390 F
damss@moravian.edu

DAMSCHRODER,
Matthew .... 814-641-3151 386 E
damschm@juniata.edu

DAN, Chong .... 704-216-6035 330 H
cdan@livingstone.edu

DANA, Robert, Q .... 207-581-1405 196 G
rdana@maine.edu

DANA, Samantha .... 253-589-4520 478 J
samantha.dana@cptc.edu

DANCE, Andrea .... 252-335-0821 333 G
andrea_dance@albemarle.edu

DANCER, Erin .... 770-426-2974 122 C
erin.dancer@life.edu

DANCHO, Michelle .... 336-757-3710 334 F
mdancho@forsythtech.edu

DANCY, Gerlinde .... 963-638-2941 114 B
dancygl@webber.edu

DANCY, Regina, M .... 704-636-6454 330 A
rdancy@hoodseminary.edu

DANDO, Mary .... 303-492-2975.. 84 B
mary.dando@colorado.edu

DANDOURAS, Spiros .... 516-686-1034 308 I
sdandour@nyit.edu

DANE, Jane, H .... 757-683-6702 469 B
jhdane@odu.edu

DANE, Stephanie .... 314-889-1467 253 E
sdane@fontbonne.edu

DANELL, Allison .... 252-328-6249 341 A
danella@ecu.edu

DANELL, James, N .... 507-354-8221 236 J
danelljc@mlc-wels.edu

DANES, Mark .... 515-271-1661 165 G
mark.danes@dmu.edu

DANFORD, Richard, K .. 740-376-4736 355 E
richard.danford@marietta.edu

DANFORTH, Brian .... 352-846-1849 111 A
bdanforth@uff.ufl.edu

DANFORTH, Dave .... 218-281-8490 244 A
danfo002@umn.edu

DANFORTH, Elizabeth ... 406-994-3836 264 C
danforth@montana.edu

DANG, Hung, D .... 805-437-8918.. 30 C
hung.dang@csuci.edu

DANG, Jessica .... 510-763-7787.. 24 C

DANG, Tuan .... 425-739-8818 481 C
tuan.dang@lwtech.edu

DANG-WILLIAMS, Thao 314-246-8757 262 C
thaodangwilliams@webster.edu

DANGELANTONIO,
Sarah .... 603-899-4278 273 E
dangelantonios@franklinpierce.edu

DANGERFIELD, Deneen . 410-777-2830 197 G
drdangerfield@aacc.edu

DANHEISER, Priscilla, R 678-547-6028 122 E danheiser_p@mercer.edu
DANICA, Kathleen 518-244-4552 313 A bouchk2@sage.edu
DANIEL, Adam 434-924-4052 472 D ard2a@virginia.edu
DANIEL, Andrea, D 706-355-5111 115 F adaniel@athenstech.edu
DANIEL, Brett 903-675-6393 451 F bdaniel@tvcc.edu
DANIEL, Carmen 251-981-3771 5 A carmen.daniel@columbiasouthern.edu
DANIEL, Chett 417-455-5750 252 E chettdaniel@crowder.edu
DANIEL, Chris 770-229-3327 125 H chris.daniel@sctech.edu
DANIEL, Chris 813-974-2972 111 C cldaniel@usf.edu
DANIEL, Eileen 585-395-5505 317 E edaniel@brockport.edu
DANIEL, Ethel 617-217-9887 206 E edaniel@baystate.edu
DANIEL, Juliet 828-225-3993 328 D admissions@daoisttraditions.edu
DANIEL, Ken 541-278-5775 371 H kdaniel@bluecc.edu
DANIEL, Kenya 404-225-4400 115 H
DANIEL, Kevin, S 719-587-7741 77 G ksdaniel@adams.edu
DANIEL, Larry 432-552-2120 456 F daniel_l@utpb.edu
DANIEL, Mary 254-298-8362 445 G mary.daniel@templejc.edu
DANIEL, Meredith 864-941-8442 411 C meredith.d@ptc.edu
DANIEL, Mick 864-977-7513 410 I mick.daniel@ngu.edu
DANIEL, Nancy 828-448-3160 339 A ndaniel@wpcc.edu
DANIEL, Robin 434-949-1018 475 B robin.daniel@southside.edu
DANIEL, Sandra 229-931-2275 120 D sandra.daniel@gsw.edu
DANIEL, Sharlene 423-775-6596 422 I sdaniel@ogs.edu
DANIEL, Tamara 870-508-6100 17 G
DANIEL, W. John 205-934-3474 8 A wdaniel@uab.edu
DANIEL, William 214-648-5308 457 A william.daniel@utsouthwestern.edu
DANIELE, Christina 845-575-3000 305 D christina.daniele@marist.edu
DANIELL, Steven 817-531-4405 451 C sdaniell@txwes.edu
DANIELLO, Lindsey 856-222-9311 281 C ldaniello@rcbc.edu
DANIELS, Alyson 207-755-5233 195 D adaniels@cmcc.edu
DANIELS, Ann 843-477-2168 409 J ann.daniels@hgtc.edu
DANIELS, Ashley 504-520-5166 193 E adaniels@xula.edu
DANIELS, Brian 865-974-6611 427 A brian.daniels@tennessee.edu
DANIELS, C. Wess 336-316-2445 329 D danielscw@guilford.edu
DANIELS, Carmen 614-287-5210 351 C cdaniels@cscc.edu
DANIELS, Christy 252-328-6212 341 A danielsc@ecu.edu
DANIELS, Debra 661-763-7710 67 G ddaniels@taftcollege.edu
DANIELS, Denise 478-289-2385 118 C dmdaneils@ega.edu
DANIELS, Dennis, E 936-261-3085 446 C dedaniels@pvamu.edu
DANIELS, Diane 617-588-1376 206 F ddaniels@bfit.edu
DANIELS, Edward 541-885-1117 374 I edward.daniels@oit.edu
DANIELS, Gerri, L 906-227-2650 228 I gdaniels@nmu.edu
DANIELS, Gregory 860-486-1094 89 D gregory.daniels@uconn.edu
DANIELS, Heather 608-265-4562 495 D sof@secfac.wisc.edu
DANIELS, III, Jack, E 608-246-6676 499 A jdanielsiii@madisoncollege.edu
DANIELS, Joan 559-737-6242 39 B joand@cos.edu
DANIELS, Julie 601-974-1443 247 B daniejh@millsaps.edu
DANIELS, Kacey 405-422-1203 369 A kacey.daniels@redlandscc.edu
DANIELS, LaMetrius 615-248-1521 426 D ldaniels@trevecca.edu
DANIELS, Linda 601-977-4462 249 C ldaniels@tougaloo.edu
DANIELS, Linda 404-385-7604 119 E linda.daniels@cpsm.gatech.edu
DANIELS, Lisa 518-608-8398 299 C ldaniels@excelsior.edu
DANIELS, Mark 425-235-2374 482 H mdaniels@rtc.edu
DANIELS, Martin, C 518-276-6813 312 C daniem@rpi.edu
DANIELS, Mary 773-995-4460 134 K mdanie30@csu.edu
DANIELS, Michael 617-585-0200 207 A michael.daniels@the-bac.edu
DANIELS, Michael 828-448-3564 339 A mdaniels@wpcc.edu
DANIELS, JR., Mitchell 317-208-5311 160 A
DANIELS, JR., Mitchell, E 765-494-9708 160 B president@purdue.edu
DANIELS, Rebecca 419-251-1821 355 G rebecca.daniels@mercycollege.edu
DANIELS, Robin 325-793-4601 439 F daniels.robin@mcm.edu
DANIELS, Ronald, J 410-516-4170 199 G president@jhu.edu
DANIELS, Sandra 212-410-8015 308 E sdaniels@nycpm.edu
DANIELS, Shedrick 847-635-1699 146 G sdaniels@oakton.edu
DANIELS, Von 870-338-6474 22 G
DANIELSON, Eric, M 301-447-5505 201 B danielson@msmary.edu
DANIELSON, Lisa, M 920-424-3007 496 C danielsn@uwosh.edu
DANIELSON, Lynda 208-459-5231 131 C ldanielson@collegeofidaho.edu
DANIELSON, Marsha 507-453-2700 239 B
DANIELSON, Michelle 507-285-7180 240 H michelle.danielson@rctc.edu
DANIELSON, Timothy 414-229-4463 496 B danieltj@uwm.edu
DANIELZUK, Nicole 308-635-6033 270 C danielzn@wncc.edu
DANIEU, Paul, F 716-851-1856 299 B danieu@ecc.edu
DANIK, Steve 410-951-3577 204 B sdanik@coppin.edu
DANILOWICZ, Bret 561-297-6350 109 J provost@fau.edu
DANINHIRSCH, Carrie 952-806-3910 242 P
DANKO, James 413-755-4812 216 A jdanko@stcc.edu
DANKO, James, M 317-940-9900 154 C president@butler.edu
DANKOVICH, Robin 915-215-4370 451 B robin.dankovich@ttuhsc.edu
DANLEY, Roger 316-295-5836 174 A rogerd@friends.edu
DANLEY, Stacy, L 803-533-3743 411 G sdanley@scsu.edu
DANNA, Sasha 530-898-6116 30 D sdanna@calstate.edu
DANNA, Stephen 518-792-5425 318 E dann1253@plattsburgh.edu
DANNEMILLER, Stanley, D 330-325-6558 357 D sdannemiller@neomed.edu
DANNEN, Troy 504-865-5500 191 F tdannen@tulane.edu
DANNENBAUM, Martha, C 979-458-8300 446 F mdannenbaum@tamu.edu
DANNENHOFFER, Patrick 914-606-8541 325 A patrick.dannenhoffer@sunywcc.edu
DANNER, Deborah 509-359-2383 479 G ddanner2@ewu.edu
DANNER, John, P 210-458-4105 455 E john.danner@utsa.edu
DANSBY, Sylvia 706-649-1278 117 I sdansby@columbustech.edu
DANSBY-SPARKS, Royce 706-864-1492 127 A royce.dansbysparks@ung.edu
DANSER, Dolores, A 717-245-1589 382 D danserd@dickinson.edu
DANTLEY, Michael 513-529-6317 356 A dantleme@miamioh.edu
DANUFF, Allan 352-854-2322 97 N danuffa@cf.edu
DANVER, Steven 866-492-5336 244 F steven.danver@mail.waldenu.edu
DANZ, Nick 715-394-8161 497 C ndanz@uwsuper.edu
DANZ, Stephanie 518-629-7158 302 C s.danz@hvcc.edu
DANZY, Jamia 585-292-3010 307 B jdanzy1@monroecc.edu
DAOAS, Doman 691-320-2480 504 C daoas@comfsm.fm
DAOOD, Christopher 262-691-5314 500 B cdaood@wctc.edu
DAOUST, Carolyn 989-358-7211 221 C daoust@alpenacc.edu
DAPICE-WONG, Stephanie 631-665-1600 322 F stephanie.wong@touro.edu
DAPICE-WONG, Stephanie 212-463-0400 322 G stephanie.wong@touro.edu
DAPP, Kelly 661-362-3983 38 D kelly.dapp@canyons.edu
DAPRA, Joe 816-322-0110 251 B joe.dapra@calvary.edu
DAPRANO, Corinne 937-229-3557 362 C cdapranp1@udayton.edu
DARA, Joshua 318-487-7291 187 E joshua.dara@lacollege.edu
DARAS, April 412-392-8118 396 G adaras@pointpark.edu
DARBANDI, Shiva 207-699-5090 195 A sdarbandi@meca.edu
DARBEAU, Ron 570-484-2576 394 E rdarbeau@lockhaven.edu
DARBONE, Davidson 337-421-6940 188 J david.darbone@sowela.edu
DARBUT, Nancy 952-446-4190 235 J darbutn@crown.edu
DARBY, Kadia 212-616-7263 301 C kadia.darby@helenefuld.edu
DARBY, Marisa 972-721-5221 452 B mdarby@udallas.edu
DARBY, Shani 212-431-2896 309 A shani.darby@nyls.edu
DARCY, Kip 810-762-7331 226 B kdarcy@kettering.edu
DARDEN, Alyssa 614-947-6685 352 J alyssa.darden@franklin.edu
DARDEN, Elbert 816-501-4275 258 I elbert.darden@rockhurst.edu
DARDEN, Joanna 901-572-2448 418 A joanna.darden@baptistu.edu
DARDEN, Thomas 215-455-1300 378 F tdarden@aspirapa.org
DARDEN-BEAUFORD, Yulonda 404-225-4488 115 H ybeauford@atlantatech.edu
DARDZINSKI, Jennifer 631-656-2178 300 B jennifer.dardzinski@ftc.edu
DARE, Akinola 478-257-5825 93 H
DARETY, Ethan 731-989-6000 419 K
DARGA, Richard 773-995-2378 134 K rdarga@csu.edu
DARGAN, Bernardo, I 919-516-4000 339 I
DARIAROW, Esmail 239-939-4766 109 A
DARIN, Jessica 805-756-6000 29 I darin@calpoly.edu
DARIN, Jessica, L 805-756-6000 29 I darin@calpoly.edu
DARKEN, Kristin 831-646-4001 52 G kdarken@mpc.edu
DARLAND, Ruth, E 606-693-5000 183 C rdarland@kmbc.edu
DARLAND, Zane 606-693-5000 183 C zdarland@kmbc.edu
DARLAND, Zane, E 606-693-5000 183 C zdarland@kmbc.edu
DARLING, Candida 801-957-4186 461 C candida.darling@slcc.edu
DARLING, Danielle 410-827-5818 198 F ddarling@chesapeake.edu
DARLING, Douglas, D 701-662-1506 346 C doug.darling@lrsc.edu
DARLING, Kyle 206-934-3869 483 C kyle.darling@seattlecolleges.edu
DARLING, Leslie 312-899-5100 149 F
DARLING, Mary 619-594-8299 33 D mdarling@sdsu.edu
DARLING, Terry 517-750-1200 231 C tdarling@arbor.edu
DARLINGTON, Sue 760-872-2000 40 I sdarlington@deepsprings.edu
DARLINGTON, Susan 215-968-8251 379 D susan.darlington@bucks.edu
DARMON, Robin 619-260-4654 72 I rdarmon@sandiego.edu
DARNELL, Beverly 865-573-4517 420 E bdarnell@johnsonu.edu
DARNELL, Kacey 254-867-3009 449 D kacey.darnell@tstc.edu
DARR, Eric, D 717-901-5111 385 H edarr@harrisburgu.edu
DARR, Jay, E 412-648-7930 400 H jay.darr@pitt.edu
DARR, Kristi 515-294-6458 163 G kdarr@iastate.edu
DARRAGH, Alex 847-467-5810 146 E
DARRAH, Joseph 610-527-0200 397 D joe.darrah@rosemont.edu
DARRAH, Thom 541-885-1600 374 I thom.darrah@oit.edu
DARRELL, Christopher 973-408-3553 277 A cdarrell@drew.edu
DARROUZET, Hunter 563-588-8192 164 E hunter.darrouzet@clarke.edu
DARROW, David 906-932-4231 224 D davidd@gogebic.edu
DARSCH, Lisa 540-665-4787 470 G ldarsch@su.edu
DARSEE, Jon 319-335-3565 163 H jon-darsee@uiowa.edu
DARST, Abbie 859-985-3019 179 I darsta@berea.edu
DART, Lucas 308-698-5270 269 I ldart@nufoundation.org
DART, Regina 575-769-4045 285 O regina.dart@clovis.edu
DARTY, Leah 334-514-5073 2 F leah.darty@istc.edu
DARTY, Roxanne 210-690-9000 436 H rdarty@hallmarkuniversity.edu
DARWIN, Mike 205-726-4241 6 E mdarwin@samford.edu
DAS, A. Andrew 630-617-3541 137 G adas@elmhurst.edu
DAS, Carolyn 352-395-5226 108 A carolyn.das@sfcollege.edu
DAS, Joggeshwar 716-829-8006 298 E dasj@dyc.edu
DAS, Sujoy 215-895-4971 382 F sd889@drexel.edu
DASBURG, Deanne 828-641-0597 327 B dasburg@brevard.edu
DASGUPTA, Nandini 510-907-2433 60 C ndasgupta@samuelmerritt.edu
DASH, Jennifer 386-481-2116 96 D dashj@cookman.edu
DASH, Nicole 940-565-3440 453 E nicole.dash@unt.edu
DASHER, Leah 912-538-3186 125 G ldasher@southeasterntech.edu
DASILVA, Jose 940-872-4002 440 F jdasilva@nctc.edu
DASILVA, Joseph 413-662-5247 213 C joseph.dasilva@mcla.edu
DASILVA, Yvonne 713-348-2697 442 F
DASTGHEIB-BEHESHTI, Babak 516-686-7437 308 I babak.beheshti@nyit.edu
DATAR, Srikant 617-495-6550 210 E sdatar@hbs.edu
DATEMA, Betsy 574-232-2408 159 H bdatema@jpu.edu
DATHER, Julie 605-668-1525 415 F jdather@mountmarty.edu
DATTA, Sumana 979-845-1957 446 F sumad@tamu.edu
DATTAGUPTA, Satya 504-865-5731 191 F dattagupta@tulane.edu
DATUIN, Bonnie Mae, M 671-735-5616 504 D bonniemae.datuin@guamcc.edu
DATZKO-BANTA, Richard 201-692-7005 277 I rdatzkobanta@fdu.edu
DAUB, Amber 903-923-2277 435 H adaub@etbu.edu
DAUBENMIRE, Jeff 740-753-6122 353 H daubenmirej@hocking.edu
DAUBER, Timothy 407-277-0311 99 D tdauber@evergladesuniversity.edu
DAUBERMAN, Barbara, A 804-752-7300 469 F bdauberman@rmc.edu

DAUBERT, Christopher, R .... 573-882-0368 261 A daubertc@missouri.edu
DAUBMANN, Karl .... 248-204-2805 227 A kdaubmann@ltu.edu
DAUGHERTY, Adam ...... 812-888-5555 162 F adaugherty@vinu.edu
DAUGHERTY, Bob .... 858-513-9240.. 68 K robert.daugherty@ashford.edu
DAUGHERTY, Carolyn ... 719-549-2830.. 80 B carolyn.daugherty@csupueblo.edu
DAUGHERTY, Caron ...... 620-343-4600 173 G cdaugherty@fhtc.edu
DAUGHERTY, Daniel ..... 934-420-2702 320 F daughed@farmingdale.edu
DAUGHERTY, Doug .... 562-903-4867.. 27 A doug.daugherty@biola.edu
DAUGHERTY, Robyn ..... 479-524-7301.. 19 H rdaugherty@jbu.edu
DAUGHERTY, Teresa, M .... 815-282-7900 148 I teresadaugherty@sacn.edu
DAUGHERTY, Terry .... 812-237-2000 156 D terry.daugherty@indstate.edu
DAUGHERTY, Vernon, D .... 828-398-7220 332 B vdaugherty@abtech.edu
DAUGHERTY, Whitney, N .... 812-888-4142 162 F wdaugherty@vinu.edu
DAUGHETY, Kathy .... 252-399-6529 326 K kdaughety@barton.edu
DAUGHT, Gary .... 423-461-8799 422 E gfdaught@milligan.edu
DAUGHTRY, Delanie ..... 919-775-5401 333 C
DAULT, Tasha .... 231-843-5805 233 A tdault@westshore.edu
DAULTON, Jonathan, G 864-242-5100 406 H
DAUM, Richard .... 267-502-2699 379 A richard.daum@brynathyn.edu
DAUNER, Jasmin .... 785-833-4320 175 E jasmin.dauner@kwu.edu
DAUSEY, David, J .... 412-396-6000 383 A dausey@duq.edu
DAUZAT, Taylor .... 318-487-7420 187 E taylor.dauzat@lacollege.edu
DAVALOZ, Dalilah .... 714-564-5527.. 58 F davaloz_dalilah@sac.edu
DAVAR, David .... 212-678-6161 303 D dadavar@jtsa.edu
DAVENPORT, Bethany ... 319-363-1323 168 F bdavenport@mtmercy.edu
DAVENPORT, Brian .... 509-359-2036 479 G bdavenport2@ewu.edu
DAVENPORT, Catherine, M .... 717-245-1231 382 D davenpor@dickinson.edu
DAVENPORT, Chari .... 425-352-8000 478 D cdavenport@cascadia.edu
DAVENPORT, Darrien .... 717-337-6011 384 D ddavenpo@gettysburg.edu
DAVENPORT, Darrien .... 717-337-6375 384 D ddavenpo@gettysburg.edu
DAVENPORT, Floyd .... 573-651-2217 259 H fdavenport@semo.edu
DAVENPORT, Jason .... 804-828-0880 473 B jedavenport@vcu.edu
DAVENPORT, John .... 309-438-2008 140 D jmdaven@ilstu.edu
DAVENPORT, Kevin .... 256-306-2574.... 1 F kevin.davenport@calhoun.edu
DAVENPORT, Kevin .... 804-524-5995 476 D pdjackson@vsu.edu
DAVENPORT, Mason ..... 410-626-2513 202 A annapolis.registrar@sjc.edu
DAVENPORT, Mike .... 270-824-8661 182 D mike.davenport@kctcs.edu
DAVENPORT, Mona ...... 217-581-6690 137 E mydavenport@eiu.edu
DAVENPORT, Robert ..... 313-577-4302 232 K hd5623@wayne.edu
DAVENPORT, Robert ..... 405-585-5301 367 B robert.davenport@okbu.edu
DAVENPORT, Robin ...... 973-618-3905 276 D rdavenport@caldwell.edu
DAVENPORT, Sara .... 315-294-8597 292 G davenport@cayuga-cc.edu
DAVENPORT, Susan, C . 609-652-4521 283 E susan.davenport@stockton.edu
DAVENPORT, Zebulun ... 610-436-3301 395 D zdavenport@wcupa.edu
DAVENPORT BROWN, Krystyna .... 802-654-2470 462 G kdavenportbr@smcvt.edu
DAVENPORT TIGNOR, Stephanie .... 804-827-7882 473 B davenportse@vcu.edu
DAVENPORTE, Cynthia .. 678-916-2604 115 I cdavenporte@johnmarshall.edu
DAVES, Renate .... 714-241-6146.. 37 J rakins1@coastline.edu
DAVEY, Daniel, K .... 757-479-3706 472 F dkdavey@vbts.edu
DAVEY, Martha .... 307-675-0822 501 G mdavey@sheridan.edu
DAVEY, Patrick .... 202-319-6907.. 92 A daveyp@cua.edu
DAVEY, Stephen .... 919-573-5350 340 C
DAVID, Craig, A .... 573-882-9570 261 A davidcr@missouri.edu
DAVID, Elizabeth .... 925-424-1420.. 35 K edavid@laspositascollege.edu
DAVID, Jerad .... 985-448-4303 192 F jerad.david@nicholls.edu
DAVID, Kim .... 478-553-2054 123 H kdavid@oftc.edu
DAVID, Kimberly, C ...... 713-798-1543 431 D kcotner@bcm.edu
DAVID, Kyle .... 774-455-7100 211 F kdavid@umassp.edu
DAVID, Marc .... 843-661-8101 409 F marc.david@fdtc.edu
DAVID, Marcella .... 312-369-7495 136 D mdavid@colum.edu
DAVID, Matthew .... 934-249-3048 320 F bksfarmingdale@bncollege.com
DAVID, Prabu .... 517-355-3410 227 F pdavid@msu.edu
DAVID, Taylor .... 866-217-9823 187 G
DAVIDOWITZ, Menachem .... 585-473-2810 321 H
DAVIDS, Cheryl .... 828-339-7018 338 B c_davids@southwesterncc.edu
DAVIDSEN, Susanna ...... 866-492-5336 244 F susanna.davidsen@mail.waldenu.edu
DAVIDSON, Anthony, R 718-817-4602 300 C ardavidson@fordham.edu
DAVIDSON, Brent .... 601-877-4063 245 A bdavidson@sodexo.com
DAVIDSON, Camille ...... 618-453-8761 150 B camille.davidson@siu.edu
DAVIDSON, Charity ...... 248-218-2011 230 B
DAVIDSON, Cheryl .... 812-877-8686 160 F clapp@rose-hulman.edu
DAVIDSON, Diana .... 870-777-5722.. 22 I diana.davidson@uaht.edu
DAVIDSON, Erin .... 817-598-6285 457 J edavidson@wc.edu
DAVIDSON, James, A ... 410-827-5846 198 F jdavidson@chesapeake.edu
DAVIDSON, Jamie .... 702-895-3627 271 D jamie.davidson@unlv.edu
DAVIDSON, Janet .... 724-925-4215 402 F davidsonj@westmoreland.edu
DAVIDSON, Janine, A ... 303-615-0060.. 81 M davidson@msudenver.edu
DAVIDSON, Jeanie .... 417-893-7143 259 I jdavidson@sbuniv.edu
DAVIDSON, Jeanne .... 435-797-0146 460 C jeanne.davidson@usu.edu
DAVIDSON, Jennifer ..... 708-456-3033 151 D jenniferdavidson@triton.edu
DAVIDSON, Jonathan ... 251-580-2222..... 1 I jonathan.davidson@coastalalabama.edu
DAVIDSON, Katrena, J .. 330-941-1712 364 H katrena.davidson@ysu.edu
DAVIDSON, Keith, S ..... 410-651-6496 203 D kdavidson@umes.edu
DAVIDSON, Laura .... 919-760-8531 331 D davidsonl@meredith.edu
DAVIDSON, Laura-Lee .. 202-274-6260.. 94 B lauralee.davidson@udc.edu
DAVIDSON, Leslie .... 608-363-2380 491 H davidsonl@beloit.edu
DAVIDSON, Maryanne .. 475-210-6392.. 89 A davidsonm6@sacredheart.edu
DAVIDSON, Megan .... 912-358-3004 125 A
DAVIDSON, Michael ..... 617-552-3358 207 C michael.davidson.3@bc.edu
DAVIDSON, Michael, E . 404-413-3154 120 E mdavidson@gsu.edu
DAVIDSON, Mitch .... 260-481-6196 160 C davidsom@pfw.edu
DAVIDSON, Nick .... 616-632-2475 221 E nwd001@aquinas.edu
DAVIDSON, Richard ...... 248-689-8282 232 C rdavidson@walshcollege.edu
DAVIDSON, Roger .... 916-485-6028.. 50 G davidsr@arc.losrios.edu
DAVIDSON, Sharon ...... 718-262-2155 295 E sdavid@york.cuny.edu
DAVIDSON, Stacy, L ..... 765-983-1744 155 A davidst@earlham.edu
DAVIDSON, Steed .... 773-947-6341 143 H sdavidson@mccormick.edu
DAVIDSON, Stephanie .. 405-692-3241 366 D stephanie.davidson@macu.edu
DAVIDSON, Stuart .... 336-272-7102 329 C
DAVIDSON, Suellen ...... 870-368-2059.. 20 E sdavidson@ozarka.edu
DAVIDSON, Tracy .... 406-657-1015 265 E tracy.davidson@rocky.edu
DAVIDSON, Tyler .... 205-349-4240.... 7 A tdavidson@stillman.edu
DAVIDSON, Veronica .... 937-294-0592 356 D veronica.davidson@themodern.edu
DAVIDSON, William ...... 301-243-2319 502 L william.davidson@dodiis.mil
DAVIDSON-BOYD, Leslie .... 909-537-3252.. 32 E lboyd@csusb.edu
DAVIE, Fred .... 212-280-1408 323 K fdavie@uts.columbia.edu
DAVIE, Karen .... 646-378-6121 310 D karen.davie@nyack.edu
DAVIE, Keith, A .... 646-564-6760 310 D keith.davie@nyack.edu
DAVIES, Becky .... 972-721-5206 452 B bdavies@udallas.edu
DAVIES, Daniel .... 702-463-2122 272 G president@wongu.org
DAVIES, Elizabeth .... 815-740-3819 152 H edavies@stfrancis.edu
DAVIES, H. Dele, O ...... 402-559-5131 269 K dele.davies@unmc.edu
DAVIES, Haldane .... 340-693-1004 513 E hdavies@uvi.edu
DAVIES, Karlha .... 209-667-3807.. 33 B kdavies@csustan.edu
DAVIES, Kathy .... 706-721-9911 116 A kadavies@augusta.edu
DAVIES, Kim .... 706-737-1738 116 A kdavies1@augusta.edu
DAVIES, Laura, J .... 607-753-2011 318 A laura.davies@cortland.edu
DAVIES, Lincoln, L .... 614-292-0574 358 D davies.473@osu.edu
DAVIES, Lorelle .... 719-502-2447.. 82 E lorelle.davies@ppcc.edu
DAVIES, Mark .... 607-436-2541 316 F mark.davies@oneonta.edu
DAVIES, Patty .... 303-352-3310.. 80 F patty.davies@ccd.edu
DAVIES, Paul .... 804-752-7399 469 F pauldavies@rmc.edu
DAVIES, Robert, O .... 989-774-3131 222 E president@cmich.edu
DAVIES, Sharon .... 404-270-5031 126 B sldavies@spelman.edu
DAVIES, Susan .... 810-762-9927 226 B sdavies@kettering.edu
DAVIES, Susan, B .... 706-721-0211 116 A sdavies@augusta.edu
DAVIES, William, E .... 301-447-5234 201 B davies@msmary.edu
DAVILA, Alba .... 787-751-0160 506 F adavila@cmpr.pr.gov
DAVILA, Alberto .... 573-651-2112 259 H adavila@semo.edu
DAVILA, Ariel .... 787-798-3001 511 B ariel.davila@uccaribe.edu
DAVILA, Cheyla .... 305-222-2812.. 99 L
DAVILA, Danielle .... 432-552-2803 456 F davila_d@utpb.edu
DAVILA, David .... 361-698-1561 435 G ddavila23@delmar.edu
DAVILA, Grace .... 713-221-8633 453 A davilag@uhd.edu
DAVILA, Heydi .... 305-266-7678 104 A h.davila@miuniversity.edu
DAVILA, Ivan .... 787-841-2000 509 J idavila@pucpr.edu
DAVILA, Michael .... 870-460-1110.. 22 C davila@uamont.edu
DAVILA RIVERA, Hector, M .... 787-765-4210 505 K
DAVIN, David .... 847-214-7143 137 F ddavin@elgin.edu
DAVINGMAN, Stephanie .... 217-351-2200 147 C sdavingman@parkland.edu
DAVINO, Rich .... 508-626-4625 213 A rdavino@framingham.edu
DAVIS, Abby .... 479-356-2033.. 18 C adavis@atu.edu
DAVIS, Abigail, H .... 706-886-6831 126 D abdavis@tfc.edu
DAVIS, Adam .... 844-837-7489.. 22 E
DAVIS, Alan, B .... 205-853-1200.... 2 G adavis@jeffersonstate.edu
DAVIS, Alana .... 804-752-7227 469 F adavis@rmc.edu
DAVIS, Alex .... 919-760-8809 331 D amdavis@meredith.edu
DAVIS, Andrew .... 334-347-2623.... 2 A adavis@escc.edu
DAVIS, Andrew .... 713-743-3009 452 D adavis5@central.uh.edu
DAVIS, Andrew .... 816-584-6411 258 C andrew.davis@park.edu
DAVIS, Andrew .... 541-383-7592 372 A apdavis@cocc.edu
DAVIS, Angiah .... 678-359-5076 120 F adavis1@gordonstate.edu
DAVIS, Anita .... 860-297-4251.. 89 B anita.davis@trincoll.edu
DAVIS, Anthony .... 718-262-5228 295 E adavis13@york.cuny.edu
DAVIS, Anthony, J .... 704-216-6044 330 H adavis@livingstone.edu
DAVIS, Anthony, K .... 803-323-4503 414 D davisa@winthrop.edu
DAVIS, Audrey .... 301-546-0124 201 E davisac@pgcc.edu
DAVIS, Ayanna .... 510-204-0733.. 36 I adavis@cdsp.edu
DAVIS, Becky .... 903-923-2136 435 H bdavis@etbu.edu
DAVIS, Betsy .... 360-385-4948 481 G betsy@nwswb.edu
DAVIS, Billy .... 936-261-1550 446 C bcdavis@pvamu.edu
DAVIS, Blake .... 214-768-3738 444 D bbdavis@smu.edu
DAVIS, Brad .... 707-522-2824.. 63 D bdavis@santarosa.edu
DAVIS, Brad .... 405-789-7661 369 I brad.davis@swcu.edu
DAVIS, Bradley .... 814-824-2559 389 G bdavis2@mercyhurst.edu
DAVIS, Bradley, J .... 408-741-2421.. 75 C bradley.davis@wvm.edu
DAVIS, Brealle .... 423-461-8335 422 E bkdavis@milligan.edu
DAVIS, Brent .... 559-730-3912.. 39 B brentd@cos.edu
DAVIS, Brian .... 870-236-6901.. 18 J
DAVIS, Brian .... 870-236-6901.. 18 J bdavis@crc.edu
DAVIS, Brian .... 803-778-6612 406 I davisjb@cctech.edu
DAVIS, Britt .... 910-893-1215 327 D davisb@campbell.edu
DAVIS, Brittany .... 662-846-4675 245 G bdavis@deltastate.edu
DAVIS, Brittany .... 334-833-4428.... 5 G finaid@hawks.huntingdon.edu
DAVIS, Bryan .... 951-343-4721.. 27 G bdavis@calbaptist.edu
DAVIS, Bryan, P .... 229-928-1361 120 D bryan.davis@gsw.edu
DAVIS, Bryson .... 270-745-2051 186 C bryson.davis@wku.edu
DAVIS, Carenado .... 919-532-5759 338 G cdavis19@waketech.edu
DAVIS, Carissa .... 708-656-8000 145 C carissa.davis@morton.edu
DAVIS, Carole .... 269-965-3931 225 H davisc@kellogg.edu
DAVIS, Carolyn .... 601-877-6246 245 A cadavis@alcorn.edu
DAVIS, Catherine, C ..... 609-497-7882 280 C student.relations@ptsem.edu
DAVIS, Chad .... 701-477-7847 346 J cdavis@tm.edu
DAVIS, Charity .... 330-325-6365 357 D cdavis6@neomed.edu
DAVIS, III, Charles, E .. 540-887-7240 468 G cedavis@marybaldwin.edu
DAVIS, Charles, N .... 706-542-1704 126 G cndavis@uga.edu

DAVIS, Nevaler .... 813-253-7068 102 B
ndavis5@hccfl.edu
DAVIS, Nick .... 812-877-8116 160 F
davis11@rose-hulman.edu
DAVIS, Nyla .... 850-201-6048 112 C
nyla.davis@tcc.fl.edu
DAVIS, Octavius .... 706-355-5069 115 F
odavis@athenstech.edu
DAVIS, Patrice .... 843-574-6010 412 I
patrice.davis@tridenttech.edu
DAVIS, Patricia .... 207-780-5911 197 D
patdavis@maine.edu
DAVIS, Patricia .... 970-860-8180 434 G
pdavis@dcccd.edu
DAVIS, Patricia, A .... 251-380-3063.... 6 H
pdavis@shc.edu
DAVIS, SR., Patrick ...... 731-424-3520 424 E
pdavis@jscc.edu
DAVIS, Patti .... 410-386-8066 198 D
pdavis@carrollcc.edu
DAVIS, Paul, J .... 641-784-5422 166 E
pjdavis@graceland.edu
DAVIS, Paul, R .... 530-226-4719.. 64 E
pdavis@simpsonu.edu
DAVIS, Paula, M .... 269-387-8411 233 B
paula.davis@wmich.edu
DAVIS, Peggy .... 804-524-5030 476 D
pdavis@vsu.edu
DAVIS, Pete .... 701-477-7862 346 J
pdavis@tm.edu
DAVIS, Phylesia .... 870-543-8611.. 21 B
pdavis@seark.edu
DAVIS, Raeanne .... 212-237-8604 294 D
radavis@jjay.cuny.edu
DAVIS, Ralph .... 323-241-5261.. 49 E
davisrw@lasc.edu
DAVIS, Ralph .... 605-394-2493 416 H
ralph.davis@sdsmt.edu
DAVIS, Ralph, U .... 843-661-1110 409 G
rdavis@fmarion.edu
DAVIS, Rance .... 315-229-5551 314 D
rdavis@stlawu.edu
DAVIS, Randy .... 502-213-2122 182 C
randall.davis@kctcs.edu
DAVIS, Rebecca, F .... 512-637-1949 442 I
rebeccad@stedwards.edu
DAVIS, Reginald .... 601-484-8804 247 A
rdavis21@meridiancc.edu
DAVIS, Rhonda .... 817-722-1618 438 G
rhonda.davis@tku.edu
DAVIS, Rick .... 850-973-9492 104 L
davisr@nfc.edu
DAVIS, Rick .... 617-373-2134 217 I
DAVIS, Rick .... 703-993-8624 467 E
rdavi4@gmu.edu
DAVIS, Rick, C .... 402-280-1785 266 H
richarddavis@creighton.edu
DAVIS, JR., Robert, W . 570-941-7500 401 F
robert.davis@scranton.edu
DAVIS, Robin .... 804-257-5710 476 F
DAVIS, Rodney, L .... 573-999-2145 175 A
DAVIS, Rodrigo .... 727-712-5720 107 E
davis.rod@spcollege.edu
DAVIS, Roger, W .... 724-480-3400 381 H
roger.davis@ccbc.edu
DAVIS, Rosario .... 512-245-9222 450 C
rd31@txstate.edu
DAVIS, Sandra, S .... 803-535-1218 411 B
davisss@octech.edu
DAVIS, Scott .... 575-562-2425 286 B
scott.davis@enmu.edu
DAVIS, Shanda .... 320-308-5538 241 A
shanda.davis@sctcc.edu
DAVIS, Sharon .... 803-765-6029 406 D
sdavis@allenuniversity.edu
DAVIS, Sharon .... 254-526-1346 432 D
sharon.davis@ctcd.edu
DAVIS, Sheila, J .... 706-542-9167 126 G
sjames@uga.edu
DAVIS, Shelly .... 207-893-7726 196 C
sdavis@sjcme.edu
DAVIS, Sheri .... 401-874-5654 405 E
sdavis@uri.edu
DAVIS, Sherri .... 205-929-6357.... 2 H
sdavis@lawsonstate.edu
DAVIS, Sherri .... 828-398-7900 332 B
sherrijdavis@abtech.edu
DAVIS, Sherry .... 812-221-1714 162 E
sherrydavis@vbc.edu
DAVIS, Sherry .... 254-659-7818 437 A
sdavis@hillcollege.edu
DAVIS, Stephanie .... 615-547-1387 419 C
sdavis@cumberland.edu
DAVIS, Stephen .... 360-475-7805 481 I
sdavis2@olympic.edu
DAVIS, Stephen .... 609-652-4803 283 E
stephen.davis@stockton.edu
DAVIS, Stephen .... 301-295-3062 503 C
stephen.davis@usuhs.edu
DAVIS, Steve .... 509-527-5777 486 B
davissp@whitman.edu
DAVIS, Steven .... 707-638-5270.. 68 B
steven.davis@tu.edu
DAVIS, Steven, J .... 208-496-3305 130 I
daviss@byui.edu
DAVIS, Stewart .... 256-549-8603.... 2 B
sdavis@gadsdenstate.edu
DAVIS, Stuart .... 760-862-1333.. 38 E
stdavis@collegeofthedesert.edu
DAVIS, Sue .... 225-768-1802 187 B
sue.davis@franu.edu
DAVIS, Susan, M .... 434-924-4639 472 D
smd5r@virginia.edu
DAVIS, Suzanne .... 618-664-7000 138 F
suzanne.davis@greenville.edu
DAVIS, Suzanne, E .... 315-268-6493 295 F
sdavis@clarkson.edu
DAVIS, Taisheika .... 225-771-2790 191 B
taisheika_davis@subr.edu
DAVIS, Taishieka .... 225-771-4530 191 A
taishieka_davis@subr.edu
DAVIS, Tamara .... 317-274-8362 156 G
tamsdavi@iu.edu
DAVIS, Tamara, S .... 317-274-8362 157 D
tamsdavi@iu.edu
DAVIS, Tammy .... 325-574-7695 458 D
tdavis@wtc.edu
DAVIS, Teresa .... 336-433-5570 341 D
tmdavis4@ncat.edu
DAVIS, Terry Daily .... 314-340-3688 254 A
davist@hssu.edu
DAVIS, Theresa, A .... 626-395-4638.. 28 J
theresa.davis@caltech.edu
DAVIS, Thom .... 661-654-2287.. 30 B
tdavis31@csub.edu
DAVIS, Thomas .... 520-206-4769.. 15 B
tdavis53@ppima.edu
DAVIS, Tiffany .... 206-726-5099 479 E
tdavis@cornish.edu
DAVIS, Tom .... 334-670-3981.... 7 C
tomdavis@troy.edu
DAVIS, Traci .... 309-796-5408 133 G
davist@bhc.edu
DAVIS, Tracy .... 951-763-0500.. 55 B
DAVIS, Tracy .... 713-222-5323 453 A
davisjam@uhd.edu
DAVIS, Troy .... 714-484-7271.. 54 B
tdavis@cypresscollege.edu
DAVIS, Troy .... 413-748-3108 218 I
tdavis10@springfield.edu
DAVIS, Ty .... 770-457-2021 121 D
DAVIS, Wain .... 618-393-2982 139 E
davist@iecc.edu
DAVIS, Warren .... 972-860-2944 434 G
wldavis@dcccd.edu
DAVIS, Warren .... 972-860-2994 435 A
jarreddavis@dcccd.edu
DAVIS, Wartyna .... 973-720-2731 284 J
davisw@wpunj.edu
DAVIS, Wayne .... 214-333-5163 434 C
wayned@dbu.edu
DAVIS, Wendy .... 520-515-3623.. 11 M
davisd@cochise.edu
DAVIS, Wendy .... 501-812-2273.. 23 B
wdavis@uaptc.edu
DAVIS, Wendy .... 330-363-6347 348 C
wendy.davis@aultmancollege.edu
DAVIS, Wesley .... 701-477-7853 346 J
wdavis1@tm.edu
DAVIS, Wesley .... 828-669-8012 331 K
wesley.davis@montreat.edu
DAVIS, Whitney .... 478-757-5170 127 F
wdavis@wesleyancollege.edu
DAVIS, William .... 708-534-4105 138 E
wdavis3@govst.edu
DAVIS, William .... 830-792-7415 443 E
deanoffaculty@schreiner.edu
DAVIS, William .... 610-359-6500 382 A
wdavis@dccc.edu
DAVIS, Zabe .... 662-562-3314 248 D
DAVIS-AJAMI,
Mary Lynn .... 812-855-7089 156 G
mdavisaj@iu.edu
DAVIS-BAXTER, Angela . 704-636-6023 330 A
adavisbaxter@hoodseminary.edu
DAVIS-EYENE, Mishawn 857-701-1230 215 G
mdeyene@rcc.mass.edu
DAVIS-FREEMAN,
Juana .... 803-934-3464 410 G
jdavis@morris.edu
DAVIS FREEMAN,
Louisa, M .... 413-755-4333 216 A
ldavisfreeman@stcc.edu
DAVIS-HAYNES, Angela 770-689-4779 115 C
ahaynes@aii.edu
DAVIS-JOHNSON, Max . 208-426-3033 130 H
maxdavis-johnson@boisestate.edu
DAVIS JONES, Chrissy . 800-222-4222 385 B
DAVIS-KAHL, Stephanie 309-556-3350 140 F
sdaviska@iwu.edu
DAVIS-KEPHART, Renee 334-386-7230.... 5 C
rkephart@faulkner.edu
DAVIS-LOWE, Eda .... 407-582-3057 113 I
edavislowe@valenciacollege.edu
DAVIS-SAMUELS,
Ivanetta .... 615-327-6141 421 D
isamuel@mmc.edu
DAVIS-STREET, Jeanean 508-531-6151 212 D
jeanean.davisstreet@bridgew.edu
DAVISON, Brent .... 423-652-4832 420 F
bedavison@king.edu
DAVISON, Frieda, M ..... 864-503-5610 414 A
fdavison@uscupstate.edu
DAVISON, James .... 252-335-0821 333 G
james_davison99@albemarle.edu
DAVISON, Jane, M .... 989-774-1870 222 E
matty1jm@cmich.edu
DAVISON, Kimberly, K . 972-985-3781 433 I
kdavison@collin.edu
DAVISON, Natalie .... 208-459-5188 131 C
ndavison@collegeofidaho.edu
DAVISON, Scott, A .... 606-783-2273 184 C
s.davison@moreheadstate.edu
DAVITT, Jeffrey .... 904-819-6489.. 99 E
jdavitt@flagler.edu
DAVITT, Kristin .... 412-647-6504 400 H
davitt@pitt.edu
DAVITZ, Pamela, K .... 314-505-7010 252 A
davitzp@csl.edu
DAVOLT, David .... 208-376-7731 130 G
ddavolt@boisebible.edu
DAVOUD, Mohammad .. 912-478-7412 120 C
mdavoud@georgiasouthern.edu
DAVRAY, Niranjan .... 315-228-7995 296 E
ndavray@colgate.edu
DAVROS, Harry .... 214-637-3530 457 H
hdavros@wadecollege.edu
DAW, Michael .... 415-442-6682.. 43 I
mdaw@ggu.edu
DAWE, Chris .... 660-562-1348 257 E
cdawe@nwmissouri.edu
DAWE, Richard, L .... 870-368-2006.. 20 E
rdawe@ozarka.edu
DAWES, Daniel .... 404-752-1833 123 E
ddawes@msm.edu
DAWES, Elliott .... 646-312-4542 292 L
elliott.dawes@baruch.cuny.edu
DAWES, Trevor, A .... 302-831-2231.. 91 C
lib-vplm@udel.edu
DAWKINS, Lisa .... 304-357-4374 487 J
lisadawkins@ucwv.edu
DAWKINS, Norman .... 212-431-2142 309 A
norman.dawkins@nyls.edu
DAWKINS, Sandra, C ... 662-252-8000 248 G
sdawkins@rustcollege.edu
DAWLEY, Anna Marie ... 315-268-6475 295 F
adawley@clarkson.edu
DAWN, Russell .... 708-771-8300 136 E
russell.dawn@cuchicago.edu
DAWSEY, Brian .... 912-358-4154 125 A
dawseyb@savannahstate.edu
DAWSON, Barbara, E .... 304-293-4874 490 E
barbara.dawson@mail.wvu.edu
DAWSON, Bradley .... 703-591-7042 466 M
bdawson@fxua.edu
DAWSON, Brandon .... 860-231-5430.. 90 A
bdawson@usj.edu
DAWSON, Bridgette ...... 740-699-3804 348 E
bdawson@belmontcollege.edu
DAWSON, Caroline .... 209-386-6730.. 52 A
DAWSON, Cindy .... 423-472-7141 424 B
cdawson@clevelandstatecc.edu
DAWSON, Dani .... 619-239-0391.. 34 G
ddawson@cwsl.edu
DAWSON, Darren .... 256-824-1000.... 8 B
president@uah.edu
DAWSON, Greg .... 615-248-1507 426 D
gdawson@trevecca.edu
DAWSON, J. Lin .... 404-880-8123 117 C
jldawson@cau.edu
DAWSON, Keith .... 574-520-4480 157 E
khdawson@iusb.edu
DAWSON, Kevin .... 202-806-6100.. 92 F
DAWSON, Leslie .... 509-533-3527 479 D
leslie.dawson@sfcc.spokane.edu
DAWSON, Marcus .... 517-629-0224 221 A
mdawson@albion.edu
DAWSON, Marsha .... 607-274-3011 302 G
mdawson@ithaca.edu
DAWSON, Patrick .... 410-455-2356 203 B
pdawson@umbc.edu
DAWSON, Rachel .... 660-596-7478 259 M
rdawson1@sfccmo.edu
DAWSON, Randall .... 210-486-2534 429 B
rdawson@alamo.edu
DAWSON, Renita .... 919-735-5151 338 H
rddawson@waynecc.edu
DAWSON, Teresa, U ..... 256-765-4328.... 8 E
tdawson2@una.edu
DAWSON, JR.,
Thomas, E .... 410-951-3792 204 B
thdawson@coppin.edu
DAWSON-SCULLY, Ken . 800-541-6682 105 A
DAWTON, Dennis .... 215-965-4073 390 E
academic@moore.edu
DAY, Alexandra, H .... 609-258-8771 280 D
ahday@princeton.edu
DAY, Barbara .... 828-726-2471 332 G
bday@cccti.edu
DAY, Barton .... 953-923-3201 449 D
bart.day@tstc.edu
DAY, Charles .... 518-262-3777 289 L
dayc1@amc.edu
DAY, David .... 412-536-1070 386 H
david.day@laroche.edu
DAY, Deborah, A .... 540-231-7999 476 C
alumni@vt.edu
DAY, Ian .... 734-432-5495 227 C
iday@madonna.edu
DAY, Jeffrey .... 561-912-2166.. 99 D
jeday@evergladesuniversity.edu
DAY, John, R .... 404-413-2564 120 E
jday@gsu.edu
DAY, Lawrence .... 315-792-3099 324 B
lday@utica.edu
DAY, Mark .... 949-376-6000.. 47 D
mday@lcad.edu
DAY, Mellani, J .... 303-963-3434.. 78 H
mday@ccu.edu
DAY, Michael .... 812-941-2244 157 F
micaday@ius.edu
DAY, Michael .... 760-744-1150.. 56 B
DAY, Michelle .... 406-768-6351 263 F
mday@fpcc.edu
DAY, Mitzi .... 231-591-3800 224 A
mitziday@ferris.edu
DAY, Patricia .... 518-828-4181 297 B
day@sunycgcc.edu
DAY, Patrick, K .... 408-924-5900.. 34 A
DAY, Richard .... 216-397-1904 353 O
rday@jcu.edu
DAY, Rondall, H .... 470-578-6074 121 M
rday9@kennesaw.edu
DAY, Sharon .... 417-447-7603 257 G
days@otc.edu
DAY, Stuart .... 913-897-4903 177 J
day@ku.edu
DAY, Thelma .... 323-953-4000.. 49 A
dayt@lacitycollege.edu
DAY-HAIRSTON, Beth ... 478-825-6856 118 F
beth.dayhairston@fvsu.edu
DAYAL, Ravinder .... 916-361-5100.. 34 K
DAYHOFF, Brenda, K .... 301-447-5207 201 B
b.k.dayhoff@msmary.edu
DAYHOFF, Sharon, S .... 717-337-6276 384 D
sdayhoff@gettysburg.edu
DAYNES, Gary .... 252-399-6343 326 K
gdaynes@barton.edu
DAYRIES, Sonje .... 831-459-2686.. 71 A
sdayries@ucsc.edu
DAYTON, Nancy .... 765-998-5204 161 C
nndayton@taylor.edu
DAYTON-JOHNSON,
Jeffrey .... 831-647-4647 462 E
jdaytonjohnson@miis.edu
DAYZIE, Merle .... 928-724-6950.. 12 D
mtdayzie@dinecollege.edu
DE, Arijit .... 856-256-4507 281 F
de@rowan.edu
DE ARMOND, Maureen 515-271-3133 165 J
maureen.dearmond@drake.edu

DEAVER, Robin .... 910-678-8250 334 E
deaverr@faytechcc.edu
DEBACCO, Mark .... 323-860-0789.. 50 B
DEBECK, Adam .... 574-239-8338 156 A
adebeck@hcc-nd.edu
DEBEER, Katie .... 413-782-1478 220 A
katie.debeer@wne.edu
DEBENEDETTI, Pablo .... 609-258-5480 280 D
pdebene@princeton.edu
DEBENEDICTIS, Katie .... 419-530-5660 363 B
katie.debenedictis@utoledo.edu
DEBERARD, Scott .... 435-797-1462 460 C
scott.deberard@usu.edu
DEBERNARDI, Maureen 617-254-2610 218 E
admissionsandrecords@sjs.edu
DEBERNARDI, Maureen 617-779-4369 218 E
maureen.debernardi@sjs.edu
DEBERRY, Marilyn .... 803-376-5827 406 D
myoung@allenuniversity.edu
DEBERRY, Ron .... 757-826-1883 464 G
rdeberry@ascent.edu
DEBIAS, Patti .... 773-256-0728 143 F
pdebias@lstc.edu
DEBIASE, Paul .... 212-217-3750 299 D
paul_debiase@fitnyc.edu
DEBILZAN, Vern .... 434-528-5276 477 B
DEBLOIS, Nicole .... 207-795-2270 195 B
debloini@mchp.edu
DEBNER, Stephanie ...... 503-251-5757 377 B
sdebner@uws.edu
DEBOARD, John .... 580-581-2237 365 D
jdeboard@cameron.edu
DEBOBES, Derek .... 508-793-3336 208 D
ddebobes@holycross.edu
DEBOCK, Devin .... 918-293-4944 368 B
devin.debock@okstate.edu
DEBOEF, Cindy, S .... 231-777-0303 228 G
cindy.deboef@muskegoncc.edu
DEBOEF, Ryan .... 417-836-8500 256 G
ryandeboef@missouristate.edu
DEBOER, Eileen .... 318-487-7222 187 E
eileen.deboer@lacollege.edu
DEBOER, John .... 406-243-4970 263 K
john.deboer@umontana.edu
DEBOER, Keith .... 616-222-1247 223 C
keith.deboer@cornerstone.edu
DEBOER, Michael .... 334-386-7547.... 5 C
mdeboer@faulkner.edu
DEBOER, Missy .... 989-837-4339 229 B
deboerme@northwood.edu
DEBOLT, Ken .... 315-781-3146 301 F
debolt@hws.edu
DEBOLT, Patricia .... 918-631-2308 371 C
patricia-zumwalt@utulsa.edu
DEBOLT, Peg .... 260-359-4068 156 C
pdebolt@huntington.edu
DEBONA, OSB, Guerric 812-357-6549 161 A
gdebona@saintmeinrad.edu
DEBONI, Toni .... 805-437-8962.. 30 C
toni.deboni@csuci.edu
DEBORD, Cris .... 304-293-2545 490 E
cris.debord@mail.wvu.edu
DEBORD, Kristy, L .... 770-720-9146 124 G
kristy.debord@reinhardt.edu
DEBORD, Toni Lynn ..... 412-563-6673 125 F
tdebord@southuniversity.edu
DEBRAGA, Angie .... 775-775-2231 271 A
angie.debraga@gbcnv.edu
DEBRAGGIO,
Michael, J .... 315-859-4654 300 H
mdebragg@hamilton.edu
DEBRECENI, Brian .... 951-493-6753.. 77 B
bdebreceni@youngamericans.org
DEBRO, Angela .... 256-372-5230.... 1 A
angela.debro@aamu.edu
DEBRUM, David .... 692-625-6416 504 G
ddebrum@cmi.edu
DEBURE, Olivier .... 727-864-8366.. 98 J
debureoc@eckerd.edu
DEBURRO, Jennifer .... 207-602-2132 197 E
jdeburro@une.edu
DEBUS, Casey .... 307-532-8311 501 B
casey.debus@ewc.wy.edu
DEC, Matthew .... 937-319-6082 347 G
mdec@antiochcollege.edu
DEC, Ted .... 631-687-5155 314 A
tdec@sjcny.edu
DECAIRE, Maryann .... 847-578-8810 148 F
maryann.decaire@rosalindfranklin.edu
DECAPUA-RINCK,
Nicole .... 201-761-6023 283 A
ndecapuarinck@saintpeters.edu

DECARIE, Linette, A ...... 617-353-7118 207 E
decarie@bu.edu
DECARLO, Robert, L ..... 516-877-3184 289 I
decarlo@adelphi.edu
DECARO, Peter .... 718-862-7379 304 M
pdecaro01@manhattan.edu
DECAROLIS, Crystal ...... 845-905-4632 297 G
crystal.decarolis@culinary.edu
DECAROLIS, Donna, M . 215-895-1795 382 F
donna.marie.decarolis@drexel.edu
DECARVALHO,
Meghan, M .... 401-341-2348 405 D
meghan.decarvalho@salve.edu
DECATUR, Jane .... 508-626-4585 213 A
jdecatur@framingham.edu
DECATUR, Sean .... 740-427-5111 354 I
decatur@kenyon.edu
DECAY, Jarlene .... 972-860-8071 434 G
jdecay@dcccd.edu
DECELLE, Michael, P .... 603-641-4107 274 F
mike.decelle@unh.edu
DECENT, Bridgette .... 901-678-5502 426 G
bdecent@memphis.edu
DECERO, OSF, Linda .... 610-358-4213 391 A
decerol@neumann.edu
DECESARE, Renee .... 617-552-4400 207 C
renee.decesare@bc.edu
DECEW, Dave .... 603-428-2292 273 G
ddecew@nec.edu
DECHAMBEAU,
Aimee, L .... 330-972-7488 361 H
aimee@uakron.edu
DECHARINTE, Janeen .... 815-836-5263 142 F
decharja@lewisu.edu
DECHIARO, Thomas ...... 215-895-1434 382 F
tdechiaro@drexel.edu
DECICCO, Stephanie ...... 773-291-6100 135 E
sdecicco@ccc.edu
DECKARD, Marty .... 361-582-2469 457 E
marty.deckard@victoriacollege.edu
DECKER, Ann .... 772-462-7240 102 F
adecker@irsc.edu
DECKER, Ann .... 772-462-4772 102 F
DECKER, Craig .... 719-255-4338.. 84 C
cdecker@uccs.edu
DECKER, David, R .... 614-947-6017 352 J
david.decker@franklin.edu
DECKER, Douglas .... 724-983-0700 388 B
ddecker@laurel.edu
DECKER, Douglas, S ..... 724-439-4900 388 A
ddecker@laurel.edu
DECKER, Evan .... 510-215-3977.. 40 B
edecker@contracosta.edu
DECKER, Jarron, P .... 518-276-6216 312 C
deckej3@rpi.edu
DECKER, John .... 989-964-4612 230 E
jdecker1@svsu.edu
DECKER, Marlene .... 563-876-3353 165 H
mdecker@dwci.edu
DECKER, SVD, Mike ..... 563-876-3353 165 H
midecker@dwci.edu
DECKER, Nancy .... 724-983-0700 388 B
ndecker@laurel.edu
DECKER, Nancy, M .... 724-439-4900 388 A
ndecker@laurel.edu
DECKER, Randy .... 903-589-7143 438 C
rdecker@jacksonville-college.edu
DECKER, Stephanie .... 973-684-6868 280 A
sdecker@pccc.edu
DECKER, Steven .... 715-788-7113 499 H
steve.decker@northwoodtech.edu
DECKER, Timothy .... 845-298-0755 298 D
tdecker@sunydutchess.edu
DECKER, William, C ..... 501-916-3328.. 22 A
wcdecker@ualr.edu
DECKER, William, C ..... 501-916-3302.. 22 A
wcdecker@ualr.edu
DECKERT, Glenn .... 978-867-4736 210 B
glenn.deckert@gordon.edu
DECKINGA, Mike .... 219-864-2400 159 N
mdeckinga@midamerica.edu
DECLASS, SVD, Sonny .. 563-876-3353 165 H
edeclass@dwci.edu
DECOCINIS, Anthony ..... 717-815-6579 403 F
adecocinis@ycp.edu
DECONNO, David .... 518-580-5718 315 F
ddeconno@skidmore.edu
DECOSMO, Andrea .... 303-404-5117.. 81 A
andrea.decosmo@frontrange.edu
DECOSTA, Leah .... 617-552-4700 207 C
leah.decosta@bc.edu
DECOSTER, Daisy .... 201-761-6465 283 A
ddecoster@saintpeters.edu

DECOSTER, Terry .... 918-540-6311 366 F
terry.decoster@neo.edu
DECOTEAU, Brian .... 701-221-1604 347 A
bdecoteau@uttc.edu
DECOTEAU, Jolene .... 701-255-3285 347 A
jolene.decoteau@uttc.edu
DECOTEAU, Katina .... 701-255-3285 347 A
kdecoteau@uttc.edu
DECOTEAU, Robert .... 360-392-4293 481 F
rdecoteau@nwic.edu
DECOURCY, Michael ..... 502-597-5550 183 D
michael.decourcy@kysu.edu
DECOURSEY, Paul, A .... 515-574-1055 167 A
decoursey@iowacentral.edu
DECRISTO, James .... 336-734-2862 343 D
decristoj@uncsa.edu
DECRISTO, Jim .... 336-734-2862 343 D
decristoj@uncsa.edu
DECRISTOFARO,
Richard .... 617-984-1776 218 C
rdecristofaro@quincycollege.edu
DECROSTRA, Joseph ..... 412-396-5180 383 A
decrostra@duq.edu
DECUIR, Bobbie .... 337-482-1000 193 B
bobbie@louisiana.edu
DECUIR, Karla .... 281-396-3792 453 B
decuirk@uhv.edu
DECUIR, JR.,
Winston, G .... 225-578-2111 189 E
wdecuirjr@lsu.edu
DECUIR, JR.,
Winston, G .... 225-578-2111 189 D
DEDDO, Gary .... 980-495-3978 329 B
DEDEAUX, Ebby .... 601-925-3310 247 C
ededeaux@mc.edu
DEDIEMAR, Jeanette ..... 210-784-1109 447 E
jdediemar@tamusa.edu
DEDOMENICO-PAYNE,
Melissa .... 540-868-7000 474 C
DEDOMINICI, Peter .... 703-329-9100.. 93 H
DEDONATO, Joy .... 516-572-0670 307 E
joy.dedonato@ncc.edu
DEDWYLDER, Jason ..... 601-477-4075 246 G
jason.dedwylder@jcjc.edu
DEDWYLDER, Kari .... 601-477-4040 246 G
kari.dedwylder@jcjc.edu
DEE, Edward .... 718-862-7597 304 M
edee02@manhattan.edu
DEE, Edward .... 718-779-1499 311 E
edee@plazacollege.edu
DEE, Kay, C .... 812-877-8502 160 F
dee@rose-hulman.edu
DEE, Shawn, G .... 336-334-4822 335 A
sgdee@gtcc.edu
DEE, Tina .... 231-777-0660 228 G
tina.dee@muskegoncc.edu
DEEB, Bassam, M .... 716-827-2423 323 G
deebb@trocaire.edu
DEEB, Tiffni .... 612-659-6600 239 A
tiffni.deeb@minneapolis.edu
DEEDS, Brad .... 530-541-4660.. 47 E
deeds@ltcc.edu
DEEDS, Leeland .... 314-935-4259 262 A
ldeeds@wustl.edu
DEEG, Richard .... 215-204-7443 399 B
DEEGAN, Michele .... 484-664-3130 390 H
deanofacademiclife@muhlenberg.edu
DEEK, Fadi, P .... 973-596-3220 279 E
fadi.deek@njit.edu
DEEKEN, Lynnae .... 425-388-9502 480 B
ldeeken@everettcc.edu
DEEL, David .... 276-498-5227 464 D
ddeel@acp.edu
DEEL, Ritchie .... 276-523-2400 474 D
rdeel@mecc.edu
DEEL, Susan, M .... 989-463-7176 221 B
deel@alma.edu
DEELY, Pamela .... 630-829-6047 133 E
pdeely@ben.edu
DEEM, Marie .... 412-536-1128 386 H
marie.deem@laroche.edu
DEEMER, Cindy .... 231-995-1058 229 A
cdeemer@nmc.edu
DEEN, Christopher .... 907-564-8282.... 9 F
cdeen@alaskapacific.edu
DEEN, Michael .... 903-813-2306 430 H
mdeen@austincollege.edu
DEER, Susan .... 845-574-4280 312 H
sdeer@sunyrockland.edu
DEES, Margaret .... 904-256-7020 102 H
mdees@ju.edu
DEES, Meg, K .... 704-637-4394 327 I
mkdees12@catawba.edu

DEES-BURNETT,
Keichanda .... 816-235-5628 261 B
deesk@umkc.edu
DEESE, Phyllis .... 903-823-3355 446 A
phyllis.deese@texarkanacollege.edu
DEESS, Eugene, P .... 973-596-3110 279 E
eugene.p.deess@njit.edu
DEETER, Daniel, P .... 864-597-4232 414 E
deeterdp@wofford.edu
DEETZ, Kristi, R .... 812-888-5333 162 F
kdeetz@vinu.edu
DEEULIS, Chris .... 810-762-3000 232 A
cdeeulis@umich.edu
DEEVERS, Shari .... 269-965-3931 225 H
deevers@kellogg.edu
DEFALCO, Cindy .... 609-343-4900 275 D
DEFALCO, Julie .... 860-832-2551.. 85 G
julie.defalco@ccsu.edu
DEFATTA, Jerry .... 601-266-5013 249 F
jerry.defatta@usm.edu
DEFAZIO, Harmony, R .. 520-626-9211.. 16 D
defazioh@arizona.edu
DEFAZIO, Jeannie .... 330-490-7332 363 E
jdefazio@walsh.edu
DEFEDE, Kathryn .... 559-925-3145.. 75 B
kathryndefede@whccd.edu
DEFEIS, Evelyn .... 973-684-5900 280 A
edefeis@pccc.edu
DEFELICE, Jonathan, P . 603-641-7010 274 A
jdefelice@anselm.edu
DEFELICE, Stacey .... 516-876-3009 318 C
defelices@oldwestbury.edu
DEFEO, William .... 252-335-0821 333 G
william_defeo@albemarle.edu
DEFFENBACHER, Mark .. 559-453-2239.. 43 A
mark.deffenbacher@fresno.edu
DEFILIPPIS, Brian, J ..... 410-704-2358 204 E
bdefilippis@towson.edu
DEFILIPPIS, Nunzio .... 818-333-3558.. 53 J
nunzio.defilippis@nyfa.edu
DEFLORIO, Mel .... 802-831-1037 463 C
mdeflorio@vermontlaw.edu
DEFLORIO, Mel .... 802-485-2969 462 F
mdeflori@norwich.edu
DEFOOR, Keith .... 706-379-3111 128 C
kdefoor@yhc.edu
DEFORD, Victoria .... 763-424-0955 240 A
vdeford@nhcc.edu
DEFORE, Jody .... 678-359-5990 120 F
jody@gordonstate.edu
DEFORE, Matt .... 205-726-4021.... 6 E
mdefore@samford.edu
DEFOREST, Kristin, A .... 607-746-4590 320 D
deforeka@delhi.edu
DEFORREST, Matthew ... 704-378-1238 330 D
mdeforrest@jcsu.edu
DEFRAIN, Steven, R ...... 610-917-1430 401 G
srdefrain@valleyforge.edu
DEFRANCO, Jeff .... 530-541-4660.. 47 E
defranco@ltcc.edu
DEFRATES, Bruce .... 509-359-2314 479 G
bdefrates@ewu.edu
DEFREECE, Michele, T .. 607-746-4652 320 D
defreemt@delhi.edu
DEFREITAS, Jack .... 660-263-3900 251 D
jackdefreitas@cccb.edu
DEFRONZO, Jennier ...... 508-626-4923 213 A
jdefronzo@framingham.edu
DEFUSCO-SULLIVAN,
Andrea .... 978-762-4000 215 D
adefusco@northshore.edu
DEGAIN, Sabrina .... 336-506-4161 332 A
sabrina.degain@alamancecc.edu
DEGAISH, Ann .... 361-825-2481 447 C
ann.degaish@tamucc.edu
DEGARMO, David, L ..... 417-862-9533 253 F
ddegarmo@globaluniversity.edu
DEGEARE, Chris .... 636-481-3467 254 C
cdegear1@jeffco.edu
DEGENHARDT, Brian ..... 660-626-2304 250 A
bdegenhardt@atsu.edu
DEGENHARDT, Nancy ... 412-578-6423 380 B
nadegenhardt@carlow.edu
DEGENHART,
Mary Louise .... 314-446-8302 260 H
mary.degenhart@stlcop.edu
DEGEORGE, Dave .... 608-363-2039 491 H
degeorge@beloit.edu
DEGERMAN, Roger .... 336-316-2123 329 D
degermanre@guilford.edu
DEGEYTER, Julienne ..... 206-934-5300 483 D
DEGEYTER, Julienne ..... 530-754-2293.. 69 B
jdegeyter@ucdavis.edu

DELISLE, Joseph .... 781-239-2571 214 G
jdelisle@massbay.edu
DELITTO, Anthony .... 412-383-6560 400 H
delitto@pitt.edu
DELIZIO, Carissa .... 401-456-8126 405 A
cdelizio@ric.edu
DELL, Irve .... 507-786-3816 243 D
dell@stolaf.edu
DELL, Kyle .... 336-316-2207 329 D
kdell@guilford.edu
DELL, Rebekah .... 517-607-2233 225 C
rdell@hillsdale.edu
DELL, Robert .... 831-656-3671 502 M
dell@nps.edu
DELL, Troy .... 301-687-4471 204 C
tadell@frostburg.edu
DELLA COLETTA,
Cristina .... 858-534-6270.. 70 C
cdellacoletta@ucsd.edu
DELLA POSTA,
Joseph, B .... 315-445-4564 303 I
dellapjb@lemoyne.edu
DELLA ROCCA, Jodi ...... 518-262-4303 289 L
dellarj@amc.edu
DELLACONTRADA,
John .... 716-645-6969 316 C
dellacon@buffalo.edu
DELLAPIETRA, Lynn ...... 215-968-8272 379 D
lynn.dellapietra@bucks.edu
DELLAPORTA, Pamela ... 718-933-6700 307 A
pdellaporta@monroecollege.edu
DELLAROCAS, Chris ...... 617-358-0831 207 E
dell@bu.edu
DELLASALA, Kristen ...... 845-569-3439 307 D
kristen.dellasala@msmc.edu
DELLATORRE, Bonnie ... 714-449-7495.. 51 B
bdellatorre@ketchum.edu
DELLE, James .... 717-871-7462 395 A
james.delle@millersville.edu
DELLE, James, A .... 717-871-7462 395 A
james.delle@millersville.edu
DELLI GATTI, Barbara ... 510-780-4500.. 47 K
bdelligatti@lifewest.edu
DELLICARPINI,
Dominic, F .... 717-815-1303 403 F
dcarpini@ycp.edu
DELLINGER, Dewey .... 704-922-6207 334 G
dellinger.dewey@gaston.edu
DELLINGER, Elaine, C ... 540-828-5605 464 L
edelling@bridgewater.edu
DELLINGER, Jade .... 239-489-9313 101 A
jdellinger@fsw.edu
DELLINGER, Tim .... 731-425-2610 424 E
tdellinger@jscc.edu
DELLINGER ACEITUNO,
Leslie .... 305-284-4025 113 C
leslie@miami.edu
DELLO BUONO,
Ricardo .... 718-862-7527 304 M
ricardo.dellobuono@manhattan.edu
DELLWO, Sarah .... 406-447-6908 264 B
sarah.dellwo@helenacollege.edu
DELL'AQUILO, Bobbie .. 516-686-7851 308 I
rdellaqu@nyit.edu
DELL'OLIO, Pam .... 559-251-4215.. 27 I
bookkeeper@calchristiancollege.edu
DELL'OLIVER, Carol, A . 503-943-7134 377 A
delloliv@up.edu
DELL'OMO, Gregory ..... 609-896-5001 281 B
gdellomo@rider.edu
DELMAR, Cindy .... 585-345-6813 300 F
cmdelmar@genesee.edu
DELMARK, Cary .... 281-649-3703 437 B
cdelmark@hbu.edu
DELMONT, Angie .... 815-825-9686 141 F
adelmont@kish.edu
DELO, Carl .... 718-409-7412 320 G
cdelo@sunymaritime.edu
DELOACH, Brian .... 912-478-7288 120 C
briandeloach@georgiasouthern.edu
DELOACH, C. Gregory .. 678-547-6620 122 E
deloach_cg@mercer.edu
DELOATCH, Jameson .... 540-373-2200 466 C
jdeloatch@evcc.edu
DELONG, Allen .... 207-786-8305 194 A
adelong@bates.edu
DELONG, Brian, C .... 610-799-1179 388 D
bdelong2@lccc.edu
DELONG, Cliff .... 605-455-6079 415 H
cdelong@olc.edu
DELONG, Lori .... 251-442-2302.... 8 C
ldelong@umobile.edu
DELONG, Rhonda .... 313-317-6800 225 B
rdelong@hfcc.edu
DELONGORIA, Maria .... 718-270-4850 294 G
mdelongoria@mec.cuny.edu
DELONGPRE JOHNSTON,
Dedee, I .... 336-758-3256 344 C
DELONIS, Alex .... 765-361-6375 163 B
delonisa@wabash.edu
DELOREN, Dianne .... 505-467-6807 288 H
diannedeloren@swc.edu
DELORENZO, Michael ... 217-333-1300 152 B
michaeld@illinois.edu
DELORENZO, Robin ...... 518-861-2513 305 C
robind@mariacollege.edu
DELORME, Teresa .... 701-477-7862 346 J
tdelorme@tm.edu
DELORT, Greg .... 785-539-3571 176 A
gdelort@mccks.edu
DELOS REYES DAVIS,
Mark .... 831-459-0111.. 71 A
DELP, Mark Damien ..... 510-356-4760.. 77 F
DELP, Michael .... 850-644-1281 110 C
mdelp@fsu.edu
DELPLANQUE,
Jean-Pierre .... 530-754-8380.. 69 B
delplanque@ucdavis.edu
DELPRETE, Angela .... 440-375-7230 354 K
adelprete@lec.edu
DELPRIORE, Michael .... 717-464-7050 387 F
DELQUADRI, Sheila ...... 509-574-4655 486 D
sdelquadri@yvcc.edu
DELTONDO, Bruce .... 719-587-7227.. 77 G
bdeltond@adams.edu
DELUCA, Anthony, L ..... 516-876-3177 318 C
delucaa@oldwestbury.edu
DELUCA, Cynthia, A ...... 813-974-3077 111 C
deluca@usf.edu
DELUCA, Eileen .... 239-985-3498 101 A
eileen.deluca@fsw.edu
DELUCA, Mick .... 310-206-1753.. 69 E
mdeluca@recreation.ucla.edu
DELUCA, Thomas .... 541-737-4279 375 A
DELUCA, Vincent, J ...... 212-817-7500 293 F
vdeluca@gc.cuny.edu
DELUCCHI, Jennifer ...... 916-568-3039.. 50 F
deluccj@losrios.edu
DELUCIA, Andrea .... 619-574-5809.. 42 J
adelucia@fst.edu
DELUCIA, Melissa .... 203-773-8538.. 85 D
mdelucia@albertus.edu
DELUNAS, Linda .... 219-980-6643 157 C
ldelunas@iun.edu
DELVA, Jorge .... 617-353-3760 207 E
jdelva@bu.edu
DELVECCHIO, Edie .... 201-200-3159 279 D
edelvecchio@njcu.edu
DELVISCIO, Gregory ...... 607-777-2175 316 B
gregdelv@binghamton.edu
DEMA, Anne, C .... 816-415-5912 262 F
demaa@william.jewell.edu
DEMAEGD, Gwen .... 574-239-8349 156 A
gdemaegd@hcc-nd.edu
DEMAGGIO, Steve .... 530-895-2327.. 27 C
demaggiost@butte.edu
DEMAGISTRIS, Jared ..... 518-736-3622 300 D
jdmagis@fmcc.edu
DEMANT, Timothy .... 509-777-3600 486 C
tdemant@whitworth.edu
DEMARAIS, Melanie .... 508-767-7332 206 A
demarais@assumption.edu
DEMARCO, Anthony ...... 610-607-6294 396 H
ademarco@racc.edu
DEMARCO, Deborah ...... 508-856-2903 212 C
deborah.demarco@umassmed.edu
DEMARCO, Joanne .... 914-888-5215 306 C
jdemarco1@mercy.edu
DEMARCO, Patricia ...... 508-286-3458 220 B
demarco_patricia@wheatoncollege.edu
DEMARCO, Rosanna ..... 617-287-7500 211 H
rosanna.demarco@umb.edu
DEMARCO, Tom .... 610-519-4200 401 K
tom.demarco@villanova.edu
DEMARCO FUENTES,
Wendy .... 212-817-7187 293 F
wdemarco@gc.cuny.edu
DEMARESKI, Roger .... 610-330-5133 387 C
demaresr@lafayette.edu
DEMARK, Sarah .... 801-274-3280 461 E
sarah.demark@wgu.edu
DEMARS, Kelly .... 512-617-5700 433 B
DEMARS, Kerry .... 708-802-6154 138 C
kdemars@foxcollege.edu
DEMART-KRAUS, Gina .. 440-646-8334 363 C
gdemart@ursuline.edu
DEMARTE, Daniel, T ..... 716-338-1060 303 A
danieldemarte@mail.sunyjcc.edu
DEMARTINO, Amanda ... 609-771-2231 276 I
demartia@tcnj.edu
DEMAS, Christopher ..... 423-354-2588 425 A
cddemas@northeaststate.edu
DEMATTEO, Jeanne .... 925-631-4123.. 59 I
jdematte@stmarys-ca.edu
DEMAYO PUGNO,
Courtney .... 419-448-2510 353 E
cdemayo@heidelberg.edu
DEMBROSKI, Ben .... 414-847-3285 494 C
bendembroski@miad.edu
DEMBSKEY, Evan .... 269-467-9945 224 C
edembskey@glenoaks.edu
DEMCIE, Christine .... 716-829-7874 298 E
demciec@dyc.edu
DEMEDEIROS, Joe .... 512-233-1443 442 I
joed@stedwards.edu
DEMEDICIS, David .... 540-834-1026 473 I
ddemedicis@germanna.edu
DEMEL, Tammy .... 470-578-6383 121 M
tdemel@kennesaw.edu
DEMELIA, Andrew .... 401-232-6082 404 A
ademelia@bryant.edu
DEMELLO, Ken .... 509-533-3407 479 D
kenneth.demello@ccs.spokane.edu
DEMELO, Amy .... 417-269-3667 252 D
amy.demelo@coxcollege.edu
DEMENT, Gregory .... 713-221-8280 453 A
dementg@uhd.edu
DEMENT, Jennifer .... 503-491-7385 374 B
jennifer.dement@mhcc.edu
DEMENT, Laura .... 303-373-2008.. 83 G
ldement@rvu.edu
DEMENT, Paul .... 732-263-5679 279 A
pdement@monmouth.edu
DEMENT, Randal .... 806-720-7508 439 D
randal.dement@lcu.edu
DEMERITT, Dan .... 207-581-1865 196 G
DEMERITT, Daniel .... 207-581-5864 196 F
dan.demeritt@maine.edu
DEMERRITT, Stan .... 806-716-2360 443 G
sdemerritt@southplainscollege.edu
DEMERS, Amanda .... 410-287-1005 198 E
mdemers@cecil.edu
DEMERS, Ben .... 323-241-5401.. 49 E
demersbk@lasc.edu
DEMERS, David .... 207-621-3417 196 F
david.demers@maine.edu
DEMERS, John .... 516-773-5000 503 H
demersj@usmma.edu
DEMERS, Lisa .... 336-316-2178 329 D
ldemers@guilford.edu
DEMERS, Susan, S .... 727-791-2501 107 E
demers.susan@spcollege.edu
DEMERSE, Kate .... 608-342-1854 496 E
demersek@uwplatt.edu
DEMERSSEMAN, Anne ... 308-432-6224 268 D
ademersseman@csc.edu
DEMETRIOU, Sophia ..... 212-925-6625 293 D
sdemetriou@ccny.cuny.edu
DEMETRULIAS, Diana ... 617-731-3500 210 G
DEMEZZO, Robert, C .... 203-392-5886.. 86 A
demezzor1@southernct.edu
DEMICHAEL, Mark .... 765-677-2317 158 B
mark.demichael@indwes.edu
DEMING, Brett .... 970-247-7491.. 80 J
deming_b@fortlewis.edu
DEMING, Els .... 253-840-8401 482 E
edeming@pierce.ctc.edu
DEMING, Faith .... 845-434-5750 321 E
DEMIR, Kristin .... 517-884-6142 227 F
DEMIRBAG,
Jocelyn Romero .... 808-984-3471 130 D
jocelyn.romerodemirbag@
uhfoundation.org
DEMISHKEVICH, Maya .. 410-386-8157 198 D
mdemishkevich@carrollcc.edu
DEMISSIE, Kitaw .... 718-270-1056 317 B
kitaw.demissie@downstate.edu
DEMISSIE, Yoseph .... 313-496-2959 232 E
ykidane1@wcccd.edu
DEMKO, Amy .... 513-244-4408 356 F
amy.demko@msj.edu
DEMMERLE, Jennifer ..... 216-987-4709 351 E
jennifer.demmerle@tri-c.edu
DEMMERS, Dan .... 559-638-0300.. 67 D
dan.demmers@reedleycollege.edu
DEMMINGS, Elizabeth ... 765-658-4220 154 J
betsydemmings@depauw.edu
DEMMONS, Daniel, C ... 401-865-1755 404 F
ddemmons@providence.edu
DEMO, Tina .... 860-509-9549.. 88 B
tdemo@hartsem.edu
DEMOND, Ramon, S .... 260-399-7700 162 B
rdemond@sf.edu
DEMORST, Wendi .... 310-434-4271.. 63 C
demorst_wendi@smc.edu
DEMORY, Yolanda, F .... 757-446-8498 466 D
demoryyf@evms.edu
DEMPSEY, Greg .... 206-934-5201 483 D
greg.dempsey@seattlecolleges.edu
DEMPSEY, John, R .... 910-695-3700 337 H
dempseyj@sandhills.edu
DEMPSEY, Kristin .... 607-778-5407 317 D
dempseyks@sunybroome.edu
DEMPSEY, Matthew .... 972-273-3501 435 B
mdempsey@dcccd.edu
DEMPSEY, Ron .... 812-749-1213 159 O
rdempsey@oak.edu
DEMPSEY, Van, O .... 910-962-3354 343 C
dempseyv@uncw.edu
DEMPSEY-SWOPES,
Danielle .... 785-670-1906 178 C
danielle.dempsey-swopes@washburn.
edu
DEMPSTER, Douglas, J . 512-471-9601 455 A
ddempster@austin.utexas.edu
DEMPSTER, Joan .... 310-506-6997.. 56 G
joan.dempster@pepperdine.edu
DEMPSTER, John .... 215-885-2360 389 C
jdempster@manor.edu
DEMSETZ, Laura .... 650-574-6581.. 62 K
demsetz@smccd.edu
DEMUTH, Paul .... 651-423-8370 238 A
paul.demuth@dctc.edu
DEMUTH, Paul .... 651-450-3536 238 E
pdemuth@inverhills.edu
DEN DULK, Kevin .... 616-526-6234 222 C
krd33@calvin.edu
DENARD, Carolyn .... 478-445-8652 119 B
carolyn.denard@gcsu.edu
DENARD, Letitia, J .... 404-270-5143 126 B
ldenard@spelman.edu
DENARDIS, Nick .... 313-577-4540 232 K
ndenardis@wayne.edu
DENARO, Jessica .... 914-606-8571 325 A
jessica.denaro@sunywcc.edu
DENASHA, Lydia .... 715-634-4790 492 L
ldenasha@lco.edu
DENBESTE, Michelle ..... 509-963-1400 478 E
michelle.denbeste@cwu.edu
DENBOW, Rick .... 325-738-3349 449 D
rick.denbow@tstc.edu
DENCH, Emma .... 617-496-1464 210 E
dench@fas.harvard.edu
DENDY, Phillip, B .... 512-499-4652 454 H
pdendy@utsystem.edu
DENEAU, Kathleen .... 517-884-1136 227 F
deneauk@msu.edu
DENEEN, Mary, C .... 757-683-3211 469 B
mdeneen@odu.edu
DENENMARK, Lisa .... 415-575-6282.. 28 I
ldenenmark@ciis.edu
DENEUI, Dan .... 541-552-6913 376 B
deneuid@sou.edu
DENG, Qi .... 909-895-7138.. 45 H
kiki@huca.edu
DENG, Yi .... 215-895-6824 382 F
yd362@drexel.edu
DENGEL, Daniel .... 215-204-7276 399 B
daniel.dengel@temple.edu
DENHAM, Andrew, C .... 202-885-8601.. 94 D
adenham@wesleyseminary.edu
DENHAM, Cynthia .... 256-840-4133.... 3 F
cynthia.denham@snead.edu
DENHAM, Mark .... 313-993-3250 231 E
denhamma@udmercy.edu
DENICOLA, Maura .... 201-355-1433 277 J
denicolaa@felician.edu
DENIO, John .... 401-232-6046 404 A
jdenio@bryant.edu
DENIS, Tony .... 352-854-2322.. 97 N
denist@cf.edu
DENISTON, Paul .... 719-255-4665.. 84 C
pdenisto@uccs.edu
DENIUS, Homer .... 410-293-9320 504 A
DENKENBERGER, Amie . 937-481-2271 364 A
amie_denkenberger@wilmington.edu
DENLEY, Tristan .... 404-962-3060 127 D
tristan.denley@usg.edu
DENMAN, Barbara .... 301-546-0185 201 E
denmanbx@pgcc.edu
DENMAN, Brian, S .... 254-710-2663 431 E
brian_denman@baylor.edu

DENMAN, Philip .... 253-833-9111 480 I
pdenman@greenriver.edu
DENMARK, Stephanie ... 850-484-1605 105 H
sdenmark@pensacolastate.edu
DENNARD, Shajuana .... 256-761-8849.... 7 B
sdennard@talladega.edu
DENNEY, Amber .... 317-278-7703 157 D
ambdenne@iu.edu
DENNEY, Carolyn .... 509-527-2890 485 C
carolyn.denney@wallawalla.edu
DENNEY, Jon .... 650-723-2300.. 66 E
DENNEY, Karen .... 828-627-4546 335 C
kdenney@haywood.edu
DENNEY, Mark .... 281-283-2100 452 E
denney@uhcl.edu
DENNEY, Tammy .... 903-675-6306 451 F
tdenney@tvcc.edu
DENNIE, Deidra .... 859-233-8300 185 C
ddennie@transy.edu
DENNIN, Michael .... 949-824-7761.. 69 D
mdennin@uci.edu
DENNING, Jacob .... 303-292-0015.. 80 H
jdenning@denvercollegeofnursing.edu
DENNING, CSC,
John, F .... 508-565-1301 219 A
jdenning@stonehill.edu
DENNING, Rusty .... 864-941-8417 411 C
denning.r@ptc.edu
DENNING, Timothy .... 404-413-2000 120 E
DENNIS, Alecia .... 614-251-4500 358 B
DENNIS, Anne .... 515-643-6640 168 D
adennis@mercydesmoines.org
DENNIS, Diana .... 815-753-2111 146 B
ddennis@niu.edu
DENNIS, Edward, J .... 212-986-4343 275 I
edward-dennis@berkeleycollege.edu
DENNIS, Edward, J .... 212-986-4343 291 E
edward-dennis@berkeleycollege.edu
DENNIS, Elizabeth .... 740-753-6449 353 H
dennise31771@hocking.edu
DENNIS, Fay .... 831-476-9424.. 42 F
scextension@fivebranches.edu
DENNIS, James .... 615-329-8775 419 H
jdennis@fisk.edu
DENNIS, Jennifer .... 580-581-2339 365 D
jdennis@cameron.edu
DENNIS, Kale .... 720-890-8922.. 81 I
registrar@itea.edu
DENNIS, Larinee .... 405-585-4253 367 B
larinee.dennis@okbu.edu
DENNIS, Larry .... 850-644-5804 110 C
larry.dennis@cci.fsu.edu
DENNIS, Michelle .... 312-662-4000 132 G
DENNIS, Pam .... 704-406-4298 329 A
pdennis@gardner-webb.edu
DENNIS, Paul .... 909-384-8286.. 60 F
pdennis@sbccd.cc.ca.us
DENNIS, Peggy .... 419-372-8495 348 G
fayed@bgsu.edu
DENNIS, Sarah .... 281-649-3350 437 B
sdennis@hbu.edu
DENNIS, Terry .... 863-680-4148 100 H
vdennis@flsouthern.edu
DENNIS, Vicki .... 318-678-6000 187 H
vdennis@bpcc.edu
DENNIS, Yolanda .... 508-588-9100 215 A
ydennis@massasoit.mass.edu
DENNISON, Anne .... 207-699-5054 195 A
adennison@meca.edu
DENNISON, Corley .... 304-558-0261 489 H
corley.dennison@wvhepc.edu
DENNISON, Lori, R .... 315-859-4412 300 H
ldenniso@hamilton.edu
DENNISON, Marla, K .... 651-631-5395 244 D
mkdennison@unwsp.edu
DENNISON, Mary .... 507-285-7233 240 H
mary.dennison@rctc.edu
DENNISON, Wayne .... 812-877-8858 160 F
dennison@rose-hulman.edu
DENNO, Linda .... 520-626-2422.. 16 D
ldenno@arizona.edu
DENON, Gregory .... 978-934-2418 212 B
gregory_denon@uml.edu
DENSE, Angela .... 417-865-2815 253 D
densea@evangel.edu
DENSMORE, Timothy .... 607-844-8222 322 D
tad@tompkinscortland.edu
DENSON, Frederick .... 912-358-3028 125 A
densonf@savannahstate.edu
DENSON, Jeff .... 510-845-5373.. 29 B
jeff@cjc.edu
DENSON, John .... 205-665-6237.... 8 D
jdenson1@montevallo.edu
DENSON, Kiwana .... 361-698-2411 435 G
kdenson@delmar.edu
DENSON, Rob .... 515-964-6638 165 A
rjdenson@dmacc.edu
DENT, David, D .... 202-994-6706.. 92 D
ddent@gwu.edu
DENT, Deborah .... 601-979-4299 246 F
deborah.f.dent@jsums.edu
DENT, Sara .... 304-829-7744 487 A
sdent@bethanywv.edu
DENTINO, Daniel .... 740-283-6346 352 I
ddentino@franciscan.edu
DENTLER, James .... 330-337-6403 347 D
registrar@awc.edu
DENTON, Aaron .... 252-985-5276 339 D
adenton@ncwc.edu
DENTON, Amy .... 800-686-1883 222 G
adenton@cleary.edu
DENTON, Andrew .... 952-446-4112 235 J
dentona@crown.edu
DENTON, Andrew, C 612-343-4745 242M
acdenton@northcentral.edu
DENTON, Carol .... 704-922-6484 334 G
denton.carol@gaston.edu
DENTON, Christine .... 808-739-8597 128 E
christine.denton@chaminade.edu
DENTON, Melissa .... 913-234-0750 172 K
melissa.denton@cleveland.edu
DENTON, SaVana .... 580-477-7712 371 D
DENVER, Genae .... 785-539-3571 176 A
gdenver@mccks.edu
DENYS, Mark .... 215-204-7500 399 B
mark.denys@temple.edu
DEOLALIKAR, Anil .... 951-827-2310.. 70 B
anil.deolalikar@ucr.edu
DEOLIVEIRA,
Shushawna .... 718-270-4744 317 B
shushawna.deoliveira@downstate.edu
DEORSEY, Ellen, M .... 802-654-2212 462 G
edeorsey@smcvt.edu
DEPACE, Paul .... 401-874-2725 405 E
pauldepace@uri.edu
DEPAOLA, John .... 518-262-6008 289 L
depaolj@amc.edu
DEPAOLA, Natacha .... 312-567-3009 140 A
depaola@iit.edu
DEPAS, Jacob .... 920-465-2000 495 F
depasj@uwgb.edu
DEPASS, Donald .... 607-431-4112 301 A
depassd@hartwick.edu
DEPAULL, Mark .... 607-753-2111 318 A
mark.depaull@cortland.edu
DEPEDER, Suzanne .... 312-362-8648 136 H
sdepeder@depaul.edu
DEPEW, Chris .... 845-434-5750 321 E
cdepew@sunysullivan.edu
DEPEW, Dennis, R .... 423-439-4289 419 G
depewd@etsu.edu
DEPEW, Monette .... 620-450-2211 177 B
monetted@prattcc.edu
DEPINET, Andrea .... 419-372-8844 348 G
adepine@bgsu.edu
DEPINTO, Michael .... 908-526-1200 281 A
michael.depinto@raritanval.edu
DEPOUTOT, Al .... 727-376-6911 112 G
adepoutot@trinitycollege.edu
DEPOY, Bryan .... 440-375-7028 354 K
bdepoy@lec.edu
DEPPONG, Greg, J .... 517-355-5020 227 F
deppong@msu.edu
DEPRETTO-BEHAN,
Melissa .... 215-895-6154 382 F
med87@drexel.edu
DEPREY, Brynn .... 201-216-9901 277 B
brynn.deprey@eicollege.edu
DEPRINZIO, OSA,
Kevin .... 610-519-5431 401 K
kevin.deprinzio@villanova.edu
DEPRON, Dianna .... 225-771-5050 191 B
dianna_gilbert@subr.edu
DEPTA, Linda .... 269-488-4821 225 G
ldepta@kvcc.edu
DEPTULA, Bill .... 603-428-2296 273 G
wdeptula@nec.edu
DEPUE, Joel .... 978-869-1122 439 G
DEPUTY, Meghan .... 386-312-4169 107 C
meghandeputy@sjrstate.edu
DER, Brenda .... 410-837-4813 204 F
bder@ubalt.edu
DERAMUS, Danny .... 501-279-4339.. 19 C
dderamus@harding.edu
DERBY, Andre .... 954-532-9614 102 E
DERBY, Dustin, C .... 563-884-5682 169 F
dustin.derby@palmer.edu
DERBY-TALBOT, Ryan ... 760-572-2000.. 40 I
rdt@deepsprings.edu
DERBYSHIRE, Lynne ..... 401-874-4732 405 E
derbyshire@uri.edu
DERCOLE, Steve .... 212-237-8000 294 D
DERDA, Bob .... 412-392-6157 396 G
rderda@pointpark.edu
DERDEN, Wade .... 501-760-4203.. 20 A
wade.derden@np.edu
DERDERIAN, Todd .... 508-767-7392 206 A
tderderi@assumption.edu
DERDIARIAN, Armine ... 805-678-5029.. 74 A
aderdiarian@vcccd.edu
DERDIK, Ari .... 347-619-9074 326 F
DEREGHSIAN, Armineh . 323-953-4000.. 49 A
deregha@lacitycollege.edu
DEREMER, Dennis .... 970-204-8255.. 81 A
dennis.deremer@frontrange.edu
DEREMER, Lee .... 717-560-8278 387 E
lderemer@lbc.edu
DERIA, Jamilla .... 413-545-3517 211 G
jderia@umass.edu
DERICO, Sherika .... 205-929-6437.... 2 H
sderico@lawsonstate.edu
DERIEUX, Anne .... 206-726-5171 479 E
aderieux@cornish.edu
DERIGGI, Nancy .... 914-923-2699 311 A
DERING, Allison .... 337-421-6955 188 J
allison.dering@sowela.edu
DERK, Malcolm .... 570-372-4571 398 F
derk@susqu.edu
DERMER, Shannon .... 708-534-8396 138 E
sdermer@govst.edu
DERMISHYAN, Sima ..... 916-877-7977.. 59 E
sima@sui.edu
DERMODY, Sean, B ...... 518-564-2539 318 E
dermodsb@plattsburgh.edu
DEROCHE, Jessica .... 940-498-6282 440 F
jderoche@nctc.edu
DEROCHE, Jessica .... 972-899-8402 440 F
jderoche@nctc.edu
DEROCHER, Cynthia ..... 989-358-7394 221 C
derocherc@alpenacc.edu
DEROCHI, Jack .... 803-323-2275 414 D
derochij@winthrop.edu
DEROCHI, Jack .... 803-323-2204 414 D
derochij@winthrop.edu
DEROSA, John .... 203-837-9806.. 86 B
derosaj@wcsu.edu
DEROSA, Michael .... 510-879-9280.. 60 C
mderosa@samuelmerritt.edu
DEROSE, Angela .... 203-287-3032.. 88 E
DEROSE, Michelle .... 616-632-2826 221 E
derosmic@aquinas.edu
DEROSE, Paul .... 602-285-7517.. 13 F
paul.derose@phoenixcollege.edu
DEROUIN, Erika .... 719-587-7901.. 77 G
ederouin@adams.edu
DERR, Colleen .... 765-677-3467 158 B
colleen.derr@indwes.edu
DERR, Gary, L .... 802-656-2212 463 A
gary.derr@uvm.edu
DERR, Matthew, A .... 802-586-7711 462 I
mderr@sterlingcollege.edu
DERRICK, Ann .... 512-381-7252 430 G
aderrick@escoffier.edu
DERRICK, Damon .... 936-468-4305 445 E
derrickdc@sfasu.edu
DERRICK, Diahann .... 541-881-5827 376 F
dderrick@tvcc.cc
DERRICK, Joey .... 803-777-3205 413 A
jcderric@mailbox.sc.edu
DERRICO, Cindy .... 805-437-3340.. 30 C
cindy.derrico@csuci.edu
DERRITT, Shawn .... 913-288-7437 175 B
sderritt@kckcc.edu
DERRIVAN, Kevin .... 617-217-9000 206 E
DERRY, John .... 972-241-3371 434 D
DERSTINE, Andria .... 440-775-8665 357 G
andria.derstine@oberlin.edu
DERUBBO, Jeff .... 724-938-4415 393 E
derubbo@calu.edu
DERUITER, Mark .... 269-749-7133 229 J
mderuiter@olivetcollege.edu
DERWOSTYP, William ... 832-813-6281 439 C
william.derwostyp@lonestar.edu
DESAI, Amanda .... 508-213-2092 217 H
amanda.desai@nichols.edu
DESAI, Rebekah .... 512-637-1924 442 I
rebekahn@stedwards.edu
DESALVO, Dianne, S ..... 989-774-4308 222 E
desal1ds@cmich.edu
DESALVO, Stephen .... 718-429-6600 324 D
stephen.desalvo@vaughn.edu
DESANCTIS, Greg .... 908-526-1200 281 A
greg.desanctis@raritanval.edu
DESANCTIS, Marielena .. 303-556-2400.. 80 F
marielena.desanctis@ccd.edu
DESANDRE, Carolynn .... 706-867-2778 127 A
carolynn.desandre@ung.edu
DESANTIS, Charles, E ... 202-687-1787.. 92 E
ced33@georgetown.edu
DESANTIS, Melanie .... 617-989-4590 219 F
desantism@wit.edu
DESANTIS, Melissa .... 303-724-1748.. 84 D
melissa.desantis@ucdenver.edu
DESANTIS, Susan .... 239-489-9234 101 A
susan.desantis@fsw.edu
DESANTIS, Victor, S ..... 717-871-5742 395 A
victor.desantis@millersville.edu
DESAUTELS-POLIQUIN,
Lisa .... 207-859-1243 196 D
desautelsl@thomas.edu
DESCH, Andrew, P .... 920-748-8849 494 J
descha@ripon.edu
DESCHENES, Marilyn, E 401-865-2074 404 F
mdeschen@providence.edu
DESHAW, Carla, M .... 315-655-7147 292 H
cmdeshaw@cazenovia.edu
DESHIELDS, Richard ..... 406-874-6226 263 H
deshieldsr@milescc.edu
DESHLER, Kirsten .... 805-893-4588.. 70 E
kirsten.deshler@ia.ucsb.edu
DESHONG, Jelanie .... 718-270-1490 317 B
jelanie.deshong@downstate.edu
DESHOTEL, Al .... 713-522-7911 454 G
deshotak@stthom.edu
DESHPANDE, Satish ...... 269-387-5067 233 B
satish.deshpande@wmich.edu
DESIMIO, Angelica .... 816-802-3461 254 D
adesimio@kcai.edu
DESIMONE, Barbara ...... 716-614-6220 309 G
desimone@niagaracc.suny.edu
DESJARDINS, Karla .... 860-932-4000.. 87 E
kdesjardins@qvcc.edu
DESJARDINS, Linda ...... 413-775-1105 214 E
desjardins@gcc.mass.edu
DESJEANS, Karen .... 413-552-2168 214 F
kdesjeans@hcc.edu
DESMARAIS, Mark .... 603-342-3009 273 C
mdesmarais@ccsnh.edu
DESMARAIS, Rachel, M 252-492-2061 338 F
desmarais@vgcc.edu
DESMARTEAU, Doug ..... 620-901-6245 171 D
desmarteau@allencc.edu
DESMOND, Bill .... 309-796-5437 133 G
desmondw@bhc.edu
DESMOND, Daneisha .... 336-744-0900 327 E
frontoffice@carolina.edu
DESMOND, Jill .... 414-382-6067 491 F
jill.desmond@alverno.edu
DESMOND, Nell .... 540-887-7225 468 G
hdesmond@marybaldwin.edu
DESOLYN, Foy .... 409-747-3277 456 E
defoy@utmb.edu
DESORMEAUX, Amy ..... 337-482-1325 193 B
amyd@louisiana.edu
DESOUZA, Priscila .... 650-543-3786.. 51 G
priscila.desouza@menlo.edu
DESPAIN, Trenton .... 540-261-8453 471 B
trenton.despain@svu.edu
DESPATHY, Carol .... 603-206-8136 272 L
cdespathy@ccsnh.edu
DESPLAS, Edward .... 505-566-3253 288 D
desplase@sanjuancollege.edu
DESRAVINES, Melissa ... 212-280-1531 323 K
finaid@utsnyc.edu
DESROCHES, Reginald .. 713-348-0000 442 F
rdr@rice.edu
DESROSIERS, Candace .. 281-649-3049 437 B
cdesrosiers@hbu.edu
DESRUISSEAUX, Lisa .... 617-984-1619 218 C
ldesruisseaux@quincycollege.edu
DESSA, Grace .... 561-912-1211.. 99 D
gdessa@evergladesuniversity.edu
DESSER, Kari .... 360-417-6291 482 C
kdesser@pencol.edu
DESSOYE, Jane, F .... 570-408-3839 403 A
jane.dessoye@wilkes.edu
DESTEFANO,
Joanne, M .... 607-255-4242 297 F
jmd11@cornell.edu
DESTEIGUER, John .... 405-425-5100 367 C
john.desteiguer@oc.edu

DESTEPHANO, Andrew .. 212-986-4343 291 E afd@berkeleycollege.edu
DESTEPHANO, Andrew .. 212-986-4343 275 I afd@berkeleycollege.edu
DESTER, Lisa .... 518-743-2232 320 A desterl@sunyacc.edu
DESVIGNE, LaVora .... 718-482-5114 294 F ldesvigne@lagcc.cuny.edu
DESWERT, David .... 413-585-2200 218 H ddeswert@smith.edu
DETAMPEL, SuAnn .... 920-465-2302 495 F detampes@uwgb.edu
DETAR, Eric .... 315-279-5378 303 G edetar@keuka.edu
DETEMPLE, Jon Jay ...... 610-526-6119 385 D jdetemple@harcum.edu
DETER, Daniel .... 434-592-4172 468 E ddeter@liberty.edu
DETER, Michael .... 419-517-8894 355 C mdeter@lourdes.edu
DETERMANN, Nic .... 641-585-8164 170 I nic.determann@waldorf.edu
DETIEGE, Jacques, J ..... 504-283-8822 186 I jdetiege@dillard.edu
DETLAFF, Alan .... 713-743-7819 452 D ajdettlaff@uh.edu
DETLEFSEN, Karen .... 215-898-7225 400 F karen.detlefsen@provost.upenn.edu
DETLEV, Angela .... 703-993-8969 467 E adetlev@gmu.edu
DETRICK, Jeffrey .... 979-230-3383 431 I
DETRIE, Pam .... 901-843-3835 423 A detriep@rhodes.edu
DETROW, David, A .... 540-432-4110 466 B detrowd@emu.edu
DETTELBACH, Michael .. 781-736-4052 208 A dettelbach@brandeis.edu
DETTELIS, Mary .... 716-896-0700 324 E mdettelis@villa.edu
DETTLOFF, Kathy .... 410-455-1720 203 B dettloff@umbc.edu
DETTMER, Sharon, A .... 315-655-7258 292 H sdettmer@cazenovia.edu
DETTY, Aaron .... 619-388-3400.. 60 I adetty@sdccd.edu
DETUCCIO, James .... 352-588-8920 107 D james.detuccio@saintleo.edu
DETWILER, David .... 970-248-1303.. 78 J detwiler@coloradomesa.edu
DETWILER, Rita .... 434-544-8300 471 L detwiler@lynchburg.edu
DETWILER, Robert .... 419-783-2358 351 K rdetwiler@defiance.edu
DETWILER, Tim .... 616-988-3790 226 E tdetwiler@kuyper.edu
DEUCHARS, Julie .... 503-399-5000 372 B julie.deuchars@chemeketa.edu
DEUCK, Brenda .... 315-279-5339 303 G bdueck@keuka.edu
DEUERLIEN, Silje .... 310-303-7382.. 51 C sdeuerlien@marymountcalifornia.edu
DEUTER, Clayton .... 605-995-7132 415 E clayton.deuter@mitchelltech.edu
DEUTSCH, Cynthia .... 434-832-7618 473 E deutschc@centralvirginia.edu
DEUTSCH, Gail, S .... 714-449-7459.. 51 B gdeutsch@ketchum.edu
DEUTSCH, Josef .... 347-558-8422 322 A
DEUTSCH, Robin, J .... 804-862-6100 470 C rdeutsch@rbc.edu
DEUTSCH, Yeruchem .... 718-963-9770 323 L ed@utsb.org
DEUTSCHER, Taylor ...... 785-227-3380 172 A deutscherta@bethanylb.edu
DEUTSCHMAN, Robert .. 636-481-3386 254 C rdeutsch2@jeffco.edu
DEVANE, Lisa .... 910-879-5516 332 D ldevane@bladencc.edu
DEVANEY, Chevy .... 315-781-3700 301 F devaney@hws.edu
DEVANEY, Margaret ...... 540-831-6903 469 D mdevaney@radford.edu
DEVASAGAYAM, Raj ...... 516-876-3292 318 C raj@oldwestbury.edu
DEVASAGAYAM, Raj ...... 732-263-5550 279 A raj@monmouth.edu
DEVAUGHN, Misty .... 662-720-7200 248 C mwdevaughn@nemcc.edu
DEVAULT, John .... 304-367-4644 489 K jdevault3@fairmontstate.edu
DEVEAU, Caroline .... 860-297-2139.. 89 B caroline.deveau@trincoll.edu
DEVEAU, Shawn .... 617-287-5800 211 H shawn.deveau@umb.edu
DEVENNEY, Michael ..... 215-503-3509 399 E michael.devenney@jefferson.edu
DEVENS, Robert .... 512-232-7615 455 A rdevens@utpress.utexas.edu
DEVER, David .... 310-434-4384.. 63 C dever_david@smc.edu
DEVER, Lydia .... 770-426-2709 122 C ldever@life.edu
DEVER, Michael .... 517-629-0960 221 A mdever@albion.edu
DEVER, Rhea .... 906-227-2330 228 I rdever@nmu.edu
DEVEREAUX, Kent .... 410-337-6040 199 B president@goucher.edu
DEVEREAUX, Rebecca ... 305-626-3666 100 D rebecca.devereaux@fmuniv.edu
DEVEREUX, Mandy .... 503-370-6924 377 F mdevereux@willamette.edu
DEVERICKS, Lynne Marie .... 856-222-9311 281 C ldevericks@rcbc.edu
DEVERO, Susan .... 479-308-2289.. 17 A susan.devero@acheedu.org
DEVERS, Monica, C ...... 612-330-1000 234 A devers@augsburg.edu
DEVERY, Dennis .... 609-777-5693 284 C ddevery@tesu.edu
DEVERY, Fletcher .... 251-380-4000.... 6 H fdevery@shc.edu
DEVIER, David .... 269-467-9945 224 C ddevier@glenoaks.edu
DEVILBISS, Mark .... 203-582-8721.. 88 G mark.devilbiss@quinnipiac.edu
DEVINE, Annie .... 419-251-1866 355 G annie.devine@mercycollege.edu
DEVINE, Erica .... 781-768-7847 218 D erica.devine@regiscollege.edu
DEVINE, Flora .... 912-358-4000 125 A devinef@savannahstate.edu
DEVINE, Linda, W .... 813-253-6203 113 H ldevine@ut.edu
DEVINE, Shawn .... 360-475-7106 481 I sdevine@olympic.edu
DEVINEY, Will .... 918-631-2559 371 C will-deviney@utulsa.edu
DEVINNE, Christine .... 440-646-8101 363 C cdevinne@ursuline.edu
DEVINO, Nancy .... 281-283-3016 452 E devino@uhcl.edu
DEVINO, Terrence .... 617-732-1608 209 D devinot@emmanuel.edu
DEVITO, Don .... 952-806-3910 242 P
DEVITO, Rose, M .... 617-984-1620 218 C rdevito@quincycollege.edu
DEVITO, Theresa .... 413-565-1000 206 D tdevito@baypath.edu
DEVITT, Amanda .... 860-231-5322.. 90 A adevitt@usj.edu
DEVIVO, Sharon, B .... 718-429-6600 324 D sharon.devivo@vaughn.edu
DEVKOTA, Tripti .... 704-403-1639 327 C tripti.devkota@atriumhealth.org
DEVLESCHOWARD, Brian .... 269-783-2706 231 A bdevleschoward@swmich.edu
DEVLIN, Bruce .... 434-791-5600 464 I bdevlin@wffservices.com
DEVLIN, Bruce .... 434-791-5780 464 I bdevlin@wffservices.com
DEVLIN, Catherine .... 413-775-1147 214 E devlinc@gcc.mass.edu
DEVLIN, George, A .... 803-705-4417 406 G george.devlin@benedict.edu
DEVLIN, Kathy .... 704-378-6776 330 D kdevlin@jcsu.edu
DEVLIN, Kimberly .... 607-436-3024 316 F kimberly.devlin@oneonta.edu
DEVLIN, Maura .... 413-565-1000 206 D mdevlin@baypath.edu
DEVLIN, Thomas, C ...... 510-642-3461.. 69 A tcd@berkeley.edu
DEVOE, Kelsey, R .... 508-793-2276 208 D krdevoe@holycross.edu
DEVOGE, Savala .... 218-281-8507 244 A devog007@crk.umn.edu
DEVOLL, Karlin .... 432-837-8652 450 B kdevoll@sulross.edu
DEVOND, Lesa .... 937-376-6163 349 J ldevond@centralstate.edu
DEVONISH, Cheryl .... 203-857-7024.. 87 D cdevonish@norwalk.edu
DEVONISH, Natalie .... 609-343-4972 275 D ndevonis@atlantic.edu
DEVORA-JONES, Kayla .. 361-354-2532 432 K kdjones@coastalbend.edu
DEVORE, Debra .... 740-392-6868 356 G
DEVORE, Lauren .... 713-646-1828 443 I ldevore@stcl.edu
DEVRIES, Jill .... 701-845-7160 345 G jill.devries@vcsu.edu
DEVRIES, Kristen .... 269-387-8785 233 B kristen.devries@wmich.edu
DEVRIES, Susann .... 270-745-6422 186 C susann.devries@wku.edu
DEVRIEZE, Craig, J .... 563-333-6294 169 G devriezecraigj@sau.edu
DEW, Deb .... 608-363-2618 491 H dewd@beloit.edu
DEW, JR., James Kenneth .... 504-282-4455 190 F jdew@nobts.edu
DEW, Wendi, M .... 407-582-3841 113 I wdew@valenciacollege.edu
DEWAAL, Rachel .... 615-514-2787 422 H rdewaal@nossi.edu
DEWALD, Daryll .... 509-358-7521 485 D daryll.dewald@wsu.edu
DEWALD, Luke .... 920-206-2339 493 C luke.dewald@mbu.edu
DEWALD, Marylou .... 785-248-2550 176 I marylou.dewald@ottawa.edu
DEWALT, Daniel .... 310-506-7427.. 56 G danny.dewalt@pepperdine.edu
DEWALT, Marie .... 304-876-5299 490 A mdewalt@shepherd.edu
DEWALT, Molly .... 509-777-4272 486 C mdewalt@whitworth.edu
DEWALT, Sheryl .... 207-947-4591 194 B sdewalt@bealcollege.edu
DEWAN, Craig .... 315-792-3393 324 B cpdewan@utica.edu
DEWAN, Julie .... 315-731-5716 306 K jdewan@mvcc.edu
DEWAN, Mantosh .... 315-464-4513 317 C dewanm@upstate.edu
DEWAN, Rajiv .... 315-443-2736 321 G rdewan@syr.edu
DEWAR, Cynthia .... 415-239-3292.. 36 K cdewar@ccsf.edu
DEWBERRY, Angela, B . 704-894-2227 328 E andewberry@davidson.edu
DEWBERRY, Thomas .... 541-683-5141 373 B cdewberry@gutenberg.edu
DEWBRE, Dane .... 806-716-2211 443 G ddewbre@southplainscollege.edu
DEWBRE, Jeri Ann .... 806-894-9611 443 G jdewbre@southplainscollege.edu
DEWEASE, Brandon .... 601-481-1340 247 A bdewease@meridiancc.edu
DEWEERD, Crystal .... 801-542-7600 459 B
DEWEERDT, Daniel .... 414-288-4740 493 E daniel.deweerdt@marquette.edu
DEWEERTH, Jennifer ..... 315-731-5818 306 K jdeweerth@mvcc.edu
DEWEERTH, Stephen, P 610-758-5308 388 E spd416@lehigh.edu
DEWEES, Bridget, P ...... 803-535-5793 407 D bdewees@claflin.edu
DEWEES, Deborah .... 360-560-3353 485 I deborah.dewees@wwu.edu
DEWELL, Roger .... 325-649-8825 437 G rdewell@hputx.edu
DEWESE, Jerima .... 914-251-6000 319 B
DEWEY, Greg .... 518-694-7255 289 J greg.dewey@acphs.edu
DEWEY, Marvin, L .... 724-847-6880 384 C marvin.dewey@geneva.edu
DEWEY, Matthew .... 806-742-2136 450 F mdewey@ttu.edu
DEWEY, Michael .... 936-294-1325 450 A mld072@shsu.edu
DEWEY, Robin .... 410-386-4699 200 F rdewey@mcdaniel.edu
DEWEY, Tom .... 706-419-1105 118 A tom.dewey@covenant.edu
DEWINTER, Naomi .... 563-288-6003 166 A
DEWIS, John .... 760-938-6176.. 40 I jdewis@deepsprings.edu
DEWIT, Robert .... 562-985-5091.. 31 D robert.dewit@csulb.edu
DEWITT, Amy .... 304-876-5480 490 A adewitt@shepherd.edu
DEWITT, David, C .... 812-941-2569 157 F davdewit@ius.edu
DEWITT, Jeffrey .... 785-864-0938 177 J jeff.dewitt@ku.edu
DEWITT, Kelly .... 479-308-2207.. 17 A kelly.dewitt@acheedu.org
DEWITT, Linda .... 918-610-0027 365 I ldewitt@communitycarecollege.edu
DEWITT, Siobhan, K ...... 412-578-6651 380 B skdewitt@carlow.edu
DEWITT, William .... 828-641-0116 327 B dewittwm@brevard.edu
DEWOODY, Susan .... 405-585-5805 367 B susan.dewoody@okbu.edu
DEWYRE, Lynne .... 440-646-8370 363 C lynne.dewyre@ursuline.edu
DEXHEIMER, David .... 573-629-3124 253 J david.dexheimer@hlg.edu
DEXTER, Brian .... 509-542-4727 479 A bdexter@columbiabasin.edu
DEXTER, Kimberly .... 508-626-4951 213 A kdexter@framingham.edu
DEXTER, Kimberly .... 508-215-5859 213 A kdexter@framingham.edu
DEY, Anind .... 206-685-9937 485 A anind@uw.edu
DEY, Anita .... 989-964-4236 230 E adey@svsu.edu
DEY, Farouk .... 410-516-0874 199 G fdey@jhu.edu
DEY, Farouk .... 650-723-1983.. 66 E fdey@stanford.edu
DEY, Saibal .... 301-295-3449 503 C saibal.dey@usuhs.edu
DEYAMPERT, Fredi .... 906-487-7301 224 B fredi.deyampert@finlandia.edu
DEYKIN, Eugene .... 413-265-2586 208 E keykine@elms.edu
DEYO, Abigail .... 608-785-8558 496 A adeyo@uwlax.edu
DEYO, Sarah .... 225-214-6975 187 B sarah.deyo@franu.edu
DEYOUNG, Michael ...... 702-968-2006 272 C mdeyoung@roseman.edu
DEYOUNG, Paul, D .... 503-777-7290 375 G paul.deyoung@reed.edu
DEYOUNG, Renee .... 231-348-6618 228 H rdeyoung@ncmich.edu
DEYTON, Patricia, H ..... 617-521-3876 218 G patricia.deyton@simmons.edu
DEZARN, Andrew .... 859-251-4569 180 F andrew.dezarn@frontier.edu
DEZEEUW, Julie .... 920-693-1222 498 H julie.dezeeuw@gotoltc.edu
DEZEMBER, John .... 276-964-7332 475 C john.dezember@sw.edu
DEZENBERG, Maria .... 804-862-6100 470 C mdezenberg@rbc.edu
DEZURA, Mia, S .... 540-868-7087 474 C mleggettdezura@lfcc.edu
DHALIWAL, Jasbir .... 901-678-1592 426 G jdhaliwl@memphis.edu
DHANARINE, Rebecca .. 864-231-2000 406 F rdhanarine@andersonuniversity.edu
DHANKHER, Veena .... 413-552-2543 214 F vdhankher@hcc.edu
DHANWADA, Kavita ...... 708-524-6403 137 C kdhanwada@dom.edu
DHARMARAJ, Premkumar .... 626-448-0023.. 46 G
DHAWAN, Atam, P .... 973-596-8566 279 E atam.p.dhawan@njit.edu
DHAWAN, Reetika .... 928-344-7650.. 11 A reetika.dhawan@azwestern.edu
DHILLON, Harpal .... 510-254-3756.. 48 C hdhillon@lincolnuca.edu
DHILLON, Mona .... 415-869-2900 210 H mona.dhillon@hult.edu
DHILLON, Upinder, S ... 607-777-2314 316 B dhillon@binghamton.edu
DHILLON, Vineeta .... 707-654-1283.. 32 A vdhillon@csum.edu
DHINOJWALA, Ali .... 330-972-6246 361 H ali4@uakron.edu
DHUPELIA, Aarti .... 312-261-3484 145 D adhupelia@nl.edu
DI BARTOLO-BECKMAN, Adriana .... 909-621-8277.. 63 F
DI BENEDETTO, Eileen, M .... 212-854-7732 291 A edibened@barnard.edu
DI DIO, Stephen .... 718-631-6044 295 C sdidio@qcc.cuny.edu
DI FRANCESCO, Gabriele .... 661-824-2977.. 53 H gdifrancesco@ntps.edu

DIEHL, Melissa, M .... 570-577-3776 379 C
melissa.diehl@bucknell.edu
DIEHL, Nathan .... 610-896-1298 385 I
ndiehl@haverford.edu
DIEHM, Perry .... 405-789-6400 369 H
pdiehm@snu.edu
DIEKMAN, Larry .... 269-467-9945 224 C
ldiekman@glenoaks.edu
DIEKMANN, Beth .... 507-285-7259 240 H
beth.diekmann@rctc.edu
DIEL-HUNT, Sarah .... 309-268-8593 138 H
sarah.dielhunt@heartland.edu
DIEMER, Maria .... 815-394-5112 148 D
mdiemer@rockford.edu
DIENES, Tye, A .... 518-388-6000 323 J
DIENGER, Rebecca, J ... 715-836-4423 495 E
diengerj@uwec.edu
DIENNO, Linda .... 703-370-6600 476 E
DIEP, Kyle .... 847-735-5035 142 A
diep@lakeforest.edu
DIERINGER, Deanna, L . 907-474-6629.. 10 A
dldieringer@alaska.edu
DIERMEIER, Daniel .... 615-322-7311 428 A
DIERS, Jody .... 970-248-1536.. 78 J
jmdiers@coloradomesa.edu
DIERSING, Robert .... 361-593-3964 447 D
robert.diersing@tamuk.edu
DIETER, Mary .... 765-658-4286 154 J
marydieter@depauw.edu
DIETERICH, Scott .... 718-409-7204 320 G
sdieterich@sunymaritime.edu
DIETERLY, Cathy .... 954-492-5353.. 97 G
cdieterly@citycollege.edu
DIETERLY, Cindy .... 401-841-6594 503 A
cindy.dieterly@usnwc.edu
DIETERLYL, Catherine ... 305-428-5700 104 F
DIETRICH, Kim, E .... 260-399-7700 162 B
kdietrich@sf.edu
DIETRICH, Nathan .... 916-278-3725.. 32 D
nathan.dietrich@csus.edu
DIETRICH, Robb .... 570-321-4401 389 B
dietrich@lycoming.edu
DIETRICH, Robert .... 617-373-4827 217 I
DIETRICH, Sandra, L .... 919-866-5674 338 G
sldietrich@waketech.edu
DIETZ, Elizabeth .... 606-693-5000 183 C
edietz@kmbc.edu
DIETZ, Fred .... 940-397-4533 440 C
fred.dietz@msutexas.edu
DIETZ, Jonathan .... 620-792-9271 171 I
dietzj@bartonccc.edu
DIETZ, Kelley .... 919-508-2220 344 E
kelley.dietz@peace.edu
DIETZ, Maya .... 618-374-5162 147 E
maya.dietz@principia.edu
DIETZ, Timothy, D .... 240-567-7998 200 G
tim.dietz@montgomerycollege.edu
DIETZ, Timothy, N .... 530-226-4103.. 64 E
tdietz@simpsonu.edu
DIETZE, Jane .... 401-867-3986 403 J
jane_dietze@brown.edu
DIETZEL, Lea .... 231-348-6667 228 H
ldietzel@ncmich.edu
DIETZOLD, Heather 850-729-6922 104M
dietzolh@nwfsc.edu
DIEU, Mindie .... 514-463-5902 373 D
dieum@lanecc.edu
DIEUDONNE, Jose .... 484-664-3464 390 H
josedieudonne@muhlenberg.edu
DIEUJUSTE, Slandie ...... 413-748-3131 218 I
sdieujuste@springfield.edu
DIEUJUSTE, Slandie ...... 508-588-9100 215 A
sdieujus1@massasoit.mass.edu
DIEZ, Mickey .... 936-468-3401 445 E
DIEZ ROUX, Ana, V ..... 215-571-4013 382 F
ana.v.diezroux@drexel.edu
DIFFEN, Marta .... 830-792-7201 443 E
mdiffen@schreiner.edu
DIFFENDERFER, Jason .. 914-633-2373 302 E
jdiffenderfer@iona.edu
DIFFEY, Stephanie .... 662-472-9101 246 D
scdiffey@holmescc.edu
DIFFEY, Steve .... 662-472-9068 246 D
sdiffey@holmescc.edu
DIFILIPO, JR.,
Stephen, J .... 717-871-4086 395 A
steve.difilipo@millersville.edu
DIFINI, Marcelo .... 858-653-3000.. 29 D
mdifini@calmu.edu
DIFINO, Heather .... 315-268-6477 295 F
hdifino@clarkson.edu
DIFONZO, Kari .... 781-283-2360 219 E
cmacgreg@wellesley.edu

DIFRANCO, Heidi .... 803-641-3397 413 B
heidid@usca.edu
DIGATE, Andrew .... 815-753-0122 146 B
adigate1@niu.edu
DIGATE, Russell, J .... 718-990-6411 313 G
digater@stjohns.edu
DIGENNARO, Linda ...... 856-256-4107 281 F
digennaro@rowan.edu
DIGGORY, Parker .... 518-580-8340 315 F
kdiggory@skidmore.edu
DIGGS, Amanda .... 334-670-5782.... 7 C
amdiggs@troy.edu
DIGGS, Christina .... 212-217-3900 299 D
christina_diggs@fitnyc.edu
DIGGS, Jeannie (Carol) 507-433-0571 240 G
jeannie.diggs@riverland.edu
DIGGS, Tina .... 740-203-8012 351 C
tdiggs4@cscc.edu
DIGIOACCHINO,
Dominic .... 973-803-5000 280 B
ddigioacchino@pillar.edu
DIGIRONIMO, Joseph ... 215-468-8800 386 C
director@culinaryarts.edu
DIGMAN, Jo-Ann .... 314-539-5358 259 A
jdigman1@stlcc.edu
DIGMANN, Ashley .... 605-995-2891 415 A
ashley.digmann@dwu.edu
DIGORIO, Jeremy .... 386-822-7022 112 A
jdigorio@stetson.edu
DIGRAZIA, Lauren .... 919-962-8289 342 C
lauren.digrazia@unc.edu
DIGREGORIO, Antonia .. 516-876-3156 318 C
digregorioa@oldwestbury.edu
DILAURO, Nanette .... 212-854-2154 291 A
ndilauro@barnard.edu
DILBECK, Cindy .... 805-546-3118.. 40 F
cynthia_dilbeck@cuesta.edu
DILBECK, David .... 479-394-7622.. 23 C
ddilbeck@uarichmountain.edu
DILBECK, LeAnn .... 479-394-7622.. 23 C
ldilbeck@uarichmountain.edu
DILBECK, Mackenzie ..... 405-325-0311 370 K
DILENO, Susan .... 440-646-8114 363 C
susan.dileno@ursuline.edu
DILENO, Susan .... 213-477-2535.. 52 I
sdileno@msmu.edu
DILES, David, L .... 540-464-7251 476 B
dilesdl@vmi.edu
DILGER, Patrick .... 203-392-6586.. 86 A
dilgerp1@southernct.edu
DILL, Bonnie, T .... 301-405-0949 202 H
btdill@umd.edu
DILL, Chris .... 601-605-3363 246 D
cdill@holmescc.edu
DILL, Debbie .... 864-388-8000 410 A
DILL, Deborah .... 325-649-8610 437 G
ddill@hputx.edu
DILL, Herb .... 440-375-7555 354 K
hdill@lec.edu
DILL, Jeremy .... 207-741-5821 195 H
jdill@smccme.edu
DILL, Ken .... 864-644-5431 412 D
kdill@swu.edu
DILL, Marian .... 423-614-8304 420 H
mdill@leeuniversity.edu
DILL, Tracy .... 218-755-4022 237 F
tracy.dill@bemidjistate.edu
DILLA, Bethany .... 541-684-7282 371 I
bdilla@bushnell.edu
DILLANE, Robert, J .... 717-867-6060 388 C
dillane@lvc.edu
DILLARD, Anthony .... 740-474-8896 358 A
adillard@ohiochristian.edu
DILLARD, Coralyn .... 806-291-3763 457 I
dillardc@wbu.edu
DILLARD, Helene .... 530-752-1605.. 69 B
hrdillard@ucdavis.edu
DILLARD, Paulette .... 919-719-3860 340 B
pdillard@shawu.edu
DILLBECK, Michael .... 641-472-1187 168 C
sdillbeck@miu.edu
DILLBECK, Susan .... 641-472-1187 168 C
sdillbeck@miu.edu
DILLE, Wayne .... 641-628-5336 164 D
dille@central.edu
DILLENGER, Jennifer .... 864-587-4295 412 F
dillengerj@smcsc.edu
DILLER, Lisa .... 423-236-2417 423 F
ldiller@southern.edu
DILLER, Matthew .... 212-636-6875 300 C
diller@fordham.edu
DILLEY, Darlene .... 435-652-7704 460 B
darlene.dilley@dixie.edu

DILLIHAY, Elliot .... 843-746-5100.. 93 H
DILLINER, Kathleen, L .. 615-297-7545 417 G
DILLINGHAM, Sabine .... 240-895-4192 202 B
sldillingham@smcm.edu
DILLION, Shaquille .... 903-927-3214 458 F
sdillion@wileyc.edu
DILLMAN, Ray .... 405-703-8226 366 D
ray.dillman@macu.edu
DILLMAN, Stephanie, C 610-861-1566 390 F
dillmans@moravian.edu
DILLON, Anastacia .... 503-768-7095 373 E
adillon@lclark.edu
DILLON, Diana .... 605-856-2355 415 J
diana.dillon@sintegleska.edu
DILLON, Ellen .... 308-635-6787 270 C
dillone@wncc.edu
DILLON, Jennifer .... 216-397-1976 353 O
jdillon@jcu.edu
DILLON, John .... 603-641-7349 274 A
jdillon@anselm.edu
DILLON, John .... 610-683-4002 394 D
dillon@kutztown.edu
DILLON, Jordan, P .... 276-326-4201 464 J
jdillon@bluefield.edu
DILLON, Karen .... 641-269-4481 166 G
dillonka@grinnell.edu
DILLON, Katherine, E .... 914-594-4527 309 B
katherine_dillion@nymc.edu
DILLON, Kendall .... 515-263-6129 166 F
kdillon@grandview.edu
DILLON, Mark .... 978-867-4900 210 B
mark.dillon@gordon.edu
DILLON, Mary Ellen ...... 704-922-6475 334 G
dillon.maryellen@gaston.edu
DILLON, Michele, M ...... 603-862-2062 274 F
michele.dillon@unh.edu
DILLON, Patricia .... 215-951-1430 387 A
dillonp@lasalle.edu
DILLON, Paul .... 410-455-2872 203 B
pdillon@umbc.edu
DILLON, Sarah .... 715-675-3331 499 F
dillon@ntc.edu
DILLON, T. Kevin .... 713-500-3535 456 B
kevin.dillon@uth.tmc.edu
DILLOW, Al .... 217-245-3168 139 C
al.dillow@ic.edu
DILLOW, Katie .... 414-382-6127 491 F
katie.dillow@alverno.edu
DILLS-ALLEN,
Michael, C .... 530-898-5142.. 30 D
mcdills-allen@csuchico.edu
DILLSWORTH, Gary .... 716-926-8920 301 E
gdillsworth@hilbert.edu
DILORENZO, Judith ...... 518-629-7204 302 C
j.dilorenzo@hvcc.edu
DILORENZO, Kenneth ... 787-264-1912 508 F
kenneth_dilorenzo@intersg.edu
DILORENZO, Molly .... 617-735-9876 209 D
dilorenzom@emmanuel.edu
DILORENZO, Vicki .... 518-694-7331 289 J
vicki.dilorenzo@acphs.edu
DILS, Keith .... 724-738-2292 395 C
keith.dils@sru.edu
DILUCA, Susan, A .... 502-895-3411 183 H
sdiluca@lpts.edu
DILUSTRO, John .... 252-398-6220 328 C
dilusj@chowan.edu
DILWORTH, Paulette, P 205-934-0541.... 8 A
ppddei@uab.edu
DIMAGGIO, Jacqueline . 864-250-8179 409 I
jacqui.dimaggio@gvltec.edu
DIMANNA, Nicholas ..... 303-410-2416.. 83 J
nicholas.dimanna@spartan.edu
DIMARCO, Erin .... 302-356-6924.. 91 E
erin.j.dimarco@wilmu.edu
DIMARCO, Scott, R .... 570-662-4689 394 F
sdimarco@mansfield.edu
DIMARIA, David .... 410-455-2624 203 B
dimaria@umbc.edu
DIMARINO, Nicholas .... 610-558-5626 391 A
dimarinn@neumann.edu
DIMARIO, Joseph, X ..... 847-578-8494 148 F
joseph.dimario@rosalindfranklin.edu
DIMARZIO, Denise .... 508-678-2811 214 B
denise.dimarzio@bristolcc.edu
DIMARZO, Dean .... 845-569-3219 307 D
dean.dimarzo@msmc.edu
DIMATTIA, Andrea .... 570-504-9634 384 B
adimattia@som.geisinger.edu
DIMATTIO, David .... 563-588-6300 164 E
DIMATTIO,
Mary Jane, K .... 570-941-7400 401 F
maryjane.dimattio@scranton.edu

DIMAURO, Alfredo .... 860-253-3031.. 86 C
adimauro@asnuntuck.edu
DIMAURO, Giorgio .... 212-854-7430 291 A
gdimauro@barnard.edu
DIMAURO, Michael ...... 315-781-3691 301 F
dimauro@hws.edu
DIMEMMO, Kristine ...... 951-222-8265.. 59 D
kristine.dimemmo@rcc.edu
DIMENT, Gregory, S ..... 269-337-7149 225 F
greg.diment@kzoo.edu
DIMET, Emily .... 989-328-1245 228 D
emily.dimet@montcalm.edu
DIMICK, Jeff .... 405-425-5116 367 C
jeff.dimick@oc.edu
DIMIDIK, George .... 937-481-2543 364 A
george_dimidik@wilmington.edu
DIMING, Mianta' .... 219-980-6620 157 C
mdiming@iun.edu
DIMINO, Solweig .... 973-300-2215 284 A
sdimino@sussex.edu
DIMITCH, Jessica .... 701-662-1546 346 C
jessica.l.dimitch@lrsc.edu
DIMITRI, Nick .... 510-215-3848.. 40 B
ndimitri@contracosta.edu
DIMITRIOU, Kathy .... 313-845-9650 225 B
kdimitriou@hfcc.edu
DIMITROV, Danielle, E . 718-982-2335 293 E
danielle.dimitrov@csi.cuny.edu
DIMITROVA, Diana .... 604-274-3306 302 G
ddimitrova@ithaca.edu
DIMOFF, Danielle .... 419-372-2356 348 G
ddimoff@bgsu.edu
DIMOLITSAS, Spiros ..... 202-687-3730.. 92 E
seniorvp@georgetown.edu
DIMON, Denise .... 619-260-6824.. 72 I
dimon@sandiego.edu
DIMOND, David .... 914-632-5400 307 A
ddimond@monroecollege.edu
DIMURA, Maria .... 704-461-6717 326 L
mariadimura@bac.edu
DIN, Kristine .... 508-565-1411 219 A
kdin@stonehill.edu
DINALLO, JR.,
Benjamin .... 201-559-3507 277 J
dinallob@felician.edu
DINAN, Richard .... 856-225-2910 281 G
richard.dinan@rutgers.edu
DINAN, Susan .... 516-877-3803 289 I
sdinan@adelphi.edu
DINANI, Thandi .... 615-460-6342 418 B
thandi.dinani@belmont.edu
DINDY, Bill .... 706-854-4718 121 F
bdindy@helms.edu
DINE, Andrea, B .... 781-736-3620 208 A
dine@brandeis.edu
DINEEN-THACKERAY,
Lorrie .... 707-654-1086.. 32 A
ldineen-thackeray@csum.edu
DINEGAR, Leonard .... 303-860-5600.. 84 A
leonard.dinegar@cu.edu
DINEHART, Laura .... 305-348-3790 110 A
laura.dinehart@fiu.edu
DINELLA, Amy .... 352-245-4119 112 E
amy.dinella@taylorcollege.edu
DINEROS, Jedrek .... 717-358-3860 383 I
jdineros@fandm.edu
DINERSTEIN, Robert ..... 202-274-4004.. 91 F
rdiners@american.edu
DING, Xiaoting .... 626-289-7719.. 24 H
registrar@amu.edu
DINGER, Julie .... 580-349-1402 367 F
julie.dinger@opsu.edu
DINGES, Danielle .... 406-874-6182 263 H
dingesd@milescc.edu
DINGLE, Terry .... 843-661-8321 409 F
terry.dingle@fdtc.edu
DINGMAN, Heather .... 907-852-1768.... 9 H
heather.dingman@ilisagvik.edu
DINGMANN, Brian .... 218-935-0417 244 G
brian.dingmann@wetcc.edu
DINGMANN, Melissa .... 218-477-2085 239 E
melissa.dingmann@mnstate.edu
DINGUS-EASON,
Jeannine .... 401-456-8110 405 A
jdinguseason@ric.edu
DINH, Chris .... 616-957-8619 222 B
crd081@calvinseminary.edu
DINH, Katie .... 941-281-6784 387 D
kdinh@lecom.edu
DINKENS, Sedaric .... 903-730-4890 438 D
sdinkens@jarvis.edu
DINKINS, Elizabeth .... 502-272-7958 179 H
edinkins@bellarmine.edu

DOBI, Hanko, H .... 203-932-7191.. 89 H hdobi@newhaven.edu
DOBIE, Elizabeth, A ...... 607-871-2137 290 B dobie@alfred.edu
DOBISH, Rodney, W ..... 412-396-4781 383 A dobish@duq.edu
DOBIYANSKI, Victoria, E .... 979-845-4728 446 F vdobiyanski@tamu.edu
DOBKIN, Bethami .... 801-832-2550 461 F bdobkin@westminstercollege.edu
DOBRANSKY, Mary .... 402-557-7160 265 J mary.dobransky@bellevue.edu
DOBRIN, Ben .... 757-455-3412 477 C bdobrin@vwu.edu
DOBRINSKY, Herbert, C .... 212-960-0850 326 D dobrinsk@yu.edu
DOBROWSKI, Pauline ... 508-565-1363 219 A pdobrowski@stonehill.edu
DOBSON, Alyssa .... 724-738-2220 395 C alyssa.dobson@sru.edu
DOBSON, Catherine ...... 417-208-0636 254 E cdobson@kcumb.edu
DOBSON, Laura .... 828-328-7028 330 F laura.dobson@lr.edu
DOCETT, AJ .... 678-916-2665 115 I ajdoucett@johnmarshall.edu
DOCHERTY, Karen .... 480-517-8432.. 13 G karen.docherty@riosalado.edu
DOCKENDORF, Amy, L . 605-256-5130 416 F amy.dockendorf@dsu.edu
DOCKENS, Samuel .... 409-880-8195 449 F sjdockens@lit.edu
DOCKERY, David, S ...... 817-921-8600 445 A provost@swbts.edu
DOCKERY, Jonathan ..... 847-317-7083 151 C jsdockery@tiu.edu
DOCKERY, Rachael, M .. 417-836-8507 256 G rmdockery@missouristate.edu
DOCKERY, Sheila .... 910-788-6250 338 A sheila.dockery@sccnc.edu
DOCKERY, Tim .... 239-280-1695.. 95 M timothy.dockery@avemaria.edu
DOCKING, Jeffrey, R ..... 517-265-5161 220 G jdocking@adrian.edu
DOCKINS, Tiffany .... 601-979-3950 246 F tiffany.h.dockins@jsums.edu
DOCKTER, Jason .... 217-786-4947 143 B jason.dockter@llcc.edu
DOCTOR, John .... 650-738-4166.. 62 L doctorj@smccd.edu
DOCTOR, OFM, John .... 217-228-5432 147 F docotjo@quincy.edu
DOCTOR, OFM, John .... 218-228-5432 147 F doctojo@quincy.edu
DODANI, Sunita .... 757-446-7944 466 D dodanis@evms.edu
DODD, Daran .... 828-694-1832 332 E d_dodd@blueridge.edu
DODD, Paul .... 530-754-7806.. 69 B pdodd@ucdavis.edu
DODD, Shelley .... 307-766-4273 501 I shelley@uwyo.edu
DODD, Tim .... 806-742-3031 450 F tim.dodd@ttu.edu
DODDROE, Josh .... 480-857-5521.. 12 O josh.doddroe@cgc.edu
DODDS, David, L .... 701-777-5529 345 B david.dodds@und.edu
DODDS, Jon .... 304-367-4275 489 K jon.dodds@fairmontstate.edu
DODGE, Darla .... 775-445-4231 271 F darla.dodge@wnc.edu
DODGE, Gail .... 757-683-3277 469 B gdodge@odu.edu
DODGE, Georgina .... 301-405-2838 202 H gdodge1@umd.edu
DODGE, Kevin .... 301-387-3328 199 A kevin.dodge@garrettcollege.edu
DODGE, Lauren .... 217-854-5509 133 I lauren.dodge@blackburn.edu
DODGE, Marvin .... 435-586-7721 460 A marvindodge@suu.edu
DODGE, Michelle .... 503-847-2560 377 B mdodge@uws.edu
DODGE, Norma Jean .... 620-417-1171 177 F normajean.dodge@sccc.edu
DODGE, Randall .... 858-695-8587 156 B rdodge@horizonuniversity.edu
DODGE, Rhonda, M ..... 727-816-3401 105 F dodger@phsc.edu
DODMAN, Michael, J ... 202-685-3924 502 K
DODOSH, Gabrielle .... 316-942-4291 176 E dodoshg@newmanu.edu
DODRILL, Stella .... 304-647-6310 490 C sdodrill@osteo.wvsom.edu
DODSON, Jennifer .... 269-467-9945 224 C jdodson@glenoaks.edu
DODSON, Jerry .... 254-442-5152 432 I jerry.dodson@cisco.edu
DODSON, Preston .... 910-893-1310 327 D dodsonp@campbell.edu
DODSON, Renee .... 620-278-2173 177 H
DODSON, Shelley .... 765-973-8332 157 A midodson@iue.edu
DODSON, Wendy, B ..... 910-246-2868 337 H dodsonw@sandhills.edu
DODSON-REED, Candace .... 410-455-2065 203 B cdodreed@umbc.edu
DOEBLE, Gina .... 239-489-9029 101 A gdoeble@fsw.edu
DOEBLER, Jennifer .... 207-699-5035 195 A jdoebler@meca.edu
DOEHNE, Ben .... 612-351-0631 236 E bdoehne@ipr.edu
DOELL, Elaine .... 910-962-3855 343 C doelle@uncw.edu
DOELL, Margaret .... 719-587-8383.. 77 G mjdoell@adams.edu
DOEPKER, Joel .... 636-584-6527 253 B joel.doepker@eastcentral.edu
DOERFLER, Debra .... 760-744-1150.. 56 B ddoerfler@palomar.edu
DOERGE, Rebecca, W ... 412-268-5124 380 C rwdoerge@andrew.cmu.edu
DOERING, Douglas .... 207-699-5082 195 A doug@meca.edu
DOERING, Laura, J .... 515-294-0760 163 G ljdoeri@iastate.edu
DOERMANN, Thomas ... 319-363-1323 168 F tdoermann@mtmercy.edu
DOERR, Roger .... 402-463-2402 267 C rdoerr@hastings.edu
DOGBEVIA, Moses .... 402-461-7466 267 C mdogbevia@hastings.edu
DOGGETT, Jeffrey .... 978-837-5207 216 F doggettj@merrimack.edu
DOGONNIUCK, Theodore .... 516-773-5000 503 H dogonniuckt@usmma.edu
DOHERTY, Elizabeth ...... 401-863-7845 403 J elizabeth_doherty@brown.edu
DOHERTY, Jennifer .... 818-836-5038 142 F dohert@lewisu.edu
DOHERTY, Kathleen, T .. 717-780-2496 385 B ktdohert@hacc.edu
DOHERTY, Kenneth .... 313-577-3756 232 K ken-doherty@wayne.edu
DOHERTY, Kevin .... 620-421-6700 175 F kevind@labette.edu
DOHERTY, Kevin .... 773-371-5404 134 D kdoherty@ctu.edu
DOHERTY, Kristal .... 864-250-8417 409 I kristal.doherty@gvltec.edu
DOHERTY, Leanna, J .... 620-421-6700 175 F leannan@labette.edu
DOHERTY, Mark .... 650-325-5621.. 59 J
DOHERTY, Mary Ann .... 951-571-6928.. 59 B maryann.doherty@mvc.edu
DOHERTY, Sharon .... 651-690-6783 243 A sldoherty@stkate.edu
DOHERTY, Tiffany .... 603-513-1328 274 G tiffany.doherty@granite.edu
DOHNALIK, Judith .... 254-298-8600 445 G j.dohnalik@templejc.edu
DOI, Keiko .... 626-396-2439.. 26 B keiko.doi@artcenter.edu
DOIRON, Gail, M .... 978-665-3101 212 E gdoiron@fitchburgstate.edu
DOLAK, Lisa, A .... 315-443-1860 321 G ladolak@syr.edu
DOLAN, Abby .... 714-816-0366.. 68 E abby.dolan@trident.edu
DOLAN, Cathy .... 212-616-7278 301 C
DOLAN, Christy .... 502-863-8022 180 H christy_dolan@georgetowncollege.edu
DOLAN, Daniel .... 212-237-8900 294 D ddolan@jjay.cuny.edu
DOLAN, Elizabeth .... 610-758-1888 388 E bdk3@lehigh.edu
DOLAN, Gayle .... 617-277-3915 207 D dolang@bgsp.edu
DOLAN, Jill, S .... 609-258-3040 280 D jsdolan@princeton.edu
DOLAN, Kevin .... 617-732-2144 216 D kevin.dolan@mcphs.edu
DOLAN, Kevin .... 215-951-1010 387 A dolank@lasalle.edu
DOLAN, Matthew .... 202-319-5142.. 92 A
DOLAN, Sarah .... 617-984-1666 218 C sdolan@quincycolleg.edu
DOLAN, Scott .... 518-464-8500 299 C
DOLAN, Scott .... 614-234-1076 356 E sdolan@mccn.edu
DOLAN, Stacey, L .... 312-788-1147 152 J sdolan@vandercook.edu
DOLAN, Tammy .... 701-328-4116 345 A tammy.dolan@ndus.edu
DOLAN, Tim .... 808-956-3711 129 E timdolan@hawaii.edu
DOLAN, Timothy .... 808-376-7801 129 C info@uhfoundation.org
DOLAN, Tina, M .... 781-283-3501 219 E cdolan@wellesley.edu
DOLAN-WILSON, Allison .... 978-556-3624 215 E adolanwilson@necc.mass.edu
DOLBERRY, Carol .... 229-732-5962 115 B caroldolberry@andrewcollege.edu
DOLBOW, Dana .... 386-738-6691 112 A ddolbow@stetson.edu
DOLBOW, David .... 702-567-1920 270 I
DOLCI, Elizabeth .... 802-635-1482 463 G elizabeth.dolci@northernvermont.edu
DOLD, Julie .... 315-257-2350 319 A doldjm@potsdam.edu
DOLDER-ZIEKE, Beth, D .... 608-796-3828 497 O bdzieke@viterbo.edu
DOLE, Danny .... 307-766-1121 501 I
DOLE, Robin, L .... 610-499-4352 402 G rldole@widener.edu
DOLEHANTY, Cherie ..... 765-973-8558 157 A cdolehan@iue.edu
DOLEN, Tom .... 408-864-8764.. 42 H dolentom@deanza.edu
DOLEZAL, Marlo .... 316-677-1690 178 E mdolezal@watc.edu
DOLEZAL, Vernon .... 316-295-5679 174 A vernon_dolezal@friends.edu
DOLHEIMER, Mary, E ... 717-815-1274 403 F mdolheim@ycp.edu
DOLINAR, Jon .... 216-987-4354 351 E jon.dolinar@tri-c.edu
DOLIVE, Mark .... 817-515-2113 445 F mark.dolive@tccd.edu
DOLL, Bill .... 828-395-1676 335 D wdoll@isothermal.edu
DOLL, Christopher .... 740-366-9383 349 F doll.4@cotc.edu
DOLL, Christopher .... 563-589-3215 170 G cdoll@dbq.edu
DOLL, DeAnn .... 863-583-9050 110 B
DOLL, DeAnne .... 641-673-2118 171 C dollde@wmpenn.edu
DOLLA, Marie .... 718-779-1499 311 E mdolla@plazacollege.edu
DOLLAR, Andrew .... 256-216-5364.... 4 C andrew.dollar@athens.edu
DOLLINS, David .... 814-393-2306 393 G ddollins@clarion.edu
DOLLYHITE, Ronald ...... 336-838-6149 339 B radollyhite367@wilkescc.edu
DOLPH, Annette .... 708-709-3502 147 D adolph@prairiestate.edu
DOLPHIN, Jen .... 712-274-5110 168 E dolphinj@morningside.edu
DOLS, Kenn .... 218-855-8132 237 G kenneth.dols@clcmn.edu
DOLSON, Scott .... 812-855-4848 156 G
DOLSON, Scott, M .... 812-855-0866 156 F sdolson@iu.edu
DOLTER, Kathryn .... 319-398-5630 167 J kathryn.dolter@kirkwood.edu
DOMACK, Alicia .... 414-277-7351 494 D domack@msoe.edu
DOMAN-FLYGARE, Sarah .... 763-424-0755 240 A sdoman-flygare@nhcc.edu
DOMANN, Britney .... 816-604-1317 255 C britney.domann@mcckc.edu
DOMANN, Moira .... 503-768-7680 373 E clb@lclark.edu
DOMAS, Matthew .... 662-562-3494 248 D
DOMBROSKI, Harry ...... 817-272-2882 454 I harry.dombroski@uta.edu
DOMBROWSKI, Kirk ..... 802-656-2918 463 A kirk.dombrowski@uvm.edu
DOMECK, Craig .... 561-803-2318 105 C craig_domeck@pba.edu
DOMENE, Douglas, S ... 714-879-3901.. 45 G dsdomene@hiu.edu
DOMENECH, Roxanna ... 787-766-1717 510 G rdomenech1@uagm.edu
DOMENECH, Roxanna, D .... 787-766-1717 510 G rdomenech1@uagm.edu
DOMENICI, Bob .... 650-574-6161.. 62 K
DOMES, Chris, E .... 610-558-5501 391 A cdomes@neumann.edu
DOMIANO, Sam .... 985-549-2282 193 A sdomiano@selu.edu
DOMINGO, Courtney, N .... 808-956-6486 129 C cmnd@hawaii.edu
DOMINGO, Junior .... 626-914-8656.. 36 J jdomingo@citruscollege.edu
DOMINGUEZ, Aaron ..... 202-319-5244.. 92 A provost@cua.edu
DOMINGUEZ, Israel ...... 949-582-4777.. 65 D idominguez@saddleback.edu
DOMINGUEZ, Mary .... 805-922-6966.. 24 I mary.dominguez@hancockcollege.edu
DOMINGUEZ, Norberto . 787-296-0453 507 J dominguez@inter.edu
DOMINGUEZ, Vanessa . 805-922-6966.. 24 I vdominguez@hancockcollege.edu
DOMINGUEZ, Victoria .. 626-914-8794.. 36 J vdominguez@citruscollege.edu
DOMINGUEZ-FLORES, Noraida .... 787-998-8997 509 M ndominguez@eeapr.org
DOMINICIS, Erick .... 305-237-6583 104 E edominic@mdc.edu
DOMINICK, Jay .... 609-258-5601 280 D jdominick@princeton.edu
DOMINICK, Tara .... 541-881-5928 376 F tdominick@tvcc.cc
DOMINIQUE, Ezechiel ... 203-857-7154.. 87 D
DOMINQUEZ, Jesse ...... 940-552-6291 457 C jdominguez@vernoncollege.edu
DOMINY, Carol .... 478-218-3700 116 G cjones@centralgatech.edu
DOMINY, Robert .... 478-757-3579 116 G rdominy@centralgatech.edu
DOMKE-DAMONTE, Darla, J .... 843-349-2129 408 A ddamonte@coastal.edu
DOMMER, David .... 919-658-7854 340 G ddommer@umo.edu
DOMNWACHUKWU, Chinaka .... 909-537-5600.. 32 E chinaka.domnwachukwu@csusb.edu
DOMZALSKI, Jim .... 570-740-0342 389 A jdomzalski@luzerne.edu
DOMÍNGUEZ FLORES, Noraida .... 787-764-0000 513 B noraida.dominguez@upr.edu
DON, John .... 864-231-2100 406 F jdon@andersonuniversity.edu
DONA, David .... 541-383-7209 372 A ddona@cocc.edu
DONAGER, Sedef .... 617-989-4590 219 F donagers@wit.edu
DONAGHUE, Jennifer, H .... 202-994-4477.. 92 D iso@gwu.edu
DONAGHY, Maureen ..... 856-225-6131 281 G maureen.donaghy@rutgers.edu
DONAHOE, Frances ...... 570-389-4652 393 D fdonahoe@bloomu.edu
DONAHUE, Bob .... 614-947-6010 352 J robert.donahue@franklin.edu
DONAHUE, Brian .... 509-359-6345 479 G bdonahue@ewu.edu
DONAHUE, Colin .... 818-677-2333.. 32 C colin.donahue@csun.edu
DONAHUE, Darrell .... 304-293-2395 490 E darrell.donahue@mail.wvu.edu
DONAHUE, Gerard .... 610-902-8546 379 G gd7006@cabrini.edu
DONAHUE, James, P .... 423-652-6002 420 F jpd@king.edu
DONAHUE, Lorraine ...... 814-262-3822 393 A ldonahue@pennhighlands.edu
DONAHUE, Maura, S .... 740-368-3350 359 G msdonahue@owu.edu
DONAHUE, Nancy .... 865-694-6541 425 B ndonahue@pstcc.edu

DOSREIS, Catrina, S ..... 919-530-6198 341 E
cdosreis@nccu.edu
DOSS, Brad ..... 507-433-0523 240 G
brad.doss@riverland.edu
DOSS, Justin ..... 409-212-5724 431 A
DOSS, Katherine ..... 210-486-3936 429 A
kbeaumont@alamo.edu
DOSS, Khalilah ..... 812-464-1757 162 C
kdoss2@usi.edu
DOSS, Lauren ..... 205-726-2915.... 6 E
ledoss@samford.edu
DOSS, Mara, R ..... 301-546-0767 201 E
dossmr@pgcc.edu
DOSS, Peggy ..... 870-460-1020.. 22 C
dossp@uamont.edu
DOSTER, Betty ..... 704-687-5769 342 D
betty.doster@uncc.edu
DOSTER, Robert ..... 201-684-7870 280 H
rdoster@ramapo.edu
DOSTER, Ronda ..... 937-258-8251 353 N
DOSUMU, Samuel ..... 970-564-6222.. 82 J
samuel.dosumu@pueblocc.edu
DOTSON, Aaron ..... 907-786-1800.... 9 J
addotson@alaska.edu
DOTSON, Barry ..... 912-538-3141 125 G
bdotson@southeasterntech.edu
DOTSON, Carolyn ..... 731-352-4020 418 C
dotsonc@bethelu.edu
DOTSON, Chadwick, S . 276-244-1240 464 E
cdotson@asl.edu
DOTSON, Dana ..... 606-368-6040 178 G
danadotson@alc.edu
DOTSON, Donald ..... 334-229-6995.... 4 A
ddotson@alasu.edu
DOTSON, Kaitlin ..... 912-443-5874 125 B
kdotson@savannahtech.edu
DOTSON, Kit ..... 423-461-8708 422 E
kdotson@milligan.edu
DOTSON, Mark ..... 706-379-3111 128 C
mcdotson@yhc.edu
DOTSON, Ricky ..... 817-531-4874 451 C
rdotson@txwes.edu
DOTSON, Robert, L ..... 812-888-4102 162 F
rdotson@vinu.edu
DOTSON, Samantha ..... 360-596-5361 484 D
ssoto@spscc.edu
DOTSON, Tawny, M ..... 530-741-6707.. 77 E
tdotson@yccd.edu
DOTSON, Tom ..... 614-222-3280 351 B
tdotson@ccad.edu
DOTTER, Anne ..... 913-469-8500 174 I
adotter@jccc.edu
DOTTER, Diana ..... 206-546-4101 484 B
ddotter@shoreline.edu
DOTTS, Janene ..... 903-675-6215 451 F
janene.dotts@tvcc.edu
DOTY, Angela ..... 541-684-7289 371 I
adoty@bushnell.edu
DOTY, Brett ..... 901-321-4321 418 G
bdoty@cbu.edu
DOTY, Heather ..... 309-694-5494 139 B
heather.doty@icc.edu
DOTY, Jessica ..... 701-777-0500 345 B
jessica.doty@und.edu
DOTY, Kate ..... 317-955-6000 159 K
DOTY, Laura ..... 916-660-7655.. 64 D
ldoty@sierracollege.edu
DOTY, Laura ..... 304-829-7601 487 A
ldoty@bethanywv.edu
DOTY, Laura ..... 304-829-7142 487 A
ldoty@bethanywv.edu
DOTY, Steve ..... 212-799-5000 303 E
DOUCET, Derek ..... 802-443-3108 462 E
ddoucet@middlebury.edu
DOUCET, Gayle ..... 318-678-6000 187 H
gdoucet@bpcc.edu
DOUCET, John ..... 985-448-4385 192 F
john.doucet@nicholls.edu
DOUCETT, Sandra, L ..... 413-585-2686 218 H
sdoucett@smith.edu
DOUCETTE, Dennis ..... 858-566-1200.. 40 J
dennis@disd.edu
DOUCETTE, Donald, S .. 563-336-3304 165 K
ddoucette@eicc.edu
DOUCETTE, Kari ..... 218-262-6735 238 D
karidoucette@hibbing.edu
DOUCETTE, Margot ..... 858-566-1200.. 40 J
margot@disd.edu
DOUCETTE, Mary ..... 775-327-2120 271 A
mary.doucette@gbcnv.edu
DOUCETTPERRY, Maria . 775-784-1547 271 E
mdoucettperry@unr.edu

DOUD, Megan, F ..... 734-647-6000 231 H
mdoud@umich.edu
DOUET, Lelanya ..... 337-482-1278 193 B
ldouet@louisiana.edu
DOUGAL, Ian ..... 617-746-1990 210 H
ian.dougal@hult.edu
DOUGALL, Jennifer, L .. 330-325-6484 357 D
jdougall@neomed.edu
DOUGHARTY,
W. Houston ..... 516-463-6933 301 G
w.houston.dougharty@hofstra.edu
DOUGHERTY, Bill, W .... 608-246-6223 499 A
wdougherty@madisoncollege.edu
DOUGHERTY, Brian, C . 812-244-4009 160 F
brian.dougherty@rhventures.org
DOUGHERTY,
Christopher ..... 215-248-7130 381 A
doughertyc@chc.edu
DOUGHERTY, Clint, C .. 760-355-6207.. 45 K
clint.dougherty@imperial.edu
DOUGHERTY, Dennis ..... 610-647-4400 385 L
ddougherty1@immaculata.edu
DOUGHERTY,
Dennis, A ..... 626-395-3646.. 28 J
dadougherty@caltech.edu
DOUGHERTY, Gabe ..... 503-838-9396 377 D
doughertyg@wou.edu
DOUGHERTY, III,
Jim, R 570-326-3761 392W
jdoughe3@pct.edu
DOUGHERTY, Kaitlyn .... 734-432-5832 227 C
kdougherty@madonna.edu
DOUGHERTY, Kathleen . 603-899-4178 273 E
doughertyk@franklinpierce.edu
DOUGHERTY, Kathleen . 989-463-7176 221 B
doughertyka@alma.edu
DOUGHERTY, Kevin ..... 541-737-8748 375 A
deanofstudents@oregonstate.edu
DOUGHERTY, Lisa ..... 201-360-4111 278 C
ldougherty@hccc.edu
DOUGHERTY, Mark ..... 864-646-1871 412 H
mdougher@tctc.edu
DOUGHERTY,
Michele, R ..... 215-955-6656 399 E
michele.dougherty@jefferson.edu
DOUGHERTY, Rebecca .. 414-464-9777 498 B
dougherty.rebecca@wspp.edu
DOUGHERTY, Sharon ..... 215-248-7036 381 A
doughertys@chc.edu
DOUGHERTY,
Susan-Ellis ..... 301-314-1713 202 H
sdougher@umd.edu
DOUGHERTY, Tracy, D . 806-371-5106 429 E
tsdougherty@actx.edu
DOUGHERTY, Troy, J ... 208-496-9220 130 I
doughertyt@byui.edu
DOUGHERTY, Veronica . 410-287-1947 198 E
vdougherty@cecil.edu
DOUGHERTY DURHAM,
Danielle ..... 208-459-5004 131 C
ddurham@collegeofidaho.edu
DOUGHMAN, Siham ..... 617-373-2000 217 I
DOUGHTIE, Michael ..... 973-877-3000 277 G
mdoughti@essex.edu
DOUGHTY, JR., Clyde .. 301-860-3559 204 A
cdoughty@bowiestate.edu
DOUGHTY, JR.,
David, C 757-594-7050 465M
doughty@cnu.edu
DOUGHTY, Delbert ..... 903-223-3073 448 A
del.doughty@tamut.edu
DOUGHTY, Ellen ..... 207-581-5840 196 F
edoughty@maine.edu
DOUGHTY, Harry ..... 504-286-5312 191 C
hdoughty@suno.edu
DOUGHTY, Karen ..... 432-335-6701 441 A
kdoughty@odessa.edu
DOUGLAS, Alicia, R ..... 816-501-4306 258 I
alicia.douglas@rockhurst.edu
DOUGLAS, Amy, K ..... 334-844-3604.... 4 D
douglak@auburn.edu
DOUGLAS, Andrew ..... 410-516-8770 199 G
douglas@jhu.edu
DOUGLAS, Bernadine ... 305-891-8182.. 96 A
bdouglas@barry.edu
DOUGLAS, Blake ..... 702-895-2399 271 D
blake.douglas@unlv.edu
DOUGLAS, Brianna ..... 843-383-8175 408 B
bbuncedouglas@coker.edu
DOUGLAS, C.D ..... 402-375-7213 268 F
cddougl1@wsc.edu
DOUGLAS, Dana ..... 504-286-5000 191 C
ddouglas@suno.edu

DOUGLAS, Darcy ..... 713-646-1803 443 I
ddouglas@stcl.edu
DOUGLAS, Denise ..... 440-365-5222 355 B
DOUGLAS, Derek ..... 773-702-3627 151 E
drbdouglas@uchicago.edu
DOUGLAS, Hallie ..... 203-773-6678.. 85 D
hdouglas@albertus.edu
DOUGLAS, Jamie ..... 765-361-5592 163 B
douglasj@wabash.edu
DOUGLAS, Jasmine ..... 404-627-2681 116 C
jasmine.douglas@beulah.edu
DOUGLAS, Jerome, N ... 610-917-1403 401 G
jndouglas@valleyforge.edu
DOUGLAS, Joan ..... 281-495-0078 437 E
DOUGLAS, Kristen ..... 678-664-0529 128 A
kristen.douglas@westgatech.edu
DOUGLAS, Kristin ..... 309-794-3443 133 C
kristindouglas@augustana.edu
DOUGLAS, Laura, L ..... 508-678-2811 214 B
laura.douglas@bristolcc.edu
DOUGLAS, Lee ..... 562-938-4209.. 48 F
ldouglas@lbcc.edu
DOUGLAS, Mary ..... 870-508-6101.. 17 G
mdouglas@asumh.edu
DOUGLAS, Michelle ..... 850-644-7950 110 C
mbdouglas@fsu.edu
DOUGLAS, Natacha ..... 636-227-2100 255 A
DOUGLAS, Pam ..... 336-517-2209 327 A
pdouglas@bennett.edu
DOUGLAS, Roger ..... 360-438-4375 482 I
ddouglas@stmartin.edu
DOUGLAS, Tiffanie ..... 972-860-4256 434 H
tdouglas@dcccd.edu
DOUGLASS, David ..... 208-459-5259 131 C
ddouglass@collegeofidaho.edu
DOUGLASS, Debbie ..... 559-730-3736.. 39 B
debbied@cos.edu
DOUGLASS, James ..... 507-433-0611 240 G
james.douglass@riverland.edu
DOUGLASS, Laura ..... 978-998-7750 209 E
ldouglas@endicott.edu
DOUGLIS, Evan ..... 518-276-6460 312 C
douglis@rpi.edu
DOUGNAC, Carlos ..... 352-273-4000 111 A
cdougnac@ufl.edu
DOULIS, Peter ..... 215-871-6900 395 G
peterd@pcom.edu
DOUMA, Debbie ..... 850-484-1705 105 H
ddouma@pensacolastate.edu
DOUMA, Jason ..... 605-331-6750 417 C
jason.douma@usiouxfalls.edu
DOUMA, Ross ..... 712-722-6234 165 I
ross.douma@dordt.edu
DOURLEIN, Peter ..... 520-621-9414.. 16 D
dourlein@arizona.edu
DOURTE, Melinda ..... 509-793-2001 478 B
melindad@bigbend.edu
DOURTY, Brian ..... 972-883-6600 455 B
brian.dourty@utdallas.edu
DOUSSETT, Courtney .... 760-776-7339.. 38 E
cdoussett@collegeofthedesert.edu
DOUTHIRT COHEN,
Beth ..... 301-624-2711 198 I
bdcohen@frederick.edu
DOUTHIT, James ..... 828-262-3020 340 I
douthitjr1@appstate.edu
DOUTHIT, Tricia ..... 303-273-3383.. 79 J
tdouthit@mines.edu
DOVE, Bill ..... 719-389-6093.. 78 I
william.dove@coloradocollege.edu
DOVE, Gary ..... 276-656-5494 474 G
gdove@patrickhenry.edu
DOVE, John ..... 843-349-5296 409 J
john.dove@hgtc.edu
DOVE, Shirley ..... 254-442-5134 432 I
shirley.dove@cisco.edu
DOVE, Tangila ..... 210-486-5000 428 H
DOVI, Anthony ..... 201-684-7305 280 H
adovi@ramapo.edu
DOVIAK, Jason ..... 607-587-4630 319 F
doviakjm@alfredstate.edu
DOW, Steven, R ..... 402-465-2255 268 G
sdow@nebrwesleyan.edu
DOWD, Bonnie Ann ..... 619-388-6975.. 60 H
bdowd@sdccd.edu
DOWD, Carolyn, R ..... 817-554-5950 439 H
cdowd@messengercollege.edu
DOWD, Denny ..... 214-333-5102 434 C
denny@dbu.edu
DOWD, Jay ..... 843-953-1411 407 C
jdowd1@citadel.edu
DOWD, Nathan ..... 608-663-2837 492 F
ndowd@edgewood.edu

DOWD, Sarah ..... 843-574-6624 412 I
sarah.dowd@tridenttech.edu
DOWD, Sean, R ..... 973-596-3041 279 E
sean.r.dowd@njit.edu
DOWD-HIGGINS,
Caroline ..... 812-327-4884 158 D
cdowdhiggins@ivytech.edu
DOWDALL, Alexandria .. 810-762-0293 228 F
alexandria.dowdall@mcc.edu
DOWDELL-WHITE,
Ambe ..... 712-325-3371 167 I
adowdellwhite@iwcc.edu
DOWDLE, Deedie ..... 765-658-4416 154 J
deediedowdle@depauw.edu
DOWDY, Chris ..... 214-376-1000 441 F
cdowdy@pqc.edu
DOWDY, Jamie ..... 903-923-2296 435 H
etbu@bkstr.com
DOWE, Peter ..... 585-395-2531 317 E
pdowe@brockport.edu
DOWELL, Adrian, E ..... 402-280-4483 266 H
adriandowell@creighton.edu
DOWELL, Aileen ..... 912-478-3326 120 C
adowell@georgiasouthern.edu
DOWELL, David ..... 606-337-3196 180 C
DOWELL, Elise ..... 212-678-8950 303 D
eldowell@jtsa.edu
DOWELL, Greg ..... 434-592-3888 468 E
dgdowell@liberty.edu
DOWELL, Luke ..... 620-417-1012 177 F
luke.dowell@sccc.edu
DOWEN, Chris ..... 303-315-2550.. 84 D
chris.dowen@ucdenver.edu
DOWER, David ..... 202-885-3278.. 91 F
dower@american.edu
DOWER, Julia ..... 603-542-7744 273 B
jdower@ccsnh.edu
DOWER, Kellori ..... 714-564-5600.. 58 F
dower_kellori@sac.edu
DOWERY, Yolanda ..... 404-527-7702 121 L
ydowery@itc.edu
DOWLAND, Pam ..... 812-357-6515 161 A
pdowland@saintmeinrad.edu
DOWLESS, Donald, V ... 706-233-7201 125 C
chimes@shorter.edu
DOWLING, Audra ..... 765-455-9204 157 B
aedowlin@iu.edu
DOWLING, Beth ..... 603-428-2239 273 G
edowling@nec.edu
DOWLING, Casey ..... 318-487-7137 187 E
casey.dowling@lacollege.edu
DOWLING, Diana ..... 928-776-2391.. 16 J
diana.dowling@yc.edu
DOWLING, Gage ..... 318-487-7154 187 E
gage.dowling@lacollege.edu
DOWLING, Joseph, B ... 714-895-7711.. 38 A
jdowling@gwc.cccd.edu
DOWLING, Rosemary ... 617-747-2292 206 H
housing@berklee.edu
DOWLING, Timothy, F .. 302-831-3699.. 91 C
tdowling@udel.edu
DOWLING, Victoria ..... 262-524-7132 492 A
vdowling@carrollu.edu
DOWN, Cody ..... 808-543-8024 128 G
cdown@hpu.edu
DOWN, Ron ..... 402-643-7133 266 G
ronald.down@cune.edu
DOWNER, James ..... 814-472-3286 397 F
jdowner@francis.edu
DOWNES, Harry, W ..... 302-857-7911.. 90 E
hdownes@desu.edu
DOWNES, John ..... 770-426-2646 122 C
jdownes@life.edu
DOWNES, Kathy ..... 316-978-3586 178 D
kathy.downes@wichita.edu
DOWNES, Kelly ..... 618-437-5321 147 I
downes@rlc.edu
DOWNEY, Christina ..... 765-455-9385 157 B
downeyca@iuk.edu
DOWNEY, John, A ..... 540-453-2200 473 D
downeyj@brcc.edu
DOWNEY, John, P ..... 610-499-1265 402 G
jpdowney@widener.edu
DOWNEY, Liesl, V ..... 773-442-4248 146 A
l-downey@neiu.edu
DOWNEY, Mechell ..... 405-382-9260 369 F
m.downey@sscok.edu
DOWNEY, Nancy ..... 207-859-4503 194 D
nancy.downey@colby.edu
DOWNEY, Nora ..... 610-785-6582 397 E
ndowney@scs.edu
DOWNEY, Patricia ..... 412-365-1199 380 G
downey@chatham.edu

DRINKARD, Sharon ...... 434-395-2209 468 F
drinkardsf@longwood.edu
DRINKEN, Brandee .... 715-425-4597 496 F
brandee.drinken@uwrf.edu
DRINKWINE, Marlene ... 562-938-4406.. 48 F
mdrinkwine@lbcc.edu
DRISCOLL, Alisa .... 714-289-2098.. 36 B
driscoll@chapman.edu
DRISCOLL, Daniel .... 630-889-6609 145 E
ddriscoll@nuhs.edu
DRISCOLL, Debbie .... 434-544-8125 471 L
driscoll@lynchburg.edu
DRISCOLL, Lori .... 850-769-1551 101 N
ldriscoll@gulfcoast.edu
DRISCOLL, Mary .... 803-641-3448 413 B
maryc@usca.edu
DRISCOLL, Mary Erina .. 781-768-7000 218 D
DRISCOLL, Michael, A .. 724-357-2200 394 C
michael.driscoll@iup.edu
DRISCOLL, Michael, J ... 301-447-5068 201 B
m.j.driscoll@msmary.edu
DRISCOLL, Micheline .... 718-368-5436 294 E
mdriscoll@kbcc.cuny.edu
DRISCOLL, Michelle ...... 816-501-3608 250 F
michelle.driscoll@avila.edu
DRISCOLL, Robert, G ..... 401-865-2090 404 F
rdriscol@providence.edu
DRISCOLL, Shellie .... 909-599-5433.. 48 A
sdriscoll@lifepacific.edu
DRISH, Michael .... 413-545-0222 211 G
mdrish@umass.edu
DRISKELL, Chad .... 601-266-6525 249 F
chad.driskell@usm.edu
DRISKELL, Lindsay .... 502-213-2141 182 C
lindsay.driskell@kctcs.edu
DRISTAS, Natalie .... 703-522-1617 468 H
natalie.dristas@marymount.edu
DRIVER, Berry .... 502-897-4807 184 G
bdriver@sbts.edu
DRIVER, Dale .... 678-839-6587 127 C
ddriver@westga.edu
DRIVER, Ken .... 503-581-8600 372 H
kdriver@corban.edu
DRIVER, Louise .... 406-683-7511 264 A
louise.driver@umwestern.edu
DRODDY, Jason .... 225-578-2154 189 E
jdroddy@lsu.edu
DRODDY, Sara .... 740-283-6340 352 I
sdroddy@franciscan.edu
DROEGEMUELLER,
Heidi .... 651-641-3528 236 G
hdroegemueller001@luthersem.edu
DROLL, Charlotte .... 570-389-4921 393 D
cdroll@bloomu.edu
DRONGOWSKI, OP,
Stanley .... 616-632-8900 221 E
sad004@aquinas.edu
DROOG, Sue .... 712-722-6017 165 I
sue.droog@dordt.edu
DROPKIN, Keith .... 617-559-8783 210 F
kdropkin@hebrewcollege.edu
DROSS, Megan .... 904-361-6213 101 B
megan.dross@fscj.edu
DROST, Donald .... 732-906-2568 278 G
ddrost@middlesexcc.edu
DROST, Jack .... 256-824-7407.... 8 B
jack.drost@uah.edu
DROST, Michelle .... 715-425-3073 496 F
michelle.drost@uwrf.edu
DROUILLARD, Shelly .... 419-530-4341 363 B
shelly.drouillard@utoledo.edu
DROVER, Michelle .... 563-884-5106 169 F
michelle.drover@palmer.edu
DROWNE, Kate .... 573-341-4687 261 D
kdrowne@mst.edu
DROZ-RAMOS, Marcus . 787-480-2442 506 C
mdroz@sanjuan.pr
DRUCKENMILLER,
Patrick .... 907-474-6939.. 10 A
psdruckenmiller@alaska.edu
DRUCKER, David .... 508-541-1508 209 A
ddrucker@dean.edu
DRUCKER, Monique .... 203-582-8723.. 88 G
monique.drucker@quinnipiac.edu
DRUEKE, Tim .... 803-323-4862 414 D
drueket@winthrop.edu
DRUFFEL, Ginger .... 509-335-4200 485 D
gkdruffel@wsu.edu
DRUGOVICH,
Margaret, L .... 607-431-4990 301 A
president@hartwick.edu
DRUIN, Allison .... 718-687-5543 311 F
adruin@pratt.edu
DRUM, Amanda .... 361-825-2835 447 C
amanda.drum@tamucc.edu
DRUM, Tim .... 864-587-4282 412 F
drumt@smcsc.edu
DRUMBL, Michelle .... 540-458-8502 477 D
mdrumbl@wlu.edu
DRUMM, Jennifer .... 303-384-2604.. 79 J
jdrumm@mines.edu
DRUMM, Kevin .... 607-778-5100 317 D
drummke@sunybroome.edu
DRUMM, Meaghan, M .. 585-475-5520 312 F
mmdsfa@rit.edu
DRUMM, Mitch .... 216-368-6269 349 D
mitchell.drumm@case.edu
DRUMMER, Carlee .... 518-828-4181 297 B
carlee.drummer@sunycgcc.edu
DRUMMER, Ebony .... 216-987-4069 351 E
ebony.drummer@tri-c.edu
DRUMMER, Nephtalin ... 253-680-7150 477 I
ndrummer@batestech.edu
DRUMMOND, Carl .... 260-481-6116 160 C
drummond@pfw.edu
DRUMMOND, Connie ... 405-682-1611 367 D
cdrummond@occc.edu
DRUMMOND, Cynthia .. 281-401-5327 439 C
cynthia.drummond@lonestar.edu
DRUMMOND, Gordon ... 480-212-1704.. 15 O
gordon@sessions.edu
DRUMMOND, Hugh ...... 508-849-3345 205 H
hdrummond@annamaria.edu
DRUMMOND, Marcy ..... 323-953-4000.. 49 A
drummomj@lacitycollege.edu
DRUMMOND, Nancy ..... 503-517-1018 377 C
ndrummond@warnerpacific.edu
DRUMMOND, Sara .... 206-726-5035 479 E
sdrummond@cornish.edu
DRUPKA, Agnieszka ...... 201-216-9901 277 B
agnieszka.drupka@eicollege.edu
DRURY, Connie .... 618-634-3277 149 G
connied@shawneecc.edu
DRURY, Cooper, C .... 573-884-3971 261 A
drury@missouri.edu
DRURY, David .... 760-355-6323.. 45 K
david.drury@imperial.edu
DRURY, Leesa .... 218-751-8670 242 O
leesadrury@oakhills.edu
DRURY, Scott .... 864-644-5013 412 D
sdrury@swu.edu
DRURY, Shana .... 940-552-6291 457 C
sdrury@vernoncollege.edu
DRYDEN, Barbara .... 386-226-6000.. 99 A
DRYDEN, Deidra .... 540-261-8501 471 B
deidra.dryden@svu.edu
DRYDEN, Gary .... 502-213-2646 182 C
gary.dryden@kctcs.edu
DRYDEN, JR., Gary ...... 502-213-2646 182 C
gary.dryden@kctcs.edu
DRYDEN, Jonathan, N .. 440-366-4052 355 B
DRYDEN, Tracy .... 608-789-6179 500 C
drydent@westerntc.edu
DRYE, Theresa .... 856-256-4139 281 F
drye@rowan.edu
DRYE-DANCY, Kimberly 336-517-1374 327 A
DRYER, Christy .... 410-287-1013 198 E
cdryer@cecil.edu
DRYER, Michael .... 215-951-2677 399 E
michael.dryer@jefferson.edu
DRYER, Peter .... 602-489-5300.. 10 F
peter.dryer@arizonachristian.edu
DU, Brody .... 972-780-3600 454 A
brody.du@untdallas.edu
DU, Wendy .... 619-298-1829.. 65 K
wdu@ssu.edu
DU MONT, Malia .... 845-758-7800 290 I
mdumont@bard.edu
DU VIVIER, Derick .... 503-494-5657 374 H
derik@ohsu.edu
DUA, Sumeet .... 318-257-2871 192 D
dua@latech.edu
DUARTE, Ivette .... 305-348-2423 110 A
fduartei@fiu.edu
DUARTE, Kelly .... 207-221-4772 197 E
kduarte@une.edu
DUARTE, Khioverny ...... 732-743-3800.. 93 H
DUARTE, Maria .... 575-492-2141 289 F
mduarte@usw.edu
DUARTE, Mark, A .... 671-735-2266 504 F
mduarte@triton.uog.edu
DUARTE, Mirna .... 559-443-8680.. 67 B
mirna.duarte@fresnocitycollege.edu
DUARTE, Nelly .... 787-620-2040 505 C
duarten@aupr.edu
DUBAK, Izabela .... 630-889-6576 145 E
idubak@nuhs.edu
DUBAL, Deepa .... 859-233-8515 185 C
ddubal@transy.edu
DUBBE, Della .... 406-447-6943 264 B
della.dubbe@helenacollege.edu
DUBE, Vicki .... 401-874-5275 405 E
vdube@uri.edu
DUBENION, Brian .... 484-365-7705 388 H
ddubenion@lincoln.edu
DUBIEL, Mandy .... 517-629-0600 221 A
adubiel@albion.edu
DUBINSKY, Julie .... 816-415-5085 262 F
dubinskyj@william.jewell.edu
DUBINSKY, Zalman ...... 973-267-8005 280 F
DUBITSKY, Pamela .... 301-624-2754 198 I
pdubitsky@frederick.edu
DUBLON, Felice .... 312-629-6800 149 F
fdublon@saic.edu
DUBMAN, Jillian .... 978-232-2013 209 E
jdubman@endicott.edu
DUBOFF, Brian .... 505-428-1343 288 E
brian.duboff@sfcc.edu
DUBOIS, Darcy .... 401-456-8240 405 A
ddubois1@ric.edu
DUBOIS, Glenn .... 804-819-4903 473 C
gdubois@vccs.edu
DUBOIS, Raymond .... 843-792-2842 410 C
duboisrn@musc.edu
DUBON, Oscar .... 510-642-7294.. 69 A
vcei@berkeley.edu
DUBOSE, Alexis, W ...... 843-355-4165 414 C
dubosea@wiltech.edu
DUBOSE, Cheryl .... 843-355-4162 414 C
dubosec@wiltech.edu
DUBOSKY, Patricia .... 701-671-2612 346 D
patricia.dubosky@ndscs.edu
DUBRAY, Robert, R ...... 412-365-2716 380 G
rdubray@chatham.edu
DUBRON, Denise .... 718-522-9073 290 E
ddubron@asa.edu
DUBROY, Tashni-Ann ... 202-806-6100.. 92 F
DUBUC, Lisa .... 716-614-6798 309 G
dubuc@niagaracc.suny.edu
DUBUIS, Dina .... 734-432-5309 227 C
ddubuis@madonna.edu
DUBUQUE, Betsy .... 508-531-2100 212 D
edubuque@bridgew.edu
DUBUQUE, Melissa ...... 573-288-6343 252 F
mdubuque@culver.edu
DUCA, Jacqueline .... 706-737-1632 116 A
jduca@augusta.edu
DUCHARME, Gaylene .... 406-338-5441 263 A
gatk@bfcc.edu
DUCHARME, Lisa .... 413-572-8370 213 F
lducharme@westfield.ma.edu
DUCHENEAUX,
Stephanie .... 325-574-6502 458 D
sducheneaux@wtc.edu
DUCHETTE, Katharine .... 207-741-5726 195 H
kduchette@smccme.edu
DUCHSCHERER, Eric, D 315-267-2350 319 A
duchsced@potsdam.edu
DUCIOAME, Lynn .... 940-397-4676 440 C
lynn.ducioame@msutexas.edu
DUCK, Joseph, T .... 617-628-5000 219 C
joseph.duck@tufts.edu
DUCKETT, Danny .... 423-746-5318 426 C
dduckett@tnwesleyan.edu
DUCKETT, Randy .... 803-641-3480 413 B
randyd@usca.edu
DUCKHAM, James .... 765-285-1832 153 H
jaduckham@bsu.edu
DUCKWORTH, Anthony . 229-500-2847 114 H
anthony.duckworth@asurams.edu
DUCKWORTH, Brad ...... 715-346-2694 497 A
brad.duckworth@uwsp.edu
DUCLOS-BARRETT,
Victoria .... 401-341-2345 405 D
duclosv@salve.edu
DUCOFFE, Robert .... 262-595-2261 496 D
ducoffe@uwp.edu
DUCOTE, Melissa .... 318-342-5141 193 C
ducote@ulm.edu
DUCSAY, Teresa .... 412-809-5275 396 E
barbour.teresa@ptcollege.edu
DUDA, David .... 215-489-2356 382 B
david.duda@delval.edu
DUDA, Heather .... 330-829-6127 362 E
dudahe@mountunion.edu
DUDA, Teri .... 201-967-9667 275 I
td@berkeleycollege.edu
DUDAS, Bertalan .... 814-866-8142 387 D
bdudas@lecom.edu
DUDAS, Jon .... 520-626-6350.. 16 D
jondudas@arizona.edu
DUDGEON, Ashley .... 859-846-4421 184 B
adudgeon@midway.edu
DUDGEON, David .... 305-899-3727.. 96 A
ddudgeon@barry.edu
DUDGEON, Hollis .... 502-863-8056 180 H
hollis_dudgeon@georgetowncollege.
edu
DUDGEON, Mark .... 614-287-2508 351 C
mdudgeon@cscc.edu
DUDICH, Jason .... 317-788-3301 161 H
dudichj@uindy.edu
DUDLEY, Brad .... 256-228-6001.... 3 B
fricksb@nacc.edu
DUDLEY, Brad, D .... 310-506-4184.. 56 G
brad.dudley@pepperdine.edu
DUDLEY,
Christopher, H .... 336-841-9127 329 F
cdudley@highpoint.edu
DUDLEY, Jacklyn .... 270-809-3774 184 D
jdudley@murraystate.edu
DUDLEY, Jason .... 239-985-8368 101 A
jason.dudley@fsw.edu
DUDLEY, John .... 605-658-3830 416 D
john.dudley@usd.edu
DUDLEY, Kaitlin .... 404-297-9522 120 B
DUDLEY, Kristine .... 603-206-8161 272 L
kdudley@ccsnh.edu
DUDLEY, Manuel .... 336-334-4822 335 A
mcdudley@gtcc.edu
DUDLEY, Roland, Q ...... 417-268-6108 250 G
rdudley@gobbc.edu
DUDLEY, Sharese .... 219-980-6791 157 C
shaadudl@iun.edu
DUDLEY, Waller, T .... 540-458-8470 477 D
wdudley@wlu.edu
DUDLEY, William, C ..... 540-458-8700 477 D
president@wlu.edu
DUDONIS, Shirlin .... 510-666-8248.. 24 D
registrar@aimc.edu
DUDONIS, Shirlin .... 510-666-8248.. 24 D
DUDT, Susan .... 770-426-2700 122 C
sdudt@life.edu
DUDUIT, Angie .... 740-351-3322 360 F
aduduit@shawnee.edu
DUDUIT, James .... 864-231-2000 406 F
jduduit@andersonuniversity.edu
DUDZIK, Kim .... 619-660-4453.. 44 D
kim.dudzik@gcccd.edu
DUELL, Charles .... 303-914-6517.. 83 C
charles.duell@rrcc.edu
DUELLMAN, Scott .... 314-977-8283 259 F
scott.duellman@slu.edu
DUELLMAN, Scott .... 314-977-3862 259 F
scott.duellman@slu.edu
DUENAS, Hector .... 305-273-4499.. 97 K
hector@cbt.edu
DUENAS, Miguel .... 323-265-8835.. 48 J
duenasma@elac.edu
DUENAS, Tina .... 530-242-7622.. 64 C
tduenas@shastacollege.edu
DUENKEL, Priscilla .... 865-981-5302 425 B
pduenkel@pstcce.edu
DUERK, Jeffrey .... 305-284-6318 113 C
jeffrey.duerk@miami.edu
DUERR, Larry .... 414-382-6173 491 F
larry.duerr@alverno.edu
DUERR, William .... 864-250-7000.. 93 H
DUERWACHTER,
Kathleen, A .... 608-796-3072 497 O
kaduerwachter@viterbo.edu
DUESING, Jason .... 816-414-3740 256 C
jduesing@mbts.edu
DUET, Jodi .... 985-448-7946 188 C
jodi.duet@fletcher.edu
DUETSCH, Craig .... 773-995-2042 134 K
cduetsch@csu.edu
DUETT, Belinda, G .... 334-833-4519.... 5 G
bduett@hawks.huntingdon.edu
DUEWEKE, Jerome .... 317-940-8000 154 C
DUEÑAS, Felicia .... 805-289-6562.. 74 B
fduenas@vcccd.edu
DUEÑEZ, Nydia .... 213-738-6871.. 66 B
deanofstudents@swlaw.edu
DUFAU, Nancy .... 410-704-5822 204 E
ndufau@towson.edu
DUFAULT-HUNTER,
David, R .... 818-677-3700.. 32 C
ddh@csun.edu

DUFF, Evan 252-985-5136 339 D eduff@ncwc.edu
DUFF, John 727-341-7176 107 E duff.john@spcollege.edu
DUFFEL, Cary Beth 901-751-8453 421 G
DUFFIE, Cecil 903-923-2455 458 F cduffie@wileyc.edu
DUFFIE, James 561-868-3077 105 D duffiej@palmbeachstate.edu
DUFFIE, James, E 561-868-3077 105 D duffiej@palmbeachstate.edu
DUFFIELD, Stacy 701-231-7012 345 F stacy.duffield@ndsu.edu
DUFFINS, Varo, L 610-328-8360 398 G vduffin1@swarthmore.edu
DUFFY, Brian 215-972-2030 392 T bduffy@pafa.edu
DUFFY, Camisha 270-809-3155 184 D cduffy@murraystate.edu
DUFFY, Chris 813-974-0658 111 C cduffy@usf.edu
DUFFY, Chrissie 334-222-6591 2 I cduffy@lbwcc.edu
DUFFY, Deborah 215-717-6387 400 E deduffy@uarts.edu
DUFFY, Dolly 574-631-2788 162 A eduffy@nd.edu
DUFFY, Elizabeth 240-629-7886 198 I eduffy@frederick.edu
DUFFY, James, P 717-337-6240 384 D jpduffy@gettysburg.edu
DUFFY, Julia, A 203-254-4000 87 I jduffy@fairfield.edu
DUFFY, Kelly 315-470-5922 291 I kellyduffy@crouse.org
DUFFY, Kelly 937-481-2243 364 A
DUFFY, Kevin 609-586-4800 278 F duffyk@mccc.edu
DUFFY, Kristine 518-743-2237 320 A duffyk@sunyacc.edu
DUFFY, Matthew 218-726-8829 243 G duffy@d.umn.edu
DUFFY, Michael 517-265-5161 220 G mduffy@adrian.edu
DUFFY, Rachelle, M 517-265-5161 220 G rduffy@adrian.edu
DUFFY, Raymond 610-519-4237 401 K raymond.duffy@villanova.edu
DUFFY, Stephen, M 956-326-2543 446 E sduffy@tamiu.edu
DUFFY, Susan 781-239-6425 206 B sduffy@babson.edu
DUFFY, Thomas 845-431-8305 298 D thomas.duffy1@sunydutchess.edu
DUFFY, II, William, R 563-425-5221 170 H duffyw@uiu.edu
DUFORT, Linda 630-617-3059 137 G dufortl@elmhurst.edu
DUFOUR, Graciela 815-836-5270 142 F dufourgr@lewisu.edu
DUFOUR, Jeanna 253-583-4328 478 J jeanna.dufour@cptc.edu
DUFOUR, Jeff 518-694-7395 289 J jeff.dufour@acphs.edu
DUFRESNE, Edwidge 478-825-6200 118 F edwidge.dufresne@fvsu.edu
DUFRESNE, Sarah 989-686-9386 223 J sarahdufresne@delta.edu
DUGAN, James 816-654-7219 254 E jdugan@kcumb.edu
DUGAN, Jennifer 606-218-5219 186 B jenniferdugan@upike.edu
DUGAN, Lyndsey 304-367-4135 489 K lyndsey.dugan@fairmontstate.edu
DUGAN, Marnei 800-747-2687 144 H mdugan@monmouthcollege.edu
DUGAN, Mary 775-784-3941 271 E mdugan@unr.edu
DUGAN, Robert 315-470-6667 319 D rcdugan@esf.edu
DUGAR, Curtis 570-422-3460 394 A cdugar@esu.edu
DUGAS, Alisha 314-838-8858 261 F adugas@ugst.edu
DUGAT, Nathan 713-525-2152 454 G registrar@stthom.edu
DUGGAN, Gary 413-572-5243 213 F gduggan@westfield.ma.edu
DUGGAN, Michael 617-824-8351 209 C michael_duggan@emerson.edu
DUGGAN, Sean 806-742-2661 450 F s.duggan@ttu.edu
DUGGIN, Josh 731-286-3338 424 D duggin@dscc.edu
DUGUID, Brent 601-643-8261 245 F brent.duguid@colin.edu
DUGUID, Iain 215-887-5511 402 E iduguid@wts.edu
DUGUID, James 864-231-2000 406 F jduguid@andersonuniversity.edu
DUGUID, Stephanie 601-643-5341 245 F stephanie.duguid@colin.edu
DUHAI, Karen 800-287-8822 154 A duhaika@bethanyseminary.edu
DUHAME-SCHMIDT, Donna, L 248-522-3505 229 C dlduhame@oaklandcc.edu
DUHE, Christen 601-928-6205 247 E christen.duhe@mgccc.edu
DUHON, Gail 616-222-1431 223 C gail.duhon@cornerstone.edu
DUHON, Stacey, D 318-274-6174 192 C duhons@gram.edu
DUIJVESTEIJN, Adria 978-542-7524 213 E adria.duijvesteijn@salemstate.edu
DUININK, Leslie 641-628-7643 164 D duininkl@central.edu
DUITCH, Suri 504-865-5555 191 F sduitch@tulane.edu
DUKE, Alex 310-393-0411 56 C
DUKE, Christopher 615-329-8505 419 H cduke@fisk.edu
DUKE, Del, G 870-235-4171 21 C dgduke@saumag.edu
DUKE, Jaime 406-265-3582 264 E jaime.duke@msun.edu
DUKE, Labin, L 262-646-6517 494 F lduke@nashotah.edu
DUKE, Robert 626-815-5441 26 F rrduke@apu.edu
DUKE, Russell 980-495-3978 329 B
DUKE, Steven, T 402-472-8845 269 H sduke@nebraska.edu
DUKE, Todd 765-973-8611 157 A mtduke@iu.edu
DUKERICH, Janet, M 512-471-3007 455 A janet.dukerich@austin.utexas.edu
DUKES, Bonita 386-822-8808 112 A bdukes@stetson.edu
DUKES, Charlene, M 240-567-5264 200 G president@montgomerycollege.edu
DUKES, Earnstein 806-742-2261 450 F earnstein.dukes@ttu.edu
DUKES, Gary 503-838-8221 377 D dukesg@wou.edu
DUKES, Keith 301-736-3631 200 C
DUKES, Kristen 251-460-6294 9 A kdukes@southalabama.edu
DUKES, Kristin Nicole 814-332-3100 378 A
DUKES, Marsha, B 229-245-6490 127 E mbdukes@valdosta.edu
DULABAUM, Mary 847-628-2089 141 C mdulabaum@judsonu.edu
DULANEY, Kimberly 540-831-5000 469 D kddulaney@radford.edu
DULANEY, Wes 931-540-2617 424 C wdulaney@columbiastate.edu
DULANY, Ann 740-284-5254 352 I adulany@franciscan.edu
DULATRE, Mary 978-762-4000 215 D mdulatre@northshore.edu
DULAY, Sarah 708-237-5050 146 D sdulay@nc.edu
DULEY, Melody 775-445-4235 271 F melody.duley@wnc.edu
DULGAR, Laura 623-935-8808 13 A laura.dulgar@estrellamountain.edu
DULIAN, Morgan 907-474-6631 10 A madulian@alaska.edu
DULIN, Amy 704-669-4420 333 E dulin@clevelandcc.edu
DULIN, Scott 617-236-8877 209 G sdulin@fisher.edu
DULL, Chad 507-453-1443 239 B chad.dull@southeastmn.edu
DULLEA, Robert 206-296-2590 484 A dullea@seattleu.edu
DULUDE, Ryan 802-654-0505 463 F rxd04120@ccv.vsc.edu
DUMANCELA, Fanny 718-518-4434 294 B fdumancela@hostos.cuny.edu
DUMAS, Marine 805-898-2915 42 D mdumas@fielding.edu
DUMAS, Maureen 401-598-2350 404 D maureen.dumas@jwu.edu
DUMAS, Theresa 662-254-3618 248 B theresa.dumas@mvsu.edu
DUMAS-DYER, Heather 408-554-4900 63 B hdumasdyer@scu.edu
DUMAS SERFES, Pamela 860-439-5226 87 H pdserfes@conncoll.edu
DUMAUAL, Roberto 718-522-9073 290 E rdumaual@asa.edu
DUMAY, Harry, E 413-265-2293 208 E hdumay@elms.edu
DUMBLETON, Eric 415-565-4616 69 C dumbletoneric@uchastings.edu
DUMDEI, Mike 903-823-3107 446 A michael.dumdei@texarkanacollege.edu
DUMIRE, William 724-852-3382 402 C wdumire@waynesburg.edu
DUMITRU, Dariu 661-362-2607 51 D ddumitru@masters.edu
DUMONT, Betsy 209-228-3612 70 A edumont@ucmerced.edu
DUMONT, Christine 401-341-2189 405 D dumontc@salve.edu
DUMONT, Sara, E 202-885-1321 91 F dumont@american.edu
DUMONTELLE, Janine 714-997-6533 36 B jpdumont@chapman.edu
DUMOUCHEL, Jerrett 904-632-3307 101 B jerrett.dumouchel@fscj.edu
DUMPSON, Kimberly, C 401-456-8460 405 A kdumpson@ric.edu
DUNAGAN, Pam 706-368-6397 116 B pdunagan@berry.edu
DUNAJ, Joshua 951-552-8330 27 G jdunaj@calbaptist.edu
DUNAVIN, Callie 870-733-6840 17 F cdunavin@asumidsouth.edu
DUNAWAY, Donna, H 615-230-3551 425 E donna.dunaway@volstate.edu
DUNAWAY, Gregory 304-293-4611 490 E gregory.dunaway@mail.wvu.edu
DUNBAR, Andrea 312-935-4232 140 G adunbar@icsw.edu
DUNBAR, Deirdre, M 262-554-2010 494 A
DUNBAR, Dorlena 516-572-7759 307 E dorlena.dunbar@ncc.edu
DUNBAR, Erin 715-232-2314 497 B dunbare@uwstout.edu
DUNBAR, Joan 313-577-1912 232 K aj0824@wayne.edu
DUNBAR, John 770-533-7028 122 B jdunbar@laniertech.edu
DUNBAR, Kelly 215-619-7314 390 C kdunbar@mc3.edu
DUNBAR, Melanie 814-866-8160 387 D mdunbar@lecom.edu
DUNBAR, Nelia 575-835-5783 286 K nelia.dunbar@nmt.edu
DUNBAR, Scott 701-662-1525 346 C scott.dunbar@lrsc.edu
DUNBAR, Wayne 951-785-2000 47 C
DUNBAR, William, J 262-554-2010 494 A
DUNBAR-JACOB, Jacqueline 412-624-2400 400 H dunbar@pitt.edu
DUNBAR-SMALLEY, Sandra 407-303-7894 95 B sandra.dunbar-smalley@ahu.edu
DUNCAN, Alfonzo 803-327-7402 407 F aduncan@clintoncollege.edu
DUNCAN, Andrew 603-524-3207 272 K aduncan@ccsnh.edu
DUNCAN, Benton 701-231-7033 345 F benton.duncan@ndsu.edu
DUNCAN, Bernadine 936-261-3564 446 C bduncan@pvamu.edu
DUNCAN, Charles 919-508-2395 344 E cduncan@peace.edu
DUNCAN, Chelsea 810-762-3322 232 A chelswin@umich.edu
DUNCAN, Christine 505-224-3479 285 N cduncan@cnm.edu
DUNCAN, Christopher 973-353-5255 282 B chris.duncan@rutgers.edu
DUNCAN, Darrell 615-966-6166 421 B darrell.duncan@lipscomb.edu
DUNCAN, Dennis, L 574-372-5100 155 F duncandl@grace.edu
DUNCAN, Geordon 540-828-5706 464 L gduncan@bridgewater.edu
DUNCAN, Heather 904-620-1000 111 B heather.duncan@unf.edu
DUNCAN, Hilary 812-237-6131 156 D hilary.duncan@indstate.edu
DUNCAN, Holly 864-596-9704 408 F holly.duncan@converse.edu
DUNCAN, Issac 270-686-4324 179 J issac.duncan@brescia.edu
DUNCAN, J. Ligon 601-923-1600 248 F lduncan@rts.edu
DUNCAN, Jan 903-593-8311 448 G jduncan@texascollege.edu
DUNCAN, Jay, R 770-720-5543 124 G jrd@reinhardt.edu
DUNCAN, Jenny 918-293-5488 368 B jenny.duncan@okstate.edu
DUNCAN, Jerelyn 903-923-2464 458 F jduncan@wileyc.edu
DUNCAN, Jim 901-843-3946 423 A duncanjb@rhodes.edu
DUNCAN, John 313-883-8599 230 C duncan.john@shms.edu
DUNCAN, John 864-977-7156 410 I john.duncan@ngu.edu
DUNCAN, K. Michael 843-953-6356 408 C duncanm@cofc.edu
DUNCAN, Kimberly 818-785-2726 35 E kimberly.duncan@casalomacollege.edu
DUNCAN, Krystal 650-574-6440 62 K duncank@smccd.edu
DUNCAN, Laura 334-833-8339 5 G lduncan@hawks.huntingdon.edu
DUNCAN, Lynette 479-524-7225 19 H lduncan@jbu.edu
DUNCAN, Marlina 508-856-2179 212 C marlina.duncan@umasmed.edu
DUNCAN, Martina 207-725-3797 194 C mduncan@bowdoin.edu
DUNCAN, Matthew 408-554-4583 63 B mduncan@scu.edu
DUNCAN, Megan 314-505-7593 252 A duncanm@csl.edu
DUNCAN, Michael, W 724-847-6528 384 C mwduncan@geneva.edu
DUNCAN, Paul 330-337-6403 347 D
DUNCAN, Randall, S 262-243-5700 492 E randall.duncan@cuaa.edu
DUNCAN, Randy 704-687-7323 342 D rduncan@uncc.edu
DUNCAN, Robert 419-267-1202 357 E rduncan@northweststate.edu
DUNCAN, Robin 951-552-8948 27 G rduncan@calbaptist.edu
DUNCAN, Susan 662-915-6900 249 D sduncan@olemiss.edu
DUNCAN, Teresa, S 865-481-2000 425 C duncants@roanestate.edu
DUNCAN, Teresa, S 865-882-4648 425 C duncants@roanestate.edu
DUNCAN, Tim 504-282-4455 190 F
DUNCAN, Tim 504-280-6102 190 B tduncan@uno.edu
DUNCAN, Todd 513-556-4200 361 J todd.duncan@uc.edu
DUNCAN, William, H 916-660-7000 64 D president@sierracollege.edu
DUNCAN-POITIER, Johanna 518-320-1276 315 H johanna.duncan-poitier@suny.edu
DUNCAN RAINES, Lisa 757-594-7846 465 M duncanl@cnu.edu
DUNCAN-RAMIREZ, Rebecca 412-809-5278 396 E ramirez.rebecca@ptcollege.edu
DUNCAN SMITH, Shá 408-554-5131 63 B tssmith@scu.edu
DUNCKLEE, Mary 508-565-3360 219 A stonehillbkstr@fheg.follett.com
DUNCOMBE, Kemmoree 989-275-5000 226 D kemmoree.duncombe@kirtland.edu
DUNCOMBE, Markita 954-771-0376 103 S
DUNEGAN, Kent 432-837-8103 450 B kdunegan@sulross.edu
DUNGEE-ANDERSON, Elizabeth 757-823-8668 469 A eddungee-anderson@nsu.edu
DUNHAM, Adrianne 860-773-1371 87 G amarkham@tunxis.edu
DUNHAM, Andrew 517-629-0216 221 A ddunham@albion.edu
DUNHAM, Andrew, M 517-629-0477 221 A ddunham@albion.edu
DUNHAM, David 209-228-7732 70 A ddunham@ucmerced.edu

DUNHAM, Dennis .... 405-974-2374 370 I
ddunham1@uco.edu
DUNHAM, Douglas, N .. 816-501-4617 258 I
douglas.dunham@rockhurst.edu
DUNHAM, Mark, E .... 660-263-3900 251 D
markdunham@cccb.edu
DUNHAM, Nikki .... 313-577-2116 232 K
gz1101@wayne.edu
DUNHAM, Stephen, S .. 814-867-4088 391 G
ssd13@psu.edu
DUNHAM, Steven .... 704-687-0756 342 D
steven.dunham@uncc.edu
DUNHAM, Thomas .... 773-907-4477 135 C
tdunham@ccc.edu
DUNHAM STRAND,
Amy .... 616-632-8900 221 E
stranamy@aquinas.edu
DUNIFUN, Rachel .... 607-255-2138 297 F
red26@cornell.edu
DUNIWAY, Robert .... 206-296-2105 484 A
rduniway@seattleu.edu
DUNKELMAN, James .... 562-907-4205.. 76 B
jdunkelman@whittier.edu
DUNKER, Eric .... 303-797-5859.. 77 I
eric.dunker@arapahoe.edu
DUNKERTON, David, W 304-877-6428 486 G
david.dunkerton@abc.edu
DUNKLE, John, H .... 847-491-2151 146 E
j-dunkle@northwestern.edu
DUNKLE, Mike .... 402-471-2505 268 C
mdunkle@nscs.edu
DUNKLEBERGER,
Robert, L .... 570-321-4278 389 B
dunkleberger@lycoming.edu
DUNKLEY, Eugene .... 618-664-6543 138 F
eugene.dunkley@greenville.edu
DUNKLEY, Jessica, L ..... 513-585-0032 350 D
jessica.dunkley@thechristcollege.edu
DUNKLIN, Kendrick .... 904-470-8202.. 98 L
DUNLAP, Brandy .... 828-726-2225 332 G
bdunlap@cccti.edu
DUNLAP, Christopher ... 815-224-0450 140 E
chris_dunlap@ivcc.edu
DUNLAP, Doug .... 620-901-6261 171 D
ddunlap@allencc.edu
DUNLAP, John .... 617-287-7050 211 F
jdunlap@umassp.edu
DUNLAP, Lanee .... 903-886-5738 447 B
lanee.dunlap@tamuc.edu
DUNLAP, Michael, P ..... 920-565-1000 493 A
dunlapmp@lakeland.edu
DUNLAP, Ruth .... 662-562-3202 248 D
rdunlap@northwestms.edu
DUNLAP, Scott .... 973-720-3232 284 J
dunlaps@wpunj.edu
DUNLAP, Stacey .... 870-512-7811.. 18 A
stacey_dunlap@asun.edu
DUNLAP, Susan, L .... 516-726-5816 503 H
dunlaps@usmma.edu
DUNLAVY, Patrick .... 440-826-3623 348 D
pdunlavy@bw.edu
DUNLAY, Robert, W ...... 402-280-2600 266 H
robertdunlay@creighton.edu
DUNLEAVY, Aidan .... 316-295-5214 174 A
aidan_dunleavy@friends.edu
DUNLEAVY, James, F .... 610-861-5463 391 C
jdunleavy@northampton.edu
DUNLOP, Kath .... 413-597-4286 220 D
kdk2@williams.edu
DUNN, Alaina .... 650-417-2055.. 55 L
adunn@paloaltou.edu
DUNN, Amy .... 202-379-7808.. 93 H
DUNN, Andrew .... 714-438-4611.. 37 I
wdunniii@cccd.edu
DUNN, Ashley .... 818-778-5518.. 49 G
dunnae@lavc.edu
DUNN, Barbara .... 870-543-5957.. 21 B
bdunn@seark.edu
DUNN, Barry, H .... 605-688-4111 417 A
barry.dunn@sdstate.edu
DUNN, Becky .... 816-271-4200 257 A
DUNN, Brad .... 512-863-1944 445 C
dunnb@southwestern.edu
DUNN, Charissa .... 918-335-6822 368 E
cdunn@okwu.edu
DUNN, Chris .... 816-271-4200 257 A
DUNN, Christopher .... 617-482-3103 211 G
cdunn@admin.umass.edu
DUNN, Corey .... 404-471-6176 114 G
cdunn@agnesscott.edu
DUNN, Daniel .... 312-329-4451 144 I
daniel.dunn@moody.edu
DUNN, Darren .... 970-351-2362.. 84 F
darren.dunn@unco.edu
DUNN, Deborah .... 734-432-5457 227 C
ddunn@madonna.edu
DUNN, Derrek .... 256-372-5104.... 1 A
derrek.dunn@aamu.edu
DUNN, Derrek, B .... 410-651-6348 203 D
ddunn@umes.edu
DUNN, Doug .... 606-693-5000 183 C
ddunn@kmbc.edu
DUNN, Elizabeth .... 607-436-2520 316 F
elizabeth.dunn@oneonta.edu
DUNN, Elizabeth .... 607-436-3458 316 F
elizabeth.dunn@oneonta.edu
DUNN, Florence .... 559-325-3600.. 28 D
fdunn@chsu.edu
DUNN, Gary .... 831-459-2628.. 71 A
gmdunn@ucsc.edu
DUNN, Jaime .... 410-626-2500 202 A
jaime.dunn@sjc.edu
DUNN, James .... 559-325-3600.. 28 D
jdunn@chsu.edu
DUNN, James, J .... 336-758-4240 344 C
jdunn@vergercapital.com
DUNN, Jena .... 361-991-9403 445 D
DUNN, Jenny, R .... 864-587-4271 412 F
dunnj@smcsc.edu
DUNN, Jim .... 918-335-6234 368 E
jdunn@okwu.edu
DUNN, Jimmy .... 559-325-3600.. 28 D
jdunn@chsu.edu
DUNN, John, B .... 617-552-3350 207 C
jack.dunn@bc.edu
DUNN, Judi, B .... 402-552-6123 266 E
dunn@clarksoncollege.edu
DUNN, Keith .... 601-974-1010 247 B
keith.dunn@millsaps.edu
DUNN, Kelly .... 715-682-1351 494 G
kdunn@northland.edu
DUNN, Kevin .... 617-627-2816 219 C
kevin.dunn@tufts.edu
DUNN, Kevin .... 859-246-6716 181 F
kevin.dunn@kctcs.edu
DUNN, Kristin .... 405-382-9525 369 F
k.dunn@sscok.edu
DUNN, Linda .... 801-581-6996 459 O
linda.dunn@alumni.utah.edu
DUNN, Lisa .... 602-274-1885.. 14 O
ldunn@pihma.edu
DUNN, Louise .... 940-565-4307 453 E
louise.dunn@unt.edu
DUNN, Marilee .... 801-957-4490 461 C
marilee.dunn@slcc.edu
DUNN, Michael, K .... 240-895-4105 202 B
mkdunn@smcm.edu
DUNN, Molly .... 740-588-1224 365 B
mdunn@zanestate.edu
DUNN, Patricia, A .... 815-599-3408 139 A
pat.dunn@highland.edu
DUNN, Paul .... 860-701-7739.. 88 D
dunn_p@mitchell.edu
DUNN, Paul .... 360-650-3472 485 I
paul.dunn@wwu.edu
DUNN, Robin .... 410-626-2540 202 A
robin.dunn@sjc.edu
DUNN, Roderick .... 501-374-6305.. 20 G
roderick.dunn@shortercollege.edu
DUNN, Rose Ellen .... 609-497-7818 280 C
rose.ellen.dunn@ptsem.edu
DUNN, Shari .... 704-687-5723 342 D
shari.dunn@uncc.edu
DUNN, Sharon .... 318-813-2941 189 I
sharon.dunn@lsuhs.edu
DUNN, Stanley .... 518-276-8433 312 C
dunns6@rpi.edu
DUNN, Susan, C .... 407-582-6871 113 I
sdunn18@valenciacollege.edu
DUNN, Timothy .... 212-659-3604 303 H
tdunn@tkc.edu
DUNN, Tracy .... 859-233-8148 185 C
tdunn@transy.edu
DUNN, Tracy .... 803-705-4694 406 G
tracy.dunn@benedict.edu
DUNN, W. Brent .... 417-836-6666 256 G
brentdunn@missouristate.edu
DUNN CARLTON,
Heather .... 209-667-6635.. 33 B
hdunncarlton@csustan.edu
DUNN CARPENTER,
Christina .... 913-758-6267 178 B
christina.dunn_carpenter@stmary.edu
DUNN-RAMSAY, Sheri .. 910-410-1907 337 B
srdunn-ramsay@richmondcc.edu
DUNNAGAN, Tim .... 208-426-3917 130 H
timdunnagan@boisestate.edu
DUNNE, Colleen .... 360-412-6155 482 I
cdunne@stmartin.edu
DUNNE, Jennifer .... 617-333-2271 208 G
jdunne1213@curry.edu
DUNNE, Nicole .... 831-646-3007.. 52 G
ndunne@mpc.edu
DUNNE, Timothy .... 207-741-5506 195 H
tdunne@smccme.edu
DUNNE-CASCIO,
Colleen .... 541-962-3476 372 I
ccascio@eou.edu
DUNNING, Carol .... 312-553-2500 135 A
cdunning6@ccc.edu
DUNNING, Eric .... 920-403-1346 495 B
eric.dunning@snc.edu
DUNNING, Jim .... 805-756-5551.. 29 I
jdunning@calpoly.edu
DUNNING, John .... 402-375-7107 268 F
jodunni1@wsc.edu
DUNNING, Kathy .... 251-442-2281.... 8 C
kdunning@umobile.edu
DUNNING, Scott .... 765-973-8435 157 A
sdunning@iu.edu
DUNNING, Sue .... 863-638-2937 114 B
dunnings@webber.edu
DUNNINGTON, Renee ... 614-236-6701 349 B
rdunning@capital.edu
DUNNIVANT, Stephen ... 954-201-7350.. 96 F
DUNNUCK, John .... 954-201-7405.. 96 F
jdunnuck@broward.edu
DUNPHY, Francis, J ...... 215-204-7000 399 B
francis.dunphy@temple.edu
DUNPHY, Michael .... 330-490-7123 363 E
mdunphy@walsh.edu
DUNPHY-CULP, Bryan .. 215-646-7300 385 A
dunphy-culp.b@gmercyu.edu
DUNSCOMBE, William .. 908-709-7570 284 D
dunscombe@ucc.edu
DUNSEATH, Jennifer ..... 401-254-3275 405 C
jdunseath@rwu.edu
DUNSMORE, Tara .... 410-857-2798 200 F
tdunsmore@mcdaniel.edu
DUNSTAN, Dani .... 208-282-3343 131 G
dunsdani@isu.edu
DUNSTON, Julie .... 618-453-3430 150 B
dunston@siu.edu
DUNSTON, Karen .... 503-352-2713 375 C
dunstonk@pacificu.edu
DUNSTON, Rita .... 540-654-1265 471 N
rdunston@umw.edu
DUNSWORTH,
Richard, L .... 479-979-1242.. 23 I
rdunsworth@ozarks.edu
DUNTLEY, Mark .... 503-768-7082 373 E
duntley@lclark.edu
DUNTON, Renee .... 207-947-4591 194 B
rdunton@bealcollege.edu
DUONG, Tom .... 714-903-2762.. 68 G
DUPAUL, Stephanie .... 804-287-6442 472 C
sdupaul@richmond.edu
DUPAY, Abbie .... 812-941-2115 157 F
aedupay@ius.edu
DUPEE, Daniel, J .... 315-786-2401 303 C
ddupee@sunyjefferson.edu
DUPIER, Jo .... 606-539-4208 185 E
jo.dupier@ucumberlands.edu
DUPLANTIS, Josh .... 251-990-0445.... 1 I
joshua.duplantis@coastalalabama.edu
DUPLER, Terry .... 719-587-7208.. 77 G
dtdupler@adams.edu
DUPLESSIS, Tamika ...... 504-941-8500 188 B
tduple@dcc.edu
DUPLESSIS, Tamika ...... 504-671-5055 188 B
tduple@dcc.edu
DUPONT, Jeffrey .... 970-247-7153.. 80 J
dupont_j@fortlewis.edu
DUPONT, Joseph .... 617-552-3430 207 C
joseph.dupont@bc.edu
DUPONT, Michael .... 817-515-3015 445 F
michael.dupont@tccd.edu
DUPONT, Randall .... 318-427-4489 189 F
rdupont@lsua.edu
DUPONT, Richard .... 203-332-5991.. 86 F
rdupont@hcc.commnet.edu
DUPRA, JoAnn .... 870-543-5993.. 21 B
jdupra@seark.edu
DUPRAS, Tosha .... 407-823-6725 110 E
tosha.dupras@ucf.edu
DUPRE, Tara .... 985-549-2001 193 A
tara.dupre@selu.edu
DUPRE, Terry, G .... 985-448-4031 192 F
terry.dupre@nicholls.edu
DUPREE, Carol .... 325-794-4401 432 I
carol.dupree@cisco.edu
DUPREE, Jason, M .... 580-774-7081 370 A
jason.dupree@swosu.edu
DUPREE, Kathy .... 281-212-1610 452 E
dupree@uhcl.edu
DUPREE, Leslie, M .... 309-794-7626 133 C
lesliedupree@augustana.edu
DUPREE, Paul .... 704-216-7114 337 F
paul.dupree@rccc.edu
DUPREE, Paul, J .... 859-858-3511 179 D
pdupree@asbury.edu
DUPREE JONES, Kim .... 503-413-7694 373 F
kim.jones@linfield.edu
DUPRIEST, Barclay, F ... 804-752-7371 469 F
bdupries@rmc.edu
DUPUIS, Chad .... 315-781-3103 301 F
dupuisc@hws.edu
DUPUIS, Mishelle .... 910-938-6251 333 F
dupuism@coastalcarolina.edu
DURAJ, Jonathan .... 937-327-7817 364 D
jduraj@wittenberg.edu
DURALL, Changamire ... 504-520-7490 193 E
cdurall1@xula.edu
DURAN, Adrianna .... 915-779-8031 457 F
DURAN, Armando .... 626-585-7148.. 56 D
axduran@pasadena.edu
DURAN, Cristina .... 505-454-3456 286 J
duranc@nmhu.edu
DURAN, Jennie Marie .. 518-320-1851 315 H
DURAN, Michael, S ...... 505-984-6000 288 C
msduran@sjc.edu
DURAN, Richard, P ...... 210-829-6968 453 C
rduran@uiwtx.edu
DURAN, Veronica .... 520-494-5481.. 11 K
veronica.duran@centralaz.edu
DURAN-CERDA,
Dolores .... 520-206-4999.. 15 B
dcerda@pima.edu
DURAND,
Alain-Philippe .... 520-621-9294.. 16 D
adurand@arizona.edu
DURAND, David .... 415-455-8088.. 53 B
DURAND, Gene .... 707-527-4011.. 63 D
DURANT, Brian, M .... 315-255-1743 292 G
bdurant@cayuga-cc.edu
DURANT, Joyce, M .... 843-661-1301 409 G
jdurant@fmarion.edu
DURANT, Leroy, A .... 803-535-5341 407 D
ldurant@claflin.edu
DURANT, Natalie .... 860-768-5565.. 89 G
ndurant@hartford.edu
DURANT, Richard .... 909-794-1084.. 39 E
DURANT DANCEL,
Samantha .... 415-703-9577.. 28 B
sdurant@cca.edu
DURANT-JONES, Lisa ... 585-389-2775 307 F
ldurant4@naz.edu
DURANTE, Angela .... 773-298-3000 149 D
DURAZO, Marco, A .... 805-482-2755.. 59 G
rector@stjohnsem.edu
DURBAK, Andres .... 773-907-4708 135 C
adurbak@ccc.edu
DURBEN, Katherine .... 414-288-5470 493 E
katherine.durben@marquette.edu
DURBIN, Bryce .... 706-236-2282 116 B
bdurbin@berry.edu
DURBIN, Daniel .... 502-852-5555 186 A
daniel.durbin.1@louisville.edu
DURBIN, Kelly .... 505-428-1814 288 E
kelly.durbin@sfcc.edu
DURBIN, Rachel .... 503-494-7800 374 H
finaid@ohsu.edu
DURDELLA, Caroline ..... 562-908-3412.. 58 L
cdurdella@riohondo.edu
DURDEN, Lori, S .... 912-871-1638 123 J
ldurden@ogeecheetech.edu
DURDEN, Robert .... 434-218-4540 472 D
uvimco@uvimco.org
DURDEN, Tracey .... 734-432-5673 227 C
tdurden@madonna.edu
DUREN, Brad .... 580-349-1498 367 F
duren@opsu.edu
DURFEE, Carissa .... 617-989-4086 219 F
durfeec@wit.edu
DURFEE, Jeffrey, A .... 904-620-2820 111 B
jdurfee@unf.edu
DURGIN, Tricia .... 208-885-6469 132 F
triciadurgin@uidaho.edu
DURGLO, Dan .... 406-275-4972 265 F
dan_durglo@skc.edu

D'AMBROSIO, Steve ..... 856-227-7200 276 E
sdambrosio@camdencc.edu
D'AMBROSIO, Teresa ... 206-239-4500 478 H
D'AMBROSIO, Vincent .. 352-588-8432 107 D
vincent.dambrosio@saintleo.edu
D'AMICO, Doreen .... 212-410-8054 308 E
ddamico@nycpm.edu
D'AMICO, Gabrielle ...... 570-408-4510 403 A
gabrielle.damico@wilkes.edu
D'AMICO, Janna .... 517-265-5161 220 G
jdamico@adrian.edu
D'AMIL, Bonita .... 646-378-6153 310 D
bonita.damil@nyack.edu
D'AMORE, Jonathan ..... 802-654-2000 462 G
jdamore@smcvt.edu
D'AMOUR, Angela .... 805-565-7089.. 76 A
adamour@westmont.edu
D'ANDREA, Jennifer ..... 860-685-3196.. 90 B
jdandrea@wesleyan.edu
D'ANDREA, Jennifer ...... 845-341-4179 310 G
jennifer.dandrea@sunyorange.edu
D'ANGELO, Frank .... 928-771-4885.. 16 J
frank.dangelo@yc.edu
D'ANGELO, Kathryn, P . 215-204-6545 399 B
kathryn.dangelo@temple.edu
D'ANGELO, Louann ...... 413-572-5622 213 F
ldangelo@westfield.ma.edu
D'ANNA, Debora .... 828-641-0594 327 B
debora.danna@brevard.edu
D'APRIX, Kathleen .... 315-498-6088 310 F
k.a.daprix@sunyocc.edu
D'AQUILA, Richard .... 847-491-8400 146 E
richard.daquila@northwestern.edu
D'AQUINO, Erik .... 386-506-3810.. 98 D
erik.d'aquino@daytonastate.edu
D'ARCANGELO, Deb ..... 609-984-1100 284 C
D'ARCY, Kelly .... 580-745-2948 369 G
kdarcy@se.edu
D'ARCY, Kim .... 949-582-4206.. 65 D
kdarcy@saddleback.edu
D'ARGENIO, John .... 518-783-2450 315 E
dargenio@siena.edu
D'COSTA, Richard .... 787-761-0640 511 E
rdcostaofrey@utcpr.edu
D'CUNHA, Fidelis .... 313-496-2536 232 E
fdcunha2@wcccd.edu
D'EATH, Kelly .... 256-549-8266.... 2 B
kdeath@gadsdenstate.edu
D'ELIA, Christopher ...... 225-578-8574 189 E
cdelia@lsu.edu
D'EMILIO, Deanne, H ... 215-641-5548 385 A
demilio.d@gmercyu.edu
D'EMILIO, Matthew ...... 412-628-4256 380 C
mdemilio@andrew.cmu.edu
D'ITALIA, Alexandra ..... 213-738-5729.. 66 B
aditalia@swlaw.edu
D'MONTE, Loreto .... 909-593-3511.. 71 C
ldmonte@laverne.edu
D'OLIVO, Amy .... 908-852-1400 276 G
dolivoa@centenaryuniversity.edu
D'SA, Vinessa .... 314-838-8858 261 F
vdsa@ugst.edu
D'SOUZA, Gerard .... 936-261-2212 446 C
gedsouza@pvamu.edu

E

EACKER, Anne .... 888-576-3348.. 46 I
EADE, Chuck .... 218-477-2131 239 E
chuck.eade@mnstate.edu
EADES, Annemarie .... 678-839-6100 127 C
aeades@westga.edu
EADES, Timothy .... 405-491-6600 369 H
teades@snu.edu
EADIE, Danielle .... 716-839-8337 298 A
dseadie@daemen.edu
EADS, Amy .... 423-869-6751 421 A
amy.eads@lmunet.edu
EADS, Jessica, L .... 516-463-6318 301 G
jessica.l.eads@hofstra.edu
EADS, Sonja .... 606-759-7141 182 E
sonja.eads@kctcs.edu
EADY, Daniel, P .... 214-768-3999 444 D
deady@smu.edu
EADY, Niya .... 404-225-4452 115 H
neady@atlantatech.edu
EAFFORD, Felisa .... 216-987-5229 351 E
felisa.eafford@tri-c.edu
EAGAN, Johanna .... 303-384-2589.. 79 J
jeagan@mines.edu
EAGAN, John .... 617-333-2974 208 G
jeagan1008@curry.edu
EAGAN, Paige .... 269-488-4468 225 G
peagan@kvcc.edu
EAGEN, Michael, J .... 413-545-2554 211 G
meagen@provost.umass.edu
EAGER, Pamela .... 412-268-2135 380 C
eager@cmu.edu
EAGER, Trenton .... 251-405-7034.... 1 E
teager@bishop.edu
EAGLE, Steve .... 513-745-3741 364 G
0565mgr@fheg.follett.com
EAGLE, Teresa .... 304-746-8924 489 M
thardman@marshall.edu
EAHEART, Maggie .... 773-298-3301 149 D
eaheart@sxu.edu
EAKER, David .... 602-275-7133.. 15 M
EAKER, Jodie .... 815-772-7218 145 B
jeaker@morrisontech.edu
EAKIN, Amber .... 757-382-9900.. 93 H
EAKINS, Lewis .... 208-282-2515 131 G
eakilewi@isu.edu
EANES, Berenecea, J .... 718-262-2350 295 E
bjeanes@york.cuny.edu
EANNACE, Maryrose ...... 315-786-2235 303 C
meannace@sunyjefferson.edu
EANOCHS, LaDonna ...... 601-877-6123 245 A
lweanochs@alcorn.edu
EAPEN, Jacob .... 215-751-8029 381 I
jeapen@ccp.edu
EAR, Saovra .... 206-934-6964 483 C
saovra.ear@seattlecolleges.edu
EARHART, Alan .... 956-665-3572 455 D
alan.earhart@utrgv.edu
EARICK, Mary .... 505-454-3146 286 J
maryearick@nmhu.edu
EARL, Brittany .... 417-328-1500 259 I
bearl@sbuniv.edu
EARL, Bryan .... 313-593-5070 231 I
earlb@umich.edu
EARL, Danielle .... 914-961-8313 314 H
dearl@svots.edu
EARL, Olen .... 404-727-8346 118 E
olen.earl@emory.edu
EARL, Todd .... 417-328-1843 259 I
tearl@sbuniv.edu
EARL, Twyler .... 405-789-6400 369 H
tearl@snu.edu
EARL-REPLOGLE,
Melanie .... 417-873-7444 252 G
mearl@drury.edu
EARLE, David .... 620-278-2173 177 H
EARLE, Heather, A .... 603-646-9442 273 D
heather.a.earle@dartmouth.edu
EARLE, Jonathan, H ...... 225-578-2735 189 E
jearle@lsu.edu
EARLE, Shannon, C ...... 828-250-3913 342 B
searle@unca.edu
EARLE, Steven, R .... 562-903-4740.. 27 A
steve.earle@biola.edu
EARLEY, Jeff .... 540-231-6905 476 C
jearley@vt.edu
EARLEY, Rita .... 828-766-1290 336 A
rearley@mayland.edu
EARLY, Amy .... 503-399-6239 372 B
amy.early@chemeketa.edu
EARLY, Johnnie .... 850-599-3301 109 I
johnnie.early@famu.edu
EARLY, Lisa .... 410-951-3666 204 B
learly@coppin.edu
EARLY, Patrick .... 785-670-1711 178 C
patrick.early@washburn.edu
EARNEST, Bruce .... 251-442-2325.... 8 C
bearnest@umobile.edu
EARNEST, Greta .... 212-217-4370 299 D
greta_earnest@fitnyc.edu
EARNEST, Melissa .... 309-672-5513 144 C
mearnest@methodistcol.edu
EARNEST, Mike .... 907-474-7500.. 10 A
wmearnest@alaska.edu
EARNEST, Sarah .... 978-232-2042 209 E
searnest@endicott.edu
EARP, Christy .... 336-838-6117 339 B
cbearp774@wilkescc.edu
EARP, Samantha .... 413-585-2618 218 H
searp@smith.edu
EASLEY, Dawn .... 763-576-4268 237 E
dawn.easley@anokatech.edu
EASLEY, II, Jacob .... 212-463-0400 322 G
jacob.easley@touro.edu
EASLEY, II, Jacob .... 212-463-0400 322 F
jacob.easley@touro.edu
EASLEY, John .... 870-733-6841.. 17 F
jaeasley@asumidsouth.edu
EASLEY, Mike .... 704-233-8299 344 F
m.easley@wingate.edu
EASOM, Lauren .... 478-445-5384 119 B
lauren.easom@gcsu.edu
EASON, Rod .... 641-472-1204 168 C
reason@miu.edu
EASON, Wayne .... 601-635-2111 246 A
weason@eccc.edu
EASTBERG, Jodi .... 414-382-6231 491 F
jodi.eastberg@alverno.edu
EASTER, Michael .... 573-518-2188 256 D
mreaster@mineralarea.edu
EASTER-PILCHER,
Andrea .... 801-626-6159 461 A
aeasterpilcher@weber.edu
EASTERBROOK,
Jonathan .... 860-768-5096.. 89 G
easterbro@hartford.edu
EASTERLING, Mayson ... 864-231-2000 406 F
measterling@andersonuniversity.edu
EASTERLING,
W. Samuel .... 515-294-9988 163 G
wse@iastate.edu
EASTERWOOD, Allyson . 601-266-5005 249 F
allyson.easterwood@usm.edu
EASTHAM, Sabine .... 270-384-8236 183 G
easthams@lindsey.edu
EASTHAM, Yvette .... 270-707-3731 182 B
yvette.eastham@kctcs.edu
EASTIN, Elizabeth .... 602-383-8228.. 16 C
eeastin@uat.edu
EASTIN, Graig, R .... 518-276-6247 312 C
eastig@rpi.edu
EASTIN, Todd, B .... 602-243-8245.. 14 A
todd.eastin@southmountaincc.edu
EASTLICK, Beth .... 919-681-0405 328 F
beth.eastlick@duke.edu
EASTMAN, Diana .... 605-394-2497 416 H
diana.eastman@sdsmt.edu
EASTMAN, Doug .... 802-224-3009 463 D
doug.eastman@vsc.edu
EASTMAN, Karen .... 423-697-4791 424 A
karen.eastman@chattanoogastate.edu
EASTMAN, Katharine, G 617-333-2935 208 G
garrett.eastman@curry.edu
EASTMAN, Ken .... 405-744-5064 367 G
ken.eastman@okstate.edu
EASTMAN, Lori .... 518-580-5640 315 F
leastman@skidmore.edu
EASTMAN, Michele, A .. 301-405-5025 202 H
meastman@umd.edu
EASTMAN, Mindy, R ..... 641-422-4363 168 G
eastmmin@niacc.edu
EASTMAN, Nancy .... 816-802-3466 254 D
neastman@kcai.edu
EASTMAN, Rayshawn .... 513-244-4467 356 F
rayshawn.eastman@msj.edu
EASTON, Celia, A .... 585-245-5541 318 B
easton@geneseo.edu
EASTON, Nancy .... 773-442-4650 146 A
n-easton@neiu.edu
EASTON, Patricia .... 909-607-3318.. 37 C
patricia.easton@cgu.edu
EASTON, Rebecca .... 806-371-5982 429 E
rreaston@actx.edu
EASTON, Stephen, D ..... 701-483-2326 345 C
steve.easton@dickinsonstate.edu
EASTON-BROOKS,
Donald .... 775-682-7853 271 E
deastonbrooks@unr.edu
EASTRIDGE, Julie .... 641-844-5571 167 G
julie.eastridge@iavalley.edu
EASTRIDGE, Julie .... 641-844-5571 167 E
julie.eastridge@iavalley.edu
EASTRIDGE, June .... 702-992-2863 271 B
june.eastridge@nsc.edu
EASTWICK, Thomas .... 201-327-8877 277 F
teastwick@eastwick.edu
EASTWICK, Thomas ...... 973-661-0600 277 E
teastwick@eastwick.edu
EASTWICK, Thomas, M . 201-327-8877 277 D
EATMAN, Lynne .... 318-670-6000 191 D
EATON, Adrienne .... 848-932-9503 282 A
eaton@smlr.rutgers.edu
EATON, Amy .... 503-943-8615 377 A
eaton@up.edu
EATON, Andrew .... 856-222-9311 281 C
aeaton@rcbc.edu
EATON, Brett .... 336-758-5237 344 C
eatonbd@wfu.edu
EATON, Charlee .... 603-899-4097 273 E
eatonc@franklinpierce.edu
EATON, Emily .... 309-467-6826 138 A
eeaton@eureka.edu
EATON, Janet .... 419-517-8987 355 C
jeaton@lourdes.edu
EATON, Patrick, D .... 662-720-7165 248 C
pdeaton@nemcc.edu
EATON, Robert .... 401-456-8776 405 A
reaton@ric.edu
EATON, Rosalyn .... 507-786-3615 243 D
reaton@stolaf.edu
EATON, Stephanie .... 314-516-5765 261 C
stephanie@umsl.edu
EATON, Tim .... 812-888-4450 162 F
teaton@vinu.edu
EATON, Timothy, W ...... 405-912-9456 368 J
teaton@ru.edu
EAVENSON, Dave .... 910-630-7182 331 E
deavenson@methodist.edu
EAVES, Philip, J .... 330-569-5103 353 G
eavespj@hiram.edu
EAVES, Robert .... 803-934-3229 410 G
reaves@morris.edu
EAVES, Stephen .... 615-460-8118 418 B
stephen.eaves@belmont.edu
EAVES-MCLENNAN,
Kristi .... 919-760-8455 331 D
eavesk@meredith.edu
EBARB, Lisa .... 318-675-6505 189 I
lisa.ebarb@lsuhs.edu
EBBING, Jeff .... 319-208-5060 170 D
jebbing@scciowa.edu
EBBOTT, Mary .... 508-793-2335 208 D
mebbott@holycross.edu
EBBS, George, H .... 757-594-7184 465 M
george.ebbs@cnu.edu
EBEL, Malia, M .... 603-526-3375 272 H
malia.ebel@colby-sawyer.edu
EBENHACK, Kori .... 541-956-7196 376 A
kebenhack@roguecc.edu
EBER, Hayley .... 212-353-4220 297 E
hayley.eber@cooper.edu
EBERHARDT, David .... 205-226-4731.... 4 F
deberhar@bsc.edu
EBERHARDT, Russell .... 605-698-3966 416 B
reberhardt@swcollege.edu
EBERHART, Becky, J ..... 847-866-3938 138 D
becky.eberhart@garrett.edu
EBERHART, John .... 269-782-1207 231 A
jeberhart@swmich.edu
EBERL, Jason .... 314-977-2500 259 F
jason.eberl@slu.edu
EBERLE, Jeanette .... 863-638-2978 114 B
eberleja@webber.edu
EBERLE, John .... 615-248-1234 426 D
jeberle@trevecca.edu
EBERLE, Matt .... 480-245-7969.. 12 M
matt.eberle@tricityministries.org
EBERLE, Sarah, D .... 701-355-8126 347 C
sdeberle@umary.edu
EBERLY, Jamie .... 402-872-2436 268 E
jeberly@peru.edu
EBERSOLE, Erin .... 301-934-7621 198 G
erebersole@scmd.edu
EBERSOLE, Susan .... 718-960-8000 294 A
susan.ebersole@lehman.cuny.edu
EBERT, Chris .... 559-791-2370.. 47 A
chris.ebert@portervillecollege.edu
EBERT, Jason .... 920-693-1732 498 H
jason.ebert@gotoltc.edu
EBERT, Loretta .... 518-783-2550 315 E
lebert@siena.edu
EBERT, Stacy .... 281-756-5601 429 D
sebert@alvincollege.edu
EBERT, Tina, L .... 417-268-6006 250 G
tebert@gobbc.edu
EBERT-HOLBERG, Olga . 865-539-7283 425 B
odeberthiberg@pstcc.edu
EBERTH, Denise .... 269-927-8704 226 F
deberth@lakemichigancollege.edu
EBERTS, Keirsten .... 260-665-4675 161 E
ebertsk@trine.edu
EBERTZ, Susan J, S ..... 563-589-0265 171 A
library@wartburgseminary.edu
EBLEN-ZAYAS, Melissa . 507-222-5367 234 G
meblenza@carleton.edu
EBNER, Laura .... 773-244-5726 145 G
lmebner@northpark.edu
EBNER, Timothy, J .... 801-581-5808 459 O
tim.ebner@utah.edu
EBONG, Imeh .... 661-654-3344.. 30 B
iebong@csub.edu
EBRAHIMPOUR, Maling 401-874-4244 405 E
mebrahimpour@uri.edu
EBRON, Kienesha .... 252-618-6675 334 D
ebronk@edgecombe.edu
ECABERT, Gayle .... 859-371-9393 179 G
gecabert@beckfield.edu

EDWARDS, Karen .... 251-460-7092.... 9 A
cedwards@southalabama.edu
EDWARDS, Karen, K ..... 641-269-3703 166 G
edwardsk@grinnell.edu
EDWARDS, Karin .... 360-992-2101 478 I
kedwards@clark.edu
EDWARDS, Katherine .... 415-422-5209.. 72 J
kedwards3@usfca.edu
EDWARDS, Katie .... 817-598-6479 457 J
kedwards@wc.edu
EDWARDS, Keith .... 518-243-4196 291 D
edwardsk@ellismedicine.org
EDWARDS, Lacy .... 863-638-1431 114 B
EDWARDS, Lauralea ...... 801-957-4888 461 C
lauralea.edwards@slcc.edu
EDWARDS, Lola .... 229-430-1702 114 I
ledwards@albanytech.edu
EDWARDS, Luanne .... 419-447-6442 361 D
EDWARDS, Mark, H ...... 315-655-7334 292 H
medwards@cazenovia.edu
EDWARDS, Mary, A ...... 304-336-8000 490 B
edwardsm@westliberty.edu
EDWARDS, Mary Ann ... 304-336-8000 490 B
edwardsm@westliberty.edu
EDWARDS, Michael ...... 641-673-2120 171 C
edwardsml@wmpenn.edu
EDWARDS, Natasha ...... 718-489-2035 313 E
nedwards2@sfc.edu
EDWARDS, Nigel .... 850-599-3183 109 I
nigel.edwards@famu.edu
EDWARDS, Paul .... 804-861-6100 470 C
pedwards@rbc.edu
EDWARDS, JR.,
Quinton, T .... 662-915-3785 249 D
qtedward@olemiss.edu
EDWARDS, Romney ...... 314-340-3340 254 A
edwardro@hssu.edu
EDWARDS, Ronald .... 718-482-5080 294 F
rsedwards@lagcc.cuny.edu
EDWARDS, Rosie .... 334-514-5063.... 2 F
rosie.edwards@istc.edu
EDWARDS, Sarah .... 270-706-8447 181 G
sarah.edwards@kctcs.edu
EDWARDS, Scarlet .... 919-866-5457 338 G
stedwards@waketech.edu
EDWARDS, Sharon .... 931-393-1663 424 F
sedwards@mscc.edu
EDWARDS, Shawn .... 843-953-6989 407 C
shawn.edwards@citadel.edu
EDWARDS, Sheryl .... 870-235-5090.. 21 C
saedwards@saumag.edu
EDWARDS, Stephen ...... 719-884-5000.. 82 B
sfedwards@nbc.edu
EDWARDS, Steve .... 912-583-3218 116 E
sedwards@bpc.edu
EDWARDS, Susan .... 617-254-2610 218 E
susan.edwards@sjs.edu
EDWARDS, Susan, L ..... 937-775-2312 364 E
susan.edwards@wright.edu
EDWARDS, Tamika .... 501-975-8543.. 20 F
tedwards@philander.edu
EDWARDS, Terry .... 334-386-7940.... 5 C
tedwards@faulkner.edu
EDWARDS, Thomas ...... 207-859-1362 196 D
edwardst@thomas.edu
EDWARDS, Tim .... 205-652-3457.... 9 B
tedwards@uwa.edu
EDWARDS, Timothy ...... 208-882-1566 132 C
timedwards@nsa.edu
EDWARDS, Tina, L .... 260-982-5001 159 J
tledwards@manchester.edu
EDWARDS, Tony .... 740-392-6868 356 G
tony.edwards@mvnu.edu
EDWARDS, Tracy .... 405-945-3376 368 C
tracy.edwards@okstate.edu
EDWARDS, Verneda ...... 785-594-6451 171 F
EDWARDS, Wanda .... 910-275-6364 335 E
wedwards@jamessprunt.edu
EDWARDS, Wayne .... 516-876-3207 318 C
edwardsw@oldwestbury.edu
EDWARDS-GILBERT,
Gretchen .... 909-607-9100.. 63 F
EDWARDS LANGE,
Sheila .... 206-934-4144 483 A
sheila.edwardslange@seattlecolleges.edu
EDWARDS LANGE,
Sheila .... 253-692-5646 485 A
sredward@uw.edu
EDWARDS-NEFF,
Denise .... 626-815-6000.. 26 F
EDWARDSON, Anton ..... 907-852-1776.... 9 H
anton.edwardson@ilisagvik.edu

EDWIN, Shirin .... 651-793-1727 238 I
shirin.edwin@metrostate.edu
EDYTHE, Abdullah, E .... 904-620-5408 111 B
e.abdullah@unf.edu
EE, Marvin .... 254-295-8620 453 D
mee@umhb.edu
EFTHIMIOU, Chris .... 718-289-5169 293 B
chris.efthimiou@bcc.cuny.edu
EFTHYMIOU,
Lampeto (Betty) .... 718-631-6611 295 C
lefthymiou@qcc.cuny.edu
EFURD, Melissa .... 479-308-2284.. 17 A
melissa.efurd@arcomedu.org
EGAN, Beth-Anne .... 860-253-3030.. 86 C
began@asnuntuck.edu
EGAN, Brian .... 973-684-5999 280 A
began@pccc.edu
EGAN, Carolyn .... 850-644-4440 110 C
cegan@fsu.edu
EGAN, Eric .... 760-921-5520.. 56 A
eegan@paloverde.edu
EGAN, Jodi .... 575-654-0963 435 E
humanresources@diu.edu
EGAN, Jonathon .... 562-947-8755.. 65 I
jonathonegan@scuhs.edu
EGAN, Kristen .... 847-628-2017 141 C
kristen.egan@judsonu.edu
EGAN, Maryan .... 239-590-1130 109 K
megan@fgcu.edu
EGAN, Michael .... 309-794-8965 133 C
mikeegan@augustana.edu
EGAN, Michelle .... 574-284-4601 160 I
mlegan@saintmarys.edu
EGAN, Russi .... 530-541-4660.. 47 E
egan@ltcc.edu
EGAN, Thomas .... 215-572-2900 378 E
egant@arcadia.edu
EGBE, Daniel .... 501-370-5268.. 20 F
degbe@philander.edu
EGBE, Emmanuel .... 718-270-5170 294 G
egbe@mec.cuny.edu
EGBERT, Edwin, C .... 605-342-0317 415 C
eegbert@jwc.edu
EGBERT, Jean .... 651-385-6349 239 B
jegbert@southeastmn.edu
EGBERT, Jeb .... 949-783-4800.. 74 L
jegbert@westcoastuniversity.edu
EGENESS, Cynthia .... 651-690-6864 243 A
cnegeness@stkate.edu
EGERSON, Veronica, V . 414-464-9777 498 B
egerson.veronica@wspp.edu
EGGEBRECHT, Erin .... 815-967-7302 148 C
eeggebrecht@rockfordcareercollege.edu
EGGENSPERGER,
Martin .... 870-248-4000.. 18 F
martin.eggensperger@blackrivertech.edu
EGGER, Thomas, J .... 314-505-7011 252 A
eggert@csl.edu
EGGERS, Marilyn .... 909-558-7658.. 48 E
meggers@llu.edu
EGGERS, Ron .... 252-399-6417 326 K
reggers@barton.edu
EGGERS, Troy .... 212-854-5939 297 C
te99@columbia.edu
EGGERS-BUTTES,
Jessica, H .... 260-399-7700 162 B
jbuttes@sf.edu
EGGERT, Mary .... 414-930-3354 494 E
eggertm@mtmary.edu
EGGIMAN, Jessica .... 864-596-9055 408 F
jessica.eggiman@converse.edu
EGGIMANN, Becky .... 630-752-5646 153 C
becky.eggimann@wheaton.edu
EGGLESTON, Chad .... 254-299-8672 439 E
ceggleston@mclennan.edu
EGGLESTON, Joseph ..... 562-947-8755.. 65 I
josepheggleston@scuhs.edu
EGGLESTON,
Kathryn, K .... 972-238-6364 435 C
keggleston@dcccd.edu
EGGLESTON, Kevin .... 724-938-1626 393 E
eggleston@calu.edu
EGGLESTON, Meghan ... 276-656-0285 474 G
meggleston@patrickhenry.edu
EGGLESTON, Tami .... 618-537-4481 144 A
EGGLESTON, Tami .... 618-537-6926 144 A
teggleston@mckendree.edu
EGLE, Don .... 903-233-3290 439 A
donegle@letu.edu
EGLSAER, Richard .... 936-294-1001 450 A
eglsaer@shsu.edu

EGUARAS, Agnes .... 818-240-1000.. 43 G
aeguaras@glendale.edu
EHLER, Gina, M .... 262-524-7247 492 A
gehler@carrollu.edu
EHLERS, Chris .... 918-781-7233 365 C
ehlersc@bacone.edu
EHLERS, Kathleen .... 617-670-4501 209 G
kehlers@fisher.edu
EHLERS, Pam .... 405-744-2122 367 G
pam.ehlers@okstate.edu
EHLERT, Alycia .... 386-506-3769.. 98 D
alycia.ehlert@daytonastate.edu
EHLING, Andrew .... 620-242-0582 176 B
ehlinga@mcpherson.edu
EHLING, Andrew .... 505-454-3351 286 J
aehling@nmhu.edu
EHLING, William .... 252-328-6387 341 A
ehlingw16@ecu.edu
EHMAN, Amanda .... 740-245-7443 363 A
amandae@rio.edu
EHMANN, Sue-Ann .... 276-656-0206 474 G
sehmann@patrickhenry.edu
EHMEN, Stacy, L .... 217-443-8746 136 G
stacy@dacc.edu
EHMIG, Ashley .... 503-244-0726 371 E
EHMKE, Pamela .... 620-432-0400 176 D
pehmke@neosho.edu
EHNOT, Jillian .... 406-791-5307 265 H
jillian.ehnot@uprovidence.edu
EHRESMAN, Terry .... 620-278-4264 177 H
tehresman@sterling.edu
EHRHARDT, Emily .... 319-399-8663 164 F
eehrhardt@coe.edu
EHRLICH, Anne .... 717-337-6921 384 D
aehrlich@gettysburg.edu
EHRLICH, Brian .... 321-674-8832 100 C
behrlich@fit.edu
EHRLICH, Robert .... 660-626-2297 250 A
rehrlich@atsu.edu
EHRMAN, James, E .... 717-866-5775 383 F
james.ehrman@evangelical.edu
EHRMAN, Jim .... 206-876-6100 483 H
ehrman@theseattleschool.edu
EHRMAN, Sheryl .... 408-924-3800.. 34 A
sheryl.ehrman@sjsu.edu
EHST, Suzanne .... 574-535-7839 155 E
sehst@goshen.edu
EICHELROTH, Kathleen . 508-929-8098 213 G
keichelroth@worcester.edu
EICHENBERGER, Julie ... 620-223-2700 173 I
juliee@fortscott.edu
EICHENSTEIN, Joseph ... 732-985-6533 280 E
EICHER, Michael .... 614-292-9858 358 D
eicher@osu.edu
EICHHORN, Gregory ..... 203-932-7492.. 89 H
geichhorn@newhaven.edu
EICHHORN, Kristen, C .. 315-312-3152 318 D
kristen.eichhorn@oswego.edu
EICHHORST, Amy .... 301-405-2102 202 H
aeich@umd.edu
EICHINGER, Stephen ..... 212-517-0400 305 E
EICHLER, Richard .... 212-854-2878 297 C
re1@columbia.edu
EICHNER, John .... 716-614-6431 309 G
jeichner@niagaracc.suny.edu
EICHOLTZ, Kristin .... 610-282-1100 382 C
kristin.eicholtz@desales.edu
EICHORST, Christopher . 509-777-4780 486 C
ceichorst@whitworth.edu
EICKE, Dustin .... 308-635-6026 270 C
eicked@wncc.edu
EICKEN, Hajo .... 907-474-7331.. 10 A
heicken@alaska.edu
EICKHOFF, Chad, A ...... 928-523-8558.. 14 H
chad.eickhoff@nau.edu
EICKHOFF, Jeffrey .... 402-643-4052 269 A
sggs@sggs.edu
EICKHOLT, Marcia .... 419-227-3141 362 F
marcia@unoh.edu
EICKHORST, Lindsay ..... 309-268-8031 138 H
lindsay.eickhorst@heartland.edu
EICKMAN, Joseph .... 715-394-8461 497 C
jeickman@uwsuper.edu
EID, Haitham .... 504-286-5010 191 C
heid@suno.edu
EID, Hanan .... 626-264-8880.. 71 F
EIDE, Kevin .... 414-955-4888 493 F
keide@mcw.edu
EIDELMAN, Lipa .... 732-370-1560 275 G
EIDGAHY, Saeid .... 714-564-6606.. 58 F
eidgahy_saeid@sac.edu
EIDSON, Kevin .... 615-966-7190 421 B
kevin.eidson@lipscomb.edu

EIDSON, Kristi .... 270-686-4216 179 J
kristi.eidson@brescia.edu
EIDSON, Natasha .... 580-349-1356 367 F
natasha.eidson@opsu.edu
EIDSON, Paul .... 406-799-1515 262 I
dreidson@apollos.edu
EIDSON, Scott .... 406-604-4320 262 I
drscott@apollos.edu
EIDSON, Steve .... 229-430-6619 114 I
seidson@albanytech.edu
EIFERT, Robert .... 217-824-4004 142 C
reifert@lakeland.cc.il.us
EIGHMY, Sunny .... 641-628-5272 164 D
eighmys@central.edu
EIGHMY, Taylor .... 210-458-4101 455 E
taylor.eighmy@utsa.edu
EIGNER, Tony .... 864-977-3219 410 I
tony.eigner@ngu.edu
EIKE, Claire .... 312-629-9379 149 F
ceike@saic.edu
EIKENBERRY, Michael .. 317-940-8940 154 C
meikenbe@butler.edu
EILER, Claire .... 610-917-1461 401 G
cmeiler@valleyforge.edu
EILERS, Kay .... 414-229-7194 496 B
kceilers@uwm.edu
EILOLA, William, T .... 419-772-2261 358 C
w-eilola@onu.edu
EIMER, Greg, A .... 217-735-7222 142 H
geimer@lincolncollege.edu
EIMERS, Mardy, T .... 573-882-4077 261 A
eimersm@missouri.edu
EINFELD, Aaron .... 616-957-7035 222 B
aaron@calvinseminary.edu
EINHELLIG, Frank, E ..... 417-836-5119 256 G
frankeinhellig@missouristate.edu
EINOLF, Karl, W .... 260-422-5561 156 E
kweinolf@indianatech.edu
EINSPAHR, Kent .... 402-643-7315 266 G
kent.einspahr@cune.edu
EINSTEIN, Heath, A .... 817-257-7490 448 F
h.einstein@tcu.edu
EIS, Linda .... 417-625-3797 256 F
eis-l@mssu.edu
EISELE, Chad, E .... 434-223-6151 467 F
ceisele@hsc.edu
EISEMAN, Margaret .... 412-396-6061 383 A
eiseman@duq.edu
EISEN, Jeffrey, M .... 919-658-7759 340 G
jeisen@umo.edu
EISEN, Karen .... 718-780-0343 291 K
karen.eisen@brooklaw.edu
EISENBACH, Regina ...... 760-750-4253.. 33 A
regina@csusm.edu
EISENBEISER, Colleen ... 410-777-1249 197 G
ckeisenbeiser@aacc.edu
EISENBERG, Ann .... 734-487-0341 223 K
aeisenbe@emich.edu
EISENBERG, Eric .... 813-974-2804 111 C
eisenberg@usf.edu
EISENBERG, Judith .... 718-289-5132 293 B
judith.eisenberg@bcc.cuny.edu
EISENBERGER, Israel .... 845-362-3053 291 B
EISENHART, Pamela ...... 717-337-6010 384 D
peisenha@gettysburg.edu
EISENHAUER, James ..... 218-879-0743 238 B
james.eisenhauer@fdltcc.edu
EISENHAUER, Jay .... 304-829-7465 487 A
jeisenhauer@bethanywv.edu
EISENHAUER, Joseph .... 313-993-1204 231 E
eisenhjg@udmercy.edu
EISENHAUER, Ryan, L .. 575-624-8291 287 B
eisenhauer@nmmi.edu
EISENHAUER, Thomas .. 816-415-5990 262 F
eisenhauer@william.jewell.edu
EISENHOUR, Lyn .... 425-352-8548 478 D
leisenhour@cascadia.edu
EISENMAN, Ann .... 563-244-7040 165 L
aeisenman@eicc.edu
EISENMENGER,
Paul, W .... 309-341-7212 141 G
pweisenmenger@knox.edu
EISENSTEIN, Laya .... 718-268-4700 312 A
EISENSTEIN, Paul .... 614-823-1609 359 H
peisenstein@otterbein.edu
EISENTRAGER, Pete .... 816-235-2665 261 B
eisentragerp@umkc.edu
EISGRUBER,
Cristopher, L .... 609-258-3026 280 D
eisgrube@princeton.edu
EISLER, David, L .... 231-591-2500 224 A
davideisler@ferris.edu

EISMEIER, Michael .... 301-445-2783 202 G meismeier@usmd.edu
EISNER, Alan .... 508-793-7368 208 C aeisner@clarku.edu
EISNER, SND, Janet ...... 617-735-9825 209 D president@emmanuel.edu
EISSES, Effie .... 360-650-7610 485 I eissese@wwu.edu
EITEL, Christa .... 561-297-0884 109 J ceitel@fau.edu
EITEL, Norine .... 660-626-2391 250 A neitel@atsu.edu
EIZENGA, Shannon .... 510-549-4718.. 66 G seizenga@sksm.edu
EJIGIRI, Damien .... 225-771-3103 191 B
EJIMA, Tricia, R .... 808-956-4304 129 E ejimat@hawaii.edu
EKANGER, Holger .... 716-338-1332 303 A holgerekanger@mail.sunyjcc.edu
EKARIUS, John .... 215-503-5017 399 E john.ekarius@jefferson.edu
EKE, Kenoye .... 903-730-4890 438 D keke@jarvis.edu
EKKER, David, A .... 757-822-7197 475 E dekker@tcc.edu
EKLUND, Julie .... 715-425-3962 496 F uwrf@bkstr.com
EKMAN, Tom .... 615-230-3350 425 E thomas.ekman@volstate.edu
EKNESS, Ray .... 406-243-4088 263 K ray.ekness@umontana.edu
EKOUE TOTOU, Patrick . 415-883-2211.. 39 A pekouetotou@marin.edu
EKSTROM, Rodney .... 603-535-2217 275 A raekstrom@plymouth.edu
EL-AMIN, Aisha .... 312-413-3450 151 G aelami2@uic.edu
EL-BURKI, Imaani .... 610-328-7360 398 G ielburk1@swarthmore.edu
EL-DWEIK, Majed .... 573-681-5134 254 G dweikm@lincolnu.edu
EL FATTAL, David .... 805-652-5536.. 73 I delfattal@vcccd.edu
EL HACHEM, Peter .... 315-859-4129 300 H pelhache@hamilton.edu
EL-HAGGAN, Ahmed ..... 410-951-3896 204 B aelhaggan@coppin.edu
EL-HASHEMY, Shehab .. 503-552-1848 374 D selhashemy@nunm.edu
EL JAMAL, Haaneen ..... 914-694-4606 296 B heljamal@riversidehealth.org
EL-KHOURY, Nadim ...... 413-748-3925 218 I nel-khoury@springfield.edu
EL-KHOURY, Rodolphe . 305-284-9092 113 C rxe66@miami.edu
EL-OSERY, Aly .... 575-835-5481 286 K aly.elosery@nmt.edu
EL-REWINI, Hesham ..... 703-284-1550 468 H hesham.el-rewini@marymount.edu
EL-SHEIKH, Eman .... 850-474-3074 111 F eelsheikh@uwf.edu
ELA, Mohamed .... 609-258-3000 280 D mela@princeton.edu
ELACHKO, Nicole .... 412-362-8500 396 D nelachko@pims.edu
ELAM, JR., Harry, J ...... 323-259-2691.. 54 I
ELAM, Michael, A .... 252-536-7217 335 B melam@halifaxcc.edu
ELAM, Nicole .... 205-391-2211.... 3 E
ELAM, Terry .... 574-807-7168 154 B terry.elam@bethelunivesity.edu
ELAN HELSPER, Lauren 562-860-2451.. 35 H lelanhelsper@cerritos.edu
ELAND, Tom .... 612-659-6286 239 A thomas.eland@minneapolis.edu
ELARDE, Chris .... 914-923-2804 311 A
ELAZIER, Molly .... 209-382-4508.. 70 A melazier@ucmerced.edu
ELBASSIOUNY, Samir ... 908-835-2334 284 H selbassiouny@warren.edu
ELBE, Michael .... 217-641-4101 141 A melbe@jwcc.edu
ELBERT, Erickia .... 336-285-3771 341 D edelbert@ncat.edu
ELDAHAN, Wanda .... 423-869-6023 421 A wanda.eldahan@lmunet.edu
ELDAYRIE, Elias, G .... 352-273-1788 111 A eldayrie@ufl.edu
ELDEMIRE, Flavia .... 803-255-4742 406 D feldemire@allenuniversity.edu
ELDER, Britni .... 501-450-3181.. 23 H belder@uca.edu
ELDER, Darla .... 814-732-2743 394 B delder@edinboro.edu
ELDER, Gregory .... 229-500-3076 114 H gregory.elder@asurams.edu
ELDER, Jill .... 605-718-2411 417 D jill.elder@wdt.edu
ELDER, Keith .... 601-925-3202 247 C kelder@mc.edu
ELDER, Kelly .... 412-268-8977 380 C kelder@andrew.cmu.edu
ELDER, Shelia .... 404-962-3002 127 D shelia.elder@usg.edu
ELDER, Steve .... 501-205-8893.. 18 H selder@cbc.edu
ELDERS, Candice .... 269-927-8198 226 F celders@lakemichigancollege.edu
ELDREDGE, Keith .... 718-817-4350 300 C eldredge@fordham.edu
ELDRIDGE, Audrey .... 208-562-3509 131 E audreyeldridge@cwi.edu
ELDRIDGE, Connie .... 847-574-5264 142 B celdridge@lfgsm.edu
ELDRIDGE, Gwenn .... 765-602-2415 158 D geldridge6@ivytech.edu
ELDRIDGE, Jacqueline .. 501-420-1252.. 16 L jacqueline.eldridge@arkansasbaptist.edu
ELDRIDGE, Jonathan ..... 415-485-9619.. 39 A jeldridge@marin.edu
ELDRIDGE, Karen .... 865-981-8207 421 C karen.eldridge@maryvillecollege.edu
ELDRIDGE, Paul, J .... 951-343-4492.. 27 G peldridge@calbaptist.edu
ELDRIDGE, Ray .... 615-966-5946 421 B ray.eldridge@lipscomb.edu
ELDRIDGE, Ricky .... 310-506-4702.. 56 G richard.eldridge@pepperdine.edu
ELDRIDGE, Sara .... 507-786-3885 243 D eldrid1@stolaf.edu
ELEDGE, Jean .... 423-473-3795 420 H jeledge@leeuniversity.edu
ELEFF, Zev .... 847-982-2500 138 I eleff@htc.edu
ELEFF, Zev .... 215-635-7300 384 E president@gratz.edu
ELENICH, Richard .... 906-487-2763 228 A rjelenic@mtu.edu
ELENWO, Elizabeth .... 619-549-3974.. 65 G elizabeth.elenwo@socalsem.edu
ELFRING, Lisa, K .... 520-621-1671.. 16 D elfring@arizona.edu
ELFRINK, Stephanie ...... 314-529-9370 255 B selfrink@maryville.edu
ELGARICO, Michael ...... 805-493-3049.. 29 C elgarico@callutheran.edu
ELGENDY, Rick .... 202-885-8670.. 94 D relgendy@wesleyseminary.edu
ELI, Lisa, G .... 407-582-6649 113 I leli@valenciacollege.edu
ELIAS, Ingrid .... 818-345-8879.. 39 D
ELIAS, Jack .... 401-863-3336 403 J jack_elias@brown.edu
ELIAS, Michael .... 610-896-1228 385 I melias@haverford.edu
ELIAS, Stephanny, J ..... 617-333-2010 208 G selias0104@curry.edu
ELIAS, Steven, M .... 970-247-7010.. 80 J selias@fortlewis.edu
ELIASSON-CREEK, Fia ... 253-833-9111 480 I feliasson-creek@greenriver.edu
ELIAV, Eli .... 585-275-5688 323 M eli_eliav@urmc.rochester.edu
ELICKER, Beth .... 207-699-5045 195 A belicker@meca.edu
ELIMIMIAN, Jonathan ... 256-761-6277.... 7 B jelimimian@talladega.edu
ELISH-PIPER, Laurie ..... 815-753-9055 146 B laurieep@niu.edu
ELIZA, Lourdes .... 787-852-1430 507 C leliza@hccpr.edu
ELIZABETH TOMPSON, Mary .... 432-837-8130 450 B mxt15av@sulross.edu
ELIZONDO, Laura, M .... 956-326-2213 446 E laura@tamiu.edu
ELIZONDO, Maria, G .... 956-872-3559 443 H marye@southtexascollege.edu
ELKESHK, Abed .... 718-405-3300 296 F abed.elkeshk@mountsaintvincent.edu
ELKINS, Abby .... 704-991-0226 338 C aelkins9340@stanly.edu
ELKINS, Brian .... 308-635-6012 270 C elkinsb@wncc.edu
ELKINS, Dan .... 309-438-7018 140 D delkins@ilstu.edu
ELKINS, Germaine .... 910-695-3706 337 H elkinsg@sandhills.edu
ELKINS, Julie, B .... 617-228-2436 214 C jelkins@bhcc.mass.edu
ELKINS, Lindsay .... 901-722-3378 423 G lelkins@sco.edu
ELKINS, Mark .... 904-596-2445 112 F melkins@tbc.edu
ELKINS, Mary Jane .... 434-949-1051 475 B mary.elkins@southside.edu
ELKINS, Paula, S .... 706-886-6831 126 D pelkins@tfc.edu
ELKINS, Penny, L .... 478-301-2120 122 E elkins_pl@mercer.edu
ELKINS, Susan .... 803-777-7695 413 A selkins@mailbox.sc.edu
ELKS, Martha .... 404-752-1881 123 E melks@msm.edu
ELLARD, Katherine .... 662-472-9134 246 D kellard@holmescc.edu
ELLARD, Mark, D .... 662-329-7145 248 A mdellard@muw.edu
ELLARD, Michael .... 609-771-3121 276 I ellardm@tcnj.edu
ELLARD, Owen, H .... 210-567-2413 456 C ellard@uthscsa.edu
ELLEITHY, Khaled, M .... 203-576-4703.. 89 C elleithy@bridgeport.edu
ELLEN, Kim .... 714-463-7547.. 51 B ekim@ketchum.edu
ELLENBERG, George, B . 850-474-2035 111 F gellenberg@uwf.edu
ELLENBERG, Kristi .... 304-205-6622 488 D kristi.ellenberg@bridgevalley.edu
ELLENS, Timothy, L ...... 616-526-6475 222 C tje6@calvin.edu
ELLER, Greg .... 850-872-3857 101 N geller@gulfcoast.edu
ELLERBE, Laverne .... 757-822-1994 475 E lellerbe@tcc.edu
ELLERKER, Charla .... 863-784-7176 108 F charla.ellerker@southflorida.edu
ELLERMAN, Paige, L ..... 513-244-4393 356 F paige.ellerman@msj.edu
ELLERTSON, Chris .... 847-735-5001 142 A ellertson@lakeforest.edu
ELLERTSON, Shari .... 208-426-1614 130 H shariellertson@boisestate.edu
ELLIBEE, Margaret .... 501-812-2216.. 23 B mellibee@uaptc.edu
ELLIFF POUND, Lee ...... 417-625-9355 256 F pound-l@mssu.edu
ELLIG, Tracy .... 406-994-5607 264 C tellig@montana.edu
ELLIMAN, JR., Donald, M .... 303-556-2400.. 84 D
ELLINGER, John, M ...... 419-372-2006 348 G johne@bgsu.edu
ELLINGHUYSEN, Conner .... 712-749-2078 164 C ellinghuysenc@bvu.edu
ELLINGHUYSEN, Scott .. 507-457-5696 241 F sellinghuysen@winona.edu
ELLINGSON, Mike .... 701-231-7307 345 F michael.ellingson@ndsu.edu
ELLINGTON, Michael, A 304-293-2702 490 E michael.ellington@mail.wvu.edu
ELLINWOOD, Dawn, M . 802-654-2566 462 G dellinwood@smcvt.edu
ELLINWOOD, Suzanne .. 970-248-1337.. 78 J sellinwo@coloradomesa.edu
ELLIOT, Jillian .... 415-575-6194.. 28 I jelliot@ciis.edu
ELLIOT, Robert .... 646-717-9764 300 E elliot@gts.edu
ELLIOT, Ryan .... 314-968-5963 262 C relliott@webster.edu
ELLIOT BROWN, Karin, A .... 323-343-3820.. 31 E kbrown5@calstatela.edu
ELLIOT-CHESLEK, Theresa .... 509-335-3564 485 D telliot@wsu.edu
ELLIOTT, Anita .... 704-406-4247 329 A arelliott@gardner-webb.edu
ELLIOTT, Brandi .... 912-260-4415 125 D brandi.elliott@sgsc.edu
ELLIOTT, Brynn .... 308-635-6186 270 C elliot1@wncc.edu
ELLIOTT, Charles, G ...... 901-435-1627 420 I charles_elliott@loc.edu
ELLIOTT, Cheryl .... 404-727-6115 118 E celliot@emory.edu
ELLIOTT, Chris .... 409-880-2292 449 F celliott@lit.edu
ELLIOTT, Clifton, R .... 843-355-4138 414 C elliottr@wiltech.edu
ELLIOTT, Crystal .... 309-677-3223 134 A celliott@bradley.edu
ELLIOTT, Deborah, M .... 315-786-2416 303 C delliott@sunyjefferson.edu
ELLIOTT, Erica .... 765-677-2075 158 B erica.elliott@indwes.edu
ELLIOTT, Fatina .... 318-670-9376 191 D felliott@susla.edu
ELLIOTT, Jacquelyn .... 520-494-5200.. 11 K jackie.elliott@centralaz.edu
ELLIOTT, James .... 312-329-4166 144 I jim.elliott@moody.edu
ELLIOTT, Jason .... 206-239-4500 478 H
ELLIOTT, Jeffrey .... 703-416-1441 466 A library@divinemercy.edu
ELLIOTT, John .... 860-486-2317.. 89 D john.elliott@uconn.edu
ELLIOTT, John, P .... 412-624-6127 400 H jelliott@cfo.pitt.edu
ELLIOTT, CPPS, Karen ... 513-244-4844 356 F karen.elliott@msj.edu
ELLIOTT, Katharine .... 601-376-4950 246 C kathy.elliott@hindscc.edu
ELLIOTT, Ken .... 601-968-8972 245 B kelliott@belhaven.edu
ELLIOTT, Kenneth .... 856-225-6244 281 G kenneth.elliott@rutgers.edu
ELLIOTT, Kiersten .... 310-434-4173.. 63 C elliott_kiersten@smc.edu
ELLIOTT, Lisa .... 254-299-8640 439 E lelliott@mclennan.edu
ELLIOTT, Mark .... 615-248-1271 426 D melliott@trevecca.edu
ELLIOTT, Mark .... 570-577-3200 379 C mark.elliott@bucknell.edu
ELLIOTT, Mary .... 303-869-5522.. 79 J mfelliot@mines.edu
ELLIOTT, Megan, C .... 812-877-8458 160 F elliott3@rose-hulman.edu
ELLIOTT, Melissa, J ...... 940-552-6291 457 C mjelliott@vernoncollege.edu
ELLIOTT, Michael .... 860-297-2000.. 89 B michael.elliott@trincoll.edu
ELLIOTT, Michael, A ..... 404-727-6062 118 E mellio2@emory.edu
ELLIOTT, Michael, S ..... 870-297-4261.. 89 B michael.elliott@trincoll.edu
ELLIOTT, Monica .... 843-355-4191 414 C elliottm@wiltech.edu
ELLIOTT, Patrena .... 910-272-3300 337 D pelliott@robeson.edu
ELLIOTT, Patrick .... 443-412-2345 199 D paelliott@harford.edu
ELLIOTT, Patrick .... 607-777-2043 316 B pelliott@binghamton.edu
ELLIOTT, Peter .... 863-784-7218 108 F peter.elliott@southflorida.edu
ELLIOTT, Rennae .... 256-726-7533.... 6 C elliott@oakwood.edu
ELLIOTT, Rob .... 715-675-3331 499 F elliottr@ntc.edu
ELLIOTT, Robert .... 843-574-6171 412 I robert.elliott@tridenttech.edu
ELLIOTT, Robert, T .... 915-831-6761 436 A relliot3@epcc.edu
ELLIOTT, Sally .... 336-593-5402 334 F selliott@forsythtech.edu
ELLIOTT, Scott .... 618-985-3741 140 H scottelliott@jalc.edu
ELLIOTT, Sherman .... 602-639-7500.. 12 J
ELLIOTT, Stanley .... 252-527-6223 335 G
ELLIOTT, Steven .... 402-375-7208 268 F stellio1@wsc.edu
ELLIOTT, Susan .... 901-321-3251 418 G susan.elliott@cbu.edu
ELLIOTT, Tammy .... 323-860-0789.. 50 B
ELLIOTT, Theresa .... 352-638-9821.. 96 B telliott@beaconcollege.edu
ELLIOTT, Tracy .... 239-590-7600 109 K telliott@fgcu.edu
ELLIOTT, Zachary .... 540-261-4921 471 B zach.elliott@svu.edu
ELLIOTT LITTLE, Lisa .... 678-839-6399 127 C lelliott@westga.edu
ELLIS, Althia .... 305-629-2929 107 H aellis@sanignaciouniversity.edu

ELLIS, Audrey .... 978-556-3966 215 E
aellis@necc.mass.edu

ELLIS, Bethany .... 781-283-2001 219 E
be100@wellesley.edu

ELLIS, Bobby .... 229-430-3816 114 I
bellis@albanytech.edu

ELLIS, Brad .... 303-373-2008.. 83 G
bellis@rvu.edu

ELLIS, Brent, D .... 517-750-1200 231 C
bellis@arbor.edu

ELLIS, Bret .... 801-626-7660 461 A
bretellis@weber.edu

ELLIS, Brian, F .... 405-325-6211 370 K
be@ou.edu

ELLIS, III, Carlton .... 419-866-0261 361 B

ELLIS, Carmen .... 910-755-7351 332 F
ellisc@brunswickcc.edu

ELLIS, Cheryl .... 580-327-8530 367 A
clellis@nwosu.edu

ELLIS, Christi .... 417-667-8181 252 B
cellis@cottey.edu

ELLIS, Christopher, E .... 515-964-0601 166 D
ellisc@faith.edu

ELLIS, Christy .... 270-686-4536 182 F
christy.ellis@kctcs.edu

ELLIS, David, A .... 513-529-3638 356 A
ellisda2@miamioh.edu

ELLIS, Dechelle .... 704-463-3411 339 E
dechelle.ellis@sodexo.com

ELLIS, Denise .... 402-826-8251 267 A
denise.ellis@doane.edu

ELLIS, Diane .... 870-307-7284.. 19 I
diane.ellis@lyon.edu

ELLIS, Donna .... 505-566-3209 288 D
ellisdon@sanjuancollege.edu

ELLIS, Eddie .... 803-376-5828 406 D
eellis@allenuniversity.edu

ELLIS, Emily .... 910-938-6234 333 F
ellise@coastalcarolina.edu

ELLIS, Erin .... 225-214-6990 187 B
erin.ellis@franu.edu

ELLIS, Favor .... 802-586-7711 462 I

ELLIS, Greg .... 903-593-8311 448 G
gellis@texascollege.edu

ELLIS, Gwen .... 423-461-8492 422 E
ghellis@milligan.edu

ELLIS, Heidi, B .... 903-813-2235 430 H
hellis@austincollege.edu

ELLIS, Jan .... 614-287-2640 351 C
jellis@cscc.edu

ELLIS, Jason .... 325-674-2305 428 F
jwe95i@acu.edu

ELLIS, Jerry .... 918-647-1388 365 E
jellis@carlalbert.edu

ELLIS, John .... 518-454-5166 296 G
ellisj@strose.edu

ELLIS, Jon .... 860-515-3881.. 85 E
jeellis@charteroak.edu

ELLIS, Karen .... 870-762-3158.. 17 B
kellis@smail.anc.edu

ELLIS, Kathy .... 863-680-4106 100 H
kellis@flsouthern.edu

ELLIS, Keely .... 970-675-3219.. 79 H
keely.ellis@cncc.edu

ELLIS, Keith .... 402-872-2365 268 E
kellis@peru.edu

ELLIS, Kristie .... 505-566-3408 288 D
ellisk@sanjuancollege.edu

ELLIS, Larry .... 607-729-1581 298 B
lellis@davisny.edu

ELLIS, Larry .... 570-585-9210 381 B
lellis@clarkssummitu.edu

ELLIS, Mark .... 308-865-8767 269 I
ellismr@unk.edu

ELLIS, Monica .... 508-831-5000 220 F

ELLIS, Pamela .... 828-395-1456 335 D
pellis@isothermal.edu

ELLIS, Pelema .... 603-862-1234 274 F
pelema.ellis@unh.edu

ELLIS, R. Darin .... 313-577-2024 232 K
rdellis@wayne.edu

ELLIS, Randall .... 804-819-4922 473 C
rellis@vccs.edu

ELLIS, Reggie .... 310-434-3780.. 63 C
ellis_reggie@smc.edu

ELLIS, Reuben .... 818-394-3316.. 76 E
reuben.ellis@woodbury.edu

ELLIS, Rod .... 714-772-3330.. 25 M

ELLIS, Rodney, A .... 318-670-9312 191 D
rellis@susla.edu

ELLIS, Ronald, L .... 951-343-4210.. 27 G
jarmentrout@calbaptist.edu

ELLIS, Rose, R .... 860-932-4140.. 87 E
rellis@qvcc.edu

ELLIS, Sabrina .... 212-998-1205 309 F
sabrina.ellis@nyu.edu

ELLIS, Samuel .... 207-216-4434 195 J
sellis@yccc.edu

ELLIS, Shannon .... 775-784-6196 271 E
elliss@unr.edu

ELLIS, Sharmina .... 302-292-6100.. 93 H

ELLIS, Susan .... 580-774-6039 370 A
susan.ellis@swosu.edu

ELLIS, Teneisha .... 970-351-1333.. 84 F
teneisha.ellis@unco.edu

ELLIS, Tom, M .... 423-425-4687 427 C
tom-ellis@utc.edu

ELLIS, Wade .... 626-914-8897.. 36 J
wellis@citruscollege.edu

ELLIS, William .... 828-766-1227 336 A
wellis@mayland.edu

ELLIS, William, C .... 918-495-7308 368 F
wellis@oru.edu

ELLIS FOSTER,
Stephanie .... 703-284-6478 468 H
sfoster@marymount.edu

ELLIS-HILL, Ralonda ..... 216-987-5544 351 E
ralonda.ellis-hill@tri-c.edu

ELLISON, Brian .... 510-925-4282.. 25 K

ELLISON, Cynthia, S ..... 804-524-5845 476 D
cellison@vsu.edu

ELLISON, Diane .... 585-475-7284 312 F
dmeges@rit.edu

ELLISON, Jared .... 732-743-3800.. 93 H

ELLISON, Maderia .... 928-532-6743.. 14 J
maderia.ellison@npc.edu

ELLISON, Marjorie .... 573-288-6541 252 F
mellison@culver.edu

ELLISON, Mark .... 828-339-4229 338 B
m_ellison@southwesterncc.edu

ELLISON, Ron .... 209-946-7372.. 71 E
rellison1@pacific.edu

ELLISON, Ronald .... 360-792-6050 481 I

ELLISON, Season .... 218-755-3355 237 F
season.ellison@bemidjistate.edu

ELLISOR, Kimberly, M .. 843-661-1190 409 G
kellisor@fmarion.edu

ELLRICH, Lisa .... 207-778-7054 196 I
ellrich@maine.edu

ELLSPERMANN, Sue, J . 317-921-4980 158 D
sellspermann@ivytech.edu

ELLSWORTH, Laura, R .. 301-546-0553 201 E
ellswolr@pgcc.edu

ELLSWORTH, Tim .... 731-661-5215 426 F
tellsworth@uu.edu

ELLWANGER, Carolyn ... 712-279-5484 164 B
carolyn.ellwanger@briarcliff.edu

ELLWOOD, JoAnn .... 540-868-7000 474 C

ELM, Dana .... 203-596-2153.. 87 B
delm@nv.edu

ELMAN, Beth .... 712-362-7947 167 B
belman@iowalakes.edu

ELMBORG, James .... 205-348-2719.... 7 G
jkelmborg@ua.edu

ELMENDORF, Douglas .. 617-495-1122 210 E
doug_elmendorf@hks.harvard.edu

ELMORE, Amanda .... 864-646-1401 412 H
amandal.elmore@tctc.edu

ELMORE, Amelia .... 910-592-8081 337 G
aelmore@sampsoncc.edu

ELMORE, Amy .... 270-534-3118 183 B
amy.elmore@kctcs.edu

ELMORE, Bryan .... 334-844-3664.... 4 D
elmorbj@auburn.edu

ELMORE, Chris .... 336-272-7102 329 C
chris.elmore@greensboro.edu

ELMORE, Dana .... 601-925-3371 247 C
elmore@mc.edu

ELMORE, Donna .... 803-535-1202 411 B
elmored@octech.edu

ELMORE, Garland, C ..... 317-274-5555 157 D

ELMORE, George .... 803-780-1211 414 B
gelmore@voorhees.edu

ELMORE, Kenneth .... 617-353-4126 207 E
kennmore@bu.edu

ELMORE, Mary .... 704-403-3218 327 C
mary.elmore@atriumhealth.org

ELMORE, R. Duane .... 814-863-0273 391 G
rde9@psu.edu

ELMORE, Robert .... 513-875-3344 350 C
robert.elmore@chatfield.edu

ELMORE, Trent .... 910-893-1635 327 D
telmore@campbell.edu

ELMORE, Wendy .... 409-882-3077 449 H
wendy.elmore@lsco.edu

ELMS, Alicia, C .... 804-752-3205 469 F
aliciaelms@rmc.edu

ELMS, Sherry .... 209-384-6000.. 52 A

ELNASHAI, Amr .... 713-743-5797 452 D
elnashai@uh.edu

ELNESS, Jodi, M .... 320-308-5087 241 A
jelness@sctcc.edu

ELNICK, William .... 215-572-2172 378 E
elnickb@arcadia.edu

ELNICKI, Patrice .... 716-614-5933 309 G
pelnicki@niagaracc.suny.edu

ELOFIR, Stacy .... 410-704-4414 204 E
selofir@towson.edu

ELOI-EVANS, Sasha ...... 585-245-5620 318 B

ELOIZARD, SCC,
Monique .... 973-957-0188 275 C
criss@acs350.org

ELOWSKY, Joel .... 314-505-7106 252 A
elowskyj@csl.edu

ELROD, David .... 706-272-4473 118 B
delrod@daltonstate.edu

ELROD, David .... 615-966-5887 421 B
david.elrod@lipscomb.edu

ELROD, Eileen, R .... 408-554-4136.. 63 B
eelrod@scu.edu

ELROD, Susan .... 574-520-4220 157 E
slelrod@iusb.edu

ELS, Jason .... 606-546-1231 185 D
jels@unionky.edu

ELSBERRY, Meagan ...... 561-237-7233 103 W
melsberry@lynn.edu

ELSE, George .... 610-989-1200 401 I
gelse@vfmac.edu

ELSEN, Jake .... 615-244-5848 423 C

ELSENBAUMER, Ronald 260-481-6103 160 C
chancellor@pfw.edu

ELSENER, Daniel, J .... 317-955-6100 159 K
delsener@marian.edu

ELSHAYEB, Tarek, A ..... 704-687-7859 342 D
telshaye@uncc.edu

ELSMORE, Kathleen ...... 610-989-1330 401 I
kelsmore@vfmac.edu

ELSTER, Eric .... 301-295-3017 503 C
eric.elster@usuhs.edu

ELSTON, Ken, D .... 336-841-2848 329 F
kelston@highpoint.edu

ELSTON, Timothy, G ..... 803-321-5110 410 H
timothy.elston@newberry.edu

ELSTONE, Paul .... 541-346-2166 376 H
pelstone@uoregon.edu

ELSWICK, Clark .... 575-562-4490 286 B
clark.elswick@enmu.edu

ELTON, Nathan .... 302-831-8574.. 91 C
nelton@udel.edu

ELTRINGHAM, TJ .... 570-955-1487 387 B
eltringhamj@lackawanna.edu

ELUFIEDE, Babafemi ..... 229-500-2255 114 H
babafemi.elufiede@asurams.edu

ELUSKIE, Robert .... 616-538-2330 224 E
beluskie@gracechristian.edu

ELVARD, Lesly .... 410-888-9048 200 E
lelvard@muih.edu

ELVERSON, Katie .... 412-536-1079 386 H
katie.elverson@laroche.edu

ELVOVE, Naomi .... 415-257-1380.. 41 C
naomi.elvove@dominican.edu

ELWELL, David .... 617-253-3795 216 B

ELWELL, Marcene .... 308-635-7431 270 C
elwellm1@wncc.edu

ELY, Mike .... 573-897-5000 260 A

ELY, SJ, Peter .... 206-296-6158 484 A
ely@seattleu.edu

ELY, Susan .... 559-325-3600.. 28 D
sely@chsu.edu

ELY, Tim .... 610-526-1862 385 D
tely@harcum.edu

ELY, Tim .... 610-526-1862 385 D
tely@harucm.edu

EMAMI, Azita .... 206-221-2472 485 A
emamia@uw.edu

EMANUEL, Catherine, B 770-720-9232 124 G
cbe@reinhardt.edu

EMANUEL, Stashia .... 502-597-5117 183 D
stashia.emanuel@kysu.edu

EMBACHER, Barbara ...... 507-433-0659 240 G
barb.embacher@riverland.edu

EMBERTON,
Sherilyn, R .... 260-359-4050 156 C
semberton@huntington.edu

EMBLER, Marc .... 843-863-7000 407 B
membler@csuniv.edu

EMBRY, Jason .... 303-444-0202.. 82 A

EMBRY, Kelli .... 501-760-4349.. 20 A
kelli.embry@np.edu

EMBRY, Robin .... 803-323-2229 414 D
embryr@winthrop.edu

EMDY, Jim .... 831-476-9424.. 42 F
librarian@fivebranches.edu

EMEHISER, Theresa ...... 623-245-4600.. 16 B
temehiser@uti.edu

EMEKA, Amon .... 518-580-8111 315 F
aemeka@skidmore.edu

EMENGER, Nancy, E ..... 801-626-6017 461 A
nemenger@weber.edu

EMERICK, Brian, J .... 740-368-3177 359 G
bjemeric@owu.edu

EMERICK, Kenneth .... 301-687-4880 204 C
kmemerick@frostburg.edu

EMERICK, Laura .... 740-389-4636 355 F
emerickl@mtc.edu

EMERICK, Mary .... 781-280-3624 215 B
emerickm@middlesex.mass.edu

EMERICK, Sandra, M .... 330-325-6759 357 D
semerick@neomed.edu

EMERSON, Adam .... 413-236-2132 214 A
aemerson@berkshirecc.edu

EMERSON, Brian .... 716-896-0700 324 E
bemerson@villa.edu

EMERSON, Colleen .... 401-341-2908 405 D
emersonc@salve.edu

EMERSON, Dana .... 714-241-6184.. 37 J
demerson3@coastline.edu

EMERSON, Matthew ...... 405-585-4426 367 B
matthew.emerson@okbu.edu

EMERSON, Michael .... 630-617-3178 137 G
michael.emerson@elmhurst.edu

EMERSON, Mitchell, R .. 623-572-3501 144 F
memers@midwestern.edu

EMERSON, Peter .... 985-549-3894 193 A
peter.emerson@selu.edu

EMERSON, Steve .... 208-467-8528 132 E
sdemerson@nnu.edu

EMERSON, Steve .... 951-343-4415.. 27 G
semerson@calbaptist.edu

EMERSON, Tonsha .... 662-243-2664 246 B
temerson@eastms.edu

EMERSON, Yolanda ...... 562-908-3457.. 58 L
yemerson@riohondo.edu

EMERSON, Yolanda ...... 562-908-3409.. 58 L
yemerson@riohondo.edu

EMERT, John .... 765-285-1024 153 H
jemert@bsu.edu

EMERY, Donna .... 512-472-4133 443 F
donna.emery@ssw.edu

EMERY, Lisa .... 903-813-2423 430 H
lemery@austincollege.edu

EMERY, Matthew .... 870-236-6901.. 18 J
memery@crc.edu

EMERY, Melissa .... 269-927-6114 226 F
memery@lakemichigancollege.edu

EMERY, P. Michael .... 713-221-5806 453 A
emeryp@uhd.edu

EMILIO, Linda .... 909-469-8421.. 75 I
lemilio@westernu.edu

EMIRU, Tadael .... 916-691-7913.. 50 H
emirut@crc.losrios.edu

EMISON, Barry .... 662-407-1409 246 E
blemison@iccms.edu

EMISON, David .... 410-293-1901 504 A
emison@usna.edu

EMMA, Janine .... 732-255-0400 279 F
jemma@ocean.edu

EMMANUEL, Steven ...... 757-455-3405 477 C
semmanuel@vwu.edu

EMMER, Karen .... 520-515-5417.. 11 M
emmerk@cochise.edu

EMMICK, Joe .... 847-866-3923 138 D
joe.emmick@garrett.edu

EMMIL, Bruce .... 701-224-5758 346 A
bruce.emmil@bismarckstate.edu

EMMONS, Carol-Ann ..... 312-567-3827 140 A
emmons@iit.edu

EMMONS, Larry, K .... 989-964-2558 230 E
lkemmons@svsu.edu

EMMONS, Lee .... 270-534-3084 183 B
lee.emmons@kctcs.edu

EMORY, Cynthia, M ...... 717-264-2192 403 C
cynthia.emory@wilson.edu

EMORY, Julie, W .... 252-398-6252 328 C
emoryj@chowan.edu

EMORY, Rose .... 800-323-5692 347 I
rose.emory@artacademy.edu

EMORY, Sid .... 803-793-5147 408 G
emorys@denmarktech.edu

EMPET, Audriana, L 570-326-3761 392W
alm56@pct.edu
EMR, Linda .... 201-879-7206 275 H
lemr@bergen.edu
EMRICH, Whitney .... 601-974-1000 247 B
whitney.emrich@millsaps.edu
EMRICH, Whitney .... 601-974-1105 247 B
whitney.emrich@millsaps.edu
EMSELLEM, Dawn .... 401-341-2336 405 D
dawn.emsellem@salve.edu
EMSWELLER, Dave .... 419-434-4578 362 D
emsweller@findlay.edu
EMSWELLER, David, W . 419-434-4578 362 D
emsweller@findlay.edu
ENAMAIT, John .... 704-991-0220 338 C
jenamait1211@stanly.edu
ENAYAT, Sharmeen ...... 619-574-5819.. 42 J
senayat@sandiego.edu
ENCARNACION, Zaneta . 619-482-6301.. 66 A
ENCINA, Rosalinda .... 210-486-4609 428 I
rencina@alamo.edu
ENCISO, Martha .... 657-278-8655.. 31 C
maenciso@fullerton.edu
ENDEAN, Kristopher ..... 480-245-7993.. 12M
kristopher.endean@ibcs.edu
ENDERS, Jessica .... 760-773-2508.. 38 E
jenders@collegeofthedesert.edu
ENDERS, Naulayne, R ... 606-474-3276 181 B
nenders@kcu.edu
ENDICOTT, Alicia .... 660-359-3948 257 D
aendicott@mail.ncmissouri.edu
ENDICOTT, Daniel, D .... 904-620-2019 111 B
dendicot@unf.edu
ENDICOTT, David .... 218-894-5172 237 G
david.endicott@clcmn.edu
ENDICOTT, Jon .... 559-453-3484.. 43 A
jon.endicott@fresno.edu
ENDICOTT, Patricia .... 812-749-1435 159 O
pendicott@oak.edu
ENDLER, Dean, K .... 979-845-0099 446 F
d-endler@tamu.edu
ENDRASKE, Mark, C ..... 530-226-4108.. 64 E
mendraske@simpsonu.edu
ENDRES, David .... 513-231-2223 348 B
dendres@athenaeum.edu
ENDRES, Judy .... 507-389-7351 241 C
judy.endres@southcentral.edu
ENDRIJONAS, Erika, A .. 626-585-7201.. 56 D
eendrijonas@pasadena.edu
ENDSLEY, Kara .... 919-530-5597 341 E
kendsley@nccu.edu
ENDY, Michael .... 817-598-6211 457 J
mendy@wc.edu
ENDY, Stephanie .... 216-368-2000 349 D
stephanie.endy@case.edu
ENFIELD, Jeff .... 708-239-4803 151 A
jeff.enfield@trnty.edu
ENG, Michelle .... 415-575-6100.. 28 I
meng@ciis.edu
ENGBRECHT, Jason .... 507-786-3849 243 D
engbrech@stolaf.edu
ENGBROCK, M. Jeff ...... 409-944-1215 436 E
mengbrock@gc.edu
ENGDAHL, Anna .... 701-252-3467 347 B
amunns@uj.edu
ENGE, Whitney .... 616-233-2593 223 E
whitney.enge@davenport.edu
ENGEBRETSON, Daniel . 605-658-3761 416 D
daniel.engebretson@usd.edu
ENGEBRETSON, Pam .... 651-779-3994 237 H
pam.engebretson@century.edu
ENGEBRETSON, Pat ...... 605-256-5798 416 F
patrick.engebretson@dsu.edu
ENGEL, Angela .... 309-438-3305 140 D
akengel@ilstu.edu
ENGEL, Christen .... 706-721-7406 116 A
cengel@augusta.edu
ENGEL, Deidre .... 712-279-5448 164 B
deidre.engel@briarcliff.edu
ENGEL, Karen .... 650-306-3145.. 62 J
engelk@smccd.edu
ENGEL, Renata, S .... 814-863-6726 391 G
rse1@psu.edu
ENGEL, Richard, R .... 530-752-9960.. 69 B
rrengel@ucdavis.edu
ENGEL, Steven .... 912-478-0357 120 C
sengel@georgiasouthern.edu
ENGELBACH, Karl, M .... 530-754-7237.. 69 B
kmengelbach@ucdavis.edu
ENGELBERT, Bryce .... 402-826-8617 267 A
bryce.engelbert@doane.edu
ENGELBOURG, Karen .... 617-358-4560 207 E
engelbou@bu.edu
ENGELBRIDE, Ed .... 518-956-8140 316 A
eengelbride@albany.edu
ENGELDINER, Lyle .... 831-755-6706.. 44 G
lengeldinger@hartnell.edu
ENGELHARDT, Nichole .. 573-897-5120 260 A
ENGELHART, Brian, W .. 260-422-5561 156 E
bwengelhart@indianatech.edu
ENGELKEMIER, John ..... 312-329-2145 144 I
john.engelkemier@moody.edu
ENGELLANT, Roxanne ... 406-683-7305 264 A
roxanne.engellant@umwestern.edu
ENGELMAN, Kevin .... 843-349-5393 409 J
kevin.engelman@hgtc.edu
ENGELMAN, Mike .... 615-966-7617 421 B
mike.engelman@lipscomb.edu
ENGELMANN, Kathleen . 203-576-4253.. 89 C
kengelma@bridgeport.edu
ENGELSCHALL,
Emily, D .... 951-827-2587.. 70 B
emily.engelschall@ucr.edu
ENGELSEN, Karen .... 760-245-4271.. 74 D
karen.engelsen@vvc.edu
ENGELSMA, Chris .... 616-432-3406 230 A
chris.engelsma@prts.edu
ENGEN, Stuart .... 701-671-2446 346 D
stuart.engen@ndscs.edu
ENGERMAN, Kimarie .... 340-692-4110 513 E
kengerm@uvi.edu
ENGFER, Tom .... 323-856-7747.. 25 G
tengfer@afi.com
ENGH, Ellen .... 319-352-8499 170 J
ellen.engh@wartburg.edu
ENGISCH, Kathy .... 937-775-2611 364 E
kathrin.engisch@wright.edu
ENGLAND, Christy .... 850-245-0466 109 H
christy.england@flbog.edu
ENGLAND, Jerry .... 615-547-1240 419 C
jengland@cumberland.edu
ENGLAND, Kirk, R .... 805-437-3763.. 30 C
kirk.england@csuci.edu
ENGLAND, Rebecca ...... 276-244-1231 464 E
bengland@asl.edu
ENGLAND, Richard .... 217-581-2017 137 E
rengland@eiu.edu
ENGLAND, Susan .... 865-974-2444 427 B
sengla10@utk.edu
ENGLAR, Samantha .... 618-537-6548 144 A
smenglar@mckendree.edu
ENGLE, Cathy .... 360-417-6347 482 C
cengle@pencol.edu
ENGLE, Chris .... 810-762-0242 228 F
chris.engle@mcc.edu
ENGLE, Jason .... 509-544-4935 479 A
jengle@columbiabasin.edu
ENGLE, Joshua .... 580-774-3767 370 A
joshua.engle@swosu.edu
ENGLE, Patricia, A .... 248-370-4223 229 I
pengle@oakland.edu
ENGLE, Sara .... 406-377-9441 263 D
sengle@dawson.edu
ENGLEHARDT,
Richard, E .... 606-693-5000 183 C
registrar@kmbc.edu
ENGLEHARDT, Thomas . 617-349-8598 211 C
ENGLEHART, Kathy .... 207-453-5117 195 F
kenglehart@kvcc.me.edu
ENGLER, Russell .... 617-451-0010 217 F
ENGLERT, Patrick .... 502-272-8323 179 H
penglert@bellarmine.edu
ENGLESTATTER,
Pauline, A .... 301-447-5086 201 B
englesta@msmary.edu
ENGLIN, Peter, D .... 515-294-5636 163 G
penglin@iastate.edu
ENGLISH, Ana .... 928-317-6000.. 11 A
ENGLISH, Ana .... 928-317-6092.. 11 A
ana.english@azwestern.edu
ENGLISH, Andrew .... 870-307-7225.. 19 I
andrew.english@lyon.edu
ENGLISH, Andrew .... 864-489-7151 410 B
aenglish@limestone.edu
ENGLISH, Andy .... 515-961-1547 170 B
andy.english@simpson.edu
ENGLISH, Ashley .... 334-808-6539.... 7 C
englisha@troy.edu
ENGLISH, Cara .... 480-285-1761.. 12 B
ENGLISH, Chris .... 910-788-6270 338 A
ENGLISH, Claude .... 816-584-6492 258 C
claude.english@park.edu
ENGLISH, Cyndy .... 504-865-5738 191 F
cenglish@tulane.edu
ENGLISH, David, A .... 740-587-6262 352 A
englishda@denison.edu
ENGLISH, David, J .... 919-962-1000 340 H
ENGLISH, Eva .... 406-353-2607 262 H
eenglish@ancollege.edu
ENGLISH, Garrett .... 951-552-8865.. 27 G
genglish@calbaptist.edu
ENGLISH, JR.,
Herbert, L .... 760-252-2411.. 26 G
ENGLISH, Jennifer .... 508-929-8110 213 G
jenglish1@worcester.edu
ENGLISH, Jill .... 616-392-8555 233 E
jill@westernsem.edu
ENGLISH, John .... 610-989-1200 401 I
jenglish@vfmac.edu
ENGLISH, Josh .... 661-362-2245.. 51 D
jenglish@masters.edu
ENGLISH, Kelly .... 910-275-6370 335 E
kenglish@jamessprunt.edu
ENGLISH, Kent .... 907-564-8350.... 9 F
kbenglish@alaskapacific.edu
ENGLISH, Kristen .... 309-457-2210 144 H
kenglish@monmouthcollege.edu
ENGLISH, Lindsay .... 216-987-3610 351 E
lindsay.english@tri-c.edu
ENGLISH, Mechelle .... 803-508-7263 406 C
ENGLISH, Sarah, H .... 845-575-3000 305 D
sarah.english@marist.edu
ENGLISH, Susan .... 616-632-8900 221 E
ENGLOT, Peter .... 973-353-5541 282 B
peter.englot@rutgers.edu
ENGLUND, Elizabeth ..... 425-352-8432 478 D
eenglund@cascadia.edu
ENGLUND, Kristin .... 773-244-6248 145 G
kenglund@northpark.edu
ENGLUND, Tim .... 509-963-1866 478 E
tim.englund@cwu.edu
ENGSTROM, Dan, M ..... 724-938-4407 393 E
engstrom@calu.edu
ENGSTROM, Larry .... 775-682-8803 271 E
engstrom@unr.edu
ENGSTROM, Mark .... 734-462-4400 230 G
mengstro@schoolcraft.edu
ENGSTROM, Rick .... 425-889-6397 481 H
rick.engstrom@northwestu.edu
ENLOE, Greg .... 240-567-7977 200 G
greg.enloe@montgomerycollege.edu
ENNA, Christina .... 701-228-5458 346 B
bookcell@dakotacollege.edu
ENNELLO-BUTLER,
Deanna .... 518-694-7305 289 J
deanna.ennello-butler@acphs.edu
ENNES, Felicia .... 570-702-8981 386 D
fennes@johnson.edu
ENNIS, Daniel .... 919-684-6600 328 F
daniel.ennis@duke.edu
ENNIS, Daniel, J .... 843-349-2089 408 A
dennis@coastal.edu
ENNIS, Greg .... 319-363-1323 168 F
gennins@mtmercy.edu
ENNIS, Jackie .... 252-399-6571 326 K
jennis@barton.edu
ENNIS, Lisa .... 334-699-2266.... 1 B
lennis@acom.edu
ENNS-REMPEL, Kevin .... 559-453-2225.. 43 A
kevin.enns-rempel@fresno.edu
ENO, Alisha .... 303-765-3102.. 81 G
aeno@iliff.edu
ENOKAWA, Jerilyn .... 808-734-9899 129 H
jilorenz@hawaii.edu
ENOMA, Benjamin .... 212-463-0400 322 F
benjamin.enoma@touro.edu
ENOMA, Benjamin .... 212-463-0400 322 G
benjamin.enoma@touro.edu
ENOS, Chris .... 785-670-1153 178 C
chris.enos@washburn.edu
ENOS, Kelly .... 818-364-7758.. 49 C
enoskw@lamission.edu
ENRIGHT, Jan Brue ...... 605-256-5205 416 F
jan.enright@dsu.edu
ENRIGHT, John .... 213-613-2200.. 65 E
john_enright@sciarc.edu
ENRIGHT, Lauren .... 971-236-9231 372 E
ENRIGHT, Nancy .... 973-275-2545 283 C
nancy.enright@shu.edu
ENRIGHT, Patrick .... 973-328-5700 276 J
penright@ccm.edu
ENRIGHT, Sara .... 401-825-1084 404 C
senright@ccri.edu
ENRIGHT, Sherri .... 214-378-1617 434 F
senright@dcccd.edu
ENRIQUEZ, Anita, B ...... 671-735-2994 504 F
abe@triton.uog.edu
ENRIQUEZ, Igrí .... 787-765-3560 506 K
enriquez@edpuniversity.edu
ENROTH, Kevin .... 662-325-7404 247 F
enroth@osp.msstate.edu
ENS, Terry .... 620-947-3121 177 I
terryens@tabor.edu
ENSER, Jason .... 802-728-1434 464 A
jenser@vtc.edu
ENSER, Pamela .... 518-580-4709 320 E
pamela.enser@esc.edu
ENSING, Kim .... 805-922-6966.. 24 I
kensing@hancockcollege.edu
ENSLEY, Cynthia .... 252-638-7201 334 A
ensleyc@cravencc.edu
ENSLEY, Dana .... 706-379-3111 128 C
ddensley@yhc.edu
ENSLIN, Jon .... 920-403-3016 495 B
jon.enslin@snc.edu
ENSMINGER, Michelle .. 806-743-9196 451 A
michelle.ensminger@ttuhsc.edu
ENSOR, Jerry .... 252-493-7541 336 H
jensor@email.pittcc.edu
ENSOR, Pat .... 713-221-8011 453 A
ensorp@uhd.edu
ENTERS, David, T .... 262-243-5700 492 E
dave.enters@cuw.edu
ENTIN, Pauline .... 508-999-8352 212 A
pentin@umassd.edu
ENTINGER, Julienne, N . 651-628-3380 244 D
jnentinger@unwsp.edu
ENTLER, David .... 952-829-4193 234 B
david.entler@bethfel.org
ENTREKIN, Cindy .... 256-215-4246.... 1 G
centrekin@cacc.edu
ENTRINGER, Chris, E .... 844-642-2338 169 A
entringc@nicc.edu
ENTZ, Susan .... 603-862-3765 274 F
susan.entz@unh.edu
ENYEDI, Alexander .... 518-564-2000 318 E
ENZ, Jeff .... 760-355-6577.. 45 K
jeff.enz@imperial.edu
ENZLER, Mario .... 713-525-2120 454 G
enzlerm@stthom.edu
ENZOR, Sharon, B .... 662-685-4771 245 C
senzor@bmc.edu
EODICE, Michelle, A ..... 405-325-2937 370 K
meodice@ou.edu
EOFF, Shirley .... 325-942-2722 450 E
shirley.eoff@angelo.edu
EPHREM, Alex .... 718-933-6700 307 A
EPLEY, Pamela .... 312-755-2250 137 H
EPLING, Larry .... 606-218-5293 186 B
larryepling@upike.edu
EPLION, David .... 812-941-2269 157 F
deplion@ius.edu
EPP, Adam .... 425-889-5263 481 H
adam.epp@northwestu.edu
EPP, Michelle .... 651-696-6062 236 I
mepp@macalester.edu
EPPEHIMER, Trevor ...... 704-636-6743 330 A
teppehimer@hoodseminary.edu
EPPER, Rhonda .... 719-846-5541.. 83 L
rhonda.epper@trinidadstate.edu
EPPERLY, Dustin .... 740-474-8896 358 A
depperly@ohiochristian.edu
EPPINETTE, Chance, W . 318-342-5021 193 C
eppinette@ulm.edu
EPPINGER, Beth .... 479-788-7334.. 21 G
beth.eppinger@uafs.edu
EPPLER, Michelle .... 402-557-7010 265 J
michelle.eppler@bellevue.edu
EPPLEY, Douglas .... 724-537-4555 397 I
douglas.eppley@stvincent.edu
EPPLEY, Douglas .... 724-532-5034 398 A
douglas.eppley@stvincent.edu
EPPLING, Chris .... 706-865-2134 126 E
ceppling@truett.edu
EPPLING, Marcie, T ...... 256-824-6443.... 8 B
marcie.eppling@uah.edu
EPPS, Aaron .... 402-437-2823 269 C
aepps@southeast.edu
EPPS, Bruce .... 614-236-6461 349 B
bepps@capital.edu
EPPS, Charmica, D .... 804-524-5595 476 D
cepps@vsu.edu
EPPS, Eric, L .... 815-835-6322 149 E
eric.epps@svcc.edu
EPPS, JoAnne, A .... 215-204-4775 399 B
provost@temple.edu
EPPS, Margaret, W .... 919-684-8978 328 F
margaret.epps@duke.edu
EPSTEIN, Bonnie .... 212-678-8997 303 D
boepstein@jtsa.edu
EPSTEIN, Catherine, A .. 413-542-2334 205 G
cepstein@amherst.edu

EPSTEIN, Joanne .... 352-335-2332.. 94 E
joanne.epstein@acupuncturist.edu
EPSTEIN, Keith .... 860-723-0062.. 85 F
epsteink@ct.edu
EPSTEIN, Meryl .... 480-212-1704.. 15 O
EPSTEIN, Michael, M .... 213-738-6774.. 66 B
mepstein@swlaw.edu
EPSTEIN, Richard .... 856-225-6117 281 G
repstein@camden.rutgers.edu
EPSTEIN, Scott .... 616-554-5691 223 E
sepstein1@davenport.edu
EPSTEIN, Shira .... 212-678-8030 303 D
shestein@jtsa.edu
EPSTEIN, Shlomo, Z ..... 718-438-1002 306 D
EPSTEIN, Sue .... 518-587-2100 320 E
EPSTEIN, Warren .... 719-502-2666.. 82 E
warren.epstein@ppcc.edu
EPTING, Bert .... 864-231-2000 406 F
bepting@andersonuniversity.edu
EQUINOA, Kim .... 805-893-3858.. 70 E
kim.equinoa@sa.ucsb.edu
ERARDI, Lauren .... 203-582-3686.. 88 G
lauren.erardi@quinnipiac.edu
ERARIO, Vince .... 678-264-8808 122 C
vince.erario@life.edu
ERATO, Michael, J .... 414-425-8300 495 A
merato@shsst.edu
ERB, Bill .... 801-863-8972 460 D
erbbi@uvu.edu
ERB, Brian, I .... 706-236-2234 116 B
berb@berry.edu
ERB, Daniel, E .... 336-841-9229 329 F
derb@highpoint.edu
ERB, Daniel, E .... 336-841-4595 329 F
derb@highpoint.edu
ERB, Linda .... 305-289-1121.. 98 E
linda@dolphins.org
ERBE, Jarrod .... 414-443-8800 498 A
jarrod.erbe@wlc.edu
ERBE, John .... 703-370-6600 476 E
jerbe@vts.edu
ERBELE, Cindy .... 706-865-2134 126 E
cerbele@truett.edu
ERBES, Melody .... 818-575-6800.. 68 C
melody.erbes@tuw.edu
ERBES, Paul, K .... 563-589-0221 171 A
perbes@wartburgseminary.edu
ERCKERT, Joseph .... 973-290-4449 282 I
jerckert@steu.edu
ERDLE, Jennie .... 585-785-1263 299 F
jennie.erdle@flcc.edu
ERDMAN, Al .... 813-253-7015 102 B
aerdman2@hccfl.edu
ERDMAN, Brian, J .... 773-508-7592 143 C
berdman@luc.edu
ERDMAN, Jennifer .... 410-532-5123 201 D
jerdman@ndm.edu
ERDMANN, Alex .... 407-582-1389 113 I
aerdmann@valenciacollege.edu
ERDMANN, Joel .... 251-460-7121.... 9 A
jerdmann@southalabama.edu
ERDMANN, Paul .... 620-441-5264 173 C
paul.erdmann@cowley.edu
ERDMANN, Stephanie ... 406-771-4305 264 F
stephanie.erdmann@gfcmsu.edu
EREMITA, Nicholas .... 301-985-7000 203 E
ERFAN, Shahir .... 718-482-5501 294 F
serfan@lagcc.cuny.edu
ERFFMEYER, Kenneth .... 616-526-6097 222 C
kde2@calvin.edu
ERFOURTH, Stavroula ... 989-729-3431 221 K
serfou01@baker.edu
ERGIN, Laure .... 302-831-7364.. 91 C
lbergin@udel.edu
ERICKSEN, Janet, S ...... 320-589-6020 244 B
ericksja@morris.umn.edu
ERICKSON, Angela .... 507-933-7595 236 A
aerick13@gustavus.edu
ERICKSON, Brian .... 307-754-6210 501 H
brian.erickson@nwc.edu
ERICKSON, Chris .... 952-829-1919 234 B
chris.erickson@bethfel.org
ERICKSON, Christine .... 209-667-3177.. 33 B
cerickson2@csustan.edu
ERICKSON, Deb .... 619-849-2323.. 57 J
deberickson@pointloma.edu
ERICKSON, Elly .... 845-451-1468 297 G
elly.erickson@culinary.edu
ERICKSON, Ethan, E ..... 785-532-5416 175 C
eerickson@ksu.edu
ERICKSON, Gary .... 314-838-8858 261 F
gerickson@ugst.edu
ERICKSON, Jennifer ...... 320-308-5940 241 A
jennifer.erickson@sctcc.edu
ERICKSON, Jennifer ...... 915-215-4145 451 B
jennifer.erickson@ttuhsc.edu
ERICKSON, Jessica .... 707-256-7205.. 53 E
jerickson@napavalley.edu
ERICKSON, Jon .... 320-762-4405 237 C
jon.erickson@alextech.edu
ERICKSON, Karen .... 701-224-5424 346 A
karen.erickson@bismarckstate.edu
ERICKSON, Kevin .... 402-486-2504 269 F
kevin.erickson@ucollege.edu
ERICKSON, Kim .... 909-652-6021.. 35 L
kim.erickson@chaffey.edu
ERICKSON, Lauren .... 402-467-9052 267 A
lauren.erickson@doane.edu
ERICKSON, Lori .... 423-439-4457 419 G
ericksol@etsu.edu
ERICKSON, Marc .... 706-419-1645 118 A
marc.erickson@covenant.edu
ERICKSON, Mark .... 845-451-1295 297 G
mark.erickson@culinary.edu
ERICKSON, Mark, H ...... 610-861-5458 391 C
merickson@northampton.edu
ERICKSON, Maureen ..... 845-905-4613 297 G
maureen.erickson@culinary.edu
ERICKSON, Michael .... 619-660-4000.. 44 D
ERICKSON, Michele ...... 509-452-5100 482 B
merickson@pnwu.edu
ERICKSON, Michelle ..... 617-735-9825 209 D
erickson@emmanuel.edu
ERICKSON, Paul, J .... 608-342-1194 496 E
ericksop@uwplatt.edu
ERICKSON, Ron .... 651-423-8232 238 A
ron.erickson@dctc.edu
ERICKSON, Siri, C .... 507-933-7446 236 A
sericks5@gustavus.edu
ERICKSON, Steve .... 218-846-3721 239 C
steve.erickson@minnesota.edu
ERICKSON, Susan .... 757-455-3220 477 C
serickson@vwu.edu
ERICKSON-PESETSKI,
Stacy, L .... 260-982-5391 159 J
slerickson-pesetski@manchester.edu
ERICSON, III, Ed .... 479-238-8669.. 19 H
eericson@jbu.edu
ERICSON, Kendra .... 712-279-3149 169 H
kendra.ericson@stlukescollege.edu
ERICSON, Laura .... 715-833-6232 498 E
lericson2@cvtc.edu
ERICSON, Todd, M .... 608-796-3856 497 O
tmericson@viterbo.edu
ERIKSEN, Jennifer .... 704-337-2217 339 F
eriksenj@queens.edu
ERIKSEN, John .... 714-438-4680.. 37 I
jeriksen@cccd.edu
ERIQUEZZO, Michael ..... 413-737-7000 205 F
ERJAVEC, Patricia .... 719-549-3213.. 82 J
patty.erjavec@pueblocc.edu
ERLACHER, Ryan .... 678-466-4672 117 D
ryanerlacher@clayton.edu
ERLANGER, Esrael .... 718-645-0536 306 J
ERMATINGER, James .... 217-206-6512 152 A
jerma2@uis.edu
ERMER, Scott .... 319-398-4944 167 J
scott.ermer@kirkwood.edu
ERMER, Scott .... 716-851-1977 299 B
ermer@ecc.edu
ERMOLI, Victor .... 912-525-5000 124 I
vermoli@scad.edu
ERNE, Richard .... 208-459-5179 131 C
rerne@collegeofidaho.edu
ERNEST, Matthew, S ..... 914-968-6200 314 C
mernest@archny.org
ERNEST, Ralynn .... 614-825-6255 347 E
rernest@aiam.edu
ERNST, Chris .... 502-456-6506 185 A
cernst@sullivan.edu
ERNST, Donna .... 502-852-6538 186 A
donna.ernst@louisville.edu
ERNST, Jennifer .... 509-574-4641 486 D
jernst@yvcc.edu
ERNST, Joshua, R .... 206-934-4710 483 B
josh.ernst@seattlecolleges.edu
ERNST, Nathan .... 630-515-6342 144 F
nernst@midwestern.edu
ERNST, Robert, D .... 734-647-8160 231 H
robernst@umich.edu
ERNST-LEONARD,
Amber .... 305-809-3531.. 97 O
amber.ernstleonard@cfk.edu
ERNSTBERGER, Jon .... 706-880-8155 122 A
jernstberger@lagrange.edu
ERNSTER, Michael .... 563-884-5667 169 F
mike.ernster@palmer.edu
ERNSTING, Brian .... 603-888-1311 273 I
bernsting@rivier.edu
ERNY, Michael .... 850-729-6051 104 M
ernym@nwfsc.edu
ERO-TOLLIVER, Isi .... 757-727-5239 467 G
isi.erotolliver@hamptonu.edu
ERPELDING, Augustine . 623-845-4526.. 13 C
augustine.erpelding@gccaz.edu
ERPENBACH, Steve .... 605-688-4151 417 A
steve.erpenbach@sdstatefoundation.org
ERPESTAD, Hanna .... 218-733-7667 238 G
hanna.erpestad@lsc.edu
ERRECA, Lori .... 619-388-3207.. 60 I
lerreca@sdccd.edu
ERRICO, James .... 845-398-4000 314 G
ERRTHUM, Amy .... 563-588-6683 164 E
amy.errthum@clarke.edu
ERSING, Rachel .... 716-829-8092 298 E
ersingr@dyc.edu
ERSKINE, Tina .... 207-454-1002 195 I
terskine@wccc.me.edu
ERSTE, SR., Mark, A ..... 740-284-5234 352 I
merste@franciscan.edu
ERTEL, Mia .... 978-646-7111 210 C
mertel@gcts.edu
ERTEL, Rebecca .... 937-376-6495 349 J
rertel@centralstate.edu
ERTEL, Stefanie .... 910-221-2224 331 B
sertel@manna.edu
ERTEL, Steve .... 615-343-8506 428 A
steve.ertel@vanderbilt.edu
ERUZIONE, Vincent .... 617-333-2202 208 G
veruzion@curry.edu
ERVIN, Archie .... 404-385-3686 119 E
archie.ervin@vpid.gatech.edu
ERVIN, Carrie .... 765-983-1758 155 A
ervinca@earlham.edu
ERVIN, Elonda .... 812-237-8513 156 D
elonda.ervin@indstate.edu
ERVIN, Jennifer .... 404-880-8051 117 C
jervin@cau.edu
ERVIN, Kathryn .... 816-584-6289 258 C
katie.ervin@park.edu
ERVIN, Korrie .... 910-898-9603 336 D
ervink@montgomery.edu
ERVIN, Larry .... 865-981-8222 421 C
larry.ervin@maryvillecollege.edu
ERVIN, Leisa .... 662-325-7353 247 F
lbryant@audit.msstate.edu
ERVIN, Timothy, R .... 217-786-9605 143 B
tim.ervin@llcc.edu
ERWIN, Betsy .... 802-831-1225 463 C
berwin@vermontlaw.edu
ERWIN,
Charlotte Katherine ..... 303-735-5437.. 84 B
katherine.erwin@colorado.edu
ERWIN, Craig .... 512-863-1472 445 C
erwinc@southwestern.edu
ERWIN, Curtis .... 804-828-7666 473 B
cgerwin@vcu.edu
ERWIN, Deidre .... 262-524-7201 492 A
derwin@carrollu.edu
ERWIN, Gary .... 313-993-1254 231 E
erwingj@udmercy.edu
ERWIN, John .... 508-856-8200 212 C
john.erwin@umassmed.edu
ERWIN, John, O .... 616-985-2230 359 L
jerwin@pcj.edu
ERWIN, Leslie .... 419-251-1710 355 G
leslie.erwin@mercycollege.edu
ERWIN, Lisa .... 218-726-8501 243 G
laerwin@d.umn.edu
ERWIN, Paul .... 205-975-8970.... 8 A
perwin@uab.edu
ERWIN, R. Guy .... 717-338-3000 400 D
president@uls.edu
ERWIN, Ryan .... 903-923-2226 435 H
rerwin@etbu.edu
ERWIN, Shari .... 918-293-4966 368 B
shari.erwin@okstate.edu
ERWIN, Steve .... 620-235-4231 177 A
serwin@pittstate.edu
ERWIN, Steve .... 661-362-5917.. 38 D
steve.erwin@canyons.edu
ERWIN-SVOBODA, Cal .. 360-532-9020 480 G
ESAU, Sheri .... 620-327-8147 174 E
sheri.esau@hesston.edu
ESCAGY, Marsha .... 718-270-6984 294 G
mescagy@mec.cuny.edu
ESCAJEDA, Jackie .... 408-855-5038.. 75 D
jacqueline.escajeda@missioncollege.edu
ESCALANTE, Angie .... 787-765-5974 511 D
aescalante@pupr.edu
ESCALANTE, Eddie .... 626-571-8811.. 73 E
eddiee@uwest.edu
ESCALANTE, John .... 773-442-4110 146 A
j-escalante3@neiu.edu
ESCALANTE, Maria .... 800-567-2344 492 C
mescalante@menominee.edu
ESCALERA, Liya .... 617-287-5862 211 H
liya.escalera@umb.edu
ESCALERA, Liya .... 617-228-2173 214 C
lescalera@bhcc.mass.edu
ESCALERA MUÑOZ,
Jorge .... 787-620-2040 505 C
jescalera@aupr.edu
ESCALLIER, Lori, A .... 718-270-7632 317 B
lori.escallier@downstate.edu
ESCAMILLA, Cynthia, S . 210-829-3136 453 C
cyescami@uiwtx.edu
ESCAMILLA, Mark .... 361-698-1203 435 G
mescamilla@delmar.edu
ESCAMILLA, Phil .... 916-577-2200.. 76 D
pescamilla@jessup.edu
ESCH, Marj .... 989-275-5000 226 D
marj.esch@kirtland.edu
ESCH, Rod .... 970-351-3192.. 84 F
rodney.esch@unco.edu
ESCHBACH, Jeanne .... 607-962-9335 320 C
eschbach@corning-cc.edu
ESCHENBAUM, Matt .... 303-871-4256.. 84 E
matt.eschenbaum@du.edu
ESCHENBERG, Ardis ...... 808-235-7402 130 E
ardise@hawaii.edu
ESCHENBRENNER,
Nancy .... 860-773-1304.. 87 G
neschenbrenner@tunxis.edu
ESCHER, Nancy .... 401-341-2157 405 D
nancy.escher@salve.edu
ESCHHOLZ, Ingrid .... 303-315-2600.. 84 D
ingrid.eschholz@ucdenver.edu
ESCLAVON, Annette .... 972-241-3371 434 D
ESCOBAR, Fabio .... 716-270-6688 299 B
escobar@ecc.edu
ESCOBAR, Jorge, L .... 408-270-6452.. 62 F
jorge.escobar@sjeccd.edu
ESCOBAR, Luis .... 650-738-4124.. 62 L
escobarluis@smccd.edu
ESCOBAR, Maria .... 408-855-5147.. 75 D
maria.escobar@missioncollege.edu
ESCOBEDO, Beatriz .... 619-934-0797.. 61 B
ESCOBEDO, Maria .... 805-591-6220.. 40 F
maria_escobedo@cuesta.edu
ESCOE, Gigi .... 513-556-9193 361 J
gisela.escoe@uc.edu
ESCOE, Gisela .... 513-556-9193 361 J
gisela.escoe@uc.edu
ESCOFFERY, Ciaran .... 212-799-5000 303 E
ESCOLAS, Roger .... 614-222-3264 351 B
rescolas@ccad.edu
ESHELMAN, Steve .... 561-803-2022 105 C
steve_eshelman@pba.edu
ESHLEMAN, Kristen .... 860-297-2525.. 89 B
kristen.eshleman@trincoll.edu
ESHLEMAN, Kristen ...... 704-894-2583 328 E
kreshleman@davidson.edu
ESHLEMAN, Robert .... 406-656-9950 265 I
reshleman@yellowstonechristian.edu
ESKAM, Shannon .... 307-268-2596 500 U
seskam@caspercollege.edu
ESKANDARI, Sepehr ..... 406-657-2367 264 D
sepehr.eskandari@msubillings.edu
ESKER, Brian .... 312-899-5177 149 F
besker@saic.edu
ESKEW, Natalie .... 872-972-2042.. 17 E
neskew@astate.edu
ESKINS, Katrina .... 304-696-7096 489 M
eskinsk@marshall.edu
ESKOW, Karen .... 410-704-2128 204 E
keskow@towson.edu
ESKOW, Robin .... 619-260-2928.. 72 I
reskow@sandiego.edu
ESKRIDGE, Steve .... 206-546-4553 484 B
seskridge@shoreline.edu
ESLAND, Melanie .... 248-689-8282 232 C
mesland@walshcollege.edu
ESLINGER, Elise .... 507-222-5597 234 G
eeslinger@carleton.edu
ESMAEILI, Ali .... 956-872-7270 443 H
esmaeili@southtexascollege.edu

EVANS, Bill ... 402-481-3967 265 K
bill.evans@bryanhealthcollege.edu

EVANS, Bobbi ... 415-771-7020 .. 61 C
bevans@sfai.edu

EVANS, Brenda ... 978-934-5021 212 B
brenda_evans@uml.edu

EVANS, Brian ... 502-863-8223 180 H
brian_evans@georgetowncollege.edu

EVANS, Brian ... 651-641-8766 235 I
bevans@csp.edu

EVANS, Brian ... 423-697-2417 424 A
brian.evans@chattanoogastate.edu

EVANS, Charlotte ... 402-554-2772 270 A
cevans@unomaha.edu

EVANS, Charlotte ... 402-554-2772 269 K
charlotte.evans@unmc.edu

EVANS, Chas ... 601-635-2111 246 A
cevans@eccc.edu

EVANS, Chris, P ... 713-831-7863 454 G
evanscp@stthom.edu

EVANS, Chuck ... 205-226-4640 .... 4 F
cwevans@bsc.edu

EVANS, Crystal-Rae ... 414-410-4683 491 I
cevans2@stritch.edu

EVANS, Damian ... 262-595-2540 496 D
damian.evans@uwp.edu

EVANS, Damon ... 301-314-0013 202 H
devans16@umd.edu

EVANS, Dana ... 601-718-5900 .. 93 H

EVANS, David ... 209-667-3153 .. 33 B
devans@csustan.edu

EVANS, David ... 406-756-3066 263 E
devans@fvcc.edu

EVANS, David ... 972-273-3561 435 B
devans@dcccd.edu

EVANS, Dianne ... 936-261-1905 446 C
dtevan@pvamu.edu

EVANS, Donna ... 937-319-0211 347 G
devans@antiochcollege.edu

EVANS, Edward ... 718-489-2008 313 E
eevans3@sfc.edu

EVANS, Edward ... 361-825-2693 447 C
ed.evans@tamucc.edu

EVANS, Eric ... 440-375-7056 354 K
erevans@lec.edu

EVANS, Eric ... 602-384-2555 .. 11 F
eric.evans@bryanuniversity.edu

EVANS, Eric ... 606-546-1653 185 D
eevans@unionky.edu

EVANS, Eric, D ... 781-981-7000 216 B

EVANS, Erik ... 570-389-4047 393 D
eevans@bloomu.edu

EVANS, Frederick M, G 803-536-7133 411 G
fevans6@scsu.edu

EVANS, Gail ... 909-469-3796 .. 75 I
devans@westernu.edu

EVANS, Garry, W ... 214-491-6271 433 I
gevans@collin.edu

EVANS, Gary ... 607-753-2302 318 A
gary.evans@cortland.edu

EVANS, George ... 618-545-3010 141 E
gevans@kaskaskia.edu

EVANS, JR., Gilbert, L .. 386-312-4127 107 C
gilbertevans@sjrstate.edu

EVANS, Greg ... 423-652-4707 420 F
gaevans1@king.edu

EVANS, Greg ... 541-463-5340 373 D
evansg@lanecc.edu

EVANS, Ivan ... 858-534-2247 .. 70 C
ercprovost@ucsd.edu

EVANS, J. David ... 470-578-6194 121 M
devans@kennesaw.edu

EVANS, Jami ... 606-451-6726 182 G
jami.evans@kctcs.edu

EVANS, Janet, D ... 412-392-3824 396 G
jevans@pointpark.edu

EVANS, Jason ... 401-508-1880 404 D
jason.evans@jwu.edu

EVANS, Jennifer, M ... 717-867-6271 388 C
jevans@lvc.edu

EVANS, Jessica ... 618-235-2700 150 E
jessica.evans@swic.edu

EVANS, Jessica ... 254-968-9682 446 D
jevans@tarleton.edu

EVANS, Jill ... 208-496-9812 130 I
evansj@byui.edu

EVANS, John ... 901-678-2209 426 G
jevans@memphis.edu

EVANS, Johnny ... 912-279-5960 117 F
jevans@ccga.edu

EVANS, June ... 301-546-8235 201 E
evansjl1@pgcc.edu

EVANS, Kamira ... 610-892-1504 393 B
kevans@pit.edu

EVANS, Kathleen ... 315-312-2823 318 D
kathleen.evans@oswego.edu

EVANS, Katie ... 281-649-3000 437 B
kevans@hbu.edu

EVANS, Katina ... 619-201-8700 .. 60 G
katina.evans@sdcc.edu

EVANS, Keigan ... 229-500-3062 114 H
keigan.evans@asurams.edu

EVANS, Kenne ... 817-515-3055 445 F
kenneth.evans1@tccd.edu

EVANS, Kenneth, R ... 405-208-5032 367 E
kevans@okcu.edu

EVANS, Kris ... 413-585-2840 218 H
kevans@smith.edu

EVANS, Layna ... 214-333-5275 434 C
layna@dbu.edu

EVANS, Liz ... 412-392-5945 396 G
eevans@pointpark.edu

EVANS, III, Louis, D ... 713-221-2766 453 A
evansl@uhd.edu

EVANS, Marcheta, P ... 973-748-9000 276 A
marcheta_evans@bloomfield.edu

EVANS, Mario ... 843-574-6053 412 I
mario.evans@tridenttech.edu

EVANS, Marisa, L ... 814-886-6336 390 G
mevans@mtaloy.edu

EVANS, Mark ... 845-938-5502 503 I
mark.evans@westpoint.edu

EVANS, Melissa ... 315-386-7123 320 B
evansm@canton.edu

EVANS, Melissa ... 660-562-1110 257 E
mevans@nwmissouri.edu

EVANS, Michael ... 402-872-2239 268 E
mevans@peru.edu

EVANS, Michael ... 603-665-2450 274 C
m.evans@snhu.edu

EVANS, Michael, L ... 806-743-2738 451 A
michael.evans@ttuhsc.edu

EVANS, Mike ... 503-399-2391 372 B
mike.evans@chemeketa.edu

EVANS, Murry ... 510-849-8200 .. 55 G

EVANS, Nancy ... 484-365-5167 388 H
nevans@lincoln.edu

EVANS, Nate ... 704-406-4254 329 A
njevans@gardner-webb.edu

EVANS, Nicole ... 907-852-1782 .... 9 H
nicole.evan@ilisagvik.edu

EVANS, Nita ... 909-667-4411 .. 37 G

EVANS, Oliver, H ... 937-775-3035 364 E
oliver.evans@wright.edu

EVANS, Patricia ... 310-265-6143 .. 60 B
patricia.evans@usw.salvationarmy.org

EVANS, Pervis ... 432-335-6412 441 A
pevans@odessa.edu

EVANS, Philesha ... 409-772-8695 456 E
paevans@utmb.edu

EVANS, Philip ... 540-665-4515 470 G
pevans@su.edu

EVANS, Piper ... 212-228-1888 312 B

EVANS, Rhonda ... 978-869-1122 439 G

EVANS, Rick ... 818-677-6285 .. 32 C
rick.evans@csun.edu

EVANS, Robbie ... 760-252-2411 .. 26 G
revans@barstow.edu

EVANS, Runan ... 859-246-6305 181 F
runan.evans@kctcs.edu

EVANS, Russell ... 405-208-5276 367 E
revans@okcu.edu

EVANS, Ruth ... 215-572-2187 378 E
evansr@arcadia.edu

EVANS, Sammara ... 864-503-7352 414 A
sammarae@uscupstate.edu

EVANS, Sara ... 610-359-5302 382 A
sevans28@dccc.edu

EVANS, Sarah ... 317-931-2303 154 G
sevans@cts.edu

EVANS, Sharmyne ... 678-622-0390 123 D
sharmyne.evans@morehouse.edu

EVANS, Sherry, L ... 405-325-3916 370 K
sevans@ou.edu

EVANS, Sidney ... 443-885-3144 201 A
sidney.evans@morgan.edu

EVANS, Sidney, S ... 540-458-8754 477 D
sevans@wlu.edu

EVANS, Susan ... 276-223-4740 476 A
sevans@wcc.vccs.edu

EVANS, Susan ... 406-756-3822 263 E

EVANS, Suzanne, M ... 386-312-4041 107 C
suzanneevans@sjrstate.edu

EVANS, Tara ... 307-766-4019 501 I
tevans15@uwyo.edu

EVANS, Terry ... 502-863-8038 180 H
terry_evans@georgetowncollege.edu

EVANS, Terry, R ... 904-620-2624 111 B
terry.evans@unf.edu

EVANS, Thomas, M ... 210-829-3900 453 C
tevans@uiwtx.edu

EVANS, Tiffany ... 785-462-3984 173 B

EVANS, Todd ... 865-539-7164 425 B
jtevans@pstcc.edu

EVANS, Toner ... 205-726-2484 .... 6 E
jevans1@samford.edu

EVANS, Tracy, L ... 304-929-5480 488 G
tevans@newriver.edu

EVANS, Virginia, H ... 434-982-2249 472 D
veb5u@virginia.edu

EVANS, W. Franklin ... 304-336-8000 490 B
president@westliberty.edu

EVANS, William, B ... 617-552-4445 207 C
william.evans@bc.edu

EVANS-DINNEEN,
Laurie ... 907-564-8880 .... 9 F
levansdinneen@alaskapacific.edu

EVANS GOODCHILD,
Joy ... 231-995-1084 229 A
jevans@nmc.edu

EVANS JONES, Cheryl .. 706-821-8230 124 B
cevansjones@paine.edu

EVANS-PLANTS, Penny . 706-232-5374 116 B
peplants@berry.edu

EVANS TAYLOR,
Genevieve ... 818-677-2121 .. 32 C
genevieve.evanstaylor@csun.edu

EVANS WILSON, Kelly .. 937-313-3832 352 J
kelly.evans-wilson@franklin.edu

EVANSON, Mary ... 515-294-3959 163 G
mevanson@foundation.iastate.edu

EVE, Debra ... 406-353-2607 262 H
deve@ancollege.edu

EVELAND, Jessica, A ... 614-292-1132 358 D
eveland.9@osu.edu

EVELAND, Peter ... 909-580-9661 .. 34 D

EVELYN, Tom ... 864-294-2151 409 H
tom.evelyn@furman.edu

EVENER, Julie ... 800-241-1027 .. 72 G
jevener@usa.edu

EVENSON, Amanda ... 479-380-2266 .. 17 A
amande.evenson@arcomedu.org

EVENSON, Brad ... 620-278-4221 177 H
bevenson@sterling.edu

EVENSON, Shane ... 715-645-7037 499 H
shane.evenson@northwoodtech.edu

EVENSON, Tresse ... 605-274-5520 414 G
tresse.evenson@augie.edu

EVENSVOLD, Marty ... 620-251-7700 173 A
evensvold.marty@coffeyville.edu

EVERETT, Dennis ... 850-718-2216 .. 97 E
everettd@chipola.edu

EVERETT, Dennis, F ... 850-718-2216 .. 97 E
everettd@chipola.edu

EVERETT, Frankie ... 541-956-7104 376 A
feverett@roguecc.edu

EVERETT, Jim ... 208-459-5268 131 C
jeverett@collegeofidaho.edu

EVERETT, John ... 512-404-4871 430 J
jeverett@austinseminary.edu

EVERETT, John, C ... 704-636-6545 330 A
jeverett@hoodseminary.edu

EVERETT, Julia ... 256-228-6001 .... 3 B
everettj@nacc.edu

EVERETT, Kaitlin ... 732-255-0400 279 F
keveratt@ocean.edu

EVERETT, Kelly ... 229-931-2351 125 E
keverett@southgatech.edu

EVERETT, Leonard ... 352-854-2322 .. 97 N
everettl@cf.edu

EVERETT, Marcia, K ... 330-471-8335 355 D
meverett@malone.edu

EVERETT, Margaret ... 401-254-3030 405 C
meverett@rwu.edu

EVERETT, Mark ... 561-697-9200 125 F
maeverett@southuniversity.edu

EVERETT, Patricia ... 734-432-5388 227 C
peverett@madonna.edu

EVERETT, Sophia ... 205-391-2326 .... 3 E
severett@sheltonstate.edu

EVERETT, Steve ... 212-817-7000 293 F
provost@gc.cuny.edu

EVERETT, Susan ... 918-631-2602 371 C
susan-everett@utulsa.edu

EVERETT, Thomas ... 912-537-8875 116 E

EVERETT, Todd ... 614-234-5177 356 E
teverett@mccn.edu

EVERETT-HAYNES,
La Monica ... 619-594-0232 .. 33 D
leveretthaynes@sdsu.edu

EVERETT-HENSLEY,
Elaine ... 361-572-6440 457 E
elaine.hensley@victoriacollege.edu

EVERHART, Bruce ... 312-329-2040 144 I
bruce.everhart@moody.edu

EVERHART, Clinton, D .. 501-686-5113 .. 22 B
cdeverhart@uams.edu

EVERHART, Kim ... 937-775-5414 364 E
kim.everhart@wright.edu

EVERHEART, Jazmine ... 863-680-3004 100 H
jeverheart@flsouthern.edu

EVERITT, David ... 508-793-7397 208 C
deveritt@clarku.edu

EVERS, Cynthia ... 202-806-6100 .. 92 F

EVERS-MANLY, Shirley . 601-304-4302 245 A
severs-manly@alcorn.edu

EVERSLEY BRADWELL,
Nicole ... 607-274-3124 302 G
neversley@ithaca.edu

EVERSOLE, Malinda ... 276-223-4869 476 A
meversole@wcc.vccs.edu

EVERSON, Melvin ... 770-962-7580 121 E
meverson@gwinnetttech.edu

EVERTS, Sheri ... 828-262-2040 340 I
evertssn@appstate.edu

EVERY, Janice, S ... 620-421-6700 175 F
janicec@labette.edu

EVETOVICH, Tammy ... 608-342-1261 496 E
evetovicht@uwplatt.edu

EVEY, Rachel ... 509-682-6415 485 H
revey@wvc.edu

EWALD, Doug, A ... 402-559-6300 270 A
doug.ewald@unmc.edu

EWALD, Douglas ... 402-599-6300 269 K
doug.ewald@unmc.edu

EWALD, Jennifer ... 203-254-4000 .. 87 I
jewald@fairfield.edu

EWALD, Stanley ... 503-251-5717 377 B
sewald@uws.edu

EWART, Dan ... 208-885-2127 132 F
dewart@uidaho.edu

EWELL, Clint ... 928-776-2166 .. 16 J
clint.ewell@yc.edu

EWELL, Robbi ... 619-388-3870 .. 60 I
rewell@sdccd.edu

EWEN, Amy ... 401-598-4370 404 D
amy.ewen@jwu.edu

EWEN, Bernadette ... 812-877-8697 160 F
ewen@rose-hulman.edu

EWEN, Kurt ... 713-718-8176 437 C
kurt.ewen@hccs.edu

EWERS, Matt ... 307-681-6022 501 G
mewers@sheridan.edu

EWIN, Tammy ... 330-972-5766 361 H
tewin@uakron.edu

EWING, April ... 706-821-8307 124 B
aewing@paine.edu

EWING, Deborah ... 979-230-3632 431 I
deborah.ewing@brazosport.edu

EWING, Greg ... 812-535-1191 160 H
greg.ewing@smwc.edu

EWING, James ... 954-262-8082 105 A
jewing@nova.edu

EWING, Jennifer ... 619-201-8967 .. 65 G
jennifer.ewing@socalsem.edu

EWING, Matthew ... 208-426-4231 130 H
mnewing@boisestate.edu

EWING, Mel ... 406-683-7382 264 A
mel.ewing@umwestern.edu

EWING, Michele, Y ... 410-337-6000 199 B
michele.ewing@goucher.edu

EWING, Mike, J ... 320-363-5605 235 F
mjewing@csbsju.edu

EWING, Nadia ... 574-284-4560 160 I
newing@saintmarys.edu

EWING, II, Rick, M ... 419-289-5893 347 J
pewing@ashland.edu

EWING, Rob ... 510-845-5373 .. 29 B
rob@cjc.edu

EWING, Sarah ... 814-871-7618 384 A
ewing003@gannon.edu

EWING, Sunnie ... 901-722-3231 423 G
sewing@sco.edu

EWING, Terry ... 918-610-8303 368 G
terry.ewing@ptstulsa.edu

EWING-MORGAN,
Dawn ... 718-960-8111 294 A
dawn.ewing-morgan@lehman.cuny.edu

EXANTUS, Yveline ... 617-405-5912 218 C
yexantus@quincycollege.edu

FANGMEYER, Len, J ..... 308-865-8555 269 I
fangmeyerlj@unk.edu
FANN, Erin .... 843-921-6916 411 A
efann@netc.edu
FANNAN, Lisa, L .... 816-604-2314 255 F
lisa.fannan@mcckc.edu
FANNIN, Larry .... 801-878-1053 272 C
lfannin@roseman.edu
FANNIN, Nichole .... 678-839-5035 127 C
nfannin@westga.edu
FANNING, Daniel .... 218-733-6945 238 G
daniel.fanning@lsc.edu
FANNING, Eli .... 518-262-6008 289 L
FANNING, Rick .... 517-884-0101 227 F
rickfanning@msu.edu
FANNING, Rita .... 267-341-3651 385 J
rfanning@holyfamily.edu
FANT, JR., Gene, C ...... 864-977-7018 410 I
gene.fant@ngu.edu
FANT, Tyson .... 404-835-6138 423 B
tfant@richmont.edu
FANT PEGUES,
Charlotte .... 662-915-7705 249 D
cfant@olemiss.edu
FANTAUZZI, Maricelly .. 787-852-1430 507 C
mfantauzzi@hccpr.edu
FANTER, Jeff .... 317-921-4502 158 D
jfanter@ivytech.edu
FANTILLO, Karina .... 415-422-5368.. 72 J
kgfantillo@usfca.edu
FANTINI, Maria .... 856-351-2601 283 B
mfantini@salemcc.edu
FANTOZZI, Joseph .... 212-650-7865 293 D
jfantozzi@ccny.cuny.edu
FANTOZZI, Joseph .... 212-472-1500 309 D
bursaroffice@nysid.edu
FANTUZZI, Angela .... 925-473-7628.. 40 D
afantuzzi@losmedanos.edu
FANUCCHI, Tina .... 773-577-8100 136 F
tfanucchi@coynecollege.edu
FANUZZI, Robert .... 718-390-4266 313 G
fanuzzir@stjohns.edu
FAOUR, Sheila .... 318-675-6001 189 I
sheila.faour@lsuhs.edu
FAOUR, William, G .... 423-305-7783 418 F
bill.faour@chattanoogacollege.edu
FARABEE, Lars, C .... 336-841-9604 329 F
lfarabee@highpoint.edu
FARAD, Timothy .... 303-329-6355.. 79 L
FARADAY, Christine ...... 516-572-7401 307 E
christine.faraday@ncc.edu
FARAGALLA, Sameh .... 973-661-0600 277 E
sfaragalla@eastwick.edu
FARAHANI, Eric .... 631-656-2144 300 B
eric.farahani@ftc.edu
FARAHANI, Gohar .... 301-846-2451 198 I
gfarahani@frederick.edu
FARANDA, Nicholas ...... 914-261-9758 308 A
farandan@newschool.edu
FARBANIEC, David .... 845-257-3196 316 E
farbanid@newpaltz.edu
FARCHMIN, Eileen .... 863-638-1431 114 B
FARFAN, Erika, M .... 740-427-5571 354 I
farfane@kenyon.edu
FARGASON, Renee .... 850-245-0466 109 H
renee.fargason@flbog.edu
FARGNOLI, Stephanie ... 518-320-1100 315 H
FARHA, Darron, C .... 219-464-6702 162 D
darron.farha@valpo.edu
FARHAT, Joseph .... 860-832-3187.. 85 G
josephfarhat@ccsu.edu
FARIA, Mary .... 512-492-3054 430 A
mfaria@aoma.edu
FARIAS, Teddy .... 281-998-6150 443 B
teddy.farias@sjcd.edu
FARIDIAN, Fred .... 650-685-6616.. 44 F
ffaridian@gurnick.edu
FARINA, Amanda .... 910-275-6126 335 E
afarina@jamessprunt.edu
FARINA, Jonathan .... 973-761-9388 283 C
jonathan.farina@shu.edu
FARINA, Matthew, R ..... 212-592-2126 315 C
mfarina@sva.edu
FARINELLI, Robert .... 814-262-6474 393 A
rfarinelli@pennhighlands.edu
FARKAS, Esther .... 718-252-0847 326 B
FARKAS, John .... 814-886-6331 390 G
jfarkas@mtaloy.edu
FARLAND, Lisa .... 310-338-7896.. 51 A
lisa.farland@lmu.edu
FARLAY, Grace, R .... 800-686-1883 222 G
FARLESS, John, A .... 812-228-5157 162 C
jafarless@usi.edu

FARLEY, Barbara, A ...... 217-245-3001 139 C
barbara.farley@ic.edu
FARLEY, Catherine .... 805-922-6966.. 24 I
catherine.farley@hancockcollege.edu
FARLEY, Christy .... 602-872-2555.. 14 H
christy.farley@nau.edu
FARLEY, Dwayne .... 617-879-7805 213 B
dfarley@massart.edu
FARLEY, Emy .... 507-222-4290 234 G
efarley@carleton.edu
FARLEY, Gregory .... 605-642-6341 416 E
gregory.farley@bhsu.edu
FARLEY, Jerry, B .... 785-670-1022 178 C
jerry.farley@washburn.edu
FARLEY, Kathleen .... 401-341-2206 405 D
kathleen.farley2@salve.edu
FARLEY, Margaret .... 307-624-7010 501 B
margaret.farley@ewc.wy.edu
FARLEY, Patrick .... 301-891-4551 205 A
pfarley@wau.edu
FARLEY, Rebecca .... 559-934-2913.. 75 A
rebeccafarley@whccd.edu
FARLEY, Ryan .... 801-957-4681 461 C
ryan.farley@slcc.edu
FARLEY, Troy .... 616-331-3311 224 G
farleytr@gvsu.edu
FARLOW, Carolyn .... 515-965-7067 165 A
cdfarlow@dmacc.edu
FARLOW, Rita .... 727-302-6526 107 E
farlow.rita@spcollege.edu
FARMER, Blake .... 304-384-6056 489 J
bfarmer@concord.edu
FARMER, Bradley .... 614-287-2787 351 C
bfarmer@cscc.edu
FARMER, Brenda .... 605-856-8186 415 J
FARMER, David .... 910-695-3914 337 H
farmerdj@sandhills.edu
FARMER, Elizabeth, M .. 412-624-6304 400 H
efarmer@pitt.edu
FARMER, Joyce .... 610-282-1100 382 C
joyce.farmer@desales.edu
FARMER, Kris .... 785-243-1435 172 L
krisfarmer@cloud.edu
FARMER, Lindsey .... 910-695-3907 337 H
farmerl@sandhills.edu
FARMER, Lisa .... 775-673-7025 271 C
ldfarmer@tmcc.edu
FARMER, Melanie .... 304-384-6314 489 J
mfarmer@concord.edu
FARMER, Pam .... 864-977-2021 410 I
pam.farmer@ngu.edu
FARMER, Patricia, J, B .. 315-229-5265 314 D
pfarmer@stlawu.edu
FARMER, Patrick .... 618-664-7079 138 F
patrick.farmer@greenville.edu
FARMER, Scott .... 432-552-2983 456 F
farmer_s@utpb.edu
FARMER, Stephen .... 434-924-3728 472 D
smf4t@virignia.edu
FARMER, Tod Allen .... 817-594-6271 457 J
tafarmer@wc.edu
FARMER, Yolanda .... 815-280-6691 141 B
yfarmer@jjc.edu
FARMER, Yvonne .... 314-889-1419 253 E
yfarmer@fontbonne.edu
FARMER-DIXON,
Cherae .... 615-327-6207 421 D
cdixon@mmc.edu
FARMER-KAISER, Mary . 337-482-6965 193 B
kaiser@louisiana.edu
FARMER-NEAL,
Rochonda .... 254-710-3684 431 E
rochonda_farmer-neal@baylor.edu
FARMER NOONAN,
Erin .... 617-735-9991 209 D
farmer@emmanuel.edu
FARMIGA, Adriana .... 212-353-4200 297 E
adriana.farmiga@cooper.edu
FARNAM, Boyd, A .... 248-370-3110 229 I
farnam@oakland.edu
FARNAN, Christiane ...... 518-783-2353 315 E
FARNAN, JR.,
Joseph, J .... 302-356-6817.. 91 E
ashley.r.mundy@wilmu.edu
FARNEY, Kirk .... 630-752-5016 153 C
kirk.farney@wheaton.edu
FARNSWORTH, August . 541-956-7203 376 A
afarnsworth@roguecc.edu
FARNSWORTH, Scott .... 928-776-2234.. 16 J
scott.farnsworth@yc.edu
FARNSWORTH, Tracy .... 208-795-4266 131 F
FARNSWORTH, Vicki ..... 423-425-1755 427 C
vicki-farnsworth@utc.edu

FARNSWORTH, Ward .... 512-232-1120 455 A
wf@law.utexas.edu
FARQUHAR,
Sherry Leigh .... 334-833-4562.... 5 G
internships@hawks.huntingdon.edu
FARQUHARSON,
Donald .... 816-523-9140 262 D
don.f@wellspring.edu
FARQUHARSON, Hope .. 951-487-6752.. 53 A
hfarquharson@msjc.edu
FARR, Matthew .... 856-222-9311 281 C
mfarr@rcbc.edu
FARR, Paul .... 229-931-2482 125 E
pfarr@southgatech.edu
FARR, Sharon .... 573-288-6633 252 F
sfarr@culver.edu
FARR, Shawn .... 717-728-2275 380 E
shawnfarr@centralpenn.edu
FARRAH, Anne .... 800-818-6136.. 55 L
afarrah@palaoltou.edu
FARRAR, Carol .... 951-222-8493.. 59 D
carol.farrar@rcc.edu
FARRAR, Griffen .... 712-325-3487 167 I
gfarrar@iwcc.edu
FARRAR, JR.,
James, D .... 540-458-8417 477 D
jdfarrar@wlu.edu
FARRELL, Allison .... 315-445-4275 303 I
cudaal@lemoyne.edu
FARRELL, Chris .... 814-631-9633 393 A
cfarrell@pennhighlands.edu
FARRELL, Cynthia, H .... 724-589-2178 399 D
cfarrell@thiel.edu
FARRELL, Diane .... 706-864-1951 127 A
diane.farrell@ung.edu
FARRELL, Dina .... 971-722-2851 375 D
dina.farrell@pcc.edu
FARRELL, Dolly .... 239-590-7638 109 K
dofarrell@fgcu.edu
FARRELL, Donna .... 423-323-3191 425 A
FARRELL, Erin, P .... 317-788-2127 161 H
farrelle@uindy.edu
FARRELL, Gregory .... 212-220-1379 293 A
gfarrell@bmcc.cuny.edu
FARRELL, Jill .... 305-899-3649.. 96 A
jfarrell@barry.edu
FARRELL, Jillian .... 864-578-8770 411 F
jfarrell@sherman.edu
FARRELL, Kathleen .... 914-251-6090 319 B
kathleen.farrell@purchase.edu
FARRELL, Kathy .... 402-472-9500 269 J
kfarrell2@unl.edu
FARRELL, Kevin .... 570-961-4725 389 D
kfarrell@marywood.edu
FARRELL, Lauren, M ..... 724-925-4079 402 F
farrelll@westmoreland.edu
FARRELL, Lisa, M .... 636-584-6558 253 B
lisa.farrell@eastcentral.edu
FARRELL, Maggie .... 702-895-2286 271 D
maggie.farrell@unlv.edu
FARRELL, Natasha .... 315-445-4460 303 I
farrelnt@lemoyne.edu
FARRELL, Neil .... 631-632-6350 317 A
neil.farrell@stonybrook.edu
FARRELL, Patricia .... 918-781-7394 365 C
farrellp@bacone.edu
FARRELL, Robert, B ...... 570-941-6213 401 F
robert.farrell@scranton.edu
FARRELL, Shawn .... 909-537-3015.. 32 E
shawn.farrell@csusb.edu
FARRELL, Stephanie ...... 856-256-5300 281 F
farrell@rowan.edu
FARRELL, Thomas 585-275-1837 323M
farrellt@rochester.edu
FARRELL, Tony .... 858-513-9240.. 68 K
courtney.farrell@ashford.edu
FARREN, Chelsea .... 215-248-7011 381 A
farrenc@chc.edu
FARRIER, Jasmine .... 502-852-6924 186 A
j.farrier@louisville.edu
FARRINGTON, Keisha ... 214-860-2032 434 I
kfarrington@dcccd.edu
FARRINGTON, Lisa, E ... 202-806-6100.. 92 F
FARRINGTON, Mary ...... 919-267-1640 330 B
FARRINGTON, Susan .... 903-510-2371 452 A
susan.farrington@tjc.edu
FARRIOR, Andy .... 361-582-2547 457 E
andy.farrior@victoriacollege.edu
FARRIS, G. Corey .... 304-293-5811 490 E
corey.farris@mail.wvu.edu
FARRIS, Kent .... 662-728-7751 248 C
FARRIS, Kristie .... 423-697-3143 424 A
kristie.farris@chattanoogastate.edu

FARRIS, Michael .... 434-832-7891 473 E
farrism@centralvirginia.edu
FARRIS, Michael, P ...... 540-338-1776 469 C
chancellor@phc.edu
FARRIS, Rachel .... 251-981-3771.... 5 A
rachel.farris@columbiasouthern.edu
FARRIS, Thomas, N ...... 848-445-1640 282 A
tfarris@rutgers.edu
FARROW, Joseph .... 530-752-3113.. 69 B
jafarrow@ucdavis.edu
FARRY, Gavin .... 847-578-3252 148 F
gavin.farry@rosalindfranklin.edu
FARSAD, Sarah .... 212-396-6863 294 C
sf957@hunter.cuny.edu
FARTHING, Scott .... 949-582-4907.. 65 D
sfarthing@saddleback.edu
FARVARDIN, Nariman ... 201-216-5213 283 D
president@stevens.edu
FARVOUR, Jennifer, K .. 920-923-8725 493 D
jkfarvour37@marianuniversity.edu
FARWELL, Kamrhan ...... 573-882-4523 260 I
FARWELL, Kamrhan, M . 573-882-4523 261 A
farwellk@missouri.edu
FARWELL, Keenan .... 207-778-7009 196 I
keenan.farwell@maine.edu
FARWELL, Susan .... 217-732-3168 142 G
FARYNIAK, Karen, N ..... 717-245-1323 382 D
faryniak@dickinson.edu
FASANELLA, Karen .... 973-748-9000 276 A
karen_fasanella@bloomfield.edu
FASANO, Frank .... 415-338-2125.. 33 E
ffasano@sfsu.edu
FASSERO, Matt .... 913-360-7420 171 J
mfassero@benedictine.edu
FASSETT, Lori .... 989-386-6692 228 B
lfassett1@midmich.edu
FASSINO, Dina .... 715-425-4306 496 F
dina.fassino@uwrf.edu
FAST, Doreen .... 620-229-6223 177 G
doreen.fast@sckans.edu
FAST, Katie .... 541-737-4514 375 A
FASTNOW, Chris .... 406-994-2870 264 C
cfastnow@montana.edu
FATERI, Fardad .... 786-534-0500.. 99 L
FATH, Stephen, J .... 713-500-5202 456 B
stephen.j.fath@uth.tmc.edu
FATHALLAH, Fadi .... 530-754-9707.. 69 B
fathallah@ucdavis.edu
FATHERLY, Sarah .... 704-337-2568 339 F
fatherlys@queens.edu
FATIMA, Nasrin .... 607-777-2365 316 B
nfatima@binghamton.edu
FATKIN, Beth .... 316-942-4291 176 E
fatkinb@newmanu.edu
FATOOL, Kirk .... 765-448-1986 155 B
FATTA, Libby .... 805-289-6474.. 74 B
lfatta@vcccd.edu
FATTOUH, Said .... 713-221-8059 453 A
fattouhs@uhd.edu
FAUCETT, Trinity .... 919-718-7291 333 C
tfaucett@cccc.edu
FAUCHET, Philippe, M .. 615-322-0720 428 A
philippe.m.fauchet@vanderbilt.edu
FAUCI, Darcy .... 607-777-2131 316 B
dfauci@binghamton.edu
FAUDREE, Donna .... 574-807-7752 154 B
donna.faudree@betheluniversity.edu
FAUGHANAN, Timothy . 607-777-2275 316 B
tfaughn@binghamton.edu
FAUGHT, Jerry .... 580-481-5243 457 I
jerry.faught@wbu.edu
FAUGHT, Norma .... 575-392-5018 287 A
nfaught@nmjc.edu
FAULCONER, Christian . 801-422-4690 458 H
christian_faulconer@byu.edu
FAULK, Randy .... 361-570-4397 453 B
faulkr@uhv.edu
FAULKNER, B. Keith ..... 276-244-1283 464 E
bkfaulkner@asl.edu
FAULKNER, Brenda .... 254-968-9044 446 D
faulkne@tarleton.edu
FAULKNER, Doug .... 618-664-6626 138 F
doug.faulkner@greenville.edu
FAULKNER,
Jacqueline, A .... 901-333-5722 425 D
jfaulkner@southwest.tn.edu
FAULKNER, Jessica ...... 501-205-8800.. 18 H
jfaulkner@cbc.edu
FAULKNER, Karen, R .... 812-888-5640 162 F
kfaulkner@vinu.edu
FAULKNER, Keith .... 434-592-5351 468 E
bkfaulkner@liberty.edu

FELIX, Vivienne .... 724-503-1001 402 B
vfelix@washjeff.edu
FELKER, Sharon, M ...... 303-963-3369.. 78 H
sfelker@ccu.edu
FELKER, Steven .... 757-825-2716 475 D
felkers@tncc.edu
FELL, Julie .... 319-335-0224 163 H
julie-fell@uiowa.edu
FELL, Katherine, R .... 419-434-4510 362 D
fell@findlay.edu
FELL, Vince .... 806-743-7013 451 A
vince.fell@ttuhsc.edu
FELLEGY, Anna .... 218-879-0878 238 B
afellegy@fdltcc.edu
FELLER, Cory .... 218-683-8633 240 B
cory.feller@northlandcollege.edu
FELLER, David, C .... 414-955-8424 493 F
dfeller@mcw.edu
FELLER, Scott, E .... 765-361-6221 163 B
fellers@wabash.edu
FELLINGER, Jennifer ..... 616-395-7860 225 D
fellinger@hope.edu
FELSER, Francis, J .... 716-250-7500 292 A
fjfelser@bryantstratton.edu
FELSKE, Eileen .... 973-618-3419 276 D
efelske@caldwell.edu
FELT, Bryan .... 973-761-9492 283 C
bryan.felt@shu.edu
FELTHOUSEN, Robert .... 541-956-7147 376 A
rfelthousen@roguecc.edu
FELTNER, Michael, E .... 310-506-4280.. 56 G
michael.feltner@pepperdine.edu
FELTON, David .... 251-405-7118.... 1 E
dfelton@bishop.edu
FELTON, Dean .... 310-287-4499.. 49 H
feltond@wlac.edu
FELTON, JR.,
Herman, J .... 903-927-3201 458 F
seventeen@wileyc.edu
FELTON, III, James ...... 609-771-2423 276 I
feltonj@tcnj.edu
FELTON, Rob .... 503-554-2129 373 A
rfelton@georgefox.edu
FELTON, Shawn .... 607-255-5241 297 F
admissions@cornell.edu
FELTON, Shawn .... 239-590-7511 109 K
sfelton@fgcu.edu
FELTON, Terence .... 630-466-7900 152 K
tfelton@waubonsee.edu
FELTS, Cynthia .... 812-488-1046 161 G
cf128@evansville.edu
FELTS, Jessica .... 706-583-2893 115 F
jfelts@athenstech.edu
FELTS, Joanna .... 559-251-4215.. 27 I
jfelts@calchristiancollege.edu
FELTS, Ronald .... 661-726-1911.. 68 J
ron.felts@uav.edu
FELTY, Darren .... 843-958-5813 412 I
darren.felty@tridenttech.edu
FELTY, James .... 717-867-6698 388 C
felty@lvc.edu
FELVER, Richard .... 413-236-2151 214 A
rfelver@berkshirecc.edu
FEMINELLA,
Catherine, A .... 610-499-4392 402 G
cafeminella@widener.edu
FEMINO, Donny .... 978-232-5201 209 E
dfemino@endicott.edu
FEML, Nicole, A .... 315-267-2128 319 A
conantna@potsdam.edu
FENCSIK, Alissa .... 510-204-0727.. 36 I
afencsik@cdsp.edu
FENDER, Samantha .... 828-689-1126 331 C
sfender@mhu.edu
FENDERS, Nancy .... 207-941-7153 194 F
fendersn@husson.edu
FENDRICH, Chris .... 719-549-2611.. 80 B
chris.fendrich@csupueblo.edu
FENG, Alice .... 858-784-8469.. 64 A
FENG, Jin .... 641-269-4464 166 G
fengjin@grinnell.edu
FENG, Xiaodong .... 916-686-8066.. 29 E
FENG, Xiaodong .... 916-686-7400.. 29 E
FENLASON, Julie .... 320-762-4531 237 C
julief@alextech.edu
FENLASON, Laurie .... 413-585-2170 218 H
lfenlaso@smith.edu
FENLON, Matt .... 617-287-5000 211 H
matt.fenlon@umb.edu
FENN, Jennifer .... 360-596-5444 484 D
jfenn@spscc.edu
FENNEBERG, Leanna ...... 609-896-5313 281 B
lfenneberg@rider.edu
FENNELL, Angelia .... 903-593-8311 448 G
afennell@texascollege.edu
FENNELL, Barbara .... 432-686-4250 440 B
bfennell@midland.edu
FENNELL, Catherine ...... 610-896-1221 385 I
cfennell@haverford.edu
FENNELL, Dwight .... 903-593-8311 448 G
dfennell@texascollege.edu
FENNELL, Katie .... 740-376-4369 355 E
katie.cretin@marietta.edu
FENNELL, Sabrina .... 716-839-8228 298 A
sfennell@daemen.edu
FENNER, Felicia .... 706-821-8320 124 B
ffenner@paine.edu
FENNERN, Nikki .... 847-628-2521 141 C
nikki.fennern@judsonu.edu
FENNESSY, Greg .... 803-812-7354 413 E
fennesj@mailbox.sc.edu
FENNING, Julie .... 218-793-2463 240 B
julie.fenning@northlandcollege.edu
FENOGLIO, Sharon .... 314-516-6788 261 C
fenoglios@umsl.edu
FENRICH, Eileen .... 202-687-0100.. 92 E
FENRICK, David .... 651-641-3517 236 G
dfenrick001@luthersem.edu
FENSKE, Susanne .... 814-393-2351 393 G
sfenske@clarion.edu
FENSTERMACHER, Erin . 610-606-4612 380 D
erin.fenstermacher@cedarcrest.edu
FENTIMAN, Angela .... 805-493-3839.. 29 C
FENTON, Kimberly .... 716-286-8566 309 H
kfenton@niagara.edu
FENTRESS, Brittany .... 209-667-3395.. 33 B
bfentress@csustan.edu
FENTRESS, Craig, M ...... 240-500-2352 199 C
cmfentress@hagerstowncc.edu
FENVES, Gregory, L ...... 404-727-6013 118 E
president@emory.edu
FENWICK, Brad .... 620-665-3417 174 G
fenwickb@hutchcc.edu
FENWICK, Garland .... 540-423-9046 473 I
gfenwick@germanna.edu
FENWICK, Jim .... 818-947-2508.. 49 G
fenwicjl@lavc.edu
FERALDI, Corey .... 803-641-3280 413 B
coreyf@usca.edu
FERALDI, Patricia, A ..... 716-673-3553 316 D
patricia.feraldi@fredonia.edu
FERBER, David .... 402-399-2319 266 F
dferber@csm.edu
FERBER, Moshe .... 718-601-3523 326 C
mosheferber@ytariverdale.org
FERBER, Paul .... 636-481-3420 254 C
pferber@jeffco.edu
FERBRACHE, Jeanne ..... 402-559-3937 269 K
jferbrache@unmc.edu
FERDARKO, Mark .... 770-792-6100 122 C
mark.ferdarco@life.edu
FERDINAND, Jason .... 256-726-7277..... 6 C
jferdinand@oakwood.edu
FERDON, Joel .... 704-991-0261 338 C
jferdon0525@stanly.edu
FEREBEE, Cheryl .... 678-916-2615 115 I
cferebee@johnmarshall.edu
FEREBEE, Ryan .... 804-524-5297 476 D
rferebee@vsu.edu
FEREDE, Mulugeta .... 512-475-6600 455 A
mferede@utexas.edu
FEREIRA, James .... 864-231-2000 406 F
jfereira@andersonuniversity.edu
FERENCE, Jonathan, D .. 570-408-4271 403 A
jonathan.ference@wilkes.edu
FERENCHAK, Greg .... 903-785-7661 441 D
gferenchak@parisjc.edu
FERGEL, Mike .... 701-349-5421 346 I
mfergel@trinitybiblecollege.edu
FERGUS, Roy .... 516-299-2277 304 E
roy.fergus@liu.edu
FERGUSON, Annette ...... 281-425-6887 438 I
aferguson@lee.edu
FERGUSON, Barclay ...... 414-955-8740 493 F
bferguson@mcw.edu
FERGUSON, Brooke .... 540-857-6323 475 G
bferguson@virginiawestern.edu
FERGUSON, Charity, F .. 270-384-8100 183 G
fergusonc@lindsey.edu
FERGUSON, Chris .... 209-946-2011.. 71 E
FERGUSON, Colin .... 276-656-0349 474 G
cferguson@patrickhenry.edu
FERGUSON, Conner ...... 304-462-6116 489 L
conner.ferguson@glenville.edu
FERGUSON, Cristie .... 903-693-2005 441 C
cferguson@panola.edu
FERGUSON, Darla .... 321-433-7080.. 98 I
fergusond@easternflorida.edu
FERGUSON, David .... 765-285-8971 153 H
dferguson@bsu.edu
FERGUSON, Douglas, J 610-359-7399 382 A
dferguson4@dccc.edu
FERGUSON, Glenda ...... 478-757-5241 127 F
gferguson@wesleyancollege.edu
FERGUSON, Jason .... 434-832-7797 473 E
fergusonj@centralvirginia.edu
FERGUSON, Jason .... 434-223-6327 467 F
jferguson@hsc.edu
FERGUSON, Jason .... 228-497-7800 247 E
jason.ferguson@mgccc.edu
FERGUSON, Jennifer ..... 757-822-7330 475 E
jferguson@tcc.edu
FERGUSON, Joseph, C . 915-831-7730 436 A
jfergu11@epcc.edu
FERGUSON, Julie .... 570-941-4330 401 F
julie.ferguson@scranton.edu
FERGUSON, Karen .... 304-326-1465 487 I
karen.ferguson@salemu.edu
FERGUSON, Karen .... 800-462-7845.. 80 A
FERGUSON, Keith .... 256-233-8215.... 4 C
keith.ferguson@athens.edu
FERGUSON, Kenlanna ... 269-337-7191 225 F
kenlanna.feguson@kzoo.edu
FERGUSON, Kenneth ..... 540-636-2900 465 L
ken.ferguson@christendom.edu
FERGUSON, Kim .... 914-395-2371 315 A
kferguson@sarahlawrence.edu
FERGUSON, Larry .... 606-326-2042 181 D
larry.ferguson@kctcs.edu
FERGUSON, Lee .... 903-923-2048 435 H
lferguson@etbu.edu
FERGUSON, Lisa .... 270-789-5109 180 A
lgferguson@campbellsville.edu
FERGUSON, Lisa, M ..... 740-284-5894 352 I
lferguson@franciscan.edu
FERGUSON, Mark .... 202-319-5188.. 92 A
cua-architecture@cua.edu
FERGUSON, Mark .... 973-290-4238 282 I
mferguson@steu.edu
FERGUSON, Megan, R .. 605-342-0317 415 C
library@jwc.edu
FERGUSON, Melissa ...... 937-294-0592 356 D
melissa.ferguson@themodern.edu
FERGUSON, Melody, A . 253-535-7077 482 A
fergusma@plu.edu
FERGUSON, Nancy .... 706-542-6147 126 G
nferg@uga.edu
FERGUSON, Noreen ...... 248-204-3106 227 A
nferguson@ltu.edu
FERGUSON, Oliver .... 952-446-4486 235 J
fergusono@crown.edu
FERGUSON, Pam .... 309-672-5510 144 C
pmferguson@methodistcol.edu
FERGUSON, Pamela ...... 973-720-2615 284 J
fergusonp4@wpunj.edu
FERGUSON, Paul, W ..... 626-812-3075.. 26 F
president@apu.edu
FERGUSON, Randi .... 856-225-6760 281 G
randi.ferguson@camden.rutgers.edu
FERGUSON, Randy .... 276-656-0229 474 G
rferguson@patrickhenry.edu
FERGUSON, JR.,
Roy, W .... 540-828-5307 464 L
rferguson@bridgewater.edu
FERGUSON, Sam .... 325-793-4631 439 F
ferguson.sam@mcm.edu
FERGUSON, Sarah .... 972-860-4854 434 F
sferguson@dcccd.edu
FERGUSON, Sarah .... 303-385-1070 359 F
FERGUSON, Sarah .... 830-372-8002 449 A
sferguson@tlu.edu
FERGUSON, Stephanie .. 575-492-2643 287 A
sferguson@nmjc.edu
FERGUSON, Timothy ...... 859-572-7770 184 E
fergusont2@nku.edu
FERGUSON, Vicki .... 925-969-2005.. 40 C
vferguson@dvc.edu
FERGUSON, Vicky .... 254-519-5720 447 A
vferguson@tamuct.edu
FERGUSON STEGER,
Emily .... 406-243-2311 263 K
emily.steger@umontana.edu
FERLAND, Chris .... 478-445-3350 119 B
chris.ferland@gcsu.edu
FERLAND, William, R ... 401-825-1210 404 C
wferland@ccri.edu
FERLAZZO, Mike .... 570-577-2000 379 C
mike.ferlazzo@bucknell.edu
FERLEGER, Naomi, A .... 845-575-3000 305 D
naomi.ferleger@marist.edu
FERMAN, Pamela .... 716-375-2351 313 C
pferman@sbu.edu
FERME, Valerio .... 513-556-2588 361 J
provost@uc.edu
FERNÁNDEZ, Camelia ... 787-728-1515 513 D
cameliac.fernandez@sagrado.edu
FERNÁNDEZ, Ramón ..... 787-264-1912 508 F
ramon_fernandez@sangerman.inter.edu
FERNÁNDEZ MORAL,
Leticia .... 787-751-0500 513 B
leticia.fernandez@upr.edu
FERN, Abigail .... 620-235-4122 177 A
afern@pittstate.edu
FERNALD, Julian, L ...... 831-459-4341.. 71 A
jfernald@ucsc.edu
FERNANDER, Kevin, A .. 561-868-3143 105 D
fernandk@palmbeachstate.edu
FERNANDES, Brian .... 845-848-7807 298 C
brian.fernandes@dc.edu
FERNANDES, Jamie .... 404-894-7162 119 E
jamie.fernandes@business.gatech.edu
FERNANDES, Jane .... 937-767-1286 347 G
FERNANDES, Joseph .... 617-745-3000 209 B
FERNANDES, Kim .... 816-604-1418 255 C
kim.fernandes@mcckc.edu
FERNANDES, Sidney ..... 813-974-7927 111 C
sfernand@health.usf.edu
FERNANDEZ, Angela ..... 937-512-2917 360 G
angela.fernandez@sinclair.edu
FERNANDEZ,
Damian, J .... 727-864-8211.. 98 J
president@eckerd.edu
FERNANDEZ, Dianne ..... 509-865-8600 481 A
FERNANDEZ, Edel .... 507-389-7200 241 C
edel.fernandez@southcentral.edu
FERNANDEZ, Edith .... 702-992-2358 271 B
edith.fernandez@nsc.edu
FERNANDEZ, Ernie .... 305-284-8281 113 C
erniefernandez@miami.edu
FERNANDEZ, Eva .... 718-997-2867 295 B
eva.fernandez@qc.cuny.edu
FERNANDEZ, Frank .... 614-236-6504 349 B
ffernand@capital.edu
FERNANDEZ, Henry, B .. 954-486-7728 113 B
uftlchancellor@uftl.edu
FERNANDEZ, Hilary .... 212-353-4100 297 E
FERNANDEZ, Jazmine ... 954-776-4476 103 B
jazminef@keiseruniversity.edu
FERNANDEZ, Jeffrey ..... 508-289-2325 220 E
jfernandez@whoi.edu
FERNANDEZ, Jorge .... 973-748-9000 276 A
jorge_fernandez@bloomfield.edu
FERNANDEZ, Jose .... 973-684-6107 280 A
jfernandez@pccc.edu
FERNANDEZ, Julie .... 843-863-7914 407 B
jfernandez@csuniv.edu
FERNANDEZ, Marco, A . 915-831-6498 436 A
mferna56@epcc.edu
FERNANDEZ, Marla .... 660-785-4130 260 F
mfernandez@truman.edu
FERNANDEZ, Mayra ...... 509-453-0374 482 D
mayra.fernandez@perrytech.edu
FERNANDEZ, Miguel ..... 802-443-5792 462 E
fernande@middlebury.edu
FERNANDEZ, Mike .... 615-966-5186 421 B
mike.fernandez@lipscomb.edu
FERNANDEZ,
Rodolfo, J .... 305-284-4085 113 C
rudyfernandez@miami.edu
FERNANDEZ, Serafin ..... 707-524-1704.. 63 D
sfernandez2@santarosa.edu
FERNANDEZ, Terry .... 202-885-2554.. 91 F
tfernan@american.edu
FERNANDEZ, Yaniris ..... 413-559-5781 210 D
ymfpr@hampshire.edu
FERNANDEZ-TORRES,
Luis, C .... 305-474-6014 107 F
fernandez@stu.edu
FERNANDO, Gihan .... 202-885-1829.. 91 F
gihan@american.edu
FERNANDO, Lionel .... 910-362-7890 332 H
lsfernando826@mail.cfcc.edu
FERNANDO, Rukshan ... 626-969-3434.. 26 F
FERNETTE, Eric .... 713-500-3110 456 B
eric.fernette@uth.tmc.edu
FERNHALL, Bo .... 312-996-6695 151 G
fernhall@uic.edu
FERNIANY, Will .... 205-975-5362.... 8 A
ferniany@uab.edu
FERNOS, Manuel, J ...... 787-766-1912 508 C
mfernos@inter.edu

FIELDS, Petra ... 704-991-0231 338 C
pfields7679@stanly.edu
FIELDS, Scott ... 603-230-3500 272 I
sfields@ccsnh.edu
FIELDS, Stanley ... 708-656-8000 145 C
stanley.fields@morton.edu
FIELDS, Stephenie ... 817-594-5471 457 J
sfields@wc.edu
FIELDS, Todd, E ... 972-881-5174 433 I
tfields@collin.edu
FIELDS, Valerie ... 318-342-5215 193 C
fields@ulm.edu
FIELDS, W. Bradley ... 859-238-5485 180 B
brad.fields@centre.edu
FIELER, Vickie, K ... 603-594-2567 274 B
vfieler@sjhnh.org
FIER, Luke ... 540-671-6981 465 L
luke.fier@christendom.edu
FIER, Sara ... 507-537-7150 241 D
sara.fier@smsu.edu
FIERKE, Carol, A ... 781-736-2101 208 A
carolfierke@brandeis.edu
FIERO, Diane ... 661-362-3424.. 38 D
diane.fiero@canyons.edu
FIERRO, Jose, L ... 562-860-2451.. 35 H
jfierro@cerritos.edu
FIERRO, Melissa ... 432-837-8166 450 B
melissa.fierro@sulross.edu
FIESE, Richard ... 325-646-8600 437 G
rfiese@hputx.edu
FIEZ, Terri ... 303-492-7401.. 84 B
terri.fiez@colorado.edu
FIFE, Dustin ... 970-943-2278.. 85 C
dfife@western.edu
FIFER, Tom ... 660-831-4219 256 I
fifert@moval.edu
FIGA, Jan ... 305-899-3768.. 96 A
jfiga@barry.edu
FIGARI, Charles, A ... 713-500-8400 456 B
charles.a.figari@uth.tmc.edu
FIGLER, Daniel, J ... 252-862-1226 337 C
djfigler@roanokechowan.edu
FIGLIANO, Fred ... 334-808-6509.... 7 C
ffigliano@troy.edu
FIGLIO, David, N ... 847-491-3828 146 E
figlio@northwestern.edu
FIGORA, Luke ... 847-467-6171 146 E
luke.figora@northwestern.edu
FIGUEIRA, Josh ... 801-422-2049 130 I
figueira@byui.edu
FIGUEIREDO, Kevin ... 617-747-8681 206 H
studentfinancialservices@berklee.edu
FIGUEIREDO, Rosa ... 978-681-0800 216 C
FIGUEROA, Agnes ... 253-680-7080 477 I
afigueroa@batestech.edu
FIGUEROA, Angel ... 787-753-6000 507 D
a_figueroa@icprjc.edu
FIGUEROA, Carolina ... 781-891-2855 206 G
cfigueroa@bentley.edu
FIGUEROA, Eduardo ... 787-882-2065 510 C
technoloa_industrial@unitecpr.net
FIGUEROA, Fernando ... 859-442-1175 181 H
fernando.figueroa@kctcs.edu
FIGUEROA, Gisela ... 956-295-3379 449 C
gisela.figueroa@tsc.edu
FIGUEROA, Jennifer, E . 570-577-1028 379 C
j.figueroa@bucknell.edu
FIGUEROA, Juan, A ... 787-786-3030 511 A
jfigueroa@ucb.edu.pr
FIGUEROA, Maria, V ... 787-743-7979 510 H
ut_mfigueroa@suagm.edu
FIGUEROA, Marilyn ... 787-728-1515 513 D
marilyn.figueroa@sagrado.edu
FIGUEROA, Mark ... 503-768-7676 373 E
figueroa@lclark.edu
FIGUEROA, Maruth ... 858-534-3844.. 70 C
mafigueroa@ucsd.edu
FIGUEROA, Shannon ... 409-880-7819 449 G
shannon.figueroa@lamar.edu
FIGUEROA, Vitaliano ... 608-785-8062 496 A
vfigueroa@uwlax.edu
FIGUEROA, William ... 787-758-2525 512 F
william.figueroa2@upr.edu
FIGUEROA, Wilma ... 787-279-1912 508 A
wfigueroa@bayamon.inter.edu
FIGUEROA-RODRÍGUEZ,
Carina ... 787-993-8897 512 A
carina.figueroa@upr.edu
FIGURSKI, Eric ... 620-331-4100 174 H
efigurski@indycc.edu
FIJAL, Amanda ... 773-702-7659 151 E
afijal@uchicago.edu

FIKE, David, J ... 415-442-7059.. 43 I
dfike@ggu.edu
FIKE, Janet ... 304-214-8837 488 J
jfike@wvncc.edu
FIKE, Nancy ... 810-762-9925 226 B
nfike@kettering.edu
FIKE-CURRY, Esther ... 407-831-9816.. 97 F
efike@citycollege.edu
FILA, Jennifer ... 607-436-2491 316 F
jennifer.fila@oneonta.edu
FILA, Susan ... 310-434-4746.. 63 C
fila_susan@smc.edu
FILAK, Andrew ... 513-558-7333 361 J
andrew.filak@uc.edu
FILARDI, Salvatore ... 203-582-8800.. 88 G
salvatore.filardi@quinnipiac.edu
FILARDO, Amy ... 443-840-5215 198 H
afilardo@ccbcmd.edu
FILE, Carter ... 620-665-3505 174 G
filec@hutchcc.edu
FILE, Jayme ... 785-738-9037 176 F
jfile@ncktc.edu
FILEMYR, Ann ... 505-467-6823 288 H
annfilemyr@swc.edu
FILES, Sylvia ... 310-233-4011.. 49 B
filesss@lahc.edu
FILIATREAU, Amy ... 561-237-7000 103W
afiliatreau@lynn.edu
FILION, Diane ... 816-235-1107 261 B
filiond@umkc.edu
FILIPCHUK, Danielle ... 567-661-7970 359 I
danielle_filipchuk@owens.edu
FILIPETTO, Frank ... 817-735-2221 454 B
frank.filipetto@unthsc.edu
FILIPPONE, Anne ... 610-902-8407 379 G
anne.filippone@cabrini.edu
FILKO, Jeffrey, D ... 407-582-1709 113 I
jfilko@valenciacollege.edu
FILLER, Daniel, M ... 215-571-4705 382 F
daniel.m.filler@drexel.edu
FILLING-BROWN,
Michelle ... 610-902-8502 379 G
mlf57@cabrini.edu
FILLINGER, Barbara ... 734-973-3560 232 D
bfillinger@wccnet.edu
FILLION, Jennifer ... 810-762-0474 228 F
jennifer.fillion@mcc.edu
FILLPOT, Jim ... 909-652-7676.. 35 L
jim.fillpot@chaffey.edu
FILOSA, Bruce ... 718-951-5366 293 C
bfilosa@brooklyn.cuny.edu
FILOWITZ, Mark ... 657-278-2945.. 31 C
mfilowitz@fullerton.edu
FILS, Guerda ... 212-938-5883 319 E
gfils@sunyopt.edu
FILS AIME, Andel, P ... 407-582-1388 113 I
afilsaime4@valenciacollege.edu
FILSON, Cori ... 518-580-5355 315 F
cfilson@skidmore.edu
FILSON, David ... 215-887-5511 402 E
dfilson@wts.edu
FINALY, Roy ... 818-575-6800.. 68 C
yoram.neumann@tuw.edu
FINALY, Roy ... 818-575-6800.. 68 C
roy.finaly@tuw.edu
FINCANNON, Angie, L .. 260-422-5561 156 E
alfincannon@indianatech.edu
FINCH, Amanda ... 607-436-2513 316 F
amanda.finch@oneonta.edu
FINCH, Amy ... 731-286-3347 424 D
finch@dscc.edu
FINCH, Christopher ... 201-559-6084 277 J
finchc@felician.edu
FINCH, Jim ... 626-396-2456.. 26 B
jim.finch@artcenter.edu
FINCH, Joanna ... 314-246-7114 262 C
joannafinch84@webster.edu
FINCH, Judy ... 503-768-7328 373 E
finchj@lclark.edu
FINCH, Kathryn ... 912-688-6922 123 J
kfinch@ogeecheetech.edu
FINCH, Kim ... 985-545-1500 188 E
FINCH, Manicia ... 314-340-3383 254 A
finchm@hssu.edu
FINCH, Marissa ... 315-792-4575 324 B
mmfinch@utica.edu
FINCH, Tony ... 662-720-7304 248 C
tfinch@nemcc.edu
FINCH, Tracy ... 870-972-2031.. 17 E
tfinch@astate.edu
FINCH-SIMPSON,
Hedda, T ... 340-692-4228 513 E
hfinch@uvi.edu

FINCHAM, Brian, S ... 515-964-0601 166 D
finchamb@faith.edu
FINCHER, David, B ... 660-263-3900 251 D
president@cccb.edu
FINCHER, Ken ... 541-885-1118 374 I
ken.fincher@oit.edu
FINCHER, Louise ... 276-944-6342 466 L
lfincher@ehc.edu
FINCK, Brandy ... 207-621-3037 196 H
brandy.finck@maine.edu
FINDLEN, Sean, T ... 207-786-6328 194 A
sfindlen@bates.edu
FINDLEY, Lauren ... 256-782-5265.... 6 A
lsthomas@jsu.edu
FINDLEY, Mike, T ... 402-280-5746 266 H
mikefindley@creighton.edu
FINDTNER, Rob ... 503-838-8601 377 D
findtnr@wou.edu
FINE, David ... 303-605-5234.. 81 M
dfine2@msudenver.edu
FINE, Kimberly ... 910-788-6305 338 A
kimberly.fine@sccnc.edu
FINEGAN, SC, Carol, M 718-405-3349 296 F
carol.finegan@mountsaintvincent.edu
FINEGOLD, David ... 412-365-1160 380 G
finegold@chatham.edu
FINELLI, Chris ... 910-962-3787 343 C
finellic@uncw.edu
FINGER, Mary ... 724-838-4211 398 C
mfinger@setonhill.edu
FINGEROTE, Paul ... 510-845-5373.. 29 B
FINHOLT, Thomas, A ... 734-647-3576 231 H
finholt@umich.edu
FINK, Brenda ... 626-914-8830.. 36 J
bfink@citruscollege.edu
FINK, Ernest ... 718-409-5265 320 G
efink@sunymaritime.edu
FINK, Gayle, M ... 301-860-3403 204 A
gfink@bowiestate.edu
FINK, Michael ... 909-652-6453.. 35 L
michael.fink@chaffey.edu
FINK, Michael ... 912-525-5000 124 I
mfink@scad.edu
FINK, Pete ... 815-235-6121 139 A
pete.fink@highland.edu
FINK, Tim ... 231-843-5919 233 A
tfink@westshore.edu
FINKE, John ... 317-955-6202 159 K
jfinke@marian.edu
FINKEL, Barry ... 323-469-3300.. 24 P
FINKEL, Max ... 215-884-8942 403 D
registrar@woninstitute.edu
FINKELSTEIN, Eric, M ... 718-990-2417 313 G
finkelse@stjohns.edu
FINKELSTEIN, Jerry ... 212-229-1671 308 A
finkelsj@newschool.edu
FINKELSTEIN, Laura ... 703-526-6861 468 H
laura.finkelstein@marymount.edu
FINKEN, Mark ... 303-369-5151.. 82 I
mark.finken@plattcolorado.edu
FINLAY, Amy ... 313-593-5151 231 I
akaraban@umich.edu
FINLAY, Cheryl, S ... 412-383-4473 400 H
cfinlay@pitt.edu
FINLAY, Stephen ... 580-387-7303 366 E
sfinlay@mscok.edu
FINLAYSON, Al ... 218-733-7600 238 G
alan.finlayson@lsc.edu
FINLAYSON,
Alexander (Sandy) ... 215-572-3823 402 E
sfinlayson@wts.edu
FINLAYSON, Jeanne ... 508-565-1337 219 A
jfinlayson@stonehill.edu
FINLAYSON, Matthew ... 860-701-3540.. 88 D
finlayson_m@mitchell.edu
FINLEY, Adam ... 817-598-8831 457 J
afinley@wc.edu
FINLEY, Brad ... 309-694-8557 139 B
bfinley@icc.edu
FINLEY, Bryan ... 212-659-7200 303 H
bfinley@tkc.edu
FINLEY, David ... 229-931-2068 125 E
dfinley@southgatech.edu
FINLEY, David, R ... 231-348-6601 228 H
dfinley@ncmich.edu
FINLEY, Gerald ... 662-846-4740 245 G
gfinley@deltastate.edu
FINLEY, Jerry ... 806-716-2340 443 G
jfinley@southplainscollege.edu
FINLEY, Rebecca ... 215-503-9000 399 E
rebecca.finley@jefferson.edu
FINLEY, Terence ... 314-340-5770 254 A
finleyt@hssu.edu

FINN, Alan ... 765-285-1033 153 H
atfinn@bsu.edu
FINN, Alicia, A ... 603-641-7600 274 A
afinn@anselm.edu
FINN, Erin ... 215-503-1040 399 E
erin.finn@jefferson.edu
FINN, Erin, M ... 215-503-1040 399 E
erin.finn@jefferson.edu
FINN, Janice ... 267-620-4112 378 E
finn@arcadia.edu
FINN, Kevin ... 248-204-4100 227 A
kfinn@ltu.edu
FINN, Laurie Ann ... 757-352-4036 470 B
lfinn@regent.edu
FINN, Mary, A ... 517-355-2192 227 F
mfinn@msu.edu
FINN, Mary Beth ... 801-883-8336 459 A
FINN, Nancy ... 617-585-0200 207 A
nancy.finn@the-bac.edu
FINN, Nathan ... 864-977-7011 410 I
nathan.finn@ngu.edu
FINN, Robert ... 207-454-1011 195 I
rfinn@wccc.me.edu
FINN, Troy ... 603-862-1234 274 F
troy.finn@unh.edu
FINN, William ... 708-974-5727 145 A
finn@morainevalley.edu
FINNEGAN, John ... 612-625-1179 243 F
finne001@umn.edu
FINNEGAN, Lorna ... 708-216-5448 143 C
lfinnegan2@luc.edu
FINNEGAN, Paul, J ... 617-495-1000 210 E
FINNEGAN, Robert ... 802-828-2800 463 F
rjf12090@ccv.vsc.edu
FINNEL, Kristen ... 360-442-2501 481 D
kfinnel@lowercolumbia.edu
FINNELL, JoRene ... 831-646-4272.. 52 G
jfinnell@mpc.edu
FINNELLY, Ryan ... 210-999-8490 451 E
rfinnell@trinity.edu
FINNEMORE, Cathi ... 207-236-8581 196 B
cfinnemore@mainemedia.edu
FINNEN, Mary ... 646-660-6549 292 L
mary.finnen@baruch.cuny.edu
FINNERAN,
Christina, M ... 207-725-3897 194 C
cfinnera@bowdoin.edu
FINNERN, Julie ... 651-638-6400 234 D
j-finnern@bethel.edu
FINNERTY, Bob ... 585-475-4733 312 F
refuns@rit.edu
FINNERTY, James, M ... 716-878-4324 317 F
finnerjm@buffalostate.edu
FINNERTY, Mary Beth ... 518-782-6818 315 E
mfinnerty@siena.edu
FINNEY, Andy ... 208-769-3266 132 D
andy_finney@nic.edu
FINNEY, George ... 214-768-3950 444 D
gfinney@smu.edu
FINNEY, Jack ... 540-231-6122 476 C
jfinney@vt.edu
FINNEY, Jennifer ... 979-230-3395 431 I
jennifer.finney@brazosport.edu
FINNEY, Lesley, M ... 717-361-1445 383 C
finneylm@etown.edu
FINNEY, Maureen ... 716-926-8854 301 E
mfinney@hilbert.edu
FINNEY, Sarah ... 206-296-6390 484 A
sfinney@seattleu.edu
FINNEY, Terry ... 870-972-2398.. 17 E
tfinney@astate.edu
FINNIN, Meredith ... 212-752-1530 304 A
meredith.finnin@limcollege.edu
FINO, Danielle ... 508-289-3624 220 E
dfino@whoi.edu
FINO, Mike ... 760-757-2121.. 52 F
mfino@miracosta.edu
FINO, Mireli, W ... 617-474-3250 212 C
mireli.fino@umassmed.edu
FINTON, Tabby ... 612-343-4743 242M
tjfinton@northcentral.edu
FINUF, Danny, D ... 304-326-1522 487 I
dan.finuf@salemu.edu
FINZO, Katie ... 417-865-2815 250 E
finzok@evangel.edu
FIOCCHI, Robbie ... 509-420-4545 480 E
robbie@gather4him.net
FIOCHETTA, Joseph ... 570-484-2083 394 E
jfiochetta@lockhaven.edu
FIORE, Douglas, J ... 515-643-6600 168 D
dfiore@mercydesmoines.org
FIORE, Elizabeth ... 914-323-5171 305 B
elizabeth.fiore@mville.edu

FITZGERALD-BOCARSLY, Patricia ...... 973-972-5233 282 A bocarsly@njms.rutgers.edu
FITZGIBBON, Cecelia .... 215-965-4000 390 E cfitzgibbon@moore.edu
FITZGIBBON, James ..... 510-231-5000.. 46 J james.x.fitzgibbon@kp.org
FITZGIBBONS, SJ, John, P ...... 303-458-4190.. 83 E president@regis.edu
FITZHUGH, Clayton ...... 215-503-1418 399 E clayton.fitzhugh@jefferson.edu
FITZHUGH, Stephen ...... 802-485-2025 462 F fitzhugh@norwich.edu
FITZMAURICE, Patricia .. 212-752-1530 304 A patricia.fitzmaurice@limcollege.edu
FITZPATRICK, Allison ... 570-369-1937 391 C afitzpatrick@northampton.edu
FITZPATRICK, Catherine 973-353-1882 282 B catherine.fitzpatrick@rutgers.edu
FITZPATRICK, Colleen ... 802-443-3177 462 E cfitzpatrick@middlebury.edu
FITZPATRICK, Daniel ..... 304-384-5276 489 J dfitzpatrick@concord.edu
FITZPATRICK, Holly ...... 413-775-1813 214 E fitzpatrickh@gcc.mass.edu
FITZPATRICK, James, D 203-254-4000.. 87 I jfitzpatrick@fairfield.edu
FITZPATRICK, Jane .... 606-783-2053 184 C j.fitzpatrick@moreheadstate.edu
FITZPATRICK, Kenneth .. 209-476-7840.. 67 E kfitzpatrick@clc.edu
FITZPATRICK, Laura ...... 432-264-5039 437 F lfitzpatrick@howardcollege.edu
FITZPATRICK, Mary Anne ...... 803-777-4621 413 A fitzpatm@mailbox.sc.edu
FITZPATRICK, Nivla .... 310-506-4210.. 56 G nivla.fitzpatrick@pepperdine.edu
FITZPATRICK, Patrick "Fitz" ...... 206-934-3646 483 B patrick.fitzpatrick@seattlecolleges.edu
FITZPATRICK, Paula, A . 508-767-7550 206 A pfitzpat@assumption.edu
FITZPATRICK, Ralph ...... 502-852-6026 186 A ralph.fitzpatrick@louisville.edu
FITZPATRICK, Sharon ... 405-945-3292 368 C sharon.fitzpatrick@okstate.edu
FITZPATRICK, Tamara ... 209-476-7840.. 67 E tfitzpatrick@clc.edu
FITZPATRICK, Timothy, J ...... 352-273-1325 111 A timf@ufl.edu
FITZPATRICK, Tod .... 702-895-5120 271 D tod.fitzpatrick@unlv.edu
FITZPATRICK, Tracy .... 914-251-6105 319 B tracy.fitzpatrick@purchase.edu
FITZSIMMONS, Debra, L ...... 724-357-2202 394 C dfitzsim@iup.edu
FITZSIMMONS, Joanne . 518-445-2324 289 K jfitz@albanylaw.edu
FITZSIMMONS, Katie ..... 701-328-4109 345 A katie.fitzsimmons@ndus.edu
FITZSIMMONS, Linda .... 207-454-1033 195 I lfitzsimmons@wccc.me.edu
FITZSIMMONS, Stephanie ...... 732-224-2369 276 B sfitzsimmons@brookdalecc.edu
FITZSIMMONS, Tracy .... 540-665-4505 470 G tfitzsim@su.edu
FITZSIMONS, Orla .... 914-674-7574 306 C ofitzsimons@mercy.edu
FIVECOAT, Frederick ..... 610-892-1519 393 B ffivecoat@pit.edu
FIXSEN, Liz ...... 785-738-9060 176 F lfixsen@ncktc.edu
FLAA, Carol ...... 701-224-5519 346 A carol.flaa@bismarckstate.edu
FLACK, Anna ...... 631-451-4008 321 C flacka@sunysuffolk.edu
FLACK, Tamala ...... 315-228-7014 296 E tflack@colgate.edu
FLADELAND, Diane .... 701-355-8140 347 C dflade@umary.edu
FLADRY, Robert ...... 303-753-6046.. 83 F rfladry@rmcad.edu
FLAGEL, Jennifer ...... 781-891-2740 206 G jflagel@bentley.edu
FLAGG, Chuck, S .... 248-232-4811 229 C csflagg@oaklandcc.edu
FLAGSTAD, Paul ...... 952-446-4152 235 J flagstadp@crown.edu
FLAHERTY, Anne, G ...... 217-581-3221 137 E agflaherty@eiu.edu
FLAHERTY, John ...... 212-817-7761 293 F jflaherty@gc.cuny.edu
FLAHERTY, Kathryn .... 843-857-4227 408 B kflaherty@coker.edu
FLAHERTY, Mary ...... 585-594-6533 312 E flahertym@roberts.edu
FLAHERTY, Pamela, B ... 781-280-3631 215 B flahertyp@middlesex.mass.edu
FLAIG, Thomas ...... 303-724-8155.. 84 D thomas.flaig@ucdenver.edu
FLAKUS, Zack ...... 605-626-3005 416 G zack.flakus@northern.edu
FLAMER, Keith ...... 707-476-4170.. 58 I keith-flamer@redwoods.edu
FLAMER, Thelma ...... 301-243-2178 502 L thelma.flamer@dodiis.mil
FLAMINIO, Becca .... 630-844-5475 133 D bflaminio@aurora.edu
FLAMM, Andrew, R .... 574-372-5100 155 F drew.flamm@grace.edu
FLANAGAN, Chris .... 206-517-4541 483 F cflanagan@sieam.edu
FLANAGAN, Erin ...... 619-388-3453.. 60 I eflanaga@sdccd.edu
FLANAGAN, Gareth .... 617-451-0010 217 F
FLANAGAN, Hilary .... 206-220-6088 484 A hflanagan@seattleu.edu
FLANAGAN, J. Kelly ..... 801-863-8943 460 D kelly.flanagan@uvu.edu
FLANAGAN, James .... 212-247-3434 304 L jflanagan@mandl.edu
FLANAGAN, James, P ... 603-641-6025 274 A jflanagan@anselm.edu
FLANAGAN, John .... 510-642-3414.. 69 A jgflanagan@berkeley.edu
FLANAGAN, Jon ...... 414-443-8826 498 A jon.flanagan@wlc.edu
FLANAGAN, Joseph ...... 716-375-2375 313 C jflan@sbu.edu
FLANAGAN, Karla .... 979-209-7445 431 H karla.flanagan@blinn.edu
FLANAGAN, Liesl ...... 314-529-9360 255 B lflanagan@maryville.edu
FLANAGAN, Lori ...... 314-516-5661 261 C flanagamlo@umsl.edu
FLANAGAN, Mary Jane . 989-774-7393 222 E flana1mj@cmich.edu
FLANAGAN, Melissa ..... 770-962-7580 121 E mflanagan@gwinnetttech.edu
FLANARY, Trevor ...... 800-607-6377.. 60 C tflanary@samuelmerritt.edu
FLANDERS, Lorene .... 251-460-7021.... 9 A lflanders@southalabama.edu
FLANIGAN, Alyce .... 256-352-8295.... 3 I alyce.malcolm@wallacestate.edu
FLANIGAN, Carol .... 312-915-7267 143 C cflanigan1@luc.edu
FLANIGAN, Karen .... 480-988-8884.. 12 O karen.flanigan@cgc.edu
FLANIGAN, Rod ...... 520-515-4516.. 11 M flaniganr@cochise.edu
FLANIGAN, Virginia ...... 973-877-3056 277 G vflaniga@essex.edu
FLANIK, Greg, G ...... 440-826-2700 348 D gflanik@bw.edu
FLANNERY, Brenda ...... 507-389-9423 239 D brenda.flannery@mnsu.edu
FLANNERY, Chad ...... 618-252-5400 149 I chad.flannery@sic.edu
FLANNERY, John .... 608-246-6052 499 A jflannery1@madisoncollege.edu
FLANNERY, Kathleen ..... 620-235-4769 177 A kflannery@pittstate.edu
FLANNERY, Kim ...... 262-595-2301 496 D bookstore@uwp.edu
FLANNERY, Patrick .... 517-607-2239 225 C pflannery@hillsdale.edu
FLANNERY, Teresa .... 631-632-6265 317 A teresa.flannery@stonybrook.edu
FLASH, Kevin ...... 916-558-2254.. 50 J flashk@scc.losrios.edu
FLASH, Lacretia ...... 617-266-1400 206 H lflash@berklee.edu
FLATEN, Mike ...... 218-262-6749 238 D mikeflaten@hibbing.edu
FLATLEY, Kate ...... 314-889-1447 253 E kflatley@fontbonne.edu
FLATT, Jennifer ...... 912-201-8000 125 F jflatt@southuniversity.edu
FLATT, Larry ...... 931-393-1720 424 F lflatt@mscc.edu
FLATTERY, Tim ...... 313-664-7696 222 H tflattery@collegeforcreativestudies.edu
FLATZ, Connor ...... 914-968-6200 314 C
FLAUGHER, Amanda ...... 989-317-4760 230 D aflaugher@sagchip.edu
FLAX-HYMAN, Cheryl, L ...... 850-747-3215 101 N cflax-hyman@gulfcoast.edu
FLAYTON, Brad ...... 605-331-6575 417 C brad.flayton@usiouxfalls.edu
FLEAGLE, Steven, R ...... 319-384-0595 163 H steve-fleagle@uiowa.edu
FLECK, Alicia ...... 860-632-3012.. 88 C afleck@holyapostles.edu
FLECK, Lauren ...... 410-287-1087 198 E lfleck@cecil.edu
FLECK, Mary ...... 972-721-4054 452 B mfleck@udallas.edu
FLECK, Theresa ...... 636-227-2100 255 A
FLEEGER, Christina, M . 724-287-8711 379 E christine.fleeger@bc3.edu
FLEEGER, Christina, M . 724-287-8711 379 E tina.fleeger@bc3.edu
FLEENER, Katie ...... 559-453-7121.. 43 A katie.fleener@fresno.edu
FLEENOR, James ...... 478-757-5140 127 F jfleenor@wesleyancollege.edu
FLEENOR, Rick ...... 606-539-4154 185 E rick.fleenor@ucumberlands.edu
FLEETWOOD, Nick .... 619-596-2766.. 26 D nfleetwood@ata.edu
FLEISCHER, Amy ...... 805-756-2132.. 29 I afleisch@calpoly.edu
FLEISCHER ROWLAND, Theresa ...... 925-485-5244.. 35 I trowland@clpccd.org
FLEISCHMAN, Linda ...... 704-337-2543 339 F fleischmanl@queens.edu
FLEISCHMAN, Robert ...... 507-389-5567 239 D robert.fleischman@mnsu.edu
FLEISCHMAN, Robert .... 231-591-3797 224 A robertfleischman@ferris.edu
FLEISCHMANN, Anne .... 916-660-8000.. 64 D afleischmann@sierracollege.edu
FLEISCHMANN, Kenneth ...... 314-446-8104 260 H kenneth.fleischmann@stlcop.edu
FLEISHMAN, Michael .... 301-860-4331 204 A mfleishman@bowiestate.edu
FLEITAS, Dionisio .... 214-333-5481 434 C dionisio@dbu.edu
FLEMING, A.L ...... 229-500-3286 114 H al.fleming@asurams.edu
FLEMING, Alicia ...... 773-235-5572 146 F alicia.fleming@oakpoint.edu
FLEMING, Allyson .... 615-327-6235 421 D afleming@mmc.edu
FLEMING, Amanda .... 910-962-3122 343 C flemingac@uncw.edu
FLEMING, Andrea .... 419-251-2182 355 G andrea.fleming@mercycollege.edu
FLEMING, Angela ...... 607-962-9458 320 C aflemin2@corning-cc.edu
FLEMING, April ...... 239-489-9319 101 A april.fleming@fsw.edu
FLEMING, Candace, C .. 973-655-4040 279 B flemingc@montclair.edu
FLEMING, David ...... 269-782-1201 231 A dfleming@swmich.edu
FLEMING, David ...... 540-654-1058 471 N dflemin3@umw.edu
FLEMING, Elizabeth ...... 413-565-1000 206 D lfleming@baypath.edu
FLEMING, Ian ...... 678-872-8007 119 D ifleming@highlands.edu
FLEMING, J. Christopher ...... 757-683-3685 469 B jcflemin@odu.edu
FLEMING, Jennifer .... 479-498-6020.. 18 C jfleming@atu.edu
FLEMING, John ...... 512-245-2308 450 C jf18@txstate.edu
FLEMING, OP, John Mary ...... 615-256-5486 417 G education@op-tn.org
FLEMING, Julie ...... 704-406-4491 329 A jcfleming@gardner-webb.edu
FLEMING, Justin ...... 507-786-3615 243 D flemingj@stolaf.edu
FLEMING, Katherine ...... 212-998-3660 309 F katherine.fleming@nyu.edu
FLEMING, Kelli ...... 304-358-2000 487 D kelli.fleming@future.edu
FLEMING, Kevin ...... 951-739-7880.. 59 C kevin.fleming@norcocollege.edu
FLEMING, Kirsty ...... 562-985-4128.. 31 D kirsty.fleming@csulb.edu
FLEMING, Lyesha, J ..... 570-422-3896 394 A lfleming@esu.edu
FLEMING, Mark ...... 973-655-5225 279 B flemingm@montclair.edu
FLEMING, Michael ...... 510-430-2350.. 52 E mifleming@mills.edu
FLEMING, Philip ...... 714-484-7394.. 54 B pfleming@cypresscollege.edu
FLEMING, Rita ...... 870-230-5820.. 19 D fleminr@hsu.edu
FLEMING, Sarahi, S ...... 863-667-5253 108 K esfleming@seu.edu
FLEMING, Tawny .... 707-826-4273.. 33 C tb36@humboldt.edu
FLEMING, Thomas, O ... 310-338-2738.. 51 A tfleming@lmu.edu
FLEMING, Tracey .... 773-777-7900 135 G tfleming22@ccc.edu
FLEMING, Tricia ...... 610-526-6001 385 D tfleming@harcum.edu
FLEMING, Wanda .... 601-877-6188 245 A wcfleming@alcorn.edu
FLEMING-RANDLE, Marche ...... 316-978-5932 178 D marche.fleming-randle@wichita.edu
FLEMMING, Damon ...... 805-756-1302.. 29 I dmf@calpoly.edu
FLENIKEN, Tracey .... 940-668-4207 440 F tfleniken@nctc.edu
FLENNER, Ronald, W .... 757-446-5829 466 D flennerw@evms.edu
FLESCHNER, Julius .... 706-368-7732 119 D jfleschn@highlands.edu
FLESHLER, David .... 216-368-2399 349 D david.fleshler@case.edu
FLESNER, Brian ...... 402-826-8228 267 A brian.flesner@doane.edu
FLETCHER, Antonio .... 770-229-3370 125 H antonio.fletcher@sctech.edu
FLETCHER, Bill ...... 502-852-4740 186 A bill.fletcher@louisville.edu
FLETCHER, Brandi .... 931-372-3317 426 B bhill@tntech.edu
FLETCHER, Carol ...... 575-562-2611 286 B carol.fletcher@enmu.edu
FLETCHER, Francis .... 916-608-6500.. 50 I
FLETCHER, James .... 920-424-3030 496 C fletcher@uwosh.edu
FLETCHER, Jennifer ...... 304-473-8017 491 D fletcher.j@wvwc.edu
FLETCHER, Kiely ...... 312-996-5563 151 G kfletch@uic.edu
FLETCHER, Lauronda ..... 610-399-2224 393 F lfletcher@cheyney.edu
FLETCHER, Leah ...... 816-584-6407 258 C leah.fletcher@park.edu
FLETCHER, Linda ...... 256-469-7333.... 5 H students@hbc1.edu
FLETCHER, Linda ...... 252-492-2061 338 F fletcherl@vgcc.edu
FLETCHER, Martha .... 615-675-5264 428 C mfletcher@welch.edu
FLETCHER, Randy .... 321-433-7380.. 98 I fletcherr@easternflorida.edu
FLETCHER, Rob ...... 773-291-6143 135 E
FLETCHER, Scott ...... 503-768-6001 373 E graddean@lclark.edu
FLETCHER, T-Ray .... 812-749-1576 159 O tfletcher@oak.edu
FLETCHER, Thomas .... 570-389-5161 393 D tfletche@bloomu.edu
FLEURY, Karl ...... 715-425-3133 496 F karl.fleury@uwrf.edu
FLEURY, Sam ...... 573-875-8700 251 I
FLEWELLEN, Vincent ..... 314-246-8250 262 C vincentflewellen@webster.edu
FLEWELLING, Travis ..... 252-246-1210 339 C tflewelling@wilsoncc.edu
FLICK, Chuck ...... 540-568-3825 468 C flickco@jmu.edu
FLICK, Ethan ...... 810-984-3881 230 F
FLICK, Kay ...... 508-849-3228 205 H kflick@annamaria.edu
FLICK, Matt ...... 937-294-0592 356 D matt.flick@themodern.edu
FLICK, Zeke ...... 641-683-5282 166 I zeke.flick@indianhills.edu
FLICKEMA, Aubree .... 847-628-1572 141 C aubree.flickema@judsonu.edu

FLICKER, John .... 928-350-4100.. 15 L
john.flicker@prescott.edu
FLICKER, Thomas .... 315-279-5217 303 G
help@keuka.edu
FLICKINGER, Annette .... 317-921-4341 158 D
alamb37@ivytech.edu
FLICKINGER, Catherine . 516-686-7792 308 I
catherine.flickinger@nyit.edu
FLIDER, Robert .... 217-300-5348 152 B
rflider@illinois.edu
FLIGER, Jerry .... 409-933-8229 433 H
jfliger@com.edu
FLINDERS, Tracy, W ..... 801-422-3142 458 H
tracy_flinders@byu.edu
FLING, Corey .... 619-849-2583.. 57 J
coreyfling@pointloma.edu
FLINK, Janet .... 860-231-5272.. 90 A
jflink@usj.edu
FLINK, Sara .... 413-265-2447 208 E
flinks@elms.edu
FLINN, Cara .... 479-979-1467.. 23 I
cflinn@ozarks.edu
FLINN, Eileen .... 724-805-2897 398 A
eileen.flinn@stvincent.edu
FLINT, Juanita .... 972-860-4694 434 F
juanitazf@dcccd.edu
FLINT, Mary Ann .... 601-643-8414 245 F
maryann.flint@colin.edu
FLINT, Michelle .... 508-793-4378 208 C
mflint@clarku.edu
FLINT, Randy .... 714-546-7600.. 37 J
FLINT, Tora .... 310-577-3000.. 76 I
registrar@yosan.edu
FLINT, Wendy .... 503-554-2332 373 A
wflint@georgefox.edu
FLINT-HAMILTON,
Kimberly .... 315-229-5011 314 D
kflint@stlawu.edu
FLINTJER, Nathan .... 845-451-1405 297 G
nathan.flintjer@culinary.edu
FLINTOFT, Rebecca .... 303-273-3050.. 79 J
rflintof@mines.edu
FLIPSE, Vanessa .... 785-628-4494 173 H
vmflipse@fhsu.edu
FLOCK, Gretchen .... 724-805-2209 397 I
gretchen.flock@email.stvincent.edu
FLOCKEN, Lise .... 760-757-2121.. 52 F
lflocken@miracosta.edu
FLOM, Sheldon .... 541-917-4999 373 G
floms@linnbenton.edu
FLOOD, Derrick .... 252-536-7237 335 B
dflood@halifaxcc.edu
FLOOD, Kathy .... 619-574-5805.. 42 J
kflood@fst.edu
FLOOD, Malia .... 619-421-6700.. 66 A
mflood@swccd.edu
FLOOD, Michael .... 404-752-1500 123 E
mflood@msm.edu
FLOOD, Moira .... 414-382-6082 491 F
moira.flood@alverno.edu
FLOOD, Thomas .... 718-489-5443 313 E
thomasflood@sfc.edu
FLOOD, Tim .... 760-757-2121.. 52 F
tflood@miracosta.edu
FLOOD, Tom .... 336-278-6549 328 J
tflood@elon.edu
FLOOD-WEINER,
Christie .... 614-253-3502 358 B
weinerc@ohiodominican.edu
FLORA, David .... 606-783-9404 184 C
d.flora@moreheadstate.edu
FLORA, Kristin, C .... 317-738-8784 155 D
kflora@franklincollege.edu
FLORA, William, F .... 423-439-6872 419 G
floraw@etsu.edu
FLORAK, Mike .... 740-284-5860 352 I
mflorak@franciscan.edu
FLOREA, Carleen .... 716-896-0700 324 E
cflorea@villa.edu
FLORENCE, Brad .... 563-876-3353 165 H
bflorence@dwci.edu
FLORENDO, Heather ..... 808-844-2310 130 A
heather.florendo@hawaii.edu
FLORENTINE, Dennis ..... 908-835-2326 284 H
dflorentine@warren.edu
FLORES, Al .... 915-215-4491 451 B
FLORES, Andrew .... 254-501-5800 447 A
dps@tamuct.edu
FLORES, Anita .... 509-865-8600 481 A
FLORES, Anna .... 480-517-8171.. 13 G
anna.flores@riosalado.edu
FLORES, Aubrey .... 775-784-4805 271 E
aubreyf@unr.edu

FLORES, Austin .... 419-267-1364 357 E
aflores@northweststate.edu
FLORES, Brian .... 713-221-8978 453 A
floresbr@uhd.edu
FLORES, Chio .... 509-682-6805 485 H
cflores@wvc.edu
FLORES, Daniel .... 830-372-8110 449 A
danflores@tlu.edu
FLORES, David, R .... 530-752-3619.. 69 B
FLORES, Eddie .... 575-538-6321 289 G
flores4@wnmu.edu
FLORES, Elizabeth .... 616-632-2868 221 E
floreeli@aquinas.edu
FLORES, Esmarelda .... 210-431-6520 441 B
emflores@lake.ollusa.edu
FLORES, Fernando .... 915-831-6391 436 A
fflore63@epcc.edu
FLORES, Harold .... 305-821-3333 100 E
hflores@fnu.edu
FLORES, Hector .... 409-880-8305 449 G
hector.flores@lamar.edu
FLORES, Javier .... 325-942-2047 450 E
javier.flores@angelo.edu
FLORES, Jorge .... 210-486-2505 429 B
flores375@alamo.edu
FLORES, Juan, S .... 915-831-7866 436 A
jflor242@epcc.edu
FLORES, Maria, E .... 787-743-7979 510 H
ut_mflores@suagm.edu
FLORES, Marilyn .... 714-564-6975.. 58 F
flores_marilyn@sac.edu
FLORES, Mark .... 510-885-3791.. 31 A
mark.flores@csueastbay.edu
FLORES, Maureen, E ..... 781-891-2818 206 G
mflores@bentley.edu
FLORES, Mayra .... 787-746-1400 507 B
FLORES, Michael .... 702-610-1853 271 E
floresm@unr.edu
FLORES, Michael .... 775-784-4901 270 J
FLORES, Mike .... 210-485-0020 428 G
rflores@alamo.edu
FLORES, Minerva .... 707-468-3011.. 51 F
mflores@mendocino.edu
FLORES, Monica .... 707-468-3280.. 51 F
monicaflores@mendocino.edu
FLORES, Nanette .... 413-755-4418 216 A
nflores@stcc.edu
FLORES, Ricardo .... 301-891-4017 205 A
rflore01@wau.edu
FLORES, Robert, E .... 863-453-6661 108 F
robert.flores@southflorida.edu
FLORES, Rolando .... 575-646-3748 287 C
rolflo@nmsu.edu
FLORES, Sonja .... 214-887-5193 435 F
sflores@dts.edu
FLORES, Wanda .... 787-850-0000 512 D
wanda.flores@upr.edu
FLORES-CHURCH,
Adriana .... 562-860-2451.. 35 H
achurch@cerritos.edu
FLORES-LOPEZ, Brenda 423-236-2277 423 F
bfloreslopez@southern.edu
FLORES-MEDINA,
Donna .... 505-454-5328 286 F
dflores@luna.edu
FLORES-MILLS, Maria ... 704-337-2227 339 F
floresm@queens.edu
FLORES ROBERTS,
Teresa .... 909-621-8519.. 57 E
pam_jones@pitzer.edu
FLORES-SOTO, Yaly ...... 305-595-9500.. 94 G
dean@amcollege.edu
FLOREY, Nancy .... 717-947-6098 392 V
neflorey@pacollege.edu
FLOREZ-NEVAREZ, Tina 254-519-8015 447 A
t.flores@tamuct.edu
FLORIAN, Greg, E .... 217-875-7200 148 A
gflorian@richland.edu
FLORIAN, James, S ...... 520-621-3680.. 16 D
florianj@arizona.edu
FLORIAN, Kelley .... 804-627-5300 464 K
kelley_florian@bshsi.org
FLORIAN, Tim .... 812-357-6222 161 A
tflorian@saintmeinrad.edu
FLORIO, Gina .... 718-990-2638 313 G
floriog@stjohns.edu
FLORIO, Joseph .... 708-656-8000 145 C
joseph.florio@morton.edu
FLOROS, John .... 575-646-2035 287 C
president.floros@nmsu.edu
FLORY, Julie .... 314-935-5408 262 A
julie.flory@wustl.edu

FLOT, Garry .... 504-398-2347 192 A
gflot@uhcno.edu
FLOT, Rob .... 323-259-2500.. 54 I
flot@oxy.edu
FLOTRON, Rich .... 573-518-2341 256 D
rflotron@mineralarea.edu
FLOTTE, Terence, R .... 508-856-8000 212 C
terry.flotte@umassmed.edu
FLOUHOUSE, Steve .... 606-326-2055 181 D
steve.flouhouse@kctcs.edu
FLOURNOY, Carrie .... 318-257-3785 192 D
flournoy@latech.edu
FLOURNOY, Eric .... 706-385-1459 124 E
FLOURNOY, Jacob .... 361-593-2410 447 D
jacob.flournoy@tamuk.edu
FLOWER, Hannah .... 912-525-5000 124 I
hcrocket@scad.edu
FLOWER, Mark .... 212-621-3789 294 D
mflower@jjay.cuny.edu
FLOWER KIM, Laura ..... 626-395-6330.. 28 J
laura.flowerkim@caltech.edu
FLOWERS, Brenda .... 972-708-7340 435 E
FLOWERS, Carly .... 207-834-7571 197 A
carly.flowers@maine.edu
FLOWERS, Carol, A .... 404-727-0833 118 E
caflowe@emory.edu
FLOWERS, George .... 334-844-4700.... 4 D
flowegt@auburn.edu
FLOWERS, Jim .... 678-466-4316 117 D
jimflowers@clayton.edu
FLOWERS, Kathleen ...... 315-781-3825 301 F
kflowers@hws.edu
FLOWERS, Ken .... 269-927-4103 226 F
flowers@lakemichigancollege.edu
FLOWERS, Laura .... 615-550-3168 428 E
laura@williamsoncc.edu
FLOWERS, Madison ...... 617-745-3675 209 B
madison.flowers@enc.edu
FLOWERS, Marshall ...... 276-326-4355 464 J
mflowers@bluefield.edu
FLOWERS, Patricia, J .... 850-644-0415 110 C
pjflowers@fsu.edu
FLOWERS, Rachel .... 239-280-2500.. 95M
rachel.flowers@avemaria.edu
FLOWERS, Robert .... 315-781-3827 301 F
flowers@hws.edu
FLOWERS, Robert .... 610-758-4570 388 E
rof2@lehigh.edu
FLOWERS, Shannon ...... 843-383-8000 408 B
sflowers@coker.edu
FLOWERS, Tessa .... 601-477-4845 246 G
tessa.flowers@jcjc.edu
FLOWERS, Vanessa .... 904-770-3650.. 72 G
vflowers@usa.edu
FLOWERS-FIELDS, Ellen 301-934-2251 198 G
eflowers-fields@csmd.edu
FLOYD, Andrew .... 229-500-3281 114 H
andrew.floyd@asurams.edu
FLOYD, Dawn .... 828-328-7040 330 F
dawn.floyd@lr.edu
FLOYD, Gina .... 706-233-7205 125 C
gfloyd@shorter.edu
FLOYD, James, C .... 615-898-2025 422 C
james.floyd@mtsu.edu
FLOYD, James, J .... 909-621-8351.. 37 D
james.floyd@cmc.edu
FLOYD, Kevin .... 803-691-3685 410 D
floydk@midlandstech.edu
FLOYD, Krystal .... 334-727-8540.... 7 D
kfloyd@tuskegee.edu
FLOYD, Morris .... 316-942-4291 176 E
floydm@newmanu.edu
FLOYD, Myron .... 919-515-2011 342 A
FLOYD, Polly, K .... 850-263-3261.. 95 P
pkfloyd@baptistcollege.edu
FLOYD, Shawnda .... 972-378-1607 435 B
shawndafloyd@dcccd.edu
FLOYD, Shawnda .... 214-378-1601 434 E
FLOYD, Stuart .... 864-977-7669 410 I
stuart.floyd@ngu.edu
FLOYD, Tony .... 828-689-1141 331 C
tony_floyd@mhu.edu
FLOYD, Wesley .... 662-720-7594 248 C
wcfloyd@nemcc.edu
FLOYD-SMITH, Tamara . 334-727-8953.... 7 D
tfloyd@tuskegee.edu
FLUECKIGER,
Joseph, T .... 413-542-2220 205 G
jflueckiger@amherst.edu
FLUECKIGER,
Urs Peter (Upe) .... 806-742-2184 450 F
upe.flueckiger@ttu.edu

FLUET, Gregoire, J .... 845-569-3154 307 D
gregoire.fluet@msmc.edu
FLUG, Kenneth .... 845-848-4104 298 C
kenneth.flug@dc.edu
FLUGSTAD, Bjorn .... 928-523-4240.. 14 H
bjorn.flugstad@nau.edu
FLUGUM, Deborah .... 818-677-6567.. 32 C
deborah.flugum@csun.edu
FLUHARTY, Steven, J ... 215-898-7320 400 F
sasdean@sas.upenn.edu
FLUKE, Donald, W .... 574-372-5100 155 F
dwfluke@grace.edu
FLUKER, Roderick .... 334-727-8014.... 7 D
FLUNKER, Thomas, G ... 507-933-7449 236 A
tflunker@gustavus.edu
FLURY, Ron .... 575-624-7328 286 C
ron.flury@roswell.enmu.edu
FLUSCHE, Sara .... 940-668-3351 440 F
sflusche@nctc.edu
FLUTE, Sylvan .... 605-698-3966 416 B
sjflute@swcollege.edu
FLY, Pam .... 918-444-2060 366 G
fly@nsuok.edu
FLYING, Eva .... 406-638-3111 263 G
flyinge@lbhc.edu
FLYNN, Chris .... 540-231-6557 476 C
flynnc@vt.edu
FLYNN, Christie .... 253-964-6553 482 E
cflynn@pierce.ctc.edu
FLYNN, Cynthia .... 516-773-5000 503 H
flynnc@usmma.edu
FLYNN, Daniel .... 561-297-0268 109 J
flynnd@fau.edu
FLYNN, Eric, F .... 203-285-2371.. 86 E
eflynn@gatewayct.edu
FLYNN, Jackie .... 708-444-4500 138 C
FLYNN, Jackie .... 412-391-7021 401 J
jflynn@vti.edu
FLYNN, James .... 412-237-3124 381 D
jflynn@ccac.edu
FLYNN, Jay .... 434-381-6239 471 I
jflynn@sbc.edu
FLYNN, Jeff .... 208-562-3220 131 E
jeffflynn@cwi.edu
FLYNN, Joan .... 410-617-5161 200 B
jflynn@loyola.edu
FLYNN, Joanna, K 570-326-3761 392W
jflynn@pct.edu
FLYNN, John, J .... 212-769-5055 312 D
dean-rggs@amnh.org
FLYNN, Kacie .... 707-826-5159.. 33 C
kacie.flynn@humboldt.edu
FLYNN, Linda .... 973-353-3848 282 B
lflynn@sn.rutgers.edu
FLYNN, Linda .... 973-353-3848 282 A
lflynn@sn.rutgers.edu
FLYNN, Lucille .... 732-571-3502 279 A
lflynn@monmouth.edu
FLYNN, Mari .... 570-945-8335 386 F
mari.flynn@keystone.edu
FLYNN, Maura .... 716-926-8822 301 E
mflynn@hilbert.edu
FLYNN, Mindi .... 940-552-6291 457 C
mflynn@vernoncollege.edu
FLYNN, Stuart .... 817-257-8282 448 F
s.flynn@tcu.edu
FLYNN, Terence .... 319-296-4269 166 H
terence.flynn@hawkeyecollege.edu
FLYNN, Thomas, V .... 505-565-1413 219 A
tflynn@stonehill.edu
FOCARETO, Nicole .... 724-503-1001 402 B
nfocareto@washjeff.edu
FOCKLER, Cassandra .... 717-337-6207 384 D
cfockler@gettysburg.edu
FOCKLER, Debra .... 509-359-6348 479 G
dfockler@ewu.edu
FOCO, Jonathan .... 989-686-9228 223 J
jonathanfoco@delta.edu
FODRAN, Kimberly .... 562-985-5146.. 31 D
kimberly.fodran@csulb.edu
FOECKLER, Michael, S .. 540-636-2900 465 L
mfoeckler@christendom.edu
FOEHL, Brooks, L .... 413-597-4408 220 D
brooks.l.foehl@williams.edu
FOELSCH, Joseph .... 212-772-4540 294 C
jf1128@hunter.cuny.edu
FOGA, Thomas .... 609-586-4800 278 F
fogat@mccc.edu
FOGARTY, John .... 850-644-1346 110 C
john.fogarty@med.fsu.edu
FOGARTY, Timothy, P .... 814-393-1939 393 G
tfogarty@clarion.edu

FOGEL, Andy .... 785-670-2770 178 C
andy.fogel@washburn.edu
FOGERSON, Kathy, J .... 217-333-3070 151 F
kfogerso@uillinois.edu
FOGERTY, Jennifer .... 215-503-6335 399 E
jennifer.fogerty@jefferson.edu
FOGG, W. Neal .... 401-598-1890 404 D
neal.fogg@jwu.edu
FOGGATT, Stephen .... 406-657-1641 264 D
stephen.foggatt@msubillings.edu
FOGGS, Ranodore, M ... 618-537-6911 144 A
rmfoggs@mckendree.edu
FOGLE, Elizabeth .... 419-720-6670 359 M
elizabeth.fogle@proskills.edu
FOGLE, Nicole .... 336-838-6424 339 B
nefogle753@wilkescc.edu
FOGLEMAN, Tony .... 704-669-4117 333 E
foglemana728@clevelandcc.edu
FOHL, Dana .... 859-622-6973 180 E
dana.fohl@eku.edu
FOHRMAN, Jonathan .... 760-757-2121.. 52 F
jfohrman@miracosta.edu
FOISY, Andre .... 518-464-8720 299 C
afoisy@excelsior.edu
FOISY, Brian, R .... 208-885-6174 132 F
brianfoisy@uidaho.edu
FOK, Kristie .... 602-286-8062.. 13 B
kristie.fok@gatewaycc.edu
FOLAN, Amy, G .... 989-774-3043 222 E
folan1ag@cmich.edu
FOLAN, Kate .... 781-899-5500 218 B
kfolan@psjs.edu
FOLDEN, Jenn .... 740-588-1225 365 B
jfolden@zanestate.edu
FOLDS-BENNETT,
Trisha .... 276-328-0121 472 E
folds-bennett@uvawise.edu
FOLES, Shawn .... 618-664-6694 138 F
shawn.foles@greenville.edu
FOLEY, Chris .... 812-855-2953 156 G
cfoley@iu.edu
FOLEY, Chris, J .... 812-855-2953 156 F
cfoley@iu.edu
FOLEY, Ed .... 816-604-1176 255 C
ed.foley@mcckc.edu
FOLEY, Erin .... 541-885-1013 374 I
erin.foley@oit.edu
FOLEY, Henry .... 516-686-7650 308 I
president@nyit.edu
FOLEY, Joseph .... 508-767-7456 206 A
jfoley@assumption.edu
FOLEY, Kathleen .... 570-674-6304 390 B
kfoley@misericordia.edu
FOLEY, Lee .... 859-371-9393 179 G
lfoley@beckfield.edu
FOLEY, Marie .... 973-761-9282 283 C
marie.foley@shu.edu
FOLEY, Mark, D .... 205-348-9545.... 7 F
mfoley@uasystem.edu
FOLEY, Mary .... 620-792-9278 171 I
foleym@bartonccc.edu
FOLEY, Ryan .... 912-688-6061 123 J
rfoley@ogeecheetech.edu
FOLEY, Teresa .... 860-253-3137.. 86 C
tfoley@asnuntuck.edu
FOLGER, Susan .... 802-831-1237 463 C
sfolger@vermontlaw.edu
FOLK, Janice .... 207-326-2280 196 A
janice.folk@mma.edu
FOLK, Kevin .... 417-862-9533 253 F
kfolk@globaluniversity.edu
FOLKESTAD, William ..... 719-549-2865.. 80 B
william.folkestad@csupueblo.edu
FOLKS, Liesl .... 520-626-8121.. 16 D
liesl@arizona.edu
FOLKS, Lonnie .... 314-529-9288 255 B
lfolks@maryville.edu
FOLLETT, Naomi .... 530-541-4660.. 47 E
FOLLIARD, Peter .... 605-274-5233 414 G
peter.folliard@augie.edu
FOLLICK, David .... 516-572-7346 307 E
david.follick@ncc.edu
FOLLICK, Edwin .... 714-533-1495.. 64 I
edfollick@southbaylo.edu
FOLLONI, Laura .... 508-531-1343 212 D
lfolloni@bridgew.edu
FOLLOWELL, Coleen ..... 562-985-4121.. 31 D
coleen.followell@csulb.edu
FOLLOWELL, Wendell ... 859-256-3100 181 C
wendell.followell@kctcs.edu
FOLSE, Dick .... 309-556-3058 140 F
dfolse@iwu.edu
FOLSE, Vickie .... 309-556-3052 140 F
vfolse@iwu.edu
FOLSE, Vickie .... 309-556-3051 140 F
nursing@iwu.edu
FOLSOM, Michele .... 716-888-8367 292 F
folsom@canisius.edu
FOLT, Carol, L .... 213-740-2311.. 73 D
president@usc.edu
FOLTZ, Amber .... 540-869-0799 474 C
afoltz@lfcc.edu
FOLTZ, Kathy .... 805-893-4774.. 70 E
foltz@lifesci.ucsb.edu
FOMENKO, Juliana .... 215-972-2003 392 T
jfomenko@pafa.edu
FON, Lael .... 415-575-6100.. 28 I
lfon@ciis.edu
FONDILLER, Jennifer .... 212-854-2817 291 A
jfondill@barnard.edu
FONG, Chun, M .... 626-917-9482.. 36 G
chunmingfong@cesna.edu
FONG, Lindy .... 323-780-6738.. 48 J
fonglw@elac.edu
FONG, Matt .... 402-461-7786 267 C
mfong@hastings.edu
FONG, Steve .... 503-552-1584 374 D
sfong@nunm.edu
FONG, Valerie .... 650-949-7135.. 42 I
fongvalerie@fhda.edu
FONG, Wyman .... 952-485-5261.. 35 I
wfong@clpccd.org
FONG, Wyman .... 925-485-5261.. 35 J
wfong@clpccd.org
FONJWENG, Godlove .... 936-261-2119 446 C
gtfonjweng@pvamu.edu
FONNVILLE, Shawn .... 325-574-7645 458 D
sfonville@wtc.edu
FONOIMOANA, David ... 808-675-3565 128 D
david.fonoimoana@byuh.edu
FONSECA, Anthony .... 413-265-2280 208 E
fonsecaa@elms.edu
FONTÁNEZ, Awilda .... 787-523-6000 507 D
afontanez@icprjc.edu
FONT, Iris, J .... 787-740-4282 511 B
iris.font@uccaribe.edu
FONT-GUZMÁN,
Jacqueline .... 540-432-4398 466 B
jackie.font@emu.edu
FONTAINE, Andrea .... 208-562-3000 131 E
andreafontaine@cwi.edu
FONTAINE, Chris .... 903-510-2496 452 A
chris.fontaine@tjc.edu
FONTAINE, David .... 315-792-3050 324 B
dsfontaine@utica.edu
FONTAINE, Deborah ...... 904-633-8163 101 B
deborah.fontaine@fscj.edu
FONTAINE, Linda .... 512-492-3014 430 A
lfontaine@aoma.edu
FONTAINE, Paul, V .... 401-865-1575 404 F
fontaine@providence.edu
FONTAINE, Sheryl .... 657-278-2651.. 31 C
sfontaine@fullerton.edu
FONTANA, Janine .... 641-628-5229 164 D
fontanaj@central.edu
FONTANA, Jeanette .... 209-575-6498.. 77 A
fontanaj@mjc.edu
FONTANET-MALDONADO,
Julio, E .... 787-751-1912 509 A
jfontane@juris.inter.edu
FONTANEZ, Awilda .... 787-753-6000 507 D
afontanez@icprjc.edu
FONTENETTE, Edward ... 870-575-8410.. 22 D
fontenettee@uapb.edu
FONTENOT, Karen .... 985-549-2101 193 A
kfontenot@selu.edu
FONTENOT, Lana .... 337-521-9026 188 I
lana.fontenot@solacc.edu
FONTENOT, Olufunke .... 478-825-6330 118 F
olufunke.fontenot@fvsu.edu
FONTENOT, Olufunke .... 478-825-6374 118 F
olufunke.fontenot@fvsu.edu
FONTENOT, Patrick .... 210-486-4431 428 I
pfontenot@alamo.edu
FONTENOT, Roxane ...... 337-475-5090 192 E
rfontenot@mcneese.edu
FONTES, Mary .... 218-793-2460 240 B
mary.fontes@northlandcollege.edu
FONTOURA, Ana, M ..... 201-692-2653 277 I
ana_maria_fontoura66@fdu.edu
FONTS, Raul, A .... 401-865-2754 404 F
rfonts@providence.edu
FONZO, Crescenzo .... 201-761-6412 283 A
cfonzo@saintpeters.edu
FOOS, Jacque .... 419-559-2370 361 C
jafoos@terra.edu
FOOS, Jordan .... 605-668-1392 415 F
jordan.foos@mountmarty.edu
FOOSE, David .... 913-234-0650 172 K
david.foose@cleveland.edu
FOOSE, Tanya .... 440-934-3101 357 I
tfoose@ohiobusinesscollege.edu
FOOTE, Amy .... 661-362-3574.. 38 D
amy.foote@canyons.edu
FOOTE, Bruce .... 815-740-3403 152 H
bfoote@stfrancis.edu
FOOTE, Chandra .... 716-286-8549 309 H
cjf@niagara.edu
FOOTE, Jeffrey, C .... 518-255-5830 319 C
footejc@cobleskill.edu
FOOTE, Monica, W .... 718-939-5100 304 C
mfoote@libi.edu
FOOTE, Nicola .... 412-624-6880 400 H
nfoote@pitt.edu
FORAN, Joanne .... 978-837-5000 216 F
FORBEAR, Lori .... 815-836-5498 142 F
lforbear@lewisu.edu
FORBES, Claudia .... 303-352-3035.. 80 F
claudia.forbes@ccd.edu
FORBES, DeChelle .... 410-951-3390 204 B
dforbes@coppin.edu
FORBES, Digna .... 615-327-6204 421 D
dforbes@mmc.edu
FORBES, J. Thomas ...... 812-855-5700 156 F
forbesjt@iu.edu
FORBES, J.T .... 812-855-5700 156 G
forbesjt@iu.edu
FORBES, John .... 559-325-5219.. 67 A
john.forbes@cloviscollege.edu
FORBES, Lindi .... 620-421-6700 175 F
lindif@labette.edu
FORBES, Lindi, D .... 620-421-6700 175 F
lindif@labette.edu
FORBES, Lisa, R .... 402-486-2897 269 F
lisa.r.forbes@ucollege.edu
FORBES, Scott .... 713-500-3289 456 B
scott.forbes@uth.tmc.edu
FORBES, Tonya .... 269-965-3931 225 H
forbest@kellogg.edu
FORBES, Valery, E .... 612-624-2244 243 F
veforbes@umn.edu
FORBES BERTHOUND,
Diane .... 410-706-7727 203 A
dforbes@umaryland.edu
FORBUS, Amy .... 501-450-1426.. 19 E
forbus@hendrix.edu
FORCE, Daniel .... 402-486-2534 269 F
daniel.force@ucollege.edu
FORCE, Maria .... 973-408-3515 277 A
mforce@drew.edu
FORCE, Rex .... 208-282-3848 131 G
forcrex@isu.edu
FORCH, Aron .... 847-317-6400 151 C
agforch@tiu.edu
FORD, Allison .... 985-448-4002 192 F
allison.ford@nicholls.edu
FORD, Amy .... 580-559-5725 365 K
aford@ecok.edu
FORD, Andrea .... 202-274-2303.. 94 C
andrea.ford@potomac.edu
FORD, Ashlie .... 830-372-8064 449 A
aford@tlu.edu
FORD, Beth .... 216-373-5351 357 F
bford@ndc.edu
FORD, Cathy .... 567-661-7398 359 I
catherine_ford@owens.edu
FORD, Charlotte .... 205-665-6110.... 8 D
cford6@montevallo.edu
FORD, Chris .... 270-686-4291 179 J
chris.ford@brescia.edu
FORD, Christopher .... 434-797-8598 473 G
christopher.ford@danville.edu
FORD, Claudia, J .... 315-267-2184 319 A
fordcj@potsdam.edu
FORD, Daryl .... 401-254-3215 405 C
dford@rwu.edu
FORD, David .... 925-631-4818.. 59 I
dford@stmarys-ca.edu
FORD, Deborah, L .... 262-595-2211 496 D
deborah.ford@uwp.edu
FORD, Debra .... 402-280-2551 266 H
debraford@creighton.edu
FORD, Erin .... 307-268-2621 500 U
erin.ford@caspercollege.edu
FORD, Glenn .... 503-847-2570 377 B
gford@uws.edu
FORD, Gregory .... 504-286-5381 191 C
FORD, Henri .... 305-243-5677 113 C
hford@med.miami.edu
FORD, James .... 805-893-2706.. 70 E
j.ford@summer.ucsb.edu
FORD, Jeff .... 417-690-3290 251 H
jford@cofo.edu
FORD, Jermaine .... 337-521-9049 188 I
jermaine.ford@solacc.edu
FORD, Jesse .... 617-670-4536 209 G
jford02@fisher.edu
FORD, Josh .... 575-492-2183 289 F
jford@usw.edu
FORD, Kelsey .... 314-837-6777 258 K
kford@stlchristian.edu
FORD, Kimberly .... 843-863-7050 407 B
kcford@csuniv.edu
FORD, Kimberly .... 330-337-6403 347 D
ie@awc.edu
FORD, Kristie, A .... 518-580-5425 315 F
kford@skidmore.edu
FORD, Lacy .... 803-777-7798 413 A
ford@mailbox.sc.edu
FORD, Lynne, E .... 843-953-6531 408 C
fordl@cofc.edu
FORD, Madeline .... 718-518-4211 294 B
mford@hostos.cuny.edu
FORD, Mark, C .... 913-971-3614 176 C
mford@mnu.edu
FORD, Mary Beth .... 412-396-2061 383 A
fordmb@duq.edu
FORD, Michael .... 312-341-2322 148 E
mford@roosevelt.edu
FORD, Miriam .... 914-674-7860 306 C
mford@mercy.edu
FORD, Nadine .... 919-536-7200 334 C
fordn@durhamtech.edu
FORD, Ricky, G .... 662-720-7730 248 C
rgford@nemcc.edu
FORD, Rochelle .... 336-278-5724 328 J
rford9@elon.edu
FORD, Shamika .... 215-885-2360 389 C
sford@manor.edu
FORD, Sharhonda, L .... 305-626-3103 100 D
sharhonda.ford@fmuniv.edu
FORD, Sherry .... 970-943-7052.. 85 C
sford@western.edu
FORD, Sue .... 518-262-6008 289 L
FORD, Tami .... 619-594-4723.. 33 D
tford2@sdsu.edu
FORD, Terrance .... 972-224-5481 444 B
FORD, Theresa .... 724-503-1001 402 B
tford@washjeff.edu
FORD, Tracey .... 336-770-3283 343 D
fordt@uncsa.edu
FORD, Tracey, D .... 419-783-2354 351 K
tford@defiance.edu
FORD, Tracy .... 601-968-8840 245 B
tford@belhaven.edu
FORD FISHER,
Margaret .... 713-718-8011 437 C
margaret.fordfisher@hccs.edu
FORD-KEE, Dianthia ...... 662-254-3550 248 B
dfkee@mvsu.edu
FORD-THOMAS,
Manisha .... 314-977-5510 259 F
manisha.fordthomas@slu.edu
FORDE, Althea .... 718-960-8066 294 A
althea.forde@lehman.cuny.edu
FORDE, Christopher ...... 617-544-8657 139 G
fordec@iecc.edu
FORDE, Dermot, M .... 419-372-9475 348 G
dforde@bgsu.edu
FORDE, Dorothy .... 256-726-7287.... 6 C
deforde@oakwood.edu
FORDE, Nokoia .... 484-365-7275 388 H
nforde@lincoln.edu
FORDE, Timothy .... 502-597-6044 183 D
timothy.forde@kysu.edu
FORDHAM, Traci .... 971-722-4667 375 D
traci.fordham@pcc.edu
FORDHAM, Tracy .... 941-377-4880 104 D
tfordham@meridian.edu
FORDIS, JR.,
C. Michael .... 713-798-8256 431 D
fordis@bcm.edu
FORDYCE, Amanda .... 440-375-7015 354 K
afordyce@lec.edu
FORE, Marilyn, J .... 843-349-5201 409 J
marilyn.fore@hgtc.edu
FORE, Shonna .... 417-328-1689 259 I
sfore@sbuniv.edu
FORE, Sue .... 252-249-1851 336 F
sfore@pamlicocc.edu
FOREHAND, Cynthia, J . 802-656-8060 463 A
cynthia.forehand@uvm.edu

FOREMAN, Adam .... 601-484-8615 247 A
tforeman@meridiancc.edu
FOREMAN, Artie .... 601-635-2111 246 A
aforeman@eccc.edu
FOREMAN, David .... 610-328-8625 398 G
dforema1@swarthmore.edu
FOREMAN, Erin .... 260-982-5945 159 J
erforeman@manchester.edu
FOREMAN, Hank, T .... 828-262-2040 340 I
foremanht@appstate.edu
FOREMAN, Kyle .... 509-793-2299 478 B
kylef@bigbend.edu
FOREMAN, Margo .... 515-294-0143 163 G
mrforma@iastate.edu
FOREMAN, Michelle ..... 717-477-1475 395 B
mtforeman@ship.edu
FOREMAN, Mika .... 817-598-6354 457 J
mforeman@wc.edu
FOREMAN, Pamela, B ... 804-257-5821 476 F
pforeman@vuu.edu
FOREMAN, Todd .... 518-956-8120 316 A
todd.foreman@albany.edu
FORESE, Joseph .... 770-426-2741 122 C
joseph.forese@life.edu
FOREST, Colleen .... 805-437-8537.. 30 C
colleen.forest@csuci.edu
FOREST, Mark .... 609-771-2247 276 I
forestm@tcnj.edu
FOREST, Rebecca .... 978-630-9597 215 C
r_forest@mwcc.mass.edu
FORESTER, David .... 252-536-7213 335 B
dforester@halifaxcc.edu
FORESTER, Erin .... 706-778-8500 124 D
FORESTER, Robin .... 334-244-3676.... 4 E
rforeste@aum.edu
FORESTER, Sherri, L ..... 270-901-1115 182 H
sherri.forester@kctcs.edu
FORGER, James, B .... 517-355-4583 227 F
forger@msu.edu
FORGERY, Glendon .... 806-457-4200 436 C
FORGETTE, Adrienne ...... 505-566-3217 288 D
forgettea@sanjuancollege.edu
FORGUES, Chalea .... 657-278-7758.. 31 C
ceforgues@fullerton.edu
FORGUES, David .... 657-278-8351.. 31 C
dforgues@fullerton.edu
FORINA, Olga .... 718-517-7722 314 F
FORISTER, J. Glenn ...... 817-735-2762 454 B
glenn.forister@unthsc.edu
FORKNER, Peter .... 781-891-2274 206 G
pforkner@bentley.edu
FORLINES, Jon .... 615-675-5299 428 C
jforlines@welch.edu
FORLINES, Susan .... 615-675-5259 428 C
susan@welch.edu
FORMAN, Robert, J ...... 718-990-7552 313 G
formanj@stjohns.edu
FORMAN, Robin .... 504-865-5261 191 F
rforman@tulane.edu
FORMAN, Scheherazade, W .... 301-546-0884 201 E
formansw@pgcc.edu
FORMICA, Melinda .... 203-582-3735.. 88 G
melinda.formica@quinnipiac.edu
FORNERIS, Glenda .... 815-802-8835 141 D
gforneris@kcc.edu
FORNEY, Heather .... 605-773-3455 416 C
heather.forney@sdbor.edu
FORNIERI, Diane, K ...... 516-323-3204 306 M
dfornieri@molloy.edu
FORNWALT, Lisa .... 256-215-4301.... 1 G
lfornwalt@cacc.edu
FOROUDASTAN, Hooshang .... 434-381-6130 471 I
hforoudastan@sbc.edu
FORRAY, April .... 414-930-3627 494 E
forraya@mtmary.edu
FORREST, Anderson ...... 610-372-4721 396 H
aforrest@racc.edu
FORREST, Barbara .... 205-665-6055.... 8 D
forrestb@montevallo.edu
FORREST, Christian .... 248-204-2204 227 A
cforrest@ltu.edu
FORREST, Christy .... 336-249-8186 334 B
christy_forrest@davidsondavie.edu
FORREST, Danae .... 585-567-9493 302 B
danae.forrest@houghton.edu
FORREST, Jeffrey .... 661-362-3144.. 38 D
jeffrey.forrest@canyons.edu
FORREST, Lisa .... 704-894-2599 328 E
liforrest@davidson.edu
FORREST, Tyler .... 423-425-4393 427 C
tyler-forrest@utc.edu
FORRESTER, Cynthia ..... 913-758-6114 178 B
cynthia.forrester@stmary.edu
FORRESTER, Djuna .... 903-463-8759 436 G
forresterd@grayson.edu
FORRESTER, Don .... 812-221-1714 162 E
donforrester@vbc.edu
FORRESTER, Jill, M ...... 717-245-1669 382 D
forrestj@dickinson.edu
FORRESTER, Maureen ... 781-891-2000 206 G
mforrester@bentley.edu
FORRESTER, Michael, P 864-592-4805 412 E
forresterm@sccsc.edu
FORRESTER, Risa .... 405-425-5106 367 C
risa.forrester@oc.edu
FORRIDER, Timothy ...... 330-337-6403 347 D
FORRY, Jennifer .... 617-735-9746 209 D
forryj@emmanuel.edu
FORSBERG, LeAnn .... 817-257-7516 448 F
leann.forsberg@tcu.edu
FORSHEE, Jennifer .... 208-282-2566 131 G
jennforshee@isu.edu
FORSMAN, Nneka .... 336-744-0900 327 E
nneka.forsman@carolina.edu
FORSSTROM, Janice, M 978-762-4000 215 D
jforsstr@northshore.edu
FORSTE, Renata .... 801-422-1801 458 H
renata_forste@byu.edu
FORSTEIN, David .... 303-373-2008.. 83 G
dforstein@rvu.edu
FORSTEIN, David .... 303-373-2008.. 83 G
president@rvu.edu
FORSTER, Dan .... 413-572-5365 213 F
dforster@westfield.ma.edu
FORSTER, Jerry .... 304-352-0020 487 J
jerryforster@ucwv.edu
FORSTER, Kathy .... 716-673-3341 316 D
kathy.forster@fredonia.edu
FORSYTH, Anne, S .... 805-525-4417.. 67 K
aforsyth@thomasaquinas.edu
FORSYTH, Nate .... 641-648-4611 167 F
nate.forsyth@iavalley.edu
FORSYTHE, Micah .... 406-586-3585 263 I
micah.forsythe@montanabiblecollege.edu
FORSYTHE, Robert, E .... 313-577-4501 232 K
robert.forsythe@wayne.edu
FORSYTHE, Ryan .... 508-929-8498 213 G
rforsythe@worcester.edu
FORT, Jill .... 316-942-4291 176 E
fortj@newmanu.edu
FORT, Lindsay .... 763-424-0736 240 A
lfort@nhcc.edu
FORT, Rebecca, L .... 330-471-8313 355 D
rfort@malone.edu
FORTE, Allana .... 904-256-7549 102 H
aforte@ju.edu
FORTE, Marcel .... 831-582-4796.. 32 B
mforte@csumb.edu
FORTE, Paul, D .... 828-262-2030 340 I
fortepd@appstate.edu
FORTE, Teresa (Terrie) .. 413-747-0204 208 B
teresa.forte@cambridgecollege.edu
FORTHMAN, Emily .... 618-634-3223 149 G
emilyf@shawneecc.edu
FORTHMAN, Jennifer .... 870-245-5299.. 20 D
forthmanj@obu.edu
FORTHOFER, Scott .... 406-496-4500 265 A
sforthofer@mtech.edu
FORTHUBER, Mary .... 443-352-5625 202 E
mforthuber@stevenson.edu
FORTIER, Breean .... 617-373-2416 217 I
FORTIER, Breean .... 617-585-1740 217 E
FORTIN, Elizabeth .... 207-453-5858 195 F
efortin@kvcc.me.edu
FORTINI, Mary-Ellen ..... 408-554-4806.. 63 B
mfortini@scu.edu
FORTINI, Nick .... 619-201-8676.. 60 G
nfortini@sdcc.edu
FORTINI, Robert .... 413-662-5099 213 C
r.fortini@mcla.edu
FORTINO, Matthew .... 212-924-5900 321 F
mfortino@swedishinstitute.edu
FORTIS SANTIAGO, Yaihara, M .... 646-888-3705 304 J
fortissy@mskcc.org
FORTMAN, Brian, J .... 864-833-8287 411 D
bjfortman@presby.edu
FORTMAN, Susan .... 516-323-4311 306 M
sfortman@molloy.edu
FORTNER, Everette .... 434-243-7755 472 D
ewf5db@virginia.edu
FORTNER, James .... 404-385-7590 119 E
james.fortner@business.gatech.edu
FORTNER, Melissa .... 706-865-2134 126 E
mfortner@truett.edu
FORTNEY, Patrick .... 308-635-6339 270 C
fortneyp@wncc.edu
FORTRESS, Marty .... 517-750-1200 231 C
marty.fortress@arbor.edu
FORTSCH, Peggy .... 319-226-2031 163 C
peggy.fortsch@allencollege.edu
FORTSON, Carolyn .... 803-793-5213 408 G
fortsonc@denmarktech.edu
FORTSON, Daniel .... 415-442-7000.. 43 I
dfortson@ggu.edu
FORTSON, Jill .... 325-674-2653 428 F
jill.fortson@acu.edu
FORTUNATO, Frank .... 904-264-2172 106 K
frank.fortunato@om.org
FORTUNE, André .... 678-839-6423 127 C
afortune@westga.edu
FORTUNE, Angelene ..... 828-328-7387 330 F
angelene.fortune@lr.edu
FORTUNE, Diana .... 518-891-2915 310 A
dfortune@nccc.edu
FORTUNE, Sarah, E ...... 812-888-4587 162 F
sfortune@vinu.edu
FOSCHIA, Christine ...... 724-805-2524 397 I
chris.foschia@stvincent.edu
FOSCHIA, Christine, L .. 724-805-2524 398 A
christine.foschia@stvincent.edu
FOSDYCK, Rick .... 641-683-5117 166 I
rick.fosdyck@indianhills.edu
FOSHEE, Brian, E .... 901-843-3870 423 A
foshee@rhodes.edu
FOSHEE, Kenneth, H ..... 205-348-2857.... 7 G
ken.foshee@ua.edu
FOSS, Ben .... 941-487-4777 110 D
bfoss@ncf.edu
FOSS, Laura .... 845-687-5211 323 H
fossl@sunyulster.edu
FOSS, Lisa, H .... 320-308-4028 240 I
lhfoss@stcloudstate.edu
FOSSETT, Christine .... 360-623-8451 478 F
christine.fossett@centralia.edu
FOSSETTE, Regina .... 501-812-2724.. 23 B
rfossette@uaptc.edu
FOSSUM, Dallas .... 218-299-4533 235 H
dfossum@cord.edu
FOSSUM, Michael, E .... 409-740-4408 446 F
fossum@tamug.edu
FOSSUM, Scott .... 605-995-7178 415 E
scott.fossum@mitchelltech.edu
FOSTER, Alan .... 580-628-6435 366 J
alan.foster@noc.edu
FOSTER, Alicia .... 315-792-7347 321 B
alicia.foster@sunypoly.edu
FOSTER, Anderle .... 601-426-6346 249 A
afoster@southeasternbaptist.edu
FOSTER, Andrew .... 203-773-8542.. 85 D
afoster@albertus.edu
FOSTER, Angelique .... 303-860-5600.. 84 A
angelique.foster@cu.edu
FOSTER, Ashley .... 434-200-3070 465 D
FOSTER, Ben .... 315-786-2291 303 C
bfoster@sunyjefferson.edu
FOSTER, Cherie, A .... 248-341-2117 229 C
cafoster@oaklandcc.edu
FOSTER, Claire .... 757-352-4219 470 B
cfoster@regent.edu
FOSTER, Colleen .... 575-835-5352 286 K
colleen.foster@nmt.edu
FOSTER, Curt .... 413-552-2203 214 F
cfoster@hcc.edu
FOSTER, Dava .... 334-347-2623.... 2 A
dfoster@escc.edu
FOSTER, David, F .... 603-646-3839 273 D
david.f.foster@dartmouth.edu
FOSTER, Diane .... 610-359-5100 382 A
dfoster@dccc.edu
FOSTER, Donna .... 864-941-8430 411 C
foster.d@ptc.edu
FOSTER, Doug .... 803-777-0707 413 A
drdofster@mailbox.sc.edu
FOSTER, Dyrell, W .... 925-424-1001.. 35 K
dfoster@laspositascollege.edu
FOSTER, Greg .... 607-255-2723 297 F
gjf48@cornell.edu
FOSTER, Gretchen .... 308-635-6183 270 C
fosterg2@wncc.edu
FOSTER, Isaac .... 646-378-6125 310 D
isaac.foster@nyack.edu
FOSTER, Jackie .... 910-362-7019 332 H
jfoster@cfcc.edu
FOSTER, Jan .... 864-663-0052 410 I
jan.foster@ngu.edu
FOSTER, Janet .... 562-985-5459.. 31 D
janet.foster@csulb.edu
FOSTER, Jasmine .... 661-362-3101.. 38 D
jasmine.foster@canyons.edu
FOSTER, Jean .... 714-992-7001.. 54 C
jfoster@fullcoll.edu
FOSTER, Jeanie .... 817-735-0217 454 B
jeanie.foster@unthsc.edu
FOSTER, Jennifer .... 515-964-6692 165 A
jlfoster1@dmacc.edu
FOSTER, Jimmie .... 717-358-3953 383 I
jfoster1@fandm.edu
FOSTER, Jimmie, A .... 843-953-7199 408 C
fosterja@cofc.edu
FOSTER, Karen .... 318-342-5236 193 C
kfoster@ulm.edu
FOSTER, Kathryn, A ...... 609-771-1855 276 I
foster@tcnj.edu
FOSTER, Kimberly .... 504-865-5000 191 F
FOSTER, Lauren .... 828-898-2496 330 E
fosterl@lmc.edu
FOSTER, Lisa .... 559-453-3443.. 43 A
lisa.foster@fresno.edu
FOSTER, Matt .... 630-942-3993 135 I
fosterm5@cod.edu
FOSTER, Meezie .... 302-225-6235.. 91 B
fosterm@gbc.edu
FOSTER, Meichele, A .... 573-882-5394 261 A
fosterma@missouri.edu
FOSTER, Melissa .... 205-226-4736.... 4 F
FOSTER, Michelle, R ..... 407-582-2008 113 I
mrfoster@valenciacollege.edu
FOSTER, Misty .... 405-789-7661 369 I
misty.foster@swcu.edu
FOSTER, Morris, W .... 757-683-3460 469 B
mfoster@odu.edu
FOSTER, Nicola .... 212-346-1949 311 A
nfoster@pace.edu
FOSTER, Pam .... 785-670-1509 178 C
pam.foster@washburn.edu
FOSTER, Paul .... 406-657-1705 264 D
paul.foster4@msubillings.edu
FOSTER, Paul, C .... 513-556-9021 361 J
paul.foster@uc.edu
FOSTER, Quisa .... 404-880-8742 117 C
qfoster@cau.edu
FOSTER, Rachel .... 414-847-3211 494 C
rachelfoster@miad.edu
FOSTER, Robert .... 304-647-6285 490 C
rfoster@osteo.wvsom.edu
FOSTER, Rodney .... 714-432-5531.. 38 B
rfoster@occ.cccd.edu
FOSTER, Ruby .... 714-463-7559.. 51 B
rfoster@ketchum.edu
FOSTER, Shelby .... 510-659-6200.. 54 J
sfoster@ohlone.edu
FOSTER, Stacey .... 314-539-5185 259 A
sfoster@stlcc.edu
FOSTER, Stephen .... 281-487-1170 448 E
sfoster@txchiro.edu
FOSTER, Stephen, P ...... 603-535-2188 275 A
spfoster@plymouth.edu
FOSTER, Tim .... 559-730-3902.. 39 B
timf@cos.edu
FOSTER, Timothy, J ...... 309-341-7814 141 G
tfoster@knox.edu
FOSTER, Todd .... 803-705-4565 406 G
todd.foster@benedict.edu
FOSTER, Tracy .... 920-206-2393 493 C
tracy.foster@mbu.edu
FOSTER ZSIGA, Erin ..... 207-786-6215 194 A
efoster@bates.edu
FOSTON, Amia .... 317-940-8000 154 C
FOTI, Bill .... 336-316-2199 329 D
wfoti@guilford.edu
FOTOPLES, Dan .... 216-397-1559 353 O
dfotoples@jcu.edu
FOTOUHI, Farshad .... 313-577-3776 232 K
fotouhi@wayne.edu
FOUBERG, Andi .... 605-688-4151 417 A
FOUBERG, Erin .... 605-626-2558 416 G
erin.fouberg@northern.edu
FOUBERG, Erin .... 605-626-2524 416 G
erin.fouberg@northern.edu
FOUBERT, John .... 731-661-5373 426 F
jfoubert@uu.edu
FOUCART, Steve .... 417-836-4563 256 G
stevefoucart@missouristate.edu
FOUCHT, Craig .... 919-735-5151 338 H
cfoucht@waynecc.edu
FOUGERE, John .... 573-592-4585 262 G
john.fougere@williamwoods.edu

FOUGERES, Michel .... 727-864-7987.. 98 J
fougermw@eckerd.edu
FOULKROD,
Marianna, K .... 317-788-3302 161 H
mfoulkrod@uindy.edu
FOUNTAIN, Barbara ...... 951-639-5212.. 53 A
bfountain@msjc.edu
FOUNTAIN, Brent .... 662-325-0849 247 F
bjf2@msstate.edu
FOUNTAIN, Cheryl, A ... 904-620-2496 111 B
fountain@unf.edu
FOUNTAIN, Jennifer ...... 253-566-5159 484 E
jfountain@tacomacc.edu
FOUNTAIN, Richard ...... 850-474-2866 111 F
rfountain@uwf.edu
FOUNTAIN, Sydney .... 620-947-3121 177 I
sydneyshields@tabor.edu
FOUNTAIN, Wesley .... 910-672-1685 341 C
wtfountain01@uncfsu.edu
FOUNTAIN WILLIAMS,
Leslie .... 360-623-8647 478 F
leslie.fountainwilliams@centralia.edu
FOUNTAIN WILLIAMS,
Leslie .... 212-616-7227 301 C
lfountainwilliams@heleneful.edu
FOURNET, Rachel .... 225-768-1739 187 B
rachel.fournet@franu.edu
FOURNIER, Jody .... 614-236-6445 349 B
jfournier@capital.edu
FOURNIER, Katie .... 207-778-7042 196 I
katie.b.fournier@maine.edu
FOURNIER, Nicole .... 207-768-9589 197 C
nicole.l.fournier@maine.edu
FOURNIER, Robert .... 313-577-4280 232 K
rob.fournier@wayne.edu
FOURNIER, Robyn .... 949-359-0045.. 29 A
FOURNIER, Susan .... 617-353-4076 207 E
fournism@bu.edu
FOUSE, Kathryn .... 254-295-4678 453 D
kfouse@umhb.edu
FOUSE, Steve .... 417-447-7776 257 G
fouses@otc.edu
FOUST, Dane, R .... 410-543-6080 204 D
drfoust@salisbury.edu
FOUST, John .... 585-785-1599 299 F
john.foust@flcc.edu
FOUST, Julia .... 708-239-4608 151 A
julia.foust@trnty.edu
FOUST, Lori, N .... 717-358-4438 383 I
lori.foust@fandm.edu
FOUT, Jason .... 773-380-6780 133 F
FOUTY, Dennis .... 832-842-4603 452 C
dfouty@uh.edu
FOUTY, Dennis .... 832-842-4603 452 D
dfouty@uh.edu
FOWL, Steve .... 410-617-2327 200 B
sfowl@loyola.edu
FOWLER, Bill .... 870-864-7146.. 21 A
bfowler@southark.edu
FOWLER, Carlton .... 816-604-4101 255 H
carlton.fowler@mcckc.edu
FOWLER, Charles .... 865-471-3200 418 E
cfowler@cn.edu
FOWLER, Charlotte .... 760-471-1316.. 72 H
FOWLER, Craig .... 828-227-7282 343 E
cfowler@wcu.edu
FOWLER, David .... 334-386-7415.... 5 C
dfowler@faulkner.edu
FOWLER, Dominique .... 804-257-5219 476 F
dmfowler@vuu.edu
FOWLER, Gregory .... 301-985-7000 203 E
FOWLER, Heather, L ..... 570-577-1188 379 C
h.fowler@bucknell.edu
FOWLER, James, R .... 401-341-2908 405 D
jim.fowler@salve.edu
FOWLER, Jason .... 850-201-7773 112 C
jason.fowler@tcc.fl.edu
FOWLER, Jason .... 919-761-2252 340 D
jfowler@sebts.edu
FOWLER, Jeffrey .... 314-977-2849 259 F
jeff.fowler@slu.edu
FOWLER, Judy .... 214-818-1301 433 O
jfowler@criswell.edu
FOWLER, Justin .... 503-552-1517 374 D
jfowler@nunm.edu
FOWLER, Kelly .... 909-274-5414.. 52 J
kfowler@mtsac.edu
FOWLER, Kristy .... 949-214-3064.. 39 K
kristy.fowler@cui.edu
FOWLER, Liesl, A .... 309-794-7211 133 C
lieslfowler@augustana.edu
FOWLER, Lisa .... 303-914-6302.. 83 C
lisa.fowler@rrcc.edu
FOWLER, Logan .... 208-792-2200 132 A
ljfowler@lcsc.edu
FOWLER, Matt .... 618-262-8641 139 I
fowlerm@iecc.edu
FOWLER, Michael .... 304-793-6869 490 C
mfowler@osteo.wvsom.edu
FOWLER, Mike .... 502-451-0815 185 A
mfowler@sullivan.edu
FOWLER, Paul .... 337-550-1433 189 G
pfowler@lsue.edu
FOWLER, Paul .... 404-727-0512 118 E
pgfowle@emory.edu
FOWLER, Peter .... 617-989-4082 219 F
fowlerp@wit.edu
FOWLER, Peter, A .... 518-388-6176 323 J
FOWLER, Rhonda .... 734-487-2587 223 K
rfowler@emich.edu
FOWLER, Robert .... 315-866-0300 301 D
fowlerrc@herkimer.edu
FOWLER, S. Kevin .... 903-510-2307 452 A
kfow@tjc.edu
FOWLER, Sandra .... 530-661-5700.. 77 D
FOWLER, Sky .... 618-252-5400 149 I
sky.fowler@sic.edu
FOWLER, T. Mark .... 434-223-6164 467 F
mfowler@hsc.edu
FOWLER, Tammy .... 901-572-2774 418 A
tammy.fowler@baptistu.edu
FOWLER, Vivia, L .... 478-757-5212 127 F
vfowler@wesleyancollege.edu
FOWLER, Walter, B .... 412-365-1105 380 G
wfowler@chatham.edu
FOWLER, Wes .... 319-398-7797 167 J
wes.fowler@kirkwood.edu
FOWLES, Gareth .... 561-237-7601 103 W
gfowles@lynn.edu
FOWLES, Michelle, R .... 818-947-2437.. 49 G
fowlesmr@lavc.edu
FOWLKES, April .... 215-242-7704 381 A
fowlkesa@chc.edu
FOWLKES, Bruce, M ..... 309-467-6423 138 A
bfowlkes@eureka.edu
FOWLKES, Carl .... 410-455-3377 203 B
cfowlkes@umbc.edu
FOWLKES, Rodney .... 937-769-1356 347 H
rfowlkes@antioch.edu
FOX, Alisha .... 423-472-7141 424 B
afox@clevelandstatecc.edu
FOX, Allen .... 435-652-7938 460 B
fox@dixie.edu
FOX, Amanda .... 205-665-6040.... 8 D
foxat@montevallo.edu
FOX, Amanda .... 516-572-7436 307 E
amanda.fox@ncc.edu
FOX, Amber .... 218-935-0417 244 G
amber.fox@wetcc.edu
FOX, Amelia .... 334-514-4018..... 2 F
amelia.fox@istc.edu
FOX, Andrew .... 314-529-9584 255 B
afox@maryville.edu
FOX, Ashley .... 270-789-5216 180 A
amfarmer@campbellsville.edu
FOX, Carole, M .... 512-463-9471 449 E
carole.fox@tsus.edu
FOX, Charles .... 318-626-1565 189 I
charles.fox@lsuhs.edu
FOX, Charles .... 313-883-8563 230 C
fox.charles@shms.edu
FOX, Christian, A .... 801-422-8417 458 H
cfox@byu.edu
FOX, Chuck .... 817-735-5030 454 B
chuck.fox@unthsc.edu
FOX, Dan .... 303-273-3231.. 79 J
dfox@mines.edu
FOX, David .... 570-561-1818 397 H
fr.david.fox@stots.edu
FOX, Debbie .... 225-768-1727 187 B
deborah.fox@franu.edu
FOX, Debbie .... 502-272-7777 179 H
dfox@bellarmine.edu
FOX, Deborah .... 785-442-6010 174 F
dfox@highlandcc.edu
FOX, Djuan .... 727-341-3334 107 E
fox.djuan@spcollege.edu
FOX, Donnie, S .... 606-337-1530 180 C
president@ccbbc.edu
FOX, Douglas .... 325-942-2333 450 E
doug.fox@angelo.edu
FOX, Gary .... 601-936-5553 246 C
gmfox@hindscc.edu
FOX, Janelle .... 843-863-8052 407 B
jmfox@csuniv.edu
FOX, Jeanne, E .... 574-807-7243 154 B
jeanne.fox@betheluniversity.edu
FOX, Jennifer .... 252-222-6081 333 A
jenniferl2176@carteret.edu
FOX, John .... 410-455-2591 203 B
johnfox@umbc.edu
FOX, Kathleen .... 989-275-5000 226 D
kathleen.fox@kirtland.edu
FOX, Kelly .... 404-894-4615 119 E
kelly.fox@gatech.edu
FOX, Kimberley .... 215-965-4035 390 E
kifox@moore.edu
FOX, Laurie .... 585-245-5577 318 B
fox@geneseo.edu
FOX, Levi .... 417-328-2072 259 I
lfox@sbuniv.edu
FOX, Linda, K .... 706-542-4879 126 G
lkfox@uga.edu
FOX, Lori .... 646-313-8000 295 D
lori.fox@cuny.edu
FOX, Mark .... 704-669-4175 333 E
foxm@clevelandcc.edu
FOX, II, Mark, O .... 864-833-8232 411 D
mfox@presby.edu
FOX, Mary David .... 864-503-5040 414 A
mdfox@uscupstate.edu
FOX, Matthew .... 413-782-1410 220 A
mfox@wne.edu
FOX, Melanie .... 828-251-6700 342 B
mrfox@unca.edu
FOX, Melissa .... 607-753-2305 318 A
melissa.fox@cortland.edu
FOX, Michael .... 716-851-1639 299 B
ascfoxm@ecc.edu
FOX, Michael, J .... 207-941-7000 194 F
foxm@husson.edu
FOX, Michael, J .... 757-221-1693 465 N
mjfox1@wm.edu
FOX, Michelle .... 406-604-4300 262 I
mfox@apollos.edu
FOX, Miranda .... 802-635-1257 463 G
FOX, Pamela .... 540-887-7026 468 G
pfox@marybaldwin.edu
FOX, Paul .... 254-710-2900 431 E
paul_fox@baylor.edu
FOX, Pete .... 989-686-9565 223 J
petefox@delta.edu
FOX, Ray .... 208-535-5378 131 B
ray.fox@cei.edu
FOX, Richard .... 718-368-4799 294 E
rfox@kbcc.cuny.edu
FOX, Robert .... 502-852-6745 186 A
bob.fox@louisville.edu
FOX, Robin .... 262-472-5821 497 D
foxr@uww.edu
FOX, Ronald, E .... 304-336-8021 490 B
ronald.fox@westliberty.edu
FOX, Rusty .... 575-528-7221 287 F
rfox@nmsu.edu
FOX, Sandra .... 541-885-1107 374 I
sandra.fox@oit.edu
FOX, Teresa .... 330-490-7503 363 E
tfox@walsh.edu
FOX, Tim .... 954-771-0376 103 S
tfox@knoxseminary.edu
FOX, Toyin .... 618-985-2828 140 H
toyinfox@jalc.edu
FOX-GARRITY, Bonnie .. 716-829-8122 298 E
garrityb@dyc.edu
FOX-WILSON, Jessica ... 608-363-2647 491 H
foxjs@beloit.edu
FOXMAN, Philip, R .... 814-332-5383 378 A
pfoxman@allegheny.edu
FOXMAN, Ruth .... 860-231-5221.. 90 A
rfoxman@usj.edu
FOXWORTH, Derrick ..... 971-722-4980 375 D
derrick.foxworth@pcc.edu
FOXX, LaMisa, M .... 919-530-7361 341 E
lmccoy@nccu.edu
FOXX-DAWODU,
Paulette, R .... 301-546-0995 201 E
foxxdapr@pgcc.edu
FOY, Allsion .... 864-294-3464 409 H
allison.foy@furman.edu
FOY, Geoffrey, E .... 253-535-7126 482 A
foy@plu.edu
FOY, Joseph .... 414-382-6044 491 F
joseph.foy@alverno.edu
FOY, Morna, K .... 608-267-9066 498 C
president@wtcsystem.edu
FOY, Richard .... 715-425-3505 496 F
richard.foy@uwrf.edu
FOY-BURROUGHS,
Wanda .... 704-378-1023 330 D
wfburroughs@jcsu.edu
FOYE, Shanen .... 949-675-4451.. 46 C
shanen@idi.edu
FOYLE, Kevin, J .... 713-500-4472 456 B
kevin.j.foyle@uth.tmc.edu
FOZARD, John, D .... 405-692-3176 366 D
president@macu.edu
FRAASE, Justin .... 605-626-3007 416 G
justin.fraase@northern.edu
FRABONI, David .... 260-665-4310 161 E
FRACE, Lisa .... 517-355-5016 227 F
lfrace@msu.edu
FRACKER, Julie .... 248-645-3300 223 D
jfracker@cranbrook.edu
FRACTION, Lynette, M .. 651-290-6310 242 L
lynette.fraction@mitchellhamline.edu
FRADEN, Rena .... 209-946-2023.. 71 E
rfraden@pacific.edu
FRADEN, Sarah .... 904-538-1000.. 93 H
FRAGALE, Stephen .... 518-381-1378 315 B
fragalsa@sunysccc.edu
FRAGOSO, Marcos .... 210-805-3014 453 C
fragoso@uiwtx.edu
FRAHM, Karyn .... 661-726-1911.. 68 J
karyn.frahm@uav.edu
FRAIK, Jennifer .... 218-755-2053 237 F
jennifer.fraik@bemidjistate.edu
FRAIMAN, Keren .... 312-322-1728 150 F
FRAINIER, Janine, L ..... 317-940-9228 154 C
jfrainie@butler.edu
FRAIRE, John .... 831-582-4363.. 32 B
jfraire@csumb.edu
FRAIRE-CUELLAR,
Martha .... 512-245-2367 450 C
mf29@txstate.edu
FRAKES, Jamie .... 870-762-3126.. 17 B
jfrakes@smail.anc.edu
FRAKES, Robert .... 661-654-3986.. 30 B
rfrakes1@csub.edu
FRALEY, Bill .... 304-384-6334 489 J
bfraley@concord.edu
FRALEY, James .... 217-420-6765 144 G
jfraley@millikin.edu
FRALEY, Meghann .... 740-245-7267 363 A
mfraley@rio.edu
FRALEY, Priscilla .... 606-368-6045 178 G
priscillafraley@alc.edu
FRALEY, Taryn .... 806-457-4200 436 C
tfraley@fpctx.edu
FRALIC, Bradley .... 713-348-4927 442 F
bradley.w.fralic@rice.edu
FRALING, III, Matthew . 410-951-3000 204 B
mfraling@coppin.edu
FRALIX, Brandon .... 973-748-9000 276 A
brandon_fralix@bloomfield.edu
FRAME, Adrienne, O .... 407-823-6960 110 E
adrienne.frame@ucf.edu
FRAME, Brenda .... 507-280-2814 240 H
brenda.frame@rctc.edu
FRAME, Charles .... 952-358-9211 239 G
charles.frame@normandale.edu
FRAME, J. Davidson ..... 703-516-0035 471 M
davidson.frame@umtweb.edu
FRAME, Michael .... 315-792-7400 321 B
mframe@sunypoly.edu
FRAME, Rose .... 620-450-2169 177 B
rosef@prattcc.edu
FRAME, Sandra, O .... 304-457-6324 486 E
frameso@ab.edu
FRAMPTON, Danica, D . 512-448-8418 442 I
danicad@stedwards.edu
FRAMPTON, Travis .... 830-792-7371 443 E
provost@schreiner.edu
FRANCA, Whitney, R ..... 405-325-1693 370 K
wfranca@ou.edu
FRANCE, Lucy .... 406-243-4742 263 K
lucy.france@umontana.edu
FRANCE, Melissa, H ..... 918-631-2516 371 C
melissa-france@utulsa.edu
FRANCESCHINI,
Geralynn .... 202-885-2121.. 91 F
geralynn@american.edu
FRANCHAK, Jen .... 513-529-3831 356 A
jen.franchak@miamioh.edu
FRANCIES, Karen .... 281-649-3450 437 B
kfrancies@hbu.edu
FRANCIOSI, Adrienne .... 617-243-2214 211 B
afranciosi@lasell.edu
FRANCIS, Aisha .... 617-588-1342 206 F
afrancis@bfit.edu
FRANCIS, Anthony .... 618-537-4481 144 A

FREDERICK, Harmony ... 661-255-1050.. 28 G
hfrederick@calarts.edu
FREDERICK, Jeff .... 704-233-8123 344 F
j.frederick@wingate.edu
FREDERICK, Jeff .... 910-521-6439 343 B
jeff.frederick@uncp.edu
FREDERICK, Julia .... 337-482-6700 193 B
julia.frederick@louisiana.edu
FREDERICK, Lesley, J ... 217-786-2597 143 B
lesley.frederick@llcc.edu
FREDERICK, Linda, D ... 504-286-5106 191 C
lfrederick@suno.edu
FREDERICK, Lori .... 337-482-6293 193 B
lori.frederick@louisiana.edu
FREDERICK, Matthew .... 276-944-6221 466 L
mfrederick@ehc.edu
FREDERICK, Michelle .... 202-885-2689.. 91 F
afrederi@american.edu
FREDERICK, Pam .... 540-423-9125 473 I
pfrederick@germanna.edu
FREDERICK, Richard ..... 662-252-8000 248 G
rfrederick@rustcollege.edu
FREDERICK, Robert .... 256-824-7200.... 8 B
robert.frederick@uah.edu
FREDERICK, Robert, J ... 319-273-6857 164 A
robert.frederick@uni.edu
FREDERICK, Robert, R .. 701-788-4794 345 D
robert.frederick@mayvillestate.edu
FREDERICK, Steven .... 518-327-6317 311 C
sfrederick@paulsmiths.edu
FREDERICK, Tammy ...... 303-473-8046 491 D
frederick_t@wvwc.edu
FREDERICK, Tammy ...... 304-473-8440 491 D
frederick_t@wvwc.edu
FREDERICK, Todd .... 805-546-3118.. 40 F
tfrederi@cuesta.edu
FREDERICK, Wayne .... 202-806-2500.. 92 F
wfrederick@howard.edu
FREDERICKS, Jason ...... 908-526-1200 281 A
jason.fredericks@raritanval.edu
FREDERICKS, Kimberly . 518-292-1782 313 A
fredek1@sage.edu
FREDERICKS, Rachel ..... 931-598-3208 423 D
rlfreder@sewanee.edu
FREDERICKSON, Cliff .... 206-546-4101 484 B
cfrederickson@shoreline.edu
FREDERICKSON, Derek . 954-771-0376 103 S
FREDERICKSON, Joel .... 651-638-6317 234 D
frejoe@bethel.edu
FREDERIKSEN, Jens ...... 615-329-8762 419 H
jfrederiksen@fisk.edu
FREDETTE, Brenda .... 724-938-4169 393 E
fredette@calu.edu
FREDETTE, Emile .... 802-728-1292 464 A
efredett@vtc.edu
FREDETTE, Melissa .... 617-746-1990 210 H
melissa.fredette@hult.edu
FREDIE, Michael, C .... 860-444-8503 503 G
michael.s.fredie@uscga.edu
FREDOTOVIC, Ivana .... 305-237-7450 104 E
ifredoto@mdc.edu
FREDRICH, Dolores .... 516-463-1800 301 G
dolores.fredrich@hofstra.edu
FREDRICH, Rachel, R .... 507-354-8221 236 J
fredrirr@mlc-wels.edu
FREDRICK, Kay .... 605-626-2518 416 G
kay.fredrick@northern.edu
FREDRICK, Travis .... 803-780-1360 414 B
tfredrick@voorhees.edu
FREDRICKSEN,
Donovan .... 903-923-2229 435 H
dfredricksen@etbu.edu
FREDRICKSON, Angela . 402-375-7220 268 F
anfredr1@wsc.edu
FREDRICKSON, Kurt ...... 626-584-5654.. 43 B
kurtf@fuller.edu
FREDRICKSON, Lang .... 323-856-7600.. 25 G
lfredrickson@afi.com
FREDRICKSON-LAOUINI,
Kendra .... 909-447-2592.. 37 E
kfredrickson-laouini@cst.edu
FREDRIKSON, Dawn ..... 708-974-5202 145 A
fredrikson@morainevalley.edu
FREDSON, Janice .... 509-682-6505 485 H
jfredson@wvc.edu
FREE, Carolyn, G .... 803-536-8402 411 G
cfree@scsu.edu
FREE, Rhona, C .... 860-231-5221.. 90 A
rfree@usj.edu
FREEBOURN, Randal ..... 904-256-8000 102 H
rfreebo@ju.edu
FREEBURG, Beth .... 605-658-3850 416 D
beth.freeburg@usd.edu

FREED, Curt .... 970-542-3105.. 81 N
curt.freed@morgancc.edu
FREED, Doug .... 309-298-1965 153 A
da-freed@wiu.edu
FREED, Rebekah .... 402-643-7405 266 G
rebekah.freed@cune.edu
FREED, Sarah .... 610-436-3411 395 D
sfreed@wcupa.edu
FREED, Ty .... 812-888-5308 162 F
tfreed@vinu.edu
FREEDLAND,
Gregory, E .... 717-871-5874 395 A
gregory.freedland@millersville.edu
FREEDMAN, Colaiv .... 971-770-0613 114 E
administrator@ygmiami.com
FREEDMAN, Daniel .... 845-257-3728 316 E
freedmad@newpaltz.edu
FREEDMAN, Eric .... 312-369-8222 136 D
efreedman@colum.edu
FREEDMAN, Michael ..... 301-985-7200 203 E
michael.freedman@umuc.edu
FREEDMAN, Michael, J 716-286-8584 309 H
mfreedman@niagara.edu
FREEDMAN, Phyllis, D . 304-326-1390 487 I
pfreedman@salemu.edu
FREEDMAN, Wendy, A .. 845-437-5700 324 C
wefreedman@vassar.edu
FREELAND, Brian .... 304-724-3700 486 F
bfreeland@apus.edu
FREELAND, Melissa ...... 843-792-4364 410 C
freelan@musc.edu
FREELANDER, Chichi .... 405-491-6396 369 H
cfreelan@snu.edu
FREELS, Cindy .... 573-288-6511 252 F
cfreels@culver.edu
FREEMAN, Abby .... 402-472-9531 269 J
abby.freeman@unl.edu
FREEMAN, Abby .... 313-496-2997 232 E
afreema2@wcccd.edu
FREEMAN, Adam .... 813-974-9047 111 C
adamfreeman@usf.edu
FREEMAN, Angela .... 404-752-1657 123 E
afreeman@msm.edu
FREEMAN, Catharine ..... 319-296-4041 166 H
catharine.freeman@hawkeyecollege.edu
FREEMAN, Cecily .... 901-722-3290 423 G
cfreeman@sco.edu
FREEMAN, Craig .... 253-272-1126 481 E
cfreeman@ncad.edu
FREEMAN, Deborah ...... 209-946-7362.. 71 E
dfreeman@pacific.edu
FREEMAN, Douglas ...... 607-274-1415 302 G
dfreeman@ithaca.edu
FREEMAN, Eddie .... 817-272-2106 454 I
efreeman@uta.edu
FREEMAN, Gary .... 402-461-7752 267 C
gfreeman@hastings.edu
FREEMAN, Ginger, C .... 615-898-2922 422 C
ginger.freeman@mtsu.edu
FREEMAN, Heather .... 731-425-2602 424 E
hfreeman@jscc.edu
FREEMAN, Heather .... 225-771-7827 191 A
heather_freeman@sus.edu
FREEMAN, Heather .... 225-771-4955 191 B
heather_freeman@subr.edu
FREEMAN, Irving .... 724-552-2880 387 D
ifreeman@lecom.edu
FREEMAN, Jack .... 435-652-7552 460 B
jfreeman@dixie.edu
FREEMAN, Jackie .... 435-652-7612 460 B
freeman@dixie.edu
FREEMAN, Jamee .... 910-272-3375 337 D
jfreeman@robeson.edu
FREEMAN, Jason .... 252-789-0304 335 H
jason.freeman@martincc.edu
FREEMAN, Jeremy .... 315-229-5286 314 D
jfreeman@stlawu.edu
FREEMAN, Jerrid .... 918-444-2010 366 G
freema22@nsuok.edu
FREEMAN, Jim .... 417-690-3248 251 H
jfreeman@cofo.edu
FREEMAN, Karen .... 315-786-2404 303 C
kfreeman@sunyjefferson.edu
FREEMAN, Kevin .... 405-974-2446 370 I
kfreeman7@uco.edu
FREEMAN, Linda .... 916-900-2850.. 26 C
lfreeman@asher.edu
FREEMAN, Lisa .... 202-885-1000.. 91 F
lisaf@american.edu
FREEMAN, Lisa .... 413-572-5204 213 F
lfreeman@westfield.ma.edu
FREEMAN, Lisa, C .... 815-753-9500 146 B
lfreeman1@niu.edu

FREEMAN, Marcus .... 302-622-8000.. 90 D
FREEMAN, Michael .... 410-951-3933 204 B
mfreeman@coppin.edu
FREEMAN, Michael .... 831-656-3218 502 M
mfreeman@nps.edu
FREEMAN, Michelle, K . 773-577-8100 136 F
mfreeman@coynecollege.edu
FREEMAN, Mike .... 712-274-5464 168 E
freemanm@morningside.edu
FREEMAN, Mitch .... 360-416-7771 484 C
mitch.freeman@skagit.edu
FREEMAN, Sharon .... 662-254-3811 248 B
sharonf@mvsu.edu
FREEMAN, Sheila, D ..... 662-685-4771 245 C
sfreeman@bmc.edu
FREEMAN, Sherryta .... 610-330-5530 387 C
freemasy@lafayette.edu
FREEMAN, Stacy .... 912-538-3129 125 G
sfreeman@southeasterntech.edu
FREEMAN, JR., Steven . 925-473-7491.. 40 D
sfreeman@losmedanos.edu
FREEMAN, Susan .... 863-680-4206 100 H
sfreeman@flsouthern.edu
FREEMAN, Susan, L ...... 312-942-9511 148 G
susan_l_freeman@rush.edu
FREEMAN, Tanisha .... 940-898-3845 451 D
tfreeman1@twu.edu
FREEMAN, Terhan .... 216-475-7520 360 B
terhan.freeman@remingtoncollege.edu
FREEMAN, William .... 360-676-2772 481 F
wfreeman@nwic.edu
FREEMAN, Yancy .... 423-425-4303 427 C
yancy-freeman@utc.edu
FREEMAN-PATTON,
Dena .... 310-243-3877.. 30 E
dfreemanpatton@csudh.edu
FREEMAN-TAYLOR,
Tierra .... 502-597-5932 183 D
tierra.freeman@kysu.edu
FREEMON, Iris, A .... 214-378-1809 434 E
FREEMYER, Sara .... 816-271-4287 257 A
sfreemyer1@missouriwestern.edu
FREER, Doug .... 909-537-5130.. 32 E
dfreer@csusb.edu
FREER, Michael .... 651-290-6322 242 L
michael.freer@mitchellhamline.edu
FREER, Michael .... 320-308-3203 240 I
mwfreer@stcloudstate.edu
FREER, Wayne .... 845-687-5053 323 H
freerw@sunyulster.edu
FREESE, Jalesa, C .... 920-565-1000 493 A
freesej@lakeland.edu
FREESE, Woodrow .... 508-793-7510 208 C
wfreese@clarku.edu
FREESTONE, Julie .... 801-832-2573 461 F
jfreestone@westminstercollege.edu
FREET, Dan .... 314-516-5157 261 C
freetd@umsl.edu
FREEZE, Kimberly .... 541-956-7117 376 A
kfreeze@roguecc.edu
FREI, Jennifer .... 541-463-5306 373 D
freij@lanecc.edu
FREIBERG, Brittany .... 815-921-4502 148 B
b.freiberg@rockvalleycollege.edu
FREIBERGER, Amy, M .. 918-631-3727 371 C
amy-freiberger@utulsa.edu
FREIBURGER, Chevy ..... 641-628-7637 164 D
freiburgerc@central.edu
FREIBURGER, Lisa .... 616-234-4025 224 F
lfreiburger@grcc.edu
FREIBURGER, Tina .... 414-229-6134 496 B
freiburg@uwm.edu
FREID, Laura .... 207-699-5011 195 A
lfreid@meca.edu
FREIDEL NELSON,
Kelsey .... 605-668-1270 415 F
kelsey.nelson@mountmarty.edu
FREIDHOFF, Rob .... 229-253-4077 127 E
rcfreidhoff@valdosta.edu
FREIJE, Margaret .... 508-793-2541 208 D
mfreije@holycross.edu
FREILER, Dan .... 717-396-7833 392 U
dfreiler@pcad.edu
FREIRE, Bethany .... 952-996-1303 234 B
bethany.freire@bethfel.org
FREIRE, Kenneth .... 952-996-1316 234 B
kenneth.freire@bethfel.org
FREITAG, Nancy .... 312-413-2411 151 G
nfreitag@uic.edu
FREITAG, Rodd, D .... 715-836-2542 495 E
freitard@uwec.edu
FREIWALD, Susan .... 415-422-6304.. 72 J
freiwald@usfca.edu

FREKING, Lisa .... 651-450-3551 238 E
lfreking@inverhills.edu
FREKING, Lise .... 651-423-8000 238 A
lfreking@inverhills.edu
FRELICH, Daryl .... 202-250-2282.. 92 C
daryl.frelich@gallaudet.edu
FRENCH, Alexandra .... 808-956-5495 129 E
afrench@hawaii.edu
FRENCH, Alexandra, S .. 808-956-5495 129 E
afrench@hawaii.edu
FRENCH, Amanda .... 949-376-6000.. 47 D
afrench@lcad.edu
FRENCH, Angie .... 870-248-4000.. 18 F
angie.french@blackrivertech.edu
FRENCH, Brian .... 406-243-2311 263 K
brian.french@umontana.edu
FRENCH, Christopher .... 860-297-5204.. 89 B
christopher.french@trincoll.edu
FRENCH, Cortney .... 603-513-1345 274 G
cortney.french@granite.edu
FRENCH, Dan .... 409-880-8603 449 G
dfrench2@lamar.edu
FRENCH, Dan .... 419-251-1967 355 G
dan.french@mercycollege.edu
FRENCH, Daniel, J .... 315-443-9732 321 G
djfrench@syr.edu
FRENCH, Daphne .... 912-260-4233 125 D
daphne.french@sgsc.edu
FRENCH, JR.,
George, T .... 404-880-8500 117 C
caupresident@cau.edu
FRENCH, Haley .... 918-495-6890 368 F
hfrench@oru.edu
FRENCH, Heather .... 314-446-8632 260 H
heather.french@stlcop.edu
FRENCH, Heather .... 314-889-1410 253 E
hfrench@fontbonne.edu
FRENCH, Jeffrey .... 210-486-2105 429 B
jfrench21@alamo.edu
FRENCH, Joy .... 303-724-2516.. 84 D
joy.french@ucdenver.edu
FRENCH, Kelly .... 859-344-3619 185 B
frenchk@thomasmore.edu
FRENCH, Mary Ann ...... 617-353-5168 207 E
mafrench@bu.edu
FRENCH, CSSP,
Raymond .... 412-396-5286 383 A
french@duq.edu
FRENCH-HART, Holly ..... 318-678-6000 187 H
hfrench@bpcc.edu
FRENCH-HOLLOWAY,
Michelle .... 310-954-4056.. 52 I
mfrench@msmu.edu
FRENDO, Cristina .... 313-593-5156 231 I
vatalaro@umich.edu
FRENK, Julio .... 305-284-5155 113 C
jfrenk@miami.edu
FRENZA, Linda .... 909-469-5356.. 75 I
lfrenza@westernu.edu
FRERE, Leslie .... 540-828-5380 464 L
lfrere@bridgewater.edu
FRERICHS, Chris .... 515-961-1711 170 B
chris.frerichs@simpson.edu
FRESA, Kerin .... 215-871-6864 395 G
kerinf@pcom.edu
FRESCAS, Christina, C .. 915-831-6735 436 A
ccasta16@epcc.edu
FRESE, Philip .... 814-393-2600 393 G
pfrese@clarion.edu
FRESHOUR, Brett .... 724-552-4372 398 C
bfreshour@setonhill.edu
FRESHOUR, Missy .... 928-523-3611.. 14 H
missy.freshour@nau.edu
FRESHWATER,
Laurie, A .... 252-222-6281 333 A
freshwaterl@carteret.edu
FRESQUEZ, Jessica .... 650-508-3640.. 54 G
jfresquez@ndnu.edu
FRESQUEZ, Julie .... 951-343-4302.. 27 G
jfresquez@calbaptist.edu
FRESSE, Daliana .... 787-815-0000 511 H
daliana.fresse@upr.edu
FREUDENHEIM, Lisa ..... 617-451-0010 217 F
FREUND, Caroline .... 858-534-1946.. 70 C
clfreund@ucsd.edu
FREUND, Debra .... 860-512-3107.. 86 G
dfreund@manchestercc.edu
FREUND, Scott .... 401-739-5000 404 E
sfreund@neit.edu
FREVILLE, Ben .... 708-524-6557 137 C
freville@dom.edu
FREW, Jeremy .... 517-796-8409 225 E
frewjeremy@jccmi.edu

FREW, Stuart ... 706-355-5052 115 F sfrew@athenstech.edu
FREWALDT, Megan ... 605-626-3007 416 G megan.frewaldt@northern.edu
FREY, Carolyn, A ... 859-238-5275 180 B carrie.frey@centre.edu
FREY, Eva, R ... 253-535-7159 482 A eva.frey@plu.edu
FREY, Isabel, D ... 516-463-4779 301 G isabel.d.frey@hofstra.edu
FREY, James ... 229-931-2039 125 E jfrey@southgatech.edu
FREY, Jason ... 773-896-2400 134 L jason.frey@ctschicago.edu
FREY, Jason ... 773-896-2400 134 L
FREY, Len, T ... 870-972-3303.. 17 E lfrey@astate.edu
FREY, Mandy ... 605-367-4236 417 B mandy.frey@southeasttech.edu
FREY, Melissa ... 304-724-3700 486 F mfrey@apus.edu
FREY, Melissa ... 503-589-7652 372 B melissa.frey@chemeketa.edu
FREY, Michelle ... 660-263-4100 257 B michellefrey@macc.edu
FREY, Sarah ... 209-228-4400.. 70 A
FREY, Steven ... 936-294-2739 450 A saf001@shsu.edu
FREY, Susan, M ... 570-348-6211 389 D sfrey@marywood.edu
FREY, Tim ... 402-826-8648 267 A timothy.frey@doane.edu
FREYBERG, Ian ... 606-539-4219 185 E
FREYTAG, Cathy ... 585-567-9315 302 B cathy.freytag@houghton.edu
FREYTES, Liza ... 787-279-1912 508 A lfreytes@bayamon.inter.edu
FRIANT, Jakim ... 910-362-7212 332 H jfriant@cfcc.edu
FRIAR, Shirley ... 334-724-4667.... 7 D sfriar@tuskegee.edu
FRIAR, Tobyn, L ... 773-508-8636 143 C tfriar@luc.edu
FRIAS, Frank ... 206-546-4613 484 B ffrias@shoreline.edu
FRICK, Jeffrey ... 724-503-1001 402 B jfrick@washjeff,.edu
FRICK, Lillian ... 989-386-6605 228 B lfrick@midmich.edu
FRICK, Richard, A ... 201-692-2001 277 I rfrick@fdu.edu
FRICK, Wanda ... 910-898-9637 336 D frickw@montgomery.edu
FRICK CARDELLE, Rachel ... 978-630-9161 215 C rfrickcardelle@mwcc.mass.edu
FRICK-RUPPERT, Jennifer, E ... 828-641-0788 327 B jefrick@brevard.edu
FRICKE, Erik ... 805-965-0581.. 63 A fricke@sbcc.edu
FRICKER, Ronald ... 540-231-7078 476 C rf@vt.edu
FRIDAY, Alicia ... 832-813-6738 439 C alicia.r.friday@lonestar.edu
FRIDAY, Brenda ... 570-422-3455 394 A bfriday@esu.edu
FRIDAY, Yolanda ... 909-652-7405.. 35 L yolanda.fridayl@chaffey.edu
FRIDAY-STROUD, Shawnta ... 850-599-3491 109 I shawnta.friday@famu.edu
FRIDAY-STROUD, Shawnta ... 850-599-3565 109 I shawnta.friday@famu.edu
FRIDDLE, Adrienne ... 336-249-8186 334 B adrienne_friddle@davidsondavie.edu
FRIDGE, Rob ... 417-873-7526 252 G rfridge001@drury.edu
FRIDLEY, Daryl, E ... 570-389-4005 393 D dfridley@bloomu.edu
FRIDRIKSSON, Julius ... 803-777-5931 413 A fridriks@mailbox.sc.edu
FRIDSON, Ilona ... 718-368-5109 294 E
FRIEBIS, Michael ... 607-962-9000 320 C
FRIED, Barry, J ... 608-796-3811 497 O bjfried@viterbo.edu
FRIED, Hindie ... 516-239-9002 315 D hfried@shoryoshuv.org
FRIED, Linda, P ... 212-305-9300 297 C lpfried@columbia.edu
FRIED, Marc ... 785-670-1712 178 C marc.fried@washburn.edu
FRIED, Ray ... 325-235-7320 449 D ray.fried@tstc.edu
FRIED, Sandy ... 701-224-2423 346 A sandra.fried@bismarckstate.edu
FRIED-WALKENFELD, Faye ... 212-742-8770 322 G faye.fried-walkenfeld@touro.edu
FRIEDEL, Julie ... 918-631-3838 371 C julie-friedel@utulsa.edu
FRIEDEL, Kristin, M ... 315-859-4637 300 H kfriedel@hamilton.edu
FRIEDEMAN, Elijah ... 601-366-8880 249 G efriedeman@wbs.edu
FRIEDER, Steven, W ... 414-288-7752 493 E steven.frieder@marquette.edu
FRIEDHOFF, AJ ... 314-889-1429 253 E afriedhoff@fontbonne.edu
FRIEDLANDER, Michael, J ... 540-231-2013 476 C friedlan@vt.edu
FRIEDLEN, Karen ... 414-930-3349 494 E friedlek@mtmary.edu
FRIEDLEY, Margret ... 360-623-8410 478 F margret.friedley@centralia.edu
FRIEDLI, Deidre ... 208-459-5025 131 C dfriedli@collegeofidaho.edu
FRIEDLINE, Patrick ... 312-329-4414 144 I patrick.friedline@moody.edu
FRIEDMAN, Avraham ... 847-982-2500 138 I friedman@htc.edu
FRIEDMAN, Bruce ... 610-647-4400 385 L bfriedman@immaculata.edu
FRIEDMAN, David ... 410-484-7200 201 C dfreidman@nirc.edu
FRIEDMAN, Elea ... 213-884-4133.. 24 A registrar@ajrca.edu
FRIEDMAN, Elizabeth ... 718-518-4314 294 B efriedman@hostos.cuny.edu
FRIEDMAN, Eric, M ... 201-447-7237 275 H efriedman@bergen.edu
FRIEDMAN, Erica ... 212-650-7624 293 D ericafriedman@med.cuny.edu
FRIEDMAN, Erik ... 312-369-7790 136 D efriedman@colum.edu
FRIEDMAN, Frank ... 434-977-1620 474 I ffriedman@pvcc.edu
FRIEDMAN, Jay, R ... 530-898-4890.. 30 D jfriedman1@csuchico.edu
FRIEDMAN, Jill ... 508-793-7681 208 C jifriedman@clarku.edu
FRIEDMAN, Joshua ... 305-284-4111 113 C jmfriedman@miami.edu
FRIEDMAN, Lori ... 617-989-4233 219 F friedmanl@wit.edu
FRIEDMAN, Max Paul ... 202-885-2446.. 91 F friedman@american.edu
FRIEDMAN, Melissa ... 212-280-6001 303 D mefriedman@jtsa.edu
FRIEDMAN, Robert ... 646-592-6255 326 D robert.freidman@yu.edu
FRIEDMAN, Ronald ... 260-481-5750 160 C friedmar@pfw.edu
FRIEDMAN, Sandra, V .. 516-572-7326 307 E sandra.friedman@ncc.edu
FRIEDMAN, Scott ... 708-974-5359 145 A friedmans5@morainevalley.edu
FRIEDMAN, Scott ... 310-825-8607.. 69 E friedman@idre.ucla.edu
FRIEDMAN, Yaakov ... 847-982-2500 138 I yfriedman@htc.edu
FRIEDMANN, Jonathan . 213-884-4133.. 24 A jfriedmann@ajrca.edu
FRIEDRICH, Brian ... 651-641-8211 235 I
FRIEDRICH, II, Charles 850-644-2825 110 C friedrich@fsu.edu
FRIEDRICH, David ... 617-253-2811 216 B
FRIEDRICHSEN, Steven, W ... 909-706-3911.. 75 I sfriedrichsen@westernu.edu
FRIEDT, Barbara ... 440-525-7510 354 L bfriedt@lakelandcc.edu
FRIEL, Lydia ... 215-780-1251 398 B lfriel@salus.edu
FRIEL, Wm. Jake ... 724-287-8711 379 E jake.friel@bc3.edu
FRIEND, Damian ... 303-273-3154.. 79 J dfriend@mines.edu
FRIEND, Dane ... 713-798-1544 431 D dfriend@bcm.edu
FRIEND, Dave ... 531-622-2647 267 G dkfriend@mccneb.edu
FRIEND, Jennifer ... 816-501-4076 258 I jennifer.friend@rockhurst.edu
FRIEND, John ... 251-460-7051.... 9 A jfriend@southalabama.edu
FRIEND, Micheal ... 860-701-6728 503 G micheal.friend@uscg.mil
FRIEND, Patricia ... 708-974-5551 145 A friendp5@morainevalley.edu
FRIEND, Ricky ... 205-348-1370.... 7 G rdfriend@bama.ua.edu
FRIER, Jessica ... 952-777-3134 242 N jfrier@nwhealth.edu
FRIERSON, Georita ... 973-761-9022 283 C georita.frierson@shu.edu
FRIERSON, Kenneth ... 312-935-4232 140 G kfrierson@icsw.edu
FRIES, Jane ... 970-542-3106.. 81 N jane.fries@morgancc.edu
FRIES, Ruth, A ... 651-628-3241 244 D rafries@unwsp.edu
FRIES, Tammi ... 910-814-4923 327 D fries@campbell.edu
FRIESEMA, Nathan ... 607-735-1821 298 H nfriesema@elmira.edu
FRIESEN, Brandon ... 805-893-8125.. 70 E brandon.friesen@ucsb.edu
FRIESEN, Joshua ... 864-250-8994 409 I joshua.friesen@gvltec.edu
FRIESON, Dawn ... 419-372-2865 348 G dfreison@bgsu.edu
FRIESSEN, Lisa ... 580-774-3149 370 A lisa.friessen@swosu.edu
FRIESZ, Janet ... 406-496-4868 265 A jfriesz@mtech.edu
FRIGGE, Maria ... 334-670-3736.... 7 C lfrigge@troy.edu
FRINK, Brian, T ... 920-565-1000 493 A frinkbt@lakeland.edu
FRINK, Dorothy ... 219-980-6994 157 C defrink@iun.edu
FRINK, Kandy ... 307-382-1602 501 J kfrink@westernwyoming.edu
FRISBEE, Bob ... 620-235-4365 177 A rfrisbee@pittstate.edu
FRISBEE, Sean ... 304-293-4731 490 E sean.frisbee@mail.wvu.edu
FRISBEE, Stephen ... 315-792-5399 306 K sfrisbee@mvcc.edu
FRISBIE, Kathy ... 970-542-3240.. 81 N kathy.frisbie@morgancc.edu
FRISBY, Anthony ... 215-503-8848 399 E anthony.frisby@jefferson.edu
FRISBY, Anthony ... 215-503-4990 399 E anthony.frisby@jefferson.edu
FRISCH, Kevin ... 315-279-5889 303 G kfrisch@keuka.edu
FRISCH, Kim ... 303-458-4909.. 83 E kfrisch@regis.edu
FRISENDA, Louis ... 703-247-8341 468 H louis.frisenda@marymount.edu
FRISINA, Warren ... 516-463-4783 301 G warren.frisina@hofstra.edu
FRISKEN, Amanda ... 516-876-3915 318 C friskena@oldwestbury.edu
FRISKICS, Scott ... 406-353-2607 262 H
FRISONE, Al ... 510-409-7939.. 60 C afrisone@samuelmerritt.edu
FRISQUE, Megan ... 512-863-1584 445 C frisquem@southwestern.edu
FRIST, Matthew, J ... 412-396-6063 383 A frist@duq.edu
FRITCH, John, E ... 319-273-2725 164 A john.fritch@uni.edu
FRITCH, Todd ... 941-752-5000 109 G
FRITSCH, Denise ... 859-442-1113 181 H denise.fritsch@kctcs.edu
FRITSCHI, Ramona ... 717-697-6027 389 H rfritschi@messiah.edu
FRITSKY, Wren ... 570-389-4070 393 D wfritsky@bloomu.edu
FRITZ, Cheryl ... 314-246-7055 262 C cherylfritz49@webster.edu
FRITZ, John ... 410-455-6596 203 B fritz@umbc.edu
FRITZ, Kelli ... 605-626-2550 416 G kelli.fritz@northern.edu
FRITZ, Sarah ... 608-246-6559 499 A fritz@madisoncollege.edu
FRITZ, Simon ... 315-228-7144 296 E sfritz@colgate.edu
FRITZ, Ted, P ... 412-624-0072 400 H tfritz@pitt.edu
FRITZ, Thomas, R ... 814-472-3006 397 F tfritz@francis.edu
FRITZ, Tim ... 805-969-3626.. 55 J tfritz@pacifica.edu
FRITZ, William, J ... 718-982-2400 293 E president@csi.cuny.edu
FRITZE, Kellie ... 907-474-6265.. 10 A kfritze@alaska.edu
FRITZMAN, D. Jason ... 304-243-2043 491 E jfritzman@wheeling.edu
FRIZZA-POMPA, Julio ... 619-265-0107.. 57 I jfrizza@platt.edu
FRIZZELL, Douglas ... 412-396-3234 383 A frizzelld@duq.edu
FRIZZELL, Monica ... 479-979-1215.. 23 I mfrizzell@ozarks.edu
FROEDGE, Claudia ... 270-384-8519 183 G froedgec@lindsey.edu
FROELICH, Aaron ... 906-932-4231 224 D aaronf@gogebic.edu
FROEMMING, Darold ... 937-255-6565 502 C darold.froemming@afit.edu
FROHARDT, Russell ... 210-486-4136 428 I rfrohardt@alamo.edu
FROHLICH, Denise ... 775-445-4246 271 F denise.frohlich@wnc.edu
FROHOFF, Katherine ... 816-501-4151 258 I katherine.frohoff@rockhurst.edu
FROMBGEN, Elizabeth .. 724-589-2200 399 D efrombgen@thiel.edu
FROMMELT, Steve ... 309-796-5933 133 G frommelts@bhc.edu
FRONCZEK, Walter ... 708-974-5372 145 A fronczek@morainevalley.edu
FRONHEISER, Joey ... 405-945-3250 368 C joey.fronheiser@okstate.edu
FRONK, Brynn ... 801-581-5701 459 O brynn.fronk@utah.edu
FRONTERA, Daniel ... 716-851-1832 299 B vafrontera@ecc.edu
FRONTERA AGENJO, Jose, A ... 787-841-2000 509 J jose_frontera@pucpr.edu
FRONTERHOUSE, Misti . 719-336-1511.. 81 K misti.fronterhouse@lamarcc.edu
FRONTIERA, Charlene ... 650-574-6312.. 62 K frontierac@smccd.edu
FRONTIERA, Patrick ... 310-568-6219.. 51 A patrick.frontiera@lmu.edu
FROONJIAN, John ... 609-626-3626 283 E john.froonjian@stockton.edu
FROSCH, Jeff ... 512-313-4105 433 N jeff.frosch@concordia.edu
FROSLID JONES, Karen, L ... 202-885-6155.. 91 F kfroslid@american.edu
FROST, Dana, L ... 864-644-5004 412 D dfrost@swu.edu
FROST, David ... 843-349-2227 408 A dfrost@coastal.edu
FROST, Donny ... 479-979-1000.. 23 I dfrost@ozarks.edu
FROST, Eric ... 315-464-4393 317 C froste@upstate.edu
FROST, James ... 830-303-0404 449 A frost@frostlawoffice.com
FROST, John ... 402-399-2350 266 F jfrost@csm.edu
FROST, Kimberly ... 619-482-6309.. 66 A kfrost@swccd.edu
FROST, Leanne ... 406-771-4372 264 F leanne.frost@gfcmsu.edu
FROST, Linda ... 423-425-5922 427 C linda-frost@utc.edu
FROST, Mark ... 518-783-4100 315 E mfrost@siena.edu
FROST, Mary ... 563-884-5664 169 F mary.frost@palmer.edu
FROST, Meghan, S ... 602-406-7265 266 H meghanfrost@creighton.edu
FROST, Mike ... 406-243-4711 263 K mike.frost@umontana.edu
FROST, Pamela ... 614-825-6255 347 E pfrost@aiam.edu
FROST, Richard, A ... 616-395-7800 225 D frost@hope.edu
FROST, Stacy ... 507-537-6483 241 D stacy.frost@smsu.edu
FROUDE, Bill ... 859-572-5112 184 E froudew1@nku.edu
FRUCHTHANDLER, Abraham, H ... 718-377-0777 311 G
FRUEH, Elizabeth ... 715-425-4192 496 F elizabeth.frueh@uwrf.edu
FRUGE, Alfred ... 337-562-4290 192 E ffruge@mcneese.edu

FRUGE, Cheryl .... 337-521-6670 188 I
cheryl.fruge@solacc.edu
FRUGE, Courtney .... 337-550-1201 189 G
crfruge@lsue.edu
FRUGE, Jason .... 973-300-2256 284 A
jfruge@sussex.edu
FRUITTICHER, Lee .... 478-445-5768 119 B
lee.fruitticher@gcsu.edu
FRUITTICHER, Lee .... 478-445-5650 119 B
lee.fruitticher@gcsu.edu
FRUM, Jennifer, L .... 706-542-6126 126 G
jfrum@uga.edu
FRY, Alyssa .... 614-234-4760 356 E
afry@mchs.com
FRY, Angela .... 870-574-4523.. 21 D
afry@sautech.edu
FRY, Blake .... 816-604-1412 255 C
blake.fry@mcckc.edu
FRY, Donna .... 810-237-6503 232 A
donnafry@umich.edu
FRY, Jason .... 409-747-9082 456 E
jefry@utmb.edu
FRY, John, A .... 215-895-2100 382 F
jaf@drexel.edu
FRY, Justyn .... 937-376-6386 349 J
jfry@centralstate.edu
FRY, Keener .... 307-766-4166 501 I
keener.fry@uwyo.edu
FRY, Pamela .... 405-744-5627 367 G
pamela.fry@okstate.edu
FRY-BOWERS, Eileen .... 619-260-2964.. 72 I
efrybowers@sandiego.edu
FRYAR, Ben .... 208-496-1896 130 I
fryarb@byui.edu
FRYAR, David .... 252-985-5222 339 D
dfryar@ncwc.edu
FRYDA, Megan, M .... 308-865-8934 269 I
frydamm@unk.edu
FRYE, Brandon .... 936-468-3401 445 E
FRYE, Catherine .... 803-778-6602 406 I
fryecm@cctech.edu
FRYE, Gerald .... 662-846-3000 245 G
FRYE, Harlan .... 919-209-2025 335 F
hefrye@johnstoncc.edu
FRYE, Holly .... 304-876-5402 490 A
hfrye@shepherd.edu
FRYE, Jeffrey .... 419-434-4501 362 D
frye@findlay.edu
FRYE, Karen .... 910-898-9620 336 D
fryek@montgomery.edu
FRYE, Kevin .... 937-708-5628 363 G
kfrye@wilberforce.edu
FRYE, Lela .... 352-395-5420 108 A
lela.frye@sfcollege.edu
FRYE, Ricky .... 540-545-7338 470 G
rfrye2@su.edu
FRYKBERG, Jay .... 310-342-5200.. 73 F
FRYLING, Andrea .... 616-988-3639 226 E
afryling@kuyper.edu
FRYLING, Michelle, S ... 724-357-2302 394 C
mfryling@iup.edu
FRYNS, Jennifer .... 352-854-2322.. 97 N
frynsj@cf.edu
FRYSON, David, M .... 304-293-3431 490 E
david.fryson@mail.wvu.edu
FU, Di .... 954-763-9840.. 95 J
fudi@atom.edu
FU, Siqi .... 856-225-2349 281 G
sfu@camden.rutgers.edu
FU, Xuanning .... 559-278-2636.. 31 B
xfu@csufresno.edu
FUCHKO, John .... 404-962-3025 127 D
john.fuchko@usg.edu
FUCHS, Caroline .... 718-990-5050 313 G
fuchsc@stjohns.edu
FUCHS, Kris .... 815-921-4013 148 B
k.fuchs@rockvalleycollege.edu
FUCHS, Lisa .... 402-354-7065 268 B
lisa.fuchs@methodistcollege.edu
FUCHS, Tina, M .... 503-838-8220 377 D
fuchst@wou.edu
FUCHS, W. Kent .... 352-392-1311 111 A
president@ufl.edu
FUCHSER, Kathy .... 402-562-1211 266 A
kathyfuchser@cccneb.edu
FUDALA, Amanda .... 303-871-2394.. 84 E
amanda.fudala@du.edu
FUDALLY, Steve .... 218-733-7600 238 G
steve.fudally@lsc.edu
FUENTES, Alan .... 718-933-1604 293 B
alan.fuentes@bcc.cuny.edu
FUENTES, Angel .... 510-464-3224.. 57 B
afuentes@peralta.edu
FUENTES, Angeles .... 831-582-4136.. 32 B
afuentes@csumb.edu
FUENTES, Angelica, M .. 956-295-3383 449 C
angelica.fuentes@tsc.edu
FUENTES, Fred .... 903-886-5067 447 B
fred.fuentes@tamuc.edu
FUENTES, Jonathan .... 432-553-6493 441 A
jfuentes@odessa.edu
FUENTES, Jose, A .... 787-279-1912 508 A
jfuentes@bayamon.inter.edu
FUENTES, Laysa .... 787-753-6000 507 D
lfuentes@icprjc.edu
FUENTES, Montserrat .... 512-448-8411 442 I
mfuentes@stedwards.edu
FUENTES, Ramonita ...... 787-751-0178 510 E
ue_rfuentes@uagm.edu
FUENTES, Renee .... 805-437-3608.. 30 C
renee.fuentes@csuci.edu
FUENTES, Ricky .... 575-769-4076 285 O
ricky.fuentes@clovis.edu
FUENTES, Vilma .... 352-395-5030 108 A
vilma.fuentes@sfcollege.edu
FUENTES-AFFLICK,
Elena .... 415-476-1977.. 70 D
elena.fuentes-afflick@ucsf.edu
FUENTES-ALANIS,
Dawn .... 312-553-5914 135 B
dfuentesalanis@ccc.edu
FUENTES-MARTIN, Mari 210-784-1527 447 E
mfuentes@tamusa.edu
FUENTEZ, Tammy .... 620-421-6700 175 F
tammyf@labette.edu
FUENZALIDA, Bracey .... 212-659-7200 303 H
bfuenzalida@tkc.edu
FUERST, Barbara .... 636-922-8363 258 J
bfuerst@stchas.edu
FUERST, Nathan .... 860-486-1463.. 89 D
nathan.fuerst@uconn.edu
FUEST, Cana .... 585-582-8218 298 F
canafuest@elim.edu
FUGATE, Amy .... 989-275-5000 226 D
amy.fugate@kirtland.edu
FUGATE, Edna .... 606-218-5625 186 B
ednafugate@upike.edu
FUGATE, Megan .... 620-421-6700 175 F
mfugate@labette.edu
FUGATE, Stu .... 606-487-3196 181 I
stu.fugate@kctcs.edu
FUGATE, Wesley, R ...... 717-262-2000 403 C
FUGATE-CATE, Kassie ... 620-223-2700 173 I
kassief@fortscott.edu
FUGAZZOTTO, Sam ...... 702-895-0892 271 D
sam.fugazzotto@unlv.edu
FUGETT, David .... 941-487-4877 110 D
dfugett@ncf.edu
FUGIEL, Lisa .... 413-755-4786 216 A
lfugiel@stcc.edu
FUHRMAN, Dane .... 573-876-7210 260 B
dfuhrman@stephens.edu
FUHRMAN, Heather ...... 785-442-6144 174 F
hfuhrman@highlandcc.edu
FUHRMAN, Hillary .... 330-941-2453 364 H
hlfuhrman@ysu.edu
FUHRMAN, Tim .... 509-793-2351 478 B
timf@bigbend.edu
FUHRMANN, Donald, J 814-824-2104 389 G
dfuhrmann@mercyhurst.edu
FUITH, Leanne .... 651-290-7526 242 L
leanne.fuith@mitchellhamline.edu
FUJA, Thomas, E .... 574-631-5534 162 A
tfuja@nd.edu
FUJII, Stephanie .... 303-797-5701.. 77 I
stephanie.fujii@arapahoe.edu
FUJII, Tak .... 310-287-4359.. 49 H
fujiit@wlac.edu
FUJIMOTO, Kell .... 408-924-5910.. 34 A
kell.fujimoto@sjsu.edu
FUJITA, Sherri .... 509-279-6241 479 C
sherri.fujita@scc.spokane.edu
FUJIYOSHI, Lois, M ...... 808-932-7664 129 D
lfujiyos@hawaii.edu
FULBRIGHT, Brittney ..... 757-340-2121 465 I
careercvab@centura.edu
FULBRIGHT, Kyle .... 423-746-5327 426 C
kfulbright@tnwesleyan.edu
FULBRIGHT, Marshall ... 619-644-7104.. 44 E
marshall.fulbright@gcccd.edu
FULCHER, Kerry .... 619-849-2651.. 57 J
kerryfulcher@pointloma.edu
FULCOMER, Eric, W ...... 815-226-4010 148 D
efulcomer@rockford.edu
FULFORD, Leroy .... 740-377-2520 361 E
leroy.fulford@tsbc.edu
FULFORD, Tim .... 843-574-6116 412 I
tim.fulford@tridenttech.edu
FULIGNI, Paul .... 515-294-2631 163 G
pfuligni@iastate.edu
FULK, Scott .... 219-980-6792 157 C
sfulk@iun.edu
FULK, Sheryl, E .... 812-877-8514 160 F
fulk1@rose-hulman.edu
FULKERSON, Anne .... 567-661-2073 359 I
anne_fulkerson@owens.edu
FULKERSON, Cathy .... 775-445-4405 271 F
cathy.fulkerson@wnc.edu
FULKERSON,
Christopher, D .... 336-278-5003 328 J
fulkers@elon.edu
FULKERSON, Diane .... 585-395-2156 317 E
dfulkerson@brockport.edu
FULKERSON, Laurel ...... 850-644-2525 110 C
lfulkerson@fsu.edu
FULKERSON, Steven ..... 501-686-2925.. 21 E
sfulkerson@uasys.edu
FULKS, Mark, A .... 423-439-8550 419 G
fulks@etsu.edu
FULKS, Steve .... 252-399-6570 326 K
sfulks@barton.edu
FULLANA, Yaremis, P ... 407-582-3037 113 I
yfullana@valenciacollege.edu
FULLBRIGHT, Kalyn ...... 405-585-5000 367 B
kalyn.fullbright@okbu.edu
FULLEM, Wendy .... 973-300-2120 284 A
wfullem@sussex.edu
FULLER, Andrew .... 801-302-2800 459 H
andrew.fuller@neumont.edu
FULLER, April .... 801-618-0438 458 G
afuller@ameritech.edu
FULLER, Belinda .... 304-766-3387 490 D
bfuller@wvstateu.edu
FULLER, Brad .... 269-956-3931 225 H
fullerb@kellogg.edu
FULLER, Brad .... 870-460-1050.. 22 C
fullerb@uamont.edu
FULLER, Brian, J .... 269-387-1850 233 B
brian.j.fuller@wmich.edu
FULLER, Cam .... 920-403-3030 495 B
cam.fuller@snc.edu
FULLER, Candy .... 361-354-2251 432 K
fuller_c@coastalbend.edu
FULLER, Chris .... 615-547-1336 419 C
cfuller@cumberland.edu
FULLER, Christopher ..... 207-893-7705 196 C
cfuller@sjcme.edu
FULLER, Dayna .... 251-981-3771.... 5 A
dayna.fuller@columbiasouthern.edu
FULLER, JR., Henry, M 843-953-5185 407 C
hank.fuller@citadel.edu
FULLER, Howard .... 360-383-3295 486 A
hfuller@whatcom.edu
FULLER, Jonathon .... 218-281-8345 244 A
fulle423@crk.umn.edu
FULLER, Karen .... 716-338-1034 303 A
karenfuller@mail.sunyjcc.edu
FULLER, Kyle .... 740-753-7059 353 H
fullerk@hocking.edu
FULLER, Leanna .... 412-924-1459 396 F
lfuller@pts.edu
FULLER, Mark .... 740-753-7129 353 H
fullerm@hocking.edu
FULLER, Mark .... 508-999-8004 212 A
chancellor@umassd.edu
FULLER, Marshall, R ..... 919-536-7200 334 C
fullerm@durhamtech.edu
FULLER, Melanie .... 919-508-2311 344 E
mjfuller@peace.edu
FULLER, Michael .... 903-223-3060 448 A
michael.fuller@tamut.edu
FULLER, Michael .... 541-684-7248 371 I
mfuller@bushnell.edu
FULLER, Mickey .... 405-945-8645 368 C
mickey.fuller@okstate.edu
FULLER, Peggy .... 318-678-6000 187 H
pfuller@bpcc.edu
FULLER, Roger, D .... 817-257-7199 448 F
r.fuller@tcu.edu
FULLER, Rose .... 239-590-1356 109 K
rfuller@fgcu.edu
FULLER, Sherry .... 903-510-3346 452 A
sherry.fuller@tjc.edu
FULLER, Stephanie .... 336-272-7102 329 C
stephanie.fuller@greensboro.edu
FULLER, Sunny .... 417-328-1512 259 I
sfuller@sbuniv.edu
FULLER, Swanita .... 336-322-2281 336 G
swanita.fuller@piedmontcc.edu
FULLERTON, Adam .... 712-274-5247 168 E
fullertona@morningside.edu
FULLERTON, Fred, C .... 208-467-8530 132 E
ffullerton@nnu.edu
FULLERTON, John .... 208-795-4266 131 F
FULLMAN, Leah .... 334-386-7395.... 5 C
lfullman@faulkner.edu
FULLMER, Matt .... 610-459-0905 391 A
fullmerm@neumann.edu
FULLMER, Ryan .... 310-342-5200.. 73 F
FULLWOOD, Carla .... 336-278-5017 328 J
cfullwood@elon.edu
FULMER, David .... 478-387-4890 119 F
dfulmer@gmc.edu
FULMER, Gregory, L ...... 610-921-2381 377 G
FULMER, Hal .... 334-670-3112.... 7 C
hfulmer@troy.edu
FULMER, Ingrid .... 848-445-4519 282 A
ifulmer@smlr.rutgers.edu
FULMER, Janet .... 316-284-5248 172 B
jfulmer@bethelks.edu
FULMER, Judy .... 334-670-3102.... 7 C
jfulmer@troy.edu
FULMER, Sarah .... 575-769-4085 285 O
sarah.fulmer@clovis.edu
FULOP, Ann .... 309-467-6301 138 A
afulop@eureka.edu
FULOP, Ann .... 309-467-6440 138 A
afulop@eureka.edu
FULOP, Timothy .... 434-791-5630 464 I
tfulop@averett.edu
FULTINEER, Scheri .... 401-454-6100 405 B
sfultine@risd.edu
FULTON, Dean .... 360-752-8378 478 A
dfulton@btc.edu
FULTON, Deborah, M .... 540-231-0735 476 C
dfulton@vt.edu
FULTON, DoVeanna .... 757-823-8408 469 A
provost@nsu.edu
FULTON, Jodie .... 541-956-7200 376 A
jfulton@roguecc.edu
FULTON, Lori .... 509-452-5100 482 B
lfulton@pnwu.edu
FULTON, Neil .... 605-658-3508 416 D
neil.fulton@usd.edu
FULTON, Tara Lynn .... 603-862-1506 274 F
taralynn.fulton@unh.edu
FULTON, Tom .... 412-924-1434 396 F
tfulton@pts.edu
FULTZ, Angela .... 606-759-7141 182 E
angela.fultz@kctcs.edu
FULTZ, Bob .... 502-863-8029 180 H
bob_fultz@georgetowncollege.edu
FULTZ, Larenda .... 731-286-3234 424 D
fultz@dscc.edu
FULTZ, Rob .... 423-614-8420 420 H
rfultz@leeuniversity.edu
FULWOOD, III, Sam ...... 202-885-1000.. 91 F
sfulwood@american.edu
FUNARO, Janette .... 925-969-2347.. 40 C
jfunaro@dvc.edu
FUNASAKI, Eric, T .... 432-837-8109 450 B
etf14xz@sulross.edu
FUNDERBURG,
Stephanie .... 617-873-0238 208 B
stephanie.funderburg@
cambridgecollege.edu
FUNDERBURK, Annette . 334-290-3265.... 2 F
annette.funderburk@istc.edu
FUNDERBURK, Dana ..... 660-626-2391 250 A
FUNG, Eileen .... 415-422-6083.. 72 J
fung@usfca.edu
FUNK, Andrea .... 805-765-9300.. 62 N
FUNK, Chad .... 916-484-8452.. 50 G
funkc@arc.losrios.edu
FUNK, David .... 903-510-3078 452 A
dfun@tjc.edu
FUNK, Julie .... 520-626-8550.. 16 D
juliefunk@arizona.edu
FUNK, Ray .... 509-574-4722 486 D
rfunk@yvcc.edu
FUNK, Tiger .... 435-586-7888 460 A
funk@suu.edu
FUNK-BAXTER, Kathryn 210-784-2000 447 E
kbaxter@tamusa.edu
FUNKE, Rebecca .... 515-964-6328 165 A
rsfunke@dmacc.edu
FUNSTON, Terry Lyn .... 815-825-9338 141 F
tfunston@kish.edu
FUQUA, Amy .... 605-642-6221 416 E
amy.fuqua@bhsu.edu
FUQUA, Julie .... 850-718-2478.. 97 E
fuquaj@chipola.edu

GALARDI, Karen .... 267-341-3208 385 J
kgalardi@holyfamily.edu
GALATIC, John .... 304-434-8000 488 E
john.galatic@easternwv.edu
GALATIC, John .... 304-384-5190 489 J
jgalatic@concord.edu
GALBARY, Tiffany .... 406-395-4875 265 G
tgalbary@stonechild.edu
GALBAVY, Colton .... 406-395-4875 265 G
cgalbavy@stonechild.edu
GALBIERZ, Todd .... 636-922-8359 258 J
tgalbierz@stchas.edu
GALBRAITH, Drew .... 860-297-2057.. 89 B
drew.galbraith@trincoll.edu
GALBRAITH, Gretchen ... 315-267-2231 319 A
galbragr@potsdam.edu
GALBRAITH, II, Jay, R . 407-582-3420 113 I
jgalbraith1@valenciacollege.edu
GALBRAITH, Jennifer .... 909-274-4600.. 52 J
jgalbraith@mtsac.edu
GALBRAITH, Joan .... 973-805-8099 277 A
jgalbrai@drew.edu
GALBRAITH, Joseph, P . 864-656-4233 407 E
joegalb@clemson.edu
GALBREATH, Dodd .... 615-966-1771 421 B
dodd.galbreath@lipscomb.edu
GALBREATH, Susan, C . 615-966-5952 421 B
susan.galbreath@lipscomb.edu
GALCHINSKY, Michael .. 404-413-2578 120 E
mgalchinsky@gsu.edu
GALDIERI, Viriginia ...... 201-684-7506 280 H
vgaldier@ramapo.edu
GALE, Andrea .... 909-607-1236.. 37 D
andrea.gale@cmc.edu
GALE, Jason .... 615-297-7545 417 G
galej@aquinascollege.edu
GALE, Jennifer, D .... 610-917-1488 401 G
jdgale@valleyforge.edu
GALE, Jesse .... 610-526-6526 379 B
jgale@brynmawr.edu
GALE, Mary .... 952-885-5437 242 N
mgale@nwhealth.edu
GALE, Nicole, L .... 410-651-6458 203 D
nlgale@umes.edu
GALEA, Sandro .... 617-358-1840 207 E
sgalea@bu.edu
GALEANO, Angela .... 410-951-3931 204 B
agaleano@coppin.edu
GALER, Sara .... 317-788-3583 161 H
galers@uindy.edu
GALER, Scott, W .... 208-496-4310 130 I
galers@byui.edu
GALEY, Frank .... 435-797-1167 460 C
frank.galey@usu.edu
GALGON, Aquila .... 209-946-2421.. 71 E
agalgon@pacific.edu
GALIANI, Colette .... 415-257-1392.. 41 C
colette.galiani@dominican.edu
GALIANO-WILLIAMS,
Matthew .... 617-745-3000 209 B
GALICIA, Delia .... 805-482-2755.. 59 G
dgalicia@stjohnsem.edu
GALICK, Rob .... 847-925-6380 138 G
rgalick@harpercollege.edu
GALICKI, Stan .... 601-974-1405 247 B
galics@millsaps.edu
GALIME, Steve .... 518-956-8030 316 A
sgalime@albany.edu
GALINSKI, Bonnie .... 978-542-2532 213 E
bonnie.galinski@salemstate.edu
GALIPEAU, Jennifer ...... 401-598-1813 404 D
jennifer.galipeau@jwu.edu
GALIPEAU-KONATE,
Bethany .... 540-542-6285 470 G
bgalipea@su.edu
GALIPO, Anna .... 216-421-7957 350 H
avgalipo@cia.edu
GALITZ, Todd .... 718-951-5099 293 C
todd.galitz@brooklyn.cuny.edu
GALL, Connie .... 405-692-3258 366 D
connie.gall@macu.edu
GALL, Cory .... 309-341-5273 134 B
cgall@sandburg.edu
GALL, Rob .... 707-765-1836.. 52 B
GALLAGHER, Amber .... 949-582-4860.. 65 D
agallagher4@saddleback.edu
GALLAGHER, Amie .... 908-526-1200 281 A
amie.gallagher@raritanval.edu
GALLAGHER, Amy .... 217-735-7201 142 H
agallagher@lincolncollege.edu
GALLAGHER, Bonnie ..... 845-431-8631 298 D
bonnie.gallagher@sunydutchess.edu
GALLAGHER, Connie .... 610-558-5501 391 A
gallaghc@neumann.edu
GALLAGHER, Daniel ..... 518-485-3390 296 G
gallaghd@strose.edu
GALLAGHER, Ed .... 256-766-6610.... 5 E
egallagher@hcu.edu
GALLAGHER, Elizabeth .. 925-631-4223.. 59 I
egallagh@stmarys-ca.edu
GALLAGHER,
Geraldine M, P .... 407-582-3155 113 I
ggallagher@valenciacollege.edu
GALLAGHER, Heather ..... 973-300-2110 284 A
hgallagher@sussex.edu
GALLAGHER, CSC,
James, T .... 503-943-8011 377 A
gallaghe@up.edu
GALLAGHER, Jennifer ... 410-810-7765 205 B
jrunyon2@washcoll.edu
GALLAGHER, Joanna .... 215-646-7300 385 A
gallagher.j@gmercyu.edu
GALLAGHER, John .... 573-341-4286 261 D
gallagherjo@mst.edu
GALLAGHER, Judith ...... 817-515-7702 445 F
judith.gallagher@tccd.edu
GALLAGHER, Karen .... 607-753-4717 318 A
karen.gallagher@cortland.edu
GALLAGHER, Kathleen .. 215-503-6959 399 E
kathleen.gallagher@jefferson.edu
GALLAGHER, Kathy .... 503-375-7181 372 H
kgallagher@corban.edu
GALLAGHER, Kelsey ..... 201-216-9901 277 B
GALLAGHER, Leslie, D . 281-425-6301 438 I
lgallagher@lee.edu
GALLAGHER, Lori .... 610-606-4609 380 D
lori.gallagher@cedarcrest.edu
GALLAGHER, Lori .... 713-525-3592 454 G
irishstudies@stthom.edu
GALLAGHER, Mary .... 323-953-4000.. 49 A
gallagmp@lacitycollege.edu
GALLAGHER,
Mary Beth .... 276-223-4765 476 A
mgallagher@wcc.vccs.edu
GALLAGHER, Maureen .. 914-395-2385 315 A
mgallagh@sarahlawrence.edu
GALLAGHER, Miles, P .. 717-871-7210 395 A
miles.gallagher@millersville.edu
GALLAGHER, Patricia .... 781-292-2416 210 A
patricia.gallagher@olin.edu
GALLAGHER, Patrick ..... 412-624-4200 400 H
pdg@pitt.edu
GALLAGHER, Patrick ..... 908-709-7045 284 D
gallagher@ucc.edu
GALLAGHER, Peg .... 773-298-3703 149 D
gallagher@sxu.edu
GALLAGHER, Scott .... 573-592-4337 262 G
scott.gallagher@williamwoods.edu
GALLAGHER, Steve .... 650-723-2300.. 66 E
GALLAGHER, Steve .... 336-631-1217 343 D
gallaghers@uncsa.edu
GALLAGHER, Susan ...... 410-777-2124 197 G
sgallagher5@aacc.edu
GALLAGHER, Susan ...... 503-312-5425 374 A
susan.gallagher@mtangel.edu
GALLAGHER, Terri .... 724-480-3427 381 H
terri.gallagher@ccbc.edu
GALLAGHER, Thomas ... 406-243-7852 263 K
tom.gallagher@umontana.edu
GALLAGHER-LEPAK,
Susan .... 920-465-2034 495 F
galaghs@uwgb.edu
GALLAHER, Connie .... 614-251-4690 358 B
connie.gallaher@ohiodominican.edu
GALLANT, Darren .... 207-786-6216 194 A
dgallant@bates.edu
GALLANT, Suzanna .... 207-755-5396 195 D
sgallant@cmcc.edu
GALLARDO, Ignacio ...... 805-893-4412.. 70 E
ignacio.gallardo@ucsb.edu
GALLARDO, Joanne .... 574-533-7000 155 E
joannekg@goshen.edu
GALLARDO, Mark .... 573-341-4981 261 D
gallardom@mst.edu
GALLARDO, Ruben, C .. 915-831-6306 436 A
rgalla16@epcc.edu
GALLARDO, Yoli .... 509-313-6115 480 F
gallardoy@gonzaga.edu
GALLE, Gillian .... 802-468-1344 463 E
gillian.galle@castleton.edu
GALLEGO, Pete, P .... 432-837-8000 450 B
president@sulross.edu
GALLEGOS,
Christopher, M .... 210-829-6012 453 C
cmgalle2@uiwtx.edu
GALLEGOS, Jeremy .... 316-295-5871 174 A
jeremy_gallegos@friends.edu
GALLEGOS, Joel, A .... 704-687-7755 342 D
jagalleg@uncc.edu
GALLEGOS, John .... 916-348-4689.. 41 H
jgallegos@epic.edu
GALLEGOS, Jose Alfred 323-242-5511.. 49 E
gallegja@lasc.edu
GALLEGOS, Renee, D .... 562-463-7271.. 58 L
rdgallegos@riohondo.edu
GALLEN, Peter, C .... 864-592-4680 412 E
gallenp@sccsc.edu
GALLENBERG, Dale .... 715-425-3841 496 F
dale.gallenberg@uwrf.edu
GALLERY, Tracy .... 800-955-2527 174 C
tgallery@grantham.edu
GALLEY, Amy .... 307-382-1645 501 J
agalley@westernwyoming.edu
GALLIANETTI, David, D . 920-565-1000 493 A
gallianettidd@lakeland.edu
GALLICHIO, Kathy .... 973-300-2100 284 A
kgallichio@sussex.edu
GALLIE, Alain .... 770-220-7908 119 A
agallie@gcuniv.edu
GALLIE, Alain .... 770-559-0580 124 A
GALLIGAN, Chad .... 623-935-8075.. 13 A
chad.galligan@estrellamountain.edu
GALLIGAN, Kathleen ..... 503-206-3217 377 B
kgalligan@uws.edu
GALLIGAN, Laura .... 401-598-2163 404 D
laura.galligan@jwu.edu
GALLIHER, Shelbey .... 310-338-7854.. 51 A
shelbey.galliher@lmu.edu
GALLIHUGH, Joel .... 313-993-1235 231 E
gallihja@udmercy.edu
GALLIMORE, Alec, D .... 734-647-7008 231 H
rasta@umich.edu
GALLIMORE, Jennie ...... 419-372-7581 348 G
jgallim@bgsu.edu
GALLIMORE, Sarah .... 717-815-6470 403 F
sgallimo@ycp.edu
GALLINA, Nancy .... 212-463-0400 322 F
nancy.gallina@touro.edu
GALLINA, Nancy .... 212-463-0400 322 G
nancy.gallina@touro.edu
GALLINI, Brian .... 503-370-6402 377 F
bgallini@willamette.edu
GALLION, Melanie .... 843-525-8224 412 G
mgallion@tcl.edu
GALLIPEAU, Jean, B ..... 315-443-3765 321 G
jbgallip@syr.edu
GALLIVAN, Mary .... 505-224-4000 285 N
mgallivan@cnm.edu
GALLMAN, Kathleen ...... 252-638-7233 334 A
gallmank@cravencc.edu
GALLO, James .... 215-646-7300 385 A
gallo.j@gmercyu.edu
GALLO, John, D .... 724-847-6796 384 C
jdgallo@geneva.edu
GALLO, Kathleen .... 516-463-4074 301 G
kathleen.gallo@hofstra.edu
GALLO, Kelly .... 562-902-3316.. 65 I
kellygallo@scuhs.edu
GALLO, Maria .... 715-425-3201 496 F
maria.gallo@uwrf.edu
GALLO, Nancy .... 973-300-2181 284 A
ngallo@sussex.edu
GALLO-MURPHY,
Meredith .... 773-907-4650 135 C
mgallo-murphy@ccc.edu
GALLOF, Bernard .... 770-720-5551 124 G
bernard.gallof@reinhardt.edu
GALLONIO, Anthony ..... 401-454-6636 405 B
agalloni@risd.edu
GALLOT, JR., Richard ... 318-274-3811 192 C
prez@gram.edu
GALLOWAY, Carolina .... 806-651-5309 448 B
cgalloway@wtamu.edu
GALLOWAY, David .... 808-675-3368 128 D
david.galloway@byuh.edu
GALLOWAY, David .... 651-603-6263 235 I
galloway@csp.edu
GALLOWAY, Heather ..... 512-245-2266 450 C
hg02@txstate.edu
GALLOWAY, Jeanne ...... 425-602-3007 477 H
jgalloway@bastyr.edu
GALLOWAY, Jeannie ..... 606-368-6113 178 G
jeanniegalloway@alc.edu
GALLOWAY, Merrill ...... 606-589-3079 183 A
merrill.galloway@kctcs.edu
GALLOWAY, Pamela ..... 919-760-8360 331 D
davisp@meredith.edu
GALLOWAY, Peter .... 610-436-1015 395 D
pgalloway@wcupa.edu
GALLOWAY, Robert .... 713-646-2927 443 I
rgalloway@stcl.edu
GALLOWAY, Robin .... 319-296-4292 166 H
robin.galloway@hawkeyecollege.edu
GALLOWAY, Sean .... 717-358-4210 383 I
sean.galloway@fandm.edu
GALLOWAY, Sheila .... 910-755-7312 332 F
galloways@brunswickcc.edu
GALLOWAY, Stephen .... 714-997-6765.. 36 B
sgalloway@chapman.edu
GALLOWAY-PERRY,
Rulisa .... 212-237-8701 294 D
rgalloway@jjay.cuny.edu
GALLOWGLAS, Robin ..... 916-484-8401.. 50 G
gallowr@arc.losrios.edu
GALLUCCI, Kathleen ..... 585-275-2121 323 M
GALLUZZO, Benjamin .... 315-268-2387 295 F
bgalluzz@clarkson.edu
GALOPE, Richard .... 909-382-4034.. 60 D
rgalope@sbccd.cc.ca.us
GALOYAN, Nazy .... 408-864-8292.. 42 H
galoyannazy@deanza.edu
GALT, Cindy .... 561-433-2330 108 J
GALTNEY, Alfred .... 601-877-6124 245 A
agaltney@alcorn.edu
GALUKYAN, Armine .... 626-585-7201.. 56 D
agalukyan@pasadena.edu
GALVAN, Adriana .... 310-206-3961.. 69 E
agalvan@college.ucla.edu
GALVAN, Betty .... 210-528-7183 441 B
bagalvan@ollusa.edu
GALVAN, Dennis, C ...... 541-346-5851 376 H
dgalvan@uoregon.edu
GALVAN, Efren .... 714-432-5774.. 38 B
egalvan@occ.cccd.edu
GALVAN, Jaime, B .... 787-891-0925 507 K
jgalvan@aguadilla.inter.edu
GALVAN, Juan, M .... 956-872-5051 443 H
GALVAN, Margarita, M . 361-593-3209 447 D
margarita.galvan@tamuk.edu
GALVAN, Michael .... 903-223-3013 448 A
michael.galvan@tamut.edu
GALVAN, Ovidio .... 713-221-8967 453 A
galvano@uhd.edu
GALVAN, Racheal .... 785-309-3147 177 E
racheal.galvan@salinatech.edu
GALVAN, Sonia .... 443-412-2545 199 D
sgalvan@harford.edu
GALVANONI, Mark .... 630-889-6661 145 E
mgalvanoni@nuhs.edu
GALVEZ, Jocelin .... 870-584-1163.. 22 F
GALVIN, Carroll .... 410-532-5314 201 D
cgalvin@ndm.edu
GALVIN, Elizabeth .... 401-341-2904 405 D
elizabeth.galvin@salve.edu
GALVIN, Garrett .... 619-574-5801.. 42 J
ggalvin@fst.edu
GALVIN, Jeanne .... 718-631-6220 295 C
jgalvin@qcc.cuny.edu
GALVIN, Mary, E .... 574-631-6456 162 A
mgalvin2@nd.edu
GALVIN, Michael .... 973-655-7761 279 B
galvinm@montclair.edu
GALVIN, Sophia .... 954-201-7350.. 96 F
GALVINHILL, Paul .... 508-793-3363 208 D
pgalvin@holycross.edu
GALYEAN, Paul .... 903-589-7135 438 C
pgalyean@jacksonville-college.edu
GAMBA, Melissa .... 267-502-6038 379 A
GAMBERG, Amy .... 502-597-5509 183 D
prexyassistant@kysu.edu
GAMBILL, Jon .... 816-501-2436 250 F
jon.gambill@avila.edu
GAMBILL, Todd .... 864-388-8182 410 A
tgambill@lander.edu
GAMBINO, Ellen, M ...... 845-431-8954 298 D
egambino@sunydutchess.edu
GAMBLE, Desiree .... 360-442-2202 481 D
dgamble@lowercolumbia.edu
GAMBLE, Gregory .... 856-225-6388 281 G
gambleg@camden.rutgers.edu
GAMBLE, Jim .... 616-538-2330 224 E
jgamble@gracechristian.edu
GAMBLE, Richard .... 423-775-6596 422 I
rgamble@ogs.edu
GAMBLE, Rob .... 408-855-5255.. 75 D
rob.gamble@missioncollege.edu
GAMBLE, Thomas, J ...... 518-861-2579 305 C
tgamble@mariacollege.edu
GAMBOA, Anthony .... 773-481-8752 135 G
agamboa@ccc.edu

GARCIA, Sharon .... 630-466-7900 152 K
sgarcia@waubonsee.edu
GARCIA, Smiley .... 806-743-8973 451 A
smiley.garcia@ttuhsc.edu
GARCIA, Steve .... 909-748-8477.. 72 F
steve_garcia@redlands.edu
GARCIA, Sunshine .... 805-437-3776.. 30 C
sunshine.garcia@csuci.edu
GARCIA, T. David .... 724-938-4020 393 E
garcia@calu.edu
GARCIA, Tara .... 657-278-5312.. 31 C
tgarcia@fullerton.edu
GARCIA, Tara .... 785-628-4231 173 H
tngarcia@fhsu.edu
GARCIA, Teresa .... 781-283-2237 219 E
tgarcia@wellesley.edu
GARCIA, Tina .... 303-352-6958.. 80 F
tina.garcia@ccd.edu
GARCIA, Tomas .... 409-938-1211 433 H
GARCIA, Tony .... 608-663-3274 492 F
tgarcia@edgewood.edu
GARCIA, Valentin .... 559-925-3331.. 75 B
valgarcia@whccd.edu
GARCIA, Valeria .... 813-974-6987 111 C
vgarcia@usf.edu
GARCIA, Veronica .... 210-486-5000 428 H
GARCIA, Veronica .... 210-486-5230 428 G
vgarcia2@alamo.edu
GARCIA, Viviana .... 760-750-4040.. 33 A
vivigarcia@csusm.edu
GARCIA, Vladimir .... 787-725-8120 506 M
vgarcia0068@eap.edu
GARCIA, Washington .... 386-822-8960 112 A
GARCIA, Wendy .... 870-584-1139.. 22 F
wgarcia@cccua.edu
GARCIA, Zahira .... 787-620-2040 505 C
zgarcia@aupr.edu
GARCIA BARRIOS,
Ramon, D .... 787-850-9335 512 D
ramon.garcia1@upr.edu
GARCIA BEDOLLA, Lisa 510-642-6000.. 69 A
GARCIA-CAMPOS,
Georgina .... 323-860-0789.. 50 B
GARCIA-GARIBAY,
Miguel .... 310-825-1042.. 69 E
mgarciagaribay@college.ucla.edu
GARCIA-GUZMAN,
Yessica .... 732-255-0400 279 F
ygarcia-guzman@ocean.edu
GARCIA-LEON, Jose ...... 212-799-5000 303 E
GARCIA-MILLER, Maria . 209-478-0800.. 45 I
mgarcia@humphreys.edu
GARCIA-MURILLO,
Martha .... 402-554-2380 270 A
mgarciamurillo@unomaha.edu
GARCIA-PRAJER, Renee 336-721-2600 340 A
renee.garcia-prajer@salem.edu
GARCIA-REYES, Ana, I .. 718-518-4313 294 B
agreyes@hostos.cuny.edu
GARCIA-RITTGERS,
Andrea .... 650-306-3193.. 62 J
garcia-rittgersa@smccd.edu
GARCON, Reginald .... 301-891-4485 205 A
rgarcon@wau.edu
GARCÍA, Rafael, I .... 787-766-1717 510 G
rigarcia@uagm.edu
GARCÍA, Tary .... 787-264-1912 508 F
tdgarcia@sangerman.inter.edu
GARCÍA, Tary .... 787-264-1912 508 F
tdgarcia@intersg.edu
GARD, Evelyn .... 203-332-5191.. 86 F
egard@housatonic.edu
GARD, Evelyn .... 203-285-2127.. 86 E
egard@gatewayct.edu
GARD, Julee, A .... 815-740-3372 152 H
jgard@stfrancis.edu
GARDE, Shekhar .... 518-276-6298 312 C
gardes@rpi.edu
GARDEA, Oscar, M .... 415-338-2897.. 33 E
omgardea@sfsu.edu
GARDEN, Oliver .... 225-578-3202 189 E
GARDI, Kerri .... 610-683-4647 394 D
gardi@kutztown.edu
GARDIER PATERSON,
Mary, T .... 570-340-6018 389 D
paterson@marywood.edu
GARDIN, Carey, C .... 920-923-7617 493 D
cgardin@marianuniversity.edu
GARDINA, Jackie .... 805-765-9300.. 62 N
GARDINA, Susan .... 717-947-6094 392 V
sgardina2@pacollege.edu
GARDINER, Alicia, J ..... 207-859-4127 194 D
alicia.gardiner@colby.edu
GARDINER, Lori .... 801-422-4597 458 H
lori@byu.edu
GARDING, Ed .... 406-657-2326 264 D
edward.garding@msubillings.edu
GARDNER, Amy .... 607-431-4120 301 A
gardnera@hartwick.edu
GARDNER, Andrew .... 910-898-9670 336 D
gardnera@montgomery.edu
GARDNER, Andy .... 704-669-4041 333 E
gardnera@clevelandcc.edu
GARDNER, Betina .... 859-622-5036 180 E
betina.gardner@eku.edu
GARDNER, Bonnie .... 636-584-6502 253 B
bonnie.gardner@eastcentral.edu
GARDNER, Bonnie, S ... 636-584-6502 253 B
bonnie.gardner@eastcentral.edu
GARDNER, Brian .... 978-468-7111 210 C
bgardner3@gcts.edu
GARDNER, Chris .... 910-410-1731 337 B
csgardner@richmondcc.edu
GARDNER, Chris, L ...... 864-597-4236 414 E
gardnercl@wofford.edu
GARDNER, Christina ..... 619-849-2246.. 57 J
christinagardner@pointloma.edu
GARDNER,
Christopher, L .... 864-597-4000 414 E
gardnercl@wooford.edu
GARDNER, Clinton .... 202-274-2303.. 94 C
GARDNER, Daniel .... 718-862-7399 304 M
dgardner01@manhattan.edu
GARDNER, Denise .... 865-974-4373 427 B
d.gardner@utk.edu
GARDNER, Donna .... 816-415-7622 262 F
gardnerd@william.jewell.edu
GARDNER, Eileen .... 251-442-2234.... 8 C
egardner@umobile.edu
GARDNER, Greg .... 405-682-7879 367 D
ggardner@occc.edu
GARDNER, Gretchen ..... 412-809-5302 396 E
gardner.gretchen@ptcollege.edu
GARDNER, Jared .... 541-888-7316 376 C
jgardner@socc.edu
GARDNER, Joe Barry .... 503-768-7123 373 E
jgardner@lclark.edu
GARDNER, Kasey .... 916-558-2402.. 50 J
gardnek@scc.losrios.edu
GARDNER, Kasey .... 530-661-5700.. 77 D
GARDNER, Kathleen ...... 989-774-3111 222 E
gardn2k@cmich.edu
GARDNER, Kathy .... 314-446-8389 260 H
kathy.gardner@stlcop.edu
GARDNER, Kevin .... 502-852-6356 186 A
kevin.gardner@louisville.edu
GARDNER, Laurie, A ..... 207-778-7272 196 I
lgardner@maine.edu
GARDNER, Lisa .... 208-426-1698 130 H
lisagardner@boisestate.edu
GARDNER, Lizz .... 312-850-7889 135 H
egardner17@ccc.edu
GARDNER, Marie .... 785-242-2067 176 D
mgardner@neosho.edu
GARDNER, Marilyn .... 617-322-3566 211 A
marilyn_gardner@laboure.edu
GARDNER, Mary Jo .... 651-450-3835 238 E
mgardner@inverhills.edu
GARDNER, Melissa .... 330-823-6092 362 E
gardnemf@mountunion.edu
GARDNER, Mike .... 484-460-6067 390 H
mikegardner@muhlenberg.edu
GARDNER, Nathan .... 518-262-5251 289 L
gradnen@amc.edu
GARDNER, Pamela, K ... 802-656-3450 463 A
pamela.k.gardner@uvm.edu
GARDNER, Phil .... 864-977-7014 410 I
phil.gardner@ngu.edu
GARDNER, Richard .... 212-924-5900 321 F
rgardner@swedishinstitute.edu
GARDNER, Ron .... 559-297-4500.. 45 N
rgardner@iot.edu
GARDNER, Sarah .... 415-485-3239.. 41 C
sarah.gardner@dominican.edu
GARDNER, Scott .... 208-496-4012 130 I
gardners@byui.edu
GARDNER,
Stephanie, F .... 501-686-5689.. 22 B
sfgardner@uams.edu
GARDNER, Susan .... 541-737-0123 375 A
susan.gardner@oregonstate.edu
GARDNER, Suzanne ...... 727-341-3160 107 E
gardner.suzanne@spcollege.edu
GARDNER, Tyshawn ...... 205-366-8838.... 7 A
tgardner@stillman.edu
GARDNER, William .... 301-546-0652 201 E
gardnewx@pgcc.edu
GARDNER SMITH,
Catie, K .... 651-696-6315 236 I
GARDUZA, Ericka .... 281-487-1170 448 E
egarduza@txchiro.edu
GARDZINA, Matt .... 614-222-4014 351 B
mgardzina@ccad.edu
GAREIS, Martha .... 970-521-6662.. 82 C
martha.gareis@njc.edu
GARELICK, Rhonda .... 212-229-8916 308 A
garelicr@newschool.edu
GAREY, Bryan .... 540-231-7457 476 C
bgarey@vt.edu
GAREY, Kelly .... 503-552-1603 374 D
kgarey@nunm.edu
GARGIULO, Colette .... 201-489-5836 278 D
GARGIULO, Donald .... 213-252-5100.. 23 K
dgargiulo@alu.edu
GARGIULO, Leslie .... 213-252-5100.. 23 K
lgargiulo@alu.edu
GARIBALDI,
Antoine, M .... 313-993-1455 231 E
garibaldi@udmercy.edu
GARIEPY, Maria .... 508-929-8784 213 G
mgariepy1@worcester.edu
GARIMELLA, Suresh ...... 802-656-7878 463 A
suresh.garimella@uvm.edu
GARLAND, Colleen .... 740-427-5154 354 I
garland1@kenyon.edu
GARLAND, Elizabeth ..... 503-370-6209 377 F
ecarson@willamette.edu
GARLAND, Philip .... 619-260-4724.. 72 I
pgarland@sandiego.edu
GARLAND, Rebecca, R . 815-740-3648 152 H
rgarland@stfrancis.edu
GARLAND, Tom .... 813-988-5131.. 99 R
garlandt@floridacollege.edu
GARLAND, Zanne .... 828-771-2038 344 D
zgarland@warren-wilson.edu
GARLIC, Brandy .... 410-532-5195 201 D
bgarlic@ndm.edu
GARLICK, Bill .... 517-483-1780 226 H
garliw@lcc.edu
GARLICK, Rebecca .... 979-743-5222 431 H
bgarlick@blinn.edu
GARLICK, Stella .... 304-263-6262 487 F
GARLING, Brittany .... 712-749-2065 164 C
garling@bvu.edu
GARLING, Jessica .... 712-749-2500 164 C
garlingj@bvu.edu
GARLITZ, John .... 541-962-3114 372 I
jgarlitz@eou.edu
GARMAN, Deanna .... 423-585-6897 425 F
deanna.garman@ws.edu
GARN, Gregg, A .... 405-325-1267 370 K
garn@ou.edu
GARN, Jonathan .... 989-686-9160 223 J
jonathangarn@delta.edu
GARNAR, Martin, L ...... 413-542-2000 205 G
GARNER, Alison .... 617-585-1100 217 E
GARNER, Amber .... 662-720-7256 248 C
acgarner@nemcc.edu
GARNER, Amy .... 937-327-7457 364 D
daltona@wittenberg.edu
GARNER, Brian .... 615-329-8690 419 H
bgarner@fisk.edu
GARNER, Cindy .... 901-722-3223 423 G
cgarner@sco.edu
GARNER, David, B .... 215-572-3811 402 E
dgarner@wts.edu
GARNER, Gregg .... 615-879-2022 420 C
GARNER, Jeffrey .... 239-590-1083 109 K
jgarner@fgcu.edu
GARNER, John .... 334-670-3712.... 7 C
jcgarner@troy.edu
GARNER, John .... 205-348-7880.... 7 F
jgarner@uasystem.edu
GARNER, III, Joseph .... 573-221-3675 253 J
GARNER, Josh .... 770-720-5928 124 G
josh.garner@reinhardt.edu
GARNER, Latonya .... 662-254-3421 248 B
lcgarner@mvsu.edu
GARNER, Lyn .... 281-998-6150 443 B
lyn.garner@sjcd.edu
GARNER, Michael .... 859-846-5839 184 B
michael.garner@midway.edu
GARNER, Porter .... 979-845-7514 446 F
porter-garner@tamu.edu
GARNER, Regina .... 214-860-8561 435 A
garnerre@dcccd.edu
GARNER, Sam .... 402-363-5620 270 D
sgarner@york.edu
GARNER, Tim .... 256-782-8220.... 6 A
tgarner@jsu.edu
GARNER-FERRIS,
Chelsea .... 941-351-5100 106 J
GARNETT, Heather .... 434-544-8431 471 L
garnett_h@lynchburg.edu
GARNSEY-HARTER, Ann 206-546-4101 484 B
agarnsey@shoreline.edu
GAROFALO, Giovanni ... 412-365-1292 380 G
g.garofalo@chatham.edu
GARONE, Wilson .... 206-296-6148 484 A
wgarone@seattleu.edu
GARR, Bethany .... 864-596-9595 408 F
healthservices@converse.edu
GARRANT, Ines .... 617-358-0513 207 E
igarrant@bu.edu
GARRELL, Robin, L .... 212-817-7000 293 F
GARREN, Cynthia .... 863-784-7177 108 F
cynthia.garren@southflorida.edu
GARREN, Mary Ann ...... 870-762-3168.. 17 B
mgarren@smail.anc.edu
GARRETSON, Angela, R 973-596-3101 279 E
angela.r.garretson@njit.edu
GARRETT, Allen .... 619-201-8700.. 60 G
algarrett@sdcc.edu
GARRETT, Allison .... 620-341-5551 173 F
agarrett@emporia.edu
GARRETT, JR.,
Alphonso .... 410-651-6411 203 D
agarrett@umes.edu
GARRETT, Bonnie, J ..... 410-777-2503 197 G
bjgarrett@aacc.edu
GARRETT, Candace .... 256-761-6590.... 7 B
cgarrett@talladega.edu
GARRETT, Craig .... 504-282-4455 190 F
cgarrett@nobts.edu
GARRETT, Daniel .... 605-225-1634 415 I
GARRETT, Deb .... 309-467-3721 138 A
GARRETT, Don .... 325-674-2213 428 F
dlg09a@acu.edu
GARRETT, Geoff .... 213-740-6422.. 73 D
dean@marshall.usc.edu
GARRETT, Gina .... 870-307-7557.. 19 I
gina.garrett@lyon.edu
GARRETT, Glenda .... 214-860-8591 435 A
ghall@dcccd.edu
GARRETT, Helen .... 206-685-2553 485 A
helenbg@uw.edu
GARRETT, JR.,
James, H .... 412-268-2000 380 C
garrett@andrew.cmu.edu
GARRETT, Jason .... 731-661-5365 426 F
jgarrett@uu.edu
GARRETT, Katrina .... 601-484-8724 247 A
kgarret2@meridiancc.edu
GARRETT, Kevin .... 304-384-5340 489 J
garrettad@concord.edu
GARRETT, Kristi .... 205-860-7845.... 7 A
kgarrett@stillman.edu
GARRETT, Krystal .... 217-351-2533 147 C
kgarrett@parkland.edu
GARRETT, LaCharlotte ... 504-284-5435 191 C
lgarrett@suno.edu
GARRETT, Leonard .... 214-860-3697 435 A
lgarrett@dcccd.edu
GARRETT, Lynn .... 407-404-6060 108 D
garrettl@seminolestate.edu
GARRETT, Mark .... 270-901-1065 182 H
mark.garrett@kctcs.edu
GARRETT, Natasha .... 412-536-1296 386 H
natasha.garrett@laroche.edu
GARRETT, Nicole, L ...... 919-658-7896 340 G
ngarrett@umo.edu
GARRETT, P.B .... 443-352-5955 202 E
pbgarrett@stevenson.edu
GARRETT, Paul .... 864-977-7035 410 I
paul.garrett@ngu.edu
GARRETT, Rachele .... 936-468-2403 445 E
nixonhr@sfasu.edu
GARRETT, Rick .... 765-641-4156 153 G
ragarrett@anderson.edu
GARRETT, Robert, J ...... 208-496-1124 130 I
garrettr@byui.edu
GARRETT, Robin .... 254-526-1733 432 D
robin.garrett@ctcd.edu
GARRETT, Scott .... 216-687-5119 350 J
s.garrett1@csuohio.edu
GARRETT, Shana .... 866-492-5336 244 F
shana.garrett@mail.waldenu.edu
GARRETT, Teresa .... 434-381-6205 471 I
tgarrett@sbc.edu
GARRETT, Todd, L .... 913-971-3278 176 C
tgarrett@mnu.edu

GAUDELLI, William .... 610-758-3221 388 E
wig318@lehigh.edu
GAUDETTE, Helen .... 212-217-5380 299 D
helen_gaudette@fitnyc.edu
GAUDREAU, Alison, K .. 248-364-6117 229 I
agaudreau@oakland.edu
GAUGER, John .... 434-582-8946 468 E
jmgauger@liberty.edu
GAUGHAN, Cheryl .... 619-849-2499.. 57 J
cherylgaughan@pointloma.edu
GAUGHF, Natalie, W ..... 601-845-6436 249 E
nwgaughf1@umc.edu
GAUL, Julie, M .... 412-578-6042 380 B
jmgaul@carlow.edu
GAULDEN, Susan .... 201-684-7500 280 H
sgaulden@ramapo.edu
GAUNCE, Lori .... 606-759-7141 182 E
lori.gaunce@kctcs.edu
GAUNDER, Alisa .... 512-863-1418 445 C
gaundera@southwestern.edu
GAUNTT, Kamille .... 706-865-2134 126 E
kgauntt@truett.edu
GAURMER, Terry .... 303-458-1629.. 83 E
tgaurmer@regis.edu
GAURON, Patricia, M ... 978-556-3000 215 E
pgauron@necc.mass.edu
GAUS, Gregory, J .... 630-515-7307 144 F
ggausx@midwestern.edu
GAUSE, Genell .... 843-661-8351 409 F
genell.gause@fdtc.edu
GAUSSOIN, Kristofer ..... 505-224-4746 285 N
kgaussoin@cnm.edu
GAUSTAD, Gabrielle, G . 607-871-2953 290 B
gaustad@alfred.edu
GAUTAM, Mridul .... 775-327-2363 271 E
mgautam@unr.edu
GAUTHIER, Theresa ...... 585-785-1304 299 F
theresa.gauthier@flcc.edu
GAUTIER, Angela .... 575-835-6619 286 K
angela.gautier@nmt.edu
GAUVAIN, Ignatius .... 570-561-1818 397 H
ignatius.gauvain@stots.edu
GAUVIN, Keith, R .... 203-837-9202.. 86 B
gauvink@wcsu.edu
GAVARRA-OH,
Mary Anne .... 818-710-2234.. 49 D
gavarrm@piercecollege.edu
GAVENTA, Sarah .... 512-404-4885 430 J
sgaventa@austinseminary.edu
GAVER, Bob .... 402-363-5721 270 D
bagaver@york.edu
GAVIGAN, Lisa .... 508-286-3799 220 B
gavigan_lisa@wheatoncollege.edu
GAVIN, Andrew .... 262-595-2485 496 D
gavin@uwp.edu
GAVIN, Carrie .... 850-599-3076 109 I
carrie.gavin@famu.edu
GAVIN, Diane .... 210-486-2431 429 B
dgavin7@alamo.edu
GAVIN, Joseph .... 713-718-6015 437 C
joseph.gavin@hccs.edu
GAVIN, Laurence .... 910-678-8382 334 E
gavinl@faytechcc.edu
GAVIN, M. F. Chip .... 207-621-3173 196 F
chip.gavin@maine.edu
GAVIN, Michael .... 414-297-6760 499 C
gavinmj@matc.edu
GAVIN, Michael, H .... 989-686-9000 223 J
GAVIN, Mike .... 828-395-1295 335 D
mgavin@isothermal.edu
GAVIN, Paul .... 319-363-1323 168 F
pgavin@mtmercy.edu
GAVIN, Paula .... 386-752-1822 100 B
paula.gavin@fgc.edu
GAVINI, Srinivas, R ..... 225-771-2277 191 B
reddy_gavini@subr.edu
GAVLICK, Christopher ... 718-636-3579 311 F
cgavlick@pratt.edu
GAVLIK, Deborah .... 937-512-3060 360 G
deborah.gavlik@sinclair.edu
GAW, Kevin .... 401-232-6090 404 A
kgaw@bryant.edu
GAWEL, Matthew .... 207-893-6609 196 C
mgawel@sjcme.edu
GAWELEK, Mary Ann .... 419-824-3809 355 C
mgawelek@lourdes.edu
GAWENDA, Matt .... 312-922-1884 143 G
mgawenda@maccormac.edu
GAWLICK, Craig .... 650-949-7777.. 42 I
GAWLIK, Terry .... 208-885-0216 132 F
tlg@uidaho.edu

GAWRONSKI, JR.,
Michael .... 845-341-4284 310 G
michael.gawronski@sunyorange.edu
GAWTHROP, Larry .... 810-762-0235 228 F
larry.gawthrop@mcc.edu
GAWU, Helena .... 409-984-6216 449 I
arthurh@lamarpa.edu
GAXIOLA-ROWLES,
Thomas .... 559-443-8612.. 67 B
thom.gaxiola@fresnocitycollege.edu
GAY, Aaron .... 859-246-6565 181 F
aaron.gay@kctcs.edu
GAY, Bob .... 304-724-3700 486 F
rgay@apus.edu
GAY, Claudine .... 617-495-1566 210 E
fasdean@fas.harvard.edu
GAY, Cliff .... 478-289-2025 118 C
cgay@ega.edu
GAY, John .... 410-386-8434 198 D
jgay@carrollcc.edu
GAY, Michelle .... 704-403-1758 327 C
michelle.gay@atriumhealth.org
GAY MIYOSHI, Erin ...... 440-684-6022 363 C
erin.miyoshi@ursuline.edu
GAYA, Liliam .... 787-250-1912 508 D
lgaya@intermetro.edu
GAYER, Richard, H .... 213-262-3939.. 46 D
GAYLOR, IV, Charles .... 919-735-5151 338 H
cpgaylor@waynecc.edu
GAYMON, Joffery .... 334-844-6428.... 4 D
jag0124@auburn.edu
GAYNOR, Dona, E .... 321-674-8102 100 C
dgaynor@fit.edu
GAYNOR, Julie .... 940-397-4353 440 C
julie.gaynor@msutexas.edu
GAYNOR, Lynnette .... 919-365-7711 340 E
lgaynor@sfwbc.edu
GAYNOR, Michael, M ... 610-519-4000 401 K
michael.gaynor@villanova.edu
GAYNOR, Timothy .... 919-365-7711 340 E
GAYTON, Linda .... 973-684-6104 280 A
lgayton@pccc.edu
GAZAL, Andre .... 406-586-3585 263 I
andre.gazal@montanabiblecollege.edu
GAZAL, Mary .... 724-805-2627 397 I
mary.gazal@stvincent.edu
GAZAL, Mary .... 724-805-2555 398 A
mary.gazal@stvincent.edu
GAZZALE, Bob .... 323-856-7600.. 25 G
bgazzale@afi.com
GAZZARA HESS,
Margaret .... 508-588-9100 215 A
mhess2@massasoit.mass.edu
GAZZILLO, Sara .... 201-684-7610 280 H
sgazzill@ramapo.edu
GEAGHAN, Tom .... 216-687-4745 350 J
t.geaghan@csuohio.edu
GEAR, Lisa, L .... 213-738-6834.. 66 B
admissions@swlaw.edu
GEARAN, Dan .... 603-428-2372 273 G
dgearan@nec.edu
GEARHART, Gregory, L . 717-691-6007 389 H
gearhart@messiah.edu
GEARHART, Victoria ..... 301-687-4714 204 C
vmgearhart@frostburg.edu
GEARHART TURNER,
Patti .... 817-531-5820 451 C
pturner@txwes.edu
GEARING-KALILL,
Allison .... 413-565-1000 206 D
agkalill@baypath.edu
GEARY, Cale .... 724-838-4282 398 C
cgeary@setonhill.edu
GEARY, Colette .... 718-862-7200 304 M
cgeary01@manhattan.edu
GEARY, Gregg .... 562-903-4834.. 27 A
gregg.geary@biola.edu
GEARY, Jason .... 848-932-9360 282 A
jgeary@mgsa.rutgers.edu
GEARY, MaryLee .... 303-678-3642.. 81 A
marylee.geary@frontrange.edu
GEARY, Parrish .... 916-484-8172.. 50 G
gearyp@arc.losrios.edu
GEARY, Ronald .... 815-921-4011 148 B
r.geary@rockvalleycollege.edu
GEASEY, David, W .... 607-436-3314 316 F
david.geasey@oneonta.edu
GEBBIE, Joe .... 703-284-5960 468 H
jgebbie@marymount.edu
GEBEKE, Mike .... 309-438-8851 140 D
mdgebek@ilstu.edu
GEBHARDT, Matthias .... 951-763-0500.. 55 B
GEBHARDT, Maureen .... 978-927-0585 209 E
mgebhard@endicott.edu

GEBHARDT, Michael, B 215-204-6542 399 B
michael.gebhardt@temple.edu
GEBKE, Jill .... 314-446-8140 260 H
jill.gebke@stlcop.edu
GEBLER, Ryan, L .... 920-832-6584 493 B
ryan.l.gebler@lawrence.edu
GEBO, John .... 607-844-8222 322 D
geboj@tompkinscortland.edu
GEBREMICHAEL, Miliite 651-793-1876 238 I
miliite.gebremichael@metrostate.edu
GEBRU, Amanuel .... 805-553-4065.. 73 J
agebru@vcccd.edu
GEDDINGS, Scarlet .... 803-535-1243 411 B
geddingss@octech.edu
GEDDIS, Catherine .... 610-328-8397 398 G
cgeddis1@swarthmore.edu
GEDLINSKE, Paul .... 920-424-0404 496 C
gedlinsk@uwosh.edu
GEDNALSKE, Julie .... 605-331-6683 417 C
julie.gednalske@usiouxfalls.edu
GEDRO, Julie .... 585-224-3222 320 E
julie.gedro@esc.edu
GEDULDIG, Liza .... 802-651-5938 462 A
lgeduldig@champlain.edu
GEE, E. Gordon .... 304-293-5531 490 E
gordon.gee@mail.wvu.edu
GEE, Henry .... 562-692-0921.. 58 L
GEE, Henry .... 310-900-1600.. 39 F
emartinez@compton.edu
GEE, Robert .... 909-794-1084.. 39 E
GEE, Terry .... 619-594-2853.. 33 D
tgee@sdsu.edu
GEEHAN, Margaret .... 518-629-7151 302 C
m.geehan@hvcc.edu
GEEL, Donna .... 207-454-1013 195 I
dgeel@wccc.me.edu
GEER, Cynthia .... 513-745-3119 364 G
geer@xavier.edu
GEER, John, G .... 615-936-6366 428 A
john.geer@vanderbilt.edu
GEER, Kimberly .... 425-739-8119 481 C
kimberly.geer@lwtech.edu
GEER, Nathan .... 503-375-8192 372 H
ngeer@corban.edu
GEETER, Andy .... 229-732-5934 115 B
andygeeter@andrewcollege.edu
GEETER, Candy .... 248-341-2138 229 C
crgeeter@oaklandcc.edu
GEETTER, Erika .... 617-353-2326 207 E
egeetter@bu.edu
GEFELL, Michele, D ...... 315-786-2271 303 C
mgefell@sunyjefferson.edu
GEFFERT, Bryn .... 802-656-2020 463 A
bryn.geffert@uvm.edu
GEGENHEIMER BALDASSARO,
Sarah .... 202-994-5152.. 92 D
sarahgb@gwu.edu
GEHBAUER, Daryl .... 636-481-3120 254 C
dgehbaue@jeffco.edu
GEHLERT, Sarah .... 213-740-2311.. 73 D
GEHLERT, Sarah .... 803-777-5292 413 A
sgehlert@mailbox.sc.edu
GEHLHAUSEN, Keith ..... 812-488-2943 161 G
kg77@evansville.edu
GEHRICH, Michael, D .... 317-381-6016 162 F
mgehrich@vinu.edu
GEHRING, Dennis .... 319-363-1323 168 F
dgehring@mtmercy.edu
GEHRING, Patrick, D .... 253-535-7119 482 A
gehrinpd@plu.edu
GEHRINGER, Steve .... 610-409-3598 401 H
sgehringer@ursinus.edu
GEHRKE, Sean .... 206-543-9956 485 A
sjgehrke@uw.edu
GEHRKE, Shelly .... 620-341-5421 173 F
rgehrke@emporia.edu
GEHRMAN ROTTIER,
Laura .... 715-346-3903 497 A
laura.gehrman.rottier@uwsp.edu
GEIBEL, Randy .... 631-656-2157 300 B
GEIER, Cathy .... 202-884-9545.. 94 A
geierc@trinitydc.edu
GEIER, Doug .... 415-369-5275.. 43 I
dgeier@ggu.edu
GEIER, Marisa .... 360-442-2391 481 D
mgeier@lowercolumbia.edu
GEIGER, Debra .... 912-443-5700 125 B
dgeiger@savannahtech.edu
GEIGER, Douglas .... 773-838-7984 135 F
dgeiger3@ccc.edu
GEIGER, Hope .... 918-631-2715 371 C
hope-geiger@utulsa.edu

GEIGER, James .... 814-393-2818 393 G
jgeiger@clarion.edu
GEIGER, Karen .... 610-527-0200 397 D
karen.geiger@rosemont.edu
GEIGER, Martha .... 513-936-1691 362 A
martha.geiger@uc.edu
GEIGER, Tad .... 847-970-4902 152 I
tgeiger@usml.edu
GEIKEN, Jason .... 479-968-0400.. 18 C
jgeiken@atu.edu
GEIL, Carol .... 641-844-5747 167 G
carol.geil@iavalley.edu
GEIL, Toi .... 307-766-2187 501 I
GEIS, Jodi .... 828-327-7000 333 B
jgeis@manufacturingsolutionscenter.org
GEISER, Laura .... 314-977-2543 259 F
laura.geiser@slu.edu
GEISER-GETZ, Glenn .... 585-245-5531 318 B
geisergetz@geneseo.edu
GEISLER, Allison .... 218-322-2323 238 F
allison.geisler@itascacc.edu
GEISLER, Michael, E ..... 914-323-5230 305 B
michael.geisler@mville.edu
GEISLER, Norman, L ..... 714-966-8500.. 74 C
info@ves.edu
GEISMAN, Cami .... 225-342-6950 192 B
cami.geisman@ulsystem.edu
GEISSLER, Nancy .... 217-228-5432 147 F
geissna@quincy.edu
GEIST, Alan .... 937-766-7768 349 E
geista@cedarville.edu
GEIST, Amanda .... 630-466-7900 152 K
ageist@waubonsee.edu
GELAYE, Enku .... 404-727-5693 118 E
enku.gelaye@emory.edu
GELB, Edward .... 919-573-5350 340 C
assessment@shepherds.edu
GELBACK-DIAZ, Christy 317-921-4746 158 D
cgelback@ivytech.edu
GELDZAHLER, Daniel .... 718-633-4715 311 L
GELERNTER, Mark .... 303-315-1020.. 84 D
mark.gelernter@ucdenver.edu
GELINA, Denise .... 573-875-8700 251 I
GELINAS, Cynthia, B .... 803-641-3609 413 B
cindyg@usca.edu
GELL, Barry .... 518-255-5440 319 C
gellbf@cobleskill.edu
GELLE, Mark .... 507-786-3294 243 D
gelle@stolaf.edu
GELLER, Jack, M .... 813-253-6262 113 H
jgeller@ut.edu
GELLER, Laurie .... 701-858-3310 345 E
laurie.geller@minotstateu.edu
GELLER, Mary, A .... 320-363-5601 235 F
mgeller@csbsju.edu
GELLER, Steve .... 952-358-8954 239 G
steve.geller@normandale.edu
GELLES, Karen .... 934-420-2040 320 F
gelleska@farmingdale.edu
GELLMAN, Sarah, M ..... 724-946-7340 402 D
gellmasm@westminster.edu
GELO, Erica .... 218-879-0746 238 B
erica@fdltcc.edu
GELSTON, Nicole .... 860-486-5796.. 89 D
nicole.gelston@uconn.edu
GELWICKS, Carla .... 360-383-3222 486 A
cgelwick@whatcom.edu
GELY, Gilda .... 616-554-5183 223 E
gilda.gely@davenport.edu
GEMEDA, Mekbib, L ..... 757-446-7151 466 D
gemedam@evms.edu
GEMME, Terese .... 203-392-5499.. 86 A
gemmet1@southernct.edu
GEMMELL, Ann .... 651-290-6434 242 L
ann.gemmell@mitchellhamline.edu
GEMMER, Pete .... 513-936-1632 362 A
peter.gemmer@uc.edu
GEMPERLEIN,
Monica, P .... 919-334-1520 338 G
mpgemperlein@waketech.edu
GEMPERLINE, Paul .... 252-328-6073 341 A
gemperlinep@ecu.edu
GENANDT, James .... 785-320-4500 175 G
jamesgenandt@manhattantech.edu
GENARD, Daniel, J .... 757-683-3090 469 B
dgenard@odu.edu
GENARD, Giovanna, M . 757-683-3580 469 B
ggenard@odu.edu
GENARDO, Patricia .... 630-889-6597 145 E
pgenardo@nuhs.edu
GENDRON, Dennis .... 206-296-5556 484 A
gendron@seattleu.edu

GENDRON, Dennis .... 615-327-6894 421 D
dgendron@mmc.edu
GENECIN, Paul .... 203-432-0076.. 90 C
paul.genecin@yale.edu
GENELIUS, Sandy .... 413-542-5785 205 G
sgenelius@amherst.edu
GENERALS, Donald .... 215-751-8000 381 I
ggenerals@ccp.edu
GENES, Marna .... 408-924-1550.. 34 A
marna.genes@sjsu.edu
GENESE, Carol .... 914-632-5400 307 A
cgenese@monroecollege.edu
GENETTI, Carol .... 805-893-2013.. 70 E
cgenetti@graddiv.ucsb.edu
GENFI, Henrieta .... 973-618-3589 276 D
hgenfi@caldwell.edu
GENGLER, Charles, E ... 713-221-8017 453 A
GENIG, Dennis .... 734-462-4400 230 G
dgenig@schoolcraft.edu
GENIN, Larisa .... 316-978-3200 178 D
larisa.genin@wichita.edu
GENNA, Angela .... 602-285-7357.. 13 F
angela.genna@phoenixcollege.edu
GENNARO, Gwen .... 719-255-3153.. 84 C
ggennaro@uccs.edu
GENNETTE, Heather ...... 785-243-1435 172 L
hgennette@cloud.edu
GENO, Amanda .... 413-565-1150 206 D
ageno@baypath.edu
GENO, Rita, B .... 802-468-1203 463 E
rita.geno@castleton.edu
GENONI, Mia, R .... 804-289-8468 472 C
mgenoni@richmond.edu
GENOVESE, Erin .... 309-677-3160 134 A
egenovese@bradley.edu
GENT, Barbara .... 606-248-0142 183 A
barbara.gent@kctcs.edu
GENT, Pamela .... 814-393-2413 393 G
pgent@clarion.edu
GENTEMAN, Kurt .... 706-769-1472 115 E
GENTHON, Paulette ...... 402-556-4456 269 G
paulettegenthon@ucha.edu
GENTILE, Julie .... 330-941-3700 364 H
jgentile@ysu.edu
GENTILE, Kim .... 330-972-6345 361 H
gentile@uakron.edu
GENTILE, Linda .... 412-268-5231 380 C
lgentile@cmu.edu
GENTILE, Maria .... 415-257-1307.. 41 C
maria.gentile@dominican.edu
GENTILE, Marla .... 828-898-3841 330 E
gentilem@lmc.edu
GENTIUS, Paula .... 919-515-2011 342 A
paula_gentius@ncsu.edu
GENTLEWARRIOR,
Sabrina .... 508-531-1429 212 D
sabrina.gentlewarrior@bridgew.edu
GENTRY, Eric, C .... 859-572-5129 184 E
egentry@nku.edu
GENTRY, Holly .... 303-914-6341.. 83 C
holly.wren@rrcc.edu
GENTRY, Jeff .... 575-562-2733 286 B
jeff.gentry@enmu.edu
GENTRY, Jeffrey .... 270-809-3420 184 D
jgentry@murraystate.edu
GENTRY, Jodi, D .... 352-392-1075 111 A
jodi-gentry@ufl.edu
GENTRY, Keil .... 703-784-2105 502 J
keil.gentry@usmc.mil
GENTRY, Rusty .... 615-868-6503 422 B
rusty.gentry@mtsa.edu
GENTRY, Susan .... 252-335-0821 333 G
susan_gentry@albemarle.edu
GENTRY, William, A ..... 336-841-9470 329 F
wgentry@highpoint.edu
GENTRY-WRIGHT,
Susan, C .... 864-833-8100 411 D
sgentry-w@presby.edu
GENTSCH, James .... 205-652-3361.... 9 B
jgentsch@uwa.edu
GENUNG, Scott .... 217-300-9788 152 B
sagenung@illinois.edu
GEOGHEGAN, Michael .. 740-264-5591 352 B
mgeoghegan@egcc.edu
GEORGE, Amanda .... 501-686-5670.. 22 B
adgeorge@uams.edu
GEORGE, Amanda .... 717-245-1556 382 D
georgea@dickinson.edu
GEORGE, Andrew, L ..... 616-526-6057 222 C
alg35@calvin.edu
GEORGE, Charles .... 503-491-6422 374 B
charles.george@mhcc.edu
GEORGE, Chris .... 507-786-3775 243 D
georgec@stolaf.edu
GEORGE, Claudia .... 770-538-4749 116 D
cgeorge@brenau.edu
GEORGE, Dean .... 304-829-7255 487 A
dgeorge@bethanywv.edu
GEORGE, Deborah .... 770-962-7580 121 E
dgeorge@gwinnetttech.edu
GEORGE, Demetria .... 225-771-2552 191 E
dgeorge@sulc.edu
GEORGE, Dionne .... 478-757-4023 127 F
dgeorge@wesleyancollege.edu
GEORGE, Emily .... 605-995-2601 415 A
emily.george@dwu.edu
GEORGE, Jennifer .... 501-882-8957.. 17 D
jlgeorge@asub.edu
GEORGE, Julie .... 859-622-1778 180 E
julie.george@eku.edu
GEORGE, Katherine .... 315-655-7287 292 H
kageorge@cazenovia.edu
GEORGE, Lee .... 612-330-1629 234 A
lgeorge@augsburg.edu
GEORGE, Lisa .... 620-327-8217 174 E
lisa.george@hesston.edu
GEORGE, Lynn, E .... 412-578-6115 380 B
legeorge@carlow.edu
GEORGE, Marianne .... 863-297-1000 106 A
mgeorge@polk.edu
GEORGE, Mertha, V ...... 601-877-6154 245 A
mgeorge@alcorn.edu
GEORGE, Michel .... 503-768-7850 373 E
mgeorge@lclark.edu
GEORGE, Regina .... 251-460-6050.... 9 A
reginageorge@southalabama.edu
GEORGE, Rick .... 303-492-6591.. 84 B
rick.george@colorado.edu
GEORGE, Safiya .... 561-297-3206 109 J
sgeorge@health.fau.edu
GEORGE, Sheila .... 202-885-8657.. 94 D
sgeorge@wesleyseminary.edu
GEORGE, Susan .... 304-473-8080 491 D
george@wvwc.edu
GEORGE, Tami .... 910-272-3541 337 D
tgeorge@robeson.edu
GEORGE, Tondelaya, K . 315-470-6810 319 D
tkgeorge@esf.edu
GEORGE, Tracey .... 615-322-6310 428 A
tracey.george@vanderbilt.edu
GEORGE, Travis .... 386-752-1822 100 B
travis.george@fgc.edu
GEORGE, Tree .... 318-257-3036 192 D
tgeorge@latech.edu
GEORGE, William, D ..... 570-577-1228 379 C
wdgeorge@bucknell.edu
GEORGE-MERRILL,
Pamela .... 216-397-1908 353 O
pgeorgemerrill@jcu.edu
GEORGE-TAYLOR,
Mosunmola .... 423-697-5731 424 A
mosunmola.georgetaylor@
chattanoogastate.edu
GEORGE-WEINSTEIN,
Mindy .... 215-871-6654 395 G
mindygw@pcom.edu
GEORGES, Jane .... 619-260-4550.. 72 I
jgeorges@sandiego.edu
GEORGESON, Jeff .... 352-254-4119 112 E
GEORGIEV, Nancy .... 864-294-3274 409 H
nancy.georgiev@furman.edu
GEORGIOPOULOS,
Michael .... 407-823-5338 110 E
michaelg@ucf.edu
GEORGIOU, Tina .... 212-343-1234 306 G
tgeorgiou@mcny.edu
GEPPERTH, James .... 800-517-0857 355 A
GERACE, Christopher .... 716-250-7500 292 A
cpgerace@bryantstratton.edu
GERACITANO, Jenna ..... 503-847-2584 377 B
jgeracitano@uws.edu
GERAGHTY, James .... 718-430-2000 290 A
GERAMI, Keyvan .... 314-286-3670 258 F
kgerami@ranken.edu
GERAMI, Michelle .... 409-933-8351 433 H
mgerami@com.edu
GERARD, Debra .... 714-480-7450.. 58 E
gerard_debra@rsccd.edu
GERARD, Matthew, C ... 402-280-1773 266 H
matthewgerard@creighton.edu
GERARD, Phil .... 864-242-5100 406 H
GERARD, Stacey .... 252-940-6241 332 C
stacey.gerard@beaufortccc.edu
GERASSIMIDES, Gus ...... 859-985-3158 179 I
gerassimidesg@berea.edu
GERATY, Bob .... 309-556-3953 140 F
bgeraty@iwu.edu
GERATY, Brent, G .... 909-748-8076.. 72 F
brent_geraty@redlands.edu
GERATY, Larry .... 951-785-2160.. 47 C
lgeraty@lasierra.edu
GERBASI, Iris .... 714-997-6676.. 36 B
gerbasi@chapman.edu
GERBER, Cheryl .... 724-946-6173 402 D
gerberca@westminster.edu
GERBER, Dan .... 816-523-9140 262 D
dan.g@wellspring.edu
GERBER, Elizabeth, L .... 815-599-3421 139 A
liz.gerber@highland.edu
GERBER, Gary .... 870-245-5129.. 20 D
gerberg@obu.edu
GERBER, Molly .... 215-955-1061 399 E
molly.gerber@jefferson.edu
GERBER, Natalie .... 716-673-3529 316 D
natalie.gerber@fredonia.edu
GERBER, Nathan .... 801-863-7973 460 D
nathan.gerber@uvu.edu
GERBER, Randy .... 937-481-2222 364 A
randy_gerber@wilmington.edu
GERBER, Stephen, D .... 574-372-5100 155 F
gerbersd@grace.edu
GERBER, Sue .... 201-200-3042 279 D
sgerber@njcu.edu
GERBERICH, Brian .... 214-887-5174 435 F
bgerberich@dts.edu
GERBOTH, Karen .... 937-327-6141 364 D
kgerboth@wittenberg.edu
GERBRACHT, Tonya ...... 319-273-6520 164 A
tonya.gerbracht@uni.edu
GERDES, Christine, M .. 734-936-2254 231 H
cmgerdes@umich.edu
GERDES, Nathan .... 641-472-1177 168 C
gerdes-nathan@aramark.com
GERDRUM, Kacie .... 541-684-7288 371 I
kgerdrum@bushnell.edu
GERDTS, Adam .... 646-592-6863 326 D
adam.gerdts@yu.edu
GERDTS, Daniel .... 507-344-7777 234 C
dgerdts@blc.edu
GERE, Nicholas .... 207-602-2011 197 E
ngere@une.edu
GEREAUX, Teresa, T ..... 540-375-2282 470 E
gereaux@roanoke.edu
GERENZ, Eileen .... 978-762-4000 215 D
egerenz@northshore.edu
GERG, Julie .... 607-844-8222 322 D
gergj@tompkinscortland.edu
GERGER, Daniel .... 212-217-3315 299 D
daniel_gerger@fitnyc.edu
GERGER, Rick .... 314-246-8708 262 C
rickgerger06@webster.edu
GERHARD, Gesine .... 515-271-3939 165 J
gesine.gerhard@drake.edu
GERHARD, Ronald .... 925-485-5206.. 35 I
rgerhard@clpccd.org
GERHARDSON, Ashley .. 479-308-2311.. 17 A
ashley.gerhardson@arcomedu.org
GERHARDT, Cassie .... 701-777-4200 345 B
cassie.gerhardt@und.edu
GERHARDT, Lyndsay ..... 585-345-6800 300 F
lagerhardt@genesee.edu
GERHART, Stacey .... 714-879-3901.. 45 G
sgerhart@hiu.edu
GERIA, Kellyann, R .... 215-699-5700 387 H
kgeria@lsb.edu
GERICS, Aron .... 810-762-0200 228 F
aron.gerics@mcc.edu
GERIG, Jill .... 912-478-5367 120 C
jgerig@georgiasouthern.edu
GERIGUIS, David .... 951-785-2002.. 47 C
dgerigui@lasierra.edu
GERIK, Debbie .... 254-659-7704 437 A
debgerik@hillcollege.edu
GERING, Carol .... 541-346-3428 376 H
cgering2@uoregon.edu
GERING, Jonathan, C ... 316-284-5241 172 B
jgering@bethelks.edu
GERINGER, Sandra .... 251-626-3303.... 7 E
sgeringer@ussa.edu
GERISCH, Carl .... 541-888-7707 376 C
carl.gerisch@socc.edu
GERKE-CORRIGAN,
Shannon .... 920-735-4796 498 F
gerkecor@fvtc.edu
GERKEN, Heather .... 203-432-1660.. 90 C
heather.gerken@yale.edu
GERKEN, Jeffrey .... 518-437-4794 316 A
jgerken@albany.edu
GERKEN, Kevin .... 419-267-1226 357 E
kgerken@northweststate.edu
GERKEN, Stacey .... 715-346-3553 497 A
sgerken@uwsp.edu
GERKIN, Jeff .... 865-974-1501 427 B
jgerkin@utk.edu
GERKIN, Jeffrey, G .... 865-974-3131 427 B
jgerkin@utk.edu
GERKIN GUERRANT,
Emily .... 517-355-3853 227 F
emilyg@msu.edu
GERL, Beth .... 901-321-3531 418 G
bgerl@cbu.edu
GERLACH, Alysa .... 617-373-5144 217 I
GERLACH, David, M ..... 217-735-7200 142 H
dgerlach@lincolncollege.edu
GERLACH, Karen .... 202-884-9203.. 94 A
gerlachk@trinitydc.edu
GERLING, Nikki .... 319-385-8021 167 H
nikki.gerling@iw.edu
GERLOFF, Jill .... 817-531-6502 451 C
gerloff@txwes.edu
GERMAIN, Lauren .... 315-464-5193 317 C
germainl@upstate.edu
GERMAN, Deborah .... 407-266-1000 110 E
deborah.german@ucf.edu
GERMAN, James .... 916-278-5344.. 32 D
james.german@csus.edu
GERMAN, Lisa .... 256-352-8306.... 3 I
lisa.german@wallacestate.edu
GERMANA, Katie .... 212-799-5000 303 E
GERMANO, Dorothy ...... 707-986-4153.. 44 J
GERMANO, William .... 516-796-4800 310 B
wgermano@nycc.edu
GERMANY, Carole, H ... 601-635-6201 246 A
cgermany@eccc.edu
GERMANY, Debbie .... 803-754-4100 408 E
GERMANY, Sylvia .... 256-726-8328.... 6 C
germany@oakwood.edu
GERMIC, Stephen .... 616-632-2151 221 E
sag004@aquinas.edu
GERNANDER, Scott, R .. 281-478-2771 443 A
scottr.gernander@sjcd.edu
GERNER, Steven, W ...... 262-243-5700 492 E
steven.gerner@cuw.edu
GERODIMOS, Ashley .... 219-989-2414 160 D
afclark@pnw.edu
GEROSIMO, Veronica .... 201-360-4198 278 C
vgerosimo@hccc.edu
GEROUX, Joni .... 715-833-6397 498 E
jgeroux3@cvtc.edu
GEROW, Gary .... 207-941-7907 194 F
gerowg@husson.edu
GERRAIN, Dawn .... 518-608-8271 299 C
dgerrain@excelsior.edu
GERRETSEN, Amy, L ..... 920-748-8353 494 J
gerretsena@ripon.edu
GERRISH, James .... 973-290-4479 282 I
jgerrish@steu.edu
GERRY, Bobbi, J .... 208-885-6111 132 F
bgerry@uidaho.edu
GERSBACHER, Holly ..... 937-327-6374 364 D
gersbacherh@wittenberg.edu
GERSON, Stanton, L ..... 216-368-2825 349 D
stanton.gerson@case.edu
GERSTENBERGER, Julie 806-716-2019 443 G
jgerstenberger@southplainscollege.edu
GERSTENBERGER,
Shawn .... 702-895-1565 271 D
shawn.gerstenberger@unlv.edu
GERSTL-PEPIN, Cynthia 413-545-2705 211 G
cgerstlp@umass.edu
GERSTMAN, Josh .... 206-878-3710 481 B
jgerstman@highline.edu
GERSTMAYR, Andrew .... 973-748-9000 276 A
andrew_gerstmayr@bloomfield.edu
GERSTNER, Glenn .... 718-990-7474 313 G
gerstneg@stjohns.edu
GERTLER, Sara .... 909-667-4413.. 37 G
sgertler@claremontlincoln.edu
GERTNER, Kimberly, A . 843-953-5758 408 C
gertnerka@cofc.edu
GERTSON, Katherine ..... 212-799-5000 303 E
GERTZ, Genie .... 202-651-5653.. 92 C
genie.gertz@gallaudet.edu
GERVAIS, Shayne .... 724-938-5700 393 E
gervais@calu.edu
GERWITZ, Jim .... 573-518-2134 256 D
jgerwitz@mineralarea.edu
GERZINA, Holly, A .... 330-325-6740 357 D
hgerzina@neomed.edu
GESELE, Scott 757-594-7863 465M
scott.gesele@cnu.edu

GESO, Cristina .... 215-955-8164 399 E
cristina.geso@jefferson.edu
GESSLER, Benjamin ...... 740-283-6466 352 I
bgessler@franciscan.edu
GESSNER, Bob, F .... 407-582-1321 113 I
rgessner@valenciacollege.edu
GESTRING, Sheila, K ..... 605-658-5641 416 D
sheila.gestring@usd.edu
GETACHEW, Mimi .... 703-892-5100.. 93 H
GETCHELL, Glenn .... 706-236-2215 116 B
ggetchell@berry.edu
GETFORD, Patty .... 352-335-2332.. 94 E
GETMAN, Meghan .... 315-792-7264 321 B
meghan.getman@sunypoly.edu
GETSINGER, Joseph ...... 856-415-6209 281 D
jgetsinger@rcsj.edu
GETTLE, Darla .... 717-464-7050 387 F
GETTY, Marc, D .... 304-326-1258 487 I
mgetty@salemu.edu
GETTYS, Rob .... 269-471-3215 221 D
rgettys@andrews.edu
GETZ, Rob .... 610-902-8147 379 G
rag44@cabrini.edu
GETZ, Roger .... 207-768-9595 197 C
roger.getz@maine.edu
GEVITZ, Norman .... 660-626-2726 250 A
ngevitz@atsu.edu
GEWEKE, Christina .... 319-273-7505 164 A
christina.geweke@uni.edu
GEWOLB, Matthew .... 212-431-2352 309 A
matthew.gewolb@nyls.edu
GEYER, Andrea .... 260-399-7700 162 B
ageyer@sf.edu
GEYER, Eileen .... 978-232-2129 209 E
egeyer@endicott.edu
GEYER, Enid .... 518-262-6008 289 L
geyere@amc.edu
GEYER, Jon .... 614-236-6955 349 B
jgeyer@capital.edu
GEYER, Mariann, K .... 412-392-3805 396 G
mgeyer@pointpark.edu
GFELLER, Josh .... 785-320-4550 175 G
joshgfeller@manhattantech.edu
GHADESSI, Touba .... 508-286-8200 220 B
GHAFFAR, Abdul .... 910-521-6577 343 B
abdul.ghaffar@uncp.edu
GHALI, Ghali, E .... 318-675-5240 189 I
ghali.ghali@lsuhs.edu
GHAN, Mark .... 775-445-4468 271 F
mark.ghan@wnc.edu
GHANEM, Salma .... 312-362-8875 136 H
sghanem@depaul.edu
GHANNADIAN,
F. Frank .... 813-253-6221 113 H
fghannadian@ut.edu
GHARAKHANIAN,
Anahid .... 213-738-6786.. 66 B
agharakhanian@swlaw.edu
GHAZARIAN, Esther, A . 781-768-7280 218 D
esther.ghazarian@regiscollege.edu
GHAZARIAN, Garo .... 818-766-8151.. 39 H
GHAZARYAN, Ashot .... 510-925-4282.. 25 K
ashot.ghazaryan@aua.am
GHERBI, Naima .... 860-439-2411.. 87 H
nghe@conncoll.edu
GHIDIU, Katherine, E .... 585-292-2320 307 B
kghidiu@monroecc.edu
GHIDOTTI, Lisa .... 540-831-5000 469 D
lghidotti@radford.edu
GHILONI, Adam .... 864-646-1583 412 H
aghiloni@tctc.edu
GHINASSI, Frank .... 848-932-3818 282 A
ghinassi@ubhc.rutgers.edu
GHOLSON, Robert, D .... 601-266-4466 249 F
robert.gholson@usm.edu
GHOLSON, Shari .... 270-534-3372 183 B
shari.gholson@kctcs.edu
GHOLSTON, Kim .... 215-895-2582 382 F
kjg88@drexel.edu
GHORAYEB, Samir .... 409-984-6484 449 I
samir.ghorayeb@lamarpa.edu
GHORI, Zaid .... 650-738-7088.. 62 L
ghoriz@smccd.edu
GHORMOZ, Jacquelyn .. 570-504-9073 384 B
jghormoz@som.geisinger.edu
GHORPADE, Anuja .... 518-694-7337 289 J
anuja.ghorpade@acphs.edu
GHOSAL, Bobby .... 601-928-6207 247 E
bobby.ghosal@mgccc.edu
GHOSH, Avijit .... 217-333-3077 151 F
ghosha@uillinois.edu
GHOSH, Avijit .... 217-265-0263 151 F
ghosha@uillinois.edu

GHOSH, Guru .... 540-231-3205 476 C
gghosh@vt.edu
GHOSH, Jayati .... 989-964-4064 230 E
jghosh@svsu.edu
GHOSH, Melanie Mala . 617-627-2000 219 C
mala.ghosh@tufts.edu
GHOSH, Monica .... 808-956-7205 129 E
monicag@hawaii.edu
GHOSH, Sibdas .... 412-578-6072 380 B
sghosh@carlow.edu
GHOSH, Soumitra .... 312-362-8610 136 H
GHOUS, Mostafa .... 831-386-7100.. 44 G
mghous@hartnell.edu
GHOUSSAINI, Nizar ...... 402-280-2700 266 H
GHRAYEB, Omar .... 815-753-0494 146 B
oghrayeb@niu.edu
GIACOBBE, Jeff .... 973-655-5373 279 B
giacobbej@montclair.edu
GIACOMAZZI, Andrew .. 208-426-1368 130 H
agiacom@boisestate.edu
GIACOMAZZI, James .... 925-424-1281.. 35 K
jgiacomazzi@laspositascollege.edu
GIACOMELLI, Jodi .... 814-871-7741 384 A
organ002@gannon.edu
GIACOMETTI, Dena .... 773-838-7799 135 F
dgiacometti@ccc.edu
GIACOMINI, Mike .... 661-395-4203.. 46 L
mike.giacomini@bakersfieldcollege.edu
GIAGO, Don .... 605-455-6044 415 H
dgiago@olc.edu
GIAGO, Don .... 605-455-6000 415 H
dgiago@olc.edu
GIAMBONA, Mary Ellen 518-525-6850 306 B
GIAMBRA, Leonard, M . 860-701-6679 503 G
leonard.m.giambra@uscg.mil
GIAMPAOLI, Michael .... 702-463-2122 272 G
mgiampaoli@wongu.org
GIAMPIETRO, Michael .. 413-565-1000 206 D
mgiampietro@baypath.edu
GIANCATARINO, Kate ... 610-519-6285 401 K
kate.giancatarino@villanova.edu
GIANCOLI, Adriana .... 607-735-1770 298 H
agiancoli@elmira.edu
GIANNELLIS,
Emmanuel, P .... 607-255-7200 297 F
epg2@cornell.edu
GIANNESCHI, Matt .... 970-945-8691.. 78 L
mgianneschi@coloradomtn.edu
GIANNET, Stanley, M ... 727-816-3490 105 F
giannes@phsc.edu
GIANNETTINO, Val .... 319-208-5065 170 D
vgiannettino@scciowa.edu
GIANNETTO, Michael .... 802-387-4767 462 C
GIANNINI, Amy .... 617-585-1201 217 E
amy.giannini@necmusic.edu
GIANNINI, John .... 856-256-5414 281 F
giannini@rowan.edu
GIANNINI, Renee .... 209-664-6652.. 33 B
rgiannini@csustan.edu
GIANNOBILE,
William, V .... 617-495-1000 210 E
william_giannobile@hsdm.harvard.edu
GIANNOTTI, Louis, J .... 410-293-1400 504 A
giannott@usna.edu
GIANOLI, Mary Beth ..... 317-955-6697 159 K
sgianoli@marian.edu
GIANOUSSOPAULOUS,
Denise .... 909-593-3511.. 71 C
GIARDULLO, Kelly .... 781-891-2014 206 G
kgiardullo@bentley.edu
GIATAS, Domna .... 207-621-3495 196 H
domna.giatas@maine.edu
GIAUQUE, Margie, T .... 218-755-2038 237 F
margie.giauque@bemidjistate.edu
GIBAJA, Marcia .... 904-256-7077 102 H
mgibaja@ju.edu
GIBB, Deborah .... 212-229-5667 308 A
gibbd@newschool.edu
GIBB, Katharine .... 864-503-5444 414 A
kgibb@uscupstate.edu
GIBB, Randy .... 602-639-7500.. 12 J
GIBBINGS, Emily .... 413-579-3040 213 F
egibbings@westfield.ma.edu
GIBBISON, Godfrey .... 843-953-3596 408 C
gibbisonga@cofc.edu
GIBBON, Lori .... 316-942-4291 176 E
gibbonl@newmanu.edu
GIBBONS, Arthur .... 845-758-7442 290 I
gibbons@bard.edu
GIBBONS, Dennis .... 315-792-5361 306 K
dgibbons@mvcc.edu
GIBBONS, Jeremy .... 910-362-7054 332 H
jgibbons@cfcc.edu

GIBBONS, Kristie .... 540-261-4100 471 B
kristie.gibbons@svu.edu
GIBBONS, Megan .... 781-768-7843 218 D
megan.gibbons@regiscollege.edu
GIBBONS, Meghan .... 240-567-7185 200 G
meghan.gibbons@montgomerycollege.edu
GIBBONS, Michael .... 478-471-2458 122 F
michael.gibbons@mga.edu
GIBBONS, Peter .... 304-724-3700 486 F
pgibbons@apus.edu
GIBBONS, Susan .... 203-432-1810.. 90 C
susan.gibbons@yale.edu
GIBBONS, Thomas, F ... 312-503-3011 146 E
tgibbons@northwestern.edu
GIBBONS, Tom .... 401-841-4008 503 A
gibbonst@usnwc.edu
GIBBS, Benjamin .... 972-721-5203 452 B
bgibbs@udallas.edu
GIBBS, Charles .... 404-880-8566 117 C
cgibbs@cau.edu
GIBBS, Chymeka .... 229-293-2100 128 B
chymeka.gibbs@wiregrass.edu
GIBBS, Danny .... 615-366-3921 423 H
danny.gibbs@tbr.edu
GIBBS, Donna .... 360-650-3482 485 I
donna.gibbs@wwu.edu
GIBBS, Hilary, H .... 229-259-5503 127 E
hhgibbs@valdosta.edu
GIBBS, J. D .... 252-527-6223 335 G
jdgibbs27@lenoircc.edu
GIBBS, Jamie .... 252-249-1851 336 F
jgibbs@pamlicocc.edu
GIBBS, Jeffery .... 407-971-5172 108 D
gibbsj@seminolestate.edu
GIBBS, Jeremiah .... 317-788-2058 161 H
gibbsj@uindy.edu
GIBBS, Jim .... 806-651-3287 448 B
jgibbs@wtamu.edu
GIBBS, Kelly .... 510-549-4702.. 66 G
kgibbs@sksm.edu
GIBBS, Lincoln .... 231-591-2273 224 A
lincolngibbs@ferris.edu
GIBBS, Martin .... 208-792-2325 132 A
mlgibbs@lcsc.edu
GIBBS, Robert, C .... 512-428-1060 442 I
rgibbs@stedwards.edu
GIBBS, Ryan .... 806-716-2207 443 G
rgibbs@southplainscollege.edu
GIBBS, Sarah .... 919-209-2086 335 F
sfgibbs@johnstoncc.edu
GIBBS, Shawn, G .... 979-436-9322 446 F
sgibbs@tamu.edu
GIBBS, Susan .... 620-227-9327 173 D
sgibbs@dc3.edu
GIBBS, Tanya, R .... 203-285-2061.. 86 E
tgibbs@gatewayct.edu
GIBBS, Thomas, C .... 314-434-4044 252 C
GIBBS DRAYTON,
Marilyn .... 803-535-5309 407 D
mgibbs@claflin.edu
GIBBS-EMENAKA,
Stephanie .... 215-545-6400 391 E
sgibbs-emenaka@peirce.edu
GIBERT, Lisa .... 360-992-2677 478 I
lgibert@clark.edu
GIBERTI, Bruno .... 805-756-2246.. 29 I
bgiberti@calpoly.edu
GIBISCH, Elizabeth .... 256-824-6926.... 8 B
elizabeth.gibisch@uah.edu
GIBLER, Linda .... 210-341-1366 440 H
lgibler@ost.edu
GIBLER, Rhonda, K .... 573-882-2094 261 A
giblerr@missouri.edu
GIBLIN, Frank .... 248-370-2395 229 I
giblin@oakland.edu
GIBLIN, Harvey, M .... 512-691-1717 430 E
hgiblin@aii.edu
GIBLIN, Patrick .... 314-246-7174 262 C
patrickgiblin61@webster.edu
GIBLIN, Tara .... 714-432-5093.. 38 B
tgiblin@occ.cccd.edu
GIBNEY, Glenn .... 912-344-3248 120 C
ggibney@georgiasouthern.edu
GIBNEY, Regan .... 412-578-6654 380 B
rpgibney@carlow.edu
GIBOUT, Holly .... 847-970-4929 152 I
hgibout@usml.edu
GIBRALTER, Jonathan ... 315-364-3265 324 I
president@wells.edu
GIBSON, Amy, B .... 630-515-7198 144 F
agibso@midwestern.edu
GIBSON, Andrea .... 386-506-3337.. 98 D
andrea.gibson@daytonastate.edu

GIBSON, Annie, K .... 757-683-3152 469 B
akmorris@odu.edu
GIBSON, Ashley, M ...... 918-270-6405 368 G
ashley.gibson@ptstulsa.edu
GIBSON, Bernard .... 805-289-6121.. 74 B
agibson@vcccd.edu
GIBSON, Brenda .... 503-375-7110 372 H
bgibson@corban.edu
GIBSON, Brian .... 504-278-6420 188 G
bgibson@nunez.edu
GIBSON, Brian .... 801-581-8305 459 O
brian.gibson@utah.edu
GIBSON, Camille .... 936-261-5205 446 C
cbgibson@pvamu.edu
GIBSON, Cedrick .... 904-779-4045 101 B
cedrick.gibson@fscj.edu
GIBSON, Chris .... 650-574-6161.. 62 K
GIBSON, Christoper, P . 518-783-2302 315 E
cgibson@siena.edu
GIBSON, Christopher .... 650-738-4343.. 62 L
gibsonc@smccd.edu
GIBSON, Clayton .... 940-565-2055 453 E
clayton.gibson@unt.edu
GIBSON, Crystal, L .... 240-895-4295 202 B
clgibson@smcm.edu
GIBSON, Dan .... 214-333-5931 434 C
danielg@dbu.edu
GIBSON, David, J .... 802-443-5834 462 E
djgibson@middlebury.edu
GIBSON, David, W .... 432-837-8707 450 B
dgibson@sulross.edu
GIBSON, Denise .... 505-454-2500 286 F
GIBSON, Donald 718-862-7440 304M
dgibson01@manhattan.edu
GIBSON, Donald .... 207-768-9560 197 C
donald.gibson@maine.edu
GIBSON, Donna, S .... 212-639-2109 304 J
gibsond@mskcc.org
GIBSON, Dwight .... 847-317-7005 151 C
dgibson@tiu.edu
GIBSON, Edie, B .... 731-881-7508 427 D
edgibson@utm.edu
GIBSON, Gloria, J .... 773-442-5400 146 A
gjgibson@neiu.edu
GIBSON, Howard, O ..... 903-923-1620 458 F
hgibson@wileyc.edu
GIBSON, J. Murray .... 850-410-6161 109 I
jmgibson@eng.famu.fsu.edu
GIBSON, Jane .... 901-375-4400 422 A
janegibson@midsouthchristian.edu
GIBSON, Janell .... 251-981-3771.... 5 A
janell.gibson@columbiasouthern.edu
GIBSON, Jeanine .... 203-332-5000.. 86 F
GIBSON, Jeff .... 319-895-4357 164 G
jgibson@cornellcollege.edu
GIBSON, Jeff .... 417-625-9727 256 F
gibson-j@mssu.edu
GIBSON, Jeffrey .... 580-559-5204 365 K
jgibson@ecok.edu
GIBSON, Jeremy .... 978-837-5306 216 F
gibsonj@merrimack.edu
GIBSON, Jody .... 402-844-7112 268 H
jody@northeast.edu
GIBSON, Jonathan .... 503-517-1806 377 E
jgibson@westernseminary.edu
GIBSON, Joseph .... 843-574-6311 412 I
joe.gibson@tridenttech.edu
GIBSON, Keith, E .... 540-464-7334 476 B
gibsonke@vmi.edu
GIBSON, Kelly .... 913-971-3392 176 C
krgibson@mnu.edu
GIBSON, Kody .... 602-850-8000.. 15 A
GIBSON, Lloyd .... 914-674-7159 306 C
lgibson@mercy.edu
GIBSON, Lynn .... 662-685-4771 245 C
lgibson@bmc.edu
GIBSON, Mandi .... 713-646-1702 443 I
mgibson@stcl.edu
GIBSON, Marc .... 318-675-4928 189 I
marc.gibson@lsuhs.edu
GIBSON, Maribeth .... 601-366-8880 249 G
mgibson@wbs.edu
GIBSON, Matthew .... 816-926-4400 253 I
GIBSON, Michael .... 256-840-4124.... 3 F
michael.gibson@snead.edu
GIBSON, Murray .... 850-410-6161 110 C
jmgibson@fsu.edu
GIBSON, Nathan .... 719-255-3075.. 84 C
ngibson@uccs.edu
GIBSON, Nola, R .... 601-974-1132 247 B
gibsonk@millsaps.edu
GIBSON, Pamela .... 910-486-3930 334 E
gibsonp@faytechcc.edu

GIBSON, Peggy .... 276-523-2400 474 D
pgibson@mecc.edu
GIBSON, Rick .... 734-764-1817 231 H
gibsonrl@umich.edu
GIBSON, Rob .... 620-341-6694 173 F
rgibson1@emporia.edu
GIBSON, Robert .... 541-552-7672 376 B
GIBSON, Ryan .... 606-368-6130 178 G
ryangibson@alc.edu
GIBSON, Ryan, W .... 217-581-1904 137 E
rwgibson@eiu.edu
GIBSON, Sally .... 816-271-4369 257 A
sgibson14@missouriwestern.edu
GIBSON, Shanan .... 386-226-7283.. 99 A
shanan.gibson@erau.edu
GIBSON, Stacey .... 208-282-3964 131 G
gibssta2@isu.edu
GIBSON, Susan .... 404-880-8757 117 C
sgibson@cau.edu
GIBSON, Tammy .... 706-379-3111 128 C
tgibson@yhc.edu
GIBSON, Tera .... 325-670-1077 436 I
tera.gibson@hsutx.edu
GIBSON, Thomas .... 715-346-2123 497 A
GIBSON, Tim .... 212-659-7207 303 H
tgibson@tkc.edu
GIBSON, Tim .... 405-692-3287 366 D
tim.gibson@macu.edu
GIBSON, Todd, D .... 724-458-2147 384 G
tdgibson@gcc.edu
GIBSON, Tonia, R .... 270-824-1739 182 D
tonia.gibson@kctcs.edu
GIBSON, Willietta .... 336-273-4431 327 A
GIBSON-GAYLE, Gale .... 718-489-5240 313 E
ggibson-gayle@sfc.edu
GIBSON SHEFFIELD,
Gail .... 802-387-6797 462 C
gailsheffield@landmark.edu
GIBSON-SHREVE, Lada . 330-494-6170 360 K
lshreve@starkstate.edu
GIDDARIE, Thanh .... 978-762-4000 215 D
ngiddari@northshore.edu
GIDDENS, Elizabeth ...... 619-260-4823.. 72 I
egiddens@sandiego.edu
GIDDENS, Jean .... 804-828-5174 473 B
jgiddens@vcu.edu
GIDDINGS, Matthew ..... 701-224-5789 346 A
matthew.giddings@bismarckstate.edu
GIDEON, Amy, C .... 615-868-6503 422 B
amy@mtsa.edu
GIDEON, Ryan .... 320-363-5225 235 F
rgideon001@csbsju.edu
GIDJUNIS, Rebecca ...... 610-341-1576 383 B
rgidjuni@eastern.edu
GIE, Lori .... 504-520-5730 193 E
lgie@xula.edu
GIELOW, Bob .... 617-559-8847 210 F
bgielow@hebrewcollege.edu
GIELOW, Bob .... 617-559-8610 210 F
bgielow@hebrewcollege.edu
GIENGER, Crystal .... 985-448-7909 188 C
crystal.gienger@fletcher.edu
GIER, David .... 734-764-0584 231 H
dgier@umich.edu
GIER, Matt .... 208-459-5846 131 C
mgier@collegeofidaho.edu
GIERBOLINI-SANTIAGO,
Rafael, L .... 787-993-8855 512 A
rafael.gierbolini@upr.edu
GIERI, Joe .... 505-454-3168 286 J
jgieri@nmhu.edu
GIEROK, Ed .... 503-554-2090 373 A
egierok@georgefox.edu
GIESCHEN, Charles, A .. 260-452-2104 154 I
charles.gieschen@ctsfw.edu
GIESE, Martin .... 218-751-8670 242 O
martingiese@oakhills.edu
GIESE, Melissa .... 816-604-1492 255 C
melissa.giese@mcckc.edu
GIESE, Michael .... 202-885-2200.. 91 F
mgiese@american.edu
GIESE, Ralph .... 719-255-4327.. 84 C
rgiese@uccs.edu
GIESECKE, Guy, B .... 601-815-7020 249 E
ggiesecke@umc.edu
GIESECKE, Marian, K .... 806-651-2055 448 B
mgiesecke@wtamu.edu
GIESEKE, Amy .... 515-961-1615 170 B
amy.gieseke@simpson.edu
GIESEKE, Elizabeth .... 763-488-2757 238 C
elizabeth.gieseke@hennepintech.edu
GIESS, Melissa .... 717-358-4391 383 I
mgiess@fandm.edu
GIETZEN, Garett .... 209-228-9780.. 70 A
ggietzen@ucmerced.edu
GIFFEN, Scott .... 618-664-6768 138 F
scott.giffen@greenville.edu
GIFFORD, Darcy .... 734-487-5375 223 K
dgiffor2@emich.edu
GIFFORD, Eva .... 704-978-1344 336 C
eeisnaugle@mitchellcc.edu
GIFFORD, Kirk .... 208-496-3807 130 I
giffordk@byui.edu
GIFFORD, Rachel .... 870-838-2902.. 17 B
rgifford@smail.anc.edu
GIFFORD, Rhonda .... 724-938-1510 393 E
gifford@calu.edu
GIFFORD, Roy .... 859-572-6565 184 E
giffordr2@nku.edu
GIFFROW, Tammy .... 281-756-3598 429 D
tgiffrow@alvincollege.edu
GIGER, Lisa .... 662-846-4035 245 G
lgiger@deltastate.edu
GIGLIOTTI, Chandra, M 410-827-5812 198 F
cgigliotti@chesapeake.edu
GIGLIOTTI, Kate .... 413-662-5074 213 C
kate.gigliotti@mcla.edu
GIGLIOTTI, Ralph .... 848-932-3965 282 A
ralph.gigliotti@rutgers.edu
GIGOT, Jeremy .... 620-276-9570 174 B
jeremy.gigot@gcccks.edu
GIGUETTE, Marguerite .. 504-520-7525 193 E
mgiguett@xula.edu
GIL, Andres .... 305-348-2494 110 A
andres.gil@fiu.edu
GIL, Sean .... 951-827-6063.. 70 B
sean.gil@ucr.edu
GIL GARCIA, Ana .... 773-878-8756 149 A
GILBECK, Paula .... 715-836-2637 495 E
GILBERT, Aerin .... 410-923-4585.. 93 H
GILBERT, Alan .... 718-951-5116 293 C
agilbert@brooklyn.cuny.edu
GILBERT, Bryan .... 512-313-4117 433 N
bryan.gilbert@concordia.edu
GILBERT, Charlene .... 419-530-2413 363 B
charlene.gilbert@utoledo.edu
GILBERT, Cherry .... 206-281-2009 483 G
cyueh@spu.edu
GILBERT, Corynn .... 541-684-7222 371 I
cgilbert@bushnell.edu
GILBERT, David, H .... 414-906-4670 496 B
dhg@uwm.edu
GILBERT, Demetrius ...... 501-374-6305.. 20 G
demetrius.gilbert@shortercollege.edu
GILBERT, Doris, J .... 936-261-3180 446 C
djgilbert@pvamu.edu
GILBERT, Emily, R .... 806-371-5403 429 E
e0400185@actx.edu
GILBERT, Faye .... 207-581-1951 196 G
faye.gilbert@maine.edu
GILBERT, Jan .... 308-367-5252 270 B
jgilbert3@unl.edu
GILBERT, Jarett .... 541-506-6025 372 F
jgilbert@cgcc.edu
GILBERT, Jerome, A ..... 304-696-3977 489 M
gilbert@marshall.edu
GILBERT, Jessica .... 518-381-1336 315 B
gilberjv@sunysccc.edu
GILBERT, Jon .... 252-737-4502 341 A
gilbertjo18@ecu.edu
GILBERT, Karen .... 404-471-6435 114 G
kgilbert@agnesscott.edu
GILBERT, Kelsey .... 207-974-4623 195 E
kgilbert@emcc.edu
GILBERT, Koshaneke ..... 225-771-2552 191 E
GILBERT, Larry .... 940-498-6282 440 F
lgilbert@nctc.edu
GILBERT, Linda, K .... 610-499-1168 402 G
lkgilbert@widener.edu
GILBERT, Michael .... 860-486-2265.. 89 D
michael.gilbert@uconn.edu
GILBERT, Michael .... 213-624-1200.. 42 B
mgilbert@fidm.edu
GILBERT, Mindy .... 615-514-2787 422 H
mgilbert@nossi.edu
GILBERT, Natalie .... 918-631-3247 371 C
nag4481@utulsa.edu
GILBERT, Peter, J .... 920-832-7353 493 B
peter.j.gilbert@lawrence.edu
GILBERT, Rhonda .... 319-226-2011 163 C
rhonda.gilbert@allencollege.edu
GILBERT, Robert .... 352-392-1784 111 A
ragilber@ufl.edu
GILBERT, Stacy .... 318-257-4730 192 D
stacyc@latech.edu
GILBERT, Trent .... 205-226-4694.... 4 F
trgilber@bsc.edu
GILBERT-BELL,
Lawanna .... 318-342-1039 193 C
lbell@ulm.edu
GILBERT-DEPRON,
Dianna .... 225-771-5050 191 A
dianna_gilbert@subr.edu
GILBERTSON, Jake .... 619-849-2253.. 57 J
jakegilbertson@pointloma.edu
GILBERTSON, Rick .... 605-331-6633 417 C
rick.gilbertson@usiouxfalls.edu
GILBERTSON, Sandi ...... 701-671-2904 346 D
sandi.gilbertson@ndscs.edu
GILBES SANTAELLA,
Fernando .... 787-265-3828 512 E
decano.arci@uprm.edu
GILCHRIST, Christi .... 208-562-2710 131 E
christigilchrist@cwi.edu
GILCHRIST, Sandra .... 941-487-4597 110 D
gilchrist@ncf.edu
GILCHRIST, Tamra .... 360-442-2621 481 D
tgilchrist@lowercolumbia.edu
GILCREASE, Kathy .... 936-294-1012 450 A
gilcrease@shsu.edu
GILCREAST, Emily .... 401-598-1953 404 D
emily.gilcreast@jwu.edu
GILDEA-BRODERICK,
Kate .... 801-957-4914 461 C
kate.gildea@slcc.edu
GILDNER, Justin .... 828-771-3029 344 D
jgildner@warren-wilson.edu
GILE, Jason .... 630-620-2105 146 C
jgile@faculty.seminary.edu
GILE, Joseph .... 316-942-4291 176 E
gilej@newmanu.edu
GILER, Will .... 516-463-5019 301 G
will.giler@hofstra.edu
GILES, Daniel .... 330-337-6403 347 D
bookstore@awc.edu
GILES, Kim .... 530-339-3664.. 64 C
kgiles@shastacollege.edu
GILES, Quincy .... 215-574-9600 385 K
GILES, Roger, W .... 870-235-4008.. 21 C
rwgiles@saumag.edu
GILES, Roni .... 724-480-3401 381 H
roni.giles@ccbc.edu
GILES, Wayne .... 312-996-5939 151 G
wgiles@uic.edu
GILFERT, Christy .... 239-985-3475 101 A
christy.gilfert@fsw.edu
GILFILLAN, Margaret .... 412-392-3994 396 G
mgilfillan@pointpark.edu
GILGALLON, James .... 570-208-8103 386 G
jamesgilgallon@kings.edu
GILGER, Jeffrey .... 209-228-4343.. 70 A
jgilger@ucmerced.edu
GILGOUR, Joe .... 573-518-2146 256 D
jgilgour@mineralarea.edu
GILKERSON,
Tammeil, Y .... 408-270-6471.. 62 G
tammeil.gilkerson@evc.edu
GILKEY, Shannon .... 859-256-3100 181 C
shannon.gilkey@kctcs.edu
GILL, Allison .... 978-837-5175 216 F
gilla@merrimack.edu
GILL, Alyson .... 828-898-8962 330 E
gilla@lmc.edu
GILL, Americus .... 434-592-7106 468 E
amgill@liberty.edu
GILL, Barbara, A .... 301-314-8350 202 H
bgill@umd.edu
GILL, Beth .... 903-813-2226 430 H
bgill@austincollege.edu
GILL, Casey .... 937-327-7801 364 D
gillc@wittenberg.edu
GILL, Coner .... 210-202-3700.. 93 H
GILL, Coner .... 512-568-3300.. 93 H
GILL, D. Chris .... 216-373-5181 357 F
dcgill@ndc.edu
GILL, Dana .... 616-395-7782 225 D
gill@hope.edu
GILL, Davie .... 727-341-4314 107 E
gill.davie@spcollege.edu
GILL, Jason .... 860-632-3020.. 88 C
jgill@holyapostles.edu
GILL, Jason .... 847-866-3987 138 D
jason.gill@garrett.edu
GILL, Lanae .... 313-993-1230 231 E
gillla@udmercy.edu
GILL, Lee, A .... 864-656-4238 407 E
lagill@clemson.edu
GILL, Mark, A .... 859-846-5364 184 B
mgill@midway.edu
GILL, Michele .... 402-844-7292 268 H
micheleg@northeast.edu
GILL, Nancy .... 805-437-8456.. 30 C
nancy.gill@csuci.edu
GILL, Paula .... 615-460-8637 418 B
paula.gill@belmont.edu
GILL, Ruth, F .... 410-334-2928 205 D
rgill@worwic.edu
GILL, Shelly .... 318-473-6417 189 F
sgill@lsua.edu
GILL, Steven .... 609-258-3466 280 D
sgill@princeton.edu
GILLAM, Jeremy .... 501-450-5004.. 23 H
jgillam@uca.edu
GILLAN, Darlene .... 617-879-7050 213 B
dgillan@massart.edu
GILLAN, Maria .... 973-684-5904 280 A
mgillan@pccc.edu
GILLAND, Laura .... 704-637-4410 327 I
lgwimpey@catawba.edu
GILLARD, Natalie .... 575-461-4413 286 G
natalieg@mesalands.edu
GILLASPIE, Ray .... 270-824-8592 182 D
ray.gillaspie@kctcs.edu
GILLE, Chaudron .... 706-864-1602 127 A
chaudron.gille@ung.edu
GILLECE, Nancy, E .... 301-696-3710 199 E
gillece@hood.edu
GILLEN, Dan .... 319-296-4268 166 H
daniel.gillen@hawkeyecollege.edu
GILLEN, Edward .... 401-841-2438 503 A
edward.gillen@usnwc.edu
GILLERLAIN, Kelly, T .... 757-822-5201 475 E
kgillerlain@tcc.edu
GILLESPIE, Aftin .... 719-587-7661.. 77 G
aftingillespie@adams.edu
GILLESPIE, Andrew, R ... 334-844-5009.... 4 D
arg0014@auburn.edu
GILLESPIE, Anne .... 319-363-1323 168 F
agillespie@mtmercy.edu
GILLESPIE, Bart .... 678-839-6582 127 C
bgillesp@westga.edu
GILLESPIE, Christine ..... 201-612-7488 275 H
cgillespie@bergen.edu
GILLESPIE, Dave .... 402-941-6545 267 L
gillespie@midlandu.edu
GILLESPIE, Deena .... 928-524-7365.. 14 J
deena.gillespie@npc.edu
GILLESPIE, Denise .... 225-768-1755 187 B
denise.gillespie@franu.edu
GILLESPIE, Denise .... 662-620-5368 246 E
dlgillespie@iccms.edu
GILLESPIE, Greg .... 805-652-5502.. 73 I
ggillespie@vcccd.edu
GILLESPIE, John .... 718-270-2262 317 B
john.gillespie@downstate.edu
GILLESPIE, Jon .... 210-829-3971 453 C
jong@uiwtx.edu
GILLESPIE, Joseph .... 215-885-2360 389 C
jgillespie@manor.edu
GILLESPIE, Kendra .... 703-284-1554 468 H
kendra.gillespie@marymount.edu
GILLESPIE, Lydia .... 503-255-0332 374 C
lydiagillespie@multnomah.edu
GILLESPIE, Melanie .... 864-646-2083 412 H
mgilles7@tctc.edu
GILLESPIE, Michele, K .. 336-758-5000 344 C
gillesmk@wfu.edu
GILLETT, Charisse, L .... 859-280-1230 183 F
cgillett@lextheo.edu
GILLETTE, Allyson .... 952-446-4177 235 J
gillettea@crown.edu
GILLETTE, John .... 608-785-9402 500 C
gillettej@westerntc.edu
GILLETTE, John .... 509-533-8378 479 B
john.gillette@ccs.spokane.edu
GILLETTE, John .... 509-533-8378 479 D
john.gillette@ccs.spokane.edu
GILLETTE, Kimberly .... 218-477-2959 239 E
kimberly.gillette@mnstate.edu
GILLETTE, Lynn .... 906-635-2211 226 G
lgillette@lssu.edu
GILLETTE, Susan .... 410-706-5353 203 A
sgillett@umaryland.edu
GILLEY, Michael .... 276-523-2400 474 D
mgilley@mecc.edu
GILLEY, Pam .... 318-255-7950 192 D
pam@latechalumni.org
GILLEY, Ryan .... 513-529-2107 356 A
gilleyrl@miamioh.edu
GILLIAM, Brock .... 803-641-3550 413 B
brockg@usca.edu

GILLIAM, Dara .... 405-695-5533 366 B
dgilliam@familyoffaith.edu
GILLIAM, Dara .... 405-273-5331 366 B
dgilliam@familyoffaith.edu
GILLIAM, Franklin, D .... 336-334-5266 343 A
chancellor@uncg.edu
GILLIAM, Glenna .... 479-308-2209.. 17 A
glenna.gilliam@arcomedu.org
GILLIAM, Janice .... 865-938-8186 419 B
janice.gilliam@thecrowncollege.edu
GILLIAM, Julie .... 336-322-2152 336 G
julie.gilliam@piedmontcc.edu
GILLIAM, Karla .... 864-941-8629 411 C
gilliam.k@ptc.edu
GILLIAM, Kevin .... 616-988-3695 226 E
kgilliam@kuyper.edu
GILLIAM, Melissa .... 773-795-5432 151 E
mgilliam@bsd.uchicago.edu
GILLIAM, Rebecca .... 318-670-9353 191 D
rgilliam@susla.edu
GILLIAM, Thomas, J ..... 850-484-1500 105 H
tgilliam@pensacolastate.edu
GILLIAM, Tom .... 850-484-1500 105 H
tgilliam@pensacolastate.edu
GILLIAM-HOLMES,
Sheraine .... 931-221-7179 417 H
gilliams@apsu.edu
GILLIAM-HOLMES,
Sheraine .... 214-752-5532 453 E
sheraine.gilliam@untsystem.edu
GILLIAM JOHNSON,
Patrice .... 302-857-6000.. 90 E
pgjohnson@desu.edu
GILLIAM-WILLIAMS,
Bennie .... 314-340-3506 254 A
gilliamb@hssu.edu
GILLIARD, Dewayne, J .. 410-651-2200 203 D
GILLIARD, Heidi .... 503-399-5237 372 B
heidi.gilliard@chemeketa.edu
GILLIE, Esther .... 757-352-4182 470 B
egillie@regent.edu
GILLIE, Lynn, L .... 607-735-1804 298 H
lgillie@elmira.edu
GILLIES, Cheryl .... 626-396-2278.. 26 B
cheryl.gillies@artcenter.edu
GILLIES, Pamela .... 646-768-5300 300 G
GILLIES, Shawne .... 617-266-2030 217 D
gilliess@neco.edu
GILLIGAN, William .... 617-824-8525 209 C
william_gilligan@emerson.edu
GILLILAN, Kevin .... 406-994-4788 264 C
kevin.gillilan@montana.edu
GILLILAND, Austin, A ... 617-228-2420 214 C
agillila@bhcc.edu
GILLILAND, Brandon ..... 305-284-2258 113 C
bgilliland@miami.edu
GILLILAND,
Brandon, M .... 716-673-3253 316 D
brandon.gilliland@fredonia.edu
GILLILAND, Christie ...... 253-833-9111 480 I
cgilliland@greenriver.edu
GILLILAND, Cody .... 406-586-3585 263 I
cody.gilliland@montanabiblecollege.edu
GILLILAND, Jane, A ...... 607-871-2159 290 B
gilliland@alfred.edu
GILLILAND, Mary, K ..... 520-494-5210.. 11 K
maryk.gilliland@centralaz.edu
GILLIN, Douglas, P ...... 828-262-7781 340 I
gillindp@appstate.edu
GILLING RAYNOR,
Beatrice .... 718-951-5778 293 C
braynor@brooklyn.cuny.edu
GILLINS, Dawn .... 914-606-6844 325 A
dawn.gillins@sunywcc.edu
GILLIS, Arthur .... 225-743-8500 188 H
agillis@rpcc.edu
GILLIS, Diane .... 617-984-1700 218 C
GILLIS, Lynette .... 512-313-5301 433 N
lynette.gillis@concordia.edu
GILLIS-OLION, Marion .. 910-672-2525 341 C
molion@uncfsu.edu
GILLISPIE, James .... 540-868-7042 474 C
jgillispie@lfcc.edu
GILLISS, Buster .... 701-224-5512 346 A
buster.gilliss@bismarckstate.edu
GILLISS, Catherine .... 415-476-1805.. 70 D
catherine.gilliss@ucsf.edu
GILLMAN, Howard, A .... 949-824-5111.. 69 D
chancellor@uci.edu
GILLMAN, Sally .... 605-688-6094 417 A
sally.gillman@sdstate.edu
GILLOOLY, Jeffrey .... 508-793-7512 208 C
jgillooly@clarku.edu
GILLS, Twyla .... 713-785-5995 432 L

GILLUM, Deborah .... 574-807-7015 154 B
deborah.gillum@bethel university.edu
GILLUS, Raynaldo .... 662-254-3636 248 B
raynaldo.gillus@mvsu.edu
GILMAN, Isaac .... 503-352-1401 375 C
gilmani@pacificu.edu
GILMAN, James, T .... 203-932-7015.. 89 H
jgilman@newhaven.edu
GILMAN, Regis, M .... 252-328-9317 341 A
gilmanr16@ecu.edu
GILMAN, Wendy .... 518-255-5520 319 C
gilmanwc@cobleskill.edu
GILMARTIN, Kevin, M .. 626-395-6100.. 28 J
kmg@hss.caltech.edu
GILMER, Christopher .... 304-424-8200 490 F
president@wvup.edu
GILMER, Ray .... 240-567-7970 200 G
ray.gilmer@montgomerycollege.edu
GILMORE, Blaine .... 859-572-6449 184 E
gilmoreb@nku.edu
GILMORE, Bradley .... 706-802-5479 119 D
bgilmore@highlands.edu
GILMORE, Brent .... 562-938-4311.. 48 F
bgilmore@lbcc.edu
GILMORE, Calvin, L ...... 336-272-7102 329 C
gilmorec@greensboro.edu
GILMORE, Darwin .... 850-718-2270.. 97 E
gilmored@chipola.edu
GILMORE, David .... 617-989-4328 219 F
gilmored@wit.edu
GILMORE, Derrick, C .... 205-349-4240.... 7 A
dgilmore@stillman.edu
GILMORE, Don .... 661-362-2811.. 51 D
dgilmore@masters.edu
GILMORE, Donna .... 239-590-7582 109 K
dgilmore@fgcu.edu
GILMORE, Eric, J .... 402-280-2100 266 H
ericgilmore@creighton.edu
GILMORE, Grover, C ..... 216-368-2270 349 D
gcg@case.edu
GILMORE, John, W .... 609-497-7700 280 C
john.gilmore@ptsem.edu
GILMORE, Katrina .... 661-654-3330.. 30 B
kgilmore2@csub.edu
GILMORE, Paul .... 848-932-0990 282 A
paul.gilmore@rutgers.edu
GILMORE, Robert .... 914-323-5357 305 B
robert.gilmore@mville.edu
GILMORE, Thomas .... 712-325-3288 167 I
tgilmore@iwcc.edu
GILMORE, Wayne .... 617-353-8289 207 E
waygil@bu.edu
GILMORE-CLEVELAND,
Sherie .... 925-631-4552.. 59 I
sbg2@stmarys-ca.edu
GILMORE ENGLISH,
Jessica .... 425-235-2463 482 H
jgilmoreenglishl@rtc.edu
GILMOUR, Davie, J .... 570-320-8010 391 G
djg120@psu.edu
GILMOUR, Davie Jane .. 570-326-3761 392W
dgilmour@pct.edu
GILORMINI, Dominique 787-766-1912 509 A
dgilormini@inter.edu
GILORMINI-DE GRACIA,
Dominique, A .... 787-763-4203 507 J
dgilormini@inter.edu
GILPERT, Jessica .... 610-647-4400 385 L
jgilpert@immaculata.edu
GILPIN, Sandy .... 505-566-3022 288 D
gilpins@sanjuancollege.edu
GILREATH, Scott .... 765-677-6515 158 B
scott.gilreath@indwes.edu
GILROY, Janice .... 914-606-6610 325 A
janice.gilroy@sunywcc.edu
GILROY, Maryellen .... 518-783-2328 315 E
mgilroy@siena.edu
GILSON, Jannie .... 508-588-9100 215 A
jgilson1@massasoit.mass.edu
GILSTRAP, Donald .... 205-348-7561.... 7 G
dlgilstrap@ua.edu
GILTNER, Greg .... 405-425-5501 367 C
greg.giltner@oc.edu
GILTNER, Scott .... 573-288-6382 252 F
sgiltner@culver.edu
GIMNESS, Erik .... 253-964-6529 482 E
egimness@pierce.ctc.edu
GINDER, Greg .... 317-955-6018 159 K
gginder@marian.edu
GINDICESSI, Beth .... 415-503-6285.. 61 D
egindicessi@sfcm.edu
GINES, D. Scott .... 302-857-6030.. 90 E
dgines@desu.edu

GINEVAN, Douglas, W .. 207-786-6093 194 A
dginevan@bates.edu
GINGERELLA, David ...... 508-999-8051 212 A
dgingerella@umassd.edu
GINGERICH, Jeff .... 570-941-7520 401 F
jeffrey.gingerich@scranton.edu
GINGERICH, Tamara ..... 219-464-6196 162 D
tamara.gingerich@valpo.edu
GINGLES, Haley, N .... 336-750-3152 344 A
gingleshn@wssu.edu
GINGRAS, Gregory .... 510-879-9267.. 60 C
ggingras@samuelmerritt.edu
GINN, Bryan .... 678-225-7500 395 G
bginn@pcom.edu
GINN, Julie .... 781-239-2734 214 G
jginn@massbay.edu
GINN, Mark .... 828-262-2070 340 I
ginnmc@appstate.edu
GINNETTI, Jennifer .... 215-646-7300 385 A
ginnetti.j@gmercyu.edu
GINSBERG, Amy .... 973-720-2594 284 J
ginsberga3@wpunj.edu
GINSBERG, Mark .... 703-993-5399 467 E
mginsber@gmu.edu
GINSBERG, Richard .... 718-289-5770 293 B
richard.ginsberg@bcc.cuny.edu
GINSBERG, Rick .... 785-864-4297 177 J
ginsberg@ku.edu
GINSBURG, Charles, M 214-648-8597 457 A
charles.ginsburg@utsouthwestern.edu
GINTER, Judy .... 859-985-3767 179 I
ginterj@berea.edu
GINTER, Matthew .... 419-434-5624 362 D
ginterm@findlay.edu
GINTNER, Robin .... 541-867-8516 374 F
robin.gintner@oregoncoast.edu
GINTY, Kevin .... 773-508-2204 143 C
kginty@luc.edu
GIOGLIO, Tom .... 570-484-2102 394 E
tmg252@lockhaven.edu
GIOIOSO, JR.,
Domenic .... 603-526-3698 272 H
domenic.gioioso@colby-sawyer.edu
GIONFRIDDO, Elizabeth 508-213-2113 217 H
elizabeth.gionfriddo@nichols.edu
GIORDANI, Robert .... 410-704-3508 204 E
rgiordani@towson.edu
GIORDANO, Amy .... 567-661-7883 359 I
amy_giordano@owens.edu
GIORDANO,
Christopher .... 810-762-3434 232 A
giordanc@umich.edu
GIORDANO, Matthew .... 716-896-0700 324 E
giordano@villa.edu
GIORDANO,
Nicholas, J .... 334-844-5737.... 4 D
njg0003@auburn.edu
GIORDANO, Steve .... 615-547-1225 419 C
sgiordano@cumberland.edu
GIORDANO, Victoria ..... 863-680-5080 100 H
vgiordano@flsouthern.edu
GIOVAGNOLI, Michelle . 570-208-5847 386 G
michellegiovagnoli@kings.edu
GIOVANNELLI, Tony ..... 724-964-8811 391 B
tgiovannelli@ncstrades.edu
GIOVANNINI,
Eugene, V .... 817-515-5201 445 F
chancellors.office@tccd.edu
GIPE, Jason .... 919-658-7637 340 G
jgipe@umo.edu
GIPKO, Jesse .... 740-699-9500 348 E
jgipko@belmontcollege.edu
GIPSON, Amy .... 386-822-7220 112 A
agipson@stetson.edu
GIPSON, Cory .... 903-730-4890 438 D
cgipson@jarvis.edu
GIPSON, Dee .... 239-304-7977.. 95 M
dee.gipson@avemaria.edu
GIPSON, Keith .... 719-846-5577.. 83 L
keith.gipson@trinidadstate.edu
GIPSON, Maurice .... 573-882-3394 260 I
mdgipson@missouri.edu
GIPSON, Maurice, D .... 573-882-3394 261 A
mdgipson@missouri.edu
GIPSON, Pamela .... 540-515-3749 464 L
pgipson@bridgewater.edu
GIPSON, Patrick .... 773-602-5524 135 D
pgipson2@ccc.edu
GIPSON, Richard .... 817-257-2787 448 F
r.gipson@tcu.edu
GIPSON, Tim .... 760-872-2000.. 40 I
tgipson@deepsprings.edu
GIPSON, William .... 215-898-0809 400 F
wgipson@exchange.upenn.edu

GIRALDO, Luis .... 805-965-0581.. 63 A
lggiraldo@sbcc.edu
GIRALDO, Maribel .... 914-594-4696 309 B
mgiraldo2@nymc.edu
GIRANDOLA, Joe .... 513-562-8743 347 I
president@artacademy.edu
GIRARD, Angela .... 562-985-5146.. 31 D
angela.girard@csulb.edu
GIRARD, Angie .... 509-452-5100 482 B
agirard@pnwu.edu
GIRARD, David .... 719-384-6818.. 82 D
david.girard@ojc.edu
GIRARD, Don .... 310-434-4287.. 63 C
girard_donald@smc.edu
GIRARD, Joseph, C ...... 401-841-2245 503 A
joseph.girard@usnwc.edu
GIRARD, Preble .... 337-475-5243 192 E
preble@mcneese.edu
GIRARD, Samantha .... 619-216-6762.. 66 A
sgirard@swccd.edu
GIRARD-MALLEY,
Jenny .... 510-436-1081.. 45 E
girard-malley@hnu.edu
GIRARDEAU, Cathy .... 912-650-5672 125 F
cgirardeau@southuniversity.edu
GIRARDOT, Steven .... 404-385-7344 119 E
steven.girardot@gatech.edu
GIRARDOT, Steven .... 404-894-5551 119 E
steven.girardot@gatech.edu
GIRAUD, Gerald .... 307-754-6235 501 H
gerald.giraud@nwc.edu
GIRELLI, Carl, A .... 434-947-8126 469 E
cgirelli@randolphcollege.edu
GIRGIS, Ibrahim .... 304-326-1259 487 I
ibrahim.girgis@salemu.edu
GIRNUS, Josh, C .... 253-535-7476 482 A
girnusjc@plu.edu
GIROD, Douglas, A ...... 785-864-3131 177 J
dgirod@ku.edu
GIROD, Mark .... 503-838-8471 377 D
girodm@wou.edu
GIROIR, Elizabeth .... 337-482-5930 193 B
elizabeth.giroir@louisiana.edu
GIRON, Jenny .... 915-831-6571 436 A
jgiron6@epcc.edu
GIROUX, Jenifer .... 401-456-8990 405 A
jgiroux@ric.edu
GIRTEN, Kathryn .... 765-973-8201 157 A
kathcruz@iue.edu
GIRTON, Kaitlin .... 718-390-3100 324 F
GISH, Jennifer .... 518-337-5694 296 G
gishj@strose.edu
GISH, Joanne .... 805-565-6066.. 76 A
jgish@westmont.edu
GISS, Gary .... 315-279-2969 303 G
ggiss@keuka.edu
GISSELER, Adam .... 815-825-2086 141 F
agisseler@kish.edu
GISSENDANNER,
Cindy, H .... 410-704-5456 204 E
cgissendanner@towson.edu
GISSY, Cynthia .... 304-424-8259 490 F
cindy.gissy@wvup.edu
GIST, Vicki .... 406-265-3706 264 E
gist@msun.edu
GITAU, Peter .... 530-895-2511.. 27 C
GITLIN, Laura, N .... 267-359-5957 382 F
laura.n.gitlin@drexel.edu
GITTELL, Ross .... 401-232-6008 404 A
rgitt@bryant.edu
GITTENS, Brian, E .... 501-603-1159.. 22 B
bgittens@uams.edu
GITTENS, Carol Ann ..... 925-631-4012.. 59 I
cgittens@stmarys-ca.edu
GITTENS, Cheryl .... 608-262-5175 495 D
cheryl.gittens@wisc.edu
GITTINGS, Carl, W .... 304-457-6243 486 E
gittingscw@ab.edu
GITTINGS-CARLSON,
Laura .... 406-657-2240 264 D
l.gittingscarlson@msubillings.edu
GITTLEMAN, John, L .... 706-542-2968 126 G
ecohead@uga.edu
GIUFFI, Krista .... 312-942-2569 148 G
krista_m_giuffi@rush.edu
GIUFFRIDA, Andrea ...... 210-567-4219 456 C
giuffrida@uthscsa.edu
GIUFRE, Matt .... 845-257-3910 316 E
giufrem@newpaltz.edu
GIUNTA, Bridget .... 570-408-4134 403 A
bridget.giunta@wilkes.edu
GIUSTI, Linda .... 916-577-2305.. 76 D
lgiusti@jessup.edu

GMITTER, Elizabeth .... 312-850-4595 135 H
egmitter@ccc.edu
GNADINGER, Cindy ...... 262-524-7246 492 A
cgnadinger@carrollu.edu
GNAN, Peter, D .... 708-209-3192 136 E
peter.gnan@cuchicago.edu
GNARRA, James .... 941-782-5957 387 D
jgnarra@lecom.edu
GNINGUE, Serigne .... 718-960-8000 294 A
GOATELY, Virginia .... 518-442-5080 316 A
vgoatley@albany.edu
GOBEN, Jason .... 606-693-5000 183 C
jgoben@kmbc.edu
GOBER, Jaclyn .... 215-572-5511 402 E
jgober@wts.edu
GOBER, Steve .... 859-858-3581 179 C
GOBER, T. Kale .... 602-639-7500.. 12 J
GOBERIS, Lisa .... 303-273-3230.. 79 J
lgoberis@mines.edu
GOBERISH, John, S ...... 724-480-3450 381 H
john.goberish@ccbc.edu
GOBERMAN, Alex .... 419-372-7710 348 G
goberma@bgsu.edu
GOBIEL, Eric .... 508-213-2351 217 H
eric.gobiel@nichols.edu
GOBLE, Bryen-Lynn ...... 606-886-3863 181 E
bryen.goble@kctcs.edu
GOBLE, Luke .... 503-517-1074 377 C
lgoble@warnerpacific.edu
GOBLIRSCH, James ...... 507-457-5045 241 F
jgoblirsch@winona.edu
GOCHENAUER, Kristan . 262-691-5211 500 B
kgochenauer@wctc.edu
GOCHENAUR,
Heather, K .... 260-982-5873 159 J
hkgochenaur@manchester.edu
GOCHIS, Cheryl .... 254-710-2000 431 E
cheryl_gochis@baylor.edu
GOCHIS, Suzanne .... 816-604-1033 255 C
suzanne.gochis@mcckc.edu
GOCIAL, Tammy .... 314-529-6893 255 B
tgocial@maryville.edu
GOCKLEY, Daniel, L ...... 214-458-6200 455 E
daniel.gockley@utsa.edu
GODARD, Michael .... 573-651-2063 259 H
mgodard@semo.edu
GODBEE, Sara .... 443-334-2688 202 E
sgodbee@stevenson.edu
GODDARD, Amy .... 405-224-3140 371 B
agoddard@usao.edu
GODDARD, Courtney .... 660-543-4157 260 G
cgoddard@ucmo.edu
GODDARD, Deanna ...... 507-457-2493 241 F
dgoddard@winona.edu
GODDARD, Jerry .... 661-946-2274.. 74 H
GODDARD, Lisa .... 916-306-1628.. 67 F
lgoddard@sum.edu
GODDARD, Nick .... 303-352-3053.. 80 F
nick.goddard@ccd.edu
GODDARD, Scott, D ..... 304-637-1352 487 C
goddards@dewv.edu
GODDARD MCGUIRK,
Lisa .... 814-871-7664 384 A
mcguirk001@gannon.edu
GODDEN, Barb .... 712-325-3320 167 I
bgodden@iwcc.edu
GODDING, Courtney ..... 325-793-6548 439 F
godding.courtney@mcm.edu
GODDING, Jesse .... 972-825-4811 444 J
jgodding@sagu.edu
GODEK, Jim .... 949-376-6000.. 47 D
jgodek@lcad.edu
GODES, Iris .... 508-541-1547 209 A
igodes@dean.edu
GODFREY, Rodney .... 662-241-7636 248 A
ragodfrey@muw.edu
GODFREY, SJ,
Timothy, S .... 415-422-6272.. 72 J
tgodfrey@usfca.edu
GODFREY-DAWSON,
Angela, R .... 252-335-0821 333 G
adawson@albemarle.edu
GODIN, Eric .... 305-625-6576 107 F
egodin@stu.edu
GODINA, Rafael .... 773-838-7516 135 F
rgodina1@ccc.edu
GODINEZ, Bobby .... 323-780-6722.. 48 J
godinerj@elac.edu
GODLESKI, Kasha .... 315-445-4772 303 I
godleska@lemoyne.edu
GODLESKI, Mark, G ...... 315-445-4520 303 I
godlesmg@lemoyne.edu

GODLEY, Amanda, J ..... 412-624-2137 400 H
agodley@pitt.edu
GODMAN, Christi .... 859-442-1684 181 H
christi.godman@kctcs.edu
GODNEY, Elmer .... 979-209-7575 431 H
elmer.godney@blinn.edu
GODO, James .... 630-637-5809 145 F
jwgodo@noctrl.edu
GODOY, Cuauhtemoc ... 787-622-8000 511 D
cgodoy@pupr.edu
GODOY, Sarah .... 360-650-3164 485 I
sarah.godoy@wwu.edu
GODSEY, R. Kirby .... 478-330-5612 122 E
godsey_rk@mercer.edu
GODULA, Amanda .... 724-552-1369 398 C
agodula@setonhill.edu
GODWIN, Donald, A ..... 505-272-0907 288 J
dgodwin@salud.unm.edu
GODWIN, Donald, R .... 619-260-4588.. 72 I
donald.godwin@sandiego.edu
GODWIN, Hilary .... 206-543-1144 485 A
hgodwin@uw.edu
GODWIN, Lewis .... 301-846-2674 198 I
lgodwin@frederick.edu
GODWIN, Norman .... 334-844-5774.... 4 D
godwinh@auburn.edu
GODWIN, Wendell .... 580-559-5274 365 K
wgodwin@ecok.edu
GODWYLL, Francis .... 309-298-1690 153 A
fe-godwyll@wiu.edu
GODZWA, Alicia .... 540-362-6660 467 H
agodzwa@hollins.edu
GOEBEL, Dan .... 585-395-5537 317 E
dgoebel@brockport.edu
GOEBELBECKER, Eric .... 407-303-9798.. 95 B
eric.goebelbecker@ahu.edu
GOEBELER, Stefanie ...... 803-695-3687 410 D
goebelers@midlandstech.edu
GOEL, Meeta .... 661-722-6300.. 26 A
mgoel@avc.edu
GOELDNER, Jason .... 715-365-4534 499 E
jgoeldner@nicoletcollege.edu
GOELLER, Linda .... 405-382-9210 369 F
l.goeller@sscok.edu
GOELLNER, Erik .... 401-598-1251 404 D
erik.goellner@jwu.edu
GOELLNER, Marilyn ...... 814-732-1778 394 B
mgoellner@edinboro.edu
GOEMAN, Peter .... 919-573-5350 340 C
pgoeman@shepherds.edu
GOEN, Brandon .... 806-720-7313 439 D
brandon.goen@lcu.edu
GOEN, Jennifer .... 239-590-1020 109 K
jgoen@fgcu.edu
GOEPPINGER,
Kathleen, H .... 630-515-7300 144 F
drgoeppinger@midwestern.edu
GOERTZEN, Karen .... 503-375-7104 372 H
kgoertzen@corban.edu
GOERTZEN, Leroy .... 503-375-7103 372 H
lgoertzen@corban.edu
GOES, Paulo .... 520-621-2125.. 16 D
pgoes@arizona.edu
GOETCHIUS, Stephen .... 860-215-9002.. 87 F
sgoetchius@threerivers.edu
GOETCHIUS,
Stephen, H .... 860-215-9002.. 87 F
sgoetchius@threerivers.edu
GOETSCH, John .... 661-946-2274.. 74 H
GOETSCH, Steven .... 603-641-7500 274 A
sgoetsch@anselm.edu
GOETTL, Randi .... 651-450-3884 238 E
rgoettl@inverhills.edu
GOETZ, Beth .... 765-285-5131 153 H
bgoetz@bsu.edu
GOETZ, Michael, A .... 414-847-3305 494 C
mikegoetz@miad.edu
GOETZ, Michele .... 619-594-1862.. 33 D
mgoetz@sdsu.edu
GOETZ, Whitney .... 423-439-1000 419 G
GOFF, David .... 303-724-7304.. 84 D
david.goff@ucdenver.edu
GOFF, Jay .... 202-994-6710.. 92 D
jwgoff@gwu.edu
GOFF, Karen .... 440-775-8462 357 G
kgoff@oberlin.edu
GOFF, Kim .... 916-558-2054.. 50 J
goffk@scc.losrios.edu
GOFF, Margot, H .... 979-845-7293 446 F
margot_goff@tamu.edu
GOFF, Pamela .... 304-326-1304 487 I
pgoff@salemu.edu

GOFF, Patricia, A .... 401-865-1031 404 F
pgoff@providence.edu
GOFF, Sue .... 503-594-3110 372 C
sue.goff@clackamas.edu
GOFF, Travis .... 785-864-3143 177 J
kuathletics@ku.edu
GOFF-CREWS, Kimberly 203-432-6602.. 90 C
kimberly.goff-crews@yale.edu
GOFFE, Lorraine .... 814-863-6188 391 G
lag5792@psu.edu
GOFFE-MCNISH, Jackie . 845-431-8445 298 D
mcnish@sunydutchess.edu
GOFORTH, Cheri, D ...... 501-686-5850.. 22 B
goforthcherid@uams.edu
GOFORTH, Glen .... 936-633-5240 429 J
ggoforth@angelina.edu
GOGA, Nedzad .... 718-636-3599 311 F
ngoga@pratt.edu
GOGAL, Mark .... 910-521-4615 343 B
mark.gogal@uncp.edu
GOGERTY, Andrew .... 515-964-0601 166 D
gogertya@faith.edu
GOGGIN, Nan .... 317-278-9470 157 D
ngoggin@iu.edu
GOGOLA, Eva .... 313-593-5495 231 I
egronows@umich.edu
GOGU, Longin .... 281-290-3772 439 C
longin.gogu@lonestar.edu
GOGUE, Jay .... 334-844-4650.... 4 D
president@auburn.edu
GOH, Michael .... 612-624-0594 243 F
mgoh@umn.edu
GOHDE, Amanda .... 715-645-7042 499 H
amanda.gohde@northwoodtech.edu
GOHEEN, Peter .... 207-551-5765 195 G
pgoheen@nmcc.edu
GOHL, Pam .... 605-331-6652 417 C
pam.gohl@usiouxfalls.edu
GOHMANN, Jennifer ..... 502-585-9911 184 H
jgohmann@spalding.edu
GOIN, JR., Randy .... 717-720-4010 393 C
rgoin@passhe.edu
GOINES, Daniel (Dee) ... 972-780-3600 454 A
daniel.goines@untdallas.edu
GOINES, Pamela .... 513-792-8625 362 A
pamela.goines@uc.edu
GOINGS, Andrea .... 419-995-8302 360 C
goings.a@rhodesstate.edu
GOINGS, Tyson .... 419-358-3306 348 F
goingst@bluffton.edu
GOINS, Jennifer .... 804-627-5300 464 K
jennifer_goins@bshsi.org
GOINS, Jessica, D .... 864-488-4590 410 B
jgoins@limestone.edu
GOINS, Jody .... 423-869-6725 421 A
jody.goins@lmunet.edu
GOINS, LaKeya .... 205-366-8150.... 7 A
lgoins@stillman.edu
GOINS, Melissa .... 936-633-5215 429 J
mgoins@angelina.edu
GOINS, Scot .... 678-916-2652 115 I
sgoins@johnmarshall.edu
GOINS, Scott, E .... 337-475-5456 192 E
sgoins@mcneese.edu
GOINS, Suzanne .... 251-460-6111.... 9 A
sgoins@southalabama.edu
GOKCEK, Gigi .... 415-482-2427.. 41 C
gigi.gokcek@dominican.edu
GOKE-PARIOLA,
Abiodun .... 630-637-5356 145 F
agokepariola@noctrl.edu
GOLA, Kate .... 413-585-2200 218 H
kgola@smith.edu
GOLABEK, Sue .... 843-208-8144 413 C
sgolabek@uscb.edu
GOLAN, Linda .... 754-312-2898 103 R
GOLAND, Lois .... 518-782-6673 315 E
lgoland@siena.edu
GOLAR, Norman .... 205-349-4240.... 7 A
ngolar@stillman.edu
GOLATO, Andrea .... 512-245-2581 450 C
a_g554@txstate.edu
GOLAY, David, R .... 757-446-5890 466 D
golaydr@evms.edu
GOLBA, Gina .... 816-802-3397 254 D
ggolba@kcai.edu
GOLD, Chris .... 310-660-3735.. 41 E
cgold@elcamino.edu
GOLD, E .... 212-964-2830 306 F
egold@mtj.edu
GOLD, Ellen .... 734-487-1107 223 K
egold@emich.edu

GOLD, Harriet, B .... 270-384-8018 183 G
goldh@lindsey.edu
GOLD, Jeffery, P .... 402-559-4201 269 K
jeffrey.gold@unmc.edu
GOLD, Jeffrey .... 402-472-7117 269 H
jeffrey.gold@nebraska.edu
GOLD, Jered .... 626-396-2251.. 26 B
jered.gold@artcenter.edu
GOLD, Julie .... 518-783-4239 315 E
jgold@siena.edu
GOLD, Kimberly .... 919-807-7100 331 L
GOLDAMMER, Diana ..... 605-995-2997 415 A
diana.goldammer@dwu.edu
GOLDBART, Paul, M ...... 631-632-6265 317 A
provost@stonybrook.edu
GOLDBERG, Amy .... 212-674-5300 301 B
GOLDBERG, Amy, J ...... 215-707-5078 399 B
amy.goldberg@temple.edu
GOLDBERG, David .... 517-265-5161 220 G
dgoldberg@adrian.edu
GOLDBERG, Dovid .... 440-943-5300 360 A
dgoldberg@telsheyeshiva.edu
GOLDBERG, Elaine .... 646-565-6136 322 F
elaine.goldberg@touro.edu
GOLDBERG, Elaine .... 646-565-6136 322 G
elaine.goldberg@touro.edu
GOLDBERG, Maureen ... 805-965-0581.. 63 A
mmgoldberg@pipeline.sbcc.edu
GOLDBERG, Robert .... 909-621-8132.. 57 K
robert.goldberg@pomona.edu
GOLDBERG, Steven .... 706-446-4482 116 A
stgoldberg@augusta.edu
GOLDBERG, Yisroel ...... 973-267-9404 280 F
financialaid@rca.edu
GOLDBERGBELLE,
Jonathan .... 217-206-8319 152 A
jgold1@uis.edu
GOLDBERGER, David .... 845-783-9901 324 A
GOLDBERGER, Jo .... 212-229-5192 308 A
jogo@newschool.edu
GOLDBLUM, Tom .... 610-989-1329 401 I
tgoldblum@vfmac.edu
GOLDEN, Andrew, K ..... 609-258-4136 280 D
agolden@princeton.edu
GOLDEN, Beverley .... 903-566-7303 456 A
bgolden@uttyler.edu
GOLDEN, Cheryl .... 316-942-4291 176 E
goldenc@newmanu.edu
GOLDEN, Chris .... 423-614-8020 420 H
cgolden@leeuniversity.edu
GOLDEN, Cynthia .... 412-624-3335 400 H
goldenc@pitt.edu
GOLDEN, Denise .... 814-871-7663 384 A
golden007@gannon.edu
GOLDEN, Kathie, S .... 662-254-3800 248 B
ksgolden@mvsu.edu
GOLDEN, Kendra, J ...... 509-527-4952 486 B
golden@whitman.edu
GOLDEN, Leslie, B .... 407-582-3466 113 I
lgolden@valenciacollege.edu
GOLDEN, Matthew .... 973-596-5286 279 E
matthew.golden@njit.edu
GOLDEN, Michelle .... 901-761-9494 419 A
GOLDEN, Paul .... 570-586-2400 381 B
pgolden@clarkssummitu.edu
GOLDEN, Rebecca .... 386-752-1822 100 B
rebecca.golden@fgc.edu
GOLDEN, Robert, N ...... 608-263-4910 495 D
rngolden@wisc.edu
GOLDEN, Teresa .... 580-745-2286 369 G
tgolden@se.edu
GOLDEN-BATTLE, Julia . 617-732-2058 216 D
julia.golden-battle@mcphs.edu
GOLDEN-BOTTI, Julie ... 561-297-4204 109 J
goldenj@fau.edu
GOLDENBERG,
David, H .... 860-768-4055.. 89 G
goldenber@hartford.edu
GOLDENBERG, Isabel ... 202-741-2656.. 92 D
iag@gwu.edu
GOLDENBERG, Jay .... 646-216-2862 308 G
jgoldenberg@nycda.edu
GOLDENBERG, Mary ..... 847-491-2005 146 E
m-goldenberg@northwestern.edu
GOLDEY, Ellen, S .... 859-238-5226 180 B
ellen.goldey@centre.edu
GOLDFEIZ, Emanuel ..... 410-653-0433 201 C
GOLDGEIER, Eileen ...... 401-863-9900 403 J
eileen_goldgeier@brown.edu
GOLDHABER,
Yochanan .... 718-232-7800 325 H
GOLDIN, Michael .... 269-467-9945 224 C
mgoldin@glenoaks.edu

GONZALEZ, Anna, K ..... 314-935-5949 262 A anna.gonzalez@wustl.edu
GONZALEZ, Aurelia .... 209-575-7707.. 77 A gonzaleza@mjc.edu
GONZALEZ, Aurora .... 787-738-2161 512 C aurora.gonzalez2@upr.edu
GONZALEZ, Beatriz .... 305-237-3310 104 E bgonza6@mdc.edu
GONZALEZ, Carla .... 313-664-7431 222 H cgonzalez@collegeforcreativestudies.edu
GONZALEZ, Carlos, J .... 787-622-8000 511 D gonzalez@pupr.edu
GONZALEZ, Carlos, R ... 818-364-7778.. 49 C gonzalcr@lamission.edu
GONZALEZ, Celia .... 787-844-8181 513 A celia.gonzalez@upr.edu
GONZALEZ, Claudia ...... 305-348-2111 110 A clgonzal@fiu.edu
GONZALEZ, Danielle ..... 413-597-2681 220 D dg3@williams.edu
GONZALEZ, Deena .... 509-313-4780 480 F gonzalez@gonzaga.edu
GONZALEZ, Diane, R .... 909-869-4051.. 30 A dianeg@cpp.edu
GONZALEZ, Edith .... 212-817-7530 293 F egonzalez@gc.cuny.edu
GONZALEZ, Elba .... 773-878-3194 149 A
GONZALEZ, Ernesto ...... 305-821-3333 100 E egonzalez@fnu.edu
GONZALEZ, Fernando ... 787-665-7910 506 D fgonzalez@columbiacentral.edu
GONZALEZ, Francisco .. 619-660-4621.. 44 D francisco.gonzalez@gcccd.edu
GONZALEZ, George ...... 281-998-6177 442 K george.gonzalez@sjcd.edu
GONZALEZ, Gina, D ..... 956-326-2206 446 E gina@tamiu.edu
GONZALEZ, Griselda ..... 212-217-3363 299 D griselda_gonzalez@fitnyc.edu
GONZALEZ, JR., Guillermo, E .... 956-326-2232 446 E guillermo.gonzalez@tamiu.edu
GONZALEZ, JR., Guillermo, F .... 956-326-3023 446 E guillermo@tamiu.edu
GONZALEZ, Herman ..... 602-787-6601.. 13 E herman.gonzalez@paradisevalley.edu
GONZALEZ, Ian .... 414-288-1766 493 E ian.gonzalez@marquette.edu
GONZALEZ, Iris .... 787-878-5475 507 L ibgonzalez@arecibo.inter.edu
GONZALEZ, Irma .... 760-921-5552.. 56 A irma.gonzalez@paloverde.edu
GONZALEZ, Isabel .... 954-201-7072.. 96 F igonzal2@broward.edu
GONZALEZ, Jaime .... 787-620-2040 505 C carroyo@aupr.edu
GONZALEZ, Jaime .... 787-620-2040 505 C jgonzalez@aupr.edu
GONZALEZ, Jean .... 714-867-5009.. 65 A jgonzalez@southcoastcollege.com
GONZALEZ, Jeandelize . 787-850-9347 512 D jeandelize.gonzalez@upr.edu
GONZALEZ, Jennifer ..... 305-629-2929 107 H jgonzalez@sanignaciouniversity.edu
GONZALEZ, Jennifer ..... 201-216-9901 277 B jennifer.gonzalez@eicollege.edu
GONZALEZ, Jenny .... 773-577-8100 136 F jgonzalez@coynecollege.edu
GONZALEZ, Jeremy ...... 312-553-5641 135 B jgonzalez@ccc.edu
GONZALEZ, Jesse .... 714-480-7401.. 58 E gonzalez_jesse@rsccd.edu
GONZALEZ, Jorge, G .... 269-337-7220 225 F jorge.gonzalez@kzoo.edu
GONZALEZ, Jose .... 787-840-2575 509 I jogonzalez@psm.edu
GONZALEZ, Joselyn ...... 214-860-2447 434 I joselyngonzalez@dcccd.edu
GONZALEZ, Juan, E ...... 972-883-2234 455 B jgonzal@utdallas.edu
GONZALEZ, Julio .... 951-571-6409.. 59 B julio.gonzalez@mvc.edu
GONZALEZ, Junius .... 516-686-1462 308 I junius.gonzalez@nyit.edu
GONZALEZ, Karen .... 787-766-1717 510 G um_kgonzalez@uagm.edu
GONZALEZ, Karilys .... 787-257-0000 512 B karilys.gonzalez@upr.edu
GONZALEZ, Kenneth ..... 915-831-2640 436 A kgonz179@epcc.edu
GONZALEZ, Kiebelle ..... 787-766-1717 510 G
GONZALEZ, Leonore ..... 212-220-8044 293 A lgonzalez@bmcc.cuny.edu
GONZALEZ, Lizbeth ...... 603-578-8900 272 M lgonzalez@ccsnh.edu
GONZALEZ, Luis .... 805-678-5949.. 74 A lgonzalez@vcccd.edu
GONZALEZ, Mari, G ..... 787-743-7979 510 H mggonzalez@suagm.edu
GONZALEZ, Maria .... 951-372-7137.. 59 C maria.gonzalez@norcocollege.edu
GONZALEZ, Maria De La Luz .... 559-925-3244.. 75 B mariadelaluzgonzalez@whccd.edu
GONZALEZ, Marilyn ...... 787-882-2065 510 C mgonzalez@unitecpr.edu
GONZALEZ, Maritza ...... 916-306-1628.. 67 F mgonzalez@sum.edu
GONZALEZ, Martha .... 210-784-2059 447 E martha.gonzalez@tamusa.edu
GONZALEZ, Matthew .... 860-632-3010.. 88 C mgonzalez@holyapostles.edu
GONZALEZ, Melissa ..... 806-291-3662 457 I gonzalez@wbu.edu
GONZALEZ, Melissa ..... 281-312-1644 439 C melissa.gonzalez@lonestar.edu
GONZALEZ, Miguel, A .. 281-283-3705 452 E gonzalezmig@uhcl.edu
GONZALEZ, Millie .... 787-863-2390 508 B millie.gonzalez@fajardo.inter.edu
GONZALEZ, Millie .... 508-626-4651 213 A vgonzalez@framingham.edu
GONZALEZ, Natalie .... 214-379-5438 441 F ngonzalez@pqc.edu
GONZALEZ, Orlando ...... 787-766-1912 507 J ogonzale@inter.edu
GONZALEZ, Paco .... 316-942-4291 176 E gonzalezp@newmanu.edu
GONZALEZ, Patricia ...... 787-250-1912 508 D pgonzalez@metro.inter.edu
GONZALEZ, Paulette, B 718-990-6521 313 G gonzalep@stjohns.edu
GONZALEZ, Ramon, F .. 787-758-2525 512 F ramon.gonzalez5@upr.edu
GONZALEZ, Raul .... 305-899-3000.. 96 A rgonzalez@barry.edu
GONZALEZ, Reyes .... 773-878-7502 149 A rgonzalez@staugustine.edu
GONZALEZ, Richard ...... 239-992-4624.. 96 E
GONZALEZ, Rick .... 424-207-3727.. 55 C rgonzalez@otis.edu
GONZALEZ, Ricky .... 763-433-1137 237 D ricardo.gonzalez@anokaramsey.edu
GONZALEZ, Robert, A ... 505-277-2903 288 J ragonzalez@unm.edu
GONZALEZ, Roberto ..... 310-287-4314.. 49 H
GONZALEZ, Roberto, O 310-287-4248.. 49 H gonzalro@wlac.edu
GONZALEZ, Rocelia, T .. 904-620-2870 111 B rrgonz@unf.edu
GONZALEZ, Roenice ..... 914-367-8208 314 C roenice.gonzalez@archny.org
GONZALEZ, Ruth .... 860-738-6315.. 87 C rgonzalez@nwcc.edu
GONZALEZ, Samantha .. 860-512-2663.. 86 G sgonzalez@manchestercc.edu
GONZALEZ, Sandra .... 787-882-2065 510 C sgonzalez@unitecpr.edu
GONZALEZ, Sergio .... 401-863-5402 403 J sergio_gonzalez@brown.edu
GONZALEZ, Sonia .... 562-860-2451.. 35 H smgonzalez@cerritos.edu
GONZALEZ, Sophia .... 210-486-2247 429 B fklein@alamo.edu
GONZALEZ, Stacy .... 518-244-4557 313 A gonzas@sage.edu
GONZALEZ, Susana ...... 281-998-6129 442 K susana.gonzalez@sjcd.edu
GONZALEZ, Taima .... 786-391-1167.. 95 G
GONZALEZ, Tania .... 209-228-4400.. 70 A
GONZALEZ, Tanya .... 785-532-4797 175 C tgonzale@ksu.edu
GONZALEZ, Ted .... 254-526-1668 432 D ted.gonzalez@ctcd.edu
GONZALEZ, Tina .... 212-799-5000 303 E
GONZALEZ, Tomas .... 585-785-1469 299 F tomas.gonzalez@flcc.edu
GONZALEZ, Victor .... 956-872-2336 443 H vgonzalez99@southtexascollege.edu
GONZALEZ, Victor .... 787-257-0000 512 B
GONZALEZ, Widalys ..... 787-884-3838 505 D wgonzalez@atenascollege.edu
GONZALEZ, Wilson .... 610-861-1554 390 F gonzalezw02@moravian.edu
GONZALEZ, Yaitzaenid .. 787-765-3560 506 K ygonzalez@edpuniversity.edu
GONZALEZ, Zoila .... 787-894-2828 513 C zoila.gonzalez@upr.edu
GONZALEZ-DE JESUS, Naydeen .... 414-297-6436 499 C gonzan43@matc.edu
GONZALEZ-LEVY, Sandra .... 305-348-7235 110 A sandra.gonzalez-levy@fiu.edu
GONZALEZ MEDINA, CMF, Ruben, A .... 787-848-5265 509 J ruben_gonzalez@pucpr.edu
GONZALEZ-MELENDEZ, Saraliz .... 787-857-3600 507 M sgonzalez@br.inter.edu
GONZALEZ PACHECO, Monica .... 787-863-2390 508 B monica.gonzalez@fajardo.inter.edu
GONZALEZ-ZAMBRANA, Zorymar .... 787-780-5134 509 E
GOO, Brian .... 408-855-5204.. 75 D brian.goo@missioncollege.edu
GOO, Shannon .... 617-217-9000 206 E
GOOCH, Cheryl .... 518-381-1382 315 B goochcrg@sunysccc.edu
GOOCH, Darlene .... 919-962-4388 342 C darlene_gooch@unc.edu
GOOCH, Jackie .... 256-233-8211.... 4 C jackie.gooch@athens.edu
GOOCH, Janet, L .... 660-785-4105 260 F jquinzer@truman.edu
GOOCH, Josh .... 620-665-3594 174 G goochj@hutchcc.edu
GOOCH, Zanetta .... 615-963-7401 426 A zgooch@tnstate.edu
GOOCH-GRAYSON, Cynthia .... 531-622-2649 267 G cgooch@mccneb.edu
GOOD, Amy .... 641-752-4643 167 G amy.good@iavalley.edu
GOOD, Andrew .... 818-364-7800.. 49 C gooda@lamission.edu
GOOD, Darrin, S .... 402-465-2217 268 G president@nebrwesleyan.edu
GOOD, Gayle, A .... 402-363-5621 270 D gagood@york.edu
GOOD, Glenn .... 352-392-3261 111 A ggood@coe.ufl.edu
GOOD, Jason .... 941-359-7690 106 J jgood@ringling.edu
GOOD, Lisa .... 717-396-7833 392 U lgood@pcad.edu
GOOD, Michael, L .... 801-581-5701 459 O president@utah.edu
GOOD, Michael, L .... 801-581-7480 459 O michael.good@hsc.utah.edu
GOOD, Rhonda .... 717-337-6015 384 D rgood@gettysburg.edu
GOOD, RT .... 561-237-7458 103 W rgood@lynn.edu
GOOD KAUFMANN, Cynthia .... 574-535-7351 155 E cynthiagk@goshen.edu
GOOD LUCK, Aldean .... 406-638-3118 263 G goodluckav@lbhc.edu
GOODALE, Brian .... 518-587-2100 320 E brian.goodale@esc.edu
GOODALE, Nathan .... 315-859-4615 300 H ngoodale@hamilton.edu
GOODALE, Timothy, A .. 252-335-3767 341 B tagoodale@ecsu.edu
GOODBERLET, Amy ...... 314-744-7699 256 E amy.goodberlet@mobap.edu
GOODBURN, Amy .... 402-472-3751 269 J agoodburn1@unl.edu
GOODE, David .... 662-692-1508 248 C dtgoode@nemcc.edu
GOODE, Greg, J .... 812-237-7778 156 D greg.goode@indstate.edu
GOODE, Jacqueline .... 610-399-2038 393 F jgoode@cheyney.edu
GOODE, Jess .... 312-567-3970 140 A jgoode1@iit.edu
GOODE, Jodi .... 325-646-8075 437 G jgoode@hputx.edu
GOODE, Kevin .... 814-866-8406 387 D kgoode@lecom.edu
GOODE, Mike .... 704-894-2143 328 E migoode@davidson.edu
GOODE, Tyler .... 828-339-4394 338 B t_goode@southwesterncc.edu
GOODELL, Adam .... 201-879-3673 275 H agoodell@bergen.edu
GOODELL, Adam .... 201-879-7033 275 H agoodell@bergen.edu
GOODEN, Amoaba .... 330-672-2442 354 A agooden@kent.edu
GOODEN, Benny, L ...... 479-308-2294.. 17 A benny.gooden@acheedu.org
GOODEN, Carlos .... 773-995-3526 134 K cgooden@csu.edu
GOODENOW, Andrew ... 816-235-1107 261 B goodenowa@umkc.edu
GOODFELLOW, Geoffrey .... 312-949-7016 139 D ggoodfel@ico.edu
GOODFELLOW, Tim ...... 503-554-2585 373 A tgoodfellow@georgefox.edu
GOODFRIEND, Kimberly .... 972-883-2201 455 B kimberly.goodfriend@utdallas.edu
GOODGAME, Henry ...... 470-639-0400 123 D henry.goodgame@morehouse.edu
GOODGE, Samuel .... 304-829-7905 487 A sgoodge@bethanywv.edu
GOODHEART, Marc .... 617-496-9480 210 E marc_goodheart@harvard.edu
GOODHIND, Deborah ... 413-545-5542 211 G deb.goodhind@umass.edu
GOODHUE LYNCH, Mary .... 508-588-9100 215 A mgoodhuel@massasoit.mass.edu
GOODING, Betsy .... 903-434-8137 440 G bgooding@ntcc.edu
GOODING, JR., Dale, E 330-972-5908 361 H dale2@uakron.edu
GOODING, Michelle ..... 305-899-3058.. 96 A migooding@barry.edu
GOODING, Sharon .... 817-257-4748 448 F s.gooding@tcu.edu
GOODJOHN, Bunny ...... 434-947-8126 469 E bgoodjohn@randolphcollege.edu
GOODKIND, Hilary .... 650-574-6196.. 62 K goodkindh@smccd.edu
GOODLAND, Jennifer .... 719-336-1541.. 81 K jennifer.goodland@lamarcc.edu
GOODLING, Barry, G .... 717-796-5064 389 H bgoodlin@messiah.edu
GOODMAN, Adam .... 205-853-1200.... 2 G akgoodman@jeffersonstate.edu
GOODMAN, Ann .... 575-646-1722 287 C anng@nmsu.edu
GOODMAN, Brent .... 619-849-2371.. 57 J brentgoodman@pointloma.edu
GOODMAN, Carl .... 301-860-3460 204 A cgoodman@bowiestate.edu
GOODMAN, David, M ... 617-552-3900 207 C david.goodman@bc.edu
GOODMAN, Dennis, S .. 573-341-4284 261 D dgoodman@mst.edu
GOODMAN, Elizabeth .... 651-641-8277 235 I goodman@csp.edu
GOODMAN, Elodie .... 509-533-3694 479 D elodie.goodman@sfcc.spokane.edu
GOODMAN, Grayson .... 407-303-1631.. 95 B grayson.goodman@ahu.edu
GOODMAN, Guy, H .... 602-243-8000.. 14 A guy.goodman@southmountaincc.edu
GOODMAN, Gwen .... 518-327-6242 311 C ggoodman@paulsmiths.edu
GOODMAN, Hunter, P .. 937-229-4915 362 C hgoodman1@udayton.edu
GOODMAN, Jacque .... 641-844-5640 167 E jacque.goodman@iavalley.edu
GOODMAN, James .... 808-455-0668 130 C goodmanj@hawaii.edu
GOODMAN, Jeremy ...... 781-292-2373 210 A jeremy.goodman@olin.edu
GOODMAN, Jim .... 432-837-8077 450 B jxg20jfq@sulross.edu
GOODMAN, Lena, C ..... 920-433-6638 491 G lena.goodman@bellincollege.edu
GOODMAN, Marc, P ..... 310-506-4607.. 56 G marc.goodman@pepperdine.edu
GOODMAN, Mark .... 646-565-6000 322 F mark.goodman6@touro.edu
GOODMAN, Mark .... 646-565-6000 322 G mark.goodman6@touro.edu
GOODMAN, Matthew .... 207-741-5507 195 H mgoodman@smccme.edu
GOODMAN, Michael ..... 504-865-5725 191 F mgoodman@tulane.edu
GOODMAN, Michael ..... 508-999-9231 212 A mgoodman@umassd.edu
GOODMAN, Patricia ..... 574-535-7700 155 E pgoodman@goshen.edu

GORTER, Tracy .... 712-324-5061 169 C
tgorter@nwicc.edu
GORTMAKER, Jessica ... 701-845-7710 345 G
jessica.gortmaker@vcsu.edu
GOSAI, Mayur .... 301-243-2336 502 L
mayur.gosai@dodiis.mil
GOSCH, Judy .... 865-539-7233 425 B
jagosch@pstcc.edu
GOSE, Becca .... 541-737-2474 375 A
GOSE, Carrie .... 307-766-1121 501 I
GOSHA, Kortne .... 850-599-3868 109 I
kortne.gosha@famu.edu
GOSHORN, Mark, A ...... 859-344-3352 185 B
goshorm@thomasmore.edu
GOSIER, Michelle .... 585-385-8064 313 F
mgosier@sjfc.edu
GOSLIN, Elle .... 860-932-4000.. 87 E
egoslin@qvcc.edu
GOSNELL, Victor .... 434-947-8308 469 E
vgosnell@randolphcollege.edu
GOSNEY, Sue .... 213-356-5330.. 65 E
sue_gosney@sciarc.edu
GOSS, Barbara .... 205-853-1200.... 2 G
bgoss@jeffersonstate.edu
GOSS, Gary .... 518-458-5439 296 G
gossg@strose.edu
GOSS, Leah .... 303-352-3121.. 80 F
leah.goss@ccd.edu
GOSS, Nathan, R .... 770-534-6162 116 D
ngoss@brenau.edu
GOSS, Peter .... 971-722-4490 375 D
peter.goss@pcc.edu
GOSS, Rebecca .... 509-533-8449 479 C
rebecca.goss@scc.spokane.edu
GOSS, Steven .... 718-862-7862 304 M
sgoss01@manhattan.edu
GOSSAGE, Steve .... 443-352-5469 202 E
sgossage@stevenson.edu
GOSSELIN, Grant, M ..... 617-552-3100 207 C
grant.gosselin@bc.edu
GOSSEN, Larry .... 308-367-5200 270 B
larry.gossen@unl.edu
GOSSEN, Timothy .... 507-457-1597 243 C
tgossen@smumn.edu
GOSSETT, Betty .... 716-673-3321 316 D
betty.gossett@fredonia.edu
GOSSETT, Elsa .... 425-739-8200 481 C
elsa.gossett@lwtech.edu
GOSSETT, Greg .... 972-707-8600 457 G
GOSSETT, John .... 828-398-7112 332 B
johndgossett@abtech.edu
GOSWAMI, Jaya, S .... 361-593-2170 447 D
jaya.goswami@tamuk.edu
GOSZ, Mike .... 312-567-3198 140 A
gosz@iit.edu
GOSZ, Sharon .... 414-229-5346 496 B
schetney@uwm.edu
GOTANDA, John .... 808-544-0203 128 G
president@hpu.edu
GOTCHER, Mike .... 931-372-3366 426 B
mgotcher@tntech.edu
GOTCHER, Robert .... 414-425-8300 495 A
GOTELLI, Luis .... 787-728-1515 513 D
luis.gotelli@sagrado.edu
GOTHAM, Kerry .... 585-395-2068 317 E
kgotham@brockport.edu
GOTHARD, Mathew, J .. 303-963-3223.. 78 H
mgothard@ccu.edu
GOTJEN, Lynne .... 207-795-7166 195 B
gotjenly@mchp.edu
GOTSCH, Sarah, A .... 574-631-3903 162 A
sgotsch@nd.edu
GOTSCHALL, Matthew ... 308-398-7300 266 A
mgotschall@cccneb.edu
GOTSMAN, Craig .... 973-596-5488 279 E
craig.gotsman@njit.edu
GOTT, Jared .... 731-989-6649 419 K
jgott@fhu.edu
GOTTARDY, John .... 716-645-2450 316 C
johngott@buffalo.edu
GOTTDIENER, Yitzchok . 718-941-8000 306 E
GOTTLIEB, Jane .... 212-799-5000 303 E
GOTTLIEB, Mel .... 213-884-4133.. 24 A
mgottlieb@ajrca.edu
GOTTLIEB, Neal .... 732-431-1600 284 B
GOTTSCHALK,
Katherine .... 765-983-1267 155 A
gottska@earlham.edu
GOTTSCHALK, Mark ...... 806-894-9611 443 G
mgottschalk@southplainscollege.edu
GOTTSHALL, Lori .... 954-771-0376 103 S
lgottshall@knoxseminary.edu

GOTTULA, Todd .... 308-865-8454 269 I
gottulatm@unk.edu
GOTZMAN, Ron .... 763-417-8250 235 A
rgotzman@centralseminary.edu
GOUDEAU, Arthur .... 281-487-1170 448 E
agoudeau@txchiro.edu
GOUDEAU, LaTasha ...... 713-221-8162 453 A
goudeaul@uhd.edu
GOUDY, Senta .... 304-424-8000 490 F
senta.goudy@wvup.edu
GOUGER, Tammy .... 585-395-2126 317 E
tgouger@brockport.edu
GOUGH, Allison .... 808-544-1109 128 G
agough@hpu.edu
GOUGH, Annette .... 732-571-3402 279 A
gough@monmouth.edu
GOUGH, Christopher .... 203-332-5022.. 86 F
cgough@hcc.commnet.edu
GOUGH, Darby .... 816-501-3660 250 F
darby.gough@avila.edu
GOUGH, Pam .... 251-981-3771.... 5 A
pam.gough@columbiasouthern.edu
GOUGH, Richard, J ...... 843-525-8247 412 G
rgough@tcl.edu
GOUGHNOUR, Karla ..... 417-328-1823 259 I
kgoughnour@sbuniv.edu
GOULD, Amanda .... 413-565-1000 206 D
agould@baypath.edu
GOULD, Bryan, M .... 253-879-3355 484 G
bmgould@pugetsound.edu
GOULD, Deborah, M .... 413-545-2554 211 G
dmgould@admin.umass.edu
GOULD, Greg .... 406-275-4991 265 F
greg_gould@skc.edu
GOULD, Janet .... 336-316-2135 329 D
jgould@guilford.edu
GOULD, Jenkin .... 413-755-4061 216 A
jgould@stcc.edu
GOULD, Kenneth .... 718-951-3136 293 C
kgould@brooklyn.cuny.edu
GOULD, Kyle .... 765-998-4635 161 C
kygould@taylor.edu
GOULD, Mark .... 978-837-5072 216 F
gouldm@merrimack.edu
GOULD, Nicholas .... 202-779-9399.. 92 C
nicholas.gould@gallaudet.edu
GOULD, Rachel .... 607-274-3306 302 G
rgould@ithaca.edu
GOULD, Robert .... 612-330-1582 234 A
gouldr@augsburg.edu
GOULD, Shari .... 814-860-5151 387 D
sgould@lecom.edu
GOULD, Shari .... 814-732-1294 394 B
sgould@edinboro.edu
GOULD, Terri .... 989-686-9081 223 J
tlgould@delta.edu
GOULD, Thomas .... 252-493-7406 336 H
tgould@email.pittcc.edu
GOULD, Trent .... 601-266-5253 249 F
trent.gould@usm.edu
GOULET, Bonnie .... 203-576-8752.. 87 B
bgoulet@nv.edu
GOULET, Caroline .... 210-283-6924 453 C
goulet@uiwtx.edu
GOULET, Stephen, P ..... 508-793-7598 208 C
sgoulet@clarku.edu
GOURDINE, Raji .... 334-876-9292.... 2 D
ragi.gourdine@wccs.edu
GOURJI, Konstantin ...... 650-685-6616.. 44 F
kgourji@gurnick.edu
GOURLEY, Bridget, L .... 765-658-4359 154 J
bgourley@depauw.edu
GOURLEY, Kristin .... 865-981-8215 421 C
kristin.gourley@maryvillecollege.edu
GOURNEAU, Haven .... 406-768-6300 263 F
hgourneau@fpcc.edu
GOURNEAU, Kim .... 218-755-3948 237 F
kim.gourneau@bemidjistate.edu
GOURNIAK, Allison .... 419-289-5622 347 J
agournia@ashland.edu
GOUSE, Richard, I .... 401-739-5000 404 E
rgouse@neit.edu
GOUVEIA, Jan .... 808-956-6405 129 E
jgouveia@hawaii.edu
GOUVEIA, Jan, N .... 808-956-6405 129 C
jgouveia@hawaii.edu
GOUVEIA, JR.,
Leonard, R .... 808-956-8259 129 E
lgouveia@hawaii.edu
GOVAN, Jennifer .... 212-678-3022 322 C
govan@tc.columbia.edu
GOVEA, Lewis .... 707-965-6303.. 55 I
lgovea@puc.edu

GOVEA, Rene .... 815-479-7619 143 I
rgovea@mchenry.edu
GOVEA, Sam .... 972-860-4216 434 F
sgovea@dcccd.edu
GOVENDER, Yogani ...... 787-250-1912 508 D
ygovender@metro.inter.edu
GOVER, Bruce .... 606-679-8501 182 G
bruce.gover@kctcs.edu
GOVER, Kristie .... 904-256-7070 102 H
kgover1@ju.edu
GOVINDARAJU,
Venugopal .... 716-645-3321 316 C
vpr@buffalo.edu
GOVINDARAJULU,
Chitti .... 765-455-9275 157 B
cgovinda@iu.edu
GOVINDASWAMY,
Parvadha .... 636-584-6627 253 B
parvadha.govindaswamy@eastcentral.edu
GOVITZ, Leanne .... 989-686-9490 223 J
leannegovitz@delta.edu
GOVITZ, Scott .... 989-386-6624 228 B
sgovitz@midmich.edu
GOW, Joe .... 608-785-8004 496 A
jgow@uwlax.edu
GOWAN, Mary, A .... 706-864-1800 127 A
mary.gowan@ung.edu
GOWANS, Faye .... 803-822-3251 410 D
gowansf@midlandstech.edu
GOWDY, Stephen .... 616-538-2330 224 E
sgowdy@gracechristian.edu
GOWEN, Karla .... 312-553-2500 135 A
kgowen@ccc.edu
GOWER, Ana Maria ...... 510-628-8034.. 48 C
agower@lincolnuca.edu
GOWER, Molly .... 574-284-4886 160 I
mgower@saintmarys.edu
GOWER, Paula .... 405-585-5410 367 B
paula.gower@okbu.edu
GOWER, Rena .... 618-544-8657 139 G
gowerr@iecc.edu
GOWER, Ryan .... 618-393-2982 139 E
gowerry@iecc.edu
GOWING, Wendi .... 303-762-6887.. 80 I
wendi.gowing@denverseminary.edu
GOYETTE, John .... 805-525-4417.. 67 K
jgoyette@thomasaquinas.edu
GOYETTE, Sylvain .... 815-836-5974 142 F
goyettsy@lewisu.edu
GOYUNYAN, Gevorg ..... 510-925-4282.. 25 K
gevorg@aua.am
GOZA, Franklin .... 262-472-1712 497 D
gozaf@uww.edu
GOZIK, Nick .... 617-552-3827 207 C
nick.gozik@bc.edu
GOZIK, Nick .... 336-278-6700 328 J
ngozik@elon.edu
GOZUM, Allan .... 937-769-1304 347 H
agozum@antioch.edu
GRABER, Brent .... 574-296-6221 153 F
it@ambs.edu
GRABER, David .... 402-375-7257 268 F
dagrabe1@wsc.edu
GRABER, Linda .... 866-931-4300 258 H
linda.graber@rockbridge.edu
GRABHER, Karen .... 262-595-2211 496 D
grabher@uwp.edu
GRABLE, Bettye .... 850-599-3379 109 I
bettye.grable@famu.edu
GRABOWSKI, Jeremiah . 716-829-8392 298 E
grabowsj@dyc.edu
GRABOWSKI, John, F ... 410-777-2231 197 G
jfgrabowski@aacc.edu
GRABOWSKI, Mark .... 417-328-1556 259 I
mgrabowski@sbuniv.edu
GRABOWSKI,
Rodney, M .... 716-645-2925 316 C
rodneyg@buffalo.edu
GRABSKI, Joanna .... 480-727-1568.. 10 J
joanna.grabski@asu.edu
GRACE, Anna .... 503-253-3443 374 G
anna.grace@ocom.edu
GRACE, Audrey .... 781-768-7000 218 D
GRACE, Chris .... 641-472-1104 168 C
stuact@miu.edu
GRACE, Janet .... 620-441-5564 173 C
janet.grace@cowley.edu
GRACE, Melissa, H .... 850-474-3423 111 F
mgrace@uwf.edu
GRACE, Michelle, M ..... 847-543-2274 136 A
mgrace@clcillinois.edu
GRACE, Nabil, F .... 248-204-2500 227 A
ngrace@ltu.edu

GRACE, Sherie .... 256-228-6001.... 3 B
graces@nacc.edu
GRACE, Susan .... 513-487-1217 361 F
susan.grace@myunion.edu
GRACIA, Edward .... 787-844-8181 513 A
edward.gracia@upr.edu
GRACIA, Hector .... 787-780-0070 505 F
graciah@caribbean.edu
GRACIA, Jessica, L ..... 508-565-1301 219 A
jlgracia@stonehill.edu
GRACIANI, Ruben .... 540-568-4850 468 C
graciarg@jmu.edu
GRACIAS, Vicente, H .... 732-235-6300 282 A
graciavh@rbhs.rutgers.edu
GRACYALNY, David .... 410-225-2220 200 D
dgracyal@mica.edu
GRADDY, Elizabeth .... 213-740-6715.. 73 D
graddy@usc.edu
GRADDY, Kathryn .... 781-736-8616 208 A
kgraddy@brandeis.edu
GRADOWSKI, Charles ... 484-365-8049 388 H
cgradowski@lincoln.edu
GRADY, Amber, N .... 870-759-4188.. 23 J
agrady@williamsbu.edu
GRADY, Catherine .... 937-229-1000 362 C
GRADY, Darryl .... 910-592-8081 337 G
dgrady@sampsoncc.edu
GRADY, Helene .... 443-997-3359 199 G
hgrady1@jhu.edu
GRADY, Jessica .... 781-283-2088 219 E
jg101@wellesley.edu
GRADY, Jonathan .... 909-869-3850.. 30 A
jgrady@cpp.edu
GRADY, Meghan .... 610-606-4666 380 D
meghan.grady@cedarcrest.edu
GRADY, Sandra, K .... 518-861-2579 305 C
sgrady@mariacollege.edu
GRADY, Sara .... 508-929-8130 213 G
sara.grady@worcester.edu
GRADY, Sarah .... 718-409-7262 320 G
sgrady@sunymaritime.edu
GRADY, Susan .... 817-202-6755 444 I
sgrady@swau.edu
GRAEBERT, James, K .... 414-288-3048 493 E
james.graebert@marquette.edu
GRAEF, Jon .... 206-726-5028 479 E
jgraef@cornish.edu
GRAEM, David .... 903-675-6364 451 F
dgraem@tvcc.edu
GRAESER, Kristin .... 717-736-4103 385 B
kgraeser@hacc.edu
GRAF, Amanda .... 540-636-2900 465 L
agraf@christendom.edu
GRAF, Bob .... 651-696-6280 236 I
rgraf@macalester.edu
GRAF, Mel .... 401-598-4949 404 D
mary.graf@jwu.edu
GRAFALS, Rosana .... 787-738-2161 512 C
rosana.grafals@upr.edu
GRAFF, Brenda .... 217-641-4530 141 A
bgraff@jwcc.edu
GRAFF, Eric .... 614-885-5585 359 L
egraff@pcj.edu
GRAFF, Eric, S .... 614-885-5585 359 L
egraff@pcj.edu
GRAFF, Jennifer .... 920-424-0775 496 C
graff@uwosh.edu
GRAFF, Leslie .... 901-321-3271 418 G
leslie.graff@cbu.edu
GRAFF, Michael .... 440-525-7060 354 L
mgraff@lakelandcc.edu
GRAFF, Nadja .... 212-463-0400 322 F
nadja.graff@touro.edu
GRAFF, Nadja .... 212-463-0400 322 G
ngraff@touro.edu
GRAFF, Robin .... 914-606-7756 325 A
robin.graff@sunywcc.edu
GRAFFAGNINO, Jason .. 706-865-2134 126 E
jgraffagnino@truett.edu
GRAFFEO, Mary Ann .... 719-389-6000.. 78 I
GRAFFIUS, Jeffrey .... 740-374-8716 363 F
jgraffius@wscc.edu
GRAFIUS, Brandon .... 313-831-5200 223 L
bgrafius@etseminary.edu
GRAFTON, Anthony .... 870-307-7315.. 19 I
anthony.grafton@lyon.edu
GRAFTON, Anthony, K .. 870-307-7315.. 19 I
anthony.grafton@lyon.edu
GRAFTON, David .... 860-509-9536.. 88 B
dgrafton@hartsem.edu
GRAFTON, Donald .... 541-485-1780 374 E
donaldgrafton@newhope.edu

GRANT, Tyler .... 574-807-7124 154 B
tyler.grant@betheluniversity.edu
GRANT, Tyler, C .... 574-807-7124 154 B
tyler.grant@betheluniversity.edu
GRANT, Velvet, L .... 757-683-3159 469 B
vlgrant2@odu.edu
GRANT-BRINKLEY,
Kedra .... 210-805-5814 453 C
kegrant@uiwtx.edu
GRANTHAM, Kimberly .. 901-678-2930 426 G
kimberly.grantham@memphis.edu
GRANTHAM, Lisa, P ..... 512-448-8774 442 I
lisag@stedwards.edu
GRANZOW, Daniel .... 636-922-8508 258 J
dgranzow@stchas.edu
GRAPENTHIEN, Robert .. 847-925-6245 138 G
rgrapent@harpercollege.edu
GRASELL, James, F ...... 610-660-1299 397 G
jgrasell@sju.edu
GRASSADONIA, Jane .... 570-577-2000 379 C
jmg064@bucknell.edu
GRASSEL, OSB, Martin . 503-845-3326 374 A
martin.grassel@mtangel.edu
GRASSI, Janel .... 417-447-2601 257 G
grassij@otc.edu
GRASSMAN, Sandy .... 216-373-5283 357 F
sgrassman@ndc.edu
GRASSO, Dominico .... 313-593-5500 231 I
grasso@umich.edu
GRASSO, Eliot .... 541-683-5141 373 B
GRASSO, Richard .... 718-489-3450 313 E
richardgrasso@sfc.edu
GRATE, Cammy .... 803-516-4510 411 G
cgrate2@scsu.edu
GRATSON, Emily .... 616-949-5300 223 C
emily.gratson@cornerstone.edu
GRATZ, Bruce, A .... 507-344-7367 234 C
bruce.gratz@blc.edu
GRAU, Beverly .... 479-619-3103.. 20 C
bgrau@nwacc.edu
GRAU, Isidro .... 713-221-8494 453 A
graui@uhd.edu
GRAU, Kurt .... 405-208-5240 367 E
kmgrau@okcu.edu
GRAU, Leeann .... 740-389-4636 355 F
graul@mtc.edu
GRAU, Melissa .... 269-927-6172 226 F
grau@lakemichigancollege.edu
GRAU, Monica, C .... 607-436-2255 316 F
monica.grau@oneonta.edu
GRAUBERGER, Renee ... 602-383-8228.. 16 C
rgrauberger@uat.edu
GRAUMAN, Greg .... 808-543-8061 128 G
ggrauman@hpu.edu
GRAUSE, Candice .... 850-201-6219 112 C
candice.grause@tcc.fl.edu
GRAVATT, Tomi .... 217-234-5253 142 C
tgravatt@lakelandcollege.edu
GRAVDAHL, Jeanette .... 605-698-3966 416 B
jgravdahl@swcollege.edu
GRAVEEN, Melody .... 951-571-6291.. 59 B
melody.graveen@mvc.edu
GRAVEL, Matthew .... 413-755-4623 216 A
mgravel@stcc.edu
GRAVEL, Tammy .... 508-373-5682 216 D
tammy.gravel@mcphs.edu
GRAVELLE, Andrea .... 410-386-8419 198 D
agravelle@carrollcc.edu
GRAVERATTE,
Jacqueline .... 989-317-4760 230 D
jgraveratte@sagchip.edu
GRAVES, Becky .... 256-352-8159.... 3 I
becky.graves@wallacestate.edu
GRAVES, Bennie .... 979-830-4701 431 H
bennie.graves@blinn.edu
GRAVES, Carla .... 985-867-2232 190 K
humanresources@sjasc.edu
GRAVES, Carla .... 904-470-8237.. 98 L
carla.graves@ewc.edu
GRAVES, Cheryl .... 719-884-5000.. 82 B
cagraves@nbc.edu
GRAVES, Devin .... 620-441-5595 173 C
devin.graves@cowley.edu
GRAVES, Elizabeth, E .... 859-238-5200 180 B
elizabeth.graves@centre.edu
GRAVES, Frank .... 254-299-8126 439 E
fgraves@mclennan.edu
GRAVES, Howard .... 434-797-8460 473 G
howard.graves@danville.edu
GRAVES, Howard, E ...... 516-463-6429 301 G
howard.e.graves@hofstra.edu
GRAVES, Jacqueline, N . 606-783-2211 184 C
jngraves@moreheadstate.edu
GRAVES, Jeana .... 740-377-2520 361 E
jeana.graves@tsbc.edu
GRAVES, Kathleen .... 563-884-5102 169 F
kathleen.graves@palmer.edu
GRAVES, Lauren .... 502-597-6229 183 D
lauren.graves@kysu.edu
GRAVES, Lisa, E .... 269-337-4400 233 D
GRAVES, Loreatha, D .... 336-285-2702 341 D
loretha@ncat.edu
GRAVES, Mallis .... 859-442-1608 181 H
mallis.graves@kctcs.edu
GRAVES, Marquita, J .... 336-750-3331 344 A
gravesmj@wssu.edu
GRAVES, Randy .... 918-647-1370 365 E
rggraves@carlalbert.edu
GRAVES, Randy, K .... 269-471-3854 221 D
gravesr@andrews.edu
GRAVES, Robbie .... 731-661-5008 426 F
rgraves@uu.edu
GRAVES, Sara .... 256-824-6064.... 8 B
sara.graves@uah.edu
GRAVES, Sara, J .... 256-824-6064.... 8 B
sara.graves@uah.edu
GRAVES, Scott .... 907-564-8342.... 9 F
sgraves@alaskapacific.edu
GRAVES, Thomas, K ...... 623-572-6375 144 F
tgraves@midwestern.edu
GRAVES, William .... 316-942-4291 176 E
gravesw@newmanu.edu
GRAVES, William, R ...... 515-294-2682 163 G
graves@iastate.edu
GRAVES, William, T ...... 318-342-1961 193 C
graves@ulm.edu
GRAVES-BAYAZITOGLU,
Rebecca .... 609-258-3000 280 D
GRAVETT, Erika .... 760-750-4437.. 33 A
egravett@csusm.edu
GRAVETT, Sharon, L ..... 229-333-5950 127 E
sgravett@valdosta.edu
GRAVIETTE,
Kimberly, K .... 402-461-7387 267 C
kgraviette@hastings.edu
GRAVINA, Kevin .... 303-273-3351.. 79 J
kgravina@mines.edu
GRAVLEY-STACK, Kara .. 218-477-4000 239 E
kara.gravleystack@mnstate.edu
GRAY, Amanda .... 816-995-2806 258 G
amanda.gray@researchcollege.edu
GRAY, Amy .... 630-844-5467 133 D
agray@aurora.edu
GRAY, Amy .... 815-280-2246 141 B
amgray@jjc.edu
GRAY, Brandy .... 315-792-3228 324 B
bgray@utica.edu
GRAY, Charlotte .... 417-967-5466 260 D
GRAY, Charlotte .... 417-777-5062 250 H
cgray@texascountytech.edu
GRAY, Chris .... 913-469-8500 174 I
chrisgray@jccc.edu
GRAY, Chris .... 815-455-8673 143 I
cgray1@mchenry.edu
GRAY, Christine .... 303-722-5724.. 81 L
cgray@lincolntech.edu
GRAY, Corey .... 402-643-3651 266 G
corey.gray@cune.edu
GRAY, Courtney .... 903-730-4890 438 D
cgray@jarvis.edu
GRAY, David, R .... 540-868-7154 474 C
dgray@lfcc.edu
GRAY, Ellen .... 518-243-3517 291 D
graye@ellismedicine.org
GRAY, Gary .... 570-422-3689 394 A
ggray2@esu.edu
GRAY, Gregory, S .... 334-727-8011.... 7 D
gsgray@tuskegee.edu
GRAY, Hannah .... 972-279-6511 429 F
hgray@amberton.edu
GRAY, Holly .... 662-862-8381 246 E
ehgray@iccms.edu
GRAY, Isabel .... 856-227-7200 276 E
igray@camdencc.edu
GRAY, James .... 205-247-8001.... 7 A
jgray@stillman.edu
GRAY, Jeff .... 870-733-6731.. 17 F
wjgray@asumidsouth.edu
GRAY, Jeff .... 478-387-4781 119 F
jgray@gmc.edu
GRAY, Jeffrey, L .... 718-817-4750 300 C
gray@fordham.edu
GRAY, Jennifer .... 405-425-1936 367 C
jennifer.gray@oc.edu
GRAY, Jim .... 413-585-2426 218 H
jwgray@smith.edu
GRAY, John .... 910-755-7434 332 F
grayj@brunswickcc.edu
GRAY, John, C .... 302-295-1139.. 91 E
john.c.gray@wilmu.edu
GRAY, Julianna, R .... 607-871-2256 290 B
gray@alfred.edu
GRAY, Karol .... 804-828-1200 473 B
kgray8@vcu.edu
GRAY, Kathleen .... 718-489-5340 313 E
kgray4@sfc.edu
GRAY, Kelly, A .... 419-755-4823 357 B
kgray@ncstatecollege.edu
GRAY, Kent .... 281-487-1170 448 E
kgray@txchiro.edu
GRAY, Kilen .... 502-895-3411 183 H
kgray@lpts.edu
GRAY, Kristen .... 616-395-7945 225 D
gray@hope.edu
GRAY, Kristina .... 309-341-5456 134 B
kgray@sandburg.edu
GRAY, Lisa .... 410-455-8478 203 B
lisamgray@umbc.edu
GRAY, Lisa, G .... 410-546-6390 204 D
lggray@salisbury.edu
GRAY, Lloyd .... 601-974-1000 247 B
lloyd.gray@millsaps.edu
GRAY, Lydia, E .... 718-862-7231 304 M
lydia.gray@manhattan.edu
GRAY, Marisa .... 443-885-4714 201 A
marisa.gray@morgan.edu
GRAY, Michaelle .... 580-387-7000 366 E
mgray@mscok.edu
GRAY, Michaelle .... 580-387-7131 366 E
mgray@mscok.edu
GRAY, Michelle .... 541-956-7084 376 A
mgray@roguecc.edu
GRAY, Mike .... 606-546-4151 185 D
mgray@unionky.edu
GRAY, Monita, M .... 920-832-6697 493 B
monita.m.gray@lawrence.edu
GRAY, Neil .... 903-566-7368 456 A
ngray@uttyler.edu
GRAY, Nicholas .... 765-361-6188 163 B
grayn@wabash.edu
GRAY, Peter, W .... 931-598-1274 423 D
pwgray@sewanee.edu
GRAY, Rebecca .... 254-968-9473 446 D
rgray@tarleton.edu
GRAY, Ronald .... 828-448-6068 339 A
rgray@wpcc.edu
GRAY, Ronald, A .... 201-559-3541 277 J
grayr@felician.edu
GRAY, Sarah .... 309-649-6265 150 G
sarah.gray@src.edu
GRAY, Scott .... 402-844-7036 268 H
sgray7@northeast.edu
GRAY, Sean .... 319-385-6271 167 H
sean.gray@iw.edu
GRAY, Seneca .... 503-768-6781 373 E
seneca@lclark.edu
GRAY, Shashuna .... 540-891-3037 473 I
sgray@germanna.edu
GRAY, Shaun .... 207-741-5580 195 H
sgray@smccme.edu
GRAY, Shawn .... 409-880-8466 449 G
shawn.gray@lamar.edu
GRAY, Sheryl .... 865-471-3240 418 E
sgray@cn.edu
GRAY, Simon .... 716-285-1212 309 H
sgray@niagara.edu
GRAY, Tiffany .... 206-296-6070 484 A
grayt@seattleu.edu
GRAY, Tiffiney .... 662-252-8000 248 G
tgray@rustcollege.edu
GRAY, Tim .... 303-937-4420.. 78 C
tim.gray@augustineinstitute.org
GRAY, Timothy .... 704-216-6284 330 H
tgray@livingstone.edu
GRAY, Toni, B .... 806-371-2912 429 E
tbgray@actx.edu
GRAY, Tracy .... 858-695-8587 156 B
tgray@horizonuniversity.edu
GRAY, Tuesday, A .... 225-216-8403 187 G
grayt@mybrcc.edu
GRAY, Velma .... 901-435-1676 420 I
velma_gray@loc.edu
GRAY, William .... 417-777-5062 250 H
bgray@texascountytech.edu
GRAY-DEVINE, Sherry ... 580-387-7212 366 E
sgray@mscok.edu
GRAY-VICKREY, Peg ..... 254-519-5447 447 A
gray-vickrey@tamuct.edu
GRAYBEAL, David .... 252-399-6599 326 K
jdgraybeal@barton.edu
GRAYBEAL, Susan .... 423-354-2549 425 A
segraybeal@northeaststate.edu
GRAYBILL, Jody, D .... 570-577-3351 379 C
jody.graybill@bucknell.edu
GRAYBILL, Mark, S ...... 610-499-1008 402 G
msgraybill@widener.edu
GRAYLEE, Laleh .... 657-278-2304.. 31 C
lgraylee@fullerton.edu
GRAYS, Rodney, F .... 301-447-7411 201 B
grays@msmary.edu
GRAYS, Shantay .... 713-718-5115 437 C
shantay.grays@hccs.edu
GRAYSON, Denise, R .... 605-256-5152 416 F
denise.grayson@dsu.edu
GRAYSON, Micki .... 951-571-6382.. 59 B
micki.clowney@mvc.edu
GRAZIANO, Carl .... 570-961-7899 387 B
grazianoc@lackawanna.edu
GRAZIANO, Lisa .... 716-851-1499 299 B
grazianol@ecc.edu
GRAZIOSO, Amanda ..... 603-535-2260 275 A
ajgrazioso@plymouth.edu
GRAZULIS, Michele ...... 617-373-2000 217 I
GRAZZINI-OLSON,
Nancy .... 952-851-0066 233 G
GRDEN, Nancy .... 757-683-6140 469 B
ngrden@odu.edu
GREAGOFF, Amy .... 337-550-1416 189 G
agreagof@lsue.edu
GREANEY, Brendan .... 419-995-8416 360 C
greaney.b@rhodesstate.edu
GREANEY, Bryan .... 917-493-4448 305 A
bgreaney@msmnyc.edu
GREANEY, KC .... 707-778-4188.. 63 D
kgreaney@santarosa.edu
GREATHOUSE, Jo .... 979-230-3234 431 I
jo.greathouse@brazosport.edu
GREAVES, Matthew, C .. 202-687-3488.. 92 E
mcg3@georgetown.edu
GREAVES, Valerie .... 734-973-3345 232 D
vgreaves@wccnet.edu
GREAVES-BENJAMIN,
Lana .... 301-891-4541 205 A
lgbenjam@wau.edu
GREBIN, Kevin .... 605-331-6772 417 C
kevin.grebin@usiouxfalls.edu
GREBINOSKI, Jeff .... 920-498-7193 499 G
jeffrey.grebinoski@nwtc.edu
GRECO, Anne .... 215-751-8217 381 I
agreco@ccp.edu
GRECO, Frank, M .... 412-365-1680 380 G
greco@chatham.edu
GRECO, Gary .... 310-660-3593.. 41 E
ggreco@elcamino.edu
GRECO, Gil .... 541-683-5141 373 B
ggreco@gutenberg.edu
GRECO, Jared, K .... 530-226-4101.. 64 E
jgreco@simpsonu.edu
GRECO, Juneann .... 570-340-6004 389 D
greco@marywood.edu
GRECO, Michelle .... 504-671-5091 188 B
mgreco@dcc.edu
GRECO, Michelle .... 504-671-6006 188 B
mgreco@dcc.edu
GRECO, Peter .... 801-832-2005 461 F
pgreco@westminstercollege.edu
GRECO, Richard .... 413-781-7822 216 A
rdgreco@stcc.edu
GRECOL, Joseph .... 216-373-5407 357 F
jgrecol@ndc.edu
GREDEN, Leigh .... 734-487-2211 223 K
lgreden@emich.edu
GREEAR, Amy .... 276-523-7480 474 D
agreear@mecc.edu
GREELEY, Darryl .... 480-423-6522.. 13 H
darryl.greeley@scottsdalecc.edu
GREEN, Adam, S .... 423-439-4211 419 G
greenas@etsu.edu
GREEN, Adrienne .... 601-977-7819 249 C
agreen3@tougaloo.edu
GREEN, Andre .... 850-599-3400 109 I
andre.green@famu.edu
GREEN, Andrew .... 443-997-1288 199 G
andrew.green@jhu.edu
GREEN, Ashley .... 817-722-1612 438 G
ashley.green@tku.edu
GREEN, Becky .... 806-457-4200 436 C
bgreen@fpctx.edu
GREEN, Bernice .... 334-727-8011.... 7 D
GREEN, Bevley .... 251-460-6796.... 9 A
bwgreen@southalabama.edu

GREENLEE, Mitchelle .... 619-574-5806.. 42 J
mgreenlee@fst.edu
GREENLEE, Pam, S .... 815-939-5211 147 A
pgreenle@olivet.edu
GREENLEE, Zach .... 314-744-7639 256 E
greenleez@mobap.edu
GREENMAN, David .... 716-286-8590 309 H
dgreenman@niagara.edu
GREENO, Darren .... 360-416-7729 484 C
darren.greeno@skagit.edu
GREENO, Jimmie .... 215-972-2303 392 T
jgreeno@pafa.edu
GREENO, John, G .... 412-396-5103 383 A
greenoj@duq.edu
GREENO, Stephanie ...... 845-434-5750 321 E
sgreeno@sunysullivan.edu
GREENSLADE, Ernestine 978-556-3862 215 E
egreenslade@necc.mass.edu
GREENSLADE-SMITH,
Toni .... 614-292-8266 358 D
greenslade-smith.1@osu.edu
GREENSTEIN, Amy .... 212-343-1234 306 G
agreenstein@mcny.edu
GREENSTEIN, Benjamin 401-254-3043 405 C
bgreenstein@rwu.edu
GREENSTEIN, Daniel ..... 717-720-4010 393 C
chancellor@passhe.edu
GREENSTEIN, Kerry .... 434-381-6221 471 I
kgreenstein@sbc.edu
GREENTHAL, Joseph, T 607-587-3938 319 F
greentjt@alfredstate.edu
GREENUP, Troy .... 562-907-4287.. 76 B
greenup@whittier.edu
GREENWALD, J. Patrick 716-888-8216 292 F
greenwal@canisius.edu
GREENWALD, Kellye ..... 301-696-3714 199 E
greenwald@hood.edu
GREENWALD, Reesa ..... 973-275-2828 283 C
reesa.greenwald@shu.edu
GREENWALD, Richard ... 203-254-4000.. 87 I
rgreenwald@fairfield.edu
GREENWALT, Dawn .... 937-529-2201 361 G
dgreenwalt@united.edu
GREENWALT, Riane, B .. 618-650-2852 150 C
rgreenw@siue.edu
GREENWAY, Adam, W .. 817-921-8710 445 A
presoffice@swbts.edu
GREENWAY, Janet .... 605-995-7194 415 E
janet.greenway@mitchelltech.edu
GREENWAY, Jill .... 605-995-3023 415 E
jill.greenway@mitchelltech.edu
GREENWAY,
Kimberly, A .... 256-765-4223.... 8 E
kagreenway@una.edu
GREENWAY, Lidell .... 229-468-2240 128 B
lidell.greenway@wiregrass.edu
GREENWAY, Pamela ..... 864-596-9050 408 F
pamela.greenway@converse.edu
GREENWELL, Brian .... 330-490-7282 363 E
bgreenwell@walsh.edu
GREENWELL, Natalie, G 972-985-3768 433 I
ngreenwell@collin.edu
GREENWOD, Steve .... 209-932-2815.. 71 E
sgreenwood@pacific.edu
GREENWOOD, Brandon 501-370-5317.. 20 F
bgreenwood@philander.edu
GREENWOOD, Diane ..... 610-409-3316 401 H
dgreenwood@ursinus.edu
GREENWOOD, Gail .... 423-472-7141 424 B
ggreenwood@clevelandstatecc.edu
GREENWOOD, Grant ..... 325-793-4785 439 F
greenwood.grant@mcm.edu
GREENWOOD, Marisol . 469-454-3400.. 93 H
GREENWOOD, Nichole . 801-832-2027 461 F
nhg@westminstercollege.edu
GREENWOOD, Paul ...... 813-257-3095 113 H
GREENWOOD-BLACKSHEAR,
Sheila .... 410-706-2281 203 A
sheila.blackshear@umaryland.edu
GREER, Bradley .... 864-424-8039 413 H
greerm@mailbox.sc.edu
GREER, Carrie .... 636-481-3220 254 C
cgreer4@jeffco.edu
GREER, Charles .... 951-827-3093.. 70 B
charles.greer@ucr.edu
GREER, Christine, G ..... 906-227-1700 228 I
cgreer@nmu.edu
GREER, Gregg .... 806-291-3406 457 I
greerg@wbu.edu
GREER, Jay .... 616-988-1000 223 A
GREER, Jennifer .... 859-257-2000 185 F
jgr357@uky.edu
GREER, Jeremy .... 870-245-5526.. 20 D
greerj@obu.edu
GREER, Karla, J .... 972-860-7173 434 H
kgreer@dcccd.edu
GREER, Kimberly .... 510-885-3711.. 31 A
kim.greer@csueastbay.edu
GREER, Kimberly .... 209-667-3203.. 33 B
kgreer@csustan.edu
GREER, Marisa .... 606-546-1730 185 D
mgreer@unionky.edu
GREER, Melodie .... 267-502-2407 379 A
melodie.greer@brynathyn.edu
GREER, Michael, D .... 501-526-8963.. 22 B
mgreer@uams.edu
GREER, Nyssa .... 712-329-4743 167 I
ngreer@iwcc.edu
GREER, Rebecca .... 914-361-6220 307 C
rgreer@montefiore.org
GREER, Sheree .... 606-474-3186 181 B
sgreer@kcu.edu
GREER, Sherman, D ..... 901-333-4101 425 D
sdgreer@southwest.tn.edu
GREER, T. Richard .... 585-594-6160 312 E
greerr@roberts.edu
GREER, Todd .... 251-442-2218.... 8 C
tgreer@umobile.edu
GREER, William .... 734-763-3571 231 H
wggreer@umich.edu
GREER, William, B .... 423-461-8710 422 E
bgreer@milligan.edu
GREGERSEN, Denise ..... 707-545-3647.. 26 H
denise@berginu.edu
GREGERSON, Robert, G 724-836-9911 400 H
rgregers@pitt.edu
GREGERSON, Sandra .... 832-813-6835 439 C
sandra.g.gregerson@lonestar.edu
GREGG, Carla .... 712-274-5463 168 E
gregg@morningside.edu
GREGG, Claire .... 864-596-9213 408 F
claire.gregg@converse.edu
GREGG, Cody .... 361-698-1931 435 G
cgregg2@delmar.edu
GREGG, Kori .... 620-441-5245 173 C
kori.gregg@cowley.edu
GREGG, Marisa .... 508-793-2720 208 D
GREGG, Phyllis .... 312-362-8850 136 H
pgregg@depaul.edu
GREGG, Rachel .... 619-594-2078.. 33 D
rgregg@sdsu.edu
GREGG, Robert, S .... 609-652-4542 283 E
robert.gregg@stockton.edu
GREGG, Tara .... 402-465-2488 268 G
tgregg@nebrwesleyan.edu
GREGO, Laura .... 704-290-5261 337 I
GREGOIRE, David, P ..... 518-564-2090 318 E
david.gregoire@plattsburgh.edu
GREGOIRE, JR.,
Paul, E .... 504-282-4455 190 F
pgregoire@nobts.edu
GREGOIRE, Tom .... 614-292-9426 358 D
gregoire.5@osu.edu
GREGOR, Jeffrey .... 630-870-7900 152 K
jgregor@waubonsee.edu
GREGORIO, Anthony ..... 504-280-6068 190 B
agregor1@uno.edu
GREGORSKI, Ryan .... 231-843-5985 233 A
rgregorski@westshore.edu
GREGORY, Alison .... 703-284-1673 468 H
alison.gregory@marymount.edu
GREGORY, Anne .... 260-982-5285 159 J
aggregory@manchester.edu
GREGORY, Anne .... 219-989-2360 160 D
anne.gregory@pnw.edu
GREGORY,
Archimandrite .... 530-467-3544.. 60 A
frg@spots.edu
GREGORY, Barb .... 410-386-8232 198 D
bgregory@carrollcc.edu
GREGORY, Brent .... 601-635-6200 246 A
bgregory@eccc.edu
GREGORY, Carolyn .... 216-368-5276 349 D
carolyn.gregory@case.edu
GREGORY, Charles .... 630-829-6004 133 E
cgregory@ben.edu
GREGORY, Charlie .... 308-635-6740 270 C
gregor43@wncc.edu
GREGORY, Christopher . 508-626-4510 213 A
cgregory@framingham.edu
GREGORY, Dan .... 320-308-4909 240 I
ddgregory@stcloudstate.edu
GREGORY, Dan .... 512-313-3000 433 N
daniel.gregory@concordia.edu
GREGORY, Danyelle ...... 740-826-8211 356 H
dgregory@muskingum.edu
GREGORY, David .... 617-747-6495 206 H
dgregory@berklee.edu
GREGORY, David .... 615-460-6538 418 B
david.gregory@belmont.edu
GREGORY, David, L ...... 606-783-5100 184 C
d.gregory@moreheadstate.edu
GREGORY, Deborah ...... 315-279-5135 303 G
dgregory@keuka.edu
GREGORY, Denise .... 205-726-2725.... 6 E
djgregor@samford.edu
GREGORY, Derek .... 570-961-7839 387 B
gregoryd@lackawanna.edu
GREGORY, Elizabeth ..... 660-263-4100 257 B
elizabethgregory@macc.edu
GREGORY, Ellen, D .... 859-846-6046 184 B
egregory@midway.edu
GREGORY, James, W .... 386-226-6000.. 99 A
GREGORY, Janna .... 207-834-7504 197 A
janna.gregory@maine.edu
GREGORY, Katherine .... 617-552-2867 207 C
katherine.gregory@bc.edu
GREGORY, Kimberly ..... 252-335-0821 333 G
kimberly_gregory73@albemarle.edu
GREGORY, Lesha .... 816-604-4339 255 H
lesha.gregory@mcckc.edu
GREGORY, Matthew ...... 617-322-3506 211 A
matthew_gregory@laboure.edu
GREGORY, Melissa .... 240-567-5036 200 G
melissa.gregory@montgomerycollege.edu
GREGORY, Miraglia ...... 707-654-4528.. 53 E
mgregory@napavalley.edu
GREGORY, Patrick .... 334-386-7259.... 5 C
pgregory@faulkner.edu
GREGORY, Rhonda .... 615-230-3675 425 E
rhonda.gregory@volstate.edu
GREGORY, Sadie .... 410-951-1295 204 B
srgregory@coppin.edu
GREGORY, Seamus .... 715-682-1395 494 G
sgregory@northland.edu
GREGORY, Tony .... 864-424-8000 413 H
gregorga@mailbox.sc.edu
GREGORYK, Kerry .... 701-845-7480 345 G
kerry.gregoryk@vcsu.edu
GREGSON, Joanna .... 253-535-7126 482 A
gregson@plu.edu
GREIG, Carl .... 903-223-3062 448 A
carl.greig@tamut.edu
GREIMAN, Judith .... 631-632-6302 317 A
judith.greiman@stonybrook.edu
GREIMAN, Judith .... 631-632-6538 317 A
judith.greiman@stonybrook.edu
GREINER, Gary .... 219-981-4291 157 C
gagreine@iu.edu
GREINER, Stephanie ..... 515-271-1386 165 G
stephanie.greiner@dmu.edu
GREISDORF, Steven ...... 978-646-4052 210 C
sgreisdorf@gcts.edu
GREITZ MILLER,
Roxanne .... 714-628-2628.. 36 B
rgmiller@chapman.edu
GRELINGER, Adam .... 316-942-4291 176 E
grelingera@newmanu.edu
GREMMELS, Gillian .... 515-271-4776 165 J
gillian.gremmels@drake.edu
GRENDER, Teresa .... 606-368-6044 178 G
teresagrender@alc.edu
GRENIER, Christine .... 630-617-3071 137 G
cgrenier@elmhurst.edu
GRENLUND, Lauren ...... 217-735-7238 142 H
lgrenlund@lincolncollege.edu
GRENNAN, Jon .... 845-451-1323 297 G
jon.grennan@culinary.edu
GRENZ, Jonathan .... 561-803-2295 105 C
jon_grenz@pba.edu
GRESCH, Mary .... 206-543-8222 485 A
mgresch@uw.edu
GRESHAM, Joanne .... 209-476-7840.. 67 E
jgresham@clc.edu
GRESHAM, Jonathan ..... 423-636-7300 426 E
jgresham@tusculum.edu
GRESHAM, Kathryn .... 828-641-0324 327 B
greshakb@brevard.edu
GRESHAM, Ralph .... 209-476-7840.. 67 E
rgresham@clc.edu
GRESS, Andrew .... 515-643-6637 168 D
agress@mercydesmoines.org
GRESS, Vicky .... 217-333-4885 152 B
gress@illinois.edu
GRESS, Vicky .... 217-333-4493 152 B
gress@illinois.edu
GRETCH, Jim .... 406-791-5320 265 H
jim.gretch@uprovidence.edu
GRETEN-HARRISON,
Derek .... 703-370-6600 476 E
dgreten-harrison@vts.edu
GRETEN-HARRISON,
Derek .... 703-370-6600 476 E
GRETINA, Lauren .... 718-518-4284 294 B
lgretina@hostos.cuny.edu
GREUBEL, Deb .... 540-887-7370 468 G
dgreubel@marybaldwin.edu
GREUFE, Sandra .... 641-648-4611 167 F
sandra.greufe@iavalley.edu
GREVE, Jennifer .... 402-844-7062 268 H
jenniferg@northeast.edu
GREVE, Scott .... 740-284-5891 352 I
sgreve@franciscan.edu
GREVING, John .... 402-465-2486 268 G
jgreving@nebrwesleyan.edu
GREW-GILLEN, Cheryl .. 701-777-4200 345 B
cheryl.grewgillen@und.edu
GREWAL, Daman .... 650-574-6550.. 62 I
grewald@smccd.edu
GREWAL, Parwinder ...... 956-665-3883 455 D
parwinder.grewal@utrgv.edu
GREY, Cynthia .... 727-302-6724 107 E
grey.cynthia@spcollege.edu
GREY, Gregory, D .... 410-334-2933 205 D
ggrey@worwic.edu
GREY, Marge .... 209-946-2311.. 71 E
mgrey@pacific.edu
GREY, Mary .... 413-796-2267 220 A
mgrey@wne.edu
GREY, Pam .... 408-864-8209.. 42 H
greypam@deanza.edu
GREY, Shenequa .... 225-771-2552 191 E
GREY GILBERT,
Jeannette .... 406-994-4284 264 C
jeannette.greygilbert@montana.edu
GREYDANUS, John .... 541-737-9099 375 A
john.greydanus@oregonstate.edu
GRGICAK, Catherine ..... 856-225-6142 281 G
cmg369@camden.rutgers.edu
GRIBBEN, Les .... 212-817-7414 293 F
lgribben@gc.cuny.edu
GRIBBIN, David .... 478-289-2047 118 C
dgribbin@ega.edu
GRIBBLE, Kari .... 608-663-2328 492 F
kgribble@edgewood.edu
GRIBBLE, Kari .... 608-663-2305 492 F
kgribble@edgewood.edu
GRIBBLE, Scott .... 308-632-6933 269 E
GRIBBLE, Shannon, L ... 301-687-7588 204 C
slgribble@frostburg.edu
GRIBBONS, Barry, C ...... 818-947-2321.. 49 G
gribbobc@lavc.edu
GRIBLIN, Diana .... 316-942-4291 176 E
griblind@newmanu.edu
GRICAR, Jeff .... 713-718-7431 437 C
jeff.gricar@hccs.edu
GRICE, Ronnie, D .... 785-532-1131 175 C
raker@ksu.edu
GRICE, Sharon .... 319-895-4162 164 G
sgrice@cornellcollege.edu
GRIECCI, Christina .... 800-877-4723 208 B
GRIEFF, Jamie .... 203-576-4961.. 89 C
GRIEGER, Mary .... 414-425-8300 495 A
mgrieger@shsst.edu
GRIEGO, Esperanza .... 505-467-6593 288 H
esperanzagriego@swc.edu
GRIEGO, Orlando .... 575-624-8020 287 B
GRIEGO, Orlando .... 815-740-3452 152 H
ogriego@stfrancis.edu
GRIER, Consuelo .... 425-564-2232 477 J
consuelo.grier@bellevuecollege.edu
GRIER, Derek .... 703-445-9056 472 G
GRIER, Ed .... 804-828-1062 473 B
egrier@vcu.edu
GRIER, Ed .... 408-554-4523.. 63 B
egrier@scu.edu
GRIER, Judith .... 757-789-1753 473 H
jgrier@es.vccs.edu
GRIES, Kathie .... 269-782-1425 231 A
kgries@swmich.edu
GRIES, Zachery, W .... 563-588-7136 168 A
zachery.gries@loras.edu
GRIESHEIMER, Tina .... 303-797-5901.. 77 I
tina.griesheimer@arapahoe.edu
GRIESSE, Sarah .... 612-330-1489 234 A
griesse@augsburg.edu
GRIEVE, Kimberly .... 605-658-3555 416 D
kimberly.grieve@usd.edu

GRIEVE, Robyn .... 408-260-0208.. 42 E daom@fivebranches.edu
GRIEWISCH, Carl .... 828-898-8862 330 E griewischc@lmc.edu
GRIFFEL, Michael, M ..... 541-346-2667 376 H mgriffel@uoregon.edu
GRIFFEN, Emily .... 413-542-2265 205 G egriffen@amherst.edu
GRIFFENBERG, William 210-784-4357 447 E william.griffenberg@tamusa.edu
GRIFFEY, Stacy .... 320-222-5200 240 F
GRIFFIN, Amy .... 317-917-5956 158 E agriffin76@ivytech.edu
GRIFFIN, Bruce .... 925-485-5247.. 35 I bgriffin@clpccd.org
GRIFFIN, Bryan, L .... 989-774-7112 222 E griff3bl@cmich.edu
GRIFFIN, Cathy .... 908-526-1200 281 A cathy.griffin@raritanval.edu
GRIFFIN, Clifton, P .... 410-548-3894 204 D cpgriffin@salisbury.edu
GRIFFIN, Colton .... 304-333-3688 489 K colton.griffin@fairmontstate.edu
GRIFFIN, Dan .... 731-661-5120 426 F dgriffin@uu.edu
GRIFFIN, David .... 617-824-8495 209 C david_griffin@emerson.edu
GRIFFIN, David .... 903-923-2340 435 H dgriffin@etbu.edu
GRIFFIN, Derika .... 256-395-2211.... 3 G
GRIFFIN, Donitha .... 334-876-9302.... 2 D donitha.griffin@wccs.edu
GRIFFIN, Elaine .... 615-966-5818 421 B elaine.griffin@lipscomb.edu
GRIFFIN, Erica .... 618-252-5400 149 I erica.griffin@sic.edu
GRIFFIN, George .... 229-386-3229 126 A ggriffin@southernregional.edu
GRIFFIN, Gerald .... 616-395-7785 225 D griffing@hope.edu
GRIFFIN, Heather .... 502-895-3411 183 H hgriffin@lpts.edu
GRIFFIN, James .... 860-906-5076.. 86 D jgriffin@capitalcc.edu
GRIFFIN, James .... 281-542-2089 443 A james.griffin@sjcd.edu
GRIFFIN, Jasmyn .... 785-320-4574 175 G jasmyngriffin@manhattantech.edu
GRIFFIN, Jason .... 567-661-2692 359 I jason_griffin@owens.edu
GRIFFIN, Jeff, D .... 504-816-8018 190 F jgriffin@nobts.edu
GRIFFIN, Jessica .... 252-246-1271 339 C jgriffin@wilsoncc.edu
GRIFFIN, Jill, G .... 812-488-2829 161 G jg121@evansville.edu
GRIFFIN, Joe .... 765-973-8633 157 A joegrif@iue.edu
GRIFFIN, Joel .... 864-941-8553 411 C griffin.j@ptc.edu
GRIFFIN, Joseph .... 410-617-2200 200 B jgriffin@loyola.edu
GRIFFIN, Kara .... 775-682-9013 271 E karag@unr.edu
GRIFFIN, Karen .... 813-253-7002 102 B kgriffin@hccfl.edu
GRIFFIN, Kenneth .... 765-674-6901 158 B ken.griffin@indwes.edu
GRIFFIN, Kotosha .... 757-455-3400 477 C kgriffin@vwu.edu
GRIFFIN, Lance .... 626-584-5423.. 43 B lancegriffin@fuller.edu
GRIFFIN, Larry .... 901-375-4400 422 A larrygriffin@midsouthchristian.edu
GRIFFIN, Leslie .... 662-846-4400 245 G lgriffin@deltastate.edu
GRIFFIN, Lisa .... 229-217-4144 126 A lgriffin@southernregional.edu
GRIFFIN, Lonnie .... 912-443-4174 125 B lgriffin@savannahtech.edu
GRIFFIN, Lori .... 253-912-3633 482 E lgriffin@pierce.ctc.edu
GRIFFIN, Louise .... 603-862-0152 274 F louise.griffin@unh.edu
GRIFFIN, Lynn .... 843-383-8071 408 B lgriffin@coker.edu
GRIFFIN, Mark .... 973-353-1458 282 B markg@newark.rutgers.edu
GRIFFIN, Mark .... 785-628-4026 173 H magriffin2@fhsu.edu
GRIFFIN, Meghan .... 863-667-5004 108 K mlgriffin@seu.edu
GRIFFIN, Micah .... 256-372-5601.... 1 A micha.griffin@aamu.edu
GRIFFIN, Michael .... 574-239-8307 156 A mgriffin@hcc-nd.edu
GRIFFIN, Michael .... 212-636-6520 300 C mgriffin19@fordham.edu
GRIFFIN, Mike .... 218-281-8679 244 A griffinm@crk.umn.edu
GRIFFIN, Neil .... 626-966-4576.. 25 H neil@jamagency.com
GRIFFIN, Neil .... 864-592-4897 412 E griffinn@sccsc.edu
GRIFFIN, Patricia, L ...... 785-628-5377 173 H pgriffin@fhsu.edu
GRIFFIN, CM, Patrick, J .... 718-990-6311 313 G griffinp@stjohns.edu
GRIFFIN, Peree, E .... 713-500-8444 456 B peree.e.griffin@uth.tmc.edu
GRIFFIN, Ragan, K .... 724-357-2218 394 C rgriffin@iup.edu
GRIFFIN, Rob .... 713-348-4009 442 F rob.griffin@rice.edu
GRIFFIN, Robert .... 401-254-3498 405 C rgriffin@rwu.edu
GRIFFIN, Robert .... 518-442-5142 316 A rpgriffin@albany.edu
GRIFFIN, Robert .... 901-375-4400 422 A robertgriffin@midsouthchristian.edu
GRIFFIN, Ryan .... 615-244-5848 423 C r.griffin@sae.edu
GRIFFIN, Sharon, R .... 919-516-4132 339 I srgriffin@st-aug.edu
GRIFFIN, Stephanie .... 847-467-3289 146 E stephanie.griffin@northwestern.edu
GRIFFIN, Stephen, L ...... 651-962-6855 244 E stephen.griffin@stthomas.edu
GRIFFIN, Terranze .... 973-353-5533 282 B terranze.griffin@rutgers.edu
GRIFFIN, Tim .... 602-639-7500.. 12 J
GRIFFIN, Timothy .... 724-799-2900.. 93 H
GRIFFIN, Timothy .... 201-216-5107 283 D timothy.griffin@stevens.edu
GRIFFIN, Troyline .... 706-821-8244 124 B tgriffin@paine.edu
GRIFFIN-DESTA, Jerlena .... 707-664-2880.. 34 B
GRIFFIN-SMITH, Elizabeth .... 972-721-5000 452 B egriffin@udallas.edu
GRIFFIN-SOBEL, Joyce, P .... 212-616-7284 301 C jgriffinsobel@helenefuld.edu
GRIFFING, Joan .... 316-295-5849 174 A joan_griffing@friends.edu
GRIFFIS, Emma .... 303-273-3067.. 79 J egriffis@mines.edu
GRIFFIS, Kathie .... 832-813-6737 439 C kathie.griffis@lonestar.edu
GRIFFIS, Sarah .... 617-305-1721 219 B sgriffis@suffolk.edu
GRIFFITH, Anne .... 574-631-4106 162 A agriffit@nd.edu
GRIFFITH, Belinda .... 404-270-6618 126 B bgriff14@spelman.edu
GRIFFITH, III, Charles .. 859-323-5079 185 F charleshgriffith@uky.edu
GRIFFITH, Claire .... 434-381-6479 471 I cgriffith@sbc.edu
GRIFFITH, Cynthia .... 281-756-3601 429 D cgriffith@alvincollege.edu
GRIFFITH, Darcell .... 302-831-6741.. 91 C darcellg@udel.edu
GRIFFITH, Debra .... 408-741-2438.. 75 E debra.griffith@westvalley.edu
GRIFFITH, Dede .... 254-298-8282 445 G dede.griffith@tempkejc.edu
GRIFFITH, Donald .... 559-453-3485.. 43 A donald.griffith@fresno.edu
GRIFFITH, Jackie .... 302-857-6707.. 90 E jgriffith@desu.edu
GRIFFITH, Jennifer .... 601-477-4029 246 G jennifer.griffith@jcjc.edu
GRIFFITH, Jimmy .... 828-726-2245 332 G jgriffith@cccti.edu
GRIFFITH, Jolene .... 641-782-1456 170 F griffith@swcciowa.edu
GRIFFITH, Kayin .... 503-554-2322 373 A kgriffith@georgefox.edu
GRIFFITH, Kelly .... 205-391-2211.... 3 E
GRIFFITH, Kelly .... 360-417-6201 482 C kgriffith@pencol.edu
GRIFFITH, Kevin .... 574-520-4879 157 E kevgriff@iusb.edu
GRIFFITH, Lauren .... 904-256-7535 102 H lgriffi9@ju.edu
GRIFFITH, Luther, T ...... 434-381-6325 471 I lgriffith@sbc.edu
GRIFFITH, Margo .... 907-474-6600.. 10 A margo.griffith@alaska.edu
GRIFFITH, Mary .... 615-547-1200 419 C mgriffith@cumberland.edu
GRIFFITH, Michell .... 845-938-4379 503 I michell.griffith@westpoint.edu
GRIFFITH, Rebecca (Becki) .... 817-515-1581 445 F rebecca.griffith@tccd.edu
GRIFFITH, Robert .... 417-447-8922 257 G griffitr@otc.edu
GRIFFITH, Roger, D ...... 304-647-6563 488 G rgriffith@newriver.edu
GRIFFITH, Ryan .... 209-946-2090.. 71 E rgriffith@pacific.edu
GRIFFITH, Sarah .... 360-442-2520 481 D sgriffith@lowercolumbia.edu
GRIFFITH, Shane .... 423-614-8505 420 H sgriffith@leeuniversity.edu
GRIFFITH, Tashika .... 727-341-4738 107 E griffith.tashika@spcollege.edu
GRIFFITH-KLINE, Cheri . 704-687-7077 342 D cgriffit@uncc.edu
GRIFFITHS, Doreen .... 918-631-4010 371 C doreen-griffiths@utulsa.edu
GRIFFITHS, James .... 602-489-5300.. 10 F james.griffiths@arizonachristian.edu
GRIFFITHS, José -Marie .... 605-256-5112 416 F presidentsoffice@dsu.edu
GRIFFITHS, Mary Ellen . 315-279-5237 303 G mgriffit@keuka.edu
GRIFFO, Nicole .... 716-926-8943 301 E ngriffo@hilbert.edu
GRIFFOR, Karl .... 520-452-2644.. 11 M griffork@cochise.edu
GRIFFUS, Randall .... 706-272-2509 118 B rgriffus@daltonstate.edu
GRIFFY, Loretta .... 931-221-7634 417 H griffyl@apsu.edu
GRIGG, Alan .... 313-993-1475 231 E griggae@udmercy.edu
GRIGG, Dan, G .... 260-422-5561 156 E dggrigg@indianatech.edu
GRIGG, Eddie, G .... 704-334-6882 328 B egrigg@charlottechristian.edu
GRIGG, James, J .... 803-323-2261 414 D griggj@winthrop.edu
GRIGG, Laurie, M .... 608-258-2401 499 A lmgrigg@madisoncollege.edu
GRIGGS, Brandon .... 254-519-5748 447 A griggs@tamuct.edu
GRIGGS, Jessica .... 318-342-3118 193 C mckee@ulm.edu
GRIGGS, Joyce .... 917-493-4113 305 A jgriggs@msmnyc.edu
GRIGGS, LaSonya .... 607-844-8222 322 D lag@tompkinscortland.edu
GRIGGS, Peter .... 530-242-7514.. 64 C pgriggs@shastacollege.edu
GRIGGS, Robert, J .... 605-367-8355 417 B robert.griggs@southeasttech.edu
GRIGGS, Ron .... 402-461-7337 267 C ron.griggs@hastings.edu
GRIGGS, Ronald, K .... 740-427-5632 354 I griggs@kenyon.edu
GRIGSBY, Bryon .... 717-290-8701 387 G
GRIGSBY, Bryon, L .... 610-861-1364 390 F grigsbyb@moravian.edu
GRIGSBY, Rebekah .... 903-923-2212 435 H rgrigsby@etbu.edu
GRILL, Joshua, L .... 570-577-3223 379 C josh.grill@bucknell.edu
GRILL, Larry .... 909-607-0175.. 37 F larry_grill@kgi.edu
GRILLO, Matthew .... 207-768-2792 195 G nmgrillo@nmcc.edu
GRILLO, Richard .... 305-442-9223 104 G rgrillo@mru.edu
GRILLO, Robert .... 305-348-2738 110 A robert.grillo@fiu.edu
GRIM, L. Dewey .... 443-518-4047 199 F lgrim@howardcc.edu
GRIMALDO, Cruz .... 510-642-6000.. 69 A
GRIMES, Brittany .... 309-341-5221 134 B bgrimes@sandburg.edu
GRIMES, Daniel .... 574-296-6266 153 F dbgrimes@ambs.edu
GRIMES, Deborah .... 252-527-6223 335 G ddgrimes39@lenoircc.edu
GRIMES, Donnie .... 606-539-4197 185 E donnie.grimes@ucumberlands.edu
GRIMES, Harley, G .... 252-335-3961 341 B hggrimes@ecsu.edu
GRIMES, Howard .... 210-458-7689 455 E howard.grimes@utsa.edu
GRIMES, Jana, L .... 641-269-4818 166 G grimesjana@grinnell.edu
GRIMES, Kathleen, A .... 518-580-5700 315 F kgrimes@skidmore.edu
GRIMES, Kendra, S .... 804-752-7374 469 F kendragrimes@rmc.edu
GRIMES, Kristen .... 951-487-3002.. 53 A kgrimes@msjc.edu
GRIMES, Paul .... 620-235-4598 177 A paul.grimes@pittstate.edu
GRIMES, Robert (Bud), D .... 731-881-7615 427 D bgrimes@utm.edu
GRIMES, Sidney, A .... 212-217-4040 299 D sidney_grimes@fitnyc.edu
GRIMES, Terri, A .... 815-599-3514 139 A terri.grimes@highland.edu
GRIMES-HILLMAN, Michelle .... 714-432-5015.. 38 B mgrimes@cccd.edu
GRIMM, Constance .... 319-296-4439 166 H constance.grimm@hawkeyecollege.edu
GRIMM, Gary .... 503-370-6814 377 F ggrimm@willamette.edu
GRIMM, Josh .... 225-578-1899 189 E jgrimm@lsu.edu
GRIMM, Randy .... 816-322-0110 251 B randy.grimm@calvay.edu
GRIMM, Rich .... 864-977-7010 410 I rich.grimm@ngu.edu
GRIMM, Tonya .... 660-626-2076 250 A tgrimm@atsu.edu
GRIMMER, Brett .... 618-374-5180 147 E brett.grimmer@principia.edu
GRIMMER, Kevin, M ..... 315-792-7520 321 B grimmek@sunypoly.edu
GRIMMETT, Branden ..... 310-258-8779.. 51 A branden.grimmett@lmu.edu
GRIMMETT, Wanda .... 870-543-5907.. 21 B wgrimmett@seark.edu
GRIMSHAW, Carrie .... 508-213-2234 217 H carrie.grimshaw@nichols.edu
GRIMSON, W. Eric, L ... 617-253-5415 216 B
GRIMSRUD, Bob .... 605-718-2953 417 D robert.grimsrud@wdt.edu
GRINAGE, Leslie .... 212-854-5262 291 A lgrinage@barnard.edu
GRINBERG, Nancy .... 443-518-4160 201 E ngrinberg@pgcc.edu
GRINDE, Jane .... 701-328-4217 345 A jane.grinde@ndus.edu
GRINDLE, Blaine, D ...... 585-292-2814 307 B bgrindle@monroecc.edu
GRINDSTAFF, Chad .... 423-636-7300 426 E cgrindstaff@tusculum.edu
GRINER, Andrea .... 478-757-3551 116 G agriner@centralgatech.edu
GRINNAN, Susan .... 804-706-5035 474 B sgrinnan@jtcc.edu
GRINNELL, Nevin .... 972-860-8201 434 G
GRIPP, Kristine .... 216-791-5000 350 I kristine.gripp@cim.edu
GRIPPE, Al .... 847-376-7099 146 G agrippe@oakton.edu
GRIPPO, Marisa .... 870-235-4038.. 21 C mcgrippo@saumag.edu
GRISHAM, Bob .... 360-438-4368 482 I bgrisham@stmartin.edu
GRISHOW, Kevin .... 909-387-1608.. 60 F kgrishow@sbccd.cc.ca.us
GRISSIM, Robert .... 256-551-3145.... 2 E robert.grissim@drakestate.edu
GRISWOLD, Al .... 800-222-4222 385 B
GRISWOLD, Emmett ...... 229-430-3511 114 I egriswold@albanytech.edu
GRISWOLD, Lauren .... 208-426-1428 130 H laurengriswold@boisestate.edu
GRISWOLD, Matt .... 608-609-6033.. 81 M mgriswo2@msudenver.edu
GRISWOLD, Oliver .... 207-893-7644 196 C ogriswold@sjcme.edu
GRISWOLD, Richard, M 617-585-0200 207 A richard.griswold@the-bac.edu

GRISWOLD, Robyn .... 603-578-8900 272 M
GRISWOLD, Stephanie .. 708-239-4820 151 A
stephanie.griswold@trnty.edu
GRIVETTI, Gino .... 414-410-4722 491 I
ggrivetti@stritch.edu
GRIZANTI, Robert .... 716-896-0700 324 E
bgrizanti@villa.edu
GRIZZELL, Kyle .... 513-562-6262 347 I
kgrizzell@artacademy.edu
GRIZZLE, Debra, F .... 706-245-7226 118 D
dgrizzle@ec.edu
GRIZZLE, Jerry, W .... 575-624-8001 287 B
supt@nmmi.edu
GRIZZLE, Kendra .... 620-278-4280 177 H
kgrizzle@sterling.edu
GROB, Lance .... 425-640-1459 480 A
GROCE, Jeanetta .... 903-875-7316 440 D
jeanetta.groce@navarrocollege.edu
GROCOCK, Trent, A ...... 574-631-8966 162 A
tgrocock@nd.edu
GRODE-HANKS, Carol .. 605-995-3023 415 E
carol.grode-hanks@mitchelltech.edu
GRODEN, Joanna .... 312-996-9450 151 G
jgroden@uic.edu
GRODSKY, Jennifer .... 202-393-7272 207 E
jgrodsky@bu.edu
GRODZICKER, Terri, I ... 516-367-6890 296 C
GROEN, Gwen .... 641-648-4611 167 F
gwen.groen@iavalley.edu
GROENER, Michael .... 510-436-1520.. 45 E
groener@hnu.edu
GROENEVELD, Bill .... 805-565-6849.. 76 A
procurement@westmont.edu
GROENEWOLD,
Suzanne .... 603-542-7744 273 B
sgroenewold@ccsnh.edu
GROENNERT, Harvey .... 618-394-2200 142 C
hgroennert@lakeland.cc.i.us
GROFF, David .... 541-885-1116 374 I
david.groff@oit.edu
GROFF, Theresa .... 303-797-5625.. 77 I
theresa.groff@arapahoe.edu
GROGAN,
Jacqueline, H .... 718-990-6176 313 G
groganj@stjohns.edu
GROGAN, John Paul ..... 802-656-0123 463 A
john.grogan@uvm.edu
GROGAN, Karen .... 304-327-4086 489 I
kgrogan@bluefieldstate.edu
GROGG, Ben .... 785-539-3571 176 A
bgrogg@mccks.edu
GROGG, Sam .... 516-877-3810 289 I
sgrogg@adelphi.edu
GROH, Sara .... 315-228-6134 296 E
sgroh@colgate.edu
GROLEAU, Ron, W .... 815-224-0482 140 E
ron_groleau@ivcc.edu
GROMAKOV, Max .... 800-686-1883 222 G
GROMATZKY, Steven ...... 913-360-7511 171 J
sgromatzky@benedictine.edu
GROMIS, Jeffrey .... 610-341-1775 383 B
jgromis@eastern.edu
GRONA, Marion .... 940-552-6291 457 C
mgrona@vernoncollege.edu
GROND, Greta .... 712-707-7248 169 D
ggrond@nwciowa.edu
GRONDA, Hellene .... 503-223-8188 375 F
hellene.gronda@processwork.edu
GRONDIN, Megan .... 817-722-1741 438 G
megan.grondin@tku.edu
GRONERT, Scott .... 414-229-5895 496 B
sgronert@uwm.edu
GRONEWALD, Kate .... 903-233-3291 439 A
kategronewald@letu.edu
GRONLUND, Robin .... 802-651-5911 462 A
rgronlund@champlain.edu
GRONNIGER, Eileen, C . 785-442-6010 174 F
egronniger@highlandcc.edu
GRONO, Anthony .... 718-817-4943 300 C
grono@fordham.edu
GRONSKY, Jennifer .... 215-503-8189 399 E
jennifer.gronsky@jefferson.edu
GRONSKY, Jennifer, M . 215-503-8189 399 E
jennifer.gronsky@jefferson.edu
GROOBY, Stuart .... 302-857-6000.. 90 E
sgrooby@desu.edu
GROOM, Ruth .... 513-529-9210 356 A
groomra@miamioh.edu
GROOMS, Catherine ..... 661-362-5151.. 38 D
catherine.grooms@canyons.edu
GROOMS, Daniel, L ...... 515-294-9860 163 G
dgrooms@iastate.edu
GROOMS, Kenya .... 312-922-1884 143 G
kgrooms@maccormac.edu
GROPP, Jonathan .... 864-231-2000 406 F
jgropp@andersonuniversity.edu
GROPPER, Daniel .... 561-297-3635 109 J
dgropper@fau.edu
GROS, Kathy, R .... 504-865-3237 190 C
kgros@loyno.edu
GROSBY, Karen .... 954-262-5885 105 A
grosby@nsu.nova.edu
GROSCH, Darren .... 323-953-4000.. 49 A
groschda@lacitycollege.edu
GROSE, Kelly .... 304-734-6636 488 D
kelly.grose@bridgevalley.edu
GROSPITCH, Eric .... 785-670-2100 178 C
eric.grospitch@washburn.edu
GROSS, Amanda, R .... 716-839-8210 298 A
agross@daemen.edu
GROSS, Bryan, J .... 413-782-1233 220 A
bryan.gross@wne.edu
GROSS, Calvin .... 859-985-3274 179 I
grossj@berea.edu
GROSS, Candace .... 870-512-7716.. 18 A
candace_gross@asun.edu
GROSS, Carla, E .... 717-796-1800 389 H
cgross@messiah.edu
GROSS, Charles .... 406-447-5480 263 B
cgross@carroll.edu
GROSS, Daryl, J .... 323-343-3080.. 31 E
dgross4@calstatela.edu
GROSS, Dawn .... 508-999-8665 212 A
dgross1@umassd.edu
GROSS, Dolores .... 915-831-6484 436 A
dgross2@epcc.edu
GROSS, Erik, E .... 603-862-1584 274 F
erik.gross@unh.edu
GROSS, Heidi .... 307-681-6400 501 G
hgross@sheridan.edu
GROSS, Henry .... 706-649-1883 117 I
hgross@columbustech.edu
GROSS, Laura .... 518-255-5531 319 C
grossll@cobleskill.edu
GROSS, Lois .... 516-739-1545 308 F
studentservices@nyctcm.edu
GROSS, Michael .... 732-987-2373 278 A
mgross@georgian.edu
GROSS, Michael, L .... 610-921-7672 377 G
mgross@albright.edu
GROSS, Monika .... 301-860-4091 204 A
mgross@bowiestate.edu
GROSS, Scott .... 606-487-3528 181 I
scott.gross@kctcs.edu
GROSS, Steven .... 973-698-4944.. 16 G
steven.gross@phoenix.edu
GROSS, Susan .... 201-216-8142 283 D
susan.gross@stevens.edu
GROSS, Tim .... 770-426-2658 122 C
tgross@life.edu
GROSS METHNER,
Sara, E .... 651-962-6901 244 E
gros6968@stthomas.edu
GROSSE, Barry .... 706-721-0900 116 A
agrosse@augusta.edu
GROSSE, Kerry, J .... 414-955-8874 493 F
kegrosse@mcw.edu
GROSSI, OSB, Anthony 724-537-4554 397 I
anthony.grossi@email.stvincent.edu
GROSSKOPF, John .... 850-973-1601 104 L
grosskopfj@nfc.edu
GROSSMAN, David .... 714-992-7046.. 54 C
dgrossman@fullcoll.edu
GROSSMAN, LuAnn .... 605-331-6738 417 C
luann.grossman@usiouxfalls.edu
GROSSMAN, Michal ...... 732-414-2834 285 H
GROSSMAN, Pam .... 215-898-7014 400 F
grossman@gse.upenn.edu
GROSSMAN, Seth .... 202-885-2121.. 91 F
sethg@american.edu
GROSSMAN BLOOM,
Stacie .... 212-998-1212 309 F
GROSVENOR, Ari .... 978-921-4242 217 B
ari.grosvenor@montserrat.edu
GROSVENOR, Christy .... 303-762-6902.. 80 I
christy.grosvenor@denverseminary.edu
GROTE, Justin .... 614-287-3853 351 C
jgrote5@cscc.edu
GROTE, Lisa .... 605-626-2521 416 G
lisa.grote@northern.edu
GROTEGUT, Chris, J ...... 920-565-1000 493 A
grotegutcj@lakeland.edu
GROTH, Clayton .... 608-249-6611 492 H
cgroth@herzing.edu
GROTH, Dennis .... 812-856-1079 156 F
iuldean@indiana.edu
GROTH, Kathy .... 219-464-5114 162 D
kathy.groth@valpo.edu
GROTHE, Malcolm .... 206-934-6808 483 A
malcolm.grothe@seattlecolleges.edu
GROTTON, Chris .... 207-941-7785 194 F
grottonc@husson.edu
GROTZINGER, John, P . 626-395-6005.. 28 J
grotz@gps.caltech.edu
GROUNDS, Cynthia ...... 785-749-8418 174 D
cynthia.grounds@bie.edu
GROURKE, Stephen, J .. 610-526-1389 378 D
stephen.grourke@theamericancollege.edu
GROVE, Allison, A .... 570-326-3761 392 W
aab14@pct.edu
GROVE, Amber .... 208-376-7731 130 G
agrove@boisebible.edu
GROVE, Jessica .... 314-539-5000 259 A
GROVE, Laurie .... 717-396-7188 399 C
grove@stevenscollege.edu
GROVE, Luke, J .... 515-574-1062 167 A
grove@iowacentral.edu
GROVE, Melinda, F .... 330-972-8574 361 H
mgrove@uakron.edu
GROVE, Russell .... 208-376-7731 130 G
rgove@boisebible.edu
GROVE, Shannon, D ..... 814-886-6391 390 G
sgrove@mtaloy.edu
GROVE, Theresa .... 229-333-5800 127 E
tjgrove@valdosta.edu
GROVEMAN, Susan ...... 661-763-7942.. 67 G
sgroveman@taftcollege.edu
GROVENSTEIN,
Elizabeth .... 919-807-7070 331 L
GROVER, Arthur, G .... 610-660-1111 397 G
agrover@sju.edu
GROVER, Carol .... 315-781-3339 301 F
groverc@hws.edu
GROVER, Dustin .... 918-540-6202 366 F
dugrover@neo.edu
GROVER, Felicia .... 904-470-8013.. 98 L
GROVER, Jim .... 817-272-1021 454 I
grover@uta.edu
GROVER-BISKER, Edna . 573-341-4292 261 D
egroverb@mst.edu
GROVER-ROOSA,
Janice .... 307-382-1701 501 J
jgrover@westernwyoming.edu
GROVES, Allen .... 315-443-1870 321 G
GROVES, Allen, W .... 434-924-7429 472 D
awg8vd@virginia.edu
GROVES, JR., David ..... 217-443-8864 136 G
dgroves@dacc.edu
GROVES, Devany .... 904-620-2506 111 B
dgroves@unf.edu
GROVES, Emily .... 405-789-7661 369 I
emily.groves@swcu.edu
GROVES, Katharina .... 719-389-6000.. 78 I
GROVES, Kathy .... 573-592-1106 262 G
kathy.groves@williamwoods.edu
GROVES, Loren .... 307-681-6460 501 G
lgroves@sheridan.edu
GROVES, Robert, M ...... 202-687-6400.. 92 E
provost@georgetown.edu
GROVES, Shelley .... 405-789-7661 369 I
shelley.groves@swcu.edu
GROVES, Suzanne .... 817-515-1541 445 F
suzanne.groves@tccd.edu
GROVES, William .... 937-769-1345 347 H
bgroves@antioch.edu
GROVES-SCOTT,
Victoria .... 501-450-3175.. 23 H
vickigs@uca.edu
GROW, David .... 801-274-3280 461 E
dgrow@wgu.edu
GROW, Tamera, J .... 660-562-1146 257 E
tammi@nwmissouri.edu
GROYSMAN, Natasga .... 954-492-5353.. 97 G
ngroysman@citycollege.edu
GROZA, Adam .... 909-687-1450.. 43 D
adamgroza@gs.edu
GRREEN-ROGERS,
Martine Kei .... 336-770-3243 343 D
GRUBB, Autumn .... 863-680-5118 100 H
agrubb@flsouthern.edu
GRUBB, Derek .... 303-914-6516.. 83 C
derek.grubb@rrcc.edu
GRUBB, John .... 423-354-5144 425 A
jmgrubb@northeaststate.edu
GRUBB, Kevin .... 610-519-4060 401 K
kevin.c.grubb@villanova.edu
GRUBB, Lillie .... 620-223-2700 173 I
lillieg@fortscott.edu
GRUBBS, Laurie .... 850-644-3296 110 C
lgrubbs@fsu.edu
GRUBBS, Norris, C .... 504-282-4455 190 F
provostadmin@nobts.edu
GRUBE, AJ .... 828-227-3028 343 E
agrube@wcu.edu
GRUBE, Sean .... 540-231-9811 476 C
grube@vt.edu
GRUBER, Ann Marie ..... 440-525-7840 354 L
agruber@lakelandcc.edu
GRUBER,
Christopher, J .... 704-894-2710 328 E
chgruber@davidson.edu
GRUBER, Elizabeth .... 570-484-2858 394 E
egruber@lockhaven.edu
GRUBER, Jay .... 202-687-7014.. 92 E
jg1502@georgetown.edu
GRUBISIC, Charles, M .. 920-565-1000 493 A
grubisiccm@lakeland.edu
GRUCZELAK, Jennifer ... 415-575-6100.. 28 I
jgruczelak@ciis.edu
GRUDZINSKI, Shanelle . 402-844-7215 268 H
shanelle@northeast.edu
GRUENER, David .... 409-266-9923 456 E
dcgruene@utmb.edu
GRUENIG, Gwendolyn .. 907-450-8190.... 9 I
gdgruenig@alaska.edu
GRUENWALD, John ...... 610-399-2051 393 F
jgruenwald@cheyney.edu
GRUETT, Jon .... 636-584-6575 253 B
jon.gruett@eastcentral.edu
GRUHLER, Sarah .... 360-992-2406 478 I
sgruhler@clark.edu
GRUICHICH, Dawn .... 480-732-7050.. 12 O
dawn.gruichich@cgc.edu
GRUITS, Christopher, A 215-898-5828 400 F
GRUNBLATT, Akiva .... 718-268-4700 312 A
GRUNDEN, Cynthia .... 312-369-7125 136 D
cgrunden@colum.edu
GRUNDEN, Ken .... 614-837-4088 363 D
grundenk@valorcollege.edu
GRUNDER, Mark .... 989-358-7376 221 C
grunderm@alpenacc.edu
GRUNDER, Ty, J .... 563-333-5736 169 G
grundertyj@sau.edu
GRUNDIG, John .... 863-680-6212 100 H
jgrundig@flsouthern.edu
GRUNDY, Christy .... 419-289-5306 347 J
cgrundy@ashland.edu
GRUNDY, Dallas, A ...... 330-972-8877 361 H
dgrundy@uakron.edu
GRUNDY, Margaret, S .. 434-982-6409 472 D
mg8r@virginia.edu
GRUNEIRO, Nieves .... 973-328-5400 276 J
ngruneiro@ccm.edu
GRUNEWALD, Jeff .... 920-693-1119 498 H
jeffrey.grunewald@gotoltc.edu
GRUNKEMEYER, Heidi .. 402-280-1272 266 H
heidigrunkemeyer@creighton.edu
GRUNKLEE, David .... 319-296-4042 166 H
david.grunklee@hawkeyecollege.edu
GRUNLOH, Jean Anne .. 217-234-5329 142 C
jgrunloh@lakeland.cc.il.us
GRUNOW, Tamie, L ...... 513-556-1015 361 J
grunowtl@ucmail.uc.edu
GRUNWALD, Gerald ...... 215-503-8982 399 E
gerald.grunwald@jefferson.edu
GRUPP, Laurie .... 203-254-4000.. 87 I
lgrupp@fairfield.edu
GRUS, Shannon .... 573-897-5000 260 A
GRUSE, Douglas .... 518-244-4593 313 A
grused@sage.edu
GRUSKA, Julie .... 320-363-3395 243 B
jgruska@csbsju.edu
GRUSKA, Julie, E .... 320-363-3395 235 F
jgruska@csbsju.edu
GRUSKOS, Cynthia .... 732-224-2204 276 B
cgruskos@brookdalecc.edu
GRUSZKA, Bill .... 678-466-4351 117 D
billgruska@clayton.edu
GRUTZIK, Cynthia .... 415-338-2686.. 33 E
cgrutzik@sfsu.edu
GRUVER, Nolan .... 509-533-8481 479 B
nolan.gruver@ccs.spokane.edu
GRUVER, Nolan .... 509-434-8481 479 D
nolan.gruver@ccs.spokane.edu
GRUVER, Randi .... 515-574-1148 167 A
gruver@iowacentral.edu
GRUYS, Melissa .... 260-481-6461 160 C
gruysm@pfw.edu

GUNS, Michael 608-663-6714 492 F mguns@edgewood.edu
GUNTER, Mary 479-968-0332 18 C mgunter@atu.edu
GUNTER, Precious 239-745-4366 109 K pgunter@fgcu.edu
GUNTER, Rée 203-837-8691 86 B gunterr@wcsu.edu
GUNTER, Robert 205-929-6442 2 H rgunter@lawsonstate.edu
GUNTER, Steve 828-766-1320 336 A sgunter@mayland.edu
GUNTER-SMITH, Pamela, J 717-815-1221 403 F collegepresident@ycp.edu
GUNTHER, Amanda 724-805-2933 397 I amanda.gunther@email.stvincent.edu
GUNTHER, Elisabeth 209-500-8502 70 A egunther@ucmerced.edu
GUNTHER, Janet 270-707-3833 182 B janet.gunther@kctcs.edu
GUNTHER, John 619-849-2235 57 J johngunther@pointloma.edu
GUNTHER, Karah, L 804-828-6879 473 B klgunther@vcu.edu
GUNTHORPE, Sydney, D 505-224-4427 285 N sydney@cnm.edu
GUNWALL, Claire 701-328-4140 345 A claire.gunwall@ndus.edu
GUNZENHAUSER, Bonnie 216-397-1940 353 O bgunzenhauser@jcu.edu
GUO, Lan 816-415-5032 262 F guol@william.jewell.edu
GUORDANO, Deborah 212-517-0400 305 E
GUPCHUP, Gireesh 618-536-3465 150 A gireesh.gupchup@siu.edu
GUPTA, Akhil 401-598-1954 404 D akhil.gupta@jwu.edu
GUPTA, Priya 213-738-6777 66 B psgupta@swlaw.edu
GUPTA, Sanjay 517-355-8379 227 F gupta@broad.msu.edu
GUPTA, Sunil, B 718-482-5301 294 F sbgupta@lagcc.cuny.edu
GURDINEER, Allison 914-674-7601 306 C agurdineer@mercy.edu
GURECKI, Christopher, M 920-923-8950 493 D cmgurecki64@marianuniversity.edu
GUREK, Shannon 413-538-2040 217 C sgurek@mtholyoke.edu
GURGEL, Richard, L 507-354-8221 236 J gurgelrl@mlc-wels.edu
GURLAND, Suzanne 802-443-5323 462 E sgurland@middlebury.edu
GURLER, Dan 415-575-6125 28 I dgurler@ciis.edu
GURLEY, Dustin, H 919-209-2116 335 F dcgurley@johnstoncc.edu
GURLEY, Mary Ellen 706-272-4438 118 B megurley@daltonstate.edu
GURNAK, John 773-508-7476 143 C jgurnak@luc.edu
GURNEY, Holly 207-741-5545 195 H hgurney@smccme.edu
GURROLA, Andrea 505-224-4000 285 N agurrola1@cnm.edu
GURSKI, Kelsea 217-206-7797 152 A kgurs2@uis.edu
GURSKIS, Daniel, A 973-655-5104 279 B gurskisd@montclair.edu
GURTATOWSKI, Jill 859-985-3968 179 I gurtowskij@berea.edu
GURULE, Dan 816-531-5223 251 K
GUSKIEWICZ, Kevin, M 919-962-1365 342 C chancellor@unc.edu
GUST, Jonathan 610-519-6508 401 K jonathan.gust@villanova.edu
GUSTAFSON, Anita, O 478-301-2915 122 E gustafson_ao@mercer.edu
GUSTAFSON, Bridget 701-228-5657 346 B bridget.gustafson@dakotacollege.edu
GUSTAFSON, Christine, A 603-641-7250 274 A cgustafson@anselm.edu
GUSTAFSON, Crandon 858-566-1200 40 J cgustafson@disd.edu
GUSTAFSON, Eric 508-626-4012 213 A egustafson1@framingham.edu
GUSTAFSON, Eric 704-847-5600 340 F egustafson@ses.edu
GUSTAFSON, Jacqueline 951-552-8372 27 G jgustafson@calbaptist.edu
GUSTAFSON, Katherine 813-419-5100 233 C gustafsk@cooley.edu
GUSTAFSON, Katie 218-879-0808 238 B katie.gustafson@fdltcc.edu
GUSTAFSON, Katie 802-828-8714 463 B katie.gustafson@vcfa.edu
GUSTAFSON, Terri 231-995-1076 229 A tgustafson@nmc.edu
GUSTAVSON, Leif 503-352-1431 375 C gustavson@pacificu.edu
GUSTER, Stephanie 423-236-2020 423 F sguster@southern.edu
GUSTIN HAMROCK, Sarah 717-796-1800 389 H sgustinhamrock@messiah.edu
GUTFREUND, Dina 718-252-6333 326 B
GUTFREUND, Meir Chaim 718-252-6333 326 B
GUTH, Carrie 904-620-2518 111 B carrie.guth@unf.edu
GUTH, Erin 608-363-2175 491 H guthe@beloit.edu
GUTH, Virginia 847-628-1151 141 C gguth@judsonu.edu
GUTH, Wendee 309-999-4656 139 B wendee.guth@icc.edu
GUTHIER, Mark, C 608-262-4463 495 D mcguthier@wisc.edu
GUTHMAN, John, C 516-463-6791 301 G john.c.guthman@hofstra.edu
GUTHMILLER, Janet 402-472-1344 269 K janet.guthmiller@unmc.edu
GUTHORN, Amanda 215-951-1300 387 A guthorn@lasalle.edu
GUTHREY, Janna 870-248-4000 18 F janna.guthrey@blackrivertech.edu
GUTHRIE, Amanda 806-720-7327 439 D amanda.guthrie@lcu.edu
GUTHRIE, Belinda 408-554-4113 63 B bguthrie@scu.edu
GUTHRIE, JR., Charles, D 330-972-5575 361 H cguthrie@uakron.edu
GUTHRIE, Chris 615-322-9800 428 A chris.guthrie@vanderbilt.edu
GUTHRIE, Edward, L 302-356-6870 91 E edward.l.guthrie@wilmu.edu
GUTHRIE, Erin 206-685-9956 485 A eguthrie@uw.edu
GUTHRIE, Grant 601-318-6193 249 H grant.guthrie@wmcarey.edu
GUTHRIE, Gregory 641-472-1125 168 C gguthrie@miu.edu
GUTHRIE, Kasie 979-230-3204 431 I kasie.guthrie@brazosport.edu
GUTHRIE, Ken 423-425-4714 427 C kenneth-guthrie01@utc.edu
GUTHRIE, Lauren 877-248-6724 12 K lguthrie@hmu.edu
GUTHRIE, Mary 847-317-7114 151 C mcguthrie@tiu.edu
GUTHRIE, Owen 907-455-2071 10 A obguthrie@alaska.edu
GUTIERREZ, Alfonso 305-428-5700 104 F capes@aii.edu
GUTIERREZ, Allen 817-722-1700 438 G
GUTIERREZ, Ann, E 956-326-2346 446 E ann.gutierrez@tamiu.edu
GUTIERREZ, Anthony 805-546-3289 40 F agutierr@cuesta.edu
GUTIERREZ, Brian, G 817-257-7815 448 F brian.gutierrez@tcu.edu
GUTIERREZ, Edna, I 787-720-1022 505 E registrador@atlanticu.edu
GUTIERREZ, Eduardo 305-271-6555 95 C
GUTIERREZ, Eric 212-961-3380 290 H egutierrez3@bankstreet.edu
GUTIERREZ, Glenn 989-275-5000 226 D glenn.gutierrez@kirtland.edu
GUTIERREZ, Jason, L 719-333-2072 503 D jason.gutierrez.ctr@usafa.edu
GUTIERREZ, Javier 651-523-3076 236 B jgutierrez@hamline.edu
GUTIERREZ, Jorge 310-660-6172 41 E jgutierrez@elcamino.edu
GUTIERREZ, Jose 801-818-8900 459 J jgutierrez@provocollege.edu
GUTIERREZ, Juan 714-432-5725 38 B jgutierrez@occ.cccd.edu
GUTIERREZ, Lily 505-467-6603 288 H lilygutierrez@swc.edu
GUTIERREZ, Marisol 915-778-4001 444 H
GUTIERREZ, Martin 530-741-6939 77 E mgutierr@yccd.edu
GUTIERREZ, Mercedes 213-891-2173 48 I gutiermc4@laccd.edu
GUTIERREZ, Michael 916-558-2101 50 J gutierm@scc.losrios.edu
GUTIERREZ, Moises 562-938-4750 48 F mgutierrez@lbcc.edu
GUTIERREZ, Nancy, A 704-687-0081 342 D ngutierr@uncc.edu
GUTIERREZ, Omar 559-489-2232 67 B omar.gutierrez@fresnocitycollege.edu
GUTIERREZ, Robert 408-274-7900 62 G robert.gutierrez@evc.edu
GUTIERREZ, Robert 408-288-3104 62 H robert.gutierrez@sjcc.edu
GUTIERREZ, Robert 570-577-3310 379 C robert.gutierrez@bucknell.edu
GUTIERREZ, Roberto 305-348-2494 110 A robert.gutierrez@fiu.edu
GUTIERREZ, Roberto 541-880-2210 373 C gutierrezr@klamathcc.edu
GUTIERREZ, Tiffany 518-694-7254 289 J tiffany.gutierrez@acphs.edu
GUTIERREZ, Tim 505-277-0963 288 J tguiterr@unm.edu
GUTIERREZ-SANDOVAL, Yvonne 562-938-4631 48 F ygutierrez@lbcc.edu
GUTKIN, Jeffrey 973-290-4046 282 I jgutkin@steu.edu
GUTKNECHT, Joy 541-867-8515 374 F joy.gutknecht@oregoncoast.edu
GUTKNECHT, June 239-590-1227 109 K jgutknec@fgcu.edu
GUTKNECHT, Leah, K 319-273-2846 164 A leah.gutknecht@uni.edu
GUTMAN, Zack 303-329-6355 79 L clinicdirector@cstcm.edu
GUTMANN, Amy 215-898-7221 400 F president@upenn.edu
GUTMANN, Mark 239-939-4766 109 A
GUTOSKEY, David, P 410-543-6040 204 D dpgutoskey@salisbury.edu
GUTOW, Amy 207-326-2441 196 A amy.gutow@mma.edu
GUTTENTAG, Christoph, O 919-684-2898 328 F christoph.guttentag@duke.edu
GUTTERUD, Molly 866-766-0331 54 D mgutterud@ncu.edu
GUTTMAN, Minerva 201-692-2890 277 I minerva_guttman@fdu.edu
GUTTMAN, Stephen, J 610-758-4204 388 E sjg2@lehigh.edu
GUVARA, Walter 818-766-8151 39 H
GUY, Elmer 505-387-7370 286 I eguy@navajotech.edu
GUY, Georgina 949-582-4738 65 D gguy@saddleback.edu
GUY, Kathleen 404-261-1441 123 K kguy1@oglethorpe.edu
GUY, Kip 859-257-5290 185 F kip.guy@uky.edu
GUY, Stephanie 206-934-7935 483 D stephanie.guy@seattlecolleges.edu
GUY, Sunethra 901-381-3939 428 B sunethra@visible.edu
GUY, Todd 562-903-6000 27 A todd.guy@biola.edu
GUY-ANDERSON, Adrian 504-816-4713 186 I aguy@dillard.edu
GUY-LEVAR, Sarah 218-235-2169 241 E sarah.guy-levar@vcc.edu
GUY-SHEFTAL, Beverly 404-270-5624 126 B bsheftal@spelman.edu
GUYETTE, Daniel 269-387-5810 233 B daniel.guyette@wmich.edu
GUYETTE, Joyce 864-379-8858 409 E jguyette@erskine.edu
GUYETTE, Randy 828-835-4265 338 E rguyette@tricountycc.edu
GUYTON, Deirdre 304-327-4569 489 I dguyton@bluefieldstate.edu
GUYTON, Sondra 910-879-5634 332 D sguyton@bladencc.edu
GUZMÁN LÓPEZ, Osvaldo 787-765-9882 511 F osvaldo.guzmanlopez@upr.edu
GUZMAN, Abel 661-395-4011 46 L
GUZMAN, Alejandro 818-523-9026 49 C guzmana4@lamission.edu
GUZMAN, Amanda 575-492-2176 289 F aguzman@usw.edu
GUZMAN, Andre 509-793-2077 478 B andreg@bigbend.edu
GUZMAN, Andrew 213-740-7331 73 D andrewgu@usc.edu
GUZMAN, Ariel 787-751-0160 506 F aguzman@cmpr.pr.gov
GUZMAN, Jill 973-720-2257 284 J guzmanj21@wpunj.edu
GUZMAN, John 718-963-4112 291 J jguzman@boricuacollege.edu
GUZMAN, Juan 308-865-8127 269 I guzmanj@unk.edu
GUZMAN, Juan (Johnny), C 830-591-7264 444 G jcguzman@swtjc.edu
GUZMAN, Karina 703-284-6541 468 H karina.guzman@marymount.edu
GUZMAN, Katheleen 405-325-4652 370 K kguzman@ou.edu
GUZMAN, Laura 949-214-3099 39 K laura.guzman@cui.edu
GUZMAN, Maricia 308-635-6348 270 C guzmanm@wncc.edu
GUZMAN, Nanette 386-226-7695 99 A nanette.guzman@erau.edu
GUZMAN, Richard 787-844-8181 513 A richard.guzman@upr.edu
GUZMAN, Ruben 949-451-5220 65 C rguzman@ivc.edu
GUZMAN, Tobias 970-351-1944 84 F tobias.guzman@unco.edu
GUZMAN-AGUILAR, Mariella 530-661-7759 77 D mguzman@yccd.edu
GUZMAN-LOPEZ, Evelyn 787-480-2410 506 C eguzman@sanjuan.pr
GUZMAN QUILES, Jaydee, A 787-720-4476 511 C secretariapresidente@mizpa.edu
GUZMAN-TREVINO, Susan 254-298-8340 445 G susan.guzmantrevino@templejc.edu
GUZZARDO, Joseph 215-670-9060 391 E jguzzardo@peirce.edu
GUZZI, Martin 607-778-5245 317 D guzzimj@sunybroome.edu
GUZZI, Michael, A 530-898-4336 30 D maguzzi@csuchico.edu
GUZZO, Linda 860-906-5132 86 D lguzzo@capitalcc.edu
GUZZO, Sarah 757-233-8785 477 C sguzzo@vwu.edu
GWALTNEY, Darrell 615-460-5552 418 B darrell.gwaltney@belmont.edu
GWALTNEY, Tammy 618-985-3741 140 H tammygwaltney@jalc.edu
GWARTNEY, Kurt 918-270-6470 368 G kurt.gwartney@ptstulsa.edu
GWIAZDA, Jane 617-266-2030 217 D gwiazdj@neco.edu
GWIN, Matthew 201-216-3346 283 D matthew.gwin@stevens.edu
GWINN, Janice 304-357-4383 487 J janicegwinn@ucwv.edu
GWINN, Lois 251-405-7295 1 E lgwinn@bishop.edu
GWINNER, Kevin, P 785-532-7227 175 C kgwinner@ksu.edu
GWYN, Lori 580-774-7010 370 A lori.gwyn@swosu.edu
GWYNN, Douglas 443-885-3647 201 A douglas.gwynn@morgan.edu
GWYTHER, Chelsea 617-243-2152 211 B cgwyther@lasell.edu
GYLLIN, John 407-708-4577 108 D gyllinj@seminolestate.edu
GYORKE, Allan 305-284-6101 113 C a.gyorke@miami.edu

H

HA, Corey 585-245-5584 318 B ha@geneseo.edu
HA, Kevin 760-328-5554 51 E
HA, Viet, X 864-833-8193 411 D vxha@presby.edu
HA, Won 415-476-6296 70 D won.ha@ucsf.edu

HAGG, Scott ... 760-750-4825 33 A shagg@csusm.edu
HAGGARD, Bill ... 828-251-6474 342 B bhaggard@unca.edu
HAGGARD, David, L ... 423-775-7207 418 D david.haggard@bryan.edu
HAGGARD, Lisa ... 870-733-6741 17 F lhaggard@asumidsouth.edu
HAGGARD, Luanne ... 816-279-7000 250 B luanne.haggard@abtu.edu
HAGGARD, Michael ... 518-355-4000 421 G mhaggard@mabtsne.edu
HAGGENMILLER, Karen 858-784-8469 64 A
HAGGERTY, Blake ... 973-596-2912 279 E blake.haggerty@njit.edu
HAGGERTY, Christina ... 815-455-8694 143 I chaggerty@mchenry.edu
HAGGERTY, Emily ... 440-684-6107 363 C emily.haggerty@ursuline.edu
HAGGERTY, Roy ... 541-737-4811 375 A roy.haggerty@oregonstate.edu
HAGGERTY, Trish ... 607-587-3933 319 F haggerpm@alfredstate.edu
HAGGETT, Rosemary, R 214-752-5535 453 E rosemary.haggett@untsystem.edu
HAGGINS, Debra, L ... 757-727-5340 467 G debra.haggins@hamptonu.edu
HAGGINS, Isaac ... 800-517-0857 355 A
HAGGINS, Tanya ... 800-518-0857 355 A
HAGGLUND, Kristofer ... 573-884-6705 261 A hagglundk@missouri.edu
HAGGRAY, Annette ... 703-845-6222 474 F
HAGGY, Marisa ... 218-879-0879 238 B mhaggy@fdltcc.edu
HAGIN, Linwood ... 864-663-0069 410 I linwood.hagin@ngu.edu
HAGMAN, Tracy ... 217-641-4106 141 A thagman@jwcc.edu
HAGOOD, Joel ... 205-387-0511 1 D joel.hagood@bscc.edu
HAGOOD, Matthew ... 305-348-2820 110 A matthew.hagood@fiu.edu
HAGOOD, Thomas, C ... 801-585-9604 459 O
HAGOPIAN, Tara ... 401-752-2640 404 B
HAGREEN, Sarah ... 585-292-2352 307 B shagreen@monroecc.edu
HAGUE, Martin ... 314-505-7313 252 A haguem@csl.edu
HAGY, Joseph ... 540-863-2925 473 F jhagy@dslcc.edu
HAH, Megan ... 626-289-7719 24 H mhah@amu.edu
HAHKA, Curt ... 906-487-7380 224 B curt.hahka@finlandia.edu
HAHN, Ben ... 907-564-8289 9 F bhahn@alaskapacific.edu
HAHN, David ... 520-621-6595 16 D dwhahn@arizona.edu
HAHN, Derek ... 507-433-0569 240 G derek.hahn@riverland.edu
HAHN, Karen ... 352-588-8522 107 D karen.hahn@saintleo.edu
HAHN, Kathryn ... 612-330-1013 234 A hahn@augsburg.edu
HAHN, Kelli ... 269-927-6701 226 F khahn@lakemichigancollege.edu
HAHN, Lenell ... 573-986-6012 259 H lhahn@semo.edu
HAHN, Lisa ... 516-572-7169 307 E lisa.hahn@ncc.edu
HAHN, Marc, B ... 816-654-7102 254 E mhahn@kcumb.edu
HAHN, Marcela ... 212-875-4400 290 H mhahn@bankstreet.edu
HAHN, Mary Joan ... 509-313-6095 480 F hahn@gonzaga.edu
HAHN, Rob ... 414-443-8944 498 A rob.hahn@wlc.edu
HAHN, Sarah ... 530-752-8990 69 B shahn@shcs.ucdavis.edu
HAHN, Stephen ... 713-792-2121 456 D
HAHN, Tony ... 812-888-5101 162 F thahn@vinu.edu
HAHN, Troy ... 718-997-3009 295 B troy.hahn@qc.cuny.edu
HAHN SCHNIPPER, Jenny ... 636-922-8244 258 J jschnipper@stchas.edu
HAHUES, Sven ... 239-590-1337 109 K shahues@fgcu.edu
HAIDLE, Shirley ... 541-881-5842 376 F shaidle@tvcc.cc
HAIDLE, Sue, E ... 740-368-3104 359 G sehaidle@owu.edu
HAIGHT, Aaron ... 616-331-3585 224 G haighta@gvsu.edu
HAIGLER, Steve ... 831-646-4040 52 G shaigler@mpc.edu
HAILE, Amy ... 207-221-4228 197 E ahaile@une.edu
HAILE, Bob, A ... 309-649-6331 150 G bob.haile@src.edu
HAILE, Dawit ... 804-524-1141 476 D dhaile@vsu.edu
HAILE, Gregory Adam ... 954-201-7401 96 F
HAILE, Haley ... 870-307-7425 19 I
HAILEY, Christine ... 512-245-2119 450 C ceh138@txstate.edu
HAILEY, Maryann ... 903-875-7305 440 D maryann.hailey@navarrocollege.edu
HAILEY, Mechele ... 620-227-9377 173 D mhailey@dc3.edu
HAILEY, Rachel ... 434-961-6547 474 I rhailey@pvcc.edu
HAILEY, Robert, C ... 504-862-8064 191 F rhailey@tulane.edu
HAILEY PENN, Carla ... 973-353-5541 282 B carla.hpenn@rutgers.edu
HAIN, Brooke ... 410-857-2546 200 F bhain@mcdaniel.edu
HAIN, Cathy ... 585-475-2627 312 F cathy.hain@rit.edu
HAIN, Peggy, S ... 402-465-2137 268 G phain@nebrwesleyan.edu
HAIN, Tom ... 432-552-2780 456 F hain_t@utpb.edu
HAINES, Amanda ... 360-623-8428 478 F amanda.haines@centralia.edu
HAINES, Asher ... 704-687-8693 342 D ahaines3@uncc.edu
HAINES, Chris, M ... 480-423-6310 13 H chris.haines@scottsdalecc.edu
HAINES, Chuck ... 805-893-8541 70 E chuck.haines@ucsb.edu
HAINES, Darla, V ... 260-982-5949 159 J dvhaines@manchester.edu
HAINES, Gary ... 719-884-5000 82 B gwhaines@nbc.edu
HAINES, Lynne ... 912-650-5673 125 F lhaines@southuniversity.edu
HAINES, Rhonda ... 315-792-7100 321 B rhaines@sunypoly.edu
HAINES, Terry ... 913-266-8601 176 I terry.haines@ottawa.edu
HAINGRAY, Donald ... 585-567-9287 302 B donald.haingray@houghton.edu
HAINLINE, Benjamin ... 580-628-6250 366 J ben.hainline@noc.edu
HAIR, Neil, F ... 585-475-6322 312 F nfhbbu@rit.edu
HAIR, Shannon ... 434-797-8495 473 G shannon.hair@danville.edu
HAIRE, Helen, M ... 319-273-2712 164 A helen.haire@uni.edu
HAIRE, Jacqueline ... 254-526-1903 432 D jacqueline.haire@ctcd.edu
HAIRR, Blair ... 910-592-8081 337 G ahairr@sampsoncc.edu
HAIRSTON, Creasie ... 312-996-3219 151 G cfh@uic.edu
HAIRSTON, Gertrude, J . 410-651-6404 203 D gjhairston@umes.edu
HAISCH, Craig ... 503-883-2675 373 F chaisch@linfield.edu
HAISMA, Dale ... 616-632-3037 221 E haismdal@aquinas.edu
HAIZLIP, Kim ... 402-354-7000 268 B kimberly.haizlip@methodistcollege.edu
HAJ-HARIRI, Hossein ... 803-777-7356 413 A hhh@mailbox.sc.edu
HAJDER, Michelle ... 866-492-5336 244 F michelle.hajder@mail.waldenu.edu
HAJELA, Prabhat ... 518-276-6487 312 C hajelap@rpi.edu
HAJIR, Farshid ... 413-545-6330 211 G hajir@provost.umass.edu
HAJIR, Tracy, F ... 410-543-6012 204 D tfhajir@salisbury.edu
HAJJAR, Souraya ... 915-831-4143 436 A shajjar@epcc.edu
HAKALA, Curtis ... 304-434-8000 488 E curtis.hakala@easternwv.edu
HAKE, Eric ... 704-637-4293 327 I erhake@catawba.edu
HAKEEM, Nasir ... 909-607-7415 37 C nasir.hakeem@cgu.edu
HAKES, Joseph ... 312-567-7124 140 A jhakes@iit.edu
HAKIM, George ... 810-762-3223 232 A geohak@umich.edu
HAKIM, Iman, A ... 520-626-7083 16 D ihakim@arizona.edu
HAKKAKIAN, Eliyahu ... 410-484-7200 201 C
HALABE, Anjali ... 304-293-8768 490 E anjali.halabe@mail.wvu.edu
HALADA, Robert ... 402-471-2505 268 C rhalada@nscs.edu
HALARIS, Dimitris ... 914-633-2649 302 E dhalaris@iona.edu
HALAS, Wally ... 203-254-4000 87 I whalas@fairfield.edu
HALASZ, Tom ... 252-328-6050 341 A halaszt18@ecu.edu
HALBERSTADT, Joseph . 718-438-1002 306 D
HALBERSTAM, Lisa ... 646-565-6326 322 G lisa.halberstam@touro.edu
HALBERSTAM, Lisa ... 646-565-6326 322 F lisa.halberstam@touro.edu
HALBERT, Jay ... 325-942-2355 450 E jay.halbert@angelo.edu
HALBESLEBEN, Jonathon ... 205-348-6330 7 G jrhalbesleben@ua.edu
HALBROOK, Anna ... 501-208-5310 23 A halbrook@uaccm.edu
HALCOMB, Jonda ... 361-698-1219 435 G jhalcomb@delmar.edu
HALCUMB, Cambrea ... 573-840-9658 260 E chalcumb@trcc.edu
HALDEMAN, Bill ... 612-626-5148 243 F
HALE, Ann ... 409-772-9796 456 E aehale@utmb.edu
HALE, Barry ... 903-923-2021 435 H bhale@etbu.edu
HALE, Cassandra ... 417-455-5675 252 E cassandrahale@crowder.edu
HALE, Charles, R ... 805-893-8354 70 E ssdean@ltsc.ucsb.edu
HALE, Dale ... 901-321-3264 418 G dale.hale@cbu.edu
HALE, Dana ... 601-643-8658 245 F dana.hale@colin.edu
HALE, David, B ... 804-289-8150 472 C dhale2@richmond.edu
HALE, Don ... 404-413-3025 120 E dhale@gsu.edu
HALE, Georgia ... 479-788-7030 21 G georgia.hale@uafs.edu
HALE, Jason ... 806-742-1480 450 F jason.hale@ttu.edu
HALE, Jean, M ... 724-946-7368 402 D halejm@westminster.edu
HALE, Jeff, A ... 504-520-5797 193 E jhale@xula.edu
HALE, Jerold ... 423-425-4633 427 C jerold-hale@utc.edu
HALE, Jimmie ... 864-488-4519 410 B jhale@limestone.edu
HALE, Kandi ... 207-941-7138 194 F halek@husson.edu
HALE, Kathy ... 913-234-0649 172 K kathy.hale@cleveland.edu
HALE, Kayla ... 918-631-2565 371 C kayla-hale@utulsa.edu
HALE, Kimberly ... 217-228-5432 147 F haleki@quincy.edu
HALE, LaToya ... 443-394-3377 93 H
HALE, Mallie ... 256-824-6501 8 B mallie.hale@uah.edu
HALE, Mario ... 760-921-5409 56 A mario.hale@paloverde.edu
HALE, Mark ... 214-333-5503 434 C markh@dbu.edu
HALE, Melina ... 773-702-2102 151 E mhale@uchicago.edu
HALE, Mike ... 503-552-1555 374 D
HALE, Nori ... 785-242-5200 176 I nori.hale@ottawa.edu
HALE, Philip, D ... 773-508-7452 143 C phale@luc.edu
HALE, Ryan ... 941-408-1405 109 G haler@scf.edu
HALE, Shawn ... 803-780-1129 414 B shale@voorhees.edu
HALE, Ted ... 860-906-5053 86 D thale@capitalcc.edu
HALE, Tracy ... 507-457-2319 241 F
HALE, Tricia, A ... 229-333-5940 127 E tahale@valdosta.edu
HALEAMAU-KAM, Raynette (Kalei) ... 808-969-8804 129 I haleamau@hawaii.edu
HALES, Brent ... 814-865-4028 391 G bdh5347@psu.edu
HALES, Cassie ... 319-352-8553 170 J cassie.hales@wartburg.edu
HALES, Erin ... 714-463-7554 51 B ehales@ketchum.edu
HALES, Jessica ... 410-334-2808 205 D jhales@worwic.edu
HALES, Mike ... 859-572-5207 184 E halesm1@nku.edu
HALES, Reagan ... 806-371-5000 429 E r0107362@actx.edu
HALEY, Christopher ... 207-326-2232 196 A christopher.haley@mma.edu
HALEY, Donna ... 678-839-6438 127 C dhaley@westga.edu
HALEY, John ... 315-445-4520 303 I haleyjr@lemoyne.edu
HALEY, John, R ... 315-445-4689 303 I haleyjr@lemoyne.edu
HALEY, Meghan ... 610-527-0200 397 D meghan.haley@rosemont.edu
HALEY, Melissa ... 847-578-8756 148 F melissa.haley@rosalindfranklin.edu
HALEY, Tara ... 904-633-8285 101 B tara.haley@fscj.edu
HALEY, Ted ... 508-767-7215 206 A thaley@assumption.edu
HALEY, Terence ... 256-824-6674 8 B terence.haley@uah.edu
HALEY-THOMSON, Lisa 518-454-5239 296 G thomsonl@strose.edu
HALGREN, Cara ... 701-777-2724 345 B cara.halgren@und.edu
HALIBURTON, William .. 870-575-8000 22 D
HALIBURTON, Willie ... 503-725-4406 375 E willie@pdx.edu
HALICKI, Shannon, D ... 304-336-8075 490 B shalicki@westliberty.edu
HALIEMUN, Cynthia ... 217-228-5432 147 F haliecy@quincy.edu
HALING, Linda ... 920-424-3322 496 C
HALKITIS, Perry, N ... 732-235-9700 282 A perry.halkitis@rutgers.edu
HALL, Allyson ... 860-465-5283 85 H hallal@easternct.edu
HALL, Amber, L ... 501-450-3663 23 H amberh@uca.edu
HALL, Amy ... 225-214-6979 187 B amy.hall@franu.edu
HALL, Anders, W ... 615-322-2451 428 A anders.hall@vanderbilt.edu
HALL, Andrew ... 404-523-8520 126 B ahall@follett.com
HALL, Andy ... 423-585-6801 425 F robert.hall@ws.edu
HALL, Andy ... 423-585-6801 425 F andy.hall@ws.edu
HALL, Andy ... 425-889-5212 481 H andy.hall@northwestu.edu
HALL, Benjamin ... 740-362-3448 355 H bhall@mtso.edu
HALL, Bobby, L ... 806-291-3401 457 I hallb@wbu.edu
HALL, Brad ... 903-886-5043 447 B brad.hall@tamuc.edu
HALL, Brian ... 207-768-2707 195 G nbhall@nmcc.edu
HALL, Brian ... 312-850-7899 135 H bhall44@ccc.edu
HALL, Carol ... 860-515-3889 85 E chall@charteroak.edu
HALL, Carol ... 860-515-3880 85 E chall@charteroak.edu
HALL, Carrie, M ... 510-430-2050 52 E cmilliga@mills.edu
HALL, Cassie ... 406-447-4572 263 B chall@carroll.edu
HALL, Chaundra ... 501-686-2921 21 E chall@uasys.edu
HALL, Cheryl ... 985-549-5312 193 A chall@selu.edu
HALL, Chris ... 410-827-5859 198 F chall@chesapeake.edu
HALL, Chris ... 618-537-6833 144 A chall@mckendree.edu
HALL, Christina ... 973-618-3670 276 D chall@caldwell.edu

HALL, Christopher 803-934-3216 410 G
chall@morris.edu
HALL, Cynthia 530-283-0202 42 A
chall@frc.edu
HALL, Daniel, B 323-241-5467 49 E
halldb@lasc.edu
HALL, Danielle 517-371-5140 233 C
halld@cooley.edu
HALL, David 501-279-4407 19 C
dhall@harding.edu
HALL, David 340-693-1000 513 E
dhall@uvi.edu
HALL, David, A 417-836-8444 256 G
dhall@missouristate.edu
HALL, Deborah, P 706-880-8232 122 A
dhall4@lagrange.edu
HALL, Dennis 817-531-6504 451 C
dhall@txwes.edu
HALL, Derek 906-227-2716 228 I
halld@nmu.edu
HALL, Devon 910-410-1912 337 B
dghall@richmondcc.edu
HALL, Donald 585-273-5000 323 M
donald.hall@rochester.edu
HALL, Frank 603-428-2320 273 G
fhall@nec.edu
HALL, Frank 435-586-1934 460 A
frankhall1@suu.edu
HALL, Gene 503-517-1119 377 C
ghall@warnerpacific.edu
HALL, Gwen 610-526-1441 378 D
gwendolyn.hall@theamericancollege.edu
HALL, Gwenn 318-345-9126 188 D
ghall@ladelta.edu
HALL, Haley 520-795-0787 10 I
HALL, Haley 803-535-1255 411 B
hallht@octech.edu
HALL, Heather 251-445-9400 9 A
heatherhall@southalabama.edu
HALL, Hollie, M 607-587-4200 319 F
hallhm@alfredstate.edu
HALL, Jack, C 386-312-4293 107 C
jackhall@sjrstate.edu
HALL, Jackie 606-487-3180 181 I
jackie.hall@kctcs.edu
HALL, James 934-420-2479 320 F
jim.hall@farmingdale.edu
HALL, James 585-475-2295 312 F
jchcms@rit.edu
HALL, James, R 864-597-4351 414 E
halljr@wofford.edu
HALL, Jami 706-272-4428 118 B
jhall@daltonstate.edu
HALL, Jean 914-323-5412 305 B
jean.hall@mville.edu
HALL, Jeff 229-931-2066 120 D
jeff.hall@gsw.edu
HALL, Jeffrey 229-500-3024 114 H
jeffrey.hall@asurams.edu
HALL, Jeffrey, B 706-419-1121 118 A
hall@covenant.edu
HALL, Jennifer 606-368-6053 178 G
jenniferhall@alc.edu
HALL, Jennifer 334-222-6591 2 I
jmh@lbwcc.edu
HALL, Jennifer 330-829-6644 362 E
halljene@mountunion.edu
HALL, Jessica 478-934-3458 122 F
jessica.hall@mga.edu
HALL, Jessica 614-251-4372 358 B
hallj@ohiodominican.edu
HALL, Jim 934-420-2457 320 F
jim.hall@farmingdale.edu
HALL, Jo 336-727-7102 329 C
jo.hall@greensboro.edu
HALL, JoAnn 920-922-8611 499 D
jhall@morainepark.edu
HALL, SR., John 888-532-7282 56 E
HALL, John, D 817-272-2102 454 I
jhall@uta.edu
HALL, Jon Mark 812-464-1846 162 C
jmhall@usi.edu
HALL, Jona 740-374-8716 363 F
jhall@wscc.edu
HALL, Karla 502-213-2507 182 C
karla.hall@kctcs.edu
HALL, Karyn 936-468-3806 445 E
khall@sfasu.edu
HALL, Keith, E 626-969-3434 26 F
HALL, Kellie, M 701-477-7862 346 J
kmhall@tm.edu
HALL, Kelly 619-482-6310 66 A
khall@swccd.edu
HALL, Kelly 610-606-4666 380 D
kelly.hall@cedarcrest.edu
HALL, Kenneth 570-484-2598 394 E
khall@lockhaven.edu
HALL, Kevin 651-603-6165 235 I
khall@csp.edu
HALL, Kim 360-416-7601 484 C
kim.hall@skagit.edu
HALL, Kim, B 865-251-1800 423 E
khall@south.edu
HALL, Kristin, E 845-758-7531 290 I
hall@bard.edu
HALL, Kristy 276-523-2400 474 D
khall@mecc.edu
HALL, Lareese, M 207-859-5100 194 D
lareese.hall@colby.edu
HALL, Lasella 508-999-9220 212 A
lhall1@umassd.edu
HALL, Lataria 559-442-8267 67 B
lataria.hall@fresnocitycollege.edu
HALL, Lawanda 951-571-6317 59 B
lawanda.hall@mvc.edu
HALL, Lawrence 860-832-2298 85 G
halllaw@ccsu.edu
HALL, Ledawn 973-877-3596 277 G
lhall8@essex.edu
HALL, Lemond 850-201-6652 112 C
lemond.hall@tcc.fl.edu
HALL, Les 803-545-5048 413 A
les.hall@uscmed.sc.edu
HALL, Linda 434-544-8126 471 L
hall.l@lynchburg.edu
HALL, Linda, M 585-292-2103 307 B
lhall38@monroecc.edu
HALL, Lisa 423-236-2900 423 F
lisahall@southern.edu
HALL, Lori 207-741-5501 195 H
lhall@smccme.edu
HALL, Lori 503-594-3162 372 C
lori.hall@clackamas.edu
HALL, Lydia 803-327-8000 414 F
lhall@yorktech.edu
HALL, Lyndon 252-492-2061 338 F
halll@vgcc.edu
HALL, Lynn 812-866-7385 155 G
hall@hanover.edu
HALL, Margaret 213-738-5771 66 B
library@swlaw.edu
HALL, Mark 919-545-8043 333 C
mhall@cccc.edu
HALL, Marsha 210-486-2866 429 B
mhall13@alamo.edu
HALL, Mary 828-232-5109 342 B
mhall7@unca.edu
HALL, Matthew 805-893-8989 70 E
matthall@ucsb.edu
HALL, Matthew 502-897-4897 184 G
mhall@sbts.edu
HALL, Matthew, J 407-823-1007 110 E
matthew.hall@ucf.edu
HALL, Maurice 609-771-1855 276 I
hallmau@tcnj.edu
HALL, Michael 570-484-2452 394 E
mhall@lockhaven.edu
HALL, Michael, R 336-841-9235 329 F
mhall@highpoint.edu
HALL, Michael, W 540-654-1635 471 N
mhall2@umw.edu
HALL, Michelle 985-549-2077 193 A
mhall@selu.edu
HALL, Michelle 620-278-4211 177 H
mhall@sterling.edu
HALL, Michelle 404-364-8336 123 K
mhall@oglethorpe.edu
HALL, Myrna 303-458-4160 83 E
mhall004@regis.edu
HALL, Nicole 312-629-6100 149 F
nhall1@saic.edu
HALL, Nicole 336-334-4174 343 A
nrhall@uncg.edu
HALL, Norma 317-788-3206 161 H
hallne@uindy.edu
HALL, Norman, D 530-226-4130 64 E
nhall@simpsonu.edu
HALL, Otis 918-587-6789 370 H
otis.hall@tws.edu
HALL, Pamela 313-845-6410 225 B
phall@hfcc.edu
HALL, Patricia 479-394-7622 23 C
phall@uarichmountain.edu
HALL, Paulakay 423-775-7308 418 D
phall7036@bryan.edu
HALL, Persephone 860-439-2646 87 H
phall3@conncoll.edu
HALL, Philip, D 843-792-8979 410 C
hallpd@musc.edu
HALL, Rachelle 623-845-3235 13 C
rachelle.hall@gccaz.edu
HALL, Rakin 215-572-2900 378 E
hallr@arcadia.edu
HALL, Raymond, D 810-762-3335 232 A
raydhall@umich.edu
HALL, Rebecca, S 269-337-7090 225 F
rebecca.hall@kzoo.edu
HALL, Renardo, A 717-871-5840 395 A
renardo.hall@millersville.edu
HALL, Renee 662-621-4858 245 D
rsanford@coahomacc.edu
HALL, Ricardo 610-758-3890 388 E
rih217@lehigh.edu
HALL, Rickey 206-685-0518 485 A
vpomad@uw.edu
HALL, Rikki 925-473-7501 40 D
rhall@losmedanos.edu
HALL, Riley 208-496-1301 130 I
hallr@byui.edu
HALL, Robert 716-829-7657 298 E
hallrm@dyc.edu
HALL, Robert 512-223-1053 430 I
robert.hall@austincc.edu
HALL, Robin 828-448-3107 339 A
rhall@wpcc.edu
HALL, Rodney 804-524-2954 476 D
rhall@vsu.edu
HALL, Ron 865-251-1800 423 E
rhall@south.edu
HALL, Ronnie, L 806-651-3000 448 B
rhall@wtamu.edu
HALL, Sandy 325-674-2273 428 F
halls@acu.edu
HALL, Schernavia 205-348-3091 7 G
schernavia.m.hall@ua.edu
HALL, Scott 757-189-1752 473 H
shall@es.vccs.edu
HALL, Seth 318-342-1015 193 C
shall@ulm.edu
HALL, Steve, W 713-467-4501 444 E
HALL, Steven 309-341-7823 141 G
shall@knox.edu
HALL, Steven, A 617-358-0476 207 E
sahall@bu.edu
HALL, Susan 856-415-2185 281 D
shall@rcsj.edu
HALL, Susan, L 585-292-2179 307 B
shall60@monroecc.edu
HALL, Tami 870-307-7203 19 I
tami.hall@lyon.edu
HALL, Tammy 501-279-8756 19 C
thall@harding.edu
HALL, Teri 316-978-3021 178 D
teri.hall@wichita.edu
HALL, Terry 225-771-2552 191 E
thall@sulc.edu
HALL, Tim 337-475-5787 192 E
thall16@mcneese.edu
HALL, Tim 618-650-2871 150 C
timhall@siue.edu
HALL, Tim 205-726-2771 6 E
thall5@samford.edu
HALL, Timothy 914-674-7307 306 C
thall@mercy.edu
HALL, Timothy 252-638-0156 334 A
hallt@cravencc.edu
HALL, Tina 870-230-5348 19 D
hallt@hsu.edu
HALL, Tom 913-469-8500 174 I
thall44@jccc.edu
HALL, Tonya, S 804-524-3222 476 D
tshall@vsu.edu
HALL, Tracy, A 336-316-2349 329 D
thall@guilford.edu
HALL, Tracy, D 901-333-4200 425 D
tdhall@southwest.tn.edu
HALL, Watasha 773-252-6464 146 F
watasha.hall@oakpoint.edu
HALL, Wendy 360-442-2491 481 D
whall@lowercolumbia.edu
HALL, William 714-997-6891 36 B
whall@chapman.edu
HALL, William, B 401-341-2132 405 D
hallb@salve.edu
HALL, William, C 617-984-1760 218 C
whall@quincycollege.edu
HALL, William, J 603-862-1287 274 F
bill.hall@unh.edu
HALL, William, M 256-824-6933 8 B
william.hall@uah.edu
HALL-BAKER, Tre'Shawn 310-434-4170 63 C
hall-baker_treshawn@smc.edu
HALL-JONES, Jenny 740-593-1000 358 K
hallj1@ohio.edu
HALL-PETERSON, Georgette 610-358-4540 391 A
hallpetg@neumann.edu
HALL-YATES, Joyce 419-448-3049 361 D
hallyatesjc@tiffin.edu
HALLADAY, Choi 206-934-4114 483 A
choi.halladay@seattlecolleges.edu
HALLADAY, Chris 610-758-3900 388 E
pch214@lehigh.edu
HALLADAY, Ona 716-829-8304 298 E
halladay@dyc.edu
HALLAK, Nadia 312-939-0111 137 D
HALLAM, Lindsey 907-260-7422 9 D
HALLAM, Matt 513-721-7944 353 C
mhallam@gbs.edu
HALLE, Kevin 402-375-7234 268 F
kehalle1@wsc.edu
HALLEEN, Jan 952-886-7580 242 N
jhalleen@nwhealth.edu
HALLEEN, Tom 562-777-4053 27 A
tom.halleen@biola.edu
HALLER, Alan 517-355-1623 227 F
halleral@msu.edu
HALLER, Amy 815-455-8768 143 I
ahaller@mchenry.edu
HALLER, Brian 212-220-8013 293 A
bhaller@bmcc.cuny.edu
HALLER, Ellizabeth 605-626-2601 416 G
elizabeth.haller@northern.edu
HALLER, John, G 305-284-3970 113 C
jgh22@miami.edu
HALLER, Karen 308-535-3720 267 J
hallerk@mpcc.edu
HALLER, Ryan, M 972-721-5000 452 B
rhaller@udallas.edu
HALLERAN, Donna 608-265-3443 495 D
donna.halleran@wisc.edu
HALLETT, David 503-399-6593 372 B
david.hallett@chemeketa.edu
HALLETT-ADAMS, Chere 603-899-4038 273 E
hallettadamsc@franklinpierce.edu
HALLEY, Crystal 870-460-1033 22 C
halleyc@uamont.edu
HALLEY, Marcus 860-297-2013 89 B
marcus.halley@trincoll.edu
HALLEY, Maureen 508-849-3344 205 H
mhalley@annamaria.edu
HALLICK, Lesley, M 503-352-2123 375 C
hallick@pacificu.edu
HALLIDAY, Robert, M 315-792-3122 324 B
rhalliday@utica.edu
HALLISSEY, Kathleen 201-684-7869 280 H
khallis1@ramapo.edu
HALLMAN, Cheryl, A 856-225-6046 281 G
challman@camden.rutgers.edu
HALLMAN, Janet, S 253-879-8620 484 G
jhallman@pugetsound.edu
HALLMAN, Joseph, M 608-342-1584 496 E
hallmanjo@uwplatt.edu
HALLMAN, Taniya 641-472-1144 168 C
registrar@miu.edu
HALLMARK, James 979-458-6072 446 B
jhallmark@tamus.edu
HALLMARK, Tim 931-540-2712 424 C
thallmark2@columbiastate.edu
HALLOCK, Hiltòn 907-564-8261 9 F
hhallock@alaskapacific.edu
HALLORAN, Elizabeth 651-690-6093 243 A
emhalloran531@stkate.edu
HALLORAN, Monica 708-524-6054 137 C
mhallora@dom.edu
HALLOWELL, David 484-664-3433 390 H
davidhallowell@muhlenberg.edu
HALLSMITH, George 617-228-2401 214 C
gchallsm@bhcc.mass.edu
HALLSTROM, Peggy 605-626-3011 416 G
peggy.hallstrom@northern.edu
HALM, Steven 515-271-1515 165 G
steven.halm@dmu.edu
HALMA, Jane 201-761-6012 283 A
HALPERIN, Edward 914-594-4900 322 F
edward_halperin@nymc.edu

HALPERIN, Edward ...... 914-594-4900 322 G
edward_halperin@nymc.edu
HALPERIN, Edward, C .. 914-594-4900 309 B
edward_halperin@nymc.edu
HALPERIN, Michael ...... 607-735-1895 298 H
registrar@elmira.edu
HALPERIN, Rebecca ...... 718-405-3332 296 F
rebecca.halperin@mountsaintvincent.edu
HALPERN, Daphne .... 718-636-3537 311 F
dhalpern@pratt.edu
HALPERN, Leslie, F ...... 646-592-4372 326 D
leslie.halpern@yu.edu
HALPERN, Linda, C ...... 540-568-7770 468 C
halperlc@jmu.edu
HALPIN, John .... 415-452-7013.. 36 K
jhalpin@ccsf.edu
HALPIN-ROBBINS, Kathleen .... 413-565-1000 206 D
khrobbins@baypath.edu
HALSEY, Mark, D .... 845-752-2336 290 I
halsey@bard.edu
HALSMER, Hillary .... 307-332-2930 502 A
hhalsmer@wyomingcatholic.edu
HALSTEAD, Barbara, E .. 407-582-3250 113 I
bhalstead@valenciacollege.edu
HALSTEAD, Michele ...... 845-257-3210 316 E
halsteam@newpaltz.edu
HALSTEAD, Stead .... 541-684-7276 371 I
chalstead@bushnell.edu
HALSTED, Lauren .... 619-660-4675.. 44 D
lauren.halsted@gcccd.edu
HALSTED, Steve .... 406-771-4367 264 F
shalsted@gfcmsu.edu
HALT, Michelle .... 575-538-6328 289 G
michelle.halt@wnmu.edu
HALTERMAN, Rick .... 423-236-2871 423 F
halterman@southern.edu
HALTON, Curtis .... 404-225-4491 115 H
chalton@atlantatech.edu
HALUPA, Colleen .... 903-923-2038 435 H
chalupa@etbu.edu
HALUSCHAK, Rich .... 626-396-2308.. 26 B
rich.haluschak@artcenter.edu
HALVERSON, James ...... 847-628-1123 141 C
jhalverson@judsonu.edu
HALVERSON, Mark .... 801-626-8022 461 A
markhalverson@weber.edu
HALVERSON, Michael, S .... 312-915-7283 143 C
mhalverson@luc.edu
HALVERSON, Paul, K .... 317-274-4242 157 D
pkhalver@iupui.edu
HALVERSTADT, Adrian .. 620-862-5252 171 H
adrian.halverstadt@barclaycollege.edu
HALVORSON, Corabeth . 608-822-2316 500 A
chalverson@swtc.edu
HALVORSON, Daisy ...... 605-229-8453 415 I
daisy.halvorson@presentation.edu
HALVORSON, J. Derek .. 706-419-1117 118 A
derek.halvorson@covenant.edu
HALVORSON, Kurt .... 218-935-0417 244 G
kurt.halvorson@wetcc.edu
HALVORSON, Lloyd .... 701-662-1681 346 C
lloyd.halvorson@lrsc.edu
HAM, Brandy .... 432-335-6651 441 A
bham@odessa.edu
HAM, Dwight .... 661-362-2733.. 51 D
dham@masters.edu
HAM, Gary .... 978-762-4000 215 D
gham@northshore.edu
HAM, Jeoung, H .... 636-327-4645 256 B
reg@midwest.edu
HAM, Michelle .... 912-279-5744 117 F
mham@ccga.edu
HAM, Nicole .... 252-940-6204 332 C
nicole.ham@beaufortccc.edu
HAM, Paige .... 919-735-5151 338 H
peham@waynecc.edu
HAMACHER, Lori .... 719-389-6710.. 78 I
lori.hamacher@coloradocollege.edu
HAMAD, James .... 630-844-4910 133 D
jhamad@aurora.edu
HAMADA, Larisa .... 562-985-8256.. 31 D
larisa.hamada@csulb.edu
HAMADEH, Yousef, A .... 423-425-5703 427 C
yousef-hamadeh@utc.edu
HAMAKAWA, Curt .... 413-782-1223 220 A
curt.hamakawa@wne.edu
HAMANN, Dick .... 407-708-2258 108 D
hamannd@seminolestate.edu
HAMANN, Leah .... 701-255-3285 347 A
lhamann@uttc.edu
HAMANN, Melanie .... 573-840-9665 260 E
mhamann@trcc.edu
HAMBERGER, Elizabeth . 934-420-2479 320 F
studyabroad@farmingdale.edu
HAMBEY, Anthony .... 205-226-4850.... 4 F
ahambey@bsc.edu
HAMBLIN, Carolyn .... 928-758-3926.. 14 F
chamblin@mohave.edu
HAMBLIN, John .... 503-491-7384 374 B
john.hamblin@mhcc.edu
HAMBLIN, Veronica ...... 660-263-3900 251 D
veronicahamblin@cccb.edu
HAMBRICK, Angie, Z .... 253-535-8108 482 A
hambriaz@plu.edu
HAMBRIGHT, Beverly .... 850-718-2223.. 97 E
hambrightb@chipola.edu
HAMBY, Dan .... 270-707-3790 182 B
dan.hamby@kctcs.edu
HAMBY, Jamie .... 423-472-7141 424 B
jhamby@clevelandstatecc.edu
HAMBY, Kyle .... 214-818-1306 433 O
khamby@criswell.edu
HAMEL, Dale, M .... 508-626-4580 213 A
dhamel@framingham.edu
HAMEL, John .... 508-849-3306 205 H
jhamel@annamaria.edu
HAMEL, Kayte .... 815-825-9447 141 F
khamel@kish.edu
HAMEL, Lowell .... 269-473-2222 221 D
HAMEL, Nicholas .... 207-755-5284 195 D
nhamel@cmcc.edu
HAMELINE, Walter .... 718-390-3488 324 F
whamelin@wagner.edu
HAMEN, Laurie .... 320-363-5505 235 F
csbpres@csbsju.edu
HAMER, Lawrence .... 219-989-2606 160 D
hamerl@pnw.edu
HAMERSKY, Steve .... 316-942-4291 176 E
hamerskys@newmanu.edu
HAMES, Anne .... 731-352-4066 418 C
hamesa@bethelu.edu
HAMES, Joe .... 731-352-4000 418 C
hamesj@bethelu.edu
HAMID, Faisal .... 510-356-4760.. 77 F
HAMID, Hadi .... 803-571-4022 408 G
hamidh@denmarktech.edu
HAMIL, T. J .... 706-245-7226 118 D
thamil@ec.edu
HAMILL, Chad, S .... 928-523-3849.. 14 H
chad.hamill@nau.edu
HAMILL, Nancy, G .... 510-987-9720.. 70 E
nancy.hamill@ucop.edu
HAMILL, Robert .... 440-646-8301 363 C
bob.hamill@ursuline.edu
HAMILL, Tara .... 732-247-5241 279 C
thamill@nbts.edu
HAMILL, Timothy .... 267-341-3514 385 J
thamill@holyfamily.edu
HAMILTON, Aaron .... 772-546-5534 102 C
HAMILTON, Alice .... 785-442-6025 174 F
ahamilton@highlandcc.edu
HAMILTON, Alice, M .... 843-953-3313 408 C
hamiltonam1@lowcountrygradcenter.org
HAMILTON, Alicia .... 972-825-4612 444 J
ahamilton@sagu.edu
HAMILTON, Allana .... 615-366-1505 423 H
ahamilton@tbr.edu
HAMILTON, Amber .... 806-371-5303 429 E
ahbrookshire@actx.edu
HAMILTON, Andrew ...... 212-998-2345 309 F
andrew.hamilton@nyu.edu
HAMILTON, Andrew ...... 641-269-3800 166 G
hamiltoa@grinnell.edu
HAMILTON, Andrew ...... 336-334-5000 343 A
a_hamilt@uncg.edu
HAMILTON, Andrew, P . 719-333-2299 503 D
paul.hamilton@usafa.edu
HAMILTON, Angela, M . 724-480-3440 381 H
angela.hamilton@ccbc.edu
HAMILTON, Ann .... 213-763-7000.. 49 F
HAMILTON, Ann .... 661-362-3310.. 38 D
ann.hamilton@canyons.edu
HAMILTON, Anna .... 270-706-8649 181 G
ahamilton0062@kctcs.edu
HAMILTON, Barbara ...... 870-837-4003.. 21 D
bhamilto@sautech.edu
HAMILTON, Becky .... 812-488-2163 161 G
bh9@evansville.edu
HAMILTON, Billie Jo ..... 813-974-3039 111 C
bjhamilton@usf.edu
HAMILTON, Billy .... 979-458-6421 446 B
bhamilton@tamus.edu
HAMILTON, Brian .... 863-680-4203 100 H
bhamilton@flsouthern.edu
HAMILTON, Cara .... 864-646-1797 412 H
chamilt5@tctc.edu
HAMILTON, Christine ... 913-758-6242 178 B
christine.hamilton@stmary.edu
HAMILTON, Crystal .... 270-852-3130 183 E
clhamilton@kwc.edu
HAMILTON, Daniel, W .. 702-895-1876 271 D
daniel.hamilton@unlv.edu
HAMILTON, David, L .... 413-542-2167 205 G
dhamilton@amherst.edu
HAMILTON, DaVina ...... 904-256-7067 102 H
dhamilt3@ju.edu
HAMILTON, Debbie .... 713-718-5041 437 C
debbie.hamilton@hccs.edu
HAMILTON, Debra .... 919-267-1640 330 B
HAMILTON, Eboni .... 512-505-3044 438 A
elhamilton@htu.edu
HAMILTON, JR., Elbert . 713-629-1500 457 D
HAMILTON, Eldrie .... 318-274-6321 192 C
hamiltoneb@gram.edu
HAMILTON, Eric .... 843-574-6272 412 I
eric.hamilton@tridenttech.edu
HAMILTON, Erin .... 502-895-3411 183 H
ehamilton@lpts.edu
HAMILTON, Ethan .... 619-849-2621.. 57 J
ethanhamilton@pointloma.edu
HAMILTON, Glenn .... 708-524-6795 137 C
hamilton@dom.edu
HAMILTON, Glenn, R .... 859-858-3511 179 D
glenn.hamilton@asbury.edu
HAMILTON, Guy .... 206-546-4101 484 B
ghamilton@shoreline.edu
HAMILTON, Heather ...... 303-273-3951.. 79 J
hhamilton@mines.edu
HAMILTON, Jared .... 508-213-2045 217 H
jared.hamilton@nichols.edu
HAMILTON, Jeff .... 740-351-3393 360 F
jhamilton@shawnee.edu
HAMILTON, Jeffrey, S ... 254-710-2657 431 E
jeffrey_hamilton@baylor.edu
HAMILTON, Jody .... 919-546-8416 340 B
jhamilton@shawu.edu
HAMILTON, Julia .... 252-638-7317 334 A
hamiltonj@cravencc.edu
HAMILTON, Karen .... 310-578-1080 347 H
khamilton1@antioch.edu
HAMILTON, Kate .... 517-264-7143 230 H
khamilton@sienaheights.edu
HAMILTON, Keith, J ..... 907-822-3201.... 9 D
keith@akcc.org
HAMILTON, Kelly .... 949-794-9090.. 66 D
khamilton@stanbridge.edu
HAMILTON, Ken .... 903-589-7130 438 C
khamilton@jacksonville-college.edu
HAMILTON, Kevin .... 217-332-5833 152 B
kham@illinois.edu
HAMILTON, Laura .... 501-202-7937.. 18 E
laura.hamilton@baptist-health.org
HAMILTON, Leah .... 214-245-3199 139 C
leah.hamilton@ic.edu
HAMILTON, JR., Leroy .. 502-597-6641 183 D
leroy.hamilton@kysu.edu
HAMILTON, LoriRae ...... 719-846-5524.. 83 L
lorirae.hamilton@trinidadstate.edu
HAMILTON, Louis, I ...... 973-642-7664 279 E
louis.i.hamilton@njit.edu
HAMILTON, Margaret .... 541-463-5200 373 D
hamiltonm@lanecc.edu
HAMILTON, Marty .... 423-236-2806 423 F
mlhamil@southern.edu
HAMILTON, Matthew .... 276-326-4602 464 J
mhamilton@bluefield.edu
HAMILTON, Michael ..... 757-240-2206 470 D
michael.hamilton@rivhs.com
HAMILTON, Michelle .... 618-985-3741 140 H
michellehamilton@jalc.edu
HAMILTON, Nakeysha ... 216-373-5316 357 F
nhamilton@ndc.edu
HAMILTON, Nardos ...... 516-572-7759 307 E
nardos.hamilton@ncc.edu
HAMILTON, Penny .... 585-785-1201 299 F
penny.hamilton@flcc.edu
HAMILTON, Richard ...... 360-442-2263 481 D
rhamilton@lowercolumbia.edu
HAMILTON, Ronald ...... 304-434-8000 488 E
ron.hamilton@easternwv.edu
HAMILTON, Ryan .... 419-267-1273 357 E
rhamilton@northweststate.edu
HAMILTON, Salina .... 386-481-2628.. 96 D
hamiltonsd@cookman.edu
HAMILTON, Shadel .... 813-221-6302 107 D
shadel.hamilton@saintleo.edu
HAMILTON, Shelley ...... 760-921-5483.. 56 A
shamilton@paloverde.edu
HAMILTON, Tina .... 201-216-9901 277 B
tina.hamilton@eicollege.edu
HAMILTON, William ...... 352-588-6610 107 D
william.hamilton02@saintleo.edu
HAMILTON-DRAGER, Catrina .... 717-254-8935 382 D
hamiltoc@dickinson.edu
HAMILTON-GOLDEN, Barbara .... 201-447-7113 275 H
bagolden@bergen.edu
HAMILTON-HONEY, Emily .... 315-386-7071 320 B
hamiltone@canton.edu
HAMILTON SLANE, Sandra .... 530-242-7799.. 64 C
sslane@shastacollege.edu
HAMLETT, Rebecca .... 816-415-7620 262 F
hamlettr@william.jewell.edu
HAMLETT, Tiffany .... 816-995-2844 258 G
tiffany.hamlett@researchcollege.edu
HAMLETT, Willie .... 626-815-3890.. 26 F
whamlett@apu.edu
HAMLIN, Annemarie ..... 541-383-7523 372 A
ahamlin@cocc.edu
HAMLIN, April .... 541-956-7255 376 A
ahamlin@roguecc.edu
HAMLIN, John .... 337-550-1301 189 G
jhamlin@lsue.edu
HAMLIN, Toby .... 518-608-8218 299 C
thamlin@excelsior.edu
HAMLUK, Brian, F .... 716-645-2982 316 C
bfhamluk@buffalo.edu
HAMM, Ashley .... 806-743-1445 451 A
ashley.hamm@ttuhsc.edu
HAMM, Bernard, C .... 804-828-1233 473 B
bchamm2@vcu.edu
HAMM, Darryl .... 562-951-4500.. 31 B
dhamm@calstate.edu
HAMM, Doug .... 920-693-1648 498 H
douglas.hamm@gotoltc.edu
HAMM, Jennifer .... 828-327-7000 333 B
jhamm@cvcc.edu
HAMM, Jolene .... 540-857-7311 475 G
jhamm@virginiawestern.edu
HAMM, Lee, L .... 504-988-5462 191 F
lhamm@tulane.edu
HAMM, Michelle .... 404-471-5443 114 G
mhamm@agnesscott.edu
HAMM, Reggie .... 678-359-5103 120 F
reggieh@gordonstate.edu
HAMM, Rod .... 620-947-3121 177 I
rodneyhamm@tabor.edu
HAMMACK, Brian .... 641-683-4270 166 I
brian.hammack@indianhills.edu
HAMMACK, Mike .... 325-670-1278 436 I
mhammack@hsutx.edu
HAMMAN, John .... 240-567-9006 200 G
john.hamman@montgomerycollege.edu
HAMMAR, Matt .... 503-554-2162 373 A
mhammar@georgefox.edu
HAMMAT, Jennifer, R ... 812-464-1862 162 C
jhammat@usi.edu
HAMMEKE, Curtis .... 785-628-4050 173 H
chammeke@fhsu.edu
HAMMEL, Kevin .... 936-294-3974 450 A
kxh058@shsu.edu
HAMMEL, Rachel .... 330-490-7452 363 E
rhammel@walsh.edu
HAMMER, Adam .... 320-762-4901 237 C
adam.hammer@alextech.edu
HAMMER, Bradley, C .... 419-434-6922 362 D
hammer@findlay.edu
HAMMER, Brian .... 802-257-7751 462 H
brian.hammer@sit.edu
HAMMER, Debbie .... 610-989-1200 401 I
dhammer@vfmac.edu
HAMMER, Elizabeth ...... 504-520-5141 193 E
eyhammer@xula.edu
HAMMER, Jaime, S ...... 334-844-5176.... 4 D
jsh0073@auburn.edu
HAMMER, Joyce .... 360-623-8486 478 F
joyce.hammer@centralia.edu
HAMMER, Kathryn .... 716-839-8364 298 A
khammer@daemen.edu
HAMMER, Katie .... 617-715-5940 216 B
HAMMER, Kimberley ..... 757-455-3205 477 C
khammer@vwu.edu
HAMMER, Larry .... 828-227-7216 343 E
hammer@wcu.edu

HANKINS, Jeff .... 501-660-1004.. 17 C
jhankins@asusystem.edu
HANKINS, Kim .... 815-455-8778 143 I
khankins@mchenry.edu
HANKINS, Orlando, E ... 919-516-4860 339 I
oehankins@st-aug.edu
HANKINS, Paul .... 479-788-7431.. 21 G
paul.hankins@uafs.edu
HANKINSON, Carol, A .. 252-862-1239 337 C
cahankinson@roanokechowan.edu
HANKINSON, Holbrook 765-658-4800 154 J
HANKINSON, Holbrook 765-658-4538 154 J
holbrookhankinson@depauw.edu
HANKS, Mary .... 205-652-3668.... 9 B
mhanks@uwa.edu
HANKS, Timothy .... 337-482-6449 193 B
timothy.hanks@louisiana.edu
HANLEY, Darla, S .... 617-747-2664 206 H
dhanley@berklee.edu
HANLEY, James .... 215-204-5578 399 B
sm693@bncollege.com
HANLEY, Peggy .... 318-274-6546 192 C
peggy@gram.edu
HANLEY, Rodney, S ...... 906-635-2202 226 G
rhanley@lssu.edu
HANLEY, Theodore .... 713-718-8566 437 C
theodore.hanley@hccs.edu
HANLEY, Tim .... 414-288-7141 493 E
timothy.hanley@marquette.edu
HANLEY-MAXWELL,
Cheryl .... 217-333-6677 152 B
cherylhm@illinois.edu
HANLON, Andra .... 540-665-4500 470 G
HANLON, Chris .... 610-921-2381 377 G
HANLON, Christopher .. 410-532-5369 201 D
chanlon@ndm.edu
HANLON, Erin .... 617-322-3531 211 A
erin_hanlon@laboure.edu
HANLON, Philip, J .... 603-646-2223 273 D
philip.j.hanlon@dartmouth.edu
HANLON, Susan, C ...... 330-972-7442 361 H
hanlon@uakron.edu
HANN, Nancy .... 614-234-1135 356 E
nhann@mccn.edu
HANNA, Aaron .... 210-431-3335 442 J
ahanna1@stmarytx.edu
HANNA, Abigail .... 262-551-8500 492 B
ahanna@carthage.edu
HANNA, Bashar, W .... 570-484-2000 394 E
basharhanna@lockhaven.edu
HANNA, Bashar, W .... 570-389-4526 393 D
bhanna@bloomu.edu
HANNA, Bryce .... 970-943-2126.. 85 C
bhanna@western.edu
HANNA, Chris .... 616-432-3407 230 A
chris.hanna@prts.edu
HANNA, Dorothy .... 785-833-4468 175 E
dahanna@kwu.edu
HANNA, Heather .... 406-657-2131 264 D
heather.hanna@msubillings.edu
HANNA, Jandy .... 304-647-6366 490 C
jhanna@osteo.wvsom.edu
HANNA, Jenette .... 620-441-5214 173 C
jenette.hanna@cowley.edu
HANNA, Kim .... 931-372-3203 426 B
khanna@tntech.edu
HANNA, Mae .... 513-732-5332 362 B
mae.hanna@uc.edu
HANNA, Mark .... 708-239-4705 151 A
mark.hanna@trnty.edu
HANNA, Rame .... 508-831-5000 220 F
HANNA, Randy .... 850-770-2102 110 C
rhanna@fsu.edu
HANNAFORD, Bo, S ..... 580-327-8406 367 A
bshannaford@nwosu.edu
HANNAFORD, Erin, E ... 717-867-6071 388 C
hannafor@lvc.edu
HANNAFORD, Tara .... 580-327-8540 367 A
tlhannaford@nwosu.edu
HANNAH, Felisa .... 559-791-2316.. 47 A
felisa.hannah@portervillecollege.edu
HANNAH, Jason .... 913-344-1216 171 F
HANNAH, Katie .... 269-783-2185 231 A
khannah@swmich.edu
HANNAH, Kimberly .... 413-265-2293 208 E
hannahk@elms.edu
HANNAH, Marcus .... 334-876-9360.... 2 D
marcus.hannah@wccs.edu
HANNAH, Russ .... 870-972-3303.. 17 E
rhannah@astate.edu
HANNAH-JEFFERSON,
Floressa .... 601-979-2127 246 F
floressa.j.hannah-jefferson@jsums.edu

HANNAN, Christopher .. 319-291-2705 166 H
christopher.hannan@hawkeyecollege.edu
HANNAN, James .... 315-445-4100 303 I
hannanjp@lemoyne.edu
HANNAN, Michael .... 814-732-2729 394 B
hannan@edinboro.edu
HANNAR, Christine .... 636-949-4625 254 H
channar@lindenwood.edu
HANNE, Benjamin, C .... 620-229-6371 177 G
ben.hanne@sckans.edu
HANNERS, Rodney .... 323-442-9775.. 73 D
rod.hanners@med.usc.edu
HANNES, Sarah .... 307-778-1178 501 E
shannes@lccc.wy.edu
HANNIGAN, Robyn .... 315-268-6544 295 F
rhanniga@clarkson.edu
HANNIGAN, Scott .... 501-279-4407.. 19 C
shannigan@harding.edu
HANNING, Chris .... 610-430-4178 395 D
channing@wcupa.edu
HANNMANN, Richard .... 518-608-8198 299 C
rhannmann@excelsior.edu
HANNO, Dennis, M ...... 508-286-8244 220 B
hanno_dennis@wheatoncollege.edu
HANNON, Daniel .... 914-323-5253 305 B
dan.hannon@mville.edu
HANNON, Dominic .... 716-878-4631 317 F
hannondj@buffalostate.edu
HANNON, James .... 330-672-0566 354 A
jhannon5@kent.edu
HANNON, Jim, M .... 563-333-6359 169 G
hannonjamesm@ambrose.sau.edu
HANNON, Ken .... 210-341-1366 440 H
khannon@ost.edu
HANNON, Kristin .... 330-490-7226 363 E
khannon@walsh.edu
HANNON, Kristina .... 909-388-6900.. 60 D
HANNON, Lauretta .... 706-295-6273 120 A
lhannon@gntc.edu
HANNON, Lauretta .... 404-756-4666 115 G
lhannon@atlm.edu
HANNON, Ron .... 408-848-4895.. 43 E
rhannon@gavilan.edu
HANNUM, Joshua .... 520-795-0787.. 10 I
president@asaom.edu
HANNUM, Natalie .... 925-473-7401.. 40 D
nhannum@losmedanos.edu
HANOFEE, Rosemarie ... 845-434-5750 321 E
rhanofee@sunysullivan.edu
HANOLD, John, W .... 814-863-0768 391 G
jhh6@psu.edu
HANRAHAN, Chelsea .... 603-428-2291 273 G
chanrahan@nec.edu
HANRAHAN, Neil, S ..... 212-998-4581 309 F
nsh2@nyu.edu
HANRAHAN, Susan, N . 870-972-3112.. 17 E
hanrahan@astate.edu
HANRAHAN,
Thomas, M .... 717-867-6030 388 C
hanrahan@lvc.edu
HANS, Peter .... 919-962-1000 340 H
HANSARD, Jamie .... 806-742-1482 450 F
jamie.hansard@ttu.edu
HANSBARGER, Tom ...... 845-938-2715 503 I
tom.hansbarger@westpoint.edu
HANSBURG, David .... 303-273-3300.. 79 J
hansburg@mines.edu
HANSCOM, Marcus .... 401-254-3345 405 C
mhanscom@rwu.edu
HANSELMAN, Jennifer .. 413-572-8702 213 F
jhanselman@westfield.ma.edu
HANSEN, Andy .... 605-229-8378 415 I
andrew.hansen@presentation.edu
HANSEN, Anne, W .... 518-564-2090 318 E
hansenaw@plattsburgh.edu
HANSEN, Blaine, J .... 828-898-8838 330 E
hansenb@lmc.edu
HANSEN, Chelsie .... 402-554-2541 270 A
chelsiehansen@unomaha.edu
HANSEN, Cheryl .... 712-279-1633 164 B
cheryl.hansen@briarcliff.edu
HANSEN, Chris .... 423-236-2802 423 F
chansen@southern.edu
HANSEN, Christian .... 207-453-5128 195 F
chansen@kvcc.me.edu
HANSEN, Christopher ... 978-867-4500 210 B
chris.hansen@gordon.edu
HANSEN, Cynthia .... 641-269-3099 166 G
hansency@grinnell.edu
HANSEN, Dan .... 605-688-4237 417 A
dan.hansen@sdstate.edu

HANSEN, Dan .... 405-491-6309 369 H
dhansen@snu.edu
HANSEN, David .... 843-574-6021 412 I
david.hansen@tridenttech.edu
HANSEN, David .... 605-367-7568 416 C
dave.hansen@sdbor.edu
HANSEN, Dean .... 662-915-1945 249 D
dlhansen@olemiss.edu
HANSEN, Eric .... 325-481-8300 437 F
ehansen@howardcollege.edu
HANSEN, Gregg .... 978-468-7111 210 C
ghansen@gcts.edu
HANSEN, Jill .... 815-825-9517 141 F
jhansen1@kish.edu
HANSEN, John .... 515-576-7201 167 A
hansen_j@iowacentral.edu
HANSEN, John .... 307-532-8304 501 B
john.hansen@ewc.wy.edu
HANSEN, Jon .... 308-432-6231 268 D
jhansen@csc.edu
HANSEN, Jory .... 605-995-2151 415 A
jory.hansen@dwu.edu
HANSEN, Katherine .... 425-235-2356 482 H
khansen@rtc.edu
HANSEN, Kathy .... 320-363-5307 235 F
kghansen@csbsju.edu
HANSEN, Kenneth .... 402-559-5301 269 K
hansenkl@unmc.edu
HANSEN, Kent, A .... 909-558-2644.. 48 E
khansen@claysonlaw.com
HANSEN, Kevin .... 319-398-5625 167 J
kevin.hansen@kirkwood.edu
HANSEN, Kristine .... 651-793-1300 238 I
kristine.hansen@metrostate.edu
HANSEN, Lynn .... 407-823-2362 110 E
lynn.hansen@ucf.edu
HANSEN, Mandy .... 719-255-7528.. 84 C
mhansen2@uccs.edu
HANSEN, Marie .... 207-973-1081 194 F
hansenm@my.husson.edu
HANSEN, Matt .... 563-333-6261 169 G
hansenmattb@sau.edu
HANSEN, Micah .... 605-367-5550 417 B
micah.hansen@southeasttech.edu
HANSEN, Michele, J ...... 317-278-2618 157 D
mjhansen@iupui.edu
HANSEN, Milton .... 706-864-1941 127 A
milton.hansen@ung.edu
HANSEN, Monica .... 509-542-4614 479 A
mhansen@columbiabasin.edu
HANSEN, Niels .... 518-276-6196 312 C
hansen3@rpi.edu
HANSEN, Noah .... 619-594-4808.. 33 D
nhansen@sdsu.edu
HANSEN, Peter .... 210-436-3324 442 J
phansen@stmarytx.edu
HANSEN, Randy .... 301-985-7000 203 E
HANSEN, Richard, A ...... 334-844-8348.... 4 D
rah0019@auburn.edu
HANSEN, Sarah .... 319-335-3557 163 H
sarah-hansen@uiowa.edu
HANSEN, Sharon .... 610-409-3175 401 H
shansen@ursinus.edu
HANSEN, Shelley .... 530-541-4660.. 47 E
hansen@ltcc.edu
HANSEN, Sherri .... 435-283-7251 461 B
sherri.hansen@snow.edu
HANSEN, Susan .... 860-727-6782.. 88 A
shansen@goodwin.edu
HANSEN, Terry .... 432-264-5600 437 F
thansen@howardcollege.edu
HANSEN, Zeynep .... 208-426-3314 130 H
zeynephansen@boisestate.edu
HANSEN-KIEFFER,
Kristin, M .... 717-796-5234 389 H
khansen@messiah.edu
HANSEN-THOMAS,
Holly .... 940-898-3415 451 D
hhansenthomas@twu.edu
HANSEN-THOMAS,
Holly .... 940-898-2749 451 D
hhansenthomas@twu.edu
HANSENS-PASSERI,
Catherine .... 410-651-9314 203 D
chpasseri@umes.edu
HANSLEY, Emily .... 704-748-5259 334 G
hansley.emily@gaston.edu
HANSON, Andrew .... 208-792-2218 132 A
ahanson@lcsc.edu
HANSON, Andrew .... 702-895-2267 271 D
andrew.hanson@unlv.edu
HANSON, Anita .... 218-879-0805 238 B
anita.hanson@fdltcc.edu

HANSON, Brenda .... 406-756-3843 263 E
bhanson@fvcc.edu
HANSON, Charlene .... 401-841-6541 503 A
charlene.hanson@usnwc.edu
HANSON, Cheryl .... 208-282-2533 131 G
hanscher@isu.edu
HANSON, Christina, R .. 717-796-1800 389 H
chanson@messiah.edu
HANSON, Courtney .... 414-288-3577 493 E
courtney.hanson@marquette.edu
HANSON, Cyndi .... 402-241-6405 268 H
cyndih@northeast.edu
HANSON, Denise .... 319-226-2012 163 C
denise.hanson@allencollege.edu
HANSON, Eric .... 540-261-8400 471 B
eric.hanson@svu.edu
HANSON, Gary, A .... 310-506-4405.. 56 G
gary.hanson@pepperdine.edu
HANSON, Jana .... 605-688-6305 417 A
jana.hanson@sdstate.edu
HANSON, Janet, K .... 507-786-3018 243 D
jhanson@stolaf.edu
HANSON, Julie .... 970-945-8691.. 78 L
HANSON, Ken .... 817-202-6519 444 I
ken.hanson@swau.edu
HANSON, Kent .... 763-433-1179 237 D
kent.hanson@anokaramsey.edu
HANSON, Kent .... 763-576-4700 237 E
kent.hanson@anokatech.edu
HANSON, Kristen .... 386-506-4506.. 98 D
kristen.hanson@daytonastate.edu
HANSON, Leon .... 903-675-6349 451 F
lhanson@tvcc.edu
HANSON, Lisa .... 309-341-5212 134 B
lhanson@sandburg.edu
HANSON, Margaret .... 513-556-5858 361 J
margaret.hanson@uc.edu
HANSON, Mark .... 920-206-2342 493 C
mark.hanson@mbu.edu
HANSON, Megan .... 810-762-9781 226 B
mhanson@kettering.edu
HANSON, Michelle .... 605-331-6714 417 C
michelle.hanson@usiouxfalls.edu
HANSON, Patti, L .... 641-422-4170 168 G
hansopat@niacc.edu
HANSON, Peter .... 513-875-3344 350 C
peter.hanson@chatfield.edu
HANSON, Rhoda .... 503-842-8222 376 E
rhodahanson@tillamookbaycc.edu
HANSON, Richard .... 605-256-5136 416 F
richard.hanson@dsu.edu
HANSON, Sara .... 860-343-5883.. 87 A
shanson@mxcc.edu
HANSON, Steven, D .... 517-355-2352 227 F
hansons@msu.edu
HANSON, Susanah .... 724-266-3838 400 B
shanson@tsm.edu
HANSON, Tonya .... 952-358-8213 239 G
tonya.hanson@normandale.edu
HANSON, Virginia .... 773-577-8100 136 F
vhanson@coynecollege.edu
HANSS, Patrick, G .... 315-386-7222 320 B
hanssp@canton.edu
HANSTAD, Kari .... 701-483-2326 345 C
kari.hanstad@dickinsonstate.edu
HANSTEN, LaDeane .... 209-588-5087.. 76 K
hanstenl@yosemite.edu
HANTL, Bill .... 216-881-1700 358 J
bhantl@ohiotech.edu
HANTON, Tracy .... 215-496-6175 381 I
thanton@ccp.edu
HANUSCIN, R. Douglas 419-755-4871 357 B
dhanusci@ncstatecollege.edu
HANYCZ, Colleen, M .... 215-951-1010 387 A
president@lasalle.edu
HANYCZ, Colleen, M .... 513-745-3502 364 G
president@xavier.edu
HANZLIK, Gilbert .... 804-524-3698 476 D
ghanzik@vsu.edu
HAO, David .... 713-525-3570 454 G
haodq@stthom.edu
HAO, Lan .... 626-914-8521.. 36 J
lhao@citruscollege.edu
HAPNER, Leslie .... 850-873-3511 101 N
lhapner@gulfcoast.edu
HAPPE, Doyle .... 713-529-2778 432 C
happe@paralegal.edu
HAPPEL, Harriet .... 661-362-3653.. 38 D
harriet.happel@canyons.edu
HAPSMITH, Linda, M ... 907-474-1849.. 10 A
lhapsmith@alaska.edu
HARA, Lou .... 785-749-8440 174 D
lhara@haskell.edu

HARMON, Jeff .... 208-732-6210 131 D
jharmon@csi.edu
HARMON, Jeff .... 501-916-5907.. 22 A
jwharmon@ualr.edu
HARMON, John .... 541-885-1106 374 I
john.harmon@oit.edu
HARMON, Kate .... 503-244-0726 371 E
kateharmon@achs.edu
HARMON, Kerri .... 302-857-1037.. 91 A
kerri.harmon@dtcc.edu
HARMON, Kevin .... 701-858-3299 345 E
kevin.harmon@minotstateu.edu
HARMON, Kiara .... 617-537-6547 144 A
HARMON, Ladelle .... 828-652-0626 336 B
ladelleh@mcdowelltech.edu
HARMON, LaVerne, T ... 302-356-6818.. 91 E
president@wilmu.edu
HARMON, Martino .... 734-764-5132 231 H
harmonma@umich.edu
HARMON, Meghan .... 716-926-8828 301 E
mharmon@hilbert.edu
HARMON, Melanie, B ... 260-982-5211 159 J
mbharmon@manchester.edu
HARMON, Melissa .... 910-678-8244 334 E
harmonm@faytechcc.edu
HARMON, Nathaniel, S . 417-268-6007 250 G
nharmon@gobbc.edu
HARMON, Patricia .... 304-929-5460 488 G
pharmon@newriver.edu
HARMON, Samantha ..... 917-225-2716 292 H
sharmon@cazenovia.edu
HARMON, Steve, K .... 956-326-2180 446 E
harmon@tamiu.edu
HARMON, Suzanne .... 937-393-3431 360 H
sharmon3@sscc.edu
HARMON, Terrence .... 336-770-3374 343 D
harmont@uncsa.edu
HARMON, Travis .... 256-766-6610.... 5 E
tharmon@hcu.edu
HARMON-FRANCIS,
Barbara .... 201-684-7543 280 H
bharmonf@ramapo.edu
HARMS, Cory, L .... 515-294-2591 163 G
clharms@iastate.edu
HARMS, Craig, A .... 785-532-5500 175 C
caharms@ksu.edu
HARMS, Dennis .... 708-239-4819 151 A
dennis.harms@trnty.edu
HARMS, Matthew .... 562-860-2451.. 35 H
mharms@cerritos.edu
HARMSEN, Mark .... 254-526-1365 432 D
mark.harmsen@ctcd.edu
HARNACKE, Jacob .... 217-735-7294 142 H
jharnacke@lincolncollege.edu
HARNE, George, A .... 713-522-7911 454 G
harneg@stthom.edu
HARNER, Kristy .... 423-614-8110 420 H
kharner@leeuniversity.edu
HARNER, Mike .... 517-607-2303 225 C
mharner@hillsdale.edu
HARNISCH, Joe .... 402-941-6143 267 L
harnischj@midlandu.edu
HARNISH, Eric .... 661-362-3429.. 38 D
eric.harnish@canyons.edu
HARNOIS, Deborah .... 508-856-2660 212 C
deborahl.harnois@umassmed.edu
HARNUM, Donald, P .... 609-896-5054 281 B
harnum@rider.edu
HAROLD, Martin .... 858-653-6740.. 46 H
mharold@jpcatholic.com
HARP, Dennis .... 406-377-9425 263 D
dharp@dawson.edu
HARP, Elizabeth, R .... 815-282-7900 148 I
bethharp@sacn.edu
HARP, Jeff .... 405-974-2800 370 I
jharp@uco.edu
HARP, John, W .... 319-895-4234 164 G
jharp@cornellcollege.edu
HARP, Randy .... 903-886-5351 447 B
randy.harp@tamuc.edu
HARP, Samuel .... 508-289-2955 220 E
sharp@whoi.edu
HARP-STEPHENS,
Becky .... 859-246-6498 181 F
becky.harp@kctcs.edu
HARPE, Cicely .... 706-771-4156 115 J
charpe@augustatech.edu
HARPE, John Michael .. 803-356-5906 406 D
jmharpe@allenuniversity.edu
HARPER, Alexie .... 571-483-8002.. 93 F
HARPER, April .... 704-991-0114 338 C
aharper6224@stanly.edu
HARPER, Candace .... 601-403-1365 248 E
charper@prcc.edu
HARPER, Charles .... 615-460-6403 418 B
charles.harper@belmont.edu
HARPER, Christine .... 859-257-3458 185 F
christine.harper@uky.edu
HARPER, Daniel .... 512-463-6449 449 E
daniel.harper@tsus.edu
HARPER, Daniel, S .... 901-321-3577 418 G
dharper3@cbu.edu
HARPER, David .... 410-827-5806 198 F
dharper@chesapeake.edu
HARPER, David .... 412-396-5589 383 A
harperd1@duq.edu
HARPER, Donna, L .... 540-568-3705 468 C
harperdl@jmu.edu
HARPER, Doreen, C ...... 205-934-5360.... 8 A
dcharper@uab.edu
HARPER, Heather .... 615-230-3519 425 E
heather.harper@volstate.edu
HARPER, Holly .... 620-441-5240 173 C
holly.harper@cowley.edu
HARPER, Jimmy .... 912-260-4314 125 D
jimmy.harper@sgsc.edu
HARPER, Joann .... 706-245-7226 118 D
jharper@ec.edu
HARPER, John .... 507-389-7433 241 C
john.harper@southcentral.edu
HARPER, Josh .... 503-255-0332 374 C
jharper@multnomah.edu
HARPER, Karla .... 937-376-6444 349 J
kharper@centralstate.edu
HARPER, Kathy .... 573-651-2552 259 H
kharper@semo.edu
HARPER, Kimberly, P ... 540-828-5393 464 L
kharper@bridgewater.edu
HARPER, Kristin .... 205-226-4720.... 4 F
kharper@bsc.edu
HARPER, Lauren .... 409-933-8690 433 H
lharper1@come.edu
HARPER, Lisa .... 405-974-2553 370 I
lharper@uco.edu
HARPER, Lisa, D .... 859-858-3511 179 D
lisa.harper@asbury.edu
HARPER, Marie .... 304-724-3700 486 F
mharper@apus.edu
HARPER, Marjoree .... 318-678-6000 187 H
mharper@bpcc.edu
HARPER, Mary, J .... 812-465-1026 162 C
mjharper@usi.edu
HARPER, Pam .... 270-706-8434 181 G
pamela.harper@kctcs.edu
HARPER, Randy .... 870-574-4590.. 21 D
rharper@sautech.edu
HARPER, Ross .... 620-421-6700 175 F
rossh@labette.edu
HARPER, Sandra .... 325-793-3800 439 F
harper.sandra@mcm.edu
HARPER, Stephany .... 304-462-6171 489 L
stephany.harper@glenville.edu
HARPER, Teresa, B .... 502-213-2121 182 C
teresa.harper@kctcs.edu
HARPER, Vernon .... 661-654-2154.. 30 B
vharper@csub.edu
HARPER HAGAN, Mary 305-284-4476 113 C
mharperh@miami.edu
HARPER-LANE, Destiny . 210-486-2157 429 B
dharper24@alamo.edu
HARPHAM, Edward .... 972-883-6729 455 B
harpham@utdallas.edu
HARPHAM, Jennifer, E . 330-972-5860 361 H
jharpham@uakron.edu
HARPIN, Kimberlee .... 815-802-8472 141 D
kharpin@kcc.edu
HARPINE, Annette .... 910-938-6789 333 F
harpinea@coastalcarolina.edu
HARPOLE, Jessica .... 662-329-7129 248 A
jjharpole@muw.edu
HARPOLE, Theresa .... 662-476-5274 246 B
tharpole@eastms.edu
HARPOOL, David .... 866-776-0331.. 54 D
president@ncu.edu
HARPOOL, David .... 866-776-0331.. 54 D
dharpool@ncu.edu
HARPS, Trynette Lottie . 231-777-0559 228 G
trynette.lottie-harps@muskegoncc.edu
HARPST, Steve .... 845-341-4230 310 G
steve.harpst@sunyorange.edu
HARPSTER, Tanya .... 570-484-2460 394 E
tlh106@lockhaven.edu
HARR, Jon .... 423-652-4773 420 F
jharr@king.edu
HARR, Shannon, L .... 606-783-2529 184 C
s.harr@moreheadstate.edu
HARRA, Alice .... 503-517-7421 375 G
harraa@reed.edu
HARRAL, Judy .... 361-825-2495 447 C
judy.harral@tamucc.edu
HARRAL, Kevin .... 650-949-7223.. 42 I
harralkevin@foothill.edu
HARRAWOOD, Hank ..... 803-323-2129 414 D
harrawoodh@winthrop.edu
HARRELL, Alfred, E .... 225-771-3911 191 B
alfred_harrell@sus.edu
HARRELL, III, Alfred, E 225-771-3911 191 A
alfred_harrell@sus.edu
HARRELL, Angela .... 260-399-7700 162 B
aharrell@sf.edu
HARRELL, Brandan .... 706-204-2209 119 D
bharrell@highlands.edu
HARRELL, Brenda .... 904-470-8081.. 98 L
b.harrell@ewc.edu
HARRELL, Brian .... 478-934-3027 122 F
brian.harrell@mga.edu
HARRELL, Bryant, L ...... 860-727-6756.. 88 A
bharrell@goodwin.edu
HARRELL, David, L .... 865-539-7378 425 B
dlharrell@pstcc.edu
HARRELL, Evelyn .... 504-286-5234 191 C
eharrell@suno.edu
HARRELL, II, Ivan, L .... 253-566-5100 484 E
iharrell@tacomacc.edu
HARRELL, Jessica .... 336-506-4113 332 A
jessica.harrell@alamancecc.edu
HARRELL, Jonathan .... 757-352-4453 470 B
jonahar@regent.edu
HARRELL, Joseph, H .... 513-558-4635 361 J
joseph.harrell@uc.edu
HARRELL, Katie .... 605-668-1293 415 F
katie.harrell@mountmarty.edu
HARRELL, Katie .... 605-668-1491 415 F
katie.harrell@mountmarty.edu
HARRELL, Kim .... 252-862-1288 337 C
kharrell@roanokechowan.edu
HARRELL, Kimberley ..... 916-691-7117.. 50 H
kimberley.harrell@crc.losrios.edu
HARRELL, Lee .... 941-359-7532 106 J
lharrell@ringling.edu
HARRELL, Lisa .... 229-430-3396 114 I
lharrell@albanytech.edu
HARRELL, Pamela, J ..... 919-209-2048 335 F
pjharrell@johnstoncc.edu
HARRELL, Shereada ...... 850-599-3700 109 I
shereada.harrell@famu.edu
HARRELL, Tracy .... 870-850-3121.. 21 B
tharrell@seark.edu
HARRELL, Zach .... 212-229-5150 308 A
harrellz@newschool.edu
HARRELSON, Chris .... 505-566-3284 288 D
harrelsonc@sanjuancollege.edu
HARRI, Ed .... 360-383-3230 486 A
eharri@whatcom.edu
HARRI, Robert .... 563-387-2103 168 B
harrro01@luther.edu
HARRIER, Briana, K .... 515-964-0601 166 D
harrierb@faith.edu
HARRIES, Peter, J .... 919-515-1989 342 A
pjharrie@ncsu.edu
HARRIG, Tina, L .... 920-832-6541 493 B
tina.l.harrig@lawrence.edu
HARRIGAN, Tammy ...... 401-598-1012 404 D
tammy.harrigan@jwu.edu
HARRIGAN-CRUZ,
Anide .... 954-492-5353.. 97 G
aharrigancruz@citycollege.edu
HARRIGER, Christine .... 540-362-6609 467 H
harrigerce@hollins.edu
HARRILL, Thad .... 828-395-1624 335 D
tharrill@isothermal.edu
HARRIMAN, Melinda .... 805-565-6045.. 76 A
mharriman@westmont.edu
HARRIMAN, Tayler .... 510-594-3633.. 28 B
tayler.harriman@cca.edu
HARRING, Christopher . 410-225-2255 200 D
charring@mica.edu
HARRING, Kathleen ...... 484-664-3125 390 H
president@muhlenberg.edu
HARRINGTON, Angela .. 973-278-5400 291 E
angela-harringt@berkeleycollege.edu
HARRINGTON, Angela ..... 973-278-5400 275 I
angela-harringt@berkeleycollege.edu
HARRINGTON, Billie ..... 864-578-8770 411 F
bharrington@sherman.edu
HARRINGTON, Bonnie .. 215-751-8253 381 I
bharrington@ccp.edu
HARRINGTON,
Constance .... 240-965-2494 198 C
cpharrington@captechu.edu
HARRINGTON, David .... 603-428-2440 273 G
dharrington@nec.edu
HARRINGTON, Donna ... 505-467-6831 288 H
donnaharrington@swc.edu
HARRINGTON, Heather . 901-321-3260 418 G
hharring@cbu.edu
HARRINGTON, Jaclyn ... 315-866-0300 301 D
harringjp@herkimer.edu
HARRINGTON, Jamee ... 541-956-7017 376 A
jharrington@roguecc.edu
HARRINGTON,
Jermaine .... 215-368-5000 390 A
jharrington@missio.edu
HARRINGTON, Jessica . 757-455-3107 477 C
jharrington@vwu.edu
HARRINGTON, Kahlil .... 323-953-4000.. 49 A
harrinkg@lacitycollege.edu
HARRINGTON, Kim .... 404-894-2499 119 E
kim.harrington@ohr.gatech.edu
HARRINGTON,
Kimberly .... 704-216-6151 330 H
kharrington@livingstone.edu
HARRINGTON, Krista .... 843-574-6077 412 I
krista.harrington@tridentttech.edu
HARRINGTON, Lynn ..... 708-974-5704 145 A
harrington@morainevalley.edu
HARRINGTON, Mark, R 716-888-3749 292 F
harring4@canisius.edu
HARRINGTON, Melinda 620-276-9514 174 B
melinda.harrington@gcccks.edu
HARRINGTON, Michael . 934-420-2053 320 F
michael.harrington@farmingdale.edu
HARRINGTON,
Michael, J .... 415-422-2790.. 72 J
harrington@usfca.edu
HARRINGTON, Rob .... 605-331-6645 417 C
rob.harrington@usiouxfalls.edu
HARRINGTON, Ryan ..... 573-518-2236 256 D
rkharrin@mineralarea.edu
HARRINGTON, Sean, P . 540-464-7132 476 B
harringtonsp@vmi.edu
HARRINGTON,
Sherre, L .... 706-236-2285 116 B
sharrington@berry.edu
HARRINGTON, Stacey ... 314-977-7124 259 F
stacey.harrington@slu.edu
HARRINGTON, Thomas . 504-280-1154 190 B
trharrin@uno.edu
HARRINGTON-HOPE,
Sharon .... 617-243-2145 211 B
sharrington-hope@lasell.edu
HARRIOTT, Danielle ...... 815-965-8616 148 C
dharriott@rockfordcareercollege.edu
HARRIS, Alexis .... 251-981-3771.... 5 A
alexis.harris@columbiasouthern.edu
HARRIS, Alice .... 304-424-8224 490 F
alice.harris@wvup.edu
HARRIS, Allatia .... 281-459-7140 442 K
allatia.harris@sjcd.edu
HARRIS, Alvin .... 501-370-5284.. 20 F
aharris@philander.edu
HARRIS, Andrew .... 312-341-3500 148 E
aharris52@roosevelt.edu
HARRIS, Andrew .... 415-338-1471.. 33 E
a1harris@sfsu.edu
HARRIS, Angie .... 717-245-1556 382 D
harrisa@dickinson.edu
HARRIS, Angie .... 865-981-8201 421 C
angie.harris@maryvillecollege.edu
HARRIS, Anna-Lize .... 201-216-5208 283 D
anna-lize.harris@stevens.edu
HARRIS, Anne .... 641-269-3000 166 G
harrisanne@grinnell.edu
HARRIS, Anthony .... 802-828-2800 463 F
ajh03150@ccv.vsc.edu
HARRIS, April .... 540-261-8400 471 B
april.harris@svu.edu
HARRIS, Becky .... 214-638-0484 438 E
bharris@kdstudio.com
HARRIS, Bennie .... 803-503-5200 414 A
HARRIS, Bennie, L .... 404-752-1955 123 E
bharris@msm.edu
HARRIS, Beryl .... 410-951-6280 204 B
bharris@coppin.edu
HARRIS, Beth .... 203-287-3023.. 88 E
HARRIS, Bethany, W ..... 434-949-1007 475 B
bethany.harris@southside.edu
HARRIS, Beverly .... 757-823-2409 469 A
bbharris@nsu.edu
HARRIS, Bill .... 972-708-7340 435 E
bill_harris@diu.edu

HARRIS, Caleb .... 208-882-1566 132 C charris15@nsa.edu
HARRIS, Carol, B .... 605-342-0317 415 C charris@jwc.edu
HARRIS, Caroline .... 252-536-7265 335 B charris@halifaxcc.edu
HARRIS, Charles, S ...... 434-791-5701 464 I csharris@averett.edu
HARRIS, Chelsia .... 615-966-6650 421 B chelsia.harris@lipscomb.edu
HARRIS, Chelsy .... 719-502-3034.. 82 E chelsy.harris@ppcc.edu
HARRIS, Chonnea .... 661-726-1911.. 68 J chonnea.harris@uav.edu
HARRIS, Chris .... 949-214-3169.. 39 K chris.harris@cui.edu
HARRIS, Christina .... 530-422-7923.. 74 G charris@weimar.edu
HARRIS, Christine .... 320-762-4435 237 C christine.harris@alextech.edu
HARRIS, Clark .... 307-772-4245 501 E charris@lccc.wy.edu
HARRIS, Clark .... 580-628-6201 366 J president@noc.edu
HARRIS, Clayton .... 216-987-4425 351 E clayton.harris@tri-c.edu
HARRIS, Corrine .... 704-233-8979 344 F c.harris@wingate.edu
HARRIS, Craig .... 540-857-7797 475 G charris@virginiawestern.edu
HARRIS, Crystal .... 816-271-5827 257 A crharris@missouriwestern.edu
HARRIS, Danielle .... 828-627-4507 335 C ldharris@haywood.edu
HARRIS, Dannie .... 913-758-6219 178 B dannie.harris@stmary.edu
HARRIS, Darnell .... 559-638-0300.. 67 D darnell.harris@reedleycollege.edu
HARRIS, Darrell, A .... 904-264-2172 106 K dharris@iws.edu
HARRIS, David .... 320-308-4866 240 I djharris@stcloudstate.edu
HARRIS, David .... 718-268-4700 312 A
HARRIS, David .... 843-574-6615 412 I david.harris@tridenttech.edu
HARRIS, David, P .... 909-558-7600.. 48 E dpharris@llu.edu
HARRIS, David, R .... 518-388-6101 323 J harrisd@union.edu
HARRIS, David, W .... 319-273-2470 164 A david.harris@uni.edu
HARRIS, Dawn .... 225-771-2680 191 B dawn_harris@subr.edu
HARRIS, Debbie .... 804-751-9191 465 K dharris@ccc-va.com
HARRIS, Delores, R .... 919-530-6681 341 E dharr226@nccu.edu
HARRIS, Denise, M .... 716-878-5811 317 F harrisdm@buffalostate.edu
HARRIS, Derrell .... 912-287-5855 117 E dharris@coastalpines.edu
HARRIS, Dianne .... 206-543-5340 485 A dsh1@uw.edu
HARRIS, Dina .... 574-520-4131 157 E dlharris@iusb.edu
HARRIS, Doris, M .... 301-546-0129 201 E harrisdm@pgcc.edu
HARRIS, Eboneigh .... 940-397-4567 440 C eboneigh.harris@msutexas.edu
HARRIS, Erica .... 606-539-4167 185 E erica.harris@ucumberlands.edu
HARRIS, Eugenia .... 903-813-2371 430 H eharris@austincollege.edu
HARRIS, SR., Forrest, E .... 615-256-1463 417 F officeofthepresident@abcnash.edu
HARRIS, Frank .... 520-795-0787.. 10 I admissions@asaom.edu
HARRIS, G. Duncan .... 860-906-5100.. 86 D gharris@capitalcc.edu
HARRIS, Gail .... 423-746-5208 426 C gharris@tnwesleyan.edu
HARRIS, Gary, L .... 202-806-2550.. 92 F gharris@howard.edu
HARRIS, Gheretta .... 231-591-3947 224 A gherettaharris@ferris.edu
HARRIS, Hayley .... 607-274-3011 302 G hharris@ithaca.edu
HARRIS, Hubert, D .... 804-524-1085 476 D hharris@vsu.edu
HARRIS, J. Loyd .... 850-747-3211 101 N lharris@gulfcoast.edu
HARRIS, James, T .... 619-260-4520.. 72 I president@sandiego.edu
HARRIS, Jason .... 919-301-6500.. 93 H
HARRIS, Jayne .... 251-343-8200.... 6 D
HARRIS, Jean .... 941-487-4570 110 D jharris@ncf.edu
HARRIS, Jeff .... 205-226-4700.... 4 F jharris@bsc.edu
HARRIS, Jeff .... 575-674-2391 285 L jharris@burrell.edu
HARRIS, Jessica .... 618-650-5609 150 C jesharr@siue.edu
HARRIS, Jewell .... 601-979-1773 246 F jewell.e.harris@jsums.edu
HARRIS, Jim .... 301-405-4568 202 H harrisjf@umd.edu
HARRIS, John .... 515-271-1472 165 G john.harris@dmu.edu
HARRIS, John .... 601-635-2111 246 A jharris@eccc.edu
HARRIS, John .... 518-244-4582 313 A harrisj8@sage.edu
HARRIS, Kendra, L .... 340-692-4151 513 E kendra.harris@uvi.edu
HARRIS, Kenneth, E .... 313-831-5200 223 L kharris@etseminary.edu
HARRIS, Kevin .... 931-372-6144 426 B kharris@tntech.edu
HARRIS, Kim .... 865-882-4695 425 C harriskb@roanestate.edu
HARRIS, Kim .... 662-720-7193 248 C kkharris@nemcc.edu
HARRIS, Krista .... 785-227-3380 172 A harriskm@bethanylb.edu
HARRIS, Kristi .... 660-359-3948 257 D kharris@mail.ncmissouri.edu
HARRIS, Kristie .... 941-487-5020 110 D klharris@ncf.edu
HARRIS, Kristin .... 940-855-2203 457 C kharris@vernoncollege.edu
HARRIS, Kurt .... 435-586-1991 460 A harrisk@suu.edu
HARRIS, Lakeisha, L ..... 410-651-6507 203 D llharris@umes.edu
HARRIS, Lamel .... 408-288-3736.. 62 H lamel.harris@sjcc.edu
HARRIS, Liesl, W .... 205-853-1200.... 2 G lwharris@jeffersonstate.edu
HARRIS, Link .... 325-794-4411 432 I link.harris@cisco.edu
HARRIS, Lisa .... 318-357-6441 192 G
HARRIS, Lisa .... 763-433-1292 237 D lisa.harris@anokaramsey.edu
HARRIS, Lori .... 757-233-8786 477 C lharris@vwu.edu
HARRIS, Marc .... 717-867-6208 388 C harris@lvc.edu
HARRIS, Marie .... 253-964-6500 482 E mharris@pierce.ctc.edu
HARRIS, Marilyn .... 417-873-7854 252 G mharris016@drury.edu
HARRIS, Marion .... 334-872-2533.... 6 F
HARRIS, Mark .... 626-398-2222.. 76 C
HARRIS, Mark .... 631-451-4231 321 C harrism@sunysuffolk.edu
HARRIS, Mark .... 414-416-8417 496 B mtharris@uwm.edu
HARRIS, Mark .... 414-290-7272 496 B mtharris@uwm.edu
HARRIS, Mark, T .... 414-416-8417 496 B mtharris@uwm.edu
HARRIS, Marty .... 626-968-1328.. 47 G
HARRIS, Mary .... 317-931-4440 154 G mharris@cts.edu
HARRIS, Mary, E .... 512-223-7705 430 I mharris3@austincc.edu
HARRIS, Mary Ann .... 202-274-5426.. 94 B mharris@udc.edu
HARRIS, Mary Beth .... 785-227-3380 172 A harrismb@bethanylb.edu
HARRIS, Maurice, A ...... 315-443-4734 321 G maharr17@syr.edu
HARRIS, Mel .... 703-812-4757 468 D mharris@leland.edu
HARRIS, Melvin .... 256-726-7374.... 6 C mharris@oakwood.edu
HARRIS, Michael .... 615-963-5000 426 A
HARRIS, Michelle .... 828-627-4521 335 C mlharris@haywood.edu
HARRIS, Monty .... 575-234-9215 287 E mwharris@nmsu.edu
HARRIS, Nick, L .... 504-816-4704 186 I nharris@dillard.edu
HARRIS, Noelle .... 401-232-6045 404 A nharris@bryant.edu
HARRIS, Patricia .... 662-252-8000 248 G pharris@rustcollege.edu
HARRIS, Patricia .... 616-988-3624 226 E pharris@kuyper.edu
HARRIS, Patrick .... 406-447-4380 263 B pharris@carroll.edu
HARRIS, Perry .... 205-853-1200.... 2 G pharris3@jeffersonstate.edu
HARRIS, Peter .... 860-512-3203.. 86 G pharris@manchestercc.edu
HARRIS, Phaedra .... 850-644-2525 110 C
HARRIS, Randall .... 601-857-3889 246 C randall.harris@hindscc.edu
HARRIS, Randy .... 814-866-8416 387 D rharris@lecom.edu
HARRIS, Renard .... 843-953-5079 408 C harrisr@cofc.edu
HARRIS, Rhonda, L .... 757-683-4007 469 B rlharris@odu.edu
HARRIS, Richard .... 479-508-3310.. 18 C rharris1@atu.edu
HARRIS, Richard, C .... 516-671-2215 324 G rharris@webb.edu
HARRIS, Rob .... 417-328-1827 259 I rharris@sbuniv.edu
HARRIS, Robin .... 252-335-0821 333 G robin_harris@albemarle.edu
HARRIS, Rotesha .... 404-880-6389 117 C rharris@cau.edu
HARRIS, Sarah .... 559-737-5478.. 39 B sarahha@cos.edu
HARRIS, Sedwick .... 610-861-4558 391 C sharris@northampton.edu
HARRIS, Sharlene, J ..... 340-693-1361 513 E sharris@uvi.edu
HARRIS, Siabhon .... 757-822-7261 475 E smharris@tcc.edu
HARRIS, Skip .... 802-651-5961 462 A sharris@champlain.edu
HARRIS, Stephen .... 512-499-4351 454 H sharris@utsystem.edu
HARRIS, Steven .... 773-583-4450 146 A
HARRIS, Susan .... 360-867-6100 480 C harriss@evergreen.edu
HARRIS, Susan, G .... 434-924-7120 472 D sgh4c@virginia.edu
HARRIS, Suzann .... 615-248-1201 426 D sharris3@trevecca.edu
HARRIS, Terral .... 912-279-5726 117 F tharris@ccga.edu
HARRIS, Terrance .... 805-756-2311.. 29 I tharris@calpoly.edu
HARRIS, Thomas, W ...... 859-257-1933 185 F tom.harris@uky.edu
HARRIS, Todd, D .... 910-630-7155 331 E toharris@methodist.edu
HARRIS, Toi .... 713-798-6590 431 D toih@bcm.edu
HARRIS, Tonya .... 870-838-2913.. 17 B tharris@smail.anc.edu
HARRIS, Tosca .... 620-901-6306 171 D harris@allencc.edu
HARRIS, Tracy .... 240-725-5300 198 G taharris1@csmd.edu
HARRIS, Tracy .... 601-979-2433 246 F ltracy.l.harris@jsums.edu
HARRIS, Travaris .... 847-925-6738 138 G tharris@harpercollege.edu
HARRIS, Victoria .... 314-340-5750 254 A harrisv@hssu.edu
HARRIS, Walter .... 888-576-3348.. 46 I
HARRIS, Wendy .... 410-462-8300 198 B wharris@bccc.edu
HARRIS, Wendy .... 901-435-1477 420 I wendy_harris@loc.edu
HARRIS, Windell .... 803-786-3343 408 D wharris@columbiasc.edu
HARRIS, Yolanda .... 719-502-4689.. 82 E yolanda.harris@ppcc.edu
HARRIS, Yvonne .... 916-278-6402.. 32 D y.harris@csus.edu
HARRIS-BRACKETT, Betsy .... 770-962-7580 121 E bharris@gwinnetttech.edu
HARRIS-CALDWELL, Jeanne .... 949-582-4607.. 65 D jharriscaldwell@saddleback.edu
HARRIS COHEN, David . 626-264-8880.. 71 F
HARRIS-DAVIS, Devin ... 502-863-7073 180 H devin_harris-davis@georgetowncollege.edu
HARRIS-HOOKER, Sandra .... 404-752-1725 123 E sharris-hooker@msm.edu
HARRIS-JOLLY, Stephanie .... 229-500-3442 114 H stephanie.harris-jolly@asurams.edu
HARRIS KISUNZU, Cheryl .... 301-891-4116 205 A
HARRIS-LOTT, Yvonne .. 800-462-7845.. 80 A
HARRISON, Amanda ..... 480-285-1761.. 12 B
HARRISON, B. Timothy 618-537-6962 144 A btharrison@mckendree.edu
HARRISON, Bertran .... 713-313-7011 449 B
HARRISON, Bob .... 526-947-8755.. 65 I bobharrison@scuhs.edu
HARRISON, Carol .... 301-934-7552 198 G caharrison@csmd.edu
HARRISON, Charles ...... 918-293-5130 368 B charles.harrison10@okstate.edu
HARRISON, Crystal .... 920-498-5541 499 G crystal.harrison@nwtc.edu
HARRISON, Cynthia, F . 914-968-6200 314 C
HARRISON, David .... 336-770-3273 343 D harrisondl@uncsa.edu
HARRISON, David, T .... 614-287-2402 351 C dth@cscc.edu
HARRISON, Earnestine .. 480-517-8381.. 13 G earnestine.harrison@riosalado.edu
HARRISON, Elgloria ...... 718-960-8000 294 A
HARRISON, Emily, P .... 804-752-7211 469 F emilyharrison@rmc.edu
HARRISON, Erika .... 713-221-5771 453 A harrisone@uhd.edu
HARRISON, Faimous .... 209-513-9403.. 33 B fharrison@csustan.edu
HARRISON, Fiona .... 626-395-6601.. 28 J fiona@srl.caltech.edu
HARRISON, Gerald .... 931-221-7904 417 H harrisongj@apsu.edu
HARRISON, Heidi .... 610-647-4400 385 L hharrison2@immaculata.edu
HARRISON, Hiroko .... 574-239-8341 156 A hharrison@hcc-nd.edu
HARRISON, J.T .... 256-766-6610.... 5 E jharrison@hcu.edu
HARRISON, Jada, L ...... 334-683-2313.... 3 A jharrison@marionmilitary.edu
HARRISON, Janice .... 508-565-1096 219 A jaharrison@stonehill.edu
HARRISON, Jim .... 478-553-2108 123 H jharrison@oftc.edu
HARRISON, Jim, H .... 920-206-2396 493 C jim.harrison@mbu.edu
HARRISON, Jonathan .... 800-348-3481 419 K jharrison@fhu.edu
HARRISON, Justin .... 858-513-9240.. 68 K justin.harrison@ashford.edu
HARRISON, Kathy, L ..... 417-268-1026 250 E harrisonk@evangel.edu
HARRISON, Kelly, G ..... 904-620-1707 111 B n00874366@unf.edu
HARRISON, Kenneth ..... 334-291-4963.... 1 H kenneth.harrison@cv.edu
HARRISON, Kevin .... 714-895-8983.. 38 A kharrison@gwc.cccd.edu
HARRISON, Kevin .... 714-895-8983.. 38 B kharrison21@gwc.cccd.edu
HARRISON, Kim, W ...... 931-363-9876 427 E kharr423@utsouthern.edu
HARRISON, Lee .... 423-461-8719 422 E lharrison@milligan.edu
HARRISON, Lonnie .... 575-492-2168 289 F lharrison@usw.edu
HARRISON, M. Blake .... 270-852-3460 183 E bharrison@kwc.edu
HARRISON, Malou .... 305-237-7248 104 E mharriso@mdc.edu
HARRISON, Matthew ..... 214-818-1312 433 O mharrison@criswell.edu
HARRISON, Merrell, J .. 606-783-2035 184 C m.harrison@moreheadstate.edu
HARRISON, Michael ..... 334-347-2623.... 2 A mharrison@escc.edu
HARRISON, Michael ..... 585-395-2317 317 E mharriso@brockport.edu
HARRISON, Nancy .... 530-541-4660.. 47 E harrison@ltcc.edu
HARRISON, Pam .... 601-484-8690 247 A pharriso@meridiancc.edu
HARRISON, Rebecca ..... 256-766-6610.... 5 E rharrison@hcu.edu
HARRISON, Renee .... 336-757-3215 334 F rharrison@forsythtech.edu

HARRISON, Rodger 425-564-2224 477 J
rodger.harrison@bellevuecollege.edu
HARRISON, Rodney, A 816-414-3700 256 C
rharrison@mbts.edu
HARRISON, Ryan 313-664-7678 222 H
rharrison@collegeforcreativestudies.edu
HARRISON, Sandra 310-506-6500 56 G
sandra.k.harrison@pepperdine.edu
HARRISON, Scott 219-464-5335 162 D
scott.harrison@valpo.edu
HARRISON, Shannon 516-877-3486 289 I
sharrison@adelphi.edu
HARRISON, Stephanie 989-686-9276 223 J
stephanieharrison@delta.edu
HARRISON, Steven 567-661-7575 359 I
steven_harrison@owens.edu
HARRISON, Suzan 727-864-8212 98 J
harrisms@eckerd.edu
HARRISON, Tammiko 601-979-2345 246 F
tammiko.l.harrison@jsums.edu
HARRISON, Teresa 256-331-5215 3 C
teresah@nwscc.edu
HARRISON, Teresa 757-925-6782 474 H
tharrison@pdc.edu
HARRISON, Tim 510-215-3847 40 B
tharrison@contracosta.edu
HARRISON, Todd 903-875-7600 440 D
todd.harrision@navarrocollege.edu
HARRISON, Tracey 601-925-3239 247 C
tharriso@mc.edu
HARRISON, Valerie, I 215-204-8922 399 B
valerie.harrison@temple.edu
HARRISON, Violet 803-376-5702 406 D
vharrison@allenuniversity.edu
HARRISON-MERCER, Sheryl, E 678-916-2681 115 I
sharrison@johnmarshall.edu
HARRISS, Frankie 808-245-8229 130 B
frankieh@hawaii.edu
HARRISS, Harriet 718-399-4304 311 F
hharriss@pratt.edu
HARROD, Joseph 502-897-4215 184 G
jharrod@sbts.edu
HARROD, Ryan 301-387-3043 199 A
ryan.harrod@garrettcollege.edu
HARROZ, JR., Joseph 405-325-3916 370 K
jharroz@ou.edu
HARSHBARGER, Beth 612-343-4473 242 M
HARSHBARGER, John 440-775-8470 357 G
john.harshbarger@oberlin.edu
HARSHMAN, Cris 828-254-1921 332 B
charshman@abtech.edu
HARSTON, Julie 615-966-5717 421 B
julie.harston@lipscomb.edu
HART, Aaron, J 281-283-7600 452 E
harta@uhcl.edu
HART, Bianca 215-248-7021 381 A
hartb@chc.edu
HART, Brad 912-538-3121 125 G
brhart@southeasterntech.edu
HART, Carol 904-264-2172 106 K
chart@iws.edu
HART, Charlene 775-784-4040 271 E
crhart@unr.edu
HART, Charles 601-643-8358 245 F
charles.hart@colin.edu
HART, Chenita 352-854-2322 97 N
hartc@cf.edu
HART, Chris 502-585-9911 184 H
chart@spalding.edu
HART, Chris 410-837-5739 204 F
chart@ubalt.edu
HART, Christi 503-491-6961 374 B
christi.hart@mhcc.edu
HART, Daniel 856-225-6741 281 G
daniel.hart@rutgers.edu
HART, Deanna 562-860-2451 35 H
dhart@cerritos.edu
HART, Debra 304-696-2597 489 M
hart70@marshall.edu
HART, Erick 585-395-2579 317 E
ehart@brockport.edu
HART, Erin 814-871-5603 384 A
hart022@gannon.edu
HART, Erin 336-285-2470 341 D
ehhart@ncat.edu
HART, Eyvonne 912-486-7784 123 J
ehart@ogeecheetech.edu
HART, George, K 401-825-2233 404 C
ghart3@ccri.edu
HART, Geraldine 516-463-6605 301 G
geraldine.hart@hofstra.edu
HART, James, R 904-264-2172 106 K
president@iws.edu
HART, James, T 804-862-6100 470 C
jhart@rbc.edu
HART, Jeni, L 573-884-1402 261 A
hartjl@missouri.edu
HART, Jennifer 717-871-7001 395 A
jennifer.hart@millersville.edu
HART, Jill 914-674-7362 306 C
jhart2@mercy.edu
HART, Jimmy, W 615-898-5131 422 C
jimmy.hart@mtsu.edu
HART, John 937-766-3400 349 E
johnhart@cedarville.edu
HART, Jon 605-995-2152 415 A
jon.hart1@dwu.edu
HART, Joy 502-852-6976 186 A
jlhart01@louisville.edu
HART, Julie 315-498-2214 310 F
hartj@sunyocc.edu
HART, Kelly 304-876-5016 490 A
khart08@shepherd.edu
HART, Kristin 718-997-3760 295 B
kristin.hart@qc.cuny.edu
HART, Kristy 916-608-6993 50 I
hartk@flc.losrios.edu
HART, La Toya 601-979-7030 246 F
latoya.m.hart@jsums.edu
HART, Mandy 254-298-8634 445 G
mandy.hart@templejc.edu
HART, Melanie 212-229-5400 308 A
melanie.hart@newschool.edu
HART, Melissa 605-642-6549 416 E
melissa.hart@bhsu.edu
HART, Michael 207-741-5500 195 H
mhart@smccme.edu
HART, Mischon 765-641-4083 153 G
mnhart@anderson.edu
HART, Patrick 718-658-0006 308 C
HART, Richard, H 909-558-4540 48 E
rhart@llu.edu
HART, Richard, L 214-768-4301 444 D
rlhart@smu.edu
HART, Samatha 570-577-2000 379 C
samatha.hart@bucknell.edu
HART, Sara 724-805-2064 397 I
sara.hart@stvincent.edu
HART, Sara 724-805-2064 398 A
sara.hart@stvincent.edu
HART, Susan 615-343-6604 428 A
susan.hart@vanderbilt.edu
HART, Thomas 412-396-6002 383 A
hartt1@duq.edu
HART, OSB, Thomas 724-805-2322 398 A
thomas.hart@stvincent.edu
HART, Tim 316-978-6192 178 D
tim.hart@wichita.edu
HART, Tracy 859-572-1493 184 E
harttr@nku.edu
HART RUTHENBECK, Robin 740-427-5136 354 I
hartruthenbeck1@kenyon.edu
HART-STEFFES, Jeanne, S 413-782-3111 220 A
HART-THORE, Dawn 504-278-6332 188 G
dhart@nunez.edu
HARTE, Barry 703-284-3847 468 H
barry.harte@marymount.edu
HARTE, Tim 610-526-5000 379 B
HARTE WEYANT, Meghan 901-843-3997 423 A
weyantm@rhodes.edu
HARTENBURG, Dale 706-721-3356 116 A
dhartenburg@augusta.edu
HARTENBURG, Gary 281-649-3630 437 B
ghartenburg@hbu.edu
HARTER, Jill 314-446-8346 260 H
jill.harter@stlcop.edu
HARTER, Kris 937-298-3399 354 J
kris.harter@kc.edu
HARTER, Michelle 912-583-3245 116 E
mharter@bpc.edu
HARTFIELD, Colleen 601-857-3751 246 C
colleen.hartfield@hindscc.edu
HARTFORD, Sharon, M 509-527-4323 485 B
sharon.hartford@wwcc.edu
HARTFORD, Stephanie 618-985-2828 140 H
stephaniehartford@jalc.edu
HARTGE, Gary 352-395-5835 108 A
gary.hartge@sfcollege.edu
HARTHORN, Karen, M 651-962-6353 244 E
kmharthorn@stthomas.edu
HARTIGAN, Gretchen 617-358-6361 207 E
hartigan@bu.edu
HARTIGAN, Sheenah 732-255-0400 279 F
shartigan@ocean.edu
HARTING, Troy, R 719-333-4130 503 D
troy.harting@usafa.edu
HARTING, William 317-955-6015 159 K
bharting@marian.edu
HARTJE, Sandra 206-281-2111 483 G
HARTL, Derek 563-387-1433 168 B
hartde01@luther.edu
HARTL, Renae 563-387-1244 168 B
hartre01@luther.edu
HARTLAUB, Elizabeth 859-441-4500 181 H
elizabeth.hartlaub@kctcs.edu
HARTLESS, Megan 540-453-2209 473 D
hartlessm@brcc.edu
HARTLEY, Brian 618-664-6821 138 F
brian.hartley@greenville.edu
HARTLEY, Carolyn 219-980-7205 157 C
cjhartle@iun.edu
HARTLEY, Greg, L 916-348-4689 41 H
ghartley@epic.edu
HARTLEY, James 870-762-1020 17 B
jehartley@smail.anc.edu
HARTLEY, Julie 801-321-7101 459 N
jhartley@ushe.edu
HARTLEY, Katherine 909-537-5000 32 E
katherine.hartley@csusb.edu
HARTLEY, Laura 316-942-4291 176 E
hartleyl@newmanu.edu
HARTLEY, Laura, C 206-281-2508 483 G
lhartley@spu.edu
HARTLEY, Leslie 205-387-0511 1 D
leslie.hartley@bscc.edu
HARTLEY, Roger 410-837-5359 204 F
rhartley@ubalt.edu
HARTLEY, Timothy 330-337-6403 347 D
thartley@awc.edu
HARTLEY, Vaughn 304-473-8367 491 D
hartley.v@wvwc.edu
HARTLEY-HUTTON, Kelley 260-481-6643 160 C
hartleyk@pfw.edu
HARTLINE, Michael 850-644-4405 110 C
mhartline@cob.fsu.edu
HARTMAN, Brandi, P 864-488-4617 410 B
bhartman@limestone.edu
HARTMAN, C. Max 650-306-3132 62 J
hartmanmax@smccd.edu
HARTMAN, Carolyn, S 910-962-4103 343 C
hartmanc@uncw.edu
HARTMAN, Chris, T 215-885-2360 389 C
chartman@manor.edu
HARTMAN, Christine 717-796-1800 389 H
chartman@messiah.edu
HARTMAN, Cynthia 740-389-4636 355 F
hartmanc@mtc.edu
HARTMAN, Dean, A 706-880-8246 122 A
dhartman@lagrange.edu
HARTMAN, Fritz 574-535-7423 155 E
fritzdh@goshen.edu
HARTMAN, Greg 979-458-6000 446 B
HARTMAN, Greg 979-458-8679 446 F
ghartman@tamu.edu
HARTMAN, James 609-896-5016 281 B
jhartman@rider.edu
HARTMAN, Joseph 972-825-4774 444 J
jhartman@sagu.edu
HARTMAN, Joseph 978-934-2168 212 B
joseph_hartman@uml.edu
HARTMAN, Joshua 617-627-3248 219 C
joshua.hartman@tufts.edu
HARTMAN, Katie 740-593-2600 358 K
hartmank@ohio.edu
HARTMAN, Kerry 701-627-4738 346 F
khartm@nhsc.edu
HARTMAN, Kevin 414-229-4594 496 B
hartman@uwm.edu
HARTMAN, Kimberly 727-712-5876 107 E
hartman.kimberly@spcollege.edu
HARTMAN, Laurie 315-792-7400 321 B
laurie.hartman@sunypoly.edu
HARTMAN, Paulla 641-844-5767 167 G
paulla.hartman@iavalley.edu
HARTMAN, Rob 803-754-4100 408 E
HARTMAN, Robin 714-879-3901 45 G
rhartman@hiu.edu
HARTMAN, Sarah 806-291-1045 457 I
harmans@wbu.edu
HARTMAN, Sherry 410-287-1025 198 E
shartman@cecil.edu
HARTMAN, Stephanie 304-358-2000 487 D
stephanie@future.edu
HARTMAN, Thomas 336-506-4201 332 A
thomas.hartman@alamancecc.edu
HARTMANN, Angela 361-570-4374 453 B
hartmanna@uhv.edu
HARTMANN, Lori, L 859-238-5371 180 B
lori.hartmann@centre.edu
HARTMANN, Richard 714-992-7044 54 C
rhartmann@fullcoll.edu
HARTMANN, Steve 631-451-4000 321 D
hartmas@sunysuffolk.edu
HARTMANN, Wendy 636-584-6712 253 B
wendy.hartmann@eastcentral.edu
HARTNESS, Darrin, L 336-249-8186 334 B
darrin_hartness@davidsondavie.edu
HARTNET, Amelia 309-298-1971 153 A
af-hartnett@wiu.edu
HARTNETT, Mary 716-839-8451 298 A
mhartnet@daemen.edu
HARTNETT, Ryan 716-896-0700 324 E
hartnettr@villa.edu
HARTO, Diana, L 304-336-8139 490 B
diana.harto@westliberty.edu
HARTOG, III, John 712-324-5061 169 C
jhartog@nwicc.edu
HARTOG, Paul, A 515-964-0601 166 D
hartogp@faith.edu
HARTON, Mary Kay 847-925-6221 138 G
mharton@harpercollege.edu
HARTS, Melissa, L 727-816-3466 105 F
hartsm@phsc.edu
HARTSELL, Amy 540-432-4100 466 B
springer@emu.edu
HARTSELL, Angela 239-489-9427 101 A
ahartsell1@fsw.edu
HARTSHORN, Kevin 610-861-1374 390 F
hartshornk@moravian.edu
HARTSHORN, Tricia 620-242-0441 176 B
hartshot@mcpherson.edu
HARTSOCK, Michael 217-424-6265 144 G
mhartsock@millikin.edu
HARTSON, Michelle 931-431-9700 422 G
mhartson@nci.edu
HARTSON, Michelle 931-431-9700 422 G
financialaid@nci.edu
HARTUNG, Benjamin 716-673-3111 316 D
benjamin.hartung@fredonia.edu
HARTWELL, John 435-797-2060 460 C
john.hartwell@usu.edu
HARTWELL, Richard, H 610-361-2336 391 A
hartwelr@neumann.edu
HARTWELL, Stephanie 313-577-2519 232 K
gr2312@wayne.edu
HARTWIG, Ryan 303-963-3426 78 H
rhartwig@ccu.edu
HARTY, Kristin 412-365-2769 380 G
kharty@chatham.edu
HARTY, Molly 610-902-8131 379 G
mh10962@cabrini.edu
HARTZ, James 270-686-4630 182 F
jim.hartz@kctcs.edu
HARTZ, Rachel 570-348-6211 389 D
rhartz@marywood.edu
HARTZ, Ronald, G 671-735-5555 504 D
ronald.hartz@guamcc.edu
HARTZELL, Jay, C 512-471-1232 455 A
president@utexas.edu
HARTZELL, Rick 563-425-5293 170 H
hartzellr53@uiu.edu
HARTZLER, Murray, G 843-661-1237 409 G
mhartzler@fmarion.edu
HARTZLER, Tracy 505-224-4415 285 N
thartzler@cnm.edu
HARTZSCH, Hannah 413-737-7000 205 F
HARVEN, Gabriel 925-969-2082 40 C
gharven@dvc.edu
HARVEY, Andrew 301-387-3025 199 A
andrew.harvey@garrettcollege.edu
HARVEY, Angel 919-267-1640 330 B
HARVEY, Ashley 850-718-2487 97 E
harveya@chipola.edu
HARVEY, Barron, H 202-806-1500 92 F
bharvey@howard.edu
HARVEY, Binti 909-621-8152 63 F
bharvey@scrippscollege.edu
HARVEY, Cameron 901-381-3939 428 B
cameron@visible.edu
HARVEY, Christopher 727-398-8407 107 E
harvey.chris@spcollege.edu
HARVEY, Diana 510-987-0700 68 L
HARVEY, Diana 510-642-6448 69 A
diana.harvey@berkeley.edu

HARVEY, Donna, J .... 812-941-2026 157 F
djharvey@ius.edu
HARVEY, Erik .... 518-891-2915 310 A
eharvey@nccc.edu
HARVEY, George .... 919-761-2203 340 D
harvey@sebts.edu
HARVEY, Janice .... 870-248-4000.. 18 F
janice.harvey@blackrivertech.edu
HARVEY, Jay .... 800-227-2013 248 F
jharvey@rts.edu
HARVEY, Jennifer .... 515-271-3751 165 J
jennifer.harvey@drake.edu
HARVEY, John .... 503-768-7861 373 E
johnharvey@lclark.edu
HARVEY, Katie .... 304-769-0011 491 A
kharvey@wvjc.edu
HARVEY, Kem .... 864-592-4795 412 E
harveyk@sccsc.edu
HARVEY, Kim .... 585-389-2023 307 F
kharvey8@naz.edu
HARVEY, Laurie .... 516-686-7711 308 I
lharve05@nyit.edu
HARVEY, Linda .... 718-780-0382 291 K
linda.harvey@brooklaw.edu
HARVEY, Marcus .... 816-604-4121 255 H
marcus.harvey@mcckc.edu
HARVEY, Marilyn .... 951-639-5436.. 53 A
mharvey@msjc.edu
HARVEY, Melissa .... 715-682-1230 494 G
mharvey@northland.edu
HARVEY, Michael .... 410-778-7202 205 B
mharvey2@washcoll.edu
HARVEY, Michael .... 864-592-4991 412 E
harveym@sccsc.edu
HARVEY, Peter, W .... 509-527-5145 486 B
harvey@whitman.edu
HARVEY, Roberta .... 856-256-5140 281 F
harvey@rowan.edu
HARVEY, Ryan, D .... 740-826-8051 356 H
harvey@muskingum.edu
HARVEY, Sally .... 480-858-9100.. 15 Q
s.harvey@scnm.edu
HARVEY, Sandra .... 318-678-6000 187 H
sharvey@bpcc.edu
HARVEY, Sandra .... 704-468-2155 327 G
sandra.harvey@carolinascollege.edu
HARVEY, Sandra .... 704-403-3202 327 C
sandra.harvey@atriumhealth.org
HARVEY, Sarah, J .... 260-359-4010 156 C
sharvey@huntington.edu
HARVEY, Scott .... 864-646-1556 412 H
sharvey@tctc.edu
HARVEY, Shannon, S ... 814-865-2044 391 G
sxs205@psu.edu
HARVEY, Sonja, K .... 217-786-4913 143 B
sonja.harvey@llcc.edu
HARVEY, Stephanie .... 503-517-1026 377 C
sdharvey@warnerpacific.edu
HARVEY, Stephen .... 212-731-3419 302 D
stephen.harvey@mssm.edu
HARVEY, Stewart, A .... 207-581-2668 196 G
stewarth@maine.edu
HARVEY, William, R ..... 757-727-5231 467 G
presidentsoffice@hamptonu.edu
HARVEY-LIVINGSTON,
Kim .... 903-566-7197 456 A
klivingston@uttyler.edu
HARVEY-MANUS,
Kimberly .... 636-481-3200 254 C
kharvey@jeffco.edu
HARVEY-SMITH,
Alicia, B .... 412-809-5303 396 E
harveysmith.alicia@ptcollege.edu
HARVILL, James .... 979-830-4165 431 H
james.harvill@blinn.edu
HARVILLE, Beth .... 417-873-4085 252 G
bharville@drury.edu
HARWARD, Brian .... 814-332-3027 378 A
bharward@allegheny.edu
HARWELL, Anthony .... 816-322-0110 251 B
anthony.harwell@calvary.edu
HARWELL, Jeff .... 626-584-5629.. 43 B
jharwell@fuller.edu
HARWELL, Neal .... 870-248-4000.. 18 F
neal.harwell@blackrivertech.edu
HARWOOD, Alexander .. 323-343-3000.. 31 E
HARWOOD, Gina .... 718-960-8245 294 A
gina.harwood@lehman.cuny.edu
HARWOOD, Jessica .... 864-587-4000 412 F
harwoodj@smcsc.edu
HARWOOD, Kenneth ..... 703-284-1580 468 H
kharwood@marymount.edu
HARWOOD, Mike .... 541-346-8267 376 H
maharwoo@uoregon.edu
HARWOOD, Scott .... 518-891-2915 310 A
sharwood@nccc.edu
HARWOOD, Yvonne .... 806-720-7497 439 D
yvonne.harwood@lcu.edu
HARWOOD-ROM,
Melissa .... 479-575-5004.. 21 F
melissa@uark.edu
HARZMAN, Kirby .... 405-733-7387 369 E
kharzman@rose.edu
HASAN, Nash .... 704-461-6257 326 L
nashhasan@bac.edu
HASAN, NS .... 703-591-7042 466 M
nshasan@fxua.edu
HASAN, Zia .... 803-535-5219 407 D
hasan@claflin.edu
HASANADKA, Lakshmi . 317-921-4564 158 D
lhasanadka@ivytech.edu
HASART, Lisa .... 360-992-2488 478 I
lnelson@clark.edu
HASBROUCK, Douglas .. 718-409-3938 320 G
dhasbrouck@sunymaritime.edu
HASCALL, Corey .... 207-780-4883 197 D
corey.hascall@maine.edu
HASCHAK, David .... 814-886-6459 390 G
dhaschak@mtaloy.edu
HASE, Heath .... 816-415-7641 262 F
haseh@william.jewell.edu
HASE, Steven, V .... 704-847-5600 340 F
shase@ses.edu
HASEGAWA, Betsy .... 206-934-5300 483 D
betsy.hasegawa@seattlecolleges.edu
HASELEY, Amanda .... 716-614-6271 309 G
ahaseley@niagaracc.suny.edu
HASELHORST, Christina 620-227-9541 173 D
chaselhorst@dc3.edu
HASELOFF, Greg, K .... 859-858-3511 179 D
greg.haseloff@asbury.edu
HASENKAMP, Mindy .... 509-533-3500 479 D
HASENPFLUG, Kathy ..... 541-737-0123 375 A
HASH, Jennifer .... 303-722-5724.. 81 L
jhash@lincolntech.edu
HASH, Joe .... 559-934-2452.. 75 A
joehash@whccd.edu
HASH, Joshua .... 209-575-7910.. 76 J
hashj@yosemite.edu
HASHEM, Esra .... 661-654-3578.. 30 B
ehashem1@csub.edu
HASHEMI, Mahasti .... 848-445-0345 282 A
mhashemi@sas.rutgers.edu
HASHIM, Sharief .... 570-372-4272 398 F
hashim@susqu.edu
HASHIRO, Kimberly, M 808-956-6855 129 C
hashirok@hawaii.edu
HASHIZUME, John .... 415-485-3227.. 41 C
john.hashizume@dominican.edu
HASHLEY, Douglas .... 406-791-5966 265 H
doug.hashley@uprovidence.edu
HASIK, Michelle .... 815-802-8552 141 D
mhasik@kcc.edu
HASKELL, Chet .... 415-994-7246 347 H
chaskell1@antioch.edu
HASKETT, Danielle .... 541-440-4670 376 G
danielle.haskett@umpqua.edu
HASKEY, Glennita .... 928-724-6736.. 12 D
ghaskey@dinecollege.edu
HASKIN, Kevin .... 831-646-4048.. 52 G
khaskin@mpc.edu
HASKINS, Clemette .... 909-445-2590.. 37 E
chaskins@cst.edu
HASKINS, Eileen, T .... 401-598-1035 404 D
eileen.haskins@jwu.edu
HASKINS, Kirk .... 785-594-6451 171 F
HASKINS, Michael .... 251-460-6211..... 9 A
mhaskins@southalabama.edu
HASLAG, Dan .... 660-562-1183 257 E
dhaslag@nwmissouri.edu
HASLAM, Kent .... 406-243-5348 263 K
kent.haslam@umontana.edu
HASLAM, Kevin .... 256-765-4397..... 8 E
khaslam@una.edu
HASLAM, Kevin, R .... 256-765-5018..... 8 E
khaslam@una.edu
HASLAM, Lacey .... 513-562-8743 347 I
lacey.haslam@artacademy.edu
HASLER, Dan .... 765-494-4600 160 B
djhasler@purdue.edu
HASLER, Paul .... 715-346-3059 497 A
phasler@uwsp.edu
HASLER, Susan .... 410-617-1619 200 B
sahasler@loyola.edu
HASS, Amy, M .... 352-392-1358 111 A
amhass@ufl.edu
HASS, Chris, J .... 352-392-4792 111 A
cjhass@ufl.edu
HASS, Martha .... 518-694-7238 289 J
martha.hass@acphs.edu
HASSABELNABY,
Hassan .... 859-572-6642 184 E
hassabelnh1@nku.edu
HASSAN, Ali .... 408-554-5739.. 63 B
ahassan@scu.edu
HASSANPOUR, Zinat ..... 704-403-1698 327 C
zinat.hassanpour@atriumhealth.org
HASSE, Rachel .... 503-251-5738 377 B
rhasse@uws.edu
HASSELL, Kaytee .... 903-510-2200 452 A
kaytee.hassell@tjc.edu
HASSELL, Rusty .... 706-385-1503 124 E
rusty.hassell@point.edu
HASSEMER, Holly .... 715-831-7331 498 E
hhassemer1@cvtc.edu
HASSEN, Marjorie .... 207-725-3281 194 C
mhassen@bowdoin.edu
HASSENBEIN, Ashley ..... 570-702-8953 386 D
ahassenbein@johnson.edu
HASSENPLUG, Eric .... 920-206-2305 493 C
eric.hassenplug@mbu.edu
HASSENZAHL,
David, M .... 530-898-6121.. 30 D
dhassenzahl@csuchico.edu
HASSENZAHL,
David, M .... 530-898-3865.. 30 D
dhassenzahl@csuchico.edu
HASSENZAHL, Roger .... 765-285-1532 153 H
rahassenzahl@bsu.edu
HASSETT, Danny .... 214-333-5118 434 C
dannyh@dbu.edu
HASSEVOORT, Darrin .... 423-697-3383 424 A
darrin.hassevoort@chattanoogastate.
edu
HASSINGER, Steven .... 717-728-2262 380 E
stevehassinger@centralpenn.edu
HASSUMANI, Sabrina ... 713-743-2755 452 D
shassumani@uh.edu
HASTIE, Cole .... 425-889-5208 481 H
cole.hastie@northwestu.edu
HASTINGS, Aaron .... 615-732-7847 422 B
aaron.hastings@mtsa.edu
HASTINGS, Benjamin .... 405-974-2000 370 I
bhastings@uco.edu
HASTINGS, Billy .... 269-749-7668 229 J
bhastings@olivetcollege.edu
HASTINGS, Brad .... 508-541-1508 209 A
bhastings@dean.edu
HASTINGS, Brian .... 402-458-1100 269 J
bhastings@nufoundation.org
HASTINGS, Dana, M ..... 785-532-6221 175 C
dhasting@ksu.edu
HASTINGS, JudeAnne ... 574-239-8372 156 A
jhastings@hcc-nd.edu
HASTINGS, Mark .... 501-882-4523.. 17 D
mahastings@asub.edu
HASTINGS, Mary .... 918-631-3639 371 C
mary-hastings@utulsa.edu
HASTINGS, Michelle .... 314-446-8338 260 H
michelle.hastings@stlcop.edu
HASTINGS, Nancy .... 312-329-4415 144 I
nancy.hastings@moody.edu
HASTINGS, Peter .... 978-837-5357 216 F
hastingsp@merrimack.edu
HASTINGS, Ron .... 909-384-8542.. 60 F
rhastings@sbccd.cc.ca.us
HASTINGS, Sarah .... 309-556-3059 140 F
iwu@bkstr.com
HASZ, David .... 952-829-1896 234 B
david.hasz@bethanygu.edu
HATCH, Joy, A .... 304-367-4927 489 K
joy.hatch@fairmontstate.edu
HATCH, Mark .... 719-389-6805.. 78 I
mhatch@coloradocollege.edu
HATCH, Mary .... 847-214-7421 137 F
mhatch@elgin.edu
HATCH, Melanie .... 229-500-2813 114 H
melanie.hatch@asurams.edu
HATCH, Tamara, T .... 540-568-2350 468 C
hatchtt@jmu.edu
HATCH, Tracy .... 651-793-1910 238 I
tracy.hatch@metrostate.edu
HATCHEL, Doni, S .... 910-898-9613 336 D
codyd@montgomery.edu
HATCHER, Barb, D .... 540-365-4231 467 B
bhatcher@ferrum.edu
HATCHER, Betty, K .... 252-638-3745 334 A
hatcherb@cravencc.edu
HATCHER, Lance .... 443-885-3117 201 A
lance.hatcher@morgan.edu
HATCHER, Melanie .... 903-785-7661 441 D
mhatcher@parisjc.edu
HATCHER, Michelle .... 913-253-5000 177 D
HATCHER, Norma Jean . 910-275-6163 335 E
nhatcher@jamessprunt.edu
HATCHER, Oeida .... 434-544-8344 471 L
hatcher@lynchburg.edu
HATCHER, Pam .... 859-246-6788 181 F
pam.hatcher@kctcs.edu
HATCHER, Richard .... 614-287-2870 351 C
rhatche1@cscc.edu
HATCHER, Robert .... 212-817-7029 293 F
rhatcher@gc.cuny.edu
HATCHER, Spencer .... 510-204-0716.. 36 I
shatcher@cdsp.edu
HATCHETT, Patricia, A .. 336-322-2153 336 G
patricia.hatchett@piedmontcc.edu
HATCHETT, Steven .... 512-505-3041 438 A
shatchett@htu.edu
HATFIELD, Amy .... 859-442-1701 181 H
amy.hatfield@kctcs.edu
HATFIELD, Amy .... 360-475-7555 481 I
ahatfield@olympic.edu
HATFIELD, Chad .... 914-961-8313 314 H
hatfield@svots.edu
HATFIELD, David .... 606-368-6105 178 G
HATFIELD, Karen .... 352-588-8460 107 D
karen.hatfield@saintleo.edu
HATFIELD, Mark .... 662-720-7270 248 C
mahatfield@nemcc.edu
HATFIELD, Misty .... 803-778-6641 406 I
hatfieldmf@cctech.edu
HATFIELD, Mitzi .... 615-514-2787 422 H
admissions@nossi.edu
HATFIELD, Stan .... 618-235-2700 150 E
stan.hatfield@swic.edu
HATHAWAY, Joel .... 314-434-4044 252 C
joel.hathaway@covenantseminary.edu
HATHAWAY, William, L 757-352-4320 470 B
agast@regent.edu
HATHCOCK, Michele ..... 828-398-7203 332 B
mhathcock@abtech.edu
HATHMAN, Laurie, E .... 816-501-4144 258 I
laurie.hathman@rockhurst.edu
HATHORN, Dana, M ..... 757-822-2180 475 E
dsingleton@tcc.edu
HATHORN, Janine, M ... 540-458-8672 477 D
jhathorn@wlu.edu
HATHORN, Pamela .... 918-444-3800 366 G
hathorn@nsuok.edu
HATLEN, Mary .... 920-748-8318 494 J
hatlenm@ripon.edu
HATLEY, Anita, L .... 501-370-5314.. 20 F
ahatley@philander.edu
HATLEY, Jennifer .... 704-991-0193 338 C
jhatley9287@stanly.edu
HATMAKER, Amy .... 361-570-4374 453 B
hatmakera@uhv.edu
HATTEBERG, Greg, A .... 214-887-5101 435 F
ghatteberg@dts.edu
HATTEN, Gerrie .... 805-756-5893.. 29 I
ghatten@calpoly.edu
HATTO, Susan .... 989-328-1254 228 D
susanh@montcalm.edu
HATTON, Jay .... 703-784-2105 502 J
jay.hatton@usmc.mil
HATTON, John .... 314-577-8353 259 F
john.hatton@slu.edu
HATTON, Karl .... 706-233-7310 125 C
khatton@shorter.edu
HATTON, Martin .... 662-329-7231 248 A
mlhatton@muw.edu
HATTON, Nora .... 620-235-4276 177 A
nhatton@pittstate.edu
HATTON-FICKLIN,
Brenda .... 501-370-5271.. 20 F
HATTORI-UCHIMA,
Margaret .... 671-735-2653 504 F
muchima@triton.uog.edu
HAUB, Elaine .... 812-941-2284 157 F
ehaub@ius.edu
HAUBENREISER, Jenny . 541-737-9355 375 A
HAUBER, Susan, C .... 319-296-4004 166 H
susan.hauber@hawkeyecollege.edu
HAUCK, Nancy .... 435-652-7844 460 B
hauck@dixie.edu
HAUCK, Sadie .... 570-389-4208 393 D
shauck@bloomu.edu
HAUCK, Steven .... 605-882-5284 415 D
haucks@lakeareatech.edu
HAUF, Todd .... 701-483-2570 345 C
todd.hauf@dickinsonstate.edu

HAUFF, Brian .... 417-865-2815 253 D
hauffb@evangel.edu
HAUFT, Amy, G .... 314-935-6525 262 A
ahauft@wustl.edu
HAUG, Christopher .... 610-459-0905 391 A
haugc@neumann.edu
HAUG, Jannelle .... 845-569-3249 307 D
jannelle.haug@msmc.edu
HAUGABROOK, Adrian . 603-665-7254 274 C
a.haugabrook@snhu.edu
HAUGE, Todd, W .... 410-293-1600 504 A
hauge@usna.edu
HAUGEN, Dolores .... 253-566-6090 484 E
dhaugen@tacomacc.edu
HAUGEN, Donna, M ..... 516-572-7809 307 E
donna.haugen@ncc.edu
HAUGEN, Doug .... 530-938-5295.. 39 C
haugen@siskiyous.edu
HAUGEN, Doug .... 530-938-5295.. 39 C
HAUGEN, Jay .... 314-977-2269 259 F
jay.haugen@slu.edu
HAUGEN, Jon .... 641-673-1398 171 C
haugenj@wmpenn.edu
HAUGEN, Regina .... 270-858-6510 182 G
regina.haugen@kctcs.edu
HAUGER, Sara .... 317-921-4607 158 E
shauger3@ivytech.edu
HAUGH, Kevin .... 610-902-8258 379 G
kevin.o.haugh@cabrini.edu
HAUGHEY, Caitlin .... 617-305-1999 219 B
chaughey@suffolk.edu
HAUGHIE, Jennifer, A ... 717-477-1235 395 B
jahaughie@ship.edu
HAUGHT, Patrick .... 651-523-2664 236 B
phaught01@hamline.edu
HAUGHT, Paul .... 901-321-3230 418 G
phaught@cbu.edu
HAUGLAND, Gary .... 701-662-1557 346 C
gary.haugland@lrsc.edu
HAUGO, Gary .... 218-477-2948 239 E
gary.haugo@mnstate.edu
HAUN, Phil .... 401-841-6431 503 A
phil.haun@usnwc.edu
HAUNGS, Megan .... 516-739-1545 308 F
admin_dean@nyctcm.edu
HAUPT, Benjamin .... 314-505-7040 252 A
hauptb@csl.edu
HAUS, David .... 207-941-7124 194 F
hausd@husson.edu
HAUS, Teri .... 970-943-2196.. 85 C
thaus@western.edu
HAUSCHILD, Karen .... 843-953-5404 408 C
hauschildkb@cofc.edu
HAUSE, Jeffrey, P .... 402-280-3581 266 H
jeffreyhause@creighton.edu
HAUSER, Carrie .... 248-476-1122 227 E
chauser@msp.edu
HAUSER, Dan .... 336-841-9057 329 F
dhauser@highpoint.edu
HAUSER, John .... 704-922-6475 334 G
hauser.john@gaston.edu
HAUSER, Joseph, H ...... 901-722-3228 423 G
jhauser@sco.edu
HAUSER, LuAnn .... 620-432-0353 176 D
lhauser@neosho.edu
HAUSER, Melanie .... 712-749-2111 164 C
hauser@bvu.edu
HAUSER, Stephen, C .... 608-246-2101 499 A
shauser@madisoncollege.edu
HAUSFELD, Patricia ...... 631-691-8733 302 F
phausfeld@idti.edu
HAUSLER, Mike .... 406-447-6932 264 B
mike.hausler@helenacollege.edu
HAUSMAN, Gary, M ..... 831-242-5200 502 F
HAUSSER, Ginger .... 615-353-3144 424 G
ginger.hausser@nscc.edu
HAUTANEN, JR.,
David, L .... 240-895-5000 202 B
dlhautanen@smcm.edu
HAUTER, Asia .... 678-466-4467 117 D
asiahauter@clayton.edu
HAUVER, Dottie .... 508-793-2327 208 D
dhauver@holycross.edu
HAVARD, Mary, G .... 409-772-8779 456 E
mghavard@utmb.edu
HAVE, Ron .... 651-681-7410 234 B
ron_have@freightmasters.com
HAVEARD, Melanie, J ... 850-474-2555 111 F
mhaveard@uwf.edu
HAVELY, Candace .... 319-296-4229 166 H
candace.havely@hawkeyecollege.edu
HAVEN, John .... 678-839-6410 127 C
jhaven@westga.edu
HAVENS, Brandi .... 806-874-3571 432 J
brandi.havens@clarendoncollege.edu
HAVENS, Bruce .... 417-862-9533 253 F
bhavens@globaluniversity.edu
HAVENS, Chris .... 214-333-5555 434 C
christopher@dbu.edu
HAVENS, Debra .... 254-526-1214 432 D
debra.havens@ctcd.edu
HAVENS, Donna .... 610-519-4933 401 K
donna.havens@villanova.edu
HAVENS, Luisa .... 540-231-4623 476 C
lmhavens@vt.edu
HAVERDINK, Jeff .... 616-526-7744 222 C
jdh9@calvin.edu
HAVERDINK, Marlon ..... 712-707-7200 169 D
marlon@nwciowa.edu
HAVERKAMPF, Kelly ...... 715-365-4917 499 E
khaverkampf@nicoletcollege.edu
HAVERLY, Mark 660-596-7407 259M
mhaverly@sfccmo.edu
HAVERSTIC, Margaret ... 417-667-8181 252 B
mhaverstic@cottey.edu
HAVERSTICK, Jim .... 618-235-2700 150 E
jim.haverstick@swic.edu
HAVERTY, April .... 414-955-4844 493 F
ahaverty@mcw.edu
HAVERTY, Cris .... 617-243-2131 211 B
chaverty@lasell.edu
HAVERTY, John .... 785-670-2330 178 C
john.haverty@washburn.edu
HAVHOLM, Karen, G .... 715-836-3405 495 E
havholkg@uwec.edu
HAVIGHORST,
Deborah, S .... 708-709-7918 147 D
dhavighorst@prairiestate.edu
HAVILAND, Bobbie .... 620-901-6291 171 D
haviland@allencc.edu
HAVRON, Tom .... 620-223-2700 173 I
tomha@fortscott.edu
HAWAYEK, Jose .... 787-758-2525 512 F
jose.hawayek@upr.edu
HAWES, Heather .... 404-270-5068 126 B
hhawes@spelman.edu
HAWES, Jeffrey .... 309-854-1835 133 G
hawesj@bhc.edu
HAWES, Jeffry .... 309-796-5000 133 G
HAWES, Susan .... 207-947-4591 194 B
shawes@bealcollege.edu
HAWGOOD, Sam .... 415-476-6582.. 70 D
sam.hawgood@ucsf.edu
HAWK, Kelly .... 423-869-6618 421 A
kelly.hawk@lmunet.edu
HAWK, Mary .... 402-465-2139 268 G
mhawk@nebrwesleyan.edu
HAWKER, James .... 863-784-7192 108 F
james.hawker@southflorida.edu
HAWKES, Mark .... 605-256-5177 416 F
mark.hawkes@dsu.edu
HAWKES, Mark .... 605-256-5274 416 F
mark.hawkes@dsu.edu
HAWKES, Nicole, A ...... 909-869-3214.. 30 A
nahawkes@cpp.edu
HAWKINBERRY,
Jennifer .... 800-263-1549 486 E
HAWKINBERRY,
Jennifer, C .... 304-457-6203 486 E
hawkinberryjc@ab.edu
HAWKINS, Audrey .... 903-675-6357 451 F
ahawkins@tvcc.edu
HAWKINS, Billy, C .... 256-761-6212.... 7 B
bhawkins@talladega.edu
HAWKINS, Brandy .... 325-942-2259 450 E
brandy.hawkins@angelo.edu
HAWKINS, Christie .... 405-744-4244 367 G
christie.hawkins@okstate.edu
HAWKINS, Christy .... 434-961-5333 474 I
chawkins@pvcc.edu
HAWKINS, Corey .... 314-862-3456 253 E
chawkins@fontbonne.edu
HAWKINS, Eileen .... 410-209-6037 198 B
ehawkins@bccc.edu
HAWKINS, Irene .... 302-857-6261.. 90 E
ihawkins@desu.edu
HAWKINS, JR., Jack ...... 334-670-3200.... 7 C
jhawkins@troy.edu
HAWKINS, Jacqueline ... 270-706-8538 181 G
jhawkins0045@kctcs.edu
HAWKINS, Jahquan, C . 248-232-4405 229 C
jchawkin@oaklandcc.edu
HAWKINS, Jeffrey .... 717-720-4070 395 A
jhawkins@passhe.edu
HAWKINS, Jodi .... 401-874-2141 405 E
jhawkins@uri.edu
HAWKINS, Joe .... 407-303-9380.. 95 B
joe.hawkins@ahu.edu
HAWKINS, Josh .... 502-852-7002 186 A
josh.hawkins@louisville.edu
HAWKINS, Julie .... 601-318-6298 249 H
jhawkins@wmcarey.edu
HAWKINS,
Katherine, W .... 757-683-4423 469 B
kwhawkin@odu.edu
HAWKINS, Kennosha .... 229-430-3510 114 I
khawkins@albanytech.edu
HAWKINS, Kristy .... 757-340-2121 465 I
directoredcvab@centura.edu
HAWKINS, Lauren .... 218-869-5748 186 F
lhawkins@centenary.edu
HAWKINS, Lawrence ..... 615-226-3990 420 J
HAWKINS, LeAllen .... 469-454-3400.. 93 H
HAWKINS, Marcia .... 606-546-1700 185 D
mhawkins@unionky.edu
HAWKINS, Margaret, E . 941-752-5307 109 G
hawkinm@scf.edu
HAWKINS, Martin, E ..... 972-224-5481 444 B
HAWKINS, Mary, B .... 402-557-7005 265 J
mary.hawkins@bellevue.edu
HAWKINS, Matt .... 317-921-4882 158 D
matthawkins@ivytech.edu
HAWKINS, Melissa .... 617-274-3355 216 D
melissa.hawkins@mcphs.edu
HAWKINS, Michael .... 601-968-5940 245 B
mhawkins@belhaven.edu
HAWKINS, Michael .... 704-669-6000 333 E
HAWKINS, Michele .... 561-297-3069 109 J
mhawkins@fau.edu
HAWKINS, Nadine .... 973-290-4705 282 I
nhawkins@steu.edu
HAWKINS, Ray .... 662-915-7234 249 D
rahawkin@olemiss.edu
HAWKINS, Reynani .... 559-325-5295.. 67 A
reynani.hawkins@cloviscollege.edu
HAWKINS, Robin .... 773-995-3755 134 K
rhawkins@csu.edu
HAWKINS, Ronald, E .... 434-592-4030 468 E
rehawkins@liberty.edu
HAWKINS, JR.,
Ronnie, D .... 325-942-2073 450 E
ronnie.hawkins@angelo.edu
HAWKINS, Ryan .... 618-393-2982 139 E
hawkinsr@iecc.edu
HAWKINS, Tony .... 301-846-2491 198 I
thawkins@frederick.edu
HAWKINS, Vernon, L .... 922-860-4221 434 F
vhawkins@dcccd.edu
HAWKINS-HILKE,
Annika .... 802-860-2711 462 A
ahawkinshilke@champlain.edu
HAWKINS-WILDING,
Susan .... 262-865-8614 158 D
shawkinswilding@ivytech.edu
HAWKINSON, Carrie ..... 309-341-5360 134 B
chawkinson@sandburg.edu
HAWKINSON,
Kenneth, S .... 610-683-4102 394 D
hawkinson@kutztown.edu
HAWKINSON, Paul .... 828-669-8012 331 K
paul.hawkinson@montreat.edu
HAWKS, Matt .... 407-646-2104 106 L
mhawks@rollins.edu
HAWLEY, Bill .... 660-543-4710 260 G
hawley@ucmo.edu
HAWLEY, Dawn .... 360-752-8574 478 A
dhawley@btc.edu
HAWLEY, Eric .... 435-797-8146 460 C
eric.hawley@usu.edu
HAWLEY, Harold .... 843-349-5279 409 J
harold.hawley@hgtc.edu
HAWLEY, Jana .... 940-565-2925 453 E
jana.hawley@unt.edu
HAWLEY, Michelle .... 207-755-5370 195 D
mhawley@cmcc.edu
HAWLEY, Michelle .... 323-343-3830.. 31 E
mhawley@calstatela.edu
HAWLEY, Pamela .... 410-455-2832 203 B
mcinnis@umbc.edu
HAWLEY, Thomas, A .... 231-843-5803 233 A
tahawley@westshore.edu
HAWORTH, John .... 423-697-2692 424 A
john.haworth@chattanoogastate.edu
HAWORTH, Timothy ...... 310-338-7760.. 51 A
thaworth@lmu.edu
HAWSEY, David .... 765-983-1600 155 A
hawseda@earlham.edu
HAWTHORNE, Julia ...... 217-353-2082 147 C
jhawthorne@parkland.edu
HAWTHORNE, Laura ..... 434-982-2791 472 D
lfh4c@virginia.edu
HAWTHORNE, Pat .... 909-869-3968.. 30 A
pthawthorne@cpp.edu
HAWTON, Noelle .... 651-201-1801 237 B
noelle.hawton@minnstate.edu
HAXTON, Lori .... 660-626-2236 250 A
lhaxton@atsu.edu
HAY, April .... 812-237-2020 156 D
april.hay@indstate.edu
HAY, David, P .... 859-858-3511 179 D
david.hay@asbury.edu
HAY, Kuniko .... 510-981-2933.. 56 I
khay@peralta.edu
HAY, Laura .... 912-583-3202 116 E
lhay@bpc.edu
HAY, Mary .... 828-771-2088 344 D
mhay@warren-wilson.edu
HAY, Sharon, L .... 401-865-2750 404 F
sharhay@providence.edu
HAY, Tobi .... 518-564-2000 318 E
HAYASHI, Lori Lei .... 808-455-0213 130 C
lhayashi@hawaii.edu
HAYASHI, Lori Lei .... 808-455-0657 130 C
lhayashi@hawaii.edu
HAYASHIDA, Peter, A ... 951-827-5203.. 70 B
peter.hayashida@ucr.edu
HAYDARI, Shahram ...... 978-934-6546 212 B
shahram_haydari@uml.edu
HAYDEN, Angie, N .... 410-572-8712 205 D
ahayden@worwic.edu
HAYDEN, Bryan .... 504-864-7241 190 C
blhayden@loyno.edu
HAYDEN, Cathy, C .... 601-857-3322 246 C
cchayden@hindscc.edu
HAYDEN, Chris .... 617-585-1181 217 E
chris.hayden@necmusic.edu
HAYDEN, Donna .... 601-877-6182 245 A
dhayden@alcorn.edu
HAYDEN, Jeffrey .... 413-552-2587 214 F
jhayden@hcc.edu
HAYDEN, Laura .... 617-287-7600 211 H
laura.hayden@umb.edu
HAYDEN, Ruby .... 425-739-8208 481 C
ruby.hayden@lwtech.edu
HAYDEN, Tom .... 615-353-3584 424 G
thomas.hayden@nscc.edu
HAYDEN-ROY, Patrick ... 402-465-2440 268 G
phr@nebrwesleyan.edu
HAYDON, Darrell .... 210-829-6004 453 C
haydon@uiwtx.edu
HAYE, Jack .... 540-338-1776 469 C
president@phc.edu
HAYE, Melissa .... 304-327-4145 489 I
mhaye@bluefieldstate.edu
HAYEK, Cheryl .... 515-650-3198 163 E
cheryllhayek@theartofeducation.edu
HAYEK, John .... 512-463-7281 449 E
john.hayek@tsus.edu
HAYEK, Mario .... 903-886-5178 447 B
mario.hayek@tamuc.edu
HAYEN, Christopher, M 518-388-6358 323 J
hayenc@union.edu
HAYEN, Janet .... 605-995-2648 415 A
janet.hayen@dwu.edu
HAYES, Alastair .... 802-828-8600 463 B
alastair.hayes@vcfa.edu
HAYES, Amy .... 706-865-2134 126 E
ahayes@truett.edu
HAYES,
Andrea (Andy), S .... 573-882-2824 261 A
hayesas@missouri.edu
HAYES, Ann, C .... 717-867-6416 388 C
hayes@lvc.edu
HAYES, Anne, C .... 336-517-2243 327 A
anne.hayes@bennett.edu
HAYES, Blair .... 301-985-7940 203 E
blair.hayes@umuc.edu
HAYES, Carla .... 803-641-3645 413 B
carlah@usca.edu
HAYES, Caroline .... 617-746-1990 210 H
caroline.hayes@hult.edu
HAYES, Clint .... 606-451-6601 182 G
clint.hayes@kctcs.edu
HAYES, Dale .... 772-462-7809 102 F
lhayes@irsc.edu
HAYES, Dan .... 434-791-7252 464 I
dhayes@averett.edu
HAYES, Daniel, J .... 315-267-2147 319 A
hayesdj@potsdam.edu
HAYES, David .... 800-686-1883 222 G
dhayes@cleary.edu

HEASTON, Frances .... 918-587-6789 370 H
fran.heaston@tws.edu
HEATH, Aaron .... 816-322-0110 251 B
aaron.heath@calvary.edu
HEATH, Cantey .... 803-777-3106 413 A
canteyh@mailbox.sc.edu
HEATH, Carl .... 817-274-4284 431 F
cheath@bhcarroll.edu
HEATH, Cassandra .... 208-459-5099 131 C
cheath@collegeofidaho.edu
HEATH, Cassandra .... 562-903-6000.. 27 A
HEATH, Cheryl, A .... 307-675-0811 501 G
cheath@sheridan.edu
HEATH, David, A .... 212-938-5650 319 E
dheath@sunyopt.edu
HEATH, Deb .... 920-232-6027 498 F
heath@fvtc.edu
HEATH, Donna, R .... 336-334-5092 343 A
drheath@uncg.edu
HEATH, Janie, H .... 859-257-1701 185 F
jheath@uky.edu
HEATH, Janine .... 573-840-9698 260 E
jheath@trcc.edu
HEATH, Jason .... 502-897-4106 184 G
jheath@sbts.edu
HEATH, Jesse .... 405-789-7661 369 I
jesse.heath@swcu.edu
HEATH, Joan, L .... 512-245-2133 450 C
jh06@txstate.edu
HEATH, John .... 608-785-9464 500 C
heathj@westerntc.edu
HEATH, Kathy .... 207-326-2339 196 A
kathy.heath@mma.edu
HEATH, Kelly .... 314-246-7881 262 C
kellyheath89@webster.edu
HEATH, Marie .... 904-470-8933.. 98 L
m.heath@ewc.edu
HEATH, Melanie .... 801-321-7101 459 N
mheath@ushe.edu
HEATH, Michael .... 215-368-5000 390 A
mheath@missio.edu
HEATH, Sherri .... 706-583-2818 115 F
sheath@athenstech.edu
HEATH-MCKENZIE,
Angelicia .... 404-527-5725 121 L
aheath@itc.edu
HEATHERLY, Cole .... 843-383-8360 408 B
HEATHERLY, David, L .... 910-938-6211 333 F
heatherlyd@coastalcarolina.edu
HEATLIE, Pam .... 313-436-9194 231 I
pheatlie@umich.edu
HEATON, Angela .... 419-995-8813 360 C
heaton.a@rhodesstate.edu
HEATON, Benjamin .... 801-626-7928 461 A
benjaminheaton@weber.edu
HEATON, Dennis .... 641-470-1399 168 C
dheaton@miu.edu
HEATON, Haidee .... 573-288-6434 252 F
hheaton@culver.edu
HEATON, Jill .... 775-784-1740 271 E
jheaton@unr.edu
HEATON, Jill .... 775-831-1314 272 D
jheaton@sierranevada.edu
HEATON, Mandy .... 503-777-7289 375 G
heatonm@reed.edu
HEATON, Pamela, C ..... 513-558-4177 361 J
heatonp@ucmail.uc.edu
HEATON, Tim .... 605-688-5117 417 A
timothy.heaton@sdstate.edu
HEATOR, Martin .... 734-462-4400 230 G
mheator@schoolcraft.edu
HEAVENER, Mac .... 904-596-2400 112 F
macheavener@tbc.edu
HEAVENER, Matthew ...... 904-596-2420 112 F
mheavener@tbc.org
HEAVENER, Michael ..... 904-596-2400 112 F
miheavener@tbc.edu
HEAVEY, Chris .... 702-895-3301 271 D
chris.heavey@unlv.edu
HEAVIN, Jessica .... 918-595-7269 370 C
jessica.heavin@tulsacc.edu
HEAVY RUNNER, Joely . 701-255-3285 347 A
jheavyrunner@uttc.edu
HEBARD, John .... 907-474-6831.. 10 A
jahebard@alaska.edu
HEBBARD, Matthew ...... 956-872-2147 443 H
mshebbar@southtexascollege.edu
HEBERLE, Julia, F .... 610-921-7581 377 G
jheberle@albright.edu
HEBERT, Bill .... 309-694-8970 139 B
bill.hebert@icc.edu
HEBERT, Carolyn .... 860-515-3880.. 85 E
chebert@charteroak.edu
HEBERT, Gurdeep .... 559-325-5378.. 67 A
gurdeep.hebert@cloviscollege.edu
HEBERT, Jaimie .... 337-482-6454 193 B
jaimie.hebert@louisiana.edu
HEBERT, Jason .... 575-835-5832 286 K
jason.hebert@nmt.edu
HEBERT, Joseph .... 281-998-6150 443 C
joseph.hebert@sjcd.edu
HEBERT, Karen .... 803-934-3196 410 G
khebert@morris.edu
HEBERT, Katie .... 508-626-4575 213 A
khebert@framingham.edu
HEBERT, Lisa .... 903-463-8651 436 G
hebertl@grayson.edu
HEBERT, Richard .... 203-576-4804.. 89 C
rhebert@bridgeport.edu
HEBERT, Sarah .... 603-542-7744 273 B
shebert@ccsnh.edu
HEBERT, Trace .... 615-966-5325 421 B
trace.hebert@lipscomb.edu
HEBERT-MACCARO,
Karen .... 781-239-4355 206 B
maccaro@babson.edu
HEBRA, Jada .... 603-665-7173 274 C
j.hebra@snhu.edu
HEBREARD, Dana .... 616-632-8900 221 E
HECHANOVA, JR.,
Manuel, B .... 671-735-2620 504 F
mannyh@triton.uog.edu
HECHT, Amy .... 850-644-5590 110 C
ahecht@fsu.edu
HECHT, Bill .... 901-321-3396 418 G
whecht@cbu.edu
HECHT, Boruch .... 973-267-9404 280 F
HECHT, Jason .... 828-398-7900 332 B
HECHT, Pinchas .... 718-645-0536 306 J
HECIMOVIC, Katrina, M 608-342-1155 496 E
hecimovick@uwplatt.edu
HECK, Annie .... 541-737-0790 375 A
annie.heck@oregonstate.edu
HECK, Julia .... 734-487-0074 223 K
emu_ombuds@emich.edu
HECKAMAN, Daniel, A .. 218-477-2300 239 E
daniel.heckaman@mnstate.edu
HECKAMAN, Judith, M . 717-560-8278 387 E
jheckaman@lbc.edu
HECKENDORN, Sally ..... 717-245-1518 382 D
heckendo@dickinson.edu
HECKENLAIBLE, Anna ... 605-331-6651 417 C
anna.heckenlaible@usiouxfalls.edu
HECKENLAIBLE, John ... 623-845-3809.. 13 C
john.heckenlaible@gccaz.edu
HECKER, James, B .... 334-953-2044 502 D
HECKLER, Pamela .... 410-706-5631 203 A
phecker@umaryland.edu
HECKMAN, Mary Ellen .. 610-372-4721 396 H
mheckman@racc.edu
HECKMAN, Michael ...... 513-244-4593 356 F
michael.heckman@msj.edu
HECKMANN, John .... 815-753-2900 146 B
jheckmann@niu.edu
HECKSTALL, Jaime, P ... 252-862-1255 337 C
jheckstall6664@roanokechowan.edu
HECTOR, Gerald .... 407-823-2387 110 E
gerald.hector@ucf.edu
HECTOR, Leticia .... 909-384-8535.. 60 F
lhector@sbccd.cc.ca.us
HEDAL, Laura .... 425-352-8186 478 D
lhedal@cascadia.edu
HEDAYAT, Nasser .... 407-582-3326 113 I
nhedayat@valenciacollege.edu
HEDBERG, Rick .... 701-858-4483 345 E
rick.hedberg@minotstateu.edu
HEDBERG, William, B ... 518-956-8030 316 A
whedberg@albany.edu
HEDDEN, Gregory .... 419-559-2302 361 C
ghedden01@terra.edu
HEDDLESTON, George .. 423-425-4363 427 C
george-heddleston@utc.edu
HEDDLESTON,
Patrick, D .... 330-823-6599 362 E
heddlepd@mountunion.edu
HEDEEN, Deborah .... 207-834-7500 197 A
HEDEGARD, Heidi .... 603-862-0967 274 E
heidi.hedegard@usnh.edu
HEDGE, Dennis .... 605-688-4173 417 A
dennis.hedge@sdstate.edu
HEDGEPATH, Donna ..... 270-789-5231 180 A
drhedgepath@campbellsville.edu
HEDGEPETH, Amy .... 919-278-2673 340 B
amy.hedgepeth@shawu.edu
HEDGES, Jennifer .... 217-234-5217 142 C
jhedges@lakeland.cc.il.us
HEDGES, Jerris, R .... 808-692-0899 129 E
jerris@hawaii.edu
HEDGES, Tammy .... 901-678-2843 426 G
thedges@memphis.edu
HEDIN, Norma .... 214-333-5599 434 C
norma@dbu.edu
HEDLUN, Erin .... 417-865-2815 250 E
hedlune@evangel.edu
HEDLUN, Erin .... 417-865-2815 253 D
hedlune@evangel.edu
HEDLUN, Randy, J .... 417-862-9533 253 F
rhedlun@globaluniversity.edu
HEDLUND, Traci .... 816-960-2008 251 G
billing@cityvision.edu
HEDMAN, Miranda .... 228-497-7639 247 E
miranda.hedman@mgccc.edu
HEDMAN, Shawn .... 507-537-6292 241 D
shawn.hedman@smsu.edu
HEDRICK, Noemi .... 952-829-1479 234 B
noemi.hedrick@bethfel.org
HEDRICK, Van .... 940-668-7347 440 F
vhedrick@nctc.edu
HEDSTROM, Lori .... 843-953-7777 407 C
lhedstro@citadel.edu
HEEKE, Dave .... 520-621-4622.. 16 D
dheeke@arizona.edu
HEEMSTRA, John .... 605-995-7204 415 E
john.heemstra@mitchelltech.edu
HEERDINK, Joe .... 270-831-9615 182 D
joe.heerdink@kctcs.edu
HEERDINK, Joe .... 270-831-9615 182 A
joe.heerdink@kctcs.edu
HEEREN, Diana .... 210-999-7163 451 E
dheeren@trinity.edu
HEEREN, Matthew .... 660-626-2522 250 A
mheeren@atsu.edu
HEERMAN, Heather, L .. 508-565-1301 219 A
hheerman@stonehill.edu
HEERMANN, Keith .... 417-862-9533 253 F
kheermann@globaluniversity.edu
HEERSINK, Heather .... 719-587-7759.. 77 G
heather_heersink@adams.edu
HEERSINK, Jordan .... 303-963-3388.. 78 H
joheersink@ccu.edu
HEETLAND, David, L ..... 847-866-3970 138 D
david.heetland@garrett.edu
HEFFERN, Tim .... 562-938-4346.. 48 F
theffern@lbcc.edu
HEFFERNAN, Emily .... 941-487-4225 110 D
eheffernan@ncf.edu
HEFFERNAN, Tom .... 262-524-7343 492 A
theffernan@carrollu.edu
HEFFNER, Brian .... 231-995-1014 229 A
bheffner@nmc.edu
HEFFRON, Timothy .... 740-284-5177 352 I
theffron@franciscan.edu
HEFLIN, Sherry .... 717-815-1257 403 F
sheflin@ycp.edu
HEFNER, Alana .... 254-968-9078 446 D
hefner@tarleton.edu
HEFNER, Beth .... 770-533-6607 122 B
bhefner@laniertech.edu
HEFNER, Kelli .... 662-720-7411 248 C
kehefner@nemcc.edu
HEFNER, Todd .... 417-667-8181 252 B
thefner@cottey.edu
HEFTKA, Chris .... 815-479-7661 143 I
cheftka@mchenry.edu
HEFTON, Ryan .... 214-333-5424 434 C
ryanh@dbu.edu
HEGAB, Hisham .... 318-257-4647 192 D
hhegab@latech.edu
HEGARTY, Joseph .... 207-509-7292 196 E
jhegarty@unity.edu
HEGARTY, Mary .... 714-564-6904.. 58 F
hegarty_mary@sac.edu
HEGEDUS, Stephen .... 203-392-5900.. 86 A
schoolofeducation@southernct.edu
HEGEMAN, Jay .... 301-687-4738 204 C
jhegeman@frostburg.edu
HEGENBARTH, Chris ..... 218-235-2164 241 E
chris.hegenbarth@vcc.edu
HEGER, Laura .... 570-389-4179 393 D
lheger@bloomu.edu
HEGGEMEYER, Terri ...... 402-844-7263 268 H
terrih@northeast.edu
HEGGOY, Liv .... 540-868-4091 474 C
lheggoy@lfcc.edu
HEGLUND, Emily .... 903-670-2664 451 F
emily.heglund@tvcc.edu
HEGWER, Kim .... 757-352-4127 470 B
HEGWOOD, Johnetta .... 310-342-5290.. 73 F
HEHL, Jim .... 239-590-1313 109 K
jhehl@fgcu.edu
HEIDA, Debbie .... 706-236-2227 116 B
dheida@berry.edu
HEIDBREDER, Kay, K .... 540-231-6293 476 C
heidbred@vt.edu
HEIDEMAN, Carl, E ...... 616-395-7670 225 D
heideman@hope.edu
HEIDEMAN, Gail .... 618-664-6609 138 F
gail.heideman@greenville.edu
HEIDEMAN, James .... 714-539-6561.. 66 F
HEIDEMANN, Molly ...... 513-529-8600 356 A
mheidemann@miamioh.edu
HEIDENDAL, Egon .... 660-562-1965 257 E
egon@nwmissouri.edu
HEIDENFELDER, Jason . 630-829-1389 133 E
jheidenfelder@ben.edu
HEIDENREICH, Kari .... 262-472-1921 497 D
heidenreka12@uww.edu
HEIDENREICH, Lisa ...... 651-290-7678 242 L
lisa.heidenreich@mitchellhamline.edu
HEIDER, Don .... 408-554-7898.. 63 B
dheider@scu.edu
HEIDERICH, Gail .... 504-526-4745 190 E
gailh@nationsu.edu
HEIDICK, Venesa, A ...... 979-845-1059 446 F
vheidick@tamu.edu
HEIDINGSFIELD,
Michael, J .... 512-499-4688 454 H
mheidingsfield@utsystem.edu
HEIDKE, Stephen .... 314-392-2372 256 E
heidkesj@mobap.edu
HEIDLE, Wayne .... 714-463-7589.. 51 B
wheidle@ketchum.edu
HEIDRICH, Mark .... 208-459-5199 131 C
mheidrich@collegeofidaho.edu
HEIDRICK, Judy .... 785-738-9058 176 F
jheidrick@ncktc.edu
HEIDT, Mason .... 276-244-1226 464 E
mheidt@asl.edu
HEIDT, Matthew .... 716-926-8792 301 E
mheidt@hilbert.edu
HEIDTKE, Staci, L .... 715-836-5358 495 E
heidtksl@uwec.edu
HEIFNER, Bryan .... 432-335-6512 441 A
bheifner@odessa.edu
HEIGHES, Robert .... 734-487-0892 223 K
rheighes@emich.edu
HEIGHT, Linda, L .... 248-204-2159 227 A
lheight@ltu.edu
HEIGLE, Chris .... 870-838-2945.. 17 B
cheigle@smail.anc.edu
HEIKKILA, Christina ...... 910-362-7313 332 H
cheikkila@cfcc.edu
HEIKKINEN, Melinda .... 651-523-2100 236 B
mheikkinen@hamline.edu
HEIL, Elissa .... 717-262-2018 403 C
elissa.heil@wilson.edu
HEIL, Mark .... 208-426-1200 130 H
markheil@boisestate.edu
HEIL, Marti .... 517-884-1008 227 F
heil@msu.edu
HEIL, Scott .... 951-827-3296.. 70 B
scott.heil@ucr.edu
HEILAND, Donna .... 718-636-3744 311 F
dheiland@pratt.edu
HEILBRON, Shawn, R ... 631-632-7205 317 A
shawn.heilbron@stonybrook.edu
HEILGEIST, Pete .... 360-650-3127 485 I
pete.heilgeist@wwu.edu
HEILMAN, Carl, R .... 620-792-9301 171 I
heilmanc@bartonccc.edu
HEILMAN, Todd .... 212-774-0704 305 E
theilman@mmm.edu
HEILSTEDT, Sally .... 425-739-8233 481 C
sally.heilstedt@lwtech.edu
HEIM, Bret .... 251-380-3871.... 6 H
HEIM, Dianna .... 717-264-2064 403 C
dianna.heim@wilson.edu
HEIM, Edward .... 610-796-2838 378 C
edward.heim@alvernia.edu
HEIM, Peggy, M .... 610-799-1532 388 D
pheim@lccc.edu
HEIM, Reanna .... 712-325-3207 167 I
rheim@iwcc.edu
HEIMANN, Anne .... 402-552-3100 266 E
heimannanne@clarksoncollege.edu
HEIMBAUGH, Sharon .... 773-442-5805 146 A
s-heimbaugh@neiu.edu
HEIMBURGER, David, F 314-977-3139 259 F
david.heimburger@slu.edu
HEIMLICH, Dana .... 973-278-5400 275 I
dana-heimlich@berkeleycollege.edu

HENDERSHOT, Stephanie, N .... 412-262-6251 397 B hendershot@rmu.edu
HENDERSON, Alexis ..... 708-239-4808 151 A alexis.henderson@trnty.edu
HENDERSON, Allan .... 816-322-0110 251 B allan.henderson@calvary.edu
HENDERSON, Amy .... 410-287-1910 198 E ahenderson@cecil.edu
HENDERSON, Andre ..... 412-237-2224 381 D ahenderson@ccac.edu
HENDERSON, April .... 650-949-7777.. 42 I
HENDERSON, Ashley .... 610-409-3718 401 H ahenderson@ursinus.edu
HENDERSON, Brad .... 660-596-7250 259 M rhenderson9@sfccmo.edu
HENDERSON, Brad .... 806-291-3616 457 I brad.henderson@wbu.edu
HENDERSON, Brian ...... 479-979-1304.. 23 I bhenderson@ozarks.edu
HENDERSON, Brian ...... 276-656-0313 474 G bhenderson@patrickhenry.edu
HENDERSON, Brittany ... 206-726-5174 479 E bhenderson@cornish.edu
HENDERSON, Brittney ... 678-664-0515 128 A brittney.henderson@westgatech.edu
HENDERSON, Carol, E .. 404-727-3127 118 E carol.e.henderson@emory.edu
HENDERSON, Carolyn .. 256-551-3226.... 2 E carolyn.henderson@drakestate.edu
HENDERSON, Charles ... 212-517-0400 305 E
HENDERSON, Chiquita, A .... 727-816-3205 105 F henderc@phsc.edu
HENDERSON, Christina 515-271-1501 165 G christina.henderson@dmu.edu
HENDERSON, Christine 773-371-5450 134 D chenderson@ctu.edu
HENDERSON, Cynthia ... 903-223-3053 448 A cynthia.henderson@tamut.edu
HENDERSON, Darren ... 219-473-4346 154 D dhenderson@ccsj.edu
HENDERSON, Eddie, W 806-651-2600 448 B ehenderson@wtamu.edu
HENDERSON, George ... 704-330-4806 333 D george.henderson@cpcc.edu
HENDERSON, Howard ... 580-349-1380 367 F howardh@opsu.edu
HENDERSON, James ...... 262-472-1918 497 D
HENDERSON, James, B 225-342-6950 192 B jim.henderson@ulsystem.edu
HENDERSON, Jennifer .. 210-999-7561 451 E jhender4@trinity.edu
HENDERSON, Joe, T ..... 731-881-3506 427 D jhende33@utm.edu
HENDERSON, John .... 951-827-1012.. 70 B
HENDERSON, June .... 317-738-8028 155 D jhenderson@franklincollege.edu
HENDERSON, Keli .... 724-938-5985 393 E henderson_k@calu.edu
HENDERSON, Ken .... 617-373-4798 217 I
HENDERSON, Kyle, W .. 740-427-5729 354 I hendersonk@kenyon.edu
HENDERSON, Lacey ...... 903-886-5108 447 B lacey.henderson@tamuc.edu
HENDERSON, Laretta .... 217-581-2524 137 E lhenderson2@eiu.edu
HENDERSON, Lenneal, J .... 804-524-1162 476 D lhenderson@vsu.edu
HENDERSON, Lisa .... 440-826-2767 348 D lhenders@bw.edu
HENDERSON, Mantra .... 662-254-3495 248 B mlhenderson@mvsu.edu
HENDERSON, Margaret . 202-885-1000.. 91 F maggieh@american.edu
HENDERSON, Mark .... 818-610-6551.. 49 G henderme@laccd.edu
HENDERSON, Mark .... 818-833-3333.. 49 C hendersml@elac.edu
HENDERSON, Mark .... 412-624-4141 400 H hendersm@pitt.edu
HENDERSON, Michelle . 760-252-2411.. 26 G mhenderson@barstow.edu
HENDERSON, Nancy ...... 319-296-4448 166 H nancy.henderson@hawkeyecollege.edu
HENDERSON, Paul .... 207-602-2302 197 E phenderson@une.edu
HENDERSON, Peter .... 410-455-3263 203 B phenders@umbc.edu
HENDERSON, Sarah ...... 309-457-2190 144 H shenderson@monmouthcollege.edu
HENDERSON, Sean .... 559-442-8295.. 67 B sean.henderson@fresnocitycollege.edu
HENDERSON, Silvester . 510-466-5379.. 57 A shenderson@peralta.edu
HENDERSON, Stacie ..... 334-727-8643.... 7 D shenderson@tuskegee.edu
HENDERSON, Sue .... 201-200-3111 279 D shenderson@njcu.edu
HENDERSON, Susan ..... 843-383-8264 408 B shenderson@coker.edu
HENDERSON, Taja-Nia . 973-353-5834 282 B tajania@law.rutgers.edu
HENDERSON, Tammy .... 850-484-1766 105 H thenderson@pensacolastate.edu
HENDERSON, Tracy ...... 870-886-6741.. 23 J
HENDERSON, Triss .... 217-353-2101 147 C thenderson@parkland.edu
HENDERSON, Virginia .. 601-968-8778 245 B vhenderson@belhaven.edu
HENDERSON-BROWN, Tessa .... 415-239-3530.. 36 K thenders@ccsf.edu
HENDERSON-GASSER, Ellen .... 217-357-3129 134 B ehenderson@sandburg.edu
HENDLER, Gail .... 708-216-5303 143 C ghendler@luc.edu
HENDREY, Elizabeth ...... 718-997-5900 295 B elizabeth.hendrey@qc.cuny.edu
HENDRICK, Kathy .... 903-463-8716 436 G hendrickk@grayson.edu
HENDRICK, Ron .... 806-742-2184 450 F ron.hendrick@ttu.edu
HENDRICK, Sarah .... 661-654-3370.. 30 B shendrick@csub.edu
HENDRICK, Sarah .... 860-932-4096.. 87 E shendrick@qvcc.edu
HENDRICKS, Andrew .... 317-738-8121 155 D ahendricks@franklincollege.edu
HENDRICKS, Bill .... 214-887-5252 435 F bhendricks@dts.edu
HENDRICKS, Cher .... 330-972-5060 361 H chendricks@uakron.edu
HENDRICKS, Constance 334-727-8282.... 7 D chendricks@tuskegee.edu
HENDRICKS, Cynthia, L 651-696-6145 236 I chendric@macalester.edu
HENDRICKS, Dawn .... 570-321-4022 389 B henddawn@lycoming.edu
HENDRICKS, Jeff .... 336-278-5587 328 J jhendrick4@elon.edu
HENDRICKS, Jeff .... 270-852-8977 182 F jhendricks0008@kctcs.edu
HENDRICKS, Julie .... 805-893-4581.. 70 E julie.hendricks@dcs.ucsb.edu
HENDRICKS, Lynn Nicole .... 203-582-8753.. 88 G lynn.hendricks@quinnipiac.edu
HENDRICKS, Mark .... 916-278-1999.. 32 D mark.hendricks@csus.edu
HENDRICKS, Michael .... 864-294-3231 409 H michael.hendricks@furman.edu
HENDRICKS, Michelle, M .... 570-577-2404 379 C michelle.jones@bucknell.edu
HENDRICKS, Richard .... 703-233-7469 125 C rhendricks@shorter.edu
HENDRICKS, Richard, J 708-974-5203 145 A hendricksr4@morainevalley.edu
HENDRICKS, Susan ...... 765-455-9288 157 B shendric@iu.edu
HENDRICKS, Taylor Ann .... 641-422-4001 168 G
HENDRICKS, Tom, M ... 248-232-4312 229 C tmhendri@oaklandcc.edu
HENDRICKSEN, David ... 502-456-6504 185 A dhendricksen@sullivan.edu
HENDRICKSON, Anthony, R .... 402-280-2852 266 H anthonyhendrickson@creighton.edu
HENDRICKSON, Brittney .... 417-447-8656 259 I bhendrickson@sbuniv.edu
HENDRICKSON, SJ, Daniel, S .... 402-280-2770 266 H president@creighton.edu
HENDRICKSON, Jennifer .... 678-407-5818 119 C jhendrickson@ggc.edu
HENDRICKSON, Kathy .. 763-424-0881 240 A kathy.hendrickson@nhcc.edu
HENDRICKSON, Ken ..... 936-294-1031 450 A his_keh@shsu.edu
HENDRICKSON, Kristine .... 401-341-2148 405 D hendrick@salve.edu
HENDRICKSON, Loretta 607-962-9291 320 C hendrickson@corning-cc.edu
HENDRICKSON, Nathan 541-880-2273 373 C hendrickson@klamathcc.edu
HENDRICKSON, Philip .. 402-643-7358 266 G philip.hendrickson@cune.edu
HENDRICKSON, Ryan, C .... 217-581-2220 137 E rchendrickson@eiu.edu
HENDRICKSON, Sandy . 425-889-5232 481 H sandy.hendrickson@northwestu.edu
HENDRICKSON, Scott ... 906-487-7307 224 B
HENDRICKSON, Vicki, A .... 918-631-2526 371 C vicki-hendrickson@utulsa.edu
HENDRIKSMA, Jane, E . 616-526-6117 222 C jhendrik@calvin.edu
HENDRIX, Andrew .... 803-641-3490 413 B andrewh@usca.edu
HENDRIX, Dean, D .... 210-458-4889 455 E dean.hendrix@utsa.edu
HENDRIX, Grace .... 208-882-1566 132 C ghendrix@nsa.edu
HENDRIX, Jill .... 704-922-6521 334 G hendrix.jill@gaston.edu
HENDRIX, Joan .... 228-267-8643 247 E joan.hendrix@mgccc.edu
HENDRIX, Kristi .... 706-886-6831 126 D khendrix@tfc.edu
HENDRIX, Mary .... 304-876-5107 490 A mhendrix@shepherd.edu
HENDRIX, Mary Helen .. 803-822-3077 410 D hendrixca@midlandstech.edu
HENDRIX, Sherri .... 517-750-1200 231 C shendrix@arbor.edu
HENDRYX, Julie, A .... 260-422-5561 156 E jahendryx@indianatech.edu
HENEGAR, Kellie .... 618-545-3025 141 E khenegar@kaskaskia.edu
HENEISE, Rachael .... 417-777-5062 250 H rhammon@texascountytech.edu
HENESSEE, Valerie .... 319-385-6290 167 H valerie.henessee@iw.edu
HENFER, Marsha .... 773-442-5412 146 A m-henfer@neiu.edu
HENG-MOSS, Tiffany ..... 402-472-2797 269 J thengmoss2@unl.edu
HENGGELER, Christina . 678-946-1105 119 D chenggel@highlands.edu
HENICK, Steven, T .... 410-777-2429 197 G sthenick@aacc.edu
HENKE, Brian .... 816-802-3493 254 D bhenke@kcai.edu
HENKE, Corrine .... 208-426-4045 130 H chenke@boisestate.edu
HENKE, Hilary .... 309-779-7700 151 B
HENKEL, Mandy .... 608-822-2475 500 A mhenkel@swtc.edu
HENKEL, Taylor .... 650-543-3885.. 51 G taylor.henkel@menlo.edu
HENKELMAN, Amy .... 415-257-1304.. 41 C amy.henkelman@dominican.edu
HENKLE, Jeannie .... 509-682-6718 485 H jhenkle@wvc.edu
HENLEY, Amy .... 701-777-2135 345 B amy.henley@und.edu
HENLEY, Antonio .... 704-330-1320 330 D ahenley@jcsu.edu
HENLEY, Brian .... 916-278-7766.. 32 D brian.henley@csus.edu
HENLEY, Charles .... 936-294-4719 450 A ceh071@shsu.edu
HENLEY, Keldon .... 870-245-5405.. 20 D henleyk@obu.edu
HENLEY, Kyle .... 213-740-7000.. 73 D khenley@adm.usc.edu
HENLEY, Marilynn, D ... 602-614-2337.. 10 D
HENLEY, Marsia .... 215-751-8902 381 I mhenley@ccp.edu
HENLEY, Wade .... 301-860-3744 204 A whenley@bowiestate.edu
HENNEN, Thomas, J ..... 563-333-6151 169 G hennenthomasj@sau.edu
HENNESSEY, Brendan ... 575-562-2424 286 B brendan.hennessey@enmu.edu
HENNESSEY, David .... 617-243-2478 211 B dhennessey@lasell.edu
HENNESSEY-GREENE, Megan .... 508-910-6958 212 A mhennesseygreene@umassd.edu
HENNESSY, Bill .... 701-349-5779 346 I bhennessy@trinitybiblecollege.edu
HENNESSY, Catherine ... 516-463-6820 301 G catherine.hennessy@hofstra.edu
HENNESSY, John, L ...... 650-723-2300.. 66 E
HENNESSY, Kelly .... 609-771-3455 276 I hennessk@tcnj.edu
HENNESSY, Lynne, M ... 203-773-8529.. 85 D lhennessy@albertus.edu
HENNIGAN, Ed .... 570-740-0399 389 A ehennigan@luzerne.edu
HENNIGES, Amy .... 920-465-2380 495 F hennigea@uwgb.edu
HENNING, Amy .... 215-572-2900 378 E henninga@arcadia.edu
HENNING, Anna .... 563-588-8000 166 C ahenning@emmaus.edu
HENNING, Arnold .... 217-206-6600 152 A ahenn6@uis.edu
HENNING, Cynthia .... 307-778-1185 501 E chenning@lccc.wy.edu
HENNING, John .... 732-571-4484 279 A jhenning@monmouth.edu
HENNING, Kana .... 773-508-3489 143 C kwibben@luc.edu
HENNING, Kent, L .... 515-263-2802 166 F khenning@grandview.edu
HENNING, Patricia .... 505-277-6128 288 J henning@unm.edu
HENNING, Stefanie .... 617-747-2246 206 H careercenter@berklee.edu
HENNING, Stephanie .... 407-646-2258 106 L shenning@rollins.edu
HENNING, Volker .... 509-527-2615 485 C volker.henning@wallawalla.edu
HENNINGER, Ed .... 541-962-3672 372 I eahenninger@eou.edu
HENNINGSEN, James, D .... 352-873-5835.. 97 N jim.henningsen@cf.edu
HENRICH, IHM, Mary ... 610-647-4400 385 L mhenrich@immaculata.edu
HENRICH, William, L .... 210-567-2050 456 C henrich@uthscsa.edu
HENRICKSON, Melanie, L .... 410-777-2237 197 G mlscherer@aacc.edu
HENRIE, Stephen, E ...... 313-577-5929 232 K fj9065@wayne.edu
HENRIKSEN, J.L .... 509-533-7295 479 C jl.henriksen@scc.spokane.edu
HENRIKSEN, Melanie .... 503-552-1702 374 D president@nunm.edu
HENRIKSEN, Smokey .... 406-338-5441 263 A smokeyh@bfcc.edu
HENRIQUES, Richard .... 402-486-2121 269 F richard.henriqes@ucollege.edu
HENRIQUES, Shilo .... 508-588-9100 215 A shenrique@massasoit.mass.edu
HENRY, Amber .... 314-392-2224 256 E amber.henry@mobap.edu
HENRY, Amir .... 336-750-8033 344 A henryaa@wssu.edu
HENRY, Amy .... 404-894-7475 119 E amy.henry@oie.gatech.edu
HENRY, Ashley .... 434-200-7029 465 D ashley.henry@centracollege.edu
HENRY, Barb .... 404-364-8443 123 K bhenry@oglethorpe.edu
HENRY, Barbara, L .... 419-372-4825 348 G bhenry@bgsu.edu
HENRY, Brian .... 847-543-2264 136 A bhenry1@clcillinois.edu
HENRY, Carolyn, J .... 573-882-3768 261 A henryc@missouri.edu
HENRY, Charles, E .... 713-313-4343 449 B henryce@tsu.edu
HENRY, Christy, S .... 478-757-5219 127 F chenry@wesleyancollege.edu
HENRY, Cynthia .... 850-599-3225 109 I cynthia.henry@famu.edu
HENRY, Deena, H .... 919-209-2017 335 F dhhenry@johnstoncc.edu
HENRY, Donna, P .... 276-328-0122 472 E dph3p@uvawise.edu
HENRY, Donna, P .... 276-328-0122 472 D dph3p@virginia.edu
HENRY, Douglas, V .... 254-710-4860 431 E douglas_henry@baylor.edu
HENRY, Etta, A .... 757-683-5889 469 B ehenry@odu.edu
HENRY, Frank, M .... 405-325-6151 370 K fhenry@ou.edu

HERNANDEZ, Elizabeth . 305-284-2777 104 C
elizabeth.hernandez@hcahealthcare.com
HERNANDEZ, Eric .... 773-252-5133 146 F
eric.hernandez@oakpoint.edu
HERNANDEZ, Erika .... 281-459-7680 443 B
erika.hernandez@sjcd.edu
HERNANDEZ, Evelyn ..... 360-475-7600 481 I
ehernandez@olympic.edu
HERNANDEZ, Frank ...... 817-257-7663 448 F
frank.hernandez@tcu.edu
HERNANDEZ, Gabe .... 409-747-2148 456 E
glhernan@utmb.edu
HERNANDEZ, Grace ...... 806-742-2121 450 F
grace.hernandez@ttu.edu
HERNANDEZ, Grace ...... 323-415-5445.. 48 J
hernang4@elac.edu
HERNANDEZ, Heriberto 956-721-5802 438 H
heriberto.hernandez@laredo.edu
HERNANDEZ, Jesus ...... 248-689-8282 232 C
jherna3@walshcollege.edu
HERNANDEZ, Jill .... 509-963-1858 478 E
jill.hernandez2@cwu.edu
HERNANDEZ, John .... 949-451-5210.. 65 B
johnhernandez@ivc.edu
HERNANDEZ, John, C .. 949-451-5210.. 65 C
johnhernandez@ivc.edu
HERNANDEZ, Jose .... 323-860-1153.. 53 D
joseh@mi.edu
HERNANDEZ, Jose .... 310-434-4455.. 63 C
hernandez_jose@smc.edu
HERNANDEZ, Jose .... 858-635-4772.. 24 K
HERNANDEZ, Juan .... 410-337-6000 199 B
juan.hernandez@goucher.edu
HERNANDEZ, Justin, J . 660-944-2851 251 J
justin@conception.edu
HERNANDEZ, Karla .... 305-348-4163 110 A
karla.hernandez5@fiu.edu
HERNANDEZ, Leonor .... 956-295-3436 449 C
leonor.barrera@tsc.edu
HERNANDEZ, Linda .... 903-730-4890 438 D
lhernandez@jarvis.edu
HERNANDEZ, Lino .... 787-738-2161 512 C
lino.hernandez@upr.edu
HERNANDEZ, Lisa .... 951-343-4767.. 27 G
lihernandez@calbaptist.edu
HERNANDEZ, Lisa, H ... 412-397-5968 397 B
hernandezl@rmu.edu
HERNANDEZ, Loana .... 361-664-2981 432 K
lhernandez@coastalbend.edu
HERNANDEZ, Lola .... 806-894-9611 443 G
lhernandez@southplainscollege.edu
HERNANDEZ, Luis .... 915-747-5308 455 C
lehernan@utep.edu
HERNANDEZ, Luz, A ..... 787-890-2681 511 G
luz.hernandez6@upr.edu
HERNANDEZ, Luz, S ..... 787-620-2040 505 C
lhernandez@aupr.edu
HERNANDEZ,
Madelline .... 818-364-7618.. 49 C
hernanm@lamission.edu
HERNANDEZ, Maria, M 787-758-2525 512 F
maria.hernandez15@upr.edu
HERNANDEZ, Marisa .... 989-837-4337 229 B
toschkof@northwood.edu
HERNANDEZ,
Mary Lou .... 520-494-5200.. 11 K
marylou.hernandez@centralaz.edu
HERNANDEZ, Melissa ... 210-458-4140 455 E
melissa.hernandez@utsa.edu
HERNANDEZ, Mina .... 760-757-2121.. 52 F
HERNANDEZ, Miranda .. 831-242-5291 502 F
HERNANDEZ, Myrna ..... 330-263-2011 351 A
mhernandez@wooster.edu
HERNANDEZ, Nina .... 908-709-7127 284 D
hernandez@ucc.edu
HERNANDEZ, Oscar, O . 956-295-3451 449 C
oscar.hernandez@tsc.edu
HERNANDEZ, JR.,
Pablo .... 956-872-8372 443 H
phernan@southtexascollege.edu
HERNANDEZ, JR.,
Pablo .... 956-872-2182 443 H
phernan@southtexascollege.edu
HERNANDEZ, Page .... 281-649-3487 437 B
phernandez@hbu.edu
HERNANDEZ, Paul .... 978-630-9288 215 C
phernandez@mwcc.mass.edu
HERNANDEZ, Ramon .... 860-832-1619.. 85 G
hernandez@ccsu.edu
HERNANDEZ, Ramon .... 787-841-2000 509 J
ramon_hernandezcruz@pucpr.edu
HERNANDEZ, Raul .... 787-284-1912 508 E
rhernand@ponce.inter.edu
HERNANDEZ, Rebecca .. 503-554-2147 373 A
rhernandez@georgefox.edu
HERNANDEZ, Richard ... 760-252-2411.. 26 G
rhernandez@barstow.edu
HERNANDEZ, Rosa .... 305-821-3333 100 E
rhernandez@fnu.edu
HERNANDEZ, Samuel ... 787-882-2065 510 C
shernandez@unitecpr.edu
HERNANDEZ, Samuel ... 210-688-3101 432 H
HERNANDEZ, Sofia .... 956-296-1445 455 D
sofia.hernandez@utrgv.edu
HERNANDEZ, Sorangel . 818-947-2324.. 49 G
hernansp@lavc.edu
HERNANDEZ, Sylvia ..... 718-997-3460 295 B
sylvia.hernandez@qc.cuny.edu
HERNANDEZ, Theran .... 214-376-1000 441 F
thernandez@pqc.edu
HERNANDEZ,
Thomas, J .... 585-395-2510 317 E
thernand@brockport.edu
HERNANDEZ, Todd .... 419-267-1310 357 E
thernandez@northweststate.edu
HERNANDEZ, Victor, M 787-841-2000 509 J
capellania@pucpr.edu
HERNANDEZ, Victor, M 787-894-2828 513 C
victor.hernandez23@upr.edu
HERNANDEZ, Wanda .... 646-565-6000 322 G
wanda.hernandez@touro.edu
HERNANDEZ, Wanda .... 646-565-6000 322 F
wanda.hernandez@touro.edu
HERNANDEZ, West .... 307-754-6103 501 H
west.hernandez@nwc.edu
HERNANDEZ, Yvette ..... 830-591-7318 444 G
yvetteh@swtjc.edu
HERNANDEZ JARVIS,
Lorna .... 253-879-3207 484 G
lhernandezjarvis@pugetsound.edu
HERNANDEZ MEJIA,
Jesus, O .... 507-933-7687 236 A
jhernan2@gustavus.edu
HERNANDEZ NUNEZ,
Maria, L .... 787-884-3838 505 D
mlhernandez@atenascollege.edu
HERNANDEZ PRIMMER,
Marianly .... 954-776-4476 103 B
HERNANDEZ-STEVENSON,
Britney .... 270-824-8671 182 D
britney.hernandezstevenson@kctcs.edu
HERNDON, Brooke .... 802-831-1078 463 C
bherndon@vermontlaw.edu
HERNDON, Craig .... 804-819-4782 473 C
cherndon@vccs.edu
HERNDON, Doug .... 916-484-8101.. 50 G
herndod@arc.losrios.edu
HERNDON,
Kimmetha, D .... 205-726-2198.... 6 E
kherndon@samford.edu
HERNDON, OSB, Linda 913-360-7553 171 J
lherndon@benedictine.edu
HERNDON, Linda, M .... 229-226-1621 126 C
lherndon@thomasu.edu
HERNDON,
Michael (Mike) .... 817-515-1502 445 F
michael.herndon@tccd.edu
HERNDON, Nicole .... 501-760-4300.. 20 A
nicole.herndon@np.edu
HERNDON, Renee .... 205-929-3419.... 2 H
rherndon@lawsonstate.edu
HERNDON, Steven, T ... 937-229-3317 362 C
sherndon1@udayton.edu
HERNE, Jaclyn .... 716-839-8245 298 A
jherne@daemen.edu
HERNESS, Scott .... 973-655-4368 279 B
hernesss@montclair.edu
HEROD, Kevin .... 256-761-8757.... 7 B
krherod@talladega.edu
HEROLD, Dale .... 352-638-9778.. 96 B
dherold@beaconcollege.edu
HERON, Keith .... 212-217-4210 299 D
keith_heron@fitnyc.edu
HERONIMUS, Katie .... 507-372-3455 239 F
katie.heronimus@mnwest.edu
HEROY, Darci .... 503-370-6195 377 F
dheroy@willamette.edu
HERR, Audrey .... 717-871-7612 395 A
aherr@ssi.millersville.edu
HERR, Beth, J .... 402-280-5769 266 H
bherr@creighton.edu
HERR, Don .... 850-201-6168 112 C
don.herr@tcc.fl.edu
HERR, Duane .... 410-777-2346 197 G
dpherr@aacc.edu
HERR, Robert .... 518-327-6031 311 C
rherr@paulsmiths.edu
HERRELL, Kate .... 636-627-2555 254 H
kherrell@lindenwood.edu
HERRELL, Ron .... 419-783-2376 351 K
rherrell@defiance.edu
HERREN, Johnna .... 618-985-3741 140 H
johnnaherren@jalc.edu
HERREN, Melissa .... 405-945-3297 368 C
melissa.herren@okstate.edu
HERRERA, Antoinette .... 408-274-7900.. 62 G
antoinette.herrera@evc.edu
HERRERA, Clarissa, L ... 651-450-3657 238 E
clarissa.herrera@dctc.edu
HERRERA, Clarissa, L ... 651-423-8244 238 A
clarissa.herrera@dctc.edu
HERRERA, Cynthia .... 805-652-5944.. 73 I
cynthia_herrera@vcccd.edu
HERRERA, Gilberto .... 787-890-2681 511 G
gilberto.herrera@upr.edu
HERRERA, Gregory .... 212-229-5323 308 A
herrerag@newschool.edu
HERRERA, Jesse .... 605-394-1828 416 H
jesse.herrera@sdsmt.edu
HERRERA, Jorge, D ...... 512-404-4829 430 J
jherrera@austinseminary.edu
HERRERA, José .... 319-273-2517 164 A
jose.herrera@uni.edu
HERRERA, Nelly .... 512-463-1808 449 E
netty.herrera@tsus.edu
HERRERA, Rick .... 956-364-5002 449 D
rick.herrera@tstc.edu
HERRERA, Xochil .... 303-360-4788.. 80 E
xochil.herrera@ccaurora.edu
HERRERA LINDSTROM,
Cynthia, E .... 312-996-3719 151 G
cynthiar@uic.edu
HERRERO, Veronica ...... 312-553-2500 135 A
vherrero@ccc.edu
HERRICK, Alice .... 207-326-2445 196 A
alice.herrick@mma.edu
HERRICK, George .... 304-367-4883 489 K
george.herrick@fairmontstate.edu
HERRICK, James, S ...... 619-594-0213.. 33 D
herrick1@sdsu.edu
HERRICK, Jessica .... 989-328-1228 228 D
jessicah@montcalm.edu
HERRICK, Jim .... 619-594-8236.. 33 D
herrick1@sdsu.edu
HERRICK-PHELPS,
Johnna .... 802-865-5488 462 A
jherrickphelps@champlain.edu
HERRIDGE, Curt .... 214-768-4197 444 D
herridge@smu.edu
HERRIFORD, Steven, R . 317-781-5767 161 H
sherriford@uindy.edu
HERRIG, Becky .... 563-588-6321 164 E
becky.herrig@clarke.edu
HERRIN, Andraea .... 803-376-5758 406 D
aherrin@allenuniversity.edu
HERRIN, Brice .... 229-732-5980 115 B
briceherrin@andrewcollege.edu
HERRIN, Bridget .... 619-388-2509.. 60 J
bherrin@sdccd.edu
HERRIN, Carl .... 508-929-8263 213 G
cherrin@worcester.edu
HERRIN, Madison .... 912-583-3178 116 E
mherrin@bpc.edu
HERRIN, Timothy, D ..... 704-233-8150 344 F
herrin@wingate.edu
HERRIN, William .... 209-946-2650.. 71 E
wherrin@pacific.edu
HERRING, Angela .... 252-246-1363 339 C
aherring@wilsoncc.edu
HERRING, April .... 410-386-8444 198 D
aherring@carrollcc.edu
HERRING, Charles .... 410-704-2505 204 E
cherring@towson.edu
HERRING, Jack .... 360-650-4900 485 I
jack.herring@wwu.edu
HERRING, Jeff, C .... 801-585-0928 459 O
jeff.herring@utah.edu
HERRING, Natalie .... 217-206-8660 152 A
nherr4@uis.edu
HERRING, Nathan .... 765-677-2257 158 B
nathan.herring@indwes.edu
HERRING, Paula .... 229-333-2109 128 B
paula.herring@wiregrass.edu
HERRING, Robin .... 717-262-2017 403 C
rherring@wilson.edu
HERRING, Ryan .... 208-562-3227 131 E
ryanherring@cwi.edu
HERRING, Susan .... 215-968-8364 379 D
susan.herring@bucks.edu
HERRINGER,
Gretchen, B .... 413-585-2550 218 H
gherringer@smith.edu
HERRINGTON, Ashley ... 928-344-7501.. 11 A
ashley.herrington@azwestern.edu
HERRINGTON, James ... 816-654-7910 254 E
jherrington@kcumb.edu
HERRINGTON, Jere .... 662-562-3214 248 D
recruiting@northwestms.edu
HERRINGTON, Kristine . 904-620-1672 111 B
k.herrington@unf.edu
HERRINGTON, Marla .... 318-342-5320 193 C
lindsey@ulm.edu
HERRINGTON,
Theophilus .... 713-313-7827 449 B
theo.herrington@tsu.edu
HERRMAN, Kathy .... 785-628-4251 173 H
kaherrman@fhsu.edu
HERRMANN, Anthony ... 914-323-5406 305 B
anthony.herrmann@mville.edu
HERRMANN, Bryan .... 320-589-6113 244 B
herrmanb@morris.umn.edu
HERRMANN, John, L .... 740-284-5215 352 I
jherrmann@franciscan.edu
HERRMANN, Mark .... 907-474-7116.. 10 A
mlherrmann@alaska.edu
HERRMANN, Matthew ... 910-938-6236 333 F
herrmannm@coastalcarolina.edu
HERRMANN, Tracy .... 513-745-5689 362 A
tracy.herrmann@ec.edu
HERROD, Lindsay .... 724-925-4059 402 F
herrodl@westmoreland.edu
HERRON, Alex .... 512-313-3000 433 N
alexandra.herron@concordia.edu
HERRON, Crystal .... 314-286-0236 258 F
cherron@ranken.edu
HERRON, Jeffrey .... 732-906-2515 278 G
jherron@middlesexcc.edu
HERRON, John .... 804-752-7244 469 F
johnherron@rmc.edu
HERRON, Kimberly .... 903-785-7661 441 D
kimberlyherron@parisjc.edu
HERRON, Kyle .... 843-953-9888 407 C
jherron@citadel.edu
HERRON, Margaret .... 785-242-5200 176 I
margaret.herron@ottawa.edu
HERRON, Martin, T .... 515-964-0601 166 D
herronm@faith.edu
HERRON, Matthew .... 410-777-2707 197 G
mtherron@aacc.edu
HERRON, Robert .... 251-626-3303.... 7 E
rherron@ussa.edu
HERSCH, Lisa .... 301-687-7085 204 C
ldhersch@frostburg.edu
HERSCH, Tonya .... 415-457-8811.. 39 A
thersch@marin.edu
HERSCHEDE, Kathryn, J 610-499-4101 402 G
kjherschede@widener.edu
HERSETH SANDLIN,
Stephanie .... 605-274-4111 414 G
stephanie.hersethsandlin@augie.edu
HERSHBERGER, Bernie . 207-725-3069 194 C
bhershbe@bowdoin.edu
HERSHBERGER, Del ...... 620-327-8602 174 E
del.hershberger@hesston.edu
HERSHENSON, Jay .... 718-997-5648 295 B
jay.hershenson@qc.cuny.edu
HERSHEY, April .... 717-464-7050 387 F
HERSHEY, J. David .... 717-396-7833 392 U
dhershey@pcad.edu
HERSHEY, Jean .... 717-947-6150 392 V
jlhershe@pacollege.edu
HERSHKOWITZ, Meyer . 845-207-0330 290 F
HERSHOCK, Martin .... 313-593-5490 231 I
mhershoc@umich.edu
HERSKER, Alan, L .... 315-267-3445 319 A
herskeal@potsdam.edu
HERSKOWITZ, Issac ...... 212-463-0400 322 G
issac.herskowitz@touro.edu
HERSKOWITZ, Issac ...... 212-463-0400 322 F
issac.herskowitz@touro.edu
HERSKOWITZ,
Mordechai .... 732-367-1060 275 K
HERSON, Mendy .... 973-267-9404 280 F
ymmherson@rca.edu
HERSON, Moshe .... 973-267-9404 280 F
rabbiherson@rca.edu
HERT, Darlene .... 406-657-2320 264 D
dhert@msubillings.edu
HERTEL, James .... 210-999-7551 451 E
jhertel@trinity.edu
HERTEL, Jeffrey .... 616-395-7770 225 D
hertelj@hope.edu

HICKMAN, Wesley, T .... 803-777-7440 413 A
whickman@mailbox.sc.edu
HICKMAN-GODOY,
Julie .... 804-752-7259 469 F
juliehickmangodoy@rmc.edu
HICKMAN HOLLAND,
Heather .... 415-749-4540.. 61 C
hhickman@sfai.edu
HICKOX, Chad .... 509-527-4274 485 B
chad.hickox@wwcc.edu
HICKS, Allisha .... 252-536-5469 335 B
ahicks@halifaxcc.edu
HICKS, Ann .... 773-244-4908 145 G
ahicks@northpark.edu
HICKS, Barbara .... 941-487-4380 110 D
bhicks@ncf.edu
HICKS, OSB,
Boniface, N .... 724-532-6662 398 A
boniface.hicks@stvincent.edu
HICKS, Brenda, D .... 620-229-6387 177 G
brenda.hicks@sckans.edu
HICKS, Brian, A .... 336-734-7191 334 F
bhicks@forsythtech.edu
HICKS, Bruce .... 310-287-4307.. 49 H
hicksbr@wlac.edu
HICKS, Bruno .... 706-272-4420 118 B
bhicks@daltonstate.edu
HICKS, Bryan .... 256-372-4014.... 1 A
byran.hicks@aamu.edu
HICKS, Cassandra .... 573-334-6825 259 G
chicks@sehcollege.edu
HICKS, JR., Cecil .... 402-554-3664 270 A
chicks@unomaha.edu
HICKS, Chris .... 903-675-6212 451 F
chicks@tvcc.edu
HICKS, Dennis .... 765-973-8270 157 A
dehicks@iue.edu
HICKS, Derrick .... 973-748-9000 276 A
derrick_hicks@bloomfield.edu
HICKS, Diana .... 916-484-8654.. 50 G
hicksd@arc.losrios.edu
HICKS, Douglas, A .... 404-784-8300 118 E
douglas.hicks@emory.edu
HICKS, Elena, D .... 214-768-4115 444 D
ehicks@smu.edu
HICKS, J. David .... 423-652-4782 420 F
jdhicks@king.edu
HICKS, Janet, K .... 570-586-2400 381 B
jhicks@clarkssummitu.edu
HICKS, Janice .... 432-335-6412 441 A
jhicks@odessa.edu
HICKS, Jennifer .... 706-295-6371 119 D
jhicks@highlands.edu
HICKS, Jim .... 423-425-4246 427 C
jim-hicks@utc.edu
HICKS, Joel .... 318-677-3100 192 G
hicksj@nsula.edu
HICKS, Juanita .... 404-962-3265 127 D
juanita.hicks@usg.edu
HICKS, Julie .... 252-492-2061 338 F
hicksj@vgcc.edu
HICKS, Kasey .... 717-728-2272 380 E
kaseyhicks@centralpenn.edu
HICKS, Lori .... 502-597-6415 183 D
lori.hicks@kysu.edu
HICKS, Mandy .... 812-258-9510 154 E
mhicks@cariscollege.edu
HICKS, Megan .... 319-895-4828 164 G
mhicks@cornellcollege.edu
HICKS, Mona, L .... 561-803-2174 105 C
mona_hicks@pba.edu
HICKS, Renee, G .... 985-493-2556 192 F
renee.hicks@nicholls.edu
HICKS, Rick .... 714-895-8270.. 38 A
rhick@gwc.cccd.edu
HICKS, Samantha .... 843-349-2348 408 A
shicks@coastal.edu
HICKS, Scott .... 434-592-4808 468 E
smhicks@liberty.edu
HICKS, Shawn .... 619-644-7163.. 44 E
shawn.hicks@gcccd.edu
HICKS, Stephanie .... 334-833-4571.... 5 G
stephanie.hicks@hawks.huntingdon.edu
HICKS, Timothy, J .... 315-859-4790 300 H
thicks@hamilton.edu
HICKS, Travis .... 209-381-6047.. 52 A
HICKS KONVALINKA,
April .... 407-823-4663 110 E
april.hickskonvalinka@ucf.edu
HICKS-MCGOWAN,
Jennifer .... 945-938-6104 503 I
jennifer.hicksmcgowan@westpoint.edu
HICSWA, Stefani .... 406-657-2300 264 D
stefani.hicswa@msubillings.edu

HIDALGO, Troy .... 337-475-5748 192 E
shidalgo@mcneese.edu
HIDLEBAUGH, Laura ..... 319-234-5748 166 H
laura.hidlebaugh@hawkeyecollege.edu
HIEBERT, Sandra .... 620-327-8231 174 E
sandra.hiebert@hesston.edu
HIEDEMAN, Ann .... 218-477-2066 239 E
ann.hiedeman@mnstate.edu
HIEDEMANN, Kathryn ... 216-421-7411 350 H
kjheidemann@cia.edu
HIEL, Edwin .... 619-388-3400.. 60 I
ehiel@sdccd.edu
HIEMENZ, Karen, A ...... 320-308-5017 241 A
khiemenz@sctcc.edu
HIEN, Denise .... 848-445-0749 282 A
denise.hien@smithers.rutgers.edu
HIESTAND, Nathaniel .... 320-308-5009 241 A
nhiestand@sctcc.edu
HIETAPELTO, Amy .... 218-726-7281 243 G
lsbe@d.umn.edu
HIETSCH, Stephen .... 315-229-5896 314 D
shietsch@stlawu.edu
HIETT, Lee Ann .... 713-266-6594 436 B
HIGA, Pat .... 949-582-4585.. 65 D
phiga@saddleback.edu
HIGA-KING, Jennifer ..... 808-845-9110 130 A
higaking@hawaii.edu
HIGASHI, Lori .... 541-485-1780 374 E
lorihigashi@enewhope.edu
HIGBEE, Isabelle .... 601-974-1220 247 B
higbeie@millsaps.edu
HIGDON, Beth .... 641-784-5064 166 E
mhigdon@graceland.edu
HIGDON, Hal, L .... 417-447-2602 257 G
higdonh@otc.edu
HIGDON, Jude .... 802-440-4485 461 G
judehigdon@bennington.edu
HIGDON, Leon .... 334-244-3028.... 4 E
lhigdon@aum.edu
HIGGINBOTHAM,
Amanda .... 610-921-7636 377 G
ahigginbotham@albright.edu
HIGGINBOTHAM,
Carmenita .... 804-828-2787 473 B
artsdean@vcu.edu
HIGGINBOTHAM,
Debra .... 940-397-4120 440 C
debra.higginbotham@msutexas.edu
HIGGINBOTHAM, Karen 212-472-1500 309 D
deanofstudents@nysid.edu
HIGGINBOTHAM, Ray .... 931-393-1737 424 F
rhigginbotham@mscc.edu
HIGGINS, Brandon .... 903-823-3024 446 A
brandon.higgins@texarkanacollege.edu
HIGGINS, Carla .... 419-783-2571 351 K
chiggins@defiance.edu
HIGGINS, Carolyn .... 212-752-1530 304 A
carolyn.higgins@limcollege.edu
HIGGINS, Colette .... 808-235-7339 130 E
chiggins@hawaii.edu
HIGGINS, Cory .... 801-618-5171 128 D
cory.higgins@byuh.edu
HIGGINS, Dalton .... 918-335-6865 368 E
dhiggins@okwu.edu
HIGGINS, Dawn .... 603-271-6484 273 A
dhiggins@ccsnh.edu
HIGGINS, Elizabeth .... 207-780-4632 197 D
bhiggins@maine.edu
HIGGINS, Holly .... 207-699-5047 195 A
hhiggins@meca.edu
HIGGINS, Holly .... 800-650-4772.. 38 F
hhiggins@issaonline.edu
HIGGINS, Joe .... 617-715-2616 216 B
HIGGINS, Kacey .... 325-670-1368 436 I
kacey.higgins@hsutx.edu
HIGGINS, Kerena .... 360-650-2040 485 I
kerena.higgins@wwu.edu
HIGGINS, Kevin .... 626-398-2222.. 76 C
HIGGINS, Lori .... 972-860-4746 434 F
lhiggins@dcccd.edu
HIGGINS, Rhonda .... 440-934-3101 357 I
HIGGINS, Ronnell, A .... 203-432-9455.. 90 C
ronnell.higgins@yale.edu
HIGGINS, Sandra .... 718-260-5700 295 A
shiggins@citytech.cuny.edu
HIGGINS, Terri .... 641-782-1431 170 F
thiggins@swcciowa.edu
HIGGINS, Thomas, J .... 518-564-3013 318 E
higgintj@plattsburgh.edu
HIGGINS, Wendy .... 707-654-1194.. 32 A
whiggins@csum.edu
HIGGINSON, Jason .... 252-744-2201 341 A
higginsonj@ecu.edu

HIGGS, Fred .... 713-348-5923 442 F
higgs@rice.edu
HIGGS, Jessica .... 309-677-2700 134 A
jhiggs@bradley.edu
HIGGS, John .... 724-480-3558 381 H
john.higgs@ccbc.edu
HIGGS, Michael .... 903-813-2342 430 H
mhiggs@austincollege.edu
HIGGS HYPPOLITE,
Belinda .... 405-325-0311 370 K
HIGH, Andrew .... 310-289-5123.. 74 I
andrew.high@wcui.edu
HIGH, Elizabeth .... 910-788-6367 338 A
elizabeth.high@sccnc.edu
HIGH, Jennifer .... 252-399-6397 326 K
jmhigh@barton.edu
HIGH, Lucrecia, A .... 252-451-8387 336 E
lahigh756@nashcc.edu
HIGHAM, Pamela, S ..... 814-332-3576 378 A
phigham@allegheny.edu
HIGHERS, Cami .... 918-444-4200 366 G
highersc@nsuok.edu
HIGHFILL, Katie .... 417-447-4820 257 G
highfilk@otc.edu
HIGHFILL, Melanie .... 559-638-0300.. 67 D
melanie.highfill@reedleycollege.edu
HIGHLEY, Melinda, C .... 606-783-2033 184 C
m.highley@moreheadstate.edu
HIGHSMITH, Stephen ... 610-902-1070 379 G
smh395@cabrini.edu
HIGHSMITH, Vanessa ... 818-702-1387.. 56 G
vanessa.highsmith@pepperdine.edu
HIGHTOWER, Darlene ... 405-744-3555 367 G
darlene.hightower@okstate.edu
HIGHTOWER, Jodie .... 870-612-2016.. 22 H
jodie.hightower@uaccb.edu
HIGHTOWER, Zachary ... 706-886-6831 126 D
zhightower@tfc.edu
HIGHTOWER-MITCHELL,
Damara .... 803-780-1234 414 B
dhmitchell@voorhees.edu
HIGINBOTHAM,
Lynn, E .... 212-998-4444 309 F
lynn.higinbotham@nyu.edu
HIGLEY, William, J .... 570-586-2400 381 B
whigley@clarkssummitu.edu
HIJEK, Barbara .... 754-312-2898 103 R
HILBELINK, Amy .... 865-251-1800 423 E
ahilbelink@south.edu
HILBERT, Jim .... 651-290-6423 242 L
jim.hilbert@mitchellhamline.edu
HILBERT, Stephen .... 216-987-3501 351 E
stephen.hilbert@tri-c.edu
HILBURN, Nancy .... 843-574-6564 412 I
nancy.hilburn@tridenttech.edu
HILDEBRAND, Carol ...... 415-485-9306.. 39 A
childebrand@marin.edu
HILDEBRAND, Garrick .. 972-780-3600 454 A
garrick.hildebrand@untdallas.edu
HILDEBRANDT, Kristin .. 414-229-6031 496 B
hildebra@uwm.edu
HILDEN, Scott .... 734-677-5306 232 D
sjhilden@wccnet.edu
HILDERBRAND, Carey .. 801-274-3280 461 E
carey.hilderbrand@wgu.edu
HILDRETH, Brandon ...... 559-730-3879.. 39 B
brandonhi@cos.edu
HILDRETH, SR.,
James E.K .... 615-327-6904 421 D
jhildreth@mmc.edu
HILES, Jason .... 602-639-7500.. 12 J
HILFERTY, Bridget .... 610-499-1344 402 G
bhilferty@widener.edu
HILGEDICK, Brianne ..... 660-248-6210 251 E
bhilgedi@centralmethodist.edu
HILGERSOM, Karin .... 775-673-7025 271 C
khilgersom@tmcc.edu
HILKE, David .... 805-493-3960.. 29 C
dhilke@callutheran.edu
HILL, Adriane .... 212-870-1212 309 E
ahill@nyts.edu
HILL, Alan, P .... 765-658-4199 154 J
alanhill@depauw.edu
HILL, Amanda .... 215-545-6400 391 E
amhill@peirce.edu
HILL, Amber .... 928-524-7311.. 14 J
amber.hill@npc.edu
HILL, Andrew .... 906-227-2531 228 I
anhill@nmu.edu
HILL, Angela .... 409-880-8188 449 F
ajhill@lit.edu
HILL, Araceli .... 214-954-3610 447 B
araceli.hill@tamuc.edu

HILL, Ben .... 319-384-3400 163 H
benjamin-hill-1@uiowa.edu
HILL, Benjamin .... 540-831-2311 469 D
bhill59@radford.edu
HILL, Benjamin .... 920-929-2136 499 D
bhill@morainepark.edu
HILL, Bernard .... 706-585-0028 124 E
bernard.hill@point.edu
HILL, Beth .... 520-515-3613.. 11 M
hillb@cochise.edu
HILL, Beverly .... 479-619-2679.. 20 C
bhill3@nwacc.edu
HILL, Brad .... 252-618-6640 334 D
hillb@edgecombe.edu
HILL, Brandon .... 765-677-2200 158 B
brandon.hill@indwes.edu
HILL, Brandon .... 580-559-5208 365 K
bhill@ecok.edu
HILL, Brian .... 412-268-1939 380 C
brianhill@cmu.edu
HILL, Brian, W .... 540-231-5107 466 K
bhill@vcom.vt.edu
HILL, Calvin, R .... 413-748-3552 218 I
chill@springfield.edu
HILL, Carol .... 580-349-1566 367 F
carol.hill@opsu.edu
HILL, Cassandra .... 815-753-0380 146 B
chill14@niu.edu
HILL, Charles .... 920-424-3190 496 C
hill@uwosh.edu
HILL, Cheryl .... 434-223-6219 467 F
chill@hsc.edu
HILL, Christina .... 704-669-4545 333 E
bellch@clevelandcc.edu
HILL, Christopher, D .... 404-413-2572 120 E
chill@gsu.edu
HILL, Christopher, J ..... 412-392-4707 396 G
chill@pointpark.edu
HILL, Craig, C .... 214-768-2534 444 D
craighill@smu.edu
HILL, Craig, R .... 352-392-1336 111 A
craighill@ufl.edu
HILL, Crystal .... 252-985-5202 339 D
chill@ncwc.edu
HILL, Curtis .... 435-865-8621 460 A
hillc@suu.edu
HILL, David .... 973-290-4345 282 I
dhill@steu.edu
HILL, Deana .... 570-484-2014 394 E
dhill@lockhaven.edu
HILL, Diane .... 973-353-1634 282 B
dianeh@newark.rutgers.edu
HILL, Doree .... 252-222-6282 333 A
hilld@carteret.edu
HILL, Doris .... 651-793-1852 238 I
doris.hill@metrostate.edu
HILL, Edward .... 314-340-3352 254 A
hille@hssu.edu
HILL, Eileen .... 831-479-6458.. 27 D
eihill@cabrillo.edu
HILL, Emilee .... 863-667-5280 108 K
echill@seu.edu
HILL, Emily .... 319-335-1684 163 H
emily-hill@uiowa.edu
HILL, G. Richard .... 801-626-7313 461 A
grhill@weber.edu
HILL, Gary .... 573-681-5496 254 G
hillg@lincolnu.edu
HILL, Gladys .... 205-391-2457.... 3 E
ghill@sheltonstate.edu
HILL, Heather .... 704-330-6730 333 D
heather.hill@cpcc.edu
HILL, Holly, L .... 904-826-8636.. 99 E
hhill@flagler.edu
HILL, Jacqueline .... 305-623-4281 100 D
jacqueline.hill@fmuniv.edu
HILL, Jamie .... 309-796-5284 133 G
hillj@bhc.edu
HILL, Janeen, M .... 714-628-7223.. 36 B
jhill@chapman.edu
HILL, Jeff .... 608-249-6611 492 H
HILL, Jennifer .... 256-352-8032.... 3 I
jennifer.hill@wallacestate.edu
HILL, Jerell .... 626-529-8500.. 55 F
HILL, Jody .... 901-334-5809 421 E
jhill@memphisseminary.edu
HILL, John .... 310-243-2056.. 30 E
johill@csudh.edu
HILL, Johnny .... 919-546-8612 340 B
jhill@shawu.edu
HILL, Jonathan, H .... 212-346-1810 311 A
HILL, Joslyn .... 405-425-5476 367 C
joslyn.hill@oc.edu

HILL, Joyce .... 575-439-3879 287 D
joyhill@nmsu.edu
HILL, Kameshia .... 601-979-1325 246 F
kameshia.m.hill@jsums.edu
HILL, Karen .... 310-665-6910.. 55 C
khill@otis.edu
HILL, Kari, M .... 608-342-1555 496 E
hillkar@uwplatt.edu
HILL, Katherine .... 303-352-6938.. 80 F
katy.hill@ccd.edu
HILL, Katrina .... 937-298-3399 354 J
katrina.hill@kc.edu
HILL, Kelli .... 309-268-8100 138 H
kelli.hill@heartland.edu
HILL, Ken .... 207-801-5630 194 E
khill@coa.edu
HILL, Kimberly .... 252-527-6223 335 G
krhill01@lenoircc.edu
HILL, Leah .... 252-985-5293 339 D
lhill@ncwc.edu
HILL, Leia .... 601-484-8786 247 A
lhill@meridiancc.edu
HILL, Lena .... 540-458-8418 477 D
lmhill@wlu.edu
HILL, Leroy .... 619-201-8959.. 65 G
leroy.hill@socalsem.edu
HILL, Lisa .... 410-337-6000 199 B
lisa.hill@goucher.edu
HILL, Lisa .... 252-940-6223 332 C
lisa.hill@beaufortccc.edu
HILL, Malcolm .... 207-786-6066 194 A
mhill@bates.edu
HILL, Mark .... 651-641-8223 235 I
hill@csp.edu
HILL, Mark, J .... 315-470-6670 319 D
mjhill@esf.edu
HILL, Mary .... 202-806-6100.. 92 F
HILL, Mary, M .... 989-774-3331 222 E
hill1mm@cmich.edu
HILL, Mathew, B .... 651-631-5362 244 D
mbhill@unwsp.edu
HILL, Melinda .... 910-898-9634 336 D
hillm@montgomery.edu
HILL, Melissa .... 509-865-0411 481 A
hill_m@heritage.edu
HILL, Melissa, D .... 812-941-2359 157 F
mhill02@ius.edu
HILL, Michael .... 610-328-8067 398 G
mhill1@swarthmore.edu
HILL, Michael .... 903-468-3104 447 B
michael.hill@tamuc.edu
HILL, Michael, E .... 919-530-5214 341 E
mhill73@nccu.edu
HILL, Michelle, D .... 757-823-8135 469 A
mdhill@nsu.edu
HILL, Mike .... 704-687-1054 342 D
athleticdirector@uncc.edu
HILL, Miriam .... 651-638-6415 234 D
m-hill@bethel.edu
HILL, Nicholas .... 803-535-5689 407 D
nhill@claflin.edu
HILL, Nicole, R .... 717-477-1373 395 B
nrhill@ship.edu
HILL, Penny .... 518-629-7294 302 C
p.hill@hvcc.edu
HILL, Peter .... 774-392-1646 220 E
phill@whoi.edu
HILL, Redgina .... 574-284-4834 160 I
rhill@saintmarys.edu
HILL, Reggie .... 314-516-6471 261 C
reggiehill@umsl.edu
HILL, Reinhold, R .... 812-348-7226 157 D
reihill@iupuc.edu
HILL, Robert, A .... 617-353-3560 207 E
rahill@bu.edu
HILL, Rory .... 216-397-3015 353 O
rhill@jcu.edu
HILL, Samantha .... 850-484-4680 105 H
smhill@pensacolastate.edu
HILL, Sandra, B .... 973-720-2565 284 J
hills21@wpunj.edu
HILL, Sarah .... 217-234-5338 142 C
shill@lakeland.cc.il.us
HILL, Sean .... 618-468-6000 142 E
shill@lc.edu
HILL, Shane .... 806-894-9611 443 G
shill@southplainscollege.edu
HILL, Shannon .... 805-546-3279.. 40 F
shannon_hill@cuesta.edu
HILL, Sharon .... 770-229-3454 125 H
sharon.hill@sctech.edu
HILL, Sheila, M .... 706-771-4840 115 J
shill@augustatech.edu
HILL, Sherri .... 203-837-8774.. 86 B
hills@wcsu.edu
HILL, Soni .... 513-569-4215 350 F
soni.hill@cincinnatistate.edu
HILL, Stacy .... 509-777-3842 486 C
shill@whitworth.edu
HILL, Stephanie .... 937-376-6591 349 J
shill2@centralstate.edu
HILL, Stephen, E .... 801-422-8153 458 H
steve_hill@byu.edu
HILL, Tim .... 541-440-4707 376 G
tim.hill@umpqua.edu
HILL, Tina .... 717-262-2012 403 C
tina.hill@wilson.edu
HILL, Toni, E .... 301-546-0688 201 E
hillte@pgcc.edu
HILL, Tonya, L .... 217-443-8772 136 G
thill@dacc.edu
HILL, Travis, R .... 315-859-4023 300 H
thill@hamilton.edu
HILL, W. Timothy .... 801-422-7011 458 H
7714@byu.edu
HILL, Walter, A .... 334-727-8157.... 7 D
hillwa@tuskegee.edu
HILL, Wayne, R .... 330-972-2148 361 H
whill@uakron.edu
HILL, Wes .... 252-246-1339 339 C
whill@wilsoncc.edu
HILL, William .... 713-646-1764 443 I
whill@synermarkprop.com
HILL, II, William, L .... 215-965-4022 390 E
whill@moore.edu
HILL, Wynn, N .... 208-496-9200 130 I
hillw@byui.edu
HILL, Yasmine .... 334-699-2266.... 1 B
yhill@acom.edu
HILL, Z. JoAnna .... 303-292-0015.. 80 H
zhill@denvercollegeofnursing.edu
HILL, Zach .... 651-638-6050 234 D
z-hill@bethel.edu
HILL-CHEATOM, Petrina 716-851-1120 299 B
cheatom@ecc.edu
HILL-CLARKE, Kandi ..... 901-678-5495 426 G
kyhill@memphis.edu
HILL-FARON, Jennifer ... 850-484-4443 105 H
jhillfaron@pensacolastate.edu
HILL-HANNA, Shantey .. 718-940-5759 314 A
shill4@sjcny.edu
HILL-HANNA, Shantey .. 631-687-1445 314 A
shill4@sjcny.edu
HILL-STANFORD, Holly . 417-328-1725 259 I
hhill@sbuniv.edu
HILLA, Jose .... 707-664-2880.. 34 B
HILLARD, Cecilia, J .... 414-955-8493 493 F
chillard@mcw.edu
HILLE, Jim .... 817-257-7031 448 F
j.hille@tcu.edu
HILLEBRAND, Kayli .... 714-556-3610.. 73 H
kayli.hillebrand@vanguard.edu
HILLER, Renee .... 906-487-2800 228 A
rlhiller@mtu.edu
HILLER-FREUND,
Darby, L .... 937-327-7930 364 D
hillerd@wittenberg.edu
HILLERMAN, Donnie ..... 660-359-3948 257 D
dhillerman@mail.ncmissouri.edu
HILLERY, Barbara .... 516-876-3257 318 C
hilleryb@oldwestbury.edu
HILLESLAND, Michelle .. 253-589-5586 478 J
michelle.hillesland@cptc.edu
HILLGROVE, Jennifer .... 303-751-8700.. 78 D
hillgrove@belrea.edu
HILLIARD, Aaron .... 269-488-4409 225 G
ahilliard@kvcc.edu
HILLIARD, Dianne .... 775-445-3288 271 F
dianne.hilliard@wnc.edu
HILLIARD, Eva .... 510-879-9200.. 60 C
ehilliard@samuelmerritt.edu
HILLIKER, Tommy .... 866-931-4300 258 H
tommy.hilliker@rockbridge.edu
HILLIS, Ed .... 512-863-1066 445 C
hillise@southwestern.edu
HILLIS, Greg .... 575-439-3624 287 D
ghillis@nmsu.edu
HILLIS, Michael .... 805-493-3422.. 29 C
mhillis@callutheran.edu
HILLMAN, Elizabeth, L .. 510-430-2094.. 52 E
bhillman@mills.edu
HILLMAN, George .... 214-887-5261 435 F
ghillman@dts.edu
HILLMAN, Kenna .... 562-938-4016.. 48 F
khillman@lbcc.edu
HILLMAN, Luce .... 802-656-1079 463 A
luce.hillman@uvm.edu
HILLMER, Paul .... 651-641-8215 235 I
hillmer@csp.edu
HILLS, Fred .... 254-299-8602 439 E
fhills@mclennan.edu
HILLS, Megan .... 319-385-6391 167 H
megan.hills@iw.edu
HILLS, Warren, L .... 269-387-3895 233 B
warren.l.hills@wmich.edu
HILLS, Wilfredo .... 787-743-7979 510 H
wihill@suagm.edu
HILLSTROM, Maury ...... 310-377-5501.. 51 C
mhillstrom@marymountcalifornia.edu
HILLYER, Rebecca .... 503-399-8677 372 B
rebecca.hillyer@chemeketa.edu
HILMEY, David .... 716-375-2603 313 C
dhilmey@sbu.edu
HILPRE-FRISCHMAN,
Christina .... 612-767-7055 233 H
christina@alfredadler.edu
HILT, Michael .... 402-554-2232 270 A
mhilt@unomaha.edu
HILTNER, Erin .... 970-248-1908.. 78 J
ehiltner@coloradomesa.edu
HILTON, Adriel .... 504-286-5000 191 C
ahilton@suno.edu
HILTON, Adriel .... 724-830-1076 398 C
ahilton@setonhill.edu
HILTON, Don .... 254-267-7007 441 K
dhilton@rangercollege.edu
HILTON, III, Earl, M ..... 336-334-7686 341 D
hiltone@ncat.edu
HILTON, James, L .... 734-764-9358 231 H
hilton@umich.edu
HILTON, Stacey .... 928-717-7775.. 16 J
stacey.hilton@yc.edu
HILTON, Warren .... 610-683-4327 394 D
hilton@kutztown.edu
HILTON-MORROW,
Wendy .... 309-794-7313 133 C
wendyhilton-morrow@augustana.edu
HILTS, Deb, B .... 607-431-4171 301 A
hiltsd@hartwick.edu
HILVO, Wendy, A .... 920-923-8122 493 D
wahilvo37@marianuniversity.edu
HILWIG, Stephanie .... 719-587-7771.. 77 G
stephaniehilwig@adams.edu
HILYER, Billy, D .... 334-386-7414.... 5 C
bhilyer@faulkner.edu
HIMBEAULT-TAYLOR,
Simone .... 734-764-5132 231 H
shtaylor@umich.edu
HIMBER, Richard .... 985-549-5322 193 A
richard.himber@selu.edu
HIMELEIN, Melissa .... 828-250-3896 342 B
himelein@unca.edu
HIMELFARB, Igor .... 510-250-6113.. 48 C
ihimelfarb@lincolnuca.edu
HIMES, A.C. (Buddy) .... 936-468-2801 445 E
himesac@sfasu.edu
HIMES, Christine .... 312-567-3933 140 A
chimes@iit.edu
HIMES, Shane .... 814-472-3372 397 F
shimes@francis.edu
HIMMELBERGER,
Stacey, J .... 315-859-4416 300 H
shimmelb@hamilton.edu
HIMMELREICH, Ellen .... 607-735-1855 298 H
ehimmelreich@elmira.edu
HIMMELSTEIN, Amos .... 323-259-1347.. 54 I
himmelstein@oxy.edu
HIMON, Kemia .... 410-857-2234 200 F
khimon@mcdaniel.edu
HIMSEL, Christian, R .... 262-243-5700 492 E
christian.himsel@cuw.edu
HINCH, Virginia (Gini) .. 509-359-2329 479 G
vhinch@ewu.edu
HINCKLEY, R. Shane .... 979-458-1729 446 F
shane.hinckley@tamu.edu
HIND, Jonathan, T .... 315-859-4116 300 H
jhind@hamilton.edu
HINDE, Liz .... 303-615-1444.. 81 M
ehinde@msudenver.edu
HINDE, RJ .... 865-974-0684 427 B
rhinde@utk.edu
HINDS, Thomas .... 412-924-1369 396 F
thinds@pts.edu
HINDS-BRUSH,
Kimberly .... 301-687-4121 204 C
kmhindsbrush@frostburg.edu
HINE, Cheryl .... 260-481-6129 160 C
hinec@pfw.edu
HINE, Christopher .... 661-336-5040.. 46 K
christopher.hine@kccd.edu
HINE, James .... 415-502-3037.. 70 D
jim.hine@ucsf.edu
HINE, Mark, L .... 434-592-3240 468 E
mhine@liberty.edu
HINEBAUGH, Kearstin .. 301-387-3000 199 A
kearstin.hinebaugh@garrettcollege.edu
HINEMAN, Sheri .... 712-274-5335 168 E
hineman@morningside.edu
HINERMAN, Nate .... 415-442-7000.. 43 I
HINES, CharMaine .... 313-469-2720 232 E
chines1@wcccd.edu
HINES, Cory .... 325-649-8000 437 G
president@hputx.edu
HINES, Craig .... 312-662-4111 132 G
chines@adler.edu
HINES, Domonique .... 229-500-2909 114 H
domonique.hines@asurams.edu
HINES, Florence .... 315-229-5226 314 D
fhines@stlawu.edu
HINES, Jacquelyn .... 313-831-5200 223 L
jhines@etseminary.edu
HINES, Jean, C .... 804-289-8181 472 C
jhines@richmond.edu
HINES, Joseph .... 908-497-4317 284 D
joseph.hines@ucc.edu
HINES, Kenneth, D .... 919-658-7755 340 G
dhines@umo.edu
HINES, M'Lyn .... 860-932-4056.. 87 E
mhines@qvcc.edu
HINES, Nancy .... 509-777-4638 486 C
nhines@whitworth.edu
HINES, Nancy, A .... 563-333-6377 169 G
hinesnancya@sau.edu
HINES, Patrick .... 919-536-7200 334 C
hinesp@durhamtech.edu
HINES, Rakesia .... 334-229-6810.... 4 A
rhines@alasu.edu
HINES, Ruth .... 857-701-1645 215 G
rhines@rcc.mass.edu
HINES, Scott .... 650-433-3855.. 55 L
shines@paloaltou.edu
HINES, Shanna .... 410-669-9200 200 D
shines@mica.edu
HINES, Susan .... 434-395-2921 468 F
hinessr@longwood.edu
HINES, Terri .... 719-598-0200.. 80 D
HINES, Wendy .... 828-565-4069 335 C
whines@haywood.edu
HINES-GAITHER,
Krishauna .... 336-316-2473 329 D
hinesgaitherkl@guilford.edu
HINEY, Delaine, S .... 712-362-0428 167 B
dhiney@iowalakes.edu
HINGA, Beth, D .... 308-865-8541 269 I
hingabd@unk.edu
HINGA, Gilbert .... 308-865-8528 269 I
hingag2@unk.edu
HINGELBERG, Julie .... 313-664-7494 222 H
julieh@collegeforcreativestudies.edu
HINGORANI, Kamal .... 334-229-4123.... 4 A
khingorani@alasu.edu
HINKEL, Nate .... 844-837-7489.. 22 E
HINKEL, Nate .... 501-686-2951.. 21 E
nhinkel@uasys.edu
HINKLE, Adrian .... 405-789-7661 369 I
adrian.hinkle@swcu.edu
HINKLE, Christina .... 949-582-4605.. 65 D
chinkle@saddleback.edu
HINKLE, Jason .... 661-362-3420.. 38 D
jason.hinkle@canyons.edu
HINKLE, Katerina .... 419-434-4200 364 C
hinklek@winebrenner.edu
HINKLE, Lance .... 405-744-5237 367 G
lance.hinkle@okstate.edu
HINKLE, Sandy, L .... 573-651-2250 259 H
shinkle@semo.edu
HINKLE, Sara .... 610-436-3511 395 D
shinkle@wcupa.edu
HINKLEY, Richard .... 434-592-3077 468 E
rdhinkle@liberty.edu
HINKS, David .... 919-515-6500 342 A
dhinks@ncsu.edu
HINKSON, Avis .... 909-621-8017.. 57 K
avis.hinkson@pomona.edu
HINMAN, Lisa .... 503-581-8600 372 H
lhinman@corban.edu
HINOJOSA, Felix .... 915-831-2623 436 A
fhinojo3@epcc.edu
HINOJOSA, Jason .... 801-585-2677 459 O
jason.hinojosa@utah.edu

HINOJOSA, Joanne .... 909-384-8595.. 60 F jhinojosa@sbccd.cc.ca.us
HINOJOSA, Maggie .... 956-665-2321 455 D maggie.hinojosa@utrgv.edu
HINOJOSA-SEGURA, Veronica .... 512-499-4271 454 H vhinojosasegura@utsystem.edu
HINRICHSEN, Jacqueline .... 402-826-2161 267 A jackie.hinrichsen@doane.edu
HINSHAW, Dana .... 620-665-3322 174 G hinshawd@hutchcc.edu
HINSHAW, Garrett, D .... 828-327-7000 333 B ghinshaw@cvcc.edu
HINSHAW, Jeffrey .... 310-660-3160.. 41 E jhinshaw@elcamino.edu
HINSHAW, Lynn .... 828-898-3473 330 E hinshaw@lmc.edu
HINSHAW, Stephanie .... 800-280-0307 153 E stephanie.hinshaw@ace.edu
HINSON, Bobby .... 850-201-6071 112 C bobby.hinson@tcc.fl.edu
HINSON, Brett .... 615-966-5642 421 B brett.hinson@lipscomb.edu
HINSON, Michael .... 704-991-0300 338 C mhinson4851@stanly.edu
HINSON, Natalie .... 910-788-6361 338 A natalie.hinson@sccvnc.edu
HINTERBERGER, Karl .... 716-286-8323 309 H khinterberger@niagara.edu
HINTERSTOISSER, Tanja .... 802-651-5896 462 A thinterstoisser@champlain.edu
HINTON, Aaron .... 704-406-4101 329 A ahinton2@gardner-webb.edu
HINTON, Armenta .... 717-736-4102 385 B aehinton@hacc.edu
HINTON, Audra .... 501-374-6305.. 20 G audra.hinton@shortercollege.edu
HINTON, C. Royce .... 801-524-8174 459 E hintoncr@ldsbc.edu
HINTON, Conner .... 504-816-8072 190 F chinton@nobts.edu
HINTON, Gregory .... 206-934-3600 483 B gregory.hinton@seattlecolleges.edu
HINTON, Jeff .... 903-223-3005 448 A jeff.hinton@tamut.edu
HINTON, Marie .... 410-209-6072 198 B mhinton@bccc.edu
HINTON, Mary, D .... 540-362-6321 467 H presoffc@hollins.edu
HINTON, Samuel .... 803-793-5154 408 G hintons@denmarktech.edu
HINTON, Toby, R .... 770-534-6257 116 D thinton@brenau.edu
HINTON, Wendy .... 570-208-5900 386 G wendyhinton@kings.edu
HINTON-RIVERA, Jake .. 775-327-2116 271 A jake.hinton-rivera@gbcnv.edu
HINTZ, Alex .... 612-343-4400 242 M ajhintz@northcentral.edu
HINTZ, Carol .... 816-235-1621 261 B hintzc@umkc.edu
HINTZ, Debra .... 231-843-5850 233 A dhintz@westshore.edu
HINTZ, Sharon .... 908-835-2356 284 H hintz@warren.edu
HINTZE, Nate .... 207-725-4244 194 C nhintze@bowdoin.edu
HINZE, Jodey .... 281-649-3130 437 B jhinze@hbu.edu
HIONIDES, David .... 214-818-1374 433 O dhionides@criswell.edu
HIOTT, Henry .... 843-321-1502 410 B hhiott@limestone.edu
HIPES, Barrett .... 212-799-5000 303 E
HIPOLITO, Melvin .... 808-984-3245 130 D mh2350@hawaii.edu
HIPOLITO, Veronica ...... 480-732-7309.. 12 O veronica.hipolito@cgc.edu
HIPP, Joye, G .... 803-786-3178 408 D joyehipp@columbiasc.edu
HIPP, Julie .... 630-844-6503 133 D jhipp@aurora.edu
HIPPEN, Kristi .... 309-457-2327 144 H khippen@monmouthcollege.edu
HIPPISLEY, Andrew .... 316-978-6659 178 D andrew.hippisley@wichita.edu
HIPPS, Kathy .... 423-636-7320 426 E khipps@tusculum.edu
HIRATA, Heather .... 808-932-7369 129 D hiratah@hawaii.edu
HIRNING, Bernell .... 701-774-4231 346 E bernell.hirning@willistonstate.edu
HIRSCH, Alex .... 907-474-7931.. 10 A ahirsch@alaska.edu
HIRSCH, Andy .... 610-328-8534 398 G ahirsch1@swarthmore.edu
HIRSCH, Michael .... 512-505-3125 438 A mlhirsch@htu.edu
HIRSCH, Samuel .... 215-751-8160 381 I shirsch@ccp.edu
HIRSCH, Sarah .... 949-258-7091.. 38 B shirsch3@occ.cccd.edu
HIRSCHFELD, Adam ...... 614-251-4234 358 B hirschfa@ohiodominican.edu
HIRSCHFELD, Chloe ...... 970-542-3126.. 81 N chloe.hirschfeld@morgancc.edu
HIRSCHHORN, Charles . 310-665-6800.. 55 C
HIRSCHI, Jill .... 406-657-1009 265 E jill.hirschi@rocky.edu
HIRSCHLER, Dave .... 740-474-8896 358 A dhirschler@ohiochristian.edu
HIRSCHY, Margaret .... 419-434-4260 364 C hirschym@findlay.edu
HIRSH, Rae, A .... 412-578-6014 380 B rahirsh@carlow.edu
HIRSHMAN, Elliot .... 443-334-2203 202 E
HIRSHON, Arnold .... 216-368-5292 349 D arnold.hirshon@case.edu
HIRST, Liz .... 850-644-1085 110 C lehirst@fsu.edu
HIRST, Martha, K .... 718-817-3120 300 C mhirst1@fordham.edu
HIRST, Steve .... 903-886-5523 447 B steve.hirst@tamuc.edu
HIRT, Samuel .... 540-261-8400 471 B samuel.hirt@svu.edu
HIRT, Sonia, A .... 706-542-8113 126 G sonia.hirt@uga.edu
HIRTLE, Christopher ...... 413-572-5455 213 F chris@westfield.ma.edu
HISCANO, Lisa .... 908-965-2358 284 D hiscano@ucc.edu
HISE, Jeremy .... 580-628-6200 366 J jeremy.hise@noc.edu
HISER, Larry, R .... 740-376-4665 355 E larry.hiser@marietta.edu
HISEY, Richard, M .... 617-747-2018 206 H rhisey@berklee.edu
HISLE, W. Lee .... 860-439-2650.. 87 H wlhis@conncoll.edu
HISLOP, Charlotte .... 619-298-1829.. 65 K
HISSONG, Wesley .... 315-786-6517 303 C whissong@sunyjefferson.edu
HITCHCOCK, Harold .... 937-778-7979 352 D
HITCHCOCK, Marina ...... 570-561-1818 397 H
HITCHCOCK, Patrick ...... 508-831-5577 220 F phitchcock@wpi.edu
HITCHCOCK, Richard .... 907-796-6493.. 10 B rhitchc1@alaska.edu
HITCHELL, Dan .... 860-297-4224.. 89 B dan.hitchell@trincoll.edu
HITCHMAN, Evan .... 315-268-4300 295 F ehitchma@clarkson.edu
HITE, Griffin .... 256-765-4400.... 8 E una@bkstr.com
HITE, Lisa .... 618-252-5400 149 I lisa.hite@sic.edu
HITE, Robert .... 415-458-3726.. 41 C
HITE, Stu .... 620-235-4624 177 A skhite@pittstate.edu
HITECHEW, Chris .... 423-323-3191 425 A
HITES, Michael, H .... 214-768-3805 444 D hites@smu.edu
HITT, Anne .... 248-370-3804 229 I hitt@oakland.edu
HITT, Jennifer .... 508-793-7318 208 C jhitt@clarku.edu
HITT, Richard, J .... 863-784-7036 108 F richard.hitt@southflorida.edu
HITT-MAYO, Jennifer .... 901-321-3465 418 G jhitt@cbu.edu
HITTLE, Ann .... 509-452-5100 482 B ahittle@pnwu.edu
HITZEMAN, Adam .... 312-922-1884 143 G ahitzeman@maccormac.edu
HITZEMAN, Katrina .... 503-253-3443 374 G katrina.hitzeman@ocom.edu
HIVELY, Karla, R .... 304-457-6317 486 E hivelykr@ab.edu
HIX, Ann .... 303-273-3052.. 79 J ahix@mines.edu
HIX, Patty .... 803-754-4100 408 E
HIXON, Courtney .... 270-809-2146 184 D chixon@murraystate.edu
HIXON, Sharon .... 706-272-4594 118 B shixon@daltonstate.edu
HIXSON, Kim .... 301-687-4120 204 C tkhixson@frostburg.edu
HIXSON, Tom .... 909-687-1500.. 43 D tomhixson@gs.edu
HIYANE-BROWN, Kathi . 360-383-3330 486 A presoffice@whatcom.edu
HJALTALIN, Lisa .... 509-434-5275 479 B lisa.hjaltalin@ccs.spokane.edu
HJALTALIN, Lisa .... 509-434-5210 479 D lisa.hjaltalin@ccs.spokane.edu
HJALTALIN, Lisa .... 509-434-5210 479 C lisa.hjaltalin@ccs.spokane.edu
HJELLUM, Wilma .... 531-622-2723 267 G whjellum@mccneb.edu
HJERPE, Karen .... 724-938-4167 393 E hjerpe@calu.edu
HJERPE, Kelsey .... 602-386-4115.. 10 F kelseyhjerpe@arizonachristian.edu
HLADIS, Jirka .... 303-245-4702.. 82 A jirka@naropa.edu
HLAVACEK, Chris .... 919-761-2100 340 D chlavacek@sebts.edu
HLAVACEK, Tracy .... 605-882-5284 415 D tracy.hlavacek@lakeareatech.edu
HLAVENKA, Lawrence ... 201-689-7057 275 H lhlavenka@bergen.edu
HLAVIN, Karen .... 847-543-2384 136 A adr016@clcillinois.edu
HLEBASKO, Julie .... 951-571-6332.. 59 B julie.hlebasko@mvc.edu
HLEBOWITSH, Peter ...... 205-348-6052.... 7 G peter.hleb@ua.edu
HLINAK, Matthew, J ...... 773-612-5797 137 C mhlinak@dom.edu
HLUBB, Emma .... 931-424-7366 427 E ehlubb@utsouthern.edu
HLUBB, James, R .... 931-424-7379 427 E jhlubb@utsouthern.edu
HLUCH, Dale, A .... 330-325-6191 357 D dhluch@neomed.edu
HO, Co .... 714-992-7021.. 54 C cho@fullcoll.edu
HO, Henry .... 615-353-3231 424 G henry.ho@nscc.edu
HO, Katy, W .... 971-722-4005 375 D kho@pcc.edu
HO, Nan .... 925-424-1182.. 35 K nho@laspositascollege.edu
HO, Sam .... 408-223-6798.. 62 F sam.ho@sjeccd.edu
HO, Sandra .... 603-427-7614 272 J sho@ccsnh.edu
HO, Shuk-Mei .... 501-686-7000.. 22 B
HO-A, Carla .... 303-492-3224.. 84 B carla.ho-a@colorado.edu
HOAG, David, A .... 863-638-7209 114 A david.hoag@warner.edu
HOAG, Jamie, D .... 508-793-2011 208 D jhoag@holycross.edu
HOAG, William .... 857-701-1380 215 G whoag@rcc.mass.edu
HOAGLAND, Andrea ..... 517-483-1077 226 H hoaglana@lcc.edu
HOAGLAND, Christopher .... 610-341-5934 383 B 0713mgr@follett.com
HOANG, Ann, D .... 973-596-5798 279 E ann.d.hoang@njit.edu
HOANG, Christina .... 714-816-0366.. 68 E christina.hoang@trident.edu
HOANG, Harold, T .... 800-443-9266 503 D harold.hoang@usafa.edu
HOANG, Minh-Ha .... 619-260-4506.. 72 I mhoang@sandiego.edu
HOANG, SVD, Thang .... 563-876-3353 165 H hcthang@dwci.edu
HOANG POE, Linh .... 808-734-9570 129 H lhoang@hawaii.edu
HOARD, Phil .... 317-896-9324 161 F phoard@ubca.org
HOBAN, Elizabeth .... 973-328-5160 276 J ehoban@ccm.edu
HOBAN, Patricia, K .... 503-375-5477 377 F phoban@willamette.edu
HOBART, Denise .... 320-733-2500 347 F
HOBART, Paul .... 231-591-2376 224 A paulhobart@ferris.edu
HOBART, Will .... 361-825-2616 447 C will.hobart@tamucc.edu
HOBBS, Bill .... 301-696-3622 199 E hobbs@hood.edu
HOBBS, Brenna .... 541-440-4617 376 G brenna.hobbs@umpqua.edu
HOBBS, Clinton, G .... 478-757-5161 127 F chobbs@wesleyancollege.edu
HOBBS, David .... 503-943-7306 377 A hobbsd@up.edu
HOBBS, III, James, P ... 504-671-5510 188 B jhobbs@dcc.edu
HOBBS, Jeanie .... 817-598-6267 457 J jhobbs@wc.edu
HOBBS, Jennifer .... 212-229-5600 308 A hobbsj@newschool.edu
HOBBS, Jessica, W ...... 910-630-7005 331 E jhobbs@methodist.edu
HOBBS, Lynn .... 410-626-2504 202 A lynn.hobbs@sjc.edu
HOBBS, Morgan .... 215-972-2199 392 T mhobbs@pafa.edu
HOBBS, Patrick, E .... 732-445-8610 282 A patrick.hobbs@rutgers.edu
HOBBS, Phillip, M .... 205-853-1200.... 2 G mhobbs@jeffersonstate.edu
HOBBS, Ryan .... 435-879-4653 460 B ryan.hobbs@dixie.edu
HOBBS, Tameka, B .... 305-626-3955 100 D tameka.hobbs@fmuniv.edu
HOBBS, Tommy .... 205-929-3521.... 2 H thobbs@lawsonstate.edu
HOBBS, Valerie .... 503-253-3443 374 G valerie.hobbs@ocom.edu
HOBBS, III, William ...... 305-430-1166 100 D william.hobbs@fmuniv.edu
HOBBY, Brett .... 713-221-5075 453 A hobbyb@uhd.edu
HOBBY-MEARS, Michelle .... 949-480-4134.. 64 G mhobby@soka.edu
HOBERMAN, Chaim ...... 516-255-4700 311 J
HOBERMAN, Evan .... 646-565-6000 322 F evan.hoberman@touro.edu
HOBERMAN, Evan .... 646-565-6000 322 G evan.hoberman@touro.edu
HOBGOOD, Kathy, B .... 864-656-1151 407 E kbhob@clemson.edu
HOBGOOD, Sarah .... 757-594-8763 465 M sarah.hobgood@cnu.edu
HOBIN, Caron, T .... 413-565-1333 206 D chobin@baypath.edu
HOBLER, Dean .... 419-998-3103 362 F dahobler@unoh.edu
HOBLET, Kent, H .... 662-325-1418 247 F hoblet@cvm.msstate.edu
HOBSON, Aaron .... 608-890-0158 495 D aaron.hobson@wisc.edu
HOBSON, Elizabeth .... 847-214-6945 137 F ehobson@elgin.edu
HOBSON, Jack .... 657-278-2935.. 31 C jhobson@fullerton.edu
HOBSON, Lynn, M .... 620-341-5267 173 F lhobson@emporia.edu
HOBSON, Paula Lee ...... 607-431-4026 301 A hobsonp@hartwick.edu
HOBSON, Sheila .... 301-860-3451 204 A shobson@bowiestate.edu
HOBSON, Tricia .... 405-422-1235 369 A hobsont@redlandscc.edu
HOBUS, Mary .... 785-594-6451 171 F
HOBYAK, Michael, S .... 215-785-0111 392 S
HOCHMAN, Alex .... 415-422-2437.. 72 J ahochman@usfca.edu
HOCHNER, Rose .... 713-500-3824 456 B rose.hochner@uth.tmc.edu
HOCHSTEIN, Dale .... 212-517-0571 305 E phochstein@mmm.edu
HOCHSTEIN, Jessica ..... 402-399-2664 266 F jhochstein@csm.edu
HOCHSTETLER, Stephanie .... 574-807-7354 154 B stephanie.hochstetler@betheluniversity.edu
HOCK, Joan .... 215-489-2975 382 B joan.hock@delval.edu
HOCKADAY, David .... 660-473-6089 259 M dhockaday@sfccmo.edu
HOCKENBERRY, Frederick .... 301-846-2544 198 I fhockenberry@frederick.edu
HOCKENHULL, Ben .... 440-775-6727 357 G ben.hockenhull@oberlin.edu
HOCKER, Michael, B .... 956-296-1445 455 D michael.hocker@utrgv.edu
HOCKMAN, Joan .... 814-371-2090 399 H jhockman@triangle-tech.edu

HOFSTETTER, Dale .... 513-745-8308 362 A
hofsteda@uc.edu
HOFSTROM, Hillary, E .. 570-326-3761 392W
heh1@pct.edu
HOGAN, Amy .... 785-242-5200 176 I
amy.hogan@ottawa.edu
HOGAN, Anne .... 901-678-2350 426 G
anne.hogan@memphis.edu
HOGAN, Bill .... 206-296-5451 484 A
hoganw@seattleu.edu
HOGAN, Cara .... 432-335-6404 441 A
chogan@odessa.edu
HOGAN, Carrie .... 518-783-2554 315 E
chogan@siena.edu
HOGAN, Cheryl .... 231-843-5864 233 A
clhogan@westshore.edu
HOGAN, Christopher, J 828-262-3180 340 I
hogancj@appstate.edu
HOGAN, Edward .... 314-792-6100 254 F
HOGAN, Gina .... 626-914-8855.. 36 J
ghogan@citruscollege.edu
HOGAN, Gregory .... 207-221-4321 197 E
ghogan@une.edu
HOGAN, James .... 704-878-4321 336 C
jhogan@mitchellcc.edu
HOGAN, Jennifer .... 810-762-3000 232 A
jhogan@umich.edu
HOGAN, Jennifer .... 315-781-3388 301 F
hogan@hws.edu
HOGAN, John .... 501-760-4200.. 20 A
john.hogan@np.edu
HOGAN, Jordyn .... 260-481-0186 160 C
newmanj@pfw.edu
HOGAN, Judith .... 781-280-3816 215 B
hoganj@middlesex.mass.edu
HOGAN, Kay .... 850-973-1605 104 L
hogank@nfc.edu
HOGAN, Kimberly .... 860-343-5731.. 87 A
khogan@mxcc.edu
HOGAN, Kristen .... 212-853-1795 291 A
khogan@barnard.edu
HOGAN, Lesley .... 425-235-7873 482 H
lhogan@rtc.edu
HOGAN, Matthew .... 718-522-2300 313 E
HOGAN, Melissa .... 847-330-4503 148 E
mhogan03@roosevelt.edu
HOGAN, Pashia .... 423-354-2425 425 A
phhogan@northeaststate.edu
HOGAN, Patrick, N .... 301-445-1927 202 G
phogan@usmd.edu
HOGAN, Paul .... 603-271-6484 273 A
phogan@ccsnh.edu
HOGAN, Robert .... 908-709-7151 284 D
robert.hogan@ucc.edu
HOGAN, Ryan .... 229-333-5791 127 E
rmhogan@valdosta.edu
HOGAN, Sharon, K .... 503-943-8677 377 A
hogans@up.edu
HOGAN, Susan, S .... 413-597-4204 220 D
susan.s.hogan@williams.edu
HOGAN, Travis .... 303-360-4722.. 80 E
travis.hogan@ccaurora.edu
HOGAN, Whitney .... 207-725-3184 194 C
HOGANS, Karen .... 352-435-6358 103 U
hogansk@lssc.edu
HOGENCAMP, Kelly ...... 909-607-2981.. 63 F
khogenca@scrippscollege.edu
HOGENSON, Liz .... 763-424-0902 240 A
lhogenson@nhcc.edu
HOGGARD, Justin .... 361-354-2200 432 K
jhoggard@coastalbend.edu
HOGGATT, Michael .... 405-682-1611 367 D
michael.d.hoggatt@occc.edu
HOGLE, Paul .... 216-791-5000 350 I
paul.hogle@cim.edu
HOGUE, Dale, A .... 719-333-2163 503 D
dale.hogue@usafa.edu
HOGUE, Eric .... 303-963-3093.. 78 H
ehogue@ccu.edu
HOGUE, Jason .... 402-872-2429 268 E
jhogue@peru.edu
HOGUE, Laurel .... 660-543-4984 260 G
lhogue@ucmo.edu
HOGUE, Matthew, L ..... 843-349-2813 408 A
dhogue@coastal.edu
HOGUE, Michael, D ...... 909-558-1300.. 48 E
mhogue@llu.edu
HOGUE, Natasa .... 786-331-1000 104 H
library@maufl.edu
HOGUE, Terri .... 303-273-3000.. 79 J
HOGUE, Tiffany .... 254-710-3555 431 E
tiffany_hogue@baylor.edu
HOHAM, Lindsey .... 315-228-7438 296 E
lhoham@colgate.edu
HOHBERG, Tonian .... 213-624-1200.. 42 B
thohberg@fidm.edu
HOHENSTEIN, Heather .. 218-235-2172 241 E
heather.hohenstein@vcc.edu
HOHERTZ, Cherie, L ..... 972-721-5040 452 B
chohertz@udallas.edu
HOHL, Kathleen, M ...... 414-410-4202 491 I
kghohl@stritch.edu
HOHMAN, Adam .... 260-982-5235 159 J
arhohman@manchester.edu
HOHN, Daniel .... 303-797-5753.. 77 I
daniel.hohn@arapahoe.edu
HOI, Samuel .... 410-225-2237 200 D
president@mica.edu
HOIE, Steffanie .... 619-260-7414.. 72 I
shoie@sandiego.edu
HOILAND, Eric .... 530-893-7528.. 27 C
hoilander@butte.edu
HOILAND, Erin .... 360-412-6149 482 I
ehoiland@stmartin.edu
HOILMAN, Sandra, K .... 828-448-6025 339 A
shoilman@wpcc.edu
HOIT, Marc, I .... 919-515-0141 342 A
mark_hoit@ncsu.edu
HOJAN, Elizabeth, M .... 262-554-2010 494 A
HOJAN-CLARK, Jane ..... 212-853-0469 297 C
jh3574@columbia.edu
HOJSACK, Dana .... 619-849-2678.. 57 J
danahojsack@pointloma.edu
HOKANSON, SND,
Karen .... 617-735-9976 209 D
hokanson@emmanuel.edu
HOKE, Chris .... 701-252-3467 347 B
choke@uj.edu
HOKE, Cynthia .... 912-358-4000 125 A
hokec@savannahstate.edu
HOKE, Franklin .... 212-327-8998 312 G
fhoke@rockefeller.edu
HOKE, Kay .... 765-658-4394 154 J
kayhoke@depauw.edu
HOKE, Thomas .... 407-708-2224 108 D
hoket@seminolestate.edu
HOKOANA, Lui .... 808-984-3636 130 D
lhokoana@hawaii.edu
HOLADAY, Stephanie .... 304-326-1311 487 I
stephanie.holaday@salemu.edu
HOLAHAN, Barbara .... 516-686-7755 308 I
bholahan@nyit.edu
HOLAHAN, Cindy .... 262-524-7361 492 A
cholahan@carrollu.edu
HOLAK, Susan, L .... 718-982-2920 293 E
schoolofbusiness@csi.cuny.edu
HOLAN, Craig .... 618-650-2560 150 C
cholan@siue.edu
HOLANDA, Shelly .... 800-686-1883 222 G
sholanda@cleary.edu
HOLBECK, Michael .... 605-688-4455 417 A
michael.holbeck@sdstate.edu
HOLBERG, John .... 706-419-1565 118 A
john.holberg@covenant.edu
HOLBROOK, Catherine . 413-662-5231 213 C
catherine.holbrook@mcla.edu
HOLBROOK, Jamirae .... 606-539-4120 185 E
HOLBROOK, Jennifer .... 870-230-5275.. 19 D
holbroj@hsu.edu
HOLBROOK, Karen .... 941-359-4340 111 C
kholbrook@usf.edu
HOLBROOK, Peter .... 419-448-5864 361 D
holbrookpj@tiffin.edu
HOLBROOK, Tim .... 404-712-0353 118 E
tholbrook@emory.edu
HOLCOMB, David .... 254-295-4184 453 D
dholcomb@umhb.edu
HOLCOMB, David .... 423-775-7136 418 D
dholcomb8093@bryan.edu
HOLCOMB, Debra .... 903-510-2380 452 A
debra.holcomb@tjc.edu
HOLCOMB, John .... 216-687-5548 350 J
j.p.holcomb@csuohio.edu
HOLCOMB, John, P .... 216-687-9370 350 J
j.p.holcomb@csuohio.edu
HOLCOMB, Mark, E ...... 815-939-5236 147 A
mholcomb@olivet.edu
HOLCOMB, Rich, S .... 734-647-5574 231 H
rsholcom@umich.edu
HOLCOMB, Robert .... 707-527-4615.. 63 D
rholcomb@santarosa.edu
HOLCOMB, Todd .... 319-296-4201 166 H
todd.holcomb@hawkeyecollege.edu
HOLCOMB-MCCOY,
Cheryl .... 202-885-3720.. 91 F
cholcomb@american.edu
HOLCOMBE, Andrea ...... 904-620-2552 111 B
andrea.holcombe@unf.edu
HOLCOMBE, Bobby .... 864-424-8024 413 H
reholcom@mailbox.sc.edu
HOLCOMBE, Kara .... 503-554-2189 373 A
kholcombe@georgefox.edu
HOLCOMBE, Randall ..... 808-586-3013 129 E
rfh6979@hawaii.edu
HOLDEMAN, Lisa, K ..... 713-743-8408 452 C
lkholdeman@uh.edu
HOLDEMAN, Lisa, K ..... 713-743-0945 452 D
lkholdeman@uh.edu
HOLDEN, Andrea .... 413-265-2454 208 E
holdena@elms.edu
HOLDEN, Brad .... 541-278-5783 371 H
bholden@bluecc.edu
HOLDEN, Cheryl .... 509-542-4761 479 A
cholden@columbiabasin.edu
HOLDEN, Christy .... 719-846-5550.. 83 L
christy.holden@trinidadstate.edu
HOLDEN, Dave .... 618-664-6750 138 F
dave.holden@greenville.edu
HOLDEN, Ginger .... 209-954-5040.. 61 G
gholden@deltacollege.edu
HOLDEN, Joan .... 773-508-2530 143 C
jholde1@luc.edu
HOLDEN, Joseph, M .... 714-966-8500.. 74 C
info@ves.edu
HOLDEN, Kimberly .... 706-771-4819 115 J
kimberly.holden@augustatech.edu
HOLDEN, Kurt, A .... 937-775-2056 364 E
kurt.holden@wright.edu
HOLDEN, Larry .... 615-327-6339 421 D
lholden@mmc.edu
HOLDEN, Leslie .... 540-365-4460 467 B
lholden@ferrum.edu
HOLDEN, Randy .... 336-334-3376 343 A
rmholden@uncg.edu
HOLDEN, Ronald .... 330-823-2138 362 E
holdenrf@mountunion.edu
HOLDEN, Wesley .... 772-546-5534 102 C
wesleyholden@hsbc.edu
HOLDEN-DUFFY,
Cheryl .... 410-651-6460 203 D
clduffy@umes.edu
HOLDER, Amy .... 931-393-1643 424 F
aholder@mscc.edu
HOLDER, Beth .... 910-521-6221 343 B
beth.holder@uncp.edu
HOLDER, Candace .... 336-386-3382 338 D
holderc@surry.edu
HOLDER, Connie .... 573-518-2119 256 D
cholder@mineralarea.edu
HOLDER, Debra .... 817-274-4284 431 F
dholder@bhcarroll.edu
HOLDER, Kenneth .... 251-405-7172.... 1 E
kholder@bishop.edu
HOLDER, Mike .... 405-744-7231 367 G
mike.holder@okstate.edu
HOLDER, Mitchell .... 660-359-3948 257 D
mholder@mail.ncmissouri.edu
HOLDERMAN, John .... 918-631-3092 371 C
john-holderman@utulsa.edu
HOLDING, Frederick ..... 910-962-1123 343 C
holdingf@uncw.edu
HOLDNAK, John, R .... 850-872-3800 101 N
jholdnak@gulfcoast.edu
HOLFORD, Kenneth ...... 219-989-2446 160 D
cholford@pnw.edu
HOLGARD, Austin, J ..... 701-355-8297 347 C
ajholgard@umary.edu
HOLIDAY, Jana .... 978-468-7111 210 C
jholiday@gordonconwell.edu
HOLIDAY-GOODMAN,
Monica .... 419-383-1933 363 B
monica.holiday-goodman@utoledo.edu
HOLIFIELD, Brenda .... 870-780-1227.. 17 B
bholifield@smail.anc.edu
HOLIGROCKI, Rick .... 805-493-3528.. 29 C
rholigrocki@callutheran.edu
HOLL, Karolina .... 315-792-3179 324 B
kmholl@utica.edu
HOLLAAR, Jean .... 218-477-2070 239 E
jean.hollaar@mnstate.edu
HOLLADAY, Allison .... 570-321-4220 389 B
holladay@lycoming.edu
HOLLAND, Beth .... 828-726-2200 332 G
bholland@cccti.edu
HOLLAND, Colleen .... 417-455-5588 252 E
colleenholland@crowder.edu
HOLLAND, Frederick ..... 888-775-1514.. 68 I
HOLLAND, Hailey .... 208-535-5622 131 B
hailey.holland@cei.edu
HOLLAND, Jeff .... 304-424-8229 490 F
jeff.holland@wvup.edu
HOLLAND, Karen .... 330-569-5109 353 G
hollandk@hiram.edu
HOLLAND, Kevin .... 940-552-6291 457 C
kholland@vernoncollege.edu
HOLLAND, Kimberly ...... 334-727-8881.... 7 D
kholland@tuskegee.edu
HOLLAND, Leslie .... 901-722-3238 423 G
lholland@sco.edu
HOLLAND, Linda .... 501-354-7565.. 23 A
holland@uaccm.edu
HOLLAND, Mario .... 405-466-3370 366 C
mario.holland@langston.edu
HOLLAND, Mary .... 937-775-5200 364 E
mary.holland@wright.edu
HOLLAND, Richard .... 863-583-9050 110 B
HOLLAND, Sam .... 214-768-2880 444 D
sholland@smu.edu
HOLLAND, Scott .... 800-287-8822 154 A
hollasc@bethanyseminary.edu
HOLLAND, Sharon .... 301-295-3578 503 C
sharon.holland@usuhs.edu
HOLLAND, Steven, C .... 520-621-1556.. 16 D
sholland@arizona.edu
HOLLAND, Tina .... 225-768-1710 187 B
tina.holland@franu.edu
HOLLAND, Tracey .... 845-437-7360 324 C
trholland@vassar.edu
HOLLAND, Wentreal ...... 312-922-1884 143 G
wholland@maccormac.edu
HOLLANDER, Lisa .... 219-464-6882 162 D
lisa.hollander@valpo.edu
HOLLANDSWORTH,
Heather .... 540-365-4282 467 B
hhollandsworth@ferrum.edu
HOLLAWAY, Jamie .... 319-352-8521 170 J
jamie.hollaway@wartburg.edu
HOLLEMAN, Clate .... 662-472-9087 246 D
cholleman@holmescc.edu
HOLLEMON, John .... 434-223-7154 467 F
jhollemon@hsc.edu
HOLLENBAUGH, David . 724-805-2590 398 A
david.hollenbaugh@stvincent.edu
HOLLENBAUGH, David . 724-805-2590 397 I
david.hollenbaugh@stvincent.edu
HOLLENBECK, Nicole .... 480-627-5384.. 15 N
nhollenbeck@taliesin.edu
HOLLENBECK, Peter ...... 765-494-9709 160 B
phollenb@purdue.edu
HOLLENBERGER, Leah .. 802-635-1251 463 G
leah.hollenberger@northernvermont.
edu
HOLLENHORST, Steven . 360-650-3521 485 I
steve.hollenhorst@wwu.edu
HOLLER, Stacy .... 301-387-3045 199 A
stacy.holler@garrettcollege.edu
HOLLER, Steven .... 503-251-0332 374 C
sholler@multnomah.edu
HOLLERAN, Meghan ..... 660-263-4100 257 B
meghanh@macc.edu
HOLLERICH, Mary .... 612-330-1603 234 A
holleric@augsburg.edu
HOLLEY, Angela, M ...... 757-683-4401 469 B
amholley@odu.edu
HOLLEY, Betty .... 937-971-2860 359 K
bholley@payneseminary.edu
HOLLEY, Chelsea .... 404-270-5279 126 B
chelsea.holley@spelman.edu
HOLLEY, John .... 256-306-2865.... 1 F
john.holley@calhoun.edu
HOLLEY, Stephanie .... 972-780-3600 454 A
stephanie.holley@untdallas.edu
HOLLEY, Steven .... 909-607-9192.. 37 B
steven.holley@claremont.edu
HOLLEY, Steven .... 662-915-7200 249 D
vcaf@olemiss.edu
HOLLEY, Suzy .... 813-253-7116 102 B
sholley7@hccfl.edu
HOLLEY, Tracy, S .... 540-365-4216 467 B
tholley@ferrum.edu
HOLLEY-WALKER,
Danielle, R .... 202-806-8000.. 92 F
danielle.holley-walker@howard.edu
HOLLIDAY, Chrissy .... 719-549-2645.. 80 B
chrissy.holliday@csupueblo.edu
HOLLIDAY, Deann .... 425-352-8324 478 D
dholliday@cascadia.edu
HOLLIDAY, Greg .... 256-233-8106.... 4 C
greg.holliday@athens.edu
HOLLIDAY, Lisa, C .... 503-370-6574 377 F
lcjones@willamette.edu

HOLT, Christine .... 870-777-5722.. 22 I
christine.holt@uaht.edu
HOLT, Christine, J .... 573-882-2011 261 A
holtcj@umsystem.edu
HOLT, Claudette .... 501-205-8840.. 18 H
cholt@cbc.edu
HOLT, Daniel .... 816-415-5977 262 F
holtd@william.jewell.edu
HOLT, Felicia, P .... 336-322-2101 336 G
felicia.holt@piedmontcc.edu
HOLT, Gail, W .... 413-542-2296 205 G
finaid@amherst.edu
HOLT, Greg .... 931-372-6062 426 B
gholt@tntech.edu
HOLT, Herman .... 828-250-3880 342 B
hholt@unca.edu
HOLT, Jody .... 308-865-8702 269 I
holtj@unk.edu
HOLT, Karen .... 210-297-7638 430 L
HOLT, Mary Margaret ... 405-325-7370 370 K
marymholt@ou.edu
HOLT, Melissa .... 573-288-6417 252 F
mholt@culver.edu
HOLT, Mike .... 303-871-2463.. 84 E
mholt@du.edu
HOLT, Rosalind .... 770-216-2960 121 I
rholt@ict.edu
HOLT, Ruth Ann .... 931-540-2750 424 C
rholt@columbiastate.edu
HOLT, Ryan, C .... 828-641-0505 327 B
holtrc@brevard.edu
HOLT, Sam .... 580-387-7311 366 E
sholt@mscok.edu
HOLT, Shari .... 870-743-3000.. 20 B
sholt@northark.edu
HOLT, Tina .... 706-419-1275 118 A
tina.holt@covenant.edu
HOLT, II, William, G ..... 334-953-5613 502 D
HOLTE, Lane .... 920-924-3163 499 D
lholte@morainepark.edu
HOLTEN, Kathryn .... 828-641-0322 327 B
holtenki@brevard.edu
HOLTGRAVE, David .... 518-402-0281 316 A
dholtgrave@albany.edu
HOLTGREIVE, Shaun ..... 989-774-3346 222 E
holtg1s@cmich.edu
HOLTGREN, Shawn, M . 574-807-7215 154 B
holtgrs@betheluniversity.edu
HOLTHAUS, Barbara ...... 217-641-4104 141 A
bholthaus@jwcc.edu
HOLTHAUS, Cynthia ..... 785-670-1560 178 C
cynthia.holthaus@washburn.edu
HOLTHOUSER,
David, M .... 704-894-2220 328 E
daholthouser@davidson.edu
HOLTMAN, Kaity .... 660-944-2823 251 J
communications@conception.edu
HOLTMANN, Miranda ... 503-251-5712 377 B
mholtmann@uws.edu
HOLTMEYER, Donna ..... 217-228-5432 147 F
holtmda@quincy.edu
HOLTMYER-JONES,
Larissa .... 515-294-6511 163 G
larissah@foundation.iastate.edu
HOLTON, Benjamin .... 404-894-1420 119 E
benjamin.holton@health.gatech.edu
HOLTON, Kristina .... 541-917-4416 373 G
holtonk@linnbenton.edu
HOLTROP, Steve .... 712-722-6214 165 I
steve.holtrop@dordt.edu
HOLTSCHNEIDER, CM,
Dennis, H .... 312-362-8712 136 H
dholtsch@depaul.edu
HOLTSCLAW, Roger ...... 423-869-7006 421 A
roger.holtsclaw@lmunet.edu
HOLTSCLAW, Sarah .... 937-481-2401 364 A
sarah_holtsclaw@wilmington.edu
HOLTZ, Daniel, F .... 320-222-5205 240 F
daniel.holtz@ridgewater.edu
HOLTZ, Edwin .... 712-325-3227 167 I
eholtz@iwcc.edu
HOLTZ, Ryan .... 410-706-7481 203 A
rholtz@umaryland.edu
HOLTZCLAW, Mike .... 650-574-6161.. 62 K
HOLTZCLAW, Rhonda ... 239-590-1037 109 K
rholtzcl@fgcu.edu
HOLTZHAUSEN, Derina . 409-880-8137 449 G
derina.holtzhausen@lamar.edu
HOLUBIK, Donna .... 734-487-0455 223 K
dholubik@emich.edu
HOLUP, Theresa .... 419-824-3809 355 C
tholup@lourdes.edu
HOLVERTON, Laura .... 408-848-4743.. 43 E
HOLVEY BOWLES,
Joanna .... 315-228-7216 296 E
jholveybowles@colgate.edu
HOLWERDA, Jane .... 620-227-9359 173 D
jholwerda@dc3.edu
HOLWICK, Jana, W .... 770-426-2697 122 C
jana.holwick@life.edu
HOLYFIELD, Patrick ...... 704-991-0235 338 C
pholyfield8286@stanly.edu
HOLZ, Marina .... 914-594-4110 309 B
mholz@nymc.edu
HOLZ, Richard .... 303-273-3003.. 79 J
rholz@mines.edu
HOLZ-CLAUSE, Mary ..... 218-281-8343 244 A
mhclause@umn.edu
HOLZBERLEIN, Anne ..... 405-974-2770 370 I
aholzberlein@uco.edu
HOLZHEUSER,
Christina .... 361-825-3065 447 C
christina.holzheuser@tamucc.edu
HOLZMER, OSF,
M. Anita .... 260-399-7700 162 B
aholzmer@sf.edu
HOMAN, Elizabeth, S .... 443-518-4073 199 F
ehoman@howardcc.edu
HOMAN, Judi .... 901-375-4400 422 A
judihoman@midsouthchristian.edu
HOMAN, Pamela .... 605-274-5016 414 G
pamela.homan@augie.edu
HOMAN, Vimla .... 708-524-6490 137 C
vhoman@dom.edu
HOMANY, Garry .... 216-397-1982 353 O
ghomany@jcu.edu
HOMARD, Jennifer .... 352-395-5493 108 A
jen.homard@sfcollege.edu
HOMER, Cory .... 973-300-2116 284 A
chomer@sussex.edu
HOMER, Rollin .... 626-396-2263.. 26 B
rollin.homer@artcenter.edu
HOMER, Stephanie .... 503-338-2428 372 D
shomer@clatsopcc.edu
HOMFELDT, Mike .... 541-880-2244 373 C
homfeldt@klamathcc.edu
HOMICH, John .... 617-627-6333 219 C
john.homich@tufts.edu
HOMOLKA, Karen, K ..... 217-245-3094 139 C
khomolk@ic.edu
HOMS, Raul .... 787-288-1118 510 I
HOMSEY, David .... 518-631-9852 295 F
dhomsey@clarkson.edu
HONADEL, Tim .... 661-362-3699.. 38 D
tim.honadel@canyons.edu
HONAKER, Lisa .... 609-652-4505 283 E
lisa.honaker@stockton.edu
HONAN, David .... 607-255-8945 297 F
HONAN, Lisa .... 203-932-7264.. 89 H
lhonan@newhaven.edu
HONDA, Herminia .... 323-409-6301.. 50 A
hhonda@dhs.lacounty.gov
HONDA, Hirosuke .... 207-621-3216 196 H
hirosuke.honda@maine.edu
HONEBRINK, Emily .... 952-446-4112 235 J
honebrinke@crown.edu
HONEGAN, Rhonda ...... 404-270-5075 126 B
rhonegan@spelman.edu
HONEYCUTT,
Andrew, E .... 714-772-3330.. 25 M
HONEYCUTT, Del Rey ... 716-375-2310 313 C
dhoneycu@sbu.edu
HONEYCUTT, Steven ..... 336-334-4182 343 A
steve_honeycutt@uncg.edu
HONG, Barbara, S .... 956-326-2134 446 E
barbara.hong@tamiu.edu
HONG, Benjamin .... 909-671-4038.. 34 F
HONG, Ireen .... 213-293-1771.. 75 G
HONG, Luoluo .... 404-385-8772 119 E
vp_sewb@gatech.edu
HONG, Marcus .... 502-895-3411 183 H
mhong@lpts.edu
HONG, Mary, F .... 443-518-3823 199 F
mhong@howardcc.edu
HONG, Michael .... 323-860-1122.. 53 D
hongm@mi.edu
HONG, Rebecca .... 310-338-7371.. 51 A
rebecca.hong@lmu.edu
HONG, Sung Wook .... 512-444-8082 448 H
whong@thsu.edu
HONG, Tran .... 951-343-3907.. 27 G
thong@calbaptist.edu
HONG, Ye (Solar) .... 218-755-3773 237 F
ye.hong@bemidjistate.edu
HONG, Z. George .... 718-817-0029 300 C
zhong4@fordham.edu
HONIGFORD, Kevin ...... 317-921-4749 158 D
khonigford@ivytech.edu
HONNELL, Cherie .... 503-494-7878 374 H
acad@ohsu.edu
HONORA, Angela .... 504-816-5308 186 I
ahonora@dillard.edu
HONOREE, Nicole .... 504-568-2587 189 H
nhonor@lsuhsc.edu
HOO, Karlene .... 509-313-6117 480 F
hook@gonzaga.edu
HOOD, Amanda .... 601-643-8619 245 F
amanda.hood@colin.edu
HOOD, Chester .... 850-599-3796 109 I
chester.hood@famu.edu
HOOD, David .... 973-655-4280 279 B
hoodd@montclair.edu
HOOD, Donna .... 828-395-1404 335 D
dhood@isothermal.edu
HOOD, Jean .... 817-272-5554 454 I
jmhood@uta.edu
HOOD, Jim, W .... 336-316-2146 329 D
president@guilford.edu
HOOD, Marcia .... 229-500-2116 114 H
marcia.hood@asurams.edu
HOOD, Mattie .... 850-599-3203 109 I
mattie.hood@famu.edu
HOOD, Mike .... 903-233-4115 439 A
mikehood@letu.edu
HOOD, Scott, W .... 207-725-3256 194 C
shood@bowdoin.edu
HOOD, Tim .... 989-386-6602 228 B
thood@midmich.edu
HOOD, W.C. (Chip) .... 864-656-3414 407 E
chip@clemson.edu
HOOGEWERF, Arlene .... 616-526-8668 222 C
ahoogewe@calvin.edu
HOOK, Amy .... 617-353-2399 207 E
amyhook@bu.edu
HOOKE, Ruthanna .... 703-370-6600 476 E
HOOKER, John .... 352-395-5722 108 A
john.hooker@sfcollege.edu
HOOKER, Kendricks ...... 608-243-4088 499 A
khooker@madisoncollege.edu
HOOKER, Steven, P ...... 619-594-6516.. 33 D
shooker@sdsu.edu
HOOKS, Deborah .... 850-484-2116 105 H
dhooks@pensacolastate.edu
HOOKS, Jeffery .... 269-783-2159 231 A
jhooks@swmich.edu
HOOKS, Karin .... 440-366-7102 355 B
HOOKS, Rebecca .... 704-216-3488 337 F
rebecca.hooks@rccc.edu
HOOLE, Thomas .... 978-934-3509 212 B
thomas_hoole@uml.edu
HOOPER, Brooke .... 757-446-7439 466 D
hooperab@evms.edu
HOOPER, Bryan .... 850-201-8169 112 C
bryan.hooper@tcc.fl.edu
HOOPER, Christy .... 615-966-1000 421 B
christy.hooper@lipscomb.edu
HOOPER, Cynthia .... 713-623-2040 430 E
HOOPER, Dave .... 434-395-2099 468 F
hooperdv@longwood.edu
HOOPER, Elizabeth, A ... 253-535-7337 482 A
hooperea@plu.edu
HOOPER, Heath .... 706-292-3906 125 C
hhooper@shorter.edu
HOOPER, Mary, A .... 404-880-8363 117 C
mhooper@cau.edu
HOOPER, Nicholas .... 269-927-8763 226 F
nhooper@lakemichigancollege.edu
HOOPER, Ryan .... 607-436-2317 316 F
ryan.hooper@oneonta.edu
HOOPER, Stephanie ...... 304-336-8899 490 B
stephanie.hooper@westliberty.edu
HOOPER-PORTER,
Tracey .... 740-588-1377 365 B
tporter2@zanestate.edu
HOOPES, Jill .... 316-284-5326 172 B
jhoopes@bethelks.edu
HOOPES, Robbin .... 513-569-1511 350 F
robbin.hoopes@cincinnatistate.edu
HOOPES, Tom .... 913-360-7529 171 J
thoopes@benedictine.edu
HOOPS, Lisa .... 937-778-7955 352 D
lhoops@edisonohio.edu
HOOPS, Tony .... 316-284-5279 172 B
thoops@bethelks.edu
HOORMAN, Rachel .... 504-865-2011 190 C
rchoorma@loyno.edu
HOORNBEEK, Corbin .... 626-815-5328.. 26 F
choornbeek@apu.edu
HOOT, Dustin .... 414-847-3233 494 C
dustinhoot@miad.edu
HOOTEN, Jon .... 805-922-6966.. 24 I
jon.hooten@hancockcollege.edu
HOOTS, Cathy .... 336-750-2265 344 A
hoots@wssu.edu
HOOVER, Amy, K .... 712-778-2466 266 H
amyhoover@creighton.edu
HOOVER, Curtis .... 212-752-1530 304 A
curtis.hoover@limcollege.edu
HOOVER, Diane .... 541-956-7011 376 A
dhoover@roguecc.edu
HOOVER, Douglas .... 724-938-4096 393 E
hoover@calu.edu
HOOVER, Jean, B .... 717-262-2007 403 C
jhoover@wilson.edu
HOOVER, John .... 202-685-3924 502 K
HOOVER, Josie .... 202-664-5682.. 94 D
jhoover@wesleyseminary.edu
HOOVER, Karelyn .... 909-274-4570.. 52 J
khoover@mtsac.edu
HOOVER, Kathleen .... 610-558-5560 391 A
hooverk@neumann.edu
HOOVER, Kelly .... 410-704-2516 204 E
khoover@towson.edu
HOOVER, Kevin .... 559-325-3600.. 28 D
khoover@chsu.edu
HOOVER, Lisa .... 214-637-3530 457 H
lhoover@wadecollege.edu
HOOVER, Myrna .... 850-644-6089 110 C
mhoover@fsu.edu
HOOVER, Nick .... 937-481-2369 364 A
nick_hoover@wilmington.edu
HOOVER, Robert .... 563-588-6338 164 E
robert.hoover@clarke.edu
HOOVER, Sandy .... 903-923-2086 435 H
shoover@etbu.edu
HOOVER, Susan .... 405-425-5961 367 C
susan.hoover@oc.edu
HOOVER, Tom .... 318-257-2477 192 D
thoover@cloud.latech.edu
HOOVER-ERBIG,
Andrea .... 757-455-3136 477 C
ahoover@vwu.edu
HOOYMAN, Jamie .... 660-562-1120 257 E
jhooyman@nwmissouri.edu
HOPE, Alana .... 510-780-4500.. 47 K
ahope@lifewest.edu
HOPE, Deryle .... 864-503-5769 414 A
dhope@uscupstate.edu
HOPE, Henry .... 404-471-6355 114 G
hhope@agnesscott.edu
HOPE, John .... 251-981-3771.... 5 A
john.hope@columbiasouthern.edu
HOPE, Joseph, S .... 315-228-7422 296 E
jshope@colgate.edu
HOPE, Laura .... 909-652-6131.. 35 L
laura.hope@chaffey.edu
HOPE, Mindy .... 308-535-3773 267 J
hopem@mpcc.edu
HOPE, Oral .... 212-431-2300 309 A
oral.hope@nyls.edu
HOPES, Diana, L .... 972-549-6476 433 I
dhopes@collin.edu
HOPEWELL, Mitch .... 661-362-2683.. 51 D
mhopewell@masters.edu
HOPEY, Christopher, E . 978-837-5110 216 F
christopher.hopey@merrimack.edu
HOPKIN, Fran .... 435-797-8380 460 C
fran.hopkin@usu.edu
HOPKINS, Alex .... 816-654-7000 254 E
HOPKINS,
Alexander, M .... 713-798-4262 431 D
ahopkins@bcm.edu
HOPKINS, Barry .... 773-256-0734 143 F
bhopkins@jkmlibrary.org
HOPKINS, Barry .... 773-256-0734 143 H
bhopkins@jkmlibrary.org
HOPKINS, Boone, J ...... 864-596-9050 408 F
boone.hopkins@converse.edu
HOPKINS, Brandon .... 312-553-3193 135 B
bhopkins19@ccc.edu
HOPKINS, Carla .... 301-860-3939 204 A
alumni@bowiestate.edu
HOPKINS, Christi .... 620-242-0414 176 B
hopkinsc@mcpherson.edu
HOPKINS, David .... 903-675-6214 451 F
david.hopkins@tvcc.edu
HOPKINS, Dawn .... 302-857-6000.. 90 E
HOPKINS, Drew, W .... 609-984-3430 284 C
dhopkins@tesu.edu
HOPKINS, Ebonnie .... 408-274-7900.. 62 G
ebonnie.hopkins@evc.edu

HOSTETLER, Chad .... 304-457-6320 486 E hostetlercs@ab.edu
HOSTETLER, Marna, M . 812-464-1824 162 C mmhostetle@usi.edu
HOSTETLER, Tim, J .... 423-775-7262 418 D hostetti@bryan.edu
HOSTETTER, Larry .... 270-686-4236 179 J larry.hostetter@brescia.edu
HOSTETTER, Mayme ...... 212-228-1888 312 B
HOTALEN, Allison .... 706-886-6831 126 D ahotalen@tfc.edu
HOTALING, Marcus, S .. 518-388-6161 323 J hotalinm@union.edu
HOTCHKISS, David, C ... 414-955-8715 493 F dhotchkiss@mcw.edu
HOTCHKISS, Gregory .... 973-278-5400 275 I gkh@berkeleycollege.edu
HOTCHKISS, Gregory .... 212-986-4343 291 E gkh@berkeleycollege.edu
HOTCHKISS, Valerie ...... 615-322-4782 428 A valerie.hotchkiss@vanderbilt.edu
HOTELLING, Ben .... 937-395-5712 354 J ben.hotelling@kc.edu
HOTELLING, Benjamin .. 937-395-5712 354 J ben.hotelling@kc.edu
HOTEZ, Peter, J .... 713-798-1199 431 D hotez@bcm.edu
HOTOVY, Steve .... 402-471-2505 268 C shotovy@nscs.edu
HOTTEL, Haven .... 910-893-1421 327 D hottelh@campbell.edu
HOTTINGER, Sara .... 843-349-2473 408 A shottinge@coastal.edu
HOTTMAN, Winston .... 214-818-1313 433 O whottman@criswell.edu
HOTZFIELD, Brian .... 773-298-3096 149 D hotzfield@sxu.edu
HOTZLER, Russell, K .... 718-260-5400 295 A rhotzler@citytech.cuny.edu
HOU, Cheng Yu .... 714-480-7489.. 58 E hou_chengyu@rsccd.edu
HOUCHEN-CLAGETT, Denise, A .... 910-755-7472 332 F houchen-clagettd@brunswickcc.edu
HOUCHIN, Janeane .... 785-833-4462 175 E janeane.houchin@kwu.edu
HOUCHINS, Jessyca ..... 858-566-1200.. 40 J jhouchins@disd.edu
HOUCK, Beth .... 864-977-7200 410 I beth.houck@ngu.edu
HOUCK, Chad .... 760-384-6201.. 46 M chad.houck@cerrocoso.edu
HOUCK, Clarence, M .... 803-934-3235 410 G chouck@morris.edu
HOUCK, Eric .... 707-256-7542.. 53 E eric.houck@napavalley.edu
HOUCK, Laurie .... 407-646-2124 106 L lhouck@rollins.edu
HOUDE, Dorothy .... 671-734-1812 504 E
HOUDE, Joe .... 858-653-6740.. 46 H jhoude@jpcatholic.edu
HOUDER, Nathalie .... 603-358-2014 274 H nathalie.houder@keene.edu
HOUDYSCHELL, Jendonnae .... 304-696-6704 489 M houdyschell2@marshall.edu
HOUFER, Michael .... 651-747-4085 237 H michael.houfer@century.edu
HOUFF, Bekah .... 260-982-5243 159 J rlhouff@manchester.edu
HOUGE, Melanie .... 406-791-5976 265 H melanie.houge@uprovidence.edu
HOUGH, Andy .... 314-744-7623 256 E andy.hough@mobap.edu
HOUGH, Barbara, J ...... 518-276-6426 312 C houghb2@rpi.edu
HOUGH, Brad .... 636-227-2100 255 A
HOUGH, Jennifer, A ..... 724-946-7339 402 D houghja@westminster.edu
HOUGH, Kendra .... 318-345-9187 188 D khough@ladelta.edu
HOUGH, Melanie, J ...... 419-772-2027 358 C m-hough@onu.edu
HOUGH, Samara .... 810-237-6648 232 A samaralw@umich.edu
HOUGH, Tony .... 803-738-7695 410 D hought@midlandstech.edu
HOUGHTON, Brian .... 808-675-3209 128 D brian.houghton@byuh.edu
HOUGHTON, David .... 405-585-4400 367 B david.houghton@okbu.edu
HOUGLAND, Dawn .... 312-341-3531 148 E dhougland@roosevelt.edu
HOUK, Christopher .... 270-686-4241 179 J chris.houk@brescia.edu
HOUK, Claire .... 785-827-5541 175 E
HOUK, Suzanne, N .... 724-458-2208 384 G snhouk@gcc.edu
HOULE, Dylan .... 650-543-4097.. 51 G dylan.houle@menlo.edu
HOULIHAN, Janet, M ... 714-895-8307.. 38 A jhoulihan@gwc.cccd.edu
HOULIHAN, Jill .... 501-760-4206.. 20 A jill.houlihan@np.edu
HOULT, Kevin, J .... 334-844-3466.... 4 D kjh0029@auburn.edu
HOULTON, Benjamin, Z 607-255-2241 297 F calsdean@cornell.edu
HOUP, Trena .... 803-777-0460 413 A thoup@sc.edu
HOUPT, Andrew, M .... 724-589-2175 399 D ahoupt@thiel.edu
HOURIGAN, Christopher, P .... 401-456-8998 405 A chourigan@ric.edu
HOUSE, Dan .... 919-515-4211 342 A dlhouse@ncsu.edu
HOUSE, Deandre .... 601-857-3353 246 C deandre.house@hindscc.edu
HOUSE, H. Wayne .... 888-777-7675 480 D hwhouse@faithseminary.edu
HOUSE, Kamesia .... 910-672-1325 341 C kmhouse@uncfsu.edu
HOUSE, Kandy .... 580-774-3260 370 A kandy.house@swosu.edu
HOUSE, Karen .... 978-542-6120 213 E karen.house@salemstate.edu
HOUSE, Kevin .... 509-244-6851 479 C kevin.house@scc.spokane.edu
HOUSE, Stephanie .... 208-769-3368 132 D stephanie.house@nic.edu
HOUSE, Steven .... 336-278-6290 328 J shouse@elon.edu
HOUSE, Vicki .... 325-670-1276 436 I vhouse@hsutx.edu
HOUSEHOLDER, Mary .. 616-395-7413 225 D householder@hope.edu
HOUSEKNECHT, Karen .. 207-602-2872 197 E khouseknecht@une.edu
HOUSEMAN, Jennifer ... 215-951-1070 387 A houseman@lasalle.edu
HOUSENICK, Joseph ..... 570-408-4630 403 A joseph.housenick@wilkes.edu
HOUSER, Janet .... 303-458-1843.. 83 E jhouser@regis.edu
HOUSER, John .... 575-562-2123 286 B john.houser@enmu.edu
HOUSER, Katie .... 843-953-5606 408 C houserkk@cofc.edu
HOUSER, Kay .... 910-788-6219 338 A kay.houser@sccnc.edu
HOUSER, Kris .... 217-245-3832 139 C kris.houser@ic.edu
HOUSER, Nate .... 785-594-8316 171 F
HOUSER, Robert .... 970-351-1759.. 84 F robert.houser@unco.edu
HOUSEWORTH, Julie .... 573-592-4260 262 G julie.houseworth@williamwoods.edu
HOUSHMAND, Ali .... 856-256-4100 281 F presidenthoushmand@rowan.edu
HOUSHOLDER, Suahil .. 765-641-4115 153 G srhousholder@anderson.edu
HOUSLEY, Brooks .... 334-387-3877.... 4 B brookshousley@amridgeuniversity.edu
HOUSLEY, Harold .... 903-875-7307 440 D harold.housley@navarrocollege.edu
HOUSLEY, Heather, L ... 404-413-2070 120 E heatherh@gsu.edu
HOUSLEY, La Royce ..... 310-954-4191.. 52 I ldodd@msmu.edu
HOUSMAN, Naomi .... 215-635-7300 384 E nhousman@gratz.edu
HOUSMAN, Yosef .... 732-367-1060 275 K yhousman@bmg.edu
HOUSTON, Adam .... 760-921-5463.. 56 A ahouston@paloverde.edu
HOUSTON, Angela .... 620-331-4100 174 H ahouston@indycc.edu
HOUSTON, Angela .... 601-318-6231 249 H lhouston@wmcarey.edu
HOUSTON, Annazette .... 865-539-7401 425 B ahouston1@pstcc.edu
HOUSTON, Anne .... 610-330-5150 387 C houstona@lafayette.edu
HOUSTON, Don .... 408-855-5428.. 75 D don.houston@wvm.edu
HOUSTON, Doris .... 309-438-5677 140 D dmhous2@ilstu.edu
HOUSTON, Doug .... 636-584-6732 253 B doug.houston@eastcentral.edu
HOUSTON, Douglas ...... 559-243-7102.. 66 H douglas.houston@scccd.edu
HOUSTON, Douglas, B . 530-741-6971.. 77 C dhouston@yccd.edu
HOUSTON, Hope .... 781-891-2450 206 G hhouston@bentley.edu
HOUSTON, Jason .... 509-328-4220 480 F houston@gonzaga.edu
HOUSTON, Jean .... 707-765-1836.. 52 B
HOUSTON, Julia .... 662-407-1512 246 E jfhouston@iccms.edu
HOUSTON, Kathryn .... 816-235-6211 261 B houstonk@umkc.edu
HOUSTON, Kristen .... 206-876-6100 483 H khouston@theseattleschool.edu
HOUSTON, Michael ...... 662-621-4853 245 D mhouston@coahomacc.edu
HOUSTON, Michelle ..... 631-499-7100 304 C mhouston@libi.edu
HOUSTON, Nainsi .... 740-826-8260 356 H nhouston@muskingum.edu
HOUSTON, Rachel .... 704-403-1228 327 C rachel.houston@atriumhealth.org
HOUSTON, Raymond .... 914-606-6789 325 A raymond.houston@sunywcc.edu
HOUSTON, Rick .... 978-867-4130 210 B ric.houston@gordon.edu
HOUSTON, Sue .... 419-372-2211 348 G shousto@bgsu.edu
HOUSTON, Vinson .... 256-782-5993.... 6 A vhouston@jsu.edu
HOUSTON-BROWN, Clive .... 909-469-7037.. 75 I choustonbrown@westernu.edu
HOUT-REILLY, Daniel .... 216-791-5000 350 I daniel.hout-reilly@cim.edu
HOUTMAN, Anne .... 765-983-1211 155 A earlhampresident@earlham.edu
HOUZE, Shea, K .... 865-974-3179 427 B shouze@utk.edu
HOVAN, Steve .... 724-357-2100 394 C steven.hovan@iup.edu
HOVATER, Richard .... 910-323-5614 327 F rhovater@ccbs.edu
HOVATTER, Angela, L ... 301-687-4301 204 C ahovatter@frostburg.edu
HOVEKAMP, Tina .... 541-383-7295 372 A thovekamp@cocc.edu
HOVELL, Ashley .... 651-255-6162 243 E ahovell@unitedseminary.edu
HOVEN, Christina .... 716-286-8372 309 H ccuttone@niagara.edu
HOVEN, Kierstin .... 218-755-4135 237 F kierstin.hoven@bemidjistate.edu
HOVENGA, Danielle .... 918-631-3303 371 C danielle-hovenga@utulsa.edu
HOVERSTEN, Mark .... 919-515-8347 342 A mark_hoversten@ncsu.edu
HOVESTOL, Dan .... 406-586-3585 263 I dan.hovestol@montanabiblecollege.edu
HOVEY, Ann .... 541-867-8541 374 F ann.hovey@oregoncoast.edu
HOVEY, Jeff .... 314-977-8375 259 F jeff.hovey@slu.edu
HOVEY, Mark .... 860-685-2337.. 90 B mhovey@wesleyan.edu
HOVEY, Rebecca .... 413-585-2697 218 H rhovey@smith.edu
HOW, Christine .... 402-557-7002 265 J chow@bellevue.edu
HOW, John .... 406-994-2001 264 C john.how@montana.edu
HOWAR, Julie .... 309-690-6909 139 B julie.howar@icc.edu
HOWARD, Alan .... 903-693-2023 441 C ahoward@panola.edu
HOWARD, Ann .... 202-884-9608.. 94 A howarda@trinitydc.edu
HOWARD, April .... 540-986-1800 464 C ahoward@an.edu
HOWARD, Armando ...... 718-270-6484 294 G ahoward@mec.cuny.edu
HOWARD, Assuanta ...... 718-730-7403 294 F ahoward@lagcc.cuny.edu
HOWARD, Ayanna .... 614-292-2836 358 D howard.1727@osu.edu
HOWARD, Barry .... 615-514-2787 422 H bhoward@nossi.edu
HOWARD, Bobby .... 870-743-3000.. 20 B robert.howard@northark.edu
HOWARD, Brandy .... 925-969-2048.. 40 C bhoward@dvc.edu
HOWARD, Catherine ..... 903-823-3285 446 A catherine.howard@texarkanacollege.edu
HOWARD, Cedric, B ..... 716-673-3271 316 D cedric.howard@fredonia.edu
HOWARD, Chad, E .... 479-248-7236.. 19 B choward@ecollege.edu
HOWARD, Charles, L ... 215-898-8456 400 F choward@upenn.edu
HOWARD, Christopher . 609-652-4785 283 E christopher.howard@stockton.edu
HOWARD, Christopher, B .... 412-397-6400 397 B president@rmu.edu
HOWARD, Cindy .... 816-268-5424 257 C choward@nts.edu
HOWARD, Dale, S .... 330-490-7303 363 E dhoward@walsh.edu
HOWARD, Daniel .... 601-925-3350 247 C drhoward@mc.edu
HOWARD, David .... 601-979-6944 246 F david.c.howard@jsums.edu
HOWARD, DeAndre ...... 864-587-4632 412 F howardd@smcsc.edu
HOWARD, Donna .... 443-885-4680 201 A donna.howard@morgan.edu
HOWARD, Doris .... 415-503-6214.. 61 D finaid@sfcm.edu
HOWARD, Doug .... 615-460-6306 418 B doug.howard@belmont.edu
HOWARD, Drew .... 863-680-4266 100 H ahoward@flsouthern.edu
HOWARD, JR., Eddie, J .... 859-572-6447 184 E howarde10@nku.edu
HOWARD, Erica .... 931-598-1229 423 D eohoward@sewanee.edu
HOWARD, Ezra .... 662-621-4083 245 D ehoward@coahomacc.edu
HOWARD, Garth .... 832-813-6737 439 C garth.e.howard@lonestar.edu
HOWARD, Gary, E .... 859-858-3511 179 D gary.howard@asbury.edu
HOWARD, Gene .... 205-726-2366.... 6 E wehoward@samford.edu
HOWARD, Genevieve .... 360-992-2217 478 I ghoward@clark.edu
HOWARD, Gregory .... 804-257-5717 476 F gmhoward@vuu.edu
HOWARD, Jay, R .... 317-940-9874 154 C jrhoward@butler.edu
HOWARD, Jeffery, S ..... 423-439-4210 419 G howardjs@etsu.edu
HOWARD, Jessica .... 503-399-6591 372 B jessica.howard@chemeketa.edu
HOWARD, John .... 303-273-3646.. 79 J jkhoward@mines.edu
HOWARD, Jordan .... 620-768-2909 173 I jordanh@fortscott.edu
HOWARD, Joseph, E .... 610-499-4000 402 G jehoward1@widener.edu
HOWARD, Joy .... 503-517-1212 377 C jhoward@warnerpacific.edu
HOWARD, Karleen .... 251-380-4000.... 6 H kphoward@shc.edu
HOWARD, Katrina .... 912-427-5876 117 E khoward@coastalpines.edu
HOWARD, Kimberly, A . 802-656-4296 463 A kimberly.howard@uvm.edu
HOWARD, LaMarcus ..... 734-487-2470 223 K lhoward7@emich.edu
HOWARD, Lelia .... 267-502-2680 379 A lelia.howard@brynathyn.edu
HOWARD, Lonnie .... 409-880-8185 449 F llhoward@lit.edu
HOWARD, Martin, J ..... 617-353-2290 207 E mjhoward@bu.edu
HOWARD, Mary Ann .... 478-757-5137 127 F mhoward@wesleyancollege.edu
HOWARD, Michael .... 617-627-3331 219 C michael.howard@tufts.edu
HOWARD, Michael, P ... 518-564-3140 318 E mhowa001@plattsburgh.edu
HOWARD, Predita .... 478-934-3092 122 F predita.howard@mga.edu
HOWARD, Randy, B ..... 386-226-6000.. 99 A randy.howard@erau.edu
HOWARD, II, Ruben ..... 847-635-1807 146 G rhoward@oakton.edu

HUBBARD, James .... 309-268-8452 138 H
jim.hubbard@heartland.edu
HUBBARD, Karen .... 208-769-4372 132 D
klhubbard@nic.edu
HUBBARD, Laura, E ..... 716-645-5124 316 C
laurahub@buffalo.edu
HUBBARD, Michael ...... 205-366-8817.... 7 A
mhubbard@stillman.edu
HUBBARD, Nancy .... 434-544-8720 471 L
hubbard_na@lynchburg.edu
HUBBARD, Stacey .... 217-420-6743 144 G
shubbard@millikin.edu
HUBBARD, Susan, G .... 334-844-4790.... 4 D
hubbasg@auburn.edu
HUBBARD, Tatum .... 432-552-3102 456 F
hubbard_t@utpb.edu
HUBBARD, Vaniethia ..... 714-564-6084.. 58 F
hubbard_vaniethia@sac.edu
HUBBARD, William, C .. 803-777-6857 413 A
whubbard@email.sc.edu
HUBBARD, Zackary .... 704-216-3555 337 F
zackary.hubbard@rccc.edu
HUBBARD JACKSON,
Chris .... 636-922-8271 258 J
chubbard@stchas.edu
HUBBELL, Sarah .... 269-488-4207 225 G
shubbell@kvcc.edu
HUBBERT, Daron .... 951-343-4229.. 27 G
dhubbert@calbaptist.edu
HUBBS, Cathy .... 202-885-3998.. 91 F
hubbs@american.edu
HUBBS, Jocelyn .... 541-684-7291 371 I
jhubbs@bushnell.edu
HUBER, Amy .... 973-803-5000 280 B
ahuber@pillar.edu
HUBER, E. Kim .... 303-315-2252.. 84 D
HUBER, Heidi .... 410-857-2769 200 F
hhuber@mcdaniel.edu
HUBER, Jeff .... 859-371-9393 179 G
HUBER, John .... 937-512-3041 360 G
john.huber3526@sinclair.edu
HUBER, Karrie, K .... 701-355-8226 347 C
kkhuber@umary.edu
HUBER, Lindsey .... 309-341-5213 134 B
lhuber@sandburg.edu
HUBER, Lydia .... 361-572-6461 457 E
lydia.huber@victoriacollege.edu
HUBER, Lynn .... 336-278-5709 328 J
lhuber@elon.edu
HUBER, Matthew .... 847-635-1740 146 G
mahuber@oakton.edu
HUBER, Morgan .... 605-995-7250 415 E
morgan.huber@mitchelltech.edu
HUBER, Patricia, B .... 540-674-3601 474 E
phuber@nr.edu
HUBERMAN, Jeffrey, H . 309-677-2360 134 A
huberman@bradley.edu
HUBERMAN, Steven ...... 212-463-0400 322 F
steven.huberman@touro.edu
HUBERS, Todd, K .... 616-526-8754 222 C
thubers@calvin.edu
HUBERT, Christine .... 330-941-2000 364 H
cmhubert@ysu.edu
HUBERT, David .... 801-957-4280 461 C
david.hubert@slcc.edu
HUBERT, Lydia .... 229-468-2460 128 B
lydia.hubert@wiregrass.edu
HUBIN, Josh .... 620-242-0400 176 B
hubinj@mcpherson.edu
HUBIN, Kert .... 303-245-4797.. 82 A
khubin@naropa.edu
HUBRIC, Kim .... 610-921-2381 377 G
HUCKABA, Sam .... 850-644-4404 110 C
shuckaba@fsu.edu
HUCKABY, Cathy .... 561-904-3000.. 93 H
HUCKSTEAD, Seth .... 616-432-3411 230 A
seth.huckstead@prts.edu
HUDAK, David .... 614-247-8670 358 D
dhudak@osu.edu
HUDAK, Jane, E .... 484-664-3300 390 H
janehudak@muhlenberg.edu
HUDAK, Randy .... 440-826-2475 348 D
rhudak@bw.edu
HUDAK, Sharon .... 570-674-6295 390 B
shudak@misericordia.edu
HUDANICK, Richard ...... 636-584-6500 253 B
richard.hudanick@eastcentral.edu
HUDDLESTON, Ryan ..... 925-473-7328.. 40 D
rhuddleston@4cd.edu
HUDDLESTON, Sean, L . 317-543-3235 159 L
HUDDLESTON, Tim .... 870-759-4105.. 23 J
thuddleston@williamsbu.edu

HUDDY, Patrick .... 303-369-5151.. 82 I
patrick.huddy@plattcolorado.edu
HUDGENS, James .... 404-894-7325 119 E
james.hudgens@gtri.gatech.edu
HUDGENS, Kevin .... 719-502-2000.. 82 E
kevin.hudgens@ppcc.edu
HUDGIK, Mark .... 413-552-2592 214 F
mhudgik@hcc.edu
HUDGIN, Denise .... 419-251-1324 355 G
denise.hudgin@mercycollege.edu
HUDGINS, Karen .... 904-819-6252.. 99 E
khudgins@flagler.edu
HUDGINS, Molly .... 636-949-4192 254 H
mhudgins@lindenwood.edu
HUDGINS, V. Lavoyed .. 859-985-3240 179 I
hudginsv@berea.edu
HUDNELL, Jason .... 501-760-4374.. 20 A
jason.hudnell@np.edu
HUDOCK, Amy .... 843-722-5556 412 I
amy.hudock@tridenttech.edu
HUDSICK, Walter .... 360-752-8333 478 A
whudsick@btc.edu
HUDSON, Adair .... 864-488-4370 410 B
ahudson@limestone.edu
HUDSON, Angela .... 501-686-2504.. 21 E
ahudson@uasys.edu
HUDSON, Ashley .... 503-777-7259 375 G
hashley@reed.edu
HUDSON, Barbara .... 256-840-4147.... 3 F
barbara.hudson@snead.edu
HUDSON, Bo .... 918-293-4912 368 B
steven.w.hudson@okstate.edu
HUDSON, Bobby .... 615-230-3445 425 E
bobby.hudson@volstate.edu
HUDSON, Cindy .... 773-244-5691 145 G
cehudson2@northpark.edu
HUDSON, David, D .... 714-895-8104.. 38 A
dhudson@gwc.cccd.edu
HUDSON, David, J .... 434-243-0900 472 D
djh2t@virginia.edu
HUDSON, Dean, P .... 843-349-2739 408 A
dhudson@coastal.edu
HUDSON, Donald, M .... 609-652-4883 283 E
donald.hudson@stockton.edu
HUDSON, Edith .... 414-288-3633 493 E
edith.hudson@marquette.edu
HUDSON, El Pagnier .... 305-348-2190 110 A
elpagnier.hudson@fiu.edu
HUDSON, Elizabeth .... 617-373-2170 217 I
HUDSON, Garien .... 419-559-2525 361 C
ghudson01@terra.edu
HUDSON, Gregory .... 501-370-5295.. 20 F
gahudson@philander.edu
HUDSON, Holly .... 979-845-0544 446 F
studyabroad@tamu.edu
HUDSON, Jennifer, M .. 713-646-1819 443 I
jhudson@stcl.edu
HUDSON, John .... 713-221-8664 453 A
hudsonj@uhd.edu
HUDSON, Karen .... 615-550-3165 428 E
karen.hudson@williamsoncc.edu
HUDSON, Kevin .... 256-765-4274.... 8 E
kchudson@una.edu
HUDSON, Lea Ann .... 404-471-6402 114 G
lhudson@agnesscott.edu
HUDSON, Lori .... 304-336-8990 490 B
lori.hudson@westliberty.edu
HUDSON, Lyla .... 843-792-8721 410 C
hudsonly@musc.edu
HUDSON, Mark, A .... 217-581-7711 137 E
mahudson@eiu.edu
HUDSON, Matthew .... 417-447-8102 257 G
hudsonm@otc.edu
HUDSON, Mattie .... 256-352-8170.... 3 I
mattie.hudson@wallacestate.edu
HUDSON, Merissa .... 850-769-1551 101 N
mhudson@gulfcoast.edu
HUDSON, Michael, J .... 630-637-5661 145 F
mjhudson@noctrl.edu
HUDSON, Rob .... 719-502-3193.. 82 E
rob.hudson@ppcc.edu
HUDSON, Sean .... 773-907-4428 135 C
shudson52@ccc.edu
HUDSON, Sean .... 716-827-2567 323 G
hudsons@trocaire.edu
HUDSON, Sheila .... 707-864-7000.. 64 H
sheila.hudson@solano.edu
HUDSON, Shirley .... 972-524-3341 445 B
shirley.hudson@swcc.edu
HUDSON, Sid .... 405-224-3140 371 B
shudson@usao.edu
HUDSON, Stephanie ..... 601-857-3280 246 C
stephanie.hudson@hindscc.edu

HUDSON, Stephanie ..... 864-379-8718 409 E
hudson@erskine.edu
HUDSON, Thomas .... 601-979-2323 246 F
thomas.k.hudson@jsums.edu
HUDSON, Tijuana, R .... 803-535-5197 407 D
thudson@claflin.edu
HUDSON, Tim .... 931-221-7779 417 H
hudsont@apsu.edu
HUDSON, Violina .... 684-699-9155 504 B
HUDSON, JR., William . 850-599-3183 109 I
william.hudsonjr@famu.edu
HUDSON HOSEK,
Hilary .... 312-567-3012 140 A
hhudsonhosek@iit.edu
HUDSPETH, Donald .... 585-475-7077 312 F
don.hudspeth@croatia.rit.edu
HUDSPETH, Josie .... 541-885-1392 374 I
josie.hudspeth@oit.edu
HUDSPETH, William ...... 770-426-2833 122 C
william.hudspeth2@life.edu
HUEBER, Charlie .... 830-792-7278 443 E
deanofstudents@schreiner.edu
HUEBNER, Casey .... 425-576-5807 481 C
casey.huebner@lwtech.edu
HUEBNER, Erinn .... 616-538-2330 224 E
ehuebner@gracechristian.edu
HUEBNER, Janet .... 319-352-8227 170 J
janet.huebner@wartburg.edu
HUEBNER, Mj .... 269-337-7172 225 F
mj.huebner@kzoo.edu
HUEBNER, JR.,
Thomas .... 601-484-8618 247 A
thuebner@meridiancc.edu
HUEBNER, Tim .... 901-843-3653 423 A
huebner@rhodes.edu
HUEBOTTER, Chris .... 573-288-6542 252 F
chuebotter@culver.edu
HUEG, Kurt .... 650-949-7394.. 42 I
huegkurt@foothill.edu
HUELSBECK, Tom, A ..... 253-535-7200 482 A
tom.huelsbeck@plu.edu
HUENEMANN, Kurt .... 419-448-2351 353 E
keh@heidelberg.edu
HUERTA, Cindy .... 915-779-8031 457 F
HUERTA, Homer, J .... 512-428-1385 442 I
homerh@stedwards.edu
HUERTA, Patricia .... 312-362-8601 136 H
phuerta@depaul.edu
HUERTA, Paul .... 312-341-4167 148 E
phuerta@roosevelt.edu
HUERTA, Yvette, V .... 915-831-2654 436 A
yhuerta@epcc.edu
HUERTAS, Carmelo, V .. 973-353-5581 282 B
carmelo.huertas@rutgers.edu
HUERTAS, Felix, R .... 787-743-7979 510 H
fhuertas@suagm.edu
HUERTAS, Linda .... 773-481-8453 135 G
lhuertas@ccc.edu
HUERTAS, Roxanne .... 856-225-6532 281 G
roxanne.huertas@camden.rutgers.edu
HUERTAS GONZÁLEZ,
Félix, R .... 787-257-7373 510 F
fhuertas@uagm.edu
HUESER, Kyle .... 712-274-6400 171 B
kyle.hueser@witcc.edu
HUESTON, William, J ... 414-955-8220 493 F
whueston@mcw.edu
HUET, Yvette .... 704-687-8696 342 D
ymhuet@uncc.edu
HUETH, Jeremy .... 303-860-5600.. 84 A
HUEWITT, Kenneth .... 713-313-7011 449 B
HUEY, Keith .... 248-218-2124 230 B
khuey@rochesteru.edu
HUEY, Marcy .... 205-348-4132.... 7 G
mhuey@ua.edu
HUFF, Eugene .... 925-229-6850.. 40 A
ehuff@4cd.edu
HUFF, Julie .... 334-844-5777.... 4 D
hilljul@auburn.edu
HUFF, Kim .... 803-535-1204 411 B
huffk@octech.edu
HUFF, Mary .... 502-272-8359 179 H
mhuff@bellarmine.edu
HUFF, Michael .... 256-824-6633.... 8 B
michael.huff@uah.edu
HUFF, Michael .... 216-987-4294 351 E
michael.huff@tri-c.edu
HUFF, Peter .... 630-829-6664 133 E
phuff@ben.edu
HUFF, Tim, T .... 405-744-5459 367 G
tim.huff@okstate.edu
HUFFAKER, Joshua .... 470-322-1200 423 E
jhuffaker@south.edu

HUFFER, Sarah .... 434-200-3070 465 D
HUFFINE, David, M .... 404-378-8821 117 G
HUFFMAN, Donald .... 440-366-7397 355 B
HUFFMAN, Jodi .... 704-922-6250 334 G
huffman.jodi@gaston.edu
HUFFMAN, Keith .... 740-362-3380 355 H
khuffman@mtso.edu
HUFFMAN, Lisa .... 940-898-2204 451 D
lhuffman1@twu.edu
HUFFMAN, Mari, L .... 419-866-0261 361 B
mlhuffman@stautzenberger.com
HUFFMAN, Monica, R .. 660-543-4106 260 G
mhuffman@ucmo.edu
HUFFMAN, Rebecca ...... 276-328-0139 472 E
reg5a@uvawise.edu
HUFFMAN, Robin .... 260-399-7700 162 B
rhuffman@sf.edu
HUFFMAN, Tammy, S .. 740-588-1212 365 B
thuffman@zanestate.edu
HUFFMAN, Xander .... 510-430-3127.. 66 G
xhuffman@sksm.edu
HUFFORD, Larry .... 406-243-2632 263 K
larry.hufford@umontana.edu
HUFFSTETLER, Edward .. 304-384-5241 489 J
ehuffstetler@concord.edu
HUFFSTUTLER, Steven .. 618-650-5234 150 C
shuffst@siue.edu
HUFNAGEL, Michele, A 412-536-1096 386 H
michele.hufnagel@laroche.edu
HUFTALIN, Deneece ...... 801-957-4226 461 C
deneece.huftalin@slcc.edu
HUFTON, Maren .... 805-756-6770.. 29 I
mhufton@calpoly.edu
HUG-ENGLISH, Cheryl .. 775-784-6122 271 E
cherylh@med.unr.edu
HUGANIR, Gail .... 717-815-1425 403 F
ghuganir@ycp.edu
HUGGINS, Derrick, E .... 803-777-3150 413 A
dhuggins@mailbox.sc.edu
HUGGINS, Jennifer .... 815-802-8702 141 D
jhuggins@kcc.edu
HUGGINS, Jonathan ..... 706-236-2217 116 B
jhuggins@berry.edu
HUGGINS, Lance .... 816-654-7702 254 E
lhuggins@kcumb.edu
HUGGINS, Michael .... 254-968-9781 446 D
mhuggins@tarleton.edu
HUGGINS, Regina, M ... 919-866-5408 338 G
rmhuggins@waketech.edu
HUGGINS, Tim .... 864-977-7272 410 I
tim.huggins@ngu.edu
HUGHES, Adam .... 765-658-4293 154 J
adamhughes@depauw.edu
HUGHES, Alan .... 706-236-2202 116 B
rhughes@berry.edu
HUGHES, Andrew .... 775-673-7240 271 C
ahughes@tmcc.edu
HUGHES, Angela .... 865-694-6400 425 B
arhughes1@pstcc.edu
HUGHES, Bernice .... 229-391-5130 114 F
bhughes@abac.edu
HUGHES, Blanche, M ... 970-491-1101.. 79 N
blanche.hughes@colostate.edu
HUGHES, Bonnie .... 506-865-8588 481 A
hughes_b@heritage.edu
HUGHES, JR., Byron, A 540-231-6272 476 C
bahughes@vt.edu
HUGHES, Carol .... 312-362-8592 136 H
chughe23@depaul.edu
HUGHES, Carolyn .... 319-352-8642 170 J
carolyn.hughes@wartburg.edu
HUGHES, Cathie .... 423-775-6596 422 I
HUGHES, Chris .... 870-236-6901.. 18 J
chughes@crc.edu
HUGHES, Christopher ... 251-380-2292.... 6 H
chughes@shc.edu
HUGHES, Christy .... 812-866-7012 155 G
hughes@hanover.edu
HUGHES, Cory .... 410-290-7100 200 A
HUGHES, David .... 435-586-7735 460 A
hughes@suu.edu
HUGHES, Deborah .... 786-279-2643 290 E
dhughes@asa.edu
HUGHES, DeVetta .... 843-574-6199 412 I
devetta.hughes@tridenttech.edu
HUGHES, Dorothy .... 934-420-2166 320 F
hughesd@farmingdale.edu
HUGHES, Doug .... 509-544-8310 479 A
djhughes@columbiabasin.edu
HUGHES, Ed .... 901-334-5812 421 E
ehughes@memphisseminary.edu
HUGHES, Ernie, T .... 660-785-4133 260 F
ehughes@truman.edu

HUMS, Jason .... 619-216-6761.. 66 A
jhums@swccd.edu
HUNDLEY, Christina ..... 602-787-6622.. 13 E
christina.hundley@paradisevalley.edu
HUNDLEY, Stephen, P .. 317-278-2090 157 D
shundley@iupui.edu
HUNDLEY, Theresa ...... 620-421-6700 175 F
theresah@labette.edu
HUNEYCUTT, Richy .... 252-527-6223 335 G
rshuneycutt78@lenoircc.edu
HUNG TRUONG,
Michael .... 714-903-2762.. 68 G
HUNGER, Suzanne .... 406-265-3568 264 E
suzanne.hunger@msun.edu
HUNGERFORD, Amy ..... 212-854-8296 297 C
aeh2217@columbia.edu
HUNGERFORD,
H. Daniel .... 716-375-2017 313 C
dhungerf@sbu.edu
HUNHOFF, Christian ..... 605-668-5126 415 F
christian.hunhoff@mountmarty.edu
HUNHOLZ, Ben .... 734-973-3517 232 D
bhunholz@wccnet.edu
HUNKERSTORM,
Louisa .... 307-855-2235 501 A
lhunker@cwc.edu
HUNN, Jonathan .... 636-949-4528 254 H
jhunn@lindenwood.edu
HUNN, Martha, S .... 843-349-2962 408 A
mhunn@coastal.edu
HUNN, II, Marvin, T .... 214-887-5281 435 F
mhunn@dts.edu
HUNNELL, Matt .... 740-474-8896 358 A
mhunnell@ohiochristian.edu
HUNNEWELL, Haley ...... 269-749-7570 229 J
hhunnewell@olivetcollege.edu
HUNNEWELL, Lila .... 617-358-4913 207 E
lilawell@bu.edu
HUNNICUTT, Lew, K ..... 252-451-8221 336 E
lkhunnicutt002@nashcc.edu
HUNSADER, Tricia ...... 423-636-7305 426 E
thunsader@tusculum.edu
HUNSAKER, Deanna ..... 660-626-2019 250 A
dhunsaker@atsu.edu
HUNSAKER, Jessica ...... 865-354-3000 425 C
hunsakerjl@roanestate.edu
HUNSAKER, Marc .... 706-236-2292 116 B
mhunsaker@berry.edu
HUNSBERGER, Jill .... 734-484-1322 223 K
jhunsberg1@emich.edu
HUNSBERGER, Mark, A 260-422-5561 156 E
mahunsberger@indianatech.edu
HUNSICKER, Donald ...... 617-585-0200 207 A
don.hunsicker@the-bac.edu
HUNSINGER PATTEN,
Rachael .... 610-359-5131 382 A
rpatten@dccc.edu
HUNSTAD, Carla, J .... 719-333-0056 503 D
carla.hunstad@usafa.edu
HUNSUCKER, Scott, E .. 704-233-8221 344 F
scotth@wingate.edu
HUNT, Ana .... 501-812-2206.. 23 B
ahunt@uaptc.edu
HUNT, Angela .... 503-338-2306 372 D
ahunt@clatsopcc.edu
HUNT, Bill (William) ...... 918-495-7750 368 F
whunt@oru.edu
HUNT, Blanchie .... 870-762-1020.. 17 B
bhunt@smail.anc.edu
HUNT, Corey .... 304-367-4658 489 K
corey.hunt@fairmontstate.edu
HUNT, Darnell .... 310-267-4304.. 69 E
dhunt@soc.ucla.edu
HUNT, Dave .... 319-398-1251 167 J
dave.hunt@kirkwood.edu
HUNT, Dave .... 816-501-4890 258 I
dave.hunt@rockhurst.edu
HUNT, Deborah .... 914-826-9258 306 C
dhunt4@mercy.edu
HUNT, Denise .... 256-782-5151.... 6 A
dhunt@jsu.edu
HUNT, Denise .... 760-921-5510.. 56 A
dhunt@paloverde.edu
HUNT, Donlad, E .... 530-752-5589.. 69 B
HUNT, Dwayne .... 530-741-6700.. 77 C
HUNT,
Dwayne (Dalexh) .... 530-741-6705.. 77 E
dhunt1@yccd.edu
HUNT, Emily .... 806-651-5330 448 B
ehunt@wtamu.edu
HUNT, Faith .... 203-254-4000.. 87 I
fhunt@fairfield.edu
HUNT, Felicia .... 626-395-2923.. 28 J
fhunt@caltech.edu

HUNT, Gerri .... 336-342-4261 337 E
huntg0780@rockinghamcc.edu
HUNT, Gerry .... 405-208-5582 367 E
ghunt@okcu.edu
HUNT, James .... 870-230-5134.. 19 D
huntj@hsu.edu
HUNT, James .... 850-644-4041 110 C
jhunt@fsu.edu
HUNT, Janet .... 501-337-5000.. 18 B
jhunt@asutr.edu
HUNT, Janette .... 727-341-3229 107 E
hunt.janette@spcollege.edu
HUNT, Jeff .... 303-963-3254.. 78 H
jhunt@ccu.edu
HUNT, Jeff .... 864-592-4727 412 E
huntj@sccsc.edu
HUNT, Jennifer .... 765-641-4063 153 G
jehunt@anderson.edu
HUNT, Karen .... 304-829-7591 487 A
khunt@bethanywv.edu
HUNT, Katerine .... 352-854-2322.. 97 N
huntk@cf.edu
HUNT, Kristen, H .... 901-843-3730 423 A
huntk@rhodes.edu
HUNT, Laura .... 575-492-2189 289 F
lhunt@usw.edu
HUNT, Lisa .... 910-521-6357 343 B
lisa.hunt@uncp.edu
HUNT, Lori .... 509-533-7378 479 C
lori.hunt@scc.spokane.edu
HUNT, Louis, D .... 919-515-1428 342 A
ldhunt@ncsu.edu
HUNT, Mark .... 334-386-7140.... 5 C
mhunt@faulkner.edu
HUNT, Mary .... 860-231-5738.. 90 A
mhunt@usj.edu
HUNT, Michelle .... 760-750-8362.. 33 A
mihunt@csusm.edu
HUNT, Patrick, G .... 240-895-4307 202 B
pghunt@smcm.edu
HUNT, Philip .... 701-231-7987 345 F
philip.hunt@ndsu.edu
HUNT, Rusty .... 252-527-6223 335 G
rthunt78@lenoircc.edu
HUNT, Scott, H .... 801-422-6446 458 H
scott_hunt@byu.edu
HUNT, Shane .... 208-282-2601 131 G
shanehunt@isu.edu
HUNT, Shari .... 315-866-0300 301 D
huntsl@herkimer.edu
HUNT, Sherrica .... 251-405-7043.... 1 E
shunt@bishop.edu
HUNT, Skyler .... 304-357-4741 487 J
skylerhunt@ucwv.edu
HUNT, Sonia .... 937-376-6649 349 J
shunt@centralstate.edu
HUNT, Steve .... 310-434-4689.. 63 C
hunt_steve@smc.edu
HUNT, Steve .... 828-327-7000 333 B
shunt@cvcc.edu
HUNT, Steven .... 910-272-3600 337 D
shunt@robeson.edu
HUNT, T. Jill .... 270-809-3763 184 D
thunt2@murraystate.edu
HUNT, Terry, L .... 520-621-3015.. 16 D
tlhunt@arizona.edu
HUNT, Thomas, M .... 805-437-3352.. 30 C
thomas.hunt@csuci.edu
HUNT, Tolif, R .... 319-273-3217 164 A
tolif.hunt@uni.edu
HUNT, Valerie .... 206-934-4085 483 C
valerie.hunt@seattlecolleges.edu
HUNT, Wendy .... 402-465-2135 268 G
whunt@nebrwesleyan.edu
HUNT-BULL, Nicholas ... 518-327-6247 311 C
nhuntbull@paulsmiths.edu
HUNTER, Alison .... 619-482-6414.. 66 A
ahunter@swccd.edu
HUNTER, Amy .... 413-585-2245 218 H
ahunter65@smith.edu
HUNTER, Ben .... 812-855-4296 156 F
bdhunter@iu.edu
HUNTER, Ben .... 208-885-6534 132 F
bhunter@uidaho.edu
HUNTER, Chip .... 509-335-3596 485 D
chip.hunter@wsu.edu
HUNTER, David .... 570-348-6211 389 D
dhunter@marywood.edu
HUNTER, Derek .... 919-739-7020 338 H
mdhunter@waynecc.edu
HUNTER, Evie .... 215-489-4471 382 B
evelia.hunter@delval.edu

HUNTER, Gayle .... 386-752-1822 100 B
gayle.hunter@fgc.edu
HUNTER, Gerald, E .... 757-823-8011 469 A
gehunter@nsu.edu
HUNTER, Gill .... 859-622-8010 180 E
gill.hunter@eku.edu
HUNTER, Grant .... 402-984-8825 267 C
ghunter@hastings.edu
HUNTER, James .... 270-707-3713 182 B
james.hunter@kctcs.edu
HUNTER, Jane .... 520-621-5168.. 16 D
jhunter2@arizona.edu
HUNTER, Jasmine .... 225-771-2552 191 E
jhunter@sulc.edu
HUNTER, Jeff, C .... 304-462-6113 489 L
jeff.hunter@glenville.edu
HUNTER, Jessica, S 570-326-3761 392W
jhunter@pct.edu
HUNTER, Joseph .... 503-883-2202 373 F
jhunter3@linfield.edu
HUNTER, Kierstyn .... 413-236-2101 214 A
khunter@berkshirecc.edu
HUNTER, Kim .... 513-244-4248 356 F
kim.hunter@msj.edu
HUNTER, Kymm .... 803-705-4519 406 G
kymm.hunter@benedict.edu
HUNTER, Lai-Monte .... 870-307-7313.. 19 I
laimonte.hunter@lyon.edu
HUNTER, Larry, T .... 614-236-6641 349 B
lhunter2@capital.edu
HUNTER, LeAnn .... 509-452-5100 482 B
lhunter@pnwu.edu
HUNTER, Lorna .... 410-778-7114 205 B
lhunter2@washcoll.edu
HUNTER, Lynn .... 781-239-3111 214 G
lhunter@massbay.edu
HUNTER, Maggie .... 510-430-3220.. 52 E
mhunter@mills.edu
HUNTER, Marc .... 405-382-9950 369 F
m.hunter@sscok.edu
HUNTER, Martin, J .... 410-543-6150 204 D
mjhunter@salisbury.edu
HUNTER, Patti .... 805-565-6076.. 76 A
phunter@westmont.edu
HUNTER, Rebecca .... 212-229-5620 308 A
hunterr@newschool.edu
HUNTER, Richie .... 541-346-3134 376 H
richieh@uoregon.edu
HUNTER, Richie, C .... 518-276-2800 312 C
hunter3@rpi.edu
HUNTER, Rosey .... 509-313-3564 480 F
hunterr2@gonzaga.edu
HUNTER, Sandra .... 252-638-7249 334 A
hunters@cravencc.edu
HUNTER, Sean .... 614-947-6103 352 J
sean.hunter@franklin.edu
HUNTER, Teressa .... 405-466-3274 366 C
teressa.hunter@langston.edu
HUNTER, Tiffany .... 937-328-6025 350 G
huntert@clarkstate.edu
HUNTER, Timothy .... 704-216-3694 337 F
timothy.hunter@rccc.edu
HUNTER, Tracie .... 310-434-4871.. 63 C
hunter_tracie@smc.edu
HUNTER, William .... 670-237-6719 505 A
william.hunter@marianas.edu
HUNTER-MCKINNEY,
Shaunna, E .... 434-223-6193 467 F
shunter@hsc.edu
HUNTHAUSEN,
Stephanie .... 406-447-6993 264 B
stephanie.hunthausen@helenacollege.edu
HUNTINGTON, Lucas .... 225-768-1732 187 B
lucas.huntington@franu.edu
HUNTINGTON, Robert ... 419-448-2202 353 E
president@heidelberg.edu
HUNTLEY, Brian .... 315-268-6723 295 F
bhuntley@clarkson.edu
HUNTLEY, Celestine ...... 954-201-7350.. 96 F
HUNTLEY, Deborah, R .. 989-964-4296 230 E
huntley@svsu.edu
HUNTLEY, Julie .... 918-495-7040 368 F
jhuntley@oru.edu
HUNTLEY, Kristy .... 403-205-3338 205 F
kristy.huntley@aic.edu
HUNTLEY, Steve, E .... 904-264-2172 106 K
steve.huntley@iws.edu
HUNTOON,
Jacqueline, E .... 906-487-2440 228 A
jeh@mtu.edu
HUNTSINGER, Trish ...... 828-395-1297 335 D
thuntsinger@isothermal.edu

HUNZER, Kathleen .... 715-425-0720 496 F
kathleen.hunzer@uwrf.edu
HUNZIGER, Lucas .... 785-442-6180 174 F
lhunziger@highlandcc.edu
HUO,
Xiaoming (Sharon) ..... 931-372-3463 426 B
xhuo@tntech.edu
HUOPPI, Jennifer .... 860-465-4357.. 85 H
huoppij@easternct.edu
HUPFER, Mary, A .... 812-464-1627 162 C
mhupfer@usi.edu
HUPKE, Jennifer .... 219-989-2953 160 D
jhupke@pnw.edu
HUPP, Stephen .... 304-424-8273 490 F
stephen.hupp@wvup.edu
HUPPE, Alicia, L .... 972-377-1749 433 I
ahuppe@collin.edu
HUPPERT, Susan .... 515-271-1384 165 G
susan.huppert@dmu.edu
HURBANIS, Julie, T ...... 651-696-6475 236 I
jhurbani@macalester.edu
HURD, Amy .... 309-438-2157 140 D
arhurd@ilstu.edu
HURD, Anne, J .... 336-272-7102 329 C
anne.hurd@greensboro.edu
HURD, Brian .... 216-397-1974 353 O
bhurd@jcu.edu
HURD, Catherine .... 336-273-4431 327 A
HURD, Karen .... 315-312-3627 318 D
karen.hurd@oswego.edu
HURD, Phillip .... 713-743-8000 452 C
pwhurd@uh.edu
HURD, Roy .... 707-546-4000.. 41 G
rhurd@empcol.edu
HURD, Sherie .... 707-546-4000.. 41 G
shurd@empcol.edu
HURD-CRANK, Cathy .... 606-886-3863 181 E
cathy.hurdcrank@kctcs.edu
HURDA, Lisa .... 608-757-7704 498 D
lhurda@blackhawk.edu
HURDT, Emily .... 704-669-4321 333 E
hurdte@clevelandcc.edu
HURIER, Joanna .... 617-587-5787 217 D
hurierj@neco.edu
HURLBERT, Jeffrey .... 202-685-3924 502 K
HURLBUT, Bradford, D . 201-692-2170 277 I
hurlbut@fdu.edu
HURLBUT, Jeffrey .... 949-451-5546.. 65 C
jhurlbut@ivc.edu
HURLEY, Charles, T ...... 574-631-7495 162 A
hurley.32@nd.edu
HURLEY, Deanne .... 440-646-8320 363 C
dhurley@ursuline.edu
HURLEY,
Donald (Shane) .... 210-431-5531 441 B
dshurley@ollusa.edu
HURLEY, Elizabeth .... 617-521-2000 218 G
HURLEY, James .... 617-627-4337 219 C
james.hurley@tufts.edu
HURLEY, James .... 254-968-9100 446 D
president@tarleton.edu
HURLEY, Jeff .... 513-244-4465 356 F
jeff.hurley@msj.edu
HURLEY, John, J .... 716-888-2100 292 F
hurleyj@canisius.edu
HURLEY, Kristin, M ...... 301-447-5372 201 B
k.hurley@msmary.edu
HURLEY, Leah, A .... 214-648-7986 457 A
leah.hurley@utsouthwestern.edu
HURLEY, Rachel .... 937-529-2201 361 G
rehurley@united.edu
HURLEY, Roberta .... 864-597-4044 414 E
hurleyrl@wofford.edu
HURLEY, Ronald .... 201-200-3127 279 D
rhurley@njcu.edu
HURLEY, Sam .... 903-928-3288 451 F
shurley@tvcc.edu
HURLEY, Wanda .... 601-635-2111 246 A
whurley@eccc.edu
HURLOW, Julia .... 765-998-4924 161 C
julia_hurlow@taylor.edu
HURN, Jeffrey .... 785-442-6077 174 F
jhurn@highlandcc.edu
HURN, Patricia, D .... 734-764-7185 231 H
phurn@umich.edu
HURNS, Kimberly .... 734-973-3488 232 D
khurns@wccnet.edu
HURRELL, Rockie .... 719-502-2007.. 82 E
rockie.hurrell@ppcc.edu
HURREN, Lee .... 575-562-2443 286 B
HURSE, Jeremy .... 828-669-8012 331 K
jeremy.hurse@montreat.edu

HYUN, Timothy .... 253-752-2020 480 D
librarian@faithseminary.edu

I

IACONO, Anthony, J ..... 973-328-5031 276 J
tiacono@ccm.edu
IACONO, Neil .... 562-985-4031.. 31 D
neil.iacono@csulb.edu
IACOVOU, Charles, L .... 336-758-4579 344 C
iacovou@wfu.edu
IACUESSA, Michelle, A . 845-569-3217 307 D
michelle.iacuessa@msmc.edu
IANNAZZI, Michael, L .. 203-371-7899.. 89 A
iannazzim@sacredheart.edu
IANNELLI, Angela .... 973-290-4436 282 I
aiannelli@steu.edu
IANNELLI, Clare .... 281-998-6150 443 C
clare.iannelli@sjcd.edu
IANNELLI, Clare .... 281-998-6150 443 B
clare.iannelli@sjcd.edu
IANNELLI, Clare .... 281-478-2756 443 A
clare.iannelli@sjcd.edu
IANNELLI, Clare .... 281-998-1357 442 K
clare.iannelli@sjcd.edu
IANNELLO, Lisa .... 607-431-4061 301 A
iannellol@hartwick.edu
IANNESSA, Katherine .... 512-499-4204 454 H
kiannessa@utsystem.edu
IANNI, Danielle, D .... 716-888-2500 292 F
iannid@canisius.edu
IANNINI, Joseph .... 212-217-3359 299 D
joseph_iannini@fitnyc.edu
IANNO, Daniel .... 315-792-5356 306 K
dianno@mvcc.edu
IANNONE, Frank .... 321-674-8113 100 C
fiannone@fit.edu
IANNUZZI, Maria Lise .. 909-447-2552.. 37 E
miannuzzi@cst.edu
IATRIDIS, Ioanna .... 530-339-3610.. 64 C
iiatridis@shastacollege.edu
IAVARONE, William ...... 309-794-7357 133 C
williamiavarone@augustana.edu
IBANEZ, Beatriz .... 937-481-2231 364 A
beatriz.ibanez@wilmington.edu
IBARRA, Clotilde .... 212-343-1234 306 G
cibarra@mcny.edu
IBARRA, Ruben .... 909-448-4959.. 71 C
ssmith3@laverne.edu
IBARRA MORA, Ivan, A 650-362-3997.. 24 G
IBE, Basil .... 310-233-4160.. 49 B
ibebo@lahc.edu
IBEANUSI, Victor .... 850-599-3550 109 I
victor.ibeanusi@famu.edu
IBRAHIM, Olla .... 425-640-1957 480 A
olla.ibrahim@edcc.edu
IBSEN, Brian .... 907-786-1263.... 9 J
bpibsen@alaska.edu
ICE, Jerry .... 617-873-0224 208 B
jerry.ice@cambridgecollege.edu
ICE, Richard .... 320-363-5503 235 F
rice@csbsju.edu
ICE, Richard .... 320-363-5503 243 B
rice@csbsju.edu
ICENHOWER, Nathan .... 541-684-7221 371 I
nicenhower@bushnell.edu
ICHIGAYA, Frank .... 925-473-7391.. 40 D
fichigaya@losmedanos.edu
ICHSAN, Tony .... 509-527-5999 486 B
ichsan@whitman.edu
ICKES, Jessica .... 321-674-7569 100 C
jickes@fit.edu
IDE, Susan .... 248-218-2059 230 B
side@rochesteru.edu
IDELL, Steven .... 903-565-5515 456 A
sidell@uttyler.edu
IDETA, Lori .... 808-956-3290 129 E
ideta@hawaii.edu
IDZERDA, Yves .... 406-994-7838 264 C
idzerda@physics.montana.edu
IERIEN, Kim .... 503-281-4181 372 G
IEVERS, Teresa .... 253-589-6039 478 J
teresa.ievers@cptc.edu
IFERT JOHNSON,
Danette .... 269-337-7162 225 F
danette.johnson@kzoo.edu
IFLAND, Rick .... 805-565-6007.. 76 A
rifland@westmont.edu
IFRAH, Joseph .... 443-548-6037 201 C
jifrah@nirc.edu
IFTEKHARUDDIN, Khan 757-683-4271 469 B
kiftekha@odu.edu
IGHODARO, Osaro, O ... 602-243-8036.. 14 A
osaro.ighodaro@southmountaincc.edu

IGWIKE, Richard .... 504-816-4830 186 I
rigwike@dillard.edu
IHEANYI-IGWE,
Agametochukwu .... 541-684-7314 371 I
aiheanyiigwe@bushnell.edu
IHEKWEAZU,
Stanley, N .... 803-536-8860 411 G
sihekwea@scsu.edu
IHEKWEAZU,
Stanley, N .... 803-536-8392 411 G
sihekwea@scsu.edu
IHRER, Kenneth .... 212-650-7400 293 D
kihrer@ccny.cuny.edu
IHRIG, Stacy .... 515-574-1138 167 A
ihrig@iowacentral.edu
IHRKE, Barbara .... 765-677-1578 158 B
barbara.ihrke@indwes.edu
IKACH, Yugo .... 724-938-1589 393 E
ikach@calu.edu
IKEGAMI, Robin .... 916-558-2337.. 50 J
ikegamr@scc.losrios.edu
IKEM, Fidelis, M .... 601-979-2411 246 F
fidelis.ikem@jsums.edu
IKHARO, Sadiq .... 510-466-7336.. 57 C
sikharo@peralta.edu
ILARDI, Kristin .... 949-794-9090.. 66 D
ILES, Linda .... 530-221-4275.. 64 B
finaid@shasta.edu
ILIAKIS-DOHERTY,
Sophia .... 360-417-6219 482 C
sdoherty@pencol.edu
ILICETO, Thomas .... 212-229-5101 308 A
ilicetot@newschool.edu
ILIEVA, Vessela, K .... 801-863-5183 460 D
vessela.ilieva@uvu.edu
ILINCA, Ingrid .... 573-592-5323 262 E
ingrid.ilinca@westminster-mo.edu
ILLICH, Paul .... 402-323-3415 269 C
pillich@southeast.edu
ILLIES, Diane .... 320-308-5572 241 A
diane.illies@sctcc.edu
IM, Dou Ho .... 562-926-1023.. 58 A
IM, Manyul, E .... 203-576-4234.. 89 C
manyulim@bridgeport.edu
IM, Sam .... 215-887-5511 402 E
sim@wts.edu
IMAFUJI, Elizabeth .... 765-641-4441 153 G
elimafuji@anderson.edu
IMASUEN, Edwin .... 252-536-7239 335 B
eimasuen@halifaxcc.edu
IMBRAGULIO, Lisa .... 205-726-4172.... 6 E
lcimbrag@samford.edu
IMBRESCIA, Janelle ...... 724-653-2192 382 E
janelle@dec.edu
IMBRESCIA, Jeffrey, D .. 724-653-2200 382 E
jimbrescia@dec.edu
IMBRESCIA, Julian .... 724-653-2213 382 E
julian@dec.edu
IMBRIALE, William .... 718-409-5879 320 G
wimbriale@sunymaritime.edu
IMBRIGLIO, Sarah .... 908-526-1200 281 A
sarah.imbriglio@raritanval.edu
IMBROCK, Ryan .... 419-783-2302 351 K
rimbrock@defiance.edu
IMEL, Travis .... 202-651-5064.. 92 C
travis.imel@gallaudet.edu
IMES, Amber .... 480-994-9244.. 15 R
amberi@swiha.edu
IMES, Jean .... 352-854-2322.. 97 N
imesj@cf.edu
IMES, Melissa, J .... 717-262-2000 403 C
melissa.imes@wilson.edu
IMHOFF, Dan .... 608-822-2401 500 A
dimhoff@swtc.edu
IMHOFF, Donna .... 216-987-5125 351 E
donna.imhoff@tri-c.edu
IMHOFF, Maren, E .... 212-327-8682 312 G
imhoff@rockefeller.edu
IMLER, Mary Elizabeth .. 815-740-2274 152 H
mimler@stfrancis.edu
IMMLER, Eric .... 410-386-4639 200 F
eimmler@mcdaniel.edu
IMPERATO, Pascal .... 718-270-1056 317 B
pascal.imperato@downstate.edu
IMPERIALE, Michael, J . 734-763-3472 231 H
imperial@umich.edu
INABINET, Chad, E .... 231-843-5965 233 A
ceinabinet@westshore.edu
INAFUKU, Derek .... 808-845-9123 130 A
dinafuku@hawaii.edu
INAKE, Rachael .... 808-455-0676 130 C
rinake@hawaii.edu
INBASEKARAN, Pamela 212-228-1888 312 B

INBODY, Brian, L .... 620-432-0300 176 D
binbody@neosho.edu
INCANDELA, Joe .... 805-893-8270.. 70 E
incandela@research.ucsb.edu
INCANDELA, Joseph ..... 630-829-6247 133 E
jincandela@ben.edu
INCANDELA, Marybeth .. 934-420-2107 320 F
marybeth.incandela@farmingdale.edu
INCERA, Vivian .... 956-665-8726 455 D
vivian.incera@utrgv.edu
INCH, Edward .... 507-389-1111 239 D
INCH, Megan .... 336-841-9166 329 F
minch@highpoint.edu
INCIARDI, Kristin .... 215-545-6400 391 E
kinciardi@peirce.edu
INCITTI, Merri, S .... 304-367-4832 489 K
merri.incitti@fairmontstate.edu
INCORVAIA, James, A .. 310-204-1666.. 58 K
INDIATSI, John .... 713-221-5777 453 A
indiatsij@uhd.edu
INES, Caryn, L .... 603-535-2981 275 A
clines1@plymouth.edu
INFANTI, Steven, M ...... 717-901-5146 385 H
sinfanti@harrisburgu.edu
INFUSINO, Melissa .... 562-938-3217.. 48 F
minfusino@lbcc.edu
INGALLS, Brett .... 919-573-5350 340 C
bingalls@shepherds.edu
INGALLS, Dianne, J ...... 603-646-3001 273 D
dianne.j.ingalls@dartmouth.edu
INGALLS, Erica .... 303-404-5332.. 81 A
erica.ingalls@frontrange.edu
INGALLS, Jenna .... 800-607-6377.. 60 C
jingalls@samuelmerritt.edu
INGALLS SAUFLEY,
Leigh .... 207-780-4141 197 D
INGARGIOLA, Janet ...... 217-709-0920 142 D
INGARGIOLA, Janet, M 217-443-8760 136 G
jingarg@dacc.edu
INGBER, Marc .... 303-556-2870.. 84 D
marc.ingber@ucdenver.edu
INGBRITSEN, Sherry ..... 941-355-9080.. 98 H
INGE, Brittany .... 502-213-5155 182 C
brittany.inge@kctcs.edu
INGERMAN, Bret .... 850-201-6082 112 C
bret.ingerman@tcc.fl.edu
INGERSOLL,
Christopher .... 407-823-6424 110 E
christopher.ingersoll@ucf.edu
INGERSOLL, Julia .... 610-526-6132 385 D
jingersoll@harcum.edu
INGLAND, Susan .... 620-417-1400 177 F
susan.ingland@sccc.edu
INGLE, Jeffery, S .... 865-981-8199 421 C
jeff.ingle@maryvillecollege.edu
INGLE, Karen .... 616-331-3688 224 G
inglek@gvsu.edu
INGLE, III, Kenneth ...... 704-216-3577 337 F
ken.ingle@rccc.edu
INGLE, Kent .... 863-667-5002 108 K
kingle@seu.edu
INGLEHART, Hope .... 770-593-2257 121 A
higlehart@gupton-jones.edu
INGLES, Susan, L .... 414-410-4236 491 I
slingles@stritch.edu
INGLES, Terri .... 309-690-6945 139 B
tingles@icc.edu
INGLESIAS, Kaylynn, C . 315-684-6046 321 A
inglesike@morrisville.edu
INGLISH, Darla .... 940-397-4321 440 C
darla.inglish@msutexas.edu
INGMIRE, Eric .... 785-442-6020 174 F
eingmire@highlandcc.edu
INGMIRE, Mac .... 217-732-3168 142 G
INGMIRE, Randall .... 217-234-5253 142 C
ringmire@lakelandcollege.edu
INGRAFFIA STRONG,
Deborah .... 775-445-3334 271 F
deborah.ingraffia@wnc.edu
INGRAHAM, Barry .... 207-768-2706 195 G
bingraham@nmcc.edu
INGRAHAM, Melissa ..... 602-489-5300.. 10 F
melissa.ingraham@arizonachristian.edu
INGRAHAM, Timothy .... 978-468-7111 210 C
tingraham@gcts.edu
INGRAM, Archinya .... 803-327-7402 407 F
aingram@clintoncollege.edu
INGRAM, Beth .... 815-753-0493 146 B
bingram@niu.edu
INGRAM, Beverly .... 318-487-7694 187 E
beverly.ingram@lacollege.edu
INGRAM, Bill .... 501-420-1200.. 16 L
bill.ingram@arkansasbaptist.edu

INGRAM, Brian, C .... 731-881-7069 427 D
cingram@utm.edu
INGRAM, Casey .... 318-257-4917 192 D
casey@latech.edu
INGRAM, Clark .... 603-880-8308 274 D
INGRAM, David .... 817-461-8741 430 B
dingram@abu.edu
INGRAM, Donnie .... 803-327-7402 407 F
dingram@clintoncollege.edu
INGRAM, Donnie, L ...... 563-333-5826 169 G
ingramdonniel@sau.edu
INGRAM, Geoff .... 951-785-2000.. 47 C
gingram@lasierra.edu
INGRAM, Iris .... 714-480-7342.. 58 E
ingram_iris@rsccd.edu
INGRAM, Iris, I .... 714-480-7340.. 58 F
ingram_iris@rsccd.edu
INGRAM, J. Kevin .... 785-539-3571 176 A
kingram@mccks.edu
INGRAM, John .... 412-536-1181 386 H
john.ingram@laroche.edu
INGRAM, Joyce .... 850-412-5146 109 I
joyce.ingram@famu.edu
INGRAM, Joyce .... 850-412-5156 109 I
joyce.ingram@famu.edu
INGRAM, Kimberly .... 360-623-8444 478 F
kimberly.ingram@centralia.edu
INGRAM, Krista .... 315-228-7797 296 E
kingram@colgate.edu
INGRAM,
Lashawanda, T .... 315-386-7128 320 B
ingraml@canton.edu
INGRAM, Maleka .... 866-492-5336 244 F
maleka.ingram@mail.waldenu.edu
INGRAM, Mark, T .... 205-934-0766.... 8 A
mingram@uab.edu
INGRAM, Mary, H .... 256-352-7820.... 3 I
mary.ingram@wallacestate.edu
INGRAM, Raymond .... 937-971-2862 359 K
ringram@payneseminary.edu
INGRAM, SR.,
Roderick, L .... 330-325-6673 357 D
ringram@neomed.edu
INGRAM, Trent .... 870-248-4000.. 18 F
trent.ingram@blackrivertech.edu
INGRAM, William .... 615-460-6568 418 B
william.ingram@belmont.edu
INGRAM-WALLACE,
Brenda, J .... 610-921-7585 377 G
bingramwallace@albright.edu
INGS, Margaret Ann ..... 617-824-8299 209 C
margaret_ann_ings@emerson.edu
INIGUEZ, Alicia .... 408-285-1761.. 12 B
INIGUEZ, Edmond .... 719-549-3206.. 82 J
edmond.iniguez@pueblocc.edu
INIGUEZ, Maria .... 509-682-6400 485 H
miniguez@wvc.edu
INKSTER, Kathy .... 606-546-1616 185 D
kyinkster@unionky.edu
INLOW, Laura .... 618-468-3255 142 E
linlow@lc.edu
INMAN, Barbara, L .... 757-727-5264 467 G
barbara.inman@hamptonu.edu
INMAN, Don .... 630-942-2972 135 I
inmand@cod.edu
INMAN, John, G .... 724-458-2176 384 G
jginman@gcc.edu
INMAN, Lisa, D .... 919-536-7200 334 C
inmanl@durhamtech.edu
INMAN, Stan, D .... 801-585-5028 459 D
sinman@sa.utah.edu
INMAN, Steve, G .... 814-868-8258 387 D
sinman@mch1.org
INMAN, Tim .... 541-346-3440 376 H
tbinman@uoregon.edu
INNERST, Sean .... 303-937-4420.. 78 C
INNIGER, Alyssa, K ...... 507-344-7874 234 C
alyssa.inniger@blc.edu
INNISS, Tasha .... 404-270-5897 126 B
tinniss@spelman.edu
INOUYE, Carolyn .... 805-678-5803.. 74 A
cinouye@vcccd.edu
INOUYE, Susan, K .... 808-956-8155 129 C
susani@hawaii.edu
INOWAY-RONNIE, Eden 608-265-5975 495 D
eden.inowayronnie@wisc.edu
INSELL, Courtney .... 731-989-6011 419 K
cinsell@fhu.edu
INSKEEP, Kathryn .... 802-258-3101 462 H
kathryn.inskeep@sit.edu
INSKO, Thomas .... 541-962-3512 372 I
tinsko@eou.edu

IWAMA, Ken .... 219-980-6700 157 C
kiwama@iun.edu
IWAMIYA, Shigeo .... 617-305-2500 219 B
siwamiya@suffolk.edu
IWAMURA, Jane .... 626-571-8811.. 73 E
janei@uwest.edu
IWANAGA-BECKER,
Kelly .... 847-635-1973 146 G
kbecker@oakton.edu
IWANCZUK, Lukasz ...... 248-392-9210 231 D
liwanczuk@sscms.edu
IWANE, David .... 213-615-7268.. 36 E
diwane@thechicagoschool.edu
IWANENKO, JR.,
Walter .... 814-871-7401 384 A
iwanenko001@gannon.edu
IWASA, David .... 509-257-2542 485 C
david.iwasa@wallawalla.edu
IWATA, Chris .... 916-558-2552.. 50 J
iwatac@scc.losrios.edu
IYENGAR, Sundararaj .... 305-348-3549 110 A
undararaj.iyengar@fiu.edu
IYER, Anand .... 757-727-5071 467 G
anand.iyer@hamptonu.edu
IYER, Aruna .... 860-701-5161.. 88 D
iyer_a@mitchell.edu
IYER, Chitra .... 561-297-3076 109 J
IYER, Nalini .... 206-296-6161 484 A
niyer@seattleu.edu
IYER, Rupa .... 254-459-5449 446 D
iyer@tarleton.edu
IYER, Sandhya, L .... 603-646-0101 273 D
sandhya.l.iyer@dartmouth.edu
IZADIAN, Ali .... 657-278-2122.. 31 C
izadian@fullerton.edu
IZAGUIRRE, Minelia ...... 281-998-6150 443 B
mini.izaguirre@sjcd.edu
IZBRAND, Joe .... 210-458-8754 455 E
joe.izbrand@utsa.edu
IZQUIERDO, Julio .... 516-572-7700 307 E
julio.izquierdo@ncc.edu
IZUMI, Yoshiko .... 714-867-5009.. 65 A
yizumi@southcoastcollege.com
IZZI, Michael .... 818-677-1200.. 32 C

J

JABAR, Abdul .... 212-346-1521 311 A
ajabar@pace.edu
JABAUT, Gregory .... 617-573-8034 219 B
gjabaut@suffolk.edu
JABBOUR, Alice .... 804-862-6100 470 C
ajabbour@rbc.edu
JABLONSKI, Allison ...... 434-544-8266 471 L
jablonski@lynchburg.edu
JABLONSKI, Erin .... 570-577-2000 379 C
erin.jablonski@bucknell.edu
JABLONSKI, Jack .... 608-262-4046 495 C
jjablonski@uwsa.edu
JABLONSKI, John .... 518-743-2236 320 A
jablonski@sunyacc.edu
JABLONSKY, Carol .... 516-686-1014 308 I
cjablons@nyit.edu
JABOUR, Albert .... 214-768-3054 444 D
ajabour@smu.edu
JABRASSIAN, Vic .... 213-613-2200.. 65 E
vic@sciarc.edu
JABS, Carol, A .... 708-209-3145 136 E
carol.jabs@cuchicago.edu
JACCARINO, David .... 305-626-3766 100 D
david.jaccarino@fmuniv.edu
JACHIM-MOORE,
Darrell .... 585-292-2185 307 B
djachim-moore@monroecc.edu
JACHIM-MOORE,
Darrell, K .... 585-292-2185 307 B
djachim-moore@monroecc.edu
JACHNA, Timothy, J .... 513-556-9808 361 J
timothy.jachna@uc.edu
JACK, Adam .... 724-852-3211 402 C
ajack@waynesburg.edu
JACK, Eric .... 205-934-8800.... 8 A
ejack@uab.edu
JACK, Grilly .... 691-320-3795 504 C
gjack@comfsm.fm
JACK, Jill .... 319-399-8023 164 F
jjack@coe.edu
JACK, Laura .... 315-228-7407 296 E
ljack@colgate.edu
JACK, Syrion .... 973-877-3477 277 G
sjack1@essex.edu
JACKANICZ, Jeffrey .... 415-405-4061.. 33 E
jjackanicz@sfsu.edu
JACKLIN, Lori .... 714-463-7541.. 51 B
ljacklin@ketchum.edu
JACKLITSCH, Anthony ... 845-341-4715 310 G
JACKLOSKY, Robert ...... 718-405-3301 296 F
robert.jacklosky@mountsaintvincent.edu
JACKMAN, Guy .... 305-595-9500.. 94 G
finaid@amcollege.edu
JACKO, Mariusz .... 787-250-1912 508 D
mjacko@intermetro.com
JACKSON, Adrian .... 210-486-2712 429 B
ajackson202@alamo.edu
JACKSON, Alicia .... 229-500-2156 114 H
alicia.jackson@asurams.edu
JACKSON, SR.,
Alonzo, K .... 301-736-3631 200 C
alonzo.jackson@msbbcs.edu
JACKSON, Amy .... 620-450-2135 177 B
amyj@prattcc.edu
JACKSON, Angela .... 434-949-1004 475 B
angela.jackson@southside.edu
JACKSON, Anthony .... 225-771-5781 191 B
anthony_jackson@subr.edu
JACKSON, Antonio .... 910-678-0058 334 E
jacksona@faytechcc.edu
JACKSON, Arrick, L ...... 218-477-4377 239 E
arrick.jackson@mnstate.edu
JACKSON, Athena .... 713-743-9915 452 D
anjackson7@uh.edu
JACKSON, Barcus .... 816-604-1180 255 C
barcus.jackson@mcckc.edu
JACKSON, Bradley, A .... 513-585-0116 350 D
bradley.jackson@thechristcollege.edu
JACKSON, Brenda .... 910-695-3731 337 H
jacksonbr@sandhills.edu
JACKSON, Brenda .... 251-578-1313.... 3 D
bjackson@rstc.edu
JACKSON, Brenda, W ... 504-586-5274 191 C
bjackson@suno.edu
JACKSON, Brent .... 724-838-4215 398 C
jbjackson@setonhill.edu
JACKSON, Brian .... 434-797-8410 473 G
brian.jackson@danville.edu
JACKSON, Brian, K .... 609-652-4900 283 E
brian.jackson@stockton.edu
JACKSON, Bridgett .... 334-291-4972.... 1 H
bridgett.jackson@cv.edu
JACKSON, Bryan .... 870-541-7858.. 19 G
JACKSON, Bryant .... 605-658-6199 416 D
bryant.jackson@usd.edu
JACKSON, Cameron ...... 704-233-8739 344 F
c.jackson@wingate.edu
JACKSON, Carlissa .... 925-631-4754.. 59 I
cj10@stmarys-ca.edu
JACKSON, Casanna .... 904-256-7267 102 H
cjackso29@ju.edu
JACKSON, Cheryl .... 903-730-4890 438 D
cjackson@jarvis.edu
JACKSON, Chris .... 213-615-7284.. 36 E
cjackson4@thechicagoschool.edu
JACKSON, Corey .... 415-476-1000.. 70 D
corey.jackson@ucsf.edu
JACKSON, Corey, A .... 610-566-1776 403 B
cjackson@williamson.edu
JACKSON, Courtney ...... 508-270-4005 214 G
cjackson@massbay.edu
JACKSON, Craig .... 478-757-3508 116 G
cjackson@centralgatech.edu
JACKSON, Craig .... 541-440-7729 376 G
craig.jackson@umpqua.edu
JACKSON, Craig, R .... 909-558-4545.. 48 E
cjackson@llu.edu
JACKSON, Dalen, C .... 502-863-8300 179 F
dalen.jackson@bsk.edu
JACKSON, Danielle .... 406-353-2607 262 H
djackson@ancollege.edu
JACKSON, Darryl .... 256-372-4854.... 1 A
darryl.jackson1@aamu.edu
JACKSON, JR., David ... 850-599-3505 109 I
david.jackson@famu.edu
JACKSON, David, H ...... 941-309-0166 106 J
djackson@ringling.edu
JACKSON, JR.,
David, H .... 919-530-6230 341 E
JACKSON, Deanne .... 573-341-4362 261 D
registrar@mst.edu
JACKSON, Deborah, C .. 617-873-0112 208 B
deborah.jackson@cambridgecollege.edu
JACKSON, Debra .... 661-654-3420.. 30 B
djackson9@csub.edu
JACKSON, Debra .... 309-677-3085 134 A
dsjackson@bradley.edu
JACKSON, Deidra, A ..... 229-391-5001 114 F
JACKSON, Deirdre .... 910-630-7150 331 E
dejackson@methodist.edu
JACKSON, Derek, A ...... 785-532-6453 175 C
derekaj@ksu.edu
JACKSON, Dexter .... 334-214-4815.... 1 H
dexter.jackson@cv.edu
JACKSON, Diana, K ...... 510-231-5000.. 46 J
diana.k.jackson@kp.org
JACKSON, Diane, V .... 803-793-5329 408 G
guinyardjackson@denmarktech.edu
JACKSON, Equilla .... 936-261-1890 446 C
eqjackson@pvamu.edu
JACKSON, Eric .... 208-467-8061 132 E
ericjackson@nnu.edu
JACKSON, Erica .... 804-257-5848 476 F
emjackson@vuu.edu
JACKSON, Ericka .... 313-577-1981 232 K
emjackson@wayne.edu
JACKSON, Eugene .... 973-877-3276 277 G
ejackson@essex.edu
JACKSON, Faith .... 201-200-2340 279 D
fjackson@njcu.edu
JACKSON, Gary .... 662-325-3036 247 F
gary@ext.msstate.edu
JACKSON, Gayla .... 251-626-3303.... 7 E
gjackson@ussa.edu
JACKSON, Gregory .... 256-372-8653.... 1 A
gregory.jackson@aamu.edu
JACKSON, Gregory .... 508-626-4698 213 A
gjackson@framingham.edu
JACKSON, Guy .... 307-742-3776 502 B
gjackson@wyotech.edu
JACKSON, Heidi .... 308-635-6395 270 C
jacksonh@wncc.edu
JACKSON, J. Brooks ..... 319-335-8064 163 H
brooks-jackson@uiowa.edu
JACKSON, Jacob .... 425-235-5846 482 H
jackson.jacob@rtc.edu
JACKSON, Jacqueline ... 443-412-2333 199 D
jajackson@harford.edu
JACKSON, Jay .... 864-592-4723 412 E
jacksonj@sccsc.edu
JACKSON, Jean .... 919-760-8556 331 D
jacksonj@meredith.edu
JACKSON, Jerry .... 606-539-4250 185 E
jerry.jackson@ucumberlands.edu
JACKSON, Jim, C .... 580-581-2460 365 D
jjackson@cameron.edu
JACKSON, John .... 916-577-2210.. 76 D
jjackson@jessup.edu
JACKSON, John .... 540-231-8508 476 C
johnj1@vt.edu
JACKSON, JR., John, L 215-898-4407 400 F
dean@asc.upenn.edu
JACKSON, Julie .... 662-846-4151 245 G
jjackson@deltastate.edu
JACKSON, Justin .... 973-408-3957 277 A
jjackson@drew.edu
JACKSON, Karina .... 443-412-2114 199 D
kjackson@harford.edu
JACKSON, Kashanta ...... 662-846-4690 245 G
kjackson@deltastate.edu
JACKSON, Kathy .... 512-492-3118 442 I
kathyj@stedwards.edu
JACKSON, Keith .... 334-876-9238.... 2 D
keith.jackson@wccs.edu
JACKSON, Keith .... 304-293-4532 490 E
keith.jackson@mail.wvu.edu
JACKSON, Kelly .... 910-592-8081 337 G
kjackson@sampsoncc.edu
JACKSON, Kelly .... 970-339-6583.. 77 H
kelly.jackson@aims.edu
JACKSON, Kelly .... 903-813-2468 430 H
kjackson@austincollege.edu
JACKSON, Ken, L .... 208-496-1610 130 I
jacksonken@byui.edu
JACKSON, Kenneth .... 219-989-2366 160 D
kjackson@pnw.edu
JACKSON, Kevin, P .... 254-710-1314 431 E
JACKSON, Kevin, P .... 254-710-1616 431 E
kevin_p_jackson@baylor.edu
JACKSON, Kim .... 509-793-2067 478 B
kimj@bigbend.edu
JACKSON, Kimberly ...... 252-940-6252 332 C
kimberly.jackson@beaufortccc.edu
JACKSON, Kirk .... 918-335-6833 368 E
kjackson@okwu.edu
JACKSON, Kremiere ...... 509-963-1425 478 E
kremiere.jackson@cwu.edu
JACKSON, Kris .... 405-789-7661 369 I
kris.jackson@swcu.edu
JACKSON, Lachanna ..... 513-569-1230 350 F
lachanna.jackson@cincinnatistate.edu
JACKSON, LaTisha .... 501-370-5229.. 20 F
ljackson@philander.edu
JACKSON, LaToya .... 916-660-7102.. 64 D
ljackson7@sierracollege.edu
JACKSON, LaToya .... 646-313-8000 295 D
latoya.jackson@guttman.cuny.edu
JACKSON, LaTrelle .... 937-775-3494 364 E
latrelle.jackson@wright.edu
JACKSON, Laura .... 601-925-3865 247 C
ljackson@mc.edu
JACKSON, Laura .... 903-565-5936 456 A
laurajackson@uttyler.edu
JACKSON, Lauren .... 318-357-5961 192 G
potterl@nsula.edu
JACKSON, Leah .... 318-357-4553 192 G
jacksonl@nsula.edu
JACKSON, Leah .... 440-375-7200 354 K
ljackson@lec.edu
JACKSON, Lee, M .... 773-907-4360 135 C
ljackson410@ccc.edu
JACKSON, Lenora .... 404-270-5209 126 B
lenoraj@spelman.edu
JACKSON, Leon .... 928-724-6774.. 12 D
lejackson@dinecollege.edu
JACKSON, Les .... 256-765-4357.... 8 E
aljackson@una.edu
JACKSON, Linda .... 804-257-5807 476 F
lrjackson@vuu.edu
JACKSON, Linda, Y .... 512-505-3006 438 A
lyjackson@htu.edu
JACKSON, Lisa .... 972-524-3341 445 B
lisa.jackson@swcc.edu
JACKSON, Lisa .... 225-743-8500 188 H
ljackson@rpcc.edu
JACKSON, Lisa .... 301-985-7077 203 E
lisa.jackson@umuc.edu
JACKSON, Loreto .... 617-228-2088 214 C
lmjackson@bhcc.mass.edu
JACKSON, Marcus .... 512-505-3005 438 A
mwjackson@htu.edu
JACKSON, Margaret, W 931-363-9836 427 E
mjacks93@utsouthern.edu
JACKSON, Marilyn .... 415-338-1293.. 33 E
mjackson@sfsu.edu
JACKSON, Mark .... 610-519-4110 401 K
m.w.jackson@villanova.edu
JACKSON, Mary .... 504-286-5388 191 C
mjackson@suno.edu
JACKSON, Mary Anne ... 816-235-1808 261 B
jacksonmar@umkc.edu
JACKSON, Mckenzie ...... 910-630-7108 331 E
mjackson@methodist.edu
JACKSON, Melodie, R ... 717-361-1404 383 C
jacksonmr@etown.edu
JACKSON, Meredith ...... 256-840-4163.... 3 F
meredith.jackson@snead.edu
JACKSON, Micah .... 773-380-6780 133 F
mjackson@bexleyseabury.edu
JACKSON, Michael .... 858-646-3100.. 62M
mjackson@sbpdiscovery.org
JACKSON, Michael, D ... 256-766-6610.... 5 E
mjackson@hcu.edu
JACKSON, Mike .... 717-871-4292 395 A
michael.jackson@millersville.edu
JACKSON, Mike .... 918-463-2931 365 J
mike.jackson@connorsstate.edu
JACKSON, Milan, A ...... 610-917-1402 401 G
majackson@valleyforge.edu
JACKSON, Miles .... 360-992-2934 478 I
mjackson@clark.edu
JACKSON, Monica .... 202-885-2155.. 91 F
monica@american.edu
JACKSON, Myesha .... 619-216-6631.. 66 A
mjackson@swccd.edu
JACKSON, Nan .... 850-484-1721 105 H
njackson@pensacolastate.edu
JACKSON, Nancy .... 334-833-4482.... 5 G
hcbookstore@hawks.huntingdon.edu
JACKSON, Natalie .... 419-372-0464 348 G
njackson@bgsu.edu
JACKSON, Nick .... 903-434-8147 440 G
njackson@ntcc.edu
JACKSON, Nicole .... 706-641-5245 117 I
njackson@columbustech.edu
JACKSON, Pat .... 618-985-3741 140 H
patjackson@jalc.edu
JACKSON, Patrick, T ..... 202-885-6194.. 91 F
ptjack@american.edu
JACKSON, Paul .... 603-880-8308 274 D
tmc@thomasmorecollege.edu

JACKSON, Paul 585-245-6128 318 B jackson@geneseo.edu
JACKSON, Peggy 870-612-2030 22 H peggy.jackson@uaccb.edu
JACKSON, Philip 870-972-3362 17 C pjackson@asusystem.edu
JACKSON, Raymond, L 817-272-3186 454 I jackson@uta.edu
JACKSON, Richard 615-687-6892 417 F rjackson@abcnash.edu
JACKSON, Rickey 928-524-7350 14 J rickey.jackson@npc.edu
JACKSON, Robert 270-809-3763 184 D rjackson@murraystate.edu
JACKSON, Robert 901-678-8324 426 G rjax@memphis.edu
JACKSON, Robert, D 847-578-3248 148 F robert.jackson@rosalindfranklin.edu
JACKSON, Rodney 404-627-2681 116 C rodney.jackson@beulah.edu
JACKSON, Ron 864-592-4817 412 E jacksonr@sccsc.edu
JACKSON, Ronald 718-951-5352 293 C rcjackson@brooklyn.cuny.edu
JACKSON, Rose Mary 501-882-4407 17 D rmjackson@asub.edu
JACKSON, Ruth 207-859-4350 194 D ruth.jackson@colby.edu
JACKSON, Ruth 405-466-3424 366 C ruth.jackson@langston.edu
JACKSON, Sally 509-533-3123 479 D sally.jackson@sfcc.spokane.edu
JACKSON, Scarlett 863-638-7297 114 A scarlett.jackson@warner.edu
JACKSON, Shanna, L 615-353-3236 424 G shanna.jackson@nscc.edu
JACKSON, Sharon, S 804-752-3747 469 F sjackson@rmc.edu
JACKSON, Shawn, L 773-907-4450 135 C sljackson@ccc.edu
JACKSON, Shelbra 919-735-5151 338 H sbjackson@waynecc.edu
JACKSON, Sherri 904-256-7212 102 H sjackso@ju.edu
JACKSON, Sherry 865-354-3000 425 C jacksons3@roanestate.edu
JACKSON, Shirley, J 202-806-7565 92 F sjackson@howard.edu
JACKSON, Shirley Ann 518-276-6211 312 C president@rpi.edu
JACKSON, Smith 336-278-5837 328 J jacksons@elon.edu
JACKSON, Stacey, N 248-246-2612 229 C snjackso@oaklandcc.edu
JACKSON, Stacy, N 313-447-3905 232 K stacy.jackson@wayne.edu
JACKSON, Stanley 410-455-1336 203 B jacksons@umbc.edu
JACKSON, Stephanie 912-525-5000 124 I sjackson@scad.edu
JACKSON, Stephen, B 858-534-6514 70 C s7jackson@ucsd.edu
JACKSON, Tambra 317-274-2290 157 D tambjack@iupui.edu
JACKSON, Tammi 919-760-8516 331 D tdjacson@meredith.edu
JACKSON, Terell 256-551-3117 2 E terell.jackson@drakestate.edu
JACKSON, Teresa 314-652-0300 258 M tjackson@slchc.edu
JACKSON, Tom 336-256-0543 341 D htjackson@ncat.edu
JACKSON, JR., Tom 707-826-3311 33 C tom.jackson@humboldt.edu
JACKSON, Tondaleya 803-705-4726 406 G tondaleya.jackson@benedict.edu
JACKSON, Tony 803-712-7430 413 E tonyjack@mailbox.sc.edu
JACKSON, Tonya 850-561-2888 109 I tonya.jackson@famu.edu
JACKSON, Torie 304-424-8000 490 F torie.jackson@wvup.edu
JACKSON, Tracey 504-520-7364 193 E tjacks33@xula.edu
JACKSON, Trevor 443-412-2286 199 D tjackson@harford.edu
JACKSON, Twana 304-929-6716 488 G tjackson@newriver.edu
JACKSON, Tyrone 323-343-2800 31 E tjackso4@calstatela.edu
JACKSON, Tyrone 662-246-6301 247 D tjackson@msdelta.edu
JACKSON, Veronica, G 843-355-4150 414 C grahamjacksonv@wiltech.edu
JACKSON, Vince, E 912-287-5818 117 E vjackson@costalpines.edu
JACKSON, Vincent 213-763-7035 49 F vjackson@lattc.edu
JACKSON, Wayne 407-823-2716 110 E wayne.jackson@ucf.edu
JACKSON, Wendy 704-216-6158 330 H wjackso@livingstone.edu
JACKSON, William 904-819-6310 99 E wjackson@flagler.edu
JACKSON, William 301-891-4475 205 A wjackson@wau.edu
JACKSON, William 217-234-5296 142 C wjackson60312@lakeland.cc.il.us
JACKSON, Zena 817-515-3010 445 F zena.jackson@tccd.edu
JACKSON-BECK, Lauren, A 315-267-2477 319 A jacksola@potsdam.edu
JACKSON-DAVIS, Dorothy, G 601-877-6460 245 A djdavis@alcorn.edu
JACKSON-ELMOORE, Cynthia 517-355-2326 227 F jacks174@msu.edu
JACKSON-ELMOORE, Cynthia 805-756-2186 29 I cp-provost@calpoly.edu
JACKSON-GOODE, Cecelia 410-617-2524 200 B cjackson-goode@loyola.edu
JACKSON-NEWSOM, Julia 336-334-3218 343 A j_jackso@uncg.edu
JACKSON-STENLUND, Laura 785-227-3380 172 A stenlundl@bethanylb.edu
JACKSON-WILLIAMS, Loretta 601-984-5006 249 E ljackson@umc.edu
JACOB, Bill 907-786-4622 9 J uaa.administrative.services@alaska.edu
JACOB, Jeffrey, S 212-678-8000 303 D jejacob@jtsa.edu
JACOB, Karen 978-478-3400 218 A kjacob@northpoint.edu
JACOB, Patrick 501-212-6608 18 H pjacob@cbc.edu
JACOB, Ric 859-846-5419 184 B rjacob@midway.edu
JACOB, Robert, W 570-577-1791 379 C rjw003@bucknell.edu
JACOB, Sinu 718-368-4645 294 E sinu.jacob@kbcc.cuny.edu
JACOB, Stephen 626-350-1500 28 F
JACOB, Sybil 810-762-9514 226 B sjacob@kettering.edu
JACOB ARRIOLA, Kimberly, R 404-727-2600 118 E kjacoba@emory.edu
JACOBOWITZ, Chanie 732-367-1060 275 K cjacobowitz@bmg.edu
JACOBS, Amy 646-565-6276 322 G amy.jacobs@touro.edu
JACOBS, Amy 646-565-6276 322 F amy.jacobs@touro.edu
JACOBS, Andrew 334-386-7657 5 C ajacobs@faulkner.edu
JACOBS, Bonita 706-864-1993 127 A president@ung.edu
JACOBS, Brandi, D 304-696-3328 489 M jacobs2@marshall.edu
JACOBS, Carmela 785-320-4530 175 G carmelajacobs@manhattantech.edu
JACOBS, Cathleen 412-536-1033 386 H cathleen.jacobs@laroche.edu
JACOBS, Cecilia 254-968-1620 446 D cjacobs@tarleton.edu
JACOBS, Christine 314-977-8482 259 F christine.jacobs@health.slu.edu
JACOBS, Courtney 910-272-3231 337 D cjacobs@robeson.edu
JACOBS, Craig, M 610-892-1509 393 B cjacobs@pit.edu
JACOBS, Danny, O 503-494-8252 374 H president@ohsu.edu
JACOBS, Dennis, C 718-817-3040 300 C dcjacobs@fordham.edu
JACOBS, Derya, A 412-397-6363 397 B jacobs@rmu.edu
JACOBS, Diane 412-237-3064 381 D djacobs@ccac.edu
JACOBS, Douglas 530-891-6900 27 E
JACOBS, Holly, A 330-941-2340 364 H hajacobs@ysu.edu
JACOBS, Jay 802-656-5841 463 A jason.jacobs@uvm.edu
JACOBS, Jenny 573-897-5000 260 A
JACOBS, Jo-Ann 718-270-6024 294 G jo-ann@mec.cuny.edu
JACOBS, Josh 740-376-4711 355 E jej002@marietta.edu
JACOBS, Joshua 740-376-4711 355 E jej002@marietta.edu
JACOBS, Joshua 217-228-5432 147 F jacobwi@quincy.edu
JACOBS, Judy 620-792-9349 171 I jacobsj@bartonccc.edu
JACOBS, Kelvin 910-521-6000 343 B
JACOBS, Ken 830-792-7450 443 E security2@schreiner.edu
JACOBS, Kevin 708-239-4735 151 A kevin.jacobs@trnty.edu
JACOBS, Kristen 401-254-3428 405 C kjacobs@rwu.edu
JACOBS, Lacie 910-788-6442 338 A lacie.jacobs@sccnc.edu
JACOBS, Latrissa 817-984-0550 93 H
JACOBS, Laura 479-575-7910 21 F laura@uark.edu
JACOBS, Leah 409-747-4862 456 E lejacobs@utmb.edu
JACOBS, Mark 480-965-2354 10 J mark.jacobs@asu.edu
JACOBS, Mary, R 513-875-3344 350 C mary.jacobs@chatfield.edu
JACOBS, Michael 585-292-3369 307 B mjacobs20@monroecc.edu
JACOBS, Morenika 425-235-2352 482 H mjacobs@rtc.edu
JACOBS, Nicole 410-617-2271 200 B nmjacobs@loyola.edu
JACOBS, Sheila 479-508-3317 18 C sjacobs3@atu.edu
JACOBS, Tina 405-422-1454 369 A tina.jacobs@redlandscc.edu
JACOBS, Tomeka 909-447-2536 37 E tjacobs@cst.edu
JACOBS, Walt 408-924-5300 34 A walt.jacobs@sjsu.edu
JACOBS, Will 610-757-8702 378 D will.jacobs@theamericancollege.edu
JACOBS ANDERSON, Laura 503-370-6206 377 F ljacobsa@willamette.edu
JACOBS WILKE, Alexandra 315-267-2918 319 A jacobsam@potsdam.edu
JACOBSEN, Brandy 318-670-9371 191 D bjacobsen@susla.edu
JACOBSEN, Christie 610-625-7797 390 F jacobsen@moravian.edu
JACOBSEN, Gabe 206-281-2043 483 G jacobseng@spu.edu
JACOBSEN, Joyce, P 315-781-3309 301 F jacobsen@hws.edu
JACOBSEN, Linda 775-445-4262 271 F linda.jacobsen@wnc.edu
JACOBSEN, Ruth 206-281-2114 483 G rjacobsen@spu.edu
JACOBSEN, Stan 828-641-0554 327 B jacobssf@brevard.edu
JACOBSEN, Valarie 513-745-1983 364 G jacobsenv@xavier.edu
JACOBSMA, Kelly, G 616-395-7738 225 D jacobsma@hope.edu
JACOBSON, Anne Marie 970-204-8375 81 A annemarie.jacobson@frontrange.edu
JACOBSON, Annie 231-845-3329 233 A ajacobson@westshore.edu
JACOBSON, Bob 510-642-6000 69 A bjacobson@berkeley.edu
JACOBSON, Bryan 701-349-3621 346 I bjacobson@trinitybiblecollege.edu
JACOBSON, Cynthia 620-901-6213 171 D jacobson@allencc.edu
JACOBSON, Karin 620-432-0333 176 D kjacobson@neosho.edu
JACOBSON, Kristie 765-998-4956 161 C kristie_jacobson@taylor.edu
JACOBSON, Leigh Ann 570-408-4608 403 A leighann.jacobson@wilkes.edu
JACOBSON, Mark 804-862-6100 470 C mjacobson@rbc.edu
JACOBSON, Mark 414-416-9503 496 B markj@uwm.edu
JACOBSON, Mary 763-433-1315 237 D mary.jacobson@anokaramsey.edu
JACOBSON, Mary 763-433-1315 237 E mary.jacobson@anokaramsey.edu
JACOBSON, Renee, R 231-995-1256 229 A hjacobson@nmc.edu
JACOBSON, Ron 718-817-1000 300 C rjacobson@fordham.edu
JACOBSON, Ronald 509-777-4574 486 C rjacobson@whitworth.edu
JACOBSON, Steven 707-638-5270 68 B steven.jacobson@tu.edu
JACOBSON, Terra 708-974-5467 145 A jacobsont6@morainevalley.edu
JACOBSON, Tim 952-995-1471 238 C tim.jacobson@hennepintech.edu
JACOBSON-SCHULTE, Marah 612-330-1034 234 A jacobsm@augsburg.edu
JACOBSON-SCHULTE, Patrick 712-279-5504 164 B patrick.jacobson-schulte@briarcliff.edu
JACOBY, JoAnn 719-389-6070 78 I jjacoby@coloradocollege.edu
JACOBY, Susan 202-651-5005 92 C susan.jacoby@gallaudet.edu
JACOT, Jaclyn 509-279-6235 479 C jaclyn.jacot@scc.spokane.edu
JACQUE, Mark 410-837-6875 204 F mjacque@ubalt.edu
JACQUES, Kevin 256-765-5760 8 E kljacques@una.edu
JACQUES, Theresa 901-321-2474 418 G tjacque2@cbu.edu
JACQUES, Theresa, K 906-487-2936 228 A tjacques@mtu.edu
JACQUES, Therese 314-889-1434 253 E tjacques@fontbonne.edu
JACSO, Jeff 812-237-3525 156 D jeff.jacso@indstate.edu
JACZYNSKI, Linda 610-519-4080 401 K linda.jaczynski@villanova.edu
JADALLA, Kholood 714-533-3946 34 C ssa@calums.edu
JADALLAH, Edward 843-349-2773 408 A ejadalla@coastal.edu
JADHAV, Esther, D 859-858-3511 179 D esther.jadhav@asbury.edu
JADIN, Jason 507-280-2816 240 H jason.jadin@rctc.edu
JADLOS, Melissa 585-385-8164 313 F mjadlos@sjfc.edu
JADUSHLEVER, Renee 510-430-2033 52 E reneejad@mills.edu
JAECKEL, Andrea 928-350-4006 15 L andrea.jaeckel@prescott.edu
JAEGER, David 239-590-2315 109 K djaeger@fgcu.edu
JAEGER, Meridith 920-498-6995 499 G meridith.jaeger@nwtc.edu
JAEGER, Naftali 516-239-9002 315 D rnj@shoryoshuv.org
JAEGER, Timothy, J 949-214-3179 39 K tim.jaeger@cui.edu
JAEN, Ulysses 239-687-5501 95 L ujaen@avemarialaw.edu
JAFERIAN, Warren 978-232-2272 209 E wjaferia@endicott.edu
JAFFE, Dan, T 512-471-2877 455 A vp-research-sr@utexas.edu
JAFFE, David, L 561-237-7099 103 W djaffe@lynn.edu
JAFFE, Denise 802-387-1682 462 C denisejaffe@landmark.edu
JAFFE, Robert 718-482-5037 294 F rjaffe@lagcc.cuny.edu
JAFFE, Victoria 602-206-8115 272 L vjaffe@ccsnh.edu
JAFFE, Yaakov 347-619-9074 326 F
JAFFE GROPACK, Stacy 631-632-6265 317 A stacy.jaffegropack@stonybrookmedicine.edu
JAFFEE, Victoria 949-214-3042 39 K victori.jaffe@cui.edu
JAFFER, Nori 212-687-3730 275 I naj@berkeleycollege.edu
JAFFER, Nori 212-687-3730 291 E naj@berkeleycollege.edu
JAGANATHAN, Shiva 512-471-3833 455 A irris@austin.utexas.edu
JAGENDORF, Susan 518-255-5558 319 C jagends@cobleskill.edu

JAGER, Tim .... 712-274-5313 168 E
jager@morningside.edu
JAGERSON, Todd .... 651-450-3373 238 E
tjagerson@inverhills.edu
JAGERSON, Todd .... 651-423-8000 238 A
todd.jagerson@dctc.edu
JAGGARD, Meredith ..... 415-581-8879.. 69 C
jaggardmeredith@uchastings.edu
JAGGARS, Damon, E .... 614-292-4241 358 D
jaggars.1@osu.edu
JAGGER, Kathleen, S .... 316-942-4291 176 E
jaggerk@newmanu.edu
JAGGERS, Dametraus .... 610-436-3260 395 D
djaggers@wcupa.edu
JAGNE-SHAW,
Marcel, E .... 410-651-7859 203 D
mjagneshaw@umes.edu
JAGODZINSKE, Scott .... 785-833-4529 175 E
campus.ministry@kwu.edu
JAGOE, Christopher, J .. 570-408-4989 403 A
christopher.jagoe@wilkes.edu
JAGORD, Mary-Jo .... 716-878-6001 317 F
jagordmj@buffalostate.edu
JAGUSZTYN, Nicole .... 813-253-7090 102 B
njagusztyn@hccfl.edu
JAH, Cassaundra .... 575-758-8914 286 H
cassaundraj@midwiferycollege.edu
JAHANIAN, Farnam ..... 412-268-2201 380 C
president@andrew.cmu.edu
JAHNKE, Tamera, S .... 417-836-5249 256 G
tamerajahnke@missouristate.edu
JAIME, Andres .... 210-431-5579 441 B
aijaime@ollusa.edu
JAIME-SANCHEZ,
Norma .... 541-276-1260 371 H
njaime@bluecc.edu
JAIN, Madhu .... 312-939-0111 137 D
madhu@eastwest.edu
JAKE, Charles .... 419-530-8411 363 B
charles.jake@utoledo.edu
JAKOBSEN, Lindsey ..... 605-642-6111 416 E
lindsey.jakobsen@bhsu.edu
JAKUBOWSKI, Laura ..... 802-468-6072 463 E
laura.jakubowski@castleton.edu
JAKUBS, Deborah .... 919-660-5800 328 F
deborah.jakubs@duke.edu
JAKWAY, Julie .... 941-752-5326 109 G
jakwayj@scf.edu
JALBERT, Kenneth .... 401-739-5000 404 E
kjalbert@neit.edu
JALOMO, Romero .... 831-755-6822.. 44 G
rjalomo@hartnell.edu
JALOWIEC, Tammi .... 218-679-2860 242 U
JALSEVAC, Paul .... 540-636-2900 465 L
pjalsevac@christendom.edu
JAMEISON, Linda .... 864-646-1562 412 H
ljameiso@tctc.edu
JAMERSON, Joseph ...... 904-264-2172 106 K
joe.jamerson@iws.edu
JAMERSON, JR.,
Londell .... 816-604-1453 255 C
londell.jamerson@mcckc.edu
JAMERSON, Sun Kyong 440-366-7569 355 B
JAMES, JR.,
Advergus, D .... 334-727-8088.... 7 D
ajames@tuskegee.edu
JAMES, Anisa .... 606-546-1704 185 D
ajames@unionky.edu
JAMES, April .... 706-245-7226 118 D
ajames@ec.edu
JAMES, Arthur .... 972-860-3364 435 B
ajames@dcccd.edu
JAMES, Beverly .... 803-786-3107 408 D
bjames@columbiasc.edu
JAMES, Blake .... 305-284-6381 113 C
bjames@miami.edu
JAMES, Brian .... 706-245-7226 118 D
bjames@ec.edu
JAMES, Catherine .... 269-965-3931 225 H
jamesc@kellogg.edu
JAMES, Cheryl .... 505-747-2162 287 H
cheryl.james@nnmc.edu
JAMES, Christene .... 209-667-3077.. 33 B
cajames@csustan.edu
JAMES, Deborah .... 804-862-6100 470 C
djames@rbc.edu
JAMES, Denise .... 708-209-3337 136 E
denise.james@cuchicago.edu
JAMES, Derrick .... 504-286-5295 191 C
djames@suno.edu
JAMES, Ella .... 870-338-6474.. 22 G
JAMES, Eric .... 775-784-4013 271 E
ejames@police.unr.edu
JAMES, Erika, H .... 215-898-4715 400 F
ehjames@wharton.upenn.edu
JAMES, Errin .... 870-633-4480.. 19 A
ejames@eacc.edu
JAMES, III, Frank .... 215-368-5000 390 A
fjames@missio.edu
JAMES, Glenn, E .... 210-829-3940 453 C
gjames@uiwtx.edu
JAMES, Gwendolyn .... 509-533-8883 479 C
gwendolyn.james@scc.spokane.edu
JAMES, II, Hubert, L .... 386-481-2524.. 96 D
jamesh@cookman.edu
JAMES, Jacqueline .... 404-270-5111 126 B
jjames@spelman.edu
JAMES, Janet, C .... 972-238-6974 435 C
jjames@dcccd.edu
JAMES, Jeff .... 412-397-2424 397 B
jamesj@rmu.edu
JAMES, Jennifer, N .... 718-270-5083 294 G
jenjames@mec.cuny.edu
JAMES, Jeremy .... 334-556-2361.... 2 C
jjames@wallace.edu
JAMES, Jill .... 856-351-2910 283 B
jjames@salemcc.edu
JAMES, Karen .... 310-204-1666.. 58 K
JAMES, Karlon .... 405-466-3299 366 C
karlon.james@langston.edu
JAMES, Keith .... 701-483-2391 345 C
keith.w.james@dickinsonstate.edu
JAMES, Kelly .... 785-890-3641 176 H
kelly.james@nwktc.edu
JAMES, Kelly .... 815-394-5045 148 D
kjames@rockford.edu
JAMES, Kesha .... 205-929-6450.... 2 H
kjames@lawsonstate.edu
JAMES, Kevin, E .... 404-458-6085 123 F
JAMES, Kevin, L .... 336-334-7632 341 D
kljames@ncat.edu
JAMES, Kim .... 972-825-4634 444 J
kjames@sagu.edu
JAMES, Kimberly .... 860-773-1504.. 87 G
kjames@tunxis.edu
JAMES, Latoya .... 561-433-2330 108 J
JAMES, Lisa .... 719-502-2056.. 82 E
lisa.james@ppcc.edu
JAMES, Lisa .... 256-726-7270.... 6 C
ljames@oakwood.edu
JAMES, Makila .... 202-685-4242 502 K
makila.james.civ@ndu.edu
JAMES, Mark .... 806-874-3571 432 J
mark.james@clarendoncollege.edu
JAMES, Mary, B .... 503-777-7250 375 G
mjames@reed.edu
JAMES, Matricia .... 716-375-2000 313 C
mjames@sbu.edu
JAMES, Matthew .... 504-282-4455 190 F
JAMES, Megan .... 601-974-1225 247 B
JAMES, Michael .... 620-947-3121 177 I
michaeljames@tabor.edu
JAMES, Michelle .... 412-536-1139 386 H
michelle.james@laroche.edu
JAMES, Mike .... 956-665-2451 455 D
mike.james@utrgv.edu
JAMES, Naja .... 310-377-5501.. 51 C
njames@marymountcalifornia.edu
JAMES, Nancy .... 916-660-8300.. 64 D
njames3@sierracollege.edu
JAMES, Novia .... 520-383-0054.. 16 A
njames@tocc.edu
JAMES, Patrick .... 256-824-6942.... 8 B
patrick.james@uah.edu
JAMES, Patrick .... 312-629-6600 149 F
pjames@saic.edu
JAMES, Peggy .... 262-595-2101 496 D
james@uwp.edu
JAMES, Penny .... 402-354-7225 268 B
penny.james@methodistcollege.edu
JAMES, Regina .... 225-771-2552 191 E
rjames@sulc.edu
JAMES, Reuben .... 310-900-1600.. 39 F
JAMES, Robert .... 252-451-8308 336 E
rmjames752@nashcc.edu
JAMES, Ruben .... 310-900-1600.. 39 F
rjames@elcamino.edu
JAMES, Ruby, F .... 217-420-6029 144 G
rubyjames@millikin.edu
JAMES, Shashanta .... 269-387-6000 233 B
shanta.james@wmich.edu
JAMES, Shauna .... 256-765-4279.... 8 E
sljames@una.edu
JAMES, Steven .... 802-322-1676 462 B
steven.james@goddard.edu
JAMES, Susan, M .... 757-822-1084 475 E
sjames@tcc.edu
JAMES, Sylvia .... 253-964-6710 482 E
JAMES, Timmy .... 256-331-6281.... 3 C
timmy.james@nwscc.edu
JAMES, Tracy .... 636-481-3187 254 C
tjames@jeffco.edu
JAMES, Vernon .... 719-549-3035.. 82 J
vernon.james@pueblocc.edu
JAMES, W. Brian .... 706-245-7226 118 D
bjames@ec.edu
JAMES BLACKWELL,
Leanna .... 413-565-1000 206 D
ljamesblackwell@baypath.edu
JAMESON, Chandler ..... 559-325-3600.. 28 D
cjameson@chsu.edu
JAMESON, J, L .... 215-898-6796 400 F
ljameson@mail.med.upenn.edu
JAMESON, Maisha .... 510-464-3236.. 57 B
mjameson@peralta.edu
JAMESON, Naima .... 510-356-4760.. 77 F
JAMESON, Sean .... 914-395-2494 315 A
sjameson@sarahlawrence.edu
JAMESON, Susan .... 507-389-7211 241 C
susan.jameson@southcentral.edu
JAMGOCHIAN, Amy .... 415-455-8088.. 53 B
JAMIESON, Richard, J .. 216-368-3720 349 D
rjj@case.edu
JAMIESON, Steve .... 314-434-4044 252 C
steve.jamieson@covenantseminary.edu
JAMIESON-DRAKE,
David .... 919-684-0736 328 F
david.jamieson.drake@duke.edu
JAMISON, Calvin, D ..... 972-883-2213 455 B
cjamison@utdallas.edu
JAMISON, Hope .... 678-916-2682 115 I
hjamison@johnmarshall.edu
JAMISON, Larry, W .... 814-393-1926 393 G
ljamison@cuf-inc.org
JAMISON, Leslie .... 609-343-5004 275 D
ljamison@atlantic.edu
JAMISON, Lucretzia ...... 773-451-3798 135 D
ljamison@ccc.edu
JAMISON, Matt .... 303-678-3845.. 81 A
matt.jamison@frontrange.edu
JAMISON, Timothy .... 617-253-1000 216 B
JAMISON, Todd .... 507-222-4292 234 G
tjamison@carleton.edu
JAMISON, Wendy .... 319-398-5693 167 J
wendy.jamison@kirkwood.edu
JAMKHANDI,
Sudhakar, R .... 304-327-4000 489 I
sjamkhandi@bluefieldstate.edu
JAMOUS, Daniel .... 617-732-2885 216 D
daniel.jamous@mcphs.edu
JAMOUS, Danielly .... 401-739-5000 404 E
djamous@neit.edu
JAMSEN, Nina .... 909-537-7138.. 32 E
nina.jamsen@csusb.edu
JANARO, Walter, A .... 540-636-2900 465 L
walter@christendom.edu
JANCHENKO, Michael ... 312-329-4495 144 I
michael.janchenko@moody.edu
JANDREAU, Jami .... 207-780-5250 197 D
jami.jandreau@maine.edu
JANELLE, Sherri .... 304-876-5043 490 A
sjanelle@shepherd.edu
JANELLE, William, P ..... 603-862-1903 274 F
william.janelle@unh.edu
JANES, Jennifer .... 607-431-4013 301 A
janesj@hartwick.edu
JANESCH, Cynthia, D ... 570-577-3763 379 C
cindy.janesch@bucknell.edu
JANEWAY, Grey .... 423-869-6306 421 A
JANG, Michelle .... 714-533-1495.. 64 I
michelle@southbaylo.edu
JANG, Sung Shik .... 770-220-7900 119 A
sungjang@gcuniv.edu
JANGER, Edward .... 718-780-0314 291 K
edward.janger@brooklaw.edu
JANIESCH, Mark .... 636-481-3130 254 C
mjaniesc@jeffco.edu
JANIGA, Nicholas .... 914-594-4567 309 B
nicholas_janiga@nymc.edu
JANIS, Debra .... 715-425-4971 496 F
debra.janis@uwrf.edu
JANIS, Ely .... 413-662-5242 213 C
ely.janis@mcla.edu
JANIS, Robert, J .... 312-362-8762 136 H
bjanis@depaul.edu
JANIS, Sharon .... 605-455-6064 415 H
JANIS, Sofia, A .... 412-359-1000 400 A
sjanis@triangle-tech.edu
JANITZ, Suzanne .... 607-431-4244 301 A
janitzs@hartwick.edu
JANKE, Louise, L .... 608-785-8604 496 A
ljanke@uwlax.edu
JANKOWSKI, Kara, K .... 920-748-8742 494 J
jankowskik@ripon.edu
JANKOWSKI, Mark .... 518-587-2100 320 E
mark.jankowski@esc.edu
JANKOWSKI NIEMCZURA,
Leslie .... 614-222-3225 351 B
ljankowski@ccad.edu
JANNEY, Cindy .... 507-389-1011 239 D
cynthia.janney@mnsu.edu
JANNEY, Dell Ann .... 573-288-6388 252 F
djanney@culver.edu
JANNEY, Justin .... 912-478-5224 120 C
jjjanney@georigasouthern.edu
JANOSIK, MaryAnn .... 847-925-6290 138 G
mjanosik@harpercollege.edu
JANOSKY, Amanda .... 716-896-0700 324 E
ajanosky@villa.edu
JANOSKY, Janine, E ..... 773-838-7511 135 F
jjanosky@ccc.edu
JANOUSH, Andrea .... 601-857-3201 246 C
andrea.janoush@hindscc.edu
JANOW, Merit, E .... 212-854-4604 297 C
mj60@columbia.edu
JANOWIAK, Steve .... 219-464-5000 162 D
JANOWSKI, Lori .... 212-772-4482 294 C
lori.janowski@hunter.cuny.edu
JANOYAN, Kerop .... 909-448-4366.. 71 C
kjanoyan@laverne.edu
JANS, Briget .... 832-842-3701 452 D
bajans@uh.edu
JANS, Roger .... 201-684-7231 280 H
rjans@ramapo.edu
JANSEN, Erica .... 808-518-4791 129 B
ericajansen@pacrim.edu
JANSEN, James, S .... 402-280-1804 266 H
jimjansen@creighton.edu
JANSEN, Shelley .... 970-943-2101.. 85 C
sjansen@western.edu
JANSKY, Madison .... 218-299-6557 239 C
madison.jansky@minnesota.edu
JANSMA, Dana .... 269-337-7210 225 F
dana.jansma@kzoo.edu
JANSMA, Pamela .... 303-556-2557.. 84 D
pamela.jansma@ucdenver.edu
JANSSEN, Emma .... 360-417-6503 482 C
ejanssen@pencol.edu
JANSSEN, Jill, M .... 815-599-3412 139 A
jill.janssen@highland.edu
JANSSEN, Michelle, L ... 765-361-6365 163 B
janssenm@wabash.edu
JANSSEN-ROBINSON,
Aimee .... 812-535-5219 160 H
a.janssen-robinson@smwc.edu
JANSSEN WOLFORD,
Jessica .... 402-941-6523 267 L
janssen@midlandu.edu
JANSSON, Jimilea .... 580-628-6771 366 J
jimilea.jansson@noc.edu
JANUARY, Shennell ...... 703-445-9056 472 G
JANUSCH, Barry .... 360-475-7458 481 I
bjanusch@olympic.edu
JANUSZIEWICZ,
Jason, R .... 724-946-7119 402 D
januszjr@westminster.edu
JANZ, Curtis .... 479-788-7591.. 21 G
curtis.janz@uafs.edu
JANZ, Jeff .... 414-297-6043 499 C
janzjc@matc.edu
JANZ, Kenneth .... 507-457-2299 241 F
kjanz@winona.edu
JANZ, Mary .... 414-288-7208 493 E
mary.janz@marquette.edu
JANZEN, Amy .... 405-425-5907 367 C
amy.janzen@oc.edu
JANZEN, David .... 620-947-3121 177 I
JANZEN, Scott .... 574-296-6213 153 F
registrar@ambs.edu
JAQUES, Kate .... 916-484-8406.. 50 G
jaquesk@arc.losrios.edu
JAQUEZ, Abraham .... 210-924-4338 431 C
abe.jaquez@bua.edu
JAQUILLARD, Jenny ..... 800-869-7223 124 I
jjaquill@scad.edu
JARA, Blanca .... 708-656-8000 145 C
blanca.jara@morton.edu
JARAMILLO, Brooke ...... 229-333-2100 128 B
brooke.jaramillo@wiregrass.edu
JARAMILLO, Ed .... 360-416-7719 484 C
ed.jaramillo@skagit.edu

JEMISON-POLLARD,
Dianne .... 713-313-7139 449 B
dianne.jemison-pollard@tsu.edu
JEMMOTT, Jill .... 203-576-4000.. 89 C
jjemott@bridgeport.edu
JENCKS, Doyle .... 580-477-7736 371 D
doyle.jencks@wosc.edu
JENDRASZAK, Stephen . 612-330-1182 234 A
jendra@augsburg.edu
JENE, Beverly .... 802-322-1650 462 B
beverly.jene@goddard.edu
JENEFSKY, Cyd .... 209-946-2300.. 71 E
cjenefsky@pacific.edu
JENEMANN, David .... 802-656-8209 463 A
david.jenemann@uvm.edu
JENERETTE, Kim .... 937-766-7866 349 E
kimjenerette@cedarville.edu
JENIK, Jeff .... 803-641-3258 413 B
jeffj@usca.edu
JENIOUS, Anita .... 615-322-4705 428 A
anita.jenious@vanderbilt.edu
JENISON, Jenae .... 641-628-5138 164 D
jenisonj@central.edu
JENKENS, A. Lawrence . 508-999-9286 212 A
lawrence.jenkens@umassd.edu
JENKINS, Adam .... 620-229-6091 177 G
adam.jenkins@sckans.edu
JENKINS, Anthony, L .... 410-951-1290 204 B
anjenkins@coppin.edu
JENKINS, Brandon .... 919-739-6841 338 H
bmjenkins@waynecc.edu
JENKINS, Brent .... 317-632-5553 159 I
bjenkins@lincolntech.edu
JENKINS, Bryan .... 919-807-7147 331 L
jenkinsb@nccommunitycolleges.edu
JENKINS, Cara .... 610-436-3513 395 D
cjenkins@wcupa.edu
JENKINS, Caren .... 304-462-6182 489 L
caren.jenkins@glenville.edu
JENKINS, Carri, P .... 801-422-1166 458 H
carri_jenkins@byu.edu
JENKINS, Celia .... 520-515-5491.. 11 M
jenkinsc@cochise.edu
JENKINS, Cheryl, S ...... 919-760-8338 331 D
jenkinsc@meredith.edu
JENKINS, D. Scott .... 972-578-5579 433 I
sjenkins@collin.edu
JENKINS, David .... 229-931-2724 120 D
david.jenkins@gsw.edu
JENKINS, David, A .... 502-852-7997 186 A
d.jenkins@louisville.edu
JENKINS, DeAnna .... 214-333-5402 434 C
deannaj@dbu.edu
JENKINS, Diane .... 301-736-3631 200 C
djenkins@msbbcs.edu
JENKINS, Dora .... 912-921-2900.. 93 H
JENKINS, Ernest .... 919-530-7639 341 E
ernest.jenkins@nccu.edu
JENKINS, Garry .... 612-625-4841 243 F
gjenkins@umn.edu
JENKINS, Gloria .... 574-284-4571 160 I
gjenkins@saintmarys.edu
JENKINS, H. E .... 713-942-5079 454 G
jenkinhe@stthom.edu
JENKINS, Jacqueline .... 212-217-4000 299 D
jacqueline_jenkins1@fitnyc.edu
JENKINS, Jan .... 479-968-0456.. 18 C
ejenkins@atu.edu
JENKINS, Jason .... 701-777-6345 345 B
jjenkins@nd.gov
JENKINS, Jeffrey, L ...... 812-877-8209 160 F
jenkins@rose-hulman.edu
JENKINS, SR.,
Jimmy, R .... 704-216-6098 330 H
jjenkins@livingstone.edu
JENKINS, Jo Ann .... 708-608-4199 145 A
jenkinsj52@morainevalley.edu
JENKINS, Joanna .... 215-965-4059 390 E
jjenkins@moore.edu
JENKINS, CSC, John, I . 574-631-3903 162 A
jenkins.1@nd.edu
JENKINS, Katrina .... 407-646-2115 106 L
kejenkins@rollins.edu
JENKINS, Keith .... 585-475-7404 312 F
kbjgpt@rit.edu
JENKINS, Keith .... 936-294-1759 450 A
rca_kej@shsu.edu
JENKINS, Kevin .... 870-307-7220.. 19 I
kevin.jenkins@lyon.edu
JENKINS, Lidia .... 415-239-3267.. 36 K
ljenkins@ccsf.edu
JENKINS, Lucy .... 603-578-8900 272 M
ljenkins@ccsnh.edu
JENKINS, Malia .... 619-201-8728.. 60 G
malia.jenkins@sdcc.edu
JENKINS, Marjorie .... 864-455-7992 413 F
mjenkins@greenvillemed.sc.edu
JENKINS, Melanie .... 919-735-5151 338 H
mkjenkins@waynecc.edu
JENKINS, Melanie .... 435-283-7000 461 B
melanie.jenkins@snow.edu
JENKINS, Melanie .... 804-484-1581 472 C
mjenkin3@richmond.edu
JENKINS, Michelle .... 314-529-9625 255 B
mjenkins@maryville.edu
JENKINS, Mike .... 903-983-8189 438 F
mjenkins@kilgore.edu
JENKINS, Nicole, T .... 434-924-3176 472 D
nt4jw@virginia.edu
JENKINS, Patricia .... 865-354-3000 425 C
jenkinsp@roanestate.edu
JENKINS, Paul .... 603-899-4142 273 E
jenkinsp@franklinpierce.edu
JENKINS, Pernell .... 334-229-4234.... 4 A
pjenkins@alasu.edu
JENKINS, Rebecca .... 419-434-5692 362 D
jenkinsr1@findlay.edu
JENKINS, Rita, H .... 713-942-9505 437 D
rjenkins@hgst.edu
JENKINS, Robert .... 909-384-8662.. 60 F
rjenkins@sbccd.cc.ca.us
JENKINS, Robert .... 713-500-3334 456 B
robert.jenkins@uth.tmc.edu
JENKINS, Rod .... 972-708-7369 435 E
rod_jenkins@diu.edu
JENKINS, Rodney .... 928-776-2280.. 16 J
rodney.jenkins@yc.edu
JENKINS, Ronny .... 202-319-5492.. 92 A
jenkinsr@cua.edu
JENKINS, Safia .... 504-286-5101 191 C
sjenkins@suno.edu
JENKINS, Scott .... 402-643-7482 266 G
finaid@cune.edu
JENKINS, Sherry .... 606-546-1701 185 D
spartin2@unionky.edu
JENKINS, Sonja .... 478-218-3308 116 G
sjenkins@centralgatech.edu
JENKINS, Spencer .... 801-321-7101 459 N
sjenkins@ushe.edu
JENKINS, Stancia, J ..... 402-472-5270 269 H
sjenkins@nebraska.edu
JENKINS, Stephanie ...... 606-589-3086 181 E
sjenkins0074@kctcs.edu
JENKINS, Stephen .... 541-737-4771 375 A
JENKINS, Steve .... 619-201-8716.. 60 G
steve.jenkins@sdcc.edu
JENKINS, Steven .... 740-392-6868 356 G
steven.jenkins@mvnu.edu
JENKINS, Sylvia .... 708-974-5201 145 A
president@morainevalley.edu
JENKINS, Timothy, S .... 219-464-5411 162 D
tim.jenkins@valpo.edu
JENKINS, Vanessa, C ... 757-823-8173 469 A
vcjenkins@nsu.edu
JENKINS-EVANS, Janie . 802-387-6814 462 C
janiejenkinsevans@landmark.edu
JENKS, Ann, M .... 269-337-7297 225 F
ann.jenks@kzoo.edu
JENKS, Catherine .... 678-839-6449 127 C
cjenks@westga.edu
JENKS, David .... 478-475-8630 122 F
david.jenks@mga.edu
JENKS, Dean .... 503-517-1093 377 C
djenks@warnerpacific.edu
JENKS, Laura .... 617-358-5207 207 E
ljenks@bu.edu
JENKS, Rick .... 815-921-4360 148 B
r.jenks@rockvalleycollege.edu
JENKS, Wayne .... 919-761-2277 340 D
wjenks@sebts.edu
JENNESS, Jennier .... 701-845-7276 345 G
jennifer.jenness@vcsu.edu
JENNESS, Valerie .... 949-824-6503.. 69 D
jenness@uci.edu
JENNETTE, Judy .... 252-789-0310 335 H
judy.jennette@martincc.edu
JENNETTEN, Tory .... 309-677-2259 134 A
tory@fsmail.bradley.edu
JENNINGS, Amani .... 732-987-2601 278 A
ajennings@georgian.edu
JENNINGS, Arbolina, L . 713-313-7661 449 B
jennings_al@tsu.edu
JENNINGS, Barbara .... 641-844-5522 167 E
barb.jennings@iavalley.edu
JENNINGS, Bill .... 541-880-2202 373 C
jenningsb@klamathcc.edu
JENNINGS, Bill .... 541-880-2247 373 C
jenningsb@klamathcc.edu
JENNINGS, Charla .... 870-743-3000.. 20 B
charlam@northark.edu
JENNINGS, Chris .... 626-387-5763.. 26 F
cjennings@apu.edu
JENNINGS, Chris .... 213-624-1200.. 42 B
cjennings@fidm.edu
JENNINGS, David, C ..... 646-378-6117 310 D
david.jennings@nyack.edu
JENNINGS, Eli .... 808-518-4791 129 B
elijennings@pacrim.edu
JENNINGS, Eva .... 510-748-2318.. 57 A
ejennings@peralta.edu
JENNINGS, Jamie .... 541-880-2228 373 C
jennings@klamathcc.edu
JENNINGS, Jarvis .... 423-585-6845 425 F
jarvis.jennings@ws.edu
JENNINGS, Jody .... 864-977-7158 410 I
jody.jennings@ngu.edu
JENNINGS, John .... 415-955-2100.. 24 J
jjennings@alliant.edu
JENNINGS, Linda .... 603-366-5260 272 K
ljennings@ccsnh.edu
JENNINGS, Logan .... 423-652-4895 420 F
ljennings@king.edu
JENNINGS, Lynn .... 252-335-0821 333 G
lynn_jennings@albemarle.edu
JENNINGS, Michael, E .. 864-294-2149 409 H
michael.jennings3@furman.edu
JENNINGS, Robert .... 402-559-5899 269 K
robert.jennings@unmc.edu
JENNINGS, Sarah, E ..... 870-235-4040.. 21 C
sejennings@saumag.edu
JENNINGS, Susan .... 423-697-2576 424 A
susan.jennings@chattanoogastate.edu
JENNINGS, Thomas, W 540-458-8233 477 D
tjennings@wlu.edu
JENNINGS-ROGGENSACK,
Colleen .... 480-965-5062.. 10 J
cjr@asu.edu
JENNISON, Barry .... 423-697-2614 424 A
barry.jennison@chattanoogastate.edu
JENNISON, Bridget .... 815-226-3374 148 D
bjennison@rockford.edu
JENNUM, Joe .... 909-274-4630.. 52 J
jjennum@mtsac.edu
JENNY, Paul .... 415-476-4148.. 70 D
paul.jenny@ucsf.edu
JENRETTE, John .... 310-423-8294.. 35 G
JENSCHKE, Danielle ...... 830-792-7217 443 E
admissions@schreiner.edu
JENSEMA, Ryan .... 412-924-1384 396 F
rjensema@pts.edu
JENSEN, Al .... 360-752-8571 478 A
ajensen@btc.edu
JENSEN, Anna .... 812-856-2548 156 G
anjensen@iu.edu
JENSEN, Anna, K .... 812-856-2548 156 F
anjensen@iu.edu
JENSEN, Brenda .... 808-236-3533 128 G
bjensen@hpu.edu
JENSEN, Carla .... 989-463-7421 221 B
jensencr@alma.edu
JENSEN, Carlos .... 858-534-0096.. 70 C
avcei@ucsd.edu
JENSEN, Christine .... 408-298-2181.. 62 H
JENSEN, Christopher .... 270-745-5065 186 C
christopher.jensen@wku.edu
JENSEN, Chuck .... 970-339-6509.. 77 H
chuck.jensen@aims.edu
JENSEN, Dan .... 817-735-2500 454 B
danny.jensen@unthsc.edu
JENSEN, David, H .... 512-404-4821 430 J
djensen@austinseminary.edu
JENSEN, Douglas, J ...... 701-224-5431 346 A
douglas.j.jensen@bismarckstate.edu
JENSEN, Dustin .... 701-252-3467 347 B
dustin.jensen@uj.edu
JENSEN, Eric .... 707-545-3647.. 26 H
JENSEN, Gail .... 951-487-3040.. 53 A
gjensen@msjc.edu
JENSEN, Gail, M .... 402-280-3727 266 H
gailjensen@creighton.edu
JENSEN, Grant .... 801-422-2290 458 H
grant_jensen@byu.edu
JENSEN, Holly .... 520-626-5620.. 16 D
hollyjensen@arizona.edu
JENSEN, Jamie .... 218-299-6882 239 C
jaime.jensen@minnesota.edu
JENSEN, Jed .... 307-681-6100 501 G
jjensen@sheridan.edu
JENSEN, DPM,
Jeffrey, L .... 623-572-3451 144 F
jjensen1@midwestern.edu
JENSEN, Jennifer .... 401-341-2209 405 D
jennifer.jensen@salve.edu
JENSEN, Jennifer, M ..... 610-758-3705 388 E
jmj313@lehigh.edu
JENSEN, John .... 410-706-4358 203 A
jjensen@umaryland.edu
JENSEN, John, A .... 540-458-8604 477 D
jensenj@wlu.edu
JENSEN, Joshua .... 509-527-5768 486 B
jensenj@whitman.edu
JENSEN, Kae .... 208-562-3336 131 E
kaejensen@cwi.edu
JENSEN, Karen .... 907-474-7224.. 10 A
kjensen@alaska.edu
JENSEN, Katie .... 425-388-9581 480 B
kjensen@everettcc.edu
JENSEN, Kevin .... 607-255-9043 297 F
finaid-director@cornell.edu
JENSEN, Kirsten .... 218-477-2175 239 E
kirsten.jensen@mnstate.edu
JENSEN, Laura .... 970-491-5939.. 79 N
l.jensen@colostate.edu
JENSEN, Lauren, J .... 616-526-6106 222 C
lauren.jensen@calvin.edu
JENSEN, Laurie .... 575-624-7157 286 C
laurie.jensen@roswell.enmu.edu
JENSEN, Mary, K .... 717-690-8600 466 B
mary.jensen@emu.edu
JENSEN, Megan .... 509-574-4635 486 D
mjensen@yvcc.edu
JENSEN, Michael .... 208-562-3160 131 E
michaeljensen2@cwi.edu
JENSEN, Michael, A ...... 801-422-4327 458 H
jensen@byu.edu
JENSEN, Michelle .... 785-833-4316 175 E
kmichelj@kwu.edu
JENSEN, Nathan .... 714-432-5909.. 38 B
njensen@occ.cccd.edu
JENSEN, Paul .... 708-456-0300 151 D
pauljensen@triton.edu
JENSEN, Paul, E .... 215-895-2200 382 F
jensenpe@drexel.edu
JENSEN, Riki .... 989-328-1220 228 D
riki.jensen@montcalm.edu
JENSEN, Sam .... 734-481-5125 223 K
ajensen2@emich.edu
JENSEN, Scott .... 316-978-3693 178 D
scott.jensen@wichita.edu
JENSEN, Scott .... 435-879-4603 460 B
scott.jensen@dixie.edu
JENSEN, Sol .... 815-753-2253 146 B
sjensen1@niu.edu
JENSEN, Steve, M .... 563-588-8000 166 C
smjensen@emmaus.edu
JENSEN, Steven, M .... 330-471-8521 355 D
sjensen@malone.edu
JENSEN, Trisha .... 801-832-2598 461 F
tjensen@westminstercollege.edu
JENSEN, Tyler .... 307-675-0777 501 G
tjensen@sheridan.edu
JENSEN, Valerie .... 408-855-5464.. 75 D
valerie.jensen@missioncollege.edu
JENSEN, Vince .... 626-256-4673.. 37 A
vjensen@coh.org
JENSON, Doug .... 909-274-5517.. 52 J
djenson@mtsac.edu
JENSON, Hal, B .... 269-337-4400 233 D
JENSON, John .... 671-735-2694 504 F
jjenson@triton.uog.edu
JENSON, Todd .... 405-912-9475 368 J
tjenson@ru.edu
JENT, Laura .... 931-540-2521 424 C
ljent1@columbiastate.edu
JENUWINE, Daniel, J ..... 248-341-2134 229 C
djjenuwi@oaklandcc.edu
JEON, Isaac .... 323-643-0301.. 25 F
JEON, John .... 213-487-0110.. 41 D
JEON, John .... 213-487-0150.. 41 D
JEONG, Wooseob .... 620-341-5203 173 F
wjeong1@emporia.edu
JEPPESEN, Vicki .... 715-675-3331 499 F
jeppesen@ntc.edu
JEPSON, Darla .... 815-802-8832 141 D
djepson@kcc.edu
JERABEK, Megan .... 610-436-2205 395 D
mjerabek@wcupa.edu
JERALDS, Jeri Ann .... 314-837-6777 258 K
jjeralds@stlchristian.edu
JERDAN, David .... 215-968-8184 379 D
david.jerdan@bucks.edu

JOHNSON, Alesa .... 606-451-6693 182 G
alesa.johnson@kctcs.edu
JOHNSON, Alex .... 617-643-6496 217 A
ajohnson@mghihp.edu
JOHNSON, Alex .... 918-335-6295 368 E
ajohnson@okwu.edu
JOHNSON, Alex .... 216-987-4853 351 E
alex.johnson@tri-c.edu
JOHNSON, Alexandra, C .... 540-828-8051 464 L
ajohnson7@bridgewater.edu
JOHNSON, Allie .... 207-755-5224 195 D
ajohnson@cmcc.edu
JOHNSON, Alverneece .. 985-545-1500 188 E
JOHNSON, Amanda .... 479-880-4520.. 18 C
ajohnson94@atu.edu
JOHNSON, Amber .... 314-977-2921 259 F
amber.johnson@slu.edu
JOHNSON, Amy .... 919-966-4045 342 C
vcsa@unc.edu
JOHNSON, Amy .... 731-286-3398 424 D
ajohnson@dscc.edu
JOHNSON, Amy, D .... 423-439-8661 419 G
johnsoad@etsu.edu
JOHNSON, Andre .... 510-885-2164.. 31 A
andre.johnson@csueastbay.edu
JOHNSON, Andre .... 972-860-8365 434 H
andrejohnson@dcccd.edu
JOHNSON, Andrew .... 860-465-0009.. 85 H
johnsonan@easternct.edu
JOHNSON, Andrew .... 610-799-1155 388 D
ajohnson23@lccc.edu
JOHNSON, Andy .... 479-788-7106.. 21 G
andy.johnson@uafs.edu
JOHNSON, Angela .... 303-797-5715.. 77 I
angela.johnson@arapahoe.edu
JOHNSON, Angela .... 334-808-6261.... 7 C
ajohnson@troy.edu
JOHNSON, Angela .... 617-588-1367 206 F
ajohnson@bfit.edu
JOHNSON, Angela .... 216-987-4213 351 E
angela.johnson@tri-c.edu
JOHNSON, Ann .... 801-618-0438 458 G
ajohnson@ameritech.edu
JOHNSON, Anne .... 651-423-8281 238 A
anne.johnson@dctc.edu
JOHNSON, Antoinette ... 757-925-6340 474 H
ajohnson@pdc.edu
JOHNSON, April .... 334-670-3402.... 7 C
acjohnson@troy.edu
JOHNSON, Arminta .... 352-365-3510 103 U
johnsona@lssc.edu
JOHNSON, Arvid, C ...... 815-740-3369 152 H
ajohnson@stfrancis.edu
JOHNSON, Ashlee .... 314-392-2305 256 E
johnsona@mobap.edu
JOHNSON, Ashlee .... 314-392-2305 256 E
ashlee.johnson@mobap.edu
JOHNSON, Barbara .... 609-777-4351 284 C
bjohnson@tesu.edu
JOHNSON, Barbara, J ... 479-968-0319.. 18 C
bjohnson@atu.edu
JOHNSON, Barry .... 408-864-5678.. 42 H
johnsonbarry@deanza.edu
JOHNSON, Barry .... 704-406-4440 329 A
bjohnson@gardner-webb.edu
JOHNSON, Bart .... 218-322-2388 238 F
bart.johnson@itascacc.edu
JOHNSON, Becky .... 903-983-8223 438 F
rjohnson@kilgore.edu
JOHNSON, Betsy .... 419-372-2651 348 G
betsyj@bgsu.edu
JOHNSON, Bill .... 952-446-4352 235 J
johnsonb@crown.edu
JOHNSON, Bonnie .... 641-673-1036 171 C
johnsonb@wmpenn.edu
JOHNSON, Brad .... 910-630-7609 331 E
bjohnson@methodist.edu
JOHNSON, Brad .... 417-328-1805 259 I
bjohnson@sbuniv.edu
JOHNSON, Brad .... 360-650-6400 485 I
brad.johnson@wwu.edu
JOHNSON, Brandi .... 978-232-3096 209 E
bjohnson@endicott.edu
JOHNSON, Brandon ...... 931-372-3636 426 B
bjjohnson@tntech.edu
JOHNSON, Brenda .... 510-780-4500.. 47 K
bjohnson@lifewest.edu
JOHNSON, Brenda .... 510-981-2830.. 56 I
bjohnson@peralta.edu
JOHNSON, Brenda .... 325-793-4857 439 F
johnson.brenda@mcm.edu
JOHNSON, Brent .... 239-280-1598.. 95 M
brent.johnson@avemaria.edu
JOHNSON, Brian .... 504-314-2486 191 F
johnson@tulane.edu
JOHNSON, Brian, L ...... 503-517-1246 377 C
president@warnerpacific.edu
JOHNSON, Bridgett .... 281-312-1631 439 C
bridgett.johnson@lonestar.edu
JOHNSON, Brooke .... 708-209-3163 136 E
brooke.johnson@cuchicago.edu
JOHNSON, Bruce .... 520-621-1081.. 16 D
brucej@arizona.edu
JOHNSON, Bruce .... 972-524-3341 445 B
john634@att.net
JOHNSON, Bryan .... 256-215-4311.... 1 G
bmjohnson@cacc.edu
JOHNSON, Bryan .... 610-526-1582 378 D
bryan.johnson@theamericancollege.edu
JOHNSON, Calvin, M .... 334-844-4546.... 4 D
johncal@auburn.edu
JOHNSON, Candace ..... 936-261-1566 446 C
cajohnson@pvamu.edu
JOHNSON, Carla .... 831-759-6006.. 44 G
cjohnson@hartnell.edu
JOHNSON, Carla .... 662-246-6301 247 D
cjohnson@msdelta.edu
JOHNSON, Carley .... 215-717-6380 400 E
cajohnson@uarts.edu
JOHNSON, Carlos .... 843-349-2876 408 A
JOHNSON, Carol .... 906-227-2947 228 I
carjohns@nmu.edu
JOHNSON, Carol .... 704-878-3225 336 C
cjohnson@mitchellcc.edu
JOHNSON, Casie .... 507-453-2663 239 B
cjohnson@southeastmn.edu
JOHNSON, Cassandra .. 903-927-3201 458 F
cmjohnson@wileyc.edu
JOHNSON, Cassandra, M .... 903-927-3201 458 F
cmjohnson@wileyc.edu
JOHNSON, Cassandra, M .... 903-927-3336 458 F
cmjohnson@wileyc.edu
JOHNSON, Catherine .... 585-785-1212 299 F
catherine.johnson@flcc.edu
JOHNSON, Catherine .... 207-780-4141 197 D
catherine.johnson@maine.edu
JOHNSON, Cathy .... 478-218-3309 116 G
cajohnson@centralgatech.edu
JOHNSON, Charlene ..... 803-780-1234 414 B
cjohnson@voorhees.edu
JOHNSON, Charlene ..... 803-780-1039 414 B
cjohnson@voorhees.edu
JOHNSON, Charles .... 912-260-4338 125 D
charles.johnson@sgsc.edu
JOHNSON, Charles, R .. 812-888-4208 162 F
president@vinu.edu
JOHNSON, Charlotte ..... 870-584-1115.. 22 F
cjohnson@cccua.edu
JOHNSON, Charlotte ..... 619-260-4588.. 72 I
studentaffairs@sandiego.edu
JOHNSON, Chris .... 303-762-6924.. 80 I
chris.johnson@denverseminary.edu
JOHNSON, Chris .... 202-319-4494.. 92 A
johnsoncp@cua.edu
JOHNSON, Chris .... 315-443-1899 321 G
cejohns@syr.edu
JOHNSON, Christine ..... 509-434-5006 479 B
christine.johnson@ccs.spokane.edu
JOHNSON, Christine ..... 509-434-5006 479 C
christine.johnson@ccs.spokane.edu
JOHNSON, Christine, L 859-858-3581 179 C
JOHNSON, Christol ...... 214-860-2627 434 I
christoljohnson@dcccd.edu
JOHNSON, Christopher 805-965-0581.. 63 A
ckjohnson2@sbcc.edu
JOHNSON, Christopher 940-898-3206 451 D
cjohnson44@twu.edu
JOHNSON, Cindi Beth .. 651-255-6137 243 E
cbjohnson@unitedseminary.edu
JOHNSON, Cindy .... 620-235-4175 177 A
cynthia.johnson@pittstate.edu
JOHNSON, Cindy, K ..... 816-604-1011 255 C
cindy.johnson@mcckc.edu
JOHNSON, Clayton .... 919-267-1640 330 B
JOHNSON, Clint .... 816-604-6775 255 D
clint.johnson@mcckc.edu
JOHNSON, Coleman ..... 806-743-2900 451 A
coleman.johnson@ttuhsc.edu
JOHNSON, Connie .... 719-598-0200.. 80 D
cjohnson@coloradotech.edu
JOHNSON, Cornelia ...... 302-857-1126.. 91 A
cornelia@dtcc.edu
JOHNSON, Cornelius .... 214-860-2496 434 I
cjohnson@dcccd.edu
JOHNSON, Cornelius, H .... 434-797-8454 473 G
cornelius.johnson@danville.edu
JOHNSON, Craig .... 847-491-3741 146 E
JOHNSON, Craig .... 320-222-5202 240 F
craig.johnson@ridgewater.edu
JOHNSON, Cretia .... 740-386-4195 355 F
johnsonc@mtc.edu
JOHNSON, Croslena ..... 864-646-1568 412 H
cjohnso5@tctc.edu
JOHNSON, Cuthrell ...... 336-750-2230 344 A
johnsonc@wssu.edu
JOHNSON, Cynthia .... 360-688-2290 482 I
cjohnson@stmartin.edu
JOHNSON, Dacia .... 218-736-1512 239 C
dacia.johnson@minnesota.edu
JOHNSON, Danette .... 804-524-5070 476 D
dljohnson@vsu.edu
JOHNSON, Danette .... 865-539-5340 425 B
djohnson11@pstcc.edu
JOHNSON, Daniel .... 803-812-7353 413 E
johns943@mailbox.sc.edu
JOHNSON, Daniel .... 206-934-6709 483 D
daniel.johnson@seattlecolleges.edu
JOHNSON, Daniel .... 701-662-1515 346 C
dan.johnson@lrsc.edu
JOHNSON, Daniel .... 918-444-4211 366 G
johnso89@nsuok.edu
JOHNSON, Daniel, W ... 414-443-8952 498 A
daniel.johnson@wlc.edu
JOHNSON, Danny .... 714-895-8344.. 38 A
djohnson@gwc.cccd.edu
JOHNSON, Dara .... 765-455-9533 157 B
darnjohn@iu.edu
JOHNSON, Darryl .... 206-934-5437 483 C
darryl.johnson@seattlecolleges.edu
JOHNSON, Darryl .... 336-517-2358 327 A
djohnson@bennett.edu
JOHNSON, Daryl .... 651-793-1227 238 I
daryl.johnson@metrostate.edu
JOHNSON, Dave .... 310-506-4798.. 56 G
david.m.johnson@pepperdine.edu
JOHNSON, David .... 606-368-6031 178 G
davidjohnson@alc.edu
JOHNSON, David .... 812-855-8908 156 G
vpem@indiana.edu
JOHNSON, David .... 510-436-2501.. 57 C
dmjohnson@peralta.edu
JOHNSON, David .... 256-824-6288.... 8 B
david.johnson@uah.edu
JOHNSON, David .... 314-838-8858 261 F
djohnson@ugst.edu
JOHNSON, David .... 716-338-1280 303 A
davejohnson@mail.sunyjcc.edu
JOHNSON, David, B ..... 812-855-8908 156 F
dj44@indiana.edu
JOHNSON, David, J ...... 513-745-3202 364 G
johnsond8@xavier.edu
JOHNSON, David, N ..... 919-209-2050 335 F
dnjohnson@johnstoncc.edu
JOHNSON, Dañáe .... 229-226-1621 126 C
djohnson@thomasu.edu
JOHNSON, Deadre .... 202-885-2721.. 91 F
deadrej@american.edu
JOHNSON, Dean, L ...... 906-487-2668 228 A
dean@mtu.edu
JOHNSON, Debbie .... 218-733-6904 238 G
debra.johnson@lsc.edu
JOHNSON, Deborah ...... 618-634-3374 149 G
deborahj@shawneecc.edu
JOHNSON, Deborah ...... 484-365-7429 388 H
dejohnson@lincoln.edu
JOHNSON, Deidre .... 410-951-2654 204 B
deijohnson@coppin.edu
JOHNSON, Deirdra, G .. 410-334-2902 205 D
djohnson@worwic.edu
JOHNSON, Delores .... 574-535-7507 155 E
drjohnson@goshen.edu
JOHNSON, Demetrius ... 301-860-3391 204 A
djohnson@bowiestate.edu
JOHNSON, Denise .... 425-889-7829 481 H
denise.johnson@northwestu.edu
JOHNSON, Derrick .... 559-244-2612.. 67 B
derrick.johnson@fresnocitycollege.edu
JOHNSON, Deshawn ..... 248-204-2117 227 A
djohnson@ltu.edu
JOHNSON, Diana .... 479-725-4681.. 20 C
djohnson@nwacc.edu
JOHNSON, Donald .... 912-201-8000 125 F
dojohnson@southuniversity.edu
JOHNSON, Donielle, R . 972-860-7372 434 H
doniellejohnson@dcccd.edu
JOHNSON, Donna .... 318-383-5758 192 D
donnaj@latech.edu
JOHNSON, Donte .... 804-751-9191 465 K
JOHNSON, Dorianne ..... 314-340-3534 254 A
johnsdor@hssu.edu
JOHNSON, Doug .... 315-228-6624 296 E
djohnson@colgate.edu
JOHNSON, Doug .... 317-274-4860 157 D
johnsodo@indiana.edu
JOHNSON, Doug .... 785-460-5411 173 B
doug.johnson@colbycc.edu
JOHNSON, Douglas, P . 207-581-1392 196 G
douglasj@maine.edu
JOHNSON, Dreand .... 816-604-1206 255 C
dreand.johnson@mcckc.edu
JOHNSON, Dustin .... 715-394-8122 497 C
djohns75@uwsuper.edu
JOHNSON, E. Patrick .... 847-467-6993 146 E
dean-epj@northwestern.edu
JOHNSON, Eartha .... 504-816-4723 186 I
ejohnson@dillard.edu
JOHNSON, Edward .... 732-224-2899 276 B
edjohnson@brookdalecc.edu
JOHNSON, Elise .... 586-498-4119 227 B
johnsonem@macomb.edu
JOHNSON, Elizabeth ..... 203-596-4638.. 88 F
ejohnson@post.edu
JOHNSON, Ellen, V ...... 814-332-3100 378 A
JOHNSON, Emily .... 651-450-3241 238 E
ejohnson@inverhills.edu
JOHNSON, Eric .... 906-227-2313 228 I
ericjohn@nmu.edu
JOHNSON, Eric .... 907-260-7422.... 9 D
JOHNSON, Eric .... 815-224-0440 140 E
eric_johnson@ivcc.edu
JOHNSON, Eric .... 219-464-5085 162 D
eric.johnson@valpo.edu
JOHNSON, Eric .... 813-253-7560 102 B
ejohnson71@hccfl.edu
JOHNSON, Eric, C .... 617-627-5484 219 C
eric.johnson@tufts.edu
JOHNSON, Eric, P .... 218-299-3447 235 H
johnson@cord.edu
JOHNSON, Eric, S .... 207-859-4460 194 D
eric.johnson@colby.edu
JOHNSON, Eric, W .... 219-464-5000 162 D
JOHNSON, Erica .... 406-657-1029 265 E
erica.johnson@rocky.edu
JOHNSON, Erica .... 801-832-2206 461 F
eljohnson@westminstercollege.edu
JOHNSON, Erik .... 541-885-1151 374 I
erik.johnson3@oit.edu
JOHNSON, Erin .... 865-981-8011 421 C
erin.johnson@maryvillecollege.edu
JOHNSON, Erin, E .... 260-422-5561 156 E
eejohnson@indianatech.edu
JOHNSON, Ethan .... 912-287-4027 117 E
ejohnson@coastalpines.edu
JOHNSON, Ezra .... 952-446-4115 235 J
johnsonez@crown.edu
JOHNSON, Faith .... 320-222-7645 240 F
JOHNSON, Feng-Ling ... 320-308-5272 240 I
feng-ling.johnson@stcloudstate.edu
JOHNSON, Frank .... 620-947-3121 177 I
frankj@tabor.edu
JOHNSON, G. Michael . 816-654-7641 254 E
mjohnson@kcumb.edu
JOHNSON, Gail .... 605-642-6054 416 E
gail.johnson@bhsu.edu
JOHNSON, Gary .... 828-328-7112 330 F
gary.johnson@lr.edu
JOHNSON, George .... 210-486-2174 429 B
gjohnson@alamo.edu
JOHNSON, George, W .. 803-535-5077 407 D
geojohnson@claflin.edu
JOHNSON, Glen .... 276-739-2467 475 F
gjohnson@vhcc.edu
JOHNSON, Glenn .... 304-929-1495 487 J
glennjohnson@ucwv.edu
JOHNSON, Greg .... 251-442-2269.... 8 C
gjohnson@umobile.edu
JOHNSON, Greg, L .... 651-631-5363 244 D
gljohnson@unwsp.edu
JOHNSON, Gregg .... 412-392-3898 396 G
gjohnson@pointpark.edu
JOHNSON, Hannah .... 662-685-4771 245 C
hjohnson@bmc.edu
JOHNSON, Harper .... 719-255-3594.. 84 C
hjohnson@uccs.edu
JOHNSON, Harrison, P . 601-979-2300 246 F
harrison.p.johnson@jsums.edu

JOHNSON, Patrick .... 240-567-5288 200 G
patrick.johnson@montgomerycollege.edu
JOHNSON, Patrick, H ... 615-327-6061 421 D
pjohnson@mmc.edu
JOHNSON, Paul .... 850-729-6493 104 M
johns467@nwfsc.edu
JOHNSON, Paul .... 404-727-7707 118 E
rpaul.johnson@emory.edu
JOHNSON, Paul, C .... 303-273-3280.. 79 J
presoffice@mines.edu
JOHNSON, Paula, A ..... 781-283-2237 219 E
pjohnson@wellesley.edu
JOHNSON, Paula, J ...... 858-534-2552.. 70 C
pjjohnson@ucsd.edu
JOHNSON, Paulette, M . 269-471-3275 221 D
paulettej@andrews.edu
JOHNSON, Peggy, A ..... 814-865-2631 391 G
paj6@psu.edu
JOHNSON, Philip .... 906-487-7201 224 B
philip.johnson@finlandia.edu
JOHNSON, Phill .... 334-244-3202.... 4 E
pjohns23@aum.edu
JOHNSON, Quenetta ..... 252-985-5369 339 D
qjohnson@ncwc.edu
JOHNSON, Quentin, R .. 434-949-1000 475 B
quentin.johnson@southside.edu
JOHNSON, R .... 504-283-8822 186 I
rjohnson@dillard.edu
JOHNSON, Rachel .... 916-660-8103.. 64 D
rjohnson45@sierracollege.edu
JOHNSON, Rachel .... 320-589-6300 244 B
rmjohnson@morris.umn.edu
JOHNSON, Ralph .... 301-891-4109 205 A
rejohnson@wau.edu
JOHNSON, Ralph, F ...... 706-542-7369 126 G
rfj@uga.edu
JOHNSON, Ramon .... 502-597-6655 183 D
ramon.johnson@kysu.edu
JOHNSON, Rana .... 812-237-8954 156 D
rana.johnson@indstate.edu
JOHNSON, Randee .... 843-525-8250 412 G
rjohnson@tcl.edu
JOHNSON, Randi .... 406-377-9401 263 D
rjohnson@dawson.edu
JOHNSON, Randolph .... 864-644-5220 412 D
rjohnson@swu.edu
JOHNSON, Raniyah ...... 408-223-6768.. 62 G
raniyah.johnson@evc.edu
JOHNSON, Rebecca ...... 541-737-2111 375 A
pres.office@oregonstate.edu
JOHNSON, Rebecca, J .. 703-784-2105 502 J
JOHNSON, Regynold .... 773-291-6100 135 E
JOHNSON, Renita .... 704-922-6312 334 G
johnson.renita@gaston.edu
JOHNSON, Richard .... 870-236-6901.. 18 J
rjohnson@crc.edu
JOHNSON, Richard, A .. 864-597-4090 414 E
johnsonra@wofford.edu
JOHNSON, Rick .... 307-778-1135 501 E
rjohnson@lccc.wy.edu
JOHNSON, Robby .... 580-349-2611 367 F
JOHNSON, Robert .... 916-691-4323.. 50 H
johnsor3@crc.losrios.edu
JOHNSON, Robert .... 928-524-7695.. 14 J
robert.johnson@npc.edu
JOHNSON, Robert .... 973-972-4538 282 A
rjohnson@njms.rutgers.edu
JOHNSON, Robert, E .... 413-782-1243 220 A
robert.johnson@wne.edu
JOHNSON, Robert, E .... 913-667-5715 172 I
rjohnson@cbts.edu
JOHNSON, Roberta, L .. 515-294-0109 163 G
rljohns@iastate.edu
JOHNSON, Rochelle ...... 208-459-5894 131 C
rjohnson@collegeofidaho.edu
JOHNSON, Roderick ..... 931-540-2553 424 C
rjohnson63@columbiastate.edu
JOHNSON, Rodney .... 937-766-4114 349 E
johnsonr@cedarville.edu
JOHNSON, Roger .... 540-261-8400 471 B
roger.johnson@svu.edu
JOHNSON, Ronnie, J .... 903-586-2501 431 B
ronnie.johnson@bmats.edu
JOHNSON, Rory .... 707-465-2300.. 58 I
rory-johnson@redwoods.edu
JOHNSON, Ruben .... 505-566-3279 288 D
johnsonr@sanjuancollege.edu
JOHNSON, Ruben .... 972-860-8161 434 G
rjohnson@dcccd.edu
JOHNSON, JR.,
Rushton, W .... 865-694-6552 425 B
rwjohnson2@pstcc.edu
JOHNSON, Russell, R ... 207-859-4776 194 D
margaret.mcfadden@colby.edu
JOHNSON, Ryan .... 501-205-8815.. 18 H
rjohnson@cbc.edu
JOHNSON, Sabrina, J ... 920-923-8082 493 D
sjjohnson41@marianuniversity.edu
JOHNSON, Samantha ... 334-808-6580.... 7 C
johnson@troy.edu
JOHNSON, Samantha ... 979-209-7281 431 H
samantha.johnson@blinn.edu
JOHNSON, Sandra .... 661-726-1911.. 68 J
sandra.johnson@uav.edu
JOHNSON, Sandra, S ... 585-475-2267 312 F
ssjvsa@rit.edu
JOHNSON, Saphronia ... 770-426-2733 122 C
saphronia.johnson@life.edu
JOHNSON, Sarah .... 419-448-3039 361 D
depughst@tiffin.edu
JOHNSON, Scott .... 715-682-1369 494 G
skjohnson@northland.edu
JOHNSON, Scott .... 831-479-5663.. 27 D
scjohnso@cabrillo.edu
JOHNSON, Scott .... 714-449-7438.. 51 B
scottjohnson@ketchum.edu
JOHNSON, Scott .... 419-448-2280 353 E
sjohnson@heidelberg.edu
JOHNSON, Scott .... 336-838-6141 339 B
sajohnson366@wilkescc.edu
JOHNSON, Sean .... 701-252-3467 347 B
sean.johnson@uj.edu
JOHNSON, Sean .... 707-664-4032.. 34 B
spjohnson@sonoma.edu
JOHNSON, Seth .... 716-375-2382 313 C
sjohnson@sbu.edu
JOHNSON, Sharon .... 314-516-6817 261 C
sharon_johnson@umsl.edu
JOHNSON, Shatealy ...... 912-443-5347 125 B
sjohnson@savannahtech.edu
JOHNSON, Sheila, G .... 405-744-6321 367 G
sheila.johnson@okstate.edu
JOHNSON, Sheila, M .... 727-376-6911 112 G
registrar@trinitycollege.edu
JOHNSON, Shelley .... 850-599-3017 109 I
shelley.johnson@famu.edu
JOHNSON, Sherrick, L . 706-771-4008 115 J
sjohnson@augustatech.edu
JOHNSON, Sonia .... 870-236-6901.. 18 J
sjohnson@crc.edu
JOHNSON, Sonja .... 910-362-7021 332 H
sjohnson@cfcc.edu
JOHNSON, Sonya .... 803-705-4815 406 G
sonya.johnson@benedict.edu
JOHNSON, Stacey .... 718-368-1193 304 C
sjohnson@libi.edu
JOHNSON, Stacy .... 248-689-8282 232 C
JOHNSON, Stephanie .... 573-875-7357 251 I
sgjohnson@ccis.edu
JOHNSON, Stephanie .... 605-882-5472 415 D
stephanie.johnson@lakeareatech.edu
JOHNSON, Stephanie .... 704-886-6500.. 93 H
JOHNSON, Stephen .... 626-812-3020.. 26 F
sjohnson@apu.edu
JOHNSON, Stephen .... 214-305-9500 428 F
scj98d@acu.edu
JOHNSON, Steve .... 504-280-6303 190 B
sgjohnso@uno.edu
JOHNSON, Steve .... 913-360-7415 171 J
stevej@benedictine.edu
JOHNSON, Steve .... 580-774-3016 370 A
steve.johnson@swosu.edu
JOHNSON, Steven .... 906-635-2160 226 G
sjohnson18@lssu.edu
JOHNSON, Steven .... 603-665-2799 274 C
s.johnson5@snhu.edu
JOHNSON, Steven, L .... 937-512-2525 360 G
president@sinclair.edu
JOHNSON, Susan .... 775-831-1314 272 D
sjohnson@sierranevada.edu
JOHNSON, Susan, E ..... 651-631-5333 244 D
snjohnson@unwsp.edu
JOHNSON, Suzanne ...... 253-833-9111 480 I
sjohnson@greenriver.edu
JOHNSON, Tamara .... 847-925-6103 138 G
jt03888@harpercollege.edu
JOHNSON, Tamara .... 312-662-4043 132 G
tajohnson@adler.edu
JOHNSON, Tammy .... 304-696-3161 489 M
johnson73@marshall.edu
JOHNSON, Tara .... 229-500-2007 114 H
tara.johnson@asurams.edu
JOHNSON, Tara .... 863-680-4110 100 H
tjohnson@flsouthern.edu
JOHNSON, Tardis .... 212-217-3082 299 D
tardis_johnson@fitnyc.edu
JOHNSON, TaRita .... 616-526-6484 222 C
tdj4@calvin.edu
JOHNSON, Tasha .... 252-527-6223 335 G
tvjohnson90@lenoircc.edu
JOHNSON, Ted .... 858-822-5949.. 70 C
edjohnson@ucsd.edu
JOHNSON, Teisha .... 312-949-7407 139 D
tjohnson@ico.edu
JOHNSON, Terrence ..... 231-843-5874 233 A
tjohnson@westshore.edu
JOHNSON, Terri .... 512-863-1342 445 C
tjohnson@southwestern.edu
JOHNSON, Theodore ..... 630-889-6512 145 E
tjohnson@nuhs.edu
JOHNSON, Thomas .... 323-343-3488.. 31 E
tjohnson@cslanet.calstatela.edu
JOHNSON, Thomas .... 641-628-5272 164 D
johnsont@central.edu
JOHNSON, Thomas, A .. 409-882-3314 449 H
thomas.johnson@lsco.edu
JOHNSON, Tianna .... 507-457-1635 243 C
tpjohnso@smumn.edu
JOHNSON, Tiffany .... 870-972-3025.. 17 E
tijohnson@astate.edu
JOHNSON, Tiffany .... 512-313-4109 433 N
tiffany.johnson@concordia.edu
JOHNSON, Tim .... 918-495-7149 368 F
tjohnson@oru.edu
JOHNSON, Timothy .... 336-334-5636 343 A
tjjohns3@uncg.edu
JOHNSON, Timothy .... 843-953-5770 408 C
johnsonts@cofc.edu
JOHNSON, Timothy, R . 870-864-8421.. 21 A
JOHNSON, Todd, K .... 757-683-3464 469 B
tjohnso@odu.edu
JOHNSON, Toni .... 419-755-9028 357 B
tjohnson@ncstatecollege.edu
JOHNSON, Tonjanita ..... 205-348-8347.... 7 F
tjohnson@uasystem.edu
JOHNSON, Tony .... 903-983-8102 438 F
tjohnson@kilgore.edu
JOHNSON, Toya .... 312-850-7267 135 H
tjohnson616@ccc.edu
JOHNSON, Tracci .... 818-252-5114.. 76 E
tracci.johnson@woodbury.edu
JOHNSON, Tracey .... 618-634-3271 149 G
traceyj@shawneecc.edu
JOHNSON, Tracy .... 214-860-2033 434 I
tracy.johnson@dcccd.edu
JOHNSON, Travis, T ..... 803-536-8480 411 G
tjohns41@scsu.edu
JOHNSON, Trent .... 270-534-3302 183 B
trent.johnson@kctcs.edu
JOHNSON, Tricia .... 303-404-5022.. 81 A
tricia.johnson@frontrange.edu
JOHNSON, Troy .... 334-244-3110.... 4 E
ljohns90@aum.edu
JOHNSON, Troy .... 817-272-5401 454 I
troy.johnson@uta.edu
JOHNSON, Trygve, D .... 616-395-7966 225 D
johnsont@hope.edu
JOHNSON, Ursa .... 540-365-4323 467 B
ujohnson@ferrum.edu
JOHNSON, Valen, E ...... 979-845-8817 446 F
vejohnson@tamu.edu
JOHNSON, Valerie .... 919-719-5061 340 B
valerie.johnson@shawu.edu
JOHNSON, Veronica ..... 773-947-6319 143 H
vjohnson@mccormick.edu
JOHNSON, Victoria, D .. 504-865-5591 191 F
victoria@tulane.edu
JOHNSON, Vivian .... 937-529-2201 361 G
vjohnson@united.edu
JOHNSON, Wallace .... 909-384-8502.. 60 F
wjohnson@sbccd.cc.ca.us
JOHNSON, Walter .... 630-942-2800 135 I
JOHNSON, Walter .... 864-977-2007 410 I
walter.johnson@ngu.edu
JOHNSON, Wayne .... 847-317-7001 151 C
wjohnson@tiu.edu
JOHNSON, Wendy .... 225-743-8500 188 H
wjohnson@rpcc.edu
JOHNSON, Wesley .... 910-892-3178 329 E
JOHNSON, Wesley, T ... 407-582-1118 113 I
wjohnson55@valenciacollege.edu
JOHNSON, William .... 510-885-4602.. 31 A
william.johnson@csueastbay.edu
JOHNSON, William .... 734-973-3490 232 D
billjohnson@wccnet.edu
JOHNSON, William, H .. 203-254-4000.. 87 I
wjohnson@fairfield.edu
JOHNSON, William, P .. 314-977-2788 259 F
william.johnson@slu.edu
JOHNSON, Willie .... 715-232-1151 497 B
johnsonw@uwstout.edu
JOHNSON, Zak .... 218-755-2226 237 F
zachary.johnson@bemidjistate.edu
JOHNSON, Zakia .... 443-518-4079 199 F
zjohnson@howardcc.edu
JOHNSON-BAILEY,
Juanita .... 706-542-2846 126 G
jjb@uga.edu
JOHNSON-CASSULO,
Nancy .... 208-459-5680 131 C
njohnsoncassulo@collegeofidaho.edu
JOHNSON-CHANDLER,
Sabrina .... 718-262-2719 295 E
sjohnson25@york.cuny.edu
JOHNSON-COLEMAN,
Sasha .... 803-793-5197 408 G
johnson-coleman@denmarktech.edu
JOHNSON-DEBAUFRE,
Melanie .... 973-408-3823 277 A
mjjohnso@drew.edu
JOHNSON-HOUSTON,
Debbie, L .... 337-475-5716 192 E
djohnsonhouston@mcneese.edu
JOHNSON JONES,
Sylvia, M .... 847-543-2404 136 A
cps086@clcillinois.edu
JOHNSON MATHERSON,
Akua, J .... 919-530-6204 341 E
amathers@nccu.edu
JOHNSON-MILLS,
Jessica .... 818-401-1151.. 39 D
jjohnsonmills@columbiacollege.edu
JOHNSON RENVALL,
Poppy .... 505-224-4435 285 N
pjohnsonrenvall@cnm.edu
JOHNSON-ROSS,
Debora .... 319-352-8284 170 J
debora.johnsonross@wartburg.edu
JOHNSON SHAHEED,
Karen .... 301-860-3555 204 A
kshaheed@bowiestate.edu
JOHNSON-SHAHEED,
Karen .... 301-860-3504 204 A
kshaheed@bowiestate.edu
JOHNSON SUSKI,
Katharine .... 515-294-0815 163 G
ksuski@iastate.edu
JOHNSON-VARNEY,
Suzanne .... 740-351-3410 360 F
svarney@shawnee.edu
JOHNSON-WALKER,
Heather .... 334-556-2397.... 2 C
hwalker@wallace.edu
JOHNSON-WEEKS,
Demetria .... 713-313-7940 449 B
weeks_dj@tsu.edu
JOHNSRUD, Jason .... 202-462-2101.. 93 A
johnsrud@iwp.edu
JOHNSSON,
Magnus, H .... 804-827-1363 473 B
johnssonm@vcu.edu
JOHNSTON, Alysia .... 620-223-2700 173 I
alysiaj@fortscott.edu
JOHNSTON, Angela ...... 330-263-2141 351 A
ajohnston@wooster.edu
JOHNSTON, Ann .... 970-943-2493.. 85 C
afjohnston@western.edu
JOHNSTON, Barbara, A 972-985-3732 433 I
bjohnston@collin.edu
JOHNSTON, Brian, A .... 202-319-6425.. 92 A
johnston@cua.edu
JOHNSTON, Carol .... 213-477-2617.. 52 I
cjohnston@msmu.edu
JOHNSTON, Caroline .... 321-674-7400 100 C
cjohnston@fit.edu
JOHNSTON, Chad .... 318-678-6000 187 H
cjohnston@bpcc.edu
JOHNSTON, Cheryl, L .. 724-847-6577 384 C
cljohnst@geneva.edu
JOHNSTON,
Christine, D .... 309-457-2444 144 H
cjohnston@monmouthcollege.edu
JOHNSTON,
Christopher .... 216-987-5378 351 E
christopher.johnston@tri-c.edu
JOHNSTON, Cynthia ..... 843-349-7835 409 J
cynthia.johnston@hgtc.edu
JOHNSTON, David .... 707-468-3091.. 51 F
djohnston@mendocino.edu
JOHNSTON, Delaney ..... 812-221-1714 162 E
djohnston@vbc.edu

JOHNSTON, Dusty, R ... 940-552-6291 457 C
drj@vernoncollege.edu
JOHNSTON, Elizabeth ... 214-637-3530 457 H
ejohnston@wadecollege.edu
JOHNSTON, Elizabeth ... 412-237-8195 381 D
ejohnston@ccac.edu
JOHNSTON, Jacqueline 516-877-6004 289 I
jjohnston@adelphi.edu
JOHNSTON, James .... 940-397-4000 440 C
james.johnston@msutexas.edu
JOHNSTON, Jamie, M .. 770-720-9238 124 G
jmj@reinhardt.edu
JOHNSTON, Janan .... 212-986-4343 291 E
janan-johnston@berkeleycollege.edu
JOHNSTON, Janan .... 973-278-5400 275 I
janan-johnston@berkeleycollege.edu
JOHNSTON, Jason .... 207-768-9652 197 C
jason.johnston@maine.edu
JOHNSTON, Jeremy ...... 903-923-2010 435 H
jjohnston@etbu.edu
JOHNSTON, Jerome .... 281-649-3467 437 B
jrjohnston@hbu.edu
JOHNSTON, Jessica ...... 773-834-2500 150 K
jjohnston@ttic.edu
JOHNSTON, Jessica, R . 309-457-2125 144 H
jjohnston@monmouthcollege.edu
JOHNSTON, Judy .... 912-279-5705 117 F
jjohnston@ccga.edu
JOHNSTON, Julie, L ..... 530-251-8820.. 47 F
jjohnston@lassencollege.edu
JOHNSTON, Justin .... 585-343-0055 300 F
jmjohnston@genesee.edu
JOHNSTON, Kara .... 303-963-3320.. 78 H
kjohnston@ccu.edu
JOHNSTON, Kathy .... 636-481-3280 254 C
kjohnsto@jeffco.edu
JOHNSTON, Ken .... 312-567-5850 140 A
johnston@iit.edu
JOHNSTON, Kerri .... 978-934-3933 212 B
kerri_johnston@uml.edu
JOHNSTON, Kristen ...... 316-677-1647 178 E
kjohnston@watc.edu
JOHNSTON, Kyle .... 518-891-2915 310 A
kyle.johnston@nccc.edu
JOHNSTON, Lisa .... 727-864-8206.. 98 J
johnstln@eckerd.edu
JOHNSTON, Marsha ..... 314-838-8858 261 F
mjohnston@ugst.edu
JOHNSTON, Mary .... 618-842-3711 139 F
johnstonm@iecc.edu
JOHNSTON, Michael ..... 850-484-1717 105 H
mjohnston@pensacolastate.edu
JOHNSTON, Michael ..... 530-898-5201.. 30 D
mpjohnston@csuchico.edu
JOHNSTON, Michelle .... 912-279-5705 117 F
president@ccga.edu
JOHNSTON, Molly .... 218-235-2119 241 E
molly.johnston@vcc.edu
JOHNSTON, Pamela ...... 850-201-6150 112 C
pamela.johnston@tcc.fl.edu
JOHNSTON, Phil .... 615-460-6964 418 B
phil.johnston@belmont.edu
JOHNSTON, Roxanne .... 706-233-7464 125 C
rjohnston@shorter.edu
JOHNSTON, Ruth .... 575-646-9875 287 C
ruthj@nmsu.edu
JOHNSTON,
S. Claiborne .... 512-495-5000 455 A
dellmedschool@utexas.edu
JOHNSTON, Sal .... 562-907-4204.. 76 B
sjohnston@whittier.edu
JOHNSTON, Sandra ...... 815-455-9793 143 I
sjohnston@mchenry.edu
JOHNSTON, Sharon ...... 979-830-4115 431 H
sharon.johnston@blinn.edu
JOHNSTON, Susan .... 903-823-3260 446 A
susan.johnston@texarkanacollege.edu
JOHNSTON, Timothy ..... 530-242-7669.. 64 C
tjohnston@shastacollege.edu
JOHNSTON, Will .... 919-761-2100 340 D
wjohnston@sebts.edu
JOHNSTONE, Jason, L .. 936-468-1672 445 E
jljohnstone@sfasu.edu
JOINER, Haywood .... 318-473-6466 189 F
hjoiner@lsua.edu
JOINER, Jennie .... 315-279-5259 303 G
jjoiner@keuka.edu
JOINER, Karen .... 360-442-2861 481 D
kjoiner@lowercolumbia.edu
JOINER, Steve .... 615-966-7141 421 B
steve.joiner@lipscomb.edu
JOKELA, Janet .... 217-337-2398 152 B
jokela@illinois.edu
JOKERST, Doreen .... 303-492-7311.. 84 B
doreen.jokerst@colorado.edu
JOKI, Jody .... 906-353-8400 226 C
jjoki@kbocc.edu
JOKL, Todd .... 585-475-5392 312 F
tsjpgd@rit.edu
JOLER-LABBE, Michelle 207-859-1240 196 D
hr@thomas.edu
JOLICOEUR, Paul .... 910-775-4675 343 B
paul.jolicoeur@uncp.edu
JOLLEY, Kassandra .... 413-538-2756 217 C
kjolley@mtholyoke.edu
JOLLEY, Kate .... 707-527-4421.. 63 D
kjolley@santarosa.edu
JOLLEY, Kim .... 864-503-7417 414 A
JOLLEY, Renee, W .... 804-257-5756 476 F
rwjolley@vuu.edu
JOLLIFFE, Vicki, M .... 724-439-4900 388 A
vjolliffe@laurel.edu
JOLLY, Carole .... 714-449-7451.. 51 B
cjolly@ketchum.edu
JOLLY, Connie .... 843-574-6150 412 I
connie.jolly@tridenttech.edu
JOLLY, Jim .... 248-204-2414 227 A
jjolly@ltu.edu
JOLLY, Laura .... 515-294-5380 163 G
ljolly@iastate.edu
JOLLY, Lawson .... 352-588-8354 107 D
lawson.jolly@saintleo.edu
JOLLY, Melody .... 714-850-4800.. 67 H
jolly@taftu.edu
JONAS, Lisa .... 415-703-9595.. 28 B
ljonas@cca.edu
JONAS, Scott .... 443-997-3715 199 G
scott.jonas@jhu.edu
JONES, A. Fitzgerald ..... 678-715-2200.. 93 H
JONES, Aaron .... 417-873-6819 252 G
ajones11@drury.edu
JONES, Adrianne .... 215-871-6711 395 G
adriannjo@pcom.edu
JONES, Alan .... 410-532-5393 201 D
ajones17@ndm.edu
JONES, Alan, E .... 601-984-1010 249 E
aejones@umc.edu
JONES, Alana .... 303-315-2109.. 84 D
alana.jones@ucdenver.edu
JONES, Alesia, M .... 250-934-5321.... 8 A
amjones@uab.edu
JONES, Alexander .... 585-594-6202 310 C
jones_alexander@roberts.edu
JONES, Alexander .... 585-594-6200 312 E
jones_alexander@roberts.edu
JONES, Alice, L .... 757-683-4388 469 B
aljones@odu.edu
JONES, Alisa .... 972-860-7026 434 H
alisajones@dcccd.edu
JONES, Alison .... 317-632-5553 159 I
ajones@lincolntech.edu
JONES, Almarie .... 856-415-2154 281 D
ajones@rcsj.edu
JONES, Alton .... 918-465-1739 366 A
ajones725@eosc.edu
JONES, Amanda .... 641-269-4872 166 G
jonesama@grinnell.edu
JONES, Amber .... 806-457-4200 436 C
ajones@fpctx.edu
JONES, Amy .... 231-995-1245 229 A
amjones@nmc.edu
JONES, Amy .... 734-462-4400 230 G
ajones2@schoolcraft.edu
JONES, Andrea .... 601-979-0779 246 F
andrea.e.jones@jsums.edu
JONES, Andrea .... 225-578-8281 189 E
ajones9@lsu.edu
JONES, Andrea .... 404-413-1351 120 E
andreajones@gsu.edu
JONES, Andrew .... 562-951-4500.. 29 H
gajones@calstate.edu
JONES, Andrew, B .... 317-738-8080 155 D
ajones1@franklincollege.edu
JONES, Angela .... 501-882-8845.. 17 D
agjones@asub.edu
JONES, Angela .... 850-474-2846 111 F
ajones1@uwf.edu
JONES, Angie .... 717-295-1100 403 I
JONES, Anne .... 843-921-6994 411 A
ajones@netc.edu
JONES, Anni .... 603-271-6484 273 A
JONES, Anthony .... 850-201-6036 112 C
anthony.jones@tcc.fl.edu
JONES, Anthony .... 256-761-6304.... 7 B
amjones@talladega.edu
JONES, Anthony .... 801-581-7466 459 O
anthony.p.jones@utah.edu
JONES, Anthony, E .... 724-589-2000 399 D
ajones@thiel.edu
JONES, Arvis, C .... 915-831-2712 436 A
ajones22@epcc.edu
JONES, Ashley .... 404-962-3041 127 D
ashley.jones@usg.edu
JONES, Ashley .... 253-272-1126 481 E
ajones@ncad.edu
JONES, Barry .... 931-221-7330 417 H
JONES, Ben .... 440-775-8624 357 G
ben.jones@oberlin.edu
JONES, Bernette .... 336-272-7102 329 C
bernette.jones@greensboro.edu
JONES, Bert .... 804-819-4917 473 C
bjones@vccs.edu
JONES, Bill, H .... 803-754-4100 408 E
JONES, Blake .... 573-518-2224 256 D
bajones@mineralarea.edu
JONES, III, Bob .... 864-242-5100 406 H
JONES, Bobby .... 850-201-6035 112 C
bobby.jones@tcc.fl.edu
JONES, Bradley .... 317-738-8033 155 D
bjones@franklincollege.edu
JONES, Brenda .... 414-847-3231 494 C
brendajones@miad.edu
JONES, Brent .... 772-546-5534 102 C
JONES, Brent .... 334-670-3783.... 7 C
brentjones@troy.edu
JONES, Brian .... 507-389-2422 239 D
brian.jones@mnsu.edu
JONES, Brian .... 252-493-7200 336 H
cbjones@email.pittcc.edu
JONES, Brian, M .... 843-953-7478 407 C
bjones16@citadel.edu
JONES, Brittany .... 256-331-5319.... 3 C
bjones@nwscc.edu
JONES, Bryan, D .... 857-701-1200 215 G
bdjones@rcc.mass.edu
JONES, C. Darryl .... 510-231-5000.. 46 J
darryl.jones@kp.org
JONES, C. Stephen .... 410-704-4053 204 E
csjones@towson.edu
JONES, Camie .... 334-302-1005.... 3 A
cjones@marionmilitary.edu
JONES, Candace .... 626-585-7725.. 56 D
cdjones@pasadena.edu
JONES, Candace .... 626-585-7172.. 56 D
cdjones@pasadena.edu
JONES, JR., Carnell ...... 401-874-9500 405 E
carnell@uri.edu
JONES, Carol .... 404-756-4000 115 G
JONES, Carol .... 706-272-4545 118 B
cjones@daltonstate.edu
JONES, Cassandra .... 706-419-1117 118 A
cassandra.jones@covenant.edu
JONES, Cassandra .... 240-567-4248 200 G
cassandra.jones@montgomerycollege.edu
JONES, Cassie .... 434-791-5684 464 I
cwjones@averett.edu
JONES, Catherine .... 815-479-7751 143 I
cjones60@mchenry.edu
JONES, Cathy .... 301-846-2458 198 I
cjones@frederick.edu
JONES, Cathy .... 704-330-1461 330 D
cjones2@jcsu.edu
JONES, Cecelia .... 903-730-4890 438 D
cjones@jarvis.edu
JONES, Charles .... 662-621-4175 245 D
cjones@coahomacc.edu
JONES, Charlotte .... 740-284-5787 352 I
cjones@franciscan.edu
JONES, Cheri .... 502-852-4494 186 A
cheri.jones@louisville.edu
JONES, Cheryl .... 806-371-5044 429 E
cheryl.jones@actx.edu
JONES, Chris .... 641-472-1105 168 C
cjones@miu.edu
JONES, Chris .... 641-472-1219 168 C
cjones@miu.edu
JONES, Chris .... 434-582-8783 468 E
jjones774@liberty.edu
JONES, Christina .... 770-216-2960 121 I
cjones@ict.edu
JONES, Christopher ...... 978-927-2300 210 B
chris.jones@gordon.edu
JONES, Christopher ...... 570-288-8400 383 G
christopherj@fortisinstitute.edu
JONES, Christopher, L .. 909-748-8289.. 72 F
christopher_jones@redlands.edu
JONES, Cindy .... 252-527-6223 335 G
cwjones29@lenoircc.edu
JONES, Clayton .... 225-578-8200 189 E
chj1@lsu.edu
JONES, Clayton, W .... 585-292-2192 307 B
cjones@monroecc.edu
JONES, Clifton .... 254-519-5424 447 A
cwjones@tamuct.edu
JONES, Cody .... 205-665-6130.... 8 D
ccjones@montevallo.edu
JONES, Cody .... 717-720-4010 393 C
codyjones@passhe.edu
JONES, Colleen .... 847-628-1510 141 C
colleen.jones@judsonu.edu
JONES, Cooper .... 707-826-3666.. 33 C
JONES, Cravor .... 304-327-4016 489 I
cjones@bluefieldstate.edu
JONES, Cristen .... 202-722-8111.. 93 H
JONES, Crystal .... 765-455-9415 157 B
crmjones@iu.edu
JONES, Crystal .... 937-328-6145 350 G
jonesc@clarkstate.edu
JONES, Cynthia .... 956-665-8287 455 D
cynthia.jones@utrgv.edu
JONES, Dan, L .... 423-439-4841 419 G
jonesdl4@etsu.edu
JONES, Darci .... 814-824-2233 389 G
djones@mercyhurst.edu
JONES, Darin .... 360-538-4234 480 G
djones@ghc.edu
JONES, Darnell .... 816-501-4117 258 I
darnell.jones@rockhurst.edu
JONES, Darrell, C .... 714-879-3901.. 45 G
dcjones@hiu.edu
JONES, Darren .... 301-736-3631 200 C
darren.jones@msbbcs.edu
JONES, Darren .... 501-977-2191.. 23 A
jones@uaccm.edu
JONES, Darryl .... 201-714-7100 278 C
JONES, David .... 507-389-2121 239 D
david.jones@mnsu.edu
JONES, David .... 443-550-6012 198 G
dvjones1@csmd.edu
JONES, David .... 920-465-2300 495 F
jonesd@uwgb.edu
JONES, David .... 307-766-3495 501 I
dljones@uwyo.edu
JONES, David, R .... 301-784-5000 197 F
djones@allegany.edu
JONES, Dawn .... 903-983-8205 438 F
djones1@kilgore.edu
JONES, Deborah .... 270-852-3302 183 E
deborah.jones@kwc.edu
JONES, Deborah, J .... 409-772-1510 456 E
debjjone@utmb.edu
JONES, Denise .... 708-456-0300 151 D
denisejones@triton.edu
JONES, Diana .... 641-784-5412 166 E
dianaj@gracelend.edu
JONES, Don .... 410-669-9200 200 D
JONES, Donald .... 860-768-4751.. 89 G
djones@hartford.edu
JONES, Donald, A .... 502-371-8330 179 E
djones@ata.edu
JONES, Donald, E .... 803-754-4100 408 E
JONES, Doug .... 423-636-7322 426 E
djones@tusculum.edu
JONES, Douglas .... 831-656-3658 502 M
dwjones@nps.edu
JONES, Douglas, W .... 805-565-6048.. 76 A
vpfinance@westmont.edu
JONES, Dwane .... 202-274-7182.. 94 B
dwane.jones@udc.edu
JONES, Eddie, V .... 989-964-4909 230 E
evjones@svsu.edu
JONES, Edward .... 312-329-4354 144 I
edward.jones@moody.edu
JONES, JR., Edward ..... 202-274-7441.. 94 B
ejones@udc.edu
JONES, Elliot .... 318-257-4217 192 D
elliotj@latech.edu
JONES, Elliot .... 248-218-2036 230 B
ejones@rochesteru.edu
JONES, Elwin .... 251-981-3771.... 5 A
elwin.jones@columbiasouthern.edu
JONES, Emily, M .... 413-542-2267 205 G
ejones@amherst.edu
JONES, Eric .... 641-628-5420 164 D
jonese@central.edu
JONES, Ericka .... 512-505-3035 438 A
edjones@htu.edu
JONES, Erin .... 619-260-4523.. 72 I
ekjones@sandiego.edu

JONES, Erna .... 704-330-1408 330 D
epjones@jcsu.edu
JONES, Esther .... 508-793-7141 208 C
esjones@clarku.edu
JONES, II, Eugene, G .... 407-582-1635 113 I
ejones102@valenciacollege.edu
JONES, Faye, M .... 615-353-3556 424 G
faye.jones@nscc.edu
JONES, Gabriel .... 615-244-5848 423 C
JONES, Garry .... 407-679-0100 101 K
gjones@fullsail.com
JONES, Garry .... 662-243-2643 246 B
gjones@eastms.edu
JONES, Garth .... 909-448-1502.. 71 C
gjones@laverne.edu
JONES, Gary .... 405-425-5904 367 C
gary.jones@oc.edu
JONES, Gena, W .... 575-646-1694 287 C
genaj@nmsu.edu
JONES, George .... 610-399-2082 393 F
gejones@cheyney.edu
JONES, Gerald .... 850-201-6140 112 C
gerald.jones@tcc.fl.edu
JONES, Gerald .... 334-386-7600..... 5 C
gjones@faulkner.edu
JONES, Gina, G .... 803-323-2194 414 D
jonesgg@winthrop.edu
JONES, Gordon .... 208-426-2975 130 H
gojones@boisestate.edu
JONES, Grady .... 843-383-8000 408 B
g.jones@coker.edu
JONES, Gregg .... 636-584-6507 253 B
gregg.jones@eastcentral.edu
JONES, Gregory .... 504-520-7449 193 E
gjones24@xula.edu
JONES, Gregory .... 615-460-6793 418 B
JONES, Griff .... 805-969-3626.. 55 J
gjones@pacifica.edu
JONES, Harold .... 903-675-6256 451 F
hjones@tvcc.edu
JONES, Hollie .... 718-270-5010 294 G
hjones@mec.cuny.edu
JONES, J. Pernell .... 610-341-5948 383 B
pjones1@eastern.edu
JONES, J. Preston .... 305-623-1423 100 D
preston.jones@fmuniv.edu
JONES, James .... 920-565-1000 493 A
jonesj3@lakeland.edu
JONES, James, C .... 334-699-2266..... 1 B
jjones@acom.edu
JONES, Jamie .... 319-363-1323 168 F
jjones@mtmercy.edu
JONES, Jamie .... 434-949-1068 475 B
jamie.jones@southside.edu
JONES, Jan-Erik .... 540-261-8400 471 B
je.jones@svu.edu
JONES, Janet .... 937-512-3890 360 G
janet.jones@sinclair.edu
JONES, Janice .... 270-707-3707 182 B
jjones0004@kctcs.edu
JONES, Jarian, R .... 770-220-7926 119 A
library@gcuniv.edu
JONES, Jason .... 850-245-0466 109 H
jason.jones@flbog.edu
JONES, Jeannette .... 830-372-6061 449 A
jjones@tlu.edu
JONES, Jeff .... 909-687-1750.. 43 D
jeffjones@gs.edu
JONES, Jeff .... 903-693-1112 441 C
jjones@panola.edu
JONES, Jeffrey .... 610-399-2042 393 F
jjones@cheyney.edu
JONES, Jen .... 254-295-8645 453 D
jen.jones@umhb.edu
JONES, Jennifer .... 920-465-2111 495 F
jonesj@uwgb.edu
JONES, Jennifer .... 815-455-8770 143 I
jjones@mchenry.edu
JONES, Jennifer .... 828-327-7000 333 B
jjones555@cvcc.edu
JONES, Jennifer .... 252-536-7254 335 B
JONES, Jenny .... 859-246-6653 181 F
jenny.jones@kctcs.edu
JONES, Jenny .... 512-542-7830 446 B
jjones@tamus.edu
JONES, Jenny, B .... 662-472-9035 246 D
jbailey@holmescc.edu
JONES, Jenny, L .... 404-880-8549 117 C
jjones@cau.edu
JONES, Jeremy .... 541-962-3553 372 I
jdjones1@eou.edu
JONES, Jerry .... 254-519-5446 447 A
jerry.jones@tamuct.edu

JONES, Jessica .... 252-246-1221 339 C
jjones@wilsoncc.edu
JONES, Jessie .... 573-592-5039 262 E
jessica.jones@westminster-mo.edu
JONES, Jim .... 517-787-0800 225 E
jonesjamesl@jccmi.edu
JONES, Jim .... 972-860-8058 434 G
s.jimjones@dcccd.edu
JONES, Jimmy .... 903-657-6543 448 D
jjones@tbi.edu
JONES, Joanne .... 912-260-4664 125 D
joanne.jones@sgsc.edu
JONES, John .... 269-965-3931 225 H
JONES, John .... 817-598-6345 457 J
jdjones@wc.edu
JONES, John .... 904-596-2304 112 F
jjones@tbc.edu
JONES, John .... 316-978-7751 178 D
john.jones@wichita.edu
JONES, John .... 765-677-2387 158 B
john.jones@indwes.edu
JONES, John .... 479-788-7456.. 21 G
john.jones@uafs.edu
JONES, John .... 615-329-8681 419 H
jjones@fisk.edu
JONES, III, John, E .... 717-245-1322 382 D
jonesjohn@dickinson.edu
JONES, John, P .... 520-621-1112.. 16 D
jpjones@arizona.edu
JONES, III, John, R ...... 205-996-0132..... 8 A
jrjones3@uab.edu
JONES, John, S .... 772-546-5534 102 C
johnjones@hsbc.edu
JONES, Johnny .... 281-949-1800.. 93 H
JONES, Johnny .... 937-708-3747 363 G
jjonesd@wilberforce.edu
JONES, Jon .... 417-268-6049 250 G
jjones@gobbc.edu
JONES, Josefvon .... 336-506-4289 332 A
jjones827@alamancecc.edu
JONES, Joseph .... 678-359-5468 120 F
jjones1@gordonstate.edu
JONES, Joseph .... 559-453-2010.. 43 A
fpupres@fresno.edu
JONES, Josh .... 785-864-6414 177 J
joshjones@ku.edu
JONES, Joshua .... 309-677-1000 134 A
jejones@bradley.edu
JONES, Joshua .... 864-503-5093 414 A
jjones3@uscupstate.edu
JONES, Joy .... 386-481-2959.. 96 D
jonesjo@cookman.edu
JONES, Joy .... 304-865-6102 487 H
joy.jones@ovu.edu
JONES, Joyce .... 404-962-3105 127 D
joyce.jones@usg.edu
JONES, Judy .... 979-532-6561 458 E
judyj@wcjc.edu
JONES, Julie .... 215-895-1910 382 F
jaj358@drexel.edu
JONES, K. Russell .... 479-968-0490.. 18 C
rjones@atu.edu
JONES, Karen .... 607-777-4775 316 B
kjones@binghamton.edu
JONES, Kathy .... 713-348-5460 442 F
kjones@rice.edu
JONES, Katie .... 704-330-6758 333 D
katie.jones@cpcc.edu
JONES, Katrina .... 716-338-1446 303 A
katrinajones@mail.sunyjcc.edu
JONES, Keisha .... 336-249-8186 334 B
keisha_jones@davidsondavie.edu
JONES, Keith .... 859-233-8181 185 C
kjones@transy.edu
JONES, Kelly .... 802-586-7711 462 I
kjones@sterlingcollege.edu
JONES, Ken .... 919-735-5151 338 H
kwjones@waynecc.edu
JONES, Kenneth, E .... 615-329-8681 419 H
kjones@fisk.edu
JONES, Kent .... 256-228-6001..... 3 B
jonesk@nacc.edu
JONES, Kevin .... 518-736-3622 300 D
kevin.jones@fmcc.suny.edu
JONES, Kevin .... 803-754-4100 408 E
JONES, Kevin .... 740-474-8896 358 A
kjones7@ohiochristian.edu
JONES, Kim .... 530-895-6144.. 27 C
joneski@butte.edu
JONES, Kim .... 270-831-9617 182 A
kim.jones@kctcs.edu
JONES, Kim .... 270-824-8649 182 D
kim.jones@kctcs.edu

JONES, Kim .... 903-823-3004 446 A
kimberly.jones@texarkanacollege.edu
JONES, Kimberly, W ...... 305-626-3629 100 D
kimberly.jones@fmuniv.edu
JONES, Kona .... 217-875-7211 148 A
kona@richland.edu
JONES, Kristen .... 425-564-2260 477 J
kristen.jones@bellevuecollege.edu
JONES, Kristine .... 919-497-3217 330 I
kjones@louisburg.edu
JONES, Lacretia .... 504-520-7593 193 E
ljames6@xula.edu
JONES, Lance .... 386-752-1822 100 B
christopher.jones@fgc.edu
JONES, Lance .... 303-458-3673.. 83 E
ljones007@regis.edu
JONES, Larry .... 443-885-3405 201 A
larry.jones@morgan.edu
JONES, Latia .... 786-331-1000 104 H
ljones@maufl.edu
JONES, Laura, A .... 928-523-9084.. 14 H
laura.jones@nau.edu
JONES, Laura, B .... 734-764-7423 231 H
laurabj@umich.edu
JONES, Lee .... 713-425-3100 433 C
JONES, Leonard .... 360-650-2953 485 I
leonard.jones@wwu.edu
JONES, II, LeRoy .... 773-995-2438 134 K
ljones27@csu.edu
JONES, Leslie .... 757-401-6125 477 G
JONES, Leslie .... 313-883-8512 230 C
jones.leslie@shms.edu
JONES, Leslie, M .... 504-398-2252 192 A
lmjones@uhcno.edu
JONES, Levi .... 816-268-5414 257 C
ljones@nts.edu
JONES, Lewis .... 256-726-8039..... 6 C
ljones@oakwood.edu
JONES, Liesl, B .... 410-462-8300 198 B
ljones@bccc.edu
JONES, Lisa .... 970-675-3210.. 79 H
lisa.jones@cncc.edu
JONES, Lisa .... 845-257-3216 316 E
jonesl@newpaltz.edu
JONES, Liz .... 706-368-7509 119 D
lijones@highlands.edu
JONES, Logan .... 816-271-4476 257 A
jones@missouriwestern.edu
JONES, Luke .... 208-426-1001 130 H
lukeajones@boisestate.edu
JONES, Maggie .... 334-222-6591..... 2 I
mjones@lbwcc.edu
JONES, Marcus .... 225-342-6950 192 B
marcus.jones@ulsystem.edu
JONES, Margaret .... 914-422-4043 311 A
mjones@pace.edu
JONES, Marian .... 704-378-1074 330 D
myjones@jcsu.edu
JONES, Marie .... 828-641-0768 327 B
jonesmf@brevard.edu
JONES, Marlon .... 216-421-7424 350 H
mjjones@cia.edu
JONES, Marlynn .... 904-620-2513 111 B
marlynn.jones@unf.edu
JONES, Mary .... 805-289-6346.. 74 B
mjones@vcccd.edu
JONES, OP, Mary .... 517-264-7109 230 H
mjones@sienaheights.edu
JONES, Mary, O .... 845-575-3000 305 D
mary.jones@marist.edu
JONES, Matthew .... 630-829-6135 133 E
mjones@ben.edu
JONES, Mautra .... 405-466-2937 366 C
mautra.jones@langston.edu
JONES, Megan .... 732-571-3465 279 A
mjones@monmouth.edu
JONES, Megan .... 423-323-0226 425 A
majones@northeaststate.edu
JONES, Melanie, E .... 803-327-8012 414 F
mjones@yorktech.edu
JONES, Melinda, L .... 901-678-2690 426 G
mljones6@memphis.edu
JONES, Melissa, A .... 910-678-8474 334 E
jonesma@faytechcc.edu
JONES, Meredith .... 580-559-5668 365 K
mjones@ecok.edu
JONES, Michael .... 918-444-3211 366 G
jones361@nsuok.edu
JONES, Michael .... 518-292-8615 313 A
jonesm4@sage.edu
JONES, Michael .... 321-674-7297 100 C
jonesm@fit.edu

JONES, Michael .... 909-607-8585.. 37 F
michael_jones@kgi.edu
JONES, Mike .... 434-544-8538 471 L
jones.mj@lynchburg.edu
JONES, Molly .... 513-618-1933 350 E
mjones@ccms.edu
JONES, Monterrio .... 803-934-3226 410 G
mjones@morris.edu
JONES, Nancy .... 714-241-6209.. 37 J
njones@coastline.edu
JONES, Nancy, L .... 404-527-7767 121 L
nljones@itc.edu
JONES, Natalie .... 207-780-5113 197 D
natalie.jones@maine.edu
JONES, III, Nathaniel ... 510-522-7221.. 57 A
nathanieljones@peralta.edu
JONES, Ned, J .... 518-783-2423 315 E
jones@siena.edu
JONES, Nedra, W .... 804-524-6706 476 D
nwjones@vsu.edu
JONES, Neil .... 478-445-5596 119 B
neil.jones@gcsu.edu
JONES, Nicholas, P .... 814-865-2505 391 G
provost@psu.edu
JONES, Nicholaus .... 215-780-1417 398 B
njones@salus.edu
JONES, Nicole .... 619-660-4302.. 44 D
nicole.jones@gcccd.edu
JONES, Niki .... 870-633-4480.. 19 A
njones@eacc.edu
JONES, Nina .... 662-915-7690 249 D
nina@olemiss.edu
JONES, Nolan .... 972-825-7970 444 J
nojones@sagu.edu
JONES, Norm, E .... 615-329-8663 419 H
nejones@fisk.edu
JONES, Norman .... 706-821-8232 124 B
njones@paine.edu
JONES, Olivia .... 919-530-7713 341 E
ojones@nccu.edu
JONES, Orion .... 419-434-4544 362 D
orion.jones@findlay.edu
JONES, Otis, C .... 800-443-9266 503 D
JONES, Pamela .... 956-295-3622 449 C
pamela.jones@tsc.edu
JONES, Para, M .... 330-494-6170 360 K
pjones@starkstate.edu
JONES, Parago .... 303-329-6355.. 79 L
dean@cstcm.edu
JONES, Pat .... 318-357-6441 192 G
JONES, Patrice .... 703-892-5100.. 93 H
JONES, Paul .... 478-825-6315 118 F
president@fvsu.edu
JONES, Paul .... 414-288-5276 493 E
paul.jones@marquette.edu
JONES, Phil .... 772-546-5534 102 C
philjones@hsbc.edu
JONES, Phyllis .... 314-838-8858 261 F
pjones@ugst.edu
JONES, Polly .... 864-379-8833 409 E
pjones@erskine.edu
JONES, R Clifford .... 256-726-7365..... 6 C
rcjones@oakwood.edu
JONES, Randy .... 805-565-7048.. 76 A
rjones@westmont.edu
JONES, Randy, P .... 214-768-2146 444 D
rpjones@smu.edu
JONES, Razel .... 615-963-5000 426 A
JONES, Rebecca .... 503-255-0332 374 C
beccajones@multnomah.edu
JONES, Renee .... 310-665-6800.. 55 C
rjones@otis.edu
JONES, Rilla .... 662-620-5031 246 E
rkjones@iccms.edu
JONES, Robert .... 903-823-3154 446 A
robert.jones@texarkanacollege.edu
JONES, Robert .... 508-999-8552 212 A
rjones@umassd.edu
JONES, Robert .... 401-232-6027 404 A
rjones10@bryant.edu
JONES, Robert .... 503-517-1862 377 E
rjones@westernseminary.edu
JONES, III, Robert .... 804-330-0111 465 H
JONES, Robert, H .... 864-656-3940 407 E
provost@clemson.edu
JONES, Robert, J .... 217-333-6290 151 F
rjjones@illinois.edu
JONES, Robert, J .... 217-333-6290 152 B
chancellor@illinois.edu
JONES, Robin .... 334-291-4927..... 1 H
robin.jones@cv.edu
JONES, Robin .... 205-348-5490..... 7 G
rjones@uasystem.edu

JOSEPH, Kevin .... 785-864-4060 177 J
k.joseph@ku.edu
JOSEPH, Laly .... 212-614-6153 311 D
laly.joseph@mountsinai.org
JOSEPH, Laura .... 934-420-2003 320 F
laura.joseph@farmingdale.edu
JOSEPH, Laurel .... 281-756-3513 429 D
ljoseph@alvincollege.edu
JOSEPH, Mark .... 740-284-5870 352 I
mjoseph@franciscan.edu
JOSEPH, Michael .... 312-369-7114 136 D
mijoseph@colum.edu
JOSEPH, Michiko .... 808-689-2707 129 F
msjoseph@hawaii.edu
JOSEPH, Nicole .... 208-282-2123 131 G
rosenico@isu.edu
JOSEPH, Noson .... 718-601-3523 326 C
njoseph@ytariverdale.org
JOSEPH, Patricia .... 484-365-8152 388 H
joseph@lincoln.edu
JOSEPH, Rabi .... 707-654-1782.. 32 A
JOSEPH, Sonya, F .... 407-582-7734 113 I
sjoseph@valenciacollege.edu
JOSEPH, Stephen, M ..... 724-287-8711 379 E
steve.joseph@bc3.edu
JOSEPH, Susan .... 914-361-6221 307 C
soojoseph@montefiore.org
JOSEPH, Susan .... 423-697-3136 424 A
susan.joseph@chattanoogastate.edu
JOSEPH-KEMPLIN,
Mitch .... 614-234-2341 356 E
mjoseph-kemplin@mccn.edu
JOSEPHSON, David .... 973-655-6956 279 B
josephsond@montclair.edu
JOSEPHSON, Kimberlee 717-867-6109 388 C
josephson@lvc.edu
JOSEY, Peige .... 334-222-6591.... 2 I
pjosey@lbwcc.edu
JOSHEE, Jeet .... 562-985-4106.. 31 D
jeet.joshee@csulb.edu
JOSHEE, Jeet .... 562-985-8330.. 31 D
jeet.joshee@csulb.edu
JOSHI, Chetan .... 301-314-7069 202 H
cajoshi@umd.edu
JOSHI, Maulin .... 973-618-3519 276 D
mjoshi@caldwell.edu
JOSHUA, Donald .... 212-280-1462 323 K
djoshua@uts.columbia.edu
JOSHUA, Kazi .... 509-527-5158 486 B
joshuake@whitman.edu
JOSHUA, Querencia ...... 281-756-3688 429 D
qjoshua@alvincollege.edu
JOSLEYN, Alyshia .... 206-546-4101 484 B
ajosleyn@shoreline.edu
JOSLIN, Jennifer .... 417-873-6850 252 G
jjoslin@drury.edu
JOSLIN, Michael .... 661-362-3260.. 38 D
michael.joslin@canyons.edu
JOSLIN, Randall .... 530-251-8836.. 47 F
rjoslin@lassencollege.edu
JOSLYN-SIEMIATKOSKI,
Dan .... 512-472-4133 443 F
dan.joslyn-siemiatkoski@ssw.edu
JOSS, Jamie .... 321-674-7209 100 C
jjoss@fit.edu
JOSSELL, Steven .... 662-621-4304 245 D
sjossell@coahomacc.edu
JOSSERAND,
Tamara, M .... 909-748-8840.. 72 F
tamara_josserand@redlands.edu
JOST, Steve, A .... 301-860-4212 204 A
sjost@bowiestate.edu
JOSUWEIT, Samuel .... 570-389-4000 393 D
JOUGHIN, Sarah .... 207-581-3437 196 G
joughin@maine.edu
JOURDAN, Dawn .... 301-405-8000 202 H
djourdan@umd.edu
JOURDAN, Lee Ann ...... 317-738-8755 155 D
ljourdan@franklincollege.edu
JOURNET, Nancy .... 708-344-4700 143 A
njournet@lincolntech.edu
JOUTZ, Marguerite .... 401-863-9212 403 J
marguerite_joutz@brown.edu
JOUVENAS, Anthony ..... 334-556-2474.... 2 C
ajouvenas@wallace.edu
JOVANOVIC, Jasna .... 805-756-2033.. 29 I
jjovanov@calpoly.edu
JOVEN, Robert .... 203-582-3468.. 88 G
robert.joven@quinnipiac.edu
JOVICIC, Mila .... 310-204-1666.. 58 K
JOWERS, Angel .... 205-652-3547.... 9 B
ajowers@uwa.edu
JOWERS, Rebecca .... 214-887-5000 435 F
JOY, Alonzo, F .... 202-806-6100.. 92 F
JOY, Cory .... 727-376-6911 112 G
anthony.abell@trinitycollege.edu
JOY, Lilia .... 270-831-9641 182 A
lilia.joy@kctcs.edu
JOY, Steaven .... 731-426-7523 420 G
sjoy@lanecollege.edu
JOYCE, Christine .... 317-632-5553 159 I
cjoyce@lincolntech.edu
JOYCE, Christopher, J .. 781-891-2003 206 G
cjoyce@bentley.edu
JOYCE, Daniel .... 215-951-1881 387 A
joyced@lasalle.edu
JOYCE, SJ, Daniel, R .... 610-660-3291 397 G
djoyce@sju.edu
JOYCE, David, C .... 828-641-0826 327 B
president@brevard.edu
JOYCE, Gerard .... 610-282-1100 382 C
gerard.joyce@desales.edu
JOYCE, Jeff .... 828-641-0170 327 B
joycejj@brevard.edu
JOYCE, Kelly .... 215-895-1891 382 F
kelly.a.joyce@drexel.edu
JOYCE, Kelly .... 812-866-7160 155 G
joyce@hanover.edu
JOYCE, Kevin .... 914-674-7775 306 C
kjoyce@mercy.edu
JOYCE, Kimberly .... 410-287-1022 198 E
kjoyce@cecil.edu
JOYCE, Michelle .... 574-631-2786 162 A
mjoyce@nd.edu
JOYNER, Angela, M ...... 540-831-5370 469 D
ajoyner9@radford.edu
JOYNER, Barry .... 912-478-5322 120 C
joyner@georgiasouthern.edu
JOYNER, Chartarra .... 336-285-2941 341 D
cmjoyne2@ncat.edu
JOYNER, Laurie, M .... 773-298-3000 149 D
joyner@sxu.edu
JOYNER, Marie .... 973-408-3097 277 A
mjoyner@drew.edu
JOYNER, Stephen .... 561-868-3033 105 D
joyners@palmbeachstate.edu
JOYNER, SR., Stephen . 704-330-1406 330 D
sjoyner@jcsu.edu
JOYNER-GRAHAM,
JoAnn .... 718-270-4832 294 G
jjoyner@mec.cuny.edu
JOYNES, Stephanie, N .. 434-223-6325 467 F
sjoynes@hsc.edu
JOYNES-STURGIS,
Jicola, R .... 410-651-7018 203 D
jrsturgis@umes.edu
JUÁREZ, JR.,
José (Beto), R .... 954-262-6101 105 A
jjuarez@nova.edu
JU MILLER, Grace .... 765-998-4734 161 C
grace_miller2@taylor.edu
JUARBE, Lorraine .... 787-763-6425 507 J
ljuarbe@inter.edu
JUARBE REY, Myriam ... 787-720-4476 511 C
asistenciaeconomica@mizpa.edu
JUAREZ, Anabel .... 972-273-3084 435 B
JUAREZ, Cindy .... 760-776-7441.. 38 E
cjuarez@collegeofthedesert.edu
JUAREZ, Elisa .... 520-494-5426.. 11 K
elisa.juarez@centralaz.edu
JUAREZ, III, Fred .... 956-326-2448 446 E
fredjuarez@tamiu.edu
JUAREZ, Raelene .... 209-588-5087.. 76 K
juarezr@yosemite.edu
JUAREZ, Reina .... 858-534-3755.. 70 C
rjuarez@ucsd.edu
JUDAH, Courtney .... 541-506-6151 372 F
cjudah@cgcc.edu
JUDD, Matthew .... 909-274-4425.. 52 J
mjudd@mtsac.edu
JUDD, Summer .... 731-989-6662 419 K
sjudd@fhu.edu
JUDD, Tim .... 270-789-5027 180 A
tmjudd@campbellsville.edu
JUDE, II, Willie .... 262-595-2591 496 D
jude@uwp.edu
JUDGE, Gwenn .... 315-443-1870 321 G
JUDGE, Jeffrey .... 952-358-8585 239 G
jeff.judge@normandale.edu
JUDGE, John .... 202-319-5160.. 92 A
judge@cua.edu
JUDGE, Joseph .... 610-282-1100 382 C
jjudge@follett.com
JUDGE, Kristin, O .... 215-572-2928 378 E
judgek@arcadia.edu
JUDGE, Lisa .... 440-826-2106 348 D
ljudge@bw.edu
JUDGE, Sheila .... 504-816-4370 186 I
sjudge@dillard.edu
JUDGE CRIPE,
Stephanie .... 317-940-9351 154 C
sjudge@butler.edu
JUDKINS, Brooke .... 760-750-8782.. 33 A
bjudkins@csusm.edu
JUDKINS, Jason .... 760-245-4271.. 74 D
jason.judkins@vvc.edu
JUDSON, Dan .... 617-559-8638 210 F
djudson@hebrewcollege.edu
JUDSON, Frank .... 570-585-9444 381 B
fjudson@clarkssummitu.edu
JUDY, Allison .... 308-635-6081 270 C
judya2@wncc.edu
JUDY, Joyce, M .... 802-828-2800 463 F
jmj10300@ccv.vsc.edu
JUELE, Lilia .... 845-574-4480 312 H
ljuele@sunyrockland.edu
JUELG, Earl .... 832-246-0055 439 C
butch@lonestar.edu
JUENGER, Mike .... 618-235-2700 150 E
michael.juenger@swic.edu
JUERGENS, Kristin, A ... 414-464-9777 498 B
juergens.kristin@wspp.edu
JUERGENS, Valorie .... 269-467-9945 224 C
vjuergens@glenoaks.edu
JUGOVICH, Shelly .... 218-748-2416 240 E
shelly.jugovich@mesabirange.edu
JUKKALA, Clint, A .... 215-972-7623 392 T
cjukkala@pafa.edu
JUKOSKI, Mary Ellen .... 860-215-9001.. 87 F
mjukoski@threerivers.edu
JULIA, Jake .... 847-491-2912 146 E
jjulia@northwestern.edu
JULIAN, Betsy .... 541-383-7205 372 A
bjulian@cocc.edu
JULIAN, Charity .... 812-749-1235 159 O
cjulian@oak.edu
JULIAN, Elizabeth, A ..... 706-771-4049 115 J
ejulian@augustatech.edu
JULIAN, JR., James ...... 617-287-7050 211 F
evp@umassp.edu
JULIAN, Janelle .... 314-719-8057 253 E
jjulian@fontbonne.edu
JULIAN, Jeff .... 847-925-6183 138 G
jjulian1@harpercollege.edu
JULIAN, Karen, M .... 651-962-6176 244 E
kmjulian@stthomas.edu
JULIAN, Leisa .... 765-973-8348 157 A
lejulian@iu.edu
JULIAN, Tijuana, S .... 417-873-7215 252 G
tjulian@drury.edu
JULIANI, Justine .... 253-879-2720 484 G
jjuliani@pugetsound.edu
JULICH, Daniel .... 863-638-7639 114 A
daniel.julich@warner.edu
JULICH PEREZ, April .... 617-258-0385 216 B
JULIEN, Earlye, A .... 563-884-5476 169 F
earlye.julien@palmer.edu
JULIUS, Greg .... 805-482-2755.. 59 G
greg@stjohnsem.edu
JULIUS, James .... 760-757-2121.. 52 F
jjulius@miracosta.edu
JUMONVILLE, Jennifer .. 504-314-2602 191 F
jjumonvi@tulane.edu
JUMP, Jonathon, D ...... 765-361-6206 163 B
jumpj@wabash.edu
JUMPER, Cynthia .... 806-743-3280 451 A
cynthia.jumper@ttuhsc.edu
JUMPER, G. Robin .... 850-263-3261.. 95 P
grjumper@baptistcollege.edu
JUNCO, Maite .... 646-664-9100 292 K
JUNE, Robert .... 414-443-8867 498 A
robert.june@wlc.edu
JUNE, Vincent .... 337-521-8909 188 I
vincent.june@solacc.edu
JUNEAU-BUTLER,
Allyson .... 801-649-5230 459 G
admissions@midwifery.edu
JUNEK, Shauna .... 605-642-6203 416 E
shauna.junek@bhsu.edu
JUNG, Alan .... 205-726-2716.... 6 E
apjung@samford.edu
JUNG, Anne, S .... 518-861-2532 305 C
ajung@mariacollege.edu
JUNG, Barnabas .... 951-763-0500.. 55 B
JUNG, Chul Heon .... 562-926-1023.. 58 A
ptsamedia@ptsa.edu
JUNG, Jackie .... 213-740-2311.. 73 C
JUNG, Jimmy .... 856-256-4230 281 F
jungj@rowan.edu
JUNG-MATHEWS,
Anne, M .... 603-535-2458 275 A
amjung@plymouth.edu
JUNGBLUT, Heather, L . 563-588-7103 168 A
heather.jungblut@loras.edu
JUNGERS, Christin .... 740-284-7220 352 I
cjungers@franciscan.edu
JUNGKUNTZ, David ...... 360-752-8355 478 A
djungkun@btc.edu
JUNKER, OP, Gianna .... 615-297-7545 417 G
srgianna@aquinascollege.edu
JUNKERMAN,
Charles, L .... 650-723-6866.. 66 E
clj@stanford.edu
JUNKIN, Chip .... 410-857-2256 200 F
cjunkin@mcdaniel.edu
JUNN, Ellen .... 209-667-3201.. 33 B
president@csustan.edu
JUNOR, Bill .... 914-251-6460 319 B
bill.junor@purchase.edu
JUNOR, Laura, J .... 202-685-4379 502 K
laura.j.junor.civ@ndu.edu
JUNQUERA, Belinda ...... 787-766-1717 510 G
junquerab1@uagm.edu
JUNTUNEN, Cindy .... 701-777-2674 345 B
cindy.juntunen@und.edu
JURAN, Victor .... 651-690-6826 243 A
vbjuran@stkate.edu
JURAS, Jennifer .... 415-703-9522.. 28 B
jjuras@cca.edu
JURAS, Kenneth .... 845-687-5108 323 H
jurask@sunyulster.edu
JURKOVIC, Frank .... 727-341-4732 107 E
jurkovic.frank@spcollege.edu
JURNAK, Sheila .... 505-277-6331 288 J
sjurnak@unm.edu
JURSZA-WILLIAMS,
Tammy .... 607-871-2123 290 B
jurszawilliams@alfred.edu
JUSINO, Lidis, L .... 787-284-1912 508 E
ljusino@ponce.inter.edu
JUSKEVICE, Leigh .... 207-509-7208 196 E
ljuskevice@unity.edu
JUSKIEWICZ, Scott .... 406-496-4523 265 A
sjuskiewicz@mtech.edu
JUSSEAUME, Yvette ...... 323-856-7721.. 25 G
yjusseaume@afi.com
JUSSEL, Adam .... 414-229-4632 496 B
jussel@uwm.edu
JUST, Eric .... 785-670-1860 178 C
eric.just@washburn.edu
JUSTESEN, Bryan, H ...... 208-356-1320 130 I
justesenb@byui.edu
JUSTESON, Rebecca ...... 530-898-6421.. 30 D
rjusteson@csuchico.edu
JUSTICE, Brooke .... 270-901-1001 182 H
brooke.palmer@kctcs.edu
JUSTICE, Della, M .... 850-263-3261.. 95 P
dmjustice@baptistcollege.edu
JUSTICE, Elizabeth .... 405-585-4256 367 B
elizabeth.justice@okbu.edu
JUSTICE, Gary .... 606-218-5306 186 B
garyjustice@upike.edu
JUSTICE, Greg .... 260-481-6785 160 C
justiceg@pfw.edu
JUSTICE, Jessica .... 606-546-1214 185 D
jjustice@unionky.edu
JUSTICE, LaMica .... 601-977-7720 249 C
ljustice@tougaloo.edu
JUSTICE, Lillian .... 310-660-6960.. 41 E
ljustice@elcamino.edu
JUSTICE, Richard .... 317-299-0333 161 D
richard@tcmi.org
JUSTINGER, Doreen ...... 716-250-7500 292 A
dajustinger@bryantstratton.edu
JUSTINIANO, Jonna ...... 510-501-5075.. 58 H
jjustiniano@reachinst.org
JUSTISON, Brian, K .... 217-424-6300 144 G
bjustison@millikin.edu
JUSTNYA, Erin .... 806-743-3451 451 A
erin.justyna@ttuhsc.edu
JUSZCZYK, Casey .... 815-479-7524 143 I
cjuszczyk@mchenry.edu
JUTKIEWICZ, Richard .... 215-885-2360 389 C
rjutkiewicz@manor.edu
JUVERA, Kelly .... 520-515-3612.. 11 M
juverak@cochise.edu

K

KA-TANDIA, Nogaye ..... 607-962-9000 320 C
president@corning-cc.edu

KANAKIS, Chris .... 312-942-2831 148 G
chris_kanakis@rush.edu
KANALIS, Mike .... 724-938-5417 393 E
kanalis@calu.edu
KANARAS, Elizabeth ...... 610-902-8283 379 G
KANAREK, Berel .... 914-736-1500 310 E
KANAREK, E .... 914-736-1500 310 E
KANBAR, Hiam .... 831-242-5618 502 F
hiam.n.kanbar@dliflc.edu
KANDEL-CISCO, Brooke 317-940-8000 154 C
KANDER, Ron .... 215-951-0252 399 E
kanderr@philau.edu
KANDLER, Mike .... 850-769-1551 101 N
mkandler@gulfcoast.edu
KANDOGAN, Yener .... 810-762-3160 232 A
yener@umich.edu
KANDUS-FISHER,
Christopher .... 617-747-2231 206 H
studentaffairs@berklee.edu
KANE, Andrew .... 609-258-3469 280 D
kane@princeton.edu
KANE, Barry, S .... 212-854-1458 297 C
barry@columbia.edu
KANE, Brian .... 610-785-6265 397 E
bkane@scs.edu
KANE, Chris .... 610-690-5529 398 G
ckane1@swarthmore.edu
KANE, Colleen .... 715-422-5510 499 B
colleen.kane@mstc.edu
KANE, Daniel .... 315-312-4142 318 D
daniel.kane@oswego.edu
KANE, Daniel, C .... 207-768-9475 197 C
daniel.c.kane@maine.edu
KANE, Gina .... 315-781-3064 301 F
kane@hws.edu
KANE, Hillary .... 213-738-6825.. 66 B
hkane@swlaw.edu
KANE, Jane .... 908-709-7169 284 D
jane.kane@ucc.edu
KANE, Jesse .... 718-270-6245 294 G
jkane@mec.cuny.edu
KANE, Katherine, J .... 864-938-3913 411 D
kjkane@presby.edu
KANE, Kathleen .... 856-227-7200 276 E
kkane@camdencc.edu
KANE, Kerri .... 413-755-4115 216 A
kpkane@stcc.edu
KANE, Kevin, M .... 610-499-4555 402 G
kmkane1@widener.edu
KANE, Kim .... 707-638-5280.. 68 B
kim.kane@tu.edu
KANE, Laura .... 580-581-5502 365 D
laurak@cameron.edu
KANE, Marie .... 210-485-0020 428 G
KANE, Micah .... 650-543-3744.. 51 G
bot@menlo.edu
KANE, Michael .... 650-738-4248.. 62 L
kanem@smccd.edu
KANE, Michael, J .... 859-858-3511 179 D
mike.kane@asbury.edu
KANE, Robert, C .... 202-685-3927 502 K
robert.kane@ndu.edu
KANE, Ryan .... 920-748-8115 494 J
KANE, Ryan, D .... 407-582-3421 113 I
rkane8@valenciacollege.edu
KANE, Sara, F .... 863-638-7602 114 A
sara.kane@warner.edu
KANE, Scott .... 570-662-4345 394 F
skane@mansfield.edu
KANE, Scott .... 570-389-4000 393 D
KANE, Sylvia .... 714-556-3610.. 73 H
KANE, Tara .... 734-432-5429 227 C
tkane@madonna.edu
KANE, Thomas .... 781-891-2340 206 G
tkane@bentley.edu
KANE, Thomas, F .... 570-674-6223 390 B
tkane@misericordia.edu
KANE, Vicki .... 814-944-5643 403 I
vicki.kane@yti.edu
KANE, Victoria .... 323-650-7777.. 47 J
KANE, Wendy .... 432-685-4695 440 B
wkane@midland.edu
KANELOS, Gwen, E .... 708-209-3101 136 E
gwen.kanelos@cuchicago.edu
KANEPS, Katherine, D ... 610-330-5200 387 C
kanepsk@lafayette.edu
KANEVSKAYA, Svetlana 212-752-1530 304 A
svetlana.kanevskaya@limcollege.edu
KANG, David .... 303-492-4212.. 84 B
david.kang@colorado.edu
KANG, Hanna .... 703-206-0508 465 O
hannak@ccdc.edu
KANG, Hyo Jeong .... 714-533-1495.. 64 I
hjkang@southbaylo.edu
KANG, Kathy, Y .... 310-739-0132.. 40 H
KANG, Mia .... 770-220-7906 119 A
academic@gcuniv.edu
KANG, Min .... 806-743-3600 451 A
min.kang@ttuhsc.edu
KANG, Richard .... 213-740-2311.. 73 C
KANG, Soonhae .... 714-527-0691.. 41 J
KANG, YeJoon .... 770-232-2717 124 F
KANG, Yunn .... 215-702-4271 380 A
ykang@cairn.edu
KANG, Yunn .... 215-702-4461 380 A
ykang@cairn.edu
KANGAS, Richard .... 218-322-2319 238 F
richard.kangas@itascacc.edu
KANGETHE, Patrick .... 857-701-1552 215 G
pkangethe@rcc.mass.edu
KANIA, Dan .... 314-371-0236 258 F
KANIA, Ed .... 407-646-2117 106 L
ekania@rollins.edu
KANIA, Ellie, L .... 540-464-7322 476 B
kaniael@vmi.edu
KANIATOBE, Phillip ...... 505-984-6144 288 C
phillip.kaniatobe@sjc.edu
KANICH, Amy .... 814-886-6483 390 G
akanich@mtaloy.edu
KANIKKEBERG,
Dee Dee .... 208-885-6571 132 F
deedeek@uidaho.edu
KANIPES, Margaret .... 336-285-2030 341 D
mikanipe@ncat.edu
KANIS, David .... 773-995-2497 134 K
dkanis@csu.edu
KANMORE, John .... 575-562-2511 286 B
john.kanmore@enmu.edu
KANN, Andrea .... 212-824-2208 301 B
akann@huc.edu
KANNAN, Govind .... 478-825-4613 118 F
govindak@fvsu.edu
KANNARKAT, Mily .... 757-446-8910 466 D
kannarmj@evms.edu
KANNE, Lynn .... 206-934-4072 483 C
lynn.kanne@seattlecolleges.edu
KANNENBERG, Karen ... 314-392-2337 256 E
karen.kannenberg@mobap.edu
KANNENWISCHER,
Susan .... 614-222-4001 351 B
skannenwischer@ccad.edu
KANOY, David .... 910-362-7695 332 H
dkanoy@cfcc.edu
KANTARDJIEFF,
Katherine .... 831-582-4401.. 32 B
kkantardjieff@csumb.edu
KANTENWEIN, Heidi, L . 260-422-5561 156 E
hlkantenwein@indianatech.edu
KANTERMAN, Kathy ...... 401-254-3531 405 C
kkanterman@rwu.edu
KANTNER, Joanne .... 815-825-9450 141 F
mkantner@kish.edu
KANTNER, John .... 904-620-1360 111 B
j.kantner@unf.edu
KANTNER, John .... 904-620-2455 111 B
j.kantner@unf.edu
KANTNER, Michael .... 856-256-4566 281 F
kantner@rowan.edu
KANTO, Kind .... 691-330-2620 504 C
kank@comfsm.fm
KANTOR, Ali .... 617-521-1038 218 G
ali.kantor@simmons.edu
KANTOR, Rebecca .... 303-315-6343.. 84 D
rebecca.kantor@ucdenver.edu
KANU, Andrew .... 804-524-5930 476 D
akanu@vsu.edu
KANWAR, Vik .... 213-738-6845.. 66 B
vkanwar@swlaw.edu
KANWISCHER, Charlie .. 419-372-9395 348 G
ckanwis@bgsu.edu
KAO, Chi-Chang .... 650-723-2300.. 66 E
KAO, Patrick .... 415-422-5380.. 72 J
pk@usfca.edu
KAOPUIKI, Ryon .... 260-982-5000 159 J
rdkaopuiki@manchester.edu
KAOUDIS, Kathryn .... 303-352-3356.. 80 F
kathy.kaoudis@ccd.edu
KAPASI, Zoher, F .... 843-792-3328 410 C
kapasi@musc.edu
KAPFHAMMER, Sean ..... 410-777-2836 197 G
srkapfhammer@aacc.edu
KAPILESHWARI,
Sameer .... 336-334-5536 343 A
s_kapile@uncg.edu
KAPINUS, Carolyn .... 940-898-3301 451 D
ckapinus@twu.edu
KAPLA, Dale, P .... 906-227-2920 228 I
dkapla@nmu.edu
KAPLAN, Alan .... 608-263-8025 495 D
akaplan@uwhealth.org
KAPLAN, Judith .... 216-987-4613 351 E
judith.kaplan@tri-c.edu
KAPLAN, Keith, B .... 315-267-2141 319 A
kaplankb@potsdam.edu
KAPLAN, Leonard, I ...... 973-596-3638 279 E
leonard.i.kaplan@njit.edu
KAPLAN, Mark .... 352-392-4574 111 A
mark.kaplan@ufl.edu
KAPLAN, Richard .... 617-732-2808 216 D
richard.kaplan@mcphs.edu
KAPLAN, Ronald, S ...... 847-578-8538 148 F
ronald.kaplan@rosalindfranklin.edu
KAPLAN, Steven, H ...... 203-932-7276.. 89 H
skaplan@newhaven.edu
KAPLINSKY, Yoheved ... 212-799-5000 303 E
KAPOUN, Jim .... 717-815-1353 403 F
jkapoun@ycp.edu
KAPP, Alisha .... 217-854-5511 133 I
alisha.kapp@blackburn.edu
KAPPANADZE,
Margaret .... 607-735-1867 298 H
mkappanadze@elmira.edu
KAPPEL, Stephanie .... 304-214-8801 488 J
skappel@wvncc.edu
KAPPENMAN, Angi .... 605-256-5134 416 F
angi.kappenman@dsu.edu
KAPPES, Christiaan .... 412-321-8383 379 F
dean@bcs.edu
KAPRIVE, Mark .... 561-803-2542 105 C
mark_kaprive@pba.edu
KAPSAL, Sean .... 859-344-3698 185 B
kapsals@thomasmore.edu
KAPTAIN, Laurence .... 303-352-3559.. 84 D
laurence.kaptain@ucdenver.edu
KAPUR, Anup .... 609-771-2859 276 I
kapura@tcnj.edu
KAPUR, Sonia .... 503-552-1933 374 D
skapur@nunm.edu
KAPURCH, Jason .... 508-929-8045 213 G
jkapurch@worcester.edu
KARABETSOS,
Michael, L .... 517-264-7109 230 H
mkarabet@sienaheights.edu
KARACAL, Cem .... 618-650-2861 150 C
skaraca@siue.edu
KARAFA, Andy .... 716-673-3173 316 D
andy.karafa@fredonia.edu
KARAFIN, Diana, L .... 212-998-4426 309 F
diana.karafin@nyu.edu
KARAGEZIAN, Vardan ... 818-240-6900.. 25 J
karagezian@amsc.edu
KARAGIANNIS, Aliki, E . 508-565-1537 219 A
akaragiannis@stonehill.edu
KARAGOSIAN, Nico ...... 740-593-4764 358 K
nico@ohio.edu
KARAHADIAN, Milton ... 619-849-2649.. 57 J
miltonkarahadian@pointloma.edu
KARAKASHIAN, Ara ...... 201-360-4696 278 C
akarakashian@hccc.edu
KARAM, Robert .... 270-384-7309 183 G
karamr@lindsey.edu
KARAM, Vanessa .... 626-571-8811.. 73 E
vanessak@uwest.edu
KARAMAN, Ana .... 503-838-8137 377 D
karamana@wou.edu
KARAMOL, Mark .... 567-661-7988 359 I
mark_karamol@owens.edu
KARANFIL, Tanju .... 864-656-7701 407 E
tkaranf@clemson.edu
KARANJA, Benson, M .. 404-627-2681 116 C
benson.karanja@beulah.edu
KARANJA, Peter .... 404-627-2681 116 C
peter.karanja@beulah.edu
KARAPANAGIOTIS,
Nicole .... 856-225-6574 281 G
nicole.karapanagiotis@rutgers.edu
KARAS, Jane, A .... 406-756-3801 263 E
jkaras@fvcc.edu
KARAS, Jennifer .... 303-871-6793.. 84 E
jkaras@du.edu
KARAS, Tara .... 941-487-5001 110 D
tkaras@ncf.edu
KARAS, Timothy .... 707-468-3071.. 51 F
tkaras@mendocino.edu
KARASEK, III,
Raymond, N .... 401-825-2298 404 C
mkarasek@ccri.edu
KARASINSKI, Tracy .... 401-825-2305 404 C
tkarasinski@ccri.edu
KARASS, Alan .... 706-507-8681 117 H
karass_alan@columbusstate.edu
KARATAN, Ece .... 828-262-7459 340 I
karatane@appstate.edu
KARAVOLAS, Susan ...... 518-694-7278 289 J
susan.karavolas@acphs.edu
KARAZIM, Jan .... 517-483-1461 226 H
karazimj@lcc.edu
KARBAN, Janel .... 920-498-5409 499 G
janel.karban@nwtc.edu
KARCH, Amanda .... 518-828-4181 297 B
amanda.karch@sunycgcc.edu
KARCH, Lisa .... 218-477-2699 239 E
lisa.karch@mnstate.edu
KARDAN, Sel .... 213-621-2200.. 38 C
KARDOW, Vivian, D ..... 409-772-2636 456 E
vdkardow@utmb.edu
KARGES, Teri .... 843-863-7050 407 B
tkarges@csuniv.edu
KARIM, Alema .... 401-456-9538 405 A
akarim@ric.edu
KARIM, Anwar .... 240-567-3212 200 G
anwar.karim@montgomerycollege.edu
KARIMBUX, Nadeem .... 617-636-6636 219 C
nadeem.karimbux@tufts.edu
KARIMIGEVARI, Reza .... 503-352-7276 375 C
karimir@pacificu.edu
KARIOTIS, Angela .... 732-224-2109 276 B
akariotis@brookdalecc.edu
KARIUKI, Benson .... 903-730-4890 438 D
bkariuku@jarvis.edu
KARLBERG,
Anne Marie .... 360-383-3302 486 A
amkarlberg@whatcom.edu
KARLE, Christie .... 949-794-9090.. 66 D
ckarle@stanbridge.edu
KARLGAARD, Joseph .... 713-348-4077 442 F
joe.karlgaard@rice.edu
KARLIN, Angela .... 785-864-4700 177 J
akarlin@ku.edu
KARLIN, Barbara, H ...... 415-442-7882.. 43 I
bkarlin@ggu.edu
KARLIN, Craig .... 785-628-4222 173 H
ckarlin@fhsu.edu
KARLOFF, Michael .... 402-461-7473 267 C
mkarloff@hastings.edu
KARMAN, John .... 502-852-1108 186 A
john.karman@louisville.edu
KARMANOVA, Tatiana ... 909-537-3986.. 32 E
tkarma@csusb.edu
KARMELEK, Mary .... 212-229-5600 308 A
karmelem@newschool.edu
KARMIS, Beth .... 312-949-7415 139 D
bkarmis@ico.edu
KARMON, Rachel .... 937-433-3410 352 G
rkarmon@fortiscollege.edu
KARNES, Christy .... 202-379-7808.. 93 H
KARNES, Michael, S ..... 585-753-3700 307 B
mkarnes@monroecc.edu
KARNOWSKI,
Thomas, J .... 202-685-3929 502 K
thomas.j.karnowski.civ@ndu.edu
KAROL, Gloria .... 315-792-5486 306 K
gkarol@mvcc.edu
KAROLEWICS, Vicki .... 256-352-8130.... 3 I
vicki.karolewics@wallacestate.edu
KAROLYI, Andrew .... 607-255-2153 297 F
gak56@cornell.edu
KAROUSATOS, Natalie .. 615-898-2700 422 C
sm8348@bncollege.com
KARP, Adam .... 916-484-8307.. 50 G
karpa@arc.losrios.edu
KARP, Dan .... 440-826-2328 348 D
dkarp@bw.edu
KARP, Debra .... 262-595-2208 496 D
karp@uwp.edu
KARP, Emily .... 212-237-8488 294 D
ekarp@jjay.cuny.edu
KARP, Jeff .... 913-234-0634 172 K
jeff.karp@cleveland.edu
KARPALO, Nikolay .... 610-526-1644 385 D
facilities@harcum.edu
KARPEN, Jim .... 641-472-0778 168 C
jkarpen@miu.edu
KARPER, Barb .... 315-445-4525 303 I
karperbm@lemoyne.edu
KARPILO, Lacy .... 541-962-3635 372 I
lkarpilo@eou.edu
KARPINSKI,
Michaelene .... 716-896-0700 324 E
karpinskim@villa.edu

KAY, Peggy .... 916-278-6862.. 32 D
peggy.kay@csus.edu
KAY COQUEMONT,
Kathryn .... 651-696-6220 236 I
KAY-WONG, Chelsea .... 808-932-7442 129 D
ckwong@hawaii.edu
KAYE, Alan .... 318-675-6124 189 I
alan.kaye@lsuhs.edu
KAYE, Johanna .... 503-554-2235 373 A
kayej@georgefox.edu
KAYE, Joyce .... 212-592-2011 315 C
jkaye3@sva.edu
KAYKAYOGLU, Ediz ...... 509-963-1404 478 E
ediz.kaykayoglu@cwu.edu
KAYLOR, Debbie .... 208-426-4351 130 H
debbiekaylor@boisestate.edu
KAYLOR, Sean, P .... 845-575-3000 305 D
sean.kaylor@marist.edu
KAYNAMA, Shohreh, A . 410-704-6309 204 E
skaynama@towson.edu
KAYNARD, Meryl, R .... 212-220-1237 293 A
mkaynard@bmcc.cuny.edu
KAYS, Brenda, S .... 903-983-8100 438 F
bkays@kilgore.edu
KAYSEN-LUZBETAK,
Angie .... 815-280-2885 141 B
akaysen@jjc.edu
KAZANECKI-KEMPTER,
Diane .... 934-420-2065 320 F
diane.kazanecki-kempter@farmingdale.edu
KAZANJIAN, Marina ..... 251-626-3303.... 7 E
mkazanjian@ussa.edu
KAZARIAN, Julie .... 508-929-8077 213 G
jkazarian@worcester.edu
KAZDA, Jim .... 609-258-3000 280 D
jkazda@princeton.edu
KAZDA, Kathleen .... 262-691-5464 500 B
kkazda@wctc.edu
KAZEN, James, D .... 210-567-0390 456 C
kazen@uthscsa.edu
KAZEN, Tom .... 708-239-4866 151 A
thomas.kazen@trnty.edu
KAZER, Meredith, W ..... 203-254-4150.. 87 I
mkazer@fairfield.edu
KAZEROUNIAN, Kazem . 860-486-2221.. 89 D
kazem.kazerounian@uconn.edu
KAZMIR, Darin .... 361-582-2417 457 E
darin.kazmir@victoriacollege.edu
KAZUMA, Clement .... 680-488-2471 505 B
clementk@palau.edu
KAZYAKA, Carrie .... 619-297-9700.. 68 A
ckazyaka@tjsl.edu
KEADY, Thomas, J .... 617-552-6795 207 C
thomas.keady@bc.edu
KEAL, Aaron, J .... 620-421-6700 175 F
aaronk@labette.edu
KEALA, David .... 808-675-3572 128 D
david.keala@byuh.edu
KEALEY, Jarrett .... 856-222-9311 281 C
jkealey@rcbc.edu
KEAN, Christopher, S ... 719-333-9338 503 D
christopher.kean@usafa.edu
KEAN, Joy .... 970-943-2114.. 85 C
jkean@western.edu
KEAN, Linda .... 781-239-4284 206 B
kean@babson.edu
KEAN, Linda .... 252-328-1283 341 A
keanl@ecu.edu
KEANE, Cath .... 360-992-2071 478 I
ckeane@clark.edu
KEANE, Christopher ...... 509-335-3574 485 D
chris.keane@wsu.edu
KEANE, James .... 508-854-4425 215 F
jkeane@qcc.mass.edu
KEANE, James .... 610-896-1023 385 I
jkeane@haverford.edu
KEANE, John .... 212-752-1530 304 A
john.keane@limcollege.edu
KEANE, Timothy .... 619-260-4886.. 72 I
tkeane@sandiego.edu
KEAR, Mindy .... 765-285-8101 153 H
mindywagnerkear@bsu.edu
KEARN, Tim .... 559-297-4500.. 45 N
tkearn@iot.edu
KEARNEY, Janice .... 870-575-8283.. 22 D
kearneyj@uapb.edu
KEARNEY, Jennifer .... 813-988-5131.. 99 R
library@floridacollege.edu
KEARNEY, Joseph, D .... 414-288-1955 493 E
joseph.kearney@marquette.edu
KEARNEY, Kimberly ...... 540-261-8542 471 B
kim.kearney@svu.edu
KEARNEY, Matt .... 573-651-2039 259 H
mkearney@semo.edu
KEARNS, Chris .... 406-994-2828 264 C
chris.kearns@montana.edu
KEARNS, Jennifer .... 619-388-2759.. 60 J
jnkearns@sdccd.edu
KEARNS, Joanne .... 973-328-5044 276 J
jkearns@ccm.edu
KEARNS, Kevin .... 716-673-3758 316 D
kevin.kearns@fredonia.edu
KEARNS, Michelle .... 801-863-8976 460 D
michelle.kearns@uvu.edu
KEARNS-BARRETT,
Marybeth .... 508-793-2448 208 D
mkearns@holycross.edu
KEAS, Lenora .... 361-698-1207 435 G
lkeas@delmar.edu
KEASLER, Robert, L ...... 540-665-4533 470 G
rkeasler@su.edu
KEAST, Cindy .... 620-665-3565 174 G
keastc@hutchcc.edu
KEATING, Colleen .... 518-454-5197 296 G
keatingc@strose.edu
KEATING, Frederick ...... 856-415-2100 281 D
fkeating@rcsj.edu
KEATING, Jeffery .... 909-469-5205.. 75 I
keating@westernu.edu
KEATING, Joseph .... 740-588-1396 365 B
jkeating@zanestate.edu
KEATING, Kathy .... 616-234-4953 224 F
kkeating@grcc.edu
KEATING, Lisa .... 518-458-5383 296 G
keatingl@strose.edu
KEATING, Scott .... 717-560-8211 387 E
skeating@lbc.edu
KEATING, Tina .... 760-471-1316.. 72 H
KEATING, Tina .... 760-471-1316.. 72 H
tkeating@usk.edu
KEATING POLSON,
Alicia .... 425-564-1000 477 J
presidentoffice@bellevuecollege.edu
KEATON, Alicia .... 407-823-2827 110 E
alicia.keaton@ucf.edu
KEATON, Theodore .... 803-376-5835 406 D
tkeaton@allenuniversity.edu
KEATY, Anthony .... 781-899-5500 218 B
akeaty@psjs.edu
KEBOS, Linus .... 692-625-3394 504 G
KEBREAB, Ermias .... 530-754-9707.. 69 B
ekebreab@ucdavis.edu
KECHICHIAN,
Avedis (Avo) .... 909-448-4034.. 71 C
akechichian2@laverne.edu
KECK, Julie, L .... 740-695-9500 348 E
jkeck@belmontcollege.edu
KECK, Kathleen .... 518-327-6223 311 C
kkeck@paulsmiths.edu
KECK, Kay .... 269-965-3931 225 H
keckk@kellogg.edu
KECK, III, Ray, M .... 903-886-5014 447 B
ray.keck@tamuc.edu
KECKLEY, Kim .... 540-665-4841 470 G
kkeckley@su.edu
KEDROSKI, Cristie .... 850-729-5210 104 M
kedroskc@nwfsc.edu
KEDROWSKI, Karen ...... 218-748-2418 238 D
kkedrowski@nhed.edu
KEDROWSKI, Karen ...... 218-748-2418 238 H
kkedrowski@nhed.edu
KEDSKI, Cathy .... 508-830-5042 213 D
ckedski@maritime.edu
KEE, Josh .... 870-235-4321.. 21 C
jrkee@saumag.edu
KEE, Shomari .... 859-572-5198 184 E
kees1@nku.edu
KEEBLER, Patrick .... 440-826-3745 348 D
pkeebler@bw.edu
KEECH, Brian, T .... 215-895-2244 382 F
brian.keech@drexel.edu
KEECH, Renee .... 860-465-4596.. 85 H
keechr@easternct.edu
KEECH, Roland .... 301-934-2251 198 G
rlkeech@csmd.edu
KEEDY, Thomas, E .... 765-361-6227 163 B
keedyt@wabash.edu
KEEFE, Andrea, B .... 401-865-1534 404 F
aricci@providence.edu
KEEFE, Maureen .... 617-879-7705 213 B
mkeefe@massart.edu
KEEFER, Charles .... 620-450-2120 177 B
charlesk@prattcc.edu
KEEFER, Elizabeth, J .... 216-368-5555 349 D
elizabeth.keefer@case.edu
KEEFER, Jeffrey .... 845-434-5750 321 E
jkeefer@sunysullivan.edu
KEEFER, Jessica .... 303-384-2601.. 79 J
jkeefer@mines.edu
KEEFER, Maureen, H .... 412-397-6484 397 B
keefer@rmu.edu
KEEGAN, Bridget, M ..... 402-280-4015 266 H
bmkeegan@creighton.edu
KEEGAN, Joe .... 518-354-5282 310 A
jkeegan@nccc.edu
KEEGAN, Lisa .... 570-577-2000 379 C
lak032@bucknell.edu
KEEGAN, Thomas .... 360-416-7997 484 C
thomas.keegan@skagit.edu
KEEHN, Aybuke .... 928-344-7699.. 11 A
aybuke.keehn@azwestern.edu
KEEHN, Jay .... 513-861-6400 361 F
jay.keehn@myunion.edu
KEEL, Beverly .... 615-898-5150 422 C
beverly.keel@mtsu.edu
KEEL, Brooks, A .... 706-721-2301 116 A
president@augusta.edu
KEEL, Darla .... 901-678-5755 426 G
darkeel@memphis.edu
KEEL, Dave .... 804-758-6731 475 A
dkeel@rappahannock.edu
KEELE, Kevin .... 213-624-1200.. 42 B
kkeele@fidm.edu
KEELER, Bruce .... 714-241-6257.. 37 J
bkeeler@coastline.edu
KEELER, Calvin .... 302-831-2524.. 91 C
ckeeler@udel.edu
KEELER, Karen .... 603-206-8002 272 L
kkeeler@ccsnh.edu
KEELER-STROM,
Michela .... 402-844-7122 268 H
michela@northeast.edu
KEELEY, Brian .... 360-383-3375 486 A
bkeeley@whatcom.edu
KEELEY, Edward, J .... 608-663-2223 492 F
ekeeley@edgewood.edu
KEELEY, Eileen, M .... 704-894-2422 328 E
eikeeley@davidson.edu
KEELEY, Gloria .... 312-996-2860 151 G
gkeeley@uic.edu
KEELING, Amy .... 865-354-3000 425 C
keelinga@roanestate.edu
KEELING, Nicholas .... 602-384-2555.. 11 F
KEELS, Carl .... 301-736-3631 200 C
drkeels@msbbcs.edu
KEELS, Carl, E .... 301-736-3631 200 C
drkeels@msbbcs.edu
KEELY, Brian .... 641-585-8791 170 I
keelyb@waldorf.edu
KEEN, Cathy .... 352-395-5829 108 A
cathy.keen@sfcollege.edu
KEEN, Larry .... 910-678-8321 334 E
keenl@faytechcc.edu
KEEN, Mike .... 423-775-7111 418 D
mkeen8126@bryan.edu
KEEN, Ralph .... 312-413-2267 151 G
rkeen01@uic.edu
KEEN, Russell .... 706-721-2301 116 A
rukeen@augusta.edu
KEEN, Suzanne .... 315-859-4607 300 H
skeen@hamilton.edu
KEENAHAN, Patty .... 585-340-9638 296 D
pkeenahan@crcds.edu
KEENAN, Claudine .... 609-652-3593 283 E
claudine.keenan@stockton.edu
KEENAN, Erika .... 602-285-7842.. 13 F
erika.keenan@phoenixcollege.edu
KEENAN, Fran .... 603-578-8900 272 M
KEENAN, SJ, James, F . 617-552-3880 207 C
james.keenan.2@bc.edu
KEENAN, John .... 978-542-6400 213 E
john.keenan@salemstate.edu
KEENAN, Laurie .... 518-464-8575 299 C
laurie@excelsior.edu
KEENAN, Mary .... 218-726-7009 243 G
mkeenan@d.umn.edu
KEENAN, Maura .... 215-780-1266 398 B
mkeenan@salus.edu
KEENAN, Ruth .... 281-998-6368 442 K
ruth.keenan@sjcd.edu
KEENAN, Stuart .... 605-995-2647 415 A
stuart.keenan@dwu.edu
KEENAN, Timothy .... 920-924-3420 499 D
tkeenan@morainepark.edu
KEENE, David .... 502-456-6504 185 A
dkeene@sullivan.edu
KEENE, Frances .... 540-231-8056 476 C
fbabb@vt.edu
KEENE, Jennifer .... 714-744-2102.. 36 B
keene@chapman.edu
KEENE, Jennifer .... 702-895-3401 271 D
jennifer.keene@unlv.edu
KEENE, John .... 973-353-3899 282 B
john.keene@rutgers.edu
KEENE, Kristen .... 615-898-2728 422 C
kristen.keene@mtsu.edu
KEENE, Vickie .... 276-498-5230 464 D
vkeene@acp.edu
KEENE, Vincent .... 276-326-4209 464 J
vkeene@bluefield.edu
KEENER, Barb .... 419-755-4539 357 B
bkeener@ncstatecollege.edu
KEENER, Gary, S .... 540-863-2900 473 F
gkeener@dslcc.edu
KEENER, John, F .... 434-947-8367 469 E
jkeener@randolphcollege.edu
KEENEY, Madonna .... 815-599-3449 139 A
madonna.keeney@highland.edu
KEENEY, Michael, S ...... 843-953-5843 407 C
mkeeney@citadel.edu
KEENUM, Mark, E .... 662-325-3221 247 F
president@msstate.edu
KEENUM, Nancy .... 256-306-2850.... 1 F
nancy.keenum@calhoun.edu
KEERY, Nina .... 781-239-2463 214 G
nkeery@massbay.edu
KEESE, Russelle .... 502-597-5759 183 D
russelle.keese@kysu.edu
KEESE, Wallace .... 478-825-6931 118 F
keesew@fvsu.edu
KEETER, Amanda .... 512-313-3000 433 N
amanda.keeter@concordia.edu
KEETER, Howell, W .... 417-690-2370 251 H
dock@cofo.edu
KEETER, Tara .... 252-536-7223 335 B
tkeeter618@halifaxcc.edu
KEETON, Tim .... 913-971-3607 176 C
tkeeton@mnu.edu
KEEVE, Michael .... 757-823-8180 469 A
mokeeve@nsu.edu
KEEVY, Joline .... 912-358-4147 125 A
keevyj@savannahstate.edu
KEEVY, Lindsay .... 360-442-2667 481 D
lkeevy@lowercolumbia.edu
KEFAUVER, Lucy .... 304-336-8378 490 B
lucy.kefauver@westliberty.edu
KEGEL, Gregory, D .... 406-265-3720 264 E
kegel@msun.edu
KEGELMAN, Nancy .... 732-224-2221 276 B
nkegelman@brookdalecc.edu
KEGLEY, Jacquelyn .... 661-654-2249.. 30 B
jkegley@csub.edu
KEGLEY, Kristy .... 850-629-3250.. 93 H
KEHL, Kevin .... 501-279-4529.. 19 C
kkehl@harding.edu
KEHL, Maria .... 760-921-5415.. 56 A
maria.kehl@paloverde.edu
KEHL, Susan .... 501-279-4941.. 19 C
skehl@harding.edu
KEHNEMOUYI,
Muhammad .... 240-567-4406 200 G
muhammad.kehnemouyi@montgomerycollege.edu
KEHOE, Jillian .... 718-409-7236 320 G
KEHOE-ROBINSON,
Colleen, R .... 910-275-6332 335 E
ckehoe-robinson@jamessprunt.edu
KEHRING, Justin .... 262-691-5221 500 B
jkehring@wctc.edu
KEHRLI, Katherine .... 206-934-4386 483 C
kathrine.kehrli@seattlecolleges.edu
KEIB, Carrie .... 419-521-6802 347 J
ckeib@ashland.edu
KEIBLER, Michael .... 402-375-7198 268 F
mikeibl1@wsc.edu
KEIFFER, Greggory .... 281-649-3132 437 B
gkeiffer@hbu.edu
KEIGHER, Craig .... 815-802-8402 141 D
ckeigher@kcc.edu
KEILEN, Sean .... 831-459-3700.. 71 A
keilen@ucsc.edu
KEILERS, Vikki .... 903-233-4141 439 A
vikkikeilers@letu.edu
KEILFRIDER, Debbie ..... 215-785-0111 392 S
KEILLOR BERG, Linda .. 952-888-4777 242 N
KEIM, Jodi .... 928-428-8231.. 12 F
jodi.keim@eac.edu
KEINATH, Richelle .... 307-766-1121 501 I
KEINER, Louis, E .... 843-349-2226 408 A
lkeiner@coastal.edu

KELLY, Inesha, B .... 773-291-6275 135 E
ikelly1@ccc.edu
KELLY, Janet .... 478-218-3319 116 G
jkelly@centralgatech.edu
KELLY, Jarrod .... 252-985-5261 339 D
jkelly@ncwc.edu
KELLY, Jeffrey, M .... 443-352-4012 202 E
jkelly@stevenson.edu
KELLY, Jeneen .... 914-323-5337 305 B
jeneen.kelly@mville.edu
KELLY, Jennifer .... 617-451-0010 217 F
KELLY, Jennifer .... 808-518-4791 129 B
jenniferkelly@pacrim.edu
KELLY, Jennifer .... 318-357-6441 192 G
KELLY, Jess, P .... 972-860-7141 434 H
jesskelly@dcccd.edu
KELLY, John .... 617-735-9710 209 D
kellyjo@emmanuel.edu
KELLY, John .... 561-297-3450 109 J
president@fau.edu
KELLY, John .... 870-512-7824.. 18 A
john_kelly@asun.edu
KELLY, Julie, A .... 860-444-8508 503 G
julie.a.kelly@uscg.mil
KELLY, Kathleen .... 617-585-1154 217 E
kathleen.kelly@necmusic.edu
KELLY, Kathleen .... 518-244-2030 313 A
kellyk5@sage.edu
KELLY, Kathy .... 513-244-4418 356 F
kathy.kelly@msj.edu
KELLY, Kelly .... 608-822-2305 500 A
kkelly@swtc.edu
KELLY, Kevin .... 617-236-5402 209 G
kkelly@fisher.edu
KELLY, Kevin .... 860-215-9325.. 87 F
kkelly@threerivers.edu
KELLY, Kevin, P .... 410-269-5087 203 A
kkelly@umaryland.edu
KELLY, Kirk .... 503-725-6246 375 E
kkelly@pdx.edu
KELLY, Kristi .... 815-836-5538 142 F
kellykj@lewisu.edu
KELLY, Kyle .... 775-831-1314 272 D
kkelly@sierranevada.edu
KELLY, Laura .... 315-312-3151 318 D
laura.kelly@oswego.edu
KELLY, Lauren, E .... 407-582-8125 113 I
lkelly22@valenciacollege.edu
KELLY, Lee .... 904-725-0525.. 97 P
KELLY, Lee .... 718-997-4455 295 B
lee.kelly@qc.cuny.edu
KELLY, Leslie, E .... 207-834-7522 197 A
lesliek@maine.edu
KELLY, Liisa .... 910-843-5304 331 A
lkelly@nabc.edu
KELLY, Lisa .... 732-906-2564 278 G
lkelly@middlesexcc.edu
KELLY, Lynn .... 912-260-4324 125 D
lynn.kelly@sgsc.edu
KELLY, Maisha .... 215-895-2000 382 F
KELLY, Marie, C .... 508-565-1169 219 A
mkelly1@stonehill.edu
KELLY, Marisa .... 617-573-8120 219 B
mjkelly@suffolk.edu
KELLY, Mark .... 269-927-8100 226 F
kelly@lakemichigancollege.edu
KELLY, Maureen .... 708-235-7556 138 E
mkelly7@govst.edu
KELLY, Michael .... 813-974-1442 111 C
michaelskelly@usf.edu
KELLY, Michele .... 734-462-4400 230 G
mkelly@schoolcraft.edu
KELLY, Mickie .... 828-669-8012 331 K
KELLY, Paige .... 276-739-2461 475 F
pkelly@vhcc.edu
KELLY, Patricia .... 662-246-6417 247 D
pkelly@msdelta.edu
KELLY, Patrick .... 304-336-8510 490 B
patrick.kelly@westliberty.edu
KELLY, Peter .... 540-654-1464 471 N
pkelly3@umw.edu
KELLY, Peter, T .... 570-389-4674 393 D
pkelly@bloomu.edu
KELLY, Rob .... 410-617-2842 200 B
rkelly1@loyola.edu
KELLY, Rosemary .... 910-678-8325 334 E
kellyr@faytechcc.edu
KELLY, Ryan, J .... 517-750-1200 231 C
jo776328@arbor.edu
KELLY, Sandra .... 803-777-2808 413 A
sjkelly@mailbox.sc.edu
KELLY, Sandra, J .... 803-777-2808 413 A
sandra-kelly@sc.edu
KELLY, Sara .... 585-395-2369 317 E
skelly@brockport.edu
KELLY, Sarah, E .... 914-323-5304 305 B
sarah.kelly@mville.edu
KELLY, Sarah, J .... 330-972-6134 361 H
sarah30@uakron.edu
KELLY, Sean .... 210-458-6463 455 E
sean.kelly@utsa.edu
KELLY, Stephanie .... 317-788-6099 161 H
spkelly@uindy.edu
KELLY, Steve .... 757-401-6125 477 G
KELLY, Susan .... 617-287-7050 211 F
skelly@umassp.edu
KELLY, Thomas, M .... 312-915-6875 143 C
tkelly4@luc.edu
KELLY, Tiffany .... 719-389-6772.. 78 I
tkelly@coloradocollege.edu
KELLY, Todd .... 719-549-2013.. 80 B
todd.kelly@csupueblo.edu
KELLY, Tracy .... 716-338-1042 303 A
tracykelly@mail.sunyjcc.edu
KELLY, Troy .... 703-284-1614 468 H
bstore@marymount.edu
KELLY, Valerie, I .... 330-672-0020 354 A
vkelly@kent.edu
KELLY, William, G .... 860-444-8285 503 G
william.g.kelly@uscg.mil
KELLY BATES, Martha ... 847-578-8582 148 F
martha.bates@rosalindfranklin.edu
KELLY-BOWRY, Tanya ... 303-831-6192.. 84 A
tanya.kellybowry@cu.edu
KELLY KLEESE,
Christine .... 919-536-7200 334 C
kleesec@durhamtech.edu
KELLY-RILEY, Diane ...... 208-885-5013 132 F
dkr@uidaho.edu
KELLY-VERGONA,
Barbara .... 973-957-0188 275 C
registrar@acs350.org
KELM, Mary Helen .... 903-675-6338 451 F
mary.kelm@tvcc.edu
KELMAN, Ari .... 530-752-7783.. 69 B
KELMAN, Jake .... 650-543-3798.. 51 G
jake.kelman@menlo.edu
KELMER, JR.,
Kenneth, J .... 207-768-2715 195 G
sm8407@bncollege.com
KELSAY, Missy .... 662-562-3319 248 D
KELSCH, Anne .... 701-777-3325 345 B
anne.kelsch@und.edu
KELSCH, Tyler .... 303-546-3569.. 82 A
tkelsch@naropa.edu
KELSER, Sandra, B .... 334-833-4409.... 5 G
skelser@hawks.huntingdon.edu
KELSEY, Ashley, A .... 276-244-1283 464 E
aakelsey@asl.edu
KELSEY, Barb .... 608-789-6199 500 C
kelseyb@westerntc.edu
KELSEY, Cathie .... 303-765-3103.. 81 G
ckelsey@iliff.edu
KELSEY, Katie, M .... 402-280-1715 266 H
katiekelsey@creighton.edu
KELSEY, Mark, N .... 276-244-1285 464 E
mkelsey@asl.edu
KELSEY, Ross .... 281-998-6150 443 C
ross.kelsey@sjcd.edu
KELSO, Abby .... 360-867-6300 480 C
kelso@evergreen.edu
KELSO, Amanda .... 919-684-2174 328 F
amanda.kelso@duke.edu
KELSO, Anne-Marie ...... 541-881-5838 376 F
akelso@tvcc.cc
KELSO, Donovan .... 405-945-3243 368 C
donovak@okstate.edu
KELTON, Emily .... 303-273-3148.. 79 J
ekelton@mines.edu
KELVEY, Bill .... 410-386-8214 198 D
bkelvey@carrollcc.edu
KEMENY, Paul, C .... 724-458-2025 384 G
pckemeny@gcc.edu
KEMNETZ, Larry .... 773-252-6464 146 F
larry.kemnetz@oakpoint.edu
KEMNITZ, Carl .... 760-750-4050.. 33 A
ckemnitz@csusm.edu
KEMNITZ, Marcie .... 308-398-7400 266 A
mkemnitz@cccneb.edu
KEMP, Arnold .... 312-899-1294 149 F
akemp@saic.edu
KEMP, Camilla .... 810-762-9937 226 B
ckemp@kettering.edu
KEMP, Darcy .... 413-755-4558 216 A
dkemp@stcc.edu
KEMP, Dawn .... 317-632-5553 159 I
dkemp@lincolntech.edu
KEMP, Gloria .... 501-686-6128.. 22 B
kempgloriad@uams.edu
KEMP, John .... 864-294-3717 409 H
john.kemp@furman.edu
KEMP, Katie .... 847-317-8177 151 C
katiek@tiu.edu
KEMP, Nathan, R .... 309-341-7255 141 G
nkemp@knox.edu
KEMP, Nicholas .... 352-365-3526 103 U
kempn@lssc.edu
KEMP, Rick .... 480-517-8000.. 13 G
KEMP, Rick .... 480-517-8508.. 13 G
rick.kemp@riosalado.edu
KEMP, Shirley .... 304-829-7485 487 A
skemp@bethanywv.edu
KEMP, Stephen .... 515-292-9694 163 D
stephen.kemp@antiochschool.edu
KEMP, Steve .... 760-366-5283.. 40 E
skemp@cmccd.edu
KEMP, Tracy .... 614-287-5380 351 C
tkemp@cscc.edu
KEMPE, Amy, P .... 401-825-2028 404 C
apkempe@ccri.edu
KEMPE, Michael, A .... 330-325-6481 357 D
mkempe@neomed.edu
KEMPEL, Leo, C .... 517-355-5114 227 F
kempel@egr.msu.edu
KEMPER, Heather .... 501-279-4276.. 19 C
hkemper@harding.edu
KEMPER, James .... 740-588-1209 365 B
jkemper@zanestate.edu
KEMPER, Kenneth, B .... 616-538-2330 224 E
preskemper@gracechristian.edu
KEMPER, Lori, A .... 623-572-3202 144 F
lorik@midwestern.edu
KEMPER, Steven .... 848-932-1395 282 A
skemper@mgsa.rutgers.edu
KEMPER-PELLE, Cathy .. 541-956-7000 376 A
ckemperpelle@roguecc.edu
KEMPF, Cory .... 715-394-8366 497 C
ckempf1@uwsuper.edu
KEMPF, Kimberly .... 802-387-6723 462 C
kimberlykempf@landmark.edu
KEMPNER, Brandon .... 505-454-3286 286 J
bkempner@nmhu.edu
KEMPSTER, James .... 718-636-3471 311 F
jkempster@pratt.edu
KEMPTON, Daniel .... 740-283-6228 352 I
dkempton@franciscan.edu
KENAN, Tonya .... 910-275-6181 335 E
tkenan@jamessprunt.edu
KENAUSIS, Veronica ...... 203-837-9109.. 86 B
kenausisv@wcsu.edu
KENCH, Brian .... 203-932-7115.. 89 H
bkench@newhaven.edu
KENDALL, Anthony .... 513-487-1203 361 F
anthony.kendall@myunion.edu
KENDALL, Curtis, L ...... 540-828-5476 464 L
ckendall@bridgewater.edu
KENDALL, David .... 574-535-7030 155 E
davidk15@goshen.edu
KENDALL, Donna .... 781-891-3441 206 G
dkendall@bentley.edu
KENDALL, Joel .... 580-774-3252 370 A
joel.kendall@swosu.edu
KENDALL, Justin .... 620-862-5252 171 H
justin.kendall@barclaycollege.edu
KENDALL, Kenny .... 315-470-7749 291 I
kennethkendall@crouse.org
KENDALL, Mark .... 909-607-9660.. 57 K
mark.kendall@pomona.edu
KENDALL, Rex .... 812-237-6100 156 D
rkendall@indstatefoundation.org
KENDALL-LEKKA,
Meitaka .... 692-625-3394 504 G
mkendall@cmi.edu
KENDE, Ashley .... 201-216-9901 277 B
KENDER, Joseph, P ...... 610-660-2309 397 G
jkender@sju.edu
KENDERDINE, Linda ..... 410-706-5036 203 A
lcassard@umaryland.edu
KENDI, Ibram, X .... 617-353-2230 207 E
kendi@bu.edu
KENDIG, P. Tysen .... 860-486-6713.. 89 D
tysen.kendig@uconn.edu
KENDJORIA, Barrett ...... 864-656-4013 407 E
bkendjo@clemson.edu
KENDRA-DILL, Zach .... 704-922-6223 334 G
kendra-dill.zachary@gaston.edu
KENDREX, Bradley .... 480-461-7000.. 13 D
KENDREX, Bradley, S ... 480-732-7379.. 12 O
bradley.kendrex@cgc.edu
KENDRICK, Bethany ...... 620-421-6700 175 F
bethanyk@labette.edu
KENDRICK, Curtis .... 607-777-4550 316 B
kendrick@binghamton.edu
KENDRICK, Ebony .... 336-517-8632 327 A
KENDRICK, Emory .... 478-757-2038 127 F
ekendrick@wesleyancollege.edu
KENDRICK, Haley .... 704-406-3957 329 A
hkendrick@gardner-webb.edu
KENDRICK, Kaetrena, D 803-323-2232 414 D
kendrickk@winthrop.edu
KENDRICK, Kevin .... 334-229-6500.... 4 A
kkendrick@alasu.edu
KENDRICK, Lorna .... 510-879-3347.. 60 C
lkendrick@samuelmerritt.edu
KENDRICK, Marsha .... 405-692-3241 366 D
marsha.kendrick@macu.edu
KENDRICK, Samantha ... 616-222-1428 223 C
KENERSON, Laura .... 401-874-5271 405 E
lkenerson@uri.edu
KENFIELD, Mikal, C ...... 218-299-3872 235 H
kenfield@cord.edu
KENIMER, Ann, L .... 979-845-4016 446 F
a-kenimer@tamu.edu
KENISTON, Joseph, C .. 315-229-1858 314 D
jkeniston@stlawu.edu
KENISTON, Josh .... 603-646-0458 273 D
josh.keniston@dartmouth.edu
KENISTON, Leonda .... 434-961-5380 474 I
lkeniston@pvcc.edu
KENLEY, David .... 605-256-5270 416 F
david.kenley@dsu.edu
KENMILLE, Cleo .... 406-275-4864 265 F
cleo_kenmille@skc.edu
KENN, Jim .... 617-559-8688 210 F
jkenn@hebrewcollege.edu
KENNA-SCHENK, Becca 360-951-3733 485 I
becca.kenna-schenk@wwu.edu
KENNAMER, Mike .... 256-228-6001.... 3 B
kennamerm@nacc.edu
KENNEALLY, Steve, P ... 724-847-6692 384 C
spkennea@geneva.edu
KENNEDY, Aaron .... 575-461-4413 286 G
aaronk@mesalands.edu
KENNEDY, Anne .... 503-357-6151 375 C
KENNEDY, Bill .... 406-657-2244 264 D
foundation@msubillings.edu
KENNEDY, Brianne .... 619-388-3513.. 60 I
bkennedy@sdccd.edu
KENNEDY, Calhoun, L .. 864-597-4200 414 E
kennedycl@wofford.edu
KENNEDY, Carol, M ..... 570-577-1511 379 C
carol.kennedy@bucknell.edu
KENNEDY, Catherine, B 401-739-5000 404 E
ckennedy@neit.edu
KENNEDY,
Catherine, C .... 727-394-6202 107 E
kennedy.catherine@spcollege.edu
KENNEDY, Chrisitne ..... 312-942-5836 148 G
christine_kennedy@rush.edu
KENNEDY, Christopher . 843-661-1557 409 G
ckennedy@fmarion.edu
KENNEDY, Colleen .... 773-371-5417 134 D
ckennedy@ctu.edu
KENNEDY, Damon .... 432-685-4524 440 B
dkennedy@midland.edu
KENNEDY, Dana .... 330-263-2317 351 A
dakennedy@wooster.edu
KENNEDY, David .... 919-684-3363 328 F
david.kennedy@duke.edu
KENNEDY, Deborah ...... 540-674-3690 474 E
dkennedy@nr.edu
KENNEDY, Dennis .... 518-629-8085 302 C
d.kennedy1@hvcc.edu
KENNEDY, Elizabeth .... 816-271-4237 257 A
president@missouriwestern.edu
KENNEDY, Elizabeth ...... 802-485-2218 462 F
ekennedy@norwich.edu
KENNEDY, Ellen .... 413-236-1003 214 A
ekennedy@berkshirecc.edu
KENNEDY, Erica .... 216-397-4598 353 O
ekennedy@jcu.edu
KENNEDY, Gary .... 318-257-4287 192 D
kennedy@latech.edu
KENNEDY, Helen .... 724-422-2808 379 F
hkennedy@bcs.edu
KENNEDY, James .... 714-241-5708.. 58 F
kennedy_james@sac.edu
KENNEDY, James .... 714-241-5708.. 58 G
kennedy_james@sac.edu

KENNEDY, James, D .... 304-896-7408 488 I doug.kennedy@southernwv.edu
KENNEDY, Jason .... 951-571-6931.. 59 B jason.kennedy@mvc.edu
KENNEDY, Jay .... 617-747-2150 206 H academicaffairs@berklee.edu
KENNEDY, Jeanne .... 252-527-6223 335 G jmkennedy48@lenoircc.edu
KENNEDY, Jennifer .... 734-432-5856 227 C jkennedy@madonna.edu
KENNEDY, Jodi .... 912-478-1435 120 C jmiddleton@georgiasouthern.edu
KENNEDY, Jody .... 662-329-7396 248 A jwkennedy@muw.edu
KENNEDY, John .... 413-545-8500 211 G jkennedy@admin.umass.edu
KENNEDY, John, M ...... 315-386-7513 320 B kennedyjm@canton.edu
KENNEDY, Julia .... 704-463-1360 339 E julia.kennedy@pfeiffer.edu
KENNEDY, Julie .... 205-929-6333.... 2 H jkennedy@lawsonstate.edu
KENNEDY, Karen, M ..... 574-631-5878 162 A karen.kennedy@nd.edu
KENNEDY, Katherine, J . 617-353-4745 207 E kkennedy@bu.edu
KENNEDY, Kathleen ...... 504-520-7421 193 E kkenned1@xula.edu
KENNEDY, Keith .... 386-506-3562.. 98 D keith.kennedy@daytonastate.edu
KENNEDY, Kenneth .... 417-625-9741 256 F kennedy-k@mssu.edu
KENNEDY, Linda .... 949-480-4072.. 64 G lkennedy@soka.edu
KENNEDY, Lola .... 803-376-5791 406 D lkennedy@allenuniversity.edu
KENNEDY, Lori, B .... 610-758-4665 388 E lbk4@lehigh.edu
KENNEDY, Marcus .... 205-366-8817.... 7 A mkennedy@stillman.edu
KENNEDY, Marina .... 415-503-6230.. 61 D mkennedy@sfcm.edu
KENNEDY, Mary, M .... 207-725-3067 194 C mkennedy@bowdoin.edu
KENNEDY, Matthew ...... 732-255-0400 279 F mkennedy@ocean.edu
KENNEDY, Melba .... 225-743-8500 188 H mkennedy@rpcc.edu
KENNEDY, Melissa .... 269-782-1241 231 A mkennedy03@swmich.edu
KENNEDY, Mike .... 815-455-8569 143 I mkennedy297@mchenry.edu
KENNEDY, Mike .... 864-596-9390 408 F mike.kennedy@converse.edu
KENNEDY, Missty .... 334-844-7771.... 4 D kennem1@auburn.edu
KENNEDY, Missy .... 910-962-2049 343 C kennedym@uncw.edu
KENNEDY, Nancy .... 716-614-6792 309 G verstrea@niagaracc.suny.edu
KENNEDY, Norma .... 478-289-2028 118 C nkennedy@ega.edu
KENNEDY, Paul, W .... 585-594-6469 312 E kennedy_paul@roberts.edu
KENNEDY, Rachel, A .... 574-807-7462 154 B rachel.kennedy@betheluniversity.edu
KENNEDY, Rebecca ...... 205-975-4041.... 8 A rekenn@uab.edu
KENNEDY, Ron .... 434-592-5079 468 E rkennedy@liberty.edu
KENNEDY, Roxie .... 816-802-3358 254 D rkennedy@kcai.edu
KENNEDY, Scott .... 949-451-5200.. 65 C skennedy@ivc.edu
KENNEDY, Sean .... 856-566-6221 281 F
KENNEDY, Shannon ...... 804-758-6701 475 A
KENNEDY, SSJ, Sheila .. 215-248-7104 381 A kennedys@chc.edu
KENNEDY, Taurean .... 212-343-1234 306 G tkennedy@mcny.edu
KENNEDY, Timothy, R .. 507-933-6395 236 A tkennedy@gustavus.edu
KENNEDY, II, William "Rusty" .... 859-846-5456 184 B wkennedy@midway.edu
KENNEDY-FLETCHER, Jackie .... 812-855-7087 156 G jacfletc@indiana.edu
KENNEDY-JONES, Danielle .... 334-229-4202.... 4 A botliaison@alasu.edu
KENNEDY-PHILLIPS, Lance, C .... 814-863-8721 391 G lck7@psu.edu
KENNEDY-RATAJACK, Kathy, S .... 302-356-2481.. 91 E kathy.s.kennedy-ratajack@wilmu.edu
KENNEDY-WITTHAR, Shawna, J .... 806-651-2227 448 B switthar@wtamu.edu
KENNELL, Deena .... 308-432-6388 268 D dkennell@csc.edu
KENNELL, Scott .... 734-432-5604 227 C skennell@madonna.edu
KENNELLY, Raymond ..... 815-836-5520 142 F kennelra@lewisu.edu
KENNEMER, Kelly .... 903-813-2277 430 H kkennemer@austincollege.edu
KENNER, Carole .... 609-771-2848 276 I kennerc@tcnj.edu
KENNER, Corry, G .... 701-662-1505 346 C corry.kenner@lrsc.edu
KENNER, Rosaland .... 803-793-5196 408 G kennerr@denmarktech.edu
KENNERKNECHT, Megan .... 585-785-1277 299 F megan.kennerknecht@flcc.edu
KENNERLY, A. Chris ...... 740-427-5160 354 I kennerlyc@kenyon.edu
KENNERLY, JR., John, F .... 864-379-8788 409 E kennerly@erskine.edu
KENNETT-HENSEL, Pamela .... 504-280-6193 190 B pkennett@uno.edu
KENNEY, Christopher ... 802-654-2200 462 G ckenney@smcvt.edu
KENNEY, Eileen .... 918-595-8144 370 C eileen.kenney@tulsacc.edu
KENNEY, Heather .... 904-646-2296 101 B heather.a.kenney@fscj.edu
KENNEY, Jason .... 316-322-3232 172 D jkenney2@butlercc.edu
KENNEY, Jennie .... 303-273-3399.. 79 J jkenney@mines.edu
KENNEY, Kristie .... 256-761-6233.... 7 B kkenney@talladega.edu
KENNEY, Patrick, J .... 480-727-2634.. 10 J pkenney@asu.edu
KENNEY, Rob .... 815-802-8173 141 D rkenney@kcc.edu
KENNEY, Steven, H ...... 985-448-4041 192 F steven.kenney@nicholls.edu
KENNEY, JR., Steven, H .... 985-448-4001 192 F steven.kenney@nicholls.edu
KENNEY, Sue, B .... 443-334-2547 202 E skenney@stevenson.edu
KENNEY, Tamara .... 607-871-2134 290 B kenney@alfred.edu
KENNINGTON, Janet, S 410-334-2942 205 D jkennington@worwic.edu
KENNON, Cheryl .... 817-257-6122 448 F c.kennon@tcu.edu
KENNON, Susan .... 434-544-8218 471 L kennon@lynchburg.edu
KENNY, Carol Ann .... 914-633-2122 302 E ckenny@iona.edu
KENNY, Cathleen .... 718-636-3784 311 F ckenny@pratt.edu
KENNY, Eddie .... 270-852-3146 183 E ekenny@kwc.edu
KENNY, James .... 323-415-5374.. 48 J kennyja@elac.edu
KENNY, John .... 702-254-7577 272 A john.kenny@northwestcareercollege.edu
KENNY, Patrick .... 702-254-7577 272 A patrick.kenny@northwestcareercollege.edu
KENNY, Stephanie .... 702-254-7577 272 A stephanie.kenny@northwestcareercollege.edu
KENNY, Tammy .... 810-984-3881 230 F
KENNY, Thomas .... 702-254-7577 272 A thomas.kenny@northwestcareercollege.edu
KENOLIO, Ellen .... 808-689-2755 129 F kenolio@hawaii.edu
KENT, Allen .... 601-643-8314 245 F allen.kent@colin.edu
KENT, Andrea .... 251-460-6261.... 9 A akent@southalabama.edu
KENT, Angela .... 402-878-2380 267 D angela.kent@littlepriest.edu
KENT, Cassy .... 585-785-1486 299 F cassy.kent@flcc.edu
KENT, Christopher .... 864-578-8770 411 F ckent@sherman.edu
KENT, Jennifer .... 410-857-2205 200 F jkent@mcdaniel.edu
KENT, Jennifer .... 361-582-2560 457 E jennifer.kent@victoriacollege.edu
KENT, Jonathan .... 607-871-2406 290 B kentj@alfred.edu
KENT, K. Craig .... 434-924-9308 472 D ck8aq@hscmail.mcc.virginia.edu
KENT, Kathryn .... 229-217-4206 126 A kkent@southernregional.edu
KENT, Kimberly .... 563-884-5176 169 F kent_k@palmer.edu
KENT, Lyn .... 918-595-7742 370 C lyn.kent@tulsacc.edu
KENT, Rebekah .... 218-894-5172 237 G rebekah.kent@clcmn.edu
KENT, Shayna .... 831-459-3966.. 71 A skent1@ucsc.edu
KENT, Stephen .... 651-290-7522 242 L stephen.kent@mitchellhamline.edu
KENT, Tom .... 518-793-5250 320 A kentt@sunyacc.edu
KENTON, Jay .... 503-838-8888 377 D kentonj@wou.edu
KENTON, Katrina .... 513-244-4327 356 F katrina.kenton@msj.edu
KENWORTHY, Anne ...... 901-321-4213 418 G anne.kenworthy@cbu.edu
KENYON, Carl .... 814-944-5643 403 G carl.kenyon@yti.edu
KENYON, Charles, B ..... 315-364-3312 324 I ckenyon@wells.edu
KENYON, Gina .... 815-752-8990 146 B gkenyon@niu.edu
KENYON, Jane .... 253-879-3610 484 G jkenyon@pugetsound.edu
KENYON, Melaine .... 716-839-8290 298 A mkenyon@daemen.edu
KENYON, Steven .... 508-678-2811 214 B steve.kenyon@bristolcc.edu
KENZOR, Jennifer .... 812-877-8217 160 F seddelme@rose-hulman.edu
KEOGH, Kristina .... 941-359-7582 106 J kkeogh@ringling.edu
KEOGH, Lily .... 402-354-7263 268 B lily.keogh@methodistcollege.edu
KEOGH GEORGE, Stacy 509-777-3851 486 C sgeorge@whitworth.edu
KEOHANE, Ellen, J .... 508-793-2477 208 D ekeohane@holycross.edu
KEON, Thomas, L .... 219-989-2204 160 D tkeon@pnw.edu
KEOPUHIWA, Thomas .. 808-734-9522 129 H keopuhiw@hawaii.edu
KEOUGH, Diana .... 856-225-6053 281 G diana.keough@camden.rutgers.edu
KEOUGH, Shawn .... 503-845-3579 374 A shawn.keough@mtangel.edu
KEOUGH, Wendy .... 269-471-3611 221 D keoughw@andrews.edu
KEOWN, Maureen .... 718-817-4160 300 C mkeown@fordham.edu
KEPFORD, Joyce .... 605-688-4442 417 A joyce.kepford@sdstate.edu
KEPHART, Joy .... 828-835-4212 338 E jkephart@tricountycc.edu
KEPHART, Noah .... 515-964-0601 166 D kephartn@faith.edu
KEPLEY, Bruce .... 812-258-9510 154 E bkepley@cariscollege.edu
KEPPNER, Dana .... 217-641-4241 141 A dkeppner@jwcc.edu
KERBEL, Matthew .... 610-519-4553 401 K matthew.kerbel@villanova.edu
KERBS, Nancy .... 417-667-8181 252 B nkerbs@cottey.edu
KERBY, Molly .... 270-745-6952 186 C molly.kerby@wku.edu
KERBY, Steve .... 410-386-4686 200 F skerby@mcdaniel.edu
KERCE, Walter .... 413-552-2155 214 F wkerce@hcc.edu
KERCH, Matthew .... 205-348-9364.... 7 G mkerch@ua.edu
KERDA, Stephen, J .... 301-243-2167 502 L stephen.kerda@dodiis.mil
KERDOLFF, Russell, A .. 859-572-6455 184 E kerdolff@nku.edu
KEREN, Hila .... 213-738-6755.. 66 B hkeren@swlaw.edu
KERESTLY, Charles, E ... 325-942-2246 450 E ed.kerestly@angelo.edu
KERFOOT, Adina .... 731-424-2603 424 E akerfoot@jscc.edu
KERKAERT, Debra .... 507-537-6093 241 D deb.kerkaert@smsu.edu
KERLIN, Julie, M .... 404-413-1405 120 E jkerlin1@gsu.edu
KERLIN, Scott .... 510-780-4500.. 47 K skerlin@lifewest.edu
KERMAN, Lucy, E .... 215-895-2123 382 F lucy.e.kerman@drexel.edu
KERMES, Anita .... 916-278-6980.. 32 D anita.kermes@csus.edu
KERN, Alexander .... 617-373-2728 217 I
KERN, Jessica .... 606-759-7141 182 E jessica.kern@kctcs.edu
KERN, Linda .... 770-538-4722 116 D lkern@brenau.edu
KERN, Rhonda .... 763-433-1362 237 D rhonda.kern@anokaramsey.edu
KERN, Tony .... 218-281-8257 244 A akern@umn.edu
KERNAN, William .... 503-838-8154 377 D kernanb@wou.edu
KERNER, Kelly, K .... 706-542-2002 126 G kkerner@uga.edu
KERNER, Walter .... 212-217-3400 299 D walter_kerner@fitnyc.edu
KERNICK, Rhonda .... 432-264-5100 437 F rkernick@howardcollege.edu
KERNIN, Richard, P ...... 716-286-8044 309 H rpk@niagara.edu
KERNS, Connie .... 620-792-9273 171 I kernsc@bartonccc.edu
KERNS, Robert .... 301-387-3003 199 A robert.kerns@garrettcollege.edu
KERO, Miriam .... 218-263-2969 238 D miriamkero@hibbing.edu
KEROUAC, Luke .... 435-652-7513 460 B kerouac@dixie.edu
KERP, Lauri .... 860-444-8308 503 G bookstore@uscga.edu
KERR, Adrian .... 239-565-8100 101 A adrian.kerr@fsw.edu
KERR, Alecia .... 412-536-1059 386 H alecia.kerr@laroche.edu
KERR, Anne, B .... 863-680-4100 100 H akerr@flsouthern.edu
KERR, Brian .... 718-631-6262 295 C bkerr@qcc.cuny.edu
KERR, Colleen .... 206-219-2415 485 D colleen.kerr@wsu.edu
KERR, Courtney, A .... 757-446-5798 466 D kerrca@evms.edu
KERR, Elizabeth .... 716-896-0700 324 E ekerr@villa.edu
KERR, Emily, C .... 706-886-6831 126 D eraynor@tfc.edu
KERR, Jean .... 309-556-3212 140 F jkerr@iwu.edu
KERR, Julie .... 601-925-7759 247 C jkerr@mc.edu
KERR, Kathleen .... 315-312-3214 318 D
KERR, Kathleen, G .... 302-831-4663.. 91 C kkerr@udel.edu
KERR, Kristie .... 612-343-4741 242M kekerr@northcentral.edu
KERR, Mary Frances ..... 404-471-6325 114 G mfkerr@agnesscott.edu
KERR, Mickey .... 254-295-4618 453 D mkerr@umhb.edu
KERR, Peter .... 303-963-3163.. 78 H pakerr@ccu.edu
KERR, Shelly, K .... 541-346-3227 376 H skerr@uoregon.edu
KERR, Stephen .... 617-732-2093 216 D stephen.kerr@mcphs.edu
KERR, Susan .... 478-445-1196 119 B susan.kerr@gcsu.edu
KERR-MCCURRY, Norah 732-224-2628 276 B nmccurry@brookdalecc.edu
KERRES, Johnna .... 563-336-3308 165 K jkerres@eicc.edu
KERRICK, Ken .... 209-946-2251.. 71 E kkerrick@pacific.edu
KERRIGAN, Adrian .... 516-572-0601 307 E adrian.kerrigan@ncc.edu
KERRIGAN, Dana .... 610-989-1364 401 I dkerrigan@vfmac.edu
KERRIGAN, John, E ...... 408-554-4968.. 63 B jekerrigan@scu.edu
KERRIGAN, Noreen .... 718-430-2000 290 A

KERRIGAN, Rochelle ..... 773-252-6464 146 F
rochelle.kerrigan@oakpoint.edu
KERRUISH, Diane .... 847-214-7374 137 F
dkerruish@elgin.edu
KERRY, Bill .... 607-274-3353 302 G
wkerry@ithaca.edu
KERRY, Susan, E .... 906-487-1060 228 A
skerry@mtu.edu
KERSCHNER, Joseph, E 414-955-8213 493 F
jkerschner@mcw.edu
KERSEY, Robert, N .... 843-953-5542 408 C
kerseyr@cofc.edu
KERSH, Rogan .... 336-758-3128 344 C
kersh@wfu.edu
KERSHAW, Josephine ... 870-743-3000.. 20 B
josephine.kershaw@northark.edu
KERSHNER, Scott, M .... 570-372-4220 398 F
kershner@susqu.edu
KERSTEN, Andrew .... 314-516-5404 261 C
kerstenan@umsl.edu
KERSTEN, Belen .... 559-730-3794.. 39 B
belenk@cos.edu
KERSTEN, David, W ...... 773-244-6235 145 G
dwkersten@northpark.edu
KERSTEN, James, B ...... 515-574-1132 167 A
kersten@iowacentral.edu
KERSTENS, Margaret ..... 832-813-6272 439 C
margaret.kerstens@lonestar.edu
KERTULIS-TARTAR,
Gina .... 706-272-4516 118 B
gkertulistartar@daltonstate.edu
KERTZ, Nancy, K .... 515-643-6615 168 D
nkertz@mercydesmoines.org
KERWICK, Sean .... 201-360-4023 278 C
skerwick@hccc.edu
KERWIN, David, M .... 206-543-4150 485 A
dkerwin@uw.edu
KERWIN, Kevin .... 559-791-2403.. 47 A
kevin.kerwin@portervillecollege.edu
KERWIN, Linda .... 716-827-2454 323 G
kerwinl@trocaire.edu
KERWITZ, Ann .... 815-921-4001 148 B
a.kerwitz@rockvalleycollege.edu
KERYLOW, Tiffany .... 802-387-6725 462 C
tiffanykerylow@landmark.edu
KESARIS, Thomas .... 610-660-1836 397 G
tkesaris@sju.edu
KESERAUSKIS, Beth ...... 314-446-8207 260 H
beth.keserauskis@stlcop.edu
KESHVALA, Seelpa .... 281-290-3940 439 C
seelpa.h.keshvala@lonestar.edu
KESICKI, Michael .... 814-871-5873 384 A
kesicki001@gannon.edu
KESLER, David .... 734-462-4400 230 G
dkesler@schoolcraft.edu
KESLER, Laurie .... 662-720-7259 248 C
lgkesler@nemcc.edu
KESNER, Idalene, F .... 812-855-8489 156 F
ikesner@indiana.edu
KESNER, Idalene, F .... 812-855-8489 156 G
ikesner@indiana.edu
KESSEL, Monica .... 352-588-8646 107 D
monica.kessel@saintleo.edu
KESSELMAN, Harvey ..... 609-652-4521 283 E
harvey.kesselman@stockton.edu
KESSIE, Michael .... 941-487-4212 110 D
mkessie@ncf.edu
KESSINGER, David .... 618-664-7109 138 F
david.kessinger@greenville.edu
KESSINGER, Jason .... 812-288-8878 159 M
jkessinger@mid-america.edu
KESSINGER, Whitney ..... 513-244-4389 356 F
whitney.kessinger@msj.edu
KESSLER, Brian .... 910-893-1776 327 D
kesslerb@campbell.edu
KESSLER, Mary .... 812-488-2579 161 G
mk43@evansville.edu
KESSLER, Michael .... 701-231-7494 345 F
michael.r.kessler@ndsu.edu
KESSLER, Richard .... 212-580-0210 308 A
kesslerr@newschool.edu
KESSLER, Sheryl .... 215-972-7600 392 T
skessler@pafa.edu
KESSLER, Susan, B .... 386-312-4021 107 C
susankessler@sjrstate.edu
KESSLER-CLEARY,
Timothy .... 973-618-3484 276 D
tcleary@caldwell.edu
KESTENBAUM, Yoel ...... 845-782-1380 326 G
KESTER, Jaimee .... 570-484-2357 394 E
jlk7206@lockhaven.edu
KESTER, John .... 910-410-1778 337 B
jikester@richmondcc.edu

KESTER, Kelly .... 360-383-3245 486 A
kkester@whatcom.edu
KESTER, Lori .... 303-273-3639.. 79 J
lkester@mines.edu
KESTERSON, Donald ..... 863-784-7132 108 F
donald.kesterson@southflorida.edu
KESTERSON, Ronald, L . 865-694-6608 425 B
rkesterson@pstcc.edu
KESTNER-RICKETTS,
Laura .... 309-794-7338 133 C
laurakestnerricketts@augustana.edu
KETCHEN, John .... 865-573-4517 420 E
jketchen@johnsonu.edu
KETCHER, Sam .... 417-690-2211 251 H
ketcher@cofo.edu
KETCHESON, Kathi, A ... 503-725-3425 375 E
ketchesonk@pdx.edu
KETCHUM, Kendra .... 210-458-4011 455 E
KETELS, Margo .... 563-589-3765 170 G
mketels@dbq.edu
KETJEN, William .... 330-823-2293 362 E
ketjenwl@mountunion.edu
KETSDEVER, Andrew ..... 541-322-3100 375 A
andrew.ketsdever@osucascades.edu
KETTEMAN, P. Greg ...... 615-675-5312 428 C
gketteman@welch.edu
KETTENBEIL, Kenneth ... 313-593-5140 231 I
kketten@umich.edu
KETTERING, Rocky .... 706-507-8954 117 H
kettering_rocky@columbusstate.edu
KETTERING-LANE,
Denise .... 800-287-8822 154 A
kettede@bethanyseminary.edu
KETTERLING, Jayme ...... 208-732-6552 131 D
jketterling@csi.edu
KETTERLING, Kate .... 612-343-4442 242 M
kaketter@northcentral.edu
KETTERMAN, Beth .... 252-744-2212 341 A
kettermane@ecu.edu
KETTERMAN, Lynn .... 301-687-4090 204 C
lketterman@frostburg.edu
KETTINGER, Kevin .... 585-567-9350 302 B
kevin.kettinger@houghton.edu
KETTINGER, Kirk .... 585-594-6415 312 E
kettinger_kirk@roberts.edu
KETTLER, Karen .... 304-336-8070 490 B
kkettler@westliberty.edu
KETTLER, Ryan, J .... 615-772-1184 282 A
r.j.kettler@rutgers.edu
KETTLEWELL, Kelly .... 570-577-1604 379 C
kelly.kettlewell@bucknell.edu
KETTNER, Valrey, V .... 701-231-9608 345 F
val.kettner@ndsu.edu
KEUFFEL, Elizabeth .... 603-641-7203 274 A
ekeuffel@anselm.edu
KEUSS, Theresa .... 314-516-4602 261 C
keusst@umsl.edu
KEVARI, Jacob .... 951-571-6421.. 59 B
jacob.kevari@mvc.edu
KEVIL, Chris .... 318-675-4102 189 I
chris.kevil@lsuhs.edu
KEVIL, Tim .... 903-875-7443 440 D
tim.kevil@navarrocollege.edu
KEVORKIAN, Meline .... 954-262-8523 105 A
melinek@nova.edu
KEVORKIAN,
Theresa, R .... 305-684-6020 321 A
kevorktr@morrisville.edu
KEW-FICKUS, Olivia ...... 615-343-2746 428 A
olivia.m.kew-fickus@vanderbilt.edu
KEY, Charles .... 865-471-3447 418 E
ckey@cn.edu
KEY, Dan .... 641-844-5741 167 G
dan.key@iavalley.edu
KEY, Jacob .... 276-326-4211 464 J
jkey@bluefield.edu
KEY, Katari .... 414-382-6324 491 F
katari.key@alverno.edu
KEYEK-FRANSSEN,
Deborah .... 801-581-5057 459 O
deblkf@utah.edu
KEYES, Brian .... 417-865-2815 253 D
keyesb@evangel.edu
KEYES, Mandy .... 479-788-7086.. 21 G
mandy.keyes@uafs.edu
KEYES, Rusty .... 601-266-4986 249 F
rusty.keyes@usm.edu
KEYNTON, Robert, S ..... 704-687-8242 342 D
rkeynton@uncc.edu
KEYS, James, A .... 910-843-5304 331 A
KEYS, Margo, A .... 715-858-1825 498 E
mkeys@cvtc.edu
KEYS, Mattie .... 918-463-2931 365 J
mattie.keys@connorsstate.edu

KEYS, Staci .... 417-667-8181 252 B
skeys@cottey.edu
KEYS, Terrance .... 585-292-3432 307 B
tkeys@monroecc.edu
KEYS, Tracy .... 910-843-5304 331 A
finance@nabc.edu
KEYSER, Tom .... 541-885-1481 374 I
tom.keyser@oit.edu
KEYTON, Debbie .... 870-512-7822.. 18 A
debbie_keyton@asun.edu
KEZEY, Katherine .... 802-828-2800 463 F
kap06170@ccv.vsc.edu
KHACHATRIAN, Gaiane . 510-925-4282.. 25 K
KHACHATRYAN,
Agun Anna .... 818-509-9970.. 43 C
KHACHATRYAN, Davit ... 949-451-5326.. 65 C
dkhachatryan@ivc.edu
KHADANGA, Dave .... 334-386-7113.... 5 C
dkhadanga@faulkner.edu
KHADEM, Farnaz .... 650-723-2300.. 66 E
KHADKA, Chandni .... 256-782-8304.... 6 A
ckhadka@jsu.edu
KHAGRAM, Sanjeev ...... 602-978-7203.. 10 J
sanjeev.khagram@thunderbird.asu.edu
KHAJARIAN, Seta .... 818-702-1036.. 56 G
seta.khajarian@pepperdine.edu
KHALDEN, Jeff .... 817-598-6485 457 J
jkhalden@wc.edu
KHALEDI, Morteza .... 817-272-3491 454 I
morteza.khaledi@uta.edu
KHALFANI, Akil .... 973-877-3000 277 G
khalfani@essex.edu
KHALILI, Kambiz .... 734-763-1291 231 H
kkhalili@umich.edu
KHAMIS, Hanan .... 508-999-8845 212 A
hkhamis@umassd.edu
KHAMOUNA, Mo .... 308-367-5213 270 B
mkhamouna1@unl.edu
KHAN, Adil .... 636-227-2100 255 A
KHAN, Ali .... 402-559-4950 269 K
ali.khan@unmc.edu
KHAN, Feroze .... 703-539-6890 471 F
fkhan@stratford.edu
KHAN, M. Rehan .... 502-852-7997 186 A
rehan.khan@louisville.edu
KHAN, M. Wasiullah .... 312-939-0111 137 D
chancellor@eastwest.edu
KHAN, Ray .... 562-916-5055.. 56 F
KHAN, Raza .... 410-386-8222 198 D
rkhan@carrollcc.edu
KHAN, Rumaana, R ...... 209-490-4591.. 24 E
rkhan@advancedcollege.edu
KHAN, Sadya .... 708-974-5283 145 A
khans46@morainevalley.edu
KHAN, Sobia .... 210-486-0947 429 C
skhan32@alamo.edu
KHAN-MARCUS,
Zaveeni .... 805-893-8411.. 70 E
zaveeni.khan-marcus@sa.ucsb.edu
KHANEJA, Gurvinder .... 201-684-7766 280 H
gkhaneja@ramapo.edu
KHANI, Anthony .... 646-717-9743 300 E
khani@gts.edu
KHANNA, Pradeep .... 217-333-9525 152 B
pkhanna@illinois.edu
KHARGONEKAR,
Pramod .... 949-824-5796.. 69 D
pkhargon@uci.edu
KHARKOVYY, Andriy ..... 269-471-3591 221 D
alumni@andrews.edu
KHARTABIL, Basim .... 407-708-4405 108 D
khartabilb@seminolestate.edu
KHASIDOVA, Albina ...... 212-776-7299 293 A
akhasidova@bmcc.cuny.edu
KHATOR, Renu .... 713-743-8820 452 C
rkhator@uh.edu
KHATOR, Renu .... 713-743-8820 452 D
rkhator@uh.edu
KHATRI, Achal .... 617-873-0235 208 B
achal.khatri@cambridgecollege.edu
KHATTAB, Ahmed .... 337-482-6166 193 B
khattab@louisiana.edu
KHAWAR, Mariam .... 607-735-1932 298 H
mkhawar@elmira.edu
KHAYUM, Mohammed .. 812-465-1617 162 C
mkhayum@usi.edu
KHELLA, Julie, T .... 562-907-4463.. 76 B
jkhella@whittier.edu
KHIDEKEL, Nelly .... 626-395-6454.. 28 J
nkhidekel@caltech.edu
KHOJA, Faiza .... 254-519-5724 447 A
fkhoja@tamuct.edu

KHOO-ROBINSON,
Cynthia .... 716-645-3313 316 C
ckr5@buffalo.edu
KHOR, Henry .... 909-895-7138.. 45 H
khor@huca.edu
KHOSLA, Pradeep, K .... 858-534-3135.. 70 C
chancellor@ucsd.edu
KHOSRAVANI, Mariam . 714-241-6159.. 37 J
mkhosravani@coastline.edu
KHOSRAVI, Ebrahim ..... 678-466-4400 117 D
ebrahimkhosravi@clayton.edu
KHOSROWPANAH,
Shahram .... 671-735-2694 504 F
khosrow@triton.uog.edu
KHOURY, Melik Peter ... 207-509-7221 196 E
mkhoury@unity.edu
KHOURY, Philip, S .... 617-253-0887 216 B
KHOZA, Lombuso, S .... 410-651-8385 203 D
lskhoza@umes.edu
KHURANA, Rakesh .... 617-495-1555 210 E
deankhurana@fas.harvard.edu
KHURANA-BAUGH,
Nikki .... 845-569-3216 307 D
nikki.khurana-baugh@msmc.edu
KHUSHMAN, Aneesh .... 215-702-4843 380 A
akhushman@cairn.edu
KIA, Norman .... 575-769-4074 285 O
norman.kia@clovis.edu
KIAMAN, Matthew .... 310-434-4397.. 63 C
kiaman_matthew@smc.edu
KIAN, David .... 561-297-3007 109 J
dkian@fau.edu
KIBBE REED, Trudie ..... 386-481-2000.. 96 D
KIBBLE, Danny .... 317-940-8000 154 C
KIBLER, Bill .... 361-825-3404 447 C
bill.kibler@tamucc.edu
KIBLER, Michele .... 614-222-4009 351 B
mkibler@ccad.edu
KIBUI, Stephen .... 562-692-0921.. 58 L
KICKER, Darrell .... 808-983-4100 128 H
KICKLIGHTER, Barry ..... 678-359-5680 120 F
bkicklighter@gordonstate.edu
KID, Terry .... 318-670-6000 191 D
KIDD, Anessa .... 334-876-9286.... 2 D
anessa.kidd@wccs.edu
KIDD, Beth Ann .... 903-675-6223 451 F
bkidd@tvcc.edu
KIDD, Jimmy .... 502-213-2446 182 C
jimmy.kidd@kctcs.edu
KIDD, Kevin .... 617-989-4095 219 F
kiddk@wit.edu
KIDD, Lisa, L .... 920-923-8115 493 D
llkidd60@marianuniversity.edu
KIDD, Nim .... 512-424-2436 446 B
nim.kidd@tdem.texas.gov
KIDD, Quentin .... 757-594-0723 465 M
qkidd@cnu.edu
KIDD, Savalas .... 937-229-2131 362 C
skidd1@udayton.edu
KIDD, Windy .... 859-280-1237 183 F
wkidd@lextheo.edu
KIDDER, Micki .... 574-631-6526 162 A
mkidder@nd.edu
KIDDIE, Thomas .... 304-766-3170 490 D
tkiddie@wvstateu.edu
KIDESS LUCEY, Tamie .. 413-748-3161 218 I
tkidessl@springfield.edu
KIDNEIGH, Gina .... 307-675-0331 501 G
gkidneigh@sheridan.edu
KIDO, Kengo .... 323-860-1173.. 53 D
kengok@mi.edu
KIDWELL, Eric, A .... 334-833-4420.... 5 G
ekidwell@hawks.huntingdon.edu
KIDWELL, John .... 870-460-1083.. 22 C
kidwell@uamont.edu
KIDWELL, Kim .... 217-333-0460 152 B
kkidwell@illinois.edu
KIDWELL, Kimberly .... 423-636-7300 426 E
kkidwell@tusculum.edu
KIEC, Michael .... 216-373-5227 357 F
mkiec@ndc.edu
KIEC, Michele .... 610-683-4500 394 D
kiec@kutztown.edu
KIECKHAFER, David, S . 608-342-1321 496 E
kieckhaferd@uwplatt.edu
KIEDIS, Thomas, L .... 717-560-8278 387 E
tkiedis@lbc.edu
KIEF, Bob .... 253-879-2820 484 G
bkief@pugetsound.edu
KIEFER, Mike .... 941-752-5000 109 G
kieferm@scf.edu
KIEFFER, Rebecca .... 585-385-8280 313 F
rkieffer@sjfc.edu

KIMBLE, Treina .... 318-342-1004 193 C
landrum@ulm.edu
KIMBRIEL, William .... 870-508-6107.. 17 G
wkimbriel@asumh.edu
KIMBROUGH, B. J .... 205-652-3531.... 9 B
bkimbrough@uwa.edu
KIMBROUGH, B.J .... 205-652-3421.... 9 B
bkimbrough@uwa.edu
KIMBROUGH, Matt .... 417-328-1767 259 I
mkimbrough@sbuniv.edu
KIMBROUGH, Qhamora 585-340-9588 296 D
qkimbrough@crcds.edu
KIMBROUGH, Walter, M .... 504-816-4640 186 I
wkimbrough@dillard.edu
KIMBROW, Terry .... 501-205-8904.. 18 H
tkimbrow@cbc.edu
KIME, Kevin .... 814-886-6481 390 G
kkime@mtaloy.edu
KIMERY, Millard .... 325-649-8173 437 G
mkimery@hputx.edu
KIMLER, Robert .... 732-224-2355 276 B
rkimler@brookdalecc.edu
KIMMEL, Amy .... 415-565-4837.. 69 C
kimmela@uchastings.edus.edu
KIMMEL, Kate .... 631-656-2145 300 B
kate.kimmel@ftc.edu
KIMMEL, Rhonda .... 262-595-2237 496 D
rhonda.kimmel@uwp.edu
KIMMEL, Stephanie .... 312-915-6065 143 C
skimmel@luc.edu
KIMMELMAN, Barbara .. 215-951-2612 399 E
barbara.kimmelman@jefferson.edu
KIMMELMAN, Scott ...... 772-462-7760 102 F
skimmelm@irsc.edu
KIMMINS, William, P ... 516-876-3179 318 C
kimminsw@oldwestbury.edu
KIMMITT, Jonathan .... 918-631-2743 371 C
jonathan-kimmitt@utulsa.edu
KIMPEL, Susan .... 731-989-6698 419 K
skimpel@fhu.edu
KIMPLE, Kelley, C .... 305-626-3794 100 D
kelley.kimple@fmuniv.edu
KIMREY, Phil .... 205-726-2736.... 6 E
ppkimrey@samford.edu
KIN, Amanda, E .... 205-853-1200.... 2 G
akin@jeffersonstate.edu
KIN, Jen .... 419-559-2388 361 C
jkin01@terra.edu
KINANE, Michael, G ..... 516-876-3162 318 C
kinanem@oldwestbury.edu
KINARD, Mary .... 205-387-0511.... 1 D
mary.kinard@bscc.edu
KINARD, Trent .... 803-812-7468 413 E
tkinard@mailbox.sc.edu
KINCAID, Heather .... 740-374-8716 363 F
hkincaid@wscc.edu
KINCAID, Jennifer .... 812-855-7559 156 F
oie@iu.edu
KINCAID, Kristine .... 602-285-7562.. 13 F
kristine.kincaid@phoenixcollege.edu
KINCANNON, Mary .... 817-257-7237 448 F
m.kincannon@tcu.edu
KINCART, Joel, B .... 518-276-6247 312 C
kincaj@rpi.edu
KINCHEN, Thomas, A ... 850-263-3261.. 95 P
takinchen@baptistcollege.edu
KINCHENS, Eulish .... 229-931-2249 125 E
ekinchens@southgatech.edu
KIND, Gene .... 970-542-3248.. 81 N
gene.kind@morgancc.edu
KIND, Jule .... 765-677-2980 158 B
jule.kind@indwes.edu
KIND-KEPPEL, Heather, M .... 847-578-3431 148 F
heather.kindkeppel@rosalindfranklin.edu
KINDBERG, Maria .... 716-338-1143 303 A
mariakindberg@mail.sunyjcc.edu
KINDER, Chad, L .... 580-774-3790 370 A
chad.kinder@swosu.edu
KINDER, Sara .... 317-738-8080 155 D
skinder@franklincollege.edu
KINDER, Terri .... 419-866-0291 361 B
tkinder@stautzenberger.com
KINDHART, Randi .... 217-228-5432 147 F
kindhra@quincy.edu
KINDL, Christine .... 724-938-5492 393 E
kindl@calu.edu
KINDLE, Darin .... 952-829-4680 234 B
darin.kindle@bethanygu.edu
KINDLE, Derek .... 608-262-3770 495 D
derek.kindle@wisc.edu

KINDLER, Andreas .... 309-677-3107 134 A
akindler@bradley.edu
KINDLER, Lisa .... 704-406-3923 329 A
lkindler@gardner-webb.edu
KINDON, Victoria .... 434-395-2001 468 F
kindonv@longwood.edu
KINEAVY, Jacqueline .... 973-684-6300 280 A
jkineavy@pccc.edu
KINEAVY, John .... 617-573-8406 219 B
jkineavy@suffolk.edu
KINEL, Janine, S .... 860-297-2255.. 89 B
janine.kinel@trincoll.edu
KINERNEY, Donna .... 240-567-8827 200 G
donna.kinerney@montgomerycollege.edu
KINERSON, Sara .... 802-635-1258 463 G
sara.kinerson@northernvermont.edu
KING, Adrienne .... 419-530-2299 363 B
adrienne.king@utoledo.edu
KING, Albert .... 419-289-5959 347 J
aking@ashland.edu
KING, Amelia .... 773-577-8100 136 F
aking@coynecollege.edu
KING, Andrew .... 207-780-5670 197 D
andrew.king@maine.edu
KING, Angela .... 303-914-6417.. 83 C
KING, Angella .... 859-246-6696 181 F
angie.king@kctcs.edu
KING, Anne .... 805-289-6503.. 74 B
aking@vcccd.edu
KING, Anthony .... 937-255-6565 502 C
anthony.king@afit.edu
KING, Art .... 646-312-4570 292 L
art.king@baruch.cuny.edu
KING, B.J .... 423-439-5884 419 G
kingbj@etsu.edu
KING, Bayard .... 212-217-4020 299 D
bayard_king@fitnyc.edu
KING, Beth .... 304-637-1243 487 C
kinge@dewv.edu
KING, Bill, L .... 972-985-3796 433 I
blking@collin.edu
KING, Blythe .... 228-896-2503 247 E
blythe.king@mgccc.edu
KING, Bob .... 210-999-8272 451 E
bob.king@trinity.edu
KING, Brenda, M .... 304-336-8076 490 B
kingbren@westliberty.edu
KING, Brian .... 916-568-3021.. 50 F
kingb@losrios.edu
KING, Brian .... 814-866-6641 387 D
bking@lecom.edu
KING, Bruce .... 510-215-4853.. 40 B
bking@contracosta.edu
KING, Bruce .... 940-668-4234 440 F
bking@nctc.edu
KING, Carolee .... 409-772-1904 456 E
caaking@utmb.edu
KING, Caroline .... 941-907-2262.. 99 D
caking@evergladesuniversity.edu
KING, Charles .... 501-370-5392.. 20 F
cking@philander.edu
KING, Charles .... 409-933-8404 433 H
cking@com.edu
KING, Charles, W .... 540-568-6434 468 C
kingcw@jmu.edu
KING, Chris, A .... 412-397-4913 397 B
kingc@rmu.edu
KING, Clifton .... 662-246-6462 247 D
cking@msdelta.edu
KING, Corey .... 920-465-2511 495 F
kingc@uwgb.edu
KING, Corinna .... 515-263-2802 166 F
cking@grandview.edu
KING, Craig .... 212-870-1238 309 E
cking@nyts.edu
KING, Curt .... 978-542-6446 213 E
curt.king@salemstate.edu
KING, D. Wayne .... 859-238-5550 180 B
wayne.king@centre.edu
KING, Dan .... 218-679-2860 242 U
KING, Dana .... 706-622-5006 125 C
dking@shorter.edu
KING, Daniel .... 570-585-9208 381 B
dking@clarkssummitu.edu
KING, Daniel, P .... 334-844-4810.... 4 D
dpk0002@auburn.edu
KING, Darin .... 701-777-4237 345 A
darin.r.king@ndus.edu
KING, David, A .... 330-471-8121 355 D
dking@malone.edu
KING, David, A .... 540-432-4440 466 B
david.king@emu.edu

KING, David, S .... 252-334-2084 331 F
david.king@macuniversity.edu
KING, Deborah .... 870-338-6474.. 22 G
KING, Del .... 404-727-7567 118 E
dking2@emory.edu
KING, Denise .... 606-886-4755 181 E
dking0024@kctcs.edu
KING, Dennis .... 785-628-4276 173 H
dking@fhsu.edu
KING, Dianne .... 864-231-2000 406 F
ldking@andersonuniversity.edu
KING, Dottie .... 812-535-5296 160 H
president@smwc.edu
KING, Elizabeth, H .... 316-978-3510 178 D
elizabeth.king@wichita.edu
KING, Elle .... 336-249-8186 334 B
elle_king@davidsondavie.edu
KING, Emily .... 702-651-7511 270 K
emily.king@csn.edu
KING, Eric .... 972-524-3341 445 B
eric.king@swcc.edu
KING, Evelyn .... 205-366-8851.... 7 A
eking@stillman.edu
KING, Fleurette .... 970-351-3012.. 84 F
fleurette.king@unco.edu
KING, Fred, L .... 304-293-3449 490 E
fred.king@mail.wvu.edu
KING, Garrett .... 580-774-3267 370 A
garrett.king@swosu.edu
KING, Gillian, M .... 315-859-4105 300 H
gking@hamilton.edu
KING, Greg .... 309-556-3248 140 F
gking@iwu.edu
KING, Greg .... 423-236-2975 423 F
gking@southern.edu
KING, Gregory .... 330-823-2282 362 E
kinggl@mountunion.edu
KING, Herbert, L .... 828-898-8785 330 E
kingl@lmc.edu
KING, Jackie, E .... 585-275-9900 323 M
jking@admin.rochester.edu
KING, Jason .... 850-484-1337 105 H
jking@pensacolastate.edu
KING, Jason .... 512-499-4465 454 H
jking@utsystem.edu
KING, Jeff .... 630-892-6431 133 D
jking@aurora.edu
KING, Jeff .... 615-230-3461 425 E
jeff.king@volstate.edu
KING, Jennifer .... 406-377-9458 263 D
jking@dawson.edu
KING, Jerry .... 903-675-6211 451 F
jking@tvcc.edu
KING, Jody .... 718-522-9073 290 E
KING, Joel .... 308-398-7315 266 A
joelking@cccneb.edu
KING, John .... 832-813-6663 439 C
john.e.king@lonestar.edu
KING, John .... 806-720-7211 439 D
john.king@lcu.edu
KING, John .... 541-552-6261 376 B
kingjo@sou.edu
KING, John, J .... 401-254-3550 405 C
jjking@rwu.edu
KING, Jovanna, J .... 864-656-0663 407 E
jovanna@clemson.edu
KING, Julie .... 803-786-3650 408 D
juking@columbiasc.edu
KING, Jyne .... 708-239-4770 151 A
jyne.king@trnty.edu
KING, Karen .... 828-898-3446 330 E
kingk@lmc.edu
KING, Karen, D .... 423-439-5654 419 G
kingk@etsu.edu
KING, Katherine .... 949-480-4161.. 64 G
kking@soka.edu
KING, Keith .... 850-474-2503 111 F
kcking@uwf.edu
KING, Kelvin .... 334-844-8888.... 4 D
kfk0014@auburn.edu
KING, Kevin .... 760-384-6367.. 46 M
kevin.king@cerrocoso.edu
KING, Khristian, J .... 716-673-3398 316 D
khristian.king@fredonia.edu
KING, Kim .... 937-971-2863 359 K
kking@payneseminary.edu
KING, Kimberly .... 239-280-2484.. 95 M
kimberly.king@avemaria.edu
KING, Kwanna .... 307-766-5272 501 I
regirtrar@uwyo.edu
KING, Laura .... 715-232-2857 497 B
kingla@uwstout.edu

KING, Laura .... 651-846-1316 241 B
laura.king@saintpaul.edu
KING, Leslie .... 718-518-4377 294 B
lking@hostos.cuny.edu
KING, Leslie .... 770-426-2713 122 C
lesliek@life.edu
KING, Linda .... 903-886-5013 447 B
linda.king@tamuc.edu
KING, Makini .... 816-235-1727 261 B
kingml@umkc.edu
KING, Maria .... 912-260-4301 125 D
maria.king@sgsc.edu
KING, Marsha, M .... 260-399-7700 162 B
mking@sf.edu
KING, Mary .... 940-552-6291 457 C
mking@vernoncollege.edu
KING, Meade, B .... 540-464-7287 476 B
mking@vmiaa.org
KING, Meredith .... 508-793-7739 208 C
meking@clarku.edu
KING, Michael .... 706-754-7711 123 G
mking@northgatech.edu
KING, Michael .... 913-360-7633 171 J
mking@benedictine.edu
KING, Mike .... 617-747-2363 206 H
enrollment@berklee.edu
KING, Mike .... 812-535-5273 160 H
mking2@smwc.edu
KING, Mikki .... 567-268-6022 361 D
kingmr@tiffin.edu
KING, Mindy .... 715-346-2321 497 A
mking@uwsp.edu
KING, Natalie .... 831-582-3609.. 32 B
nmking@csumb.edu
KING, Natasha .... 912-287-5827 117 E
nking@coastalpines.edu
KING, Nathan .... 828-669-8012 331 K
nathan.king@montreat.edu
KING, Nathaniel .... 702-992-2806 271 B
nathaniel.king@nsc.edu
KING, Nina, E .... 919-684-2431 328 F
nina.king@duke.edu
KING, Paula Kay .... 765-973-8331 157 A
pkayking@iue.edu
KING, Peter, D .... 843-661-1281 409 G
pking@fmarion.edu
KING, Phillip .... 206-546-4552 484 B
pking@shoreline.edu
KING, Phyllis .... 561-803-2807 105 C
phyllis_king@pba.edu
KING, Phyllis .... 414-229-6175 496 B
pking@uwm.edu
KING, Piper .... 505-438-8884 288 F
cfo@acupuncturecollege.edu
KING, Queen .... 661-654-2251.. 30 B
qking@csub.edu
KING, Robert .... 773-995-2002 134 K
rking31@csu.edu
KING, Robert .... 724-738-2199 395 C
robert.king@sru.edu
KING, Roch .... 251-626-3303.... 7 E
rking@ussa.edu
KING, Rochelle, D .... 704-378-1000 330 D
rdking@jcsu.edu
KING, Rodmon .... 315-312-4478 318 D
rodmon.king@oswego.edu
KING, Ronan .... 276-944-6125 466 L
rking@ehc.edu
KING, Ryan .... 207-326-0136 196 A
ryan.king@mma.edu
KING, Ryan, A .... 334-844-2930.... 4 D
rak0025@auburn.edu
KING, Sara, A .... 309-341-7315 141 G
saking@knox.edu
KING, Sasha .... 310-434-3404.. 63 C
king_sasha@smc.edu
KING, Shawn .... 509-359-6878 479 G
sking@ewu.edu
KING, Shayla .... 918-293-4950 368 B
shayla.king@okstate.edu
KING, Sheila .... 907-564-8204.... 9 F
sking@alaskapacific.edu
KING, Sheila, D .... 310-506-4151.. 56 G
sheila.king@pepperdine.edu
KING, Shelly .... 816-415-5963 262 F
kings@william.jewell.edu
KING, Stacey .... 313-993-1005 231 E
kingst1@udmercy.edu
KING, Stephanie .... 413-565-1000 206 D
sking@baypath.edu
KING, Susan, L .... 207-780-4681 197 D
susank@maine.edu

KING, Susan, R .... 919-962-1204 342 C susanking@unc.edu
KING, JR., Talmadge, E .... 415-476-2342.. 70 D talmadge.king@ucsf.edu
KING, Tamara .... 215-898-6081 400 F tamking@upenn.edu
KING, Terry .... 419-267-1251 357 E tking@northweststate.edu
KING, Theresa .... 201-684-7800 280 H 0396mgr@fheg.follett.com
KING, Thomas .... 610-896-1111 385 I tking@haverford.edu
KING, Tim .... 256-782-5020.... 6 A tbking@jsu.edu
KING, Timothy .... 714-995-9988.. 47 B
KING, Tina .... 619-482-6315.. 66 A tking@swccd.edu
KING, Tom .... 610-896-1111 379 B tking01@brynmawr.edu
KING, Tommy .... 601-318-6495 249 H pres@wmcarey.edu
KING, Trevor .... 919-761-2285 340 D registrar@sebts.edu
KING, Victor, I .... 323-343-3054.. 31 E vking@cslanet.calstatela.edu
KING, Vonnetta .... 614-837-4088 363 D kingv@valorcollege.edu
KING, William .... 734-764-0277 231 H wwking@umich.edu
KING, William .... 540-231-5992 466 K wiking1@vcom.vt.edu
KING, Yolanda .... 440-684-6085 363 C yolanda.king@ursuline.edu
KING-LEROY, Cynthia, B .... 518-783-2420 315 E kingleroy@siena.edu
KING LIU, Tsu-Jae .... 510-642-5771.. 69 A tking@eecs.berkeley.edu
KING-MEADOWS, Tyson, D .... 617-287-6505 211 H tyson.meadows@umb.edu
KING MOMON, Kendra 404-364-8318 123 K
KING NOHOS, Therese . 708-534-7096 138 E tnohos@govst.edu
KING SANDERS, Nancy 931-221-6648 417 H kingsandersn@apsu.edu
KINGAN, Michael .... 203-392-6191.. 86 A kinganm1@southernct.edu
KINGERY, Bobbi .... 217-581-7462 137 E rkingery@eiu.edu
KINGERY, Joe .... 606-218-5446 186 B joekingery@upike.edu
KINGHAM, Margret, T .. 610-566-1776 403 B mkingham@williamson.edu
KINGREY, Deb .... 337-475-5556 192 E dkingrey@mcneese.edu
KINGREY, Tiffany .... 719-549-2708.. 80 B tiffany.kingrey@csupueblo.edu
KINGSBURY, Judy .... 507-285-7216 240 H judy.kingsbury@rctc.edu
KINGSLEY, Lindsay .... 623-245-4600.. 16 B likingsley@uti.edu
KINGSLEY, Margery .... 580-581-6900 365 D margeryk@cameron.edu
KINGSLEY, Patty .... 402-463-2402 267 C pkingsley@hastings.edu
KINGSMORE, Lynette .... 208-467-8107 132 E lkingsmore@nnu.edu
KINGSTON, Linda .... 218-733-7637 238 G linda.kingston@lsc.edu
KINGSTON, Lori .... 651-793-1278 238 I lori.kingston@metrostate.edu
KINGSTON, Melissa .... 877-559-3621.. 28 H
KINGSTONE, Peter .... 973-655-4314 279 B kingstonep@montclair.edu
KINIKINI, Lea Lani .... 801-957-4228 461 C lealani.kinikini@slcc.edu
KINIMAKA, Malia .... 562-985-4296.. 31 D malia.kinimaka@csulb.edu
KINION, Veneeya .... 970-945-8691.. 78 L vkinion@coloradomtn.edu
KINJO, Erica .... 530-422-7926.. 74 G registrar@weimar.edu
KINKADE, Michael .... 503-365-4688 372 B michael.kinkade@chemeketa.edu
KINKADE, Mike .... 870-584-1320.. 22 F mkinkade@cccua.edu
KINKAID, Stephanie ..... 309-298-1977 153 A sm-kinkaid@wiu.edu
KINKEADE, Jenna .... 254-710-8353 431 E jenna_kinkeade@baylor.edu
KINLAW, George .... 773-838-7699 135 F gkinlaw@ccc.edu
KINLAW, Mark, O .... 336-342-4261 337 E kinlawm@rockinghamcc.edu
KINLEY, Billie .... 360-676-2772 481 F bjkinley@nwic.edu
KINLEY, Naomi .... 718-489-5260 313 E nkinley@sfc.edu
KINLEY, Sharon .... 360-676-2772 481 F skinley@nwic.edu
KINLOCH, Valerie .... 412-648-1773 400 H vkinlock@pitt.edu
KINNAIRD, Jennifer ...... 440-375-7115 354 K jkinnaird@lec.edu
KINNAMAN, Mindy .... 303-404-5254.. 81 A mindy.kinnaman@frontrange.edu
KINNAMON, Jeffrey .... 617-747-2240 206 H registrar@berklee.edu
KINNARD, Rob .... 510-436-1035.. 45 E kinnard@hnu.edu
KINNARD-PAYTON, Tiffany .... 330-490-7538 363 E tkpayton@walsh.edu
KINNER, David .... 828-227-7646 343 E dkinner@wcu.edu
KINNESTON, Susan ...... 920-693-1224 498 H susan.kinneston@gotoltc.edu
KINNEY, Amy, J .... 419-434-4241 364 C kinney@winebrenner.edu
KINNEY, Daniel .... 712-325-3201 167 I dkinney@iwcc.edu
KINNEY, Doug .... 315-294-8411 292 G doug.kinney@cayuga-cc.edu
KINNEY, Judith .... 410-225-5266 200 D jkinney01@mica.edu
KINNEY, Katie .... 256-765-4252.... 8 E kckinney@una.edu
KINNEY, Kevin .... 408-795-5600.. 34 A kevin.kinney@sjsu.edu
KINNEY, Lee, M .... 575-439-3605 287 D kinney@nmsu.edu
KINNEY, Mark .... 231-845-6211 233 A mkinney@westshore.edu
KINNEY, Michael .... 607-778-5031 317 D kinneym@sunybroome.edu
KINNEY, Susan .... 205-226-4645.... 4 F skinney@bsc.edu
KINNEY, Wendi .... 585-245-5501 318 B kinney@geneseo.edu
KINNISON, Mike .... 662-846-4300 245 G mkinnisn@deltastate.edu
KINNUNEN, Heather, M .... 715-682-1205 494 G hkinnunen@northland.edu
KINSEL, Gary .... 618-453-4551 150 B gkinsel@siu.edu
KINSELLA, Jill, H .... 478-301-2717 122 E kinsella_jh@mercer.edu
KINSELLA, Susan .... 352-588-8272 107 D susan.kinsella@saintleo.edu
KINSER, Rachel .... 407-438-6000 109 C
KINSERVIK, Matt .... 302-831-2101.. 91 C matthewk@udel.edu
KINSEY, Barry, C .... 734-384-4124 228 C bkinsey@monroeccc.edu
KINSEY, Chris, S .... 229-391-5001 114 F ckinsey@abac.edu
KINSEY, Daniel .... 406-353-2607 262 H dkinsey@ancollege.edu
KINSEY, Sheila, C .... 910-630-7668 331 E skinsey@methodist.edu
KINSHUK, ... 940-565-2731 453 E kinshuk@unt.edu
KINSLEY, Chris .... 941-487-4444 110 D ckinsley@ncf.edu
KINTO, Diana .... 409-882-3362 449 H diana.kinto@lsco.edu
KINTZ, David .... 847-697-1000 137 F dkintz@elgin.edu
KINYATTI, Njoki .... 718-262-2021 295 E nkinyatti@york.cuny.edu
KINZEL, Lisa .... 303-384-2470.. 79 J lkinzel@mines.edu
KINZER, Esther .... 951-785-2175.. 47 C ekinzer@lasierra.edu
KINZER, Greg .... 903-813-2361 430 H gkinzer@austincollege.edu
KINZER, Jay .... 620-227-9204 173 D jkinzer@dc3.edu
KINZER, Marlin, L .... 605-394-2375 416 H marlin.kinzer@sdsmt.edu
KINZIGER, Linda .... 920-748-8358 494 J kinzigerl@ripon.edu
KINZLER, Robert, J .... 215-951-1048 387 A kinzler@lasalle.edu
KINZY, Terri .... 309-438-5677 140 D kinzy20@ilstu.edu
KINZY, Terri, G .... 269-387-8294 233 B terri.kinzy@wmich.edu
KIP, Margaret .... 215-898-6636 400 F mkip@upenn.edu
KIPFER, Jamie, D .... 540-458-8455 477 D jkipfer@wlu.edu
KIPFER, Julie .... 406-994-5737 264 C jkipfer@montana.edu
KIPNES, Ethan .... 540-458-8427 477 D ekipnes@wlu.edu
KIPP, Tom, E .... 414-410-4156 491 I tekipp@stritch.edu
KIPPENHAN, Heidi .... 701-228-5669 346 B heidi.kippenhan@dakotacollege.edu
KIPPES, John .... 605-995-2160 415 A john.kippes@dwu.edu
KIRALLA, John .... 310-338-2366.. 51 A john.kiralla@lmu.edu
KIRALLA, Laura .... 310-665-6961.. 55 C lkiralla@otis.edu
KIRBY, Claire .... 704-687-7292 342 D ckirby@uncc.edu
KIRBY, Claire, J .... 704-687-7292 342 D ckirby@uncc.edu
KIRBY, Dawn .... 239-590-1094 109 K dkirby@fgcu.edu
KIRBY, SJ, Donald .... 315-445-4110 303 I kirby@lemoyne.edu
KIRBY, Elizabeth .... 618-664-7100 138 F elizabeth.kirby@greenville.edu
KIRBY, Elizabeth, A .... 989-774-1885 222 E kirby2ea@cmich.edu
KIRBY, Emily .... 425-558-0299 479 F
KIRBY, Eric .... 435-586-7700 460 A erickirby@suu.edu
KIRBY, John .... 401-874-2957 405 E jdkirby@uri.edu
KIRBY, Joseph .... 410-455-3020 203 B kirby@umbc.edu
KIRBY, Kamisha .... 704-290-5822 337 I kkirby@spcc.edu
KIRBY, Kevin .... 859-572-6544 184 E kirby@nku.edu
KIRBY, Kevin .... 713-348-6040 442 F kevin.kirby@rice.edu
KIRBY, Kim .... 870-673-4201.. 22 G
KIRBY, Marie .... 979-209-7337 431 H marie.kirby@blinn.edu
KIRBY, Renee .... 262-595-2610 496 D kirby@uwp.edu
KIRBY, Stephanie .... 812-749-1416 159 O skirby@oak.edu
KIRBY, Vickie, S .... 903-813-2414 430 H vkirby@austincollege.edu
KIRBY, Yvonne .... 860-832-1784.. 85 G ykirby@ccsu.edu
KIRCH, Michael .... 952-358-8164 239 G michael.kirch@normandale.edu
KIRCHER, Jason .... 630-752-5011 153 C jason.kircher@wheaton.edu
KIRCHGESSNER, Justina .... 309-282-8480 144 C jkirchgessner@methodistcol.edu
KIRCHMAIER, Michael .. 617-850-1239 210 G mkirchmaier@hchc.edu
KIRCHNER, Margaret .... 206-726-5151 479 E mkirchner@cornish.edu
KIRCHNER, Tom, A .... 440-525-7138 354 L tkirchner@lakelandcc.edu
KIREMIT, Yavuz .... 617-243-2247 211 B ykiremit@lasell.edu
KIRGIS, Julianne .... 510-594-3656.. 28 B jkirgis@cca.edu
KIRGIS, Paul .... 406-243-2549 263 K paul.kirgis@umontana.edu
KIRIAKOS, Christopher . 541-485-1780 374 E christopherkiriakos@newhope.edu
KIRIAKOS, Leslie .... 541-485-1780 374 E lesliekiriakos@newhope.edu
KIRK, Artemis, G .... 202-687-7425.. 92 E agk3@georgetown.edu
KIRK, Barrie .... 803-691-3875 410 D kirkb@midlandstech.edu
KIRK, Beth, V .... 301-546-0007 201 E kirkbv@pgcc.edu
KIRK, Daniel .... 321-674-7622 100 C dkirk@fit.edu
KIRK, Daniel .... 507-457-2570 241 F daniel.kirk@winona.edu
KIRK, Donna, R .... 904-620-2819 111 B d.kirk@unf.edu
KIRK, Donnie .... 940-696-8752 457 C dkirk@vernoncollege.edu
KIRK, Eileen .... 413-265-2468 208 E kirke@elms.edu
KIRK, Ella, W .... 330-569-5150 353 G kirkew@hiram.edu
KIRK, Gary, R .... 717-254-8917 382 D kirkg@dickinson.edu
KIRK, Jeff .... 254-519-5427 447 A jeff.kirk@tamuct.edu
KIRK, Jimmy .... 415-452-5534.. 36 K jkirk@ccsf.edu
KIRK, Joe .... 330-263-2590 351 A jkirk@wooster.edu
KIRK, Kay, D .... 205-975-9762.... 8 A kdkirk@uab.edu
KIRK, Kristi .... 512-313-3000 433 N kristi.kirk@concordia.edu
KIRK, Michael .... 860-486-0715.. 89 D michael.kirk@uconn.edu
KIRK, Sarah .... 315-781-3304 301 F kirk@hws.edu
KIRK, Teresa .... 217-854-3231 133 I
KIRK, Tim .... 870-864-7154.. 21 A wtkirk@southark.edu
KIRK-HOLLAND, Marcie .... 530-752-0752.. 69 B makirk@ucdavis.edu
KIRKEIDE, Shannon .... 763-433-1897 237 D shannon.kirkeide@anokaramsey.edu
KIRKEMO, William .... 816-268-5400 257 C bkirkemo@nts.edu
KIRKEN, Robert .... 915-747-5000 455 C rakirken@utep.edu
KIRKENDALL-BAKER, Heyke .... 503-768-6235 373 E hkirkendall-baker@lclark.edu
KIRKER, Elizabeth .... 302-225-6256.. 91 B kirkere@gbc.edu
KIRKLAND, Cecil, E ...... 304-629-7161 487 I ekirkland@salemu.edu
KIRKLAND, Jillian .... 843-525-8209 412 G jkirkland@tcl.edu
KIRKLAND, Joe .... 828-669-8012 331 K jkirkland@montreat.edu
KIRKLAND, Keith .... 973-877-3070 277 G kirkland@essex.edu
KIRKLAND, Kenneth ..... 256-549-8200.... 2 B
KIRKLAND, LeeAnn ...... 478-471-2717 122 F leeann.kirkland@mga.edu
KIRKLAND, Michael ...... 229-243-3160 114 F mkirkland@abac.edu
KIRKLAND, Nick .... 601-484-8620 247 A nkirkla1@meridiancc.edu
KIRKLAND, Sandra .... 804-594-1566 474 B skirkland@jtcc.edu
KIRKLAND, Susan, M ... 336-278-5443 328 J skirkland3@elon.edu
KIRKLAND, William, B . 803-777-0066 413 A kirkland@sc.edu
KIRKLAND LEWIS, Fanita .... 386-481-2000.. 96 D
KIRKMAN, Dawayne ..... 937-328-7977 350 G kirkmans@clarkstate.edu
KIRKPATRICK, Bonnie, L .... 302-356-6804.. 91 E bonnie.l.kirkpatrick@wilmu.edu
KIRKPATRICK, Brian, J . 973-596-3427 279 E brian.j.kirkpatrick@njit.edu
KIRKPATRICK, Christopher .... 906-227-2355 228 I ckirkpat@nmu.edu
KIRKPATRICK, Daniel 575-492-2164 289 F dkirkpatrick@usw.edu
KIRKPATRICK, Elizabeth, L .... 240-500-2265 199 C elkirkpatrick@hagerstowncc.edu
KIRKPATRICK, Heather .. 650-776-7713.. 24 G
KIRKPATRICK, Holly, R . 215-572-4475 378 E kirkpath@arcadia.edu
KIRKPATRICK, Lisa, L ... 512-448-8408 442 I lisak@stedwards.edu
KIRKPATRICK, Mac .... 864-338-8090 410 A mkirkpatrick@lander.edu
KIRKPATRICK, Michael . 800-895-7411 464 E mkirkpatrick@asl.edu
KIRKPATRICK, Ron .... 951-571-6100.. 59 B
KIRKSEY, Jason .... 405-744-9154 367 G jason.kirksey@okstate.edu
KIRKSEY, Jennifer .... 740-593-1804 358 K kirkseyj@ohio.edu

KIRKWOOD, Alisia .... 562-938-4362.. 48 F
akirkwood@lbcc.edu
KIRKWOOD, Jeffrey, D . 301-243-2119 502 L
jeffrey.kirkwood@dodiis.mil
KIRKWOOD,
William, G .... 423-439-4210 419 G
kirkwood@etsu.edu
KIRLEIS, Kathleen .... 617-287-5100 211 H
kathleen.kirleis@umb.edu
KIRMER, Lisa .... 620-343-4600 173 G
lkirmer@fhtc.edu
KIRMSE, David .... 415-422-2057.. 72 J
dkirmse@usfca.edu
KIRON, Gopu .... 570-504-7929 387 B
kirong@lackawanna.edu
KIRSCH, Breanne .... 712-279-5451 164 B
breanne.kirsch@briarcliff.edu
KIRSCH, OSB, Myron ... 724-805-2111 398 A
myron.kirsch@stvincent.edu
KIRSCH, OSB, Myron ... 724-805-2111 397 I
myron.kirsch@email.stvincent.edu
KIRSCH, Ramona, R ...... 540-362-6214 467 H
kirschrr@hollins.edu
KIRSCHBAUM, Steven ... 563-588-6326 164 E
steven.kirschbaum@clarke.edu
KIRSCHEN, Alyse .... 714-449-7835.. 51 B
akirschen@ketchum.edu
KIRSCHLING, Jane, M .. 410-706-6741 203 A
kirschling@son.umaryland.edu
KIRSCHMANN, Anne ..... 414-847-3238 494 C
annekirschmann@miad.edu
KIRSCHNER, Kelly .... 727-864-8880.. 98 J
kirschkm@eckerd.edu
KIRST, Thomas .... 541-485-1780 374 E
thomaskirst@newhope.edu
KIRSTAETTER, Dawn ..... 410-462-7432 198 B
dkirstaetter@bccc.edu
KIRSTEN, Jan .... 732-255-0400 279 F
jkirsten@ocean.edu
KIRTLEY, Adam, M .... 509-522-4449 486 B
kirtleam@whitman.edu
KIRTMAN, Janet .... 212-346-1700 311 A
jkirtman@pace.edu
KIRTMAN, Lisa .... 657-278-5901.. 31 C
lkirtman@fullerton.edu
KIRVES, Carol .... 270-707-3751 182 B
carol.kirves@kctcs.edu
KIRWIN, Luanne .... 617-373-2520 217 I
KIS, Daphne .... 504-662-1946 193 D
KISA, Josi .... 503-491-6422 374 B
josi.kisa@mhcc.edu
KISCADEN, Elizabeth, J 402-280-2700 266 H
elizabethkiscaden@creighton.edu
KISER, Dan .... 828-328-7154 330 F
dan.kiser@lr.edu
KISER, Joe .... 276-328-0143 472 E
jbk5b@uvawise.edu
KISER, Liz .... 252-399-6453 326 K
epkiser@barton.edu
KISH, Anne .... 406-683-7492 264 A
anne.kish@umwestern.edu
KISH, Joy .... 828-689-1140 331 C
jkish@mhu.edu
KISH-GOODLING,
Donna, M .... 484-664-3479 390 H
donnakish-goodling@muhlenberg.edu
KISH-JOHANSEN, Deb .. 813-253-7860 102 B
dkishjohansen@hccfl.edu
KISHBAUGH, Amanda ... 570-389-4297 393 D
akishba2@bloomu.edu
KISHBAUGH, Tara .... 540-432-4000 466 B
dean-sean@emu.edu
KISHEN, Ron .... 215-895-8800 401 E
KISHIDA, Katsumi .... 908-737-0349 278 E
kkishida@kean.edu
KISHPAUGH, Jason ...... 423-869-6277 421 A
jason.kishpaugh@lmunet.edu
KISHPAUGH, Melva ...... 540-654-1084 471 N
mkishpau@umw.edu
KISLER, Jeffrey .... 215-717-6415 400 E
jkisler@uarts.edu
KISLOSKI, Roger .... 903-463-8777 436 G
kisloskir@grayson.edu
KISLYUK, Paulina .... 413-369-4044 208 F
kislyuk@csld.edu
KISONGO, Ibuchwa .... 763-424-0806 240 A
ikisongo@nhcc.edu
KISPERT, Craig, G .... 206-281-2536 483 G
ckispert@spu.edu
KISS, Boglarka .... 805-289-6232.. 74 B
bkiss@vcccd.edu
KISS, John, Z .... 336-334-5241 343 A
jzkiss@uncg.edu

KISS, Michelle .... 562-951-4700.. 29 H
mkiss@calstate.edu
KISSACK, Heather .... 719-389-6202.. 78 I
hkissack@coloradocollege.edu
KISSAL, Carol, D .... 703-993-8750 467 E
ckissal@gmu.edu
KISSEBERTH, Sara .... 419-358-3484 348 F
kisseberths@bluffton.edu
KISSEL, Chuck .... 657-278-4101.. 31 C
ckissel@fullerton.edu
KISSINGER, Sue .... 715-346-3361 497 A
skissing@uwsp.edu
KISSLER, Lance .... 509-359-4257 479 G
lkissler@ewu.edu
KISSLING, Catherine ..... 847-574-5224 142 B
ckissling@lfgsm.edu
KISSOCK, Tim .... 816-271-4466 257 A
tkissock@missouriwestern.edu
KIST, Emily .... 517-265-5161 220 G
ekist@adrian.edu
KIST-KLINE, Gail, E ...... 513-585-1414 350 D
gail.kistkline@thechristcollege.edu
KISTLER, Eric .... 843-863-7933 407 B
ekistler@csuniv.edu
KISTNER, Angie .... 618-437-5321 147 I
kistner@rlc.edu
KISTNER, Frances .... 508-373-5749 216 D
frances.kistner@mcphs.edu
KISTNER, Janet .... 850-644-7836 110 C
jkistner@fsu.edu
KISTNER, Warren .... 309-556-3237 140 F
wkistner@iwu.edu
KISTULENTZ, Steven ..... 352-588-7218 107 D
steven.kistulentz@saintleo.edu
KIT, Stephanie .... 865-974-5435 427 B
smkit@utk.edu
KITALONG,
Christopher, U .... 680-488-2746 505 B
KITAS, Chris .... 724-357-4077 394 C
ckitas@iup.edu
KITCH, Rhonda, K .... 607-255-3203 297 F
KITCHEN, Augusta .... 803-780-1159 414 B
akitchen@voorhees.edu
KITCHEN, Todd .... 479-619-4232.. 20 C
tkitchen@nwacc.edu
KITCHENS, Joann .... 701-662-1502 346 C
joann.kitchens@lrsc.edu
KITCHENS, Penny .... 478-553-2060 123 H
pkitchens@oftc.edu
KITCHIN, Steven, H ...... 401-739-5000 404 E
skitchin@neit.edu
KITCHINGS, Maribeth ... 601-974-1002 247 B
kitchme@millsaps.edu
KITE, Brian .... 310-825-7891.. 69 E
bkite@tft.ucla.edu
KITE, Eddie .... 903-675-6359 451 F
eddie.kite@tvcc.edu
KITE, Michelle .... 269-782-1302 231 A
mkite@swmich.edu
KITE, Terry .... 636-481-3273 254 C
tkite@jeffco.edu
KITHCART, Jane .... 845-687-5111 323 H
kithcarj@sunyulster.edu
KITHCART, Shawn .... 617-849-8814 211 C
KITLEY, Barry, S .... 336-841-9363 329 F
bkitley@highpoint.edu
KITTEL, Jane .... 262-691-5214 500 B
jkittel@wctc.edu
KITTELL, Joseph .... 701-255-7500 347 C
jjkittell@umary.edu
KITTELSON, Laura .... 763-576-4039 237 E
laura.kittelson@anokatech.edu
KITTERMAN, Elizabeth .. 620-421-6700 175 F
elizabethk@labette.edu
KITTLE, Daniel .... 319-352-8443 170 J
daniel.kittle@wartburg.edu
KITTNER, Missy .... 254-299-8514 439 E
mkittner@mclennan.edu
KITTREDGE, Cynthia, B . 512-472-4133 443 F
cynthia.kittredge@ssw.edu
KITTRELL-MIKELL,
Deborah .... 478-289-2368 118 C
dkittrell@ega.edu
KITTS, Kenneth, D .... 256-765-4211.... 8 E
kkitts@una.edu
KITZINGER, Denis .... 603-880-8308 274 D
dkitzinger@thomasmorecollege.edu
KITZINGER, Sara .... 603-566-5017 274 D
skitzinger@thomasmorecollege.edu
KIWUS, Christopher ...... 540-231-6291 476 C
chkiwus@vt.edu
KIYAR, Baris .... 812-855-6413 156 F
bkiyar@iu.edu

KIYOSAKI, Donna .... 808-956-7616 129 E
donnafay@hawaii.edu
KIZLINZKI, Stacy .... 918-631-2615 371 C
sdk8996@utulsa.edu
KJAR, Daniel .... 607-735-1826 298 H
dkjar@elmira.edu
KJELLEREN, Donald, J .. 413-597-2312 220 D
donald.f.kjelleren@williams.edu
KLAAS, Brian .... 816-235-1333 261 B
klaasb@umkc.edu
KLAAS, Daniel .... 770-689-4965 115 C
dklass@aii.edu
KLAASSEN, Sara .... 816-322-0110 251 B
sara.klaassen@calvary.edu
KLABE, Kimberly, S ...... 301-447-5377 201 B
klabe@msmary.edu
KLAEHN, Scott .... 651-450-3462 238 E
sklaehn@inverhills.edu
KLAFFKE, David .... 360-383-3016 486 A
dklaffke@whatcom.edu
KLAHR, Sabine, C .... 801-587-8888 459 O
s.klahr@utah.edu
KLAIBER, James, S .... 440-775-5603 357 G
jim.klaiber@oberlin.edu
KLANDERUD, Jessica ... 859-985-3000 179 I
KLAPATAUSKAS,
Kyle, J .... 563-588-7639 168 A
kyle.klapatauskas@loras.edu
KLAPPENBACK, Kirby ... 402-643-7192 266 G
kirby.klappenback@cune.edu
KLARE, Diana, G .... 719-333-2180 503 D
diane.klare@usafa.edu
KLASEK, Angie .... 402-466-4774 267 A
angie.klasek@doane.edu
KLASEN, James .... 617-588-1344 206 F
jklasen@bfit.edu
KLASKO, Stephen, K ..... 215-955-6617 399 E
stephen.klasko@jefferson.edu
KLASKOW, Sam .... 810-762-7870 226 B
sklaskow@kettering.edu
KLATT, Lori .... 360-867-5185 480 C
klattl@evergreen.edu
KLATT, Sara .... 712-274-6400 171 B
sara.klatt@witcc.edu
KLAUBER, SR.,
James, S .... 240-500-2233 199 C
jklauber@hagerstowncc.edu
KLAUS, Amanda .... 732-571-3653 279 A
aklaus@monmouth.edu
KLAUS, Chad, L .... 609-258-5498 280 D
klaus@princeton.edu
KLAUS, Courtney .... 785-242-5200 176 I
courtney.klaus@ottawa.edu
KLAUS, Larry, S .... 989-774-3081 222 E
klaus1ls@cmich.edu
KLAUS, Sky .... 575-234-9414 287 E
skyklaus@nmsu.edu
KLAUSLI, Julia .... 703-416-1441 466 A
jklausli.ips@divinemercy.edu
KLAUSMEYER, Robert ... 573-875-7304 251 I
rklausmeyer@ccis.edu
KLAVER, Lenny .... 660-359-3948 257 D
lklaver@mail.ncmissouri.edu
KLAVER, Tzipora .... 305-944-0035 104 I
KLAWE, Maria, M .... 909-921-8120.. 44 H
klawe@hmc.edu
KLAWUNN, Margaret .... 805-893-3651.. 70 E
margaret.klawunn@sa.ucsb.edu
KLEBANOV, Marina .... 718-793-2330 309 C
KLEBBA, Megan .... 913-367-5340 171 J
KLEBE, Kelli .... 719-255-3121.. 84 C
kklebe@uccs.edu
KLEE-TIESMAN,
Kerry, J .... 517-750-1200 231 C
ke497810@arbor.edu
KLEEMAN, Kathryn .... 217-206-4847 152 A
kklee1@uis.edu
KLEICH, Tammie .... 308-635-6072 270 C
kleicht@wncc.edu
KLEIMAN, Adriana .... 213-615-7295.. 36 E
akleiman@thechicagoschool.edu
KLEIN, Andrew, O .... 508-849-3313 205 H
aklein@annamaria.edu
KLEIN, Barb .... 641-648-4611 167 F
barb.klein@iavalley.edu
KLEIN, Bart .... 816-501-4780 258 I
bart.klein@rockhurst.edu
KLEIN, Cynthia .... 412-809-5100 396 E
klein.cynthia@ptcollege.edu
KLEIN, Daniel .... 617-559-8637 210 F
dklein@hebrewcollege.edu
KLEIN, David .... 818-333-3558.. 53 J
david@nyfa.edu

KLEIN, Eric .... 619-644-7390.. 44 E
eric.klein@gcccd.edu
KLEIN, Erin .... 701-252-3467 347 B
eklein@uj.edu
KLEIN, Gary .... 507-457-1489 243 C
gklein@smumn.edu
KLEIN, Janette .... 660-543-4159 260 G
jklein@ucmo.edu
KLEIN, Jim .... 502-456-6508 185 A
jklein@sullivan.edu
KLEIN, June .... 650-433-3849.. 55 L
jklein@paloaltou.edu
KLEIN, Kara .... 843-953-3721 407 C
kklein1@citadel.edu
KLEIN, Kenneth, S .... 619-239-0391.. 34 G
kklein@cwsl.edu
KLEIN, Leslie, G .... 410-358-3144 205 C
KLEIN, Lori .... 907-796-6057.. 10 B
laklein@alaska.edu
KLEIN, Lori .... 907-796-6540.. 10 B
laklein@alaska.edu
KLEIN, Mendel .... 718-384-5460 325 L
KLEIN, Michael .... 215-204-1927 399 B
mike.klein@temple.edu
KLEIN, Michelle, W ...... 504-866-7426 190 G
finance@nds.edu
KLEIN, Nate .... 319-363-1323 168 F
nklein@mtmercy.edu
KLEIN, Patti .... 651-523-2421 236 B
pklein01@hamline.edu
KLEIN, Peg .... 401-841-3665 503 A
margaret.klein@usnwc.edu
KLEIN, Phil .... 304-214-8967 488 J
pklein@wvncc.edu
KLEIN, Ray .... 812-941-2457 157 F
rayklein@ius.edu
KLEIN, Sara .... 201-216-3543 283 D
sara.klein@stevens.edu
KLEIN, Steve .... 503-352-2822 375 C
kleinsk@pacificu.edu
KLEIN, Terry .... 715-645-7048 499 H
terry.klein@northwoodtech.edu
KLEIN-WILLIAMS,
Marcella .... 805-678-5262.. 74 A
mkleinwilliams@vcccd.edu
KLEINE, Patricia, A .... 715-836-2320 495 E
kleinepa@uwec.edu
KLEINE, Todd .... 708-524-6570 137 C
tdkleine@dom.edu
KLEINER, Zev .... 347-394-1036 291 F
KLEINHANS, Randy .... 574-372-5100 155 F
kleinhrp@grace.edu
KLEINJAN, Brent .... 701-255-3285 347 A
bkleinjan@uttc.edu
KLEINKAUFMAN, Dovid 718-327-7600 325 D
info@yofr.org
KLEINMAN, Daniel, L ... 617-353-2230 207 E
dlklein@bu.edu
KLEINMAN, Kent .... 401-454-6406 405 B
kkleinman@risd.edu
KLEISER, Richele .... 559-325-3600.. 28 D
rkleiser@chsu.edu
KLEITSCH, II, Andrew ... 919-536-7200 334 C
KLEMANN, Jim .... 701-252-3467 347 B
jklemann@uj.edu
KLEMANN, M. Adam .... 330-471-8308 355 D
aklemann@malone.edu
KLEMENS, Kristina .... 262-595-2004 496 D
klemens@uwp.edu
KLEMIUK, Christy .... 817-515-7778 445 F
christy.klemiuk@tccd.edu
KLEMM, Aaron .... 909-869-3047.. 30 A
amklemm@cpp.edu
KLEMM, Jotisa .... 817-515-3083 445 F
jotisa.klemm@tccd.edu
KLEN, Joseph, R .... 765-361-6052 163 B
klenj@wabash.edu
KLENKLEN, Andy .... 202-885-8696.. 94 D
aklenklen@wesleyseminary.edu
KLEPARSKI, Tracy .... 217-351-2206 147 C
tkleparski@parkland.edu
KLEPETAR, Adam .... 413-236-2140 214 A
aklepetar@berkshirecc.edu
KLEPFER, Jennifer .... 352-854-2322.. 97 N
klepferj@cf.edu
KLEPITSCH, Heather, A . 815-282-7900 148 I
heatherklepitsch@sacn.edu
KLEPONIS, Stephen ...... 610-526-6017 385 D
skleponis@harcum.edu
KLEPPER, Scott .... 405-789-7661 369 I
scott.klepper@swcu.edu

KLESENSKI-RISPOLI, Deborah ..... 212-217-4045 299 D
deborah_klesenski@fitnyc.edu
KLESENSKI-RISPOLI, Deborah ..... 212-217-4040 299 D
deborah_klesenski@fitnyc.edu
KLESS, Teresa, M ..... 401-825-2003 404 C
tkless@ccri.edu
KLETT, Breanna ..... 562-903-4751.. 27 A
KLETTKE, Kari ..... 701-845-7534 345 G
kari.klettke@vcsu.edu
KLETTNER, Kurt ..... 304-424-8000 490 F
kurt.klettner@wvup.edu
KLETZER, Lori ..... 831-459-3885.. 71 A
cpevc@ucsc.edu
KLEVENO, Robert ..... 951-222-8000.. 59 D
robert.kleveno@rcc.edu
KLEVER, Mark ..... 530-938-5927.. 39 C
KLEWICKI, Lisa ..... 703-416-1441 466 A
lklewicki.ips@divinemercy.edu
KLEYN, Henk ..... 616-432-3400 230 A
henk.kleyn@prts.edu
KLIETHERMES, Aaron .... 573-897-5000 260 A
KLIEVER, Amanda ..... 541-917-4204 373 G
klievea@linnbenton.edu
KLIEWER, Jan ..... 580-774-3084 370 A
jan.kliewer@swosu.edu
KLIEWER, Miriam ..... 620-947-3121 177 I
miriamkliewer@tabor.edu
KLIEWER, Wayne ..... 620-947-3121 177 I
waynekliewer@tabor.edu
KLIGMAN, Linda, B ..... 267-975-2254 386 B
lindakligman@iirp.edu
KLIM, Karin ..... 609-896-5167 281 B
kklim@rider.edu
KLIMCZAK, Karen ..... 303-315-7734.. 84 D
karen.klimczak@ucdenver.edu
KLIMCZYK, Karen ..... 219-464-5015 162 D
karen.klimczyk@valpo.edu
KLIMKEWICZ, Patricia ... 518-629-7887 302 C
p.klimkewicz@hvcc.edu
KLIMKOWSKI, Ann Francis ..... 419-885-3211 355 C
aklimkowski@lourdes.edu
KLIMOFF, Dodi ..... 215-635-7300 384 E
dklimoff@gratz.edu
KLIMPT, Kelly ..... 281-756-3539 429 D
kklimpt@alvincollege.edu
KLIN, Celia ..... 607-777-2145 316 B
cklin@binghamton.edu
KLINE, Christopher ..... 815-838-0500 142 F
klinech@lewisu.edu
KLINE, David ..... 651-846-1703 241 B
david.kline@saintpaul.edu
KLINE, Elizabeth ..... 740-588-4116 365 B
ekline@zanestate.edu
KLINE, John ..... 714-816-0366.. 68 E
john.kline@trident.edu
KLINE, John ..... 847-585-2014.. 10 E
jkline@aiuniv.edu
KLINE, Kevin ..... 419-755-4521 357 B
kkline@ncstatecollege.edu
KLINE, Laura ..... 502-272-7051 179 H
lkline@bellarmine.edu
KLINE, Laura ..... 610-921-7293 377 G
lckline@albright.edu
KLINE, Loni, N 570-326-3761 392W
lnk6@pct.edu
KLINE, Richard ..... 440-375-7512 354 K
rkline@lec.edu
KLINE, Thomas ..... 262-551-6036 492 B
tkline@carthage.edu
KLINEPETER, Pamela .... 606-326-2254 181 D
pamela.klinepeter@kctcs.edu
KLING, Lenda ..... 850-201-6084 112 C
lenda.kling@tcc.fl.edu
KLING, Rory ..... 785-890-3641 176 H
rory.kling@nwktc.edu
KLINGELE, Nora ..... 217-641-4201 141 A
nklingele@jwcc.edu
KLINGEMANN, John ..... 325-942-2162 450 E
john.klingemann@angelo.edu
KLINGENBERG, Erin ..... 701-845-7424 345 G
erin.klingenberg@vcsu.edu
KLINGENSMITH, Dan .... 865-981-8278 421 C
dan.klingensmith@maryvillecollege.edu
KLINGER, Donna, J ..... 301-447-5657 201 B
d.j.klinger@msmary.edu
KLINGER, Joe ..... 708-456-0300 151 D
joeklinger@triton.edu
KLINGER, John ..... 314-505-7384 252 A
klingerj@csl.edu
KLINGER, Julie ..... 419-434-4589 362 D
julie.klinger@findlay.edu
KLINGLER, Samantha .... 309-298-2457 153 A
sj-klingler@wiu.edu
KLINGSHIRN, Connie ... 419-267-1329 357 E
cklingshirn@northweststate.edu
KLINK, Charles, J ..... 804-828-1244 473 B
cjklink@vcu.edu
KLINKENBERG, Laurel .. 217-641-4500 141 A
lklinkenberg@jwcc.edu
KLINKHAMMER, Barbara ..... 215-951-2899 399 E
barbara.klinkhammer@jefferson.edu
KLIPFEL, India ..... 605-225-1634 415 I
india.klipfel@presentation.edu
KLIPP, Todd L, C ..... 617-353-9550 207 E
tklipp@bu.edu
KLIPPENSTEIN, Stacy, S ..... 928-757-0800.. 14 F
sklippenstein@mohave.edu
KLITZ, Kelly ..... 713-525-6955 454 G
klitzk@stthom.edu
KLOBERDANZ, Jennifer 815-280-2414 141 B
jkloberd@jjc.edu
KLOBERDANZ, Mark ..... 515-271-4526 165 J
mark.kloberdanz@drake.edu
KLOBY, Kathryn ..... 320-308-3151 240 I
kathryn.kloby@stcloudstate.edu
KLOCEK, David ..... 276-376-3445 472 E
dmk8e@uvawise.edu
KLOCEK, Juliana ..... 952-830-3868 242 P
juliana.klocek@rasmussen.edu
KLOCKE, Astrid ..... 928-523-6235.. 14 H
astrid.klocke@nau.edu
KLOCKE, Julie ..... 515-964-6386 165 A
jaklocke1@dmacc.edu
KLOCKO, Tim ..... 816-942-8400 250 F
tim.klocko@avila.edu
KLOEPPEL, Brian ..... 828-227-7398 343 E
bkloeppel@wcu.edu
KLOFT, Craig ..... 563-589-3251 170 G
ckloft@dbq.edu
KLOKE, Rafeeka ..... 360-383-3330 486 A
rkloke@whatcom.edu
KLOMMHAUS, Kylee ..... 641-782-1455 170 F
klommhaus@swcciowa.edu
KLONOFF, Elizabeth ..... 407-823-5538 110 E
elizabeth.klonoff@ucf.edu
KLONOSKI, Edward ..... 860-515-3888.. 85 E
eklonoski@charteroak.edu
KLOOS, Lori ..... 320-308-5026 241 A
lkloos@sctcc.edu
KLOPFER, Dale ..... 419-372-2018 348 G
klopfer@bgsu.edu
KLOPPENBERG, Lisa ..... 408-554-4533.. 63 B
lkloppenberg@scu.edu
KLOPSCH, Vicki, P ..... 909-607-9671.. 63 F
vklopsch@scrippscollege.edu
KLOS, Laura ..... 314-446-8325 260 H
laura.klos@stlcop.edu
KLOS, Ryan ..... 815-455-8562 143 I
rklos@mchenry.edu
KLOSE, Kathryn ..... 240-684-2476 203 E
kathryn.klose@umuc.edu
KLOSS, Michelle ..... 410-386-8411 198 D
mkloss@carrollcc.edu
KLOSTERMANN, Jill ..... 618-545-3081 141 E
jklostermann@kaskaskia.edu
KLOSTERMEYER, William ..... 904-620-1327 111 B
wkloster@unf.edu
KLOTMAN, Mary, E ..... 919-684-2455 328 F
mary.klotman@duke.edu
KLOTMAN, Paul ..... 713-798-4800 431 D
president@bcm.edu
KLOTZ, Ann Marie ..... 303-444-0202.. 82 A
KLOTZ, Kristen ..... 520-621-9181.. 16 D
kbklotz@arizona.edu
KLOTZBACH, Daniel, P . 773-298-3019 149 D
klotzbach@sxu.edu
KLOTZBIER, Ed ..... 209-201-6693.. 70 A
eklotzbier@ucmerced.edu
KLUCK, Annette ..... 662-915-7474 249 D
askluck@olemiss.edu
KLUCK, Ron ..... 402-562-1253 266 A
rkluck@cccneb.edu
KLUCK, Wesley ..... 870-245-5220.. 20 D
kluckw@obu.edu
KLUCKING, Joel ..... 509-963-2323 478 E
joel.klucking@cwu.edu
KLUG, Jane ..... 605-642-6080 416 E
jane.klug@bhsu.edu
KLUG, Theodore, A ..... 507-354-8221 236 J
klugta@mlc-wels.edu
KLUGE, Cindy ..... 414-229-4586 496 B
ckluge@uwm.edu
KLUIN, Richard ..... 605-367-5692 417 B
rich.kluin@southeasttech.edu
KLUNDT, Matthew ..... 319-385-6262 167 H
matt.klundt@iw.edu
KLUNG, Robin ..... 602-489-5300.. 10 F
robin.klung@arizonachristian.edu
KLUTE, Paul ..... 706-425-3183 126 G
pklute@uga.edu
KLUTTZ-LEACH, Camille ..... 617-373-7433 217 I
KLUVER, Erica, L ..... 515-263-2816 166 F
ekluver@grandview.edu
KLUVER, Kirk, R ..... 319-335-2516 163 H
kirk-kluver@uiowa.edu
KLYMENKO, Anthony .... 201-559-6100 277 J
klymenkoa@felician.edu
KLYMENKO, Priscilla ... 201-559-6037 277 J
klymenkop@felician.edu
KLYN, Jeremy ..... 708-239-4854 151 A
jeremy.klyn@trnty.edu
KLYN DE NOVELO, Jessica ..... 641-628-7600 164 D
klynj@central.edu
KLYNE, Dov ..... 718-774-5050 322 B
KMIECH, Joseph ..... 715-425-3658 496 F
joseph.kmiech@uwrf.edu
KNAAPEN, Laura ..... 920-424-2368 496 C
knaapen@uwosh.edu
KNAB, Drew ..... 414-229-3494 496 B
knab@uwm.edu
KNABE, Alexis ..... 907-474-6533.. 10 A
asknabe@alaska.edu
KNABE, Alexis ..... 907-474-2600.. 10 A
asknabe@alaska.edu
KNAFF, Mary ..... 423-697-3371 424 A
mary.knaff@chattanoogastate.edu
KNAP, Andrew ..... 630-617-5682 137 G
andrew.knap@elmhurst.edu
KNAPE, Beth ..... 409-839-2054 449 F
bknape1@lit.edu
KNAPP, Brian, R ..... 517-750-1200 231 C
bknapp@arbor.edu
KNAPP, IV, Clair, W ..... 260-982-5245 159 J
cwknapp@manchester.edu
KNAPP, Jake ..... 916-568-3101.. 50 F
knappj@losrios.edu
KNAPP, Jeffrey ..... 518-458-5374 296 G
knappj@strose.edu
KNAPP, Jennifer ..... 615-353-3117 424 G
jennifer.knapp@nscc.edu
KNAPP, John ..... 724-503-1001 402 B
jknapp@washjeff.edu
KNAPP, Katherine ..... 713-221-5055 453 A
knappk@uhd.edu
KNAPP, Kathy ..... 607-735-1877 298 H
kknapp@elmira.edu
KNAPP, Kenyon ..... 434-582-2697 468 E
kcknapp@liberty.edu
KNAPPER, William ..... 308-635-6002 270 C
knapperw@wncc.edu
KNARR, Rob ..... 513-936-1724 362 A
robert.knarr@uc.edu
KNAUER, Cheryl ..... 410-857-2294 200 F
cknauer@mcdaniel.edu
KNAUS, Kathy ..... 720-890-8922.. 81 I
financial@itea.edu
KNAUS, Kelli ..... 440-646-8316 363 C
kknaus@ursuline.edu
KNAUSS, Tina ..... 712-325-3230 167 I
tknauss@iwcc.edu
KNAUTZ, Arcetta ..... 414-251-5203 496 B
knautz@uwm.edu
KNEALING, Todd ..... 712-279-5402 164 B
todd.knealing@briarcliff.edu
KNECHT, Doug ..... 212-875-4400 290 H
dknecht@bankstreet.edu
KNECHT, James ..... 405-744-9650 367 G
james.knecht@okstate.edu
KNECHT, Mike, W ..... 270-831-9760 182 A
mike.knecht@kctcs.edu
KNEDLER, Jacque ..... 402-280-2166 266 H
jacqueknedler@creighton.edu
KNEEBONE, Elaine ..... 870-230-5820.. 19 D
kneebone@hsu.edu
KNELLY, Kennith ..... 518-564-3622 318 E
kknel001@plattsburgh.edu
KNEPFLE, Chuck ..... 503-725-5249 375 E
knepfle@pdx.edu
KNEPP, Marcia ..... 301-387-3056 199 A
marcia.knepp@garrettcollege.edu
KNEPPE, Janiece ..... 303-914-6553.. 83 C
janiece.kneppe@rrcc.edu
KNEPPER, Karla ..... 937-512-4561 360 G
karla.knepper@sinclair.edu
KNERR, Amanda ..... 812-237-3993 156 D
amanda.knerr@indstate.edu
KNERR, Christopher ..... 413-565-1000 206 D
cknerr@baypath.edu
KNESER, Greg ..... 419-824-3759 355 C
gkneser@lourdes.edu
KNETL, Brian ..... 616-234-4000 224 F
KNETSCHE, Kelly ..... 859-238-5500 180 B
kelly.knetsche@centre.edu
KNETTER, Michael, M ... 608-265-9953 495 D
mike.knetter@supportuw.org
KNEUPPER, Julie ..... 210-431-6584 441 B
jkneupper@ollusa.edu
KNEUVEAN, Shelley ..... 785-594-8347 171 F
KNICELEY, Allen ..... 704-669-4037 333 E
kniceleya@clevelandcc.edu
KNICELY, Leah, M ..... 304-457-6242 486 E
knicelylm@ab.edu
KNIERIM, Maria-Louisa 314-529-9330 255 B
mknierim@maryville.edu
KNIEWEL, Marla ..... 402-354-7036 268 B
marla.kniewel@methodistcollege.edu
KNIFE, Christopher ..... 352-873-5808.. 97 N
knifec@cf.edu
KNIFFEN, Robyn ..... 402-399-2435 266 F
rkniffen@csm.edu
KNIFFIN, Mary ..... 513-745-4275 364 G
kniffinm@xavier.edu
KNIGGE, Dalynn ..... 732-584-6365 282 A
knigge@rutgers.edu
KNIGGE, Dalynn ..... 732-412-7397 281 G
knigge@rutgers.edu
KNIGGE, Dalynn ..... 732-584-6365 282 B
knigge@rutgers.edu
KNIGGE, David ..... 605-626-2537 416 G
david.knigge@northern.edu
KNIGHT, Aaron ..... 281-922-3403 443 C
aaron.knight@sjcd.edu
KNIGHT, Alexis ..... 985-448-7939 188 C
alexis.knight@fletcher.edu
KNIGHT, Allison, P ..... 757-446-5255 466 D
knightap@evms.edu
KNIGHT, Antonia ..... 716-286-8204 309 H
abk@niagara.edu
KNIGHT, Ashley ..... 773-325-4852 136 H
aknight@depaul.edu
KNIGHT, Aubrey, L ..... 815-740-5047 152 H
aknight@stfrancis.edu
KNIGHT, Bobbie ..... 205-929-1428.... 6 B
bknight@miles.edu
KNIGHT, Brenda ..... 239-489-9056 101 A
bknight3@fsw.edu
KNIGHT, Cindi ..... 304-647-6299 490 C
cknight@osteo.wvsom.edu
KNIGHT, Cynthia ..... 985-545-1500 188 E
KNIGHT, Danita ..... 404-471-6000 114 G
dknight@agnesscott.edu
KNIGHT, Darryl ..... 847-925-6675 138 G
dknight@harpercollege.edu
KNIGHT, Derric ..... 906-635-6244 226 G
dknight@lssu.edu
KNIGHT, Gabe ..... 563-244-7021 165 L
gknight@eicc.edu
KNIGHT, Gary, E ..... 803-705-4559 406 G
gary.knight@benedict.edu
KNIGHT, Gina, R ..... 252-335-4822 341 B
grknight@ecsu.edu
KNIGHT, Jack ..... 540-568-5242 468 C
knigh2jf@jmu.edu
KNIGHT, Jaime ..... 508-531-2337 212 D
j2knight@bridgew.edu
KNIGHT, James ..... 828-689-1122 331 C
jknight@mhu.edu
KNIGHT, John, C ..... 423-585-6882 425 F
john.knight@ws.edu
KNIGHT, Joseph ..... 601-484-8779 247 A
jknight5@meridiancc.edu
KNIGHT, Lance ..... 404-364-8542 123 K
lknight@oglethorpe.edu
KNIGHT, Leonard ..... 760-245-4271.. 74 D
leonard.knight@vvc.edu
KNIGHT, Patricia ..... 757-727-5447 467 G
patricia.knight@hamptonu.edu
KNIGHT, Sandra ..... 857-701-1290 215 G
sknight@rcc.mass.edu
KNIGHT, Saskia ..... 949-753-4774.. 71 D
KNIGHT, Stephanie ..... 352-638-9730.. 96 B
sknight@beaconcollege.edu

KNIGHT, Stephanie, L .. 214-768-4242 444 D
slknight@smu.edu

KNIGHT, Tamara .... 804-751-9191 465 K
tknight@ccc-va.com

KNIGHT, Tim .... 870-245-5528.. 20 D
knightt@obu.edu

KNIGHT, Tirzah .... 918-335-6252 368 E
tknight@okwu.edu

KNIGHT, TR .... 765-998-4902 161 C
tr.knight@taylor.edu

KNIGHT, Tracey .... 870-245-5401.. 20 D
knightte@obu.edu

KNIGHT, Victoria .... 573-592-5245 262 E
victoria.knight@westminster-mo.edu

KNIGHT, Wendy, S .... 844-642-2338 169 A
knightw@nicc.edu

KNIGHT, Wesley .... 573-288-6420 252 F
wknight@culver.edu

KNIGHT, William, E ...... 513-529-1660 356 A
knightw3@miamioh.edu

KNIGHTON, Denise .... 662-915-7792 249 D
denisek@olemiss.edu

KNIGHTON, Diana .... 205-929-1442.... 6 B
dknighton@miles.edu

KNIGHTON, Jeffery .... 678-359-5018 120 F
jknighton@gordonstate.edu

KNIGHTON, JR.,
Lewis, J .... 864-656-3184 407 E
knightl@clemson.edu

KNIGHTS, Chad .... 703-323-3387 474 F
cknights@nvcc.edu

KNIGHTS, John, E .... 407-582-5197 113 I
jknights@valenciacollege.edu

KNILEY, Mary Lynne .... 585-582-8317 298 F
marykniley@elim.edu

KNIPE, Mike .... 612-343-3541 242 M
mjknipe@northcentral.edu

KNIPFEL, Shirley, J ...... 515-294-1781 163 G
sknipfel@iastate.edu

KNIPPEL, Dianne .... 661-722-6300.. 26 A
dknippel@avc.edu

KNISLEY, Emilia .... 513-875-3344 350 C
emilia.knisley@chatfield.edu

KNISLEY, Joel .... 828-232-5121 342 B
jknisley@unca.edu

KNISLEY, Patrick .... 212-217-4320 299 D
patrick_knisley@fitnyc.edu

KNISPEL, Todd .... 620-432-0384 176 D
tknispel@neosho.edu

KNISS, Fred, L .... 540-432-4105 466 B
fred.kniss@emu.edu

KNISS, Rob .... 901-678-4825 426 G
rskniss@memphis.edu

KNITIG, Sherri .... 785-890-3641 176 H
sherri.knitig@nwktc.edu

KNOBBE, Amy .... 402-481-8847 265 K
amy.knobbe@bryanhealthcollege.edu

KNOBLICH, Julie .... 620-792-9275 171 I
knoblichj@bartonccc.edu

KNODEL, Becky .... 701-252-3467 347 B
bknodel@uj.edu

KNODLE-BRAGIEL, Lisa 503-883-2214 373 F
lbragiel@linfield.edu

KNOEPPEL, Robert, C ... 813-974-3400 111 C
rkc3@usf.edu

KNOETTGEN, Amber ..... 785-243-1435 172 L
aknoettgen@cloud.edu

KNOETTGEN, Suzi .... 785-243-1435 172 L
sknoettgen@cloud.edu

KNOLL, Eric .... 314-446-8375 260 H
eric.knoll@stlcop.edu

KNOLL, Joseph .... 617-824-8112 209 C
joseph_knoll@emerson.edu

KNOLL, Molly, H .... 641-422-4404 168 G
knollmol@niacc.edu

KNOLL-FINN, MJ .... 212-998-4553 309 F
mjknollfinn@nyu.edu

KNOLLE, Jon .... 831-646-3030.. 52 G
jknolle@mpc.edu

KNOLLENBERG, Dustin . 217-234-5253 142 C
dknollenberg@lakelandcollege.edu

KNOLTON, Cristina, C .. 213-738-5774.. 66 B
cknolton@swlaw.edu

KNOOR, Robert .... 616-957-6039 222 B
rknoor@calvinseminary.edu

KNOP, Joachim, W .... 202-994-6506.. 92 D
knop@gwu.edu

KNOPF, Lydia .... 714-879-3901.. 45 G
lknopf@hiu.edu

KNORR, Dan .... 570-389-4655 393 D
dknorr@bloomu.edu

KNOTT, Betsy .... 740-376-4480 355 E
emk004@marietta.edu

KNOTT, Blythe .... 503-768-7296 373 E
blythe@lclark.edu

KNOTT, Catherine .... 812-866-7087 155 G
knott@hanover.edu

KNOTT, Dana .... 937-769-1881 347 H
dknott@antioch.edu

KNOTT, Gail .... 308-535-3605 267 J
knottg@mpcc.edu

KNOTT, Greg .... 217-333-9334 151 F
gknott63@uillinois.edu

KNOTT, Gregory .... 217-333-9334 152 B
gknott63@uillinois.edu

KNOTT, Kevin .... 217-351-2239 147 C
kknott@parkland.edu

KNOTT, Teresa, L .... 804-828-0634 473 B
tlknott@vcu.edu

KNOTTS, Brad .... 812-749-1215 159 O
bknotts@oak.edu

KNOTTS, Chantaye .... 256-469-7333.... 5 H
deaninst@hbc1.edu

KNOTTS, Debby .... 505-277-9000 288 J
debby@unm.edu

KNOTTS, Gibbs .... 843-953-6792 408 C
knottshg@cofc.edu

KNOTTS, Joshua .... 801-618-0438 458 G
jknotts@ameritech.edu

KNOUSE, Christine .... 717-262-2016 403 C
cknouse@wilson.edu

KNOWLES, Ann .... 864-522-2000 409 H
ann.knowles@prismahealth.org

KNOWLES, Bill .... 405-382-9272 369 F
b.knowles@sscok.edu

KNOWLES, Harley .... 423-746-5201 426 C
hknowles@tnwesleyan.edu

KNOWLES, James, M ... 409-984-6432 449 I
knowlejm@lamarpa.edu

KNOWLES, Matteel .... 864-250-8177 409 I
matteel.knowles@gvltec.edu

KNOWLES, Melody, D .. 703-370-6600 476 E

KNOWLES, Monica .... 360-992-2904 478 I
mknowles@clark.edu

KNOWLES, Sada .... 405-425-5803 367 C
sada.knowles@oc.edu

KNOWLES, Tamece .... 305-348-7882 110 A
knowles@fiu.edu

KNOWLTON, Eloise .... 508-767-7487 206 A
eknowlton@assumption.edu

KNOWLTON, James ...... 510-642-5316.. 69 A
athletic.director@berkeley.edu

KNOX, Brenda .... 918-610-0027 365 I
bknox@communitycarecollege.edu

KNOX, Cecilia .... 301-546-1580 201 E
knoxca@pgcc.edu

KNOX, Craig .... 850-201-8660 112 C

KNOX, Danny .... 859-233-8287 185 C
dknox@transy.edu

KNOX, George .... 919-546-8527 340 B
george.knox@shawu.edu

KNOX, Jan .... 336-334-4822 335 A
jhknox@gtcc.edu

KNOX, Linda, B .... 219-989-3169 160 D
lbknox@pnw.edu

KNOX, Lindsay .... 503-554-2242 373 A
lknox@georgefox.edu

KNOX, Lindsay .... 503-538-8383 373 A

KNOX, Lisa .... 574-284-5318 160 I
lknox@saintmarys.edu

KNOX, Michael, J .... 806-651-2050 448 B
mknox@wtamu.edu

KNOX, Ryan .... 309-248-8189 138 H
ryan.knox@heartland.edu

KNOX, Tracey .... 970-521-6643.. 82 C
tracey.knox@njc.edu

KNOX, Wayne .... 512-505-3003 438 A
wknox@htu.edu

KNUCKLES, Jill .... 970-248-1426.. 78 J
jknuckle@coloradomesa.edu

KNUCKLES, Leator .... 410-238-9000.. 93 H

KNUDSEN, J. Todd .... 315-568-3146 310 B
tknudsen@nycc.edu

KNUDSEN, Jeffrey .... 802-831-1285 463 C
jknudsen@vermontlaw.edu

KNUDSEN, Ross .... 208-376-7731 130 G
rknudsen@boisebible.edu

KNUDSON, Chris .... 319-352-8580 170 J
chris.knudson@wartburg.edu

KNUDSON, Edward, T .. 661-722-6300.. 26 A
eknudson@avc.edu

KNUDSON, Kari .... 701-224-5604 346 A
kari.l.knudson@bismarckstate.edu

KNUDTSON, Matt .... 573-642-3361 262 E

KNUPPEL, Lisa .... 714-432-5575.. 38 B
lknuppel@occ.cccd.edu

KNUREK, Charles .... 860-253-3037.. 86 C
cknurek@asnuntuck.edu

KNUST, Alyse .... 217-424-3769 144 G
aknust@millikin.edu

KNUTEL, Phillip .... 781-239-4225 206 B
pknutel@babson.edu

KNUTH, Doug .... 775-784-6900 271 E
dknuth@unr.edu

KNUTH, Julie, J .... 260-982-5214 159 J
jjknuth@manchester.edu

KNUTSEN, Mark .... 423-697-4785 424 A
mark.knutsen@chattanoogastate.edu

KNUTSON, Jennifer .... 605-331-6611 417 C
jennifer.knutson@usiouxfalls.edu

KNUTSON, Jonathan ..... 218-855-8027 237 G
jonathan.knutson@clcmn.edu

KNUTSON, Karen .... 320-363-5922 235 F
kknutson@csbsju.edu

KNUTSON, Ryan .... 406-994-4545 264 C
ryan.knutson2@montana.edu

KNUTSON, Stephanie .... 608-789-6083 500 C
knutsons@westerntc.edu

KNUTSON, Todd .... 605-331-6813 417 C
todd.knutson@usiouxfalls.edu

KNYSAK, Elsa .... 414-955-4516 493 F
eknysak@mcw.edu

KO, Jeanne .... 212-472-1500 309 D
jeanne.ko@nysid.edu

KO, Kristina .... 202-554-0578 231 H
kdko@umich.edu

KO, Lester, D .... 717-245-1102 382 D
kole@dickinson.edu

KO, Shinsaeng .... 404-727-0825 118 E
shinsaeng.ko@emory.edu

KO, Yoo, K .... 571-730-4750 256 B
wdc@midwest.edu

KOAN, Mark .... 480-731-8895.. 12 N
mark.koan@domail.maricopa.edu

KOBALLA, JR.,
Thomas, R .... 678-547-6333 122 E
koballa_tr@mercer.edu

KOBAYASHI, Frank .... 916-484-8202.. 50 G
kobayaf@arc.losrios.edu

KOBERNUSZ, Bob .... 605-995-7128 415 E
bob.kobernusz@mitchelltech.edu

KOBES, Patricia .... 845-574-4280 312 H
pkobes@sunyrockland.edu

KOBETZ, Erin .... 305-243-6185 113 C
ekobetz@miami.edu

KOBLE, Sonya .... 701-224-5434 346 A
sonya.koble@bismarckstate.edu

KOBLER, Soheila .... 973-618-3724 276 D
skobler@caldwell.edu

KOBLER, Wendy .... 607-274-3115 302 G
wkobler@ithaca.edu

KOBMAN, Lisa .... 513-244-4979 356 F
lisa.kobman@msj.edu

KOBOLAKIS, Evan .... 516-876-3379 318 C
kobolakise@oldwestbury.edu

KOBRINSKY, Natasha ... 310-665-6837.. 55 C
nkobrinsky@otis.edu

KOBUS, Gloria .... 404-894-9396 119 E
gloria.kobus@business.gatech.edu

KOBUS, James .... 641-673-1046 171 C
james.kobus@wmpenn.edu

KOBYELSKI, Kammie .... 928-776-2032.. 16 J
kammie.kobyelski@yc.edu

KOBYLSKI, Gerald .... 845-938-5608 503 I
gerald.kobylski@westpoint.edu

KOBYLSKI, Janet .... 570-208-5900 386 G
janetkobylski@kings.edu

KOCAK, Taskin .... 504-280-4384 190 B
tkocak@uno.edu

KOCER, Ken .... 605-668-1589 415 F
kkocer@mountmarty.edu

KOCH, Amy .... 317-955-6021 159 K
akoch@marian.edu

KOCH, Bill .... 252-328-6166 341 A
kochb@ecu.edu

KOCH, Brad .... 610-328-8325 398 G
bkoch2@swarthmore.edu

KOCH, Bradley .... 610-902-8571 379 G
bradley.r.koch@cabrini.edu

KOCH, Colleen .... 352-273-7500 111 A
kochc@ufl.edu

KOCH, Don .... 618-634-3289 149 G
donk@shawneecc.edu

KOCH, Doug .... 573-651-2207 259 H
dskoch@semo.edu

KOCH, Erec .... 212-650-8166 293 D
ekoch1@ccny.cuny.edu

KOCH, Jiang Fei .... 503-338-2522 372 D
amclean@clatsopcc.edu

KOCH, Jo Ann .... 770-216-2960 121 I
jkoch@ict.edu

KOCH, John .... 607-777-6757 316 B
jkoch@binghamton.edu

KOCH, Jon .... 262-691-5227 500 B
jkoch18@wctc.edu

KOCH, Kathie .... 312-369-7436 136 D
kkoch@colum.edu

KOCH, Kevin .... 781-762-1211 209 F
kkoch@fmc.edu

KOCH, Matthew .... 919-890-7500.. 93 H

KOCH, Nicole .... 801-333-8100 459 D
nicole.koch@eaglegatecollege.edu

KOCH, Paul .... 563-333-6212 169 G
kochpaulc@sau.edu

KOCH, Paul .... 831-459-2931.. 71 A
plkoch@ucsc.edu

KOCH, Sheena .... 270-707-3921 182 B
bkshopkinsville@bncollege.com

KOCH, Thomas, L .... 520-621-2448.. 16 D
tlkoch@arizona.edu

KOCHAN, Roman .... 562-985-4047.. 31 D
roman.kochan@csulb.edu

KOCHER, Andrew .... 317-788-3493 161 H
akocher@uindy.edu

KOCHER, Craig, T .... 804-289-8500 472 C
ckocher@richmond.edu

KOCHER, Rebecca .... 937-327-7426 364 D
kocherr@wittenberg.edu

KOCHEVAR, Brenda ...... 218-749-0314 238 H
b.kochevar@mesabirange.edu

KOCHIS, Brad, A .... 740-392-6868 356 G
brad.kochis@mvnu.edu

KOCHIS, Stephen, J ...... 845-575-3000 305 D
stephen.kochis@marist.edu

KOCHMAN, Laura .... 215-965-4000 390 E

KOCHUBA, Sara .... 724-503-1001 402 B
skochuba@washjeff.edu

KOCIAN, Bryce .... 979-532-6315 458 E
brycek@wcjc.edu

KOCIAN, Justin .... 402-494-2311 268 A
jkocian@thenicc.edu

KOCIELA, Ryan .... 724-772-5520 379 E
ryan.kociela@bc3.edu

KOCIK, Piotr .... 718-518-6610 294 B
pkocik@hostos.cuny.edu

KOCIOLEK, Patrick .... 303-492-8464.. 84 B
patrick.kociolek@colorado.edu

KOCOUR, Bruce .... 865-471-3240 418 E
bkocour@cn.edu

KOCSIS, Katie, L .... 716-286-8669 309 H
kkocsis@niagara.edu

KOCZERA, Cris .... 707-826-5711.. 33 C
cej32@humboldt.edu

KODAT, Catherine .... 920-832-6528 493 B
catherine.g.kodat@lawrence.edu

KODJO, Jilou .... 770-559-0580 124 A

KOEGL, Evan, S .... 516-463-8000 301 G
evan.koegl@hofstra.edu

KOEGLER, Jason, W ..... 304-336-8302 490 B
jkoegler@westliberty.edu

KOEHLER, Christi .... 972-686-7878 442 B

KOEHLER, David .... 308-635-6021 270 C
koehlerd@wncc.edu

KOEHLER, Laurie .... 607-274-1555 302 G
lkoehler@ithaca.edu

KOEHLER, Martha Kaye 813-253-7007 102 B
mkoehler@hccfl.edu

KOEHLER, R. Brien .... 262-646-6545 494 F
rkoehler@nashotah.edu

KOEHLER, Rachael .... 641-844-5708 167 G
rachael.koehler@iavalley.edu

KOEHN, Michelle .... 316-226-2002 163 C
michelle.koehn@allencollege.edu

KOEHNEKE, Mary, A ...... 716-888-2300 292 F
mkoehneke@canisius.edu

KOELLER, Martin, E ...... 973-761-9782 283 C
martin.koeller@shu.edu

KOELTZOW, Dawn .... 309-677-2510 134 A
dkoeltzow@fsmail.bradley.edu

KOENECKE, David .... 660-626-2410 250 A
dkoenecke@atsu.edu

KOENEN, Gary .... 414-930-3534 494 E
koeneng@mtmary.edu

KOENIG, Deanna .... 612-659-6509 239 A
deanna.koenig@minneapolis.edu.edu

KOENIG, Jason, T .... 864-833-8490 411 D
jtkoenig@presby.edu

KOENIG, Linda .... 740-351-3655 360 F
lkoenig@shawnee.edu

KOENIG, Richard .... 509-335-4561 485 D
richk@wsu.edu

KOPP, David .... 305-899-3708.. 96 A
dkopp@barry.edu
KOPP, Nikki .... 715-675-3331 499 F
kopp@ntc.edu
KOPP, Sacha, E .... 402-554-2907 270 A
sacha.kopp@unomaha.edu
KOPP, Sonya .... 251-981-3771.... 5 A
sonya.kopp@columbiasouthern.edu
KOPP, Will, E .... 740-368-3108 359 G
wekopp@owu.edu
KOPP-MILLER, Barbara . 419-530-4488 363 B
barbara.kopp-miller@utoledo.edu
KOPPEL, Michael .... 202-885-8610.. 94 D
mkoppel@wesleyseminary.edu
KOPPELL, Jonathan ...... 973-655-4212 279 B
koppellj@montclair.edu
KOPPEN, Jason .... 928-774-3890.. 12 L
jkoppen@indianbible.org
KOPPI, Stefan .... 508-831-5260 220 F
skoppi@wpi.edu
KOPPISCH, Andrew .... 928-523-8893.. 14 H
andy.koppisch@nau.edu
KOPPY, Katie .... 320-625-5114 240 D
katie.koppy@pine.edu
KOPROWSKI, John .... 307-766-1121 501 I
KOPS, Christopher, P ... 414-955-8704 493 F
ckops@mcw.edu
KOPSTAIN, Eric .... 615-875-8617 428 A
eric.kopstain@vanderbilt.edu
KORALESKY, Barron ...... 413-597-3072 220 D
barron.koralesky@williams.edu
KORB, Kristi .... 417-667-8181 252 B
kkorb@cottey.edu
KORB-NICE, Jobe, S ...... 206-281-2564 483 G
jobe@spu.edu
KORBEL, Linda .... 847-635-1952 146 G
lkorbel@oakton.edu
KORBER, William .... 787-622-8000 511 D
jdavila@pupr.edu
KORD, JoLanna .... 620-341-6829 173 F
jkord@emporia.edu
KORDEK, Nicholas, M .. 315-655-7230 292 H
nmkordek@cazenovia.edu
KORDENBROCK,
William, R .... 906-487-2200 228 A
billk@mtu.edu
KORDSMEIER,
Gregory, T .... 812-941-2860 157 F
gkordsme@ius.edu
KORENEK, Rebecca .... 409-747-2210 456 E
bbkorene@utmb.edu
KORETOFF, Lisa, A .... 336-334-4822 335 A
lakoretoff@gtcc.edu
KORETSKY, Carla, M ..... 269-387-4360 233 B
carla.koretsky@wmich.edu
KORF, Abraham .... 305-673-5664 114 E
KORF, Benzion .... 305-653-8770 114 E
bkorf@lecfl.com
KORFF, Zamira .... 781-736-4047 208 A
zkorff@brandeis.edu
KORGAN, Kate, H .... 702-895-0446 271 D
kate.korgan@unlv.edu
KORINKE, Kim .... 805-378-1463.. 73 J
kkorinke@vcccd.edu
KORIR, Albert .... 417-873-7509 252 G
akorir@drury.edu
KORITARI, Andi .... 312-261-3317 145 D
andi.koritari@nl.edu
KORKLAN, Michael .... 816-604-1000 255 H
michael.korklan@mcckc.edu
KORMAN, Caryn .... 312-996-7125 151 G
caryn1@uic.edu
KORMAN, Thomas, P ... 517-750-1200 231 C
tkorman@arbor.edu
KORMANAK, Steve .... 608-757-7766 498 D
skormanak@blackhawk.edu
KORN, Megan .... 918-595-7846 370 C
megan.korn@tulsacc.edu
KORN, Randi .... 617-349-8596 211 C
lijiri@lesley.edu
KORNACKI, Kelly .... 414-425-8300 495 A
kkornacki@shsst.edu
KORNBERG, Mindy .... 206-685-4730 485 A
mindyk@uw.edu
KORNBLUH, Mark .... 313-577-2200 232 K
kornbluh@wayne.edu
KORNBLUTH, Jerry .... 516-572-7775 307 E
jerry.kornbluth@ncc.edu
KORNBLUTH, Sally .... 919-684-2631 328 F
sally.kornbluth@duke.edu
KORNEGAY, Joy .... 919-739-7091 338 H
jmkornegay@waynecc.edu
KORNER, Christoph ...... 818-394-3325.. 76 E
christoph.korner@woodbury.edu
KORNFELD, Julie .... 212-854-2691 297 C
jk3924@columbia.edu
KORNFUEHRER, Dana ... 512-313-3000 433 N
dana.kornfuehrer@concordia.edu
KORNGIEBEL, Aaron ..... 206-934-4532 483 B
aaron.korngiebel@seattlecolleges.edu
KORNKVEN, Kelly, J .... 701-788-4816 345 D
kelly.kornkven@mayvillestate.edu
KORNS, Linda .... 409-839-2022 449 F
ldkorns@lit.edu
KORNUTA, Halyna .... 310-204-1666.. 58 K
KORNWEIBEL, Karen, R 423-439-7881 419 G
kornweib@etsu.edu
KORONKIEWICZ, Talia .. 815-455-8584 143 I
tkoronkiewicz@mchenry.edu
KOROS, Shadrack .... 678-422-4100.. 93 H
KORPELA, Doreen .... 906-487-7201 224 B
doreen.korpela@finlandia.edu
KORSCHINOWSKI,
Claire .... 253-589-5516 478 J
claire.korschinowski@cptc.edu
KORST, Summer .... 206-878-3710 481 B
skorst@highline.edu
KORSTAD, John .... 918-495-6942 368 F
jkorstad@oru.edu
KORTA, Allison .... 716-614-6231 309 G
akorta@niagaracc.suny.edu
KORTCAMP, Bryan .... 661-259-3540.. 51 D
KORTE, Andrea .... 910-695-3767 337 H
kortea@sandhills.edu
KORTH, Niki .... 415-771-7020.. 61 C
nkorth@sfai.edu
KORTOKRAX, Sandy ..... 419-995-8200 360 C
kortokrax.s@rhodesstate.edu
KORUS, Daniel .... 361-698-1065 435 G
dkorus@delmar.edu
KORVER, Bill .... 910-323-5614 327 F
president@ccbs.edu
KORVICK, Lynn .... 479-788-7830.. 21 G
lynn.korvick@uafs.edu
KORZENDORFER, Kate .. 781-768-7340 218 D
kate.korzendorfer@regiscollege.edu
KOSAKA, Timothy .... 817-202-6628 444 I
tim@swau.edu
KOSAKOWSKI, Sheryl ... 413-565-1000 206 D
skosakowski@baypath.edu
KOSARUE, Lori .... 517-264-5161 220 G
lkosarue@adrian.edu
KOSARUE, Lori .... 517-264-7132 230 H
lshearer@sienaheights.edu
KOSBOTH, Michele .... 440-775-6392 357 G
mkosboth@oberlin.edu
KOSCHMEDER,
Douglas, D .... 319-352-8761 170 J
doug.koschmeder@wartburg.edu
KOSCHWANEZ, Jeanne . 760-795-6840.. 52 F
jkoschwanez@miracosta.edu
KOSCIW, Dennis .... 850-718-2244.. 97 E
kosciwd@chipola.edu
KOSER, Ashley .... 570-484-2128 394 E
amk718@lockhaven.edu
KOSHI, Deanne .... 808-245-8226 130 B
deannesy@hawaii.edu
KOSHI-LUM, Jessica ...... 425-235-2352 482 H
KOSHLAND, Cathy .... 510-643-7384.. 69 A
ckoshland@berkeley.edu
KOSHMIDER, III,
John, W .... 330-471-8326 355 D
jkoshmider@malone.edu
KOSHORK, Lori .... 206-726-5027 479 E
lkoshork@cornish.edu
KOSHUT, Thomas, M ... 256-824-6100.... 8 B
tom.koshut@uah.edu
KOSIEK, Timothy, J ...... 708-709-3702 147 D
tkosiek@prairiestate.edu
KOSIK, Jamie, F .... 304-293-7202 490 E
jamie.kosik@mail.wvu.edu
KOSINA, Joseph .... 631-451-4881 321 C
kosinaj@sunysuffolk.edu
KOSINE, Brandon .... 307-268-2550 500 U
bkosine@caspercollege.edu
KOSINSKI, Mark .... 203-285-2077.. 86 E
mkosinski@gatewayct.edu
KOSINSKI, Ross, J .... 630-515-6470 144 F
rkosin@midwestern.edu
KOSINSKY, James, A .... 708-209-3519 136 E
jim.kosinsky@cuchicago.edu
KOSKI, Janet .... 906-227-2420 228 I
jakoski@nmu.edu
KOSKI, Lynne .... 308-635-6792 270 C
koskil1@wncc.edu
KOSKI, Mary .... 309-794-7208 133 C
marykoski@augustana.edu
KOSKI, Pat .... 479-575-5900.. 21 F
pkoski@uark.edu
KOSKOFF, Max .... 607-871-2601 290 B
koskoff@alfred.edu
KOSKY, John .... 434-924-5948 472 D
jak3fa@virginia.edu
KOSKY, Kristy .... 740-695-9500 348 E
kkosky@belmontcollege.edu
KOSLOSKY, Jill .... 307-637-1154 501 E
jkoslosk@lccc.wy.edu
KOSLOW MARTIN, Jodi 708-456-0300 151 D
jodikoslowmartin@triton.edu
KOSMOSKI, Kathleen .... 912-486-7409 123 J
kkosmoski@ogeecheetech.edu
KOSOBUCKI, Dave .... 858-695-8587 156 B
dkosobucki@horizonuniversity.edu
KOSS, Kim .... 706-721-0140 116 A
kkoss@augusta.edu
KOSS, Michelle .... 586-286-2172 227 B
kossm26@macomb.edu
KOSS, Susan .... 217-443-8814 136 G
skoss@dacc.edu
KOSSE, Glenn, F .... 502-272-8328 179 H
gkosse@bellarmine.edu
KOSSO, Cynthia .... 610-861-1348 390 F
kossoc@moravian.edu
KOST, Patricia, L .... 216-368-2165 349 D
patricia.kost@case.edu
KOSTECKI, David .... 808-356-5256 128 G
dkostecki@hpu.edu
KOSTECKI, James .... 630-942-3821 135 I
kosteckij@cod.edu
KOSTELIS, Kimberly ...... 860-832-2228.. 85 G
kimberly.kostelis@ccsu.edu
KOSTEN, Linda .... 303-871-7922.. 84 E
linda.kosten@du.edu
KOSTER, Ed .... 402-761-8224 269 C
ekoster@southeast.edu
KOSTER, Jill .... 785-833-4332 175 E
jill.koster@kwu.edu
KOSTIC, Jennifer .... 937-512-4191 360 G
jennifer.kostic@sinclair.edu
KOSTIC, Ljubisa .... 619-388-6591.. 60 H
lkostic@sdccd.edu
KOSTIHOVA, Marcela .... 651-523-2252 236 B
mkostihova01@hamline.edu
KOSTJUK, Todd .... 661-362-2734.. 51 D
tkostjuk@masters.edu
KOSTRZEWSKI, Diana ... 701-777-4354 345 B
diana.kostrzewski@und.edu
KOSTYUKOV, Victoria ... 718-522-9073 290 E
vkostyukov@asa.edu
KOT, Valerie .... 832-813-6809 439 C
valerie.a.kot@lonestar.edu
KOTAKIS, Paul .... 978-921-4242 217 B
paul.kotakis@montserrat.edu
KOTCAMP, Butch .... 740-351-3429 360 F
bkotcamp@shawnee.edu
KOTCH, Amanda .... 618-842-3711 139 F
kotcha@iecc.edu
KOTECKI, Kathy .... 406-657-1660 264 D
kkotecki@msubillings.edu
KOTH, Jason .... 212-592-2259 315 C
jkoth@sva.edu
KOTH, Kent .... 206-296-2329 484 A
kothk@seattleu.edu
KOTHANDARAMAN,
Prabakar .... 315-312-3168 318 D
pk@oswego.edu
KOTHMANN, Angie .... 228-493-5300 248 E
akothmann@prcc.edu
KOTIW, Karen .... 864-250-8856 409 I
karen.kotiw@gvltec.edu
KOTLAS, Maureen .... 301-405-3960 202 H
mkotlas@umd.edu
KOTLER, A. Malkiel ...... 732-367-1060 275 K
KOTLER, Aaron .... 732-367-1060 275 K
akotler@bmg.edu
KOTLER, Yitzchok, S ..... 732-367-1060 275 K
KOTLIKOFF, Michael, I . 607-255-2364 297 F
provost@cornell.edu
KOTLINSKI, Michael, J . 717-337-6363 384 D
mkotlinski@gettysburg.edu
KOTOISUVA, Agnes ...... 692-625-3394 504 G
KOTOKLO, Mireille .... 541-440-4600 376 G
mireille.kotoklo@umpqua.edu
KOTORI, Chiaki .... 570-321-4029 389 B
kotori@lycoming.edu
KOTOWICZ, Keith, A ..... 414-847-3301 494 C
keithkotowicz@miad.edu
KOTOWSKI, Amy .... 516-364-0808 308 D
akotowski@nycollege.edu
KOTOWSKI, Kelli .... 740-597-1819 358 K
kotowskk@ohio.edu
KOTT, Elijah .... 517-321-0242 225 A
elkott@glcc.edu
KOTT, Micheal .... 708-656-8000 145 C
micheal.kott@morton.edu
KOTTAS, Kathy .... 620-786-1107 171 I
kottask@bartonccc.edu
KOTTENSTETTE, Kathy ... 970-675-3237.. 79 H
kathy.kottenstette@cncc.edu
KOTTER, David .... 303-963-3336.. 78 H
dkotter@ccu.edu
KOTTICH, Sarah .... 402-399-2427 266 F
skottich@csm.edu
KOTTON, Stevenson ...... 692-625-3394 504 G
skotton@cmi.edu
KOTTRE, Chris .... 805-581-1233.. 41 I
ckottre@eternitybiblecollege.com
KOTULA, Nadia .... 813-258-6151 102 B
nkotula@hccfl.edu
KOTWICKI, Lee .... 941-363-7218 109 G
kotwicl@scf.edu
KOTZ, David, F .... 603-646-2404 273 D
david.f.kotz@dartmouth.edu
KOTZ, Kim .... 716-896-0700 324 E
kkotz@villa.edu
KOUA, Deb .... 515-965-7025 165 A
dkkoua@dmacc.edu
KOUANCHAO, Ketmani . 626-585-7560.. 56 D
kkouanchao@pasadena.edu
KOUBA, Mary Beth .... 325-670-1679 436 I
marybeth.kouba@hsutx.edu
KOUBEK, Richard, J ..... 906-487-2200 228 A
koubek@mtu.edu
KOUGH, Katherine .... 717-262-2006 403 C
kkough@wilson.edu
KOUKOL, June .... 617-333-2091 208 G
jkoukol@curry.edu
KOULIK, Chet .... 845-451-1347 297 G
chet.koulik@culinary.edu
KOULOS, Elleni, R .... 909-448-4178.. 71 C
ekoulos@laverne.edu
KOULTOURIDES, Libby . 574-284-4581 160 I
lgray@saintmarys.edu
KOUMAS, Sokratis .... 508-999-8859 212 A
skoumas@umassd.edu
KOUREMETIS, Michael .. 617-731-3500 210 G
KOURINIAN, Christine .. 818-364-7685.. 49 C
kourinhc@laccd.edu
KOUROPOVA, Patricia .. 213-427-2200.. 35 F
KOURY, Regina .... 856-225-2828 281 G
regina.koury@rutgers.edu
KOUTSIDIS, Anastasia .. 718-997-4443 295 B
anastasia.koutsidis@qc.cuny.edu
KOVAC, Celia .... 540-458-8794 477 D
ckovac@wlu.edu
KOVAC, Jason .... 503-594-3390 372 C
jason.kovac@clackamas.edu
KOVAC, Matt .... 724-287-8711 379 E
matt.kovac@bc3.edu
KOVACH, Jacalyn, E ..... 330-325-6369 357 D
jkovach1@neomed.edu
KOVACICH, Christine, L 330-325-6551 357 D
ckovacich@neomed.edu
KOVACS, Andrea, E .... 203-773-8550.. 85 D
KOVACS, Anita .... 850-484-1728 105 H
akovacs@pensacolastate.edu
KOVACS, Charles .... 941-359-7650 106 J
ckovacs@ringling.edu
KOVACS, Edward .... 610-526-6080 385 D
ekovacs@harcum.edu
KOVACS, Gene .... 850-245-0466 109 H
gene.kovacs@flbog.edu
KOVALCHICK, Ann .... 209-228-4899.. 70 A
akovalchick@ucmerced.edu
KOVALCHICK, Eugene ... 267-341-3545 385 J
gkovalchick@holyfamily.edu
KOVALCHICK, Mary .... 610-799-1957 388 D
mkovalchick@lccc.edu
KOVALESKI, John .... 251-461-1622.... 9 A
jkovales@southalabama.edu
KOVATCH, Julie .... 503-338-2429 372 D
jkovatch@clatsopcc.edu
KOVATCH, Richard, A .... 434-982-5166 472 D
rak3e@virginia.edu
KOVEROLA, Catherine ... 814-362-5140 400 H
koverola@pitt.edu
KOVITZ, Jenn .... 541-383-7599 372 A
jkovitz@cocc.edu
KOVOLSKI, Chris .... 610-519-7450 401 K
chris.kovolski@villanova.edu

KRETZ, Bryan .... 402-363-5689 270 D
bckretz@york.edu
KREUSER, Ryan .... 715-394-8538 497 C
rkreuser@uwsuper.edu
KREUTTER, Tayler .... 585-594-6391 312 E
kreutter_tayler@roberts.edu
KREUTZER, Steven .... 973-748-9000 276 A
steven_kreutzer@bloomfield.edu
KREUZER, Charlene ...... 507-457-5090 241 F
ckreuzer@winona.edu
KREVH, Janet .... 216-397-4349 353 O
jkrevh@jcu.edu
KREYE, Judy .... 330-244-4757 363 E
jkreye@walsh.edu
KREYMER, Diana .... 718-518-4300 294 B
KREYNIS, Ilona .... 408-498-5104.. 73 B
ikreynis@cogswell.edu
KRHIN, Daniel, J .... 920-748-8394 494 J
krhind@ripon.edu
KRIARAS, Dimitrios ...... 602-384-2555.. 11 F
KRIBS, Rick, A .... 812-888-4176 162 F
rkribs@vinu.edu
KRIDLI, Ghassan .... 313-593-5290 231 I
gkridli@umich.edu
KRIEB, Dennis .... 618-468-4300 142 E
dkrieb@lc.edu
KRIEBS, John .... 641-844-5670 167 G
john.kriebs@iavalley.edu
KRIEG, Eric, J .... 716-878-5550 317 F
kriegej@buffalostate.edu
KRIEG, John .... 360-650-7405 485 I
john.krieg@wwu.edu
KRIEG, Lisa, M .... 412-268-5399 380 C
krieg@andrew.cmu.edu
KRIEGE, Bill .... 816-501-4855 258 I
bill.kriege@rockhurst.edu
KRIEGER, Andrea .... 850-484-1477 105 H
akrieger@pensacolastate.edu
KRIEGER, Gail .... 212-986-4343 275 I
gail-krieger@berkeleycollege.edu
KRIEGER, Jill, M .... 412-397-5279 397 B
krieger@rmu.edu
KRIEGER, Marcos .... 570-372-4292 398 F
kriegerm@susqu.edu
KRIEPS, Kevin .... 219-473-4330 154 D
kkrieps@ccsj.edu
KRIER, Jacob, C .... 507-344-7519 234 C
jake.krier@blc.edu
KRIESE, Theresa .... 605-995-2621 415 A
theresa.kriese@dwu.edu
KRIGEL, Belinda .... 256-233-8100.... 4 C
belinda.krigel@athens.edu
KRIKORIAN, Greg .... 410-778-7752 205 B
gkrikorian2@washcoll.edu
KRILEY, Taylor .... 785-628-4664 173 H
tkriley@fhsu.edu
KRIMMEL, Jon .... 626-815-4570.. 26 F
KRIMPELBEIN, Kristi ..... 715-232-2149 497 B
krimpelbeink@uwstout.edu
KRINER, Stephanie .... 910-788-6314 338 A
stephanie.kriner@sccnc.edu
KRINGEL, Dawny .... 575-492-2114 289 F
dkringel@usw.edu
KRINJECK, Ashley .... 814-262-6442 393 A
akrinjeck@pennhighlands.edu
KRIPP, Andrew .... 860-723-0000.. 85 F
KRISAK, Wendy .... 610-282-1100 382 C
wendy.krisak@desales.edu
KRISE, Thomas, W .... 671-735-2990 504 F
tkrise@triton.uog.edu
KRISHNAIAH, Raghu ..... 602-557-3501.. 16 G
raghu.krishnaiah@phoenix.edu
KRISHNAMOORTI,
Ramanan .... 713-743-4307 452 D
rkrishna@central.uh.edu
KRISHNAMURTHY,
Sushma .... 318-342-1041 193 C
krishnamurthy@ulm.edu
KRISHNAN, G, V .... 713-221-8478 453 A
krishnang@uhd.edu
KRISHNAN, Ramayya .... 412-268-2159 380 C
rk2x@andrew.cmu.edu
KRISHNASWAMY,
Vidya .... 972-377-1575 433 I
vkrishnaswamy@collin.edu
KRISHNASWAMY,
Vidya .... 972-860-8152 434 G
vkrishnaswamy@dcccd.edu
KRISIAK, Jeff .... 570-504-1760 387 B
krisiakj@lackawanna.edu
KRISLOV, Marvin .... 212-346-1097 311 A
president@pace.edu

KRISS, George .... 618-545-3099 141 E
gkriss@kaskaskia.edu
KRISSOFF BOEHM,
Lisa .... 508-531-2809 212 D
lkrissoffboehm@bridgew.edu
KRISTENSEN,
Douglas, A .... 308-865-8208 269 I
kristensend@unk.edu
KRISTOF-BROWN, Amy . 319-335-0866 163 H
amy-kristof-brown@uiowa.edu
KRITSCHER, Matthew .... 510-723-6743.. 35 J
mkritscher@chabotcollege.edu
KRITSKY, Gene .... 513-244-4401 356 F
gene.kritsky@msj.edu
KRIVONIAK,
Christopher .... 740-283-6860 352 I
ckrivoniak@franciscan.edu
KRIZ, Christine .... 540-868-7094 474 C
ckriz@lfcc.edu
KROBOTH, Patricia, D .. 412-624-3270 400 H
pkroboth@pitt.edu
KROEGER, Danielle, T .. 919-209-2027 335 F
dlkroeger@johnstoncc.edu
KROEGER, William .... 812-888-4227 162 F
KROEKER, Dean .... 620-241-0723 172 J
dean.kroeker@centralchristian.edu
KROENKE, Paul .... 309-677-2325 134 A
pkroenke@bradley.edu
KROGDAHL, Renate ...... 888-820-1484.. 64 F
renate.krogdahl@sofia.edu
KROGH, Mary Anne ...... 605-688-5178 417 A
maryanne.krogh@sdstate.edu
KROGMAN, Margy .... 608-796-3000 497 O
KROGOL, Jacob .... 313-317-1546 225 B
jakrogol@hfcc.edu
KROGULL, Steve .... 479-718-3314.. 21 F
skrogull@uark.edu
KROH, Lynne .... 417-862-9533 253 F
enroll@globaluniversity.edu
KROHN, Lisa .... 712-274-5100 168 E
krohn@morningside.edu
KROKROSKIA, Kimberly 417-667-8181 252 B
kkrokroskia@cottey.edu
KROL, Miroslaw .... 248-392-9995 231 D
mkrol@orchardlakeschools.com
KROL, Naz .... 814-866-8152 387 D
nkrol@lecom.edu
KROLAK, Steven .... 812-941-2470 157 F
skrolak@ius.edu
KROLICK, Sandy .... 505-747-2191 287 H
sandyk@nnmc.edu
KROLL, Ann .... 510-723-7637.. 35 K
akroll@clpccd.edu
KROLL, Dana .... 262-551-5706 492 B
dkroll@carthage.edu
KROLL, Jason .... 201-200-3344 279 D
jkroll@njcu.edu
KROLOFF, Reed .... 312-567-3000 140 A
KROMER, Neil .... 906-487-7207 224 B
neil.kromer@finlandia.edu
KROMPF, Steven .... 703-425-4143 468 B
KRONENBERGER, Judy . 513-862-5010 353 D
judy.kronenberger@email.gscollege.edu
KRONENBITTER,
Jennifer .... 607-753-2221 318 A
jennifer.kronenbitter@cortland.edu
KRONFELD, Michelle .... 608-796-3025 497 O
mlkronfeld@viterbo.edu
KRONISER, Maria .... 412-365-1862 380 G
mkroniser@chatham.edu
KRONK-WARNER,
Elizabeth .... 801-581-6571 459 O
elizabeth.warner@law.utah.edu
KROOT, Irwin .... 212-229-5671 308 A
krooti@newschool.edu
KROPF, Kevin .... 417-873-7524 252 G
kkropf@drury.edu
KROPF, Nancy, P .... 678-891-2700 120 E
nkropf@gsu.edu
KROPFF, Robert, C .... 330-972-7048 361 H
bobk@uakron.edu
KROPP, Kevin .... 518-828-4181 297 B
kevin.kropp@sunycgcc.edu
KROPP-ANDERSON,
Pamela .... 207-941-7107 194 F
kroppandersonp@husson.edu
KROSKIE, Hanna .... 502-863-7947 180 H
hanna_kroskie@georgetowncollege.edu
KROTINGER, Nicole .... 802-485-2126 462 F
nkroting@norwich.edu
KROUSE, Alisa .... 713-963-8979 125 F
akrouse@southuniversity.edu
KROUSE, Anne, M .... 610-499-4214 402 G
amkrouse@widener.edu

KROVI, Ravi .... 801-626-6006 461 A
rkrovi@weber.edu
KROWCHUK, Heidi .... 336-334-4899 343 A
hvkrowch@uncg.edu
KRPIC, Diana .... 914-694-4283 296 B
dkrpic@riversidehealth.org
KRSTIC, Miroslav .... 858-534-5556.. 70 C
mkrstic@ucsd.edu
KRUCKEBERG, Tara .... 626-395-8661.. 28 J
tkruckeb@caltech.edu
KRUCKENBERG, Erica ... 620-947-3121 177 I
KRUEGER, Brian .... 920-424-3466 496 C
KRUEGER, Bryon, D ..... 651-631-5392 244 D
bdkrueger@unwsp.edu
KRUEGER, Carr .... 801-422-3760 458 H
carr@byu.edu
KRUEGER, Christopher . 410-626-2558 202 A
chris.krueger@sjc.edu
KRUEGER, Conrad .... 210-486-0915 429 C
ckrueger@alamo.edu
KRUEGER, Dave .... 406-265-4157 264 E
david.krueger@msun.edu
KRUEGER, Dee .... 217-786-2778 143 B
debra.krueger@llcc.edu
KRUEGER, Joni .... 605-274-4015 414 G
joni.krueger@augie.edu
KRUEGER, Kate .... 315-268-2320 295 F
kkrueger@clarkson.edu
KRUEGER, Laura .... 480-423-6116.. 13 H
laura.krueger@scottsdalecc.edu
KRUEGER, Matthew ...... 218-855-8115 237 G
matthew.krueger@clcmn.edu
KRUEGER, Severa .... 920-923-8091 493 D
smkrueger36@marianuniversity.edu
KRUEGER, Todd .... 252-335-0821 333 G
todd_krueger@albemarle.edu
KRUEKEBERG, Adam .... 617-552-3300 207 C
adam.krueckeberg@bc.edu
KRUEMMLING, Brooke . 215-780-1364 398 B
bkruemmling@salus.edu
KRUG, Anita, K .... 312-567-3000 140 A
KRUG, Cherie .... 301-387-3100 199 A
cherie.krug@garrettcollege.edu
KRUG, Kirstin .... 405-491-6609 369 H
kkrug@snu.edu
KRUGER, Jenny .... 712-325-3326 167 I
jkruger@iwcc.edu
KRUGER, Matt .... 651-450-3701 238 E
mkruger@inverhills.edu
KRUGER, Michael .... 817-257-7727 448 F
michael.kruger@tcu.edu
KRUGER, Michael, J ..... 704-688-4233 248 F
mkruger@rts.edu
KRUIZENGA, Alicia .... 714-564-6970.. 58 F
kruizenga_alicia@sac.edu
KRUKONES, James .... 216-397-4762 353 O
jkrukones@jcu.edu
KRUKOVITZ, Robyn, M . 570-348-6231 389 D
rmkrukovitz@marywood.edu
KRULAK, Todd .... 205-726-4036.... 6 E
tkrulak@samford.edu
KRULL, Kimberly .... 316-322-3100 172 D
kim.krull@butlercc.edu
KRULL, Lucille .... 509-527-2145 485 C
lucy.krull@wallawalla.edu
KRUMBACH, Carol .... 562-467-5053.. 35 H
ckrumbach@cerritos.edu
KRUMBACH, Jillian .... 402-354-7129 268 B
jillian.krumbach@methodistcollege.edu
KRUMER, Walter .... 718-522-9073 290 E
wkrumer@asa.edu
KRUMHANSL, Ezra .... 502-585-9911 184 H
ekrumhansl@spalding.edu
KRUML, Susan .... 402-941-6200 267 L
kruml@midlandu.edu
KRUMM, Brenda, L .... 620-432-0364 176 D
bkrumm@neosho.edu
KRUMM, Javier .... 951-785-2295.. 47 C
jkrumm@lasierra.edu
KRUMMEN SCHRAVEN,
Ginger, B .... 920-433-6631 491 G
ginger.krummen@bellincollege.edu
KRUMMENACHER, Alan 512-404-4803 430 J
akrummenacher@austinseminary.edu
KRUMPELMAN, Jacqui . 330-363-6347 348 C
jacqui.krumpelman@aultman.com
KRUMWEIDE, Darrin ..... 323-466-6663.. 43 H
KRUPICKA, Ted .... 503-352-1515 375 C
tedk@pacificu.edu
KRUPIN, Maria .... 845-451-1385 297 G
maria.krupin@culinary.edu
KRUPITSKIY, Anna .... 201-714-7100 278 C

KRUPKA, Moshe, D ...... 646-565-6277 322 F
moshe.krupka@touro.edu
KRUPKA, Moshe, D ...... 646-565-6277 322 G
moshe.krupka@touro.edu
KRUPNICK-WALSH,
Kayla .... 415-442-7228.. 43 I
kkrupnick@ggu.edu
KRUPP, David .... 808-235-7416 130 E
krupp@hawaii.edu
KRUPP, Jason .... 727-341-3339 107 E
krupp.jason@spcollege.edu
KRUPPS, Gina .... 309-341-5264 134 B
gkrupps@sandburg.edu
KRUPPSTADT, Tom .... 877-476-8674 436 F
KRUPSKI, Eric, A .... 617-422-7298 217 F
ekrupski@nesl.edu
KRUS, Haley .... 309-677-2242 134 A
hkrus@fsmail.bradley.edu
KRUSCHINSKA, Kurt ..... 313-577-6748 232 K
registrar@wayne.edu
KRUSE, Amy .... 320-629-5129 240 D
amy.kruse@pine.edu
KRUSE, Beckie .... 262-243-5700 492 E
beckie.kruse@cuw.edu
KRUSE, Heather .... 602-285-7229.. 13 F
heather.kruse@phoenixcollege.edu
KRUSE, Janetta .... 817-598-6391 457 J
jkruse@wc.edu
KRUSE, Jerry, E .... 217-545-3625 150 B
jkruse@siumed.edu
KRUSE, Krystal .... 515-271-1447 165 G
krystal.kruse@dmu.edu
KRUSE, Liz .... 563-588-6300 164 I
liz.kruse@clarke.edu
KRUSE, Mary .... 517-264-7112 230 I
mkruse@sienaheights.edu
KRUSE, Thomas, D 563-588-4948 168
tom.kruse@loras.edu
KRUSE, Tracy, L 402-844-7056 268
tracyk@northeast.edu
KRUSEMARK, Diane 651-638-6043 234
d-krusemark@bethel.edu
KRUSEMARK, Diane 630-752-5009 153
diane.krusemark@wheaton.edu
KRUSEMARK, Stacy, L .. 605-256-5127 416
stacy.krusemark@dsu.edu
KRUSEMARK,
Stephanie .... 303-765-3106.. 81
skrusemark@iliff.edu
KRUSLING, James .... 415-442-7248.. 4
jkrusling@ggu.edu
KRUSNIAK, Bryan 660-626-2364 25
bkrusniak@atsu.edu
KRUTKA, Holly 307-766-1121 50
KRUTSCH, Jackie .... 479-308-2295.. 1
jackie.krutsch@acheedu.org
KRUWELL, Judith 936-468-3401 4
KRUZANSKY, Charles ... 518-434-4157 2
albany_office@cornell.edu
KRYLOWICZ, Brian 413-748-3345 2
bkrylowicz@springfield.edu
KRYSIAK, JR., Richard . 937-229-3766 3
rkrysiak1@udayton.edu
KRYSIAK BITTAR,
S. Mary .... 561-723-4424 G
mkrysiakbittar@svdp.edu
KRYSTYNIAK, Becky ..... 763-433-1216 D
rebecca.krystyniak@anokaramsey.e
KRYZHANOVSKAYA,
Tatyana .... 718-522-9073 E
tkryzhanovskaya@asa.edu
KRZAK, Chris .... 732-987-2785 A
ckrzak@georgian.edu
KRZANIK, Jacki .... 413-662-5421 213 C
j.krzanik@mcla.edu
KRZANOWSKI,
Roseanne .... 860-231-5647.. 90 A
rkrzanowski@usj.edu
KRZMARZICK, Tony ...... 724-830-1052 398 C
tkrzmarzick@setonhill.edu
KRZYWICKI, James .... 440-684-6119 363 C
jkrzywicki@ursuline.edu
KSACHIKIAN, Sam .... 818-988-2300.. 53 F
KTUL, Kathy .... 252-492-2061 338 F
ktul@vgcc.edu
KUAN, Jeffrey .... 909-447-2552.. 37 E
jkuan@cst.edu
KUAN TSU, Christina ... 212-854-2024 291 A
ckuantsu@barnard.edu
KUBA, Jodie, M .... 808-956-7251 129 E
jodiek@hawaii.edu
KUBA, Shawn .... 304-473-8560 491 D
kuba_s@wvwc.edu

KUBACAK, James .... 254-299-8608 439 E
jkubacak@mclennan.edu
KUBACKI, Matthew .... 718-420-4324 324 F
matthew.kubacki@wagner.edu
KUBAJAK, Jacob .... 660-944-2832 251 J
jacob@conception.edu
KUBAS, Andrew .... 651-846-1411 241 B
andrew.kubas@saintpaul.edu
KUBAT, Robert, A .... 814-863-3681 391 G
rak28@psu.edu
KUBATZKE, Trevor, A ... 269-927-8600 226 F
tkubatzke@lakemichigancollege.edu
KUBE, Marcia .... 402-481-8845 265 K
marcia.kube@bryanhealthcollege.edu
KUBERSKI, Christina ..... 815-599-3513 139 A
chris.kuberski@highland.edu
KUBES, Nathan .... 970-943-3084.. 85 C
nkubes@western.edu
KUBIAK, Adam .... 815-836-5581 142 F
akubiak@lewisu.edu
KUBIAK, Cathy .... 616-234-3971 224 F
cathykubiak@grcc.edu
KUBIAK, Sheryl .... 313-577-4400 232 K
ao1692@wayne.edu
KUBIK, Rachel .... 714-432-5834.. 38 B
rkubik@occ.cccd.edu
KUBINAK, Lois, A .... 610-921-7612 377 G
lkubinak@albright.edu
KUBISTA, Ray .... 360-752-8312 478 A
rkubista@btc.edu
KUBO, Takeo .... 408-288-3733.. 62 H
takeo.kubo@sjcc.edu
KUBUS, Tom .... 585-271-3657 313 B
tom.kubus@stbernards.edu
KUCER, MSA, Peter, S .. 860-632-3063.. 88 C
pkucer@holyapostles.edu
KUCERA, Karil .... 507-786-3129 243 D
kucera@stolaf.edu
KUCERA, Kevin .... 734-487-8892 223 K
kkucera@emich.edu
KUCERA, Victoria .... 402-461-2414 266 A
vkucera@cccneb.edu
KUCHESKY, Anicia .... 617-322-3513 211 A
anicia_kuchesky@laboure.edu
KUCHIBHOTLA, Anand .. 844-872-8680.. 73 A
KUCHIBHOTLA,
Mamatha .... 844-872-8680.. 73 A
KUCHTA,
Christopher, J .... 708-709-3950 147 D
ckuchta@prairiestate.edu
KUCIC, Terry .... 814-371-2090 400 A
tkucic@triangle-tech.edu
KUCIK, Maggie .... 317-955-6213 159 K
mkucik@marian.edu
KUCINE, Allan, R .... 631-632-8950 317 A
allan.kucine@stonybrookmedicine.edu
KUCKO, Jane .... 918-631-3225 371 C
jane-kucko@utulsa.edu
KUDLA-POLAY, Zoe ...... 309-341-5230 134 B
zkudla@sandburg.edu
KUE, Mailee .... 401-232-6448 404 A
mkue@bryant.edu
KUEBLER, Daniel .... 740-284-5268 352 I
dkuebler@franciscan.edu
KUEBLER, Jared .... 805-525-4417.. 67 K
jkuebler@thomasaquinas.edu
KUECKER, Aaron .... 708-239-4839 151 A
aaron.kuecker@trnty.edu
KUEHLER, Robert .... 303-837-2112.. 84 A
robert.kuehler@cu.edu
KUEHNER, Holly .... 850-872-3804 101 N
hkuehner@gulfcoast.edu
KUEHNL, Kody .... 614-947-6104 352 J
kody.kuehnl@franklin.edu
KUEHNLE, Melissa .... 863-784-7251 108 F
melissa.kuehnle@southflorida.edu
KUENNEN, Connie .... 844-642-2338 169 A
kuennenc@nicc.edu
KUENNEN, Dondi .... 321-674-7229 100 C
dkuennen@fit.edu
KUENSTNER, Debby ...... 781-283-5770 219 E
dkuenstner@wellesley.edu
KUENTZEL, Jeffrey .... 313-577-3398 232 K
jkuentzel@wayne.edu
KUETHER, Eva .... 414-297-6897 499 C
kuethere@matc.edu
KUETHER, Shawna .... 920-424-0283 496 C
KUFFEL, Cesalee .... 989-275-5000 226 D
cesalee.kuffel@kirtland.edu
KUFFEL, Lorne .... 205-348-7200.... 7 G
lkuffel@ua.edu
KUFFREY, Casey .... 770-484-1204 122 D
casey.kuffrey@lutherrice.edu
KUFUOR, Edward .... 718-522-9071 290 E
ekufuor@asa.edu
KUGLER, Angela .... 425-558-0299 479 F
KUGLER, Jeffrey .... 717-477-1451 395 B
jwkugler@ship.edu
KUGLER, Sharon .... 203-432-1128.. 90 C
sharon.kugler@yale.edu
KUHAJDA,
Kimberlee, A .... 440-826-2251 348 D
kkuhajda@bw.edu
KUHAR, Anissa .... 815-394-5025 148 D
akuhar@rockford.edu
KUHAR, Marilyn .... 617-228-3290 214 C
mkkuhar@bhcc.mass.edu
KUHL, Jaromy .... 850-474-2688 111 F
jkuhl@uwf.edu
KUHL, Sue .... 303-861-1151.. 80 G
skuhl@concorde.edu
KUHLENGEL HORVATH,
Tina .... 352-392-2171 111 A
tinah@housing.ufl.edu
KUHLHORST,
Michelle, L .... 260-399-7700 162 B
mkuhlhorst@sf.edu
KUHLMAN, Ann .... 203-432-9686.. 90 C
ann.kuhlman@yale.edu
KUHLMAN, Gregory ...... 718-951-5174 293 C
kuhlman@brooklyn.cuny.edu
KUHLMANN, Diana, E .. 620-341-5173 173 F
dkuhlman@emporia.edu
KUHLMANN, Kathy .... 636-481-3131 254 C
kkuhlman@jeffco.edu
KUHN, Bill .... 952-446-4162 235 J
kuhnb@crown.edu
KUHN, Chuck .... 616-988-1000 223 A
chuck.k@compass.edu
KUHN, Darlene .... 205-726-2727.... 6 E
dfkuhn@samford.edu
KUHN, David .... 307-742-3776 502 B
dkuhn@wyotech.edu
KUHN, Helen .... 217-245-3013 139 C
registrar@ic.edu
KUHN, Jens-Uwe .... 805-965-0581.. 63 A
jkuhn@sbcc.edu
KUHN, Joel, A .... 260-422-5561 156 E
jakuhn@indianatech.edu
KUHN, Karl, A .... 920-565-1000 493 A
kuhnka@lakeland.edu
KUHN, Kathryn, A .... 414-955-6501 493 F
kkuhn@mcw.edu
KUHN, Lisa .... 410-386-8032 198 D
lkuhn@carrollcc.edu
KUHN, Paul .... 732-247-5241 279 C
pkuhn@nbts.edu
KUHN, Rachel .... 773-371-5415 134 D
rkuhn@ctu.edu
KUHN-SCHNELL,
Tamara .... 217-786-2353 143 B
tammy.schnell@llcc.edu
KUHNER, Matthew .... 585-271-3657 313 B
matthew.kuhner@stbernards.edu
KUHNLENZ, Fritz .... 617-747-2012 206 H
alumniaffairs@berklee.edu
KUHR, Brittanie .... 419-783-2411 351 K
bkuhr@defiance.edu
KUHR, Werner .... 303-384-2312.. 79 J
wkuhr@mines.edu
KUIPER, Forrest .... 907-474-7681.. 10 A
fjkuiper@alaska.edu
KUIPERS, David .... 229-931-2004 125 E
dkuipers@southgatech.edu
KUJAWA, Lisa, R .... 248-204-2403 227 A
lkujawa@ltu.edu
KUJAWA, Tricia, A .... 217-786-2211 143 B
tricia.kujawa@llcc.edu
KUKAINIS, Maris .... 856-227-7200 276 E
mkukainis@camdencc.edu
KUKLINSKI, Danny .... 414-410-4839 491 I
dpkuklinski@stritch.edu
KUKREJA, Sunil .... 253-879-3207 484 G
kukreja@pugetsound.edu
KUKUK, Carley .... 715-232-2346 497 B
kukukc@uwstout.edu
KUKULIES, Emily Ann .. 808-845-9219 130 A
kukulies@hawaii.edu
KULA, Stan .... 973-300-2100 284 A
skula@sussex.edu
KULAGA, Jon .... 740-474-8896 358 A
KULESZA, Darrell .... 508-541-1864 209 A
dkulesza@dean.edu
KULESZA, Randy .... 814-866-8423 387 D
rkulesza@lecom.edu
KULICK, Steven, W .... 315-445-4560 303 I
kulicksw@lemoyne.edu
KULIK, Dmitry .... 202-462-2101.. 93 A
kulik@iwp.edu
KULIS, Carol .... 858-653-3000.. 29 D
ckulis@calmu.edu
KULKA, Maria .... 269-782-1472 231 A
mkulka01@swmich.edu
KULKARNI, Sanjeev ...... 609-258-3020 280 D
kulkarni@princeton.edu
KULKE, Erik .... 262-551-5916 492 B
ekulke@carthage.edu
KULL, Christian .... 607-962-9540 320 C
ckull1@corning-cc.edu
KULL, Edward .... 718-817-1000 300 C
ekull@fordham.edu
KULL, F. Jon .... 603-646-1552 273 D
f.jon.kull@dartmouth.edu
KULL, Stephen .... 815-394-4365 148 D
skull@rockford.edu
KULLAR, Pardeep .... 510-780-4500.. 47 K
pkullar@lifewest.edu
KULP, Amanda .... 904-620-1944 111 B
amanda.kulp@unf.edu
KULP, Holly .... 570-208-5900 386 G
hollykulp@kings.edu
KULTAN-PFAUTZ,
Natissa .... 610-341-5936 383 B
nkultan@eastern.edu
KUM, Byung-Dal .... 714-995-9988.. 47 B
KUMAR, Manish .... 773-583-4050 146 A
KUMAR, Mukul .... 617-746-1990 210 H
mukul.kumar@hult.edu
KUMAR, Neeraj .... 312-341-3587 148 E
nkumar@roosevelt.edu
KUMAR, Poonam .... 409-880-7398 449 G
poonam.kumar@lamar.edu
KUMAR, R. Thulasi .... 540-231-1428 476 C
tkumar@vt.edu
KUMAR, Rajesh .... 914-674-7798 306 C
rkumar@mercy.edu
KUMAR, Senthil .... 352-588-8351 107 D
senthil.kumar@saintleo.edu
KUMAR, Sunil .... 410-516-3355 199 G
provost@jhu.edu
KUMAR, Vijay .... 215-898-7244 400 F
kumar@seas.upenn.edu
KUMARASAMY, Sundar 617-373-4810 217 I
KUMLER, Kurt .... 412-391-4100 396 G
kkumler@pointpark.edu
KUMLER, Kurt .... 412-268-2922 380 C
kkumler@andrew.cmu.edu
KUMM, David .... 402-643-7222 266 G
david.kumm@cune.edu
KUMMERMAN, Howard . 714-484-7126.. 54 B
hkummerman@cypresscollege.edu
KUMP, Lee .... 814-863-1274 391 G
lrk4@psu.edu
KUMP, Melissa .... 406-496-4108 265 A
mkump@mtech.edu
KUMPALA, Cody .... 906-217-4300 222 A
cody.kumpala@baycollege.edu
KUMPF, Dan .... 805-289-6285.. 74 B
dkumpf@vcccd.edu
KUNA, Monica .... 215-968-8003 379 D
monica.kuna@bucks.edu
KUNCE, Kim, M .... 708-709-3684 147 D
kkunce@prairiestate.edu
KUNDELL, Ken, F .... 410-543-6043 204 D
kfkundell@salisblury.edu
KUNDINGER, Amy .... 920-403-4223 495 B
amy.kundinger@snc.edu
KUNE, Natacha, F .... 206-543-1240 485 A
fookune@uw.edu
KUNERT, Charles .... 503-552-1742 374 D
ckunert@nunm.edu
KUNERT, Erin .... 219-464-5333 162 D
erin.kunert@valpo.edu
KUNES, Melissa, J .... 814-867-0647 391 G
mjk5@psu.edu
KUNG, Bethany, E .... 202-994-6046.. 92 D
bcobb@gwu.edu
KUNJUMMEN, Raju .... 563-588-8000 166 C
rkunjummen@emmaus.edu
KUNKA, Jennifer .... 843-661-1520 409 G
jkunka@fmarion.edu
KUNKEL, Anthony .... 985-448-4336 192 F
anthony.kunkel@nicholls.edu
KUNKEL, JoAnn .... 605-658-3622 416 D
joann.kunkel@usd.edu
KUNKEL, Karl .... 608-785-8113 496 A
kkunkel@uwlax.edu
KUNKEL, Roberta .... 408-274-7900.. 62 G
roberta.kunkel@evc.edu
KUNKEL, Tony .... 320-308-3064 240 I
abkunkel@stcloudstate.edu
KUNKEL-JORDAN,
Laurie .... 414-382-6300 491 F
laurie.kunkel-jordan@alverno.edu
KUNKO, Bill .... 575-492-2501 287 A
bkunko@nmjc.edu
KUNKO, Tina .... 575-492-2782 287 A
tkunko@nmjc.edu
KUNO, Phyllis .... 701-349-5407 346 I
phylliskuno@trinitybiblecollege.edu
KUNOVICH, Sheri .... 214-768-1285 444 D
kunovich@smu.edu
KUNSMAN, Kip .... 410-777-2961 197 G
kakunsman@aacc.edu
KUNST, Malia .... 619-388-7834.. 61 A
mkunst@sdccd.edu
KUNTZ, Bliss .... 402-486-2514 269 F
bliss.kuntz@ucollege.edu
KUNTZ, Daniel .... 805-493-3855.. 29 C
kuntz@callutheran.edu
KUNTZ, David .... 216-987-4790 351 E
david.kuntz@tri-c.edu
KUNTZ, F. Douglas ...... 570-321-4116 389 B
kuntz@lycoming.edu
KUNTZ, Jason .... 717-391-7322 399 C
kuntz@stevenscollege.edu
KUNTZ, Jim .... 215-335-0800 388 G
KUNTZ, John .... 973-300-2252 284 A
jkuntz@sussex.edu
KUNTZ, Kristi .... 217-333-6677 152 B
kakuntz@illinois.edu
KUNTZ, Nicole .... 570-321-4081 389 B
kuntzn@lycoming.edu
KUNTZ, Twyla .... 701-349-5438 346 I
twyla@trinitybiblecollege.edu
KUNTZ, Wayne .... 228-897-4361 247 E
wayne.kuntz@mgccc.edu
KUNZ, Amy, S .... 808-956-7161 129 C
amykunz@hawaii.edu
KUNZ, Erin .... 701-788-5240 345 D
erin.kunz@mayvillestate.edu
KUNZ, Jason .... 410-837-4482 204 F
jkunz.ubpolice@ubalt.edu
KUNZ, Leonard .... 908-852-1400 276 G
kunzl01@centenaryuniversity.edu
KUNZINGER, Michael ... 434-582-7390 468 E
mmkunzin@liberty.edu
KUO, David .... 215-871-7128 395 G
davidku@pcom.edu
KUO, David .... 215-871-6690 395 G
davidku@pcom.edu
KUO, Kent .... 541-737-3525 375 A
kent.kuo@oregonstate.edu
KUO, Ling Ling .... 626-571-8811.. 73 E
linglingk@uwest.edu
KUO, Peter, J .... 415-439-2350.. 25 E
pjkuo@act-sf.org
KUO, Zheng-jie .... 510-763-7787.. 24 C
KUPERMAN, Eli .... 732-367-1060 275 K
ekuperman@bmg.edu
KUPERMAN, Tina .... 310-900-1600.. 39 F
KUPERSMITH, Peter, A . 215-489-2254 382 B
peter.kupersmith@delval.edu
KUPETS, Keith .... 229-333-6051 127 E
1493mgr@follett.com
KUPFERMAN, Francine . 617-228-2316 214 C
fskupfer@bhcc.edu
KUPIEC, Suzanne .... 908-737-4804 278 E
skupiec@kean.edu
KUPO, Leilani .... 775-784-4898 271 E
lkupo@unr.edu
KUPPER, Jodi .... 402-471-2505 268 C
jkupper@nscs.edu
KUPPINGER, Karen .... 585-389-2100 307 F
kkuppin9@naz.edu
KURACINA, William ...... 903-886-5166 447 B
william.kuracina@tamuc.edu
KURAPATI, Raaj .... 901-678-2121 426 G
kurapati@memphis.edu
KURDA, Linda .... 907-543-4502.. 10 A
lrcurda@alaska.edu
KURIMAY, Mary Beth ... 610-436-6931 395 D
mkurimay@wcupa.edu
KURISKY, Brian .... 757-455-3216 477 C
bkurisky@vwu.edu
KURKER-STEWART,
Nicole .... 860-768-5101.. 89 G
kurkerste@hartford.edu
KUROKAWA, Linda .... 760-757-2121.. 52 F
lkorokawa@miracosta.edu
KUROWSKI, Gail .... 231-995-1283 229 A
gkurowski@nmc.edu

KURPIUS, David, D ...... 573-882-6686 261 A
kurpius@missouri.edu
KURR, Brigitte .... 918-610-0027 365 I
bkurr@communitycarecollege.edu
KURTH, Ann .... 203-737-6785.. 90 C
ann.kurth@yale.edu
KURTINITIS, Sandra, L . 443-840-1015 198 H
skurtinitis@ccbcmd.edu
KURTZ, Andrew .... 419-372-0623 348 G
kurtz@bgsu.edu
KURTZ, Diane, L .... 517-750-1200 231 C
dkurtz@arbor.edu
KURTZ, James, E .... 651-696-6711 236 I
jkurtz2@macalester.edu
KURTZ, Josef .... 617-735-9979 209 D
kurtzj@emmanuel.edu
KURTZ, Rick .... 507-389-7369 241 C
rick.kurtz@southcentral.edu
KURTZ, Steve .... 208-769-7835 132 D
steve.kurtz@nic.edu
KURTZ, Terri .... 361-572-6463 457 E
terri.kurtz@victoriacollege.edu
KURTZ, Terry .... 440-775-8692 357 G
terry.kurtz@oberlin.edu
KURTZ HOFFMAN,
Linda, A .... 330-471-8145 355 D
lhoffman@malone.edu
KURTZ-SHAW, Brad ...... 208-467-8539 132 E
bradshaw@nnu.edu
KURZY, Tracy .... 626-256-4673.. 37 A
tkurzy@coh.org
KUSCH, Bruce, C .... 801-524-8113 459 E
bkusch@ldsbc.edu
KUSCH, Joshua .... 740-392-6868 356 G
josh.kusch@mvnu.edu
KUSER, Janet .... 617-236-5458 209 G
jkuser@fisher.edu
KUSH, Lynn, A .... 215-871-6815 395 G
lynnku@pcom.edu
KUSHMIDER, Kristin ...... 303-724-8488.. 84 D
kristin.kushmider@ucdenver.edu
KUSHNER, Cynthia .... 440-366-7610 355 B
KUSHNER, Mark .... 415-771-7020.. 61 C
mkushner@sfai.edu
KUSHNER, Melissa .... 610-647-4400 385 L
mkushner@immaculata.edu
KUSHNER, Mikhel, A .... 410-706-1852 203 A
mikhel.kushner@umaryland.edu
KUSHNER, Tiffany .... 908-852-1400 276 G
kushnert@centenaryuniversity.edu
KUSKOWSKI, David ...... 864-656-5297 407 E
dkuskow@clemson.edu
KUSPA, Adam .... 713-798-1060 431 D
akuspa@bcm.edu
KUSS, Charlotte .... 850-729-4935 104 M
kussc@nwfsc.edu
KUSSE, Debra .... 585-475-3947 312 F
dskpur@rit.edu
KUSUMI, Kenro .... 480-965-8065.. 10 J
kenro.kusumi@asu.edu
KUTATELADZE, Andrei .. 303-871-2995.. 84 E
akutatel@du.edu
KUTCH, Jason .... 219-464-5917 162 D
jason.kutch@valpo.edu
KUTCHER, Gene .... 609-895-5152 281 B
ekutcher@rider.edu
KUTCHER, Kevin .... 856-351-2612 283 B
kkutcher@salemcc.edu
KUTCHMAN, Michael .... 814-472-3035 397 F
mkutchman@francis.edu
KUTHY, Anna .... 270-686-4277 179 J
anna.kuthy@brescia.edu
KUTI, Morakinyo .... 937-376-6598 349 J
mkuti@centralstate.edu
KUTINAC, Linda .... 575-674-2201 285 L
lkutinac@burrell.edu
KUTLENIOS, Rose, M ... 304-336-8108 490 B
rose.kutlenios@westliberty.edu
KUTNER, Sender .... 847-982-2500 138 I
kutner@htc.edu
KUTNEY, Joshua, P ...... 920-565-1000 493 A
kutneyjp@lakeland.edu
KUTZKE, Mike .... 320-222-5218 240 F
mike.kutzke@ridgewater.edu
KUVAAS, Laura .... 320-222-6090 240 F
KUWITZKY, Chris .... 785-670-4963 178 C
chris.kuwitzky@washburn.edu
KUYKENDALL, Brad ...... 915-532-3737 458 B
KUYKENDALL, John ...... 317-788-3778 161 H
kuykendallj@uindy.edu
KUYKENDALL, John ...... 870-575-8489.. 22 D
kuykendallj@upab.edu

KUYKENDALL, John ...... 870-575-8498.. 22 D
kuykendallj@uapb.edu
KUYKENDALL, John ...... 843-863-7026 407 B
jkuykendall@csuniv.edu
KUYKENDALL, Michelle 208-467-8521 132 E
mlkuykendall@nnu.edu
KUYKENDALL, Robin .... 575-769-4994 285 O
robin.kuykendall@clovis.edu
KUZMA, Marta .... 203-432-2606.. 90 C
marta.kuzma@yale.edu
KUZNACIC, Katharine .... 262-472-1918 497 D
KVAAL, Kimberly .... 512-448-8413 442 I
kimkvaal@stedwards.edu
KVIGNE, Eric .... 530-752-1247.. 69 B
epkvigne@ucdavis.edu
KWAI, Joshladd .... 216-687-3910 350 J
j.kwai@csuohio.edu
KWAK, Kun .... 909-623-0302.. 59 H
KWAK, Kyueil .... 770-220-7908 119 A
kkwak@gcuniv.edu
KWAK, Nojin .... 716-645-2368 316 C
vpinted@buffalo.edu
KWAN, Billy .... 212-472-1500 309 D
libraryinfo@nysid.edu
KWANBUNBUMPEN,
Ada .... 204-286-5244 191 C
akwanbunbumpen@suno.edu
KWANDRANS, Karen ..... 716-614-6472 309 G
kkwandrans@niagaracc.suny.edu
KWANG CHUNG, Sae ... 714-222-1110.. 27 F
KWAPONG, Sam .... 619-849-2524.. 57 J
samkwapong@pointloma.edu
KWASIGROH, Catherine 731-661-5281 426 F
ckwasigroh@uu.edu
KWASIKPUI, Tremaine .. 713-221-8563 453 A
kwasikpuit@uhd.edu
KWASITSU, Lishi .... 503-517-1023 377 C
lkwasitsu@warnerpacific.edu
KWENDA, Maxwell .... 509-313-6948 480 F
kwenda@gonzaga.edu
KWESKIN, Amy, B .... 314-935-9842 262 A
amy.b.kweskin@wustl.edu
KWIATKOWSKI, Amy .... 415-955-2100.. 24 J
akwiatkowski@alliant.edu
KWIATKOWSKI,
Anthony .... 773-907-4784 135 C
akwiatkowski@ccc.edu
KWIATKOWSKI, Christa 304-367-4796 489 K
christa.kwiatkowski@fairmontstate.edu
KWIECIEN, Garth .... 510-531-4911.. 57 C
KWIECIEN, Garth .... 415-452-7768.. 36 K
gkwiecien@ccsf.edu
KWIECINSKA, Karolina .. 860-297-4203.. 89 B
karolina.kwiecinska@trincoll.edu
KWILINSKI, Kathie .... 206-934-7965 483 D
kathie.kwilinski@seattlecolleges.edu
KWIST, Sabrina, T .... 925-473-7314.. 40 D
skwist@losmedanos.edu
KWOFIE, Winnie .... 510-885-4149.. 31 A
winnie.kwofie@csueastbay.edu
KWOLEK, Katherine .... 617-585-0200 207 A
katherine.kwolek@the-bac.edu
KWON, Jenny .... 415-565-4627.. 69 C
kwonjenny@uchastings.edu
KWONG, Davina .... 202-651-5005.. 92 C
davina.kwong@gallaudet.edu
KYLE, Brandon .... 908-621-8807.. 57 E
KYLE, Eric .... 417-447-7602 257 G
kylee@otc.edu
KYLE, James, R .... 619-596-2766.. 26 D
jkyle@ata.edu
KYLE, Jean .... 507-433-0568 240 G
jean.kyle@riverland.edu
KYLE, Katherine .... 678-407-5770 119 C
kkyle@ggc.edu
KYLE, Michael .... 507-786-3025 243 D
kylem@stolaf.edu
KYLE, Roberta .... 508-929-8811 213 G
rkyle@worcester.edu
KYNARD, Olivia, L .... 413-538-7000 214 F
okynard@hcc.edu
KYNOR, James .... 719-589-7075.. 83 L
james.kynor@trinidadstate.edu
KYOORE, Jude .... 636-481-3210 254 C
jkyoore@jeffco.edu
KYPRIANE, Schemanun 530-464-3544.. 60 A
mky@spots.edu
KYPRIOS, Linda, A .... 972-881-5726 433 I
lkyprios@collin.edu
KYPUROS, Javier .... 903-566-7267 456 A
jkypuros@uttyler.edu
KYRIAKIDES, Michelle .. 516-463-6060 301 G
michelle.kyriakides@hofstra.edu

KYTE, Rachel .... 617-627-4172 219 C
rachel.kyte@tufts.edu
KYTE, Richard, L .... 608-796-3704 497 O
rlkyte@viterbo.edu

L

LA BARBERA,
Christopher .... 781-239-3114 214 G
clabarbera@massbay.edu
LA BELLE, Brian .... 312-488-6062.. 36 E
blabelle@thechicagoschool.edu
LA BELLE-HAMER,
Nettie .... 907-474-5837.. 10 A
nalabellehamer@alaska.edu
LA BRANCHE, Mark, D . 931-363-9802 427 E
mlb@utsouthern.edu
LA CHAPELLE,
Jacqueline .... 337-550-1282 189 G
jlachape@lsue.edu
LA MAZZA, Bernadette . 480-732-7019.. 12 O
bernadette.la.mazza@cgc.edu
LA PIERRE, Mary .... 518-562-4125 296 A
mary.lapierre@clinton.edu
LA POINT, Kris .... 262-554-2010 494 A
LA POINT, Kristine, L .... 773-975-1295 494 A
LA ROCCA, Chris .... 252-492-2061 338 F
laroccac@vgcc.edu
LA TORRA, Grace .... 206-876-6100 483 H
glatorra@theseattleschool.edu
LA VOY, Sharon, A .... 301-405-3828 202 H
slavoy@umd.edu
LABA, Laura .... 847-543-2200 136 A
llaba@clcillinois.edu
LABADIE, Nicole .... 713-525-3129 454 G
labadin@stthom.edu
LABADIE, Tracy .... 269-488-4223 225 G
tlabadie@kvcc.edu
LABAN, Danielle .... 312-261-3162 145 D
dlaban@nl.edu
LABANG, Yaw .... 903-593-8311 448 G
ylabang@texascollege.edu
LABARBERA, Mark .... 219-464-6894 162 D
mark.labarbera@valpo.edu
LABARBERA, Paul .... 845-758-7940 290 I
labarbera@bard.edu
LABAT, Nichole .... 985-545-1500 188 E
LABAT, Tony .... 415-351-3574.. 61 C
tlabat@sfai.edu
LABATTE, Rhonda .... 605-698-3966 416 B
rlabatte@swcollege.edu
LABAUGH, Amy, R .... 208-496-1155 130 I
labaugha@byui.edu
LABAY, Theodore .... 251-405-7240.... 1 E
tlabay@bishop.edu
LABBERTON, Mark, A ... 626-584-5201.. 43 B
LABE, Geoffey .... 610-896-1806 385 I
glabe@haverford.edu
LABELL, Yitzi .... 301-649-7077 205 E
ylabell@yeshiva.edu
LABENSKI, Paula .... 570-740-0388 389 A
plabenski@luzerne.edu
LABKOWSKI, Zalman .... 718-774-3430 292 J
LABOE, Mark .... 773-325-4004 136 H
mlaboe@depaul.edu
LABOE, Timothy .... 313-883-8556 230 C
laboe.timothy@shms.edu
LABONTE, Angela .... 603-342-3041 273 C
alabonte@ccsnh.edu
LABONTE, Gene, R .... 978-542-6542 213 E
gene.labonte@salemstate.edu
LABONTE, Jason .... 631-656-2113 300 B
jason.labonte@ftc.edu
LABONTE, Kim .... 618-650-2789 150 A
klabont@siue.edu
LABONTE, Robert .... 978-630-9272 215 C
r_labonte@mwcc.mass.edu
LABOR, Jennifer .... 918-465-1828 366 A
jlabor@eosc.edu
LABORDE, Bridget .... 985-545-1500 188 E
LABOUNTY, Jennifer ..... 714-992-7085.. 54 C
jlabounty@fullcoll.edu
LABOY, Gloryber .... 787-751-0160 506 F
glaboy@cmpr.pr.gov
LABOY FUSTER, Rafael . 787-720-4476 511 C
relacionespublicas@mizpa.edu
LABRAKE, Matthew .... 201-360-4038 278 C
mlabrake@hccc.edu
LABRANCHE, Matthew .. 413-782-1503 220 A
matthew.labranche@wne.edu
LABRANCHE, Michael ... 504-398-2241 192 A
mlabrake@uhcno.edu
LABRIE, Lori, A .... 713-313-7040 449 B
labrie_la@tsu.edu

LABRIOLA, Elisabeth, S 860-439-2064.. 87 H
elisabeth.labriola@conncoll.edu
LABRON, Wendy .... 617-735-9778 209 D
labronw@emmanuel.edu
LABROSSE, Tonya, B .... 603-535-2846 275 A
tblabrosse@plymouth.edu
LABROZZI, Ryan .... 304-637-1253 487 C
labrozzir@dewv.edu
LABRY, Daniel .... 877-476-8674 436 F
LABS, Jeff .... 715-365-4406 499 E
jlabs@nicoletcollege.edu
LABUDE, Mark .... 318-342-1040 193 C
labude@ulm.edu
LACASCIO, Joe .... 508-286-3405 220 B
lacascio_joe@wheatoncollege.edu
LACEFIELD, Hyla .... 650-306-3460.. 62 J
lacefieldh@smccd.edu
LACEY, Doris .... 256-469-7333.... 5 H
finaid@hbc1.edu
LACEY, Kasi .... 573-592-5269 262 E
kasi.lacey@westminster-mo.edu
LACEY, Kristin .... 864-596-9031 408 F
kristin.lacey@converse.edu
LACEY, Mark .... 904-632-3319 101 B
mark.lacey@fscj.edu
LACEY, Pete .... 810-989-5561 230 F
placey@sc4.edu
LACEY, Roshae .... 601-877-6333 245 A
rlacey@alcorn.edu
LACH, Carolyn .... 773-244-5506 145 G
clach@northpark.edu
LACH, John .... 202-994-1000.. 92 D
jlach@gwu.edu
LACHANCE, Andrea .... 607-753-5430 318 A
andrea.lachance@cortland.edu
LACHANCE, Beatrice ..... 615-547-1222 419 C
blachance@cumberland.edu
LACHANCE,
Elizabeth, A .... 585-385-8410 313 F
llachance@sjfc.edu
LACHANCE, Ian .... 518-629-4571 302 C
i.lachance@hvcc.edu
LACHANCE, Kelly .... 918-683-4581 365 C
LACHANCE, Laurie, G ... 207-859-1201 196 D
president@thomas.edu
LACHAPELLE, Christelle 860-447-1911.. 87 H
clachapel@conncoll.edu
LACHAPELLE, Laurie ..... 978-762-4000 215 D
llachape@northshore.edu
LACHENAUER,
Heather, A .... 972-721-5363 452 B
hlachenauer@udallas.edu
LACHENBRUCH, Mary ... 406-449-9158 263 J
mlachenbruch@montana.edu
LACHER, Henry .... 502-897-4703 184 G
hlacher@sbts.edu
LACHICA-CHAVEZ,
Cassandra, M .... 915-831-2580 436 A
clachica@epcc.edu
LACHINA, David .... 443-885-3144 201 A
david.lachina@morgan.edu
LACK, Nicole .... 916-278-7322.. 32 D
LACKEY, Chad .... 704-878-3360 336 C
clackey@mitchellcc.edu
LACKEY, Laura, W .... 478-301-4106 122 E
lackey_l@mercer.edu
LACKEY, Miles .... 910-962-3383 343 C
lackeym@uncw.edu
LACKEY, Russell, L .... 515-263-6004 166 F
rlackey@grandview.edu
LACKIE, Mary .... 501-450-3197.. 23 H
mlackie@uca.edu
LACKLAND, Jonathan .... 309-438-5677 140 D
jwlackl@ilstu.edu
LACKNER, Elisabeth ...... 718-631-6279 295 C
elackner@qcc.cuny.edu
LACKNER, Sandra .... 828-395-1429 335 D
slackner@isothermal.edu
LACKOVIC, Michael, P .. 920-565-1000 493 A
lackovicmp@lakeland.edu
LACLAIR, Elizabeth .... 803-508-7413 406 C
laclaire@atc.edu
LACOCK, Kerri .... 724-503-1001 402 B
klacock@washjeff.edu
LACOMBA, AJ .... 732-987-2352 278 A
ajlacomba@georgian.edu
LACOMBE, Chris .... 801-957-5190 461 C
chris.lacombe@slcc.edu
LACORAZZA, Stephen .... 978-867-4048 210 B
stephen.lacorazza@gordon.edu
LACORTE, Bonnie .... 216-881-1700 358 J
blacorte@ohiotech.edu

LACOUR, Brian 206-543-3392 485 A balacour@uw.edu
LACOURSE, Michael 435-652-7506 460 B lacourse@dixie.edu
LACOURSE, William 410-455-2598 203 B lacourse@umbc.edu
LACRETA, James 781-736-2231 208 A jlacreta@brandeis.edu
LACRO, Erika, L 808-956-7038 129 C lacro@hawaii.edu
LACRO, Erika, L 808-956-7038 129 G lacro@hawaii.edu
LACROIX, Luke 619-260-4777 72 I lukelacroix@sandiego.edu
LACROIX, Nicole 360-538-4000 480 G
LACROIX, Roland, J 207-581-4053 196 G rjlacroix@maine.edu
LACSINA, Abbie 253-879-3502 484 G alacsina@pugetsound.edu
LACY, Charles, F 702-968-2016 272 C clacy@roseman.edu
LACY, Constance 972-780-3600 454 A constance.lacy@untdallas.edu
LACY, Dominic 202-651-5005 92 C dominic.lacy@gallaudet.edu
LACY, Herbert, E 410-293-1881 504 A lacy@usna.edu
LACY, Kirk 928-704-4373 14 F klacy@mohave.edu
LACY, Sherea 616-538-2330 224 E slacy@gracechristian.edu
LACY SORENSON, Melanie 908-621-8198 57 E melanie_lacy@pitzer.edu
LACZ, Sarah 973-748-9000 276 A sarah_lacz@bloomfield.edu
LADANY, Nicholas 404-364-8320 123 K nladany@oglethorpe.edu
LADD, Brittany 203-576-4022 89 C bladd@bridgeport.edu
LADD, Cindy 952-358-8223 239 G cindy.ladd@normandale.edu
LADD, Janet 410-386-8113 198 D jladd@carrollcc.edu
LADDEN, Kevin 215-489-2472 382 B kevin.ladden@delval.edu
LADENBURGER, Ed 252-222-6179 333 A ladenburgerj@carteret.edu
LADER, Donald 816-279-7000 250 B don.lader@abtu.edu
LADERBERG, Sharon 757-233-8736 477 C sladerberg@vwu.edu
LADIPO, Folorunso 614-234-5622 356 E fladipo@mccn.edu
LADITKA, Doug 517-629-0350 221 A dladitka@albion.edu
LADNER, Bobby 903-730-4890 438 D bladner@jarvis.edu
LADNER, Hilda 520-206-7215 15 B hladner@pima.edu
LADRIGAN-WHELPLEY, Theresa 401-341-7282 405 D theresa.whelpley@salve.edu
LADUCER, Karen 313-664-7672 222 H kladucer@collegeforcreforcreativestudies.edu
LADUCER, Wanda 701-477-7875 346 J wladucer@tm.edu
LADUE, Chad 518-891-2915 310 A cladue@nccc.edu
LADUE, John 573-840-9654 260 E jladue@trcc.edu
LADWIG, Laura 616-432-3415 230 A laura.ladwig@prts.edu
LAENEN, Carol 231-348-6839 228 H claenen@ncmich.edu
LAERMER, Gary 212-346-1200 311 A
LAFAILLE, Pierre 713-623-2040 430 E pilafaille@aii.edu
LAFANTASIE, Jordana 304-473-8130 491 D lafantasie.j@wvwc.edu
LAFARR, Michael, J 303-871-2000 84 E
LAFAVE, Alan 701-845-7122 345 G alan.lafave@vcsu.edu
LAFAYETTE, Moira 608-757-7750 498 D mlafayette@blackhawk.edu
LAFERLA, Frank 949-824-5315 69 D laferla@uci.edu
LAFEVOR, Kim 256-216-5359 4 C kim.lafevor@athens.edu
LAFFERTY, Danielle 704-463-3221 339 E danielle.lafferty@pfeiffer.edu
LAFFERTY, Iris 858-513-9240 68 K iris.lafferty@ashford.edu
LAFFERTY, Jason 773-602-5465 135 D
LAFFERTY, Kevin 813-253-6214 113 H klafferty@ut.edu
LAFFERTY, William, J 717-337-6912 384 D wlaffert@gettysburg.edu
LAFFITTE, Ron 704-463-3401 339 E ron.laffitte@pfeiffer.edu
LAFFOON-JACKSON, Julia 270-707-3885 182 B julia.laffoon@kctcs.edu
LAFLAM, Tina 802-387-1674 462 C tlaflam@landmark.edu
LAFLAMME, Jacques 401-739-5000 404 E jlaflamme@neit.edu
LAFLASH, Debra, A 508-854-4551 215 F dal@qcc.mass.edu
LAFLER, Renata 303-273-3823 79 J rlafler@mines.edu
LAFLEUR, Jennifer 410-462-7405 198 B jlafleur@bccc.edu
LAFLEUR, Laura 337-421-6948 188 J laura.lafleur@sowela.edu
LAFLEUR, Rebecca 914-323-5293 305 B rebecca.lafleur@mville.edu
LAFONTAINE, Francine 734-764-1361 231 H laf@umich.edu
LAFONTAINE, Joni 701-477-7862 346 J jlafontaine@tm.edu
LAFONTANA, Kathryn 440-646-8101 363 C kathryn.lafontana@ursuline.edu
LAFOREST, Beth 734-462-4400 230 G blafores@schoolcraft.edu
LAFORGE, William (Bill) 662-846-4000 245 G wlaforge@deltastate.edu
LAFRANCE, Dawn 315-228-7385 296 E dlafrance@colgate.edu
LAFRANCE, George 505-387-7477 286 I glefrance@navajotech.edu
LAFRANCE, Herard 954-427-8830 104 K
LAGAL, Billy 361-570-4865 453 B lagalb@uhv.edu
LAGARDERE, Fabiola 305-629-2929 107 H flagardere@sanignaciouniversity.edu
LAGATTA, Andrea 315-792-7273 321 B andrea.lagatta@sunypoly.edu
LAGATTA, Regina 518-629-7736 302 C r.lagatta@hvcc.edu
LAGO, Baldomero 801-863-7301 460 D lagoba@uvu.edu
LAGORIO, Grant 541-956-7378 376 A glagorio@roguecc.edu
LAGRAND, James 717-796-1800 389 H jlagrand@messiah.edu
LAGRASSA, Michael 508-999-9180 212 A mlagrassa@umassd.edu
LAGRONE, Lynn 319-296-4015 166 H lynn.lagrone@hawkeyecollege.edu
LAGROW, Jeff 309-694-5127 139 B jeff.lagrow@icc.edu
LAGUARDIA COOPER, Beth 304-724-3700 486 F blaguardia@apus.edu
LAGUE, Lorna, J 218-935-0417 244 G lorna.lague@wetcc.edu
LAGUERRE-BROWN, Caroline 202-994-2360 92 D clbrown@gwu.edu
LAGUILLES, Raldy 413-748-3244 218 I rlaguilles@springfield.edu
LAGUNA BORREGO, Maryam 305-237-3118 104 E mlaguna@mdc.edu
LAGUNEZ, David 972-241-3371 434 D
LAH, Cindy 614-236-6742 349 B clah@capital.edu
LAHAIE, Goeffrey 541-880-2392 373 C lahaieg@klamathcc.edu
LAHAIE, Jeanne 541-880-2231 373 C lahaie@klamathcc.edu
LAHAIE, Ute 330-490-7453 363 E ulahaie@walsh.edu
LAHART, Amy 570-674-6320 390 B alahart@misericordia.edu
LAHART, Edward 570-504-9668 384 B elahart@som.geisinger.edu
LAHM, Terry, D 614-236-6108 349 B tlahm@capital.edu
LAHODA, Anne, L 412-397-5235 397 B lahoda@rmu.edu
LAHR, Sheri, K 580-327-8550 367 A sklahr@nwosu.edu
LAHTI, Michele 209-667-3131 33 B mlahti@csustan.edu
LAI, Chun 215-887-5511 402 E clai@wts.edu
LAIDACKER, Crystal 972-241-3371 434 D claidacker@dallas.edu
LAIDLAW, Shawn 201-684-6836 280 H slaidlaw@ramapo.edu
LAIN, Jill 214-860-8845 435 A jilllain@dcccd.edu
LAINE, Vance 309-268-4355 142 H vlaine@lincolncollege.edu
LAING, Joyce 941-727-2273 112 B
LAING, Latoya 312-341-3616 148 E llaing@roosevelt.edu
LAINO, Nicholas 315-866-0300 301 D lainonf@herkimer.edu
LAINSBURY, Kristen 765-983-1512 155 A lainskr@earlham.edu
LAIRD, Curt 614-287-2786 351 C claird@cscc.edu
LAIRD, Kimberly 903-566-7044 456 A klaird@uttyler.edu
LAIRD, Nicole 870-230-5076 19 D lairdn@hsu.edu
LAIRD, Stephen 509-452-5100 482 B slaird@pnwu.edu
LAIRD, Whitney 270-831-9627 182 A whitney.laird@kctcs.edu
LAIRMORE, Michael, D 530-752-1361 69 B mdlairmore@ucdavis.edu
LAJOIE, Evviva 716-645-2965 316 C evvivawe@buffalo.edu
LAJOIE, Roger 603-524-3207 272 K rlajoie@ccsnh.edu
LAJUBUTU, Oyebanjo, A 419-372-7816 348 G lajubuo@bgsu.edu
LAKE, Claude 205-391-2996 3 E clake@sheltonstate.edu
LAKE, Diana 360-475-7831 481 I dlake@olympic.edu
LAKE, Erinn 814-732-2856 394 B lakee@edinboro.edu
LAKE, Erinn 814-732-2724 394 B lakee@edinboro.edu
LAKE, Kathryn 740-427-5113 354 I lakek@kenyon.edu
LAKE, Kathy 231-591-2113 224 A kathylake@ferris.edu
LAKE, Kendra 231-348-6715 228 H klake@ncmich.edu
LAKE, Kendra 810-989-5642 230 F kklake@sc4.edu
LAKE, Lauren 607-871-2412 290 B lakel@alfred.edu
LAKE, Lyndon, J 315-267-2573 319 A lakelj@potsdam.edu
LAKE, Michael, P 850-644-2478 110 C mlake@admin.fsu.edu
LAKE, Patti 406-683-7031 264 A patricia.lake@umwestern.edu
LAKE, Rebecca 361-570-4835 453 B laker@uhv.edu
LAKE, Stephanie, S 919-866-5927 338 G sslake@waketech.edu
LAKE, Todd 615-460-6628 418 B todd.lake@belmont.edu
LAKE-KING, Shirley, L 340-693-1400 513 E sking@uvi.edu
LAKEN, Michael, J 630-515-6148 144 F mlaken@midwestern.edu
LAKETA, Dave 815-740-3464 152 H dlaketa@stfrancis.edu
LAKEY, David, L 512-852-3194 454 H dlakey@utsystem.edu
LAKHANI, Aliza 617-373-2000 217 I
LAKHANI, Vikash 760-744-1150 56 B vlakhani@palomar.edu
LAKIN, Jessica 973-408-3263 277 A jlakin@drew.edu
LAKIS, James 570-321-4141 389 B lakis@lycoming.edu
LAKOTA, Kimberly 440-646-8312 363 C klakota@ursuline.edu
LAKSHMANASWAMY, Rajkumar 915-215-4158 451 B rajkumar.lakshmanaswamy@ttuhsc.edu
LAKSHMINARAYANAN, Sambhavi 718-270-5122 294 G slakshminarayanan@mec.cuny.edu
LALA, Andrea 518-608-8153 299 C alala@excelsior.edu
LALANDE, Emmanuel 803-705-4684 406 G emmanuel.lalande@benedict.edu
LALCHANDANI, Atam 775-831-1314 272 D kyoung@sierranevada.edu
LALIBERTE, Michael, R 607-746-4090 320 D lalibemr@delhi.edu
LALLO, Christian 410-225-2300 200 D clallo@mica.edu
LALLY, Jay 321-674-8278 100 C jlally@fit.edu
LALLY, Kim, B 937-229-3902 362 C klally1@udayton.edu
LALLY, Mary 617-573-8430 219 B mlally@suffolk.edu
LALLY, Shiela 617-236-4422 209 G slally@fisher.edu
LALONDE, Catherine 518-327-6056 311 C clalonde@paulsmiths.edu
LALONDE, Joseph, C 337-550-1470 189 G jlalonde@lsue.edu
LALONDE, Matthew 518-255-5215 319 C lalondmm@cobleskill.edu
LALOVIC-HAND, Mira 856-256-4146 281 F lalovic-hand@rowan.edu
LALTRELLO, Rob 678-872-8088 119 D rlaltrel@highlands.edu
LALUMENDRE, Rob 815-939-5350 147 A rlalumen@olivet.edu
LALUZERNE, Joe 619-849-2317 57 J jlaluzer@pointloma.edu
LALUZERNE, Shannon, S 920-923-7661 493 D slaluzerne@marianuniversity.edu
LAM, Clement 408-855-5332 75 D clement.lam@wvm.edu
LAM, Felix 212-650-8173 293 D flam@ccny.cuny.edu
LAM, Mariam 951-827-5672 70 B mariam.lam@ucr.edu
LAM, Ming-huei 323-357-6234 48 J lamm2@elac.edu
LAM, Mirasari 817-202-6233 444 I miral@swau.edu
LAM, Philip 212-517-3929 315 G p.lam@sia.edu
LAM, Sarah 315-792-5321 306 K slam@mvcc.edu
LAM, Trang 503-943-7331 377 A lam@up.edu
LAM YUEN, Peteru, K 684-699-9155 504 B p.lamyuen@amsamoa.edu
LAMAGNA, Dan 570-504-1579 387 B lamagnad@lackawanna.edu
LAMANNA, Richard 718-289-5355 293 B richard.lamanna@bcc.cuny.edu
LAMAR, Melissa 860-773-1407 87 G mlamar@tunxis.edu
LAMAR, Sharmaine 610-690-5675 398 G slamar1@swarthmore.edu
LAMARAND, Donita, M 757-446-6009 466 D lamaradm@evms.edu
LAMARCH, Jessica 906-217-4086 222 A jessica.lamarch@baycollege.edu
LAMARCHE, Gilles 770-426-2674 122 C gilles.lamarche@life.edu
LAMARCHE, Paul 609-258-4999 280 D lamarche@princeton.edu
LAMB, Barry, P 217-786-2334 143 B barry.lamb@llcc.edu
LAMB, Colin 620-276-9683 174 B colin.lamb@gcccks.edu
LAMB, Cory 641-683-5141 166 I cory.lamb@indianhills.edu
LAMB, Craig 585-345-6969 300 F crlamb@genesee.edu
LAMB, Craig 704-216-3500 337 F craig.lamb@rccc.edu
LAMB, David 215-368-5000 390 A dlamb@missio.edu
LAMB, Duane 205-348-8092 7 G dlamb@fa.ua.edu
LAMB, Earnest 218-477-2764 239 E earnest.lamb@mnstate.edu
LAMB, Jeffrey, N 714-564-6080 58 F lamb_jeffrey@sac.edu
LAMB, Jennifer 276-326-4397 464 J jlamb@bluefield.edu
LAMB, Jon 734-462-4400 230 G jlamb@schoolcraft.edu
LAMB, Keith 940-397-4291 440 C keith.lamb@msutexas.edu
LAMB, Kelly 816-331-5700 258 D

LAMB, Kevin, D .... 859-238-5367 180 B
kevin.lamb@centre.edu
LAMB, Kyle .... 731-989-6020 419 K
klamb@fhu.edu
LAMB, Linda .... 315-866-0300 301 D
lamblc@herkimer.edu
LAMB, Margaret .... 619-388-6957.. 60 H
mlamb@sdccd.edu
LAMB, Mary .... 707-468-3071.. 51 F
mlamb@mendocino.edu
LAMB, Marybeth .... 508-531-1353 212 D
marybeth.lamb@bridgew.edu
LAMB, Melissa .... 912-427-5840 117 E
mlamb@coastalpines.edu
LAMB, Michael .... 316-978-3804 178 D
mike.lamb@wichita.edu
LAMB, Molly .... 217-206-8622 152 A
mehle01s@uis.edu
LAMB, Scott .... 434-592-6836 468 E
scottlamb@liberty.edu
LAMB, Stephen, R .... 706-446-3147 116 A
stelamb@augusta.edu
LAMB, Susan .... 925-969-2001.. 40 C
slamb@dvc.edu
LAMBA, Sandy .... 707-864-7000.. 64 H
sandy.lamba@solano.edu
LAMBA, Sangeeta .... 973-972-4823 282 A
lambasa@njms.rutgers.edu
LAMBDIN, Brandon ...... 423-746-5337 426 C
bslambdin@tnwewsleyan.edu
LAMBE, Joan .... 212-772-5462 294 C
joan.lambe@hunter.cuny.edu
LAMBERSON, Diane ...... 281-649-3090 437 B
dlamberson@hbu.edu
LAMBERSON, Jeffrey ..... 843-953-7962 407 C
jlamber6@citadel.edu
LAMBERSON, Shannon . 817-531-5817 451 C
sklamberson@txwes.edu
LAMBERT, Alli .... 802-656-0518 463 A
alli.lambert@uvm.edu
LAMBERT, Ame .... 503-725-4410 375 E
alamber2@pdx.edu
LAMBERT, Angela .... 304-327-4480 489 I
alambert@bluefieldstate.edu
LAMBERT, Anne .... 713-525-2160 454 G
lambera@stthom.edu
LAMBERT, Bill .... 909-274-4215.. 52 J
wlambert@mtsac.edu
LAMBERT, Brooke .... 402-557-7087 265 J
blambert@bellevue.edu
LAMBERT, Buddy .... 918-540-6451 366 F
georgml@neo.edu
LAMBERT, Charla .... 516-367-6890 296 C
LAMBERT, Chip .... 276-326-4603 464 J
clambert@bluefield.edu
LAMBERT, Chris .... 757-352-4091 470 B
clambert@regent.edu
LAMBERT, Christopher .. 267-341-3309 385 J
clambert@holyfamily.edu
LAMBERT, Christopher .. 414-425-8300 495 A
clambert@shsst.edu
LAMBERT, Cindy .... 806-874-3571 432 J
cindy.lambert@clarendoncollege.edu
LAMBERT, David .... 740-377-2520 361 E
david.lambert@tsbc.edu
LAMBERT, Dewayne ...... 985-545-1500 188 E
LAMBERT, Elizabeth ...... 607-735-1806 298 H
llambert@elmira.edu
LAMBERT, Ian .... 313-664-1474 222 H
ilambert@collegeforcreativestudies.edu
LAMBERT, James .... 540-261-4122 471 B
james.lambert@svu.edu
LAMBERT, James .... 802-468-6052 463 E
james.lambert@castleton.edu
LAMBERT, James .... 419-372-9970 348 G
jlamber@bgsu.edu
LAMBERT, Jay .... 361-570-4290 453 B
lambertj1@uhv.edu
LAMBERT, Kathy .... 919-508-2028 344 E
kplambert@peace.edu
LAMBERT, Kelley .... 276-326-4260 464 J
klambert@bluefield.edu
LAMBERT, Kevin .... 606-589-2145 183 A
LAMBERT, III, Lake .... 812-866-7056 155 G
lambert@hanover.edu
LAMBERT, Lee, D .... 520-206-4747.. 15 B
llambert@pima.edu
LAMBERT, Lori, A .... 513-745-3203 364 G
lambert@xavier.edu
LAMBERT, Patrick .... 845-398-4396 314 G
plambert@stac.edu
LAMBERT, Robyn .... 573-288-6640 252 F
rlambert@culver.edu
LAMBERT, Sarah .... 423-775-6596 422 I
slambert@ogs.edu
LAMBERT, Stacey .... 617-327-6777 220 C
stacey_lambert@williamjames.edu
LAMBERT, Tamatha .... 478-471-2700 122 F
LAMBERT, Toni .... 434-949-1017 475 B
toni.lambert@southside.edu
LAMBERT-JONES,
Rythee .... 301-405-1247 202 H
LAMBERTH, Lucy .... 601-484-8776 247 A
lmorgan1@meridiancc.edu
LAMBERTON, Jill .... 765-361-6154 163 B
lambertj@wabash.edu
LAMBETH, Gregory .... 208-885-6716 132 F
lambeth@uidaho.edu
LAMBLEY, Jennifer .... 605-367-5990 417 B
jennifer.lambley@southeasttech.edu
LAMBORN, Kim .... 503-251-5798 377 B
klamborn@uws.edu
LAMBOY, Camille .... 787-743-7979 510 H
calamboy@suagm.edu
LAMBOY, Edwin .... 212-650-5697 293 D
elamboy@ccny.cuny.edu
LAMBOY, Maritza .... 787-834-9595 510 D
mlamboy@uaa.edu
LAMBRAKIS, Christine .. 602-286-8227.. 13 B
christine.lambrakis@gatewaycc.edu
LAMBRECHT, Anne, K ... 989-463-7225 221 B
lambrechtak@alma.edu
LAMBRECHT,
Jessica, N .... 920-565-1000 493 A
lambrechtjn@lakeland.edu
LAMBRECHT, John .... 708-456-0300 151 D
johnlambrecht@triton.edu
LAMBRECHTSEN, Karen 916-577-2200.. 76 D
klambrechtsen@jessup.edu
LAMBRIGHT, Jonathan .. 912-358-4172 125 A
lambrij@savannahstate.edu
LAMBROPOULOUS,
Despina .... 978-556-3614 215 E
dlambropoulos@necc.mass.edu
LAMBRUNO, Joyce .... 270-707-3844 182 B
joyce.lambruno@kctcs.edu
LAMELZA, George .... 417-447-2664 257 G
lamelzag@otc.edu
LAMENS, Gigi .... 631-687-4500 314 A
glamens@sjcny.edu
LAMERS, Chet .... 920-498-5723 499 G
chet.lamers@nwtc.edu
LAMICA, Lauren .... 413-545-3016 211 G
llamica@finaid.umass.edu
LAMICA, Thomas .... 805-922-6966.. 24 I
thomas.lamica@hancockcollege.edu
LAMIMAN, Lynne .... 972-708-7536 435 E
LAMIOTTE, Jonathan ..... 860-215-9323.. 87 F
jlamiotte@threerivers.edu
LAMIQUIZ, Jason .... 509-453-0374 482 D
jason.lamiquiz@perrytech.edu
LAMM, Edward .... 920-403-3007 495 B
edward.lamm@snc.edu
LAMM, Gary .... 254-295-4545 453 D
glamm@umhb.edu
LAMMERS, Amanda ...... 770-534-6108 116 D
alammers@brenau.edu
LAMMERS, Jenna .... 618-545-3044 141 E
jlammers@kaskaskia.edu
LAMMERS, Shelley .... 402-844-7282 268 H
shelley@northeast.edu
LAMMONS, Anthony ..... 951-343-4309.. 27 G
alammons@calbaptist.edu
LAMONS, Jerisia .... 270-706-8841 181 G
jlamons0001@kctcs.edu
LAMONT, Becky .... 812-488-2680 161 G
bl164@evansville.edu
LAMONTAGNE, Ramona 815-836-5291 142 F
lamontra@lewisu.edu
LAMOTT, Eric, E .... 651-641-8729 235 I
lamott@csp.edu
LAMOUREUX, Leila .... 781-239-4702 206 B
llamoureux@babson.edu
LAMOUREUX, AA,
Richard, E .... 508-767-7033 206 A
re.lamoureux@assumption.edu
LAMPE, Lawrence, P ..... 513-556-2201 361 J
lampelp@ucmail.uc.edu
LAMPE, Paul .... 636-584-6581 253 B
paul.lampe@eastcentral.edu
LAMPEREZ, Eddie .... 480-423-6300.. 13 H
eddie.lamperez@scottsdalecc.edu
LAMPERT, Jackie .... 701-766-4415 344 G
LAMPERT-SHEPEL,
Elina .... 212-463-0400 322 G
elina.lampert-shepel@touro.edu
LAMPHERE, Scott .... 617-243-2115 211 B
slamphere@lasell.edu
LAMPHIER, Denise .... 641-628-5279 164 D
lamphierd@centrla.edu
LAMPING, Patrick .... 859-442-4175 181 H
patrick.lamping@kctcs.edu
LAMPKIN, Reggie .... 706-867-4518 127 A
reggie.lampkin@ung.edu
LAMPKIN-WILLIAMS,
Ann .... 313-593-5321 231 I
lampkin@umich.edu
LAMPKIN-WILLIAMS,
Ann .... 313-593-5090 231 I
lampkin@umich.edu
LAMPLEY, Dearl .... 615-790-4419 424 C
dlampley@columbiastate.edu
LAMPLEY, Katherine ...... 781-891-2243 206 G
klampley@bentley.edu
LAMPMAN, Claudia ...... 907-786-1619.... 9 J
cblampman@alaska.edu
LAMPO, Jane .... 816-654-7109 254 E
jlampo@kcumb.edu
LAMPO, Jane .... 816-654-7282 254 E
jlampo@kcumb.edu
LAMPSON, Dawayne ..... 715-682-1399 494 G
dlampson@northland.edu
LAMSMA, Matt .... 509-313-4100 480 F
lamsma@gonzaga.edu
LAMUNYON, Craig .... 909-869-3898.. 30 A
cwlamunyon@cpp.edu
LAMURAGLIA, Rose ...... 619-388-3488.. 60 I
rlamurag@sdccd.edu
LANA, Peter .... 585-389-2344 307 F
plana0@naz.edu
LANAGAN, Keni .... 865-981-8308 421 C
keni.lanagan@maryvillecollege.edu
LANAHAN, Richard .... 570-208-6069 386 G
richardlanahan@kings.edu
LANCASTER, Amy, E ...... 864-597-4430 414 E
lancasterae@wofford.edu
LANCASTER, Brad .... 717-337-6377 384 D
blancast@gettysburg.edu
LANCASTER, Brian .... 620-223-2700 173 I
brianl@fortscott.edu
LANCASTER, David .... 304-424-8346 490 F
david.lancaster@wvup.edu
LANCASTER, Dennis ...... 417-255-7900 256 H
dennislancaster@missouristate.edu
LANCASTER, Dennis ...... 417-255-7900 256 G
dennislancaster@missouristate.edu
LANCASTER, James .... 630-844-5144 133 D
jlancast@aurora.edu
LANCASTER, James .... 323-953-4000.. 49 A
lancasj@lacitycollege.edu
LANCASTER, Jennifer .... 718-489-5323 313 E
jlancaster@sfc.edu
LANCASTER, Kelly .... 406-604-4300 262 I
klancaster@apollos.edu
LANCASTER, Kim .... 270-745-4346 186 C
kim.lancaster@wku.edu
LANCASTER, Kimberley . 561-790-9006 105 D
lancastk@palmbeachstate.edu
LANCASTER, Loren .... 406-874-6171 263 H
lancasterl@milescc.edu
LANCASTER, Mary Beth 251-809-1500.... 1 I
mary.lancaster@coastalalabama.edu
LANCASTER, Paula, E ... 989-774-6995 222 E
lanca1pe@cmich.edu
LANCASTER, Rich .... 484-365-7252 388 H
rlancaster@lincoln.edu
LANCASTER, Robin .... 501-882-4547.. 17 D
rglancaster@asub.edu
LANCE, Amanda .... 870-777-5722.. 22 I
amanda.lance@uaht.edu
LANCE, Cindy .... 870-777-5722.. 22 I
cindy.lance@uaht.edu
LAND, Christopher .... 508-289-2900 220 E
cland@whoi.edu
LAND, Elizabeth .... 504-280-6723 190 B
eland@uno.edu
LAND, Kelly .... 706-778-8500 124 D
LAND, Matt .... 260-665-4143 161 E
landm@trine.edu
LAND, Richard, D .... 704-847-5600 340 F
pginn@ses.edu
LAND, Roderic .... 801-957-4024 461 C
roderic.land@slcc.edu
LANDA, Carrie .... 617-353-3569 207 E
clanda@bu.edu
LANDA, Keith .... 914-251-6435 319 B
keith.landa@purchase.edu
LANDAETA, Carolina ..... 305-629-2929 107 H
clandaeta@sanignaciouniversity.edu
LANDAU, Joshua .... 717-815-6632 403 F
jlandau@ycp.edu
LANDEN, Jenny .... 505-428-1837 288 E
jenny.landen@sfcc.edu
LANDEN, Marcia .... 601-266-4119 249 F
marcia.landen@usm.edu
LANDEN, Robyn .... 307-268-2362 500 U
rlanden@caspercollege.edu
LANDENBERGER, Lacey 316-295-5407 174 A
lacey_landenberger@friends.edu
LANDENBERGER,
Rebecca .... 906-217-4266 222 A
becky.landenberger@baycollege.edu
LANDENBERGER, Toni .. 402-228-8286 269 C
tlandenberger@southeast.edu
LANDENBURGER,
Marguerite .... 540-665-4618 470 G
mlandenb@su.edu
LANDER, Janice .... 303-273-3266.. 79 J
jslander@mines.edu
LANDER, Laura .... 903-730-4890 438 D
llander@jarvis.edu
LANDER, Maria .... 704-290-5267 337 I
mlander@spcc.edu
LANDER, Marissa .... 410-857-2223 200 F
mlander@mcdaniel.edu
LANDEROS, Ramiro ...... 714-744-7865.. 36 B
landeros@chapman.edu
LANDERS, Ben .... 865-251-1800 423 E
blanders@south.edu
LANDERS, Joanne .... 973-290-4720 282 I
jlanders@steu.edu
LANDERS, Mary, G .... 336-256-2014 343 A
mglander@uncg.edu
LANDERS, Michael .... 903-875-7488 440 D
michael.landers@navarrocollege.edu
LANDERS, Tyler, R .... 262-243-5700 492 E
tyler.landers@cuw.edu
LANDEVER, Gwen .... 913-758-6243 178 B
gwen.landever@stmary.edu
LANDGAARD, Jodi .... 507-372-3403 239 F
jodi.landgaard@mnwest.edu
LANDGRAF, Tanya .... 712-749-2212 164 C
landgraft@bvu.edu
LANDGREN, Peter .... 513-556-6703 361 J
peter.landgren@uc.edu
LANDING, Haydee .... 787-725-8120 506 M
hlandiing0030@eap.edu
LANDINO,
Christopher, S .... 570-422-7952 394 A
clandino@esu.edu
LANDIS, Amy .... 303-273-3871.. 79 J
amylandis@mines.edu
LANDIS, Bethany, L ...... 517-750-1200 231 C
blandis@arbor.edu
LANDIS, David .... 620-278-4235 177 H
dlandis@sterling.edu
LANDIS, Jean, W .... 215-951-1020 387 A
landis@lasalle.edu
LANDIS, Jennifer .... 717-299-7754 399 C
LANDIS, Kristi .... 712-324-5061 169 C
klandis@nwicc.edu
LANDIS, Michelle .... 928-344-7526.. 11 A
michelle.landis@azwestern.edu
LANDIS, Michelle .... 928-317-6000.. 11 A
LANDIS, Sarah .... 540-828-5334 464 L
slandis@bridgewater.edu
LANDIS, Susan .... 540-665-4513 470 G
slandis@su.edu
LANDISS, Leslie .... 615-966-6194 421 B
leslie.landiss@lipscomb.edu
LANDOWSKI, Anthony .. 608-757-7726 498 D
alandowski@blackhawk.edu
LANDPHAIR, Juliette ..... 540-654-1656 471 N
jlandpha@umw.edu
LANDRAU-ESPINOSA,
Barbara .... 787-993-8856 512 A
barbara.landrau@upr.edu
LANDREMAN, Lisa .... 503-370-6139 377 F
llandreman@willamette.edu
LANDRETH, Paige .... 405-945-3200 368 C
paige.n.landreth@okstate.edu
LANDRIEU, Josefina ..... 651-793-1300 238 I
josefina.landrieu@metrostate.edu
LANDRIEU, Madeleine .. 504-861-5550 190 C
landrieu@loyno.edu
LANDRITH, James .... 864-231-2000 406 F
wlandrith@andersonuniversity.edu
LANDRUM, Kay .... 817-598-6499 457 J
klandrum@wc.edu
LANDRUM, Zalika .... 773-602-5116 135 D
zlandrum@ccc.edu
LANDRY, Abbie .... 318-357-4403 192 G
landry@nsula.edu

LANDRY, Brett .... 972-721-5276 452 B
cobdean@udallas.edu
LANDRY, Debborah .... 918-444-2060 366 G
landryd@nsuok.edu
LANDRY, Fred .... 318-869-5136 186 F
flandry@centenary.edu
LANDRY, Julie .... 414-930-3185 494 E
landryj@mtmary.edu
LANDRY, Lisa, C .... 337-482-5430 193 B
ldlandry@louisiana.edu
LANDRY, Nicole .... 414-930-3663 494 E
landryn@mtmary.edu
LANDRY, Patrick .... 337-482-6402 193 B
pml@louisiana.edu
LANDRY, Shawntel, D ... 800-280-0307 153 E
shawntel.landry@ace.edu
LANDRY, Stephen .... 973-761-7386 283 C
stephen.landry@shu.edu
LANDRY-THOMAS,
Kerii .... 225-771-2142 191 E
klandry-thomas@sulc.edu
LANDS, Jon .... 850-478-8496 105 G
jlands@pcci.edu
LANDSAW, Christy .... 918-444-2192 366 G
landsaw@nsuok.edu
LANDWER, Allan, J .... 325-670-5894 436 I
alandwer@hsutx.edu
LANDWERMEYER,
Elizabeth .... 817-515-3049 445 F
elizabeth.landwermeyer@tccd.edu
LANDY, Margo .... 415-338-3982.. 33 E
margolandy@sfsu.edu
LANE, Austin, A .... 618-453-2341 150 B
austin.lane@siu.edu
LANE, Betsy .... 760-355-6525.. 45 K
betsy.lane@imperial.edu
LANE, Beverly .... 614-885-5585 359 L
bslane@pcj.edu
LANE, Bradley .... 310-434-4702.. 63 C
lane_bradley@smc.edu
LANE, Charles, E .... 352-392-9122 111 A
charlielane@ufl.edu
LANE, Dean .... 202-462-2101.. 93 A
dlane@iwp.edu
LANE, Deborah .... 405-744-6384 367 G
debbie.lane@okstate.edu
LANE, Deborah .... 865-573-4517 420 E
dlane@johnsonu.edu
LANE, Diane, L .... 217-362-6416 144 G
dlane@millikin.edu
LANE, Edwin, H .... 816-415-7587 262 F
lanee@william.jewell.edu
LANE, Eric .... 951-343-4689.. 27 G
elane@calbaptist.edu
LANE, Gower .... 845-451-1309 297 G
gower.lane@culinary.edu
LANE, Jill .... 618-468-4900 142 E
jlane@lc.edu
LANE, Jill .... 678-466-4194 117 D
jilllane@clayton.edu
LANE, John .... 713-221-8292 453 A
lanej@uhd.edu
LANE, Jon .... 940-397-4241 440 C
jon.lane@msutexas.edu
LANE, Joseph .... 304-829-7311 487 A
jlane@bethanywv.edu
LANE, Kelsi-Leandra ..... 315-445-4194 303 I
lanekl@lemoyne.edu
LANE, Kimberly, A .... 864-833-8379 411 D
kalane@presby.edu
LANE, Kristi .... 218-855-8054 237 G
kristi.lane@clcmn.edu
LANE, Krystle .... 918-463-2931 365 J
kdlane@connorsstate.edu
LANE, LaTia .... 773-291-6100 135 E
LANE, Laura .... 248-476-1122 227 E
llane@msp.edu
LANE, Marguerite .... 516-323-4014 306 M
mlane@molloy.edu
LANE, Mary Ellen .... 508-856-4018 212 C
maryellen.lane@umassmed.edu
LANE, Michael .... 516-686-7723 308 I
mlane@nyit.edu
LANE, Natalie .... 307-382-1673 501 J
nlane@westernwyoming.edu
LANE, Nathan .... 561-803-2754 105 C
nathan_lane@pba.edu
LANE, Phillip .... 618-985-2828 140 H
philliplane@jalc.edu
LANE, Rick .... 217-206-6678 152 A
rlane3@uis.edu
LANE, Robert, J .... 515-961-1417 170 B
bob.lane@simpson.edu
LANE, Rona .... 212-237-8000 294 D
LANE, Sean .... 256-824-6200.... 8 B
sean.lane@uah.edu
LANE, Shamica .... 252-335-3251 341 B
sdlane@ecsu.edu
LANE, Stephanie .... 707-826-3132.. 33 C
sml19@humboldt.edu
LANE, Thomas, A .... 785-532-6237 175 C
talane@ksu.edu
LANE, Tracey, R .... 817-722-1621 438 G
tracey.lane@tku.edu
LANE, Tracy .... 252-246-1202 339 C
tlane@wilsoncc.edu
LANE, Troy .... 865-974-6631 427 B
tlane15@utk.edu
LANE RASMUS, Fran, R 253-535-7141 482 A
lanerafr@plu.edu
LANEAR, John .... 866-776-0331.. 54 D
provost@ncu.edu
LANEEL TANNER, Beth . 732-247-5241 279 C
btanner@nbts.edu
LANESSKOG, Stig .... 909-621-8026.. 37 B
stig.lanesskog@claremont.edu
LANEVE, Melissa .... 508-849-3205 205 H
mlaneve@annamaria.edu
LANEY, Brenda .... 816-501-4122 258 I
brenda.laney@rockhurst.edu
LANEY, Candy .... 406-874-6165 263 H
laneyc@milescc.edu
LANFEAR, Jeffery .... 773-325-8308 136 H
jlanfear@depaul.edu
LANFORD, Coty .... 540-863-2861 473 F
clanford@dslcc.edu
LANFORD, Julie .... 864-587-4233 412 F
lanfordj@smcsc.edu
LANG, Angela .... 740-374-8716 363 F
alang1@wscc.edu
LANG, Bob .... 970-248-1754.. 78 J
bllang@coloradomesa.edu
LANG, Christopher .... 660-543-4673 260 G
crlang@ucmo.edu
LANG, Heather .... 971-722-4008 375 D
heather.lang@pcc.edu
LANG, Jennifer, R .... 718-780-0679 291 K
jennifer.lang@brooklaw.edu
LANG, Jessica .... 646-312-3870 292 L
jessica.lang@baruch.cuny.edu
LANG, Katherine .... 580-559-5424 365 K
klang@ecok.edu
LANG, Lisa .... 901-435-1200 420 I
lisa_lang@loc.edu
LANG, Lisa, K .... 502-597-5945 183 D
lisa.lang@kysu.edu
LANG, Mandy .... 715-422-5446 499 B
mandy.lang@mstc.edu
LANG, Mary, K .... 330-569-5137 353 G
langmk@hiram.edu
LANG, Milton .... 510-659-6107.. 54 J
mlang@ohlone.edu
LANG, Mindy .... 212-353-4212 297 E
lang@cooper.edu
LANG, Suzanne .... 517-353-5300 227 F
langsu@msu.edu
LANG-RAYMOND,
Michelle .... 503-517-1190 377 C
mlang@warnerpacific.edu
LANGAN, Brooke .... 570-422-3619 394 A
blangan1@esu.edu
LANGAN, Elena .... 631-761-7100 322 F
elangan@tourolaw.edu
LANGAN, Elena .... 631-761-7100 322 G
elangan@tourolaw.edu
LANGAN, Frances .... 570-945-8000 386 F
fran.langan@keystone.edu
LANGAN, Nicole .... 570-945-8274 386 F
nicole.langan@keystone.edu
LANGDON, Dawn .... 410-462-8352 198 B
dlangdon@bccc.edu
LANGDON, Dawn .... 304-243-2304 491 E
finaid@wheeling.edu
LANGDON, Deb .... 740-389-4636 355 F
langdond@mtc.edu
LANGDON, Heather, H .. 828-262-2093 340 I
langdonhh@appstate.edu
LANGDON, James .... 608-262-4048 495 C
jlangdon@uwsa.edu
LANGDON, Nikolette ..... 502-213-2400 182 C
nikolette.langdon@kctcs.edu
LANGDON, Steven, D ... 573-334-6825 259 G
slangdon@sehcollege.edu
LANGE, Denice .... 480-285-1761.. 12 B
LANGE, Don .... 817-272-3571 454 I
donlange@uta.edu
LANGE, Janet .... 309-677-2523 134 A
lange@bradley.edu
LANGE, Janet .... 309-677-2374 134 A
lange@fsmail.bradley.edu
LANGE, Jeff .... 309-438-3383 140 D
jwlange@ilstu.edu
LANGE, Karen, M .... 651-962-6120 244 E
kmlange@stthomas.edu
LANGE, Mark .... 608-262-3253 495 C
mark.lange@business.wisconsin.edu
LANGE, Paul .... 800-553-4674 156 B
plange@horizonuniversity.edu
LANGE, Richard .... 915-215-4300 451 B
richard.lange@ttuhsc.edu
LANGE, Robert, A .... 423-439-4641 419 G
langer@etsu.edu
LANGE, Robert, J .... 757-594-7015 465 M
robert.lange@cnu.edu
LANGE, Shane .... 815-224-0219 140 E
shane_lange@ivcc.edu
LANGE, Steven .... 320-629-5155 240 D
steve.lange@pine.edu
LANGE, Tom, J .... 715-831-7285 498 E
tlange8@cvtc.edu
LANGE, Tyana .... 660-785-7468 260 F
tyana@truman.edu
LANGE, Tyler .... 206-616-5631 485 A
langet2@uw.edu
LANGELL, John .... 330-325-6255 357 D
LANGEMAK, Elizabeth ... 215-951-1145 387 A
langemak@lasalle.edu
LANGEMEIER, Ryan .... 507-379-3335 240 G
ryan.langemeier@riverland.edu
LANGEN, Jill .... 989-729-3350 221 F
jill.langen@baker.edu
LANGENBERG, Todd ...... 410-704-4679 204 E
tlangenberg@towson.edu
LANGENEGGER, Joyce .. 979-209-8991 431 H
joyce.langenegger@blinn.edu
LANGENMAYR,
Kimberly .... 516-323-3952 306 M
klangenmayr@mollloy.edu
LANGER, Dan .... 608-262-4766 495 D
dan.langer@wisc.edu
LANGER, Katherine .... 803-323-4746 414 D
langerk@winthrop.edu
LANGER, Manfred .... 740-377-2520 361 E
manfred.langer@tsbc.edu
LANGER, Patricia .... 651-696-6211 236 I
LANGERBEIN, Helmut ... 870-235-4200.. 21 C
hblangerbein@saumag.edu
LANGEVIN, OP,
Dominic .... 202-495-3820.. 93 D
dean@dhs.edu
LANGEVIN, Duetta .... 909-274-4230.. 52 J
dlangevin@mtsac.edu
LANGEVIN, Patrice .... 909-607-2226.. 57 E
patrice_langevin@pitzer.edu
LANGFORD, Allison ...... 417-328-2093 259 I
alangford@sbuniv.edu
LANGFORD, Chris .... 503-253-3443 374 G
clangford@ocom.edu
LANGFORD, Curt .... 806-742-3641 450 F
curt.langford@ttu.edu
LANGFORD, Debra .... 304-876-5216 490 A
dlangfor@shepherd.edu
LANGFORD, Jeremy, W 312-915-6159 143 C
jlangford@luc.edu
LANGFORD, Joel, C ...... 770-720-5585 124 G
jcl@reinhardt.edu
LANGFORD, Pamela ...... 909-537-7454.. 32 E
plangfor@csusb.edu
LANGFORD, Russ .... 417-862-9533 253 F
rlangford@globaluniversity.edu
LANGHAM, Gay .... 601-643-8307 245 F
gay.langham@colin.edu
LANGHAM, Julie .... 706-595-0166 115 J
jlangham@augustatech.edu
LANGHART, Alex .... 662-915-1101 249 D
langhart@olemiss.edu
LANGHART, Maura .... 662-915-2760 249 D
mmwakefi@olemiss.edu
LANGKILDE, Tracy .... 814-865-9591 391 G
tll30@psu.edu
LANGLANDS, Bryan ...... 502-863-8153 180 H
bryan_langlands@georgetowncollege.
edu
LANGLEY, Anne .... 860-486-4035.. 89 D
anne.langley@uconn.edu
LANGLEY, Clint .... 334-214-4853.... 1 H
clint.langley@cv.edu
LANGLEY, Dorothy .... 903-730-4890 438 D
dlangley@jarvis.edu
LANGLEY, Maia .... 502-418-5638 182 C
maia.langley@kctcs.edu
LANGLEY, Seth .... 718-270-7763 317 B
seth.langley@downstate.edu
LANGLEY, Terrell .... 541-917-4999 373 G
langlet@linnbenton.edu
LANGLEY, Trinette, B .... 252-399-6626 326 K
tboone@barton.edu
LANGLEY-TURNBAUGH,
Samantha .... 859-572-7528 184 E
langleys1@nku.edu
LANGLOIS, Jon .... 406-377-9465 263 D
jlanglois@dawson.edu
LANGLOIS, Mary Ann ... 716-888-2103 292 F
langloim@canisius.edu
LANGMAN, Juliet .... 210-458-4011 455 E
LANGOLF, Judi .... 810-762-9585 226 B
jlangolf@kettering.edu
LANGONI, Kerri .... 505-566-3515 288 D
langonik@sanjuancollege.edu
LANGREHR, Andrew ...... 314-539-5364 259 A
alangrehr@stlcc.edu
LANGRIDGE, Nick .... 540-568-3197 468 C
langrinl@jmu.edu
LANGROCK, Adela .... 802-443-3440 462 E
alangroc@middlebury.edu
LANGSTON, Carol .... 409-944-1302 436 E
clangston@gc.edu
LANGSTON, Emily .... 410-972-3303 202 A
emily.langston@sjc.edu
LANGSTON, James .... 209-476-7840.. 67 E
jlangston@clc.edu
LANGSTON, Jessica ...... 918-463-2931 365 J
jessica.langston@connorsstate.edu
LANGSTON, Randall ...... 660-543-4811 260 G
rlangston@ucmo.edu
LANGSTRAAT, Jim .... 503-352-1621 375 C
jim.langstraat@pacificu.edu
LANGSTRAAT, Nate .... 360-383-3350 486 A
nlangstraat@whatcom.edu
LANGTEAU, Paula .... 605-229-8405 415 I
presidentsoffice@presentation.edu
LANGVARDT, Guy .... 213-740-2311.. 73 C
LANGWELL, Teri .... 806-457-4200 436 C
tlangwell@fpctx.edu
LANHAM, Chuck .... 360-650-3917 485 I
chuck.lanham@wwu.edu
LANHAM, Heather .... 937-778-7803 352 D
hlanham@edisonohio.edu
LANHAM, Jeff .... 740-245-7485 363 A
jlanham@rio.edu
LANHAM, Terri .... 270-686-4548 182 F
terri.lanham@kctcs.edu
LANHAM, Tracey, M ..... 239-513-1122 102 D
tlanham@hodges.edu
LANIER, Lisa .... 912-871-1606 123 J
llanier@ogeecheetech.edu
LANIER, Mark .... 910-962-3030 343 C
lanierm@uncw.edu
LANIER, Stephen, M ..... 313-577-5600 232 K
stephen.lanier@wayne.edu
LANIER, Walter .... 414-297-7710 499 C
lanierw@matc.edu
LANIER-SHIPP,
Elizabeth .... 314-516-4753 261 C
laniershippe@umsl.edu
LANKISCH, Karen .... 513-732-5200 362 B
karen.lankisch@uc.edu
LANN, Jennifer .... 802-387-6764 462 C
jlann@landmark.edu
LANNEN, Dan .... 610-282-1100 382 C
daniel.lannen@desales.edu
LANNERS, Brandon .... 607-255-6224 297 F
LANNERT, Mitchell .... 317-931-2313 154 G
mlannert@cts.edu
LANNING, Brek .... 828-565-4027 335 C
bwlanning@haywood.edu
LANNING, Crystal .... 715-425-3246 496 F
crystal.lanning@uwrf.edu
LANNING, Stephanie .... 785-670-1574 178 C
stephanie.lanning@washburn.edu
LANOUE, David .... 870-235-4004.. 21 C
davidlanoue@saumag.edu
LANOUE, Kevin .... 540-568-4777 468 C
lanoueka@jmu.edu
LANPHER, Jim .... 803-754-4100 408 E
LANSING, Corey .... 231-439-6349 228 H
clansing@ncmich.edu
LANSING, Travis .... 801-957-4009 461 C
travis.lansing@slcc.edu
LANSIQUOT,
Beverley, A .... 340-692-4117 513 E
beverley.lansiquot@uvi.edu

LANTER, Jennifer .... 920-735-2520 498 F
lanter@fvtc.edu
LANTHIER, Eric .... 617-243-2433 211 B
elanthier@lasell.edu
LANTHIER-BANDY,
Julie .... 760-744-1150.. 56 B
jlanthierbandy@palomar.edu
LANTIS, Glenda .... 541-318-3753 372 A
glantis@cocc.edu
LANTTA, Lissa .... 608-757-7708 498 D
mlantta@blackhawk.edu
LANTZ, Dana .... 330-941-2216 364 H
cdlantz@ysu.edu
LANTZ, David .... 301-387-3011 199 A
david.lantz@garrettcollege.edu
LANTZ, Mary Jan .... 409-944-1281 436 E
mlantz@gc.edu
LANTZ, Susan .... 570-372-4415 398 F
lantzs@susqu.edu
LANYON, Scott .... 612-625-2809 243 F
slanyon@umn.edu
LANZA, Michael .... 718-951-5220 293 C
mlanza@brooklyn.cuny.edu
LANZEROTTI, Robert ..... 309-794-7374 133 C
robertlanzerotti@augustana.edu
LANZI, Lesley .... 518-736-3622 300 D
lesley.lanzi@fmcc.suny.edu
LANZO, Caryn .... 216-802-3143 350 J
c.lanzo@csuohio.edu
LAO, Lixing .... 703-323-5690 477 A
LAOYZA, Matt .... 507-389-5308 239 D
matthew.laoyza@mnsu.edu
LAP, James .... 718-260-5565 295 A
jlap@citytech.cuny.edu
LAPAYOVER, Alan .... 215-576-0800 396 I
alapayover@rrc.edu
LAPERLE, Kimberly .... 508-856-8992 212 C
kimberlymuri.laperle@umassmed.edu
LAPHAM, Steve .... 301-891-0103 205 A
slapham@wau.edu
LAPIANA, William, P .... 212-431-2840 309 A
william.lapiana@nyls.edu
LAPIDUS, Chaim, D ...... 443-548-6063 201 C
cdl@nirc.edu
LAPIDUS, Richard, S .... 978-665-3101 212 E
rlapidus@fitchburgstate.edu
LAPIER, Terrance .... 407-265-8383.. 96 H
LAPIER, Terrence .... 561-381-4990.. 96 G
LAPIERRE DREGER,
Miah .... 860-906-5010.. 86 D
mlapierre-dreger@capitalcc.edu
LAPIKAS, Ken .... 814-724-0700 388 A
klapikas@laurel.edu
LAPIKAS, Sonya, L .... 724-589-2172 399 D
slapikas@thiel.edu
LAPINSKI, Scott .... 432-552-2629 456 F
lapinski_s@utpb.edu
LAPLANT, James, T ...... 229-333-5800 127 E
jtlaplant@valdosta.edu
LAPLANTE, Brian .... 518-445-2381 289 K
blapl@albanylaw.edu
LAPLANTE, Jane .... 701-858-3855 345 E
jane.laplante@minotstateu.edu
LAPLANTE, Kim .... 920-498-5487 499 G
kim.laplante@nwtc.edu
LAPLANTE, Melissa .... 603-342-3086 273 C
mlaplante@ccsnh.edu
LAPLANTE, Mike .... 970-943-7038.. 85 C
mlaplante@western.edu
LAPOINTE, Lacey .... 817-735-5126 454 B
lacey.lapointe@unthsc.edu
LAPOINTE, Laurence ...... 860-465-5113.. 85 H
lapointel@easternct.edu
LAPOINTE, Michael .... 219-980-7106 157 C
mslapoin@iun.edu
LAPOINTE, Robert .... 312-567-7135 140 A
lapointe@iit.edu
LAPORTE, Christopher .. 860-773-1362.. 87 G
claporte@tunxis.edu
LAPORTE, Laura .... 518-736-3622 300 D
llaporte@fmcc.suny.edu
LAPORTE, Sandra .... 312-567-5199 140 A
laporte@iit.edu
LAPOS, Christopher ...... 570-389-4740 393 D
clapos@bloomu.edu
LAPOTASKY, Michael .... 215-596-8800 401 E
LAPP, Beverly, K .... 574-296-6267 153 F
bklapp@ambs.edu
LAPP, Ian .... 617-989-4590 219 F
ian.lapp@wit.edu
LAPP, Katherine, N .... 617-495-1524 210 E
katie_lapp@harvard.edu

LAPPIN, Julie, M .... 909-537-5002.. 32 E
jlappin@csusb.edu
LAPPLE, James, H .... 212-327-8371 312 G
james.lapple@rockefeller.edu
LAPPS, Brian .... 615-366-4438 423 H
brian.lapps@tbr.edu
LAPRADE, Kimberly ...... 602-639-7500.. 12 J
LAPRADE, Shane .... 508-565-1970 219 A
slaprade@stonehill.edu
LAPRAY, Kim .... 208-732-6299 131 D
klapray@csi.edu
LAPRISE, Coleen .... 207-741-5715 195 H
claprise@smccme.edu
LAPRISE, John .... 423-585-6829 425 F
john.laprise@ws.edu
LAPSLEY, Jacqueline, E 609-497-7815 280 C
academic.dean@ptsem.edu
LAQUEY, Karen .... 325-649-8805 437 G
klaquey@hputx.edu
LARA, Dan .... 541-867-8506 374 F
dan.lara@oregoncoast.edu
LARA, Gabriel .... 847-543-2288 136 A
glara3@clcillinois.edu
LARA, Holly .... 307-532-8330 501 B
holly.lara@ewc.wy.edu
LARA, Larry .... 714-992-7025.. 54 C
llara@fullcoll.edu
LARA, Maria .... 650-306-3125.. 62 J
lara@smccd.edu
LARA, Rosa .... 717-720-4010 393 C
rlara@passhe.edu
LARA, Veronica .... 512-448-8575 442 I
sm8415@bncollege.com
LARANGE, Shannon ...... 413-775-1410 214 E
larange@gcc.mass.edu
LARAY SEALEY,
Alphonso .... 804-257-5742 476 F
LARDNER, Emily .... 206-878-3710 481 B
elardner@highline.edu
LARDNER, Patrick .... 803-777-2036 413 A
lardnerp@mailbox.sc.edu
LARDY, Greg .... 701-231-7660 345 F
gregory.lardy@ndsu.edu
LARDY, Greg .... 701-231-7426 345 F
gregory.lardy@ndsu.edu
LAREAU, Martin .... 708-596-2000 149 H
mlareau@ssc.edu
LAREY, Franklin .... 309-556-3061 140 F
flarey@iwu.edu
LAREZ, Joseph .... 509-961-4674 481 A
larez_j@heritag.edu
LARGE, Kevin .... 410-462-7628 198 B
klarge@bccc.edu
LARGE, Ron .... 509-313-6767 480 F
large@gonzaga.edu
LARGEN, Kristin, K .... 563-589-0200 171 A
klargen@wartburgseminary.edu
LARGENT, Liz .... 405-682-1611 367 D
llargent@occc.edu
LARGENT, Mark, A .... 517-353-5380 227 F
largent@msu.edu
LARGENT, Trudy .... 510-466-7252.. 57 C
tlargent@peralta.edu
LARICK, Duane, K .... 919-515-2196 342 A
duane_larick@ncsu.edu
LARIMORE, Jennifer ...... 715-425-4603 496 F
jennifer.larimore@uwrf.edu
LARIOS, Daphne .... 509-542-4562 479 A
klarios@columbiabasin.edu
LARIOS, Jose .... 828-669-8012 331 K
jose.larios@montreat.edu
LARIOS, Jose .... 828-669-8012 331 K
jlarios14@montreat.edu
LARIOS, Liza .... 718-631-6356 295 C
llarios@qcc.cuny.edu
LARIVE, Cynthia .... 831-459-2058.. 71 A
chancellor@ucsc.edu
LARIVEE, Lisa .... 802-322-1644 462 B
lisa.larivee@goddard.edu
LARKAN, Kara .... 210-999-7479 451 E
klarkans@trinity.edu
LARKIN, Anne .... 508-856-4250 212 C
anne.larkin@umassmed.edu
LARKIN, SSJ,
Mary Josephine .... 215-248-7055 381 A
mjlarkin@chc.edu
LARKIN, Susan .... 757-233-8809 477 C
slarkin@vwu.edu
LARKIN, Willie .... 608-663-2348 492 F
wlarkin@edgewood.edu
LAROBINA, Michael, D . 203-371-7859.. 89 A
larobinam@sacredheart.edu

LAROCCA, Cherie, K ..... 504-278-6273 188 G
clarocca@nunez.edu
LAROCHE, Adrienne ...... 207-741-5994 195 H
alaroche@smccme.edu
LAROCHELLE, Josee ...... 518-564-2130 318 E
jlaro007@plattsburgh.edu
LAROCQUE, Edward, A . 260-399-7700 162 B
elarocque@sf.edu
LAROCQUE,
Monique, M .... 207-581-3143 196 G
mlarocque@maine.edu
LAROCQUE, Sandra ...... 701-477-7913 346 J
slarocqu@tm.edu
LAROI, Heather .... 608-265-3195 495 C
hlaroi@uwsa.edu
LAROSE, Sydney .... 408-846-4980.. 43 E
LAROSEE, Howie .... 617-879-7938 213 B
hlarosee@massart.edu
LARRABEE, Ashley .... 361-825-3020 447 C
ashley.larrabee@tamucc.edu
LARRAT, Paul .... 401-874-5003 405 E
larrat@uri.edu
LARRIVEE, Linda .... 508-929-8333 213 G
llarrivee@worcester.edu
LARROUSSE, William .... 267-502-6034 379 A
william.larrousse@brynathyn.edu
LARRY, Latasha .... 773-291-6210 135 E
llarry4@ccc.edu
LARSEN, Carlton .... 423-869-6484 421 A
carl.larsen@lmunet.edu
LARSEN, Chris .... 714-533-1495.. 64 I
chrislarsen@southbaylo.edu
LARSEN, Christoffer ...... 785-227-3380 172 A
larsencl@bethanylb.edu
LARSEN, Curt .... 801-957-4186 461 C
curt.larsen@slcc.edu
LARSEN, Cynde .... 608-822-2642 500 A
clarsen@swtc.edu
LARSEN, Daniel .... 630-466-7900 152 K
dlarsen@waubonsee.edu
LARSEN, David .... 253-833-9111 480 I
dlarsen@greenriver.edu
LARSEN, Jennifer .... 402-559-4837 269 K
jlarsen@unmc.edu
LARSEN, Jon-Erik .... 503-352-7221 375 C
jon-erik@pacificu.edu
LARSEN, Kelly Jo .... 918-444-2120 366 G
larsenk@nsuok.edu
LARSEN, Kerstin .... 609-258-9289 280 D
klarsen@princeton.edu
LARSEN, Kevin, W .... 252-334-2044 331 F
kevin.larsen@macuniversity.edu
LARSEN, Kevin, W .... 252-334-2009 331 F
kevin.larsen@macuniversity.edu
LARSEN, Marci .... 435-283-7013 461 B
marci.larsen@snow.edu
LARSEN, Matt .... 701-231-5614 345 F
matt.larsen@ndsu.edu
LARSEN, Rachel .... 916-691-7207.. 50 H
larsenr@crc.losrios.edu
LARSEN, Sarah .... 713-743-7948 452 D
sclarsen@central.uh.edu
LARSEN, Susan .... 575-562-2211 286 B
susan.larsen@enmu.edu
LARSEN, Whitney, M ..... 540-261-8530 471 B
whitney.larsen@svu.edu
LARSON, Ann .... 972-707-8600 457 G
LARSON, Barb .... 308-398-7359 266 A
blarson@cccneb.edu
LARSON, Bruce .... 360-650-3319 485 I
bruce.larson@wwu.edu
LARSON, Cate .... 651-631-0204 233 I
clarson@aaaom.edu
LARSON, Chelsea .... 701-777-4409 345 B
chelsea.larson@und.edu
LARSON, Craig .... 763-424-0733 240 A
clarson@nhcc.edu
LARSON, Dale, C .... 214-887-5021 435 F
dlarson@dts.edu
LARSON, Dan .... 541-737-3626 375 A
dan.larson@oregonstate.edu
LARSON, David .... 864-231-2000 406 F
dlarson@andersonuniversity.edu
LARSON, Debra .... 618-537-6816 144 A
dlarson@mckendree.edu
LARSON, Debra, S .... 530-898-6101.. 30 D
dslarson@csuchico.edu
LARSON, Denise .... 570-955-1479 387 B
larsond@lackawanna.edu
LARSON, Doreen .... 937-778-7801 352 D
dlarson@edisonohio.edu
LARSON, Elena .... 916-278-6845.. 32 D
larsone@csus.edu

LARSON, Erik .... 570-961-0700 387 B
larsone@lackawanna.edu
LARSON, Gary .... 630-752-5990 153 C
gary.larson@wheaton.edu
LARSON, George .... 918-465-1750 366 A
glarson@eosc.edu
LARSON, Greg .... 239-590-1500 109 K
LARSON, Heidi .... 701-252-3467 347 B
hlarson@uj.edu
LARSON, Jamie .... 409-880-7126 449 G
jamie.larson@lamar.edu
LARSON, Jan .... 605-995-2614 415 A
jan.larson@dwu.edu
LARSON, Jason .... 480-314-2102.. 15 P
LARSON, Jennifer .... 701-845-7401 345 G
jennifer.larson@vcsu.edu
LARSON, Jens .... 509-359-6584 479 G
jlarson@ewu.edu
LARSON, Jon, H .... 732-255-0330 279 F
jlarson@ocean.edu
LARSON, Kristin .... 906-635-2453 226 G
klarsen1@lssu.edu
LARSON, Laura .... 651-633-4311 243 E
llarson@unitedseminary.edu
LARSON, Lawrence .... 401-863-1422 403 J
lawrence_larson@brown.edu
LARSON, Lesley .... 570-321-4456 389 B
larsonl@lycoming.edu
LARSON, Lisa .... 207-974-4691 195 E
llarson@emcc.edu
LARSON, Lois .... 651-793-1411 238 I
lois.larson@metrostate.edu
LARSON, Lori .... 218-736-1514 239 C
lori.larson@minnesota.edu
LARSON, Paul, V .... 805-565-6286.. 76 A
plarson@westmont.edu
LARSON, R. Alan .... 434-799-2271 471 D
LARSON, Rebecca .... 630-752-5566 153 C
rebecca.a.larson@wheaton.edu
LARSON, Robert .... 718-390-3100 324 F
LARSON, Robert .... 503-255-0332 374 C
rlarson@multnomah.edu
LARSON, Ruth .... 315-470-4716 319 D
rlarson@esf.edu
LARSON, Samantha ...... 712-325-3341 167 I
slarson@iwcc.edu
LARSON, Sandra .... 847-578-3400 148 F
sandra.larson@rosalindfranklin.edu
LARSON, Scott .... 806-720-7266 439 D
scott.larson@lcu.edu
LARSON, Shane .... 970-945-8691.. 78 L
LARSON, Shane .... 712-325-3402 167 I
LARSON, Shane .... 620-441-5246 173 C
shane.larson@cowley.edu
LARSON, Susan, J .... 218-299-3001 235 H
larson@cord.edu
LARSON, Thomas .... 309-694-5225 139 B
thomas.larson@icc.edu
LARSON, Thomas, R ..... 423-652-4765 420 F
trlarson@king.edu
LARSON, Trudy .... 775-784-7103 271 E
tlarson@unr.edu
LARUE, Clint .... 405-425-5191 367 C
clint.larue@oc.edu
LARUE, Shanda .... 270-686-4252 179 J
shanda.larue@brescia.edu
LARUE, Wesley .... 901-678-2732 426 G
wtlarue@memphis.edu
LARUSSO,
Christopher, P .... 716-880-2377 305 G
christopher.p.larusso@medaille.edu
LASAKOW, Paul, H .... 757-822-1527 475 E
plasakow@tcc.edu
LASCEK, Natalie .... 717-396-7833 392 U
nlascek@pcad.edu
LASCH, Chris .... 480-860-2700.. 15 N
clasch@taliesin.edu
LASCH, Jackie, D .... 407-582-3302 113 I
jlasch@valenciacollege.edu
LASECKI, Matthew .... 215-646-7300 385 A
lasecki.m@gmercyu.edu
LASEY, Brian .... 479-968-0261.. 18 C
blasey@atu.edu
LASH, Chris .... 847-628-1565 141 C
christopher.lash@judsonu.edu
LASH, Elysia .... 919-278-2665 340 B
elysia.lash@shawu.edu
LASH, Jonathan .... 413-559-5521 210 D
jlpr@hampshire.edu
LASH, Julie .... 317-274-2548 157 D
jlash@iupui.edu
LASHER, Marie .... 603-456-2656 273 H
mlasher@magdalen.edu

LASHER, Robert, W .... 603-646-3095 273 D
robert.w.lasher@dartmouth.edu
LASHLEY, Edwin, L .... 410-543-6222 204 D
ellashley@salisbury.edu
LASHLEY, Janeisa .... 410-337-6000 199 B
janeisa.lashley@goucher.edu
LASHLEY, Jeffery .... 660-263-4100 257 B
jeffl@macc.edu
LASHLEY, Kent .... 405-733-7306 369 E
klashley@rose.edu
LASHLEY, Marsha .... 660-831-4115 256 I
lashleym@moval.edu
LASHLEY, Maudry .... 718-270-4995 294 G
mlashley@mec.cuny.edu
LASHURE, Faith .... 630-466-7900 152 K
flashure@waubonsee.edu
LASICH, Deb .... 303-273-3097.. 79 J
dlasich@mines.edu
LASINSKI, Jon .... 907-796-6497.. 10 B
jlasinski@alaska.edu
LASITER, Paul .... 406-243-4606 263 K
paul.lasiter@mso.umt.edu
LASITS, Mary .... 260-422-5560 156 E
mlasits@indianatech.edu
LASKER, Y. Mayer .... 718-377-0777 311 G
LASKEY, Dina .... 541-888-7400 376 C
dina.laskey@socc.edu
LASKIN, Emily .... 626-396-2455.. 26 B
emily.laskin@artcenter.edu
LASKOFSKI, Mike .... 703-993-4573 467 E
mlaskofs@gmu.edu
LASKOWSKI, Anne .... 860-685-2006.. 90 B
alaskowski@wesleyan.edu
LASKY, Sarah .... 716-851-1994 299 B
lasky@ecc.edu
LASLEY, Steven, T .... 615-460-6404 418 B
steve.lasley@belmont.edu
LASPISA, Matt .... 845-434-5750 321 E
mlaspisa@sunysullivan.edu
LASPROGATA, Eva .... 206-296-6368 484 A
lasprogg@seattleu.edu
LASSETTER, Jane, H ...... 801-422-7198 458 H
jane_lassetter@byu.edu
LASSETTER, Jerry .... 919-761-2266 340 D
jlassetter@sebts.edu
LASSIAL, Erin .... 315-386-7608 320 B
lassiale@canton.edu
LASSITER, Carllos .... 903-813-2228 430 H
classiter@austincollege.edu
LASSITER, Catherine ..... 919-866-7106 338 G
cblassiter@waketech.edu
LASSITER, Colleen .... 706-233-7337 125 C
classiter@shorter.edu
LASSITER, Donald, L ..... 910-630-7081 331 E
lassiter@methodist.edu
LASSITER, Elbert, J .... 336-633-0009 337 A
ejlassiter@randolph.edu
LASSITER, Ingrid .... 404-270-5383 126 B
ilassite@spelman.edu
LASSITER, John .... 706-295-6511 120 A
jlassiter@gntc.edu
LASSITER, Keith .... 704-233-8098 344 F
k.lassiter@wingate.edu
LASSITER, Teresa, C ..... 252-335-8740 341 B
tclassiter@ecsu.edu
LASSITER, Timothy .... 252-862-1351 337 C
tmlassiter6983@roanokechowan.edu
LASSITER-COUNTS,
Leigh .... 501-450-1373.. 19 E
lassiter-counts@hendrix.edu
LASSNER, David .... 808-956-8207 129 E
david@hawaii.edu
LASSNER, David, K .... 808-956-8207 129 C
david@hawaii.edu
LASSNER, Jennifer .... 319-335-2123 163 H
jennifer-lassner@uiowa.edu
LASSO, Megan .... 406-994-4391 264 C
megan.lasso@montana.edu
LAST, Brad .... 435-652-7858 460 B
blast@dixie.edu
LAST, Brett .... 734-487-3044 223 K
blast@emich.edu
LASTER, Braylin .... 731-426-7500 420 G
LASTRA, Lauren .... 805-969-3626.. 55 J
llastra@pacifica.edu
LASTRA, Sarai .... 787-743-7979 510 H
LASZCZ, Amy .... 504-671-5456 188 B
alaszc@dcc.edu
LATA, Fran .... 303-373-2008.. 83 G
flata@rvu.edu
LATCOVICH, Mark, A .... 440-943-7600 360 E
mal@dioceseofcleveland.org
LATESSA, Kenneth .... 804-862-6100 470 C
klatessa@rbc.edu
LATHAM, Amy .... 662-562-3201 248 D
a_latham@northwestms.edu
LATHAM, Chris .... 256-233-8291.... 4 C
chris.latham@athens.edu
LATHAM, Heather .... 410-626-2511 202 A
heather.latham@sjc.edu
LATHAM, Jessica .... 910-898-9617 336 D
lathamj@montgomery.edu
LATHAM, Linda .... 336-734-7412 334 F
llatham@forsythtech.edu
LATHAM, Lindsay, S ...... 336-272-7102 329 C
lindsay.latham@greensboro.edu
LATHAM, Mike .... 252-451-8327 336 E
dmlatham118@nashcc.edu
LATHAM, Sarah .... 831-459-3778.. 71 A
sclatham@ucsc.edu
LATHAM, Scott .... 713-942-5036 454 G
slatham@stthom.edu
LATHAM, Sheila .... 701-858-4145 345 E
sheila.latham@minotstateu.edu
LATHAM, William .... 202-274-5210.. 94 B
william.latham@udc.edu
LATHROP, Jessica .... 608-262-2326 495 C
jlathrop@uwsa.edu
LATHROP, Justin .... 863-667-5000 108 K
jjlathrop@seu.edu
LATHROP, Sam .... 217-228-5432 147 F
lathrsa@quincy.edu
LATIF, Niaz .... 219-989-2469 160 D
nlatif@pnw.edu
LATIF, Niaz .... 219-989-3251 160 D
nlatif@pnw.edu
LATIF, Saima .... 213-624-1200.. 42 B
slatif@fidm.edu
LATIMER, Cassandra, H 717-264-2784 403 C
cassandra.latimer@wilson.edu
LATIMER, Margaret .... 240-567-7711 200 G
margaret.latimer@montgomerycollege.edu
LATIMER, Tanisha .... 864-250-8107 409 I
tanisha.latimer@gvltec.edu
LATINO, Niki .... 303-871-2712.. 84 E
niki.latino@du.edu
LATINO-NEWMAN,
Tracy .... 916-278-6989.. 32 D
tracy.newman@csus.edu
LATIOLAIS, Scott .... 253-589-5546 478 J
scott.latiolais@cptc.edu
LATONA, Erin .... 712-324-5066 169 C
elatona@nwicc.edu
LATORELLA, Jacqueline 813-253-6219 113 H
jlatorella@ut.edu
LATOUF, Christina .... 646-660-6114 292 L
christina.latouf@baruch.cuny.edu
LATOUR, Bill .... 217-641-4290 141 A
blatour@jwcc.edu
LATOUR, Jennifer, B ..... 757-594-8589 465 M
jennifer.latour@cnu.edu
LATOUR, Mickey .... 870-972-2085.. 17 E
mlatour@astate.edu
LATOUR, Terry, S .... 814-393-1931 393 G
tlatour@clarion.edu
LATSCH, Wolfram .... 206-221-4308 485 A
latsch@uw.edu
LATSHAW, Todd, M .... 717-867-6330 388 C
latshaw@lvc.edu
LATSON, Stephen .... 318-670-6000 191 D
LATTA, Bruce, J .... 410-293-1801 504 A
latta@usna.edu
LATTA, Jonathan .... 209-946-2211.. 71 E
jlatta@pacific.edu
LATTA, Michael .... 812-877-8975 160 F
mlatta@rose-hulman.edu
LATTA, Timothy .... 301-243-2123 502 L
LATTER, George .... 336-273-4431 327 A
LATTIMER, Heather .... 408-924-3600.. 34 A
heather.lattimer@sjsu.edu
LATTIMORE, Mark .... 478-825-6296 118 F
lattimorem@fvsu.edu
LATTIMORE, Vergel, L .. 704-636-6823 330 A
vlattimore@hoodseminary.edu
LATTING, John .... 404-727-6036 118 E
john.latting@emory.edu
LATTY, Erika .... 207-509-7297 196 E
elatty@unity.edu
LATZ, II, Gil, I .... 614-688-1178 358 D
latz.9@osu.edu
LAU, Bradley, A .... 503-554-2316 373 A
blau@georgefox.edu
LAU, Eric .... 505-277-1444 288 J
elau@unm.edu
LAU, Lawrence .... 310-577-3000.. 76 I
lau@yosan.edu
LAU, Margaret .... 805-922-6966.. 24 I
mlau@hancockcollege.edu
LAU, Pam .... 217-351-2542 147 C
plau@parkland.edu
LAU, Terence .... 530-898-6272.. 30 D
tjlau@csuchico.edu
LAUB, Joe .... 212-484-1108 294 D
jlaub@jjay.cuny.edu
LAUBE, Philip .... 740-826-8101 356 H
plaube@muskingum.edu
LAUBER, David .... 630-752-5054 153 C
david.lauber@wheaton.edu
LAUBER, Ray .... 620-341-5077 173 F
rlauber@emporia.edu
LAUCHNER, Kerri .... 805-493-3225.. 29 C
klauchne@callutheran.edu
LAUD, Sher-Ron .... 252-398-6500 328 C
LAUDENSLAGER,
Kristin .... 610-282-1100 382 C
kristin.laudenslager@desales.edu
LAUDER, Frank .... 617-873-0137 208 B
finaid@cambridgecollege.edu
LAUDERDALE, Wendy ... 985-549-2239 193 A
wlauderdale@selu.edu
LAUDERMILK, Erin .... 620-278-4340 177 H
elaudermilk@sterling.edu
LAUDNER, Kevin .... 719-255-4490.. 84 C
klaudner@uccs.edu
LAUEN, Wendy .... 815-479-7528 143 I
wlauen@mchenry.edu
LAUER, Andrew, J .... 646-592-4410 326 D
andrewlauer@yu.edu
LAUER, Betty .... 508-854-2765 215 F
blauer@qcc.mass.edu
LAUER, Bonnie .... 570-740-0734 389 A
blauer@luzerne.edu
LAUER, Casey, S .... 785-532-2578 175 C
cslauer@ksu.edu
LAUER, Joel .... 210-436-3791 442 J
jlauer@stmarytx.edu
LAUER, John .... 719-389-6200.. 78 I
jlauer@coloradocollege.edu
LAUER, Karla .... 941-752-5694 109 G
lauerk@scf.edu
LAUFFER, Shannon .... 515-650-3198 163 E
shannonlauffer@theartofeducation.edu
LAUG, Adam .... 641-269-3200 166 G
laugadam@grinnell.edu
LAUGHEAD, Ross .... 210-485-0059 428 G
rlaughead@alamo.edu
LAUGHLIN, Jennifer .... 214-638-0484 438 E
jenlaughlin@kdstudio.com
LAUGHLIN, Karen, L ...... 850-644-2740 110 C
klaughlin@admin.fsu.edu
LAUGHLIN, Robert .... 504-941-8211 189 H
rlaugh@lsuhsc.edu
LAUGHLIN, Ronda .... 360-752-8334 478 A
rlaughlin@btc.edu
LAUGHLIN, Russ .... 817-202-6462 444 I
laughlinr@swau.edu
LAUGHRAN, Patrick .... 508-626-4357 213 A
plaughran@framingham.edu
LAUMBATTUS, Doug ..... 217-234-5253 142 C
dlaumbattus@lakelandcollege.edu
LAUNDERVILLE, OSB,
Dale .... 320-363-3389 243 B
dlaunderville@csbsju.edu
LAUNTZ, Timothy .... 814-641-3192 386 E
launtzt@juniata.edu
LAUR, Dave .... 906-217-4031 222 A
dave.laur@baycollege.edu
LAURDSEN, Lindsay ..... 801-426-8234 459 M
LAUREANO, José .... 732-906-2509 278 G
jlaureano@middlesexcc.edu
LAUREL, Jera .... 863-638-7209 114 A
jera.laurel@warner.edu
LAURENCE, David .... 928-776-7666.. 16 J
david.laurence@yc.edu
LAURENT, Dianna .... 985-867-2415 190 K
dlaurent@sjasc.edu
LAURENT, Timothy .... 319-363-1323 168 F
tlaurent@mtmercy.edu
LAURENTE, Theresa ...... 803-536-7200 411 G
tlaurent@scsu.edu
LAURENZ, Jamie .... 575-562-2312 286 B
jamie.laurenz@enmu.edu
LAURENZI, Kellie, L ...... 412-397-5201 397 B
laurenzi@rmu.edu
LAURIE, Sean .... 516-323-4820 306 M
slaurie@molloy.edu
LAURITA, Brandi .... 419-434-4663 362 D
ankney@findlay.edu
LAURITSEN, Jess .... 763-488-2605 238 C
jessica.lauritsen@hennepintech.edu
LAURSEN, Tod .... 518-320-1100 315 H
LAURSEN, Tod .... 315-792-7400 321 B
tod.laursen@sunypoly.edu
LAUSCH, Mark, C .... 516-572-7664 307 E
mark.lausch@ncc.edu
LAUSE, Thomas .... 419-434-4521 362 D
lause@findlay.edu
LAUTERBACH, Lisa .... 734-487-1118 223 K
counseling.services@emich.edu
LAUX, Beth .... 310-506-4532.. 56 G
beth.laux@pepperdine.edu
LAUX, Donald .... 406-238-7293 265 E
donald.laux@rocky.edu
LAVAL, Jennifer .... 559-442-8206.. 67 B
jennifer.laval@fresnocitycollege.edu
LAVALLEY, David .... 203-672-6646.. 85 D
dlavalley@albertus.edu
LAVALLEY, Kenneth, J .. 603-862-4343 274 F
ken.lavalley@unh.edu
LAVARIEGA MONFORTI,
Jessica .... 805-493-3555.. 29 C
jlavariega@callutheran.edu
LAVEIST, Thomas .... 504-865-5000 191 F
LAVENDER, Bernadette .. 770-426-2633 122 C
bernadette.lavender@life.edu
LAVENDER, Carol .... 281-649-3300 437 B
clavender@hbu.edu
LAVENDER, Michael, K . 828-652-0681 336 B
michaell@mcdowelltech.edu
LAVERDURE, Andrea ..... 701-477-7862 346 J
LAVERGNE, Joseph .... 337-421-6951 188 J
joseph.lavergne@sowela.edu
LAVERGNE, Paul .... 718-429-6600 324 D
paul.lavergne@vaughn.edu
LAVERY, Hugh, J .... 215-955-6834 399 E
hugh.lavery@jefferson.edu
LAVERY, Kyle .... 217-735-7382 142 H
klavery@lincolncollege.edu
LAVES, Beth .... 270-745-5308 186 C
beth.laves@wku.edu
LAVIAL, Pierre .... 772-466-4822.. 95 N
pierre.lavial@aviator.edu
LAVIGNE, Brent .... 574-807-7120 154 B
brent.lavigne@betheluniversity.edu
LAVIGNE, Robert, W ..... 508-213-2217 217 H
robert.lavigne@nichols.edu
LAVIN, Gabrielle .... 215-965-4027 390 E
glavin@moore.edu
LAVIN, Lindsie .... 413-565-1000 206 D
llavin@baypath.edu
LAVIN, Luke .... 406-756-3839 263 E
llavin@fvcc.edu
LAVIN, Theresa .... 303-352-6625.. 80 F
theresa.lavin@ccd.edu
LAVINDER,
Katherine, W .... 610-758-4159 388 E
kwl211@lehigh.edu
LAVINE, Danielle .... 860-509-9511.. 88 B
dlavine@hartsem.edu
LAVINE, Deborah .... 336-770-1333 343 D
lavined@uncsa.edu
LAVINE, Natasha .... 404-756-4000 115 G
LAVOIE, Chuck .... 802-468-1250 463 E
chuck.lavoie@castleton.edu
LAVOIE, Donna .... 314-977-2244 259 F
donna.lavoie@slu.edu
LAW, Cameron .... 916-278-5556.. 32 D
c.law@csus.edu
LAW, David .... 323-685-6196.. 67 J
LAW, Donna .... 435-865-8182 460 A
law@suu.edu
LAW, Kristie .... 317-543-3235 159 L
LAW, Mike .... 503-253-3443 374 G
mlaw@ocom.edu
LAW, Nancy .... 903-983-8101 438 F
nlaw@kilgore.edu
LAW, Renee .... 954-201-7482.. 96 F
rlaw@broward.edu
LAW, Scott .... 515-271-3860 165 J
scott.law@drake.edu
LAW, Shirley .... 646-313-8000 295 D
shirley.law@guttman.cuny.edu
LAW, Theresa .... 505-454-3198 286 J
tlaw@nmhu.edu
LAWDERMILT, Sherry .... 218-755-2832 237 F
sherry.lawdermilt@bemidjistate.edu
LAWERANCE, Adrea ...... 406-243-4911 263 K
adrea.lawerance@umontana.edu

LAWHORN, Janice .... 928-428-8509.. 12 F
janice.lawhorn@eac.edu
LAWHORNE, Angela ...... 757-569-6064 474 H
alawhorne@pdc.edu
LAWHORNE, Jeffrey, L .. 540-464-7156 476 B
lawhornejl@vmi.edu
LAWKIS, Nicholas .... 251-460-7277.... 9 A
nlawkis@southalabama.edu
LAWLER, Ann .... 563-441-4173 166 B
alawler@eicc.edu
LAWLER, Hannah .... 310-434-3472.. 63 C
lawler_hannah@smc.edu
LAWLER, John .... 518-276-6266 312 C
lawlej4@rpi.edu
LAWLER, Michael, J ..... 509-452-5100 482 B
president@pnwu.edu
LAWLER-SAGARIN,
Kimberly .... 630-617-3202 137 G
ksagarin@elmhurst.edu
LAWLESS, Jacob .... 248-218-2080 230 B
jlawless@rochesteru.edu
LAWLESS, Kimberly .... 814-865-2526 391 G
klr5825@psu.edu
LAWLESS, Perry .... 985-448-4417 192 F
perry.lawless@nicholls.edu
LAWLESS-ANDRIC,
Dana .... 330-672-1980 354 A
dlawless@kent.edu
LAWLEY, John .... 404-727-9626 118 E
jlawley@emory.edu
LAWLOR, Michael .... 916-691-7215.. 50 H
lawlorm@crc.losrios.edu
LAWLOR, Sarah .... 406-447-4515 263 B
slawlor@carroll.edu
LAWLOR, William .... 402-559-5838 269 K
wlawlor@unmc.edu
LAWRENCE, Alvin .... 352-392-1575 111 A
alaw@ufl.edu
LAWRENCE, Amy .... 559-453-3453.. 43 A
amy.lawrence@fresno.edu
LAWRENCE, Barbara ...... 336-316-2196 329 D
blawrenc@guilford.edu
LAWRENCE, Charles ...... 206-296-6384 484 A
lawrence@seattleu.edu
LAWRENCE, Cherrelle ... 252-492-2061 338 F
lawrencec@vgcc.edu
LAWRENCE, Courtney ... 701-255-3285 347 A
clawrence@uttc.edu
LAWRENCE, Craig, D .... 205-929-3427.... 2 H
clawrence@lawsonstate.edu
LAWRENCE, Dan .... 303-360-4740.. 80 E
dan.lawrence@ccaurora.edu
LAWRENCE, Dana, J ..... 972-438-6932 441 E
LAWRENCE, David .... 616-233-2595 223 E
david.lawrence@davenport.edu
LAWRENCE, David, A .... 740-245-7032 363 A
lawrence@rio.edu
LAWRENCE, Deborah .... 518-244-2466 313 A
lawred@sage.edu
LAWRENCE, Deborah .... 317-955-6208 159 K
dlawrence@marian.edu
LAWRENCE, Derrick ...... 605-698-3966 416 B
dlawrence@swcollege.edu
LAWRENCE, Diana .... 502-456-6506 185 A
dlawrence@sullivan.edu
LAWRENCE, Gail .... 325-235-7333 449 D
gail.lawrence@tstc.edu
LAWRENCE, Gary .... 805-893-3781.. 70 E
gary@ucen.ucsb.edu
LAWRENCE, Jamie .... 270-789-5227 180 A
jwlawrence@campbellsville.edu
LAWRENCE, Jason .... 860-231-5700.. 90 A
jmlawrence@usj.edu
LAWRENCE, Jennifer ...... 318-678-6000 187 H
jelawrence@bpcc.edu
LAWRENCE, John, D ..... 515-294-5390 163 G
jdlaw@iastate.edu
LAWRENCE, Kalista .... 812-535-5102 160 H
kalista.lawrence@smwc.edu
LAWRENCE, Kendra .... 504-520-7388 193 E
klawren4@xula.edu
LAWRENCE, Kevin .... 757-388-2862 470 F
klawrence@sentara.edu
LAWRENCE, Lara .... 660-263-3900 251 D
laralawrence@cccb.edu
LAWRENCE, Larry, D ..... 501-450-3196.. 23 H
larryl@pplant.uca.edu
LAWRENCE, Lesa .... 218-755-4142 237 F
lesa.lawrence@bemidjistate.edu
LAWRENCE, Leslie .... 518-276-6287 312 C
lawrel@rpi.edu
LAWRENCE, Maricel ...... 406-243-2311 263 K
maricel.lawrence@umontana.edu
LAWRENCE, Mark .... 757-352-4295 470 B
marklaw@regent.edu
LAWRENCE, Maureen .... 718-522-2300 313 E
LAWRENCE, Melanie ..... 404-727-1886 118 E
melanie.lawrence@emory.edu
LAWRENCE, Paul .... 412-624-6620 400 H
plawrence@cfo.pitt.edu
LAWRENCE, Randall, K . 817-554-5950 439 H
rlawrence@messengercollege.edu
LAWRENCE, Ross .... 406-874-6172 263 H
lawrencer@milescc.edu
LAWRENCE, Sharee .... 478-825-6282 118 F
lawrencs@fvsu.edu
LAWRENCE, Tena .... 701-252-3467 347 B
tlawrenc@uj.edu
LAWRENCE, Tom .... 864-646-1429 412 H
tlawrenc@tctc.edu
LAWRENCE, Tonya .... 662-605-3413 246 D
tlawrence@holmescc.edu
LAWRENCE, Torrey .... 208-885-6448 132 F
tlawrence@uidaho.edu
LAWRENCE KEANE,
Loretta .... 212-217-4700 299 D
loretta_keane@fitnyc.edu
LAWRIE, Jeanne .... 863-638-2918 114 B
LAWRIE, Joshua .... 419-372-2011 348 G
jlawrie@bgsu.edu
LAWS, David .... 423-869-6418 421 A
david.laws@lmunet.edu
LAWS,
Donna Jean (DJ) .... 864-656-5616 407 E
djlaws@clemson.edu
LAWS, Frank .... 601-968-8978 245 B
flaws@belhaven.edu
LAWS, Michaele, D .... 423-439-8245 419 G
lawsm@etsu.edu
LAWS, Mishelle .... 562-985-8356.. 31 D
mishelle.laws@csulb.edu
LAWS, Paige .... 870-633-4480.. 19 A
plaws@eacc.edu
LAWS, Tyler .... 502-863-8182 180 H
tyler_laws@georgetowncollege.edu
LAWSON, Abby .... 803-934-3298 410 G
alawson@morris.edu
LAWSON, Andrea .... 805-756-2511.. 29 I
alawso07@calpoly.edu
LAWSON, Angela .... 615-230-3576 425 E
angela.lawson@volstate.edu
LAWSON, Carey .... 337-457-6135 189 G
clawson@lsue.edu
LAWSON, Cassandra .... 415-452-7689.. 36 K
clawson@ccsf.edu
LAWSON, Cynthia .... 212-229-8970 308 A
lawsonc@newschool.edu
LAWSON, Dan .... 419-289-5244 347 J
dlawson@ashland.edu
LAWSON, Daniel, L ...... 415-422-4222.. 72 J
lawson@usfca.edu
LAWSON, Danny, L ...... 423-323-0234 425 A
dllawson@northeaststate.edu
LAWSON, Darren, P ...... 864-242-5100 406 H
LAWSON, Deneen .... 864-242-5100 406 H
LAWSON, Diana .... 616-331-7100 224 G
lawsond1@gvsu.edu
LAWSON, Donald .... 864-424-8040 413 H
lawsondr@mailbox.sc.edu
LAWSON, Earl .... 831-582-3062.. 32 B
elawson@csumb.edu
LAWSON, Ernest .... 336-334-4822 335 A
elawson@gtcc.edu
LAWSON, Jacob .... 918-463-2931 365 J
jacob.lawson@connorsstate.edu
LAWSON, Jason .... 270-789-5031 180 A
jklawson@campbellsville.edu
LAWSON, Jeffrey .... 828-227-7495 343 E
LAWSON, Jill .... 606-387-3236 182 G
jill.lawson@kctcs.edu
LAWSON, John .... 847-925-6330 138 G
jlawson@harpercollege.edu
LAWSON, Kelvin .... 904-281-9800 109 I
kelvin.lawson@famu.edu
LAWSON, Kenneth .... 360-416-7732 484 C
kenneth.lawson@skagit.edu
LAWSON, Laura .... 848-932-3517 282 A
ljlawson@sebs.rutgers.edu
LAWSON, Melanie .... 713-313-7762 449 B
lawson_mw@tsu.edu
LAWSON, Michael, S .... 919-761-2100 340 D
mlawson@sebts.edu
LAWSON, Patricia .... 312-893-7120 137 H
plawson@erikson.edu
LAWSON, Patricia, P .... 804-523-5375 474 A
plawson@reynolds.edu
LAWSON, Peter .... 541-880-2363 373 C
lawson@klamathcc.edu
LAWSON, Raymond ...... 847-635-1979 146 G
rlawson@oakton.edu
LAWSON, Rebecca, L ... 843-661-1841 409 G
rlawson@fmarion.edu
LAWSON, Regina, G ..... 336-758-6066 344 C
lawsonrg@wfu.edu
LAWSON, Sarah .... 317-813-2300 158 C
LAWSON, Steve .... 859-985-3050 179 I
lawsonst@berea.edu
LAWSON, Tamara, F ..... 305-474-2418 107 F
tlawson@stu.edu
LAWSON, Thomas .... 661-255-1050.. 28 G
tlawson@calarts.edu
LAWSON, Tonia .... 850-872-3843 101 N
tlawson@gulfcoast.edu
LAWSON, Valerie, S ..... 276-376-4523 472 E
vas7k@uvawise.edu
LAWSON, Victoria .... 206-221-6075 485 A
lawson@uw.edu
LAWSON, Von .... 951-487-3440.. 53 A
vlawson@msjc.edu
LAWSON-BORDERS,
Gracie .... 202-806-7694.. 92 F
gracie.lawsonborders@howard.edu
LAWTER, JR., Vernon ... 352-746-6721.. 97 N
lawterv@cf.edu
LAWTON, Elizabeth .... 603-366-5299 272 K
elawton@ccsnh.edu
LAWTON, Kenneth, B .... 570-662-4913 394 F
klawton@mansfield.edu
LAWTON, Margaret, M . 843-377-2423 407 A
mlawton@charlestonlaw.edu
LAWTON-RAUH,
Amy, L .... 864-656-9867 407 E
apfa@clemson.edu
LAWVER, Miranda .... 906-932-4231 224 D
mirandal@gogebic.edu
LAWYER, Becky .... 952-885-5458 242 N
blawyer@nwhealth.edu
LAWYER, Mary, K .... 518-783-4288 315 E
mlawyer@siena.edu
LAXAMANA, Grace .... 650-289-3336.. 59 J
grace.laxamana@stpsu.edu
LAXMI, Priti .... 210-297-9634 430 L
pxlaxmi@baptisthealthsystem.com
LAY, Bethany .... 931-540-2837 424 C
blay@columbiastate.edu
LAY, Brian, K .... 734-384-4188 228 C
blay@monroeccc.edu
LAY, Delma .... 432-552-2102 456 F
lay_d@utpb.edu
LAYCOCK, Sharon .... 318-487-5443 187 J
sharonlaycock@cltcc.edu
LAYE, Don .... 229-430-3577 114 I
dlaye@albanytech.edu
LAYER, Paul .... 907-450-8019.... 9 I
pwlayer@alaska.edu
LAYISH, Michael, D ...... 781-239-4022 206 B
mlayish@babson.edu
LAYMAN, Amy, T .... 717-358-4263 383 I
amy.layman@fandm.edu
LAYMAN, Leslie .... 773-907-4059 135 C
llayman1@ccc.edu
LAYMAN, Sarah .... 405-224-3140 371 B
slayman@usao.edu
LAYMON, Steven, E ...... 540-362-6000 467 H
laymonse@hollins.edu
LAYNE, Barbara .... 978-542-8036 213 E
barbara.layne@salemstate.edu
LAYNE, Donnell .... 951-571-6118.. 59 B
donnell.layne@mvc.edu
LAYNE, Michael .... 909-384-8987.. 60 F
mlayne@sbccd.cc.ca.us
LAYNE, Preston .... 276-523-7491 474 D
playne@mecc.edu
LAYNE, Rebecca .... 540-665-4500 470 G
LAYNE, Ron .... 910-246-4109 337 H
layner@sandhills.edu
LAYTHAM, D. Brent ...... 410-864-4202 202 C
blaytham@stmarys.edu
LAYTON, Bruce .... 847-491-5680 146 E
b-layton@northwestern.edu
LAYTON, Christopher .... 281-873-0262 433 J
c.layton@commonwealth.edu
LAYTON, Dave, B .... 724-847-6508 384 C
dblayton@geneva.edu
LAYTON, Rebecca .... 601-928-6230 247 E
rebecca.layton@mgccc.edu
LAYTON, III,
William, C .... 207-859-4342 194 D
bill.layton@colby.edu
LAYZELL, Dan .... 319-895-4242 164 G
dlayzell@cornellcollege.edu
LAYZELL, Daniel .... 225-578-4342 189 E
dlayzell@lsu.edu
LAZARO, Helena, C ...... 323-259-2500.. 54 I
LAZARUS, Natalia .... 310-656-8070.. 50 E
LAZIC, Boris .... 617-973-1177 219 B
blazic@suffolk.edu
LAZO, Ryan .... 970-247-7080.. 80 J
alumni@fortlewis.edu
LAZU, Carlos .... 787-850-9804 512 D
carlos.lazu@upr.edu
LAZZARI, John (JW) ..... 775-445-3259 271 F
john.lazzari@wnc.edu
LAZZELL, Robert .... 920-206-2345 493 C
robert.lazzell@mbu.edu
LE, Hao .... 713-313-7950 449 B
hao.le@tsu.edu
LE, Hung, V .... 310-506-4307.. 56 G
hung.le@pepperdine.edu
LE, Michael, S .... 707-826-5489.. 33 C
michael.le@humboldt.edu
LE, Trangthithuy .... 714-995-9988.. 47 B
LE MASTERS, Philip ...... 325-793-3898 439 F
plemasters@mcm.edu
LE ROY, Michael, K ...... 616-526-6100 222 C
president@calvin.edu
LE SAUX, Catherine ...... 812-866-7399 155 G
lesaux@hanover.edu
LEA, Brette, E .... 512-223-7611 430 I
blea@austincc.edu
LEA, Jernice .... 215-590-8231 388 H
jlea@lincoln.edu
LEA, Kizzy .... 336-734-7540 334 F
klea@forsythtech.edu
LEA, Rachel .... 503-517-1092 377 C
rlea@warnerpacific.edu
LEACH, Barbara .... 815-825-2086 141 F
bleach1@kish.edu
LEACH, Evan .... 610-436-2930 395 D
eleach@wcupa.edu
LEACH, Faith, M .... 518-564-2090 318 E
LEACH, Jane, L .... 972-548-6884 433 I
jleach@collin.edu
LEACH, John .... 404-727-4317 118 E
john.blanchard.leach@emory.edu
LEACH, Karen, L .... 315-859-4524 300 H
kleach@hamilton.edu
LEACH, Les .... 610-690-6877 398 G
lleach1@swarthmore.edu
LEACH, R. Gavin .... 906-227-2200 228 I
gleach@nmu.edu
LEACH, Robert .... 404-225-4541 115 H
rleach@atlantatech.edu
LEACH, Robin .... 719-549-3310.. 82 J
robin.leach@pueblocc.edu
LEACH, Stephen, E .... 304-367-4692 488 H
stephen.leach@pierpont.edu
LEACHMAN, Joyce .... 773-947-6283 143 H
jleachman@mccormick.edu
LEADBETER, Marci .... 410-532-5390 201 D
mleadbeter@ndm.edu
LEADEM, Evan .... 503-943-8088 377 A
leadem@up.edu
LEADER, Lizette .... 985-545-1500 188 E
LEADLEY, Robert .... 734-462-4400 230 G
rleadley@schoolcraft.edu
LEAFGREEN, Melet .... 214-648-6335 457 A
melet.leafgreen@utsouthwestern.edu
LEAFSTEDT, Jill .... 805-437-2792.. 30 C
jill.leafstedt@csuci.edu
LEAGUE, Timothy .... 410-386-8052 198 D
tleague@carrollcc.edu
LEAHEY, James, P .... 859-238-5224 180 B
jamey.leahey@centre.edu
LEAHY, Daniel .... 781-768-7559 218 D
daniel.leahy@regiscollege.edu
LEAHY, Mindy, S .... 563-884-5647 169 F
mindy.leahy@palmer.edu
LEAHY, Patrick, F .... 732-571-3402 279 A
president@monmouth.edu
LEAHY, Thomas .... 515-643-6621 168 D
tleahy@mercydesmoines.org
LEAHY, S.J.,
William, P .... 617-552-3250 207 C
william.leahy@bc.edu
LEAK, Arthur .... 765-641-4162 153 G
ajleak@anderson.edu
LEAK, Monica .... 703-812-4757 468 D
mleak@leland.edu
LEAKE, Dawn, M .... 575-674-2284 285 L
dleake@burrell.edu

LEE, James, S .... 626-448-0023.. 46 G
president@itsla.edu
LEE, Janice .... 626-571-8811.. 73 E
janicel@uwest.edu
LEE, Jason .... 937-766-7674 349 E
jasonlee@cedarville.edu
LEE, Jay .... 970-521-6607.. 82 C
jay.lee@njc.edu
LEE, Jean .... 201-216-3667 283 D
jean.lee@stevens.edu
LEE, Jeffrey, C .... 904-808-7492 107 C
jeffreylee@sjrstate.edu
LEE, Jenna .... 940-898-3031 451 D
jlee11@twu.edu
LEE, Joanne .... 406-496-4769 265 A
jlee@mtech.edu
LEE, John .... 703-812-4757 468 D
jlee@leland.edu
LEE, Jonathan .... 310-233-4471.. 49 B
leej@lahc.edu
LEE, Jonathan .... 210-486-1097 429 C
jlee@alamo.edu
LEE, JongOh .... 909-447-6305.. 37 E
jolee@cst.edu
LEE, Joni, C .... 501-916-5698.. 22 A
jclee@ualr.edu
LEE, Joseph .... 251-380-3865.... 6 H
jlee@shc.edu
LEE, Judy .... 718-818-6470 314 F
jlee@edaff.com
LEE, Julian .... 626-455-0312.. 58 J
LEE, Ka Yee, C .... 773-702-8810 151 E
kayeelee@uchicago.edu
LEE, Kang Won .... 714-592-7878.. 44 I
kwlee@haven.edu
LEE, Karen .... 619-849-2535.. 57 J
karenlee@pointloma.edu
LEE, Karen .... 630-752-5004 153 C
karen.lee@wheaton.edu
LEE, Karen .... 808-845-9225 130 A
karenlee@hawaii.edu
LEE, Karyn .... 626-316-5331.. 63 E
klee2@saybrook.edu
LEE, Katrina .... 919-739-6736 338 H
kklee@waynecc.edu
LEE, Kenneth .... 603-645-9691 274 C
k.lee7@snhu.edu
LEE, Kenya, N .... 646-312-3322 292 L
kenya.lee@baruch.cuny.edu
LEE, Kirk, D .... 972-377-1793 433 I
kdlee@collin.edu
LEE, Kwang Hoon .... 213-381-0081.. 46 E
khlee@irus.edu
LEE, Kyu, H .... 253-752-2020 480 D
klee@faithseminary.edu
LEE, Kyu Hae .... 562-926-1023.. 58 A
office@ptsa.edu
LEE, Kyuboem .... 215-368-5000 390 A
klee@missio.edu
LEE, Kyung Hun .... 770-220-7910 119 A
LEE, LeBlanc .... 210-486-0560 429 C
lleblanc7@alamo.edu
LEE, Lenetta .... 484-365-7222 388 H
llee@lincoln.edu
LEE, Lily .... 240-567-5272 200 G
lily.lee@montgomerycollege.edu
LEE, Lisa .... 212-410-8007 308 E
llee@nycpm.edu
LEE, Mai Soua .... 559-730-3826.. 39 B
maisoual@cos.edu
LEE, Malisa .... 559-278-4639.. 31 B
malisal@csufresno.edu
LEE, Marion .... 210-690-9000 436 H
mlee2@hallmarkuniversity.edu
LEE, Mary W, L .... 630-515-7311 144 F
mleexx@midwestern.edu
LEE, Matt .... 225-578-2111 189 D
LEE, Matt .... 225-578-7155 189 E
mlee@lsu.edu
LEE, Matthew .... 913-722-0272 175 A
matt.lee@kansaschristian.edu
LEE, Meesun .... 714-525-0088.. 43 J
LEE, Miae .... 888-777-7675 480 D
mlee@faithseminary.edu
LEE, Michael .... 509-542-4399 479 A
mlee@columbiabasin.edu
LEE, Michael .... 641-683-5295 166 I
michael.lee@indianhills.edu
LEE, Michael .... 717-477-1211 395 B
mjlee@ship.edu
LEE, Michael, J .... 216-368-4306 349 D
michael.j.lee6@case.edu

LEE, Michele .... 864-424-8038 413 H
michele@mailbox.sc.edu
LEE, Michelle .... 910-362-7777 332 H
mlee@cfcc.edu
LEE, Mike .... 916-686-7300.. 29 E
LEE, Mike, C .... 818-947-2336.. 49 G
leemc@lavc.edu
LEE, Min .... 714-525-0088.. 43 J
gmu@gm.edu
LEE, Miwon .... 323-643-0301.. 25 F
LEE, Myung Chul .... 562-926-1023.. 58 A
mclee@ptsa.edu
LEE, Natasha .... 510-849-8200.. 55 G
LEE, Norman .... 315-294-8412 292 G
norman.lee@cayuga-cc.edu
LEE, Ok-Hee .... 218-477-2095 239 E
okheelee@mnstate.edu
LEE, Ouk Sup .... 703-712-7073 477 E
LEE, Patricia, A .... 843-355-4127 414 C
leepa@wiltech.edu
LEE, Patrick .... 210-486-3282 429 A
plee18@alamo.edu
LEE, Paula .... 225-216-8732 187 G
leep@mybrcc.edu
LEE, Phyllis .... 815-967-7306 148 C
plee@rockfordcareercollege.edu
LEE, Randall .... 601-635-6375 246 A
rlee@eccc.edu
LEE, Randolph .... 860-297-2413.. 89 B
randolph.lee@trincoll.edu
LEE, Rebecca .... 270-901-1019 182 H
rebecca.lee@kctcs.edu
LEE, Richard .... 607-436-2517 316 F
richard.lee@oneonta.edu
LEE, Richard .... 910-678-8287 334 E
leeri@faytechcc.edu
LEE, Samuel .... 951-372-7199.. 59 C
samuel.lee@norcocollege.edu
LEE, Sang Meyng .... 562-926-1023.. 58 A
sangmeynglee@msn.com
LEE, Sanghoon .... 323-643-0301.. 25 F
president@aeu.edu
LEE, Sanghoon .... 323-643-0301.. 25 F
dean@aeu.edu
LEE, Sara .... 216-368-2000 349 D
hirschfeld.lee@case.edu
LEE, Sarah, K .... 972-549-6417 433 I
sklee@collin.edu
LEE, Seung Deok .... 213-487-0110.. 41 D
president@dula.edu
LEE, Shane .... 605-394-2347 416 H
shane.lee@sdsmt.edu
LEE, Sheng Chien, R .... 956-326-2323 446 E
sheng.lee@tamiu.edu
LEE, Stacey .... 317-788-6095 161 H
lees@uindy.edu
LEE, Staci .... 760-921-5512.. 56 A
staci.lee@paloverde.edu
LEE, Stephen .... 570-484-2087 394 E
slee@lockhaven.edu
LEE, Stephen .... 435-652-7651 460 B
stephen.lee@dixie.edu
LEE, Stephen .... 304-293-0141 490 E
stephen.lee@mail.wvu.edu
LEE, Steven .... 757-446-5221 466 D
leect@evms.edu
LEE, Sunny .... 510-642-6000.. 69 A
LEE, Susan .... 406-791-5318 265 H
susan.lee@uprovidence.edu
LEE, Taehoon .... 909-623-0302.. 59 H
LEE, Tammy .... 206-281-2701 483 G
tammylee@spuu.edu
LEE, Teresa .... 785-670-1538 178 C
teresa.lee@washburn.edu
LEE, Terri, S .... 919-209-2125 335 F
tslee@johnstoncc.edu
LEE, Theresa .... 865-974-4337 427 B
artscidean@utk.edu
LEE, Thomas .... 863-297-1000 106 A
LEE, Tiffany .... 562-944-0351.. 27 A
tiffany.lee@biola.edu
LEE, Tiffany .... 484-365-7608 388 H
tlee@lincoln.edu
LEE, Timothy .... 315-445-4300 303 I
leetm@lemoyne.edu
LEE, Tony .... 310-825-1633.. 69 E
tlee@ucpd.ucla.edu
LEE, Traci .... 480-314-2102.. 15 P
LEE, Treva, A .... 504-520-7653 193 E
tlee@xula.edu
LEE, Trisha .... 907-796-6294.. 10 B
tclee@alaska.edu

LEE, Trudy .... 573-651-2332 259 H
tglee@semo.edu
LEE, Tyjaun .... 816-604-4205 255 C
tyjaun.lee@mcckc.edu
LEE, Tyjaun .... 816-604-4203 255 H
tyjaun.lee@mcckc.edu
LEE, Valerie .... 276-523-2400 474 D
vlee@mecc.edu
LEE, Vina .... 845-672-0550 299 E
LEE, W. P. Andrew .... 214-648-8712 457 A
wpandrew.lee@utsouthwestern.edu
LEE, Willie .... 201-761-7125 283 A
wlee@saintpeters.edu
LEE, Yung-Jae .... 415-458-3786.. 41 C
yung-jae.lee@dominican.edu
LEE, Zelda .... 803-535-5348 407 D
zlee@claflin.edu
LEE-BARBER, Jill .... 404-413-1655 120 E
jleebarber@gsu.edu
LEE-LEWIS, Sherri .... 310-434-4419.. 63 C
lee-lewis_sherri@smcv.edu
LEE MURPHY, Karen .... 954-201-7350.. 96 F
LEE SANG, Brian .... 202-885-6108.. 91 F
leesang@american.edu
LEE-YUAN, Mona .... 516-739-1545 308 F
clinicdirector@nyctcm.edu
LEEBRON, David, W .... 713-348-5050 442 F
president@rice.edu
LEEBRON TUTELMAN,
Elizabeth .... 215-204-8660 399 B
elizabeth.leebron@temple.edu
LEECK, Henry .... 618-437-5321 147 I
leeckh@rlc.edu
LEEDER, Mike .... 229-931-2222 120 D
mike.leeder@gsw.edu
LEEDS CARSON, Ben .... 831-459-4512.. 71 A
blc@ucsc.edu
LEEDY, David .... 212-659-7290 303 H
dleedy@tkc.edu
LEEDY, David .... 212-659-0741 303 H
dleedy@tkc.edu
LEEDY, Debbie .... 623-845-4770.. 13 C
debbie.leedy@gccaz.edu
LEEK, Danielle .... 617-228-3364 214 C
drleek@bhcc.edu
LEEK, Danielle, R .... 804-371-3000 474 A
dleek@reynolds.edu
LEEMAN, Julia .... 847-585-2267.. 10 E
jleeman@careered.com
LEEMAN BARTZIS,
Opal .... 517-353-8920 227 F
bartziso@msu.edu
LEENHOUTS, Dave .... 636-922-8740 258 J
dleenhouts@stchas.edu
LEENHOUTS, James ...... 828-898-8730 330 E
leenhoutsj@lmc.edu
LEEPER, Karla .... 706-721-7406 116 A
kleeper@augusta.edu
LEES, David .... 215-991-2015 387 A
leesp@lasalle.edu
LEES, Jill .... 812-855-7621 156 G
jmlees@iu.edu
LEES, Melissa .... 410-617-6769 200 B
mklees@loyola.edu
LEFAUVE, Linda, M .... 704-894-2124 328 E
lilefauve@davidson.edu
LEFEBVRE, Carol .... 706-721-8611 116 A
clefebvr@augusta.edu
LEFEBVRE, Ray .... 617-287-5000 211 H
raymond.lefebvre@umb.edu
LEFEVER-DAVIS, Shirley 316-978-3301 178 D
shirley.lefever-davis@wichita.edu
LEFEVRE, Lisa .... 970-521-6615.. 82 C
lisa.lefevre@njc.edu
LEFEW, Susan .... 304-357-4713 487 J
susanlefew@ucwv.edu
LEFFEL, Lisa .... 414-443-8796 498 A
lisa.leffel@wlc.edu
LEFFELMAN, Jeremy ..... 218-755-4222 237 F
jeremy.leffelman@bemidjistate.edu
LEFFLER, Lyvier .... 972-686-7878 442 B
LEFLER, Jennifer .... 952-358-8200 239 G
jennifer.lefler@normandale.edu
LEFRANCOIS, Paul, R ... 864-488-4527 410 B
plefrancois@limestone.edu
LEFTHERIS, Julie .... 850-245-0466 109 H
julie.leftheris@flbog.edu
LEFTON, Tonya .... 303-384-2332.. 79 J
tlefton@mines.edu
LEFTWICH, Lukas, D ..... 812-855-0973 156 F
lleftwic@indiana.edu
LEGASPI, Lorenze .... 619-388-2990.. 60 J
llegaspi@sdccd.edu

LEGAULT, Greg .... 785-227-3380 172 A
legaultg@bethanylb.edu
LEGG, David .... 865-573-4517 420 E
dlegg@johnsonu.edu
LEGG, Hal, S .... 607-436-2748 316 F
hal.legg@oneonta.edu
LEGG, Jamie, W .... 910-630-7028 331 E
jlegg@methodist.edu
LEGG, Margaret, A .... 423-775-7210 418 D
leggma@bryan.edu
LEGGETT, Terri .... 252-789-0204 335 H
terri.leggett@martincc.edu
LEGGETT, Vi .... 330-363-6183 348 C
vi.leggett@aultman.com
LEGGETTE COLLINS,
Priscilla .... 315-386-7315 320 B
leggettep@canton.edu
LEGNER, Christine .... 813-757-2108 102 B
clegner@hccfl.edu
LEGRAND, Tom .... 864-488-8274 410 B
tslegrand@limestone.edu
LEGRANDE, Tomika .... 804-827-8737 473 B
tplegrande@vcu.edu
LEGRO, Jeffrey .... 804-289-8153 472 C
jlegro@richmond.edu
LEHFELDT, Elizabeth ..... 216-687-5559 350 J
e.lehfeldt@csuohio.edu
LEHKER, Michael .... 956-665-2291 455 D
michael.lehker@utrgv.edu
LEHMACHER, Andrea .... 847-635-1806 146 G
alehmacher@oakton.edu
LEHMAN, Amy .... 831-479-6100.. 27 D
LEHMAN, Amy .... 831-479-6285.. 27 D
amlehman@cabrillo.edu
LEHMAN, Andrew .... 717-720-4030 393 C
alehman@passhe.edu
LEHMAN, Ann .... 716-375-2435 313 C
alehman@sbu.edu
LEHMAN, Ann .... 540-231-7676 476 C
aelehman@vt.edu
LEHMAN, Brennan .... 660-562-1187 257 E
blehman@nwmissouri.edu
LEHMAN, Caelee .... 816-995-2879 258 G
caelee.lehman@researchcollege.edu
LEHMAN, DeWayne ...... 617-287-5302 211 H
dewayne.lehman@umb.edu
LEHMAN, Ed .... 540-432-4390 466 B
lehmanem@emu.edu
LEHMAN, John, B .... 906-487-1832 228 A
jblehman@mtu.edu
LEHMAN, Sandra .... 801-957-4227 461 C
sandra.lehman@slcc.edu
LEHMAN, Tracey, A ...... 541-885-1291 374 I
tracey.lehman@oit.edu
LEHMAN, William, H .... 262-554-2010 494 A
LEHMKUHL, Dennis ...... 859-341-5800 185 B
LEHMKUHL, James .... 937-778-8600 352 D
LEHMKUHL, James .... 937-778-8600 352 D
jlehmkuhl@edisonohio.edu
LEHMPUHL, David .... 719-549-2340.. 80 B
david.lehmpuhl@csupueblo.edu
LEHNER, Eric, J .... 757-479-3706 472 F
elehner@vbts.edu
LEHNER, Jennifer .... 800-818-6136.. 55 L
jlehner@paloaltou.edu
LEHNERTZ, Rod .... 319-335-3565 163 H
rodney-lehnertz@uiowa.edu
LEHOCKY, John, F .... 847-970-4810 152 I
jlehocky@usml.edu
LEHOTAK, Ed .... 402-557-7050 265 J
ed.lehotak@bellevue.edu
LEHR, David .... 434-395-4952 463 F
lehrdl@longwood.edu
LEHR, Randy .... 916-660-7900.. 64 D
rlehr1@sierracollege.edu
LEHRBERGER, Paula ..... 610-499-1226 402 G
pjlehrberger@widener.edu
LEHRE, Elaine .... 906-248-8422 221 M
elehre@bmcc.edu
LEHRFELD, David .... 971-236-9231 372 E
LEHRIAN, Amanda .... 863-674-6010 101 A
alehrian@fsw.edu
LEHRLING, Tony .... 580-745-2186 369 G
tlehrling@se.edu
LEHRMAN, Susan .... 856-256-5225 281 F
lehrman@rowan.edu
LEHUA, Connie .... 415-485-9361.. 39 A
clehua@marin.edu
LEHWALD, Annie .... 816-501-4276 258 I
anne.lehwald@rockhurst.edu
LEI, Lei .... 973-353-1169 282 B
llei@business.rutgers.edu

LEONARD, Kelly .... 865-981-8246 421 C
kelly.leonard@maryvillecollege.edu
LEONARD, Kevin .... 618-650-5047 150 C
kleonar@siue.edu
LEONARD, Kim .... 913-722-0272 175 A
LEONARD, Lindsey .... 319-352-8526 170 J
lindsey.leonard@wartburg.edu
LEONARD, Lou .... 412-365-1842 380 G
l.leonard@chatham.edu
LEONARD, Marjolie ...... 631-632-6280 317 A
marjolie.leonard@stonybrook.edu
LEONARD,
Mary Kathleen .... 814-871-7430 384 A
leonard010@gannon.edu
LEONARD, Raychelle .... 928-724-6683.. 12 D
rleonard@dinecollege.edu
LEONARD, Robert .... 256-824-2233.... 8 B
robert.leonard@uah.edu
LEONARD, Robert .... 252-492-2061 338 F
leonardr@vgcc.edu
LEONARD, Roberta .... 724-589-2024 399 D
rleonard@thiel.edu
LEONARD, Sanejo .... 916-306-1628.. 67 F
sleonard@sum.edu
LEONARD, Steve .... 317-738-8316 155 D
sleonard@franklincollege.edu
LEONARD, Tammy .... 972-721-5336 452 B
tleonard@udallas.edu
LEONARD, Tammy .... 214-388-5466 435 D
tleonard@dallasinstitute.edu
LEONARD, Timothy .... 410-704-3936 204 E
tleonard@towson.edu
LEONARD, Trish .... 602-639-7500.. 12 J
LEONARD, Vee .... 239-590-1101 109 K
vleonard@fgcu.edu
LEONARD, William, J ... 610-361-5217 391 A
leonardw@neumann.edu
LEONE, Cataldo .... 617-358-6621 207 E
cleone@bu.edu
LEONE, Charles .... 215-204-7900 399 B
charles.leone@temple.edu
LEONE, Gerard .... 617-287-7050 211 F
gleone@umassp.edu
LEONE, John .... 518-828-4181 297 B
john.leone@sunycgcc.edu
LEONE, Lucian .... 269-782-1490 231 A
lleone@swmich.edu
LEONE, Thomas, A .... 410-706-7032 203 A
tleone@police.umaryland.edu
LEONETTI, Marc .... 401-254-3843 405 C
mleonetti@rwu.edu
LEONHART, Alex .... 717-396-7833 392 U
aleonhart@pcad.edu
LEONI, Amy .... 740-284-7214 352 I
aleoni@franciscan.edu
LEONOR, JR.,
Samuel, E .... 951-785-2090.. 47 C
sleonor@lasierra.edu
LEOPARD, Tim .... 205-348-4530.... 7 G
tleopard@fa.ua.edu
LEOPOLD, Emily .... 617-588-1347 206 F
eleopold@bfit.edu
LEOPOLD, Joseph .... 727-341-3719 107 E
leopold.joseph@spcollege.edu
LEOPOLD, Lillian .... 619-482-6564.. 66 A
lleopold@swccd.edu
LEOUSIS, Kim .... 251-442-2290.... 8 C
kleousis@umobile.edu
LEPAGE, Sharon .... 808-440-4263 128 E
slepage@chaminade.edu
LEPHART, Scott, M .... 859-323-1100 185 F
scott.lephart@uky.edu
LEPICK, Vicki .... 808-518-4791 129 B
vickilepick@pacrim.edu
LEPLEY, Suzanne .... 269-337-7177 225 F
suzanne.lepley@kzoo.edu
LEPOWSKY, Steven .... 860-679-2808.. 89 D
slepowsky@uchc.edu
LEPPER, Charles .... 801-957-4285 461 C
charles.lepper@slcc.edu
LEPPER, David .... 989-275-5000 226 D
david.lepper@kirtland.edu
LEPRE, Dave .... 575-835-5091 286 K
dave.lepre@nmt.edu
LEPRE, Lyn .... 540-831-5401 469 D
president@radford.edu
LERCH, Derek .... 530-283-0202.. 42 A
dlerch@frc.edu
LERER, Nava .... 516-877-3236 289 I
lerer@adelphi.edu
LERMAN, Linda .... 203-857-7211.. 87 D
llerman@norwalk.edu
LERNER, Barbara .... 940-898-2739 451 D
blerner@twu.edu
LEROY, Francois .... 859-572-7976 184 E
leroy@nku.edu
LEROY, Lindsay .... 910-962-2684 343 C
leroyl@uncw.edu
LEROY, Richard, S .... 805-437-1662.. 30 C
richard.leroy@csuci.edu
LEROY, Terri .... 620-421-6700 175 F
terril@labette.edu
LESAK, Zack .... 412-244-3240 386 A
LESAN, Thomas, L .... 641-782-1443 170 F
lesan@swcciowa.edu
LESANE, II, Cornell, B .. 508-793-3622 208 D
clesane@holycross.edu
LESANE, Steven .... 919-546-8534 340 B
slesane@shawu.edu
LESCARBEAU, Lisa .... 413-662-5205 213 C
lisa.lescarbeau@mcla.edu
LESCAULT, JR.,
Maurice, A .... 434-971-3291 502 I
maurice.a.lescault.civ@mail.mil
LESCHES, Elchonon .... 718-363-2034 322 B
LESCINSKI, CSJ, Joan ... 563-333-6213 169 G
officeofthepresident@sau.edu
LESEN, Beth .... 562-985-5587.. 31 D
beth.lesen@csulb.edu
LESESNE, David, L .... 804-752-7305 469 F
davidlesesne@rmc.edu
LESH, Aja .... 626-815-6000.. 26 F
alesh@apu.edu
LESHIN, Laurie .... 508-831-5200 220 F
president@wpi.edu
LESHINSKIE, Eric .... 480-731-8000.. 12 N
eric.leshinskie@domail.maricopa.edu
LESHKEVICH, Peter .... 734-973-3729 232 D
pleshkev@wccnet.edu
LESHKOWICH,
Ann Marie .... 508-793-2335 208 D
aleshkow@holycross.edu
LESHOK, Laura .... 734-462-4400 230 G
lleshok@schoolcraft.edu
LESIAK, Erin .... 308-398-7406 266 A
erinlesiak@cccneb.edu
LESLEY, Kimberly .... 215-965-8582 390 E
klesley@moore.edu
LESLIE, Benjamin, C ..... 704-406-4239 329 A
bleslie@gardner-webb.edu
LESLIE, Bethany .... 330-823-8440 362 E
lesliebe@mountunion.edu
LESLIE, Brian .... 321-674-8038 100 C
bleslie@fit.edu
LESLIE, Colleen, M .... 617-253-7086 216 B
LESLIE, Howard .... 973-278-5400 291 E
hdl@berkeleycollege.edu
LESLIE, Howard .... 973-278-5400 275 I
hdl@berkeleycollege.edu
LESLIE, Jon .... 303-492-2537.. 84 B
jon.leslie@colorado.edu
LESLIE, Julie .... 419-251-1598 355 G
julie.leslie@mercycollege.edu
LESLIE, Ken .... 802-635-1315 463 G
ken.leslie@northernvermont.edu
LESLIE, Meinya .... 404-225-4712 115 H
LESLIE, Robert .... 704-978-5410 336 C
rleslie@mitchellcc.edu
LESLIE, Robin .... 704-463-3442 339 E
robin.leslie@pfeiffer.edu
LESLIE, Sarah-Jane .... 609-258-3035 280 D
sjleslie@princeton.edu
LESMEISTER, Heather ... 417-625-9365 256 F
lesmeister-h@mssu.edu
LESPERANCE, Dawn ...... 208-792-2318 132 A
sdlesperance@lcsc.edu
LESPERANCE, Katherine 920-465-2464 495 F
lesperka@uwgb.edu
LESPERANCE, Wayne .... 603-428-2908 273 G
wlesperance@nec.edu
LESSANE JENKINS,
Wanda .... 910-672-1145 341 C
wljenkins@uncfsu.edu
LESSARD, Kelley .... 508-830-5014 213 D
klessard@maritime.edu
LESSARD, Richard .... 617-732-2880 216 D
richard.lessard@mcphs.edu
LESSEIG, Lisa .... 912-279-5737 117 F
llesseig@ccga.edu
LESSEM, Louis, A .... 313-577-2268 232 K
louis.lessem@wayne.edu
LESSER, Cheryl .... 570-740-0200 389 A
clesser@luzerne.edu
LESSER, Mary .... 828-328-7078 330 F
mary.lesser@lr.edu
LESSITER, Julie .... 318-795-4238 190 A
julie.lessiter@lsus.edu
LESSNE, Eric .... 203-392-6050.. 86 A
lessnee1@southernct.edu
LESSNER, Kimberly .... 903-510-2383 452 A
kles@tjc.edu
LESTER, Cancee .... 936-591-9075 441 C
clester@panola.edu
LESTER, Dennis .... 831-656-3432 502 M
dennis.lester@nps.edu
LESTER, Dyan, E .... 276-964-7677 475 C
dyan.lester@sw.edu
LESTER, Gillian .... 212-854-2675 297 C
glester@law.columbia.edu
LESTER, Jason .... 561-803-2402 105 C
jason_lester@pba.edu
LESTER, John .... 912-478-6397 120 C
jlester@georgiasouthern.edu
LESTER, John .... 334-670-3923.... 7 C
jlester@troy.edu
LESTER, Karen, K .... 218-477-2062 239 E
lesterka@mnstate.edu
LESTER, Melinda .... 888-532-7282.. 56 E
LESTER, Mike .... 507-285-7254 240 H
mike.lester@rctc.edu
LESTER, Richard, K .... 617-253-7704 216 B
LESTER, Ron .... 405-491-6356 369 H
rlester@snu.edu
LESTER, Tammy .... 252-451-8371 336 E
ttlester342@nashcc.edu
LESTER, Tina, M .... 479-575-6765.. 21 F
tlester@uark.edu
LESUEUR, Mary .... 662-252-8000 248 G
mlesueur@rustcollege.edu
LESZKO, Dennis .... 203-837-8214.. 86 B
leszkod@wcsu.edu
LETANG, Alick .... 203-392-5652.. 86 A
letanga1@southernct.edu
LETCHER, Owen .... 925-485-5277.. 35 I
oletcher@clpccd.org
LETCHWORTH, Deemie . 601-643-8403 245 F
deemie.letchworth@colin.edu
LETCHWORTH, Megan .. 928-350-1006.. 15 L
megan.letchworth@prescott.edu
LETELLIER, Lisa .... 580-559-5173 365 K
lletellier@ecok.edu
LETELLIER, Travis .... 605-658-3424 416 D
travis.letellier@usd.edu
LETENDRE, Donald, E .... 319-335-8794 163 H
donald-letendre@uiowa.edu
LETENDRE, Guy .... 801-626-6569 461 A
guyletendre@weber.edu
LETENDRE, Linell, A ..... 719-333-4270 503 D
linell.letendre@usafa.edu
LETH-STEENSEN, Ted ..... 413-565-1000 206 D
tlethsteensen@baypath.edu
LETIZIA, Katelyn .... 716-926-8942 301 E
kletizia@hilbert.edu
LETO, Leah .... 201-761-6102 283 A
lleto@saintpeters.edu
LETOURNEAU, Diana .... 315-268-7608 295 F
dletourn@clarkson.edu
LETT-BREWINGTON,
La Wanza .... 757-683-4109 469 B
llettbre@odu.edu
LETTER, Leon .... 734-384-4282 228 C
lletter@monroeccc.edu
LETTIERE, Barbara .... 610-647-4400 385 L
blettiere@immaculata.edu
LETTINI, Gabriella .... 510-549-4714.. 66 G
glettini@sksm.edu
LETTINI, Pat .... 516-876-3191 318 C
lettinip@oldwestbury.edu
LETTKO, James .... 518-464-8500 299 C
jlettko@excelsior.edu
LEUENBERGER, Deniz ... 508-531-1201 212 D
dleuenberger@bridgew.edu
LEUGERS, Lucinda .... 928-692-3041.. 14 F
lleugers@mohave.edu
LEUMA, Elizabeth .... 684-699-9155 504 B
e.leuma@amsamoa.edu
LEUNER, Jean .... 334-244-3658.... 4 E
jleuner@aum.edu
LEUNG, David .... 818-767-0888.. 76 E
david.leung@woodbury.edu
LEUNG, Katheryn .... 626-917-9482.. 36 G
kleung@cesna.edu
LEUNG-ROGALA,
Bridget .... 508-849-3490 205 H
blrogala@annamaria.edu
LEUTZINGER, Eugene ... 319-296-4457 166 H
eugene.leutzinger@hawkeyecollege.edu
LEVA, Gennaro, J .... 215-204-2452 399 B
levagj@temple.edu
LEVAN, Gretchen, L ...... 610-917-1478 401 G
gllevan@valleyforge.edu
LEVAN, Kent, G .... 314-977-7143 259 F
kent.levan@slu.edu
LEVAN, Stephanie .... 843-863-7382 407 B
slevan@csuniv.edu
LEVANDA, Eric .... 334-833-4335.... 5 G
elevanda@hawks.huntingdon.edu
LEVANDER, Caroline ..... 717-348-4228 442 F
clevande@rice.edu
LEVANDOSKI, Mark .... 641-269-3450 166 G
levandos@grinnell.edu
LEVANTE, Shela .... 413-236-3070 214 A
slevante@berkshirecc.edu
LEVARIO GUTIERREZ,
Estela .... 775-337-5647 271 C
elevario@tmcc.edu
LEVAS, Frances .... 617-731-3500 210 G
flevas@hchc.edu
LEVASSEUR, Katherine .. 802-224-3000 463 D
LEVATO, Peggy, S .... 315-379-3871 320 B
levatop@canton.edu
LEVEN, Carol .... 212-217-4700 299 D
carol_leven@fitnyc.edu
LEVEN, Scott .... 417-447-6985 257 G
levens@otc.edu
LEVENS, Michael, P ...... 248-689-8282 232 C
mlevens@walshcollege.edu
LEVENSON, Gary, M ...... 540-464-7314 476 B
levensongm@vmi.edu
LEVENSON, Stephanie ... 216-397-1886 353 O
LEVEQUE, Karen .... 312-362-8091 136 H
kleveque@depaul.edu
LEVEQUE, Rod .... 909-448-4708.. 71 C
rleveque@laverne.edu
LEVER, Timothy .... 973-720-2843 284 J
levert@wpunj.edu
LEVERENZ, Jeffrey .... 262-691-5301 500 B
jleverenz@wctc.edu
LEVERETTE, Craig, C ..... 972-377-1551 433 I
cleverette@collin.edu
LEVERGOOD, Bill, J ...... 417-268-6113 250 G
blevergoodl@gobbc.edu
LEVERICH, Ellen .... 585-245-5626 318 B
eleverich@geneseo.edu
LEVERITT, Chad .... 979-230-3037 431 I
chad.leveritt@brazosport.edu
LEVERS, David, W .... 718-289-5157 293 B
david.levers@bcc.cuny.edu
LEVESQUE, Andrew .... 860-231-5238.. 90 A
ajlevesque@usj.edu
LEVESQUE, Heather, A .. 423-439-5378 419 G
levesque@etsu.edu
LEVESQUE, Jeanne .... 617-552-4787 207 C
jeanne.levesque@bc.edu
LEVESQUE, Maurice ...... 336-278-6455 328 J
levesque@elon.edu
LEVESQUE, Neil .... 603-222-4109 274 A
nlevesque@anselm.edu
LEVESQUE, Paige .... 704-355-6676 327 G
paige.levesque@carolinascollege.edu
LEVETT, Kerry .... 425-352-8378 478 D
klevett@cascadia.edu
LEVEY, Lynn .... 508-793-7194 208 C
llevey@clarku.edu
LEVICKI, Glenn .... 843-525-8276 412 G
glevicki@tcl.edu
LEVIN, Amy .... 818-677-2138.. 32 C
amy.levin@csun.edu
LEVIN, Gary, M .... 305-760-7500 103 V
LEVIN, Hannah .... 952-222-0699 234 B
hannah.levin@bethfel.org
LEVIN, Holly .... 208-426-2694 130 H
hollylevin@boisestate.edu
LEVIN, Jason .... 801-274-3280 461 E
jason.levin@wgu.edu
LEVIN, Jonathan .... 650-723-2300.. 66 E
jdlevin@stanford.edu
LEVIN, Lubbe .... 310-794-0810.. 69 E
llevin@chr.ucla.edu
LEVIN, Marc .... 410-888-9048 200 E
mlevin@muih.edu
LEVIN, Rob .... 207-801-5623 194 E
rlevin@coa.edu
LEVIN, Shmuel, Y .... 773-463-7738 150 J
LEVIN, Yitzchok .... 773-463-7738 150 J
yzlevin@telshe.edu
LEVIN-STANKEVICH,
Brian .... 509-359-6200 479 G
LEVINE, Heidi .... 515-961-1617 170 B
heidi.levine@simpson.edu

LEWIS, Stacy .... 415-422-5540.. 72 J
lewiss@usfca.edu
LEWIS, Stephanie .... 909-384-8534.. 60 F
slewis@sbccd.cc.ca.us
LEWIS, Susan .... 325-674-2024 428 F
lewiss@acu.edu
LEWIS, Susan .... 541-506-6047 372 F
slewis@cgcc.edu
LEWIS, Tammy .... 718-951-5024 293 C
tlewis@brooklyn.cuny.edu
LEWIS, Ted .... 304-327-4161 489 I
tlewis@bluefieldstate.edu
LEWIS, Tiffany .... 765-677-2102 158 B
tiffany.lewis@indwes.edu
LEWIS, Tracie, O .... 336-285-4491 341 D
tolewis@ncat.edu
LEWIS, Trevor .... 305-626-3750 100 D
trevor.lewis@fmuniv.edu
LEWIS, Trevor, C .... 215-898-1135 400 F
lewistc@upenn.edu
LEWIS, Walter .... 518-587-2100 320 E
walter.lewis@esc.edu
LEWIS, JR., Wayne, D .. 585-567-9310 302 B
wayne.lewis@houghton.edu
LEWIS, Whitney .... 404-364-8309 123 K
wlewis@oglethorpe.edu
LEWIS, Wick .... 520-452-2619.. 11 M
lewisw@cochise.edu
LEWIS, Zachary .... 314-446-8402 260 H
zachary.lewis@stlcop.edu
LEWIS-BHOLA,
Prudence .... 305-626-3180 100 D
prudence.bhola@fmuniv.edu
LEWIS-GUMP, Kelly ...... 248-645-3300 223 D
kgump@cranbrook.edu
LEWIS-JASPER, Vera ..... 409-944-1496 436 E
vlewis@gc.edu
LEWLESS, Scott .... 989-686-9042 223 J
scottlewless@delta.edu
LEWMAN, Marguerite .... 530-251-8834.. 47 F
mlewman@lassencollege.edu
LEWTER, John, A .... 731-881-7710 427 D
jlewter@utm.edu
LEWTER, Richard .... 804-758-6840 475 A
rlewter@rappahannock.edu
LEWTER, Roblyn .... 703-539-6890 471 F
LEWTON-YATES,
Jennifer .... 601-974-1327 247 B
yatesjl@millsaps.edu
LEY, David .... 907-745-3201.... 9 C
dley@akbible.edu
LEY-SOTO, Javier .... 305-237-3694 104 E
jleysoto@mdc.edu
LEYBA, John .... 706-864-1958 127 A
john.leyba@ung.edu
LEYBA-RUIZ, Teresa ..... 623-845-3010.. 13 C
teresa.leyba-ruiz@gccaz.edu
LEYKAM, Scott, R .... 503-943-8420 377 A
leykam@up.edu
LEYSHON, Lisa .... 208-282-3111 131 G
leyslisa@isu.edu
LEYVA-PUEBLA,
Ricardo .... 206-934-3890 483 C
ricardo.leyvapuebla@seattlecolleges.
edu
LEZHEO, Kao .... 206-934-3851 483 C
kao.lezheo@seattlecolleges.edu
LE'AU, Samoa .... 816-531-5223 251 K
LE'I, Emilia .... 684-699-9155 504 B
e.lei@amsamoa.edu
LI, Haipeng .... 209-228-7632.. 70 A
hli58@ucmerced.edu
LI, Joanne .... 305-348-2751 110 A
joli@fiu.edu
LI, Joanne .... 402-554-2419 270 A
joli@unomaha.edu
LI, King .... 217-300-2424 152 B
kingli@illinois.edu
LI, Kuiyuan .... 850-473-7716 111 F
kli@uwf.edu
LI, Luchen .... 410-337-6000 199 B
luchen.li@goucher.edu
LI, Ming .... 269-387-2966 233 B
ming.li@wmich.edu
LI, Peter .... 361-593-4340 447 D
peter.li@tamuk.edu
LI, Rui .... 610-430-4959 395 D
rli@wcupa.edu
LI, Sharon, F .... 415-422-2790.. 72 J
lis@usfca.edu
LI, Xiaofan .... 312-567-3135 140 A
lix@iit.edu
LI, Xiaohong .... 661-763-7978.. 67 G
xli@taftcollege.edu
LI, Xiaonong .... 661-763-7978.. 67 G
xli@taftcollege.edu
LI, Xun .... 954-776-4476 103 B
xli@keiseruniversity.edu
LI, Yan .... 425-352-8633 478 D
yli@cascadia.edu
LI, Yi .... 212-237-8801 294 D
yili@jjay.cuny.edu
LI, Zhan .... 203-254-4070.. 87 I
zli2@fairfield.edu
LI-BUGG, Cherry .... 714-808-4787.. 54 A
clibugg@nocccd.edu
LI-ROSI, AnaMaria .... 239-280-7398.. 95 M
anamaria.lirosi@avemaria.edu
LIANG, Bruce .... 860-679-7214.. 89 D
bliang@uchc.edu
LIANG, Heng .... 707-621-7000.. 41 A
LIANG, John Paul .... 713-780-9777 429 G
jpliang@acaom.edu
LIANG, Mark .... 714-564-6040.. 58 F
liang_mark@sac.edu
LIANG, Sara .... 608-663-2277 492 F
sliang@edgewood.edu
LIANTONIO, Richard ..... 913-253-5000 177 D
LIAO, Min-Ken .... 864-294-2248 409 H
minken.liao@furman.edu
LIAO-TROTH, Matthew .. 727-341-3323 107 E
liaotroth.matthew@spcollege.edu
LIAUTAUD, Danielle ...... 973-720-2121 284 J
liautaudd@wpunj.edu
LIBBY, Betsy .... 207-755-5250 195 D
blibby@cmcc.edu
LIBBY, Grace .... 860-913-2264.. 88 A
glibby@goodwin.edu
LIBENGOOD, Desiree .... 612-343-4796 242 M
dslibeng@northcentral.edu
LIBERATI, Dennis .... 267-295-2314 402 A
dliberati@walnuthillcollege.edu
LIBERATORI, Ellen, A .... 607-746-4612 320 D
liberaem@delhi.edu
LIBERATOSCIOLI,
Daniel .... 267-295-2316 402 A
president@walnuthillcollege.edu
LIBERATOSCIOLI,
Peggy .... 267-295-2315 402 A
pl@walnuthillcollege.edu
LIBERATOSCIOLI,
Peggy .... 267-295-2325 402 A
pl@walnuthillcollege.edu
LIBERIO, Lydia, G .... 213-252-5100.. 23 K
lliberio@alu.edu
LIBERMAN, Ira .... 718-438-1002 306 D
LIBERTO, Salvadore ...... 251-460-7725.... 9 A
sliberto@southalabama.edu
LIBERTO, Terri .... 412-536-1813 386 H
terri.liberto@laroche.edu
LIBERTY, Bob .... 254-526-1310 432 D
bob.liberty@ctcd.edu
LIBERTY, Cynthia .... 336-770-3333 343 D
libertyc@uncsa.edu
LIBERTY, Paul .... 703-993-8860 467 E
pliberty@gmu.edu
LIBET, Alice, Q .... 843-792-4930 410 C
libeta@musc.edu
LIBUNAO, Arte .... 949-783-4800.. 74 L
alibunao@westcoastuniversity.edu
LIBUTTI, Dean .... 401-874-4408 405 E
dean@uri.edu
LIBUTTI, Ken .... 561-868-3239 105 D
libuttik@palmbeachstate.edu
LIBUTTI, Steven, K .... 732-235-8064 282 A
steven.libutti@cinj.rutgers.edu
LICARI, Frank .... 702-990-4433 272 C
flicari@roseman.edu
LICARI, Michael .... 931-221-7011 417 H
LICATA, Betty Jo .... 330-941-3064 364 H
bjlicata@ysu.edu
LICATA, Christine, M .... 585-475-2953 312 F
cmlnbt@rit.edu
LICHT, Daniel .... 914-395-2301 315 A
dlicht@sarahlawrence.edu
LICHT, Jodi, N .... 212-752-1530 304 A
jodi.licht@limcollege.edu
LICHT, William .... 920-206-2320 493 C
william.licht@mbu.edu
LICHTBLAU, Jobey .... 710-231-7672 345 F
jobey.lichtblau@ndsu.edu
LICHTENSTEIN, Mark .... 315-470-4748 319 D
malichte@esf.edu
LICHTI, Benjamin .... 316-284-5349 172 B
blichti@bethelks.edu
LICHTMAN, Jeffrey .... 212-463-0400 322 G
jeff.lichtman@touro.edu
LICHTVELD, Maureen .... 412-624-3001 400 H
mlichtve@pitt.edu
LIDDELL, Peter, E .... 315-294-8861 292 G
liddell@cayuga-cc.edu
LIDDELL, Tammy .... 206-296-6052 484 A
liddellt@seattleu.edu
LIDDELL, Wendy .... 509-248-7100 480 H
LIDDICOAT, Al .... 805-756-2844.. 29 I
aliddico@calpoly.edu
LIDDLE, Ken .... 713-348-2287 442 F
kliddle@rice.edu
LIDDY, Colette .... 973-618-3209 276 D
cliddy@caldwell.edu
LIDERS, Gunta .... 585-275-5373 323 M
gliders@orpa.rochester.edu
LIDGUS, Jonathan .... 314-516-5911 261 C
lidgusj@umsl.edu
LIDINGTON, Siobhan ...... 203-773-8550.. 85 D
slidington@albertus.edu
LIDSKY, Lyrissa, B .... 573-882-3246 261 A
lidskyl@missouri.edu
LIDSTONE, Rena .... 409-772-5714 456 E
rllidsto@utmb.edu
LIDTKE, Suzanne .... 262-547-1211 492 A
slidtke@carrollu.edu
LIDY, Paul .... 217-362-6410 144 G
plidy@millikin.edu
LIEBEGOTT, Kris .... 570-955-1530 387 B
liebegott@lackawanna.edu
LIEBENGOOD, Kelly .... 903-233-3372 439 A
kellyliebengood@letu.edu
LIEBER, Barbara .... 217-641-4535 141 A
blieber@jwcc.edu
LIEBER, Steve .... 480-461-7066.. 13 D
steven.lieber@mesacc.edu
LIEBERMAN,
Devorah, A .... 909-448-4900.. 71 C
dlieberman@laverne.edu
LIEBERMAN, Matthew ... 646-565-6067 322 F
matthew.lieberman@touro.edu
LIEBERMAN, Matthew ... 646-565-6067 322 G
matthew.lieberman@touro.edu
LIEBERT, Jane .... 913-758-6126 178 B
jane.liebert@stmary.edu
LIEBESKIND, Lanny, S .. 404-727-6604 118 E
chemll1@emory.edu
LIEBHABER, Karen .... 870-248-4000.. 18 F
karenl@blackrivertech.edu
LIEBHABER, Sharon ...... 215-635-7300 384 E
LIEBLICH, Kathleen .... 516-876-3242 318 C
lieblichk@oldwestbury.edu
LIEBLING, Mark .... 231-995-1342 229 A
mliebling@nmc.edu
LIEBOWITZ, Debra, J .... 203-582-7576.. 88 G
debra.liebowitz@qu.edu
LIEBOWITZ, Ronald, D . 781-736-2000 208 A
president@brandeis.edu
LIEBSCH, Anita .... 303-963-3365.. 78 H
aliebsch@ccu.edu
LIEBST, Anne .... 479-788-7205.. 21 G
anne.liebst@uafs.edu
LIEBURN, Scott .... 920-924-6459 499 D
slieburn@morainepark.edu
LIECHTI, Brian .... 828-771-3006 344 D
bliechti@warren-wilson.edu
LIECHTY, Benjamin, A .. 765-455-9595 157 B
baliecht@iuk.edu
LIECHTY, Dan .... 574-535-7563 155 E
dankl@goshen.edu
LIECHTY, Jeanne, M ..... 574-535-7401 155 E
jeannem@goshen.edu
LIEDERBACH, Mark .... 919-761-2100 340 D
mliederbach@sebts.edu
LIEDTKA, Theresa .... 423-425-4506 427 C
theresa-liedtka@utc.edu
LIEDTKE, Richard, W .... 785-670-1812 178 C
richard.liedtke@washburn.edu
LIEF, Charles, G .... 303-245-4804.. 82 A
president@naropa.edu
LIEF, Nathan, P .... 651-696-6140 236 I
nlief@macalester.edu
LIEN, Thuy .... 858-513-9240.. 68 K
thuy.lien@ashford.edu
LIERZ, Rachel .... 913-469-8500 174 I
rachellierz@jccc.edu
LIESEN, Joseph .... 573-288-6480 252 F
jliesen@culver.edu
LIESEN, Kristen .... 217-228-5432 147 F
liesekr@quincy.edu
LIESKE, Barb .... 219-464-6717 162 D
barb.lieske@valpo.edu
LIESMAN, Laura .... 732-987-2685 278 A
lliesman@georgian.edu
LIESTMAN, Daniel .... 509-865-8520 481 A
liestman_d@heritage.edu
LIETO, Mary .... 914-923-2690 311 A
mlieto@pace.edu
LIETZ, Cynthia .... 602-496-0600.. 10 J
clietz@asu.edu
LIEU, Mark .... 510-659-6276.. 54 J
mlieu@ohlone.edu
LIFKA, David .... 607-254-8621 297 F
lifka@cornell.edu
LIFSEY, Britt .... 678-359-5108 120 F
brittl@gordonstate.edu
LIFTON, Richard, P .... 212-327-8080 312 G
rickl@rockefeller.edu
LIGAS, Mark .... 203-254-4025.. 87 I
mligas@fairfield.edu
LIGEIKIS, David .... 607-778-5575 317 D
ligeikisd@sunybroome.edu
LIGHT, Aaron .... 417-447-8802 257 G
lighta@otc.edu
LIGHT, Barb .... 906-635-2745 226 G
bjlight@lssu.edu
LIGHT, Brad .... 336-334-4355 343 A
uncg@bkstore.com
LIGHT, Cathy, A .... 626-395-6304.. 28 J
clight@caltech.edu
LIGHT, Cathy, A .... 412-268-5345 380 C
calight@andrew.cmu.edu
LIGHT, Logan .... 501-279-4332.. 19 C
hlight@harding.edu
LIGHT, Wesley .... 717-477-1121 395 B
wwlight@ship.edu
LIGHTCAP, Lisa .... 610-282-1100 382 C
lisa.lightcap@desales.edu
LIGHTCAP, Rhonda .... 516-671-0379 324 G
rlightcap@webb.edu
LIGHTCAP, Stephen .... 215-717-6375 400 E
slightcap@uarts.edu
LIGHTFOOT, Carolyn, A 281-425-6455 438 I
clightfo@lee.edu
LIGHTFOOT, David .... 434-832-7643 473 E
lightfootd@centralvirginia.edu
LIGHTFOOT, Stacy, G ... 423-425-4141 427 C
stacy-lightfoot@utc.edu
LIGHTNER, Michael .... 303-860-5600.. 84 A
lightner@cu.edu
LIGHTNER, Robin .... 513-745-5660 362 A
robin.lightner@uc.edu
LIGHTSEY, Pamela .... 773-256-3000 144 B
LIGHTY, JoAnn .... 208-426-1450 130 H
joannlighty@boisestate.edu
LIGMAN, Scott .... 509-527-2395 485 C
scott.ligman@wallawalla.edu
LIGNAROLO, Giancarlo . 305-821-3333 100 E
ljanvier@fnu.edu
LIGON, Jay .... 318-257-4321 192 D
ligon@latech.edu
LIGON, Theresa .... 713-780-9777 429 G
LIGUORI, Gary .... 401-874-9330 405 E
gliguori@uri.edu
LIKELY, Nygil .... 269-927-8752 226 F
nlikely@lakemichigancollege.edu
LIKEN, Fiona, B .... 706-542-6020 126 G
fliken@uga.edu
LIKENS, Erin .... 601-643-8316 245 F
erin.likens@colin.edu
LIKINS, Michelle .... 706-754-7819 123 G
mlikins@northgatech.edu
LIKINS, Sarah .... 540-362-6281 467 H
likinsse@hollins.edu
LIKNESS, Tabitha .... 605-668-1603 415 F
tabitha.likness@mountmarty.edu
LILES, Jeffrey .... 419-824-3829 355 C
jliles@lourdes.edu
LILES, Tammy .... 859-246-6449 181 F
tammy.liles@kctcs.edu
LILFORD, Grant .... 912-583-3103 116 E
glilford@bpc.edu
LILIENTHAL, Ronda .... 615-248-1245 426 D
rlilienthal@trevecca.edu
LILJEGREN, Donna .... 630-947-8914 133 D
dliljegren@aurora.edu
LILJEGREN, Lisa .... 262-243-5700 492 E
lisa.liljegren@cuw.edu
LILLARD, Laura .... 423-648-2675 423 B
llillard@richmont.edu
LILLARD, Shanetta, S ... 973-761-7161 283 C
shannetta.lillard@shu.edu
LILLARD, Tom .... 540-831-6172 469 D
tlillard@radford.edu
LILLBACK, Peter, A .... 215-572-3811 402 E
plillback@wts.edu

LILLEBO, Troy .... 816-235-6585 261 B lillebot@umkc.edu

LILLEHAUGEN, Sandi .... 701-662-1543 346 C sandra.lillehaugen@lrsc.edu

LILLES, Anthony .... 650-289-3344.. 59 J anthony.lilles@stpsu.edu

LILLEY, Lisa .... 256-331-5368.... 3 C lisa.lilley@nwscc.edu

LILLIE, Deb .... 319-385-6210 167 H deb.lillie@iw.edu

LILLQUIST, Erik .... 973-275-4811 283 C erik.lillquist@shu.edu

LILLQUIST, Mark .... 863-297-1083 106 A mlilquist@polk.edu

LILLY, Flavius .... 410-706-7767 203 A flilly@umaryland.edu

LILLY, Ryan .... 865-981-8033 421 C bookstore@maryvillecollege.edu

LIM, Adriene .... 301-405-1668 202 H

LIM, Bob .... 408-924-1000.. 34 A

LIM, Choong .... 808-735-4831 128 E clim@chaminade.edu

LIM, David .... 213-386-0080.. 45 A

LIM, Paul, J .... 213-385-2322.. 76 F paul1911@wmu.edu

LIM, Paul, S .... 213-385-2322.. 76 F sunglim@wmu.edu

LIM, Rosy .... 323-731-2383.. 55 H rosylim@psuca.edu

LIM, Sulgi .... 413-597-2214 220 D sl3@williams.edu

LIM, Teik .... 817-272-2101 454 I teik.lim@uta.edu

LIM, Xieng .... 425-739-8264 481 C xieng.lim@lwtech.edu

LIM-TEPPER, Noriko ...... 415-338-1948.. 33 E noriko@sfsu.edu

LIMA, Kristin .... 925-473-7405.. 40 D klima@losmedanos.edu

LIMAS MARTINEZ, Maricela .... 323-259-2500.. 54 I

LIMAYEM, Moez .... 813-974-4281 111 C mlimayem@usf.edu

LIMBACH, Patrick, A ..... 513-558-0026 361 J pat.limbach@uc.edu

LIMBAUGH, James, M . 310-287-4325.. 49 H limbaujm@wlac.edu

LIMOGES, Brian .... 605-658-3308 416 D brian.limoges@usd.edu

LIMON, Gissella .... 312-850-7168 135 H glimon7@ccc.edu

LIMPER, Leslie .... 503-352-2871 375 C limp5635@pacificu.edu

LIN, Anne .... 410-532-5545 201 D alin@ndm.edu

LIN, Chia-Yen .... 619-260-4598.. 72 I linc@sandiego.edu

LIN, Janice .... 219-464-5333 162 D janice.lin@valpo.edu

LIN, Jerry .... 409-880-8760 449 G jerry.lin@lamar.edu

LIN, Kathleen .... 626-571-5110.. 48 D kathleenlin@les.edu

LIN, Shu-Chiang .... 512-444-8082 448 H sclin@thsu.edu

LIN, Stephanie .... 480-750-4470.. 15 N

LIN, Yi-Chun Tricia ...... 203-392-6864.. 86 A lyny4@southernct.edu

LIN, Ying .... 205-226-4622.... 4 F ylin@bsc.edu

LIN-COOK, Wendy .... 973-655-4259 279 B lincookw@montclair.edu

LINAKER, Kathleen .... 608-785-9102 500 C linakerk@westerntc.edu

LINAM, Gail .... 214-333-5372 434 C gaill@dbu.edu

LINAMEN, Larry .... 951-552-8744.. 27 G llinamen@calbaptist.edu

LINARD, Stephanie .... 850-729-6466 104 M linards@nwfsc.edu

LINCE, Amy .... 989-386-6601 228 B alince@midmich.edu

LINCE, Tiburcio .... 254-968-1714 446 D lince@tarleton.edu

LINCOLN, Holly .... 636-481-3230 254 C hlincoln@jeffco.edu

LINCOLN, Jonathan .... 973-720-2858 284 J lincolnj@wpunj.edu

LINCOLN, Michael .... 973-278-5400 275 I mil@berkeleycollege.edu

LINCOLN, Timothy .... 512-404-4873 430 J tlincoln@austinseminary.edu

LIND, Elise .... 800-996-6422 238 F e.lind@nhed.edu

LIND, Josh .... 715-232-1233 497 B lindjo@uwstout.edu

LIND, Joy .... 605-575-2063 417 C joy.lind@usiouxfalls.edu

LIND, Kellie .... 707-965-7500.. 55 I klind@puc.edu

LIND, Sonja .... 909-537-3204.. 32 E sonja.lind@csusb.edu

LIND, Steven .... 415-442-6622.. 43 I slind@ggu.edu

LIND, Werner .... 276-326-4267 464 J wlind@bluefield.edu

LIND, William .... 843-953-5011 407 C wlind@citadel.edu

LIND-AYRES, Justin ...... 612-330-1746 234 A lindayre@augsburg.edu

LIND-GONZALEZ, Patricia .... 934-420-2298 320 F lindgop@farmingdale.edu

LINDAHL, Roberta, D .... 503-943-7321 377 A lindahl@up.edu

LINDBERG, Brad .... 641-269-3250 166 G lindbergb@grinnell.edu

LINDBERGH, Tracy .... 480-858-9100.. 15 Q t.lindbergh@scnm.edu

LINDBLAD, Gary .... 562-903-4770.. 27 A gary.lindblad@biola.edu

LINDBLOM, Timothy ..... 256-782-8488.... 6 A tlindblom@jsu.edu

LINDBURG, Jaci .... 402-554-2020 270 A jlindburg@nebraska.edu

LINDEBORG, Ruth .... 610-526-5157 379 B rlindebo@brynmawr.edu

LINDELL, Andrea .... 866-492-5336 244 F andrea.lindell@mail.waldenu.edu

LINDELL, Calvin, O .... 606-474-3273 181 B colindell@kcu.edu

LINDELL, Melissa, M .... 315-268-6716 295 F mlindell@clarkson.edu

LINDEMANN, Susan, K . 269-337-7308 225 F susan.lindemann@kzoo.edu

LINDEN, Erika .... 515-271-1526 165 G erika.linden@dmu.edu

LINDEN, Kristin .... 310-338-2868.. 51 A kristen.linden@lmu.edu

LINDEN, Stephen, M .... 248-232-4674 229 C smlinden@oaklandcc.edu

LINDENBAUM, Sharon .. 816-235-2650 261 B lindenbaums@umkc.edu

LINDENBERG, Beren ..... 305-809-3109.. 97 O beren.lindenberg@cfk.edu

LINDENFELD, Laura ...... 631-632-7403 317 A laura.lindenfeld@stonybrook.edu

LINDENMAYER, Kathleen .... 203-837-8266.. 86 B lindenmayerk@wcsu.edu

LINDENMEYR, Adele ..... 610-519-4606 401 K adele.lindenmeyr@villanova.edu

LINDER, Meloney .... 701-777-2038 345 B meloney.linder@und.edu

LINDER, Patty .... 863-297-1000 106 A plinder@polk.edu

LINDERMAN, Regan ...... 209-667-3440.. 33 B rlinderman@csustan.edu

LINDERS, Annette .... 623-845-3377.. 13 C annette.linders@gccaz.edu

LINDGREN, Robert, R ... 804-752-7211 469 F rlindgren@rmc.edu

LINDGREN, Teresa .... 606-783-2449 184 C t.lindgren@moreheadstate.edu

LINDHOLM, Mary, C .... 512-232-2959 455 A lindholm@austin.utexas.edu

LINDLEY, Holly .... 650-433-3881.. 55 L hlindley@paloaltou.edu

LINDLEY, Kelli .... 208-467-8825 132 E klindley@nnu.edu

LINDLEY, Korey .... 714-484-7464.. 54 B klindley@cypresscollege.edu

LINDLEY, Korey .... 949-451-5435.. 65 C klindley@ivc.edu

LINDLEY, Lori .... 814-871-7522 384 A lindley001@gannon.edu

LINDLEY, Steve .... 507-786-3521 243 D lindley@stolaf.edu

LINDNER, Angela .... 352-273-1102 111 A alindner@aa.ufl.edu

LINDNER, Bill .... 850-644-7572 110 C blindner@fsu.edu

LINDNER, Janet .... 203-432-8588.. 90 C janet.lindner@yale.edu

LINDO, Patricia .... 860-512-3613.. 86 G plindo@manchestercc.edu

LINDOERFER, Brian ...... 303-735-0716.. 84 B brian.lindoerfer@colorado.edu

LINDON, Jennifer .... 606-487-3100 181 I jennifer.lindon@kctcs.edu

LINDON-BURGETT, Dana .... 405-733-7433 369 E dlindon@rose.edu

LINDOW, Claudio .... 718-262-5337 295 E clindow@york.cuny.edu

LINDOW, Tracy .... 901-722-3230 423 G tlindow@sco.edu

LINDQUIST, Cynthia, A . 701-766-4055 344 G president@littlehoop.edu

LINDQUIST, Kelsey .... 510-436-1245.. 45 E lindquist@hnu.edu

LINDQUIST, Kimberly ... 734-384-4101 228 C klindquist@monroeccc.edu

LINDQUIST, Robert .... 256-824-2882.... 8 B robert.lindquist@uah.edu

LINDQUIST, Vern, L ...... 217-786-2885 143 B vern.lindquist@llcc.edu

LINDQUIST, Will .... 816-415-7655 262 F lindquistw@william.jewell.edu

LINDSAY, Charles, W ... 607-735-1790 298 H clindsay@elmira.edu

LINDSAY, Dawn, S .... 410-777-1177 197 G dslindsay@aacc.edu

LINDSAY, Deb .... 561-732-4424 107 G dlindsay@svdp.edu

LINDSAY, Dennis .... 541-684-7253 371 I dlindsay@bushnell.edu

LINDSAY, Jenny .... 610-647-4400 385 L jlindsay2@immaculata.edu

LINDSAY, Jonathan .... 410-337-6000 199 B jonathan.lindsay@goucher.edu

LINDSAY, Marsha, N .... 412-809-5293 396 E lindsay.marsha@ptcollege.edu

LINDSAY, Michael .... 765-998-5000 161 C president@taylor.edu

LINDSAY, Nathan .... 406-243-4689 263 K nathan.lindsay@umontana.edu

LINDSAY, Shawn .... 417-626-1234 257 F lindsay.shawn@occ.edu

LINDSAY, Terry .... 229-500-2000 114 H

LINDSAY, Thomas .... 312-553-5600 135 B tlindsay6@ccc.edu

LINDSETH, Jenna .... 715-425-4972 496 F jenna.lindseth@uwrf.edu

LINDSEY, Chuck .... 239-590-7168 109 K clindsey@fgcu.edu

LINDSEY, Connie .... 773-947-6300 143 H clindsey@mccormick.edu

LINDSEY, Dana .... 352-395-4409 108 A dana.lindsey@sfcollege.edu

LINDSEY, Haley .... 620-227-9313 173 D hlindsey@dc3.edu

LINDSEY, Heidie .... 337-482-6272 193 B hlindsey@louisiana.edu

LINDSEY, Jill .... 540-545-7324 470 G jlindsey@su.edu

LINDSEY, John .... 918-781-7200 365 C lindseyj@bacone.edu

LINDSEY, Jonathan .... 602-274-1885.. 14 O jlindsey@pihma.edu

LINDSEY, Jordan .... 503-375-7156 372 H jlindsey@corban.edu

LINDSEY, Melissa .... 320-308-5377 241 A mlindsey@sctcc.edu

LINDSEY, Pam .... 217-420-6774 144 G plindsey@millikin.edu

LINDSEY, Patrick, O ..... 313-577-4228 232 K patrick.lindsey@wayne.edu

LINDSEY, Rochelle .... 404-752-5223 123 E rlindsey@msm.edu

LINDSEY, Shannon .... 785-628-4462 173 H sdlindsey@fhsu.edu

LINDSEY, Steve .... 602-557-7537.. 16 G steve.lindsey@phoenix.edu

LINDSEY, Terryl .... 918-293-5388 368 B terryl.lindsey@okstate.edu

LINDSEY, JR., Trumanue .... 612-659-6474 239 A trumanue.lindsey@minneapolis.edu

LINDSEY, Valarie .... 773-252-5318 146 F valarie.lindsey@oakpoint.edu

LINDSKOOG, Marie .... 765-455-9468 157 B mlindsko@iuk.edu

LINDSTAEDT, William ... 415-476-4986.. 70 D bill.lindstaedt@ucsf.edu

LINDSTEDT, John .... 508-856-2198 212 C john.lindstedt@umassmed.edu

LINDSTROM, Chris .... 207-581-1640 196 G chris.lindstrom@maine.edu

LINDSTROM, Derrick ..... 651-450-3618 238 E derrick.lindstrom@inverhills.edu

LINDSTROM, Kevin .... 763-576-4076 237 E klindstrom@anokaramsey.edu

LINDSTROM, Lauren ...... 530-752-4663.. 69 B lelindstrom@ucdavis.edu

LINDSTROM, Lynne .... 563-884-5313 169 F lynne.lindstrom@palmer.edu

LINDSTROM, Peter .... 303-352-6785.. 80 F peter.lindstrom@ccd.edu

LINDSTROM, Richard, W .... 323-563-5832.. 36 C richardlindstrom@cdrewu.edu

LINDSTROM, Ryan .... 801-863-8303 460 D lindstry@uvu.edu

LINDSTROM, Yvonne .... 313-578-0328 231 E lindstym@udmercy.edu

LINDUSKA, Kim .... 712-749-2243 164 C linduskak@bvu.edu

LINDZEY, Jonathan .... 570-484-2204 394 E jlindzey@lockhaven.edu

LINE, Josh .... 740-389-4636 355 F linej@mtc.edu

LINEBACH, Jared .... 706-233-7294 125 C jlinebach@shorter.edu

LINEBACK, Carla .... 802-258-3266 462 H carla.lineback@worldlearning.org

LINEBERGER, Susanne, B .... 386-312-4050 107 C susannelineberger@sjrstate.edu

LINEBERRY, Gene, T ..... 859-323-6630 185 F gt.lineberry@uky.edu

LINEBURG, Robert .... 540-831-5228 469 D rlineburg@radford.edu

LINEGAR, Malinda .... 308-432-6399 268 D mlinegar@csc.edu

LINEHAN, Rob .... 765-998-4905 161 C rblinehan@taylor.edu

LINEHAN, Stephen .... 781-899-5500 218 B rev.linehan@psjs.edu

LINEMAN, Hope, E .... 814-393-1270 393 G hlineman@clarion.edu

LINENBURG, Savannah, C .... 812-888-6222 162 F slinenburg@vinu.edu

LINFANTE, Patrick .... 973-761-9328 283 C patrick.linfante@shu.edu

LINFORD, Jon, F .... 208-496-1123 130 I linfordj@byui.edu

LINGEN, Scott .... 701-224-5441 346 A scott.lingen@bismarckstate.edu

LINGENFELTER, Monica 304-876-5286 490 A mlingenf@shepherd.edu

LINGER, Frederick, S .... 740-427-5250 354 I lingerf@kenyon.edu

LINGLE, Earl, W .... 336-841-9552 329 F elingle@highpoint.edu

LINGLE, Richard .... 816-279-7000 250 B richard.lingle@abtu.edu

LINGNER, Jackie .... 321-674-8053 100 C jlingner@fit.edu

LINGO, Amy .... 502-852-6411 186 A amy.lingo@louisville.edu

LINGRELL, Scot .... 912-478-1863 120 C slingrell@georgiasouthern.edu

LINK, Christine, A .... 626-914-8821.. 36 J clink@citruscollege.edu

LINK, Eric .... 701-777-2049 345 B eric.link@und.edu

LINK, Gerred .... 559-791-2428.. 47 A gerred.link@portervillecollege.edu

LINK, Hilary, L .... 814-332-5380 378 A hlink@allegheny.edu

LINK, James .... 805-525-4417.. 67 K jlink@thomasaquinas.edu

LINK, John .... 314-968-6982 262 C johnlink24@webster.edu

LINK, Laura .... 612-874-3700 237 A llink@mcad.edu

LINK, Lisa .... 616-222-1426 223 C lisa.link@cornerstone.edu

LINK, Matthew .... 253-879-3244 484 G mlink@pugetsound.edu

LINK, Robert .... 419-434-4528 362 D link@findlay.edu

LINK, Stephen .... 202-687-1747.. 92 E spl8@georgetown.edu

LINK, Tonya .... 701-355-8245 347 C tmlink@umary.edu

LINK, Whitney .... 701-671-2507 346 D whitney.link@ndscsd.edu

LINKER, Maureen .... 313-593-5445 231 I mlinker@umich.edu

LINKER, Maureen .... 313-593-5621 231 I
mlinker@umich.edu
LINKS, Jonathan .... 410-516-6880 199 G
jlinks1@jhu.edu
LINMAN, Eric .... 503-255-0332 374 C
elinman@multnomah.edu
LINN, Brooke .... 503-552-1716 374 D
blinn@nunm.edu
LINN, Joseph .... 785-628-4277 173 H
jlinn@fhsu.edu
LINN, Richard, T .... 716-827-3451 323 G
linnr@trocaire.edu
LINN-ADDISON,
Margaret .... 303-964-3657.. 83 E
mlinnaddison@regis.edu
LINNANE, SJ, Brian, F . 410-617-2201 200 B
president@loyola.edu
LINNELL, Michael .... 701-858-3065 345 E
michael.linnell@minotstateu.edu
LINNEMAN, Scott .... 360-650-7207 485 I
scott.linneman@wwu.edu
LINNEWEBER,
Travis, W .... 765-658-4175 154 J
travislinneweber@depauw.edu
LINO, Paulette .... 510-723-2665.. 35 J
plino@chabotcollege.edu
LINSEBIGLER, Tommie . 406-275-4985 265 F
tommie_linsebigler@skc.edu
LINSENMEYER,
Machelle .... 304-793-6871 490 C
alinsenmeyer@osteo.wvsom.edu
LINSEY, Troy .... 678-513-5202 122 B
tlinsey@laniertech.edu
LINSON, Marci .... 417-690-2636 251 H
linson@cofo.edu
LINSON, Robert .... 202-885-6013.. 91 F
rlinson@american.edu
LINSTRA, Ralph .... 434-582-2427 468 E
rlinstra@liberty.edu
LINTNER, Tim .... 803-641-3564 413 B
tlintner@usca.edu
LINTON, Greg .... 865-573-4517 420 E
glinton@johnsonu.edu
LINTON, Jill .... 814-732-1346 394 B
jlinton@edinboro.edu
LINTON, Julie, M .... 864-455-8203 413 F
julie.linton@prismahealth.org
LINTON, Richard, H ...... 919-515-2668 342 A
richard_linton@ncsu.edu
LINTZ, Brian .... 410-386-8249 198 D
blintz@carrollcc.edu
LINVILLE, Allison .... 406-756-3822 263 E
LINVILLE, David .... 423-439-4219 419 G
linville@etsu.edu
LINVILLE, Joe .... 304-896-7366 488 I
joe.linville@southernwv.edu
LINZEY, Scott .... 912-525-5000 124 I
slinzey@scad.edu
LION, Benjamin .... 314-392-2211 256 E
benjamin.lion@mobap.edu
LIOSATOS, Alex .... 920-565-1000 493 A
liosatosa@lakeland.edu
LIOTTA, Robert .... 301-295-9172 503 C
robert.liotta@usuhs.edu
LIOTTA, Sheila, A .... 401-865-2600 404 F
sadamus@providence.edu
LIPAN, Petruta .... 314-977-3571 259 F
petruta.lipan@slu.edu
LIPE, Kaiwipuni .... 808-956-2697 129 E
kaiwipun@hawaii.edu
LIPECKA, Evy .... 773-256-3000 144 B
LIPHART, Kristin .... 920-693-1854 498 H
kristin.liphart@gotoltc.edu
LIPITZ, Jon .... 410-225-2516 200 D
jlipitz@mica.edu
LIPITZ, Michael .... 312-996-2695 151 G
mlipitz@uic.edu
LIPIZ GONZALEZ,
Elaine .... 714-992-7088.. 54 C
elipizgonzalez@fullcoll.edu
LIPMAN, Elizabeth, D ... 610-799-1165 388 D
elipman@lccc.edu
LIPMAN, Howard .... 305-348-6298 110 A
howard.lipman@fiu.edu
LIPP, Evan, E .... 978-232-2005 209 E
elipp@endicott.edu
LIPP, Jacob .... 713-226-5585 453 A
lippp@uhd.edu
LIPPARD, Rodney .... 803-641-3460 413 B
rodneyl@usca.edu
LIPPE, Diane .... 954-262-4932 105 A
lipped@nova.edu
LIPPENS, Susan 419-720-6670 359M
susan.lippens@proskills.edu

LIPPERT, Patricia, A ...... 812-488-2152 161 G
pl23@evansville.edu
LIPPERT, Robert .... 559-453-2189.. 43 A
robert.lippert@fresno.edu
LIPPIELLO, Stephen ...... 412-536-1047 386 H
steve.lippiello@laroche.edu
LIPPMAN, Fred .... 954-262-1508 105 A
flippman@nsu.nova.edu
LIPPMAN, Stuart .... 646-565-6726 322 G
stuart.lippman@touro.edu
LIPPMAN, Stuart .... 646-565-6726 322 F
stuart.lippman@touro.edu
LIPSCHUETZ, Angie .... 415-817-4205.. 33 E
alipschuetz@sfsu.edu
LIPSCOMB, Benjamin .... 585-567-9374 302 B
benjamin.lipscomb@houghton.edu
LIPSCOMB, Natasha ...... 704-216-3622 337 F
natasha.lipscomb@rccc.edu
LIPSCOMB, Tom .... 336-517-2304 327 A
tlipscomb@bennett.edu
LIPSETT, Teresa .... 787-743-7979 510 H
ut_tlipsett@suagm.edu
LIPSKIER, Hershel .... 973-267-9404 280 F
info@rca.edu
LIPSKY, Andrew .... 508-626-4640 213 A
alipsky@framingham.edu
LIPSTREU, Tiffany .... 614-823-1414 359 H
tlipstreu@otterbein.edu
LIPTAK, Kathy .... 304-384-6303 489 J
liptakka@concord.edu
LIPTAK, Victoria .... 617-585-0200 207 A
LIRLEY, Sean .... 719-336-1543.. 81 K
sean.lirley@lamarcc.edu
LISCHKE, Douglas, E .... 434-982-3485 472 D
del8s@virginia.edu
LISCHWE, Sheila, T ...... 864-656-1661 407 E
slischw@clemson.edu
LISCIO, Gina .... 315-792-7288 321 B
gina.liscio@sunypoly.edu
LISCO, Heather .... 812-258-9510 154 E
financialaid@cariscollege.edu
LISEA, Scott .... 805-565-6170.. 76 A
slisea@westmont.edu
LISHEN, Wendy .... 301-295-1667 503 C
wendy.lishen@usuhs.edu
LISHNER, Ryan .... 303-233-4697.. 79 K
LISK, Patti .... 540-423-9824 473 I
plisk@germanna.edu
LISLE, Kristy .... 650-949-7209.. 42 I
lislekristy@foothill.edu
LISLE, Tara .... 432-264-5646 437 F
tlisle@howardcollege.edu
LISNER, Lydia .... 804-627-5300 464 K
lydia_lisner@bshsi.org
LISONBEE, Stephen .... 435-586-5418 460 A
lisonbee@suu.edu
LISS, Donna .... 660-785-4163 260 F
dliss@truman.edu
LISS, Joshua .... 267-341-3100 385 J
jliss@holyfamily.edu
LISS, Katrina .... 618-664-7014 138 F
katrina.liss@greenville.edu
LISS, Tony .... 212-650-8261 293 D
tliss@ccny.cuny.edu
LIST, Allison .... 631-687-5198 314 A
alist@sjcny.edu
LIST, Edith .... 618-374-5068 147 E
edith.list@principia.edu
LISTAU, Lynsey .... 850-484-2128 105 H
llistau@pensacolastate.edu
LISTER, Basil .... 816-604-4206 255 H
basil.lister@mcckc.edu
LISTER, Philip .... 505-224-4000 285 N
plister@cnm.edu
LISTER, Tommy .... 626-584-5338.. 43 B
tommylister@fuller.edu
LISTERMAN, Robin .... 704-463-3062 339 E
robin.listerman@pfeiffer.edu
LISTON, Brenda .... 614-947-6532 352 J
brenda.liston@franklin.edu
LISTON, Jed .... 406-243-5211 263 K
jed.liston@umontana.edu
LISTWAK, Jeffrey, A ...... 412-397-5263 397 B
listwak@rmu.edu
LISZKA, Justin .... 336-272-7102 329 C
justin.liszka@greensboro.edu
LITA SARMIENTO,
Maria .... 201-714-7100 278 C
msarmiento2@hccc.edu
LITANT, Josiah .... 507-453-1420 239 B
josiah.litant@southeastmn.edu
LITCHFIELD, Brad .... 609-896-5000 281 B
blitchfield@rider.edu

LITCHFIELD, Charles ..... 719-255-3678.. 84 C
clitchfi@uccs.edu
LITCHMAN, Jennifer, B . 410-706-3477 203 A
jlitchman@umaryland.edu
LITHERLAND, Steve, E .. 757-822-1944 475 E
slitherland@tcc.edu
LITKE, Russ .... 419-995-8342 360 C
litke.r@rhodesstate.edu
LITMAN, Kay .... 610-372-4721 396 H
klitman@racc.edu
LITSITSA, Anna .... 650-433-3807.. 55 L
alitsitsa@paloaltou.edu
LITT, Eleni .... 212-229-8947 308 A
litte@newschool.edu
LITT, Jacquelyn, S .... 848-932-3047 282 A
jlitt@echo.rutgers.edu
LITTEN, Lyndsi .... 559-737-4892.. 39 B
lyndsil@cos.edu
LITTERAL, Samuel, M ... 304-896-7426 488 I
samuel.litteral@southernwv.edu
LITTERER, Denise .... 419-372-2081 348 G
denisel@bgsu.edu
LITTKY, Dennis .... 401-752-2640 404 B
LITTLE, Andrew, P .... 410-777-2227 197 G
aplittle1@aacc.edu
LITTLE, Bernard .... 630-466-7900 152 K
blittle@waubonsee.edu
LITTLE, Chris .... 530-895-2400.. 27 C
littlech@butte.edu
LITTLE, Christopher .... 765-983-1400 155 A
littlech@earlham.edu
LITTLE, Crystal .... 619-594-5901.. 33 D
little@sdsu.edu
LITTLE, F. Shanon .... 707-664-2358.. 34 B
LITTLE, Jennifer .... 864-592-4808 412 E
littlej@sccsc.edu
LITTLE, Jennifer .... 541-349-7487 371 I
jlittle@bushnell.edu
LITTLE, Joseph .... 606-368-6059 178 G
LITTLE, Lara .... 704-463-3353 339 E
lara.little@pfeiffer.edu
LITTLE, Laura .... 570-702-8946 386 D
llittle@johnson.edu
LITTLE, Leeann .... 918-335-6234 368 E
llittle@okwu.edu
LITTLE, Michael .... 678-466-4477 117 D
michaellittle@clayton.edu
LITTLE, Michael .... 678-466-4478 117 D
michaellittle@clayton.edu
LITTLE, Pamela .... 919-866-5805 338 G
pmlittle@waketech.edu
LITTLE, Rebecca, K .... 812-888-4220 162 F
rlittle@vinu.edu
LITTLE, Scott .... 601-968-5956 245 B
slittle@belhaven.edu
LITTLE, Shay .... 912-478-2795 120 C
slittle@georgiasouthern.edu
LITTLE, Sylvester .... 863-292-3762 106 A
slittle@polk.edu
LITTLE-BERRY, Terri ...... 850-599-3183 109 I
ruthie.littleberry@famu.edu
LITTLE-PALMER, Tanya . 770-689-5088 430 E
tlittle-palmer@aii.edu
LITTLE WHITEMAN,
Iona .... 701-627-4738 346 F
ilittl@nhsc.edu
LITTLEBEAR, Richard ..... 406-477-6215 263 C
rlbear@cdkc.edu
LITTLEFIELD,
Elizabeth, S .... 804-523-5181 474 A
blittlefield@reynolds.edu
LITTLEFOX, Allie .... 510-430-2232.. 52 E
afox@mills.edu
LITTLEJOHN, Dee .... 214-887-5006 435 F
dlittlejohn@dts.edu
LITTLEJOHN, Quincina .. 973-748-9000 276 A
quincina_littlejohn@bloomfield.edu
LITTLEJOHN, Sylvia .... 803-738-7764 410 D
littlejohns@midlandstech.edu
LITTLES, Kathy .... 925-631-4021.. 59 I
kl30@stmarys-ca.edu
LITTLETON, Robert, A ... 423-652-6022 420 F
ralittle@king.edu
LITTLETON STEIB,
Larissa .... 504-762-3000 188 B
llsteib@dcc.edu
LITTMAN, Jared, E .... 718-990-2920 313 G
littmanj@stjohns.edu
LITTRELL, Johnny .... 931-540-2840 424 C
jlittrell@columbiastate.edu
LITTRELL, Meghann .... 513-732-5327 362 B
meghann.littrell@uc.edu
LITVACK, Steven, B .... 201-489-5836 278 D

LITWACK, Kim .... 414-229-4189 496 B
litwack@uwm.edu
LITWILLER, Hannah ...... 620-241-0723 172 J
hannah.litwiller@centralchristian.edu
LITWIN, Daveen, H .... 603-646-3780 273 D
daveen.h.litwin@dartmouth.edu
LITZ, Kerri .... 410-225-2277 200 D
klitz@mica.edu
LITZIN, Louise .... 928-724-6633.. 12 D
louise@dinecollege.edu
LIU, Bei .... 408-733-1878.. 71 B
LIU, Chris .... 816-235-1301 261 B
y.liu@umkc.edu
LIU, Eric .... 641-472-7000 168 C
bliu@miu.edu
LIU, Fengshan .... 302-857-6646.. 90 E
fliu@desu.edu
LIU, Frank .... 626-917-9482.. 36 G
frankliu@cesna.edu
LIU, Keming .... 718-270-4951 294 G
kliu@mec.cuny.edu
LIU, Monika .... 415-452-5730.. 36 K
mliu@ccsf.edu
LIU, Samuel .... 626-571-5110.. 48 D
samuelliu@les.edu
LIU, Shuang .... 410-777-1868 197 G
sliu4@aacc.edu
LIU, Susan .... 626-448-0023.. 46 G
LIU, Tina .... 626-917-9482.. 36 G
tinaliu@cesna.edu
LIU, Xiaoqing .... 618-453-4321 150 B
xiaoqing.liu@siu.edu
LIU, Ying .... 561-297-2719 109 J
yingliu@fau.edu
LIU, Yun Lin (Cynthia) . 631-499-7100 304 C
clin@libi.edu
LIU, Yuxiang .... 646-592-6008 326 D
yuxiang.liu@yu.edu
LIU, Yuxing .... 512-454-1188 430 A
info@aoma.edu
LIVELY, Alisa .... 304-473-8431 491 D
lively_a@wvwc.edu
LIVELY, Amanda .... 478-538-3160 125 G
alively@southeasterntech.edu
LIVELY, David .... 847-491-2094 146 E
david.lively@northwestern.edu
LIVELY, Kathryn, J .... 603-646-3113 273 D
kathryn.j.lively@dartmouth.edu
LIVENGOOD, Matthew .. 816-995-2901 258 G
matthew.livengood@researchcollege.edu
LIVERMAN, Deborah, L . 617-715-5329 216 B
LIVERS, Regina .... 513-569-5735 350 F
regina.livers@cincinnatistate.edu
LIVESAY, Dennis .... 316-978-6513 178 D
dennis.livesay@wichita.edu
LIVESEY, Jim .... 713-718-7864 437 C
jim.livesey@hccs.edu
LIVINGOOD, Rick .... 540-296-4695 471 K
rick.livingood@ufairfax.edu
LIVINGOOD,
Susannah, B .... 405-325-5065 370 K
slivingood@ou.edu
LIVINGS-VEALS, Sandy . 504-486-7411 193 E
LIVINGSTON, Carolyn ... 507-222-4248 234 G
clivingston@carleton.edu
LIVINGSTON, David, J .. 815-836-5230 142 F
dlivingston@lewisu.edu
LIVINGSTON, Esther ...... 859-985-3065 179 I
livginstone@berea.edu
LIVINGSTON, Jane .... 850-644-2525 110 C
jane.livingston@fsu.edu
LIVINGSTON, Jane .... 574-631-9700 162 A
jlivingston@nd.edu
LIVINGSTON, Jeff .... 201-200-2064 279 D
jlivingston@njcu.edu
LIVINGSTON, Karin .... 713-743-4415 452 C
klivingston@uh.edu
LIVINGSTON, Karin .... 832-842-4415 452 D
klivingston@uh.edu
LIVINGSTON, Karin .... 713-221-8004 453 A
livingstonk@uhd.edu
LIVINGSTON, Lynette .... 715-858-1849 498 E
livingston3@cvtc.edu
LIVINGSTON, Michelle .. 614-234-2821 356 E
mlivingston@mccn.edu
LIVINGSTON, Omar .... 203-332-5049.. 86 F
olivingston@housatonic.edu
LIVINGSTON, Randy ...... 650-724-0213.. 66 E
livingston@stanford.edu
LIVINGSTON, Shannon . 715-675-3331 499 F
livingst@ntc.edu

LOGAN, Logan .... 334-683-2362.... 3 A
llogan@marionmilitary.edu
LOGAN, Mark .... 562-860-2451.. 35 H
mlogan@cerritos.edu
LOGAN, Martin .... 425-352-8262 478 D
mlogan@cascadia.edu
LOGAN, Matt .... 601-403-1111 248 E
mlogan@prcc.edu
LOGAN, Melissa .... 412-924-1373 396 F
mlogan@pts.edu
LOGAN, Michael, F .... 336-334-4104 343 A
mflogan@uncg.edu
LOGAN, Mikaela .... 276-376-3430 472 E
mra4p@uvawise.edu
LOGAN, Mike .... 712-274-6400 171 B
mike.logan@witcc.edu
LOGAN, Steven .... 903-510-2127 452 A
steven.logan@tjc.edu
LOGAN, Traci .... 617-587-5711 217 D
logant@neco.edu
LOGAN-BENNETT, Lorie 410-704-2386 204 E
lloganbennett@towson.edu
LOGGINS, Jeffery .... 662-254-3325 248 B
jloggins@mvsu.edu
LOGGINS, Ron .... 402-375-7030 268 F
rologgi1@wc.edu
LOGSDON, Phillip .... 859-985-3000 179 I
LOGUE, Heather .... 847-317-8192 151 C
hlogue@tiu.edu
LOGUE, Jean .... 918-444-2230 366 G
loguej@nsuok.edu
LOH, Albert .... 510-628-8028.. 48 C
aloh@lincolnuca.edu
LOHAN-BREMER,
Maureen .... 845-257-3256 316 E
lbremerm@newpaltz.edu
LOHDEN, Bethany, L .... 636-584-6503 253 B
bethany.lohden@eastcentral.edu
LOHER, Steven .... 314-889-1493 253 E
sloher@fontbonne.edu
LOHMAN, Brenda, J ..... 573-882-0291 261 A
blohman@missouri.edu
LOHMANN, Courtney .... 925-631-4577.. 59 I
ccarmign@stmarys-ca.edu
LOHMANN, Janet .... 207-725-3228 194 C
jlohmann@bowdoin.edu
LOHOCZKY, Maria .... 863-297-1000 106 A
mlehoczky@polk.edu
LOHR, Joel .... 860-509-9502.. 88 B
jlohr@hartsem.edu
LOHR, Nathan .... 317-788-3349 161 H
lohrn@uindy.edu
LOHREY, Adam .... 937-481-2266 364 A
adam_lohrey@wilmington.edu
LOHSE, MaryPat .... 617-349-8669 211 C
mlohse@lesley.edu
LOHSTROH, Tracy .... 618-634-3203 149 G
tracyl@shawneecc.edu
LOILAND, Sharon .... 701-777-3178 345 B
sharon.loiland@und.edu
LOIODICE, Melissa .... 413-236-1022 214 A
mloiodice@berkshirecc.edu
LOISEAU, Marvin .... 617-588-1368 206 F
mloiseau@bfit.edu
LOJOWSKY, MacAdam . 707-468-3081.. 51 F
mlojowsky@mendocino.edu
LOKENI, Lokeni .... 684-699-9155 504 B
l.lokeni@amsamoa.edu
LOKKEN, Pamela, S ...... 314-935-5752 262 A
lokken@wustl.edu
LOKKO, Lesley .... 212-650-7284 293 D
llokko@ccny.cuny.edu
LOKMAN, Lawrence, H . 814-863-1028 391 G
lhl11@psu.edu
LOKUTA, Sharon .... 260-422-5561 156 E
slokuta@indianatech.edu
LOLI, Stephany .... 510-626-5300.. 63 E
LOLL, Andrea .... 618-544-8657 139 E
lolla@iecc.edu
LOLLAND, Sonja .... 530-741-6793.. 77 C
slolland@yccd.edu
LOLLATHIN, Eric .... 740-245-7438 363 A
ericl@rio.edu
LOMBARD, Anne, E ...... 315-470-6658 319 D
aelombard@esf.edu
LOMBARD-SIMS,
Danielle .... 501-603-1315.. 22 B
dlombardsims@uams.edu
LOMBARDI, Annie .... 845-398-4016 314 G
alombard@stac.edu
LOMBARDI, Mark .... 314-529-9330 255 B
president@maryville.edu
LOMBARDI, Phillip .... 401-232-6374 404 A
plombard@bryant.edu
LOMBARDI, Ryan, T ..... 607-255-7595 297 F
ryan.lombardi@cornell.edu
LOMBARDO, Joann .... 860-486-5519.. 89 D
joann.lombardo@uconn.edu
LOMBARDO, John .... 631-851-6225 321 C
lombarj@sunysuffolk.edu
LOMBARDO, Kristina .... 904-826-8583.. 99 E
klombardo@flagler.edu
LOMBARDO, Michael ..... 503-777-7542 375 G
lombardm@reed.edu
LOMBARDO, Roberto .... 386-506-3159.. 98 D
roberto.lombardo@daytonastate.edu
LOMBARDO, Tony .... 225-578-2111 189 D
LOMBARDO, Tony .... 225-578-0552 189 E
lauramorrow@lsu.edu
LOMBARDO-BEAVER,
Natalie .... 814-234-7755 398 E
LOMBELLA, James, P .... 860-773-1419.. 87 G
jlombella@acc.commnet.edu
LOMBELLA, James, P .... 860-723-0625.. 86 C
lombellaj@ct.edu
LOMELI, Nestor .... 559-925-3135.. 75 B
nestorlomeli@whccd.edu
LOMIDZE, Kote .... 202-464-6973 462 H
kote.lomidze@worldlearning.org
LOMONACO, Barbara .... 859-238-5200 180 B
LOMONACO, Barbara .... 401-454-6655 405 B
blomonac@risd.edu
LOMONACO, Bethany .... 978-837-5616 216 F
lomonacob@merrimack.edu
LONDON, Allen, S .... 478-301-2715 122 E
london_a@mercer.edu
LONDON, April .... 847-866-3902 138 D
LONDON, Lauren .... 734-487-1055 223 K
llondon2@emich.edu
LONDON, Manuel .... 631-632-8304 317 A
manuel.london@stonybrook.edu
LONDON, Michael, E ..... 415-422-4400.. 72 J
melondon@usfca.edu
LONDON, Samuel .... 256-726-7223.... 6 C
slondon@oakwood.edu
LONDON, Tim .... 812-237-6311 156 D
tim.london@indstate.edu
LONDON, William .... 816-584-6226 258 C
william.london@park.edu
LONDONO, Hernan .... 305-899-4019.. 96 A
hlondono@barry.edu
LONDRAVILLE, Erin .... 315-268-7810 295 F
elondrav@clarkson.edu
LONDRE, Tristan .... 660-359-3948 257 D
tlondre@mail.ncmissouri.edu
LONE HILL, Karen .... 605-455-6100 415 H
klonehill@olc.edu
LONERGAN, Dennis ...... 718-862-7349 304 M
dennis.lonergan@manhattan.edu
LONERGAN, Elizabeth ... 315-786-2252 303 C
elonergan@sunyjefferson.edu
LONEY, Teresa, A .... 816-604-1517 255 C
teresa.loney@mcckc.edu
LONEY, Timothy .... 218-235-2149 241 E
timothy.loney@vcc.edu
LONG, Adam .... 864-503-5863 414 A
LONG, Adina .... 336-734-7272 334 F
along@forsythtech.edu
LONG, Angi .... 920-832-6579 493 B
angi.long@lawrence.edu
LONG, Antonio .... 678-466-4000 117 D
antoniolong@clayton.edu
LONG, Blake .... 662-720-7448 248 C
bdlong@nemcc.edu
LONG, Bobby .... 803-321-5282 410 H
bobby.long@newberry.edu
LONG, Brenda .... 706-233-7461 125 C
blong@shorter.edu
LONG, Brenda, J .... 252-222-6151 333 A
longb@carteret.edu
LONG, Bridget, T .... 617-495-3401 210 E
bridget_long@gse.harvard.edu
LONG, Brittney .... 402-399-2454 266 F
blong@csm.edu
LONG, Bronson .... 706-368-7618 119 D
blong@highlands.edu
LONG, Bruce .... 972-241-3371 434 D
blong@dallas.edu
LONG, Carol .... 310-434-4762.. 63 C
long_carol@smc.edu
LONG, Carol .... 503-375-6623 377 F
clong@willamette.edu
LONG, Christina .... 620-665-3521 174 G
longc@hutchcc.edu
LONG, Christopher, P ... 517-355-4597 227 F
cplong@msu.edu
LONG, Curt .... 563-588-6657 164 E
curt.long@clarke.edu
LONG, Cynthia .... 563-884-5157 169 F
cynthia.long@palmer.edu
LONG, Dallas .... 309-438-3139 140 D
dlong@ilstu.edu
LONG, Daniel .... 334-347-2623.... 2 A
dlong@escc.edu
LONG, Daniel .... 313-664-7675 222 H
dlong@collegeforcreativestudies.edu
LONG, Doreen .... 603-428-2303 273 G
dlong@nec.edu
LONG, Durwin .... 715-836-4899 495 E
longd@uwec.edu
LONG, Dustin .... 910-272-3566 337 D
dulong@robeson.edu
LONG, Emily .... 612-330-1558 234 A
long10@augsburg.edu
LONG, Gardner .... 423-697-5767 424 A
gardner.long@chattanoogastate.edu
LONG, Gerard, E .... 210-562-6285 456 C
longg@uthscsa.edu
LONG, Gregory .... 407-708-2174 108 D
longg@seminolestate.edu
LONG, James .... 316-295-5527 174 A
james_long@friends.edu
LONG, James .... 559-453-3439.. 43 A
james.long@fresno.edu
LONG, Jan .... 951-785-3531.. 47 C
jlong@lasierra.edu
LONG, Janet, R .... 610-499-4105 402 G
jrlong@widener.edu
LONG, II, JD .... 314-935-5582 262 A
jlongii@wustl.edu
LONG, Jeanine .... 229-227-2668 126 A
jlong@southernregional.edu
LONG, Jeff .... 575-562-2221 286 B
jeff.long@enmu.edu
LONG, Jeff .... 601-403-1041 248 E
jlong@prcc.edu
LONG, Jessica .... 336-757-7416 334 F
jlong@forsythtech.edu
LONG, Jodi .... 352-395-5680 108 A
jodi.long@sfcollege.edu
LONG, John .... 302-931-2200.. 91 C
jwl@udel.edu
LONG, Juliet .... 541-956-7279 376 A
jlong@roguecc.edu
LONG, Justin .... 239-985-8361 101 A
justin.long@fsw.edu
LONG, Karen, S .... 518-276-6216 312 C
longks@rpi.edu
LONG, Kelly .... 970-491-5932.. 79 N
kelly.long@colostate.edu
LONG, Kenneth .... 231-777-0560 228 G
kenneth.long@muskegoncc.edu
LONG, Kenneth, A .... 570-422-3201 394 A
kenlong@esu.edu
LONG, Kevin .... 240-567-7972 200 G
kevin.long@montgomerycollege.edu
LONG, Laura .... 770-720-5514 124 G
laura.long@reinhardt.edu
LONG, Laurel .... 256-824-2285.... 8 B
laurel.long@uah.edu
LONG, Lauren .... 703-993-2909 467 E
llong3@gmu.edu
LONG, Leann .... 423-585-6772 425 F
leann.long@ws.edu
LONG, Linda .... 713-942-9505 437 D
llong@hgst.edu
LONG, Lisa .... 265-761-6215.... 7 B
lelong@talladega.edu
LONG, Marcus .... 605-668-1514 415 F
marcus.long@mountmarty.edu
LONG, Matt .... 972-708-7340 435 E
helpdesk@diu.edu
LONG, Matthew .... 707-778-3930.. 63 D
mlong@santarosa.edu
LONG, Nathan .... 626-316-5310.. 63 E
nlong@saybrook.edu
LONG, Nicholas, K .... 989-774-3334 222 E
long1n@cmich.edu
LONG, Nigel .... 410-888-9048 200 E
nlong@muih.edu
LONG, Rebecca .... 740-245-7376 363 A
rlong@rio.edu
LONG, Samuel, C .... 517-321-0242 225 A
slong@glcc.edu
LONG, Shawn .... 470-578-3132 121 M
slong70@kennesaw.edu
LONG, Sheryl .... 336-721-2774 340 A
sheryl.long@salem.edu
LONG, Susan .... 501-686-5731.. 22 B
longsusanl@uams.edu
LONG, Tamara .... 325-674-2949 428 F
tnb99a@acu.edu
LONG, Terry .... 660-562-1706 257 E
tlong@nwmissouri.edu
LONG, Todd .... 419-559-2360 361 C
tlong08@terra.edu
LONG-COFFEE,
Michelle .... 310-287-4597.. 49 H
longcofm@wlac.edu
LONGACRE, Jeffrey .... 301-295-1917 503 C
jeffrey.longacre@usuhs.edu
LONGACRE, Teri, E .... 713-743-4669 452 D
elkins@central.uh.edu
LONGAKER, Frank .... 540-444-4101 471 K
flongaker@ufairfax.edu
LONGAKER, Frank, E .... 540-986-1800 464 C
frank@an.edu
LONGBELLA, Jody .... 218-894-5128 237 G
jody.longbella@clcmn.edu
LONGBRAKE, John .... 805-893-2191.. 70 E
john.longbrake@ucsb.edu
LONGENECKER, Penni .. 717-947-6093 392 V
pelongen@pacollege.edu
LONGHOFER, Kristi .... 661-946-2274.. 74 H
LONGHTA, Karie, L .... 217-786-2263 143 B
karie.longhta@llcc.edu
LONGIE, Candace .... 701-477-7862 346 J
clongie@tm.edu
LONGJOHN, Gerald ...... 616-222-1423 223 C
gerald.longjohn@cornerstone.edu
LONGLEY, Darryl .... 860-768-4153.. 89 G
longley@hartford.edu
LONGLEY, Katie .... 413-265-2322 208 E
longleyk@elms.edu
LONGLEY, Ross .... 479-308-2356.. 17 A
ross.longleu@arcomedu.org
LONGMIRE, Carla .... 205-247-8927.... 7 A
clongmirer@stillman.edu
LONGMIRE, Kolleen ...... 615-514-2787 422 H
klongmire@nossi.edu
LONGMUIR, Marcus ..... 212-229-5300 308 A
longmuim@newschool.edu
LONGO, Jose Miguel ... 315-792-7165 321 B
longojm@sunypoly.edu
LONGO, Laura .... 732-224-2259 276 B
llongo@brookdalecc.edu
LONGO, Rick .... 718-636-3514 311 F
rlongo@pratt.edu
LONGO, Rick .... 215-717-6618 400 E
rlongo@uarts.edu
LONGO, Timothy .... 434-924-7166 472 D
tjl8x@virginia.edu
LONGORIA, Erin .... 361-825-2621 447 C
erin.longoria@tamucc.edu
LONGORIA, Estrellita .... 610-957-6113 398 G
elongor1@swarthmore.edu
LONGORIA, Hossiella .... 305-899-3950.. 96 A
hlongoria@barry.edu
LONGSDORF, Brittany ... 207-753-6906 194 A
blongsdo@bates.edu
LONGWORTH, Rhonda .. 734-487-3200 223 K
rkinney@emich.edu
LONGYEAR, JR.,
George, E .... 203-436-4899.. 90 C
george.longyear@yale.edu
LONON, Justin .... 214-378-1816 434 E
justin.lonon@dcccd.edu
LONOWSKI, Jerrold ...... 575-624-8421 287 B
lonowsk@nmmi.edu
LOO, Chih .... 256-824-2243.... 8 B
chih.loo@uah.edu
LOOBY, Lynn, S .... 508-213-2215 217 H
lynn.looby@nichols.edu
LOOMER, Peter, M .... 210-567-3160 456 C
loomer@uthscsa.edu
LOOMER, Tim .... 805-565-6832.. 76 A
tloomer@westmont.edu
LOOMIS, Ryan .... 406-447-6944 264 B
ryan.loomis@helenacollege.edu
LOOMIS, Susan .... 207-326-2345 196 A
susan.loomis@mma.edu
LOOMIS HUBBELL,
Loren .... 203-392-5722.. 86 A
loomishubbl1@southernct.edu
LOONAN, John .... 843-805-5507 408 C
LOONEY, Erin .... 423-614-8200 420 H
elooney@leeuniversity.edu
LOONEY, JoAnn .... 646-564-6734 310 D
joann.looney@nyack.edu

LORENZ, Kristen .... 304-876-5212 490 A
klorenz@shepherd.edu
LORENZ, Michael .... 317-208-5311 160 A
LORENZ, Michael .... 402-280-2775 266 H
michaellorenz@creighton.edu
LORENZEN, Chris .... 307-268-3088 500 U
christopher.lorenzen@caspercollege.edu
LORENZO, Janice .... 787-891-0925 507 K
jalorenzo@aguadilla.inter.edu
LORENZO, Susan .... 650-738-4253.. 62 L
lorenzo@smccd.edu
LORENZONI, Paul .... 718-678-8485 306 C
plorenzoni@mercy.edu
LORETO, David, P .... 716-878-3694 317 F
loretodp@buffalostate.edu
LORGAN, Jason .... 530-752-9075.. 69 B
jplorgan@ucdavis.edu
LORGE-GROVER,
Christina .... 715-422-5526 499 B
christina.lorgegrover@mstc.edu
LORIA, Anne .... 716-250-7500 292 A
alloria@bryantstratton.edu
LORICK, Piper .... 803-750-2510.. 93 H
LORIMER, David, W .... 606-693-5000 183 C
dlorimer@kmbc.edu
LORIMER, Steve, A .... 606-693-5000 183 C
slorimer@kmbc.edu
LORIMER, Steve, E .... 606-693-5000 183 C
slorimer@kmbc.edu
LORIMER, Thomas .... 606-693-5000 183 C
tlorimer@kmbc.edu
LORINCZOVA, Klaudia .. 315-279-5699 303 G
klorincz@keuka.edu
LORING, Trish .... 603-271-6984 273 A
tloring@ccsnh.edu
LORING, Trish .... 603-271-6484 273 A
tloring@ccsnh.edu
LORIUS, Billie Jo .... 701-328-4107 345 A
billiejo.lorius@ndus.edu
LORKOVICH, Malinda ... 312-996-4366 151 G
mlork@uic.edu
LORMAND, Sarah, J ..... 315-448-5040 314 B
sarah.lormand@sjhcon.edu
LORTA, Danielle .... 510-780-4500.. 47 K
dlorta@lifewest.edu
LORTON-ROWLAND,
Julie .... 317-921-4715 158 D
jlorton@ivytech.edu
LORTZ, Peter .... 206-934-3701 483 B
peter.lortz@seattlecolleges.edu
LOSASSO, Joseph .... 609-652-4235 283 E
joe.losasso@stockton.edu
LOSCHIAVO, Linda .... 718-817-3570 300 C
loschiavo@fordham.edu
LOSCHIAVO, Melissa .... 770-426-2741 122 C
melissa.loschiavo@life.edu
LOSO, Chris .... 860-231-5323.. 90 A
closo@usj.edu
LOSS, Jeffrey .... 570-577-2000 379 C
jeffrey.loss@bucknell.edu
LOSTON WILLIAMS,
Adena .... 210-486-2900 429 B
aloston@alamo.edu
LOTANO, Vincent .... 908-709-7046 284 D
vincent.lotano@ucc.edu
LOTHRINGER,
Robert, L .... 214-768-3531 444 D
rlothringer@smu.edu
LOTITO, Tom .... 757-382-9900.. 93 H
LOTKOWICTZ, Bob .... 315-464-4448 317 C
lotkowir@upstate.edu
LOTRIONTE, John, D .... 901-321-3550 418 G
jlotrion@cbu.edu
LOTSU, Adamma .... 773-291-6100 135 E
LOTT, Cari .... 620-242-0400 176 B
LOTT, Ileo .... 847-635-1660 146 G
ilott@oakton.edu
LOTT, Jesse .... 315-655-7161 292 H
jlott@cazenovia.edu
LOTT, Shevallanie .... 757-727-5251 467 G
shevallanie.lott@hamptonu.edu
LOTT, Stephanie .... 785-532-6220 175 C
slott@ksu.edu
LOTTERIO, Marco .... 661-824-2977.. 53 H
mlotterio@ntps.edu
LOTTO, Benjamin .... 845-437-7437 324 C
lotto@vassar.edu
LOTURCO, Jennifer .... 212-217-4000 299 D
jennifer_loturco@fitnyc.edu
LOTZ, Cindy .... 309-556-3536 140 F
clotz@iwu.edu
LOTZ, Erin .... 928-350-2307.. 15 L
elotz@prescott.edu
LOTZ, Hailey .... 850-484-1714 105 H
hlotz@pensacolastate.edu
LOTZE, Conrad .... 304-724-3700 486 F
clotze@apus.edu
LOTZER, Gina .... 651-641-3456 236 G
glotzer001@luthersem.edu
LOU, Kris .... 503-370-5328 377 F
klou@willamette.edu
LOUALLEN, Cheryl .... 937-481-2337 364 A
cheryl_louallen@wilmington.edu
LOUCHOUARN, Patrick . 979-845-4016 446 F
loup@tamu.edu
LOUCKS, Susan .... 718-940-5564 314 A
sloucks@sjcny.edu
LOUDEN, Jennifer .... 410-617-2861 200 B
jhlouden@loyola.edu
LOUDEN, Sandy .... 731-352-4095 418 C
loudens@bethelu.edu
LOUDER, Corey .... 660-626-2203 250 A
clouder@atsu.edu
LOUDERMILK, Jennifer . 706-295-1715 120 A
jloudermilk@gntc.edu
LOUDERMILK, Jessica .. 210-784-1612 447 E
jloudermilk@tamusa.edu
LOUDIN, Rose Ellen ..... 304-473-8600 491 D
loudin_r@wvwc.edu
LOUFEK, Michelle .... 321-433-7765.. 98 I
loufekm@easternflorida.edu
LOUGEE, Wendy, P .... 612-624-1807 243 F
wlougee@umn.edu
LOUGHLIN, Stephen, J . 585-271-3657 313 B
stephen.loughlin@stbernards.edu
LOUGHMAN, Ann .... 518-262-5435 289 L
loughma@amc.edu
LOUGHREN, Joseph ..... 718-997-5910 295 B
joseph.loughren@qc.cuny.edu
LOUIMA, Gariot .... 937-767-6082 347 G
glouima@antiochcollege.edu
LOUIS, Germaine .... 703-993-1918 467 E
chhsdean@gmu.edu
LOUIS, Lindsay .... 508-213-2372 217 H
lindsay.louis@nichols.edu
LOUIS, Louisana .... 727-341-3640 107 E
louis.louisana@spcollege.edu
LOUIS, Michael .... 314-505-7301 252 A
louism@csl.edu
LOUIS, Naomi .... 937-328-6031 350 G
louisn@clarkstate.edu
LOUNDER, Lee .... 406-265-3711 264 E
lee.lounder@msun.edu
LOUNEY, Mark .... 617-747-2682 206 H
publicsafety@berklee.edu
LOUNSBERY, Monica .... 562-985-4691.. 31 D
monica.lounsbery@csulb.edu
LOURO, Jeffrey .... 508-999-8171 212 A
jlouro@umassd.edu
LOUTHAN, Katherine ..... 314-529-9671 255 B
mlouthan@maryville.edu
LOUTTIT, Julianne, E .... 724-287-8711 379 E
juli.louttit@bc3.edu
LOUTTIT, Kristen .... 724-938-4404 393 E
louttit@calu.edu
LOVAS, Judy .... 973-300-2100 284 A
jlovas@sussex.edu
LOVATO, Heather .... 575-769-4039 285 O
heather.lovato@clovis.edu
LOVATO, Stella .... 210-486-0000 429 C
slovato@alamo.edu
LOVATO, Stella .... 210-486-0903 429 C
slovato@alamo.edu
LOVATO, Todd .... 505-428-1217 288 E
todd.lovato@sfcc.edu
LOVE, Andrea .... 225-771-2552 191 E
alove@sulc.edu
LOVE, Brandolyn .... 843-355-4131 414 C
loveb@wiltech.edu
LOVE, C Bryan .... 803-584-3446 413 E
bryanlov@mailbox.sc.edu
LOVE, Casey .... 504-862-8315 191 F
mkane1@tulane.edu
LOVE, Ceshia .... 713-221-8454 453 A
lovec@uhd.edu
LOVE, Charles .... 864-503-5733 414 A
clove@uscupstate.edu
LOVE, Cindy .... 919-516-5082 339 I
clove@st-aug.edu
LOVE, David .... 413-597-4237 220 D
dlove@williams.edu
LOVE, Deborah .... 336-273-4431 327 A
LOVE, Eric .... 574-631-2859 162 A
elove1@nd.edu
LOVE, Jamica, N .... 540-464-7230 476 B
lovejn@vmi.edu
LOVE, Jan .... 404-727-6324 118 E
jlove3@emory.edu
LOVE, Jennifer .... 325-942-2116 450 E
jenny.love@angelo.edu
LOVE, Kathy, S .... 912-443-3024 125 B
klove@savannahtech.edu
LOVE, Kensey .... 740-753-7007 353 H
lovek@hocking.edu
LOVE, Latonya, J .... 713-500-6054 456 B
latanya.d.jones@uth.tmc.edu
LOVE, Marla .... 607-255-1115 297 F
dean_of_students@cornell.edu
LOVE, Paula .... 903-730-4890 438 D
plove@jarvis.edu
LOVE, Vanessa .... 412-391-4100 396 G
vlove@pointpark.edu
LOVE-SMITH, Ashley ..... 310-206-6361.. 69 E
alovesmith@volunteer.ucla.edu
LOVE-VAUGHN,
Devonia .... 318-257-2532 192 D
dlvaughn@latech.edu
LOVEDAY, Joyce .... 253-589-5500 478 J
joyce.loveday@cptc.edu
LOVEDAY, Travis, C .... 865-694-6415 425 B
tcloveday@pstcc.edu
LOVEJOY, Jonathan ...... 210-832-5668 453 C
lovejoy@uiwtx.edu
LOVEJOY, Mike .... 469-348-2500 433 M
LOVELACE, Amber .... 256-395-2211.... 3 G
alovelace@suscc.edu
LOVELACE, Rhonda .... 501-370-5297.. 20 F
rlovelace@philander.edu
LOVELACE, Vanessa .... 717-290-8723 387 G
LOVELADY, III, Artis ..... 832-252-4617 432 L
artis@cbshouston.edu
LOVELAND, David, A .... 607-746-4013 320 D
lovelada@delhi.edu
LOVELESS, Cecelia .... 360-438-6138 482 I
cloveless@stmartin.edu
LOVELESS, Debra .... 937-327-6131 364 D
registrar@wittenberg.edu
LOVELESS, Jill .... 304-214-8856 488 J
jloveless@wvncc.edu
LOVELESS, Stephanie .... 706-368-7736 119 D
sloveless@highlands.edu
LOVELL, Cheryl, D .... 719-587-7341.. 77 G
president@adams.edu
LOVELL, Dave .... 800-553-4674 156 B
dlovell@horizonindy.org
LOVELL, Diana .... 580-774-3766 370 A
diana.lovell@swosu.edu
LOVELL, Donna .... 650-723-2300.. 66 E
dlovell@stanford.edu
LOVELL, Janet .... 706-754-7833 123 G
jlovell@northgatech.edu
LOVELL, Kenya .... 386-481-2275.. 96 D
lovellk@cookman.edu
LOVELL, Matthew, D ..... 812-877-8318 160 F
lovellmd@rose-hulman.edu
LOVELL, Michael, R ...... 414-288-7223 493 E
michael.lovell@marquette.edu
LOVELL, Sharon .... 540-568-2705 468 C
lovellse@jmu.edu
LOVELY, Christine .... 530-752-1011.. 69 B
LOVELY, Courtney .... 561-803-2337 105 C
courtney_lovely@pba.edu
LOVERIN, David .... 559-730-3722.. 39 B
davidl@cos.edu
LOVETT, Julie .... 817-257-7132 448 F
j.n.lovett@tcu.edu
LOVETT, Lisa .... 303-492-4129.. 84 B
lisa.lovett@colorado.edu
LOVETT, Myra .... 318-342-1266 193 C
mlovett@ulm.edu
LOVETT, Patricia .... 270-686-4336 179 J
patricia.lovett@brescia.edu
LOVETTE-COLYER,
Michael .... 619-260-4600.. 72 I
mlovettecolyer@sandiego.edu
LOVIK, Eric .... 540-831-5099 469 D
elovik@radford.edu
LOVIN, Eddie .... 662-846-4150 245 G
elovin@deltastate.edu
LOVIN, Eddie .... 615-547-1231 419 C
elovin@cumberland.edu
LOVITT, Del .... 913-469-8500 174 I
dlovitt@jccc.edu
LOVITT, Timmothy .... 425-388-9142 480 B
tlovitt@everettcc.edu
LOVORN, Beth .... 228-497-7685 247 E
beth.lovorn@mgccc.edu
LOVORN, Michael .... 507-457-6620 243 C
mlovorn@smumn.edu
LOVSETH, Stephanie ..... 618-374-5215 147 E
stephanie.lovseth@principia.edu
LOVSTUEN, Brenda, C .. 319-895-4292 164 G
blovstuen@cornellcollege.edu
LOW, Avrum Yehuda .... 718-600-8897 325 J
LOW,
Catherine Yu-Ling ...... 808-371-5443 129 A
cfo@orientalmedicine.edu
LOW, Daniel .... 626-398-2222.. 76 C
LOW, Douglas .... 812-749-1280 159 O
dlow@oak.edu
LOW, George, S .... 678-407-5200 119 C
gslow@ggc.edu
LOW, Greg .... 949-794-9090.. 66 D
glow@stanbridge.edu
LOW, Hershel .... 718-600-8897 325 J
LOW, Rochel .... 718-600-8897 325 J
LOW, Ryan .... 207-581-5846 196 F
ryan.low@maine.edu
LOW, Wai Hoa .... 808-521-2288 129 A
whlow@orientalmedicine.edu
LOWDEN, Jay .... 530-740-1703.. 77 E
jlowden@yccd.edu
LOWDEN, Kyle .... 217-854-3231 133 I
LOWDEN, Paul .... 616-732-1194 223 E
plowden@davenport.edu
LOWDEN, Rob .... 317-278-7533 156 G
rlowden@iu.edu
LOWDEN, Rob .... 317-278-7533 156 F
rlowden@iu.edu
LOWDER, Diane, M ...... 804-752-7218 469 F
dianelowder@rmc.edu
LOWDER, Michael .... 405-789-7661 369 I
michael.lowder@swcu.edu
LOWDER, Theresa .... 859-985-3313 179 I
lowdert@berea.edu
LOWDERMILK,
Robert, S .... 336-342-4261 337 E
lowdermilkb@rockinghamcc.edu
LOWE, Allyson, M .... 716-827-2480 323 G
lowea@trocaire.edu
LOWE, Brenda .... 806-720-7307 439 D
brenda.lowe@lcu.edu
LOWE, Carmen .... 617-627-4239 219 C
carmen.lowe@tufts.edu
LOWE, Carrie Beth .... 865-573-4517 420 E
cblowe@johnsonu.edu
LOWE, Charles .... 973-720-2200 284 J
lowec1@wpunj.edu
LOWE, Charm .... 864-592-4624 412 E
lowec@sccsc.edu
LOWE, JR., Eugene, Y .. 847-491-8409 146 E
eyljr@northwestern.edu
LOWE, Grant .... 706-419-1360 118 A
grant.lowe@covenant.edu
LOWE, James .... 765-285-2805 153 H
jlowe@bsu.edu
LOWE, James, R .... 860-486-0566.. 89 D
jim.lowe@uconn.edu
LOWE, Jeanette .... 706-595-0166 115 J
jlowe@augustatech.edu
LOWE, Jerron .... 303-871-4238.. 84 E
jerron.lowe@du.edu
LOWE, Jody .... 662-915-7911 249 D
jplowe@olemiss.edu
LOWE, John-Martin ...... 402-552-3001 269 K
jjlowe@unmc.edu
LOWE, Judy .... 423-697-2686 424 A
judy.lowe@chattanoogastate.edu
LOWE, Kathy .... 707-638-5200.. 68 B
LOWE, Kristen, M .... 585-292-2000 307 B
LOWE, Larry .... 803-705-4573 406 G
larry.lowe@benedict.edu
LOWE, Megan .... 318-342-3041 193 C
lowe@ulm.edu
LOWE, Melinda .... 662-241-6088 248 A
mslowe@muw.edu
LOWE, Melissa .... 502-456-0058 185 A
mlowe@sullivan.edu
LOWE, Nathan .... 541-962-3098 372 I
nlowe@eou.edu
LOWE, Pamela .... 847-578-8786 148 F
pamela.lowe@rosalindfranklin.edu
LOWE, Patricia .... 617-552-3334 207 C
patricia.lowe@bc.edu
LOWE, Rick, D .... 910-630-7027 331 E
rlowe@methodist.edu
LOWE, Rosemary .... 870-762-3182.. 17 B
rlowe@smail.anc.edu
LOWE, Scott .... 208-426-5439 130 H
scottlowe@boisestate.edu

LUEBBERT, Paula, J ...... 217-782-1086 143 B
paula.luebbert@llcc.edu
LUEBKE, Miriam .... 651-651-8825 235 I
luebke@csp.edu
LUECKE, Chris .... 435-797-2452 460 C
chris.luecke@usu.edu
LUECKE, Julie .... 608-663-2372 492 F
jluecke@edgewood.edu
LUEKEN, Joel .... 605-394-2352 416 H
joel.lueken@sdsmt.edu
LUEKENGA, Chris .... 970-943-2616.. 85 C
cluekenga@western.edu
LUEKENGA, Julie .... 303-718-5307.. 77 H
julie.luekenga@aims.edu
LUELLEN, Jannie .... 662-252-8000 248 G
jluellen@rustcollege.edu
LUER, Mark, S .... 618-650-5153 150 C
mluer@siue.edu
LUERA, Kayla .... 785-890-3641 176 H
kayla.luera@nwktc.edu
LUESSE, Amy .... 952-446-4122 235 J
luessea@crown.edu
LUETH, Brian .... 269-488-4777 225 G
blueth@kvcc.edu
LUETH, Erica, S .... 253-535-7385 482 A
erica.lueth@plu.edu
LUETKEHANS, Lara .... 724-357-2219 394 C
lara.luetkehans@iup.edu
LUEVANO, Margaret, Y . 512-471-7885 455 A
mluevano@austin.utexas.edu
LUFF, Libby .... 615-514-2787 422 H
lfunke@nossi.edu
LUFF, Paula .... 765-285-5344 153 H
pcluff@bsu.edu
LUFKIN, Daniel .... 817-515-4501 445 F
daniel.lufkin@tccd.edu
LUFKIN, MB .... 603-358-2181 274 H
mb.lufkin@keene.edu
LUFKINS, Lorraine .... 218-935-0417 244 G
lorraine.lufkins@wetcc.edu
LUFT, John, P .... 717-796-1800 389 H
jluft@messiah.edu
LUGDON, Shannon .... 207-834-7800 197 A
shannon.lugdon@maine.edu
LUGO, Daniel, G .... 704-337-2216 339 F
president@queens.edu
LUGO, Efrain .... 787-620-2040 505 C
elugo@aupr.edu
LUGO, Eric .... 646-660-6095 292 L
eric.lugo@baruch.cuny.edu
LUGO, Javier .... 787-894-2828 513 C
javier.lugo3@upr.edu
LUGO, Nilsa, L .... 787-850-9337 512 D
nilsa.lugo@upr.edu
LUGO, Victoria .... 562-860-2451.. 35 H
vlugo@cerritos.edu
LUGO, Victoria .... 626-529-8500.. 55 F
LUGO CARDONA,
Jennifer .... 787-250-0000 511 F
jennifer.lugo1@upr.edu
LUGO-VÉLEZ, Samuel ... 787-993-8878 512 A
samuel.lugo1@upr.edu
LUHTA, Brad .... 440-375-7585 354 K
bluhta@lec.edu
LUI, Joyce .... 408-288-3177.. 62 H
joyce.lui@sjcc.edu
LUIKART, Nancy .... 563-288-6073 166 A
nluikart@eicc.edu
LUINENBURG, Amber ... 507-372-3499 239 F
amber.luinenburg@mnwest.edu
LUING, Kevin, L .... 973-278-5400 291 E
kevin@berkeleycollege.edu
LUING, Kevin, L .... 973-278-5400 275 I
kevin@berkeleycollege.edu
LUING, Tim .... 973-278-5400 275 I
tim@berkeleycollege.edu
LUING, Tim .... 212-986-4343 291 E
tim@berkeleycollege.edu
LUIS, Silvio .... 202-646-1337.. 93 B
LUJAN, Annette .... 719-846-5679.. 83 L
annette.lujan@trinidadstate.edu
LUJAN, Linda .... 719-336-1511.. 81 K
linda.lujan@lamarcc.edu
LUKAC, Dan .... 513-244-4617 356 F
dan.lukac@msj.edu
LUKACH, Matt .... 701-777-1234 345 B
matthew.lukach@und.edu
LUKACSKO, Debbie .... 201-684-7535 280 H
dlukacsk@ramapo.edu
LUKAS, Sofia .... 678-450-0550 121 I
slukas@ict.edu
LUKAS, Veronica .... 718-281-5196 295 C
vlukas@qcc.cuny.edu
LUKASIEWICZ, Mark ..... 516-463-5213 301 G
mark.lukasiewicz@hofstra.edu
LUKASKIEWICZ, Robert . 860-297-2279.. 89 B
robert.lukaskiewicz@trincoll.edu
LUKE, Amy .... 807-956-9704 129 E
aluke@hawaii.edu
LUKE, Amy, M .... 808-956-8207 129 C
aluke@hawaii.edu
LUKE, Don, J .... 570-326-3761 392 W
dluke@pct.edu
LUKE, Emily .... 304-829-7630 487 A
eluke@bethanywv.edu
LUKE, Kristie .... 580-745-2176 369 G
kluke@se.edu
LUKE, Kristin .... 931-393-1930 424 F
kluke@mscc.edu
LUKE, Learie, B .... 803-536-7180 411 G
lluke@scsu.edu
LUKE, Sarah .... 207-801-5670 194 E
sluke@coa.edu
LUKE, Victoria .... 308-367-5204 270 B
vluke1@unl.edu
LUKEHART, Debra .... 641-269-3400 166 G
lukehart@grinnell.edu
LUKES, Don .... 812-855-4206 156 G
dlukes@iu.edu
LUKES, Donald, S .... 812-855-4206 156 F
dlukes@iu.edu
LUKKES, Nathan .... 605-773-3455 416 C
nathan.lukkes@sdbor.edu
LUKOWSKI, Kristin .... 810-762-9748 226 B
klukowski@kettering.edu
LUKSA, Jennifer .... 570-674-6224 390 B
jluksa@misericordia.edu
LUKSAN, Abel .... 402-461-5177 267 E
LUKSENBURG, Dana ..... 800-371-6105.. 14 G
dana@nationalparalegal.edu
LULGJURAJ, Diana .... 718-817-4914 300 C
dlulgjuraj2@fordham.edu
LULING, Jennifer .... 267-341-3479 385 J
jluling@holyfamily.edu
LULLO, Ronald .... 708-656-8000 145 C
ronald.lullo@morton.edu
LUM, Grande, H .... 650-543-3757.. 51 G
grande.lum@menlo.edu
LUM, Jeannie .... 808-735-4761 128 E
jeannie.lum@chaminade.edu
LUM, Jennifer, T .... 626-395-5940.. 28 J
jennifer.lum@caltech.edu
LUMAN, Karl .... 601-366-8880 249 G
kluman@wbs.edu
LUMPE, Mike .... 614-885-5585 359 L
mlumpe@pcj.edu
LUMPKIN, Collier .... 336-721-2600 340 A
collier.lumpkin@salem.edu
LUMPKIN, Maria .... 478-825-6291 118 F
maria.lumpkinj@fvsu.edu
LUMPKIN, Melissa .... 205-726-4459.... 6 E
mlumpki1@samford.edu
LUMPKIN, Robert .... 773-291-6100 135 E
LUMSDEN, Mark .... 321-674-8493 100 C
mlumsden@fit.edu
LUMZY, Arthur .... 972-780-3600 454 A
arthur.lumzy@untdallas.edu
LUNA, Andrew .... 931-221-6184 417 H
lunaa@apsu.edu
LUNA, Carmen, M .... 787-766-1717 510 G
cmluna@uagm.edu
LUNA, Cyndie .... 559-442-4600.. 67 B
cyndie.luna@fresnocitycollege.edu
LUNA, David .... 520-515-5485.. 11 M
lunad@cochise.edu
LUNA, Edna, G .... 931-363-9824 427 E
eluna7@utsouthern.edu
LUNA, Javier .... 760-355-6448.. 45 K
javier.luna@imperial.edu
LUNA, Mickey .... 314-977-3948 259 F
mickey.luna@slu.edu
LUNA, Naelys .... 561-297-2056 109 J
ndiaz10@fau.edu
LUNA, Olga .... 787-758-6260 507 J
oluna@inter.edu
LUNA, Raul .... 509-453-0374 482 D
raul.luna@perrytech.edu
LUNA, Reyes .... 909-869-3983.. 30 A
rjluna@cpp.edu
LUNA, Shirley .... 936-468-2605 445 E
sluna@sfasu.edu
LUNA, Victoria .... 210-341-1366 440 H
LUNBECK, Jo .... 501-660-1030.. 17 C
jlunbeck@asusystem.edu
LUNCEFORD, Casey ...... 772-462-2505 102 F
cluncefo@irsc.edu
LUND, Annette .... 801-863-3000 460 D
annette.lund@uvu.edu
LUND, Brenda .... 360-438-4307 482 I
blund@stmartin.edu
LUND, Christopher .... 412-359-1000 400 A
clund@triangle-tech.edu
LUND, James .... 760-480-8474.. 75 J
jlund@wscal.edu
LUND, Jon .... 563-387-1428 168 B
lundjon@luther.edu
LUND, Lisa .... 989-328-1284 228 D
lisal@montcalm.edu
LUND, Robin .... 210-486-4134 428 I
rlund4@alamo.edu
LUNDAY, Bobbi, J .... 701-662-1501 346 C
bobbi.lunday@lrsc.edu
LUNDAY, Tammy .... 605-688-4157 417 A
tammy.lunday@sdstate.edu
LUNDBERG, Alessandra 860-932-4170.. 87 E
alundberg@qvcc.edu
LUNDBERG, Erik .... 734-615-4445 231 H
lerikl@umich.edu
LUNDBERG, Phil .... 503-253-3443 374 G
phil.lundberg@ocom.edu
LUNDBERG, Stacey .... 218-335-4222 236 F
stacey.lundberg@lltc.edu
LUNDBLAD, Jeffrey, K .. 773-244-5542 145 G
jlundblad@northpark.edu
LUNDBURG, Wesley ..... 619-388-7834.. 61 A
wlundburg@sdccd.edu
LUNDE, Allen, K .... 530-898-4412.. 30 D
aklunde@csuchico.edu
LUNDE, Beth .... 757-822-1711 475 E
blunde@tcc.edu
LUNDE, Beth .... 757-789-1789 473 H
blunde@tcc.edu
LUNDE-STOCKERO,
Beth .... 906-487-3310 228 A
blunde@mtu.edu
LUNDEEN, Kate .... 414-382-6103 491 F
kate.lundeen@alverno.edu
LUNDELL, Judy .... 850-973-9416 104 L
lundellj@nfc.edu
LUNDGREN, Angie .... 336-734-7157 334 F
alundgren@forsythtech.edu
LUNDGREN, Jennifer .... 816-235-1107 261 B
lundgrenj@umkc.edu
LUNDGREN, LouAnne ... 505-224-3936 285 N
llundgren1@cnm.edu
LUNDQUIST, Harvey ..... 907-260-7422.... 9 D
LUNDQUIST, Lisa, M .... 678-547-6308 122 E
lundquist_lm@mercer.edu
LUNDQUIST, Lynn .... 651-641-8232 235 I
lundquist@csp.edu
LUNDSTREM, Karen ...... 718-260-5043 295 A
klundstrem@citytech.cuny.edu
LUNDSTROM, Alicia ...... 601-318-6709 249 H
alundstrom@wmcarey.edu
LUNDSTROM, Joel .... 712-792-8308 165 A
jtlundstrom@dmacc.edu
LUNDY, Jennifer .... 724-838-4236 398 C
jlundy@setonhill.edu
LUNDY, Michael, D ...... 913-684-0014 503 E
LUNDY, Rae .... 903-927-3296 458 F
rlundy@wileyc.edu
LUNDY, Rae .... 903-923-3296 458 F
rlundy@wileyc.edu
LUNDY, Rae .... 903-927-3296 458 F
rlundy@wileyc.edu
LUNG, Melissa .... 614-236-6011 349 B
LUNN, Ardelia, M .... 334-727-8147.... 7 D
alunn@tuskegee.edu
LUNN, D. Paul .... 919-513-6210 342 A
paul_lunn@ncsu.edu
LUNN, Sheri, V .... 651-628-3321 244 D
svlunn@unwsp.edu
LUNNERMON, II,
James, G .... 410-651-7606 203 D
jglunnermonii@umes.edu
LUNSFORD, Jessica ...... 334-347-2623.... 2 A
jlunsford@escc.edu
LUNSFORD, Justin, P ... 260-982-5280 159 J
jplunsford@manchester.edu
LUNSFORD, Sam .... 206-934-6968 483 C
sam.lunsford@seattlecolleges.edu
LUNSFORD, Tracey .... 317-738-8090 155 D
tlunsford@franklincollege.edu
LUNT, Andrew .... 575-538-6181 289 G
andrew.lunt@wnmu.edu
LUNTSFORD, Becky ...... 850-474-2449 111 F
rluntsford@uwf.edu
LUOMA, Jeffrey .... 203-773-8573.. 85 D
jluoma@albertus.edu
LUOMA, Jeffrey, E .... 203-773-8550.. 85 D
LUONG, Carmen .... 718-482-5511 294 F
carmenl@lagcc.cuny.edu
LUONG, Huan .... 972-860-8102 434 G
hluong@dcccd.edu
LUONGO, Ann Marie .... 516-323-3200 306 M
presidents-office@molloy.edu
LUPACHINO, Keri .... 860-832-2204.. 85 G
lupachinok@ccsu.edu
LUPER, Brian .... 848-445-6950 282 A
bluper@oit.rutgers.edu
LUPIANI, Blanca, M ..... 979-845-4274 446 F
blupiani@tamu.edu
LUPIEN, Todd .... 575-624-8110 287 B
todd@nmmi.edu
LUPTAK, Marcia .... 847-214-6917 137 F
mluptak@elgin.edu
LUPTON, Brendan .... 847-970-4891 152 I
blupton@usml.edu
LUPU, Peter .... 623-845-3747.. 13 C
peter.lupu@gccaz.edu
LUQUETTE, Heidi .... 503-842-8222 376 E
heidiluquette@tillamookbaycc.edu
LUQUIRE, Heath .... 704-991-0122 338 C
rluquire5455@stanly.edu
LURZ, Carol .... 910-938-6343 333 F
lurzc@coastalcarolina.edu
LUSHBAUGH, Jeffery .... 609-777-3083 284 C
jlushbaugh@tesu.edu
LUSHNIAK, Boris, D ..... 301-405-2437 202 H
lushniak@umd.edu
LUSK, Brian .... 540-831-6327 469 D
blusk@radford.edu
LUSK, Carol .... 615-966-5256 421 B
carol.lusk@lipscomb.edu
LUSK, D. Claude .... 806-291-3436 457 I
luskc@wbu.edu
LUSK, Kent .... 312-553-5628 135 B
klusk1@ccc.edu
LUSK, Laurel .... 330-244-4762 363 E
llusk@walsh.edu
LUSK, Susie .... 304-384-5323 489 J
lusks@concord.edu
LUSSIER, Michel .... 207-741-5519 195 H
mlussier@smccme.edu
LUSSON, Keith .... 312-369-7283 136 D
klusson@colum.edu
LUSTER, Pamela, T .... 619-388-2721.. 60 J
pluster@sdccd.edu
LUSTER, Stacey .... 508-929-8022 213 G
sluster@worcester.edu
LUSTIG, Derek .... 315-781-3123 301 F
lustig@hws.edu
LUTAT, Daniel .... 712-362-0491 167 B
dlutat@iowalakes.edu
LUTCHEN, Kenneth, R ... 617-353-2800 207 E
klutch@bu.edu
LUTER, Gary, S .... 813-253-3333 113 H
gluter@ut.edu
LUTES, David .... 703-284-5993 468 H
david.lutes@marymount.edu
LUTES, Nicholas .... 253-680-7123 477 I
nlutes@batestech.edu
LUTGEN, Roxanne .... 715-675-3331 499 F
lutgen@ntc.edu
LUTGRING, Ray .... 812-488-2589 161 G
rl5@evansville.edu
LUTHER, Kathleen .... 314-505-7258 252 A
lutherk@csl.edu
LUTHER, Raminder .... 978-542-6000 213 E
raminder.luther@salemstate.edu
LUTNER, Rachel .... 216-687-2223 350 J
r.lutner@csuohio.edu
LUTOLF, Colleen .... 718-960-8000 294 A
LUTON, Sally .... 315-498-2466 310 F
lutons@sunyocc.edu
LUTRICK, Candace .... 972-825-4650 444 J
clutrick@sagu.edu
LUTRICK, Donny .... 972-825-4824 444 J
dlutrick@sagu.edu
LUTTJEBOER, Jared .... 219-864-2400 159 N
jluttjeboer@midamerica.edu
LUTTON, Margaret, K .... 817-515-5140 445 F
margaret.lutton@tccd.edu
LUTTRELL, Cindy .... 919-866-5005 338 G
clluttrell@waketech.edu
LUTUS, Peter, E .... 302-356-6920.. 91 E
peter.e.lutus@wilmu.edu
LUTY, Paul, J .... 503-943-8874 377 A
luty@up.edu
LUTZ, Andrew, J .... 563-333-5842 169 G
lutzandrewj@sau.edu

LUTZ, JR., Ben 865-573-4517 420 E blutz@johnsonu.edu
LUTZ, Bob 561-803-2552 105 C bob_lutz@pba.edu
LUTZ, Brock 517-607-2561 225 C blutz@hillsdale.edu
LUTZ, Bryan 740-753-6489 353 H lutzb@hocking.edu
LUTZ, Carrie 812-237-8764 156 D carrie.lutz@indstate.edu
LUTZ, Cathleen, A 570-321-4069 389 B lutz@lycoming.edu
LUTZ, Cheryl 717-391-3595 399 C lutz@stevenscollege.edu
LUTZ, John, M 615-875-8895 428 A john.lutz@vanderbilt.edu
LUTZ, Kimberley 843-661-8005 409 F kimberley.lutz@fdtc.edu
LUTZ, Nate, K 612-874-3780 237 A nate_lutz@mcad.edu
LUTZ, Todd 254-519-5708 447 A todd.lutz@tamuct.edu
LUVIS-NUÑEZ, Agustina 787-763-6700 507 A decanatura@se-pr.edu
LUX, J.D 317-916-7977 158 D jdlux@ivytech.edu
LUX, Jace 270-745-4295 186 C jace.lux@wku.edu
LUX, Jace, T 270-745-2551 186 C jace.lux@wku.edu
LUXNER, Catherine 570-961-4703 389 D luxner@marywood.edu
LUXTON, Andrea, T 269-471-3100 221 D aluxton@andrews.edu
LUYCKX, April 214-637-3530 457 H aluyckx@wadecollege.edu
LUZ, Ana 402-461-7300 267 C ana.luz@hastings.edu
LUZURIAGA, Katherine 508-856-6282 212 C katherine.luzuriaga@umassmed.edu
LUZURIAGA VOIGHT, Suzana, H 513-556-0364 361 J susana.luzuriaga@uc.edu
LUZZI, David 617-373-4160 217 I
LY, Geisce 415-267-6521 36 K gly@ccsf.edu
LY, Geisce 415-267-6521 36 K jly@ccsf.edu
LY, Michael 714-867-5009 65 A mcly@southcoastcollege.com
LY, Pearl 619-388-2801 60 J ply@sdccd.edu
LYALL, Rachel 610-861-1304 390 F lyallr@moravian.edu
LYBECKER, Donna 208-282-2592 131 G lybedonn@isu.edu
LYBYER, Debra 208-792-2313 132 A dlybyer@lcsc.edu
LYDEN MURPHY, Diane 315-443-5582 321 G dlmurphy@syr.edu
LYDON, Carol Ann 828-694-1882 332 E ca_lydon@blueridge.edu
LYDON, Christopher, P 202-319-5305 92 A lydon@cua.edu
LYDUM, Randi 503-838-8094 377 D lydumr@wou.edu
LYKE, Alan, D 719-884-5000 82 B adlyke@nbc.edu
LYKE, Heather, R 412-648-8230 400 H lykeh@pitt.edu
LYKINS, Karen 931-372-3084 426 B klykins@tntech.edu
LYLE, William 215-489-4987 382 B william.lyle@delval.edu
LYM, Brian 212-772-4161 294 C blym@hunter.cuny.edu
LYMAN, Barbara, G 845-257-3280 316 E provost@newpaltz.edu
LYMAN, Katie 319-398-4947 167 J katie.lyman@kirkwood.edu
LYMANSTALL, Judy 419-783-2300 351 K jlymanstall@defiance.edu
LYN, Janice 985-448-4563 192 F janice.lyn@nicholls.edu
LYN, Rodney 404-413-1133 120 E ryn1@gsu.edu
LYNCH, Alice, D 804-752-3039 469 F alicelynch@rmc.edu
LYNCH, Alicia 515-271-1457 165 G alicia.lynch@dmu.edu
LYNCH, Andrea 626-256-4673 37 A alynch@coh.org
LYNCH, Andrea 609-586-4800 278 F lyncha@mccc.edu
LYNCH, Chad 531-622-2929 267 G celynch@mccneb.edu
LYNCH, Christopher 951-827-6374 70 B christopher.lynch@ucr.edu
LYNCH, Christopher 405-974-2328 370 I clynch6@uco.edu
LYNCH, Cynthia 414-847-3340 494 C cynthialynch@miad.edu
LYNCH, Darlene 219-980-6614 157 C darlynch@iun.edu
LYNCH, Deborah 407-708-2147 108 D lynchd@seminolestate.edu
LYNCH, Diane 908-852-1400 276 G diane.lynch@centenaryuniversity.edu
LYNCH, Diane 973-761-9175 283 C diane.lynch@shu.edu
LYNCH, Dianne 573-876-7210 260 B president@stephens.edu
LYNCH, Jacqueline 708-456-0300 151 D jacquelinelynch@triton.edu
LYNCH, James 912-279-5713 117 F jlynch@ccga.edu
LYNCH, James 508-588-9100 215 A jlynch@massasoit.mass.edu
LYNCH, James 315-792-5316 306 K jlynch@mvcc.edu
LYNCH, Joanna 502-213-2410 182 C joanna.morris@kctcs.edu
LYNCH, Joe 717-337-6518 384 D jlynch@gettysburg.edu
LYNCH, Kelly 781-239-4220 206 B klynch@babson.edu
LYNCH, Laura 912-279-4548 117 F llynch@ccga.edu
LYNCH, Malkia 757-340-2121 465 I mlynch@centura.edu
LYNCH, Marilyn, K 972-860-4181 434 F mklynch@dcccd.edu
LYNCH, Marlon, C 517-355-1855 227 F lynchmc@msu.edu
LYNCH, Michael 678-916-2661 115 I mlynch@johnmarshall.edu
LYNCH, Michael 781-239-4528 206 B mlynch4@babson.edu
LYNCH, Molly 703-257-6664 474 F mlynch@nvcc.edu
LYNCH, Patricia 336-334-9725 343 A pmlynch2@uncg.edu
LYNCH, Paul, F 315-445-4551 303 I lynchpf@lemoyne.edu
LYNCH, Richard 972-708-7340 435 E dick_lynch@diu.edu
LYNCH, Stacy 318-345-9322 188 D stacyainsworth@ladelta.edu
LYNCH, Stephanie, J 202-687-4560 92 E sjl28@georgetown.edu
LYNCH, Stephen, J 401-865-2233 404 F sjlynch@providence.edu
LYNCH, III, Thomas 617-973-1175 219 B tlynch@suffolk.edu
LYNCH, Timothy 718-631-6344 295 C tlynch@qcc.cuny.edu
LYNCH, Timothy, G 734-764-0304 231 H timlynch@umich.edu
LYNCH, Viron 941-359-7518 106 J vlynch@ringling.edu
LYNCH, Viron 615-963-5000 426 A
LYNCH, Wayne 716-614-5980 309 G wlynch@niagaracc.suny.edu
LYNCH GADALETA, Margaret, A 401-456-8387 405 A mlynchgadaleta@ric.edu
LYNCH-SOSA, Jill 402-472-7488 269 J jlynch-sosa@nebraskamed.com
LYNCHESKI, Marc 949-376-6000 47 D mlyncheski@lcad.edu
LYNDON, Laura 510-436-1658 45 E lyndon@hnu.edu
LYNDS, Daniel 760-744-1150 56 B dlynds@palomar.edu
LYNETT, Christopher 617-243-2211 211 B clynett@lasell.edu
LYNG-GLIDDI, Diana, L 518-327-6314 311 C dlyngglidi@paulsmiths.edu
LYNHAM, Sandra 207-741-5923 195 H slynham@smccme.edu
LYNN, Brent 806-291-3672 457 I lynnb@wbu.edu
LYNN, Christine 330-490-7617 363 E clynn@walsh.edu
LYNN, David 405-425-5645 367 C david.lynn@oc.edu
LYNN, Jeff 256-234-6346 1 G jlynn@cacc.edu
LYNN, Jolene 816-423-4671 166 E jlynn1@graceland.edu
LYNN, Laura 866-492-5336 244 F laura.lynn@mail.waldenu.edu
LYNN, Mac 504-526-4745 190 E macl@nationsu.edu
LYNN, Martha 206-546-4101 484 B mlynn@shoreline.edu
LYNN, Marty 504-526-4745 190 E martyl@nationsu.edu
LYNN, Marvin 503-725-4697 375 E marvinlynn@pdx.edu
LYNN, Steffanie 218-262-7246 238 D steffanie.lynn@hibbing.edu
LYNN, Steve 803-777-2128 413 A lynns@mailbox.sc.edu
LYNN, Vicki 501-450-1494 19 E lynn@hendrix.edu
LYNN, Vivian 732-255-0400 279 F vlynn@ocean.edu
LYNNE, Chris 602-557-5760 16 G chris.lynne@phoenix.edu
LYNSKY, Michael 215-489-2905 382 B michael.lynsky@delval.edu
LYON, Brett 712-274-5234 168 E lyon@morningside.edu
LYON, Brooke 256-782-5449 6 A bbell@jsu.edu
LYON, James 706-721-8106 116 A jlyon@augusta.edu
LYON, Jonathan 978-837-5280 216 F lyonj@merrimack.edu
LYON, L. Andrew 714-997-6930 36 B lyon@chapman.edu
LYON, Larry 504-282-4455 190 F
LYON, Larry 254-710-3588 431 E larry_lyon@baylor.edu
LYON, Leah 580-559-5259 365 K llyon@ecok.edu
LYON, Mary Eilleen 616-331-2221 224 G lyonme@gvsu.edu
LYON, Matthew 865-585-5318 421 A matthew.lyon@lmunet.edu
LYON, Melissa 714-895-8284 38 A mlyon@gwc.cccd.edu
LYON, Misty 910-678-8413 334 E lyonm@faytechcc.edu
LYON, Mollie 515-271-1400 165 G mollie.lyon@dmu.edu
LYON, Rachele 541-888-7259 376 C rachele.lyon@socc.edu
LYON, Tammy 910-938-6247 333 F lyont@coastalcarolina.edu
LYON, Wade 620-417-1064 177 F wade.lyon@sccc.edu
LYONS, Andrea 423-425-2345 427 C andrea-lyons@utc.edu
LYONS, Angelica 323-473-5673 74 L alyons@westcoastuniversity.edu
LYONS, Becky 406-657-2168 264 D blyons@msubillings.edu
LYONS, Bridget 540-665-4646 470 G blyons@su.edu
LYONS, Bruce 410-455-1000 203 B blyons@umbc.edu
LYONS, Cheryl, C 501-450-3140 23 H clyons@uca.edu
LYONS, Cindy 434-947-8722 469 E clyons@randolphcollege.edu
LYONS, Cindy, G 858-534-5448 70 C cglyons@ucsd.edu
LYONS, Florence 229-500-2805 114 H florence.lyons@asurams.edu
LYONS, Heather 910-695-3701 337 H lyonsh@sandhills.edu
LYONS, Heather 425-640-1088 480 A
LYONS, James 408-551-1691 63 B jlyons@scu.edu
LYONS, Jason, C 757-594-8175 465 M jason.lyons@cnu.edu
LYONS, Joseph 804-524-6453 476 D jlyons@vsu.edu
LYONS, Kendall 214-818-1311 433 O klyons@criswell.edu
LYONS, Laura 808-956-5971 129 E lelyons@hawaii.edu
LYONS, Leah, T 615-898-2534 422 C leah.lyons@mtsu.edu
LYONS, Marybeth 315-792-7505 321 B smbl@sunypoly.edu
LYONS, Matt 202-664-5703 94 D mlyons@wesleyseminary.edu
LYONS, Melanie, N 616-526-7745 222 C mnl2@calvin.edu
LYONS, Patrick, G 973-761-9498 283 C patrick.lyons@shu.edu
LYONS, Paul 909-580-9661 34 D
LYONS, Phillip 936-294-1700 450 A icc_pml@shsu.edu
LYONS, Richard, K 510-643-2027 69 A lyons@haas.berkeley.edu
LYONS, Sarah 218-733-5975 238 G sarah.lyons@lsc.edu
LYONS, Sarah 800-567-2344 492 C salyons@menominee.edu
LYONS, Shane 304-293-5621 490 E shlyons@mail.wvu.edu
LYONS, Shawn 859-233-8551 185 C slyons@transy.edu
LYONS, Sheena 410-704-5074 204 E slyons@towson.edu
LYONS, Steve 218-723-6167 235 G slyons@css.edu
LYONS, Tricia 781-239-5840 206 B plyons@babson.edu
LYSACK, Catherine 313-577-1574 232 K c.lysack@wayne.edu
LYSIAK, Amber 503-251-5747 377 B alysiak@uws.edu
LYSNE, Josh, D 218-299-3645 235 H jlysne@cord.edu
LYSNE, Marit 507-222-4080 234 G mlysne@carleton.edu
LYTHGOE, Maren 801-524-8103 459 E mlythgoe@ldsbc.edu
LYTLE, Anne 212-772-4246 294 C alytle@hunter.cuny.edu
LYTLE, Daniel 715-233-5358 498 E dlytle@cvtc.edu
LYTLE, Dixie 361-358-2838 432 K
LYTLE, James, R 570-586-2400 381 B jlytle@clarkssummitu.edu
LYTLE, Jesse 610-896-1000 385 I jlytle@haverford.edu
LYTLE, Roy 505-566-3990 288 D lytler@sanjuancollege.edu
LYTTLE, Darylnet 757-683-3132 469 B dlyttle@odu.edu
LYZUN, Nancy 317-940-8029 154 C nlyzun@butler.edu
L'ALLIER, Kristi 763-424-0725 240 A k.l'allier@nhcc.edu
L'AMOREAUX, Neal 330-972-7535 361 H neal@uakron.edu
L'ECUYER, John 304-243-2090 491 E jlecuyer@wheeling.edu
L'ESPERANCE, Mark 540-568-6572 468 C lesperme@jmu.edu

M

MA, Carolyn 808-932-8116 129 D csjma@hawaii.edu
MA, Cynthia 408-532-5567 34 E
MA, Elise 516-739-1545 308 F financial_aid@nyctcm.edu
MA, Jennifer 510-464-3420 57 B jenniferma@peralta.edu
MA, Patricia 215-965-4069 390 E pma@moore.edu
MA, Qing 626-289-7719 24 H qma@amu.edu
MA, Steven 941-782-5946 387 D sma@lecom.edu
MA, Wei 928-532-6164 14 J wei.ma@npc.edu
MA, Wonsuk 918-495-6868 368 F wma@oru.edu
MA, Yanli 630-617-3653 137 G yanlima@elmhurst.edu
MA, Yue 773-298-5516 149 D ma@sxu.edu
MAAS, Lisa 920-498-6829 499 G lisa.maas@nwtc.edu
MAAS, Lisa 931-372-3384 426 B lmaas@tntech.edu
MAAS, Lyndsay 805-965-0581 63 A lmmaas@sbcc.edu
MAAS, Paula 646-909-2358 308 A maasp@newschool.edu
MAAS, Tammy 307-778-1258 501 E tmaas@lccc.wy.edu

MAAS-STEED, Deaun ..... 405-692-3263 366 D
deaun.maas-steed@macu.edu
MAASJO, Brian .... 212-772-4852 294 C
bm514@hunter.cuny.edu
MAASS, Kern .... 504-865-3039 190 C
kdmaass@loyno.edu
MABE, Charles .... 252-334-2043 331 F
charles.mabe@macuniversity.edu
MABE, Scotty .... 910-410-1684 337 B
samabe@richmondcc.edu
MABERY, Dan .... 918-444-2017 366 G
mabery@nsuok.edu
MABERY, Mary, V .... 504-526-4745 190 E
registrar@nationsu.edu
MABEUS, Amy .... 319-385-6478 167 H
amy.mabeus@iw.edu
MABOKELA, Reitumetse 217-333-1828 152 B
mabokela@illinois.edu
MABRY, Tom, R .... 719-333-2229 503 D
tom.mabry@usafa.edu
MAC PHERSON, Garry .. 805-893-3132.. 70 E
gmacpherson@ucsb.edu
MACALESTER, Tom .... 704-461-6721 326 L
tommacalester@bac.edu
MACAN, Drew .... 386-822-7472 112 A
dmacan@stetson.edu
MACAPINLAC, Jonas, D 671-735-2944 504 F
jmac@triton.uog.edu
MACARTHUR, John .... 661-362-2210.. 51 D
jmacarthur@masters.edu
MACARTHUR, John .... 989-463-7241 221 B
macarthurjr@alma.edu
MACARTHUR, Sharon ... 718-990-6360 313 G
macarths@stjohns.edu
MACAULAY, Barbara ..... 508-373-5897 216 D
barbara.macaulay@mcphs.edu
MACAULAY,
Jennifer, M .... 508-565-1238 219 A
jmacaulay@stonehill.edu
MACAULEY, Robert .... 201-200-3171 279 D
rmacauley@njcu.edu
MACCARONE, Ellen, M . 509-313-6136 480 F
maccarone@gonzaga.edu
MACCARTHY,
Stephen, J .... 215-898-8724 400 F
smaccar@upenn.edu
MACCARTNEY, Teresa ... 404-962-3016 127 D
teresa.maccartney@usg.edu
MACCARTNEY, Teresa ... 404-962-3000 127 D
chancellor@usg.edu
MACCHI, Thomas, J ..... 215-572-2942 378 E
macchit@arcadia.edu
MACCHIARELLA, Sue, A 386-226-7740.. 99 A
macchis1@erau.edu
MACCHIAVELLI, Raul, E 787-832-4040 512 E
decanodirector.cca@upr.edu
MACCLAREN, Jon .... 802-387-6721 462 C
jmacclaren@landmark.edu
MACCLAREN, Jon, A ..... 802-387-6721 462 C
jonmacclaren@landmark.edu
MACCORMACK,
Jennifer .... 206-616-7933 485 A
jmaccorm@uw.edu
MACCUISH, Spencer ..... 805-581-1233.. 41 I
smaccuish@eternitybiblecollege.com
MACCULLOCH, Heather . 646-312-5045 292 L
heather.macculloch@baruch.cuny.edu
MACDONALD, Amy .... 919-866-5076 338 G
ajmacdonald@waketech.edu
MACDONALD, Ashley .... 207-454-1020 195 I
amacdonald@wccc.me.edu
MACDONALD, Beth .... 701-228-2277 346 B
beth.macdonald@dakotacollege.edu
MACDONALD, Brian ...... 610-282-1100 382 C
brian.macdonald@desales.edu
MACDONALD, David, E 419-772-2200 358 C
d-macdonald@onu.edu
MACDONALD, Elizabeth 636-949-4396 254 H
emacdonald@lindenwood.edu
MACDONALD, Ellen ...... 510-501-5075.. 58 H
MACDONALD, Gregory . 610-330-5069 387 C
macdonag@lafayette.edu
MACDONALD, Heather .. 708-344-4700 143 A
hmacdonald@lincolntech.edu
MACDONALD, Ian .... 518-458-5396 296 G
macdonai@strose.edu
MACDONALD, Jody .... 207-974-4633 195 E
jmacdonald@emcc.edu
MACDONALD, Kent .... 989-837-4203 229 B
MACDONALD, Kerry ...... 802-828-8613 463 B
kerry.macdonald@vcfa.edu
MACDONALD, Laura ...... 732-571-7563 279 A
lembrey@monmouth.edu
MACDONALD, Lauren ... 925-631-4232.. 59 I
lmm24@stmarys-ca.edu
MACDONALD, Lisa .... 781-239-3147 214 G
lmacdonald@massbay.edu
MACDONALD, Paul .... 843-661-1160 409 G
pmacdonald@fmarion.edu
MACDONALD,
Randall, M .... 863-680-4165 100 H
rmacdonald1@flsouthern.edu
MACDONALD, Sam .... 303-329-6355.. 79 L
MACDONALD, Sarah ..... 410-626-2514 202 A
skmacdonald@sjc.edu
MACDONALD,
Shauna, M .... 610-519-4895 401 K
shauna.macdonald@villanova.edu
MACDONALD, Thomas . 617-254-2610 218 E
thomas.macdonald@sjs.edu
MACDONALD, William .. 218-299-4358 235 H
macdonal@cord.edu
MACDONALD-DENNIS,
Christopher .... 413-662-5300 213 C
christopher.macdonald-dennis@mcla.edu
MACDONNELL, Lisa ...... 313-993-1455 231 E
macdonnl@udmercy.edu
MACDONNELL, Tony ..... 703-416-1441 466 A
campusministry@divinemercy.edu
MACE, Christina, M ...... 570-340-6058 389 D
cmace@marywood.edu
MACE, Drema .... 304-647-6380 490 C
dmace@osteo.wvsom.edu
MACE, Melissa .... 314-529-6857 255 B
mmace@maryville.edu
MACE, Melissa .... 816-271-4200 257 A
mace@missouriwestern.edu
MACEK, Kate .... 216-421-8019 350 H
kemacek@cia.edu
MACELI, Peter .... 914-633-2466 302 E
pmaceli@iona.edu
MACEMORE, Kristen ..... 336-838-6122 339 B
khmacemore969@wilkescc.edu
MACEO,
Thandabantu, B .... 317-738-8785 155 D
tmaceo@franklincollege.edu
MACFARLAND, Joseph . 410-626-2511 202 A
joseph.macfarland@sjc.edu
MACFARLANE, Lisa .... 603-862-1234 274 F
lisa.macfarlane@unh.edu
MACGILLIVRAY,
Diane, N .... 617-373-2520 217 I
MACGREGOR,
Carol Ann .... 504-865-2011 190 C
camacgre@loyno.edu
MACH, Thomas .... 937-766-7770 349 E
macht@cedarville.edu
MACHA, Barry .... 940-397-6225 440 C
barry.macha@msutexas.edu
MACHACEK, Jennifer, L 920-748-8185 494 J
machacekj@ripon.edu
MACHADO, Alyson .... 808-544-1126 128 G
amachado@hpu.edu
MACHADO, Daniel .... 845-368-7200 314 I
MACHADO, Jessica ...... 540-654-1266 471 N
jmachado@umw.edu
MACHADO, Jorge, E ..... 305-760-7500 103 V
MACHADO, Miguel .... 713-798-4951 431 D
MACHAMER, Ann .... 408-223-6728.. 62 F
ann.machamer@sjeccd.edu
MACHAMER, Claire .... 336-770-3293 343 D
machamerc@uncsa.edu
MACHANDE, Ken .... 540-654-1457 471 N
kmachand@umw.edu
MACHEN, Chase .... 903-463-8608 436 G
machenc@grayson.edu
MACHEN, Paul .... 210-486-2252 429 B
MACHERY, Edouard ...... 412-624-1052 400 H
machery@pitt.edu
MACHIA, Michael .... 580-628-6291 366 J
michael.machia@noc.edu
MACHIRA, Mary, A .... 801-626-6839 461 A
marymachira@weber.edu
MACHLIS, Gedelyah ...... 718-232-7800 325 H
MACHUCA, José, E .... 787-257-7373 510 F
jemachuca@uagm.edu
MACHUCA, José, E .... 787-766-1717 510 G
jemachuca@uagm.edu
MACHUCA, Yesenia ...... 787-710-8999 506 G
yesenia.machuca@dewey.edu
MACHUGA, Steve .... 860-685-2138.. 90 B
smachuga@wesleyan.edu
MACIAS, Benjamin .... 626-914-8611.. 36 J
bmacias@citruscollege.edu
MACIAS, Sandra .... 650-961-9300.. 55 L
smacias@paloaltou.edu
MACIAS, Tom .... 760-757-2121.. 52 F
tmacias@miracosta.edu
MACIAS, Trinidad .... 210-805-2539 453 C
trmacias@uiwtx.edu
MACIEL, Anthony .... 949-582-4882.. 65 D
amaciel@saddleback.edu
MACIK-FREY, Marilyn ... 985-448-4170 192 F
marilyn.macik-frey@nicholls.edu
MACINTOSH, Mandy ..... 626-584-5201.. 43 B
mandymacintosh@fuller.edu
MACINTYRE, Rich .... 215-248-7138 381 A
macintyre@chc.edu
MACK, Alicia Graf .... 212-799-5000 303 E
MACK, Anthony .... 213-283-4258.. 36 E
amack2@thechicagoschool.edu
MACK, Craig .... 617-732-2929 216 D
craig.mack@mcphs.edu
MACK, Henry .... 229-500-2197 114 H
henry.mack@asurams.edu
MACK, Jeffrey .... 229-500-2197 114 H
jeffrey.mack@asurams.edu
MACK, Joseph .... 607-431-4209 301 A
mackj@hartwick.edu
MACK, Josh, C .... 641-422-4436 168 G
mackjosh@niacc.edu
MACK, Kari .... 845-687-5214 323 H
mackk@sunyulster.edu
MACK, Kimberly, J .... 252-536-7273 335 B
kmack219@halifaxcc.edu
MACK, Qing Lin .... 860-253-3041.. 87 G
qmack@acc.commnet.edu
MACK, Rachel .... 859-251-4700 180 F
rachel.mack@frontier.edu
MACK, Rob .... 617-627-3323 219 C
robert.mack@tufts.edu
MACK, Sherri .... 724-287-8711 379 E
sherri.mack@bc3.edu
MACK, Susan .... 513-585-0365 350 D
susan.mack@thechristcollege.edu
MACK, Tonya .... 530-741-6987.. 77 C
tmack@yccd.edu
MACKAY, Cynthia .... 603-342-3054 273 C
cmackay@ccsnh.edu
MACKAY, Janet .... 970-675-3276.. 79 H
janet.mackay@cncc.edu
MACKAY, Jeff .... 503-883-2436 373 F
jmackay@linfield.edu
MACKE, Aaron, M .... 651-962-6470 244 E
ammacke@stthomas.edu
MACKE, Nick .... 617-585-1229 217 E
nick.macke@necmusic.edu
MACKEITH, Peter .... 479-575-2702.. 21 F
mackeith@uark.edu
MACKEN, Jen .... 303-914-6303.. 83 C
MACKENZIE, Ellen .... 410-955-3540 199 G
emacken1@jhu.edu
MACKENZIE, Lorie .... 315-229-5600 314 D
lmackenzie@stlawu.edu
MACKENZIE, Lorie, R ... 315-229-5600 314 D
lmackenzie@stlawu.edu
MACKERETH, Anne .... 952-885-5417 242 N
amackereth@nwhealth.edu
MACKERSIE, Chris .... 517-483-1813 226 H
mackersc@lcc.edu
MACKESY, Francis, J .... 904-620-2800 111 B
f.mackesy@unf.edu
MACKEY, Brian .... 406-657-2309 264 D
bmackey@msubillings.edu
MACKEY, Geoffrey .... 724-266-3838 400 B
gmackey@tsm.edu
MACKEY, George .... 501-374-6305.. 20 G
gmackey@shortercollege.edu
MACKEY, Josh .... 928-523-6144.. 14 H
joshua.mackey@nau.edu
MACKEY, Roberta .... 850-729-5337 104 M
mackeyr@nwfsc.edu
MACKEY, Stephen .... 831-582-4749.. 32 B
smackey@csumb.edu
MACKEY, Teresa, L .... 601-635-6202 246 A
tmackey@eccc.edu
MACKEY, Tonja .... 903-823-3028 446 A
tonja.mackey@texarkanacollege.edu
MACKEY, Will .... 719-884-5000.. 82 B
MACKIE, Charlie .... 913-259-4657 178 B
charlie.mackey@stmary.edu
MACKIE, Jennifer .... 805-765-9300.. 62 N
MACKIE-MASON,
Jeffrey .... 510-642-3773.. 69 A
jmmason@berkeley.edu
MACKILLOP, Jane .... 718-960-4681 294 A
jane.mackillop@lehman.cuny.edu
MACKIN, Gail .... 509-963-1403 478 E
gail.mackin@cwu.edu
MACKINNON, Fern .... 978-934-4660 212 B
fern_mackinnon@uml.edu
MACKINNON, George .... 414-955-2850 493 F
gmackinnon@mcw.edu
MACKINNON, Jessica ... 708-524-6289 137 C
jmack@dom.edu
MACKINNON, Joseph .... 508-362-2131 214 D
jmackinnon@capecod.edu
MACKINNON, Nate .... 775-784-3430 270 J
nmackinnon@nshe.nevada.edu
MACKINNON, Neil, J .... 706-721-4014 116 A
nmackinnon@augusta.edu
MACKINNON, Pam .... 415-439-2365.. 25 E
pammackinnon@act-sf.org
MACKINNON, Thomas .. 570-941-7723 401 F
thomas.mackinnon@scranton.edu
MACKINTOSH, Kathryn . 781-283-2335 219 E
kmackint@wellesley.edu
MACKLER, Dan .... 818-333-3558.. 53 J
dan@nyfa.edu
MACKLIN, Charles .... 425-388-9990 480 B
cmacklin@everettcc.edu
MACLAINE, Julie, A ...... 740-588-1201 365 B
jmaclaine@zanestate.edu
MACLAREN, James, M .. 717-867-6211 388 C
maclaren@lvc.edu
MACLEAN, Mark .... 715-394-8052 497 C
mmaclean@uwsuper.edu
MACLEAN, Sean .... 714-556-3610.. 73 H
MACLEISH, Padraic .... 760-872-2000.. 40 I
padraicm@deepsprings.edu
MACLEOD, Kellye .... 952-851-0066 233 G
MACLEOD, Melissa, A .. 724-458-2050 384 G
mamacleod@gcc.edu
MACLEOD, Robert .... 813-974-6015 111 C
rmacleod@usf.edu
MACLEOD WALLS,
Elizabeth .... 816-415-5026 262 F
macleodwallse@william.jewell.edu
MACMASTER, Donald .... 989-358-7246 221 C
macmastd@alpenacc.edu
MACMILLAN, John .... 831-459-0111.. 71 A
MACMILLAN FOX,
Rebecca .... 305-284-2648 113 C
rfox@miami.edu
MACNEIL, Jacqueline .... 727-864-7856.. 98 J
macneijm@eckerd.edu
MACNEILL, Andrew .... 619-388-2799.. 60 J
amacneil@sdccd.edu
MACNEILL, Shirley .... 409-984-6365 449 I
macneisb@lamarpa.edu
MACNEW, James .... 267-341-3261 385 J
jmacnew@holyfamily.edu
MACNOW, Andrea .... 203-285-2000.. 86 E
MACON, Kenneth .... 334-523-3670.. 93 H
MACON, Kyle .... 931-393-1623 424 F
kmacon@mscc.edu
MACONI, Steve, M .... 800-444-1839 476 B
smaconi@vmiaa.org
MACOPSON, Elmer, R ... 828-652-0603 336 B
elmerm@mcdowelltech.edu
MACPHERSON, Andrew . 319-398-5669 167 J
andrew.macpherson@kirkwood.edu
MACPHERSON,
Heidi, R .... 585-395-2361 317 E
hmacpherson@brockport.edu
MACRAE, Gaylene .... 509-533-7000 479 C
MACRAE, Pamela .... 207-621-3255 196 H
pamela.macrae@maine.edu
MACREYNOLDS,
William, K .... 336-727-7102 329 C
bill.macreynolds@greensboro.edu
MACRISS, Bill .... 916-278-7550.. 32 D
b.macriss@csus.edu
MACRO, Venessa .... 515-271-3710 165 J
venessa.macro@drake.edu
MACTAGGART, Julie ..... 563-589-3619 170 G
jmactaggart@dbq.edu
MACUR, Kenneth, M ..... 716-880-2202 305 G
kenneth.m.macur@medaille.edu
MACVEY, Mark .... 760-480-8474.. 75 J
mmacvey@wscal.edu
MACY, Dawn .... 657-278-7450.. 31 C
dmacy@fullerton.edu
MACZKA, Eric .... 402-941-6201 267 L
maczka@midlandu.edu
MACZKIEWICZ,
Keith, A .... 203-254-4000.. 87 I
kmaczkiewicz@fairfield.edu
MADAIO, Carolyn .... 718-990-6302 313 G
madaioc@stjohns.edu

MADAIO-O'BRIEN, Melanie ... 617-353-7138 207 E asmelmad@bu.edu

MADAN, Vibhas ... 215-895-2124 382 F madanv@drexel.edu

MADANAT, Hala ... 619-594-3754 .. 33 D hmadanat@sdsu.edu

MADAR, Sandra ... 330-829-6129 362 E madarsi@mountunion.edu

MADAS, Yesenia ... 732-224-2215 276 B ymadas@brookdalecc.edu

MADDAHI, Dariush (David) ... 888-243-2493 .. 53 G

MADDALENA, Robin ... 508-767-7272 206 A r.maddalena@assumption.edu

MADDEN, Christopher .. 214-648-0702 457 A christopher.madden@utsouthwestern.edu

MADDEN, Danielle ... 202-884-9525 .. 94 A maddend@trinitydc.edu

MADDEN, Dean, R ... 603-646-4091 273 D dean.r.madden@dartmouth.edu

MADDEN, Fred, H ... 856-415-2272 281 D fmadden@rcsj.edu

MADDEN, Jennifer ... 503-883-2252 373 F jrmadden@linfield.edu

MADDEN, Madeline ... 361-354-2520 432 K mmadden@coastalbend.edu

MADDEN, Margaret ... 518-783-2307 315 E mmadden@siena.edu

MADDEN, Mary Lou ... 907-796-6050 .. 10 B mlmadden@alaska.edu

MADDEN, Meggan ... 618-374-5155 147 E meggan.madden@principia.edu

MADDEN, Paul ... 740-351-3270 360 F pmadden@shawnee.edu

MADDEN, Richard ... 931-363-9844 427 E rmadden3@utsouthern.edu

MADDEN, Sally, J ... 847-578-3266 148 F sally.madden@rosalindfranklin.edu

MADDEN, Susan ... 240-567-5274 200 G susan.madden@montgomerycollege.edu

MADDEN, Susan ... 917-493-4115 305 A smadden@msmnyc.edu

MADDEN, Vicky, L ... 606-474-3118 181 B vmadden@kcu.edu

MADDIRALA, James, S . 340-693-1013 513 E james.maddirala@uvi.edu

MADDOX, Gregory, H ... 713-313-7889 449 B maddox_gh@tsu.edu

MADDOX, Kelley, L ... 770-534-6270 116 D kmaddox@brenau.edu

MADDOX, Kim ... 479-979-1201 .. 23 I kmaddox@ozarks.edu

MADDOX, Natasha ... 606-759-7141 182 E natasha.maddox@kctcs.edu

MADDOX, Nedra ... 704-669-4142 333 E maddox@clevelandcc.edu

MADDOX, Nicole ... 706-880-8243 122 A nmaddox@lagrange.edu

MADDOX, Rob, W ... 240-895-3000 202 B rwmaddox@smcm.edu

MADDOX, Tangella ... 917-493-4456 305 A tmaddox@msmnyc.edu

MADDOX, Timothy ... 252-527-6223 335 G tdmaddox07@lenoircc.edu

MADDOX-POWELL, Gloria ... 817-515-5259 445 F gloria.maddox-powell@tccd.edu

MADDUX, Pat ... 563-588-6366 164 E pat.maddux@clarke.edu

MADDUX, Susan ... 864-294-2140 409 H susan.maddux@furman.edu

MADDY, Angela ... 620-792-9226 171 I maddya@bartonccc.edu

MADDY, Luther ... 208-792-2400 132 A lmmaddy@lcsc.edu

MADELONE LINCOLN, Laura ... 607-436-2526 316 F laura.lincoln@oneonta.edu

MADER, Mary ... 603-641-7174 274 A mmader@anselm.edu

MADER, Pamela ... 909-621-8856 .. 57 E pamela_mader@pitzer.edu

MADERA, Pablo ... 413-265-2278 208 E maderap@elms.edu

MADERER, Jason ... 412-268-1151 380 C

MADERO, Flor ... 325-942-2031 450 E flor.madero@angelo.edu

MADIA, Sherrie ... 267-341-3348 385 J smadia@holyfamily.edu

MADIGAN, David ... 617-373-4517 217 I

MADIGAN, James ... 617-373-3376 217 I

MADIGAN, Kay ... 330-652-9919 352 E kaymadigan@eticollege.edu

MADIGAN, Kaye ... 320-762-4684 237 C kayem@alextech.edu

MADIGAN, Marc ... 906-932-4231 224 D marcm@gogebic.edu

MADISON, JR., Chet ... 916-278-6851 .. 32 D

MADISON, Stephen, S .. 817-515-1002 445 F stephen.madison@tccd.edu

MADISON-CANNON, Sabrina ... 541-346-1000 376 H smadison@uoregon.edu

MADLOCK, Calvin ... 510-466-5398 .. 57 C cmadlock@peralta.edu

MADLOCK, Krystal ... 319-352-8434 170 J krystal.madlock@wartburg.edu

MADONNA, Richard ... 860-439-2044 .. 87 H rich.madonna@conncoll.edu

MADOR, Jonathan, M ... 336-841-9370 329 F jmador@highpoint.edu

MADORE, Keith ... 860-253-3041 .. 86 C kmadore@asnuntuck.edu

MADORE, Keith ... 860-253-3041 .. 87 G kmadore@acc.commnet.edu

MADORIN, Jeanne ... 336-334-5167 343 A j_madori@uncg.edu

MADRAMOOTOO, Narinedat ... 916-484-8108 .. 50 G madramn@arc.losrios.edu

MADRIAN, Brigitte ... 801-422-4122 458 H brigitte_madrian@byu.edu

MADRID, Carlos ... 671-735-2156 504 F madridc@triton.uog.edu

MADRID, Corina ... 575-492-2186 289 F cmadrid@usw.edu

MADRIGAL, Alexandra .. 973-803-5000 280 B amadrigal@pillar.edu

MADRIGAL, Daniel ... 909-607-2760 .. 44 H dmadrigal@hmc.edu

MADRIGAL, Richard ... 949-359-0045 .. 29 A

MADSEN, Jan, E ... 402-280-2131 266 H janmadsen@creighton.edu

MADSEN, Monte ... 210-688-3101 432 H

MADSEN, Patrick ... 704-687-0784 342 D pmadsen@uncc.edu

MADSEN, Reva ... 210-688-3101 432 H

MADSEN, Ruthanne ... 617-824-8600 209 C ruthanne_madsen@emerson.edu

MADSEN, Thor ... 816-414-3700 256 C academicdean@mbts.edu

MADSON, Brieanna ... 801-818-8900 459 J bmadson@provocollege.edu

MADSON, Greg ... 406-791-5359 265 H gregory.madson@uprovidence.edu

MADSON, Gregory ... 406-791-5359 265 H gregory.madson@uprovidence.edu

MADUKO, John ... 218-299-6504 239 C john.maduko@minnesota.edu

MADULI, Ed ... 408-741-2082 .. 75 C ed.maduli@wvm.edu

MADUTA, John ... 360-992-2505 478 I jmaduta@clark.edu

MAEA, Cheri ... 540-834-1980 473 I cmaea@germanna.edu

MAEDA, Donna, K ... 651-696-6581 236 I maeda@macalester.edu

MAEDER, Deb ... 402-481-8065 265 K deb.maeder@bryanhealthcollege.edu

MAENE, Sara ... 304-876-5112 490 A smaene@shepherd.edu

MAENNLE, Erin ... 828-689-1435 331 C erinmaennle1@mhu.edu

MAESTAS, Ashley, A ... 719-587-7011 .. 77 G

MAESTAS, Belen ... 719-587-7321 .. 77 G bmaestas@adams.edu

MAESTAS, Michael ... 785-864-2277 177 J mvm1@ku.edu

MAESTAS, Reynaldo ... 505-454-3323 286 J reynaldo@nmhu.edu

MAESTAS, Stacy ... 307-778-1240 501 E smaestas@lccc.wy.edu

MAFFEI, Melody ... 209-667-3623 .. 33 B mmaffei@csustan.edu

MAFFIA, Robert ... 201-216-3542 283 D robert.maffia@stevens.edu

MAFFLY-KIPP, Laurie ... 314-935-8901 262 A maffly-kipp@wustl.edu

MAGALDI, Thomas, G .. 646-888-6639 304 J magaldit@mskcc.org

MAGALLON, Eric ... 626-914-8624 .. 36 J emagallon@citruscollege.edu

MAGANA, Elbi ... 818-677-2121 .. 32 C elbi.magana@csun.edu

MAGARO, Lori ... 253-879-3202 484 G lmagaro@pugetsound.edu

MAGAYA, Amuhelang ... 732-987-2729 278 A amagaya@georgian.edu

MAGAZU, Daniel ... 508-626-4539 213 A dmagazu@framingham.edu

MAGAZU, Jessica ... 678-331-4276 122 C jessica.magzu@life.edu

MAGAZZU, Tammi ... 781-768-7291 218 D

MAGBIE-CARR, Shawna 704-886-6500 .. 93 H

MAGDZIARZ, Wayne ... 312-915-6403 143 C wmagdzi@luc.edu

MAGEE, Colin ... 270-824-8674 182 D colin.magee@kctcs.edu

MAGEE, Edward ... 304-558-0281 489 H edward.magee@wvhepc.edu

MAGEE, Jeanette ... 323-241-5274 .. 49 E mageejm@lasc.edu

MAGEE, Jennifer ... 214-637-3530 457 H jmagee@wadecollege.edu

MAGEE, John ... 734-432-5656 227 C jmagee@madonna.edu

MAGEE, Michael ... 610-785-2213 397 E mmagee@scs.edu

MAGEEHON, Ali ... 541-888-7417 376 C ali.mageehon@socc.edu

MAGENAU, Keller ... 805-678-5116 .. 74 A kmagenau@vcccd.edu

MAGENNIS, Joe ... 401-598-4467 404 D joe.magennis@jwu.edu

MAGERS, Ron ... 304-243-8162 491 E rmagers@wheeling.edu

MAGET, Douglas ... 212-854-5204 291 A dmaget@barnard.edu

MAGGARD, Bryan ... 337-482-5393 193 B athleticdirector@louisiana.edu

MAGGARD, Ginger ... 620-862-5252 171 H

MAGGARD, Trent ... 620-862-5252 171 H trent.maggard@barclaycollege.edu

MAGGART, Christina ... 765-641-4111 153 G clmaggart@anderson.edu

MAGGELAKIS, Sophia ... 585-475-2483 312 F sxmsma@rit.edu

MAGGIO, Chris ... 318-357-6441 192 G maggioc@nsula.edu

MAGGIO, Marielena ... 216-368-2519 349 D mxm346@case.edu

MAGGIONI, Susan ... 781-239-2461 214 G smaggioni@massbay.edu

MAGGIORE, Ray ... 516-876-2031 318 C maggiorer@oldwestbury.edu

MAGGITTI, Patrick, G ... 610-519-4521 401 K patrick.maggitti@villanova.edu

MAGGITTI, Sara ... 610-902-8561 379 G sara.t.maggitti@cabrini.edu

MAGGS, Mark ... 814-234-7755 398 E mmaggs@southhills.edu

MAGILL, M. Elizabeth ... 434-924-3728 472 D mem2a@virginia.edu

MAGINNIS, JR., Edward ... 301-405-4939 202 H maginnis@umd.edu

MAGLARAS, Constantinos ... 212-854-4240 297 C cm479@columbia.edu

MAGLIONE, Antonio ... 518-562-4131 296 A antonio.maglione@clinton.edu

MAGLOIRE, Yves, M ... 516-628-5007 318 C magloirey@oldwestbury.edu

MAGLONE, Alyssa ... 618-393-2982 139 E maglonea@iecc.edu

MAGNAN, Carolyn ... 860-832-3715 .. 85 G magnanc@ccsu.edu

MAGNER, Brent ... 402-363-5657 270 D bnmagner@york.edu

MAGNER, Kevin ... 714-867-5009 .. 65 A kjmagner@southcoastcollege.com

MAGNER, Michael ... 978-837-5019 216 F magnerm@merrimack.edu

MAGNONI, Dee ... 848-932-7129 282 A dee.magnoni@rutgers.edu

MAGNUS, Keith, B ... 317-940-9385 154 C kmagnus@butler.edu

MAGNUSON, Amy ... 850-644-8868 110 C amagnuson@admin.fsu.edu

MAGNUSON, Kelly, J ... 320-222-6094 240 F kelly.magnuson@ridgewater.edu

MAGNUSON, Kendyl ... 760-744-1150 .. 56 B kmagnuson@palomar.edu

MAGNUSON, Terry ... 919-962-1319 342 C tmagnuson@unc.edu

MAGNUSSON, Selena ... 706-295-6866 120 A smagnusson@gntc.edu

MAGO, Pedro ... 304-293-4157 490 E pedro.mago@mail.wvu.edu

MAGORIAN, Cortney ... 916-660-7391 .. 64 D cmagorian@sierracollege.edu

MAGORIAN, Kathy ... 605-668-1535 415 F kathy.magorian@mountmarty.edu

MAGRETTA, Dawn ... 734-462-4400 230 G dmagrett@schoolcraft.edu

MAGRO, Edward ... 401-232-6528 404 A emagro@bryant.edu

MAGRO, Kate ... 561-803-2661 105 C

MAGRUDER, Brent ... 812-749-1216 159 O bmagruder@oak.edu

MAGUET, Kathryn, L ... 570-577-3700 379 C kathryn.maguet@bucknell.edu

MAGUINA HELLER, Marie ... 563-589-3115 170 G

MAGUIRE, Angelique ... 618-842-3711 139 F maguirea@iecc.edu

MAGUIRE, Mary ... 916-278-7255 .. 32 D maguirem@csus.edu

MAGUIRE, Robert ... 973-278-5400 275 I robert-maguire@berkeleycollege.edu

MAGUIRE, Robert ... 973-278-5400 291 E robert-maguire@berkeleycollege.edu

MAGURK, Michael ... 518-327-6090 311 C mmagurk@paulsmiths.edu

MAGUSIAK, Henry ... 724-738-4898 395 C henry.magusiak@sru.edu

MAHADY, Sarah ... 812-535-5143 160 H sarah.mahady@smwc.edu

MAHAFFEY, Patricia ... 858-534-4378 .. 70 C pmahaffey@ucsd.edu

MAHAFFY, Kevin ... 312-329-4134 144 I kevin.mahaffy@moody.edu

MAHALINGAM, Shankar ... 256-824-6474 .... 8 B shankar.mahalingam@uah.edu

MAHAN, Christine, P ... 610-341-1706 383 B cmahan@eastern.edu

MAHAN, Forest, E ... 803-508-7247 406 C mahanf@atc.edu

MAHAN, Karl ... 806-720-7122 439 D karl.mahan@lcu.edu

MAHAN, Kim, B ... 806-371-5050 429 E kbmahan@actx.edu

MAHAN, Lisa ... 317-738-8020 155 D lmahan@franklincollege.edu

MAHAN, Mickie ... 417-455-5533 252 E mickiemahan@crowder.edu

MAHANY, Patrick ... 310-665-6995 .. 55 C pmahany@otis.edu

MAHAR, Alissa ... 503-594-3009 372 C alissa.mahar@clackamas.edu

MAHAR, Eddie ... 903-785-7661 441 D emahar@parisjc.edu

MAHAR, Kate ... 530-242-7769 .. 64 C kmahar@shastacollege.edu

MAHARAJ, Peter ... 714-484-7109 .. 54 B pmaharaj@cypresscollege.edu

MAHARAJ, Peter, S ... 619-388-6939 .. 60 H pmaharaj@sdccd.edu

MAHARAS, Marian ... 303-404-5285 .. 81 A marian.maharas@frontrange.edu

MAHDAVI, Pardis ... 480-727-7632 .. 10 J pardis.mahdavi@asu.edu

MAHDY, Ahmed ... 361-825-3881 447 C ahmed.mahdy@tamucc.edu

MAHER, Brian ... 212-986-4343 291 E bdm@berkeleycollege.edu

MAHER, Brian ... 973-278-5400 275 I bdm@berkeleycollege.edu

MAHER, Brian ... 605-773-3455 416 C

MAHER, Elizabeth (Beth) ... 510-464-3221 .. 57 B emaher@peralta.edu

MAHER, Hannah ... 309-457-2317 144 H hmaher@monmouthcollege.edu

MAHER, CM, James ... 716-286-8350 309 H president@niagara.edu

MAHER, Jeffrey ... 207-725-3178 194 C jmaher@bowdoin.edu

MAHER, Jerelyn ... 309-676-7611 134 A jmaher2@fsmail.bradley.edu

MAHER, John ... 304-696-4748 489 M maherj@marshall.edu

MAHER, Judith ... 724-805-2900 397 I judith.maher@email.stvincent.edu

MAHER, Judith ... 724-805-2581 398 A judith.maher@stvincent.edu

MAHER, Shannon ... 212-217-4330 299 D shannon_maher@fitnyc.edu

MAHER, Tracy .... 701-854-8039 346 H
tracy.maher@sittingbull.edu
MAHER, Walter .... 210-829-3939 453 C
maher@uiwtx.edu
MAHER, William, J .... 716-888-2986 292 F
maherw@canisius.edu
MAHFOOD, OP,
Sebastian, P .... 860-632-3085.. 88 C
smahfood@holyapostles.edu
MAHINDRA, Ankush ..... 310-665-6916.. 55 C
amahindra@otis.edu
MAHINDRA, Ankush ..... 310-665-6800.. 55 C
amahindra@otis.edu
MAHITAB, Frank .... 478-825-6754 118 F
mahitabf@fvsu.edu
MAHLBERG, Raye .... 918-610-0027 365 I
rmahlberg@communitycarecollege.edu
MAHLE-GRISEZ, Lisa .... 937-512-2882 360 G
lisa.mahle-grisez@sinclair.edu
MAHLER, Craig .... 615-675-5292 428 C
cmahler@welch.edu
MAHLMANN, Jaclyn ..... 361-825-2321 447 C
jaclyn.mahlmann@tamucc.edu
MAHLMEISTER,
Kenneth, J .... 718-990-5883 313 G
mahlmeik@stjohns.edu
MAHMOOD, Ghazanfar . 209-490-4591.. 24 E
gmahmood@advancedcollege.edu
MAHMOUD, Ghina .... 856-256-5747 281 F
najjar@rowan.edu
MAHMUD, Faisal .... 703-993-1000 467 E
MAHN, Mojdeh .... 661-362-3346.. 38 D
mojdeh.mahn@canyons.edu
MAHNKE, Corrynn .... 715-836-2327 495 E
mahnkecm@uwec.edu
MAHON, Cathryn, A ..... 843-953-5432 408 C
mahonc@cofc.edu
MAHON,
Gwendolyn, M .... 973-972-4892 282 A
mahongm@shp.rutgers.edu
MAHON, James .... 718-960-8675 294 A
james.maho@lehman.cuny.edu
MAHON, Patricia, G ...... 605-394-2416 416 H
patricia.mahon@sdsmt.edu
MAHONE-LEIWS,
Gerald .... 254-526-1166 432 D
gerald.mahone-lewis@ctcd.edu
MAHONEY, Angela .... 336-770-3317 343 D
mahoneya@uncsa.edu
MAHONEY, Erin, A .... 765-658-4278 154 J
emahoney@depauw.edu
MAHONEY, Joanie .... 315-470-6681 319 D
jmahoney@esf.edu
MAHONEY, John .... 530-898-3276.. 30 D
jmahoney@csuchico.edu
MAHONEY, JR., John ... 617-552-3100 207 C
john.mahoney.2@bc.edu
MAHONEY, Kathryn ...... 303-352-6165.. 80 F
kathryn.mahoney@ccd.edu
MAHONEY, Kevin, B ..... 215-662-2203 400 F
kevin.mahoney@uphs.upenn.edu
MAHONEY, Kim .... 907-786-1110.... 9 J
kmahone1@alaska.edu
MAHONEY, Leo .... 440-366-7218 355 B
MAHONEY, Lynn .... 415-338-1381.. 33 E
president@sfsu.edu
MAHONEY, Melissa .... 804-862-6100 470 C
mmahoney@rbc.edu
MAHONEY, Peter, E ...... 330-569-5416 353 G
mahoneype@hiram.edu
MAHONEY, Peter, E ...... 724-805-2241 397 I
peter.mahoney@email.stvincent.edu
MAHONEY, Sharon, A .. 508-767-7322 206 A
shmahone@assumption.edu
MAHONEY, Thomas ...... 609-771-2734 276 I
tmahoney@tcnj.edu
MAHONEY, Trina .... 208-885-4387 132 F
tmahoney@uidaho.edu
MAHONEY, Yemi .... 765-973-8474 157 A
ymahoney@iu.edu
MAHONY, Daniel, F ...... 618-536-3471 150 A
president@siu.edu
MAHONY, James .... 517-264-3525 220 G
jmahony@adrian.edu
MAHOWALD, Rose .... 310-660-3111.. 41 E
rmahowald@elcamino.edu
MAI, Brent .... 904-620-2615 111 B
brent.mai@unf.edu
MAI, Christy .... 502-863-8031 180 H
christy_mai@georgetowncollege.edu
MAI, Laura .... 309-268-8103 138 H
laura.mai@heartland.edu
MAI, Uyen .... 909-274-4121.. 52 J
umai@mtsac.edu

MAIDEN, Michael .... 732-263-5285 279 A
mmaiden@monmouth.edu
MAIDOU, Nikoleta .... 617-850-1231 210 G
nmaidou@hchc.edu
MAIENSHEIN,
Richard, W .... 215-887-5511 402 E
rmaienshein@wts.edu
MAIER, Kim .... 608-822-2463 500 A
kmaier@swtc.edu
MAIER, Mark .... 517-607-2648 225 C
mmaier@hillsdale.edu
MAIER-O'SHEA,
Kathryn .... 773-244-5582 145 G
kmaier@northpark.edu
MAIERHOFER, Jean ...... 763-488-2633 238 C
jean.maierhofer@hennepintech.edu
MAILE, Kristin .... 914-395-2560 315 A
kmaile@sarahlawrence.edu
MAILEY, Sharon .... 304-876-5344 490 A
smailey@shepherd.edu
MAILLEY, Kimberly .... 718-940-5987 314 A
kmailley@sjcny.edu
MAIMONE, Charles .... 919-515-2155 342 A
camaimon@ncsu.edu
MAIN, Jean .... 860-773-1494.. 87 G
jmain@tunxis.edu
MAIN, Jeremy .... 314-434-4044 252 C
jeremy.main@covenantseminary.edu
MAIN, Mary, E .... 540-458-8920 477 D
mmain@wlu.edu
MAIN, Nathan .... 269-927-8169 226 F
nmain@lakemichigancollege.edu
MAINE, Kate .... 706-864-1950 127 A
kate.maine@ung.edu
MAINOUS, Rosalie .... 940-898-2401 451 D
rmainous@twu.edu
MAINUS, Michael .... 520-383-0061.. 16 A
mmainus@tocc.edu
MAIO, James .... 315-792-5401 306 K
jmaio@mvcc.edu
MAISENBACHER,
Melissa .... 863-667-5010 108 K
mamaisenbacher@seu.edu
MAISON, Amy .... 229-225-3977 126 A
amaison@southernregional.edu
MAISTO, Jeremy, A .... 717-867-6215 388 C
maisto@lvc.edu
MAITINO, Jennifer .... 617-333-3165 208 G
jmaitino0615@curry.edu
MAITLAND, Gillian .... 315-786-2234 303 C
gmaitland@sunyjefferson.edu
MAITLEN, Caitlyn .... 641-782-1453 170 F
maitlen@swcciowa.edu
MAIXNER, Ron .... 218-751-8670 242 O
ronmaixner@oakhills.edu
MAIZE, David .... 210-883-1000 453 C
maize@uiwtx.edu
MAIZES, Beth .... 707-386-4153.. 44 J
MAJAK, Julieta .... 845-257-3295 316 E
majakj@newpaltz.edu
MAJCHRZAK, Monika ... 503-847-2626 377 B
mohernandez@uws.edu
MAJEBE, Mary Cissy .... 828-225-3993 328 D
president@daoisttraditions.edu
MAJEED, Hameedah ...... 281-756-3584 429 D
hmajeed@alvincollege.edu
MAJEKOBAJE, Abolade . 503-847-2601 377 B
bmajekobaje@uws.edu
MAJEROVIC, Chaim ...... 516-239-9002 315 D
rcm@shoryoshuv.org
MAJESKI, Mark .... 541-917-4245 373 G
majeskm@linnbenton.edu
MAJETTE, Yolanda .... 252-398-6249 328 C
majety@chowan.edu
MAJEWSKI, Deborah ..... 508-999-9293 212 A
dmajewski@umassd.edu
MAJEWSKI, John .... 805-893-4327.. 70 E
majewski@ltsc.ucsb.edu
MAJEWSKI, Marc .... 415-338-2596.. 33 E
majewski@sfsu.edu
MAJEWSKI, Michelle, E 920-923-7617 493 D
mmajewski@marianuniversity.edu
MAJID, Anouar .... 206-221-4447 197 E
amajid@une.edu
MAJKA, David, R .... 412-397-5443 397 B
majka@rmu.edu
MAJOCHA, Kristen .... 724-938-5891 393 E
majocha@calu.edu
MAJOR, Blair .... 252-789-0323 335 H
bm07738@martincc.edu
MAJOR, Carla .... 504-762-3003 188 B
cmajor@dcc.edu
MAJOR, Carrie .... 865-251-1800 423 E
cmajor@south.edu

MAJOR, Debbie .... 602-274-1885.. 14 O
dmajor@pihma.edu
MAJOR, Heather .... 215-572-2900 378 E
majorh@arcadia.edu
MAJORS, Cristina .... 615-550-3170 428 E
cris@williamsoncc.edu
MAJZNER, Kathy .... 561-803-2080 105 C
kathy_majzner@pba.edu
MAKARCZUK, Meghan .. 914-323-5484 305 B
meghan.makarczuk@mville.edu
MAKARECHI, Pejman .... 215-503-7841 399 E
pejman.makarechi@jefferson.edu
MAKAROFF, JR.,
Christopher, A .... 513-529-4432 356 A
makaroca@miamioh.edu
MAKATCHE, Jaime .... 620-242-0487 176 B
makatchej@mcpherson.edu
MAKEE, Susan .... 603-271-6484 273 A
smakee@ccsnh.edu
MAKEVICH, John .... 760-757-2121.. 52 F
jmakevich@miracosta.edu
MAKHIJA, Anil, K .... 614-292-7899 358 D
makhija.1@osu.edu
MAKI, David, W .... 906-227-1262 228 I
dmaki@nmu.edu
MAKI, Kristen .... 508-856-1870 212 C
kristen.maki@umassmed.edu
MAKI, Laura .... 209-575-6173.. 77 A
makil@mjc.edu
MAKI, William .... 651-201-1732 237 B
MAKIN, Linda .... 801-863-8457 460 D
linda.makin@uvu.edu
MAKIN, Richard, C .... 814-359-2793 380 F
MAKINEN, Bryan .... 859-622-2421 180 E
bryan.makinen@eku.edu
MAKINSTER, Jamie .... 315-781-3304 301 F
makinster@hws.edu
MAKIYA, George .... 832-562-1782 153 E
george.makiya@ace.edu
MAKOFSKE, Rose .... 215-619-7383 390 C
rmakofsk@mc3.edu
MAKOW, Grace .... 213-884-4133.. 24 A
gmakow@ajrca.edu
MAKOWSKI, Susan .... 609-896-5250 281 B
smakowski@rider.edu
MAKREZ ALLEN,
Heather .... 978-934-4809 212 B
heather_makrezallen@uml.edu
MAKRIS, Sara .... 866-492-5336 244 F
sara.makris@laureate.net
MAL, Frances .... 973-748-9000 276 A
frances_mal@bloomfield.edu
MAL, Mirlen .... 617-333-2193 208 G
mirlen.mal@curry.edu
MALAFA, Jeanette .... 217-652-6467 153 A
j-malafa@wiu.edu
MALAGIERE, Kenneth .... 732-255-0400 279 F
kmalagiere@ocean.edu
MALAGON, Blanca .... 305-284-2605 113 C
bmalagon@miami.edu
MALAGON, Kelli Jo ...... 213-252-5100.. 23 K
kmalagon@alu.edu
MALAGRINO, Tony .... 562-985-4131.. 31 D
tony.malagrino@csulb.edu
MALANDRA, Theresa .... 215-951-1619 387 A
malandrat1@lasalle.edu
MALANI, Upendra .... 703-284-1491 468 H
upendra.malani@marymount.edu
MALASKI, Donna .... 269-965-3931 225 H
malaskid@kellogg.edu
MALASPINA, Margaret .. 860-906-5096.. 86 D
mmalaspina@capitalcc.edu
MALAT, Heide .... 651-690-6805 243 A
hlmalat@stkate.edu
MALAT, Jennifer .... 804-828-8295 473 B
malatj@vcu.edu
MALATESTA, Addy .... 570-408-4020 403 A
adelene.malatesta@wilkes.edu
MALATESTA,
Matthew, J .... 518-388-6026 323 J
malatesm@union.edu
MALATRAS, Jim .... 518-320-1355 315 H
chancellor@suny.edu
MALAVE, Cesar, O .... 979-845-2217 446 F
dean@qatar.tamu.edu
MALAVE, Gladys .... 787-765-1915 509 B
gmalave@opto.inter.edu
MALAVE, Tania .... 787-850-9387 512 D
tania.malave@upr.edu
MALAVE-LASSO, Mara .. 787-480-2418 506 C
mamalave@sanjuan.pr
MALAVET, Carmen .... 787-840-2575 509 I
cmalavet@psm.edu

MALBAURN, Scott .... 541-552-8484 376 B
malbaurns@sou.edu
MALBROUGH, Russell .. 631-451-4630 321 C
malbror@sunysuffolk.edu
MALBY, Jeff .... 406-238-7376 265 E
jeff.malby@rocky.edu
MALCOLM, Amir .... 973-353-3569 282 B
am2777@afc.rutgers.edu
MALCOLM, John .... 617-824-8544 209 C
john_malcolm@emerson.edu
MALCOLM, John .... 216-791-5000 350 I
john.malcolm@cim.edu
MALCOLM, Kathy .... 309-796-5038 133 G
malcolmk@bhc.edu
MALCOLM, Kim .... 309-694-8815 139 B
kmalcolm@icc.edu
MALCOLM, Lorna, A ..... 212-220-801 293 A
lmalcolm@bmcc.cuny.edu
MALCOLM, Molly Beth . 512-223-7683 430 I
mollybeth.malcolm@austincc.edu
MALCOM-PIQUEUX,
Lindsey, E .... 626-395-1567.. 28 J
malcom@caltech.edu
MALDAR, Mustafa .... 832-230-5555 440 E
maldar@na.edu
MALDONADO, Amelia ... 787-850-9327 512 D
amelia.maldonado1@upr.edu
MALDONADO,
Bernadette .... 301-405-1995 202 H
blm@umd.edu
MALDONADO, Candice . 325-481-8300 437 F
cdraper@howardcollege.edu
MALDONADO, Carlos ... 760-773-2566.. 38 E
cmaldonado@collegeofthedesert.edu
MALDONADO, Cesar .... 713-718-5059 437 C
cesar.maldonado@hccs.edu
MALDONADO, Gilda ..... 619-388-2817.. 60 J
gmaldona@sdccd.edu
MALDONADO, Heather . 315-279-5000 303 G
MALDONADO, Ileana 787-725-8120 506M
imaldonado@eap.edu
MALDONADO, Israel ..... 718-270-3161 317 B
israel.maldonado@downstate.edu
MALDONADO, Leticia ... 650-949-7777.. 42 I
MALDONADO,
Lilliam, Y .... 787-894-6918 513 C
lilliam.maldonado1@upr.edu
MALDONADO,
Maria del Carmen ...... 787-751-0160 506 F
mcmaldon@cmpr.pr.gov
MALDONADO, Marisela 281-649-3186 437 B
momaldonado@hbu.edu
MALDONADO, Michelle 570-941-7560 401 F
michelle.maldonado@scranton.edu
MALDONADO, Orlando . 787-751-0160 506 F
omaldonado@cmpr.pr.gov
MALDONADO, Victor .... 787-878-5475 507 L
vmaldonado@arecibo.inter.edu
MALDONADO, Víctor .... 787-815-0000 511 H
victor.maldonado1@upr.edu
MALDONADO, Wanda ... 787-758-4417 511 F
rector.rcm@upr.edu
MALDONADO, Wanda ... 787-758-2525 512 F
wanda.maldonado1@upr.edu
MALDONADO, Yesenia . 630-889-6546 145 E
ymaldonado@nuhs.edu
MALDONADO-RIVERA,
Irving .... 787-743-3038 509 N
imaldonado@sanjuanbautista.edu
MALDONADO-ROJAS,
Jose, E .... 787-288-1118 510 I
MALDOON, Gladys .... 718-960-1984 294 A
gladys.maldoon@lehman.cuny.edu
MALE, Taylor .... 989-328-1275 228 D
taylor.male@montcalm.edu
MALECHA, Gary, L .... 503-943-7452 377 A
malecha@up.edu
MALECHA, Ryan .... 731-989-6022 419 K
rmalecha@fhu.edu
MALEK RICHARD,
Christine, S .... 904-620-3983 111 B
christine.malek.richard@unf.edu
MALEKI, Soroush .... 206-934-6070 483 B
soroush.maleki@seattlecolleges.edu
MALEKZADEH, Ali .... 312-341-3800 148 E
amalekzadeh@roosevelt.edu
MALEPEAI-RHODES,
Alexis .... 208-562-3505 131 E
alexisrhodes@cwi.edu
MALESZEWSKI, Joseph . 850-412-5479 109 I
joseph.maleszewski@famu.edu
MALEY, Beth .... 859-344-3513 185 B
maleyb@thomasmore.edu

MANGELSON, Mike .... 801-618-0438 458 G
mmangelson@ameritech.edu

MANGHAM, Kirk .... 757-490-1241 464 B
kmangham@auto.edu

MANGIACAPRA,
Vincent, P .... 203-932-7058.. 89 H
vmangiacapra@newhaven.edu

MANGINE, John, J .... 814-332-4356 378 A
jmangine@allegheny.edu

MANGINO, Christine .... 718-631-6222 295 C
cmangino@qcc.cuny.edu

MANGIONE, Amy .... 518-445-2361 289 K
amang@albanylaw.edu

MANGIONE, Lisa .... 864-250-8461 409 I
lisa.mangione@gvltec.edu

MANGIONE, Terri .... 310-338-3756.. 51 A
terri.mangione@lmu.edu

MANGLONA-PROPST,
Daisy .... 670-237-6792 505 A
daisy.propst@marianas.edu

MANGOLD, Maria .... 406-243-2311 263 K
maria.mangold@umontana.edu

MANGOLD, Nancy .... 510-885-3291.. 31 A
nancy.mangold@csueastbay.edu

MANGOLD, Thomas ...... 401-841-7886 503 A
thomas.mangold@usnwc.edu

MANGUAL, Marlene ...... 787-766-1912 507 J
mmanguals@inter.edu

MANGUM, Genita, D .... 717-736-4144 385 B
gdmangum@hacc.edu

MANGUM, Linda .... 336-285-3769 341 D
lmangum@ncat.edu

MANGUM, Sarah .... 530-752-2427.. 69 B
semangum@ucdavis.edu

MANGUM, Steve .... 865-974-5061 427 B
smangum@utk.edu

MANGUM, Vincent .... 404-756-4006 115 G
vmangum@atlm.edu

MANGUM, William .... 770-426-2833 122 C
william.mangum@life.edu

MANGUS, Christy .... 269-782-1473 231 A
cmangus@swmich.edu

MANHARDT, Joseph ..... 207-741-5598 195 H
jmanhardt@smccme.edu

MANIACI, Vincent, M ... 413-205-3202 205 F
vincent.maniaci@aic.edu

MANIAGO, Vanessa ...... 702-968-2872 272 C
vmaniago@roseman.edu

MANIATIS, Marc .... 203-932-7200.. 89 H
mmaniatis@newhaven.edu

MANICKAM, Joseph ...... 620-327-8233 174 E
joseph.manickam@hesston.edu

MANIER, Tracy, L .... 512-448-8602 442 I
tracym@stedwards.edu

MANIGAULT, Kimberly .. 412-237-3001 381 D
kmanigault@ccac.edu

MANIGO, Jocelyn .... 610-436-3238 395 D
jmanigo@wcupa.edu

MANIGO, Venis .... 803-777-4115 413 A
venis.manigo@sc.edu

MANILAY, Jol .... 209-946-2236.. 71 E
jmanilay@pacific.edu

MANION, Amy .... 262-695-3459 500 B
amanion@wctc.edu

MANION, Andrew, P ...... 608-663-2240 492 F
amanion@edgewood.edu

MANION, Christine .... 414-297-6508 499 C
manionc@matc.edu

MANION, Sheila, M ...... 314-977-2306 259 F
sheila.manion@slu.edu

MANIS, Christopher ...... 619-388-6546.. 60 H
cmanis@sdccd.edu

MANIS, Salia .... 417-873-7879 252 G

MANISCALCO, Steven ... 607-436-2735 316 F
steven.maniscalco@oneonta.edu

MANJONE, Joe .... 251-981-3771.... 5 A
joe.manjone@columbiasouthern.edu

MANKEY, Richanne, C .. 419-783-2300 351 K
rmankey@defiance.edu

MANKO, Tammy, P ...... 724-357-2235 394 C
tammy.manko@iup.edu

MANKOWICH, James .... 205-929-3498.... 2 H
jmankowich@lawsonstate.edu

MANLEY, Colleen .... 315-229-5988 314 D
cmanley@stlawu.edu

MANLEY, James .... 845-451-1760 297 G
james.manley@culinary.edu

MANLEY, Jennifer .... 360-596-5305 484 D
jmanley@spscc.edu

MANLEY, John .... 252-335-3266 341 B
jhmanley@ecsu.edu

MANLEY, Lisa .... 860-913-2078.. 88 A
lmanley@goodwin.edu

MANLEY-ROOK,
Stephanie .... 252-493-7383 336 H
sgmrook@email.pittcc.edu

MANN, Andrea .... 678-225-7507 395 G
andreama1@pcom.edu

MANN, Barbara .... 678-407-5818 119 C
bmann@ggc.edu

MANN, Brian .... 813-253-7022 102 B
bmann@hccfl.edu

MANN, Carola .... 863-583-9050 110 B

MANN, Charles, G .... 301-696-3611 199 E
mann@hood.edu

MANN, Christy .... 870-512-7867.. 18 A
christy_mann@asun.edu

MANN, Daniel .... 217-333-9299 152 B
danmann@illinois.edu

MANN, Douglas, F .... 423-775-7201 418 D
dmann7365@bryan.edu

MANN, Eric .... 251-626-3303.... 7 E
emann@ussa.edu

MANN, Erin .... 615-230-3214 425 E
erin.mann@volstate.edu

MANN, Henry, J .... 614-292-5711 358 D
mann.414@osu.edu

MANN, Janet .... 202-687-1307.. 92 E
mannj2@georgetown.edu

MANN, Karen .... 315-279-5289 303 G
kmann@keuka.edu

MANN, Kevin, J .... 410-543-6202 204 D
kjmann@salisbury.edu

MANN, Lara, G .... 317-788-3368 161 H
mannlg@uindy.edu

MANN, Laura .... 507-457-5069 241 F
lmann@winona.edu

MANN, Lynde .... 256-228-6001.... 3 B
mannl@nacc.edu

MANN, Steve .... 732-247-5241 279 C
smann@nbts.edu

MANN, Thomas .... 401-232-6977 404 A
tmann@bryant.edu

MANN, Tommy .... 239-432-7336 101 A
tmann2@fsw.edu

MANNARA, Kevin .... 585-385-8196 313 F
kmannara@sjfc.edu

MANNELLA, Stephen ..... 610-436-2242 395 D
smannella@wcupa.edu

MANNER, Kimberly, E ... 818-364-7635.. 49 C
mannerke@lamission.edu

MANNERING,
Susan, M .... 302-225-6232.. 91 B
manners@gbc.edu

MANNINEN, Kevin .... 906-487-7371 224 B
kevin.manninen@finlandia.edu

MANNING, Amelia .... 603-314-1416 274 C
a.manning@snhu.edu

MANNING, Beth .... 810-762-3150 232 A
bmanning@umich.edu

MANNING, Carmen, K .. 715-836-3671 495 E
manninck@uwec.edu

MANNING, Colleen .... 713-646-1729 443 I
cmanning@stcl.edu

MANNING, Danielle ...... 508-793-7443 208 C
damanning@clarku.edu

MANNING, Dawn .... 252-493-7633 336 H
dmanning@email.pittcc.edu

MANNING, Dianne .... 413-662-5249 213 C
dianne.manning@mcla.edu

MANNING, Gaye .... 870-574-4509.. 21 D
gmanning@sautech.edu

MANNING, Jennifer ...... 815-753-9676 146 B
manning@niu.edu

MANNING, Jessica .... 214-305-9454 428 F
jxm15c@acu.edu

MANNING, Jessica .... 325-942-2021 450 E
jessica.manning@angelo.edu

MANNING, John, F .... 617-495-4601 210 E
jmanning@law.harvard.edu

MANNING, Karen .... 910-695-3995 337 H
manningk@sandhills.edu

MANNING, Kirk .... 845-398-4066 314 G
kmanning@stac.edu

MANNING, Mark .... 315-498-2622 310 F
m.r.manning@sunyocc.edu

MANNING, Mike .... 765-674-6901 158 B
mike.manning@indwes.edu

MANNING, Noel, T .... 704-406-4631 329 A
ntmanning@gardner-webb.edu

MANNING, R. Douglas . 714-564-6900.. 58 F
manning_r-douglas@sac.edu

MANNING, Robert .... 217-228-5432 147 F
manniro@quincy.edu

MANNING, Scott .... 570-372-4256 398 F
manning@susqu.edu

MANNING, Stephanie ... 870-235-4399.. 21 C
sdmanning@saumag.edu

MANNING, Sylvia .... 909-469-5200.. 75 I
smanning@westernu.edu

MANNING, Tina .... 912-427-5814 117 E
tmanning@coastalpines.edu

MANNING, Veronica ..... 870-512-7890.. 18 A
veronica_manning@asun.edu

MANNING, Vivian .... 360-992-2104 478 I
vmanning@clark.edu

MANNINO, Sam .... 502-459-3535 185 A
smannino@sullivan.edu

MANNISTO, Richard ...... 414-443-8788 498 A
rich.mannisto@wlc.edu

MANNIX, Kristin .... 507-281-7770 240 H
kristin.mannix@rctc.edu

MANNO, Kim .... 740-366-9135 349 F
manno.18@osu.edu

MANNO, Mariann, M .... 508-856-2323 212 C
admissions@umassmed.edu

MANNS, Jennifer .... 970-207-4500.. 85 A

MANNS, Jill, R .... 260-982-5050 159 J
jrmanns@manchester.edu

MANOGIN, Toni, L .... 225-771-2273 191 B
toni_manogin@sus.edu

MANOLIS, Lilly .... 617-327-6777 220 C
lilly_manolis@williamjames.edu

MANOR, Scott .... 954-771-0376 103 S
smanor@knoxseminary.edu

MANORA, JR., Wade .... 706-867-2720 127 A
wade.manora@ung.edu

MANORD, Wayne .... 256-352-8116.... 3 I
wayne.manord@wallacestate.edu

MANORE, David .... 315-792-7280 321 B
david.manore@sunypoly.edu

MANRING, Noah, D ...... 573-882-0693 261 A
manringn@missouri.edu

MANRIQUE, Santos .... 620-231-3690 173 I
santosm@fortscott.edu

MANRIQUEZ, Chris ...... 310-243-3655.. 30 E
cmanriquez@csudh.edu

MANROSE, Mark .... 310-665-6851.. 55 C
mmanrose@otis.edu

MANRY, J. Mark .... 248-218-2120 230 B
mmanry@rochesteru.edu

MANRY, Mark .... 248-218-2120 230 B
mmanry@rochesteru.edu

MANRY, Robert .... 785-628-4513 173 H
rjmanry@fhsu.edu

MANSELL, Chrisa .... 662-846-4050 245 G
cmansell@deltastate.edu

MANSER,
Jacqueline, M .... 330-490-7117 363 E
jmanser@walsh.edu

MANSFIELD, Amy .... 616-234-4226 224 F
amymansfield@grcc.edu

MANSFIELD, Amy .... 616-698-7111 223 E

MANSFIELD, Jerry .... 614-234-5800 356 E
jerry.mansfield@mchs.com

MANSFIELD,
Michael, P .... 207-236-8581 196 B
mmansfield@mainemedia.edu

MANSFIELD, Robin .... 908-737-4880 278 E
rmansfie@kean.edu

MANSKI, Marion .... 203-576-4815.. 89 C
mmanski@bridgeport.edu

MANSO, Jose, R .... 212-694-1000 291 J
jmanso@boricuacollege.edu

MANSON, Rachel .... 484-365-7807 388 H
rmanson@lincoln.edu

MANSON, Robert .... 714-564-6247.. 58 F
manson_robert@sac.edu

MANSOUR, Deena .... 406-243-2988 263 K
deena.mansour@umontana.edu

MANSOUR, Ruchana ..... 347-394-1036 291 F

MANSUETO, Anthony .... 214-860-2693 434 I
anthony.mansueto@dcccd.edu

MANSUR, Jay .... 859-858-2305 179 C

MANTELLA,
Philomena, V .... 616-331-2100 224 G
president@gvsu.edu

MANTER, Debbie .... 972-708-7340 435 E
alumni@diu.edu

MANTERNACH, Dean .... 402-354-7058 268 B
dean.manternach@methodistcollege.
edu

MANTHA, Jordan .... 913-971-3676 176 C
jhmantha@mnu.edu

MANTHE, Theodore, E .. 507-344-7745 234 C
ted.manthe@blc.edu

MANTHEY, Tom .... 406-657-2085 264 D
tom.manthey@msubillings.edu

MANTILLA, Andrea .... 814-886-6388 390 G
amantilla@mtaloy.edu

MANTLO, Ryan .... 910-362-7042 332 H
rmantlo@cfcc.edu

MANTOCK, Todd .... 918-270-6451 368 G
todd.mantock@ptstulsa.edu

MANTON, Mark, H .... 303-329-6355.. 79 L

MANTONI, Thomas .... 610-282-1100 382 C
thomas.mantoni@desales.edu

MANTOOTH, Brooks, E . 620-665-3497 174 G
mantoothb@hutchcc.edu

MANTOOTH, James, D . 731-881-7053 427 D
jdmantooth@utm.edu

MANTOOTH, Liz .... 910-362-7067 332 H
lmantooth@cfcc.edu

MANTOVANI, Theresa ... 407-265-8383.. 96 H

MANTRANA, Manuel ..... 214-860-3633 435 A
manuelmantrana@dcccd.edu

MANTZ, Erika .... 603-862-1567 274 F
erika.mantz@unh.edu

MANTZ, Tim .... 610-902-8765 379 G
tm10760@cabrini.edu

MANUEL, Barbara .... 276-739-2432 475 F
bmanuel@vhcc.edu

MANUEL, Beulah .... 301-891-4184 205 A
bmanuel@wau.edu

MANUEL, Cora .... 510-430-2255.. 52 E

MANUEL, Elizabeth .... 304-558-0655 489 H
elizabeth.manuel@wvhepc.edu

MANUEL, Jeff .... 205-652-3682.... 9 B
jmanuel@uwa.edu

MANUEL, Marilyn, G .... 504-286-5020 191 C
mmanuel@suno.edu

MANUEL, Mark .... 859-246-6673 181 F
mark.manuel@kctcs.edu

MANUEL, Mary .... 661-362-3184.. 38 D
mary.manuel@canyons.edu

MANUEL, Nicole .... 337-521-8898 188 I
nicole.manuel@solacc.edu

MANUEL, Robert, L .... 317-788-3211 161 H
rmanuel@uindy.edu

MANUEL, Thomas, E .... 859-238-5361 180 B
thomas.manuel@centre.edu

MANUEL, Warde .... 734-764-9416 231 H
wardemanuelad@umich.edu

MANUKIN, Jeff .... 724-222-5330 391 F

MANULI, Nunziatina, A . 718-990-2401 313 G
manulin@stjohns.edu

MANZ, Jonathan .... 503-517-1225 377 C
jmanz@warnerpacific.edu

MANZANARES, Mark .... 719-587-8138.. 77 G
markmanzanares@adams.edu

MANZANAREZ,
Magdaleno .... 575-538-6229 289 G
magdaleno.manzanarez@wnmu.edu

MANZANERA, Ignacio ... 770-426-2873 122 C
ignacio.manzanera@life.edu

MANZANO, Anna .... 310-665-6951.. 55 C
amanzano@otis.edu

MANZANO, David .... 575-835-6997 286 K
david.manzano@nmt.edu

MANZANO, Florentino .. 818-947-2691.. 49 G
manzanf@lavc.edu

MANZANO, Lester, J .... 773-508-7067 143 C
lmanzan@luc.edu

MANZKE, Robert .... 715-346-3738 497 A
rmanzke@uwsp.edu

MANZO, Dana .... 352-638-9751.. 96 B
dmanzo@beaconcollege.edu

MANZO, Pablo .... 916-856-3400.. 50 F
manzop@losrios.edu

MANZO, Serena .... 206-281-2598 483 G
serenamanzo@spu.edu

MAO, Ruixuan .... 847-214-7440 137 F
rmao@elgin.edu

MAPIRA, Happiness ...... 614-251-7641 358 B
mapirah@ohiodominican.edu

MAPLE, Makala .... 402-844-7268 268 H
makala@northeast.edu

MAPLES, Greg .... 731-989-6002 419 K
gmaples@fhu.edu

MAPLES, Joellen .... 585-385-3727 313 F
jmaples@sjfc.edu

MAPLES, John .... 806-720-7478 439 D
john.maples@lcu.edu

MAPLES, Stephen .... 775-784-4700 271 E
smaples@unr.edu

MAPSTON, Austin .... 406-657-1024 265 E
mapstona@rocky.edu

MARA, Mary .... 206-239-4500 478 H

MARA, Stacy, J .... 920-832-6557 493 B
stacy.j.mara@lawrence.edu

MARKOWITZ, Marianne 315-448-5040 314 B
marianne.markowitz@sjhcon.edu
MARKOWITZ, Michael .. 267-341-3286 385 J
mmarkowitz@holyfamily.edu
MARKOWITZ, Sheila ..... 620-341-5211 173 F
smarkowi@emporia.edu
MARKS, Andrea .... 210-567-7103 456 C
marksa@uthscsa.edu
MARKS, Andy .... 219-473-4295 154 D
amarks@ccsj.edu
MARKS, David .... 201-879-7999 275 H
dmarks1@bergen.edu
MARKS, Dennis .... 503-883-2602 373 F
dmarks@linfield.edu
MARKS, Erica .... 845-257-3240 316 E
markse@newpaltz.edu
MARKS, Farah .... 434-947-8056 469 E
fmarks@randolphcollege.edu
MARKS, Howard .... 432-685-4726 440 B
hmarks@midland.edu
MARKS, Jeffrey .... 760-750-4062.. 33 A
jmarks@csusm.edu
MARKS, John .... 414-382-6360 491 F
john.marks@alverno.edu
MARKS, Lilly .... 303-724-5369.. 84 D
lilly.marks@ucdenver.edu
MARKS, Mary Beth .... 504-280-7014 190 B
mmarks1@uno.edu
MARKS, Michelle .... 303-556-2400.. 84 D
chancellor@ucdenver.edu
MARKS, Nick .... 603-822-5434 274 G
nicholas.marks@granite.edu
MARKS, Patrice .... 908-526-1200 281 A
patrice.marks@raritanval.edu
MARKS, Rachelle .... 410-778-7710 205 B
rmarks2@washcoll.edu
MARKS, Sandra .... 562-860-2451.. 35 H
smarks@cerritos.edu
MARKSON, Alison, W ... 617-333-2120 208 G
amarkson1109@curry.edu
MARKSON, Sephora ..... 510-649-2400.. 44 B
MARKULY, Mark .... 206-296-5330 484 A
markulym@seattleu.edu
MARKUM, Michael .... 254-298-8291 445 G
mmarkum@templejc.edu
MARKUSON, Lori .... 847-465-0575 145 D
lori.markuson@nl.edu
MARKWOOD, Chris ...... 706-507-8950 117 H
markwood_chris@columbusstate.edu
MARKWORTH, Ruth ...... 414-425-8300 495 A
rmarkworth@shsst.edu
MARLAIRE, Colin .... 866-776-0331.. 54 D
cmarlaire@ncu.edu
MARLAIRE, Natalyn, M . 715-852-1399 498 E
nmarlaire@cvtc.edu
MARLER, Eric .... 808-675-3708 128 D
eric.marler@byuh.edu
MARLETTE, Marnie, S ... 336-841-4683 329 F
mmarlett@highpoint.edu
MARLEY, Chad .... 307-778-1346 501 E
cmarley@lccc.wy.edu
MARLIN, John .... 973-328-5090 276 J
jmarlin@ccm.edu
MARLO,
Francis (Frank) .... 202-462-2101.. 93 A
fmarlo@iwp.edu
MARLOW, Amber .... 715-634-4790 492 L
marlowa@lco.edu
MARLOW, Dan .... 816-279-7000 250 B
dan@abtu.edu
MARLOW, J.J .... 712-274-5424 168 E
marlow@morningside.edu
MARLOW, Mike .... 928-523-5353.. 14 H
mike.marlow@nau.edu
MARLOW, Peter .... 619-260-7460.. 72 I
petermarlow@sandiego.edu
MARLOW, Thomas, J ... 718-390-4352 313 G
marlowt@stjohns.edu
MARLOWE,
Channing, H .... 205-391-2256.... 3 E
cmarlowe@sheltonstate.edu
MARLOWE, June .... 314-991-6245 134 E
jmarlowe@chamberlain.edu
MARLOWE, Wendy, C ... 252-451-8243 336 E
wcmarlowe937@nashcc.edu
MARMARELLI, Beth .... 313-593-5542 231 I
bethmar@umich.edu
MARMOLEJO, William .. 818-710-2955.. 49 D
marmolwa@piercecollege.edu
MARNEY, Dylan .... 573-288-6351 252 F
dmarney@culver.edu
MARNEY, Katherine ...... 573-288-6478 252 F
kmarney@culver.edu
MARNICH, Darlene .... 412-392-3474 396 G
dmarnich@pointpark.edu
MAROHL, Matthew .... 507-786-3092 243 D
marohl@stolaf.edu
MAROLDO, Brian .... 516-686-7449 308 I
bmaroldo@nyit.edu
MARONEY,
Christopher, S .... 315-684-6465 321 A
maronecs@morrisville.edu
MARONEY, Dustin .... 520-494-5237.. 11 K
dustin.maroney@centralaz.edu
MARONEY, Dustin .... 480-517-8418.. 13 G
dustin.maroney@riosalado.edu
MAROUN, Sarah .... 518-891-2915 310 A
smaroun@nccc.edu
MAROZICK, Jeff .... 415-485-9467.. 39 A
jmarozick@marin.edu
MARPLES, Sarah .... 818-833-3558.. 53 J
sarah.marples@nyfa.edu
MARQUARDT,
Benjamin .... 315-858-0945 302 A
MARQUARDT, Brian ...... 231-591-3755 224 A
brianmarquardt@ferris.edu
MARQUARDT,
Christopher .... 315-229-5250 314 D
cmarquardt@stlawu.edu
MARQUARDT, Robert .... 405-585-5504 367 B
robert.marquardt@okbu.edu
MARQUARDT, Shelly ..... 714-547-9625.. 28 A
smarquardt@calcoast.edu
MARQUES, Jeffrey .... 413-775-1700 214 E
marquesj@gcc.mass.edu
MARQUES, Joan .... 818-394-3391.. 76 E
joan.marques@woodbury.edu
MARQUEZ, Andrew .... 520-792-1506 457 I
andrew.marquez@wbu.edu
MARQUEZ, Angela .... 303-360-4932.. 80 E
angela.marquez@ccaurora.edu
MARQUEZ, Celia .... 408-848-4800.. 43 E
MARQUEZ, Dianne .... 575-492-2841 287 A
dmarquez@nmjc.edu
MARQUEZ, Jacqueline .. 781-283-2687 219 E
jm100@wellesley.edu
MARQUEZ, Krishna .... 787-746-1400 507 B
kmarquez@huertas.edu
MARQUEZ, Loren, L ..... 757-455-3338 477 C
lmarquez@vwu.edu
MARQUEZ, Mat .... 212-659-3604 303 H
mat_marquez@tkc.edu
MARQUEZ, Moses .... 505-454-5312 286 F
mmarquez@luna.edu
MARQUEZ, Nelson .... 863-734-1509 114 B
marqueznj@webber.edu
MARQUEZ, Nora .... 650-433-3865.. 55 L
nmarquez@paloaltou.edu
MARQUEZ, Patricia .... 619-260-7795.. 72 I
pmarquez@sandiego.edu
MARQUEZ, Raymond ..... 805-482-2755.. 59 G
rmarquez@stjohnsem.edu
MARQUEZ-HUDSON,
Christine .... 303-615-0065.. 81 M
cmarqu37@msudenver.edu
MARQUINEZ,
Romualdo .... 904-632-3374 101 B
rmarquin@fscj.edu
MARQUIS, Susan .... 310-393-0411.. 56 C
smarquis@rand.org
MARR, Jay, D .... 502-456-6506 185 A
jmarr@sullivan.edu
MARR, Jena .... 405-422-1265 369 A
jena.marr@redlandscc.edu
MARR, Kelly .... 603-206-8004 272 L
kmarr@ccsnh.edu
MARR, Ronda .... 209-946-2206.. 71 E
rmarr@pacific.edu
MARR, Ryan "Bud" .... 515-643-6679 168 D
rmarr@mercydesmoines.org
MARR, Shannon .... 406-771-4408 264 F
shannon.marr1@gfcmsu.edu
MARRA, Chelsea .... 315-786-6544 303 C
cmarra@sunyjefferson.edu
MARRA, Michele, L ...... 740-376-4718 355 E
mm011@marietta.edu
MARRANT, Dale .... 913-234-0612 172 K
dale.marrant@cleveland.edu
MARRAPESE, Patricia .... 607-777-2510 316 B
pmarra@binghamton.edu
MARRAPODI,
Michael, E .... 617-873-0652 208 B
michael.marrapodi@cambridgecollege.edu
MARRERO, Antonio .... 718-951-5000 293 C
MARRERO, Argelio .... 860-906-5125.. 86 D
amarrero@capitalcc.edu
MARRERO, Kyle .... 912-478-5211 120 C
kmarrero@georgiasouthern.edu
MARRERO, Luis, A .... 787-766-1717 510 G
lumarrero@uagm.edu
MARRERO, Rafael .... 787-780-0070 505 F
rmarrero@caribbean.edu
MARRERO, Rene .... 787-841-2000 509 J
rene_marrero@pucpr.edu
MARRERO, Tara .... 510-531-4911.. 57 C
MARRERO, Wanda, I ..... 787-723-4481 506 A
wanda.marrero@ceaprc.edu
MARRERO, Wilma .... 787-765-1915 509 B
wmarrero@opto.inter.edu
MARRERO CARRER,
Darwin, J .... 787-764-0000 513 B
darwin.marrero@upr.edu
MARRERO-HERNÁNDEZ,
Angel .... 787-993-8852 512 A
angel.marrero@upr.edu
MARRETT, Clifford .... 860-465-0306.. 85 H
marrettc@easternct.edu
MARRI, Anand .... 765-285-5452 153 H
armarri@bsu.edu
MARRIN, John .... 308-635-6001 270 C
marrinj1@wncc.edu
MARRINER, Nigel, R ..... 716-878-4811 317 F
marrinnr@buffalostate.edu
MARRIOTT, Carol .... 585-343-0055 300 F
cmarriott@genesee.edu
MARRIOTT, Douglas ...... 818-947-2929.. 49 G
marriodc@lavc.edu
MARRIOTT, Jean .... 410-386-8121 198 D
jmarriott@carrollcc.edu
MARRIOTT, Karin .... 951-487-3060.. 53 A
kmarriott@msjc.edu
MARRIOTT, Martin .... 920-206-2310 493 C
marty.marriott@mbu.edu
MARRIOTT, Russell .... 214-818-1318 433 O
rmarriott@criswell.edu
MARROCCO, Susan .... 941-752-5201 109 G
marrocs@scf.edu
MARROCHELLO, Drew ... 617-353-4631 207 E
marroand@bu.edu
MARRON, Timothy .... 206-296-5990 484 A
marront@seattleu.edu
MARRON, Victoria .... 281-425-6501 438 I
vmarron@lee.edu
MARROW, Cary .... 806-894-9611 443 G
cmarrow@southplainscollege.edu
MARROW, Victor .... 252-536-7283 335 B
vmarrow@halifaxcc.edu
MARRS, Chris .... 979-691-2069 431 H
chris.marrs@blinn.edu
MARRS, Ezell .... 317-543-3235 159 L
MARRS, Rick .... 310-506-4261.. 56 G
rick.marrs@pepperdine.edu
MARRS, Sherrie .... 606-218-5261 186 B
sherriemarrs@upike.edu
MARS, Bonnie, J .... 724-946-6216 402 D
marsbj@westminster.edu
MARSALA, Ebony .... 617-552-3300 207 C
ebony.marsala@bc.edu
MARSALEK, Lisa .... 419-783-2587 351 K
lmarsalek@defiance.edu
MARSALIS, Joyce .... 865-354-3000 425 C
marsalisje@roanestate.edu
MARSALIS, Wynton .... 212-799-5000 303 E
MARSCH, Charlotte .... 417-328-1803 259 I
cmarsch@sbuniv.edu
MARSCHKE, Robyn .... 719-255-3640.. 84 C
rmarschk@uccs.edu
MARSDEN, Janet .... 740-427-5158 354 I
marsden1@kenyon.edu
MARSDEN, John, P ...... 859-846-5310 184 B
jmarsden@midway.edu
MARSDEN, Michael ...... 773-298-3000 149 D
MARSDEN, Robert .... 610-647-4400 385 L
rmarsden@immaculata.edu
MARSELIAN, Zareh .... 805-493-3119.. 29 C
marselia@callutheran.edu
MARSH, Anne .... 540-828-8024 464 L
atmarsh@bridgewater.edu
MARSH, Barry .... 843-349-7557 409 J
barry.marsh@hgtc.edu
MARSH, Bonnie .... 724-439-4900 388 A
bmarsh@laurel.edu
MARSH, Brent .... 662-915-7705 249 D
MARSH, Cecilia .... 660-359-3948 257 D
cmarsh@mail.ncmissouri.edu
MARSH, Clay, B .... 304-293-1024 490 E
cbmarsh@hsc.wvu.edu
MARSH, Dawn, E .... 517-264-7190 230 H
dmarsh1@sienaheights.edu
MARSH, Douglas, K ..... 574-631-4200 162 A
marsh.14@nd.edu
MARSH, Dyremple .... 302-857-6400.. 90 E
dmarsh@desu.edu
MARSH, Eric .... 585-785-1293 299 F
eric.marsh@flcc.edu
MARSH, III, F. Chapin . 954-453-9228.. 34 H
MARSH, Gregory .... 409-880-2100 449 G
gregory.marsh@lamar.edu
MARSH, James, G .... 254-710-2467 431 E
jim_marsh@baylor.edu
MARSH, Janet .... 517-607-2240 225 C
jmarsh@hillsdale.edu
MARSH, Jed .... 609-258-7860 280 D
jmarsh@princeton.edu
MARSH, Jerry .... 570-702-8927 386 D
jmarsh@johnson.edu
MARSH, Jolee .... 910-678-8217 334 E
marshj@faytechcc.edu
MARSH, Kent .... 719-255-3505.. 84 C
kmarsh@uccs.edu
MARSH, Marilyn .... 215-324-0746 383 B
mmarsh@eastern.edu
MARSH, Marlee .... 803-786-3932 408 D
mmarsh@columbiasc.edu
MARSH, Maureen .... 410-516-8132 199 G
mmarsh9@jhu.edu
MARSH, Nicole, Y .... 510-379-4053.. 48 C
librarian@lincolnuca.edu
MARSH, Wendy .... 503-517-1220 377 C
wmarsh@warnerpacific.edu
MARSH-PEEK, Angela ... 269-488-4793 225 G
amarshpeek@kvcc.edu
MARSHAK, Helen Hopp 909-558-4578.. 48 E
hhoppmarshak@llu.edu
MARSHAK, Sofia .... 425-235-2464 482 H
smarshak@rtc.edu
MARSHALECK, Allison .. 610-341-4375 383 B
amarshal@eastern.edu
MARSHALL, Alycia .... 410-777-2776 197 G
aamarshall@aacc.edu
MARSHALL, Amy .... 510-986-6984.. 57 B
amarshall@peralta.edu
MARSHALL, Amy .... 706-886-6831 126 D
amarshall@tfc.edu
MARSHALL, Ave .... 404-270-5288 126 B
amarshall@spelman.edu
MARSHALL, Ben .... 813-253-7125 102 B
rmarshall10@hccfl.edu
MARSHALL, Bleuzette .... 513-556-6262 361 J
bleuzette.marshall@uc.edu
MARSHALL, Bryon .... 609-586-4800 278 F
marshalb@mccc.edu
MARSHALL, Cameron ... 434-223-6148 467 F
cmarshall@hsc.edu
MARSHALL, Charles ...... 919-962-1219 342 C
charles.marshall@unc.edu
MARSHALL, Chebon ..... 661-255-1050.. 28 G
cmarshall@calarts.edu
MARSHALL, Christina ... 714-997-6517.. 36 B
cmarsh@chapman.edu
MARSHALL,
Christopher .... 813-529-2640 502 L
christopher.marshall@centcom.mil
MARSHALL, Connie ...... 423-279-7632 425 A
MARSHALL, Connie ...... 423-323-0238 425 A
cmarshall@northeaststate.edu
MARSHALL, Courtney ... 316-978-3830 178 D
courtney.marshall@wichita.edu
MARSHALL, Darren .... 801-957-4782 461 C
darren.marshall@slcc.edu
MARSHALL, Darwina ..... 405-692-3196 366 D
MARSHALL, Dave .... 218-235-2125 241 E
david.marshall@vcc.edu
MARSHALL, David .... 909-537-5032.. 32 E
dmarshall@csusb.edu
MARSHALL, David, B .... 805-893-2785.. 70 E
david.marshall@ucsb.edu
MARSHALL, Debbie .... 858-695-8587 156 B
dmarshall@horizonuniversity.edu
MARSHALL, Donald .... 605-688-4173 417 A
donald.marshall@sdstate.edu
MARSHALL, Elaine .... 864-503-5331 414 A
emarshall@uscupstate.edu
MARSHALL, Ella .... 843-383-8060 408 B
emarshall@coker.edu
MARSHALL, Erica, A ..... 260-359-4290 156 C
emarshall@huntington.edu
MARSHALL, Filomela .... 609-633-6460 284 C
pmarshall@tesu.edu
MARSHALL, J, A .... 413-205-3263 205 F
ja.marshall@aic.edu

MARSHALL, James .... 559-278-2448.. 31 B
jamesm@csufresno.edu
MARSHALL, JaNice .... 216-987-3260 351 E
janice.marshall@tri-c.edu
MARSHALL, Jeff .... 706-272-2611 118 B
jmarshall@daltonstate.edu
MARSHALL, Joan .... 732-247-5241 279 C
jmarshall@nbts.edu
MARSHALL, John .... 970-248-1498.. 78 J
marshall@coloradomesa.edu
MARSHALL, Jon .... 620-901-6212 171 D
marshall@allencc.edu
MARSHALL, Justin, W .. 989-837-4279 229 B
marshall@northwood.edu
MARSHALL, Karen .... 828-395-1163 335 D
kmarshall@isothermal.edu
MARSHALL, Katherine ... 716-270-2661 299 B
marshallk@ecc.edu
MARSHALL, Kent .... 708-974-5390 145 A
marshallk34@morainevalley.edu
MARSHALL, Kevin .... 909-460-2000.. 71 C
gholmes@laverne.edu
MARSHALL, Kim .... 870-762-1020.. 17 B
kmarshall@smail.anc.edu
MARSHALL, Kimberley .. 470-639-0982 123 D
kimberley.marshall@morehouse.edu
MARSHALL, Lea .... 916-361-5100.. 34 K
MARSHALL, Lianna .... 417-269-3401 252 D
MARSHALL, Lori .... 856-256-4197 281 F
marshall@rowan.edu
MARSHALL, Lynette, L .. 319-335-3305 163 H
lynette-marshall@foriowa.org
MARSHALL, Marianne ... 262-551-8500 492 B
mmarshall@carthage.edu
MARSHALL, Maura .... 603-641-7028 274 A
mmarshall@anselm.edu
MARSHALL, Michael, L . 540-464-7230 476 B
marshallml@vmi.edu
MARSHALL, Mike .... 502-272-8180 179 H
mmarshall2@bellarmine.edu
MARSHALL, Molly, T ..... 913-667-5721 172 I
mtmarshall@cbts.edu
MARSHALL, Molly, T .... 651-255-6162 243 E
mtmarshall@unitedseminary.edu
MARSHALL, Paul .... 518-736-3622 300 D
pmarshall@fmcc.edu
MARSHALL, II,
Sherman .... 605-856-5880 415 J
MARSHALL, Sheryll .... 843-921-6939 411 A
smarshall@netc.edu
MARSHALL, Steven .... 951-372-7040.. 59 C
steven.marshall@norcocollege.edu
MARSHALL, Steven .... 208-376-7731 130 G
smarshall@boisebible.edu
MARSHALL, Steven .... 610-282-1100 382 C
steven.marshall@desales.edu
MARSHALL, Susan .... 401-598-4988 404 D
susan.marshalled.d@jwu.edu
MARSHALL, Susan, D ... 423-652-6006 420 F
sdmarsha@king.edu
MARSHALL, Tammy ...... 615-547-1359 419 C
tmarshall@cumberland.edu
MARSHALL, Tim .... 214-378-1856 434 E
tmarshall@dcccd.edu
MARSHALL, Timothy ..... 772-462-7997 102 F
tmarshall@irsc.edu
MARSHALL, Todd .... 315-792-5400 306 K
tmarshall@mvcc.edu
MARSHALL, Todd .... 419-289-5353 347 J
tmarsha5@ashland.edu
MARSHALL, William ...... 218-322-2340 238 F
william.marshall@itascacc.edu
MARSHALL BIGGINS,
Cynthia .... 903-593-8311 448 G
cmarshall-biggins@texascollege.edu
MARSHALL-BIGGINS,
Cynthia .... 903-593-8311 448 G
cmarshall-biggins@texascollege.edu
MARSHALL-CHAPMAN,
Sophia .... 903-927-3219 458 F
smarshallchapman@wileyc.edu
MARSHBURN, Kevin ..... 800-263-1549 486 E
MARSILI, Amanda .... 401-254-3774 405 C
amarsili@rwu.edu
MARSON, Jason .... 419-448-3300 361 D
marsonjm@tiffin.edu
MARSON, Wendy .... 651-450-3392 238 A
wmarson@inverhills.edu
MARSON, Wendy .... 651-450-3392 238 E
wmarson@inverhills.edu
MARSTELLER, Diane ...... 330-652-9919 352 E
dianemarsteller@eticollege.edu
MARSTELLER, Jill, A ..... 610-409-3582 401 H
jmarsteller@ursinus.edu
MARSTELLER-KOWALEWSKI,
Brenda .... 801-626-7737 461 A
bkowalewski@weber.edu
MARSWILLO,
Joseph, S .... 973-642-4568 279 E
joseph.s.marswillo@njit.edu
MARTE, Maria .... 973-684-5993 280 A
mmarte@pccc.edu
MARTEL, David, W .... 434-924-7821 472 D
dwm5x@virginia.edu
MARTEL, Kristie, A .... 724-847-5751 384 C
kamartel@geneva.edu
MARTEL, Sherrie .... 503-552-1518 374 D
smartel@nunm.edu
MARTEL-FOLEY, Joseph 617-989-4590 219 F
MARTELL, Corey .... 860-343-5701.. 87 A
cmartell@mxcc.edu
MARTELL, Loida .... 859-280-1256 183 F
lmartell@lextheo.edu
MARTELL, Marilyn .... 979-862-7020 446 F
mmartell@tamu.edu
MARTELLARO, John ...... 816-235-1592 261 B
martellaroj@umkc.edu
MARTELLO, Michael ...... 716-338-1055 303 A
michaelmartello@mail.sunyjcc.edu
MARTEN, Timothy .... 217-544-6464 149 C
timothy.marten@sjcs.edu
MARTENS, Anne .... 301-405-4280 202 H
amartens@umd.edu
MARTENSEN, Brian .... 507-389-1111 239 D
MARTERER, Aaron, C .... 803-777-5555 413 A
marterer@sc.edu
MARTEZ, Eboni, L .... 864-455-7992 413 F
emartez@greenvillemed.sc.edu
MARTH, Brian .... 312-369-7933 136 D
bmarth@colum.edu
MARTHERS, Paul, P ...... 404-727-3533 118 E
paul.p.marthers@emory.edu
MARTI, Tammy, S .... 563-588-7142 168 A
tammy.marti@loras.edu
MARTI, Vionex .... 787-738-2161 512 C
vionex.marti@upr.edu
MARTICH, Luisa .... 718-289-5732 293 B
luisa.martich@bcc.cuny.edu
MARTICKE, Nathan .... 816-584-6844 258 C
nathan.marticke@park.edu
MARTIGNETTI, Rick .... 239-280-2424.. 95 M
fr.rick.martignetti@avemaria.edu
MARTIN, Aaron .... 570-372-4120 398 F
martinaaron@susqu.edu
MARTIN, Abigail .... 850-245-0466 109 H
abigail.martin@flbog.edu
MARTIN, Abigail .... 671-735-2942 504 F
martinarp@triton.uog.edu
MARTIN, Akilah .... 281-756-3830 429 D
amartin@alvincollege.edu
MARTIN, Alan, B .... 304-293-7398 490 E
alan.martin@mail.wvu.edu
MARTIN, Allison .... 318-678-6000 187 H
amartin@bpcc.edu
MARTIN, Allyson .... 724-266-3838 400 B
amartin@tsm.edu
MARTIN, Alvin .... 213-884-4133.. 24 A
amartin@ajrca.edu
MARTIN, Alyssa .... 701-355-8020 347 C
amartin@umary.edu
MARTIN, Amanda .... 615-966-1962 421 B
amanda.martin@lipscomb.edu
MARTIN, Andrew, D ..... 314-935-5100 262 A
admartin@wustl.edu
MARTIN, Angela, A .... 515-574-1064 167 A
martin_a@iowacentral.edu
MARTIN, Angela, S .... 859-257-9830 185 F
angie.martin@uky.edu
MARTIN, Angelo .... 570-372-4136 398 F
martinma@susqu.edu
MARTIN, Angie .... 608-785-9454 500 C
martina@westerntc.edu
MARTIN, Anita .... 501-337-5000.. 18 B
amartin@asutr.edu
MARTIN, Anne .... 864-231-2000 406 F
amartin@andersonuniversity.edu
MARTIN, SR., Anthony . 708-709-7834 147 D
manthony@prairiestate.edu
MARTIN, Arlana .... 903-886-5041 447 B
arlana.martin@tamuc.edu
MARTIN, Barbara .... 601-877-6230 245 A
bmartin@alcorn.edu
MARTIN, Ben .... 325-649-8022 437 G
benmartin@hputx.edu
MARTIN, Benjamin .... 270-384-7479 183 G
martinb@lindsey.edu
MARTIN, Bethany, A ..... 315-386-7555 320 B
martinb@canton.edu
MARTIN, Bonnie .... 518-255-5402 319 C
martinbg@cobleskill.edu
MARTIN, Brad .... 704-894-2612 328 E
bcmartin@davidson.edu
MARTIN, Brandon .... 816-235-1020 261 B
martinbran@umkc.edu
MARTIN, Brian .... 765-641-4199 153 G
bhmartin@anderson.edu
MARTIN, Bridgit .... 920-403-3963 495 B
bridgit.martin@snc.edu
MARTIN, Brint .... 757-727-5425 467 G
alumni@hamptonu.edu
MARTIN, Bronwyn .... 601-605-3314 246 D
bmartin@holmescc.edu
MARTIN, Byron .... 219-464-6760 162 D
byron.martin@vlapo.edu
MARTIN, Callie .... 808-934-2503 129 I
calliev@hawaii.edu
MARTIN, Cameron, K ... 801-375-5125 459 K
MARTIN, Carla, M .... 870-575-8873.. 22 D
martinm@uapb.edu
MARTIN,
Carolyn (Biddy), A ..... 413-542-2234 205 G
president@amherst.edu
MARTIN, Cathy .... 615-329-1907 419 H
camartin@fisk.edu
MARTIN, Cecelia .... 503-847-2581 377 B
cmartin@uws.edu
MARTIN, Chad .... 580-774-3024 370 A
chad.martin@swosu.edu
MARTIN, Charles .... 340-693-1511 513 E
cmartin@uvi.edu
MARTIN, Charlie .... 727-376-6911 112 G
cmartin@trinitycollege.edu
MARTIN, Chicora .... 510-430-3189.. 52 E
chimartin@mills.edu
MARTIN, Chris .... 904-997-2924 101 B
chris.martin@fscj.edu
MARTIN, Chris .... 318-257-4526 192 D
cmartin@latech.edu
MARTIN, Chris .... 573-651-2322 259 H
cmartin@semo.edu
MARTIN, Christa, S ...... 931-540-2644 424 C
cmartin@columbiastate.edu
MARTIN, Christopher .... 208-769-3340 132 D
camartin@nic.edu
MARTIN, Christy .... 503-255-0332 374 C
cmartin@multnomah.edu
MARTIN, Courtney, E ... 330-385-1070 359 F
cmartin@ovct.edu
MARTIN, Crystle .... 310-660-3593.. 41 E
cmartin@elcamino.edu
MARTIN, Curt .... 970-248-1396.. 78 J
cumartin@coloradomesa.edu
MARTIN, Curtis, E .... 706-821-8312 124 B
cmartin@paine.edu
MARTIN, Cynthia .... 603-428-2214 273 G
cmartin@nec.edu
MARTIN, D. Michael ..... 909-687-1600.. 43 D
michaelmartin@gs.edu
MARTIN, Dale .... 318-357-5030 192 G
dale@nsula.edu
MARTIN, Dan, J .... 412-268-2349 380 C
djmartin@cmu.edu
MARTIN, Daniel .... 305-223-4561 107 B
MARTIN, Daniel, J .... 206-281-2114 483 G
dmartin@spu.edu
MARTIN, David .... 409-880-8471 449 G
dmartin28@lamar.edu
MARTIN, David .... 831-646-4060.. 52 G
dmartin@mpc.edu
MARTIN, David .... 323-469-3300.. 24 P
dmartin@amda.edu
MARTIN, David .... 203-837-9600.. 86 B
martind@wcsu.edu
MARTIN, David .... 718-420-4341 324 F
dmartin@wagner.edu
MARTIN, David .... 254-968-9644 446 D
dvmartin@tarleton.edu
MARTIN, David, L .... 570-941-7400 401 F
david.martin2@scranton.edu
MARTIN, David, W .... 605-394-1269 416 H
david.martin@sdsmt.edu
MARTIN, Dawn .... 757-423-2095 467 A
MARTIN, Deborah .... 661-336-5124.. 46 K
debmarti@kccd.edu
MARTIN, Deborah .... 312-629-6800 149 F
dmartin@saic.edu
MARTIN, Debra .... 310-954-4030.. 52 I
dmartin@msmu.edu
MARTIN, Debra .... 662-246-6263 247 D
dmartin@msdelta.edu
MARTIN, Deidre .... 229-391-4907 114 F
dmartin@abac.edu
MARTIN, Denise .... 919-777-7784 333 C
dmartin@cccc.edu
MARTIN, Dillon .... 719-384-6890.. 82 D
dillon.martin@ojc.edu
MARTIN, Donna .... 904-548-4414 101 B
donna.martin@fscj.edu
MARTIN, Donna .... 337-475-5493 192 E
dmartin@mcneese.edu
MARTIN, Dorothy .... 207-768-2806 195 G
ndmartin@nmcc.edu
MARTIN, Doug .... 757-446-5035 466 D
martinsd@evms.edu
MARTIN, Dustin .... 765-641-4150 153 G
dlmartin@anderson.edu
MARTIN, Earl, F .... 515-271-2191 165 J
earl.martin@drake.edu
MARTIN, III, Earl Joe ... 225-752-4230 187 D
jmartin@iticollege.edu
MARTIN, Elwyn .... 870-230-5135.. 19 D
emartin@hsu.edu
MARTIN, Eric .... 212-752-1530 304 A
eric.martin@limcollege.edu
MARTIN, Etienne .... 614-287-2491 351 C
emarti10@cscc.edu
MARTIN, Frank, C .... 803-536-8388 411 G
fmartin@scsu.edu
MARTIN, Gale .... 610-526-6143 385 D
gmartin@harcum.edu
MARTIN, Galen .... 770-962-7580 121 E
gmartin@gwinnetttech.edu
MARTIN, Gary .... 561-237-7157 103 W
gmartin@lynn.edu
MARTIN, Gary, D .... 651-696-6735 236 I
gmartin6@macalester.edu
MARTIN, George .... 508-541-1815 209 A
gmartin@dean.edu
MARTIN, Gerald .... 610-436-1074 395 D
gmartin2@wcupa.edu
MARTIN, Greg .... 515-964-6368 165 A
gcmartin@dmacc.edu
MARTIN, Greta, R .... 301-546-0402 201 E
martingr@pgcc.edu
MARTIN, SR.,
Harold, L .... 336-334-7940 341 D
hmartin@ncat.edu
MARTIN, Heather .... 601-643-8404 245 F
heather.martin@colin.edu
MARTIN, Heidi .... 248-476-1122 227 E
hmartin@msp.edu
MARTIN, Holly .... 636-922-8356 258 J
hmartin@stchas.edu
MARTIN, Irene .... 860-343-5740.. 87 A
imartin@mxcc.edu
MARTIN, Jackie .... 601-643-8323 245 F
jackie.martin@colin.edu
MARTIN, Jake .... 903-593-8311 448 G
jmartin@texascollege.edu
MARTIN, James .... 913-684-3280 503 E
MARTIN, James, J .... 501-882-8851.. 17 D
jjmartin@asub.edu
MARTIN, James, R .... 208-282-2341 131 G
martjame@isu.edu
MARTIN, II, James, R .. 412-624-9811 400 H
jrmartin@pitt.edu
MARTIN, Jamie .... 602-787-6500.. 13 E
jamie.martin@paradisevalley.edu
MARTIN, Janette .... 208-795-4266 131 F
MARTIN, Jeania .... 704-991-0370 338 C
jmartin8295@stanly.edu
MARTIN, Jeanne .... 210-366-2701 441 J
MARTIN, Jeffrey .... 508-999-8058 212 A
jeff.martin@umassd.edu
MARTIN, Jeffrey, L .... 401-456-8840 405 A
jmartin1@ric.edu
MARTIN, Jenni .... 509-533-7075 479 C
jenni.martin@scc.spokane.edu
MARTIN, Jenni .... 509-533-7075 479 B
jenni.martin@ccs.spokane.edu
MARTIN, Jennifer .... 940-898-3406 451 D
jmartin@twu.edu
MARTIN, Jeremiah .... 312-915-6709 143 C
jmartin17@luc.edu
MARTIN, Jeremy, A .... 513-556-1826 361 J
jeremy.martin@uc.edu
MARTIN, Jerrold .... 312-553-2500 135 A
jlmartin@ccc.edu

MARTIN, Jill .... 571-633-9651 472 A
jill.martin@uona.edu
MARTIN, Jo Leda .... 303-963-3206.. 78 H
jomartin@ccu.edu
MARTIN, Joel, W .... 718-390-3131 324 F
joel.martin@wagner.edu
MARTIN, John, J .... 609-258-3000 280 D
jjmartin@princeton.edu
MARTIN, Joshua .... 508-854-7513 215 F
jmartin@qcc.mass.edu
MARTIN, Joshua .... 972-825-4821 444 J
jmartin@sagu.edu
MARTIN, Joshua .... 740-264-5591 352 B
jmartin@egcc.edu
MARTIN, Juanita, K ...... 330-972-7082 361 H
juanita@uakron.edu
MARTIN, Karen .... 419-289-5604 347 J
kmarti44@ashland.edu
MARTIN, Karla .... 740-264-5591 352 B
kmartin@egcc.edu
MARTIN, Kathleen .... 413-748-3070 218 I
kmartin5@springfield.edu
MARTIN, Kathy .... 540-375-2262 470 E
kmartin@roanoke.edu
MARTIN, Keith .... 918-343-7706 369 B
kmartin@rsu.edu
MARTIN, Keith .... 713-743-1449 452 D
kmartin@uh.edu
MARTIN, Kelsey, A .... 580-327-8478 367 A
kamartin@nwosu.edu
MARTIN, Kelsey, C .... 310-794-9507.. 69 E
kcmartin@mednet.ucla.edu
MARTIN, Kenneth, M .... 717-815-1211 403 F
kmartin@ycp.edu
MARTIN, Kevin .... 215-407-0584 392 T
kmartin@pafa.edu
MARTIN, Kevin .... 703-591-7042 466 M
kevin@fxua.edu
MARTIN, Kimberly .... 731-352-7646 418 C
martink@bethelu.edu
MARTIN, Kristina .... 617-585-1725 217 E
kristina.martin@necmusic.edu
MARTIN, Kyle, R .... 208-496-1450 130 I
martink@byui.edu
MARTIN, Kylie .... 413-748-3227 218 I
kmartin@springfield.edu
MARTIN, Lara .... 561-237-7459 103 W
lmartin@lynn.edu
MARTIN, Larry .... 657-278-4380.. 31 C
larrymartin@fullerton.edu
MARTIN, Laura .... 304-877-6428 486 G
financialaid@abc.edu
MARTIN, Leandra .... 913-722-0272 175 A
leandra.martin@kansaschristian.edu
MARTIN, Linda .... 206-934-5300 483 D
MARTIN, Linda .... 505-224-4000 285 N
lmartin@cnm.edu
MARTIN, Linda, C .... 865-974-3843 427 A
lcmartin@tennessee.edu
MARTIN, Lisa .... 254-710-2611 431 E
lisa_m_martin@baylor.edu
MARTIN, Lisa .... 864-941-8393 411 C
martin.l@ptc.edu
MARTIN, Llanet .... 818-778-5764.. 49 G
martinl7@lavc.edu
MARTIN, Lori .... 225-578-2031 189 E
lkemp1@lsu.edu
MARTIN, Machelle .... 916-278-6078.. 32 D
martin.machelle@csus.edu
MARTIN, Maegan .... 580-477-7875 371 D
maegan.martin@wosc.edu
MARTIN, Marc .... 510-780-4500.. 47 K
mmartin@lifewest.edu
MARTIN, Mariel .... 518-580-8212 315 F
mariel@skidmore.edu
MARTIN, Mark .... 757-352-4040 470 B
marybun@regent.edu
MARTIN, Mark, A .... 989-837-4497 229 B
martinm@northwood.edu
MARTIN, Marty .... 571-633-9651 472 A
marty.martin@uona.edu
MARTIN,
Marty (Dewey) .... 314-246-7560 262 C
deweymartin21@webster.edu
MARTIN, Mary .... 541-506-6028 372 F
mmartin@cgcc.edu
MARTIN, Maureen .... 734-647-6000 231 H
mmartin@umich.edu
MARTIN, Micah .... 704-406-2135 329 A
mmartin8@gardner-webb.edu
MARTIN, Michael .... 707-654-1000.. 32 A
MARTIN, Michael .... 216-397-4199 353 O
mmartin@jcu.edu
MARTIN, Michael, V ..... 239-590-1055 109 K
president@fgcu.edu
MARTIN, Michelle .... 309-672-5515 144 C
mmartin@methodistcol.edu
MARTIN, Michelle .... 478-825-6436 118 F
michelle.martin@fvsu.edu
MARTIN, Michelle .... 417-328-1826 259 I
mnmartin@sbuniv.edu
MARTIN, Michelle .... 972-580-7600 431 F
mmartin@bhcarroll.edu
MARTIN, Mirta, M .... 304-367-4151 489 K
mirta.martin@fairmontstate.edu
MARTIN, Natalie .... 501-202-6200.. 18 E
MARTIN, Natasha .... 206-398-4039 484 A
nmartin@seattleu.edu
MARTIN, Pat .... 610-328-8451 398 G
pmartin1@swarthmore.edu
MARTIN, Paul, W .... 518-276-8711 312 C
martip@rpi.edu
MARTIN, Paula .... 618-537-6952 144 A
phmartin@mckendree.edu
MARTIN, Rafael, O .... 972-883-3550 455 B
rafael.martin@utdallas.edu
MARTIN, II, Ralph, C .... 617-373-2101 217 I
MARTIN, Randy .... 870-972-2093.. 17 E
rmartin@astate.edu
MARTIN, Renee .... 318-626-6730 190 A
sm8267@bncollege.com
MARTIN, Renee .... 303-963-3384.. 78 H
rmartin@ccu.edu
MARTIN, Rich .... 315-279-5645 303 G
rmartin@keuka.edu
MARTIN, Robert .... 505-424-2301 286 E
MARTIN, Robyn .... 520-515-3688.. 11 M
martinrc@cochise.edu
MARTIN, Ronald .... 773-843-7553 135 F
rmartin@ccc.edu
MARTIN, Roneida .... 847-543-2641 136 A
rmartin@clcillinois.edu
MARTIN, Rosa, L .... 706-821-8365 124 B
rmartin@paine.edu
MARTIN, Rosemary .... 816-604-1587 255 C
rosemary.martin@mcckc.edu
MARTIN, Russell .... 864-941-8669 411 C
martin.r@ptc.edu
MARTIN, Sandra, E .... 870-235-4041.. 21 C
sandrasmith@saumag.edu
MARTIN, Sarah .... 509-533-3680 479 D
sarah.martin@sfcc.spokane.edu
MARTIN, Sean .... 860-439-2058.. 87 H
sean.martin@conncoll.edu
MARTIN, Shadi .... 775-682-8714 271 E
shadim@unr.edu
MARTIN, Shane .... 206-296-2595 484 A
martins@seattleu.edu
MARTIN, Sharon, L ...... 304-293-9091 490 E
sharon.martin@mail.wvu.edu
MARTIN, Shaun .... 503-338-2393 372 D
smartin@clatsopcc.edu
MARTIN, Sherry .... 910-272-3343 337 D
smartin@robeson.edu
MARTIN, Stacey .... 325-670-1253 436 I
smartin@hsutx.edu
MARTIN, Staci .... 903-983-8200 438 F
smartin@kilgore.edu
MARTIN, Steve .... 336-770-3322 343 D
martinw@uncsa.edu
MARTIN, Steve .... 850-478-8496 105 G
smartin@pcci.edu
MARTIN, Steven, J .... 419-772-2277 358 C
s-martin.11@onu.edu
MARTIN, Susan .... 352-588-8117 107 D
susan.martin04@saintleo.edu
MARTIN, Susie .... 310-377-5501.. 51 C
smartin@marymountcalifornia.edu
MARTIN, Terry .... 479-575-3836.. 21 F
MARTIN, Thomas, J ...... 413-345-1247 211 G
thojmartin@umass.edu
MARTIN, Thomas, K ..... 972-758-3817 433 I
tmartin@collin.edu
MARTIN, Tim .... 843-574-6326 412 I
tim.martin@tridenttech.edu
MARTIN, Timothy, J ..... 515-574-1097 167 A
martin@iowacentral.edu
MARTIN, Timothy, R ...... 508-767-7373 206 A
timartin@assumption.edu
MARTIN, Tod .... 501-279-4403.. 19 C
registrar@harding.edu
MARTIN, Todd .... 660-263-4100 257 B
toddmartin@macc.edu
MARTIN, Tom .... 859-622-2383 180 E
tom.martin@eku.edu
MARTIN, Tom .... 361-593-2139 447 D
katdm00@tamuk.edu
MARTIN, Tony, L .... 336-386-3222 338 D
martint@surry.edu
MARTIN, Tracey .... 281-949-1800.. 93 H
MARTIN, Traci .... 410-337-6191 199 B
tmartin@goucher.edu
MARTIN, Tracy .... 602-489-5300.. 10 F
tracy.martin@arizonachristian.edu
MARTIN, Traycee, F ...... 229-333-5710 127 E
tmartin@valdosta.edu
MARTIN, Troy .... 617-745-3865 209 B
troy.martin@enc.edu
MARTIN, Troy .... 801-863-8183 460 D
troy.martin@uvu.edu
MARTIN, Valerie, G ...... 570-372-4288 398 F
vmartin@susqu.edu
MARTIN, Vicki, J .... 414-297-6320 499 C
martinv@matc.edu
MARTIN, Victor .... 661-654-2222.. 30 B
vmartin4@csub.edu
MARTIN, Wayne .... 973-754-7192 280 A
wmartin@pccc.edu
MARTIN, Wendy .... 207-859-1111 196 D
martinw@thomas.edu
MARTIN, Willadean .... 972-860-4817 434 F
wmartin@dcccd.edu
MARTIN-BROWN,
Karen .... 352-371-2833.. 98 G
director@dragonrises.edu
MARTIN-HALL,
Margaret, J .... 870-575-8064.. 22 D
hallm@uapb.edu
MARTIN LONG, Kim ..... 504-280-1278 190 B
kmlong@uno.edu
MARTIN LOPIT,
Maribeth .... 206-281-2448 483 G
martinm3@spu.edu
MARTIN-OSORIO,
Carol, J .... 615-353-3268 424 G
carol.martin-osorio@nscc.edu
MARTIN PARISIEN,
Terri .... 701-477-7862 346 J
tparisien@tm.edu
MARTIN-REND, Jill .... 814-653-8265 379 E
jill.martin-rend@bc3.edu
MARTIN SCOUFIELD,
Ali .... 216-687-2048 350 J
a.martinscoufield@csuohio.edu
MARTIN THORNTON,
Renee .... 951-222-8048.. 59 D
renee.martin-thornton@rcc.edu
MARTIN TSE, Jennifer ... 315-464-4604 317 C
registrar@upstate.edu
MARTIN-VEGA,
Louis, A .... 919-515-2311 342 A
louis_martin-vega@ncsu.edu
MARTINDALE, Judy .... 801-863-8932 460 D
judy.martindale@uvu.edu
MARTINDALE, Trey .... 615-494-8909 422 C
trey.martindale@mtsu.edu
MARTINE, Jason .... 407-926-2000.. 93 H
MARTINE, Jason .... 407-618-5900.. 93 H
MARTINEAU, Jim .... 503-594-3271 372 C
jmartineau@clackamas.edu
MARTINEAU,
Michael, D .... 801-581-7481 459 O
mike.martineau@utah.edu
MARTINELLE, Lorraine .. 413-572-8014 213 F
lmartinelle@westfield.ma.edu
MARTINELLI, Diana .... 304-293-5746 490 E
diana.martinelli@mail.wvu.edu
MARTINELLI, Joseph ..... 973-275-2733 283 C
joseph.martinelli@shu.edu
MARTINELLI,
Rosemaria .... 512-471-2694 455 A
rmartinelli@austin.utexas.edu
MARTINELLI-FERNANDEZ,
Susan .... 309-298-1828 153 A
martinelli-fernandez@wiu.edu
MARTINES, Ian .... 210-436-3996 442 J
imartines@stmarytx.edu
MARTINES, James .... 702-651-7488 270 K
james.martines@csn.edu
MARTINEZ, Abelardo .... 787-758-2525 512 F
abelardo.martinez@upr.edu
MARTINEZ, Adrienne .... 303-615-1333.. 81 M
amart475@msudenver.edu
MARTINEZ, Alicia .... 860-701-5000.. 88 D
martinez_a@mitchell.edu
MARTINEZ, Amy .... 559-934-2203.. 75 A
amymartinez@whccd.edu
MARTINEZ, Ana .... 718-518-4407 294 B
anmartinez@hostos.cuny.edu
MARTINEZ, Annemieke . 202-806-6100.. 92 F
MARTINEZ, Art .... 512-499-4296 454 H
amartinez@utsystem.edu
MARTINEZ, Auris .... 787-878-5475 507 L
amartinez@arecibo.inter.edu
MARTINEZ, Brenda .... 510-466-7203.. 57 C
bmartinez@peralta.edu
MARTINEZ, Carla .... 714-895-8705.. 38 A
cmartinez@gwc.cccd.edu
MARTINEZ, Carlos .... 817-531-4959 451 C
cmartinez@txwes.edu
MARTINEZ, Carlos .... 210-458-4011 455 E
MARTINEZ, Carmen .... 650-508-3746.. 54 G
cmartinez@ndnu.edu
MARTINEZ, Chanel .... 213-427-2200.. 35 F
MARTINEZ, Charles ...... 512-471-7255 455 A
dean.education@austin.utexas.edu
MARTINEZ, Christina ..... 806-742-0012 450 F
christina.martinez@ttu.edu
MARTINEZ, Christy .... 505-467-6811 288 H
christymartinez@swc.edu
MARTINEZ, Connie .... 210-486-3960 429 A
cacovio@alamo.edu
MARTINEZ, Cristina ...... 787-257-0000 512 B
cristina.martinezlebron@upr.edu
MARTINEZ, Cynthia ...... 909-607-0121.. 37 F
cynthia_martinez@kgi.edu
MARTINEZ, Daniel .... 760-776-7212.. 38 E
damartinez@collegeofthedesert.edu
MARTINEZ, Danny .... 310-338-2893.. 51 A
danny.martinez@lmu.edu
MARTINEZ, Debra .... 517-353-3922 227 F
oie.debramartinez@msu.edu
MARTINEZ, Denise .... 254-968-9924 446 D
dmartinez@tarleton.edu
MARTINEZ, Diana .... 630-942-3007 135 I
martinezd59@cod.edu
MARTINEZ, Diana .... 602-285-7821.. 13 F
dr.martinez@phoenixcollege.edu
MARTINEZ, Diana, S ..... 210-458-8000 455 E
diana.martinez1@utsa.edu
MARTINEZ, Edward .... 631-451-4176 321 D
martineze@sunysuffolk.edu
MARTINEZ, Elena, M ..... 956-326-2433 446 E
emartinez@tamiu.edu
MARTINEZ, Elias, L ...... 512-245-1555 450 C
elm170@txstate.edu
MARTINEZ, Elizabeth .... 505-438-8884 288 F
librarians@acupuncturecollege.edu
MARTINEZ, Elizabeth .... 787-841-2000 509 J
elizabeth_martinez@pucpr.edu
MARTINEZ, Ernie .... 559-265-5711.. 67 B
ernie.martinez@fresnocitycollege.edu
MARTINEZ, Federico ..... 305-629-2929 107 H
MARTINEZ, Geraldine ... 575-528-7244 287 F
gerri66@nmsu.edu
MARTINEZ, German .... 609-497-7779 280 C
facilities-security@ptsem.edu
MARTINEZ, Gilbert .... 815-836-5442 142 F
gmartinez9@lewisu.edu
MARTINEZ, Graciela ...... 361-698-1192 435 G
gmartinez@delmar.edu
MARTINEZ, Haydee .... 508-999-8148 212 A
hmartinez@umassd.edu
MARTINEZ, Hector .... 787-284-1912 508 E
hmartin@ponce.inter.edu
MARTINEZ, Hector .... 787-284-1912 508 E
hemart@ponce.inter.edu
MARTINEZ, Jacqueline .. 212-938-5500 319 E
jmartinez@sunyopt.edu
MARTINEZ, Janice, A .... 787-765-1915 509 B
jamartinez@opto.inter.edu
MARTINEZ, Jeffrey .... 909-748-8400.. 72 F
jeff_martinez@redlands.edu
MARTINEZ, Jenny, S .... 650-723-2300.. 66 E
MARTINEZ, Jerry .... 979-230-3215 431 I
jerry.martinez@brazosport.edu
MARTINEZ, Jesse .... 208-885-7716 132 F
jessem@uidaho.edu
MARTINEZ, Jesus .... 787-738-2161 512 C
jesus.martinez5@upr.edu
MARTINEZ, Joaquin ...... 443-840-1021 198 H
jmartinez@ccbcmd.edu
MARTINEZ, Jordan .... 951-552-8967.. 27 G
jmartinez@calbaptist.edu
MARTINEZ, Jose .... 510-592-9688.. 54 F
jose.martinez@npu.edu
MARTINEZ, Jose, D ...... 787-288-1118 510 I
MARTINEZ, JR.,
Jose, F .... 210-832-3294 453 C
jfmartin@uiwtx.edu
MARTINEZ, Juan .... 334-683-2333.... 3 A
jmartinez@marionmilitary.edu

MARTINEZ, Juan ... 787-894-2828 513 C
juan.martinez8@upr.edu
MARTINEZ, Juan ... 716-851-1257 299 B
martinez@ecc.edu
MARTINEZ, Kara ... 806-716-4600 443 G
kmartinez@southplainscollege.edu
MARTINEZ, Kate ... 646-745-8328 291 A
kmartine@barnard.edu
MARTINEZ, Kimberly ... 303-861-1151.. 80 G
kmartinez@concorde.edu
MARTINEZ, Kristen ... 617-236-5400 209 G
kmartinez@fisher.edu
MARTINEZ, Kymm ... 651-962-6486 244 E
kymm.martinez@stthomas.edu
MARTINEZ, Leticia ... 928-344-7644.. 11 A
leticia.martinez@azwestern.edu
MARTINEZ, Lisette ... 215-955-6000 399 E
MARTINEZ, Lissette ... 619-260-4659.. 72 I
lissettemartinez@sandiego.edu
MARTINEZ, Loretta ... 505-277-5035 288 J
lpmartinez@salud.unm.edu
MARTINEZ, Luis, E ... 786-331-1000 104 H
lmartinez@maufl.edu
MARTINEZ, Luisa ... 904-620-5800 111 B
luisa.martinez@unf.edu
MARTINEZ, Luz, E ... 787-894-2828 513 C
luz.martinez6@upr.edu
MARTINEZ, Manuel ... 614-251-4671 358 B
martinem1@ohiodominican.edu
MARTINEZ, Marco ... 915-532-3737 458 B
MARTINEZ, Maria ... 787-751-0178 510 E
ac_mmartinez@uagm.edu
MARTINEZ, Maria ... 415-338-7264.. 33 E
mlmartinez@sfsu.edu
MARTINEZ, Maria ... 361-593-2129 447 D
maria.martinez2@tamuk.edu
MARTINEZ, Maria ... 918-465-1711 366 A
mmartinez@eosc.edu
MARTINEZ, Marilyn ... 787-863-2390 508 B
marilyn.martinez@fajardo.inter.edu
MARTINEZ, Marina ... 408-848-4800.. 43 E
MARTINEZ, Mario ... 909-748-8790.. 72 F
mario_martinez@redlands.edu
MARTINEZ, Mark ... 716-829-7836 298 E
martinem@dyc.edu
MARTINEZ, Marla ... 512-232-7903 455 A
marla.martinez@austin.utexas.edu
MARTINEZ, Marvin ... 505-224-4585 285 N
mmartinez188@cnm.edu
MARTINEZ, Marvin ... 714-480-7450.. 58 E
martinez_marvin@rsccd.edu
MARTINEZ, Mary, A ... 989-774-3253 222 E
marti14m@cmich.edu
MARTINEZ, Melinda ... 949-214-3134.. 39 K
melinda.martinez@cui.edu
MARTINEZ, Miriam ... 787-284-1912 508 E
mmartine@ponce.inter.edu
MARTINEZ, Monica ... 760-245-4271.. 74 D
monica.martinez@vvc.edu
MARTINEZ, Nina ... 502-456-6505 185 A
nmartinez@sullivan.edu
MARTINEZ, Olivia ... 610-566-1776 403 B
omartinez@williamson.edu
MARTINEZ, Pablo ... 305-223-4561 107 B
pmartinez@sjvcs.edu
MARTINEZ, Paola ... 626-969-3434.. 26 F
MARTINEZ, Patti ... 915-747-5999 455 C
pdmartinez@utep.edu
MARTINEZ, Pedro ... 707-826-4402.. 33 C
pedro.martinez@humboldt.edu
MARTINEZ, Rachel ... 361-570-4260 453 B
martinezr@uhv.edu
MARTINEZ, Rachel ... 503-768-7685 373 E
rachelmartinez@lclark.edu
MARTINEZ, Raul, J ... 972-985-3725 433 I
rjmartinez@collin.edu
MARTINEZ, Rick ... 512-863-1914 445 C
rickmartinez@southwestern.edu
MARTINEZ, Rolando ... 312-850-7291 135 H
rmartinez610@ccc.edu
MARTINEZ, Roman ... 305-237-0012 104 E
rmartin9@mdc.edu
MARTINEZ, Rosa, J ... 787-864-2222 508 C
rosa.martinez@guayama.inter.edu
MARTINEZ, Ruben, O ... 407-303-9372.. 95 B
ruben.martinez@ahu.edu
MARTINEZ, Sandra ... 951-571-6267.. 59 B
sandra.martinez@mvc.edu
MARTINEZ, Sarai ... 773-371-5454 134 D
smartinez@ctu.edu
MARTINEZ, Sergio ... 956-665-3439 455 D
sergio.martinez@utrgv.edu
MARTINEZ, Siria ... 530-668-2536.. 77 D
smartinez@yccd.edu
MARTINEZ, Sirimarie ... 787-765-1915 509 B
smartinez@opto.inter.edu
MARTINEZ, Steve ... 830-591-7280 444 G
srmartinez@swtjc.edu
MARTINEZ, Tara ... 612-659-6761 239 A
tara.martinez@minneapolis.edu
MARTINEZ, Terry ... 315-859-4020 300 H
tmartine@hamilton.edu
MARTINEZ, Terry, M ... 315-859-4020 300 H
tmartine@hamilton.edu
MARTINEZ, Veronica ... 408-848-4725.. 43 E
vmartinez@gavilan.edu
MARTINEZ, Vesta, M ... 817-515-7795 445 F
vesta.martinez@tccd.edu
MARTINEZ, Vilma ... 787-264-0409 508 F
vilma_martinez_toro@intersg.edu
MARTINEZ, Xochitl, E ... 909-448-4509.. 71 C
xmartinez@laverne.edu
MARTINEZ-DAVIS, Iris .. 845-344-6222 310 G
MARTINEZ DE DIOS,
Heri ... 787-720-0596 505 E
hmartinez@atlanticu.edu
MARTINEZ-DOANE,
Karol ... 410-225-2284 200 D
kmartinez@mica.edu
MARTINEZ FIGUEROA,
Myriam ... 787-250-0000 511 F
myriam.martinez5@upr.edu
MARTINEZ-GONZALEZ,
Liduvina ... 212-938-4033 319 E
lgonzalez@sunyopt.edu
MARTINEZ-LOPEZ,
Carmen Leonor ... 914-606-6795 325 A
carmen.martinez-lopez@sunywcc.edu
MARTINEZ-POWLESS,
Eva ... 414-297-6080 499 C
marte17b@matc.edu
MARTINEZ-SAENZ,
Miguel ... 718-489-5220 313 E
president@sfc.edu
MARTINEZ-SANDOVAL,
Yvonne ... 928-776-2307.. 16 J
yvonne.sandoval@yc.edu
MARTINEZ STLUKA,
Rena ... 714-992-7077.. 54 C
rmartinezstluka@fullcoll.edu
MARTINEZ-WOODRUFF,
Regina ... 254-526-1397 432 D
regina.martinez-woodruff@ctcd.edu
MARTINI, Louis ... 609-777-5696 284 C
lmartini@tesu.edu
MARTINI-HAUSNER,
Mary ... 315-279-5368 303 G
mmartini@keuka.edu
MARTINI-JOHNSON,
Lisa, A ... 610-799-1754 388 D
lmartinijohnson@lccc.edu
MARTINIS, Susan ... 217-244-2405 152 B
martinis@illinois.edu
MARTINO, Andrew, P ... 410-546-6902 204 D
apmartino@salisbury.edu
MARTINO, Bill ... 212-592-2212 315 C
wmartino@sva.edu
MARTINO, Gregory ... 215-972-2079 392 T
gmartino@pafa.edu
MARTINOV, Willam ... 516-299-3720 304 E
william.martinov@liu.edu
MARTINS, Kevin ... 401-232-6364 404 A
kmartins@bryant.edu
MARTINS, Sandra ... 630-942-2174 135 I
martinss14@cod.edu
MARTINSEN, Daniel ... 254-299-8333 439 E
dmartinsen@mclennan.edu
MARTINSEN, Michael ... 440-775-5782 357 G
mike.martinsen@oberlin.edu
MARTINSON, Ben ... 651-846-1473 241 B
benjamin.martinson@saintpaul.edu
MARTINSON, Brady ... 773-244-6203 145 G
bmartinson@northpark.edu
MARTIR, Jaime ... 787-710-8999 506 G
jaime.martir@dewey.edu
MARTLAND, Paul ... 845-344-6222 310 G
paul.martland@sunyorange.edu
MARTNER, James, E ... 630-942-2543 135 I
martner@cod.edu
MARTOCCI, DeAnne ... 518-629-7154 302 C
d.martocci@hvcc.edu
MARTON, Nathan ... 716-829-7583 298 E
martonn@dyc.edu
MARTONE, Eric ... 914-674-7618 306 C
emartone@mercy.edu
MARTORANA,
Anne Marie ... 617-368-1418 217 F
amartorana@nesl.edu
MARTOZA, Roberta ... 209-932-2933.. 71 E
rmartoza@pacific.edu
MARTS, Chad ... 757-490-1241 464 B
cmarts@auto.edu
MARTUNAS, Cheryl, A .. 508-831-5000 220 F
MARTY, Angela, L ... 630-515-6120 144 F
amarty@midwestern.edu
MARTY, Judith ... 305-463-7210.. 98 F
MARTY, Patrick ... 570-326-3761 392 W
pmarty@pct.edu
MARTZ, Ben ... 304-876-5176 490 A
bmartz@shepherd.edu
MARTZ, Ben ... 304-876-5007 490 A
bmartz@shepherd.edu
MARTZ, Diane ... 585-385-7309 313 F
dmartz@sjfc.edu
MARTÍNEZ, David, J ... 503-554-2646 373 A
dmartinez@georgefox.edu
MARTÍNEZ, María, T ... 787-728-1515 513 D
mariat.martinez@sagrado.edu
MARTÍNEZ, Vilma ... 787-264-0409 508 F
vilma_martinez_toro@intersg.edu
MARTÍNEZ, Vilma ... 787-264-1912 508 F
vilma_martinez_toro@intersg.edu
MARTÍNEZ RIVERA,
Waleska ... 787-751-0160 506 F
wmartinez@cmpr.pr.gov
MARUCCI, Kimberly ... 610-892-1500 393 B
MARUCHA, Phillip, T ... 503-494-8801 374 H
marucha@ohsu.edu
MARUJO, John ... 617-989-4590 219 F
MARUTZKY, Deborah ... 307-766-5612 501 I
MARUYAMA, Kenichi ... 480-461-7758.. 13 D
kenichi.maruyama@mesacc.edu
MARVANOVA, Marketa .. 460-243-2417 263 K
marketa.marvanova@umontana.edu
MARVASHTI, Lisa ... 540-654-1378 471 N
lchinn@umw.edu
MARVIN, Corey ... 760-384-6201.. 46 M
cmarvin@cerrocoso.edu
MARX, Christopher ... 616-451-3511 223 E
cmarx@davenport.edu
MARX, Christopher ... 845-688-7167 323 H
marxc@sunyulster.edu
MARX, Christopher ... 845-802-7167 323 H
marxc@sunyulster.edu
MARX, David ... 570-941-7673 401 F
david.marx@scranton.edu
MARX, Drew ... 270-831-9632 182 A
drew.marx@kctcs.edu
MARX, Lisa, M ... 410-778-7261 205 B
lmarx2@washcoll.edu
MARXUACH-TORROS,
Gilberto ... 787-727-7033 513 D
gilberto.marxuach@sagrado.edu
MARYATT, Victoria ... 916-608-6925.. 50 I
maryatv@flc.losrios.edu
MARYE, Erica ... 859-442-1163 181 H
erica.marye@kctcs.edu
MARYMONT, John ... 251-341-3030.... 9 A
jmarymont@southalabama.edu
MARZAN, Marissa ... 559-297-4500.. 45 N
mmarzan@iot.edu
MARZANO, Maria ... 212-517-0428 305 E
mmarzano@mmm.edu
MARZCAK, Kelly ... 906-932-4231 224 D
kellym@gogebic.edu
MARZILLI, T. Scott ... 713-221-8007 453 A
marzillis@uhd.edu
MARZLUFF, Elaine ... 641-269-3100 166 G
marzluff@grinnell.edu
MARZO, Sam, J ... 708-216-9183 143 C
smarzo@luc.edu
MARZULLO, Frank ... 708-656-8000 145 C
frank.marzullo@morton.edu
MARZULLO, Keith ... 301-405-2033 202 H
marzullo@umd.edu
MASAU, Traci ... 618-545-3030 141 E
tmasau@kaskaskia.edu
MASCARENAS, Malinda 303-404-5630.. 81 A
malinda.mascarenas@frontrange.edu
MASCARI, OP, Michael 314-256-8855 250 D
mascari@ai.edu
MASCARINA, David ... 818-252-3399.. 76 E
david.mascarina@woodbury.edu
MASCARO, Elizabeth ... 951-487-3210.. 53 A
emascaro@msjc.edu
MASCARO, Jennifer ... 207-262-7836 196 H
jennifer.mascaro@maine.edu
MASCARO, Juan, C ... 828-641-0951 327 B
mascarjc@brevard.edu
MASCARO, Maria, S ... 787-841-2000 509 J
exalumnos@pucpr.edu
MASCETTI, Kris ... 205-665-6392.... 8 D
kmascett@montevallo.edu
MASCHMAN, Greg, D ... 402-465-2116 268 G
gdm@nebrwesleyan.edu
MASCI, Kristin ... 570-702-8922 386 D
kalfieri@johson.edu
MASCIA, Frank ... 732-987-2256 278 A
fmascia@georgian.edu
MASCIANTONIO, John .. 215-596-8531 401 E
j.mascia@usciences.edu
MASEK, Jessie ... 805-893-3938.. 70 E
jessie.masek@ucsb.edu
MASEK, Phyllis ... 573-592-5363 262 E
phyllis.masek@westminster-mo.edu
MASELLI, Gennaro ... 914-606-6856 325 A
gennaro.maselli@sunywcc.edu
MASENTHIN,
Kimberly, R ... 262-243-5700 492 E
kimberly.masenthin@cuw.edu
MASHARIKI, Opio ... 912-358-3449 125 A
ssuathletics@savannahstate.edu
MASHBURN, Scott ... 423-746-5203 426 C
smashburn@tnwesleyan.edu
MASHEK, Randy, D ... 844-642-2338 169 A
mashekr@nicc.edu
MASHUDA, Patrick, M .. 252-398-6484 328 C
mashup@chowan.edu
MASI, Jessica ... 207-216-4401 195 J
jmasi@yccc.edu
MASINGILA, Joanna, O 315-443-4751 321 G
jomasing@syr.edu
MASINI, Blase, E ... 773-442-4899 146 A
b-masini@neiu.edu
MASINI, Marco ... 630-829-6006 133 E
mmasini@ben.edu
MASK, Caleb ... 706-419-1280 118 A
caleb.mask@covenant.edu
MASK, Renae ... 901-375-4400 422 A
renaemask@midsouthchristian.edu
MASKELL, David ... 281-487-1170 448 E
dmaskell@txchiro.edu
MASKEY, Cynthia, L ... 217-786-2436 143 B
cynthia.maskey@llcc.edu
MASLENNIKOVA, Lena .. 864-663-0258 410 I
lena.maslennikova@ngu.edu
MASLEY, Kelly ... 989-463-7146 221 B
masley@alma.edu
MASLOW, Tamara ... 718-327-7600 325 D
tmaslow@yofr.org
MASMAN, T. Todd ... 419-824-3873 355 C
tmasman@lourdes.edu
MASON, Amy ... 340-457-6274 486 E
masonar@ab.edu
MASON, Angel ... 706-236-2260 116 B
amason@berry.edu
MASON, Aprile ... 423-869-7145 421 A
aprile.mason@lmunet.edu
MASON, Ashley ... 903-988-7520 438 F
amason@kilgore.edu
MASON, Bobby ... 512-245-3078 450 C
bjm257@txstate.edu
MASON, Bobby, J ... 405-325-3546 370 K
bjm@ou.edu
MASON, Chip ... 601-968-8945 245 B
cmason@belhaven.edu
MASON, Chuck ... 802-443-5717 462 E
cmason@middlebury.edu
MASON, Clif ... 402-557-7512 265 J
clif.mason@bellevue.edu
MASON, Eric ... 419-995-8265 360 C
mason.e@rhodesstate.edu
MASON, Eric ... 303-605-7258.. 81 M
emason9@msudenvr.edu
MASON, Erin ... 765-285-1722 153 H
MASON, Geri ... 402-557-7020 265 J
geri.mason@bellevue.edu
MASON, Gregory ... 618-634-3325 149 G
gregm@shawneecc.edu
MASON, JR., Herman ... 803-780-1229 414 B
hmason@voorhees.edu
MASON, Holly ... 740-366-9219 349 F
mason.536@cotc.edu
MASON, James ... 314-792-6152 254 F
mason@kenrick.edu
MASON, James ... 617-879-7691 213 B
jmason@massart.edu
MASON, Jeff ... 617-217-9000 206 E
MASON, Jesse ... 763-424-0712 240 A
jmason@nhcc.edu

MASON, Justin .... 406-683-7536 264 A
justin.mason@umwestern.edu
MASON, Karol, V .... 212-237-8000 294 D
MASON, Kathryn .... 609-652-4282 283 E
kathryn.mason@stockton.edu
MASON, Keri .... 217-743-2051 143 B
keri.mason@llcc.edu
MASON, Linda .... 423-585-6809 425 F
linda.mason@ws.edu
MASON, Martha .... 907-450-8383.. 10 A
mjmason@alaska.edu
MASON, Matthew .... 717-560-8200 387 E
mmason@lbc.edu
MASON, Melanie .... 443-352-4371 202 E
mmason5@stevenson.edu
MASON, Merle .... 650-508-3739.. 54 G
mmason@ndnu.edu
MASON, Patience .... 678-225-7534 395 G
patiencema@pcom.edu
MASON, Paul .... 325-793-3850 439 F
mason.paul@mcm.edu
MASON, Rachel .... 562-860-2451.. 35 H
rmason@cerritos.edu
MASON, Reni .... 318-487-7503 187 E
reni.mason@lacollege.edu
MASON, Rick .... 606-589-2145 183 A
rick.mason@kctcs.edu
MASON, Rochelle .... 719-389-6800.. 78 I
rmason@coloradocollege.edu
MASON, Ron .... 203-837-8736.. 86 B
masonr@wcsu.edu
MASON, JR., Ronald .... 202-274-6016.. 94 B
ronald.mason@udc.edu
MASON, Shawna .... 479-308-2210.. 17 A
shawna.mason@arcomedu.org
MASON, Stacey, W .... 864-488-4540 410 B
smason@limestone.edu
MASON, Starla .... 307-778-1118 501 E
smason@lccc.wy.edu
MASON, Steven, D .... 903-233-3200 439 A
stevenmason@letu.edu
MASON, Terrell .... 540-374-4300.. 93 H
MASON, Terry .... 641-269-3230 166 G
masonter@grinnell.edu
MASON, Tisa .... 785-628-4231 173 H
tisa.mason@fhsu.edu
MASON, Tonya .... 240-567-5052 200 G
tonya.mason@montgomerycollege.edu
MASON, Traci .... 352-873-5808.. 97 N
masont@cf.edu
MASON-GARNER,
Felicia .... 803-780-1259 414 B
fgarner@voorhees.edu
MASON-KINSEY,
Natalie, L .... 818-677-2077.. 32 C
natalie.masonkinsey@csun.edu
MASOUD, Summer .... 575-674-2266 285 L
smasoud@burrell.edu
MASOUM, Nazi .... 949-794-9090.. 66 D
nazim@stanbridge.edu
MASRI, Safwan, M .... 212-854-8716 297 C
smm1@columbia.edu
MASS, Emily .... 772-462-7361 102 F
emass@irsc.edu
MASS, Gregory .... 973-596-5745 279 E
gregory.mass@njit.edu
MASS-FEARY, Maureen . 585-785-1364 299 F
maureen.massfeary@flcc.edu
MASSA, Gary, R .... 513-745-3335 364 G
massag@xavier.edu
MASSA, James .... 914-968-6200 314 C
bishop.james.massa@archny.org
MASSA-MCKINLEY,
Lilly .... 502-272-8154 179 H
lmassamckinley@bellarmine.edu
MASSAGEE, Danielle ..... 719-365-8291.. 83 N
danielle.massagee@uchealth.org
MASSAGUE, Joan .... 646-888-6639 304 J
j-massague@ski.mskcc.org
MASSANELLI, Randy ..... 479-575-7964.. 21 F
jrmassan@uark.edu
MASSARI, Lydia, I .... 787-751-0178 510 E
ac_lmassari@uagm.edu
MASSARO, Chris, J .... 615-898-2450 422 C
chris.massaro@mtsu.edu
MASSARO, Patrick .... 315-386-7838 320 B
massarop@canton.edu
MASSE, Carol .... 414-847-3270 494 C
carolmasse@miad.edu
MASSE, Tracy .... 716-839-8504 298 A
tmasse@daemen.edu
MASSELL, Laura .... 802-654-0532 463 F
lxm09190@ccv.vsc.edu

MASSENBURG,
Shirley, B .... 504-520-5229 193 E
sbmoses@xula.edu
MASSENGALE, Rick .... 870-743-3000.. 20 B
rick.massengale@northark.edu
MASSERINI, John .... 928-523-2672.. 14 H
john.masserini@nau.edu
MASSEY, Anne .... 413-545-9853 211 G
dean@isenberg.umass.edu
MASSEY, April .... 202-274-5194.. 94 B
amassey@udc.edu
MASSEY, Beverly .... 254-442-5116 432 I
beverly.massey@cisco.edu
MASSEY, Carissa .... 717-396-7833 392 U
cmassey@pcad.edu
MASSEY, David .... 419-517-3509 355 C
dmassey@lourdes.edu
MASSEY, Erin .... 610-328-8193 398 G
career@swarthmore.edu
MASSEY, Jeff .... 318-473-6423 189 F
jmassey@lsua.edu
MASSEY, John, D .... 817-921-8640 445 A
jmassey@swbts.edu
MASSEY, Jonathan .... 734-764-1315 231 H
drjrm@umich.edu
MASSEY, Julie .... 920-403-3014 495 B
julie.massey@snc.edu
MASSEY, Kristine .... 972-273-3283 435 B
kmassey@dcccd.edu
MASSEY, Laura .... 971-722-7700 375 D
laura.massey@pcc.edu
MASSEY, Leigh Ann ...... 202-685-2137 502 K
masseybl@ndu.edu
MASSEY, Michael .... 919-209-2087 335 F
mtmassey@johnstoncc.edu
MASSEY, Pamela, L ...... 501-450-3237.. 23 H
pamm@uca.edu
MASSEY, Perry, A .... 910-672-1475 341 C
pmassey@uncfsu.edu
MASSEY, Rachel .... 504-280-4436 190 B
rdmassey@uno.edu
MASSEY, Susan, A .... 904-264-2172 106 K
susan.massey@iws.edu
MASSEY, Tanya .... 405-744-9158 367 G
tanya.massey@okstate.edu
MASSEY-GARRETT,
Tamara .... 334-244-3754.... 4 E
tmassey2@aum.edu
MASSEY-SAMPSON,
Lamonte, J .... 704-216-6933 330 H
sampson@livingstone.edu
MASSIAH-ARTHUR,
Lesley, A .... 718-817-3023 300 C
massiah@fordham.edu
MASSIE, Charles .... 541-880-2339 373 C
massie@klamathcc.edu
MASSINGILL, Judson .... 713-683-3817 443 D
MASSINGILL, Linda .... 713-683-3817 443 D
MASSINI, Stephen, M ... 717-531-6614 391 G
smm83@psu.edu
MASSMAN, Joseph .... 816-654-7105 254 E
jmassman@kcumb.edu
MASSOGLIA, Mike .... 336-734-7177 334 F
mmassoglia@forsythtech.edu
MASSOT, Devon .... 407-646-1943 106 L
dmassot@rollins.edu
MASSOUD, Yehia .... 201-216-3461 283 D
yehia.massoud@stevens.edu
MASSRI, Al .... 479-619-2202.. 20 C
amassri@nwacc.edu
MAST, Gabriel .... 360-416-7797 484 C
gabriel.mast@skagit.edu
MAST, Maura, B .... 718-817-4700 300 C
mmast@fordham.edu
MAST, Russell, F .... 606-783-2870 184 C
r.mast@moreheadstate.edu
MASTASCUSA, Martin ... 610-526-5266 379 B
mmastasc@brynmawr.edu
MASTEL, Chad, L .... 651-641-8815 235 I
MASTELLER, John, Q .... 805-525-4417.. 67 K
jmasteller@thomasaquinas.edu
MASTER, Sarah, L .... 818-364-7788.. 49 C
mastersl@lamission.edu
MASTERS, Bradley .... 318-345-9239 188 D
bmasters@ladelta.edu
MASTERS, Carolynn ...... 401-456-8014 405 A
cmasters@ric.edu
MASTERS, Chris .... 479-394-7622.. 23 C
cmasters@uarichmountain.edu
MASTERS, Deborah, C .. 415-338-1681.. 33 E
dmasters@sfsu.edu
MASTERS, Hannah .... 417-667-8181 252 B
hmasters@cottey.edu

MASTERS, Kathy .... 318-342-1022 193 C
masters@ulm.edu
MASTERS, Mark .... 559-323-2100.. 61 F
mmasters@sjcl.edu
MASTERS, Michael .... 706-272-4461 118 B
mmasters@daltonstate.edu
MASTERS, Peggy .... 256-824-2771.... 8 B
peggy.masters@uah.edu
MASTERS, Summer .... 816-584-6367 258 C
summer.masters@park.edu
MASTERSON, Ana .... 928-692-3016.. 14 F
amasterson@mohave.edu
MASTERSON, Dan .... 785-227-3380 172 A
masterson@bethanylb.edu
MASTERSON, Doug .... 601-266-4714 249 F
doug.masterson@usm.edu
MASTERSON, John, A ... 620-901-6341 171 D
masterson@allencc.edu
MASTERSON, Joshua .... 502-863-7035 180 H
joshua_masterson@georgetowncollege.edu
MASTERSON, Julie, J .... 417-836-5335 256 G
juliemasterson@missouristate.edu
MASTERSON, Lisanne ... 828-694-1806 332 E
lmasterson@blueridge.edu
MASTERSON, JR.,
Thomas, J .... 989-774-1850 222 E
maste1tj@cmich.edu
MASTIN, Lorie .... 360-867-5371 480 C
mastinl@evergreen.edu
MASTON, Tammy .... 716-829-7810 298 E
mastont@dyc.edu
MASTRANGELO, Ryan ... 207-778-7048 196 I
ryan.mastrangelo@maine.edu
MASTRO, Denise .... 619-298-1829.. 65 K
MASUCCI, Michele, M .. 215-204-6875 399 B
michele.masucci@temple.edu
MASUDA, Danielle .... 808-735-4718 128 E
danielle.masuda@chaminade.edu
MASZAROS, Sue .... 615-460-5496 418 B
sue.maszaros@belmont.edu
MASZCZAK, Melissa, A 609-777-5660 284 C
mmaszczak@tesu.edu
MATA, Carolyn .... 404-364-8320 123 K
cmata@oglethorpe.edu
MATA, Luis .... 615-244-5848 423 C
MATA, Margot .... 830-591-7223 444 G
mhmata@swtjc.edu
MATANYI, Eric .... 708-209-3255 136 E
eric.matanyi@cuchicago.edu
MATAS, Francine .... 805-969-3626.. 55 J
fmatas@pacifica.edu
MATASAR, Richard .... 504-314-7612 191 F
rmatasar@tulane.edu
MATAVA, Robert, J .... 703-658-4304 465 L
rmatava@christendom.edu
MATCHAN, Steven .... 626-585-7489.. 56 D
sxmatchan@pasadena.edu
MATCHETT, Laura .... 231-995-1704 229 A
lmatchett@nmc.edu
MATCHIN, Patricia .... 575-624-8203 287 B
matchin@nmmi.edu
MATEJCIK, Mark, M ...... 216-916-7515 354 A
mmatejci@kent.edu
MATEN, Lionel .... 662-915-7705 249 D
lmaten@olemiss.edu
MATEO, Aurorisa .... 787-743-7979 510 H
amateo@suagm.edu
MATEO, Frances .... 623-845-3147.. 13 C
frances.mateo@gccaz.edu
MATERRE, Denise, W .... 413-585-2025 218 H
dmaterre@smith.edu
MATES, Ilene .... 610-436-2128 395 D
emates@wcupa.edu
MATHAI, Cynthia .... 503-517-1810 377 E
cmathai@westernseminary.edu
MATHEMA,
Shubhashish .... 603-542-7744 273 B
smathema@ccsnh.edu
MATHENA, Cindy .... 605-394-4800 415 G
MATHENEY, H. Scott .... 630-617-3025 137 G
hscottm@elmhurst.edu
MATHENY, Chris .... 920-735-2401 498 F
matheny@fvtc.edu
MATHENY, Jacqueline .. 716-827-2450 323 G
mathenyj@trocaire.edu
MATHENY, Samuel .... 215-871-6170 395 G
samuelmat@pcom.edu
MATHENY, Stephen ...... 828-395-1293 335 D
smatheny@isothermal.edu
MATHER, Claudia .... 855-239-1886 171 I
matherc@bartonccc.edu

MATHERLY, Barron .... 919-962-1091 342 C
matherly@unc.edu
MATHERLY, Cheryl, A ... 610-758-2981 388 E
cam716@lehigh.edu
MATHERN, Rebecca ...... 541-737-4331 375 A
rebecca.mathern@oregonstate.edu
MATHES, Cassie .... 319-273-2761 164 A
cassie.mathes@uni.edu
MATHES, Kevin .... 570-577-1446 379 C
kmathes@bucknell.edu
MATHESON, Regina, M 563-333-5838 169 G
mathesonreginam@sau.edu
MATHEW, Roy .... 915-747-5117 455 C
rmathew@utep.edu
MATHEWS, Angela .... 507-786-3231 243 D
mathews@stolaf.edu
MATHEWS, Becky .... 785-833-4303 175 E
becky.mathews@kwu.edu
MATHEWS, Bruce .... 808-932-7036 129 D
bmathews@hawaii.edu
MATHEWS, Christopher 952-446-4202 235 J
mathewsc@crown.edu
MATHEWS, Darren .... 941-309-4058 106 J
dmathews@ringling.edu
MATHEWS, Gary .... 512-404-4806 430 J
gmathews@austinseminary.edu
MATHEWS, Jennifer .... 508-565-1915 219 A
jmathews@stonehill.edu
MATHEWS, John .... 215-968-8211 379 D
john.mathews@bucks.edu
MATHEWS, Josh .... 503-517-1876 377 E
jmathews@westernseminary.edu
MATHEWS, Karen .... 937-376-6076 349 J
kmathews@centralstate.edu
MATHEWS, Kimberly ..... 714-564-6224.. 58 F
mathews_kimberly@sac.edu
MATHEWS, Lakeisha ..... 410-837-4030 204 F
lmathews@ubalt.edu
MATHEWS, Marc .... 859-233-8100 185 C
mmathews@transy.edu
MATHEWS, Marsha .... 865-882-4517 425 C
mathewsmr@roanestate.edu
MATHEWS, Michael ...... 303-333-4224.. 78 A
MATHEWS, Michael ...... 918-495-6812 368 F
mmathews@oru.edu
MATHEWS, Mike .... 971-722-2831 375 D
mike.mathews@pcc.edu
MATHEWS, Nancy, E .... 802-656-4280 463 A
nancy.mathews@uvm.edu
MATHEWS, Rajan, G ..... 646-378-6153 310 D
president@nyack.edu
MATHEWS, Robert .... 920-498-5701 499 G
robert.mathews@nwtc.edu
MATHEWS, Shannon ...... 912-358-3202 125 A
mathewss@savannahstate.edu
MATHEWS, Steven .... 252-493-7750 336 H
smathews@email.pittcc.edu
MATHEWSON, Dan, B ... 864-597-4560 414 E
mathewsondb@wofford.edu
MATHIAS, Ann .... 520-626-7864.. 16 D
annmathias@arizona.edu
MATHIAS, Duane, A ..... 719-884-5000.. 82 B
damathias@nbc.edu
MATHIAS, Jim, N .... 410-651-7789 203 D
jnmathias@umes.edu
MATHIAS, Michael .... 301-687-4436 204 C
mbmathias@frostburg.edu
MATHIESEN, Gaylan ...... 218-739-3375 236 H
gmathiesen@lbs.edu
MATHIEU, Dickens .... 860-297-2253.. 89 B
dickens.mathieu@trincoll.edu
MATHIEU, Rick .... 704-337-2701 339 F
mathieur@queens.edu
MATHIS, Clay, P .... 361-593-5400 447 D
clay.mathis@tamuk.edu
MATHIS, Jeff .... 813-988-5131.. 99 R
development@floridacollege.edu
MATHIS, Jennifer .... 870-759-4139.. 23 J
jmathis@williamsbu.edu
MATHIS, Jennifer, M .... 864-388-8307 410 A
jmathis@lander.edu
MATHIS, Jim .... 307-742-3776 502 B
jmathis@wyotech.edu
MATHIS, Kassie .... 334-347-2623.... 2 A
kmathis@escc.edu
MATHIS, Malissa .... 501-916-3110.. 22 A
mktrantham@ualr.edu
MATHIS, Maureen .... 610-660-1306 397 G
mmathis@sju.edu
MATHIS, Michael .... 817-735-0224 454 B
michael.mathis@unthsc.edu
MATHIS, Michele, W .... 336-322-2237 336 G
michele.mathis@piedmontcc.edu

MATHIS, Molly .... 256-765-4343... 8 E mjmathis@una.edu
MATHIS, RJ .... 478-825-6316 118 F rj.mathis@fvsu.edu
MATHIS, Sharale .... 413-552-2226 214 F smathis@hcc.edu
MATHIS, Sharese .... 517-264-7606 230 H smathis@sienaheights.edu
MATHIS, Shawn .... 501-450-1333.. 19 E mathis@hendrix.edu
MATHIS, Teri .... 229-391-5045 114 F terimathis@abac.edu
MATHIS, William .... 419-372-8603 348 G wmathis@bgsu.edu
MATHISEN, Germaine ... 834-842-3446 452 D glmathisen@uh.edu
MATHISON, Karyssa ..... 253-566-5169 484 E kmathison@tacomacc.edu
MATHOV, Sara .... 503-251-5739 377 B smathov@uws.edu
MATHUR, Guarav .... 202-651-5520.. 92 C gaurav.mathur@gallaudet.edu
MATIAS, Audeliz .... 518-587-2100 320 E
MATIAS, Madelyn .... 717-871-7001 395 A
MATIAS-ORTIZ, Andres . 914-674-7458 306 C amatiasortiz@mercy.edu
MATIC, Katharina .... 717-245-1010 382 D matick@dickinson.edu
MATICH, Michael .... 734-432-5441 227 C mmatich@madonna.edu
MATIIA, Mike, M .... 717-337-6530 384 D mmattia@gettysburg.edu
MATIKA, Susan .... 908-709-7548 284 D matika@ucc.edu
MATISON, Kim .... 253-566-5194 484 E kmatison@tacomacc.edu
MATITIA, Abraham .... 440-943-5300 360 A
MATKIN, Gary, W .... 949-824-5525.. 69 D gmatkin@uci.edu
MATKIN, H. Neil .... 972-758-3800 433 I nmatkin@collin.edu
MATLIN, David .... 808-956-7301 129 E athdir@hawaii.edu
MATLOCK, Debra .... 312-996-7084 151 G mdebra@uic.edu
MATLOCK, Haley .... 580-559-5697 365 K hmatlock@ecok.edu
MATLOCK, Monica .... 907-563-7575.... 9 E monica.matlock@alaskacareercollege.edu
MATNEY, Ross .... 540-674-3613 474 E rmatney@nr.edu
MATONAK, Jessica, M . 724-287-8711 379 E jessica.matonak@bc3.edu
MATOS, Awilda .... 787-834-9595 510 D amatos@uaa.edu
MATOS, Bethany .... 559-934-2217.. 75 A bethanymatos@whccd.edu
MATOS, Carol .... 917-493-4450 305 A cmatos@msmnyc.edu
MATOS, Dania .... 209-228-3510.. 70 A
MATOS, Daniel .... 212-484-1303 294 D dmatos@jjay.cuny.edu
MATOS, Elsa .... 787-890-2681 511 G elsa.matos@upr.edu
MATOS, Emily .... 787-844-8181 513 A emily.matos@upr.edu
MATOS, Jose .... 787-751-0160 506 F jamatos@cmpr.pr.gov
MATOS, Jose .... 787-758-2525 512 F jose.matos5@upr.edu
MATOS, Juan Carlos .... 718-817-0664 300 C jmatos6@fordham.edu
MATOS, LaKeitta .... 918-343-7573 369 B lmatos@rsu.edu
MATOS, Lillian .... 787-780-0070 505 F lmatos@caribbean.edu
MATOS, Ron .... 518-783-2376 315 E rmatos@siena.edu
MATOS RODRIGUEZ, Felix, V .... 646-664-9100 292 K
MATOSO, Michael, J .... 925-631-4399.. 59 I mjm37@stmarys-ca.edu
MATOT, Diana .... 802-651-5975 462 A dmatot@champlain.edu
MATOTT, Benjamin .... 315-386-7448 320 B matot104@canton.edu
MATROS, Karen .... 870-245-5573.. 20 D matrosk@obu.edu
MATSEN, Maureen .... 757-594-7585 465 M maureen.matsen@cnu.edu
MATSON, Christine, B .. 671-735-0231 504 D christine.matson@guamcc.edu
MATSUBARA, Melissa ... 808-544-0288 128 G mmatsubara@hpu.edu
MATSUDA, Matt .... 848-932-0990 282 A mmatsuda@echo.rutgers.edu
MATSUDA, Seiichi .... 713-348-4002 442 F matsuda@rice.edu
MATSUKADO, Kevin, G . 808-544-1407 128 G kmatsukado@hpu.edu
MATSUMORI, Dylan ...... 602-384-2555.. 11 F
MATSUMOTO, David ..... 510-809-1444.. 45 M
MATSUMOTO, Mark ...... 209-228-4047.. 70 A mmatsumoto@ucmerced.edu
MATSUNAGA, Sachiko .. 831-755-6700.. 44 G smatsunaga@hartnell.edu
MATSUNO, Kenichi .... 781-239-4363 206 B matsuno@babson.edu
MATSUO, Monica .... 626-396-2268.. 26 B monica.matsuo@artcenter.edu
MATSUOKA, Jon .... 808-983-4100 128 H
MATT, Andrew .... 814-732-1564 394 B amatt@edinboro.edu
MATT, Kathleen .... 302-831-8370.. 91 C ksmatt@udel.edu
MATTACOLA, Carl, G .... 336-334-5744 343 A cgmattac@uncg.edu
MATTALIANO, John ...... 732-906-4187 278 G jmattaliano@middlesexcc.edu
MATTEI, Vivien .... 787-284-1912 508 E vmattei@ponce.inter.edu
MATTEK, Barb .... 414-443-8662 498 A barbara.mattek@wlc.edu
MATTEO, Elizabeth .... 610-790-1981 378 C elizabeth.matteo@alvernia.edu
MATTEO, Jim .... 609-258-1447 280 D jsmatteo@princeton.edu
MATTER, Shawn .... 765-677-2869 158 B shawn.matter@indwes.edu
MATTERAZZO, Susan .... 860-832-3002.. 85 G matterazzo@ccsu.edu
MATTERN, Amy .... 925-424-1383.. 35 K amattern@laspositascollege.edu
MATTERN, Retha .... 701-224-2439 346 A retha.mattern@bismarckstate.edu
MATTES, Bilita, S .... 717-901-5134 385 H bmattes@harrisburgu.edu
MATTES, Marty .... 360-596-5227 484 D mmattes@spscc.edu
MATTESON, Christi, G .. 904-264-2172 106 K christi.matteson@iws.edu
MATTESON, Kimberly .... 563-333-6339 169 G mettesonkimberly@sau.edu
MATTESON, Ryan .... 805-756-7676.. 29 I rmatteso@calpoly.edu
MATTESON, Susan, A ... 574-807-7824 154 B sue.matteson@betheluniversity.edu
MATTEY, Melissa, L ...... 443-518-4208 199 F mmattey@howardcc.edu
MATTHEIS, Lacey .... 417-690-3223 251 H lmattheis@cofo.edu
MATTHES, Kevin .... 575-538-6715 289 G kevin.matthes@wnmu.edu
MATTHES, Peter .... 319-335-3714 163 H peter-matthes@uiowa.edu
MATTHES, Peter, R .... 319-335-3549 163 H peter-matthes@uiowa.edu
MATTHEW, Dayna, B .... 202-994-1114.. 92 D lawdeanmatthew@gwu.edu
MATTHEW, Kathryn .... 281-283-3020 452 E matthew@uhcl.edu
MATTHEW CORPUS, Ben .... 863-583-9050 110 B
MATTHEWS, Adrienne ... 256-726-7398.... 6 C amatthews@oakwood.edu
MATTHEWS, Ann .... 573-840-9669 260 E amatthews@trcc.edu
MATTHEWS, Anne .... 541-888-7612 376 C amatthews@socc.edu
MATTHEWS, Buffy .... 601-928-6211 247 E buffy.matthews@mgccc.edu
MATTHEWS, Cissy .... 409-944-1203 436 E cmatthews@gc.edu
MATTHEWS, Daniel .... 405-273-5331 366 B dmatthews@familyoffaith.edu
MATTHEWS, Daniel, J ... 405-273-5331 366 B dmatthews@familyoffaith.edu
MATTHEWS, Daniell, C . 412-397-6237 397 B matthews@rmu.edu
MATTHEWS, Dennis, T .. 252-399-6345 326 K dtmatthews@barton.edu
MATTHEWS, Dennis, W 215-968-8301 379 D dennis.matthews@bucks.edu
MATTHEWS, Dirk .... 312-369-7620 136 D dmatthews@colum.edu
MATTHEWS, Dustin .... 641-472-1163 168 C dmatthews@miu.edu
MATTHEWS, Elizabeth ... 760-750-4195.. 33 A ematthew@csusm.edu
MATTHEWS, Ellen .... 903-510-2379 452 A emat@tjc.edu
MATTHEWS, Ellery .... 718-636-3603 311 F matthews@pratt.edu
MATTHEWS, Elyse .... 212-961-3390 290 H ematthews@bankstreet.edu
MATTHEWS, Emily .... 215-335-0800 388 G
MATTHEWS, Gary, C ..... 858-534-6820.. 70 C gcmatthews@ucsd.edu
MATTHEWS, Grant .... 541-463-5618 373 D matthewsg@lanecc.edu
MATTHEWS, Greg .... 802-485-2013 462 F gmatthe2@norwich.edu
MATTHEWS, John, D ..... 864-242-5100 406 H
MATTHEWS, Joseph ...... 706-864-1786 127 A joseph.matthews@ung.edu
MATTHEWS, Joyce .... 240-567-7493 200 G joyce.matthews@montgomerycollege.edu
MATTHEWS, Kenneth ..... 320-308-5382 241 A kenneth.matthews@sctcc.edu
MATTHEWS, Kismet ...... 252-792-1521 335 H
MATTHEWS, Lawrence .. 419-358-3409 348 F matthewsl@bluffton.edu
MATTHEWS, Leon .... 704-330-6524 333 D leon.matthews@cpcc.edu
MATTHEWS, Lindy, L ..... 254-267-7075 441 K lmatthews@rangercollege.edu
MATTHEWS, Matt .... 352-854-2322.. 97 N matthewm@cf.edu
MATTHEWS, Matt .... 423-425-4719 427 C matt-matthews@utc.edu
MATTHEWS, Paul .... 614-236-6211 349 B pmatthews@capital.edu
MATTHEWS, Penny .... 805-437-8909.. 30 C penny.matthews@csuci.edu
MATTHEWS, Robert .... 810-232-2511 228 F robert.matthews@mcc.edu
MATTHEWS, Robin .... 252-672-7506 334 A matthewsr@cravencc.edu
MATTHEWS, Ronald, A . 610-341-5890 383 B ron.matthews@eastern.edu
MATTHEWS, Samuel, W 405-273-5331 366 B smatthews@familyoffaith.edu
MATTHEWS, Sasha .... 757-401-6125 477 G
MATTHEWS, Stephanie .. 417-836-6603 256 G stephaniematthews@missouristate.edu
MATTHEWS, Stephen, P 518-564-3824 318 E matthesp@plattsburgh.edu
MATTHEWS, Steve, M ... 972-758-3895 433 I stevematthews@collin.edu
MATTHEWS, Thomas ..... 216-368-2188 349 D thomas.matthews@case.edu
MATTHEWS, Tim .... 859-622-8678 180 E tim.matthews@eku.edu
MATTHEWS, Tracey, D .. 256-782-5428.... 6 A tdmatthews@jsu.edu
MATTHEWS, Valencia, E .... 850-599-3430 109 I valencia.matthews@famu.edu
MATTHEWS, Victor .... 417-836-5529 256 G victormatthews@missouristate.edu
MATTHEWSON, Mansfield .... 616-234-3851 224 F mmatthew@grcc.edu
MATTHIAS, Ryan .... 402-643-7374 266 G ryan.matthias@cune.edu
MATTIACCI, John, A ..... 215-625-5400 399 B john.mattiacci@temple.edu
MATTILA, Lisa .... 413-236-1609 214 A lmattila@berkshirecc.edu
MATTINGLY, Bruce .... 607-753-4312 318 A bruce.mattingly@cortland.edu
MATTINGLY, Carole ...... 270-831-9786 182 A carole.mattingly@kctcs.edu
MATTINGLY, Chris .... 931-424-4060 427 E cmattin3@utsouthern.edu
MATTINGLY, Linda .... 843-953-6859 407 C linda.mattingly@citadel.edu
MATTIOLI, Kathy, L .... 740-283-6267 352 I kmattioli@franciscan.edu
MATTIS, JR., George, E 276-223-4744 476 A gmattis@wcc.vccs.edu
MATTIS, Jacqueline .... 973-353-5213 282 B jacqueline.mattis@rutgers.edu
MATTIS-PINARD, Rebecca .... 212-517-0562 305 E rpinard@mmm.edu
MATTISON, Debra .... 651-213-4282 236 C dmattison@hazeldenbettyford.edu
MATTISON, Emily .... 765-674-6901 158 B emily.mattison@indwes.edu
MATTISON, Sue .... 515-271-3751 165 J sue.mattison@drake.edu
MATTSON, Craig .... 708-239-4881 151 A craig.mattson@trnty.edu
MATTSON, Joanne .... 314-889-4514 253 E jmattson@fontbonne.edu
MATTSON, Michelle ...... 937-327-7915 364 D mattsonm@wittenberg.edu
MATULA, John .... 281-756-3719 429 D jmatula@alvincollege.edu
MATULIA, Michael, K ... 352-323-3643 103 U matuliam@lssc.edu
MATURI, Donna .... 781-280-3200 215 B
MATUSIK, Sharon .... 303-735-5113.. 84 B sharon.matusik@colorado.edu
MATVEY, Jessica .... 218-262-7384 238 D jessicamatvey@hibbing.edu
MATWEYCHUK, Karen ... 610-647-4980 385 L kmatweychuk@immaculata.edu
MATYE EDWARDS, Lisa 303-797-5601.. 77 I lisa.matyeedwards@arapahoe.edu
MATYNKA, Paul, J .... 248-232-4662 229 C pjmatynk@oaklandcc.edu
MATZ, Chris .... 325-942-2222 450 E chris.matz@angelo.edu
MATZ, Kurt, M .... 574-520-5522 157 E kumatz@iusb.edu
MATZ, Robert .... 573-221-3675 253 J
MATZ, Tina .... 517-787-0800 225 E matztinam@jccmi.edu
MATZKE, Brian .... 616-632-2073 221 E matzkbri@aquinas.edu
MATZKE, William .... 989-358-7259 221 C matzkew@alpenacc.edu
MATZKIN, Michael .... 641-472-7000 168 C webmaster@miu.edu
MATZNER, Alan .... 507-537-6010 241 D alan.matzner@smsu.edu
MAU, Jeremy .... 563-588-8000 166 C jmau@emmaus.edu
MAUCH, Elizabeth, K .... 785-227-3380 172 A president@bethanylb.edu
MAUCH, Tom .... 909-274-4380.. 52 J tmauch@mtsac.edu
MAUCK, Megan, J .... 330-588-2586 355 D mmauck@malone.edu
MAUDSLEY, Laura .... 360-676-2772 481 F lmaudsley@nwic.edu
MAUE, Deb .... 630-844-7572 133 D dmaue@aurora.edu
MAUER, JR., Gerard, M .... 202-685-4260 502 K gerard.m.mauer.civ@ndu.edu
MAUER, Rachel .... 215-489-2977 382 B rachel.mauer@delval.edu
MAUHS-PUGH, Thomas 802-468-6413 463 E thomas.mauhspugh@castleton.edu
MAUI, Lorraine, C .... 670-237-6708 505 A lorraine.maui@marianas.edu
MAUK, Andy .... 910-962-7638 343 C mauka@uncw.edu
MAUK, Teresa .... 401-598-4478 404 D teresa.mauk@jwu.edu
MAULDIN, Brad .... 575-562-2393 286 B bradley.mauldin@enmu.edu
MAULDIN, Teena, P ..... 704-463-3031 339 E teena.mauldin@pfeiffer.edu
MAULTSBY, Bill .... 910-788-6310 338 A bill.maultsby@sccnc.edu
MAUN, Duane, F .... 717-901-5120 385 H dmaun@harrisburgu.edu
MAUNE, Dietrich .... 540-568-7002 468 C maunedx@jmu.edu
MAUNEY, Richard .... 773-371-5442 134 D rmauney@ctu.edu
MAUNSELL, Jody .... 802-828-8724 463 B jody.maunsell@vcfa.edu
MAURANA, Cheryl, A ... 414-955-8075 493 F cmaurana@mcw.edu
MAURANO, Steven, J ... 401-865-2775 404 F smaurano@providence.edu
MAURER, Amanda, C ... 813-974-4126 111 C amaurer@usf.edu
MAURER, Amybeth .... 847-214-7423 137 F amaurer@elgin.edu
MAURER, Caroline .... 206-281-2366 483 G cmaurer@spu.edu
MAURER, Charles .... 212-757-1190 290 D cmaurer@aami.edu

MAURER, Erin .... 864-231-2000 406 F
emaurer@andersonuniversity.edu
MAURER, Gaylyn .... 541-885-1800 374 I
gaylyn.maurer@oit.edu
MAURER, Lynn .... 409-880-8508 449 G
lmaurer@lamar.edu
MAURER, Paul, J .... 828-669-8012 331 K
president@montreat.edu
MAURER, Ryan .... 937-327-6114 364 D
rmaurer@wittenberg.edu
MAURER, Stace .... 503-760-3131 371 G
stace@birthingway.edu
MAURER, Tena .... 570-389-4000 393 D
MAURER, William, M ... 949-824-6802.. 69 D
wmmaurer@uci.edu
MAURICE, JR.,
John, W .... 252-334-2004 331 F
president@macuniversity.edu
MAURIELLO, Thomas .... 718-862-7241 304 M
thomas.mauriello@manhattan.edu
MAURIN, Kay .... 985-549-2507 193 A
kay.maurin@selu.edu
MAURO, Ann Marie ...... 732-263-5271 279 A
amauro@monmouth.edu
MAURO, Anthony .... 724-938-1653 393 E
mauro@calu.edu
MAURO, Brian .... 973-443-8343 277 I
brian_mauro@fdu.edu
MAURO, Laurie .... 304-263-6262 487 F
lmauro@martinsburgcollege.edu
MAURO, Linda .... 212-986-4343 291 E
lsp@berkeleycollege.edu
MAURO, Steven, A .... 814-871-7605 384 A
mauro003@gannon.edu
MAUS, Sharon .... 610-861-1536 390 F
mauss@moravia.edu
MAUST, Donielle, R ..... 304-293-4245 490 E
donielle.maust@mail.wvu.edu
MAUST, Heather .... 740-857-1311 360 D
hmaust@rosedale.edu
MAUST, Scott .... 309-341-7892 141 G
smaust@knox.edu
MAUSZYCKI, Christine .. 605-995-2737 415 A
christine.mauszycki@dwu.edu
MAUZY, Stephanie .... 314-446-8419 260 H
stephanie.hoffmann@stlcop.edu
MAVALVALA, Nergis ..... 617-253-8900 216 B
MAVITY-MADDALENA,
Julie, A .... 920-565-1000 493 A
mavmadja@lakeland.edu
MAVRINAC, Mary Ann .. 585-275-4461 323 M
maryann.mavrinac@rochester.edu
MAVROS, Jeff .... 309-438-2181 140 D
jmavros@ilstu.edu
MAW, Elizabeth .... 415-561-6555.. 58 B
MAWUNTU, Valencia .... 269-471-3484 221 D
valencia@andrews.edu
MAX, Claire .... 831-459-2991.. 71 A
cemax@ucsc.edu
MAX, Rosemary .... 248-370-4730 229 I
rmax@oakland.edu
MAX, Sheryl .... 816-995-2842 258 G
sheryl.max@researchcollege.edu
MAXEINER, Amy .... 309-796-5043 133 G
maxeinera@bhc.edu
MAXEY, Evie .... 864-231-2000 406 F
emaxey@andersonuniversity.edu
MAXEY, JoAnn .... 501-686-2515.. 21 E
jmaxey@uasys.edu
MAXEY, Larry .... 619-388-5940.. 60 J
lmaxey@sdccd.edu
MAXEY, Michael, C ...... 540-375-2200 470 E
maxey@roanoke.edu
MAXEY, Susan .... 606-783-2317 184 C
s.maxey@moreheadstate.edu
MAXFIELD, John .... 303-963-3228.. 78 H
jmaxfield@ccu.edu
MAXFIELD, Sylvia .... 401-865-1224 404 F
maxfield@providence.edu
MAXIE, Donell .... 662-254-3577 248 B
donell.maxie@mvsu.edu
MAXIE, Leslie .... 502-272-3101 179 H
lmaxie@bellarmine.edu
MAXSON, Amanda .... 901-843-3885 423 A
registrar@rhodes.edu
MAXSON, Kathi .... 605-718-2401 417 D
katherine.maxson@wdt.edu
MAXWELL, Barbara, A .. 509-527-5208 486 B
maxwelba@whitman.edu
MAXWELL, Ben .... 864-587-4251 412 F
maxwellb@smcsc.edu
MAXWELL, Brandon, T . 404-687-4522 117 G
maxwellb@ctsnet.edu
MAXWELL, Cathy .... 303-292-0015.. 80 H
cmaxwell@denvercollegeofnursing.edu
MAXWELL, Chris .... 706-245-7226 118 D
cmaxwell@ec.edu
MAXWELL, Colin .... 800-477-2254.. 29 G
cmaxwell@calsouthern.edu
MAXWELL, Daniel .... 713-743-5390 452 D
dmmaxwell@central.uh.edu
MAXWELL, Drew .... 414-847-3317 494 C
drewmaxwell@miad.edu
MAXWELL, James .... 423-869-6298 421 A
james.maxwell@lmunet.edu
MAXWELL, James .... 972-524-3341 445 B
jamxw@swcc.edu
MAXWELL, Jewerl .... 978-867-4118 210 B
jewerl.maxwell@gordon.edu
MAXWELL, Kate .... 410-827-5802 198 F
kmaxwell@chesapeake.edu
MAXWELL, Kim .... 970-542-3192.. 81 N
kim.maxwell@morgancc.edu
MAXWELL, Logan .... 903-463-2646 436 G
maxwelll@grayson.edu
MAXWELL, Mardell .... 832-842-9058 452 D
mrmaxwell@central.uh.edu
MAXWELL, Monique ..... 703-445-9056 472 G
MAXWELL, Noel .... 907-745-3201.... 9 C
nmaxwell@akbible.edu
MAXWELL, Sharon .... 630-844-5630 133 D
smaxwell@aurora.edu
MAXWELL, Sharon .... 214-818-1353 433 O
smaxwell@criswell.edu
MAXWELL, Tanisha .... 925-473-7421.. 40 D
tmaxwell@losmedanos.edu
MAXWELL, Valarie .... 940-397-4346 440 C
valarie.maxwell@msutexas.edu
MAXWELL-DOHERTY,
Melissa .... 805-493-3330.. 29 C
revmmmd@callutheran.edu
MAY, Barbara .... 320-363-5401 243 B
bmay@csbsju.edu
MAY, Barbara .... 320-363-5401 235 F
bmay@csbsju.edu
MAY, Bryan .... 803-778-7841 406 I
maybw@cctech.edu
MAY, Caleb .... 785-539-3571 176 A
caleb.may@mccks.edu
MAY, Cathryn .... 601-635-6238 246 A
cmay@eccc.edu
MAY, Charles, A .... 573-882-7744 261 A
mayc@missouri.edu
MAY, Christopher, V .... 314-977-3167 259 F
christopher.may@slu.edu
MAY, David .... 509-359-7900 479 G
dmay@ewu.edu
MAY, David, J .... 603-862-2727 274 F
david.may@unh.edu
MAY, Gary, S .... 530-752-2065.. 69 B
chancellor@ucdavis.edu
MAY, Ginny, A .... 248-218-2018 230 B
gmay@rochesteru.edu
MAY, Janet .... 713-718-8570 437 C
janet.may2@hccs.edu
MAY, Joanna .... 413-584-2700 218 H
MAY, Joe, D .... 214-378-1601 434 E
jmay@dcccd.edu
MAY, Karen .... 314-340-3880 254 A
mayk@hssu.edu
MAY, Libby .... 603-645-9698 274 C
l.may@snhu.edu
MAY, MaryAnn .... 334-699-2266.... 1 B
mmay@acom.edu
MAY, Michael .... 724-738-4573 395 C
michael.may@sru.edu
MAY, Mindy .... 937-766-7855 349 E
mkmay@cedarville.edu
MAY, Nina .... 609-586-4800 278 F
mayn@mccc.edu
MAY, Nita .... 903-434-8113 440 G
nmay@ntcc.edu
MAY, Robert, E .... 276-739-2436 475 F
rmay@vhcc.edu
MAY, Ronald .... 253-964-6736 482 E
rmay@pierce.ctc.edu
MAY, Sarah, E .... 478-301-2413 122 E
may_se@mercer.edu
MAY, Susan .... 618-985-2828 140 H
susanmay@jalc.edu
MAY, Susan, A .... 920-735-5731 498 F
may@fvtc.edu
MAY, Tammie .... 816-604-4018 255 C
tammie.may@mcckc.edu
MAY, Walter, P .... 770-720-5540 124 G
wpm@reinhardt.edu
MAY-RICCIUTI, Heather . 304-829-7335 487 A
hricciuti@bethanywv.edu
MAYAN, Kathy .... 410-386-8110 198 D
kmayan@carrollcc.edu
MAYBANK, Denise, B ... 646-664-9100 292 K
MAYDEN, Sharrie .... 702-895-0970 271 D
sharrie.mayden@unlv.edu
MAYEA, Bethany .... 810-989-5537 230 F
blmayea@sc4.edu
MAYER, Cathy .... 847-735-5054 142 A
cmayer@lakeforest.edu
MAYER, Charles .... 336-249-8186 334 B
cmayer@davidsondavie.edu
MAYER, Connie .... 518-445-2393 289 K
cmaye@albanylaw.edu
MAYER, Fritz .... 303-871-6338.. 84 E
frederick.mayer@du.edu
MAYER, Jason .... 425-235-5555 482 H
jmayer@rtc.edu
MAYER, Kasey .... 913-288-7240 175 B
kmayer@kckcc.edu
MAYER, Kathy .... 608-262-1605 495 C
kmayer@uwsa.edu
MAYER, Kerry .... 707-476-4326.. 58 I
kerry-mayer@redwoods.edu
MAYER, Louis .... 201-216-8761 283 D
louis.mayer@stevens.edu
MAYER, Lynn .... 202-319-5220.. 92 A
mayer@cua.edu
MAYER, Patrick .... 606-451-6702 182 G
patrick.mayer@kctcs.edu
MAYER, Susan .... 623-845-3849.. 13 C
susan.mayer@gccaz.edu
MAYER, Thomas .... 803-793-5197 408 G
mayert@denmarktech.edu
MAYERS, Brock .... 804-257-5875 476 F
bmayers@vuu.edu
MAYERS, Kendra .... 804-342-3939 476 F
kmayers@vuu.edu
MAYERSKI, Christopher 570-408-7890 403 A
christopher.mayerski@wilkes.edu
MAYES, Carey, J .... 512-464-8822 442 I
careym@stedwards.edu
MAYES, David .... 501-882-4432.. 17 D
dmmayes@asub.edu
MAYES, John, A .... 203-432-8049.. 90 C
john.mayes@yale.edu
MAYES, Larry, D .... 336-334-9876 343 A
ldmayes@uncg.edu
MAYES, LaVerne .... 215-871-6560 395 G
lavernema@pcom.edu
MAYES, Lisa .... 757-683-6746 469 B
lmayes@odu.edu
MAYES, Nathan .... 660-284-4800 254 B
MAYEUX, Liza .... 225-490-1664 187 B
liza.mayeux@franu.edu
MAYFIEDL MULLEN,
Jana .... 805-565-6144.. 76 A
jmayfield@westmont.edu
MAYFIELD, Amanda, B . 860-439-2088.. 87 H
amanda.mayfield@conncoll.edu
MAYFIELD, Charles .... 660-562-1138 257 E
mayfield@nwmissouri.edu
MAYFIELD, Donny .... 423-746-5253 426 C
dmayfield@tnwesleyan.edu
MAYFIELD, Janet .... 314-392-2355 256 E
mayfij@mobap.edu
MAYFIELD, Pamela .... 254-867-3118 449 D
pamela.mayfield@tstc.edu
MAYFIELD-BURFORD,
Rosetta .... 901-321-3119 418 G
rmayfie1@cbu.edu
MAYHER, Michael, E .... 440-525-7255 354 L
mmayher@lakelandcc.edu
MAYHEW, Alyssa .... 281-931-7717 121 I
amayhew@ict.edu
MAYHEW, Sam .... 423-439-4286 419 G
mayhew@etsu.edu
MAYHEW, Susan, L ...... 276-498-5201 464 D
slmayhew@acp.edu
MAYLE, Chad, A .... 304-457-6410 486 E
mayleca@ab.edu
MAYLE, Tony .... 740-376-3287 355 E
aam006@marietta.edu
MAYLOR, Andrew .... 978-837-5000 216 F
maylora@merrimack.edu
MAYNARD, Charmel ..... 305-284-9587 113 C
cmaynard@miami.edu
MAYNARD, Chris .... 936-294-1006 450 A
maynard@shsu.edu
MAYNARD, Craig .... 309-467-6305 138 A
cmaynard@eurka.edu
MAYNARD, Francyenne 972-273-3015 435 B
fmaynard@dcccd.edu
MAYNARD, Gene .... 916-348-4689.. 41 H
gmaynard@epic.edu
MAYNARD, Kimberly, L 304-896-7345 488 I
kimberly.maynard@southernwv.edu
MAYNARD, Nelly .... 773-821-2453 134 K
nmaynard@csu.edu
MAYNARD, Thurmond .. 301-696-3546 199 E
maynard@hood.edu
MAYNARD-ERRAMI,
Nickcole .... 434-381-6478 471 I
nmaynarderrami@sbc.edu
MAYNARD NELSON,
Jeanette .... 612-767-7043 233 H
jeanette@alfredadler.edu
MAYNARD-REID,
Pedrito .... 509-527-2028 485 C
pedrito.maynard-reid@wallawalla.edu
MAYNC, Tania .... 213-740-2311.. 73 C
MAYNE, Kevin .... 802-387-6716 462 C
kevinmayne@landmark.edu
MAYNES, Leslie .... 515-271-2011 165 J
leslie.maynes@drake.edu
MAYO, Christy .... 616-234-5722 232 B
christy.mayo@vai.edu
MAYO, Dan .... 252-493-7531 336 H
dmayo@email.pittcc.edu
MAYO, Jacqueline .... 704-403-1326 327 C
jacqueline.mayo@atriumhealth.org
MAYO, Jennifer .... 919-739-6721 338 H
jbmayo@waynecc.edu
MAYO, Julia .... 503-517-1856 377 E
jmayo@westernseminary.edu
MAYO, Karen .... 859-246-6525 181 F
karen.mayo@kctcs.edu
MAYO, Kathy .... 252-249-1851 336 F
kmayo@pamlicocc.edu
MAYO, Kelly .... 847-491-3741 146 E
tgsdean@northwestern.edu
MAYO, Michele .... 252-940-6233 332 C
michele.mayo@beaufortccc.edu
MAYO, Michelle, L .... 919-530-7149 341 E
mlmayo@nccu.edu
MAYO, Michelle, P .... 585-292-2370 307 B
mmayo@monroecc.edu
MAYO, Rachel .... 831-786-4710.. 27 D
ramayo@cabrillo.edu
MAYO, Sandra .... 206-281-2515 483 G
mayos@spu.edu
MAYOR, Ryan .... 651-846-1305 241 B
ryan.mayer@saintpaul.edu
MAYOR-GLENN,
Jennifer, A .... 801-972-3596 459 O
j.mayer-glenn@partners.utah.edu
MAYORAL, Eliza .... 480-245-7930.. 12 M
eliza.mayoral@ibcs.edu
MAYRAND, Leslie .... 325-486-6247 450 E
leslie.mayrand@angelo.edu
MAYRL, Matt .... 608-262-1165 495 D
matthew.mayrl@wisc.edu
MAYROSE, James .... 716-878-5550 317 F
mayrosj@buffalostate.edu
MAYS, Beth, A .... 410-777-2480 197 G
bamays@aacc.edu
MAYS, Cathy .... 434-381-6448 471 I
cdmays@sbc.edu
MAYS, Elizabeth .... 714-772-3330.. 25 M
MAYS, Florence .... 803-822-3419 410 D
maysf@midlandstech.edu
MAYS, Justin .... 678-466-5544 117 D
justinmays@clayton.edu
MAYS, Justin .... 417-667-8181 252 B
jmays@cottey.edu
MAYS, Lisa .... 937-433-3410 352 G
lmays@fortiscollege.edu
MAYS, Nathaniel .... 617-349-8539 211 C
nmays@lesley.edu
MAYS, Susan .... 615-550-3161 428 E
susan@williamsoncc.edu
MAYS, Theresa .... 334-420-4296.... 3 H
tmays@trenholmstate.edu
MAYS, Thomas .... 301-546-7594 201 E
maysto@pgcc.edu
MAYS-JACKSON, Debra 601-979-2323 246 F
debra.mays-jackson@jsums.edu
MAYSE, Tiffany .... 859-572-5806 184 E
masyset@nku.edu
MAYSENT, Patty .... 858-249-5534.. 70 C
pmaysent@ucsd.edu
MAZA, Antonio .... 703-416-1441 466 A
amaza@divinemercy.edu
MAZA, Octavio .... 786-331-1000 104 H
octavio.maza@maufl.edu

MCCALL, Suzanne .... 479-964-0898.. 18 C
smccall@atu.edu
MCCALLEY, Greg .... 607-844-8222 322 D
jgm006@tompkinscortland.edu
MCCALLIE, Kathleen, D . 918-270-6441 368 G
kathy.mccallie@ptstulsa.edu
MCCALLIN, Julia, M ..... 626-395-3230.. 28 J
julia.mccallin@caltech.edu
MCCALLISTER, Mark ...... 352-392-0371 111 A
markm@ufl.edu
MCCALLUM, Jodee .... 952-358-8271 239 G
jodee.mccallum@normandale.edu
MCCALLUM, Rex, M ...... 409-772-3639 456 E
remccall@utmb.edu
MCCALLUM BEATTY,
Krista .... 517-353-1720 227 F
kristamb@msu.edu
MCCAMBRIDGE, Wendy 630-942-2269 135 I
mccambridgew@cod.edu
MCCAMBRY, Al .... 850-769-1551 101 N
amccambr1@gulfcoast.edu
MCCAMEY, Marilyn .... 206-934-3198 483 C
marilyn.mccamey@seattlecolleges.edu
MCCAMIS, Jennifer .... 937-775-5703 364 E
jennifer.mccamis@wright.edu
MCCAMISH, Daniel .... 937-481-2280 364 A
daniel_mccamish@wilmington.edu
MCCAMPBELL LIEN,
Margaret .... 540-535-3531 470 G
mmccampb@su.edu
MCCANDLESS, Ann .... 724-287-8711 379 E
ann.mccandless@bc3.edu
MCCANDLESS, John ...... 513-529-2223 356 A
mccandjm@miamioh.edu
MCCANDLESS, Michael . 209-384-6185.. 52 A
mccandless.m@mccd.edu
MCCANDLESS,
Raymond .... 419-434-4565 362 D
mccandless@findlay.edu
MCCANN, Bonnie .... 614-947-6017 352 J
bonnie.mccann@franklin.edu
MCCANN, Elizabeth .... 949-582-4481.. 65 D
emccann@saddleback.edu
MCCANN, Erin .... 201-761-7362 283 A
emccann@saintpeters.edu
MCCANN, Kevin .... 802-860-2754 462 A
kmccann@champlain.edu
MCCANN, Maggie .... 225-768-1783 187 B
maggie.mccann@franu.edu
MCCANN, Mitch .... 805-922-6966.. 24 I
mitch.mccann@hancockcollege.edu
MCCANN, Paul, A .... 217-581-2979 137 E
pmccann@eiu.edu
MCCARDLE, Elizabeth .... 386-752-1822 100 B
elizabeth.mccardle@fgc.edu
MCCAREY, Christine ...... 508-362-2131 214 D
cmccarey@capecod.edu
MCCARGO, Donavan ..... 610-683-1396 394 D
mccargo@kutztown.edu
MCCARLEY, Erin .... 503-842-8222 376 E
erinmccarley@tillamookbaycc.edu
MCCARN, Sarah .... 912-525-5000 124 I
smccarn@scad.edu
MCCARRAGHER,
Timothy, M .... 330-972-5976 361 H
mccarra@uakron.edu
MCCARRELL, Kyle .... 708-239-4797 151 A
kyle.mccarrell@trnty.edu
MCCARRICK, Ashley ...... 914-594-4900 309 B
amccarri@nymc.edu
MCCARRICK,
Richard, G .... 914-594-4503 309 B
richard_mccarrick@nymc.edu
MCCARRIE, Ashley .... 267-502-2400 379 A
MCCARRON, Anne .... 414-382-6068 491 F
anne.mccarron@alverno.edu
MCCARRON, Cathy .... 508-362-2131 214 D
MCCARRY, Tim .... 325-670-1434 436 I
facilities@hsutx.edu
MCCARTAN, Brian .... 206-616-2021 485 A
bpmcc@uw.edu
MCCARTER, Iika .... 662-329-7103 248 A
itmccarter@muw.edu
MCCARTHY, Alison .... 860-773-1487.. 87 G
amccarthy@tunxis.edu
MCCARTHY, Anne .... 651-523-2335 236 B
amccarthy02@hamline.edu
MCCARTHY, Anne .... 402-375-7215 268 F
anmccar1@wsc.edu
MCCARTHY, Barbara ..... 914-773-3741 311 A
bmccarthy@pace.edu
MCCARTHY, Brendan .... 904-256-7550 102 H
bmccart3@ju.edu
MCCARTHY, Brian .... 480-858-9100.. 15 Q
b.mccarthy1@scnm.edu
MCCARTHY, Carlie .... 530-283-0202.. 42 A
cmccarthy@frc.edu
MCCARTHY, Casey, J .... 218-755-3888 237 F
casey.mccarthy@bemidjistate.edu
MCCARTHY, Charles ..... 610-604-7700.. 93 H
MCCARTHY, Colby .... 973-408-3112 277 A
finaid@drew.edu
MCCARTHY, Cynthia ..... 732-987-2254 278 A
cmccarthy@georgian.edu
MCCARTHY, Daniel .... 985-549-2055 193 A
dmccarthy@selu.edu
MCCARTHY, David, M ... 301-447-5333 201 B
dmccarth@msmary.edu
MCCARTHY, Dennis, K .. 805-525-4417.. 67 K
dmccarthy@thomasaquinas.edu
MCCARTHY, Diane .... 508-289-2502 220 E
dmccarthy@whoi.edu
MCCARTHY, Dominica .. 972-860-4689 434 F
dmccarthy@dcccd.edu
MCCARTHY, Douglas .... 602-285-7245.. 13 F
douglas.mccarthy@phoenixcollege.edu
MCCARTHY, Faith .... 530-221-4275.. 64 B
registrar@shasta.edu
MCCARTHY, Faith .... 530-221-4275.. 64 B
fmccarthy@shasta.edu
MCCARTHY, Ginny .... 708-216-3245 143 C
vmccarthy@luc.edu
MCCARTHY, James .... 978-921-4242 217 B
jim.mccarthy@montserrat.edu
MCCARTHY, John .... 740-593-9336 358 K
mccarthj@ohio.edu
MCCARTHY, John, C ..... 202-319-5259.. 92 A
mccartjc@cua.edu
MCCARTHY, John, J ..... 413-545-6223 211 G
jmccarthy@provost.umass.edu
MCCARTHY, Joseph, J .. 412-624-0790 400 H
jjmcc@pitt.edu
MCCARTHY, Kate .... 530-898-6650.. 30 D
kmccarthy@csuchico.edu
MCCARTHY, Kate .... 802-635-1458 463 G
kathleen.mccarthy@northernvermont.
edu
MCCARTHY,
Katherine, M .... 315-470-4945 319 D
kmccar10@esf.edu
MCCARTHY, Kevin .... 704-330-6907 333 D
kevin.mccarthy@cpcc.edu
MCCARTHY, Kevin .... 757-822-7042 475 E
kmccarthy@tcc.edu
MCCARTHY, Kevin .... 315-568-3267 310 B
kmccarthy@nycc.edu
MCCARTHY, Kevin .... 803-508-7337 406 C
mccarthk@atc.edu
MCCARTHY, Kevin, D .... 425-235-2235 482 H
kmccarthy@rtc.edu
MCCARTHY, Kristin, C .. 617-422-7418 217 F
kmccarthy@nesl.edu
MCCARTHY, Marsha ...... 908-737-7100 278 E
mmccarth@kean.edu
MCCARTHY, Maureen .... 765-285-1042 153 H
mmccarthy@bsu.edu
MCCARTHY, Maureen .... 215-968-8058 379 D
maureen.mccarthy@bucks.edu
MCCARTHY, Megan .... 270-686-4255 179 J
megan.mccarthy@brescia.edu
MCCARTHY, Melissa ..... 401-874-2599 405 E
mcmel@uri.edu
MCCARTHY, Michael, R 978-556-3924 215 E
mmccarthy1@necc.mass.edu
MCCARTHY, Michelle .... 607-587-3917 319 F
mccartma@alfredstate.edu
MCCARTHY, Patricia ...... 724-357-7544 394 C
mccarthy@iup.edu
MCCARTHY, Patrick .... 619-594-1643.. 33 D
pmccarthy@sdsu.edu
MCCARTHY, Piper .... 775-445-3270 271 F
piper.mccarthy@wnc.edu
MCCARTHY, Robert .... 207-221-4365 197 E
rmccarthy2@une.edu
MCCARTHY, Rosemary .. 412-536-1173 386 H
rosemary.mccarthy@laroche.edu
MCCARTHY, Ryan .... 718-289-5338 293 B
ryan.mccarthy@bcc.cuny.edu
MCCARTHY, Sherry .... 712-279-3158 169 H
sherry.mccarthy@stlukescollege.edu
MCCARTHY, William ...... 973-353-3292 282 B
wm307@scj.rutgers.edu
MCCARTNEY, Cliff .... 865-573-4517 420 E
cmccartney@johnsonu.edu
MCCARTNEY, Jill .... 740-427-5811 354 I
mccartney1@kenyon.edu
MCCARTNEY, Kathleen .. 413-585-2100 218 H
kmccartney@smith.edu
MCCARTNEY,
William, G .... 765-496-2267 160 B
mccart@purdue.edu
MCCARTNEY, JR.,
William, L .... 252-328-6050 341 A
mccartneyw@ecu.edu
MCCARTY, Alison .... 781-239-2506 214 G
amccarty1@massbay.edu
MCCARTY, Kevin .... 512-245-5500 450 C
km20@txstate.edu
MCCARTY, Lori .... 706-272-4462 118 B
lmccarty@daltonstate.edu
MCCARTY, Michael .... 502-897-4720 184 G
mmccarty@sbts.edu
MCCARTY, Nolan .... 609-258-4796 280 D
MCCARTY, Philips, R .... 212-217-4100 299 D
philips_mccarty@fitnyc.edu
MCCARTY, Rich .... 860-528-4111.. 88 A
rmccarty@goodwin.edu
MCCARTY, Rich, M .... 203-576-2354.. 89 C
rmccarty@bridgeport.edu
MCCARTY, Steve .... 270-831-9803 182 A
steve.mccarty@kctcs.edu
MCCARTY, Susan .... 212-772-4850 294 C
susan.mccarty@hunter.cuny.edu
MCCARVER, Viva .... 419-372-8421 348 G
vivam@bgsu.edu
MCCARVILLE, Jeanie ..... 515-965-7120 165 A
jamccarville1@dmacc.edu
MCCARY, Jennifer, Q .... 419-372-2147 348 G
jmccary@bgsu.edu
MCCASKEY, Mary .... 931-372-3503 426 B
mamccaskey@tntech.edu
MCCASKILL, John .... 803-535-1264 411 B
mccaskill@octech.edu
MCCASKILL, Sharrell ..... 202-651-5642.. 92 C
sharrell.mccaskill@gallaudet.edu
MCCASLAND, Shannon . 970-339-6563.. 77 H
shannon.mccasland@aims.edu
MCCASLIN, Blake .... 423-745-7504 426 C
bmccaslin@tnwesleyan.edu
MCCASLIN, Jaime .... 814-871-7330 384 A
mccaslin007@gannon.edu
MCCASLIN, James .... 270-901-1112 182 H
james.mccaslin@kctcs.edu
MCCASLIN, Julie .... 423-746-5214 426 C
jmccaslin@tnwesleyan.edu
MCCASLIN, Sharon .... 314-889-4567 253 E
smccaslin@fontbonne.edu
MCCAULEY, David, W ... 304-473-8322 491 D
mccauley@wvwc.edu
MCCAULEY, Dennis .... 215-968-8394 379 D
dennis.mccauley@bucks.edu
MCCAULEY, Juli .... 806-743-2848 450 F
juli.mccauley@ttuhsc.edu
MCCAULEY, Justin .... 508-531-1277 212 D
jmccauley@bridgew.edu
MCCAULEY, Justin .... 402-878-2380 267 D
justin.mccauley@littlepriest.edu
MCCAULEY, Karen .... 404-962-3056 127 D
karen.mccauley@usg.edu
MCCAULEY, Laurie, K ... 734-763-3311 231 H
mccauley@umich.edu
MCCAULEY, Linda .... 404-727-7976 118 E
linda.mccauley@emory.edu
MCCAULEY, Linda .... 559-737-6194.. 39 B
lindam@cos.edu
MCCAULEY, Michele ..... 269-749-7141 229 J
mmccauley@olivetcollege.edu
MCCAULEY JUGOVICH,
Shelly .... 218-748-2416 238 H
s.mccauley@mesabirange.edu
MCCAULEY-JUGOVICH,
Shelly .... 218-748-2416 238 H
s.mccauley@mesabirange.edu
MCCAULLEY, Michelle .. 573-875-8700 251 I
MCCAUSLAND, Bill .... 813-974-1868 111 C
mccausland@usf.edu
MCCAW, Ian .... 434-582-2100 468 E
ijmccaw@liberty.edu
MCCAW, Shawn .... 314-889-4686 253 E
smccaw@fontbonne.edu
MCCAY, Megan .... 601-266-4059 249 F
megan.mccay@usm.edu
MCCAY, T. Dwayne .... 321-674-8099 100 C
tdmccay@fit.edu
MCCHESENEY-YOUNG,
Mary .... 510-204-0731.. 36 I
mmcchesneyyoung@gtu.edu
MCCHESNEY-YOUNG,
Mary .... 510-204-0731.. 36 I
mmcchesney-young@cdsp.edu
MCCHORD, Jennifer, J .. 859-858-3511 179 D
jennifer.mcchord@asbury.edu
MCCHURCH, Bob .... 309-796-5013 133 G
mcchurchb@bhc.edu
MCCLAFFERTY, Joseph . 406-496-4804 265 A
jmcclafferty@mtech.edu
MCCLAIN, Barbara, L .... 304-326-1234 487 I
bmcclain@salemu.edu
MCCLAIN, Carol, M ...... 803-934-3430 410 G
cmcclain@morris.edu
MCCLAIN, Elizabeth ...... 479-308-2286.. 17 A
elizabeth.mcclain@acheedu.org
MCCLAIN, Elman .... 773-244-5222 145 G
memcclain@northpark.edu
MCCLAIN, James, W ..... 870-838-2910.. 17 B
jmcclain@smail.anc.edu
MCCLAIN, Janet .... 617-585-0200 207 A
janet.mcclain@the-bac.edu
MCCLAIN, Jeremy .... 601-266-5017 249 F
jeremy.mcclain@usm.edu
MCCLAIN, Jessica .... 352-854-2322.. 97 N
MCCLAIN, Lisa, L .... 504-520-7593 193 E
lmcclain@xula.edu
MCCLAIN, Michael .... 803-981-7126 414 F
mmclain@yorktech.edu
MCCLAIN, Paula, D .... 919-681-1560 328 F
pmmclain@duke.edu
MCCLAIN, Rance .... 479-308-2382.. 17 A
rance.mcclain@arcomedu.org
MCCLAIN, Samantha, E 515-574-1080 167 A
mcclain@iowacentral.edu
MCCLAIN, Tamara .... 630-942-2422 135 I
mccalint57@cod.edu
MCCLANAHAN, Barry .... 717-477-1701 395 B
bkmcca@ship.edu
MCCLANAHAN, Denise . 434-961-5275 474 I
dmcclanahan@pvcc.edu
MCCLANAHAN,
Elizabeth .... 540-231-2265 476 C
elizabeth.mcclanahan@vtf.org
MCCLANAHAN, Keith .... 870-762-3151.. 17 B
kmcclanahan@smail.anc.edu
MCCLANE, Curtis .... 423-775-6596 422 I
cmcclane@ogs.edu
MCCLARNON, Ryan .... 317-738-8758 155 D
rmclarnon@franklincollege.edu
MCCLAY, Kelly .... 609-343-4939 275 D
mcclay@atlantic.edu
MCCLAY, Liam .... 352-395-5199 108 A
liam.mcclay@sfcollege.edu
MCCLEARN, Keith .... 706-419-1209 118 A
keith.mcclearn@covenant.edu
MCCLEARY, Jillian .... 563-884-5726 169 F
jillian.mccleary@palmer.edu
MCCLEARY, Tim .... 406-638-3121 263 G
baaxpaa@lbhc.edu
MCCLELLAN, Amy .... 937-393-3431 360 H
amcclellan@sscc.edu
MCCLELLAN, Amy .... 937-393-3431 360 H
MCCLELLAN, Ann, K ..... 603-535-3500 275 A
akmcclellan@plymouth.edu
MCCLELLAN, Jane .... 201-200-3196 279 D
jmcclellan@njcu.edu
MCCLELLAN, Laura .... 276-739-2425 475 F
lmcclellan@vhcc.edu
MCCLELLAN, Mark .... 870-733-6722.. 17 F
mpmcclellan@asumidsouth.edu
MCCLELLAN, Mia .... 619-482-6542.. 66 A
mmcclellan@swccd.edu
MCCLELLAN, Scott .... 206-220-8229 484 A
mcclells@seattleu.edu
MCCLELLAN, Teri .... 352-381-3625 108 A
teri.mcclellan@sfcollege.edu
MCCLELLAND, Jeremy ... 214-860-2351 434 I
jmcclelland@dcccd.edu
MCCLELLAND, Karin ...... 925-631-4013.. 59 I
klm14@stmarys-ca.edu
MCCLELLAND, Paul .... 740-826-8468 356 H
paulm@muskingum.edu
MCCLELLON, Leslie, R .. 313-670-9300 191 D
lmcclellon@susla.edu
MCCLENAGAN,
Cindy, M .... 806-291-3410 457 I
cindym@wbu.edu
MCCLENAHAN, Lindsey 415-422-6423.. 72 J
lmcclenahan@usfca.edu
MCCLENDON, Dawn ...... 541-278-5937 371 H
ddifuria@bluecc.edu
MCCLENDON, Karen ..... 916-686-8602.. 29 E
MCCLENDON, Michael .. 918-631-2742 371 C
michael-mcclendon@utulsa.edu
MCCLENDON, Michael .. 918-631-2200 371 C
michael-mcclendon@utulsa.edu

MCCLENDON, Vivienne . 281-283-3931 452 E
mcclendonv@uhcl.edu
MCCLENNEY, Elizabeth .. 540-375-2293 470 E
mcclenney@roanoke.edu
MCCLENNY, Bradley ...... 903-463-8749 436 G
mcclennyb@grayson.edu
MCCLIN, Raul .... 787-761-0640 511 E
online@utcpr.edu
MCCLINTICK, Wes .... 208-885-7994 132 F
mcclintick@uidaho.edu
MCCLINTOCK, Angela ... 314-838-8858 261 F
amcclintock@ugst.edu
MCCLINTOCK,
Elizabeth, A .... 412-578-6018 380 B
eamcclintock@carlow.edu
MCCLINTOCK, Grace ..... 831-459-4300.. 71 A
grace@ucsc.edu
MCCLINTOCK, Jonathan 314-838-8858 261 F
jmcclintock@ugst.edu
MCCLINTOCK,
Melvin, A .... 240-895-4309 202 B
mamcclintock@smcm.edu
MCCLINTOCK, Patty ...... 812-237-2305 156 D
patty.mcclintock@indstate.edu
MCCLINTOCK-COMEAUX,
Marta .... 724-938-5246 393 E
mcclintock@calu.edu
MCCLINTON, Angela ..... 281-646-1109 431 G
angela.mcclinton@thebibleseminary.edu
MCCLINTON, Flandus ... 225-771-5550 191 B
flandus_mcclinton@sus.edu
MCCLINTON, Flandus ... 225-771-5550 191 A
flandus_mcclinton@sus.edu
MCCLINTON, Leon .... 405-744-9164 367 G
leon.mcclinton@okstate.edu
MCCLINTON, Lisa, R ..... 252-335-8792 341 B
lrmcclinton@ecsu.edu
MCCLINTON, Martin ...... 239-483-6798 101 A
martin.mcclinton@fsw.edu
MCCLOSKEY, Dan, E ..... 646-664-8910 292 K
daniel.mccloskey@cuny.edu
MCCLOSKEY, Erin .... 814-472-3938 397 F
emccloskey@francis.edu
MCCLOSKEY, James, M 302-356-6880.. 91 E
james.m.mccloskey@wilmu.edu
MCCLOSKEY, John, R .... 610-796-8226 378 C
john.mccloskey@alvernia.edu
MCCLOSKEY, JR.,
John, R .... 610-796-3005 378 C
john.mccloskey@alvernia.edu
MCCLOUD, Alyssa .... 973-761-9107 283 C
alyssa.mccloud@shu.edu
MCCLOUD, Amber .... 806-291-3430 457 I
amber.mccloud@wbu.edu
MCCLOUD, Barbara, L .. 630-515-7687 144 F
bmcclo@midwestern.edu
MCCLOUD, Clarence ..... 386-506-6301.. 98 D
clarence.mccloud@daytonastate.edu
MCCLOUD, Mark .... 731-881-3715 427 D
mmcclou5@utm.edu
MCCLOUD, Mickey .... 913-469-8500 174 I
mccloud@jccc.edu
MCCLOY, Eric .... 610-341-1372 383 B
eric.mccloy@eastern.edu
MCCLUNG, bruce, d ...... 336-334-5789 343 A
bdmcclun@uncg.edu
MCCLUNG, Steven .... 256-782-8773.... 6 A
smcclung1@jsu.edu
MCCLURE, Cami .... 208-885-5541 132 F
camim@uidaho.edu
MCCLURE, Chris .... 919-962-1000 340 H
MCCLURE, Dan .... 503-338-2460 372 D
dmcclure@clatsopcc.edu
MCCLURE, Erin .... 361-593-2760 447 D
erin.mcclure@tamuk.edu
MCCLURE, Gina .... 731-881-7888 427 D
gmcclure@utm.edu
MCCLURE, Jennifer .... 847-214-7319 137 F
jmcclure@elgin.edu
MCCLURE, Joe .... 859-233-8118 185 C
jmcclure@transy.edu
MCCLURE, Judy .... 828-766-1272 336 A
jmmclure@mayland.edu
MCCLURE, Kelly .... 580-581-2255 365 D
kmcclure@cameron.edu
MCCLURE, Krista .... 801-426-8234 459 M
kmcclure@ucdh.edu
MCCLURE, Michael .... 337-482-6224 193 B
michael.mcclure@louisiana.edu
MCCLURE, Mike .... 541-956-7237 376 A
mmclure@roguecc.edu
MCCLURE, Monica .... 920-403-3365 495 B
monica.mcclure@snc.edu
MCCLURE, Shannon ...... 417-865-2815 253 D
mcclures@evangel.edu
MCCLURE, Stuart .... 314-434-4044 252 C
stuart.mcclure@covenantseminary.edu
MCCLURE, Tonya .... 478-757-3467 116 G
tmcclure@centralgatech.edu
MCCLURE, William .... 718-997-5790 295 B
wmclure@qc.cuny.edu
MCCLURKEN, Jeff .... 540-654-1475 471 N
jmcclurk@umw.edu
MCCLURKEN, Jeffrey ..... 540-654-1475 471 N
jmcclurk@umw.edu
MCCLUSKEY, Cindy .... 815-825-9324 141 F
cmccluskey@kish.edu
MCCLUSKEY, Jennifer ... 314-529-9561 255 B
jmccluskey@maryville.edu
MCCLUSKEY, Peter .... 860-773-1442.. 87 G
pmccluskey@tunxis.edu
MCCLYMONT, Jay, W .... 717-796-1800 389 H
jmcclymont@messiah.edu
MCCOEY, Margaret .... 215-951-1130 387 A
mccoey@lasalle.edu
MCCOIN, Baleigh .... 903-785-7661 441 D
bmccoin@parisjc.edu
MCCOLGIN,
Cathleen, C .... 315-866-0300 301 D
mccolgicc@herkimer.edu
MCCOLLOUGH,
William, A .... 352-392-1202 111 A
amccollough@aa.ufl.edu
MCCOLLUM, Brian .... 202-885-8617.. 94 D
bmccollum@wesleyseminary.edu
MCCOLLUM, Jennifer .... 503-554-2100 373 A
jmccollum@georgefox.edu
MCCOLLUM, Ricky .... 718-429-6600 324 D
ricky.mccollum@vaughn.edu
MCCOLLUM, Scott .... 937-512-3068 360 G
scott.mccullum@sinclair.edu
MCCOLLUM,
Shannon, M .... 530-895-2484.. 27 C
mccollumsh@butte.edu
MCCOLLUM, Walter .... 866-492-5336 244 F
walter.mccollum@mail.waldenu.edu
MCCOMAS, Katherine .... 607-255-9970 297 F
kam19@cornell.edu
MCCOMAS, Michael ...... 304-710-3453 488 F
mccomas2@mctc.edu
MCCOMB, Veronica .... 401-232-6000 404 A
vmccomb@bryant.edu
MCCOMBE, John, P ...... 937-229-4615 362 C
jmccombe1@udayton.edu
MCCOMBE WALLER,
Sandy .... 301-624-2826 198 I
smccombewaller@frederick.edu
MCCOMBS, Jonathan .... 614-947-6169 352 J
jonathan.mccombs@franklin.edu
MCCOMMON, John .... 731-425-2652 424 E
jmccommon@jscc.edu
MCCONAHA, Kristen ..... 425-267-0154 480 B
kmcconaha@everettcc.edu
MCCONAHAY, Mark .... 812-855-2654 156 F
mcconaha@indiana.edu
MCCONAHAY, Mark .... 812-855-2654 156 G
mcconaha@indiana.edu
MCCONATHY, Terry, M . 318-257-4262 192 D
tmm@latech.edu
MCCONICO, Shannon ... 229-333-2110 128 B
shannon.mcconico@wiregrass.edu
MCCONKEY, Deborah .... 916-348-4689.. 41 H
dmcconkey@epic.edu
MCCONKEY, Nancy .... 402-437-2604 269 C
nmcconkey@southeast.edu
MCCONNAUGHAY,
Kelly .... 309-677-2383 134 A
kdm@bradley.edu
MCCONNAUGHHAY,
Dennis .... 314-837-6777 258 K
MCCONNELL, Cary .... 617-573-8575 219 B
cmcconnell@suffolk.edu
MCCONNELL, Cheryl, A 610-660-1000 397 G
emoran@sju.edu
MCCONNELL, Frank, J .. 706-864-1606 127 A
mac.mcconnell@ung.edu
MCCONNELL, George .... 218-755-2027 237 F
george.mcconnell@bemidjistate.edu
MCCONNELL, Jason ...... 423-869-6333 421 A
jason.mcconnell@lmunet.edu
MCCONNELL, Joyce, E .. 970-491-6211.. 79 N
presofc@colostate.edu
MCCONNELL, Karen, E .. 253-535-7656 482 A
mcconnke@plu.edu
MCCONNELL, Karl .... 856-227-7200 276 E
kmcconnell@camdencc.edu
MCCONNELL, Kathleen .. 607-844-8222 322 D
km124@tompkinscortland.edu
MCCONNELL, KJ .... 740-376-4465 355 E
kj.mcconnell@marietta.edu
MCCONNELL, Penny, J . 217-443-8747 136 G
pmcconn@dacc.edu
MCCONNELL, Rachel ..... 215-368-5000 390 A
rmcconnell@missio.edu
MCCONNELL, Sheppard 405-224-3140 371 B
smcconnell@usao.edu
MCCONNELL-BLACK,
Karnell .... 503-777-7270 375 G
kblack@reed.edu
MCCONNER, Mary .... 901-321-3547 418 G
mmcconn1@cbu.edu
MCCONNICO, Kelly .... 336-758-5000 344 C
mcconnkm@wfu.edu
MCCONOUGHEY, Gina .. 815-455-8996 143 I
gmcconoughey@mchenry.edu
MCCONVILLE, Haley ...... 203-773-8577.. 85 D
hmcconville@albertus.edu
MCCONVILLE, Haley ...... 978-921-4242 217 B
haley.mcconville@montserrat.edu
MCCONVILLE,
Jennifer, A .... 308-367-5259 270 B
jmcconville2@unl.edu
MCCOOK, Sonya .... 336-506-4278 332 A
sonya.mccook@alamancecc.edu
MCCOOL, Jeff .... 575-492-4711 287 A
jmccool@nmjc.edu
MCCOOL, Kayleigh .... 662-562-3200 248 D
MCCOOL, Kyle .... 314-246-7497 262 C
kylemccool50@webster.edu
MCCORCLE, Michael ..... 417-865-2815 253 D
mccorclem@evangel.edu
MCCORD, A. Janelle ..... 513-569-1688 350 F
MCCORD, Janelle .... 513-569-1688 350 F
MCCORD, Marian .... 603-862-1234 274 F
marian.mccord@unh.edu
MCCORD-FITHIAN,
Regina, L .... 812-888-6947 162 F
rmccord-fithian@vinu.edu
MCCORKLE, Candy .... 269-387-1000 233 B
candy.s.mccorkle@wmich.edu
MCCORKLE, Kimberly .... 850-474-2035 111 F
kmccorkle@uwf.edu
MCCORKLE, Kimberly .... 423-439-1000 419 G
MCCORMAC, Greg .... 916-608-6615.. 50 I
mccormg@flc.losrios.edu
MCCORMACK, Amy .... 219-473-4333 154 D
amccormack@ccsj.edu
MCCORMACK, Beth .... 802-831-1237 463 C
bmccormack@vermontlaw.edu
MCCORMACK, Brian ...... 956-295-3585 449 C
brian.mccormack@tsc.edu
MCCORMACK, Cathleen 717-720-4070 394 C
cmccormack@passhe.edu
MCCORMACK,
Dawn, M .... 615-898-5005 422 C
dawn.mccormack@mtsu.edu
MCCORMACK, Jeff .... 405-425-5469 367 C
jeff.mccormack@oc.edu
MCCORMACK, Jennifer . 214-887-5088 435 F
jmccormack@dts.edu
MCCORMACK, Jim .... 570-389-4062 393 D
jmccorma@bloomu.edu
MCCORMACK, John .... 708-596-2000 149 H
jmccormack@ssc.edu
MCCORMACK, Merita .... 703-416-1441 466 A
studentsuccess@divinemercy.edu
MCCORMACK, Teresa .... 802-468-1111 463 E
teresa.mccormack@castleton.edu
MCCORMICK, Adrienne . 803-323-2220 414 D
mccormicka@winthrop.edu
MCCORMICK, Brad .... 423-697-3264 424 A
brad.mccormick@chattanoogastate.edu
MCCORMICK, Brian .... 319-296-4050 166 H
brian.mccormick@hawkeyecollege.edu
MCCORMICK, Cathleen . 717-720-4070 393 F
cmccormick@passhe.edu
MCCORMICK,
Cecilia, M .... 717-361-1000 383 C
mccormickcecilia@etown.edu
MCCORMICK, Charlie .... 830-792-7345 443 E
president@schreiner.edu
MCCORMICK, David ...... 312-567-4972 140 A
dmccormick@iitri.org
MCCORMICK, Elizabeth . 918-631-5796 371 C
elizabeth-mccormick@utulsa.edu
MCCORMICK, Heath ...... 610-921-6680 377 G
hmccormick@albright.edu
MCCORMICK, Jim, S .... 303-963-3363.. 78 H
jimmccormick@ccu.edu
MCCORMICK, Jonathan . 909-687-1482.. 43 D
jonathanmccormick@gs.edu
MCCORMICK, Joseph .... 301-846-2548 198 I
jmccormick@frederick.edu
MCCORMICK, Justin ...... 479-979-1234.. 23 I
jmccormick@ozarks.edu
MCCORMICK, Karla, S .. 334-844-4183.... 4 D
ksm0010@auburn.edu
MCCORMICK, Kevin, M . 630-515-6053 144 F
kmccor@midwestern.edu
MCCORMICK, Kimberly . 615-366-4429 423 H
kimberly.mccormick@tbr.edu
MCCORMICK, Lauren .... 979-230-3489 431 I
lauren.mccormick@brazosport.edu
MCCORMICK, Lisa .... 830-792-7312 443 E
library@schreiner.edu
MCCORMICK, Lucas ...... 785-227-3380 172 A
mccormicklf@bethanylb.edu
MCCORMICK, Lynn .... 617-989-4590 219 F
mccormickl@wit.edu
MCCORMICK, Mark .... 732-906-2517 278 G
mmccormick@middlesexcc.edu
MCCORMICK, Mark .... 205-366-8831.... 7 A
mmccormick@stillman.edu
MCCORMICK, OSU,
Mary .... 440-943-7600 360 E
mmccormick@dioceseofcleveland.org
MCCORMICK,
Michael, R .... 315-386-7222 320 B
mccormic@canton.edu
MCCORMICK, Mike .... 805-756-2100.. 29 I
mmccor21@calpoly.edu
MCCORMICK, Noemi ..... 801-689-2160 459 I
MCCORMICK, Patrick, T 509-313-6715 480 F
mccormick@gonzaga.edu
MCCORMICK, CSC,
Peter, M .... 574-631-7800 162 A
mccormick.23@nd.edu
MCCORMICK, Reenie .... 410-334-2939 205 D
rmccormick@worwic.edu
MCCORMICK, Robert ..... 312-362-6627 136 H
bmccormi@depaul.edu
MCCORMICK, Sara .... 505-747-2161 287 H
sara.mccormick@nnmc.edu
MCCORMICK, Silas .... 217-732-3168 142 G
pres@lincolnchristian.edu
MCCORN, Lester, A .... 803-327-7402 407 F
MCCORRY, Laurie, K ..... 617-228-2465 214 C
lkmccorry@bhcc.mass.edu
MCCORRY, Margaret ..... 908-737-0580 278 E
mmccorry@kean.edu
MCCORRY-ANDALIS,
Catherine, M .... 915-747-5648 455 C
cmandalis@utep.edu
MCCORVEY, Ann .... 704-894-2859 328 E
anmccorvey@davidson.edu
MCCORY, Denise .... 216-987-4034 351 E
MCCOSKER, Lynn .... 856-351-2624 283 B
lmccosker@salemcc.edu
MCCOTTER, Suzanne ..... 609-771-1855 276 I
mccottes@tcnj.edu
MCCOURRY, Maurine .... 517-607-2401 225 C
mmccourry@hillsdale.edu
MCCOURT,
MaryFrances .... 215-898-1005 400 F
mfmccourt@upenn.edu
MCCOWAN, Carla .... 217-333-3701 152 B
cmccowan@illinois.edu
MCCOWN, Amber .... 239-489-9226 101 A
amccown@fsw.edu
MCCOY, Ann .... 660-543-4272 260 G
mccoy@ucmo.edu
MCCOY, Becky .... 479-387-3820.. 21 F
remccoy@uark.edu
MCCOY, Chris .... 940-565-2224 453 E
chris.mccoy@untsystem.edu
MCCOY, Danielle .... 309-672-5513 144 C
dmcoy@methodistcol.edu
MCCOY, David, M .... 804-289-8718 472 C
dmccoy2@richmond.edu
MCCOY, Holly, M .... 724-738-2650 395 C
holly.mccoy@sru.edu
MCCOY, Isaac .... 205-247-8149.... 7 A
imccoy@stillman.edu
MCCOY, James .... 229-732-5950 115 B
jamesmccoy@andrewcollege.edu
MCCOY, James .... 702-651-5602 270 K
james.mccoy@csn.edu
MCCOY, James .... 336-721-2600 340 A
james.mccoy@salem.edu
MCCOY, JR., James, F . 813-393-3675 125 F
jmccoy@southuniversity.edu
MCCOY, John .... 724-266-3838 400 B
jmccoy@tsm.edu

MCCOY, Jonathan .... 828-689-1366 331 C
jonathan_mccoy@mhu.edu
MCCOY, Julie .... 803-938-3821 413 G
jmccoy@uscsumter.edu
MCCOY, Karen, A .... 651-962-6926 244 E
mcco7879@stthomas.edu
MCCOY, Kathleen .... 941-487-4900 110 D
kmccoy@ncf.edu
MCCOY, Kelly .... 229-931-2320 120 D
kelly.mccoy@gsw.edu
MCCOY, Kevin .... 785-227-3380 172 A
mccoyk@bethanylb.edu
MCCOY, Marilyn .... 847-491-4335 146 E
mmccoy@northwestern.edu
MCCOY, Melissa .... 601-977-7783 249 C
mmccoy@tougaloo.edu
MCCOY, Meredith .... 802-442-5401 461 G
MCCOY, Mike .... 620-229-6104 177 G
mike.mccoy@sckans.edu
MCCOY, Mike .... 256-216-3300.... 4 C
mike.mccoy@athens.edu
MCCOY, Nathaniel .... 309-268-4304 142 H
nmccoy@lincolncollege.edu
MCCOY, Robert .... 907-474-7500.. 10 A
rpmccoy@alaska.edu
MCCOY, Ryan .... 303-404-5238.. 81 A
ryan.mccoy@frontrange.edu
MCCOY, Sue .... 916-484-8211.. 50 G
mccoys@arc.losrios.edu
MCCOY, Tammie, M .... 662-329-7299 248 A
tmmccoy@muw.edu
MCCOY, Tammy .... 615-815-8360 422 F
MCCOY, Ted .... 641-673-1090 171 C
mccoyt@wmpenn.edu
MCCOY, William .... 617-745-3000 209 B
MCCOY, William, K .... 570-577-1609 379 C
bill.mccoy@bucknell.edu
MCCOY, Zaire .... 407-646-2385 106 L
zmccoy@rollins.edu
MCCOY-WILSON,
Sonya .... 404-225-4672 115 H
smccoy-wilson@atlantatech.edu
MCCRACKEN, Bobbi ...... 951-827-3303.. 70 B
bobbi.mccracken@ucr.edu
MCCRACKEN, Fawn .... 952-446-4325 235 J
mccrackenf@crown.edu
MCCRACKEN, Maria .... 909-599-5433.. 48 A
mmccracken@lifepacific.edu
MCCRACKIN, Tara .... 616-254-9303 224 A
taramccrackin@ferris.edu
MCCRAE, Byron, P .... 704-894-2225 328 E
bymccrae@davidson.edu
MCCRARY, Katy .... 386-754-4344 100 B
kathryn.mccrary@fgc.edu
MCCRARY, Lauren .... 270-686-4236 179 J
lauren.mccrary@brescia.edu
MCCRARY, Vicki .... 541-956-7000 376 A
vmccrary@roguecc.edu
MCCRARY, Victor .... 202-274-7443.. 94 B
victor.mccrary@udc.edu
MCCRAW, Bethany, J ...... 254-710-1715 431 E
bethany_mccraw@baylor.edu
MCCRAW, Liz .... 580-745-2080 369 G
lmccraw@se.edu
MCCRAW, Patti, H .... 864-488-4571 410 B
pmccraw@limestone.edu
MCCRAY, Corey, L .... 757-569-6712 474 H
cmccray@pdc.edu
MCCRAY, Suzanne .... 479-575-4883.. 21 F
smccray@uark.edu
MCCRAY, Sylvia .... 215-574-9600 385 K
sylvia.mccray@hussiancollege.edu
MCCRAY-ROBERTS,
Patty .... 253-566-5050 484 E
pmccray-roberts@tacomacc.edu
MCCREA, Douglas .... 609-896-5196 281 B
dmccrea@rider.edu
MCCREA, Larry .... 816-604-1000 255 D
MCCREADY, Randall ...... 412-624-7180 400 H
mccready@pitt.edu
MCCREARY, Beverly ...... 808-956-9429 129 E
bmccrear@hawaii.edu
MCCREARY, Micah, L ... 732-247-5241 279 C
mmccreary@nbts.edu
MCCREARY, William ...... 419-530-3990 363 B
william.mccreary@utoledo.edu
MCCREE, Bernard, L ...... 610-683-4032 394 D
mccree@kutztown.edu
MCCREERY, John .... 440-375-7225 354 K
jmccreery@lec.edu
MCCREIGHT,
Christopher, J .... 330-569-6094 353 G
mccreightcj@hiram.edu
MCCREIGHT, Megan ..... 719-365-8292.. 83 N
megan.mccreight@uchealth.org
MCCREIGHT, Robert ...... 785-738-9031 176 F
rmccreight@ncktc.edu
MCCRELESS, Penny .... 859-344-3356 185 B
mccrelp@thomasmore.edu
MCCRILLIS, Neal, R ...... 312-413-1468 151 G
nealrm@uic.edu
MCCRIMMON, Samuel .. 315-445-4778 303 I
mccrimsi@lemoyne.edu
MCCROHAN, Betty, A .... 979-532-6304 458 E
bettym@wcjc.edu
MCCRORY, Davis .... 540-654-1042 471 N
dmccrory@umw.edu
MCCRORY, Heidi, H ...... 864-294-2475 409 H
heidi.mccrory@furman.edu
MCCROSKEY, Lorie, L ... 336-633-1118 337 A
llmccroskey@randolph.edu
MCCROW, Rich .... 661-395-4694.. 46 L
rmccrow@bakersfieldcollege.edu
MCCUBBIN, Todd, A ...... 573-882-6017 261 A
mccubbint@missouri.edu
MCCUDDEN, Suzanne ... 253-833-9111 480 I
smccudden@greenriver.edu
MCCUE, Cindy .... 934-420-2319 320 F
cynthia.mccue@farmingdale.edu
MCCUE, Jennie .... 949-582-4500.. 65 D
jmccue@saddleback.edu
MCCUEN, Jan .... 714-997-6862.. 36 B
mccuen@chapman.edu
MCCUIEN-SMITH,
Cassandra .... 501-450-3173.. 23 H
cmccuien@uca.edu
MCCUISTION, Kim .... 682-703-7067 446 D
mccuistion@tarleton.edu
MCCULLA, Justin .... 937-328-7819 350 G
mccullaj@clarkstate.edu
MCCULLAR, Bryan, L .... 785-833-4398 175 E
bryan.mccullar@kwu.edu
MCCULLEN, Ann, S .... 904-620-2100 111 B
amccullen@unf.edu
MCCULLEY, Becky .... 214-633-4805 457 A
becky.mcculley@utsouthwestern.edu
MCCULLEY, Heather ...... 530-226-4943.. 64 E
hmcculley@simpsonu.edu
MCCULLEY, Justin .... 276-964-2555 475 C
justin.mcculley@sw.edu
MCCULLOCH, Greg .... 618-252-5400 149 I
greg.mcculloch@sic.edu
MCCULLOCH, Sonja ...... 912-260-4402 125 D
sonja.mcculloch@sgsc.edu
MCCULLOH, Edna .... 330-490-7191 363 E
emcculloh@walsh.edu
MCCULLOH, Julie, A ..... 509-313-6591 480 F
mccullohj@gonzaga.edu
MCCULLOH, Thayne, M 509-313-6102 480 F
president@gonzaga.edu
MCCULLOUGH, Bryan ... 336-249-8186 334 B
bryan_mccullough@davidsondavie.edu
MCCULLOUGH,
Catherine .... 802-728-1247 464 A
cmccullough@vtc.edu
MCCULLOUGH,
Cheryl, J .... 803-327-7402 407 F
cmccullough@clintoncollege.edu
MCCULLOUGH, Dana .... 414-847-3236 494 C
danamccullough@miad.edu
MCCULLOUGH, Dona .... 312-662-4000 132 G
MCCULLOUGH,
Jonathan, W .... 903-434-8115 440 G
jmccullough@ntcc.edu
MCCULLOUGH, Karen ... 785-628-4260 173 H
kamccullough@fhsu.edu
MCCULLOUGH, Laura ... 912-478-5234 120 C
lmccullough@georgiasouthern.edu
MCCULLOUGH, Laura ... 304-205-6611 488 D
laura.mccullough@bridgevalley.edu
MCCULLOUGH,
Phenicia .... 657-278-4637.. 31 C
pmccullough@fullerton.edu
MCCULLOUGH, Richard 850-644-1085 110 C
president@fsu.edu
MCCULLOUGH,
Robert, R .... 216-368-5445 349 D
robert.mccullough@case.edu
MCCULLOUGH, Scott ..... 507-529-2789 240 H
scott.mccullough@rctc.edu
MCCULLOUGH, Tami ..... 262-472-6704 497 D
mccullot@uww.edu
MCCULLOUGH, Telara ... 509-527-5941 486 B
mccullti@whitman.edu
MCCULLUM, BJ .... 217-234-5253 142 C
bmccullum@lakelandcollege.edu
MCCULLY, Clare .... 617-724-6399 217 A
cmccully@mghihp.edu
MCCUNE, Jennifer .... 661-654-3405.. 30 B
jmccune@csub.edu
MCCUNE, Kathryn .... 606-539-4316 185 E
MCCUNE, LB .... 810-762-9629 226 B
lbmccune@kettering.edu
MCCUNE, Roger .... 304-485-5487 487 G
MCCURDY, Clantha .... 617-391-6098 211 E
cmccurdy@dhe.mass.edu
MCCURDY, Debra, L ..... 410-462-7799 198 B
dlmccurdy@bccc.edu
MCCURDY, Eugene, M .. 608-796-3921 497 O
emmccurdy@viterbo.edu
MCCURDY, Katie .... 850-872-3814 101 N
kmccurdy2@gulfcoast.edu
MCCURDY, Megan .... 870-235-4094.. 21 C
meganmccurdy@saumag.edu
MCCURDY, Solynn .... 206-296-6116 484 A
mccurdys@seattleu.edu
MCCURLEY, Lisa .... 603-427-7878 272 J
MCCURREN, Cynthia ..... 810-762-3420 232 A
mccurrec@umich.edu
MCCURRY, David .... 864-503-5509 414 A
dmccurry@uscupstate.edu
MCCURRY, Elizabeth ..... 985-448-4521 192 F
liz.mccurry@nicholls.edu
MCCURRY, Faith .... 803-535-1230 411 B
mccurryf@octech.edu
MCCURRY, Michael .... 202-885-8600.. 94 D
mmccurry@wesleyseminary.edu
MCCURRY, Rickey .... 702-895-2810 271 D
rickey.mccurry@unlv.edu
MCCURRY, Roslyn .... 770-229-3404 125 H
roslyn.mccurry@sctech.edu
MCCURTY, Kenyetta ...... 334-387-3877.... 4 B
kenyettamccurty@amridgeuniversity.edu
MCCUSKEY, Beth .... 765-494-4600 160 B
MCCUTCHEN, Michael ... 731-989-6901 419 K
mmccutchen@fhu.edu
MCCUTCHEON, Andy ..... 661-362-3387.. 38 D
andy.mccutcheon@canyons.edu
MCCUTCHEON, John ..... 805-893-8320.. 70 E
jmccutch@athletics.ucsb.edu
MCDADE, Kate .... 216-987-4710 351 E
kate.mcdade@tri-c.edu
MCDADE, Lucinda .... 909-625-8767.. 37 C
lucinda.mcdade@cgu.edu
MCDAID, James .... 617-879-7960 213 B
jmcdaid@massart.edu
MCDAID, Justin .... 913-469-8500 174 I
jmcdaid@jccc.edu
MCDANIEL, Allison .... 210-297-9664 430 L
MCDANIEL, Amy .... 636-481-3465 254 C
amcdanie@jeffco.edu
MCDANIEL, Anna, M .... 352-273-6324 111 A
annammcdaniel@ufl.edu
MCDANIEL, Becky .... 620-235-4769 177 A
remcdaniel@pittstate.edu
MCDANIEL, Brienne ...... 678-359-5133 120 F
briennem@gordonstate.edu
MCDANIEL, Cleve .... 575-835-5606 286 K
cleve.mcdaniel@nmt.edu
MCDANIEL, Clifton .... 817-461-8741 430 B
cmcdaniel@abu.edu
MCDANIEL, Cynthia ...... 973-748-9000 276 A
cindy_mcdaniel@bloomfield.edu
MCDANIEL, Diane .... 765-677-2436 158 B
diane.mcdaniel@indwes.edu
MCDANIEL, Donna .... 903-823-3220 446 A
donna.mcdaniel@texarkanacollege.edu
MCDANIEL, Gary .... 402-643-7233 266 G
gary.mcdaniel@cune.edu
MCDANIEL, Jennifer ...... 951-571-6965.. 59 B
jennifer.mcdaniel@mvc.edu
MCDANIEL, Joy .... 580-387-7000 366 E
jmcdaniel@mscok.edu
MCDANIEL, Juley .... 620-223-2700 173 I
juleym@fortscott.edu
MCDANIEL, Kristina, D . 573-840-9695 260 E
kristinamcdaniel@trcc.edu
MCDANIEL, Laura .... 701-231-8330 345 F
laura.mcdaniel@ndsu.edu
MCDANIEL, Mary .... 620-341-5223 173 F
mmcdanie@emporia.edu
MCDANIEL, Mick, R ...... 607-844-8222 322 D
mcdanim@tompkinscortland.edu
MCDANIEL, Nivenitie .... 678-872-4203 119 D
nmcdanie@highlands.edu
MCDANIEL, Sonya .... 770-962-7580 121 E
smcdaniel@gwinnetttech.edu
MCDANIEL, Wendy .... 479-394-7622.. 23 C
wmcdaniel@uarichmountain.edu
MCDANIEL-SMITH,
Nicole, L .... 302-356-6928.. 91 E
nicole.l.mcdaniel-smith@wilmu.edu
MCDANIELS,
Preselfannie .... 601-979-2455 246 F
preselfannie.w.mcdaniels@jsums.edu
MCDANIELS, Rob, M .... 573-882-9370 261 A
mcdanielsr@missouri.edu
MCDANIELS WILSON,
Cathy .... 614-236-6114 349 B
cmcdanielswilson@capital.edu
MCDAVID, Cristina, C .. 304-696-2248 489 M
mcdavidc@marshall.edu
MCDEAVITT, James .... 713-798-4951 431 D
MCDEDE, Savanna .... 858-566-1200.. 40 J
smcdede@disd.edu
MCDERMIT, Meisha ...... 570-484-2123 394 E
mmcdermi@lockhaven.edu
MCDERMOTT,
Anastacia, M .... 563-588-7056 168 A
anastacia.mcdermott@loras.edu
MCDERMOTT, Anne .... 401-341-2140 405 D
anne.mcdermott@salve.edu
MCDERMOTT, Brian ...... 907-564-8323.... 9 F
bmcdermott@alaskapacific.edu
MCDERMOTT, Brian ...... 308-398-7387 266 A
bmcdermott@cccneb.edu
MCDERMOTT, Christine 315-568-3105 310 B
cmcdermott@nycc.edu
MCDERMOTT, Colleen ... 920-424-1210 496 C
mcdermot@uwosh.edu
MCDERMOTT, David ...... 617-287-7050 211 F
dmcdermott@umassp.edu
MCDERMOTT, Joan .... 415-422-6623.. 72 J
jmcdermott2@usfca.edu
MCDERMOTT, John, R .. 563-588-7132 168 A
john.mcdermott@loras.edu
MCDERMOTT, Loren ...... 914-323-5299 305 B
loren.mcdermott@mville.edu
MCDERMOTT,
Madonna, K .... 651-962-6750 244 E
mkmcdermott@stthomas.edu
MCDERMOTT, Marty ...... 231-777-0462 228 G
marty.mcdermott@muskegoncc.edu
MCDERMOTT, Patrice .... 410-455-3150 203 B
mcdermot@umbc.edu
MCDERMOTT, Patrick .... 941-377-4880 104 D
pmcdermott@meridian.edu
MCDERMOTT, Randi ...... 208-426-1493 130 H
randimcdermott@boisestate.edu
MCDERMOTT, Suzan ..... 315-386-7611 320 B
mcdermotts@canton.edu
MCDERMOTT, Teresa ..... 360-475-7480 481 I
tmcdermott@olympic.edu
MCDERMOTT, Tom .... 410-516-8028 199 G
tmcderm1@jhu.edu
MCDERMOTT,
Virginia, M .... 336-841-9384 329 F
vmcdermo@highpoint.edu
MCDERMOTT,
Walter, M .... 434-223-6112 467 F
wmcdermott@hsc.edu
MCDEVITT, Richard, K .. 704-406-2361 329 A
rmcdevitt@gardner-webb.edu
MCDEVITT, Steven .... 603-641-7574 274 A
smcdevitt@anselm.edu
MCDONAGH, David, L .. 646-888-6639 304 J
mcdonagd@sloankettering.edu
MCDONALD, Angela, R . 610-660-1265 397 G
amcdonal@sju.edu
MCDONALD, Ann .... 508-626-4993 213 A
amcdonald3@framingham.edu
MCDONALD, Barbara .... 218-723-6041 235 G
president@css.edu
MCDONALD, Bridgette .. 678-466-5400 117 D
bridgettemcdonald@clayton.edu
MCDONALD, Carleigh ... 415-703-9500.. 28 B
c.mcdonald@cca.edu
MCDONALD, Charles .... 518-292-1725 313 A
mcdonc@sage.edu
MCDONALD,
Christopher .... 949-451-5679.. 65 C
cmcdonald@ivc.edu
MCDONALD, Clay .... 636-227-2100 255 A
MCDONALD, Damita ..... 410-532-5546 201 D
dmcdonald1@ndm.edu
MCDONALD, Danielle ... 813-974-6677 111 C
dmcdonald@usf.edu
MCDONALD, Dave .... 503-838-8919 377 D
mcdonald@wou.edu
MCDONALD, Debbie ..... 626-966-4576.. 25 H
info@agu.edu

MCFEELY, Gareth .... 617-353-9888 207 E
garethmc@bu.edu
MCFETRIDGE, Travis ..... 541-881-5599 376 F
tmcfetri@tvcc.cc
MCFETRIDGE, Travis ..... 541-881-5825 376 F
tmcfetri@tvcc.cc
MCFRAZIER, Michael, L 936-261-2111 446 C
mlmcfrazier@pvamu.edu
MCFRY, Kevin .... 256-549-8242.... 2 B
kmcfry@gadsdenstate.edu
MCGADNEY, Andrew ..... 309-341-7210 141 G
camcgadney@knox.edu
MCGADNEY, C. Andrew 207-859-4114 194 D
andy.mcgadney@colby.edu
MCGAHAN, Chris .... 919-515-7277 342 A
chris_mcgahan@ncsu.edu
MCGAHEE, Thayer .... 803-641-2823 413 B
thayerm@usca.edu
MCGAHERAN, Amy .... 315-268-3788 295 F
amcgaher@clarkson.edu
MCGALLIARD, Mike ...... 501-279-4640.. 19 C
mmcgalliard@harding.edu
MCGANN, Joesph .... 860-465-4514.. 85 H
mcgannj@easternct.edu
MCGANN, Matthew .... 413-542-2328 205 G
admissions@amherst.edu
MCGANN, Robert .... 610-861-5506 391 C
rmcgann@northampton.edu
MCGARRITY, DeShawn . 518-631-2262 315 B
mcgarrdn@sunysccc.edu
MCGARRY, Robert .... 815-825-9811 141 F
rmcgarry@kish.edu
MCGARRY, Sean, T .... 434-971-3303 502 I
sean.t.mcgarry.mil@mail.mil
MCGARRY, Timothy ...... 516-876-3303 318 C
mcgarryt@oldwestbury.edu
MCGARRY, William .... 315-268-6689 295 F
wmcgarry@clarkson.edu
MCGARVEY, Betty Sue .. 901-572-2585 418 A
bettysue.mcgarvey@baptistu.edu
MCGARVEY, Kristy .... 303-357-5842.. 80 I
kristy.mcgarvey@denverseminary.edu
MCGARVEY, Suzi .... 660-263-4100 257 B
suzim@macc.edu
MCGARVEY,
Vicki Lewis .... 215-204-5665 399 B
vicki.mcgarvey@temple.edu
MCGAUGH, Becky, E .... 928-523-6415.. 14 H
becky.mcgaugh@nau.edu
MCGAUGHEY, Jodie .... 325-670-1508 436 I
jmcgaughey@hsutx.edu
MCGAUGHEY, Kelly ...... 850-474-2400 111 F
kmcgaughey1@uwf.edu
MCGAUGHY, Mac .... 704-687-8548 342 D
jmcgaug1@uncc.edu
MCGAW, Darin .... 207-454-1003 195 I
dmcgaw@wccc.me.edu
MCGEADY, John .... 512-471-3391 455 A
john.mcgeady@austin.utexas.edu
MCGEE, Alex .... 470-578-3880 121 M
amcgee32@kennesaw.edu
MCGEE, Angel .... 318-487-5443 187 J
angelmcgee@cltcc.edu
MCGEE, Brian, R .... 217-228-5432 147 F
president@quincy.edu
MCGEE, Christina .... 913-288-7489 175 B
chmcgee@kckcc.edu
MCGEE, Darryl .... 731-425-2550 420 G
dmcgee@lanecollege.edu
MCGEE, Ed .... 434-832-7742 473 E
mcgeee@centralvirginia.edu
MCGEE, Glenn .... 203-479-4192.. 89 H
gmcgee@newhaven.edu
MCGEE, Gregory, R .... 859-858-3511 179 D
gregory.mcgee@asbury.edu
MCGEE, Isaiah, R .... 803-535-5679 407 D
imcgee@claflin.edu
MCGEE, James .... 404-756-4443 115 G
MCGEE, James .... 708-534-4900 138 E
jmcgee@govst.edu
MCGEE, John .... 770-426-2805 122 C
john.mcgee@life.edu
MCGEE, John .... 816-322-0110 251 B
john.mcgee@calvary.edu
MCGEE, Keith .... 601-877-6678 245 A
kmcgee@alcorn.edu
MCGEE, Laura .... 847-925-6686 138 G
lmcgee@harpercollege.edu
MCGEE, Lucy .... 800-895-7411 464 E
lmcgee@asl.edu
MCGEE, Marjorie .... 352-854-2322.. 97 N
mcgeem@cf.edu
MCGEE, Melandie .... 985-545-1500 188 E
MCGEE, Michael .... 828-328-7127 330 F
michael.mcgee@lr.edu
MCGEE, Robby .... 910-362-7191 332 H
rmcgee@cfcc.edu
MCGEE, Sharon, J .... 423-439-4221 419 G
mcgees@etsu.edu
MCGEE, Shawn .... 229-500-3026 114 H
shawn.mcgee@asurams.edu
MCGEE, Steve, G .... 817-257-7930 448 F
s.mcgee@tcu.edu
MCGEE, Steve, R .... 512-245-2533 450 C
steve.mcgee@tsus.edu
MCGEE, Summer .... 336-721-2605 340 A
summer.mcgee@salem.edu
MCGEE, Summer, J ...... 203-479-4104.. 89 H
smcgee@newhaven.edu
MCGEE, Tammy .... 612-381-3370 235 K
tmcgee@dunwoody.edu
MCGEE, Thomas .... 412-365-1837 380 G
t.mcgee@chatham.edu
MCGEE, Tim .... 217-245-3060 139 C
timothy.mcgee@ic.edu
MCGEE, Tom .... 815-479-7764 143 I
tmcgee@mchenry.edu
MCGEE-YUROFF, Carrie 203-857-7000.. 87 D
MCGEHEE, Janice .... 208-562-3163 131 E
janicemcgehee@cwi.edu
MCGEHEE, JR.,
Robert, E .... 501-686-5454.. 22 B
rem@uams.edu
MCGHEE, Danielle .... 512-505-3079 438 A
dmcghee@htu.edu
MCGHEE, JR.,
James, D .... 804-752-3736 469 F
jamesmcghee@rmc.edu
MCGHEE, Lisa .... 870-762-3174.. 17 B
lmcghee@smail.anc.edu
MCGHEE, Marianne, S .. 804-523-5810 474 A
mmcghee@reynolds.edu
MCGHEE, Megan .... 615-248-1627 426 D
mmcghee@trevecca.edu
MCGHEE, Sandra, W ...... 540-375-2287 470 E
mcghee@roanoke.edu
MCGHEE, Stephanie ...... 417-667-8181 252 B
smcghee@cottey.edu
MCGHEE, Tanya .... 252-444-0739 334 A
mcgheet@cravencc.edu
MCGHEE, Tony .... 276-964-5668 475 C
tony.mcghee@sw.edu
MCGILL, Angela .... 972-881-5151 433 I
amcgill@collin.edu
MCGILL, Antoinette .... 510-780-4500.. 47 K
amcgill@lifewest.edu
MCGILL, Bret .... 256-306-2861.... 1 F
bret.mcgill@calhoun.edu
MCGILL, Diana .... 859-572-5860 184 E
mcgill@nku.edu
MCGILL, Elizabeth, A .... 570-348-6211 389 D
emcgill@marywood.edu
MCGILL, Jason, T .... 402-280-5750 266 H
jasonmcgill@creighton.edu
MCGILL, Jean .... 860-913-2070.. 88 A
jmcgill@goodwin.edu
MCGILL, Lawrence .... 410-888-9048 200 E
lmcgill@muih.edu
MCGILL, Peggy .... 305-289-1121.. 98 E
MCGILL, Shaniece .... 510-626-5300.. 63 E
MCGILL, Shawna .... 575-769-4954 285 O
shawna.mcgill@clovis.edu
MCGILL, Sheila .... 405-466-2957 366 C
srmcgill@langston.edu
MCGILL, Shelia, R .... 405-466-3283 366 C
srmcgill@langston.edu
MCGILLICUDDY, Maren 207-509-7136 196 E
mmcgillicuddy@unity.edu
MCGILLICUDDY,
Suzanne .... 212-217-3800 299 D
suzanne_mcgillicuddy@fitnyc.edu
MCGILLIS, Bill .... 619-260-2982.. 72 I
wmcgillis@sandiego.edu
MCGILLOWAY,
Samantha .... 978-762-4000 215 D
smcgillo@northshore.edu
MCGILVRAY, Richard .... 716-827-4338 323 G
mcgilvrayr@trocaire.edu
MCGING, Christine .... 651-779-3368 237 H
christine.mcging@century.edu
MCGINLEY, Christina .... 215-968-8224 379 D
christina.mcginley@bucks.edu
MCGINLEY, Lynn .... 409-772-8909 456 E
lmmcginl@utmb.edu
MCGINLEY, William ...... 440-826-8014 348 D
wmcginle@bw.edu
MCGINN, BJ .... 515-433-5050 165 A
bjmcginn@dmacc.edu
MCGINNESS, Colleen .... 517-607-2304 225 C
cmcginness@hillsdale.edu
MCGINNIS, Blake .... 870-759-4170.. 23 J
bmcginnis@williamsbu.edu
MCGINNIS, Brianna ...... 410-386-8304 198 D
bmcginnis@carrollcc.edu
MCGINNIS, Carrie .... 270-809-3437 184 D
cmcginnis2@murraystate.edu
MCGINNIS, Erik .... 704-463-3001 339 E
erik.mcginnis@pfeiffer.edu
MCGINNIS, Grace .... 708-709-3519 147 D
gmcginnis@prairiestate.edu
MCGINNIS, Kim, M ...... 203-332-5183.. 86 F
kmcginnis@hcc.commnet.edu
MCGINNIS,
Maurice (Max) .... 585-594-6409 312 E
mcginnis_max@roberts.edu
MCGINNIS, Michael ...... 802-485-2310 462 F
mmcginni@norwich.edu
MCGINNIS, Sharon, R .. 910-938-6231 333 F
mcginniss@coastalcarolina.edu
MCGINNIS GONZALEZ,
Sherri .... 312-996-2398 151 G
smcginn@uic.edu
MCGINNISS, Michael .... 701-777-0588 345 B
michael.mcginniss@und.edu
MCGINNISS, Michael .... 215-951-1360 387 A
mcginnis@lasalle.edu
MCGINTY, Evelyn, J ...... 936-261-1725 446 C
ejmcginty@pvamu.edu
MCGINTY, Rachel .... 845-848-4034 298 C
rachel.mcginty@dc.edu
MCGIVERN, Martha .... 312-362-8998 136 H
martha.mcgivern@depaul.edu
MCGIVNEY, R, J .... 860-768-4401.. 89 G
rmcgivney@hartford.edu
MCGIVNEY-BURELLE,
Jean .... 208-282-4143 131 G
jeanmcgivneyburel@isu.edu
MCGLADDERY, Nicole ... 805-581-1233.. 41 I
nmcgladdery@eternitybiblecollege.com
MCGLADDERY, Ryan ..... 805-581-1233.. 41 I
rmcgladdery@eternitybiblecollege.com
MCGLADE, Jackie .... 304-243-2281 491 E
jmcglade@wheeling.edu
MCGLAMERY, Matt .... 970-247-7065.. 80 J
mcglamery_m@fortlewis.edu
MCGLAMERY, Orien, S . 970-247-7317.. 80 J
mcglamery_o@fortlewis.edu
MCGLASHAN, Holland .. 352-854-2322.. 97 N
mcglashh@cf.edu
MCGLAUFLIN, Nicole .... 712-279-5494 164 B
nicole.mcglauflin@briarcliff.edu
MCGLINCHEY, Tom .... 714-879-3901.. 45 G
tmcglinchey@hiu.edu
MCGLOTHLAN, Mary ..... 509-375-7105 372 H
mmcglothlan@corban.edu
MCGLOTHLIN, Jason .... 276-498-5247 464 D
jmcglothlin@acp.edu
MCGLOTHLIN,
Michael, G .... 276-498-4190 464 D
mmcglothlin@acp.edu
MCGLOUGHLIN,
Stephen .... 916-691-7589.. 50 H
mcglous@crc.losrios.edu
MCGODMAN, Kandi ...... 916-348-4689.. 41 H
kmcgodman@epic.edu
MCGOFF, Michael, F ..... 607-777-2143 316 B
mmcgoff@binghamton.edu
MCGOLDRICK, John ...... 215-951-1015 387 A
mcgoldri@lasalle.edu
MCGOLDRICK, Rowena . 860-515-3751.. 85 E
rmcgoldrick@charteroak.edu
MCGOLDRICK, Sean ...... 775-784-6514 271 E
smcgoldrick@unr.edu
MCGONAGLE,
William, B .... 281-283-2160 452 E
mcgonagle@uhcl.edu
MCGONIGLE, Erin .... 410-455-2691 203 B
emcgonigle@umbc.edu
MCGONIGLE, Gregory ... 404-727-4429 118 E
gregory.mcgonigle@emory.edu
MCGONIGLE, Mary .... 610-519-4070 401 K
mary.mcgonigle@villanova.edu
MCGONIGLE, Robert ..... 570-208-5875 386 G
rbmcgoni@kings.edu
MCGORRY, Marian .... 610-359-5394 382 A
mmcgorry@dccc.edu
MCGOVERN, Kathy .... 610-896-1089 385 I
kmcgovern@haverford.edu
MCGOVERN, Kevin .... 617-879-5982 216 D
kevin.mcgovern@mcphs.edu
MCGOVERN, Martin, P . 508-565-1321 219 A
mmcgovern@stonehill.edu
MCGOVERN, Michael ...... 718-933-6700 307 A
MCGOWAN, Annie .... 979-458-2905 446 F
al-mcgowan@tamu.edu
MCGOWAN, Christina ... 203-254-4000.. 87 I
cmcgowan@fairfield.edu
MCGOWAN, John .... 205-348-5610.... 7 G
john.mcgowan@ua.edu
MCGOWAN, John .... 585-345-6999 300 F
jmmcgowan@genesee.edu
MCGOWAN, Joumana ... 626-914-8881.. 36 J
jmcgowan@citruscollege.edu
MCGOWAN, Katie .... 610-526-6062 385 D
cmcgowan@harcum.edu
MCGOWAN, Kevin .... 239-687-5335.. 95 L
kmcgowan@avemarialaw.edu
MCGOWAN, Kyle .... 208-282-3198 131 G
mcgokyle@isu.edu
MCGOWAN, Kyle, D ...... 615-322-6850 428 A
kyle.mcgowan@vanderbilt.edu
MCGOWAN, Mary, M .... 585-385-8066 313 F
mmcgowan@sjfc.edu
MCGOWAN, Matthew .... 617-984-1700 218 C
MCGOWAN, Michelle .... 229-271-4045 125 E
mmcgowan@southgatech.edu
MCGOWAN, Paul .... 617-552-3055 207 C
paul.mcgowan.2@bc.edu
MCGOWAN, Stephanie .. 201-559-3551 277 J
mcgowans@felician.edu
MCGRADY, Patricia .... 973-957-0188 275 C
treasurer@acs350.org
MCGRADY, Ronald, L ... 330-325-6799 357 D
rmcgrady@neomed.edu
MCGRADY, Tracy .... 417-447-8152 257 G
mcgradyt@otc.edu
MCGRAIL, Frederick, J .. 610-758-4487 388 E
fjm208@lehigh.edu
MCGRAIL, James .... 603-862-0927 274 E
james.mcgrail@usnh.edu
MCGRANE, Wendy .... 417-625-9801 256 F
mcgrane-w@mssu.edu
MCGRANN, Michael ...... 718-940-5741 314 A
mmgrann@sjcny.edu
MCGRATH, Abigail .... 312-567-3497 140 A
amcgrat1@iit.edu
MCGRATH, Beth .... 201-216-3389 283 D
cos.mcgrath@stevens.edu
MCGRATH, Bill .... 239-992-4624.. 96 E
MCGRATH, Cheryl .... 617-824-8328 209 C
cheryl_mcgrath@emerson.edu
MCGRATH, Christina ..... 719-549-3308.. 82 J
christina.mcgrath@pueblocc.edu
MCGRATH, Elizabeth ..... 563-588-6414 164 E
beth.mcgrath@clarke.edu
MCGRATH, Elizabeth ..... 660-944-3105 251 J
MCGRATH, Frank .... 239-687-5331.. 95 L
fmcgrath@avemarialaw.edu
MCGRATH, Greg .... 802-485-2225 462 F
gmcgrath@norwich.edu
MCGRATH, James .... 517-371-5140 233 C
mcgrathj@cooley.edu
MCGRATH, Jane .... 312-362-5765 136 H
jmcgrath@depaul.edu
MCGRATH, Karen .... 607-431-4130 301 A
mcgrathk@hartwick.edu
MCGRATH, Kat .... 518-608-8374 299 C
kmcgrath@excelsior.edu
MCGRATH, Mark .... 267-331-2853 381 A
mcgrathm@chc.edu
MCGRATH, Nicole .... 203-932-7077.. 89 H
nmcgrath@newhaven.edu
MCGRATH, Riley, C ...... 715-836-5521 495 E
mcgratrc@uwec.edu
MCGRATH, Teresa .... 978-232-2290 209 E
tmcgrath@endicott.edu
MCGRATH, Thomas ...... 508-565-1086 219 A
tmcgrath@stonehill.edu
MCGRATH, Tim .... 714-895-8178.. 38 A
tmcgrath@gwc.cccd.edu
MCGRATH-ROTHENBERG,
Alexis .... 914-674-7607 306 C
arothenberg@mercy.edu
MCGRAW, Bryan .... 630-752-5928 153 C
bryan.mcgraw@wheaton.edu
MCGRAW, Darryl .... 919-508-2418 344 E
ddmcgraw@peace.edu
MCGRAW, Larry .... 325-670-1269 436 I
mcgraw@hsutx.edu
MCGRAW, Matthew .... 540-863-2866 473 F
mmcgraw@dslcc.edu
MCGRAW, Packy .... 518-694-7257 289 J
packy.mcgraw@acphs.edu

MCKENNA, Timothy, J .. 319-273-3241 164 A
tim.mckenna@uni.edu
MCKENNA, Tori .... 860-439-2314.. 87 H
tori.mckenna@conncoll.edu
MCKENNA-JONES, Amy 573-518-2146 256 D
mjones@mineralarea.edu
MCKENZIE, Alicia .... 508-213-2020 217 H
alicia.mckenzie@nichols.edu
MCKENZIE, Andre, A .... 718-990-1892 313 G
mckenzia@stjohns.edu
MCKENZIE, Bruce .... 937-778-7855 352 D
bmckenzie@edisonohio.edu
MCKENZIE, Chris, D ..... 252-399-6314 326 K
cdmckenzie@barton.edu
MCKENZIE, Connie, L ... 757-965-8500 466 D
mckenzcl@evms.edu
MCKENZIE, Deborah ..... 803-705-4589 406 G
deborah.mckenzie@benedict.edu
MCKENZIE, Helen, R ..... 814-866-8130 387 D
hmckenzie@lecom.edu
MCKENZIE, JoAnn .... 404-727-6052 118 E
jmckenz@emory.edu
MCKENZIE, Justin .... 484-365-8134 388 H
cio@lincoln.edu
MCKENZIE, Laura .... 208-282-2979 131 G
mckelaur@isu.edu
MCKENZIE, Mary Beth .. 978-665-3123 212 E
memckenzie@fitchburgstate.edu
MCKENZIE, Michael ...... 828-262-2130 340 I
mckenziemj@appstate.edu
MCKENZIE, Rene .... 541-956-7129 376 A
rmckenzie@roguecc.edu
MCKENZIE, Sarah .... 334-808-6128.... 7 C
smckenzie93530@troy.edu
MCKENZIE, Steve .... 707-476-4385.. 58 I
MCKENZIE, Vandeen ..... 575-646-6014 287 C
vmckenzi@nmsu.edu
MCKEON, John .... 850-729-4929 104 M
mckeonj@nwfsc.edu
MCKEON, Margaret .... 215-871-6826 395 G
margaremc@pcom.edu
MCKEON, Michael .... 518-442-5435 316 A
mmckeon@albany.edu
MCKEOWN, Joshua, S .. 315-312-2118 318 D
joshua.mckeown@oswego.edu
MCKEOWN, Robert .... 716-614-6201 309 G
mckeown@niagaracc.suny.edu
MCKERALL, Deborah ..... 936-294-3548 450 A
dam004@shsu.edu
MCKERNAN, Sarah .... 620-341-5551 173 F
smckerna@emporia.edu
MCKERNAN-WALLEY,
Jillian .... 315-229-5512 314 D
jmckwall@stlawu.edu
MCKERNON, Bill .... 620-341-5331 173 F
wmckerna@emporia.edu
MCKETHAN, Lisa, H ...... 254-710-3817 431 E
lisa_mckethan@baylor.edu
MCKETHER, Willie ...... 419-530-5529 363 B
willie.mckether@utoledo.edu
MCKIBBON, Chris .... 402-844-7015 268 H
chris@northeast.edu
MCKIE, Angi .... 319-335-3531 163 H
angi-mckie@uiowa.edu
MCKIM, Heather .... 970-248-1950.. 78 J
hmckim@coloradomesa.edu
MCKINDRA, Freeman ..... 731-426-7500 420 G
MCKINION, Randall .... 937-766-7986 349 E
rmkinion@cedarville.edu
MCKINLEY, Bob .... 817-598-6256 457 J
bmckinley@wc.edu
MCKINLEY, Colleen .... 562-860-2451.. 35 H
cmckinley@cerritos.edu
MCKINLEY, Erica .... 662-915-7014 249 D
mckinley@olemiss.edu
MCKINLEY, Kathy .... 919-536-7244 334 C
mckinleyk@durhamtech.edu
MCKINLEY, Kristin, L .... 920-832-6532 493 B
kristin.l.mckinley@lawrence.edu
MCKINLEY, Robert .... 210-485-0020 428 G
MCKINLEY, Ronald .... 510-981-2800.. 56 I
MCKINNEY, Amy .... 209-588-5100.. 76 K
MCKINNEY, Anya .... 865-251-1800 423 E
library@south.edu
MCKINNEY, Bryan .... 870-245-5513.. 20 D
mckinneyb@obu.edu
MCKINNEY, Bryan .... 870-245-5250.. 20 D
mckinneyb@obu.edu
MCKINNEY, David, C .... 888-491-8686.. 75 F
davidmckinney@westcliff.edu
MCKINNEY, Gail .... 303-797-5647.. 77 I
gail.mckinney@arapahoe.edu

MCKINNEY, Jason .... 315-279-5434 303 G
jmckinney@keuka.edu
MCKINNEY, Jermaine ... 386-481-2358.. 96 D
mckinneyj@cookman.edu
MCKINNEY, Jill .... 317-940-8312 154 C
jsmckinn@butler.edu
MCKINNEY, Joan, C ..... 270-789-5214 180 A
jmckinney@campbellsville.edu
MCKINNEY, Marion .... 610-436-3307 395 D
mmckinney@wcupa.edu
MCKINNEY, Marion, R .. 804-524-5961 476 D
mmckinney@vsu.edu
MCKINNEY, Mica .... 435-797-1156 460 C
mica.mckinney@usu.edu
MCKINNEY, Michael ..... 724-589-2600 399 D
mmckinney@thiel.edu
MCKINNEY, Mitchell, S 330-972-6433 361 H
mmckinney@uakron.edu
MCKINNEY, Monica ...... 919-760-8056 331 D
mckinneym@meredith.edu
MCKINNEY, Nancy .... 803-732-5355 410 D
mckinneyn@midlandstech.edu
MCKINNEY, Nick .... 509-777-4596 486 C
nmckinney@whitworth.edu
MCKINNEY, Paul .... 662-325-7428 247 F
kpm137@msstate.edu
MCKINNEY, Rebekah ..... 417-255-7949 256 H
MCKINNEY, Robert .... 337-482-5308 193 B
mckinney@louisiana.edu
MCKINNEY, Roger .... 866-492-5336 244 F
roger.mckinney@laureate.net
MCKINNEY, Ronnie .... 334-244-3668.... 4 E
ronnie@aum.edu
MCKINNEY, Scott .... 304-473-8041 491 D
mckinney.s@wvwc.edu
MCKINNEY, Shortie ...... 978-934-4460 212 B
shortie_mckinney@uml.edu
MCKINNEY, Teresa .... 713-313-7011 449 B
MCKINNEY, Teresa, F ... 423-425-4141 427 C
teresa-mckinney@utc.edu
MCKINNEY, Ulreen .... 321-674-7472 100 C
ujones@fit.edu
MCKINNISS, Mike .... 805-565-6819.. 76 A
mmckinniss@westmont.edu
MCKINNON, Brad .... 256-766-6610.... 5 E
bmckinnon@hcu.edu
MCKINNON, Charles ..... 770-962-7580 121 E
cmckinnon@gwinnetttech.edu
MCKINNON, Georgia .... 980-495-3978 329 B
MCKINNON, Laura .... 817-515-4521 445 F
laura.mckinnon@tccd.edu
MCKINNON, Maureen ... 816-501-4831 258 I
maureen.mckinnon@rockhurst.edu
MCKINNON, Will .... 801-863-8922 460 D
will.mckinnon@uvu.edu
MCKINNON-HOWE,
Leah .... 617-585-1284 217 E
leah.mckinnon-howe@necmusic.edu
MCKINNY, Terry .... 864-488-8907 410 B
atmckinney@limestone.edu
MCKINSEY-MABRY,
Kimberly .... 585-292-1616 307 B
kmckinseymabry@monroecc.edu
MCKINSEY-MABRY,
Kimberly .... 585-262-1616 307 B
kmckinseymabry@monroecc.edu
MCKINSON-BECKFORD,
Simone .... 716-286-7353 309 H
sbeckford@niagara.edu
MCKINZIE, Jena .... 830-372-8155 449 A
jmckinzie@tlu.edu
MCKIRDY, Pam .... 434-791-5618 464 I
MCKISSICK, Issac .... 864-466-1065 412 E
mckissicki@sccsc.edu
MCKISSON, Kevin .... 281-669-4711 442 K
kevin.mckisson@sjcd.edu
MCKISSON, Kevin .... 281-998-6150 443 C
kevin.mckisson@sjcd.edu
MCKISSON, Kevin .... 281-669-4711 442 K
kevin.mckisson@sjcd.edu
MCKISSON, Kevin .... 281-998-6150 443 B
kevin.mckisson@sjcd.edu
MCKISSON, Kevin, R .... 281-669-4711 443 A
kevin.mckisson@sjcd.edu
MCKITTRICK, Jerry .... 314-744-5345 256 E
mckittrickj@mobap.edu
MCKLOSKEY, Brian .... 412-237-3056 381 D
bmckloskey@ccac.edu
MCKNIGHT, Carla, L ..... 407-582-1756 113 I
cmcknight5@valenciacollege.edu
MCKNIGHT, Colleen ..... 301-846-2446 198 I
cmcknight@frederick.edu

MCKNIGHT, Cynthia ..... 440-684-6102 363 C
cmcknigh@ursuline.edu
MCKNIGHT, John .... 860-439-2035.. 87 H
jmcknight@conncoll.edu
MCKNIGHT, John .... 610-896-1232 385 I
jmcknight@haverford.edu
MCKNIGHT, Natalie .... 617-353-2852 207 E
njmck@bu.edu
MCKNIGHT, Oscar .... 419-289-5065 347 J
omcknigh@ashland.edu
MCKNIGHT, Sandra ...... 216-987-4832 351 E
sandra.mcknight@tri-c.edu
MCKNIGHT, Scott .... 210-233-1102 433 A
MCKNIGHT, Steven, H .. 571-858-3000 476 C
shm@vt.edu
MCKNIGHT, Tanner .... 870-633-4480.. 19 A
tmcknight@eacc.edu
MCKNIGHT-TUTEIN,
Gillian .... 303-352-3059.. 80 F
gillian.mcknight-tutein@ccd.edu
MCKONE, Kevin .... 601-643-8369 245 F
kevin.mckone@colin.edu
MCKOWN, Johnette ...... 254-299-8601 439 E
jmckown@mclennan.edu
MCKOY, Cynthia .... 910-879-5566 332 D
cmckoy@bladencc.edu
MCKUSICK, Jim .... 816-235-2182 261 B
honors@umkc.edu
MCLAIN, Andrea .... 617-984-1713 218 C
amclain@quincycollege.edu
MCLAIN, Chris .... 425-739-8265 481 C
chris.mclain@lwtech.edu
MCLAIN, Kimberly .... 607-778-5024 317 D
mclainkb@sunybroome.edu
MCLAIN, Mandy .... 336-725-8344 327 H
mclainm@carolinau.edu
MCLAIN, Rebecca .... 704-922-6352 334 G
mclain.rebecca@gaston.edu
MCLALLEN, Peter .... 626-398-2222.. 76 C
MCLAMB, Alvin .... 803-327-7402 407 F
amclamb@clintoncollege.edu
MCLANE, Margaret .... 518-485-3334 296 G
mclanem@strose.edu
MCLANEY, Carl .... 323-563-4854.. 36 C
carlmclaney@cdrewu.edu
MCLAREN, Donna .... 585-594-6114 312 E
mclaren_donna@roberts.edu
MCLAREN, Robert .... 808-956-8531 129 E
rmclaren@hawaii.edu
MCLAREN-POOLE, Kate . 508-531-6502 212 D
kate.mclaren@bridgew.edu
MCLARIO, Lisa .... 770-381-7200 121 B
MCLARTY, Meridith .... 972-860-4823 434 F
mmclarty@dcccd.edu
MCLARY, Laura .... 540-362-7433 467 H
mclaryla@hollins.edu
MCLARY, Laura, A .... 503-943-7255 377 A
mclary@up.edu
MCLAUGHLAN, Craig .... 309-438-7018 140 D
ccmclau@ilstu.edu
MCLAUGHLIN, Adam .... 319-385-6490 167 H
adam.mclaughlin@iw.edu
MCLAUGHLIN, Annette . 718-817-4350 300 C
lmclaughlin9@fordham.edu
MCLAUGHLIN,
Bryan, S .... 402-280-2386 266 H
bmclaughlin@creighton.edu
MCLAUGHLIN, Cate ...... 617-521-2000 218 G
MCLAUGHLIN, Chris ..... 541-962-3516 372 I
cjmclaughlin@eou.edu
MCLAUGHLIN, Colin ..... 724-805-2176 398 A
colin.mclaughlin@stvincent.edu
MCLAUGHLIN,
David, B .... 419-207-5555 347 J
dmclaugh@ashland.edu
MCLAUGHLIN, Edward .. 267-341-3031 385 J
emclaughlin2@holyfamily.edu
MCLAUGHLIN,
Edward, K .... 804-828-6692 473 B
athleticsdir@vcu.edu
MCLAUGHLIN,
Francis, X .... 718-817-4300 300 C
mclaughlin@fordham.edu
MCLAUGHLIN, Jennifer . 215-335-0800 388 G
jmcloughlin@lincolntech.edu
MCLAUGHLIN, Joyce .... 978-934-4237 212 B
joyce_mclaughlin@uml.edu
MCLAUGHLIN, Keith ..... 708-656-8000 145 C
keith.mclaughlin@morton.edu
MCLAUGHLIN, Kerry ..... 718-933-6700 307 A
kmclaughlin@monroecollege.edu
MCLAUGHLIN, Kevin .... 216-791-5000 350 I
kevin.mclaughlin@cim.edu

MCLAUGHLIN, Kevin .... 401-863-9525 403 J
kevin_mclaughlin@brown.edu
MCLAUGHLIN, Laura, L 217-581-7264 137 E
lmclaughlin@eiu.edu
MCLAUGHLIN,
Laurie, L .... 612-626-1499 243 F
mclau001@umn.edu
MCLAUGHLIN, LaVerne 229-500-3468 114 H
laverne.mclaughlin@asurams.edu
MCLAUGHLIN, Lisa .... 701-854-8023 346 H
lisa.mclaughlin@sittingbull.edu
MCLAUGHLIN, Mark ..... 610-785-6216 397 E
mmclaughlin@scs.edu
MCLAUGHLIN, Mark ..... 513-745-3409 364 G
mclaughlin@xavier.edu
MCLAUGHLIN,
Maureen .... 215-248-7137 381 A
mclaughlinm1@chc.edu
MCLAUGHLIN, Nora ...... 503-777-7774 375 G
nora.mclaughlin@reed.edu
MCLAUGHLIN, Paula .... 843-676-8590 409 F
paula.mclaughlin@fdtc.edu
MCLAUGHLIN, Robert ... 775-241-4445 270 E
MCLAUGHLIN, Robert ... 973-761-7405 283 C
robert.mclaughlin@shu.edu
MCLAUGHLIN, Robert ... 713-798-4613 431 D
rmclaughlin@bcm.edu
MCLAUGHLIN, Sean, M 614-823-1576 359 H
smclaughlin@otterbein.edu
MCLAUGHLIN, Steve ..... 612-874-3759 237 A
smclaughlin@mcad.edu
MCLAUGHLIN,
Steven, W .... 404-894-6825 119 E
swm@gatech.edu
MCLAUGHLIN, Tim .... 850-478-8496 105 G
tmclaughlin@pcci.edu
MCLAUGHLIN, William . 585-785-1561 299 F
william.mclaughlin@flcc.edu
MCLAUGHLIN VIGNIER,
Loretta .... 973-720-2104 284 J
mclaughlinvignierl@wpunj.edu
MCLAUGHLIN VIGNIER,
Loretta, C .... 973-720-3636 284 J
mclaughlinvignierl@wpunj.edu
MCLAUGHLIN-VOLPE,
Tracy .... 617-873-0150 208 B
tracy.mclaughlin@cambridgecollege.
edu
MCLAURY, Brenton .... 918-631-2999 371 C
brenton-mclaury@utulsa.edu
MCLEAN, Amber .... 906-635-2382 226 G
amclean@lssu.edu
MCLEAN, Angela .... 406-449-9131 263 J
amclean@montana.edu
MCLEAN, Beverly .... 925-631-4600.. 59 I
bam12@stmarys-ca.edu
MCLEAN, Brandon .... 402-844-7102 268 H
brandon@northeast.edu
MCLEAN, Connie .... 309-796-5369 133 G
mcleanc@bhc.edu
MCLEAN, David .... 970-491-3366.. 79 N
david.mclean@colostate.edu
MCLEAN, Jake .... 309-341-7303 141 G
jrmclean@knox.edu
MCLEAN, Janna .... 574-807-7191 154 B
janna.mclean@betheluniversity.edu
MCLEAN, Jennifer .... 570-326-3761 392 W
jmclean@pct.edu
MCLEAN, Kirk .... 202-319-6065.. 92 A
mclean@cua.edu
MCLEAN, Mark .... 985-448-7925 188 C
mark.mclean@fletcher.edu
MCLEAN, Michael, F ...... 805-525-4417.. 67 K
mmclean@thomasaquinas.edu
MCLEAN, Monique .... 202-884-9097.. 94 A
mcleanmo@trinitydc.edu
MCLEAN, Natalie .... 336-273-4431 327 A
nmclean@bennett.edu
MCLEAN, Pat .... 417-690-3441 251 H
mclean@cofo.edu
MCLEAN, Robert .... 443-997-8767 199 G
bobmclean@jhu.edu
MCLEAN, Selvin .... 321-674-7715 100 C
smclean@fit.edu
MCLEAN, William .... 804-289-6010 472 C
smcinvest@richmond.edu
MCLEER, Karen .... 608-342-1081 496 E
mcleerk@uwplatt.edu
MCLELLAN, Amy .... 415-442-5285.. 43 I
amclellan@ggu.edu
MCLELLAN, Colleen ...... 734-432-5880 227 C
cmclellan@madonna.edu
MCLELLAN, Mark .... 940-369-7487 453 E
mark.mclellan@unt.edu

MCNATT,
Rosemary Bray .... 510-549-4724.. 66 G
rbraymcnatt@sksm.edu
MCNAUGHTON, Laura .. 605-658-5641 416 D
laura.mcnaughton@usd.edu
MCNAUGHTON, Victor .. 202-806-1106.. 92 F
vmcnaughton@howard.edu
MCNAUL, Kathleen, V ... 570-326-3761 392W
kmcnaul@pct.edu
MCNEAL, Latanya, L ..... 561-993-1156 105 D
mcneall@palmbeachstate.edu
MCNEAL, Lisa .... 912-279-4505 117 F
lmcneal@ccga.edu
MCNEAL, Nadine .... 731-989-6644 419 K
nmcneal@fhu.edu
MCNEAL, Ryan .... 912-681-5667 123 J
rmcneal@ogeecheetech.edu
MCNEALEY, Eloise .... 256-469-7333.... 5 H
dev@hbc1.edu
MCNEALEY, Ernest .... 803-376-5701 406 D
emcnealey@allenuniversity.edu
MCNEAR, Marie .... 334-229-4200.... 4 A
mmcnear@alasu.edu
MCNEELEY, Wendy .... 325-649-8619 437 G
wmcneeley@hputx.edu
MCNEELY, Ann Marie ... 828-448-3509 339 A
amcneely@wpcc.edu
MCNEELY, Shelley .... 608-785-9880 500 C
mcneelys@westerntc.edu
MCNEELY, Stanton, F .... 504-398-2109 192 A
smcneely@uhcno.edu
MCNEELY COBHAM,
Afeni .... 616-234-4000 224 F
MCNEESE, Laura .... 918-595-7643 370 C
laura.mcneese@tulsacc.edu
MCNEESE, Tim, D .... 402-363-5683 270 D
tdmcnesse@york.edu
MCNEIL, Beth .... 765-494-2900 160 B
MCNEIL, Carlene .... 407-708-2683 108 D
mcneilc@seminolestate.edu
MCNEIL, J. Derek .... 206-876-6100 483 H
dmcneil@theseattleschool.edu
MCNEIL, Jaquelyn .... 941-752-5231 109 G
mcneilj@scf.edu
MCNEIL, Jinawa .... 410-951-3610 204 B
jmcneil@coppin.edu
MCNEIL, Jinawa .... 978-665-3140 212 E
jmcnei12@fitchburgstate.edu
MCNEIL, Krista .... 847-866-3907 138 D
krista.mcneil@garrett.edu
MCNEIL, JR.,
Lawrence, R .... 301-860-3590 204 A
lmcneil@bowiestate.edu
MCNEIL, Mia .... 810-766-6718 232 A
miamc@umich.edu
MCNEIL, Stephanie .... 704-216-6953 330 H
smcneil@livingstone.edu
MCNEILL, Amanda .... 505-368-3524.. 12 D
amcneill@dinecollege.edu
MCNEILL, Andy .... 417-690-3200 251 H
purch@cofo.edu
MCNEILL, Kathy .... 210-999-8425 451 E
kmcneill@trinity.edu
MCNEILL, MaNina .... 919-546-8617 340 B
manina.manina@shawu.edu
MCNEILL, Savonne .... 704-922-6420 334 G
mcneill.savonne@gaston.edu
MCNEILL, Warren .... 806-720-7212 439 D
warren.mcneill@lcu.edu
MCNELEY, Kim .... 816-235-8648 261 B
mcneleyk@umkc.edu
MCNELLEY, Eric .... 610-341-1736 383 B
emcnell@eastern.edu
MCNEW, Regina .... 865-694-6650 425 B
rdmcnew@pstcc.edu
MCNICHOLS, Michaels .. 317-921-4710 158 D
mmcnichols@ivytech.edu
MCNICOL, Greg, L .... 915-747-7182 455 C
gmcnicol@utep.edu
MCNIECE, Jennifer .... 325-649-8179 437 G
jmcniece@hputx.edu
MCNIEL, Christina .... 352-371-2833.. 98 G
admissions@dragonrises.edu
MCNIER, Michelle .... 989-463-7423 221 B
mcniermI@alma.edu
MCNITT, Zakary .... 517-787-0800 225 E
mcnittzakaryt@jccmi.edu
MCNULTY, Charlie .... 863-667-5000 108 K
ckmcnulty@seu.edu
MCNULTY, George .... 906-932-4231 224 D
MCNULTY, Jenny .... 907-786-1707.... 9 J
jmcnulty@alaska.edu
MCNULTY, LeeAnne ...... 805-922-6966.. 24 I
leeanne.mcnulty@hancockcollege.edu
MCNULTY, Mary Kate ... 215-572-2877 378 E
mcnultym@arcadia.edu
MCNULTY, Michael .... 267-341-3281 385 J
mmcnulty@holyfamily.edu
MCNULTY, Patrick .... 312-942-6849 148 G
patrick_j_mcnulty@rush.edu
MCNULTY, Paul, J .... 724-458-2500 384 G
pjmcnulty@gcc.edu
MCNULTY, Timothy .... 412-268-7778 380 C
tpm@andrew.cmu.edu
MCNUTT, Jon .... 323-259-1343.. 54 I
jmcnutt@oxy.edu
MCNUTT, Kraig .... 214-887-5141 435 F
kmcnutt@dts.edu
MCNUTT, Paula, M .... 563-333-6112 169 G
mcnuttpaulam@sau.edu
MCPARTLAND, Terence . 203-672-6647.. 85 D
tmcpartland@albertus.edu
MCPARTLON, Shannon . 313-664-7460 222 H
smcpartlon@collegeforcreativestudies.edu
MCPHAIL, Christine ...... 919-516-4000 339 I
MCPHAIL, Craig .... 828-898-2483 330 E
mcphail@lmc.edu
MCPHAIL, Julie .... 319-656-2447 170 A
MCPHAIL, P. Curtis ...... 864-597-4261 414 E
mcphailpc@wofford.edu
MCPHATTER, Anna .... 443-885-3922 201 A
anna.mcphatter@morgan.edu
MCPHATTER, George ..... 818-785-2726.. 35 E
george.mcphatter@casalomacollege.edu
MCPHATTER, Renee ...... 202-994-0679.. 92 D
rmcphatt@gwu.edu
MCPHEARSON, Petra, R 731-881-7800 427 D
prencher@utm.edu
MCPHEE, Debra .... 212-636-6616 300 C
dmcphee1@fordham.edu
MCPHEE, Myra, M .... 305-626-3626 100 D
myra.mcphee@fmuniv.edu
MCPHEE, Sidney, A ...... 615-898-2623 422 C
sidney.mcphee@mtsu.edu
MCPHEE, Sydney .... 615-220-7853 424 F
smcphee@mscc.edu
MCPHEETERS, Andrew .. 503-768-7936 373 E
mcpheete@lclark.edu
MCPHERON, Bruce .... 614-292-6164 358 D
mcpheron.24@osu.edu
MCPHERON, Lisa .... 714-992-7014.. 54 C
mcpheron@fullcoll.edu
MCPHERSON, Brisco ..... 405-224-3140 371 B
bmcpherson@usao.edu
MCPHERSON,
Christopher, A .... 304-336-8274 490 B
christopher.mcpherson@westliberty.edu
MCPHERSON, John .... 765-285-5600 153 H
jmcphers@bsu.edu
MCPHERSON, Kevin ...... 312-488-6051.. 36 E
kmcpherson1@tcsedsystem.edu
MCPHERSON, Michael .. 305-809-3280.. 97 O
michael.mcpherson@cfk.edu
MCPHERSON, Michael .. 940-565-5206 453 E
michael.mcpherson@unt.edu
MCPHERSON, Nancy ..... 816-268-5402 257 C
nmcpherson@nts.edu
MCPHERSON, Robert .... 713-743-5003 452 D
bmcph@uh.edu
MCPHERSON, Tim .... 423-648-2421 423 B
tmcpherson@richmont.edu
MCPHERSON, Timothy .. 816-268-5430 257 C
tmcpherson@nts.edu
MCPHERSON, Walter ..... 910-814-3470 333 C
wmcpherson@cccc.edu
MCPHERSON-MYERS,
Penny .... 856-256-4086 281 F
mcphersonp@rowan.edu
MCPHILLIPS, Michael .... 740-351-3046 360 F
mmcphillips@shawnee.edu
MCQUADE, Eileen .... 805-565-6117.. 76 A
mcquade@westmont.edu
MCQUADE, Robert, K .... 574-631-6161 162 A
mcquade.10@nd.edu
MCQUAID, David, P ..... 614-292-2635 358 D
mcquaid.11@osu.edu
MCQUARIE, Audra .... 602-557-6151.. 16 G
audra.mcquarie@phoenix.edu
MCQUARTERS, Alfred .... 503-491-6422 374 B
alfred.mcquarters@mhcc.edu
MCQUEEN, Candice ...... 615-966-1787 421 B
candice.mcqueen@lipscomb.edu
MCQUEEN, Mary .... 361-698-1317 435 G
mmcqueen2@delmar.edu
MCQUEEN, Rebecca ..... 270-852-3289 183 E
rmcqueen@kwc.edu
MCQUEENEY, Chris, B .. 315-568-3352 310 B
cmcqueeney@nycc.edu
MCQUERRY, Marcia ...... 405-585-5100 367 B
marcia.mcquerry@okbu.edu
MCQUESTEN, Pam .... 608-363-2470 491 H
mcquestenp@beloit.edu
MCQUILKIN, Scott .... 509-777-3200 486 C
president@whitworth.edu
MCQUILLAN, Shawn, A 412-365-1591 380 G
s.mcquillan@chatham.edu
MCQUILLEN, Troy .... 319-398-5569 167 J
troy.mcquillen@kirkwood.edu
MCQUINN, Robert .... 847-467-2469 146 E
r-mcquinn@northwestern.edu
MCRAE, Kevin .... 406-449-9154 263 J
kmcrae@montana.edu
MCRAE, Martin .... 903-589-7129 438 C
mmcrae@jacksonville-college.edu
MCRAE, Mary, S .... 972-378-8790 433 I
mmcrae@collin.edu
MCRAE-BRUNSON,
Marcela, C .... 870-235-4025.. 21 C
mdbrunson@saumag.edu
MCREE, Matt .... 706-245-3115 118 D
mmcree@ec.edu
MCRELL, Michael .... 620-341-5214 173 F
mcrellmi@emporia.edu
MCREYNOLDS, Ginny .... 916-558-2407.. 50 J
mcreynv@scc.losrios.edu
MCREYNOLDS, Julie ..... 618-453-7935 150 B
jcima@siu.edu
MCREYNOLDS, Karla ..... 573-288-6544 252 F
kmcreynolds@culver.edu
MCREYNOLDS, Shawn .. 276-223-4810 476 A
smcreynolds@wcc.vccs.edu
MCRINA, Rhonda .... 319-296-4463 166 H
rhonda.mcrina@hawkeyecollege.edu
MCROBBIE, Michael, A . 812-855-4613 156 G
iupres@iu.edu
MCRORIE, Sally, E .... 850-644-1765 110 C
smcrorie@fsu.edu
MCSHAN, Braxton .... 504-816-4669 186 I
bmcshan@dillard.edu
MCSHANE, Janet 718-862-7948 304M
janet.mcshane@manhattan.edu
MCSHANE, S.J.,
Joseph, M .... 718-817-3000 300 C
president@fordham.edu
MCSHEFFERY, Ed .... 724-938-4299 393 E
mcsheffery@calu.edu
MCSHERRY, Bernard ..... 201-200-2020 279 D
bmcsherry@njcu.edu
MCSHERRY, Rod .... 210-458-4101 455 E
MCSPADDEN, Daniel, L 513-745-3756 364 G
mcspaddend@xavier.edu
MCSTEEN, Patti .... 740-593-1800 358 K
mcsteenp@ohio.edu
MCSWAIN, Ann .... 573-681-5400 254 G
mcswaina@lincolnu.edu
MCSWAIN, Arletha .... 386-481-2094.. 96 D
mcswaina@cookman.edu
MCSWAIN, Roderick ..... 251-405-7013.... 1 E
rmcswain@bishop.edu
MCSWEEN, Amanda ...... 806-743-6431 451 A
amanda.mcsween@ttuhsc.edu
MCTIERNAN, Kerri-Ann . 516-572-7537 307 E
kerriann.mctiernan@ncc.edu
MCTIERNAN, Susan ...... 401-254-3444 405 C
smctiernan@rwu.edu
MCTYIER, James (Jay) .. 812-941-2454 157 F
jmctyier@ius.edu
MCVAY, Janine .... 413-565-1000 206 D
jmcvay@baypath.edu
MCVAY, John .... 509-527-2121 485 C
john.mcvay@wallawalla.edu
MCVAY, John, R .... 575-624-8150 287 B
mcvay@nmmi.edu
MCVEAN, Aaron .... 650-358-6803.. 62 I
mcveana@smccd.edu
MCVEY, Greg .... 352-395-5536 108 A
greg.mcvey@sfcollege.edu
MCVEY, Josh .... 575-461-4413 286 G
joshm@mesalands.edu
MCVEY, Troy .... 671-734-6912 504 F
tmcvey@triton.uog.edu
MCVICKER, Libby .... 618-395-7777 139 E
mcvickero@iecc.edu
MCWAINE, DeRhonda ... 281-998-6150 443 A
derhonda.mcwaine@sjcd.edu
MCWELL, Andre .... 712-274-5318 168 E
mcwell@morningside.edu
MCWHERTER, Karen ...... 731-661-5337 426 F
kmcwhert@uu.edu
MCWHORTER,
Shirlyon, J .... 305-348-2785 110 A
shirlyon.mcwhorter@fiu.edu
MCWHORTER, Thomas . 213-740-5445.. 73 D
faodean@usc.edu
MCWILLIAMS, Brendan . 617-735-9986 209 D
mcwilliamsb@emmanuel.edu
MCWILLIAMS, Diana ..... 972-686-7878 442 B
MCWILLIAMS, Gene ...... 610-558-5504 391 A
genemcw@neumann.edu
MCWILLIAMS, Joe .... 208-496-7010 130 I
mcwilliamsj@byui.edu
MCWILLIAMS,
Josette, A .... 207-581-1512 196 G
josette.mcwilliams@maine.edu
MCWILLIAMS, Mindy .... 202-687-8041.. 92 E
mcwillie@georgetown.edu
MCWILLIAMS, Rachel ... 252-985-5343 339 D
rmcwilliams@ncwc.edu
MCWILLIAMS,
Stephen, T .... 610-519-4095 401 K
stephen.mcwilliams@villanova.edu
MCWILLIAMS, Susan .... 207-228-8258 197 D
susan.mcwilliams@maine.edu
MCWORTHY, Chance .... 319-363-1323 168 F
cmcworthy@mtmercy.edu
MCZEE, Taran .... 859-246-6438 181 F
taran.mczee@kctcs.edu
MEA, William .... 614-236-6872 349 B
wmea@capital.edu
MEAD, Ann Marie .... 609-896-5000 281 B
amead@rider.edu
MEAD, Craig .... 907-786-1480.... 9 J
MEAD, Molly .... 816-235-6595 261 B
meadmo@umkc.edu
MEAD, Shawnboda .... 662-915-2933 249 D
sdmead@olemiss.edu
MEADE, Elizabeth .... 610-606-4612 380 D
president@cedarcrest.edu
MEADE, Joseph .... 215-951-1010 387 A
meade@lasalle.edu
MEADE, Melissa .... 360-596-5364 484 D
mmeade@spscc.edu
MEADE, OSB,
Pachomius .... 660-944-2950 251 J
pachomius@conception.edu
MEADE, Phil .... 718-429-6600 324 D
phil.meade@vaughn.edu
MEADER, Eric .... 207-755-5348 195 D
emeader@cmcc.edu
MEADERDS, Genesis ..... 541-962-3496 372 I
gmeaderds@eou.edu
MEADOR, Cherie .... 708-974-5633 145 A
meadorc@morainevalley.edu
MEADOR, Earl .... 318-371-3035 188 F
earlmeador@nltcc.edu
MEADOR, Ryan .... 816-604-1076 255 C
ryan.meador@mcckc.edu
MEADOWS, Aaron .... 843-953-5049 407 C
smeadows@citadel.edu
MEADOWS, Courtney .... 618-395-1169 139 H
meadowsc@iecc.edu
MEADOWS, David, D .... 814-641-0714 386 E
meadowd@juniata.edu
MEADOWS, David, J ..... 412-578-8842 380 B
djmeadows@carlow.edu
MEADOWS, Ed .... 850-484-1700 105 H
emeadows@pensacolastate.edu
MEADOWS, Leslie .... 334-244-3657.... 4 E
lmeadows@aum.edu
MEADOWS, Lorelle .... 906-487-2827 228 A
lameadows@mtu.edu
MEADOWS, Melissa ...... 760-252-2411.. 26 G
mmeadows@barstow.edu
MEADOWS, Michelle ..... 434-395-2429 468 F
meadowsme@longwood.edu
MEADOWS, Ricky .... 252-638-4550 334 A
millardj@cravencc.edu
MEADOWS, Steve .... 304-384-5180 489 J
meadows@concord.edu
MEADOWS, Terry .... 479-788-7891.. 21 G
terry.meadows@uafs.edu
MEADS, Lisa .... 252-335-0821 333 G
lisa_meads@albemarle.edu
MEAGER, Kevin .... 419-227-3141 362 F
klmeager@unoh.edu
MEAGHER, Jo-Ann .... 978-630-9101 215 C
j_meagher@mwcc.mass.edu
MEAGHER, Kathy .... 301-387-3095 199 A
kathy.meagher@garrettcollege.edu

MEAGHER, Paula, G 915-831-4530 436 A pmeagher@epcc.edu
MEALER, Donna 731-286-3312 424 D mealer@dscc.edu
MEALIE, Monica 225-771-3282 191 B monica_mealie@subr.edu
MEALY, Stephanie 414-277-7224 494 D
MEANEY, Dorothy 617-627-2979 219 C dorothy.meaney@tufts.edu
MEANEY, Heather, L 518-381-1250 315 B meaneyhl@sunysccc.edu
MEANEY, Kevin, M 540-568-3501 468 C meaneykm@jmu.edu
MEANEY, Sarah 630-617-3191 137 G sarah.meaney@elmhurst.edu
MEANOR, Michael 570-706-8659 181 G michaelj.meanor@kctcs.edu
MEANOR, Nicole 470-578-7629 121 M nmeanor@kennesaw.edu
MEANS, Amanda 740-351-3229 360 F ameans@shawnee.edu
MEANS, Amanda 216-373-6470 357 F ameans@ndc.edu
MEANS, Ben 217-228-5432 147 F meansbe@quincy.edu
MEANS, John 661-336-5036 46 K jmeans@kccd.edu
MEANY, Birgit 907-852-1818 9 H birgit.meany@ilisagvik.edu
MEANY, David 509-359-6335 479 G dmeany@ewu.edu
MEARA, Mark 856-222-9311 281 C mmeara@rcbc.edu
MEARIG, Sayaka 541-485-1780 374 E sayakamearig@newhope.edu
MEARNS, Geoffrey, S 765-285-5555 153 H gsmearns@bsu.edu
MEARS, Jamie 806-665-8801 432 J jamie.mears@clarendoncollege.edu
MEARS, Kathy 850-645-1328 110 C kmears@fsu.edu
MEARS, Laura 301-846-2429 198 I lmears@frederick.edu
MEASAMER, Ronnie 919-718-7409 333 C rmeasamer@cccc.edu
MEASE, Ervin, J 610-799-1112 388 D emease@lccc.edu
MEBANE, August 336-750-2832 344 A mebanea@wssu.edu
MECHAM, Melissa 206-239-4500 478 H
MECHAM, Melissa, E 206-239-4500 478 H
MECHE, Eddie 225-342-6950 192 B eddie.meche@ulsystem.edu
MECHE, Lance 972-825-4747 444 J lmeche@sagu.edu
MECHLER, Heather, S 505-918-7302 288 J hsmechler@unm.edu
MECKEL, David 415-703-9561 28 B dmeckel@cca.edu
MECKLEY, Phil 785-833-4354 175 E pmeckley@kwu.edu
MEDA, Pat 626-529-8261 55 F pmeda@pacificoaks.edu
MEDAGLIA, Kimberly 847-317-4004 151 C kjmedaglia@tiu.edu
MEDASTIN, Jean-Jacques 937-376-6302 349 J jmedastin@centralstate.edu
MEDBERY, Russell 603-526-3870 272 H rmedbery@colby-sawyer.edu
MEDBURY, Doug 425-235-2352 482 H dmedbury@rtc.edu
MEDDERS, Elizabeth 817-735-2483 454 B elizabeth.medders@unthsc.edu
MEDDERS, Mike, W 903-566-7393 456 A mmedders@uttyler.edu
MEDEARIS, Cheryl 605-856-5880 415 J cheryl.medearis@sintegleska.edu
MEDEARIS, Jessica 763-433-1103 237 D jessica.medearis@anokaramsey.edu
MEDEIROS, Madeline 805-546-3123 40 F mmedeiro@cuesta.edu
MEDEL, Michael 805-965-0581 63 A medel@sbcc.edu
MEDEMA, Pamela, S 815-835-6378 149 E pamela.s.medema@svcc.edu
MEDENBLIK, Julius, T 616-957-6024 222 B jmedenblik@calvinseminary.edu
MEDFORD, Edna 202-806-6700 92 F
MEDFORD, Lienne 864-596-9082 408 F lienne.medford@converse.edu
MEDFORD, Lienne, F 864-596-9082 408 F lienne.medford@converse.edu
MEDFORD, Mike 404-687-4576 117 G medfordm@ctsnet.edu
MEDI, Srini 480-557-2000 16 G srini.medi@phoenix.edu
MEDINA, Celia 787-815-0000 511 H celia.medina@upr.edu
MEDINA, Erica 325-793-4801 439 F medina.erica@mcm.edu
MEDINA, Gabriela 787-764-0000 513 B gabriela.medina2@upr.edu
MEDINA, Griselda 432-552-2700 456 F medina_g@utpb.edu
MEDINA, Heather 609-652-4831 283 E heather.medina@stockton.edu
MEDINA, Herbert, A 503-943-7105 377 A medinah@up.edu
MEDINA, Kathryn 510-723-6751 35 J kmedina@chabotcollege.edu
MEDINA, Kimberly 970-248-1958 78 J kmedina@coloradomes.edu
MEDINA, Lisa 760-750-4802 33 A lmmedina@csusm.edu
MEDINA, Lisa 760-750-4813 33 A lmmedina@csusm.edu
MEDINA, Lourdes, E 787-766-1717 510 G lmedina@suagm.edu
MEDINA, Maxiel 212-410-8486 308 E mmedina@nycpm.edu
MEDINA, Nancy 773-442-5255 146 A n-medina4@neiu.edu
MEDINA, Nathan 312-329-4177 144 I nathan.medina@moody.edu
MEDINA, Noemy 801-863-7408 460 D noemym@uvu.edu
MEDINA, Raúl 787-264-0406 508 F rimedina@intersg.edu
MEDINA, Ricco 262-646-6528 494 F rmedina@nashotah.edu
MEDINA, Robert 818-778-5787 49 G medinara@lavc.edu
MEDINA, Susan 402-399-2458 266 F smedina@csm.edu
MEDINA, Tinnah 559-278-2373 31 B tinnahcm@mail.fresnostate.edu
MEDINA, Widylia 787-890-2681 511 G widylia.medina@upr.edu
MEDINA-MARTIN, Flavio 661-362-3559 38 D flavio.medina-martin@canyons.edu
MEDINA MONTES, Isamari 787-848-5739 510 B imedinam@csifpr.org
MEDINA-ORTIZ, Roberto 787-622-8000 511 D rmedina@pupr.edu
MEDIO, Brittany 609-652-4733 283 E brittany.medio@stockton.edu
MEDIONTE-PHILIPS, Krista 607-777-4010 316 B kmediont@binghamton.edu
MEDLEY, Dawn 313-577-1090 232 K dawn.medley@wayne.edu
MEDLEY, Mike 435-896-9714 461 B michael.medley@snow.edu
MEDLEY, Ticily 817-515-4742 445 F ticily.medley@tccd.edu
MEDLEY-WEEKS, Clarice 214-379-5565 441 F cweeks@pqc.edu
MEDLIN, Melissa, T 256-765-4276 8 E mtmedlin@una.edu
MEDLIN, Ramanda 704-463-3067 339 E ramanda.medlin@pfeiffer.edu
MEDLIN, Rian 661-362-3426 38 D rian.medlin@canyons.edu
MEDRANO, Jennifer 801-832-2126 461 F jmedrano@westminstercollege.edu
MEDRANO, Joel 714-712-7900 46 B
MEDRO, Alfred 619-265-0107 57 I amedro@platt.edu
MEDVETZ, Betsy 603-428-2477 273 G bmedvetz@nec.edu
MEDVIC, Laura, A 717-358-4168 383 I laura.medvic@fandm.edu
MEDWICK, Peter 215-972-2017 392 T pmedwick@pafa.edu
MEE, Christine, L 843-349-2091 408 A christin@coastal.edu
MEE, David 910-893-1291 327 D dmee@campbell.edu
MEECE, Jill 606-451-6625 182 G jill.meece@kctcs.edu
MEEDZAN, Nancy 978-232-2389 209 E nmeedzan@endicott.edu
MEEHAN, Barry 603-578-8900 272 M bmeehan@ccsnh.edu
MEEHAN, Gabriel 916-558-2097 50 J meehang@scc.losrios.edu
MEEHAN, Jenna 215-619-7457 390 C jmeehan1@mc3.edu
MEEHAN, Lisa 425-739-8155 481 C lisa.meehan@lwtech.edu
MEEHAN, Martin, T 617-287-7050 211 F umasspresident@umassp.edu
MEEK, Charles Ronald 340-693-1421 513 E charles.meek@uvi.edu
MEEK, Christopher 701-483-2565 345 C christopher.meek@dickinsonstate.edu
MEEK, Grayson 254-299-8652 439 E gmeek@mclennan.edu
MEEK, Marshall 785-670-1830 178 C mmeek@wualumni.org
MEEK, Michelle 606-886-3863 181 E michelle.meek@kctcs.edu
MEEK, Scott 602-787-7902 13 E scott.meek@paradisevalley.edu
MEEK, Tracey 518-587-2100 320 E tracey.meek@esc.edu
MEEKER, April, M 605-642-6092 416 E april.meeker@bhsu.edu
MEEKER, Kimberly 660-359-3948 257 D kmeeker@mail.ncmissouri.edu
MEEKER, Melissa 618-537-6834 144 A mlmeeker@mckendree.edu
MEEKER, Steve, L 605-642-6385 416 E steve.meeker@bhsu.edu
MEEKMA, Glenn 269-471-3484 221 D meekma@andrews.edu
MEEKS, Andy 859-572-5575 184 E meeksa@nku.edu
MEEKS, Chris 575-624-7155 286 C chris.meeks@roswell.enmu.edu
MEEKS, Donna, W 757-683-3072 469 B dmeeks@odu.edu
MEEKS, Harry, L 812-888-4511 162 F hmeeks@vinu.edu
MEEKS, John 813-253-7957 102 B jmeeks@hccfl.edu
MEEKS, Mark 478-445-5851 119 B mark.meeks@gcsu.edu
MEEKS, Ronald 662-685-4771 245 C rmeeks@bmc.edu
MEEKS, Susan 478-387-4801 119 F smeeks@gmc.edu
MEEKS, Tom 216-373-5206 357 F tmeeks@ndc.edu
MEENTS-DECAIGNY, Ellen 312-362-7298 136 H emeentsd@depaul.edu
MEEROFF, Diego 561-868-3128 105 D meeroffd@palmbeachstate.edu
MEETZE-HOLCOMBE, Tracy 843-661-1558 409 G tmeetzeholcombe@fmarion.edu
MEFFORD, Angel 660-596-7218 259 M amefford@sfccmo.edu
MEFFORD, Megan 707-826-4142 33 C mefford@humboldt.edu
MEGAHED, Nivine 312-261-3232 145 D nivine.megahed@nl.edu
MEGAN, Piccus 413-565-1000 206 D mpiccus@baypath.edu
MEGAW, Shelly 507-389-7289 241 C shelly.megaw@southcentral.edu
MEGGERT, Shannon 615-244-5848 423 C s.meggert@sae.edu
MEGGETT, Paul 828-262-2751 340 I meggettpa@appstate.edu
MEGGIE, Derrick 803-777-0112 413 A meggie@mailbox.sc.edu
MEGGS, Christi 843-921-6908 411 A cmeggs@netc.edu
MEGHREBLIAN, Caren 510-925-4282 25 K cmeghreblian@aua.am
MEGNA, Robert, L 518-320-1364 315 H robert.megna@suny.edu
MEHALKO, Dana 434-791-6898 464 I dmehalko@averett.edu
MEHAN, Uppinder 270-534-3388 183 B uppinder.mehan@kctcs.edu
MEHAS, Shayna 336-278-6096 328 J smehas@elon.edu
MEHDIZADEH, Mojdeh 925-229-6858 40 A modjeh@4cd.edu
MEHEGAN, Moxie 802-586-7711 462 I
MEHLBERGER, Scott 818-299-5500 74 L smehlberger@westcoastuniversity.edu
MEHLHOFF, Monte 605-626-7781 416 G monte.mehlhoff@northern.edu
MEHLHORN, Joey 731-881-7012 427 D jmehlhor@utm.edu
MEHLIG, Lisa 815-921-4070 148 B l.mehlig@rockvalleycollege.edu
MEHLINGER, Linda 443-885-4501 201 A linda.mehlinger@morgan.edu
MEHRER, Susanne 603-646-2236 273 D susanne.mehrer@dartmouth.edu
MEHRHOFF, Jay 636-584-6585 253 B jay.mehrhoff@eastcentral.edu
MEHRINGER, Marty 610-527-0200 397 D marty.mehringer@rosemont.edu
MEHROTRA, Anuj 202-994-1152 92 D anuj_m@gwu.edu
MEHTA, Raj 513-556-6252 361 J raj.mehta@uc.edu
MEHUS, Joseph 701-788-4802 345 D joseph.mehus@mayvillestate.edu
MEIDL, Barb 704-216-3605 337 F barb.meidl@rccc.edu
MEIDLINGER, Jeannie 507-453-2743 239 B jeannie.meidlinger@southeastmn.edu
MEIER, Andreea 843-863-7095 407 B ameier@csuniv.edu
MEIER, Beth, A 919-760-8427 331 D meierb@meredith.edu
MEIER, Heather 215-641-6603 390 C hmeier@mc3.edu
MEIER, Jared 970-248-1945 78 J jmeier@coloradomesa.edu
MEIER, John 610-330-5927 387 C meierj@lafayette.edu
MEIER, Karen, F 757-683-5026 469 B kmeier@odu.edu
MEIER, Lori 712-279-3518 169 H lori.meier@stlukescollege.edu
MEIER, Veronica 402-872-2218 268 E vmeier@peru.edu
MEIER PFEIFER, Donna 620-672-2700 177 B donnamp@prattcc.edu
MEIGHEN, Bethany 919-962-1000 340 H
MEIGS, Katrina 802-224-3000 463 D
MEIGS, Mike 727-341-3313 107 E meigs.mike@spcollege.edu
MEIKLEJOHN, Scott 207-725-3460 194 C smeiklej@bowdoin.edu
MEILMAN, Philip, W 202-687-6985 92 E pwm9@georgetown.edu
MEIN, Dina 810-762-7812 226 B dmein@kettering.edu
MEINDERS, Darin 417-268-6065 250 G dmeinders@gobbc.edu
MEINDL, Lidia 212-463-0400 322 F lidia.meindl@touro.edu
MEINDL, Lidia 212-463-0400 322 G lidia.meindl@touro.edu
MEINECKE, Dale 325-649-8804 437 G dmeinecke@hputx.edu
MEINEKE, John 309-796-5053 133 G meinekej@bhc.edu
MEINERT, Anita 641-673-1063 171 C meinerta@wmpenn.edu
MEINERT, David 641-673-1702 171 C meinertd@wmpenn.edu
MEINERT, David, B 417-836-4408 256 G davidmeinert@missouristate.edu
MEINTJES, James 817-735-2530 454 B james.meintjes@unthsc.edu
MEIRICK, Craig, R 844-642-2338 169 A meirickc@nicc.edu
MEIS, Aaron 513-745-2941 364 G meisa@xavier.edu
MEIS, Gail, N 404-471-6306 114 G gmeis@agnesscott.edu
MEIS, John 229-226-1621 126 C jmeis@thomasu.edu
MEISCH, Karen 931-221-7971 417 H meischk@apsu.edu
MEISEL, Joseph 401-863-2162 403 J joseph_meisel@brown.edu
MEISEL, Seth 262-472-1013 497 D meisels@uww.edu
MEISELS, Yesoscher 718-600-8897 325 J
MEISENZAHL, Dan 808-956-8856 129 E dmeisenz@hawaii.edu
MEISENZAHL, Dan, T 808-956-5941 129 C dmeisenz@hawaii.edu
MEISNER, Jolene 570-662-4696 394 F jmeisner@mansfield.edu
MEISSEN, Randall 352-588-7321 107 D randall.meissen@saintleo.edu

MEISSNER, John .... 724-964-8811 391 B
MEISTER, Bobbi .... 712-274-5606 168 E
meisterb@morningside.edu
MEISTER, Tony .... 660-944-2899 251 J
tmeister@conception.edu
MEITZNER, June .... 507-285-7213 240 H
june.meitzner@rctc.edu
MEIXELL, Mary .... 401-598-1471 404 D
mary.meixell@jwu.edu
MEJABI, Patricia .... 610-372-4721 396 H
pmejabi@racc.edu
MEJIA, Andres .... 619-934-0797.. 61 B
MEJIA, Juan, E .... 903-510-2380 452 A
juan.mejia@tjc.edu
MEJIA, Laurie .... 626-966-4576.. 25 H
lauriemejia@agu.edu
MEJIA MARTINEZ,
Marcela .... 714-997-6711.. 36 B
mamartin@chapman.edu
MEJIAS, Ida, A .... 787-250-1912 508 D
iamejias@metro.inter.edu
MEJIAS, Jackeline .... 787-765-1915 509 B
jmejias@opto.inter.edu
MEJIAS, Nelson .... 787-753-6335 507 D
nmejias@icprjc.edu
MEJIAS-ORTIZ, Juan, R 787-763-6700 507 A
jrmejias@se-pr.edu
MEJIAS-ORTIZ, Juan, R 787-763-6700 507 A
presidencia@se-pr.edu
MEKARI, Marie .... 212-217-3702 299 D
marie_mekari@fitnyc.edu
MELANCON, Girard .... 225-216-8055 187 G
melancong@mybrcc.edu
MELANCON, Kimberly ... 225-768-1710 187 B
kimberly.melancon@franu.edu
MELANSON, Christine ... 207-509-7141 196 E
cmelanson@unity.edu
MELARAGNI, Robert ..... 617-670-4401 209 G
rmelaragni@fisher.edu
MELARAGNO, Steven .... 401-254-3667 405 C
smelaragno@rwu.edu
MELBOURNE, Barbara ... 563-884-5290 169 F
barbara.melbourne@palmer.edu
MELBY, Darlene .... 530-938-5220.. 39 C
dmelby@siskiyous.edu
MELBY, Diane .... 210-434-6711 441 B
dmelby@ollusa.edu
MELCHER, Chris .... 706-721-4018 116 A
cmelcher@augusta.edu
MELCHER, Mike .... 806-291-1000 457 I
MELCHER, Mike .... 806-291-3431 457 I
melcherp@wbu.edu
MELCHER, Rick, W .... 610-921-7748 377 G
rmelcher@albright.edu
MELCHERT, Russell, B .. 816-235-1607 261 B
melchertr@umkc.edu
MELCHIOR, Lisa .... 507-389-7354 241 C
lisa.melchior@southcentral.edu
MELCHIOR, Paul, M ...... 703-784-2105 502 J
MELCHIOR, Vonda .... 813-253-7107 102 B
vmelchior@hccfl.edu
MELCHOR, Paul .... 912-279-5833 117 F
pmelchor@ccga.edu
MELDE, Vicki .... 903-223-3025 448 A
vicki.melde@tamut.edu
MELDER, Renee .... 318-487-7340 187 E
renee.melder@lacollege.edu
MELE MAI, Debbie .... 360-676-2772 481 F
dmelemai@nwic.edu
MELEG, Mike .... 309-796-5002 133 G
melegm@bhc.edu
MELEN, Pia .... 714-533-1495.. 64 I
pmelen@southbaylo.edu
MELENDEZ, Andre .... 315-792-7100 321 B
jmelendez@sunypoly.edu
MELENDEZ, Astrid, Y .... 787-884-3838 505 D
amelendez@atenascollege.edu
MELENDEZ, Gabriel ...... 787-725-8120 506 M
programaextension@eap.edu
MELENDEZ, Georgianna 617-287-4877 211 H
georgianna.melendez@umb.edu
MELENDEZ, Jennifer ..... 212-472-1500 309 D
registration@nysid.edu
MELENDEZ, Jennifer ..... 914-395-2689 315 A
jmelendez@sarahlawrence.edu
MELENDEZ, Keimily ...... 787-665-7910 506 D
kmelendez@columbiacentral.edu
MELENDEZ, Luis .... 914-632-5400 307 A
lmelendez@monroecollege.edu
MELENDEZ, Marlene ..... 575-674-2223 285 L
mmelendez@burrell.edu
MELENDEZ, Nildalee ..... 787-743-3038 509 N
nildaleemr@sanjuanbautista.edu
MELENDEZ, Rafael .... 787-725-6500 505 G
rmelendez@albizu.edu
MELENDEZ, Roy, S .... 530-226-4750.. 64 E
rmelendez@simpsonu.edu
MELENDEZ LEON,
Leonardo .... 787-720-4476 511 C
registraduria@mizpa.edu
MELENDEZ-ORTEGA,
Maria, M .... 787-857-3600 507 M
mmmelendez@br.inter.edu
MELENDEZ ORTIZ,
Victor, M .... 787-725-8120 506 M
vmelendez@eap.edu
MELENDY, Lisa, M .... 413-597-2477 220 D
lisa.m.melendy@williams.edu
MELERO, Calixto .... 575-646-2098 287 C
calixto1@nmsu.edu
MELGAREJO, Ricardo .... 787-780-0070 505 F
rmelgarejo@caribbean.edu
MELIKECHI,
Noureddine .... 978-934-3840 212 B
noureddine_melikechi@uml.edu
MELIN, Paulina .... 718-940-5566 314 A
pmelin@sjcny.edu
MELINCIANU, Peter ...... 206-517-4541 483 F
peter@seattlecontroller.com
MELIS, Mike, F .... 804-828-6610 473 B
mfmelis@vcu.edu
MELKONIAN, Carol .... 609-343-5117 275 D
cmelkoni@atlantic.edu
MELKONIAN,
Madeleine .... 718-405-3236 296 F
madeleine.melkonian@
mountsaintvincent.edu
MELLEN, Emily .... 409-882-3917 449 H
emily.mellen@lsco.edu
MELLICHAMP,
James, F .... 706-776-0100 124 D
president@piedmont.edu
MELLING, Alice .... 206-934-3693 483 B
alice.melling@seattlecolleges.edu
MELLINGER, Keith .... 540-654-1052 471 N
kmelling@umw.edu
MELLIZA, Alex .... 916-306-1628.. 67 F
amelliza@sum.edu
MELLO, Catherine .... 402-559-4385 269 K
catherine.mello@unmc.edu
MELLO, Heath, M .... 402-472-7156 269 H
hmello@nebraska.edu
MELLO, James .... 740-284-5369 352 I
jmello@franciscan.edu
MELLO, Lynne .... 401-254-3436 405 C
lmello@rwu.edu
MELLON, James, P .... 808-932-7467 129 D
mellon@hawaii.edu
MELLOR, Kariena .... 253-589-5588 478 J
kariena.mellor@cptc.edu
MELLOR, Tracey .... 617-747-6600 206 H
studyabroad@berklee.edu
MELLOTT, David, M ...... 317-931-2303 154 G
dmellott@cts.edu
MELLOTT, Ramona, N ... 928-523-7145.. 14 H
ramona.mellott@nau.edu
MELMED, Shlomo .... 310-423-8294.. 35 G
MELNICK, Patrick .... 216-221-8584 357 C
MELNYK, Bernadette ..... 614-292-4844 358 D
melnyk.15@osu.edu
MELO, Amberr .... 409-880-7011 449 G
MELOAN, Andrea .... 816-415-7831 262 F
meloana@william.jewell.edu
MELOCHE, Kyle .... 410-857-2275 200 F
kmeloche@mcdaniel.edu
MELOHUSKY, Lisa .... 716-673-3649 316 D
lisa.melohusky@fredonia.edu
MELONSON, Christie .... 210-829-3129 453 C
melonson@uiwtx.edu
MELOY, Michelle .... 856-225-2724 281 G
mlmeloy@rutgers.edu
MELROE LEHRMAN,
Bethany .... 605-995-2706 415 A
bethany.melroe@dwu.edu
MELSON, Ben .... 713-792-2121 456 D
MELSON, Rick .... 937-766-7810 349 E
rickmelson@cedarville.edu
MELSON, Vollie, D .... 410-777-1494 197 G
vmelson@aacc.edu
MELTON, Angela .... 402-471-2505 268 C
amelton@nscs.edu
MELTON, Brice .... 828-327-7000 333 B
bmelton@cvcc.edu
MELTON, Chad, W .... 517-750-1200 231 C
cmelton@arbor.edu
MELTON, Cindy .... 601-925-3250 247 C
cmelton@mc.edu
MELTON, David, V .... 617-364-3510 207 B
dmelton@boston.edu
MELTON, Ellen, C .... 512-233-1400 442 I
ellencm@stedwards.edu
MELTON, Eric, E .... 405-325-3701 370 K
emelton@ou.edu
MELTON, Jerry .... 318-274-3831 192 C
meltonj@gram.edu
MELTON, Judi .... 214-329-4447 430 K
judi.melton@bgu.edu
MELTON, Judi .... 214-329-4447 430 K
MELTON, Judy .... 828-652-0645 336 B
judym@mcdowelltech.edu
MELTON, Julie .... 217-875-7211 148 A
jmelton@richland.edu
MELTON, Leslie, J .... 740-368-3152 359 G
ljdelerm@owu.edu
MELTON, Mark, A .... 919-516-4029 339 I
mamelton@st-aug.edu
MELTON, Matthew .... 423-614-8115 420 H
mmelton@leeuniversity.edu
MELTON, Randy, G .... 517-750-1200 231 C
ra766788@arbor.edu
MELTON, Ryan .... 541-684-7470 371 I
rmelton@bushnell.edu
MELTON, JR., Samuel .. 662-254-3434 248 B
smelton@mvsu.edu
MELTON, Steve .... 828-297-3811 332 G
smelton@cccti.edu
MELTON, Susan, B .... 252-862-1228 337 C
sbmelton1310@roanokechowan.edu
MELTON, Toni .... 901-381-3939 428 B
toni@visible.edu
MELUSKY, Marie, B ...... 814-472-3126 397 F
mmelusky@francis.edu
MELVILLE, John .... 252-638-7260 334 A
melvillej@cravencc.edu
MELVIN, Dana .... 724-653-2216 382 E
dmelvin@dec.edu
MELVIN, Julie .... 216-421-7447 350 H
jrmelvin@cia.edu
MELVIN, Kari .... 301-846-2442 198 I
kmelvin@frederick.edu
MELVIN, Lee, H .... 716-645-5970 316 C
leemelvi@buffalo.edu
MELVIN, Marilee, A ...... 630-752-5517 153 C
marilee.melvin@wheaton.edu
MELVIN, Matt .... 785-864-4381 177 J
mattmelvin@ku.edu
MELVIN, Stephanie .... 202-884-9700.. 94 A
melvins@trinitydc.edu
MELZER, Libby .... 614-234-5213 356 E
emelzer@mccn.edu
MEMMOTT, Brian .... 208-496-4829 130 I
memmottb@byui.edu
MENA, Clara .... 203-285-2123.. 86 E
cmena@gatewayct.edu
MENA, Robert .... 213-738-6716.. 66 B
studentaffairs@swlaw.edu
MENA, Salvador .... 848-932-8576 282 A
salvador.mena@rutgers.edu
MENA, Terry .... 773-442-4600 146 A
t-mena2@neiu.edu
MENADIER, Judy .... 352-854-2322.. 97 N
menadiej@cf.edu
MENARD, Jennifer .... 508-678-2811 214 B
jennifer.menard@bristolcc.edu
MENARD, Richard, R .... 401-841-7004 503 A
richard.menard@usnwc.edu
MENARD, Tim .... 218-281-8585 244 A
menar021@umn.edu
MENARD, William .... 401-739-5000 404 E
bmenard@neit.edu
MENCARELLI, Brent, T .. 574-372-5100 155 F
mencarb@grace.edu
MENCARINI, Steven ...... 336-316-2465 329 D
mencarinism@guilford.edu
MENCER, Curt .... 404-752-1500 123 E
cmencer@msm.edu
MENCH, Matthew .... 865-974-5321 427 B
mmench@utk.edu
MENCHACA, Patricia ..... 760-744-1150.. 56 B
pmenchaca@palomar.edu
MENCHION, Byron .... 850-644-1803 110 C
bmenchion@fsu.edu
MENDELSON, Eleonor ... 831-476-9424.. 42 F
admissions@fivebranches.edu
MENDENHALL, James .... 918-463-2931 365 J
james.mendenhall@connorsstate.edu
MENDES, Godfrey .... 614-947-6027 352 J
godfrey.mendes@frankli.edu
MENDES, Steve .... 203-857-7011.. 87 D
smendes@norwalk.edu
MENDES, Susy .... 212-237-8449 294 D
smendes@jjay.cuny.edu
MENDEZ, Angel .... 787-878-5475 507 L
amendez@arecibo.inter.edu
MENDEZ, Boamari .... 787-701-5100 506 D
bmendez@columbiacentral.edu
MENDEZ, Celia .... 787-257-0000 512 B
celia.mendez@upr.edu
MENDEZ, David .... 787-743-7979 510 H
edmendez@suagm.edu
MENDEZ, Elisaida .... 216-421-7463 350 H
emendez@cia.edu
MENDEZ, Jannette .... 787-856-0945 506 D
jmendez@columbiacentral.edu
MENDEZ, José, F .... 787-766-1717 510 G
jmendez@uagm.edu
MENDEZ, José, F .... 787-751-0178 510 F
jmendez@uagm.edu
MENDEZ, Jose, F .... 787-751-2262 510 E
jmendez@uagm.edu
MENDEZ, Magaly .... 787-815-0000 511 H
magaly.mendez@upr.edu
MENDEZ, Mike .... 651-423-8319 238 A
mike.mendez@dctc.edu
MENDEZ, Pedro .... 209-575-6332.. 77 A
mendezp@mjc.edu
MENDEZ, Rafael .... 787-257-0000 512 B
MENDEZ, Sheri .... 775-784-4252 271 E
smendez@unr.edu
MENDEZ ESCUDERO,
Margarita .... 787-250-0000 511 F
margarita.mendez@upr.edu
MENDEZ-GRANT,
Monica .... 940-898-3700 451 D
mmendezgrant@twu.edu
MENDEZ-GRANT,
Monica .... 940-898-3010 451 D
mmendezgrant@twu.edu
MENDEZ-HERNANDEZ,
Santiago .... 787-296-1101 208 B
santiago.mendez-hernandez@
cambridgecollege.edu
MENDIETA, Juan .... 305-237-7611 104 E
jmendiet@mdc.edu
MENDINI, Shauna .... 435-865-8185 460 A
mendini_s@suu.edu
MENDIOLA, Francisco .. 691-320-2480 504 C
mendiolaf@comfsm.fm
MENDIOLA, Mark .... 671-735-2260 504 F
mendiolam@triton.uog.edu
MENDOLA, Richard, A .. 404-727-6861 118 E
rich.mendola@emory.edu
MENDOLARO,
Angela, J .... 407-582-3011 113 I
amendolaro@valenciacollege.edu
MENDONCA, James ...... 401-456-8888 405 A
jmendonca@ric.edu
MENDOZA, Cesar .... 773-878-4014 149 A
MENDOZA, Gaylyn .... 254-267-7040 441 K
gmendoza@rangercollege.edu
MENDOZA, Graciano .... 408-848-4715.. 43 E
MENDOZA, Graciano .... 650-306-3274.. 62 J
mendozag@smccd.edu
MENDOZA, Johnny .... 800-785-0585.. 39 D
MENDOZA, Jorge .... 218-335-4218 236 F
jorge.mendoza@lltc.edu
MENDOZA, Kimberlee .... 806-291-1100 457 I
mendozak@wbu.edu
MENDOZA, Mark .... 605-394-4800 415 G
MENDOZA, Mynor .... 760-252-2411.. 26 G
mmendoza@barstow.edu
MENDOZA, Pablo .... 678-696-2462 127 A
pablo.mendoza@ung.edu
MENDOZA, Patricia .... 714-432-5562.. 38 B
pmendoza31@occ.cccd.edu
MENDOZA, Raul .... 787-891-0925 507 K
rmendoza@aguadilla.inter.edu
MENDOZA, Rick .... 310-879-0554.. 66 C
rmendoza@spartan.edu
MENDOZA, Stephanie ... 415-503-6280.. 61 D
security@sfcm.edu
MENDOZA, Sylvia, F .... 201-360-4201 278 C
smendoza@hccc.edu
MENDOZA, Tracey .... 210-829-3837 453 C
temendo2@uiwtx.edu
MENDOZA-BAUTISTA,
Maria .... 920-748-8190 494 J
mendoza-bautistam@ripon.edu
MENDOZA-MILLER,
Marylou .... 559-278-2032.. 31 B
maryloum@csufresno.edu
MENDOZA-WELCH,
Maxine .... 903-886-5851 447 B
maxine.mmendo@tamu.edu

MENEAR, Anne, P 660-263-3900 251 D annemenear@cccb.edu
MENEAR, Shelley 301-387-3037 199 A shelley.menear@garrettcollege.edu
MENEELY, Emily 252-334-2020 331 F emily.meneely@macuniversity.edu
MENEELY, J. Andy 252-334-2087 331 F andy.meneely@macuniversity.edu
MENELEY, Theresa 713-221-8612 453 A meneleyt@uhd.edu
MENENDEZ, Jacqueline, R 305-284-5505 113 C jmenendez@miami.edu
MENENDEZ, Megan 303-867-1155.. 83 K menendez@taft.edu
MENENDEZ, Mirizza 305-442-9223 104 G mmenendez@mru.edu
MENENDEZ, Rasel 310-287-4379.. 49 H menendrm2@wlac.edu
MENEZES, Jill 217-206-6651 152 A jmene1@uis.edu
MENGEL, David 513-745-3101 364 G mengel@xavier.edu
MENGEL, Stanley 312-862-3217.. 68 E stanley.mengel@kirkland.com
MENGELLE, Ervens 614-885-5585 359 L emengelle@pcj.edu
MENGHINI, Becci 919-843-0594 342 C becci_menghini@unc.edu
MENGHINI, Jared 570-208-5868 386 G jaredmenghini@kings.edu
MENGLER, Thomas, M 210-436-3722 442 J tmengler@stmarytx.edu
MENICE, Paul 207-786-6254 194 A pmenice@bates.edu
MENIFEE, Delorean, J 570-372-4293 398 F menifee@susqu.edu
MENIFIELD, Charles 973-353-5093 282 B charles.menifield@rutgers.edu
MENJARES, Pete 714-556-3610.. 73 H officeoftheprovost@vanguard.edu
MENJARES, Pete 714-556-3610.. 73 H
MENJIVAR, Claudia, I 650-574-6146.. 62 K menjivarc@smccd.edu
MENK, David, A 507-933-6539 236 A dmenk@gustavus.edu
MENKE, Adriana 305-237-0656 104 E amenke@mdc.edu
MENKE, Donna 800-658-4308 267 J menked@mpcc.edu
MENKE, Scott 262-595-2076 496 D menke@uwp.edu
MENN, Esther 773-256-0721 143 F emenn@lstc.edu
MENNECHEY, Pamela 407-708-2380 108 D mennecheyp@seminolestate.edu
MENNEKE, Beth, R 314-505-7761 252 A mennekeb@csl.edu
MENNELL, Betsy 801-626-6002 461 A betsymennell@weber.edu
MENNELL, Jennifer 828-251-6500 342 B jmennell@unca.edu
MENNELLA, Hillary 562-860-2451.. 35 H hmennella@cerritos.edu
MENNICKE, Sue 717-358-7187 383 I sue.mennicke@fandm.edu
MENON, Sanjay, T 318-797-5234 190 A sanjay.menon@lsus.edu
MENON, Sathyapal 415-442-7080.. 43 I smenon@ggu.edu
MENON, Shaily 203-932-7257.. 89 H smenon@newhaven.edu
MENON, Thila 800-477-2254.. 29 G tmenon@calsouthern.edu
MENSA-WILMOT, Kojo 470-578-6000 121 M
MENSAH, Elfrida 336-285-4319 341 D elfridam@ncat.edu
MENSAH, Ernesta 323-860-0789.. 50 B
MENSAH, Kartet 828-771-3816 344 D
MENSCH, Deserie 254-519-5722 447 A d.mensch@tamuct.edu
MENSCHING, Ron 630-889-6606 145 E rmensching@nuhs.edu
MENSE, Tobias 334-244-3838.... 4 E tmense@aum.edu
MENTA, Vijay 802-443-2929 462 E vmenta@middlebury.edu
MENY, Jennifer 860-253-3090.. 86 C jmeny@asnuntuck.edu
MENZ, Harald 304-829-7915 487 A hmenz@bethanywv.edu
MENZEL, Carol, A 410-334-2946 205 D cmenzel@worwic.edu
MENZEMER, Craig, C 330-972-7911 361 H ccmenze@uakron.edu
MENZER, Paul 540-887-7058 468 G pmenzer@marybaldwin.edu
MEONSKE, Kali, A 330-325-6492 357 D kmeonske@neomed.edu
MERANDA, Seth 402-643-7220 266 G seth.meranda@cune.edu
MERAR, Roland 670-234-5498 505 A roland.merrar@marianas.edu
MERCADEL, Robert 504-520-7396 193 E rmercade@xula.edu
MERCADO, Claudia 847-925-6622 138 G cmercado@harpercollege.edu
MERCADO, Héctor 787-264-1912 508 F hector_mercado@intersg.edu
MERCADO, Harry 787-740-3555 511 B harry.mercado@uccaribe.edu
MERCADO, Jose 660-543-4560 260 G mercado@ucmo.edu
MERCADO, Juan Carlos 212-925-6625 293 D jmercado@ccny.cuny.edu
MERCADO, Lemuel 770-228-7383 125 H lemuel.mercado@sctech.edu
MERCADO, Maritza 718-522-9073 290 E mmercado@asa.edu
MERCADO, Waddy 787-841-2000 509 J waddy_mercado@pucpr.edu
MERCADO-COTA, Teresa 714-564-6105.. 58 F mercado-cota_teresa@sac.edu
MERCADO-LÓPEZ, Damaris 787-763-6700 507 A dmercado@se-pr.edu
MERCANTINI, Jonathan 908-737-0437 278 E jmercant@kean.edu
MERCANTINI, Rachel 828-395-4201 335 D rmercantini@isothermal.edu
MERCED, Ana 787-743-4041 506 D asmerced@columbiacentral.edu
MERCED, Melissa 718-368-4911 294 E melissa.merced@kbcc.cuny.edu
MERCER, Connie 423-478-7702 422 J cmercer@ptseminary.edu
MERCER, Debbie, K 785-532-5525 175 C dmercer@ksu.edu
MERCER, Frank 386-506-4461.. 98 D frank.mercer@daytonastate.edu
MERCER, Holly 620-227-9285 173 D hmercer@dc3.edu
MERCER, John 513-745-4890 364 G mercerjl@xavier.edu
MERCER, John, D 850-872-3807 101 N jmercer@gulfcoast.edu
MERCER, Louie 386-506-4433.. 98 D louie.mercer@daytonastate.edu
MERCER, Roberta 740-377-2520 361 E bobby.mercer@tsbc.edu
MERCER, Sally 724-480-3379 381 H sally.mercer@ccbc.edu
MERCER, Shannon 850-718-2362.. 97 E mercershan@chipola.edu
MERCHANT, Debra, S 513-556-4119 361 J debra.merchant@uc.edu
MERCHANT, Deneene 614-287-5539 351 C dmerchant1@cscc.edu
MERCHANT, Jason 773-702-8523 151 E merchant@uchicago.edu
MERCHANT, Josh 248-370-4287 229 I joshuamerchant@oakland.edu
MERCHANT, Maeesha 213-621-2200.. 38 C
MERCHANT, Susan 518-608-8420 299 C smerchant@excelsior.edu
MERCHLEWITZ, Ann, E 507-457-1587 243 C amerchle@smumn.edu
MERCIER, Diane 617-585-0200 207 A diane.mercier@the-bac.edu
MERCIER, Nichole, R 314-747-1903 262 A nmercier@wustl.edu
MERCIER, Rose 410-857-2452 200 F rmercier@mcdaniel.edu
MERCIER, Stace, L 601-266-8525 249 F stace.mercier@usm.edu
MERCIER, Taylor 210-690-9000 436 H tmercier@hallmarkuniversity.edu
MERCK, Dana 252-222-6021 333 A merckd@carteret.edu
MERCKX, Frank 973-408-3391 277 A fcmerckx@drew.edu
MERCUIRIO, Sherry 614-947-6581 352 J sherry.mercurio@franklin.edu
MERCURIO, Sherry 614-947-6581 352 J sherry.mercurio@franklin.edu
MEREDITH, David 419-530-5731 363 B david.meredith@utoledo.edu
MEREDITH, Derek 252-335-0821 333 G derek_meredith@albemarle.edu
MEREDITH, Joyce 740-587-6515 352 A meredithj@denison.edu
MEREDITH, Kim 678-547-6584 122 E meredith_kc@mercer.edu
MEREDITH, Nic 415-503-6289.. 61 D nmeredith@sfcm.edu
MEREDITH, Peggy 502-895-3411 183 H pmeredith@lpts.edu
MEREDITH, Rence 616-331-3856 224 G meredlaw@gvsu.edu
MEREDITH, Stephanie 304-336-8117 490 B smeredith@westliberty.edu
MEREDITH, Steve 435-586-7700 460 A stevenmeredith@suu.edu
MEREDITH, Steven 435-586-1914 460 A stevenmeredith@suu.edu
MEREN ACIERTO, Ei 626-448-0023.. 46 G
MERESSI, Tesfay 508-999-8542 212 A tmeressi@umassd.edu
MERFALEN, Vincent 670-237-6764 505 A vincent.merfalen@marianas.edu
MERGEN, Amy 419-251-1842 355 G amy.mergen@mercycollege.edu
MERGET, Kathleen 845-451-1776 297 G kathy.merget@culinary.edu
MERGUIE, John 501-450-3111.. 23 H jmerguie@uca.edu
MERHAR, Sarah 218-262-6713 238 D sarahmerhar@hibbing.edu
MERIAN, Dan 313-593-5151 231 I dmerian@umich.edu
MERIANO, John 203-582-8763.. 88 G john.meriano@quinnipiac.edu
MERIANS, Linda 646-313-8000 295 D linda.merians@guttman.cuny.edu
MERICA, Michael 928-226-4212.. 11 O michael.merica@coconino.edu
MERIDA, Cindy 657-278-4697.. 31 C cmerida@fullerton.edu
MERIDETH, Christine 405-425-5094 367 C christine.merideth@oc.edu
MERILLAT, Jason, C 610-566-1776 403 B jmerillat@williamson.edu
MERILLAT, Melinda 932-252-0745 432 L melinda.merillat@cbshouston.edu
MERINAR, Whitney 803-321-5125 410 H whitney.merinar@newberry.edu
MERINO, Robert 281-998-6150 442 K robert.merino@sjcd.edu
MERINO, Robert 281-998-6342 443 A robert.merino@sjcd.edu
MERINO, Robert 281-998-6342 443 B robert.merino@sjcd.edu
MERINO, Robert 281-998-6342 443 C robert.merino@sjcd.edu
MERINO CONTINO, Deanna 562-907-4274.. 76 B dmerinoc@whittier.edu
MERIWETHER, Jason 707-826-3361.. 33 C jason.meriwether@humboldt.edu
MERIWETHER, Mimi 803-786-3856 408 D mmeriwether@columbiasc.edu
MERJIL, Mark 909-384-8900.. 60 F mmerjil@sbccd.cc.ca.us
MERK, Shannon 712-279-3346 169 H shannon.merk@stlukescollege.edu
MERKEL, Luz 509-777-4225 486 C lmerkel@whitworth.edu
MERKEL, SJ, Tom 402-280-1771 266 H tommerkel2@creighton.edu
MERKIN, Yitzchok 301-962-5111 205 E ymerkin@yeshiva.edu
MERKL, Linda 970-521-6606.. 82 C linda.merkl@njc.edu
MERKLE, Ben 208-882-1566 132 C bmerkle@nsa.edu
MERKLE, Jean 605-658-3665 416 D jean.merkle@usd.edu
MERKLE, Joseph, F 717-815-1460 403 F jmerkle@ycp.edu
MERKLE, Patricia 315-568-3277 310 B pmerkle@nycc.edu
MERKLIN, Lynn 269-471-6066 221 D merklin@andrews.edu
MERKOW, Russ 425-739-8436 481 C russ.merkow@lwtech.edu
MERKT, Dan 518-608-8371 299 C dmerkt@excelsior.edu
MERLE, Robin 212-484-1156 294 D rmerle@jjay.cuny.edu
MERLO, Barbara 254-526-1999 432 D barbara.merlo@ctcd.edu
MERLO, Scott, R 269-387-5555 233 B scott.merlo@wmich.edu
MERMANN-JOZWIAK, Elisabeth 570-577-1561 379 C emmj001@bucknell.edu
MERMELSTEIN, Joanne 978-837-5117 216 F mermelsteinj@merrimack.edu
MEROPOL, Ian 617-243-2150 211 B imeropol@lasell.edu
MERRELL, Davis 361-698-1715 435 G dmerrell@delmar.edu
MERRELL, Howard 671-734-1812 504 E hmerrell@piu.edu
MERRELL, Kathy 671-734-1812 504 E
MERRELL, Tom 415-422-2613.. 72 J merrellt@usfca.edu
MERRICK, Mark 419-530-5453 363 B mark.merrick@utoledo.edu
MERRICK, Robyn, M 225-771-5497 191 A robyn_merrick@sus.edu
MERRICK, Robyn, M 225-771-2000 191 B robyn_merrick@sus.edu
MERRIFIELD, Ann 573-875-7210 251 I
MERRILL, Chad 828-694-1704 332 E chadm@blueridge.edu
MERRILL, Dale 657-278-4497.. 31 C dmerrill@fullerton.edu
MERRILL, Joanne 603-897-8257 273 I jmerrill@rivier.edu
MERRILL, Justin 808-237-5140 128 F
MERRILL, Miriam 909-621-8016.. 57 K miriam.merrill@pomona.edu
MERRILL, Peter 802-586-7711 462 I pmerrill@sterlingcollege.edu
MERRILL, Ryan 508-910-6884 212 A rmerrill1@umassd.edu
MERRILL, Scott, M 508-793-2438 208 D smerrill@holycross.edu
MERRILL, Timothy 804-523-5131 474 A tmerrill@reynolds.edu
MERRILL, Traci 619-260-7967.. 72 I tmerrill@sandiego.edu
MERRILL-SANDS, Deborah, M 603-862-1983 274 F deborah.merrill-sands@unh.edu
MERRIMAN, Gary 909-599-5433.. 48 A gmerriman@lifepacific.edu
MERRIT, Nancy 412-383-3549 400 H nmm107@pitt.edu
MERRITT, Amanda 828-898-8772 330 E merritta@lmc.edu
MERRITT, Bradley 910-521-6000 343 B
MERRITT, Brett 678-717-3755 127 A brett.merritt@ung.edu
MERRITT, Brian, S 828-652-0630 336 B
MERRITT, Cheryl 909-607-7853.. 37 F cheryl_merritt@kgi.edu
MERRITT, Jeffrey 919-866-7206 338 G jlmerritt@waketech.edu
MERRITT, Kevin 304-485-5487 487 G kmerritt@msc.edu
MERRITT, Maribea 432-552-2020 456 F
MERRITT, Michelle 309-457-2113 144 H mmerritt@monmouthcollege.edu
MERRITT, Nathan 626-584-5364.. 43 B nathanmerritt@fuller.edu
MERRITT, Pearl, E 325-696-0503 451 A pearl.merritt@ttuhsc.edu
MERRITT, Scott 318-869-5708 186 F smerritt@centenary.edu
MERRITT, Shondrika 646-909-8302 308 A merritts@newschool.edu
MERRITT, Terence 503-845-3564 374 A terence.merritt@mtangel.edu
MERRITT MILLER, Beth 805-756-5759.. 29 I bamerrit@calpoly.edu
MERRY, Dave 617-573-8000 219 B dmerry@suffolk.edu
MERRY, Kelly 409-944-1303 436 E kmerry@gc.edu
MERRYMAN, Ed 408-554-5076.. 63 B emerryman@scu.edu
MERRYMAN, Jason 423-236-2875 423 F jasonmerryman@southern.edu
MERRYMAN, Jon 870-245-5506.. 20 D merrymanj@obu.edu
MERSCHBROCK, Kenneth, L 913-722-0272 175 A drkenny@kansaschristian.edu

MERTENS, Daniel .... 701-662-1654 346 C
danial.mertens@lrsc.edu
MERTENS, Peter .... 718-518-6731 294 B
pmertens@hostos.cuny.edu
MERTES, Michael .... 802-387-7179 462 C
michaelmertes@landmark.edu
MERTES, Scott .... 989-386-6607 228 B
smertes@midmich.edu
MERTH, Paula, B .... 651-290-6376 242 L
paula.merth@mitchellhamline.edu
MERTZ, Jennifer, L .... 610-758-3181 388 E
jlm207@lehigh.edu
MERTZ, Jessica .... 714-533-3946.. 34 C
personnel@calums.edu
MERTZ, Jessica, M .... 714-533-3946.. 34 C
jessica.mertz@calums.edu
MERTZ KUCKKAHN, Penny .... 715-365-4526 499 E
amaki@nicoletcollege.edu
MERVIUS, Sandra .... 516-463-4335 301 G
sandra.mervius@hofstra.edu
MERWIN, Elizabeth .... 817-272-2776 454 I
elizabeth.merwin@uta.edu
MERY, Pam .... 415-239-3227.. 36 K
pmery@ccsf.edu
MERZ, Marcie, L .... 215-898-6171 400 F
mmerz@dev.upenn.edu
MERZ, Nan .... 408-554-4007.. 63 B
nmerz@scu.edu
MESA, Norma .... 805-969-3626.. 55 J
nmesa@pacifica.edu
MESA, Tina .... 210-486-3901 429 A
emesa@alamo.edu
MESACK, Megan .... 313-664-7666 222 H
mmesack@collegeforcreativestudies.edu
MESARA, Gulden .... 626-256-4673.. 37 A
gmesara@coh.org
MESARIS, Nikilos (Nik) . 951-487-3073.. 53 A
nmesaris@msjc.edu
MESCH, Brenden, D ...... 469-365-1902 433 I
bmesch@collin.edu
MESCHINO, Barbara ...... 312-850-7424 135 H
bmeschino@ccc.edu
MESE, Connie .... 970-542-3159.. 81 N
connie.mese@morgancc.edu
MESEHA, Manal .... 973-300-2754 284 A
mmeseha@sussex.edu
MESERVE, Linda .... 970-491-5105.. 79 N
linda.meserve@colostate.edu
MESERVE, Mary .... 207-786-6097 194 A
mmeserve@bates.edu
MESHKATY, Shahra .... 619-260-2298.. 72 I
meshkaty@sandiego.edu
MESICS, Linda, L .... 610-799-1585 388 D
lmesics@lccc.edu
MESLENER, Jennifer ...... 301-387-3022 199 A
jennifer.meslener@garrettcollege.edu
MESONAS, Lenny .... 908-526-1200 281 A
lenny.mesonas@raritanval.edu
MESQUITA, Cezar .... 360-650-4350 485 I
cezar.mesquita@wwu.edu
MESSA, Emily .... 832-842-8184 452 C
eamessa@uh.edu
MESSA, Emily .... 832-842-8184 452 D
eamessa@uh.edu
MESSAC, Achille .... 202-806-6565.. 92 F
messac@howard.edu
MESSATZZIA, Amanda .. 410-334-2908 205 D
amessatzzia@worwic.edu
MESSER, Emily .... 256-782-5003.... 6 A
emesser@jsu.edu
MESSER, Emily, W .... 256-782-5363.... 6 A
emesser@jsu.edu
MESSER, Lucas .... 480-423-6303.. 13 H
lucas.messer@scottsdalecc.edu
MESSER, Thomas, C ..... 904-596-2411 112 F
tmesser@tbc.org
MESSER-KNODE, Gena . 252-985-5151 339 D
gknode@ncwc.edu
MESSERVY, Steven .... 256-824-6881.... 8 B
steven.messervy@uah.edu
MESSIER, John, D .... 207-778-7457 196 I
john.messier@maine.edu
MESSIER, Matthew .... 617-984-1700 218 C
MESSINA, John, A .... 330-972-6594 361 H
jam125@uakron.edu
MESSINA, Joseph, P ..... 205-348-7007.... 7 G
jpmessina@ua.edu
MESSINA, Kimberlee ...... 509-533-3535 479 D
kimberlee.messina@sfcc.spokane.edu
MESSINA, Kimberlee ..... 509-434-5107 479 B
kimberlee.messina@sfcc.spokane.edu
MESSINA, Michael .... 239-477-3594 101 A
mmessina7@fsw.edu
MESSINA, Pamela .... 973-443-8938 277 I
pamela_messina@fdu.edu
MESSINA, Rosalia .... 503-847-2555 377 B
rmessina@uws.edu
MESSINGER, Jacque ..... 903-785-7661 441 D
jmessinger@parisjc.edu
MESSINGER, Lori .... 865-974-3351 427 B
lmessing@utk.edu
MESSINGSCHLAGER, Mark .... 859-344-3506 185 B
messinm@thomasmore.edu
MESSITTE, Zachariah, P 920-748-8118 494 J
messittez@ripon.edu
MESSMAN-MANDICOTT, Lea .... 301-687-4890 204 C
lmessman@frostburg.edu
MESSMORE, Ryan .... 603-456-2656 273 H
MESSNER, Bob .... 717-780-2333 385 B
rhmessne@hacc.edu
MESSNER, Leonard, V .. 312-949-7108 139 D
lmessner@ico.edu
MESSNER, Robert, H ..... 717-780-2333 385 B
rhmessne@hacc.edu
MESSNER, Stephanie .... 312-949-7013 139 D
smessner@ico.edu
MESSNER, Tom .... 904-646-2175 101 B
tom.messner@fscj.edu
MESSPLAY, Paul .... 540-654-1410 471 N
pmesspla@umw.edu
MESTAN, Michael, A ..... 315-568-3100 310 B
mmestan@nycc.edu
MESTETH, Leslie .... 605-455-6033 415 H
lmesteth@olc.edu
MESTLER, Nathan, M .... 480-245-7993.. 12 M
nathan.mestler@ibcs.edu
MESTLER, Nathan, M .... 480-245-7994.. 12 M
nathan.mestler@ibcs.edu
MESTRES, Ibrahim .... 787-780-0070 505 F
imestres@caribbean.edu
MESYEF, Masha .... 866-680-2756 459 G
fundraising@midwifery.edu
MESYEF, Masha .... 801-649-5230 459 G
marketing@midwifery.edu
MESYEF, Whitney .... 866-680-2756 459 G
financialaid@midwifery.edu
METAJ, Dee .... 317-278-5644 157 D
metaj@iupui.edu
METCALF, Amanda .... 304-367-4241 489 K
amanda.metcalf@fairmontstate.edu
METCALF, Courtney ...... 620-223-2700 173 I
courtneym@fortscott.edu
METCALF, Dustin .... 208-467-8665 132 E
dmetcalf@nnu.edu
METCALF, Gary .... 559-453-2089.. 43 A
gary.metcalf@fresno.edu
METCALF, Kyle .... 603-578-8900 272 M
METCALF, Linda .... 817-531-7530 451 C
lmetcalf@txwes.edu
METCALF, Michael .... 608-663-3285 492 F
mmetcalf@edgewood.edu
METCALFE, Allen .... 508-830-5063 213 D
ametcalfe@maritime.edu
METCALFE, Sharon .... 740-392-6868 356 G
sharon.metcalfe@mvnu.edu
METE, T.J .... 772-466-4822.. 95 N
tj.mete@aviator.edu
METESH, John, J .... 406-496-4159 265 A
jmetesh@mtech.edu
METH, Clifford .... 646-565-6133 322 G
yehudah.meth2@touro.edu
METH, Clifford .... 646-565-6133 322 F
yehudah.meth2@touro.edu
METHE, Deborah .... 413-265-2485 208 E
methed@elms.edu
METHVIN, Jennifer .... 501-882-8956.. 17 D
jlmethvin@asub.edu
METIANU, Mihaela .... 561-297-3049 109 J
mmetianu@fau.edu
METILLY, Paul .... 617-254-2610 218 E
paul.metilly@sjs.edu
METIVIER SCOTT, Shelly .... 508-999-8407 212 A
shelly.scott@umassd.edu
METRESS, Heather, B .... 706-721-5052 116 A
hmetress@augusta.edu
METS, Lisa, A .... 727-864-8221.. 98 J
metsla@eckerd.edu
METSGAR, Christopher . 651-450-3520 238 E
cmetsgar@inverhills.edu
METTEN, Michelle .... 618-252-5400 149 I
michelle.metten@sic.edu
METTILLE, Teege .... 262-524-7221 492 A
tmettill@carrollu.edu
METTLACH, Deborah ..... 314-362-6289 253 G
deborah.mettlach@barnesjewishcollege.edu
METTS, Amanda .... 252-399-6315 326 K
ahmetts@barton.edu
METTS, Deanna .... 931-372-3045 426 B
dmetts@tntech.edu
METZ, Bernice .... 712-279-5400 164 B
bernice.metz@briarcliff.edu
METZ, Catherine, A .... 765-361-6418 163 B
metzc@wabash.edu
METZ, Christine .... 516-562-3403 298 G
cmetz@northwell.edu
METZ, Gregory .... 513-745-5720 362 A
gregory.metz@uc.edu
METZ, Robert, C .... 517-264-7117 230 H
rmetz@sienaheights.edu
METZ, Roxanne .... 949-582-4824.. 65 D
rmetz@saddleback.edu
METZ, Starla .... 727-341-4368 107 E
metz.starla@spcollege.edu
METZ, Susan .... 201-216-5245 283 D
susan.metz@stevens.edu
METZ, Terry .... 651-523-2160 236 B
tmetz01@hamline.edu
METZ, Tim .... 323-860-1129.. 53 D
tmetz@mi.edu
METZ, Tim .... 828-227-3046 343 E
tdmetz@wcu.edu
METZER, Stacy .... 515-574-1148 167 A
mentzer_s@iowacentral.edu
METZGAR, Johanna ...... 650-723-2300.. 66 E
METZGAR, Kim .... 724-805-2601 398 A
kim.metzgar@stvincent.edu
METZGER, Amanda .... 585-385-8005 313 F
ametzger@sjfc.edu
METZGER, Carl .... 407-823-5555 110 E
carl.metzger@ucf.edu
METZGER, David, D ...... 757-683-4865 469 B
dmetzger@odu.edu
METZGER, Elizabeth ..... 505-277-5111 288 J
emetzger@unm.edu
METZGER, Jeff .... 419-251-6122 355 G
jeff.metzger@mercycollege.edu
METZGER, Liz .... 812-237-3088 156 D
liz.metzger@indstate.edu
METZGER, Matthew, R .. 574-372-5100 155 F
metzgemr@grace.edu
METZGER, Michael, D ... 716-673-3109 316 D
michael.metzger@fredonia.edu
METZGER, Nan .... 414-930-3338 494 E
metzgern@mtmary.edu
METZGER, Peggy .... 707-826-4321.. 33 C
mam7001@humboldt.edu
METZGER, Rob .... 757-490-1241 464 B
rmetzger@auto.edu
METZGER, Thomas .... 702-968-2013 272 C
tmetzger@roseman.edu
METZGER, Tina .... 804-627-5300 464 K
METZINGER, Harry .... 856-222-9311 281 C
hmetzinger@rcbc.edu
METZINGER, Michelle ... 913-758-6115 178 B
michelle.metzinger@stmary.edu
METZLER, Christopher .. 717-299-7794 399 C
metzler@stevenscollege.edu
METZO, Vincent .... 212-924-5900 321 F
vmetzo@swedishinstitute.edu
MEULEMANS, Nicole ..... 651-423-8403 238 A
nicole.meulemans@dctc.edu
MEUNKS, Chris .... 573-897-5000 260 A
MEUSCHKE, Daylene .... 661-362-5329.. 38 D
daylene.meuschke@canyons.edu
MEUWISSEN, Daniel, J . 651-962-5100 244 E
djmeuwissen@stthomas.edu
MEWIN, Jon .... 510-885-2775.. 31 A
jon.medwin@csueastbay.edu
MEY, Craig, A .... 715-836-3263 495 E
meyca@uwec.edu
MEYER, Adam .... 212-799-5000 303 E
MEYER, AJ .... 937-327-6471 364 D
meyera@wittenberg.edu
MEYER, Alexis .... 414-955-8246 493 F
alemeyer@mcw.edu
MEYER, Angela .... 573-651-2292 259 H
admeyer@semo.edu
MEYER, Ann .... 312-329-4417 144 I
ann.meyer@moody.edu
MEYER, Carrie .... 765-998-4554 161 C
crmeyer@taylor.edu
MEYER, Chris .... 405-733-7913 369 E
cmeyer@rose.edu
MEYER, Christine .... 304-876-5526 490 A
cmeyer@shepherd.edu
MEYER, Christopher, G . 559-278-3936.. 31 B
cmeyer@csufresno.edu
MEYER, David .... 816-414-3700 256 C
dmeyer@mbts.edu
MEYER, David, D .... 504-865-5930 191 F
meyer@tulane.edu
MEYER, Donald, J .... 319-352-8517 170 J
donald.meyer@wartburg.edu
MEYER, Dulcie .... 315-781-3082 301 F
dmeyer@hws.edu
MEYER, Eddie .... 860-727-6906.. 88 A
emeyer@goodwin.edu
MEYER, Eric, T .... 512-471-3821 455 A
dean@ischool.utexas.edu
MEYER, Fredric, B .... 507-538-0554 235 B
MEYER, Fredric, B .... 507-284-3268 235 C
MEYER, Gary .... 414-288-6350 493 E
gary.meyer@marquette.edu
MEYER, Gregg, A .... 508-531-1237 212 D
gmeyer@bridgew.edu
MEYER, Gregor .... 312-788-1132 152 J
gmeyer@vandercook.edu
MEYER, Guy .... 520-417-4095.. 11 M
meyerg@cochise.edu
MEYER, Heidi .... 612-625-2008 243 F
meyer119@umn.edu
MEYER, Hilary .... 708-456-0300 151 D
hilarymeyer@triton.edu
MEYER, Jacque .... 513-244-4232 356 F
jacque.meyer@msj.edu
MEYER, Jay .... 847-543-2717 136 A
jmeyer@clcillinois.edu
MEYER, Jean, C .... 610-526-1466 378 D
jean.meyer@theamericancollege.edu
MEYER, Jennifer .... 818-785-2726.. 35 E
MEYER, Jill .... 414-277-7365 494 D
MEYER, John .... 414-443-8910 498 A
john.meyer@wlc.edu
MEYER, John, D .... 239-513-1122 102 D
jmeyer@hodges.edu
MEYER, John, E .... 507-354-8221 236 J
meyerjd@mlc-wels.edu
MEYER, Josh .... 540-857-6311 475 G
jmeyer@virginiawestern.edu
MEYER, Kathy .... 701-483-2535 345 C
kathleen.meyer@dickinsonstate.edu
MEYER, Katie .... 270-706-8443 181 G
cmeyer0015@kctcs.edu
MEYER, Kelli, A .... 203-576-4487.. 89 C
kmeyer@bridgeport.edu
MEYER, Kimberly, J ...... 574-807-7021 154 B
kimberly.meyer@betheluniversity.edu
MEYER, Kyle, P .... 402-559-7428 269 K
kpmeyer@unmc.edu
MEYER, Lara .... 509-527-4928 486 B
meyerla@whitman.edu
MEYER, Larry .... 859-572-6117 184 E
meyerl3@nku.edu
MEYER, Marilyn, S .... 801-863-6797 460 D
marilyn.meyer@uvu.edu
MEYER, Mathys .... 606-218-5467 186 B
mathysmeyer@upike.edu
MEYER, Matthew .... 919-807-7155 331 L
meyerm@nccommunitycolleges.edu
MEYER, Merry .... 845-758-7005 290 I
sm568@bncollege.com
MEYER, Michael .... 808-844-2308 130 A
mmeyer@hawaii.edu
MEYER, Michele .... 407-691-1754 106 L
mmeyer@rollins.edu
MEYER, Patricia .... 240-629-7905 198 I
pmeyer@frederick.edu
MEYER, Patricia .... 513-745-1996 364 G
meyerp@xavier.edu
MEYER, Rich .... 434-381-6110 471 I
rmeyer@sbc.edu
MEYER, Richard .... 314-246-7429 262 C
richardmeyer33@webster.edu
MEYER, Rick .... 909-599-5433.. 48 A
rmeyer@lifepacific.edu
MEYER, Robert .... 907-564-8890.... 9 F
rmeyer@alaskapacific.edu
MEYER, Scott .... 701-252-3467 347 B
scott.meyer@uj.edu
MEYER, Sheree .... 916-278-6502.. 32 D
meyers@csus.edu
MEYER, Steve .... 307-742-3776 502 B
smeyer@wyotech.edu
MEYER, Stuart .... 904-256-7647 102 H
smcmeek@ju.edu

MILAM, Elizabeth .... 864-656-3431 407 E
milamm@clemson.edu
MILAM, Jennifer .... 410-386-8417 198 D
jmilam@carrollcc.edu
MILAM, John .... 540-868-7249 474 C
jmilam@lfcc.edu
MILAM, Linda .... 918-781-7275 365 C
milaml@bacone.edu
MILAM, Rebecca .... 865-694-6566 425 B
bmilam@pstcc.edu
MILAN, Jordan .... 715-394-8213 497 C
jmilan@uwsuper.edu
MILANI, Andrea .... 513-569-1555 350 F
andrea.milani@cincinnatistate.edu
MILANI, Rachel .... 218-262-7258 238 D
rachelmilani@hibbing.edu
MILANICH, Timothy, R . 216-368-4306 349 D
timothy.milanich@case.edu
MILANO, Angela .... 916-484-8050.. 50 G
milanoa@arc.losrios.edu
MILANO-HIGHTOWER,
Alyssa .... 360-442-2241 481 D
amilanohightower@lowercolumbia.edu
MILAS, T. Patrick .... 732-247-5241 279 C
MILASINOVIC, Milan ...... 216-221-8584 357 C
milan.milasinovic@thencc.edu
MILASZEWSKI, Bruncha 775-824-3819 271 C
bmilaszewski@tmcc.edu
MILAVETZ, Barry .... 701-777-4278 345 B
barry.milavetz@und.edu
MILAZZO, Theresa .... 404-727-7404 118 E
theresa.milazzo@emory.edu
MILBERG, Craig .... 503-370-6561 377 F
cmilberg@willamette.edu
MILBERG, William .... 212-229-5901 308 A
milbergw@newschool.edu
MILBOURNE, Lauren ..... 805-922-6966.. 24 I
lauren.milbourne@hancockcollege.edu
MILBRETT, Juanita .... 507-389-5860 239 D
juanita.milbrett@mnsu.edu
MILBURN, Jaime, E ...... 740-368-3206 359 G
jemilbur@owu.edu
MILBURN, John .... 661-362-3245.. 38 D
john.milburn@canyons.edu
MILBURN DOAN,
Natalie .... 740-368-2000 359 G
nmdoan@owu.edu
MILBY, John .... 864-294-2111 409 H
john.milby@furman.edu
MILBY, Kevin, S .... 859-238-5534 180 B
kevin.milby@centre.edu
MILBY, Megan, H .... 859-238-5516 180 B
megan.milby@centre.edu
MILCZARSKI, Vivian ...... 845-569-3523 307 D
vivian.milczarski@msmc.edu
MILDENHALL, Joseph ... 602-639-7500.. 12 J
MILEHAM, Trisha .... 219-464-5099 162 D
trisha.mileham@valpo.edu
MILEK, Joseph .... 814-863-2521 391 G
jmm9228@psu.edu
MILEM, Jeffrey .... 805-893-3917.. 70 E
jmilem@education.ucsb.edu
MILEM, Jill .... 936-468-2401 445 E
jmilem@sfasu.edu
MILES, Abbie .... 773-995-2040 134 K
amiles24@csu.edu
MILES, Arletha .... 914-773-3856 311 A
lmiles@pace.edu
MILES, Belinda, S .... 914-606-6707 325 A
belinda.miles@sunywcc.edu
MILES, Byron .... 208-535-5387 131 B
byron.miles@cei.edu
MILES, Catherine .... 225-771-6231 191 B
catherine_miles@sus.edu
MILES, Daniel .... 740-283-6777 352 I
dmiles@franciscan.edu
MILES, David, A .... 201-692-2227 277 I
dmiles@fdu.edu
MILES, Deborah .... 912-279-5750 117 F
dmiles@ccga.edu
MILES, Deidra .... 978-934-4807 212 B
deidra_miles@uml.edu
MILES, Donald .... 814-472-3029 397 F
dmiles@francis.edu
MILES, Donna .... 405-224-3140 371 B
dmiles@usao.edu
MILES, Elizabeth .... 503-253-3443 374 G
elizabeth.miles@ocom.edu
MILES, Jenifer .... 512-505-3040 438 A
jpmiles@htu.edu
MILES, Jessica .... 217-443-8769 136 G
jmiles@dacc.edu
MILES, John, D .... 770-720-9102 124 G
john.miles@reinhardt.edu
MILES, Keith .... 850-599-3413 109 I
keith.miles@famu.edu
MILES, Kim .... 941-377-4880 104 D
kmiles@meridian.edu
MILES, Leon .... 319-471-6260 415 B
lmiles@ilt.edu
MILES, Lloyd .... 301-985-7237 203 E
lloyd.miles@umuc.edu
MILES, Martin .... 757-727-5635 467 G
martin.miles@hamptonu.edu
MILES, Mary, E .... 248-942-3331 229 C
memiles@oaklandcc.edu
MILES, Mary Elizabeth .. 502-852-6688 186 A
maryelizabeth.miles@louisville.edu
MILES, Michelle .... 304-769-0011 491 A
mmiles@wvjc.edu
MILES, Sandra .... 904-818-6238.. 99 E
smiles@flagler.edu
MILES, Sarah, L .... 508-831-4180 220 F
smiles@wpi.edu
MILES, Thomas .... 773-702-9495 151 E
tmiles@law.uchicago.edu
MILES, Tom .... 478-445-2090 119 B
tom.miles@gcsu.edu
MILES, Travis .... 660-785-4242 260 F
tmiles@truman.edu
MILES, Vickie .... 334-670-3732.... 7 C
vmiles@troy.edu
MILEWICZ, Mark .... 910-521-6630 343 B
mark.milewicz@uncp.edu
MILEY, Melinda .... 843-953-5426 408 C
mileym@cofc.edu
MILFORD, Dorie .... 540-373-2200 466 C
dmilford@evcc.edu
MILI, Fatma .... 704-687-8450 342 D
fmili@uncc.edu
MILICI, JR., Roger, A ... 212-636-6545 300 C
milici@fordham.edu
MILIONI, Barbara .... 417-268-6008 250 G
bmilioni@gobbc.edu
MILIONI, Emily .... 417-268-6068 250 G
emilioni@gobbc.edu
MILIONI, Mark, L .... 417-268-6008 250 G
mmilioni@gobbc.edu
MILIONIS, Daren .... 503-375-7012 372 H
dmilionis@corban.edu
MILIOTIS, David .... 507-457-1421 243 C
dmilioti@smumn.edu
MILJEVICH, Greg .... 715-365-4486 499 E
gmiljevich@nicoletcollege.edu
MILKEWICZ, Ciera .... 541-888-7339 376 C
cmilkewicz@socc.edu
MILKOVICH, Patrice ...... 619-575-6176.. 66 A
pmilkovich@swccd.edu
MILKOWSKI, Rose .... 312-629-6182 149 F
rmilkowski@saic.edu
MILKOWSKI, Tracy .... 414-847-3239 494 C
tracymilkowski@miad.edu
MILLAN, Iris .... 773-481-8765 135 G
imillan3@ccc.edu
MILLAR, Janet .... 661-654-3366.. 30 B
jmillar@csub.edu
MILLARD, Cristi .... 801-957-4145 461 C
cristi.millard@slcc.edu
MILLARD, David .... 805-546-3205.. 40 F
david_millard1@cuesta.edu
MILLARD, Jill .... 704-290-5887 337 I
jmillard@spcc.edu
MILLARD, Jim .... 252-638-7266 334 A
millardj@cravencc.edu
MILLARD, Kent .... 937-529-2201 361 G
kmillard@united.edu
MILLARD, Rachel .... 316-295-5719 174 A
millard@friends.edu
MILLARD, Sandy .... 919-209-2011 335 F
sbmillard@johnstoncc.edu
MILLAS, Nikoletta .... 610-896-1032 385 I
nmillas@haverford.edu
MILLEA, Matthew, J ...... 315-470-6649 319 D
mjmillea@esf.edu
MILLEN, Jonathan .... 207-283-0171 197 E
jmillen@une.edu
MILLEN, Michelle, L ..... 972-548-6677 433 I
mmillen@collin.edu
MILLENBAH, Kelly, F .... 517-355-0234 227 F
millenba@msu.edu
MILLENBINE, Donnie .... 618-437-5321 147 I
millenbined@rlc.edu
MILLENDER, Angelia ..... 651-779-3368 237 H
angelia.millender@century.edu
MILLER, Adam .... 509-527-5778 486 B
millera@whitman.edu
MILLER, Al .... 251-442-2357.... 8 C
amiller@umobile.edu
MILLER, Alexander .... 740-587-0810 352 A
MILLER, Allyson .... 214-333-2212 434 C
allysonm@dbu.edu
MILLER, Alyce .... 818-710-4332.. 49 D
millerae@piercecollege.edu
MILLER, Amber, D .... 213-740-2531.. 73 D
dean@dornsife.usc.edu
MILLER, Amy .... 616-732-1157 223 E
amy.miller@davenport.edu
MILLER, Amy .... 931-372-3634 426 B
almiller@tntech.edu
MILLER, Andrea .... 940-565-2095 453 E
andrea.miller@unt.edu
MILLER, Andrew .... 719-549-3353.. 82 J
andrew.miller@pueblocc.edu
MILLER, Andrew, M ...... 269-337-7542 225 F
andrew.miller@kzoo.edu
MILLER, Andy .... 530-898-6116.. 30 D
MILLER, III, Andy .... 601-366-8880 249 G
amiller@wbs.edu
MILLER, Angela .... 601-718-5900.. 93 H
MILLER, Angela .... 502-456-6771 185 A
anmiller@sullivan.edu
MILLER, Angela .... 937-512-2526 360 G
angela.miller5594@sinclair.edu
MILLER, Angela, M .... 608-342-1555 496 E
millerang@uwplatt.edu
MILLER, Angie .... 970-675-3235.. 79 H
angela.miller@cncc.edu
MILLER, Anita .... 617-287-5000 211 H
anita.miller@umb.edu
MILLER, Anita .... 580-477-2000 371 D
MILLER, Ann .... 440-826-3308 348 D
amiller@bw.edu
MILLER, Anthony .... 763-424-0822 240 A
amiller@nhcc.edu
MILLER, Anthony .... 540-545-7257 470 G
amiller@su.edu
MILLER, April, D .... 606-783-2857 184 C
ad.miller@moreheadstate.edu
MILLER, Ave .... 770-962-7580 121 E
amiller@gwinnetttech.edu
MILLER, B.J .... 202-685-2906 502 K
bj.miller.civ@ndu.edu
MILLER, Barbara, K .... 320-308-5447 240 I
barbara.miller@stcloudstate.edu
MILLER, Baruch .... 718-269-4080 292 I
MILLER, Becky .... 913-360-7410 171 J
beckymiller@benedictine.edu
MILLER, Becky .... 812-298-2361 158 D
rmiller@ivytech.edu
MILLER, Bert .... 580-559-5760 365 K
bmiller@ecok.edu
MILLER, Beth .... 330-337-6403 347 D
bmiller@awc.edu
MILLER, Bethany .... 859-622-0269 180 E
bethany.miller@eku.edu
MILLER, Bethany .... 562-903-4886.. 27 A
bethany.miller@biola.edu
MILLER, Bethany, L ...... 651-696-6265 236 I
bmille14@macalester.edu
MILLER, Betsy .... 575-538-6118 289 G
millerb@wnmu.edu
MILLER, Bill .... 830-372-8120 449 A
bmiller@tlu.edu
MILLER, Bo .... 601-968-8777 245 B
bmiller@belhaven.edu
MILLER, Bob .... 610-526-7878 379 B
rmiller03@brynmawr.edu
MILLER, Boise .... 570-484-2287 394 E
bmiller1@lockhaven.edu
MILLER, Boise .... 570-484-2255 394 E
bmiller1@lockhaven.edu
MILLER, Brandon .... 918-444-4677 366 G
mille218@nsuok.edu
MILLER, Brett .... 304-473-8462 491 D
miller_bt@wvwc.edu
MILLER, Brian .... 616-732-1195 223 E
bmiller@davenport.edu
MILLER, Brian .... 562-906-4572.. 27 A
brian.miller@biola.edu
MILLER, Brian .... 408-855-5247.. 75 D
brian.miller@missioncollege.edu
MILLER, Brian .... 414-277-6947 494 D
MILLER, Brian .... 252-493-7421 336 H
bmiller@email.pittcc.edu
MILLER, Brian, E .... 219-989-2994 160 D
mill1817@pnw.edu
MILLER, Bridget .... 267-620-4834 378 E
millerb@arcadia.edu
MILLER, Brittney .... 325-942-2248 450 E
brittney.miller@angelo.edu
MILLER, Caitlin .... 450-620-2122 177 B
caitlinm@prattcc.edu
MILLER, Cameron .... 419-866-0261 361 B
MILLER, Carey .... 412-365-1552 380 G
cmiller8@chatham.edu
MILLER, Carey .... 307-754-6114 501 H
carey.miller@nwc.edu
MILLER, Carolann .... 631-656-2134 300 B
carolann.miller@ftc.edu
MILLER, Carolyn .... 318-670-6000 191 D
MILLER, Catherine .... 203-857-3342.. 87 D
cmiller@norwalk.edu
MILLER, Chad .... 812-488-2050 161 G
cm121@evansville.edu
MILLER, Chad, N .... 651-286-7474 244 D
cnmiller@unwsp.edu
MILLER, Chana .... 908-354-6057 285 J
MILLER, Chandra .... 580-559-5262 365 K
chalmil@ecok.edu
MILLER, Chanti .... 612-359-6491 234 A
millerch@augsburg.edu
MILLER, Charles .... 337-521-8990 188 I
charles.miller@solacc.edu
MILLER, Cheryl .... 503-552-1510 374 D
cmiller@nunm.edu
MILLER, Chris .... 623-845-3841.. 13 C
c.miller@gccaz.edu
MILLER, Chris .... 760-744-1150.. 56 B
cmiller@palomar.edu
MILLER, Chris .... 847-317-7036 151 C
cmiller@tiu.edu
MILLER, Chris .... 864-656-2161 407 E
lcmille@clemson.edu
MILLER, Chris, E 570-326-3761 392W
cmiller@pct.edu
MILLER, Christi .... 806-291-3526 457 I
millerc@wbu.edu
MILLER, Christina .... 719-587-7506.. 77 G
crmiller@adams.edu
MILLER, Christine, M .... 916-278-6331.. 32 D
millercm@csus.edu
MILLER, Cindy .... 314-838-8858 261 F
cmiller@ugst.edu
MILLER, Clinton .... 901-251-7100.. 93 H
MILLER, Clinton .... 423-417-3550.. 93 H
MILLER, Colin 612-343-4400 242M
MILLER, Cory .... 952-886-7569 242 N
cmiller@nwhealth.edu
MILLER, Dale .... 518-381-1280 315 B
millerdj@sunysccc.edu
MILLER, Daniel .... 406-994-4410 264 C
danmiller@montana.edu
MILLER, Daniel .... 478-757-5146 127 F
dmiller@wesleyancollege.edu
MILLER, Daniel, P .... 570-321-4139 389 B
millerda@lycoming.edu
MILLER, Darlene .... 973-877-3101 277 G
dmiller@essex.edu
MILLER, David .... 205-226-4723.... 4 F
wdmiller@bsc.edu
MILLER, David .... 606-546-1291 185 D
dkmiller@unionky.edu
MILLER, David .... 312-362-8720 136 H
miller@cdm.depaul.edu
MILLER, David .... 623-845-3707.. 13 C
david.miller@gccaz.edu
MILLER, David .... 316-978-5821 178 D
david.miller@wichita.edu
MILLER, David .... 605-256-5675 416 F
david.miller@dsu.edu
MILLER, David, J .... 715-836-3871 495 E
milleda@uwec.edu
MILLER, David, L .... 865-974-9080 427 A
davidmiller@tennessee.edu
MILLER, Davin .... 706-721-5426 116 A
davmiller@augusta.edu
MILLER, Dawn .... 337-482-6471 193 B
dawn.miller@louisiana.edu
MILLER, Dawn .... 612-330-1216 234 A
millerd1@augsburg.edu
MILLER, Deb .... 904-620-1416 111 B
deb.miller@unf.edu
MILLER, Deborah .... 410-617-2020 200 B
dherman@loyola.edu
MILLER, Deborah, L ...... 419-772-2464 358 C
d-miller@onu.edu
MILLER, Debra .... 815-753-1375 146 B
dmiller20@niu.edu

MILLER, Delana .... 831-479-6100.. 27 D demiller@cabrillo.edu
MILLER, Derek .... 334-699-2266.... 1 B dmiller@southeasthealth.org
MILLER, Diane .... 419-530-5529 363 B diane.miller@utoledo.edu
MILLER, Dianna .... 956-721-5232 438 H dmiller@laredo.edu
MILLER, Dion .... 718-482-5741 294 F dmiller@lagcc.cuny.edu
MILLER, Don .... 314-514-3103 147 E don.miller@principia.edu
MILLER, Don .... 562-908-3402.. 58 L dmiller@riohondo.edu
MILLER, Don, M .... 336-322-2154 336 G don.miller@piedmontcc.edu
MILLER, Doug .... 417-626-1234 257 F miller.doug@occ.edu
MILLER, Doug .... 713-348-6770 442 F doug.miller@rice.edu
MILLER, Drew .... 936-294-1720 450 A adm007@shsu.edu
MILLER, E. John .... 701-231-7933 345 F ej.miller@ndsu.edu
MILLER, Elizabeth .... 562-860-2451.. 35 H emiller@cerritos.edu
MILLER, Elizabeth .... 920-403-3117 495 B elizabeth.miller@snc.edu
MILLER, Elizabeth, K ..... 651-638-6215 234 D e-miller@bethel.edu
MILLER, Ellen .... 317-791-5932 161 H emiller@uindy.edu
MILLER, Emily, A .... 606-474-3212 181 B emilyamiller@kcu.edu
MILLER, Emma .... 228-896-2506 247 E emma.miller@mgccc.edu
MILLER, Eric .... 724-847-6634 384 C emiller@geneva.edu
MILLER, Eric .... 304-865-6161 487 H eric.miller@ovu.edu
MILLER, Erika .... 830-372-8077 449 A emiller@tlu.edu
MILLER, Fayneese, S .... 651-523-2202 236 B president@hamline.edu
MILLER, Frank .... 314-286-3390 258 F fdmiller@ranken.edu
MILLER, Fred .... 828-669-8012 331 K
MILLER, Gary, L .... 330-972-7869 361 H president@uakron.edu
MILLER, George, C .... 901-722-3217 423 G gmiller@sco.edu
MILLER, III, George, E . 757-823-8015 469 A gemiller@nsu.edu
MILLER, Glen .... 503-399-6520 372 B glen.miller@chemeketa.edu
MILLER, Glenn .... 816-268-5400 257 C gamiller@mmsmidwest.com
MILLER, Glynis .... 512-223-7850 430 I glynis.miller@austincc.edu
MILLER, Grant, T .... 208-467-8059 132 E gtmiller@nnu.edu
MILLER, Gregory, J .... 330-471-8119 355 D gmiller@malone.edu
MILLER, Gretchen .... 260-665-4312 161 E millerg@trine.edu
MILLER, Gretchen .... 414-229-3067 496 B gemiller@uwm.edu
MILLER, JR., H. Samuel .... 828-227-7147 343 E sammiller@wcu.edu
MILLER, Heather .... 662-846-4311 245 G hmiller@deltastate.edu
MILLER, Heather, C ...... 704-233-8632 344 F h.miller@wingate.edu
MILLER, Holly .... 321-674-8871 100 C hmiller@fit.edu
MILLER, J. Scott .... 801-422-2779 458 H scott_miller@byu.edu
MILLER, Jack .... 619-574-6909.. 55 E jmiller@pacificcollege.edu
MILLER, Jaime, M .... 708-709-3513 147 D jmmiller@prairiestate.edu
MILLER, James .... 630-637-5513 145 F jlmiller@noctrl.edu
MILLER, James .... 435-652-7625 460 B miller_j@dixie.edu
MILLER, James, A .... 256-824-2481.... 8 B james.miller@uah.edu
MILLER, Jan .... 205-652-3421.... 9 B jmiller@uwa.edu
MILLER, Jan .... 205-652-3675.... 9 B jmiller@uwa.edu
MILLER, Jason .... 419-289-5621 347 J jmille70@ashland.edu
MILLER, Jean .... 309-438-8322 140 D jmmill5@ilstu.edu
MILLER, Jeanette .... 206-934-3727 483 B jeanette.miller@seattlecolleges.edu
MILLER, Jeff .... 970-247-7525.. 80 J jkmiller2@fortlewis.edu
MILLER, Jeff .... 314-529-9353 255 B jeffmiller@maryville.edu
MILLER, Jeff .... 320-222-5218 240 F
MILLER, Jeffrey, A .... 412-396-5081 383 A millerjeff@duq.edu
MILLER, Jen .... 602-787-6500.. 13 E jen.miller@paradisevalley.edu
MILLER, Jeremy .... 740-857-1311 360 D jmiller@rosedale.edu
MILLER, Jerry .... 707-524-1506.. 63 D jmiller@santarosa.edu
MILLER, Jess .... 541-440-4698 376 G jess.miller@umpqua.edu
MILLER, Jessica .... 724-357-2621 394 C jemiller@iup.edu
MILLER, Jim .... 412-396-6000 383 A
MILLER, Jo Ann .... 770-426-2819 122 C joann.miller@life.edu
MILLER, Joannie .... 541-888-7298 376 C joannie.miller@socc.edu
MILLER, Jodi .... 410-516-6330 199 G jodimiller@jhu.edu
MILLER, John .... 585-582-8212 298 F johnmiller@elim.edu
MILLER, John .... 802-831-1334 463 C jmiller@vermontlaw.edu
MILLER, John .... 256-840-4195.... 3 F john.miller@snead.edu
MILLER, John .... 803-705-4788 406 G john.miller@benedict.edu
MILLER, Jonathan .... 413-597-2502 220 D jm30@williams.edu
MILLER, Jonathan, L ..... 978-556-3818 215 E jmiller@necc.mass.edu
MILLER, Joseph .... 773-244-6232 145 G jmiller2@northpark.edu
MILLER, Joseph .... 803-323-2191 414 D
MILLER, Joseph .... 361-825-5967 447 C joseph.miller@tamucc.edu
MILLER, Joseph, C .... 706-880-8253 122 A jcmiller@lagrange.edu
MILLER, Joshua .... 205-665-6245.... 8 D millerjd@montevallo.edu
MILLER, Joshua .... 660-263-3900 251 D joshuamiller@cccb.edu
MILLER, Julie, H .... 313-577-2034 232 K julie.h.miller@wayne.edu
MILLER, Julie, L .... 317-940-9714 154 C jlmille5@butler.edu
MILLER, June, B .... 301-447-5188 201 B jmiller@msmary.edu
MILLER, Justin .... 941-487-4649 110 D jumiller@ncf.edu
MILLER, Kara .... 248-218-2038 230 B kmiller@rochesteru.edu
MILLER, Karen .... 507-223-7252 239 F karen.miller@mnwest.edu
MILLER, Karen .... 404-639-0999 123 D karen.miller@morehouse.edu
MILLER, Karen .... 270-824-8680 182 D karen.miller@kctcs.edu
MILLER, Karen .... 216-987-3471 351 E karen.miller@tri-c.edu
MILLER, Karen, A .... 770-216-2960 121 I kam@ict.edu
MILLER, Karissa .... 941-359-7970 106 J karissa@ringling.edu
MILLER, Karla .... 256-372-4871.... 1 A karla.miller@aamu.edu
MILLER, Kathryn .... 863-583-9050 110 B
MILLER, SSJ, Kathryn ... 215-248-7167 381 A kmiller@chc.edu
MILLER, Katie .... 252-335-0821 333 G kathryn_miller@albemarle.edu
MILLER, Kausha .... 859-246-6417 181 F kausha.miller@kctcs.edu
MILLER, KC .... 480-994-9244.. 15 R kc@swiha.edu
MILLER, Keila .... 606-487-3287 181 I keila.miller@kctcs.edu
MILLER, Keith .... 864-250-8175 409 I keith.miller@gvltec.edu
MILLER, Kelly .... 217-581-2223 137 E kpmiller@eiu.edu
MILLER, Kelly, M .... 317-788-3437 161 H kmiller@uindy.edu
MILLER, Kelly, M .... 361-825-2621 447 C kelly.miller@tamucc.edu
MILLER, Kelsey .... 410-778-7745 205 B kmiller8@washcoll.edu
MILLER, Ken .... 407-646-2999 106 L kmiller@rollins.edu
MILLER, Kenneth .... 740-857-1311 360 D kmiller@rosedale.edu
MILLER, Kevin .... 847-866-3920 138 D kevin.miller@garrett.edu
MILLER, Kevin .... 434-223-6161 467 F kmiller@hsc.edu
MILLER, Kevin, D .... 973-408-3109 277 A theoadm@drew.edu
MILLER, Kevin, D .... 973-408-3646 277 A kmiller@drew.edu
MILLER, Kevin, J .... 716-878-5601 317 F millerkj@buffalostate.edu
MILLER, Kevyn .... 480-517-8076.. 13 G kevyn.miller@riosalado.edu
MILLER, Khadijah, O ..... 757-823-2864 469 A komiller@nsu.edu
MILLER, Kimela .... 575-835-5881 286 K kimela.miller@nmt.edu
MILLER, Kris .... 615-966-5722 421 B kris.miller@lipscomb.edu
MILLER, Kristen .... 603-342-3002 273 C kmiller@ccsnh.edu
MILLER, Kristine .... 435-797-3646 460 C kristine.miller@usu.edu
MILLER, Kyren .... 701-224-2450 346 A kyren.miller@bismarckstate.edu
MILLER, Lance .... 620-276-9789 174 B lance.miller@gcccks.edu
MILLER, Larry .... 410-706-7776 203 A larry.miller@umaryland.edu
MILLER, Larry .... 864-250-8058 409 I larry.miller@gvltec.edu
MILLER, Laura, M .... 717-796-1800 389 H lmiller@messiah.edu
MILLER, Laurence .... 724-357-2229 394 C llmiller@iup.edu
MILLER, Libby .... 865-471-3200 418 E lmiller@cn.edu
MILLER, Lindsay .... 605-658-6250 416 D lindsay.miller@usd.edu
MILLER, Lisa .... 561-237-7000 103 W lmiller@lynn.edu
MILLER, Lisa .... 620-450-2185 177 B lisam@prattcc.edu
MILLER, Lisa .... 708-210-5767 149 H lmiller@ssc.edu
MILLER, Lisa .... 318-342-5441 193 C lmiller@ulm.edu
MILLER, Lisa .... 516-323-3046 306 M lmiller@molloy.edu
MILLER, Lor, M .... 844-642-2338 169 A millerd1533@nicc.edu
MILLER, Lori .... 215-702-4335 380 A lmiller@cairn.edu
MILLER, Marc .... 870-230-5377.. 19 D millermd@hsu.edu
MILLER, Marc, L .... 520-621-1498.. 16 D marc.miller@law.arizona.edu
MILLER, Marcia, K .... 316-284-5315 172 B mmiller@bethelks.edu
MILLER, Mark .... 620-862-5252 171 H
MILLER, Mark .... 318-869-5117 186 F mmiller@centenary.edu
MILLER, Mark .... 740-376-4811 355 E mark.miller@marietta.edu
MILLER, Martin, J .... 724-287-8711 379 E martin.miller@bc3.edu
MILLER, Matt .... 724-287-8711 379 E matt.miller@bc3.edu
MILLER, Matt .... 989-386-6600 228 B mmiller@midmich.edu
MILLER, Matthew .... 903-875-7422 440 D matt.miller@navarrocollege.edu
MILLER, Megan .... 434-395-2064 468 F millermp@longwood.edu
MILLER, Megan, M .... 603-526-3409 272 H megan.miller@colby-sawyer.edu
MILLER, Megan, M .... 978-542-7537 213 E megan.miller@salemstate.edu
MILLER, Melinda .... 615-248-1650 426 D mmiller@trevecca.edu
MILLER, Melinda, A ...... 315-386-7085 320 B millerm@canton.edu
MILLER, Melissa, C ...... 615-898-5179 422 C melissa.miller@mtsu.edu
MILLER, Melissa, C ...... 386-312-4106 107 C melissamiller@sjrstate.edu
MILLER, Melvin .... 803-705-4461 406 G melvin.miller@benedict.edu
MILLER, Merlin, R .... 660-562-1836 257 E merlin@nwmissouri.edu
MILLER, Merrill .... 315-228-1000 296 E mmiller@colgate.edu
MILLER, Michael .... 617-420-1820 218 F
MILLER, Michael .... 805-893-2118.. 70 E mike.miller@sa.ucsb.edu
MILLER, Michael .... 239-280-2401.. 95 M michael.miller@avemaria.edu
MILLER, Michael .... 817-257-7577 432 A michael.miller@tcu.edu
MILLER, Michael, J .... 718-289-5548 293 B michael.miller@bcc.cuny.edu
MILLER, Mike .... 660-562-1014 257 E mmiller@nwmissouri.edu
MILLER, Mike .... 805-893-2118.. 70 E mike.miller@sa.ucsb.edu
MILLER, Mike .... 317-955-6254 159 K mmiller@marian.edu
MILLER, Mindy .... 704-637-4394 327 I mmmiller17@catawba.edu
MILLER, Miryom, R .... 845-434-5240 326 J mmiller@ygzm.edu
MILLER, Mitch .... 608-757-7659 498 D mmiller80@blackhawk.edu
MILLER, Molly .... 614-947-6541 352 J molly.miller@franklin.edu
MILLER, Nancy .... 307-754-6243 501 H nancy.miller@nwc.edu
MILLER, Natasha .... 240-965-2469 198 C nmiller@captechu.edu
MILLER, Nora, R .... 662-329-7100 248 A nrmiller@muw.edu
MILLER, Pamela .... 605-274-0770 414 G pamela.miller@augie.edu
MILLER, Pat .... 517-629-0318 221 A pmiller@albion.edu
MILLER, Pat .... 405-912-9015 368 J pmiller@ru.edu
MILLER, Patrick .... 903-813-2307 430 H pmiller@austincollege.edu
MILLER, Paul .... 662-243-1902 246 B pmiller@eastms.edu
MILLER, Paul .... 336-278-5882 328 J millerp@elon.edu
MILLER, Pearlie .... 334-876-9277.... 2 D pearlie.miller@wccs.edu
MILLER, Pete .... 423-354-2448 425 A pwmiller@northeaststate.edu
MILLER, Peter .... 516-671-7373 324 G pmiller@webb.edu
MILLER, Phil .... 803-754-4100 408 E
MILLER, Phillip, G .... 412-397-6914 397 B millerp@rmu.edu
MILLER, Randall .... 304-260-4380 488 C rmiller@blueridgectc.edu
MILLER, Rebecca .... 707-654-1000.. 32 A
MILLER, Richard .... 855-702-7434 186 E
MILLER, Richard .... 718-613-8590 317 B richard.miller@downstate.edu
MILLER, Rita .... 508-531-1295 212 D rmiller@bridgew.edu
MILLER, Rob .... 913-758-6160 178 B rob.miller@stmary.edu
MILLER, Robert .... 270-809-3399 184 D rmiller47@murraystate.edu
MILLER, JR., Robert, L . 908-852-1400 276 G robert.miller@centenaryuniversity.edu
MILLER, Robert, P .... 302-356-2477.. 91 E robert.p.miller@wilmu.edu
MILLER, Robert, R .... 540-828-5383 464 L rmiller@bridgewater.edu
MILLER, Rod .... 501-450-1423.. 19 E miller@hendrix.edu
MILLER, Rodney, E .... 316-978-3389 178 D rodney.miller@wichita.edu
MILLER, Rodney, E .... 706-419-1190 118 A miller@covenant.edu
MILLER, Roger .... 512-647-8792 449 D roger.miller@tstc.edu
MILLER, Ronald .... 201-447-7157 275 H rmiller1@bergen.edu
MILLER, JR., Ronald, E 843-661-1678 409 G rmiller@fmarion.edu
MILLER, Ronda .... 517-483-1452 226 H miller53@lcc.edu
MILLER, Roy .... 865-573-4517 420 E rmiller@johnsonu.edu

MILLER, Russell, L .... 281-283-2295 452 E
millerr@uhcl.edu
MILLER, Ryan .... 979-830-4282 431 H
ryan.miller@blinn.edu
MILLER, Ryan .... 561-586-0121 101 O
MILLER, Sandy, A .... 716-888-8222 292 F
mille267@canisius.edu
MILLER, Sarah .... 913-971-3838 176 C
smmiller@mnu.edu
MILLER, Sarah .... 661-722-6300.. 26 A
MILLER, Sarah .... 304-865-6200 487 H
sarah.m.miller@ovu.edu
MILLER, Scott .... 308-398-7355 266 A
scottmiller@cccneb.edu
MILLER, Scott .... 580-774-3187 370 A
scott.miller@swosu.edu
MILLER, Scott .... 814-732-2400 394 B
millerse@edinboro.edu
MILLER, Scott .... 814-732-2460 394 B
millerse@edinboro.edu
MILLER, Scott .... 307-855-2113 501 A
smiller@cwc.edu
MILLER, Scott, D .... 757-455-3215 477 C
president@vwu.edu
MILLER, Shae .... 417-328-7210 259 I
shaemiller@sbuniv.edu
MILLER, Shannon .... 408-924-4300.. 34 A
shannon.miller@sjsu.edu
MILLER, Shari, K .... 716-673-3438 316 D
shari.miller@fredonia.edu
MILLER, Sharyne .... 910-962-7261 343 C
millersa@uncw.edu
MILLER, Shawn .... 208-426-4454 130 H
shawnomiller@boisestate.edu
MILLER, Shawn .... 315-379-3820 320 B
millers@canton.edu
MILLER, Shawn .... 425-352-8135 478 D
smiller@cascadia.edu
MILLER, Shealynn .... 336-725-8344 327 H
MILLER, Simone .... 662-472-9144 246 D
smiller@holmescc.edu
MILLER, Simone .... 909-469-5608.. 75 I
simone.miller@westernu.edu
MILLER, ESQ, Sonya, A 305-626-3678 100 D
sonya.miller@fmuniv.edu
MILLER, Stacey .... 860-832-1652.. 85 G
stacey.miller@ccsu.edu
MILLER, Staci .... 662-246-6314 247 D
smiller@msdelta.edu
MILLER, Stephanie .... 256-215-4251.... 1 G
stmiller01@cacc.edu
MILLER, Stephanie .... 405-682-7897 367 D
smiller@occc.edu
MILLER, Stephen .... 812-941-2101 157 F
sfmiller@ius.edu
MILLER, Stephen .... 240-684-2037 203 E
stephen.miller@umuc.edu
MILLER, Steve .... 912-871-1801 123 J
smiller@ogeecheetech.edu
MILLER, Steve .... 925-631-4970.. 59 I
scmiller@stmarys-ca.edu
MILLER, Steve .... 513-745-5736 362 A
steve.miller2@uc.edu
MILLER, Steven .... 601-266-5001 249 F
steven.g.miller@usm.edu
MILLER, Steven .... 848-932-8714 282 A
stmiller@rutgers.edu
MILLER, Stormy, C .... 415-485-9601.. 39 A
smiller@marin.edu
MILLER, Susan .... 610-436-2442 395 D
smiller2@wcupa.edu
MILLER, Svetlana .... 516-629-6260 324 G
lmiller@webb.edu
MILLER, Sylvia .... 870-460-1034.. 22 C
millersm@uamont.edu
MILLER, Tabitha .... 252-789-0246 335 H
tabitha.miller@martincc.edu
MILLER, Tamsin .... 865-882-4640 425 C
miller@roanestate.edu
MILLER, Tara .... 641-648-4611 167 F
tara.miller@iavalley.edu
MILLER, Teresa .... 518-320-1388 315 H
teresa.miller@suny.edu
MILLER, Terry .... 605-642-6562 416 E
terry.miller@bhsu.edu
MILLER, Thomas, K ...... 919-513-5006 342 A
tkm@ncsu.edu
MILLER, Tia .... 603-862-0700 274 E
tia.miller@usnh.edu
MILLER, Tiffany .... 310-287-4521.. 49 H
millerts@wlac.edu
MILLER, Timothy .... 209-476-7840.. 67 E
tmiller@stocktonacademy.org
MILLER, Timothy, M ..... 540-568-3685 468 C
millertm@jmu.edu
MILLER, Tina .... 602-787-7081.. 13 E
tina.miller@paradisevalley.edu
MILLER, Tina .... 906-248-8437 221 M
tinamiller@bmcc.edu
MILLER, Tod .... 775-445-4282 271 F
todm@unr.edu
MILLER, Tracy .... 734-462-4400 230 G
tmiller@schoolcraft.edu
MILLER, Troy .... 717-815-1218 403 F
tmiller15@ycp.edu
MILLER, Troy .... 215-248-7004 381 A
millert@chc.edu
MILLER, Troy, A .... 716-645-6136 316 C
tam45@buffalo.edu
MILLER, Tyrus .... 949-824-5133.. 69 D
tyrusm@uci.edu
MILLER, Valerie .... 740-593-9853 358 K
millerv@ohio.edu
MILLER, Van .... 940-668-3333 440 F
vmiller@nctc.edu
MILLER, Victoria .... 619-388-2699.. 60 J
vmiller@sdccd.edu
MILLER, Vince .... 229-333-5941 127 E
vincemiller@valdosta.edu
MILLER, Vince .... 208-282-1045 131 G
millvinc@isu.edu
MILLER, Vincia .... 704-216-6009 330 H
MILLER, Wayne, C .... 606-783-2158 184 C
w.miller@moreheadstate.edu
MILLER, Wendy .... 847-214-7308 137 F
wmiller@elgin.edu
MILLER, Wendy .... 415-239-3370.. 36 K
wmiller@ccsfs.edu
MILLER, William .... 904-256-7030 102 H
wmiller5@ju.edu
MILLER, William .... 605-668-1584 415 F
bill.miller@mountmarty.edu
MILLER, Wynter .... 701-483-2340 345 C
wynter.miller@dickinsonstate.edu
MILLER, Yolanda, D ..... 662-621-4101 245 D
ymiller@coahomacc.edu
MILLER DIVINE,
Christine .... 678-407-5437 119 C
cmillerdivine@ggc.edu
MILLER-GALAZ,
Michelle .... 559-791-2432.. 47 A
michelle.miller@portervillecollege.edu
MILLER-GONZALEZ,
Emily, B .... 732-263-5393 279 A
emillerg@monmouth.edu
MILLER-HERNANDEZ,
Leangela .... 559-730-3795.. 39 B
leangelam@cos.edu
MILLER-LUGO, Karl .... 210-458-4011 455 E
MILLER-MCNEILL,
Laurie .... 914-606-6804 325 A
laurie.millermcneill@sunywcc.edu
MILLER NEVELS,
Andrea .... 773-244-5740 145 G
anevels@northpark.edu
MILLER-SCANDLE,
Tabbi .... 570-941-5824 401 F
tabbi.miller-scandle@scranton.edu
MILLER-SCHACHINGER,
Susanne .... 616-234-5825 232 B
susanne.miller@vai.edu
MILLER-SCHUSTER,
Danielle .... 309-438-5451 140 D
dnmille@ilstu.edu
MILLER-THORN, Jill .... 631-656-2122 300 B
jill.millerthorn@ftc.edu
MILLER-WIETECHA,
Lynn .... 248-204-2383 227 A
lmillerwi@ltu.edu
MILLER-YOW, Ronnie ... 501-370-5344.. 20 F
rmiller-yow@philander.edu
MILLER-YOW, Ronnie ... 501-370-5297.. 20 F
rmiller-yow@philander.edu
MILLERBERG, Reid .... 808-675-3514 128 D
reid.millerberg@byuh.edu
MILLET, Matthew, B ...... 412-397-6405 397 B
millet@rmu.edu
MILLET, Michelle .... 216-397-3053 353 O
mmillet@jcu.edu
MILLET, Peter, E .... 615-327-6015 421 D
pmillet@mmc.edu
MILLICAN, Joni .... 903-223-3054 448 A
businessoffice@tamut.edu
MILLICAN, Tony .... 931-393-1613 424 F
tmillican@mscc.edu
MILLIER, Deborah .... 706-245-7226 118 D
dmillier@ec.edu
MILLIGAN, Aretha .... 901-843-3000 423 A
milligana@rhodes.edu
MILLIGAN, Barry .... 937-775-2953 364 E
barry.milligan@wright.edu
MILLIGAN, Kristen .... 760-776-7428.. 38 E
kmilligan@collegeofthedesert.edu
MILLIGAN, Troy .... 405-422-1206 369 A
milligant@redlandscc.edu
MILLIKEN, Chris .... 719-549-2212.. 80 B
chris.milliken@csupueblo.edu
MILLIKEN, James, B ..... 512-499-4201 454 H
chancellor@utsystem.edu
MILLIKEN, Michelle ...... 910-592-8081 337 G
mmilliken@sampsoncc.edu
MILLIKEN, Roberta .... 740-774-7207 358 K
MILLIKEN, Ronald, P .... 207-778-7105 196 I
milliken@maine.edu
MILLIKEN, Stephanie .... 270-534-3394 183 B
stephanie.milliken@kctcs.edu
MILLIKIN, Mary .... 918-343-7605 369 B
mmillikin@rsu.edu
MILLIMAN, Robert, W .. 316-284-5239 172 B
rmilliman@bethelks.edu
MILLION, Christina, C .. 404-413-2190 120 E
cmillion@gsu.edu
MILLION, Kimberly .... 317-788-3488 161 H
0224mgr@follett.com
MILLIRON, Maureen ..... 239-687-5303.. 95 L
mmmilliron@avemarialaw.edu
MILLISON, Jeffrey .... 703-323-5690 477 A
MILLLER, Susan .... 219-989-2254 160 D
stmiller@pnw.edu
MILLNER, Kate .... 701-224-5666 346 A
katharine.millner@bismarckstate.edu
MILLNER, Musco .... 315-792-3046 324 B
mumillne@utica.edu
MILLNER, Tanya, C .... 410-777-2332 197 G
tcmillner@aacc.edu
MILLORA, Lisa .... 408-924-1000.. 34 A
MILLOY, Leslie .... 415-239-3554.. 36 K
lmilloy@ccsf.edu
MILLS, Alicia .... 508-831-5000 220 F
MILLS, Allison .... 217-786-2290 143 B
allison.mills@llcc.edu
MILLS, Andrea .... 615-966-5737 421 B
andrea.mills@lipscomb.edu
MILLS, Brian .... 541-681-7304 371 I
bmills@bushnell.edu
MILLS, Caroline .... 864-294-2191 409 H
caroline.mills@furman.edu
MILLS, Chavonda, J ..... 678-407-5602 119 C
cmills9@ggc.edu
MILLS, Cheryll .... 757-789-1730 473 H
cmills@es.vccs.edu
MILLS, Chris .... 610-896-1039 385 I
cmills@haverford.edu
MILLS, Christopher .... 410-287-1034 198 E
cmills@cecil.edu
MILLS, Dean, S .... 719-333-2877 503 D
dean.mills@usafa.edu
MILLS, Diana .... 410-334-2884 205 D
dmills@worwic.edu
MILLS, Edward .... 916-278-6060.. 32 D
emills@csus.edu
MILLS, Edward, D .... 912-478-1193 120 C
edmills@georgiasouthern.edu
MILLS, F. Joe .... 931-221-7444 417 H
millsj@apsu.edu
MILLS, Foy .... 806-720-7402 439 D
foy.mills@lcu.edu
MILLS, Frank .... 340-693-1067 513 E
fmills@uvi.edu
MILLS, Geofrey .... 724-357-7889 394 C
gtmills@iup.edu
MILLS, JR., Gordon ...... 251-460-7859.... 9 A
gmills@southalabama.edu
MILLS, Jacala .... 802-387-6732 462 C
jacalamills@landmark.edu
MILLS, Joe .... 304-336-5189 490 B
jmills@westliberty.edu
MILLS, John .... 606-368-6121 178 G
johnmills@alc.edu
MILLS, John, W .... 802-635-1240 463 G
MILLS, Josie .... 303-797-5813.. 77 I
josie.mills@arapahoe.edu
MILLS, Josie .... 303-797-5702.. 77 I
josie.mills@arapahoe.edu
MILLS, Juline .... 413-572-5300 213 F
MILLS, Juline .... 413-572-8691 213 F
jmills@westfield.ma.edu
MILLS, Kathy .... 315-787-4005 300 A
MILLS, Kelley .... 817-515-5043 445 F
kelley.mills@tccd.edu
MILLS, Kevin .... 209-932-3014.. 71 E
kmills@pacific.edu
MILLS, Leslie .... 361-825-2628 447 C
leslie.mills@tamucc.edu
MILLS, Lillian .... 512-471-4607 455 A
lillian.mills@mccombs.utexas.edu
MILLS, Linda, G .... 212-992-9712 309 F
linda.mills@nyu.edu
MILLS, Mark .... 215-898-1453 400 F
millsme@upenn.edu
MILLS, Martin .... 512-245-2501 450 C
mm79@txstate.edu
MILLS, Marvin, J .... 240-567-5371 200 G
marvin.mills@montgomerycollege.edu
MILLS, Matthew .... 913-253-5060 177 D
matthew.mills@spst.edu
MILLS, Michael .... 240-567-6001 200 G
michael.mills@montgomerycollege.edu
MILLS, Michael .... 940-397-4590 440 C
michael.mills@msutexas.edu
MILLS, Pamela .... 718-960-8764 294 A
pamela.mills@lehman.cuny.edu
MILLS, Rebecca .... 802-651-5965 462 A
rmills@champlain.edu
MILLS, Richard, G .... 603-646-0459 273 D
richard.g.mills@dartmouth.edu
MILLS, Sandra .... 513-487-1104 361 F
sandra.mills@myunion.edu
MILLS, Shala .... 845-257-3550 316 E
millss@newpaltz.edu
MILLS, Shirley, D .... 803-777-2001 413 A
smills@mailbox.sc.edu
MILLS, Thomas .... 817-515-1011 445 F
thomas.mills@tccd.edu
MILLS, William, R .... 617-552-8661 207 C
william.mills@bc.edu
MILLS CAMPBELL,
Dawn .... 803-705-4383 406 G
dawn.campbell@benedict.edu
MILLS-DICK, Melissa .... 413-559-5316 210 D
memdv@hampshire.edu
MILLS-LEMIRE, Denise .. 218-733-7600 238 G
denise.mills-lemire@lsc.edu
MILLSAP, Pamela .... 409-984-6211 449 I
millsappa@lamarpa.edu
MILLSAPPS, Michael ..... 970-339-6376.. 77 H
michael.millsapps@aims.edu
MILLSAPS, Brooke .... 828-771-3015 344 D
bmillsaps@warren-wilson.edu
MILLWOOD, Kent .... 864-231-2049 406 F
kmillwood@andersonuniversity.edu
MILNARICH, Sarah .... 361-354-2741 432 K
shmilnarich@coastalbend.edu
MILNE, Arryn .... 410-864-4075 202 C
amilne@stmarys.edu
MILNE, Erin .... 413-662-5049 213 C
erin.milne@mcla.edu
MILNE, Sheila .... 252-399-6326 326 K
smilne@barton.edu
MILNER, Andrea .... 517-265-5161 220 G
amilner@adrian.edu
MILNER, Devika, M ...... 305-284-6858 113 C
dmilner@miami.edu
MILNER, Eric .... 401-341-2218 405 D
eric.milner@salve.edu
MILNER, Jocelyn, L ...... 608-263-5658 495 D
jocelyn.milner@wisc.edu
MILNER, Melissa .... 719-587-8171.. 77 G
mmilner@adams.edu
MILO, Elaine .... 978-542-8031 213 E
elaine.milo@salemstate.edu
MILO, Jennifer .... 760-750-7108.. 33 A
jmilo@csusm.edu
MILON, Ronald, A .... 212-217-3070 299 D
ronald_milon@fitnyc.edu
MILONE-NUZZO, Paula 617-726-8002 217 A
pmilone-nuzzo@mghihp.edu
MILOWSKI, Nicholas, B 718-817-4975 300 C
nmilowski@fordham.edu
MILROY, Melodie .... 406-657-1022 265 E
melodie.milroy@rocky.edu
MILSOM, Penny .... 443-840-5426 198 H
mmilsom@ccbcmd.edu
MILTENBERGER, Chad .. 509-758-1711 485 B
chad.miltenberger@wwcc.edu
MILTER, Rebecca .... 678-916-2621 115 I
rmilter@johnmarshall.edu
MILTON, Alice .... 205-929-6306.... 2 H
amilton@lawsonstate.edu
MILTON, David .... 651-450-3522 238 E
dmilton@inverhills.edu
MILTON, David .... 651-450-3534 238 A
dmilton@inverhills.edu

MITCHELL, Clayton .... 215-503-7268 399 E
clayton.mitchell@jefferson.edu

MITCHELL, Clifton .... 229-226-1621 126 C
cmitchell@thomasu.edu

MITCHELL, Connie .... 803-754-4100 408 E

MITCHELL, Cordelia ...... 501-374-6305.. 20 G
cordelia.mitchell@shortercollege.edu

MITCHELL, Courtney ..... 443-412-2379 199 D
cmitchell@harford.edu

MITCHELL, Craig .... 206-517-4541 483 F
cmitchell@sieam.edu

MITCHELL, Damon .... 314-529-9252 255 B
dmitchell@maryville.edu

MITCHELL, David .... 415-503-6218.. 61 D
dlmitchell@sfcm.edu

MITCHELL, David, B ...... 301-405-5726 202 H
dmitche5@umd.edu

MITCHELL, Dawn .... 318-357-5960 192 G
dawnmitchell@nsula.edu

MITCHELL, Delmer .... 217-222-8020 147 F

MITCHELL, Dennis .... 480-461-7213.. 13 D
dennis.mitchell@mesacc.edu

MITCHELL, Dennis .... 212-854-7161 297 C
dmitchell@columbia.edu

MITCHELL, Dennis, A .... 212-854-1754 297 C

MITCHELL, Dian .... 478-471-6684 122 F
dian.mitchell@mga.edu

MITCHELL, JR.,
Donald (DJ) .... 502-272-8000 179 H

MITCHELL, Donna .... 740-245-7303 363 A
mitchell@rio.edu

MITCHELL, III,
Earnest, L .... 731-426-7604 420 G
emitchell@lanecollege.edu

MITCHELL, Eleanor .... 717-245-1864 382 D
mitchele@dickinson.edu

MITCHELL, Emilie .... 916-691-7142.. 50 H
mitchee@crc.losrios.edu

MITCHELL, Erica .... 901-321-3318 418 G
erica.mitchell@cbu.edu

MITCHELL, Erik, T .... 858-534-2230.. 70 C

MITCHELL, Glendon, G . 801-587-3784 459 O
gmitchell@purchasing.utah.edu

MITCHELL, Gloria .... 903-927-3304 458 F
gemitchell@wileyc.edu

MITCHELL, Gregory .... 843-477-2032 409 J
greg.mitchell@hgtc.edu

MITCHELL,
Gwendolyn, F .... 803-536-8212 411 G
gmitche3@scsu.edu

MITCHELL, Heather .... 850-201-6067 112 C
heather.mitchell@tcc.fl.edu

MITCHELL, Jada .... 678-466-4076 117 D
jadamitchell@clayton.edu

MITCHELL, James .... 517-483-1673 226 H
mitch94@lcc.edu

MITCHELL, James, M .... 334-876-9230.... 2 D
james.mitchell@wccs.edu

MITCHELL, Jennifer ...... 229-732-5946 115 B
jennifermitchell@andrewcollege.edu

MITCHELL, Joan .... 801-274-3280 461 E
jmitchell@wgu.edu

MITCHELL, Joann .... 215-898-6630 400 F
joannm@upenn.edu

MITCHELL, Joanne .... 310-665-6963.. 55 C
jmitchell@otis.edu

MITCHELL, Johnnie .... 501-337-5000.. 18 B
jmitchell@asutr.edu

MITCHELL, Jon .... 731-352-4280 418 C

MITCHELL, Joshua .... 610-769-1322 388 D
jmitchell10@lccc.edu

MITCHELL, Joshua .... 262-547-1211 492 A
jmitchell@carrollu.edu

MITCHELL, Jud .... 870-574-4726.. 21 D
jmitchel@sautech.edu

MITCHELL, Judy .... 815-280-2207 141 B
jmitchel@jjc.edu

MITCHELL, Karen .... 615-230-3505 425 E
karen.mitchell@volstate.edu

MITCHELL, Katharyne .... 831-459-2919.. 71 A
kmitch@ucsc.edu

MITCHELL, Kathryn .... 661-722-6300.. 26 A
kmitchel18@avc.edu

MITCHELL, Keith .... 580-581-2211 365 D
kmitchel@cameron.edu

MITCHELL, Ken, H .... 919-209-2112 335 F
khmitchell@johnstoncc.edu

MITCHELL, Kerrie .... 575-492-2560 287 A
kmitchell@nmjc.edu

MITCHELL, Kerry .... 623-845-3693.. 13 C
kerry.mitchell@gccaz.edu

MITCHELL, Kim .... 502-456-6508 185 A
kmitchell@sullivan.edu

MITCHELL, Kimberly, A . 309-655-2230 149 B
kim.mitchell@osfhealthcare.org

MITCHELL, Lisa .... 602-557-1732.. 16 G
lisa.mitchell@phoenix.edu

MITCHELL, Lori .... 540-674-3790 474 E
lmitchell@nr.edu

MITCHELL, Maria .... 610-372-4721 396 H
mmitchell@racc.edu

MITCHELL, Mark .... 540-338-1776 469 C

MITCHELL, Marquita ..... 214-379-5412 441 F
mmitchell@pqc.edu

MITCHELL, Matt .... 573-592-5301 262 E
matt.mitchell@westminster-mo.edu

MITCHELL, Melanie .... 508-793-2011 208 D

MITCHELL, Melissa .... 308-432-6221 268 D
mmitchell@csc.edu

MITCHELL, Michael .... 251-460-6172.... 9 A
mmitchell@southalabama.edu

MITCHELL, Michele .... 601-403-1440 248 E
mmitchell@prcc.edu

MITCHELL, Michelle ...... 731-352-4239 418 C
mitchellm@bethelu.edu

MITCHELL, Mitch .... 812-288-8878 159 M
mmitchell@mid-america.edu

MITCHELL, Mitch .... 336-750-3356 344 A
mitchellja@wssu.edu

MITCHELL, Nancy .... 636-584-6617 253 B
nancy.mitchell@eastcentral.edu

MITCHELL, Nancy, L ...... 509-527-5168 486 B
mitchenl@whitman.edu

MITCHELL, Naomi .... 318-345-9150 188 D
nmitchell@ladelta.edu

MITCHELL, Pamela .... 860-512-2605.. 86 G
pmitchell1@manchestercc.edu

MITCHELL, Paula .... 915-831-6375 436 A
pmitche8@epcc.edu

MITCHELL, Peg, P .... 302-356-6810.. 91 E
peg.p.mitchell@wilmu.edu

MITCHELL, JR.,
Randolph .... 904-470-8150.. 98 L
randolph.mitchell@ewc.edu

MITCHELL, JR., Robert . 504-816-4864 186 I
rvmitchell@dillard.edu

MITCHELL, Robin .... 563-288-6103 166 A
rmitchell@eicc.edu

MITCHELL, Roland .... 225-578-2156 189 E
rwmitch@lsu.edu

MITCHELL, Sandra .... 651-690-6649 243 A
slmitchell224@stkate.edu

MITCHELL, Scott .... 815-226-4026 148 D
smitchell@rockford.edu

MITCHELL, Scott .... 510-809-1444.. 45 M

MITCHELL, Sharon, L .... 716-645-2720 316 C
smitch@buffalo.edu

MITCHELL, Sheila .... 731-661-5953 426 F
smitchell@uu.edu

MITCHELL, Stephen .... 517-265-5161 220 G
smitchell@adrian.edu

MITCHELL, Steve .... 903-823-3269 446 A
steven.mitchell@texarkanacollege.edu

MITCHELL, Tedd, L .... 806-742-0012 450 F
tedd.mitchell@ttuhsc.edu

MITCHELL, Tedd, L .... 806-742-0012 450 D

MITCHELL, Thomas .... 814-732-2743 394 B
tmitchell@edinboro.edu

MITCHELL, Thomas, J .... 352-392-5407 111 A
tmitchell@uff.ufl.edu

MITCHELL, Thomas, R .. 956-326-2240 446 E
tmitchell@tamiu.edu

MITCHELL, Trapper .... 608-342-1183 496 E
mitchellt@uwplatt.edu

MITCHELL, Tucker .... 843-661-1332 409 G
cmitchell@fmarion.edu

MITCHELL, Venita .... 573-592-4235 262 G
venita.mitchell@williamwoods.edu

MITCHELL, Venita .... 434-791-5627 464 I
vmitchell@averett.edu

MITCHELL, Vicki .... 740-588-1386 365 B
vmitchell@zanestate.edu

MITCHELL, Victor .... 860-314-4709.. 87 G
vmitchell@tunxis.edu

MITCHELL, William .... 508-588-9100 215 A
wamitchell@massasoit.mass.edu

MITCHELL, JR.,
Zane, W .... 812-465-7137 162 C
zwmitchell@usi.edu

MITCHELL-FERRIS,
Peggy .... 479-964-0532.. 18 C
pmitchellferris@atu.edu

MITCHELSON, Ron .... 252-744-2201 341 A
mitchelsonr@ecu.edu

MITCHEM, Brandi .... 478-445-2313 116 G
bmitchem@centralgatech.edu

MITCHUM, M.G .... 843-574-6995 412 I
mg.mitchum@tridenttech.edu

MITERKO, Lori, A .... 716-880-2288 305 G
lori.a.miterko@medaille.edu

MITHANI, Amynah .... 667-208-7545 199 G
amithan1@jhu.edu

MITJANS, Dolores .... 787-882-2065 510 C
dmitjans@unitecpr.edu

MITNICK, Eric .... 508-985-1169 212 A
emitnick@umassd.edu

MITRA, Sabyasachi .... 352-392-2398 111 A
sabymitra@warrington.ufl.edu

MITSLER, Julee .... 636-949-4913 254 H
jmitsler@lindenwood.edu

MITSUI, Mark .... 971-722-4365 375 D
mark.mitsui@pcc.edu

MITTELSTAEDT, John .... 937-229-3349 362 C
jmittelstaedt1@udayton.edu

MITTEN, Richard .... 646-312-2076 292 L
richard.mitten@baruch.cuny.edu

MITTLEMAN,
Michael, H .... 215-780-1280 398 B
president@salus.edu

MITTLER, Tiina .... 626-852-8047.. 36 J
tmittler@citruscollege.edu

MITTMAN, Paul, A .... 480-858-9100.. 15 Q
p.mittman@scnm.edu

MITTON, Gregory, S ..... 484-664-3175 390 H
gregmitton@muhlenberg.edu

MITTON, Lynda .... 816-960-2008 251 G
dean@cityvision.edu

MITTS, Maryann .... 417-667-8181 252 E
mmitts@cottey.edu

MITTUCH, Maggie, A .... 253-879-3673 484 G
mmittuch@pugetsound.edu

MITZEL, Bobbi .... 307-675-0703 501 G
rmitzel@sheridan.edu

MITZEL, Thomas, M ...... 270-852-3104 183 E
tom.mitzel@kwc.edu

MIX, Catherine .... 937-229-4311 362 C
cmix01@udayton.edu

MIX, Julie, L .... 253-535-7101 482 A
mixjl@plu.edu

MIX, Kerry .... 409-839-2048 449 F
kmix@lit.edu

MIXON, Lonnie .... 407-303-8192.. 95 B
lonnie.mixon@ahu.edu

MIXON, Stewart .... 843-792-5050 410 C
mixonsa@musc.edu

MIXSON, Frank .... 562-860-2451.. 35 H
fmixson@cerritos.edu

MIYAKE, Christina .... 212-563-6647 323 I
c.lmiyake@uts.edu

MIYASHIRO, James .... 619-260-7690.. 72 I
publicsafety@sandiego.edu

MIYASHIRO, Jane .... 310-660-3401.. 41 E
jmiyashiro@elcamino.edu

MIYASHIRO, Ross .... 310-660-3472.. 41 E
rmiyashiro@elcamino.edu

MIZAK, Pat .... 941-893-2858 106 J
pmizak@ringling.edu

MIZE, Kyle, C .... 325-649-8049 437 G
kmize@hputx.edu

MIZELL, Claire .... 903-510-2939 452 A
cmiz@tjc.edu

MIZELL, Hunter .... 843-863-7000 407 B
hmizell@csuniv.edu

MIZELL, Nathan .... 252-789-0232 335 H
nathan.mizell@martincc.edu

MIZNER, Kevin .... 559-730-3868.. 39 B
kevinm@cos.edu

MIZZY, Danianne .... 973-655-4301 279 B
mizzyd@montclair.edu

MIÑANA, Rogelio .... 215-571-3194 382 F
rogelio.minana@drexel.edu

MLLER, Justin (Jay) .... 859-257-3887 185 F
justin.miller1@uky.edu

MLODZIK, Leigh .... 515-961-1699 170 B
leigh.mlodzik@simpson.edu

MLYNARCZYK, Chuck ... 866-582-8448 108 B

MLYNSKI, Melissa .... 217-206-7148 152 A
mmlyn2@uis.edu

MMEJE,
Kenechukwu (K.C.) ..... 214-768-2821 444 D
kmmeje@smu.edu

MNOOKIN, Jennifer, L .. 310-825-8202.. 69 E
mnookin@law.ucla.edu

MO, Huanbiao .... 404-413-1082 120 E
hmo@gsu.edu

MOAK, Marvin .... 601-629-6805 246 C
memoak@hindscc.edu

MOANANU, Letupu .... 684-699-9155 504 B
l.moananu@amsamoa.edu

MOATS, Kyle .... 417-836-5244 256 G
kylemoats@missouristate.edu

MOAVENI, Saeed .... 801-863-8237 460 D
saeed.moaveni@uvu.edu

MOAWAD, Greg .... 503-494-6004 374 H
moawad@ohsu.edu

MOBELINI, Deronda ...... 606-487-3409 181 I
deronda.mobelini@kctcs.edu

MOBERG,
Christopher, R .... 989-774-2481 222 E
mober1cr@cmich.edu

MOBERLY, Jonathon ..... 402-643-7430 266 G
jonathon.moberly@cune.edu

MOBERLY, Richard .... 402-472-1256 269 J
moberly@unl.edu

MOBLEY, Jill .... 870-307-7226.. 19 I
jill.mobley@lyon.edu

MOBLEY, Karen .... 912-871-1638 123 J
kmobley@ogeecheetech.edu

MOBLEY, Katie .... 802-654-0505 463 F
kjf06010@ccv.vsc.edu

MOBLEY, Wade .... 763-544-9501 235 L

MOBRAY, Todd .... 620-792-9245 171 I
mobrayt@bartonccc.edu

MOCARSKI, Richard, A . 308-865-8496 269 I
mocarskira@unk.edu

MOCCIA, Mario .... 575-646-7630 287 C
moccia@nmsu.edu

MOCHUN, Katelynn .... 508-213-2277 217 H
katelynn.mochun@nichols.edu

MOCK, Kenrick .... 907-786-1956.... 9 J
kjmock@alaska.edu

MOCK, Lisa .... 701-228-5432 346 B
lisa.mock@dakotacollege.edu

MOCK, Melissa .... 209-384-6199.. 52 A

MOCK, Robert, C .... 410-651-6101 203 D
rcmock@umes.edu

MOCTEZUMA, Edgar ..... 713-522-7911 454 G
mocteze@stthom.edu

MODDELMOG, Debra .... 775-784-6805 271 E
dmoddelmog@unr.edu

MODELANE, Dan .... 508-541-1614 209 A
dmodelane@dean.edu

MODENA, Shawn .... 478-825-6100 118 F
modenas@fvsu.edu

MODENSTEIN, Susan .... 212-592-2208 315 C
smodenstein@sva.edu

MODERO, Thomas .... 646-565-6163 322 F
thomas.modero@touro.edu

MODERO, Thomas .... 646-565-6163 322 G
thomas.modero@touro.edu

MODESTOU,
Jennifer, A .... 319-335-0705 163 H
jennifer-modestou@uiowa.edu

MODIC, Jeannette, L ..... 240-895-2260 202 B
jlmodic@smcm.edu

MODICA, Joseph .... 909-748-8692.. 72 F
joseph_modica@redlands.edu

MODICA, Joseph, B .... 610-341-5826 383 B
jmodica@eastern.edu

MODICA, Kathy .... 870-864-7107.. 21 A
kmodica@southark.edu

MODIG, James, E .... 785-864-3493 177 J
jmodig@ku.edu

MODISETTE, Jan .... 903-589-7300 438 C
jmodisette@jacksonville-college.edu

MODLIN, Andrew, S ...... 336-841-9605 329 F
amodlin@highpoint.edu

MODLIN, Eli, J .... 410-548-3316 204 D
ejmodlin@salisbury.edu

MODLIN, Jason .... 252-985-5404 339 D
jmodlin@ncwc.edu

MODROVSKY, Amanda . 570-408-5534 403 A
amanda.modrovsky@wilkes.edu

MODRY-CARON, Irah .... 260-481-6375 160 C
modryi@pfw.edu

MOE, Karine, F .... 651-696-6160 236 I
moe@macalester.edu

MOE, Keri, L .... 915-831-6526 436 A
kmoe@epcc.edu

MOE, Rolin .... 650-738-7149.. 62 L
moer@smccd.edu

MOEDER, Brenda .... 660-543-4515 260 G
moeder@ucmo.edu

MOEGGENBERG, Rich ... 517-607-2250 225 C
rmoeggenberg@hillsdale.edu

MOEHLING, Carolyn ..... 848-932-8662 282 A
cmoehling@echo.rutgers.edu

MOELLER, Darin .... 712-274-6400 171 B
darin.moeller@witcc.edu

MOELLER, Lon, D .... 386-226-6000.. 99 A
moellerl@erau.edu

MONGILLO, Anne, M .... 516-463-6776 301 G
anne.mongillo@hofstra.edu
MONGO, Karen .... 972-273-3593 435 B
kmongo@dcccd.edu
MONHEIT, Yidel .... 718-853-2442 325 K
MONIACI, Steve .... 281-649-3096 437 B
smoniaci@hbu.edu
MONIODIS, Paul .... 410-837-5270 204 F
pmoniodis@ubalt.edu
MONIZ, Jeffrey .... 808-689-2303 129 F
jmoniz@hawaii.edu
MONIZ, Richard .... 843-349-5269 409 J
richard.moniz@hgtc.edu
MONJURE, Derek .... 208-882-1566 132 C
dmonjure@nsa.edu
MONK, Gordon .... 225-578-3849 189 E
gordon@lsualumni.org
MONK, Matthew .... 802-828-8556 463 B
matthew.monk@vcfa.edu
MONK, Suzanne .... 601-318-6767 249 H
smonk@wmcarey.edu
MONK, Virginia .... 903-875-7619 447 B
virginia.monk@tamuc.edu
MONK-MORGAN, Kaye . 316-978-3010 178 D
kaye.monk@wichita.edu
MONKS, Birgit .... 909-652-6876.. 35 L
birgit.monks@chaffey.edu
MONLUX, Carrie .... 530-879-4050.. 27 C
monluxca@butte.edu
MONNES, Mark, J .... 419-755-4824 357 B
mmonnes@ncstatecollege.edu
MONNIG, Amber .... 660-248-6280 251 E
armonnig@centralmethodist.edu
MONNIG, Donna .... 660-263-4100 257 B
donnamonnig@macc.edu
MONNIN, Donald .... 716-896-0700 324 E
monnind@villa.edu
MONNIN, Erica .... 212-752-1530 304 A
erica.monnin@limcollege.edu
MONNOT, Charles .... 405-208-5295 367 E
cmonnot@okcu.edu
MONOD, Kelly .... 941-752-5491 109 G
monodk@scf.edu
MONRO, Glenn .... 214-887-5173 435 F
gmonro@dts.edu
MONROE, Alicia .... 856-256-4284 281 F
monroe@rowan.edu
MONROE, Alicia .... 713-798-2312 431 D
alicia.monroe@bcm.edu
MONROE, Dana .... 919-546-8220 340 B
dmonroe@shawu.edu
MONROE, Darin .... 815-921-3822 148 B
d.monroe@rockvalleycollege.edu
MONROE, Jill .... 619-849-2298.. 57 J
jillmonroe@pointloma.edu
MONROE, Joseph, W ... 859-257-5770 185 F
joe.monroe@uky.edu
MONROE, JP .... 541-346-2085 376 H
jpmonroe@uoregon.edu
MONROE, Kara .... 317-921-4882 158 D
kmonroe@ivytech.edu
MONROE, Kareema .... 718-270-4900 294 G
MONROE, Tonya, C ...... 336-328-1751 337 A
tcmonroe@randolph.edu
MONROE, William .... 713-743-9007 452 D
wmonroe@uh.edu
MONROE-DAVIS,
Sandra .... 757-823-2916 469 A
sfmonroe-davis@nsu.edu
MONROY, Mandy .... 620-331-2480 174 H
mmonroy@indycc.edu
MONS, Marie .... 404-894-4582 119 E
marie.mons@finaid.gatech.edu
MONTA, Anthony .... 574-239-8385 156 A
amonta@hcc-nd.edu
MONTAGUE, Emma .... 508-678-2811 214 B
emma.montague@bristolcc.edu
MONTAGUE, Evan, L .... 989-774-1912 222 E
monta3e@cmich.edu
MONTAGUE, Kathleen ... 518-694-7256 289 J
kathleen.montague@acphs.edu
MONTAGUE, Lynne .... 978-542-6134 213 E
lynne.montague@salemstate.edu
MONTAGUE,
Marlena, O .... 671-735-5612 504 D
marlena.montague@guamcc.edu
MONTAGUE, Orinthia .... 615-230-3500 425 E
orinthia.montague@volstate.edu
MONTAGUE,
Orinthia, T .... 607-844-8222 322 D
otm@tompkinscortland.edu
MONTALBANO,
Anthony .... 207-602-2863 197 E
amontalbano@une.edu

MONTALBANO, Ivonne . 713-221-8060 453 A
montalbanoi@uhd.edu
MONTALBANO, JoAnn .. 985-867-2237 190 K
rouquette@sjasc.edu
MONTALTO, Karen .... 856-222-9311 281 C
kmontalto@rcbc.edu
MONTALVO, Carmen .... 787-878-5475 507 L
cmontalv@arecibo.inter.edu
MONTALVO, Cynthia ..... 201-559-6036 277 J
montalvoc@felician.edu
MONTALVO, Devyn .... 863-638-2964 114 B
montalvods@webber.edu
MONTALVO, Elsa .... 432-552-2795 456 F
montalvo_e@utpb.edu
MONTALVO, Irene .... 254-501-5852 447 A
i.montalvo@tamuct.edu
MONTALVO, Luis .... 617-585-0200 207 A
luis.montalvo@the-bac.edu
MONTALVO-COLÓN,
Sonia, I .... 787-751-1912 509 A
smontalv@juris.inter.edu
MONTALVO-CUMMINGS,
Jessica .... 361-698-1170 435 G
jmontalvo@delmar.edu
MONTANA, Michael ...... 717-262-2002 403 C
michael.montana@wilson.edu
MONTANARO,
Marilee, K .... 618-537-6838 144 A
mkmontanaro@mckendree.edu
MONTANEZ, Isabel .... 787-764-0000 513 B
isavel.montanez@upr.edu
MONTANEZ, Robert ...... 916-691-7326.. 50 H
montanr2@crc.losrios.edu
MONTANEZ-LOPEZ,
Nilda .... 787-798-3001 511 B
nilda.montanez@uccaribe.edu
MONTANO, Estavan ...... 312-341-2125 148 E
emontano02@roosevelt.edu
MONTANO, Mark .... 715-634-4790 492 L
mmontano@lco.edu
MONTANY, Lisa, M ...... 260-356-4014 156 C
lmontany@huntington.edu
MONTAS, Keiselim, A ... 603-646-4000 273 D
keiselim.a.montas@dartmouth.edu
MONTAVON, Joshua ...... 801-832-2502 461 F
jmontavon@westminstercollege.edu
MONTAÑO, Estevan ...... 708-524-6873 137 C
emontano@dom.edu
MONTEAGUDO, Rene .... 305-284-5511 113 C
rxm981@miami.edu
MONTECALVO, Frank .... 814-472-3002 397 F
fmontecalvo@francis.edu
MONTECALVO, Marisa .. 914-594-4236 309 B
marisa_montecalvo@nymc.edu
MONTEFUSCO, Luis ...... 609-343-5635 275 D
lmontefu@atlantic.edu
MONTEIRO, Alessandra 508-588-9100 215 A
amontei24@massasoit.mass.edu
MONTEIRO, Beth .... 307-855-2254 501 A
bmonteir@cwc.edu
MONTEIRO, JR.,
D. Paul .... 202-806-2510.. 92 F
paul.monteiro@howard.edu
MONTEIRO, Paul .... 202-806-6100.. 92 F
MONTEITH, Kellie .... 828-227-7147 343 E
monteith@wcu.edu
MONTEJANO, Rachel .... 210-784-1372 447 E
rachel.montejano@tamusa.edu
MONTEMAYOR, Roland 408-288-3146.. 62 H
roland.montemayor@sjcc.edu
MONTENEGRO, Luis ..... 718-289-5939 293 B
luis.montenegro@bcc.cuny.edu
MONTENEGRO-SPENCER,
Delmy .... 909-389-3355.. 60 E
dspencer@craftonhills.edu
MONTERO, Alfred .... 507-222-4311 234 G
amontero@carleton.edu
MONTERO, Grecia .... 609-771-3132 276 I
montero@tcnj.edu
MONTERO, Joel .... 787-720-1022 505 E
admisiones@atlanticu.edu
MONTEROSO,
Catherine .... 304-336-8231 490 B
cmonteroso@westliberty.edu
MONTES, Angel .... 213-356-5321.. 65 E
angel_montes@sciarc.edu
MONTES, Anibal .... 787-844-8181 513 A
anibal.montes@upr.edu
MONTES, Nathania .... 630-942-3324 135 I
MONTES, Porfirio .... 787-863-2390 508 B
porfirio.montes@fajardo.inter.edu
MONTES, Rebecca .... 707-468-3009.. 51 F
rmontes@mendocino.edu

MONTES, Sofia .... 956-665-3650 455 D
sofia.montes@utrgv.edu
MONTES, Susan, R .... 305-284-6021 113 C
smontes@miami.edu
MONTES-HELU, Mario .. 520-383-0076.. 16 A
mmontes@tocc.edu
MONTESINO,
María del C .... 787-720-1022 505 E
recaudaciones@atlanticu.edu
MONTEVIRGEN, Alexis .. 818-719-6408.. 49 D
MONTEZ, Daniel .... 956-447-6635 443 H
dmontez@southtexascollege.edu
MONTEZ, Nicholas .... 619-482-6306.. 66 A
nmontez@swccd.edu
MONTGOMERY, Alan .... 772-462-7860 102 F
jmontgom@irsc.edu
MONTGOMERY,
Alisa, L .... 336-322-2213 336 G
alisa.montgomery@piedmontcc.edu
MONTGOMERY, Cassie . 806-345-5600 429 E
c0353116@actx.edu
MONTGOMERY, Cathy .. 912-427-6265 117 E
cmontgomery@coastalpines.edu
MONTGOMERY, Christy 985-545-1500 188 E
MONTGOMERY, Cindy .. 229-226-1621 126 C
cmontgomery@thomasu.edu
MONTGOMERY, Dale .... 479-636-9222.. 20 C
dmontgom@nwacc.edu
MONTGOMERY, Daron .. 603-641-7107 274 A
dmontgomery@anselm.edu
MONTGOMERY, Don ..... 928-757-0821.. 14 F
dmontgomery@mohave.edu
MONTGOMERY,
Edward, B .... 269-387-2351 233 B
edward.montgomery@wmich.edu
MONTGOMERY, Erin ...... 863-298-6837 106 A
emontgomery@polk.edu
MONTGOMERY, Jeff ...... 937-393-3431 360 H
jlmontgo@sscc.edu
MONTGOMERY, John ..... 951-343-4963.. 27 G
jmontgomery@calbaptist.edu
MONTGOMERY, John .... 734-432-5574 227 C
jmontgomery@madonna.edu
MONTGOMERY, John .... 575-562-4002 286 B
john.montgomery@enmu.edu
MONTGOMERY,
Joseph, D .... 330-823-2295 362 E
montgojd@mountunion.edu
MONTGOMERY,
Kara, H .... 724-946-7363 402 D
montgokh@westminster.edu
MONTGOMERY, Katrina 512-505-3060 438 A
kkmontgomery@htu.edu
MONTGOMERY, Keisha . 803-705-4601 406 G
keisha.montgomery@benedict.edu
MONTGOMERY,
Laura, M .... 630-752-5227 153 C
laura.montgomery@wheaton.edu
MONTGOMERY, Lisa ..... 312-567-3777 140 A
montgomeryl@iit.edu
MONTGOMERY, Mark ... 315-792-7100 321 B
MONTGOMERY, Mark ... 610-526-1518 378 D
mark.montgomery@
theamericancollege.edu
MONTGOMERY, Martha 254-442-5114 432 I
martha.montgomery@cisco.edu
MONTGOMERY, Nancy . 949-451-5273.. 65 C
nmontgomery@ivc.edu
MONTGOMERY, Robby . 575-835-5816 286 K
robby.montgomery@nmt.edu
MONTGOMERY, Robert . 248-232-4808 229 C
rjmontgo@oaklandcc.edu
MONTGOMERY,
Tamara, F .... 225-771-2200 191 B
tamara_montgomery@subr.edu
MONTGOMERY,
Tamara, F .... 225-771-2200 191 A
tamara_montgomery@subr.edu
MONTGOMERY, Tina .... 936-261-1000 446 C
tlmontgomery@pvamu.edu
MONTGOMERY,
Toni-Marie .... 847-491-7552 146 E
t-montgomery@northwestern.edu
MONTGOMERY, Tony ... 662-476-5062 246 B
tmontgomery@eastms.edu
MONTGOMERY,
Walter, C .... 336-322-2258 336 G
walter.montgomery@piedmontcc.edu
MONTGOMERY, Wayne . 202-274-6065.. 94 B
MONTGOMERY, Wendy 301-405-6279 202 H
wmont@umd.edu
MONTGOMERY RICE,
Valerie .... 404-752-1740 123 E
vmrice@msm.edu

MONTI, Joseph .... 407-644-1408 106 L
jmonti@rollins.edu
MONTICCIOLO, Cheryl .. 516-686-1080 308 I
cheryl.monticciolo@nyit.edu
MONTICELLO, Anthony . 908-737-4843 278 E
amontice@kean.edu
MONTIEL, Arthuro .... 956-488-5808 443 H
amontiel@southtexascollege.edu
MONTILEAUX, Kateri ..... 605-455-6142 415 H
kmontileaux@olc.edu
MONTILLA, Elaine .... 212-817-7000 293 F
MONTILLA, Hector .... 787-834-9595 510 D
h.montilla@uaa.edu
MONTILLA, Lisannie ..... 240-567-5264 200 G
lisannie.montilla@montgomerycollege.
edu
MONTOYA, Carlos .... 925-473-7341.. 40 D
cmontoya@losmedanos.edu
MONTOYA, David .... 760-744-1150.. 56 B
MONTOYA, Denise .... 505-426-2240 286 J
montoyad@nmhu.edu
MONTOYA, Jimi .... 505-747-2139 287 H
jimi.montoya@nnmc.edu
MONTOYA, Michael ...... 505-454-2534 286 F
mimontoya@luna.edu
MONTOYA, Mitzi .... 505-277-6471 288 J
mitzimontoya@unm.edu
MONTOYA, Sharon .... 928-428-8289.. 12 F
sharon.montoya@eac.edu
MONTOYA, Valerie .... 505-346-2351 288 I
valerie.montoya@bie.edu
MONTPLAISIR, Daniel ... 909-869-4789.. 30 A
dmontplaisir@cpp.edu
MONTREAL, Steven, R .. 262-243-5700 492 E
steven.montreal@cuw.edu
MONTROSE, Lee .... 910-410-1813 337 B
ljmontrose@richmondcc.edu
MONTROSS, Julia, H .... 989-774-3332 222 E
montr1jh@cmich.edu
MONTS, William .... 864-231-2000 406 F
wmonts@andersonuniversity.edu
MONYPENY, Derek .... 760-366-3791.. 40 E
dmonypeny@cmccd.edu
MOO-YOUNG, Keith ...... 518-276-2244 312 C
mooyoh2@rpi.edu
MOODY, Bryan .... 847-578-3206 148 F
bryan.moody@rosalindfranklin.edu
MOODY, Jeff, T .... 866-294-3974 154 H
jeff.moody@ccr.edu
MOODY, Kari .... 920-465-2226 495 F
moodyk@uwgb.edu
MOODY, Kay .... 866-294-3974 154 H
kay.moody@ccr.edu
MOODY, Kelly .... 212-678-3755 322 C
ksm2182@tc.columbia.edu
MOODY, Krystal .... 903-927-3312 458 F
kmoody@wileyc.edu
MOODY, Kyle .... 620-241-0723 172 J
kyle.moody@centralchristian.edu
MOODY, Michelle, L 757-594-8819 465M
mlmoody@cnu.edu
MOON, Alan .... 903-693-1113 441 C
amoon@panola.edu
MOON, Beverly .... 662-846-4873 245 G
bmoon@deltastate.edu
MOON, Don .... 434-592-3235 468 E
donmoon@liberty.edu
MOON, Harry, K .... 954-262-0510 105 A
hmoon@nova.edu
MOON, Hope .... 440-366-7183 355 B
MOON, Hyon, J .... 949-480-4139.. 64 G
hmoon@soka.edu
MOON, Josh .... 920-465-2069 495 F
moonj@uwgb.edu
MOON, Joshua .... 605-626-3336 416 G
joshua.moon@northern.edu
MOON, Lisa .... 866-492-5336 244 F
lisa.moon@mail.waldenu.edu
MOON, Lisa, T .... 804-257-5605 476 F
ltmoon@vuu.edu
MOON, Pat .... 256-766-6610.... 5 E
pmoon@hcu.edu
MOON, Randy .... 251-460-6871.... 9 A
rmoon@southalabama.edu
MOON, Rose .... 828-726-2269 332 G
rmoon@cccti.edu
MOON, Sandra .... 502-895-3411 183 H
smoon@lpts.edu
MOON, Sarah .... 585-785-1373 299 F
sarah.moon@flcc.edu
MOON, Shin .... 973-618-3230 276 D
smoon@caldwell.edu

MOORE, Rose Marie ..... 405-422-1262 369 A
rosemarie.moore@redlandscc.edu
MOORE, Rudell .... 937-708-5734 363 G
rmoore@wilberforce.edu
MOORE, Russell .... 303-492-2890.. 84 B
rmoore@colorado.edu
MOORE, Rustin .... 614-688-8749 358 D
moore.66@osu.edu
MOORE, Sandra .... 510-215-4908.. 40 B
smoore@contracosta.edu
MOORE, Sandra .... 803-535-1237 411 B
mooresj@octech.edu
MOORE, Sara .... 212-517-3929 315 G
s.moore@sothebysinstitute.com
MOORE, Sarah .... 541-885-1023 374 I
sarah.moore@oit.edu
MOORE, Scott .... 559-278-0333.. 31 B
scottm@csufresno.edu
MOORE, Scott .... 216-397-4531 353 O
moore@jcu.edu
MOORE, Shamus .... 580-774-3001 370 A
shamus.moore@swosu.edu
MOORE, Shaun, A .... 248-370-4414 229 I
samoore@oakland.edu
MOORE, Shelby .... 713-646-1884 443 I
smoore@stcl.edu
MOORE, Shelley .... 318-797-5234 190 A
shelley.moore@lsus.edu
MOORE, Shelly .... 724-480-3492 381 H
shelly.moore@ccbc.edu
MOORE, Sheri .... 925-424-1002.. 35 K
slmoore@laspositascollege.edu
MOORE, Sherry .... 570-484-2153 394 E
snm152@lockhaven.edu
MOORE, Stacey .... 803-327-8014 414 F
smoore@yorktech.edu
MOORE, Steve .... 248-218-2430 230 B
smoore4@rochesteru.edu
MOORE, Stuart .... 307-382-1618 501 J
smoore@westernwyoming.edu
MOORE, Susan .... 508-929-8117 213 G
smoore5@worcester.edu
MOORE, Susan .... 585-245-5502 318 B
moores@geneseo.edu
MOORE, Susan .... 910-272-3345 337 D
smoore@robeson.edu
MOORE, Tammy .... 563-588-6374 164 E
tammy.moore@clarke.edu
MOORE, Tanya .... 919-962-6229 342 C
tanya_moore@unc.edu
MOORE, Teresa .... 903-813-2451 430 H
temoore@austincollege.edu
MOORE, Terrell .... 240-965-2452 198 C
tmoore@captechu.edu
MOORE, Thad .... 410-778-7231 205 B
tmoore2@washcoll.edu
MOORE, Thomas, F ...... 304-457-6238 486 E
mooretf@ab.edu
MOORE, Timothy .... 617-353-0750 207 E
mooretj@bu.edu
MOORE, Timothy .... 847-214-7651 137 F
tmoore@elgin.edu
MOORE, Timothy .... 772-462-4701 102 F
timmoore@irsc.edu
MOORE, Timothy .... 518-255-5323 319 C
mooretw@cobleskill.edu
MOORE, Tina .... 217-234-5346 142 C
tmoore@lakeland.cc.il.us
MOORE, Tom .... 870-972-2985.. 17 E
tmoore@astate.edu
MOORE, Tomeka, L .... 601-877-6118 245 A
tmoore1@alcorn.edu
MOORE, Tony .... 936-261-9370 446 C
tamoore@pvamu.edu
MOORE, Tony .... 503-399-6505 372 B
tony.moore@chemeketa.edu
MOORE, Tonya .... 770-454-9270.. 93 H
MOORE, Tonya .... 678-359-5719 120 F
tmoore@gordonstate.edu
MOORE, Torrey .... 662-246-6330 247 D
tmoore@msdelta.edu
MOORE, Tracey .... 501-420-1240.. 16 L
tracey.moore@arkansasbaptist.edu
MOORE, Traci .... 256-726-7353.... 6 C
tmoore@oakwood.edu
MOORE, Vicki .... 319-895-4378 164 G
vmoore@cornellcollege.edu
MOORE, Vincent .... 757-823-2199 469 A
vmmoore@nsu.edu
MOORE, Virginia .... 304-357-4957 487 J
virginiamoore@ucwv.edu
MOORE, Warren .... 252-527-6223 335 G
wcmoore39@lenoircc.edu
MOORE, Wes .... 214-333-5331 434 C
wesm@dbu.edu
MOORE, William .... 229-500-2027 114 H
william.moore@asurams.edu
MOORE, Zachery .... 814-865-6563 391 G
zpm100@psu.edu
MOORE-BOHANNON,
Anita .... 630-466-7900 152 K
amoorebohannon@waubonsee.edu
MOORE-GARCIA,
Beverly .... 305-237-8902 104 E
bmoorega@mdc.edu
MOORE JOHNSON,
Monica .... 662-621-4156 245 D
mmjohnson@coahomacc.edu
MOORE-JONES,
Yolanda, V .... 919-536-7201 334 C
jonesym@durhamtech.edu
MOORE-WILK, Meghan . 718-997-5559 295 B
meghan.moorewilk@qc.cuny.edu
MOOREFIELD, Jennifer . 864-250-6482 409 I
jennifer.moorefield@gvltec.edu
MOORHEAD, Cari, A .... 603-862-3007 274 F
cari.moorhead@unh.edu
MOORHEAD, Jill .... 614-222-3291 351 B
jmoorhead@ccad.edu
MOORMAN, Jack .... 336-334-7500 341 D
MOORMAN, Nate .... 706-245-7226 118 D
nmoorman@ec.edu
MOORMON, Josh .... 818-333-3558.. 53 J
josh.mormon@nyfa.edu
MOORS, Dean .... 402-460-2153 266 A
dmoors@cccneb.edu
MOORTI, Sujata .... 802-443-5735 462 E
smoorti@middlebury.edu
MOORWOOD, Woody ... 626-815-3855.. 26 F
wmoorwood@apu.edu
MOOS, Michael .... 317-917-3623 159 L
mmoos@martin.edu
MOOS, William .... 402-472-3011 269 J
bmoos@huskers.com
MOOSALLY, Michelle .... 713-221-8254 453 A
moosallym@uhd.edu
MOOSBRUGGER, Bob .... 419-372-7052 348 G
moosbrr@bgsu.edu
MOOT, Bradley .... 212-678-8035 303 D
brmoot@jtsa.edu
MOOTHART, Kathy .... 319-385-6209 167 H
kathy.moothart@iw.edu
MOOTISPAW, Angel ...... 937-393-3431 360 H
amootispaw@sscc.edu
MOOTS, Russ .... 919-365-7711 340 E
MOOTZ, Allison, C .... 215-885-2360 389 C
amootz@manor.edu
MOQTADERI, Emily .... 718-951-5074 293 C
emily.moqtaderi@brooklyn.cuny.edu
MOQUAY, Alexandra ..... 480-800-5449.. 15 N
amoquay@taliesin.edu
MORA, Cecilio .... 559-934-2430.. 74 N
ceciliomora@whccd.edu
MORA, Claudia, I .... 512-232-0884 455 A
claudia.mora@jsg.utexas.edu
MORA, Flora .... 808-984-3517 130 D
fmora@hawaii.edu
MORA, Michelle .... 818-240-1000.. 43 G
mmora@glendale.edu
MORA, Priscilla .... 805-378-4121.. 73 J
pmora@vcccd.edu
MORA, Priscilla .... 805-965-0581.. 63 A
mora@sbcc.edu
MORA, Vanessa .... 787-815-0000 511 H
vanessa.mora@upr.edu
MORA-ALVAREZ,
Gabriela .... 626-968-1328.. 47 G
MORA-HERAS, Karen 787-998-8997 509M
kmora@eeapr.org
MORADILLOS-DELGADO,
Alicia .... 787-834-9595 510 D
amora@uaa.edu
MORAIS, Emir .... 508-849-3363 205 H
emorais@annamaria.edu
MORALE, Mary .... 937-708-5663 363 G
mmorale@wilberforce.edu
MORALES, Adelina, C ... 325-942-2073 450 E
adelina.morales@angelo.edu
MORALES, Aurea .... 718-963-4112 291 J
amorales@boricuacollege.edu
MORALES, Awilda .... 787-761-0640 511 E
oficialderegistroacademico@utcpr.edu
MORALES, Betsy .... 787-265-3807 512 E
decasac@uprm.edu
MORALES, Carlos .... 817-515-5024 445 F
carlos.morales@tccd.edu
MORALES, David .... 409-984-6304 449 I
moralesdp@lamarpa.edu
MORALES, David .... 801-274-3280 461 E
david.morales@wgu.edu
MORALES, Emily .... 630-844-7836 133 D
emorales@aurora.edu
MORALES, Erica .... 713-221-8443 453 A
moralese@uhd.edu
MORALES, Gaddiel .... 787-844-8181 513 A
gaddiel.morales@upr.edu
MORALES, Gary .... 787-264-1912 508 F
gary_morales_rodriguez@intersg.edu
MORALES, Gilbert .... 314-968-7424 262 C
moralesg@webster.edu
MORALES, Ileana .... 787-878-5475 507 L
imorales@arecibo.inter.edu
MORALES, James .... 435-797-1712 460 C
james.morales@usu.edu
MORALES, Jessica .... 575-538-6139 289 G
jessica.morales@wnmu.edu
MORALES, Julie .... 575-538-6238 289 G
moralesj@wnmu.edu
MORALES, Karen, G ...... 787-841-2000 509 J
karen_morales@pucpr.edu
MORALES, Karla .... 620-417-1011 177 F
karla.moralesesc@sccc.edu
MORALES, Kathy .... 954-453-9228.. 34 H
MORALES, Kristie .... 407-265-8383.. 96 H
MORALES, Lilliam .... 787-850-9376 512 D
lilliam.morales@upr.edu
MORALES, Nancy .... 787-882-2065 510 C
nmorales@unitecpr.edu
MORALES, Nora .... 361-354-2239 432 K
moralesn@coastlbend.edu
MORALES, Ofelia, A ...... 303-492-8223.. 84 B
ofelia.morales@colorado.edu
MORALES, Patricia .... 949-824-6701.. 69 D
patricia.morales@uci.edu
MORALES, Rachel .... 207-780-5758 197 D
rachel.morales@maine.edu
MORALES, Ray .... 917-493-4445 305 A
rmorales@msmnyc.edu
MORALES, Ray .... 212-678-8000 303 D
ramorales@jtsa.edu
MORALES, Robert .... 805-965-0581.. 63 A
moralesr@sbcc.edu
MORALES, Rosalie .... 787-780-0070 505 F
rmorales@caribbean.edu
MORALES, Stephanie .... 907-852-1763.... 9 H
registration@ilisagvik.edu
MORALES, Sulmarie ...... 787-264-1912 508 F
smorales@intersg.edu
MORALES, Taina .... 732-906-2524 278 G
tmorales@middlesexcc.edu
MORALES, Tamara .... 787-765-3560 506 K
tmorales@edpuniversity.edu
MORALES, Tomas .... 909-537-5002.. 32 E
president_morales@csusb.edu
MORALES-DIAZ,
Enrique .... 413-572-8580 213 F
emoralesdiaz@westfield.ma.edu
MORALES-MATIAS,
Marjorie .... 787-890-2681 511 G
marjorie.morales1@upr.edu
MORALES-ORTIZ,
Javier .... 440-826-2452 348 D
jmorales@bw.edu
MORALES-RODRIGUEZ,
Sandra, M 787-857-3600 507M
smmorales@br.inter.edu
MORALES TORRES,
Jessica, A .... 787-764-0000 513 B
jessica.morales1@upr.edu
MORAMARCO, Jacques 310-453-8300.. 41 F
jacques@emperors.edu
MORAN, Al .... 850-201-6079 112 C
alan.moran@tcc.fl.edu
MORAN, Awilda .... 787-720-1022 505 E
recursos@atlanticu.edu
MORAN, Bradley .... 907-474-7210.. 10 A
sbmoran@alaska.edu
MORAN, Brandon .... 631-656-2157 300 B
brandon.moran@ftc.edu
MORAN, Chris .... 308-865-8191 269 I
morancl@unk.edu
MORAN, Christine .... 443-352-4710 202 E
cmoran2@stevenson.edu
MORAN, Demetria .... 401-456-8031 405 A
dmoran@ric.edu
MORAN, Eileen, P .... 940-565-3687 453 E
eileen.moran@unt.edu
MORAN, Ellen, L .... 412-624-7355 400 H
emoran@pitt.edu
MORAN, James .... 203-576-4773.. 89 C
jmoran@bridgeport.edu
MORAN, Jason, E .... 814-641-3419 386 E
moranj@juniata.edu
MORAN, Jessina .... 209-381-6410.. 52 A
MORAN, Kathy .... 518-464-8784 299 C
kmoran@excelsior.edu
MORAN, Kelly, C .... 814-393-2000 393 G
kmoran@clarion.edu
MORAN, Lady .... 931-221-1013 417 H
moranl@apsu.edu
MORAN, Laura, P .... 615-353-3217 424 G
laura.moran@nscc.edu
MORAN, Mark .... 425-869-6843 421 A
mark.moran@lmunet.edu
MORAN, Martin, O .... 301-447-5223 201 B
m.o.moran@msmary.edu
MORAN, Meghan .... 973-618-3352 276 D
mmoran@caldwell.edu
MORAN, Mike .... 478-289-2377 118 C
mmoran@ega.edu
MORAN, Patrick .... 307-766-5586 501 I
pmoran5@uwyo.edu
MORAN, Paul .... 570-208-5948 386 G
pjmoran@kings.edu
MORAN, Raymond .... 775-784-1641 271 E
rmoran@unr.edu
MORAN, Sheri .... 239-513-1122 102 D
MORAN, Virginia .... 760-245-4271.. 74 D
virginia.moran@vvc.edu
MORANDI, Marc .... 413-662-5221 213 C
m.morandi@mcla.edu
MORANO, Joe .... 845-451-1314 297 G
joe.morano@culinary.edu
MORANO, Nancy .... 914-633-2494 302 E
nmorano@iona.edu
MORANSKI, Karen .... 707-664-3222.. 34 B
MORAVEC, Todd, A ...... 518-564-2072 318 E
moraveta@plattsburgh.edu
MORAVITZ, Judy .... 909-667-4411.. 37 G
jmoravitz@claremontlincoln.edu
MORAY, Yvonne .... 212-472-1500 309 D
resumes@nysid.edu
MORBER, Timothy, T ..... 330-471-8279 355 D
tmorber@malone.edu
MORDEN, Erik .... 909-384-8671.. 60 F
emorden@sbccd.cc.ca.us
MOREA, John .... 757-822-1932 475 E
jmorea@tcc.edu
MOREAU, Bill .... 503-256-3180 377 B
bmoreau@uws.edu
MOREAU, Joe .... 650-949-6120.. 42 H
moreaujoe@fhda.edu
MOREAU, Joseph .... 650-949-6119.. 42 G
moreaujoe@fhda.edu
MOREAU, Scott .... 630-752-5933 153 C
scott.moreau@wheaton.edu
MORECI, Rick .... 773-325-4283 136 H
rmoreci@depaul.edu
MOREFIELD, Bill, R ...... 423-318-2735 425 F
bill.morefield@ws.edu
MOREHEAD, David .... 254-710-4072 431 E
david_morehead@baylor.edu
MOREHEAD, Jere, W .... 706-542-1214 126 G
president@uga.edu
MOREHEAD, Krystal ..... 704-379-6800.. 93 H
MOREHOUSE, Troy .... 207-941-7109 194 F
morehouset@husson.edu
MOREIRA, Antonio, R ... 410-455-6576 203 B
moreira@umbc.edu
MORELAND, Anna .... 610-519-4651 401 K
anna.moreland@villanova.edu
MORELAND, Jeremy, L .. 305-628-6720 107 F
jlmoreland@stu.edu
MORELAND, Kristen ...... 317-921-4858 158 D
kmoreland@ivytech.edu
MORELAND, Milton, C . 859-238-5220 180 B
milton.moreland@centre.edu
MORELL, Christina .... 434-924-8958 472 D
cm5c@virginia.edu
MORELLI, Colby .... 360-867-6205 480 C
morellic@evergreen.edu
MORELLO, Chanell .... 828-327-7000 333 B
cmorello@cvcc.edu
MORELLO, JR., Joseph 650-738-4271.. 62 L
morelloj@smccd.edu
MORELOCK, Luann .... 309-655-7353 149 B
MORELOS, Alfredo .... 318-274-1010 192 C
sm107@bncollege.com
MORENA, Pat .... 212-650-7997 293 D
pmorena@ccny.cuny.edu
MORENCY, Maurice .... 212-752-1530 304 A
maurice.morency@limcollege.edu

MORENO, Camille ... 916-691-7541 .. 50 H
morenoc@crc.losrios.edu
MORENO, Edward, J ... 210-486-3803 429 A
emoreno131@alamo.edu
MORENO, Jose ... 410-857-2791 200 F
jmoreno@mcdaniel.edu
MORENO, Judith ... 207-755-5265 195 D
jmoreno@cmcc.edu
MORENO, Kathy ... 432-837-8443 450 B
kam15ki@sulross.edu
MORENO, Laura ... 785-227-3380 172 A
morenoc@bethanylb.edu
MORENO, Linda ... 773-298-3379 149 D
moreno@sxu.edu
MORENO, Marissa ... 832-556-4047 438 I
mmoreno@lee.edu
MORENO, Melissa ... 805-683-8292 .. 63 A
melissa.moreno@sbcc.edu
MORENO, Melissa ... 650-738-4111 .. 62 L
morenomelissa@smccd.edu
MORENO, Nancy ... 713-798-8200 431 D
nmoreno@bcm.edu
MORENO, Patricia ... 281-873-0262 433 J
p.moreno@commonwealth.edu
MORENO, Valerie ... 360-992-2888 478 I
vmoreno@clark.edu
MORENO ORAMA,
Fernando ... 787-841-2000 509 J
fernando_moreno@pucpr.edu
MORENO-RIAÑO,
Gerson ... 616-222-1428 223 C
president@cornerstone.edu
MORENZ, Angie ... 217-854-5536 133 I
angie.morenz@blackburn.edu
MORENZ, Tim ... 217-854-5759 133 I
tim.morenz@blackburn.edu
MORERA-GONZÁLEZ,
Angel ... 787-993-8871 512 A
angel.morera1@upr.edu
MORESCHI, Robert, W .. 540-464-7212 476 B
moreschirw@vmi.edu
MORESCHI, Tracy, L ... 503-255-0332 374 C
tmoreschi@multnomah.edu
MOREST, Vanessa ... 914-606-6712 325 A
vanessa.morest@sunywcc.edu
MORETON, April, L ... 651-286-7773 244 D
almoreton@unwsp.edu
MORETZ, Drew ... 919-962-7096 340 H
jkappler@northcarolina.edu
MORETZ, Patsy ... 334-387-3877 .... 4 B
patsymoretz@amridgeuniversity.edu
MOREY, Ann, N ... 818-677-3266 .. 32 C
ann.morey@csun.edu
MOREY, Casey ... 207-509-7298 196 E
cmorey@unity.edu
MOREY, Debby ... 404-727-4583 118 E
dmorey@emory.edu
MOREY, Joshua ... 951-343-4235 .. 27 G
jmorey@calbaptist.edu
MOREY, Megan ... 413-597-4217 220 D
megan.e.morey@williams.edu
MOREY, Robin ... 404-727-8561 118 E
robin.morey@emory.edu
MORGAN, Adrienne ... 585-275-7814 323 M
morgan.levy@rochester.edu
MORGAN, Amanda ... 864-388-8971 410 A
amorgan@lander.edu
MORGAN, Andrea ... 303-273-3021 .. 79 J
asalazar@mines.edu
MORGAN, Annie ... 866-492-5336 244 F
ann.morgan@mail.waldenu.edu
MORGAN, Anthony ... 707-826-5555 .. 33 C
anthony.morgan@humboldt.edu
MORGAN, Barb ... 910-630-7005 331 E
bamorgan@methodist.edu
MORGAN, Betsy ... 608-785-8042 496 A
bmorgan@uwlax.edu
MORGAN, Brandee ... 405-945-3315 368 C
brandee.morgan@okstate.edu
MORGAN, Bruce ... 910-630-7005 331 E
bmorgan@methodist.edu
MORGAN, Bruce, A ... 423-775-7233 418 D
bruce.morgan@bryan.edu
MORGAN, Camella ... 253-833-9111 480 I
cmorgan@greenriver.edu
MORGAN, Carlene, J ... 919-516-4084 339 I
cjmorgan@st-aug.edu
MORGAN, Cassie ... 912-478-5421 120 C
cnmorgan@georgiasouthern.edu
MORGAN, Catherine, A 423-439-4300 419 G
morganca1@etsu.edu
MORGAN, Chris ... 951-343-4369 .. 27 G
cmorgan@calbaptist.edu
MORGAN, Chris ... 717-361-1407 383 C
morganc@etown.edu
MORGAN, David ... 765-361-6382 163 B
morgand@wabash.edu
MORGAN, David, A ... 423-775-7597 418 D
morganda@bryan.edu
MORGAN, Deborah ... 918-540-6312 366 F
demorgan@neo.edu
MORGAN, Derek ... 303-273-3288 .. 79 J
dmorgan@mines.edu
MORGAN, Derrick ... 972-780-3600 454 A
derrick.morgan@untdallas.edu
MORGAN, Elizabeth ... 909-621-8101 .. 37 D
elizabeth.morgan@cmc.edu
MORGAN, Elle ... 413-748-3628 218 I
ellemorgan@springfield.edu
MORGAN, Gilbert ... 443-885-3658 201 A
gilbert.morgan@morgan.edu
MORGAN, Ginny ... 510-841-9230 .. 76 G
vmorgan@wi.edu
MORGAN, Gus ... 423-461-8968 422 E
gmorgan@milligan.edu
MORGAN, Hal, D ... 602-557-1270 .. 16 G
hal.morgan@phoenix.edu
MORGAN, Heath ... 660-831-4087 256 I
morganh@moval.edu
MORGAN, Helen ... 912-525-5000 124 I
hmorgan@scad.edu
MORGAN, J. Reid ... 336-758-5122 344 C
jrm@wfu.edu
MORGAN, Janie, M ... 608-785-8495 496 A
jspencer@uwlax.edu
MORGAN, Jason ... 919-278-2676 340 B
jmorgan@shawu.edu
MORGAN, Jason ... 410-462-7402 198 B
jmorgan@bccc.edu
MORGAN, Jason ... 256-306-2545 .... 1 F
jason.morgan@calhoun.edu
MORGAN, Jeff ... 501-279-4305 .. 19 C
jrmorgan@harding.edu
MORGAN, Jeff ... 713-743-3455 452 D
jjmorgan@central.uh.edu
MORGAN, Jeffrey ... 480-265-8017 250 A
jmorgan@atsu.edu
MORGAN, Jim ... 575-461-4413 286 G
jimm@mesalands.edu
MORGAN, John ... 928-717-7721 .. 16 J
john.morgan@yc.edu
MORGAN, John ... 203-582-5359 .. 88 G
john.morgan@quinnipiac.edu
MORGAN, Joseph ... 732-906-4260 278 G
jmorgan@middlesexcc.edu
MORGAN, Joseph, A ... 606-783-2022 184 C
j.morgan@moreheadstate.edu
MORGAN, Joshua ... 575-492-2771 287 A
jmorgan@nmjc.edu
MORGAN, Joshua, D ... 916-660-7272 .. 64 D
jmorgan@sierracollege.edu
MORGAN, Karen ... 704-378-1000 330 D
kmorgan@jcsu.edu
MORGAN, Karrie ... 605-331-6672 417 C
karrie.morgan@usiouxfalls.edu
MORGAN, Katie ... 859-846-5303 184 B
kmorgan2@midway.edu
MORGAN, Katrice ... 865-974-2498 427 B
kmorgan4@utk.edu
MORGAN, Kelly ... 910-898-9604 336 D
morgank@montgomery.edu
MORGAN, Kristi ... 865-251-1800 423 E
kmorgan@south.edu
MORGAN, Kristy ... 903-233-4410 439 A
kristymorgan@letu.edu
MORGAN, Larry ... 402-554-3735 270 A
lmorgan@unomaha.edu
MORGAN, Leroy ... 419-448-2090 353 E
lmorgan@heidelberg.edu
MORGAN, JR., Leroy ... 706-821-8235 124 B
lmorgan@paine.edu
MORGAN, Louis ... 423-614-8567 420 H
lmorgan@leeuniversity.edu
MORGAN, Lucas ... 318-798-4107 190 A
lucas.morgan@lsus.edu
MORGAN, Mark, D ... 910-962-3719 343 C
morganm@uncw.edu
MORGAN, Matt ... 215-893-5252 381 J
matt.morgan@curtis.edu
MORGAN, Melissa ... 717-901-5173 385 H
mmorgan@harrisburgu.edu
MORGAN, Michael ... 901-843-3810 423 A
morganm@rhodes.edu
MORGAN, Michael, D ... 205-726-2727 .... 6 E
mmorgan@samford.edu
MORGAN, Michelle ... 216-397-1525 353 O
MORGAN, Mollie ... 870-508-6191 .. 17 G
mmorgan@asumh.edu
MORGAN, Natasha ... 432-685-4534 440 B
nmorgan@midland.edu
MORGAN, Patricia ... 707-256-7305 .. 53 E
pmorgan@napavalley.edu
MORGAN, Patricia ... 315-470-8851 291 I
patriciamorgan@crouse.org
MORGAN, Patrick ... 912-358-4332 125 A
morganp@savannahstate.edu
MORGAN, Rachel, A ... 651-631-5249 244 D
ramorgan@unwsp.edu
MORGAN, Rebecca ... 714-432-5670 .. 38 B
rmorgan23@occ.cccd.edu
MORGAN, Robert ... 618-536-2118 150 B
robert.d.morgan@siu.edu
MORGAN, Robin, W ... 302-831-2101 .. 91 C
morgan@udel.edu
MORGAN, Romena ... 434-528-5276 477 B
rmorgan@vul.edu
MORGAN, Samuel ... 559-638-0300 .. 67 D
samuel.morgan@reedleycollege.edu
MORGAN, Scott ... 360-867-6913 480 C
sustainabilitydirector@evergreen.edu
MORGAN, Scott ... 605-698-3966 416 B
smorgan@swcollege.edu
MORGAN, Sherelle ... 276-326-4305 464 J
smorgan@bluefield.edu
MORGAN, Sonja ... 253-566-5322 484 E
smorgan@tacomacc.edu
MORGAN, Stephanie ... 907-564-8261 .... 9 F
smorgan@alaskapacific.edu
MORGAN, Susan ... 863-297-1016 106 A
smorgan@polk.edu
MORGAN, Tasha ... 864-644-5501 412 D
tmorgan@swu.edu
MORGAN, Timothy ... 217-443-8803 136 G
tmorgan@dacc.edu
MORGAN, Tracy ... 603-641-7402 274 A
tmorgan@anselm.edu
MORGAN, Wendy ... 304-637-1341 487 C
morganw@dewv.edu
MORGAN, William, E ... 972-438-6932 441 E
wmorgan@parker.edu
MORGAN AGARD,
Nicole ... 201-684-7503 280 H
nmagard@ramapo.edu
MORGAN-CURTIS,
Samantha ... 615-963-5000 426 A
MORGAN DAVIS,
Pamela ... 940-397-4785 440 C
pamela.morgan@msutexas.edu
MORGAN-RUSSELL,
Simon ... 419-372-2340 348 G
smorgan@bgsu.edu
MORGAN-ZAYACHEK,
Eileen ... 607-436-2855 316 F
eileen.morgan@oneonta.edu
MORGANSTEIN, Penny . 212-472-1500 309 D
info@nysid.edu
MORGANTE, Nicole ... 315-464-8812 317 C
morgantm@upstate.edu
MORGENTHALER,
Diane, S ... 203-392-6300 .. 86 A
morgenthald1@southernct.edu
MORI, Darryl ... 626-396-4288 .. 26 B
darryl.mori@artcenter.edu
MORIARITY, Marlene ... 830-372-8009 449 A
mmoriarity@tlu.edu
MORIARTY, Deb ... 717-358-3971 383 I
dmoriart@fandm.edu
MORIARTY, John ... 305-899-3957 .. 96 A
jmoriarty@barry.edu
MORIARTY, Martha ... 843-521-3137 413 C
mamoriar@uscb.edu
MORIARTY, Maureen ... 802-831-1265 463 C
mmoriarty@vermontlaw.edu
MORIARTY, Michael, J . 860-515-3760 .. 85 E
mjmoriarty@charteroak.edu
MORIARTY, Sean ... 315-312-5500 318 D
sean.moriarty@oswego.edu
MORICLE, Jeanne ... 304-327-4117 489 I
jmoricle@bluefieldstate.edu
MORICONI, Jill ... 814-254-0400 381 C
jmoriconi@pa.gov
MORIKANG, Marilyn ... 408-741-2056 .. 75 E
marilyn.morikang@westvalley.edu
MORIKANG, Marilyn ... 408-288-3119 .. 62 H
marilyn.morikang@sjcc.edu
MORIKANG, Marilyn ... 408-288-3187 .. 62 H
marilyn.morikang@sjcc.edu
MORILLO, Janell ... 559-278-0276 .. 31 B
janellt@csufresno.edu
MORIMOTO, Yash ... 505-428-1765 288 E
yash.morimoto@sfcc.edu
MORIN, Anna ... 508-373-5649 216 D
anna.morin@mcphs.edu
MORIN, Brian ... 503-845-3102 374 A
brian.morin@mtangel.edu
MORIN, Jeff ... 414-847-3210 494 C
jeffreymorin@miad.edu
MORIN, Jodie ... 712-749-2097 164 C
morinj@bvu.edu
MORIN, Karen, M ... 570-577-3293 379 C
karen.morin@bucknell.edu
MORIN, Roland ... 765-361-6096 163 B
morinr@wabash.edu
MORIN, Sheila ... 701-477-7862 346 J
smorin1@tm.edu
MORIN, Shirley ... 701-477-7862 346 J
smorin@tm.edu
MORIN, Stephen, J ... 203-932-7268 .. 89 H
smorin@newhaven.edu
MORIOKA, Brennon ... 808-956-7727 129 E
bmorioka@hawaii.edu
MORISON, William ... 802-635-1240 463 G
MORISSEAU, Natalia ... 973-353-5872 282 B
natalia.morisseau@rutgers.edu
MORITA, Denise ... 510-649-2469 .. 44 B
dmorita@gtu.edu
MORITZ, Lynne, M ... 231-995-1900 229 A
lmoritz@nmc.edu
MORLEY, Deborah, G ... 610-499-4087 402 G
dgmorley@widener.edu
MORLEY, John ... 312-850-7230 135 H
jmorley@ccc.edu
MORLEY, Kathleen ... 254-710-2061 431 E
kathleen_morley@baylor.edu
MORLEY, Maureen ... 212-938-5945 319 E
mmorley@sunyopt.edu
MORLEY, Sandy ... 517-264-7193 230 H
smorley@sienaheights.edu
MORLEY, Yvonne, Y ... 859-238-5220 180 B
yvonne.morley@centre.edu
MORLEY-MOWER,
Cynthia ... 213-763-7074 .. 49 F
morleycn@lattc.edu
MORLIER, Peggy, M ... 770-720-5628 124 G
mmm@reinhardt.edu
MORMANDO, Karin, W . 215-204-8556 399 B
karin.west@temple.edu
MORNINGSTAR, Kevin .. 760-750-4775 .. 33 A
kmorningstar@csusm.edu
MORNINGSTAR, Madge 304-876-5358 490 A
mmorning@shepherd.edu
MORO, Nicole ... 617-228-1913 214 C
nmoro@bhcc.mass.edu
MORO, Simonetta ... 347-966-1096 194 G
smoro@idsva.edu
MORODOMI, Joyce, K .. 559-323-2100 .. 61 F
jmorodomi@sjcl.edu
MOROLES, Jose ... 956-872-4207 443 H
jmorole1@southtexascollege.edu
MORONEY, Donney ... 414-410-4329 491 I
dmoroney@stritch.edu
MORONG, Andrew ... 207-755-5273 195 D
amorong@cmcc.edu
MOROSKO, Linda ... 330-494-6170 360 K
lmorosko@starkstate.edu
MOROSOFF, Wendy ... 914-251-6370 319 B
wendy.morosoff@purchase.edu
MOROWSKI, James, R .. 701-788-4619 345 D
james.morowski@mayvillestate.edu
MOROZOWICH, Mark ... 202-319-5683 .. 92 A
morozowich@cua.edu
MORPHEW,
Christopher ... 410-516-7820 199 G
christopher.morphew@jhu.edu
MORPHEW, Vonnie ... 254-659-7502 437 A
ymorphew@hillcollege.edu
MORR, Alex ... 617-873-0475 208 B
alex.morr@cambridgecollege.edu
MORRA, Elizabeth ... 202-216-4365 340 H
emorra@northcarolina.edu
MORRAH, Ed ... 336-322-2121 336 G
ed.morrah@piedmontcc.edu
MORREALE, David ... 609-258-3000 280 D
MORREALE, Robert ... 716-286-8344 309 H
rmorreale@niagara.edu
MORREALE, Thirza ... 315-228-6776 296 E
tmorreale@colgate.edu
MORRELL, Christopher . 217-424-6360 144 G
cmorrell@millikin.edu
MORRELL, Erin ... 203-773-8541 .. 85 D
emorrell@albertus.edu

MORRELL, Kathleen ...... 814-262-6423 393 A
kmorrell@pennhighlands.edu
MORRELL, Matthew, D . 763-417-8250 235 A
mmorrell@centralseminary.edu
MORREN, Glen .... 313-664-1162 222 H
gmorren@collegeforcreativestudies.edu
MORRILL, Deborah, H .. 210-567-6395 456 C
morrill@uthscsa.edu
MORRILL, Donald, D .... 813-258-7409 113 H
dmorrill@ut.edu
MORRIN, Matthew .... 207-734-7562 197 C
matthew.morrin@maine.edu
MORRIN, Matthew .... 207-834-7562 197 A
matthew.morrin@maine.edu
MORRIS, Adam .... 562-903-4714.. 27 A
adam.morris@biola.edu
MORRIS, Adam .... 417-455-5740 252 E
adammorris@crowder.edu
MORRIS, Adam .... 360-475-7100 481 I
amorris@olympic.edu
MORRIS, Amanda .... 912-287-6584 117 E
amorris@coastalpines.edu
MORRIS, Amanda .... 270-685-3131 179 J
amanda.morris@brescia.edu
MORRIS, Amy .... 785-432-0444 176 D
amorris@neosho.edu
MORRIS, Andrew .... 585-389-2113 307 F
amorris8@naz.edu
MORRIS, Anne .... 734-432-5653 227 C
amorris@madonna.edu
MORRIS, Ashley .... 912-443-5783 125 B
amorris@savannahtech.edu
MORRIS, Barrett .... 818-677-2077.. 32 C
barrett.morris@csun.edu
MORRIS, Ben .... 252-940-6374 332 C
ben.morris@beaufortccc.edu
MORRIS, Brenda .... 903-468-3020 447 B
brenda.morris@tamuc.edu
MORRIS, Brenna .... 864-231-2000 406 F
bmorris@andersonuniversity.edu
MORRIS, Brett, E .... 706-867-2991 127 A
brett.morris@ung.edu
MORRIS, Callum .... 740-386-4231 355 F
morrisc@mtc.edu
MORRIS, Carlene .... 785-830-2702 174 D
cmorris@haskell.edu
MORRIS, Carlton, E ...... 334-724-8784.... 7 D
cmorris@tuskegee.edu
MORRIS, Chad .... 661-654-3267.. 30 B
cmorris@csub.edu
MORRIS, Chad, T .... 540-375-4926 470 E
morris@roanoke.edu
MORRIS, Charlotte, P .... 334-727-8501.... 7 D
interimpresident@tuskegee.edu
MORRIS, Clark .... 816-415-5997 262 F
morrisc@william.jewell.edu
MORRIS, Clark, W .... 816-415-5997 262 F
morrisc@william.jewell.edu
MORRIS, Claudia .... 352-365-3523 103 U
morrisc@lssc.edu
MORRIS, Craig .... 651-846-1348 241 B
craig.morris@saintpaul.edu
MORRIS, Daryl .... 334-244-3295.... 4 E
dmorris@aum.edu
MORRIS, David .... 205-853-1200.... 2 G
dmorris@jeffersonstate.edu
MORRIS, Desmond .... 972-780-3600 454 A
desmond.morris@untdallas.edu
MORRIS, Dodd .... 616-949-5300 223 C
MORRIS, Donna .... 325-574-7914 458 D
dmorris@wtc.edu
MORRIS, Dottie .... 603-358-2206 274 H
dmorris@keene.edu
MORRIS, Doug .... 317-940-8000 154 C
MORRIS, Earl .... 435-797-1939 460 C
torch.morris@usu.edu
MORRIS, Elizabeth .... 951-343-4507.. 27 G
emorris@calbaptist.edu
MORRIS, Gary .... 315-312-2255 318 D
gary.morris@oswego.edu
MORRIS, Gary .... 304-462-6111 489 L
gary.morris@glenville.edu
MORRIS, Geri .... 419-998-3106 362 F
geri@unoh.edu
MORRIS, Greg .... 214-860-2677 434 I
cmorris@dcccd.edu
MORRIS, Greg .... 972-860-5094 434 I
cmorris@dcccd.edu
MORRIS, Heather .... 716-338-1056 303 A
heathermorris@mail.sunyjcc.edu
MORRIS, Heather .... 614-251-4561 358 B
morrish@ohiodominican.edu

MORRIS, Henry .... 507-389-1150 239 D
henry.morris@mnsu.edu
MORRIS, Jaime .... 620-341-5457 173 F
jmorri12@emporia.edu
MORRIS, James, H .... 512-448-1271 442 I
jmorris9@stedwards.edu
MORRIS, Jason .... 325-674-2830 428 F
morrisj@acu.edu
MORRIS, Jeff .... 620-252-7177 173 A
morris.jeff@coffeyville.edu
MORRIS, Jeffery, B .... 785-532-6415 175 C
jbmorris@ksu.edu
MORRIS, Jessica .... 610-921-7552 377 G
jmorris@albright.edu
MORRIS, John .... 334-844-4645.... 4 D
jmm0264@auburn.edu
MORRIS, John .... 617-627-3232 219 C
john.morris@tufts.edu
MORRIS, John, P .... 843-953-1325 408 C
morrisjp2@cofc.edu
MORRIS, Joseph .... 303-797-5801.. 77 I
joseph.morris@arapahoe.edu
MORRIS, Julia, M .... 304-457-6205 486 E
auviljm@ab.edu
MORRIS, Justin .... 620-278-4324 177 H
jmorris@sterling.edu
MORRIS, Kate .... 408-554-4533.. 63 B
klmorris@scu.edu
MORRIS, Kathryn .... 317-940-9903 154 C
kmorris@butler.edu
MORRIS, Kathryn, A ..... 315-229-5892 314 D
kmorris@stlawu.edu
MORRIS, Kelli .... 256-326-2602.... 1 F
kelli.morris@calhoun.edu
MORRIS, Kellie .... 207-755-5294 195 D
kmorris@cmcc.edu
MORRIS, Kelly .... 912-443-5880 125 B
kmorris@savannahtech.edu
MORRIS, Kevin .... 281-922-3479 443 C
kevin.morris@sjcd.edu
MORRIS, Kevin .... 936-294-1794 450 A
kmorris@shsu.edu
MORRIS, Kizzy .... 610-399-2279 393 F
kmorris@cheyney.edu
MORRIS, Kyle .... 307-742-3776 502 B
kmorris@wyotech.edu
MORRIS, Larry .... 405-491-6314 369 H
MORRIS, Laura, M .... 302-295-1179.. 91 E
laura.m.morris@wilmu.edu
MORRIS, Lawrence, J ... 202-319-5100.. 92 A
morrisl@cua.edu
MORRIS, Loren, L .... 620-665-3523 174 G
morrisl@hutchcc.edu
MORRIS, Matthew .... 417-836-5233 256 G
mattmorris@missuristate.edu
MORRIS, Max .... 605-668-1464 415 F
maxwell.morris@mountmarty.edu
MORRIS, Michael .... 805-437-8881.. 30 C
michael.morris@csuci.edu
MORRIS, Mike .... 208-376-7731 130 G
mmorris@boisebible.edu
MORRIS, Nora .... 763-433-1632 237 E
nora.morris@anokaramsey.edu
MORRIS, Nora .... 763-433-1632 237 D
nora.morris@anokaramsey.edu
MORRIS, Paul .... 435-652-7504 460 B
pmorris@dixie.edu
MORRIS, Regina .... 573-840-9606 260 E
rmorris@trcc.edu
MORRIS, Renea .... 303-871-2711.. 84 E
renea.morris@du.edu
MORRIS, Robert .... 815-280-2884 141 B
romorris@jjc.edu
MORRIS, Sam .... 919-761-2372 340 D
admissions@sebts.edu
MORRIS, Sara, R .... 716-888-2120 292 F
morriss@canisius.edu
MORRIS, Sheila .... 405-382-9501 369 F
s.morris@sscok.edu
MORRIS, Stephanie .... 716-286-8539 309 H
smorris@niagara.edu
MORRIS, Steve .... 270-789-5017 180 A
srmorris@campbellsville.edu
MORRIS, Steve .... 606-546-1201 185 D
smorris@unionky.edu
MORRIS, Tama .... 704-337-2363 339 F
morrist@queens.edu
MORRIS, Thomas .... 304-896-7407 488 I
tom.morris@southernwv.edu
MORRIS, Tommy .... 256-824-6576.... 8 B
tommy.morris@uah.edu
MORRIS, Tracy, L .... 304-293-1788 490 E
tracy.morris@mail.wvu.edu

MORRIS, Trevor .... 806-291-3636 457 I
morrist@wbu.edu
MORRIS, Valerie, B .... 843-953-8222 408 C
morrisv@cofc.edu
MORRIS, Vicky .... 252-399-6330 326 K
vamorris@barton.edu
MORRIS, Vicky, A .... 252-399-6300 326 K
vamorris@barton.edu
MORRIS, Wanda .... 310-900-1600.. 39 F
wmorris@elcamino.edu
MORRIS, Wendy .... 410-857-2521 200 F
wmorris@mcdaniel.edu
MORRIS, William .... 336-517-2236 327 A
rwmorris@bennett.edu
MORRIS-SHEPARD,
Fenita, T .... 919-530-6105 341 E
fmorris7@nccu.edu
MORRISETT, J. Gregory 212-255-8587 297 F
techdean@cornell.edu
MORRISETTE, Joanna .... 919-735-5151 338 H
jmmorrisette@waynecc.edu
MORRISON, Aaron .... 978-927-0585 209 E
MORRISON, Alison .... 202-379-7808.. 93 H
MORRISON, Amy .... 425-739-8200 481 C
amy.morrison@lwtech.edu
MORRISON, Andrew ...... 740-588-1388 365 B
amorrison@zanestate.edu
MORRISON, Andrew ...... 757-727-5486 467 G
andrew.morrison@hamptonu.edu
MORRISON, Barry, F .... 401-232-6017 404 A
bmorriso@bryant.edu
MORRISON, Cammie ..... 856-225-2949 281 G
cammor@camden.rutgers.edu
MORRISON, Dan .... 848-932-4371 282 A
dan.morrison@rutgers.edu
MORRISON, Darrell ...... 816-271-4226 257 A
morrison@missouriwestern.edu
MORRISON, Debbie ...... 231-439-6306 228 H
d.morrison@follett.com
MORRISON, Edwina ...... 406-449-9150 263 J
emorrison@montana.edu
MORRISON,
Elizabeth, N .... 630-515-7600 144 F
emorri@midwestern.edu
MORRISON,
Hassel Andre .... 507-786-3503 243 D
morrison@stolaf.edu
MORRISON, Jason .... 870-574-4501.. 21 D
jmorriso@sautech.edu
MORRISON, Jean .... 617-353-2230 207 E
morrison@bu.edu
MORRISON, Jennifer .... 503-244-0726 371 E
jennifermorrison@achs.edu
MORRISON, Jennifer, K 508-767-7007 206 A
jemorrison@assumption.edu
MORRISON, Jessica ..... 559-730-3755.. 39 B
jessicamo@cos.edu
MORRISON, John .... 856-351-2628 283 B
jmorrison@salemcc.edu
MORRISON, Julia .... 662-243-1941 246 B
jmorrison2@eastms.edu
MORRISON, Julia .... 707-476-4172.. 58 I
julia-morrison@redwoods.edu
MORRISON, Julie .... 623-845-4761.. 13 C
julie.morrison@gccaz.edu
MORRISON, Julie .... 734-973-5010 232 D
jmorriso@wccnet.edu
MORRISON, Laura .... 252-335-0821 333 G
laura_morrison@albemarle.edu
MORRISON, Lexi .... 215-717-6362 400 E
lmorrison@uarts.edu
MORRISON, Lisa .... 712-325-3287 167 I
lmorrison@iwcc.edu
MORRISON, Marjorie .... 216-987-4529 351 E
marjorie.morrison@tri-c.edu
MORRISON, Melanie ..... 650-433-3895.. 55 L
mmorrison@paloaltou.edu
MORRISON, Michael .... 980-495-3978 329 B
MORRISON, Michael, L 812-888-5736 162 F
mmorrison@vinu.edu
MORRISON, Monica ..... 225-743-8500 188 H
mmorrison@rpcc.edu
MORRISON, Nancy, J ... 212-998-4924 309 F
nancy.morrison@nyu.edu
MORRISON, Pamela ..... 916-558-2088.. 50 J
morrisp@scc.losrios.edu
MORRISON,
Rebecca, L .... 414-955-4949 493 F
rmorriso@mcw.edu
MORRISON, Regina ...... 650-738-4350.. 62 L
morrison@smccd.edu
MORRISON, Robert .... 312-261-3372 145 D
rob.morrison@nl.edu

MORRISON, Rod .... 419-448-2391 353 E
rmorriso@heidelberg.edu
MORRISON, Roderick ... 253-566-5000 484 E
rmorrison@tacomacc.edu
MORRISON, Rodney ..... 302-831-0746.. 91 C
rodmo@udel.edu
MORRISON, Roxanne ... 619-260-7579.. 72 I
roxannemorrison@sandiego.edu
MORRISON, Sarah .... 740-366-9209 349 F
morrison.415@cotc.edu
MORRISON, Sarah, B ... 276-656-0322 474 G
sbmorrison@patrickhenry.edu
MORRISON, Scott .... 775-445-4401 271 F
scott.morrison@wnc.edu
MORRISON, Scott, D .... 540-828-5376 464 L
smorriso@bridgewater.edu
MORRISON, Thomas, A 812-855-6992 156 G
morrisot@iu.edu
MORRISON, Thomas, A 812-855-6992 156 F
morrisot@iu.edu
MORRISON, Tiffany ...... 312-850-7070 135 H
tmorrison2@ccc.edu
MORRISON, Valerie, A . 904-620-2900 111 B
n00140121@unf.edu
MORRISON, William ..... 508-588-9100 215 A
wmorrison@massasoit.mass.edu
MORRISON-FRONCKOWIAK,
Lisa, T .... 716-878-4500 317 F
morrislt@buffalostate.edu
MORRISON-MONGER,
Heather .... 865-524-8079 420 B
heather.monger@huhs.edu
MORRISON-SHETLAR,
Alison .... 434-544-8200 471 L
president@lynchburg.edu
MORRISON-WILLAIMS,
Suzanne .... 954-492-5353.. 97 G
smw@citycollege.edu
MORRISS, Andrew, P .... 216-272-9187 446 F
amorriss@tamu.edu
MORRISSEY, Ann, M .... 401-874-4402 405 E
morrissey@uri.edu
MORRISSEY, Kelly, A .... 401-333-7173 404 C
kamorrissey@ccri.edu
MORRISSEY, Sharon ..... 804-819-4972 473 C
smorrissey@vccs.edu
MORRISSEY, Shawn ...... 508-856-2265 212 C
shawn.morrissey@umassmed.edu
MORRO, Robert .... 610-519-4589 401 K
robert.morro@villanova.edu
MORROBEL-SOSA,
Anny .... 608-262-8839 495 C
amorrobel@uwsa.edu
MORRONE, Anastasia ... 317-274-3479 156 G
amorrone@iu.edu
MORRONE,
Anastasia (Stacy) .... 812-856-8010 156 F
amorrone@iu.edu
MORRONE, Anthony ..... 702-992-2156 271 B
finaid@nsc.edu
MORROW, Andrea .... 567-661-7104 359 I
andrea_morrow@owens.edu
MORROW, Barbara, A ... 314-340-5763 254 A
morrowb@hssu.edu
MORROW, Bill, J .... 302-857-1245.. 91 A
bmorrow@dtcc.edu
MORROW, David .... 267-295-2357 402 A
dmorrow@walnuthillcollege.edu
MORROW, Donnie .... 828-835-4287 338 E
dmorrow@tricountycc.edu
MORROW, Dorothy .... 402-557-7296 265 J
dorothy.morrow@bellevue.edu
MORROW, Eric .... 254-968-9141 446 D
morrow@tarleton.edu
MORROW, Erik .... 512-472-4133 443 F
emorrow@ssw.edu
MORROW, Frances .... 330-490-7312 363 E
fmorrow@walsh.edu
MORROW, Jeff .... 509-574-4691 486 D
jmorrow@yvcc.edu
MORROW, Marjann ...... 325-574-7608 458 D
mmorrow@wtc.edu
MORROW, Michael .... 651-523-1660 236 G
mmorrow001@luthersem.edu
MORROW, Nick .... 904-620-1537 111 B
nick.morrow@unf.edu
MORROW, Rebecca ...... 304-793-6591 490 C
rmorrow@osteo.wvsom.edu
MORROW, Wanda .... 713-646-1825 443 I
wmorrow@stcl.edu
MORSCHES, Michael ..... 708-974-5310 145 A
morschesm@morainevalley.edu
MORSE, Alicia .... 410-777-2587 197 G
ammorse@aacc.edu

MORSE, Andrew .... 319-273-2570 164 A
andrew.morse@uni.edu
MORSE, Cary .... 508-853-2300 215 F
csmorse@qcc.mass.edu
MORSE, Charles, C .... 508-831-5540 220 F
cmorse@wpi.edu
MORSE, Julie .... 517-750-1200 231 C
MORSE, MaryKate .... 503-554-6150 373 A
mkmorse@georgefox.edu
MORSE, Micael .... 903-589-7114 438 C
mmorse@jacksonville-college.edu
MORSE, Paris .... 231-995-2822 229 A
pmorse@nmc.edu
MORSE, Ryan, K .... 413-545-3464 211 G
rkmorse@umass.edu
MORSE, Saul .... 518-608-8472 299 C
smorse@excelsior.edu
MORSE, Stephen .... 478-471-2724 122 F
stephen.morse@mga.edu
MORSE, Susan .... 740-427-5926 354 I
morses@kenyon.edu
MORSE, Terry .... 410-706-2456 203 A
tmorse@umaryland.edu
MORSMAN, Elaine .... 607-587-4061 319 F
morsmaem@alfredstate.edu
MORSOVILLO, Michael . 708-524-6793 137 C
morsomike@dom.edu
MORTALI, Jill, M .... 603-646-3007 273 D
jill.m.mortali@dartmouth.edu
MORTAZAVI, Mansour .. 870-575-7140.. 22 D
mortazavim@uapb.edu
MORTELA, Cecilia .... 805-267-1690.. 47 H
cecilia.mortela@lauruscollege.edu
MORTENSEN, Alan .... 217-234-5253 142 C
amortens@lakelandcollege.edu
MORTENSEN, Brad, L .... 801-626-6001 461 A
bmortensen@weber.edu
MORTENSEN, John .... 435-797-1110 460 C
john.mortensen@usu.edu
MORTENSEN, Norm ...... 304-734-6680 488 D
norm.mortensen@bridgevalley.edu
MORTENSEN, Stacey ..... 701-627-4738 346 F
smorte@nhsc.edu
MORTENSON, Gary .... 254-710-1161 431 E
gary_mortenson@baylor.edu
MORTIMER, Gayle .... 620-862-5252 171 H
gayle.mortimer@barclaycollege.edu
MORTIMER, Ian .... 585-475-6637 312 F
ijmoem@rit.edu
MORTIMER, Jarron .... 919-516-4000 339 I
MORTLEY, Preston .... 323-241-5059.. 49 E
mortlepc@lasc.edu
MORTON, Amy .... 508-831-6556 220 F
ammorton@wpi.edu
MORTON, Ben .... 907-786-1214.... 9 J
bmorton4@alaska.edu
MORTON, Bradley .... 973-684-6626 280 A
bmorton@pccc.edu
MORTON, Brandon .... 972-273-3392 434 F
bmorton@dcccd.edu
MORTON, Cassandra .... 909-748-8391.. 72 F
cassandra_morton@redlands.edu
MORTON, Christina ...... 412-392-4207 396 G
cmorton@pointpark.edu
MORTON, Doug .... 919-515-8851 342 A
dgmorton@ncsu.edu
MORTON, Jack .... 512-936-8202 453 E
jack.morton@untsystem.edu
MORTON, James, P ...... 910-362-7555 332 H
jpmorton634@mail.cfcc.edu
MORTON, Jordan .... 661-362-2234.. 51 D
jmorton@masters.edu
MORTON, Josh .... 605-274-4316 414 G
josh.morton@augie.edu
MORTON, Lindsay .... 707-965-6613.. 55 I
lmorton@puc.edu
MORTON, Lynn, M .... 828-771-2070 344 D
president@warren-wilson.edu
MORTON, Mary, B .... 607-746-4430 320 D
mortonmb@delhi.edu
MORTON, Matt .... 949-376-6000.. 47 D
mmorton@lcad.edu
MORTON, Pierre .... 603-899-4045 273 E
mortonp@franklinpierce.edu
MORTON, Sally, C .... 480-965-4087.. 10 J
scmorton@asu.edu
MORTON, Tracy, L .... 757-446-5800 466 D
mortontl@evms.edu
MORVICE, Michael .... 714-432-5741.. 38 B
mmorvice@occ.cccd.edu
MORY, Scott .... 412-268-2135 380 C
mory@cmu.edu
MOSBO BALLESTRO,
Julie .... 979-862-1239 446 F
jmosbo@tamu.edu
MOSBURG, Calleb, N ... 580-327-8415 367 A
cnmosburg@nwosu.edu
MOSBY, Christel .... 602-639-7500.. 12 J
MOSBY, Dorothy, E ...... 413-538-3093 217 C
deanfac@mtholyoke.edu
MOSBY, Gary .... 913-288-7305 175 B
gmosby@kckcc.edu
MOSBY, John .... 206-878-3710 481 B
jmosby@highline.edu
MOSBY-WILSON,
Shatiqua, A .... 504-286-5030 191 C
swilson@suno.edu
MOSCA, David .... 443-367-0035 202 G
dmosca@usmd.edu
MOSCATO, Robin, A ..... 609-258-3330 280 D
moscato@princeton.edu
MOSCHELLA, Jayne ...... 972-438-6932 441 E
jmoschella@parker.edu
MOSCHENROSS, Sarah . 641-269-3702 166 G
moschenr@grinnell.edu
MOSCHINA, Justin .... 949-214-3613.. 39 K
justin.mochina@cui.edu
MOSCOVITZ, Yechezkel . 718-269-4080 292 I
MOSELEY, Bruce .... 315-228-7451 296 E
bmoseley@colgate.edu
MOSELEY, Cassandra .... 541-346-2090 376 H
cmoseley@uoregon.edu
MOSELEY, John .... 573-681-5042 254 G
moseleyj@lincolnu.edu
MOSEMAN, Dennis .... 774-243-3489 216 D
dennis.moseman@mcphs.edu
MOSER, Brett .... 701-252-3467 347 B
brett.moser@uj.edu
MOSER, Drew .... 765-998-5384 161 C
drmoser@taylor.edu
MOSER, Gary .... 661-336-5143.. 46 K
gmoser@kccd.edu
MOSER, Gary .... 707-654-1224.. 32 A
gmoser@csum.edu
MOSER, Jeremy .... 714-556-3610.. 73 H
jeremy.moser@vanguard.edu
MOSER, Kristin, M .... 319-273-3103 164 A
kristin.moser@uni.edu
MOSER, Patrick .... 503-838-8063 377 D
moserp@wou.edu
MOSER, Rachael .... 757-352-4858 470 B
rachwri@regent.edu
MOSER, Stephanie .... 417-873-7527 252 G
smoser@drury.edu
MOSER, Steven .... 601-266-5002 249 F
steven.moser@usm.edu
MOSER, Tina, L .... 724-738-2000 395 C
tina.moser@sru.edu
MOSER, Tracy, S .... 662-685-4771 245 C
tmoser@bmc.edu
MOSES, Aaron .... 817-202-6771 444 I
mosesa@swau.edu
MOSES, Bruce .... 520-206-4514.. 15 B
bmoses3@pima.edu
MOSES, Carl .... 515-263-2805 166 F
cmoses@grandview.edu
MOSES, Charles .... 415-422-2508.. 72 J
cmoses1@usfca.edu
MOSES, Henry .... 615-327-6266 421 D
hmoses@mmc.edu
MOSES, Jocelyn .... 302-225-6241.. 91 B
mosesj@gbc.edu
MOSES, Justin, L .... 757-823-8670 469 A
jlmoses@nsu.edu
MOSES, Michele, N ...... 303-492-5491.. 84 B
michele.moses@colorado.edu
MOSES, Rhonda .... 704-378-1000 330 D
rmoses@jcsu.edu
MOSES-HOLMES,
Jeanette .... 803-934-3989 410 G
jholmes@morris.edu
MOSESON, Mottie .... 732-367-1060 275 K
mmoseson@bmg.edu
MOSHAVI, Dan .... 408-924-3400.. 34 A
dan.moshavi@sjsu.edu
MOSHER, April .... 417-667-8181 252 B
amosher@cottey.edu
MOSHER, George .... 312-329-4268 144 I
george.mosher@moody.edu
MOSHER, Mike .... 641-844-5551 167 E
mike.mosher@iavalley.edu
MOSHER, Tricia .... 614-891-3200 357 A
MOSIER, Allison .... 814-871-7357 384 A
mosier007@gannon.edu
MOSIER, Greg .... 913-288-7123 175 B
gmosier@kckcc.edu
MOSIER, Gregory .... 775-784-4912 271 E
greg.mosier@unr.edu
MOSIER, Julianna .... 559-243-7132.. 66 H
julianna.mosier@scccd.edu
MOSIER, Roger .... 212-854-6031 291 A
rmosier@barnard.edu
MOSKALA, Jiri .... 269-471-3648 221 D
moskala@andrews.edu
MOSKE, Amanda .... 701-777-4358 345 B
amanda.moske@und.edu
MOSKOVITS, Chrissy .... 863-638-7508 114 A
chrissy.moskovits@warner.edu
MOSKOVITZ, Joy .... 908-737-7030 278 E
jmoskovi@kean.edu
MOSKOWITZ,
Yechezkel .... 347-619-9074 326 F
MOSLEY, Alisa .... 601-979-2944 246 F
alisa.mosley@jsums.edu
MOSLEY, Ben .... 208-459-5031 131 C
bmosley@collegeofidaho.edu
MOSLEY, Crystal .... 410-951-3579 204 B
cmosley@coppin.edu
MOSLEY, Dawn .... 302-857-6272.. 90 E
dmosley@desu.edu
MOSLEY, Eartha, J .... 803-536-7048 411 G
emosley1@scsu.edu
MOSLEY, Julie .... 479-788-7404.. 21 G
julie.mosley@uafs.edu
MOSLEY, Lisa .... 203-785-3680.. 90 C
lisa.mosley@yale.edu
MOSLEY, Yohlunda, M . 219-989-2367 160 D
ymosley@pnw.edu
MOSQUEDA, Laura .... 323-442-6411.. 73 D
deanksom@usc.edu
MOSQUEDA, Leticia ...... 212-659-7200 303 H
lmosqueda@tkc.edu
MOSQUEDA, Rolando ... 702-651-4245 270 K
rolando.mosqueda@csn.edu
MOSS, Alan .... 918-465-1802 366 A
amoss@eosc.edu
MOSS, Carol, L .... 216-368-8769 349 D
carol.moss@case.edu
MOSS, Dana .... 802-485-2176 462 F
dmoss1@norwich.edu
MOSS, Elizabeth .... 410-455-2540 203 B
emoss@umbc.edu
MOSS, Jenny .... 812-866-7397 155 G
moss@hanover.edu
MOSS, Joshua .... 951-343-5045.. 27 G
jmoss@calbaptist.edu
MOSS, Kylee, B .... 260-982-5222 159 J
kbmoss@manchester.edu
MOSS, Latoya .... 912-525-5000 124 I
lmoss@scad.edu
MOSS, Orianna, M .... 786-331-1000 104 H
omaza@maufl.edu
MOSS, Pamela .... 901-722-3318 423 G
pmoss@sco.edu
MOSS, Paula .... 816-501-4418 258 I
paula.moss@rockhurst.edu
MOSS, Sara .... 870-512-7874.. 18 A
sara_moss@asun.edu
MOSS, Sarah .... 712-722-6078 165 I
sarah.moss@dordt.edu
MOSS, Scarlett .... 512-863-1012 445 C
mosssj@southwestern.edu
MOSS-LINNEAR, Kim .... 817-515-5379 445 F
kim.moss-linnear@tccd.edu
MOSSER, Daniel .... 304-214-8800 488 J
dmosser@wvncc.edu
MOSSER, Jack .... 269-337-4400 233 D
MOSSETTE, Mary Beth .. 559-442-8286.. 67 B
marybeth.mossette@fresnocitycollege.edu
MOSSEY, Christopher ... 215-893-5252 381 J
MOSSMAN, Mark .... 309-298-1066 153 A
ma-mossman@wiu.edu
MOST, Renee .... 612-330-1176 234 A
mostr@augsburg.edu
MOSTERT, Rich .... 559-325-6413.. 67 A
richard.mostert@cloviscollege.edu
MOTA, Jesus .... 509-542-4424 479 A
jmota@columbiabasin.edu
MOTE, Nicole .... 918-463-2931 365 J
MOTE, Tanya .... 360-596-5229 484 D
tmote@spscc.edu
MOTHERSBAUGH, Erik .. 312-949-7405 139 D
emothersbaugh@ico.edu
MOTHERSHEAD, Peggy . 641-784-5224 166 E
peggym@graceland.edu
MOTHERSHED, Lorraine 607-735-1728 298 H
lmothershed@elmira.edu
MOTHERWELL, Mary ..... 734-487-2229 223 K
mmotherwe@emich.edu
MOTL, Lori .... 870-245-5110.. 20 D
motll@obu.edu
MOTLEY, Clay .... 239-590-7440 109 K
cmotley@fgcu.edu
MOTLEY, Darlene .... 412-365-2970 380 G
dmotley@chatham.edu
MOTLEY JOHNSON,
Evangeline .... 615-327-6505 421 D
emotley@mmc.edu
MOTSCHENBACHER,
Russell .... 406-771-4362 264 F
r.motschenbacher1@gfcmsu.edu
MOTT, Asena .... 863-784-7041 108 F
asena.mott@southflorida.edu
MOTT, Jennifer .... 832-813-6512 439 C
jennifer.mott@lonestar.edu
MOTT, Joanna .... 541-885-1000 374 I
joanna.mott@oit.edu
MOTT, Judy .... 859-985-3521 179 I
mottj@berea.edu
MOTT, Molly .... 315-386-7425 320 B
mottma@canton.edu
MOTT, Sandee .... 940-898-2378 451 D
smott3@twu.edu
MOTTEN, Luisa .... 206-934-6782 483 D
luisa.motten@seattlecolleges.edu
MOTTER, Kristi .... 256-824-4158.... 8 B
kristi.motter@uah.edu
MOTTER, Shannon .... 928-524-7324.. 14 J
shannon.motter@npc.edu
MOTTET, Timothy .... 719-549-2951.. 80 B
presidents.office@csupueblo.edu
MOTTLER, Christopher .. 301-295-3654 503 C
christopher.mottler@usuhs.edu
MOTTLEY, Juanita, D .... 530-898-5241.. 30 D
jmottley@csuchico.edu
MOTTO, Angela .... 570-577-2000 379 C
angela.motto@bucknell.edu
MOTTS, Pauline .... 817-722-1656 438 G
pauline.motts@tku.edu
MOTUPALLI, Chaitanya . 510-649-2400.. 44 B
MOTYKA, Konrad .... 914-888-5315 306 C
kmotyka@mercy.edu
MOTYKA, Matthew, D ... 413-585-2204 218 H
mmotyka@smith.edu
MOTYL, Anthony .... 413-748-3959 218 I
amotyl@springfield.edu
MOTYL, Lynne, M .... 724-738-2070 395 C
lynne.motyl@sru.edu
MOTZER, Bill .... 402-465-2551 268 G
wmotzer@nebrwesleyan.edu
MOUCH, Sarah .... 740-362-3335 355 H
smouch@mtso.edu
MOUDGIL, Virinder, K .. 248-204-2000 227 A
president@ltu.edu
MOUDY, Cheryl .... 918-540-6213 366 F
cheryl.moudy@neo.edu
MOUGHARBEL, Amal .... 888-488-4968.. 46 F
amougharbel@itu.edu
MOULD, Megan .... 570-961-7895 387 B
mouldm@lackawanna.edu
MOULDS, Perry .... 615-460-6434 418 B
perry.moulds@belmont.edu
MOULTON, Jeff .... 225-578-6916 189 E
jmoulton@lsu.edu
MOULTON, Katie .... 508-213-2402 217 H
katie.moulton@nichols.edu
MOULTON, Linda .... 508-999-8188 212 A
lmoulton@umassd.edu
MOULTON, Patricia, L .. 802-728-1251 464 A
pmoulton@vtc.edu
MOULTRIE, Cynthia ...... 610-399-2131 393 F
cmoultrie@cheyney.edu
MOULTRIE, Nikki .... 925-969-2036.. 40 C
nmoultrie@dvc.edu
MOUNDS, Paul .... 860-512-3634.. 86 G
pmounds@manchestercc.edu
MOUNGA, DJ .... 605-229-8366 415 I
djmounga@presentation.edu
MOUNT, Charles .... 480-732-7281.. 12 O
charles.mount@cgc.edu
MOUNT, Jeanine .... 617-732-2192 216 D
jeanine.mount@mcphs.edu
MOUNT, Judy .... 316-677-1619 178 E
jmount@watc.edu
MOUNT, Marianne, E .... 304-724-5000 487 B
mmount@cdu.edu
MOUNT, Melissa .... 970-247-7080.. 80 J
mmount@fortlewis.edu

MOUNTAIN, Carel .... 916-558-2275.. 50 J mountac@scc.losrios.edu
MOUNTAIN, Mark, C .... 815-928-5794 147 A mcmountain@olivet.edu
MOUNTJOY, Jeff .... 520-452-2601.. 11 M mountjoyj@cochise.edu
MOUNTJOY, Shane .... 402-363-5614 270 D mountjoy@york.edu
MOUNTS, William .... 912-279-5851 117 F wmounts@ccga.edu
MOURA, Edison .... 830-703-4840 450 B emoura@sulross.edu
MOURAD, Roger .... 734-677-5328 232 D mou@wccnet.edu
MOURADIAN, Maral ...... 732-235-4772 282 A mouradmm@rwjms.rutgers.edu
MOURAS, Tamara .... 251-981-3771.... 5 A tamara.mouras@columbiasouthern.edu
MOUREY, Andrea .... 315-498-2173 310 F a.l.mourey@sunyocc.edu
MOURITSEN, Matthew .. 801-626-6063 461 A mmouritsen@weber.edu
MOURNIGHAN, Jim ...... 401-341-2200 405 D jim.mournighan@salve.edu
MOURTZANOS, Emmanuel .... 661-395-4406.. 46 L emmanuel.mourtzanos@bakersfieldcollege.edu
MOUSER, Lisa .... 636-922-8319 258 J lmouser@stchas.edu
MOUSSEAU, Juliet .... 619-574-5802.. 42 J jmousseau@fst.edu
MOUTENOT, Amy .... 561-912-1211.. 99 D amoutenot@evergladesuniversity.edu
MOUTON, Charles, P .... 409-772-4793 456 E cpmouton@utmb.edu
MOUTRAY, Tonya .... 518-244-2406 313 A moutrt@sage.edu
MOUTTET, Nate .... 206-281-2652 483 G natem@spu.edu
MOW, Lauren .... 269-782-1316 231 A lmow@swmich.edu
MOWATT, Alex .... 508-849-3394 205 H amowatt@annamaria.edu
MOWDY, Cheryl .... 205-348-4530.... 7 G cmowdy@fa.ua.edu
MOWEN, David .... 540-375-2283 470 E mowen@roanoke.edu
MOWERY, Carson .... 636-584-6583 253 B carson.mowery@eastcentral.edu
MOWERY, Chris .... 423-472-7141 424 B cmowery@clevelandstatecc.edu
MOWERY, Richard .... 570-784-3123 393 D frmowery@bloomu.edu
MOWRER, Julie .... 808-932-7826 129 D jmowrer@hawaii.edu
MOWRY, Cynthia .... 253-589-5570 478 J cynthia.mowry@cptc.edu
MOWRY, Harold .... 308-432-6227 268 D hmowry@csc.edu
MOXLEY, Gary, D .... 585-475-4515 312 F gdmcps@rit.edu
MOY, James, S .... 813-974-7380 111 C moy@usf.edu
MOYA, Will .... 212-986-4343 275 I will@berkeleycollege.edu
MOYA, Will .... 212-986-4343 291 E will@berkeleycollege.edu
MOYANO, Angelica, B .. 954-607-4344 112 J angelica@uinternational.edu
MOYE, Robert, L .... 478-757-2083 127 F rmoye@wesleyancollege.edu
MOYER, Alyson .... 307-742-3776 502 B amoyer@wyotech.edu
MOYER, Andrew .... 215-489-4665 382 B andrew.moyer@delval.edu
MOYER, Anna .... 618-235-2700 150 E anna.moyer@swic.edu
MOYER, Christina, L ..... 610-799-1136 388 D cmoyer@lccc.edu
MOYER, Cole .... 510-215-3928.. 40 B cmoyer@contracosta.edu
MOYER, Cole .... 510-430-3131.. 52 E cmoyer@mills.edu
MOYER, Jason, R .... 330-471-8456 355 D jmoyer@malone.edu
MOYER, Lorraine .... 912-279-5757 117 F lmoyer@ccga.edu
MOYICH, Kelly .... 636-255-2275 254 H kmoyich@lindenwood.edu
MOYLAN, Christina .... 604-274-1465 302 G cmoylan@ithaca.edu
MOYLAN, Deana, K ...... 713-500-3279 456 B deana.k.moylan@uth.tmc.edu
MOYLAN, Shannon .... 607-735-1782 298 H smoylan@elmira.edu
MOZAFFARIAN, Dariush .... 617-636-3702 219 C dariush.mozaffarian@tufts.edu
MOZEE, JR., Sam .... 601-979-1400 246 F sam.mozee@jsums.edu
MOZELESKI, Dee Dee ... 212-650-7396 293 D dmozeleski@ccny.cuny.edu
MOZIE-ROSS, Yvette ..... 410-455-3799 203 B mozie@umbc.edu
MOZLEY, Peter .... 575-835-5311 286 K peter.mozley@nmt.edu
MOZOLIK, Erik .... 414-464-9777 498 B mozolik.erik@wspp.edu
MOZQUEDA, Andrea ..... 909-607-0896.. 37 F andrea_mozqueda@kgi.edu
MOZRALL, Jacqueline ... 585-475-7181 312 F jrmeie@rit.edu
MRASEK, Jean .... 817-257-5566 448 F j.mrasek@tcu.edu
MRKSICH, Milan, T .... 847-491-3485 146 E vp-research@northwestern.edu
MROCZKOWSKI, Mark .. 863-583-9050 110 B
MROZIK, Jacek .... 701-858-3110 345 E jacek.mrozik@minotstateu.edu
MROZOWSKI, Cheryl .... 401-847-6650 405 D cheryl.mrozowski@salve.edu
MRSNY, Jason .... 402-375-7195 268 F jamrsny1@wsc.edu
MRVOS, Dessa .... 412-396-1653 383 A mrvosds@duq.edu
MUASAU, Jarad .... 719-365-8218.. 83 N jarad.muasau@uchealth.org
MUCCI, Karen .... 510-885-2784.. 31 A karen.mucci@csueastbay.edu
MUCH, Kari .... 507-389-1455 239 D karen.much@mnsu.edu
MUCHANE, Mary, W ..... 704-894-2644 328 E mamuchane@davidson.edu
MUCHANE, Mur .... 336-758-4016 344 C mmuchane@wfu.edu
MUCHER, Walter .... 787-738-2161 512 C walter.mucher@upr.edu
MUCHIRI, Rosalind .... 301-860-4335 204 A rmuchiri@bowiestate.edu
MUDD, Michael, A .... 508-929-8746 213 G mmudd@worcester.edu
MUDD, Summer .... 702-895-5381 271 D summer.mudd@unlv.edu
MUDLOFF, Scott .... 316-942-9491 176 E mudloffs@newmanu.edu
MUECK, Robert .... 410-626-6931 202 A robert.mueck@sjc.edu
MUEGGE, Dave .... 417-836-4040 256 G davemuegge@missouristate.edu
MUEHSAM, Mitchell ...... 936-294-1254 450 A mmuehsam@shsu.edu
MUELLENBACH, Joanne 559-325-3600.. 28 D jmuellenbach@chsu.edu
MUELLER, II, Alfred, G . 610-558-5508 391 A muellera@neumann.edu
MUELLER, Beverley, D .. 757-594-7002 465 M bmueller@cnu.edu
MUELLER, Brian .... 602-639-7500.. 12 J
MUELLER, Bruce .... 734-764-1817 231 H muellerb@umich.edu
MUELLER, Don .... 562-860-2451.. 35 H dmueller@cerritos.edu
MUELLER, Edward, A .... 603-862-3272 274 F edward.mueller@unh.edu
MUELLER, Erin, R .... 773-298-3319 149 D emueller@sxu.edu
MUELLER, Janis .... 810-762-9500 226 B jmueller1@kettering.edu
MUELLER, Jennifer .... 320-308-3023 240 I jjmueller@stcloudstate.edu
MUELLER, Jeremy .... 618-985-2828 140 H jeremymueller@jalc.edu
MUELLER, Joanna .... 605-668-1514 415 F joanna.mueller@mountmarty.edu
MUELLER, Joe, B .... 307-675-0501 501 G jbmueller@sheridan.edu
MUELLER, SJ, Joseph ... 510-549-5040.. 63 B jmueller@scu.edu
MUELLER, Kate .... 714-241-6160.. 37 J kmueller@coastline.edu
MUELLER, Lloyd .... 503-338-2412 372 D lmueller@clatsopcc.edu
MUELLER, Michael .... 956-665-2121 455 D michael.mueller@utrgv.edu
MUELLER, Michelle .... 734-477-8976 232 D mimueller@wccnet.edu
MUELLER, OSU, Pam ... 270-686-4319 179 J pam.mueller@brescia.edu
MUELLER, Shelia .... 412-536-1180 386 H sheila.mueller@laroche.edu
MUELLER, Stacy .... 513-244-4524 356 F stacy.mueller@msj.edu
MUELLER, Steven, P ..... 949-214-3386.. 39 K steve.mueller@cui.edu
MUELLER, Teri .... 405-425-5104 367 C teri.mueller@oc.edu
MUELLER, Tony .... 909-748-8288.. 72 F tony_mueller@redlands.edu
MUELLER, Valerie .... 252-335-0821 333 G valerie_mueller50@albemarle.edu
MUENCH, Kim .... 414-382-6091 491 F kim.muench@alverno.edu
MUENCH, Wendy .... 303-360-4738.. 80 E wendy.muench@ccaurora.edu
MUENKS, Kathy .... 573-681-5050 254 G muenksk@lincolnu.edu
MUERTZ, Julie, A .... 618-235-2700 150 E julie.muertz@swic.edu
MUGG, Heather .... 404-727-9326 118 E hmugg@emory.edu
MUGGEO, Louis .... 845-398-4174 314 G lmuggeo@stac.edu
MUGGLI, Darrin .... 913-360-7961 171 J dmuggli@benedictine.edu
MUGRAUER, Darrah ...... 215-489-2236 382 B darrah.mugrauer@delval.edu
MUGRIDGE, Rebecca ..... 518-442-3568 316 A rmugridge@albany.edu
MUHA, Beth .... 202-885-2451.. 91 F bmuha@american.edu
MUHA, David .... 609-771-2132 276 I muhad@tcnj.edu
MUHA, Mark .... 616-977-5300 223 C mark.muha@cornerstone.edu
MUHA, Priscilla .... 707-654-1275.. 32 A pmuha@csum.edu
MUHAMMAD, Darrick, D .... 313-496-2650 232 E dmuhamm1@wcccd.edu
MUHAMMAD, Toni .... 803-376-5780 406 D tmuhammad@allenuniversity.edu
MUHL, Erica .... 213-740-6267.. 73 D artdean@usc.edu
MUHL, Erica .... 617-266-1400 206 H
MUHLEMAN, Aimee .... 309-796-5505 133 G muhlemana@bhc.edu
MUHLFELDER, Leslie, F 610-330-5060 387 C muhlfell@lafayette.edu
MUHSIN, Karen .... 504-671-6138 188 B kmuhsi@dcc.edu
MUHVIC, Marie .... 203-365-4824.. 89 A muhvicm@sacredheart.edu
MUI, Eva Marie, L .... 671-735-8889 504 D evamarie.mui@guamcc.edu
MUIR, Bernard .... 650-723-2300.. 66 E
MUIR, Eleanor .... 717-796-1800 389 H emuir@messiah.edu
MUIR, Janette .... 703-993-8891 467 E jmuir@gmu.edu
MUIR, Thorton .... 770-426-2624 122 C tmuir@life.edu
MUJICA, Andrea, J .... 641-422-4438 168 G andrea.mujica@niacc.edu
MUKHERJEE, Avinandan .... 304-696-2659 489 M mukherjeea@marshall.edu
MUKHERJEE, Chaitali ... 415-476-1683.. 70 D chaitali.mukherjee@ucsf.edu
MUKHERJEE, Mohini .... 848-932-7015 282 A mohinim@global.rutgers.edu
MUKHERJEE, Sue .... 717-477-7447 395 B smukherjee@ship.edu
MUKOOZA, Margaret, N .... 803-934-3439 410 G mmukooza@morris.edu
MULADORE, James, G .. 989-964-4190 230 E jgm@svsu.edu
MULARKEY, Terry, J ..... 954-262-7555 105 A tmularkey@nova.edu
MULCAIRE, Carrie .... 831-479-3566.. 27 D camulcai@cabrillo.edu
MULDER, Lori .... 616-395-7817 225 D mulderl@hope.edu
MULDER, Mark, R .... 253-535-7251 482 A muldermr@plu.edu
MULDOON, Kevin .... 215-572-4076 378 E muldoonk@arcadia.edu
MULDOWNEY, Jennifer . 617-243-2000 211 B jmuldowney@lasell.edu
MULERO, Daritza .... 787-258-1501 506 D dmulero@columbiacentral.edu
MULFORD, Joe .... 320-629-5140 240 D joe.mulford@pine.edu
MULFORD, Shannon, L 417-268-6037 250 G smulford@gobbc.edu
MULHALL, Lawrence, P 864-833-8300 411 D lmulhall@presby.edu
MULHERIN, April, C ..... 207-778-7081 196 I april.mulherin@maine.edu
MULHERN, John .... 480-461-7627.. 13 D john.mulhern@mesacc.edu
MULHERN, Maureen ..... 845-398-4067 314 G mmulhern@stac.edu
MULHERN, Michelle, M .... 330-325-6259 357 D mmulhern@neomed.edu
MULHOLLAND, Angela, B .... 843-953-5502 408 C mulhollandab@cofc.edu
MULHOLLAND, Colleen, S .... 319-273-2717 164 A colleen.mulholland@uni.edu
MULIK, James .... 425-640-1610 480 A james.mulik@edcc.edu
MULIK, Jim .... 425-640-1610 480 A james.mulik@edcc.edu
MULINEX, Stacey .... 614-287-5128 351 C smulinex@cscc.edu
MULKA, Christine .... 616-988-3626 226 E cmulka@kuyper.edu
MULKIN, Alan .... 315-386-7777 320 B mulkina@canton.edu
MULL, Diane .... 803-754-4100 408 E
MULL, D'Andra .... 352-392-1265 111 A dmull@ufsa.ufl.edu
MULL, Stephen, D .... 434-924-8612 472 D sdm9rg@virginia.edu
MULLAHY, Michael .... 617-725-4140 219 B mmullahy@suffolk.edu
MULLALY, Victoria .... 312-752-2080 145 D vmullaly@nl.edu
MULLANE, Patrick .... 216-397-4495 353 O pmullane@jcu.edu
MULLANEY, William, P . 607-962-9232 320 C mullaney@corning-cc.edu
MULLEN, Bill .... 706-233-7336 125 C bmullen@shorter.edu
MULLEN, Brian .... 828-227-7629 343 E bmullen@wcu.edu
MULLEN, Daniel .... 916-306-1628.. 67 F dmullen@sum.edu
MULLEN, Eric .... 616-234-3673 224 F emullen@grcc.edu
MULLEN, Frank .... 508-541-1574 209 A fmullen@dean.edu
MULLEN, Greg .... 864-656-2222 407 E gmullen@clemson.edu
MULLEN, Jeff .... 501-977-2125.. 23 A mullen@uaccm.edu
MULLEN, John .... 785-227-3380 172 A mullenj@bethanylb.edu
MULLEN, Kate .... 518-327-6480 311 C kmullen@paulsmiths.edu
MULLEN, Ken .... 209-946-2345.. 71 E kmullen@pacific.edu
MULLEN, Laurie .... 410-704-2084 204 E lmullen@towson.edu
MULLEN, Megan .... 585-224-3222 320 E megan.mullen@esc.edu
MULLEN, Michael .... 610-361-5222 391 A mullenm@neumann.edu
MULLEN, Michael, C ..... 260-422-5561 156 E mcmullen@indianatech.edu
MULLEN, Steven .... 716-851-1294 299 B mullens@ecc.edu
MULLENIX, Elizabeth, R .... 513-529-6010 356 A mullener@miamioh.edu
MULLENS, Deborah, K .. 304-473-8181 491 D mullens_d@wvwc.edu
MULLENS, Mary .... 781-280-3200 215 B
MULLENS, Michelle ...... 405-789-6400 369 H mmullens@snu.edu
MULLENS, Rob, A .... 541-346-5455 376 H athleticdirector@uoregon.edu
MULLER, Beth .... 973-300-2338 284 A bmuller@sussex.edu
MULLER, Brook .... 704-687-0090 342 D brookmuller@uncc.edu
MULLER, Dalia, A .... 716-645-3020 316 C daliamul@buffalo.edu
MULLER, David .... 212-241-8716 302 D

MULLER, Eugene .... 212-752-1530 304 A
eugene.muller@limcollege.edu
MULLER, Jacquelyn, P . 724-458-3302 384 G
jpmuller@gcc.edu
MULLER, Joseph .... 860-253-3055.. 86 C
jmuller@asnuntuck.edu
MULLER, Kathy, A .... 712-362-0433 167 B
kmuller@iowalakes.edu
MULLER, Kim .... 806-651-2345 448 B
kmuller@wtamu.edu
MULLER, Kimberly .... 906-635-2170 226 G
kmuller@lssu.edu
MULLER, Marcus .... 320-589-6011 244 B
mull0262@morris.umn.edu
MULLER, Robert .... 847-947-5065 145 D
rmuller@nl.edu
MULLER, Stephen .... 434-582-3459 468 E
swmuller@liberty.edu
MULLER, Susan .... 815-836-5245 142 F
smuller1@lewisu.edu
MULLER, Tammy .... 828-327-7000 333 B
tmuller@cvcc.edu
MULLER, Wade .... 541-278-5971 371 H
wmuller@bluecc.edu
MULLER-BORER,
Barbara .... 252-744-2546 341 A
mullerborerb@ecu.edu
MULLGRAV, Shalonda .. 912-358-3389 125 A
mullgravs@savannahstate.edu
MULLIGAN, Barbara ...... 845-569-3112 307 D
barbara.mulligan@msmc.edu
MULLIGAN, Christina ... 718-780-7520 291 K
MULLIGAN, Jason .... 815-394-5061 148 D
jmulligan@rockford.edu
MULLIGAN, Leah .... 936-294-1047 450 A
lrw001@shsu.edu
MULLIGAN, Maura .... 617-989-4232 219 F
mulliganm@wit.edu
MULLIGAN, Rob .... 916-608-6736.. 50 I
mulligr@flc.losrios.edu
MULLIGAN, Tricia .... 914-633-2429 302 E
tmulligan@iona.edu
MULLIGAN-NGUYEN,
Erin .... 361-825-5785 447 C
erin.mulligan-nguyen@tamucc.edu
MULLIKEN, Ken, R .... 920-923-7604 493 D
mulliken@marianuniversity.edu
MULLIKIN, Demeri, C .... 563-588-7407 168 A
demeri.mullikin@loras.edu
MULLIKIN, Heath .... 864-644-5015 412 D
hmullikin@swu.edu
MULLIN, Allyson .... 610-796-8317 378 C
allyson.mullin@alvernia.edu
MULLIN, Beth .... 334-291-4975.... 1 H
beth.mullin@cv.edu
MULLIN, Chris .... 978-934-4232 212 B
christopher_mullin@uml.edu
MULLIN, James .... 320-363-2882 243 B
sjpresident@csbsju.edu
MULLIN, Joseph .... 630-942-4278 135 I
mullin@cod.edu
MULLIN, Mark, E .... 573-341-4175 261 D
memullin@mst.edu
MULLIN-SAWICKI,
Gretchen .... 603-271-6484 273 A
gmullin-sawicki@ccsnh.edu
MULLINAX, Kenneth ..... 334-229-4104.... 4 A
kmullinax@alasu.edu
MULLINEAUX, J .... 707-527-4011.. 63 D
MULLINS, April .... 276-223-4897 476 A
amullins@wcc.vccs.edu
MULLINS, Beth .... 731-286-3358 424 D
lamullins@dscc.edu
MULLINS, Brian .... 859-622-2821 180 E
brian.mullins@eku.edu
MULLINS, Cathy .... 603-358-2281 274 H
catherine.mullins@keene.edu
MULLINS, Greg .... 360-867-6243 480 C
mullinsg@evergreen.edu
MULLINS, Joseph, W .... 770-720-5946 124 G
jwm@reinhardt.edu
MULLINS, Kathryn .... 616-234-4000 224 F
MULLINS, Kerry .... 908-852-1400 276 G
kerry.mullins@centenaryuniversity.edu
MULLINS, Megan .... 304-877-6428 486 G
officeofpresident@abc.edu
MULLINS, Rachel .... 501-977-2174.. 23 A
mullins@uaccm.edu
MULLINS, Stephanie, B 205-934-5121.... 8 A
smullins@uab.edu
MULLINS, Steve .... 714-879-3901.. 45 G
smullins@hiu.edu
MULLINS, Turan .... 314-529-9434 255 B
tmullins@maryville.edu
MULLION, Carrie .... 760-921-5440.. 56 A
carrie.mullion@paloverde.edu
MULLIS, Ben .... 478-275-6589 123 I
MULLIS, Christina .... 513-875-3344 350 C
christina.mullis@chatfield.edu
MULLIS,
Clarence (Tres) .... 717-337-6498 384 D
tmullis@gettysburg.edu
MULLIS, Jay .... 478-274-7879 123 I
jmullis@oftc.edu
MULLIS, Riann .... 620-432-0377 176 D
rmullis@neosho.edu
MULLNER, Joel, W .... 412-578-6119 380 B
jwmullner@carlow.edu
MULLOWNEY, Bill, J .... 407-582-3411 113 I
bmullowney@valenciacollege.edu
MULREADY, Maritza ..... 716-286-8350 309 H
mmulready@niagara.edu
MULROONEY, James .... 860-832-2660.. 85 G
mulrooneyj@ccsu.edu
MULROY, Kevin .... 323-259-2542.. 54 I
kmulroy@oxy.edu
MULROY-BOWDEN,
Linda, A .... 608-342-1845 496 E
mulroy@uwplatt.edu
MULROY-DEGENHART,
Carmella .... 814-865-7611 391 G
qum11@psu.edu
MULRYAN, Michael ...... 714-879-3901.. 45 G
mdmulryan@hiu.edu
MULTARI, James .... 516-323-3060 306 M
jmultari@molloy.edu
MULVANEY, John .... 215-702-4504 380 A
jmulvaney@cairn.edu
MULVANEY, Stacy .... 478-445-1549 119 B
stacy.mulvaney@gcsu.edu
MULVEY, Bern .... 417-667-8181 252 B
bmulvey@cottey.edu
MULVEY, Kristin .... 815-280-2353 141 B
kmulvey@jjc.edu
MULVEY, Nick .... 262-551-5982 492 B
nmulvey@carthage.edu
MULVEY, Susan .... 978-762-4000 215 D
smulvey@northshore.edu
MULVIHILL, Patrick .... 612-330-1000 234 A
mulvihil@augsburg.edu
MULVIHILL, Patrick .... 412-392-4784 396 G
pmulvihill@pointpark.edu
MULVILLE, Matthew, H . 716-888-2220 292 F
mulville@canisius.edu
MUMA, Richard, D .... 316-978-3987 178 D
richard.muma@wichita.edu
MUMFORD, Debra .... 502-895-3411 183 H
dmumford@lpts.edu
MUMM, Michele .... 320-308-4066 240 I
michelem@stcloudstate.edu
MUMOLO, Dominic .... 949-376-6000.. 47 D
dmumolo@lcad.edu
MUMPER, Michael .... 717-867-6340 388 C
mumper@lvc.edu
MUMPER, Russell, J ..... 205-348-4566.... 7 G
mumper@ua.edu
MUNA, Esther, A .... 671-735-5700 504 D
gccpresident@guamcc.edu
MUNA-LANDA, Laura .... 909-621-8036.. 37 B
laura.muna-landa@claremont.edu
MUNCASTER, Karen ...... 617-552-3090 207 C
karen.muncaster@bc.edu
MUNCH, Leah .... 718-405-3341 296 F
leah.munch@mountsaintvincent.edu
MUNCHEL,
Christopher, T .... 765-285-5608 153 H
cmunchel@bsu.edu
MUNCY, Alison .... 615-230-3526 425 E
alison.muncy@volstate.edu
MUNDAHL, Daniel, L .... 507-344-7739 234 C
daniel.mundahl@blc.edu
MUNDAY, Lynn .... 765-618-2778 158 B
lynn.munday@indwes.edu
MUNDELL, Chris .... 614-222-4015 351 B
cmundell@ccad.edu
MUNDRANE, Michael .... 860-486-1777.. 89 D
michael.mundrane@uconn.edu
MUNDY, Alison .... 510-649-2400.. 44 B
MUNDY, Amy .... 361-582-2518 457 E
amy.mundy@victoriacollege.edu
MUNDY, Ashley, R .... 302-356-6817.. 91 E
ashley.r.mundy@wilmu.edu
MUNDY, Lindsey .... 612-351-0631 236 E
lmundy@ipr.edu
MUNDY, Renee .... 570-961-7861 387 B
mundyr@lackawanna.edu
MUNDY, Tiina .... 910-879-5556 332 D
tmundy@bladencc.edu
MUNERA, Marcela .... 786-534-0500.. 99 L
MUNET-PABON,
Katherine .... 212-237-8000 294 D
MUNEZ, Angela .... 559-453-2170.. 43 A
angela.munez@fresno.edu
MUNFORD, Michael ...... 507-537-7858 241 D
michael.munford@smsu.edu
MUNGER, Michael .... 518-381-1200 315 B
mungermg@sunysccc.edu
MUNGO, T. Rein .... 843-349-2577 408 A
tmungo@coastal.edu
MUNHOFEN, Troy .... 402-494-2311 268 A
tmunhofen@thenicc.edu
MUNIER, Robert .... 508-289-3335 220 E
rmunier@whoi.edu
MUNILLO, Rebecca .... 661-763-7870.. 67 G
rmunillo@taftcollege.edu
MUNIN, Art .... 920-424-3100 496 C
munina@uwosh.edu
MUNIN, Eugene .... 239-304-7998.. 95 M
eugene.munin@avemaria.edu
MUNIVE, Lisa .... 715-634-4790 492 L
lmunive@lco.edu
MUNIZ, Ernesto .... 870-733-6810.. 17 F
ejmuniz@asumidsouth.edu
MUNIZ, Hancy .... 787-891-0925 507 K
hrmuniz@aguadilla.inter.edu
MUNIZ, Herman .... 787-257-0744 512 B
herman.muniz@upr.edu
MUNIZ, Jorge .... 574-520-4170 157 E
deanarts@iusb.edu
MUNIZ GARCIA, Maria . 787-651-2000 509 J
mmuniz@pucpr.edu
MUNIZ-MUNOZ,
Waleska .... 787-780-5134 509 E
MUNJAL, Monica .... 415-575-6263.. 28 I
mmunjal@ciis.edu
MUNLEY, David .... 978-478-3400 218 A
dmunley@northpoint.edu
MUNN, Jim .... 208-732-6860 131 D
jimmunn@csi.edu
MUNN SANCHEZ,
Edward .... 314-516-5245 261 C
munne@umsl.edu
MUNNELL, Barbra, M ... 724-458-3824 384 G
bmmunnell@gcc.edu
MUNNS, Heather .... 305-626-3149 100 D
heather.munns@fmuniv.edu
MUNOA, Miguel .... 956-326-2301 446 E
miguel.munoa@tamiu.edu
MUNOZ, Alicia .... 619-660-4226.. 44 D
alicia.munoz@gcccd.edu
MUNOZ, Celia .... 954-763-9840.. 95 J
MUNOZ, Elias .... 323-563-4800.. 36 C
MUNOZ, Jason .... 661-362-3232.. 38 D
jason.munoz@canyons.edu
MUNOZ, Jesse .... 661-362-3155.. 38 D
jesse.munoz@canyons.edu
MUNOZ, Joe .... 325-942-2073 450 E
joe.munoz@angelo.edu
MUNOZ, Julio .... 787-284-1912 508 E
jcmunoz@ponce.inter.edu
MUNOZ, Kellee .... 620-276-9574 174 B
kellee.munoz@gcccks.edu
MUNOZ, Linda .... 806-335-4352 429 E
linda.munoz27@actx.edu
MUNOZ, Raquel .... 323-357-3630.. 36 C
raquelmunoz@cdrewu.edu
MUNOZ, Rene .... 717-871-4457 395 A
rene.munoz@millersville.edu
MUNOZ BARRETO,
Jonathan .... 787-265-3862 512 E
decano.estudiantes@uprm.edu
MUNOZ COLON, Harry . 787-720-4476 511 C
serviciocristiano@mizpa.edu
MUNOZ-GIL, Enrique .... 787-622-8000 511 D
emunoz@pupr.edu
MUNOZ LANDRON,
Ileana .... 787-725-8120 506 M
ileanamunozlandron@eap.edu
MUNOZ-VETTER,
Kristine .... 972-721-5149 452 B
kmunozvetter@udallas.edu
MUNRO, Alex .... 717-299-7776 399 C
munro@stevenscollege.edu
MUNRO, Cindy, L .... 305-284-2107 113 C
cmunro@miami.edu
MUNRO, Shannon, M ... 570-326-3761 392 W
smm20@pct.edu
MUNRO, Stuart, J .... 508-767-7041 206 A
smunro@assumption.edu
MUNRO, Timothy, J ..... 518-580-5569 315 F
tmunro@skidmore.edu
MUNRO-STASIUK,
Mandy .... 330-672-3225 354 A
mmunrost@kent.edu
MUNROE, Anthony .... 212-220-1230 293 A
MUNROE, Rick .... 662-846-4706 245 G
rmunroe@deltastate.edu
MUNSCH, Patty .... 631-451-4572 321 C
munschp@sunysuffolk.edu
MUNSCHY, Karl .... 706-729-2179 116 A
kmunschy@augusta.edu
MUNSEY, Matt .... 540-887-7211 468 G
mmunsey@marybaldwin.edu
MUNSIL, Len .... 602-386-4103.. 10 F
len.munsil@arizonachristian.edu
MUNSON, JR.,
David, C .... 585-475-2394 312 F
dcmpro@rit.edu
MUNSON, Janet .... 309-649-6273 150 G
janet.munson@src.edu
MUNSON, Pamela .... 518-564-2100 318 E
munsonpj@plattsburgh.edu
MUNSON, Scott .... 303-860-5600.. 84 A
scott.munson@cu.edu
MUNSON, Steve .... 202-885-2395.. 91 F
smunson@american.edu
MUNTZ, Donna .... 740-374-8716 363 F
dmuntz@wscc.edu
MUN~OZ, Mike .... 562-938-4121.. 48 F
mmunoz@lbcc.edu
MURABITO, William ..... 716-614-5905 309 G
wmurabito@niagaracc.suny.edu
MURACA, Paul .... 713-798-6617 431 D
muraca@bcm.edu
MURACZEWSKI, Ashley 413-565-1000 206 D
amuraczewksi@baypath.edu
MURALI, Viji .... 530-752-4998.. 69 B
vpiet-sup@ucdavis.edu
MURALIDHARAN,
Aparna .... 212-875-4400 290 H
amuralidharan@bankstreet.edu
MURATA, Nathan .... 808-956-7703 129 E
nmurata@hawaii.edu
MURCH, Aimee .... 716-896-0700 324 E
murcha@villa.edu
MURCRAY, Ted .... 951-343-4760.. 27 G
tmurcray@calbaptist.edu
MURDAUGH, Jim .... 850-201-8660 112 C
jim.murdaugh@tcc.fl.edu
MURDEN, Romell .... 773-481-8451 135 G
rmurden@ccc.edu
MURDEN MCCLURE,
Tori .... 502-585-9911 184 H
tmcclure@spalding.edu
MURDOCH, Jessica ...... 978-665-3338 212 E
jmurdoch@fitchburgstate.edu
MURDOCH, William, G . 909-558-6604.. 48 E
wmurdoch@llu.edu
MURDOCH-KINCH,
Carol, A .... 317-274-5403 157 D
caramurd@iu.edu
MURDOCK, Alan, K ...... 336-734-7757 334 F
amurdock@forsythtech.edu
MURDOCK, Chip .... 934-481-2335 364 A
chip_murdock@wilmington.edu
MURDOCK, Janine .... 740-283-6223 352 I
jmurdock@franciscan.edu
MURDOCK, Melvin .... 918-595-7262 370 C
melvin.murdock1@tulsacc.edu
MURDOCK, Rebecca ..... 402-557-7136 265 J
rebecca.murdock@bellevue.edu
MURDZAK, Karen .... 814-732-1020 394 B
kmurdzak@edinboro.edu
MURGA, Margaret .... 252-536-7242 335 B
mmurga673@halifaxcc.edu
MURGA, Mario .... 617-327-6777 220 C
mario_murga@williamjames.edu
MURIANKA, Luke .... 315-858-0940 302 A
lmurianka@hts.edu
MURILLO, Alice .... 617-228-2102 214 C
amurillo@bhcc.mass.edu
MURILLO, Kindred .... 805-730-4011.. 63 A
MURILLO, Luis .... 619-594-7931.. 33 D
luis.murillo@sdsu.edu
MURILLO, Omar .... 408-855-5195.. 75 D
omar.murillo@missioncollege.edu
MURILLO, Renee .... 303-914-6345.. 83 C
renee.archuleta@rrcc.edu
MURISON, Sarah, A ..... 724-847-6674 384 C
samuriso@geneva.edu
MURKA, Adam .... 937-512-2947 360 G
adam.murka@sinclair.edu

MURLEY, Tiffany .... 580-349-1578 367 F
tiffany.murley@opsu.edu
MURNANE, Ryan .... 757-352-4891 470 B
ryanmur@regent.edu
MURO, Andres .... 915-831-4161 436 A
amuro5@epcc.edu
MURPHEY, Rodney .... 561-799-8105 109 J
rmurphey@fau.edu
MURPHREE, David .... 806-291-3641 457 I
dmurphree@wbu.edu
MURPHREE, Karen .... 912-623-2465 118 C
kmurphree@ega.edu
MURPHREY,
Hiram Todd .... 252-638-7263 334 A
murphret@cravencc.edu
MURPHY, Alexandra .... 312-362-7964 136 H
amurphy1@depaul.edu
MURPHY, Alison .... 518-828-4181 297 B
alison.murphy@sunycgcc.edu
MURPHY, Allison .... 503-517-1807 377 E
amurphy@westernseminary.edu
MURPHY, Amanda .... 561-364-3064.. 96 C
amandakm@baptisthealth.net
MURPHY, Amy .... 508-793-3880 208 D
amurphy@holycross.edu
MURPHY, Amy .... 815-280-1418 141 B
amurphy@jjc.edu
MURPHY, Amy .... 618-252-5400 149 I
amy.murphy@sic.edu
MURPHY, Angela .... 910-362-7014 332 H
amurphy@cfcc.edu
MURPHY, Ann, B .... 303-615-1113.. 81 M
murphann@msudenver.edu
MURPHY, Becca .... 269-337-7192 225 F
becca.murphy@kzoo.edu
MURPHY, Beverly, J .... 336-322-2128 336 G
beverly.murphy@piedmontcc.edu
MURPHY, Brent, D .... 574-232-2408 159 H
bmurphy@jpu.edu
MURPHY, Bret .... 775-327-2286 271 A
bret.murphy@gbcnv.edu
MURPHY, Brian .... 802-440-4335 461 G
brianmurphy@bennington.edu
MURPHY, Brian .... 530-895-2987.. 27 C
murphybr@butte.edu
MURPHY, Brian .... 914-606-6846 325 A
brian.murphy@sunywcc.edu
MURPHY, Brian .... 936-468-2803 445 E
bmurphy@sfasu.edu
MURPHY, Brian .... 360-416-7690 484 C
brian.murphy@skagit.edu
MURPHY, Britt Anne .... 501-450-1303.. 19 E
johnsen@hendrix.edu
MURPHY, Bruce .... 908-852-1400 276 G
MURPHY, Caitlin .... 814-641-3182 386 E
murphyc@juniata.edu
MURPHY, Catherine .... 615-460-6418 418 B
catherine.murphy@belmont.edu
MURPHY, Chad .... 309-649-6266 150 G
chad.murphy@src.edu
MURPHY, Cheryl .... 610-282-1100 382 C
cheryl.murphy@desales.edu
MURPHY, Chetara .... 718-270-6067 294 G
cmurphy@mec.cuny.edu
MURPHY, Chris .... 662-720-7280 248 C
cdmurphy@nemcc.edu
MURPHY, Chris .... 805-756-5692.. 29 I
cmurph18@calpoly.edu
MURPHY, Christine .... 718-940-5800 314 A
cmurphy@sjcny.edu
MURPHY, Chuck .... 610-921-7520 377 G
cmurphy@albright.edu
MURPHY, Chuck .... 509-313-6139 480 F
murphyc@gonzaga.edu
MURPHY, Colleen .... 514-234-5213 356 E
creliford@mccn.edu
MURPHY, Colleen .... 919-508-2206 344 E
cfmurphy@peace.edu
MURPHY, Colleen, K .... 781-891-2354 206 G
cmurphy@bentley.edu
MURPHY, Corinne .... 270-745-4664 186 C
corinne.murphy@wku.edu
MURPHY, David .... 608-262-1234 495 D
dlmurphy3@wisc.edu
MURPHY, Davis .... 530-251-8890.. 47 F
dmurphy@lassencollege.edu
MURPHY, Denise .... 301-687-4457 204 C
dmurphy@frostburg.edu
MURPHY, Doris .... 716-839-8272 298 A
dmurphy@daemen.edu
MURPHY, Doug .... 312-329-8911 144 I
doug.murphy@moody.edu

MURPHY, Eileen .... 845-398-4316 314 G
emurphy@stac.edu
MURPHY, Eric .... 812-749-1440 159 O
emurphy@oak.edu
MURPHY, Erin .... 509-452-5100 482 B
emurphy@pnwu.edu
MURPHY, Gail .... 239-732-3953 101 A
gail.murphy@fsw.edu
MURPHY, Gregory .... 818-677-2201.. 32 C
gregory.murphy@csun.edu
MURPHY, OSB, Isaac .... 603-641-7010 274 A
imurphy@anselm.edu
MURPHY, Jack .... 773-481-8124 135 G
jmurphy@ccc.edu
MURPHY, James, H .... 573-341-4292 261 D
murphyj@mst.edu
MURPHY, Jamie .... 814-866-8117 387 D
jmurphy@lecom.edu
MURPHY, Jenni .... 916-278-4433.. 32 D
jmurphy@csus.edu
MURPHY, Jennifer .... 318-840-3566.. 88 C
jmurphy@holyapostles.edu
MURPHY, Jessica, C .... 972-883-3536 455 B
ugdean@utdallas.edu
MURPHY, Jill .... 303-273-3259.. 79 J
jmurphy@mines.edu
MURPHY, Jim .... 973-748-9000 276 A
jim_murphy@bloomfield.edu
MURPHY, John .... 203-837-8395.. 86 B
murphyj@wcsu.edu
MURPHY, John .... 317-921-4243 158 D
jmmurphy@ivytech.edu
MURPHY, John .... 210-458-3026 455 E
john.murphy@utsa.edu
MURPHY, Joshua .... 603-703-8484 272 L
jmurphy@ccsnh.edu
MURPHY, Justin .... 812-749-1373 159 O
jmurphy@oak.edu
MURPHY, Kathy .... 256-549-8200.... 2 B
MURPHY, Kelly .... 406-756-3801 263 E
kmurphy@fvcc.edu
MURPHY, Kelsey, L .... 724-847-6643 384 C
klmurphy@geneva.edu
MURPHY, Kevin .... 607-735-1750 298 H
kmurphy@elmira.edu
MURPHY, Kevin .... 934-420-2009 320 F
murphykw@farmingdale.edu
MURPHY, Kevin .... 239-304-7827.. 95 M
kevin.murphy@avemaria.edu
MURPHY, Laura .... 508-929-8649 213 G
lmurphy@worcester.edu
MURPHY, Leah .... 712-324-5061 169 C
lmurphy@nwicc.edu
MURPHY, Lillie .... 225-743-8500 188 H
lmurphy@rpcc.edu
MURPHY, Linda .... 574-232-2408 159 H
MURPHY, Lynda .... 940-898-3405 451 D
lmurphy@twu.edu
MURPHY, M. Patrick .... 336-278-7640 328 J
murphyp@elon.edu
MURPHY, Mark .... 402-465-2254 268 G
mam@nebrwesleyan.edu
MURPHY, Mark .... 401-232-6406 404 A
mmurphy27@bryant.edu
MURPHY, Mary .... 612-343-4406 242 M
mlmurphy@northcentral.edu
MURPHY, Mary Joan .... 212-854-2091 291 A
mmurphy@barnard.edu
MURPHY, Maryanne .... 215-972-7600 392 T
MURPHY, Marybeth .... 201-216-3469 283 D
marybeth.murphy@stevens.edu
MURPHY, Maureen .... 301-934-7625 198 G
mmurphy@csmd.edu
MURPHY, Michael .... 508-678-2811 214 B
michael.murphy@bristolcc.edu
MURPHY, Michael .... 845-398-4118 314 G
mmurphy@stac.edu
MURPHY, Miguel .... 305-237-7740 104 E
mmurphy3@mdc.edu
MURPHY, Mollie .... 202-685-3951 502 K
murphyma@ndu.edu
MURPHY, Moses .... 802-656-8830 463 A
moses.murphy@uvm.edu
MURPHY, Nicole .... 765-998-4625 161 C
nicole_murphy@taylor.edu
MURPHY, Patrick .... 570-961-2513 389 D
mpmurphy@marywood.edu
MURPHY, Patty .... 305-284-3276 113 C
pxm491@miami.edu
MURPHY, Paul .... 805-922-6966.. 24 I
pmurphy@hancockcollege.edu
MURPHY, Paul .... 617-726-0422 217 A
pwmurphy@mghihp.edu

MURPHY, Paul .... 937-512-2518 360 G
paul.murphy@sinclair.edu
MURPHY, Penny .... 217-234-5253 142 C
pmurphy52829@lakelandcollege.edu
MURPHY, Pollie .... 757-727-5201 467 G
pollie.muphy@hamptonu.edu
MURPHY, Pollie .... 757-727-5237 467 G
pollie.murphy@hamptonu.edu
MURPHY, Rebecca .... 330-672-8533 354 A
rmurph20@kent.edu
MURPHY, Sarah .... 402-354-7000 268 B
sarah.murphy@methodistcollege.edu
MURPHY, Scott .... 888-556-8226 134 E
MURPHY, Sean .... 213-738-6762.. 66 B
it@swlaw.edu
MURPHY, Shar .... 530-257-6181.. 47 F
smurphy@lassencollege.edu
MURPHY, Stephen .... 203-432-4486.. 90 C
stephen.murphy@yale.edu
MURPHY, Susan .... 706-379-3111 128 C
samurphy@yhc.edu
MURPHY, Tara .... 781-283-2378 219 E
tm100@wellesley.edu
MURPHY, Taylor .... 910-630-7485 331 E
tamurphy@methodist.edu
MURPHY, Thomas .... 516-876-3215 318 C
murphyt@oldwestbury.edu
MURPHY, Thomas .... 305-284-6650 113 C
txm747@miami.edu
MURPHY, Thomas, H .... 215-898-7581 400 F
tom.murphy@isc.upenn.edu
MURPHY, Tim .... 254-442-5000 432 I
MURPHY, Todd .... 610-436-3102 395 D
tmurphy@wcupa.edu
MURPHY, Todd .... 714-432-5896.. 38 B
todd.murphy@mail.cccd.edu
MURPHY, Traci .... 716-839-8587 298 A
tmurphy@daemen.edu
MURPHY, Velissa .... 606-886-7332 181 E
vmurphy0001@kctcs.edu
MURPHY, William .... 617-552-1272 207 C
william.murphy@bc.edu
MURPHY, William .... 845-574-4362 312 H
wmurphy@sunyrockland.edu
MURPHY ALEXANDER,
Coleen .... 845-758-7431 290 I
murphy@bard.edu
MURPHY-MORIARITY,
Kathy .... 802-485-2292 462 F
kmurphym@norwich.edu
MURPHY-MORRIS,
Jayne, I .... 973-290-4245 282 I
jmmorris@steu.edu
MURPHY-NORRIS,
Carmel .... 540-453-2237 473 D
murphynorrisc@brcc.edu
MURPHY-STETZ,
Katherine .... 312-567-3080 140 A
murphy@iit.edu
MURR, Christopher .... 512-245-3975 450 C
cm18@txstate.edu
MURRAH, Matt .... 214-333-5160 434 C
matt@dbu.edu
MURRAY, Aaron .... 850-729-5260 104 M
murraya8@nwfsc.edu
MURRAY, Abby .... 773-442-5216 146 A
a-murray3@neiu.edu
MURRAY, Ashley .... 919-508-2209 344 E
ammurray@peace.edu
MURRAY, Benjamin .... 612-238-4526 243 C
bmurray@smumn.edu
MURRAY, Bob .... 231-591-2850 224 A
robertmurray@ferris.edu
MURRAY, Carol .... 845-341-4700 310 G
carol.murray@sunyorange.edu
MURRAY, Carol .... 406-338-5441 263 A
c_murray@bfcc.edu
MURRAY,
Christopher, D .... 406-994-2513 264 C
chris.murray@msuaf.org
MURRAY, Damon .... 704-922-2242 334 G
murray.damon@gaston.edu
MURRAY, David .... 616-234-3535 224 F
commdept@grcc.edu
MURRAY, David .... 415-703-9533.. 28 E
dmurray@cca.edu
MURRAY, Deborah .... 423-614-8118 420 H
debmurray@leeuniversity.edu
MURRAY, Dennis, J .... 845-575-3000 305 D
dennis.murray@marist.edu
MURRAY, Edwin .... 504-568-4810 189 H
emurr1@lsuhsc.edu
MURRAY, Eric .... 425-352-8810 478 D
emurray@cascadia.edu

MURRAY, Erika, S .... 678-916-2603 115 I
emurray@johnmarshall.edu
MURRAY, Ginger .... 217-234-5253 142 C
gmurray@lakelandcollege.edu
MURRAY, Jay .... 203-837-8286.. 86 B
murrayj@wcsu.edu
MURRAY, Jennifer .... 315-781-3740 301 F
murray@hws.edu
MURRAY, Jennifer .... 315-267-2492 319 A
murrayjm@potsdam.edu
MURRAY, Jill, A .... 570-504-1575 387 B
murrayj@lackawanna.edu
MURRAY, John, D .... 305-899-3021.. 96 A
jdmurray@barry.edu
MURRAY, Jonathan .... 706-225-5300.. 93 H
MURRAY, Julie, N .... 785-864-3131 177 J
jnmurray@ku.edu
MURRAY, Karen .... 914-594-4882 309 B
karen_murrary@nymc.edu
MURRAY, Karen .... 254-968-9992 446 D
kmurray@tarleton.edu
MURRAY, Kathleen .... 509-527-5132 486 B
kmurray@whitman.edu
MURRAY, Kim .... 434-381-6202 471 I
kmurray@sbc.edu
MURRAY, Lynne .... 785-594-8308 171 F
president@bakeru.edu
MURRAY, Maggie .... 336-342-4261 337 E
murraym7639@rockinghamcc.edu
MURRAY, Mark, J .... 904-264-2172 106 K
mark.murray@iws.edu
MURRAY, Melissa .... 802-656-2925 463 A
melissa.murray@uvm.edu
MURRAY, Michelle .... 508-793-2414 208 D
mmurray@holycross.edu
MURRAY, Nancy .... 978-665-3530 212 E
nmurray5@fitchburgstate.edu
MURRAY, Peter, J .... 410-706-2461 203 A
pmurray@umaryland.edu
MURRAY, Richard .... 808-932-7644 129 D
ramurray@hawaii.edu
MURRAY, Richard .... 914-633-2013 302 E
rmurray@iona.edu
MURRAY, Richard, M .... 626-395-4951.. 28 J
murray@caltech.edu
MURRAY, Rick .... 508-259-2512 220 E
rickmurray@whoi.edu
MURRAY, Rita .... 212-517-0416 305 E
rmurray@mmm.edu
MURRAY, Robert .... 845-398-4125 314 G
rmurray@stac.edu
MURRAY, Rodney, B .... 215-596-8789 401 E
r.murray@usciences.edu
MURRAY, Rolande .... 410-951-3010 204 B
rmurray@coppin.edu
MURRAY, Sally .... 617-333-2929 208 G
sally.murray@curry.edu
MURRAY, Sarah, A .... 859-238-5376 180 B
sarah.murray@centre.edu
MURRAY, Sean .... 888-491-8686.. 75 F
seanmurray@westcliff.edu
MURRAY, Shailagh, J .... 212-854-3229 297 C
sjm2245@columbia.edu
MURRAY, Sharon .... 518-292-1753 313 A
murras2@sage.edu
MURRAY, Suzette .... 630-466-7900 152 K
smurray@waubonsee.edu
MURRAY, Thomas .... 773-508-2398 143 C
tmurray3@luc.edu
MURRAY, Timothy, S .... 845-575-3000 305 D
tim.murray@marist.edu
MURRAY, Tom, L .... 405-789-7661 369 I
tom.murray@swcu.edu
MURRAY, Tracey, L .... 410-951-3980 204 B
tmurray@coppin.edu
MURRAY, Valerie, M .... 412-397-6423 397 B
murrayv@rmu.edu
MURRAY-HANSEN,
Ashley .... 402-465-2129 268 G
amurray3@nebrwesleyan.edu
MURRAY-LUKE,
Shanna .... 601-318-6668 249 H
smurray-luke@wmcarey.edu
MURRELL, Terry .... 712-274-6400 171 B
terry.murrell@witcc.edu
MURRET, Patricia .... 504-865-5448 190 C
pmurret@loyno.edu
MURREY, Brett .... 903-468-8687 447 B
brett.murrey@tamuc.edu
MURRY, Kim .... 620-901-6221 171 D
murry@allencc.edu
MURRY, Melanie .... 901-678-2155 426 G
mmurry@memphis.edu

N

NADEL-CADAXA, Yael ... 415-565-4600.. 69 C nadelyael@uchastings.edu
NADEN, Michelle ... 509-527-2147 485 C michelle.naden@wallawalla.edu
NADER, John, S ... 934-420-2239 320 F president@farmingdale.edu
NADERSHAHI, Nader ... 415-929-6425.. 71 E nnadersh@pacific.edu
NADLER, Jerry ... 914-594-4500 309 B jnadler@nymc.edu
NADOL, Anne, K ... 215-204-7308 399 B anne.nadol@temple.edu
NADOLSKI, OSFS, Kevin ... 610-282-1100 382 C kevin.nadolski@desales.edu
NADOLSKI, Mike ... 269-927-8109 226 F mnadolski@lakemichigancollege.edu
NAEEM, Mohammed ... 301-295-9213 503 C mohammed.naeem@usuhs.edu
NAEGELE, Chris ... 618-985-3741 140 H chrisnaegele@jalc.edu
NAEGELI, Dan ... 940-565-2686 453 E naegeli@unt.edu
NAE`OLE, Davileigh ... 808-984-3519 130 D davileig@hawaii.edu
NAFFZIGER, Sandra ... 831-582-5100.. 32 B snaffziger@csumb.edu
NAFIE, John ... 909-558-4562.. 48 E jnafie@llu.edu
NAGAGE, Champa ... 617-228-2115 214 C cnagage@bhcc.mass.edu
NAGAI, Judy ... 209-932-2864.. 71 E jnagai@pacific.edu
NAGAI, Nelson ... 657-278-2413.. 31 C nnagai@fullerton.edu
NAGANATHAN, Nagi, G 541-885-1000 374 I nagi.naganathan@oit.edu
NAGARE, Melissa ... 562-902-3386.. 65 I melissanagare@scuhs.edu
NAGASAWA, Wendy ... 206-934-5300 483 D
NAGDEMAN, Ryan ... 312-942-8708 148 G ryan_nagdeman@rush.edu
NAGEL, Brenda, K ... 701-255-7500 347 C bknagel@umary.edu
NAGEL, Lisa ... 567-661-2688 359 I lisa_nagel@owens.edu
NAGEL, Lonnie ... 361-593-2420 447 D lonnie.nagel@tamuk.edu
NAGEL, Michele ... 212-217-4630 299 D michele_nagel@fitnyc.edu
NAGEL, Suzie ... 269-387-2150 233 B suzie.nagel@wmich.edu
NAGELKIRK, Jessica ... 503-552-1966 374 D jnagelkirk@nunm.edu
NAGENGAST, Dana ... 909-621-8512.. 44 H dnagengast@hmc.edu
NAGIM, Jennifer ... 850-474-2463 111 F
NAGLAK, Steve ... 314-837-6777 258 K snaglak@stlchristian.edu
NAGLE, Kristen ... 732-987-2245 278 A knagle@georgian.edu
NAGLE, Ryen ... 708-974-5679 145 A nagler@morainevalley.edu
NAGLE-KUCH, Abbey ... 563-884-5137 169 F abbey.nagle-kuch@palmer.edu
NAGUWA, Jennifer ... 808-845-9119 130 A jnaguwa@hawaii.edu
NAGY, Lisa ... 817-272-6080 454 I nagy@uta.edu
NAGY, Mary Anne ... 732-571-3417 279 A mnagy@monmouth.edu
NAGY, Paul ... 813-253-7162 102 B pnagy@hccfl.edu
NAGY, Sharon ... 864-656-1455 407 E snagy@clemson.edu
NAGY, Zsuzsanna ... 973-290-4134 282 I znagy@steu.edu
NAHABEDIAN, Audrey .. 978-656-3223 215 B nahabediana@middlesex.mass.edu
NAHIDI, Sam ... 310-825-1728.. 69 E snahidi@saonet.ucla.edu
NAHLEN, John ... 760-245-4271.. 74 D john.nahlen@vvc.edu
NAHRGANG, Rick ... 507-453-2726 239 B rnahrgang@southeastmn.edu
NAIDU, Santhana ... 812-877-8550 160 F naidu1@rose-hulman.edu
NAIFEH, Zeak ... 580-581-2217 365 D znaifeh@cameron.edu
NAIL, Lance ... 956-665-3315 455 D lance.nail@utrgv.edu
NAIL, Steven ... 864-231-2000 406 F snail@andersonuniversity.edu
NAILLER, Katie ... 212-650-6507 293 D knailler@ccny.cuny.edu
NAILS, Dana ... 731-425-2628 424 E dnails@jscc.edu
NAIMI, Haleh ... 818-710-1310.. 27 H
NAIMI, Susan ... 818-710-1310.. 27 H
NAIR, Ajay ... 215-572-2900 378 E presidentnair@arcadia.edu
NAIR, Murali ... 734-487-0077 223 K mnair@emich.edu
NAIRN, Jason ... 814-472-3001 397 F jnairn@francis.edu
NAIRN, Roderick ... 303-315-2102.. 84 D roderick.nairn@ucdenver.edu
NAIRN, Tori ... 606-368-6134 178 G torinairn@alc.edu
NAISH, Cheri ... 951-487-3409.. 53 A cnaish@msjc.edu
NAJAM, Adil ... 617-358-7238 207 E anajam@bu.edu
NAJARIAN, David ... 704-637-4335 327 I dnajaria@catawba.edu
NAJERA, Alex ... 909-537-5138.. 32 E alex.najera@csusb.edu
NAJJAR, Yasar ... 508-626-4769 213 A ynajjar@framingham.edu
NAKADOMARI, Therese 808-689-2414 129 F therese@hawaii.edu
NAKAGAWA, Deborah ... 808-956-0321 129 G debn@hawaii.edu
NAKAMA, Debra ... 808-984-3515 130 D debran@hawaii.edu
NAKAMOTO, Rose ... 408-551-3583.. 63 B rnakamotoi@scu.edu
NAKAMURA, Aaron ... 509-527-2656 485 C aaron.nakamura@wallawalla.edu
NAKAMURA, Mayumi ... 804-752-3607 469 F mayuminakamura@rmc.edu
NAKAMURA, Tim ... 760-568-3352.. 38 E tnakamura@collegeofthedesert.edu
NAKANO, Mark, E ... 714-463-7504.. 51 B mnakano@ketchum.edu
NAKASONE, Nancy, K ... 808-689-2521 129 F nancynak@hawaii.edu
NAKATA, Glen ... 260-481-6804 160 C gnakata@pfw.edu
NAKONECHNYI, Alex ... 513-244-4264 356 F alex.nakonechnyi@msj.edu
NAKUTIS, Kristine ... 931-221-1400 417 H nakutisk@apsu.edu
NALEPA, Laurie ... 818-947-2498.. 49 G nalepal@lavc.edu
NALEVANKO, Gina ... 724-805-2251 398 A gina.nalevanko@stvincent.edu
NALLEY, Doug ... 919-761-2400 340 D dnalley@sebts.edu
NALLY, Angela, D ... 765-658-4800 154 J
NALYWAYKO, Serge ... 845-451-1409 297 G serge.nalywayko@culinary.edu
NAMUMNART, Jared ... 808-237-5145 128 F jaredn@hmi.edu
NAMUO, Clyne ... 602-285-7433.. 13 F clyne.namuo@phoenixcollege.edu
NANCE, Agnieszka ... 504-862-3348 191 F anance@tulane.edu
NANCE, Damon ... 951-372-7041.. 59 C damon.nance@norcocollege.edu
NANCE, Donna ... 817-531-6579 451 C dnance@txwes.edu
NANCE, Eva ... 574-631-1097 162 A nance.1@nd.edu
NANCE, Kristy ... 910-775-4347 343 B kristy.nance@uncp.edu
NANCE, Summer ... 864-488-8251 410 B snance@limestone.edu
NANCE, Teresa, A ... 610-519-4077 401 K terry.nance@villanova.edu
NANDOR, Sarah ... 314-246-7109 262 C nandor@webster.edu
NANNEN, Tampa, J ... 903-510-3324 452 A tnan@tjc.edu
NANNERY, Tracy ... 716-250-7500 292 A tbnannery@bryantstratton.edu
NANNEY, Ana ... 985-448-7940 188 C ana.nanney@fletcher.edu
NANNEY, Chris ... 704-669-4062 333 E nanney@clevelandcc.edu
NANNI, Louis, M ... 574-631-6123 162 A nanni.3@nd.edu
NANTZ, Samantha ... 606-546-1207 185 D snantz@unionky.edu
NAPARLO, Michael ... 732-224-2395 276 B mnaparlo@brookdalecc.edu
NAPIER, Audrey ... 334-229-4316.... 4 A anapier@alasu.edu
NAPIER, Katherine ... 404-752-1500 123 E knapier@msm.edu
NAPIER, Stacey ... 512-664-9043 454 H snapier@utsystem.edu
NAPOLEON, Jose ... 954-500-2987.. 95 O
NAPOLEON, Nawa'a ... 808-734-9517 129 H nawaa@hawaii.edu
NAPOLES, Gerald ... 832-813-6648 439 C gerald.napoles@lonestar.edu
NAPOLI, Brandon ... 831-479-5040.. 27 D brnapoli@cabrillo.edu
NAPOLI, Kim ... 208-459-5147 131 C knapoli@collegeofidaho.edu
NAPPER, Stan ... 281-649-3232 437 B snapper@hbu.edu
NAQUIN, Rose ... 504-520-7301 193 E xubooks@xula.edu
NARCISSE, Margaretta, S ... 913-253-5097 177 D margaretta.narcisse@spst.edu
NARDI, Peter, A ... 410-293-1585 504 A nardi@usna.edu
NARDIN, Gail ... 212-752-1530 304 A gail.nardin@limcollege.edu
NARDINO, Carol ... 802-387-6877 462 C cnardino@landmark.edu
NARDO, Rachel ... 435-797-3046 460 C rachel.nardo@usu.edu
NARDONE, Christopher 518-828-4181 297 B christopher.nardone@sunycgcc.edu
NARDONE, Mary, S ... 617-552-0346 207 C mary.nardone@bc.edu
NARDONE, Paul ... 570-674-8130 390 B pnardone@misericordia.edu
NARDUCCI, Julie ... 951-785-2578.. 47 C jnarducc@lasierra.edu
NARKIEWICZ, Geralyn .. 906-635-2228 226 G gnarkiewicz@lssu.edu
NARLESKI, Greg ... 413-549-4600 210 D gansa@hampshire.edu
NARMONTAS, Steven ... 413-782-1778 220 A steven.narmontas@wne.edu
NARVAEZ, Maria ... 213-477-2908.. 52 I mnarvaez@msmu.edu
NARVEKAR, Medha ... 215-898-7005 400 F narvekar@upenn.edu
NAS, Paula ... 810-424-5486 232 A pnas@umflint.edu
NASE, Christina ... 856-415-2297 281 D cnase@rcsj.edu
NASE, Laura ... 617-745-3000 209 B
NASH, Amy ... 724-938-5570 393 E nash@calu.edu
NASH, Bob ... 714-241-6143.. 37 J bnash@coastline.edu
NASH, Brian ... 712-324-5061 169 C bnash@nwicc.edu
NASH, Diana ... 212-774-0724 305 E dnash@mmm.edu
NASH, Gail ... 731-989-6072 419 K gnash@fhu.edu
NASH, Julie ... 978-934-4191 212 B julie_nash@uml.edu
NASH, Katie ... 608-265-1988 495 D katie.nash@wisc.edu
NASH, Kylie ... 256-372-5230.... 1 A
NASH, Laura ... 203-254-4000.. 87 I lnash@fairfield.edu
NASH, Leon ... 231-439-6443 228 H lnash3@ncmich.edu
NASH, Lillian ... 301-405-2583 202 H lnash1@umd.edu
NASH, Meghann ... 409-944-1238 436 E mnash@gc.edu
NASH, Mika ... 610-527-0200 397 D mika.nash@rosemont.edu
NASH, Milton ... 240-567-7794 200 G milton.nash@montgomerycollege.edu
NASH, Myranda ... 828-641-0089 327 B nashmh@brevard.edu
NASH, Peggy ... 812-535-5296 160 H peggy.nash@smwc.edu
NASH, Robert ... 870-235-4075.. 21 C robertnash@saumag.edu
NASH, Robert, B ... 509-420-4545 480 E bob@gather4him.net
NASH, Stephen ... 972-708-7573 435 E admissions-director@diu.edu
NASH, Steve ... 269-471-3284 221 D snash@andrews.edu
NASH, Timothy, G ... 989-837-4129 229 B tgnash@northwood.edu
NASH, Victoria ... 262-691-5495 500 B vnash@wctc.edu
NASH, William ... 256-782-8351.... 6 A bnash@jsu.edu
NASHUA, Lisa ... 909-652-6542.. 35 L lisa.nashua@chaffey.edu
NASHUA, Loy ... 562-938-4398.. 48 F lnashua@lbcc.edu
NASIM, Aashir ... 804-828-8947 473 B anasim@vcu.edu
NASON, Bradley, A ... 406-657-1018 265 E nasonb@rocky.edu
NASON, Stephen, S ... 207-509-7284 196 E snason@unity.edu
NASORI, Renee ... 619-644-7000.. 44 E renee.nasori@gcccd.edu
NASR, Nabil ... 585-475-5106 312 F nasr@rit.edu
NASSAR, Sayed ... 248-370-3781 229 I nassar@oakland.edu
NASSE, Jeffrey ... 954-201-7350.. 96 F
NASSER, Abdul ... 310-900-1600.. 39 F skibui@compton.edu
NASSER, Dawn, S ... 217-443-8755 136 G dnasser@dacc.edu
NASSER, Edward, D ... 520-621-5449.. 16 D enasser@arizona.edu
NASSER, Ryn ... 919-613-5577 328 F ryn.nasser@duke.edu
NASSIM, Sami ... 401-341-2480 405 D sami.nassim@salve.edu
NASSOUR, Kelly ... 956-665-3844 455 D kelly.nassour@utrgv.edu
NAST, Paul ... 479-524-7296.. 19 H pnast@jbu.edu
NATAF, Daniel, D ... 410-777-2407 197 G ddnataf@aacc.edu
NATAL, Yesenia ... 787-882-2065 510 C ynatal@unitecpr.edu
NATALE, Joel, A ... 610-558-5635 391 A natalej@neumann.edu
NATALI, Glenn ... 724-480-3361 381 H glenn.natali@ccbc.edu
NATALI, Jeanne, B ... 757-822-7296 475 E jnatali@tcc.edu
NATALI, Tony ... 574-807-7259 154 B tony.natali@betheluniversity.edu
NATALICCHIO, Gino, Q . 787-288-1118 510 I
NATALY, Mark ... 508-678-2811 214 B mark.nataly@bristolcc.edu
NATELBORG, Christopher ... 503-491-6422 374 B christopher.natelborg@mhcc.edu
NATHAN, Sean ... 808-734-9124 129 H smnathan@hawaii.edu
NATHAN, Susan ... 603-626-9267 274 C s.nathan@snhu.edu
NATHAN, Vini ... 334-844-4285.... 4 D vzn0007@auburn.edu
NATHANIEL, Shiran ... 712-274-5295 168 E nathaniel@morningside.edu
NATHANSON, Andrea ... 413-755-4889 216 A anathanson@stcc.edu
NATHANSON, Mike ... 352-435-5027 103 U nathansm@lssc.edu
NATION, Ramie ... 785-594-4530 171 F
NATION, Travis ... 206-296-2002 484 A nationt@seattleu.edu
NATIVIDAD, Rory ... 562-860-2451.. 35 H rnatividad@cerritos.edu
NATTER, Gretchen ... 717-337-6490 384 D gnatter@gettysburg.edu
NATTINGER, Ann ... 414-955-8495 493 F anatting@mcw.edu
NAU, Sharon ... 406-756-3845 263 E snau@fvcc.edu
NAUGHTON, Blake ... 970-491-6281.. 79 N blake.naughton@colostate.edu
NAUGHTON, John ... 614-251-4721 358 B naughtoj@ohiodominican.edu
NAUGHTON, John ... 614-251-6654 358 B naughtoj@ohiodominican.edu
NAUGHTON, Randy, L .. 623-935-8295.. 13 A randy.naughton@estrellamountain.edu
NAUGLE, Deemie ... 214-333-5291 434 C deemie@dbu.edu
NAUGLE, Lori ... 419-372-0113 348 G lnaugle@bgsu.edu
NAULT, Ray ... 386-822-8946 112 A renault@stetson.edu

NEITZEL, Scott 608-262-4464 495 C sneitzel@uwsa.edu
NELANT, Dan 317-805-1788 487 I dan.nelant@salemu.edu
NELEN, Carla 814-886-6411 390 G cnelen@mtaloy.edu
NELHUEBEL, Robin, M 757-240-2200 470 D robin.nelhuebel@rivhs.com
NELKENBAUM, Avrohom Yaakov 718-645-0536 306 J
NELL, Sharon, D 512-448-8620 442 I sharonn@stedwards.edu
NELLE, Nora 215-517-2659 378 E nellen@arcadia.edu
NELLER, Irene 805-565-6016.. 76 A ineller@westmont.edu
NELLESEN, Gary 909-274-4850.. 52 J gnellesen@mtsac.edu
NELLIS, Ginny 802-258-3283 462 H ginny.nellis@worldlearning.org
NELLIS, Leah 765-455-9441 157 B lmnellis@iu.edu
NELMS, Amber 662-720-7458 248 C afnelms@nemcc.edu
NELMS, Kristi 217-854-5594 133 I kristi.nelms@blackburn.edu
NELONS, Dee 253-680-7143 477 I dnelons@batestech.edu
NELSEN, Jeff, A 515-574-1115 167 A nelsen@iowacentral.edu
NELSEN, Kyle 402-375-7274 268 F kynelse1@wsc.edu
NELSEN, Robert, S 916-278-7737.. 32 D nelsen@csus.edu
NELSON, Adam 781-239-2664 214 G anelson@massbay.edu
NELSON, Alex 310-233-4312.. 49 B nelsonaw@lahc.edu
NELSON, Allan 302-857-1707.. 91 A anelso11@dtcc.edu
NELSON, Andrew 515-433-5020 165 A adnelson@dmacc.edu
NELSON, Andrew, J 715-836-5368 495 E nelsonan@uwec.edu
NELSON, Andy 712-274-5148 168 E nelsona@morningside.edu
NELSON, Angela 414-955-4708 493 F annelson@mcw.edu
NELSON, Annella 318-675-7013 189 I annella.nelson@lsuhs.edu
NELSON, Anthony, C 919-530-6175 341 E acnelson@nccu.edu
NELSON, April 580-477-7896 371 D april.nelson@wosc.edu
NELSON, Beth 281-756-3509 429 D bnelson@alvincollege.edu
NELSON, Bill 785-227-3380 172 A nelsonbn@bethanylb.edu
NELSON, Brandi 701-662-1509 346 C brandi.nelson@lrsc.edu
NELSON, Breck 618-664-7111 138 F breck.nelson@greenville.edu
NELSON, Brian 612-381-3042 235 K bnelson@dunwoody.edu
NELSON, Camille 808-956-8111 129 E
NELSON, Carol 909-274-5431.. 52 J cnelson@mtsac.edu
NELSON, Chris 870-633-4480.. 19 A cnelson@eacc.edu
NELSON, Christina 253-680-7180 477 I cnelson@batestech.edu
NELSON, Christopher 757-388-2900 470 F cnelson@sentara.edu
NELSON, Christopher 956-872-6715 443 H cnelson@southtexascollege.edu
NELSON, Daniel 651-638-6241 234 D dc-nelson@bethel.edu
NELSON, David 704-637-4414 327 I davidnelson@catawba.edu
NELSON, David 312-662-4151 132 G dnelson@adler.edu
NELSON, David 352-733-1700 111 A nelsodr@ufl.edu
NELSON, Denise 619-849-2477.. 57 J denisenelson@pointloma.edu
NELSON, Dexter 405-208-5000 367 E danelson@okcu.edu
NELSON, Diane 415-422-2444.. 72 J dlnelson3@usfca.edu
NELSON, Dirk 806-651-3501 448 B jdnelson@wtamu.edu
NELSON, Donald 684-699-9155 504 B
NELSON, Doug 563-387-1862 168 B nelsondg@luther.edu
NELSON, Douglas 909-869-3419.. 30 A dnelson1@cpp.edu
NELSON, Eboni, S 860-570-5127.. 89 D eboni.nelson@uconn.edu
NELSON, Eric 805-565-6003.. 76 A enelson@westmont.edu
NELSON, Eric 267-341-3205 385 J enelson@holyfamily.edu
NELSON, Evelyn, C 561-237-7816 103W enelson@lynn.edu
NELSON, Fred 605-642-6848 416 E fred.nelson@bhsu.edu
NELSON, Gena, C 315-267-2330 319 A nelsongc@potsdam.edu
NELSON, Glen 208-282-3540 131 G nelsglen@isu.edu
NELSON, Glen 831-582-3397.. 32 B gnelson@csumb.edu
NELSON, Greg 415-884-3100.. 39 A gnelson@marin.edu
NELSON, Gwynth 803-536-8542 411 G gnelson3@scsu.edu
NELSON, Hart 314-539-5311 259 A hartnelson@stlcc.edu
NELSON, Holly 503-399-5145 372 B holly.nelson@chemeketa.edu
NELSON, James, H 606-693-5000 183 C jnelson@kmbc.edu
NELSON, Jamie 360-442-2134 481 D jrnelson@lowercolumbia.edu
NELSON, Jay 763-576-4054 237 D jnelson@anokatech.edu
NELSON, Jay 763-576-4054 237 E jnelson@anokatech.edu
NELSON, Jeff 218-235-2193 241 E jeff.nelson@vcc.edu
NELSON, Jennifer 770-975-4000 117 B jnelson@chattahoocheetech.edu
NELSON, Jesselyn 517-355-6560 227 F nelso343@msu.edu
NELSON, Jessica 801-585-5950 459 O jessica.nelson@utah.edu
NELSON, Jessica 570-674-6330 390 B jnelson@misericordia.edu
NELSON, Jill 701-231-8211 345 F jill.r.nelson@ndsu.edu
NELSON, Jillian 309-438-2592 140 D jyoun11@ilstu.edu
NELSON, Jim 479-619-2282.. 20 C jnelson3@nwacc.edu
NELSON, Jim 304-327-4000 489 I jnelson@bluefieldstate.edu
NELSON, Joan 713-348-4759 442 F joan.m.nelson@rice.edu
NELSON, Johnathan, K 606-783-5158 184 C j.nelson@moreheadstate.edu
NELSON, Joseph, B 803-533-3740 411 G jnelso12@scsu.edu
NELSON, Karen 706-419-1288 118 A karen.nelson@covenant.edu
NELSON, Karen 724-653-2191 382 E knelson@dec.edu
NELSON, Karen, L 617-585-0200 207 A karen.nelson@the-bac.edu
NELSON, Kathy 937-328-6006 350 G nelsonk@clarkstate.edu
NELSON, Kim 701-671-2131 346 D kim.j.nelson@ndscs.edu
NELSON, Kim 360-438-4576 482 I knelson@stmartin.edu
NELSON, Kim 507-433-0664 240 G kimberly.nelson@riverland.edu
NELSON, Kimberly 410-951-3816 204 B kinelson@coppin.edu
NELSON, Kirk 225-768-1793 187 B timothy.nelson@franu.edu
NELSON, Kristy 989-686-9422 223 J kristynelson@delta.edu
NELSON, KT 531-622-2739 267 G ktnelson@mccneb.edu
NELSON, Kurt, D 570-577-1183 379 C kurt.nelson@bucknell.edu
NELSON, Lindsey, C 207-859-4622 194 D lindsey.nelson@colby.edu
NELSON, Lisa 570-740-0732 389 A lnelson@luzerne.edu
NELSON, Louis 434-924-3728 472 D ln6n@virginia.edu
NELSON, Louise, C 310-206-1355.. 69 E lnelson@conet.ucla.edu
NELSON, Maisie 606-546-1583 185 D mnelson@unionky.edu
NELSON, Mandy 208-426-1294 130 H mandynelson@boisestate.edu
NELSON, Margaret 718-289-5608 293 B margaret.nelson@bcc.cuny.edu
NELSON, Mark 607-255-8791 297 F
NELSON, Mark 218-646-3756 239 C mark.nelson@minnesota.edu
NELSON, Mark 303-797-5654.. 77 I mark.nelson@arapahoe.edu
NELSON, Mark 205-348-4786.... 7 G mnelson@ua.edu
NELSON, Mark 252-940-6213 332 C mark.nelson@beaufortccc.edu
NELSON, Merritt 402-941-6141 267 L nelson@midlandu.edu
NELSON, Michele 262-691-5520 500 B mnelson58@wctc.edu
NELSON, Michelle 262-691-3484 500 B mnelson63@wctc.edu
NELSON, Michelle 973-313-6053 283 C michell.nelson@shu.edu
NELSON, Mike 256-765-4440.... 8 E mnelson7@una.edu
NELSON, Nancy 414-227-3123 496 B nln@uwm.edu
NELSON, Paul 630-829-6000 133 E
NELSON, Peter, C 312-996-3259 151 G nelson@uic.edu
NELSON, Phil 909-469-5661.. 75 I pnelson@westernu.edu
NELSON, Randy 605-575-6585 417 C randy.nelson@usiouxfalls.edu
NELSON, Rebecca 773-244-5759 145 G rnelson1@northpark.edu
NELSON, Rencelly 691-320-2480 504 C rencelly@comfsm.fm
NELSON, Rhonda, L 701-788-4208 345 D rhonda.nelson@mayvillestate.edu
NELSON, Robyn 818-299-5500.. 74 L rnelson@westcoastuniversity.edu
NELSON, Ryan 218-477-5869 239 E ryan.nelson@mnstate.edu
NELSON, Sandra 717-901-5117 385 H snelson@harrisburgu.edu
NELSON, Sandra, H 773-256-0676 143 F sandra.nelson@lstc.edu
NELSON, Sarah 715-425-3500 496 F sarah.nelson@uwrf.edu
NELSON, Sasha 970-682-1118.. 79 H sasha.nelson@cncc.edu
NELSON, Scott Bernard 503-883-2498 373 F scott.nelson@linfield.edu
NELSON, Sean 608-262-1311 495 C snelson@uwsa.edu
NELSON, Seth 757-560-0040 409 E seth.nelson@erskine.edu
NELSON, Shad 361-593-2454 447 D shad.nelson@tamuk.edu
NELSON, Shannan 605-274-5330 414 G shannan.nelson@augie.edu
NELSON, Shannon 718-793-2330 309 C
NELSON, Stacy 707-965-6231.. 55 I snelson@puc.edu
NELSON, Steve 504-568-4009 189 H snelso1@lsuhsc.edu
NELSON, Steven 201-692-2477 277 I snelson@fdu.edu
NELSON, Suzanne 267-502-2482 379 A suzanne.nelson@brynathyn.edu
NELSON, Suzy 617-253-8566 216 B
NELSON, Tammy 207-768-2747 195 G tnelson@nmcc.edu
NELSON, Tiana 303-534-6290.. 79 M tiana.kennedy@colostate.edu
NELSON, Tim 301-891-4046 205 A tnelson@wau.edu
NELSON, Tony 270-707-3777 182 B tony.nelson@kctcs.edu
NELSON, Tony 931-372-3234 426 B tnelson@tntech.edu
NELSON, Trista 269-467-9945 224 C tnelson@glenoaks.edu
NELSON, Veronica 775-289-3589 271 A veronica.nelson@gbcnv.edu
NELSON, Wesley 704-461-6545 326 L wesleynelson@bac.edu
NELSON, Wilbert 602-285-7174.. 13 F wilbert.nelson@phoenixcollege.edu
NELSON, William, L 800-867-2243.. 55 D wnelson@pacific-college.edu
NELSON FISHER, Anne 218-855-8221 237 G anne.nelsonfisher@clcmn.edu
NELSON-HENSLEY, Susan 740-695-9500 348 E snelsonhensley@belmontcollege.edu
NELSON MOELLER, Rachel 610-330-5810 387 C moellerr@lafayette.edu
NELSON NASH, Denise 909-607-7180.. 63 F dnelnash@scrippscollege.edu
NEMBHARD, Harriet 319-335-5766 163 H harriet-nembhard@uiowa.edu
NEMEC, Mark, R 203-254-4000.. 87 I mnemec@fairfield.edu
NEMECZ, Attila 252-940-6387 332 C attila.nemecz@beaufortccc.edu
NEMETI, Jami 417-862-9533 253 F jnemeti@globaluniversity.edu
NEMITZ, James, W 304-647-6200 490 C jnemitz@osteo.wvsom.edu
NENNINGER, Sarah 417-873-7317 252 G snenninger@drury.edu
NENON, Tom 901-678-2119 426 G tnenon@memphis.edu
NEPA, Beth 315-781-3315 301 F nepa@hws.edu
NEPOMUCENO, Tina 708-209-3545 136 E tina.nepomuceno@cuchicago.edu
NEPPER, Terry, S 806-651-2747 448 B tnepper@wtamu.edu
NEPPL, Susan 952-885-5387 242 N sneppl@nwhealth.edu
NEPTUNE, Miriam 212-854-0408 291 A mneptune@barnard.edu
NEPTUNE RIVERA, Vivian 787-999-9531 513 B vneptune@law.upr.edu
NERE, Jeremy 715-394-8306 497 C jnere@uwsuper.edu
NERGER, Janice, L 970-491-6974.. 79 N janice.nerger@colostate.edu
NERIA, Angela 620-235-4603 177 A aneria@pittstate.edu
NERIANI, Kelly 937-328-6075 350 G nerianik@clarkstate.edu
NERO, Christopher 701-228-5461 346 B christopher.nero@dakotacollege.edu
NERONHA, Christopher 401-865-2774 404 F cneronha@providence.edu
NERY, Annebelle 760-776-7442.. 38 E anery@collegeofthedesert.edu
NESBARY, Dale, K 231-777-0311 228 G dale.nesbary@muskegoncc.edu
NESBIT, Jim 937-298-3399 354 J jim.nesbit@kc.edu
NESBIT, Ryan, A 706-542-1361 126 G rnesbit@uga.edu
NESBITT, Chris 704-216-3756 337 F chris.nesbitt@rccc.edu
NESBITT, Joan, M 573-341-4111 261 D nesbittj@mst.edu
NESBITT, Sean 970-945-8691.. 78 L
NESBITT, Shawna 214-648-2168 457 A shawna.nesbitt@utsouthwestern.edu
NESBITT, Stephanie, R 315-792-5292 324 B srnesbit@utica.edu
NESBITT, Thomas 518-244-4623 313 A nesbit@sage.edu
NESBY, Robin 718-951-5000 293 C
NESHEIM, Jeff 303-797-5075.. 77 I jeffrey.nesheim@arapahoe.edu
NESHEIM-KAUFFMAN, Rhonda, K 641-422-4232 168 G rhonda.nesheim-kauffman@niacc.edu
NESMITH, Chris 803-812-7330 413 E cnesmit@mailbox.sc.edu
NESMITH, Mark, A 304-326-1473 487 I mnesmith@salemu.edu
NESMITH, Robert, M 859-238-5356 180 B bob.nesmith@centre.edu
NESS, Claudia, L 509-527-5040 486 B nesscl@whitman.edu
NESS, Deborah 708-209-3115 136 E deb.ness@cuchicago.edu
NESS, Eric 570-389-4517 393 D eness@bloomu.edu
NESS, Melvin, M 646-565-6015 322 F melvin.ness@touro.edu
NESS, Mevin, M 646-565-6015 322 G melvin.ness@touro.edu
NESS, Phil 419-448-2384 353 E philness@heidelberg.edu
NESS, Shanda 323-259-2500.. 54 I sness@oxy.edu

NG, Peh .... 320-589-6015 244 B
pehng@morris.umn.edu
NG, Wendy .... 510-885-3161.. 31 A
wendy.ng@csueastbay.edu
NGHIEM, Nghi .... 323-265-8689.. 48 J
nghiemnx@elac.edu
NGIRAIRIKL,
Isumechraard, K .... 680-488-2471 505 B
ingirairikl@palau.edu
NGIRAMENGIOR, Todd . 680-488-2471 505 B
toddn@palau.edu
NGO, Ann, V .... 651-638-6400 234 D
NGO, Vincent .... 619-388-7485.. 61 A
vngo@sdccd.edu
NGOM, Mbare .... 443-885-3095 201 A
mbare.ngom@morgan.edu
NGUH, Jonas .... 800-856-9544 265 H
jonas.nguh@uprovidence.edu
NGUMA, Elibariki .... 956-872-2515 443 H
bariki@southtexascollege.edu
NGUYEN, Alice .... 801-302-2800 459 H
anguyen@neumont.edu
NGUYEN, Anhtu .... 714-539-6561.. 66 F
NGUYEN, Binh .... 510-659-6441.. 54 J
bnguyen@ohlone.edu
NGUYEN, Binh .... 510-659-6438.. 54 J
bnguyen@ohlone.edu
NGUYEN, Chau .... 702-463-2122 272 G
cnguyen@wongu.org
NGUYEN, Chris .... 888-820-1484.. 64 F
chris.nguyen@sofia.edu
NGUYEN, Christine .... 714-241-6144.. 37 J
cnguyen@coastline.edu
NGUYEN, Danny .... 408-855-5417.. 75 D
danny.nguyen@missioncollege.edu
NGUYEN, Diane .... 713-771-5336 121 I
dnguyen@ict.edu
NGUYEN, Hieu .... 909-621-8335.. 44 H
htnguyen@hmc.edu
NGUYEN, Hieu .... 808-739-8577 128 E
hnguyen@chaminade.edu
NGUYEN, Hoa .... 419-448-2228 353 E
hnguyen@heidelberg.edu
NGUYEN, Hung .... 714-564-6339.. 58 F
nguyen_hung@sac.edu
NGUYEN, Kay .... 714-895-8727.. 38 A
kvnguyen@gwc.cccd.edu
NGUYEN, Linh .... 617-217-9216 206 E
lnguyen@baystate.edu
NGUYEN, Loan .... 510-981-2808.. 56 I
lnguyen@peralta.edu
NGUYEN, SVD,
Long Phi .... 563-876-3353 165 H
lnguyen@dwci.edu
NGUYEN, Mai .... 978-934-2049 212 B
mai_nguyen@uml.edu
NGUYEN, Marion .... 360-491-4700 482 I
NGUYEN, Michael .... 805-756-2246.. 29 I
mnguyen@calpoly.edu
NGUYEN, Michael .... 303-605-5435.. 81 M
mnguye31@msudenver.edu
NGUYEN, Perla .... 800-477-2254.. 29 G
NGUYEN, Philip .... 714-903-2762.. 68 G
NGUYEN, Son .... 310-233-4584.. 49 B
nguyens@lahc.edu
NGUYEN, Son Xuan .... 714-903-2762.. 68 G
NGUYEN, Tai .... 504-278-6483 188 G
tnguyen@nunez.edu
NGUYEN, Tamie .... 323-343-5808.. 31 E
tnguyen10@cslanet.calstatela.edu
NGUYEN, Thuy .... 650-949-7200.. 42 I
nguyenthuy@foothill.edu
NGUYEN, Thuy .... 714-432-5816.. 38 B
tnguyen@occ.cccd.edu
NGUYEN, Tina .... 408-274-7900.. 62 G
tina.nguyen@evc.edu
NGUYEN, Trinh .... 925-473-7315.. 40 D
trnguyen@losmedanos.edu
NGUYEN, Trung .... 817-257-5557 448 F
trung.nguyen@tcu.edu
NGUYEN,
Truongson (Sonny) .... 619-388-7358.. 61 A
tvnguyen@sdccd.edu
NGUYEN, Tuyen .... 714-628-4844.. 58 G
nguyen_tuyen@sccollege.edu
NGUYEN, Van .... 734-462-4400 230 G
tnguyen@schoolcraft.edu
NGUYEN, Vannee, C ..... 850-474-3177 111 F
vcao@uwf.edu
NGUYEN, SCJ, Vien ...... 414-425-8300 495 A
vnguyen@shsst.edu
NGWAFU, Peter .... 229-500-2279 114 H
peter.ngwafu@asurams.edu

NHIRA, Tafadzwa .... 410-238-9000.. 93 H
NHO, Heung-sung .... 470-218-6032 124 F
heungsung.nho@runiv.edu
NHUNDU, Tapiwanashe 860-297-2072.. 89 B
tapiwanashe.nhundu@trincoll.edu
NIALIS, Ellen .... 714-879-3901.. 45 G
egnialis@hiu.edu
NICA, Claude .... 310-665-6870.. 55 C
cnica@otis.edu
NICASTRO, Eric .... 814-860-5125 387 D
enicastro@lecom.edu
NICE-WEBB, Kiva .... 573-592-6213 262 E
kiva.webb@westminster-mo.edu
NICELY, Kathleen .... 415-864-7326.. 61 D
knicely@sfcm.edu
NICELY, Nancy .... 303-871-4948.. 84 E
nancy.nicely@du.edu
NICELY, Nancy .... 303-871-4848.. 84 E
nancy.nicely@du.edu
NICELY, Tim .... 540-453-2371 473 D
nicelyt@brcc.edu
NICHOL, Charlene .... 330-672-2210 354 A
cnicho22@kent.edu
NICHOL, Kristi .... 816-654-7107 254 E
knichol@kcumb.edu
NICHOL, Victoria .... 303-273-3763.. 79 J
vnichol@mines.edu
NICHOLAS, Angela .... 434-961-5245 474 I
anicholas@pvcc.edu
NICHOLAS, David, R ..... 530-221-4275.. 64 B
sbcadm@shasta.edu
NICHOLAS, Donna, R ... 530-221-4275.. 64 B
donna@shasta.edu
NICHOLAS, Jason .... 906-227-2379 228 I
janichol@nmu.edu
NICHOLAS, Jim .... 530-895-6154.. 27 C
nicholaswi@butte.edu
NICHOLAS, Jonah .... 925-485-5253.. 35 I
jnicholas@clpccd.org
NICHOLAS, Jonah .... 925-229-6944.. 40 A
jnicholas@4cd.edu
NICHOLAS, Kedrick .... 337-475-5610 192 E
knicholas@mcneese.edu
NICHOLAS, Marc .... 334-556-2223.... 2 C
mnicholas@wallace.edu
NICHOLAS, Mark .... 508-626-4670 213 A
mnicholas1@framingham.edu
NICHOLAS-EDWARDS,
Brenita .... 740-392-6868 356 G
brenita.nicholas@mvnu.edu
NICHOLLS, Gregory, K .. 610-660-1090 397 G
gnicholl@sju.edu
NICHOLS, Aaron, F .... 802-656-3425 463 A
aaron.nichols@uvm.edu
NICHOLS, Andrew, W .... 808-956-8965 129 E
nicholsa@hawaii.edu
NICHOLS, Becky .... 816-501-2428 250 F
rebecca.nichols@avila.edu
NICHOLS, Brenda, S ..... 409-880-8398 449 G
brenda.nichols@lamar.edu
NICHOLS, Brian .... 859-257-3609 185 F
bnichols@uky.edu
NICHOLS, Carolee .... 910-843-5304 331 A
NICHOLS, Dana, J .... 706-295-6328 119 D
dnichols@highlands.edu
NICHOLS, Daniel .... 202-885-2534.. 91 F
dnichols@american.edu
NICHOLS, Denise .... 757-727-5221 467 G
denise.nichols@hamptonu.edu
NICHOLS, Drew .... 512-428-1042 442 I
drewn@stedwards.edu
NICHOLS, Eric .... 410-617-2000 200 B
ernichols@loyola.edu
NICHOLS, III, George ... 610-526-1301 378 D
george.nichols@theamericancollege.
edu
NICHOLS, Greg .... 305-626-3799 100 D
cio@fmuniv.edu
NICHOLS, Gregory, A ... 785-309-3182 177 E
greg.nichols@salinatech.edu
NICHOLS, JR.,
Harold, E .... 864-833-8296 411 D
henichols@presby.edu
NICHOLS, Jason, D ...... 573-629-3211 253 J
jnichols@hlg.edu
NICHOLS, Jennifer .... 704-922-6231 334 G
nichols.jennifer@gaston.edu
NICHOLS, Jim .... 434-592-3655 468 E
jmnichols1@liberty.edu
NICHOLS, Jody .... 715-425-3982 496 F
jody.nichols@uwrf.edu
NICHOLS, Justin .... 910-843-5304 331 A

NICHOLS, Karen .... 504-520-7692 193 E
knichola@xula.edu
NICHOLS, Keegan .... 479-968-0276.. 18 C
knichols@atu.edu
NICHOLS, Kelly .... 205-934-4488.... 8 A
nicholsk@uab.edu
NICHOLS, Lanell .... 325-942-2012 450 E
lanell.nichols@angelo.edu
NICHOLS, Laurie .... 805-437-8425.. 30 C
laurie.nichols@csuci.edu
NICHOLS, Laurie .... 605-642-6111 416 E
laurie.nichols@bhsu.edu
NICHOLS, Lesley .... 617-824-8281 209 C
lesley_nichols@emerson.edu
NICHOLS, Leslie, A .... 937-481-2200 364 A
leslie_nichols@wilmington.edu
NICHOLS, Linda .... 337-482-6491 193 B
linda.nichols@louisiana.edu
NICHOLS, Linda .... 307-268-2220 500 U
lnichols@caspercollege.edu
NICHOLS, Nichole .... 636-227-2100 255 A
NICHOLS, Pat .... 805-525-4417.. 67 K
pnichols@thomasaquinas.edu
NICHOLS, Rachel .... 828-328-7306 330 F
rachel.nichols@lr.edu
NICHOLS, Randall .... 207-725-3474 194 C
rnichols@bowdoin.edu
NICHOLS, Reginald .... 781-280-3536 215 B
NICHOLS, Ronald .... 540-674-3639 474 E
rnichols@nr.edu
NICHOLS, Sam .... 501-450-1340.. 19 E
nichols@hendrix.edu
NICHOLS, Scott, G .... 617-353-5777 207 E
nichols@bu.edu
NICHOLS, Shane .... 847-866-3866 138 D
shane.nichols@garrett.edu
NICHOLS, Sheila .... 850-484-1428 105 H
snichols@pensacolastate.edu
NICHOLS, Sheryl .... 352-638-9724.. 96 B
snichols@beaconcollege.edu
NICHOLS, Steve .... 417-269-3045 252 D
steve.nichols@coxcollege.edu
NICHOLS, Timothy .... 406-243-2541 263 K
timothy.nichols@umontana.edu
NICHOLS, Tracy .... 940-397-4277 440 C
tracy.nichols@msutexas.edu
NICHOLS, Warren .... 409-933-8271 433 H
wnichols@com.edu
NICHOLS, William .... 724-847-6544 384 C
wjnichol@geneva.edu
NICHOLSON,
Ann-Henley .... 609-497-3673 280 C
NICHOLSON, Debra ...... 620-276-9575 174 B
debra.nicholson@gcccks.edu
NICHOLSON, Emily .... 518-485-3818 296 G
nicholse@strose.edu
NICHOLSON, Eugene .... 919-516-4000 339 I
enicholas@st-aug.edu
NICHOLSON,
Jacqueline .... 585-475-2411 312 F
NICHOLSON, Judd .... 202-687-4402.. 92 E
nicholsonj@georgetown.edu
NICHOLSON, Karen .... 718-862-7374 304 M
karen.nicholson@manhattan.edu
NICHOLSON, Kim .... 765-677-2131 158 B
kim.nicholson@indwes.edu
NICHOLSON, Kristal ...... 903-875-7361 440 D
kristal.nicholson@navarrocollege.edu
NICHOLSON, Marie .... 828-689-1151 331 C
mnicholson@mhu.edu
NICHOLSON, Robin ...... 319-235-3516 163 C
robin.nicholson@unitypoint.org
NICHOLSON, Sylvia .... 336-517-2102 327 A
snicholson@bennett.edu
NICHOLSON, Tammy .... 706-295-6328 119 D
tnichols@highlands.edu
NICHOLSON, Teresa ..... 641-585-8147 170 I
teresa.nicholson@waldorf.edu
NICHOLSON, Tim .... 828-835-4261 338 E
tnicholson@tricountycc.edu
NICHOLSON, Vickie ...... 251-578-1313.... 3 D
vickien@rstc.edu
NICHOLSON ANGLE,
Jan, C .... 540-365-4285 467 B
jcnicholson@ferrum.edu
NICHOLSON-PREUSS,
Mari .... 713-221-8236 453 A
nicholsonpreussm@uhd.edu
NICK, Sara, J .... 715-833-6275 498 E
snick1@cvtc.edu
NICKE, Glenda .... 309-796-4822 133 G
nickeg@bhc.edu

NICKEL, Graig .... 785-864-9525 177 J
g491n194@ku.edu
NICKEL, Heather .... 816-531-5223 251 K
NICKEL, Jamie .... 866-766-0331.. 54 D
jnickel@ncu.edu
NICKELL, Barbara, J ..... 785-833-4390 175 E
bmarsh@kwu.edu
NICKELL, Jane Ellen ..... 814-332-2800 378 A
jnickell@allegheny.edu
NICKELL, Julie .... 713-798-4951 431 D
nickell@bcm.edu
NICKELL, Roberta .... 620-901-6214 171 D
nickell@allencc.edu
NICKELS, Ken .... 309-796-5048 133 G
nickelsk@bhc.edu
NICKELS, Lisa .... 415-503-6231.. 61 D
lnickels@sfcm.edu
NICKELS, Taylor .... 844-922-8228.. 91 G
NICKENS, Tawanna .... 217-351-2390 147 C
tnickens@parkland.edu
NICKERSON, Becky .... 402-280-3118 266 H
beckynickerson@creighton.edu
NICKERSON, Floyd, W .. 972-599-3159 433 I
fnickerson@collin.edu
NICKERSON, Jon .... 607-587-4750 319 F
nickerjd@alfredstate.edu
NICKERSON, Lori .... 508-999-8004 212 A
lori.nickerson@umassd.edu
NICKERSON, Matt .... 435-865-1955 460 A
nickerson@suu.edu
NICKERSON, Molly .... 660-284-4800 254 B
NICKERSON, Nathaniel . 203-432-1345.. 90 C
nathaniel.nickerson@yale.edu
NICKERSON, Sherita ..... 325-674-6802 428 F
sherita.nickerson@acu.edu
NICKITAS, Donna .... 856-225-2248 281 G
snc-dean@rutgers.edu
NICKLAUS, Mark, B ...... 920-748-8186 494 J
nicklausm@ripon.edu
NICKLAUS, Megan .... 719-389-6424.. 78 I
megan.nicklaus@coloradocollege.edu
NICKLE, Bonita .... 800-477-2254.. 29 G
bnickle@calsouthern.edu
NICKLE, Mary Anne .... 641-236-2202 167 E
maryanne.nickle@iavalley.edu
NICKLESS, Peter .... 315-568-3310 310 B
pnickless@nycc.edu
NICKLIN, Jessica .... 860-768-5365.. 89 G
nicklin@hartford.edu
NICKLOW, John, W ...... 504-280-6723 190 B
president@uno.edu
NICKODEMUS, Matt ...... 435-652-7542 460 B
matt.nickodemus@dixie.edu
NICKOLS, Sharon .... 217-333-6677 152 B
nickrich@illinois.edu
NICKS, Leanna .... 336-841-9313 329 F
lnicks@highpoint.edu
NICKSA, Gary, W .... 617-353-6500 207 E
nicksa@bu.edu
NICOL, Patricia .... 617-824-8123 209 C
patricia_nicol@emerson.edu
NICOLAI, Michael .... 312-629-9411 149 F
mnicolai@saic.edu
NICOLAS, Valcik .... 806-742-2166 450 F
nicolas.valcik@ttu.edu
NICOLET, Todd .... 919-962-3192 342 C
todd_nicolet@unc.edu
NICOLETTI, Katherine .... 508-213-2238 217 H
katherine.nicoletti@nichols.edu
NICOLETTI, Marian .... 585-475-7298 312 F
mmnadm@rit.edu
NICOLOV, Pressian .... 310-434-4765.. 63 C
nicolov_pressian@smc.edu
NICOSIA, Patricia .... 830-703-4836 450 B
pnicosia@sulross.edu
NICOTERA, Phillip .... 713-718-7628 437 C
phillip.nicotera@hccs.edu
NICULESCU, Jeremy ...... 503-777-7560 375 G
niculescuj@reed.edu
NIDO, Nellie .... 407-823-5346 110 E
nellie.nido@ucf.edu
NIE, Ling-Ling .... 404-894-6088 119 E
linglingnie@gatech.edu
NIECE, Matthew .... 208-426-1604 130 H
matthewniece@boisestate.edu
NIED, Danielle .... 313-228-7367 296 E
dnied@colgate.edu
NIEDENS, Rosemary ..... 316-942-4291 176 E
niedensr@newmanu.edu
NIEDERHAUSER,
Victoria .... 865-974-7584 427 B
vniederh@utk.edu

NOEL, Fred ... 406-275-4800 265 F
fred_noel@skc.edu
NOEL, JR., J. Andrew ... 607-255-8832 297 F
jan16@cornell.edu
NOEL, James ... 925-685-1230.. 40 C
jnoel@dvc.edu
NOEL, Norma ... 575-646-7793 287 C
nnoel@nmsu.edu
NOEL, Sangeeta ... 718-631-6262 295 C
NOEL, Terry ... 724-532-5095 397 I
terry.noel@email.stvincent.edu
NOEL, Terry ... 724-805-2095 398 A
terry.noel@stvincent.edu
NOEL-ELKINS, Amelia ... 309-438-3842 140 D
anoelel@ilstu.edu
NOELDNER, Troy ... 701-777-6366 345 B
troy.noeldner@und.edu
NOEVERE, Michelle ... 252-249-1851 336 F
mnoevere@pamlicocc.edu
NOFSINGER, John ... 907-786-4126.... 9 J
jnofsinger@alaska.edu
NOFZIGER, Marcie ... 260-359-4073 156 C
mnofziger@huntington.edu
NOGLE, Ryan ... 716-851-1281 299 B
nogle@ecc.edu
NOGUERA, Pedro ... 213-740-5756.. 73 D
rsoedean@usc.edu
NOHLGREN, Bethany ... 845-758-7292 290 I
nohlgren@bard.edu
NOJIMA, Stacy ... 408-741-4616.. 75 E
stacy.nojima@westvalley.edu
NOLAN, David ... 817-257-6863 448 F
d.nolan@tcu.edu
NOLAN, Dawn ... 516-572-7487 307 E
dawn.nolan@ncc.edu
NOLAN, Holly ... 281-283-2480 452 E
nolan@uhcl.edu
NOLAN, Josh ... 440-775-8401 357 G
josh.nolan@oberlin.edu
NOLAN, Judy ... 914-251-6067 319 B
judy.nolan@purchase.edu
NOLAN, Kevin ... 617-732-2900 216 D
kevin.nolan@mcphs.edu
NOLAN, Kevin ... 773-838-7526 135 F
knolan@ccc.edu
NOLAN, Lisa, K ... 706-542-3461 126 G
lisa.nolan@uga.edu
NOLAN, Nikol ... 785-462-3984 173 B
NOLAN, Sarah ... 608-265-5600 495 D
sarah.nolan@wisc.edu
NOLAN, Shay ... 270-534-3089 183 B
shay.nolan@kctcs.edu
NOLAN, Tiffany ... 573-681-5582 254 G
nolant@lincolnu.edu
NOLAN, Todd ... 941-782-5987 387 D
tnolan@lecom.edu
NOLAN-CHAVEZ, Holly . 805-922-6966.. 24 I
hchavez@hancockcollege.edu
NOLAN-WEISS,
Sharon, E ... 716-645-2266 316 C
senolan@buffalo.edu
NOLAND, Brian, E ... 423-439-4211 419 G
president@etsu.edu
NOLASCO, Maria ... 787-841-2000 509 J
mnolasco@pucpr.edu
NOLES, Jody ... 334-291-4922.... 1 H
jody.noles@cv.edu
NOLING-AUTH, Jamie ... 503-554-2321 373 A
jnolingauth@georgefox.edu
NOLL, Cheryl ... 912-650-5648 125 F
cnoll@southuniversity.edu
NOLLAN, Damond ... 919-530-6399 341 E
dnollan@nccu.edu
NOLLAN, Damond, L ... 919-530-6399 341 E
dnollan@nccu.edu
NOLLAN, Richard ... 806-743-1048 451 A
richard.nollan@ttuhsc.edu
NOLTE, Beth ... 573-681-5194 254 G
noltem@lincolnu.edu
NOLTE, JR., Harold, E .. 620-227-9378 173 D
hnolte@dc3.edu
NOLTE, Jim ... 802-828-8512 463 B
jim.nolte@vcfa.edu
NOLTEMEYER, Patrick ... 336-278-7904 328 J
pnoltemeyer@elon.edu
NOLTING, Carol ... 816-268-5400 257 C
cnolting@nts.edu
NOMURA, Christopher .. 208-885-1146 132 F
ctnomura@uidaho.edu
NONDORF, James, G ... 773-702-1234 151 E
jnondorf@uchicago.edu
NONEMAKER, Scott ... 315-792-3100 324 B
scnonema@utica.edu

NOOK, Mark, A ... 319-273-2566 164 A
mark.nook@uni.edu
NOOKS, Karyn ... 478-825-6520 118 F
karyn.nooks@fvsu.edu
NOOKS, Kirk ... 678-359-5015 120 F
presidentnooks@gordonstate.edu
NOON, Edward ... 414-443-8871 498 A
skip.noon@wlc.edu
NOON, Jennifer ... 973-443-8544 277 I
jennifer_noon@fdu.edu
NOON, Molly ... 712-325-3306 167 I
mnoon@iwcc.edu
NOONAN, Claire ... 708-524-6860 137 C
cnoonan@dom.edu
NOONAN, Daniel ... 203-576-4000.. 89 C
dnoonan@bridgeport.edu
NOONAN, John ... 919-660-4252 328 F
john.noonan@duke.edu
NOONAN, Mary Alma ... 920-832-7694 493 B
maryalma.noonan@lawrence.edu
NOONE, Anne ... 570-208-5899 386 G
aenoone@kings.edu
NOONE, Pamela, K ... 570-577-7136 379 C
noone@bucknell.edu
NOONKESTER, Myron ... 601-318-6118 249 H
myron.noonkester@wmcarey.edu
NOORI, Edris ... 315-866-0300 301 D
nooried@herkimer.edu
NORBY, Teri, L ... 651-631-5365 244 D
tlnorby@unwsp.edu
NORCIA MARSHALL,
Lisa ... 201-200-2335 279 D
lnorcia@njcu.edu
NORCINI, Heather ... 610-341-5890 383 B
hnorcini@eastern.edu
NORCROSS, Celia ... 413-236-1601 214 A
cnorcross@berkshirecc.edu
NORCROSS, Dawn ... 315-684-6038 321 A
norcrodm@morrisville.edu
NORCROSS, Paul, W ... 315-464-4361 317 C
norcrossp@upstate.edu
NORCROSS, William ... 413-662-5529 213 C
william.norcross@mcla.edu
NORD, Elonda ... 701-665-4639 346 C
elonda.nord@lrsc.edu
NORD, Elonda ... 701-662-1513 346 C
elonda.nord@lrsc.edu
NORD, Sheldon, C ... 503-375-7000 372 H
snord@corban.edu
NORDBERG, Erik ... 731-881-7070 427 D
enordber@utm.edu
NORDBY, Chelsea ... 503-847-2619 377 B
cnordby@uws.edu
NORDBY, Shawn ... 402-461-5344 267 E
snordby@marylanning.org
NORDEEN, Mark ... 307-855-2140 501 A
mark.nordeen@cwc.edu
NORDICK, Pat ... 218-299-6821 239 C
pat.nordick@minnesota.edu
NORDIN, Becky ... 612-659-6712 239 A
becky.nordin@minneapolis.edu
NORDIN, Thom ... 763-433-1424 237 D
thom.nordin@anokaramsey.edu
NORDLAND, Jeffrey ... 585-245-5606 318 B
nordland@geneseo.edu
NORDMANN, Andrea ... 817-257-5520 448 F
a.nordmann@tcu.edu
NORDONE, Ron ... 610-282-1100 382 C
ronald.nordone@desales.edu
NORDSTROM, Amanda . 906-524-8111 226 C
NORDSTROM, Steve ... 615-966-5002 421 B
steve.nordstrom@lipscomb.edu
NORDT, Lee, C ... 254-710-3361 431 E
lee_nordt@baylor.edu
NORELLI, Melinda ... 908-965-6090 284 D
melinda.norelli@ucc.edu
NOREN, Patricia ... 516-572-7396 307 E
patricia.noren@ncc.edu
NOREUIL, Margaret ... 608-663-2820 492 F
mnoreuil@edgewood.edu
NORIEGA, David ... 619-876-4260.. 68 H
NORIN, Casandra ... 620-417-1161 177 F
casandra.norin@sccc.edu
NORISE, Hershey ... 773-602-5484 135 D
hnorise@ccc.edu
NORITA, Mark ... 760-750-4679.. 33 A
mnorita@csusm.edu
NORLAND, Gretchen ... 785-227-3380 172 A
norlandg@bethanylb.edu
NORLEN, Tracy, C ... 206-281-2977 483 G
tcnorlen@spu.edu
NORLIEN, Cheryl, A ... 320-222-5638 240 F
cheryl.norlien@ridgewater.edu

NORMAN, Antony ... 606-783-2002 184 C
adnorman@moreheadstate.edu
NORMAN, David ... 903-813-2499 430 H
dnorman@austincollege.edu
NORMAN, Donald ... 559-453-2287.. 43 A
donald.norman@fresno.edu
NORMAN, Elizabeth ... 325-670-1222 436 I
enorman@hsutx.edu
NORMAN, Emily ... 402-844-7151 268 H
enorman1@northeast.edu
NORMAN, Eric ... 931-221-7341 417 H
normane@apsu.edu
NORMAN, Josh, L ... 217-581-6077 137 E
jlnorman@eiu.edu
NORMAN, Linda ... 615-343-8876 428 A
linda.norman@vanderbilt.edu
NORMAN, Lindsay ... 706-236-2209 116 B
lnorman@berry.edu
NORMAN, Margie, A ... 903-813-2247 430 H
mnorman@austincollege.edu
NORMAN, Naomi ... 706-542-2187 126 G
nnorman@uga.edu
NORMAN, Peter, E ... 815-599-3465 139 A
pete.norman@highland.edu
NORMAN, Rashawn ... 775-784-6516 271 E
norman@unr.edu
NORMAN, Robert ... 701-858-3058 345 E
robert.norman.1@minotstateau.edu
NORMAN, Stan ... 870-759-4101.. 23 J
snorman@williamsbu.edu
NORMAN, Terry, W ... 608-796-3900 497 O
twnorman@viterbo.edu
NORMAN, Tom ... 507-389-1268 239 D
thomas.norman-1@mnsu.edu
NORMAN-MARZELLA,
Nancy ... 410-287-1541 198 E
nnormormanmarzella@cecil.edu
NORMAND, Jason ... 318-427-4442 189 F
jason@lsua.edu
NORMAND, Sarah ... 603-341-7621 274 C
s.normand@snhu.edu
NORMANDIN, Karen ... 207-453-5129 195 F
president@kvcc.me.edu
NORMANDY, Elizabeth .. 910-521-6180 343 B
elizabeth.normandy@uncp.edu
NORMANN, Karen, R ... 484-664-3496 390 H
karennormann@muhlenberg.edu
NORMENT, Heather ... 843-383-8010 408 B
NORMORE, Clinton ... 660-626-2827 250 A
cnormore@atsu.edu
NORNHOLM, Rick ... 619-594-1889.. 33 D
rnornholm@sdsu.edu
NORNHOLM, Rick ... 619-594-1889.. 33 D
nornholm@sdsu.edu
NORONHA, Gloria ... 617-327-6777 220 C
gloria_noronha@williamjames.edu
NOROUZI, Jessica ... 206-934-3828 483 C
jessica.norouzi@seattlecolleges.edu
NORQUIST, Bruce, R ... 312-329-4192 144 I
bruce.norquist@moody.edu
NORQUIST, Michelle ... 616-988-3660 226 E
mnorquist@kuyper.edu
NORRED, Jonathan ... 706-649-5601 117 I
jnorred@columbustech.edu
NORRIE, James ... 717-815-1423 403 F
jnorrie@ycp.edu
NORRIS, Adam ... 504-280-6939 190 B
amnorris@uno.edu
NORRIS, Darrell ... 517-787-8439 225 E
norrisdarrellr@jccmi.edu
NORRIS, David ... 512-621-4850 430 G
dnorris@escoffier.edu
NORRIS, JR., Davy ... 318-257-3798 192 D
dnorris@latech.edu
NORRIS, Debbie ... 601-925-3225 247 C
dnorris@mc.edu
NORRIS, Debbie ... 601-925-3260 247 C
dnorris@mc.edu
NORRIS, Dena ... 816-604-1527 255 C
dena.norris@mcckc.edu
NORRIS, Emily ... 502-585-9911 184 H
enorris@spalding.edu
NORRIS, Heather ... 828-262-2070 340 I
hulburthm@appstate.edu
NORRIS, Helen ... 714-744-7848.. 36 B
hnorris@chapman.edu
NORRIS, Jeffery, S ... 434-223-6123 467 F
jnorris@hsc.edu
NORRIS, Jessica ... 314-529-9332 255 B
jessica.norris@maryville.edu
NORRIS, Jo Anna ... 202-319-6913.. 92 A
norrisj@cua.edu

NORRIS, John ... 704-330-1448 330 D
jnorris@jcsu.edu
NORRIS, Joye ... 417-836-4127 256 G
joyenorris@missouristate.edu
NORRIS, Katherine ... 630-637-5100 145 F
klnorris@noctrl.edu
NORRIS, Katie ... 870-368-2300.. 20 E
NORRIS, Lee ... 336-334-3110 343 A
clnorris@uncg.edu
NORRIS, Mark, M ... 574-372-5100 155 F
norrismm@grace.edu
NORRIS, Marly ... 415-482-1944.. 41 C
marly.norris@dominican.edu
NORRIS, Michael, C ... 563-884-5469 169 F
michael.norris@palmer.edu
NORRIS, Nancy, E ... 828-448-3150 339 A
nnorris@wpcc.edu
NORRIS, Pamela ... 202-994-6255.. 92 D
pamnorris@gwu.edu
NORRIS, Renee ... 717-867-6283 388 C
norris@lvc.edu
NORRIS, Robert, F ... 630-752-5559 153 C
bob.norris@wheaton.edu
NORRIS, Shawn ... 225-752-4233 187 D
admissions@iticollege.edu
NORRIS, Taylor ... 828-398-7200 332 B
taylornorris@abtech.edu
NORRIS, Terry ... 702-651-5813 270 K
terry.norris@csn.edu
NORRIS, Tiffany ... 205-226-4600.... 4 F
tdnorris@bsc.edu
NORRIS, Todd ... 574-284-4610 160 I
tnorris@saintmarys.edu
NORRIS HALL, Sarah ... 206-543-6277 485 A
sahall@uw.edu
NORRIS-PAULISON,
Robin ... 828-694-1746 332 E
r_paulison@blueridge.edu
NORSTROM, Carolyn ... 317-208-5311 160 A
NORTH, Donald ... 225-771-2552 191 E
dnorth@sulc.edu
NORTH, Jon, D ... 913-971-3600 176 C
jonnorth@mnu.edu
NORTH, Keith ... 406-657-1078 265 E
keith.north@rocky.edu
NORTH, Linda ... 334-745-6437.... 3 G
lnorth@suscc.edu
NORTH, Matthew ... 412-396-4075 383 A
northm@duq.edu
NORTH, Mike ... 865-228-2303 425 B
mnorth@pstcc.edu
NORTH, Paula ... 918-293-5240 368 B
paula.north@okstate.edu
NORTH, Quinn ... 719-884-5000.. 82 B
qinorth@nbc.edu
NORTH, Stephanie ... 503-244-0726 371 E
NORTH, Stephanie, M .. 304-336-8311 490 B
northsm@westliberty.edu
NORTH, Stephen ... 337-521-8914 188 I
stephen.north@solacc.edu
NORTHAM, Andrea ... 507-457-5024 241 F
anortham@winona.edu
NORTHCUT, Kathryn ... 573-341-7276 261 D
northcut@mst.edu
NORTHCUTT, David ... 706-419-1214 118 A
david.northcutt@covenant.edu
NORTHCUTT, Larry ... 903-923-2117 435 H
lnorthcutt@etbu.edu
NORTHCUTT, Melissa ... 337-475-5581 192 E
mnorthcutt@mcneese.edu
NORTHERN, Orathai ... 863-292-3645 106 A
onorthern@polk.edu
NORTHEY, Samantha ... 828-669-8012 331 K
samantha.northey@montreat.edu
NORTHINGTON,
Adrienne ... 919-735-5151 338 H
awnorthington@waynecc.edu
NORTHOVER, Michael .. 971-722-8508 375 D
michael.northover@pcc.edu
NORTHROP, Dale ... 530-422-7913.. 74 G
dnorthropsr@weimar.org
NORTHRUP, Cody ... 575-624-8316 287 B
northrup@nmmi.edu
NORTHRUP, Pam ... 251-981-3771.... 5 A
pam.northrup@columbiasouthern.edu
NORTHUP, Connie ... 913-288-7112 175 B
cnorthup@kckcc.edu
NORTON, Andrew ... 215-702-4318 380 A
anorton@cairn.edu
NORTON, Beth ... 423-697-4792 424 A
NORTON, Daniel ... 601-266-4344 249 F
daniel.norton@usm.edu

NYAGA, Doris .... 319-398-5504 167 J
doris.nyaga@kirkwood.edu
NYAMATHI, Adey .... 949-824-1514.. 69 D
anyamath@uci.edu
NYAMBANE, Gerald, G . 616-698-7111 223 E
NYARADY, Cheryl, M ... 203-576-4588.. 89 C
cnyarady@bridgeport.edu
NYARDY, OSB,
Jeffrey, S .... 724-532-6600 398 A
NYBERG, Connie .... 307-855-2207 501 A
cnyberg@cwc.edu
NYBLAD, Emily .... 847-578-3293 148 F
emily.nyblad@rosalindfranklin.edu
NYCE, Lynda .... 419-772-2542 358 C
l-nyce@onu.edu
NYE, Jamey .... 916-568-3031.. 50 F
nyej@losrios.edu
NYE, Joshua .... 412-731-6000 397 A
jnye@rpts.edu
NYE, Robert .... 585-785-1201 299 F
robert.nye@flcc.edu
NYE, Valerie .... 505-428-1506 288 E
valerie.nye@sfcc.edu
NYE, William .... 801-863-5865 460 D
nyewi@uvu.edu
NYGAARD, Steven .... 310-258-5522.. 51 A
steven.nygaard@lmu.edu
NYHAMMER, Diane .... 630-466-7900 152 K
dnyhammer@waubonsee.edu
NYIRENDA, Stanley, M . 410-651-6672 203 D
smnyirenda@umes.edu
NYNENS, Simon .... 973-642-7068 279 E
simon.nynens@njit.edu
NYQUIST, J. Paul .... 832-252-0735 432 L
paul.nyquist@cbshouston.edu
NYQUIST, Kristen .... 425-640-1459 480 A
NYRE, Joseph, E .... 973-761-9620 283 C
joseph.nyre@shu.edu
NYSTROM, Ellen .... 210-567-2640 456 C
nystrom@uthscsa.edu
NYUL, Renata .... 617-373-7666 217 I
NZEH, Okoroafor .... 706-821-8331 124 B
onzeh@paine.edu
NZEOGWU, Okeleke ...... 702-968-1659 272 C
onzeogwu@roseman.edu
NZINGA, Sekile .... 847-467-7490 146 E
s.nzinga@northwestern.edu
NÚÑEZ, Megan .... 781-283-3583 219 E
mnunez@wellesley.edu

O

OAKES, Barbee .... 702-895-5580 271 D
barbee.oakes@unlv.edu
OAKES, Brian .... 662-560-1128 248 D
boakes@northwestms.edu
OAKES, Ed .... 540-831-5173 469 D
eoakes@radford.edu
OAKES, Mary .... 312-369-6802 136 D
moakes@colum.edu
OAKES, Michael` .... 612-626-1616 243 F
OAKLAND, Aronn .... 507-389-7200 241 C
aronn.oakland@southcentral.edu
OAKS, Crockett .... 417-255-7258 256 H
OAKS, Diane, G .... 949-451-5277.. 65 C
doaks@ivc.edu
OAKS, Joni .... 660-359-3948 257 D
OAKS, Kelly .... 540-231-8771 476 C
koaks@vt.edu
OAKS SMITH, Tonya ..... 318-257-0877 192 D
tonya@latech.edu
OANES, Kari .... 218-299-6531 239 C
kari.oanes@minnesota.edu
OANES, Laura .... 507-457-6909 243 C
loanes@smumn.edu
OATES, Justin, T .... 803-323-2205 414 D
oatesjt@winthrop.edu
OATES, Richard .... 678-717-3947 127 A
richard.oates@ung.edu
OATES, Scott, F .... 804-828-9124 473 B
sfoates@vcu.edu
OATHOUT, Douglas .... 814-871-7470 384 A
oathout002@gannon.edu
OATMAN, Kim, H .... 606-783-2066 184 C
k.oatman@moreheadstate.edu
OBARE, Sherine, O .... 336-285-2805 341 D
soobare@ncat.edu
OBARE, Sherine, O .... 336-285-2800 343 A
soobare@uncg.edu
OBBINK, Kim .... 406-994-6550 264 C
kobbink@montana.edu
OBEIDI, Fida .... 303-365-8388.. 80 F
fida.obeidi@ccd.edu
OBER, Jeffrey .... 208-792-2225 132 A
jrober@lcsc.edu
OBER, Justin .... 413-236-2119 214 A
jober@berkshirecc.edu
OBER, Roxanne .... 412-346-2100 396 C
rober@pia.edu
OBER LAMBERT,
Janet, L .... 800-287-8822 154 A
oberlja@bethanyseminary.edu
OBERACKER, Lexi .... 617-451-0010 217 F
OBERFELD, Jeremy .... 312-236-9000 144 E
OBERFELDT, Kathleen ... 718-390-3435 324 F
koberfel@wagner.edu
OBERHAUSEN,
Stephanie .... 312-899-5100 149 F
OBERHAUSER, Karen .... 608-262-2748 495 D
koberhauser@wisc.edu
OBERHELMAN, Don ...... 805-756-1407.. 29 I
obe@calpoly.edu
OBERHELMAN,
Steven, M .... 979-862-6797 446 F
s-oberhelman@tamu.edu
OBERHOLTZER, Brent ... 717-867-6111 388 C
oberholt@lvc.edu
OBERLANDER, Cyril ...... 707-826-3441.. 33 C
cyril.oberlander@humboldt.edu
OBERLANDER, Cyril ...... 707-826-5877.. 33 C
cyril.oberlander@humboldt.edu
OBERLANDER, Janell .... 307-681-6201 501 G
joberlander@sheridan.edu
OBERLEITNER, Melinda 337-482-5611 193 B
melinda.oberleitner@louisiana.edu
OBERLIN, Kevin .... 864-242-5100 406 H
OBERMAN, Anne .... 320-363-5999 235 F
aoberman@csbsju.edu
OBERMARK, Julie .... 618-545-3015 141 E
jobermark@kaskaskia.edu
OBERMEISTER,
Tuvia, M .... 718-377-0777 311 G
OBERQUELL, Christian .. 406-265-3761 264 E
coberquell@msun.edu
OBERSTE, Christy .... 501-812-2243.. 23 B
coberste@uaptc.edu
OBERSTEIN, Leonard .... 410-484-7200 201 C
loberstein@nirc.edu
OBERSTEIN, Ron .... 510-780-4500.. 47 K
roberstein@lifewest.edu
OBERT, Brian .... 308-345-8109 267 J
obertb@mpcc.edu
OBI, Stacey, L .... 864-592-4618 412 E
obis@sccsc.edu
OBILADE, Sandra, O ..... 270-686-4209 179 J
sandra.obilade@brescia.edu
OBILLE LAFFERTY, Iris .. 858-513-9240.. 68 K
OBIOMON, Pamela .... 936-261-9956 446 C
phobiomon@pvamu.edu
OBISESAN, Thomas, O . 202-806-2550.. 92 F
tobisesan@howard.edu
OBLANDER,
Frances, W .... 912-650-5684 125 F
foblander@southuniversity.edu
OBOURN, Milo .... 585-395-2034 317 E
mobourn@brockport.edu
OBREZA, Thomas .... 352-392-1761 111 A
obreza@ufl.edu
OBRYCKI, Marybeth ...... 973-290-4460 282 I
mobrycki@steu.edu
OBSNIUK, Karen .... 734-432-5648 227 C
kobsniuk@madonna.edu
OBSTA, Kim .... 361-572-6410 457 E
kim.obsta@victoriacollege.edu
OCAMPO, Arturo .... 714-808-4830.. 54 A
aocampo@nocccd.edu
OCAMPO, Carlota .... 202-884-9209.. 94 A
ocampoc@trinitydc.edu
OCAMPO, Kathy .... 928-314-9559.. 11 A
katheline.ocampo@azwestern.edu
OCAMPO, Renata .... 817-202-6320 444 I
r.ocampo@swau.edu
OCASIO, Arcadio .... 787-257-0000 512 B
arcadio.ocasio@upr.edu
OCASIO, Luz .... 787-765-1915 509 B
locasio@opto.inter.edu
OCCHIOGROSSO,
Gabrielle .... 718-405-3225 296 F
gabrielle.occhiogrosso@
mountsaintvincent.edu
OCCHIOGROSSO,
Paul, F .... 212-650-8276 293 D
pocchiogrosso@ccny.cuny.edu
OCEGUERA, Gustavo ..... 951-372-7885.. 59 C
gustavo.oceguera@norcocollege.edu
OCHES, Eric .... 781-891-2937 206 G
roches@bentley.edu
OCHIE, Charles .... 229-500-2221 114 H
charles.ochie@asurams.edu
OCHOA, Eduardo, M ..... 831-582-3532.. 32 B
emochoa@csumb.edu
OCHOA, Hector .... 619-594-6881.. 33 D
provost@sdsu.edu
OCHOA, Marcia .... 831-459-2769.. 71 A
oakesprovost@ucsc.edu
OCHOA, Marilyn .... 732-906-4252 278 G
mochoa@middlesexcc.edu
OCHOA, Vanessa .... 323-265-8721.. 48 J
ochoavj@elac.edu
OCHOA, William, R .... 510-464-3592.. 57 B
wrochoa@peralta.edu
OCHS, Chaya .... 305-944-0035 104 I
OCHSENBEIN, Kim, D ... 865-981-8214 421 C
kim.ochsenbein@maryvillecollege.edu
OCHSNER, Tom, J .... 402-465-2212 268 G
tjo@nebrwesleyan.edu
OCONNELL, Amy .... 401-598-2346 404 D
amy.oconnell@jwu.edu
OCONNOR, Debra .... 516-323-4110 306 M
doconnor@molloy.edu
ODDO, Jennifer .... 330-941-3001 364 H
joddo01@ysu.edu
ODE, Joshua, J .... 989-964-7331 230 E
jjode@svsu.edu
ODEGARD, Esther .... 714-628-4931.. 58 G
odegard_esther@sccollege.edu
ODEGARD-KOESTER,
Melissa .... 573-651-2154 259 H
modegard@semo.edu
ODEH, Magdi .... 773-995-2019 134 K
modeh@csu.edu
ODEH, Omar .... 478-445-6804 119 B
omar.odeh@gcsu.edu
ODEJIMI,
Kristina Bethea .... 207-725-3490 194 C
ODELL, David .... 805-565-7164.. 76 A
dodell@westmont.edu
ODEN, Denise .... 830-591-7355 444 G
ddoden@swtjc.edu
ODEN, JR., Joe .... 304-766-3019 490 D
odenjr@wvstateu.edu
ODEN, John .... 585-567-9338 302 B
john.oden@houghton.edu
ODEN, Lorette .... 309-298-2228 153 A
ls-oden@wiu.edu
ODENTHAL, Paul .... 541-737-0123 375 A
ODENWALD, Joseph ...... 269-782-1270 231 A
president@swmich.edu
ODER, Daniel .... 816-995-2803 258 G
daniel.oder@hcahealthcare.com
ODHIAMBO, Millicent ... 573-986-6191 259 H
maodhiambo@semo.edu
ODI, Henry, U .... 610-758-5923 388 E
huo0@lehigh.edu
ODIN, Eric .... 212-217-4030 299 D
eric_odin@fitnyc.edu
ODOM, David .... 402-363-5732 270 D
dodom@york.edu
ODOM, James .... 870-762-3154.. 17 B
jodom@smail.anc.edu
ODOM, Julia, L .... 701-654-1000.. 32 A
ODOM, Lisa .... 706-295-6928 120 A
lodom@gntc.edu
ODOM, Lorraine .... 206-934-4591 483 B
lorraine.odom@seattlecolleges.edu
ODOM, Mark, R .... 325-793-4780 439 F
modom@mcm.edu
ODOM, Megan .... 530-898-5253.. 30 D
modom@csuchico.edu
ODOM, Stanyell .... 410-455-2632 203 B
stanyell_odom@umbc.edu
ODOM, Tammy .... 479-394-7622.. 23 C
todom@uarichmountain.edu
ODU, Michael .... 619-388-7800.. 61 A
ODU, Michael .... 619-482-6344.. 66 A
modu@swccd.edu
ODUCADO, Joey .... 691-320-2480 504 C
joducado@comfsm.fm
ODUKE, SJ, Charles ...... 315-445-4110 303 I
odukeco@lemoyne.edu
ODUSAMI, Kim .... 978-762-4000 215 D
OECHSLIN, Brad .... 540-362-6000 467 H
boechslin@hollins.edu
OEHLER, David .... 816-604-2385 255 F
david.oehler@mcckc.edu
OEHLER, Elizabeth .... 830-792-7303 443 E
eoehler@schreiner.edu
OEHLER, Laurie .... 281-425-6339 438 I
loehler@lee.edu
OEHLER, Robert .... 608-363-2200 491 H
oehlerr@beloit.edu
OEHLERKING, Kelly ...... 605-718-2931 417 D
kelly.oehlerking@wdt.edu
OEHLERT, Priscilla .... 713-226-5552 453 A
oehlertp@uhd.edu
OEHM, Cathy .... 785-532-5469 175 C
cathyo@ksu.edu
OELFKE, Melanie .... 903-813-2433 430 H
moelfke@austincollege.edu
OELSCHLAGER,
Sharon, G .... 412-396-5028 383 A
goedert@duq.edu
OEN, Ray .... 425-602-3000 477 H
OERLY-BENNETT,
Sandra, K .... 304-293-5242 490 E
sybennett@mail.wvu.edu
OERTEL, Ryan .... 414-443-8825 498 A
ryan.oertel@wlc.edu
OESER, Sara .... 615-966-5085 421 B
sara.oeser@lipscomb.edu
OEST, Danielle .... 608-249-6611 492 H
OESTER, Stephanie .... 541-881-5806 376 F
soester@tvcc.cc
OESTREICH, Melanie, R 610-917-2003 401 G
mroestreich@valleyforge.edu
OFE, Suellen, S .... 334-833-4515.... 5 G
ofe@hawks.huntingdon.edu
OFFBECK, Sean .... 907-260-7422.... 9 D
OFFER, Patricia .... 312-893-7113 137 H
poffer@erikson.edu
OFFERMANN, Joseph ..... 815-280-2211 141 B
joffermann@jjc.edu
OFFICER, Danielle .... 212-237-8185 294 D
dofficer@jjay.cuny.edu
OFIARA, Claire .... 734-432-5873 227 C
cofiara@madonna.edu
OFODILE, Caroline .... 201-447-9242 275 H
cofodile@bergen.edu
OFORLEA, Veronica .... 714-564-6277.. 58 F
oforlea_veronica@sac.edu
OGAWA, Michael, Y ..... 419-372-0433 348 G
mogawa@bgsu.edu
OGAWA, Tim .... 617-228-2051 214 C
togawa@bhcc.mass.edu
OGBAA, Clara .... 203-392-5760.. 86 A
ogbaac1@southernct.edu
OGBUEHI, Alphonso ..... 609-652-4876 283 E
alphonso.ogbuehi@stockton.edu
OGDEN, Alix, R .... 401-825-2387 404 C
aogden@ccri.edu
OGDEN, Denise .... 912-921-2900.. 93 H
OGDEN, Kris .... 434-832-7656 473 E
ogdenk@centralvirginia.edu
OGDEN, Matt .... 414-847-3223 494 C
mattogden@miad.edu
OGDEN, Patricia .... 912-358-3004 125 A
OGDEN, Patricia .... 858-513-9240.. 68 K
patricia.ogden@ashford.edu
OGDEN, Patrick .... 302-831-4135.. 91 C
pogden@udel.edu
OGDEN, Rachel .... 814-860-5118 387 D
rogden@lecom.edu
OGDEN, Thomas, A ...... 412-268-2328 380 C
togden@andrew.cmu.edu
OGDEN, Timothy, A ...... 260-982-5012 159 J
taogden@manchester.edu
OGEA, Angelique .... 337-475-5154 192 E
aogea@mcneese.edu
OGEA, Reggie, R .... 504-282-4455 190 F
rogea@nobts.edu
OGEKA, Alex .... 610-683-4112 394 D
ogeka@kuf.org
OGG, Laurie .... 707-664-2036.. 34 B
laurie.ogg@sonoma.edu
OGIBA, Shawn .... 212-229-5300 308 A
ogibas@newschool.edu
OGILVIE, Craig .... 406-994-4145 264 C
craig.ogilvie@montana.edu
OGILVIE, Susan .... 253-272-1126 481 E
sogilvie@ncad.edu
OGLE, Chad .... 859-572-6371 184 E
oglec1@nku.edu
OGLE, Christophor, M .. 920-748-8111 494 J
oglec@ripon.edu
OGLE, Josh .... 541-956-7039 376 A
jogle@roguecc.edu
OGLE, Kaci .... 256-782-5405.... 6 A
kogle@jsu.edu
OGLESBEE, Ariane .... 509-777-4320 486 C
aoglesbee@whitworth.edu
OGLESBY, Lamar .... 848-932-4179 282 A
lo170@ored.rutgers.edu

OLIVER, Sarah, E ... 563-333-6424 169 G
oliversarahe@sau.edu

OLIVER, Sharon, J ... 919-530-5313 341 E
soliver@nccu.edu

OLIVER, Sharon, M ... 207-581-1585 196 G
smoliver@maine.edu

OLIVER, Shawn ... 609-497-7814 280 C
shawn.oliver@ptsem.edu

OLIVER, Tamara ... 607-844-8222 322 D
tmo@tompkinscortland.edu

OLIVER, Tanya, W ... 252-862-1267 337 C
toliver@roanokechowan.edu

OLIVER, Tom ... 217-228-5432 147 F
oliveth@quincy.edu

OLIVER, Tricia ... 413-572-8575 213 F
toliver@westfield.ma.edu

OLIVER-STANLEY,
Aisha ... 212-998-1212 309 F

OLIVER-VERONESI,
Robin ... 215-746-3535 400 F
uhs-info@psu.edu

OLIVER-VERONESI,
Robin, E ... 814-865-6555 391 G
reo133@psu.edu

OLIVERAS, Esther ... 212-217-5546 299 D
esther_oliveras@fitnyc.edu

OLIVERAS, Ivette ... 787-840-2575 509 I
ivoliveras@psm.edu

OLIVERAS, Jose ... 787-844-8181 513 A
jose.oliveras2@upr.edu

OLIVERAS, Marilyn ... 787-284-1912 508 E
molivera@ponce.inter.edu

OLIVERI, Dee ... 949-582-4500.. 65 D
doliveri@saddleback.edu

OLIVERI, Mary, A ... 570-961-7855 387 B
oliverim@lackawanna.edu

OLIVERIO, Robert ... 602-489-5300.. 10 F
robert.oliverio@arizonachristian.edu

OLIVEROS, Claire ... 916-691-7487.. 50 H
claire.oliveros@crc.losrios.edu

OLIVEROS, Jon ... 847-397-0300 132 H

OLIVIA, Elizabeth ... 903-510-2362 452 A
eoli@tjc.edu

OLIVIERI-LENAHAN,
Elizabeth ... 914-633-2547 302 E
eolivieri@iona.edu

OLIVO, Christiane ... 970-542-3191.. 81 N
christiane.olivo@morgancc.edu

OLIVO, Cynthia ... 626-585-7074.. 56 D
cdolivo@pasadena.edu

OLIVO, Michael ... 516-323-4840 306 M
molivo@molloy.edu

OLKOWSKI, Mark ... 920-465-5045 495 F
olkowskm@uwgb.edu

OLLE-LAJOIE, Maureen . 715-425-3799 496 F
maureen.olle-lajoie@uwrf.edu

OLLER, Jeremy ... 405-974-5347 370 I
joller@uco.edu

OLLIFF, Kenneth ... 314-977-2925 259 F
knneth.a.olliff@slu.edu

OLLIFF, Martin ... 334-983-6556.... 7 C
molliff@troy.edu

OLLIFF, Martin ... 334-983-6556.... 7 C

OLLINGER, Nancy ... 610-902-8276 379 G
nancy.ollinger@cabrini.edu

OLLSON, Joanne ... 413-782-1343 220 A
joanne.ollson@wne.edu

OLMOS, Amanda ... 888-491-8686.. 75 F

OLMOS, Ernesto, F ... 806-371-5456 429 E
efolmos@actx.edu

OLMSTADT, William ... 318-675-5449 189 I
will.olmstadt@lsuhs.edu

OLMSTEAD, Karen, L .... 410-548-3374 204 D
klolmstead@salisbury.edu

OLMSTEAD, Patrick ... 818-401-1041.. 39 D
polmstead@columbiacollege.edu

OLMSTEAD, Steve ... 918-293-3812 368 B
steve.olmstead@okstate.edu

OLMSTED, Michelle ... 513-244-4475 356 F
michelle.omsted@msj.edu

OLNEY, Kent ... 815-939-5231 147 A
kolney@olivet.edu

OLOWUDE, Brian ... 805-893-4411.. 70 E
brian.olowude@sa.ucsb.edu

OLPHIE, Elizabeth ... 229-333-7837 127 E
ewolphie@valdosta.edu

OLSEN, Ann, E ... 502-272-8133 179 H
aolsen@bellarmine.edu

OLSEN, Chris ... 208-496-9510 130 I
olsenc@byui.edu

OLSEN, Christopher ... 812-237-2309 156 D
chris.olsen@indstate.edu

OLSEN, Danny, R ... 801-422-5648 458 H
danny_olsen@byu.edu

OLSEN, Elisa ... 713-226-5519 453 A
olsene@uhd.edu

OLSEN, Jane ... 320-308-4958 240 I
jolsen@stcloudstate.edu

OLSEN, Jeff ... 713-942-3466 454 G
jolsen@stthom.edu

OLSEN, Jennifer ... 334-347-2623.... 2 A
jolsen@escc.edu

OLSEN, Katie ... 973-328-5058 276 J
kolsen@ccm.edu

OLSEN, Keith ... 402-599-7927 269 K
keith.olsen@unmc.edu

OLSEN, Levi ... 585-343-0055 300 F
ltolsen@genesee.edu

OLSEN, Mandy ... 866-492-5336 244 F
miranda.olsen@mail.waldenu.edu

OLSEN, Micah ... 307-681-6007 501 G
molsen@sheridan.edu

OLSEN, Michelle, D ... 417-836-5274 256 G
molsen@missouristate.edu

OLSEN, Morgan, R ... 480-727-9920.. 10 J
morgan.r.olsen@asu.edu

OLSEN, Nancy ... 218-879-0715 238 B
nancy.olsen@fdltcc.edu

OLSEN, Pete ... 831-645-1362.. 52 G
polsen@mpc.edu

OLSEN, Steven, M ... 716-878-4113 317 F
olsensw@buffalostate.edu

OLSEN, Taimi ... 864-656-4542 407 E
taimio@clemson.edu

OLSHINE FRASIER,
Rachel ... 903-233-4410 439 A
rachelolshine@letu.edu

OLSON, Alexandra ... 847-735-5231 142 A
aolson@lakeforest.edu

OLSON, Barry ... 919-513-3402 342 A
barry_olson@ncsu.edu

OLSON, Ben ... 907-745-3201.... 9 C
bolson@akbible.edu

OLSON, Bob ... 904-276-6775 107 C
bobolson@sjrstate.edu

OLSON, Camron, M ... 641-422-4281 168 G
camron.olson@niacc.edu

OLSON, Cari ... 701-858-3323 345 E
cari.olson@minotstateu.edu

OLSON, Chris ... 912-478-5357 120 C
cgolson@georgiasouthern.edu

OLSON, Cynthia ... 612-381-8124 235 K
colson@dunwoody.edu

OLSON, David ... 910-962-3102 343 C
olsond@uncw.edu

OLSON, Deborah ... 863-784-7275 108 F
deborah.olson@southflorida.edu

OLSON, Dustin ... 303-273-3000.. 79 J
dolson1@mines.edu

OLSON, Eric ... 610-902-8275 379 G
eric.j.olson@cabrini.edu

OLSON, Ernest ... 309-438-1946 140 D
ewolson@ilstu.edu

OLSON, Gary, A ... 716-839-8210 298 A
golson@daemen.edu

OLSON, Heidi, L ... 320-222-5209 240 F
heidi.olson@ridgewater.edu

OLSON, Jayden ... 701-774-4546 346 E
jayden.olson@willistonstate.edu

OLSON, Jeffery, D ... 651-638-6241 234 D
jeff-olson@bethel.edu

OLSON, John ... 425-388-9555 480 B
jolson@everettcc.edu

OLSON, Jon ... 507-457-5021 241 F

OLSON, Joshua ... 906-487-1217 228 A
jolson@mtu.edu

OLSON, Julie ... 605-642-6215 416 E
julie.olson@bhsu.edu

OLSON, Keith ... 304-327-4247 489 I
kolson@bluefieldstate.edu

OLSON, Kim ... 920-996-2933 498 F
olsonk@fvtc.edu

OLSON, Kirsten, G ... 805-437-3784.. 30 C
kirsten.olson@csuci.edu

OLSON, Kris ... 218-299-3024 235 H
krisolson@cord.edu

OLSON, Kristin ... 562-938-4095.. 48 F
kolson@lbcc.edu

OLSON, Lane ... 916-348-4689.. 41 H
lolson@epic.edu

OLSON, Larry ... 740-474-8896 358 A
lolson@ohiochristian.edu

OLSON, Mary Ellen ... 920-403-3181 495 B
maryellen.olson@snc.edu

OLSON, Matthew ... 781-280-3802 215 B
olsonm@middlesex.mass.edu

OLSON, Megan ... 907-786-1764.... 9 J
msolson5@alaska.edu

OLSON, Mike ... 480-314-2102.. 15 P

OLSON, Missy ... 541-440-7865 376 G
missy.olson@umpqua.edu

OLSON, Nancy ... 507-537-6544 241 D
nancy.olson@smsu.edu

OLSON, Paul ... 701-252-3467 347 B
paul.olson@uj.edu

OLSON, Robert ... 253-833-9111 480 I
rolson@greenriver.edu

OLSON, Robin ... 614-251-4700 358 B
olsonr@ohiodominican.edu

OLSON, Roger, T ... 218-299-3682 235 H
rolson@cord.edu

OLSON, Sara ... 402-465-2159 268 G
solson@nebrwesleyan.edu

OLSON, Sara ... 863-680-3965 100 H
solson@flsouthern.edu

OLSON, Scott ... 480-245-7993.. 12 M
scott.olson@ibcs.edu

OLSON, Scott, R ... 507-457-5003 241 F
solson@winona.edu

OLSON, Sharon ... 562-985-5585.. 31 D
sharon.olson@csulb.edu

OLSON, Shelly ... 715-833-6675 498 E
solson@cvtc.edu

OLSON, Stephen ... 765-998-5119 161 C
stolson@taylor.edu

OLSON, Todd ... 202-687-6318.. 92 E
tao4@georgetown.edu

OLSON, Tomoko ... 281-998-6146 442 K
tomoko.olson@sjcd.edu

OLSON, Wendy ... 509-777-4313 486 C
wolson@whitworth.edu

OLSON, Zac ... 541-552-7672 376 B

OLSON-BUCHANAN,
Julie ... 559-278-2482.. 31 B
julieo@csufresno.edu

OLSON-KOPP, Kim ... 608-796-3267 497 O
kmolsonkopp@viterbo.edu

OLSON-LOY, Sandra ... 320-589-6013 244 B
olsonloy@morris.umn.edu

OLSON-NIKUNEN,
Shari, L ... 602-243-8035.. 14 A
shari.olson@southmountaincc.edu

OLSTEIN, Binyamin ... 847-982-2500 138 I
olstein@htc.edu

OLSZEWSKI, Gabe ... 254-710-1181 431 E
gabe_olszewski@baylor.edu

OLSZEWSKI, Kristen ... 215-489-2946 382 B
kristen.olszewski@delval.edu

OLSZEWSKI, Ryan ... 330-569-5332 353 G
ryan.olszewski@abm.com

OLTROGGE, Michael ... 402-494-2311 268 A
moltrogge@thenicc.edu

OLVER, Kristen ... 262-646-6519 494 F
kolver@nashotah.edu

OLVER, Thomas ... 989-386-6675 228 B
tolver@midmich.edu

OLVERA, Tina ... 323-466-6663.. 43 H

OLWELL, David ... 360-688-2731 482 I
dolwell@stmartin.edu

OMANN, Bernie ... 320-308-2122 240 I
bomann@stcloudstate.edu

OMAR, Richard ... 646-216-2863 308 G
romar@nycda.edu

OMAR, Sohair ... 203-575-8281.. 87 B
somar@nv.edu

OMARY, M. Bishr ... 848-445-9833 282 A
bishr.omary@rutgers.edu

OMBRELLO, Joseph ... 906-227-1188 228 I
jombrell@nmu.edu

OMEN, Shielen ... 218-679-2860 242 U

OMENITSCH, Katie ... 202-884-9301.. 94 A
omenitschka@trinitydc.edu

OMER, Aftab ... 707-765-1836.. 52 B

OMER, Nagieh ... 312-261-3004 145 D
nomer@nl.edu

OMER, Nicole ... 801-957-4209 461 C
nicole.omer@slcc.edu

OMINSKY, Paul ... 609-258-6688 280 D
pominsky@princeton.edu

OMOJOKUN,
Emmanuel ... 804-524-5322 476 D
eomojokun@vsu.edu

OMOTO, Allen ... 909-621-8218.. 57 E
dean_faculty@pitzer.edu

OMURA, Kanae ... 626-571-8811.. 73 E
kanaeo@uwest.edu

ONAPITO, Amanda ... 847-945-8800 151 C
aonapito@tiu.edu

ONDER, David ... 828-565-4077 335 C
donder@haywood.edu

ONDERDONK, John, S . 626-395-4724.. 28 J
jonderdo@caltech.edu

ONDERKO, Daniel ... 903-566-7277 456 A
donderko@uttyler.edu

ONDRIZEK, Megan, M . 305-284-3667 113 C
m.ondrizek@umiami.edu

ONEAL, Joey ... 918-631-3045 371 C
joey-oneal@utulsa.edu

ONG, Meaghan ... 314-719-3661 253 E
mong@fontbonne.edu

ONG, Teresa ... 650-949-7794.. 42 I
ongteresa@fhda.edu

ONGARO, Guilio ... 714-997-6672.. 36 B
ongaro@chapman.edu

ONISHI, Joni, Y ... 808-934-2514 129 I
jonishi@hawaii.edu

ONKEN, Marina ... 715-425-3335 496 F
marina.onken@uwrf.edu

ONNEN, Kendi ... 309-467-6303 138 A
registrar@eureka.edu

ONO, Kay ... 808-455-0453 130 C
kayono@hawaii.edu

ONO, Mika ... 909-748-6297.. 72 F
mika_ono@redlands.edu

ONODERA, Yasushi ... 479-964-0832.. 18 C
yonodera@atu.edu

ONOFRIO, Marshall ... 609-921-7100 281 B
monofrio@rider.edu

ONORATO, Suzanne ... 860-486-0744.. 89 D
suzanne.onorato@uconn.edu

ONTANEDA, Mary Kate . 920-465-2207 495 F
ontanedm@uwgb.edu

ONTIVEROS, Juan ... 512-232-4191 455 A
juan.ontiveros@austin.utexas.edu

ONTL, Lynn ... 518-255-5225 319 C
ontll@cobleskill.edu

ONUNWOR, Enyinda ... 651-846-1542 241 B
enyinda.onunwor@saintpaul.edu

ONUSKO, Mark ... 216-397-1756 353 O
monusko@jcu.edu

ONWUACHI-WILLIG,
Angela ... 617-353-3112 207 E
aow@bu.edu

ONWUNLI, Agatha ... 850-599-3115 109 I
agatha.onwunli@famu.edu

ONYEAGHALA, Raphael 507-537-6218 241 D
raphael.onyeaghala@smsu.edu

OOMMEN, Jose ... 740-397-9000 356 G
jose.oommen@mvnu.edu

OOTEN, Timothy, D ... 304-896-7658 488 I
tim.ooten@southernwv.edu

OPARAH, Chinyere ... 415-422-6136.. 72 J
jcoparah@usfca.edu

OPATZ, Patrick ... 651-779-3346 237 H
patrick.opatz@century.edu

OPAVA, William ... 617-236-8812 209 G
wopava@fisher.edu

OPDYCKE, Anita ... 312-567-7553 140 A
aopdycke@iit.edu

OPGENORTH, Timothy .. 414-229-4541 496 B
opgenort@uwm.edu

OPITZ, Brian, R ... 724-287-8711 379 E
brian.opitz@bc3.edu

OPITZ, Don ... 312-362-6426 136 H
dopitz@depaul.edu

OPITZ, Donald, D ... 724-458-2143 384 G
opitzdd@gcc.edu

OPOKU, Michael ... 763-433-1272 237 D
michael.opoku@anokaramsey.edu

OPPATT, Ron ... 864-231-2000 406 F
roppatt@andersonuniversity.edu

OPPENHEIMER,
Phillip, R ... 209-946-2561.. 71 E
poppenhe@pacific.edu

OPPERMAN, Amanda ... 415-561-6555.. 58 B

OPPERMAN, John ... 806-742-2392 450 F
john.opperman@ttu.edu

OPPERMAN, Lynne ... 214-828-8201 446 F
lopperman@tamu.edu

OPPERMAN,
Mary George ... 607-255-3621 297 F
mgo5@cornell.edu

OPPMANN, Andrew, J .. 615-898-7800 422 C
andrew.oppmann@mtsu.edu

OPPO, Delia, W ... 508-289-2681 220 E
doppo@whoi.edu

OPSATA, Rebecca ... 510-464-3213.. 57 B
ropsata@peralta.edu

OQUENDO, Carmen ... 787-250-1912 508 D
coquendo@metro.inter.edu

OQUENDO, Diane 646-660-6154 292 L diane.oquendo@baruch.cuny.edu
ORANGE, Taur, D 212-217-4170 299 D taur_orange@fitnyc.edu
ORANSKY, Elissa 949-451-5472.. 65 C eoransky@ivc.edu
ORANTE, Newin 650-738-4100.. 62 L oranten@smccd.edu
ORAVEC, Timothy 213-738-6710.. 66 B toravec@swlaw.edu
ORAVECZ, Joseph 508-531-1276 212 D joravecz@bridgew.edu
ORAVETZ, Teresa 203-332-5014.. 86 F toravetz@hcc.commnet.edu
ORCHARD, James, P 651-641-8705 235 I orchard@csp.edu
ORCHARD, Milissa, M .. 651-641-8268 235 I hrorchard@csp.edu
ORCHARD, Sue 360-442-2301 481 D sorchard@lowercolumbia.edu
ORCUTT, Jill 209-201-8531.. 70 A jorcutt2@ucmerced.edu
ORD, Anna, S 757-352-4673 470 B annashi@regent.edu
ORDONEZ, Bonnie 412-809-5336 396 E ordonez.bonnie@ptcollege.edu
ORDONEZ, Lisa, D 858-822-0830.. 70 C lordonez@ucsd.edu
OREDEIN, Ade 270-852-8607 182 F ade.oredein@kctcs.edu
OREHEK, Ashley 270-384-8250 183 G oreheka@lindsey.edu
OREIRO, David 360-676-2772 481 F doreiro@nwic.edu
ORELLANA, Victoria 201-360-4121 278 C vorellana@hccc.edu
OREM, Christopher, D .. 540-568-7208 468 C oremcd@jmu.edu
ORENDER, Patricia 386-752-1822 100 B patricia.orender@fgc.edu
ORENDORFF, Jay 415-338-2862.. 33 E jayo@sfsu.edu
ORENGA, Juan 787-746-1400 507 B
ORENGO-ORTEGA, Orlando 787-993-0000 512 A orlando.orengo@upr.edu
ORF, Michael 417-255-7272 256 H michaelorf@missouristate.edu
ORF, Robert, W 603-535-2461 275 A rorf@plymouth.edu
ORIANO, Angela 281-425-6453 438 I aoriano@lee.edu
ORIHUELA, Omar 619-482-6360.. 66 A oorihuela@swccd.edu
ORIHUELA, Ruthanne .... 303-556-3595.. 80 F ruthanne.orihuela@ccd.edu
ORIO, Julie, J 415-422-2823.. 72 J orioj@usfca.edu
ORIOLO, Michael 315-866-0300 301 D orioloma@herkimer.edu
ORIS, James, T 513-529-3734 356 A orisjt@miamioh.edu
ORITZ, Fernando 509-313-4054 480 F oritz2@gonzaga.edu
ORKIN, Michael 510-466-7308.. 57 C morkin@peralta.edu
ORKISZEWSKI, Paul 828-262-2801 340 I orkiszewskip@appstate.edu
ORLANDO, Karen 949-451-5511.. 65 C korlando@ivc.edu
ORLANDO, Matthew 207-725-3804 194 C morlando@bowdoin.edu
ORLANDO, Michael 517-264-7601 230 H morlando@sienaheights.edu
ORLANDO, Stephen, F .. 352-392-0186 111 A sfo@ufl.edu
ORLASKE, Michelle 269-782-1486 231 A mbogue@swmich.edu
ORLAUSKI, Brian 951-639-5080.. 53 A borlausk@msjc.edu
ORLIKOFF, Robert 252-744-6010 341 A orlikoffr17@ecu.edu
ORLOFF, Micah 951-639-5440.. 53 A morloff@msjc.edu
ORLOV, Ariel 312-662-4316 132 G aorlov@adler.edu
ORLUCK, Gary 701-858-4016 345 E gary.orluck@minotstateu.edu
ORMAN, Larry 601-877-6131 245 A leorman@alcorn.edu
ORMASEN, Nickolas 315-229-5908 314 D nick@stlawu.edu
ORMON, Taylor 601-925-7782 247 C tormon@mc.edu
ORMOND, Tom 717-477-1371 395 B
ORMSBEE, Christine 405-744-1000 367 G ormsbee@okstate.edu
ORNDORFF, Barry 540-858-7000 474 C
ORNDORFF, Cathy 304-293-5305 490 E cathy.orndorff@mail.wvu.edu
ORNDORFF, Robert, M . 814-865-2377 391 G rmo104@psu.edu
ORNE, Tracy 217-641-4300 141 A torne@jwcc.edu
ORNELAS, Armida 818-364-7796.. 49 C ornelaao@lamission.edu
ORNELAS, Nohemy 805-922-6966.. 24 I nornelas@hancockcollege.edu
ORNER, Lita, J 240-500-2264 199 C ljorner@hagerstowncc.edu
ORONA, Frank 505-747-2161 287 H forona@nnmc.edu
ORONA, John 210-486-2792 429 B jorona3@alamo.edu
OROPEZA, Rachel 305-809-3203.. 97 O rachel.oropeza@cfk.edu
OROS, Richard 480-517-8202.. 13 G richard.oros@riosalado.edu
OROSZ, David 216-373-5310 357 F dorosz@ndc.edu
OROSZ, Theresa 732-906-2533 278 G torosz@middlesexcc.edu
OROZ, Andres 541-867-8511 374 F andres.oroz@oregoncoast.edu
OROZCO, Daniel 512-863-1346 445 C orozcod@southwestern.edu
OROZCO, Darcy 303-753-6046.. 83 F dorozco@rmcad.edu
OROZCO, Edith 210-486-2451 429 B eorozco4@alamo.edu
OROZCO, Jessica 305-474-6863 107 F jorozco@stu.edu
OROZCO, Lisa 843-863-7954 407 B lorozco@csuniv.edu
ORR, Amy, K 843-953-7333 408 C orra@cofc.edu
ORR, Bradford 734-763-1290 231 H orr@umich.edu
ORR, Cheryl 580-477-7710 371 D cheryl.orr@newmoodle.wosc.edu
ORR, David 318-869-5087 186 F dorr@centenary.edu
ORR, Elisabeth 562-938-4446.. 48 F eorr@lbcc.edu
ORR, Ethan, R 520-621-0906.. 16 D eorr@arizona.edu
ORR, Jamar 312-341-3527 148 E jorr05@roosevelt.edu
ORR, Jay 909-607-7302.. 37 C jay.orr@cgu.edu
ORR, Jim 325-674-2659 428 F jmo10a@acu.edu
ORR, Kristy 254-710-3737 431 E kristy_orr@baylor.edu
ORR, Mandy 770-533-7012 122 B morr@laniertech.edu
ORR, Mark 916-278-6348.. 32 D athletic.director@csus.edu
ORR, Michael, T 518-580-5705 315 F morr@skidmore.edu
ORR, Ray, K 253-535-7380 482 A orrrk@plu.edu
ORR, Richard 724-589-2700 399 D rorr@thiel.edu
ORR, Robert, C 301-405-0467 202 H rorr1@umd.edu
ORR, Rodney 214-887-2976 435 F rorr@dts.edu
ORR, Shaun 208-496-9340 130 I orrs@byui.edu
ORR, Shawn 419-289-5733 347 J sorr3@ashland.edu
ORR, Stephanie, W 850-263-3261.. 95 P sworr@baptistcollege.edu
ORR, Susan, L 603-513-1310 274 G susan.orr@granite.edu
ORR, Sylvia 623-935-8413.. 13 A sylvia.orr@estrellamountain.edu
ORR, Tim 530-226-4725.. 64 E torr@simpsonu.edu
ORR, Trina 828-227-7290 343 E torr@wcu.edu
ORSCHELN, Paul 573-592-5918 262 E paul.orscheln@westminster-mo.edu
ORSINI, SPHR, Teri 704-337-2297 339 F orsinit@queens.edu
ORTA, Jose 305-223-4561 107 B jorta@sjvcs.edu
ORTA-PEREZ, Angel 951-571-6379.. 59 B angel.orta-perez@mvc.edu
ORTALE, Lynn 215-248-7030 381 A ortalel@chc.edu
ORTBERG, Jennifer, L ... 714-895-8965.. 38 A jortberg@gwc.cccd.edu
ORTEGA, Bethania 718-960-8819 294 A budget.ortega@lehman.cuny.edu
ORTEGA, Bridgett 678-916-2678 115 I bortega@johnmarshall.edu
ORTEGA, Eleazar 406-771-5136 264 F eleazar.ortega@gfcmsu.edu
ORTEGA, Elias 773-256-3000 144 B
ORTEGA, J. Martin 210-486-0721 429 C jortega@alamo.edu
ORTEGA, Janet, L 602-243-8287.. 14 A janet.ortega@southmountaincc.edu
ORTEGA, Lenin 212-463-0400 322 G lenin.ortega@touro.edu
ORTEGA, Ricardo 618-537-6533 144 A
ORTEGA, Sharon 847-397-0300 132 H
ORTEGA BELTRAN, Edwin 530-661-5729.. 77 D eortega@yccd.edu
ORTEGO, Carla 337-521-8922 188 I carla.ortego@solacc.edu
ORTEN, Mark 802-443-5626 462 E orten@middlebury.edu
ORTEZ, James 559-325-5264.. 67 A james.ortez@cloviscollege.edu
ORTIKOV, Khudoyor, S . 832-230-5555 440 E khudoyor@na.edu
ORTIZ, Angel 787-725-6500 505 G aortiz@albizu.edu
ORTIZ, Arthur 713-525-3848 454 G ortiza@stthom.edu
ORTIZ, Beni 773-442-5135 146 A b-ortiz7@neiu.edu
ORTIZ, Carmen, B 787-723-4481 506 A bethzaida.ortiz@ceaprc.edu
ORTIZ, Eduardo 787-250-1912 508 D ehortiz@metro.inter.edu
ORTIZ, Eickel 212-616-7245 301 C eickel.ortiz@helenefuld.edu
ORTIZ, Elizabeth, F 312-362-8588 136 H eortiz4@depaul.edu
ORTIZ, Fernando 714-564-5230.. 58 F ortiz_fernando@sac.edu
ORTIZ, Francisco 386-822-7300 112 A fortiz1@stetson.edu
ORTIZ, Francisco 260-665-4171 161 E ortizf@trine.edu
ORTIZ, Francisco 787-761-0640 511 E presidente@utcpr.edu
ORTIZ, Glorimar 787-738-2161 512 C glorimar.ortiz7@upr.edu
ORTIZ, Hilda, L 787-863-2390 508 B hilda.ortiz@fajardo.inter.edu
ORTIZ, Hiram 787-850-9312 512 D hiram.ortiz@upr.edu
ORTIZ, Jacqueline 772-466-4822.. 95 N
ORTIZ, Jose 201-360-4390 278 C 0188mgr@follett.com
ORTIZ, Jose 509-777-4332 486 C jortiz@whitworth.edu
ORTIZ, Juanita 405-733-7413 369 E jrortiz@rose.edu
ORTIZ, Judy 714-463-7508.. 51 B jortiz@ketchum.edu
ORTIZ, Kenneth 952-996-1313 234 B kenneth.ortiz@bethanygu.edu
ORTIZ, Kristina 212-752-1530 304 A kgibson@limcollege.edu
ORTIZ, Laura 630-466-7900 152 K lortiz@waubonsee.edu
ORTIZ, Lillian, M 508-854-4232 215 F lmortiz@qcc.mass.edu
ORTIZ, Luis 800-567-2344 492 C lortiz@menominee.edu
ORTIZ, Luis, E 787-894-2828 513 C luis.ortiz52@upr.edu
ORTIZ, Luz 787-864-2222 508 C luz.ortiz@guayama.inter.edu
ORTIZ, Madeline 787-850-9392 512 D madeline.ortiz1@upr.edu
ORTIZ, Maribel 787-758-2525 512 F maribel.ortiz5@upr.edu
ORTIZ, Mario 607-777-2311 316 B mortiz@binghamton.edu
ORTIZ, Mary Lou, D 814-865-7641 391 G mzo67@psu.edu
ORTIZ, María, C 787-766-1717 510 G um_mortiz@uagm.edu
ORTIZ, Mati 716-286-8504 309 H mortiz@niagara.edu
ORTIZ, Michael 508-830-5133 213 D mortiz@maritime.edu
ORTIZ, Michael 214-887-5391 435 F mortiz@dts.edu
ORTIZ, Mildred 787-264-1940 508 F milortiz@intersg.edu
ORTIZ, Nancy 210-297-9198 430 L nortiz@baptisthealthsystem.com
ORTIZ, Vanessa 787-257-7373 510 F ortizv2@uagm.edu
ORTIZ, Wanda 787-746-1400 507 B
ORTIZ, Zoraida 787-743-7979 510 H zortiz@suagm.edu
ORTIZ-BELTRAN, Juan .. 787-780-5134 509 E
ORTIZ-GALLEGOS, Thomasinia 505-428-1238 288 E thomasinia.ortizgall@sfcc.edu
ORTIZ GARCIA, Angel .. 787-725-6500 505 G aortiz@albizu.edu
ORTIZ-HARVEY, Cristina 646-313-8000 295 D financial.aid@guttman.cuny.edu
ORTIZ-MERCADO, Sonia 916-608-6653.. 50 I ortiz-s@flc.losrios.edu
ORTIZ-MORALES, Jonathan 787-857-3600 507 M jonathanortiz@br.inter.edu
ORTIZ-PADILLAT, Darinel 787-993-8861 512 A darinel.ortiz@upr.edu
ORTIZ PARRA, Lelis 954-322-4460 102 J ortizlelis@jmvu.edu
ORTIZ-VARGAS, Elizabeth 787-993-8922 512 A elizabeth.ortiz3@upr.edu
ORTIZ-WALTERS, Rowena 210-436-3706 442 J rortizwalters@stmarytx.edu
ORTLIEB, Evan, T 843-953-5097 407 C eortlieb@citadel.edu
ORTLOFF, Debora 585-785-1778 299 F debora.ortloff@flcc.edu
ORTLOFF, Debora 585-394-1351 299 F debora.ortloff@flcc.edu
ORTMAN, Brad 971-722-4477 375 D brad.ortman@pcc.edu
ORTON, Piper 781-283-2522 219 E
ORTON, Ty 701-483-2486 345 C ty.orton@dickinsonstate.edu
ORTQUIST-AHRENS, Leslie 859-985-3670 179 I ortquistahrensl@berea.edu
ORTSCHEID, Tory 920-465-2598 495 F ortschet@uwgb.edu
ORTÍZ, Kendra 787-786-3030 511 A kortiz@ucb.edu.pr
ORVIS, Arleen 563-387-1005 168 B orvisarl@luther.edu
ORWICK OGDEN, Sheri 419-372-7557 348 G sorwick@bgsu.edu
ORWIG, Greg 509-777-4580 486 C gorwig@whitworth.edu
ORZECHOWSKI, Michael 212-280-1301 323 K morzechowski@uts.columbia.edu
ORZEL, Linda 314-340-3624 254 A orzell@hssu.edu
ORZOLEK, Mariah 989-463-7367 221 B orzolekmv@alma.edu
OSAE-KWAPONG, John, D 516-572-7771 307 E john.osaekwapong@ncc.edu
OSAKWE, Nneka-Nora .. 229-500-2354 114 H nora.osakwe@asurams.edu
OSAKWE, Rebecca 504-520-7562 193 E rosakwe@xula.edu
OSATHANUGRAH, Vim . 702-463-2122 272 G vimo@wongu.org
OSBAHR, Diane 712-325-3235 167 I dosbahr@iwcc.edu
OSBORN, Alison 334-745-6437.... 3 G aosborn@suscc.edu
OSBORN, Aurora 850-474-2914 111 F aosborn@uwf.edu
OSBORN, Carol 719-587-7341.. 77 G cosborn@adams.edu

OSBORN, Edward, H ..... 860-465-5043.. 85 H
osborne@easternct.edu
OSBORN, Emily Lynn ... 773-702-1234 151 E
elosborn@uchicago.edu
OSBORN, Jeffrey .... 609-771-3080 276 I
josborn@tcnj.edu
OSBORN, Kevin .... 918-335-6223 368 E
kosborn@okwu.edu
OSBORN, Peter .... 616-949-5300 223 C
peter.osborn@cornerstone.edu
OSBORNE, C. Damon ... 419-434-5978 362 D
dosborne@findlay.edu
OSBORNE, Curtis .... 510-649-2477.. 44 B
cosborne@gtu.edu
OSBORNE, Daniel .... 919-365-7711 340 E
OSBORNE, Jason .... 513-529-6721 356 A
provost@miamioh.edu
OSBORNE, John .... 305-428-5700 104 F
josborne@aii.edu
OSBORNE, John .... 405-425-5463 367 C
john.osborne@oc.edu
OSBORNE, Kevin .... 336-734-7369 334 F
kosborne@forsythtech.edu
OSBORNE, Kimberly ...... 336-334-4314 343 A
k_osborn@uncg.edu
OSBORNE, Maurice .... 512-505-6433 438 A
mdosborne@htu.edu
OSBORNE, Natalie .... 912-538-3157 125 G
nosborne@southeasterntech.edu
OSBORNE, Shelley .... 704-991-0203 338 C
sosborne7501@stanly.edu
OSBOURNE, Sarah .... 207-947-4591 194 B
admissions@bealcollege.edu
OSBUN-MANLEY,
Kirsten, E .... 419-772-1998 358 C
k-osbun@onu.edu
OSBURN, Darren .... 636-922-8533 258 J
dosburn@stchas.edu
OSBURN, Monica .... 919-515-2423 342 A
monica_osburn@ncsu.edu
OSBURN, Toby .... 337-562-4249 192 E
tosburn@mcneese.edu
OSBURN, Wade .... 731-989-6067 419 K
wosburn@fhu.edu
OSEGUEDA, Roberto ..... 915-747-5680 455 C
osegueda@utep.edu
OSEGUERA, Tonantzin .. 657-278-7755.. 31 C
toseguera@fullerton.edu
OSGOOD, Jeanne .... 651-638-6035 234 D
j-osgood@bethel.edu
OSGOOD, Jeffery .... 610-738-0492 395 D
josgood@wcupa.edu
OSGUTHORPE, Rich ...... 801-422-6064 458 H
rich_osguthorpe@byu.edu
OSHIER, Mark .... 317-940-8000 154 C
OSHIRO, Cathie .... 620-792-9234 171 I
oshiroc@bartonccc.edu
OSHIRO, James .... 808-689-2663 129 F
joshiro6@hawaii.edu
OSHIRO, Wayde .... 808-455-0378 130 C
waydeo@hawaii.edu
OSHMAN, Melissa .... 909-389-3309.. 60 E
moshman@craftonhills.edu
OSHRY, Yehuda .... 845-426-3110 325 N
OSIER, Adam .... 763-544-9501 235 L
OSIKA, Elizabeth .... 317-955-6095 159 K
eosika@marian.edu
OSIRIS, Charles, E .... 805-437-3218.. 30 C
charles.osiris@csuci.edu
OSKEY, Lance, D .... 717-245-3131 503 F
lance.d.oskey.mil@mail.mil
OSKVIG, Bryant .... 202-885-1000.. 91 F
revo@american.edu
OSLER, Cheri .... 509-533-7311 479 C
cheri.osler@scc.spokane.edu
OSMAN, Md .... 213-262-3939.. 46 D
OSMOND, Tatiana .... 207-454-1094 195 I
tosmond@wccc.me.edu
OSMOTHERLY, Jason .... 800-658-4308 267 J
osmotherlyj@mpcc.edu
OSNESS, Bonnie .... 715-675-3331 499 F
osnessb@ntc.edu
OSOFSKY, Hari .... 312-503-0491 146 E
hariosofsky@law.northwestern.edu
OSOFSKY, Hari, M .... 814-863-1521 391 G
hmo8@psu.edu
OSORIO, Jonhathan ...... 808-956-0980 129 E
osorio@hawaii.edu
OSORIO, Jorge, J .... 718-990-7990 313 G
osorioj@stjohns.edu
OSORIO, Kelly .... 413-236-1641 214 A
kosorio@berkshirecc.edu
OSORIO, Michael .... 408-274-7900.. 62 G
michael.osorio@evc.edu
OSORTO, Hierald .... 607-274-3222 302 G
hosorto@ithaca.edu
OSOWICZ, Lauren .... 270-686-6415 179 J
lauren.osowicz@brescia.edu
OSSEIRAN-HANNA,
Khatmeh .... 724-357-5661 394 C
osseiran@iup.edu
OSSOWSKI, John .... 315-792-3216 324 B
jdossows@utica.edu
OSTASH, Heather .... 760-384-6249.. 46 M
hostash@cerrocoso.edu
OSTENDORF, Mari .... 206-221-5748 485 A
ostendor@uw.edu
OSTENDORF, Trevor ...... 530-541-4660.. 47 E
sm420@bncollege.com
OSTENDORFF, Stephen . 212-875-4402 290 H
sostendorff@bankstreet.edu
OSTER, Ben Zion .... 323-937-3763.. 76 H
boster@yoec.edu
OSTER, JoAnna .... 607-729-1581 298 B
joster@davisny.edu
OSTER-AALAND, Laura . 701-231-7052 345 F
laura.oster-aaland@ndsu.edu
OSTERBERG, Rick .... 781-292-2431 210 A
rick.osterberg@olin.edu
OSTERBIND, Kelly .... 251-461-7643.... 9 A
osterbind@southalabama.edu
OSTERGREN, Jennifer ... 760-750-4311.. 33 A
jostergren@csusm.edu
OSTERHOUT, Colin .... 907-796-6576.. 10 B
ctosterhout@alaska.edu
OSTERLUND, Linda .... 303-458-4100.. 83 E
losterla@regis.edu
OSTERMAN, Michael ..... 509-527-4975 486 B
ostermmg@whitman.edu
OSTERTHUN, Stu .... 402-323-3401 269 C
sosterthun@southeast.edu
OSTGAARD, Kolleen ...... 916-484-8569.. 50 G
ostgaak@arc.losrios.edu
OSTLER, Jon .... 435-283-7361 461 B
jon.ostler@snow.edu
OSTLING, Suzanne .... 540-863-2826 473 F
sostling@dslcc.edu
OSTOLAZA, Magda, E .... 787-257-7373 510 F
ue_mostolaza@uagm.edu
OSTRANDER, Gary, K .... 850-644-3347 110 C
gary@fsu.edu
OSTROM, Amy .... 480-965-6412.. 10 J
amy.ostrom@asu.edu
OSTROM, Lee .... 208-282-7903 132 F
ostrom@uidaho.edu
OSTROSKY, Jay .... 617-850-1261 210 G
jostrosky@hchc.edu
OSTROTH, Amy .... 434-381-6330 471 I
aostroth@sbc.edu
OSTROWICKI,
Jacqueline, M .... 402-472-7130 269 H
jostrowicki@nebraska.edu
OSTROWSKI, Jason ...... 208-732-6225 131 D
jostrowski@csi.edu
OSTROWSKI, Julie .... 704-923-8438 334 G
ostrowski.julie@gaston.edu
OSTROWSKI, Michael ... 931-598-1661 423 D
mtostrow@sewanee.edu
OSTWINKLE, Chris .... 815-280-6635 141 B
costwink@jjc.edu
OSWALD, Cecelia .... 484-323-3183 385 L
coswald@immaculata.edu
OSWALD, Clark .... 316-284-5233 172 B
coswald@bethelks.edu
OSWALD, Debra .... 937-512-3007 360 G
debra.oswald@sinclair.edu
OSWALD, Laurie .... 712-279-1614 164 B
laurie.oswald@briarcliff.edu
OSWALD, Scott .... 251-981-3771.... 5 A
scott.oswald@columbiasouthern.edu
OSWALD, Sharon .... 662-325-2580 247 F
soswald@cobilan.msstate.edu
OSWALD, Vicki .... 605-367-8355 417 B
vicki.oswald@southeasttech.edu
OSWALT, Natalie .... 903-693-2095 441 C
noswalt@panola.edu
OSWELL, Michelle .... 215-893-5265 381 J
michelle.oswell@curtis.edu
OSZUST, Renee .... 248-341-2153 229 C
raoszust@oaklandcc.edu
OTÓN-OLIVIERI,
Patricia .... 787-751-1912 509 A
poton@juris.inter.edu
OTERO, Deyka .... 787-894-2828 513 C
deyka.otero@upr.edu
OTERO, George .... 787-257-0000 512 B
george.otero@upr.edu
OTERO, Jorge .... 409-944-1365 436 E
jotero@gc.edu
OTHMAN, Saib .... 312-261-3164 145 D
sothman@nl.edu
OTHUON, Alberto .... 610-372-4721 396 H
aothuon@racc.edu
OTIENO, Tom .... 859-622-1393 180 E
tom.otieno@eku.edu
OTIS, Brian .... 860-486-5960.. 89 D
botis@foundation.uconn.edu
OTO, Rod, M .... 507-222-4138 234 G
roto@carleton.edu
OTRADOVEC, George .... 800-567-2344 492 C
gotradovec@menominee.edu
OTT, Alexander .... 718-289-5939 293 B
alexander.ott@bcc.cuny.edu
OTT, Amy .... 803-535-1222 411 B
otta@octech.edu
OTT, Geoffrey .... 863-667-5182 108 K
gdott@seu.edu
OTT, Kevin .... 559-791-2232.. 47 A
kevin.ott@portervillecollege.edu
OTT, Kim, A .... 928-523-1894.. 14 H
kimberly.ott@nau.edu
OTT, Luisa .... 520-494-5283.. 11 K
luisa.ott@centralaz.edu
OTT, Sandra .... 501-450-5015.. 23 H
sott@uca.edu
OTTAWAY, Mallory .... 504-398-2110 192 A
mottaway@uhcno.edu
OTTE, Bobbi .... 406-657-1086 265 E
otteb@rocky.edu
OTTE, Jennifer .... 402-363-5718 270 D
jaotte@york.edu
OTTEMAN, Marcie, M ... 989-774-3312 222 E
ottem1mm@cmich.edu
OTTEN, Daren .... 760-366-5289.. 40 E
dotten@cmccd.edu
OTTEN, Laura .... 215-951-1118 387 A
otten@lasalle.edu
OTTEN, Val .... 303-871-2647.. 84 E
val.otten@du.edu
OTTER, Kelly .... 202-687-7169.. 92 E
otter@georgetown.edu
OTTEY, Jacqueline .... 201-447-7204 275 H
jottey@bergen.edu
OTTINGER, Marie .... 334-386-7512.... 5 C
mottinger@faulkner.edu
OTTINGER, Michael ...... 505-566-3081 288 D
ottingerm@sanjuancollege.edu
OTTINO, Julio, M .... 847-491-3195 146 E
jm-ottino@northwestern.edu
OTTMAN, Ray .... 479-788-7110.. 21 G
ray.ottman@uafs.edu
OTTMAN, Stephanie ...... 918-495-7392 368 F
sottman@oru.edu
OTTO, Andy .... 785-242-2500 176 I
andy.otto@ottawa.edu
OTTO, Justin .... 509-359-7048 479 G
jotto@ewu.edu
OTTO, Richard, H .... 312-461-0600 133 A
ifitzgerald@aaart.edu
OTTO, Ryan .... 540-375-5249 470 E
otto@roanoke.edu
OTTO, Teresa .... 515-274-4111 414 G
teresa.otto@augie.edu
OTTO, Tyson .... 660-359-3948 257 D
totto@mail.ncmissouri.edu
OTTOSSON, John .... 641-673-1076 171 C
ottossonj@wmpenn.edu
OTTS, Cynthia .... 816-584-6273 258 C
cynthia.otts@park.edu
OTU, Emmanual .... 262-598-2973 496 D
otu@uwp.edu
OTUAFI, Quincey .... 801-832-2222 461 F
qotuafi@westminstercollege.edu
OTUKOLO SALTIBAN,
Belinda .... 801-863-8271 460 D
b.otukolo@uvu.edu
OTUONYE, Francis, O ... 931-372-3374 426 B
fotuonye@tntech.edu
OTUYA, Etuwe .... 678-323-7700.. 93 H
OTWELL, Ginger .... 870-230-5458.. 19 D
otwellg@hsu.edu
OTWELL, Michelle .... 386-386-7380.... 5 C
motwell@faulkner.edu
OTWORTH, Pamela .... 740-351-3208 360 F
potworth@shawnee.edu
OTY, Karla .... 580-581-7962 365 D
koty@cameron.edu
OTYENOH, Kimberly ..... 540-665-5436 470 G
kotyenoh@su.edu
OUBRÉ, Linda .... 562-907-4201.. 76 B
president@whittier.edu
OUDENHOVEN, Arnie ... 303-914-6298.. 83 C
arnie.oudenhoven@rrcc.edu
OUDSHOORN, Michael . 336-841-9000 329 F
moudshoo@highpoint.edu
OUELLETTE, Alicia .... 518-445-3305 289 K
aouel@albanylaw.edu
OUELLETTE, Andrew ...... 574-239-8305 156 A
aouellette@hcc-nd.edu
OUELLETTE, Bernie .... 207-859-1111 196 D
ouelletteb@thomas.edu
OUELLETTE, Dallas .... 301-387-3097 199 A
dallas.ouellette@garrettcollege.edu
OUELLETTE-SCHRAMM,
Jen .... 507-433-0812 240 G
jen.ouellette-schramm@riverland.edu
OUERT, Mike .... 406-994-5411 264 C
mrouert@montana.edu
OUILLET, Pierre-Yves ... 858-534-3390.. 70 C
pouillet@ucsd.edu
OUIMET, Maurice .... 802-468-1491 463 E
maurice.ouimet@castleton.edu
OUKAYAN, Tzoler .... 818-240-1000.. 43 G
toukayan@glendale.edu
OUKHEIRA BAKER,
Nadia .... 703-539-6890 471 F
OULAMINE, Saadia .... 267-256-0200.. 93 H
OULD, Jennifer .... 773-947-6307 143 H
jould@mccormick.edu
OURADA, Stephanie ..... 402-461-7733 267 C
stephanie.ourada@hastings.edu
OURS, Alan .... 912-279-5762 117 F
aours@ccga.edu
OURSO, Mark .... 225-214-1955 187 B
mark.ourso@franu.edu
OUSLEY, Allisha .... 678-422-4100.. 93 H
OUTAR, O'Neil .... 401-454-6532 405 B
ooutar@risd.edu
OUTEN, Jason .... 828-835-4229 338 E
jouten@tricountycc.edu
OUTING, Donald, A .... 610-758-2128 388 E
dao417@lehigh.edu
OUTLAW, Jennifer .... 317-791-5608 161 H
outlawj@uindy.edu
OUTLAW, Steve .... 850-201-7000 112 C
steve.outlaw@tcc.fl.edu
OUTLEY, Patrice .... 318-274-2288 192 C
outleyp@gram.edu
OUTON, Peggy, M .... 412-397-6000 397 B
outon@rmu.edu
OUTTEN, Donavan .... 314-246-6907 262 C
doutten@webster.edu
OVADIA, Steve .... 718-482-6022 294 F
sovadia@lagcc.cuny.edu
OVEDIA, Nicole, R .... 561-237-7237 103 W
novedia@lynn.edu
OVERBEE, Peyton .... 919-735-5151 338 H
OVERBY, David .... 605-688-4988 417 A
david.overby@sdstate.edu
OVERCASH, Shannon ..... 508-541-1841 209 A
sovercash@dean.edu
OVERDORF, Daniel .... 865-573-4517 420 E
doverdorf@johnsonu.edu
OVEREND, Gregory .... 203-932-7430.. 89 H
goverend@newhaven.edu
OVERHOLSER, Toni .... 937-328-8070 350 G
overholsert@clarkstate.edu
OVERHOLTZER,
Michael, H .... 646-888-6639 304 J
overhom1@mskcc.org
OVERLAUR, Kevin .... 229-245-4357 127 E
kjoverlaur@valdosta.edu
OVERMYER-VELAZQUEZ,
Mark .... 959-200-3766.. 89 D
mark.velazquez@uconn.edu
OVEROCKER, Quintin .... 828-641-0020 327 B
overocqm@brevard.edu
OVERPECK, Jonathan, T 734-764-2550 231 H
overpeck@umich.edu
OVERSTREET, Darryl ...... 580-559-5582 365 K
doverstt@ecok.edu
OVERSTREET, Kirk .... 618-985-2828 140 H
kirkoverstreet@jalc.edu
OVERSTREET, Mana ...... 615-732-7893 422 B
m.overstreet@mtsa.edu
OVERSTREET, Tammie ... 423-236-2759 423 F
toverstreet@southern.edu
OVERTON, Chrystal .... 580-477-7702 371 D
chrystal.overton@wosc.edu

O'BRIEN, Theresa .... 415-514-1455.. 70 D
theresa.obrien@ucsf.edu

O'BRIEN, William .... 848-445-1300 282 A
obrienw@echo.rutgers.edu

O'BRIEN-FOELSCH,
Molly .... 717-867-6038 388 C
mobrien@lvc.edu

O'BRIEN-KNOTTS,
Jennifer, E .... 610-758-4679 388 E
jeo211@lehigh.edu

O'BRIEN-MCMASTERS,
Vanessa .... 609-343-5670 275 D
vobmcm@atlantic.edu

O'BRUBA, Brian .... 209-228-2958.. 70 A
bobruba@ucmerced.edu

O'BRYAN, Megan .... 216-987-4737 351 E
megan.obryan@tri-c.edu

O'BRYANT, Beverly .... 410-951-2666 204 B
bobryant@coppin.edu

O'BRYANT, Teresa .... 229-931-2150 125 E
tobryant@southgatech.edu

O'BRYANT, Theresa ...... 413-662-5400 213 C
theresa.obryant@mcla.edu

O'CALLAGHAN,
Ceceilia .... 732-987-2415 278 A
cocallaghan@georgian.edu

O'CALLAGHAN, Cindy .. 617-735-9779 209 D
ocallac@emmanuel.edu

O'CARROLL, Theresa .... 708-974-5250 145 A
ocarroll@morainevalley.edu

O'CONNELL, Anne .... 847-543-2622 136 A
aoconnell@clcillinois.edu

O'CONNELL,
Catharine, E .... 217-245-3010 139 C
catharine.oconnell@ic.edu

O'CONNELL, Colleen .... 215-884-8942 403 D
planning@woninstitute.edu

O'CONNELL, Daniel ...... 978-867-4246 210 B
daniel.oconnell@gordon.edu

O'CONNELL, Danny, J .. 330-941-3549 364 H
djoconnell@ysu.edu

O'CONNELL, Heather, A 302-356-6814.. 91 E
heather.a.oconnell@wilmu.edu

O'CONNELL, Janelle ...... 325-670-1339 436 I
joconnel@hsutx.edu

O'CONNELL, John .... 260-481-6977 160 C
oconnelj@pfw.edu

O'CONNELL, Lili .... 815-455-8676 143 I
loconnell@mchenry.edu

O'CONNELL, Molly .... 920-693-1752 498 H
molly.oconnell@gototltc.edu

O'CONNELL, Patrick ...... 239-280-2461.. 95 M
patrick.oconnell@avemaria.edu

O'CONNELL, Robert, G . 617-333-2050 208 G
boconnel@curry.edu

O'CONNELL, Robin .... 816-523-9140 262 D
robin.o@wellspring.edu

O'CONNELL, Ryan .... 310-377-5501.. 51 C
roconnell@marymountcalifornia.edu

O'CONNELL, Sean, P .... 203-773-8068.. 85 D
soconnell@albertus.edu

O'CONNELL,
Shelley, M .... 319-273-7224 164 A
shelley.oconnell@uni.edu

O'CONNELL, Vincent ..... 781-239-2699 214 G
voconnell@massbay.edu

O'CONNOR, Brian .... 406-994-5016 264 C
boconnor@montana.edu

O'CONNOR, Charles, D 402-472-9339 269 J
charles.oconnor@unl.edu

O'CONNOR, Christi ...... 323-953-4000.. 49 A
oconnoca@lacitycollege.edu

O'CONNOR, Daniel, P .. 713-743-4002 452 D
doconnor2@uh.edu

O'CONNOR, Deirdre, M 570-577-3141 379 C
deirdre.oconnor@bucknell.edu

O'CONNOR, Diane .... 215-641-6416 390 C
doconnor@mc3.edu

O'CONNOR, Edward, R . 816-654-7000 254 E
eoconnor@kcumb.edu

O'CONNOR, Ellen, M ... 215-955-6835 399 E
ellen.oconnor@jefferson.edu

O'CONNOR, Gregory ..... 934-420-2170 320 F
oconnor@farmingdale.edu

O'CONNOR, Heidi .... 978-468-7111 210 C
hoconnor@gcts.edu

O'CONNOR, Isabel .... 619-388-2755.. 60 J
ioconnor@sdccd.edu

O'CONNOR, James .... 563-884-5294 169 F
james.oconnor@palmer.edu

O'CONNOR, James .... 334-844-3500.... 4 D
jmo0024@auburn.edu

O'CONNOR, Jasi .... 218-299-3549 235 H
oconnor@cord.edu

O'CONNOR, Jen .... 785-864-2640 177 J
jen.occonor@ku.edu

O'CONNOR, Jeremiah ... 508-793-2564 208 D
joconnor@holycross.edu

O'CONNOR, Julie .... 414-425-8300 495 A
joconnor@shsst.edu

O'CONNOR, Kevin .... 949-582-4788.. 65 D
koconnor@saddleback.edu

O'CONNOR, Kevin .... 800-658-4308 267 J
oconnork@mpcc.edu

O'CONNOR, Kyla .... 951-222-8649.. 59 D
kyla.oconnor@rcc.edu

O'CONNOR, Lisa, G ..... 203-582-8549.. 88 G
lisa.o'connor@quinnipiac.edu

O'CONNOR, Maria .... 216-397-4268 353 O
moconnor@jcu.edu

O'CONNOR, Maura .... 206-296-6300 484 A
oconnorm@seattleu.edu

O'CONNOR, Maureen ... 650-433-3895.. 55 L
moconnor@paloaltou.edu

O'CONNOR, Michael .... 815-802-8908 141 D
moconnor@kcc.edu

O'CONNOR, Michele .... 215-204-8276 399 B
michele.o'connor@temple.edu

O'CONNOR, Mike, K ..... 920-832-6561 493 B
mike.k.oconnor@lawrence.edu

O'CONNOR, Patricia ..... 559-278-7392.. 31 B
poconnor@csufresno.edu

O'CONNOR, Patrick ...... 617-879-7878 213 B
poconnor@massart.edu

O'CONNOR, Patrick, W 201-684-7500 280 H
poconnor@ramapo.edu

O'CONNOR, Richard ..... 413-265-2340 208 E
oconnorri@elms.edu

O'CONNOR, Rob .... 501-450-1225.. 19 E
o'connor@hendrix.edu

O'CONNOR, Robert .... 315-781-3535 301 F
oconnor@hws.edu

O'CONNOR, Samantha . 919-718-7340 333 C
socon214@cccc.edu

O'CONNOR, Shawn ...... 507-433-0564 240 G
shawn.o'connor@riverland.edu

O'CONNOR, Tennille, I . 727-816-3116 105 F
oconnot@phsc.edu

O'CONNOR, Timothy .... 212-327-8080 312 G
toconnor@rockefeller.edu

O'DANIEL, Jennifer .... 512-863-1691 445 C
odanielj@southwestern.edu

O'DAY, Steven, P .... 903-813-3001 430 H
soday@austincollege.edu

O'DELL, April .... 802-865-5734 462 A
o'dell@champlain.edu

O'DELL, Cynthia .... 219-980-6509 157 C
codell@iun.edu

O'DELL, Tammy .... 931-393-1745 424 F
todell@mscc.edu

O'DONNELL, Alicia .... 402-461-7488 267 C
aodonnell@hastings.edu

O'DONNELL, Brennan .... 718-862-7301 304 M
brennan.odonnell@manhattan.edu

O'DONNELL, Evanne ..... 530-898-5609.. 30 D
eodonnell@csuchico.edu

O'DONNELL, James ...... 480-965-3956.. 10 J
jod@asu.edu

O'DONNELL, Kathleen .. 207-778-7094 196 I
katie.odonnell@maine.edu

O'DONNELL, Loraine .... 716-829-8141 298 E
kavinokytheater@dyc.edu

O'DONNELL, Niall .... 540-636-2900 465 L
niall.odonnell@christendom.edu

O'DONNELL, SSJ,
Patricia .... 215-248-7125 381 A
podonnel@chc.edu

O'DONNELL, Patrick ...... 562-860-2451.. 35 H
podonnell@cerritos.edu

O'DONNELL, Timothy ... 540-654-1252 471 N
todonnel@umw.edu

O'DONNELL,
Timothy, T .... 540-636-2900 465 L
president@christendom.edu

O'DONNELL-RUNDLETT,
Marylou .... 617-353-5315 207 E
modonnel@bu.edu

O'DONNELL-WILSON,
Nancy .... 954-201-7414.. 96 F

O'DONOVAN, Stephen .. 254-526-1114 432 D
admissions.registrar@ctcd.edu

O'DOWD, Ann, M .... 402-280-2293 266 H
annodowd@creighton.edu

O'DOWD, Diane, K .... 949-824-0622.. 69 D
dkodowd@uci.edu

O'DRISCOLL, Daniel ...... 401-254-3510 405 C
dodriscoll@rwu.edu

O'DRISCOLL, Dean .... 509-452-5100 482 B
dodriscoll@pnwu.edu

O'DRISCOLL, Sue .... 540-545-7399 470 G
sodrisco09@su.edu

O'FARRELL, Billie .... 727-569-1401 112 G
bskinner@trinitycollege.edu

O'FARRELL, Kevin, F .... 813-527-6620 105 F
ofarrek@phsc.edu

O'FARRELL, Mark, T ..... 727-376-6911 112 G
mofarrell@trinitycollege.edu

O'FLYNN, Greg .... 305-809-3184.. 97 O
greg.oflynn@cfk.edu

O'GEARY, Amy .... 252-492-2061 338 F
ogearya@vgcc.edu

O'GRADY, Dean, P .... 315-684-6000 321 A

O'GRADY, Elaine .... 845-569-3190 307 D
elaine.ogrady@msmc.edu

O'GRADY, Tina .... 415-575-6143.. 28 I

O'GUINN, Dave .... 812-855-8188 156 G
vpsa@indiana.edu

O'GUINN, M. Dave .... 812-855-8188 156 F
mdoguinn@iu.edu

O'GWYNN, Chris .... 334-844-5061.... 4 D
ogwynca@auburn.edu

O'GWYNN, Marty .... 864-977-2093 410 I
marty.o'gwynn@ngu.edu

O'HALLORAN,
Bernadette (BJ) .... 626-584-5238.. 43 B
bjohalloran@fuller.edu

O'HALLORAN,
Kimberly, C .... 610-499-4566 402 G
kcohalloran@widener.edu

O'HALLORAN,
Teresa, E .... 715-836-2387 495 E
ohallote@uwec.edu

O'HANION, Kimberly .... 480-212-1704.. 15 O

O'HANLON, Laureen ..... 509-828-1459 479 G
lohanlon@ewu.edu

O'HARA, Amanda, T ..... 805-525-4417.. 67 K
aohara@thomasaquinas.edu

O'HARA, Bradley .... 604-482-5510 132 G
bohara@adler.edu

O'HARA, Jamie .... 401-454-6709 405 B
johara01@risd.edu

O'HARA, Kate .... 508-678-2811 214 B
kate.o'hara@bristolcc.edu

O'HARA, Kate .... 508-678-2811 214 B

O'HARA, Patrick .... 773-702-1234 151 E

O'HARA, Shawn .... 336-506-4136 332 A
shawn.ohara@alamancecc.edu

O'HARA O'CONNOR,
Erin .... 850-644-3071 110 C
eoconnor@law.fsu.edu

O'HARE, Katie .... 617-323-6662 220 C
katie_ohare@williamjames.edu

O'HARE, Lauren .... 201-761-6272 283 A
lohare@saintpeters.edu

O'HEARN, Denis .... 915-747-5666 455 C
daohearn@utep.edu

O'HERRON, Mike .... 815-965-8616 148 C
moherron@rockfordcareercollege.edu

O'HORA UHNAK,
Marilyn .... 315-781-3734 301 F
uhnak@hws.edu

O'KANE, Barbara .... 303-384-2561.. 79 J
bokane@mines.edu

O'KANE, Gail .... 612-659-6299 239 A
gail.okane@minneapolis.edu

O'KEEFE, Carolyn .... 909-537-5240.. 32 E
carolynokeefe@csusb.edu

O'KEEFE, Claire .... 239-687-5423.. 95 L
cokeefe@avemarialaw.edu

O'KEEFE, Colleen .... 201-684-7494 280 H
cokeefe3@ramapo.edu

O'KEEFE, Dean, R .... 508-565-1667 219 A
dokeefe@stonehill.edu

O'KEEFE, Erin .... 410-617-2699 200 B
eokeefe1@loyola.edu

O'KEEFE, James .... 718-390-4526 313 G
okeefej@stjohns.edu

O'KEEFE, John, L .... 610-330-5803 387 C
okeefej@lafayette.edu

O'KEEFE, Laurie .... 401-598-1000 404 D
laurie.okeefe@jwu.edu

O'KEEFE, Louise .... 256-824-2445.... 8 B
louise.okeefe@uah.edu

O'KEEFE, Martha .... 540-891-3094 473 I
mokeefe@germanna.edu

O'KEEFE, Matt, J .... 785-532-5590 175 C
mjokeefe@ksu.edu

O'KEEFE, Michael .... 781-768-7000 218 D

O'KEEFE, Mildred .... 516-876-3247 318 C
okeefem@oldwestbury.edu

O'KEEFE, Robert .... 414-930-3201 494 E
okeefer@mtmary.edu

O'KEEFE, Steve .... 618-985-3741 140 H
steveokeefe@jalc.edu

O'KELLY, Kimberly, B ... 715-836-4325 495 E
weigelkb@uwec.edu

O'LEARY, Erin .... 912-525-5000 124 I
eoleary@scad.edu

O'LEARY, Heather .... 617-573-8302 219 B
holeary@suffolk.edu

O'LEARY, Janet .... 206-239-4500 478 H

O'LEARY, Kara .... 574-284-4578 160 I
koleary@saintmarys.edu

O'LEARY, Michael .... 304-434-8000 488 E
michael.o_leary@easternwv.edu

O'LINGER, Jennifer .... 256-551-3125.... 2 E
jennifer.o'linger@drakestate.edu

O'LOUGHLIN, Paula ...... 319-399-8616 164 F
poloughlin@coe.edu

O'LYNN, Robert, G .... 606-474-3230 181 B
rolynn@kcu.edu

O'MAHONEY, Angel ...... 310-393-0411.. 56 C

O'MALLEY, Barbara ...... 909-706-7055.. 75 I
domalley@westernu.edu

O'MALLEY, Bert .... 713-798-6205 431 D
berto@bcm.edu

O'MALLEY, Marjorie ..... 617-879-7045 213 B
momalley@massart.edu

O'MALLEY, Michael ...... 512-245-2150 450 C
mo20@txstate.edu

O'MALLEY, Richard .... 979-830-4054 431 H
richard.omalley@blinn.edu

O'MALLEY, Sean, M ..... 856-225-6159 281 G
omallese@camden.rutgers.edu

O'MALLEY, Stephanie ... 303-871-2784.. 84 E
stephanie.omalley@du.edu

O'MARA, Kevin .... 910-893-1380 327 D
komara@campbell.edu

O'MARA, Kevin .... 718-270-4628 317 B
kevin.o'mara@downstate.edu

O'MARA CARVER,
Maureen .... 215-871-6704 395 G
maureenca@pcom.edu

O'MEARA, Mary Ellen .. 740-427-5112 354 I
omearam@kenyon.edu

O'MEARA, Ron .... 229-225-5200 126 A
romeara@southernregional.edu

O'NEAL, Aleshia .... 402-363-5690 270 D
ajoneal@york.edu

O'NEAL, Angela, D .... 518-629-8172 302 C
a.oneal@hvcc.edu

O'NEAL, Benjamin .... 317-738-8303 155 D
boneal@franklincollege.edu

O'NEAL, Bryan .... 312-329-4057 144 I
bryan.oneal@moody.edu

O'NEAL, Christian .... 501-916-6433.. 22 A
cxoneal@ualr.edu

O'NEAL, Dennis, L .... 254-710-3871 431 E
dennis_oneal@baylor.edu

O'NEAL, Ginger, H .... 252-335-0821 333 G
goneal@albemarle.edu

O'NEAL, Justin .... 660-596-7282 259 M
joneal@sfccmo.edu

O'NEAL, Kate .... 213-356-5386.. 65 E
kate_oneal@sciarc.edu

O'NEAL, Montrice .... 225-771-3922 191 B
dos@subr.edu

O'NEAL, Robert .... 803-535-5549 407 D
roneal@claflin.edu

O'NEAL, Sharon .... 843-525-8248 412 G
soneal@tcl.edu

O'NEIL, Alysha, M .... 573-341-4122 261 D

O'NEIL, Brian .... 410-777-2373 197 G
boneil1@aacc.edu

O'NEIL, Elizabeth .... 401-232-6000 404 A
eoneil@bryant.edu

O'NEIL, Faith .... 434-797-8458 473 G
faith.oneil@danville.edu

O'NEIL, Jill .... 605-688-6092 417 A
jill.oneil@sdstate.edu

O'NEIL, Laura, L .... 607-777-2131 316 B
loneil@binghamton.edu

O'NEIL, Patricia, S .... 312-942-5600 148 G
poneil@rush.edu

O'NEILL, Charles .... 724-830-1144 398 C
oneill@setonhill.edu

O'NEILL, Colleen .... 480-423-6177.. 13 H
colleen.oneill@scottsdalecc.edu

O'NEILL, Daniel .... 978-762-4000 215 D
daoneill@northshore.edu

O'NEILL, Dianne, M ...... 301-369-2325 198 C
dmoneill@captechu.edu

O'NEILL, F. Shawn .... 201-684-7550 280 H
soneill@ramapo.edu

O'NEILL, Gayle .... 860-215-9276 .. 87 F goneill@threerivers.edu
O'NEILL, James .... 734-432-5313 227 C joneill@madonna.edu
O'NEILL, Joan, E .... 203-432-5461 .. 90 C joan.oneill@yale.edu
O'NEILL, Kelsey .... 605-394-1203 416 H kelsey.oneill@sdsmt.edu
O'NEILL, Keven .... 718-517-7711 314 F
O'NEILL, Kevin .... 270-534-3206 183 B kevin.oneill@kctcs.edu
O'NEILL, Kim .... 360-650-3524 485 I
O'NEILL, Megan .... 970-248-1353 .. 78 J moneill@coloradomesa.edu
O'NEILL, Michael .... 610-519-7926 401 K mike.oneill@villanova.edu
O'NEILL, Stephen .... 507-786-3062 243 D oneill@stolaf.edu
O'NEILL, Thomas .... 315-228-7418 296 E toneill@colgate.edu
O'NEILL, Walter .... 616-554-5827 223 E woneill1@davenport.edu
O'NEILL, William .... 402-559-1952 269 K woneill@unmc.edu
O'QUINN, Robin .... 918-463-2931 365 J robin.oquinn@connorsstate.edu
O'REAR, Randy, G .... 254-295-4500 453 D rorear@umhb.edu
O'REGAN, Michelle .... 617-333-2970 208 G michelle.oregan@curry.edu
O'REILLY, Andrew .... 310-258-5693 .. 51 A andrew.oreilly@lmu.edu
O'REILLY, Lillian .... 718-951-5114 293 C loreilly@brooklyn.cuny.edu
O'REILLY, Maureen, A .. 603-641-7084 274 A moreilly@anselm.edu
O'REILLY, Paul, J .... 805-525-4417 .. 67 K poreilly@thomasaquinas.edu
O'REILLY, Tricia .... 510-841-9230 .. 76 G toreilly@wi.edu
O'REILLY, JR., William, R .... 781-736-4205 208 A woreilly@brandeis.edu
O'RILEY, Jane .... 318-670-9401 191 D joriley@susla.edu
O'RIORDAN, Steven .... 978-934-3185 212 B steven_oriordan@uml.edu
O'RORKE, Kevin .... 530-242-7621 .. 64 C kororke@shastacollege.edu
O'ROURKE, Brett .... 800-477-2254 .. 29 G borourke@calsouthern.edu
O'ROURKE, Brian .... 219-464-5000 162 D
O'ROURKE, Brian .... 908-526-1200 281 A brian.o'rourke@raritanval.edu
O'ROURKE, Brian, J .... 864-656-5658 407 E orourke@clemson.edu
O'ROURKE, Catherine ... 212-217-3800 299 D catherine_orourke@fitnyc.edu
O'ROURKE, Elizabeth .... 401-874-9512 405 E lorourke@uri.edu
O'ROURKE, John .... 413-565-1000 206 D jorourke@baypath.edu
O'ROURKE, Kevin .... 718-489-5496 313 E korourke@sfc.edu
O'ROURKE, Kim .... 540-231-6232 476 C orourkek@vt.edu
O'ROURKE, Krysti .... 631-656-2163 300 B krysti.orourke@ftc.edu
O'ROURKE, Mary, C ..... 443-518-4778 199 F
O'ROURKE, Patrick .... 303-492-5852 .. 84 B evc-coo@colorado.edu
O'ROURKE, Patty .... 412-281-2600 396 B porourke@pci.edu
O'ROURKE, Sheila, N ... 973-618-3341 276 D sorourke@caldwell.edu
O'RYAN, Kelly .... 802-387-6362 462 C kellyoryan@landmark.edu
O'SHEA, David .... 480-517-8689 .. 13 G david.oshea@riosalado.edu
O'SHEA, Maureen .... 508-362-2131 214 D moshea@capecod.edu
O'SHEA, William .... 503-352-1419 375 C osheawa@pacificu.edu
O'SHIELDS, Shannon .... 714-879-3901 .. 45 G soshields@hiu.edu
O'SULLIVAN, Daniel, W 410-293-1582 504 A osulliva@usna.edu
O'SULLIVAN, Eileen ...... 508-531-2921 212 D eosullivan@bridgew.edu
O'SULLIVAN, Gerry ...... 215-884-8942 403 D academicdean@woninstitute.edu
O'SULLIVAN, Joseph .... 314-516-6800 261 C osullivanj@umsl.edu
O'SULLIVAN, Kevin ...... 914-633-2120 302 E kosullivan@iona.edu
O'SULLIVAN, Margaret . 718-270-2487 317 B margaret.o'sullivan@downstate.edu
O'SULLIVAN, Patrick ...... 805-756-7244 .. 29 I posulliv@calpoly.edu
O'SULLIVAN, Rachel ..... 256-233-8100 .... 4 C rachel.osullivan@athens.edu
O'SULLIVAN, Trecia ...... 646-717-9742 300 E osullivan@gts.edu
O'TOOL, Nick .... 402-572-3650 266 D
O'TOOLE, Beth .... 605-331-6797 417 C elisabeth.otoole@usiouxfalls.edu
O'TOOLE, Jason .... 620-441-5353 173 C jason.otoole@cowley.edu
O'TOOLE, Jennifer, A .... 412-578-8725 380 B jaotoole@carlow.edu
O'TOOLE, Kayla .... 701-228-5479 346 B kayla.otoole@dakotacollege.edu
O'TOOLE, Patty .... 540-362-6588 467 H potoole@hollins.edu
O'TOOLE, Selina .... 203-932-7337 .. 89 H sotoole@newhaven.edu

P

PAAL, Christine, S .... 617-353-3608 207 E cpaal@bu.edu
PAAVOLA, Cindy, L ...... 906-227-2720 228 I cipaavol@nmu.edu
PABÓN-BATLLE, Luis .... 787-993-8868 512 A luis.pabon4@upr.edu
PABÓN PAGÁN, Jose ... 787-766-1399 511 F jose.pagan@upr.edu
PABARCUS, Deb .... 314-837-6777 258 K dpabarcus@stlchristian.edu
PABON, Jaqueline .... 787-765-1915 509 B jpabon@opto.inter.edu
PABON, Peter .... 845-848-4065 298 C peter.pabon@dc.edu
PABON GAUTIER, Maria, C .... 507-786-3334 243 D pabong1@stolaf.edu
PABON-RODRIGUEZ, Edith, C .... 787-751-1912 509 A epabon@juris.inter.edu
PACACHA, Edith .... 772-462-7340 102 F epacacha@irsc.edu
PACATTE, Bob .... 325-649-8609 437 G bpacatte@hputx.edu
PACE, Anthony, J .... 570-326-3761 392 W ajp25@pct.edu
PACE, Bobby .... 303-360-4940 .. 80 E bobby.pace@ccaurora.edu
PACE, Christy .... 870-460-1020 .. 22 C pacec@uamont.edu
PACE, Danielle .... 843-921-6932 411 A mpace@netc.edu
PACE, Derek .... 601-635-2111 246 A dpace@eccc.edu
PACE, Duane .... 423-614-8104 420 H dpace@leeuniversity.edu
PACE, Gay .... 870-460-1140 .. 22 C pace@uamont.edu
PACE, Harold .... 336-758-5000 344 C hpace@wfu.edu
PACE, James .... 229-333-5959 127 E jcpace@valdosta.edu
PACE, Jarrod .... 972-825-5469 444 J japace@sagu.edu
PACE, Jessica .... 903-693-2044 441 C jpace@panola.edu
PACE, Jessica .... 903-693-2000 441 C jpace@panola.edu
PACE, JoeAnn .... 757-493-6000 .. 93 H
PACE, Katrina .... 601-925-7645 247 C kpace@mc.edu
PACE, Kris .... 816-501-4865 258 I kristine.pace@rockhurst.edu
PACE, Lisa, L .... 843-953-4823 407 C lisa.pace@citadel.edu
PACE, Marissa .... 404-270-5160 126 B mpace@spelman.edu
PACE, Meghan .... 325-942-2083 450 E meghan.pace@angelo.edu
PACE, Roger .... 619-260-4059 .. 72 I pace@sandiego.edu
PACENTI, Elena .... 619-684-8802 .. 53 K epacenti@newschoolarch.edu
PACETTI-DONELSON, Vandy .... 251-626-3303 .... 7 E vpacettidonelson@ussa.edu
PACHECO, Andrea .... 505-467-6809 288 H registrar@swc.edu
PACHECO, Andree .... 310-900-1600 .. 39 F
PACHECO, Benito .... 505-454-3127 286 J bmpacheco@nmhu.edu
PACHECO, Christine ...... 870-235-5483 .. 21 C christinepacheco@saumag.edu
PACHECO, Edwin, R ...... 401-456-9866 405 A epacheco@ric.edu
PACHECO, Lisa .... 619-201-8962 .. 65 G lisa.pacheco@socalsem.edu
PACHECO, Michael ...... 606-218-5216 186 B michaelpacheco@upike.edu
PACHECO, Michael ...... 432-837-8000 450 B michael.pacheco@sulross.edu
PACHECO, Philicia ...... 508-678-2811 214 B philicia.pacheco@bristolcc.edu
PACHECO, Richard, M .. 913-971-3299 176 C rmpacheco@mnu.edu
PACHECO, Robert .... 817-515-5289 445 F robert.pacheco@tccd.edu
PACHECO DUNN, Tanhena .... 845-257-3172 316 E pachecot@newpaltz.edu
PACHECO DUNN, Tanhena .... 845-257-3164 316 E pachecot@newpaltz.edu
PACHMAN, Tracey .... 610-660-3140 397 G tpachman@sju.edu
PACHOLEC, Mark .... 716-270-5612 299 B pacholec@ecc.edu
PACHUAU, Lalsangkima .... 859-858-3581 179 C
PACHUTA, Stephen ...... 304-293-2521 490 E stephen.pachuta@hsc.wvu.edu
PACIELLA, Joseph, F .... 301-447-5111 201 B j.paciella@msmary.edu
PACIERO, Christine ...... 847-376-7057 146 G cpaciero@oakton.edu
PACIERO, Karen, P ...... 312-915-6435 143 C kpaciero@luc.edu
PACIONE, Anne, R .... 718-990-5800 313 G roccoa@stjohns.edu
PACK, Andrew .... 215-717-6147 400 E apack@uarts.edu
PACK, Andrew .... 503-517-1898 377 E apack@westernseminary.edu
PACK, Daniel .... 423-425-2256 427 C daniel-pack@utc.edu
PACK, Elizabeth .... 704-406-2173 329 A epack@gardner-webb.edu
PACK, Gary .... 402-552-6118 266 E
PACK, Jodi .... 903-434-8114 440 G jpack@ntcc.edu
PACK, Lee .... 828-398-7482 332 B leerpack@abtech.edu
PACKARD, Brandi .... 918-610-0027 365 I bpackard@communitycarecollege.edu
PACKARD, Francine ...... 330-821-5320 362 E packarfr@mountunion.edu
PACKARD, Katherin ...... 816-531-5223 251 K
PACKARD, Matthew, W . 850-857-6070 111 F mpackard@uwf.edu
PACKARD, Ryan .... 678-466-5499 117 D ryanpackard@clayton.edu
PACKER, Chris .... 540-261-8400 471 B chris.packer@svu.edu
PACKER, Lauren .... 717-358-4107 383 I lauren.packer@fandm.edu
PACKETT, Felicia, B ...... 804-758-6746 475 A fpackett@rappahannock.edu
PACTOL, Monica .... 916-608-6503 .. 50 I pactolm@flc.losrios.edu
PAD, Rebecca .... 313-664-7641 222 H rpad@collegeforcreativestudies.edu
PADASH, Ali .... 916-608-6648 .. 50 I padasha@flc.losrios.edu
PADDEN, Carol, A .... 858-534-6073 .. 70 C deansocsci@ucsd.edu
PADDOCK, Chris .... 415-351-3526 .. 61 C cpaddock@sfai.edu
PADDOCK, Ericka .... 909-389-3457 .. 60 E epaddock@craftonhills.edu
PADDOCK, Jean .... 330-363-6347 348 C jean.paddock@aultman.com
PADDOCK, Suzanne ...... 315-866-0300 301 D paddocksm@herkimer.edu
PADDOCK-O'REILLY, Kimberly .... 636-227-2100 255 A
PADEN, Matt .... 615-966-1904 421 B matt.paden@lipscomb.edu
PADEN, Quincy .... 312-662-4141 132 G qpaden@adler.edu
PADGETT, Brett .... 773-702-1234 151 E
PADGETT, Mila .... 803-641-3230 413 B milap@usca.edu
PADILLA, Ailin .... 787-264-1912 508 F ailin_padilla@intersg.edu
PADILLA, Carlos .... 931-393-1846 424 F cpadilla@mscc.edu
PADILLA, Diana .... 559-486-1166 .. 24 F dpadilla@agapeschools.org
PADILLA, Edgar .... 512-759-5643 449 D edgar.padilla@tstc.edu
PADILLA, Jose .... 562-907-4211 .. 76 B jpadilla@whittier.edu
PADILLA, Jose, D .... 219-464-5115 162 D
PADILLA, Lymaries ...... 787-725-6500 505 G lpadilla@albizu.edu
PADILLA, Maria .... 508-362-2131 214 D mpadilla@capecod.edu
PADILLA, Mark .... 307-382-1690 501 J mpadilla@westernwyoming.edu
PADILLA, Mayra .... 510-215-3880 .. 40 B mpadilla@contracosta.edu
PADILLA, Melissa Sue .. 617-873-0474 208 B melissasue.frasca@cambridgecollege.edu
PADILLA, Pamela .... 940-369-8289 453 E pam.padilla@unt.edu
PADILLA, Ramon .... 651-201-1454 237 B ramon.padilla@minnstate.edu
PADILLA, JR., Ramon .... 865-974-1000 427 A
PADILLA, Rene, L .... 402-280-4745 266 H renepadilla@creighton.edu
PADILLA, Sherrie .... 808-932-7451 129 D sherriep@hawaii.edu
PADILLA, Vivian, A ...... 787-786-3030 511 A vpadilla@ucb.edu.pr
PADILLA JACKSON, Olivia .... 505-224-4413 285 N opadillajackson@cnm.edu
PADILLA-WALKER, Laura .... 801-422-9053 458 H laura_walker@byu.edu
PADLAN, Jennifer .... 814-332-2312 378 A jmangus@allegheny.edu
PADMA, Ji Hyang .... 760-634-1771 .. 28 E
PADMANABHAN, Anand .... 718-817-1000 300 C anandp@fordham.edu
PADMARAJU, Lakshmikara .... 217-581-7568 137 E lpadmaraju@eiu.edu
PADOVANI, John, J ...... 607-746-4632 320 D padovajj@delhi.edu
PADUA-ANDREWS, Evelyn .... 888-488-4968 .. 46 F epaduaandrews@itu.edu
PADUAN, Jeffrey, D ...... 831-656-3241 502 M jdpaduan@nps.edu
PADUNTIN, Jack .... 626-529-8008 .. 55 F
PAEPLOW, Randall, K ... 863-784-7083 108 F randall.paeplow@southflorida.edu
PAETSCH, Claudia .... 414-288-5629 493 E claudia.paetsch@marquette.edu
PAEZ, J.C .... 815-479-7833 143 I jpaez299@mchenry.edu
PAEZ, Karen .... 971-722-4406 375 D karen.paez@pcc.edu
PAEZ, Leticia .... 915-747-8268 455 C lpaez@utep.edu
PAEZ-FIGUEROA, Jose .. 908-709-7084 284 D paez@ucc.edu
PAFFENROTH, Kim .... 914-637-2743 302 E kpaffenroth@iona.edu
PAFFRATH, Dennis .... 410-706-1101 203 A dpaffrath@umaryland.edu
PAGÁN-FALCÓN, Raúl ... 787-993-8877 512 A raul.pagan@upr.edu
PAGAN, Andres .... 787-765-1915 509 B apagan@opto.inter.edu
PAGAN, Carlos, H .... 787-844-8181 513 A carlos.pagan6@upr.edu
PAGAN, Damaris .... 787-765-1915 509 B dpagan@opto.inter.edu
PAGAN, Lorraine, M ..... 512-448-8411 442 I lorraine@stedwards.edu
PAGAN, Robert .... 718-960-8048 294 A robert.pagan@lehman.cuny.edu
PAGAN, William .... 848-445-5067 282 B william.pagan@rutgers.edu
PAGAN, William .... 848-445-5067 281 G william.pagan@rutgers.edu
PAGAN, William .... 848-445-5067 282 A william.pagan@rutgers.edu
PAGAN, Yolanda .... 787-891-0925 507 K ypagan@ns.inter.edu

PAGAN IRIZARRY, Efren .... 787-834-9595 510 D epagan@uaa.edu
PAGANELLI, John .... 508-531-1328 212 D jpaganelli@bridgew.edu
PAGANO, Amy, E .... 724-458-3850 384 G aepagano@gcc.edu
PAGANO, Diane, P .... 386-312-4267 107 C dianepagano@sjrstate.edu
PAGANO, Jeffrey, M ..... 716-839-8254 298 A jpagano@daemen.edu
PAGANO, Michael, A .... 312-413-3375 151 G mapagano@uic.edu
PAGANO, Neil .... 312-369-8218 136 D npagano@colum.edu
PAGE, Antony .... 305-348-1118 110 A antony.page@fiu.edu
PAGE, Beth .... 276-739-2401 475 F bpage@vhcc.edu
PAGE, Cynthia .... 540-453-2281 473 D pagec@brcc.edu
PAGE, David .... 504-816-4362 186 I dpage@dillard.edu
PAGE, Dawn .... 760-366-3791.. 40 E dawnpage@cmccd.edu
PAGE, Eric, J .... 860-701-6117 503 G eric.j.page@uscg.mil
PAGE, JR., Hugh, R ..... 574-631-5716 162 A hpage@nd.edu
PAGE, Jennifer .... 850-973-1603 104 L pagej@nfc.edu
PAGE, Jill .... 859-622-8757 180 E jill.page@eku.edu
PAGE, Jonathan, E .... 434-395-4808 468 F pageje@longwood.edu
PAGE, Kelli .... 209-946-2987.. 71 E kpage@pacific.edu
PAGE, LeAnne .... 910-892-3178 329 E lpage@heritagebiblecollege.edu
PAGE, Martin .... 918-631-2698 371 C martin-page@utulsa.edu
PAGE, Mary .... 610-436-2747 395 D mpage@wcupa.edu
PAGE, Michael .... 919-530-5402 341 E mpage@nccu.edu
PAGE, Michelle .... 320-589-6402 244 B pagem@morris.umn.edu
PAGE, Phillip .... 617-873-0256 208 B phillip.page@cambridgecollege.edu
PAGE, Randy .... 864-242-5100 406 H
PAGE, Richard, L .... 802-656-3114 463 A richard.page@uvm.edu
PAGE, Robert .... 912-260-4201 125 D robert.page@sgsc.edu
PAGE, Roberta .... 724-738-2021 395 C roberta.page@sru.edu
PAGE, Scott .... 503-494-8050 374 H faclog@ohsu.edu
PAGE, Susan .... 708-456-0300 151 D susanpage@triton.edu
PAGE, Yolanda .... 504-816-4368 186 I ypage@dillard.edu
PAGE-SMITH, Julie .... 231-843-5949 233 A jsmith@westshore.edu
PAGE-STADLER, Jaime .. 920-424-2181 496 C pagestad@uwosh.edu
PAGEL, Andrew, T .... 210-829-3933 453 C apagel@uiwtx.edu
PAGEL, Jessica, L .... 253-535-7414 482 A jessica.pagel@plu.edu
PAGEL, Myshie, M .... 915-831-2394 436 A mpagel@epcc.edu
PAGEL, Richard .... 714-432-5024.. 38 B rpagel@occ.cccd.edu
PAGELS, Jamie .... 231-348-6658 228 H jpagels@ncmich.edu
PAGLICCI, Michael .... 716-839-8492 298 A mpaglicc@daemen.edu
PAGNATTARO, Marisa, A .... 706-542-5806 126 G pagnatta@uga.edu
PAGOTTO, Louise .... 808-734-9565 129 H pagotto@hawaii.edu
PAGUIO, Arnold .... 510-723-6608.. 35 J apaguio@chabotcollege.edu
PAGUYO, Christina .... 303-871-6012.. 84 E christina.paguyo@du.edu
PAHL, Jennifer, K .... 989-964-4011 230 E jkpahl@svsu.edu
PAHLEN, Kayla .... 218-281-6510 244 A knott043@crk.umn.edu
PAHNKE, Thomas .... 262-547-1211 492 A tpahnke@carrollu.edu
PAHNO, Kari .... 918-836-6886 370 B kari.pahno@spartan.edu
PAI, Edward .... 310-233-4044.. 49 B paie@lahc.edu
PAICE, Elizabeth .... 574-520-4560 157 E epaice@iusb.edu
PAIGE, Brian .... 616-526-6758 222 C bp28@calvin.edu
PAIGE, Diane .... 704-272-5300 337 I dpaige@spcc.edu
PAIGE, Edward Adam ... 864-646-1362 412 H epaige@tctc.edu
PAIGE, Michael .... 978-232-2259 209 E mpaige@endicott.edu
PAIGE, Shelia .... 706-821-8364 124 B spaige@paine.edu
PAIGE, Sonji .... 617-327-6777 220 C sonji_paige@williamjames.edu
PAIGE, Squire .... 617-585-1284 217 E squire.paige@necmusic.edu
PAIGE, Tim .... 352-638-9737.. 96 B tpaige@beaconcollege.edu
PAIGE, Timothy .... 401-232-6011 404 A tpaige@bryant.edu
PAIKOWSKI, Gary .... 903-463-8707 436 G paikowskig@grayson.edu
PAIN, Karen, D .... 561-868-3325 105 D paink@palmbeachstate.edu
PAINE, Andrew .... 714-879-3901.. 45 G arpaine@hiu.edu
PAINE, Brenda .... 248-689-8282 232 C bpaine@walshcollege.edu
PAINE, Clarke, C .... 717-358-3991 383 I clarke.paine@fandm.edu
PAINE, Dorie .... 573-341-4218 261 D pained@mst.edu
PAINE, Josh .... 706-583-2552 115 F jpaine@athenstech.edu
PAINE, Wilson .... 540-365-4211 467 B wpaine@ferrum.edu
PAINLEY, Candice, K .... 330-569-5120 353 G painleyck@hiram.edu
PAINLEY, Peggy, A .... 330-569-5190 353 G painleypa@hiram.edu
PAINO, Troy .... 540-654-1301 471 N president@umw.edu
PAINTER, Amanda .... 864-206-2701 412 E paintera@sccsc.edu
PAINTER, Donald .... 863-292-3605 106 A dpainter@polk.edu
PAINTER, Jami .... 217-244-8247 151 F painterj@uillinois.edu
PAINTER, Michelle .... 760-245-4271.. 74 D michelle.painter@vvc.edu
PAINTER, Noel .... 386-822-7010 112 A npainter@stetson.edu
PAINTER, Sherry .... 901-435-1383 420 I sherry_painter@loc.edu
PAINTER, Virginia, R .... 304-696-4621 489 M painterv@marshall.edu
PAISANT, Julie .... 408-924-2250.. 34 A julie.paisant@sjsu.edu
PAISANT, Karen .... 504-280-6259 190 B kmpaisan@uno.edu
PAIT, Kevin .... 910-775-4355 343 B kevin.pait@uncp.edu
PAIT, Kevin .... 910-775-6260 343 B kevin.pait@uncp.edu
PAITSON, David .... 906-635-2625 226 G dpaitson@lssu.edu
PAIXAO, Francis .... 609-586-4800 278 F paixaof@mccc.edu
PAIZ, Teresa .... 408-288-3791.. 62 H teresa.paiz@sjcc.edu
PAJAKOWSKI, John ...... 574-239-8354 156 A jpajakowski@hcc-nd.edu
PAJE-MANALO, Leila, L 603-862-3491 274 F leila.paje-manalo@unh.edu
PAJEWSKI, Donald .... 414-410-4413 491 I dpajewski@stritch.edu
PAJIC MONGIARDO, Natasa .... 859-233-8213 185 C npajic@transy.edu
PAK, David, Y .... 703-425-4143 468 B
PAK, Rene, K .... 213-740-2111.. 73 D renepak@president.usc.edu
PAK, Su, Y .... 212-662-7100 323 K spak@uts.columbia.edu
PAK, Sujin .... 617-353-3052 207 E gspak@bu.edu
PAKHMANOV, Laura ..... 201-761-6412 283 A lpakhmanov@saintpeters.edu
PAKOWSKI, Lawrence ... 863-297-5282 106 A lpakowski@polk.edu
PALACE-NEININGER, Christine .... 585-785-1438 299 F christine.palace-neininger@flcc.edu
PALACIO, Michelle .... 305-348-1757 110 A michelle.palacio@fiu.edu
PALACIOS, Carol .... 305-377-8817.. 95 K
PALACIOS, Elizabeth ..... 254-710-1020 431 E liz_palacios@baylor.edu
PALACIOS, Francisco, E .... 671-735-5501 504 D francisco.palacios1@guamcc.edu
PALACIOS, Luz, M .... 787-786-3030 511 A lpalacios@ucb.edu.pr
PALACIOS, Omar .... 305-377-8817.. 95 K
PALACIOS, Rosanne ...... 956-326-2178 446 E rosanne.palacios@tamiu.edu
PALACIOUS, Casey .... 954-637-2268 108 E
PALAGANO, Nicole .... 973-748-9000 276 A nicole_palagano@bloomfield.edu
PALAGONIA, Michael ... 802-635-1205 463 G michael.palagonia@northernvermont.edu
PALAKAL, Mathew, J .... 317-278-7689 157 D mpalakal@iupui.edu
PALAN, Kay, M .... 205-348-8901.... 7 G kay.palan@culverhouse.ua.edu
PALANGI, Anthony .... 518-743-2246 320 A palangia@sunyacc.edu
PALAZZOLO, Dan .... 804-289-8973 472 C dpalazzo@richmond.edu
PALAZZOLO, Erin .... 575-674-2330 285 L epalazzolo@burrell.edu
PALEK, Staci-Jo .... 334-833-4402.... 5 G spalek@hawks.huntingdon.edu
PALEL, Dipte .... 310-660-3444.. 41 E dpatel@elcamino.edu
PALEN, Andrew .... 262-695-6247 500 B apalen@wctc.edu
PALEN, Lisa .... 203-575-8100.. 87 B lpalen@nv.edu
PALENCIA, Oscar .... 202-885-8664.. 94 D opalencia@wesleyseminary.edu
PALENSKE, Jamie .... 785-309-3114 177 E jamie.palenske@salinatech.edu
PALERMO, Kirk, M .... 830-591-7350 444 G kmpalermo@swtjc.edu
PALICIA, Deborah .... 973-278-5400 275 I dlp@berkeleycollege.edu
PALICIA, Deborah .... 973-278-5400 291 E dlp@berkeleycollege.edu
PALINKAS, Robert .... 847-491-8100 146 E robert.palinkas@northwestern.edu
PALIS, Jeffrey, M .... 336-841-9636 329 F jpalis@highpoint.edu
PALIS, Michael .... 856-225-6077 281 G palis@camden.rutgers.edu
PALKO, Kenneth .... 216-373-5296 357 F kpalko@ndc.edu
PALLADINO, Elena .... 413-585-2105 218 H epalladino@smith.edu
PALLADINO, Joan .... 203-837-9500.. 86 B palladino@wcsu.edu
PALLADINO, Michael .... 973-748-9000 276 A michael_palladino@bloomfield.edu
PALLADINO, Richard .... 914-633-2351 302 E rpalladino@iona.edu
PALLADINO, Robert ...... 740-283-6506 352 I rpalladino@franciscan.edu
PALLANSCH, Leona .... 210-436-3737 442 J lpallansch@stmarytx.edu
PALLARES, Amalia .... 312-355-1308 151 G amalia@uic.edu
PALLAVICINI, Maria ...... 209-946-2011.. 71 E
PALLEMONI, Sushil ...... 361-698-1131 435 G spallemoni@delmar.edu
PALLER, Alan .... 301-654-7267 202 D
PALLIN, Jeff .... 408-855-5179.. 75 D jeffrey.pallin@missioncollege.edu
PALLITO, Andrew .... 802-828-2800 463 F aap10150@ccv.vsc.edu
PALLOT, Brooke .... 305-899-1188.. 96 A bpallot@barry.edu
PALLOTO, Mike .... 805-289-6486.. 74 B mpallotto@vcccd.edu
PALM, Daniel .... 928-523-2461.. 14 H daniel.palm@nau.edu
PALM, Donald .... 804-524-5654 476 D dpalm@vsu.edu
PALM, Matt .... 419-448-2020 353 E mpalm@heidelberg.edu
PALMA, Eugene .... 516-877-3505 289 I palma@adelphi.edu
PALMA, Yazmin .... 305-273-4499.. 97 K yazmin@cbt.edu
PALMER, Alexis .... 801-863-8681 460 D palmeral@uvu.edu
PALMER, Andrew .... 859-257-5068 185 F andrew.palmer8@uky.edu
PALMER, Andrew .... 706-425-3117 115 F apalmer@athenstech.edu
PALMER, Aparna .... 303-678-3620.. 81 A aparna.palmer@frontrange.edu
PALMER, Beth .... 318-487-7301 187 E beth.palmer@lacollege.edu
PALMER, Blake, E .... 972-265-5765 452 B bepalmer@udallas.edu
PALMER, Brian .... 206-934-4547 483 B brian.palmer@seattlecolleges.edu
PALMER, Collin .... 419-530-5740 363 B collin.palmer@utoledo.edu
PALMER, Dale, J .... 404-413-3434 120 E dpalmer@gsu.edu
PALMER, Daniel .... 330-675-8823 354 A dpalmer1@kent.edu
PALMER, Daniel .... 605-677-5011 416 D daniel.palmer@usd.edu
PALMER, David .... 843-863-7930 407 B dpalmer@csuniv.edu
PALMER, David .... 315-655-7777 292 H dwpalmer@cazenovia.edu
PALMER, David .... 512-432-1400 444 C
PALMER, Doug .... 671-735-2862 504 F palmerd@triton.uog.edu
PALMER, Douglas .... 573-288-6323 252 F president@culver.edu
PALMER, Eric, F .... 804-287-6591 472 C epalmer@richmond.edu
PALMER, Gregory .... 603-428-2397 273 G gpalmer@nec.edu
PALMER, Gregory .... 361-698-1302 435 G gpalmer3@delmar.edu
PALMER, James, M .... 926-261-2175 446 C jmpalmer@pvamu.edu
PALMER, Janice .... 860-832-1791.. 85 G palmerj@ccsu.edu
PALMER, Jason .... 254-295-4698 453 D jbpalmer@umhb.edu
PALMER, Jennifer .... 706-583-2760 115 F jpalmer@athenstech.edu
PALMER, Jennifer .... 909-687-1500.. 43 D jenniferpalmer@gs.edu
PALMER, Joyce .... 315-792-5477 306 K jpalmer2@mvcc.edu
PALMER, Julio .... 787-841-2000 509 J jpalmer@pucpr.edu
PALMER, Kaitlin .... 605-642-6942 416 E kaitlin.palmer@bhsu.edu
PALMER, Kerry .... 334-670-3365.... 7 C kjpalmer@troy.edu
PALMER, Kevin .... 573-875-7329 251 I kpalmer@ccis.edu
PALMER, Kris, R .... 660-284-4800 254 B
PALMER, Kristi, L .... 317-274-8230 157 D klpalmer@iupui.edu
PALMER, Larry .... 304-243-4453 491 E lpalmer@wheeling.edu
PALMER, Laurel, S .... 269-337-7282 225 F laurel.palmer@kzoo.edu
PALMER, Lisa .... 706-771-4089 115 J lpalmer@augustatech.edu
PALMER, Martha .... 660-284-4800 254 B
PALMER, Meredith .... 973-408-3976 277 A mpalmer@drew.edu
PALMER, Phomika .... 202-274-5000.. 94 B phomika.palmer@udc.edu
PALMER, Rita .... 405-789-7661 369 I rita.palmer@swcu.edu
PALMER, Robert .... 405-789-7661 369 I robert.palmer@swcu.edu
PALMER, Ronnie .... 203-596-4531.. 88 F rpalmer@post.edu
PALMER, Sally .... 216-421-7311 350 H spalmer@cia.edu
PALMER, Sandra .... 718-281-5731 295 C spalmer@qcc.cuny.edu
PALMER, Sid, L .... 208-496-4622 130 I palmers@byui.edu
PALMER, Steven, C .... 269-387-4465 233 B steven.palmer@wmich.edu
PALMER, Susan, M .... 320-363-5298 235 F spalmer@csbsju.edu
PALMER, Trent .... 765-641-4104 153 G trpalmer@anderson.edu

PARIS, LeeAnne ... 405-425-5317 367 C leeanne.paris@oc.edu
PARIS, R. Inez ... 479-248-7236.. 19 B
PARIS, Susan ... 919-536-7200 334 C pariss@durhamtech.edu
PARISE, Leslie, V ... 802-656-0442 463 A leslie.parise@uvm.edu
PARISH, Aaron ... 214-333-5810 434 C aaron@dbu.edu
PARISH, Daniel, B ... 603-526-3729 272 H daniel.parish@colby-sawyer.edu
PARISH, Kylie, A ... 303-765-3127.. 81 G kparish@iliff.edu
PARISH, Susan ... 804-828-7247 473 B parishs@vcu.edu
PARISH-ONUKWULI, Kenya ... 251-405-7052.... 1 E konukwuli@bishop.edu
PARISHER, Deborah ... 252-618-6570 334 D parisherd@edgecombe.edu
PARISI, Joseph ... 660-248-6247 251 E jparisi@centralmethodist.edu
PARISI, Mark ... 518-454-2060 296 G parisim@strose.edu
PARISIEN, Chris ... 701-477-7814 346 J cparisien@tm.edu
PARISOT, Angel, R ... 610-917-1457 401 G arparisot@valleyforge.edu
PARISSE, Josh ... 816-501-3775 250 F josh.parisse@avila.edu
PARK, Claire ... 877-559-3621.. 28 H claire@ciat.edu
PARK, Connie ... 607-962-9229 320 C cpark3@corning-cc.edu
PARK, Daniel, W ... 858-822-1236.. 70 C dwpark@ucsd.edu
PARK, George ... 310-453-8300.. 41 F george@emperors.edu
PARK, Hojin ... 215-884-8942 403 D hojin.park@woninstitute.edu
PARK, Holly ... 251-626-3303.... 7 E hpark@ussa.edu
PARK, Hun Sung ... 213-381-0081.. 46 E office@laopendoor.org
PARK, Jack, C ... 210-567-2020 456 C parkjc@uthscsa.edu
PARK, Jae-sig ... 770-232-2717 124 F jspark@runiv.edu
PARK, Jessica, K ... 213-252-5100.. 23 K jpark@alu.edu
PARK, Jinsoo ... 973-877-3588 277 G jpark@essex.edu
PARK, Joseph, Y ... 636-327-4645 256 B miri@midwest.edu
PARK, Joshua ... 703-629-1281 473 A vp@vacu.edu
PARK, Joyce Gunhee ... 703-333-5904 477 F ghpark@wuv.edu
PARK, Kathryn ... 409-933-8201 433 H kpark@com.edu
PARK, Laura ... 801-649-5230 459 G registrar@midwifery.edu
PARK, Linda ... 315-279-5208 303 G lpark@keuka.edu
PARK, Lisa ... 703-993-2831 467 E lpark4@gmu.edu
PARK, Matthew ... 940-397-4501 440 C matthew.park@msutexas.edu
PARK, Meena ... 425-739-8251 481 C meena.park@lwtech.edu
PARK, Mimi ... 714-533-1495.. 64 I mimi@southbaylo.edu
PARK, Myung ... 253-964-7327 482 E mpark@pierce.ctc.edu
PARK, Paul Kitae ... 213-381-0081.. 46 E office@irus.edu
PARK, Roger ... 317-632-5553 159 I rpark@lincolntech.edu
PARK, Soo ... 509-543-1497 479 A spark@columbiabasin.edu
PARK, Sunny ... 806-720-7507 439 D sunny.park@lcu.edu
PARK, Un Yeong ... 508-999-8658 212 A upark@umassd.edu
PARK, Yong Hee ... 714-533-1495.. 64 I yhpark@southbaylo.edu
PARK, Young Hae ... 202-559-0434.. 92 C younghae.park@gallaudet.edu
PARKER, Amie ... 207-621-3448 196 H amie.parker@maine.edu
PARKER, Amy, E ... 407-582-1238 113 I akleeman@valenciacollege.edu
PARKER, Andrew ... 765-677-1989 158 B andrew.parker@indwes.edu
PARKER, Annette ... 507-389-7211 241 C annette.parker@southcentral.edu
PARKER, Annette ... 610-409-3591 401 H aparker@ursinus.edu
PARKER, Anthony ... 562-860-2451.. 35 H aparker@cerritos.edu
PARKER, Anthony ... 903-593-8311 448 G aparker@texascollege.edu
PARKER, Anthony, O ... 229-430-0656 114 I aparker@albanytech.edu
PARKER, Ava, L ... 561-868-3501 105 D parkera@palmbeachstate.edu
PARKER, Brandon, C ... 707-965-6699.. 55 I bparker@puc.edu
PARKER, Brian ... 330-923-9959 352 H
PARKER, Brttany ... 309-467-6345 138 A bparker@eureka.edu
PARKER, Carol ... 575-646-1727 287 C provost@nmsu.edu
PARKER, Cassandra ... 202-274-5669.. 94 B cparker@udc.edu
PARKER, Cassandra ... 334-727-8655.... 7 D cparker@tuskegee.edu
PARKER, Catherine ... 248-218-2154 230 B cparker@rochesteru.edu
PARKER, Charlie ... 253-964-6500 482 E cparker@pierce.ctc.edu
PARKER, Chip ... 417-873-7504 252 G cparker@drury.edu
PARKER, Chris ... 870-733-6047.. 17 F crparker@asumidsouth.edu
PARKER, Christine ... 401-254-3205 405 C cparker@rwu.edu
PARKER, Cindy ... 401-598-1345 404 D cindy.parker@jwu.edu
PARKER, Corey ... 404-297-9522 120 B parkerc@gptc.edu
PARKER, Craig ... 502-897-4131 184 G cparker@sbts.edu
PARKER, Cynthia ... 706-272-4477 118 B cparker@daltonstate.edu
PARKER, Dale ... 757-423-2095 467 A
PARKER, Dana ... 513-558-9964 362 B dana.parker@uc.edu
PARKER, Darnell ... 508-286-8200 220 B
PARKER, Darrell ... 864-488-4617 410 B dparker@limestone.edu
PARKER, Debra ... 419-434-5478 362 D parker@findlay.edu
PARKER, Devahn ... 619-934-0797.. 61 B
PARKER, Diane ... 617-243-2137 211 B dparker@lasell.edu
PARKER, Edith ... 319-384-1503 163 H edith-parker@uiowa.edu
PARKER, Fiona ... 817-554-5950 439 H fparker@messengercollege.edu
PARKER, Frank ... 936-294-1786 450 A fparker@shsu.edu
PARKER, Gwendolyn ... 803-778-1961 406 I
PARKER, Heath ... 334-442-4000 466 K hparker@auburn.vcom.edu
PARKER, Heather ... 352-588-8200 107 D
PARKER, Hilary ... 609-258-5574 280 D haparker@princeton.edu
PARKER, Holly ... 518-327-6300 311 C hparker@paulsmiths.edu
PARKER, Ingrid ... 312-662-4037 132 G iparker@adler.edu
PARKER, Jack ... 321-433-7090.. 98 I parkerj@easternflorida.edu
PARKER, Janet ... 312-355-4565 151 G japarker@uic.edu
PARKER, Janet ... 910-892-3178 329 E jparker@heritagebiblecollege.edu
PARKER, Janice, C ... 312-658-5100 150 I janice.parker@tbiil.edu
PARKER, Jay ... 844-837-7489.. 22 E
PARKER, Jeanette ... 270-789-5075 180 A jjparker@campbellsville.edu
PARKER, Jerry ... 515-271-2835 165 J jerry.parker@drake.edu
PARKER, Jesse ... 919-761-2310 340 D jparker@sebts.edu
PARKER, Jim ... 919-807-6976 331 L parkerj@nccommunitycolleges.edu
PARKER, Joe ... 970-491-3350.. 79 N joe.parker@colostate.edu
PARKER, JoeAnn ... 919-466-4400.. 93 H
PARKER, John ... 619-388-3400.. 60 I jparker002@sdccd.edu
PARKER, John ... 570-561-1818 397 H
PARKER, Juli ... 508-910-4582 212 A juli.parker@umassd.edu
PARKER, Julia ... 601-643-8308 245 F julia.parker@colin.edu
PARKER, Karen ... 508-678-2811 214 E karen.parker@bristolcc.edu
PARKER, Kathleen ... 320-363-2121 243 E kparker@csbsju.edu
PARKER, Kathy ... 320-363-2121 235 F kparker@csbsju.edu
PARKER, Katie ... 202-495-3830.. 93 D secretary@dhs.edu
PARKER, Keith ... 561-732-4424 107 G kparker@svdp.edu
PARKER, Kelly ... 818-345-9245.. 39 D kparker@columbiacollege.edu
PARKER, Kyle, D ... 479-308-2272.. 17 A kyle.parker@acheedu.org
PARKER, LaTonya ... 478-757-4028 127 F tparker@wesleyancollege.edu
PARKER, Laura ... 310-794-2304.. 69 E lparker@support.ucla.edu
PARKER, III, Lee ... 804-289-8405 472 C lparker@richmond.edu
PARKER, Linda, M ... 518-388-6578 323 J parkerl@union.edu
PARKER, Mae ... 641-269-4631 166 G parkerma@grinnell.edu
PARKER, Mark ... 405-208-5315 367 E mparker@okcu.edu
PARKER, Mary ... 352-392-1365 111 A maryparker@ufl.edu
PARKER, Mary Jo ... 713-221-8471 453 A parkerm@uhd.edu
PARKER, Matt ... 918-465-2361 366 A mparker@eosc.edu
PARKER, Mengie ... 765-973-8463 157 A mengpark@iue.edu
PARKER, Micah ... 712-707-7292 169 D micah.parker@nwciowa.edu
PARKER, Michelle, G ... 928-523-6500.. 14 H michelle.parker@nau.edu
PARKER, Neal ... 425-388-9392 480 E nparker@everettcc.edu
PARKER, Patsy ... 580-774-3284 370 A patsy.parker@swosu.edu
PARKER, Pennie ... 407-646-2636 106 L pparker@rollins.edu
PARKER, Philip, J ... 608-342-1235 496 E parkerp@uwplatt.edu
PARKER, Pippin ... 212-229-5859 308 A parkerp@newschool.edu
PARKER, Rob ... 504-568-2412 189 H rspark@lsuhsc.edu
PARKER, Robert ... 818-364-7772.. 49 C parkerr@lamission.edu
PARKER, Robert ... 707-256-7175.. 53 E rparker@napavalley.edu
PARKER, JR., Robert, D ... 217-383-4114 152 B rcparker@illinois.edu
PARKER, JR., Robert, J 518-388-6180 323 J parkerr@union.edu
PARKER, Robin, L ... 513-529-6734 356 A parkerrl@miamioh.edu
PARKER, Ron ... 979-230-3480 431 I ron.parker@brazosport.edu
PARKER, Sarah ... 740-374-8716 363 F sparker@wscc.edu
PARKER, Saundra ... 312-850-7176 135 H sparker66@ccc.edu
PARKER, Scott, B ... 701-430-2108 345 D scott.b.parker@mayvillestate.edu
PARKER, Sonya, L ... 270-824-8586 182 D sonya.parker@kctcs.edu
PARKER, Steven ... 218-755-4121 237 F steven.parker@bemidjistate.edu
PARKER, Terry ... 863-583-9050 110 B
PARKER, Timothy ... 510-907-2432.. 60 C tparker@samuelmerritt.edu
PARKER, Vic ... 601-857-3961 246 C victor.parker@hindscc.edu
PARKER AMES, Gwen ... 646-564-6742 310 D gwen.ames@nyack.edu
PARKER-DER BOGHOSSIAN, John ... 952-358-8358 239 G john.parker-derboghossian@normandale.edu
PARKER-JONES, Tonya . 619-934-0797.. 61 B
PARKER-KELLY, Darlene ... 323-563-9340.. 36 C darleneparkerkelly@cdrewu.edu
PARKER-LOW, Joan ... 207-859-1131 196 D joan.parkerlow@thomas.edu
PARKER-WOLERY, Amanda ... 513-562-6267 347 I aparker@artacademy.edu
PARKHILL, Jason ... 207-859-4000 194 D
PARKHURST, Abbie ... 540-828-5782 464 L aparkhur@bridgewater.edu
PARKHURST, Cindy ... 951-785-2982.. 47 C cparkhurst@lasiera.edu
PARKHURST, Jennifer ... 626-256-4673.. 37 A jparkhurst@coh.org
PARKIN, Michael ... 440-775-8410 357 G michael.parkin@oberlin.edu
PARKINSON, Curt ... 559-278-6634.. 31 B cparkinson@csufresno.edu
PARKINSON, Elizabeth .. 614-688-2048 358 D parkinson.107@osu.edu
PARKINSON, III, Henry, C ... 978-665-3160 212 E hparkinson@fitchburgstate.edu
PARKINSON, Richard ... 815-772-7218 145 B rcpark@morrisontech.edu
PARKINSON, Tracy ... 828-689-1237 331 C tracy_parkinson@mhu.edu
PARKMAN, Julie ... 315-386-7119 320 B parkman@canton.edu
PARKS, Amy ... 216-987-5137 351 E amy.parks@tri-c.edu
PARKS, Amy ... 216-987-6130 351 E amy.parks@tri-c.edu
PARKS, Ann ... 660-263-4100 257 B annp@macc.edu
PARKS, Charlotte ... 662-915-3120 249 D cpparks@olemiss.edu
PARKS, Daniel, A ... 909-869-2373.. 30 A daparks@cpp.edu
PARKS, David ... 304-473-8011 491 D parks.d@wvwc.edu
PARKS, Earl ... 202-651-5494.. 92 C earl.parks@gallaudet.edu
PARKS, Elysa ... 270-707-3761 182 B eparks0023@kctcs.edu
PARKS, Jana ... 785-594-4595 171 F
PARKS, JaNice ... 202-885-8687.. 94 D jparks@wesleyseminary.edu
PARKS, Jason ... 318-484-2184 192 G parksj@nsula.edu
PARKS, Jason ... 951-372-7017.. 59 C jason.parks@norcocollege.edu
PARKS, Jeffrey ... 281-756-3631 429 D jparks@alvincollege.edu
PARKS, Jo-Lynne ... 303-546-3570.. 82 A jparks@naropa.edu
PARKS, Lenora ... 931-221-7571 417 H parksl1@apsu.edu
PARKS, Lisa ... 541-956-7446 376 A lparks@roguecc.edu
PARKS, Marshall ... 970-351-1814.. 84 F marshall.parks@unco.edu
PARKS, Matt ... 815-753-2095 146 B mparks2@niu.edu
PARKS, Matthew ... 212-659-7200 303 H mparks@tkc.edu
PARKS, Michael ... 210-567-2791 456 C parksm@uthscsa.edu
PARKS, Patricia ... 714-816-0366.. 68 E patricia.parks@trident.edu
PARKS, Rodney ... 336-278-6677 328 J rparks4@elon.edu
PARKS, Roger ... 713-525-3151 454 G parksrw@stthom.edu
PARKS, Valerie ... 915-779-8031 457 F
PARKS, Vanasia Conley 423-425-4467 427 C vanasia-parks@utc.edu
PARKS, Wendy, E ... 630-942-2755 135 I parksw@cod.edu
PARKS, Whitney ... 660-248-6221 251 E wparks@centralmethodist.edu
PARKS-PARTON, Toni ... 217-234-5252 142 C tparks@lakelandcollege.edu
PARLACOSKI, Julie ... 732-987-2219 278 A jparlacoski@georgian.edu
PARLANGE, Marc ... 401-874-1000 405 E
PARLE, Joseph, D ... 832-252-4659 432 L joe.parle@cbshouston.edu
PARLETT, Ray, M ... 585-567-9333 302 B ray.parlett@houghton.edu
PARLETT-SWEENEY, Mary, W ... 518-782-6988 315 E mparlett-sweeney@siena.edu
PARLIER, Heather ... 828-232-5117 342 B hparlier@unca.edu
PARLOW, Matthew, J ... 714-628-2678.. 36 B parlow@chapman.edu

PATRIA, Patricia, L .... 508-831-5000 220 F
plpatria@wpi.edu
PATRICK, Beth, G .... 843-208-8138 413 C
patricbg@uscb.edu
PATRICK, Brian .... 913-288-7362 175 B
bpatrick@kckcc.edu
PATRICK, Craig .... 914-632-5400 307 A
cpatrick@monroecollege.edu
PATRICK, David .... 360-650-2884 485 I
david.patrick@wwu.edu
PATRICK, Edward .... 919-516-4127 339 I
epatrick@st-aug.edu
PATRICK, Jamie .... 919-497-3245 330 I
jpatrick@louisburg.edu
PATRICK, Julietta .... 847-635-1754 146 G
jpatrick@oakton.edu
PATRICK, Laura .... 949-376-6000.. 47 D
lpatrick@lcad.edu
PATRICK, Mary .... 805-922-6966.. 24 I
mary.patrick@hancockcollege.edu
PATRICK, Michelle, L ... 412-397-6359 397 B
patrick@rmu.edu
PATRICK, Nicole .... 662-329-7114 248 A
jnpatrick@muw.edu
PATRICK, Patricia .... 808-675-3618 128 D
patricia.patrick@byuh.edu
PATRICK, Paul, D .... 843-953-0879 408 C
patrickpd@cofc.edu
PATRICK, Thelma .... 614-234-2415 356 E
tpatrick@mccn.edu
PATRICK, Tracie, M ...... 814-641-3142 386 E
patrict@juniata.edu
PATRIQUIN, Wendy ...... 304-929-5494 488 G
wpatriquin@newriver.edu
PATSCHECK, Kathy .... 606-451-6621 182 G
PATTALITAN, Penelope . 305-821-3333 100 E
ppattalitan@fnu.edu
PATTEE, Bonnie .... 801-274-3280 461 E
bonnie.pattee@wgu.edu
PATTEN, II, Carl .... 404-527-7714 121 L
cepatten@itc.edu
PATTEN, Elizabeth .... 406-874-6192 263 H
pattene@milescc.edu
PATTEN, MaeLynn .... 401-341-2462 405 D
mae.patten@salve.edu
PATTEN, Shawn .... 941-752-5444 109 G
pattens@scf.edu
PATTEN-LEMONS,
Rebecca .... 317-921-4667 158 E
rpatten@ivytech.edu
PATTERMAN, Bambi ...... 715-319-7269 499 H
PATTERSON, Ana .... 817-202-6201 444 I
pattersonam@swau.edu
PATTERSON, Bart .... 702-992-2350 271 B
president@nsc.edu
PATTERSON, Becky .... 502-852-3385 186 A
becky.patterson@louisville.edu
PATTERSON, Betsy .... 704-878-3244 336 C
epatterson@mitchellcc.edu
PATTERSON, Brad .... 870-230-5083.. 19 D
bpatterson@hsu.edu
PATTERSON, Cam .... 501-686-7000.. 22 B
cpatters@uams.edu
PATTERSON, Carol .... 303-797-5701.. 77 I
carol.patterson@arapahoe.edu
PATTERSON, Charles, E 717-477-1301 395 B
cepatterson@ship.edu
PATTERSON, Charlotte .. 434-924-0664 472 D
cjp@virginia.edu
PATTERSON, Chrissy .... 903-983-8198 438 F
cpatterson@kilgore.edu
PATTERSON, Cindi .... 864-663-0189 410 I
cindi.patterson@ngu.edu
PATTERSON, Cynthia, A 252-638-7304 334 A
pattersonc@cravencc.edu
PATTERSON, Darrin .... 330-337-6403 347 D
maintenance@awc.edu
PATTERSON, Darrin .... 330-337-6403 347 D
maint@awc.edu
PATTERSON, David .... 605-692-9337 415 B
dpatterson@ilt.edu
PATTERSON, Donald, A 716-878-3447 317 F
patterda@buffalostate.edu
PATTERSON, Dorsey ..... 901-435-1286 420 I
dorsey_patterson@loc.edu
PATTERSON, Elice .... 202-651-5309.. 92 C
elice.patterson@gallaudet.edu
PATTERSON, Elizabeth .. 903-223-6722 448 A
elizabeth.patterson@tamut.edu
PATTERSON, Emily, A ... 316-978-3030 178 D
emily.patterson@wichita.edu
PATTERSON, Eric .... 214-654-9075 202 D
PATTERSON, Felicia, L .. 410-777-2718 197 G
flpatterson@aacc.edu
PATTERSON,
Franklin, E .... 386-481-2020.. 96 D
pattersonf@cookman.edu
PATTERSON, Hahna ...... 207-221-4418 197 E
hpatterson@une.edu
PATTERSON, Howard .... 903-566-7350 456 A
hpatterson@uttyler.edu
PATTERSON, Jackie .... 215-780-1397 398 B
jpatterson@salus.edu
PATTERSON, James .... 860-738-6482.. 87 C
jpatterson@nwcc.edu
PATTERSON,
Jana Lynn, F .... 336-278-7200 328 J
patters@elon.edu
PATTERSON, Jennifer .... 614-236-6502 349 B
jpatterson@capital.edu
PATTERSON,
Jennifer, L .... 641-422-4346 168 G
jennifer.patterson@niacc.edu
PATTERSON, Joanna ..... 866-492-5336 244 F
joanna.patterson@laureate.net
PATTERSON, John, A ..... 478-301-5537 122 E
patterson_ja@mercer.edu
PATTERSON, Joseph ..... 239-280-1595.. 95 M
joseph.patterson@avemaria.edu
PATTERSON, Karen .... 904-620-2700 111 B
karen.patterson@unf.edu
PATTERSON, Kenneth .... 505-454-2500 286 F
PATTERSON, Kenneth .... 937-481-2241 364 A
kenn.patterson@wilmington.edu
PATTERSON, Kim .... 254-299-8606 439 E
kpatterson@mclennan.edu
PATTERSON, Leni, N ..... 864-833-8284 411 D
lpatters@presby.edu
PATTERSON, Mark .... 805-437-3283.. 30 C
mark.patterson@csuci.edu
PATTERSON, Michael .... 410-225-2422 200 D
mpatters@mica.edu
PATTERSON, Michael .... 415-503-6237.. 61 D
mpatterson@sfcm.edu
PATTERSON, Michelle ... 865-354-3000 425 C
pattersonm@roanestate.edu
PATTERSON, Myrna ...... 808-845-9115 130 A
mpatters@hawaii.edu
PATTERSON, Nancy .... 423-697-2630 424 A
nancy.patterson@chattanoogastate.edu
PATTERSON, Pamela, L 703-993-1000 467 E
PATTERSON, Patty .... 954-492-5353.. 97 G
ppatterson@citycollege.edu
PATTERSON, Paul, M .... 334-844-3209.... 4 D
pmp0003@auburn.edu
PATTERSON, Ralph .... 803-321-5166 410 H
ralph.patterson@newberry.edu
PATTERSON, Robert, H . 804-752-3605 469 F
robertpatterson@rmc.edu
PATTERSON, Ron, K .... 256-765-5159.... 8 E
rpatterson1@una.edu
PATTERSON, Sarah .... 575-492-2575 287 A
spatterson@nmjc.edu
PATTERSON, Scott .... 314-446-8382 260 H
scott.patterson@stlcop.edu
PATTERSON, Shannon .. 706-771-4013 115 J
sbentley@augustatech.edu
PATTERSON, Sharna ..... 610-527-0200 397 D
sharna.patterson@rosemont.edu
PATTERSON, Sharon, E . 626-395-3937.. 28 J
sharon.patterson@caltech.edu
PATTERSON, Stacey ...... 865-974-4048 427 A
stacey.patterson@tennessee.edu
PATTERSON, Stephanie . 626-256-4673.. 37 A
spatterson@coh.org
PATTERSON, Steven ...... 703-323-3554 474 F
spatterson@nvcc.edu
PATTERSON, Teresa ...... 909-274-5512.. 52 J
tpatterson@mtsac.edu
PATTERSON, Thomas .... 334-387-3877.... 4 B
thomaspatterson@amridgeuniversity.edu
PATTERSON, Tracy .... 901-843-3856 423 A
pattersont@rhodes.edu
PATTERSON, Van .... 409-944-1205 436 E
vpatterson@gc.edu
PATTERSON, Vicki .... 832-252-4624 432 L
vicki.patterson@cbshouston.edu
PATTERSON, Wayne ...... 814-732-2703 394 B
wepatterson@edinboro.edu
PATTERSON, Zachary .... 559-730-3906.. 39 B
zacharyp@cos.edu
PATTERSON HARRIS,
Emily .... 405-466-3265 366 C
patterson.harris@okstate.edu
PATTILLO, Nicolas .... 479-788-7166.. 21 G
npattillo@uafs.edu
PATTISON, Margaret ..... 313-578-0327 231 E
peggy.pattison@udmercy.edu
PATTON, Aimee .... 816-584-6703 258 C
aimee.patton@park.edu
PATTON, Chad .... 434-949-1038 475 B
chad.patton@southside.edu
PATTON, Guy, L .... 405-321-1174 370 K
gpatton@ou.edu
PATTON, Julia, G .... 610-917-2004 401 G
jgpatton@valleyforge.edu
PATTON, Kerry .... 203-582-3087.. 88 G
kerry.patton2@quinnipiac.edu
PATTON, Laurie, L .... 802-443-5400 462 E
president@middlebury.edu
PATTON, Laurie, S .... 740-368-3026 359 G
lspatton@owu.edu
PATTON, Linda .... 404-270-5048 126 B
lpatton@spelman.edu
PATTON, Michael .... 626-529-8498.. 55 F
mpatton@pacificoaks.edu
PATTON, Paul, E .... 606-218-5262 186 B
pep@upike.edu
PATTON, Paul, N .... 518-320-1100 315 H
PATTON, Venetria .... 217-333-1529 152 B
vkpatton@illinois.edu
PATTON-OSTRANDER,
Kelley, A .... 518-580-5814 315 F
kostrand@skidmore.edu
PATTY, Stacy .... 806-720-7652 439 D
stacy.patty@lcu.edu
PATWARY, Mohsin .... 718-270-6217 294 G
mohsin@mec.cuny.edu
PATZ, Thomas .... 317-738-8183 155 D
tpatz@franklincollege.edu
PATZER, Troy .... 509-527-2586 485 C
troy.patzer@wallawalla.edu
PAUGH, Jennifer .... 734-423-2139 227 D
PAUGH, Mark .... 352-854-2322.. 97 N
paughm@cf.edu
PAUKEN, Evan .... 269-488-4215 225 G
epauken@kvcc.edu
PAUKEN, Megan .... 269-488-4755 225 G
mpauken@kvcc.edu
PAUKEN, Patrick .... 419-372-2226 348 G
paukenp@bgsu.edu
PAUKEN, Patrick .... 419-372-2550 348 G
paukenp@bgsu.edu
PAUL, Alyson .... 706-864-1900 127 A
alyson.paul@ung.edu
PAUL, Brandie .... 931-363-9879 427 E
bpaul7@utsouthern.edu
PAUL, Brandon .... 954-731-8880.. 97 Q
PAUL, Christine .... 805-493-3220.. 29 C
clpaul@callutheran.edu
PAUL, David, W .... 801-422-4887 458 H
davidwpaul@byu.edu
PAUL, Elizabeth, L .... 585-389-2004 307 F
epaul3@naz.edu
PAUL, Glenn .... 254-267-7100 441 K
gpaul@rangercollege.edu
PAUL, Jina .... 402-552-3100 266 E
pauljina@clarksoncollege.edu
PAUL, Jonathan .... 212-228-1888 312 B
PAUL, Kara .... 406-447-4401 263 B
kpaul@carroll.edu
PAUL, Keith .... 413-755-4817 216 A
kpaul@stcc.edu
PAUL, Kohle .... 770-962-7580 121 E
kpaul@gwinnetttech.edu
PAUL, Mary .... 619-849-2215.. 57 J
marypaul@pointloma.edu
PAUL, Minnu .... 910-630-7225 331 E
mpaul@methodist.edu
PAUL, Phyllis, M .... 330-941-3625 364 H
pmpaul@ysu.edu
PAUL, Rachelle .... 201-761-7302 283 A
rpaul2@saintpeters.edu
PAUL, Robert, H .... 314-516-8403 261 C
paulro@umsl.edu
PAUL, Theresa, C .... 828-227-3812 343 E
tcpaul@wcu.edu
PAUL, Tim .... 712-274-5116 168 E
pault@morningside.edu
PAUL, Tonya, D .... 419-772-3106 358 C
t-paul@onu.edu
PAULE, Romeo .... 415-949-7308.. 42 I
pauleromeo@foothill.edu
PAULE, Sara .... 765-983-1431 155 A
paulesa@earlham.edu
PAULEY, Ann .... 202-884-9725.. 94 A
pauleya@trinitydc.edu
PAULEY, Jennifer .... 740-351-3550 360 F
jpauley@shawnee.edu
PAULICK, Joe .... 305-348-4196 110 A
joseph.paulick@fiu.edu
PAULINE, Rose Lee ...... 215-951-1014 387 A
pauline@lasalle.edu
PAULINO, Avianny .... 787-761-0640 511 E
promocion@utcpr.edu
PAULK, Chavis .... 205-247-8151.... 7 A
cpaulk@stillman.edu
PAULOSKI, SP, Pam .... 773-371-5420 134 D
presoffice@ctu.edu
PAULS, Kelly .... 620-241-0723 172 J
kelly.pauls@centralchristian.edu
PAULS, Rebecca .... 304-829-7633 487 A
rpauls@bethanywv.edu
PAULSEN, Brian .... 402-844-7030 268 H
bpaulsen@northeast.edu
PAULSEN, Derek .... 859-622-3565 180 E
derek.paulsen@eku.edu
PAULSEN, Jenny .... 813-974-8944 111 C
jpaulsen@usf.edu
PAULSEN, Josh .... 972-600-2818.. 26 C
jpaulsen@asher.edu
PAULSON, Cheri .... 781-239-3845 206 B
cpaulson@babson.edu
PAULSON, Erik .... 212-752-1530 304 A
erik.paulson@limcollege.edu
PAULSON, Janis .... 888-775-1514.. 68 I
PAULSON, Kimberly .... 715-634-4790 492 L
kpaulson@lco.edu
PAULSON, Veronica ...... 605-626-2537 416 G
veronica.paulson@northern.edu
PAULUS, Bill .... 612-624-1091 243 F
paulu038@umn.edu
PAULUS, Michael .... 206-281-2414 483 G
paulusm@spu.edu
PAULUS, Michael, L ..... 419-372-2891 348 G
mpaulus@bgsu.edu
PAULY, Karen .... 704-330-6976 333 D
karen.pauly@cpcc.edu
PAULY, Katelyn .... 518-861-2565 305 C
kpauly@mariacollege.edu
PAUNAN, Crystal .... 630-953-3660 134 F
PAUSTIAN, Pamela, E ... 205-975-9376.... 8 A
paustian@uab.edu
PAUSTIAN, Tony .... 515-633-2439 165 A
adpaustian@dmacc.edu
PAUXTIS, Cody .... 760-384-6369.. 46 M
cody.pauxtis@cerrocoso.edu
PAVALKO, Eliza .... 812-855-9973 156 G
vpfaa@indiana.edu
PAVAN, Ron .... 615-547-1348 419 C
rpavan@cumberland.edu
PAVAN, Tammi .... 615-547-1228 419 C
tpavan@cumberland.edu
PAVEK, Annette .... 320-762-4411 237 C
annettep@alextech.edu
PAVELL, Cynthia .... 310-506-6023.. 56 G
cynthia.pavell@pepperdine.edu
PAVEY, Katheryne .... 251-405-7089.... 1 E
kpavey@bishop.edu
PAVEZA, Gregory .... 773-995-4517 134 K
PAVILONIS, Brigid .... 508-830-5012 213 D
bpavilonis@maritime.edu
PAVLAT, Penny .... 906-217-4099 222 A
pavlatp@baycollege.edu
PAVLIK, Angie .... 440-943-7600 360 E
apavlik@dioceseofcleveland.org
PAVLIK, Kimberly .... 561-912-1211.. 99 D
kpavlik@evergladesuniversity.edu
PAVLIS, Tim .... 203-436-9358.. 90 C
timothy.pavlis@yale.edu
PAVLOU, Paul, A .... 713-743-3562 452 D
papavlou@uh.edu
PAVLOW, Joseph .... 610-527-0200 397 D
joseph.pavlow@rosemont.edu
PAVON, Tracie .... 515-961-1630 170 B
tracie.pavon@simpson.edu
PAVRI, Shireen .... 562-985-4513.. 31 D
shireen.pavri@csulb.edu
PAVUK, Michael .... 315-858-0945 302 A
PAVY, Anna .... 270-789-5059 180 A
ampavy@campbellsville.edu
PAWAR, Ashlesha .... 563-387-1001 168 B
pawaas01@luther.edu
PAWELL, Liz .... 909-469-5202.. 75 I
lpawell@westernu.edu
PAWLAK, Erin .... 716-896-0700 324 E
epawlak@villa.edu
PAWLAK, Katherine .... 863-680-3964 100 H
kpawlak@flsouthern.edu

PAWLAK, Kurt ... 740-264-5591 352 B
kpawlak@egcc.edu
PAWLIK, Amy ... 309-268-8249 138 H
amy.munson-pawlik@heartland.edu
PAWLIKOWSKI,
Deborah, J ... 973-290-4184 282 I
dpawlikowski@steu.edu
PAWLO - JOHNSTONE,
Jennifer ... 410-337-6181 199 B
jennifer.pawlojohnstone@goucher.edu
PAXSON, Christina, H .. 401-863-2234 403 J
christina_paxson@brown.edu
PAXSON, Sherrie ... 505-566-3490 288 D
paxsons@sanjuancollege.edu
PAXTON, Ellen ... 269-399-7700 162 B
epaxton@sf.edu
PAYANZO COTTON,
Anna ... 856-222-9311 281 C
ftietz@rcbc.edu
PAYAWAL, Pamela ... 323-860-0789.. 50 B
PAYBA, Shane ... 808-984-3496 130 D
payba@hawaii.edu
PAYDAR, Nasser ... 317-274-4417 156 G
chancllr@iupui.edu
PAYDAR, Nasser, H ... 317-274-4417 157 D
paydar@iupui.edu
PAYDAR, Nasser, H ... 317-274-4417 156 F
chancllr@iupui.edu
PAYLO, Keith ... 412-392-3862 396 G
kpaylo@pointpark.edu
PAYNE, Andre ... 803-570-0028 408 G
paynea@denmarktech.edu
PAYNE, Brian, K ... 757-683-4757 469 B
bpayne@odu.edu
PAYNE, Charles, M ... 973-353-1750 282 B
charles.payne@rutgers.edu
PAYNE, Crystal ... 757-340-2121 465 I
registrarcvab@centura.edu
PAYNE, Dalry, B ... 269-471-3100 221 D
dalry@andrews.edu
PAYNE, David ... 801-734-6789 459 K
david.payne@rm.edu
PAYNE, Don ... 303-762-6900.. 80 I
academicdean@denverseminary.edu
PAYNE, Donna, G ... 585-275-2758 323 M
donna.payne@rochester.edu
PAYNE, George, M ... 240-567-2582 200 G
george.payne@montgomerycollege.edu
PAYNE, Gloria, E ... 252-335-3595 341 B
gepayne@ecsu.edu
PAYNE, JR., Harry, E .... 813-988-5131.. 99 R
president@floridacollege.edu
PAYNE, Harvey ... 703-416-1441 466 A
hpayne@divinemercy.edu
PAYNE, Heather ... 954-492-5353.. 97 G
hpayne@citycollege.edu
PAYNE, James ... 256-306-2684.... 1 F
james.payne@calhoun.edu
PAYNE, James, E ... 915-747-7781 455 C
jpayne2@utep.edu
PAYNE, Janet ... 570-321-4151 389 B
payne@lycoming.edu
PAYNE, John ... 801-422-9099 458 H
john_payne@byu.edu
PAYNE, John, F ... 671-735-5565 504 D
john.payne2@guamcc.edu
PAYNE, Karen, E ... 937-529-2201 361 G
kepayne@united.edu
PAYNE, Kathy ... 215-489-2372 382 B
kathy.payne@delval.edu
PAYNE, Kathy, O ... 904-819-6305.. 99 E
kpayne@flagler.edu
PAYNE, Kent ... 847-214-7552 137 F
kpayne@elgin.edu
PAYNE, Leslie ... 573-288-6395 252 F
lpayne@culver.edu
PAYNE, Leslie, M ... 210-567-2503 456 C
paynelm@uthscsa.edu
PAYNE, Maggie ... 701-349-5798 346 I
mpayne@trinitybiblecollege.edu
PAYNE, Maribeth ... 573-840-9007 260 E
mpayne@trcc.edu
PAYNE, Mary ... 515-271-1452 165 G
mary.payne@dmu.edu
PAYNE, Matthew ... 701-349-5415 346 I
mattpayne@trinitybiblecollege.edu
PAYNE, Melissa ... 319-398-5584 167 J
melissa.payne@kirkwood.edu
PAYNE, Molly ... 617-732-2218 216 D
molly.payne@mcphs.edu
PAYNE, Nikita, T ... 334-293-4603.... 1 C
nikita.payne@accs.edu
PAYNE, Nikki ... 314-529-6864 255 B
npayne@maryville.edu
PAYNE, Paige ... 406-447-6927 264 B
paige.payne@helenacollege.edu
PAYNE, Pamela ... 915-831-6511 436 A
ppayne1@epcc.edu
PAYNE, Stephen, C ... 202-319-5139.. 92 A
paynesl@cua.edu
PAYNE, Stephen, D ... 269-471-6534 221 D
stephen@andrews.edu
PAYNE, Tamara ... 205-853-1200.... 2 G
tlpayne@jeffersonstate.edu
PAYNE, Tara ... 603-513-1356 274 G
tara.payne@granite.edu
PAYNE, Taylor ... 217-732-3168 142 G
PAYNE, Thomas ... 931-372-3372 426 B
tpayne@tntech.edu
PAYNE, Tyran ... 928-771-6132.. 16 J
tyran.payne@yc.edu
PAYNE, Vernon ... 269-387-2136 233 B
vernon.payne@wmich.edu
PAYNE, Wesley, A ... 573-840-9698 260 E
wpayne@trcc.edu
PAYNE, William ... 775-784-6604 271 E
bpayne@cabnr.unr.edu
PAYNE CERVERA,
Brandi ... 307-778-1218 501 E
bcervera@lccc.wy.edu
PAYNE-KIRCHMEIER,
Julie, A ... 847-491-5360 146 E
vpsa@northwestern.edu
PAYNTER, Alan ... 315-781-3729 301 F
paynter@hws.edu
PAYNTER, Brooke ... 210-805-5709 453 C
paynter@uiwtx.edu
PAYNTER, Chris ... 704-330-6531 333 D
chris.paynter@cpcc.edu
PAYOVICH, Nathan ... 708-974-5330 145 A
payovichn@morainevalley.edu
PAYTON, Amanda ... 937-376-6611 349 J
apayton@centralstate.edu
PAYTON, Andy ... 812-488-2000 161 G
apayton@methodisttemple.church
PAYTON, Annie ... 256-372-4747.... 1 A
annie.payton@aamu.edu
PAYTON, Christine ... 337-521-8936 188 I
christine.payton@solacc.edu
PAYTON, Karl ... 903-233-3142 439 A
karlpayton@letu.edu
PAYTON, Kizzy ... 225-216-8404 187 G
paytonk2@mybrcc.edu
PAZ, Gabriel ... 717-867-6302 388 C
paz@lvc.edu
PAZ, Harold, L ... 614-292-6446 358 D
paz.31@osu.edu
PAZ, Veronica ... 210-366-2701 441 J
vpaz@questcollege.edu
PEABODY, William ... 845-437-7267 324 C
wipeabody@vassar.edu
PEACE, Derryle ... 903-886-5764 447 B
derryle.peace@tamuc.edu
PEACE, Donald ... 864-231-2000 406 F
dpeace@andersonuniversity.edu
PEACE, Matthew ... 386-752-1822 100 B
matthew.peace@fgc.edu
PEACH, Kyle ... 618-262-8641 139 I
peachk@iecc.edu
PEACOCK, Benjamin ... 972-860-4643 434 F
bpeacock@dcccd.edu
PEACOCK, Caleb ... 423-478-7703 422 J
cpeacock@ptseminary.edu
PEACOCK, Corey ... 307-268-2249 500 U
michael.peacock@caspercollege.edu
PEACOCK, Katie ... 425-739-8455 481 C
katie.peacock@lwtech.edu
PEACOCK, Mark ... 719-296-6108.. 82 J
mark.peacock@pueblocc.edu
PEACOCK, Melissa ... 360-676-2772 481 F
mpeacock@nwic.edu
PEACOCK, Ross ... 440-775-6927 357 G
ross.peacock@oberlin.edu
PEACOCK, Starr ... 334-387-3877.... 4 B
starrfain@amridgeuniversity.edu
PEACOCK, Steve ... 612-330-1583 234 A
peacock@augsburg.edu
PEACOCK-LANDRUM,
Linda, G ... 920-465-2163 495 F
peacockl@uwgb.edu
PEAK, Douglas, C ... 817-515-3076 445 F
douglas.peak@tccd.edu
PEAK, Lisa ... 502-410-6200 180 G
PEAL, Darryl, A ... 859-572-6630 184 E
peald1@nku.edu
PEARCE, Amy ... 314-773-0083 250 I
apearce@brookes.edu
PEARCE, Arthur, B ... 229-333-5832 127 E
apearce@valdosta.edu
PEARCE, Chris ... 336-734-7570 334 F
cpearce@forsythtech.edu
PEARCE, David ... 660-543-4365 260 G
dpearce@ucmo.edu
PEARCE, Jared ... 641-673-2107 171 C
pearcej@wmpenn.edu
PEARCE, Jennifer ... 276-944-6968 466 L
jpearce@ehc.edu
PEARCE, Julie, L ... 818-677-2366.. 32 C
julie.pearce@csun.edu
PEARCE, Kelley, H ... 256-549-8376.... 2 B
khaynes@gadsdenstate.edu
PEARCE, Kim ... 952-214-0945 242 N
kpearce@nwhealth.edu
PEARCE, Rick ... 309-268-8100 138 H
rick.pearce@heartland.edu
PEARCE, Rick ... 229-226-1621 126 C
rpearce@thomasu.edu
PEARCE, Steve ... 770-229-3293 125 H
steve.pearce@sctech.edu
PEARCY, Shelly ... 231-591-3825 224 A
shellypearcy@ferris.edu
PEARIGEN, Rob ... 601-974-1001 247 B
rob.pearigen@millsaps.edu
PEARL, Danita ... 937-708-5704 363 G
dpearl@wilberforce.edu
PEARLE, Kathleen ... 508-678-2811 214 B
kathleen.pearle@bristolcc.edu
PEARLMAN, Russ, B ... 402-280-5104 266 H
russellpearlman@creighton.edu
PEARRING, Yu Yok ... 808-932-8912 129 D
yuyok@hawaii.edu
PEARSALL, Joel, K ... 208-467-8521 132 E
president@nnu.edu
PEARSALL, Jonathan ... 617-824-8426 209 C
jonathan_pearsall@emerson.edu
PEARSALL, Kim ... 863-297-1000 106 A
kpearsall@polk.edu
PEARSALL, Roland ... 617-236-8879 209 G
rpearsall@fisher.edu
PEARSE, David ... 956-295-3517 449 C
david.pearse@tsc.edu
PEARSE, Kelly ... 262-524-7124 492 A
kgilling@carrollu.edu
PEARSEY, Lindsey, K .... 812-855-3870 156 F
lpearsey@iu.edu
PEARSON, Andre ... 201-200-3501 279 D
apearson@njcu.edu
PEARSON, Andrew, L .... 540-828-5410 464 L
apearson@bridgewater.edu
PEARSON, Annie ... 405-422-1486 369 A
annie.pearson@redlandscc.edu
PEARSON, Barry ... 914-251-6020 319 B
barry.pearson@purchase.edu
PEARSON, Bryan, J ... 814-886-6424 390 G
bpearson@mtaloy.edu
PEARSON, Christie ... 214-768-7432 444 D
cmpearson@smu.edu
PEARSON,
Christopher, A ... 810-762-3000 232 A
pear@umich.edu
PEARSON, Craig ... 641-472-1186 168 C
cpearson@miu.edu
PEARSON, David ... 951-343-4298.. 27 G
dpearson@calbaptist.edu
PEARSON, David, L ... 515-574-1234 167 A
pearson@iowacentral.edu
PEARSON, Doug, R ... 478-301-2685 122 E
pearson_dr@mercer.edu
PEARSON, Jan ... 706-233-7236 125 C
jpearson@follett.com
PEARSON, Janice, L ... 559-323-2100.. 61 F
jpearson@sjcl.edu
PEARSON, Joe ... 405-733-7973 369 E
jpearson@rose.edu
PEARSON, Karen, L ... 208-467-8663 132 E
klpearson@nnu.edu
PEARSON, Mary ... 435-865-8270 460 A
pearsonm@suu.edu
PEARSON, Matt ... 707-778-3608.. 63 D
mpearson@santarosa.edu
PEARSON, Megan ... 662-620-5090 246 E
mspearson@iccms.edu
PEARSON, Sam ... 503-589-8154 372 H
spearson@corban.edu
PEARSON, Sandy ... 415-485-3200.. 41 C
sandy.pearson@dominican.edu
PEARSON, Sarah, R ... 207-786-6247 194 A
spearson@bates.edu
PEARSON, Shelley ... 817-515-8004 445 F
shelley.pearson@tccd.edu
PEARSON, Sonya ... 702-651-7980 270 K
sonya.pearson@csn.edu
PEARSON, Stacy ... 509-335-5524 485 D
stacy.pearson@wsu.edu
PEARSON, Susan ... 509-527-4265 485 B
susan.pearson@wwcc.edu
PEARSON, Susan ... 865-354-3000 425 C
pearsonc@roanestate.edu
PEARSON, Tammi ... 909-274-4220.. 52 J
tpearson@mtsac.edu
PEARSON, Terri ... 580-477-7918 371 D
PEARSON, Tracey ... 910-630-7122 331 E
tpearson@methodist.edu
PEARSON, Virgil ... 314-340-5300 254 A
pearsonv@hssu.edu
PEARSON, Vonda ... 651-255-6115 243 E
vpearson@unitedseminary.edu
PEARSON, Yvette, E ... 972-883-4566 455 B
PEARSON-WHARTON,
Stacey ... 570-372-4238 398 F
pearsonwharton@susqu.edu
PEART, Emily, N ... 530-898-6897.. 30 D
epeart@csuchico.edu
PEART, Gwendolyn ... 704-334-6882 328 B
gpeart@charlottechristian.edu
PEART, Sandra, J ... 804-287-6086 472 C
speart@richmond.edu
PEASE, Patrick, P ... 319-273-2518 164 A
patrick.pease@uni.edu
PEASLEE, Deidra ... 651-846-1364 241 B
deidra.peaslee@saintpaul.edu
PEASTER, Rita ... 405-744-5000 367 G
PEAT, Kareem ... 718-817-3112 300 C
kpeat@fordham.edu
PEAVEY, Donna, B ... 504-282-4455 190 F
dpeavey@nobts.edu
PEAVY, Kristi ... 478-757-5200 127 F
kpeavy@wesleyancollege.edu
PEAVY, Liesa ... 770-216-2960 121 I
lpeavy@ict.edu
PEAVY, Terence ... 212-217-3801 299 D
terence_peavy@fitnyc.edu
PECCHIA, John, P ... 845-575-3000 305 D
john.pecchia@marist.edu
PECCIA, Veronica ... 845-437-5331 324 C
PECENY, Mark ... 505-277-7381 288 J
markpec@unm.edu
PECHA, David, M ... 580-327-8528 367 A
dmpecha@nwosu.edu
PECHAN, Gwen ... 904-819-6359.. 99 E
gpechan@flagler.edu
PECHENKINA, Ekaterina 718-997-5210 295 B
ekaterina.pechenkina@qc.cuny.edu
PECK, Adam ... 309-438-8110 140 D
apeck1@ilstu.edu
PECK, Daniel, A ... 408-855-5122.. 75 D
daniel.peck@missioncollege.edu
PECK, David ... 626-815-4503.. 26 F
dpeck@apu.edu
PECK, David, R ... 208-496-3963 130 I
peckdr@byui.edu
PECK, Edward ... 216-397-4218 353 O
epeck@jcu.edu
PECK, Emily ... 270-534-3244 183 B
emily.peck@kctcs.edu
PECK, James ... 414-955-4700 493 F
jpeck@mcw.edu
PECK, Jane ... 781-768-7307 218 D
jane.peck@regiscollege.edu
PECK, Jeanie ... 651-641-8709 235 I
peck@csp.edu
PECK, Kendall, D ... 208-496-1123 130 I
peckk@byui.edu
PECK, Sherry ... 614-236-6534 349 B
speck@capital.edu
PECK, Susan ... 252-335-0821 333 G
susan_peck@albemarle.edu
PECK, Travis ... 918-343-6816 369 B
tpeck@rsu.edu
PECKA, Kenneth ... 509-777-3292 486 C
kpecka@whitworth.edu
PECKHAM, Karissa ... 860-832-0030.. 85 G
kpeckham@ccsu.edu
PECKHAM, Michael ... 920-403-3360 495 B
mike.peckham@snc.edu
PECKLER, Dawn ... 815-836-5230 142 F
peckleda@lewisu.edu
PECOR, Sarah, A ... 262-243-5700 492 E
sarah.pecor@cuw.edu
PECORARO, Heather ... 508-767-7355 206 A
hl.pecoraro@assumption.edu
PECORD, Melanie ... 618-985-2828 140 H
melaniepecord@jalc.edu

PECOTA, Samuel, R ...... 707-654-1000.. 32 A
PECTOL, James, B .... 423-585-6823 425 F
james.pectol@ws.edu
PEDAWI, Evonne .... 517-884-4234 227 F
pedawi@cga.msu.edu
PEDDE, David .... 276-326-3682 464 J
dpedde@bluefield.edu
PEDDLE, Ronald .... 602-206-8220 272 L
rpeddle@ccsnh.edu
PEDE, Michael .... 315-792-5411 306 K
mpede@mvcc.edu
PEDE, Mike .... 713-743-9551 452 D
mlpede@uh.edu
PEDEN, Gary, S .... 315-470-6588 319 D
gspeden@esf.edu
PEDERSEN, Andrew .... 701-671-2314 346 D
andrew.pedersen.1@ndscs.edu
PEDERSEN, Catherine ... 757-683-4653 469 B
cpederse@odu.edu
PEDERSEN, Cindi, M .... 574-807-7239 154 B
cindi.pedersen@betheluniversity.edu
PEDERSEN, Eric .... 435-652-7977 460 B
pedersen@dixie.edu
PEDERSEN, Eric .... 360-867-6310 480 C
pedersee@evergreen.edu
PEDERSEN, Ginger, L ... 561-967-7222 105 D
pederseg@palmbeachstate.edu
PEDERSEN, Henrik .... 848-445-4795 282 A
hpederse@soe.rutgers.edu
PEDERSEN, Joy, M .... 805-756-6749.. 29 I
jmpeders@calpoly.edu
PEDERSEN, Karen, L ..... 785-532-3110 175 C
karenpedersen@ksu.edu
PEDERSEN, Mary .... 970-491-6614.. 79 N
mary.pedersen@colostate.edu
PEDERSEN, Matthew, D 801-863-8320 460 D
mpedersen@uvu.edu
PEDERSEN, Patricia, E .. 203-436-8518.. 90 C
patty.pedersen@yale.edu
PEDERSEN, Ryan .... 925-473-7404.. 40 D
rpedersen@losmedanos.edu
PEDERSON, Curtis, R ... 503-943-8046 377 A
pedersoc@up.edu
PEDERSON, Joshua ...... 507-344-7840 234 C
jpederson@blc.edu
PEDERSON, Kathy .... 507-457-1586 243 C
kpeders@smumn.edu
PEDERSON, Mark .... 765-677-2117 158 B
mark.pederson@indwes.edu
PEDERSON, Paula .... 218-736-1559 239 C
paula.pederson@minnesota.edu
PEDESCLEAUX, Desiree . 404-270-5696 126 B
dpedescl@spelman.edu
PEDLOW, Amy, M .... 716-878-6332 317 F
pedlowam@buffalostate.edu
PEDNEAU, Judy .... 276-326-4461 464 J
jpedneau@bluefield.edu
PEDONE, Melissa, D .... 321-682-4176 113 I
mpedone@valenciacollege.edu
PEDRAJA, Luis .... 508-854-4203 215 F
lpedraja@qcc.mass.edu
PEDRAZA, Jonathan, N . 262-691-5308 500 B
jpedraza2@wctc.edu
PEDRICK, Jim .... 319-385-6218 167 H
jim.pedrick@iw.edu
PEDRICK, Laura .... 414-229-3203 496 B
lpedrick@uwm.edu
PEDRO, David .... 508-910-9070 212 A
dpedro@umassd.edu
PEDRO, Joan .... 281-283-3501 452 E
pedro@uhcl.edu
PEDROTTY, Kate .... 318-869-5715 186 F
kpedrotty@centenary.edu
PEE, Charles, M .... 803-934-3294 410 G
cpee@morris.edu
PEEBLES, Lee .... 401-739-5000 404 E
lpeebles@neit.edu
PEED, Stephen .... 207-326-2451 196 A
stephen.peed@mma.edu
PEEK, Katherine .... 909-652-6333.. 35 L
kay.peek@chaffey.edu
PEEK, Patricia .... 718-817-1000 300 C
peek@fordham.edu
PEEL, Bill .... 214-932-1112 439 A
billpeel@letu.edu
PEEL, Chermae .... 432-552-3744 456 F
peel_c@utpb.edu
PEEL, Henry .... 239-489-9011 101 A
hpeel@fsw.edu
PEEL, Joe .... 318-257-3267 192 D
jpeel@latech.edu
PEELE, Natasha .... 212-410-8039 308 E
npeele@nycpm.edu
PEELER, Chris .... 704-461-6684 326 L
chrispeeler@bac.edu
PEELER, Jody .... 740-284-5216 352 I
jpeeler@franciscan.edu
PEELER, Mark, L .... 864-379-8850 409 E
mlp@erskine.edu
PEELING, Rebecca .... 561-803-2018 105 C
becky_peeling@pba.edu
PEEPLES, Jim .... 706-778-8500 124 D
jpeeples@piedmont.edu
PEEPLES, Matilda .... 404-297-9522 120 B
PEEPLES, Terry, G .... 870-245-5169.. 20 D
peeplest@obu.edu
PEEPLES, Tim .... 336-278-5613 328 J
peeples@elon.edu
PEERY, Tracy .... 276-944-6112 466 L
tpeery@ehc.edu
PEETERS, Clare .... 212-678-8080 303 D
clpeeters@jtsa.edu
PEETHALA, Sudha .... 503-255-0332 374 C
sudhapeethala@multnomah.edu
PEETZ, Ralf .... 718-982-2440 293 E
ralf.peetz@csi.cuny.edu
PEEVY, Andrea .... 985-549-3275 193 A
apeevy@selu.edu
PEEVY, DeWayne .... 773-325-7503 136 H
dpeevy@depaul.edu
PEFFER, Deb .... 313-593-5100 231 I
dkpeffer@umich.edu
PEGAH, Kris .... 941-351-7220 106 J
kpegah@ringling.edu
PEGAH, Mahmoud .... 941-359-7633 106 J
mpegah@ringling.edu
PEGG, Steven, M .... 410-777-2651 197 G
smpegg@aacc.edu
PEGGRAM, Rosemary ... 806-291-3414 457 I
peggramr@wbu.edu
PEGRAM, Mike .... 402-761-8270 269 C
mpegram@southeast.edu
PEGUES, Antonius .... 318-670-6000 191 D
PEGUES, Lisa .... 914-694-4225 296 B
lpegues@riversidehealth.org
PEGUES, Wanda .... 662-252-8000 248 G
wpegues@rustcollege.edu
PEHLMAN, Patricia, A ... 717-245-1545 382 D
pehlman@dickinson.edu
PEHRSSON,
Dale-Elizabeth .... 814-393-2220 393 G
president@clarion.edu
PEHRSSON,
Dale-Elizabeth .... 814-732-2000 394 B
PEIFER, Bruce .... 903-927-3293 458 F
bpeifer@wileyc.edu
PEIFER, Michelle .... 704-991-0393 338 C
mpeifer7924@stanly.edu
PEIFFER, Cyndi .... 641-673-1040 171 C
peifferc@wmpenn.edu
PEIFFER, Kelly .... 215-885-2360 389 C
kpeiffer@manor.edu
PEIFFER, Kelly .... 215-885-2360 389 C
admissions@manor.edu
PEIFFER, Mark .... 515-271-1475 165 G
mark.peiffer@dmu.edu
PEIPERL, Maury .... 703-993-1860 467 E
mpeiperl@gmu.edu
PEKLO, Emily .... 402-354-7274 268 B
emily.peklo@methodistcollege.edu
PEKRUL, William, A ...... 507-354-8221 236 J
pekrulwa@mlc-wels.edu
PELAEZ, Bares .... 305-348-1957 110 A
bronwen.bares@fiu.edu
PELAEZ, Indra .... 713-718-7497 437 C
indra.pelaez@hccs.edu
PELAEZ, Michelle .... 813-253-6251 113 H
mpelaez@ut.edu
PELAYO, Lula .... 210-808-4765 503 C
lula.pelayo@usuhs.edu
PELAZZA, Todd, A .... 203-254-4090.. 87 I
tapelazza@fairfield.edu
PELC, Sharon .... 308-865-8523 269 I
pelcs@unk.edu
PELCH, Aaron .... 601-974-1194 247 B
aaron.pelch@millsaps.edu
PELCHAT, Christopher .. 509-533-3500 479 D
PELCHER, Mary .... 989-317-4760 230 D
mpelcher@sagchip.edu
PELESKO, John, A .... 302-831-0740.. 91 C
pelesko@udel.edu
PELESKY, Timothy .... 301-687-3240 204 C
tdpelesky@frostburg.edu
PELHAM, Stephanie ...... 973-408-3961 277 A
spelham@drew.edu
PELIA, Clarissa .... 907-852-1820.... 9 H
clarissa.pelia@ilisagvik.edu
PELIZZA, John .... 518-244-2051 313 A
pelizj@sage.edu
PELKEY, David .... 360-596-5231 484 D
dpelkey@spscc.edu
PELLEGRIN, Angie .... 985-448-7943 188 C
angie.pellegrin@fletcher.edu
PELLEGRIN, Nathan ...... 510-466-7210.. 57 C
npellegrin@peralta.edu
PELLEGRINI, Larry .... 570-674-6307 390 B
lpellegrini@misericordia.edu
PELLEGRINI, Virginia .... 208-426-3158 130 H
virginiapellegrini@boisestate.edu
PELLEGRINO, Debra, A . 570-941-6305 401 F
debra.pellegrino@scranton.edu
PELLEGRINO, Karen ...... 610-660-1305 397 G
kpellegr@sju.edu
PELLEGRINO, Robin ...... 508-767-7599 206 A
rpellegr@assumption.edu
PELLERIN, Angela .... 318-797-5219 190 A
angela.pellerin@lsus.edu
PELLERIN, Jody .... 319-398-5409 167 J
jody.pellerin@kirkwood.edu
PELLERIN, Virginia .... 504-520-7229 193 E
vpelleri@xula.edu
PELLETIER, Corey .... 207-859-1106 196 D
pelletierc@thomas.edu
PELLETIER, Debra .... 207-834-7844 197 A
debra.pelletier1@maine.edu
PELLETIER, Jo-Ann, M .. 508-678-2811 214 B
jo-ann.pelletier@bristolcc.edu
PELLICANO, Gregory, J 215-898-7958 400 F
gpell@upenn.edu
PELLINEN, Brian .... 978-921-4242 217 B
brian.pellinen@montserrat.edu
PELLOT, Robert .... 212-938-5720 319 E
rpellot@sunyopt.edu
PELLS, Ruth .... 509-777-4665 486 C
rpells@whitworth.edu
PELLY, Michael .... 714-997-6982.. 36 B
pelly@chapman.edu
PELMAN, Javonda .... 815-588-7541 142 F
pelmanja@lewisu.edu
PELOQUIN, Andy .... 503-517-1815 377 E
apeloquin@westernseminary.edu
PELOQUIN, Elayne .... 434-544-8230 471 L
peloquin_em@lynchburg.edu
PELOQUIN-DODD,
Mary, T .... 919-515-2143 342 A
mary_peloquin-dodd@ncsu.edu
PELOSI, Lisa .... 401-598-1848 404 D
lisa.pelosi@jwu.edu
PELOSO, Elizabeth, D ... 215-746-0234 400 F
epeloso@upenn.edu
PELRINE, John .... 312-369-7045 136 D
jpelrine@colum.edu
PELTIER, Beverly .... 706-771-4171 115 J
bpeltier@augustatech.edu
PELTIER, Eileen .... 860-253-3032.. 87 G
epeltier@acc.commnet.edu
PELTIER, Eileen .... 860-253-3032.. 86 C
epeltier@commnet.edu
PELTIER, Matt .... 423-652-4740 420 F
mspeltie@king.edu
PELTO, Mauri, S .... 508-213-2201 217 H
mauri.pelto@nichols.edu
PELTON, Jeremy .... 502-897-4200 184 G
jpelton@sbts.edu
PELTON, Mark .... 478-445-5075 119 B
mark.pelton@gcsu.edu
PELTON, Vanessa .... 805-965-0581.. 63 A
pelton@sbcc.edu
PELTS, Dody .... 479-979-1422.. 23 I
dpelts@ozarks.edu
PELTZ, Kristen, S .... 660-562-1348 257 E
kpeltz@nwmissouri.edu
PELTZ, Mark .... 641-269-4940 166 G
peltzm@grinnell.edu
PELUSO, Constance ...... 718-631-6297 295 C
cpeluso@qcc.cuny.edu
PELUSO, W. Mark .... 802-443-5249 462 E
wpeluso@middlebury.edu
PELUSO-VERDEND,
Gary .... 918-270-6405 368 G
gary.peluso@ptstulsa.edu
PELUSZAK, Kris .... 215-503-1956 399 E
kris.peluszak@jefferson.edu
PEMBERTON, Barbara ... 870-245-5541.. 20 D
pembertonb@obu.edu
PEMBERTON,
Cynthia, L .... 208-792-2216 132 A
clpemberton@lcsc.edu
PEMBERTON, Paul .... 218-935-0417 244 G
paul.pemberton@wetcc.edu
PEMBROOK, Randall, G 618-650-2475 150 C
rpembro@siue.edu
PEMSTEIN, Debra, R ..... 845-758-7405 290 I
pemstein@bard.edu
PENA, Agusto, E .... 336-334-4442 343 A
aepenaes@uncg.edu
PENA, Amy, C .... 210-486-1209 429 C
apena259@alamo.edu
PENA, Andrew, M .... 915-831-6325 436 A
apena20@epcc.edu
PENA, Daniel .... 517-264-7146 230 H
dpena@sienaheights.edu
PENA, Denise .... 714-556-3610.. 73 H
PENA, Elizabeth .... 830-758-5023 450 B
epena@sulross.edu
PENA, Elizabeth, S .... 510-649-2400.. 44 B
PENA, JR., Federico ..... 402-826-8260 267 A
fred.pena@doane.edu
PENA, Fernando .... 415-338-7211.. 33 E
fernandopena@sfsu.edu
PENA, Hector .... 787-725-6500 505 G
hpena@albizu.edu
PENA, Jesus .... 610-683-4700 394 D
pena@kutztown.edu
PENA, Juanita .... 719-549-2943.. 80 B
juanita.pena@csupueblo.edu
PENA, Mauro .... 909-794-2161.. 60 E
PENA, Michelle .... 661-395-4318.. 46 L
michelle.pena@bakersfieldcollege.edu
PENA, Milly .... 914-251-6010 319 B
milly.pena@purchase.edu
PENA, Philip .... 515-961-1398 170 B
philip.pena@simpson.edu
PENALBA, Richelle .... 714-432-5869.. 38 B
rpenalba@occ.cccd.edu
PENALVA, Andrew .... 317-921-7931 158 E
apenalva@ivytech.edu
PENALVER, Eduardo, M 206-296-6000 484 A
PENAS, Angela, D .... 786-331-1000 104 H
apena@maufl.edu
PENATE, Rey .... 650-543-3932.. 51 G
rey.penate@menlo.edu
PENCE, Barry .... 563-884-5866 169 F
barry.pence@palmer.edu
PENCE, Heather .... 770-528-4545 117 B
PENCE, Kory .... 918-335-6879 368 E
kpence@okwu.edu
PENCE, Margaret .... 605-626-2254 416 G
PENCHI, Zulma .... 787-257-0000 512 B
zulma.penchi@upr.edu
PENDELTON, C. Jay .... 813-253-3333 113 H
cpendelton@ut.edu
PENDER, Moriah .... 706-233-7417 125 C
mpender@shorter.edu
PENDERGAST, Jayme .... 770-426-2858 122 C
jayme.pendergast@life.edu
PENDERGAST, Kate .... 860-768-2403.. 89 G
pendergas@hartford.edu
PENDERGAST, Marcy .... 518-629-7230 302 C
m.pendergast@hvcc.edu
PENDERGRASS, Toni ..... 505-566-3209 288 D
pendergrasst@sanjuancollege.edu
PENDERS, Brooke .... 860-768-4287.. 89 G
penders@hartford.edu
PENDHARKAR, Daya ...... 813-253-7091 102 B
dpendharkar@hccfl.edu
PENDLETON,
Christopher .... 540-261-8400 471 B
chris.pendleton@svu.edu
PENDLETON, Gail .... 510-981-2804.. 56 I
gpendleton@peralta.edu
PENDLETON, Jody .... 972-279-6511 429 F
jpendleton@amberton.edu
PENDLETON, Laura .... 509-452-5100 482 B
lpendleton@pnwu.edu
PENDLETON, Laurence .. 615-963-7925 426 A
laurence.pendleton@tnstate.edu
PENDLETON, Lorraine ... 540-891-3033 473 I
lpendleton@germanna.edu
PENDLEY, Catherine ..... 919-365-7711 340 E
catherine.pendley@sfwbc.edu
PENDSE, Ravi .... 734-763-7590 231 H
rpendse@umich.edu
PENFIELD, Randall, D ... 336-334-3944 343 A
rdpenfie@uncg.edu
PENG, Hsin (Gina) .... 310-233-4356.. 49 B
penghw@lahc.edu
PENG, Sarah .... 312-225-6288 152 J
PENG, Willie .... 657-278-2866.. 31 C
wpeng@fullerton.edu

PENGRA, Matt .... 407-679-0100 101 K
mpengra@fullsail.com
PENHALL, Colleen .... 704-687-7225 342 D
cpenhall@uncc.edu
PENICK, William .... 951-785-2100.. 47 C
wpenick@lasierra.edu
PENINGER, Heather ...... 704-403-1638 327 C
heather.peninger@atriumhealth.org
PENISTEN, Douglas ...... 918-444-4000 366 G
penisten@nsuok.edu
PENIX, Doug .... 859-442-1634 181 H
doug.penix@kctcs.edu
PENKALA, Robert .... 586-445-7636 227 B
penkalar@macomb.edu
PENKE, Ann .... 920-565-1000 493 A
penkea@lakeland.edu
PENLAND, Jennifer .... 304-876-5222 490 A
jpenland@shepherd.edu
PENLAND, Nathan .... 417-328-1828 259 I
npenland@sbuniv.edu
PENLEY, Julie .... 915-731-6715 436 A
jpenley@epcc.edu
PENLEY, Rashelle .... 828-726-2488 332 G
rpenley@cccti.edu
PENN, Courtney .... 540-375-2270 470 E
penn@roanoke.edu
PENN-MARSHALL,
Michelle .... 757-727-5267 467 G
michelle.penn-marshall@hamptonu.edu
PENN-MARSHALL,
Michelle .... 757-637-2690 467 G
michelle.pennmarshall@hamptonu.edu
PENNA, Anthony .... 617-552-3475 207 C
anthony.penna@bc.edu
PENNER, Julie .... 815-836-5667 142 F
pennerju@lewisu.edu
PENNEY, Bill .... 352-395-5160 108 A
bill.penney@sfcollege.edu
PENNEY, Samantha .... 812-237-8479 156 D
samantha.penney@indstate.edu
PENNIMAN, Sarah .... 717-361-1428 383 C
pennimans@etown.edu
PENNINGTON, Amy ...... 479-968-0407.. 18 C
apennington@atu.edu
PENNINGTON, Kevin .... 252-399-6467 326 K
knpennington@barton.edu
PENNINGTON,
Kimberly .... 828-328-7473 330 F
kimberly.pennington@lr.edu
PENNINGTON, Laura .... 276-739-2538 475 F
lpennington@vhcc.edu
PENNINGTON, Nicole ... 740-593-2551 358 K
penningj@ohio.edu
PENNINGTON, Nicole ... 740-533-4610 358 K
penningj@ohio.edu
PENNINGTON,
Sandra, L .... 801-375-5125 459 K
sandy.pennington@rm.edu
PENNINGTON, Sherry ... 417-667-8181 252 B
spennington@cottey.edu
PENNINGTON, Thomas . 479-964-0824.. 18 C
tpennington@atu.edu
PENNINI, Susan, W ...... 617-333-2165 208 G
spennini@curry.edu
PENNIX, James, A .... 540-365-4290 467 B
jpennix@ferrum.edu
PENNO, Brittany .... 620-227-9261 173 D
bgladbach@dc3.edu
PENNOCK, Kimberly ..... 508-999-8073 212 A
kpennock@umassd.edu
PENNY, Anthony .... 508-793-7389 208 C
apenny@clarku.edu
PENNY, Rick .... 440-525-7320 354 L
rpenny@lakelandcc.edu
PENPRASE, Bryan, E ..... 949-480-4184.. 64 G
bpenprase@soka.edu
PENROSE, Betsy .... 607-587-4215 319 F
penrosb@alfredstate.edu
PENROSE, Leif .... 813-253-7370 102 B
lpenrose@hccfl.edu
PENRY, Michael, A .... 919-866-5532 338 G
mapenry@waketech.edu
PENSE, Christine .... 610-861-5312 391 C
cpense@northampton.edu
PENSGARD, Sara, E ...... 540-338-1776 469 C
library@phc.edu
PENSIS, Claude .... 602-639-7500.. 12 J
PENSON, Amy, M .... 828-395-1296 335 D
apenson@isothermal.edu
PENUNURI, Christianne 619-660-4039.. 44 D
christianne.penunuri@gcccd.edu
PENWELL, Vicki .... 208-258-9334 132 B
PENYAK, Lee, M .... 269-387-5890 233 B
lee.penyak@wmich.edu

PENZENSTADLER, SSND,
Joan .... 414-930-3388 494 E
penzenj@mtmary.edu
PEOPLES, Kevin .... 706-649-1821 117 I
kpeoples@columbustech.edu
PEOPLES, Lisa .... 731-426-7500 420 G
PEOPLES, Shawn .... 217-581-3827 137 E
sdpeoples@eiu.edu
PEOPLES, VerJanis .... 225-771-2291 191 A
verjanis_peoples@subr.edu
PEOPLES, Verjanis .... 225-771-2291 191 B
verjanis_peoples@subr.edu
PEPIN, Mark .... 918-495-7236 368 F
mpepin@oru.edu
PEPITONE, Dianne .... 914-831-0367 297 A
dpepitone@cw.edu
PEPPARD, Paul, C .... 606-474-3272 181 B
pcpeppard@kcu.edu
PEPPER, Jannette, D ..... 901-722-3369 423 G
jdumas@sco.edu
PEPPER, Kelly .... 337-421-6903 188 J
kelly.pepper@sowela.edu
PEPPER, Robert .... 717-796-1800 389 H
rpepper@messiah.edu
PEPPER, Russel .... 614-236-6632 349 B
rpepper@capital.edu
PEPPERS, Marla .... 323-343-3929.. 31 E
mpepper@calstatela.edu
PEPPIN, Patricia .... 480-461-7456.. 13 D
pat.peppin@mesacc.edu
PEPPLE, Katharine, S .... 215-972-2015 392 T
kpepple@pafa.edu
PEPPLE, Michael .... 816-501-3600 250 F
michael.pepple@avila.edu
PERÉZ, Miguel .... 787-257-0000 512 B
miguel.perez8@upr.edu
PERAGALLO MONTANO,
Nilda .... 919-966-3731 342 C
npm@email.unc.edu
PERALES, Jose, J .... 585-385-8067 313 F
jperales@sjfc.edu
PERALES, Kit .... 408-864-5678.. 42 H
PERALEZ, Maisee .... 509-527-3672 485 B
maisee.peralez@wwcc.edu
PERALTA-DE LA CRUZ,
Paola .... 787-480-2455 506 C
pperalta@sanjuan.pr
PERBELLINI, Maria .... 516-686-7641 308 I
maria.perbellini@nyit.edu
PERCELL, Shannon .... 253-833-9111 480 I
spercell@greenriver.edu
PERCIVAL, Brent .... 434-243-8118 472 D
bp8x@virginia.edu
PERCUOCO, Robert, E ... 563-884-5460 169 F
robert.percuoco@palmer.edu
PERCUS, Allon .... 909-607-0744.. 37 C
allon.percus@cgu.edu
PERCY, Kerri .... 954-776-4476 103 B
kpercy@keiseruniversity.edu
PERCY, Stephen .... 503-725-4411 375 E
president@pdx.edu
PERDOMO, Jose .... 787-767-0616 511 F
josel.perdomo@upr.edu
PERDOMO RAMIREZ,
Natalia, E .... 787-725-8120 506 M
nperdomo@eap.edu
PERDUE, K. Alan .... 304-876-5009 490 A
aperdue@shepherd.edu
PERDUE, Laura .... 318-797-5257 190 A
laura.perdue@lsus.edu
PERDUE, Mark .... 217-735-7300 142 H
mperdue@lincolncollege.edu
PERDUE, Neil .... 317-788-3380 161 H
perduen@uindy.edu
PERDUE, Penny .... 708-534-4130 138 E
pperdue@govst.edu
PERDUE, Robin, A .... 843-383-8025 408 B
rperdue@coker.edu
PERDUE, Ron .... 330-490-7373 363 E
rperdue@walsh.edu
PERDUE, Tina, K .... 740-376-4730 355 E
tina.perdue@marietta.edu
PERDUE, Troy .... 931-372-3269 426 B
tperdue@tntech.edu
PERDUE, Wendy, C ...... 804-289-8740 472 C
wperdue@richmond.edu
PERDUE-SMITH, Kendra 708-596-2000 149 H
kperduesmith@ssc.edu
PEREA, Grace .... 702-254-7577 272 A
grace.perea@northwestcareercollege.edu
PEREA, Jennifer, R .... 312-362-1083 136 H
jrosato@depaul.edu

PEREBOOM, Maarten, L 410-543-6450 204 D
mlpereboom@salisbury.edu
PERECMAN, Dov .... 845-434-5240 326 J
menahel@ygzm.edu
PEREGORD,
Margaret, A .... 301-447-5627 201 B
peregord@msmary.edu
PEREIRA, Freyja .... 707-527-4512.. 63 D
fpereira@santarosa.edu
PEREIRA, Greg .... 480-517-8538.. 13 G
greg.pereira@riosalado.edu
PEREIRA, Malin .... 704-687-7197 342 D
mpereira@uncc.edu
PEREKRESTOV, Michael 315-858-0945 302 A
library@hts.edu
PERERA, Curtis .... 360-752-8330 478 A
cperera@btc.edu
PERETZ, Marc, H .... 989-964-4062 230 E
mhp@svsu.edu
PEREYRA, Moises .... 212-694-1000 291 J
mpereyra@boricuacollege.edu
PEREZ, Alex .... 559-934-2134.. 74 N
alexperez4@whccd.edu
PEREZ, Alvaro .... 787-798-6732 511 B
alvaro.perez@uccaribe.edu
PEREZ, Andrew .... 518-438-3111 305 C
andyp@mariacollege.edu
PEREZ, Awilda .... 787-766-1717 510 G
um_aperez@uagm.edu
PEREZ, Camile .... 787-766-1717 510 G
camperez@uagm.edu
PEREZ, Carlos .... 787-622-8000 511 D
cperez@pupr.edu
PEREZ, Carlos .... 787-754-8000 511 D
cperez@pupr.edu
PEREZ, Carmen, I .... 787-279-1912 508 A
cperez@bayamon.inter.edu
PEREZ, Caty .... 559-278-4036.. 31 B
catyp@csufresno.edu
PEREZ, Cesar .... 909-667-4428.. 37 G
cperez@claremontlincoln.edu
PEREZ, Daisy .... 787-892-6442 508 F
dnperez@intersg.edu
PEREZ, Debora .... 210-431-5553 441 B
daguzman@lake.ollusa.edu
PEREZ, Delva .... 787-878-6000 507 D
dperez@icprjc.edu
PEREZ, Diana .... 805-922-6966.. 24 I
dperez@hancockcollege.edu
PEREZ, Dilcie, D .... 560-860-2451.. 35 H
dilcieperez@cerritos.edu
PEREZ, Doris .... 787-891-0925 507 K
dperez@aguadilla.inter.edu
PEREZ, Doris, U .... 671-735-5517 504 D
doris.perez@guamcc.edu
PEREZ, Eduardo .... 787-279-1912 508 A
eperezd@bayamon.inter.edu
PEREZ, Eltie .... 787-894-2828 513 C
eltie.perez@upr.edu
PEREZ, Enrique .... 714-480-7460.. 58 E
perez_enrique@rsccd.edu
PEREZ, Francisco .... 787-758-2525 512 F
francisco.perez12@upr.edu
PEREZ, Gay .... 434-243-3605 472 D
bgd2j@virginia.edu
PEREZ, JR., Gilberto ..... 574-535-7434 155 E
gperez@goshen.edu
PEREZ, Gonzalo .... 609-586-4800 278 F
perezg@mccc.edu
PEREZ, Hector .... 954-637-2268 108 E
hperez@sfbc.edu
PEREZ, Hiselgis .... 305-348-2731 110 A
perezh@fiu.edu
PEREZ, Ida .... 210-431-3950 441 B
iperez@ollusa.edu
PEREZ, Ivelisse .... 787-834-9595 510 D
iperez@uaa.edu
PEREZ, Jessie .... 787-288-1118 510 I
PEREZ, Jose .... 787-738-2161 512 C
jose.pelay@upr.edu
PEREZ, Jose .... 305-821-3333 100 E
josep@fnu.edu
PEREZ, Jose .... 915-566-9621 458 B
jperez@westerntech.edu
PEREZ, Juan .... 406-275-4855 265 F
juan_perez@skc.edu
PEREZ, Julia .... 973-290-4470 282 I
jperez@steu.edu
PEREZ, Julian .... 786-391-1167.. 95 G
PEREZ, Kathryn .... 806-716-2370 443 G
kperez@southplainscollege.edu
PEREZ, Katrina .... 671-735-2957 504 F
katrina@uogendowment.org

PEREZ, Lance .... 402-472-3181 269 J
lperez1@unl.edu
PEREZ, Laura .... 323-241-5281.. 49 E
perezli2@lasc.edu
PEREZ, Linda .... 281-649-3391 437 B
lperez@hbu.edu
PEREZ, Luci .... 909-599-5433.. 48 A
lperez@lifepacific.edu
PEREZ, Lydia .... 646-565-6000 322 G
lydia.perez@touro.edu
PEREZ, Lydia .... 646-565-6000 322 F
lydia.perez@touro.edu
PEREZ, Maggie .... 305-237-7563 104 E
mperez51@mdc.edu
PEREZ,
Manuel Alejandro .... 650-306-3236.. 62 J
perezma@smccd.edu
PEREZ, Marciano .... 619-388-3498.. 60 I
mperez@sdccd.edu
PEREZ, JR., Marciano .. 619-388-3498.. 60 I
mperez@sdccd.edu
PEREZ, Margarita .... 337-482-6272 193 B
mperez@louisiana.edu
PEREZ, Maria .... 787-780-0070 505 F
mperez@caribbean.edu
PEREZ, Maria .... 787-891-0925 507 K
mperez@aguadilla.inter.edu
PEREZ, Maria del C ...... 787-284-1912 508 E
mcperezr@ponce.inter.edu
PEREZ, Mario .... 707-664-2880.. 34 B
PEREZ,
Melvin (Tony), A .... 585-292-2904 307 B
tperez7@monroecc.edu
PEREZ, Miguel .... 323-415-4123.. 48 J
perezma@elac.edu
PEREZ, Miguel, E .... 787-752-4575 512 B
miguel.perez8@upr.edu
PEREZ, Mireya .... 708-656-8000 145 C
mireya.perez@morton.edu
PEREZ, Miriam .... 787-840-2575 509 I
mperez@psm.edu
PEREZ, Monica .... 864-644-5135 412 D
mperez@swu.edu
PEREZ, Myrna .... 787-786-3030 511 A
mperez@ucb.edu.pr
PEREZ, Nancy .... 413-538-2188 217 C
nbperez@mtholyoke.edu
PEREZ, Natasha .... 316-295-5888 174 A
natasha_perez@friends.edu
PEREZ, Nicholas .... 254-415-4050.. 93 H
PEREZ, Norma .... 713-718-5040 437 C
norma.perez@hccs.edu
PEREZ, Omar .... 787-740-1611 511 B
omar.perez@uccaribe.edu
PEREZ, Orlando .... 972-780-3600 454 A
orlando.perez@untdallas.edu
PEREZ, Pablo .... 305-626-6007.. 95 A
PEREZ, Pedro .... 787-622-8000 511 D
pperez@pupr.edu
PEREZ, Peter .... 203-254-4000.. 87 I
pperez1@fairfield.edu
PEREZ, Rayetta .... 616-392-8555 233 E
rayetta@westernsem.edu
PEREZ, Robert .... 763-433-1285 237 D
robert.perez@anokarmasey.edu
PEREZ, Roger .... 559-791-2209.. 47 A
roger.perez@portervillecollege.edu
PEREZ, Scott .... 805-437-8808.. 30 C
scott.perez@csuci.edu
PEREZ, Steve .... 916-278-6331.. 32 D
steve.perez@csus.edu
PEREZ, Suleyma .... 773-442-5400 146 A
s-perez6@neiu.edu
PEREZ, Susan .... 904-620-5092 111 B
sperez@unf.edu
PEREZ, Veronica .... 210-366-2701 441 J
vperez@questcollege.edu
PEREZ, Yolanda .... 787-834-9595 510 D
yperez@uaa.edu
PEREZ-CASANOVA,
Maria, T .... 787-480-2448 506 C
mperez02@sanjuan.pr
PEREZ COLÓN, Adaliz .. 787-250-0000 511 F
adaliz.perez03@upr.edu
PEREZ DE JESUS,
Margarita .... 787-848-5739 510 B
mperez@csifpr.org
PEREZ-DORTA, Pedro ... 787-622-8000 511 D
pperez@pupr.edu
PEREZ-FRANCO, Mayte . 619-260-2395.. 72 I
mpf@sandiego.edu
PEREZ HERNÁNDEZ,
Marilu .... 787-764-0000 513 B
marilu.perez1@upr.edu

PEREZ-JOHNSTON, Angelica ...... 412-237-4535 381 D aperez-johnston@ccac.edu
PEREZ-LOPEZ, Mark ..... 910-962-3746 343 C perezlopezm@uncw.edu
PEREZ-LOPEZ, Myrna, E ...... 787-763-6700 507 A meperez@se-pr.edu
PEREZ-MEDINA, Eunice 787-250-0000 511 F eunice.perezmedina@upr.edu
PEREZ MENDEZ, Jesse . 806-742-2377 450 F jp.mendez@ttu.edu
PEREZ-RODRIGUEZ, Jose, F ...... 787-723-4481 506 A jose.perez@ceaprc.edu
PEREZ-RODRIGUEZ, Yarelis ...... 787-751-1912 509 A yarelis.perez@juris.inter.edu
PEREZ - SANTIAGO, José, A ...... 787-725-6500 505 G jperez@albizu.edu
PEREZ TOLEDO, Elizabeth ...... 787-848-5739 510 B epereztoledo@csifpr.org
PEREZ-TOPCZEWSKI, Vanessa ...... 262-650-4826 492 A vperezto@carrollu.edu
PERFETTI, Charles, A .... 412-624-7107 400 H perfetti@pitt.edu
PERFETTI, Lisa ...... 330-263-2004 351 A lperfetti@wooster.edu
PERGI, Brenan ...... 740-283-6445 352 I bpergi@franciscan.edu
PERGOLA-RIVERA, Maribelle ...... 787-993-8951 512 A maribelle.pergola@upr.edu
PERGOLIS, Robert ...... 718-940-5419 314 A rpergolis@sjcny.edu
PERGOLIZZI, Francis .... 207-973-1069 194 F pergolizzif@husson.edu
PERGOLIZZI, Vanessa ... 860-913-2160.. 88 A vpergolizzi@goodwin.edu
PERI, Jonathan ...... 215-885-2360 389 C jperi@manor.edu
PERIGARD, Julie ...... 253-272-1126 481 E jperigard@ncad.edu
PERIGARD, Kim ...... 253-272-1126 481 E kperigard@ncad.edu
PERILLO, Patty ...... 301-314-8428 202 H pperillo@umd.edu
PERINI, Don ...... 616-949-5300 223 C don.perini@cornerstone.edu
PERKINS, JR., Andrew, M ...... 336-285-4551 341 D perkins@ncat.edu
PERKINS, Anika, M ...... 662-329-7119 248 A amperkins@muw.edu
PERKINS, Becky ...... 563-588-8000 166 C bperkins@emmaus.edu
PERKINS, Bianca ...... 309-796-8240 133 G perkinsb@bhc.edu
PERKINS, Cheri ...... 318-342-5210 193 C perkins@ulm.edu
PERKINS, Chris-Tenna, M ...... 804-627-5300 464 K chris-tenna_perkins@bshsi.org
PERKINS, Dennis ...... 641-269-3700 166 G perkinsd@grinnell.edu
PERKINS, Jan ...... 214-388-5466 435 D jperkins@dallasinstitute.edu
PERKINS, Julie ...... 660-263-4100 257 B juliep@macc.edu
PERKINS, Kara ...... 562-985-8831.. 31 D k.perkins@csulb.edu
PERKINS, Keith ...... 937-376-6640 349 J kperkins@centralstate.edu
PERKINS, Kimberly ...... 843-863-7258 407 B kperkins@csuniv.edu
PERKINS, LeAnne ...... 501-660-1003.. 17 C lperkins@asusystem.edu
PERKINS, LeeAnn ...... 414-930-3548 494 E perkinsl@mtmary.edu
PERKINS, Mark ...... 307-778-1113 501 E mperkins@lccc.wy.edu
PERKINS, Mary ...... 847-214-7414 137 F mperkins@elgin.edu
PERKINS, Megan ...... 315-279-5296 303 G mryan1@keuka.edu
PERKINS, Meredith ...... 212-217-3500 299 D meredith_perkins@fitnyc.edu
PERKINS, Michele, D .... 603-428-2222 273 G mperkins@nec.edu
PERKINS, Mike ...... 707-476-4331.. 58 I mike-perkins@redwoods.edu
PERKINS, Myrna ...... 620-792-9201 171 I perkinsm@bartonccc.edu
PERKINS, Peter ...... 607-753-2518 318 A peter.perkins@cortland.edu
PERKINS, Priscilla, L .... 413-782-1531 220 A priscilla.perkins@wne.edu
PERKINS, Ryan ...... 870-762-3146.. 17 B rperkins@smail.anc.edu
PERKINS, Susan, L ...... 212-650-7000 293 D
PERKINS, Suzetta, M .... 910-672-1143 341 C sperkins@uncfsu.edu
PERKINS, Ungina ...... 704-922-2310 334 G perkins.ungina@gaston.edu
PERKINS-HOLTSCLAW, Kala ...... 423-869-7089 421 A k.perkins-holtsclaw@lmunet.edu
PERKINS JASPER, Erica 909-607-3562.. 37 D
PERKINSON, Greg ...... 541-552-6319 376 B perkinsog@sou.edu
PERKOWSKI, Henry ...... 212-678-3016 322 C hp2125@tc.columbia.edu
PERLADO, Ben ...... 661-654-2587.. 30 B bperlado@csub.edu
PERLES, Char ...... 530-938-5555.. 39 C
PERLIONI, Jason ...... 443-997-2370 199 G perlioni@jhu.edu
PERLMAN, Andrew ...... 617-573-8157 219 B aperlman@suffolk.edu
PERLMAN, Bruce, J ...... 505-277-1092 288 J bperlman@unm.edu
PERLMAN, Lynn ...... 617-277-3915 207 D perlmanl@bgsp.edu
PERLMUTTER, David ...... 806-742-3385 450 F david.perlmutter@ttu.edu
PERLMUTTER, David, H 314-362-6827 262 A perlmutterd@wustl.edu
PERLOW, Yehoshua ...... 718-438-2727 326 H
PERLOW, Yisroel ...... 718-438-2727 326 H
PERLSON, Meryl ...... 617-243-2177 211 B mperlson@lasell.edu
PERMAN, Jay, A ...... 301-445-1901 202 G jperman@usmd.edu
PERMAN, Matthew ...... 212-659-7200 303 H mperman@tkc.edu
PERNA, Laura ...... 215-898-4032 400 F lperna@gse.upenn.edu
PERNG, Becky ...... 626-571-5110.. 48 D beckyperng@les.edu
PERNICELLO, Collene ... 215-572-2840 378 E pernicelloc@arcadia.edu
PERNOT, Laurent ...... 312-369-7606 136 D lpernot@colum.edu
PEROG, Cheryl ...... 518-255-5211 319 C perogcj@cobleskill.edu
PEROO, Rama ...... 620-441-5587 173 C rama.peroo@cowley.edu
PEROW, Lauren, A ...... 814-641-3302 386 E perowl@juniata.edu
PEROZZI, Brett ...... 801-626-6008 461 A brettperozzi@weber.edu
PEROZZI, Thomas ...... 847-574-5168 142 B tperozzi@lfgsm.edu
PERR, Yechiel, I ...... 718-327-7600 325 D info@yofr.org
PERREAULT, Amy ...... 207-778-7256 196 I amy.f.perreault@maine.edu
PERREAULT, Melanie .... 410-704-4498 204 E mperreault@towson.edu
PERREIRA, Mary ...... 808-956-4650 129 G maryperr@hawaii.edu
PERRELLI, John ...... 410-337-6527 199 B john.perrelli@goucher.edu
PERRES, Irving ...... 718-232-7800 325 H
PERRET, Geraldine ...... 973-618-3536 276 D gperret@caldwell.edu
PERRETTA, Betty ...... 972-721-5000 452 B bboop@udallas.edu
PERRI, Christine ...... 619-216-6668.. 66 A cperri@swccd.edu
PERRI, Jason ...... 716-851-1421 299 B perri@ecc.edu
PERRI, Mary Lynn ...... 440-646-8329 363 C mperri@ursuline.edu
PERRI, Michael ...... 352-273-6214 111 A mperri@phhp.ufl.edu
PERRIEN, Shane ...... 402-941-6171 267 L perrien@midlandu.edu
PERRIER, Sarah ...... 412-392-8184 396 G sperrier@pointpark.edu
PERRIGO, Ryan ...... 906-353-8400 226 C rperrigo@kbocc.edu
PERRIN, Amy ...... 847-214-7217 137 F aperrin@elgin.edu
PERRIN, Brent ...... 509-452-5100 482 B bperrin@pnwu.edu
PERRIN, Brian ...... 617-236-8880 209 G bperrin@fisher.edu
PERRIN, David, H ...... 801-581-8537 459 D david.perrin@health.utah.edu
PERRIN, Gregory ...... 512-448-8452 442 I gperrin@stedwards.edu
PERRIN, Nicholas ...... 847-317-8001 151 C jmyers@tiu.edu
PERRIN, Thomas ...... 334-833-4236.... 5 G cao@hawks.huntingdon.edu
PERRIN, Tim ...... 310-506-4266.. 56 G tim.perrin@pepperdine.edu
PERRINE, Paul, C ...... 828-771-3800 344 D pperrine@warren-wilson.edu
PERRINE, Richard ...... 603-897-8206 273 I rperrine@rivier.edu
PERRINE, Zach ...... 870-612-2014.. 22 H zach.perrine@uaccb.edu
PERRINO, James, J ...... 516-877-3385 289 I jperrino@adelphi.edu
PERRINS, Robert, J ...... 310-954-4015.. 52 I rperrins@msmu.edu
PERRON, Evelyn, R ...... 603-206-8121 272 L eperron@ccsnh.edu
PERRON, Pam ...... 978-478-3400 218 A pperron@northpoint.edu
PERROTTA, Steve ...... 603-513-1341 274 G steve.perrotta@granite.edu
PERROTTA, Steven ...... 603-888-1311 273 I sperrotta@rivier.edu
PERRY, Al ...... 810-762-0417 228 F al.perry@mcc.edu
PERRY, Belvin ...... 386-481-2856.. 96 D portera@cookman.edu
PERRY, Brandon ...... 865-573-4517 420 E bperry@johnsonu.edu
PERRY, Bryan ...... 815-753-1000 146 B bperry3@niu.edu
PERRY, Carol ...... 336-342-4261 337 E perry4145@rockinghamcc.edu
PERRY, Catherine ...... 508-999-8648 212 A catherine.perry@umassd.edu
PERRY, Christine ...... 518-828-4181 297 B christine.perry@sunycgcc.edu
PERRY, Dan ...... 512-245-2396 450 C d_p93@txstate.edu
PERRY, Danny ...... 334-420-4277.... 3 H dperry@trenholmstate.edu
PERRY, David, L ...... 850-644-1240 110 C dlperry@admin.fsu.edu
PERRY, David, L ...... 919-962-8100 342 C david.perry@unc.edu
PERRY, Dwight, A ...... 312-329-4114 144 I dwight.perry@moody.edu
PERRY, Eddie ...... 253-912-2368 482 E eperry@pierce.ctc.edu
PERRY, Foster ...... 256-824-6880.... 8 B foster.perry@uah.edu
PERRY, Garth ...... 520-621-0075.. 16 D perryg@arizona.edu
PERRY, James ...... 678-664-0520 128 A james.perry@westgatech.edu
PERRY, Janet ...... 970-207-4500.. 85 A janetp@uscareerinstitute.edu
PERRY, Jason, P ...... 801-581-8514 459 O jason.perry@utah.edu
PERRY, Jennifer ...... 903-886-5666 447 B jennifer.perry@tamuc.edu
PERRY, Jennifer, E ...... 805-437-3694.. 30 C jennifer.perry@csuci.edu
PERRY, John ...... 708-534-4518 138 E jperry@govst.edu
PERRY, John, F ...... 864-503-5242 414 A johnp@uscupstate.edu
PERRY, Kedrick ...... 504-865-2306 190 C kbperry@loyno.edu
PERRY, Laura ...... 315-268-6760 295 F lperry@clarkson.edu
PERRY, Linda ...... 719-846-5541.. 83 L linda.perry@trinidadstate.edu
PERRY, Lori ...... 660-263-4100 257 B lorip@macc.edu
PERRY, Maria ...... 215-884-8942 403 D cfo@woninstitute.edu
PERRY, Marlene ...... 281-873-0262 433 J m.perry@commonwealth.edu
PERRY, Matthew ...... 281-283-3661 452 E perrym@uhcl.edu
PERRY, Melissa ...... 386-312-4088 107 C melissaperry@sjrstate.edu
PERRY, Meredith ...... 423-425-4431 427 C meredith-perry@utc.edu
PERRY, Michael ...... 321-674-7127 100 C perrymj@fit.edu
PERRY, Michael ...... 815-226-4067 148 D mperry@rockford.edu
PERRY, Michele ...... 805-553-4915.. 73 J sperry@vcccd.edu
PERRY, Missy ...... 864-941-8666 411 C perry.m@ptc.edu
PERRY, Nancy ...... 410-386-8231 198 D nperry@carrollcc.edu
PERRY, Pamela ...... 312-850-7344 135 H pperry18@ccc.edu
PERRY, Pamela ...... 319-895-4176 164 G pperry@cornellcollege.edu
PERRY, Paul ...... 231-995-1114 229 A pperry@nmc.edu
PERRY, Rhonda ...... 217-206-7796 152 A rrperry@uillinois.edu
PERRY, Robert ...... 617-879-7269 213 B rperry@massart.edu
PERRY, Roderick, D ...... 317-278-5247 157 D perryrd@iupui.edu
PERRY, Rodger ...... 704-669-4032 333 E perryr@clevelandcc.edu
PERRY, Rubye ...... 334-727-8350.... 7 D rperry@tuskegee.edu
PERRY, Stephanie, D .... 276-328-0240 472 E sdh9y@uvawise.edu
PERRY, Stuart ...... 320-363-5047 235 F sperry@csbsju.edu
PERRY, Stuart ...... 320-363-5047 243 B sperry@csbsju.edu
PERRY, Ted ...... 740-474-8896 358 A tperry@ohiochristian.edu
PERRY, Terri ...... 812-888-4103 162 F tperry@vinu.edu
PERRY, Thomas, D ...... 740-376-4408 355 E tom.perry@marietta.edu
PERRY, Tiffani ...... 662-252-8000 248 G tperry@rustcollege.edu
PERRY, Todd ...... 208-885-7179 132 F tperry@uidaho.edu
PERRY, Tom ...... 479-524-7122.. 19 H tperry@jbu.edu
PERRY, Tom ...... 740-376-4408 355 E perryt@marietta.edu
PERRY, Walter ...... 215-242-7989 381 A perryw@chc.edu
PERRY-CONLEY, Tonia .. 609-586-4800 278 F conleyt@mccc.edu
PERRY-FANTINI, Sharon ...... 419-448-3504 361 D perrynauses@tiffin.edu
PERRY KEITH, Colleen . 302-225-6260.. 91 B keithcp@gbc.edu
PERRY-MCCLURE, Kyleigh, M ...... 606-474-3200 181 B kmperrymcclure@kcu.edu
PERRY WOOTEN, Lynn . 617-521-2070 218 G
PERRYMAN, Nancy, S .. 309-655-4119 149 B nancy.s.perryman@osfhealthcare.org
PERRYMAN, Tiffany ...... 601-643-8411 245 F tiffany.perryman@colin.edu
PERSALES, David ...... 210-999-7011 451 E
PERSAUD, Axel ...... 301-405-6473 202 H apersaud@umd.edu
PERSICO, IHM, Mary .... 570-348-6231 389 D persico@marywood.edu
PERSICO, Patrice ...... 570-208-5972 386 G patricepersico@kings.edu
PERSINGER, Bill ...... 931-221-6309 417 H persingerb@apsu.edu
PERSINGER, William ..... 920-693-1297 498 H william.persinger@gotoltc.edu
PERSKY, Laura ...... 914-323-5188 305 B laura.persky@mville.edu
PERSON, Andy ...... 516-299-2851 304 D andy.person@liu.edu
PERSON, Gretchen ...... 615-322-2457 428 A religiouslife@vanderbilt.edu
PERSONS, Alexis ...... 507-433-0508 240 G alexis.persons@riverland.edu
PERTL, Brian, G ...... 920-832-6614 493 B brian.g.pertl@lawrence.edu
PERTZ, Sara ...... 715-852-1305 498 E spertz@cvtc.edu
PERUSO, Jennifer ...... 610-647-4400 385 L jperuso@immaculata.edu
PERUZZOTTI, Robert ...... 860-701-5016.. 88 D peruzzotti_r@mitchell.edu

PETERSON, Susan, K .... 785-532-6221 175 C
skp@ksu.edu
PETERSON, Thomas ...... 732-906-2512 278 G
tpeterson@middlesexcc.edu
PETERSON, Toby .... 301-696-3934 199 E
peterson@hood.edu
PETERSON, Tracy .... 303-751-8700.. 78 D
peterson@belrea.edu
PETERSON, Tyler, M ..... 205-934-8221.... 8 A
tpeterson@uab.edu
PETERSON, Val, L .... 801-863-8424 460 D
petersva@uvu.edu
PETERSON-MILLER,
Connie .... 574-520-4591 157 E
copmille@iusb.edu
PETERSON-VEATCH,
Ross .... 620-229-6090 177 G
ross.peterson-veatch@sckans.edu
PETERSSON, Arlette .... 561-586-0121 101 O
PETHE-COOK, Marlyn ... 813-253-6231 113 H
mpethe@ut.edu
PETHERBRIDGE, Julie ... 678-547-6010 122 E
petherbrid_j@mercer.edu
PETILLO, John, J .... 203-371-7900.. 89 A
petilloj@sacredheart.edu
PETIPRIN, Gary .... 502-272-8480 179 H
gpetiprin@bellarmine.edu
PETIT, Adam .... 828-395-4194 335 D
apetit@isothermal.edu
PETITT, Becky, R .... 858-822-4783.. 70 C
bpetitt@ucsd.edu
PETITT, Bill .... 972-883-2055 455 B
bpetitt@utdallas.edu
PETITT, Charles, W .... 336-714-7993 327 H
petittc@carolinau.edu
PETITTI, Mario .... 440-525-7328 354 L
mpetitti@lakelandcc.edu
PETKA, Frank .... 215-646-7300 385 A
petka.f@gmercyu.edu
PETKASH, John .... 607-962-9000 320 C
PETKUS, Edward .... 201-684-7377 280 H
epetkus@ramapo.edu
PETLEY, Kathleen .... 518-629-4557 302 C
k.petley@hvcc.edu
PETRAMALA, Sarah .... 719-384-6822.. 82 D
sarah.petramala@ojc.edu
PETRANOVICH, Sean .... 303-615-1596.. 81 M
spetran1@msudenver.edu
PETRASEK, Debbie .... 262-472-1918 497 D
PETRESCU, Claudia, A .. 785-532-7927 175 C
cpetrescu@ksu.edu
PETRI, OP, Thomas ...... 202-495-3820.. 93 D
president@dhs.edu
PETRIDIS, Heather .... 626-815-4570.. 26 F
hpetridis@apu.edu
PETRIE, Mark .... 315-279-5694 303 G
mpetrie@keuka.edu
PETRIE, Mary Beth .... 765-658-4800 154 J
PETRIKAT, Douglas .... 714-547-9625.. 28 A
dpetrikat@calcoast.edu
PETRILLO, Emilia, K ...... 410-328-8404 203 A
epetr001@umaryland.edu
PETRITIS, Paul .... 413-662-5543 213 C
paul.petritis@mcla.edu
PETRIZZO, Louis, J .... 631-451-4235 321 C
petrizl@sunysuffolk.edu
PETROKA, Louise, A ..... 203-285-2145.. 86 E
lpetroka@gatewayct.edu
PETRONE, Eileen .... 412-536-1115 386 H
eileen.petrone@laroche.edu
PETRONSKY, LeeAnn .... 716-829-7805 298 E
petronsk@dyc.edu
PETROS, William, P ...... 304-293-5212 490 E
wpetros@hsc.wvu.edu
PETROSIAN, Anahid ...... 956-872-8339 443 H
anahid@southtexascollege.edu
PETROSINO, Linda .... 607-274-3265 302 G
lpetrosino@ithaca.edu
PETROSKE, Destiny .... 360-676-2772 481 F
dpetroske@nwic.edu
PETROSKI, Mike .... 561-237-7007 103 W
mpetroski@lynn.edu
PETROSKY, Fawn .... 724-938-4453 393 E
petrosky@calu.edu
PETROSKY, Joseph, L ... 248-232-4179 229 C
jlpetros@oaklandcc.edu
PETROSYAN, Narine ...... 510-925-4282.. 25 K
narinep@aua.am
PETROSYAN, Varduhi .... 510-925-4282.. 25 K
vpetrosi@aua.am
PETROSYAN, Violetta .... 304-357-4758 487 J
violettapetrosyan@ucwv.edu
PETROVA, Elena .... 706-721-0211 116 A
epetrova@augusta.edu
PETROVICH, Douglas .... 281-646-1109 431 G
doug.petrovich@thebibleseminary.edu
PETROVICH, Jason .... 219-464-6858 162 D
jason.petrovich@valpo.edu
PETRUCCI, Michele, L ... 724-357-2295 394 C
michelep@iup.edu
PETRULAKIS, Karen ...... 781-283-2207 219 E
kpetrula@wellesley.edu
PETRUS, Robin .... 607-778-5201 317 D
petrusre@sunybroome.edu
PETRUSCH,
Suzanne, M .... 864-833-8194 411 D
spetrusch@presby.edu
PETRUSHA, Cynthia ...... 707-476-4170.. 58 I
cynthia-petrusha@redwoods.edu
PETRUZELLA, Gerol .... 413-662-5570 213 C
g.petruzella@mcla.edu
PETRUZZELLI,
Barbara, W .... 845-569-3663 307 D
barbara.petruzzelli@msmc.edu
PETRYSHAK, Bruce .... 615-898-5570 422 C
bruce.petryshak@mtsu.edu
PETSCHE, Carolyn .... 815-599-3577 139 A
carolyn.petsche@highland.edu
PETSCHENKO, Lisa .... 630-953-3694 134 F
lpetschenko@chamberlain.edu
PETTA, Tim .... 360-992-2408 478 I
tpetta@clark.edu
PETTAZZONI, Jodi, E .... 336-334-5535 343 A
jepettaz@uncg.edu
PETTEGREW, Melinda ... 816-501-4689 258 I
melinda.pettegrew@rockhurst.edu
PETTENGER, Wade, W .. 417-862-9533 253 F
wpettenger@globaluniversity.edu
PETTENGILL, Keri-Beth . 804-594-1576 474 B
kpettengill@jtcc.edu
PETTERELLI, Mark, J ..... 315-445-4444 303 I
pettermj@lemoyne.edu
PETTIBON, II,
Joseph, P .... 979-845-4016 446 F
jpp2@tamu.edu
PETTIE, Brian .... 870-512-7829.. 18 A
brian_pettie@asun.edu
PETTIFER, Geoffrey .... 609-626-6023 283 E
geoffrey.pettifer@stockton.edu
PETTIFORD, Joseph, B . 443-518-1100 199 F
jpettiford@howardcc.edu
PETTIGREW, Jason .... 605-229-8350 415 I
jason.pettigrew@presentation.edu
PETTIGREW, Yancey ...... 731-661-5134 426 F
ypettigrew@uu.edu
PETTINGILL, Jayn .... 510-845-5373.. 29 B
jayn@cjc.edu
PETTINGILL, Sara, Y ..... 502-272-8401 179 H
spettingill@bellarmine.edu
PETTIS, Carl .... 334-229-4232.... 4 A
cpettis@alasu.edu
PETTIS, Curtis .... 937-376-6201 349 J
cpettis@centralstate.edu
PETTIS-WALDEN,
Karen, M .... 804-523-5029 474 A
kpettis-walden@reynolds.edu
PETTIT, Frederick .... 570-208-5881 386 G
frederickpettit@kings.edu
PETTIT, Martin, A .... 607-746-4702 320 D
pettitma@delhi.edu
PETTIT, Paul, E .... 214-887-5102 435 F
ppettit@dts.edu
PETTIT, Stephen, D .... 864-242-5100 406 H
PETTITT, Robert .... 801-375-5125 459 K
robert.pettitt@rm.edu
PETTY, Blake .... 404-364-8400 123 K
bpetty@oglethorpe.edu
PETTY, Bradley .... 325-942-2191 450 E
bradley.petty@angelo.edu
PETTY, Clifton .... 417-873-7240 252 G
cpetty@drury.edu
PETTY, Davion, L .... 803-516-4616 411 G
dpetty@scsu.edu
PETTY, Jamie .... 706-802-5105 119 D
jpetty@highlands.edu
PETTY, Jenny .... 406-243-2311 263 K
PETTY, Jonathan .... 806-291-3588 457 I
pettyj@wbu.edu
PETTY, Marcia, L .... 202-994-6710.. 92 D
cpetty@gwu.edu
PETTY, Mark .... 605-658-6220 416 D
mark.petty@usd.edu
PETTY, Monica .... 202-885-8612.. 94 D
mpetty@wesleyseminary.edu
PETTY, Nadine .... 603-862-1234 274 F
nadine.petty@unh.edu
PETTY, Ryan .... 312-341-3500 148 E
rpetty01@roosevelt.edu
PETTY, Teresa .... 704-687-0995 342 D
tmpetty@uncc.edu
PETTY, Theresa .... 712-274-6400 171 B
theresa.petty@witcc.edu
PETTY, Warren .... 201-216-5218 283 D
warren.petty@stevens.edu
PETTY, William, J .... 864-488-8344 410 B
wpetty@limestone.edu
PETULA, Eileen, E .... 570-577-2000 379 C
PETZKE, Greg .... 704-378-1190 330 D
gpetzke@jcsu.edu
PETZNICK, Michelle, L . 641-422-4205 168 G
petznmic@niacc.edu
PETZOLD, Terri .... 270-852-3183 183 E
terri.petzold@kwc.edu
PEWE, Rich .... 517-607-2518 225 C
rpewe@hillsdale.edu
PEWITT, Shawn .... 313-577-3390 232 K
dv3831@wayne.edu
PEYER, Patrick .... 815-921-4092 148 B
p.peyer@rockvalleycollege.edu
PEYRE, Sarah .... 585-275-2121 323 M
PEYTON, Elizabeth .... 949-794-9090.. 66 D
epeyton@stanbridge.edu
PEYTON, Janice, L .... 713-313-7885 449 B
janice.peyton@tsu.edu
PEZMAN, Chris .... 713-743-9370 452 D
cwpezman@uh.edu
PEZOLD, Frank .... 361-825-2349 447 C
frank.pezold@tamucc.edu
PEZZAROSSI, Alba .... 773-481-8059 135 G
apezzarossi@ccc.edu
PEZZI, Eileen .... 315-464-7853 317 C
pezzie@upstate.edu
PEZZULLI, Michelle ...... 508-999-8974 212 A
mpezzulli@umassd.edu
PEZZULLO, Laurie .... 516-572-7832 307 E
laurie.pezzullo@ncc.edu
PEZZUTO, John .... 413-796-2323 220 A
john.pezzuto@wne.edu
PEÑA, Amy, F .... 505-747-2140 287 H
amy.pena@nnmc.edu
PEÑA, Damien, A .... 805-289-6113.. 74 B
dpena@vcccd.edu
PEÑA RIVERA, Norma .. 787-764-0000 513 B
norma.pena1@upr.edu
PEÑALOZA, Carlos .... 808-455-0215 130 C
carlospe@hawaii.edu
PFAFF, Caryl .... 715-634-4790 492 L
cpfaff@lco.edu
PFAFF, Mimi .... 303-751-8700.. 78 D
pfaff@belrea.edu
PFAHL, Michael .... 567-661-7270 359 I
michael_pfahl@owens.edu
PFANG, Raymond .... 210-486-3921 429 A
tpfang@alamo.edu
PFANNENSTIEL, Matt .... 785-227-3380 172 A
pfannenstielmm@bethanylb.edu
PFANNENSTIEL, Myra ... 316-942-4291 176 E
pfannenstielm@newmanu.edu
PFANNESTIEL, Todd ...... 315-792-3122 324 B
tjpfanne@utica.edu
PFAUTZ, Nadine .... 617-745-3812 209 B
nadine.pfautz@enc.edu
PFEFER, Mark, T .... 913-234-0796 172 K
mark.pfefer@cleveland.edu
PFEIFER, Aimee, D .... 304-293-5355 490 E
aimee.pfeifer@mail.wvu.edu
PFEIFER, Chuck .... 620-276-9521 174 B
chuck.pfeifer@gcccks.edu
PFEIFER, Gene, R .... 507-344-7315 234 C
gene.pfeifer@blc.edu
PFEIFER, Justin .... 316-677-1020 178 E
jpfeifer@watc.edu
PFEIFER, Tad .... 308-535-3684 267 J
pfeifert@mpcc.edu
PFEIFER, Terry .... 785-628-4259 173 H
tpfeifer@fhsu.edu
PFEIFFENBERGER,
Colleen .... 513-244-4296 356 F
colleen.pfeiffenberger@msj.edu
PFEIFFER, Larisa .... 301-934-7627 198 G
ljpfeiffer@csmd.edu
PFEIFFER, Patty .... 919-739-6783 338 H
pfeiffer@waynecc.edu
PFEIFFER, Tamarah .... 785-749-8404 174 D
PFLANZ, Mary .... 913-621-8764 173 E
mpflanz@donnelly.edu
PFLEGER, Heather .... 201-559-6000 277 J
PFLIPSEN, Andrew .... 320-308-5382 241 A
andrew.pflipsen@sctcc.edu
PFLIPSEN, Andrew, J .... 701-788-4770 345 D
andrew.pflipsen@mayvillestate.edu
PFOHL, Jody .... 563-588-6315 164 E
jody.pfohl@clarke.edu
PFUHL, Adam .... 651-255-6117 243 E
apfuhl@unitedseminary.edu
PHAGAN, Kathy .... 770-533-6906 122 B
kphagan@laniertech.edu
PHAGAN, Tiffany, D ...... 386-748-1364.. 99 A
phagant@erau.edu
PHAIAH, Peter .... 575-835-5187 286 K
peter.phaiah@nmt.edu
PHAKITTHONG,
Rachelle .... 715-833-6411 498 E
rphakitthong@cvtc.edu
PHAM, Chelsy .... 209-954-5300.. 61 G
chelsy.pham@deltacollege.edu
PHAM, Hong .... 916-691-7793.. 50 H
phamh@crc.losrios.edu
PHAM, SVD, Linh .... 563-876-3353 165 H
lpham@dwci.edu
PHAM, Michael .... 206-878-3710 481 B
mpham@highline.edu
PHAM, Ni .... 303-867-1155.. 83 K
pham@taft.edu
PHAM, Sandra .... 818-299-5500.. 74 L
spham@westcoastuniversity.edu
PHAM, Thinh .... 805-482-2755.. 59 G
tdpham@stjohnsem.edu
PHAM, Thomas .... 910-893-1415 327 D
tpham@campbell.edu
PHAM, Tom, C .... 617-984-1699 218 C
tpham@quincycollege.edu
PHAM, Tonga .... 716-645-5265 316 C
tongapha@buffalo.edu
PHAN, Nga .... 760-410-5334.. 72 G
nphan@usa.edu
PHAN, Tony .... 563-425-5200 170 H
phant43@uiu.edu
PHARES, Jason .... 304-462-6141 489 L
jason.phares@glenville.edu
PHARO, SCN, Diane ..... 812-357-6598 161 A
dpharo@saintmeinrad.edu
PHARR, Angela, D .... 770-720-5503 124 G
adp@reinhardt.edu
PHARR, Christine .... 414-930-3639 494 E
pharrc@mtmary.edu
PHARR, Julie .... 336-386-3452 338 D
pharrj@surry.edu
PHARR, Kathy, R .... 706-542-0054 126 G
pharr@uga.edu
PHARR, Kathy, R .... 706-542-8090 126 G
pharr@uga.edu
PHARR, Maria .... 704-290-5251 337 I
mpharr@spcc.edu
PHARRIS, Heather .... 863-680-4754 100 H
hpharris@flsouthern.edu
PHAYRE, Allison .... 360-475-7108 481 I
aphayre@olympic.edu
PHEASANT, Joel, C .... 814-641-5334 386 E
pheasaj@juniata.edu
PHELAN, Daniel, J .... 517-787-0800 225 E
phelandanielj@jccmi.edu
PHELAN, Sherry, A .... 573-840-9689 260 E
sphelan@trcc.edu
PHELAN JOHNSON,
Marcia .... 860-297-2041.. 89 B
marcia.johnson@trincoll.edu
PHELON, Kerry .... 860-701-5000.. 88 D
PHELPS, Barry .... 270-831-9678 182 A
barry.phelps@kctcs.edu
PHELPS, Bill .... 870-245-5567.. 20 D
phelpswr@obu.edu
PHELPS, Brad .... 501-660-1008.. 17 C
bphelps@asusystem.edu
PHELPS, Corey .... 405-325-0311 370 K
PHELPS, Craig .... 660-626-2391 250 A
cphelps@atsu.edu
PHELPS, Deborah .... 620-442-0430 173 C
deborah.phelps@cowley.edu
PHELPS, Esther .... 330-337-6403 347 D
ephelps@awc.edu
PHELPS, Gary, L .... 330-471-8127 355 D
gphelps@malone.edu
PHELPS, Hilary .... 860-343-5879.. 87 A
hphelps@mxcc.edu
PHELPS, Jean .... 718-262-2285 295 E
phelps@york.cuny.edu
PHELPS, Jeffrey .... 509-865-8643 481 A
PHELPS, Jodi .... 910-521-6863 343 B
jodi.phelps@uncp.edu
PHELPS, Joel .... 518-828-4181 297 B
joel.phelps@sunycgcc.edu

PHELPS, Kathy .... 239-304-7074.. 95 M kathy.phelps@avemaria.edu
PHELPS, Laura .... 904-256-7042 102 H lphelps5@ju.edu
PHELPS, Lena .... 863-784-7303 108 F lena.phelps@southflorida.edu
PHELPS, Matthew, P ..... 330-471-8370 355 D mphelps@malone.edu
PHELPS, Sherri .... 870-245-5410.. 20 D phelpss@obu.edu
PHENICIE, Christopher, N .... 864-488-4549 410 B cphenicie@limestone.edu
PHIFER-MCGHEE, Kimberly, C .... 919-530-7593 341 E kpmcghee@nccu.edu
PHILION, Thomas .... 312-853-4780 148 E tphilion@roosevelt.edu
PHILIPKOSKY, Thomas, G .... 843-953-5092 407 C tom.philipkosky@citadel.edu
PHILIPOSE, Sandy .... 903-813-2455 430 H sphilipose@austincollege.edu
PHILIPP, Diane .... 517-607-2333 225 C dphilipp@hillsdale.edu
PHILIPP, Jason .... 651-779-5834 237 H jason.philipp@century.edu
PHILIPP, Shirin .... 617-349-9600 211 C philipp@lesley.edu
PHILIPPA, Elaine .... 262-595-3215 496 D laine@uwp.edu
PHILIPS, JR., Billy, U ... 806-743-1338 451 A billy.philips@ttuhsc.edu
PHILIPSON, Randolph .. 504-314-7157 191 F rphilipson@tulane.edu
PHILLEY, Tim .... 918-495-6970 368 F tphilley@oru.edu
PHILLIP, Thomas, G ..... 262-243-5700 492 E thomas.phillip@cuw.edu
PHILLIPS, Alan .... 281-756-3514 429 D aphillips@alvincollege.edu
PHILLIPS, Allison .... 336-838-6491 339 B alphillips068@wilkescc.edu
PHILLIPS, Amanda .... 760-636-7962.. 38 E afphillips@collegeofthedesert.edu
PHILLIPS, Amanda .... 724-653-2195 382 E aphillips@dec.edu
PHILLIPS, Andre .... 608-262-3237 495 D andre.phillips@wisc.edu
PHILLIPS, Andrew, T .... 410-293-1583 504 A aphillip@usna.edu
PHILLIPS, Annie .... 940-898-4114 451 D aphillips15@twu.edu
PHILLIPS, Antoinette ..... 985-549-2258 193 A antoinette.phillips@selu.edu
PHILLIPS, Brenda .... 570-520-4290 157 E brenphil@iusb.edu
PHILLIPS, Brian .... 562-903-4897.. 27 A brian.phillips@biola.edu
PHILLIPS, Calvin .... 612-626-1616 243 F
PHILLIPS, Carrie .... 419-358-3275 348 F phillipsc@bluffton.edu
PHILLIPS, Chad .... 270-831-9614 182 A chad.phillips@kctcs.edu
PHILLIPS, Chelsea .... 405-224-3140 371 B cphillips@usao.edu
PHILLIPS, Cindy .... 912-871-8514 123 J cbphillips@ogeecheetech.edu
PHILLIPS, Clarenda .... 361-825-2722 447 C clarenda.phillips@tamucc.edu
PHILLIPS, Cynthia, R .... 718-990-1320 313 G phillipc@stjohns.edu
PHILLIPS, Danielle .... 717-337-6901 384 D dphillip@gettysburg.edu
PHILLIPS, Dave .... 619-849-2771.. 57 J davephillips@pointloma.edu
PHILLIPS, David .... 831-755-6729.. 44 G dphillips@hartnell.edu
PHILLIPS, David .... 410-516-8341 199 G dphillips@jhu.edu
PHILLIPS, David .... 801-863-8292 460 D david.phillips@uvu.edu
PHILLIPS, Dawnita .... 816-322-0110 251 B dawnita.phillips@calvary.edu
PHILLIPS, Dianna .... 304-367-4101 489 K dianna.phillips@fairmontstate.edu
PHILLIPS, Don .... 716-839-8222 298 A dphillip@daemen.edu
PHILLIPS, Donald .... 517-629-0492 221 A dphillips@albion.edu
PHILLIPS, Douglas .... 585-275-3311 323 M dphillips@admin.rochester.edu
PHILLIPS, Earnest .... 206-934-4105 483 A earnest.phillips@seattlecolleges.edu
PHILLIPS, Eddie .... 773-602-5440 135 D ephillips13@ccc.edu
PHILLIPS, Edward, J ..... 504-520-6787 193 E ephillip@xula.edu
PHILLIPS, Elaine, W ..... 405-273-5331 366 B ephillips@familyoffaith.edu
PHILLIPS, Elizabeth .... 207-454-1050 195 I ephillips@wccc.me.edu
PHILLIPS, Ellen .... 262-691-5257 500 B ephillips@wctc.edu
PHILLIPS, Faith .... 740-366-9492 349 F phillips.495@cotc.edu
PHILLIPS, Farley, A ...... 252-451-8287 336 E faphillips673@nashcc.edu
PHILLIPS, Ferna .... 617-670-4429 209 G fphillips@fisher.edu
PHILLIPS, Fred, R .... 719-884-5000.. 82 B frphillips@nbc.edu
PHILLIPS, Georgette, C . 610-758-6725 388 E gcp214@lehigh.edu
PHILLIPS, Greg .... 608-742-4473 498 D gphillips4@blackhawk.edu
PHILLIPS, Heather .... 218-477-4363 239 E phillipshe@mnstate.edu
PHILLIPS, Holli .... 540-665-4928 470 G hphillip@su.edu
PHILLIPS, Jay .... 207-786-6211 194 A jphilli2@bates.edu
PHILLIPS, Jeannette, L . 909-869-3704.. 30 A jlphillips@cpp.edu
PHILLIPS, Jeannie .... 907-474-7765.. 10 A jdphillips@alaska.edu
PHILLIPS, Jennifer .... 315-859-4243 300 H jlphillips@hamilton.edu
PHILLIPS, Jennifer, R ... 304-457-6590 486 E phillipsjr@ab.edu
PHILLIPS, Jerrett .... 580-581-8068 365 D jphillip@cameron.edu
PHILLIPS, Jesse .... 610-989-1467 401 I jphillips@vfmac.edu
PHILLIPS, Jim .... 815-599-3469 139 A jim.phillips@highland.edu
PHILLIPS, Joan .... 314-516-4528 261 C joan.phillips@umsl.edu
PHILLIPS, Joan, M .... 305-899-3532.. 96 A jphillips@barry.edu
PHILLIPS, John, M .... 386-323-5020.. 99 A john.phillips@erau.edu
PHILLIPS, Joseph, M .... 206-296-5700 484 A phillipsj@seattleu.edu
PHILLIPS, Josh .... 509-453-0374 482 D josh.phillips@perrytech.edu
PHILLIPS, Karen .... 413-775-1305 214 E phillips@gcc.mass.edu
PHILLIPS, Kathryn .... 215-517-3093 378 E phillipsk@arcadia.edu
PHILLIPS, Kendall .... 772-466-4822.. 95 N kendall.phillips@aviator.edu
PHILLIPS, Kenneth .... 603-899-4344 273 E phillipsk@franklinpierce.edu
PHILLIPS, Keri .... 865-882-4548 425 C phillipska@roanestate.edu
PHILLIPS, Kevin .... 828-898-8944 330 E phillipsk@lmc.edu
PHILLIPS, Kimberly .... 540-432-4131 466 B careerservices@emu.edu
PHILLIPS, Kristopher ..... 931-221-7127 417 H phillipsk@apsu.edu
PHILLIPS, Laurie .... 504-864-7833 190 C phillips@loyno.edu
PHILLIPS, Leonard .... 706-588-8332 124 E leonard.phillips@point.edu
PHILLIPS, Linda .... 580-581-2238 365 D lindap@cameron.edu
PHILLIPS, Luke .... 718-636-3666 311 F lphilli8@pratt.edu
PHILLIPS, Lynette, M .... 212-817-7103 293 F lphillips2@gc.cuny.edu
PHILLIPS, Mark .... 202-685-3140 502 K mark.phillips.civ@ndu.edu
PHILLIPS, Melissa, C .... 828-766-1380 336 A mcphillips@mayland.edu
PHILLIPS, Michael .... 210-690-9000 436 H mphillips@hallmarkuniversity.edu
PHILLIPS, Mike .... 334-844-2345.... 4 D jmp0133@auburn.edu
PHILLIPS, Miranda .... 409-839-2014 449 F mphillips1@lit.edu
PHILLIPS, Monika .... 870-512-7805.. 18 A monika_phillips@asun.edu
PHILLIPS, Morgan .... 520-206-2111.. 15 B mphillips23@pima.edu
PHILLIPS, Myra .... 804-524-5352 476 D mhphilli@vsu.edu
PHILLIPS, Patrick .... 541-346-3186 376 H provost@uoregon.edu
PHILLIPS, Phil, E .... 310-506-7227.. 56 G phil.phillips@pepperdine.edu
PHILLIPS, Quill .... 303-797-5830.. 77 I quill.phillips@arapahoe.edu
PHILLIPS, Rachel .... 215-965-4025 390 E rphillips@moore.edu
PHILLIPS, Renee .... 301-891-4177 205 A rphililps@wau.edu
PHILLIPS, Richard .... 903-875-7419 440 D richard.phillips@navarrocollege.edu
PHILLIPS, Richard, D .... 404-413-7000 120 E rphillips@gsu.edu
PHILLIPS, Rita .... 276-223-4831 476 A rphillips@wcc.vcss.edu
PHILLIPS, Rita, M .... 515-294-0231 163 G rphillip@iastate.edu
PHILLIPS, Robert .... 276-739-2496 475 F rphillips@vhcc.edu
PHILLIPS, SR., Robert, E .... 540-464-7390 476 B phillipsre@vmi.edu
PHILLIPS, Robert, J ...... 304-637-1292 487 C phillipsr@dewv.edu
PHILLIPS, Robin .... 314-539-5000 259 A
PHILLIPS, Rodney .... 910-323-5614 327 F rphillips@ccbs.edu
PHILLIPS, Ronald .... 281-756-3700 429 D rphillips@alvincollege.edu
PHILLIPS, Sam .... 800-877-5456 465 L sam.phillips@christendom.edu
PHILLIPS, Samanthia .... 252-618-6697 334 D phillipss@edgecombe.edu
PHILLIPS, Sara .... 518-564-2000 318 E
PHILLIPS, Sara .... 530-242-7635.. 64 C sphillips@shastacollege.edu
PHILLIPS, Sara, J .... 828-627-4529 335 C sjphillips@haywood.edu
PHILLIPS, Sarah .... 785-320-4502 175 G sarahphillips@manhattantech.edu
PHILLIPS, Sarah .... 503-352-2141 375 C phillips@pacificu.edu
PHILLIPS, Sarah, L .... 704-894-2053 328 E saphillips@davidson.edu
PHILLIPS, Sean Mike .... 310-506-6213.. 56 G sean.m.phillips@pepperdine.edu
PHILLIPS, Shaina .... 562-908-3427.. 58 L sphillips@riohondo.edu
PHILLIPS, Shannon .... 843-863-7035 407 B sphillips@csuniv.edu
PHILLIPS, Sherry .... 215-641-6562 390 C sphillips@mc3.edu
PHILLIPS, Stephanie ..... 217-641-4514 141 A sphillips@jwcc.edu
PHILLIPS, Stuart .... 706-295-6868 120 A sphillips@gntc.edu
PHILLIPS, Susan .... 909-607-7304.. 57 E susan_phillips@pitzer.edu
PHILLIPS, Syche .... 415-439-2461.. 25 E sphillips@act-sf.org
PHILLIPS, Tammie, C .... 803-323-2225 414 D phillipst@winthrop.edu
PHILLIPS, Teri, P .... 253-535-7121 482 A phillitp@plu.edu
PHILLIPS, Teri, P .... 253-535-7187 482 A phillitp@plu.edu
PHILLIPS, Terri .... 406-243-2665 263 K terri.phillips@umontana.edu
PHILLIPS, SR., Thomas, R .... 815-753-1811 146 B tphillips3@niu.edu
PHILLIPS, Timothy, P .... 412-578-6087 380 B tpphillips@carlow.edu
PHILLIPS, Valerie .... 619-596-2766.. 26 D vphillips@ata.edu
PHILLIPS, Vicki .... 229-500-3546 114 H vicki.phillips@asurams.edu
PHILLIPS, Wendy, S ...... 412-578-8861 380 B wsphillips@carlow.edu
PHILLIPS, Winfred .... 352-392-6620 111 A wphil@ufl.edu
PHILLIPS, Yancy .... 812-237-2100 156 D yancy.phillips@indstate.edu
PHILLIPS-MADSON, Robyn .... 210-283-6994 453 C rmadson@uiwtx.edu
PHILLIS, Thomas, M ...... 309-794-7279 133 C tomphillis@augustana.edu
PHILO, Kathy .... 804-751-9191 465 K kphilo@ccc-va.com
PHILOGENE, Cassandra 407-896-5869.. 95 B cassandra.philogene@ahu.edu
PHILPOTT, Ryan .... 530-541-4660.. 47 E
PHILPOTT, Sean .... 617-735-9937 209 D philpotts@emmanuel.edu
PHILSON, Grace .... 734-432-5791 227 C gphilson@madonna.edu
PHINAZEE, Karen, B ..... 919-866-6169 338 G kbphinazee@waketech.edu
PHINNEY, D. Nathan .... 712-707-7103 169 D dnathan.phinney@nwciowa.edu
PHINNEY, Nancy .... 805-565-6055.. 76 A nphinney@westmont.edu
PHIPPS, Kim, S .... 717-796-5085 389 H kphipps@messiah.edu
PHIPPS, Kylene .... 406-874-6292 263 H phippsk@milescc.edu
PHIPPS, Terry .... 972-825-4802 444 J tphipps@sagu.edu
PHIPPS, Wayne .... 706-233-4062 116 B wphipps@berry.edu
PHLEGAR, Charles, D ... 540-231-7676 476 C cphlegar@vt.edu
PHOENIX, Dru .... 505-467-6815 288 H druphoenix@swc.edu
PHOENIX-MARTIN, Shawntell .... 912-358-3004 125 A martins@savannahstate.edu
PHOU, Jenny .... 303-273-3000.. 79 J jphou@mines.edu
PHU, Jenny .... 909-274-4450.. 52 J jphu@mtsac.edu
PIACENTINI, Dean .... 973-290-4349 282 I dpiacentini@steu.edu
PIACENTINI, Katie .... 314-889-4679 253 E kpiacentini@fontbonne.edu
PIANA, Cynthia .... 615-297-7545 417 G pianac@aquinascollege.edu
PIANEZZOLA, Cristina .. 801-863-8204 460 D cristina.pianezzola@uvu.edu
PIANKA, Stephanie .... 212-998-2910 309 F stephanie.pianka@nyu.edu
PIANTA, Robert, C .... 434-243-5481 472 D rcp4p@virginia.edu
PIASECKI, David .... 734-432-5335 227 C dpiasecki@madonna.edu
PIASECKI, Joseph .... 847-578-8343 148 F joseph.piasecki@rosalindfranklin.edu
PIASSICK, Emily .... 478-301-2862 122 E piassick_ea@mercer.edu
PIATT, James, B .... 336-278-7440 328 J jpiatt@elon.edu
PIATT, Janet, M .... 423-775-7237 418 D piattja@bryan.edu
PIATT, Ronda .... 217-735-7305 142 H rpiatt@lincolncollege.edu
PIAZZA, Angela .... 574-807-7875 154 B angela.piazza@betheluniversity.edu
PIAZZA, Bradley .... 262-691-5157 500 B bpiazza@wctc.edu
PIAZZA, Daniel .... 405-682-7891 367 D daniel.c.piazza@occc.edu
PIAZZA, John .... 609-343-4911 275 D jpiazza@atlantic.edu
PIAZZA, Nick .... 815-825-9770 141 F npiazza@kish.edu
PIAZZA, Rachel .... 815-939-5331 147 A rpiazza@shet.follett.com
PIAZZA, Vincent .... 314-367-8700 260 H vincent.piazza@stlcop.edu
PIAZZOLA, Mike .... 406-683-7664 264 A mike.piazzola@umwestern.edu
PICARD, Dennis .... 207-509-7200 196 E dpicard@unity.edu
PICARD, Jennifer .... 928-692-3090.. 14 F jpicard@mohave.edu
PICARD, Matthew .... 504-398-2327 192 A mpicard@uhcno.edu
PICARD-TESSIER, Cathy, L .... 401-825-1000 404 C ctessier@ccri.edu
PICARDO, Callie .... 937-529-2201 361 G kcpicardo@united.edu
PICAZO, Leslile .... 714-895-8970.. 38 A
PICCHI, Andrea .... 559-925-3304.. 75 B andreapicchi@whccd.edu
PICCHI, Danielle .... 915-532-3737 458 B dpicchi@westerntech.edu
PICCININNI, James .... 713-525-2192 454 G jpicci@stthom.edu
PICCOLI, Benedetto .... 856-225-6356 281 G piccoli@camden.rutgers.edu

PICCOLI, Tracey .... 970-247-7464.. 80 J
piccoli_t@fortlewis.edu
PICCOLO, Jocelyn .... 912-650-6211 125 F
jpiccolo@southuniversity.edu
PICCOLO, Joe .... 301-934-7822 198 G
jpiccolo@csmd.edu
PICCOLO, Lisa .... 843-574-6195 412 I
lisa.piccolo@tridenttech.edu
PICCOLO, Nicholas .... 712-749-2656 164 C
piccolon@bvu.edu
PICHA, Kallan .... 503-943-7857 377 A
picha@up.edu
PICHA, Mike .... 863-638-7217 114 A
mike.picha@warner.edu
PICHARD, Kevin .... 850-245-0466 109 H
kevin.pichard@flbog.edu
PICHARDO, Jeannette ... 718-405-3255 296 F
jeannette.pichardo@mountsaintvincent.edu
PICHEY, Justin .... 803-786-3612 408 D
jpichey@columbiasc.edu
PICHON, Henrietta .... 575-646-3825 287 C
pichon@nmsu.edu
PICINICH, Shelly .... 615-244-5848 423 C
PICK, Katharina .... 909-607-7282.. 37 C
katharina.pick@cgu.edu
PICKARD, Angie .... 601-581-3508 247 A
apickard@meridiancc.edu
PICKARD, Anthony .... 808-675-3500 128 D
anthony.pickard@byuh.edu
PICKARD, Jeremy .... 563-288-6004 166 A
jpickard@eicc.edu
PICKEL, Wendy .... 816-501-4824 258 I
wendy.pickel@rockhurst.edu
PICKELL, Barsha .... 423-472-7141 424 B
bpickell@clevelandstatecc.edu
PICKENS, Joe .... 386-312-4111 107 C
joepickens@sjrstate.edu
PICKENS, Ronda .... 580-387-7261 366 E
rpickens@mscok.edu
PICKENS, Wanda .... 706-886-6831 126 D
wpickens@tfc.edu
PICKENS-OPOKU, Ali .... 651-779-5784 237 H
ali.pickens-opoku@century.edu
PICKERELL, Jennifer, K . 618-537-6805 144 A
jkpickerell@mckendree.edu
PICKERILL, Ted, O .... 513-529-6225 356 A
pickerto@miamioh.edu
PICKERING, Amanda ...... 315-268-3994 295 F
apickeri@clarkson.edu
PICKERING, David, J .... 815-928-5577 147 A
dpickrng@olivet.edu
PICKERING, Jeff .... 919-209-2000 335 F
jlpickering@johnstoncc.edu
PICKERING, Robert, P .. 843-953-5096 407 C
robert.pickering@citadel.edu
PICKETT, Dakiesha .... 404-756-4442 115 G
dpickett@atlm.edu
PICKETT, Himie .... 301-736-3631 200 C
himie.pickett@msbbcs.edu
PICKETT, Regina .... 281-283-2626 452 E
pickett@uhcl.edu
PICKETT, Todd .... 562-903-4754.. 27 A
todd.pickett@biola.edu
PICKHARDT, Paul .... 920-565-1000 493 A
pickhardtp@lakeland.edu
PICKRON-DAVIS,
Marcine .... 215-871-6178 395 G
marcinepi@pcom.edu
PICKRUM, Vita, C .... 302-857-6055.. 90 E
vpickrum@desu.edu
PICKUS, Keith .... 316-978-7791 178 D
keith.pickus@wichita.edu
PICKVET, Carrie, A .... 989-837-4219 229 B
pickvetc@northwood.edu
PICONE, Deborah .... 212-686-9244 290 C
PICUS, Sharon, M .... 610-683-1353 394 D
picus@kutztown.edu
PIDDINGTON, Josh, R .. 856-415-2270 281 D
jpiddington@rcsj.edu
PIECHOTA, Thomas .... 714-628-2897.. 36 B
piechota@chapman.edu
PIECORA, Annette .... 914-674-7337 306 C
apiecora@mercy.edu
PIECZYNSKI,
William, C .... 508-213-2162 217 H
william.pieczynski@nichols.edu
PIEDIMONTE, Giovanni . 504-988-3291 191 F
gpiedimonte@tulane.edu
PIEDRAS, Alex, H .... 515-263-6017 166 F
apiedras@grandview.edu
PIEHLER, Keith .... 207-941-7875 194 F
piehlerk@husson.edu
PIEHLER, Michael .... 252-726-6841 342 C
mpiehler@email.unc.edu
PIEKOS, Mark .... 815-455-8593 143 I
mpiekos@mchenry.edu
PIEKUTOWSKI,
Michelle .... 412-268-5523 380 C
mpie@andrew.cmu.edu
PIENTA-LETTA, Diane .... 973-300-2226 284 A
dpienta-lett@sussex.edu
PIEPER, John, A .... 314-446-8307 260 H
john.pieper@stlcop.edu
PIEPER, Michael .... 701-777-6862 345 B
michael.pieper@und.edu
PIEPER, Sandi, J .... 515-574-1139 167 A
pieper@iowacentral.edu
PIEPER-OLSON,
Heather .... 320-363-5964 235 F
hpieperolso@csbsju.edu
PIERATT, William .... 575-674-2201 285 L
dpieratt@burrell.edu
PIERCE, Amanda, K ...... 757-594-8851 465 M
amanda.pierce@cnu.edu
PIERCE, Bess .... 423-869-6752 421 A
bess.pierce@lmunet.edu
PIERCE, Brynn .... 541-383-7402 372 A
bpierce@cocc.edu
PIERCE, Chuck .... 901-678-3633 426 G
capierce@memphis.edu
PIERCE, Dee .... 630-752-5048 153 C
dee.pierce@wheaton.edu
PIERCE, Diane .... 575-527-7745 287 F
dpierce@nmsu.edu
PIERCE, Evan, F .... 716-286-8327 309 H
epierce@niagara.edu
PIERCE, Fred .... 906-635-2674 226 G
fpierce@lssu.edu
PIERCE, Frederic .... 607-753-2232 318 A
fred.pierce@cortland.edu
PIERCE, Greg .... 601-266-5006 249 F
greg.pierce@usm.edu
PIERCE, Janelle .... 770-962-7580 121 E
jpierce@gwinnetttech.edu
PIERCE, Jason .... 709-379-3111 128 C
jpierce@yhc.edu
PIERCE, Jason, L .... 937-229-2601 362 C
jpierce2@udayton.edu
PIERCE, Jeff .... 828-262-3190 340 I
piercewj@appstate.edu
PIERCE, Jennifer .... 856-351-2642 283 B
jpierce@salemcc.edu
PIERCE, Jerry, D .... 318-357-6588 192 G
pierce@nsula.edu
PIERCE, Jessica, A .... 504-398-2190 192 A
jpierce@uhcno.edu
PIERCE, Jill, A .... 207-859-4807 194 D
jill.pierce@colby.edu
PIERCE, Joan .... 608-785-9915 500 C
piercej@westerntc.edu
PIERCE, John .... 828-251-6742 342 B
jpierce@unca.edu
PIERCE, Jonathan .... 503-883-2553 373 F
jdpierce@linfield.edu
PIERCE, Josh .... 573-629-3014 253 J
josh.pierce@hlg.edu
PIERCE, Joshua .... 573-629-3014 253 J
joshua.pierce@hlg.edu
PIERCE, Keith .... 803-641-2838 413 B
keithp@usca.edu
PIERCE, Kellee .... 406-657-1166 265 E
piercek@rocky.edu
PIERCE, Kenneth .... 512-245-9650 450 C
krp91@txstate.edu
PIERCE, Kristen .... 505-565-1075 219 A
kpierce1@stonehill.edu
PIERCE, LaRue .... 715-836-5992 495 E
piercea@uwec.edu
PIERCE, Latoya .... 716-375-2394 313 C
lpierce@sbu.edu
PIERCE, Lori, J .... 734-764-0151 231 H
ljpierce@umich.edu
PIERCE, Malisa .... 918-270-6409 368 G
malisa.pierce@ptstulsa.edu
PIERCE, Mario .... 203-332-5015.. 86 F
mpierce@housatonic.edu
PIERCE, Marisa .... 425-640-1697 480 A
marisa.pierce@edcc.edu
PIERCE, Marisa .... 972-273-3135 435 B
marisapierce@dcccd.edu
PIERCE, Mark .... 518-736-3622 300 D
mark.pierce@fmcc.suny.edu
PIERCE, Melody, C .... 336-334-7696 341 D
mcpierce@ncat.edu
PIERCE, Michael .... 562-903-4777.. 27 A
michael.pierce@biola.edu
PIERCE, Robert 'Bob' .... 205-348-4769.... 7 G
bpierce@advance.ua.edu
PIERCE, Sean .... 718-997-4881 295 B
sean.pierce@qc.cuny.edu
PIERCE, Sharon .... 612-659-6300 239 A
sharon.pierce@minneapolis.edu
PIERCE, Sonja .... 812-288-8878 159 M
spierce@mid-america.edu
PIERCE, Stephen .... 540-338-1776 469 C
admissions@phc.edu
PIERCE, Travis, L .... 906-487-2682 228 A
tlp@mtu.edu
PIERCE, Vicki, G .... 256-765-4311.... 8 E
vgpierce@una.edu
PIERCE, Victoria .... 864-231-2000 406 F
vpierce@andersonuniversity.edu
PIERCE, William .... 419-530-5359 363 B
william.pierce@utoledo.edu
PIERCE, Yolanda .... 202-806-6100.. 92 F
PIERCE BURNETTE,
Colette .... 512-505-3001 438 A
cpburnette@htu.edu
PIERNER, Tracy, P .... 608-757-7770 498 D
tpierner@blackhawk.edu
PIEROTTI, Laura .... 201-559-3504 277 J
pierottil@felician.edu
PIERRE, Christophe ...... 201-216-5263 283 D
christophe.pierre@stevens.edu
PIERRE, David, A .... 718-990-2616 313 G
pierred@stjohns.edu
PIERRE, Devona .... 727-302-6653 107 E
pierre.devona@spcollege.edu
PIERRE, Gino .... 662-252-8000 248 G
gpierre@rustcollege.edu
PIERRE, John, K .... 225-771-2552 191 E
jpierre@sulc.edu
PIERRE, Markey .... 318-813-5151 189 I
markey@lsuhs.edu
PIERRE, Sandra, L .... 480-627-5345.. 15 N
spierre@taliesin.edu
PIERRE, Sandra, L .... 480-627-5345.. 15 N
PIERS, Sheri .... 207-893-6634 196 C
spiers@sjcme.edu
PIERSALL, Vicki .... 503-554-2161 373 A
vpiersall@georgefox.edu
PIERSOL, Jonathan .... 202-806-6100.. 92 F
PIERSOL, Jonathan .... 404-962-3300 127 D
jonathan.piersol@usg.edu
PIERSON, Ann .... 618-374-5030 147 E
ann.pierson@principia.edu
PIERSON, Carrie .... 217-424-3999 144 G
cpierson@millikin.edu
PIERSON, Connie .... 410-455-3055 203 B
krach@umbc.edu
PIERSON, Edwin .... 979-845-9999 446 F
epierson@tamu.edu
PIERSON, Gary .... 970-943-2049.. 85 C
gpierson@western.edu
PIERSON, James .... 412-365-1615 380 G
j.pierson@chatham.edu
PIERSON, Katricia .... 580-559-5213 365 K
kpierson@ecok.edu
PIERSON, Megan .... 650-723-2300.. 66 E
PIERSON, Molly .... 785-670-1065 178 C
molly.pierson@washburn.edu
PIERSON, Ryan .... 860-906-5014.. 86 D
rpierson@capitalcc.edu
PIERSON, Scott .... 715-232-5365 497 B
piersons@uwstout.edu
PIERSON, Tim, J .... 434-395-2039 468 F
piersontj@longwood.edu
PIESCO, Ryan .... 617-745-3849 209 B
ryan.piesco@enc.edu
PIESTER, Kenneth .... 661-362-2293.. 51 D
kpiester@masters.edu
PIETERSE, Carousel ...... 281-646-1109 431 G
carousel.pieterse@thebibleseminary.edu
PIETREWICZ, Brian .... 505-277-5930 283 J
bpietrewicz@unm.edu
PIETRO, Kimberly .... 716-829-7556 293 E
pietrok@dyc.edu
PIETROK, Mark .... 503-768-7065 373 E
pietrok@lclark.edu
PIETROPAULO, Jason ... 865-251-1800 423 E
jpietropaulo@south.edu
PIETROWSKI, Michael ... 505-565-1082 219 A
mpietrowski@stonehill.edu
PIETRUSZKIEWICZ,
Christopher, M .... 812-488-2151 161 G
prezp@evansville.edu
PIETRYKOWSKI, Chet ... 406-791-5283 265 H
chet.pietrykowski@uprovidence.edu
PIETRYKOWSKI,
Robert, J .... 954-262-7893 105 A
rpietrykowski@nova.edu
PIETRZAK, Dale, R .... 812-888-4141 162 F
dpietrzak@vinu.edu
PIETSCH, Amy .... 920-735-2594 498 F
pietsch@fvtc.edu
PIETTE, Kylie .... 231-591-2089 224 A
kyliepiette@ferris.edu
PIETZ, Kady .... 601-528-8446 247 E
kady.pietz@mgccc.edu
PIETZ, Vicky .... 715-675-3331 499 F
pietz@ntc.edu
PIFER, Kenneth .... 503-370-6104 377 F
kpifer@willamette.edu
PIFKO, Melissa, K .... 713-500-3268 456 B
melissa.pifko@uth.tmc.edu
PIGA, John .... 781-891-2148 206 G
jpiga@bentley.edu
PIGATTI, Kimberly .... 708-596-2000 149 H
kpigatti@ssc.edu
PIGEON, Jered .... 218-477-2721 239 E
jered.pigeon@mnstate.edu
PIGEON, Vanessa .... 713-226-5522 453 A
pigeonv@uhd.edu
PIGG, Eddie .... 334-745-6437.... 3 G
epigg@suscc.edu
PIGG, Tom .... 731-424-3520 424 E
tpigg@jscc.edu
PIGGOT, Robyn .... 508-999-8002 212 A
robyn.piggot@umassd.edu
PIGNATELLO, Robert ..... 973-443-8422 277 I
pignatello@fdu.edu
PIGNATORE, Amy .... 724-287-8711 379 E
amy.pignatore@bc3.edu
PIGORS, Aaron .... 219-980-7203 157 C
apigors@iu.edu
PIGOTT, Miguel .... 860-512-2815.. 86 G
mpigott@manchestercc.edu
PIGZA, Jennifer .... 925-631-4755.. 59 I
jpigza@stmarys-ca.edu
PIKALEK, Amy .... 608-663-2218 492 F
apikalek@edgewood.edu
PIKE, Dale .... 540-231-7108 476 C
dalepike@vt.edu
PIKLA, Christina .... 210-999-8898 451 E
cpikla@trinity.edu
PIKOWSKY, Reta .... 404-894-4181 119 E
reta.pikowsky@registrar.gatech.edu
PILARSKI, Jason .... 414-382-6151 491 F
jason.pilarski@alverno.edu
PILATI, Liz .... 206-296-1891 484 A
pilatil@seattleu.edu
PILBIN, Tory .... 978-232-2109 209 E
vpilbin@endicott.edu
PILCHICK, Yochanan ...... 718-232-7800 325 H
PILCO, Joel .... 760-634-1771.. 28 E
PILE, Judy .... 501-202-7433.. 18 E
PILEWSKI, Tim, W .... 814-732-1974 394 B
pilewski@edinboro.edu
PILGER, Dale .... 810-762-9525 226 B
dpilger@kettering.edu
PILGRIM, Antolina .... 229-333-5708 127 E
anedwards@valdosta.edu
PILGRIM, David .... 231-591-3946 224 A
davidpilgrim@ferris.edu
PILGRIM, Jacqui .... 617-422-7401 217 F
jpilgrim@nesl.edu
PILGRIM, Scott .... 864-388-8698 410 A
spilgrim@lander.edu
PILIECI, Kim .... 616-538-2330 224 E
kpilieci@gracechristian.edu
PILIERI, Thais .... 718-270-6986 294 G
tpilieri@mec.cuny.edu
PILIPZECK, Beth .... 215-596-8970 401 E
b.pilipz@usciences.edu
PILKINGTON, Annette ... 303-273-3498.. 79 J
apilking@mines.edu
PILLAI, Manila .... 800-477-2254.. 29 G
mpillai@calsouthern.edu
PILLANS, Elizabeth .... 903-875-7370 440 D
elizabeth.pillans@navarrocollege.edu
PILLAR, James .... 732-571-3585 279 A
jpillar@monmouth.edu
PILLARELLI, Tina .... 734-384-4332 228 C
tpillarelli@monroeccc.edu
PILLAY, Sasi .... 509-335-8017 485 D
sasi.k.pillay@wsu.edu
PILLING, Peter, E .... 212-854-4774 297 C
pp2542@columbia.edu
PILLO, Pam .... 203-365-7560.. 89 A
pillop@sacredheart.edu

PIZANA, Kathleen .... 574-520-4878 157 E
kpizana@iusb.edu
PIZARRO, Xavier .... 787-780-0070 505 F
xpizarro@caribbean.edu
PIZER, Lori .... 518-292-7785 313 A
inst_res@sage.edu
PIZZARDI, Frank .... 516-876-3013 318 C
pizzardif@oldwestbury.edu
PIZZO, Lauren .... 423-652-4728 420 F
lpizzo@king.edu
PIZZUTI, John .... 740-283-6238 352 I
jpizzuti@franciscan.edu
PIZZUTO, William, J ..... 203-236-9818.. 89 D
william.j.pizzuto@uconn.edu
PIÑERO, Bethzaida .... 787-701-5100 506 D
bpinero@columbiacentral.edu
PIÑERO, Ileana .... 787-751-1912 509 A
ipinero@juris.inter.edu
PJATAK, Jennifer .... 203-932-7082.. 89 H
jpjatak@newhaven.edu
PLACE, Jennifer .... 252-398-6553 328 C
placej@chowan.edu
PLACE, Nick, T .... 706-542-3924 126 G
caesdean@uga.edu
PLACER, Chandra .... 864-578-8770 411 F
cplacer@sherman.edu
PLACIDI, Kathleen .... 434-381-6596 471 I
kplacidi@sbc.edu
PLACIDO, Robert .... 207-581-5842 196 F
robert.placido@maine.edu
PLAEHN, Kris, H .... 253-535-7212 482 A
plaehnkh@plu.edu
PLAGGE, Sinead .... 360-416-7600 484 C
sinead.plagge@skagit.edu
PLAISANCE, Michelle ...... 336-272-7102 329 C
michelle.plaisance@greensboro.edu
PLAISTED, Matthew .... 805-525-4417.. 67 K
mplaisted@thomasaquinas.edu
PLANDER, Kristy .... 402-481-8849 265 K
kristy.plander@bryanhealthcollege.edu
PLANEK, John .... 815-836-5937 142 F
planekjo@lewisu.edu
PLANEY, Steve .... 724-480-3395 381 H
steve.planey@ccbc.edu
PLANK, Linda .... 214-820-3361 431 E
linda_plank@baylor.edu
PLANT, Alicia .... 404-627-2681 116 C
alicia.plant@beulah.edu
PLANT, Alisa .... 225-578-6144 189 E
alisaplant1@lsu.edu
PLANT, Maureen .... 301-447-5621 201 B
mplant@msmary.edu
PLANTE, Dawn, M .... 440-525-7327 354 L
dplante@lakelandcc.edu
PLANTEFABER, Lisa .... 413-572-5733 213 F
lplantefaber@westfield.ma.edu
PLANTY, Teresa .... 315-268-3852 295 F
tplanty@clarkson.edu
PLANTZ, Robert .... 570-585-9258 381 B
rplantz@clarkssummitu.edu
PLANTZ-MASTERS,
Shari .... 303-458-4272.. 83 E
splantzmasters@regis.edu
PLASENCIO, Eric .... 915-532-3737 458 B
PLASSE, Michelle .... 310-338-7332.. 51 A
michelle.plasse@lmu.edu
PLASSMANN, Florenz .... 740-593-2850 358 K
plassmann@ohio.edu
PLASTERS, Shana .... 336-272-7102 329 C
shana.plasters@greensboro.edu
PLATANIA, Jennifer .... 336-278-5938 328 J
jplatania@elon.edu
PLATE, William, M .... 435-797-1356 460 C
william.plate@usu.edu
PLATING, John .... 706-419-1663 118 A
john.plating@covenant.edu
PLATOVSKY, Jonathan .. 718-268-4700 312 A
PLATT, David, E .... 512-471-3518 455 A
david.platt@austin.utexas.edu
PLATT, Judy, T .... 617-353-5940 207 E
juplatt@bu.edu
PLATT, Kathleen .... 912-358-4144 125 A
plattk@savannahstate.edu
PLATT, Sharon .... 412-536-1120 386 H
sharon.platt@laroche.edu
PLATT-MOSER, Sara ...... 719-333-9532 503 D
sara.platt-moser@usafa.edu
PLATTE, Chelsea .... 231-348-6621 228 H
cplatte1@ncmich.edu
PLATUKUS, Graceann .... 570-740-0355 389 A
gplatukus@luzerne.edu
PLATZEK, Russell .... 718-262-2140 295 E
rplatzek@york.cuny.edu

PLAWECKI, Jeffrey .... 317-274-4553 157 D
jplaweck@iupui.edu
PLAYER, Kathleen, N .... 630-515-7664 144 F
kplayer@midwestern.edu
PLAZA, Erica .... 920-498-6969 499 G
erica.plaza@nwtc.edu
PLAZEK, David .... 802-635-1348 463 G
PLEAS, Dawn, E .... 620-229-6336 177 G
dawn.pleas@sckans.edu
PLEAS, Dorothy, J .... 630-637-5156 145 F
djpleas@noctrl.edu
PLEASANT, Audra .... 501-279-4145.. 19 C
apleasant@harding.edu
PLEASANT, Klint .... 248-218-2058 230 B
kpleasant@rochesteru.edu
PLEASANT, Klint, A .... 248-218-2058 230 B
kpleasant@rochesteru.edu
PLEASANT, Lori .... 850-973-9469 104 L
pleasantl@nfc.edu
PLEASANT, Rachel .... 706-778-8500 124 D
johnroberts@piedmont.edu
PLEASANT-DOINE,
Sheia, I .... 904-819-6435.. 99 E
spleasant@flagler.edu
PLEDGER, Barbara .... 607-436-2010 316 F
barbara.pledger@oneonta.edu
PLEGGENKUHLE, Jesse . 563-425-5666 170 H
pleggenkuhlej@uiu.edu
PLEHN, Michael, T .... 202-685-3924 502 K
PLEMMONS, Donna ...... 501-450-1351.. 19 E
plemmons@hendrix.edu
PLEMMONS, Eric .... 704-406-4259 329 A
eplemmons@gardner-webb.edu
PLEMMONS, Kim .... 704-403-1751 327 C
kim.plemmons@atriumhealth.org
PLENDL, Jackie .... 712-274-6400 171 B
jackie.plendl@witcc.edu
PLENSKI, Sandra .... 415-581-8863.. 69 C
plenskis@uchastings.edu
PLENTY CHIEF, Melissa 701-255-3285 347 A
mplentychief@uttc.edu
PLESSEL, Kristin .... 262-472-1918 497 D
PLESSINGER, Brian .... 860-738-6409.. 87 C
bplessinger@nwcc.edu
PLETT, Angie .... 620-278-2173 177 H
PLEVER, Steve .... 828-251-6526 342 B
splever@unca.edu
PLINER, Lauren .... 215-953-5999.. 93 H
PLINER, Susan .... 315-781-3354 301 F
pliner@hws.edu
PLINSKE, Kathleen, A ... 407-582-3400 113 I
kplinske@valenciacollege.edu
PLINSKE, Paul .... 719-549-2730.. 80 B
paul.plinske@csupueblo.edu
PLISCO, Mary .... 404-835-6135 423 B
mplisco@richmont.edu
PLOECKELMAN,
Rebecca .... 414-277-7129 494 D
ploeckel@msoe.edu
PLOEGER, Robin .... 918-631-3170 371 C
robin-ploeger@utulsa.edu
PLOEHN, Harry .... 252-328-9600 341 A
ploehnh17@ecu.edu
PLOIUM, Tina .... 701-766-4415 344 G
PLONSKY, Christine, A . 512-471-4780 455 A
cp@utexas.edu
PLOSKONKA, James ..... 216-987-5177 351 E
james.ploskonka@tri-c.edu
PLOTKIN, David .... 503-594-3020 372 C
david.plotkin@clackamas.edu
PLOTKOWSKI, Paul .... 616-331-6260 224 G
plotkowp@gvsu.edu
PLOTNER, Amy .... 315-312-3702 318 D
amy.plotner@oswego.edu
PLOTT, Richard .... 541-463-5391 373 D
plottr@lanecc.edu
PLOUFF, Chris .... 616-331-2400 224 G
plouffc@gvsu.edu
PLOUFFE, Audrey .... 406-275-4969 265 F
audrey_plouffe@skc.edu
PLOUFFE, Jeffrey .... 401-874-4198 405 E
jeffplouffe@uri.edu
PLOURD, Samantha .... 860-343-5751.. 87 A
splourd@mxcc.edu
PLOUTZ-SNYDER, Lori .. 734-764-5210 231 H
lorips@umich.edu
PLOWFIELD, Lisa .... 410-704-2132 204 E
lplowfield@towson.edu
PLOWMAN, Donde .... 865-974-2445 427 B
chancellor@utk.edu
PLUEARD, Kelley .... 541-440-7690 376 G
kelley.plueard@umpqua.edu

PLUEMER, Julie .... 608-822-2369 500 A
jpluemer@swtc.edu
PLUMB, Anne, M .... 901-572-2842 418 A
anne.plumb@baptistu.edu
PLUMB, Hylon .... 717-396-7833 392 J
hplumb@pcad.edu
PLUMB, Richard, G .... 925-631-4203.. 59 I
rplumb@stmarys-ca.edu
PLUMB, Sylvia .... 802-626-6459 463 G
sylvia.plumb@northernvermont.edu
PLUMLEY, Susan .... 304-327-4182 489 I
splumley@bluefieldstate.edu
PLUMLY, Wayne, L .... 229-245-3825 127 E
lwplumly@valdosta.edu
PLUMMER, AJ .... 319-895-4331 164 G
aplummer@cornellcollege.edu
PLUMMER, B. DaVida ... 757-727-6698 467 G
davida.plummer@hamptonu.edu
PLUMMER, Dale, H .... 610-566-1776 403 B
dplummer@williamson.edu
PLUMMER, DaVida .... 757-637-2018 467 G
davida.plummer@hamptonu.edu
PLUMMER, Eric .... 540-831-5500 469 D
eplummer@radford.edu
PLUMMER, Keith .... 215-702-4358 380 A
kplummer@cairn.edu
PLUMMER, Laura .... 915-532-3737 458 B
lplummer@westerntech.edu
PLUMMER, Lisa .... 610-282-1100 382 C
lisa.plummer@desales.edu
PLUMMER, Meredith ..... 760-366-5284.. 40 E
mplummer@cmccd.edu
PLUMMER, Troy, A .... 515-263-6050 166 F
tplummer@grandview.edu
PLUNK, Kelly .... 870-584-1104.. 22 F
kplunk@cccua.edu
PLUNKETT, Chris .... 319-385-6204 167 H
chris.plunkett@iw.edu
PLUNKETT, Gary .... 760-773-2581.. 38 E
gplunkett@collegeofthedesert.edu
PLUNKETT, Heidi .... 618-468-5110 142 E
hplunkett@lc.edu
PLUNKETT, James, C .... 215-951-1500 387 A
plunkett@lasalle.edu
PLUNKETT, John .... 636-949-4973 254 H
jplunkett@lindenwood.edu
PLUNKETT, Mary Rob ... 706-864-1625 127 A
maryrob.plunkett@ung.edu
PLURETTI, Anthony .... 610-499-4202 402 G
ampluretti@widener.edu
PLUSCHT, Patrick .... 940-565-4936 453 E
patrick.pluscht@unt.edu
PLUTCHOK, Moshe .... 718-438-5476 325 B
PLUTINO, Maria, S .... 585-385-7258 313 F
mplutino@sjfc.edu
PLYMALE, Chad .... 585-567-9480 302 B
chad.plymale@houghton.edu
POAGE, Alison .... 512-472-4133 443 F
alison.poage@ssw.edu
POAGE, Miranda .... 432-685-6754 440 B
mpoage@midland.edu
POARCH, Mark .... 828-726-2211 332 G
mpoarch@cccti.edu
POATS, Lillian, B .... 713-313-1133 449 B
poats_lb@tsu.edu
POATS, Lillian, B .... 713-313-7978 449 B
poats_lb@tsu.edu
POCHARD, Brad .... 864-294-3406 409 H
brad.pochard@furman.edu
POCHOCKI, Wendy, E ... 630-637-5808 145 F
wepochocki@noctrl.edu
POCK, Arnyce .... 301-295-9945 503 C
arnyce.pock@usuhs.edu
POCZATEK, Evelyn .... 312-947-1987 148 G
evelyn_poczatek@rush.edu
PODELL, David .... 781-239-3101 214 G
dpodell@massbay.edu
PODESCHI, Amanda ...... 217-424-3506 144 G
apodeschi@millikin.edu
PODESTÁ, Guido .... 608-262-9833 495 D
gpodesta@wisc.edu
PODESZWA, Stephen ..... 413-737-7000 205 F
PODHRADSKY, Ashley .. 605-256-5821 416 F
ashley.podhradsky@dsu.edu
PODLIN, Michael .... 206-296-6100 484 A
podlinm@seattleu.edu
PODOL, Edward .... 480-858-9100.. 15 Q
e.podol@scnm.edu
PODOLSKY, Daniel, K ... 214-648-2508 457 A
julia.kanellos@utsouthwestern.edu
PODOMINICK, Ray .... 218-235-2175 241 E
ray.podominick@vcc.edu

PODRABSKY, Jason ...... 503-725-5772 375 E
jpod@pdx.edu
PODVIN, John .... 585-276-5945 323 M
john.podvin@rochester.edu
POE, Evelyn .... 484-365-7461 388 H
epoe@lincoln.edu
POE, Katrina .... 662-325-2383 247 F
knp3@msstate.edu
POE, Mary Anne .... 731-661-5397 426 F
mpoe@uu.edu
POE, Scott .... 304-424-8212 490 F
scott.poe@wvup.edu
POE, Shawna .... 217-854-5506 133 I
shawna.poe@blackburn.edu
POEHLER, M.J .... 816-802-3393 254 D
mpoehler@kcai.edu
POEHLERT, Edward .... 760-757-2121.. 52 F
epoehlert@miracosta.edu
POEHLMAN, Lauren ...... 518-327-6291 311 C
lpoehlman@paulsmiths.edu
POELKER, Scott .... 843-574-6198 412 I
scott.poelker@tridenttech.edu
POELVOORDE, Tracy, L 309-779-7710 151 B
tracy.poelvoorde@trinitycollegeqc.edu
POESE, Debra .... 240-567-7269 200 G
debra.poese@montgomerycollege.edu
POFF, G. Elaine, N .... 954-262-7261 105 A
poff@nova.edu
POFF, Robert, C .... 812-941-2331 157 F
rcpoff@ius.edu
POGATSHNIK, Jerry ...... 859-622-8812 180 E
jerry.pogatshnik@eku.edu
POGGENDORF,
Brenda, P .... 540-375-2270 470 E
poggendorf@roanoke.edu
POGLIANO, Kit .... 858-822-5738.. 70 C
altea@ucsd.edu
POGLIANO, Kit .... 858-534-6654.. 70 C
kpogliano@ucsd.edu
POGODZINSKI, Joel ..... 414-288-1671 493 E
joel.pogodzinski@marquette.edu
POGUE, Ed .... 785-227-3380 172 A
poguee@bethanylb.edu
POHL, Charles, A .... 215-503-6988 399 E
charles.pohl@jefferson.edu
POHL, Don, J .... 314-286-3653 258 F
POHL, Jonathan .... 860-832-1945.. 85 G
pohlj@ccsu.edu
POHL, Mark .... 574-372-5100 155 F
pohlma@grace.edu
POHL, Mark, A .... 574-372-5100 155 F
pohlma@grace.edu
POHLGEERS, Linda .... 513-244-4824 356 F
linda.pohlgeers@msj.edu
POHLMAN, Jean .... 513-487-1126 361 F
jean.pohlman@myunion.edu
POHLSON, Scott .... 605-658-6261 416 D
scott.pohlson@usd.edu
POHRTE, Shannon .... 847-214-7595 137 F
spohrte@elgin.edu
POIANI, Eileen .... 201-761-6022 283 A
epoiani@saintpeters.edu
POIGER, Uta .... 617-373-5173 217 I
POIGNEE, Ieshia .... 605-856-8168 415 J
ieshia.poignee@sintegleska.edu
POINDEXTER, Jeanne ... 864-250-7000.. 93 H
POINDEXTER, Jeanne ... 423-417-3550.. 93 H
POINDEXTER, Kathi ...... 586-498-4170 227 B
poindexterk@macomb.edu
POINDEXTER, Kim .... 816-604-5230 255 E
kim.poindexter@mcckc.edu
POINDEXTER, Kimberly 816-604-6639 255 D
kim.poindexter@mcckc.edu
POINDEXTER, Wendell .. 301-846-2513 198 I
wpoindexter@frederick.edu
POINTER, Monica .... 678-715-2200.. 93 H
POINTS, Emily .... 309-694-8501 139 B
emily.points@icc.edu
POIRIER, Bill .... 603-862-3530 274 F
bill.poirier@unh.edu
POIRIER, Bill .... 603-862-0700 274 E
bill.poirier@unh.edu
POIRIER, Bill .... 603-862-3530 275 A
bill.poirier@plymouth.edu
POIRIER, J. Nicolas ...... 315-568-3197 310 B
npoirier@nycc.edu
POISSON, Craig .... 413-748-3333 218 I
cpoisson@springfield.edu
POISSON, Frances .... 978-232-2001 209 E
fpoisson@endicott.edu
POITRA, Peggy .... 218-879-0803 238 B
poitra@fdltcc.edu

POPE, Janice .... 828-262-8038 340 I
popejt@appstate.edu
POPE, Jerry .... 913-288-7100 175 B
jpope@kckcc.edu
POPE, Justin .... 434-395-4805 468 F
popejn@longwood.edu
POPE, Keisha .... 804-257-5876 476 F
klpope@vuu.edu
POPE, Keisha, L .... 804-257-5854 476 F
klpope@vuu.edu
POPE, Marion .... 910-592-8081 337 G
mpope@sampsoncc.edu
POPE, Matthew .... 865-471-3372 418 E
mpope@cn.edu
POPE, Monique .... 909-748-8337.. 72 F
monique_pope@redlands.edu
POPE, Myron, L .... 205-348-6670.... 7 G
myron.pope@ua.edu
POPE, Sandra, Y .... 304-293-1216 490 E
spope@hsc.wvu.edu
POPE, Sarah .... 804-333-6705 475 A
spope@rappahannock.edu
POPE, Sharon .... 570-372-4018 398 F
popes@susqu.edu
POPE, Stephanie .... 800-996-6422 238 F
POPE, Terri .... 216-987-3937 351 E
terri.pope@tri-c.edu
POPE-BAYNE, Claudia .. 201-761-6111 283 A
cpopebayne@saintpeters.edu
POPE-DAVIS, Donald, L 614-292-2461 358 D
pope-davis.1@osu.edu
POPE MITCHELL,
Melita .... 704-378-3593 330 D
mmitchell@jcsu.edu
POPEJOY, Cindy .... 217-732-3168 142 G
capopejoy@lincolnchristian.edu
POPELKA, David, M ...... 515-294-7007 163 G
dpopelka@iastate.edu
POPENFOOSE, Joel .... 847-628-1595 141 C
joel.popenfoose@judsonu.edu
POPESCU, Adriana .... 805-756-2622.. 29 I
popescu@calpoly.edu
POPHAM, Don .... 636-922-8636 258 J
dpopham@stchas.edu
POPHAM, Heidi .... 706-295-6928 120 A
hpopham@gntc.edu
POPHRISTIC, Vojislava . 856-256-4000 281 F
pophristic@rowan.edu
POPHRISTIC, Vojislava . 215-596-8800 401 E
POPIELARCZYK, Zsa ..... 773-907-4450 135 C
zpopiela@ccc.edu
POPIOLEK, Marcus .... 541-885-0192 374 I
marcus.popiolek@oit.edu
POPKEY, Megan .... 920-498-7186 499 G
megan.popkey@nwtc.edu
POPKO, Susan .... 408-551-3085.. 63 B
spopko@scu.edu
POPLAR, Andre' .... 248-341-2037 229 C
alpoplar@oaklandcc.edu
POPLAWSKI LEWIS,
Lisa .... 509-359-4555 479 G
lpoplawski@ewu.edu
POPLIN, Lori .... 704-991-0116 338 C
lpoplin0217@stanly.edu
POPLIN, Michelle .... 704-991-0208 338 C
mpoplin4375@stanly.edu
POPOVICH, Donna, B ... 813-253-6237 113 H
dpopovich@ut.edu
POPOVICI, Alexandru .... 914-961-8313 314 H
alpopovici@svots.edu
POPP, Laurie .... 503-491-7474 374 B
laurie.popp@mhcc.edu
POPP, Melissa, D .... 636-584-6703 253 B
melissa.popp@eastcentral.edu
POPP, Stephen .... 616-949-5300 223 C
stephen.popp@cornerstone.edu
POPP, Tari .... 269-471-3613 221 D
tari@andrews.edu
POPP, William, C .... 770-720-5568 124 G
wcp@reinhardt.edu
POPP-FINCH, Rochelle .. 772-462-7476 102 F
rfinch@irsc.edu
POPP-RADFORD, Amy .. 269-749-7172 229 J
aradfordpopp@olivetcollege.edu
POPPA, Joseph .... 914-347-3910 325 A
joseph.poppa@sunywcc.edu
POPPLEWELL, Venus .... 270-384-8189 183 G
popplewellv@lindsey.edu
POPPO, Kristin .... 607-587-3913 319 F
poppokr@alfredstate.edu
POPPRE, Beth .... 480-219-6046 250 A
bpoppre@atsu.edu
PORCA, Sanela .... 803-641-3340 413 B
sanelap@usca.edu
PORCARO, Mark, D ...... 316-978-7787 178 D
mark.porcaro@wichita.edu
PORCELLA, Adam .... 215-702-4216 380 A
aporcella@cairn.edu
PORCENA, Yves-Rose ... 404-471-6450 114 G
yporcena@agnesscott.edu
PORCHE, Demetrius ...... 504-568-4106 189 H
dporch@lsuhsc.edu
PORCHE, Saadia .... 323-953-4000.. 49 A
porchest@lacitycollege.edu
PORE, Karen .... 910-893-1266 327 D
kpore@campbell.edu
PORELL, Ryan .... 401-456-8094 405 A
rporell@ric.edu
PORFIDO, Nancy .... 609-343-5095 275 D
porfido@atlantic.edu
PORPILIA, Amy .... 864-231-2000 406 F
aporpilia@andersonuniversity.edu
PORRAS, Jose .... 575-624-8023 287 B
porras@nmmi.edu
PORRAS, Precious .... 708-524-6629 137 C
pporras@dom.edu
PORRIER, Jennifer .... 802-224-3001 463 D
jen.porrier@vsc.edu
PORTEE, Charlene .... 334-229-5053.... 4 A
dportee@alasu.edu
PORTEE, Kevin .... 803-705-4321 406 G
kevin.portee@benedict.edu
PORTELA, Stanley .... 787-752-4540 512 B
stanley.portela@upr.edu
PORTELA IRIGOYEN,
Celso, E .... 787-725-8120 506 M
cportela@centro.eap.edu
PORTELLEZ, Humberto .. 757-683-3626 469 B
hportell@odu.edu
PORTEOUS, Alexander .. 207-780-4497 197 D
alexander.porteous@maine.edu
PORTEOUS, Andrew ...... 605-331-6801 417 C
andrew.porteous@usiouxfalls.edu
PORTER, Alex .... 714-484-7313.. 54 B
aporter@cypresscollege.edu
PORTER, Andrea .... 806-651-2037 448 B
aporter@wtamu.edu
PORTER, Bobbie .... 657-278-7326.. 31 C
boporter@fullerton.edu
PORTER, Brandon .... 262-551-5941 492 B
bporter@carthage.edu
PORTER, Byron .... 540-261-4931 471 B
byron.porter@svu.edu
PORTER, Chong, U .... 916-734-9402.. 69 B
chong.porter@ucdmc.ucdavis.edu
PORTER, Christopher .... 540-857-6697 475 G
cporter@virginiawestern.edu
PORTER, Chrystal .... 617-243-2083 211 B
cporter@lasell.edu
PORTER, Cindy, L .... 914-323-5135 305 B
cindy.porter@mville.edu
PORTER, Clifford .... 757-823-8323 469 A
cporter@nsu.edu
PORTER, Connie .... 713-718-6477 437 C
connie.porter@hccs.edu
PORTER, Danielle .... 410-462-8300 198 B
dporter@bccc.edu
PORTER, David .... 731-661-5343 426 F
dporter@uu.edu
PORTER, David, S .... 401-874-2370 405 E
dporter@uri.edu
PORTER, DeeDee .... 619-388-3976.. 60 I
dporter@sdccd.edu
PORTER, Fonda .... 919-497-3205 330 I
fporter@louisburg.edu
PORTER, Hugh, E .... 503-788-6604 375 G
hporter@reed.edu
PORTER, J. Davison ...... 504-314-2188 191 F
jporter6@tulane.edu
PORTER, James, P .... 801-422-3963 458 H
james_porter@byu.edu
PORTER, Jared, L .... 859-858-3511 179 D
jared.porter@asbury.edu
PORTER, Jennifer .... 617-735-9772 209 D
porterj@emmanuel.edu
PORTER, Jennifer .... 248-218-2152 230 B
jporter1@rochesteru.edu
PORTER, John, R .... 636-949-4900 254 H
jporter@lindenwood.edu
PORTER, Kathleen .... 239-489-9091 101 A
kathleen.porter@fsw.edu
PORTER, Katlyn .... 740-588-1374 365 B
kporter2@zanestate.edu
PORTER, Kristen .... 419-251-1339 355 G
kristen.porter@mercycollege.edu
PORTER, Laurie .... 717-477-3107 395 B
PORTER, Lori .... 607-753-2201 318 A
lori.porter@cortland.edu
PORTER, Miacia .... 615-327-6806 421 D
mfporter@mmc.edu
PORTER, Michelle, C .... 605-342-0317 415 C
mporter@jwc.edu
PORTER, Molly .... 619-849-2628.. 57 J
mollyporter@pointloma.edu
PORTER, Monica .... 574-520-4872 157 E
moport@iusb.edu
PORTER, Nadine .... 240-567-5386 200 G
nadine.porter@montgomerycollege.edu
PORTER, Narda .... 276-328-0116 472 E
nnb3h@uvawise.edu
PORTER, Nicole, D .... 650-738-4121.. 62 _
portern@smccd.edu
PORTER, Nicosha .... 214-860-2476 434 I
nporter@dcccd.edu
PORTER, Paul .... 260-399-7700 162 B
pporter@sf.edu
PORTER, Rhonda .... 229-500-2153 114 H
rhonda.porter@asurams.edu
PORTER, Robyn .... 712-325-3413 167 I
rporter@iwcc.edu
PORTER, Russell .... 254-501-5823 447 A
porter@tamuct.edu
PORTER, Seth .... 719-255-3115.. 84 C
sporter9@uccs.edu
PORTER, Stephen .... 816-268-5462 257 C
sporter@nts.edu
PORTER, Susie, S .... 801-585-5693 459 D
s.porter@utah.edu
PORTER, Todd .... 212-799-5000 303 E
PORTER, Tracy .... 863-297-3743 106 A
tporter@polk.edu
PORTER, Wilma, B .... 248-232-4640 229 C
wbporter@oaklandcc.edu
PORTER BRANNON,
Towuanna .... 757-825-2700 475 D
PORTER SHABAZZ,
Tiffany .... 513-585-4399 350 D
tiffany.portershabazz@thechristcollege.edu
PORTER-UTLEY, Kristen 508-531-2418 212 D
k1porterutley@bridgew.edu
PORTERFIELD,
Deana, L .... 585-594-6100 310 C
presidentsoffice@roberts.edu
PORTERFIELD,
Deana, L .... 585-594-6100 312 E
presidentsoffice@roberts.edu
PORTERFIELD, Julie ...... 918-595-8191 370 C
julie.porterfield@tulsacc.edu
PORTERFIELD, Kent ...... 509-313-4115 480 F
porterfield@gonzaga.edu
PORTERVINT, Bernice ... 602-872-7957.. 14 A
bernice.portervint@southmountaincc.edu
PORTERVINT, Bernice ... 602-243-8364.. 14 A
bernice.portervint@southmountaincc.edu
PORTILLO, Maryam .... 925-473-7430.. 40 D
mportillo@losmedanos.edu
PORTNER, Matthew .... 419-289-5251 347 J
mportner@ashland.edu
PORTNOY, Lauren .... 610-896-4984 385 I
lportnoy@haverford.edu
PORTNOY, Robert, N .... 402-472-7450 269 J
rportnoy1@unl.edu
PORTO, JR., Jeff .... 209-667-3131.. 33 B
jporto1@csustan.edu
PORTUGAL, Elsen .... 501-623-2272.. 18 I
PORTWINE, Ronald, E .. 989-964-2064 230 E
report@svsu.edu
PORTWOOD, Craig .... 478-387-4900 119 F
aportwood@gmc.edu
PORTZ, Margaret, A ...... 610-758-5794 388 E
mak5@lehigh.edu
PORTZEL, Curt .... 310-506-4893.. 56 G
curt.portzel@pepperdine.edu
PORVAZNIK, John .... 480-377-4555.. 13 G
porvaznik@riosalado.edu
PORZUCEK, Sarah .... 716-839-8210 298 A
sporzuce@daemen.edu
POSENER, Paul .... 910-775-4253 343 B
paul.posener@uncp.edu
POSER, Susan .... 516-463-6800 301 G
president@hofstra.edu
POSEY, Doneisha .... 317-916-7819 158 D
dposey17@ivytech.edu
POSEY, Evan .... 770-484-1204 122 D
evan.posey@lutherrice.edu
POSEY, Jamie .... 832-813-6776 439 C
jamie.c.posey@lonestar.edu
POSEY, Jamie .... 423-585-6894 425 F
jamie.posey@ws.edu
POSEY, Jim .... 229-931-2302 120 D
jim.posey@gsw.edu
POSEY, Kathy .... 781-891-2177 206 G
kposey@bentley.edu
POSEY, Monica .... 513-569-1515 350 F
monica.posey@cincinnatistate.edu
POSEY, Olivia .... 601-857-3350 246 C
olivia.posey@hindscc.edu
POSHEK, Joseph .... 949-451-5650.. 65 C
jposhek@ivc.edu
POSILLICO, Joseph .... 516-686-7925 308 I
joseph.posillico@nyit.edu
POSING, Mary .... 815-802-8202 141 D
mposing@kcc.edu
POSLER, Brian .... 440-375-7200 354 K
president@lec.edu
POSLUSNY, Matthew ..... 919-760-8514 331 D
mposlusny@meredith.edu
POSNER, Kenneth .... 352-588-8992 107 D
kenneth.posner@saintleo.edu
POSNER, Marc .... 714-484-7006.. 54 B
mposner@cypresscollege.edu
POSNER, Mark .... 651-638-6383 234 D
m-posner@bethel.edu
POSPISIL, KC .... 512-313-3000 433 N
kc.pospisil@concordia.edu
POSS, Joe .... 509-313-6215 480 F
poss@gonzaga.edu
POSS, Michael .... 378-839-6452 127 C
mposs@westga.edu
POSSEHL, Kristin .... 605-367-4753 417 B
kristin.possehl@southeasttech.edu
POST, Beth .... 518-580-5750 315 F
bpost@skidmore.edu
POST, Jack .... 856-227-7200 276 E
jpost@camdencc.edu
POST, Juli .... 678-664-0530 128 A
juli.post@westgatech.edu
POST, Kari .... 802-387-6790 462 C
karipost@landmark.edu
POST, Michael, A .... 540-828-8014 464 L
mpost@bridgewater.edu
POST, Scott .... 501-760-4123.. 20 A
scott.post@np.edu
POST, Stacy .... 906-635-2684 226 G
spost1@lssu.edu
POST, Todd .... 815-802-8602 141 D
tpost@kcc.edu
POST, Tracee .... 806-651-2100 448 B
tpost@wtamu.edu
POSTEL, Gregory, C ...... 419-530-2211 363 B
gregory.postel@utoledo.edu
POSTEMA, Miles, J .... 231-591-3894 224 A
milespostema@ferris.edu
POSTER, Michael, C ..... 563-333-6032 169 G
postermichaelc@sau.edu
POSTLEWAIT, Mariah .... 717-396-7833 392 U
mpostlewait@pcad.edu
POSTMA, James .... 530-226-4129.. 64 E
jpostma@simpsonu.edu
POSTMA, Jana .... 616-988-3650 226 E
jpostma@kuyper.edu
POSTMA, Kurt .... 616-538-2330 224 E
kpostma@gracechristian.edu
POSTMA, Laura .... 906-248-8420 221 M
lpostma@bmcc.edu
POSTMUS, Judy, L .... 410-706-7794 203 A
postmus@ssw.umaryland.edu
POSTON, Linda .... 717-691-6006 389 H
poston@messiah.edu
POSTON, R. Stephen .... 704-233-8194 344 F
poston@wingate.edu
POSTON, Robin .... 901-678-5739 426 G
rposton@memphis.edu
POSTUPACK,
Mary Frances .... 570-422-7920 394 A
mpostupack@esu.edu
POTASH, David .... 773-481-8175 135 G
dpotash@ccc.edu
POTEAU, Youseline .... 305-626-3631 100 D
youseline.poteau@fmuniv.edu
POTEET, Jim .... 913-722-0272 175 A
jim.poteet@kansaschristian.edu
POTEET, Tanya, J .... 614-236-6408 349 B
tpoteet@capital.edu
POTEET, Tony .... 901-678-2619 426 G
ppoteet@memphis.edu
POTEETE-YOUNG,
Lanette .... 847-628-1097 141 C
lpoteete-young@judsonu.edu

POWERS, Susan .... 315-268-6542 295 F
spowers@clarkson.edu
POWERS, Susie .... 859-846-5340 184 B
spowers@midway.edu
POWERS, Tammy .... 928-428-8308.. 12 F
tammy.powers@eac.edu
POWERS, Tanya .... 206-878-3710 481 B
tpowers@highline.edu
POWERS, Teri .... 619-574-6909.. 55 E
tpowers@pacificcollege.edu
POWERS, Tyrone .... 410-777-7496 197 G
tpowers@aacc.edu
POWICKI, Mike .... 402-375-7520 268 F
mipowic1@wsc.edu
POWLEY, Mary, R .... 585-385-8057 313 F
mpowley@sjfc.edu
POWNALL, Phillip .... 904-819-6460.. 99 E
ppownall@flagler.edu
POYNTER, Barry .... 859-622-5012 180 E
barry.poynter@eku.edu
POYZER, Bryan .... 701-671-2872 346 D
bryan.poyzer@ndscs.edu
POZANC, Lisa .... 507-453-2402 239 B
lpozanc@southeastmn.edu
POZZA, Amy .... 804-627-5300 464 K
amy_pozza@bshsi.org
PRABA, Rashmi .... 619-594-5211.. 33 D
rpraba@sdsu.edu
PRABELL, Jon .... 859-572-5493 184 E
prabellj@nku.edu
PRABHU, Sunil .... 909-469-5550.. 75 I
sprabhu@westernu.edu
PRACHAND, Amit .... 847-467-5067 146 E
a-prachand@northwestern.edu
PRADO, Guillermo .... 305-243-2748 113 C
gprado@miami.edu
PRADO, Rosa .... 562-860-2451.. 35 H
rprado@cerritos.edu
PRAET, Diane, M .... 313-993-3313 231 E
praetdm@udmercy.edu
PRAG, Stephen .... 503-352-1563 375 C
sprag@pacificu.edu
PRAKASAM, Piram .... 231-591-5290 224 A
piramprakasam@ferris.edu
PRAKASH, Anupma .... 907-474-7096.. 10 A
aprakash@alaska.edu
PRAKASH,
Channapatana .... 334-725-2334.... 7 D
cprakash@tuskegee.edu
PRAKASH, Neeta .... 954-637-2268 108 E
nprakash@sfbc.edu
PRANGE, Raphaella ...... 217-424-6395 144 G
rpalmer@millikin.edu
PRANGER, Henriette ...... 617-732-2283 216 D
henriette.pranger@mcphs.edu
PRANKE, Greg .... 712-279-5435 164 B
greg.pranke@briarcliff.edu
PRAPAVESSI, Despina ... 925-969-2689.. 40 C
dprapavessi@dvc.edu
PRASAD, Rashmi .... 660-785-4346 260 F
rprasad@truman.edu
PRASAD, Shankar .... 401-863-3413 403 J
shankar_prasad@brown.edu
PRASLOVA, Ludmilla .... 714-556-3610.. 73 H
ludmilla.praslova@vanguard.edu
PRASTACOS, Gregory .... 201-216-8366 283 D
gregory.prastacos@stevens.edu
PRATER, Chanda, F ...... 270-852-3104 183 E
cprater@kwc.edu
PRATER, Michael .... 574-520-4319 157 E
maprater@iusb.edu
PRATER, Sarah, E .... 574-372-5100 155 F
praterse@grace.edu
PRATER, Wendi .... 337-475-5126 192 E
wprater@mcneese.edu
PRATER, Wesley .... 253-589-5813 478 J
wesley.prater@cptc.edu
PRATHER, Curtis .... 703-370-6600 476 E
PRATHER, Kanidrus ...... 706-225-5300.. 93 H
PRATHER, Kerry, N .... 317-738-8009 155 D
kprather@franklincollege.edu
PRATHER, Sean .... 925-424-1690.. 35 K
sprather@laspositascollege.edu
PRATHER, Tammy .... 662-243-1928 246 B
tprather@eastms.edu
PRATHER-JOHNSON,
Nancy, N .... 757-822-1191 475 E
nprather@tcc.edu
PRATT, Allison .... 540-831-5408 469 D
apratt6@radford.edu
PRATT, Barbara .... 908-835-2355 284 H
pratt@warren.edu
PRATT, Carla .... 785-670-1662 178 C
carla.pratt@washburn.edu
PRATT, Christy .... 574-631-7305 162 A
cpratt3@nd.edu
PRATT, Dorianna .... 207-768-9462 197 C
dorianna@maine.edu
PRATT, Edward, E .... 561-297-2126 109 J
epratt2@fau.edu
PRATT, Elizabeth .... 408-288-3142.. 62 H
elizabeth.pratt@sjcc.edu
PRATT, Gary, L .... 785-532-6520 175 C
gpratt@ksu.edu
PRATT, H. Wes .... 417-836-3736 256 G
wpratt@missouristate.edu
PRATT, Mary Jo .... 918-683-4581 365 C
PRATT, Michael .... 205-652-3565.... 9 B
mpratt@uwa.edu
PRATT, Michele .... 989-686-9822 223 J
michelepratt@delta.edu
PRATT, Mike .... 205-652-3840.... 9 B
mpratt@uwa.edu
PRATT, Rob .... 423-585-6952 425 F
robert.pratt@ws.edu
PRATT, Robert, C .... 517-750-1200 231 C
bpratt@arbor.edu
PRATT, Sally .... 213-740-8867.. 73 D
pratt@usc.edu
PRATT, Tot .... 636-584-6733 253 B
tot.pratt@eastcentral.edu
PRATT, Vallarie .... 706-712-8244 118 B
vpratt@daltonstate.edu
PRATT-CLARKE, Menah . 540-231-7500 476 C
inclusive@vt.edu
PRATT-COOK, Patricia ... 651-690-6560 243 A
pcprattcook867@stkate.edu
PRATTE, John .... 318-342-1235 193 C
pratte@ulm.edu
PRATTELLA, Todd .... 914-674-7844 306 C
tprattella@mercy.edu
PRAWIRA, Pepy .... 510-356-4760.. 77 F
PREACHER, Stephen ...... 864-644-5486 412 D
spreacher@swu.edu
PREAS, Ethan, D .... 903-468-8781 447 B
ethan.preas@tamuc.edu
PREAST, Lori .... 252-493-7700 336 H
lpreast@email.pittcc.edu
PREASTLY, Jacqueline ... 225-771-6276 191 A
jacqueline_preastly@subr.edu
PREASTLY,
Jacqueline, G .... 225-771-5808 191 B
jacqueline_preastly@subr.edu
PREBENDA, Aaron .... 410-334-2993 205 D
aprebenda@worwic.edu
PREBLE, Mark .... 508-910-6402 212 A
mpreble@umassd.edu
PRECHT, Erica .... 337-521-6985 188 I
erica.precht@solacc.edu
PRECHTER, Patricia ...... 504-398-2213 192 A
pprechter@uhcno.edu
PRECISE, Leigh .... 740-362-3121 355 H
lprecise@mtso.edu
PRECISE, Natalie .... 417-873-7874 252 G
nprecise@drury.edu
PREDMORE, Andrew ..... 812-855-2818 156 G
sapredmo@indiana.edu
PREDOEHL, Dan .... 949-582-4313.. 65 D
dpredoehl@saddleback.edu
PREECE, Barbara .... 410-617-6811 201 D
bpreece@ndm.edu
PREGEANT, Gene, E ...... 985-549-5888 193 A
gpregeant@selu.edu
PREGLIASCO, Collin ...... 916-691-7367.. 50 H
preglic@crc.losrios.edu
PREHN, James .... 312-915-6400 143 C
jprehn@luc.edu
PREIMESBERGER, Paul . 218-855-8163 237 G
paul.preimesberger@clcmn.edu
PREISIG, Florian .... 509-359-2521 479 G
fpreisig@ewu.edu
PREISMEYER, Kim .... 601-709-0966 245 B
kpreismeyer@belhaven.edu
PRELOCK, Patricia, A .... 802-656-1417 463 A
patricia.prelock@med.uvm.edu
PREMO, Jason .... 989-686-9584 223 J
jasonpremo@delta.edu
PRENDERGAST,
Jason-Anthony, K .... 305-626-3138 100 D
jason.prendergast@fmuniv.edu
PRENDERGAST,
Thomas .... 419-755-4712 357 B
tprendergast@ncstatecollege.edu
PRENEVOST, Jason .... 253-460-4462 484 E
jprenevost@tacomacc.edu
PRENKERT, Robby .... 574-807-7143 154 B
robby.prenkert@bethleuniversity.edu
PRENTICE, Dean .... 918-495-6143 368 F
dprentice@oru.edu
PRENTICE, Deborah ...... 609-258-3026 280 D
predebb@princeton.edu
PRENTICE, Marilyn .... 847-214-7992 137 F
mprentice@elgin.edu
PREOCANIN, Shelley ..... 812-866-7056 155 G
preocanins@hanover.edu
PRERO, Chana .... 305-944-0035 104 I
PRESCOTT, Angel .... 270-707-3801 182 B
angel.prescott@kctcs.edu
PRESCOTT, Barbara ...... 318-357-6171 192 G
prescottb@nsula.edu
PRESCOTT, Charles ...... 865-938-8186 419 B
charles.prescott@thecrowncollege.edu
PRESCOTT, Jay, B .... 515-263-2890 166 F
jprescott@grandview.edu
PRESCOTT, Loren, D ..... 570-408-4000 403 A
loren.prescott@wilkes.edu
PRESCOTT, Patricia, M .. 516-671-0439 324 G
pprescot@webb.edu
PRESCOTT, Romeyn ...... 518-736-3622 300 D
rprescott@fmcc.edu
PRESENT, Melissa .... 212-678-8820 303 D
mepresent@jtsa.edu
PRESENT, Wendy .... 928-776-2132.. 16 J
wendy.present@yc.edu
PRESLEY, Brian .... 276-244-1267 464 E
bpresley@asl.edu
PRESLEY, Chynna, M .... 260-359-4233 156 C
cpresley@huntington.edu
PRESLEY, David .... 205-726-4494.... 6 E
dapresle@samford.edu
PRESLEY, Evelyn, E .... 904-269-7086 101 I
PRESNELL, Deena .... 509-313-6803 480 F
presnell@gonzaga.edu
PRESNELL, Mark .... 847-491-3707 146 E
mark.presnell@northwestern.edu
PRESS, Daniel .... 408-554-4455.. 63 E
dpress@scu.edu
PRESSER, Art .... 865-524-8079 420 E
arthur.presser@huhs.edu
PRESSER, Matthew .... 914-888-5364 306 C
mpresser@mercy.edu
PRESSEY, Natalie .... 212-229-5660 308 A
presseyn@newschool.edu
PRESSIMONE,
J. Michael .... 216-373-5238 357 F
jmpressimone@ndc.edu
PRESSLEY, Diana .... 409-772-8205 456 E
dipressl@utmb.edu
PRESSLEY, Leslie .... 704-922-6366 334 G
pressley.leslie@gaston.edu
PRESSLEY, Pamela .... 510-231-5000.. 46 J
pamela.c.pressley@kp.org
PRESSLEY, Robert .... 205-391-3968.... 3 E
rpressley@sheltonstate.edu
PRESSMAN, Avrohom .... 570-346-1747 403 E
PRESSON, Dewayne ...... 314-838-8858 261 F
ithelpdesk@ugst.edu
PRESSON, Kim .... 256-782-8142.... 6 A
kpresson@jsu.edu
PRESTAGE, Fheryl, J ..... 713-718-8708 437 C
fheryl.prestage@hccs.edu
PRESTAMO, Anne .... 305-348-5726 110 A
anne.prestamo@fiu.edu
PRESTON, Alison, T ...... 512-475-7255 455 A
apreston@utexas.edu
PRESTON, April .... 615-366-4404 423 H
april.preston@tbr.edu
PRESTON, David .... 918-335-6265 368 E
dpreston@okwu.edu
PRESTON, Deborah .... 908-526-1200 281 A
deborah.preston@raritanval.edu
PRESTON, Diane .... 314-434-4044 252 C
diane.preston@covenantseminary.edu
PRESTON, Don .... 479-248-7236.. 19 B
dpreston@ecollege.edu
PRESTON, Elaine, C ...... 405-466-3202 366 C
elaine.preston@langston.edu
PRESTON, James .... 312-329-4140 144 I
james.preston@moody.edu
PRESTON, James .... 559-925-3146.. 75 B
jamespreston@whccd.edu
PRESTON, Jennifer .... 270-831-9804 182 A
jennifer.preston@kctcs.edu
PRESTON, Jon .... 678-839-6445 127 C
jpreston@westga.edu
PRESTON, Jon .... 470-578-5572 121 M
jonpreston@kennesaw.edu
PRESTON, Joseph .... 901-321-3509 418 G
jpreston@cbu.edu
PRESTON, Lisa .... 212-229-5667 308 A
lisa.preston@newschool.edu
PRESTON, Mindy .... 903-823-3198 446 A
mindy.preston@texarkanacollege.edu
PRESTON, Patrick .... 508-362-2131 214 D
ppreston@capecod.edu
PRESTON, Travis .... 661-255-1050.. 28 G
tpreston@calarts.edu
PRESTON-NELSON,
Amanda .... 209-954-5022.. 61 G
amanda.preston-nelson@deltacollege.edu
PRETE, Leanne .... 910-962-7774 343 C
pretel@uncw.edu
PRETLOW, Lester .... 706-721-2621 116 A
lpretlow@augusta.edu
PRETORIUS, Joseph, A . 260-359-4134 156 C
jpretorius@huntington.edu
PRETTI, Janet .... 208-732-6327 131 D
jpretti@csi.edu
PRETTOL, Ken .... 972-708-7340 435 E
financial-aid@diu.edu
PRETZAT, Julie .... 315-312-2285 318 D
julie.pretzat@oswego.edu
PREUSCH, Dana .... 816-268-5400 257 C
dpreusch@nts.edu
PREUSS, Timothy .... 402-643-7364 266 G
timothy.preuss@cune.edu
PREVANT, Robert .... 203-392-5350.. 86 A
prezantr1@southenct.edu
PREVATTE, Tenette .... 910-678-8346 334 E
prevattt@faytechcc.edu
PREVAUX, Steven, D .... 813-974-7777 111 C
prevaux@usf.edu
PREVITE, Pete .... 904-825-4681.. 99 E
pprevite@flagler.edu
PREVO, Jerry .... 434-582-2950 468 E
president@liberty.edu
PREVOST, Emily .... 254-295-4023 453 D
eprevost@umhb.edu
PREVOST, Suzanne, S ... 205-348-1040.... 7 G
sprevost@ua.edu
PREVOST-SHULTZ,
Justin .... 773-244-6263 145 G
jprevost@northpark.edu
PREWITT, Anthony .... 731-881-7755 427 D
aprewitt@utm.edu
PREWITT, Michael .... 304-696-3765 489 M
prewitta@marshall.edu
PREWITT, Paul .... 903-510-3273 452 A
paul.prewitt@tjc.edu
PREWITT, Steve .... 615-966-5804 421 B
steve.prewitt@lipscomb.edu
PREZIOSI, Kristine .... 928-350-2306.. 15 L
kpreziosi@prescott.edu
PRIAL, Anne .... 845-341-4286 310 G
anne.prial@sunyorange.edu
PRIBBENOW, Brad .... 218-739-3375 236 H
bpribbenow@lbs.edu
PRIBBENOW, Dean .... 630-617-3063 137 G
dpribbenow@elmhurst.edu
PRIBBENOW, Paul, C ... 612-330-1212 234 A
president@augsburg.edu
PRIBULSKY,
Christopher .... 814-262-3824 393 A
cpribulsky@pennhighlands.edu
PRIBYL, Becky .... 605-626-2640 416 G
becky.pribyl@northern.edu
PRIBYL, Kim .... 319-399-8686 164 F
kpribyl@coe.edu
PRICCI, Erica .... 570-955-1461 387 B
priccie@lackawanna.edu
PRICE, Adrienne .... 909-274-5417.. 52 J
aprice@mtsac.edu
PRICE, Alan .... 805-965-0581.. 63 A
aprice3@sbcc.edu
PRICE, Amanda .... 636-949-4477 254 H
aprice@lindenwood.edu
PRICE, Ambrose .... 512-505-6477 438 A
aprice@htu.edu
PRICE, Amy .... 920-832-7164 493 B
amy.price@lawrence.edu
PRICE, Amy, S .... 812-468-2000 162 C
asprice@usi.edu
PRICE, Angie, C .... 423-775-7269 418 D
aprice6832@bryan.edu
PRICE, Barrington .... 708-524-5930 137 C
bprice@dom.edu
PRICE, Berkeley .... 310-660-3715.. 41 E
bprice@elcamino.edu
PRICE, Bill .... 540-231-4025 466 K
bprice@vcom.vt.edu

PRICE, Bryan .... 540-458-8316 477 D
bprice@wlu.edu
PRICE, Cecil, D .... 336-758-5218 344 C
price@wfu.edu
PRICE, Cynthia, J .... 206-281-2179 483 G
cprice@spu.edu
PRICE, Danny .... 706-368-5644 116 B
dprice@berry.edu
PRICE, Dave .... 541-994-4166 374 F
dave.price@oregoncoast.edu
PRICE, David .... 214-777-6433 441 G
PRICE, Dawne .... 402-494-2311 268 A
dprice@thenicc.edu
PRICE, Deidre .... 850-729-6448 104 M
priced@nwfsc.edu
PRICE, Derrick .... 304-327-4191 489 I
dprice@bluefieldstate.edu
PRICE, Donna .... 276-739-2412 475 F
dprice@vhcc.edu
PRICE, Donna .... 276-964-7287 475 C
donna.price@sw.edu
PRICE, Donna .... 931-221-7907 417 H
priced@apsu.edu
PRICE, Douglas .... 918-595-7853 370 C
douglas.price@tulsac.edu
PRICE, Gary .... 386-481-2906.. 96 D
priceg@cookman.edu
PRICE, Greg .... 334-670-3507.... 7 C
wgprice@troy.edu
PRICE, James, B .... 610-436-3063 395 D
jprice@wcupa.edu
PRICE, Jason .... 806-457-4200 436 C
jprice@fpctx.edu
PRICE, Jeff .... 937-512-2861 360 G
jeff.price@sinclair.edu
PRICE, Jennifer .... 904-470-8844.. 98 L
j.price@ewc.edu
PRICE, Jennifer .... 518-262-5679 289 L
pricej@amc.edu
PRICE, Jerrod .... 216-791-5000 350 I
jerrod.price@cim.edu
PRICE, Jerry .... 714-997-6721.. 36 B
jprice@chapman.edu
PRICE, JoEllen .... 713-718-8891 437 C
joellen.price@hccs.edu
PRICE, Karen .... 704-461-6859 326 L
karenprice@bac.edu
PRICE, Keiko .... 404-727-2912 118 E
keiko.price@emory.edu
PRICE, Kevin, L .... 208-496-1705 130 I
priceke@byui.edu
PRICE, Leigh .... 912-478-5211 120 C
llprice@georgiasouthern.edu
PRICE, Linda, L .... 812-877-8165 160 F
price@rose-hulman.edu
PRICE, Lisa .... 618-634-3200 149 G
PRICE, JR., Major .... 419-755-9009 357 B
mprice@ncstatecollege.edu
PRICE, Marianne .... 267-341-3204 385 J
mprice@holyfamily.edu
PRICE, Maribeth, H .... 605-394-1763 416 H
maribeth.price@sdsmt.edu
PRICE, Megan .... 864-388-8019 410 A
mprice@lander.edu
PRICE, Mercedes .... 703-993-5160 467 E
mprice21@gmu.edu
PRICE, Michael .... 952-446-4161 235 J
pricem@crown.edu
PRICE, Natasha .... 229-430-0656 114 I
nprice@albanytech.edu
PRICE, Nicole .... 617-989-4590 219 F
pricen1@wit.edu
PRICE, Pam .... 609-586-4800 278 F
pricep@mccc.edu
PRICE, Park .... 208-524-3000 131 B
trustee.price@cei.edu
PRICE, Paula .... 336-334-7500 341 D
PRICE, Peggy .... 601-366-8880 249 G
pprice@wbs.edu
PRICE, Philip .... 919-718-7214 333 C
pprice@cccc.edu
PRICE, Ron .... 770-528-3988 117 B
ron.price@chattahoocheetech.edu
PRICE, Ronald, N .... 708-216-9949 143 C
rprice@luc.edu
PRICE, Rosetta .... 301-860-3829 204 A
rprice@bowiestate.edu
PRICE, Sarah .... 270-686-4501 182 F
sarah.price@kctcs.edu
PRICE, Shannon .... 408-741-2074.. 75 E
shannon.price@westvalley.edu
PRICE, Stephanie, T ...... 843-792-5733 410 C
pricstep@musc.edu
PRICE, Susan, Y .... 334-293-4551.... 1 C
susan.price@accs.edu
PRICE, Susanna .... 410-532-5318 201 D
sprice@ndm.edu
PRICE, Suzanne .... 541-684-7206 371 I
sprice@bushnell.edu
PRICE, Vincent .... 919-684-2424 328 F
president@duke.edu
PRICE, Wendy .... 410-225-4229 200 D
wprice@mica.edu
PRICE II, Rick, S .... 714-745-8577.. 51 B
PRICE-PERRY,
Cassandra, F .... 901-334-5821 421 E
cfpperry@memphisseminary.edu
PRICE PITTMAN, Audra 877-722-3285 124 I
apittman@scad.edu
PRICKEN, Stephanie ..... 215-951-1702 387 A
pricken@lasalle.edu
PRIDA, Jonas .... 412-392-4773 396 G
jprida@pointpark.edu
PRIDDY, Lynn .... 909-667-4411.. 37 G
PRIDE, Bryce .... 941-752-5000 109 G
PRIDE, Rosalind .... 573-329-5160 254 G
prider@lincolnu.edu
PRIDEAUX, Jason .... 405-974-2753 370 I
jprideaux@uco.edu
PRIDEAUX, Leslie, J ..... 319-273-2355 164 A
leslie.prideaux@uni.edu
PRIDGEN, Rachel .... 336-517-2200 327 A
rpridgen@bennett.edu
PRIEST, Barry .... 910-879-5579 332 D
bpriest@bladencc.edu
PRIEST, Jennifer .... 859-233-8239 185 C
financialaid@transy.edu
PRIEST, Terrie, H .... 910-788-6271 338 A
terrie.priest@sccnc.edu
PRIETO, Diana .... 970-491-5836.. 79 N
diana.prieto@colostate.edu
PRIETO, Eduardo .... 662-915-7211 249 D
PRIETO, Jeffrey, M .... 213-891-2188.. 48 I
prietojm@laccd.edu
PRIETO-TSEREGOUNIS,
Emily .... 530-752-0946.. 69 B
eprieto@ucdavis.edu
PRIETO-TSEREGOUNIS,
Emily .... 510-879-3346.. 60 C
epreito@samuelmerritt.edu
PRIGERSON, Gregg .... 941-359-7526 106 J
gprigers@ringling.edu
PRIGG, Benson .... 256-726-7603.... 6 C
bprigg@oakwood.edu
PRIGGE, Amy, M .... 419-772-3961 358 C
a-prigge@onu.edu
PRIHODA, Belinda .... 903-510-3318 452 A
belinda.prihoda@tjc.edu
PRIMACK, Brian, T .... 479-575-3208.. 21 F
bprimack@uark.edu
PRIMAK, David .... 718-518-4300 294 B
PRIMAS, JR., Arthur ..... 719-333-3070 503 D
arthur.primas@usafa.edu
PRIMAS, JR.,
Arthur, W .... 719-333-3070 503 D
arthur.primas@usafa.edu
PRIMAS, LaMario .... 404-225-4714 115 H
lprimas@atlantatech.edu
PRIMAVERA, Louis, H .. 631-665-1600 322 F
louis.primavera@touro.edu
PRIMAVERA, Louis, H .. 631-665-1600 322 G
louis.primavera@touro.edu
PRIME, Glenda .... 443-885-1908 201 A
glenda.prime@morgan.edu
PRIMM, Jenelle .... 501-370-5310.. 20 F
jprimm@philander.edu
PRIMO, John .... 405-733-7356 369 E
jprimo@rose.edu
PRIMOFF, Mark .... 845-758-7412 290 I
primoff@bard.edu
PRIMOZICH, Blayne, J .. 915-831-2857 436 A
bprimozi@epcc.edu
PRIMUS, Lester, S .... 410-651-6230 203 D
lsprimus@umes.edu
PRINCE, Charles .... 352-854-2322.. 97 N
princech@cf.edu
PRINCE, Christine, B .... 215-885-2360 389 C
cprince@manor.edu
PRINCE, J. Dale .... 504-568-7698 189 H
jprin2@lsuhsc.edu
PRINCE, James .... 330-263-2581 351 A
jprince@wooster.edu
PRINCE, Judith .... 864-552-4243 414 A
jprince@uscupstate.edu
PRINCE, Ken .... 812-866-7051 155 G
princek@hanover.edu
PRINCE, Pamela .... 954-453-9228.. 34 H
PRINCE, Sarah .... 202-884-9000.. 94 A
PRINCE, Tiffany .... 541-506-6103 372 F
tprince@cgcc.edu
PRINCE, Travis .... 205-226-4994.... 4 F
twprince@bsc.edu
PRINCE-RICHARD,
Celia, P .... 340-692-4132 513 E
cprince@uvi.edu
PRINCE ROSS, Tracey ... 202-884-9126.. 94 A
princetr@trinitydc.edu
PRINCIPE, JR.,
Frank, J .... 301-985-7077 203 E
frank.principe@umuc.edu
PRINDLE, Brian .... 802-656-1435 463 A
brian.prindle@uvm.edu
PRINE, Jennifer, M .... 770-720-5620 124 G
jmp1@reinhardt.edu
PRINGLE, Eboni .... 330-672-8700 354 A
epringle@kent.edu
PRINGLE, Ernest .... 803-641-3345 413 B
ernestp@usca.edu
PRINGLE, Mark .... 614-236-6813 349 B
mpringle@capital.edu
PRINGLE, Nancy .... 607-274-3083 302 G
npringle@ithaca.edu
PRINIOTAKIS, Manolis . 301-243-2118 502 L
PRINS, Samantha .... 540-568-3508 468 C
prinssc@jmu.edu
PRINTY, Sandy .... 714-879-3901.. 45 G
sprinty@hiu.edu
PRIODE, Kimberly, S .... 828-898-8769 330 E
priodek@lmc.edu
PRIOLEAU, Florence ..... 202-806-2650.. 92 F
florence.prioleau@howard.edu
PRIOLO, Bob .... 561-868-3480 105 D
priolob@palmbeachstate.edu
PRISCO, Anne .... 267-341-3220 385 J
aprisco@holyfamily.edu
PRISELAC, Thomas .... 310-423-8294.. 35 G
PRISLIN, Radmila .... 619-594-5166.. 33 D
rprislin@sdsu.edu
PRITCHARD, Alice .... 860-723-0016.. 85 F
pritcharda@ct.edu
PRITCHARD, Brett .... 256-215-4254.... 1 G
bpritchard@cacc.edu
PRITCHARD, Catherine . 910-678-8209 334 E
pritchac@faytechcc.edu
PRITCHARD, Diane .... 541-318-3772 372 A
dpritchard2@cocc.edu
PRITCHARD, Gary .... 562-860-2451.. 35 H
gpritchard@cerritos.edu
PRITCHARD, Hillary, D . 336-633-0122 337 A
hdpritchard@randolph.edu
PRITCHARD, Kathren ..... 209-575-6901.. 76 J
pritchardk@yosemite.edu
PRITCHARD, Lamar .... 713-743-1253 452 D
flpritchard@uh.edu
PRITCHARD, Laurel .... 702-895-1506 271 D
laurel.pritchard@unlv.edu
PRITCHARD, Lisa .... 636-481-3160 254 C
lpritcha@jeffco.edu
PRITCHARD, Sarah, M .. 847-491-7640 146 E
spritchard@northwestern.edu
PRITCHERT, Marcia .... 701-845-7541 345 G
marcia.pitchert@vcsu.edu
PRITCHETT, Aaron .... 601-965-7078 245 B
apritchett@belhaven.edu
PRITCHETT, Alondrea, J 334-229-4737.... 4 A
apritchett@alasu.edu
PRITCHETT, Arielle .... 806-457-4200 436 C
aboone@fpctx.edu
PRITCHETT, Asija .... 301-548-5500.. 93 H
PRITCHETT, Forrest .... 973-275-2760 283 C
forrest.pritchett@shu.edu
PRITCHETT, James .... 970-491-6274.. 79 N
james.pritchett@colostate.edu
PRITCHETT, Marie .... 586-445-7315 227 B
pritchettm@macomb.edu
PRITCHETT, Megan .... 601-925-3210 247 C
mpritchett@mc.edu
PRITCHETT, Wendell, E . 215-898-7227 400 F
provost@upenn.edu
PRITZ, Stephen, J .... 352-392-1374 111 A
spritz@ufl.edu
PRITZKER, Barry .... 518-580-5654 315 F
bpritzke@skidmore.edu
PRIZZI, Charles, V .... 516-367-6890 296 C
PROANO, Jessica .... 973-761-9078 283 C
jessica.proano@shu.edu
PROBASCO, Deseree ..... 832-813-6514 439 C
deseree@lonestar.edu
PROBST, Julliana .... 334-514-5051.... 2 F
julliana.probst@istc.edu
PROBST, Laura, K .... 218-299-4642 235 H
lprobst@cord.edu
PROBSTFELD, Carol, F .. 941-752-5201 109 G
probstc@scf.edu
PROBUS, Larry .... 509-777-4304 486 C
lprobus@whitworth.edu
PROBUS, Michael, J ...... 972-721-5000 452 B
michaelp@udallas.edu
PROCARIO-FOLEY, Carl 914-633-2632 302 E
cprocariofoley@iona.edu
PROCHASKA, Dayna ...... 254-267-7090 441 K
dprochaska@rangercollege.edu
PROCHASKA, Melissa .... 772-462-7282 102 F
mprochas@irsc.edu
PROCHELLO, Marc .... 480-314-2102.. 15 P
PROCHNOW, Allen, J .... 262-243-5700 492 E
allen.prochnow@cuw.edu
PROCOPIO, Claire .... 985-549-2135 193 A
claire.procopio@selu.edu
PROCTOR, Avis .... 847-925-6390 138 G
aproctor@harpercollege.edu
PROCTOR, Cathy .... 732-247-5241 279 C
PROCTOR, Chris .... 903-586-2501 431 B
PROCTOR, Craig .... 801-587-2191 459 O
craig.proctor@hsc.utah.edu
PROCTOR, Cynthia .... 724-925-4003 402 F
proctorc@westmoreland.edu
PROCTOR, Estella .... 512-492-3077 430 A
esears@aoma.edu
PROCTOR, Jeremiah ...... 217-732-3168 142 G
jdproctor@lincolnchristian.edu
PROCTOR, Karen .... 931-598-1232 423 D
kmproctor@sewanee.edu
PROCTOR, Kelly .... 864-388-8398 410 A
kproctor@lander.edu
PROCTOR, Kristen .... 508-854-7552 215 F
kproctor@qcc.mass.edu
PROCTOR, Lee .... 910-898-9660 336 D
proctorr@montgomery.edu
PROCTOR, Matt .... 417-626-1234 257 F
pres@occ.edu
PROCTOR, Michele .... 724-830-4986 398 C
mproctor@setonhill.edu
PROCTOR, Ross .... 870-733-6875.. 17 F
prproctor@asumidsouth.edu
PROCTOR, Tina .... 252-638-7220 334 A
proctort@cravencc.edu
PRODOEHL, Allen .... 816-322-0110 251 B
security@calvary.edu
PRODROMOU, Sarah .... 904-819-6479.. 99 E
sprodromou@flagler.edu
PROEBER, Helen .... 608-757-7623 498 D
hproeber@blackhawk.edu
PROEHL, Erinn, M .... 815-928-5553 147 A
eproehl@olivet.edu
PROFETA, Glen .... 559-730-3843.. 39 B
glenp@cos.edu
PROFFITT, Beth .... 717-358-3871 383 I
beth.proffitt@fandm.edu
PROFFITT, Juanita .... 601-643-8383 245 F
juanita.proffitt@colin.edu
PROFFITT, Samantha .... 570-372-4753 398 F
proffitt@susqu.edu
PROFFITT, Travis .... 276-944-6670 466 L
tproffitt@ehc.edu
PROFITT, Aaron .... 513-721-7944 353 C
aprofitt@gbs.edu
PROHASKA, Ed .... 415-703-9588.. 28 B
eprohaska@cca.edu
PROHN, Deborah, W .... 716-888-2919 292 F
prohnd@canisius.edu
PROJANSKY, Sarah .... 801-587-9811 459 O
sarah.projansky@utah.edu
PROKOP, Paul .... 530-754-8568.. 69 B
pjprokop@ucdavis.edu
PROKOS, John .... 617-746-1990 210 H
john.prokos@hult.edu
PROKOVICH, Jeffrey, D 724-458-3846 384 G
jdprokovich@gcc.edu
PRONOVOST, Paul .... 603-641-7243 274 A
ppronovost@anselm.edu
PROPST, Jennifer .... 828-448-6051 339 A
jpropst@wpcc.edu
PROPST, William, S ...... 310-794-6027.. 69 E
wpropst@finance.ucla.edu
PROSCIA, Domenic .... 718-429-6600 324 D
domenic.proscia@vaughn.edu
PROSCIA, Julie .... 312-662-4304 132 G
jproscia@adler.edu
PROSPER, Yamilette ...... 787-891-0925 507 K
yprosper@aguadilla.inter.edu

PROSSER, Deborah .... 407-646-2676 106 L
dprosser@rollins.edu
PROSTANO, Laura .... 914-633-2203 302 E
lprostano@iona.edu
PROSTERMAN, Daniel ... 336-721-2617 340 A
daniel.prosterman@salem.edu
PROTHERO, Charles, L . 570-945-8015 386 F
charlie.prothero@keystone.edu
PROTHROW-STITH,
Deborah .... 323-563-6981.. 36 C
dprothrowstith@cdrewu.edu
PROTO, Matt .... 207-859-4000 194 D
PROUDFOOT,
Donald, W .... 903-510-2975 452 A
dpro@tjc.edu
PROUDFOOT, Tony .... 269-387-8412 233 B
tony.proudfoot@wmich.edu
PROULX, Dave .... 401-454-6474 405 B
dproulx@risd.edu
PROULX, David .... 401-454-6764 405 B
president@risd.edu
PROULX, Dennis .... 802-468-1249 463 E
dennis.proulx@castleton.edu
PROULX, Melissa, E ..... 315-267-2086 319 A
proulxme@potsdam.edu
PROULX, Susan .... 603-427-7600 272 J
PROUTY, John .... 970-542-3166.. 81 N
john.prouty@morgancc.edu
PROUTY, Steve .... 941-752-5205 109 G
proutys@scf.edu
PROVAN, Amy .... 410-532-5379 201 D
aprovan@ndm.edu
PROVENCE, Dana .... 719-587-7639.. 77 G
dprovence@adams.edu
PROVENCHER,
Catherine, A .... 603-862-0918 274 E
catherine.provencher@usnh.edu
PROVENCIO, Angela ..... 310-243-2008.. 30 E
aprovencio@csudh.edu
PROVENCIO-VASQUEZ,
Elias .... 303-556-2400.. 84 D
PROVENZANO, Joseph . 703-908-7686 468 H
joseph.provenzano@marymount.edu
PROVENZANO, JR.,
Peter .... 248-341-2115 229 C
pmproven@oaklandcc.edu
PROVEZIS, Staci, J ...... 217-333-1353 152 B
sprovez2@illinois.edu
PROVINE, Rick, E .... 765-658-4435 154 J
provine@depauw.edu
PROVINES, Jessica .... 316-978-3440 178 D
jessica.provines@wichita.edu
PROVOST, David, J .... 802-443-5699 462 E
dprovost@middlebury.edu
PROVOST, Laura .... 603-342-3020 273 C
lprovost@ccsnh.edu
PROVOST, Mark .... 715-833-6670 498 E
mprovost@cvtc.edu
PRUCHNICKI, Jennifer .. 580-581-2209 365 D
jpruchni@cameron.edu
PRUDE, Regina .... 615-687-6901 417 F
rprude@abcnash.edu
PRUDEN, Karen, H .... 757-823-8160 469 A
khpruden@nsu.edu
PRUDENTI, A. Gail .... 516-463-4068 301 G
gail.prudenti@hofstra.edu
PRUDHOMME,
Harvey, J .... 503-370-6576 377 F
hprudhom@willamette.edu
PRUD'HOMME, Sabrina 541-522-7672 376 B
PRUD'HOMME, Sabrina 541-552-6060 376 B
prudhomms@sou.edu
PRUETT, Karen .... 706-880-8977 122 A
kpruett@lagrange.edu
PRUETT, Robert, R .... 919-658-7760 340 G
rpruett@umo.edu
PRUETT, Teresa .... 276-964-7365 475 C
teresa.pruett@sw.edu
PRUETT, Terry .... 541-776-9942 375 B
terry.p@pacificbible.edu
PRUETT, Timothy .... 419-783-2317 351 K
tpruett@defiance.edu
PRUETT, Tyler .... 510-879-9232.. 60 C
tpruett@samuelmerritt.edu
PRUIS, Angela .... 817-722-1721 438 G
angela.pruis@tku.edu
PRUITT, Beverly .... 305-284-2842 113 C
b.pruitt@miami.edu
PRUITT, Dwain, C .... 864-597-4056 414 E
pruittdc@wofford.edu
PRUITT, Glenell .... 903-730-4890 438 D
gpruitt@jarvis.edu
PRUITT, Jason .... 470-239-3103 127 A
jason.pruitt@ung.edu

PRUITT, Jolene .... 626-316-5340.. 63 E
jpruitt@saybrook.edu
PRUITT, Judy .... 612-343-4491 242 M
japruitt@northcentral.edu
PRUITT, Karl .... 205-929-6348.... 2 H
kpruitt@lawsonstate.edu
PRUITT, Kylie .... 615-248-1253 426 D
kpruitt1@trevecca.edu
PRUITT, Leah, L .... 864-587-4225 412 F
pruittl@smcsc.edu
PRUITT, Nathan .... 518-783-2342 315 E
npruitt@siena.edu
PRUITT, Nathan, K .... 919-843-4080 342 C
nknuffman@unc.edu
PRUITT, Pamela .... 609-896-5000 281 B
ppruitt@rider.edu
PRUITT, Samory, T .... 205-348-8376.... 7 G
samory.pruitt@ua.edu
PRUITT, Steven .... 561-237-7834 103 W
spruitt@lynn.edu
PRUNCHUNAS, Edward . 310-423-8294.. 35 G
PRUNEDA, Eli .... 913-360-7500 171 J
epruneda@benedictine.edu
PRUNTY, Bonnie, S ...... 607-274-3141 302 G
bprunty@ithaca.edu
PRUS, Mark .... 607-753-2207 318 A
mark.prus@cortland.edu
PRUSAK, Christopher ... 585-245-5651 318 B
prusak@geneseo.edu
PRUSHAN, Mike .... 610-526-1861 385 D
mprushan@harcum.edu
PRUSKI, Thomas .... 202-706-6843.. 94 D
tpruski@wesleyseminary.edu
PRUSS, Julie, A .... 585-395-2361 317 E
jpruss@brockport.edu
PRUTSOS, Bryce .... 760-252-2411.. 26 G
bprutsos@barstow.edu
PRUZANSKY, Aron .... 732-363-7110 285 B
PRYBUTOK, Victor .... 940-565-3957 453 E
victor.prybutok@unt.edu
PRYJMAK, Myron .... 718-409-7306 320 G
mpryjmak@sunymaritime.edu
PRYLO, Caelynn .... 518-743-2329 320 A
pryloc@sunyacc.edu
PRYOR, Adam .... 785-227-3380 172 A
pryoraw@bethanylb.edu
PRYOR, Ann .... 843-953-2060 408 C
pryoral@cofc.edu
PRYOR, Carranza .... 318-675-5406 189 I
carranza.pryor@lsuhs.edu
PRYOR, Charles .... 646-313-8000 295 D
charles.pryor@guttman.cuny.edu
PRYOR, Joanna .... 316-942-4291 176 E
pryorj@newmanu.edu
PRYOR, Julie .... 256-686-5850.. 93 H
PRYOR, Julie .... 205-453-6300.. 93 H
PRYOR, Kim .... 336-342-4261 337 E
pryork@rockinghamcc.edu
PRYOR, Marcus .... 704-991-0278 338 C
mpryor7642@stanly.edu
PRYOR, Monique .... 718-489-5520 313 E
mpryor@sfc.edu
PRYOR, Raymond .... 570-208-5828 386 G
rgpryor@kings.edu
PRYOR, Tammy, L .... 828-694-1705 332 E
t_pryor@blueridge.edu
PRYOR, Walter .... 773-995-2462 134 K
wpryor@csu.edu
PRYOR-BENNETT, Julie . 203-837-8111.. 86 B
pryorbennettj@wcsu.edu
PRYOR HARRIS, Holli .. 312-567-3167 140 A
pryor@iit.edu
PRYSOCK, James .... 614-823-1312 359 H
jprysock@otterbein.edu
PRZEKOP, Lisa .... 805-893-3641.. 70 E
lisa.przekop@sa.ucsb.edu
PRZEKURAT, Paris .... 405-422-1442 369 A
przekuratp@redlandsscc.edu
PRZYBORSKI, Carol ...... 412-321-8383 379 F
office@bcs.edu
PRZYGODA, Melitha ..... 203-392-5405.. 86 A
przygodam1@southernct.edu
PRZYMUS, Beth .... 402-562-1284 266 A
bprzymus@cccneb.edu
PRZYMUSINSKI, Lori .... 248-232-4671 229 C
laprzymu@oaklandcc.edu
PRZYWARA, Ann Marie 518-580-5765 315 F
aprzywar@skidmore.edu
PSAILA, Marisa .... 585-475-4932 312 F
mxpdar@rit.edu
PSARRIS, Kleanthis .... 718-951-5966 293 C
kpsarris@brooklyn.cuny.edu

PSOTKA, Brenda .... 412-809-5307 396 E
psotka.brenda@ptcollege.edu
PUC, Gina .... 413-662-5201 213 C
g.puc@mcla.edu
PUCCIARELLI, Matthew . 718-990-7614 313 G
pucciarm@stjohns.edu
PUCCIO, Daniel, P .... 716-880-2351 305 G
daniel.p.puccio@medaille.edu
PUCCIO, Donna .... 563-876-3353 165 H
dpuccio@dwci.edu
PUCCIO O'BRIEN, Erica 617-879-7716 213 B
erica.puccio@massart.edu
PUCHTER, Carolee .... 262-646-6514 494 F
cpuchter@nashotah.edu
PUCKETT, Adam .... 503-554-2911 373 A
apuckett@georgefox.edu
PUCKETT, Andrea .... 618-393-2982 139 E
pucketta@iecc.edu
PUCKETT, Christopher .. 303-315-6619.. 84 D
chris.puckett@ucdenver.edu
PUCKETT, Clifton .... 678-872-8006 119 D
cpuckett@highlands.edu
PUCKETT, Ed .... 281-283-2983 452 E
puckett@uhcl.edu
PUCKETT, Holly .... 434-200-5302 465 D
holly.puckett@centracollege.edu
PUCKETT, Jeffrey .... 616-395-7413 225 D
puckett@hope.edu
PUCKETT, Joan .... 812-888-4480 162 F
jpuckett@vinu.edu
PUCKETT, Katherine ...... 601-857-3624 246 C
kbpuckett@hindscc.edu
PUDDESTER,
Frederick, W .... 413-597-4421 220 D
frederick.w.puddester@williams.edu
PUENTE, Rachel .... 312-329-4189 144 I
rachel.puente@moody.edu
PUENTES, Andrew .... 209-476-7840.. 67 E
apuentes@clcm.net
PUFF, Derek .... 716-286-8055 309 H
dpuff@niagara.edu
PUFFENBARGER, Jess .. 270-534-3504 183 B
jess.puffenbarger@kctcs.edu
PUFFER, Lois .... 606-487-3503 181 I
lois.puffer@kctcs.edu
PUFFETT, Anne .... 563-425-5229 170 H
puffetta@uiu.edu
PUGEL, Mary, E .... 336-758-3005 344 C
mpugel@wfu.edu
PUGH, Benjamin .... 225-771-5021 191 B
benjamin_pugh@subr.edu
PUGH, Coleen .... 316-978-3095 178 D
coleen.pugh@wichita.edu
PUGH, Henry .... 617-243-2221 211 B
hpugh@lasell.edu
PUGH, Holly .... 804-627-5300 464 K
holly_pugh@bshsi.org
PUGH, Jason .... 601-928-6234 247 E
jason.pugh@mgccc.edu
PUGH, Judy, M .... 857-701-1280 215 G
jpugh@rcc.mass.edu
PUGH, Sandi .... 559-297-4500.. 45 N
spugh@iot.edu
PUGH-BASSETT, Lovell . 856-227-7200 276 E
lpughbassett@camdencc.edu
PUGLIESE, Heidi .... 207-326-4311 196 A
PUGLIESE, Michael .... 405-609-6622 365 G
PUGLIESI, Karen .... 928-523-2230.. 14 H
karen.pugliesi@nau.edu
PUGLISI, Michael, J ..... 276-944-6662 466 L
mpuglisi@ehc.edu
PUHAK, Robert .... 973-353-3246 282 B
rpuhak@rutgers.edu
PUHALA, Kimberly .... 508-286-3621 220 B
puhala_kimberly@wheatoncollege.edu
PUJOL, Joe .... 573-651-2408 259 H
jpujol@semo.edu
PUJOLS, Yeurys .... 201-360-4628 278 C
ypujols@hccc.edu
PULAVARTI, Srinivas .... 404-727-6123 118 E
srinivas.pulavarti@emory.edu
PULCINI, Brad, T .... 740-368-3943 359 G
btpulcin@owu.edu
PULEIO, Samuel, T .... 814-393-2280 393 G
spuleio@clarion.edu
PULEO, David .... 662-915-7407 249 D
dpuleo@olemiss.edu
PULIAFICO, Venus .... 216-368-4530 349 D
venus.puliafico@case.edu
PULICE, Jon .... 814-732-1763 394 B
jpulice@edinboro.edu
PULIDO, Jairo .... 787-250-1912 508 D
jpulido@metro.inter.edu

PULIDO, Maria .... 509-453-0374 482 D
maria.pulido@perrytech.edu
PULIDO, Miguel .... 209-667-3509.. 33 B
mpulido5@csustan.edu
PULIDO LEON,
Jose, M .... 775-784-4936 271 E
jpulidoleon@unr.edu
PULINKALA, Ivan .... 470-578-6789 121 M
ipulinka@kennesaw.edu
PULLEN, Huston .... 904-620-2479 111 B
huston.pullen@unf.edu
PULLEN, Terri .... 513-862-7761 353 D
terri.pullen@email.gscollege.edu
PULLEY, Alyssa .... 660-562-1571 257 E
apulley@nwmissouri.edu
PULLEY, D. J .... 601-318-6048 249 H
djpulley@wmcarey.edu
PULLEY, Eric .... 618-985-3741 140 H
ericpulley@jalc.edu
PULLIAM, Camden .... 816-414-3700 256 C
cpulliam@mbts.edu
PULLIAM, Cheryl .... 704-355-5093 327 G
cheryl.pulliam@carolinascollege.edu
PULLIAM, Jeff .... 870-543-5950.. 21 B
jpulliam@seark.edu
PULLIAM, Joni, L .... 315-792-3344 324 B
jpulliam@utica.edu
PULLIAM, Shane .... 307-268-2633 500 U
shane.pulliam@caspercollege.edu
PULLIN, Daniel, W .... 817-257-7511 448 F
d.pullin@tcu.edu
PULLIS, Stephen .... 313-883-8768 230 C
pullis.stephen@shms.edu
PULLIZA, Carmen .... 787-743-7979 510 H
cpulliza@suagm.edu
PULLLIAM, Cathy .... 434-797-8538 473 G
cathy.pulliam@danville.edu
PULS, Darrell .... 509-420-4545 480 E
dean@gather4him.net
PULSIFER, Joy .... 231-591-2612 224 A
joypulsifer@ferris.edu
PULSIPHER, Scott, D .... 801-274-3280 461 E
spulsipher@wgu.edu
PULTZ, Stephen, F .... 619-260-4506.. 72 I
spultz@sandiego.edu
PUMA, Lynn, M .... 716-878-5509 317 F
pumalm@buffalostate.edu
PUMARIEGA, Madeline . 305-237-8888 104 E
PUMPHREY, Dennis ...... 970-351-2245.. 84 F
dennis.pumphrey@unco.edu
PUMPHREY, Paula .... 501-374-6305.. 20 G
paula.pumphrey@shortercollege.edu
PUMPHREY, Robert .... 212-563-6647 323 I
it@uts.edu
PUMROY, B.J .... 402-461-7331 267 C
bj.pumroy@hastings.edu
PUNCHELLO-COBOS,
Catharine .... 609-984-1180 284 C
registrar@tesu.edu
PUNIELLO, Jennifer ...... 508-678-2811 214 B
jennifer.puniello@bristolcc.edu
PUNT, David .... 303-963-3185.. 78 H
dpunt@ccu.edu
PUPILLO, Melinda .... 309-794-7478 133 C
melindapupillo@augustana.edu
PUPO, Joseph .... 215-646-7300 385 A
pupo.j@gmercyu.edu
PURCELL, Anthony, B ... 205-934-2297.... 8 A
bpurcell@uab.edu
PURCELL, Chris .... 412-365-1482 380 G
c.purcell@chatham.edu
PURCELL, Chris, A .... 405-325-4122 370 K
regentspurcell@ou.edu
PURCELL, Howard, B .... 617-587-5678 217 D
purcellh@neco.edu
PURCELL, Meredith .... 815-802-8512 141 D
mpurcell@kcc.edu
PURCELL, Satch .... 949-794-9090.. 66 D
spurcell@stanbridge.edu
PURCELL, Sebastian ...... 607-753-2192 318 A
sebastian.purcell@cortland.edu
PURCELL, Stacy, R .... 757-446-6002 466 D
purcellsr@evms.edu
PURDOM, Kirk .... 662-915-7375 249 D
kirk@olemiss.edu
PURDY, Elaine .... 225-490-1616 187 B
elaine.purdy@franu.edu
PURDY, Jill .... 308-865-8421 269 I
purdyj@unk.edu
PURDY, Kim .... 479-619-4399.. 20 C
kpurdy@nwacc.edu
PURDY, Lillian .... 318-487-7110 187 E
lillian.purdy@lacollege.edu

Q

QUINLAN, Jeremiah ...... 203-432-9321.. 90 C
jeremiah.quinlan@yale.edu
QUINLAN, Melissa .... 860-913-2034.. 88 A
mquinlan@goodwin.edu
QUINLAN, Sean .... 208-885-7885 132 F
quinlan@uidaho.edu
QUINLIN, Jesse .... 970-521-6611.. 82 C
jess.quinlin@njc.edu
QUINLIVAN, Gary .... 724-537-4597 397 I
gary.quinlivan@email.stvincent.edu
QUINLIVAN, Gary, M .... 724-537-4597 398 A
gq@stvincent.edu
QUINN, Amanda .... 815-280-2693 141 B
aquinn@jjc.edu
QUINN, Anthony .... 734-384-4279 228 C
aquinn@monroeccc.edu
QUINN, Arthur .... 561-732-4424 107 G
aquinn@svdp.edu
QUINN, Bonnie .... 478-471-5184 116 G
bquinn@centralgatech.edu
QUINN, Brian .... 517-355-1855 227 F
QUINN, Brian .... 215-951-1540 387 A
quinng@lasalle.edu
QUINN, Brian, T .... 517-884-9483 227 F
quinnbri@msu.edu
QUINN, Caitlin .... 415-439-2436.. 25 E
cquinn@act-sf.org
QUINN, Consuelo .... 706-821-8262 124 B
cquinn@paine.edu
QUINN, Donna, M .... 302-356-6819.. 91 E
donna.m.quinn@wilmu.edu
QUINN, Erin .... 802-443-5253 462 E
quinn@middlebury.edu
QUINN, Felicia, K .... 302-356-6889.. 91 E
felicia.k.quinn@wilmu.edu
QUINN, Frank .... 828-328-7235 330 F
frank.quinn@lr.edu
QUINN, Gianna .... 215-646-7300 385 A
quinn.g@gmercyu.edu
QUINN, Holli .... 484-809-7770.. 93 H
QUINN, Jacqueline .... 601-643-8364 245 F
jacqueline.quinn@colin.edu
QUINN, Joe .... 510-436-1601.. 45 E
quinn@hnu.edu
QUINN, Kevin, G .... 616-632-2880 221 E
kgq001@aquinas.edu
QUINN, Kristin .... 563-333-6428 169 G
quinnkristin@sau.edu
QUINN, Laura .... 662-329-7222 248 A
lsquinn@muw.edu
QUINN, Leslie .... 913-469-8500 174 I
lquinn2@jccc.edu
QUINN, Linda .... 402-941-6280 267 L
quinn@midlandu.edu
QUINN, Melanie .... 858-653-6740.. 46 H
QUINN, Michael .... 815-394-5003 148 D
mquinn@rockford.edu
QUINN, Michael .... 206-296-5500 484 A
quinnm@seattleu.edu
QUINN, Michael, G ...... 585-292-2151 307 B
mquinn@monroecc.edu
QUINN, Michelle .... 970-351-2773.. 84 F
michelle.quinn@unco.edu
QUINN, Molly .... 319-226-2001 163 C
molly.quinn@allencollege.edu
QUINN, Patrick, A .... 315-267-2484 319 A
quinnpa@potsdam.edu
QUINN, Sarah, F .... 610-660-1230 397 G
squinn@sju.edu
QUINN, Shaman .... 307-754-6232 501 H
shaman.quinn@nwc.edu
QUINN, Stephen .... 973-618-3320 276 D
squinn@caldwell.edu
QUINN, Susan .... 585-389-2501 307 F
squinn2@naz.edu
QUINN, Susan .... 707-524-1598.. 63 D
squinn@santarosa.edu
QUINN, Teresa .... 845-437-5370 324 C
tequinn@vassar.edu
QUINN, Thomas .... 989-275-5000 226 D
tom.quinn@kirtland.edu
QUINN, Wade .... 919-735-5151 338 H
dwquinn@waynecc.edu
QUINNAN, Timothy ...... 404-835-6132 423 B
tquinnan@richmont.edu
QUINNELL, Katherine .... 254-968-9937 446 D
quinnell@tarleton.edu
QUINONES, Carlos, A ... 787-710-8999 506 G
QUINONES, Ivelisse ...... 706-580-0168 115 B
ivelissequinones@andrewcollege.edu
QUINONES, Patricia ...... 909-274-4109.. 52 J
pquinones@mtsac.edu
QUINONES, Patricia ...... 310-287-4361.. 49 H
quinonp@wlac.edu
QUINONES, Roberto ..... 562-408-6969.. 24 E
rquinones@advancedcollege.edu
QUINONES, Vanya .... 212-346-1200 311 A
QUINONES, Weyna .... 787-815-0000 511 H
QUINONES, Yesenia ..... 787-844-8181 513 A
yesenia.quinones1@upr.edu
QUINONES, Yolanda ..... 787-758-2525 512 F
yolanda.quinones@upr.edu
QUINONEZ, Julie, R ..... 419-530-6213 363 B
julie.quinonez@utoledo.edu
QUINONEZ, Virginia ..... 312-329-6623.. 36 E
vquinonez@thechicagoschool.edu
QUINTAL, Rollande .... 508-849-3340 205 H
rquintal@annamaria.edu
QUINTANA, Anita .... 509-452-5100 482 B
aquintana@pnwu.edu
QUINTANA, Elena .... 312-662-4021 132 G
equintana@adler.edu
QUINTANA, Javier .... 787-279-1912 508 A
jquintana@bayamon.inter.edu
QUINTANA, Rebecca ...... 787-780-0070 505 F
rquintana@caribbean.edu
QUINTANA, Rosaura ..... 787-815-0000 511 H
rosaura.quintana@upr.edu
QUINTANA, Sara .... 802-865-5417 462 A
squintana@champlain.edu
QUINTANA HESS,
Jessica, A .... 570-321-4318 389 B
hess@lycoming.edu
QUINTANILLA, Hector ... 817-531-4405 451 C
hquintanilla@txwes.edu
QUINTENZ, Briana .... 217-424-3758 144 G
bquintenz@millikin.edu
QUINTERO, Amanda, M 805-437-3285.. 30 C
amanda.quintero@csuci.edu
QUINTERO, Sandra .... 657-278-5366.. 31 C
squintero@fullerton.edu
QUINTYNE, Renee .... 845-398-4207 314 G
rquintyn@stac.edu
QUIONEZ, Angelica ...... 415-422-6796.. 72 J
anquinonez@usfca.edu
QUIRE, Heather .... 413-662-5231 213 C
heather.quire@mcla.edu
QUIRION, Alison .... 562-977-6006.. 42 K
alison.quirion@fremont.edu
QUIRK, Walter .... 530-226-4503.. 64 E
rquirk@simpsonu.edu
QUIRK-BAILEY, Sheila .. 309-694-5550 139 B
sheila.quirk-bailey@icc.edu
QUIROLGICO, Ray .... 626-396-2325.. 26 B
ray.quirolgico@artcenter.edu
QUIROS, Ondrea, M ..... 915-831-6615 436 A
oquiros@epcc.edu
QUIROZ, Jaime .... 562-860-2451.. 35 H
jquiroz@cerritos.edu
QUIROZ, Sally .... 806-291-3702 457 I
sally.quiroz@wbu.edu
QUIS, Steve .... 619-388-7876.. 61 A
squis@sdccd.edu
QUISTORF, Mark, W ..... 414-410-4016 491 I
mwquistorf@stritch.edu
QUIÑONES, Mickey ...... 804-289-8550 472 C
mquinones@richmond.edu
QUIÑONES SANTIAGO,
Nelson .... 787-250-0000 511 F
nelson.qui±ones2@upr.edu
QUMSIEH, Miriam .... 281-283-3005 452 E
qumsieh@uhcl.edu
QUOCK, Dan .... 509-542-4803 479 A
dquock@columbiabasin.edu
QURESHI, Elena .... 734-432-5574 227 C
equreshi@madonna.edu
QURESHI, Omar .... 510-356-4760.. 77 F
QVARNSTROM, Jeanne . 432-837-8395 450 B
jqvarnstrom@sulross.edu

R

RAAB, Jennifer, J .... 212-772-4242 294 C
jennifer.raab@hunter.cuny.edu
RAAB, Keith .... 541-737-2241 375 A
financial.aid@oregonstate.edu
RAAB, Maryrose .... 315-792-7215 321 B
maryrose.raab@sunypoly.edu
RABAGO, Cristine .... 650-543-3782.. 51 G
crabago@menlo.edu
RABB, Sydni .... 254-442-5113 432 I
sydni.rabb@cisco.edu
RABBANY, Sina, Y .... 516-463-6672 301 G
sina.y.rabbany@hofstra.edu
RABBITT, Kara, M .... 973-720-2621 284 J
rabbittk@wpunj.edu
RABBITT, Rhonda .... 570-408-2016 403 A
rhonda.rabbitt@wilkes.edu
RABE, Josh .... 217-228-5432 147 F
rabejo@quincy.edu
RABELO, Marlyn .... 973-661-0600 277 E
mrabelo@eastwick.edu
RABENOLD, Scott, A ..... 512-471-4124 455 A
srabenold@utexas.edu
RABER, II, Donald, R ... 864-833-8233 411 D
draber@presby.edu
RABERN, Don .... 719-255-3543.. 84 C
drabern@uccs.edu
RABIDEAU, Shelly, S .... 317-940-8423 154 C
srabidea@butler.edu
RABINOVICH, Sheryl .... 213-624-1200.. 42 B
srabinovich@fidm.edu
RABINOWITZ, Celia, E .. 603-358-2736 274 H
celia.rabinowitz@keene.edu
RABINOWITZ, David, B 973-290-4084 282 I
drabinowitz@steu.edu
RABINOWITZ, Eli .... 718-377-0777 311 G
erabinowitz@myrcb.org
RABITOY, Eric .... 626-914-8788.. 36 J
erabitoy@citruscollege.edu
RABITOY, Linda .... 909-667-4433.. 37 G
lrabitoy@claremontlincoln.edu
RABLE, Michelle .... 419-372-8932 348 G
marable@bgsu.edu
RABY, Don Butch .... 601-403-1300 248 E
braby@prcc.edu
RABY, James .... 803-641-3569 413 B
jamesr@usca.edu
RABY, Melissa .... 209-588-5100.. 76 K
RABY, Sherry .... 252-249-1851 336 F
sraby@pamlicocc.edu
RABY, Susan .... 315-312-2260 318 D
susan.raby@oswego.edu
RABY, Tracy .... 256-331-5462.... 3 C
tracy@nwscc.edu
RACCANELLO, Paul .... 415-485-3223.. 41 C
paul.raccanello@dominican.edu
RACE, Debbie .... 828-262-2050 340 I
racedw@appstate.edu
RACE, Tammera .... 941-487-4405 110 D
trace@ncf.edu
RACER, Jennifer .... 866-776-0331.. 54 D
jracer@ncu.edu
RACER, Jennifer .... 419-755-4040 357 B
racer.5@osu.edu
RACHAL, Michael .... 504-865-2486 190 C
rachal@loyno.edu
RACHEL, Cherie .... 479-575-4808.. 21 F
clrachel@uark.edu
RACHEL, Steven .... 575-492-2116 289 F
srachel@usw.edu
RACHFORD, Jennifer ..... 909-607-2201.. 57 K
jennifer.rachford@pomona.edu
RACHITA, David, A .... 281-283-2568 452 E
rachita@uhcl.edu
RACHOUH, Susan .... 201-216-3518 283 D
susan.rachouh@stevens.edu
RACICOT, Philip .... 603-358-2811 274 H
philip.racicot@keene.edu
RACINE, Christa .... 973-408-3650 277 A
cracine@drew.edu
RACIOPPI, Gerald .... 732-255-0315 279 F
gracioppi@ocean.edu
RACKI, James .... 508-854-7496 215 F
jracki@qcc.mass.edu
RACKLEY, Jeanette .... 910-275-6111 335 E
jrackley@jamessprunt.edu
RACKLEY, Michael .... 954-545-4500 108 E
registrar@sfbc.edu
RACKLIFFE, Jerry, J ...... 404-413-3000 120 E
jracklif@gsu.edu
RACOK, Joanne .... 978-921-4242 217 B
joanne.racok@montserrat.edu
RACOVITA, Laura .... 423-236-2638 423 F
racovita@southern.edu
RADA, Gilda .... 602-212-0501.. 14 M
grada@brightoncollege.edu
RADAK, Lisa .... 808-734-9569 129 H
lradak@hawaii.edu
RADAKOVICH, Dan .... 864-656-1935 407 E
danrad1@clemson.edu
RADANDE, Katie, W ...... 610-758-4735 388 E
kaw8@lehigh.edu
RADCLIFFE, Shelby .... 503-370-6397 377 F
sradcliffe@willamette.edu
RADCLIFFE, Timothy ..... 740-392-6868 356 G
timothy.radcliffe@mvnu.edu
RADDA, Hank .... 602-639-7500.. 12 J
RADDEN, Michael .... 256-233-8146.... 4 C
michael.radden@athens.edu
RADEMACHER, Eric .... 513-556-3304 361 J
eric.rademacher@uc.edu
RADEMAKER, Scot .... 985-448-4325 192 F
scot.rademaker@nicholls.edu
RADEMAKER II, Jim ..... 616-331-6775 224 G
rademakj@gvsu.edu
RADER, Brian .... 503-399-8074 372 B
brian.rader@chemeketa.edu
RADER, Darian .... 336-506-4056 332 A
derader420@alamancecc.edu
RADER, Emily .... 716-614-5926 309 G
erader@niagaracc.suny.edu
RADER, Sherri .... 309-649-6255 150 G
sherri.rader@src.edu
RADFORD, Marilyn .... 270-384-8022 183 G
radfordm@lindsey.edu
RADFORD, Mitchell ...... 828-641-0095 327 B
radformr@brevard.edu
RADHAKRISHNAN,
Rashmi .... 215-572-2900 378 E
radhakrishnanr@arcadia.edu
RADICE, Brad .... 205-726-4373.... 6 E
bjradice@samford.edu
RADISH, Ross .... 215-596-8800 401 E
r.radish@usciences.edu
RADKE, Cheryl .... 623-245-4600.. 16 B
cradke@uticuti.edu
RADKE, Jordan .... 719-389-7270.. 78 I
jradke@coloradocollege.edu
RADKE, Kristina .... 510-659-6534.. 54 J
kradke@ohlone.edu
RADKE, Suzette .... 712-749-2044 164 C
radkes@bvu.edu
RADNEY, Ron .... 209-228-2257.. 70 A
rradney@ucmerced.edu
RADSON, Darrell .... 630-829-6018 133 E
dradson@ben.edu
RADT, Jennifer .... 513-732-5221 362 B
jennifer.radt@uc.edu
RADTKE, Elizabeth .... 651-523-2959 236 B
bradtke@hamline.edu
RADULESCU, Eugen ...... 713-348-6725 442 F
eugen@rice.edu
RADWAN, Ahmed, Y ..... 315-792-3853 324 B
aradwan@utica.edu
RADWANSKI, Steven, E 609-652-4915 283 E
steven.radwanski@stockton.edu
RADWINE, Sam .... 213-884-4133.. 24 A
RADZIESKI, Laurel .... 570-961-7810 387 B
radzieskil@lackawanna.edu
RADZYMINSKI, Sharon . 956-665-3495 455 D
sharon.radzyminski@utrgv.edu
RAE, Janelle .... 502-585-9911 184 H
jrae@spalding.edu
RAE, Jon .... 813-988-5131.. 99 R
raej@floridacollege.edu
RAE, Lisa .... 802-258-3149 462 H
lisa.rae@worldlearning.org
RAEBEL, Christopher .... 414-277-7302 494 D
RAEBER, Michael .... 706-542-0006 126 G
mraeber@uga.edu
RAEHLL, Meghan .... 614-947-6579 352 J
meghan.raehll@franklin.edu
RAEKER-REBEK, Mary ... 866-492-5336 244 F
mary.raeker-rebek@mail.waldenu.edu
RAEL, Abenicio .... 303-404-5000.. 81 A
abenicio.rael@frontrange.edu
RAEL, Rolando .... 505-454-2500 286 F
RAEL, Sylvia .... 970-248-1029.. 78 J
srael@coloradomesa.edu
RAETHER, Julie .... 402-354-7256 268 B
julianne.raether@methodistcollege.edu
RAFALSON, Lisa .... 716-829-8489 298 E
rafalson@dyc.edu
RAFANELLO, Allyson .... 319-273-7153 164 A
allyson.rafanello@uni.edu
RAFANELLO, Nicholas .. 319-273-2333 164 A
nicholas.rafanello@uni.edu
RAFELD, Jessica .... 920-403-3071 495 B
jessica.rafeld@snc.edu
RAFFAELLE, David .... 623-845-3676.. 13 C
david.raffaelle@gccaz.edu
RAFFAELLE, Ryne .... 585-475-2055 312 F
ryne.raffaelle@rit.edu
RAFFAELLI, Kellie .... 906-487-2920 228 A
kraffael@mtu.edu
RAFFELD, Beth .... 413-585-2020 218 H
braffeld@smith.edu
RAFFENSPERGER,
Thomas .... 413-572-5233 213 F
traffensperger@westfield.ma.edu

RAMIREZ, Aurelio .... 617-879-7847 213 B aramirez@massart.edu
RAMIREZ, Corina .... 432-837-8790 450 B cramirez@sulross.edu
RAMIREZ, David .... 610-328-8059 398 G dramire1@swarthmore.edu
RAMIREZ, Desiree .... 817-735-5131 454 B desiree.ramirez@unthsc.edu
RAMIREZ, Erika .... 626-968-1328.. 47 G
RAMIREZ, Fausto .... 718-960-8593 294 A fausto.ramirez@lehman.cuny.edu
RAMIREZ, Francine, M . 909-869-6992.. 30 A fmramirez@cpp.edu
RAMIREZ, Frank .... 559-791-2278.. 47 A frank.ramirez1@portervillecollege.edu
RAMIREZ, Freddy .... 760-757-2121.. 52 F framirez@miracosta.edu
RAMIREZ, Gabriel .... 915-747-8358 455 C gramirez2@utep.edu
RAMIREZ, Greg .... 818-702-1381.. 56 G greg.g.ramirez@pepperdine.edu
RAMIREZ, Irving .... 347-964-8600 291 J iramirez@boricuacollege.edu
RAMIREZ, Jason .... 801-581-7066 459 O jasonramirez@sa.utah.edu
RAMIREZ, Jessica .... 816-604-1411 255 C jessica.ramirez@mcckc.edu
RAMIREZ, Joann .... 916-691-7112.. 50 H ramirej2@crc.losrios.edu
RAMIREZ, JR., Joe, E ... 979-845-4728 446 F joe.ramirez@tamu.edu
RAMIREZ, Jose .... 787-620-2040 505 C jramirez@aupr.edu
RAMIREZ, Jose, L .... 915-831-2634 436 A jramir20@epcc.edu
RAMIREZ, Juan .... 909-469-5622.. 75 I jramirez@westernu.edu
RAMIREZ, Katherine ...... 406-447-4388 263 B kramirez@carroll.edu
RAMIREZ, Katie .... 210-999-8819 451 E kramirez@trinity.edu
RAMIREZ, Laura .... 626-585-7734.. 56 D lramirez120@pasadena.edu
RAMIREZ, Manuel .... 787-884-3838 505 D asisteco@atenascollege.edu
RAMIREZ, Marcela, V ... 210-458-6144 455 E marcela.ramirez@utsa.edu
RAMIREZ, Mayra, I .... 787-723-4481 506 A mayra.ramirez@ceaprc.edu
RAMIREZ, Melanie .... 940-898-3534 451 D mramirez50@twu.edu
RAMIREZ, Miguel .... 305-899-3647.. 96 A maramirez@barry.edu
RAMIREZ, Minita .... 956-326-2278 446 E minita@tamiu.edu
RAMIREZ, Orlando .... 765-658-4800 154 J
RAMIREZ, Raymond .... 559-442-8200.. 67 B raymond.ramirez@fresnocitycollege.edu
RAMIREZ, Rhonda .... 510-879-9217.. 60 C rramirez@samuelmerritt.edu
RAMIREZ, Rita .... 509-793-2031 478 B ritar@bigbend.edu
RAMIREZ, Robert .... 940-898-3142 451 D rramirez9@twu.edu
RAMIREZ, Robert .... 516-572-7781 307 E robert.ramirez@ncc.edu
RAMIREZ, Rodolfo .... 530-422-7923.. 74 G rramirez@weimar.edu
RAMIREZ, Rosemary ..... 520-494-5471.. 11 K rosemary.ramirez@centralaz.edu
RAMIREZ, Ruben .... 805-922-6966.. 24 I rubenc.ramirez@hancockcollege.edu
RAMIREZ, Sam .... 361-825-2765 447 C samuel.ramirez@tamucc.edu
RAMIREZ, Sandra .... 281-998-2648 442 K sandra.ramirez@sjcd.edu
RAMIREZ, Sara, S .... 240-895-5000 202 B ssramirez@smcm.edu
RAMIREZ, Steve, D .... 512-233-1464 442 I steveramirez@stedwards.edu
RAMIREZ, Sylvia .... 787-832-6000 507 D sramirez@icprjc.edu
RAMIREZ, Sylvia .... 608-243-4587 499 A sframirez@madisoncollege.edu
RAMIREZ, Wilmer .... 303-783-3137.. 80 I wilmer.ramirez@denverseminary.edu
RAMIREZ-CARLO, III, Bolivar .... 787-620-2040 505 C bramirez@aupr.edu
RAMIREZ-FIGUEROA, Jose .... 787-620-2040 505 C jramirez@aupr.edu
RAMIREZ-GELPI, Sofia .. 805-922-6966.. 24 I sgelpi@hancockcollege.edu
RAMIREZ-PEREZ, Felicia .... 602-285-7422.. 13 F felicia.a.ramirez-perez@phoenixcollege.edu
RAMIREZ-PEREZ, Felicia .... 480-732-7093.. 12 O felicia.ramirez-perez@cgc.edu
RAMIREZ-RIVERA, Rafael .... 787-878-5475 507 L rramirez@arecibo.inter.edu
RAMKARAN, Arshaw ..... 212-650-5824 293 D aramkaran@ccny.cuny.edu
RAMKUMAR, S. Manian .... 585-475-5955 312 F smrmet@rit.edu
RAMLER, Tom .... 903-434-8175 440 G tramler@ntcc.edu
RAMM, Jennifer .... 254-295-5527 453 D jennifer.ramm@umhb.edu
RAMMING, Ronald, S ... 918-463-2931 365 J rronald@connorsstate.edu
RAMON, Deanna Rene .. 580-349-1556 367 F rene.ramon@opsu.edu
RAMON, Ralph .... 325-574-7625 458 D rramon@wtc.edu
RAMONES, Eric .... 408-741-2060.. 75 D eric.ramones@wvm.edu
RAMONES, Eric .... 408-741-2060.. 75 E eric.ramones@wvm.edu
RAMONT, John .... 760-776-7452.. 38 E jramont@collegeofthedesert.edu
RAMOS, Alan .... 865-539-7025 425 B arramos@pstcc.edu
RAMOS, Andrea .... 213-738-5574.. 66 B aramos@swlaw.edu
RAMOS, Anthony .... 847-214-7257 137 F aramos@elgin.edu
RAMOS, Antonio .... 787-284-1912 508 E aramos@ponce.inter.edu
RAMOS, Cerese .... 386-506-3240.. 98 D cerese.ramos@daytonastate.edu
RAMOS, Charlene .... 248-204-2330 227 A cramos@ltu.edu
RAMOS, Chelsea .... 718-289-5153 293 B chelsea.ayala@bcc.cuny.edu
RAMOS, Cynthia .... 602-285-7404.. 13 F cynthia.ramos@phoenixcollege.edu
RAMOS, Daisy .... 787-738-2161 512 C daisy.ramos@upr.edu
RAMOS, David, L .... 787-834-9595 510 D dramos@uaa.edu
RAMOS, Derek .... 620-276-9559 174 B derek.ramos@gcccks.edu
RAMOS, Edith .... 787-878-6000 507 D eramos@icprjc.edu
RAMOS, Efrain .... 787-891-0925 507 K eramos@aguadilla.inter.edu
RAMOS, Ernesto, V .... 787-751-0160 506 F eramos@cmpr.pr.gov
RAMOS, Freddy .... 787-764-0000 513 B freddy.ramos1@upr.edu
RAMOS, Gladys .... 787-738-2161 512 C gladys.ramos@upr.edu
RAMOS, Idalmy .... 787-264-1912 508 F iramos@intersg.edu
RAMOS, Irma .... 714-808-4810.. 54 A iramos@nocccd.edu
RAMOS, Ismael .... 787-738-2161 512 C ismael.ramos1@upr.edu
RAMOS, Jennifer .... 954-262-2134 105 A jennifer.ramos@nova.edu
RAMOS, Jennifer .... 212-228-1888 312 B
RAMOS, Joahana .... 787-844-8181 513 A joahana.ramos@upr.edu
RAMOS, John .... 406-656-9950 265 I jramos@yellowstonechristian.edu
RAMOS, Joseph .... 619-388-6411.. 60 H jramos@sdccd.edu
RAMOS, Kenneth, S ...... 713-677-7440 446 F kramos@tamu.edu
RAMOS, Mandy .... 863-638-7129 114 A mandy.ramos@warner.edu
RAMOS, Miguel .... 713-718-7444 437 C miguel.ramos@hccs.edu
RAMOS, Nancy, L .... 401-254-3455 405 C nramos@rwu.edu
RAMOS, Patricia .... 310-434-3311.. 63 C ramos_patricia@smc.edu
RAMOS, Patricia .... 718-631-6262 295 C
RAMOS, Patricia, A .... 718-289-5896 293 B patricia.ramos@bcc.cuny.edu
RAMOS, Reynaldo .... 978-542-7321 213 E reynaldo.ramos@salemstate.edu
RAMOS, Richard, O ...... 515-961-1536 170 B rich.ramos@simpson.edu
RAMOS, Rocio, M .... 323-259-2558.. 54 I ramosr@oxy.edu
RAMOS, Vanessa .... 787-725-6500 505 G varamos@albizu.edu
RAMOS, Victor .... 717-871-7500 395 A victor.ramos@millersville.edu
RAMOS, Yazmin .... 787-786-3030 511 A yramos@ucb.edu.pr
RAMOS, Yolanda .... 432-685-4733 440 B yramos@midland.edu
RAMOS-DIAZ, Mirna ...... 509-452-5100 482 B mramosdiaz@pnwu.edu
RAMPAUL, Andre .... 212-757-1190 290 D arampaul@aami.edu
RAMPERSAD, Dave .... 334-386-7100.... 5 C drampersad@faulkner.edu
RAMPP, Carrie .... 717-358-4161 383 I carrie.rampp@fandm.edu
RAMS, Richard .... 714-484-7355.. 54 B rrams@cypresscollege.edu
RAMS, Richard .... 626-914-8534.. 36 J rrams@citruscollege.edu
RAMSAMMY, Jillian .... 352-854-2322.. 97 N jillian.ramsammy@cf.edu
RAMSAMMY, Roger, A .. 518-629-4530 302 C r.ramsammy@hvcc.edu
RAMSARAN, Dave .... 570-372-4127 398 F ramsaran@susqu.edu
RAMSAY, Carl .... 870-574-4546.. 21 D cramsay@sautech.edu
RAMSAY, Darlene .... 573-341-4584 261 D ramsayd@mst.edu
RAMSAY, Kerr, C .... 336-841-9148 329 F kramsay@highpoint.edu
RAMSAY, Kimberly .... 310-377-5501.. 51 C kramsay@marymountcalifornia.edu
RAMSAY, Lara .... 509-777-4347 486 C lramsay@whitworth.edu
RAMSAY, Tim .... 616-632-2076 221 E ramsatim@aquinas.edu
RAMSBURG, David .... 304-357-4766 487 J davidramsburg@ucwv.edu
RAMSDELL, Keith .... 419-289-5397 347 J kramsdel@ashland.edu
RAMSDELL, Kerry .... 978-232-2225 209 E kramsdel@endicott.edu
RAMSDELL, Nancy, M .. 508-929-8605 213 G nramsdell@worcester.edu
RAMSDELL, Twyla .... 651-213-4180 236 C tramsdell@hazeldenbettyford.edu
RAMSDEN-MEIER, Joanna .... 319-226-2004 163 C joanna.ramsden-meier@allencollege.edu
RAMSEL, Janelle .... 303-964-5387.. 83 E jramsel@regis.edu
RAMSEY, III, James ..... 919-488-8500 330 G
RAMSEY, Jason, M .... 814-332-2761 378 A jramsey@allegheny.edu
RAMSEY, Kathy .... 785-462-3984 173 B
RAMSEY, Kimberly .... 310-377-5501.. 51 C kramsey@marymountcalifornia.edu
RAMSEY, Kyle, H .... 630-515-7352 144 F kramse@midwestern.edu
RAMSEY, Mae .... 540-362-6519 467 H mramsey@hollins.edu
RAMSEY, Marty .... 828-227-7335 343 E mramsey@wcu.edu
RAMSEY, Matthew .... 913-360-7387 171 J mramsey@benedictine.edu
RAMSEY, Nancy, A .... 865-694-6526 425 B naramsey@pstcc.edu
RAMSEY, Nate .... 773-947-6309 143 H nramsey@mccormick.edu
RAMSEY, Patricia .... 718-270-5000 294 G 6thpresident@mec.cuny.edu
RAMSEY, Paul, G .... 206-543-7718 485 A pramsey@uw.edu
RAMSEY, Rachel .... 518-337-4318 296 G ramseyr@strose.edu
RAMSEY, Richard .... 207-454-1067 195 I rramsey@wccc.me.edu
RAMSEY, Ruth .... 415-257-1393.. 41 C ruth.ramsey@dominican.edu
RAMSEY, Vickie .... 530-251-8852.. 47 F vramsey@lassencollege.edu
RAMSEY-FRANCO, Adrian, C .... 252-618-6517 334 D ramseya@edgecombe.edu
RAMSEY-HAMACHER, Paige .... 352-588-8489 107 D paige.ramsey.hamacher@saintleo.edu
RAMSEYER, Rob .... 316-295-5433 174 A rob_ramseyer@friends.edu
RAMSTAD, Erik .... 218-299-4923 235 H eramstad@cord.edu
RAMZAH, Hassan .... 402-472-4467 269 J hassan.ramzah@unl.edu
RAMÍREZ FERNÁNDEZ, Mercedes .... 585-275-6530 323M mercedes.ramirezfernandez@rochester.edu
RANABARGAR, Kerry .... 620-432-0301 176 D kranabargar@neosho.edu
RANALLI, Carlee, K ...... 240-500-2228 199 C ckranalli@hagerstowncc.edu
RANALLO-HIGGINS, Frederick .... 215-884-8942 403 D fred.ranallo.higgins@woninstitute.edu
RANCATI, Chrisanne ..... 704-637-4322 327 I crancati20@catawba.edu
RANCK, Lorrie .... 408-855-5182.. 75 D lorrie.ranck@missioncollege.edu
RAND, Jonathan .... 617-879-7263 213 B jrand@massart.edu
RAND, Patricia .... 813-253-7995 102 B prand@hccfl.edu
RAND, Paul, M .... 773-702-0689 151 E prand@uchicago.edu
RAND, Trish .... 970-339-6649.. 77 H patricia.rand@aims.edu
RANDALL, Anne .... 508-421-3804 208 C anrandall@clarku.edu
RANDALL, Brandy .... 248-370-3169 229 I brandall@oakland.edu
RANDALL, Briana .... 206-685-4139 485 A brianakr@uw.edu
RANDALL, Caroline .... 505-984-6976 288 C caroline.randall@sjc.edu
RANDALL, David .... 617-253-4052 216 B
RANDALL, John .... 949-214-3358.. 39 K john.randall@cui.edu
RANDALL, Kelli, V .... 704-216-6195 330 H krandall@livingstone.edu
RANDALL, Kim .... 617-353-9286 207 E krandall@bu.edu
RANDALL, Meridith .... 714-892-7711.. 38 A
RANDALL, Mike .... 618-468-3130 142 E mrandall@lc.edu
RANDALL, Monte .... 918-549-2806 365 H mrandall@cmn.edu
RANDALL, Nancy .... 704-233-8065 344 F nrandall@wingate.edu
RANDALL, Regina .... 614-287-5343 351 C rrandal2@cscc.edu
RANDALL, Robin .... 413-538-2023 217 C rrandall@mtholyoke.edu
RANDALL, Stacey .... 630-466-7900 152 K srandall@waubonsee.edu
RANDALL, Taylor, R ...... 801-581-3074 459 O taylor.randall@eccles.utah.edu
RANDALL, Wesley .... 940-565-2628 453 E wesley.randall@unt.edu
RANDALL-LEE, Valerie, J .... 410-677-0022 204 D vjrandall-lee@salisbury.edu
RANDAZZA, Paula .... 603-897-8303 273 I prandazza@rivier.edu
RANDAZZA, Scott .... 404-471-6000 114 G
RANDAZZO, Jennifer ..... 563-884-5141 169 F jennifer.randazzo@palmer.edu
RANDAZZO, Maria .... 315-445-4195 303 I randazmc@lemoyne.edu
RANDERS, Mary .... 503-370-6928 377 F mranders@willamette.edu
RANDHAWA, Sabah .... 360-650-3480 485 I president@wwu.edu
RANDICK, Nicole .... 612-861-7554 233 H nicole.randick@alfredadler.edu
RANDLE, Jonathan .... 601-925-3849 247 C randle@mc.edu
RANDLES, Christopher, M .... 217-351-2513 147 C crandles@parkland.edu
RANDLES, Jill, A .... 559-323-2100.. 61 F jrandles@sjcl.edu
RANDO, Robert, A .... 937-775-3409 364 E robert.rando@wright.edu
RANDOLPH, Adrian .... 847-491-3276 146 E weinberg-dean@northwestern.edu
RANDOLPH, Amber .... 973-353-5541 282 B amber.randolph@rutgers.edu

RAY, JR., Charles, A .... 504-816-8010 190 F
cray@nobts.edu
RAY, Christopher, T ...... 940-898-2852 451 D
chrisray@twu.edu
RAY, Courtney .... 770-533-7017 122 B
cray@laniertech.edu
RAY, Darby, K .... 207-786-8241 194 A
dray3@bates.edu
RAY, Dian .... 580-774-3271 370 A
dian.ray@swosu.edu
RAY, Don .... 870-768-3117.. 17 B
dray@smail.anc.edu
RAY, Emily .... 270-824-8581 182 D
emily.ray@kctcs.edu
RAY, Gary, T .... 512-245-1977 450 C
gtr21@txstate.edu
RAY, Glen .... 940-898-3505 451 D
payments@twu.edu
RAY, Jacquelyn .... 509-527-4294 485 B
jacquelyn.ray@wwcc.edu
RAY, James, U .... 803-323-2305 414 D
rayj@winthrop.edu
RAY, Jeffrey .... 828-227-2159 343 E
jeffray@wcu.edu
RAY, Jennifer .... 405-425-5150 367 C
jennifer.ray@oc.edu
RAY, Jess .... 309-438-8586 140 D
jdray@ilstu.edu
RAY, Joshua .... 801-618-0438 458 G
jray@ameritech.edu
RAY, Judy, K .... 336-841-9201 329 F
jray@highpoint.edu
RAY, Karen .... 256-551-5227.... 2 E
karen.ray@drakestate.edu
RAY, Kathlin, D .... 775-784-6500 271 E
kray@unr.edu
RAY, Ken .... 813-253-7054 102 B
kray6@hccfl.edu
RAY, Leigh, A .... 931-372-3320 426 B
lray@tntech.edu
RAY, Mandy .... 978-542-7253 213 E
mandy.ray@salemstate.edu
RAY, Marty .... 617-627-3300 219 C
marty.ray@tufts.edu
RAY, Nancy .... 704-334-6882 328 B
nray@charlottechristian.edu
RAY, Natalie .... 251-578-1313.... 3 D
nray@rstc.edu
RAY, Nicholas, T .... 812-941-2411 157 F
nicray@ius.edu
RAY, Nick .... 219-980-7202 157 C
nicray@iu.edu
RAY, Nick .... 317-274-0015 157 B
nicray@iu.edu
RAY, Nick .... 574-520-4463 157 E
nicray@iu.edu
RAY, Pamela .... 850-644-8643 110 C
pray2@fsu.edu
RAY, Phillip .... 979-458-6421 446 B
pray@tamus.edu
RAY, Ryan .... 828-766-1273 336 A
rray@mayland.edu
RAY, Sandy .... 850-484-1213 105 H
scesaretti@pensacolastate.edu
RAY, Shanna .... 615-966-5833 421 B
shanna.ray@lipscomb.edu
RAY, JR., Stephen, G ... 773-896-2400 134 L
RAY, Tracey .... 610-436-1104 395 D
tray2@wcupa.edu
RAY, Vivyen .... 973-328-5037 276 J
vray@ccm.edu
RAYBACK, Carolyn .... 503-517-1813 377 E
crayback@westernseminary.edu
RAYBUCK, Diane .... 814-732-2761 394 B
draybuck@edinboro.edu
RAYBURN, Candace ...... 817-554-5950 439 H
crayburn@messengercollege.edu
RAYBURN, Jill .... 864-977-7000 410 I
RAYBURN, T. Monroe .. 202-319-5765.. 92 A
rayburn@cua.edu
RAYFIELD, Stuart .... 404-962-3040 127 D
stuart.rayfield@usg.edu
RAYMER, John .... 617-405-5987 218 C
jraymer@quincycollege.edu
RAYMOND, Annette ...... 973-748-9000 276 A
annette_raymond@bloomfield.edu
RAYMOND, Bruce .... 719-549-2108.. 80 B
bruce.raymond@csupueblo.edu
RAYMOND, SR.,
John, R .... 414-955-8225 493 F
jraymond@mcw.edu
RAYMOND, Lisa .... 508-289-3557 220 E
lraymond@whoi.edu
RAYMOND, Sarah .... 406-496-4384 265 A
sraymond@mtech.edu
RAYMOND, Thomas, J . 504-864-7490 190 C
traymond@loyno.edu
RAYMOND, Tiffany .... 315-364-3352 324 I
traymond@wells.edu
RAYMOND, Wendy, E ... 610-896-1021 385 I
president@haverford.edu
RAYMUNDO, Laurie ...... 671-735-2184 504 F
lraymundo@triton.uog.edu
RAYNER, Jill .... 706-864-1688 127 A
jill.rayner@ung.edu
RAYNOR, Jamie .... 828-227-3052 343 E
jtraynor@wcu.edu
RAYNOR, Samantha ...... 336-256-0190 343 A
slraynor@uncg.edu
RAYNOR, Timonthy .... 203-576-4168.. 89 C
traynor@bridgeport.edu
RAYNOR, Vanessa .... 919-719-2284 340 B
vraynor@shawu.edu
RAYO, Agustín .... 617-253-2559 216 B
RAYOME, Megan .... 406-756-3822 263 E
RAZA, Ahsan .... 212-870-1228 309 E
araza@nyts.edu
RAZA, Syed .... 256-761-6200.... 7 B
sqraza@talladega.edu
RAZAFIMANJATO, Laza . 501-370-5252.. 20 F
rlaza@philander.edu
RAZI, Nahid .... 619-644-7799.. 44 E
nahid.razi@gcccd.edu
RAZZA, Paul .... 336-770-3264 343 D
razzap@uncsa.edu
RAZZAGHI, Farzaneh .... 828-227-7485 343 E
frazzaghi@email.wcu.edu
RAZZI, A. Wade .... 843-577-5245 406 E
REA, Allyson .... 434-961-5223 474 I
area@pvcc.edu
REABACK, Roslyn .... 203-932-7263.. 89 H
rreaback@newhaven.edu
REABOLD, Beth .... 480-818-0388 468 G
bsreabold@marybaldwin.edu
READ, Caitlyn .... 540-568-5152 468 C
readcl@jmu.edu
READ, Carole .... 757-789-1733 473 H
cread@es.vccs.edu
READ, Lori .... 402-643-7451 266 G
lori.read@cune.edu
READ, Melissa .... 508-541-1654 209 A
mread@dean.edu
READ, Russel .... 336-734-7651 334 F
rread@forsythtech.edu
READ, William .... 781-891-2525 206 G
wread@bentley.edu
READER, Aaron .... 206-878-3710 481 B
areader@highline.edu
READNOUR, Warren ..... 501-450-5007.. 23 H
wreadnour@uca.edu
REAGAN, Emily .... 512-471-4945 455 A
emily.reagan@utexas.edu
REAGAN, Jackie .... 580-774-3166 370 A
jackie.reagan@swosu.edu
REAGAN, Katherine, M . 423-869-6389 421 A
katherine.reagan@lmunet.edu
REAGAN, Krystal .... 618-985-2828 140 H
krystalreagan@jalc.edu
REAGAN, Melinda .... 972-279-6511 429 F
mreagan@amberton.edu
REAGEN, Nate .... 515-271-2949 165 J
nate.reagen@drake.edu
REAGIN, Cam .... 803-641-3399 413 B
camr@usca.edu
REAGINS-LILLY, Soncia 512-471-1133 455 A
vpsa@austin.utexas.edu
REAGLE, Mike .... 270-745-2037 186 C
mike.reagle@wku.edu
REAL, Yannick .... 562-860-2451.. 35 H
yreal@cerritos.edu
REAL BIRD, Sunny Day 406-657-2144 264 D
sunnyday.realbird@msubillings.edu
REALISTA, Katy .... 714-484-7142.. 54 B
krealista@cypresscollege.edu
REAM, Debbie .... 213-477-2505.. 52 I
dream@msmu.edu
REAMER, Amy .... 910-962-4075 343 C
reamera@uncw.edu
REAMER, OFM, Mark .... 518-783-2938 315 E
mreamer@siena.edu
REAMS, Amelia .... 229-219-3198 127 E
alharmon@valdosta.edu
REAMS, Angie .... 319-335-1162 163 H
angela-reams@uiowa.edu
REAMS, John, D .... 706-233-7203 125 C
jreams@shorter.edu
REAMS, Thomas .... 801-689-2160 459 I
treams@nightingale.edu
REAMY, Brian .... 301-295-1080 503 C
brian.reamy@usuhs.edu
REAMY, Sara .... 503-554-2118 373 A
sreamy@georgefox.edu
REARDON, Amy .... 310-544-6484.. 60 B
amy.reardon@usw.salvationarmy.org
REARDON, Cheryl .... 319-335-0056 163 H
cheryl-reardon@uiowa.edu
REARDON, Diana .... 803-774-3354 406 I
reardondl@cctech.edu
REARDON, Emily .... 508-213-2275 217 H
emily.reardon@nichols.edu
REARDON, Greg .... 951-343-4245.. 27 G
greardon@calbaptist.edu
REARDON, Mary .... 512-381-7253 430 G
mreardon@escoffier.edu
REARDON, Penny, E ..... 540-828-5395 464 L
preardon@bridgewater.edu
REARDON, Richard .... 802-468-1234 463 E
richard.reardon@castleton.edu
REARDON, Tim .... 401-739-5000 404 E
treardon@neit.edu
REARDON HENRY,
Melissa .... 973-720-2242 284 J
reardonhenrym@wpunj.edu
REASE MILES, LT .... 650-543-3735.. 51 G
latonya.reasemiles@menlo.edu
REASH, Brenda .... 252-222-6262 333 A
reashb@carteret.edu
REASONER, Carroll .... 319-335-2841 163 H
carroll-reasoner@uiowa.edu
REAUME, Vicki .... 734-487-2410 223 K
vreaume@emich.edu
REAVES, Ken .... 678-872-8511 119 D
kreaves@highlands.edu
REAVES, Nicole .... 919-532-5705 338 G
nreaves1@waketech.edu
REBEIN, Robert .... 317-274-8448 157 D
rrebein@iupui.edu
REBER, Christopher, M 201-360-4003 278 C
creber@hccc.edu
REBIK, Clint .... 707-826-6205.. 33 C
clint@humboldt.edu
REBMAN, Johanna .... 815-836-5050 142 F
jrebman@lewisu.edu
REBOLI, Annette .... 856-361-2800 281 F
reboli@rowan.edu
REBURN, Tom .... 218-477-2549 239 E
tom.reburn@mnstate.edu
RECA, Michael, F .... 609-896-5080 281 B
reca@rider.edu
RECALDE, Tina .... 619-388-2789.. 60 J
trecalde@sdccd.edu
RECCHIA, Karen .... 318-678-6000 187 H
krecchia@bpcc.edu
RECHTSCHAFFEN,
Joyce, A .... 202-220-1364 280 D
jrechtsc@princeton.edu
RECINOS, Alba .... 714-808-4796.. 54 A
arecinos@nocccd.edu
RECINOS, Diane .... 973-278-5400 275 I
dr@berkeleycollege.edu
RECINOS, Diane .... 973-278-5400 291 E
dr@berkeleycollege.edu
RECKER, Amy .... 531-622-2743 267 G
arecker@mccneb.edu
RECKER, Mary, A .... 937-229-4354 362 C
mpoirier1@udayton.edu
RECORD, Kim .... 336-944-6206 343 A
ksrecord@uncg.edu
RECORDS, Stefany .... 713-221-8636 453 A
recordss@uhd.edu
RECTOR, David .... 660-785-7607 260 F
daverec@truman.edu
RECTOR, David .... 425-739-8287 481 C
david.rector@lwtech.edu
RECTOR, Eric .... 540-365-4427 467 B
erector@ferrum.edu
RECTOR, Lallene, J .... 847-866-3901 138 D
ljr@garrett.edu
RECTOR, Ray .... 509-359-6612 479 G
rrector@ewu.edu
RECTOR, Rob .... 417-447-4852 257 G
rectorr@otc.edu
RECZEK, Lauren .... 716-827-2487 323 G
reczekl@trocaire.edu
RECZNIK, Joel, S .... 740-284-5236 352 I
jrecznik@franciscan.edu
REDD, Annie .... 804-524-5070 476 D
aredd@vsu.edu
REDD, Hugh .... 540-261-8400 471 B
hugh.redd@svu.edu
REDD, Leslie .... 904-256-7882 102 H
lredd@ju.edu
REDD, Randy .... 901-751-8453 421 G
rredd@mabts.edu
REDD, Rea .... 724-852-3254 402 C
rredd@waynesburg.edu
REDD, Scott .... 703-996-4054 248 F
sredd@rts.edu
REDD, Tina .... 928-634-6513.. 16 J
tina.redd@yc.edu
REDDAY, Darlene .... 605-698-3966 416 B
dredday@swcollege.edu
REDDER, Vince .... 605-995-2631 415 A
vince.redder@dwu.edu
REDDERSON, Jeff, P ..... 864-294-3262 409 H
jeff.redderson@furman.edu
REDDI, Lakshmi .... 575-646-2914 287 C
lnr@nmsu.edu
REDDICK, Chenita, R .... 410-651-8045 203 D
crreddick@umes.edu
REDDICK, Don .... 815-939-5111 147 A
dreddick@olivet.edu
REDDICK, Rinardo .... 914-606-6313 325 A
rinardo.reddick@sunywcc.edu
REDDING, Gregory .... 765-361-6310 163 B
reddingg@wabash.edu
REDDING, Victor .... 775-784-4031 271 E
vredding@unr.edu
REDDING LAPUZ,
Danni .... 650-738-4321.. 62 L
reddinglapuzd@smccd.edu
REDDINGER, Amy .... 906-217-4068 222 A
amy.reddinger@baycollege.edu
REDDINGTON, Cynthia . 757-240-2229 470 D
cynthia.reddington@rivhs.com
REDDIX, Rhoda .... 225-214-6966 187 B
rhoda.reddix@franu.edu
REDDY, Howard, J .... 850-474-3306 111 F
hreddy@uwf.edu
REDDY, Indra, K .... 979-458-7200 446 F
ireddy@tamu.edu
REDDY, Kirti .... 510-723-6641.. 35 J
kreddy@chabotcollege.edu
REDDY, Michael .... 415-476-5757.. 70 D
michael.reddy@ucsf.edu
REDDY, Narem .... 678-466-4100 117 D
naremreddy@clayton.edu
REDDY, Robert .... 617-373-3190 217 I
REDDY, Venkat .... 719-255-3436.. 84 C
chancellor@uccs.edu
REDEKER, Maureen .... 435-586-7700 460 A
maureenredeker@suu.edu
REDEKOP, Steven .... 559-453-3451.. 43 A
steven.redekop@fresno.edu
REDFEARN,
Christopher .... 701-252-3467 347 B
chris.redfearn@uj.edu
REDFERN, Amber .... 239-489-9039 101 A
aredfern@fsw.edu
REDFERN, Paul .... 315-229-5845 314 D
predfern@stlawu.edu
REDIGER, Leah .... 402-826-8118 267 A
leah.rediger@doane.edu
REDING, Jody .... 806-720-7154 439 D
jody.reding@lcu.edu
REDING, Roger .... 806-894-9611 443 G
rreding@southplainscollege.edu
REDINGER, Matthew ..... 406-791-5302 265 H
matthew.redinger@uprovidence.edu
REDINGTON, Joseph .... 570-674-6756 390 B
jredington@misericordia.edu
REDINGTON, Lyn .... 208-282-2315 131 G
redilyn@isu.edu
REDLER, Susan .... 212-431-2121 309 A
susan.redler@nyls.edu
REDLINGER,
Lawrence, J .... 972-883-6188 455 B
redling@utdallas.edu
REDMAN, Cynthia .... 773-256-3000 144 B
credman@meadville.edu
REDMAN, Donald, L ..... 717-338-3036 400 D
dredman@uls.edu
REDMAN, Jay .... 248-204-2317 227 A
jredman@ltu.edu
REDMAN, Laurel .... 480-517-8000.. 13 G
laurel.redman@riosalado.edu
REDMOND, Angie .... 641-844-5712 167 G
angie.redmond@iavalley.edu
REDMOND, James .... 805-267-1690.. 47 H
REDMOND, Jeff .... 805-267-1690.. 47 H
jeff.redmond@lauruscollege.edu
REDMOND, Kathleen .... 708-524-6818 137 C
kredmond@dom.edu

REDMOND, Michael, J . 303-458-4995.. 83 E
mredmond@regis.edu
REDMOND, Rodney .... 301-934-2251 198 G
ryredmond@csmd.edu
REDMOND, Skip .... 901-726-1977 428 D
sredmond@mooretech.edu
REDMOND, Tim .... 805-267-1690.. 47 H
timothy.redmond@lauruscollege.edu
REDMOND, Xavier .... 662-254-3478 248 B
xavier.redmond@mvsu.edu
REDONDO, Diego .... 212-237-8521 294 D
dredondo@jjay.cuny.edu
REDONNETT, Rosa .... 207-621-3419 196 F
rosar@maine.edu
REDWINE, Marian .... 405-491-6324 369 H
redwine@snu.edu
REDWINE, Mike .... 405-491-6638 369 H
mredwine@snu.edu
REECE, Amani .... 718-270-6050 294 G
areece@mec.cuny.edu
REECE, Anton .... 270-534-3082 183 B
anton.reece@kctcs.edu
REECE, Bryan .... 925-229-6820.. 40 A
breece@4cd.edu
REECE, E. Albert .... 410-706-7410 203 A
deanmed@som.umaryland.edu
REECE, James .... 610-372-1722 378 G
james.reece@berks.edu
REECE, Jeana .... 801-689-2160 459 I
jreece@nightingale.edu
REECE, Jeremy .... 870-733-6786.. 17 F
jreece@asumidsouth.edu
REECE, Jonathan .... 704-687-5703 342 D
jonathan.reece@uncc.edu
REECE, Lenora .... 214-860-2015 434 I
lenora.reece@dcccd.edu
REECE, Marc .... 678-916-2600 115 I
mreece@johnmarshall.edu
REECE, M'Shelle .... 562-938-4122.. 48 F
mreece@lbcc.edu
REECE, Ronda .... 405-945-8631 368 C
ronda.reece@okstate.edu
REECE, Scott .... 301-624-2824 198 I
sreece@frederick.edu
REECE, Sheila .... 903-785-7661 441 D
sreece@parisjc.edu
REECK, Joanne .... 612-330-1111 234 A
reeck@augsburg.edu
REED, Aaron .... 801-302-2800 459 H
aaron.reed@neumont.edu
REED, Ann, M .... 304-462-6123 489 L
ann.reed@glenville.edu
REED, Annie, G .... 818-947-2320.. 49 G
reedag@lavc.edu
REED, Arlene .... 626-585-7614.. 56 D
areed9@pasadena.edu
REED, Barrett .... 870-584-1462.. 22 F
reedb@cccua.edu
REED, Beverly .... 301-546-0494 201 E
reedbs@pgcc.edu
REED, Brady .... 530-257-6181.. 47 F
breed@lassencollege.edu
REED, Casey .... 918-631-2510 371 C
casey-reed@utulsa.edu
REED, Chad .... 540-831-5411 469 D
creed4@radford.edu
REED, Charlene, K .... 330-672-2585 354 A
creed2@kent.edu
REED, Christine .... 805-922-6966.. 24 I
creed@hancockcollege.edu
REED, Chuck .... 620-252-7125 173 A
reed.chuck@coffeyville.edu
REED, Colin .... 508-289-3855 220 E
creed@whoi.edu
REED, Corey .... 817-257-5218 448 F
corey.reed@tcu.edu
REED, Cristina .... 810-762-9584 226 B
creed@kettering.edu
REED, Crystal .... 256-331-5291.... 3 C
cingle@nwscc.edu
REED, Cynthia .... 225-771-2552 191 E
creed@sulc.edu
REED, Cynthia .... 470-578-6117 121 M
creed63@kennesaw.edu
REED, Dallas .... 973-278-5400 291 E
dfr@berkeleycollege.edu
REED, Dallas, F .... 973-278-5400 275 I
dfr@berkeleycollege.edu
REED, Dan .... 530-898-6451.. 30 D
dmreed@csuchico.edu
REED, Daniel, A .... 801-585-3366 459 O
dan.reed@utah.edu
REED, David .... 650-306-3470.. 62 J
reedd@smccd.edu
REED, David, D .... 906-487-3043 228 A
ddreed@mtu.edu
REED, Dee .... 812-535-5212 160 H
dreed@smwc.edu
REED, Diane .... 757-594-7202 465 M
dreed@cnu.edu
REED, Donald, R .... 936-261-3311 446 C
REED, Donna .... 812-941-2430 157 F
donnreed@iu.edu
REED, Donna .... 415-452-5455.. 36 K
dreed@ccsf.edu
REED, Doug .... 870-245-5167.. 20 D
reedd@obu.edu
REED, Doug .... 405-744-4244 367 G
doug.reed@okstate.edu
REED, Elaine .... 323-343-5392.. 31 E
bkscalstla@bncollege.com
REED, Elizabeth .... 215-884-8942 403 D
elizabeth.reed@woninstitute.edu
REED, Francesca .... 610-558-5615 391 A
reedf@neumann.edu
REED, George .... 719-255-4047.. 84 C
george.reed@uccs.edu
REED, Guy, L .... 602-827-2066.. 16 D
guyreed@arizona.edu
REED, Helen .... 970-351-2601.. 84 F
helen.reed@unco.edu
REED, Jeff .... 515-292-9694 163 D
jeff.reed@antiochschool.edu
REED, Jeff .... 859-985-3000 179 I
REED, Jennifer .... 740-264-5591 352 B
jreed@egcc.edu
REED, Jennifer, G .... 801-581-4033 459 O
jennifer.reed@utah.edu
REED, Jodi .... 619-660-4400.. 44 D
jodi.reed@gcccd.edu
REED, Joe .... 859-257-9734 185 F
jreed3@uky.edu
REED, Josie .... 617-585-1100 217 E
REED, Kendrick .... 864-587-4006 412 F
reedk@smcsc.edu
REED, Kesha, T .... 919-530-6976 341 E
kesha.reed@nccu.edu
REED, Kevin .... 541-346-3082 376 H
ksreed@uoregon.edu
REED, Kim .... 208-562-3114 131 E
kimreed@cwi.edu
REED, Kimberly .... 530-661-5727.. 77 D
kreed@yccd.edu
REED, Kimberly .... 530-741-6727.. 77 C
kreed@yccd.edu
REED, LaTonya .... 870-574-4504.. 21 D
lreed@sautech.edu
REED, Latoya .... 601-979-0889 246 F
latoya.t.reed@jsums.edu
REED, LaVonda .... 315-443-5525 321 G
lareed@law.syr.edu
REED, Lisa .... 770-426-2611 122 C
lisa.reed@life.edu
REED, Lori .... 507-457-5005 241 F
lreed@winona.edu
REED, Lyndsey .... 510-649-8285.. 55 G
lreed@psr.edu
REED, Mark, C .... 610-660-1200 397 G
president@sju.edu
REED, Mark, F .... 610-861-1360 390 F
reedm@moravian.edu
REED, Mark, H .... 603-646-9400 273 D
mark.h.reed@dartmouth.edu
REED, Martin .... 209-228-2977.. 70 A
mreed9@ucmerced.edu
REED, Maryanne .... 304-293-5701 490 E
provost@mail.wvu.edu
REED, Matthew .... 732-224-2265 276 B
REED, Meredith .... 504-398-2236 192 A
mreed@uhcno.edu
REED, Michael .... 504-282-4455 190 F
mreed@nobts.edu
REED, Michael, E .... 207-725-3356 194 C
mreed@bowdoin.edu
REED, Michael, J .... 570-326-3761 392 W
mjr18@pct.edu
REED, Nancy .... 901-572-2662 418 A
nancy.reed@baptistu.edu
REED, Pamela .... 806-874-3571 432 J
pamela.reed@clarendoncollege.edu
REED, Phil .... 269-749-7142 229 J
preed@olivetcollege.edu
REED, Quiana .... 864-592-4122 412 E
reedq@sccsc.edu
REED, Rahim .... 530-752-2071.. 69 B
rreed@ucdavis.edu
REED, Randle .... 302-622-8000.. 90 D
rreed@dcad.edu
REED, Randy .... 972-273-3301 435 B
randyreed@dcccd.edu
REED, Robert .... 443-334-2240 202 E
rreed1951@stevenson.edu
REED, Rod .... 765-677-2105 158 B
rod.reed@indwes.edu
REED, Sally .... 410-837-4088 204 F
sreed@ubalt.edu
REED, Sara .... 801-957-4601 461 C
sara.reed@slcc.edu
REED, Sara .... 801-957-4111 461 C
sara.reed@slcc.edu
REED, Sarah .... 415-565-4614.. 69 C
reedsarah@uchastings.edu
REED, Shannon .... 530-661-5700.. 77 D
REED, Shanoa .... 251-442-2390.... 8 C
sreed@umobile.edu
REED, Sharon .... 614-251-4593 358 B
reeds@ohiodominican.edu
REED, Shawana .... 870-235-4015.. 21 C
srreed@saumag.edu
REED, Shermain .... 214-333-5460 434 C
shermain@dbu.edu
REED, Stanton, G .... 321-682-4224 113 I
sreed21@valenciacollege.edu
REED, Stephen .... 651-793-1254 238 I
steve.reed@metrostate.edu
REED, Steve .... 417-667-8181 252 B
sreed@cottey.edu
REED, Steven .... 615-460-6619 418 B
steven.reed@belmont.edu
REED, Tammy .... 406-377-9402 263 D
treed@dawson.edu
REED, Ted .... 617-989-4590 219 F
reedt2@wit.edu
REED, Teresa .... 502-852-6907 186 A
teresa.reed@louisville.edu
REED, Teresa .... 217-228-5432 147 F
reedte@quincy.edu
REED, Terri .... 404-270-5002 126 B
treed15@spelman.edu
REED, Tiffany .... 402-375-7430 268 F
tireed1@wsc.edu
REED, Tim .... 602-489-5300.. 10 F
tim.reed@arizonachristian.edu
REED, Tracy .... 989-317-4760 230 D
treed@sagchip.edu
REED, Wendy .... 218-726-6397 243 G
wlreed@d.umn.edu
REED-BOULEY, Kenneth 402-280-2754 266 H
kennethreed-bouley@creighton.edu
REED DAVIS, Christine . 704-687-0345 342 D
crdavis@uncc.edu
REED-FRANCOIS,
Desiree .... 702-895-4729 271 D
desiree.reed@unlv.edu
REED-HENDON, Caryn .. 248-204-3144 227 A
creedhend@ltu.edu
REED-HIRSCH, Kelly ..... 903-694-4003 441 C
kreed-hirsch@panola.edu
REED-SEGRETI,
Deborah .... 516-572-7759 307 E
deborah.reed@ncc.edu
REEDER, Josh .... 909-621-8281.. 63 F
jreeder@scrippscollege.edu
REEDER, Leslie .... 334-556-2214.... 2 C
lreeder@wallace.edu
REEDER, Lynne .... 512-245-2208 450 C
blr137@txstate.edu
REEDER, Mary .... 337-421-6902 188 J
mary.reeder@sowela.edu
REEDER, Philip, P .... 412-396-4877 383 A
reederp@duq.edu
REEDER, Richard .... 631-632-7932 317 A
richard.j.reeder@stonybrook.edu
REEDER, Sean, D .... 217-581-2921 137 E
sdreeder@eiu.edu
REEDER, Shehani .... 714-744-7939.. 36 B
gunasena@chapman.edu
REEDER, Stephanie .... 815-224-0305 140 E
stephanie_reeder@ivcc.edu
REEDUS, Janice .... 815-280-6640 141 B
jreedus@jjc.edu
REEDY, Ryan, D .... 972-721-5145 452 B
rreedy@udallas.edu
REEGER, Jennifer .... 724-830-1069 398 C
jreeger@setonhill.edu
REEKS, Kevin, L .... 419-995-8081 360 C
reeks.k@rhodesstate.edu
REEL, Sally, J .... 520-626-4030.. 16 D
sreel@arizona.edu
REEL, Stephanie, L .... 314-935-0000 262 A
reel@wustl.edu
REEM, Marvin, P .... 864-242-5100 406 H
REEMER, Ronda .... 765-641-4010 153 G
rsreemer@anderson.edu
REEP, Jeff .... 937-766-7868 349 E
reepj@cedarville.edu
REER, Barbara .... 845-802-7171 323 H
reerb@sunyulster.edu
REES, John Paul .... 802-828-2800 463 F
jpr06200@ccv.vsc.edu
REES, Mary .... 805-378-1403.. 73 J
mrees@vcccd.edu
REES, Pamela, D .... 515-263-6098 166 F
prees@grandview.edu
REES, Rebecca, E .... 973-290-4721 282 I
rrees@steu.edu
REES, Shelley .... 405-224-3140 371 B
srees@usao.edu
REES, Tim .... 864-379-2131 409 E
trees@erskine.edu
REESE, Alexandra .... 614-234-5198 356 E
areese@mccn.edu
REESE, Aquirre .... 320-308-5252 241 A
aquirre.reese@sctcc.edu
REESE, Bobby .... 203-596-4548.. 88 F
breese@post.edu
REESE, Brian .... 864-388-8314 410 A
breese@lander.edu
REESE, Brian .... 717-337-6240 384 D
breese@gettysburg.edu
REESE, C. Shane .... 801-422-6201 458 H
shane_reese@byu.edu
REESE, Camille .... 704-878-3264 336 C
creese@mitchellcc.edu
REESE, Christopher ...... 562-985-2037.. 31 D
christopher.reese@csulb.edu
REESE, Cynthia .... 510-981-2851.. 56 I
creese@peralta.edu
REESE, David .... 503-768-7691 373 E
reese@lclark.edu
REESE, John .... 567-200-6829 353 B
john.reese@globaltech.edu
REESE, Kimberly .... 504-520-7575 193 E
kreese@xula.edu
REESE, Kimberly .... 336-750-3145 344 A
reesekf@wssu.edu
REESE, Nancy .... 501-450-3122.. 23 H
nancyr@uca.edu
REESE, Naomi .... 620-432-0346 176 D
nreese@neosho.edu
REESE, Pamela .... 716-488-3020 302 H
pamelareese@jbc.edu
REESE, Raymond .... 336-334-4822 335 A
rfreese@gtcc.edu
REESE, Robert, S .... 843-953-2468 408 C
reeser@cofc.edu
REESE, Suzanne .... 801-818-8900 459 J
sreese@provocolleg.edu
REESE-ULMER, Jackie ... 740-593-2000 358 K
reesulmer@ohio.edu
REESER, John, J .... 248-370-2128 229 I
jjreeser@oakland.edu
REESER, Mike .... 254-867-4891 449 D
mike.reeser@tstc.edu
REESER, Todd .... 706-565-3669 117 H
reeser_todd@columbusstate.edu
REESMAN, Melissa, J ... 260-399-7700 162 B
mreesman@sf.edu
REESOR, Lori .... 608-265-3540 495 D
lreesor@wisc.edu
REETZ, David, R .... 585-475-7108 312 F
drrcps1@rit.edu
REEVE, Scott .... 810-762-9711 226 B
sreeve@kettering.edu
REEVE-RABB, Andra ...... 912-525-5000 124 I
areeve@scad.edu
REEVES, Bert .... 404-894-1238 119 E
bert.reeves@carnegie.gatech.edu
REEVES, Brent, W .... 618-537-6938 144 A
breeves@mckendree.edu
REEVES, Bret .... 615-248-1464 426 D
breeves@trevecca.edu
REEVES, Brian .... 918-343-7983 369 B
breeves@rsu.edu
REEVES, Chip .... 989-837-4211 229 B
reevesbw@northwood.edu
REEVES, Christina .... 910-521-6301 343 B
christina.reeves@uncp.edu
REEVES, Christopher ..... 319-656-2447 170 A
chris.reeves@shilohuniversity.edu

REEVES, Darrin .... 402-872-2257 268 E
dreeves@peru.edu
REEVES, Herbert .... 334-670-3203.... 7 C
hreeves@troy.edu
REEVES, Joel .... 865-974-2333 427 B
joel.reeves@utk.edu
REEVES, Joey .... 912-478-8607 120 C
jreeves@georgiasouthern.edu
REEVES, Lisa .... 803-376-6007 406 D
lreeves@allenuniversity.edu
REEVES, Lisa .... 214-887-5025 435 F
lreeves@dts.edu
REEVES, Mark .... 678-839-5079 127 C
mreeves@westga.edu
REEVES, Michelle .... 706-880-8249 122 A
mreeves@lagrange.edu
REEVES, Richard, J .... 302-831-2021.. 91 C
rjreeves@udel.edu
REEVES, Shane .... 845-938-2000 503 I
janine.gizzi@westpoint.edu
REEVES, Shanon .... 318-274-6264 192 C
reevessh@gram.edu
REEVES, Tracey .... 352-395-5507 108 A
tracey.reeves@sfcollege.edu
REGA, Elizabeth .... 909-469-5460.. 75 I
erega@westernu.edu
REGALDO, Juan .... 909-448-4448.. 71 C
jregalado@laverne.edu
REGAN, Anna .... 732-255-0400 279 F
aregan@ocean.edu
REGAN, Brendan .... 623-845-3449.. 13 C
brendan.regan@gccaz.edu
REGAN, Joseph, P .... 312-341-2110 148 E
jregan@roosevelt.edu
REGAN, Kathleen .... 315-781-3309 301 F
regan@hws.edu
REGAN, Rich .... 312-341-3500 148 E
rregan01@roosevelt.edu
REGAN, Sheila .... 336-342-4261 337 E
regans@rockinghamcc.edu
REGE, Karen .... 443-412-2145 199 D
krege@harford.edu
REGE, Karen, M .... 443-412-2145 199 D
krege@harford.edu
REGE, Robert .... 214-648-3050 457 A
robert.rege@utsouthwestern.edu
REGE, Vidyanidhi .... 508-678-2811 214 B
vidyanidhi.rege@bristolcc.edu
REGEHR, Nanci .... 480-517-8314.. 13 G
nanci.regehr@riosalado.edu
REGEHR, Shellie .... 620-901-6299 171 D
sregehr@allencc.edu
REGENAUER, Rochelle .. 815-965-8616 148 C
REGENCIO, Eugenia ...... 973-596-3068 279 E
eugenia.regencio@njit.edu
REGER, Patricia .... 610-341-1464 383 B
preger@eastern.edu
REGER, Tim .... 515-263-6136 166 F
treger@grandview.edu
REGIER, Elaine .... 405-945-9104 368 C
elaine.regier@okstate.edu
REGIER, Jeanette .... 816-322-0110 251 B
jeanette.regier@calvary.edu
REGIER, Philip, R .... 480-965-2457.. 10 J
phil.regier@asu.edu
REGINA, Henrique .... 808-488-8570 457 I
hregina@wbu.edu
REGINATO, Justin .... 916-278-6241.. 32 D
reginato@csus.edu
REGIS, Chris, C .... 214-768-1178 444 D
cregis@smu.edu
REGIST TOMLINSON,
Tara .... 718-960-2416 294 A
tara.registtomlinson@lehman.cuny.edu
REGISTER, Kimberly ...... 770-412-4586 125 H
kimberly.register@sctech.edu
REGISTER, Patrick .... 831-459-4404.. 71 A
jpregister@ucsc.edu
REGISTER, Tammy .... 307-382-1606 501 J
tregister@westernwyoming.edu
REGJO, Kathryn .... 970-945-8691.. 78 L
REGN, Todd .... 201-200-2453 279 D
tregn@njcu.edu
REGNER, Cecile .... 857-701-1270 215 G
cregner@rcc.mass.edu
REGNER, Cecile .... 857-701-1272 215 G
cregner@rcc.mass.edu
REGUEIRO, Maria, C .... 305-821-3333 100 E
mregueiro@fnu.edu
REGUERIN, Pablo, G .... 530-752-1011.. 69 B
REGULSKA, Joanna .... 530-752-6376.. 69 B
jregulska@ucdavis.edu
REHAK, Patricia .... 361-358-2838 432 K
REHAK, Patricia .... 361-354-2728 432 K
prehak@coastalbend.edu
REHBEIN, Matt .... 615-966-6043 421 B
matt.rehbein@lipscomb.edu
REHFELD, Andrew .... 212-674-5300 301 B
REHFELD, Renee .... 830-372-6803 449 A
rrehfeld@tlu.edu
REHM, David .... 570-674-6403 390 B
drehm@misericordia.edu
REHM, Julie .... 216-523-7275 350 J
j.rehm@csuohio.edu
REHM, Mark .... 325-942-2555 450 E
mark.rehm@angelo.edu
REHM, Matthew .... 740-362-3136 355 H
mrehm@mtso.edu
REHN, Andrea .... 562-907-4200.. 76 B
arehn@whittier.edu
REHN, Lynn .... 410-228-9250 203 C
REHNELT, Wayne .... 562-860-2451.. 35 H
wrehnelt@cerritos.edu
REIBER, Carl .... 912-478-5258 120 C
creiber@georgiasouthern.edu
REICH, Amy, R .... 516-463-7580 301 G
amy.reich@hofstra.edu
REICH, Ashley .... 434-592-6709 468 E
ahageman@liberty.edu
REICH, Evan .... 843-574-6368 412 I
evan.reich@tridenttech.edu
REICH, Jacqueline .... 845-575-3000 305 D
jacqueline.reich@marist.edu
REICH, Jacqueline .... 215-248-7148 381 A
reichj@chc.edu
REICH, Lewis .... 901-722-3220 423 G
lreich@sco.edu
REICH, Patricia .... 610-330-5017 387 C
reichp@lafayette.edu
REICH, Tyler .... 503-375-6586 377 F
treich@willamette.edu
REICH PAULSEN,
Sharon .... 802-656-8585 463 A
sharon.reich.paulsen@uvm.edu
REICHARD, Jacob .... 620-223-2700 173 I
jacobr@fortscott.edu
REICHARD, Joshua .... 423-775-6596 422 I
jreichard@ogs.edu
REICHARD, Joshua .... 423-775-6596 422 I
REICHARD, Joshua .... 816-960-2008 251 G
dean@cityvision.edu
REICHARDT, Eike .... 610-799-1756 388 D
ereichardt@lccc.edu
REICHEL, Scott .... 970-339-6513.. 77 H
scott.reichel@aims.edu
REICHERT, Brett .... 678-839-4780 127 C
breicher@westga.edu
REICHERT, Greg .... 608-785-8672 496 A
greichert@uwlax.edu
REICHERT, Linda, A 570-326-3761 392W
lar22@pct.edu
REICHMAN, Harold .... 305-944-0035 104 I
REICHMUTH, Geri .... 303-292-0015.. 80 H
greichmuth@denvercollegeofnursing.
edu
REID, Adam .... 240-567-4264 200 G
adam.reid@montgomerycollege.edu
REID, Alicia .... 718-270-6406 294 G
areid@mec.cuny.edu
REID, Andrew .... 610-796-8379 378 C
andrew.reid@alvernia.edu
REID, Austin .... 803-321-5229 410 H
austin.reid@newberry.edu
REID, OP, Barbara, E ... 773-371-5420 134 D
president@ctu.edu
REID, Carol .... 678-664-0533 128 A
carol.reid@westgatech.edu
REID, Charise .... 216-421-7312 350 H
clreid@cia.edu
REID, Colette .... 757-881-5100.. 93 H
REID, Dawn .... 310-233-4287.. 49 B
reidd@lahc.edu
REID, Diana .... 860-512-2909.. 86 G
dreid@manchestercc.edu
REID, Donna, M .... 718-522-9073 290 E
dreid@asa.edu
REID, Dutchie .... 703-539-6890 471 F
dreid@stratford.edu
REID, Eric .... 601-403-1126 248 E
eried@prcc.edu
REID, Gregory .... 973-748-9000 276 A
greg_reid@bloomfield.edu
REID, Heather .... 617-747-2258 206 H
library@berklee.edu
REID, Heidi .... 913-758-6172 178 B
heidi.reid@stmary.edu
REID, Helen .... 972-932-4309 451 F
hreid@tvcc.edu
REID, James .... 325-942-2264 450 E
james.reid@angelo.edu
REID, Jodyann .... 954-545-4500 108 E
academics@sfbc.edu
REID, John .... 530-898-5555.. 30 D
jreid1@csuchico.edu
REID, Jonathan .... 518-562-4124 296 A
jonathan.reid@clinton.edu
REID, Karl .... 617-373-2000 217 I
REID, Kelly .... 601-403-1489 248 E
kareid@prcc.edu
REID, Keni .... 808-675-3701 128 D
ken.reid@byuh.edu
REID, Kevin .... 843-953-6950 407 C
kreid2@citadel.edu
REID, La Verne, M .... 919-530-5349 341 E
lreid@nccu.edu
REID, Lee .... 540-887-7212 468 G
lreid@marybaldwin.edu
REID, III, Lenzy .... 706-355-5124 115 F
lreid@athenstech.edu
REID, Lesley .... 205-348-3924.... 7 G
lwreid@ua.edu
REID, Letissa .... 860-486-2943.. 89 D
letissa.reid@uconn.edu
REID, Mark .... 308-865-8265 269 I
reidm@unk.edu
REID, Mark .... 206-281-2624 483 G
mreid@spu.edu
REID, Michael .... 509-359-6008 479 G
mreid@ewu.edu
REID, Michael, B .... 352-294-1601 111 A
michael.reid@ufl.edu
REID, Michael, L .... 406-683-7151 264 A
michael.reid@umwestern.edu
REID, Michele .... 269-965-3931 225 H
reidm@kellogg.edu
REID, Sean, F .... 401-865-2155 404 F
sean.reid@providence.edu
REID, Shannon .... 603-230-3504 272 I
sreid@ccsnh.edu
REID, Sherri .... 870-733-6020.. 17 F
sdreid@asumidsouth.edu
REID ALSTON, Melissa . 336-315-7800.. 93 H
REID-BUNCH, Jan .... 731-286-3200 424 D
REID-CHASSIAKOS,
Linda .... 818-677-3689.. 32 C
linda.reid.chassiakos@csun.edu
REID-MARTINEZ,
Kathaleen .... 918-495-7855 368 E
kreid-martinez@oru.edu
REIDY, Francis .... 352-588-8246 107 D
fran.reidy@saintleo.edu
REIDY, Joseph, P .... 202-806-6100.. 92 E
REIDY, Robert, C .... 650-723-6324.. 66 E
rcr@stanford.edu
REIDY-FOX, Kelly .... 773-298-3780 149 D
fox@sxu.edu
REIF, L. Rafael .... 617-253-0148 216 B
president@mit.edu
REIF, Richard .... 918-444-5900 366 G
reif01@nsuok.edu
REIFENHEISER, Paul ..... 607-844-8222 322 D
pr022@tompkinscortland.edu
REIFERT, Steve .... 231-591-2800 224 A
stevereifert@ferris.edu
REIG, Michael .... 215-248-7069 381 A
reigm@chc.edu
REIGEL, Dan, P .... 856-256-4200 281 F
reigel@rowan.edu
REIGEL, Heidi .... 410-857-2226 200 F
hreigel@mcdaniel.edu
REIGHARD, Erica .... 814-262-6440 393 A
ereighard@pennhighlands.edu
REIGHLEY, Twila .... 517-884-4367 227 F
reighley@msu.edu
REIGLE, Kim .... 828-689-1233 331 C
kreigle@mhu.edu
REIHER, William .... 692-625-5427 504 G
wreiher@cmi.edu
REIHL, Raeann .... 865-981-8355 421 C
raeann.reihl@maryvillecollege.edu
REIHMAN, Greg .... 610-758-3025 388 E
grr3@lehigh.edu
REIKOFSKI, Diane .... 402-844-7055 268 H
diane@northeast.edu
REILAND, Kathleen .... 714-484-7231.. 54 B
kreiland@cypresscollege.edu
REILAND, Mandi .... 281-998-6150 442 K
mandi.reiland@sjcd.edu
REILLEY, Mary Clare ..... 914-633-2686 302 E
mreilley@iona.edu
REILLO, Lissette .... 787-891-0925 507 K
lreillo@aguadilla.inter.edu
REILLY, Cathy .... 206-296-6120 484 A
reillyc@seattleu.edu
REILLY, Colleen .... 713-718-7307 437 C
colleen.reilly@hccs.edu
REILLY, David .... 973-748-9000 276 A
david_reilly1@bloomfield.edu
REILLY, John .... 303-724-0882.. 84 D
john.reilly@ucdenver.edu
REILLY, John, J .... 330-972-7753 361 H
jreilly@uakron.edu
REILLY, Joseph, R .... 973-761-9008 283 C
joseph.reilly@shu.edu
REILLY, Karen .... 269-782-1220 231 A
kreilly@swmich.edu
REILLY, Karen .... 218-736-1508 239 C
karen.reilly@minnesota.edu
REILLY, Kerin .... 212-686-9244 290 C
kreilly@aada.edu
REILLY, Lenore .... 413-538-2500 217 C
lreilly@mtholyoke.edu
REILLY, Lisa .... 304-829-7244 487 A
lreilly@bethanywv.edu
REILLY, M. B .... 513-556-1824 361 J
reillymb@ucmail.uc.edu
REILLY, Madelyn .... 412-396-5181 383 A
reillym@duq.edu
REILLY, Marianne 718-862-7891 304M
mreilly01@manhattan.edu
REILLY, Mary Beth .... 732-224-2806 276 B
mreilly@brookdalecc.edu
REILLY, Mary Jane 516-323-4702 306M
mreilly@molloy.edu
REILLY, Matthew .... 617-243-2468 211 B
mreilly@lasell.edu
REILLY, Patricia .... 617-627-2000 219 C
patricia.reilly@tufts.edu
REILLY, Ronald .... 816-604-4125 255 H
ronald.reilly@mcckc.edu
REILLY, Seamus .... 309-341-5214 134 B
sreilly@sandburg.edu
REILLY, Tim .... 706-712-8228 118 B
treilly@daltonstate.edu
REILLY, William, T .... 704-894-2765 328 E
wireilly@davidson.edu
REIM, Melanie .... 212-217-7665 299 D
melanie_reim@fitnyc.edu
REIMAN, Brock .... 330-363-6347 348 C
brock.reiman@aultman.com
REIMAN, Dennis .... 203-392-5004.. 86 A
reimand1@southernct.edu
REIMAN, Tricia .... 972-708-7552 435 E
tricia_reiman@diu.edu
REIMANN, Rick .... 518-587-2100 320 E
rick.reimann@esc.edu
REIMER, Denise .... 608-243-4484 499 A
dmreimer@madisoncollege.edu
REIMER, Martin .... 641-844-8502 167 E
martin.reimer@iavalley.edu
REIMER, Martin .... 641-648-4611 167 F
martin.reimer@iavalley.edu
REIMER, Rachel .... 515-271-1424 165 G
rachel.reimer@dmu.edu
REIMONDO, Sue .... 859-985-3212 179 I
reimondos@berea.edu
REINA, John .... 845-257-3685 316 E
reinaj@newpaltz.edu
REINA, Michelle .... 254-295-4015 453 D
mreina@umhb.edu
REINACHER, Deanna ..... 619-216-6673.. 66 A
dreinacher@swccd.edu
REINCKE, Nancy .... 515-271-2161 165 J
nancy.reincke@drake.edu
REINDERS, Gretchen ..... 608-785-8073 496 A
greinders@uwlax.edu
REINEHR, Craig .... 918-444-4700 366 G
reinehr@nsuok.edu
REINEKE, Juliann .... 419-434-4662 362 D
juliann.reineke@findlay.edu
REINEKE, Sandra .... 208-885-3165 132 F
sreineke@uidaho.edu
REINER, Christian .... 435-586-7783 460 A
christianreiner@suu.edu
REINER, Michael, D ...... 402-280-2337 266 H
michaelreiner@creighton.edu
REINERT, Duane .... 660-944-2852 251 J
dreinert@conception.edu
REINETTE ANDREWS,
Mary .... 610-527-0200 397 D
randrews@rosemont.edu

REINHARD, Ben 540-636-2900 465 L ben.reinhard@christendom.edu
REINHARD, Herb 229-333-5462 127 E hreinhar@valdosta.edu
REINHARD, Patrick 914-694-4415 296 B preinhard@riversidehealth.org
REINHARDT, Beth 217-641-4541 141 A breinhardt@jwcc.edu
REINHART, Adam 806-291-1124 457 I reinharta@wbu.edu
REINHART, Rose 410-462-7419 198 B rreinhart@bccc.edu
REINI, Aaron 218-262-7362 238 D aaronreini@hibbing.edu
REINIG, Amanda 757-455-3116 477 C areinig@vwu.edu
REINIG, Bruce 619-594-2473 33 D breinig@sdsu.edu
REININGA, Julia 864-644-5301 412 D jreininga@swu.edu
REINISCH, Lou 361-593-3108 447 D lou.reinisch@tamuk.edu
REINKE, Jeff 815-599-3406 139 A jeff.reinke@highland.edu
REINKE, Mary 414-955-4751 493 F mreinke@mcw.edu
REINKE, Stephanie 940-565-3487 453 E stephanie.reinke@unt.edu
REINL, Cindy, M 920-433-6660 491 G cindy.reinl@bellincollege.edu
REINLAND, Jeffrey, E 509-527-4312 485 B jeffrey.reinland@wwcc.edu
REINLIE, Carla 850-729-6468 104 M reinliec@nwfsc.edu
REINOEHL, Jason, K 937-229-3725 362 C jreinoehl@udayton.edu
REINOSO, Gaston 713-743-2603 452 C greinoso@uh.edu
REINOSO, Gaston 713-743-2603 452 D greinoso@uh.edu
REINSCHMIDT, Cheryl Lynn 323-259-2500 54 I
REINSEL, Kelly 330-494-6170 360 K kreinsel@starkstate.edu
REIPENHOFF, Mary, E 260-399-7700 162 B mriepenhoff@sf.edu
REIS, Gina 508-910-6505 212 A greis@umassd.edu
REIS, Jenna 605-995-7342 415 E jenna.reis@mitchelltech.edu
REISBERG, Darren 773-702-7618 151 E reisberg@uchicago.edu
REISCHE, Jim 413-597-4277 220 D jim.reische@williams.edu
REISENAUER, Eric 803-938-3862 413 G ericr@uscsumter.edu
REISER, Cyrill 818-785-2726 35 E
REISER, Sharon 805-525-4417 67 K sreiser@thomasaquinas.edu
REISH, Janean 806-874-3571 432 J janean.reish@clarendoncollege.edu
REISIG, Allison 308-635-6041 270 C wickersh@wncc.edu
REISIG, Jennifer 308-635-6550 270 C reisig1@wncc.edu
REISING, Sonia 815-455-8554 143 I sreising@mchenry.edu
REISINGER, Cynthia, E 717-815-1221 403 F creising@ycp.edu
REISMAN, Lonn 254-968-9178 446 D reisman@tarleton.edu
REISMAN, Yisroel 718-941-8000 306 E
REISNER, Jeff 716-375-2000 313 C jreisner@reisnerlawgroup.com
REISNER, John, A 937-255-3636 502 C john.reisner@afit.edu
REISS, Michael, A 718-377-0777 311 G
REISSENWEBER, Beth 940-397-4237 440 C beth.reissenweber@msutexas.edu
REISSMAN, Sallie, A 302-356-6807 91 E sallie.a.reissman@wilmu.edu
REISZ, Z 805-965-0581 63 A zreisz@sbcc.edu
REITER, Lisa 773-508-2200 143 C lreiter1@luc.edu
REITER, Sarah 802-831-1241 463 C sreiter@vermontlaw.edu
REITZ, Chris 801-524-8109 459 E creitz@ldsbc.edu
REITZ, Eric 216-421-7437 350 H ereitz@cia.edu
REITZ, Tiffany 352-638-9707 96 B treitz@beaconcollege.edu
REJHOLEC, Taryn 212-217-4700 299 D taryn_rejholec@fitnyc.edu
REKLAI, Hilda, N 680-488-2471 505 B hildan@palau.edu
REKOW, Vickie 425-889-7830 481 H vickie.rekow@northwestu.edu
REL, Ricardo 575-646-5909 287 C rrel@nmsu.edu
RELKIN, Richard 212-237-8000 294 D
RELL, Amy 303-220-1200 78 E
RELLINGER, Brian, A 740-368-3131 359 G barellin@owu.edu
RELLINGER, Thomas, D 248-218-2049 230 B trellinger@rochesteru.edu
RELYEA, Steve 562-951-4600 29 H srelyea@calstate.edu
REMBACZ, Kimberly 307-382-1661 501 J krembacz@westernwyoming.edu
REMBACZ, Mark 307-382-1871 501 J mrembacz@westernwyoming.edu
REMBOLD, Scott 202-319-6909 92 A rembold@cua.edu
REMENDER, Kathleen, A 810-762-9794 226 B kremende@kettering.edu
REMENSCHNEIDER, Mary 616-395-7252 225 D remenschneider@hope.edu
REMER, Rosalind 215-895-1203 382 F rosalind.remer@drexel.edu
REMHOF, Tamara 540-891-3013 473 I tremhof@germanna.edu
REMIAS, Bobbie 248-341-2102 229 C raremias@oaklandcc.edu
REMIERES-MORIN, Pamela 207-629-4018 195 C premieres@mccs.me.edu
REMINDER, Jodie 765-641-4316 153 G jlreminder@anderson.edu
REMINGTON, Brodie 301-405-4683 202 H brodie10@umd.edu
REMINGTON, Debra 440-375-7040 354 K dremington@lec.edu
REMINGTON, Judith, V 847-491-7456 146 E j-remington@northwestern.edu
REMLEY, Robin 727-864-7564 98 J smallerm@eckerd.edu
REMMLER, Mary, M 302-831-2082 91 C mremmler@udel.edu
REMOTTI, Steve 908-737-5018 278 E steremotti@kean.edu
REMPEL, Valerie 559-453-2319 43 A valerie.rempel@fresno.edu
REMPFER, Julie 267-341-5017 385 J jrempfer@holyfamily.edu
REMSBURG, Barbara 801-587-0851 459 O bremsburg@housing.utah.edu
REMSBURG, Mateo 740-593-4100 358 K mremsburg@ohio.edu
REMY, Jana 714-744-7934 36 B remy@chapman.edu
REN, Wei 818-575-6800 68 C
RENADETTE, Magen, M 518-564-3246 318 E mrena002@plattsburgh.edu
RENAULT, Tara, C 717-245-1390 382 D renaultt@dickinson.edu
RENBARGER, Bridgette 402-399-2646 266 F brenbarger@csm.edu
RENBARGER, Christopher 805-678-5114 74 A crenbarger@vcccd.edu
RENDA, Liz 570-702-8945 386 D lrenda@johnson.edu
RENDA, Stuart 570-945-8378 386 F stu.renda@keystone.edu
RENDER, Rachel 616-732-1198 223 E rachel.render@davenport.edu
RENDFELD, Kim 618-453-2544 150 B kim.rendfeld@siu.edu
RENDON-THOFSON, Michael 213-427-2200 35 F
RENEHAN, Colm 617-573-8444 219 B crenehan@suffolk.edu
RENER, Christine 616-331-3498 224 G renerc@gvsu.edu
RENEY, Richard 978-762-4000 215 D rreney@northshore.edu
RENFRO, Bryan 903-785-7661 441 D brenfro@parisjc.edu
RENFRO, Darcy 480-731-8000 12 N darcy.renfro@domail.maricopa.edu
RENFRO, Joe 918-540-6950 366 F joe.renfro@neo.edu
RENFROE, Sam 850-729-4944 104 M renfroes@nwfsc.edu
RENGIFO, Monica 239-687-5442 95 L mrengifo@avemarialaw.edu
RENICK, Timothy, M 404-413-2580 120 E trenick@gsu.edu
RENIFF, William, M 440-826-2212 348 D breniff@bw.edu
RENIO, Linda 808-734-9575 129 H katsudal@hawaii.edu
RENKO, Jenn 717-396-7833 392 U jrenko@pcad.edu
RENNA, Kimberly 619-574-5807 42 J krenna@fst.edu
RENNER, Blake 614-947-9236 352 J blake.renner@franklin.edu
RENNER, Catherine 641-269-4046 166 G rennerca@grinnell.edu
RENNER, Cynthia 215-489-2467 382 B cynthia.renner@delval.edu
RENNER, Lance 417-447-8202 257 G rennerl@otc.edu
RENNER, Sonja 206-934-4634 483 B sonja.renner@seattlecolleges.edu
RENNERT, Chaim 718-438-5476 325 B
RENNICKE, Dean, D 262-243-5700 492 E dean.rennicke@cuw.edu
RENNIER, Meredith 318-487-7138 187 E meredith.rennier@lacollege.edu
RENNIX, Louise 843-525-8318 412 G lrennix@tcl.edu
RENO, Adam 301-846-2560 198 I areno@frederick.edu
RENSCH, Jonathan 307-332-2930 502 A jrensch@wyomingcatholic.edu
RENSEL, Kelli 724-738-2330 395 C kelli.rensel@sru.edu
RENSHAW, Andrew 434-961-6540 474 I arenshaw@pvcc.edu
RENSHAW, Brian 502-897-4347 184 G brenshaw@sbts.edu
RENSHAW, Paul 410-827-5870 198 F prenshaw@chesapeake.edu
RENTA, Pedro 715-425-3505 496 F pedro.renta@uwrf.edu
RENTMEESTER, Matt, G 920-433-6657 491 G matt.rentmeester@bellincollege.edu
RENTSCH, Janet, M 989-964-7120 230 E jrentsch@svsu.edu
RENTSCH, Kathy 508-854-2712 215 F krentsch@qcc.mass.edu
RENTSCHLER, Gina 417-865-2815 253 D rentschlerg@evangel.edu
RENTSCHLER, Stephen 800-955-2527 174 C
RENTTO, Jessica 619-594-6018 33 D jrentto@sdsu.edu
RENTZ, Judy 916-577-2200 76 D jrentz@jessup.edu
RENTZ, Pam 850-718-2213 97 E rentzp@chipola.edu
RENWICK, Todd 775-673-7000 271 C trenwick@unr.edu
RENZ, Amy Button 785-532-5050 175 C arenz@ksu.edu
RENZ, Christopher 510-883-2084 41 B crenz@dspt.edu
RENZ, Christopher, M 510-883-2084 41 B crenz@dspt.edu
RENZ, Nolan 570-702-8912 386 D nrenz@johnson.edu
RENZULLI, Beth, W 603-526-3717 272 H brenzull@colby-sawyer.edu
REOME, Darryl 860-773-1769 87 G dreome@tunxis.edu
REPETTO, Paul 212-431-2836 309 A paul.repetto@nyls.edu
REPETTO, Sarah 213-624-1200 42 B srepetto@fidm.edu
REPKO, Lisa 215-955-0437 399 E lisa.repko@jefferson.edu
REPOLLET, Lamont 908-737-7000 278 E lrepollet@kean.edu
REPP, Ian 906-487-2354 228 A irepp@mtu.edu
REPP, Laurie 419-448-2105 353 E lrepp@heidelberg.edu
REPP, Randy 785-227-3380 172 A repprl@bethanylb.edu
REPPERT, Angela 610-398-5300 388 F areppert@lincolntech.edu
REPPETTO, Martha 212-812-4025 308 G mreppetto@nycda.edu
REPPOND, Lindsey 337-421-6917 188 J lindsey.jones@sowela.edu
REPZYNSKI, Allison 478-757-3547 116 G
REQUENA, Laura 956-872-3646 443 H lrequena@southtexascollege.edu
RERRICK, Charlotte 212-757-1190 290 D crerrick@aami.edu
RESCIGNO, Robert, W 302-295-1158 91 E robert.w.rescigno@wilmu.edu
RESENDEZ, Larry, L 818-364-7733 49 C resendcl@lamission.edu
RESENDIZ, Linda 805-378-1407 73 J lresendiz@vcccd.edu
RESER, Erin 406-657-1015 265 E erin.reser@rocky.edu
RESHEF, Shai 626-264-8880 71 F
RESIDORI, Amber 815-939-5135 147 A alresidori@olivet.edu
RESINGER, Rodney 573-518-3806 256 D rresinger@mineralarea.edu
RESMANN, Brittany 434-961-5301 474 I bresmann@pvcc.edu
RESNICK, Barry 303-867-1155 83 K resnick@taftu.edu
RESNICK, Coleen 508-541-1655 209 A cresnick@dean.edu
RESSEL, Dawn 406-243-5661 263 K dawn.ressel@umontana.edu
RESSLER, Koreen 701-854-8001 346 H koreen.ressler@sittingbull.edu
RESTEN, Paul 508-541-1629 209 A presten@dean.edu
RESTER, Aaron 312-341-7140 148 E arester@roosevelt.edu
RESTIVO, Charles 408-498-5121 73 B erestivo@cogswell.edu
RESTO, Maria de Lourdes 787-250-1912 508 D mresto@metro.inter.edu
RESTO, Richelle 703-729-8800 93 H
RESTO, Wilfredo 787-738-2161 512 C wilfredo.resto@upr.edu
RESUE, Meg 856-415-2101 281 D mresue@rcsj.edu
RESURRECCION, Yssa 202-319-6033 92 A resurreccion@cua.edu
RETANA, Ruthie 562-908-3445 58 L rretana@riohondo.edu
RETASKET, Victoria 360-676-2772 481 F vretasket@nwic.edu
RETELLE, Mary Lou 508-849-3333 205 H mretelle@annamaria.edu
RETES, Diana 714-895-8178 38 A dretes@gwc.cccd.edu
RETHEMEYER, R. Karl 413-545-4173 211 G rrethemeyer@umass.edu
RETHERFORD, Kristine 507-389-6315 239 D kristine.retherford@mnsu.edu
RETKA, James 218-683-8643 240 B james.retka@northlandcollege.edu
RETLAND, Bev 641-585-8496 170 I retlandb@waldorf.edu
RETTIG, James 410-293-6900 504 A
RETTLER, Peter, J 262-335-5706 499 D prettler@morainepark.edu
RETZLAFF, Austin 800-567-2344 492 C aretzlaff@menominee.edu
RETZLOFF, Merilee 320-762-4447 237 C merileer@alextech.edu
REULAND, Anne, C 773-508-7478 143 C aruland@luc.edu
REUNING, Charles, R 301-405-6214 202 H creuning@umd.edu
REUSCHER, Karen 315-781-3722 301 F reuscher@hws.edu
REUTER, Kellyann, M 414-277-7101 494 D reuter@msoe.edu
REUTER, William 716-851-1200 299 B reuter@ecc.edu
REVARD, Cameron 360-676-2772 481 F crevard@nwic.edu
REVEILE, Matt 916-306-1628 67 F mreveile@sum.edu
REVELEY, IV, W. Taylor 434-395-2001 468 F reveleywt@longwood.edu
REVELS, Angela 910-521-6279 343 B angela.revels@uncp.edu
REVELS, Cynthia 910-521-6855 343 B cindy.revels@uncp.edu
REVELS, Engle 910-521-6000 343 B
REVERON, Derek 401-841-3540 503 A derek.reveron@usnwc.edu

REVIERE, Mallory .... 505-277-2626 288 J
mreviere@unm.edu
REVZINA, Larisa .... 650-685-6616.. 44 F
lrevzina@gurnick.edu
REW-BIGELOW,
Monique .... 585-395-2122 317 E
mrew@brockport.edu
REWERTS, Glen .... 815-939-5277 147 A
grewerts@olivet.edu
REWIS, Nancy .... 706-290-2166 116 B
nrewis@berry.edu
REX, Barbara, A .... 805-437-3282.. 30 C
barbara.rex@csuci.edu
REX, Elizabeth .... 860-632-3033.. 88 C
erex@holyapostles.edu
REX, Judith .... 610-861-5533 391 C
jrex@northampton.edu
REX, Lisa Youngkin ...... 610-330-5060 387 C
rexl@lafayette.edu
REX, Scott .... 541-552-6745 376 B
rexs@sou.edu
REX SMITH, Amy .... 601-968-8933 245 B
arexsmith@belhaven.edu
REXFORD, Nathan .... 530-938-5336.. 39 C
REY, Holly .... 815-479-7573 143 I
hrey@mchenry.edu
REY, Michelle .... 661-362-3433.. 38 D
michelle.rey@canyons.edu
REY, Rosamil .... 787-279-1912 508 A
rrey@bayamon.inter.edu
REY ROMERO, Carlos ... 575-835-5675 286 K
carlos.romero@nmt.edu
REYELL, Sarah .... 518-564-2000 318 E
REYER, Julie .... 309-677-2709 134 A
jreyer@bradley.edu
REYES, Amy, S .... 570-321-4134 389 B
reyes@lycoming.edu
REYES, Angie .... 303-273-3525.. 79 J
areyes@mines.edu
REYES, Carlos .... 530-242-7760.. 64 C
creyes@shastacollege.edu
REYES, Christopher .... 323-259-2500.. 54 I
REYES, David .... 817-722-1623 438 G
david.reyes@tku.edu
REYES, Debra .... 575-538-6174 289 G
debra.reyes@wnmu.edu
REYES, Esmeralda .... 903-586-2518 438 C
reyese27@jacksonville-college.edu
REYES, Esmeralda .... 903-586-7110 438 C
reyese27@jacksonville-college.edu
REYES, Ginger .... 805-437-8521.. 30 C
ginger.reyes@csuci.edu
REYES, Ginny .... 785-227-3380 172 A
reyesg@bethanylb.edu
REYES, Hector .... 787-850-9342 512 D
hector.reyes@upr.edu
REYES, Idania .... 310-660-3483.. 41 E
ireyes@elcamino.edu
REYES, Ivelisse .... 787-850-9332 512 D
ivelisse.reyes1@upr.edu
REYES, Javier .... 312-413-3450 151 G
REYES, Javier .... 304-293-7800 490 E
javier.reyes@mail.wvu.edu
REYES, Jean .... 305-899-3000.. 96 A
jreyes@barry.edu
REYES, Jennifer .... 201-447-7456 275 H
jreyes@bergen.edu
REYES, Joseph .... 831-755-6950.. 44 G
jreyes@hartnell.edu
REYES, Karen .... 831-479-3503.. 27 D
kareyes@cabrillo.edu
REYES, Kasie .... 757-683-4576 469 B
kliles@odu.edu
REYES, Kyle .... 801-863-6158 460 D
kyle.reyes@uvu.edu
REYES, Livette .... 787-894-2828 513 C
livette.reyes@upr.edu
REYES, Lorenzo .... 505-566-3742 288 D
reyesl@sanjuancollege.edu
REYES, Marcos .... 787-725-6500 505 G
mreyes@albizu.edu
REYES, Maria .... 562-985-8051.. 31 D
maria.reyes@csulb.edu
REYES, Maria .... 602-285-7434.. 13 F
maria.reyes@phoenixcollege.edu
REYES, Melissa .... 949-753-4774.. 71 D
REYES, Nora .... 480-461-7444.. 13 D
nora.reyes@mesacc.edu
REYES, Otoniel .... 203-582-3660.. 88 G
otoniel.reyes@qu.edu
REYES, Paula, S .... 248-370-4423 229 I
preyes@oakland.edu
REYES, Rafael .... 212-870-1213 309 E
rreyes@nyts.edu
REYES, Ray .... 619-660-4206.. 44 D
ray.reyes@gcccd.edu
REYES, Raymond .... 509-313-6550 480 F
reyes@gonzaga.edu
REYES, Robert, G .... 214-860-2664 434 I
rreyes@dcccd.edu
REYES, Rosana .... 570-740-0336 389 A
rreyes@luzerne.edu
REYES, Rudy .... 574-631-0694 162 A
rreyes@nd.edu
REYES, Saul .... 352-854-2322.. 97 N
reyess@cf.edu
REYES, Tony .... 817-202-6232 444 I
treyes@swau.edu
REYES-GIL, Yanira .... 787-751-1912 509 A
yreyes@juris.inter.edu
REYES-GUEVARA,
Yolanda .... 210-486-4195 428 I
yreyes@alamo.edu
REYES-OSARIO,
Osmara .... 310-377-5501.. 51 C
oreyes-osario@marymountcalifornia.edu
REYMALDO, Randy .... 818-677-2128.. 32 C
randy.reynaldo@csun.edu
REYMANN, Linda .... 443-352-4203 202 E
lreymann@stevenson.edu
REYNA, Angel .... 559-675-4800.. 67 C
REYNA, Brenda .... 210-341-1366 440 H
registrar@ost.edu
REYNA, Cynthia .... 870-864-7130.. 21 A
creyna@southark.edu
REYNA, Oscar .... 361-825-5934 447 C
oscar.reyna@tamucc.edu
REYNA, Patrick .... 210-297-9663 430 L
pgreyna@baptisthealthsystem.com
REYNARD, Betty .... 409-984-6100 449 I
betty.reynard@lamarpa.edu
REYNARD, Michelle .... 216-397-1659 353 O
mreynard@jcu.edu
REYNDERS, John, C ..... 712-274-5100 168 E
reynders@morningside.edu
REYNOLDS, Allison .... 846-208-8263 413 C
ar60@uscb.edu
REYNOLDS, Amy .... 330-672-2950 354 A
areyno24@kent.edu
REYNOLDS, Benjamin ... 847-866-3936 138 D
benjamin.reynolds@garrett.edu
REYNOLDS, Beth .... 607-274-3683 302 G
breynolds@ithaca.edu
REYNOLDS, Brad .... 706-865-2134 126 E
breynolds@truett.edu
REYNOLDS, Burt .... 307-382-1621 501 J
breynolds@westernwyoming.edu
REYNOLDS, Chip .... 770-297-4511 122 B
creynolds@laniertech.edu
REYNOLDS, Chris .... 309-677-2670 134 A
reynolds@fsmail.bradley.edu
REYNOLDS, Clara .... 978-934-3567 212 B
clara_reynolds@uml.edu
REYNOLDS, Cristin .... 601-266-4466 249 F
cristin.reynolds@usm.edu
REYNOLDS, Curtis .... 352-392-1336 111 A
curtrey@ufl.edu
REYNOLDS, Daisy .... 214-818-1360 433 O
dreynolds@criswell.edu
REYNOLDS, Dan .... 662-325-0519 247 F
daniel.reynolds@msstate.edu
REYNOLDS, Debbie .... 530-895-2378.. 27 C
reynoldsde@butte.edu
REYNOLDS, Dennis .... 713-743-7896 452 D
der@uh.edu
REYNOLDS, Derrick .... 606-546-1272 185 D
dreynolds@unionky.edu
REYNOLDS, Diane, L .... 804-828-3430 473 B
dlreynol@vcu.edu
REYNOLDS, Don .... 334-386-7240.... 5 C
dreynolds2@faulkner.edu
REYNOLDS, Ed .... 940-565-3000 453 E
ed.reynolds@unt.edu
REYNOLDS, Edward .... 318-670-6000 191 D
REYNOLDS,
Elizabeth, P .... 304-293-4245 490 E
liz.reynolds@mail.wvu.edu
REYNOLDS, Ellen .... 401-874-5155 405 E
ellenreynolds@uri.edu
REYNOLDS, Gloria .... 970-351-1766.. 84 F
gloria.reynolds@unco.edu
REYNOLDS, James .... 708-456-0300 151 D
jimreynolds@triton.edu
REYNOLDS, James .... 217-424-6208 144 G
jimreynolds@millikin.edu
REYNOLDS, Jamie .... 334-727-8011.... 7 D
jreynolds@tuskegee.edu
REYNOLDS, John .... 626-624-4673.. 50 D
REYNOLDS, Joseph ...... 775-784-3226 270 J
REYNOLDS, Karl .... 918-343-7819 369 B
kreynolds@rsu.edu
REYNOLDS, Katie .... 443-412-2190 199 D
kreynolds@harford.edu
REYNOLDS, Kevin .... 859-344-3346 185 B
reynolk@thomasmore.edu
REYNOLDS, Kevin .... 503-725-3886 375 E
reynoldsk@pdx.edu
REYNOLDS, Lana .... 405-382-9200 369 F
l.reynolds@sscok.edu
REYNOLDS, Laurie .... 315-568-3103 310 B
lreynolds@nycc.edu
REYNOLDS, Loretta .... 859-985-3774 179 I
reynoldslo@berea.edu
REYNOLDS, Mark, A ..... 410-706-7461 203 A
mreynolds@umaryland.edu
REYNOLDS, Marlene ..... 419-372-9824 348 G
mreyno@bgsu.edu
REYNOLDS, Mary Beth . 304-696-2987 489 M
reynoldm@marshall.edu
REYNOLDS, Matthew ..... 209-478-0800.. 45 I
REYNOLDS, Michael ..... 704-233-8252 344 F
m.reynolds@wingate.edu
REYNOLDS, Michael, C 334-844-4367.... 4 D
reynom2@auburn.edu
REYNOLDS, Michaela .... 325-942-2335 450 E
0295mgr@follett.com
REYNOLDS, Michelle .... 410-951-3939 204 B
mreynolds@coppin.edu
REYNOLDS, Michelle .... 573-840-9077 260 E
michellereynolds@trcc.edu
REYNOLDS, Nancy, W .. 270-686-4244 179 J
nancy.reynolds@brescia.edu
REYNOLDS, Phillip .... 334-699-2266.... 1 B
preynolds@acom.edu
REYNOLDS, Randall ...... 615-460-6443 418 B
randall.reynolds@belmont.edu
REYNOLDS, Robin .... 408-554-4070.. 63 B
rreynolds@scu.edu
REYNOLDS, Russell .... 585-385-8025 313 F
rreynolds@sjfc.edu
REYNOLDS, Sean, B ..... 847-491-7326 146 E
sean.reynolds@northwestern.edu
REYNOLDS, Sharon, S .. 606-783-2527 184 C
sb.reynolds@moreheadstate.edu
REYNOLDS, Shawn .... 320-629-5161 240 D
shawn.reynolds@pine.edu
REYNOLDS,
Stephanie, C .... 315-792-5456 306 K
sreynolds@mvcc.edu
REYNOLDS, Thomas ...... 318-357-4577 192 G
reynoldst@nsula.edu
REYNOLDS, Thomas ...... 440-525-7064 354 L
treynolds17@lakelandcc.edu
REYNOLDS, Thomas, L . 704-687-7248 342 D
tlreynol@uncc.edu
REYNOLDS, Tiffany .... 239-590-1005 109 K
treynold@fgcu.edu
REYNOLDS, Torry .... 336-757-7478 334 F
treynolds@forsythtech.edu
REYNOLDS-CASPER,
ReGina .... 620-792-9364 171 I
reynoldsr@bartonccc.edu
REYNOLDS-STUMP,
Krista .... 518-262-2929 289 L
reynolk1@amc.edu
REYNOSO, Bernardo ..... 559-442-4600.. 67 E
bernardo.reynoso@fresnocitycollege.edu
REYNOSO, Ivan .... 213-427-2200.. 35 F
REZA, Fawzia .... 800-280-0307 153 E
fawzia.reza@ace.edu
REZAC, Barb .... 605-668-1292 415 F
barbara.rezac@mountmarty.edu
REZAEI, Roksana .... 801-832-2003 461 F
rrezaei@westminstercollege.edu
REZAIE, Jaleh .... 919-530-7395 341 E
jrezaie@nccu.edu
REZAK, Mary .... 509-335-5593 485 D
mary.rezak@wsu.edu
REZEK, Jon .... 252-328-1936 341 A
rezekjo17@ecu.edu
REZENDES, Elizabeth .... 203-932-7131.. 89 H
erezendes@newhaven.edu
REZENDES, Robert .... 508-678-2811 214 B
robert.rezendes@bristolcc.edu
RHAMES, Ronald .... 803-738-7600 410 D
rhamesr@midlandstech.edu
RHEA, Amanda .... 704-978-4441 336 C
ahrea@mitchellcc.edu
RHEA, Kenneth .... 585-389-2606 307 F
krhee9@naz.edu
RHEA, Kristy, K .... 540-828-5471 464 L
krhea@bridgewater.edu
RHEAD, Lori .... 608-363-2630 491 H
rheadl@beloit.edu
RHEAULT, Wendy .... 847-578-3238 148 F
wendy.rheault@rosalindfranklin.edu
RHEAUME, Steve .... 603-535-2266 275 A
srheaume@plymouth.edu
RHEE, Jinny .... 562-985-1512.. 31 D
jinny.rhee@csulb.edu
RHEE, Michael .... 212-431-2893 309 A
michael.rhee@nyls.edu
RHEE, Thomas .... 703-629-1281 473 A
president@vacu.edu
RHEIN, John .... 610-430-4163 395 D
jrhein@wcupa.edu
RHEINECKER, Connie ... 704-216-3485 337 F
connie.rheinecker@rccc.edu
RHEINECKER, Matthew . 734-432-5832 227 C
mrheinecker@madonna.edu
RHETT, Sarah .... 719-587-7631.. 77 G
sarahrhett@adams.edu
RHI-KLEINERT, Susan ... 818-710-2289.. 49 D
rhiks@piercecollege.edu
RHIE, Suok .... 714-525-0088.. 43 J
cfo@gm.edu
RHIM, Chonhee .... 323-265-8625.. 48 J
rhimcl@elac.edu
RHINE, Christine .... 610-647-4400 385 L
crhine@immaculata.edu
RHINE, Lisa .... 928-445-7300.. 16 J
lisa.rhine@yc.edu
RHINE, Randy .... 308-432-6201 268 D
rrhine@csc.edu
RHINIER, William .... 717-947-6181 392 V
wrhinier2@pacollege.edu
RHOAD, Scott .... 660-543-4123 260 G
rhoad@ucmo.edu
RHOADES, Dena .... 661-336-5100.. 46 K
RHOADES, Jeff .... 419-448-2977 353 E
jrhoade1@heidelberg.edu
RHOADES, Jeffrey .... 707-527-4811.. 63 D
jrhoades@santarosa.edu
RHOADES, IV, Mack ..... 254-710-1234 431 E
mack_rhoadesiv@baylor.edu
RHOADES, Margot .... 704-461-6733 326 L
margotrhoades@bac.edu
RHOADS, Jeffrey .... 480-461-7565.. 13 D
jeffrey.rhoads@mesacc.edu
RHOADS, Troy .... 309-298-1834 153 A
te-rhoads@wiu.edu
RHODA, Christopher ..... 207-859-1124 196 D
chris@thomas.edu
RHODE, Carolyn .... 336-506-4128 332 A
carolyn.rhode@alamancecc.edu
RHODEN, Brenda .... 256-761-6204.... 7 B
brhoden@talladega.edu
RHODEN, Deborah .... 256-840-4137.... 3 F
deborah.rhoden@snead.edu
RHODEN, Richard, R .... 337-475-5887 192 E
rrhoden@mcneese.edu
RHODEN, Rob .... 757-826-1883 464 G
rrhoden@ascent.edu
RHODES, Anthony, P .... 212-592-2071 315 C
tonyrhodes@sva.edu
RHODES, Carla .... 706-880-8240 122 A
crhodes@lagrange.edu
RHODES, David, J .... 212-592-2350 315 C
drhodes@sva.edu
RHODES, Dawn, M .... 410-706-2802 203 A
drhodes@umaryland.edu
RHODES, Eileen .... 860-906-5021.. 86 D
erhodes@capitalcc.edu
RHODES, Heather .... 281-459-7106 443 B
heather.rhodes@sjcd.edu
RHODES, Jason, F .... 410-543-6031 204 D
jfrhodes@salisbury.edu
RHODES, Jennifer .... 425-388-9509 480 B
jrhodes@everettcc.edu
RHODES, John .... 410-225-2201 200 D
jrhodes@mica.edu
RHODES, Karen .... 864-578-8770 411 F
krhodes@sherman.edu
RHODES, Kathy .... 206-934-3796 483 B
kathy.rhodes@seattlecolleges.edu
RHODES, Lisa .... 714-620-1005.. 39 G
lrhodes@concorde.edu
RHODES, Lisa .... 601-766-6422 247 E
lisa.rhodes@mgccc.edu

RHODES, Michelle .... 616-331-3234 224 G rhodesmi@gvsu.edu
RHODES, Neisha .... 209-667-3201.. 33 B nrhodes@csustan.edu
RHODES, Phil .... 254-299-8642 439 E prhodes@mclennan.edu
RHODES, Rhosetta .... 509-777-4536 486 C rrhodes@whitworth.edu
RHODES, Richard, M .... 512-223-7598 430 I rrhodes@austincc.edu
RHODES, Robert .... 325-674-2024 428 F rlr12a@acu.edu
RHODES, Shunita .... 312-788-1165 152 J srhodes@vandercook.edu
RHODES, Tammy .... 256-765-4100.... 8 E tdrhodes@una.edu
RHODES, Tasha .... 718-260-5800 295 A trhodes@citytech.cuny.edu
RHODES, Terry .... 919-962-3082 342 C asdean@unc.edu
RHODES, Tim .... 606-783-2000 184 C t.rhodes@moreheadstate.edu
RHODES, Valerie .... 972-708-7340 435 E
RHODES, Vincent, A ..... 757-446-7070 466 D rhodesva@evms.edu
RHONE, Kasey .... 918-444-2525 366 G rhone01@nsuok.edu
RHONEMUS, Sarita, A .. 304-327-4334 489 I sarhonemus@bluefieldstate.edu
RHUE, Monika .... 704-371-6741 330 D mrhue@jcsu.edu
RHYMER, Ashley .... 828-669-8012 331 K
RHYNE, Sandra .... 803-938-3761 413 G rhynes@mailbox.sc.edu
RHYNE, Teresa, L .... 757-455-3345 477 C trhyne@vwu.edu
RHYNE, Whitney .... 239-433-6943 101 A whitney.rhyne@fsw.edu
RHYNEDANCE, George .. 516-726-6048 503 H rhynedanceg@usmma.edu
RHYNER, Robyn .... 315-786-2350 303 C rrhyner@sunyjefferson.edu
RHYNHART, Hans .... 860-486-4806.. 89 D hans.rhynhart@uconn.edu
RHYNHOLD, Daniel ...... 646-592-6370 326 D rhynhold@yu.edu
RIAL, Scott .... 847-543-2652 136 A srial@clcillinois.edu
RIANO, Alexa .... 201-360-4002 278 C ariano@hccc.edu
RIBAKOW, Larry .... 443-548-6056 201 C lribakow@nirc.edu
RIBBLE, Jared .... 505-387-7490 286 I jribble@navajotech.edu
RIBEIRO, Katie .... 401-254-3161 405 C
RIBEIRO, Solange .... 612-767-7055 233 H solange.ribeiro@alfredadler.edu
RIBINSON, Gregory ...... 615-963-5000 426 A
RIBNER, Jason .... 503-917-5005 374 D jribner@nunm.edu
RIBORDY, J. Clark .... 785-242-5200 176 I clark.ribordy@ottawa.edu
RICAFRENTE, Tina .... 619-876-4250.. 68 H tricafrente@usuniversity.edu
RICARDI, Richard .... 508-849-3367 205 H rricardi@annamaria.edu
RICARDINO CSAPO, Jorge .... 303-273-3503.. 79 J ycsapo@mines.edu
RICARDO LEFRANC-MORALES, Ricardo .... 787-622-8000 511 D lefranc@iraarch.com
RICAURTE, Kelly .... 603-358-2119 274 H kricaurte@keene.edu
RICCA, Beth .... 201-684-7455 280 H bricca@ramapo.edu
RICCA, Beth, M .... 732-571-3580 279 A bricca@monmouth.edu
RICCARDI, Mark, T .... 304-724-3700 486 F mriccardi@apus.edu
RICCHEZZA, Lorraine .... 856-256-5130 281 F ricchezza@rowan.edu
RICCI, Heidi .... 763-488-2549 238 C heidi.ricci@hennepintech.edu
RICCIARDI, Jennifer, H . 617-573-8470 219 B jricciardi@suffolk.edu
RICCOBONO, Steve .... 718-636-3787 311 F sriccobo@pratt.edu
RICE, Alaina, M .... 620-417-1061 177 F alaina.rice@sccc.edu
RICE, Amy .... 208-467-8609 132 E arice@nnu.edu
RICE, Angela .... 434-592-6327 468 E amrice3@liberty.edu
RICE, Becca .... 765-285-1147 153 H rapolcz@bsu.edu
RICE, Billie Jo .... 661-395-4936.. 46 L brice@bakersfieldcollege.edu
RICE, Brian .... 937-393-3431 360 H brice@sscc.edu
RICE, Carlton .... 205-929-6389.... 2 H crice@lawsonstate.edu
RICE, Carolyn .... 828-398-7105 332 B carolynhrice@abtech.edu
RICE, Chris .... 504-865-3579 190 C crice@loyno.edu
RICE, Condoleezza .... 650-723-2300.. 66 E
RICE, Cynthia, E .... 410-706-3171 203 A crice@umaryland.edu
RICE, Deborah .... 707-826-5135.. 33 C deborah.rice@humboldt.edu
RICE, Edward .... 870-574-4500.. 21 D
RICE, Fred .... 920-924-3291 499 D frice@morainepark.edu
RICE, Gale .... 314-889-1479 253 E grice@fontbonne.edu
RICE, Heather .... 256-228-6001.... 3 B riceh@nacc.edu
RICE, Jack .... 717-361-3750 383 C ricejack@etown.edu
RICE, James, W .... 320-222-7474 240 F jim.rice@ridgewater.edu
RICE, Jennifer, K .... 301-405-5252 202 H jkr@umd.edu
RICE, Jonah .... 618-252-5400 149 I jonah.rice@sic.edu
RICE, Josh .... 423-648-6129 423 B jrice@richmont.edu
RICE, Josh .... 404-835-6129 423 B jrice@richmont.edu
RICE, Julie .... 317-299-0333 161 D julie@tcmi.org
RICE, Kathy .... 740-389-4636 355 F ricek@mtc.edu
RICE, Katlyn .... 251-580-2100.... 1 I
RICE, Kevin .... 585-395-2408 317 E krice@brockport.edu
RICE, Larry .... 918-343-7612 369 B lrice@rsu.edu
RICE, Leah, B .... 859-846-5308 184 B lbarth@midway.edu
RICE, Leila .... 978-837-5997 216 F ricelc@merrimack.edu
RICE, Malcolm .... 256-824-2613.... 8 B malcom.rice@uah.edu
RICE, Malcolm .... 256-824-2613.... 8 B malcolm.rice@uah.edu
RICE, Martin .... 765-677-2939 158 B martin.rice@indwes.edu
RICE, Monica .... 620-242-0432 176 B ricem@mcpherson.edu
RICE, Peter .... 201-684-7500 280 H price@ramapo.edu
RICE, Priscilla .... 215-968-8450 379 D priscilla.rice@bucks.edu
RICE, Rachel .... 207-768-9447 197 C rachel.rice@maine.edu
RICE, Raymond, J .... 207-768-9525 197 C raymond.rice@maine.edu
RICE, Rebekah .... 206-281-2080 483 G ricer@spu.edu
RICE, Rolondus, R .... 662-252-8000 248 G rrice@rustcollege.edu
RICE, Scott .... 217-333-0560 152 B serice@uillinois.edu
RICE, Sherwin .... 910-879-5646 332 D srice@bladencc.edu
RICE, Vance .... 662-325-6731 247 F mvr50@msstate.edu
RICE, Whit .... 256-352-8406.... 3 I whit.rice@wallacestate.edu
RICE-SPEARMAN, Lori .. 806-743-2900 451 A lori.ricespearman@ttuhsc.edu
RICELLI, Iliana .... 901-333-5000 425 D iricelli@southwest.tn.edu
RICH, Andrew .... 212-650-5967 293 D arich@ccny.cuny.edu
RICH, Carson, D .... 252-335-3229 341 B cdrich@ecsu.edu
RICH, Forrest .... 912-583-3146 116 E frich@bpc.edu
RICH, Frank .... 432-335-6507 441 A frich@odessa.edu
RICH, Jack, W .... 325-674-2013 428 F richj@acu.edu
RICH, Jason .... 518-783-2302 315 E jrich@siena.edu
RICH, Julie .... 801-626-6232 461 A jrich@weber.edu
RICH, Kathy .... 781-280-3501 215 B richk@middlesex.mass.edu
RICH, Laura .... 910-893-4364 327 D richl@campbell.edu
RICH, Marcus .... 252-985-5176 339 D mritch@ncwc.edu
RICH, Robbie .... 706-379-3111 128 C crich@yhc.edu
RICH, Scott .... 620-278-4213 177 H srich@sterling.edu
RICH, Steve, W .... 217-581-6616 137 E swrich@eiu.edu
RICH, Steven .... 617-236-8800 209 G srich@fisher.edu
RICH, Teresa .... 509-574-4667 486 D thollandrich@yvcc.edu
RICH, Virginia .... 973-618-3516 276 D vrich@caldwell.edu
RICH, Wendall .... 801-626-7443 461 A wrich@weber.edu
RICHARD, Alison, A ...... 570-372-4111 398 F arichard@susqu.edu
RICHARD, Ann-Marie .... 212-517-2771 315 G a.richard@sia.edu
RICHARD, Arthur .... 252-940-6210 332 C arthur.richard@beaufortccc.edu
RICHARD, Daryl .... 203-582-8651.. 88 G daryl.richard@quinnipiac.edu
RICHARD, Deborah .... 407-708-2487 108 D richardd@seminolestate.edu
RICHARD, Guy .... 770-852-8884 248 F grichard@rts.edu
RICHARD, Mark .... 256-840-4110.... 3 F mark.richard@snead.edu
RICHARD, Mark .... 205-665-6612.... 8 D mrichard11@montevallo.edu
RICHARD, Patricia .... 775-784-4805 271 E prichard@unr.edu
RICHARD, Reed .... 409-984-6252 449 I richardrj@lamarpa.edu
RICHARD, Renee .... 216-987-4865 351 E renee.richard@tri-c.edu
RICHARD, Robert .... 337-482-6923 193 B bookstore@louisiana.edu
RICHARD, Ryan, W .... 318-257-3693 192 D richard@latech.edu
RICHARD, Stephen .... 757-446-7165 466 D richarsw@evms.edu
RICHARD, Susan .... 337-482-6396 193 B smr@louisiana.edu
RICHARD, Valerie .... 704-403-3507 327 C valerie.richard@atriumhealth.org
RICHARDS, Caroline, B 404-880-6146 117 C crichards@cau.edu
RICHARDS, Chris .... 207-561-1619 196 G christopher.michael.richards@maine.edu
RICHARDS, Chris .... 715-346-3908 497 A crichards@uwsp.edu
RICHARDS, David .... 559-453-7195.. 43 A david.richards@fresno.edu
RICHARDS, David, E ..... 402-554-2640 270 A derichards@unomaha.edu
RICHARDS, Debbie .... 304-424-8201 490 F debbie.richards@wvup.edu
RICHARDS, Debra .... 480-212-1704.. 15 O
RICHARDS, E. Randolph .... 561-803-2058 105 C randy_richards@pba.edu
RICHARDS, Faith .... 605-455-6029 415 H frichards@olc.edu
RICHARDS, Geoffrey ..... 512-499-4336 454 H grichards@utsystem.edu
RICHARDS, Glenn .... 517-990-1453 225 E richardglennr@jccmi.edu
RICHARDS, Gwyn .... 812-855-2435 156 G grichar@indiana.edu
RICHARDS, Heraldo ...... 615-963-5620 426 A hrichards@tnstate.edu
RICHARDS, Jeni .... 949-376-6000.. 47 D jrichards@lcad.edu
RICHARDS, Jerry .... 920-924-3184 499 D jrichards2@morainepark.edu
RICHARDS, John .... 808-734-9518 129 H john.richards@hawaii.edu
RICHARDS, Kathy, A ..... 906-227-1237 228 I kathrich@nmu.edu
RICHARDS, Katie, J ...... 701-788-4675 345 D katie.richards.2@mayvillestate.edu
RICHARDS, Lee .... 740-362-3344 355 H lrichards@mtso.edu
RICHARDS, Lisa .... 508-565-1085 219 A lrichards@stonehill.edu
RICHARDS, Marilyn ...... 919-546-8529 340 B marilyn.richards@shawu.edu
RICHARDS, Mark .... 206-543-7632 485 A provost@uw.edu
RICHARDS, Mark, A ...... 801-524-8107 459 E mrichards@ldsbc.edu
RICHARDS, Marvin .... 805-969-3626.. 55 J mrichards@pacifica.edu
RICHARDS, Maryanne ... 508-830-5039 213 D mrichards@maritime.edu
RICHARDS, Matthew ..... 207-741-5927 195 H mrichards@smccme.edu
RICHARDS, Melissa ...... 315-859-4019 300 H mfrichar@hamilton.edu
RICHARDS, Michael ...... 505-272-1175 288 J mrichards@salud.unm.edu
RICHARDS, Michael, J .. 515-281-3934 163 F
RICHARDS, Michelle ..... 801-618-0438 458 G mrichards@ameritech.edu
RICHARDS, Paula .... 559-297-4500.. 45 N prichards@iot.edu
RICHARDS, Rosalie .... 386-822-7256 112 A rrichar1@stetson.edu
RICHARDS, Rosann .... 973-353-5943 282 B rcarey@newark.rutgers.edu
RICHARDS, Samantha ... 843-574-6771 412 I samantha.richards@tridenttech.edu
RICHARDS, Sandra, K ... 800-328-2660.. 95 P skrichards@baptistcollege.edu
RICHARDS, Scott .... 412-396-5140 383 A richards@duq.edu
RICHARDS, Seth .... 732-987-2541 278 A srichards@georgian.edu
RICHARDS, Steve .... 320-762-4692 237 C stever@alextech.edu
RICHARDS, Steven, N ... 540-863-2880 473 F srichards@dslcc.edu
RICHARDS, Terri .... 386-738-6682 112 A trichard@stetson.edu
RICHARDS, Terry .... 410-837-4772 204 F trichards@ubalt.edu
RICHARDS, Tom, F .... 573-882-2612 260 I richardstf@umsystem.edu
RICHARDS, Tracey .... 610-799-1779 388 D trichards1@lccc.edu
RICHARDS, Troy .... 212-217-7665 299 D troy_richards@fitnyc.edu
RICHARDS, Virginia ...... 925-473-1350.. 40 D vrichards@losmedanos.edu
RICHARDS, Virginia ...... 317-805-1783 487 I vrichards@salemu.edu
RICHARDSON, Aaron .... 601-979-3704 246 F aaron.richardson@jsums.edu
RICHARDSON, Andrea .. 334-285-5177.... 2 F andrea.richardson@istc.edu
RICHARDSON, Ann .... 206-934-4567 483 B ann.richardson@seattlecolleges.edu
RICHARDSON, Antoine, D .... 816-333-1577 251 C
RICHARDSON, Autumn . 256-766-6610.... 5 E arichardson@hcu.edu
RICHARDSON, Barbara . 520-586-1981.. 11 M richardsonbarbara@cochise.edu
RICHARDSON, Belinda, M .... 724-287-8711 379 E belinda.richardson@bc3.edu
RICHARDSON, Bernard, L .... 202-806-7280.. 92 F brichardson@howard.edu
RICHARDSON, Beverly .. 501-375-9845.. 20 F brichardson@philander.edu
RICHARDSON, Bonita L 412-237-4413 381 D brichardson@ccac.edu
RICHARDSON, Brenda .. 912-478-4636 120 C brendarichardson@georgiasouthern.edu
RICHARDSON, Brittany . 504-816-4797 186 I brichardson@dillard.edu
RICHARDSON, Casie ..... 270-824-8575 182 D casie.richardson@kctcs.edu
RICHARDSON, Christopher .... 804-355-0671 471 J crichardson@upsem.edu
RICHARDSON, Cinzia .... 973-720-2976 284 J richardsonc@wpunj.edu
RICHARDSON, Dale .... 636-481-3501 254 C drichar6@jeffco.edu
RICHARDSON, David .... 256-726-7398.... 6 C drichardson@oakwood.edu

RICHARDSON, David, E 352-392-0780 111 A
der@ufl.edu
RICHARDSON, Dawn, J 972-377-1015 433 I
drichardson@collin.edu
RICHARDSON, Debra .... 406-683-7530 264 A
debra.richardson@umwestern.edu
RICHARDSON, Denise ... 510-531-4911.. 57 C
drichardson@peralta.edu
RICHARDSON, Edie .... 830-372-8016 449 A
erichardson@tlu.edu
RICHARDSON, Ellis .... 413-236-1011 214 A
erichardson@berkshirecc.edu
RICHARDSON, Erica ...... 903-675-6371 451 F
erica.richardson@tvcc.edu
RICHARDSON, Florence 301-295-3045 503 C
florence.richardson@usuhs.edu
RICHARDSON, Greer ..... 215-951-1806 387 A
richards@lasalle.edu
RICHARDSON, Greg, C . 606-474-3250 181 B
greg@kcu.edu
RICHARDSON, Guy, L ... 601-923-1650 248 F
grichardson@rts.edu
RICHARDSON, James ... 509-682-6400 485 H
jrichardson@wvc.edu
RICHARDSON, Jennifer . 518-454-2023 296 G
richardj@strose.edu
RICHARDSON, Joe, C ... 407-582-3351 113 I
jrichardson64@valenciacollege.edu
RICHARDSON, John ..... 706-771-4111 115 J
jhrichar@augustatech.edu
RICHARDSON, Josiah ... 907-745-3201.... 9 C
RICHARDSON, Julie ...... 413-782-3111 220 A
RICHARDSON, K. Scott . 724-287-8711 379 E
scott.richardson@bc3.edu
RICHARDSON, Karen .... 609-258-6150 280 D
karenr@princeton.edu
RICHARDSON, Karry, D 573-629-3016 253 J
krichardson@hlg.edu
RICHARDSON, Kathleen 515-271-2295 165 J
kathleen.richardson@drake.edu
RICHARDSON, Kathy, B 724-946-7130 402 D
richarkb@westminster.edu
RICHARDSON, Keith ..... 215-646-7300 385 A
RICHARDSON, Keith ..... 215-489-2397 382 B
keith.richardson@delval.edu
RICHARDSON, Kevin ..... 803-934-3242 410 G
krichardson@morris.edu
RICHARDSON, Krista .... 419-995-8312 360 C
richardson.k@rhodesstate.edu
RICHARDSON, L. Song . 949-824-4158.. 69 D
srichardson@law.uci.edu
RICHARDSON, L. Song . 719-389-6000.. 78 I
RICHARDSON, Lara, K .. 803-938-3890 413 G
painterl@uscsumter.edu
RICHARDSON, Lisa, A .. 727-816-3404 105 F
richarl@phsc.edu
RICHARDSON, Lyneene 515-643-6659 168 D
lrichardson@mercydesmoines.org
RICHARDSON, Lynne .... 914-633-2256 302 E
lrichardson@iona.edu
RICHARDSON, Mary ..... 229-430-3588 114 I
mrichardson@albanytech.edu
RICHARDSON, Melanie . 360-438-4367 482 I
mrichardson@stmartin.edu
RICHARDSON, Melissa . 503-594-3300 372 C
melissa.richardson@clackamas.edu
RICHARDSON, Nicholas 718-420-4124 324 F
nrichard@wagner.edu
RICHARDSON,
Raymond .... 806-720-7230 439 D
raymond.richardson@lcu.edu
RICHARDSON, Rebecca 707-545-3647.. 26 H
becca@berginu.edu
RICHARDSON, Robert ... 317-955-6789 159 K
rrichardson@marian.edu
RICHARDSON, Robin .... 401-232-6000 404 A
rarich@bryant.edu
RICHARDSON,
Sarah, D .... 402-280-2703 266 H
sarahrichardson@creighton.edu
RICHARDSON, Scott ..... 607-587-3992 319 F
richarsa@alfredstate.edu
RICHARDSON, Scott ..... 281-283-2305 452 E
richardsons@uhcl.edu
RICHARDSON, Stephen . 312-329-4243 144 I
stephen.richardson@moody.edu
RICHARDSON, Steven ... 801-626-6001 461 A
stevenrichardson1@weber.edu
RICHARDSON, Sydney .. 336-734-7764 334 F
srichardson@forsythtech.edu
RICHARDSON, Tammi ... 660-263-4100 257 B
tamerarichardson@macc.edu
RICHARDSON, TaNeal ... 432-264-5072 437 F
trichardson@howardcollege.edu
RICHARDSON, Terry ..... 276-944-6231 466 L
trichard@ehc.edu
RICHARDSON,
Theodore .... 321-674-8123 100 C
trichardson@fit.edu
RICHARDSON,
Thomas, J .... 717-871-7085 395 A
tom.richardson@millersville.edu
RICHARDSON, Timothy . 281-283-3044 452 E
richardsont@uhcl.edu
RICHARDSON, Toni .... 843-661-8341 409 F
toni.richardson@fdtc.edu
RICHARDSON, Tracey ... 562-985-4162.. 31 D
tracey.richardson@csulb.edu
RICHARDSON, Trevor ... 405-744-5458 367 G
trevor.richardson@okstate.edu
RICHARDSON, Vanessa 575-674-2396 285 L
vrichardson@burrell.edu
RICHARDSON, Victoria . 256-469-7333.... 5 H
librn@hbc1.edu
RICHARDSON, W. Mark 510-204-0733.. 36 I
mrichardson@cdsp.edu
RICHARDSON,
William "Rusty" .... 615-547-1257 419 C
rrichardson@cumberland.edu
RICHARDSON, William . 225-578-4161 189 E
brichardson@lsu.edu
RICHARDSON-DEAN,
Tonya .... 903-670-2615 451 F
tonya.dean@tvcc.edu
RICHARDSON-ECHOLS,
Mya .... 678-466-5478 117 D
tomiiyarichardson@clayton.edu
RICHARDSON-WILKS,
Pamela .... 904-470-8012.. 98 L
p.wilks@ewc.edu
RICHART, Maria .... 585-475-5479 312 F
mjroce@rit.edu
RICHE, Cindy .... 206-934-3930 483 A
cindy.riche@seattlecolleges.edu
RICHE, Cindy .... 206-934-3930 483 B
cindy.riche@seattlecolleges.edu
RICHEMOND, Donna ..... 215-751-8131 381 I
drichemond@ccp.edu
RICHERSON, Melissa .... 805-546-3129.. 40 F
melissa_richerson@cuesta.edu
RICHES, Jonathan, S .... 610-292-9852 396 J
jonathan.riches@reseminary.edu
RICHEY, Angie .... 909-599-5433.. 48 A
arichey@lifepacific.edu
RICHEY, Anthony .... 334-244-3571.... 4 E
arichey@aum.edu
RICHEY, Barbara .... 509-359-7099 479 G
brichey@ewu.edu
RICHEY, D. Michael ...... 859-257-3911 185 F
mrichey@email.uky.edu
RICHEY, Deborah .... 518-629-4552 302 C
d.richey@hvcc.edu
RICHEY, James, H .... 321-433-7000.. 98 I
richeyj@easternflorida.edu
RICHEY, Jim .... 903-510-2468 452 A
jric@tjc.edu
RICHEY, Lance, B .... 260-399-7700 162 B
lrichey@sf.edu
RICHEY, Melody, H ...... 901-843-3730 423 A
richey@rhodes.edu
RICHEY, Patrick .... 585-389-2020 307 F
prichey1@naz.edu
RICHIE, Darren .... 863-638-2953 114 B
richieda@webber.edu
RICHIE, Darren .... 803-754-4100 408 E
RICHMAN, Aaron .... 231-773-9131 228 G
RICHMAN, Erin .... 904-256-6984 101 B
erin.richman@fscj.edu
RICHMAN, John .... 701-671-2221 346 D
john.richman@ndscs.edu
RICHMAN, Lawrence ..... 916-339-7371.. 53 C
RICHMAN, Susan .... 781-891-2660 206 G
srichman@bentley.edu
RICHMOND, Jayne, E .... 401-874-5505 405 E
jrichmond@uri.edu
RICHMOND, John, W ... 940-565-4092 453 E
john.richmond@unt.edu
RICHMOND, Kenyetta ... 336-757-7242 334 F
krichmond@forsythtech.edu
RICHMOND, Kerry .... 570-321-4202 389 B
richmond@lycoming.edu
RICHMOND,
LÆTanya, B .... 413-585-4940 218 H
lrichmon@smith.edu
RICHMOND, Michael ..... 209-946-2777.. 71 E
mrichmond@pacific.edu
RICHMOND, Michael .... 425-739-8428 481 C
michael.richmond@lwtech.edu
RICHMOND, Nicola .... 520-206-4414.. 15 B
ncrichmond@pima.edu
RICHMOND, Peggy .... 603-358-2273 274 H
mrichmon@keene.edu
RICHMOND, Randale .... 330-672-3120 354 A
rrichmo2@kent.edu
RICHMOND, Sandra, L . 570-326-3761 392W
slr8@pct.edu
RICHMOND, Sevanna ... 866-323-0233.. 58 D
RICHMOND, Theresa .... 530-938-5317.. 39 C
trichmond@siskiyous.edu
RICHNER, Gabriel .... 417-862-9533 253 F
RICHTER, Carmen .... 256-765-5215.... 8 E
crichter@una.edu
RICHTER, Jeffrey .... 610-282-1100 382 C
jeff.richter@desales.edu
RICHTER, Jerome, J ...... 701-355-8072 347 C
jjrichter@umary.edu
RICHTER, Kayla .... 507-223-1326 239 F
kayla.richter@mnwest.edu
RICHTER, Sheila, W ...... 814-824-2287 389 G
srichter@mercyhurst.edu
RICHTER, Thomas, P .... 920-923-7640 493 D
tprichter32@marianuniversity.edu
RICHTERMEYER,
Sandra .... 978-934-2850 212 B
sandra_richtermeyer@uml.edu
RICHTMAN, Meg .... 319-385-6212 167 H
meg.richtman@iw.edu
RICK, Adam .... 517-607-2645 225 C
arick@hillsdale.edu
RICK, Jennifer .... 216-397-1905 353 O
jrick@jcu.edu
RICKARD, Walter .... 718-636-3771 311 F
wrickard@pratt.edu
RICKARDS, Brenden ...... 856-415-2106 281 D
brickar1@rcsj.edu
RICKARDS, Laura .... 732-255-0400 279 F
lrickards@ocean.edu
RICKEL, Brian .... 916-691-7171.. 50 H
rickelb@crc.losrios.edu
RICKELS, Clarissa .... 541-888-2525 376 C
clarissa.rickels@socc.edu
RICKENBACKER,
Millicent .... 903-593-8311 448 G
mrickenbacker@texascollege.edu
RICKENBAKER,
Monique .... 803-705-4655 406 G
monique.rickenbaker@benedict.edu
RICKENBERG, Cassie .... 419-267-1319 357 E
crickenberg@northweststate.edu
RICKENBERG, Jason ..... 419-267-1258 357 E
jrickenberg@northweststate.edu
RICKER, Charlie .... 812-877-8470 160 F
ricker@rose-hulman.edu
RICKER, Deborah .... 301-696-3623 199 E
ricker@hood.edu
RICKER, Frances .... 303-369-5151.. 82 I
fran.ricker@plattcolorado.edu
RICKER, Jean .... 781-292-2343 210 A
jean.ricker@olin.edu
RICKER-GILBERT,
Alexander .... 904-256-7401 102 H
aricker1@ju.edu
RICKERT, Christina .... 715-346-0123 497 A
RICKETT, Robert, B .... 314-773-0083 250 I
brickett@brookes.edu
RICKETTS, Lloyd .... 609-771-2186 276 I
ricketts@tcnj.edu
RICKETTS, Nsombi, B ... 718-687-5350 311 F
nrickett@pratt.edu
RICKEY, Ron .... 413-254-2520 208 E
rickeyron@elms.edu
RICKLES, Jeff .... 601-968-8875 245 B
jrickles@belhaven.edu
RICKMAN, Blake .... 479-788-7029.. 21 G
blake.rickman@uafs.edu
RICKMAN, Richard .... 229-333-5886 127 E
RICKS, Chris .... 757-569-6722 474 H
cricks@pdc.edu
RICKS, Mary .... 731-286-3290 424 D
ricks@dscc.edu
RICKS, Melissa, K .... 479-248-7236.. 19 B
mricks@ecollege.edu
RICKS, Naima, K .... 973-290-4219 282 I
nricks@steu.edu
RICKS, Ruchelle .... 252-862-1246 337 C
rricks@roanokechowan.edu
RICKS, Sonya .... 336-517-2104 327 A
sricks@bennett.edu
RICKS, Warren .... 214-768-2083 444 D
wricks@smu.edu
RICKSECKEER, Anne ...... 575-439-3717 287 D
anricks@nmsu.edu
RICKUS, Jenna .... 765-494-4600 160 B
RICO, Antonio .... 915-779-8031 457 F
RICO, Camilla .... 360-417-6442 482 C
crico@pencol.edu
RICO-GUTIERREZ,
Luis, C .... 515-294-7427 163 G
lrico@iastate.edu
RICORDATI, Timothy ..... 630-617-3089 137 G
timothy.ricordati@elmhurst.edu
RICZKER, Nickey .... 716-338-1035 303 A
nickeyriczker@mail.sunyjcc.edu
RICZKER, Nicolette .... 716-338-1035 303 A
nickeyriczker@mail.sunyjcc.edu
RIDD-YOUNG, Kristi ...... 866-680-2756 459 G
president@midwifery.edu
RIDDELL, William .... 209-476-7840.. 67 E
w.riddell@clc.edu
RIDDELL, William .... 209-476-7840.. 67 E
wriddell@clc.edu
RIDDICK, Althea, A .... 252-335-8787 341 B
aariddick@ecsu.edu
RIDDICK, Iman .... 202-462-2101.. 93 A
iriddick@iwp.edu
RIDDICK, Rich .... 308-635-6067 270 C
riddickr@wncc.edu
RIDDICK, Vera, E .... 757-683-3689 469 B
vriddick@odu.edu
RIDDLE, Alan .... 716-375-2068 313 C
ariddle@sbu.edu
RIDDLE, Brian, T .... 724-589-2130 399 D
briddle@thiel.edu
RIDDLE, Catherine .... 518-262-3593 289 L
riddlec@amc.edu
RIDDLE, Christy .... 662-846-4336 245 G
criddle@deltastate.edu
RIDDLE, Heather .... 612-330-1177 234 A
riddle@augsburg.edu
RIDDLE, Joyce, E .... 304-462-6184 489 L
joyce.riddle@glenville.edu
RIDDLE, Kelley .... 575-538-6513 289 G
kelley.riddle@wnmu.edu
RIDDLE, Tiffany .... 509-777-4542 486 C
triddle@whitworth.edu
RIDEAUX, JR., Laarry ... 816-604-3044 255 G
larry.rideaux@mcckc.edu
RIDEAUX, Larry .... 816-604-3046 255 C
larry.rideaux@mcckc.edu
RIDEN, Ronda .... 918-338-8000 369 B
rriden@rsu.edu
RIDENER, Barbara .... 908-737-5326 278 E
bridener@kean.edu
RIDENOUR, Nancy .... 314-362-6289 253 G
nancy.ridenour@barnesjewishcollege.edu
RIDEOUT, Junior .... 910-879-5661 332 D
jrideout@bladencc.edu
RIDEOUT, Kathy 585-275-8902 323M
kathy_rideout@urmc.rochester.edu
RIDER, Abigail .... 401-874-2433 405 E
arider@uri.edu
RIDER, David, R .... 201-200-2070 279 D
drider@njcu.edu
RIDER,
Elizabeth (Betty) .... 717-361-1333 383 C
riderea@etown.edu
RIDER, Jeff .... 870-759-4194.. 23 J
jrider@williamsbu.edu
RIDER, Pamela, S .... 605-342-0317 415 C
registrar@jwc.edu
RIDER, Paul .... 515-263-2917 166 F
prider@grandview.edu
RIDER, William .... 360-532-9020 480 G
RIDGE, Matthew .... 336-249-8186 334 B
mridge5374@davidsondavie.edu
RIDGE, Sean .... 865-573-4517 420 E
sridge@johnsonu.edu
RIDGEDELL, Ken, W ...... 985-549-3856 193 A
kridgedell@selu.edu
RIDGES, Jarvis .... 404-270-5003 126 B
jarvis.ridges@spelman.edu
RIDGWAY, Dan .... 216-649-7525 354 A
dridgway@kent.edu
RIDGWAY, Kristi .... 650-574-6161.. 62 K
RIDGWAY, Lori .... 307-855-2103 501 A
lridgway@cwc.edu
RIDGWAY, Timothy .... 605-357-1309 416 D
med@usd.edu
RIDINGTON, Tom .... 610-341-1955 383 B
tom.ridington@eastern.edu

RIDLER, Chris 253-589-5529 478 J chris.ridler@cptc.edu
RIDLEY, Ellen 207-221-4419 197 E eridley@une.edu
RIDLEY, Tim 661-654-2066 30 B tridley1@csub.edu
RIDLEY, Wadell 610-660-1223 397 G wridley@sju.edu
RIDPATH, Kathy, T 540-674-3601 474 E kridpath@nr.edu
RIDPATH, Lance 304-647-6424 490 C lridpath@osteo.wvsom.edu
RIDPATH, Lisa 540-857-6310 475 G lridpath@virginiawestern.edu
RIDPATH, Tanya 540-375-2323 470 E ridpath@roanoke.edu
RIDSDALE, Carol 303-329-6355 79 L
RIEBAU, Brett 330-569-5119 353 G riebaub@hiram.edu
RIEBE, Thomas 317-921-4562 158 D triebe@ivytech.edu
RIECKER, Robin 315-866-0300 301 D rieckerra@herkimer.edu
RIEDEL, Eric 651-779-3200 237 H
RIEDEL, Martin 847-735-5055 142 A riedel@lakeforest.edu
RIEDEL CARNEY, Elizabeth 651-690-6836 243 A eacarney@stkate.edu
RIEDER, Andy 303-765-3189 81 G areider@iliff.edu
RIEDL-FARREY, Cathy, J 608-342-1435 496 E riedlfac@uwplatt.edu
RIEDMILLER, Doug 866-582-8448 108 B
RIEG, Sue 724-357-2400 394 C sue.rieg@iup.edu
RIEGER, Jim 800-477-2254 29 G jrieger@calsouthern.edu
RIEGER, Mark 239-590-7000 109 K mrieger@fgcu.edu
RIEHL, Greg 503-338-2432 372 D griehl@clatsopcc.edu
RIEKEMAN, Guy, F 770-426-2601 122 C riekeman@life.edu
RIEKERT, Jennifer 914-594-4536 309 B jennifer_riekert@nymc.edu
RIELLO, Heidi 413-662-5331 213 C heidi.riello@mcla.edu
RIEMAN, Jeff, A 419-772-3100 358 C j-rieman@onu.edu
RIENDEAU, Jason 203-931-2920 89 H jriendeau@newhaven.edu
RIERA, José-Luis 302-831-8116 91 C jriera@udel.edu
RIES, Carl 413-559-5528 210 D cmrtr@hampshire.edu
RIES, Heidi, R 937-255-3636 502 C heidi.ries@afit.edu
RIES, Tressa, C 320-308-3917 240 I tressa.ries@stcloudstate.edu
RIESNER, Robert 443-885-1552 201 A robert.riesner@morgan.edu
RIESTER, Melanie 919-536-7200 334 C riesterm@durhamtech.edu
RIESTERER, Brenda 920-693-1140 498 H brenda.riesterer@gotoltc.edu
RIESTRA, Liza 787-841-2000 509 J liza_riestra@pucpr.edu
RIESTRA, Miguel, A 787-622-8000 511 D mriestra@pupr.edu
RIESTRA-FERNANDEZ, Miguel, A 787-622-8000 511 D racosta@pupr.edu
RIETHLE, Theresa 413-565-1000 206 D triethle@baypath.edu
RIEVES, Jimmy 903-988-7536 438 F jrieves@kilgore.edu
RIEWERTS, Jaime 847-925-6368 138 G jriewert@harpercollege.edu
RIFFE, Kelley 912-443-4175 125 B kriffe@savannahtech.edu
RIFFLE, Dennis 904-596-2416 112 F driffle@tbc.org
RIGBY, Melissa, C 410-951-3848 204 B mrigby@coppin.edu
RIGDON, Kaley 563-588-6300 164 E
RIGGERT, Mark 402-557-7070 265 J bubookstore@fheg.follett.com
RIGGINS, Darius 661-654-3277 30 B driggins@csub.edu
RIGGINS, Erin 228-897-4357 247 E erin.riggins@mgccc.edu
RIGGINS, Vanessa 323-563-4842 36 C vanessariggins@cdrewu.edu
RIGGLE, Andy 866-776-0331 54 D briggle@ncu.edu
RIGGLE, Krystle 618-544-8657 139 G rigglek@iecc.edu
RIGGLE, Ron 217-786-2581 143 B ron.riggle@llcc.edu
RIGGLE YOUNG, Tracy 412-924-1423 396 F triggleyoung@pts.edu
RIGGS, Allen 435-283-7125 461 B allen.riggs@snow.edu
RIGGS, Angela 619-216-6629 66 A ariggs@swccd.edu
RIGGS, Bonnie 423-697-4465 424 A bonnie.riggs@chattanoogastate.edu
RIGGS, Dave 217-732-3168 142 G
RIGGS, David 765-677-2808 158 B david.riggs@indwes.edu
RIGGS, Eric 707-826-3256 33 C eric.riggs@humboldt.edu
RIGGS, Marie, A 517-230-0720 225 A mriggs@glcc.edu
RIGGS, Michelle 909-389-3391 60 E mriggs@craftonhills.edu
RIGGS, Paul 570-408-4600 403 A paul.riggs@wilkes.edu
RIGGS, Robert, F 214-887-5007 435 F rriggs@dts.edu
RIGGS, Wayne 850-201-8071 99 E wriggs@flagler.edu
RIGGS-GELASCO, Pamela 423-425-4704 427 C pam-gelasco@utc.edu
RIGGS-JOHNSON, Kaydee 620-229-6343 177 G kaydee.riggsjohnson@sckans.edu
RIGLING, Brian 937-775-5007 364 E brian.rigling@wright.edu
RIGNEY, Dawn 212-938-5601 319 E drigney@sunyopt.edu
RIGNEY, Joseph 612-455-3420 234 E joe.rigney@bcsmn.edu
RIGSBEE, Craig 530-895-2476 27 C rigsbeecr@butte.edu
RIGSBEE, Jason 912-525-5000 124 I jrigsbee@scad.edu
RIGSBY, Tawny 918-631-2315 371 C tawny-rigsby@utulsa.edu
RIHANEK, Christie 660-284-4800 254 B registrar@heartlandcollege.edu
RIHL LEWINSKY, Elizabeth, A 610-660-1346 397 G lewinsky@sju.edu
RIIS, Janet 406-447-5423 263 B jriis@carroll.edu
RIKALO, Heather 775-445-3241 271 F heather.rikalo@wnc.edu
RIKARD, Christy 912-486-7607 123 J crikard@ogeecheetech.edu
RIKARD, Jennifer 619-594-5220 33 D jrikard@sdsu.edu
RIKEL, Randy 806-651-2095 448 B rrikel@wtamu.edu
RIKER, David, J 210-458-6143 455 E dave.riker@utsa.edu
RILEY, Alyssa 641-782-1422 170 F ariley@swcciowa.edu
RILEY, Anne 617-287-6809 211 H anne.riley@umb.edu
RILEY, Brett 509-682-6515 485 H briley@wvc.edu
RILEY, Chris 325-674-2918 428 F cmr97t@acu.edu
RILEY, Connie 870-574-4499 21 D criley@sautech.edu
RILEY, Dean 281-649-3182 437 B driley@hbu.edu
RILEY, Doreen 216-397-4345 353 O driley@jcu.edu
RILEY, Edward 617-254-2610 218 E rev.edward.riley@sjs.edu
RILEY, Jan 334-222-6591 2 I jriley@lbwcc.edu
RILEY, Jeanette, E 401-874-2566 405 E jen_riley@uri.edu
RILEY, Jill 931-540-2573 424 C jriley9@columbiastate.edu
RILEY, Joanne 617-287-5927 211 H joanne.riley@umb.edu
RILEY, Karen 303-871-3665 84 E kriley@du.edu
RILEY, Lisa 784-682-6017 271 E lriley@unr.edu
RILEY, Lori 970-351-1890 84 F
RILEY, Mark 850-644-3500 110 C mriley@admin.fsu.edu
RILEY, Marty 423-461-8736 422 E mjriley@milligan.edu
RILEY, Marty 252-334-2025 331 F marty.riley@macuniversity.edu
RILEY, Mike 209-228-4073 70 A mriley5@ucmerced.edu
RILEY, Monica 479-788-7912 21 G monica.riley@uafs.edu
RILEY, Nicole 815-394-5111 148 D nriley@rockford.edu
RILEY, Patricia, L 410-334-2853 205 D priley@worwic.edu
RILEY, Ray 904-725-0525 97 P
RILEY, Rebecca 936-273-7222 439 C rebecca.riley@lonestar.edu
RILEY, Rhonda 913-971-3296 176 C rgriley@mnu.edu
RILEY, Robert 718-940-5796 314 A rriley@sjcny.edu
RILEY, Robert 803-376-5714 406 D
RILEY, Sarah 900-652-6176 35 L sarah.riley@chaffey.edu
RILEY, Scott 920-206-2349 493 C scott.riley@mbu.edu
RILEY, Shanda 972-780-3600 454 A shanda.riley@untdallas.edu
RILEY, Sharon 405-422-1255 369 A sharon.riley@redlandscc.edu
RILEY, Shawn, D 610-292-9852 396 J bookkeeping@reseminary.edu
RILEY, Stacy 402-761-8270 269 C sriley@southeast.edu
RILEY, Susan 513-732-5324 362 B susan.riley@uc.edu
RILEY, Tammy 409-984-6237 449 I rileytl@lamarpa.edu
RILEY, Terisa, C 479-788-7007 21 G terisa.riley@uafs.edu
RILEY, Tom 617-747-2218 206 H triley@berklee.edu
RILEY, Toni 907-564-8300 9 F triley@alaskapacific.edu
RILEY, Toni 312-567-5239 140 A triley6@iit.edu
RILEY, Tracey 617-994-4276 219 B triley@suffolk.edu
RILEY, Wanda, L 404-413-1310 120 E wriley2@gsu.edu
RILEY, Warren 504-671-5468 188 B wriley@dcc.edu
RILEY, Wayne, J 718-270-2611 317 B presidentoffice@downstate.edu
RILEY, Wendell 318-797-5108 190 A wendell.riley@lsus.edu
RILING, Dean 801-618-0438 458 G driling@ameritech.edu
RILL, Ann 812-221-1714 162 E annmarierill@vbc.edu
RILL, Josef 303-458-1638 83 E jrill@regis.edu
RILLEY, Karin 570-577-2000 379 C kwr006@bucknell.edu
RIMANDO-CHAREUNSAP, Rosie 206-934-5311 483 D rosie.rimando@seattlecolleges.edu
RIMANDO-CHAREUNSAP, Rosie 206-934-5311 483 A rosie.rimando@seattlecolleges.edu
RIMAR, Mark 314-977-3529 259 F mark.rimar@slu.edu
RIMER, Barbara, K 919-966-3215 342 C brimer@unc.edu
RIMIRCH, Bruce 680-488-2471 505 B brucer@palau.edu
RIMLER, Jesse 510-845-5373 29 B
RIMPFEL, Callie 570-674-8318 390 B crimpfel@misericordia.edu
RINALDI WINN, Mary 404-364-8412 123 K mrinaldi@oglethorpe.edu
RINARD, Patrick 727-341-3064 107 E rinard.patrick@spcollege.edu
RINCONES, Daniel 913-971-3522 176 C dsrincones@mnu.edu
RINE, Veronica 740-755-7600 349 F rine.60@cotc.edu
RINEHART, Amelia 304-293-8180 490 E amelia.rinehart@mail.wvu.edu
RINEHART, Kent, W 845-575-3000 305 D kent.rinehart@marist.edu
RINEHART, Michelle 404-894-3380 119 E michelle.rinehart@design.gatech.edu
RINEHART, Todd 303-871-3125 84 E todd.rinehart@du.edu
RINER, Meg 540-828-5636 464 L mriner@bridgewater.edu
RINEY, OSU, Judith, N 270-686-4288 179 J judith.riney@brescia.edu
RING, Andrea 785-227-3380 172 A ringan@bethanylb.edu
RING, Jackie 856-256-5153 281 F ring@rowan.edu
RING, Joshua 828-328-7927 330 F joshua.ring@lr.edu
RING, Neal 864-242-5100 406 H
RING, Patricia 508-793-3459 208 D pring@holycross.edu
RING, Tim 513-585-2402 350 D timothy.ring@thechristcollege.edu
RINGA, Melanie 914-961-8313 314 H mringa@svots.edu
RINGEL, Christopher, J 920-565-1000 493 A ringelcj@lakeland.edu
RINGEN, Kristi 215-637-7700 385 J kringen@holyfamily.edu
RINGHAM, Rebecca 701-858-3126 345 E rebecca.ringham@minotstateu.edu
RINGLE, Martin, D 503-777-7254 375 G martin.ringle@reed.edu
RINGLE, Suzanne 602-286-8110 13 B suzanne.ringle@gwmail.maricopa.edu
RINGLER, Krista 919-515-2866 342 A kmringle@ncsu.edu
RINGO, Chris 318-342-5172 193 C ringo@ulm.edu
RINGO, Teresa 936-294-1061 450 A reg_tat@shsu.edu
RINGWALD, Heather 603-899-4128 273 E ringwaldh@franklinpierce.edu
RINI, Anthony 617-373-5144 217 I
RINK, Jonathan 828-328-7249 330 F jonathan.rink@lr.edu
RINKENBAUGH, Bill 316-322-3297 172 D brinkenb@butlercc.edu
RINKENBAUGH, Heather 316-322-3345 172 D hrinkenb@butlercc.edu
RINKER, Craig 202-687-5867 92 E cmr235@georgetown.edu
RINN, Susan 830-372-8001 449 A srinn@tlu.edu
RINNE, Heather 402-872-2226 268 E hrinne@peru.edu
RIOLA, Allison 303-871-4201 84 E allison.riola@du.edu
RIOPEL, Becky 425-352-8545 478 D rriopel@cascadia.edu
RIOPKO, Colleen 410-617-1466 200 B cmriopko@loyola.edu
RIORDAN, Casey 513-562-6270 347 I casey.riordan@artacademy.edu
RIORDAN, Charles 302-831-4007 91 C riordan@udel.edu
RIORDAN, Christine, M 516-877-3838 289 I cmr@adelphi.edu
RIORDAN, Jason 816-501-4877 258 I jason.riordan@rockhurst.edu
RIORDAN, Kevin 708-596-2000 149 H kriordan@ssc.edu
RIORDAN, Mark, H 607-871-2144 290 B riordan@alfred.edu
RIORDAN, Marsha 641-673-1045 171 C riordanm@wmpenn.edu
RIORDAN, Melissa 909-869-5010 30 A mriordan@cpp.edu
RIORDAN, Phil 630-617-3050 137 G phil.riordan@elmhurst.edu
RIOS, Alfonso 323-415-5368 48 J riosa@elac.edu
RIOS, Angel 787-738-2161 512 C angel.rios7@upr.edu
RIOS, Angela, L 845-431-8953 298 D angela.rios1@sunydutchess.edu
RIOS, Charlene 509-793-2222 478 B charlener@bigbend.edu
RIOS, Charlene 509-793-2020 478 B charlener@bigbend.edu
RIOS, Christina 310-243-3789 30 E crios@csudh.edu
RIOS, Eduardo 718-368-5028 294 E eduardo.rios@kbcc.cuny.edu
RIOS, Efrain 787-844-8181 513 A efrain.rios@upr.edu

RIOS, Esther, A .... 671-735-5544 504 D
financialaid@guamcc.edu
RIOS, Irene .... 631-451-4259 321 D
riosi@sunysuffolk.edu
RIOS, Martha .... 818-364-7612.. 49 C
riosme@lamission.edu
RIOS, Yanel .... 479-394-7622.. 23 C
yrios@uarichmountain.edu
RIOS, Zilka .... 787-798-4050 511 B
zilka.rios@uccaribe.edu
RIOS-COLON,
Cristian, J .... 787-857-3600 507 M
cristianrios@br.inter.edu
RIOS-ELLIS, Britt .... 248-370-2100 229 I
RIOTTO, Karen, M .... 585-395-5484 317 E
kriotto@brockport.edu
RIOUX, Yasmin .... 563-876-3353 165 H
yrioux@dwci.edu
RIPLEY, Anneliese .... 406-683-7309 264 A
anneliese.ripley@umwestern.edu
RIPLEY, Dalie .... 734-432-5827 227 C
deripley@madonna.edu
RIPLEY, Dave .... 701-477-7862 346 J
dripley@tm.edu
RIPLEY, Judith .... 207-795-5974 195 B
ripleyj@mchp.edu
RIPPEE, Rusty .... 870-460-1018.. 22 C
rippee@uamont.edu
RIPPEN, Kelly .... 308-345-8107 267 J
rippenk@mpcc.edu
RIPPETOE, Heather .... 615-353-3636 424 G
heather.rippetoe@nscc.edu
RIPPEY, Sharon, T .... 315-859-4672 300 H
srippey@hamilton.edu
RIPPINGER, Timothy ..... 414-288-4771 493 E
timothy.rippinger@marquette.edu
RIPPLE, Jacob .... 620-227-9349 173 D
jripple@dc3.edu
RIQUELME, Joseph .... 202-885-1000.. 91 F
jriquelme@american.edu
RIQUEZ, Elizabeth .... 646-312-1390 292 L
elizabeth.riquez@baruch.cuny.edu
RISAL, Pri .... 903-468-6041 447 B
pri.risal@tamuc.edu
RISBOSKIN, John .... 570-961-7828 387 B
risboskinj@lackawanna.edu
RISCH, Thomas .... 870-972-3333.. 17 E
trisch@astate.edu
RISCHBIETER, Natalie .... 478-471-2732 122 F
natalie.rischbieter@mga.edu
RISDON, Michelle .... 530-541-4660.. 47 E
risdon@ltcc.edu
RISDON-JACKSON,
Sharlene .... 909-607-7855.. 37 F
srisdon@kgi.edu
RISELEY, Leanne .... 808-455-0440 130 C
leannech@hawaii.edu
RISEMAN, Stacy .... 508-793-2741 208 D
sriseman@holycross.edu
RISHE, Karl .... 989-686-9512 223 J
karlrishe@delta.edu
RISHWORTH, Christie ... 401-456-8520 405 A
crishworth@ric.edu
RISINGER, Jeff .... 979-845-7995 446 F
jrisinger@tamu.edu
RISLEY, Levi .... 479-308-2225.. 17 A
levi.resley@acheedu.org
RISMILLER, Lisa, S .... 937-229-4087 362 C
lrismiller1@udayton.edu
RISO, Kelly-Rue .... 802-728-1211 464 A
kriso@vtc.edu
RISSE, Duane .... 719-502-2403.. 82 E
duane.risse@ppcc.edu
RISSEL, Timothy, O .... 570-326-3761 392 W
tor1@pct.edu
RISSER, Deanna, A .... 574-296-6212 153 F
darisser@ambs.edu
RISSER, Paige .... 574-520-4445 157 E
parisser@iusb.edu
RISSLER, Heather, M .... 641-422-4319 168 G
heather.rissler@niacc.edu
RISSLER, Jacob .... 800-658-4308 267 J
risslerj@mpcc.edu
RISSLER, Jennifer .... 415-749-4586.. 61 C
jrissler@sfai.edu
RITACCO, Kevin .... 508-854-4200 215 F
kritacco@qcc.mass.edu
RITAYIK, Mary .... 845-257-3344 316 E
ritayikm@newpaltz.edu
RITCHEY, Brandon .... 740-474-8896 358 A
britchey@ohiochristian.edu
RITCHEY, Fred, L .... 903-233-4210 439 A
fredritchey@letu.edu
RITCHEY, Mary Kaye ..... 706-886-6831 126 D
mritchey@tfc.edu
RITCHEY, Philip .... 662-685-4771 245 C
pritchey@bmc.edu
RITCHEY, William, V ..... 757-594-7047 465 M
bill.ritchey@cnu.edu
RITCHIE, Chad .... 912-583-3167 116 E
critchie@bpc.edu
RITCHIE, David .... 765-998-5397 161 C
dvritchie@taylor.edu
RITCHIE, Gloria .... 412-809-5100 396 E
ritchie.gloria@ptcollege.edu
RITCHIE, Michael .... 610-282-1100 382 C
michael.ritchie@desales.edu
RITCHIE-MITCHELL,
Kedecia .... 972-773-8300.. 93 H
RITEA, Steve .... 310-825-4796.. 69 E
sritea@stratcomm.ucla.edu
RITENOUR, Lisa, L .... 330-972-6084 361 H
lritenour@uakron.edu
RITER, Jayme, S .... 716-878-4301 317 F
riterjs@buffalostate.edu
RITSCHDORFF, John ..... 845-575-3000 305 D
john.ritschdorff@marist.edu
RITSCHEL-TRIFILO,
Trish .... 806-291-3745 457 I
trifilot@wbu.edu
RITT, Elizabeth .... 630-829-1933 133 E
eritt@ben.edu
RITTENHOUSE, J, N ...... 540-828-5379 464 L
jrittenhouse@bridgewater.edu
RITTENHOUSE, Mary ..... 308-367-4124 270 B
mrittenhouse2@uni.edu
RITTER, Barbara .... 904-256-7859 102 H
britter1@ju.edu
RITTER, Gary .... 314-977-2495 259 F
gary.ritter@slu.edu
RITTER, Gretchen .... 315-443-1870 321 G
RITTER, Gretchen .... 614-292-1667 358 D
ritter.1596@osu.edu
RITTER, Joe .... 606-693-5000 183 C
finaid@kmbc.edu
RITTER, Julie .... 717-338-3007 400 D
jritter@uls.edu
RITTER, Mark .... 864-503-5939 414 A
mritter@uscupstate.edu
RITTER, Michael .... 863-638-2968 114 B
rittermj@webber.edu
RITTER, Pamela, S .... 423-439-4242 419 G
ritterp@etsu.edu
RITTER, Scott .... 608-246-6791 499 A
sritter@madisoncollege.edu
RITTER, Ted, L .... 804-257-5734 476 F
tlritter@vuu.edu
RITTER, Will .... 336-272-7102 329 C
will.ritter@greensboro.edu
RITTER SMITH, Karl ...... 425-388-9211 480 B
kritter@everettcc.edu
RITTERBROWN,
Michael .... 818-240-1000.. 43 G
michaelr@glendale.edu
RITTERBUSCH, Kristen .. 217-641-4314 141 A
kritterbusch@jwcc.edu
RITTLE, Dennis, C .... 620-441-5234 173 C
dennis.rittle@cowley.edu
RITVALSKY, Zachary ..... 717-560-8200 387 E
zritvalsky@lbc.edu
RITZ, David .... 317-632-5553 159 I
dritz@lincolntech.edu
RITZ, Robert, L .... 434-592-4800 468 E
rlritz@liberty.edu
RITZ, Steven .... 831-459-2635.. 71 A
sritz@scipp.ucsc.edu
RITZE, Nancy .... 718-289-5156 293 B
nancy.ritze@bcc.cuny.edu
RITZENHEIN, Donald ...... 586-445-7196 227 B
ritzenheind@macomb.edu
RITZERT, Marcy .... 740-826-8044 356 H
mritzert@muskingum.edu
RITZLINE, Pamela .... 330-490-7446 363 E
pritzline@walsh.edu
RITZMAN, Elizabeth ...... 708-524-6520 137 C
eritzman@dom.edu
RIVALEAU, Susan, A ..... 843-953-4973 408 C
rivaleaus@cofc.edu
RIVARA, Sara .... 503-491-7469 374 B
sara.rivara@mhcc.edu
RIVARD, Dawn .... 715-682-1812 494 G
drivard@northland.edu
RIVARD, Dean .... 903-236-4700 438 D
protect2364700@sdcglobal.net
RIVARD, Mary .... 940-552-6291 457 C
mrivard@vernoncollege.edu
RIVARD, Timothy .... 781-239-2631 214 G
trivard@massbay.edu
RIVAS, Frank .... 787-894-2828 513 C
frank.rivas@upr.edu
RIVAS, Josh .... 209-476-7840.. 67 E
jrivas@clcm.net
RIVAS, Robert .... 432-335-6311 441 A
rrivas@odessa.edu
RIVAS, Rolando .... 704-461-6561 326 L
rolandorivas@bac.edu
RIVAS, Sandra .... 951-571-6214.. 59 B
sandra.rivas@mvc.edu
RIVAS, Tony, A .... 727-816-3403 105 F
rivast@phsc.edu
RIVAULT, Mike .... 985-549-2000 193 A
RIVELAND, Bruce .... 425-739-8164 481 C
bruce.riveland@lwtech.edu
RIVENBARK, Derotha .... 918-463-2931 365 J
derotha.rivenbark@connorsstate.edu
RIVENBURG, Kevin .... 518-694-7183 289 J
kevin.rivenburg@acphs.edu
RIVENES, Teresa .... 503-842-8222 376 E
teresarivenes@tillamookbaycc.edu
RIVERA, Albert .... 609-258-3000 280 D
arivera@princeton.edu
RIVERA, Alexieyi .... 787-879-5270 511 H
alexieyi.rivera@upr.edu
RIVERA, Alfredo .... 787-891-0925 507 K
arivera@aguadilla.inter.edu
RIVERA, Ana, Y .... 787-276-8240 512 B
ana.rivera2@upr.edu
RIVERA, Anitra .... 573-341-4632 261 D
RIVERA, Ann .... 716-896-0700 324 E
riveraar@villa.edu
RIVERA, Anthony .... 787-279-1912 508 A
arivera@bayamon.inter.edu
RIVERA, Anthony, C ..... 419-772-2190 358 C
a-rivera@onu.edu
RIVERA, Arcilia .... 787-864-2222 508 C
arcilia.rivera@guayama.inter.edu
RIVERA, JR., Augustin .. 361-698-1098 435 G
ariverajr@delmar.edu
RIVERA, Basilio .... 787-764-0000 513 B
basilio.rivera@upr.edu
RIVERA, Beatriz .... 787-250-1912 508 D
brivera@metro.inter.edu
RIVERA, Carlos .... 718-319-7968 294 B
carivera@hostos.cuny.edu
RIVERA, Carlos, E .... 787-725-8120 506 M
planificacion@eap.edu
RIVERA, Carmen .... 787-725-6500 505 G
crivera@albizu.edu
RIVERA, Carmen .... 787-850-9301 512 D
carmen.rivera19@upr.edu
RIVERA, Carmen .... 787-250-1912 508 D
crivera@metro.inter.edu
RIVERA, Carmen, J .... 787-743-7979 510 H
ut_crivera@suagm.edu
RIVERA, Daisy .... 787-850-9363 512 D
daisy.rivera3@upr.edu
RIVERA, Daniel .... 651-846-1406 241 E
RIVERA, Dennise 787-288-1118 510
RIVERA, Edwin .... 787-279-1912 508 A
edrivera@bayamon.inter.edu
RIVERA, Eileen .... 787-864-2222 508 C
eileen.rivera@guayama.inter.edu
RIVERA, Elean .... 760-252-2411.. 26 G
erivera@barstow.edu
RIVERA, Eleric .... 787-738-2161 512 G
eleric.rivera@upr.edu
RIVERA, Elsandra .... 787-738-2161 512 G
elsandra.rivera@upr.edu
RIVERA, Enid .... 787-786-3030 511 A
erivera@ucb.edu.pr
RIVERA, Epifanio .... 787-725-6500 505 G
RIVERA, Epifanio .... 787-725-6500 505 G
epirivera@albizu.edu
RIVERA, Francisco .... 787-765-1915 509 B
frivera@opto.inter.edu
RIVERA, Frank .... 949-451-5237.. 65 C
frivera@ivc.edu
RIVERA, George .... 787-250-1912 508 D
griverar@metro.inter.edu
RIVERA, Gisselle .... 787-834-9595 510 D
grivera@uaa.edu
RIVERA, Guillermo .... 305-463-7210.. 98 F
RIVERA, Hannah .... 859-256-3132 181 C
hannah.rivera@kctcs.edu
RIVERA, Jaime .... 787-852-1430 507 C
jaimerivera@hccpr.edu
RIVERA, Janice .... 787-789-4251 505 E
jrivera@atlanticu.edu
RIVERA, Janis .... 765-998-5201 161 C
janis_rivera@taylor.edu
RIVERA, Jason, E .... 413-597-4139 220 D
jer6@williams.edu
RIVERA, Johana .... 718-368-6646 294 E
johana.rivera@kbcc.cuny.edu
RIVERA, Jose .... 413-755-4260 216 A
jarivera@stcc.edu
RIVERA, Jose, A .... 787-751-1912 509 A
jrivera@juris.inter.edu
RIVERA, Jose, O .... 915-747-8535 455 C
jrivera@utep.edu
RIVERA, Julian, J .... 610-989-1276 401 I
jrivera@vfmac.edu
RIVERA, Leonard .... 361-698-2404 435 G
lrivera@delmar.edu
RIVERA, Lisette .... 787-250-1912 508 D
lriverao@metro.inter.edu
RIVERA, Liza .... 347-964-8600 291 J
lrivera@boricuacollege.edu
RIVERA, Lizbeth .... 787-743-7979 510 H
lizrivera@suagm.edu
RIVERA, Luis .... 787-765-3560 506 K
luisrivera@edpuniversity.edu
RIVERA, Lydia, M .... 787-723-4481 506 A
lydia.rivera@ceaprc.edu
RIVERA, Marielis, E ...... 787-257-7373 510 F
mrivera966@uagm.edu
RIVERA, Marilys .... 787-288-1118 510 I
RIVERA, Mary Ann .... 757-388-3015 470 F
mrivera@sentara.edu
RIVERA, María .... 787-765-3560 506 K
marivera@edpuniversity.edu
RIVERA, Maximina .... 908-737-6800 278 E
mrivera@kean.edu
RIVERA, Mayra .... 787-765-3560 506 K
mrivera@edpuniversity.edu
RIVERA, Michelle .... 787-891-0925 507 K
mrivera@aguadilla.inter.edu
RIVERA, Mildred .... 787-798-3001 511 B
mildred.rivera@uccaribe.edu
RIVERA, Mildred, Y ...... 787-257-7373 510 F
myrivera@suagm.edu
RIVERA, Mildred, Y ...... 787-743-7979 510 H
myrivera@suagm.edu
RIVERA, Mishelle .... 787-841-2000 509 J
mishelle_rivera@pucpr.edu
RIVERA, Monica .... 718-951-5693 293 C
monica@brookly.cuny.edu
RIVERA, Nydia .... 787-765-3560 506 K
nrivera@edpuniversity.edu
RIVERA, Olga .... 787-753-6335 507 D
orivera@icprjc.edu
RIVERA, Pedro .... 787-878-5475 507 L
pirivera@arecibo.inter.edu
RIVERA, Pedro .... 717-299-6947 399 C
RIVERA, Peter .... 979-830-4189 431 H
peter.rivera@blinn.edu
RIVERA, Rafael .... 914-961-8313 314 H
rafael@svots.edu
RIVERA, Ramon .... 787-622-8000 511 D
rrivera@pupr.edu
RIVERA, Raymond .... 972-860-8228 434 G
rrivera@dcccd.edu
RIVERA, Rey .... 623-935-8010.. 13 A
rey.rivera@estrellamountain.edu
RIVERA, Rosa, M .... 856-225-6100 281 G
rosarive@camden.rutgers.edu
RIVERA, Schvalla .... 641-269-3100 166 G
riverasc@grinnell.edu
RIVERA, Serafin .... 787-279-2250 508 A
sriverat@bayamon.inter.edu
RIVERA, Sergio .... 210-486-3892 429 A
srivera@alamo.edu
RIVERA, Shayla, D .... 260-422-5561 156 E
sdrivera@indianatech.edu
RIVERA, Suzanne, M ..... 651-696-6207 236 I
president@macalester.edu
RIVERA, Teresita .... 787-882-2065 510 C
trivera@unitecpr.edu
RIVERA, Vanessa .... 787-725-6500 505 G
vrivera@albizu.edu
RIVERA, Veronica .... 530-938-5233.. 39 C
RIVERA, Vicki .... 269-956-3931 225 H
riverav@kellogg.edu
RIVERA, Vilma .... 787-738-2161 512 C
vilmariveraserrano@upr.edu
RIVERA, Wendy .... 818-364-7779.. 49 C
riverawc@lamission.edu
RIVERA, Yolanda .... 787-758-2525 512 F
yolanda.rivera3@upr.edu

RIVERA-CLAUDIO, Nelida 787-764-1912 507 J nerivera@inter.edu
RIVERA-FIGUEROA, Armando 323-953-4000.. 49 A riveraa2@elac.edu
RIVERA GONZÁLEZ, Sonia 787-890-2681 511 F sonia.rivera13@upr.edu
RIVERA-GONZALEZ, Sonia 787-890-2681 511 G sonia.rivera13@upr.edu
RIVERA-HAINAJ, Rosa .. 410-857-2247 200 F rhainaj@mcdaniel.edu
RIVERA LOPEZ, Soldanela 718-518-4402 294 B sriveralopez@hostos.cuny.edu
RIVERA LUGO, Yadira .. 787-766-1717 510 G um_yrivera@uagm.edu
RIVERA-MARQUEZ, Annelis 787-480-2430 506 C armarquez@sanjuan.pr
RIVERA-MARRERO, Mildred 787-798-3001 511 B mrivera@uccaribe.edu
RIVERA-MELENDEZ, Denisse 787-998-8997 509 M drivera@eeapr.org
RIVERA-MILLS, Susana . 765-285-1333 153 H sriveramills@bsu.edu
RIVERA MORET, Maritza 787-841-2000 509 J mrivera@pucpr.edu
RIVERA NEGRON, Adrian, O 787-725-8120 506 M actividadesculturales@eap.edu
RIVERA-NIEVES, Maria de Lourdes 787-725-6500 505 G marivera@albizu.edu
RIVERA-OTERO, Milagros 787-621-2835 505 C mrivera@aupr.edu
RIVERA PAGAN, Juan ... 718-963-4112 291 J jrivera@boricuacollege.edu
RIVERA RIVERA, Juan .. 787-725-6500 505 G jurivera@albizu.edu
RIVERA RUIZ, Marielis, E 787-863-2390 508 B marielis.ruiz@fajardo.inter.edu
RIVERA-RUIZ, Sharon ... 787-890-2681 511 G sharon.rivera4@upr.edu
RIVERA-SANTIAGO, Kimberly 787-993-8965 512 A kimberly.rivera@upr.edu
RIVERA-SCOTTI, Wilfredo 508-849-3406 205 H wriverascotti@annamaria.edu
RIVERA-VILLANUEVA, Nelson 787-764-0236 511 F nelson.rivera13@upr.edu
RIVERO, David, A 305-284-1650 113 C darivero@miami.edu
RIVERO, Estela 518-442-5800 316 A erivero@albany.edu
RIVERS, Andrew 202-806-2550.. 92 F andrew.rivers@howard.edu
RIVERS, Frenika 202-274-5000.. 94 B frenika.rivers@udc.edu
RIVERS, Hope, E 864-941-8301 411 C rivers.he@ptc.edu
RIVERS, Russell 803-321-2053 410 H russell.rivers@newberry.edu
RIVERS, Socrates 904-632-3356 101 B socrates.rivers@fscj.edu
RIVERS, Ted 530-221-4275.. 64 B trivers@shasta.edu
RIVERS, Verna, J 340-693-1121 513 E vrivers@uvi.edu
RIVERS-KLUTTZ, Stephanie 803-780-1062 414 B skluttz@voorhees.edu
RIVES, Cindy 318-675-5291 189 I cindy.rives@lsuhs.edu
RIVES, Lora 409-882-3343 449 H lora.rives@lsco.edu
RIVIELLO, Sylvia 732-255-0400 279 F sriviello@ocean.edu
RIX, Charles 405-425-5379 367 C charles.rix@oc.edu
RIX, Todd 843-383-8270 408 B trix@coker.edu
RIXON, Scott 206-934-4017 483 C scott.rixon@seattlecolleges.edu
RIZK, Michelle 907-450-8187.... 9 I marizk@alaska.edu
RIZZARDI, Bethany 707-826-3815.. 33 C bethany.rizzardi@humboldt.edu
RIZZARDI, Morgan, M . 724-287-8711 379 E morgan.rizzardi@bc3.edu
RIZZI, Gino 518-828-4181 297 B rizzi@sunycgcc.edu
RIZZO, Bryan 586-445-7119 227 B rizzob993@macomb.edu
RIZZO, Eric 602-557-1617.. 16 G eric.rizzo@phoenix.edu
RIZZO, Frank 949-508-2317 344 E frank.rizzo@peace.edu
RIZZO, Pete 402-375-7318 268 F perizzo1@wsc.edu
RIZZO, Rosalina, B 716-880-2339 305 G rosalina.b.rizzo@medaille.edu
RIZZO, Tracey 828-251-6315 342 B trizzo@unca.edu
RO, Eunice 934-420-2717 320 F eunice.ro@farmingdale.edu
RO, Katy 302-622-8000.. 90 D kro@dcad.edu
ROA, Bernadette 732-906-7700 278 G broa@middlesexcc.edu
ROA, Michelle 513-862-2743 353 D
ROACH, Crystal 316-295-5590 174 A crystal_roach@friends.edu
ROACH, Deb 888-378-9988 416 F deb.roach@dsu.edu
ROACH, Greg 208-496-7643 130 I roachg@byui.edu
ROACH, H. William 864-833-8217 411 D broach@presby.edu
ROACH, Janey, A 724-458-2595 384 G roachja@gcc.edu
ROACH, Kenneth 704-334-6882 328 B kroach@charlottechristian.edu
ROACH, Kristin, A 651-962-6168 244 E kris.roach@stthomas.edu
ROACH, Marshall 503-399-6243 372 B marshall.roache@chemeketa.edu
ROACH, Marybeth 302-857-1293.. 91 A marybeth.roach@dtcc.edu
ROACH, Stephen 361-593-2800 447 D stephen.roach@tamuk.edu
ROADES, Nicole 937-393-3431 360 H nroades@sscc.edu
ROAN, Matt 859-622-1000 180 E matt.roan@eku.edu
ROANE, Steve 804-333-6716 475 A sroane@rappahannock.edu
ROARK, Debbie 207-768-9755 197 C deborah.roark@maine.edu
ROARK, Donna 606-487-3128 181 I donnad.roark@kctcs.edu
ROARK, Ian 520-206-6424.. 15 B iroark@pima.edu
ROARK, Ryan 575-562-2165 286 B ryan.roark@enmu.edu
ROARKE, Susan, M 716-880-2168 305 G susan.m.roarke@medaille.edu
ROBACK, Barbara, A 315-684-6615 321 A robackba@morrisville.edu
ROBACK, Joseph, M 570-941-4385 401 F joseph.roback@scranton.edu
ROBARE, Kimberly 440-375-7509 354 K krobare@lec.edu
ROBART, Regina 618-664-7000 138 F regina.robart@greenville.edu
ROBB, Cathy 812-749-1272 159 O crobb@oak.edu
ROBB, Daniel, J 803-641-3272 413 B danr@usca.edu
ROBB, Sarah 620-432-0302 176 D sarah_robb@neosho.edu
ROBB, Stephanie 805-922-6966.. 24 I srobb@hancockcollege.edu
ROBB, Susan, E 804-827-0479 473 B sarobb@vcu.edu
ROBB SHIMKO, Molly .. 724-830-4620 398 C shimko@setonhill.edu
ROBBIE, Kimberly 510-659-6165.. 54 J krobbie@ohlone.edu
ROBBIN, Krista 518-861-2515 305 C krobben@mariacollege.edu
ROBBINS, Amanda 504-280-6590 190 B arobbin1@uno.edu
ROBBINS, Bill 920-923-7639 493 D brobbins72@marianuniversity.edu
ROBBINS, Bradley 334-244-3345.... 4 E brobbin2@aum.edu
ROBBINS, Eva 315-279-5264 303 G erobbins@keuka.edu
ROBBINS, Gene, R 401-865-2767 404 F grobbins@providence.edu
ROBBINS, Hollis 707-664-2146.. 34 B robbinsh@sonoma.edu
ROBBINS, Jill 478-387-4908 119 F jrobbins@gmc.edu
ROBBINS, Katie, A 330-471-8138 355 D krobbins@malone.edu
ROBBINS, Kristine 614-823-1232 359 H krobbins@otterbein.edu
ROBBINS, Leslie, H 915-747-8194 455 C lhrobbins@utep.edu
ROBBINS, Melanie 603-342-3093 273 C mrobbins@ccsnh.edu
ROBBINS, Michael 410-857-2242 200 F mrobbins@mcdaniel.edu
ROBBINS, Nickey, L 870-508-6108.. 17 G nrobbins@asumh.edu
ROBBINS, Paul 608-265-5296 495 D director@nelson.wisc.edu
ROBBINS, Robert, C 520-621-5511.. 16 D president@arizona.edu
ROBBINS, Rochelle 267-341-3640 385 J srobbins@holyfamily.edu
ROBBINS, Sandra 617-735-9715 209 D robbins@emmanuel.edu
ROBBINS, Steve 662-685-4771 245 C srobbins@bmc.edu
ROBBINS, Thomas, J 563-589-3507 170 G trobbins@dbq.edu
ROBBINS, Tom 574-239-8314 156 A trobbins@hcc-nd.edu
ROBBINS SMITH, Patricia 562-860-2451.. 35 H probbinsmith@cerritos.edu
ROBBINSON, Theresa ... 212-924-5900 321 F trobbinson@swedishinstitute.edu
ROBEAU, Jim 985-867-2272 190 K jrobeau@sjasc.edu
ROBECK, Mike 850-201-8546 112 C mike.robeck@tcc.fl.edu
ROBEL, Kenneth 856-351-2704 283 B krobel@salemcc.edu
ROBEL, Lauren 812-855-9011 156 G provost@indiana.edu
ROBEN, Paul, W 858-246-0473.. 70 C pwroben@ucsd.edu
ROBERGE, Tamara 603-342-3062 273 C troberge@ccsnh.edu
ROBERSON, Antoinette . 718-270-6055 294 G aroberson@mec.cuny.edu
ROBERSON, Ashley 252-492-2061 338 F robersona@vgcc.edu
ROBERSON, Chris 864-578-8770 411 F croberson@sherman.edu
ROBERSON, Deborah .... 310-243-3301.. 30 E droberson-simms@csudh.edu
ROBERSON, Glenn 765-730-0579 158 D groberso@ivytech.edu
ROBERSON, Janet 434-791-5891 464 I roberson@averett.edu
ROBERSON, Jeff 201-360-4054 278 C jrobersonjr@hccc.edu
ROBERSON, John 910-893-1205 327 D robersonj@campbell.edu
ROBERSON, Judith 225-768-1754 187 B judith.roberson@franu.edu
ROBERSON, Kim 501-337-5000.. 18 B rroberson@asutr.edu
ROBERSON, Lynwood ... 252-618-6650 334 D robersonl@edgecombe.edu
ROBERSON, Mark, A 951-552-8652.. 27 G maroberson@calbaptist.edu
ROBERSON, Morgan 252-789-0224 335 H
ROBERSON, Morgan, H 252-451-8258 336 E mhroberson492@nashcc.edu
ROBERSON, Rita, G 304-896-7425 488 I rita.roberson@southernwv.edu
ROBERSON, Robin 580-559-5467 365 K robrrob@ecok.edu
ROBERSON, TOR, Shawn 740-283-6463 352 I sroberson@franciscan.edu
ROBERSON, Stacey 803-793-5175 408 G robersons@denmarktech.edu
ROBERSON, Valerie, R .. 857-701-1280 215 G vroberson@rcc.mass.edu
ROBERSON, Wendy 651-846-1757 241 B wendy.roberson@saintpaul.edu
ROBERT, Strong 843-355-4173 414 C strongr@wiltech.edu
ROBERTS, Aaron 402-643-7233 266 G aaron.roberts@cune.edu
ROBERTS, Aaron 317-916-7827 158 E aroberts217@ivytech.edu
ROBERTS, Adam 706-880-8004 122 A aroberts@lagrange.edu
ROBERTS, Alan, P 845-687-5050 323 H robertsal@sunyulster.edu
ROBERTS, Amber 616-331-3266 224 G roberamb@gvsu.edu
ROBERTS, Bill 906-487-2921 228 A wrrobert@mtu.edu
ROBERTS, Brent 434-395-2083 468 F robertsbs2@longwood.edu
ROBERTS, Brian 602-639-7500.. 12 J
ROBERTS, Brian 918-647-1320 365 E broberts@carlalbert.edu
ROBERTS, Carmen 406-771-4392 264 F carmen.roberts@gfcmsu.edu
ROBERTS, Charlie 360-676-2772 481 F chroberts@nwic.edu
ROBERTS, Chell 619-260-4627.. 72 I croberts@sandiego.edu
ROBERTS, Cheryl, A 340-692-4192 513 E crobert@uvi.edu
ROBERTS, Christina 202-687-6335.. 92 E cdr44@georgetown.edu
ROBERTS, Christopher, B 334-844-2308.... 4 D robercr@auburn.edu
ROBERTS, Chuck 931-372-3030 426 B cproberts@tntech.edu
ROBERTS, Clint 760-750-4470.. 33 A clroberts@csusm.edu
ROBERTS, Cynthia 219-980-6636 157 C robertcs@iun.edu
ROBERTS, Daniel 985-545-1500 188 E
ROBERTS, Daniel, M 804-524-6709 476 D droberts@vsu.edu
ROBERTS, Dave 573-875-7400 251 I studentaffairs@ccis.edu
ROBERTS, David 218-736-1635 239 C david.roberts@minnesota.edu
ROBERTS, Deborah 707-664-3236.. 34 B deborah.roberts@sonoma.edu
ROBERTS, Douglas, P ... 573-341-4300 261 D robertsdp@mst.edu
ROBERTS, Dustin 870-584-1172.. 22 F droberts@cccua.edu
ROBERTS, Ed 240-567-7688 200 G edward.robert@montgomerycollege.edu
ROBERTS, Edward 828-898-8777 330 E robertse@lmc.edu
ROBERTS, Elizabeth 864-597-4300 414 E robertsew@wofford.edu
ROBERTS, Ellen 630-942-2218 135 I roberts@cod.edu
ROBERTS, Gary 269-927-8771 226 F roberts@lakemichigancollege.edu
ROBERTS, Gary, O 607-871-2177 290 B roberts@alfred.edu
ROBERTS, Gina 419-530-5812 363 B gina.roberts@utoledo.edu
ROBERTS, Gregory 716-926-8935 301 E groberts@hilbert.edu
ROBERTS, Gregory 620-227-9325 173 D groberts@dc3.edu
ROBERTS, Gregory, L ... 520-494-5446.. 11 K greg.roberts@centralaz.edu
ROBERTS, Gregory, W .. 434-982-3200 472 D gwr2g@virginia.edu
ROBERTS, Holley 478-445-6848 119 B holley.roberts@gcsu.edu
ROBERTS, Howard, V .... 606-218-5019 186 B howardroberts@upike.edu
ROBERTS, James 570-674-6758 390 B jroberts@misericordia.edu
ROBERTS, Jay 828-771-2000 344 D
ROBERTS, Jeff 931-372-3365 426 B jjroberts@tntech.edu
ROBERTS, Jeffrey 619-594-5142.. 33 D jroberts@sdsu.edu
ROBERTS, Jerilyn, C 605-394-6729 416 H jerilyn.roberts@sdsmt.edu
ROBERTS, Jerry 972-825-4870 444 J jroberts@sagu.edu
ROBERTS, Jim 315-792-5649 306 K jroberts@mvcc.edu
ROBERTS, John 903-593-8311 448 G jroberts@texascollege.edu
ROBERTS, Jonathan 501-279-4257.. 19 C jroberts@harding.edu

ROBERTS, Joy .... 816-235-1700 261 B
robertsme@umkc.edu
ROBERTS, Juanita .... 334-727-8894.... 7 D
jroberts@tuskegee.edu
ROBERTS, Julia .... 910-788-6327 338 A
julia.roberts@sccnc.edu
ROBERTS, Justin, L ...... 314-516-7673 261 C
robertsju@umsl.edu
ROBERTS, Kyle .... 651-255-6108 243 E
kroberts@unitedseminary.edu
ROBERTS, Lance .... 605-394-2256 416 H
lance.roberts@sdsmt.edu
ROBERTS, LaShawnda .. 319-385-6241 167 H
lashawnda.roberts@iw.edu
ROBERTS, Leigh .... 203-285-2143.. 86 E
lroberts@gatewayct.edu
ROBERTS, Lonnie .... 912-427-5816 117 E
lroberts@coastalpines.edu
ROBERTS, Mandy .... 918-647-1214 365 E
mroberts@carlalbert.edu
ROBERTS, Mark .... 918-495-6723 368 F
mroberts@oru.edu
ROBERTS, Mark, A .... 770-720-5503 124 G
mar@reinhardt.edu
ROBERTS, Marlene .... 715-675-3331 499 F
robertsm@ntc.edu
ROBERTS, Matt .... 843-953-5546 408 C
robertsmj1@cofc.edu
ROBERTS, Matthew .... 423-652-4780 420 F
mroberts@king.edu
ROBERTS, Melinda, R .... 812-464-1735 162 C
mrroberts1@usi.edu
ROBERTS, Melissa .... 601-266-5390 249 F
melissa.b.roberts@usm.edu
ROBERTS, Michael .... 907-773-4462 135 C
mroberts39@ccc.edu
ROBERTS, Michael, H .... 843-349-2282 408 A
mroberts@coastal.edu
ROBERTS, Michelle, A .. 662-846-4000 245 G
mroberts@deltastate.edu
ROBERTS, Mike .... 801-422-4164 458 H
mike.roberts@byu.edu
ROBERTS, Nancy .... 610-606-4640 380 D
nroberts@cedarcrest.edu
ROBERTS, Nathan .... 816-383-7100 257 A
nroberts4@missouriwestern.edu
ROBERTS, Nathan .... 337-482-6678 193 B
nathan@louisiana.edu
ROBERTS, Nathan .... 785-320-4589 175 G
nathanroberts@manhattantech.edu
ROBERTS, Patricia .... 210-436-3308 442 J
proberts6@stmarytx.edu
ROBERTS, Patrick, S ..... 330-471-8411 355 D
proberts@malone.edu
ROBERTS, Patty, J .... 318-869-5747 186 F
pjrobert@centenary.edu
ROBERTS, Paul, G .... 773-508-3163 143 C
prober2@luc.edu
ROBERTS, Phyllis .... 276-964-7588 475 C
phyllis.roberts@sw.edu
ROBERTS, Quinton .... 567-661-7418 359 I
quinton_roberts2@owens.edu
ROBERTS, Rachel .... 870-245-5593.. 20 D
robertsr@obu.edu
ROBERTS, Randy .... 620-235-4878 177 A
reroberts@pittstate.edu
ROBERTS, Roshell .... 405-682-1611 367 D
roshell.a.roberts@occc.edu
ROBERTS, Ruth .... 972-825-4656 444 J
rroberts@sagu.edu
ROBERTS, Ruth .... 215-596-8800 401 E
ROBERTS, Ryan .... 616-949-5300 223 C
ryan.roberts@cornerstone.edu
ROBERTS, Sarah .... 615-353-3275 424 G
sarah.roberts@nscc.edu
ROBERTS, Severin .... 573-876-7207 260 B
ROBERTS, Shearon .... 504-520-5747 193 E
srobert7@xula.edu
ROBERTS, Sherri .... 870-543-5952.. 21 B
sroberts@seark.edu
ROBERTS, Sonja .... 404-756-4012 115 G
sroberts@atlm.edu
ROBERTS, Stephanie ..... 912-427-5835 117 E
sroberts@coastalpines.edu
ROBERTS, Stephanie ..... 304-326-1310 487 I
sroberts@salemu.edu
ROBERTS, Stevie .... 972-524-3341 445 B
stevie.roberts@swcc.edu
ROBERTS, Teresa .... 417-626-1234 257 F
roberts.teresa@occ.edu
ROBERTS, Thomas .... 601-643-8351 245 F
tommy.roberts@colin.edu
ROBERTS, Thomas .... 785-243-1435 172 L
ROBERTS, Tom .... 239-590-7806 109 K
troberts@fgcu.edu
ROBERTS, Tracy .... 270-809-3380 184 D
troberts@murraystate.edu
ROBERTS, Valerie .... 530-938-5309.. 39 C
ROBERTS, William .... 201-692-2629 277 I
william_roberts@fdu.edu
ROBERTS, William .... 619-532-9522 503 C
william.roberts@usuhs.edu
ROBERTS, William, M ... 301-295-3013 503 C
william.roberts@usuhs.edu
ROBERTS, William, N ... 406-275-4825 265 F
nick_roberts@skc.edu
ROBERTS-BRESLIN, Jan 617-824-8912 209 C
jan_roberts_breslin@emerson.edu
ROBERTS-CAMPS, Traci 209-946-2343.. 71 E
trobertscamps@pacific.edu
ROBERTSHAW, Amy ...... 719-549-2498.. 80 B
amy.robertshaw@csupueblo.edu
ROBERTSHAW, Mia .... 415-485-9304.. 39 A
mrobertshaw@marin.edu
ROBERTSON, Alan, D .... 850-599-3270 109 I
alan.robertson@famu.edu
ROBERTSON, Anne .... 773-702-8512 151 E
awrx@uchicago.edu
ROBERTSON, Brenda ..... 972-780-3600 454 A
brenda.robertson@untdallas.edu
ROBERTSON, Bruce ...... 920-403-3045 495 B
bruce.robertson@snc.edu
ROBERTSON, Charlene . 617-732-2786 216 D
charlene.robertson@mcphs.edu
ROBERTSON, Cheryl ..... 713-221-8256 453 A
robertsonc@uhd.edu
ROBERTSON, Chuck ..... 601-477-4277 246 G
chuck.robertson@jcjc.edu
ROBERTSON, Clyde ...... 504-286-5006 191 C
crobertson@suno.edu
ROBERTSON, Craig, L .. 618-537-6856 144 A
ROBERTSON, Dalana ..... 615-322-5179 428 A
dalana.robertson@vanderbilt.edu
ROBERTSON, Don .... 270-809-6839 184 D
drobertson@murraystate.edu
ROBERTSON, Donna ..... 201-692-2196 277 I
donnamjr@fdu.edu
ROBERTSON, Emily .... 704-406-3249 329 A
erobertson@gardner-webb.edu
ROBERTSON, Ian .... 608-262-3482 495 D
engr-dean@wisc.edu
ROBERTSON, J. D .... 435-652-7576 460 B
jrobertson@dixie.edu
ROBERTSON, Jacob, M 951-552-8677.. 27 G
jmrobertson@calbaptist.edu
ROBERTSON, Janet .... 903-566-7325 456 A
jrobertson@uttyler.edu
ROBERTSON, Jeff .... 479-968-0498.. 18 C
jrobertson@atu.edu
ROBERTSON, Jen .... 603-428-2418 273 G
jrobertson@nec.edu
ROBERTSON, Jennifer ... 407-582-6150 113 I
jrobertson@valenciacollege.edu
ROBERTSON, Jill .... 303-273-3207.. 79 J
jirobert@is.mines.edu
ROBERTSON, Jim .... 845-574-4466 312 H
jrobert7@sunyrockland.edu
ROBERTSON, Joel .... 423-652-4724 420 F
jcrobert@king.edu
ROBERTSON, John .... 972-860-7709 434 E
jrobertson@dcccd.edu
ROBERTSON,
John Howard .... 601-477-4109 246 G
john.robertson@jcjc.edu
ROBERTSON, Jon, H 561-237-7701 103W
jrobertson@lynn.edu
ROBERTSON, Jordan 612-343-4440 242M
ROBERTSON, Julie .... 360-992-2076 478 I
jrobertson@clark.edu
ROBERTSON, Kristy ...... 276-328-0220 472 E
kej5c@uvawise.edu
ROBERTSON, TOR,
Luke .... 740-283-3771 352 I
lrobertson@franciscan.edu
ROBERTSON,
M.G. (Pat) .... 757-352-4036 470 B
lfinn@regent.edu
ROBERTSON, Marcia ..... 402-494-2311 268 A
ROBERTSON,
Michael, J .... 214-768-1148 444 D
robertsonm@smu.edu
ROBERTSON,
Michael, N .... 901-722-3226 423 G
mike.robertson@sco.edu
ROBERTSON, Paul .... 520-383-0079.. 16 A
probertson@tocc.edu
ROBERTSON, Prince ..... 309-556-3111 140 F
probert1@iwu.edu
ROBERTSON, Rachel ..... 801-587-9889 459 O
rachel.robertson@utah.edu
ROBERTSON, Samantha 603-271-6484 273 A
ROBERTSON, Stacey ..... 585-245-5531 318 B
robertsons@geneseo.edu
ROBERTSON, Sue .... 630-889-6527 145 E
srobertson@nuhs.edu
ROBERTSON, Tim .... 402-872-2411 268 E
trobertson@peru.edu
ROBERTSON, Tracee ..... 940-397-8948 440 C
tracee.robertson@msutexas.edu
ROBERTSON, Trey .... 601-928-6306 247 E
trey.robertson@mgccc.edu
ROBERTSON, Valerie ..... 360-596-5240 484 D
vrobertson1@spscc.edu
ROBERTSON, William ... 915-747-8200 455 C
robertson@utep.edu
ROBERTSON,
William, J .... 717-866-5775 383 F
wrobertson@evangelical.edu
ROBERTSON-JAMES,
Candace .... 215-951-1430 387 A
robertsonjames@lasalle.edu
ROBEY, Jason .... 314-434-4044 252 C
jason.robey@covenantseminary.edu
ROBICHAUD, Allyson .... 216-687-3906 350 J
a.robichaud@csuohio.edu
ROBICHAUD, Betin .... 508-213-2292 217 H
betin.robichaud@nichols.edu
ROBICHAUD, David .... 508-531-2731 212 D
drobichaud@bridgew.edu
ROBICHAUD, Jeanette .. 978-665-4646 212 E
jrobic15@fitchburgstate.edu
ROBICHAUD, Keith .... 617-333-2210 208 G
krobicha0804@curry.edu
ROBICHEAUX, Wendi .... 337-521-8932 188 I
wendi.robicheaux@solacc.edu
ROBIDOUX, Patricia ..... 909-607-0107.. 37 F
probidoux@kgi.edu
ROBIE, Candra .... 970-675-3356.. 79 H
candra.robie@cncc.edu
ROBILOTTO, Philip .... 410-706-2378 203 A
probilotto@umaryland.edu
ROBIN, Jennifer .... 203-392-5356.. 86 A
robinj2@southernct.edu
ROBIN, Tracy .... 212-229-1671 308 A
robint@newschool.edu
ROBIN, Wayne .... 508-767-7095 206 A
w.robin@assumption.edu
ROBINETT, Laura .... 402-375-7209 268 F
larobin1@wsc.edu
ROBINETTE, Kyrsten ...... 614-236-6011 349 B
ROBINS, Anthony, G ..... 412-397-6482 397 B
robins@rmu.edu
ROBINS, Diana .... 215-571-3439 382 F
dlr76@drexel.edu
ROBINS, Luke .... 360-417-6200 482 C
lrobins@pencol.edu
ROBINS, Michael .... 408-741-2187.. 75 D
michael.robins@wvm.edu
ROBINS, Michael .... 831-477-3521.. 27 D
mirobins@cabrillo.edu
ROBINS, Rochelle .... 213-884-4133.. 24 A
rrobins@ajrca.edu
ROBINSON, Alexandra .. 212-817-7112 293 F
arobinson@gc.cuny.edu
ROBINSON, Anafe .... 818-610-6515.. 49 D
robinsa@piercecollege.edu
ROBINSON, Andrea ...... 507-222-5465 234 G
arobinson@carleton.edu
ROBINSON, Andrew ...... 478-471-4394 121 F
anrobinson@helms.edu
ROBINSON,
Andristine, M .... 301-546-7422 201 E
robinsam1@pgcc.edu
ROBINSON, Angela ...... 229-430-3500 114 I
arobinson@albanytech.edu
ROBINSON, Angela .... 309-672-5513 144 C
arobinson@methodistcol.edu
ROBINSON, Ann .... 716-566-7836 298 A
arobinso@daemen.edu
ROBINSON, April .... 205-726-2803.... 6 E
alrobins@samford.edu
ROBINSON, April .... 863-297-1020 106 A
arobinson@polk.edu
ROBINSON, Ashley .... 601-979-2291 246 F
ashley.n.robinson@jsums.edu
ROBINSON, Barry .... 206-934-4349 483 C
barry.robinson2@seattlecolleges.edu
ROBINSON, Beverly ...... 912-583-3260 116 E
ROBINSON, Beverly ...... 972-825-4798 444 J
brobinson@sagu.edu
ROBINSON, Breck .... 707-826-6212.. 33 C
breck.robinson@humboldt.edu
ROBINSON, Brian .... 916-608-6849.. 50 I
robinsb@flc.losrios.edu
ROBINSON, Brigette ..... 517-990-1386 225 E
robinsobrigetta@jccmi.edu
ROBINSON, Carlos .... 405-466-3428 366 C
carlos.m.robinson@langston.edu
ROBINSON, Carrie .... 215-670-9328 391 E
cnrobinson@peirce.edu
ROBINSON,
Cassandra, M .... 301-860-4000 204 A
crobinson@bowiestate.edu
ROBINSON, Chad .... 970-943-3123.. 85 C
crobinson@western.edu
ROBINSON, Charles, F . 479-575-3836.. 21 F
ROBINSON, Charles, F . 510-987-9800.. 68 L
charles.robinson@ucop.edu
ROBINSON, Cheryl .... 407-582-3457 113 I
crobinson@valenciacollege.edu
ROBINSON, Chris .... 870-575-7950.. 22 D
ROBINSON, Chris .... 606-218-5226 186 B
chrisrobinson@upike.edu
ROBINSON, Christina ... 860-832-2364.. 85 G
christinarobinson@ccsu.edu
ROBINSON, Christine ... 704-687-5385 342 D
crobinson@uncc.edu
ROBINSON,
Christopher .... 315-268-3986 295 F
crobinso@clarkson.edu
ROBINSON,
Christopher, D .... 336-246-3900 339 B
cdrobinson877@wilkescc.edu
ROBINSON, Dave .... 641-269-9990 166 G
daver@grinnell.edu
ROBINSON, David .... 510-642-7791.. 69 A
dmrobinson@berkeley.edu
ROBINSON, David .... 212-650-8357 293 D
drobinson2@ccny.cuny.edu
ROBINSON, David, W ... 503-494-4460 374 H
provost@ohsu.edu
ROBINSON, Dawnelle ... 256-331-5310.... 3 C
dawnelle.robinson@nwscc.edu
ROBINSON,
Debra A, G .... 573-341-6154 261 D
debrar@mst.edu
ROBINSON, OSB,
Denis .... 812-357-6522 161 A
drobinson@saintmeinrad.edu
ROBINSON, Dennis ...... 972-825-4814 444 J
dbobinson@sagu.edu
ROBINSON, Derek .... 307-382-1896 501 J
derek@westernwyoming.edu
ROBINSON, Edward ...... 202-274-2300.. 94 C
library@potomac.edu
ROBINSON, Elaine .... 541-917-4854 373 G
robinse@linnbenton.edu
ROBINSON, Elwood, L . 336-750-2042 344 A
robinsonel@wssu.edu
ROBINSON, Eric .... 502-597-6646 183 D
eric.robinson@kysu.edu
ROBINSON, Erin .... 941-893-2856 106 J
erobinso@ringling.edu
ROBINSON, Evan, T ...... 402-280-1828 266 H
evanrobinson@creighton.edu
ROBINSON, Freddie ...... 804-257-5783 476 F
frobinson@vuu.edu
ROBINSON, Gail .... 901-458-8232 421 E
grobinson@memphisseminary.edu
ROBINSON, Gail, D ...... 901-334-5826 421 E
grobinson@memphisseminary.edu
ROBINSON, Gary .... 607-431-4420 301 A
robinsong@hartwick.edu
ROBINSON, Grace, G ... 805-437-3615.. 30 C
grace.robinson@csuci.edu
ROBINSON, Gregory ..... 847-214-7226 137 F
grobinson@elgin.edu
ROBINSON, Gregory ..... 702-992-2663 271 B
gregory.robinson@nsc.edu
ROBINSON, Guin .... 205-853-1200.... 2 G
grobinson@jeffersonstate.edu
ROBINSON, Henry .... 719-587-7011.. 77 G
klmarque@adams.edu
ROBINSON, Irene, M .... 281-756-3501 429 D
irobinson@alvincollege.edu
ROBINSON, Isaac .... 425-739-8456 481 C
isaac.robinson@lwtech.edu
ROBINSON, Jacqueline . 256-469-7333.... 5 H
fin@hbc1.edu
ROBINSON, James .... 281-873-0262 433 J
j.robinson@commonwealth.edu

RODGERS, Chris, T ...... 402-280-2455 266 H chrisrodgers@creighton.edu
RODGERS, Christopher . 718-817-4755 300 C chrodgers@fordham.edu
RODGERS, Coreen .... 909-621-8111.. 37 D
RODGERS, Corey .... 949-451-5409.. 65 C crodgers@ivc.edu
RODGERS, Denise, V .... 973-972-3645 282 A rodgerdv@ca.rutgers.edu
RODGERS, Frederick, B 607-871-2958 290 B rodgers@alfred.edu
RODGERS, Matt .... 334-347-2623.... 2 A mrodgers@escc.edu
RODGERS, Melinda .... 850-201-6055 112 C melinda.rodgers@tcc.fl.edu
RODGERS, Micah .... 850-973-1604 104 L rodgersm@nfc.edu
RODGERS, Michael .... 270-686-4503 182 F mike.rodgers@kctcs.edu
RODGERS, Mike .... 325-649-8055 437 G mrodgers@hputx.edu
RODGERS, Phillip .... 210-784-1320 447 E phillip.rodgers@tamusa.edu
RODGERS, Rob, G .... 412-648-0224 400 H rrodgers@cfo.pitt.edu
RODGERS, Ronald, F .... 603-862-0960 274 E ron.rodgers@usnh.edu
RODGERS, Ronda .... 509-542-4802 479 A rrodgers@columbiabasin.edu
RODGERS, Ruby .... 270-534-3184 183 B ruby.rodgers@kctcs.edu
RODGERS, Ruth .... 317-955-6321 159 K rrodgers@marian.edu
RODGERS, Victor .... 717-221-1361 385 B vrodgers@hacc.edu
RODIBAUGH, Jon .... 585-475-4485 312 F jprrar@rit.edu
RODKIN, Dan .... 352-395-4171 108 A dan.rodkin@sfcollege.edu
RODLAND, Amber .... 740-826-8171 356 H arodland@muskingum.edu
RODLER, Trina .... 323-856-7699.. 25 G trodler@afi.com
RODMAN, Gary, S .... 920-748-8343 494 J rodmang@ripon.edu
RODMAN, Michael .... 617-627-3024 219 C michael.rodman@tufts.edu
RODNEY, Chris .... 713-221-5849 453 A rodneyc@uhd.edu
RODNING, Janet, M ..... 770-720-5954 124 G jmr@reinhardt.edu
RODOCKER, Jason, L ... 540-458-8753 477 D jrodocker@wlu.edu
RODOLF, Mark .... 405-974-3611 370 I mrodolf@uco.edu
RODRIGUE, Kelly, J ...... 985-448-4154 192 F kelly.rodrigue@nicholls.edu
RODRIGUE, Morris, J .... 909-274-4230.. 52 J mrodrigue@mtsac.edu
RODRIGUES, Helena ...... 520-621-1684.. 16 D hrodrigu@arizona.edu
RODRIGUES, Leon .... 651-641-3209 236 G lrodrigues001@luthersem.edu
RODRIGUES, Nishanth .. 662-915-7206 249 D nr@olemiss.edu
RODRIGUEZ, Abel .... 787-834-9595 510 D arodriguez@uaa.edu
RODRIGUEZ, Agustin .... 787-758-2525 512 F agustin.rodriguez1@upr.edu
RODRIGUEZ, Aida, E .... 787-852-1430 507 C arodriguez@hccpr.edu
RODRIGUEZ, Alba .... 478-301-2136 122 E rodriguez_a@mercer.edu
RODRIGUEZ, Alexander 978-556-3626 215 E arodriguez@necc.mass.edu
RODRIGUEZ, Alfred ...... 210-999-7201 451 E alfred.rodriguez@trinity.edu
RODRIGUEZ, Alma .... 956-882-7657 455 D alma.rodriguez@utrgv.edu
RODRIGUEZ, Alma .... 805-289-6360.. 74 B arodriguez@vcccd.edu
RODRIGUEZ, Amy .... 217-735-7336 142 H ahaseley@lincolncollege.edu
RODRIGUEZ, Anastacia . 303-352-6564.. 80 F anastacia.rodriguez@ccd.edu
RODRIGUEZ, Anastasia . 256-782-5634.... 6 A awrodriguez@jsu.edu
RODRIGUEZ, Andy .... 970-248-1337.. 78 J arodrigu@coloradomesa.edu
RODRIGUEZ, Annabelle 956-781-6806 442 H
RODRIGUEZ, Arlene ...... 508-362-2131 214 D
RODRIGUEZ, Arlene ...... 781-280-3200 215 B
RODRIGUEZ, Armando . 787-841-2000 509 J armando_rodriguez@pucpr.edu
RODRIGUEZ, Art .... 507-222-4190 234 G adrodriguez@carleton.edu
RODRIGUEZ, Arturo ...... 805-965-0581.. 63 A amrodriguez19@sbcc.edu
RODRIGUEZ, Barbara, L .... 505-277-0735 288 J kkachirisky@unm.edu
RODRIGUEZ, Beatriz ..... 908-709-7448 284 D rodriguez@ucc.edu
RODRIGUEZ, Carlos ..... 847-970-4846 152 I crodriguez@usml.edu
RODRIGUEZ, Carlos ..... 323-343-3929.. 31 E carlos.rodriguez@calstatela.edu
RODRIGUEZ, Carlos ..... 215-780-1400 398 B crodriguez@salus.edu
RODRIGUEZ, Carmen ... 909-384-8592.. 60 F marodrig@sbccd.cc.ca.us
RODRIGUEZ, Carmen ... 305-629-2929 107 H crodriguez@sanignaciouniversity.edu
RODRIGUEZ, Carmen ... 787-878-5475 507 L clrodri@arecibo.inter.edu
RODRIGUEZ, Carmen ... 787-780-0070 505 F crodriguez@caribbean.edu
RODRIGUEZ, Carmen, B .... 787-850-9380 512 D carmen.rodriguez17@upr.edu
RODRIGUEZ, Claribel .... 787-621-2835 505 C crodriguez@aupr.edu
RODRIGUEZ, Claudia .... 787-761-0640 511 E asistenciaeconomica@utcpr.edu
RODRIGUEZ, Clemente . 713-348-6000 442 F crod@rice.edu
RODRIGUEZ, Daron ...... 303-753-6046.. 83 F drodriguez@rmcad.edu
RODRIGUEZ, David .... 949-359-0045.. 29 A
RODRIGUEZ, Dawn, M . 813-974-7297 111 C dmrodriguez@usf.edu
RODRIGUEZ, Desiree .... 504-865-3849 190 C desiree@loyno.edu
RODRIGUEZ, Diana, Z .. 909-384-4470.. 60 F drodriguez@sbccd.cc.ca.us
RODRIGUEZ, Diriee, Y .. 787-743-7979 510 H dyrodriguez@suagm.edu
RODRIGUEZ, Edgar .... 787-841-2000 509 J edrodrios@pucpr.edu
RODRIGUEZ, Edgar .... 617-989-4590 219 F rodriguezе9@wit.edu
RODRIGUEZ, Eduardo ... 509-542-4408 479 A erodriguez@columbiabasin.edu
RODRIGUEZ, Elisandra . 787-840-2575 509 I erodriguez@psm.edu
RODRIGUEZ, Elisha ...... 212-678-8206 322 C erodriguez@tc.columbia.edu
RODRIGUEZ, Elizabeth .. 561-683-1400.. 94 F lrodriguez@anho.edu
RODRIGUEZ, Elsa .... 787-753-6335 507 D e_rodriguez@icprjc.edu
RODRIGUEZ, Emilio ...... 909-537-3944.. 32 E emilio@csusb.edu
RODRIGUEZ, Emilio ...... 626-568-8850.. 48 H emilio@lacm.edu
RODRIGUEZ, Enerida .... 787-738-2161 512 C enerida.rodriguez@upr.edu
RODRIGUEZ, Ericka ...... 787-844-8181 513 A ericka.rodriguez@upr.edu
RODRIGUEZ, Evelyn ...... 787-850-9305 512 D evelyn.rodriguez3@upr.edu
RODRIGUEZ, Francisco, C .... 213-891-2201.. 48 I chancellor@email.laccd.edu
RODRIGUEZ, Gilberto ... 641-472-1170 168 C grodriguez@miu.edu
RODRIGUEZ, Glendali ... 715-232-2421 497 B rodriguezg@uwstout.edu
RODRIGUEZ, Henberto . 787-884-6000 507 D hrodriguez@icprjc.edu
RODRIGUEZ, Isaac .... 310-434-4554.. 63 C rodriguez_isaac@smc.edu
RODRIGUEZ, Israel .... 562-977-6017.. 42 K israel.rodriguez@fremont.edu
RODRIGUEZ, Israel .... 209-476-7840.. 67 E irodriguez@clc.edu
RODRIGUEZ, Israel .... 787-743-7979 510 H ut_irodriguez@suagm.edu
RODRIGUEZ, Jalibeth ... 787-841-2000 509 J jalibeth_rodriguez@pucpr.edu
RODRIGUEZ, James .... 661-654-2219.. 30 B jlrodriguez@csub.edu
RODRIGUEZ, Janeth ..... 909-652-6541.. 35 L janeth.rodriguez@chaffey.edu
RODRIGUEZ, Javier ...... 702-895-3670 271 D javier.rodriguez@unlv.edu
RODRIGUEZ, Jerry .... 915-215-4040 451 B jerry.rodriguez@ttuhsc.edu
RODRIGUEZ, Jesus, R .. 956-295-3399 449 C jroberto.rodriguez@tsc.edu
RODRIGUEZ, Jose .... 610-902-1061 379 G jose.rodriguez@cabrini.edu
RODRIGUEZ, Jose .... 718-489-5315 313 E jrodriguez2300@sfc.edu
RODRIGUEZ, Jose .... 901-843-3745 423 A rodriguezj2@rhodes.edu
RODRIGUEZ, Jose, A .... 787-279-1912 508 A jarodriguez@bayamon.inter.edu
RODRIGUEZ, Jose, C .... 972-860-7603 434 H jcrodriguez@dcccd.edu
RODRIGUEZ, Josefina ... 787-257-0000 512 B josefina.rodriguez@upr.edu
RODRIGUEZ, Juan .... 787-878-5475 507 L jcrodrig@arecibo.inter.edu
RODRIGUEZ, Katrina ..... 320-308-0121 240 I
RODRIGUEZ, Katrina ..... 970-351-2517.. 84 F katrina.rodriguez@unco.edu
RODRIGUEZ, Kevin .... 210-924-4338 431 C
RODRIGUEZ, Laura .... 423-585-6798 425 F laura.rodriguez@ws.edu
RODRIGUEZ, Leslie .... 708-524-6821 137 C lrodriguez@dom.edu
RODRIGUEZ, Lora .... 972-721-5322 452 B lbrodriguez@udallas.edu
RODRIGUEZ, Louie, F .. 951-827-5802.. 70 B gsoedean@ucr.edu
RODRIGUEZ, Lucia, M . 915-831-2848 436 A lrodr258@epcc.edu
RODRIGUEZ, Luis, R .... 787-850-9204 512 D luis.rodriguez40@upr.edu
RODRIGUEZ, Magaly .... 787-850-9361 512 D magaly.rodriguez1@upr.edu
RODRIGUEZ, Maria, E .. 410-462-7791 198 B mrodriguez@bccc.edu
RODRIGUEZ, Maria-Judith .... 858-752-4963 347 H mjrodriguez@antioch.edu
RODRIGUEZ, Maribel .... 312-553-2500 135 A mrodriguez@ccc.edu
RODRIGUEZ, Mario ...... 916-568-3058.. 50 F rodrigm3@losrios.edu
RODRIGUEZ, Marisela .. 956-721-5820 438 H marisela.rodriguez@laredo.edu
RODRIGUEZ, Mark .... 216-987-5459 351 E mark.rodriguez@tri-c.edu
RODRIGUEZ, Mary Ann 361-582-2560 457 E maryann.rodriguez@victoriacollege.edu
RODRIGUEZ, Mary Ann 503-883-2458 373 F mrodrigu1@linfield.edu
RODRIGUEZ, Mayra ...... 787-743-7979 510 H mrodrigu@suagm.edu
RODRIGUEZ, Melba ...... 812-866-7011 155 G rodriguez@hanover.edu
RODRIGUEZ, Melissa ... 478-757-5180 127 F mrodriguez@wesleyancollege.edu
RODRIGUEZ, Monica .... 510-215-3958.. 40 B mrodriguez@contracosta.edu
RODRIGUEZ, Nannette .. 531-622-2733 267 G nmrodriguez@mccneb.edu
RODRIGUEZ, Narce .... 503-352-1457 375 C nrodrigu@pacificu.edu
RODRIGUEZ, Narcedalia .... 503-357-1457 375 C nrodrigu@pacificu.edu
RODRIGUEZ, Natalie .... 213-738-6813.. 66 B narodriguez@swlaw.edu
RODRIGUEZ, Nate .... 620-901-6240 171 D rodriguez@allencc.edu
RODRIGUEZ, Nilda .... 914-422-4213 311 A nrodriguez@pace.edu
RODRIGUEZ, Norelis .... 787-704-1020 506 D norodriguez@columbiacentral.edu
RODRIGUEZ, Norma ..... 562-860-2451.. 35 H nrodriguez@cerritos.edu
RODRIGUEZ, Peter .... 713-348-5928 442 F peter.l.rodriguez@rice.edu
RODRIGUEZ, Rafael ...... 802-656-3434 463 A rrodrig1@uvm.edu
RODRIGUEZ, Raul .... 831-755-6700.. 44 G
RODRIGUEZ, Ray .... 801-618-0438 458 G rrodriguez@ameritech.edu
RODRIGUEZ, Rene .... 512-232-2780 455 A renerod@austin.utexas.edu
RODRIGUEZ, Reuban, B .... 804-828-8940 473 B rbrodriguez@vcu.edu
RODRIGUEZ, Ricardo .... 817-531-4249 451 C rrodriguez@txwes.edu
RODRIGUEZ, Ricardo .... 787-751-0178 510 E ricrodriguez@uagm.edu
RODRIGUEZ, Richard .... 559-323-2100.. 61 F rrodriguez@sjcl.edu
RODRIGUEZ, Ron .... 209-667-3709.. 33 B rrodriguez36@csustan.edu
RODRIGUEZ, Rosa .... 651-779-5786 237 H rosa.rodriguez@century.edu
RODRIGUEZ, Sandra ..... 505-747-2194 287 H sandra.rodriguez@nnmc.edu
RODRIGUEZ, Segundo .. 787-758-2525 512 F segundo.rodriguez@upr.edu
RODRIGUEZ, Seph .... 909-272-6947.. 36 E seph.rodriguez@tcsedsystem.edu
RODRIGUEZ, Sherri ...... 818-947-2726.. 49 G rodrigsa@lavc.edu
RODRIGUEZ, Silvio .... 305-237-7445 104 E srodrig2@mdc.edu
RODRIGUEZ, Sonia .... 585-475-2395 312 F smrfa@rit.edu
RODRIGUEZ, Steven ..... 949-214-3003.. 39 K steven.rodriguez@cui.edu
RODRIGUEZ, Teresita ... 310-434-4774.. 63 C rodriguez_teresita@smc.edu
RODRIGUEZ, Theresa, E .... 970-247-6983.. 80 J rodriguez_t@fortlewis.edu
RODRIGUEZ, Tiffany ..... 503-244-0726 371 E tiffanyrodriguez@achs.edu
RODRIGUEZ, Velia .... 559-730-3775.. 39 B veliar@cos.edu
RODRIGUEZ, Venessa ... 607-778-5220 317 D rodriguezvl1@sunybroome.edu
RODRIGUEZ, Wanda ..... 787-257-0000 512 B wanda.rodriguez@upr.edu
RODRIGUEZ, William .... 773-508-8890 143 C wrodriguez@luc.edu
RODRIGUEZ, Yani .... 414-410-4003 491 I yrodriguez@stritch.edu
RODRIGUEZ, Yanilda .... 787-766-1717 510 G yrodriguez98@uagm.edu
RODRIGUEZ-ANDUJAR, Glorimar .... 787-780-5134 509 E
RODRIGUEZ ANTONE, Megan .... 650-306-3418.. 62 J rodriguezm@smccd.edu
RODRIGUEZ-CHARDAVOYNE, Esther .... 718-518-4308 294 B erodriguez@hostos.cuny.edu
RODRIGUEZ-CORTES, Jesus .... 787-763-6700 507 A jrodriguez@se-pr.edu
RODRIGUEZ-CRUZ, Victor .... 787-751-1912 509 A vrodriguez@juris.inter.edu
RODRIGUEZ-DABNEY, Crystal, J .... 716-878-4102 317 F rodrigcj@buffalostate.edu
RODRIGUEZ DAVILA, Soniemi .... 787-960-4787 511 F soniemi.rodriguez@upr.edu
RODRIGUEZ-FARRAR, Hanna .... 315-228-5150 296 E hrf@colgate.edu
RODRIGUEZ-GONZALEZ, Christina .... 361-593-2132 447 D christina.rodriguez-gonzalez@tamuk.edu
RODRIGUEZ-GREGORY, Lisa .... 732-906-2550 278 G lgregory@middlesexcc.edu
RODRIGUEZ HOWELL, Daniel .... 787-850-9341 512 D daniel.rodriguez32@upr.edu
RODRIGUEZ HOWELL, Daniel .... 787-850-9343 512 D daniel.rodriguez32@upr.edu
RODRIGUEZ JAMES, Heather .... 256-726-7250.... 6 C hjames@oakwood.edu
RODRIGUEZ JOHNSON, Fatima, L .... 716-888-2118 292 F rodrig23@canisius.edu
RODRIGUEZ-LAMAS, Barbara .... 407-708-2768 108 D lamasb@seminolestate.edu
RODRIGUEZ MARTINEZ, Melanie .... 787-720-4476 511 C biblioteca@mizpa.edu
RODRIGUEZ-MOLINA, Nilda, E .... 787-480-2439 506 C nilrodriguez@sanjuan.pr

RODRIGUEZ-MORALES, Rosa, C .... 787-857-3600 507 M
rcrodriguez@br.inter.edu
RODRIGUEZ-RIVERA, Carlos .... 787-250-0000 511 F
carlos.rodriguez107@upr.edu
RODRIGUEZ-ROIG, Aida .... 787-850-9374 511 F
aida.rodriguez1@upr.edu
RODRIGUEZ ROIG, Aida, I .... 787-850-9375 512 D
aida.rodriguez1@upr.edu
RODRIGUEZ-SUAREZ, Francisco .... 217-333-1330 152 B
paco70@illinois.edu
RODRIGUEZ-VARGAS, Claribel .... 787-621-2835 505 C
crodriguez@aupr.edu
RODRIGUEZ-VINCENTY, Carmen, J .... 787-480-2438 506 C
crodriguez03@sanjuan.pr
RODRIQUEZ, Nicky, M . 866-294-3974 154 H
nicky.rodriquez@ccr.edu
RODRIQUEZ, Oscar ...... 919-278-2678 340 B
oscar.rodriquez@shawu.edu
RODRIQUEZ, Oscar, A .. 919-278-2678 340 B
oscar.rodriquez@shawu.edu
RODRÍGUEZ, Claribette . 787-751-0178 510 E
clrodriguez@uagm.edu
RODRÍGUEZ, Havidán ... 518-956-8030 316 A
presmail@albany.edu
RODRÍGUEZ, Inocencio 787-815-0000 511 H
inocencio.rodriguez@upr.edu
RODRÍGUEZ, Jose .... 787-786-3030 511 A
jorodriguez@ucb.edu.pr
RODRÍGUEZ, Julio, A ... 787-766-1717 510 G
um_jurodrigu@suagm.edu
RODRÍGUEZ, Mayra ...... 787-892-5115 508 F
mayra_rodriguez@sangerman.inter.edu
RODRÍGUEZ-DÁVILA, Soniemi .... 787-751-3601 511 F
soniemi.rodriguez@upr.edu
RODRÍGUEZ-FIGUEROA, Victor .... 787-993-8898 512 A
victor.rodriguez47@upr.edu
RODRÍGUEZ-MARTORELL, Nilsa .... 787-288-1118 510 I
RODRÍGUEZ MONTALBAN, Ramón .... 787-725-6500 505 G
rmontalban@albizu.edu
RODRÍGUEZ PÉREZ, Lourdes, C .... 787-764-0000 513 B
lourdes.rodriguez12@upr.edu
RODRÍGUEZ REYES, Zulyn .... 787-764-0000 513 B
zulyn.rodriguez@upr.edu
RODRÍGUEZ-RIVERA, Rafael, E .... 787-751-1600 509 A
rrodriguez@juris.inter.edu
ROE, Alexandria .... 608-265-0551 495 C
aroe@uwsa.edu
ROE, Elizabeth, P .... 330-471-8626 355 D
eproe@malone.edu
ROE, Laurie .... 541-956-7133 376 A
lroe@roguecc.edu
ROE, Lesa .... 214-752-8585 453 E
chancellor@unt.edu
ROE, Marc .... 406-377-9422 263 D
mroe@dawson.edu
ROE, Michael .... 845-431-8018 298 D
michael.roe@sunydutchess.edu
ROE, Robert, M .... 989-774-3933 222 E
roe1rm@cmich.edu
ROEBUCK, Alissa .... 931-393-1682 424 F
aroebuck@mscc.edu
ROEBUCK, David .... 573-592-5358 262 E
david.roebuck@westminster-mo.edu
ROEBUCK, Paris .... 910-775-4577 343 B
paris.roebuck@uncp.edu
ROEBUCK, Randy .... 316-677-9437 178 E
rroebuck@watc.edu
ROECKER, Pamela .... 781-768-7147 218 D
pamela.roecker@regiscollege.edu
ROECKER-PHELPS, Carolyn .... 937-229-3334 362 C
cphelps1@udayton.edu
ROEDEL, Glenn .... 215-780-1296 398 B
groedel@salus.edu
ROEDEL, Mark .... 903-233-3296 439 A
markroedel@letu.edu
ROEDER, Lynn, M .... 252-328-9297 341 A
roederl@ecu.edu
ROEHM, Michelle .... 336-758-5000 344 C
ROEHRICK, Randy .... 952-995-1525 238 C
randy.roehrick@hennepintech.edu
ROELFS, Melinda .... 620-235-4206 177 A
mroelfs@pittstate.edu
ROELKE, Scott .... 651-423-8297 238 A
scott.roelke@dctc.edu
ROELKE, Scott .... 651-450-3330 238 E
sroelke@inverhills.edu
ROELLKE, Christopher .. 386-822-7250 112 A
croellke@stetson.edu
ROELOFS, Lyle, D .... 859-985-3522 179 I
roelofsl@berea.edu
ROEMER, Lara .... 309-341-5219 134 B
lroemer@sandburg.edu
ROEMER, Nils .... 972-883-2984 455 B
nroemer@utdallas.edu
ROEPKE, Melinda .... 419-755-4848 357 B
mroepke@ncstatecollege.edu
ROESCH, Adam .... 618-262-8641 139 I
roescha@iecc.edu
ROESCHENTHALER, Robert .... 740-264-5591 352 B
rroeschenthaler@egcc.edu
ROESCHNTHALER, Robert .... 575-624-7000 286 C
ROESLER, Eric .... 715-346-3975 497 A
eric.roesler@uwsp.edu
ROESNER, Rebecca .... 309-556-3220 140 F
rroesner@iwu.edu
ROESSEL, Charles .... 928-724-6669.. 12 D
cmroessel@dinecollege.edu
ROESSLEIN, Tim .... 314-256-8865 250 D
roesslein@ai.edu
ROEST, Michael .... 415-503-6217.. 61 D
mroest@sfcm.edu
ROETHEL, Bryan .... 804-862-6100 470 C
broethel@rbc.edu
ROETHEMEYER, Robert, V .... 260-452-2146 154 I
robert.roethemeyer@ctsfw.edu
ROETHER, Diane .... 940-668-4338 440 F
droether@nctc.edu
ROETHLER, Don .... 701-224-5485 346 A
donald.roethler@bismarckstate.edu
ROETTGER, Linda .... 219-464-5958 162 D
linda.roettger@valpo.edu
ROEWER, Anita .... 815-455-8737 143 I
aroewer@mchenry.edu
ROGALSKI, Kathryn .... 920-498-5401 499 G
kathryn.rogalski@nwtc.edu
ROGAN, Doreen .... 207-509-7290 196 E
drogan@unity.edu
ROGAN, Doreen .... 207-216-4320 195 J
drogan@yccc.edu
ROGELSTAD, Todd .... 701-845-7209 345 G
todd.rogelstad@vcsu.edu
ROGER-GORDON, A. Patrick .... 212-346-1295 311 A
arogergordon@pace.edu
ROGERS, Amy .... 570-321-4135 389 B
rogers@lycoming.edu
ROGERS, Audra .... 620-450-2113 177 B
audrar@prattcc.edu
ROGERS, Benjamin .... 512-245-4822 450 C
br16@txstate.edu
ROGERS, Brandon .... 253-589-5727 478 J
brandon.rogers@cptc.edu
ROGERS, Brenda .... 408-741-2011.. 75 C
brenda.rogers@wvm.edu
ROGERS, Brian .... 503-494-8362 374 H
cdrcadmin@ohsu.edu
ROGERS, Bridget .... 212-659-7209 303 H
brogers@tkc.edu
ROGERS, Carl .... 770-533-6899 122 B
crogers@laniertech.edu
ROGERS, Carrie .... 218-299-3000 235 H
ROGERS, Chris .... 541-867-8549 374 F
chris.rogers@oregoncoast.edu
ROGERS, Christina .... 212-659-7200 303 H
crogers@tkc.edu
ROGERS, Christine .... 602-383-8228.. 16 C
crogers@uat.edu
ROGERS, Christopher ... 847-970-4833 152 I
crogers@usml.edu
ROGERS, Christopher ... 803-777-5643 413 A
crogers@mailbox.sc.edu
ROGERS, Cindy, A .... 972-860-8187 434 G
car3810@dcccd.edu
ROGERS, Cody .... 907-474-6026.. 10 A
cbrogers@alaska.edu
ROGERS, Craig .... 706-776-0104 124 D
crogers@piedmont.edu
ROGERS, Craig, L .... 270-789-5057 180 A
crogers@campbellsville.edu
ROGERS, David .... 602-384-2555.. 11 F
dave.rogers@bryanuniversity.edu
ROGERS, David, E .... 315-684-6044 321 A
rogersde@morrisville.edu
ROGERS, Deana .... 217-854-3231 133 I
ROGERS, Deborah .... 585-340-9588 296 D
drogers@crcds.edu
ROGERS, Deborah, A .... 215-641-6506 390 C
drogers@mc3.edu
ROGERS, Donnita .... 405-466-3262 366 C
ddrogers@langston.edu
ROGERS, Duke .... 785-227-3380 172 A
rogersk@bethanylb.edu
ROGERS, Elsa, P .... 239-513-1122 102 D
erogers@hodges.edu
ROGERS, Frederick .... 803-508-7272 406 C
rogersf@atc.edu
ROGERS, Gail .... 423-746-5202 426 C
grogers@tnwesleyan.edu
ROGERS, Gary .... 816-322-0110 251 B
gary.rogers@calvary.edu
ROGERS, Genelle .... 817-202-6214 444 I
genellerogers@swau.edu
ROGERS, Heather .... 270-901-1116 182 H
heather.rogers@kctcs.edu
ROGERS, Holly .... 518-738-8500 299 C
ROGERS, Irina .... 205-453-6300.. 93 H
ROGERS, J. Orion .... 540-831-5404 469 D
jorogers@radford.edu
ROGERS, J.R .... 707-965-7362.. 55 I
jrogers@puc.edu
ROGERS, Jack .... 724-938-4961 393 E
rogers@calu.edu
ROGERS, James .... 212-327-8506 312 G
jrogers@mail.rockefeller.edu
ROGERS, Jan .... 229-500-3056 114 H
jan.rogers@asurams.edu
ROGERS, Janet .... 765-998-5330 161 C
jnrogers@taylor.edu
ROGERS, Jason .... 615-460-6441 418 B
jason.rogers@belmont.edu
ROGERS, Jaye .... 765-641-4442 153 G
jlrogers2@anderson.edu
ROGERS, Jeff, A .... 304-457-6337 486 E
rogersja@ab.edu
ROGERS, Jevita .... 719-255-3460.. 84 C
jrogers3@uccs.edu
ROGERS, Jolene, R .... 712-362-0431 167 B
jrogers@iowalakes.edu
ROGERS, Josh .... 928-536-6227.. 14 J
joshua.rogers@npc.edu
ROGERS, Judy .... 509-313-6131 480 F
rogers2@gonzaga.edu
ROGERS, Julian .... 216-368-1723 349 D
julian.rogers@case.edu
ROGERS, Kathleen, R .... 617-521-2276 218 G
kathleen.rogers@simmons.edu
ROGERS, Katrina, S ...... 805-898-2924.. 42 D
krogers@fielding.edu
ROGERS, Kelly .... 815-280-2217 141 B
krogers@jjc.edu
ROGERS, Kim .... 580-559-5677 365 K
kimmrog@ecok.edu
ROGERS, Kimberly, R ... 510-215-3806.. 40 B
krogers@contracosta.edu
ROGERS, Lalita .... 318-670-9223 191 D
lrogers@susla.edu
ROGERS, Larson .... 617-588-1318 206 F
lrogers@bfit.edu
ROGERS, Lisa, C .... 615-898-2150 422 C
lisa.rogers@mtsu.edu
ROGERS, Lynn .... 518-782-6654 315 E
lrogers@siena.edu
ROGERS, Mark .... 478-274-7871 123 I
mwrogers@oftc.edu
ROGERS, Melissa .... 901-321-3545 418 G
cbu@bkstr.com
ROGERS, Michael .... 202-274-5986.. 94 B
michael.rogers@udc.edu
ROGERS, Michael, B ..... 607-735-1770 298 H
mrogers@elmira.edu
ROGERS, Michelle, L .... 909-748-8138.. 72 F
michelle_rogers@redlands.edu
ROGERS, Mike .... 209-946-2569.. 71 E
mrogers@pacific.edu
ROGERS, Nancy, B .... 812-237-7900 156 D
nancy.rogers@indstate.edu
ROGERS, Ogden .... 715-425-3319 496 F
ogden.rogers@uwrf.edu
ROGERS, Patricia, L ...... 218-733-7600 238 G
patricia.rogers@lsc.edu
ROGERS, Patrick .... 802-635-1417 463 G
patrick.rogers@northernvermont.edu
ROGERS, SJ, Patrick ..... 570-941-6153 401 F
patrick.rogers@scranton.edu
ROGERS, Peter .... 510-883-2083.. 41 B
progers@dspt.edu
ROGERS, Phil .... 208-459-5282 131 C
progers@collegeofidaho.edu
ROGERS, Philip .... 252-328-6212 341 A
chancelloroffice@ecu.edu
ROGERS, Randy .... 336-386-3466 338 D
rogersrj@surry.edu
ROGERS, Ray .... 512-245-2645 450 C
r_r836@txstate.edu
ROGERS, Rickey .... 870-245-5220.. 20 D
rogersr@obu.edu
ROGERS, Rodney, K ..... 419-372-2211 348 G
rrogers@bgsu.edu
ROGERS, Russell .... 201-216-5688 283 D
russell.rogers@stevens.edu
ROGERS, Sandra .... 630-889-6461 145 E
srogers@nuhs.edu
ROGERS, Sarah .... 402-872-2379 268 E
srogers@peru.edu
ROGERS, Scott .... 509-542-4834 479 A
srogers@columbiabasin.edu
ROGERS, Sonya .... 251-981-3771.... 5 A
sonya.rogers@columbiasouthern.edu
ROGERS, Stephanie ...... 318-670-9244 191 D
srogers@susla.edu
ROGERS, Steve .... 541-440-4625 376 G
steve.rogers@umpqua.edu
ROGERS, Susan .... 845-431-8952 298 D
susan.rogers1@sunydutchess.edu
ROGERS, Tammy .... 706-880-8344 122 A
trogers@lagrange.edu
ROGERS, Tamy .... 214-333-5158 434 C
tamyr@dbu.edu
ROGERS, Tarsha, M ..... 252-335-3327 341 B
tmrogers@ecsu.edu
ROGERS, Terri .... 417-328-1520 259 I
tlrogers@sbuniv.edu
ROGERS, Terri .... 580-745-2510 369 G
trogers@se.edu
ROGERS, Thomas .... 502-935-6853 182 C
thomas.rogers@kctcs.edu
ROGERS, Thomas, A ..... 719-333-6940 503 D
thomas.rogers.1@us.af.mil
ROGERS, Timothy .... 315-866-0300 301 D
rogerstd@herkimer.edu
ROGERS, Toby .... 806-720-7627 439 D
toby.rogers@lcu.edu
ROGERS, Tracy .... 719-587-7990.. 77 G
tracy_rogers@adams.edu
ROGERS-ADKINSON, Diana .... 570-389-4308 393 D
drogers@bloomu.edu
ROGERS-LOWERY, Constance .... 704-645-4803 327 I
clowery@catawba.edu
ROGG, Michael .... 660-596-7172 259 M
mrogg@sfccmo.edu
ROGGIE, Edie .... 315-786-2200 303 C
eroggie@sunyjefferson.edu
ROGGOW, Michael .... 508-588-9100 215 A
mroggow@massasoit.mass.edu
ROGSTAD, Leanne .... 763-488-2465 238 C
leanne.rogstad@hennepintech.edu
ROHALL, David .... 740-654-6711 358 K
rohall@ohio.edu
ROHAN, James, P .... 920-465-2075 495 F
rohanj@uwgb.edu
ROHAN, Robert, C .... 240-500-2367 199 C
rcrohan@hagerstowncc.edu
ROHANI, Mushka .... 425-640-1647 480 A
mushka.rohani@edcc.edu
ROHDE, Monika .... 516-686-7615 308 I
monika.rohde@nyit.edu
ROHDE, Scott .... 860-685-2809.. 90 B
srohde@wesleyan.edu
ROHDER-TONELLI, Kelly .... 815-280-2915 141 B
krohder@jjc.edu
ROHDIN, Benjamin .... 201-200-3156 279 D
brohdin@njcu.edu
ROHLEDER, John .... 651-779-3496 237 H
john.rohleder@century.edu
ROHLENA, Andrea .... 712-274-6400 171 B
andrea.rohlena@witcc.edu
ROHLENA, Mark .... 540-636-2900 465 L
mark.rohlena@christendom.edu
ROHLFING, Alexis .... 603-880-8308 274 D
arohlfing@thomasmorecollege.edu
ROHLMAN, Jessica .... 501-977-2004.. 23 A
rohlman@uaccm.edu

ROHMAN, Chad .... 708-524-6816 137 C
crohman@dom.edu
ROHMANN, LeeAnn ...... 661-940-9300.. 45 B
ROHN, Marisa .... 330-494-6170 360 K
mrohn@starkstate.edu
ROHNER, Christy .... 270-686-4243 179 J
christy.rohner@brescia.edu
ROHNER, Tom .... 312-662-4141 132 G
trohner@adler.edu
ROHR, Margie .... 973-290-4054 282 I
mrohr@steu.edu
ROHR ADAMS, Betsy .... 315-386-7951 320 B
rohradams@canton.edu
ROHRBACK, Jane, T ..... 248-204-3177 227 A
jrohrback@ltu.edu
ROHRBAUGH,
Suzanne, Y .... 336-633-0218 337 A
syrohrbaugh@randolph.edu
ROHRER, Brad .... 305-284-1256 113 C
brohrer@miami.edu
ROHRER, Thelma .... 260-982-5327 159 J
tsrohrer@manchester.edu
ROHRMAN, Patrick .... 205-940-6302 332 C
patrick.rohrman@beaufortccc.edu
ROHWER, Debbie .... 940-565-3514 453 E
debbie.rohwer@unt.edu
ROIDT, Joseph .... 605-995-2625 415 A
joseph.roidt@dwu.edu
ROIG, Katy .... 619-260-7404.. 72 I
kroig@sandiego.edu
ROJAS, Balbina, J .... 787-766-1717 510 G
barojas@uagm.edu
ROJAS, Carlos .... 787-840-2575 509 I
crojas@psm.edu
ROJAS, Daniela .... 402-399-2603 266 F
drojas@csm.edu
ROJAS, Eddy, M .... 651-962-6720 244 E
eddy.rojas@stthomas.edu
ROJAS, Eddy, M .... 937-229-4632 362 C
erojas1@udayton.edu
ROJAS, Elias .... 907-564-8081.... 9 F
erojas@alaskapacific.edu
ROJAS, Felipe, E .... 304-336-8474 490 B
felipe.rojas@westliberty.edu
ROJAS, Frank .... 626-624-4673.. 50 D
ROJAS, Gilbert .... 801-274-3280 461 E
gilbert.rojas@wgu.edu
ROJAS, Jason .... 860-297-4166.. 89 B
jason.rojas@trincoll.edu
ROJAS, Jesus .... 912-525-5000 124 I
jrojas@scad.edu
ROJAS, Legier .... 787-798-3001 511 B
legier.rojas@uccaribe.edu
ROJAS, Liliana .... 415-422-6707.. 72 J
lrojas3@usfca.edu
ROJAS, Lisa .... 731-425-8835 424 E
lrojas@jscc.edu
ROJAS, Maria .... 620-225-0186 173 D
mrojas@dc3.edu
ROJAS, Raquel .... 787-765-1915 509 B
rrojas@opto.inter.edu
ROJAS, Rebecca .... 626-529-8500.. 55 F
ROJAS, Robyn, D .... 405-325-3337 370 K
rrojas@ou.edu
ROJAS, Rodney .... 213-613-2200.. 65 E
rodney_rojas@sciarc.edu
ROJAS-DUARTE, Hilda .. 312-341-2005 148 E
hrojasduarte@roosevelt.edu
ROJAS-MORA, Norma ..... 661-395-4382.. 46 L
norma.rojas@bakersfieldcollege.edu
ROJAS SOSA,
Alejandro .... 719-549-2314.. 80 B
alejandro.rojassosa@csupueblo.edu
ROJCEWICZ, Peter .... 805-969-3626.. 55 J
projcewicz@pacifica.edu
ROKSANDIC, Stevo .... 614-234-1644 356 E
sroksandic@mchs.com
ROLAND, David, E .... 706-233-7329 125 C
droland@shorter.edu
ROLAND, Harriet, A ...... 803-533-3790 411 G
rolandha@scsu.edu
ROLAND, Kirc, J .... 360-442-2471 481 D
kroland@lowercolumbia.edu
ROLAND, Meg .... 541-917-4999 373 G
rolandm@linnbenton.edu
ROLAND, Shane .... 478-471-2414 122 F
shane.roland@mga.edu
ROLAND, Troy .... 801-883-8336 459 A
ROLAND, Yvonne .... 719-333-1309 503 D
yvonne.roland@usafa.edu
ROLDAN, Rebecca .... 310-506-7596.. 56 G
rebecca.roldan@pepperdine.edu

ROLEN, Aneisa, L .... 865-694-6403 425 B
alrolen@pstcc.edu
ROLEN, Chris .... 408-741-2055.. 75 D
chris.rolen@wvm.edu
ROLEN, Dalton Chris .... 408-741-2055.. 75 C
chris.rolen@wvm.edu
ROLEN, Scott .... 541-917-4420 373 G
rolens@linnbenton.edu
ROLEY, V. Vance .... 808-956-8377 129 E
vroley@hawaii.edu
ROLFE, Alexander .... 503-554-2414 373 A
ROLFE, Kim .... 509-526-3011 486 B
rolfekb@whitman.edu
ROLFES, Katherine .... 337-521-8906 188 I
katherine.rolfes@solacc.edu
ROLFS, Trevor .... 620-792-9378 171 I
rolfst@bartonccc.edu
ROLING, Barbara .... 563-589-0332 171 A
broling@wartburgseminary.edu
ROLL, Debbie, J .... 907-564-8220.... 9 F
droll@alaskapacific.edu
ROLL, Marcus .... 269-783-2193 231 A
mroll@swmich.edu
ROLL, Todd .... 608-342-1245 496 E
rollt@uwplatt.edu
ROLLAND, Erik .... 909-869-4869.. 30 A
erolland@cpp.edu
ROLLAND, Erik .... 909-869-2400.. 30 A
erolland@cpp.edu
ROLLE, Anthony .... 401-277-5489 405 E
anthony_rolle@uri.edu
ROLLE, Dominique .... 803-813-1144 411 G
drolle1@scsu.edu
ROLLE, Jo-Ann .... 718-270-5110 294 G
jrolle@mec.cuny.edu
ROLLE, Kevin .... 334-229-4241.... 4 A
krolle@alasu.edu
ROLLE, Kevin, A .... 334-229-6500.... 4 A
krolle@alasu.edu
ROLLEFSON, Kathy .... 641-585-8681 170 I
kathy.rollefson@waldorf.edu
ROLLER, Steven, A .... 617-228-2394 214 C
sroller@bhcc.mass.edu
ROLLING, Kristin .... 608-246-6677 499 A
krolling1@madisoncollege.edu
ROLLING, Matthew .... 402-643-4052 269 A
ROLLINGS, David .... 803-323-2191 414 D
rollingsd@winthrop.edu
ROLLINGS, Grenna .... 972-860-8181 434 G
grollings@dcccd.edu
ROLLINO, Richard .... 740-283-6223 352 I
rrollino@franciscan.edu
ROLLINS, Adam .... 423-869-6421 421 A
adam.rollins@lmunet.edu
ROLLINS, Alison .... 301-295-3357 503 C
alison.rollins@usuhs.edu
ROLLINS, Cheryl .... 443-885-4429 201 A
cheryl.rollins@morgan.edu
ROLLINS, Kate .... 402-354-7264 268 B
kate.rollins@methodistcollege.edu
ROLLINS, Kathy .... 864-379-6546 409 E
rollins@erskine.edu
ROLLINS, Maxwell .... 843-863-7956 407 B
mrollins@csuniv.edu
ROLLINS, Pam .... 334-420-4253.... 3 H
prollins@trenholmstate.edu
ROLLINS, Stephen .... 907-786-1825.... 9 J
srollins@alaska.edu
ROLLINS, Tina .... 757-727-5371 467 G
tina.rollins@hamptonu.edu
ROLLINS, Tyler .... 916-691-7052.. 50 H
rollint@crc.losrios.edu
ROLLISON, Jeffrey .... 610-647-4400 385 L
jrollison@immaculata.edu
ROLLMAN,
Catherine, A .... 804-752-7270 469 F
crollman@rmc.edu
ROLLOFF, Mary, K .... 920-433-6639 491 G
mary.rolloff@bellincollege.edu
ROLLOR, Michael .... 410-706-1875 203 A
mrollor@umaryland.edu
ROLLS, Dickie .... 620-252-7053 173 A
rolls.dickie@coffeyville.edu
ROLLS, Niccole .... 301-696-3717 199 E
rolls@hood.edu
ROLNICK, Harriet, M ..... 213-738-6690.. 66 B
scale@swlaw.edu
ROLOFF, ReBecca, K .... 651-690-6525 243 A
broloff@stkate.edu
ROLON, Reynaldo .... 787-279-1912 508 A
rrolon@bayamon.inter.edu
ROLPH, Marc .... 601-815-5133 249 E
mrolph@umc.edu

ROLSTON, Stacey .... 608-890-0960 495 C
stacey.rolston@uwss.wisconsin.edu
ROMÁN, Brenda .... 787-878-5475 507 L
broman@arecibo.inter.edu
ROM, Kjetil .... 541-881-5746 376 F
krom@tvcc.cc
ROMAGNI, Elizabeth ..... 901-321-3306 418 G
elizabeth.romagni@cbu.edu
ROMAGNI, Joanne .... 423-425-1743 427 C
joanne-romagni@utc.edu
ROMAGNOLI, Janice ..... 615-655-7274 292 H
jaromagnoli@cazenovia.edu
ROMALI, Reagan .... 310-233-4051.. 49 B
romalir@lahc.edu
ROMAN, Alberto, J .... 323-265-8663.. 48 J
vanhalkm@elac.edu
ROMAN, Allison .... 616-234-5536 232 B
alli.roman@vai.edu
ROMAN, Andrew .... 251-981-3771.... 5 A
andrew.roman@columbiasouthern.edu
ROMAN, Angela .... 231-591-2674 224 A
angelaroman@ferris.edu
ROMAN, Aris .... 787-891-0925 507 K
aroman@aguadilla.inter.edu
ROMAN, Daniel .... 773-878-4699 149 A
ROMAN, Gabriel .... 787-738-2161 512 C
gabriel.roman2@upr.edu
ROMAN, Irene .... 954-322-1612.. 99 F
ROMAN, Jennifer .... 214-329-4447 430 K
jennifer.roman@bgu.edu
ROMAN, Juan, E .... 787-841-2000 509 J
jroman@pucpr.edu
ROMAN, Judith .... 787-780-0070 505 F
judroman@caribbean.edu
ROMAN, Kristen .... 608-262-4527 495 D
kristen.roman@wisc.edu
ROMAN, Michael .... 973-384-9554 291 E
michael-roman@berkeleycollege.edu
ROMAN, Michael .... 973-384-9554 275 I
michael-roman@berkeleycollege.edu
ROMAN, Vladimir .... 787-763-6425 507 J
vroman@inter.edu
ROMAN, Yosmeriz .... 856-225-6664 281 G
yosmeriz.roman@camden.rutgers.edu
ROMAN, Yosmeriz .... 513-556-1100 361 J
yosmeriz.roman@uc.edu
ROMAN-LAGUNAS,
Victoria .... 219-980-6707 157 C
viroman@iu.edu
ROMANCZUK, Jeffrey .... 704-499-9200.. 93 H
ROMANDINI, Russ .... 513-618-1930 350 E
rromandini@ccms.edu
ROMANELLI, Ralph .... 718-631-6262 295 C
ROMANELLI, Tina .... 919-760-8554 331 D
cromanelli@meredith.edu
ROMANELLO, Mary .... 202-884-9677.. 94 A
romanellom@trinitydc.edu
ROMANO, Angela .... 845-431-8097 298 D
angela.romano@sunydutchess.edu
ROMANO, Carol .... 301-295-9002 503 C
carol.romano@usuhs.edu
ROMANO, Cenia, K ...... 787-884-3838 505 D
vpacademico@atenascollege.edu
ROMANO, Christopher .. 201-684-7309 280 H
cromano@ramapo.edu
ROMANO, Fred, D .... 630-515-6388 144 F
froman@midwestern.edu
ROMANO, Joan .... 617-989-4908 219 F
romanoj3@wit.edu
ROMANO, Judith, J ...... 864-294-3470 409 H
judith.romano@furman.edu
ROMANO, Linda .... 718-990-6865 313 G
romanol@stjohns.edu
ROMANO, Nicole .... 302-356-6846.. 91 E
nicole.romano@wilmu.edu
ROMANO, Susan .... 585-245-5731 318 B
romano@geneseo.edu
ROMANO, Victor .... 305-899-3756.. 96 A
vromano@barry.edu
ROMANO, Wendy, W .... 215-871-6300 395 G
wendyr@pcom.edu
ROMANOSKY, Neil .... 740-593-2705 358 K
romanosky@ohio.edu
ROMANS, John .... 405-744-3373 367 G
john.romans@okstate.edu
ROMANSTEIN,
Stanley, E .... 513-556-3737 361 J
stanley.romanstein@uc.edu
ROMANT, Stacy .... 414-288-3654 493 E
stacy.romant@marquette.edu
ROMAY, Melanie .... 215-717-6030 400 E
ROMBALSKI, Patrick ..... 617-792-3636 134 E
prombalski@chamberlain.edu

ROMBES, Nicholas .... 313-993-1000 231 E
rombesnd@udmercy.edu
ROME, Alan, K .... 440-943-7600 360 E
akrome@dioceseofcleveland.org
ROME, Alan, K .... 440-943-7600 360 E
cpl@dioceseofcleveland.org
ROME, Dennis .... 773-442-5420 146 A
d-rome@neiu.edu
ROME, JoAnne .... 413-552-2259 214 F
jrome@hcc.edu
ROME, Michaela .... 516-686-7403 308 I
mrome@nyit.edu
ROMEO, Beth .... 269-749-7644 229 J
bromeo@olivetcollege.edu
ROMEO, Jamie .... 860-701-3530.. 88 D
romeo_j@mitchell.edu
ROMEO TARTE, Mary ... 313-664-7451 222 H
mrtarte@collegeforcreativestudies.edu
ROMER, Andrew .... 850-474-2200 111 F
aromer@uwf.edu
ROMER-NIEMIEC, Ellen . 773-371-5445 134 D
eromer-niemiec@ctu.edu
ROMERO, Andy .... 505-747-2166 287 H
andy@nnmc.edu
ROMERO, Angel, F .... 787-765-1915 509 B
aromero@opto.inter.edu
ROMERO, Bianca .... 909-448-4693.. 71 C
bromero@laverne.edu
ROMERO, Cecilia .... 505-747-5477 287 H
cromero@nnmc.edu
ROMERO, Christina ...... 714-564-6091.. 58 F
romero_christina@sac.edu
ROMERO, Clarence .... 505-454-3369 286 J
clromero@nmhu.edu
ROMERO, Clorinda .... 575-758-8914 286 H
clorindar@midwiferycollege.edu
ROMERO, Cynthia .... 757-446-7414 466 D
romerocc@evms.edu
ROMERO, Edward, W ... 903-886-5027 447 B
edward.romero@tamuc.edu
ROMERO, Eileen .... 914-594-4495 309 B
eileen_romero@nymc.edu
ROMERO, Elizabeth .... 951-827-2750.. 70 B
elizabeth.romero@ucr.edu
ROMERO, III, Fermin ... 607-778-5657 317 D
romerof@sunybroome.edu
ROMERO, Henrietta .... 505-454-3405 286 J
hromero@nmhu.edu
ROMERO, Herminio ...... 787-622-8000 511 D
hromero@pupr.edu
ROMERO, Jessica .... 787-894-2828 513 C
jessica.romero1@upr.edu
ROMERO, Jose .... 787-864-2222 508 C
jose.romero@guayama.inter.edu
ROMERO, Julie .... 505-984-6075 288 C
julie.romero@sjc.edu
ROMERO, Lizbeth .... 787-878-5475 507 L
lromero@arecibo.inter.edu
ROMERO, Manuel .... 212-220-1238 293 A
mromero@bmcc.cuny.edu
ROMERO, Monica .... 619-388-5025.. 60 J
mdromero@sdccd.edu
ROMERO, Narda .... 914-674-7841 306 C
nromero@mercy.edu
ROMERO, Nehemias ..... 626-968-1328.. 47 G
ROMERO, Ramona, E ... 609-258-2511 280 D
ramonar@princeton.edu
ROMERO, Reyna .... 713-221-8460 453 A
romeror@uhd.edu
ROMERO, Roxane .... 602-384-2555.. 11 F
roxane.romero@bryanuniversity.edu
ROMERO, Sally .... 970-943-2150.. 85 C
sromero@western.edu
ROMERO, Van, D .... 575-835-5646 286 K
van.romero@nmt.edu
ROMERO, Victor .... 432-837-8085 450 B
vromero@sulross.edu
ROMERO, Victoria .... 909-621-8149.. 63 F
vromero@scrippscollege.edu
ROMERO-ALDAZ,
Patrick .... 303-458-4086.. 83 E
promeroaldaz@regis.edu
ROMERO-BEGLEY,
Carlita .... 559-325-3600.. 28 D
cromerobegley@chsu.edu
ROMERO-NIEVES,
Luis, E .... 787-751-1912 509 A
lromero@juris.inter.edu
ROMIG, Kenneth, J .... 724-946-7141 402 D
romigkj@westminster.edu
ROMIG, Phillip .... 303-273-3866.. 79 J
promig3@mines.edu
ROMINE, Rebecca .... 601-965-7021 245 B
rromine@belhaven.edu

ROMINES, Ellen, B .... 202-685-3911 502 K
ellen.b.romines.civ@ndu.edu
ROMIOUS, Angila .... 424-207-3753.. 55 C
aromious@otis.edu
ROMKEMA, Priscilla .... 605-642-6262 416 E
priscilla.romkema@bhsu.edu
ROMKEY, Matthew .... 515-643-6663 168 D
mromkey@mercydesmoines.org
ROMNEY, Brett .... 602-366-9699.. 16 G
brett.romney@phoenix.edu
ROMNEY, Jake .... 208-496-3947 130 I
romneyri@byui.edu
ROMO, Anthony .... 559-651-2500.. 61 H
ROMO, Nanette .... 520-515-5399.. 11 M
romon@cochise.edu
ROMO, Paul .... 623-845-3051.. 13 C
paul.romo@gccaz.edu
ROMRELL, Danae .... 208-496-7543 130 I
romrelld@byui.edu
RONAN, Donald .... 937-769-1800 347 H
dronan@antioch.edu
RONCA, Paul, L .... 804-523-5239 474 A
pronca@reynolds.edu
RONCOLATO, David ...... 814-332-5318 378 A
droncola@allegheny.edu
RONDA, Rene, S .... 787-743-7979 510 H
rsronda@suagm.edu
RONDEAU, RET.,
Ann Elisabeth .... 831-656-2511 502 M
ann.rondeau@nps.edu
RONDEAU, Heather .... 320-762-4589 237 C
heather.rondeau@alextech.edu
RONDEAU, Janet .... 518-244-2214 313 A
rondej@sage.edu
RONDINELLI, Diane .... 904-826-0084.. 72 G
drondinelli@usa.edu
RONDON, Marvin .... 910-592-8081 337 G
mrondon@sampsoncc.edu
RONEY, Kristen .... 808-932-7332 129 D
ksroney@hawaii.edu
RONEY, Kylee .... 217-362-6423 144 G
kroney@millikin.edu
RONEY, Linda .... 214-333-5147 434 C
linda@dbu.edu
RONK, Chris .... 336-725-8344 327 H
ronkc@carolinau.edu
RONKOSKI, Bob .... 636-922-8604 258 J
rronkoski@stchas.edu
RONNEBURG, Debra ..... 208-282-2602 131 G
ronndebr@isu.edu
RONNFELDT, Derek .... 253-833-9111 480 I
dronnfeltd@greenriver.edu
RONNING, Jon .... 615-868-6503 422 B
RONNING, Teresa .... 518-743-2261 320 A
ronningt@sunyacc.edu
RONNING LINDGREN,
Rachel .... 805-493-3690.. 29 C
rronning@callutheran.edu
ROOD, Denine .... 320-629-5126 240 D
denine.rood@pine.edu
ROOD, Robert .... 716-839-8503 298 A
rrood@daemen.edu
ROOD, TJ (Garrett) .... 812-237-6311 156 D
garrett.rood@indstate.edu
ROOF, Karin .... 843-953-4871 407 C
kroof1@citadel.edu
ROOF, Rick .... 434-582-2177 468 E
raroof@liberty.edu
ROOF, Steven, E .... 304-367-4363 489 K
steven.roof@fairmontstate.edu
ROOFNER, Perry, F .... 412-397-5256 397 B
roofner@rmu.edu
ROOHANI, Ben .... 312-850-7154 135 H
broohani@ccc.edu
ROOHPARVAR,
Shahrooz .... 707-826-3351.. 33 C
sr406@humboldt.edu
ROOK, Steve .... 501-332-0230.. 18 B
srook@asutr.edu
ROOK, Tony .... 252-618-6535 334 D
rookt@edgecombe.edu
ROOKE, Michael .... 860-738-6300.. 87 C
mrooke@nwcc.edu
ROOKER, Darrin .... 315-568-3063 310 B
drooker@nycc.edu
ROOKER, Suzanne .... 580-477-7944 371 D
suzanne.rooker@wosc.edu
ROOKS, Bryan .... 970-248-1252.. 78 J
brooks@coloradomesa.edu
ROOKS, James .... 616-526-8694 222 C
jrooks@calvin.edu
ROOKS, Stephanie .... 770-962-7580 121 E
srooks@gwinnetttech.edu
ROOKSBY, Jacob .... 509-313-3700 480 F
rooksby@lawschool.gonzaga.edu
ROONEY, CM, Aidan, R 716-286-8400 309 H
arooney@niagara.edu
ROONEY, Anna-Marie ... 858-784-8469.. 64 A
ROONEY, Gerard, J .... 585-385-8010 313 F
grooney@sjfc.edu
ROONEY, Jo Ann .... 312-915-6400 143 C
president@luc.edu
ROONEY, John .... 402-643-4052 269 A
ROONEY, Larry .... 802-485-2499 462 F
lrooney@norwich.edu
ROONEY, Paul .... 407-582-1100 113 I
prooney@valenciacollege.edu
ROONEY, Paula, M .... 508-541-1658 209 A
prooney@dean.edu
ROONEY, Thomas .... 561-237-7181 103 W
trooney@lynn.edu
ROOPNARINE, Darshini 315-445-4661 303 I
roopnatd@lemoyne.edu
ROOS, David .... 435-222-1252.. 83 G
droos@rvu.edu
ROOS, Jannicke .... 617-746-1990 210 H
jannicke.roos@hult.edu
ROOS, Johan .... 617-619-1900 210 H
johan.roos@hult.edu
ROOSA, Mark, S .... 310-506-4252.. 56 G
mark.roosa@pepperdine.edu
ROOSE, Craig .... 641-628-7632 164 D
roosec@central.edu
ROOSE, Robert .... 989-358-7200 221 C
rooser@alpenacc.edu
ROOSEVELT, Mark .... 505-984-6098 288 C
mroosevelt@sjc.edu
ROOT, David .... 606-539-4406 185 E
david.root@ucumberlands.edu
ROOT, Deborah .... 870-245-5510.. 20 D
rootd@obu.edu
ROOT, Jeff .... 870-245-4186.. 20 D
rootj@obu.edu
ROOT, John .... 512-245-2585 450 C
jr28@txstate.edu
ROOT, Mark, J .... 574-807-7219 154 B
rootm1@betheluniversity.edu
ROOT, Rennie, A .... 563-588-7775 168 A
rennie.root@loras.edu
ROOT, Shannon, A .... 210-832-2161 453 C
sroot@uiwtx.edu
ROOTH, Gerald, T .... 301-447-5003 201 B
rooth@msmary.edu
ROOTS, Keith, D .... 757-594-0581 465 M
keith.roots@cnu.edu
ROPELLA, Kristina .... 414-288-5460 493 E
kristina.ropella@marquette.edu
ROPER, Amy .... 803-793-5149 408 G
ropera@denmarktech.edu
ROPER, Chris .... 304-358-2000 487 D
ROPER, Craig .... 618-545-3137 141 E
croper@kaskaskia.edu
ROPER, David .... 843-349-6532 408 A
droper@coastal.edu
ROPER, Gina .... 541-881-5577 376 F
groper@tvcc.cc
ROPER, Lari .... 843-349-3658 409 J
laura.roper@hgtc.edu
ROPER, Melinda .... 805-493-3553.. 29 C
mroper@callutheran.edu
ROPER, Teri .... 501-882-8967.. 17 D
tlroper@asub.edu
ROPER-DOTEN, Emily ... 781-292-2201 210 A
emily.roper-doten@olin.edu
ROPETI, Siamaua .... 684-699-2722 504 B
s.ropeti@amsamoa.edu
ROQUEMORE, Glenn ..... 800-477-2254.. 29 G
groquemore@calsouthern.edu
RORABAUGH, Jim .... 307-532-8336 501 B
RORK, Jeanette .... 434-947-8289 469 E
jrork@randolphcollege.edu
RORKE LEVY, Pam .... 415-771-7020.. 61 C
RORRER, Caleb .... 336-342-4261 337 E
rorrerm8871@rockinghamcc.edu
ROS, Vimul .... 215-702-4553 380 A
vros@cairn.edu
ROSA, Belinda .... 787-743-7979 510 H
ac_brosa@suagm.edu
ROSA, Carmen .... 203-576-4652.. 89 C
carosa@bridgeport.edu
ROSA, Jerry .... 718-518-6561 294 B
jrosa@hostos.cuny.edu
ROSA, Jessie .... 334-244-3712.... 4 E
jrosa@aum.edu
ROSA, Joe .... 925-631-4105.. 59 I
jtr2@stmarys-ca.edu
ROSA, Maria .... 270-809-4225 184 D
mrosa1@murraystate.edu
ROSA, Peter .... 203-837-8376.. 86 B
rosap@wcsu.edu
ROSA, Sandra .... 787-279-1912 508 A
srosa@bayamon.inter.edu
ROSA, Veronica .... 603-358-2425 274 H
veronica.rosa@keene.edu
ROSA-NUNEZ,
Waleska, Y .... 787-480-2386 506 C
wrosa01@sanjuan.pr
ROSAASEN, Orlynn .... 701-777-3823 345 B
orlynn.rosaasen@und.edu
ROSACCO, Claire .... 216-987-4804 351 E
claire.rosacco@tri-c.edu
ROSADO, Akilah .... 212-875-4596 290 H
arosado@bankstreet.edu
ROSADO, Alexander ...... 787-878-5475 507 L
alrosado@arecibo.inter.edu
ROSADO, Christine .... 908-852-1440 276 G
christine.rosado@centenaryuniversity.edu
ROSADO, Ernie .... 251-981-3771.... 5 A
ernie.rosado@columbiasouthern.edu
ROSADO, Inia .... 787-878-5475 507 L
irosado@arecibo.inter.edu
ROSADO, Martin .... 787-884-6000 507 D
mrosado@icprjc.edu
ROSADO, Reinaldo .... 787-284-1912 508 E
rrosado@ponce.inter.edu
ROSADO, Renee .... 413-205-3248 205 F
renee.rosado@aic.edu
ROSADO-BERRIOS,
Carmen, C .... 787-857-3600 507 M
crosado@br.inter.edu
ROSADO-LOPEZ,
Eleane .... 787-857-3600 507 M
erosado@br.inter.edu
ROSALES, Ilian .... 619-934-0797.. 61 B
ROSAMILIO, Noel .... 203-596-8780.. 87 B
nrosamilio@nv.edu
ROSANDICH,
Thomas, J .... 251-626-3303.... 7 E
president@ussa.edu
ROSARIO, Lisanette ...... 718-518-4311 294 B
lrosario@hostos.cuny.edu
ROSARIO, Lucy .... 787-284-1912 508 E
lrsario@ponce.inter.edu
ROSARIO, Yolanda .... 787-746-1400 507 B
ROSARIO, Yoleidy .... 941-309-4023 106 J
yrosario@ringling.edu
ROSARIO, Yvette .... 718-960-8755 294 A
yvette.rosario@lehman.cuny.edu
ROSARIO DELGADO,
Victor .... 787-758-5297 513 B
victor.rosario1@upr.edu
ROSARIO-NIEVES, Ilia ... 787-841-2000 509 J
irosario@pucpr.edu
ROSARIO-PEREZ,
Glorivee .... 787-738-4660 511 F
glorivee.rosario@upr.edu
ROSARIO PEREZ,
Glorivee .... 787-738-4660 512 C
glorivee.rosario@upr.edu
ROSARIO-RODRIGUEZ,
Elizabeth .... 787-480-2444 506 C
erosario03@sanjuan.pr
ROSARIO-ROSARIO,
Yolanda .... 787-725-6500 505 G
yrosario@albizu.edu
ROSAS, Alisha .... 909-652-6115.. 35 L
alisha.rosas@chaffey.edu
ROSAS, Erudina .... 787-832-6000 507 D
erosas@icprjc.edu
ROSAS, Mirna .... 480-423-6754.. 13 H
mirna.rosas@scottsdalecc.edu
ROSAS, Olivia .... 909-537-7577.. 32 E
orosas@csusb.edu
ROSASCHI, Catherine .... 703-416-1441 466 A
registrar@divinemercy.edu
ROSATI, David, M .... 617-333-2302 208 G
david.rosati@curry.edu
ROSATI, Ross .... 612-625-5516 243 F
rosat002@umn.edu
ROSAY, Andre .... 907-786-4852.... 9 J
arosay@alaska.edu
ROSBERG, Gerald, M .... 212-854-9967 297 C
gerry.rosberg@columbia.edu
ROSBURY-HENNE,
Marcia .... 978-630-9337 215 C
ROSCH, Laura .... 417-208-0632 254 E
lrosch@kcumb.edu
ROSDAIL, Lisa .... 803-938-3794 413 G
lrosdai@uscsumter.edu
ROSE, Adam .... 501-450-3247.. 23 H
arose@uca.edu
ROSE, Alisha, D .... 901-678-2230 426 G
arose3@memphis.edu
ROSE, Billy .... 256-352-8110.... 3 I
billy.rose@wallacestate.edu
ROSE, Brian, T .... 607-777-4788 316 B
brose@binghamton.edu
ROSE, Calandra .... 580-349-1302 367 F
ROSE, Camille .... 970-521-6952.. 82 C
camille.rose@njc.edu
ROSE, Carey .... 254-298-8326 445 G
carey.rose@templejc.edu
ROSE, Carlene .... 603-524-3207 272 K
crose@ccsnh.edu
ROSE, Carrie, J .... 724-458-2134 384 G
rosecj@gcc.edu
ROSE, III, Charles, H ... 419-772-2205 358 C
c-rose.5@onu.edu
ROSE, Clayton .... 207-725-3221 194 C
crose@bowdoin.edu
ROSE, Dan, C .... 860-701-6798 503 G
dan.c.rose@uscga.edu
ROSE, Danita .... 405-682-1611 367 D
danita.a.rose@occc.edu
ROSE, Deatrea .... 620-235-6556 177 A
drose@pittstate.edu
ROSE, Don .... 620-665-3597 174 G
rosed@hutchcc.edu
ROSE, Emily .... 310-825-4606.. 69 E
erose@conet.ucla.edu
ROSE, Eric, D .... 201-216-8724 283 D
eric.rose@stevens.edu
ROSE, Erik .... 406-447-5414 263 B
erose@carroll.edu
ROSE, Gregory .... 724-925-4071 402 F
roseg@westmoreland.edu
ROSE, Gregory, S .... 740-725-6218 358 D
rose.9@osu.edu
ROSE, John .... 212-772-4242 294 C
john.rose@hunter.cuny.edu
ROSE, Julie .... 607-587-3979 319 F
roseja@alfredstate.edu
ROSE, Justin .... 217-206-6333 152 A
jrose22@uis.edu
ROSE, Justin, E .... 863-667-5386 108 K
jerose@seu.edu
ROSE, Kathleen, A .... 408-848-4712.. 43 E
krose@gavilan.edu
ROSE, Kenny .... 803-934-3211 410 G
board@morris.edu
ROSE, Kevin .... 903-434-8186 440 G
krose@ntcc.edu
ROSE, Laura .... 201-216-5000 283 D
laura.rose@stevens.edu
ROSE, Lawrence, D .... 909-537-3703.. 32 E
lrose@csusb.edu
ROSE, JR., LeRoy .... 401-598-1000 404 D
leroy.rosejr@jwu.edu
ROSE, Lesa .... 207-330-7743 195 B
rosele@mchp.edu
ROSE, Lisa .... 310-434-4402.. 63 C
rose_lisa@smc.edu
ROSE, Mark .... 754-312-2898 103 R
ROSE, Melissa .... 304-243-2233 491 E
mrose@wheeling.edu
ROSE, Melody .... 775-784-4901 270 J
ROSE, Randall .... 276-964-7278 475 C
randall.rose@sw.edu
ROSE, JR., Robert .... 703-333-5904 477 F
rrose@wuv.edu
ROSE, Ryan .... 620-432-0348 176 D
rarose@neosho.edu
ROSE, Samantha .... 334-290-3265.... 2 F
samantha.rose@istc.edu
ROSE, Saxton .... 336-631-1226 343 D
roses@uncsa.edu
ROSE, Shawn .... 970-521-6601.. 82 C
shawn.rose@njc.edu
ROSE, Steve .... 509-527-2402 485 C
steve.rose@wallawalla.edu
ROSE, Steven .... 973-684-5900 280 A
srose@pccc.edu
ROSE, Susan .... 606-539-4213 185 E
ROSE, Sylvia .... 757-727-5361 467 G
sylvia.rose@hamptonu.edu
ROSE SPAULDING,
Stephany .... 719-255-4762.. 84 C
edi@uccs.edu
ROSEBERRY, David .... 206-934-4427 483 C
david.roseberry@seattlecolleges.edu
ROSEBORO, Donyell ..... 910-962-4084 343 C
roseborod@uncw.edu

ROSEBORO-BARNES, Edwina 803-981-7162 414 F eroseboro@yorktech.edu
ROSEDALE, Jeff 914-323-5277 305 B jeff.rosedale@mville.edu
ROSEL, Evangeline 845-938-2022 503 I
ROSEMOND, Michelle 678-407-5153 119 C mrosemond@ggc.edu
ROSEN, Aaron 202-885-8674 94 D arosen@wesleyseminary.edu
ROSEN, Alesha 301-846-2630 198 I arosen@frederick.edu
ROSEN, David 201-443-8750 277 I david_rosen@fdu.edu
ROSEN, Julie 602-386-4103 10 F julie.rosen@arizonachristian.edu
ROSEN, Mike, S 713-743-8155 452 D msrosen@central.uh.edu
ROSEN, Richard 207-326-2241 196 A richard.rosen@mma.edu
ROSEN, Sara 404-413-6555 120 E srosen@gsu.edu
ROSEN, Steven, T 626-256-4673 37 A srosen@coh.org
ROSEN-METSCH, Lisa 212-854-6321 297 C lm2892@columbia.edu
ROSENBAUM, Irving 954-262-1507 105 A irv@nova.edu
ROSENBAUM, Mark 773-298-3000 149 D
ROSENBAUM, Philip 610-896-1290 385 I prosenba@haverford.edu
ROSENBAUM, Thomas, F 626-395-6301 28 J tfr@caltech.edu
ROSENBERG, Alannah 949-582-4854 65 D aorrison@saddleback.edu
ROSENBERG, Chaim 718-854-2290 291 G
ROSENBERG, David 845-731-3700 326 I
ROSENBERG, Eric 973-720-2684 284 J rosenberge@wpunj.edu
ROSENBERG, John, R 801-422-4331 458 H john_rosenberg@byu.edu
ROSENBERG, Mark 305-348-2111 110 A mark.rosenberg@fiu.edu
ROSENBERG, Randall 314-977-3827 259 F randall.rosenberg@slu.edu
ROSENBERG, Sol 718-854-2290 291 G
ROSENBERG, Travis 435-652-7522 460 B travis.rosenberg@dixie.edu
ROSENBERG, Warren 914-831-0219 297 A wrosenberg@cw.edu
ROSENBERGER, Benjamin 610-372-4721 396 H brosenberger@racc.edu
ROSENBERGER, Jeanne 408-554-4366 63 B jrosenberger@scu.edu
ROSENBERGER, Jennifer 503-847-2548 377 B jrosenberger@uws.edu
ROSENBLATT, Mark 312-996-3500 151 G mrosenbl@uic.edu
ROSENBLITH, Suzane, N 716-645-6640 316 C rosenbli@buffalo.edu
ROSENBLOOM, Stuart 312-461-0600 133 A srosenbloom@aaart.edu
ROSENBLUM, Eliyohu 718-854-2290 291 G
ROSENBOOM, David 661-255-1050 28 G david@calarts.edu
ROSENBOOM, Sharon 712-722-6740 165 I sharon.rosenboom@dordt.edu
ROSENBURGI, Melissa 207-941-7175 194 F
ROSENBURY, Laura, A 352-273-0600 111 A rosenbury@law.ufl.edu
ROSENCRANTS, Lydia 901-321-3315 418 G lrosencr@cbu.edu
ROSENDAHL, Matt 218-726-6562 243 G libaskus@d.umn.edu
ROSENFELD, Sholom 718-774-5050 322 B
ROSENGART, Sharon 973-720-3019 284 J rosengarts@wpunj.edu
ROSENGARTEN, Jeffrey 646-565-6239 322 G jeffrey.rosengarten@touro.edu
ROSENGARTEN, Jeffrey 646-565-6239 322 F jeffrey.rosengarten@touro.edu
ROSENGARTEN, Lewis 607-753-4808 318 A lewis.rosengarten@cortland.edu
ROSENGRANT, Bruce 910-672-1111 341 C
ROSENLUND, Linda 508-767-7104 206 A lrosenlund@assumption.edu
ROSENOW, Thomas, C 530-898-5556 30 D trosenow@csuchico.edu
ROSENSAFT, Jean, B 212-824-2209 301 B jrosensaft@huc.edu
ROSENSTEIN, Ilena 860-768-4418 89 G rosenstei@hartford.edu
ROSENSTEIN, Ilene 213-740-7711 73 D irosenst@usc.edu
ROSENSTIEL, Todd 503-725-9554 375 E rosensti@pdx.edu
ROSENSTOCK, Jeffrey 718-997-4995 295 B jeffrey.rosenstock@qc.cuny.edu
ROSENTEL, Edward 850-729-5368 104 M rosentee@nwfsc.edu
ROSENTHAL, Adam 954-262-5379 105 A jar1248@nova.edu
ROSENTHAL, Alisa, J 804-752-7268 469 F alisarosenthal@rmc.edu
ROSENTHAL, Amy 269-471-3411 221 D rosenthala@andrews.edu
ROSENTHAL, Austin 918-444-2202 366 G rosentha@nsuok.edu
ROSENTHAL, Bruce 859-344-3650 185 B rosentb@thomasmore.edu
ROSENTHAL, Crystal 949-854-8002 39 K
ROSENTHAL, Elijah 848-932-1994 282 A elijah.rosenthal@ruf.rutgers.edu
ROSENTHAL, Ellen 301-243-2125 502 L ellen.rosenthal@dodiis.mil
ROSENTHAL, Eric 610-861-5565 391 C erosenthal@northampton.edu
ROSENTHAL, Jean-Laurent 626-395-4068 28 J rosentha@caltech.edu
ROSENTHAL, Jeffrey, E 315-294-8499 292 G rosenthal@cayuga-cc.edu
ROSENTHAL, Julie 303-373-2008 83 G jrosenthal@rvu.edu
ROSENTHAL, Keith, M 415-485-9528 39 A kmrosenthal@marin.edu
ROSENTHAL, Ken 818-677-2561 32 C ken.rosenthal@csun.edu
ROSENTHAL, Lauren 718-933-6700 307 A lrosenthal@monroecollege.edu
ROSENTHAL, Lori 617-243-2074 211 B lrosenthal@lasell.edu
ROSENTHAL, Roseanne, K 312-225-6288 152 J rrosenthal@vandercook.edu
ROSENTHAL, Susan 305-899-3050 96 A srosenthal@barry.edu
ROSETTI, Crystal 909-607-7894 37 B crystal.rosetti@claremont.edu
ROSETTI, Patricia, H 570-961-4596 389 D rosetti@marywood.edu
ROSEVEAR, Scott, G 570-577-3647 379 C scott.rosevear@bucknell.edu
ROSEVEARE, Mark 864-592-4763 412 E rosevearem@sccsc.edu
ROSFELD, Stephen 513-556-6177 361 J stephen.rosfeld@uc.edu
ROSHAU, Kristine 541-383-7407 372 A kroshau@cocc.edu
ROSINSKI-KAUS, Donna 732-255-0400 279 F drosinski-kaus@ocean.edu
ROSIUS, Davius 863-638-2920 114 B rosius@webber.edu
ROSKO, Thomas 831-656-2441 502 M
ROSKY, Bruce 818-610-6543 49 D roskybr@piercecollege.edu
ROSMAN, Andrew 954-262-5064 105 A arosman1@nova.edu
ROSMANN, Vicki 713-780-9777 429 G
ROSNER, James 303-871-3256 84 E james.rosner@du.edu
ROSOFF, Nancy 215-572-2921 378 E rosoffn@arcadia.edu
ROSOWSKY, David, V 785-532-5110 175 C rosowsky@ksu.edu
ROSPLOCK, Valerie, R 607-735-1174 298 H vrosplock@elmira.edu
ROSS, Aaron 419-289-5048 347 J aross23@ashland.edu
ROSS, Amanda 315-268-6633 295 F aross@clarkson.edu
ROSS, Angela 804-523-5029 474 A aross@reynolds.edu
ROSS, Anissa 870-460-1036 22 C ross@uamont.edu
ROSS, Beth 617-735-9701 209 D ross@emmanuel.edu
ROSS, Casey 405-208-5979 367 E crosspetherick@okcu.edu
ROSS, Cheryl 858-822-2797 70 C caross@ucsd.edu
ROSS, Christine, C 434-223-6056 467 F cross@hsc.edu
ROSS, Christopher, R 405-744-6651 367 G chris.ross@okstate.edu
ROSS, Clint 928-774-3890 12 L cross@indianbible.org
ROSS, Corey 517-750-1200 231 C co126092@arbor.edu
ROSS, David 501-279-4930 19 C dross@harding.edu
ROSS, David 972-708-7340 435 E
ROSS, Desi 601-484-8823 247 A dross1@meridiancc.edu
ROSS, Devon, G 612-330-1588 234 A ross@augsburg.edu
ROSS, Donald, E 561-237-7782 103 W dross@lynn.edu
ROSS, Elizabeth (Liz) 865-694-6444 425 B eross@pstcc.edu
ROSS, Eric 660-263-4100 257 B ericr@macc.edu
ROSS, III, Frank, E 317-940-9570 154 C feross@butler.edu
ROSS, Gabe 916-568-3056 50 F rossg@losrios.edu
ROSS, Gary 401-841-7501 503 A gary.ross@usnwc.edu
ROSS, Gary, L 315-228-7401 296 E gross@colgate.edu
ROSS, Gerald 410-225-2399 200 D gross@mica.edu
ROSS, Gloria 662-254-3558 248 B gloria.ross@mvsu.edu
ROSS, Hannah 802-443-5229 462 E hross@middlebury.edu
ROSS, James 732-255-0400 279 F jross@ocean.edu
ROSS, James, A 734-384-4259 228 C jross@monroeccc.edu
ROSS, Jason 864-977-7026 410 I jason.ross@ngu.edu
ROSS, Jeannie 620-862-5252 171 H jeannie.ross@barclaycollege.edu
ROSS, Jeannine 207-859-1105 196 D sfs@thomas.edu
ROSS, Jeffery 816-235-6212 261 E umkccontracts@umkc.edu
ROSS, Jennifer 718-522-9073 290 E jross@asa.edu
ROSS, Jennifer, A 260-422-5561 156 E jaross@indianatech.edu
ROSS, Jeremy, B 423-439-5353 419 G rossjb@etsu.edu
ROSS, Jerry, P 530-898-6116 30 D
ROSS, Jill 540-674-3600 474 E jross@nr.edu
ROSS, Jim 252-249-1851 336 F jross@pamlicocc.edu
ROSS, Joey 714-879-3901 45 G jaross@hiu.edu
ROSS, Julia 540-231-9752 476 C rjulie@vt.edu
ROSS, Julie, S 617-627-3360 219 C j.ross@tufts.edu
ROSS, Keith, L 314-392-2355 256 E president@mobap.edu
ROSS, Kevin 714-532-7751 36 B
ROSS, Kevin, M 561-237-7823 103 W kross@lynn.edu
ROSS, Kristen 281-929-4653 443 C kristen.ross@sjcd.edu
ROSS, Laura 407-708-2511 108 D rossl@seminolestate.edu
ROSS, Laura 314-529-6893 255 B lross@maryville.edu
ROSS, Lauren 937-512-2164 360 G lauren.ross@sinclair.edu
ROSS, Leigh, A 601-984-2620 249 E laross@umc.edu
ROSS, Linda 213-738-6818 66 B accounting@swlaw.edu
ROSS, Lori, A 513-556-3483 361 J rossla@ucmail.uc.edu
ROSS, Louis 918-343-7625 369 B lross@rsu.edu
ROSS, Matthew 717-815-1359 403 F mross@ycp.edu
ROSS, Meg 662-562-3204 248 D mross@northwestms.edu
ROSS, Megan 507-285-7206 240 H megan.ross@rctc.edu
ROSS, Michael 304-865-6007 487 H michael.ross@ovu.edu
ROSS, Mikki 806-742-2121 450 F mikki.ross@ttu.edu
ROSS, Neil 785-320-4554 175 G neilross@manhattantech.edu
ROSS, Pam 864-231-2000 406 F pross@andersonuniversity.edu
ROSS, Patricia 504-762-3284 188 B paross@dcc.edu
ROSS, Patricia, A 801-585-7832 459 O p.ross@utah.edu
ROSS, Paul 602-285-7855 13 F paul.ross@phoenixcollege.edu
ROSS, JR., Quinton, T 334-229-4202 4 A president.ross@alasu.edu
ROSS, Ramsey 850-729-5358 104 M ramseyr@nwfsc.edu
ROSS, Reginald 973-720-6225 284 J rossr@wpunj.edu
ROSS, Rick 360-417-6533 482 C rross@pencol.edu
ROSS, Robin 828-327-7000 333 B rross@cvcc.edu
ROSS, Sadie 518-587-2100 320 E sadie.ross@esc.edu
ROSS, Sharon 914-961-8313 314 H sross@svots.edu
ROSS, Sheila 414-277-7238 494 D ross@msoe.edu
ROSS, Sonya 617-373-6963 217 I
ROSS, Susan 304-367-4098 489 K susan.ross@fairmontstate.edu
ROSS, Susan 570-321-4204 389 B ross@lycoming.edu
ROSS, Tausha 513-875-3344 350 C
ROSS, Teri 330-494-6170 360 K tross@starkstate.edu
ROSS, Thelma 301-546-0766 201 E rosstl1@pgcc.edu
ROSS, Trevor 360-475-7120 481 I tross@olympic.edu
ROSS, William 814-332-2316 378 A wross@allegheny.edu
ROSS-JONES, Marvel, E 716-884-9120 292 B merossjones@bryantstratton.edu
ROSS-SCOTT, Carol 607-778-5199 317 D rossca@sunybroome.edu
ROSS STAMPS, Clara 502-597-6260 183 D president@kysu.edu
ROSS STAMPS, Clara 502-597-6785 183 D clara.stamps@kysu.edu
ROSSBACH, Janet 646-660-6097 292 L janet.rossbach@baruch.cuny.edu
ROSSELL, Anita 724-222-5330 391 F arossell@penncommercial.edu
ROSSELLI, David 254-710-2561 431 E dave_rosselli@baylor.edu
ROSSER, Charice 252-536-7207 335 B crosser@halifaxcc.edu
ROSSER, Edward 404-756-4000 115 G
ROSSER, Keith 315-268-7258 295 F krosser@clarkson.edu
ROSSER, Virginia, J 419-372-9865 348 G jrosser@bgsu.edu
ROSSER-MIMS, Dionne 334-448-5112 7 C drosser-mims@troy.edu
ROSSETTI, Erin 802-626-6417 463 G
ROSSI, Jaclyn 716-286-8761 309 H jrossi@niagara.edu
ROSSI, Jamal 585-274-1010 323 M jrossi@esm.rochester.edu
ROSSI, Janelle 707-664-2158 34 B
ROSSI, John, J 626-256-4673 37 A jrossi@coh.org
ROSSI, Louis 302-831-1880 91 C rossi@udel.edu
ROSSI, Reagan 208-459-5855 131 C rrossi@collegeofidaho.edu
ROSSI, Renee 904-256-7458 102 H rrossi@ju.edu
ROSSI-LONG, Jennifer 610-436-2501 395 D jlong@wcupa.edu
ROSSIGNOL, Paul 505-438-8884 288 F paul@acupuncturecollege.edu
ROSSITER, Andrew 808-923-9741 129 E andrewro@hawaii.edu
ROSSITER, Sherry 740-593-4129 358 K bursar@ohio.edu
ROSSITER-SMITH, Carla, M 727-816-3190 105 F
ROSSITTO, Paul 860-832-1617 85 G rossitto@ccsu.edu

ROSSKY, Peter 713-348-3350 442 F peter.rossky@rice.edu
ROSSMILLER, Sheila 715-675-3331 499 F rossmiller@ntc.edu
ROSSMILLER, Zach 406-243-2311 263 K
ROSSON, Michael 718-368-5144 294 E mrosson@kbcc.cuny.edu
ROST, Gregory, S 215-898-7221 400 F gregrost@upenn.edu
ROST, Jamie, D 407-582-5412 113 I jrost@valenciacollege.edu
ROSTAD, Jerry 701-328-4113 345 A jerry.rostad@ndus.edu
ROSTAR, Jimmy 252-328-1275 341 A rostarj@ecu.edu
ROSTER, Ellen 651-846-1324 241 B ellen.roster@saintpaul.edu
ROSTRON, Stephanie 937-502-3734 363 G srostron@wilberforce.edu
ROSU, Gabriela 480-732-7012 12 O gabriela.rosu@cgc.edu
ROSZELL, Nancy, J 937-255-3636 502 C nancy.roszell@afit.edu
ROSZMAN, Deborah 419-448-3513 361 D roszmandl@tiffin.edu
ROTGER, Mariolga 787-850-9324 512 D mariolga.rotger@upr.edu
ROTGER, Mariolga 787-850-9364 512 D mariolga.rotger@upr.edu
ROTH, Adam 203-582-3325 88 G adam.roth@quinnipiac.edu
ROTH, Amy 513-875-3344 350 C amy.roth@chatfield.edu
ROTH, Ben 217-786-2773 143 B ben.roth@llcc.edu
ROTH, Beth 815-740-3216 152 H broth@stfrancis.edu
ROTH, Brenda 503-589-8189 372 H broth@corban.edu
ROTH, Brenda 810-762-3488 232 A blroth@umich.edu
ROTH, Brian 509-527-2341 485 C brian.roth@wallawalla.edu
ROTH, Cindi 304-284-4040 490 E croth@mail.wvu.edu
ROTH, Deb 620-327-8279 174 E deb.roth@hesston.edu
ROTH, Don, F 530-754-5418 69 B droth@ucdavis.edu
ROTH, Frank, A 610-758-3572 388 E far4@lehigh.edu
ROTH, James 405-208-5440 367 E jaroth@okcu.edu
ROTH, Jason 702-968-1633 272 C jroth@roseman.edu
ROTH, Jeff 310-206-8041 69 E jroth@ponet.ucla.edu
ROTH, John 510-231-5000 46 J john.roth@kp.org
ROTH, John, C 718-940-5616 314 A jroth@sjcny.edu
ROTH, Mark 843-661-8324 409 F
ROTH, Martin, S 304-357-4713 487 J
ROTH, Megan 325-674-2885 428 F mkr15a@acu.edu
ROTH, Michael 707-527-6939 63 D mroth@santarosa.edu
ROTH, Michael, S 860-685-3500 90 B mroth@wesleyan.edu
ROTH, Mike 503-589-8152 372 H mroth@corban.edu
ROTH, Neil 304-473-8312 491 D roth@wvwc.edu
ROTH, Nicholas 914-961-8313 314 H nroth@svots.edu
ROTH, Sue 503-375-7020 372 H sroth@corban.edu
ROTH, JR., Toby 989-774-3871 222 E rothj1t@cmich.edu
ROTH NICKS, Rebecca 706-880-8088 122 A rroth@lagrange.edu
ROTHAMER, Russ 970-339-6300 77 H russ.rothamer@aims.edu
ROTHAUS, Richard, M 989-774-3341 222 E rotha1r@cmich.edu
ROTHBERG, Jacob 914-736-1500 310 E
ROTHE, Justy 217-532-2181 142 C jrothe@lakelandcollege.edu
ROTHELL, Cynthia 540-373-2200 466 C crothell@evcc.edu
ROTHENBERG, Jeffrey 317-338-3879 161 B
ROTHENBERGER, Sara 860-439-2834 87 H srothenb@conncoll.edu
ROTHENBUHLER, Eric 314-246-7154 262 C erothenbuhler@webster.edu
ROTHENBUHLER, Randy 419-824-3730 355 C rrothenbuhler@lourdes.edu
ROTHMAN, Paul 410-955-3180 199 G prothma1@jhmi.edu
ROTHMAN, Paul, D 410-955-3180 199 G prothma1@jhmi.edu
ROTHMEYER, Melissa 415-955-2100 24 J
ROTHMEYER, Michelle 815-825-9807 141 F mrothmeyer@kish.edu
ROTHROCK, Dan 253-272-1126 481 E drothrock@ncad.edu
ROTHROCK, Dan 253-272-1126 481 E
ROTHSCHILD, Dovid, N 516-255-4700 311 J rdnr@mlb.edu
ROTHSCHILD, Martha, D 410-777-2701 197 G mdrothschild@aacc.edu
ROTHSTEIN, Carol 615-353-3326 424 G carol.rothstein@nscc.edu
ROTHWELL, Suzanne 573-875-7563 251 I srothwell@ccis.edu
ROTICH, Herbert, K 517-750-1200 231 C hrotich@arbor.edu
ROTKIEWICZ, Melissa, S 413-545-0333 211 G mlr@uhs.umass.edu
ROTOLO, Dee 618-453-4626 150 B drotolo@siu.edu
ROTOLO, Rene, M 718-960-8539 294 A rene.rotolo@lehman.cuny.edu
ROTONDO, Denise, M 716-888-2160 292 F rotondod@canisius.edu
ROTONDO, Mark 617-873-0675 208 B mark.rotondo@cambridgecollege.edu
ROTROFF, Kristi 419-267-1271 357 E krotroff@northweststate.edu
ROTT, Cynthia 701-231-7458 345 F cynthia.rott@ndsu.edu
ROTTENBERG, Aaron 718-854-2290 291 G
ROTTER, Bruce, E 618-474-7120 150 C brotter@siue.edu
ROTTHOFF, Kurt 973-761-9102 283 C kurt.rotthoff@shu.edu
ROTTMAN, Courtney 214-648-2288 457 A courtney.rottman@utsouthwestern.edu
ROTTWEILER, James, D 520-515-5498 11 M jdr@cochise.edu
ROTUNDO, Michael, R 906-227-2327 228 I mrotundo@nmu.edu
ROTUNNI, Lisa, M 909-869-2474 30 A lmrotunni@cpp.edu
ROTZ, Ben 918-766-4357 368 E brotz@okwu.edu
ROUBINEK, Darren 816-501-2422 250 F darren.roubinek@avila.edu
ROUGEAU, Vincent, D 508-793-2011 208 D
ROUGHTON, Dean 252-335-0821 333 G dean_roughton@albemarle.edu
ROUGHTON, Keith 912-478-0747 120 C kroughton@georgiasouthern.edu
ROULETTE, Barbara, W 240-500-2233 199 C bwroulette@hagerstowncc.edu
ROULIER, Stephen 413-748-3171 218 I sroulier@springfield.edu
ROUND, Sara 816-415-5984 262 F rounds@william.jewell.edu
ROUNDS, Claude 518-276-6601 312 C roundc@rpi.edu
ROUNDS, Dayle, G 609-497-7991 280 C dayle.rounds@ptsem.edu
ROUNDS, Michael 785-864-4419 177 J m528r913@ku.edu
ROUNDS, Michael, J 610-565-0999 403 B mrounds@williamson.edu
ROUNDS, Susan 707-621-7000 41 A
ROUNDS, Tyra 313-993-1046 231 E roundstc@udmercy.edu
ROUNDTREE, Leslie, A 773-995-2411 134 K lroundtr@csu.edu
ROUNDTREE, Naomi 541-383-7233 372 A nroundtree@cocc.edu
ROUNTREE, Hazel 575-461-4413 286 G hazelr@mesalands.edu
ROUNTREE, Jeffrey, W 540-479-1892 471 N jeff.rountree@umwf.org
ROUNTREE, Mike 478-289-2093 118 C rountree@ega.edu
ROURKE, David 415-338-1822 33 E drourke@sfsu.edu
ROURKE, SJ, Paul 203-254-4000 87 I prourke@fairfield.edu
ROUS, Philip 410-455-2598 203 B rous@umbc.edu
ROUSE, Art 252-328-6212 341 A rousew@ecu.edu
ROUSE, Douglas 908-709-7113 284 D douglas.rouse@ucc.edu
ROUSE, Kevin 828-327-7000 333 B krouse@cvcc.edu
ROUSE, Lawrence, L 252-493-7200 336 H llrouse@email.pitcc.edu
ROUSE, Linda 954-262-1408 105 A lrouse@nova.edu
ROUSE, Matthew 562-903-4769 27 A matt.rouse@biola.edu
ROUSE, Nina 920-403-4427 495 B nina.rouse@snc.edu
ROUSE, Sandra 803-321-5146 410 H sandra.rouse@newberry.edu
ROUSH, Chris, G 203-582-3641 88 G chris.roush@quinnipiac.edu
ROUSH, Clark, A 402-363-5610 270 D croush@york.edu
ROUSH, Jeffrey 785-227-3380 172 A roushjs@bethanylb.edu
ROUSH, Matt 248-204-2210 227 A mroush@ltu.edu
ROUSH, Rebecca 910-695-3704 337 H roushr@sandhills.edu
ROUSH, Richard, T 814-865-2541 391 G rtr10@psu.edu
ROUSSE, Wade 337-475-5588 192 E wrousse1@mcneese.edu
ROUSSEAU, Erica 207-602-2826 197 E erousseau1@une.edu
ROUSSEAU, Karen 413-205-3056 205 F karen.rousseau@aic.edu
ROUSSEAU, Melissa 616-526-7920 222 C mr55@calvin.edu
ROUSSEL, Hart 657-278-5429 31 C hroussel@fullerton.edu
ROUSU, Matthew 570-372-4186 398 F rousu@susqu.edu
ROUTBORT, Julia, C 518-580-5555 315 F jroutbor@skidmore.edu
ROUTENBERG, robbie 585-245-5020 318 B routenberg@geneseo.edu
ROUTH, David 919-962-0329 342 C drouth@email.unc.edu
ROUTHIER, Stacy 860-231-5661 90 A srouthier@usj.edu
ROUTT, Thalethia 859-257-9293 185 F thalethia.routt@uky.edu
ROVARIS, Dereck 225-578-5736 189 E drovaris@lsu.edu
ROVARIS, SR., Dereck 225-578-2111 189 D
ROVARIS, Jill 408-554-4501 63 B jrovaris@scu.edu
ROVETTI, Marc 510-883-2086 41 B mrovetti@dspt.edu
ROVINELLI HELLER, Nina 860-570-3649 89 D nina.heller@uconn.edu
ROVIRA-ALVAREZ, Jorge 787-993-8860 512 A jorge.rovira@upr.edu
ROVNER, Amy 206-546-4101 484 B arovner@shoreline.edu
ROWAN, Bernard 773-995-2439 134 K trowanii@csu.edu
ROWAN, Carl 703-993-3840 467 E crowan2@gmu.edu
ROWAN, John 318-473-6446 189 F jrowan@lsua.edu
ROWANE, Michael 814-866-8118 387 D mrowane@lecom.edu
ROWDEN, Molly 615-230-3352 425 E molly.rowden@volstate.edu
ROWE, Alan 229-333-7816 127 E carowe@valdosta.edu
ROWE, Brian 931-393-1544 424 F browe@mscc.edu
ROWE, David 414-297-8854 499 C rowed1@matc.edu
ROWE, Dayna 405-422-1467 369 A dayna.rowe@redlandscc.edu
ROWE, Jimmy 859-846-4357 184 B james.rowe@midway.edu
ROWE, Jonathan 410-386-8217 198 D jhoskowitz@carrollcc.edu
ROWE, Katherine, A 757-221-1693 465 N president@wm.edu
ROWE, Kenneth, D 405-325-3916 370 K kenneth-rowe@ouhsc.edu
ROWE, Mindy, S 610-917-1415 401 G msrowe@valleyforge.edu
ROWE, Nicholas 978-867-4299 210 B nicholas.rowe@gordon.edu
ROWE, Nicole 906-932-4231 224 D nicoler@gogebic.edu
ROWE, Rebecca 218-855-8145 237 G rebecca.rowe@clcmn.edu
ROWE, Sarah 765-641-4045 153 G sjrowe@anderson.edu
ROWE, Steven 773-995-4412 134 K srowe21@csu.edu
ROWE, Tim 304-877-6428 486 G academicvp@abc.edu
ROWE, Tim 304-877-6428 486 G registrar@abc.edu
ROWE-ALLEN, Ophelie 203-932-7176 89 H orallen@newhaven.edu
ROWE-JONES, Kelly 606-218-5273 186 B kellyrowe@upike.edu
ROWELL, Jeren 816-268-5401 257 C jrowell@nts.edu
ROWELL, Sam 423-354-5207 425 A ssrowell@northeaststate.edu
ROWEN, Cate 413-585-3021 218 H crowen@smith.edu
ROWETT JAMES, Kelly, A 336-285-4048 341 D karowettjames@ncat.edu
ROWH, Brett 918-825-6021 369 B browh@rsu.edu
ROWH, Mark, C 540-674-3617 474 E mrowh@nr.edu
ROWLAND, Barbara 217-228-5432 147 F rowlaba@quincy.edu
ROWLAND, Diane 207-581-1865 196 G
ROWLAND, Gordon 607-274-3734 302 G rowland@ithaca.edu
ROWLAND, Jim 918-540-6301 366 F jrowland@neo.edu
ROWLAND, Kelso 812-749-1454 159 O krowland1@oak.edu
ROWLAND, Leo 909-748-8717 72 F leo_rowland@redlands.edu
ROWLAND, Linda 706-864-1358 127 A linda.rowland@ung.edu
ROWLAND, Maia 775-831-1314 272 D mrowland@sierranevada.edu
ROWLAND, IV, Roy 863-667-5081 108 K rrowland@seu.edu
ROWLAND, Shannon 423-614-8637 420 H srowland@leeuniversity.edu
ROWLAND, Sheri 850-201-6250 112 C sheri.rowland@tcc.fl.edu
ROWLETT, Carol 540-857-7277 475 G crowlett@virginiawestern.edu
ROWLEY, Becky 505-428-1201 288 E becky.rowley@sfcc.edu
ROWLEY, Don 765-677-2313 158 B don.rowley@indwes.edu
ROWLEY, Sarah, L 248-341-2081 229 C slrowley@oaklandcc.edu
ROWLEY, Stephanie 212-678-3050 322 C sjr2192@tc.columbia.edu
ROWLEY, Sue 415-274-2200 24 B srowley@academyart.edu
ROWSER, Mayola 314-454-7055 253 G mayola.rowser@barnesjewishcollege.edu
ROWZEE, Julie 601-635-2111 246 A jrowzee@eccc.edu
ROXBURGH, Russell 631-656-2147 300 B russell.roxburgh@ftc.edu
ROXBURY, Tiese 810-762-3000 232 A troxbury@umich.edu
ROY, Alisa 704-922-6202 334 G roy.alisa@gaston.edu
ROY, Donovan 269-337-4400 233 D
ROY, Jocelyn 859-371-9393 179 G jroy@beckfield.edu
ROY, Judy, K 260-422-5561 156 E jkroy@indianatech.edu
ROY, Justin 617-322-3551 211 A justin_roy@laboure.edu
ROY, Kevin 413-748-3252 218 I
ROY, Lara 612-874-3778 237 A lara_roy@mcad.edu
ROY, Lisa 207-326-4715 196 A lisa.roy@mma.edu
ROY, Marc 856-351-2680 283 B mroy@salemcc.edu

ROY, Matthew .... 508-910-9052 212 A
mroy@umassd.edu
ROY, Melissa .... 845-574-4758 312 H
mroy@sunyrockland.edu
ROY, Michael, D .... 802-443-5490 462 E
mdroy@middlebury.edu
ROY, Omaira .... 508-286-3544 220 B
roy_omaira@wheatoncollege.edu
ROY, Rani 718-862-7755 304M
rani.roy@manhattan.edu
ROY, Tracey .... 218-322-2409 238 D
troy@itascacc.edu
ROY, Tracey .... 218-322-2409 238 F
tracey.roy@itascacc.edu
ROY, Wesley .... 401-598-1000 404 D
wesley.roy@jwu.edu
ROYAL, Angela .... 573-288-6334 252 F
aroyal@culver.edu
ROYAL, Christina .... 413-552-2700 214 F
croyal@hcc.edu
ROYAL, Rebecca .... 908-709-7042 284 D
rebecca.royal@ucc.edu
ROYCE, Richard, A .... 516-671-2356 324 G
rroyce@webb.edu
ROYCE-DAVIS,
Joanna, C .... 253-535-7206 482 A
roycedjc@plu.edu
ROYCE-DAVIS,
Joanna, C .... 253-535-7191 482 A
roycedjc@plu.edu
ROYE, Shauna .... 202-495-3837.. 93 D
sroye@dhs.edu
ROYE, Terry .... 281-425-6862 438 I
troye@lee.edu
ROYEEN, Charlotte .... 312-942-7120 148 G
charlotte_l_royeen@rush.edu
ROYER, Dara, J .... 315-443-8338 321 G
djroyer@syr.edu
ROYER, James .... 504-671-5477 188 B
jroyer@dcc.edu
ROYER, Randy .... 913-288-7188 175 B
rroyer@kckcc.edu
ROYER, Roma .... 602-429-4947.. 15 A
rroyer@ps.edu
ROYER, Tina .... 209-476-7840.. 67 E
troyer@clc.edu
ROYKO, Barry .... 216-987-0205 351 E
barry.royko@tri-c.edu
ROYO, Sebastian .... 508-793-7711 208 C
ROYSTON, Mimi .... 413-205-3448 205 F
mimi.royston@aic.edu
ROYSTON,
Rosemary, R .... 706-379-3111 128 C
rosemary@yhc.edu
ROYUK, Brent .... 402-643-7304 266 G
brent.royuk@cune.edu
ROYZMAN, Anna .... 212-799-5000 303 E
ROZADA, Mayra .... 787-891-0925 507 K
mrozada@aguadilla.inter.edu
ROZAK, Edward .... 508-830-5030 213 D
erozak@maritime.edu
ROZBORSKI, Joanne ..... 850-484-1708 105 H
jrozborski@pensacolastate.edu
ROZEBOOM, David .... 828-689-1212 331 C
david_rozeboom@mhu.edu
ROZEK, Charles, E .... 216-368-4390 349 D
cer2@case.edu
ROZELL, Liz .... 661-395-4011.. 46 L
ROZELL, Mark .... 703-993-8171 467 E
mrozell@gmu.edu
ROZELLE-STONE,
A. Rebecca .... 701-777-3302 345 B
adrian.rozelle@und.edu
ROZENEK, Carl .... 814-864-6666 384 F
ROZEWSKI, Mark .... 203-392-5456.. 86 A
rozewskim1@southernct.edu
ROZHON, Tamara .... 562-902-3304.. 65 I
tamararozhon@scuhs.edu
ROZLER, Tracy .... 716-896-0700 324 E
trozler@villa.edu
RUANO, Maritza .... 630-942-2800 135 I
RUANO, Norman .... 773-878-3894 149 A
nruano@iwe.staugustine.edu
RUARK, Matthew .... 270-852-3120 183 E
matthewru@kwc.edu
RUARTE, Daniel .... 909-599-5433.. 48 A
druarte@lifepacific.edu
RUBACK, Chad .... 847-578-8589 148 F
chad.ruback@rosalindfranlin.edu
RUBALCABA, Jacquelyn 559-325-5271.. 67 A
jacquelyn.rubalcaba@cloviscollege.edu
RUBALCAVA, Elva .... 657-278-5403.. 31 C
erubalcava@fullerton.edu
RUBALCAVA, Su-Lin ..... 805-289-6000.. 74 B
RUBEMEYER, Susan ...... 636-922-8360 258 J
srubemeyer@stchas.edu
RUBEN, Brent, D .... 848-932-7092 282 A
bruben@rutgers.edu
RUBENSTEIN, David ...... 610-758-3000 388 E
dar719@lehigh.edu
RUBIN, Adam .... 618-985-3741 140 H
adamrubin@jalc.edu
RUBIN, Beno .... 757-822-5196 475 E
brubin@tcc.edu
RUBIN, Beth .... 910-814-4377 327 D
brubin@campbell.edu
RUBIN, David .... 603-428-2509 273 G
drubin@nec.edu
RUBIN, James .... 602-787-6546.. 13 E
james.rubin@paradisevalley.edu
RUBIN, Joshua .... 718-436-2122 322 A
RUBIN, Lisa .... 770-426-2725 122 C
lrubin@life.edu
RUBIN, Lucas .... 212-966-4014 293 C
lrubin@brooklyn.cuny.edu
RUBIN, Marc, A .... 513-529-1799 356 A
rubinma@miamioh.edu
RUBIN, Moshe .... 515-239-9002 315 D
myrubin@shoryoshuv.org
RUBIN, Nancy .... 970-351-1931.. 84 F
nancy.rubin@unco.edu
RUBIN, Nancy, G .... 330-569-3211 353 G
rubinng@hiram.edu
RUBIN, Rachel .... 860-486-2337.. 89 D
rachel.rubin@uconn.edu
RUBIN, Steve .... 719-219-9636.. 78 G
srubin@cavt.edu
RUBINO, David .... 814-866-6641 387 D
drubino@lecom.edu
RUBINO, Joseph .... 410-293-1549 504 A
rubino@usna.edu
RUBINO, Karen, M .... 401-456-8849 405 A
krubino@ric.edu
RUBINO, Lorraine .... 631-632-4385 317 A
lorraine.rubino@stonybrook.edu
RUBINO, Michael, H .... 508-767-7156 206 A
rubino@assumption.edu
RUBINSTEIN, James ..... 623-572-3395 144 F
jrubinstein@midwestern.edu
RUBINSTEIN, Mark .... 603-513-1304 274 G
mark.rubinstein@granite.edu
RUBIO, Dave .... 909-384-8640.. 60 F
drubio@sbccd.cc.ca.us
RUBIO, Don .... 323-669-7555.. 48 J
derubio@lasd.org
RUBIO, Joan .... 714-463-7550.. 51 B
jrubio@ketchum.edu
RUBIO, Sara .... 310-233-4033.. 49 B
rubiosv@lahc.edu
RUBLE, Megan .... 507-933-7526 236 A
mruble@gustavus.edu
RUBLE, Michelle .... 301-934-7508 198 G
mmruble@csmd.edu
RUBRITZ, Gerald .... 814-886-6460 390 G
grubritz@mtaloy.edu
RUBY, Ashley .... 301-387-3733 199 A
ashley.ruby@garrettcollege.edu
RUBY, Kirsten, A .... 217-333-3070 151 F
RUCKEL, Stephanie .... 612-330-1550 234 A
ruckels@augsburg.edu
RUCKER, Alan, M .... 606-783-5367 184 C
a.rucker@moreheadstate.edu
RUCKER, Cedric, B .... 540-654-1200 471 N
crucker@umw.edu
RUCKER, Marty, K .... 423-585-6983 425 F
marty.rucker@ws.edu
RUCKER, Nolan .... 303-751-8700.. 78 D
rucker@belrea.edu
RUCKER, Paul .... 206-685-9223 485 A
uwalumni@uw.edu
RUCKER, Robert, E .... 662-685-4771 245 C
erucker@bmc.edu
RUCKER, Sherri, B .... 615-329-8555 419 H
srucker@fisk.edu
RUCKER, Sonia .... 573-651-2524 259 H
srucker@semo.edu
RUCKER-SHAMU,
Marian .... 301-860-3849 204 A
mshamu@bowiestate.edu
RUCKERT, Jason .... 386-226-7330.. 99 A
jason.ruckert@erau.edu
RUCKS, Lucas .... 360-538-4013 480 G
lucas.rucks@ghc.edu
RUCKS, Lucas .... 206-546-4101 484 B
lrucks@shoreline.edu
RUDA, Ryan .... 620-276-9533 174 B
ryan.ruda@gcccks.edu
RUDATSIKIRA,
Emmanuel .... 269-471-6648 221 D
rudatsikira@andrews.edu
RUDAWSKY, Donald, J . 954-262-5392 105 A
rudawsky@nova.edu
RUDD, M. David .... 901-678-2234 426 G
mdrudd@memphis.edu
RUDD, Robert .... 215-596-8800 401 E
RUDDELL, Lori .... 208-792-2216 132 A
lruddell@lcsc.edu
RUDDEN, David .... 847-214-7925 137 F
drudden@elgin.edu
RUDE, Jen, L .... 253-535-7464 482 A
rudejl@plu.edu
RUDEAU, William .... 609-771-2187 276 I
rudeau@tcnj.edu
RUDECOFF,
Christine, A .... 315-684-6055 321 A
rudecoc@morrisville.edu
RUDIGER, Brenda .... 906-487-2400 228 A
brudiger@mtu.edu
RUDIGER, Jennifer .... 715-232-5161 497 B
rudigerj@uwstout.edu
RUDIN, Mark, J .... 903-886-5011 447 B
mark.rudin@tamuc.edu
RUDISILL, Frank .... 864-503-5511 414 A
frudisill@uscupstate.edu
RUDISILL, Mark .... 630-942-4306 135 I
rudisillm@cod.edu
RUDNICK, Virginia .... 315-294-8842 292 G
vrudnick@cayuga-cc.edu
RUDNYTZKY, Nick .... 215-885-2360 389 C
nrudnytzky@manor.edu
RUDOLPH, Alan, S .... 970-491-7194.. 79 N
alan.rudolph@colostate.edu
RUDOLPH, Angela .... 304-724-5000 487 B
angela@rjpccpa.com
RUDOLPH, Cassius .... 212-870-1244 309 E
crudolph@nyts.edu
RUDOLPH, Hillel .... 305-944-0035 104 I
RUDOLPH, Leena .... 580-559-5206 365 K
leeerud@ecok.edu
RUDOLPH, Michael .... 859-257-6394 185 F
rudolph@uky.edu
RUDOVSKY, Michele ..... 650-378-6733.. 62 K
rudovskym@smccd.edu
RUDOWSKY, Catherine . 361-825-2643 447 C
catherine.rudowsky@tamucc.edu
RUDY, James .... 714-432-5017.. 38 B
jrudy7@occ.cccd.edu
RUE, Cynthia .... 239-454-5000 106 E
crue@picollege.edu
RUE, Penny .... 336-758-5943 344 C
rue@wfu.edu
RUEFF, Alicia .... 561-732-4424 107 G
arueff@svdp.edu
RUEFLE, Colleen .... 412-536-1069 386 H
colleen.ruefle@laroche.edu
RUEGG, Texas .... 903-233-4381 439 A
texasruegg@letu.edu
RUEGGER, Jacqueline .... 718-933-6700 307 A
jruegger@monroecollege.edu
RUELAS, AnnMarie .... 714-484-7369.. 54 B
aruelas@cypresscollege.edu
RUELAS, George .... 951-827-1012.. 70 B
RUELLE, Joan .... 336-278-6572 328 J
jruelle@elon.edu
RUELLE, Maggie .... 903-510-2724 452 A
mrue@tjc.edu
RUEPPEL, Cary .... 315-655-7012 292 H
carueppel@cazenovia.edu
RUESCH, Sherry .... 435-652-7551 460 B
ruesch@dixie.edu
RUETTGERS, Mary .... 618-235-2700 150 E
mary.ruettgers@swic.edu
RUFF, Corey .... 325-674-2665 428 F
clr06a@acu.edu
RUFF, Haskell .... 470-639-0999 123 D
haskell.ruff@morehouse.edu
RUFF, Joy, C .... 305-237-2090 104 E
jruff@mdc.edu
RUFF, Margaret .... 903-785-7661 441 D
mruff@parisjc.edu
RUFF, III, Raymond, H . 864-597-4171 414 E
ruffrh@wofford.edu
RUFF, Sydney .... 802-387-7223 462 C
sydneyruff@landmark.edu
RUFF, Tina .... 775-673-7135 271 C
truff@tmcc.edu
RUFF, Tina, B .... 919-536-7200 334 C
rufft@durhamtech.edu
RUFFIN, Christopher .... 601-857-3357 246 C
christopher.ruffin@hindscc.edu
RUFFIN, Derrick .... 212-924-5900 321 F
RUFFIN, Finee .... 601-477-4082 246 G
finee.ruffin@jcjc.edu
RUFFIN, Reginald .... 205-929-1100.... 6 B
rruffin@miles.edu
RUFFING, Charles, W ... 920-923-7166 493 D
cwruffing23@marianuniversity.edu
RUFFING, Rebecca .... 315-866-0300 301 D
ruffingrj@herkimer.edu
RUFFRAGE, Jo .... 315-792-7172 321 B
ruffraj@sunypoly.edu
RUFINO, Paul .... 856-415-2173 281 D
prufino@rcsj.edu
RUFLETH, Ernest .... 318-257-5500 192 D
erufleth@latech.edu
RUFO, Joseph .... 315-470-6622 319 D
jlrufo@esf.edu
RUGEMER, Ellen .... 410-857-2203 200 F
erugemer@mcdaniel.edu
RUGER, Theodore, W ... 215-898-7061 400 F
deanruger@law.upenn.edu
RUGG, Marilyn .... 315-228-7288 296 E
mrugg@colgate.edu
RUGG, Rebecca .... 312-996-2006 151 G
rugg@uic.edu
RUGGERI, Tom .... 434-961-5229 474 I
truggeri@pvcc.edu
RUGGIERO, Bruno .... 985-448-4262 192 F
bruno.ruggiero@nicholls.edu
RUGGIRELLO, John ...... 860-727-6907.. 88 A
jruggirello@goodwin.edu
RUGGLES, Jennifer .... 216-368-1723 349 D
jor15@case.edu
RUGGLES, Paul .... 910-592-8081 337 G
pruggles@sampsoncc.edu
RUGH, Susan .... 801-422-2742 458 H
susan_rugh@byu.edu
RUGLESS, Katrina .... 606-218-5291 186 B
katrinarugless@upike.edu
RUGON, Kim .... 504-286-5000 191 C
krugon@suno.edu
RUHD, Jill .... 605-256-5650 416 F
jill.ruhd@dsu.edu
RUHL, Chris .... 317-208-5311 160 A
RUHL, Christopher, A ... 765-494-4600 160 B
RUHLANDT, Karin .... 315-443-3949 321 G
kruhland@syr.edu
RUHMAN, Douglas .... 406-275-4763 265 F
douglas_ruhman@skc.edu
RUITER, Kathy .... 217-854-5525 133 I
kathleen.ruiter@blackburn.edu
RUIZ, Alfredo .... 269-471-6979 221 D
jaruiz@andrews.edu
RUIZ, Andrew .... 806-894-9611 443 G
aruiz@southplainscollege.edu
RUIZ, Angel, J .... 787-863-2390 508 B
angel.ruiz@fajardo.inter.edu
RUIZ, Angela .... 504-398-2271 192 A
aruiz@uhcno.edu
RUIZ, Carey .... 270-789-5177 180 A
cdruiz@campbellsville.edu
RUIZ, Dora .... 310-289-5123.. 74 I
dora.ruiz@wcui.edu
RUIZ, Ediltrudys .... 718-960-8421 294 A
ediltrudys.ruiz@lehman.cuny.edu
RUIZ, Elaine .... 787-798-3001 511 B
elaine.ruiz@uccaribe.edu
RUIZ, Eric .... 815-740-5070 152 H
eruiz@stfrancis.edu
RUIZ, Israel, A .... 787-840-2575 509 I
iruiz@psm.edu
RUIZ, Jesus .... 847-543-2113 136 A
jruiz20@clcillinois.edu
RUIZ, Joaquin .... 520-626-8527.. 16 D
jruiz@email.arizona.edu
RUIZ, OP, John Martin 202-495-3821.. 93 D
jruiz@dhs.edu
RUIZ, Joseph .... 361-698-1374 435 G
jruiz156@delmar.edu
RUIZ, Lucy .... 559-243-7105.. 66 H
lucy.ruiz@scccd.edu
RUIZ, Luis, A .... 787-766-1717 510 G
um_lruiz@uagm.edu
RUIZ, Luis, E .... 787-250-1912 508 D
leruiz@metro.inter.edu
RUIZ, Maria-Luisa .... 718-270-6263 294 G
mlruiz@mec.cuny.edu
RUIZ, Miguel .... 713-221-8564 453 A
ruizm@uhd.edu
RUIZ, Phyllis .... 201-216-5213 283 D
phyllis.ruiz@stevens.edu

RUIZ, Rachel .... 626-966-4576.. 25 H
studentservices@agu.edu
RUIZ, Rafael .... 787-257-0000 512 B
rafael.ruiz@upr.edu
RUIZ, Ruben .... 708-656-8000 145 C
ruben.ruiz@morton.edu
RUIZ, Sheri .... 818-364-7600.. 49 C
lamcfoundation@lamission.edu
RUIZ, Sina .... 903-875-7376 440 D
sina.ruiz@navarrocollege.edu
RUIZ, Trisha .... 713-525-2101 454 G
ruizt@stthom.edu
RUIZ, Veronica .... 787-852-1430 507 C
vernoicaruiz@hccpr.edu
RUIZ, Veronica .... 787-746-1400 507 B
vruiz@huertas.edu
RUIZ DE FIISCHLER,
Carmen .... 787-764-0000 513 B
carmen.ruiz14@upr.edu
RUIZ-ESPARZA, Emir .... 620-947-3121 177 I
emirruizesparza@tabor.edu
RUIZ-MORENO, Isabel .. 818-364-7776.. 49 C
ruizoi@lamission.edu
RULAND, Heather .... 978-630-9361 215 C
RULAND, Judith, P .... 989-964-4145 230 E
jruland@svsu.edu
RULE, Dave .... 425-602-3000 477 H
drule@bastyr.edu
RULE, Nik .... 641-673-2168 171 C
ruleng@wmpenn.edu
RULLAN TORO,
Agustin .... 787-265-3878 511 F
agustin.rullan@upr.edu
RULLAN TORO,
Agustin .... 787-832-4040 512 E
rector.uprm@upr.edu
RULNEY, Lisa .... 520-621-5977.. 16 D
lisa.rulney@arizona.edu
RULOFSON, Eric .... 307-268-2492 500 U
eric.rulofson@caspercollege.edu
RUMERY, Joyce, V .... 207-581-1655 196 G
rumery@maine.edu
RUMFORD, John .... 703-539-6890 471 F
jrumford@stratford.edu
RUMIANO, Sara .... 530-898-5270.. 30 D
srumiano@csuchico.edu
RUMLEY, Timothy .... 616-538-2330 224 E
trumley@gracechristian.edu
RUMMEL, Justin .... 570-372-4314 398 F
rummelj@susqu.edu
RUMPCA, Susan .... 218-855-8038 237 G
susan.rumpca@clcmn.edu
RUMPF, Troy .... 307-778-1142 501 E
trumpf@lccc.wy.edu
RUMPLER, Laura .... 208-769-3316 132 D
lkrumpler@nic.edu
RUMPZA, Matthew, D ... 651-696-6551 236 I
mrumpza@macalester.edu
RUMSEY, Duane .... 661-722-6300.. 26 A
drumsey@avc.edu
RUMSEY, Elizabeth ...... 218-726-7471 243 G
erumsey@d.umn.edu
RUMSEY, Tyler .... 928-776-2332.. 16 J
tyler.rumsey@yc.edu
RUND, James, A .... 480-965-2200.. 10 J
james.rund@asu.edu
RUNDELL, Isabel .... 317-896-9324 161 F
irundell@ubca.org
RUNDELL, Jay, A .... 740-362-3121 355 H
jrundell@mtso.edu
RUNDQUIST, Andy .... 651-523-2800 236 B
RUNDQUIST, Brad .... 701-777-4589 345 B
bradley.rundquist@und.edu
RUNDSTROM, Amy, L .... 308-865-8501 269 I
rundstromal@unk.edu
RUNELL HALL,
Marcella .... 413-538-3133 217 C
mhall@mtholyoke.edu
RUNESTAD, Eric, J .... 507-222-5411 234 G
erunestad@carleton.edu
RUNEY, Mim, L .... 401-598-1000 404 D
mim.runey@jwu.edu
RUNFELDT, John .... 973-877-3078 277 G
runfeldt@essex.edu
RUNGAITIS, Stacy .... 760-744-1150.. 56 B
srungaitis@palomar.edu
RUNGE, Carol .... 518-743-2313 320 A
rungec@sunyacc.edu
RUNGE, Christina .... 414-955-8487 493 F
chrunge@mcw.edu
RUNGE, Denise .... 907-786-1050.... 9 J
provost@alaska.edu
RUNGE, Marschall, S ... 734-647-9351 231 H
mrunge@umich.edu
RUNGE, Nate .... 715-830-5563 498 E
nrunge1@cvtc.edu
RUNIEWICZ, Michael, J 314-935-8976 262 A
michael_runiewicz@wustl.edu
RUNION, Robert .... 304-929-5026 488 G
rrunion@newriver.edu
RUNION, Trish .... 785-539-3571 176 A
trunion@mccks.edu
RUNKLE, Dan .... 563-589-3599 170 G
drunkle@dbq.edu
RUNKLE, Gita .... 562-463-7359.. 58 L
grunkle@riohondo.edu
RUNKSMEIER, Lori .... 860-465-5091.. 85 H
runksmeierl@easternct.edu
RUNNELS, Greg .... 574-239-8312 156 A
grunnels@hcc-nd.edu
RUNNING, Patrick .... 320-762-4483 237 C
patrickr@alextech.edu
RUNSER, Beth .... 704-461-6573 326 L
bethrunser@bac.edu
RUNYAN, Lisa .... 660-543-4914 260 G
runyan@ucmo.edu
RUNYAN, Rodney .... 936-294-2394 450 A
rcr039@shsu.edu
RUNYON, Darla, J .... 660-562-1532 257 E
drunyon@nwmissouri.edu
RUNYON, David .... 717-901-5137 385 H
drunyon@harrisburgu.edu
RUNYON, Jean .... 970-204-8100.. 81 A
jean.runyon@frontrange.edu
RUPE, Jolene, K .... 785-539-3571 176 A
jrupe@mccks.edu
RUPE, Manuel, R .... 989-774-2544 222 E
rupe1mr@cmich.edu
RUPE, Ryan, R .... 860-444-8481 503 G
ryan.r.rupe@uscg.mil
RUPERT, Kimberly .... 517-750-1200 231 C
krupert@arbor.edu
RUPERT, Molly .... 530-226-4135.. 64 E
mrupert@simpsonu.edu
RUPERT, Terry, A .... 937-481-2255 364 A
terry_rupert@wilmington.edu
RUPIPER, Russ .... 402-557-7291 265 J
russ.rupiper@bellevue.edu
RUPLEY, Larissa .... 254-710-6972 431 E
larissa_rupley@baylor.edu
RUPP, Lisa .... 541-463-5561 373 D
ruppl@lanecc.edu
RUPP, Sharon, L .... 864-424-8014 413 H
ruppsl@mailbox.sc.edu
RUPP, Sheila .... 989-356-9021 221 C
RUPPERT, Shawn .... 804-627-5300 464 K
RUPPRECHT, Stephen ... 610-902-8417 379 G
smr438@cabrini.edu
RUPRECHT, Barbara, D . 412-648-7910 400 H
bar50@pitt.edu
RURSCH, Keri .... 309-794-7721 133 C
kerirursch@augustana.edu
RUSAK, Katie .... 313-664-7861 222 H
krusak@collegeforcreativestudies.edu
RUSCH, Dan .... 704-825-6264 334 G
rusch.dan@gaston.edu
RUSCH, Kathleen, M ..... 414-464-9777 498 B
rusch.kathleen@wspp.edu
RUSCH-CURL, Kari .... 651-450-3692 238 E
krusch-curl@inverhills.edu
RUSCH-CURL, Kari .... 952-358-8776 239 G
kari.rusch-curl@normandale.edu
RUSCHE, Ernst .... 231-348-6624 228 H
erusche@ncmich.edu
RUSCHIVAL, Michael .... 303-292-0015.. 80 H
mruschival@denvercollegeofnursing.edu
RUSCHMAN, Doug .... 513-745-3185 364 G
ruschman@xavier.edu
RUSE, Elaine .... 330-941-3399 364 H
eruse@ysu.edu
RUSEN, Barbara .... 848-932-4712 282 A
brusen@docs.rutgers.edu
RUSH, Amber .... 870-368-2008.. 20 E
arush@ozarka.edu
RUSH, Amy .... 757-455-3401 477 C
arush@vwu.edu
RUSH, Bonnie, R .... 785-532-5660 175 C
brush@vet.ksu.edu
RUSH, Bryan .... 334-844-5390.... 4 D
sbr0024@auburn.edu
RUSH, Cherylyn, L .... 215-951-1948 387 A
rush@lasalle.edu
RUSH, Christopher .... 714-712-7900.. 46 B
RUSH, Denise .... 617-585-0200 207 A
denise.rush@the-bac.edu
RUSH, Dennis .... 845-569-3492 307 D
dennis.rush@msmc.edu
RUSH, Gregory, M .... 502-597-5075 183 D
gregory.rush@kysu.edu
RUSH, James .... 662-476-5386 246 B
jrush@eastms.edu
RUSH, Janet .... 402-363-5661 270 D
jgrush@york.edu
RUSH, John, H .... 563-588-8000 166 C
jrush@emmaus.edu
RUSH, John, P .... 662-325-9306 247 F
rush@devalumni.msstate.edu
RUSH, Katy .... 563-441-4046 166 B
krush@eicc.edu
RUSH, Keith .... 225-769-8820 189 C
RUSH, Kimberly .... 601-581-3506 247 A
krush5@meridiancc.edu
RUSH, Leslie .... 307-766-1121 501 I
RUSH, Mark, E .... 540-458-8904 477 D
rushm@wlu.edu
RUSH, Maureen .... 215-898-7515 400 F
mrush@publicsafety.upenn.edu
RUSH, Michele .... 863-583-9050 110 B
RUSH, Patrick .... 708-596-2000 149 H
prush@ssc.edu
RUSH, Rosalee .... 209-667-3131.. 33 B
RUSH, Tonyalle, V .... 662-562-3219 248 D
RUSHBROOK, Jill .... 860-253-3068.. 86 C
jrushbrook@asnuntuck.edu
RUSHER, Bryan .... 501-812-2256.. 23 B
brusher@uaptc.edu
RUSHFORTH, Brenda .... 909-621-8175.. 57 K
brenda.rushforth@pomona.edu
RUSHI, Purva .... 708-456-0300 151 D
purvarushi@triton.edu
RUSHIK, Julie .... 585-594-6493 312 E
rushik_julie@roberts.edu
RUSHING, Cheri .... 618-437-5321 147 I
rushing@rlc.edu
RUSHING, Dorrie .... 713-646-1898 443 I
drushing@stcl.edu
RUSHING,
James Kenneth .... 904-264-2172 106 K
krushing@iwsfla.org
RUSHING, Linda .... 870-364-6414.. 22 C
rushingl@uamont.edu
RUSHING, Mark .... 479-575-5555.. 21 F
markr@uark.edu
RUSHING, Ray .... 254-867-4893 449 D
ray.rushing@tstc.edu
RUSHLOW, Jennifer ...... 802-831-1136 463 C
jrushlow@vermontlaw.edu
RUSHMER, Bernadette .. 570-674-8028 390 B
brushmer@misericordia.edu
RUSHNAWITZ, P .... 248-968-3360 233 F
RUSHTON, Jennifer .... 706-379-3111 128 C
jlrushton@yhc.edu
RUSILOSKI, Benjamin ... 215-489-2946 382 B
president@delval.edu
RUSILOSKI, Benjamin ... 215-489-2911 382 B
benjamin.rusiloski@delval.edu
RUSINEK, Ken .... 207-985-7976 194 H
RUSINKO, Joseph .... 315-781-3304 301 F
rusinko@hws.edu
RUSKIN, Susan .... 323-856-7741.. 25 G
sruskin@afi.com
RUSLANDER, Barbara ... 518-861-2516 305 C
bruslander@mariacollege.edu
RUSS, Christina .... 425-640-1683 480 A
christina.russ@edcc.edu
RUSS, Cyrus, K .... 601-877-6114 245 A
ckruss@alcorn.edu
RUSS, Roy .... 304-793-6819 490 C
rruss@osteo.wvsom.edu
RUSS, Shelly .... 802-728-1303 464 A
sruss@vtc.edu
RUSS-WILSON, Traci, L 704-894-2201 328 E
trruss@davidson.edu
RUSSE, Sarah, R .... 630-844-4620 133 D
srusse@aurora.edu
RUSSEK, Lori .... 361-593-2678 447 D
lori.russek@tamuk.edu
RUSSEL, Michael .... 817-257-7926 448 F
m.russel@tcu.edu
RUSSEL, Philip .... 215-951-2814 399 E
philip.russel@jefferson.edu
RUSSELBURG, Morgan . 270-686-4285 179 J
morgan.russelburg@brescia.edu
RUSSELL, Adrina .... 910-670-2116 341 C
arussell@uncfsu.edu
RUSSELL, Agnes, M ...... 616-988-3656 226 E
arussell@kuyper.edu
RUSSELL, Andrew .... 315-792-7317 321 B
andrew.russell@sunypoly.edu
RUSSELL, April .... 419-448-2202 353 E
arussell@heidelberg.edu
RUSSELL, Avis .... 202-274-5400.. 94 B
avis.russell@udc.edu
RUSSELL, Babs .... 770-947-7260 128 A
babs.russell@westgatech.edu
RUSSELL, Bryan .... 270-745-5818 186 C
bryan.russell@wku.edu
RUSSELL, Bryce .... 212-812-4041 308 G
brussell@nycda.edu
RUSSELL, Carol, G .... 513-556-6169 361 J
russecg@ucmail.uc.edu
RUSSELL, Chrystina ...... 603-665-7911 274 C
c.russell@snhu.edu
RUSSELL, Craig .... 501-279-5000.. 19 C
crussell@harding.edu
RUSSELL, Danny .... 740-362-3322 355 H
drussell@mtso.edu
RUSSELL, Darcy .... 785-594-8312 171 F
RUSSELL, David, R .... 573-875-7200 251 I
RUSSELL, David, W ...... 214-648-2695 457 A
david.russell@utsouthwestern.edu
RUSSELL, Denise .... 614-236-6196 349 B
drussell@capital.edu
RUSSELL, Janet .... 909-621-8774.. 57 K
janet.russsell@pomona.edu
RUSSELL, Jarad .... 423-614-6001 420 H
jrussell@leeuniversity.edu
RUSSELL, Jeffrey .... 608-262-5823 495 D
jrussell@dcs.wisc.edu
RUSSELL, Jennie .... 314-838-8858 261 F
jrussell@ugst.edu
RUSSELL, Jennifer .... 202-685-4094 502 K
jennifer.russell@ndu.edu
RUSSELL, Jennifer, M ... 719-333-3091 503 D
jennifer.russell@usafa.edu
RUSSELL, Jill, T .... 717-867-6076 388 C
russell@lvc.edu
RUSSELL, Jim .... 914-323-5236 305 B
james.russell@mville.edu
RUSSELL, Joanna, S ..... 503-223-5100 376 D
jrussell@sumnercollege.edu
RUSSELL, Joanne .... 718-368-5661 294 E
joanne.russell@kbcc.cuny.edu
RUSSELL, Josh .... 408-274-7900.. 62 G
josh.russell@evc.edu
RUSSELL, Joyce .... 610-519-4331 401 K
joyce.russell@villanova.edu
RUSSELL, Judith .... 352-273-2505 111 A
jcrussell@ufl.edu
RUSSELL, Julia, H .... 802-656-4063 463 A
julia.russell@uvm.edu
RUSSELL, Justin .... 912-583-3161 116 E
drussell@bpc.edu
RUSSELL, Keith .... 503-399-5184 372 B
keith.russell@chemeketa.edu
RUSSELL, Kelly .... 559-278-2182.. 31 B
kellyr@csufresno.edu
RUSSELL, Kenneth .... 616-949-5300 223 C
kenneth.russell@cornerstone.edu
RUSSELL, Kevin .... 601-968-8746 245 B
krussell@belhaven.edu
RUSSELL, Kimberly .... 940-898-3863 451 D
krussell9@twu.edu
RUSSELL, Kristie .... 740-245-7191 363 A
krussell@rio.edu
RUSSELL, Leah, L .... 540-375-2211 470 E
russell@roanoke.edu
RUSSELL, Leigh .... 252-493-7354 336 H
lrussell@email.pittcc.edu
RUSSELL, Lois .... 334-229-4431.... 4 A
lrussell@alasu.edu
RUSSELL, Mark, A .... 419-772-2011 358 C
m-russell.7@onu.edu
RUSSELL, Mary .... 740-753-7080 353 H
russellm@hocking.edu
RUSSELL, Mary Jane .... 802-654-2000 462 G
ir@smcvt.edu
RUSSELL, Matt .... 704-334-6882 328 B
mrussell@charlottechristian.edu
RUSSELL, Michael .... 804-819-4995 473 C
mrusssell@vccs.edu
RUSSELL, Michelle .... 856-222-9311 281 C
mrussell@rcbc.edu
RUSSELL, Mindi .... 256-890-4989.... 1 F
mindi.russell@calhoun.edu
RUSSELL, Pam .... 304-485-5487 487 G
RUSSELL, Pamela .... 508-531-1295 212 D
prussell@bridgew.edu
RUSSELL, Pat .... 206-239-4500 478 H

RUSSELL, Patrice .... 603-641-7202 274 A
prussell@anselm.edu
RUSSELL, Patrick, J ...... 414-425-8300 495 A
prussell@shsst.edu
RUSSELL, Robb .... 562-947-8755.. 65 I
robbrussell@scuhs.edu
RUSSELL, Robert .... 605-626-7770 416 G
robert.russell@northern.edu
RUSSELL, Sharron .... 501-450-1348.. 19 E
russell@hendrix.edu
RUSSELL, Tammy .... 269-467-9945 224 C
trussell@glenoaks.edu
RUSSELL, Thad .... 559-791-2307.. 47 A
thad.russell@portervillecollege.edu
RUSSELL, Tikola .... 718-631-6314 295 C
trussell@qcc.cuny.edu
RUSSELL, Todd .... 985-867-2266 190 K
trussell@sjasc.edu
RUSSELL, Tommiann, R 315-267-2162 319 A
russeltr@potsdam.edu
RUSSELL, Traci .... 206-934-5661 483 B
traci.russell@seattlecolleges.edu
RUSSELL, William .... 860-632-3050.. 88 C
busoffice@holyapostles.edu
RUSSELL-EDWARDS,
Juanita .... 601-877-6191 245 A
juanita@alcorn.edu
RUSSETT, Gary .... 413-265-2356 208 E
russettg@elms.edu
RUSSIAKY, Rachael .... 864-977-7190 410 I
rachael.russiaky@ngu.edu
RUSSIN, Gabrielle .... 914-961-8313 314 H
grussin@svots.edu
RUSSIN, Ted .... 845-905-4427 297 G
ted.russin@culinary.edu
RUSSO, Betty, S .... 812-941-2661 157 F
bsrusso@ius.edu
RUSSO, Cecelia, M .... 718-990-6667 313 G
russoc@stjohns.edu
RUSSO, Colleen .... 718-368-5109 294 E
RUSSO, Colleen .... 801-618-0438 458 G
crusso@ameritech.edu
RUSSO, Elizabeth .... 315-279-5273 303 G
drusso@keuka.edu
RUSSO, Garth, S .... 706-542-8715 126 G
grusso@uga.edu
RUSSO, Greg .... 619-574-6909.. 55 E
grusso@pacificcollege.edu
RUSSO, Kelly .... 724-983-0700 388 B
RUSSO, Lari, C .... 516-367-6890 296 C
RUSSO, Lisa .... 213-613-2200.. 65 E
lisarusso@sciarc.edu
RUSSO, Maria .... 518-454-5121 296 G
russom@strose.edu
RUSSO, Michael .... 860-832-1904.. 85 G
michael.russo@ccsu.edu
RUSSO, Paul .... 646-592-4720 326 D
paul.russo@yu.edu
RUSSO, Richard .... 510-642-2700.. 69 A
russo@berkeley.edu
RUSSO, Ronald .... 504-762-3005 188 B
rrusso@dcc.edu
RUSSO, Thomas .... 417-873-7413 252 G
trusso@drury.edu
RUSSOM, Vaughn, N .... 715-394-8327 497 C
vrussom@follett.com
RUSSOMANNO,
Catherine .... 609-896-5121 281 B
RUSSOMANNO,
David, J .... 317-274-0802 157 D
drussoma@iupui.edu
RUSSOS, Milton, A .... 904-442-2950 101 B
mrussos@fscj.edu
RUSSOW, Rodd .... 770-537-6000 128 A
rodd.russow@westgatech.edu
RUST, Christopher .... 860-439-5328.. 87 H
christopher.rust@conncoll.edu
RUST, Jodi .... 620-227-9322 173 D
jrust@dc3.edu
RUST, Melissa .... 501-686-2532.. 21 E
mrust@uasys.edu
RUSTAD, Dan .... 507-222-4890 234 G
drustad@carleton.edu
RUSTEMEYER, Jordan ... 660-248-6292 251 E
RUSTGI, Anil .... 212-854-1754 297 C
RUSTICUS, Lisa .... 616-988-3653 226 E
lrusticus@kuyper.edu
RUTENBAR, Rob, A .... 412-624-9019 400 H
rutenbar@pitt.edu
RUTENBECK, Jeff .... 215-572-2900 378 E
rutenbeckj@arcadia.edu
RUTH, Alice, A .... 603-646-2445 273 D
alice.a.ruth@dartmouth.edu

RUTH, Andrea .... 610-225-5054 383 B
aruth@eastern.edu
RUTH, Anna .... 727-864-7966.. 98 J
ruthar@eckerd.edu
RUTH, David .... 610-861-5065 391 C
druth@northampton.edu
RUTH, Gary .... 304-887-1795 464 J
gruth@bluefield.edu
RUTH, John .... 212-353-4247 297 E
jruth@cooper.edu
RUTH, Kevin, J .... 844-283-2246.. 93 C
RUTH, Matthew .... 540-432-4118 466 B
matthew.ruth@emu.edu
RUTH, Rudy .... 610-796-8371 378 C
RUTH, Ted .... 573-341-7619 261 D
truth@mst.edu
RUTHENBECK, Julie, J .. 325-942-2255 450 E
julie.ruthenbeck@angelo.edu
RUTHER, Elliot .... 513-569-1451 350 F
elliot.ruther@cincinnatistate.edu
RUTHER, Elliott, V .... 513-569-1451 350 F
elliot.ruther@cincinnatistate.edu
RUTHERFORD, David .... 561-868-3450 105 D
rutherfd@palmbeachstate.edu
RUTHERFORD, Greg, F . 803-327-8050 414 F
grutherford@yorktech.edu
RUTHERFORD, John ..... 406-447-6935 264 B
john.rutherford@helenacollege.edu
RUTHERFORD, John, D 214-648-0400 457 A
john.rutherford@utsouthwestern.edu
RUTHERFORD, Lisa, H .. 413-542-5645 205 G
lrutherford@amherst.edu
RUTHERFORD,
Marcella, M .... 954-262-1963 105 A
rmarcell@nova.edu
RUTHERFORD, Matthew 315-268-4329 295 F
mrutherf@clarkson.edu
RUTHERFORD, Paul ...... 304-327-4403 489 I
prutherford@bluefieldstate.edu
RUTHERFORD, Tom ...... 626-398-2222.. 76 C
RUTHERFORD, Whitney 850-729-5253 104 M
rutherf2j@nwfsc.edu
RUTHERMAN, Kathy ...... 270-852-3143 183 E
krutherman@kwc.edu
RUTKOWSKE, Snow ...... 312-567-3677 140 A
srutkowske@iit.edu
RUTKOWSKI, Leslie, A . 315-470-6655 319 D
larutkow@esf.edu
RUTKOWSKI, Sandra .... 419-824-3762 355 C
srutkowski@lourdes.edu
RUTLAND, Jason .... 864-231-2000 406 F
jrutland@andersonuniversity.edu
RUTLEDGE, Brian .... 601-984-1010 249 E
brutledge@umc.edu
RUTLEDGE, Catherine ... 484-365-8087 388 H
crutledge@lincoln.edu
RUTLEDGE, Debi .... 248-218-2192 230 B
drutledge@rochesteru.edu
RUTLEDGE, Jacqueline . 817-531-6571 451 C
jrutledge@txwes.edu
RUTLEDGE, James .... 662-846-4004 245 G
jrutledge@deltastate.edu
RUTLEDGE, Janet .... 410-455-1781 203 B
jrutledge@umbc.edu
RUTLEDGE, Melissa, B . 540-378-5120 470 E
rutledge@roanoke.edu
RUTLEDGE, Peter .... 706-542-7140 126 G
borut@uga.edu
RUTLEDGE, Scott .... 765-285-5818 153 H
scott.rutledge@bsu.edu
RUTLEDGE, Valerie .... 423-425-4249 427 C
valerie-rutledge@utc.edu
RUTSKY, Lisa .... 480-947-6644.. 14 N
RUTSTEIN-RILEY, Amy .. 617-349-8401 211 C
arutstei@lesley.edu
RUTT, Charles, D .... 660-543-4370 260 G
rutt@ucmo.edu
RUTT, Douglas, L .... 314-505-7566 252 A
ruttd@csl.edu
RUTTEN, Chris .... 402-844-7051 268 H
christopherr@northeast.edu
RUTTEN, Matthew .... 218-299-3514 235 H
mrutten@cord.edu
RUTTER, Evan .... 909-621-8153.. 37 D
evan.rutter@cmc.edu
RUTTER, Jeff .... 602-489-5300.. 10 F
jeff.rutter@arizonachristian.edu
RUTTER, Jeff .... 931-221-7213 417 H
rutterj@apsu.edu
RUTTER, Sandy .... 423-697-4475 424 A
sandy.rutter@chattanoogastate.edu
RUTTLER, Megan .... 856-468-5000 281 D

RUUD, William, N .... 740-376-4701 355 E
wnr001@marietta.edu
RUYLE, Dianna 217-854-5772 133
dianna.ruyle@blackburn.edu
RUYS, Jasmine .... 661-362-3466.. 38 D
jasmine.ruys@canyons.edu
RUYS, Steve .... 661-259-7800.. 38 D
steve.ruys@canyons.edu
RUZEK, Joy .... 920-465-2222 495 F
ruzekj@uwgb.edu
RUZEK, Nicole .... 434-243-5150 472 D
nar7r@virginia.edu
RUZICH, Steve .... 708-596-2000 149 H
sruzich@ssc.edu
RUZICKA, Jim .... 402-465-2323 268 G
jruzicka@nebrwesleyan.edu
RUÍZ, Janet .... 787-766-1717 510 G
jruiz54@uagm.edu
RYALL, Patrick .... 503-768-7294 373 E
ryall@lclark.edu
RYALLS, Kenneth .... 419-251-1313 355 G
RYALS, Tara .... 334-699-2266.... 1 B
tryals@acom.edu
RYAN, Andrew, J .... 859-238-5572 180 B
andrew.ryan@centre.edu
RYAN, CSC, Brogan ...... 570-208-5900 386 G
broganryan@kings.edu
RYAN, Caroll .... 562-988-2278.. 25 L
cryan@auhs.edu
RYAN, Carrie .... 336-278-5584 328 J
cryan2@elon.edu
RYAN, Casey, J .... 215-596-8800 401 E
RYAN, Christine .... 716-827-2467 323 G
ryanc@trocaire.edu
RYAN, Clay, M .... 205-348-5863.... 7 F
cryan@uasystem.edu
RYAN, Dennis .... 757-340-2121 465 I
RYAN, Diane .... 928-717-7644.. 16 J
diane.ryan@yc.edu
RYAN, Duane .... 575-562-2112 286 B
duane.ryan@enmu.edu
RYAN, Ed .... 408-554-5182.. 63 B
eryan@scu.edu
RYAN, Erik .... 617-873-0106 208 B
erik.ryan@cambridgecollege.edu
RYAN, Gail, L .... 313-577-6595 232 K
gail.ryan@wayne.edu
RYAN, Greg .... 714-992-7092.. 54 C
gryan@fullcoll.edu
RYAN, Helen, G .... 502-272-8052 179 H
hryan@bellarmine.edu
RYAN, James .... 617-585-0200 207 A
james.ryan@the-bac.edu
RYAN, James, E .... 434-924-3337 472 D
jer6p@virginia.edu
RYAN, James, P .... 203-582-7229.. 88 G
james.ryan@quinnipiac.edu
RYAN, Jason .... 802-635-1240 463 G
RYAN, Jennifer .... 785-833-4351 175 E
jennifer.ryan@kwu.edu
RYAN, Joseph .... 859-846-5321 184 B
jryan@midway.edu
RYAN, Joseph .... 707-864-7000.. 64 H
joseph.ryan@solano.edu
RYAN, Joseph .... 505-224-3092 285 N
jeryan@cnm.edu
RYAN, Julie, A .... 928-523-9658.. 14 H
julie.ryan@nau.edu
RYAN, Kathleen .... 508-541-1515 209 A
kryan@dean.edu
RYAN, Kathleen .... 617-732-5042 216 D
kathleen.ryan@mcphs.edu
RYAN, Kathleen .... 614-823-1250 359 H
kryan@otterbein.edu
RYAN, Kelly, A .... 812-941-2208 157 F
ryanka@ius.edu
RYAN, Kimberly .... 973-300-2267 284 A
kryan@sussex.edu
RYAN, Kyle .... 781-899-5500 218 B
kryan@psjs.edu
RYAN, Larry .... 505-313-7626 288 J
larry.ryan@unmfund.org
RYAN, Marianne, P .... 773-508-2657 143 C
mryan21@luc.edu
RYAN, Mark .... 619-849-2489.. 57 J
markryan@pointloma.edu
RYAN, Matt .... 239-590-1494 109 K
mryan@fgcu.edu
RYAN, Maura, A .... 574-631-9488 162 A
mryan11@nd.edu
RYAN, Megan .... 484-664-3204 390 H
meganryan@muhlenberg.edu

RYAN, Pat .... 503-842-8222 376 E
patryan@tillamookbaycc.edu
RYAN, Patrick .... 973-720-3326 284 J
ryanp@wpunj.edu
RYAN, Patrick .... 716-270-2869 299 B
ryanp@ecc.edu
RYAN, Patrick .... 518-381-1210 315 B
ryanpc@sunysccc.edu
RYAN, Paula .... 641-628-5198 164 D
ryanp@central.edu
RYAN, Peter .... 662-325-3742 247 F
ryan@cvm.msstate.edu
RYAN, Rebecca .... 773-244-5623 145 G
rryan@northpark.edu
RYAN, Rosaleen .... 831-646-4035.. 52 G
rryan@mpc.edu
RYAN, Scott .... 817-272-3181 454 I
sdryan@uta.edu
RYAN, Sean, J .... 502-272-8376 179 H
sryan@bellarmine.edu
RYAN, Sharon .... 708-524-6299 137 C
sryan1@dom.edu
RYAN, Susan .... 386-822-7181 112 A
sryan@stetson.edu
RYAN, Thomas, J .... 856-225-6361 281 G
tomryan@camden.rutgers.edu
RYAN, Tim .... 845-452-9600 297 G
tim.ryan@culinary.edu
RYAN, Tim .... 415-452-5352.. 36 K
tryan@ccsf.edu
RYAN, Timothy, M .... 207-725-3247 194 C
tryan@bowdoin.edu
RYAN, Tom .... 727-864-8305.. 98 J
ryantj@eckerd.edu
RYAN, Virginia .... 212-853-0702 291 A
vryan@barnard.edu
RYAN, Zoe .... 215-898-5000 400 F
hello@ica.upenn.edu
RYAN-BENDER, Anna .... 215-248-7993 381 A
aryan@chc.edu
RYAN BULONE, Mary ... 419-473-2700 351 J
mryan@daviscollege.edu
RYAN HOFFMAN,
Maureen .... 802-387-4767 462 C
RYAN RODRIGUEZ,
Christina .... 714-895-8128.. 38 A
cryanrodriguez@gwc.cccd.edu
RYAN VAN ZEE,
Marynel .... 507-222-4917 234 G
mryanvanzee@carleton.edu
RYANT, Marion .... 299-500-3027 114 H
marion.ryant@asurams.edu
RYBAK, Chuck .... 920-465-2336 495 F
rybakc@uwgb.edu
RYBERG, Bill .... 253-566-5336 484 E
bryberg@tacomacc.edu
RYBIN KOOB, Amanda . 303-245-4664.. 82 A
arybinkoob@naropa.edu
RYBIOKI, Catherine ...... 828-669-8012 331 K
RYCHEL, William, E ...... 305-628-6775 107 F
wrychel@stu.edu
RYCHLEC, Timothy .... 713-221-5869 453 A
rychlect@uhd.edu
RYCRAFT, Rickianne ...... 951-639-5420.. 53 A
rrycraft@msjc.edu
RYCYNA, Mary .... 216-397-4921 353 O
mrycyna@jcu.edu
RYDER, Collette, L .... 212-327-8054 312 G
cryder@rockefeller.edu
RYDER, Ellen .... 415-422-2558.. 72 J
eryder@usfca.edu
RYDER, Jon .... 207-221-4701 197 E
jryder2@une.edu
RYDER, Michelle .... 703-284-1667 468 H
michelle.ryder@marymount.edu
RYDER, Tina .... 301-447-5038 201 B
ryder@msmary.edu
RYDL, Chareny, L .... 979-845-3158 446 F
chareny@tamu.edu
RYEA, Alan, E .... 802-656-3245 463 A
alan.ryea@uvm.edu
RYERSON, Crytsal .... 704-216-3806 337 F
crystal.ryerson@rccc.edu
RYGG, Matthew, J .... 503-943-7118 377 A
ryggm@up.edu
RYKEN, Amy .... 253-879-2810 484 G
aryken@pugetsound.edu
RYKEN, Philip, G .... 630-752-5002 153 C
philip.ryken@wheaton.edu
RYLAARSDAM, Robin ...... 651-638-6371 234 D
r-rylaarsdam@bethel.edu
RYLAND, Theresa .... 202-495-3828.. 93 D
advance@dhs.edu

ST. PIERRE, Gail, S ...... 207-786-6120 194 A
gstpierr@bates.edu
ST. PIERRE, Traci .... 207-780-4771 197 D
tracy.st@maine.edu
ST. ROMAIN, Claire ...... 337-482-0925 193 B
cstromain@louisiana.edu
ST. ROMAIN, Karen ...... 248-689-8282 232 C
kstromain@walshcollege.edu
SAINT-VICTOR, Nicole ... 708-239-4560 151 A
nicole.saint-victor@trnty.edu
SAINTJONES, Jerome .... 256-372-4863.... 1 A
jerome.saintjones@aamu.edu
SAINZ, Jose .... 540-654-1261 471 N
jsainz@umw.edu
SAIRS, Reuben .... 740-857-1311 360 D
rsairs@rosedale.edu
SAITTA, Tom .... 336-272-7102 329 C
thomas.saitta@greensboro.edu
SAJADIAN, Dalila, A ..... 641-422-4103 168 G
sajaddal@niacc.edu
SAJDAK, Jeff .... 616-957-6042 222 B
js036@calvinseminary.edu
SAJKO, Brian .... 412-237-3008 381 D
bsajko@ccac.edu
SAKAGAWA, Tamara ..... 863-292-3744 106 A
tsakagawa@polk.edu
SAKAI, Hiro .... 949-480-4008.. 64 G
sakai@soka.edu
SAKAKI, Judy .... 707-664-2156.. 34 B
SAKALLA, Khaled .... 205-940-7800.... 5 D
ksakalla@fortisinstitute.edu
SAKAMAKI, Yuri .... 661-654-3675.. 30 B
ysakamaki@csub.edu
SAKAMOTO, June .... 415-703-8291.. 69 C
sakamotoj@uchastings.edu
SAKELLARIOU, Dimitris 626-395-3208.. 28 J
dimitris@caltech.edu
SAKOSITS, Steve .... 765-983-1730 155 A
sakossi@earlham.edu
SAKRAIDA, Nicole .... 541-956-7166 376 A
nsakraida@roguecc.edu
SAKS, Deborah .... 916-558-2582.. 50 J
saksd@scc.losrios.edu
SAKS, Greg .... 657-278-5287.. 31 C
gsaks@fullerton.edu
SAKS, Michael .... 848-445-7952 282 A
chair@math.rutgers.edu
SAKSENA, P.N .... 803-323-2186 414 D
saksenapn@winthrop.edu
SALA, Andrea .... 310-660-3670.. 41 E
asala@elcamino.edu
SALA, Pete .... 315-443-5439 321 G
pesala@syr.edu
SALADIN, Lisa .... 843-792-3031 410 C
saladinl@musc.edu
SALADIN, Shawn .... 956-665-3651 455 D
shawn.saladin@utrgv.edu
SALAFSKY, David, B ..... 520-621-8297.. 16 D
salafsky@arizona.edu
SALAMY, James .... 315-866-0300 301 D
salamyjr@herkimer.edu
SALAND, Emily, V .... 845-575-3000 305 D
emily.saland@marist.edu
SALAS, Alexandra .... 610-359-5057 382 A
asalas@dccc.edu
SALAS, Angela .... 608-663-2862 492 F
asalas@edgewood.edu
SALAS, Carmen .... 773-371-5484 134 D
csalas@ctu.edu
SALAS, Leslie .... 760-744-1150.. 56 B
SALAS, Richard .... 515-271-1709 165 G
rich.salas@dmu.edu
SALASEK, Aaron .... 651-450-3611 238 E
asalasek@inverhills.edu
SALASKI, Kori .... 608-796-3185 497 O
kfsalaski@viterbo.edu
SALAY, Lawrence .... 203-285-2046.. 86 E
lsalay@gatewayct.edu
SALAZ, Alicia .... 541-346-3053 376 H
asalaz@uoregon.edu
SALAZ, Mark .... 520-494-5250.. 11 K
mark.salaz@centralaz.edu
SALAZAR, Abraham ...... 325-793-4611 439 F
salazar.abraham@mcm.edu
SALAZAR, Anna .... 323-415-4136.. 48 J
salazaal@elac.edu
SALAZAR, Freddie .... 575-769-4143 285 O
freddie.salazar@clovis.edu
SALAZAR, Jamie .... 405-491-6310 369 H
jsalazar@snu.edu
SALAZAR, S.J.,
Jose-Luis .... 718-817-4503 300 C
jsalazar8@fordham.edu
SALAZAR, Linda .... 505-454-2500 286 F
SALAZAR, Nicole .... 520-621-7739.. 16 D
hinzen@arizona.edu
SALAZAR, Rosalinda ..... 956-882-7665 455 D
rosalinda.salazar@utrgv.edu
SALAZAR, Stacey .... 410-225-2541 200 D
ssalazar@mica.edu
SALAZAR, Tony .... 303-860-5600.. 84 A
tony.salazar@cu.edu
SALAZAR, Veronikha ..... 870-230-5231.. 19 D
salazav@hsu.edu
SALAZAR, Victor, G ...... 210-431-4149 441 B
vmsalazar@ollusa.edu
SALAZAR MENDEZ,
Veronica .... 210-458-4011 455 E
SALAZAR-VALENTINE,
Marcia .... 419-372-8185 348 G
marcias@bgsu.edu
SALB, Ephraim .... 845-406-4308 325 F
rabbisalb@kessertorah.org
SALBATO, Michael .... 719-846-5653.. 83 L
michael.salbato@trinidadstate.edu
SALCEDO, Richard .... 661-654-3491.. 30 B
rsalcedo5@csub.edu
SALCIDO, Kevin, J .... 480-965-6608.. 10 J
kevin.j.salcido@asu.edu
SALCIDO, Steven, M ..... 916-278-6060.. 32 D
steven.salcido@csus.edu
SALDANA, Michelle ...... 310-954-4327.. 52 I
msaldana@msmu.edu
SALDANA-TALLEY, Jane 707-778-3931.. 63 D
lsaldana-talley@santarosa.edu
SALDIVAR, Patricia .... 956-295-3426 449 C
patricia.saldivar@tsc.edu
SALE, Rachel .... 956-872-2576 443 H
rsale@southtexascollege.edu
SALEM, Joseph .... 517-355-2341 227 F
jsalem@msu.edu
SALEM, Michael .... 845-574-4770 312 H
msalem2@sunyrockland.edu
SALEM, Susan .... 310-954-4112.. 52 I
ssalem@msmu.edu
SALEMME, Kevin .... 978-837-5377 216 F
kevin.salemme@merrimack.edu
SALERNO, Cheryl .... 918-335-6887 368 E
csalerno@okwu.edu
SALERNO, Dena .... 570-372-4302 398 F
salerno@susqu.edu
SALERNO, Janice .... 215-885-2360 389 C
jsalerno@manor.edu
SALERNO, Kerry .... 781-235-1200 206 B
SALERNO, Sarah .... 781-239-2782 214 G
ssalerno@massbay.edu
SALGADO, Juan .... 773-777-7900 135 G
jsalgado@ccc.edu
SALGADO, Juan .... 312-553-2500 135 A
jsalgado@ccc.edu
SALGADO, Nicole .... 619-660-4654.. 44 D
nicole.salgado@gcccd.edu
SALGADO, Rafael .... 787-279-1912 508 A
rsalgado@bayamon.inter.edu
SALGADO, Sergio .... 507-344-7310 234 C
ssalgado@blc.edu
SALGUERO, Jossie .... 787-766-1912 507 J
jsalguer@inter.edu
SALIBA, Matt .... 863-638-2947 114 B
salibam@webber.edu
SALIBA, Therese .... 360-867-6854 480 C
salibat@evergreen.edu
SALIBA EL HABRE,
Arlene .... 352-254-4119 112 E
SALII, Uroi, N .... 680-488-2471 505 B
usalii@palau.edu
SALIMAN, Todd .... 303-860-5600.. 84 A
officeofthepresident@cu.edu
SALINAS, Antonio .... 575-439-3601 287 D
antsalin@nmsu.edu
SALINAS, Christy .... 626-395-3651.. 28 J
cssalina@caltech.edu
SALINAS, Felix .... 210-486-4788 428 I
fsalinas26@alamo.edu
SALINAS, Francisco ...... 208-426-1411 130 H
franciscosalinas@boisestate.edu
SALINAS, Horacio .... 956-764-5798 438 H
hsalinas@laredo.edu
SALINAS, Larry .... 562-951-4792.. 29 H
lsalinas@calstate.edu
SALINAS, Laura .... 530-541-4660.. 47 E
salinas@ltcc.edu
SALINAS, Lelia .... 956-872-7209 443 H
lelias1@southtexascollege.edu
SALINAS, Nick .... 914-395-2570 315 A
nsalinas@sarahlawrence.edu
SALINAS, Patty .... 559-453-3434.. 43 A
patty.salinas@fresno.edu
SALINAS, Sergio .... 559-325-5273.. 67 A
sergio.salinas@cloviscollege.edu
SALINAS, Stacy .... 845-848-7818 298 C
stacy.salinas@dc.edu
SALINAS-HOVAR, Marta 956-665-7304 455 D
marta.salinashovar@utrgv.edu
SALING MAYER, Marni . 360-752-8325 478 A
msmayer@btc.edu
SALISBURY, Jason .... 712-279-5227 164 B
jason.salisbury@briarcliff.edu
SALISBURY, Jon .... 831-479-6187.. 27 D
josalisb@cabrillo.edu
SALISBURY, Kevin, S .... 401-333-7316 404 C
ksalisbury@ccri.edu
SALISBURY, Micheal ..... 325-942-2169 450 E
micheal.salisbury@angelo.edu
SALISBURY, Susan .... 860-297-4281.. 89 B
susan.salisbury@trincoll.edu
SALIZAR-DAVIDSON,
Hazel .... 805-493-3544.. 29 C
revhazel@callutheran.edu
SALKA, William .... 860-465-5246.. 85 H
salkaw@easternct.edu
SALKIN, Patricia .... 646-565-6522 322 G
patricia.salkin@touro.edu
SALKIN, Patricia .... 646-565-6522 322 F
patricia.salkin@touro.edu
SALLAM, Miriam .... 559-737-4842.. 39 B
mirams@cos.edu
SALLAN, Veena .... 270-686-4639 182 F
veena.sallan@kctcs.edu
SALLEE, Emily .... 816-584-6779 258 C
emily.sallee@park.edu
SALLEE, Holly, E .... 618-537-6824 144 A
hesallee@mckendree.edu
SALLEE-JUSTESEN,
Dawn .... 503-491-6422 374 B
dawn.sallee-justesen@mhcc.edu
SALLEH-BARONE,
Normah .... 708-974-5209 145 A
salleh-barone@morainevalley.edu
SALLEY, Travis .... 404-225-4612 115 H
tsalley@atlantatech.edu
SALLIS, Archer .... 662-476-8414 246 B
jsallis@eastms.edu
SALLUSTIO, Joseph ...... 909-667-4494.. 37 G
jsallustio@claremontlincoln.edu
SALMAN, Juli .... 505-426-2155 286 J
jesalman@nmhu.edu
SALMO, Jim .... 608-796-3000 497 O
SALMON, Lorraine .... 845-687-5093 323 H
salmonl@sunyulster.edu
SALMON, Matt .... 480-727-8191.. 10 J
matt.salmon@asu.edu
SALMON, Michael, G .... 212-517-0563 305 E
msalmon@mmm.edu
SALMON, Pamela .... 315-792-3011 324 B
pjsalmon@utica.edu
SALOCKS, Stephen .... 617-254-2610 218 E
rector@sjs.edu
SALOIS, Brad .... 785-827-5541 175 E
SALOME, JoAnn .... 575-835-5955 286 K
joann.salome@nmt.edu
SALOMON, Danielle ...... 310-954-4371.. 52 I
dsalomon@msmu.edu
SALOMON, Mattisyahu . 732-367-1060 275 K
SALOMON, Nasser .... 909-580-9661.. 34 D
SALOMONE, Giuseppe .. 215-895-1050 382 F
registrar@drexel.edu
SALOMONSON, Kristen . 231-591-3801 224 A
kristensalomonson@ferris.edu
SALON, Mabel .... 530-752-9795.. 69 B
masalon@ucdavis.edu
SALOVEY, Peter .... 203-432-2550.. 90 C
peter.salovey@yale.edu
SALSBURY, Lysa .... 208-885-9358 132 F
lsalsbur@uidaho.edu
SALSGIVER, Amy .... 814-393-1207 393 G
asalsgiver@clarion.edu
SALTANOVICH, Julia ..... 518-262-5522 289 L
saltanj@amc.edu
SALTER, Les .... 770-533-6901 122 B
lsalter@laniertech.edu
SALTER, Sid .... 662-325-7454 247 F
ss51@msstate.edu
SALTERS, Gregory, A .... 305-626-3713 100 D
gregory.salters@fmuniv.edu
SALTIEL, Henry .... 718-482-6120 294 F
hsaltiel@lagcc.cuny.edu
SALTING, Julia, B .... 563-333-6244 169 G
saltingjuliab@sau.edu
SALTON, Susan .... 814-332-4793 378 A
ssalton@allegheny.edu
SALTONSTALL, Margot .. 928-523-6990.. 14 H
SALTSMAN, Brian .... 607-871-2671 290 B
saltsman@alfred.edu
SALTSMAN, Terry .... 931-372-3200 426 B
tsaltsman@tntech.edu
SALVAGE, Lynn .... 718-818-6470 314 F
SALVATORE, Michael ..... 908-737-7032 278 E
msalvato@kean.edu
SALVATORIELLO,
Vincent .... 610-398-5300 388 F
vsalvatoriello@lincolntech.edu
SALVESEN, Guy .... 858-646-3100.. 62 M
gsalvesen@sbpdiscovery.org
SALVINI, Tonia .... 785-830-2753 174 D
tsalvini@haskell.edu
SALVO, Robyn .... 732-263-5228 279 A
rsalvo@monmouth.edu
SALVUCCI, Rachael .... 304-296-8282 491 B
SALYER, Sherry .... 919-962-6947 342 C
salyer@email.unc.edu
SALZBRUNN, Kimberly . 630-637-5454 145 F
ksalzbrunn@noctrl.edu
SALZER, Jean .... 414-251-7389 496 B
jeano@uwm.edu
SALZMAN, Carol .... 413-559-5521 210 D
csalzman@hampshire.edu
SALZMAN, Christine ..... 908-709-7485 284 D
csalzman@follett.com
SALZMANN, Nick .... 847-628-2492 141 C
nsalzmann@judsonu.edu
SAM, David .... 847-214-7374 137 F
dsam@elgin.edu
SAM, Mary .... 218-855-8159 237 G
mary.sam@clcmn.edu
SAM, Penselyn .... 691-320-2480 504 C
petse@comfsm.fm
SAMAHA, Ahmed .... 803-641-3411 413 B
ahmeds@usca.edu
SAMAHA, Mamoun .... 888-488-4968.. 46 F
msamaha@itu.edu
SAMAIE, Parissa .... 323-242-5536.. 49 E
samaiep@lasc.edu
SAMAN, Sarmad .... 508-678-2811 214 B
sarmad.saman@bristolcc.edu
SAMANGO, Melissa ...... 610-526-6196 385 D
msamango@harcum.edu
SAMANIEGO, Sue .... 970-675-3216.. 79 H
sue.samaniego@cncc.edu
SAMANT, Ajay .... 309-438-2251 140 D
asamant@ilstu.edu
SAMARDZIJA, Michael . 909-558-8544.. 48 E
msamardzija@llu.edu
SAMBAMURTHY,
Vallabh .... 608-262-7867 495 D
vsambamurthy@wisc.edu
SAMBDMAN, Cory, W .. 563-333-6336 169 G
1312mgr@follett.com
SAMHAT, Nayef, H .... 864-597-4010 414 E
president@wofford.edu
SAMMAKIA, Bahgat .... 607-777-4818 316 B
bahgat@binghamton.edu
SAMMARCO, Erica, C ... 716-888-2100 292 F
sammarce@canisius.edu
SAMMIS, Robert, L .... 626-914-8550.. 36 J
rsammis@citruscollege.edu
SAMMONS, Gregory, S . 607-587-3911 319 F
sammongs@alfredstate.edu
SAMMONS, Ken .... 509-313-6951 480 F
sammons@gonzaga.edu
SAMMONS, Roxana .... 607-587-4215 319 F
SAMMONS, Steve .... 503-589-8145 372 H
ssammons@corban.edu
SAMO, Tia .... 641-782-1336 170 F
samo@swcciowa.edu
SAMORA, Tracy .... 719-549-2858.. 80 B
tracy.samora@csupueblo.edu
SAMP, Mike .... 307-766-5179 501 I
bowhntr@uwyo.edu
SAMPAIO, Anna, C .... 408-554-2289.. 63 B
asampaio@scu.edu
SAMPATH, Narayan .... 413-552-2800 214 F
nsampath@hcc.edu
SAMPERTON, Amy .... 910-678-8236 334 E
samperta@faytechcc.edu
SAMPITE, Chris .... 318-869-5286 186 F
csampite@centenary.edu
SAMPLE, Bradford .... 740-474-8896 358 A
SAMPLE, Gregory, P ..... 937-775-4734 364 E
gregory.sample@wright.edu
SAMPLE, Katy .... 765-641-4408 153 G
kjsample@anderson.edu

SANDERS, Karen .... 386-506-3050.. 98 D
karen.sanders@daytonastate.edu
SANDERS, Karen .... 361-570-4850 453 B
sanderkg1@uhv.edu
SANDERS, Karen, A .... 217-786-2784 143 B
karen.sanders@llcc.edu
SANDERS, Kristie .... 912-871-1937 123 J
ksanders@ogeecheetech.edu
SANDERS, LaSha .... 678-359-5015 120 F
lashas@gordonstate.edu
SANDERS, Lisa .... 931-433-9350 424 F
lsanders@mscc.edu
SANDERS, Lisa, K .... 618-537-6865 144 A
lksanders@mckendree.edu
SANDERS, Liz .... 312-362-5289 136 H
lsander3@depaul.edu
SANDERS, Mae .... 931-393-1520 424 F
msanders@mscc.edu
SANDERS, Mark .... 318-342-7135 466 K
msanders@vlm.vcom.edu
SANDERS, Megan .... 303-384-2617.. 79 J
sanders@mines.edu
SANDERS, Melanie .... 662-243-1979 246 B
msanders@eastms.edu
SANDERS, Melinda .... 501-337-5000.. 18 B
msanders@asutr.edu
SANDERS, Nancy, A ...... 815-282-7900 148 I
nancysanders@sacn.edu
SANDERS, Rebecca .... 903-510-2084 452 A
rsan2@tjc.edu
SANDERS, Robert .... 407-646-2292 106 L
rsanders@rollins.edu
SANDERS, Salvatore, A . 330-941-3091 364 H
sasanders@ysu.edu
SANDERS, Sara .... 319-335-2625 163 H
sara-sanders@uiowa.edu
SANDERS, Shalonda ..... 229-333-5356 128 B
shalonda.sanders@wiregrass.edu
SANDERS, Susan .... 310-243-3301.. 30 E
ssanders@csudh.edu
SANDERS, Thomas .... 903-923-2075 435 H
tsanders@etbu.edu
SANDERS, Tom .... 330-337-6403 347 D
prdept@awc.edu
SANDERS, Tricia .... 218-281-8326 244 A
sand0803@umn.edu
SANDERS, Tyler .... 909-687-1759.. 43 D
tylersanders@gs.edu
SANDERS, William .... 630-844-5683 133 D
wsanders@aurora.edu
SANDERS,
Wm Gerard (Gerry), Y 210-458-4313 455 E
gerry.sanders@utsa.edu
SANDERS-FUNNYE,
Sharon .... 847-543-2383 136 A
ssandersfunnye@clcillinois.edu
SANDERS-MCMURTRY,
Kijua .... 413-538-2500 217 C
kijuasm@mtholyoke.edu
SANDERSON, Carla .... 888-556-8226 134 E
SANDERSON, Erika .... 509-527-2615 485 C
erika.sanderson@wallawalla.edu
SANDERSON,
Francie, W .... 919-866-5944 338 G
fwsanderson@waketech.edu
SANDERSON, Karri .... 402-465-2411 268 G
ksanders@nebrwesleyan.edu
SANDERSON, Larry .... 575-492-2763 287 A
lsanderson@nmjc.edu
SANDERSON, Lex .... 818-401-1032.. 39 D
lsanderson@columbiacollege.edu
SANDERSON, Robyn ..... 864-231-2000 406 F
rsanderson@andersonuniversity.edu
SANDFORD, Art .... 805-678-5198.. 74 A
asandford@vcccd.edu
SANDFORT, Jodi .... 206-616-1648 485 A
evansdean@uw.edu
SANDHEINRICH, Mark .. 608-785-8218 496 A
msandheinrich@uwlax.edu
SANDIDGE, Christa .... 208-467-8941 132 E
csandidge@nnu.edu
SANDIDGE, William ...... 434-832-7641 473 E
sandidgew@centralvirginia.edu
SANDIFER, Dylan .... 901-843-3874 423 A
sandiferd@rhodes.edu
SANDIFER, Joyce .... 504-520-5230 193 E
jsandife@xula.edu
SANDIFER, William, A .. 803-812-7302 413 E
sandifea@mailbox.sc.edu
SANDIFER, Willie .... 903-730-4890 438 D
wsandifer@jarvis.edu
SANDIGO, Laura .... 928-317-6000.. 11 A
SANDLER, Elysha .... 516-239-9002 315 D
esandler@shoryoshuv.org
SANDLER, Jennifer .... 206-878-3710 481 B
jsandler@highline.edu
SANDLER, Mike .... 303-860-5600.. 84 A
michael.sandler@cu.edu
SANDLES, Sherry .... 817-531-4401 451 C
slsandles@txwes.edu
SANDLIN, Betsy .... 931-598-1254 423 D
bsandlin@sewanee.edu
SANDLIN, Terrie .... 541-956-7283 376 A
tsandlin@roguecc.edu
SANDMANN, Laura .... 580-387-7000 366 E
lsandmann@mscok.edu
SANDNER, Michael .... 860-509-9525.. 88 B
msandner@hartsem.edu
SANDNESS, Debra .... 701-224-5524 346 A
debra.sandness@bismarckstate.edu
SANDOE, Timothy .... 717-780-2648 385 B
tlsandoe@hacc.edu
SANDOR, David, B .... 404-727-2793 118 E
david.sandor@emory.edu
SANDOR, Kathy .... 540-654-1648 471 N
kunderwo@umw.edu
SANDOVAL, Amada .... 914-395-2590 315 A
asandoval@sarahlawrence.edu
SANDOVAL, April .... 928-226-4217.. 11 O
april.sandoval@coconino.edu
SANDOVAL, Barbara, A . 360-650-7614 485 I
barbara.sandoval@wwu.edu
SANDOVAL, Belinda ...... 909-748-8164.. 72 F
belinda_sandoval@redlands.edu
SANDOVAL, Brian .... 775-784-4805 271 E
SANDOVAL, Darlene ..... 505-984-6058 288 C
darlene.sandoval@sjc.edu
SANDOVAL, Deanna ...... 303-867-1155.. 83 K
sandoval@taft.edu
SANDOVAL, Derek .... 830-591-7372 444 G
mdsandoval@swtjc.edu
SANDOVAL, John .... 719-549-2535.. 80 B
john.sandoval@csupueblo.edu
SANDOVAL, Nikki .... 301-985-7000 203 E
nikki.sandoval@umuc.edu
SANDOVAL, Paul .... 520-626-6309.. 16 D
sandovar@arizona.edu
SANDOVAL, Rudy .... 254-501-3007 432 D
rudolfo.sandoval@ctcd.edu
SANDOVAL, Yuliana .... 707-468-3110.. 51 F
ysandoval@mendocino.edu
SANDOVAL DANCS,
Jennifer .... 909-621-8111.. 37 D
jennifer.sandoval-dancs@cmc.edu
SANDRIN, Todd, R .... 602-543-4506.. 10 J
todd.sandrin@asu.edu
SANDS, Charles .... 951-343-4213.. 27 G
csands@calbaptist.edu
SANDS, Deanna .... 206-296-5696 484 A
sandsd@seattleu.edu
SANDS, Harlan, M .... 216-687-3544 350 J
harlan.sands@csuohio.edu
SANDS, Rosita .... 312-369-6286 136 D
rsands@colum.edu
SANDS, Timothy, D ...... 540-231-6231 476 C
president@vt.edu
SANDS WISE, Jonathan 502-863-8009 180 H
jonathan_sandswise@
georgetowncollege.edu
SANDSTROM, Lynne ..... 707-826-4031.. 33 C
les37@humboldt.edu
SANDSTROM,
Marlene, J .... 413-597-4171 220 D
marlene.j.sandstrom@williams.edu
SANDT, Jennifer, A .... 410-334-2911 205 D
jsandt@worwic.edu
SANDU, Terri, B .... 440-366-4215 355 B
SANDUM TUNE, Rachel 937-327-7411 364 D
rtune@wittenberg.edu
SANDY, Kirsti .... 603-358-2772 274 H
ksandy@keene.edu
SANDY, Michael .... 508-531-6183 212 D
michael.sandy@bridgew.edu
SANDY, Paula .... 716-851-1868 299 B
sandy@ecc.edu
SANELLI, Brittany .... 720-890-8922.. 81 I
vicepres@itea.edu
SANFILIPPO, Marjorie ... 727-864-7562.. 98 J
sanfilmd@eckerd.edu
SANFILIPPO, Rick .... 610-526-4600 385 D
rsanfilippo@harcum.edu
SANFORD, Debra .... 703-330-8400.. 93 H
SANFORD, Delacy .... 904-470-8290.. 98 L
dsanford@ewc.edu
SANFORD, Eric .... 316-295-5787 174 A
SANFORD, Glenn .... 281-283-3300 452 E
sanford@uhcl.edu
SANFORD, Jennifer .... 707-826-3236.. 33 C
jls7003@humboldt.edu
SANFORD, Jessica .... 765-983-1432 155 A
sanfoje@earlham.edu
SANFORD, Jonathan, J . 972-721-5203 452 B
president@udallas.edu
SANFORD, Julie .... 601-984-6200 249 E
jrsanford@umc.edu
SANFORD, Larry .... 410-228-9250 203 C
SANFORD, Mark .... 313-579-6931 232 E
msanfor1@wcccd.edu
SANFORD, Matthew ...... 607-431-4460 301 A
sanfordm@hartwick.edu
SANFORD, Sara .... 617-735-1420 216 D
sara.sanford@mcphs.edu
SANFORD, Susan, H ..... 315-470-6604 319 D
shsanfor@esf.edu
SANFTNER, Alexis .... 512-444-8082 448 H
registrar@thsu.edu
SANGER, Jeff .... 641-628-5161 164 D
sangerj@central.edu
SANGER, Tchad .... 831-459-5604.. 71 A
cpsanger@ucsc.edu
SANGHA, Gurminder ..... 559-265-5763.. 67 B
gurminder.sangha@fresnocitycollege.
edu
SANGHVI, Kamlesh .... 708-974-5522 145 A
sanghvik@morainevalley.edu
SANGHVI, Kunali .... 844-283-2246.. 93 C
SANGREY-BILLY, Cory .. 406-395-4875 265 G
csangrey@stonechild.edu
SANGSLAND, Kathryn ... 626-584-5308.. 43 B
kathrynsangsland@fuller.edu
SANGWIN, Kim .... 712-274-5428 168 E
sangwink@morningside.edu
SANIAL, Greg .... 616-331-2188 224 G
sanialg@gvsu.edu
SANJUAN, Alfredo .... 214-860-2064 434 I
aesanjuan@dcccd.edu
SANJURJO, Zenaida ...... 787-891-0925 507 K
zsanjurjo@aguadilla.inter.edu
SANKAR, Crystal .... 410-651-7685 203 D
SANKEY, Lorinda .... 402-643-7385 266 G
lorinda.sankey@cune.edu
SANKHAVARAM,
Madhavkrishna .... 361-593-5002 447 D
krishna.sankhavaram@tamuk.edu
SANKO, Jerry .... 620-450-2193 177 B
jerrys@prattcc.edu
SANKS GUIDRY,
Beverly .... 909-469-5341.. 75 I
bguidry@westernu.edu
SANNS, Aaron .... 208-496-1109 130 I
sannsa@byui.edu
SANREGRET, Suzanne ... 906-487-3070 228 A
srsangre@mtu.edu
SANSBURY, Timothy ..... 954-771-0376 103 S
tsansbury@knoxseminary.edu
SANSING, Perry .... 662-915-7014 249 D
psansing@olemiss.edu
SANSOLA, Steve .... 845-575-3000 305 D
steve.sansola@marist.edu
SANSOM, Erikka .... 304-829-7717 487 A
esansom@bethanywv.edu
SANSOM, Melvin .... 251-442-2390.... 8 C
msansom@umobile.edu
SANSOM, Randall .... 213-427-2200.. 35 F
SANSON, Jerry .... 318-473-6470 189 F
jsanson@lsua.edu
SANT, Anne, M .... 508-565-1343 219 A
asant@stonehill.edu
SANTA, Brittany, F .... 812-855-3603 156 F
bfsanta@iu.edu
SANTA MARIA,
Diane, M .... 713-500-2187 453 B
diane.m.santamaria@uth.tmc.edu
SANTAMARIA, Anthony . 973-290-4338 282 I
asantamaria@steu.edu
SANTAMARIA, Danielle . 401-598-1000 404 D
danielle.santamaria@jwu.edu
SANTAMOURIS, Beverly 502-852-6272 185 A
bgsant01@louisville.edu
SANTANA, Evelyn .... 610-526-6006 385 D
esantana@harcum.edu
SANTANA, Jesse .... 562-985-8511.. 31 D
jesse.santana@csulb.edu
SANTANA, Leslie .... 310-289-5123.. 74 I
leslie.santana@wcui.edu
SANTANA-BRAVO,
Maydel .... 305-348-1555 110 A
santanam@fiu.edu
SANTANA MARINO,
Julio .... 787-725-6500 505 G
jsantana@albizu.edu
SANTANDREA,
Margaret .... 949-794-9090.. 66 D
msantandrea@stanbridge.edu
SANTANDREA, Mona .... 512-404-4823 430 J
msantandrea@austinseminary.edu
SANTANGELO,
Victoria, R .... 718-990-1363 313 G
santangv@stjohns.edu
SANTAROSA, Michael ... 801-832-2186 461 F
msantarosa@westminstercollege.edu
SANTAVY, Adam, D ...... 330-569-6185 353 G
santavyad@hiram.edu
SANTAW, Carrie .... 352-638-9705.. 96 B
csantaw@beaconcollege.edu
SANTEE, Wendi .... 864-379-8701 409 E
santee@erskine.edu
SANTELLANO, Claudia .. 509-527-2632 485 C
claudia.santellano@wallawalla.edu
SANTERRE, Kim .... 770-228-7365 125 H
kim.santerre@sctech.edu
SANTESTEBAN, David .... 559-638-0300.. 67 D
david.santesteban@reedleycollege.edu
SANTIAGO, Adrian .... 617-327-6777 220 C
adrian_santiago@williamjames.edu
SANTIAGO, Alma, L ...... 787-841-2000 509 J
alsantiago@pucpr.edu
SANTIAGO, Barbara, I ... 787-850-9386 512 D
barbara.santiago2@upr.edu
SANTIAGO, Carlos .... 617-994-6901 211 E
commissioner@dhe.mass.edu
SANTIAGO, Carol .... 787-620-2040 505 C
csantiago@aupr.edu
SANTIAGO, Dalia .... 787-882-2065 510 C
dsantiago@unitecpr.edu
SANTIAGO, Deejay .... 949-451-5732.. 65 C
dsantiago10@ivc.edu
SANTIAGO, Delma .... 787-284-1912 508 E
dosantia@ponce.inter.edu
SANTIAGO, Edny .... 787-864-2222 508 C
ed.santiago@guayama.inter.edu
SANTIAGO, Eutimia .... 787-751-0160 506 F
esantiago@cmpr.pr.gov
SANTIAGO, Iris .... 787-743-4041 506 D
isantiago@columbiacentral.edu
SANTIAGO, Isaac .... 787-766-1912 508 C
isantiag@inter.edu
SANTIAGO, Isaac .... 787-766-1912 507 J
isantiag@inter.edu
SANTIAGO, Jaime .... 787-250-1912 508 D
jaimesantiago@metro.inter.edu
SANTIAGO, Jose, M ..... 787-786-3030 511 A
jsantiago@ucb.edu.pr
SANTIAGO, Josh .... 906-227-1062 228 I
jsantiag@nmu.edu
SANTIAGO, Judith .... 212-343-1234 306 G
jsantiago@mcny.edu
SANTIAGO, Juliane .... 919-658-7769 340 G
jsantiago@umo.edu
SANTIAGO, Karen .... 202-664-5683.. 94 D
ksantiago@wesleyseminary.edu
SANTIAGO, Kenneth ...... 773-481-8942 135 G
ksantiago6@ccc.edu
SANTIAGO, Luis .... 203-837-9004.. 86 B
santiagol@wcsu.edu
SANTIAGO, Maria .... 787-738-2161 512 C
maria.santiago25@upr.edu
SANTIAGO, Marya, Z .... 787-844-8181 513 A
marya.santiago@upr.edu
SANTIAGO, Sandra .... 787-743-4041 506 D
ssantiago@columbiacentral.edu
SANTIAGO, Teofilo .... 347-964-8600 291 J
tsantiago@boricuacollege.edu
SANTIAGO, Vanesa .... 787-279-1912 508 A
vsantiagor@bayamon.inter.edu
SANTIAGO, Victoria ...... 773-442-5301 146 A
vi-santiago@neiu.edu
SANTIAGO, Viviana .... 787-720-1022 505 E
administracion@atlanticu.edu
SANTIAGO, Viviana .... 787-720-1022 505 E
vsantiago@atlanticu.edu
SANTIAGO, Wanda .... 718-289-5352 293 B
wanda.santiago@bcc.cuny.edu
SANTIAGO, Xiomara ..... 787-738-2161 512 C
xiomara.santiago3@upr.edu
SANTIAGO, Yaritza .... 787-878-6000 507 D
ysantiago@icprjc.edu
SANTIAGO, Yinaira .... 787-284-1912 508 E
yinsant@ponce.inter.edu
SANTIAGO, Zima, E ...... 787-834-9595 510 D
zsantiago@uaa.edu
SANTIAGO GABRIELINI,
Wilma, L .... 787-250-0000 511 F
wilma.santiago1@upr.edu

SANTIAGO-GUZMAN, Cynthia ... 407-582-3253 113 I csantiagoguzman@valenciacollege.edu
SANTIAGO-LÓPEZ, Janet ... 787-763-6700 507 A recursoshumanos@se-pr.edu
SANTIAGO-LÓPEZ, Peggy ... 787-993-8877 512 A peggy.santiago@upr.edu
SANTIAGO-RIVERA, Raul, F ... 787-763-6700 507 A raul.santiago@se-pr.edu
SANTIAGO-ROSADO, Victor ... 787-857-3600 507 M vsantiago@br.inter.edu
SANTIAGO-SANTIAGO, Irma, J ... 787-993-8958 512 A irma.santiago1@upr.edu
SANTIAGO-TORO, Clarissa ... 787-723-4481 506 A clarissa.santiago@ceaprc.edu
SANTIAGO TORRES, Kareline ... 787-725-6500 505 G kasantiago@albizu.edu
SANTIAGO-VELÁZQUEZ, Birilo ... 787-890-2681 511 G birilo.santiago@upr.edu
SANTILLAN, Courtney ... 208-562-3153 131 E courtneysantillan@cwi.edu
SANTIN, Claudia ... 708-209-3228 136 E claudia.santin@cuchicago.edu
SANTINI, Sandra ... 209-664-6515.. 33 B ssantini@csustan.edu
SANTOMAURO, Kristine, M ... 302-225-6233.. 91 B santomk@gbc.edu
SANTORA, Joseph ... 718-658-0006 308 C
SANTORE, JR., Chuck .. 724-439-4900 388 A csantore@laurel.edu
SANTORO, Irma, M ... 770-720-9220 124 G ims@reinhardt.edu
SANTORO, John ... 508-626-4911 213 A jsantoro@framingham.edu
SANTOS, Ana ... 661-654-2411.. 30 B asantos20@csub.edu
SANTOS, Annette, T ... 671-735-2553 504 F atsantos@triton.uog.edu
SANTOS, April ... 314-529-9300 255 B asantos@maryville.edu
SANTOS, Carmen, M ... 787-758-2525 512 F carmen.santos4@upr.edu
SANTOS, David, M ... 860-701-6787 503 G
SANTOS, Eileen ... 202-806-6100.. 92 F
SANTOS, Elsa ... 787-850-9320 512 D elsa.santos@upr.edu
SANTOS, Eunice ... 217-333-3280 152 B eesantos@illinois.edu
SANTOS, Maggie ... 719-389-1988.. 78 I maggie.santos@coloradocollege.edu
SANTOS, Maria del, C .. 787-743-7979 510 H ut_masantos@suagm.edu
SANTOS, Matt ... 610-683-4183 394 D santos@kutztown.edu
SANTOS, Matthew ... 360-752-8396 478 A msantos@btc.edu
SANTOS, Noemi ... 787-780-0070 505 F nsantos@caribbean.edu
SANTOS, Paul ... 704-978-5409 336 C psantos@mitchellcc.edu
SANTOS, Rod ... 510-215-3921.. 40 B rsantos@contracosta.edu
SANTOS, Rosa Milagros ... 217-244-3558 152 B rsantos@illinois.edu
SANTOS, Seilyn ... 305-821-3333 100 E santoss@fnu.edu
SANTOS, Susan ... 859-442-4165 181 H susan.santos@kctcs.edu
SANTOS, Tineke ... 502-213-2109 182 C tineke.santos@kctcs.edu
SANTOS-COY, Karlos ... 714-449-7445.. 51 B karlossantoscoy@ketchum.edu
SANTOS-CRESPO, Keila . 817-202-6355 444 I keilasantos@swau.edu
SANTOS-DERIEG, Brittany ... 619-594-5201.. 33 D bsantosderieg@sdsu.edu
SANTOS-GEORGE, Arlene ... 847-543-2402 136 A asgeorge@clcillinois.edu
SANTOS-PEREZ, Kennia, I ... 787-480-2463 506 C kisantos@sanjuan.pr
SANTOS RODRIGUEZ, Maria del Carmen ... 787-725-8120 506 M msantos@eap.edu
SANTOS-SMITHHART, Xiana ... 704-216-7290 337 F xiana.smithhart@rccc.edu
SANTRY, Robert ... 802-656-8707 463 A robert.santry@uvm.edu
SANTUCCI, George ... 412-392-3498 396 G gsantucci@pointpark.edu
SANYAL, Rajib, N ... 516-877-4661 289 I rsanyal@adelphi.edu
SANYAL, Sabyasachi ... 972-721-5156 452 B ssanyal@udallas.edu
SANZARI, Kelly, J ... 724-847-6515 384 C kjsanzar@geneva.edu
SAPARILAS, John, W ... 919-866-5450 338 G jwsaparilas@waketech.edu
SAPH, Donald ... 716-614-5982 309 G dsaph@niagaracc.suny.edu
SAPIENZA, Christine ... 904-256-7679 102 H csapien@ju.edu
SAPIENZA, Matthew ... 646-664-3014 292 K matthew.sapienza@cuny.edu
SAPIENZA, Mike ... 864-231-2000 406 F msapienza@andersonuniversity.edu
SAPIO, Kevin ... 315-498-2477 310 F k.p.sapio@sunyocc.edu
SAPOZNICK, Aaron ... 718-645-0536 306 J
SAPP, Aimee ... 573-592-4391 262 G aimee.sapp@williamwoods.edu
SAPP, David, A ... 310-338-4262.. 51 A david.sapp@lmu.edu
SAPP, Rebecca ... 423-794-3071 422 E rlsapp@milligan.edu
SAPP, Robert ... 866-776-0331.. 54 D rsapp@ncu.edu
SAPP, Van ... 919-516-4354 339 I vsapp@st-aug.edu
SAPP, Vicki, T ... 716-673-3358 316 D vicki.sapp@fredonia.edu
SAPPINGTON, Eric ... 660-831-4168 256 I sappingtone@moval.edu
SARAJEDINI, Ata ... 561-297-3301 109 J asarajedini@fau.edu
SARAN, Rupam ... 718-270-4937 294 G rsaran@mec.cuny.edu
SARAO, Felix, G ... 562-908-3413.. 58 L fsarao@riohondo.edu
SARAT, Austin, D ... 413-542-2308 205 G adsarat@amherst.edu
SARATA, Andrew ... 708-974-5357 145 A sarataa@morainevalley.edu
SARAVANAPAVAN, Naomi ... 607-729-1581 298 B nsaravanapavan@davisny.edu
SARBER, John ... 765-455-9505 157 B jrsarber@iuk.edu
SARBER, Sarah ... 765-455-9316 157 B shawkins@iuk.edu
SARCEDO-MAGRUDER, Genice ... 818-710-3318.. 49 D sarcedg@piercecollege.edu
SARFF, Michelle ... 614-251-4758 358 B sarffm@ohiodominican.edu
SARGE, Sandy ... 800-867-2243.. 55 D
SARGE, Sandy ... 562-988-2278.. 25 L ssarge@auhs.edu
SARGEANT, Lynn ... 605-688-4723 417 A lynn.sargeant@sdstate.edu
SARGEANT, Marcel ... 817-202-6607 444 I sargeant@swau.edu
SARGENT, Daniel ... 315-866-0300 301 D sargentda@herkimer.edu
SARGENT, Deirdre ... 650-508-3503.. 54 G dsargent@ndnu.edu
SARGENT, Famika ... 225-771-2492 191 B famika_sargent@subr.edu
SARGENT, Frank ... 412-237-8182 381 D fsargent@ccac.edu
SARGENT, Gary ... 254-295-4242 453 D gsargent@umhb.edu
SARGENT, Jenell ... 240-895-4331 202 B ejsargent@smcm.edu
SARGENT, Madeline ... 215-455-2300 378 F madeline.sargent@aspiracitycollege.edu
SARGENT, Ryan ... 208-282-4735 131 G sargryan@isu.edu
SARGENT, Sheri ... 507-389-1112 239 D sheri.sargent@mnsu.edu
SARGENT-MARTIN, Shelia ... 304-327-4176 489 I ssmartin@bluefieldstate.edu
SARIAN, Richard ... 216-421-7432 350 H rsarian@cia.edu
SARIDAKIS, Dianne, I ... 215-885-2360 389 C dsaridakis@manor.edu
SARIN, Anurag ... 305-284-5699 113 C axs2977@miami.edu
SARISKY JONES, Susan ... 717-867-6321 388 C sjones@lvc.edu
SARKAR, Ratna ... 410-516-5925 199 G rsarkar3@jhu.edu
SARKIS, Hashim ... 617-253-4401 216 B
SARKISIAN, Jodi ... 215-898-7221 400 F jodi@upenn.edu
SARLO, Rebecca ... 727-298-8685 112 H
SARMA, Sanjay ... 617-715-4532 216 B
SARMIENTO, Reine ... 718-960-7825 294 A reine.sarmiento@lehman.cuny.edu
SARNA, Linda ... 310-825-9621.. 69 E lsarna@sonnet.ucla.edu
SARNESO, Anna ... 617-243-2243 211 B asarneso@lasell.edu
SARNI, Angela ... 414-930-3431 494 E sarnia@mtmary.edu
SARNOFF, Jonathan ... 864-488-4501 410 B jsarnoff@limestone.edu
SARR, Akua ... 617-552-9144 207 C akua.sarr@bc.edu
SARRAT, Carla ... 330-823-3847 362 E sarratca@mountunion.edu
SARRATORI, Peter ... 315-781-3647 301 F sarratori@hws.edu
SARRETT, David, C ... 804-828-7235 473 B dcsarrett@vcu.edu
SARRION-CORTES, Noemi ... 706-236-1714 116 B nsarrion@berry.edu
SARRUBBO, JR., Joe, M ... 407-582-2586 113 I jsarrubbo@valenciacollege.edu
SARTAIN, Shana ... 870-248-4000.. 18 F shana.sartain@blackrivertech.edu
SARTARELLI, Jose, V ... 910-962-3030 343 C sartarellij@uncw.edu
SARTE, Bruce ... 610-606-4635 380 D bsarte@cedarcrest.edu
SARTOR, Dan ... 423-266-4574 423 B dsartor@richmont.edu
SARTORI, Katherine ... 734-432-5417 227 C ksartori@madonna.edu
SARVEY, Sharon ... 252-399-6401 326 K sisarvey@barton.edu
SARVIS, Josephine ... 708-524-6593 137 C jsarvis@dom.edu
SARVIS, Randall, F ... 937-481-2344 364 A randy_sarvis@wilmington.edu
SARWAR, Mostofa ... 504-671-6480 188 B msarwa@dcc.edu
SASAKI, Charles, S ... 808-235-7443 130 E sasakich@hawaii.edu
SASAKI, Stefanie ... 808-845-9463 130 A sasakist@hawaii.edu
SASLOW, Lauren ... 818-710-4442.. 49 D saslowle@piercecollege.edu
SASMAL, Indrani ... 701-228-2277 346 B indrani.sasmal@dakotacollege.edu
SASMITA, SJ, I. Hadi ... 204-243-2000 491 E ihssj@wheeling.edu
SASS, Michael ... 314-446-8349 260 H michael.sass@stlcop.edu
SASS, Terricita, E ... 804-523-5296 474 A tsass@reynolds.edu
SASSAMAN, Sydnee ... 620-276-9662 174 B sydnee.sassaman@gcccks.edu
SASSE, Gary ... 401-232-6593 404 A gsasse@bryant.edu
SASSER, Craig-Ellis ... 662-720-7302 248 C cesasser@nemcc.edu
SASSER, Mackey ... 334-556-2416.... 2 C msasser@wallace.edu
SASSER, Rachelle ... 310-900-1600.. 39 F rsasser@compton.edu
SASSMAN, Jen, L ... 319-352-8262 170 J jennifer.sassman@wartburg.edu
SASSO, Mary ... 585-594-6235 312 E sasso_mary@roberts.edu
SASTRY, Hari ... 412-624-6577 400 H hsastry@cfo.pitt.edu
SATA, Leigh ... 415-703-9500.. 28 B
SATELE, Arleen ... 714-628-4717.. 58 G satele_arleen@sccollege.edu
SATER-WEE, Diane ... 614-825-6255 347 E dsater@aiam.edu
SATHER, Greg ... 218-726-6137 243 G gsather@d.umn.edu
SATHIANATHAN, Dhushy ... 562-985-4128.. 31 D dhushy.sathianathan@csulb.edu
SATKOWIAK, Ann, E ... 865-539-7153 425 B asatkowiak@pstcc.edu
SATKOWSKI, John ... 313-845-9636 225 B jssatkowski@hfcc.edu
SATO, Deirdre, C ... 212-217-5380 299 D deirdre_sato@fitnyc.edu
SATO, Heidi ... 714-816-0366.. 68 E heidi.sato@trident.edu
SATO, Sara ... 808-544-7020 128 G ssato@hpu.edu
SATO, Toshiko ... 949-480-4364.. 64 G tsato@soka.edu
SATRIANA, Dan ... 970-351-2399.. 84 F dan.satriana@unco.edu
SATTAR, Mo ... 413-565-1000 206 D msattar@baypath.edu
SATTERFIELD, Derick ... 336-342-4261 337 E satterfieldd@rockinghamcc.edu
SATTERFIELD, Jack ... 520-206-4809.. 15 B jcsatterfield@pima.edu
SATTERFIELD, Jay ... 731-989-6058 419 K jsatterfield@fhu.edu
SATTERFIELD, Kathleen . 909-706-3505.. 75 I ksatterfield@westernu.edu
SATTERFIELD, Lisa ... 828-398-2500 423 E lsatterfield@south.edu
SATTERFIELD, Rachel ... 919-684-5055 328 F rachel.satterfield@duke.edu
SATTERFIELD, Sherri ... 704-233-8810 344 F s.satterfield@wingate.edu
SATTERFIELD, Tanya ... 662-915-7692 249 D tnsatter@olemiss.edu
SATTERLEE, George ... 816-926-4400 253 I
SATTERLEE, Kevin ... 208-282-3440 131 G
SATTERLEE, Richard ... 717-815-1460 403 F
SATTERLUND, Alysson .. 858-534-4371.. 70 C asatterlund@ucsd.edu
SATTERLY, Eric ... 502-272-8098 179 H esatterly@bellarmine.edu
SATTERLY, Tom ... 970-491-0006.. 79 N tom.satterly@colostate.edu
SATTERWHITE, Dawn ... 919-761-2209 340 D dsatterwhite@sebts.edu
SATTERWHITE, Robin ... 806-716-2200 443 G rsatterwhite@southplainscollege.edu
SATZ, Debra ... 650-723-9784.. 66 E
SAUCEDA, James ... 706-355-5175 115 F jsauceda@athenstech.edu
SAUCEDA, John ... 312-329-4388 144 I john.sauceda@moody.edu
SAUCEDA, Mary ... 303-605-7350.. 81 M msauce11@msudenver.edu
SAUCEDO, Federico ... 818-240-1000.. 43 G fsaucedo@glendale.edu
SAUCIER, Jason ... 207-741-5544 195 H jsaucier@smccme.edu
SAUDER, Dustin ... 402-486-2507 269 F dustin.sauder@ucollege.edu
SAUDER, Vinita ... 402-486-2500 269 F vinita.sauder@ucollege.edu
SAUDERS, Charlette, R . 574-372-5100 155 F saudercr@grace.edu
SAUDERS, Robert, R ... 509-359-6015 479 G
SAUER, Carrie ... 405-208-5873 367 E csauer@okcu.edu
SAUER, Dietrich ... 928-226-4204.. 11 O dietrich.sauer@coconino.edu
SAUER, Greg ... 802-485-2170 462 F gsauer@norwich.edu
SAUER, Jenni ... 434-381-6231 471 I jsauer@sbc.edu
SAUER, Marty, R ... 630-637-5801 145 F mrsauer@noctrl.edu
SAUER, Meredith ... 920-693-1282 498 H meredith.sauer@gotoltc.edu
SAUERBREI, Aaron ... 319-277-2490 166 H aaron.sauerbrei@hawkeyecollege.edu
SAUERBURGER, Kate ... 314-792-7435 254 F sauerburger@kenrick.edu
SAUERS, Darlene ... 724-838-4210 398 C sauers@setonhill.edu
SAUGSTAD, Bruce ... 507-537-6038 241 D bruce.saugstad@smsu.edu
SAUL, Amy ... 610-861-1508 390 F saula@moravian.edu
SAUL, D. Eric ... 610-989-1230 401 I esaul@vfmac.edu

SAUL, John .... 315-364-3229 324 I
jsaul@wells.edu
SAUL, Sheryl .... 651-846-1384 241 B
sheryl.saul@saintpaul.edu
SAULDSBERRY,
Daviedra .... 410-462-7401 198 B
dsauldsberry@bccc.edu
SAULNIER, Timothy ...... 540-654-2468 471 N
tsaulnie@umw.edu
SAULS, Jina, M .... 276-244-1232 464 E
jsauls@asl.edu
SAULS, Steve .... 229-333-2100 128 B
SAULSBERRY, Jean .... 901-435-1727 420 I
jean_saulsberry@loc.edu
SAULSBERRY, Keith ...... 334-556-2470.... 2 C
ksaulsberry@wallace.edu
SAULSBERRY,
Lynette, M .... 478-289-2169 118 C
lsaulsberry@ega.edu
SAULSBERRY, Pamela ... 318-342-1445 193 C
saulsberry@ulm.edu
SAULSBERRY, Raquel .... 901-321-3480 418 G
rlogansa@cbu.edu
SAUMBY, Sydney .... 361-698-1080 435 G
ssaumby@delmar.edu
SAUNDERS, Aleister ...... 215-895-6203 382 F
aleister.j.saunders@drexel.edu
SAUNDERS, Amber .... 318-371-3035 188 F
ambersaunders@nltcc.edu
SAUNDERS, Catherine ... 812-535-5225 160 H
catherine.saunders@smwc.edu
SAUNDERS,
Christopher .... 615-353-3066 424 G
christopher.saunders@nscc.edu
SAUNDERS, Clark .... 860-768-4504.. 89 G
clsaunder@hartford.edu
SAUNDERS, Dee .... 503-552-1946 374 D
dsaunders@nunm.edu
SAUNDERS, Douglas ..... 606-337-3196 180 C
SAUNDERS, Gary .... 336-506-4152 332 A
gary.saunders@alamancecc.edu
SAUNDERS, Greer .... 804-819-4906 473 C
gsaunders@vccs.edu
SAUNDERS, Jennifer ..... 801-957-5009 461 C
jennifer.saunders@slcc.edu
SAUNDERS, Kara, C ...... 716-645-5725 316 C
kcs23@buffalo.edu
SAUNDERS, Kathleen .... 716-827-2445 323 G
saundersk@trocaire.edu
SAUNDERS, Keith .... 319-335-0553 163 H
keith-saunders@uiowa.edu
SAUNDERS, Kevin .... 515-271-1984 165 J
kevin.saunders@drake.edu
SAUNDERS, Marnie, M . 330-972-6590 361 H
mms129@uakron.edu
SAUNDERS, Martha, D .. 850-474-2200 111 F
msaunders@uwf.edu
SAUNDERS, Natasha ..... 540-375-2099 470 E
nsaunders@roanoke.edu
SAUNDERS, Scott, D ..... 716-673-3171 316 D
scott.saunders@fredonia.edu
SAUNDERS, Sharon .... 434-947-8704 469 E
ssaunders@randolphcollege.edu
SAUNDERS, Sharon .... 281-649-3206 437 B
ssaunders@hbu.edu
SAUNDS, Lindsay .... 706-419-1279 118 A
lindsay.saunds@covenant.edu
SAURBIER, Ann .... 304-336-8060 490 B
ann.saurbier@westliberty.edu
SAURER, James .... 717-866-5775 383 F
SAUTER, Maranah .... 706-880-8201 122 A
msauter@lagrange.edu
SAUTER, Ramona .... 408-554-4397.. 63 B
rsauter@scu.edu
SAUVIGNON, Carine ..... 508-588-9100 215 A
csauvigno@massasoit.mass.edu
SAVAGE, Daina .... 717-396-7833 392 U
dsavage@pcad.edu
SAVAGE, David .... 706-754-7815 123 G
david.savage@northgatech.edu
SAVAGE, Deana .... 432-685-4515 440 B
docsavage@midland.edu
SAVAGE, Devin .... 312-567-3615 140 A
dsavage@iit.edu
SAVAGE, James .... 337-482-6434 193 B
james.savage@louisiana.edu
SAVAGE, Jess .... 970-247-7180.. 80 J
jlsavage@fortlewis.edu
SAVAGE, Lauren .... 970-247-6073.. 80 J
lasavage@fortlewis.edu
SAVAGE, Mandara .... 804-828-6786 473 B
savagem2@vcu.edu
SAVAGE, Mary .... 860-439-2251.. 87 H
mary.savage@conncoll.edu
SAVAGE, Nesha .... 619-388-3400.. 60 I
nsavage@sdccd.edu
SAVAGE, Pam .... 314-744-5331 256 E
savagep@mobap.edu
SAVAGE, Randi .... 512-454-1188 430 A
rsavage@aoma.edu
SAVAGE, Richard, N ..... 724-458-2033 384 G
savagern@gcc.edu
SAVAGE, Ron .... 617-747-2025 206 H
rsavage@berklee.edu
SAVAGE, Scott .... 419-289-5401 347 J
ssavage2@ashland.edu
SAVAGE, Shauna .... 406-496-4422 265 A
ssavage@mtech.edu
SAVAIANO, Patrick .... 760-744-1150.. 56 B
SAVELSKI, Mariano .... 856-256-4052 281 F
savelski@rowan.edu
SAVIA, Anthony .... 301-860-3470 204 A
asavia@bowiestate.edu
SAVICKY, Kim .... 402-399-2417 266 F
ksavicky@csm.edu
SAVILLE, Vicki .... 704-330-6224 333 D
vicki.saville@cpcc.edu
SAVIN, Stuart .... 717-464-7050 387 F
SAVINO, Jeffrey .... 814-472-3006 397 F
jsavino@francis.edu
SAVINO, Stacey .... 360-538-4082 480 G
ssavino@ghc.edu
SAVITA BROWNFIELD,
Kathleen .... 408-847-4060.. 52 H
SAVITT-KING, Robin ...... 413-782-1243 220 A
robin.savitt-king@wne.edu
SAVIZKY, Ruben .... 212-353-4372 297 E
ruben.savizky@cooper.edu
SAVOCA, Marianna .... 631-632-6810 317 A
marianna.savoca@stonybrook.edu
SAVOIE, E. Joseph .... 337-482-6203 193 B
president@louisiana.edu
SAVOIE, Michael, P ...... 229-249-4894 127 E
mpsavoie@valdosta.edu
SAVOIT, Taina, J .... 337-475-5065 192 E
tsavoit@mcneese.edu
SAVRON, Doris .... 602-557-9021.. 16 G
doris.savron@phoenix.edu
SAVU, Vasemaca .... 692-625-3394 504 G
vsavu@cmi.edu
SAVUKINAS, Robert ...... 831-242-5828 502 F
SAWA, Glen .... 218-335-4200 236 F
SAWADOGO, Annette .... 906-487-7554 224 B
SAWATSKY, Kelly .... 917-493-4077 305 A
ksawatsky@msmnyc.edu
SAWATZKY, Radonna .... 580-774-3783 370 A
radonna.sawatzky@swosu.edu
SAWTELLE, III,
James (Jimmy), R ...... 318-487-5443 187 J
jsawtelle@cltcc.edu
SAWYER, Caroline .... 704-463-3026 339 E
caroline.sawyer@pfeiffer.edu
SAWYER, Donald, C ...... 203-582-8964.. 88 G
donald.sawyer@quinnipiac.edu
SAWYER, Eric .... 603-428-2407 273 G
esawyer@nec.edu
SAWYER, Gretchen .... 775-674-7686 271 C
gsawyer@tmcc.edu
SAWYER, James .... 586-445-7241 227 B
sawyerj@macomb.edu
SAWYER, Jane .... 626-529-8500.. 55 F
SAWYER, Jenny, L .... 502-852-4957 186 A
jsawyer@louisville.edu
SAWYER, Jonathan, C .. 202-319-5619.. 92 A
sawyerj@cua.edu
SAWYER, Julia .... 918-444-2210 366 G
sawyerjk@nsuok.edu
SAWYER, Katherine .... 847-635-1718 146 G
ksawyer@oakton.edu
SAWYER, LaShon, N ..... 330-569-5261 353 G
sawyerln@hiram.edu
SAWYER, Lisa .... 256-215-4536.... 1 G
lsawyer@cacc.edu
SAWYER, Lisa .... 661-362-3314.. 38 D
lisa.sawyer@canyons.edu
SAWYER, Masonne .... 336-734-7343 334 F
msawyer@forsythtech.edu
SAWYER, Mike .... 660-543-4750 260 G
msawyer@ucmo.edu
SAWYER, Nichole .... 207-454-1040 195 I
nsawyer@wccc.me.edu
SAWYER, Sarah .... 207-974-4828 195 E
ssawyer@emcc.edu
SAWYER, Scott .... 832-842-8705 452 D
ssawyer@uh.edu
SAWYER, Terrence .... 410-617-2290 200 B
tsawyer@loyola.edu
SAWYER, Wm. Gregory 707-664-2838.. 34 B
SAWYERS, Tamberly ..... 423-697-3359 424 A
tammy.sawyers@chattanoogastate.edu
SAX, Christina .... 410-888-9048 200 E
csax@muih.edu
SAX, Richard .... 740-245-7214 363 A
rsax@rio.edu
SAXBY, Christopher ...... 239-590-7924 109 K
csaxby@fgcu.edu
SAXBY, Rushelle, D ...... 252-862-1248 337 C
rsaxby@roanokechowan.edu
SAXENA, Peter .... 585-594-6800 310 C
SAXENA, Pradeep .... 585-594-6430 312 E
saxenap@roberts.edu
SAXENIAN, AnnaLee ..... 510-642-9980.. 69 A
anno@ischool.berkeley.edu
SAXON-PRICE, Melissa . 570-702-8956 386 D
msaxonprice@johnson.edu
SAXTON, Todd .... 217-641-4555 141 A
tsaxton@jwcc.edu
SAYAVONG, Phoumy .... 410-981-5014.. 56 I
psayavong@peralta.edu
SAYE, Shaydean .... 406-657-1051 265 E
shaydean.saye@rocky.edu
SAYED, Ellen, N .... 414-955-4852 493 F
esayed@mcw.edu
SAYEGH, Sharlene .... 562-985-5428.. 31 D
sharlene.sayegh@csulb.edu
SAYERS, David .... 954-545-4500 108 E
cfo@sfbc.edu
SAYERS, David .... 803-321-3353 410 H
david.sayers@newberry.edu
SAYGIN, Can .... 210-458-5264 455 E
can.saygin@utsa.edu
SAYLER, David, A .... 513-529-7286 356 A
saylerda@miamioh.edu
SAYLER, Micheal .... 734-487-1414 223 K
emu_coe@emich.edu
SAYLES, Keith .... 509-533-3514 479 D
keith.sayles@sfcc.spokane.edu
SAYLOR, JR., Allen, C .. 229-391-5001 114 F
SAYLOR, Andrea .... 517-264-3100 220 G
asaylor@adrian.edu
SAYLOR, Jessica, M ..... 701-349-5444 346 I
jsaylor@trinitybiblecollege.edu
SAYLOR, Laura .... 513-244-3263 356 F
laura.saylor@msj.edu
SAYLOR, Laurie .... 813-253-7152 102 B
lsaylor@hccfl.edu
SAYLORS, Tony .... 870-248-4000.. 18 F
tony.saylors@blackrivertech.edu
SAYRE, Cris .... 773-602-3403 135 D
csayre@ccc.edu
SAYRE, Matt .... 541-552-6273 376 B
sayrem@sou.edu
SAYRS, Elizabeth .... 740-593-1935 358 K
sayrs@ohio.edu
SBALBI,
Anthony (Tony) .... 413-755-4336 216 A
atsbalbi@stcc.edu
SBRISCIA, Amanda .... 413-552-2747 214 F
asbriscia@hcc.edu
SCACCIA, Jeff, P .... 864-833-8205 411 D
jpscaccia@presby.edu
SCAGGIANTE, Michele .. 718-270-3007 317 B
michele.scaggiante@downstate.edu
SCAGGS, Deirdre .... 859-257-3653 185 F
deirdre@uky.edu
SCAGLIONE, Agnes .... 201-692-2596 277 I
agnes@fdu.edu
SCALA, Kerry, L .... 603-862-1355 274 F
kerry.scala@unh.edu
SCALA, Natalie .... 440-375-7530 354 K
nscala@lec.edu
SCALBERG, Daniel .... 503-255-0332 374 C
dscalberg@multnomah.edu
SCALES, Barbara .... 931-393-1500 424 F
bscales@mscc.edu
SCALES, Jane .... 800-686-1883 222 G
jscales@cleary.edu
SCALES, Keyana .... 504-520-7849 193 E
kscales@xula.edu
SCALES, Lea Ann .... 978-630-9320 215 C
lscales2@mwcc.mass.edu
SCALES, Michael, D ...... 215-204-3121 399 B
michael.scales@temple.edu
SCALES, Roger .... 316-295-5551 174 A
roger_scales@friends.edu
SCALES, Valronica .... 301-314-7343 202 H
vscales@umd.edu
SCALIA, Derek .... 603-899-4152 273 E
scaliad@franklinpierce.edu
SCALLY, Alethea .... 505-984-6182 288 C
alethea.scally@sjc.edu
SCALZO, Denise .... 718-862-7178 304 M
dscalzo01@manhattan.edu
SCANDALIS, Thomas ..... 509-452-5100 482 B
tscandalis@pnwu.edu
SCANDRETT, Clyde .... 831-656-2517 502 M
cscandrett@nps.edu
SCANDRETT, Nic .... 712-279-1761 164 B
nic.scandrett@briarcliff.edu
SCANLAN, Michael .... 216-397-1596 353 O
mscanlan@jcu.edu
SCANLAN, Therese, A ... 773-252-5311 146 F
president@oakpoint.edu
SCANLON, Jennifer .... 207-725-3578 194 C
SCANLON, Jennifer .... 206-878-3710 481 B
jscanlon@highline.edu
SCANLON, John .... 201-360-4771 278 C
jscanlon@hccc.edu
SCANLON, Lina .... 684-699-9155 504 B
l.galeai-scanlan@amsamoa.edu
SCANLON, Tom .... 617-732-2775 216 D
tom.scanlon@mcphs.edu
SCANNELL, Janet .... 507-222-4077 234 G
jscannell@carleton.edu
SCANTLIN, Chelsye .... 417-967-5466 260 D
SCAPPATICCI, Jason ..... 860-906-5085.. 86 D
jscappaticci@capitalcc.edu
SCARANO, John .... 216-397-4701 353 O
jscarano@jcu.edu
SCARANO, Martin .... 603-862-2116 274 F
marty.scarano@unh.edu
SCARANTINO, Laura ...... 410-706-2562 203 A
lscarantino@umaryland.edu
SCARBORO, Gina .... 912-650-5640 125 F
gscarboro@southuniversity.edu
SCARBORO, Kim .... 850-973-1613 104 L
scarborok@nfc.edu
SCARBORO, Lynne, B .... 310-338-5236.. 51 A
lscarbor@lmu.edu
SCARBOROUGH,
Charley .... 512-472-4133 443 F
charley.scarborough@ssw.edu
SCARBOROUGH, Edesa . 813-253-3333 113 H
SCARBOROUGH,
Janna, L .... 423-439-7616 419 G
scarboro@etsu.edu
SCARBOROUGH, Scott .. 575-835-5791 286 K
scott.scarborough@nmt.edu
SCARBOROUGH,
Tara, H .... 513-556-0648 361 J
tara.scarborough@uc.edu
SCARBROUGH, Karly .... 520-515-5420.. 11 M
scarbroughk@cochise.edu
SCARBROUGH, Regina .. 516-876-3092 318 C
scarbroughr@oldwestbury.edu
SCARCELLE, Ed .... 212-229-5598 308 A
scarcele@newschool.edu
SCARFF, Colleen .... 269-387-2365 233 B
colleen.scarff@wmich.edu
SCARINGE, John .... 562-902-3330.. 65 I
johnscaringe@scuhs.edu
SCARLATO, Deborah ..... 318-869-5146 186 F
dscarlat@centenary.edu
SCARLATTA, Gabriella ... 313-593-5030 231 I
geschric@umich.edu
SCARLETT, Barbara .... 607-777-4438 316 B
scarlett@binghamton.edu
SCARLETT, Michael .... 309-794-7219 133 C
michaelscarlett@augustana.edu
SCARNATI, Brandy .... 775-824-7948 271 C
SCARSELLA, Hilary, J .... 585-271-1320 296 D
hscarsella@crcds.edu
SCATAMACCHIA, Marc .. 617-358-6401 207 E
marcs1@bu.edu
SCATES, LouAnn, P .... 704-406-4263 329 A
lscates@gardner-webb.edu
SCATTON-TESSIER,
Michelle .... 910-962-7232 343 C
scattonm@uncw.edu
SCAVONE, Victoria, R .... 248-689-8282 232 C
vscavone@walshcollege.edu
SCAVUZZO, Connie, M . 312-949-7079 139 D
cscavuzzo@ico.edu
SCEARCE, Stephanie ...... 706-295-6958 120 A
sscearce@gntc.edu
SCEGGEL, Tim .... 706-419-1517 118 A
tim.sceggel@covenant.edu
SCEPANSKY, Patricia, S 610-359-7355 382 A
pscepansky@dccc.edu
SCEPPA, Carmen .... 617-373-5543 217 I

SCHETTER, Sheila .... 920-693-1238 498 H sheila.schetter@gotoltc.edu
SCHETTINI-LYNCH, Anne Marie .... 914-633-2480 302 E aschettinilynch@iona.edu
SCHETTLER, Jim .... 661-946-2274.. 74 H
SCHETTLER, Martha, A .. 330-569-5205 353 G schettlerma@hiram.edu
SCHEUERMANN, Barry .. 419-530-4968 363 B barry.scheuermann@utoledo.edu
SCHEUERMANN, Joe ..... 504-671-5452 188 B jscheu@dcc.edu
SCHEUFENS, William .... 337-475-5711 192 E wscheufens@mcneese.edu
SCHEUTZOW, Janice ..... 585-389-2310 307 F jscheut1@naz.edu
SCHEXNEIDER, Martha, J .... 337-421-6925 188 J jo.schexneider@sowela.edu
SCHEXNIDER-FIELDS, Ingenue, S .... 504-520-6209 193 E itschexn@xula.edu
SCHEYETT, Anna, M ...... 706-542-5424 126 G amscheye@uga.edu
SCHIAVETTA, Michael ... 212-261-1701 308 I michael.schiavetta@nyit.edu
SCHIAZZA, Douglas, J .. 413-597-3696 220 D douglas.schiazza@williams.edu
SCHICK, Avi .... 732-985-6533 280 E
SCHICK, Jennifer .... 616-331-2231 224 G schickj@gvsu.edu
SCHICK, Wendell .... 419-227-3141 362 F wschick@unoh.edu
SCHIDLOVSKY, Nicholas .... 315-858-0945 302 A
SCHIEBEL, Amy .... 608-663-3414 492 F aschiebel@edgewood.edu
SCHIEBER, Amy, K .... 660-944-2847 251 J aschieber@conception.edu
SCHIEBER, Jeanette .... 660-944-2839 251 J admissions@conception.edu
SCHIEFEN, Kathleen ...... 585-345-6975 300 F kmschiefen@genesee.edu
SCHIEL, Melynie .... 760-366-3791.. 40 E
SCHIEMAN, Don .... 502-213-2451 182 C don.schieman@kctcs.edu
SCHIER, DJ (Donald) .... 716-896-0700 324 E dschier@villa.edu
SCHIFF, Emanuel .... 845-356-1980 311 H
SCHIFFER, Jason, D ...... 610-758-4200 388 E jds517@lehigh.edu
SCHIFFER, Peter .... 203-432-2647.. 90 C peter.schiffer@yale.edu
SCHIFFGENS, Hope .... 412-536-1266 386 H hope.schiffgens@laroche.edu
SCHIFFKE, Heather .... 503-552-1750 374 D hschiffke@nunm.edu
SCHIFFMAN, Jeffrey ...... 504-865-5000 191 F jschiffm@tulane.edu
SCHIFFMAN, Robyn ...... 630-942-2865 135 I
SCHILKE, Richard .... 254-519-5435 447 A rschilke@tamuct.edu
SCHILL, Matt .... 402-554-3041 270 A mschill@unomaha.edu
SCHILL, Michael, H ...... 541-346-3036 376 H pres@uoregon.edu
SCHILL, Sara .... 276-376-3432 472 E srp4b@uvawise.edu
SCHILLER-SMITH, Ali .... 410-337-6000 199 B ali.schiller-smith@goucher.edu
SCHILLI, Kara .... 636-949-4349 254 H kschilli@lindenwood.edu
SCHILLING, Dee .... 909-706-3526.. 75 I dschilling@westernu.edu
SCHILLING, JoAnna ...... 714-484-7308.. 54 B jschilling@cypresscollege.edu
SCHILLINGER, Don, N .. 318-257-3712 192 D dschill@latech.edu
SCHILT, Louis, J .... 480-212-1704.. 15 O louis@sessions.edu
SCHIMEK, Gwendolyn ... 319-895-4234 164 G gschimek@cornellcollege.edu
SCHIMER, Maria, R .... 330-325-6356 357 D maria@neomed.edu
SCHIMMEL, Kari .... 309-694-5590 139 B kari.schimmel@icc.edu
SCHIMPF, Kelly .... 856-351-2247 283 B kaschimpf@salemcc.edu
SCHINDLER, Brooke ...... 715-675-3331 499 F schindler@ntc.edu
SCHINDLER, Kerry .... 254-659-7821 437 A kschindler@hillcollege.edu
SCHINDLER, Tina .... 213-738-6813.. 66 B tschindler@swlaw.edu
SCHINELLA, Margot ...... 845-451-1261 297 G margot.schinella@culinary.edu
SCHINSTOCK, OSB, Victor .... 660-944-2992 251 J victor@conception.edu
SCHIPANI, Pamela .... 860-486-2060.. 89 D p.schipani@uconn.edu
SCHIPPERS, Dave .... 248-689-8282 232 C dschippe@walshcollege.edu
SCHIRER-SUTER, Myron 978-867-4419 210 B myron.schirer-suter@gordon.edu
SCHISSLER, John .... 330-490-7263 363 E jschissler@walsh.edu
SCHISSLER, Kathy .... 303-914-6214.. 83 C kathy.schissler@rrcc.edu
SCHIWIETZ, Michelle, B .... 214-887-5002 435 F mschiwietz@dts.edu
SCHJANG, Michael .... 360-676-2772 481 F maschjang@nwic.edu
SCHLACHTER, John .... 812-357-6142 161 A jschlachter@saintmeinrad.edu
SCHLACTER, Martin, K .. 719-333-8854 503 D martin.schlacter@usafa.edu
SCHLAFER, Tammy .... 315-470-4769 319 D tsschlaf@esf.edu
SCHLAG, Kevin .... 808-675-3735 128 D kevin@byuh.edu
SCHLAG, Paul, A .... 937-376-6668 349 J pschlag@centralstate.edu
SCHLAK, Timothy, M .... 412-397-6868 397 B schlak@rmu.edu
SCHLAM, Elisheva .... 646-565-6420 322 F elisheva.schlam@touro.edu
SCHLAM, Elisheva .... 646-565-6420 322 G elisheva.schlam@touro.edu
SCHLANG, Jamie .... 215-780-1333 398 B jschlang@salus.edu
SCHLAPP, Andrew .... 316-978-3001 178 D andy.schlapp@wichita.edu
SCHLARB, Mary .... 607-753-2209 318 A mary.schlarb@cortland.edu
SCHLATER, Nicole .... 315-498-2581 310 F schlaten@sunyocc.edu
SCHLATHER, Mary Margaret .... 304-724-5000 487 B srschlather@cdu.edu
SCHLATTER, Andy .... 802-440-4439 461 G aschlatter@bennington.edu
SCHLECT, Brenda .... 208-882-1566 132 C bschlect@nsa.edu
SCHLECT, Christopher ... 208-882-1566 132 C cschlect@nsa.edu
SCHLEEF, Debra .... 540-654-1505 471 N dschleef@umw.edu
SCHLEGEL, Alice .... 509-542-4823 479 A aschlegel@columbiabasin.edu
SCHLEGEL, Len .... 518-388-6607 323 J schlegel@union.edu
SCHLEGEL, Natalie .... 781-891-3474 206 G nschlegel@bentley.edu
SCHLEIBAUM, Michelle . 914-606-6505 325 A michelle.schleibaum@sunywcc.edu
SCHLEICH, Tamatha ...... 309-649-6632 150 G tamatha.schleich@src.edu
SCHLEICHER, Julie .... 781-239-3053 214 G jschleicher@massbay.edu
SCHLEICHER, Rolf .... 818-710-4142.. 49 D schleir@piercecollege.edu
SCHLEICHERT, Cat .... 503-491-6995 374 B catherine.schleichert@mhcc.edu
SCHLEMEYER, Lynn ...... 575-646-1837 287 C vlynns@nmsufoundation.org
SCHLENBECKER, Darlene .... 847-925-6008 138 G dschlenb@harpercollege.edu
SCHLENDER, James ...... 715-634-4790 492 L jschlender3@lco.edu
SCHLENKER, Steven ...... 215-702-4340 380 A sschlenker@cairn.edu
SCHLERETH, Jonathan ... 314-529-9236 255 B jschlereth2@maryville.edu
SCHLESINGER, Ed .... 410-516-7134 199 G tschles4@jhu.edu
SCHLESINGER, Kenneth 718-960-8577 294 A kenneth.schlesinger@lehman.cuny.edu
SCHLESINGER, Marissa 253-566-5000 484 E mschlesinger@tacomacc.edu
SCHLESINGER, Patrick .. 510-642-2866.. 69 A pschlesinger@berkeley.edu
SCHLESINGER, Philip .... 706-272-2985 118 B pschlesinger@daltonstate.edu
SCHLEY, Alisa, S .... 715-833-6266 498 E ahoepner1@cvtc.edu
SCHLICHT, Terri .... 913-469-8500 174 I tschlich@jccc.edu
SCHLICHTEMEIER, Kent . 949-854-8002.. 39 K
SCHLICKMANN, Paul .... 203-254-4000.. 87 I pschlickmann@fairfield.edu
SCHLIENTZ, Matt .... 517-607-2745 225 C mschlientz@hillsdale.edu
SCHLIMGEN, Matt .... 317-931-2382 154 G mschlimgen@cts.edu
SCHLINGMANN, Dirk .... 864-503-5663 414 A dschlingmann@uscupstate.edu
SCHLISSEL, Mark, S ...... 734-764-6270 231 H presoff@umich.edu
SCHLOER, Wolfgang ..... 404-413-2530 120 E wschloer@gsu.edu
SCHLOESSER, Brad .... 507-389-7263 241 C brad.schloesser@southcentral.edu
SCHLOESSER, Deann ..... 507-933-7495 236 A dmschloesser@gustavus.edu
SCHLOSSER, Peter .... 480-965-9801.. 10 J sclosser@asu.edu
SCHLOSSMAN, Paul ...... 818-240-1000.. 43 G pschloss@glendale.edu
SCHLOTTERHAUSEN, Lisa .... 719-336-1516.. 81 K lisa.schlotterhausen@lamarcc.edu
SCHLOTTHAUER, Scott .. 405-744-5984 367 G scott.schlotthauer@okstate.edu
SCHLUETER, Jennifer .... 614-437-1061 351 B jschlueter@ccad.edu
SCHLUETER, Margie ...... 763-433-1119 237 D margie.schlueter@anokaramsey.edu
SCHLUETER, Margie ...... 763-433-1119 237 E margie.schlueter@anokaramsey.edu
SCHLUP, Amy .... 580-559-5225 365 K aschlup@ecok.edu
SCHLUTER, Valerie .... 225-768-1795 187 B valerie.schluter@franu.edu
SCHLUTERMAN, Karen .. 479-979-1224.. 23 I kschlut@ozarks.edu
SCHMADER, Kelly, J ..... 310-206-4181.. 69 E kschmader@facnet.ucla.edu
SCHMAEFF, Robert .... 865-524-8079 420 B rschmaeff@huhs.edu
SCHMAHL, Georgina ..... 210-431-5510 441 B gschmahl@ollusa.edu
SCHMAILZL, Randy .... 531-622-2415 267 G rschmailzl@mccneb.edu
SCHMALL, Steve .... 507-285-7214 240 H steve.schmall@rctc.edu
SCHMALZEL, Katryn ...... 303-273-3260.. 79 J kschmalz@mines.edu
SCHMAND, Kathleen ..... 615-898-2773 422 C kathleen.schmand@mtsu.edu
SCHMEISER, Monte .... 310-377-5501.. 51 C mschmeiser@marymountcalifornia.edu
SCHMELCZER, Moshe ... 773-463-7738 150 J menahel@telshe.edu
SCHMELING, James ...... 202-685-3924 502 K
SCHMELTZER, Tracy ...... 919-735-5151 338 H tmschmeltzer@waynecc.edu
SCHMELZ, Kim .... 608-822-2379 500 A kschmelz@swtc.edu
SCHMELZ, Mark .... 541-346-2987 376 H mschmelz@uoregon.edu
SCHMELZER, Joy .... 978-542-6416 213 E joy.schmelzer@salemstate.edu
SCHMELZER, Judy .... 954-201-7458.. 96 F jschmelzer@broward.edu
SCHMERSAL, Cindy .... 816-501-4303 258 I cindy.schmersal@rockhurst.edu
SCHMID, Albertha .... 531-622-2354 267 G acschmid@mccneb.edu
SCHMID, Gary .... 414-443-8821 498 A gary.schmid@wlc.edu
SCHMIDEK, Celine .... 408-554-4982.. 63 B cschmidek@scu.edu
SCHMIDT, Amanda .... 706-385-1065 124 E amanda.schmidt@point.edu
SCHMIDT, Amber .... 605-256-5079 416 F amber.schmidt@dsu.edu
SCHMIDT, Amy .... 507-453-2700 239 B
SCHMIDT, Andrea .... 606-337-3196 180 C
SCHMIDT, Barbara, T .... 516-323-3015 306 M bschmidt@molloy.edu
SCHMIDT, Betsy .... 317-738-8054 155 D bschmidt@franklincollege.edu
SCHMIDT, Bradley .... 316-284-5349 172 B bschmidt@bethelks.edu
SCHMIDT, Christopher ... 270-384-8136 183 G schmidtc@lindsey.edu
SCHMIDT, Curt .... 612-659-6902 239 A curt.schmidt@minneapolis.edu
SCHMIDT, Dan .... 701-224-5735 346 A daniel.j.schmidt@bismarckstate.edu
SCHMIDT, Danielle .... 716-827-2538 323 G schmidtd@trocaire.edu
SCHMIDT, Denise .... 973-328-5245 276 J dschmidt@ccm.edu
SCHMIDT, Dobby .... 505-428-1226 288 E dobby.schmidt@sfcc.edu
SCHMIDT, Gordon .... 516-686-3802 308 I gordon.schmidt@nyit.edu
SCHMIDT, Howard .... 540-338-1776 469 C
SCHMIDT, Jacqueline .... 904-646-2300 101 B jacqueline.schmidt@fscj.edu
SCHMIDT, James, C ...... 715-836-2327 495 E jschmidt@uwec.edu
SCHMIDT, Jeffrey .... 410-704-3414 204 E jschmidt@towson.edu
SCHMIDT, Jenae, A .... 651-696-6214 236 I schmidtj@macalester.edu
SCHMIDT, Jens .... 310-204-1666.. 58 K
SCHMIDT, Joanna .... 817-257-5294 448 F joanna.schmidt@tcu.edu
SCHMIDT, Karen .... 713-718-8596 437 C karen.schmidt2@hccs.edu
SCHMIDT, Karol .... 480-517-8767.. 13 G karol.schmidt@riosalado.edu
SCHMIDT, Leslie .... 815-599-3421 139 A leslie.schmidt@highland.edu
SCHMIDT, Leslie .... 406-994-2381 264 C lschmidt@montana.edu
SCHMIDT, Liz .... 651-846-1477 241 B elizabeth.schmidt@saintpaul.edu
SCHMIDT, London .... 910-755-8393 332 F schmidtl@brunswickcc.edu
SCHMIDT, Lynn .... 765-641-4388 153 G lmschmidt@anderson.edu
SCHMIDT, Martin, A ...... 617-253-4500 216 B
SCHMIDT, Maynard .... 845-341-4205 310 G maynard.schmidt@sunyorange.edu
SCHMIDT, Mike .... 770-533-6914 122 B mschmidt@laniertech.edu
SCHMIDT, Paul .... 864-503-5036 414 A pschmidt@uscupstate.edu
SCHMIDT, Paula .... 563-588-6383 164 E paula.schmidt@clarke.edu
SCHMIDT, Rachel .... 216-687-5594 350 J r.m.schmidt@csuohio.edu
SCHMIDT, Robert .... 203-576-4792.. 89 C rschmidt@bridgeport.edu
SCHMIDT, Sara .... 605-626-2400 416 G sara.schmidt@northern.edu
SCHMIDT, Shana .... 715-833-6410 498 E sschmidt42@cvtc.edu
SCHMIDT, Sierra .... 813-988-5131.. 99 R schmidts@floridacollege.edu
SCHMIDT, Stephen .... 334-347-2623.... 2 A sschmidt@escc.edu
SCHMIDT, Steven, P ...... 330-325-6290 357 D sschmidt@neomed.edu
SCHMIDT, Stuart, J .... 920-565-1023 493 A schmidtsj@lakeland.edu
SCHMIDT, Sue .... 307-532-8207 501 B sue.schmidt@ewc.wy.edu
SCHMIDT, Tania .... 507-457-2800 241 F tschmidt@winona.edu
SCHMIDT CAMPBELL, Mary .... 404-270-5001 126 B mscampbell@spelman.edu
SCHMIDT-ROGERS, Deborah .... 773-508-3300 143 C dschmi6@luc.edu
SCHMIDTKE, Rachel ...... 812-866-7031 155 G schmidtke@hanover.edu
SCHMIEDE, Angela .... 650-543-3905.. 51 G angela.schmiede@menlo.edu
SCHMIEDEL, Mary, E ..... 202-687-3911.. 92 E schmiedm@georgetown.edu
SCHMIEG, Rose, A .... 540-665-5534 470 G rschmieg@su.edu
SCHMIEISING, David .... 740-283-6513 352 I dschmiesing@franciscan.edu
SCHMIESING, Ann .... 303-492-2890.. 84 B ann.schmiesing@colorado.edu
SCHMILL, Stuart .... 617-258-5514 216 B
SCHMISEK, Brian .... 507-457-1756 243 C bschmisek@smumn.edu
SCHMIT, Matt .... 563-441-4125 166 B mschmit@eicc.edu
SCHMIT, Matt .... 563-336-3300 165 K mschmit@eicc.edu

SCHRADER, Claudia, V . 718-368-5109 294 E
president@kbcc.cuny.edu
SCHRADER, Kacey .... 386-752-1822 100 B
kacey.schrader@fgc.edu
SCHRADER, Sarah .... 209-575-6122.. 77 A
schraders@mjc.edu
SCHRADER, Shari .... 810-424-5448 232 A
sjschrad@umich.edu
SCHRAEDER, Michael ... 214-638-0484 438 E
mschraeder@kdstudio.com
SCHRAEDER, Peter, J .... 773-508-3500 143 C
pschrae@luc.edu
SCHRAGE, Charles .... 217-206-7395 152 A
schrage.charles@uis.edu
SCHRAGE, Jim .... 661-362-3222.. 38 D
jim.schrage@canyons.edu
SCHRAM, Jacqueline, S 574-372-5100 155 F
schramjs@grace.edu
SCHRAM, Mandy .... 218-679-2860 242 U
SCHRAM, Michelle .... 716-338-1092 303 A
michellsschram@mail.sunyjcc.edu
SCHRAMM,
Christine, M .... 937-229-2229 362 C
cschramm1@udayton.edu
SCHRAMM, Dorothy ...... 610-861-5421 391 C
dschramm@northampton.edu
SCHRAMM, Jamie .... 920-683-4711 495 F
schrammj@uwgb.edu
SCHRAMM, Jamie .... 920-459-6611 495 F
schrammj@uwgb.edu
SCHRAMMEL, Debra, S . 215-670-9270 391 E
dsschrammel@peirce.edu
SCHRANTZ, John .... 937-481-2432 364 A
john_schrantz@wilmington.edu
SCHRANZ, William .... 402-643-7246 266 G
bill.schranz@cune.edu
SCHRAUTH, Jodi, S ...... 920-923-7615 493 D
jsschrauth11@marianuniversity.edu
SCHRECK, Jayne .... 800-747-2687 144 H
jayne@monmouthcollege.edu
SCHREFFLER, Ahaji .... 215-895-1704 382 F
ahaji@drexel.edu
SCHREIBER, Meredith ... 503-399-2535 372 B
meredith.schreiber@chemeketa.edu
SCHREIBER, Nancy .... 401-341-2222 405 D
nancy.schreiber@salve.edu
SCHREIBER, Pam .... 206-543-2430 485 A
pschreib@uw.edu
SCHREIBER, Rachel .... 212-229-8950 308 A
schreibr@newschool.edu
SCHREIBMAN, Andi ...... 925-424-1585.. 35 K
aschreibman@laspositascollege.edu
SCHREIER, Barry .... 319-335-7294 163 H
barry-schreier@uiowa.edu
SCHREIER, Julie .... 646-592-4305 326 D
julie.schreier@yu.edu
SCHREINER, Ashley ...... 919-496-2521 330 I
SCHREINER, Steven .... 718-862-7303 304 M
sschreiner01@manhattan.edu
SCHREINER, Susan .... 360-538-4051 480 G
susan.schreiner@ghc.edu
SCHREYER, Robert .... 609-586-4800 278 F
schreyer@mccc.edu
SCHRINER, Brian .... 305-348-3181 110 A
brian.schriner@fiu.edu
SCHROCK, Lindsey .... 740-283-6456 352 I
lschrock@franciscan.edu
SCHROCK, Lynford .... 740-857-1311 360 D
lschrock@rosedale.edu
SCHRODER, Adam .... 850-478-8496 105 G
aschroder@pcci.edu
SCHRODER, Sharon ...... 253-566-5064 484 E
sschroder@tacomacc.edu
SCHRODT, Julie .... 850-729-5307 104 M
schrodtj@nwfsc.edu
SCHROEDER, Alicia .... 937-512-5369 360 G
alicia.schroeder@sinclair.edu
SCHROEDER, Alisha ...... 406-265-4191 264 E
alisha.schroeder@msun.edu
SCHROEDER, Amanda ... 818-299-5500.. 74 L
aschroeder@westcoastuniversity.edu
SCHROEDER, Betzi .... 973-803-5000 280 B
bschroeder@pillar.edu
SCHROEDER, Brian .... 973-803-5000 280 B
brschroeder@pillar.edu
SCHROEDER, Bryon ...... 432-837-8339 450 B
bxs16zg@sulross.edu
SCHROEDER, Cynthia .... 636-949-4318 254 H
cschroeder@lindenwood.edu
SCHROEDER, David .... 203-931-2959.. 89 H
dschroeder@newhaven.edu
SCHROEDER, David, E .. 973-803-5000 280 B
dschroeder@pillar.edu
SCHROEDER, Dennis, J 818-364-7650.. 49 C
schroedj@lamission.edu
SCHROEDER, Fritz .... 410-516-8631 199 G
fschroed@jhu.edu
SCHROEDER, James ...... 214-637-3530 457 H
jschroeder@wadecollege.edu
SCHROEDER, Jennifer ... 785-243-1435 172 L
jschroeder@cloud.edu
SCHROEDER, Jennifer ... 903-886-5160 447 B
jennifer.schroeder@tamuc.edu
SCHROEDER, Joe .... 815-939-5267 147 A
schroed@olivet.edu
SCHROEDER, Kay .... 940-668-3302 440 F
kschroeder@nctc.edu
SCHROEDER, Kristi .... 319-208-5100 170 D
kschroeder@scciowa.edu
SCHROEDER, Lori .... 707-654-1000.. 32 A
SCHROEDER, Mark .... 734-432-5662 227 C
maschroeder@madonna.edu
SCHROEDER, Matt .... 419-530-1448 363 B
matt.schroeder@utoledo.edu
SCHROEDER, Michael ... 314-529-9673 255 B
mschroeder@maryville.edu
SCHROEDER, Neil .... 210-829-6000 453 C
nschroed@uiwtx.edu
SCHROEDER, Nick .... 828-327-7000 333 B
nschroeder@cvcc.edu
SCHROEDER, Nicole ...... 507-222-5478 234 G
nschroeder@carleton.edu
SCHROEDER, Rachel ...... 336-734-7646 334 F
rschroeder@forsythtech.edu
SCHROEDER, SVD,
Roger .... 773-371-5423 134 D
SCHROEDER, Ross .... 979-830-4118 431 H
ross.schroeder@blinn.edu
SCHROEDER, Ryan .... 912-478-6068 120 C
rshroeder@georgiasouthern.edu
SCHROEDER, Tracy .... 617-353-1155 207 E
tas@bu.edu
SCHROEDER-BIEK,
Julie .... 574-284-4333 160 I
jsbiek@saintmarys.edu
SCHROEDER-GREEN,
Suzanna .... 440-646-8178 363 C
sschroeder@ursuline.edu
SCHROER, Jessica .... 636-949-4920 254 H
jschroer@lindenwood.edu
SCHROER, Tara .... 785-460-5487 173 B
tara.schroer@colbycc.edu
SCHROER, Timothy .... 507-786-3615 243 D
schroert@stolaf.edu
SCHROF, Robert .... 302-857-6200.. 90 E
SCHROT, Sheree .... 231-591-3725 224 A
shereeschrot@ferris.edu
SCHROTH, Keith .... 504-568-5135 189 H
kschro@lsuhsc.edu
SCHROYER, Heath .... 337-475-5563 192 E
hschroyer@mcneese.edu
SCHRUM, Mindi-Kim ...... 505-566-3261 288 D
schrumm@sanjuancollege.edu
SCHUBERT, Beth .... 804-752-7270 469 F
bethschubert@rmc.edu
SCHUBERT, Leighton ..... 979-830-4243 431 H
leighton.schubert@blinn.edu
SCHUBERT,
Marianne, A .... 336-758-5273 344 C
schubem@wfu.edu
SCHUBERT, Melissa ...... 562-903-4555.. 27 A
melissa.b.schubert@biola.edu
SCHUBERT, Phil .... 325-674-2412 428 F
schubert@acu.edu
SCHUBERT, Ryan .... 309-672-5513 144 C
rschubert@methodistcol.edu
SCHUCH, Debra .... 717-299-7408 399 C
schuch@stevenscollege.edu
SCHUCHARDT, Bob .... 913-758-6111 178 B
robert.schuchardt@stmary.edu
SCHUCHARDT,
Maureen .... 913-758-6182 178 B
maureen.schuchardt@stmary.edu
SCHUCK, Emily .... 740-376-4712 355 E
schucke@marietta.edu
SCHUCK, John .... 856-227-7200 276 E
jschuck@camdencc.edu
SCHUCKER, Julie .... 716-614-6251 309 G
jschucker@niagaracc.suny.edu
SCHUCKMAN, Amy .... 503-517-7834 375 G
schuckma@reed.edu
SCHUELKE, Mark .... 231-591-5919 224 A
markschuelke@ferris.edu
SCHUELLER, Kenneth .... 660-543-4721 260 G
schueller@ucmo.edu
SCHUELLER, Tina .... 325-793-3819 439 F
schueller.tina@mcm.edu
SCHUEMANN,
Kahler, B .... 269-387-2360 233 B
kahler.schuemann@wmich.edu
SCHUENAMAN,
Bruce, R .... 361-593-3528 447 D
bruce.schueneman@tamuk.edu
SCHUERMER, David, A . 270-824-8633 182 D
david.schuermer@kctcs.edu
SCHUESSLER, Jennifer .. 678-839-5640 127 C
jschuess@westga.edu
SCHUESSLER VELOZ,
Nicole, A .... 619-260-7408.. 72 I
nschuessler@sandiego.edu
SCHUH, Jane .... 701-231-6542 345 F
jane.schuh@ndsu.edu
SCHUH, Mary Paula ..... 859-572-5122 184 E
schuh@nku.edu
SCHUIL, Carol .... 626-395-3368.. 28 J
carol.schuil@caltech.edu
SCHUILING, Kerri .... 906-227-2920 228 I
kschuili@nmu.edu
SCHUKEI, Chris .... 402-461-7341 267 C
cschukei@hastings.edu
SCHULER, Gwendollyn .. 512-448-8404 442 I
SCHULIST, Mike .... 262-650-4844 492 A
mschulis@carrollu.edu
SCHULL, David .... 303-963-3283.. 78 H
dschull@ccu.edu
SCHULLER, Aimee .... 330-823-2755 362 E
schullal@mountunion.edu
SCHULLER, Jennifer ...... 440-375-7255 354 K
jschuller@lec.edu
SCHULLER, Jennifer, N . 330-569-5839 353 G
schullerjn@hiram.edu
SCHULMAN, Avrohom .. 908-354-6057 285 J
SCHULMAN, Jeffrey, L .. 802-656-3075 463 A
jeffrey.schulman@uvm.edu
SCHULT, Jordan .... 715-675-3331 499 F
schult@ntc.edu
SCHULTE, Brandy .... 660-831-4108 256 I
schulteb@moval.edu
SCHULTE, Cynthia .... 641-844-5602 167 E
cindy.schulte@iavalley.edu
SCHULTE, Kristi .... 940-397-4427 440 C
kristi.schulte@msutexas.edu
SCHULTE, Mary .... 618-468-3300 142 E
mschulte@lc.edu
SCHULTE, Megan .... 419-434-4505 362 D
megan.schulte@findlay.edu
SCHULTE, Patricia .... 503-338-2425 372 D
pschulte@clatsopcc.edu
SCHULTE, Priscilla .... 907-228-4548.. 10 B
pmschulte@alaska.edu
SCHULTE, Sarah, H .... 906-487-2318 228 A
shschult@mtu.edu
SCHULTE, Sheila .... 706-867-2844 127 A
sheila.schulte@ung.edu
SCHULTE, Stacey .... 573-681-5030 254 G
schultes@lincolnu.edu
SCHULTE, Tim .... 660-831-4148 256 I
schultet@moval.edu
SCHULTE, Vickie .... 618-437-5321 147 I
schultev@rlc.edu
SCHULTE-SHOBERG,
Kim .... 715-232-1285 497 B
schulte-shobergk@uwstout.edu
SCHULTES, Debra .... 201-684-7311 280 H
dschulte@rampao.edu
SCHULTHEIS, Luke, D ... 201-692-7080 277 I
luke@fdu.edu
SCHULTHEIS, Stephen ... 678-466-5020 117 D
stephenschultheis@clayton.edu
SCHULTZ, Alex .... 303-360-4728.. 80 E
alex.schultz@ccaurora.edu
SCHULTZ, Ann .... 859-441-4500 18? H
ann.schultz@kctcs.edu
SCHULTZ, Barry .... 901-572-2772 418 A
barry.schultz@baptistu.edu
SCHULTZ, Bethany .... 208-467-8353 132 E
bhaglund@nnu.edu
SCHULTZ, Bruce .... 907-786-6108.... 9 J
brschultz@alaska.edu
SCHULTZ, Clayton .... 919-573-5350 340 C
cschultz@shepherds.edu
SCHULTZ, Craig .... 608-758-6900 498 D
cschultz31@blackhawk.edu
SCHULTZ, Diana, C .... 239-513-1122 102 D
dschultz2@hodges.edu
SCHULTZ, Eric .... 605-882-5284 415 D
eric.schultz@lakeareatech.edu
SCHULTZ, Greg .... 440-934-3101 357 I
SCHULTZ, Jennifer, A .... 815-835-6405 149 E
jennifer.a.schultz@svcc.edu
SCHULTZ, Jessica .... 309-794-7331 133 C
jessicaschultz@augustana.edu
SCHULTZ, Jessica .... 763-657-2401 238 C
jessica.schultz@hennepintech.edu
SCHULTZ, Joseph, P ...... 607-777-2187 316 B
jschultz@binghamton.edu
SCHULTZ, Katherine .... 303-492-6937.. 84 B
katherine.schultz@colorado.edu
SCHULTZ, Lynda, K ...... 920-923-8793 493 D
lkschultz@marianuniversity.edu
SCHULTZ, Marie .... 951-827-6302.. 70 B
marie.schultz@ucr.edu
SCHULTZ, Mark .... 510-592-9688.. 54 F
mark.schultz@npu.edu
SCHULTZ, Melissa .... 734-462-4400 230 G
mschultz@schoolcraft.edu
SCHULTZ, Michael .... 903-233-4441 439 A
michaelschultz@letu.edu
SCHULTZ, Peter, G .... 858-784-8469.. 64 A
SCHULTZ, Rebecca .... 920-996-2813 498 F
schultre@fvtc.edu
SCHULTZ, Roger, D ...... 434-592-4032 468 E
rschultz@liberty.edu
SCHULTZ, Roger, W ...... 951-487-3002.. 53 A
rschultz@msjc.edu
SCHULTZ, Scott .... 515-965-7123 165 A
sfschultz@dmacc.edu
SCHULTZ, Whitney .... 707-527-4011.. 63 D
SCHULTZ, William .... 651-641-8211 235 I
schultz@csp.edu
SCHULTZ, Yvonne .... 740-392-6868 356 G
yvonne.schultz@mvnu.edu
SCHULTZ-HUXMAN,
Susan .... 540-432-4100 466 B
susan.huxman@emu.edu
SCHULTZE, Christine ..... 303-329-6355.. 79 L
SCHULZ, Amy .... 916-660-7800.. 64 D
aschulz1@sierracollege.edu
SCHULZ, Amy .... 317-738-8319 155 D
aschulz@franklincollege.edu
SCHULZ, Andrew .... 520-621-7886.. 16 D
apschulz@arizona.edu
SCHULZ, Christa .... 360-416-7974 484 C
christa.schulz@skagit.edu
SCHULZ, Greg .... 714-992-7001.. 54 C
gschulz@fullcoll.edu
SCHULZ, Greg .... 626-914-8821.. 36 J
gschulz@citruscollege.edu
SCHULZ, Karyn .... 410-837-4141 204 F
kschulz@ubalt.edu
SCHULZ, Kathy, L .... 201-216-5667 283 D
kathy.schulz@stevens.edu
SCHULZ, Kirk .... 509-335-4200 485 D
presidentsoffice@wsu.edu
SCHULZ, Phyllis .... 212-817-7460 293 F
pschulz@gc.cuny.edu
SCHULZ, Robert .... 619-594-5901.. 33 D
rschulz@sdsu.edu
SCHULZ, Scott .... 623-845-3692.. 13 C
scott.schulz@gccaz.edu
SCHULZ, Scott .... 218-726-7171 243 G
sschulz1@d.umn.edu
SCHULZ, Scott .... 440-826-6970 348 D
saschulz@bw.edu
SCHULZ, Steven, D .... 641-422-4000 168 G
steve.schulz@niacc.edu
SCHULZ, Tara .... 563-884-5828 169 F
tara.schulz@palmer.edu
SCHULZ, William .... 866-492-5336 244 F
william.schulz@mail.waldenu.edu
SCHULZE, Edee .... 805-565-6028.. 76 A
eschulze@westmont.edu
SCHULZE, Janet, Y .... 610-660-2311 397 G
jschulze@sju.edu
SCHULZE, Lori, A .... 920-748-8310 494 J
schulzel@ripon.edu
SCHULZE, Rob .... 802-635-1305 463 G
rob.schulze@northernvermont.edu
SCHULZE, Robin, G .... 716-645-2711 316 C
cas-dean@buffalo.edu
SCHUMACHER, Brenda . 531-622-2406 267 G
bschumacher@mccneb.edu
SCHUMACHER,
Bryan, J .... 605-394-5102 416 H
bryan.schumacher@sdsmt.edu
SCHUMACHER,
Daniel, J .... 715-836-5858 495 E
schumadj@uwec.edu
SCHUMACHER, Denny .. 217-245-3012 139 C
dennis.schumacher@ic.edu
SCHUMACHER, Eric ...... 610-399-2599 393 F
eschumacher@cheyney.edu

SCOTT, Dave .... 626-584-5269.. 43 B
dscott@fuller.edu
SCOTT, Dave .... 360-416-7600 484 C
dave.scott@skagit.edu
SCOTT, Dave, L .... 626-584-5269.. 43 B
dscott@fuller.edu
SCOTT, David .... 850-474-3003 111 F
dscott@uwf.edu
SCOTT, David .... 719-632-7626.. 81 J
dscott@intellitec.edu
SCOTT, David .... 361-825-2661 447 C
david.scott@tamucc.edu
SCOTT, Dawn, M .... 262-524-7297 492 A
dscott@carrollu.edu
SCOTT, Deborah .... 830-792-7355 443 E
dlscott@schreiner.edu
SCOTT, Deloria .... 270-707-3823 182 B
deloria.scott@kctcs.edu
SCOTT, Derek .... 402-280-2780 266 H
derekscott@creighton.edu
SCOTT, Donna .... 512-404-4807 430 J
dscott@austinseminary.edu
SCOTT, Douglas .... 484-646-4250 394 D
dscott@kutztown.edu
SCOTT, Ed .... 850-263-3261.. 95 P
eescott@baptistcollege.edu
SCOTT, Edward .... 443-885-3050 201 A
edward.scott@morgan.edu
SCOTT, Elaine .... 408-554-4600.. 63 B
escott@scu.edu
SCOTT, Emily .... 336-272-7102 329 C
emily.scott@greensboro.edu
SCOTT, Emily, M .... 336-272-7102 329 C
emily.scott@greensboro.edu
SCOTT, Eric .... 662-216-3429 248 G
escott@rustcollege.edu
SCOTT, Eric .... 208-426-4218 130 H
ericscott@boisestate.edu
SCOTT, Eric .... 512-472-4133 443 F
eric.scott@ssw.edu
SCOTT, Garry .... 217-234-5253 142 C
gscott12070@lakelandcollege.edu
SCOTT, Gray .... 940-898-3042 451 D
grayscott@twu.edu
SCOTT, Gregory .... 865-524-8079 420 B
gregory.scott@huhs.edu
SCOTT, Harriette .... 508-588-9100 215 A
hdudley1@massasoit.mass.edu
SCOTT, Jamal .... 630-466-7900 152 K
jscott@waubonsee.edu
SCOTT, James .... 707-638-5200.. 68 B
SCOTT, James .... 575-835-5158 286 K
james.scott@nmt.edu
SCOTT, Janice, L .... 727-816-3424 105 F
cessnaj@phsc.edu
SCOTT, Jeannie, J .... 210-283-5002 453 C
scott@uiwtx.edu
SCOTT, Jennifer .... 651-638-6519 234 D
jscott@bethel.edu
SCOTT, Jeremy .... 954-637-2268 108 E
admissions@sfbc.edu
SCOTT, Jim .... 509-434-5325 479 D
jim.scott@ccs.spokane.edu
SCOTT, Jo Ann .... 662-252-8000 248 G
jscott2@rustcollege.edu
SCOTT, JoAnn .... 662-252-8000 248 G
jscott@rustcollege.edu
SCOTT, Jonathan, H ...... 229-928-1273 120 D
jonathan.scott@gsw.edu
SCOTT, Joseph .... 501-882-4411.. 17 D
jlscott@asub.edu
SCOTT, Joseph .... 937-878-7985 502 C
scottjoseph@aafes.com
SCOTT, Joyce .... 870-543-4917.. 21 B
jscott@seark.edu
SCOTT, Joylynn .... 423-236-2801 423 F
jmichals@southern.edu
SCOTT, Kathleen, E .... 937-255-3636 502 C
kathleen.scott@afit.edu
SCOTT, Kathy .... 805-965-0581.. 63 A
SCOTT, Kelly .... 970-675-3211.. 79 H
kelly.scott@cncc.edu
SCOTT, Kendall .... 918-360-9703 365 C
scottk@bacone.edu
SCOTT, Kimberly, M ..... 334-727-8011.... 7 D
SCOTT, Kristina .... 602-286-8000.. 13 B
SCOTT, Lana .... 580-477-7719 371 D
lana.scott@wosc.edu
SCOTT, Laura .... 707-864-7000.. 64 H
laura.scott@solano.edu
SCOTT, Laura, A .... 603-271-6484 273 A
lascott@ccsnh.edu

SCOTT, Linda .... 608-263-9725 495 D
ldscott@wisc.edu
SCOTT, Linda .... 559-486-1166.. 24 F
lscott@agapeschools.org
SCOTT, Linda .... 804-524-5304 476 D
lscott@vsu.edu
SCOTT, Lisa, L .... 585-785-1454 299 F
lisa.scott@flcc.edu
SCOTT, Lori .... 318-487-7401 187 E
lori.scott@lacollege.edu
SCOTT, Marc .... 740-351-3439 360 F
mscott@shawnee.edu
SCOTT, Marcia .... 805-546-3119.. 40 F
mscott@cuesta.edu
SCOTT, Matthew .... 413-205-3015 205 F
matthew.scott@aic.edu
SCOTT, Megan .... 425-889-5205 481 H
megan.scott@northwestu.edu
SCOTT, Megan, J .... 920-832-6587 493 B
megan.j.scott@lawrence.edu
SCOTT, Melody, K .... 330-471-8502 355 D
mscott@malone.edu
SCOTT, Michael .... 415-405-3943.. 33 E
mjscott@sfsu.edu
SCOTT, Michael, S .... 410-543-6456 204 D
msscott@salisbury.edu
SCOTT, Michelle, T .... 240-567-5276 200 G
michelle.scott@montgomerycollege.edu
SCOTT, Mike .... 817-257-7858 448 F
m.scott@tcu.edu
SCOTT, Patricia, A .... 410-706-7347 203 A
pscott@umaryland.edu
SCOTT, Patty .... 541-888-7401 376 C
pscott@socc.edu
SCOTT, Paul .... 912-443-5500 125 B
pscott@savannahtech.edu
SCOTT, SR., Paul .... 601-977-6180 249 C
pscott2@tougaloo.edu
SCOTT, Phyllis .... 305-899-3900.. 96 A
pscott@barry.edu
SCOTT, Raegina .... 270-824-8593 182 D
raegina.scott@kctcs.edu
SCOTT, Randa .... 512-313-3000 433 N
randa.scott@concordia.edu
SCOTT, Randolph .... 850-474-3295 111 F
rscott1@uwf.edu
SCOTT, Ray .... 662-720-7302 248 C
jrscott@nemcc.edu
SCOTT, Renae .... 208-282-2499 131 G
renaescott@isu.edu
SCOTT, Renay .... 575-646-7607 287 C
rmscott@nmsu.edu
SCOTT, Renee .... 325-793-3803 439 F
scott.renee@mcm.edu
SCOTT, Richard .... 269-965-3931 225 H
scottr@kellogg.edu
SCOTT, Richard .... 801-957-3334 461 C
richard.scott@slcc.edu
SCOTT, Rob .... 770-426-2603 122 C
rob.scott@life.edu
SCOTT, Robin .... 603-342-3016 273 C
rscott@ccsnh.edu
SCOTT, Samantha .... 626-350-1500.. 28 F
SCOTT, Sandi .... 715-232-1181 497 B
duexs@uwstout.edu
SCOTT, Sara .... 937-481-2307 364 A
sara_scott@wilmington.edu
SCOTT, Sarah .... 301-447-7415 201 B
sscott@msmary.edu
SCOTT, Sean, M .... 619-239-0391.. 34 G
sscott@cwsl.edu
SCOTT, Sharron .... 802-224-3000 463 D
SCOTT, Sharron, R .... 802-635-1208 463 G
sharron.scott@northernvermont.edu
SCOTT, Shawne .... 443-394-3339.. 93 H
SCOTT, Sheila .... 434-528-5276 477 B
SCOTT, Sherrill, B .... 731-426-7522 420 G
sbscott@lanecollege.edu
SCOTT, Stacie .... 608-363-2250 491 H
scottst@beloit.edu
SCOTT, Stacy .... 717-299-7731 399 C
SCOTT, Steven, A .... 620-235-4100 177 A
sascott@pittstate.edu
SCOTT, Susan, W .... 601-266-5000 249 F
susan.w.scott@usm.edu
SCOTT, Susanne .... 718-951-5000 293 C
sscott@brooklyn.cuny.edu
SCOTT, Tawana .... 864-877-1598 410 I
tawana.scott@ngu.edu
SCOTT, Taylor .... 401-709-8671 405 B
tscott01@risd.edu
SCOTT, Terri .... 208-459-5328 131 C
tscott@collegeofidaho.edu

SCOTT, Thomas .... 208-769-5906 132 D
ttscott@nic.edu
SCOTT, Timothy, P .... 979-845-4016 446 F
t-scott@tamu.edu
SCOTT, Todd .... 760-245-4271.. 74 D
todd.scott@vvc.edu
SCOTT, Vann .... 256-840-4188.... 3 F
vann.scott@snead.edu
SCOTT, W. Michael .... 678-466-4900 117 D
williamscott@clayton.edu
SCOTT, William, J .... 260-399-7700 162 B
bscott@sf.edu
SCOTT, Winston .... 321-674-8470 100 C
wscott@fit.edu
SCOTT,
Zaldwaynaka (Z) .... 773-995-2400 134 K
zscott21@csu.edu
SCOTT-BRAND, Tammy . 312-850-4584 135 H
tscott-brand@ccc.edu
SCOTT-GILMORE,
Jennifer .... 601-857-3395 246 C
jennifer.scottgilmore@hindscc.edu
SCOTT-JOHNSON,
Pamela .... 732-571-3405 279 A
pscottjo@monmouth.edu
SCOTT-JOHNSON,
Pamela .... 323-343-2000.. 31 E
pscottj@calstatela.edu
SCOTT-KINNEY,
Wanda, A .... 803-705-4680 406 G
wanda.scottkinney@benedict.edu
SCOTT LEE, Kristalyn .... 205-665-6001.... 8 D
klee8@montevallo.edu
SCOTTI, Frank .... 714-463-7540.. 51 B
fscotti@ketchum.edu
SCOTTO, Kathleen .... 732-235-4812 282 A
kathleen.scotto@rutgers.edu
SCOUREY, Joy .... 509-335-9711 485 D
scourey@wsu.edu
SCOVILLE, Jan .... 715-732-3888 499 G
jan.scoville@nwtc.edu
SCOVILLE, Kathy .... 518-244-2053 313 A
scovik@sage.edu
SCOVILLE, Shawn .... 541-737-3288 375 A
SCOZZAFAVA, Samuel .. 315-443-4027 321 G
sjscozza@syr.edu
SCRANAGE, Kimberly .... 859-572-7852 184 E
scranagek1@nku.edu
SCREMENTI, Lori .... 773-244-5770 145 G
lmscrementi@northpark.edu
SCREWS, Jacqueline ..... 334-291-4981.... 1 H
jackie.screws@cv.edu
SCRIBNER, Andrea .... 518-736-3622 300 D
andrea.scribner@fmcc.suny.edu
SCRIBNER, Heidi, M ...... 951-827-1012.. 70 B
SCRIMENTI, Santo, A .... 240-567-5361 200 G
santo.scrimenti@montgomerycollege.
edu
SCRIVEN, Darryl .... 315-268-6544 295 F
dscriven@clarkson.edu
SCRIVEN, Darryl .... 336-750-2400 344 A
scrivendl@wssu.edu
SCRIVEN, Gloria .... 803-934-3216 410 G
gscriven@morris.edu
SCRIVEN, Regina .... 215-780-1307 398 B
rscriven@salus.edu
SCRIVENER, Tom .... 414-229-4304 496 B
scrivene@uwm.edu
SCRIVNER, Joseph .... 205-366-8838.... 7 A
jscrivner@stillman.edu
SCROGGINS, Beth .... 503-838-8000 377 D
scrogginsb@wou.edu
SCROGGINS, Don .... 575-769-4909 285 O
don.scroggins@clovis.edu
SCROGGINS, Melinda ... 559-251-4215.. 27 I
financialaid@calchristiancollege.edu
SCROGGINS, Sarah .... 636-584-6553 253 B
sarah.scroggins@eastcentral.edu
SCROGGINS, Susan ...... 219-464-6395 162 D
susan.scroggins@valpo.edu
SCROGGINS,
William, T .... 909-274-4250.. 52 J
bscroggins@mtsac.edu
SCROGIN, Tara .... 402-559-9005 269 K
tscrogin@unmc.edu
SCRUGGS, Adina .... 423-364-3360 418 D
ascruggs8899@bryan.edu
SCRUGGS, Jeff .... 478-218-3333 116 G
jscruggs@centralgatech.edu
SCRUGGS, Philip .... 208-885-7921 132 F
pwscruggs@uidaho.edu
SCUILETTI, Linda .... 919-718-7417 333 C
lscuiletti@cccc.edu

SCULL, Nicholas .... 617-573-8000 219 B
nscull@adm.suffolk.edu
SCULLY, Amy .... 803-691-3879 410 D
scullya@midlandstech.edu
SCULLY, Beverly .... 860-701-7795.. 88 D
scully_b@mitchell.edu
SCULLY, Dale .... 559-453-7154.. 43 A
dale.scully@fresno.edu
SCULLY, Jonathan .... 413-265-2519 208 E
scullyj@elms.edu
SCULLY, Joseph, F .... 856-256-4127 281 F
scullyj@rowan.edu
SCULLY, Pamela .... 404-712-4161 118 E
pamela.scully@emory.edu
SCULLY, Pamela .... 910-678-8232 334 E
scullyp@faytechcc.edu
SCULLY, Serena .... 304-367-4151 489 K
serena.scully@fairmontstate.edu
SCURALLI, Joseph .... 973-405-2111 275 I
jss@berkeleycollege.edu
SCURALLI, Joseph .... 212-986-4343 291 E
jss@berkeleycollege.edu
SCURALLI, Joseph .... 973-405-2111 291 E
jss@berkeleycollege.edu
SCUTO, Donna, L .... 716-878-6700 317 F
scutodl@buffalostate.edu
SCUTTI, Diane .... 610-902-8415 379 G
diane.m.scutti@cabrini.edu
SEABERRY, Ben .... 408-531-6144.. 62 F
ben.seaberry@sjeccd.edu
SEABERRY, Ben .... 559-243-7321.. 66 H
ben.seaberry@scccd.edu
SEABERT, Denise .... 559-278-4004.. 31 B
dseabert@csufresno.edu
SEABOLD, Brian .... 201-216-8722 283 D
brian.seabold@stevens.edu
SEABOLD, Daniel, E ...... 516-463-5411 301 G
daniel.e.seabold@hofstra.edu
SEABOLT, Kerry .... 706-865-2134 126 E
klseabolt@truett.edu
SEABOY, Donna .... 701-854-8013 346 H
donna.seaboy@sittingbull.edu
SEABROOK-WRIGHT,
Gloria .... 803-934-3168 410 G
gwright@morris.edu
SEABROOKS, Joseph .... 972-860-8250 434 G
jseabrooks@dcccd.edu
SEACH, Kerri .... 248-204-4108 227 A
kseach@ltu.edu
SEAGA, Andrew .... 305-237-7581 104 E
aseaga@mdc.edu
SEAGER, Lori .... 719-389-6953.. 78 I
lseager@coloradocollege.edu
SEAGLE, Dennis .... 828-726-2705 332 G
dseaglejr@cccti.edu
SEAGLE, Donna .... 423-585-6933 425 F
donna.seagle@ws.edu
SEAGRAVES, Jennifer .... 919-464-2254 335 F
j_seagraves@johnstoncc.edu
SEAGRAVES, Ronda .... 512-313-4501 433 N
ronda.seagraves@concordia.edu
SEAGULL, Amon .... 903-813-3007 430 H
aseagull@austincollege.edu
SEAL, Jennifer .... 601-403-1146 248 E
jseal@prcc.edu
SEAL, John .... 510-649-2462.. 44 B
jseal@gtu.edu
SEAL, Sherry .... 706-754-7730 123 G
sseal@northgatech.edu
SEAL, Susan .... 662-325-3473 247 F
sseal@humansci.msstate.edu
SEAL, Tonia .... 601-403-1214 248 E
tmoody@prcc.edu
SEALE, Danette .... 865-471-3229 418 E
dseale@cn.edu
SEALE, Danette .... 865-471-3248 418 E
dseale@cn.edu
SEALE, Glenn .... 843-574-6519 412 I
glenn.seale@tridenttech.edu
SEALE, Michael .... 903-510-2152 452 A
michael.seale@tjc.edu
SEALES, Lisa .... 212-678-3740 322 C
ls2007@tc.columbia.edu
SEALEY, John .... 479-308-2329.. 17 A
john.sealey@arcomedu.org
SEALINE, Alma .... 217-333-0610 152 B
asealine@illinois.edu
SEALS, Lee .... 423-478-7725 422 J
lseals@ptseminary.edu
SEALS, Lisa .... 760-355-6257.. 45 K
lisa.seals@imperial.edu
SEALS, Mark .... 419-372-7622 348 G
mseals@bgsu.edu

SEALS, Nireata 505-224-4742 285 N nseals@cnm.edu
SEALS, Victoria 404-225-4600 115 H vseals@atlantatech.edu
SEALY, Gabrielle 802-865-5490 462 A gsealy@champlain.edu
SEALY, Spencer 229-732-5941 115 B spencesealy@andrewcollege.edu
SEALY, Susan 706-649-1016 117 I ssealy@columbustech.edu
SEAMAN, Chuck 615-248-1240 426 D cseaman@trevecca.edu
SEAMAN, Cynthia 610-607-6271 396 H cseaman@racc.edu
SEAMAN, Daniel, B 315-229-5601 314 D dseaman@stlawu.edu
SEAMAN, David 315-443-5533 321 G dseaman@syr.edu
SEAMAN, Diane 937-328-6014 350 G seamand@clarkstate.edu
SEAMAN, Douglas 210-431-5591 441 B dwseaman@ollusa.edu
SEAMAN, Rebecca 360-475-7767 481 I rseaman@olympic.edu
SEAMON, Mike 574-631-9701 162 A mseamon@nd.edu
SEAMS, Jennifer 304-645-6383 490 C jseams@osteo.wvsom.edu
SEAMSTER, JR., Ervin 972-524-3341 445 B
SEAMSTER, Kirsten 336-757-3396 334 F kseamster@forsythtech.edu
SEAQUIST, Carl 717-815-2084 403 F cseaquis@ycp.edu
SEARA, Maira 212-647-7223 311 F mseara@pratt.edu
SEARCY, Douglas, N 252-399-6309 326 K dsearcy@barton.edu
SEARCY, Scott 217-786-2487 143 B scott.searcy@llcc.edu
SEARCY, Yan Dominic 818-677-3317 32 C yan.searcy@csun.edu
SEARING, Linda 585-389-2870 307 F lsearin9@naz.edu
SEARLE, Natalie 802-786-5148 463 F njs12250@ccv.vsc.edu
SEARS, Andrew 816-960-2008 251 G asears@cityvision.edu
SEARS, Andrew, L 814-865-3528 391 G aus67@psu.edu
SEARS, Ashley 503-594-6140 372 C ashley.sears@clackamas.edu
SEARS, Cheryl 916-484-8320 50 G searsc@arc.losrios.edu
SEARS, David 240-567-7492 200 G david.sears@montgomerycollege.edu
SEARS, Douglas, A 617-358-4608 207 E dsears@bu.edu
SEARS, J, W 252-985-5585 339 D wsears@ncwc.edu
SEARS, Marc 336-841-9826 329 F jsears@highpoint.edu
SEARS, Melissa 859-442-1156 181 H melissa.sears@kctcs.edu
SEARS, Richard 706-507-8800 117 H
SEARS, Richard 678-839-5353 127 C rsears@westga.edu
SEARS, Steve, R 956-326-2480 446 E steve.sears@tamiu.edu
SEARS, Steven, A 401-865-2425 404 F ssears@providence.edu
SEARS, Suzanne 940-898-3748 451 D ssears1@twu.edu
SEASOR, Brooke 606-326-2092 181 D brooke.seasor@kctcs.edu
SEATON, Ann 845-758-7047 290 I aseaton@bard.edu
SEATON, Gerald 919-658-7857 340 G jseaton@umo.edu
SEATON, Matthew 815-224-0419 140 E matt_seaton@ivcc.edu
SEATON, Steve 405-692-3191 366 D steve.seaton@macu.edu
SEATON-MARTIN, Marcia 276-656-0276 474 G mseaton-martin@patrickhenry.edu
SEAVER, Catherine 518-464-8500 299 C
SEAVEY, Christopher 404-880-8064 117 C cseavey@cau.edu
SEAWORTH, Timothy 701-355-8150 347 C seaworth@umary.edu
SEAWRIGHT, Lavina 626-584-5464 43 B lavinaseawright@fuller.edu
SEAY, Lonnie 530-242-7912 64 C lseay@shastacollege.edu
SEAY, Scott 317-937-2365 154 G sseay@cts.edu
SEBAALY, Michael 208-769-3303 132 D
SEBALLOS, Shannon 928-428-8339 12 F shannon.seballos@eac.edu
SEBASTIAN, Denise 573-518-2249 256 D denise@mineralarea.edu
SEBASTIAN, J. Jayakiran 215-248-7378 400 D jsebastian@uls.edu
SEBASTIAN, John 310-338-3019 51 A john.sebastian@lmu.edu
SEBASTIAN, Juliann 402-559-4000 269 K julie.sebastian@unmc.edu
SEBASTIAN, Kelly Luce 692-625-3394 504 G ksebastian@cmi.edu
SEBASTIAN, Kurt 904-819-6291 99 E ksebastian@flagler.edu
SEBASTIAN, Pam 660-831-4142 256 I sebastianp@moval.edu
SEBASTIANI, Richard 713-221-8229 453 A sebastianir@uhd.edu
SEBEK, Lawrence 724-938-4440 393 E sebek@calu.edu
SEBER, Geoffrey 518-445-3210 289 K gsebe@albanylaw.edu
SEBOR, Rena 937-512-2919 360 G rena.sebor@sinclair.edu
SEBRING, Amy, S 757-221-1693 465 N
SECHLER, Elizabeth 304-876-5172 490 A esechler@shepherd.edu
SECHREST, Love, L 404-687-4520 117 G sechrestl@ctsnet.edu
SECHRIST, Dawndra 806-743-3223 451 A dawndra.sechrist@ttuhsc.edu
SECHRIST, John 724-653-2184 382 E jsechrist@dec.edu
SECHRIST, Jori 325-793-4772 439 F sechrist.jori@mcm.edu
SECHRIST, Shana 503-370-6236 377 F ssechrist@willamette.edu
SECHRIST, Tim 325-793-4978 439 F sechrist.tim@mcm.edu
SECKA, Lamine 760-750-4568 33 A lsecka@csusm.edu
SECKINGER, Deryl, M 478-289-2090 118 C dseckinger@ega.edu
SECOR, Scott 405-491-6335 369 H ssecor@snu.edu
SECORA, Stephen 570-674-6460 390 B ssecora@misericordia.edu
SECORD, Mark 361-354-2408 432 K secordm@coastalbend.edu
SECORD, Paul 512-863-1211 445 C secordp@southwestern.edu
SECORE, Dan 203-773-8506 85 D dsecore@albertus.edu
SECREST, Amanda 704-272-5300 337 I asecrest@spcc.edu
SECREST, Kathy, L 330-471-8415 355 D ksecrest@malone.edu
SECRIST, Tammi 304-336-8281 490 B tsecrist@westliberty.edu
SECUBAN, Gigi 740-593-2614 358 K secuban@ohio.edu
SEDA, Iris 787-264-1912 508 F iris_seda_rodriguez@intersg.edu
SEDANO, George 510-594-5033 28 B gsedano@cca.edu
SEDATOLE, Karen 404-727-6270 118 E ksedatole@emory.edu
SEDDIKI, Mohamed 973-877-3080 277 G seddiki@essex.edu
SEDEN, John 415-749-4570 61 C jseden@sfai.edu
SEDHOM, Nasser 718-522-9073 290 E nsedhom@asa.edu
SEDILLO, Dacia 575-646-5690 287 C dapachec@nmsu.edu
SEDLACEK, Bernard 531-622-2529 267 G bsedlacek@mccneb.edu
SEDLACEK, John 502-597-6582 183 D john.sedlacek@kysu.edu
SEDLACEK, Paige 607-778-5213 317 D sedlacekpm@sunybroome.edu
SEDLACK, Chris 319-208-5259 170 D csedlack@scciowa.edu
SEDLAK, Darlene, J 570-961-2412 389 D dsedlak@marywood.edu
SEDLAK, John 570-740-0234 389 A jsedlak@luzerne.edu
SEDLMEYER, Julie 209-667-3645 33 B jsedlemeyer@csustan.edu
SEDORE, Chris 617-627-6752 219 C chris.sedore@tufts.edu
SEDRICK, Greg 931-393-1828 424 F gsedrick@mscc.edu
SEDRINE, Ben 904-269-7086 101 I
SEDTAL, Lisa 409-882-3998 449 H lisa.sedtal@lsco.edu
SEDY, Paul 661-362-2200 51 D psedy@masters.edu
SEDYCIAS, Joao 201-200-3001 279 D jsedycias@njcu.edu
SEE, Jonathan 310-506-6256 56 G jonathan.see@pepperdine.edu
SEE, Leslie, C 304-260-4380 488 C lsee@blueridgectc.edu
SEE, Michael 360-992-2413 478 I msee@clark.edu
SEED, Jeff 559-934-2230 74 N jeffseed@whccd.edu
SEEGER, Matthew 313-577-5342 232 K matthew.seeger@wayne.edu
SEEGERT, Paul 206-616-3865 485 A pseegert@uw.edu
SEEKINS, Travis, P 325-670-1589 436 I seekins@hsutx.edu
SEEKLANDER, Marlene 605-882-5284 415 D marlene.seeklander@lakeareatech.edu
SEELA, Joel 320-762-4635 237 C joels@alextech.edu
SEELBACH, Brenda 540-636-2900 465 L brendaseelbach@christendom.edu
SEELEY, Lisa 903-923-2175 435 H lseeley@etbu.edu
SEELEY-CASE, Tiffany 208-732-6454 131 D tseeley@csi.edu
SEELIGSON, Michael 972-883-4464 455 B michael.seeligson@utdallas.edu
SEELY, Heather 413-236-1003 214 A hseely@berkshirecc.edu
SEELY, Tara, M 570-941-7400 401 F tara.seely@scranton.edu
SEELYE, II, Calvin, H 989-774-7471 222 E seely1ch@cmich.edu
SEEMAN, Steve, C 563-588-8000 166 C financialaid@emmaus.edu
SEERY, Denise 303-282-3414 83 H denise.seery@archden.org
SEERY, Joshua 267-295-2330 402 A jseery@walnuthillcollege.edu
SEERY, Sheila 518-956-8163 316 A sseery@albany.edu
SEESENGOOD, Robert 610-921-6610 377 G rseesengood@albright.edu
SEEVERS, JR., Gary 417-862-9533 253 F president@globaluniversity.edu
SEEVERS, Joshua 724-805-2559 398 A joshua.seevers@stvincent.edu
SEEVERS, Scott 402-643-7366 266 G scott.seevers@cune.edu
SEFCIK, Jeffrey 325-942-2041 450 E jeff.sefcik@angelo.edu
SEFCIK, Rachel 732-247-5241 279 C
SEFFERS, Tracy 304-876-5463 490 A tseffers@shepherd.edu
SEFTON, Cindy 513-569-1699 350 F cindy.sefton@cincinnatistate.edu
SEGAL, Jaime, M 908-709-7501 284 D jaime.segal@ucc.edu
SEGAL, Rick 612-455-3420 234 E rick.segal@bcsmn.edu
SEGAR, Robert, B 530-752-2172 69 B rbsegar@ucdavis.edu
SEGAR, Thomas 724-357-4040 394 C t.segar@iup.edu
SEGARRA, Barbara 787-758-2525 512 F barbara.segarra@upr.edu
SEGARRA, Carlos 787-264-1912 508 F csegarra@intersg.edu
SEGARRA, Jose 787-878-5475 507 L jsegarra@arecibo.inter.edu
SEGARRA, Nichole, A 321-682-4522 113 I nsegarra3@valenciacollege.edu
SEGAVE, Robert 585-594-6357 312 E segave_robert@roberts.edu
SEGAY, Gary 505-387-7428 286 I gsegay@navajotech.edu
SEGEL, Baruch 732-765-9126 285 C
SEGGERMAN, Richard 319-352-8215 170 J richard.seggerman@wartburg.edu
SEGGOS, Rose 518-782-6783 315 E rseggos@siena.edu
SEGLE, Zane 843-953-7083 407 C seglez1@citadel.edu
SEGOBIANO, Gina, L 618-235-2700 150 E gina.segobiano@swic.edu
SEGRAN, Sam 806-742-5151 450 F sam.segran@ttu.edu
SEGRUE, Gary 716-375-2525 313 C gsegrue@sbu.edu
SEGUIN, Debbie 715-394-8079 497 C dseguin@uwsuper.edu
SEGUIN, Nancy 989-358-7212 221 C seguinn@alpenacc.edu
SEGURA, Gary, M 310-825-4321 69 E segura@luskin.ucla.edu
SEHER, Kristy 707-476-4112 58 I kristy-seher@redwoods.edu
SEHEULT, Erin 909-558-4508 48 E eseheult@llu.edu
SEHGAL, Mani 808-543-8046 128 G msehgal@hpu.edu
SEHGAL, Varun 718-518-6641 294 B vsehgal@hostos.cuny.edu
SEHLOFF, John, M 507-344-7342 234 C john.sehloff@blc.edu
SEIBEL, Rosalie 701-662-1542 346 C rosalie.seibel@lrsc.edu
SEIBERT, Rhonda, K 844-642-2338 169 A seibertr@nicc.edu
SEIBERT, Susan 618-650-3708 150 C sseiber@siue.edu
SEIBRING, Scott 309-556-3096 140 F iwufaid@iwu.edu
SEIBRING, Steve 309-556-3135 140 F sseibrin@iwu.edu
SEIDE, Reynoso 941-727-2273 112 B
SEIDEL, Edward 307-766-4128 501 I uwpres@uwyo.edu
SEIDEL, Hayden 217-351-2283 147 C hseidel@parkland.edu
SEIDEMAN, Nancy 404-727-0640 118 E nancy.seideman@emory.edu
SEIDEN, Peggy 610-328-8553 398 G pseiden1@swarthmore.edu
SEIDENSTICKER, Duane, P 414-847-3274 494 C duaneseidensticker@miad.edu
SEIDL, David 513-529-8338 356 A seidlda@miamioh.edu
SEIDLER, Howard 803-323-2223 414 D seidlerh@winthrop.edu
SEIDLING, Luke 701-355-8237 347 C
SEIER, Nancy 610-282-1100 382 C nancy.seier@desales.edu
SEIFERLEIN, Mandy 231-591-3805 224 A mandyseiferlein@ferris.edu
SEIFERT, Alice 914-923-2616 311 A aseifert@pace.edu
SEIFERT, Annemarie 860-405-9010 89 D annemarie.seifert@uconn.edu
SEIFERT, Charles 518-783-2321 315 E seifert@siena.edu
SEIFERT, Charles, E 806-743-4200 451 A charles.seifert@ttuhsc.edu
SEIFERT, David 716-270-5348 299 B seifertd@ecc.edu
SEIFERT, Trevor 501-450-3117 23 H tseifert1@uca.edu
SEIG, Mary Theresa 218-755-3874 237 F marytheresa.seig@bemidjistate.edu
SEIGAR, Marcus 419-530-7840 363 B marcus.seigar@utoledo.edu
SEIGART, Denise 570-422-3425 394 A dseigart@esu.edu
SEIGH, William, R 206-726-5002 479 E provost@cornish.edu
SEIJO MALDONADO, Haydee 787-764-0000 513 B haydee.seijo@upr.edu
SEILER, David 512-863-1809 445 C seilerd@southwestern.edu
SEIMEARS, Matt 541-962-3672 372 I mseimears@eou.edu
SEIMERS, Jeff 907-260-7422 9 D
SEINFELD, Laura 516-299-4122 304 E laura.seinfeld@liu.edu
SEIPPEL, Danielle 608-822-2317 500 A dseippel@swtc.edu
SEIRUP, Holly, J 516-463-5318 301 G holly.j.seirup@hofstra.edu
SEITZ, Cindy, L 260-982-5213 159 J clseitz@manchester.edu
SEITZ, Greg 256-782-5368 6 A gseitz@jsu.edu

SEITZ, Gregory .... 717-299-7731 399 C
SEITZ, Thomas .... 530-226-4157.. 64 E
tseitz@simpsonu.edu
SEITZ, Tim .... 440-826-8029 348 D
tseitz@bw.edu
SEITZER, Joan, M .... 410-827-5808 198 F
jseitzer@chesapeake.edu
SEIXAS, Karyn .... 626-395-6161.. 28 J
karyn@caltech.edu
SEJDINAJ, John .... 812-855-7114 156 G
jsej@iu.edu
SEJDINAJ, John .... 812-855-7114 156 F
vpcfo@iu.edu
SEKAS, Kimberly .... 262-595-2500 496 D
sekask@uwp.edu
SEKELSKY, Mary Jo ...... 810-424-5448 232 A
maryjoss@umich.edu
SEKERAK, Robert .... 814-471-0013 393 A
rsekerak@pennhighlands.edu
SEKI, Bill, H .... 213-738-5743.. 66 B
bseki@swlaw.edu
SEKOL, Jennifer .... 570-945-8117 386 F
jennifer.sekol@keystone.edu
SEKSCIENSKI, Gregg ..... 301-687-4209 204 C
gasekscienski@frostburg.edu
SEKUL, Michelle .... 228-497-7647 247 E
michelle.sekul@mgccc.edu
SEKULICH, Brad .... 704-687-7747 342 D
sekulich@uncc.edu
SELASSIE-OKPE,
O'KenZoe .... 650-738-4100.. 62 L
selassieokpeo@smccd.edu
SELBY, David, K .... 317-788-3386 161 H
selbyd@uindy.edu
SELBY, Rosemary .... 478-553-2055 123 H
rselby@oftc.edu
SELBY, Steve .... 714-992-7081.. 54 C
sselby@fullcoll.edu
SELDEN, Pete .... 918-595-7976 370 C
peter.selden@tulsacc.edu
SELDEN, Sally .... 843-953-5007 407 C
sselden@citadel.edu
SELDES, Suzanne .... 772-462-7265 102 F
sseldes@irsc.edu
SELESKY, Melissa .... 848-445-1961 282 A
selesky@rutgers.edu
SELF, Megan .... 970-339-6210.. 77 H
megan.self@aims.edu
SELF, Rosemary .... 662-472-9079 246 D
rself@holmescc.edu
SELF, Sarah .... 865-354-3000 425 C
selfs1@roanestate.edu
SELF, Sheila .... 918-444-2120 366 G
selfsj@nsuok.edu
SELF-DAVIS, LeAnn .... 731-989-6931 419 K
ldavis@fhu.edu
SELIG, C. Wood .... 757-683-3369 469 B
wselig@odu.edu
SELIGER, Jared .... 319-226-2015 163 C
jared.seliger@allencollege.edu
SELIGMAN, Joel .... 802-656-7878 463 A
joel.seligman@uvm.edu
SELIGMAN, Richard, P . 626-395-6073.. 28 J
richard.seligman@caltech.edu
SELIGMANN, Wendy .... 828-771-3033 344 D
wseligmann@warren-wilson.edu
SELIN, Mark .... 920-403-3055 495 B
mark.selin@snc.edu
SELINKO, Katy .... 312-662-4235 132 G
kselinko@adler.edu
SELKIRK, Sara, E .... 816-654-7214 254 E
sselkirk@kcumb.edu
SELL, David, G .... 925-846-6464.. 54 E
SELL, Justin .... 605-688-6388 417 A
justin.sell@sdstate.edu
SELL, Phil .... 847-317-8031 151 C
psell@tiu.edu
SELL MATZKE, Jen .... 320-308-0121 240 I
SELLARS, Frances .... 360-676-2772 481 F
fsellars@nwic.edu
SELLARS, Telly .... 502-213-4294 182 C
telly.sellars@kctcs.edu
SELLAS, Carlos .... 787-840-2575 509 I
csellas@psm.edu
SELLAS, Erik .... 563-884-5400 169 F
erik.sellas@palmer.edu
SELLEN, Mary, K 757-594-7130 465M
mary.sellen@cnu.edu
SELLERS, Darlene .... 406-265-3527 264 E
sellersd@msun.edu
SELLERS, Emma .... 434-791-7116 464 I
elugar@averett.edu
SELLERS, Jeff .... 501-420-1206.. 16 L
jeff.sellers@arkansasbaptist.edu
SELLERS, Karen .... 401-841-6547 503 A
karen.sellers@usnwc.edu
SELLERS, Lauren .... 704-272-5331 337 I
lsellers@spcc.edu
SELLERS, Linda .... 254-442-5151 432 I
linda.sellers@cisco.edu
SELLERS, Martin .... 423-869-6815 421 A
martin.sellers@lmunet.edu
SELLERS, Matt .... 662-562-3292 248 D
msellers@northwestms.edu
SELLERS, Robert, M ...... 734-764-3982 231 H
rsellers@umich.edu
SELLERS, Terrie .... 912-408-3024 125 B
tsellers@savannahtech.edu
SELLERS, Timothy .... 315-279-5685 303 G
tsellers@keuka.edu
SELLERS BATTLE,
Crystal .... 814-641-3173 386 E
battlec@juniata.edu
SELLERS-SELIN, Ellyn .... 607-274-3177 302 G
esellersselin@ithaca.edu
SELLMAN, Carol .... 510-436-1265.. 45 E
sellman@hnu.edu
SELLMANN, James, D ... 671-735-2805 504 F
jsellman@triton.uog.edu
SELLS, Ben, R .... 870-245-5400.. 20 D
sellsb@obu.edu
SELLS, Deanna .... 573-334-6825 259 G
dsells@sehcollege.edu
SELLS, Debra, K .... 615-898-2440 422 C
debra.sells@mtsu.edu
SELLS, Maddie .... 509-453-0374 482 D
maddie.sells@perrytech.edu
SELLS, Tamatha .... 864-941-8363 411 C
sells.t@ptc.edu
SELLS, Vicki, G .... 931-598-3220 423 D
vsells@sewanee.edu
SELMAN, Brenda, V ...... 573-884-9153 261 A
selmanb@missouri.edu
SELMO, Barbara .... 617-349-8267 211 C
bselmo@lesley.edu
SELMON, John .... 231-777-0265 228 G
john.selmon@muskegoncc.edu
SELNER TAN, Anya .... 619-849-2209.. 57 J
aselnert@pointloma.edu
SELNICK, David .... 419-448-3325 361 D
selnickdj@tiffin.edu
SELORIO, Conrad .... 562-860-2451.. 35 H
cselorio@cerritos.edu
SELPH, Justin .... 941-359-7531 106 J
jselph@ringling.edu
SELTZER, Jill .... 832-230-5540 440 E
jseltzer@na.edu
SELTZER-STITT, Jennifer 801-957-4753 461 C
jen.seltzerstitt@slcc.edu
SELVAGGIO, Donna ...... 516-773-5000 503 H
selvaggiod@usmma.edu
SELWITZ, Jason .... 360-596-5409 484 D
jselwitz@spscc.edu
SEM, Daniel, S .... 262-243-5700 492 E
daniel.sem@cuw.edu
SEMAH, Charles .... 732-431-1600 284 B
SEMAN, Elizabeth .... 864-294-3474 409 H
liz.seman@furman.edu
SEMANIE, Victoria, V .... 410-864-4000 202 C
SEMENOFF, Michael ..... 310-377-5501.. 51 C
msemenoff@marymountcalifornia.edu
SEMENZA, Michael, L ... 401-341-2465 405 D
semenzam@salve.edu
SEMERARO, Steve .... 619-961-4259.. 68 A
ssemeraro@tjsl.edu
SEMICH, Robert .... 740-264-5591 352 B
rsemich@egcc.edu
SEMLEY, Lorelle .... 508-793-2769 208 D
lsemley@holycross.edu
SEMMEL, Abraham .... 718-268-4700 312 A
SEMMEL, Ralph .... 443-778-5190 199 G
ralph.semmel@jhuapl.edu
SEMMES, John .... 757-446-5676 466 D
semmesoj@evms.edu
SEMMLERSMITH, Sarah 906-487-7239 224 B
sarah.semmlersmith@finlandia.edu
SEMONES, Andy .... 229-225-3932 126 A
csemones@southernregional.edu
SEMPREBON, Gina .... 413-565-1000 206 D
gsemprebon@baypath.edu
SEMRAU, Kelly .... 863-680-4347 100 H
ksemrau@flsouthern.edu
SEN, Aparna .... 425-739-8100 481 C
aparna.sen@lwtech.edu
SENA, Al .... 505-277-6644 288 J
asena5@unm.edu
SENA, Ali .... 559-453-2236.. 43 A
ali.sena@fresno.edu
SENA, Johanna .... 617-989-4590 219 F
senaj@wit.edu
SENA, Maria .... 505-454-3269 286 J
misena@nmhu.edu
SENAPATIRATNE, Tim ... 651-255-6144 243 E
tsenapatiratne@unitedseminary.edu
SENATORE, Valerie .... 509-434-5060 479 C
valerie.senatore@ccs.spokane.edu
SENATORE, Valerie .... 509-434-5060 479 B
valerie.senatore@ccs.spokane.edu
SENCER, Stephen, D .... 404-727-2016 118 E
steve.sencer@emory.edu
SENCIL, Sabrina .... 916-691-7144.. 50 H
sencils@crc.losrios.edu
SENDERHAUF, Terye ...... 360-417-6322 482 C
tsenderhauf@pencol.edu
SENDLER, Karen .... 646-745-8310 291 A
ksendler@barnard.edu
SENDZE, Monique .... 303-273-3925.. 79 J
msendze@mines.edu
SENECAL, Molly .... 916-608-6688.. 50 I
senacam@flc.losrios.edu
SENECAUT, Tim .... 620-235-4776 177 A
tsenecaut@pittstate.edu
SENECOFF, Julie .... 215-885-2360 389 C
jsenecoff@manor.edu
SENEGAL, Pamela, G .... 336-322-2100 336 G
pamela.senegal@piedmontcc.edu
SENEQUE, Guy .... 516-877-3650 289 I
seneque@adelphi.edu
SENERIZ, Cynthia .... 805-893-8137.. 70 E
cynthia.seneriz@hr.ucsb.edu
SENESE, Jeffrey .... 352-588-8242 107 D
jeffrey.senese@saintleo.edu
SENESE, Richard .... 888-227-3552 234 F
SENESE, Vera .... 347-577-4031 294 A
elvira.senese@lehman.cuny.edu
SENFT, James .... 847-543-2975 136 A
jsenft@clcillinois.edu
SENG, Victoria .... 731-881-7854 427 D
vseng@utm.edu
SENG, Victoria, S .... 731-881-7855 427 D
vseng@utm.edu
SENGUPTA, Ayesha .... 641-472-7000 168 C
asengupta@miu.edu
SENGUPTA, Shivaji .... 347-964-8600 291 J
ssengupta@boricuacollege.edu
SENIE, Kathryn .... 413-755-4749 216 A
kcsenie2001@stcc.edu
SENIOR, Ann Marie .... 609-984-1151 284 C
amsenior@tesu.edu
SENIOR, Timothy, C ..... 610-785-6200 397 E
bsenior@scs.edu
SENKBEIL, Peter .... 949-214-3201.. 39 K
peter.senkbeil@cui.edu
SENKER, Richard .... 813-253-7144 102 B
rsenker@hccfl.edu
SENN, Kate .... 270-534-3143 183 B
catherine.senn@kctcs.edu
SENN, Michael, E .... 301-243-2122 502 L
michael.senn@dodiis.mil
SENN, Sarah .... 334-699-2266.... 1 B
ssenn@acom.edu
SENNETT, Peter .... 978-630-9160 215 C
psennett@mwcc.mass.edu
SENSENIG, Jayne .... 717-866-5775 383 F
SENSENIG, Melvin .... 610-921-7708 377 G
msensenig@albright.edu
SENSENIG, Victor .... 410-778-7201 205 B
vsensenig2@washcoll.edu
SENSER, Randie .... 212-247-3434 304 L
rsenser@mandl.edu
SENSI, Patricia .... 732-224-2234 276 B
psensi@brookdalecc.edu
SENSIBAUGH,
Cyndee, K .... 304-367-4933 488 H
cyndee.sensibaugh@pierpont.edu
SENTER, Jim .... 915-747-5347 455 C
jsenter@utep.edu
SENTER, Timothy, C ..... 662-862-8460 246 E
tcsenter@iccms.edu
SENTER, William .... 830-372-6550 449 A
wsenter@tlu.edu
SENTZ, Justin .... 717-477-1507 395 B
jasentz@ship.edu
SEO, EunJa .... 714-525-0088.. 43 J
library@gm.edu
SEO, Hillary .... 515-294-3540 163 G
hseo@iastate.edu
SEO, Sang Bae .... 636-327-4645 256 B
seoul@midwest.edu
SEPANIC, Michael, J ..... 856-225-6026 281 G
msepanic@camden.rutgers.edu
SEPEDA MCLEAN,
Sandra .... 972-438-6932 441 E
slmclean@parker.edu
SEPEHRI, Mohamad ...... 202-274-7050.. 94 B
mohamad.sepehri@udc.edu
SEPLOW, Suzanne .... 310-825-3401.. 69 E
suzanne@orl.ucla.edu
SEPPALA, Julie .... 906-487-2642 228 A
jhseppal@mtu.edu
SEPULVEDA, Dolores .... 787-891-0925 507 K
dsepulve@aguadilla.inter.edu
SEPULVEDA, Pamela ..... 562-860-2451.. 35 H
psepulveda@cerritos.edu
SEQUEIRA, Gerald .... 626-914-8517.. 36 J
gsequeira@citruscollege.edu
SERAFIMOV, Val .... 417-873-7262 252 G
vserafimov@drury.edu
SERAFIN, Julie .... 304-558-4128 489 H
julie.serafin@wvhepc.edu
SERAFIN, Renata .... 210-486-4689 428 I
rserafin@alamo.edu
SERAFINO, Candice, J .. 413-545-6253 211 G
serafino@acad.umass.edu
SERBAN, Andreea .... 714-438-4698.. 37 I
aserban@cccd.edu
SERBANTES, Jessica, A 210-829-6030 453 C
serbante@uiwtx.edu
SERBER, Michael .... 214-648-9569 457 A
michael.serber@utsouthwestern.edu
SERBY-WILKENS, Anja .. 757-455-3215 477 C
aserbywilkens@vwu.edu
SERCK, Steve .... 704-406-2707 329 A
sserck@gardner-webb.edu
SERENA, Joe .... 209-384-6000.. 52 A
SERGE, Lucia .... 305-821-3333 100 E
lserge@fnu.edu
SERGE, Susan .... 307-681-6082 501 G
sserge@sheridan.edu
SERGEANT, SR., Glenn . 501-975-8536.. 20 F
gsergeant@philander.edu
SERGENT, Ann .... 419-559-2147 361 C
asergent01@terra.edu
SERGEYEVA, Larisa .... 714-564-6806.. 58 F
sergeyeva_larisa@sac.edu
SERGIO, Tiffany .... 310-233-4208.. 49 B
sergiot@lahc.edu
SERIO, Tricia, R .... 413-545-2766 211 G
tserio@umass.edu
SERJOIE, Ara .... 336-316-2320 329 D
serjoiea@guilford.edu
SERLING, Kitty .... 816-276-4309 258 G
c.serling@researchcollege.edu
SERNA, Carlos .... 562-860-2451.. 35 H
cserna@cerritos.edu
SERNA, Edward .... 207-778-7256 196 I
edward.serna@maine.edu
SERNA, Falone .... 562-907-4820.. 76 B
fserna@whittier.edu
SERNA, Lauren .... 207-778-7058 196 I
lauren.serna@maine.edu
SERNA-WALLENDER,
Alex .... 210-999-7311 451 E
asernawa@trinity.edu
SERNOE, James .... 940-397-4000 440 C
james.sernoe@msutexas.edu
SEROVICH, Julianne ...... 813-974-1992 111 C
jserovich@usf.edu
SERPETTE, Anthony, W . 330-972-7758 361 H
serpette@uakron.edu
SERR, Jim .... 815-280-6641 141 B
jserr@jjc.edu
SERR, Russel .... 310-660-3593.. 41 E
rserr@elcamino.edu
SERRA, Ann .... 313-993-1469 231 E
serraam@udmercy.edu
SERRA, Elena .... 201-761-6366 283 A
eserra@saintpeters.edu
SERRA, Neuza .... 856-225-6005 281 G
nmserra@camden.rutgers.edu
SERRANO, Alex .... 903-223-3114 448 A
alexander.serrano@tamut.edu
SERRANO, Carlos, A ..... 718-982-2460 293 E
carlos.serrano@csi.cuny.edu
SERRANO, Fabian .... 432-264-5077 437 F
fserrano@howardcollege.edu
SERRANO, Iris .... 787-743-7979 510 H
SERRANO, Lucille .... 831-755-6900.. 44 G
lserrano@hartnell.edu

SHAFFETT, John .... 706-233-7357 125 C
jshaffett@shorter.edu
SHAFIZADEH, Kevan ..... 916-278-6366.. 32 D
SHAFKOWITZ, Marshall 479-619-8600.. 20 C
mshafkowitz@nwacc.edu
SHAFRIN, Bonnie .... 414-425-8300 495 A
bshafrin@shsst.edu
SHAFTEL, Matthew .... 740-593-1808 358 K
shaftel@ohio.edu
SHAGER, Dorian .... 765-658-4267 154 J
dshager@depauw.edu
SHAH, Gaurav .... 781-891-3467 206 G
gshah@bentley.edu
SHAH, Kashif .... 708-974-5348 145 A
shah@morainevalley.edu
SHAH, Swapnal .... 800-280-0307 153 E
swapnal.shah@ace.edu
SHAH, Vishal .... 610-738-0536 395 D
vshah@wcupa.edu
SHAH-GORDON, Ruta ... 718-420-4254 324 F
rshahgor@wagner.edu
SHAHEDIPOUR-SANDVIK,
Shadi .... 315-792-7100 321 B
sshahedipour-sandvik@sunypoly.edu
SHAHEED-SONUBI,
Taheera .... 716-851-1773 299 B
shaheed@ecc.edu
SHAHEEN, Lisa .... 212-686-9244 290 C
SHAHI,
Manvinder (Vinay) ...... 650-289-3336.. 59 J
manvinder.shahi@stpatricksseminary.org
SHAHID, Abdus .... 503-838-9331 377 D
shahida@wou.edu
SHAHID, Charles .... 937-376-6332 349 J
cshahid@centralstate.edu
SHAHID, Charles .... 937-376-6081 349 J
cshahid@centralstate.edu
SHAHID-BELLOT,
Robyn .... 617-873-1191 208 B
robyn.shahid-bellot@cambridgecollege.edu
SHAHID-BELLOT,
Robyn .... 857-701-1494 215 G
rshahid-bellot@rcc.mass.edu
SHAHIN, Hamdi .... 201-559-6076 277 J
shahinh@felician.edu
SHAHIN, Wisam .... 908-709-7024 284 D
wisam.shahin@ucc.edu
SHAHISAMAN,
Mohammad .... 951-493-6753.. 77 B
mshahisaman@yacollege.edu
SHAHRABI, Kamal .... 585-475-2411 312 F
kxscada@rit.edu
SHAHROKHI, Hossein .. 713-221-8542 453 A
shahrokhi@uhd.edu
SHAIKH, Usama .... 516-876-3175 318 C
shaikhu@oldwestbury.edu
SHAIN, Daniel .... 856-225-6144 281 G
dshain@camden.rutgers.edu
SHAIN, Sue .... 978-556-3710 215 E
sshain@necc.mass.edu
SHAIN, Yeruchim .... 732-431-1600 284 B
SHAINDLIN, Andrew ..... 401-863-3189 403 J
andrew_shaindlin@brown.edu
SHAKE, Miranda .... 217-709-0927 142 D
mshake@lakeviewcol.edu
SHAKESPEARE,
Christine .... 212-346-1200 311 A
SHAKESPEARE,
Shannon .... 516-299-3522 304 D
SHAKIBA, Trevor .... 918-333-6151 368 E
llittle@okwu.edu
SHAKIR, Salah .... 859-846-6248 184 B
sshakir@midway.edu
SHAKYA, Miroj .... 626-571-8811.. 73 E
mirojs@uwest.edu
SHALHOUB, Robert .... 973-379-2044 379 F
finance@archpitt.org
SHALLEY, Heather .... 312-329-4272 144 I
heather.shalley@moody.edu
SHAMAH, Irwin .... 347-394-1036 291 F
SHAMBARGER, Angela .. 207-221-4554 197 E
ashambarger@une.edu
SHAMBAUGH, Jeannine 330-363-5420 348 C
jeannine.shambaugh@aultman.com
SHAMBLEE, Crystal .... 410-225-4265 200 D
cshamblee@mica.edu
SHAMBLIN, Mesha .... 304-710-3401 488 F
shamblinm@mctc.edu
SHAMBURGER,
Katherine .... 318-869-5280 186 F
kshamburger@centenary.edu

SHAMES, Shauna .... 856-225-2974 281 G
shauna.shames@rutgers.edu
SHAMIM, Jina .... 415-476-8850.. 70 D
jina.shamim@ucsf.edu
SHAMOO, Yousif .... 713-348-5741 442 F
shamoo@rice.edu
SHAMS, Arian .... 714-300-0300.. 65 F
ashams@scitech.edu
SHAMS, Nazila .... 714-300-0300.. 65 F
nshams@scitech.edu
SHAMS, Parviz .... 714-300-0300.. 65 F
pshams@scitech.edu
SHAMSUD-DIN, Ayasha 503-552-1608 374 D
ashamsud-din@nunm.edu
SHANAFELT, Rebecca .... 727-816-3288 105 F
shanafr@phsc.edu
SHANAHAN, Alanna ...... 215-898-9828 400 F
athdir@upenn.edu
SHANAHAN, Brian .... 607-871-2144 290 B
shanahan@alfred.edu
SHANAHAN, James ...... 812-855-1963 156 G
jes30@indiana.edu
SHANAHAN, Jenny .... 508-531-2764 212 D
jshanahan@bridgew.edu
SHANAHAN, Kristina ..... 706-295-6332 119 D
kshanaha@highlands.edu
SHANAHAN, Michael .... 805-965-0581.. 63 A
SHANAHAN, Thomas .... 919-962-4588 340 H
tcshanahan@northcarolina.edu
SHANDA, Mark .... 859-257-1707 185 F
mark.shanda@uky.edu
SHANDERSON, Laurie ... 866-776-0331.. 54 D
lshanderson@ncu.edu
SHANDERSON, Laurie ... 309-672-5583 144 C
lshanderson@methodistcol.edu
SHANDLEY, Emily .... 203-432-2337.. 90 C
emily.shandley@yale.edu
SHANDLEY, Janet .... 206-296-5904 484 A
janshan@seattleu.edu
SHANDOR, Britnee .... 404-297-9522 120 B
SHANE, Pam .... 740-284-5193 352 I
pshane@franciscan.edu
SHANER, Megan, L .... 919-209-2201 335 F
mlshaner@johnstoncc.edu
SHANG, Ying .... 260-422-5561 156 E
yshang@indianatech.edu
SHANGLE, Max .... 770-689-4791 115 C
mshangle@aii.edu
SHANHOLTZ, Cathy ...... 540-665-5561 470 G
cshanhol2@su.edu
SHANK, Christy .... 254-526-1291 432 D
christy.shank@ctcd.edu
SHANK, Derek .... 520-494-5527.. 11 K
derek.shank@centralaz.edu
SHANK, Jeffrey, A .... 540-432-4206 466 B
jeff.shank@emu.edu
SHANK, Jennifer .... 931-372-3016 426 B
jshank@tntech.edu
SHANK, Matthew .... 703-284-1598 468 H
matthew.shank@marymount.edu
SHANK, Sherri .... 704-233-8025 344 F
s.shank@wingate.edu
SHANK, Steve .... 704-233-8691 344 F
sh.shank@wingate.edu
SHANK, Theresa, M ...... 240-500-2476 199 C
tmshank@hagerstowncc.edu
SHANKEL, James, V ...... 412-578-6258 380 B
jvshankel@carlow.edu
SHANKER, Anil .... 615-327-6460 421 D
ashanker@mmc.edu
SHANKLE, Julie .... 321-674-8202 100 C
jshankle@fit.edu
SHANKLE, Nicole .... 812-381-6002 162 F
nshankle@vinu.edu
SHANKLIN, Iris .... 404-756-4916 115 G
ishanklin@atlm.edu
SHANKMAN,
Kimberly, C .... 913-360-7413 171 J
kshankman@benedictine.edu
SHANKS, Alisa .... 303-963-3378.. 78 H
ashanks@ccu.edu
SHANKS, Brian .... 512-245-2319 450 C
bs26@txstate.edu
SHANKS, Cindy .... 918-595-8291 370 C
cindy.shanks@tulsacc.edu
SHANLEY, OP, Brian, J 718-990-6301 313 G
pres@stjohns.edu
SHANMUGARATNAM,
Carol .... 781-283-2308 219 E
cshanmug@wellesley.edu
SHANNON, David .... 405-878-6000 367 B
david.shannon@okbu.edu

SHANNON, David, R ..... 731-989-6001 419 K
dshannon@fhu.edu
SHANNON, Denise .... 313-496-2744 232 E
dshanno1@wcccd.edu
SHANNON, Erin .... 217-353-2683 147 C
eshannon@parkland.edu
SHANNON, Henry, D .... 909-652-6100.. 35 L
henry.shannon@chaffey.edu
SHANNON, John .... 260-665-4224 161 E
shannonj@trine.edu
SHANNON, JR.,
John, T .... 901-321-3250 418 G
jack.shannon@cbu.edu
SHANNON, Kelly .... 612-238-4515 243 C
kshannon@smumn.edu
SHANNON, Kim .... 864-388-8885 410 A
kshannon@lander.edu
SHANNON, LaToya .... 386-481-2942.. 96 D
shannonl@cookman.edu
SHANNON, Linda, A ..... 718-990-6578 313 G
shannonl@stjohns.edu
SHANNON, Patricia .... 610-359-2183 382 A
pshannon@dccc.edu
SHANNON, Peggy .... 619-594-4464.. 33 D
pshannon@sdsu.edu
SHANNON, S. Scott ...... 315-470-6537 319 D
sshannon@esf.edu
SHANNON, Sarah .... 406-994-3784 264 C
sarah.shannon1@montana.edu
SHANNON, Susan, K ..... 717-796-1800 389 H
sshannon@messiah.edu
SHANTON, David .... 646-660-6067 292 L
david.shanton@baruch.cuny.edu
SHAO, Alan, T .... 843-953-6651 408 C
shaoa@cofc.edu
SHAO, Chris .... 254-968-1944 446 D
shao@tarleton.edu
SHAO, Lawrence .... 724-738-2093 395 C
lawrence.shao@sru.edu
SHAO, Rodrick .... 830-372-8000 449 A
rshao@tlu.edu
SHAO, Yu-Ling .... 410-704-4011 204 E
yulingshao@towson.edu
SHAPE, Ronald .... 605-721-5214 415 G
rshape@national.edu
SHAPIRO, Claire, R ...... 901-843-3750 423 A
shapiro@rhodes.edu
SHAPIRO, Dan .... 831-582-3878.. 32 B
dshapiro@csumb.edu
SHAPIRO, David, W ...... 717-867-6060 388 C
shapiro@lvc.edu
SHAPIRO, Jeff .... 973-877-3142 277 G
shapiro@essex.edu
SHAPIRO, Joe .... 657-278-3724.. 31 C
jbshapiro@fullerton.edu
SHAPIRO, Joseph, I ...... 304-691-1700 489 M
shapiroj@marshall.edu
SHAPIRO, Philip .... 508-286-8200 220 B
SHAPIRO, Steven .... 617-349-8458 211 C
sshapir3@lesley.edu
SHAPIRO DAVIS,
Andrea .... 646-664-9100 292 K
SHAPOVAL, Sandy .... 918-270-6459 368 G
sandy.shapoval@ptstulsa.edu
SHAPPLEY, Ben .... 662-696-2312 248 C
bshappley@nemcc.edu
SHARAR, Scott .... 319-352-8318 170 J
scott.sharar@wartburg.edu
SHARBAUGH,
Sheila, M .... 302-356-3917.. 91 E
sheila.m.sharbaugh@wilmu.edu
SHARBAUGH, Tim, L .... 724-357-3011 394 G
timothy.sharbaugh@iup.edu
SHARER, C. Gregory ..... 607-753-4721 318 A
greg.sharer@cortland.edu
SHARER, Mark .... 570-577-3914 379 C
mark.sharer@bucknell.edu
SHARIAT, Vahid .... 714-816-0366.. 68 E
vahid.shariat@trident.edu
SHARIF, Zaki .... 937-376-6007 349 J
zsharif@centralstate.edu
SHARK, Steven .... 701-662-1655 346 C
steven.shark@lrsc.edu
SHARKEY, Brian .... 563-884-5306 169 F
brian.sharkey@palmer.edu
SHARKEY, Fredricka ...... 501-852-2659.. 23 H
fsharkey@uca.edu
SHARKEY, Kevin .... 724-738-3333 395 C
kevin.sharkey@sru.edu
SHARKEY, Marty .... 323-259-2934.. 54 I
msharkey@oxy.edu
SHARMA, Gulshan .... 409-772-2436 456 E
gusharma@utmb.edu

SHARMA, Malhar .... 203-576-2348.. 89 C
msharma@bridgeport.edu
SHARMA, Pam .... 304-214-8891 488 J
psharma@wvncc.edu
SHARMA, Salil .... 626-350-1500.. 28 F
SHARMA, Sanjay .... 802-656-3175 463 A
sanjay.sharma@uvm.edu
SHARMA,
Venkatanarayanan .... 973-720-2432 284 J
sharmav@wpunj.edu
SHARMAN, Sandra .... 478-289-2033 118 C
sharman@ega.edu
SHARNSKY, Brittany ...... 210-805-5832 453 C
sharnsky@uiwtx.edu
SHARON, Daniel .... 914-632-5400 307 A
dsharon@monroecollege.edu
SHARP, Andrew .... 601-477-4198 246 G
andrew.sharp@jcjc.edu
SHARP, Anthony .... 310-289-5123.. 74 I
anthony.sharp@wcui.edu
SHARP, Chris .... 806-371-5008 429 E
chris.sharp@actx.edu
SHARP, David .... 870-245-5181.. 20 D
sharpd@obu.edu
SHARP, Debbie .... 940-668-4213 440 F
dsharp@nctc.edu
SHARP, Deltha .... 870-612-2057.. 22 H
deltha.sharp@uaccb.edu
SHARP, Donna .... 918-724-6444 365 C
sharpd@bacone.edu
SHARP, Jan, T .... 865-539-7182 425 B
jtsharp@pstcc.edu
SHARP, Jason .... 620-421-6700 175 F
jasons@labette.edu
SHARP, Jason, R .... 651-631-5045 244 D
jrsharp@unwsp.edu
SHARP, John .... 979-458-6000 446 B
chancellor@tamus.edu
SHARP, Jordan .... 559-453-7104.. 43 A
jordan.sharp@fresno.edu
SHARP, Jordan .... 435-652-7544 460 B
jsharp@dixie.edu
SHARP, Kelvin .... 575-392-5004 287 A
ksharp@nmjc.edu
SHARP, Kimberly .... 601-925-3278 247 C
ksharp@mc.edu
SHARP, Kirk .... 620-223-2700 173 I
kirks@fortscott.edu
SHARP, Lara .... 413-755-4576 216 A
llsharp@stcc.edu
SHARP, Leslie .... 404-385-7590 119 E
leslie.sharp@gatech.edu
SHARP, Linda .... 573-876-7277 260 B
lsharp@stephens.edu
SHARP, Nick .... 417-690-2224 251 H
sharp@cofo.edu
SHARP, Nicole .... 812-749-1225 159 O
nsharp@oak.edu
SHARP, Randy .... 808-675-3499 128 D
randy.sharp@byuh.edu
SHARP, Samantha .... 870-633-4480.. 19 A
ssharp@eacc.edu
SHARP, Valerie .... 417-865-2815 253 D
sharpv@evangel.edu
SHARP-MCHENRY,
Lepaine .... 617-521-2000 218 G
SHARPE, Allen .... 803-732-5211 410 D
sharpea@midlandstech.edu
SHARPE, Amory .... 415-771-7020.. 61 C
asharpe@sfai.edu
SHARPE, Anna .... 706-233-4080 116 B
asharpe@berry.edu
SHARPE, Dolores .... 810-762-5698 228 F
dolores.sharpe@mcc.edu
SHARPE, Jessica .... 336-272-7102 329 C
jessica.sharpe@greensboro.edu
SHARPE, Kelli .... 615-963-1232 426 A
SHARPE, Michael .... 312-358-3132 125 A
sharpem@savannahstate.edu
SHARPE, Norean, R ...... 718-990-6800 313 G
sharpen@stjohns.edu
SHARPE, Paul .... 956-882-8221 455 D
paul.sharpe@utrgv.edu
SHARPE, Ron .... 989-275-5000 226 D
ron.sharpe@kirtland.edu
SHARPHORN, Dan .... 512-499-4462 454 H
dsharphorn@utsystem.edu
SHARPLES, Stacey .... 941-752-5256 109 G
sharpls@scf.edu
SHARPNACK, Patricia ... 440-684-6032 363 C
psharpnack@ursuline.edu
SHARPS, Chris .... 304-367-4000 489 K

SHELLEY, Jennifer, A .... 812-941-2280 157 F
jashelle@iu.edu
SHELLEY, Joseph .... 315-859-4169 300 H
jshelley@hamilton.edu
SHELLEY, Kate .... 903-813-2050 430 H
kshelley@austincollege.edu
SHELLEY, MargE .... 913-469-8500 174 I
mshelley@jccc.edu
SHELLEY, Marshall .... 303-762-6919.. 80 I
marshall.shelley@denverseminary.edu
SHELLEY, Staci .... 352-588-7560 107 D
staci.shelley@saintleo.edu
SHELLEY, Staci .... 866-492-5336 244 F
staci.shelley@laureate.net
SHELLLEY, Joe .... 315-859-4169 300 H
jshelley@hamilton.edu
SHELMERDINE,
Kathleen .... 239-687-5345.. 95 L
kshelmerdine@avemarialaw.edu
SHELPMAN, JR., David . 561-586-0121 101 O
SHELSTAD, Kyle .... 612-351-0631 236 E
kshelstad@ipr.edu
SHELTON, Alice .... 317-955-6022 159 K
ashelton@marian.edu
SHELTON, Austin .... 671-735-2918 504 F
shelton@uog.edu
SHELTON, Brad .... 541-346-2090 376 H
shelton@uoregon.edu
SHELTON, Charlita .... 509-313-4356 480 F
sheltonc@gonzaga.edu
SHELTON, Cheryl .... 810-762-0553 228 F
cheryl.shelton@edtech.mcc.edu
SHELTON, Christie .... 256-782-5540.... 6 A
cshelton@jsu.edu
SHELTON, Courtney ...... 800-280-0307 153 E
courtney.shelton@ace.edu
SHELTON, Courtney ...... 864-278-6281 412 F
sheltonc@smcsc.edu
SHELTON, Edward .... 636-649-5807 253 B
edward.shelton@eastcentral.edu
SHELTON, Jamie .... 904-256-8000 102 H
SHELTON, Joey .... 601-974-1226 247 B
sheltonjj@millsaps.edu
SHELTON, Julie .... 205-348-7917.... 7 G
jshelton@fa.ua.edu
SHELTON, Julie .... 931-363-9895 427 E
jshelt48@utsouthern.edu
SHELTON, Marc .... 503-554-2869 373 A
mshelton@georgefox.edu
SHELTON, Mark .... 508-793-2371 208 D
mshelton@holycross.edu
SHELTON, Michelle .... 610-499-4239 402 G
mmshelton@widener.edu
SHELTON, Myles .... 409-944-1200 436 E
mshelton@gc.edu
SHELTON, Nellie, R .... 864-833-8213 411 D
nshelton@presby.edu
SHELTON, Rick .... 315-792-7100 321 B
richard.shelton@sunypoly.edu
SHELTON, Robby .... 931-363-9890 427 E
rshelt19@utsouthern.edu
SHELTON, Ryan .... 219-980-6793 157 C
rydshelt@iun.edu
SHELTON, Shawna .... 509-533-4566 479 D
shawna.shelton@sfcc.spokane.edu
SHELTON, Terri .... 336-334-5495 343 A
tlshelto@uncg.edu
SHELTON, Terri, L .... 336-256-0232 343 A
shelton@uncg.edu
SHELTON, Tina .... 773-896-2400 134 L
SHEMMER, Rosalie .... 312-899-5100 149 F
SHEMWELL, Bridget ...... 870-762-3174.. 17 B
bshemwell@smail.anc.edu
SHEMWELL, James .... 870-762-3191.. 17 B
jshemwell@smail.anc.edu
SHEN, Chi .... 502-597-6083 183 D
chi.shen@kysu.edu
SHEN, Mark .... 626-571-5110.. 48 D
mys2016@les.edu
SHEN, Sunny .... 516-739-1545 308 F
academic_dean@nyctcm.edu
SHEN-AUSTIN,
Christina .... 202-250-2419.. 92 C
christina.shen-austin@gallaudet.edu
SHENBERGER, Amy .... 940-565-2354 453 E
amy.shenberger@unt.edu
SHENETTE, John .... 336-758-4623 344 C
shenettjj@wfu.edu
SHENETTE, John .... 336-758-5000 344 C
shenetjj@wfu.edu
SHENK, Hans .... 740-857-1311 360 D
hshenk@rosedale.edu

SHENNAN, Andrew .... 781-283-3583 219 E
ashennan@wellesley.edu
SHENNOY, Anitha .... 559-325-3600.. 28 D
ashennoy@chsu.edu
SHENODA, Matthew ...... 401-454-6444 405 B
mshenoda@risd.edu
SHEPARD, Anne .... 301-546-7527 201 E
sheparaf@pgcc.edu
SHEPARD, Barry .... 412-809-5338 396 E
shepard.barry@ptcollege.edu
SHEPARD, Brian .... 408-498-5135.. 73 B
bshepard@cogswell.edu
SHEPARD, Jenni .... 706-865-2134 126 E
jshepard@truett.edu
SHEPARD, Jeremy .... 617-217-9218 206 E
jshepard@baystate.edu
SHEPARD, Joseph .... 575-538-6238 289 G
joseph.shepard@wnmu.edu
SHEPARD, Kathy, J .... 717-728-2261 380 E
kathyshepard@centralpenn.edu
SHEPARD, Kirsten .... 800-686-1883 222 G
kshepard@cleary.edu
SHEPARD, Nicole .... 912-583-3298 116 E
nshepard@bpc.edu
SHEPARD, Thom .... 650-433-3814.. 55 L
tshepard@paloaltou.edu
SHEPARD, William .... 734-487-0296 223 K
bill.shepard@emich.edu
SHEPARD RAWLINS,
Cindy .... 540-231-5419 466 K
crawlins@vcom.vt.edu
SHEPARDSON,
J. Andrew .... 781-891-2161 206 G
ashepardson@bentley.edu
SHEPELOV, Sergey .... 503-491-7411 374 B
sergey.shepelov@mhcc.edu
SHEPERIS, Carl .... 210-784-2500 447 E
csheperis@tamusa.edu
SHEPHARD, Landon, P . 407-582-4877 113 I
lshephard@valenciacollege.edu
SHEPHERD, Janet .... 319-208-5053 170 D
jshepherd@scciowa.edu
SHEPHERD, Jennifer, A 603-646-2223 273 D
jennifer.a.shepherd@dartmouth.edu
SHEPHERD, Jerry .... 765-677-1903 158 B
jerry.shepherd@indwes.edu
SHEPHERD, Justin .... 404-727-0692 118 E
justin.shepherd@emory.edu
SHEPHERD, Karen .... 510-845-5373.. 29 B
SHEPHERD, Katharine ... 802-656-3424 463 A
katharine.shepherd@uvm.edu
SHEPHERD, Lewis .... 870-245-5302.. 20 D
shepherdl@obu.edu
SHEPHERD, Margaret .... 206-399-1496 485 A
mshep@uw.edu
SHEPHERD, Misty .... 407-823-2339 110 E
misty.shepherd@ucf.edu
SHEPHERD, Sara .... 252-334-2010 331 F
sara.shepherd@macuniversity.edu
SHEPHERD, Stacy .... 318-371-3035 188 F
stacyshepherd@nltcc.edu
SHEPHERD, Steve .... 417-690-2569 251 H
shepherd@cofo.edu
SHEPHERD, Sue .... 330-363-6347 348 C
admissions@aultmancollege.edu
SHEPHERD, Thomas ..... 661-946-2274.. 74 H
SHEPPARD, Andy .... 229-226-1621 126 C
asheppard@thomasu.edu
SHEPPARD, Deana .... 903-510-2261 452 A
deana.sheppard@tjc.edu
SHEPPARD, Kirsten .... 865-273-8991 421 C
kirsten.sheppard@maryvillecollege.edu
SHEPPARD, Ray .... 910-879-5542 332 D
rsheppard@bladencc.edu
SHEPPARD, Varinya ...... 315-801-3014 313 D
vsheppar@secon.edu
SHEPPLEY, Lisa .... 410-225-2237 200 D
lsheppley@mica.edu
SHEPROW, Lauren .... 631-632-4896 317 A
lauren.sheprow@stonybrook.edu
SHEPSON, Paul .... 631-632-8781 317 A
paul.shepson@stonybrook.edu
SHEPTAK, Juliann .... 724-287-8711 379 E
julie.sheptak@bc3.edu
SHER, Anna .... 831-459-4302.. 71 A
asher@ucsc.edu
SHER, Ephraim, Y .... 845-434-5240 326 J
esher@ygzm.edu
SHERADIN, Pamela .... 315-364-3260 324 I
psheradin@wells.edu
SHERAM, Norma .... 903-675-6211 451 F
nsheram@tvcc.edu

SHERAR, Megan .... 419-289-5943 347 J
msherar@ashland.edu
SHERBEYN, Aaron .... 217-234-5253 142 C
asherbeyn@lakelandcollege.edu
SHERBURNE, Gwen .... 651-523-2804 236 B
gsherburne@hamline.edu
SHERER, Sara .... 330-823-2761 362 E
sherersj@mountunion.edu
SHERER, Todd .... 404-727-5550 118 E
ttshere@emory.edu
SHERF, Thomas .... 215-702-4848 380 A
tsherf@cairn.edu
SHERFESEE,
Kimberly, B .... 843-349-2138 408 A
ksherf@coastal.edu
SHERIDAN, Andrea .... 512-475-6089 455 A
andrea.sheridan@austin.utexas.edu
SHERIDAN, Chris .... 216-368-2774 349 D
chris.sheridan@case.edu
SHERIDAN, Heidi .... 732-255-0400 279 F
hsheridan@ocean.edu
SHERIDAN, Kevin, P ..... 262-243-5700 492 E
kevin.sheridan@cuw.edu
SHERIDAN, Mark .... 806-742-1832 450 F
mark.sheridan@ttu.edu
SHERIDAN, Terence ...... 334-387-3877.... 4 B
terencesheridan@amridgeuniversity.edu
SHERIFF, Brad .... 573-651-2570 259 H
bsheriff@semo.edu
SHERIFF, Omar .... 708-596-2000 149 H
osheriff@ssc.edu
SHERIFF, Sarah, M .... 717-245-1787 382 D
sheriffs@dickinson.edu
SHERKAWY, Yasser ...... 281-495-0078 437 E
SHERLIN, Joe, H .... 423-439-4210 419 G
sherlin@etsu.edu
SHERLOCK, Julia, B ...... 989-774-3068 222 E
sherl1jb@cmich.edu
SHERLOCK, Rick .... 419-448-2171 353 E
rsherloc@heidelberg.edu
SHERMAN, Alexis .... 402-399-2365 266 F
asherman@csm.edu
SHERMAN, Alison .... 401-709-8417 405 B
asherman@risd.edu
SHERMAN, Brian .... 318-798-4117 190 A
brian.sherman@lsus.edu
SHERMAN, Courtney ..... 920-465-2033 495 F
shermanc@uwgb.edu
SHERMAN, Curt .... 402-643-7369 266 G
curt.sherman@cune.edu
SHERMAN, Daniel .... 713-500-3270 456 B
daniel.sherman@uth.tmc.edu
SHERMAN, Douglas, H . 401-739-5000 404 E
dsherman@neit.edu
SHERMAN, Erin, L .... 210-486-4932 428 I
esherman6@alamo.edu
SHERMAN, Glen .... 973-720-2761 284 J
shermang@wpunj.edu
SHERMAN, Heather .... 610-921-2381 377 G
SHERMAN, Holly .... 507-433-0606 240 G
holly.sherman@riverland.edu
SHERMAN, Hugh .... 740-593-1804 358 K
president@ohio.edu
SHERMAN, Jennifer .... 719-549-3362.. 82 J
jennifer.sherman@pueblocc.edu
SHERMAN, JR .... 239-489-9414 101 A
j.r.sherman@fsw.edu
SHERMAN, Julee .... 660-248-6203 251 E
jsherman@centralmethodist.edu
SHERMAN, Lori Ann ...... 906-524-8414 226 C
lsherman@kbocc.edu
SHERMAN, Malia .... 559-278-6777.. 31 B
msherman@csufresno.edu
SHERMAN, Mike .... 330-941-7281 364 H
msherman02@ysu.edu
SHERMAN, Moshe .... 212-463-0400 322 G
michael.sherman2@touro.edu
SHERMAN, Peter .... 970-943-3000.. 85 C
psherman@western.edu
SHERMAN, Renee .... 207-621-3041 196 H
renee.sherman@maine.edu
SHERMAN, Robin .... 207-581-5401 196 G
robin.sherman@maine.edu
SHERMAN, Rush .... 502-585-9911 184 H
rsherman@spalding.edu
SHERMAN, Sherry .... 828-766-1317 336 A
ssherman@mayland.edu
SHERMAN, Stasia .... 660-248-6239 251 E
ssherman@centralmethodist.edu
SHERMAN, Suzanne ...... 941-487-4225 110 D
sherman@ncf.edu
SHERMAN, Timothy ...... 770-612-2170.. 93 H

SHERMAN, Zahida .... 440-775-8462 357 G
zsherman@oberlin.edu
SHERMAN HECKLER,
Wendy, R .... 614-823-1556 359 H
wshermanheckler@otterbein.edu
SHERR, Karin, K .... 619-961-4240.. 68 A
ksherr@tjsl.edu
SHERRARD-HANNON,
Vida .... 360-596-5249 484 D
vsherrard-hannon@spscc.edu
SHERRICK, Rebecca, L . 630-844-5476 133 D
sherrick@aurora.edu
SHERRILL, Andrea .... 270-745-5360 186 C
andrea.sherrill@wku.edu
SHERRILL, Audrey .... 704-922-6217 334 G
sherrill.audrey@gaston.edu
SHERRILL, Erin .... 404-504-1993 123 K
esherrill@oglethorpe.edu
SHERRILL, Jason .... 517-607-2564 225 C
jsherrill@hillsdale.edu
SHERRILL, Mary Ellen .. 828-328-1741 330 F
maryellen.sherrill@lr.edu
SHERRILL, Regina, B .... 256-765-4705.... 8 E
rbsherrill@una.edu
SHERRILL, Zach .... 405-789-7661 369 I
zachary.sherrill@swcu.edu
SHERROD, Marc .... 918-836-6886 370 B
marc.sherrod@spartan.edu
SHERROD, Shalunda ..... 256-726-7340.... 6 C
ssherrod@oakwood.edu
SHERRON, Catherine .... 859-344-3387 185 B
catherine.sherron@thomasmore.edu
SHERRY, Suzanne .... 804-706-5201 474 B
ssherry@jtcc.edu
SHERSTAD, Brian, P ..... 616-538-2330 224 E
bsherstad@gracechristian.edu
SHERWOOD, David, G .. 262-646-6534 494 F
dsherwood@nashotah.edu
SHERWOOD, Emily, S .. 574-807-7023 154 B
emily.sherwood@betheluniversity.edu
SHERWOOD, Jim .... 978-934-3313 212 B
james_sherwood@uml.edu
SHERWOOD, Kim .... 316-322-3227 172 D
ksherwood@butlercc.edu
SHERWOOD,
Mary Frances .... 337-421-6926 188 J
mary.sherwood@sowela.edu
SHERWOOD, Sarah, K .. 508-767-7343 206 A
sk.sherwood@assumption.edu
SHERWOOD, Scott, S ... 719-884-5000.. 82 B
SHERWOOD, Timothy ... 443-412-2244 199 D
sherwota@harford.edu
SHERZER, Melinda .... 515-271-1461 165 G
melinda.miller@dmu.edu
SHETH, Ruchi .... 972-721-5395 452 B
rsheth@udallas.edu
SHETLEY, Shane .... 620-862-5252 171 H
SHETTY, Devdas .... 202-274-5220.. 94 B
devdas.shetty@udc.edu
SHEUCRAFT, Derrek, G . 615-353-3272 424 G
derrek.sheucraft@nscc.edu
SHEVEY, Wayne .... 414-443-8723 498 A
wayne.shevey@wlc.edu
SHEVLIN, Katie .... 434-924-4159 472 D
khr7f@virginia.edu
SHEW, Rick .... 828-759-4635 332 G
rshew@cccti.edu
SHEWAN, Thomas, F .... 512-245-2148 450 C
tfs21@txstate.edu
SHEWMAKER, Jennifer .. 325-674-2700 428 F
jws02b@acu.edu
SHEWMAKER, Stephen . 325-674-2317 428 F
sbs02a@acu.edu
SHEYBANI, Shayan .... 678-331-4571 122 C
shayan.sheybani@life.edu
SHEYTANIAN, Jennifer .. 508-541-1656 209 A
jsheytanian@dean.edu
SHI, Charlie .... 925-685-1230.. 40 C
cshi@dvc.edu
SHIAVO, Donna .... 508-531-2106 212 D
dschiavo@bridgew.edu
SHIBATA, Keri Kei .... 574-631-5559 162 A
kshibata@nd.edu
SHIBER, Cheryl .... 908-709-7511 284 D
cheryl.shiber@ucc.edu
SHIBLEY, Deborah .... 254-526-1331 432 D
deborah.shibley@ctcd.edu
SHIBLEY, Robert, G ..... 716-829-3981 316 C
rshibley@buffalo.edu
SHIDELER, Lorri, P .... 814-641-3605 386 E
shidell@juniata.edu
SHIDEMANTLE, Ronald . 304-327-4096 489 I
rshidemantle@bluefieldstate.edu

SHORT, Matt .... 918-293-5222 368 B
matt.short@okstate.edu
SHORT, Paula, M .... 713-743-5227 452 C
pmshort@uh.edu
SHORT, Paula, M .... 832-842-0550 452 D
pmshort@uh.edu
SHORT, Rosanna .... 623-935-8941.. 13 A
rosanna.short@estrellamountain.edu
SHORT, William .... 407-646-2619 106 L
wshort@rollins.edu
SHORTBULL,
Thomas, H .... 605-455-6022 415 H
tshortb@olc.edu
SHORTER, Paula .... 816-501-4633 258 I
paula.shorter@rockhurst.edu
SHORTHILL, Berkeley .... 530-226-4980.. 64 E
bshorthill@simpsonu.edu
SHORTS, Kathryn .... 541-962-3774 372 I
kshorts@eou.edu
SHORTT, Pamela .... 336-734-7224 334 F
pshortt@forsythtech.edu
SHOSTACK, Michelle ..... 848-932-7167 282 A
shostack@rutgers.edu
SHOTTS, Lesley .... 256-551-5206.... 2 E
lesley.shotts@drakestate.edu
SHOUBA, Derek .... 219-473-4305 154 D
dshouba@ccsj.edu
SHOULSON, Jeffrey .... 860-486-4037.. 89 D
jeffrey.shoulson@uconn.edu
SHOUN, Stan .... 314-286-4807 258 F
shshoun@ranken.edu
SHOUP, Angela .... 214-905-3001 455 B
angela.shoup@utdallas.edu
SHOUSE, Aimee .... 254-968-9429 446 D
ashouse@tarleton.edu
SHOUSE, Amy .... 304-724-5000 487 B
ashouse@cdu.edu
SHOWALTER, Jewel ...... 740-857-1311 360 D
jshowalter@rosedale.edu
SHOWALTER, Marybeth 540-432-4148 466 B
marybeth.showalter@emu.edu
SHOWALTER, Matthew .. 740-857-1311 360 D
mshowalter@rosedale.edu
SHOWALTER,
Rodney, J .... 540-338-1776 469 C
ie@phc.edu
SHOWERS, Dennis .... 585-245-5264 318 B
showers@geneseo.edu
SHOWERS, Kim .... 985-545-1500 188 E
SHOWERS, Shane .... 315-568-3125 310 B
sshowers@nycc.edu
SHOWERS, William .... 412-809-5268 396 E
showers.william@ptcollege.edu
SHOWS, Alicia .... 601-276-3706 249 B
showsa@smcc.edu
SHOWS, Deidre .... 601-318-6583 249 H
dede.shows@wmcarey.edu
SHOWS-PEREZ, Cindy .. 337-482-6497 193 B
cperez@louisiana.edu
SHRADER, Daniel .... 714-432-5605.. 38 B
dshrader@occ.cccd.edu
SHRADER, Matt .... 763-417-8250 235 A
mshrader@centralseminary.edu
SHRADER, Theresa .... 410-532-5155 201 D
tshrader@ndm.edu
SHREFLER, Christy, L ... 440-826-2231 348 D
chking@bw.edu
SHRESTHA, Shakil .... 510-628-8020.. 48 C
shakil@lincolnuca.edu
SHREVE, Daryl .... 413-236-1661 214 A
dshreve@berkshirecc.edu
SHREVE, Jeremy .... 828-328-7334 330 F
jeremy.shreve@lr.edu
SHREVE, Jeremy .... 919-658-7776 340 G
jshreve@umo.edu
SHREVE, Teresa .... 205-348-7829.... 7 G
tshreve@fa.ua.edu
SHREVES, Shawn .... 432-685-4690 440 B
sshreves@midland.edu
SHREWSBURY, Carrie ... 724-266-3838 400 B
cshrewsbury@tsm.edu
SHREWSBURY,
Charlene, P .... 765-658-5555 154 J
cpbrown@depauw.edu
SHRIEVE-HAWKINS,
Stephanie, E .... 415-338-7567.. 33 E
shrieve@sfsu.edu
SHRIMPTON, Nikki .... 518-587-2100 320 E
nikki.shrimpton@esc.edu
SHRIVASTAV, Rahul ...... 706-583-0690 126 G
rahuls@uga.edu
SHROCK, Joel .... 765-641-4020 153 G
jdshrock@anderson.edu

SHROFF, Nilufer, K .... 609-258-8732 280 D
nshroff@princeton.edu
SHROPSHIRE, Doug ...... 508-531-1207 212 D
dshropshire@bridgew.edu
SHROPSHIRE, James .... 641-269-4600 166 G
shropshi@grinnell.edu
SHROPSHIRE, Marty ..... 336-386-3453 338 D
shropshirem@surry.edu
SHROPSHIRE, Phyllis ... 770-426-2759 122 C
pwilliams@life.edu
SHROPSHIRE, Sandra ... 208-282-2997 131 G
shrosand@isu.edu
SHRUCK, Meghan .... 402-363-5701 270 D
mshruck@york.edu
SHRUM, Joshua, W ...... 724-805-2820 398 A
joshua.shrum@stvincent.edu
SHTAMLER, Victoriya .... 718-522-9073 290 E
vshtamler@asa.edu
SHTROMBERG, Alisa ..... 425-739-8389 481 C
alisa.shtromberg@lwtech.edu
SHUBERT, Lisa, A .... 507-344-7324 234 C
lisa.shubert@blc.edu
SHUBERT, Stephen .... 810-762-0501 228 F
stephen.shubert@mcc.edu
SHUDAK, Nicholas .... 402-375-7379 268 F
nishuda1@wsc.edu
SHUEY, Heather, M ...... 570-326-3761 392 W
hms27@pct.edu
SHUEY, Jill .... 716-286-8029 309 H
jshuey@niagara.edu
SHUEY, Lisa .... 419-559-2342 361 C
lshuey03@terra.edu
SHUEY, Timothy .... 704-406-4280 329 A
tshuey@gardner-webb.edu
SHUFFITT, Jason .... 512-313-3000 433 N
jason.shuffitt@concordia.edu
SHUFORD, Bettina .... 919-966-4045 342 C
bcshufor@email.unc.edu
SHUFORD, Eddie .... 828-652-0652 336 B
eddieshuford@mcdowelltech.edu
SHUGART, Michael .... 405-682-1611 367 D
mshugart@occc.edu
SHUGATS-CUMMINGS,
Alissa .... 716-614-5957 309 G
acummings@niagaracc.suny.edu
SHUGATS-CUMMINGS,
Alissa .... 716-614-6293 309 G
acummings@niagaracc.suny.edu
SHUKIS, Alicia .... 860-632-3033.. 88 C
ashukis@holyapostles.edu
SHULER, Hal .... 910-410-1807 337 B
whshuler@richmondcc.edu
SHULL, Roger .... 806-894-9611 443 G
rshull@southplainscollege.edu
SHULMAN, Brian .... 973-275-2168 283 C
brian.shulman@shu.edu
SHULMAN, David, J ...... 206-568-4387 483 E
SHULMAN, Yaakov .... 732-367-1060 275 K
yshulman@bmg.edu
SHULSE, Brian .... 760-872-2000.. 40 I
bdshulse@deepsprings.edu
SHULTES, Kenneth, E .... 717-245-1247 382 D
shultes@dickinson.edu
SHULTS, Christopher .... 212-220-1400 293 A
cshults@bmcc.cuny.edu
SHULTS, Kari .... 918-595-8845 370 C
kari.shults@tulsacc.edu
SHULTZ, Dee .... 970-339-6434.. 77 H
dee.shultz@aims.edu
SHULTZ, John .... 913-758-6329 178 B
john.shultz@stmary.edu
SHULTZ, Kara .... 570-389-4308 393 D
kshultz@bloomu.edu
SHULTZ, Kari .... 423-236-2484 423 F
kshultz@southern.edu
SHULTZ, Katie .... 727-341-3002 107 E
shultz.katie@spcollege.edu
SHULTZ, Megan .... 515-961-1611 170 B
megan.shultz@simpson.edu
SHULTZ, Norah .... 619-594-6881.. 33 D
nshultz@sdsu.edu
SHULTZ, JR., Walter, J . 570-326-3761 392 W
walter.shultz@pct.edu
SHUMACHER, Carrie ..... 406-768-6312 263 F
cshumacher@fpcc.edu
SHUMACK, Gareth .... 516-876-3210 318 C
shumackg@oldwestbury.edu
SHUMAKER, Carrie .... 313-593-5000 231 I
shumakr@umich.edu
SHUMAKER, Carrie .... 313-593-5454 231 I
shumakr@umich.edu
SHUMAKER, Deb .... 989-275-5000 226 D
deb.shumaker@kirtland.edu

SHUMAKER, Ryan .... 619-388-2737.. 60 J
rshumaker@sdccd.edu
SHUMAN, Jeff .... 860-253-3018.. 86 C
jshuman@asnuntuck.edu
SHUMAN, Kelli .... 336-278-5560 328 J
kshuman2@elon.edu
SHUMAN, Michaeline .... 570-372-4325 398 F
shumanm@susqu.edu
SHUMAN, Richard .... 713-525-6974 454 G
shumanr@stthom.edu
SHUMAN, Victoria .... 304-793-6898 490 C
vshuman@osteo.wvsom.edu
SHUMATE, David .... 480-245-7993.. 12 M
david.shumate@ibcs.edu
SHUMPERT, Barry .... 865-225-2365 425 B
bshumpert@pstcc.edu
SHUMPERT, Shanon ..... 410-516-8075 199 G
shanonshumpert@jhu.edu
SHUMWAY, Aaron .... 808-675-4971 128 D
aaron.shumway@byuh.edu
SHUMWAY, Karen .... 972-780-3600 454 A
karen.shumway@untdallas.edu
SHUPALA, Christine ...... 956-665-4025 455 D
christine.shupala@utrgv.edu
SHUPE, John .... 845-257-3335 316 E
shupej@newpaltz.edu
SHUPENUS, Sarah .... 217-424-6340 144 G
sshupenus@millikin.edu
SHUR, Luba .... 401-598-5155 404 D
luba.shur@jwu.edu
SHURANCE, Mike .... 949-214-3363.. 39 K
mike.shurance@cui.edu
SHURER, Brooke .... 919-760-8429 331 D
shurerb@meredith.edu
SHURLEY, Britton .... 270-534-3243 183 B
britton.shurley@kctcs.edu
SHURTLEFF, Courtney ... 508-286-3425 220 B
shurtleff_courtney@wheatoncollege.edu
SHURTZ, Mary Ann .... 703-539-6890 471 F
mshurtz@stratford.edu
SHUSHOK, JR.,
Frank, X .... 540-231-8069 476 C
vpsa@vt.edu
SHUSKO, Robin .... 301-624-2858 198 I
rshusko@frederick.edu
SHUSTER, Arthur .... 828-771-3773 344 D
ashuster@warren-wilson.edu
SHUSTRIN, Kara .... 618-650-2020 150 C
ksnyder@siue.edu
SHUTE, Paula .... 239-304-2955.. 95 M
paula.shute@avemaria.edu
SHUTT, Barbara, C .... 207-859-5415 194 D
barbara.shutt@colby.edu
SHUTT, Chris .... 831-656-2441 502 M
cmshutt@nps.edu
SHUTTER, Jamie, L .... 573-884-8383 261 A
shutterj@health.missouri.edu
SHUTTERLY, Martin .... 561-803-2200 105 C
SIAHMAKOUN, Azad ..... 812-877-8400 160 F
siahmako@rose-hulman.edu
SIAMPOS, Christa .... 314-421-0949 260 C
csiampos@siba.edu
SIBENALLER, Jim .... 773-508-7665 143 C
jsibena@luc.edu
SIBENALLER-WOODALL,
Beth .... 712-324-5061 169 C
beths@nwicc.edu
SIBERT, Kimberley .... 740-366-9233 349 F
ksibert@cotc.edu
SIBERT, Sonja .... 775-327-2355 271 A
sonja.sibert@gbcnv.edu
SIBERT, William .... 607-255-6240 297 F
controller@cornell.edu
SIBLEY, David .... 312-467-2260.. 36 E
dsibley@thechicagoschool.edu
SIBLEY, Dedra .... 321-433-7060.. 98 I
sibleyd@easternflorida.edu
SIBUMA, Bernadette ...... 781-239-2481 214 G
bsibuma@massbay.edu
SICARD, OP, Kenneth ... 401-865-2153 404 F
nkelley@providence.edu
SICARD, Rex, E .... 785-243-1435 172 L
rsicard@cloud.edu
SICIENSKY, Emily .... 931-540-2704 424 C
esiciensky@columbiastate.edu
SICILIA, IHM, Monica .. 484-323-3253 385 L
msicilia@immaculata.edu
SICILIANO, Stephen, N . 231-995-1373 229 A
ssiciliano@nmc.edu
SICONOLFI, Steven .... 215-951-1000 387 A
SIDAOUI, Mouwafac ...... 650-543-3940.. 51 G
mouwafac.sidaoui@menlo.edu

SIDAROUS, Mallory ...... 618-650-4628 150 C
msidaro@siue.edu
SIDBURY, Ben .... 704-233-8019 344 F
b.sidbury@wingate.edu
SIDDALL, David .... 641-784-5138 166 E
davids1@graceland.edu
SIDDARAJU, Raj .... 309-649-6387 150 G
raj.siddaraju@src.edu
SIDDELL, Robyn .... 334-229-4712.... 4 A
rsiddell@alasu.edu
SIDDENS, Nancy .... 217-732-3168 142 G
SIDDIQI, Melanie .... 909-652-6780.. 35 L
melanie.siddiqi@chaffey.edu
SIDDIQI, Muddassir ..... 713-718-6041 437 C
muddassir.siddiqi@hccs.edu
SIDERAS, John, F .... 216-368-4340 349 D
john.sideras@case.edu
SIDERS, Angie .... 765-455-9515 157 B
asiders@iuk.edu
SIDES, Bobbie .... 803-321-5102 410 H
bobbie.sides@newberry.edu
SIDES, Courtney, M ...... 361-570-4354 453 B
sidesc@uhv.edu
SIDES, Emilee .... 870-733-6722.. 17 F
essides@asumidsouth.edu
SIDES, Tevian .... 325-574-7640 458 D
tevian.sides@wtc.edu
SIDHU, Elda .... 702-895-5185 271 D
elda.sidhu@unlv.edu
SIDIBETH, Bakary .... 614-508-7277 353 M
SIDLE, Meg .... 606-218-5290 186 B
margaretsidle@upike.edu
SIDLE, Stuart .... 914-674-7517 306 C
ssidle@mercy.edu
SIDLER, Sherri .... 312-362-6695 136 H
ssidler@depaul.edu
SIDLER, Sherri .... 312-362-6727 136 H
ssidler@depaul.edu
SIDOR, Stanley .... 352-365-3523 103 U
sidors@lssc.edu
SIDORKIN, Alexander ... 916-278-3326.. 32 D
sidorkin@csus.edu
SIEBEN, Jeffrey .... 609-497-7789 280 C
jeffrey.sieben@ptsem.edu
SIEBENECK, Paula .... 419-995-8458 360 C
siebeneck.p@rhodesstate.edu
SIEBENMORGEN, Tom .... 501-450-1333.. 19 E
siebenmorgen@hendrix.edu
SIEBENS, Libby .... 509-682-6436 485 H
lsiebens@wvc.edu
SIEBENS, Mackie .... 845-758-7472 290 I
msiebens@bard.edu
SIEBERT, Alex .... 513-562-8749 347 I
asiebert@artacademy.edu
SIEBERT, Dave .... 847-735-5042 142 A
siebert@lakeforest.edu
SIEBERT, Florence, E .... 920-565-1000 493 A
siebertfe@lakeland.edu
SIEBERT, Katy .... 913-621-8713 173 E
ksiebert@donnelly.edu
SIEBERT, Mary Anne ..... 501-450-1372.. 19 E
siebert@hendrix.edu
SIEBUHR, Bryan .... 303-273-3092.. 79 J
bsiebuhr@mines.edu
SIEBUHR, Shantee .... 903-463-8693 436 G
siebuhrs@grayson.edu
SIECZKIEWICZ, Robert .. 570-372-4329 398 F
sieczkiewicz@susqu.edu
SIEDERS, Laura .... 906-487-7359 224 B
SIEFKEN, Rob .... 212-924-5900 321 F
rsiefken@swedishinstitute.edu
SIEGA-RIZ, Anna Maria 413-545-1079 211 G
asiegariz@umass.edu
SIEGEL, Christine .... 203-254-4000.. 87 I
csiegel@fairfield.edu
SIEGEL, Se-Ah .... 617-349-8563 211 C
SIEGFRIED, Jessica .... 435-283-7169 461 B
jessica.siegfried@snow.edu
SIEGFRIED,
Kenneth (Ziggy) .... 661-654-2200.. 30 B
ksiegfried@csub.edu
SIEGLE, Suzanne .... 248-689-8282 232 C
ssiegle@walshcollege.edu
SIEMANN, Thomas .... 510-666-8248.. 24 D
academicdirector@aimc.edu
SIEMEN, Duane .... 407-823-3010 110 E
duane.siemen@ucf.edu
SIEMENS, Henrietta .... 559-453-7100.. 43 A
henrietta.siemens@fresno.edu
SIEMER, William .... 732-571-3546 279 A
rsiemer@monmouth.edu
SIEMINSKI, Randy, B .... 315-386-7335 320 B
sieminski@canton.edu

SIEMS, Blaire ... 641-683-5115 166 I
blaire.siems@indianhills.edu
SIENA, Steven ... 516-628-5558 318 C
sienas@oldwestbury.edu
SIEREVELD, Sarah ... 318-342-5244 193 C
ssiereveld@ulm.edu
SIERKOWSKI, Dave ... 219-464-6906 162 D
dave.sierkowski@valpo.edu
SIERRA, Miguel ... 407-708-2492 108 D
sierram@seminolestate.edu
SIES, Susan ... 410-386-8325 198 D
ssies@carrollcc.edu
SIESING, Gina ... 610-526-5270 379 B
gsiesing@brynmawr.edu
SIETSEMA, Adriane ... 641-648-4611 167 F
adriane.sietsema@iavalley.edu
SIEVEN, Lauren ... 657-278-4320.. 31 C
lasieven@fullerton.edu
SIEVERDING, John ... 605-770-0700 415 E
john.sieverding@mitchelltech.edu
SIEVERS, Alex ... 812-888-4386 162 F
asievers@vinu.edu
SIEVERS, Allison ... 303-963-3437.. 78 H
asievers@ccu.edu
SIEVING, Allison ... 253-964-6531 482 E
asieving@pierce.ctc.edu
SIFERT, Jaclyn ... 641-585-8148 170 I
jaclyn.sifert@waldorf.edu
SIFFRING, Ed ... 402-643-7450 266 G
ed.siffring@cune.edu
SIFRI, Tatiana ... 630-637-5161 145 F
tsifri@noctrl.edu
SIFTAR, Michael ... 918-595-8123 370 C
michael.siftar@tulsacc.edu
SIGALA, Al ... 503-491-7548 374 B
al.sigala@mhcc.edu
SIGANDER, Max ... 503-517-1397 377 C
msigander@warnerpacific.edu
SIGANOS, Dina ... 813-868-8160.. 99 D
dsiganos@evergladesuniversity.edu
SIGAUKE, Erica ... 417-667-8181 252 B
esigauke@cottey.edu
SIGGERS, Lauretta ... 617-873-0170 208 B
lauretta.siggers@cambridgecollege.edu
SIGISMOND, Dee ... 209-384-6068.. 52 A
SIGLER, Christy ... 615-898-2185 422 C
christy.sigler@mtsu.edu
SIGLER, David, G ... 540-464-7184 476 B
siglerdg@vmi.edu
SIGLER, Haley ... 540-458-8400 477 D
siglerh@wlu.edu
SIGLER, Tim, M ... 919-573-5350 340 C
tsigler@shepherds.edu
SIGMAN, David ... 216-421-7467 350 H
dtsigman@cia.edu
SIGMAN, Stuart ... 888-820-1484.. 64 F
stuart.sigman@sofia.edu
SIGMON, Georgia ... 252-493-7834 336 H
gsigmon@email.pittcc.edu
SIGMON, JR.,
Kenneth, E ... 336-334-7600 341 D
kesigmon@ncat.edu
SIGNOR, Mary ... 212-998-6807 309 F
mary.signor@nyu.edu
SIGNORELLI, Sarah ... 716-829-8336 298 E
signores@dyc.edu
SIGNORELLO, John ... 973-761-9615 283 C
john.signorello@shu.edu
SIGWING, Marty ... 620-242-0400 176 B
sigwingm@mcpherson.edu
SII, Shelley ... 626-571-5110.. 48 D
shelley@les.edu
SIKAHEMA, Leland ... 808-675-4819 128 D
leland.sikahema@byuh.edu
SIKER, Malika ... 414-955-4493 493 F
msiker@mcw.edu
SIKER, Nancy ... 414-847-3343 494 C
nancysiker@miad.edu
SIKES, Bruce ... 479-667-4046.. 18 C
bsikes1@atu.edu
SIKES, Pamela, J ... 619-260-4595.. 72 I
psikes@sandiego.edu
SIKES, Steddon, L ... 402-363-5668 270 D
slsikes@york.edu
SIKKENGA, Jeff ... 419-289-5413 347 J
jsikkenga@ashbrook.org
SIKORA, Jacqueline ... 304-333-3652 489 K
jacqueline.sikora@fairmontstate.edu
SIKORA, Jacqueline, L .. 304-333-3652 489 K
jacqueline.sikora@fairmontstate.edu
SIKORSKY, Charles ... 703-416-1441 466 A
csikorsky@divinemercy.edu
SILAFAU-TOA, Emey ... 684-699-9155 504 B
SILAGYI, Tyler ... 716-338-1188 303 A
tylersilagyi@mail.sunyjcc.edu
SILANSKIS, Theresa ... 410-837-6838 204 F
tsilanskis@ubalt.edu
SILAS, Monique ... 205-929-6350.... 2 H
msilas@lawsonstate.edu
SILBER, Daniel ... 706-778-8500 124 D
dsilber@piedmont.edu
SILBER, Eric ... 512-313-3000 433 N
eric.silber@concordia.edu
SILBER, Jeffrey, A ... 607-255-2016 297 F
jas9@cornell.edu
SILBERMAN, Gerald ... 717-361-3737 383 C
silbermang@etown.edu
SILBERQUIT, Paul ... 410-334-2829 205 D
psilberquit@worwic.edu
SILBERSTEIN, Dara, J ... 607-777-2815 316 B
lael@binghamton.edu
SILBERSTEIN, Jeffrey ... 212-659-9091 302 D
jeffrey.silberstein@mssm.edu
SILCOX, Steve ... 269-927-7060 226 F
ssilcox@lakemichigancollege.edu
SILECCHIA, Anthony ... 419-434-5708 362 D
anthony.silecchia@findlay.edu
SILER, Cathy ... 317-955-6241 159 K
csiler@marian.edu
SILER, Keri, S ... 407-582-2867 113 I
ksiler@valenciacollege.edu
SILER, Lisa ... 870-633-4480.. 19 A
lsiler@eacc.edu
SILER, Ryan ... 920-403-3146 495 B
ryan.siler@snc.edu
SILICIANO, John, A ... 607-255-6230 297 F
jas83@cornell.edu
SILIS, Mark ... 617-253-3292 216 B
SILK, Bobby ... 931-598-1446 423 D
rjsilk@sewanee.edu
SILK, Dan ... 706-542-5813 126 G
dsilk@police.uga.edu
SILK, Elizabeth ... 708-524-6461 137 C
esilk@dom.edu
SILK, Mary, L ... 692-625-4410 504 G
msilk@cmi.edu
SILKAITIS, Carin ... 907-796-6531.. 10 B
cdsilkaitis@alaska.edu
SILL, Nancy ... 209-575-6128.. 77 A
silln@mjc.edu
SILLIMON, Laird, G ... 209-476-7840.. 67 E
lgsillimon@clc.edu
SILMAN, Shawn ... 281-459-7673 443 B
shawn.silman@sjcd.edu
SILTMAN, Kent ... 217-245-3004 139 C
kent.siltman@ic.edu
SILVA, Adelina ... 210-485-0153 428 G
asilva@alamo.edu
SILVA, Alan ... 317-955-6000 159 K
ajsilva@marian.edu
SILVA, Alyson ... 954-262-5258 105 A
asilva1@nova.edu
SILVA, Andria ... 407-646-2268 106 L
asilva2@rollins.edu
SILVA, Belinda ... 916-577-2200.. 76 D
bsilva@jessup.edu
SILVA, Betsy ... 605-642-6551 416 E
betsy.silva@bhsu.edu
SILVA, David, J ... 978-542-6246 213 E
david.silva@salemstate.edu
SILVA, Efrain ... 760-355-6249.. 45 K
efrain.silva@imperial.edu
SILVA, Elizabeth ... 619-260-2888.. 72 I
registrar@sandiego.edu
SILVA, Eneida ... 787-850-9390 512 D
eneida.silva@upr.edu
SILVA, Jack ... 401-454-6480 405 B
jsilva@risd.edu
SILVA, Jessica, L ... 401-456-8047 405 A
jsilva@ric.edu
SILVA, Joseph ... 916-686-7400.. 29 E
SILVA, Joseph ... 505-277-2241 288 J
jsilva23@unm.edu
SILVA, Mariza ... 312-922-1884 143 G
msilva@maccormac.edu
SILVA, Maureen ... 540-828-5450 464 L
msilva@bridgewater.edu
SILVA, Rito ... 361-593-3105 447 D
rito.silva@tamuk.edu
SILVA, Sonia ... 661-654-6113.. 30 B
ssilva7@csub.edu
SILVA, Stella ... 512-245-5580 450 C
ss23@txstate.edu
SILVA, Stephanie ... 510-436-1405.. 45 E
ssilva@hnu.edu
SILVA, Tammy, A ... 508-999-8486 212 A
tsilva@umassd.edu
SILVA, Tina ... 307-268-2547 500 U
tina.silva@caspercollege.edu
SILVA-BROWN, Jennifer 417-873-7213 252 G
jsilvabrown@drury.edu
SILVANO, Brian ... 949-794-9090.. 66 D
bsilvano@stanbridge.edu
SILVER, Bret ... 973-408-3227 277 A
bsilver@drew.edu
SILVER, Edward ... 201-692-7071 277 I
edsilver@fdu.edu
SILVER, Frank ... 828-652-0634 336 B
franksil@mcdowelltech.edu
SILVER, Jonathan ... 646-717-9705 300 E
silver@gts.edu
SILVERAMN, David ... 323-469-3300.. 24 P
SILVERBLATT,
Pamela, S ... 646-664-2977 292 K
pamela.silverblatt@cuny.edu
SILVERI, Annamaria ... 313-993-1170 231 E
silveran@udmercy.edu
SILVERIO, Alain ... 212-410-8046 308 E
asilverio@nycpm.edu
SILVERMAN, Claudia ... 312-939-0111 137 D
claudia@eastwest.edu
SILVERMAN, Ed ... 315-279-5120 303 G
esilverman@keuka.edu
SILVERMAN, Jennifer ... 310-338-4404.. 51 A
jennifer.silverman@lmu.edu
SILVERMAN, Lori ... 510-659-6191.. 54 J
lsilverman@ohlone.edu
SILVERMAN, Scott ... 310-434-4370.. 63 C
silverman_scott@smc.edu
SILVERMAN, Stephen ... 561-297-3357 109 J
silverman@fau.edu
SILVERS, Dominic ... 570-577-2000 379 C
dominic.silvers@bucknell.edu
SILVERS, Laurie ... 305-284-4025 113 C
SILVERS, Liz ... 828-726-2375 332 G
lsilvers@cccti.edu
SILVESTRI, Mary Ann ... 508-541-1602 209 A
msilvestri@dean.edu
SILVESTRI, Timothy ... 484-664-3178 390 H
timothysilvestri@muhlenberg.edu
SILVESTRINI, Maria ... 787-284-1912 508 E
msilvest@ponce.inter.edu
SILVESTRO, Michael ... 973-761-9138 283 C
michael.silvestro1@shu.edu
SILVEY, Greg ... 660-831-4028 256 I
silveyg@moval.edu
SILVEY, Jessica, L ... 417-836-8500 256 G
jessicasilvey@missouristate.edu
SILVIS, Kathryn ... 412-536-1297 386 H
kathryn.silvis@laroche.edu
SILVIS, Shera, L ... 843-377-4904 407 A
ssilvis@charlestonlaw.edu
SILVYN, Jeffrey ... 520-206-4678.. 15 B
jsilvyn@pima.edu
SILY, Michel ... 305-899-3781.. 96 A
msily@barry.edu
SIM, Hyun Bo ... 714-517-1945.. 26 J
SIM, Stephen ... 920-565-1000 493 A
SIMARD, Denise ... 518-564-3066 318 E
simardda@plattsburgh.edu
SIMARD, Tom ... 617-994-6918 211 E
tsimard@dhe.mass.edu
SIMARI, Robert ... 913-588-1698 177 J
rsimari@kumc.edu
SIMCOX, Mary Grace ... 717-947-6090 392 V
mrsimcox@pacollege.edu
SIMCOX, Nate ... 610-359-5190 382 A
nsimcox@dccc.edu
SIMEK, Kathy, M ... 503-943-7101 377 A
simek@up.edu
SIMENTAL, Yolanda ... 909-384-8927.. 60 F
ysimental@sbccd.cc.ca.us
SIMER, Lauren ... 864-250-8484 409 I
lauren.simer@gvltec.edu
SIMFUKWE, David ... 904-470-8174.. 98 L
dsimfukwe@ewc.edu
SIMIEN, Tammy ... 504-568-3250 189 H
tsimie@lsuhsc.edu
SIMINOE, Judith, P ... 320-308-2122 240 I
jpsiminoe@stcloudstate.edu
SIMINOFF, Laura ... 215-204-8624 399 B
lasiminoff@temple.edu
SIMIO, Frank ... 212-636-6265 300 C
simio@fordham.edu
SIMION, Karen ... 691-320-2480 504 C
ksimion@comfsm.fm
SIMIONE, Lauren, E ... 302-831-1408.. 91 C
lemurray@udel.edu
SIMKINS, Kathy ... 406-683-7566 264 A
kathy.simkins@umwestern.edu
SIMMELINK, Tara ... 253-535-8787 482 A
tara.simmelink@plu.edu
SIMMERS, Susan ... 406-657-2155 264 D
susan.simmers@msubillings.edu
SIMMERS, Susan ... 970-351-2109.. 84 F
susan.simmers@unco.edu
SIMMONDS, Donna ... 812-237-2215 156 D
donna.simmonds@indstate.edu
SIMMONDS, Thomas ... 914-674-7473 306 C
tsimmonds1@mercy.edu
SIMMONS, ADeidra ... 580-559-5239 365 K
asimmons@ecok.edu
SIMMONS, Amber ... 503-883-2200 373 F
SIMMONS, Angela, D ... 843-208-8120 413 C
SIMMONS, Barry ... 785-442-6000 174 F
SIMMONS, Benjamin ... 910-775-4341 343 B
benjamin.simmons@uncp.edu
SIMMONS, Bette, M ... 973-328-5171 276 J
bsimmons@ccm.edu
SIMMONS, Brian ... 803-754-4100 408 E
SIMMONS, Charlotte ... 405-974-2538 370 I
csimmons@uco.edu
SIMMONS, Christopher . 919-668-6285 328 F
chris.simmons@duke.edu
SIMMONS, Clay ... 940-565-4142 453 E
clay.simmons@unt.edu
SIMMONS, Dale, H ... 530-226-4143.. 64 E
dsimmons@simpsonu.edu
SIMMONS, Dan ... 580-745-2839 369 G
dsimmons@se.edu
SIMMONS, David ... 706-253-4504 117 B
dsimmons@chattahoocheetech.edu
SIMMONS, Dionne ... 661-253-7897.. 28 G
dsimmons@calarts.edu
SIMMONS, Douglas ... 603-314-1775 216 D
douglas.simmons@mcphs.edu
SIMMONS, Elaine ... 620-792-9214 171 I
simmonse@bartonccc.edu
SIMMONS, Elizabeth ... 508-830-6683 213 D
esimmons@maritime.edu
SIMMONS, Elizabeth, H 858-534-3130.. 70 C
evc@ucsd.edu
SIMMONS, Gregory ... 410-455-1452 203 B
gsimmons@umbc.edu
SIMMONS, Gwen ... 417-690-3411 251 H
simmons@cofo.edu
SIMMONS, Jacqueline .. 812-855-3312 156 G
simmonja@iu.edu
SIMMONS,
Jacqueline, A ... 812-855-3312 156 F
simmonja@iu.edu
SIMMONS, Jamar ... 504-816-4026 186 I
jsimmons@dillard.edu
SIMMONS, Jay ... 913-253-5000 177 D
SIMMONS, Jay ... 484-365-7526 388 H
jsimmons@lincoln.edu
SIMMONS, Jeffrey ... 301-447-5266 201 B
simmons@msmary.edu
SIMMONS, Jeremy ... 415-351-3510.. 61 C
jsimmons@sfai.edu
SIMMONS, Kelly, M ... 708-524-5921 137 C
ksimmons@dom.edu
SIMMONS, Kitty ... 951-785-2397.. 47 C
ksimmons@lasierra.edu
SIMMONS, Laura ... 828-694-1807 332 E
lm_simmons@blueridge.edu
SIMMONS, Loann ... 618-453-4172 150 B
lsimmons@siu.edu
SIMMONS, Lori ... 617-735-9825 209 D
simmonslo@emmanuel.edu
SIMMONS, Martha ... 719-544-0677.. 82 J
martha.simmons@pueblocc.edu
SIMMONS, Mary ... 407-888-8689 100 A
msimmons@fcim.edu
SIMMONS, Max ... 405-682-1611 367 D
msimmons@occc.edu
SIMMONS, Michelle ... 765-252-5473 158 D
msimmons@ivytech.edu
SIMMONS, Miranda ... 912-583-3176 116 E
msimmons1@bpc.edu
SIMMONS, Rasheeda ... 318-670-6000 191 D
SIMMONS, Regina ... 704-463-3404 339 E
regina.simmons@pfeiffer.edu
SIMMONS, Renita, W ... 718-951-5137 293 C
rwsimmons@brooklyn.cuny.edu
SIMMONS, Roy ... 304-205-6708 488 D
roy.simmons@bridgevalley.edu
SIMMONS, Ruth, J ... 936-261-2111 446 C
rjsimmons@pvamu.edu
SIMMONS, Shanni, E ... 812-888-4026 162 F
ssimmons@vinu.edu

SIMMONS, Shannon ..... 478-445-5149 119 B
shannon.simmons@gcsu.edu
SIMMONS, Sherry .... 262-695-3481 500 B
ssimmons9@wctc.edu
SIMMONS, Steve .... 803-508-7270 406 C
simmonss@atc.edu
SIMMONS, Tami .... 704-378-1024 330 D
tsimmons@jcsu.edu
SIMMONS, Tanya .... 804-524-5087 476 D
tsimmons@vsu.edu
SIMMONS, Thomas, E .. 419-772-2450 358 C
t-simmons@onu.edu
SIMMONS, Todd, H ...... 336-285-2606 341 D
thsimmons@ncat.edu
SIMMONS, Tonja .... 478-476-5167 116 G
tsimmons@centralgatech.edu
SIMMONS, Toye .... 713-221-8061 453 A
simmonsto@uhd.edu
SIMMONS, Traci .... 503-491-6422 374 B
traci.simmons@mhcc.edu
SIMMONS, Tracy .... 916-739-7198.. 71 E
tsimmons@pacific.edu
SIMMONS, Victoria .... 818-240-1000.. 43 G
vsimmons@glendale.edu
SIMMONS-HENRY,
Linda .... 903-593-8311 448 G
lsimmons-henry@texascollege.edu
SIMMS, Laurene .... 202-250-2587.. 92 C
laurene.simms@gallaudet.edu
SIMMS, Marcie .... 740-351-3392 360 F
msimms@shawnee.edu
SIMMS, Mary Helen ...... 318-371-3035 188 F
maryhelensimms@nltcc.edu
SIMMS, Michele .... 859-442-1690 181 H
michele.simms@kctcs.edu
SIMMS, Pat .... 501-332-0245.. 18 B
pats@asutr.edu
SIMMS, Rebecca .... 859-246-6761 181 F
rebecca.simms@kctcs.edu
SIMON, Bashe .... 718-252-7800 322 G
barbara.simon@touro.edu
SIMON, Bashe .... 212-463-0400 322 F
simonb@touro.edu
SIMON, Constance .... 313-831-5200 223 L
csimon@etseminary.edu
SIMON, Dan .... 916-388-2800.. 34 K
SIMON, Darica .... 225-216-8171 187 G
simond@mybrcc.edu
SIMON, David, F .... 215-871-6819 395 G
simond@pcom.edu
SIMON, David, R .... 920-565-1000 493 A
simondr@lakeland.edu
SIMON, Donald, E .... 718-933-6700 307 A
dsimon@monroecollege.edu
SIMON, Eric .... 410-857-2207 200 F
esimon@mcdaniel.edu
SIMON, Esan .... 860-444-8352 503 G
SIMON, Jacob .... 419-448-3421 361 D
simonja@tiffin.edu
SIMON, Jason .... 620-223-2700 173 I
jasons@fortscott.edu
SIMON, Jason, F .... 940-565-2085 453 E
jason.simon@unt.edu
SIMON, Jennifer .... 406-496-4307 265 A
jsimon@mtech.edu
SIMON, John, D .... 610-758-3156 388 E
jds414@lehigh.edu
SIMON, Marisa .... 574-239-8339 156 A
mvillano@hcc-nd.edu
SIMON, Michael .... 810-762-5640 228 F
michael.simon@mcc.edu
SIMON, Michael .... 936-633-5200 429 J
msimon@angelina.edu
SIMON, Tia .... 832-230-5156 440 E
tsimon1@na.edu
SIMON, Tim .... 402-486-2600 269 F
tim.simon@ucollege.edu
SIMON, Tina, L .... 419-372-2700 348 G
tsimon@bgsu.edu
SIMONCELLI, Andrew .... 985-448-4131 192 F
andrew.simoncelli@nicholls.edu
SIMONDS, Ken .... 760-366-5297.. 40 E
ksimonds@cmccd.edu
SIMONDS, Kurt .... 971-722-5573 375 D
kurt.simonds@pcc.edu
SIMONE, John .... 609-586-4800 278 F
simonej@mccc.edu
SIMONE, Lucian .... 203-285-2223.. 86 E
lsimone@gatewayct.edu
SIMONE, Nadia .... 626-571-8811.. 73 E
nadias@uwest.edu
SIMONEAUX, Wendy .... 225-578-8878 189 H
wsimo1@lsuhsc.edu

SIMONESCHI, Joseph ... 909-869-2008.. 30 A
jsimoneschi@cpp.edu
SIMONETTI, Joseph ...... 773-995-3689 134 K
jsimonet@csu.edu
SIMONI, Mary .... 518-276-6575 312 C
msimoni@rpi.edu
SIMONIAN, Yasmen ...... 801-626-7117 461 A
ysimonian@weber.edu
SIMONS, Austin .... 269-965-3931 225 H
simonsa2@kellogg.edu
SIMONS, Danita .... 605-718-2436 417 D
danita.simons@wdt.edu
SIMONS, Earl, G .... 718-262-3795 295 E
esimons@york.cuny.edu
SIMONS, Ernest .... 252-493-7243 336 H
esimons@email.pittcc.edu
SIMONS, Horace .... 614-837-4088 363 D
simonsh@valorcollege.edu
SIMONS, Jill .... 870-972-3574.. 17 E
jsimons@astate.edu
SIMONS, Kenneth, B ..... 414-955-4575 493 F
ksimons@mcw.edu
SIMONS, Kenni .... 253-879-3296 484 G
krsimons@pugetsound.edu
SIMONS, Lisa .... 817-598-6263 457 J
lsimons@wc.edu
SIMONS, TOR,
Matthew .... 814-472-3001 397 F
msimons@francis.edu
SIMONS, Michael, A ..... 718-990-6601 313 G
simonsm@stjohns.edu
SIMONS, Shino .... 626-812-3061.. 26 F
ssimons@apu.edu
SIMONS, Tina .... 256-840-4115.... 3 F
tina.simons@snead.edu
SIMONS, Valerie .... 303-492-5359.. 84 B
valerie.simons@colorado.edu
SIMONSEN, Jaime .... 651-201-1669 237 B
jaime.simonsen@minnstate.edu
SIMONSON, Erik .... 218-733-5915 238 G
erik.simonson@lsc.edu
SIMONSON, Richelle ..... 614-222-3211 351 B
rsimonson@ccad.edu
SIMONSON, William ...... 586-286-2110 227 B
simonsonb@macomb.edu
SIMONTON, James .... 931-393-7123 427 B
jsimonto@utsi.edu
SIMOWITZ, Aaron .... 503-370-6840 377 F
asimowitz@willamette.edu
SIMPKINS, Alice, M ...... 706-396-8111 124 B
asimpkins@paine.edu
SIMPKINS, Felix .... 708-709-3518 147 D
fsimpkins@prairiestate.edu
SIMPKINS, Will .... 303-605-5590.. 81 M
wsimpkin@msudenver.edu
SIMPLICIO, Sean, S ...... 510-325-7089 468 G
sssimplicio@marybaldwind.edu
SIMPSON, Amanda .... 760-252-2411.. 26 G
asimpson@barstow.edu
SIMPSON, Andrea .... 317-274-2195 157 D
andmsimp@iupui.edu
SIMPSON, Andy, L .... 651-631-5239 244 D
alsimpson@unwsp.edu
SIMPSON, Anita .... 580-628-6237 366 J
anita.simpson@noc.edu
SIMPSON, Betsy .... 303-963-3350.. 78 H
bsimpson@ccu.edu
SIMPSON, Brett .... 504-864-7787 190 C
bsimpson@loyno.edu
SIMPSON, Caroline .... 304-724-3700 486 F
csimpson@apus.edu
SIMPSON, JR.,
Charles, L .... 919-516-4249 339 I
clsimpson@st-aug.edu
SIMPSON, Colleen .... 920-498-5418 499 G
colleen.simpson@nwtc.edu
SIMPSON, Cynthia .... 734-432-5684 227 C
cssimpson@madonna.edu
SIMPSON, Cynthia, F ... 718-990-6333 313 G
simpsoc1@stjohns.edu
SIMPSON, Dionne .... 619-596-2766.. 26 D
dsimpson@ata.edu
SIMPSON, Donald .... 318-342-3312 193 C
dsimpson@ulm.edu
SIMPSON, Jeanna .... 417-667-8181 252 B
jbrauer@cottey.edu
SIMPSON, Jeff .... 334-241-5412.... 7 C
simpsonj@troy.edu
SIMPSON, Jeff .... 801-422-5330 458 H
jeff.simpson@byu.edu
SIMPSON, Jennifer .... 229-225-5072 126 A
jsimpson@southernregional.edu
SIMPSON, Joe .... 815-921-4752 148 B
j.simpson@rockvalleycollege.edu

SIMPSON, Kim .... 863-297-1000 106 A
ksimpson@polk.edu
SIMPSON, Kurt .... 815-599-3501 139 A
kurt.simpson@highland.edu
SIMPSON, Lawrence, J . 617-747-2150 206 H
academicaffairs@berklee.edu
SIMPSON, Lynne .... 405-466-3294 366 C
lynne.simpson@langston.edu
SIMPSON, Mark .... 512-475-7310 455 A
mark.simpson@austin.utexas.edu
SIMPSON, Mark .... 866-931-4300 258 H
mark.simpson@rockbridge.edu
SIMPSON, Matthew .... 417-447-2648 257 G
simpsonm@otc.edu
SIMPSON, Matthew .... 508-849-3462 205 H
msimpson@annamaria.edu
SIMPSON, Michael, E ... 518-564-2155 318 E
simpsome@plattsburgh.edu
SIMPSON, Philip .... 321-433-5078.. 98 I
simpsonp@easternflorida.edu
SIMPSON, Rich .... 951-343-4579.. 27 G
rsimpson@calbaptist.edu
SIMPSON, Robert .... 731-661-5219 426 F
rsimpson@uu.edu
SIMPSON, Stacy .... 618-634-3375 149 G
stacys@shawneecc.edu
SIMPSON, Steven, M ..... 248-232-4175 229 C
smsimpso@oaklandcc.edu
SIMPSON, Sun-Kyung .. 845-368-7201 314 I
SIMPSON, Tammi .... 301-696-3573 199 E
simpson@hood.edu
SIMPSON, Tammi, R .... 540-458-4111 477 D
tsimpson@wlu.edu
SIMPSON, Tera .... 479-964-0583.. 18 C
tzeigler@atu.edu
SIMPSON-LOGG,
Anastasia .... 707-468-3102.. 51 F
asimpson@mendocino.edu
SIMS, Andrea .... 909-274-4525.. 52 J
asims16@mtsac.edu
SIMS, Angela .... 505-224-4000 285 M
asims9@cnm.edu
SIMS, Angela, D .... 585-340-9680 296 D
asims@crcds.edu
SIMS, Bradford, L .... 301-369-2541 198 C
president@captechu.edu
SIMS, Damon, R .... 814-865-0909 391 G
drs37@psu.edu
SIMS, Dana .... 503-847-2597 377 B
dsims@uws.edu
SIMS, Danielle, R .... 502-213-5333 182 C
danielle.sims@kctcs.edu
SIMS, Darryl .... 920-424-1034 496 C
sims@uwosh.edu
SIMS, David .... 478-471-2780 122 F
david.sims@mga.edu
SIMS, Douglas .... 702-651-3627 270 K
douglas.sims@csn.edu
SIMS, Geoffrey .... 201-360-4045 278 C
gsims@hccc.edu
SIMS, George .... 405-208-5450 367 E
gsims@okcu.edu
SIMS, Haley .... 804-828-1645 473 B
hgsims@vcu.edu
SIMS, Hillel .... 857-701-1501 215 G
hsims@rcc.mass.edu
SIMS, Hunter .... 325-649-8115 437 G
hsims@hputx.edu
SIMS, Janet .... 910-410-1889 337 B
jmsims@richmondcc.edu
SIMS, Jaquelyn .... 310-660-3119.. 41 E
jsims@elcamino.edu
SIMS, Jeanetta .... 405-974-2000 370 I
jsims7@uco.edu
SIMS, Joel .... 406-268-3719 264 F
joel.sims@gfcmsu.edu
SIMS, Kavaris .... 405-466-3623 366 C
kavaris.sims@langston.edu
SIMS, Leslie .... 304-424-8221 490 F
leslie.sims@wvup.edu
SIMS, Lisa .... 601-477-4107 246 G
lisa.sims@jcjc.edu
SIMS, Melinda .... 405-382-9604 369 F
m.sims@sscok.edu
SIMS, Michael .... 201-200-3113 279 D
msims@njcu.edu
SIMS, Myra .... 540-362-6435 467 H
simsms@hollins.edu
SIMS, Patricia .... 256-551-3117.... 2 E
patricia.sims@drakestate.edu
SIMS, Patrick .... 336-770-3262 343 D
simsp@uncsa.edu

SIMS, Quanda, D .... 803-934-3422 410 G
qdsims@morris.edu
SIMS, Ronshekua .... 229-333-2100 128 B
SIMS, Sandra .... 303-384-2008.. 79 J
ssims@mines.edu
SIMS, Scott .... 317-931-2328 154 G
ssims@cts.edu
SIMS, Shannon .... 325-649-8069 437 G
ssims@hputx.edu
SIMS, Steve .... 724-266-3838 400 B
ssims@tsm.edu
SIMS, Tammy .... 870-235-4008.. 21 C
tdsims@saumag.edu
SIMS, Tom .... 215-885-2360 389 C
tsims@manor.edu
SIMS-AUBERT, Gail .... 920-465-2712 495 F
simsg@uwgb.edu
SIMSON, Earl, L .... 401-456-8106 405 A
esimson@ric.edu
SINA, Julie .... 310-206-8962.. 69 E
jsina@support.ucla.edu
SINA WIN, Wambli .... 918-913-2755 365 C
winw@bacone.edu
SINCHE, Melanie .... 860-231-5228.. 90 A
msinche@usj.edu
SINCLAIR, Kelli .... 630-466-7900 152 K
ksinclair@waubonsee.edu
SINCLAIR, Lisa .... 617-373-2157 217 I
SINCLAIR, Robert, L ..... 312-788-1144 152 J
rsinclair@vandercook.edu
SINCLAIR, Shannon, E .. 804-287-6683 472 C
ssinclai@richmond.edu
SINCLAIR, Taylor .... 402-471-2505 268 C
tsinclair@nscs.edu
SINCLAIR CURTIS,
Jennifer .... 530-752-0554.. 69 B
jscurtis@ucdavis.edu
SINDELAR, Richard .... 713-525-3819 454 G
sindelh@sthom.edu
SINDER, Janet .... 718-780-7975 291 K
janet.sinder@brooklaw.edu
SINDT, Christopher .... 815-836-5639 142 F
csindt@lewisu.edu
SINE-KINZ, Kristin, M .. 585-685-6192 307 B
toldham@monroecc.edu
SINELE, Jennifer .... 870-612-2009.. 22 H
jennifer.sinele@uaccb.edu
SINEWAY, Carla .... 989-317-4760 230 D
csineway@sagchip.edu
SINGELL, Larry .... 512-471-4363 455 A
lsingell@austin.utexas.edu
SINGER, Abraham .... 718-435-2105 297 D
SINGER, Israel .... 917-923-1359 322 G
israel.singer@touro.edu
SINGER, Israel .... 646-565-6000 322 F
israel.singer@touro.edu
SINGER, Jefferson .... 860-439-2010.. 87 H
jefferson.singer@conncoll.edu
SINGER, Karen .... 931-598-1890 423 D
ksinger@sewanee.edu
SINGER, Kayli .... 619-594-7903.. 33 D
ksinger2@sdsu.edu
SINGER, Mark .... 914-493-1909 309 B
mark_singer@nymc.edu
SINGER, Paula, R .... 866-492-5336 244 F
SINGER, Susan, R .... 407-646-2355 106 L
srsinger@rollins.edu
SINGER, Yossi .... 718-268-4700 312 A
SINGH, Amit, B .... 425-640-1515 480 A
amit.singh@edcc.edu
SINGH, Anita .... 916-568-3057.. 50 F
singha@losrios.edu
SINGH, Avena .... 541-888-1583 376 C
asingh@socc.edu
SINGH, Bharpur .... 209-290-0333.. 24 E
bsingh@advancedcollege.edu
SINGH, Gangaram .... 858-642-8109.. 53 I
gsingh@nu.edu
SINGH, Gurbhushan ...... 913-469-8500 174 I
gurbhushan@jccc.edu
SINGH, Hamwant (Neil) 718-429-6600 324 D
neil.singh@vaughn.edu
SINGH, Inder .... 609-586-4800 278 F
singhi@mccc.edu
SINGH, Jatinder .... 610-436-2828 395 D
jsingh@wcupa.edu
SINGH, Joanne .... 859-985-3056 179 I
singhj@berea.edu
SINGH, Judith, R .... 315-267-2188 319 A
singhjr@potsdam.edu
SINGH, Kamla .... 201-761-6082 283 A
ksingh@saintpeters.edu

SINGH, Kanwal 914-395-2303 315 A
ksingh@sarahlawrence.edu
SINGH, Kulwant 408-864-8745 42 H
singhkulwant@deanza.edu
SINGH, Lakhbir 212-343-1234 306 G
lsingh@mcny.edu
SINGH, Lindsay 239-590-7992 109 K
lsingh@fgcu.edu
SINGH, Manohar 203-392-5661 86 A
singhm6@southernct.edu
SINGH, Meharvan 708-216-0894 143 C
msingh@luc.edu
SINGH, Nanne 559-251-4215 27 I
library@calchristiancollege.edu
SINGH, Piyusha 573-875-7240 251 I
psingh@ccis.edu
SINGH, Preeti 610-558-5537 391 A
singhp@neumann.edu
SINGH, Sarabdayal 657-278-4295 31 C
ssingh@fullerton.edu
SINGH, Simran 805-893-8377 70 E
singh-s@sa.ucsb.edu
SINGH, Sudhir 301-687-4019 204 C
ssingh@frostburg.edu
SINGH, Tanuja 504-865-3034 190 C
provost@loyno.edu
SINGH CHAUHAN,
Indrajeet 212-423-2769 301 C
indrajeet.singh@helenefuld.edu
SINGH MOONILALL,
Seeta 561-912-1211 99 D
seetas@evergladesuniversity.edu
SINGHANI, Neil 516-572-7123 307 E
neil.singhani@ncc.edu
SINGLE, Karen 617-274-3352 216 D
karen.single@mcphs.edu
SINGLE, Louise, E 512-492-3114 442 I
louises@stedwards.edu
SINGLER, Melissa 910-272-3230 337 D
msingler@robeson.edu
SINGLETARY, Chip 850-201-8544 112 C
chip.singletary@tcc.fl.edu
SINGLETARY, Joshua 518-694-7896 289 J
joshua.singletary@acphs.edu
SINGLETARY, Michael 360-383-3035 486 A
msingletary@whatcom.edu
SINGLETARY, Sedrick 803-327-7402 407 F
ssingletary@clintoncollege.edu
SINGLETARY, Shawana 212-343-1234 306 G
ssingletary@mcny.edu
SINGLETON, Brian 313-496-2778 232 E
bsingle1@wcccd.edu
SINGLETON, Derrick 859-985-3339 179 I
singletonp@berea.edu
SINGLETON, Felita 503-517-1097 377 C
fsingleton@warnerpacific.edu
SINGLETON, Gena, L 713-646-1778 443 I
gsingleton@stcl.edu
SINGLETON, Ginny 601-426-6346 249 A
gsingleton@southeasternbaptist.edu
SINGLETON, Greg 252-638-7247 334 A
singletong@cravencc.edu
SINGLETON, Gregory 931-221-7005 417 H
singletong@apsu.edu
SINGLETON, Heather 757-446-7427 466 D
singleha@evms.edu
SINGLETON, Jennie 252-940-6202 332 C
jennie.singleton@beaufortccc.edu
SINGLETON, Joan 215-572-2900 378 E
singletonj@arcadia.edu
SINGLETON, John, L 817-257-7871 448 F
j.singleton@tcu.edu
SINGLETON, Lawrence 212-346-1962 311 A
lsingleton@pace.edu
SINGLETON, Rachel 601-318-6197 249 H
rsingleton@wmcarey.edu
SINGLETON, Shawn, T 859-233-8154 185 C
ssingleton@transy.edu
SINGLETON-WALKER,
Catherine 662-254-3090 248 B
cswalker@mvsu.edu
SINGLEY, Jason 510-885-3441 31 A
jason.singley@csueastbay.edu
SINHA, Kim 434-381-6530 471 I
ksinha@sbc.edu
SINHA, Monica 510-592-9688 54 F
monica@npu.edu
SINHA, Tripti 301-405-1721 202 H
tsinha@umd.edu
SINIARD, Michelle 478-218-3330 116 G
msiniard@centralgatech.edu
SINICROPE, Natalie 202-651-5547 92 C
natalie.sinicrope@gallaudet.edu
SINICROPI, Miles 315-568-3360 310 B
msinicropi@nycc.edu
SINIGAGLIA, Frank 845-434-5750 321 E
fsinigaglia@sunysullivan.edu
SINK, Britney 865-539-7242 425 B
bsink@pstcc.edu
SINK, Michael 407-823-2711 110 E
michael.sink@ucf.edu
SINN, Brad 928-350-2100 15 L
SINNAEVE, Andrea 847-628-1546 141 C
andrea.sinnaeve@judsonu.edu
SINNOT, Dawn 215-751-8085 381 I
dsinnot@ccp.edu
SINSEL, Rebecca 800-658-4308 267 J
sinselr@mpcc.edu
SINUTKO, John 805-378-1454 73 J
jsinutko@vcccd.edu
SIPE, Bryan 912-279-5819 117 F
bsipe@ccga.edu
SIPE, Gary 386-822-4210 112 A
gsipe@stetson.edu
SIPES, Jennifer, L 217-581-3221 137 E
jlsipes@eiu.edu
SIPES, Marlise 740-264-5591 352 B
mbarker@egcc.edu
SIPES, Stacie 903-875-7736 440 D
stacie.sipes@navarrocollege.edu
SIPIORA, Jennifer 508-531-1221 212 D
jennifer.pacheco@bridgew.edu
SIPPEL, Christopher 419-434-5467 362 D
sippel@findlay.edu
SIQUEIROS, Penny 478-757-5253 127 F
psiqueiros@wesleyancollege.edu
SIRAJ, Elias 757-446-5910 466 D
sirajes@evms.edu
SIRANGELO-ELBADAWY,
Catherine 201-360-4261 278 C
csirangelo@hccc.edu
SIRBU, Jerald, B 303-369-5151 82 I
jbs@plattcolorado.edu
SIRIANO, Joseph 323-469-3300 24 P
SIRIMANGKALA,
Pawena 305-899-3453 96 A
psirimangkala@barry.edu
SIRJU-JOHNSON,
Nicole 607-777-4472 316 B
njohnson@binghamton.edu
SIRKEL, Mary 918-595-7928 370 C
mary.sirkel@tulsacc.edu
SIRKIN, Tanya, A 818-947-2321 49 G
sirkinta@lavc.edu
SIROKI, David 412-536-1137 386 H
david.siroki@laroche.edu
SIRONEN, Jacqueline 419-448-2261 353 E
jsironen@heidelberg.edu
SIRVENT, Tara 559-453-8002 43 A
tara.sirvent@fresno.edu
SISCHO, Brian, C 919-515-3226 342 A
bcsischo@ncsu.edu
SISCO, Craig 405-682-7568 367 D
michael.c.sisco@occc.edu
SISCO, Julie 574-284-4574 160 I
jsisco@saintmarys.edu
SISCOE, Dee 417-836-5526 256 G
dsiscoe@missouristate.edu
SISEMORE, John 417-455-5674 252 E
johnsisemore@crowder.edu
SISK, Beth 402-399-2415 266 F
bsisk@csm.edu
SISK, Colin 724-480-3630 381 H
colin.sisk@ccbc.edu
SISK, Kari, M 304-457-6275 486 E
maxwellkl@ab.edu
SISK, Lori 801-375-5125 459 K
lori.sisk@rm.edu
SISK, Matthew 304-457-6247 486 E
siskmr@ab.edu
SISK, Megan 714-556-3610 73 H
megan.sisk@vanguard.edu
SISK, Timothy 312-329-4492 144 I
tim.sisk@moody.edu
SISKO, John, E 920-748-8109 494 J
siskoj@ripon.edu
SISLER, Kelli 301-387-3060 199 A
kelli.sisler@garrettcollege.edu
SISNEROS, Patrick 425-388-9026 480 B
psisneros@everettcc.edu
SISSEM, Amanda 814-732-2000 394 B
SISSEN, Melissa 517-264-7155 230 H
msissen@sienaheights.edu
SISSON, Brian 507-457-1638 243 C
bsisson@smumn.edu
SISSON, Cindy 309-467-3721 138 A
SISSON, George 716-338-1269 303 A
georgesisson@mail.sunyjcc.edu
SISSON, Jeanne, M 518-580-5664 315 F
jsisson@skidmore.edu
SISSON, Karen 269-337-7224 225 F
karen.sisson@kzoo.edu
SISSON, Karl 585-567-9340 302 B
karl.sisson@houghton.edu
SISSON, Philip, J 978-322-8488 215 B
sissonp@middlesex.mass.edu
SITARAMIAH, Gita 612-330-1476 234 A
sitarami@augsburg.edu
SITES, John 954-776-4476 103 B
jsites@keiseruniversity.edu
SITHARAMAN, Sri 706-507-8963 117 H
sri@columbusstate.edu
SITLINGTON, Claudia 805-553-4799 73 J
csitlington@vcccd.edu
SITTIG COSSMAN,
Lynne 210-458-2880 455 E
SITZABEE, JR.,
William, E 814-865-4402 391 G
wes25@psu.edu
SIUTA, Chris 716-926-8819 301 E
csiuta@hilbert.edu
SIUTA, Chris 716-926-8930 301 E
csiuta@hilbert.edu
SIVADASAN, Shobi 573-341-6292 261 D
shobi.sivadasan@mst.edu
SIVADON, Angela 918-595-7980 370 C
angela.sivadon@tulsacc.edu
SIVAK, Jennifer, L 240-895-4382 202 B
jlsivak@smcm.edu
SIVAKUMARAN, Thilla 870-972-3149 17 E
tsivakumaran@astate.edu
SIVAKUMARAN,
Thillainatarajan 870-972-2100 17 E
SIVE, Hazel 617-373-5089 217 I
SIVERT, Shayla 760-744-1150 56 B
ssivert@palomar.edu
SIVILLO, Jeremy 814-866-8143 387 D
jsivillo@lecom.edu
SIVORI, Jim 415-439-2305 25 E
jsivori@act-sf.org
SIWABESSY, Genevieve 530-661-4201 77 D
gsiwabes@yccd.edu
SIWABESSY, Genevieve 805-546-3276 40 F
genevieve_siwabessy@cuesta.edu
SIX, Jonathan 919-761-2100 340 D
jsix@sebts.edu
SIXTA, Jeff 913-288-7613 175 B
jsixta@kckcc.edu
SIYUM, Ben 703-591-7042 466 M
bsiyum@fxua.edu
SIZEMORE, Abby 502-863-8301 179 F
abby.sizemore@bsk.edu
SIZEMORE, Amanda 636-922-8388 258 J
asizemore@stchas.edu
SIZEMORE, Lisa 828-339-4280 338 B
l_sizemore@southwesterncc.edu
SIZEMORE, Sarah 615-244-5848 423 C
SIZEMORE, Shain 606-546-1670 185 D
ssizemore@unionky.edu
SIZER, Judith 617-873-0171 208 B
judith.sizer@cambridgecollege.edu
SJOBERG, Connie 918-495-6542 368 F
registrar@oru.edu
SJOBERG, Lisa, M 218-299-3250 235 H
sjoberg@cord.edu
SJOGREN, Michelle 859-246-6429 181 F
michelle.sjogren@kctcs.edu
SJOLANDER, Megan 616-233-3416 223 E
megan.sjolander@davenport.edu
SJOQUIST, Corey 608-785-8939 496 A
csjoquist@uwlax.edu
SJUTS, Joseph, H 816-501-3615 250 F
joe.sjuts@avila.edu
SKABROUD, Ryan 920-693-1347 498 H
ryan.skabroud@gotoltc.edu
SKACH, Peter 773-298-3548 149 D
skach@sxu.edu
SKADBERG, Ingrid 508-854-7545 215 F
iskadberg@qcc.mass.edu
SKAFF, Penny 949-582-4573 65 D
pskaff@saddleback.edu
SKAGGS, Brandon 254-295-4696 453 D
bskaggs@umhb.edu
SKAGGS, Brandon 254-295-4496 453 D
bskaggs@umhb.edu
SKAGGS, Jobie 309-677-3191 134 A
jskaggs@bradley.edu
SKALNIK, John 205-387-0511 1 D
john.skalnik@bscc.edu
SKAMRA, Brian 920-748-8174 494 J
skamrab@ripon.edu
SKANTZ, Ingrid 423-236-2833 423 F
ilskantz@southern.edu
SKARE, Donald 406-756-3822 263 E
SKARI, Lisa 503-491-7211 374 B
lisa.skari@mhcc.edu
SKARRO, Scott 701-255-3285 347 A
sskaro@uttc.edu
SKARSTEN, Fawn 810-762-3327 232 A
skarsten@umich.edu
SKATES, Kathy 229-430-3524 114 I
kskates@albanytech.edu
SKAUG, Benjamin, M 817-921-8740 445 A
bskaug@swbts.edu
SKEETE-WALKER, Dawn 718-270-1234 317 B
dawn.walker@downstate.edu
SKELCHER, Bradley 302-857-6000 90 E
SKELLON, Hilary 720-890-8922 81 I
president@itea.edu
SKELLY, Theresa 978-921-4242 217 B
theresa.skelly@montserrat.edu
SKERIK, Maryellen 630-637-5678 145 F
mjskerik@noctrl.edu
SKERRETT-LLANOS,
Carmen 787-993-8870 512 A
carmen.skerrett@upr.edu
SKEVAKIS, Anthony 410-704-2270 204 E
askevakis@towson.edu
SKEVINGTON, Deborah 504-571-1290 188 B
dskevi@dcc.edu
SKIDMORE, Alan 304-766-3261 490 D
askidmore@wvstateu.edu
SKIDMORE, Ashley 815-836-5212 142 F
skidmoas@lewisu.edu
SKIDMORE, Charlene 515-271-2999 165 J
charlene.skidmore@drake.edu
SKIDMORE, Daniel, L 315-445-4759 303 I
skidmodl@lemoyne.edu
SKIDMORE, Heather 304-424-8210 490 F
heather.skidmore@wvup.edu
SKIDMORE, Teresa 417-873-7826 252 G
tskidmore@drury.edu
SKIDMORE, Tom 317-921-4909 158 D
tskidmore2@ivytech.edu
SKILES, Adam, L 260-359-4130 156 C
askiles@huntington.edu
SKILES, Jesse 304-462-6221 489 L
jesse.skiles@glenville.edu
SKILL, Thomas, D 937-229-3511 362 C
tskill1@udayton.edu
SKILLETT, Jenei 402-826-8253 267 A
jenei.skillett@doane.edu
SKILLMAN, Josh 317-274-7200 157 D
jskillma@iupui.edu
SKINDER, Michelle 845-455-8738 143 I
mskinder@mchenry.edu
SKINKLE, Lee 417-328-1601 259 I
lskinkle@sbuniv.edu
SKINNER, Adrienne 269-467-9945 224 C
askinner@glenoaks.edu
SKINNER, Bruce 573-651-5103 259 H
bskinner@semo.edu
SKINNER, Daniel 973-748-9000 276 A
daniel_skinner@bloomfield.edu
SKINNER, Deborah 641-784-5110 166 E
dskinner@graceland.edu
SKINNER, Denese 806-371-5252 429 E
denese.skinner@actx.edu
SKINNER, Donal 740-593-2723 358 K
dcs@ohio.edu
SKINNER, Erik 916-660-7600 64 D
eskinner2@sierracollege.edu
SKINNER, Georgia 404-627-2681 116 C
georgia.skinner@beulah.edu
SKINNER, Gregory 757-524-5595 477 C
gskinner@vwu.edu
SKINNER, James 580-774-3788 370 A
james.skinner@swosu.edu
SKINNER, Kendra 573-651-2274 259 H
ksskinner@semo.edu
SKINNER, Lee 504-865-5000 191 F
leeskinner@tulane.edu
SKINNER, Loren 409-772-6615 456 E
leskinne@utmb.edu
SKINNER, Robert 304-473-8557 491 D
skinner_b@wvwc.edu
SKINNER, Sara 269-927-6851 226 F
skinner@lakemichigancollege.edu
SKINNER, Thomas 619-260-7974 72 I
tskinner@sandiego.edu
SKIPPER, Curt 601-635-2111 246 A
cskipper@eccc.edu

SKIPPER, Eric .... 843-208-8000 413 C
eskipper@uscb.edu
SKIPPER, Nick .... 850-973-9495 104 L
skippern@nfc.edu
SKIPWORTH, Stan .... 909-621-8033.. 37 B
stan.skipworth@claremont.edu
SKIPWORTH, Stan .... 909-621-8291.. 37 C
stan_skipworth@cuc.claremont.edu
SKIRA, Aaron .... 937-775-3208 364 E
aaron.skira@wright.edu
SKLAR, Jay .... 314-434-4044 252 C
jay.sklar@covenantseminary.edu
SKLEDER, Anne, A .... 770-534-6110 116 D
askleder@brenau.edu
SKLENKA, Angela .... 813-974-5711 111 C
SKLUT, John .... 509-313-3175 480 F
sklut@gonzaga.edu
SKLUT, John .... 509-313-3715 480 F
sklut@gonzaga.edu
SKLUT, John .... 509-313-3175 480 F
sklut@gonzaga.edu
SKOGLUND,
Elizabeth, A .... 410-543-6161 204 D
easkoglund@salisbury.edu
SKOGLUND, Kirk .... 816-501-4813 258 I
kirk.skoglund@rockhurst.edu
SKOMP, Elizabeth .... 386-822-7515 112 A
eskomp@stetson.edu
SKONER, Peter, R .... 814-472-3085 397 F
pskoner@francis.edu
SKORA, Sue .... 847-925-6921 138 G
sskora@harpercollege.edu
SKORTZ, Brian .... 270-686-6416 179 J
brian.skortz@brescia.edu
SKOWYRA, Jamie .... 508-213-2131 217 H
jamie.skowyra@nichols.edu
SKRABUT, Stan .... 508-541-1774 209 A
sskrabut@dean.edu
SKROCKI, Kyle .... 802-387-6887 462 C
kyleskrocki@landmark.edu
SKRYD, Jackie .... 727-302-6809 107 E
skryd.jackie@spcollege.edu
SKUKA, Eva .... 973-278-5400 275 I
esk@berkeleycollege.edu
SKUKA, Eva .... 973-278-5400 291 E
esk@berkeleycollege.edu
SKURZEWSKI-SERVANT,
Missy .... 715-422-5356 499 B
missy.skurzewskiservant@mstc.edu
SKVARLA, Jennifer .... 815-836-5201 142 F
skvarlje@lewisu.edu
SLABACH, Frederick, G . 817-531-4401 451 C
fslabach@txwes.edu
SLABAUGH, David .... 864-644-5558 412 D
dslabaugh@swu.edu
SLABAUGH, Dawnie ...... 530-938-5822.. 39 C
slabaugh@siskiyous.edu
SLABAUGH, Katie .... 765-285-1545 153 H
kslabaugh@bsu.edu
SLABODEN, Carolyn ...... 781-283-2216 219 E
cslaboden@wellesley.edu
SLABODEN, Scott .... 508-793-3644 208 D
sslabode@holycross.edu
SLABU, Claudia .... 360-442-2216 481 D
cslabu@lowercolumbia.edu
SLABY, Greg .... 216-421-7940 350 H
gslaby@cia.edu
SLACK, Judy .... 800-553-4674 156 B
jslack@horizonuniversity.edu
SLACK, Lynn .... 412-391-7021 401 J
lslack@vti.edu
SLADE, David .... 706-236-2229 116 B
dslade@berry.edu
SLADE, Heather .... 805-969-3626.. 55 J
hslade@pacifica.edu
SLADE, Lisa .... 203-332-5017.. 86 F
lslade@housatonic.edu
SLADE, Patricia .... 973-877-3209 277 G
slade@essex.edu
SLADEN, Ian .... 215-895-2185 382 F
ian.sladen@drexel.edu
SLAFF, Sara .... 410-704-4003 204 E
sslaff@towson.edu
SLAFKOSKY, Mary .... 616-632-2453 221 E
mvs002@aquinas.edu
SLAGAN, Stephanie .... 760-921-5524.. 56 A
stephanie.slagan@paloverde.edu
SLAGAN, Stephanie .... 760-921-5421.. 56 A
stephanie.slagan@paloverde.edu
SLAGELL, Jeff .... 662-846-4441 245 G
jslagell@deltastate.edu
SLAGER, Joan .... 859-251-4563 180 F
joan.slager@frontier.edu
SLAGER, Karen .... 815-802-8110 141 D
kslager@kcc.edu
SLAGHT, Charles .... 559-730-3821.. 39 B
charless@cos.edu
SLAGLE, Roger .... 828-689-1306 331 C
rslagle@mhu.edu
SLAGTER, Cynthia .... 616-526-6551 222 C
cslagter@calvin.edu
SLANIA, Heather .... 410-225-2311 200 D
hslania@mica.edu
SLATE, Kristine .... 903-233-4332 439 A
kristineslate@letu.edu
SLATE, Selina .... 706-886-6831 126 D
sslate@tfc.edu
SLATER, Alicia .... 845-575-3000 305 D
alicia.slater@marist.edu
SLATER, Bernata .... 650-358-6795.. 62 I
slaterb@smccd.edu
SLATER, Erin .... 804-752-7305 469 F
erinslater@rmc.edu
SLATER, Glenn .... 814-234-7755 398 E
SLATER, Ian .... 617-745-3000 209 B
SLATER, Ian .... 765-677-2138 158 B
ian.slater@indwes.edu
SLATER, Joseph .... 931-372-3172 426 B
jslater@tntech.edu
SLATER, Kara .... 616-395-7836 225 D
slater@hope.edu
SLATER, Larry .... 901-678-2020 426 G
lslater2@memphis.edu
SLATER, Lori .... 417-873-7267 252 G
lslater002@drury.edu
SLATER, Nikki .... 325-670-1130 436 I
nikki.slater@hsutx.edu
SLATER, Rebecca .... 309-298-4500 153 A
r-slater@wiu.edu
SLATER, Richard .... 773-291-6100 135 E
SLATER, Tracy .... 207-216-4439 195 J
tslater@yccc.edu
SLATER, Troy .... 231-348-6610 228 H
tslater@ncmich.edu
SLATER, William .... 615-675-5255 428 C
wslater@welch.edu
SLATER, Willie .... 334-724-4880.... 7 D
wslater@tuskegee.edu
SLATON, Andrea .... 479-788-7701.. 21 G
andrea.slaton@uafs.edu
SLATTERY, Katheryn ...... 815-836-5275 142 F
slatteka@lewisu.edu
SLAUGHTER, Arnie .... 859-572-5538 184 E
slaughtera@nku.edu
SLAUGHTER, Clinton .... 530-895-2366.. 27 C
slaughtercl@butte.edu
SLAUGHTER, Clinton .... 707-476-4242.. 58 I
clinton-slaughter@redwoods.edu
SLAUGHTER, Craig .... 740-427-5430 354 I
slaughterc@kenyon.edu
SLAUGHTER, John .... 254-267-7024 441 K
jslaughter@rangercollege.edu
SLAUGHTER, Lauren ..... 308-398-7548 266 A
laurenslaughter@cccneb.edu
SLAUGHTER,
Matthew, J .... 603-646-2460 273 D
matthew.j.slaughter@dartmouth.edu
SLAUGHTER, Mildred .... 361-593-2834 447 D
mildred.slaughter@tamuk.edu
SLAUGHTER, Reggie ..... 540-828-5462 464 L
rslaughter@bridgewater.edu
SLAUGHTER, Shirley ..... 510-981-2840.. 56 I
sslaughter@peralta.edu
SLAUGHTER ALLISON,
Michelle .... 619-961-4222.. 68 A
mallison@tjsl.edu
SLAVAS, Douglas .... 413-565-1000 206 D
dslavas@baypath.edu
SLAVAS, Douglas .... 413-755-4026 216 A
deslavas@stcc.edu
SLAVEN-LEE, Pamela ..... 843-271-7222.. 92 D
pamelaslavenlee@gwu.edu
SLAVENS, Joseph .... 503-255-0332 374 C
joeslavens@multnomah.edu
SLAVIN, Cheryl .... 212-824-2294 301 B
cslavin@huc.edu
SLAVIN, Dennis .... 646-660-6504 292 L
dennis.slavin@baruch.cuny.edu
SLAVIN, Joan, L .... 714-850-4800.. 67 H
slavin@taftu.edu
SLAVIN, Ken .... 210-486-0883 429 C
kslavin4@alamo.edu
SLAVIN, Lisa .... 781-239-2501 214 G
lslavin@massbay.edu
SLAVIN, Marc .... 510-628-8013.. 48 C
mslavin@lincolnuca.edu
SLAVINSKAS, Brian, R .. 312-915-8730 143 C
bslavin@luc.edu
SLAWIK, Nora .... 651-779-3338 237 H
nora.slawik@century.edu
SLAWSON, Linda .... 903-923-2137 435 H
lslawson@etbu.edu
SLAYMAKER, Valerie ..... 651-213-4746 236 C
vslaymaker@hazeldenbettyford.edu
SLAYTER, Misty .... 318-487-5443 187 J
mistyslayter@cltcc.edu
SLAYTON, Mark .... 480-947-6644.. 14 N
SLAZER, Mary .... 985-545-1500 188 E
SLEAR, Sharon .... 410-532-5321 201 D
sslear@ndm.edu
SLEASMAN, Brent, C ..... 419-434-4201 364 C
president@winebrenner.edu
SLEDGE, Dennis .... 229-430-2837 114 I
dsledge@albanytech.edu
SLEIGHT, Garth .... 406-874-6212 263 H
sleightg@milescc.edu
SLEJKO, Christa .... 972-273-3010 435 B
cslejko@dcccd.edu
SLEMMER, Duane .... 280-467-8039 132 E
dlslemmer@nnu.edu
SLENKER, Robert .... 229-931-2074 120 D
robert.slenker@gsw.edu
SLEPITZA, Ron .... 816-501-3750 250 F
ron.slepitza@avila.edu
SLEPPPY,
Christopher, G .... 317-921-4882 158 E
SLEVA, Michael .... 616-451-3511 223 E
msleva@davenport.edu
SLEZAK, Cyrill .... 801-863-6205 460 D
cslezak@uvu.edu
SLIDER, Chancey .... 318-473-6578 189 F
cslider@lsua.edu
SLIFE, JR., Harry .... 808-743-2952 451 A
harry.slife@ttuhsc.edu
SLIMAN, David .... 601-266-6633 249 F
david.sliman@usm.edu
SLINGER, Ron .... 406-874-6165 263 H
president@milescc.edu
SLINKARD, Tiffany .... 417-455-5636 252 E
tiffanyslinkard@crowder.edu
SLIWINSKI, Laura .... 858-513-9240.. 68 K
laura.sliwinski@ashford.edu
SLIWOSKI, Richard, F ... 804-828-9647 473 B
rfsliwoski@vcu.edu
SLIZEWSKI, James .... 215-489-2220 382 B
james.slizewski@delval.edu
SLOAN, Daniel .... 530-226-4125.. 64 E
dsloan@simpsonu.edu
SLOAN, Gary .... 585-785-1355 299 F
gary.sloan@flcc.edu
SLOAN, Joe .... 504-526-4745 190 E
joes@nationsu.edu
SLOAN, Joel, A .... 719-333-9115 503 D
joel.sloan@usafa.edu
SLOAN, Jon, R .... 504-526-4745 190 E
jonroy@nationsu.edu
SLOAN, Mary Anne .... 765-430-0600 158 D
msloan26@ivytech.edu
SLOAN, Noel .... 806-742-4250 450 F
noel.a.sloan@ttu.edu
SLOAN, Robert .... 281-649-3450 437 B
rsloan@hbu.edu
SLOAN, Stacey .... 303-751-8700.. 78 D
sloan@belrea.edu
SLOAN, Tim .... 801-524-1986 459 E
tim.sloan@ldsbc.edu
SLOAN, Todd .... 203-582-7525.. 88 G
todd.sloan@quinnipiac.edu
SLOAN LATTA, Marcia .. 419-434-5722 362 D
latta@findlay.edu
SLOANE, Todd .... 585-585-1836 299 F
todd.sloane@flcc.edu
SLOANE, Tomecca .... 919-760-8631 331 D
sloaneto@meredith.edu
SLOAS, Ike .... 901-843-3880 423 A
sloasi@rhodes.edu
SLOBERT, Yantee .... 585-385-8423 313 F
yslobert@sjfc.edu
SLOCKETT, Deena .... 407-303-7747.. 95 B
deena.slockett@ahu.edu
SLOCUM, Cameron .... 214-648-6404 457 A
cameron.slocum@utsouthwestern.edu
SLOCUM, Dameian .... 401-598-1000 404 D
dameian.slocum@jwu.edu
SLOCUM, Jeff .... 315-655-7192 292 H
jslocum@cazenovia.edu
SLOCUM, Stacy, S .... 585-385-8388 313 F
sslocum@sjfc.edu
SLOKA, Sandra, L .... 815-740-5026 152 H
ssloka@stfrancis.edu
SLOMOVITS, Mendel ..... 732-414-2834 285 H
SLON, Dennis .... 703-908-7600 468 H
dennis.slon@marymount.edu
SLONE, Greta .... 606-886-3863 181 E
gslone0020@kctcs.edu
SLONE, Katrina .... 606-368-6091 178 G
katrinaslone@alc.edu
SLONE, Tammy, L .... 937-766-7987 349 E
slonet@cedarville.edu
SLONIKER, Steven .... 509-574-4676 486 D
ssloniker@yvcc.edu
SLOOP, John, M .... 615-322-7360 428 A
john.m.sloop@vanderbilt.edu
SLOSS, Brian .... 715-346-4617 497 A
bsloss@uwsp.edu
SLOTA, Danielle .... 206-878-3710 481 B
dslota@highline.edu
SLOTNICK, Ruth .... 508-531-2783 212 D
ruth.slotnick@bridgew.edu
SLOTTERBACK, Carissa . 612-720-4048 400 H
cslotterback@pitt.edu
SLOVER, Todd .... 603-513-1379 274 G
todd.slover@granite.edu
SLOWE, Ashley .... 215-965-4000 390 E
SLOWENSKY, Joseph .... 714-744-7882.. 36 B
jslowens@chapman.edu
SLOWINSKI, Mandy ...... 715-346-4771 497 A
mandy.slowinski@uwsp.edu
SLUDER, Dusti .... 850-484-2232 105 H
dsluder@pensacolastate.edu
SLUDER, Richard, D ..... 615-898-2324 422 C
richard.sluder@mtsu.edu
SLUDER, Robin .... 423-478-7727 422 J
rsluder@ptseminary.edu
SLUIS, Kimberly .... 630-637-5152 145 F
kasluis@noctrl.edu
SLUPIK, Monida .... 916-348-4689.. 41 H
mslupik@epic.edu
SLUSSER, Jeney .... 941-309-4033 106 J
jslusser@ringling.edu
SLUSSER, Margaret .... 609-652-4501 283 E
margaret.slusser@stockton.edu
SLYTER, Alexis .... 417-873-7848 252 G
aslyter@drury.edu
SMAGLO, Stephanie ...... 757-233-8757 477 C
ssmaglo@vwu.edu
SMAIL, John .... 704-687-5629 342 D
jsmail@uncc.edu
SMAJIC, Alen .... 315-792-5331 306 K
asmajic@mvcc.edu
SMALARZ, Matthew ...... 215-885-2360 389 C
msmalarz@manor.edu
SMALE, Heather .... 207-454-1025 195 I
hsmale@wccc.me.edu
SMALE, Maura .... 718-260-5497 295 A
msmale@citytech.cuny.edu
SMALL, Allison .... 503-375-7193 372 H
asmall@corban.edu
SMALL, Blake .... 425-889-5235 481 H
blake.small@northwestu.edu
SMALL, Brent .... 575-562-2194 286 B
brent.small@enmu.edu
SMALL, Brent .... 502-897-4721 184 G
bsmall@sbts.edu
SMALL, Christine .... 760-384-6219.. 46 M
christine.small@cerrocoso.edu
SMALL, Cindy .... 406-265-3787 264 E
csmall@msun.edu
SMALL, Darlene .... 843-383-8039 408 B
dsmall@coker.edu
SMALL, Elizabeth .... 508-793-3759 208 D
esmall@holycross.edu
SMALL, Erika, E .... 843-349-2071 408 A
esmall@coastal.edu
SMALL, Gillian .... 201-692-7094 277 I
gsmall@fdu.edu
SMALL, Jessica .... 575-562-2218 286 B
jessica.small@enmu.edu
SMALL, Jessica .... 575-562-2118 286 C
jessica.small@enmu.edu
SMALL, Jonathan .... 504-865-5000 191 F
SMALL, LaTrice .... 501-420-1242.. 16 L
latrice.small@arkansasbaptist.edu
SMALL, Natissia .... 314-516-5128 261 C
smalln@umsl.edu
SMALL, Samuel .... 360-623-8614 478 F
samuel.small@centralia.edu
SMALL, Sonya .... 252-451-8261 336 E
sysmall345@nashcc.edu
SMALL, Steven, L .... 972-883-2355 455 B
small@utdallas.edu

SMALL, Tyvi 865-974-6270 427 B
tsmall@utk.edu
SMALL KELLOGG, Rebecca 315-786-6549 303 C
rsmallkellogg@sunyjefferson.edu
SMALLEN, Stephanie 423-746-5213 426 C
ssmallen@tnwesleyan.edu
SMALLIDGE, Dianne 617-732-1528 216 D
dianne.smallidge@mcphs.edu
SMALLING, Scott, J 315-268-6473 295 F
ssmallin@clarkson.edu
SMALLING, Steven 315-268-4368 295 F
sssmalli@clarkson.edu
SMALLING, Susan 507-786-3350 243 D
smalling@stolaf.edu
SMARR, Debbie 903-415-2592 436 G
smarrd@grayson.edu
SMARRELLA, Tony 530-226-4607 64 E
tsmarrella@simpsonu.edu
SMART, III, Clifton, M 417-836-8500 256 G
president@missouristate.edu
SMART, Gary 406-771-5140 264 F
gary.smart@gfcmsu.edu
SMART, James, G 305-284-4505 113 C
jsmart@miami.edu
SMART, Monica 325-670-1595 436 I
monica.j.smart@hsutx.edu
SMART, Robert 616-331-2281 224 G
smartr@gvsu.edu
SMART, Rod 760-355-6113 45 K
rod.smart@imperial.edu
SMART, Scott 575-562-2611 286 B
scott.smart@enmu.edu
SMART, William 615-297-7545 417 G
smartb@aquinascollege.edu
SMATRESK, Neal 940-565-4307 453 E
president@unt.edu
SMEDLEY, David 973-877-3000 277 G
dsmedley@essex.edu
SMEDLEY, Susan 660-543-4640 260 G
smedley@ucmo.edu
SMEED, Shane 816-584-6202 258 C
shane.smeed@park.edu
SMELKINSON, Michael 443-518-4522 199 F
msmelkinson@howardcc.edu
SMELSER, Dick, W 865-694-6565 425 B
rwsmelser@pstcc.edu
SMENT, Nicole 608-262-0110 495 C
nsment@uwsa.edu
SMETANKA, John 724-805-2227 397 I
john.smetanka@email.stvincent.edu
SMID, Terry 563-425-5359 170 H
smidt@uiu.edu
SMIDT, Niki 605-658-5641 416 D
niki.smidt@usd.edu
SMIGIELSKI, Kristin 217-351-2535 147 C
ksmigielski@parkland.edu
SMILEY, Ellen 318-274-3228 192 C
smileye@gram.edu
SMILEY, Joseph 727-712-5851 107 E
smiley.joseph@spcollege.edu
SMILEY, Justin 760-744-1150 56 B
jsmiley@palomar.edu
SMILEY, Scott 432-552-2605 456 F
smiley_s@utpb.edu
SMISEK, Connie 507-537-7329 241 D
connie.smisek@smsu.edu
SMITH, Adam, D 717-361-1161 383 C
smithadam1@etown.edu
SMITH, Adrian 212-343-1234 306 G
asmith@mcny.edu
SMITH, Adriana, K 864-938-3777 411 D
adsmith@presby.edu
SMITH, Alan 256-549-8601 2 B
asmith@gadsdenstate.edu
SMITH, Alan 435-797-1000 460 C
al.smith@usu.edu
SMITH, Alexa 917-493-4477 305 A
asmith@msmnyc.edu
SMITH, Alicia 732-987-2454 278 A
asmith@georgian.edu
SMITH, Alisa 419-824-3963 355 C
asmith@lourdes.edu
SMITH, Alison 330-672-3709 354 A
alisonjs@kent.edu
SMITH, Allen, D 785-827-5541 175 E
allen.smith@kwu.edu
SMITH, Altrice 804-706-5079 474 B
asmith@jtcc.edu
SMITH, Amanda 972-883-6154 455 B
als072000@utdallas.edu
SMITH, Amanda 815-921-3102 148 B
a.smith@rockvalleycollege.edu
SMITH, Amanda 806-874-3571 432 J
amanda.smith@clarendoncollege.edu
SMITH, Amber 317-788-2412 161 H
smitha008@uindy.edu
SMITH, Amber 806-291-3425 457 I
smitha@wbu.edu
SMITH, Amy 205-226-4699 4 F
acsmith3@bsc.edu
SMITH, Amy 513-745-5615 362 A
amy.smith@uc.edu
SMITH, Amy, E 716-926-8877 301 E
asmith@hilbert.edu
SMITH, Ana 520-515-3636 11 M
smitha@cochise.edu
SMITH, Andrew 423-775-7218 418 D
asmith2831@bryan.edu
SMITH, Andrew 865-471-3243 418 E
asmith@cn.edu
SMITH, Angela 229-928-1373 120 D
angela.smith@gsw.edu
SMITH, Angi 423-585-2680 425 F
angi.smith@ws.edu
SMITH, Ann 317-738-8109 155 D
asmith@franklincollege.edu
SMITH, Ann, T 859-238-5459 180 B
ann.smith@centre.edu
SMITH, Anna Mae 570-484-2209 394 E
asmith7@lockhaven.edu
SMITH, Annabelle 254-526-1205 432 D
annabelle.smith@ctcd.edu
SMITH, Anne 910-362-7028 332 H
awsmith427@mail.cfcc.edu
SMITH, Annie 864-424-8055 413 H
alsmith@mailbox.sc.edu
SMITH, April 936-468-4048 445 E
alsmith@sfasu.edu
SMITH, Ariel 478-471-4394 121 F
SMITH, Ashley 704-378-1237 330 D
apsmith2@jcsu.edu
SMITH, Astria 214-768-4738 444 D
astrias@smu.edu
SMITH, Atheria 510-981-2800 56 I
atheriasmith@peralta.edu
SMITH, Barbra 256-761-6415 7 B
bsmith@talladega.edu
SMITH, Bea, W 864-592-4448 412 E
smithbw@sccsc.edu
SMITH, Beatrice 619-574-6909 55 E
bsmith@pacificcollege.edu
SMITH, Becky 614-823-1420 359 H
rsmith@otterbein.edu
SMITH, Benny 828-227-3078 343 E
bennysmith@wcu.edu
SMITH, Beth 845-938-3808 503 I
beth.smith@westpoint.edu
SMITH, Beverly 770-720-5523 124 G
beverly.smith@reinhardt.edu
SMITH, Beverly, R 804-237-5467 476 F
brsmith@vuu.edu
SMITH, Bill 401-232-6078 404 A
bsmith8@bryant.edu
SMITH, Bill 818-345-7921 39 D
bsmith@columbiacollege.edu
SMITH, Bill 870-972-2169 17 E
billsmith@astate.edu
SMITH, Bill 703-812-4757 468 D
bsmith@leland.edu
SMITH, Blake 865-981-8264 421 C
blake.smith@maryvillecollege.edu
SMITH, JR., Bob 316-978-3444 178 D
bobby.smith@wichita.edu
SMITH, Bobby 719-549-2210 80 B
bobby.smith@csupueblo.edu
SMITH, Bonnie 850-718-2451 97 E
smithb@chipola.edu
SMITH, Brad 214-329-4447 430 K
brad.smith@bgu.edu
SMITH, Brad, D 937-766-7872 349 E
smthb@cedarville.edu
SMITH, Brad, K 608-743-4596 498 D
bsmith32@blackhawk.edu
SMITH, Bradford 601-973-5015 245 B
bmsmith@belhaven.edu
SMITH, Bradley, D 574-807-7255 154 B
bradley.smith@betheluniversity.edu
SMITH, Brenda, A 585-292-2365 307 B
bsmith2@monroecc.edu
SMITH, Brian 701-858-3210 345 E
brian.smith.2@minotstateu.edu
SMITH, Brian 443-997-5661 199 G
brismith@jhu.edu
SMITH, Brian 716-888-2785 292 F
smith@canisius.edu
SMITH, Brian 803-938-3707 413 G
bcsmith2@uscsumter.edu
SMITH, Brian, D 972-241-3371 434 D
bsmith@dallas.edu
SMITH, Brian, T 734-764-7272 231 H
btsm@umich.edu
SMITH, Brian, T 734-764-7270 231 H
btsm@umich.edu
SMITH, Brien, N 330-941-3103 364 H
bnsmith06@ysu.edu
SMITH, Brittain 508-793-2011 208 D
bsmith@holycross.edu
SMITH, Bruce 256-761-6225 7 B
bcsmith@talladega.edu
SMITH, Bruce 303-871-6103 84 E
bruce.smith@du.edu
SMITH, Bryan 270-706-8616 181 G
bryan.smith@kctcs.edu
SMITH, Bryan 419-448-2045 353 E
bsmith3@heidelberg.edu
SMITH, Bryan, F 850-599-3183 109 I
bryanf.smith@famu.edu
SMITH, Bryanna, E 360-442-2100 481 D
bsmith@lowercolumbia.edu
SMITH, Buffy 651-962-8010 244 E
bsmith@stthomas.edu
SMITH, C. Drew 870-230-5466 19 D
smithc@hsu.edu
SMITH, Cade 256-824-2274 8 B
cade.smith@uah.edu
SMITH, Carl 760-245-4271 74 D
carl.smith@vvc.edu
SMITH, Carlton 918-587-6789 370 H
carlton.smith@tws.edu
SMITH, Carol 303-273-3911 79 J
cesmith@mines.edu
SMITH, Carol 559-297-4500 45 N
clsmith@iot.edu
SMITH, Carol, L 765-658-4580 154 J
clsmith@depauw.edu
SMITH, Carola 805-965-0581 63 A
smithc@sbcc.edu
SMITH, Carola 805-965-0581 63 A
smith@sbcc.edu
SMITH, Carolyn 713-798-7640 431 D
carolyns@bcm.edu
SMITH, Carolyn, A 304-697-7550 487 E
csmith@huntingtonjuniorcollege.edu
SMITH, Caryn 847-947-5229 145 D
clsmith@nl.edu
SMITH, Ceeon, D 803-705-4558 406 G
ceeon.smith@benedict.edu
SMITH, Ceil 856-351-2644 283 B
csmith@salemcc.edu
SMITH, Charity 501-375-9845 20 F
cosmith@philander.edu
SMITH, Charles 334-727-8448 7 D
csmith1@tuskegee.edu
SMITH, Charles 256-761-6205 7 B
csmith@talladega.edu
SMITH, Charles 816-414-3700 256 C
csmith@mbts.edu
SMITH, Charles 910-678-8484 334 E
smithch@faytechcc.edu
SMITH, Charles, M 979-209-8272 431 H
charlesm@blinn.edu
SMITH, Charmaine, I 340-692-4070 513 E
hsmithc@uvi.edu
SMITH, Charmian 516-572-7376 307 E
charmian.smith@ncc.edu
SMITH, Cheryl 413-782-1542 220 A
cheryl.smith@wne.edu
SMITH, Chip 478-934-3064 122 F
chip.smith@mga.edu
SMITH, Chris 901-334-5835 421 E
csmith@memphisseminary.edu
SMITH, Christa 785-670-1873 178 C
christa.smith@washburn.edu
SMITH, Christala 580-745-3185 369 G
clsmith@se.edu
SMITH, Christie 585-245-5571 318 B
csmith@geneseo.edu
SMITH, Christine 678-466-5406 117 D
christinesmith@clayton.edu
SMITH, Christine 423-425-4646 427 C
chris-smith@utc.edu
SMITH, Christopher 870-777-5722 22 I
christopher.smith@uaht.edu
SMITH, Christopher 740-427-5415 354 I
smith5@kenyon.edu
SMITH, Chuck 612-874-3700 237 A
SMITH, Cindy 256-469-7333 5 H
admin@hbc1.edu
SMITH, Cindy 432-264-5034 437 F
csmith@howardcollege.edu
SMITH, Cindy 412-281-2600 396 B
csmith@pci.edu
SMITH, Claire 210-999-8841 451 E
csmith9@trinity.edu
SMITH, Colleen, A 928-266-4217 11 O
colleen.smith@coconino.edu
SMITH, Connie 209-476-7840 67 E
csmith@clcm.net
SMITH, Connie 207-581-1372 196 G
csmith@maine.edu
SMITH, Connor 214-333-5365 434 C
connors@dbu.edu
SMITH, Cortney 918-647-1213 365 E
clsmith@carlalbert.edu
SMITH, Courtney 859-233-8124 185 C
cesmith@transy.edu
SMITH, Courtney 973-313-6203 283 C
courtney.smith@shu.edu
SMITH, Craig 406-768-5555 263 F
csmith@fpcc.edu
SMITH, JR., Cris 251-380-2285 6 H
crsmith@shc.edu
SMITH, Crystal 973-596-3690 279 E
crystal.s.smith@njit.edu
SMITH, Crystal, M 301-546-0180 201 E
smithcm@pgcc.edu
SMITH, Cynthia 301-687-4328 204 C
colsmith@frostburg.edu
SMITH, D. Gordon 801-422-6384 458 H
smithg@law.byu.edu
SMITH, Dale, T 914-831-0311 297 A
dsmith@cw.edu
SMITH, Dan 414-443-8800 498 A
dan.smith@wlc.edu
SMITH, Dana 760-944-4449 52 F
dsmith@miracosta.edu
SMITH, Dane 202-885-8663 94 D
dsmith@wesleyseminary.edu
SMITH, Daniel 864-242-5100 406 H
SMITH, Darby 903-927-3300 458 F
dsmith3@wileyc.edu
SMITH, Darnell 210-784-5500 447 E
dsmith@tamusa.edu
SMITH, Darren, A 407-582-3015 113 I
dsmith335@valenciacollege.edu
SMITH, Darron 931-372-3149 426 B
darronsmith@tntech.edu
SMITH, Daryl 716-829-7623 298 E
smithd@dyc.edu
SMITH, David 718-260-5345 295 A
dsmith@citytech.cuny.edu
SMITH, David 718-571-7727 314 F
dsmith3@edaff.com
SMITH, David 310-568-5538 56 G
david.smith@pepperdine.edu
SMITH, David, B 518-783-2432 315 E
dsmith@siena.edu
SMITH, Davis 919-532-5770 338 G
dbsmith9@waketech.edu
SMITH, Dayle 310-338-7504 51 A
dayle.smith@lmu.edu
SMITH, Dean 504-568-5960 189 H
dgsmith@lsuhsc.edu
SMITH, Dean 919-687-3600 328 F
dean.j.smith@duke.edu
SMITH, Dean 918-631-2554 371 C
dean-smith@utulsa.edu
SMITH, Deanna 601-484-8895 247 A
dsmith40@meridiancc.edu
SMITH, Debbi 516-877-3522 289 I
smith8@adelphi.edu
SMITH, Debbie 281-998-6150 443 C
deborah.smith@sjcd.edu
SMITH, Deborah 281-998-6150 443 B
SMITH, Deborah 281-998-6150 443 A
deborah.smith@sjcd.edu
SMITH, Deborah 409-212-5724 431 A
SMITH, Debra 931-393-1690 424 F
dsmith@mscc.edu
SMITH, Del 256-372-5092 1 A
del.smith@aamu.edu
SMITH, Denise 765-973-8560 157 A
dss3@iu.edu
SMITH, Denise 914-633-2067 302 E
dsmith@iona.edu
SMITH, Denise 567-661-7250 359 I
denise_smith4@owens.edu
SMITH, Denise, D 804-662-3196 472 C
ddsmith@richmond.edu
SMITH, Dennis 530-226-4754 64 E
dsmith@simpsonu.edu

SMITH, Dennis .... 252-335-0821 333 G
dennis_smith@albemarle.edu
SMITH, Deron .... 615-966-6280 421 B
dsmith2@lipscomb.edu
SMITH, Derrek .... 256-233-8274.... 4 C
derrek.smith@athens.edu
SMITH, Derrick .... 585-785-1471 299 F
derrick.smith@flcc.edu
SMITH, Devin .... 402-643-7328 266 G
devin.smith@cune.edu
SMITH, Diana .... 303-762-6886.. 80 I
diana.smith@denverseminary.edu
SMITH, Diane .... 931-372-3554 426 B
dianesmith@tntech.edu
SMITH, Dolores .... 951-639-5230.. 53 A
dolsmith@msjc.edu
SMITH, Donald .... 530-741-6700.. 77 E
SMITH, Donald .... 623-845-3070.. 13 C
don.smith@gccaz.edu
SMITH, Donald .... 215-641-6534 390 C
dsmith4@mc3.edu
SMITH, Donald, L .... 270-745-6256 186 C
donald.smith@wku.edu
SMITH, Donna .... 601-925-3313 247 C
dsmith@mc.edu
SMITH, Donna .... 701-777-4172 345 B
donna.smith@und.edu
SMITH, Doug .... 508-565-1344 219 A
dougsmith@stonehill.edu
SMITH, Doug .... 910-695-3811 337 H
smithd@sandhills.edu
SMITH, Douglas .... 716-839-8237 298 A
dsmith@daemen.edu
SMITH, Douglas .... 765-361-6011 163 B
smithd@wabash.edu
SMITH, Drew .... 248-689-8282 232 C
dsmith4@walshcollege.edu
SMITH, Dwayne .... 203-332-5224.. 86 F
dsmith@housatonic.edu
SMITH, Dwayne .... 813-974-3151 111 C
mdsmith8@usf.edu
SMITH, III, Dwight .... 832-813-6603 439 C
dwight.smith@lonestar.edu
SMITH, E. Ashley .... 713-718-7514 437 C
edgar.smith2@hccs.edu
SMITH, Ed .... 615-550-3160 428 E
ed.smith@williamsoncc.edu
SMITH, Elaine .... 865-471-3208 418 E
esmith@cn.edu
SMITH, Elaine, L .... 516-833-8181 289 I
elsmith@adelphi.edu
SMITH, Elizabeth .... 918-631-2238 371 C
elizabeth-smith-43@utulsa.edu
SMITH, Elizabeth, F .... 603-646-3999 273 D
elizabeth.f.smith@dartmouth.edu
SMITH, Elmer, R .... 770-216-2960 121 I
ers@ict.edu
SMITH, Emmett .... 252-538-4317 335 B
esmith956@halifaxcc.edu
SMITH, Eric .... 315-464-5763 317 C
smither@upstate.edu
SMITH, Eric .... 270-789-5202 180 A
epsmith@campbellsville.edu
SMITH, Eric .... 304-357-4358 487 J
ericsmith@ucwv.edu
SMITH, Eric, D .... 805-922-6966.. 24 I
ericdsmith@hancockcollege.edu
SMITH, Eric, L .... 906-227-1314 228 I
esmith@nmu.edu
SMITH, Ericka .... 702-895-3958 271 D
ericka.smith@unlv.edu
SMITH, Erin .... 828-898-3416 330 E
smithe@lmc.edu
SMITH, Erin .... 214-333-5770 434 C
erins@dbu.edu
SMITH, Erin, T .... 724-946-7327 402 D
smithet@westminster.edu
SMITH, Eva .... 425-640-1394 480 A
esmith@edcc.edu
SMITH, JR., Frank, M .. 502-776-1443 184 F
fsmith@simmonscollegeky.edu
SMITH, Fred .... 410-706-8337 203 A
fsmith@umaryland.edu
SMITH, Frederick .... 201-200-3474 279 D
fsmith@njcu.edu
SMITH, Frederick .... 507-933-8809 236 A
fredericksmith@gustavus.edu
SMITH, Fritz .... 562-907-4951.. 76 B
fritz@whittier.edu
SMITH, Gabie .... 336-278-6490 328 J
gsmith@elon.edu
SMITH, Garrett .... 480-461-7211.. 13 D
garrett.smith@mesacc.edu
SMITH, Gary .... 716-827-2507 323 G
smithg@trocaire.edu
SMITH, Gavin .... 206-546-4792 484 B
gavinsmith@shoreline.edu
SMITH, Gene .... 910-755-7302 332 F
smithgene@brunswickcc.edu
SMITH, Gene, D .... 614-292-2477 358 D
smith.5407@osu.edu
SMITH, George .... 207-879-8955 194 G
gsmith@idsva.edu
SMITH, Gerritt .... 937-328-6062 350 G
smithg@clarkstate.edu
SMITH, Gigi .... 843-792-2228 410 C
smithgi@musc.edu
SMITH, Glenn, C .... 503-552-1514 374 D
gsmith@nunm.edu
SMITH, Grace .... 310-434-4454.. 63 C
smith_grace@smc.edu
SMITH, Greg .... 530-242-7525.. 64 C
gsmith@shastacollege.edu
SMITH, Greg .... 704-922-6476 334 G
smith.greg@gaston.edu
SMITH, Greg .... 973-408-3580 277 A
gsmith2@drew.edu
SMITH, Gregory .... 662-720-7164 248 C
gcsmith@nemcc.edu
SMITH, Gregory .... 714-449-7456.. 51 B
gsmith@ketchum.edu
SMITH, Gregory .... 610-399-2240 393 F
gsmith@cheyney.edu
SMITH, Gregory, A .... 619-388-6589.. 60 H
gsmith@sdccd.edu
SMITH, Harris .... 505-277-2112 288 J
hdsmith@unm.edu
SMITH, Heather, L .... 989-774-3197 222 E
hutch1hl@cmich.edu
SMITH, Heidi .... 714-816-0366.. 68 E
heidilinn.smith@trident.edu
SMITH, Heidi .... 713-313-1178 449 B
heidi.smith@tsu.edu
SMITH, Hilary, B .... 618-537-6981 144 A
hbsmith@mckendree.edu
SMITH, Holly .... 870-512-7841.. 18 A
holly_smith@asun.edu
SMITH, Holly .... 812-488-2241 161 G
hh98@evansville.edu
SMITH, Holly .... 253-964-6287 482 E
hsmith@pierce.ctc.edu
SMITH, Howard .... 620-235-4113 177 A
smith@pittstate.edu
SMITH, Ian .... 740-427-5181 354 I
smith18@kenyon.edu
SMITH, Idelia .... 413-552-2228 214 F
ismith@hcc.edu
SMITH, Ivan .... 301-934-7724 198 G
ilsmith1@csmd.edu
SMITH, J. Cole .... 315-443-4341 321 G
colesmit@syr.edu
SMITH, Jacqueline .... 713-221-8541 453 A
smithja@uhd.edu
SMITH, Jacquelyn, M ... 623-572-3601 144 F
jsmith@midwestern.edu
SMITH, Jake .... 608-263-2985 495 D
soas@soas.wisc.edu
SMITH, James .... 740-392-6868 356 G
james.smith@mvnu.edu
SMITH, James .... 334-241-5436.... 7 C
jesmith@troy.edu
SMITH, James .... 214-860-2232 434 I
jhsmith@dcccd.edu
SMITH, James, M .... 734-487-2211 223 K
president@emich.edu
SMITH, Jamie .... 602-557-5757.. 16 G
jamie.smith@phoenix.edu
SMITH, Jamie .... 580-581-2245 365 D
jamsmith@cameron.edu
SMITH, Jamie, M .... 941-752-5587 109 G
smithj4@scf.edu
SMITH, Janet .... 423-869-6287 421 A
janet.smith@lmunet.edu
SMITH, Janet, F .... 931-540-2510 424 C
janet.smith@columbiastate.edu
SMITH, Janet, M .... 724-946-7139 402 D
smithjm@westminster.edu
SMITH, Jared .... 704-355-4305 327 G
robert.smith2@carolinascollege.edu
SMITH, Jared .... 716-375-2622 313 C
jasmith@sbu.edu
SMITH, Jarret, L .... 540-828-5469 464 L
jlsmith@bridgewater.edu
SMITH, Jason .... 870-248-4000.. 18 F
jason.smith@blackrivertech.edu
SMITH, Jason .... 415-503-6281.. 61 D
jsmith@sfcm.edu
SMITH, Jason .... 269-687-5642 231 A
jsmith07@swmich.edu
SMITH, Jason .... 409-944-1356 436 E
jsmith@gc.edu
SMITH, Jason .... 903-823-3198 446 A
jason.smith@texarkanacollege.edu
SMITH, Jason, S .... 832-842-9064 452 C
jsmith10@uh.edu
SMITH, Jason, S .... 832-842-9064 452 D
jsmith10@uh.edu
SMITH, Jeannette .... 901-333-4737 425 D
jgsmith@southwest.tn.edu
SMITH, Jeff .... 806-720-7482 439 D
jeff.smith@lcu.edu
SMITH, Jeff .... 941-487-4353 110 D
jsmith@ncf.edu
SMITH, Jeff .... 970-339-6253.. 77 H
jeff.smith@aims.edu
SMITH, Jeffrey .... 907-260-7422.... 9 D
SMITH, Jeffrey .... 305-809-3149.. 97 O
jeffrey.smith6@cfk.edu
SMITH, Jeffrey .... 404-225-4634 115 H
jsmith@atlantatech.edu
SMITH, JR., Jeffrey .... 617-732-1652 209 D
smithj4@emmanuel.edu
SMITH, Jeffrey, N .... 716-645-4592 316 C
jeff@buffalo.edu
SMITH, Jenelle .... 251-578-1313.... 3 D
jsmith@rstc.edu
SMITH, Jennifer .... 847-925-6523 138 G
jsmith5@harpercollege.edu
SMITH, Jennifer .... 212-229-5300 308 A
jennifer.smith@newschool.edu
SMITH, Jennifer, A .... 253-535-7811 482 A
jennifer.smith@plu.edu
SMITH, Jennifer, B .... 270-745-6824 186 C
jennifer.breiwa.smith@wku.edu
SMITH, Jenny .... 828-328-7252 330 F
jenny.smith@lr.edu
SMITH, Jerry .... 928-344-7535.. 11 A
jerry.smith@azwestern.edu
SMITH, Jesse .... 661-255-1050.. 28 G
jsmith@calarts.edu
SMITH, Jesse, R .... 601-477-4100 246 G
jesse.smith@jcjc.edu
SMITH, Jessi, L .... 719-255-3963.. 84 C
jsmith20@uccs.edu
SMITH, Jessica .... 276-326-4473 464 J
jsmith@bluefield.edu
SMITH, Jill .... 859-257-8907 185 F
jhsmith@uky.edu
SMITH, Jim .... 858-513-9240.. 68 K
jim.smith@ashford.edu
SMITH, Jim .... 918-293-5234 368 B
jim.smith10@okstate.edu
SMITH, Joan .... 303-914-6410.. 83 C
joan.smith@rrcc.edu
SMITH, Joe .... 509-313-6801 480 F
smithj@gonzaga.edu
SMITH, Joel .... 308-432-6345 268 D
jsmith@csc.edu
SMITH, John .... 251-460-6171.... 9 A
johns@southalabama.edu
SMITH, John .... 515-271-2969 165 J
john.smith@drake.edu
SMITH, John, W .... 309-298-1888 153 A
jw-smith@wiu.edu
SMITH, John, W .... 931-372-6338 426 B
jwsmith@tntech.edu
SMITH, Johnny .... 252-493-7915 336 H
jmsmith@email.pittcc.edu
SMITH, Joianne, L .... 847-635-1801 146 G
joismith@oakton.edu
SMITH, Jordan .... 270-809-5706 184 D
jsmith3@murraystate.edu
SMITH, Joseph, R .... 410-651-6862 203 D
jrsmith@umes.edu
SMITH, Joshua .... 410-617-5343 200 B
jssmith2@loyola.edu
SMITH, Joshua .... 606-337-1164 180 C
joshua.smith@ccbbc.edu
SMITH, Joshua .... 714-592-7878.. 44 I
jsmith@haven.edu
SMITH, Joshua .... 254-501-5838 447 A
j.smith@tamuct.edu
SMITH, Joy, S .... 864-833-8275 411 D
jssmith@presby.edu
SMITH, Joyya .... 617-725-4110 219 B
jsmith19@suffolk.edu
SMITH, Judy .... 814-824-3650 389 G
jsmith@mercyhurst.edu
SMITH, Julie .... 503-725-3773 375 E
smithju@pdx.edu
SMITH, Juliet .... 410-822-5400 198 F
jsmith@chesapeake.edu
SMITH, Justin .... 541-917-4214 373 G
smithju@linnbenton.edu
SMITH, Kala .... 573-681-5032 254 G
smithk@lincolnu.edu
SMITH, Kalith .... 575-624-8380 287 B
ksmith@nmmi.edu
SMITH, Karan .... 252-249-1851 336 F
ksmith@pamlicocc.edu
SMITH, Karen .... 405-325-3021 370 K
karen-smith@ou.edu
SMITH, Karen .... 908-737-0585 278 E
ksmith@kean.edu
SMITH, Karen .... 410-827-5704 198 F
ksmith@chesapeake.edu
SMITH, Kari .... 575-769-4021 285 O
kari.smith@clovis.edu
SMITH, Karl .... 253-566-5127 484 E
ksmith@tacomacc.edu
SMITH, Karla .... 406-447-5501 263 B
klsmith@carroll.edu
SMITH, Kate .... 480-517-8270.. 13 G
catherine.smith@riosalado.edu
SMITH, Katelyn .... 719-587-7401.. 77 G
ksmith@adams.edu
SMITH, Kathleen, E .... 562-902-3367.. 65 I
kathleensmith@scuhs.edu
SMITH, Kathleen, S .... 405-325-3221 370 K
kathleensheasmith@ou.edu
SMITH, Kathy .... 614-234-2230 356 E
ksmith@mccn.edu
SMITH, Katrina .... 806-291-3557 457 I
smithk@wbu.edu
SMITH, Kelli .... 239-590-1900 109 K
kjsmith@fgcu.edu
SMITH, Kelli .... 718-405-3234 296 F
kelli.smith@mountsaintvincent.edu
SMITH, Kelli .... 607-777-2400 316 B
kksmith@binghamton.edu
SMITH, Kelli .... 718-429-6600 324 D
kelli.smith@vaughn.edu
SMITH, Kelly .... 619-849-2213.. 57 J
kellysmith@pointloma.edu
SMITH, Kelly, A .... 804-523-5449 474 A
ksmith@reynolds.edu
SMITH, Kelly, M .... 706-542-1914 126 G
kelly.smith@uga.edu
SMITH, Ken .... 254-295-4644 453 D
kasmith@umhb.edu
SMITH, Ken, L .... 423-478-7736 422 J
ksmith@ptseminary.edu
SMITH, Kenneth .... 508-929-8121 213 G
kenneth.smith@worcester.edu
SMITH, Kenny .... 928-428-8291.. 12 F
kenny.smith@eac.edu
SMITH, JR., Kent, J .... 405-466-3201 366 C
president@langston.edu
SMITH, Kevin .... 515-271-1400 165 G
SMITH, Kevin, L .... 785-864-4711 177 J
klsmith12@ku.edu
SMITH, Kevin, M .... 716-888-8501 292 F
smithk@canisius.edu
SMITH, Khrystal .... 864-503-5125 414 A
ksmith@uscupstate.edu
SMITH, Krista .... 229-928-1331 120 D
krista.smith@gsw.edu
SMITH, Kristen .... 870-512-7850.. 18 A
kristen_smith@asun.edu
SMITH, Kristen .... 516-686-7751 308 I
mksmith@nyit.edu
SMITH, Kristen .... 610-328-8299 398 G
registrar@swarthmore.edu
SMITH, Kristen, L .... 563-588-7042 168 A
kristen.smith@loras.edu
SMITH, Kristi .... 270-745-5352 186 C
kristi.smith@wku.edu
SMITH, Kristin .... 717-464-7050 387 F
SMITH, Kyla .... 727-867-1166.. 98 J
SMITH, Kyle .... 254-295-4591 453 D
klsmith@umhb.edu
SMITH, Kyle, A 570-326-3761 392W
kas54@pct.edu
SMITH, Kyle, D .... 337-550-1218 189 G
kdsmith@lsue.edu
SMITH, Lace, M .... 253-535-7001 482 A
smithla@plu.edu
SMITH, Lane, M .... 205-726-2905.... 6 E
SMITH, Larissa .... 434-395-2776 468 F
smithlm@longwood.edu

SMITH, Ryan .... 256-352-8233.... 3 I
ryan.smith@wallacestate.edu
SMITH, Ryan .... 309-438-2135 140 D
rlsmith@ilstu.edu
SMITH, Ryan .... 740-245-7204 363 A
rsmith@rio.edu
SMITH, Sam .... 402-363-5621 270 D
samsmith@york.edu
SMITH, Samantha .... 912-871-4779 123 J
ssmith@ogeecheetech.edu
SMITH, Samantha .... 409-882-3083 449 H
samantha.smith@lsco.edu
SMITH, Sandra, B .... 540-674-3600 474 E
ssmith@nr.edu
SMITH, Sandy .... 760-366-5296.. 40 E
ssmith@cmccd.edu
SMITH, Scott .... 906-635-6672 226 G
ssmith58@lssu.edu
SMITH, Scott, A .... 803-786-3672 408 D
scsmith@columbiasc.edu
SMITH, Scott, F .... 305-899-3085.. 96 A
sfsmith@barry.edu
SMITH, Sean .... 805-565-6063.. 76 A
sesmith@westmont.edu
SMITH, Selina .... 301-687-4187 204 C
ssmith@frostburg.edu
SMITH, Sharon .... 404-965-8118.. 10 E
ssmith2@aiuniv.edu
SMITH, Sharon, E .... 616-632-2902 221 E
smithsha@aquinas.edu
SMITH, Shawn .... 217-732-3168 142 G
SMITH,
Shawn Michelle .... 312-899-5100 149 F
SMITH, Sheila .... 615-329-8710 419 H
shsmith@fisk.edu
SMITH, Shelley .... 256-840-4128.... 3 F
shelley.smith@snead.edu
SMITH, Shelley .... 601-968-5940 245 B
sasmith@belhaven.edu
SMITH, Shelly .... 304-263-0979 488 A
SMITH, Sherri .... 304-696-2809 489 M
smithsc@marshall.edu
SMITH, Sinclair .... 215-596-8800 401 E
SMITH, Sonya .... 845-437-7583 324 C
SMITH, Stacey .... 509-777-4388 486 C
skammsmith@whitworth.edu
SMITH, Stacey .... 901-435-1351 420 I
stacey_smith@loc.edu
SMITH, Stanley .... 334-347-2623.... 2 A
ssmith@escc.edu
SMITH, Stephanie .... 312-362-7552 136 H
ssmit185@depaul.edu
SMITH, Stephanie .... 337-421-6966 188 J
stephanie.smith@sowela.edu
SMITH, Stephanie .... 606-546-1259 185 D
sasmith@unionky.edu
SMITH, Stephanie .... 928-523-3937.. 14 H
stephanie.smith@nau.edu
SMITH, Stephanie .... 415-551-9287.. 28 B
stephanie.smith@cca.edu
SMITH, Stephen .... 253-566-5055 484 E
ssmith@tacomacc.edu
SMITH, Steve .... 865-974-6600 427 B
stevensmith@utk.edu
SMITH, Steve .... 205-652-3576.... 9 B
sdsmith@uwa.edu
SMITH, Steve .... 507-389-5022 239 D
steven.smith@mnsu.edu
SMITH, Steve .... 432-264-5019 437 F
sismith@howardcollege.edu
SMITH, Steven .... 970-521-6657.. 82 C
steven.smith@njc.edu
SMITH, Steven .... 775-682-5613 271 E
ssmith@unr.edu
SMITH, Steven .... 973-378-9815 283 C
steven.smith@shu.edu
SMITH, Steven .... 915-831-6472 436 A
ssmith54@epcc.edu
SMITH, Steven .... 304-424-8000 490 F
steven.smith@wvup.edu
SMITH, Steven, E .... 516-877-3304 289 I
stsmith@adelphi.edu
SMITH, Steven, J .... 413-565-1000 206 D
ssmith@baypath.edu
SMITH, Steven, N .... 262-243-5700 492 E
steve.smith@cuw.edu
SMITH, Stuart, A .... 859-858-3511 179 D
stuart.smith@asbury.edu
SMITH, Sue .... 812-372-1623 158 D
sgsmith@ivytech.edu
SMITH, Susan .... 817-515-1225 445 F
susan.smith@tccd.edu

SMITH, Susanne .... 614-947-6160 352 J
suzanne.smith@franklin.edu
SMITH, Suzanne .... 413-755-4221 216 A
smsmith@stcc.edu
SMITH, Suzanne, R .... 229-928-1361 120 D
suzanne.smith@gsw.edu
SMITH, Sybil .... 562-947-8755.. 65 I
sybilsmith@scuhs.edu
SMITH, Tabitha .... 276-328-0131 472 E
tabitha.smith@uvawise.edu
SMITH, Tamalea .... 908-709-7093 284 D
tsmith@ucc.edu
SMITH, Tamara, J .... 770-720-5659 124 G
tjs@reinhardt.edu
SMITH, Tammy .... 716-338-1054 303 A
tammysmith@mail.sunyjcc.edu
SMITH, Tammy .... 540-674-3600 474 E
tsmith@nr.edu
SMITH, Tara .... 419-434-4035 362 D
travis@findlay.edu
SMITH, Tariva .... 678-323-7700.. 93 H
SMITH, Tawanikka .... 718-482-5590 294 F
tsmith@lagcc.cuny.edu
SMITH, Teresa .... 410-778-7204 205 B
tsmith23@washcoll.edu
SMITH, Teresa .... 207-453-5155 195 F
tsmith@kvcc.me.edu
SMITH, Teresa, A .... 856-227-7200 276 E
tasmith@camdencc.edu
SMITH, Teresa, L .... 714-879-3901.. 45 G
tlsmith@hiu.edu
SMITH, Terri .... 661-763-7817.. 67 G
tsmith@taftcollege.edu
SMITH, Terry .... 732-247-5241 279 C
tsmith@nbts.edu
SMITH, Terry .... 713-646-1708 443 I
tsmith@stcl.edu
SMITH, Thomas .... 202-319-5115.. 92 A
artsandsciences@cua.edu
SMITH, Thomas .... 314-392-2264 256 E
smitht@mobap.edu
SMITH, Thomas .... 865-573-4517 420 E
tsmith@johnsonu.edu
SMITH, Thomas, J .... 616-234-3951 224 F
tsmith@grcc.edu
SMITH, Thomas, P .... 570-941-7620 401 F
thomas.smith@scranton.edu
SMITH, Tierra .... 813-253-7160 102 B
tsmith175@hccfl.edu
SMITH, Tiffany .... 816-322-0110 251 B
tiffany.smith@calvary.edu
SMITH, Tim .... 205-226-4660.... 4 F
tsmith@bsc.edu
SMITH, Todd .... 713-831-7225 454 G
tsmith1@stthom.edu
SMITH, Tony .... 434-528-5276 477 B
SMITH, Tracee .... 601-877-6170 245 A
tracee@alcorn.edu
SMITH, Tracy, D .... 501-882-8806.. 17 D
tdsmith@asub.edu
SMITH, Travis .... 561-433-2330 108 J
SMITH, Travis .... 315-386-7300 320 B
smitht@canton.edu
SMITH, Travis, A .... 920-433-6621 491 G
travis.smith@bellincollege.edu
SMITH, Trent .... 620-276-9510 174 B
trent.smith@gcccks.edu
SMITH, Treva .... 706-867-2761 127 A
treva.smith@ung.edu
SMITH, Tricia, G .... 410-548-3999 204 D
tgarveysmith@salisbury.edu
SMITH, Trish .... 417-255-7900 256 H
SMITH, Trisha .... 202-884-9000.. 94 A
smithtri@trinitydc.edu
SMITH, Tyne .... 641-673-1703 171 C
smitht@wmpenn.edu
SMITH, Val .... 626-316-5391.. 63 E
lsmith6@saybrook.edu
SMITH, Valerie, A .... 610-328-8314 398 G
vsmith1@swarthmore.edu
SMITH, Vayta .... 707-527-4508.. 63 D
vsmith@santarosa.edu
SMITH, Vernon .... 304-724-3700 486 F
vsmith@apus.edu
SMITH, Vincent .... 541-552-7672 376 B
SMITH, Virginia .... 405-945-3214 368 C
virginia.smith@okstate.edu
SMITH, W. Randy .... 614-292-5881 358 D
smith.70@osu.edu
SMITH, Wade .... 719-587-7351.. 77 G
wsmith@adams.edu

SMITH,
Walter (Tommy), T ..... 260-470-2668 159 J
wtsmith@manchester.edu
SMITH, Wanda .... 305-237-2377 104 E
wsmith2@mdc.edu
SMITH, Wayne .... 845-341-4261 310 G
wayne.smith@sunyorange.edu
SMITH, Wendall 610-896-1000 385
w1smith@haverford.edu
SMITH, Wendy .... 305-284-4101 113 C
wendy.smith@miami.edu
SMITH, Wendy, J .... 530-226-4128.. 64 E
wsmith@simpsonu.edu
SMITH, Wendy, M .... 307-065-0412 501 G
wsmith@sheridan.edu
SMITH, Wesley .... 804-523-2296 474 A
wsmith@reynolds.edu
SMITH, William .... 860-444-8201 503 G
william.smith@uscg.mil
SMITH, William .... 760-921-5428.. 56 A
william.smith@paloverde.edu
SMITH, William, C .... 508-565-1347 219 A
wsmith1@stonehill.edu
SMITH, III, William, C . 601-984-1010 249 E
wcsmith3@umc.edu
SMITH, Willie, E .... 225-216-8403 187 G
chancellorsoffice@mybrcc.edu
SMITH, Zachary .... 336-334-3004 343 A
zrsmith3@uncg.edu
SMITH, Zelotes .... 415-458-3793.. 41 C
zelotes.smith@dominican.edu
SMITH-BATES,
Jacqui, S .... 206-281-2488 483 G
jacquisb@spu.edu
SMITH-BUTLER, Lisa ..... 843-377-2144 407 A
lsbutler@charlestonlaw.edu
SMITH-CLAY, Deborah .. 859-371-9393 179 G
dclay@beckfield.edu
SMITH-COX, Cathy, L ... 276-964-7338 475 C
cathy.smith-cox@sw.edu
SMITH DICKERSON,
Janet .... 909-621-8355.. 37 B
janet.dickerson@claremont.edu
SMITH-DUNBAR, Hope . 803-641-3786 413 B
hopes@usca.edu
SMITH-HOWELL, Deb .... 402-554-3378 270 A
dsmith-howell@unomaha.edu
SMITH-HUPP, Karen ..... 301-934-2251 198 G
kshupp@cmd.edu
SMITH-JOACHIM,
Vergina .... 501-337-5000.. 18 B
vsmith@asutr.edu
SMITH-KELLER, Keley ... 605-668-1363 415 F
keley.smith-keller@mountmarty.edu
SMITH-MACKLIN,
Alexius .... 412-578-6137 380 B
asmacklin@carlow.edu
SMITH MOORE, Karen .. 718-960-8000 294 A
karen.smithmoore@lehman.cuny.edu
SMITH-PATTERSON,
Trina .... 817-515-7059 445 F
trina.patterson@tccd.edu
SMITH-RODRIGUEZ,
Sharlise .... 914-323-3134 305 B
sharlise.smith@mville.edu
SMITH ROWE, Angela ... 617-451-0010 217 F
SMITH-SIMMONS,
Margie .... 317-274-4417 157 D
smithsim@iupui.edu
SMITH-WARD, Lori, A .. 606-474-3121 181 B
lsmithward@kcu.edu
SMITH-WELLER, Kelly ... 317-274-2451 157 D
kjbrown@iupui.edu
SMITHCAMP, Ronnette .. 831-479-6306.. 27 D
rosmithc@cabrillo.edu
SMITHEE, Deanna .... 812-535-5299 160 H
deanna.smithee@smwc.edu
SMITHER, Edward .... 803-754-4100 408 E
SMITHERS, Marc .... 585-567-9220 302 B
marc.smithers@houghton.edu
SMITHHART, Dana .... 936-633-3213 429 J
dsmithhart@angelina.edu
SMITHSON, Misty .... 620-947-3121 177 I
mistys@tabor.edu
SMOCK, Jordan .... 857-701-1230 215 G
jsmock@rcc.mass.edu
SMOKE, Gladden .... 864-596-9041 408 F
gladden.smoke@converse.edu
SMOKER, Emily .... 717-299-7731 399 C
SMOKER, Gail .... 765-973-8254 157 A
gsmoker@iue.edu
SMOKOWSKI, Peter ...... 617-353-2148 207 E
psmokows@bu.edu

SMOLEN, Jean .... 215-489-2278 382 B
jean.smolen@delval.edu
SMOLEN, Jodi .... 718-820-4917 322 G
jodi.smolen@touro.edu
SMOLEN, Jodi .... 718-820-4917 322 F
jodi.smolen@touro.edu
SMOLENSKY, Marjorie .. 309-341-5463 134 B
msmolensky@sandburg.edu
SMOLICH, James .... 916-446-1275.. 48 B
SMOLOS, Jennifer .... 661-362-3116.. 38 D
jennifer.smolos@canyons.edu
SMOLOVA, Alona .... 757-683-3080 469 B
asmolova@odu.edu
SMOLOW, Bobbie .... 914-395-2476 315 A
bsmolow@sarahlawrence.edu
SMOLOWITZ, Janice ...... 973-655-3714 279 B
smolowitzj@montclair.edu
SMOOT, Althea .... 937-971-2867 359 K
asmoot@payneseminary.edu
SMOOT, Lori .... 410-334-2898 205 D
lsmoot@worwic.edu
SMOROL, Bobbi, H .... 315-792-3128 324 B
bsmorol@utica.edu
SMOTHERS, Anthony .... 319-296-4214 166 H
anthony.smothers@hawkeyecollege.edu
SMOTHERS, SR.,
Roderick, L .... 501-370-5275.. 20 F
rsmothers@philander.edu
SMOTHERS, Traci .... 504-762-3004 188 B
tsmoth@dcc.edu
SMUCKER, April .... 419-372-2620 348 G
aprils@bgsu.edu
SMUDER, Kristin .... 813-253-7180 102 B
ksmuder@hccfl.edu
SMULSON, Erik .... 202-687-8496.. 92 E
ems62@georgetown.edu
SMUNIEWSKI, Kevin ..... 843-792-5944 410 C
smuniewk@musc.edu
SMURDON, Melissa, J . 317-940-8200 154 C
msmurdon@butler.edu
SMYDRA, Tara .... 402-844-7361 268 H
taras@northeast.edu
SMYLE, Faye .... 707-256-7155.. 53 E
fsmyle@napavalley.edu
SMYLIE, Dean .... 909-469-5469.. 75 I
dsmylie@westernu.edu
SMYRE, Russell .... 704-922-6462 334 G
smyre.russell@gaston.edu
SMYRSKI, Rose, M .... 608-342-1182 496 E
smyrskir@uwplatt.edu
SMYSER, Kathleen .... 610-527-0200 397 D
SMYTH, Alicia .... 386-226-7273.. 99 A
alicia.smyth@erau.edu
SMYTH, Conor .... 608-266-2991 498 C
conor.smyth@wtcsystem.edu
SNAPP, Michael, J .... 801-863-8219 460 D
snappmi@uvu.edu
SNAVELY, Joshua, M .... 405-466-3275 366 C
josh.snavely@langston.edu
SNEAD, Mary .... 276-739-2403 475 F
msnead@vhcc.edu
SNEDDEN, Kelly .... 316-323-6085 172 D
ksnedden@butlercc.edu
SNEDDONN, Jeff .... 208-535-5381 131 B
jeff.sneddon@cei.edu
SNEED, Brian .... 915-747-5302 455 C
bjsneed@utep.edu
SNEED, Carlos .... 651-523-2423 236 B
csneed@hamline.edu
SNEED, Gregory, W ...... 740-587-6624 352 A
sneedg@denison.edu
SNEED, Janice, B .... 318-670-9571 191 D
jsneed@susla.edu
SNEED, Kevin, B .... 813-974-2499 111 C
ksneed@usf.edu
SNEED, Mia .... 615-353-3024 424 G
mia.sneed@nscc.edu
SNEED, Stacy .... 860-297-4285.. 89 B
stacy.sneed@trincoll.edu
SNEERINGER, Christine 301-447-5135 201 B
csneeringer@msmary.edu
SNEERINGER, Gerry ...... 301-405-2996 202 H
sneeri@umd.edu
SNELGROVE, Brian .... 478-218-3300 116 G
bsnelgrove@centralgatech.edu
SNELL, Adam .... 919-496-2521 330 I
asnell@louisburg.edu
SNELL, Beverly .... 406-638-3141 263 G
snellb@lbhc.edu
SNELL, Carolyn, R .... 803-535-5338 407 D
csnell@claflin.edu
SNELL, Cynthia .... 803-754-4100 408 E

SOHNS, Dawn, R 607-746-4533 320 D
sohnsdd@delhi.edu
SOHOLT, Pam, B 701-788-4823 345 D
pam.soholt@mayvillestate.edu
SOIFER, Yitzchok 845-362-3053 291 B
ysoifer@byts.edu
SOIFFER, Stephen 718-260-5400 295 A
ssoiffer@citytech.cuny.edu
SOIGNIER, Taryn 318-257-2235 192 D
taryns@latech.edu
SOINE, Aeleah 925-631-4139.. 59 I
ahs3@stmarys-ca.edu
SOKENU, Julius 805-378-1407.. 73 J
jsokenu@vcccd.edu
SOKENU, Julius 805-553-4052.. 73 I
SOKIA, Ashley 801-957-4493 461 C
ashley.sokia@slcc.edu
SOKOL, Bryan 314-977-3929 259 F
bryan.sokol@slu.edu
SOKOL, Moshe 718-820-4800 322 G
moshe.sokol@touro.edu
SOKOL, Moshe, Z 718-820-4800 322 F
moshe.sokol@touro.edu
SOKOL, Stacey 804-862-6100 470 C
ssokol@rbc.edu
SOKOLL, Shane 512-313-4207 433 N
shane.sokoll@concordia.edu
SOKOLOSKI, Leo 570-389-4775 393 D
lsokoloski@bloomu.edu
SOLA, Peter, L 651-631-5349 244 D
plsola@unwsp.edu
SOLA-PERKINS, Bianca 708-456-0300 151 D
biancasolaperkins@triton.edu
SOLANDER, Sondra, K .. 620-432-0303 176 D
ssolander@neosho.edu
SOLANO, Maria 213-477-2536.. 52 I
msolano@msmu.edu
SOLAZZO, Daniel 513-732-5204 362 B
solazzds@ucmail.uc.edu
SOLAZZO, James 843-349-2717 408 A
jsolazzo@coastal.edu
SOLAZZO, James 843-347-3161 408 A
SOLBACH, Robin 732-987-2757 278 A
rsolbach@georgian.edu
SOLBACH, Robin 732-987-2681 278 A
rsolbach@georgian.edu
SOLBERG, Greg 301-846-2411 198 I
gsolberg@frederick.edu
SOLBERG, Janet 402-280-2731 266 H
janetsolberg@creighton.edu
SOLBERG, Janet 402-557-7095 265 J
jsolberg@bellevue.edu
SOLBERG, Laura 352-588-8218 107 D
laura.solberg@saintleo.edu
SOLBERG, Roger 814-732-2981 394 B
rsolberg@edinboro.edu
SOLDWISCH, Sandie, S 815-282-7909 149 B
sandie.soldwisch@osfhealthcare.org
SOLDWISCH, Sandie, S 815-282-7900 148 I
sandiesoldwisch@sacn.edu
SOLDZ, Stephen 617-277-3915 207 D
soldzs@bgsp.edu
SOLE, Mary, L 407-823-5496 110 E
mary.sole@ucf.edu
SOLECKI, Amanda 410-287-1003 198 E
asolecki@cecil.edu
SOLEIM, Heather, M 218-477-4060 239 E
heather.soleim@mnstate.edu
SOLEM, Thomas 701-777-0561 345 B
thoms.solem@und.edu
SOLEMBRINO, Karie 410-572-8741 205 D
ksolembrino@worwic.edu
SOLEMSAAS, Rachel, H 808-934-2504 129 I
rsolems@hawaii.edu
SOLERNOU, Sheila 203-285-2393.. 86 E
ssolernou@gatewayct.edu
SOLEY, Mary Ann 773-907-4754 135 C
msoley@ccc.edu
SOLHEIM, Derek, N 319-352-8425 170 J
derek.solheim@wartburg.edu
SOLIBAKKE, Karl 715-682-1202 494 G
ksolibakke@northland.edu
SOLIMAN, Phebe 973-328-5056 276 J
psoliman@ccm.edu
SOLINSKI, Patrick 405-682-1611 367 D
patrick.t.solinski@occc.edu
SOLIS, Amy 701-627-4738 346 F
asolis@nhsc.edu
SOLIS, Carlos 512-245-1799 450 C
crs218@txstate.edu
SOLIS, Federico 956-764-5955 438 H
fsolis@laredo.edu
SOLIS, Francisco 210-486-0063 429 C
fsolis@alamo.edu
SOLIS, Gerard 813-974-1680 111 C
gsolis@usf.edu
SOLIS, Jamie 909-448-4441.. 71 C
jsolis@laverne.edu
SOLIS, Mary 915-747-6087 455 C
mavitia@utep.edu
SOLIS, Ricardo 956-721-5101 438 H
president@laredo.edu
SOLIS, Ricardo, J 956-872-5051 443 H
SOLIS, Santiago 570-422-3463 394 A
ssolis@esu.edu
SOLIS, Shannon 559-638-0300.. 67 D
shannon.solis@reedleycollege.edu
SOLIS, Vanessa 915-215-4300 451 B
vanessa.solis@ttuhsc.edu
SOLIS, Vincent, R 775-445-4236 271 F
vincent.solis@wnc.edu
SOLIZ, Gina, M 315-228-7431 296 E
gsoliz@colgate.edu
SOLIZ, Michele 812-237-8111 156 D
michele.soliz@indstate.edu
SOLIZ, Sandra 713-525-3116 454 G
solizs@stthom.edu
SOLIZ, Ty 432-685-6467 440 B
asoliz@midland.edu
SOLKO-OLLIFF, Carol ... 785-628-4176 173 H
cmsolko@fhsu.edu
SOLLARS, David 785-670-2045 178 C
david.sollars@washburn.edu
SOLLBERGER, Robyn .... 270-789-5305 180 A
rlsollberger@campbellsville.edu
SOLLENBERGER, Mitchel 313-593-5030 231 I
msollenb@umich.edu
SOLLOSI, Nancy, B 336-334-4822 335 A
nbsollosi@gtcc.edu
SOLMAN, Amy, L 724-847-4081 384 C
alsolman@geneva.edu
SOLMS, Daniel, F 260-359-4016 156 C
dsolms@huntington.edu
SOLOCHEK, Beverly 212-217-4000 299 D
beverly_solochek@fitnyc.edu
SOLOMON, Adam 404-669-2097 124 E
adam.solomon@point.edu
SOLOMON, Bobby 662-862-8032 246 E
rtsolomon@iccms.edu
SOLOMON, Ian, H 434-924-0812 472 D
ihs8m@virginia.edu
SOLOMON, Ira 504-865-5422 191 F
isolomon@tulane.edu
SOLOMON, Ishmael 724-805-2564 397 I
ishmael.solomon@stvincent.edu
SOLOMON, Jeffrey, S ... 508-831-5288 220 F
solomon@wpi.edu
SOLOMON, Jeremy 781-239-2637 214 G
jsolomon@massbay.edu
SOLOMON, Jerome 408-498-5154.. 73 B
jsolomon@cogswell.edu
SOLOMON, Joseph 718-851-8721 325 E
SOLOMON, Kimberly .... 713-221-8138 453 A
solomonk@uhd.edu
SOLOMON, Mark 609-895-5653 281 B
masolomon@rider.edu
SOLOMON, Mary Ellen . 412-396-6668 383 A
solomon3@duq.edu
SOLOMON, Michael, J .. 734-764-4401 231 H
mjsolo@umich.edu
SOLOMON, Robert, L .... 216-368-2532 349 D
robert.l.solomon@case.edu
SOLOMON, Ronald 225-216-8267 187 G
solomonr@mybrcc.edu
SOLOMON, Samuel 781-736-8539 208 A
sasolomon@brandeis.edu
SOLOMON, Shoshana ... 973-267-9404 280 F
shoshanasolomon@rca.edu
SOLOMON, Sigrid, B .... 937-481-2270 364 A
sigrid_solomon@wilmington.edu
SOLOMON, Stephanie ... 850-558-4516 112 C
stephanie.solomon@tcc.fl.edu
SOLOMON, Steven 850-201-6549 112 C
steven.solomon@tcc.fl.edu
SOLOMON, William 772-462-7656 102 F
wsolomon@irsc.edu
SOLOMON, William, G . 478-301-2771 122 E
solomon_wg@mercer.edu
SOLOMONSON, Mike .... 928-524-7311.. 14 J
michael.solomonson@npc.edu
SOLOMONT, Alan 617-627-3453 219 C
alan.solomont@tufts.edu
SOLOMOU, Costas 585-245-5619 318 B
solomou@geneseo.edu
SOLORZANO, Fernando 562-985-4101.. 31 D
fernando.solorzano@csulb.edu
SOLOW BOUWER, Linda 707-654-1000.. 32 A
SOLOWAY, Seth 914-251-6196 319 B
seth.soloway@purchase.edu
SOLT, Michael 562-985-5306.. 31 D
michael.solt@csulb.edu
SOLTIS, Bryan 860-727-2217.. 88 A
bsoltis@goodwin.edu
SOLTIS, Corinne 206-934-6739 483 D
corinne.soltis@seattlecolleges.edu
SOLTIS, Robert, P 317-940-8960 154 C
rsoltis@butler.edu
SOLTISH, Michael 845-431-8921 298 D
soltish@sunydutchess.edu
SOLTZ-KNOWLTON, Bonnie 860-528-4111.. 88 A
SOLVERSON, Natalie ..... 608-785-8006 496 A
nsolverson@uwlax.edu
SOM, Andrew 707-654-1085.. 32 A
asom@csum.edu
SOMAN, Sherril 616-331-6821 224 G
somans@gvsu.edu
SOMER, Regina 402-461-2422 266 A
reginasomer@cccneb.edu
SOMERLAD, Tracy 910-755-7422 332 F
somerladt@brunswickcc.edu
SOMERO, Marty 970-351-2502.. 84 F
marty.somero@unco.edu
SOMERS, Charles 215-641-6538 390 C
csomers@mc3.edu
SOMERS, Christine 570-674-6314 390 B
csomers@misericordia.edu
SOMERS, Clayton 919-962-6331 342 C
clayton@unc.edu
SOMERS, Kevin 870-743-3000.. 20 B
ksomers@northark.edu
SOMERS, Micki 870-743-3000.. 20 B
msomers@northark.edu
SOMERVELL, Ron 703-591-7042 466 M
rsomervell@fxua.edu
SOMERVILLE, Charles ... 304-696-2424 489 M
somervil@marshall.edu
SOMERVILLE, Dione 567-661-7200 359 I
dione_somerville@owens.edu
SOMERVILLE, Mark 781-292-2509 210 A
mark.somerville@olin.edu
SOMERVILLE, Mary 303-556-4587.. 84 D
mary.somerville@ucdenver.edu
SOMERVILLE, Mary, M . 408-847-4060.. 52 H
SOMERVILLE, Sandi 951-719-2994.. 58 C
SOMERVILLE, Tim 951-719-2994.. 58 C
doc@golfcollege.edu
SOMMER, Carl 314-792-6140 254 F
sommer@kenrick.edu
SOMMERER, Shaun 660-219-6115 250 A
ssommerer@atsu.edu
SOMMERFELD, Janee 253-833-9111 480
jsommerfeld@greenriver.edu
SOMMERFELD, Marvin .. 913-758-6230 178 E
marvin.sommerfeld@stmary.edu
SOMMERS, Brittany 216-687-2277 350 J
b.sommers52@csuohio.edu
SOMMERS, Donald 212-960-5200 326 D
dsommers@yu.edu
SOMMERS, Greg 972-273-3518 435 E
gsommers@dcccd.edu
SOMMERS, Holly 404-727-2507 118 E
hsomme2@emory.edu
SOMMERS, Janet, B 651-631-5201 244 D
jbsommers@unwsp.edu
SOMMERS, Mary 308-865-8520 269 I
sommersm@unk.edu
SOMMERS, Rhoda 937-328-6060 350 G
sommersr@clarkstate.edu
SOMMERS, Shirley 585-389-2958 307 F
ssommer4@naz.edu
SOMMERS, William 717-262-2002 403 C
william.sommers@wilson.edu
SOMNARAIN, Emry 305-821-3333 100 E
esomnarain@fnu.edu
SOMOZA, Amarilis 305-443-9170 107 A
asomoza@sabercollege.edu
SOMPOLSKI, Robert 847-635-1690 146 G
somplski@oakton.edu
SON, Chang Ho 714-527-0691.. 41 J
SON, Eunkyung 636-327-4645 256 B
SONBOL, Dena 651-290-6398 242 L
dena.sonbol@mitchellhamline.edu
SONDAG, Lynn 415-485-3269.. 41 C
lynn.sondag@dominican.edu
SONDBERG, Brittany 336-272-7102 329 C
brittany.sondberg@greensboro.edu
SONDEJ, Julia 510-626-5300.. 63 E
SONDER, Henk, E 401-456-9577 405 A
hsonder@ric.edu
SONDEY, Joann 914-831-0288 297 A
jsondey@cw.edu
SONDEY, Stephen 973-720-2862 284 J
sondeys@wpunj.edu
SONG, A Li 516-364-0808 308 D
asong@nycollege.edu
SONG, Bokhee 636-327-4645 256 B
dbo@midwest.edu
SONG, Connie 513-231-2223 348 B
csong@athenaeum.edu
SONG, Edward 323-953-4000.. 49 A
songeb@lacitycollege.edu
SONG, Hee Sook 770-220-7925 119 A
joysong@gcuniv.edu
SONG, Jae, M 636-327-4645 256 B
midwest47@daum.net
SONG, Jae Pil 636-327-4645 256 B
jp@midwest.edu
SONG, James 636-327-4645 256 B
SONG, Sarah 818-947-2606.. 49 G
songsj@lavc.edu
SONG, Sui 925-424-1634.. 35 K
ssong@laspositascollege.edu
SONG, Sumie 773-244-5571 145 G
ssong@northpark.edu
SONG, Violet 512-492-3060 430 A
vsong@aoma.edu
SONGAO, Tracey 253-589-5595 478 J
tracey.songao@cptc.edu
SONGBIRD, Brooke 816-654-7000 254 E
SONGCO, Ken 408-855-5037.. 75 D
kenneth.songco@missioncollege.edu
SONGER, Nancy 801-581-8221 459 O
nancy.songer@utah.edu
SONGER, Zacchary 617-670-4539 209 G
zsonger@fisher.edu
SONI, Varun 213-740-6110.. 73 D
vasoni@usc.edu
SONKAYNAR, Zehra 707-527-4431.. 63 D
zsonkaynar@santarosa.edu
SONNENBERG, Jeffrey .. 847-586-4364.. 10 E
jsonnenberg@aiuniv.edu
SONNENBLICK, Carol ... 718-552-1180 295 A
csonnenblick@citytech.cuny.edu
SONNENSTEIN, Mark .... 718-933-6700 307 A
ssonnenstein@monroecollege.edu
SONNENSTRAHL, Samuel 202-651-5060.. 92 C
samuel.sonnenstrahl@gallaudet.edu
SONNTAG, Dave 509-313-6192 480 F
sonntagd@gonzaga.edu
SONNTAG, Michael 803-938-3826 413 G
sonntagm@uscsumter.edu
SONODA, Kazuhiro 509-865-8584 481 A
sonoda_k@heritage.edu
SONODA, Kazuhiro 509-865-8584 481 A
sonoda.k@heritage.edu
SONOFF, Thomas 503-594-1698 372 C
thomas.sonoff@clackamas.edu
SONRICKER, Nicholas ... 716-851-1282 299 B
sonrickern@ecc.edu
SONSTEBY, Jill 651-638-6254 234 D
jks44888@bethel.edu
SONTAG, Michael 513-244-4766 356 F
michael.sontag@msj.edu
SOO, Billy 617-552-3260 207 C
billy.soo@bc.edu
SOODSMA, Heidi 920-693-1631 498 H
heidi.soodsma@gotoltc.edu
SOOKPRASERT, Jai 562-951-4000.. 29 H
jsookprasert@calstate.edu
SOPER, Dessa 949-214-3088.. 39 K
dessa.soper@cui.edu
SOPER, Jeff, D 712-362-0422 167 B
jsoper@iowalakes.edu
SOPER, Kari 620-429-3896 173 A
soper.kari@coffeyville.edu
SOPER, Sarah 765-973-8231 157 A
saeaton@iue.edu
SOPHEA, So 646-313-8000 295 D
sophea.so@guttman.cuny.edu
SOPPE, Janelle 563-425-5339 170 H
soppej@uiu.edu
SORA, Wendy 808-956-9264 129 E
wendytak@hawaii.edu
SORBELLO, Barbara, C . 804-627-5300 464 K
barbara_sorbello@bshsi.org

SPARACINO, Debra .... 864-656-2171 407 E
dcspara@clemson.edu
SPARGEN, Dan .... 402-399-2600 266 F
dspargen@csm.edu
SPARKES, Mike .... 281-425-6327 438 I
msparkes@lee.edu
SPARKMAN, Calvin .... 951-343-4356.. 27 G
csparkman@calbaptist.edu
SPARKMAN, Susan .... 205-652-3587.... 9 B
sgt@uwa.edu
SPARKS, Audrey .... 641-585-8143 170 I
audrey.sparks@waldorf.edu
SPARKS, Brad .... 618-235-2700 150 E
bradley.sparks@swic.edu
SPARKS, Carolyn, B ...... 864-597-4160 414 E
sparkscb@wofford.edu
SPARKS, Cheryl, T .... 432-264-5030 437 F
csparks@howardcollege.edu
SPARKS, Edie .... 209-946-2011.. 71 E
SPARKS, Jane .... 760-757-2121.. 52 F
jsparks@miracosta.edu
SPARKS, Jerry .... 740-474-8896 358 A
jesparks@ohiochristian.edu
SPARKS, John .... 618-634-3230 149 G
johns@shawneecc.edu
SPARKS, Kathy, M .... 651-631-5390 244 D
kmsparks@unwsp.edu
SPARKS, Kenton .... 610-341-4383 383 B
ksparks@eastern.edu
SPARKS, Laura .... 212-353-4240 297 E
sparks@cooper.edu
SPARKS, Maria .... 518-464-8768 299 C
msparks@excelsior.edu
SPARKS, Michele, G ..... 513-529-7596 356 A
sparksm4@miamioh.edu
SPARKS, Rick .... 509-533-8833 479 D
rick.sparks@ccs.spokane.edu
SPARKS, Rick .... 509-533-8833 479 C
rick.sparks@ccs.spokane.edu
SPARKS, Rick .... 540-231-7951 476 C
rasparks@vt.edu
SPARKS, Rickey .... 815-455-8564 143 I
rsparks@mchenry.edu
SPARKS, Sarah .... 719-333-7693 503 D
sarah.sparks1@usafa.edu
SPARKS, Sonny .... 662-472-9015 246 D
sparks@holmescc.edu
SPARKS, Sonny .... 662-472-9015 246 D
ssparks@holmescc.edu
SPARKS, Stacey .... 828-689-1307 331 C
ssparks@mhu.edu
SPARKS, Steve .... 252-222-6087 333 A
sparkss@carteret.edu
SPARKS, Terrell .... 801-878-1494 272 C
tsparks@roseman.edu
SPARLING, Jennifer ...... 760-366-5294.. 40 E
jsparling@cmccd.edu
SPARLING, Steve .... 231-843-5824 233 A
ssparling@westshor.edu
SPARPANA, Eileen .... 906-217-4023 222 A
eileen.sparpana@baycollege.edu
SPARROW, Anita .... 860-512-3223.. 86 G
asparrow@manchestercc.edu
SPATAFORE, Lisa .... 267-341-3477 385 J
lspatafore@holyfamily.edu
SPATAFORE, Marisa .... 408-864-8672.. 42 H
spataforemarisa@deanza.edu
SPATARO, Keith .... 650-543-3853.. 51 G
kspataro@menlo.edu
SPATARO-WILSON,
Jennifer, A .... 540-665-5412 470 G
jspataro@su.edu
SPATES, Gerald .... 336-285-2736 341 D
gspates@ncat.edu
SPATZ, Dan .... 541-506-6034 372 F
dspatz@cgcc.edu
SPAULDING, Angela ..... 806-651-2730 448 B
aspaulding@wtamu.edu
SPAULDING, Brad .... 218-751-8670 242 O
bradspaulding@oakhills.edu
SPAULDING, II,
Henry, W .... 740-392-6868 356 G
hspauldi@mvnu.edu
SPAULDING, Melinda ..... 713-313-1361 449 B
melinda.spaulding@tsu.edu
SPAYD, Ann .... 315-787-4005 300 A
ann.spayd@flhcon.edu
SPAYD, Bonnie .... 610-607-6207 396 H
bspayd@racc.edu
SPAYER, Roger .... 847-925-6360 138 G
rspayer@harpercollege.edu
SPAZIANI, Gina .... 617-879-7053 213 B
gspaziani@massart.edu
SPEAKER, Cindy .... 315-364-3311 324 I
cspeaker@wells.edu
SPEAKMAN, Jennifer ..... 614-236-7127 349 B
jspeakman@capital.edu
SPEAKMAN, Thomas ..... 215-489-4343 382 B
thomas.speakman@delval.edu
SPEAKMAN, Wendy, S .. 260-359-4228 156 C
wspeakman@huntington.edu
SPEAKS, Michael, A ...... 315-443-0790 321 G
maspeaks@syr.edu
SPEAR, Brenda .... 602-489-5300.. 10 F
brenda.spear@arizonachristian.edu
SPEAR, Jeff .... 863-667-5000 108 K
jbspear@seu.edu
SPEAR, Nanette .... 509-434-5213 479 C
nanette.spear@ccs.spokane.edu
SPEAR, Pamela, A .... 603-526-3621 272 H
pspear@colby-sawyer.edu
SPEARIN, Rod .... 248-645-3300 223 D
rspearin@cranbrook.edu
SPEARMAN, Ashlee .... 503-517-1056 377 C
aspearman@warnerpacific.edu
SPEARMAN, Elicia .... 203-582-7722.. 88 G
elicia.spearman@quinnipiac.edu
SPEARMAN, Howard, J . 815-921-4008 148 B
h.spearman@rockvalleycollege.edu
SPEARS, Ashley .... 814-871-5592 384 A
spears005@gannon.edu
SPEARS, Ashley .... 814-732-1633 394 B
aspears@edinboro.edu
SPEARS, Brandon .... 218-679-2860 242 U
SPEARS, Curtis, L .... 210-431-3917 441 B
cspears@ollusa.edu
SPEARS, H. Keith .... 270-789-5000 180 A
SPEARS, Jacqueline, D . 913-541-1220 175 C
jdspears@ksu.edu
SPEARS, Linda, C .... 615-963-5281 426 A
lspears@tnstate.edu
SPEARS, Lori, D .... 510-841-1905.. 26 I
lspears@absw.edu
SPEARS, Marty .... 501-279-4335.. 19 C
mspears@harding.edu
SPEARS, Sylvia .... 617-824-8500 209 C
sylvia_spears@emerson.edu
SPEARS-BOYD, Amy ...... 931-540-2509 424 C
aspears@columbiastate.edu
SPEAS, Penny .... 336-517-1563 327 A
pseas@bennett.edu
SPEAS, Philip, E .... 606-693-5000 183 C
pspeas@kmbc.edu
SPECHT, Andrea .... 952-358-8866 239 G
andrea.specht@normandale.edu
SPECHT, Andy .... 805-922-6966.. 24 I
andy.specht@hancockcollege.edu
SPECHT, Mark, A .... 610-566-1776 403 B
mspecht@williamson.edu
SPECHT, Neva, J .... 828-262-3078 340 I
spechtnj@appstate.edu
SPECK, Christie .... 707-864-7000.. 64 H
christie.speck@solano.edu
SPECTAR, Jem, M .... 814-269-2090 400 H
spectar@pitt.edu
SPECTER, Robert, M ...... 202-319-5606.. 92 A
specter@cua.edu
SPECTOR, Carol .... 617-824-8586 209 C
carol_spector@emerson.edu
SPEED, Coleen .... 318-274-3338 192 C
speedc@gram.edu
SPEED, Heather .... 719-549-3082.. 82 J
heather.speed@pueblocc.edu
SPEED, Melissa .... 276-498-5237 464 D
mspeed@acp.edu
SPEED, Sam .... 318-257-4917 192 D
sspeed@latech.edu
SPEELMAN, Diana .... 814-866-6641 387 D
dspeelman@lecom.edu
SPEER, Brian .... 484-664-4332 390 H
brianspeer@muhlenberg.edu
SPEER, Brian .... 704-406-4269 329 A
bspeer@gardner-webb.edu
SPEER, Jennifer .... 615-868-6503 422 B
SPEERSCHNEIDER, Kim . 518-831-2528 305 C
kspeerschneider@mariacollege.edu
SPEHN, Steven .... 507-222-4271 234 G
sspehn@carleton.edu
SPEIDEL, Daniel .... 603-897-8576 273 I
dspeidel@rivier.edu
SPEISER, Lynn .... 419-267-1312 357 E
lspeiser@northweststate.edu
SPEISSER, Nancy .... 757-493-6946 125 F
nspeisser@southuniversity.edu
SPELL, Ashley .... 312-499-4184 149 F
aspell@saic.edu
SPELL, Bomani .... 850-599-3183 109 I
bomani.spell@famu.edu
SPELL, Paul .... 601-477-4223 246 G
paul.spell@jcjc.edu
SPELLECY, Sean .... 503-251-5727 377 B
sspellecy@uws.edu
SPELLMAN, Carlton .... 910-672-1151 341 C
cspellma@uncfsu.edu
SPELLMAN, Denise .... 504-816-4864 186 I
dspellman@dillard.edu
SPELLMAN, Marcia .... 617-559-8642 210 F
mspellman@hebrewcollege.edu
SPELLMIRE, Mark .... 310-954-4347.. 52 I
mspellmire@msmu.edu
SPELLS, Doretha, J .... 757-727-5213 467 G
doretha.spells@hamptonu.edu
SPELLS, Kaschia .... 252-246-1214 339 C
kspells@wilsoncc.edu
SPELLS, Renee .... 803-793-5174 408 G
spellsr@denmarktech.edu
SPELLS, Rhonda .... 301-546-7014 201 E
spellsrx@pgcc.edu
SPELMAN, Amy .... 309-298-1914 153 A
ae-spelman@wiu.edu
SPENCE, Charles .... 434-592-3503 468 E
cpspence@liberty.edu
SPENCE, Harlan .... 603-862-0322 274 F
harlan.spence@unh.edu
SPENCE, Jeff .... 334-347-2623.... 2 A
jspence@escc.edu
SPENCE, Jeffrey .... 920-565-1000 493 A
SPENCE, Jon, N .... 913-971-3279 176 C
jnspence@mnu.edu
SPENCE, Joseph .... 607-778-5210 317 D
spencejs@sunybroome.edu
SPENCE, Juanita, M ...... 252-335-3586 341 B
jmidgette@ecsu.edu
SPENCE, Laura .... 802-586-7711 462 I
lspence@sterlingcollege.edu
SPENCE, Thomas .... 615-460-6417 418 B
thom.spence@belmont.edu
SPENCE, Weymouth ...... 301-891-4128 205 A
wspence@wau.edu
SPENCER, A. Clayton ..... 207-786-6100 194 A
cspencer@bates.edu
SPENCER, Arlene .... 518-736-3622 300 D
aspencer@fmcc.suny.edu
SPENCER, Barbara .... 269-749-7642 229 J
bspencer@olivetcollege.edu
SPENCER, Chad, A .... 704-894-2000 328 E
SPENCER, Christine ...... 410-837-6134 204 F
cspencer@ubalt.edu
SPENCER, Cindy .... 417-667-8181 252 B
cspencer@cottey.edu
SPENCER, Deborah .... 860-231-5390.. 90 A
dspencer@usj.edu
SPENCER, Dorsey .... 315-228-7425 296 E
dspencer@colgate.edu
SPENCER, Estelle, H ..... 413-205-3461 205 F
estelle.spencer@aic.edu
SPENCER, Gene .... 610-409-3064 401 H
gspencer@ursinus.edu
SPENCER, Janett .... 256-306-2628.... 1 F
janet.spencer@calhoun.edu
SPENCER, Jed .... 801-626-6586 461 A
jedspencer@weber.edu
SPENCER, Jeremy .... 508-626-4500 213 A
jspencer1@framingham.edu
SPENCER, Joel .... 303-329-6355.. 79 L
finaid@cstcm.edu
SPENCER, JR., John ..... 304-327-4118 489 I
jspencer@bluefieldstate.edu
SPENCER, John, D .... 817-515-5079 445 F
john.spencer@tccd.edu
SPENCER, Joi .... 619-260-4540.. 72 I
joi.spencer@sandiego.edu
SPENCER, Joseph, F ..... 419-434-4791 362 D
spencer@findlay.edu
SPENCER, Julie .... 424-207-3763.. 55 C
jspencer@otis.edu
SPENCER, Keith .... 417-667-8181 252 B
kspencer@cottey.edu
SPENCER, Kyle .... 406-656-9950 265 I
kspencer@yellowstonechristian.edu
SPENCER, Lisa .... 304-647-6369 490 C
lspencer@osteo.wvsom.edu
SPENCER, Lori .... 662-846-4794 245 G
lspencer@deltastate.edu
SPENCER, Lydia .... 901-843-3850 423 A
spencerl@rhodes.edu
SPENCER, Mark .... 812-488-2569 161 G
ms628@evansville.edu
SPENCER, Mary Ellen ..... 865-694-6517 425 B
mespencer@pstcc.edu
SPENCER, Morgan .... 843-953-3706 407 C
mspence4@citadel.edu
SPENCER, Nichole .... 706-771-4035 115 J
nichole.spencer@augustatech.edu
SPENCER, Rick, E .... 630-637-5209 145 F
respencer@noctrl.edu
SPENCER, Rosa .... 334-876-9241.... 2 D
rosa.spencer@wccs.edu
SPENCER, Ruth .... 845-431-8673 298 D
ruth.spencer@sunydutchess.edu
SPENCER, Scott .... 412-392-3876 396 G
sspencer@pointpark.edu
SPENCER, Shanan .... 304-876-5276 490 A
sspencer@shepherd.edu
SPENCER, Shannon, M . 419-772-2036 358 C
s-spencer@onu.edu
SPENCER, Shawn .... 678-225-7340 395 G
shawnsp@pcom.edu
SPENCER, Stephen .... 256-233-6502.... 4 C
stephen.spencer@athens.edu
SPENCER, Susan .... 660-263-4100 257 B
susanspencer@macc.edu
SPENCER, Suzette .... 240-567-0000 200 G
suzette.spencer@montgomerycollege.edu
SPENCER, Tammy .... 352-365-3502 103 U
spencert@lssc.edu
SPENCER, Terri .... 303-368-7462.. 82 F
tspencer@pmi.edu
SPENCER, Thomas, E .... 573-882-9500 261 A
spencerte@missouri.edu
SPENCER, Tina .... 702-254-7577 272 A
tina.spencer@northwestcareercollege.edu
SPENCER, Travis .... 908-852-1400 276 G
travis.spencer@centenaryuniversity.edu
SPENCER, Yvette .... 205-226-7720.... 4 F
yspencer@bsc.edu
SPENCER-MONTEIRO,
Carol .... 508-999-8705 212 A
cspencer@umassd.edu
SPENGLER, Gregory, C . 410-706-1264 203 A
gspengler@umaryland.edu
SPENNER, Anne .... 816-235-1576 261 B
spennerae@umkc.edu
SPENSLEY, Nicole .... 803-641-3338 413 B
nicolesp@usca.edu
SPERDUTO, John .... 610-558-5611 391 A
sperdutj@neumann.edu
SPERGER, Herb .... 610-785-6284 397 E
hsperger@scs.edu
SPERICO, Jodie .... 516-877-3118 289 I
jsperico@adelphi.edu
SPERLING, Chad .... 218-793-2436 240 B
chad.sperling@northlandcollege.edu
SPERLING, Jonathan ...... 858-653-6740.. 46 H
jsperling@jpcatholic.edu
SPERLING, Mark .... 219-980-6887 157 C
masperli@iun.edu
SPERLING, Michael .... 845-905-4616 297 G
michael.sperling@culinary.edu
SPERLING, Michael .... 704-991-0357 338 C
msperling0559@stanly.edu
SPERLING, Susan, S ..... 510-723-6641.. 35 J
ssperling@chabotcollege.edu
SPERON, Sarah .... 925-631-4150.. 59 I
ses2@stmarys-ca.edu
SPEROS, Michael .... 916-278-6655.. 32 D
msperos@csus.edu
SPERRAZZA, Alexander . 570-422-3989 394 A
asperrazza@esu.edu
SPERRAZZA, Alexander . 215-646-7300 385 A
sperrazza.a@gmercyu.edu
SPERRING, Tiffany .... 614-222-6183 351 B
tsperring@ccad.edu
SPERRY, Amber .... 402-375-7370 268 F
amsperr1@wsc.edu
SPERRY, Sarah .... 412-396-5894 383 A
sperrys@duq.edu
SPESERT, Douglas .... 310-360-8888.. 26 K
SPETH, Megan .... 540-887-7323 468 G
mspeth@marybaldwin.edu
SPETKA, Rosemary, V ... 315-792-5495 306 K
rspetka@mvcc.edu
SPETS, Steve .... 906-932-4231 224 D
stevem@gogebic.edu
SPETZ, Jason .... 715-232-5076 497 B
spetzj@uwstout.edu
SPEZIANI,
Humberto, M .... 305-284-5450 113 C
hmspez@miami.edu

SPEZZA, Nicholas .... 970-204-8113.. 81 A
nicholas.spezza@frontrange.edu
SPEZZACATENA,
Maricel .... 305-273-4499.. 97 K
maricel@cbt.edu
SPICER, Christopher ..... 360-650-6144 485 I
kit.spicer@wwu.edu
SPICER, Christopher, L . 712-274-5103 168 E
spicer@morningside.edu
SPICER, Erin .... 850-484-1706 105 H
espicer@pensacolastate.edu
SPICER, Gail .... 317-543-3235 159 L
SPICER, Jacqueline .... 989-729-3431 221 K
jspice06@baker.edu
SPICER, Jacqueline .... 989-729-3350 221 F
jspice06@baker.edu
SPICER, Kerry .... 716-839-8519 298 A
kspicer@daemen.edu
SPICER, Kevin .... 508-565-1200 219 A
kspicer@stonehill.edu
SPICER, Lenora .... 602-242-6265.. 11 C
SPICER, LeRoy .... 814-234-7755 398 E
lspicer@southhills.edu
SPICER, Ruby .... 757-823-8053 469 A
rmspicer@nsu.edu
SPICKER, Brian, F .... 480-731-8098.. 12 N
brian.spicker@domail.maricopa.edu
SPIECKER, Karl .... 208-562-3000 131 E
karlspiecker@cwi.edu
SPIED, Vinell .... 973-803-5000 280 B
vspied@pillar.edu
SPIEGEL, Benjamin .... 732-367-1060 275 K
SPIEGEL, Jennifer .... 646-592-6275 326 D
jennifer.spiegel@yu.edu
SPIEGEL, Sam .... 303-273-3884.. 79 J
sspiegel@mines.edu
SPIEGELMAN, Kathy .... 617-373-2226 217 I
SPIELMAN, George, L .... 607-746-4091 320 D
spielmgl@delhi.edu
SPIERS, Cynthia, E .... 419-995-8200 360 C
spiers.c@rhodesstate.edu
SPIERS, Ruthanna .... 334-844-4710.... 4 D
blakerl@auburn.edu
SPIERS, William .... 850-201-6134 112 C
bill.spiers@tcc.fl.edu
SPIES, Dennis .... 847-970-4699 152 I
dspies@usml.edu
SPIES, Don .... 281-459-7629 443 B
don.spies@sjcd.edu
SPIES, Ingrid .... 507-457-5472 241 F
ispies@winona.edu
SPIESMAN, John .... 440-375-7426 354 K
jspiesman@lec.edu
SPIEZIO, Kim .... 304-357-4875 487 J
kimspiezio@ucwv.edu
SPIKEREIT, Damien .... 417-626-1234 257 F
spikereit.damien@occ.edu
SPILLANE, Joseph .... 404-413-2000 120 E
jspillane@gsu.edu
SPILLAR, Karen, K .... 713-500-3310 456 B
karen.k.spillar@uth.tmc.edu
SPILLER, Elizabeth .... 402-472-3751 269 J
espiller2@unl.edu
SPILLERS, James .... 619-482-6551.. 66 A
jspillers@swccd.edu
SPILLERS, Jayda .... 318-371-3035 188 F
jaydaspillers@nltcc.edu
SPILLING, Christopher .. 314-516-5285 261 C
spillingc@umsl.edu
SPILLUM, Carol .... 605-274-4090 414 G
carol.spillum@augie.edu
SPINA, Anthony .... 716-829-7648 298 E
spinaaw@dyc.edu
SPINA, Eric, F .... 937-229-4122 362 C
president19@udayton.edu
SPINA, Rachel .... 610-558-5484 391 A
spinar@neumann.edu
SPINA, Robert .... 409-880-8661 449 G
bob.spina@lamar.edu
SPINARD, John .... 617-873-0689 208 B
john.spinard@cambridgecollege.edu
SPINATO, Danielle .... 202-319-5022.. 92 A
spinato@cua.edu
SPINDLE, Bill .... 605-394-2618 416 H
william.spindle@sdsmt.edu
SPINDLE, Blair .... 405-491-6608 369 H
bspindle@snu.edu
SPINDLE, Tollya .... 405-491-6300 369 H
tspindle@snu.edu
SPINDLER, Logan .... 651-846-1741 241 B
logan.spindler@saintpaul.edu
SPINELLI, Mathew .... 860-773-1672.. 87 G
mspinelli@tunxis.edu
SPINELLI, Stephen .... 781-239-5102 206 B
spinelli@babson.edu
SPINK-FORMANSKI,
Christina .... 716-829-7775 298 E
formanst@dyc.edu
SPINKS, Sean .... 314-446-3669 254 A
spinkss@hssu.edu
SPINNATO, Amy, R .... 443-412-2258 199 D
aspinnato@harford.edu
SPINNATO, Meredith .... 617-585-0200 207 A
meredith.spinnato@the-bac.edu
SPINNER, Clifton .... 614-947-6901 352 J
clifton.spinner@franklin.edu
SPINNER, Elissa .... 617-236-8829 209 G
espinner@fisher.edu
SPINNER, Emily .... 518-243-4381 291 D
harte@ellismedicine.org
SPINNEY, Ann .... 207-768-2734 195 G
naspinne@nmcc.edu
SPINOSA, Tony .... 202-685-3946 502 K
spinosat@ndu.edu
SPINOSA DE VEGA,
Leah .... 612-330-1650 234 A
devega@augsburg.edu
SPIRA, Kathy .... 310-476-9777.. 25 I
SPIRES, Chris .... 803-641-3463 413 B
chriss@usca.edu
SPIRES, Todd .... 309-677-2830 134 A
tspires@fsmail.bradley.edu
SPIRES, Tracy, M .... 864-379-8773 409 E
tspires@erskine.edu
SPIRK, Mary Beth .... 610-861-1424 390 F
spirkm@moravian.edu
SPIRO, Deborah .... 516-572-9887 307 E
deborah.spiro@ncc.edu
SPIRO, Jonathan .... 802-468-1201 463 E
jonathan.spiro@castleton.edu
SPIROU, Costas .... 478-445-4715 119 B
costas.spirou@gcsu.edu
SPIRRISON MONTGOMERY,
Hannah .... 937-319-0128 347 G
hmontgomery@antiochcollege.edu
SPISAK-CAMERON,
Jennifer .... 919-681-0417 328 F
jennifer.cameron@dev.duke.edu
SPISSO, Johnese Maria 310-267-9315.. 69 E
jspisso@mednet.ucla.edu
SPITTAL, David, J .... 913-971-3392 176 C
president@mnu.edu
SPITTAL, Ryan, D .... 815-928-5460 147 A
rspittal@olivet.edu
SPITZ, Cody .... 575-562-2178 286 B
cody.spitz@enmu.edu
SPITZ-KILHEFNER,
Tambi .... 703-416-1441 466 A
admissions@divinemercy.edu
SPITZNAGEL, James ..... 216-397-1614 353 O
jspitz@jcu.edu
SPIVAK, Howard .... 718-951-5342 293 C
howards@brooklyn.cuny.edu
SPIVAK, Michael .... 641-472-7000 168 C
mspivak@miu.edu
SPIVAK, Victoria .... 708-524-6950 137 C
vlamick@dom.edu
SPIVEY, Susan .... 563-386-3570 169 E
SPIWAK, Doug .... 847-925-6969 138 G
dspiwak@harpercollege.edu
SPIZZIRRI, Kristin .... 903-675-6210 451 F
kspizzirri@tvcc.edu
SPOHN, Andrew .... 517-796-8410 225 E
spohnandrewb@jccmi.edu
SPOHR, Robert .... 989-328-1241 228 D
robs@montcalm.edu
SPOKAS, Megan .... 215-951-1270 387 A
spokas@lasalle.edu
SPOLTORE, Janet, D ..... 860-439-2692.. 87 H
janet.spoltore@conncoll.edu
SPOMER, Michelle .... 412-924-1350 396 F
mspomer@pts.edu
SPONN, Jeffrey, M .... 812-464-1982 162 C
jsponn@usi.edu
SPONSELLER, Eric .... 419-995-8457 360 C
sponseller.e@rhodesstate.edu
SPONSELLER, Jared ...... 740-392-6868 356 G
jared.sponseller@mvnu.edu
SPONSELLER, Kimberly . 740-283-6855 352 I
ksponseller@franciscan.edu
SPOON, Adrea .... 419-372-7857 348 G
adrea@bgsu.edu
SPOONER, Melba, C ...... 828-262-2230 340 I
spoonermc@appstate.edu
SPOONER, Michael .... 508-373-5874 216 D
michael.spooner1@mcphs.edu
SPOOR, Suzanne, J ...... 410-777-2448 197 G
sjspoor@aacc.edu
SPORBERT, Derek .... 701-777-3809 345 B
derek.sporbert@und.edu
SPORER, René .... 510-215-4006.. 40 B
rsporer@contracosta.edu
SPORER, Stephen, K ..... 563-387-1862 168 B
sporst01@luther.edu
SPORES, Jon .... 360-383-3440 486 A
jspores@whatcom.edu
SPOSATO, Aime .... 540-365-6934 467 B
asposato@ferrum.edu
SPOSATO, Amanda, L ... 724-458-2051 384 G
alsposato@gcc.edu
SPOSILI, Michael .... 518-580-5610 315 F
msposili@skidmore.edu
SPOTO, Mary .... 352-588-8244 107 D
mary.spoto@saintleo.edu
SPOTORNO, Marianne .. 707-654-1076.. 32 A
mspotorno@csum.edu
SPOTSWOOD, James .... 620-341-5403 173 F
jspotswo@emporia.edu
SPOTTS, Cyndi .... 248-204-4109 227 A
cspotts@ltu.edu
SPOTTS, Deborah .... 602-285-7667.. 13 F
deborah.spotts@phoenixcollege.edu
SPOTTS, Kristie .... 712-749-2635 164 C
spottsk@bvu.edu
SPOTTS-CONRAD,
Cindy .... 816-271-4363 257 A
spotts@missouriwestern.edu
SPOZARSKI, Deborah ... 412-391-7021 401 J
SPRADLEY, Brandon ..... 251-626-3303.... 7 E
bspradley@ussa.edu
SPRADLEY, Minou .... 619-482-6337.. 66 A
mspradley@swccd.edu
SPRADLEY, Wanda .... 434-381-6156 471 I
wspradley@sbc.edu
SPRADLIN, Chris .... 937-778-7887 352 D
cspradlin@edisonohio.edu
SPRADLIN, Michael, R . 901-751-8453 421 G
mspradlin@mabts.edu
SPRADLING, Carol .... 304-357-4747 487 J
carolspradling@ucwv.edu
SPRADLING, John .... 903-785-7661 441 D
jspradling@parisjc.edu
SPRADLING, Steve .... 330-494-6170 360 K
sspradling@starkstate.edu
SPRAGGINS, Lauren ..... 708-237-5050 146 D
SPRAGUE, Alice .... 503-399-2537 372 B
alice.sprague@chemeketa.edu
SPRAGUE, Carol .... 413-545-0698 211 G
sprague@research.umass.edu
SPRAGUE, J. Trae .... 304-462-6412 489 L
trae.sprague@glenville.edu
SPRAGUE, Jamie .... 850-474-2156 111 F
jsprague@uwf.edu
SPRAGUE, Jennifer .... 505-984-6041 288 C
jsprague@sjc.edu
SPRAGUE, Kendra .... 360-442-2121 481 D
ksprague@lowercolumbia.edu
SPRAGUE, Laura .... 518-381-1370 315 B
spraguls@sunysccc.edu
SPRAGUE, Patrick .... 251-380-4000.... 6 H
psprague@shc.edu
SPRAGUE, Viola .... 810-762-9668 226 B
vsprague@kettering.edu
SPRAKER, Matt .... 865-694-6488 425 B
smspraker@pstcc.edu
SPRANGEL, JR.,
Joseph, R .... 540-887-7067 468 G
jsprangel@marybaldwin.edu
SPRANGER, Angela, N .. 757-594-7634 465 M
angela.spranger@cnu.edu
SPRATLIN, Steve .... 256-395-2211.... 3 G
sspratlin@suscc.edu
SPRATT, Bruce, R .... 404-413-3071 120 E
bspratt@gsu.edu
SPRAW, DeeDee .... 419-434-4180 362 D
spraw@findlay.edu
SPRAW, William .... 419-434-4601 362 D
wspraw@findlay.edu
SPRECHER, Art .... 209-946-2251.. 71 E
asprecher@pacific.edu
SPREER-ALBERT,
Frances .... 518-262-5585 289 L
albertf@amc.edu
SPREHE, Dana .... 314-246-4218 262 C
danasprehe27@webster.edu
SPREITZER, Mary .... 630-637-5754 145 F
mspreitzer@noctrl.edu
SPRENGELER, Peg .... 319-398-5500 167 J
peg.sprengeler@kirkwood.edu
SPRENGER, Cathy, J ..... 717-477-1381 395 B
cjspre@ship.edu
SPRIGGS, Barry, A .... 315-684-6054 321 A
spriggbl@morrisville.edu
SPRIGGS, Janet, N .... 336-734-7201 334 F
jspriggs@forsythtech.edu
SPRING, SCC, Joseph ... 973-957-0188 275 C
president@acs350.org
SPRINGALL, Rob .... 814-863-4774 391 G
rgs5296@psu.edu
SPRINGBORG, Martin ... 651-450-3628 238 E
mspringborg@inverhills.edu
SPRINGBORN, Shelly .... 989-328-1243 228 D
shellys@montcalm.edu
SPRINGER, Cynthia .... 260-481-6677 160 C
springec@pfw.edu
SPRINGER, David, W .... 512-471-3200 455 A
dean.dwspringer@austin.utexas.edu
SPRINGER, Eric .... 815-802-8195 141 D
espringer@kcc.edu
SPRINGER, Gabe .... 618-468-3700 142 E
gspringer@lc.edu
SPRINGER, Lisa .... 212-752-1530 304 A
lisa.springer@limcollege.edu
SPRINGER, Mark .... 320-308-3093 240 I
mspringer@stcloudstate.edu
SPRINGER, Mary .... 319-399-8569 164 F
mspringer@coe.edu
SPRINGER, Patrick .... 951-487-3590.. 53 A
pspringer@msjc.edu
SPRINGER, Robert, I ..... 336-278-6644 328 J
springer@elon.edu
SPRINGER, Tracy .... 765-455-9356 157 B
tracylb@iuk.edu
SPRINGS, Chasisity ...... 803-705-4344 406 G
chasisity.springs@benedict.edu
SPRINGS, Joy, P .... 704-687-1713 342 D
jpsprings@uncc.edu
SPRINGSTON, Emily ..... 434-924-0311 472 D
pbd9af@virginia.edu
SPRINKLE, Dean, E .... 276-223-4848 476 A
dsprinkle@wcc.vccs.edu
SPROLE, JoLynn, H ...... 817-515-4563 445 F
jolynn.sprole@tccd.edu
SPROTT, David .... 307-766-4194 501 I
dsprott@uwyo.edu
SPROULL, Maria .... 412-362-8500 396 D
admissions@pims.edu
SPROULS, David .... 212-472-1500 309 D
president@nysid.edu
SPROUT, Jennifer .... 775-327-2105 271 A
jennifer.sprout@gbcnv.edu
SPROWL, Don .... 765-677-3061 158 B
don.sprowl@indwes.edu
SPROWS, Sandra .... 631-451-4252 321 D
sprowss@sunysuffolk.edu
SPRUILL, Angela .... 785-248-2314 176 I
angela.mitchell@ottawa.edu
SPRUILL, Molly .... 772-546-5534 102 C
SPRUILL, Wayne .... 615-675-5348 428 C
wspruill@welch.edu
SPRUNGER, David .... 509-526-4762 486 B
sprungde@whitman.edu
SPRUNGER, Philip, W .. 570-321-4038 389 B
sprunger@lycoming.edu
SPRUNK, Elizabeth .... 419-251-1524 355 G
elizabeth.sprunk@mercycollege.edu
SPRY, Susan .... 570-740-0407 389 A
sspry@luzerne.edu
SPUN, Brandon .... 615-815-8360 422 F
SPURGEON, Michelle .... 805-493-3157.. 29 C
spurgeon@callutheran.edu
SPURGEON-HARRIS,
Bobbie .... 405-692-3199 366 D
bobbie.spurgeon-harris@macu.edu
SPURLOCK, Chad .... 918-293-4622 368 B
chad.spurlock@okstate.edu
SPURLOCK, Patrick .... 802-257-7751 462 H
patrick.spurlock@sit.edu
SPURLOCK, Rana .... 304-214-8906 488 J
rspurlock@wvncc.edu
SPURLOCK, Rebecca ..... 432-552-2600 456 F
spurlock_r@utpb.edu
SPYCHER, Dianna .... 440-826-8061 348 D
dspycher@bw.edu
SQUAIR, Lachlan .... 607-436-3224 316 F
lachlan.squair@oneonta.edu
SQUARE, Chris .... 662-476-5347 246 B
csquare@eastms.edu
SQUIER, Ragan, A .... 315-470-6686 319 D
rasquier@esf.edu
SQUIRE, Jonathan .... 215-965-4017 390 E
jsquire@moore.edu

SQUIRES, Catherine ...... 815-753-7406 146 B
csquires@niu.edu
SQUIRES, Felicia .... 503-375-7089 372 H
fsquires@corban.edu
SQUIRES, Jason .... 252-940-6423 332 C
jason.squires@beaufortccc.edu
SQUIRES, John .... 423-472-7141 424 B
jsquires@clevelandstatecc.edu
SQUIRES, Keith .... 801-585-0804 459 O
keith.squires@utah.edu
SQUIRES, Kyle .... 480-965-2147.. 10 J
squires@asu.edu
SQUIRES, Robert .... 360-650-4446 485 I
robert.squires@wwu.edu
SQUIRES, Thomas .... 315-792-5445 306 K
tsquires@mvcc.edu
SRAMEK, Jennifer .... 361-698-1703 435 G
jsramek@delmar.edu
SRAY, Heid, J .... 724-847-6551 384 C
hjsray@geneva.edu
SRBA, Karen, V .... 304-724-3700 486 F
kvendouern-srba@apus.edu
SRIHARI, Hari .... 607-777-2336 316 B
srihari@binghamton.edu
SRIHARI, Hari .... 607-777-2871 316 B
srihari@binghamton.edu
SRIKANTA, Deepa .... 517-884-1079 227 F
srikanta@msu.edu
SRIKANTH, Rajini .... 617-287-5600 211 H
rajini.srikanth@umb.edu
SRINIVASAN, Balaji ...... 773-795-2901 151 E
balajis@uchicago.edu
SRIRAMAN, Vedaraman 512-245-1217 450 C
vs04@txstate.edu
SRONCE, Robin .... 870-235-4300.. 21 C
robinsronce@saumag.edu
SROUFE, Darren .... 812-357-6331 161 A
dsroufe@saintmeinrad.edu
SRYGLEY, David, B .... 504-526-4745 190 E
ST-GERMAIN, Pierre ...... 401-874-2698 405 E
pst-germain@uri.edu
STAAB, Eric .... 503-768-7053 373 E
ericstaab@lclark.edu
STAAB, Susan, K .... 815-282-7900 148 I
susanstaab@sacn.edu
STAATS, Raymond .... 252-638-7202 334 A
staatsr@cravencc.edu
STABILE, Carol .... 541-346-5414 376 H
cstabile@uoregon.edu
STABILE, Joseph .... 914-633-2207 302 E
jstabile@iona.edu
STACE, Peter, A .... 718-817-3200 300 C
stace@fordham.edu
STACEY, Elizabeth .... 314-529-9364 255 B
estacey@maryville.edu
STACEY, Eric .... 651-690-8778 243 A
emstacey@stkate.edu
STACEY, Marsha .... 605-394-4800 415 G
STACEY, Simon .... 410-455-2164 203 B
spstacey@umbc.edu
STACHACZ, John .... 570-408-4254 403 A
john.stachacz@wilkes.edu
STACHOWIAK, Bonni ...... 714-966-6307.. 73 H
STACHOWIAK, Sage, C . 203-392-5200.. 86 A
stachowiaks1@southernct.edu
STACHOWSKI,
Mary Albertine .... 716-896-0700 324 E
smalbertine@villa.edu
STACHURA, Hubert .... 631-656-2157 300 B
hubert.stachura@ftc.edu
STACHYRA, Karen, L ..... 219-989-2768 160 D
kstachyr@pnw.edu
STACK, Dana .... 619-388-7579.. 61 A
dstack@sdccd.edu
STACK, Eileen .... 716-926-8773 301 E
estack@hilbert.edu
STACK, Gilbert .... 212-752-1530 304 A
gilbert.stack@limcollege.edu
STACK, John .... 305-348-7266 110 A
john.stack@fiu.edu
STACK, Kim .... 401-874-4777 405 E
kstack@uri.edu
STACK, Patrick .... 314-968-6921 262 C
stackpa@webster.edu
STACK, Rachel, C .... 618-650-2345 150 C
rstack@siue.edu
STACK, Robert .... 863-837-5962 106 A
bstack@polk.edu
STACK LOMBARDO,
Jessie .... 585-245-5721 318 B
stack@geneseo.edu
STACKHOUSE, Carlotta .. 803-934-3231 410 G
cstackhouse@morris.edu
STACKHOUSE, LaToya ... 229-931-2442 120 D
latoya.stackhouse@gsw.edu
STACKHOUSE TAETZSCH,
Cindra .... 630-752-5049 153 C
cindra.taetzsch@wheaton.edu
STACKMAN, Robert .... 561-297-2270 109 J
rstackma@fau.edu
STACKMAN, William, B . 573-882-0157 261 A
william.stackman@missouri.edu
STACKPOLE, Richard ..... 513-732-5278 362 B
richard.stackpole@uc.edu
STACKPOOLE,
Roger, W .... 315-445-4174 303 I
stackprw@lemoyne.edu
STACKS, Pamela .... 408-924-2488.. 34 A
pamela.stacks@sjsu.edu
STACY, Jason .... 803-777-6383 413 A
stacyj@mailbox.sc.edu
STACY, Jeanne .... 225-216-8591 187 G
stacyj@mybrcc.edu
STACY, Mark, W .... 585-395-5149 317 E
mstacy@brockport.edu
STADICK, Anna .... 262-595-2167 496 D
stadick@uwp.edu
STADING, Gary .... 903-334-6678 448 A
gary.stading@tamut.edu
STADLER, Al .... 417-455-5712 252 E
alstadler@crowder.edu
STADLER, Megan .... 315-786-6500 303 C
mstadler@sunyjefferson.edu
STADLER, Rose .... 510-436-1089.. 45 E
stadler@hnu.edu
STAEBLER, Ned .... 313-577-2164 232 K
nedstaebler@wayne.edu
STAEHLE, Andrea .... 760-862-1326.. 38 E
astaehle@collegeofthedesert.edu
STAFFA, Adam .... 206-546-4101 484 B
astaffa@shoreline.edu
STAFFORD, Ben .... 409-984-6354 449 I
staffordbk@lamarpa.edu
STAFFORD, Courtney .... 615-550-3171 428 E
courtney.stafford@williamsoncc.edu
STAFFORD, Debra .... 509-359-6200 479 G
STAFFORD, Derek, S ..... 336-841-9433 329 F
dstaffor@highpoint.edu
STAFFORD, Gina .... 423-425-4363 427 C
gina-stafford@utc.edu
STAFFORD, Joanne .... 405-733-7373 369 E
joannestafford@rose.edu
STAFFORD, Kyle .... 918-540-6201 366 F
kyle.j.stafford@neo.edu
STAFFORD, Laura .... 419-372-2079 348 G
llstaff@bgsu.edu
STAFFORD, Mark .... 501-812-2248.. 23 B
mstafford@uaptc.edu
STAFFORD, Michael ...... 713-718-5051 437 C
michael.stafford@hccs.edu
STAFFORD,
Michael Dale .... 713-780-9777 429 G
STAFFORD, Pam .... 606-759-7141 182 E
pam.stafford@kctcs.edu
STAFFORD, Ronnie .... 843-921-6953 411 A
rstafford@netc.edu
STAFFORD, Vanessa ..... 614-781-1085 352 F
vstafford@felbrycollege.edu
STAGE, Monica .... 716-827-4342 323 G
stagem@trocaire.edu
STAGER, Karl .... 281-756-3594 429 D
kstager@alvincollege.edu
STAGGERS, Leroy .... 803-934-3211 410 G
lstaggers@morris.edu
STAGNER, Annessa .... 719-336-1519.. 81 K
annessa.stagner@lamarcc.edu
STAHL, C.J .... 215-972-2059 392 T
cstahl@pafa.edu
STAHL, Frank .... 620-450-2238 177 B
franks@prattcc.edu
STAHL, Jody .... 406-657-2278 264 D
jody.stahl@msubillings.edu
STAHL, Robert .... 516-463-6745 301 G
robert.stahl@hofstra.edu
STAHL, Stephen, D .... 440-826-2762 348 D
sstahl@bw.edu
STAHL, Ted .... 816-235-1625 261 B
stahlt@umkc.edu
STAHLE, Noel .... 641-673-1010 171 C
stahlen@wmpenn.edu
STAHLEY, Timothy .... 970-521-6655.. 82 C
timothy.stahley@njc.edu
STAHR, Jason, A .... 314-516-4934 261 C
stahrj@umsl.edu
STAIGER, Jennifer, L ..... 301-447-8387 201 B
staiger@msmary.edu
STAIHAR, Karla .... 503-357-6151 375 C
karlas@pacificu.edu
STAKE, Amy .... 301-846-2460 198 I
astake@frederick.edu
STAKER, Julie .... 319-399-8500 164 F
jstaker@coe.edu
STAKES, Robert, L .... 915-747-5683 455 C
rlstakes@utep.edu
STALDER, Michele .... 907-455-2850.. 10 A
mestalder@alaska.edu
STALDER, Rob .... 662-621-4050 245 D
rstalder@coahomacc.edu
STALEY, Avery .... 828-328-1741 330 F
avery.staley@lr.edu
STALEY, Avery .... 704-216-6080 330 H
astaley@livingstone.edu
STALEY, Joseph, L .... 281-283-2018 452 E
staleyj@uhcl.edu
STALEY, Marc, E .... 419-772-2462 358 C
m-staley@onu.edu
STALEY, Mark .... 503-251-2844 377 B
mstaley@uws.edu
STALEY, Michael .... 231-591-2635 224 A
michaelstaley@ferris.edu
STALEY, Priscilla, A ...... 214-860-2038 434 I
pstaley@dcccd.edu
STALL, Beth .... 214-860-2374 434 I
sbstall@dcccd.edu
STALLBAUMER,
Rosemary .... 619-260-4722.. 72 I
rstallbaumer@sandiego.edu
STALLCUP, Jackie, E ..... 818-677-3301.. 32 C
jackie.stallcup@csun.edu
STALLING, Undria .... 404-639-0999 123 D
undria.stalling@morehouse.edu
STALLING, Undria .... 470-639-0484 123 D
undria.stalling@morehouse.edu
STALLINGS, Amanda ..... 817-257-4684 448 F
a.stallings@tcu.edu
STALLINGS, Samaria ..... 781-239-3175 214 G
sstallings@massbay.edu
STALLINGS, Sean .... 609-771-1855 276 I
stalling@tcnj.edu
STALLINGS, Tamya .... 870-508-6166.. 17 G
tstallings@asumh.edu
STALLMAN, Amber .... 607-777-6569 316 B
stallman@binghamton.edu
STALLMAN, Jeanne .... 541-552-6221 376 B
stallman@sou.edu
STALLMAN, Scott .... 612-381-3326 235 K
sstallman@dunwoody.edu
STALLMANN, Diane .... 773-298-3089 149 D
stallmann@sxu.edu
STALLWORTH, Charles .. 205-929-1156.... 6 B
cstallworth@miles.edu
STALNAKER, Ron .... 912-478-5491 120 C
rstalnaker@georgiasouthern.edu
STALNAKER, Samantha . 817-515-1795 445 F
samantha.stalnaker@tccd.edu
STALTER, Ann, M .... 937-775-3133 364 E
ann.stalter@wright.edu
STAMBAUGH, Barbara .. 717-358-3981 383 I
barbara.stambaugh@fandm.edu
STAMBAUGH, Jeff .... 940-397-4088 440 C
jeff.stambaugh@msutexas.edu
STAMEY, Jamie .... 704-894-2678 328 E
jastamey@davidson.edu
STAMEY, Jodi .... 919-508-2362 344 E
jstamey@peace.edu
STAMM, Timothy .... 504-671-5482 188 B
tstamm@dcc.edu
STAMMEL, Andrew .... 607-436-2830 316 F
andrew.stammel@oneonta.edu
STAMOS, Michael .... 949-824-1046.. 69 D
mstamos@uci.edu
STAMP, Diane, L .... 540-568-6895 468 C
stampdl@jmu.edu
STAMP, Velma .... 843-792-3657 410 C
stampvg@musc.edu
STAMPALIA,
Jacqueline, B .... 518-276-8007 312 C
stampj@rpi.edu
STAMPER, Richard, E .... 812-877-8956 160 F
stamper1@rose-hulman.edu
STAN RAICU, Daniela ... 312-362-5460 136 H
dstan@cs.depaul.edu
STANAITIS, Judi .... 610-558-5544 391 A
stanaitj@neumann.edu
STANBROUGH,
Beverly, J .... 248-522-3811 229 C
bjstanbr@oaklandcc.edu
STANCHER, Amber .... 715-342-3114 499 B
amber.stancher@mstc.edu
STANCIL, Cynthia .... 903-730-4890 438 D
cstancil@jarvis.edu
STANCIL, Johnsie, L ..... 864-656-3208 407 E
johnsil@clemson.edu
STANCIU, Hope .... 330-490-7142 363 E
hstanciu@walsh.edu
STANDBERRY,
Cassandra .... 804-862-6100 470 C
cstandberry@rbc.edu
STANDER, Karina .... 701-858-3993 345 E
karina.stander@minotstateu.edu
STANDERFER, Mary ...... 479-394-7622.. 23 C
mstanderfer@uarichmountain.edu
STANDERFORD, Chris ... 906-227-2092 228 I
cstander@nmu.edu
STANDIFER, Alton, M ... 706-542-9167 126 G
alton@uga.edu
STANDIFIRD, Stephen ... 309-677-3167 134 A
president@bradley.edu
STANDIFORD, Chris, L . 509-313-4210 480 F
standiford@gonzaga.edu
STANDISH, Christopher 860-768-5938.. 89 G
standish@hartford.edu
STANDO, Michelle .... 734-462-4400 230 G
mstando@schoolcraft.edu
STANDRIDGE, Michelle . 502-585-9911 184 H
mstandridge@spalding.edu
STANEK, Chris .... 541-552-8786 376 B
stanek@sou.edu
STANELLE, Brett .... 478-445-5800 119 B
brett.stanelle@gcsu.edu
STANFIELD, Alan .... 770-233-6139 125 H
alan.stanfield@sctech.edu
STANFIELD, Andrea .... 678-839-6370 127 C
astanfie@westga.edu
STANFIELD, Vicki .... 409-933-8213 433 H
vstanfield@com.edu
STANFIELD, Zelda .... 919-530-7887 341 E
zstanfield@nccu.edu
STANFILL, Adrienne ...... 716-286-8339 309 H
aestanfill@niagara.edu
STANFILL, Sandy .... 731-968-5722 424 E
sstanfill@jscc.edu
STANFILL, William .... 417-667-8181 252 B
bstanfill@cottey.edu
STANFORD, Clark .... 312-996-1040 151 G
cmstan60@uic.edu
STANFORD, Erica .... 662-560-5216 248 D
STANFORD, Kathy .... 503-552-2009 374 D
kstanford@nunm.edu
STANFORD, Roger .... 608-785-9210 500 C
stanfordr@westerntc.edu
STANFORD, Stephen ...... 904-632-3142 101 B
s.stanford@fscj.edu
STANG, Kristin .... 657-278-8811.. 31 C
kstang@fullerton.edu
STANG, Megan, M .... 909-869-3768.. 30 A
mmstang@cpp.edu
STANG, Thomas .... 281-542-2042 443 A
thomas.stang@sjcd.edu
STANGE, Randy .... 913-469-8500 174 I
rstange@jccc.edu
STANGE, Von .... 319-335-3000 163 H
von-stange@uiowa.edu
STANGER, Winn .... 801-626-6876 461 A
wstanger@weber.edu
STANGLE, James, R ...... 563-333-6060 169 G
stanglejamesr@sau.edu
STANICIC, Rob .... 281-998-6150 442 K
rob.stanicic@sjcd.edu
STANIS, Karen .... 530-749-3851.. 77 E
kstanis@yccd.edu
STANISIC, Zoran .... 727-341-7135 107 E
stanisic.zoran@spcollege.edu
STANKAS, Michael .... 937-775-4008 364 E
michael.stankas@wright.edu
STANKEY, Scott .... 763-433-1396 237 D
scott.stankey@anokaramsey.edu
STANKIEWICZ, Donna ... 973-684-5218 280 A
dstankiewicz@pccc.edu
STANKIEWICZ, Jennine . 401-225-2419 200 D
jstankiewicz@mica.edu
STANKOVIC, Toni .... 206-934-3605 483 B
toni.stankovic@seattlecolleges.edu
STANKOVICH, Joseph ... 518-580-5719 315 F
jstankov@skidmore.edu
STANKOWSKI, Lisa .... 231-843-5802 233 A
lmstankowski@westshore.edu
STANKOWSKI, Rebecca 219-989-2208 160 D
stankowski@pnw.edu
STANLEY, Alicia .... 641-269-4850 166 G
stanleya@grinnell.edu

STEADMAN, Meredith ... 919-962-1000 340 H
STEADMAN, Sheryl .... 801-832-2168 461 F
ssteadman@westminstercollege.edu
STEARNS, Ana .... 716-685-9631 310 B
astearns@nycc.edu
STEARNS, Gail .... 714-628-7260.. 36 B
stearns@chapman.edu
STEARNS, Jill .... 805-546-3118.. 40 F
jill_stearns@cuesta.edu
STEARNS, Keith .... 805-546-3228.. 40 F
keith_stearns@cuesta.edu
STEARNS, Marc .... 215-503-0155 399 E
marc.stearns@jefferson.edu
STEARNS, Stephanie, L . 704-406-4236 329 A
sstearns@gardner-webb.edu
STEARNS, Susan, M ..... 515-263-2955 166 F
sstearns@grandview.edu
STEARNS MOORE, Kai .. 714-808-4829.. 54 A
kstearnsmoore@nocccd.edu
STEBBINS, Chad .... 417-625-9736 256 F
stebbins-c@mssu.edu
STEBBINS, Gerald .... 304-829-7640 487 A
gstebbins@bethanywv.edu
STEBBINS, Tim .... 202-462-2101.. 93 A
tstebbins@iwp.edu
STEBBINS, Todd, H .... 608-246-6976 499 A
stebbins@madisoncollege.edu
STEC, Gina .... 413-236-2110 214 A
gstec@berkshirecc.edu
STEC, Paul, T .... 518-783-2314 315 E
pstec@siena.edu
STEC, William, R .... 989-964-4116 230 E
wrstec@svsu.edu
STECKBAUER, Jill .... 715-422-5322 499 B
jill.steckbauer@mstc.edu
STECKLEIN, Brian .... 801-626-6787 461 A
bstecklein@weber.edu
STECKLER, Mary .... 714-564-6839.. 58 F
steckler_mary@sac.edu
STEDMAN, Bruce .... 413-369-4044 208 F
stedman@csld.edu
STEDMAN, Nicole .... 352-392-6622 111 A
nstedman@ufl.edu
STEED, Amanda .... 800-477-2254.. 29 G
asteed@calsouthern.edu
STEED, Deedra .... 870-368-2300.. 20 E
STEED, Jessica .... 817-722-1731 438 G
jessica.steed@tku.edu
STEED, Laura .... 209-946-2325.. 71 E
lsteed@pacific.edu
STEEHLER, Gail, A .... 540-375-2204 470 E
gsteehle@roanoke.edu
STEEHLER, Jack, K .... 540-375-2540 470 E
jsteehler@roanoke.edu
STEEL, Ann, E .... 717-866-5775 383 F
asteel@evangelical.edu
STEEL, Diane, M .... 559-323-2100.. 61 F
dsteel@sjcl.edu
STEEL, Virginia .... 310-825-1201.. 69 E
vsteel@library.ucla.edu
STEELANT, Wim, F .... 330-941-3009 364 H
wfsteelant@ysu.edu
STEELE, Amber .... 757-352-4928 470 B
asteele@regent.edu
STEELE, Brett .... 310-206-6469.. 69 E
brett@arts.ucla.edu
STEELE, Cherie .... 253-589-6010 478 J
cherie.steele@cptc.edu
STEELE, Christopher ...... 410-455-6841 203 B
csteele@umbc.edu
STEELE, Courtney .... 251-405-7135.... 1 E
csteele@bishop.edu
STEELE, Danielle .... 478-757-3501 116 G
dsteele@centralgatech.edu
STEELE, David .... 423-425-1785 427 C
david-steele@utc.edu
STEELE, Dawn .... 406-756-3806 263 E
dsteele@fvcc.edu
STEELE, Diane .... 913-758-6102 178 B
steeled@stmary.edu
STEELE, Donna .... 731-989-6001 419 K
dsteele@fhu.edu
STEELE, Doug .... 208-792-2211 132 A
dlsteele@lcsc.edu
STEELE, Gail, T .... 340-693-1008 513 E
gsteele@uvi.edu
STEELE, Jeffrey .... 586-498-4090 227 B
steelej40@macomb.edu
STEELE, Jennifer .... 256-378-4900.... 1 G
jsteele@cacc.edu
STEELE, Joanne .... 914-633-2691 302 E
jsteele@iona.edu
STEELE, Kandis .... 334-395-8800 125 F
ksteele@southuniversity.edu
STEELE, Kemper .... 434-961-6585 474 I
ksteele@pvcc.edu
STEELE, Laura, L .... 714-879-3901.. 45 G
llsteele@hiu.edu
STEELE, Leslie .... 615-547-1268 419 C
lsteele@cumberland.edu
STEELE, Linda, M .... 614-947-6583 352 J
linda.steele@franklin.edu
STEELE, Margaret, A ..... 570-408-4302 403 A
margaret.steele@wilkes.edu
STEELE, Michael .... 308-535-3723 267 J
steelem@mpcc.edu
STEELE, Misty .... 405-224-3140 371 B
msteele@usao.edu
STEELE, Mitzi, B .... 540-375-2249 470 E
steele@roanoke.edu
STEELE, Richard .... 704-687-5747 342 D
rsteel15@uncc.edu
STEELE, Sarah .... 910-893-1460 327 D
steeles@campbell.edu
STEELE, Sarah Jill .... 812-888-4502 162 F
ssteele@vinu.edu
STEELE, Scott .... 859-985-3490 179 I
steeles@berea.edu
STEELE, Steven .... 970-223-2669.. 81 E
ssteele@ibmc.edu
STEELE, Travis .... 260-982-5435 159 J
twsteele@manchester.edu
STEELE, Tyler .... 605-256-5318 416 F
tyler.steele@dsu.edu
STEELE, Valerie .... 212-217-4530 299 D
valerie_steele@fitnyc.edu
STEELE, Vicki .... 614-251-4706 358 B
steelev@ohiodominican.edu
STEELE-FIGUEREDO,
David, M .... 818-252-5101.. 76 E
president@woodbury.edu
STEELE-MARCELL, Lia ... 501-370-5217.. 20 F
lsteele@philander.edu
STEELE-MIDDLETON,
Amanda .... 302-831-2727.. 91 C
amsteele@udel.edu
STEELE-MOSES, Susan .. 225-490-1674 187 B
susan.steele-moses@franu.edu
STEELEY, Jodie .... 559-489-2226.. 67 B
jodie.steeley@fresnocitycollege.edu
STEELMAN, Joseph .... 770-720-5603 124 G
joseph.steelman@reinhardt.edu
STEELMAN, Megan .... 303-273-3640.. 79 J
msteelman@mines.edu
STEELMAN, Stephanie ... 601-968-8783 245 B
ssteelman@belhaven.edu
STEELMAN, Toddi, R ..... 919-613-8135 328 F
toddi.steelman@duke.edu
STEELY, Jeff .... 404-413-2000 120 E
jsteely@gsu.edu
STEELY, Kelly .... 208-562-2508 131 E
kellysteely@cwi.edu
STEEN, Brant .... 215-497-8791 379 D
brant.steen@bucks.edu
STEEN, Carrie .... 417-255-7255 256 H
carriesteen@missouristate.edu
STEEN, Clayton .... 518-587-2100 320 E
clayton.steen@esc.edu
STEEN, Franklin .... 646-565-6533 322 G
franklin.steen@touro.edu
STEEN, Franklin .... 646-565-6533 322 F
franklin.steen@touro.edu
STEEN, James .... 281-649-3208 437 B
jsteen@hbu.edu
STEEN, Kenneth, L .... 540-654-1159 471 N
ksteen@umw.edu
STEENBURGH, Chuck ... 540-283-6628 471 K
csteenburgh@an.edu
STEENIS, Paul, R .... 309-341-7145 141 G
psteenis@knox.edu
STEENSON, Greg .... 651-690-8825 243 A
gpsteenson@stkate.edu
STEENWYK, Thomas, L . 616-526-6549 222 C
steeto@calvin.edu
STEEVES, Brian .... 612-626-6300 243 F
stee0168@umn.edu
STEEVES, Myron .... 714-836-7500 151 C
msteeves@tiu.edu
STEFANAKOS, Irene ...... 617-732-2866 216 D
irene.stefanakos@mcphs.edu
STEFANICK, Susan, A ... 609-896-5065 281 B
stefanic@rider.edu
STEFANKO, Lisa .... 412-392-4727 396 G
lstefanko@pointpark.edu
STEFANONI, Andra .... 620-235-4124 177 A
astefanoni@pittstate.edu
STEFANOVIC, Tijana ...... 610-526-5632 379 B
tstefano@brynmawr.edu
STEFANOWICZ, Michael 802-654-3000 462 G
admissions@smcvt.edu
STEFFAN, Eileen .... 412-809-5211 396 E
steffan.eileen@ptcollege.edu
STEFFEL, Amy .... 757-401-6125 477 G
STEFFEN, Kaitlyn .... 218-733-7612 238 G
kaitlyn.steffen@lsc.edu
STEFFEN, Lloyd, H .... 610-758-3877 388 E
lhs1@lehigh.edu
STEFFEN, Rebecca .... 269-927-8861 226 F
steffen@lakemichigancollege.edu
STEFFEN, Wayne .... 559-453-3677.. 43 A
wayne.steffen@fresno.edu
STEFFENS, Aaron .... 563-387-1439 168 B
stefaa01@luther.edu
STEFFENSEN, Lisa .... 865-354-3000 425 C
steffensenl@roanestate.edu
STEFFY, Christina .... 610-468-1465 378 C
christina.steffy@alvernia.edu
STEG HASKETT, Allie .... 970-351-1886.. 84 F
allie.steghaskett@unco.edu
STEGALL, Kelly .... 704-290-5247 337 I
kstegall@spcc.edu
STEGER, Paul .... 314-246-7505 262 C
psteger@webster.edu
STEGGALL, Kelli .... 218-755-2504 237 F
kelli.steggall@bemidjistate.edu
STEGLICH, Leila .... 703-330-8400.. 93 H
STEGMAIER, Mary, A .... 573-882-6008 261 A
stegmaierm@missouri.edu
STEGMAN, SJ, Thomas . 617-552-6527 207 C
thomas.stegman@bc.edu
STEGNER, Joe .... 208-334-2315 132 F
jstegner@uidaho.edu
STEHLIK, Michael .... 402-826-6796 267 A
micheal.stehlik@doane.edu
STEHOUWER, Kristin ..... 989-837-4224 229 B
stehouwer@northwood.edu
STEIDEL, Michael .... 412-268-2082 380 C
ms44@andrew.cmu.edu
STEIER, Kenneth .... 646-981-4500 322 F
kenneth.steier@touro.edu
STEIER, Kenneth .... 646-981-4500 322 G
kenneth.steier@touro.edu
STEIGENGA, Timothy .... 561-799-8579 109 J
tsteigen@fau.edu
STEIGER, Gavin .... 512-245-3451 450 C
g_s339@txstate.edu
STEIGER, Gretchen .... 252-249-1851 336 F
STEILBERG, OP, John ... 314-256-8861 250 D
steilberg@ai.edu
STEIN, Anthony .... 818-299-5526.. 74 L
astein@westcoastuniversity.edu
STEIN, Barbara .... 617-627-3333 219 C
barbara.stein@tufts.edu
STEIN, Beki .... 610-796-8202 378 C
beki.stein@alvernia.edu
STEIN, Carla .... 303-678-3755.. 81 A
carla.stein@frontrange.edu
STEIN, Cliff .... 503-517-1878 377 E
cstein@westernseminary.edu
STEIN, Cynthia .... 818-766-8151.. 39 H
cstein@concorde.edu
STEIN, David .... 718-232-7800 325 H
dstein@yks.edu
STEIN, David, B .... 210-805-3591 453 C
dbstein@uiwtx.edu
STEIN, Diane .... 818-364-7867.. 49 C
steindb@lamission.edu
STEIN, Douglas .... 719-598-0200.. 80 D
dstein@coloradotech.edu
STEIN, Douglas, H .... 614-885-5585 359 L
dstein@pcj.edu
STEIN, Ellen .... 646-312-4685 292 L
ellen.stein@baruch.cuny.edu
STEIN, Jeff .... 336-278-7304 328 J
jstein@elon.edu
STEIN, John .... 404-894-7444 119 E
john.stein@gatech.edu
STEIN, Kathy .... 432-837-8770 450 B
kstein@sulross.edu
STEIN, Lisa .... 308-432-6263 268 D
lstein@csc.edu
STEIN, Marni, B .... 801-274-3280 461 E
marni.stein@wgu.edu
STEIN, Melanie .... 607-274-3113 302 G
mstein2@ithaca.edu
STEIN, N .... 732-364-1220 275 F
STEIN, Rebecca .... 215-898-7733 400 F
rstein2@upenn.edu
STEIN, Robert .... 607-871-2171 290 B
rstein@alfred.edu
STEIN, Scott .... 772-462-7691 102 F
sstein@irsc.edu
STEIN, Sheri .... 408-498-0103.. 73 B
sstein@cogswell.edu
STEIN, Sonya .... 518-327-6119 311 C
sstein@paulsmiths.edu
STEIN, Steve .... 408-420-2224.. 71 A
ststein@ucsc.edu
STEIN, Wayne .... 321-433-5150.. 98 I
steinw@easternflorida.edu
STEINACKER, Kathy .... 815-939-5359 147 A
ksteinac@olivet.edu
STEINBACK, Robin .... 951-571-6160.. 59 A
robin.steinback@mvc.edu
STEINBACK, Robin, L .... 951-571-6160.. 59 B
robin.steinback@mvc.edu
STEINBERG, Aaron .... 718-868-2300 291 C
STEINBERG, Bettie, M ... 516-562-1159 298 G
bsteinbe@northwell.edu
STEINBERG, Bryan .... 610-647-4400 385 L
bsteinberg@immaculata.edu
STEINBERG, Dean .... 608-262-2322 495 C
dstensberg@uwsa.edu
STEINBERG, Kurt, T ...... 978-921-4242 217 B
kurt.steinberg@montserrat.edu
STEINBERG, Nicole .... 215-965-8561 390 E
nsteinberg@moore.edu
STEINBERG, Scott .... 207-221-4208 197 E
ssteinberg@une.edu
STEINBERGER, Eric .... 419-559-2228 361 C
esteinberger@terra.edu
STEINCAMP, Hugo .... 520-494-5044.. 11 K
hugo.steincamp@centralaz.edu
STEINER, Earle .... 217-442-7232 136 G
esteiner@dacc.edu
STEINER, Fred .... 313-845-9621 225 B
fred@hfcc.edu
STEINER, Frederick .... 215-898-3425 400 F
fsteiner@design.upenn.edu
STEINER, Glen, D .... 708-209-3328 136 E
glen.steiner@cuchicago.edu
STEINER, Gregory, G .... 276-944-6763 466 L
gsteiner@ehc.edu
STEINER, James, D .... 563-589-3210 170 G
jsteiner@dbq.edu
STEINER, John .... 856-227-7200 276 E
jsteiner@camdencc.edu
STEINER, Karen .... 303-404-5111.. 81 A
karen.steiner@frontrange.edu
STEINER, Karl, V .... 410-455-5827 203 B
steinerk@umbc.edu
STEINER, Kimberly .... 276-964-7389 475 C
kim.steiner@sw.edu
STEINER, Lori .... 316-942-4291 176 E
steinerl@newmanu.edu
STEINER, Michael .... 863-667-5000 108 K
masteiner@seu.edu
STEINER, Michael .... 660-562-1197 257 E
msteine@nwmissouri.edu
STEINER, Michele .... 916-608-6500.. 50 I
STEINER, Michelle .... 703-284-1538 468 H
michelle.steiner@marymount.edu
STEINER, Sheila .... 360-923-8724 482 I
ssteiner@stmartin.edu
STEINER, Ted .... 216-373-5387 357 F
tsteiner@ndc.edu
STEINER-LANG, Kathy ... 314-935-5910 262 A
ksteiner@wustl.edu
STEINERT, Brandon .... 620-792-9307 171 I
steinertb@bartonccc.edu
STEINFORD, Jennifer ..... 251-981-3771.... 5 A
jennifer.steinford@columbiasouthern.
edu
STEINGRABER, Thor ...... 818-677-4400.. 32 C
thor.steingraber@csun.edu
STEINHART, Elisheva .... 305-944-0035 104 I
STEINHAUS, Paul .... 412-365-1606 380 G
psteinhaus@chatham.edu
STEINHILBER, Steven .... 770-484-1204 122 D
steven.steinhilber@lutherrice.edu
STEINHOFF, Cynthia, K 410-777-2483 197 G
cksteinhoff@aacc.edu
STEINKAMP, Sarah .... 765-658-4220 154 J
sarahsteinkamp@depauw.edu
STEINKE, Madison .... 641-673-1054 171 C
madison.steinke@wmpenn.edu
STEINKE, Paul .... 206-876-6100 483 H
psteinke@theseattleschool.edu
STEINKE, Robin .... 651-641-3211 236 G
rsteinke001@luthersem.edu

STEUER, Christopher, J 717-871-7001 395 A
chris.steuer@millersville.edu
STEUERWALD, Brian ..... 317-917-3628 159 L
bsteu@martin.edu
STEURBAUT, Margo ...... 626-395-6275.. 28 J
margo.steurbaut@caltech.edu
STEVA, Erin .... 773-995-5400 134 K
esteva@csu.edu
STEVENS, Amy .... 714-289-3143.. 36 B
amstevens@chapman.edu
STEVENS, Andrea .... 502-895-3411 183 H
astevens@lpts.edu
STEVENS, Andrea, N ..... 662-329-7431 248 A
anstevens@muw.edu
STEVENS, Andrew .... 303-373-2008.. 83 G
astevens@rvu.edu
STEVENS, Ann .... 512-471-4141 455 A
ann.stevens@austin.utexas.edu
STEVENS, April .... 906-487-7309 224 B
april.stevens@finlandia.edu
STEVENS, Bren .... 304-357-4911 487 J
brenstevens@ucwv.edu
STEVENS, Carrie .... 785-242-5200 176 I
carrie.stevens@ottawa.edu
STEVENS, Carroll .... 901-843-3730 423 A
president@rhodes.edu
STEVENS, Cathleen, M .. 585-389-2001 307 F
csteven9@naz.edu
STEVENS, David .... 603-545-4392 272 K
dstevens@ccsnh.edu
STEVENS, Debbie .... 641-673-2173 171 C
stevensd@wmpenn.edu
STEVENS, Elizabeth .... 651-690-8600 243 A
ejstevens@stkate.edu
STEVENS, Eric, A .... 660-263-3900 251 D
STEVENS, Gladstone ...... 410-864-3602 202 C
gstevens@stmarys.edu
STEVENS, Greg .... 509-434-5037 479 C
greg.stevens@ccs.spokane.edu
STEVENS, Greg .... 509-434-5037 479 D
greg.stevens@ccs.spokane.edu
STEVENS, Greg, L .... 509-434-5037 479 B
greg.stevens@ccs.spokane.edu
STEVENS, Holly, L .... 423-652-4784 420 F
hlstevens@king.edu
STEVENS, Jeff .... 607-587-3101 319 F
stevenjs@alfredstate.edu
STEVENS, John .... 435-283-7017 461 B
john.stevens@snow.edu
STEVENS, Kara .... 413-565-1000 206 D
kstevens@baypath.edu
STEVENS, Karl .... 775-327-2184 271 A
karl.stevens@gbcnv.edu
STEVENS, Kevin, T .... 312-915-6115 143 C
kstevens3@luc.edu
STEVENS, Kristina .... 860-486-0723.. 89 D
kristina.stevens@uconn.edu
STEVENS, Kristine, A ..... 816-654-7000 254 E
STEVENS, Leslie .... 701-228-5613 346 B
leslie.stevens@dakotacollege.edu
STEVENS, RSM,
Maryanne .... 402-399-2435 266 F
mstevens@csm.edu
STEVENS, Meg .... 434-791-5700 464 I
mstevens@averett.edu
STEVENS, Michael .... 802-316-6702 463 G
STEVENS, Michele .... 806-457-4200 436 C
mstevens@fpctx.edu
STEVENS, Nick .... 785-864-4914 177 J
nickstevens@ku.edu
STEVENS, Pam .... 304-876-5287 490 A
pstevens@shepherd.edu
STEVENS, Pamela .... 937-395-8601 354 J
pamela.stevens@kc.edu
STEVENS, Randy .... 909-558-4558.. 48 E
rstevens@llu.edu
STEVENS, Richard, Y ..... 919-962-2211 342 C
richardstevens@unc.edu
STEVENS, Richie .... 304-876-5370 490 A
rstevens@shepherd.edu
STEVENS, Rob .... 309-341-5457 134 B
rstevens@sandburg.edu
STEVENS, Robert .... 203-932-7435.. 89 H
rstevens@newhaven.edu
STEVENS, Sarah, E .... 812-461-5357 162 C
sestevens@usi.edu
STEVENS, Scott .... 903-923-2178 435 H
sstevens@etbu.edu
STEVENS, Scott .... 802-860-2751 462 A
stevens@champlain.edu
STEVENS, Stephanie ...... 610-399-2437 393 F
sstevens@cheyney.edu

STEVENS, Sylvia .... 513-481-1337 364 A
sylvia_stevens@wilmington.edu
STEVENS, Tanisha .... 314-516-5695 261 C
smithtn@umsl.edu
STEVENS, Timothy .... 646-592-6005 326 D
timothy.stevens@yu.edu
STEVENS, Tristan .... 715-634-4790 492 L
tstevens@lco.edu
STEVENS, Tristan .... 715-634-4790 492 L
tstevens2@lco.edu
STEVENSON, Andre, P .. 252-335-3678 341 B
apstevenson@ecsu.edu
STEVENSON, Barbra ...... 870-338-6474.. 22 G
STEVENSON, Bill .... 479-524-7119.. 19 H
wstevens@jbu.edu
STEVENSON, Courtney .. 646-313-8000 295 D
courtney.stevenson@guttman.cuny.edu
STEVENSON, Duncan .... 253-964-6612 482 E
dstevenson@pierce.ctc.edu
STEVENSON, Gene .... 928-774-3890.. 12 L
STEVENSON, Jaclyn ...... 518-828-4181 297 B
jaclyn.stevenson@sunycgcc.edu
STEVENSON, James, W . 904-997-2931 101 B
james.stevenson@fscj.edu
STEVENSON, Jennifer .... 940-565-2702 453 E
jennifer.stevenson@unt.edu
STEVENSON, Joy .... 816-235-6234 261 B
stevensonjoy@umkc.edu
STEVENSON, Karen .... 724-266-3838 400 B
karen.stevenson@tsm.edu
STEVENSON, Karen, L ... 615-353-3430 424 G
karen.stevenson@nscc.edu
STEVENSON, Keith .... 217-234-5253 142 C
kstevenson50021@lakelandcollege.edu
STEVENSON,
Kimberley, N .... 252-335-3699 341 B
knstevenson@ecsu.edu
STEVENSON, Kimberly .. 615-327-6759 421 D
kstevenson@mmc.edu
STEVENSON, Leslie, W . 804-289-8141 472 C
lsteven2@richmond.edu
STEVENSON, Mark .... 563-588-8000 166 C
mstevenson@emmaus.edu
STEVENSON, Marshall .. 410-651-6083 203 D
mfstevensonjr@umes.edu
STEVENSON, Martha ..... 610-683-4484 394 D
stevenson@kutztown.edu
STEVENSON,
Martha Ann .... 205-226-4648.... 4 F
mstevens@bsc.edu
STEVENSON,
Michael, P .... 815-835-6466 149 E
michael.p.stevenson@svcc.edu
STEVENSON, Paula .... 954-545-4500 108 E
library@sfbc.edu
STEVENSON, Raymond . 610-436-2828 395 D
rstevenson@wcupa.edu
STEVENSON, Scott, J .... 404-727-3323 118 E
sjsteve@emory.edu
STEVENSON, Tamara .... 801-832-2454 461 F
tstevenson@westminstercollege.edu
STEVENSON, Tara .... 904-826-8508.. 99 E
tstevenson@flagler.edu
STEVENSON, Valerie, O . 904-620-2920 111 B
vstevens@unf.edu
STEVENSON DUMAS,
Laura .... 904-819-6200.. 99 E
lstevenson@flagler.edu
STEVER, Matthew .... 585-785-1281 299 F
matthew.stever@flcc.edu
STEVICK, David .... 585-567-9607 302 B
david.stevick@houghton.edu
STEVICK, Thomas .... 574-520-4344 157 E
tstevick@iusb.edu
STEVINSON, Rebecca .... 218-749-7762 238 H
b.stevinson@mesabirange.edu
STEWARD, Agnes .... 253-840-8403 482 E
asteward@pierce.ctc.edu
STEWARD, Dana .... 417-328-1425 259 I
dsteward@sbuniv.edu
STEWARD, Deborah ...... 315-781-3500 301 F
steward@hws.edu
STEWARD, III, Donald .. 845-687-5191 323 H
stewardd@sunyulster.edu
STEWARD, Gary .... 405-974-5528 370 I
gsteward@uco.edu
STEWARD, Kyle .... 662-325-3221 247 F
ksteward@pres.msstate.edu
STEWARD, Regina .... 501-370-5333.. 20 F
rsteward@philander.edu
STEWARD, Terry .... 225-771-3136 191 E
tsteward@sulc.edu
STEWART, Alandrea .... 314-340-3391 254 A
stewarta@hssu.edu

STEWART, Alex .... 909-687-1602.. 43 D
alexstewart@gs.edu
STEWART, Amy .... 865-524-8079 420 B
STEWART, Anna .... 724-938-4400 393 E
stewart_a@calu.edu
STEWART, Barbara, A .... 408-554-4396.. 63 B
bstewart@scu.edu
STEWART, Barbara, E .... 608-785-5092 496 A
bstewart@uwlax.edu
STEWART, Beth .... 828-398-7633 332 B
bethstewart@abtech.edu
STEWART, Betty .... 972-338-1600 454 A
betty.stewart@untdallas.edu
STEWART, Brad, J .... 240-567-1312 200 G
brad.stewart@montgomerycollege.edu
STEWART, Bryan .... 305-237-4064 104 E
bstewar2@mdc.edu
STEWART, Caren .... 561-586-0121 101 O
STEWART, Carol, A .... 520-382-2491.. 16 D
carolstewart@arizona.edu
STEWART, Charles .... 212-650-7271 293 D
cstewart@ccny.cuny.edu
STEWART,
Chauncine, R .... 323-241-5225.. 49 E
stewarcr@lasc.edu
STEWART, Chris .... 423-236-2356 423 F
cbstewart@southern.edu
STEWART, Christine .... 410-337-6000 199 B
christine.stewart@goucher.edu
STEWART, Christy .... 618-985-2828 140 H
christystewart@jalc.edu
STEWART, Claire .... 402-472-2526 269 J
cstewart@unl.edu
STEWART, Colin .... 559-278-2741.. 31 B
costewart@csufresno.edu
STEWART, Connie .... 989-328-1249 228 D
connies@montcalm.edu
STEWART, Connie .... 731-286-7714 424 D
cstewart@dscc.edu
STEWART, David .... 217-234-5263 142 C
dstewart@lakeland.cc.il.us
STEWART, David .... 304-293-6955 490 E
david.stewart@mail.wvu.edu
STEWART, David, R .... 651-638-6225 234 D
d-stewart@bethel.edu
STEWART, Dawn .... 614-890-3000 359 H
dstewart@otterbein.edu
STEWART, Dawn .... 614-823-3529 359 H
dstewart@otterbein.edu
STEWART, Deborah .... 802-828-2800 463 F
das07200@ccv.vsc.edu
STEWART, DeShaunta ... 972-860-7156 434 H
STEWART, Donette .... 864-503-5280 414 A
dstewart@uscupstate.edu
STEWART, Doreen .... 815-967-7322 148 C
dstewart@rockfordcareercollege.edu
STEWART, Dorothy .... 313-993-1028 231 E
stewardm@udmercy.edu
STEWART, Douglas .... 601-877-2419 245 A
stewartd@alcorn.edu
STEWART, Elizabeth, D . 570-577-3108 379 C
eds019@bucknell.edu
STEWART, Emily .... 704-687-7420 342 D
estewar3@uncc.edu
STEWART, Ethny .... 916-691-7066.. 50 H
steware@crc.losrios.edu
STEWART, Gary, K .... 417-836-5534 256 G
garystewart@missouristate.edu
STEWART, Grace .... 970-675-3218.. 79 H
grace.stewart@cncc.edu
STEWART, H.D .... 828-898-8823 330 E
stewarth@lmc.edu
STEWART, Hansen .... 501-374-6305.. 20 G
STEWART, Jane .... 313-664-1533 222 H
jstewart@collegeforcreativestudies.edu
STEWART, Janeen, K ..... 319-352-8331 170 J
janeen.stewart@wartburg.edu
STEWART, Jennifer .... 314-968-7105 262 C
jstewart15@webster.edu
STEWART, Jennifer .... 417-873-6919 252 G
jstewart012@drury.edu
STEWART, Jessica .... 828-328-7254 330 F
jessica.stewart@lr.edu
STEWART, Jimmy .... 318-678-6000 187 H
jistewart@bpcc.edu
STEWART, John .... 803-780-1200 414 B
jstewart@voorhees.edu
STEWART, III, John, W 205-665-6001.... 8 D
presidentsoffice@montevallo.edu
STEWART, Josh .... 903-434-8242 440 G
jstewart@ntcc.edu
STEWART, Kaylan .... 731-989-6651 419 K
kstewart@fhu.edu

STEWART, Kiesha .... 718-368-5034 294 E
kiesha.stewart@kbcc.cuny.edu
STEWART, Lana .... 308-345-8110 267 J
stewartl@mpcc.edu
STEWART, Larry .... 248-218-2023 230 B
lstewart@rochesteru.edu
STEWART, Leah .... 859-572-6437 184 E
stewartl1@nku.edu
STEWART, Leesa .... 802-322-1652 462 B
leesa.stewart@goddard.edu
STEWART, Lisa .... 434-791-7186 464 I
lstewart@averett.edu
STEWART, Lisa .... 850-599-3730 109 I
lisa.stewart@famu.edu
STEWART, Makena .... 704-290-5840 337 I
mstewart@spcc.edu
STEWART, Malek .... 610-527-0200 397 D
malek.stewart@rosemont.edu
STEWART, Mark .... 718-270-2740 317 B
mark.stewart@downstate.edu
STEWART, Marshall, M . 573-882-2394 261 A
stewartmars@missouri.edu
STEWART, Michael .... 310-289-5123.. 74 I
mike.stewart@wcui.edu
STEWART, Michael .... 478-471-2710 122 F
michael.stewart@mga.edu
STEWART, Michelle, C .. 312-935-4232 140 G
mstewart@icsw.edu
STEWART, Mindy .... 703-812-4757 468 D
mstewart@leland.edu
STEWART, Nathan .... 262-551-5931 492 B
nstewart@carthage.edu
STEWART, Nydia .... 847-578-8482 148 F
nydia.stewart@rosalindfranklin.edu
STEWART, Paul .... 904-620-3978 111 B
p.stewart@unf.edu
STEWART, Peter .... 207-326-2181 196 A
peter.stewart@mma.edu
STEWART, Rachel .... 231-777-0461 228 G
rachel.stewart@muskegoncc.edu
STEWART, Raedorah ...... 202-885-8671.. 94 D
rcstewart@wesleyseminary.edu
STEWART, Reginald, C .. 714-997-6815.. 36 B
STEWART, Rob .... 806-742-2184 450 F
rob.stewart@ttu.edu
STEWART, Robert .... 617-552-2671 207 C
bobstewart@theq.follett.com
STEWART, Ronnie .... 706-886-6831 126 D
rstewart@tfc.edu
STEWART, Ross .... 206-281-2900 483 G
rstewart@spu.edu
STEWART, Scott .... 616-949-5300 223 C
scott.stewart@cornerstone.edu
STEWART, Sheilynda ..... 406-466-3577 366 C
sheilynda.stewart@langston.edu
STEWART, Sonja .... 931-221-7342 417 H
stewarts@apsu.edu
STEWART, Standish .... 216-987-4596 351 E
standish.stewart@tri-c.edu
STEWART, Terri .... 585-389-2840 307 F
tstewar1@naz.edu
STEWART, Thomas .... 413-538-7000 214 F
tstewart@hcc.edu
STEWART, Thomas .... 508-213-2328 217 H
thomas.stewart@nichols.edu
STEWART, Tish .... 662-472-9080 246 D
tstewart@holmescc.edu
STEWART, Todd, M .... 270-745-5276 186 C
todd.stewart@wku.edu
STEWART, Tommy .... 901-761-9494 419 A
tstewart@concorde.edu
STEWART, Toyia, K .... 312-341-2137 148 E
tkstewart@roosevelt.edu
STEWART, Trevor .... 209-575-6530.. 76 J
stewartt@yosemite.edu
STEWART, Tynelle 585-275-7532 323M
tstewar4@ur.rochester.edu
STEWART, Vicki, L .... 717-815-1287 403 F
vstewart@ycp.edu
STEWART, Wendy .... 760-757-2121.. 52 F
wstewart@miracosta.edu
STEWART, Wendy .... 253-833-9111 480 I
wstewart@greenriver.edu
STEWART, Wes .... 713-500-4963 456 B
william.w.stewart@uth.tmc.edu
STEWART GONZALEZ,
Lori .... 502-852-6153 186 A
lori.gonzalez@louisville.edu
STEWART-JAMES, Joy ... 916-278-6035.. 32 D
jsjames@csus.edu
STEWART-MAILHIOT,
Amy .... 360-688-2250 482 I
astewart-mailhiot@stmartin.edu

STOLTZFUS, Rebecca, J 574-535-7180 155 E
president@goshen.edu
STOLTZFUS, Ruth .... 574-535-7375 155 E
ruthas@goshen.edu
STOLZE, Martha, A .... 630-637-5814 145 F
mastolze@noctrl.edu
STOLZER, Alan .... 386-226-7352.. 99 A
stolzera@erau.edu
STOLZER, Donna .... 908-526-1200 281 A
donna.stolzer@raritanval.edu
STOLZER, Tess .... 213-624-1200.. 42 B
tstolzer@fidm.edu
STOMBERGER, Mary ..... 970-491-6817.. 79 N
mary.stromberger@colostate.edu
STOMPER, Jeffrey .... 847-543-2531 136 A
stomper@clcillinois.edu
STONE, Andrea .... 606-783-5272 184 C
a.fryman@moreheadstate.edu
STONE, Andrew .... 801-863-6376 460 D
andrew.stone@uvu.edu
STONE, Angie .... 256-331-5475.... 3 C
angies@nwscc.edu
STONE, Benjamin .... 414-425-8300 495 A
bstone@shsst.edu
STONE, Cedric .... 501-370-5360.. 20 F
cstone@philander.edu
STONE, Cody .... 406-994-2205 264 C
cstone@montana.edu
STONE, Daniel .... 619-574-5812.. 42 J
danielstone@fst.edu
STONE, David .... 401-841-3569 503 A
david.stone@usnwc.edu
STONE, David, A .... 248-370-2762 229 I
dstone@oakland.edu
STONE, Dawn .... 989-358-7293 221 C
stoned@alpenacc.edu
STONE, Denise .... 503-255-0332 374 C
dstone@multnomah.edu
STONE, Elizabeth .... 202-559-5079.. 92 C
elizabeth.stone@gallaudet.edu
STONE, Emily .... 925-969-2113.. 40 C
estone@dvc.edu
STONE, Greg .... 918-595-7723 370 C
greg.stone@tulsacc.edu
STONE, Gwendalyn .... 276-964-2555 475 C
gwendalyn.stone@sw.edu
STONE, Jenna .... 315-268-3790 295 F
jestone@clarkson.edu
STONE, Jennifer .... 315-228-6928 296 E
jstone@colgate.edu
STONE, John .... 661-362-2271.. 51 D
jstone@masters.edu
STONE, Karen, J .... 904-620-2828 111 B
kstone@unf.edu
STONE, Laird .... 208-732-6201 131 D
csitrustees@csi.edu
STONE, Mark .... 979-458-6450 446 B
mstone@tamus.edu
STONE, Melissa .... 313-436-9131 231 I
mjmstone@umich.edu
STONE, Meredith .... 541-888-7439 376 C
mstone@socc.edu
STONE, Patrick .... 508-362-2131 214 D
STONE, Ralinda .... 817-598-6276 457 J
rstone@wc.edu
STONE, Rhonda .... 870-248-4000.. 18 F
rhonda.stone@blackrivertech.edu
STONE, Robert .... 626-256-4673.. 37 A
rstone@coh.org
STONE, Rowena .... 417-836-5051 256 G
rowenastone@missouristate.edu
STONE, Sammy .... 229-931-2394 125 E
sstone@southgatech.edu
STONE, Scott .... 410-225-2398 200 D
sstone@mica.edu
STONE, Staci, L .... 256-782-5690.... 6 A
slstone@jsu.edu
STONE, Sue .... 229-226-1621 126 C
sstone@thomasu.edu
STONE, Susan .... 859-899-2510 180 F
sstone@frontier.edu
STONE, Tia .... 256-331-5279.... 3 C
tstone@nwscc.edu
STONE, Ty, A .... 315-786-2230 303 C
tstone@sunyjefferson.edu
STONE-MOYE, Shelly, T 336-322-2163 336 G
shelly.stone-moye@piedmontcc.edu
STONE RICHMOND,
Sally .... 540-458-8710 477 D
srichmond@wlu.edu
STONEBROOK, Kenneth 801-957-4004 461 C
kenneth.stonebrook@slcc.edu
STONECIPHER,
Amanda, G .... 812-941-2420 157 F
agstonec@ius.edu
STONEHAM, Edrel .... 361-582-2516 457 E
edrel.stoneham@victoriacollege.edu
STONEHILL, Amy .... 541-776-9942 375 B
amy.s@pacificbible.edu
STONEKING, Dawn, M .. 812-464-1932 162 C
dstoneking@usi.edu
STONER, Keith .... 419-755-4810 357 B
kstoner@ncstatecollege.edu
STONER, Kevin .... 845-687-5092 323 H
stonerk@sunyulster.edu
STONER, Melinda, J ..... 402-280-4021 266 H
registrar@creighton.edu
STONER, Melissa .... 425-352-8667 478 D
mstoner@cascadia.edu
STONER, Tamara, L ...... 302-857-6001.. 90 E
tstoner@desu.edu
STONEROCK, Krista .... 740-474-8896 358 A
kstonerock@ohiochristian.edu
STONEY, BeEtta, L .... 785-532-6221 175 C
bestoney@ksu.edu
STOOKEY, Stephen .... 806-291-1161 457 I
stookeys@wbu.edu
STOOKSBERRY, Robert . 210-436-3301 442 J
tstooksberry@stmarytx.edu
STOOPS, Lynne .... 831-459-1376.. 71 A
lstoops@ucsc.edu
STOOPS, Melinda .... 617-552-3280 207 C
melinda.stoops@bc.edu
STOOPS, Melinda .... 509-777-3701 486 C
mstoops@whitworth.edu
STOOS, Barbara .... 419-251-1702 355 G
barbara.stoos@mercycollege.edu
STOOTHOFF, Lisa .... 913-621-8726 173 E
lstoothoff@donnelly.edu
STOPHER, Brenda .... 470-578-3225 121 M
bstopher@kennesaw.edu
STOPPENBRINK, Norm . 614-837-4088 363 D
stoppenbrinkn@valorcollege.edu
STOPPER, Suzanne, T ... 570-326-3761 392 W
sstoppe2@pct.edu
STOPPLE, Jeffrey .... 805-893-2385.. 70 E
jstopple@ltsc.ucsb.edu
STORCK, Angela .... 478-289-2173 118 C
astorck@ega.edu
STORER, Andrew, J .... 906-487-2352 228 A
storer@mtu.edu
STOREY, Amy .... 315-279-5201 303 G
astorey@keuka.edu
STOREY, Bruce .... 309-796-5129 133 G
storeyb@bhc.edu
STOREY, Karen .... 906-635-2418 226 G
kstorey@lssu.edu
STOREY GROVES,
Margaret .... 802-443-5196 462 E
mgroves@middlebury.edu
STOREY LEE, Candice ... 615-343-1107 428 A
STORIE, Cheryl .... 240-582-5680 203 E
financial-affairs@umuc.edu
STORIE, Monique .... 671-735-2333 504 F
mstorie@triton.uog.edu
STORIN LINITZ, Karen ... 617-975-9324 209 D
linitzk@emmanuel.edu
STORLAZZI, Caesar, T .. 203-432-0371.. 90 C
caesar.storlazzi@yale.edu
STORM, JR., Chris, K ... 516-877-3165 289 I
cstorm@adelphi.edu
STORM, Maryam .... 818-708-9232.. 48 G
STORMER, Kevin .... 812-866-6839 155 G
stormer@hanover.edu
STORMS, Amy .... 417-626-1234 257 F
storms.amy@occ.edu
STORMS, Andy .... 417-626-1234 257 F
storms.andy@occ.edu
STORMS, Melanie .... 352-588-7805 107 D
melanie.storms@saintleo.edu
STORRAR, Scott .... 734-487-3591 223 K
sstorrar@emich.edu
STORRS, Regina, M ...... 313-593-5020 231 I
rstorrs@umich.edu
STORTI, Richard .... 559-934-2160.. 74 N
richardstorti@whccd.edu
STORY, Lachel .... 601-266-6485 249 F
lachel.story@usm.edu
STORY, Lisa, L .... 712-324-5061 169 C
lstory@nwicc.edu
STORY, Quinisha .... 770-394-8300 115 C
STORY, Sarah .... 830-372-8053 449 A
sstory@tlu.edu
STORY, Shelley .... 512-863-1281 445 C
storys@southwestern.edu
STORY-HUFFMAN, Ru ... 229-931-2259 120 D
ru.story-huffman@gsw.edu
STOSBERG, Tobey .... 816-276-4740 258 G
tobey.stosberg@researchcollege.edu
STOSKOPF, Janna .... 660-785-4111 260 F
jstoskopf@truman.edu
STOSS, Kate .... 765-285-1847 153 H
kpstoss@bsu.edu
STOTE, Kim .... 518-587-2100 320 E
STOTLER, Doug .... 618-468-6200 142 E
dstotler@lc.edu
STOTO, Robert .... 609-896-5140 281 B
stoto@rider.edu
STOTT, Roger, F .... 443-518-4463 199 F
rstott@howardcc.edu
STOTTS, Bob .... 270-789-5017 180 A
restotts@campbellsville.edu
STOTTS, James .... 404-880-8992 117 C
jstotts@cau.edu
STOTTS, Mark .... 814-864-6666 384 F
marks@glit.edu
STOTTS, Melissa .... 701-662-1538 346 C
melissa.stotts@lrsc.edu
STOUDT, Jennifer .... 610-921-7511 377 G
jstoudt@albright.edu
STOUDT, Ryan .... 989-463-7162 221 E
stoudtrr@alma.edu
STOUFFER, Vicki .... 269-749-7535 229 J
vstouffer@olivetcollege.edu
STOUFFER, Wendy, D ... 479-575-6870.. 21 F
wstouff@uark.edu
STOUGH, Edward .... 304-829-7000 487 A
estough@bethanywv.edu
STOUP, Gregory .... 530-895-2266.. 27 C
stoupgr@butte.edu
STOUP, Russ .... 618-634-3276 149 G
russs@shawneecc.edu
STOUPAS, Leslie .... 805-889-0169.. 74 E
STOUT, Alden .... 712-274-5388 168 E
stoutj@morningside.edu
STOUT, Christine .... 248-689-8282 232 C
cstout@walshcollege.edu
STOUT, David, M .... 732-224-2204 276 B
dstout@brookdalecc.edu
STOUT, Gary .... 817-531-6552 451 C
gstout@txwes.edu
STOUT, Jane .... 773-995-2548 134 K
jstout@csu.edu
STOUT, Michael .... 336-334-4822 335 A
mcstout@gtcc.edu
STOUT, Ross .... 503-370-6911 377 F
rstout@willamette.edu
STOUT, Thomas, B .... 757-822-2251 475 E
tstout@tcc.edu
STOUTE, Steve .... 312-362-7571 136 H
sstoute@depaul.edu
STOVALL, Alethea .... 402-481-3804 265 K
alethea.stovall@bryanhealthcollege.edu
STOVALL, Alfred, J .... 662-252-8000 248 G
ajstovall@rustcollege.edu
STOVALL, Chris .... 940-397-4273 440 C
chris.stovall@msutexas.edu
STOVALL, Jerry .... 229-931-2562 125 E
jstovall@southgatech.edu
STOVALL, Keith .... 601-643-8376 245 F
keith.stovall@colin.edu
STOVALL, Terri, H .... 817-921-8680 445 A
tstovall@swbts.edu
STOVALL, Tyler .... 718-817-4400 300 C
stovall1@fordham.edu
STOVALL, Tyler .... 831-459-2696.. 71 A
humanities@ucsc.edu
STOVER, Caitlin, M .... 508-767-7698 206 A
cm.stover@assumption.edu
STOVER, Dennis .... 877-954-1500 421 F
STOVER, Janice .... 620-441-5247 173 C
janice.stover@cowley.edu
STOVER, Lina .... 402-554-4196 270 A
ltraslavina@unomaha.edu
STOVER, Lizel .... 516-364-0808 308 D
lstover@nycollege.edu
STOVER, Mark .... 818-677-2271.. 32 C
mark.stover@csun.edu
STOVER, Meredith, A .... 781-239-4015 206 B
stoverm@babson.edu
STOVER, Patrick, J .... 979-845-4747 446 F
vcdean@ag.tamu.edu
STOVER, Rebecca .... 540-863-2823 473 F
rstover@dslcc.edu
STOVER, Ronalda, S ..... 803-778-6688 406 I
stoverrs@cctech.edu
STOVER, Stacey .... 734-462-4400 230 G
sstover@schoolcraft.edu
STOVER, Teri .... 903-223-3088 448 A
teri.stover@tamut.edu
STOW, George, B .... 215-951-1097 387 A
stow@lasalle.edu
STOWASSER, Melissa ... 843-574-6312 412 I
melissa.stowasser@tridenttech.edu
STOWE, Brook .... 718-522-9073 290 E
bstowe@asa.edu
STOWE, Cindy .... 501-686-5557.. 22 B
cstowe@uams.edu
STOWE, Lentz .... 252-940-6306 332 C
lentz.stowe@beaufortccc.edu
STOWE, Melissa .... 205-387-0511.... 1 D
melissa.stowe@bscc.edu
STOWE, William .... 903-983-8602 438 F
wstowe@kilgore.edu
STOWELL, Jessica .... 904-819-6322.. 99 E
jstowell@flagler.edu
STOWELL, Michael .... 864-977-7004 410 I
mike.stowell@ngu.edu
STOWERS, Ray, E .... 479-308-2285.. 17 A
ray.stowers@arcomedu.org
STOWIK, Stanley .... 401-232-6240 404 A
sstowik@bryant.edu
STOYNOFF, Stephen ..... 507-389-1242 239 D
stephen.stoynoff@mnsu.edu
STRABLE, Kim .... 336-272-7102 329 C
kim.strable@greensboro.edu
STRACK, Ashkhen .... 860-773-1489.. 87 G
astrack@tunxis.edu
STRACK, Jason .... 269-471-6571 221 D
strack@andrews.edu
STRADER, Robin .... 304-534-7892 488 H
robin.strader@pierpont.edu
STRADER, Scott .... 813-974-9232 111 C
scottstrader@usf.edu
STRAHAN, Jennifer .... 908-737-3232 278 E
jestraha@kean.edu
STRAHN-KOLLER,
Brooke .... 319-398-4969 167 J
brooke.strahn-koller@kirkwood.edu
STRAIT, Dana .... 574-284-4556 160 I
dstrait@saintmarys.edu
STRAIT, LuAnn .... 605-882-5284 415 D
straitl@lakeareatech.edu
STRAITS, Jeffrey .... 202-885-8684.. 94 D
jstraits@wesleyseminary.edu
STRAKA, Richard .... 507-389-6621 239 D
richard.straka@mnsu.edu
STRAKA, Ronald .... 952-446-4127 235 J
strakar@crown.edu
STRALEY, Cassandra ..... 614-236-6116 349 B
cstraley@capital.edu
STRANG, Bryce .... 503-943-8009 377 A
strang@up.edu
STRANG, Kathy .... 866-492-5336 244 F
katherine.strang@laureate.net
STRANGE, Adiaha .... 704-334-6882 328 B
astrange@charlottechristian.edu
STRANGE, Alan .... 219-864-2400 159 N
astrange@midamerica.edu
STRANGE, Kendra .... 864-578-8770 411 F
kstrange@sherman.edu
STRANGE, Tammy .... 303-273-3281.. 79 J
tstrange@mines.edu
STRANGE LEWIS,
Sharon .... 202-238-2446.. 92 F
STRANGE-MARTIN,
Nicole .... 202-884-9380.. 94 A
strangemartinn@trinitydc.edu
STRANGE-MARTIN,
Nicole .... 334-229-4250.... 4 A
nystrange@alasu.edu
STRANO, Kimberly .... 845-257-3215 316 E
lavoiek@newpaltz.edu
STRASBURG, Sarah .... 605-331-6793 417 C
sarah.strasburg@usiouxfalls.edu
STRASNER, Sam .... 479-498-6045.. 18 C
sstrasner@atu.edu
STRASSER, Nora .... 316-295-5818 174 A
strasser@friends.edu
STRASSFELD, Brenda .... 212-463-0400 322 G
brenda.strassfeld@touro.edu
STRATFORD, Denis .... 617-724-6340 217 A
dgstratford@mghihp.edu
STRATHEARN, Becky ..... 716-896-0700 324 E
bstrathearn@villa.edu
STRATIGAKOS,
Despina, M .... 716-645-6200 316 C
dms58@buffalo.edu
STRATTON, Chuck .... 573-840-9079 260 E
cstratton@trcc.edu
STRATTON, Gary .... 865-573-4517 420 E
gstratton@johnsonu.edu

STROUSE, Natalie .... 216-373-5298 357 F
nstrouse@ndc.edu
STROUSS, Elaine .... 724-480-3494 381 H
elaine.strouss@ccbc.edu
STROUT, Sarah .... 508-929-8119 213 G
sstrout@worcester.edu
STROW, Brian .... 561-803-2473 105 C
brian_strow@pba.edu
STROZIER, Kathlyn .... 770-229-3328 125 H
kathlyn.strozier@sctech.edu
STRUBBERG, Megen ..... 636-584-6723 253 B
megen.strubberg@eastcentral.edu
STRUBY, Shannon .... 402-354-7104 268 B
shannon.struby@methodistcollege.edu
STRUCK, Kathy .... 605-367-4625 417 B
kathryn.struck@southeasttech.edu
STRUDLER, Keith .... 973-655-5214 279 B
strudlerk@montclair.edu
STRUDWICK, Daniel .... 217-228-5432 147 F
strudda@quincy.edu
STRUEBEL, Philip .... 716-851-1588 299 B
struebel@ecc.edu
STRUNK, Brian .... 606-546-1276 185 D
bstrunk@unionky.edu
STRUNK, Lauren .... 717-245-1663 382 D
strunkl@dickinson.edu
STRUNK, Mary, C .... 518-783-2314 315 E
strunk@siena.edu
STRUPP, Kindra, L .... 812-464-1755 162 C
kstrupp@usi.edu
STRUPPA, Daniele, C .... 714-997-6611.. 36 B
struppa@chapman.edu
STRUSOWSKI, Lisa .... 302-857-1124.. 91 A
lstrusow@dtcc.edu
STRUTTON, Jill .... 281-649-3321 437 B
jstrutton@hbu.edu
STRYBOS, John .... 361-698-1243 435 G
jstrybos@delmar.edu
STRYKER, Joann .... 406-247-5752 264 D
joann.stryker@msubillings.edu
STRYKER, Joanne .... 401-454-6177 405 B
jstryker@risd.edu
STRYSICK, Michael, P ... 859-238-5710 180 B
michael.strysick@centre.edu
STRZEPEK, Jason .... 978-468-7111 210 C
jstrzepek@gordonconwell.edu
STUARD, Avis .... 504-520-7583 193 E
astuard@xula.edu
STUART, Barbara .... 802-586-7711 462 I
bstuart@sterlingcollege.edu
STUART, Cheryl .... 937-775-2556 364 E
cheryl.stuart@wright.edu
STUART, Christian .... 269-471-3310 221 D
christians@andrews.edu
STUART, Cledis, D .... 870-235-4046.. 21 C
cdstuart@sauniag.edu
STUART, Dana .... 262-524-7200 492 A
dstuart@carrollu.edu
STUART, D'Anne .... 575-646-2431 287 C
dstuart@nmsu.edu
STUART, Eddie .... 910-962-3626 343 C
stuarte@uncw.edu
STUART, Forrest .... 610-330-5055 387 C
stuartf@lafayette.edu
STUART, G. Rob .... 216-987-4757 351 E
g.rob.stuart@tri-c.edu
STUART, Lofton .... 423-425-4717 427 C
lofton-stuart@utc.edu
STUART, Nancy, M .... 860-768-4846.. 89 G
nstuart@hartford.edu
STUART, JR.,
Robert, M .... 225-578-3811 189 E
rstuart@lsufoundation.org
STUART, Stephanie .... 217-351-2200 147 C
sstuart@parkland.edu
STUART, Susan .... 913-288-7265 175 B
sstuart@kckcc.edu
STUART, T. Ramon .... 678-466-4300 117 D
STUART, Thomas .... 816-415-5973 262 F
stuartt@william.jewell.edu
STUART-CARRUTHERS,
Christine .... 956-364-4328 449 D
christine.stuart-carruthers@tstc.edu
STUBBEMAN, Nancy ..... 513-569-1501 350 F
nancy.stubbeman@cincinnatistate.edu
STUBBERT, Amanda .... 206-281-2587 483 G
amandas@spu.edu
STUBBLEFIELD,
Claudine .... 304-724-3700 486 F
cstubblefield@apus.edu
STUBBLEFIELD, Jay .... 423-869-7000 421 A
robert.stubblefield@lmunet.edu
STUBBLEFIELD, Jay .... 865-251-1800 423 E
jstubblefield@south.edu

STUBBLEFIELD,
Michael, A .... 225-771-3890 191 B
michael_stubblefield@subr.edu
STUBBS, Ben .... 850-474-2384 111 F
bstubbs@uwf.edu
STUBBS, Brent .... 912-443-4150 125 B
bstubbs@savannahtech.edu
STUBBS, Fany .... 203-857-7025.. 87 D
STUBBS, Janice .... 954-201-6464.. 96 F
STUBBS, Leah .... 502-863-8030 180 H
leah_stubbs@georgetowncollege.edu
STUBBS, Robert .... 303-492-8631.. 84 B
robert.stubbs@colorado.edu
STUBBS, Sandra .... 256-372-5230.... 1 A
sandra.stubbs@aamu.edu
STUBBS, Sidney, J .... 334-833-4416.... 5 G
oir@hawks.huntingdon.edu
STUBBS, Sidney, J .... 334-833-4431.... 5 G
registrar@hawks.huntingdon.edu
STUCHELL, Tina .... 330-823-2844 362 E
stuchetm@mountunion.edu
STUCKENBRUCK, Emily . 715-675-3331 499 F
stuckenbruck@ntc.edu
STUCKEY, Carol .... 617-732-2114 216 D
carol.stuckey@mcphs.edu
STUCKEY, Jon, C .... 717-796-5065 389 H
jstuckey@messiah.edu
STUCKEY, Lanette .... 217-709-0920 142 D
lstuckey@lakeviewcol.edu
STUCKEY, Mike .... 740-389-4636 355 F
stuckeym@mtc.edu
STUCKEY, Sheila, A .... 502-597-6867 183 D
sheila.stuckey@kysu.edu
STUCKEY, Thomas .... 574-535-7557 155 E
tstuckey@goshen.edu
STUCKY, Alan .... 940-565-2468 453 E
alan.stucky@untsystem.edu
STUCKY, Duane .... 618-536-3475 150 A
dustucky@siu.edu
STUCKY, Thomas, D .... 317-274-2016 157 D
tstucky@iupui.edu
STUCKY, Tommy .... 770-426-2616 122 C
tommy.stucky@life.edu
STUDEBAKER, Brian .... 320-589-6035 244 B
bstude@morris.umn.edu
STUDEBAKER, Kim .... 775-674-7502 271 C
kstudebaker@tmcc.edu
STUDEBAKER, Melissa .. 260-399-7700 162 B
mstudebaker@sf.edu
STUDER, Dominique .... 646-768-5300 300 G
STUDER, Garet .... 425-388-9328 480 B
gstuder@everettcc.edu
STUDER, Mary Ann .... 419-783-2553 351 K
mstuder@defiance.edu
STUDINGER, Robert .... 303-352-3193.. 80 F
bob.studinger@ccd.edu
STUEBING, David .... 757-455-8709 477 C
dstuebing@vwu.edu
STUEBNER, Susan, D .... 603-526-3451 272 H
sue.stuebner@colby-sawyer.edu
STUEMPFLE, Kristin, J .. 717-337-6011 384 D
kstuempf@gettysburg.edu
STUFF, Jerry .... 903-566-7431 456 A
jstuff@uttyler.edu
STUFFLEBEAN, Ernie .... 816-415-5969 262 F
stuffle@william.jewell.edu
STUFLICK, William .... 425-388-9212 480 B
wstuflick@everettcc.edu
STUHR-MOOTZ,
Kristin, J .... 414-955-8208 493 F
kmootz@mcw.edu
STUIFBERGEN,
Alexa, M .... 512-471-4100 455 A
astuifbergen@mail.utexas.edu
STULL, David .... 415-503-6230.. 61 D
mkennedy@sfcm.edu
STULTS, Randy .... 205-387-0511.... 1 D
randy.stults@bscc.edu
STULTZ, Shelley .... 316-322-3152 172 D
sstultz@butlercc.edu
STUM, Beth .... 409-772-0190 456 E
estum@utmb.edu
STUM, Cheryl .... 215-702-4337 380 A
cstum@cairn.edu
STUMB, IV, Paul .... 615-547-1223 419 C
pstumb@cumberland.edu
STUMBLINGBEAR,
Barbara .... 785-749-8460 174 D
barbara.stumblingbea@bie.edu
STUMBO, Christine .... 606-368-6125 178 G
christinestumbo@alc.edu
STUMBRIS, Steven, V ... 570-577-3791 379 C
steven.stumbris@bucknell.edu

STUMNE, James .... 651-779-3918 237 H
james.stumne@century.edu
STUMO, Karl, A .... 218-299-3004 235 H
kstumo@cord.edu
STUMP, Chellye .... 334-347-2623.... 2 A
cstump@escc.edu
STUMP, Sandy .... 610-921-7205 377 G
sstump@albright.edu
STUMP, Tom .... 406-994-2661 264 C
stump@montana.edu
STUMP-KURNICK,
Linda, J .... 352-392-5445 111 A
lstump@ufl.edu
STUMPF, Michelle .... 814-262-6436 393 A
mstumpf@pennhighlands.edu
STUMPFF, Lindsay .... 641-782-1555 170 F
stumpff@swcciowa.edu
STUOPIS,
Cecilia Warpinski .... 617-253-1716 216 B
STUPAR, Eric, H .... 301-243-2170 502 L
eric.stupar@dodiis.mil
STUPARICH, Chavon ..... 516-463-6809 301 G
chavon.stuparich@hofstra.edu
STURDIVANT, Alvin .... 206-296-6000 484 A
STURE, Linda .... 907-563-7575.... 9 E
linda.sture@alaskacareercollege.edu
STURGE, Paula .... 315-268-2016 295 F
psturge@clarkson.edu
STURGE-APPLE,
Melissa .... 585-275-3540 323 M
melissa.sturge-apple@rochester.edu
STURGEON, David .... 231-777-0465 228 G
david.sturgeon@muskegoncc.edu
STURGEON, Kathy, R .... 217-443-8805 136 G
ksturgeon@dacc.edu
STURGEON, Roderick .... 816-926-4400 253 I
STURGEON, Timothy, A 502-272-8131 179 H
tsturgeon@bellarmine.edu
STURGILL, David .... 859-246-6896 181 F
david.sturgill@kctcs.edu
STURGIS, Tina .... 585-275-2121 323 M
STURM, Joel .... 212-410-8047 308 E
jsturm@nycpm.edu
STURM, Neal, M .... 973-443-8689 277 I
sturm@fdu.edu
STURM-SMITH, Melissa 515-271-2835 165 J
melissa.sturm-smith@drake.edu
STURRUP, Daniel, H ..... 207-581-1799 196 G
dsturrup@maine.edu
STURTZ, Carma .... 641-628-5269 164 D
sturtzc@central.edu
STUTES, Ann, B .... 806-291-1066 457 I
stutesa@wbu.edu
STUTZ, Melissa .... 307-778-1217 501 E
mstutz@lccc.wy.edu
STUTZMAN, Karl .... 574-296-6233 153 F
kstutzman@ambs.edu
STUTZMAN,
Timothy, W .... 540-432-4197 466 B
timothy.stutzman@emu.edu
STVAN, Kenneth, J .... 315-470-6689 319 D
kjstvan@esf.edu
STYER, Daniel .... 916-558-2201.. 50 J
styerd@scc.losrios.edu
STYRON, Kelli, C .... 254-968-9081 446 D
styron@tarleton.edu
STYRON, Ken .... 251-981-3771.... 5 A
ken.styron@columbiasouthern.edu
STYRON, Kent .... 254-968-9898 446 D
wkstyron@tarleton.edu
SU, Dan .... 903-468-3048 447 B
dan.su@tamuc.edu
SU, John, J .... 414-288-3476 493 E
john.su@marquette.edu
SU, Nancy .... 212-217-3640 299 D
nancy_su@fitnyc.edu
SU, Susan .... 516-739-1545 308 F
records@nyctcm.edu
SUARA, Zulfat, A .... 615-327-6815 421 D
zsuara@mmc.edu
SUAREZ, Alberto .... 845-368-7217 314 I
alberto.suarez@use.salvationarmy.org
SUAREZ, Angelica .... 714-432-5577.. 38 B
angelica.suarez@occ.cccd.edu
SUAREZ, Francisco .... 787-841-2000 509 J
fsuarez@pucpr.edu
SUAREZ, Jeri, L .... 540-362-6000 467 H
jsuarez@hollins.edu
SUAREZ, Maria .... 520-515-5337.. 11 M
suarezm@cochise.edu
SUAREZ, Maria .... 805-922-6966.. 24 I
maria.suarez@hancockcollege.edu

SUAREZ-ESPINAL,
Cynthia .... 718-289-5914 293 B
cynthia.suarez-espinal@bcc.cuny.edu
SUAREZ-OROZCO,
Marcelo, M .... 617-287-6800 211 H
marcelo.orozco@umb.edu
SUAZO, Karelie .... 787-701-5100 506 D
ksuazo@columbiacentral.edu
SUBASI, Munevver .... 321-674-7486 100 C
msubasi@fit.edu
SUBBARAO, Italo .... 601-318-6572 249 H
isubbarao@wmcarey.edu
SUBBASWAMY,
Kumble, R .... 413-545-2211 211 G
chancellor@umass.edu
SUBE, Bob .... 805-678-5821.. 74 A
bsube@vcccd.edu
SUBHANI, Ali .... 972-516-5036 433 I
asubhani@collin.edu
SUBLETTE, Garrett .... 325-674-2655 428 F
jgs99a@acu.edu
SUBLETTE, Gaylah .... 660-626-2860 250 A
gsublette@atsu.edu
SUBOCZ, Sue .... 866-492-5336 244 F
susan.subocz@mail.waldenu.edu
SUBRAHMANYAM,
Kaven .... 323-343-2000.. 31 E
ksubrah@calstatela.edu
SUBRAMANIAM,
Chandra .... 818-677-2455.. 32 C
chandra.subramaniam@csun.edu
SUBRAMANIAM, Chelvi 310-233-4041.. 49 B
subramt@lahc.edu
SUBRAMANIAM, Ram ... 650-940-7472.. 42 I
subramaniamram@fhda.edu
SUBRAMANIAM, Ram ... 650-949-7472.. 42 I
subramaniamram@foothill.edu
SUBRAMANIAN, Ashok . 928-523-1237.. 14 H
ashok.subramanian@nau.edu
SUBREENDUTH, Sharon 912-478-5648 120 C
ssubreenduth@georgiasouthern.edu
SUCH, Tami .... 701-788-4711 345 D
tami.such@mayvillestate.edu
SUCHAN, Jennifer .... 515-294-8381 163 G
jsuchan@iastate.edu
SUCHANIC, Angela, C ... 302-356-6924.. 91 E
angela.c.suchanic@wilmu.edu
SUCHON, Donnetta .... 281-425-6400 438 I
dsuchon@lee.edu
SUCKOW, Melissa, A .... 630-515-3015 144 F
msucko@midwestern.edu
SUDA, Delight .... 671-734-1812 504 E
dsuda@piu.edu
SUDAK, Sarah .... 615-898-5342 422 C
sarah.sudak@mtsu.edu
SUDBECK, Kristine .... 402-494-2311 268 A
ksudbeck@thenicc.edu
SUDDICK, Lori .... 847-543-2200 136 A
lsuddick@clcillinois.edu
SUDEALL-HAWKINS,
Monica .... 256-551-1711.... 2 E
monica.hawkins@drakestate.edu
SUDEIKIS, Barbara .... 269-965-3931 225 H
sudeikisb@kellogg.edu
SUDERMAN, Bonnie ..... 304-336-8004 490 B
bonnie.suderman@westliberty.edu
SUDHAKAR, Rama .... 212-237-8628 294 D
rsudhakar@jjay.cuny.edu
SUDHAKAR, Samuel .... 909-537-5100.. 32 E
ssudhakar@csusb.edu
SUDIA, Tanya .... 706-721-3771 116 A
tsudia@augusta.edu
SUDLER, Clifton .... 609-343-5126 275 D
csudler@atlantic.edu
SUDLOW, Jennifer .... 215-572-4483 378 E
sudlowj@arcadia.edu
SUDMEYER, Alecia .... 207-509-7166 196 E
asudmeyer@unity.edu
SUDTELGTE, Beau .... 563-425-5959 170 H
sudtelgteb121@uiu.edu
SUEBERT, Jack .... 305-809-3195.. 97 O
jack.seubert@cfk.edu
SUEK, Ana .... 415-749-4530.. 61 C
asuek@sfai.edu
SUELFLOW, Sara, C .... 651-696-6307 236 I
suelflow@macalester.edu
SUEME, Zana .... 314-392-2230 256 E
zana.sueme@mobap.edu
SUERTH, Matthew, P .... 815-224-0550 140 E
matt_suerth@ivcc.edu
SUESS, Jack, J .... 410-455-2582 203 B
jack@umbc.edu
SUEYOSHI, Amy .... 415-338-1694.. 33 E
sueyoshi@sfsu.edu

SUN, Grace ... 404-756-8927 123 E gsun@msm.edu
SUN, Hala ... 213-381-0081.. 46 E hsun.irus@irus.edu
SUN, Joseph, S ... 215-517-2383 378 E sunj@arcadia.edu
SUN, Marcus ... 626-584-5203.. 43 B marcussun@fuller.edu
SUN, Zhen ... 512-444-8082 448 H bookkeeper@thsu.edu
SUN CHILD, Jolin ... 406-395-4875 265 G jsunchild@stonechild.edu
SUNAHARA, Wayne ... 808-845-9135 130 A waynens@hawaii.edu
SUNATA, Cem ... 805-756-6016.. 29 I csunata@calpoly.edu
SUND, Andrew, C ... 509-865-8500 481 A sund_a@heritage.edu
SUNDA-MEYA, Anderson ... 504-520-7652 193 E asundame@xula.edu
SUNDARAM, Bala ... 617-287-6055 211 H bala.sundaram@umb.edu
SUNDARAM, Sridhar ... 657-278-0000.. 31 C ssundaram@fullerton.edu
SUNDAY, Richard, S ... 212-217-3760 299 D richard_sunday@fitnyc.edu
SUNDBERG, Lori ... 319-398-5501 167 J lori.sundberg@kirkwood.edu
SUNDBERG, Lori ... 847-735-5030 142 A lsundberg@lakeforest.edu
SUNDBY, David ... 714-997-6668.. 36 B sundby@chapman.edu
SUNDBY-THORP, Valerie ... 360-596-5451 484 D vsundby-thorp@spscc.edu
SUNDEEN, Kendra, L ... 651-628-3240 244 D klsundeen@unwsp.edu
SUNDERLAND, JR., Richard ... 304-724-3700 486 F rsunderland@apus.edu
SUNDERLAND, Terri ... 618-664-7031 138 F terri.sunderland@greenville.edu
SUNDERMAN, Rick ... 614-947-6605 352 J rick.sunderman@franklin.edu
SUNDERMANN, Brigitte 970-255-2700.. 78 J bsunderm@coloradomesa.edu
SUNDERMEIER, Elisabeth ... 816-802-3376 254 D esundermeier@kcai.edu
SUNDGREN, Donald, E . 434-982-5834 472 D des5j@virginia.edu
SUNDQUIST, Jeffery ... 831-646-4036.. 52 G jsundquist@mpc.edu
SUNDQUIST, Mike ... 209-575-6081.. 77 A sundquistm@mjc.edu
SUNDSTROM, Sandy ... 503-777-7224 375 G sundstrom@reed.edu
SUNDY, Carolyn ... 606-589-3052 183 A carolyn.sundy@kctcs.edu
SUNLEAF, Arthur, W ... 563-588-7959 168 A arthur.sunleaf@loras.edu
SUNNARBORG, Avery ... 719-884-5000.. 82 B absunnarborg@nbc.edu
SUNNY, Heidi, L ... 859-858-3511 179 D heidi.sunny@asbury.edu
SUNNYGARD, John ... 303-807-9956.. 84 D john.sunnygard@ucdenver.edu
SUNNYGARD, John ... 270-745-4857 186 C john.sunnygard@wku.edu
SUNQUIST, Scott, W ... 978-468-7111 210 C sunquist@gcts.edu
SUNSER, James ... 585-345-6812 300 F presidentsoffice@genesee.edu
SUPAK, Brian ... 254-298-8609 445 G brian.supak@templejc.edu
SUPLER, Robin ... 954-262-4349 105 A rsupler@nsu.nova.edu
SUPOWITZ, Paul, A ... 412-624-2901 400 H psupowit@pitt.edu
SUPPLE, Brooke ... 301-314-8437 202 H bsupple@umd.edu
SUPPLE, Matthew ... 301-314-7781 202 H msupple@umd.edu
SUPPLEE, JR., Jack ... 859-257-8288 185 F supplee@uky.edu
SUPPLEE, Janice ... 937-766-7470 349 E suppleej@cedarville.edu
SUPPLEE, John ... 610-526-6064 385 D jsupplee@harcum.edu
SUPURGECI, Jonna ... 605-668-1298 415 F jsupurgeci@mountmarty.edu
SUR, Sarah Gilman ... 808-235-7435 130 E sgilman@hawaii.edu
SURA, Marissa ... 616-632-2843 221 E mks007@aquinas.edu
SURDOVEL, Grace ... 570-408-3102 403 A grace.surdovel@wilkes.edu
SURENDER, Sheelu, M . 316-978-5337 178 D sheelu.surender@wichita.edu
SURESH-MENON, Durga ... 617-989-4590 219 F sureshmenond@wit.edu
SURLS, Courtney ... 202-885-1334.. 91 F surls@american.edu
SUROVIEC, Alice ... 706-236-1756 116 B asuroviec@berry.edu
SURPRENANT, Aimee ... 540-231-7581 476 C asurprenant@vt.edu
SURPRENANT, Danielle . 309-298-1190 153 A de-surprenant@wiu.edu
SURPRENANT, Tess ... 816-235-6077 261 B surprenantt@umkc.edu
SURRATT, David ... 405-325-3161 370 K dsurratt@ou.edu
SURRATT, Jacob ... 336-734-7733 334 F jsurratt@forsythtech.edu
SURRELL, Jane ... 906-227-2596 228 I jasurrel@nmu.edu
SURRELL, Matt ... 662-472-9178 246 D msurrell@holmescc.edu
SURRIDGE, Mary, K ... 773-244-5710 145 G president@northpark.edu
SUSA, Angela ... 715-422-5320 499 B angela.susa@mstc.edu
SUSANA, Gil ... 619-961-4316.. 68 A gsusana@tjsl.edu
SUSANKA, Joseph ... 307-322-2930 502 A jsusanka@wyomingcatholic.edu
SUSANTO-ONG, Yuliana ... 502-597-7014 183 D yuliana.susanto@kysu.edu
SUSHINSKY, David, M .. 240-895-3381 202 B dmsushinsky@smcm.edu
SUSKI-LENCZEWSKI, Anna ... 860-832-1757.. 85 G lenczewskia@mail.ccsu.edu
SUSKIND, Robert ... 909-580-9661.. 34 D
SUSMANN, Phillip ... 802-485-2213 462 F susmann@norwich.edu
SUSMARSKI, Aaron, E .. 814-860-5101 387 D asusmarski@lecom.edu
SUSMILCH, Tyler ... 503-538-8383 373 A tsusmilch@georgefox.edu
SUSSAN, Joshua ... 718-270-6421 294 G jsussan@mec.cuny.edu
SUSSENBACH, Michelle 618-664-7025 138 F michelle.sussenbach@greenville.edu
SUSSMAN, Ronny ... 818-883-9002.. 73 G
SUTARDJI, Anne ... 510-592-9688.. 54 F anne.sutardji@npu.edu
SUTER, Charlene ... 585-292-2500 307 B csuter@monroecc.edu
SUTER, Cynthia ... 802-485-2035 462 F csuter@norwich.edu
SUTERA, Paul, J ... 914-637-2710 302 E psutera@iona.edu
SUTHERLAND, David ... 218-879-0816 238 B dsutherland@fdltcc.edu
SUTHERLAND, David ... 501-450-1254.. 19 E sutherlandd@hendrix.edu
SUTHERLAND, John ... 706-729-2260 116 A jsutherland@augusta.edu
SUTHERLAND, Kate ... 781-768-7551 218 D kate.sutherland@regiscollege.edu
SUTHERLAND, Kathleen 973-408-3100 277 A ksutherl@drew.edu
SUTHERLAND, Kelly ... 781-292-2304 210 A
SUTHERLAND, Richard . 989-358-7368 221 C sutherlr@alpenacc.edu
SUTHERLAND, Ron ... 765-998-5118 161 C rnsutherl@taylor.edu
SUTHERLIN, John ... 318-342-1413 193 C sutherlin@ulm.edu
SUTLIFF, Dani ... 912-260-4419 125 D dani.sutliff@sgsc.edu
SUTLIFF, Deborah, A ... 603-829-6027 133 E dsutliff@ben.edu
SUTLIFF, Michael ... 714-432-5122.. 38 B msutliff@occ.cccd.edu
SUTLIFFE, Nicole ... 202-651-5346.. 92 C nicole.sutliffe@gallaudet.edu
SUTLIVE, Vins, H ... 859-858-3511 179 D vins.sutlive@asbury.edu
SUTTER, Brian ... 712-325-3328 167 I bsutter@iwcc.edu
SUTTER, Frankie ... 910-592-8081 337 G fsutter@sampsoncc.edu
SUTTERFIELD, Shirley ... 251-442-2414.... 8 C ssutterfield@umobile.edu
SUTTLE, J. Lloyd ... 203-432-4453.. 90 C j.suttle@yale.edu
SUTTMEIER, Bruce ... 503-768-7100 373 E cas@lclark.edu
SUTTON, Cynthia ... 314-392-2291 256 E suttonc@mobap.edu
SUTTON, David ... 254-968-9510 446 D sutton@tarleton.edu
SUTTON, Deborah ... 252-527-6223 335 G dssutton14@lenoircc.edu
SUTTON, Dennis ... 910-275-6137 335 E dsutton@jamessprunt.edu
SUTTON, Duncan ... 310-265-6155.. 60 B duncan.sutton@usw.salvationarmy.org
SUTTON, Gary ... 843-208-8059 413 C suttong2@uscb.edu
SUTTON, Gentry ... 863-638-1426 114 A gentry.sutton@warner.edu
SUTTON, Jama ... 865-774-5800 425 F jama.sutton@ws.edu
SUTTON, Jayne ... 402-472-7131 269 H jsutton@nebraska.edu
SUTTON, Jeff ... 254-295-5044 453 D jsutton@umhb.edu
SUTTON, Jennifer ... 256-765-5558.... 8 E jballard1@una.edu
SUTTON, JerQuentin ... 732-247-5241 279 C jsutton@nbts.edu
SUTTON, Judith ... 304-485-5487 487 G jsutton@msc.edu
SUTTON, Lawrence ... 724-805-2402 398 A lawrence.sutton@stvincent.edu
SUTTON, Lori ... 309-694-5520 139 B lori.sutton@icc.edu
SUTTON, Nancy ... 217-353-2113 147 C nsutton@parkand.edu
SUTTON, Nathan ... 989-275-5000 226 D nathan.sutton@kirtland.edu
SUTTON, Pamela ... 512-223-7598 430 I psutton@austincc.edu
SUTTON, R. Anderson .. 808-956-8818 129 E rasutton@hawaii.edu
SUTTON, Renee ... 910-275-6103 335 E rsutton@jamessprunt.edu
SUTTON, Rick ... 334-699-2266.... 1 B rosutton@acom.edu
SUTTON, Scott ... 828-339-4296 338 B scotts@southwesterncc.edu
SUTTON, Shan, C ... 520-621-0717.. 16 D ssutton@arizona.edu
SUTTON, Shannon ... 309-298-2073 153 A sm-sutton@wiu.edu
SUTTON, Stephanie ... 330-494-6170 360 K ssutton@starkstate.edu
SUTTON, Steve ... 510-642-6727.. 69 A studentaffairs@berkeley.edu
SUTTON, Susan, R ... 865-882-4658 425 C suttonsr@roanestate.edu
SUTTON, Todd ... 336-790-8607 343 A tasutton@uncg.edu
SUTTON GERBER, Ronette ... 910-521-6268 343 B ronette.gerber@uncp.edu
SUTTON-LOVETT, Tommy ... 800-517-0857 355 A
SUTTON NOSS, Melinda ... 214-768-4564 444 D msnoss@smu.edu
SUTTON-SMITH, Leslie . 973-655-4376 279 B suttonsmithl@montclair.edu
SUTTON-YOUNG, Tasheka ... 718-368-5109 294 E tasheka.sutton-young@kbcc.cuny.edu
SUTTON-YOUNG, Tasheka ... 718-368-4539 294 E tasheka.sutton-young@kbcc.cuny.edu
SUTYAK, John ... 540-365-4493 467 B jsutyak@ferrum.edu
SUTZKO, Christopher ... 570-208-5874 386 G christophersutzko@kings.edu
SUWALSKY, SJ, David .. 314-977-7065 259 F david.suwalsky@slu.edu
SUZUKI, Anne ... 480-732-7000.. 12 D anne.suzuki@cgc.edu
SUZUKI, Takeo ... 423-425-4759 427 C takeo-suzuki@utc.edu
SU'ESU'E, Jessie ... 684-699-9155 504 B j.suesue@amsamoa.edu
SVACINA, Jean, M ... 443-518-1850 199 F jsvacina@howardcc.edu
SVEHLIK, Edward, T ... 304-293-2545 490 E ted.svehlik@mail.wvu.edu
SVEI, Yehuda ... 215-477-1000 399 A
SVENSSON, Vibeke ... 202-885-3980.. 91 F svensson@american.edu
SVETE, Lee ... 276-944-6660 466 L lsvete@ehc.edu
SVINARICH, Kathryn ... 810-762-7885 226 B ksvinari@kettering.edu
SVOBODA, Angela, M ... 512-448-8622 442 I asvoboda@stedwards.edu
SWAFFORD, Jeanna, C . 731-881-7629 427 D jswafford@utm.edu
SWAFFORD, Melissa ... 216-987-3195 351 E melissa.swafford@tri-c.edu
SWAGER, Sarah ... 406-243-5225 263 K sarah.swager@umontana.edu
SWAGERTY, John ... 785-833-4323 175 E john.swagerty@kwu.edu
SWAGGER, Eric ... 412-578-8712 380 B emswagger@carlow.edu
SWAGGER, Russell ... 715-634-4790 492 L rswagger@lco.edu
SWAHA, Chuck ... 540-231-7670 466 K cswaha@vcom.vt.edu
SWAID, Samar ... 501-370-5335.. 20 F sswaid@philander.edu
SWAIM, Charles ... 309-694-5422 139 B
SWAIN, Bill, F ... 302-295-1216.. 91 E bill.f.swain@wilmu.edu
SWAIN, Colleen ... 903-565-5898 456 A cswain@uttyler.edu
SWAIN, Cristal ... 970-351-1142.. 84 F cristal.wain@unco.edu
SWAIN, Heather, C ... 517-355-2262 227 F swainh@msu.edu
SWAIN, Jackie ... 406-275-4859 265 F jackie_swain@skc.edu
SWAIN, Jeffrey, D ... 305-626-3674 100 D jeffrey.swain@fmuniv.edu
SWAIN, Jennifer, L ... 607-735-1894 298 H jswain@elmira.edu
SWAIN, Matthew ... 304-842-8269 489 K mswain1@fairmontstate.edu
SWAIN, Ruth ... 541-956-7484 376 A rswain@roguecc.edu
SWAIN, Ryan ... 775-445-3322 271 F ryan.swain@wnc.edu
SWAIN, Sarah ... 910-893-1236 327 D swain@campbell.edu
SWAIN, Scott ... 216-373-5306 357 F sswain@ndc.edu
SWAIN, Scott, R ... 407-278-4557 248 F sswain@rts.edu
SWAIN-GILLIARD, LaTashia, H ... 410-651-6668 203 D lswaingilliard@umes.edu
SWAINE, Richard ... 419-383-3443 363 B richard.swaine@utoledo.edu
SWALES, Tammy ... 315-279-5000 303 G
SWALLOW, John, R ... 262-551-5858 492 B jswallow@carthage.edu
SWALLOW, Steve ... 937-529-2201 361 G slswallow@united.edu
SWALLOW, Steven ... 937-529-2201 361 G slswallow@united.edu
SWAN, Joel ... 256-761-6318.... 7 B jswan@talladega.edu
SWAN, John ... 916-577-2200.. 76 D jswan@jessup.edu
SWAN, Lilymae ... 313-993-3323 231 E swanls@udmercy.edu
SWAN, Lisa ... 262-646-6509 494 F lswan@nashotah.edu
SWAN, Lorretta ... 903-510-2349 452 A lswa@tjc.edu
SWAN, Rhonda ... 817-598-6283 457 J rswan@wc.edu
SWAN, S. Tomeka ... 410-287-1892 198 E tswan@cecil.edu
SWAN, Terry, W ... 270-384-8148 183 G swant@lindsey.edu
SWANAGAN, Diana ... 706-233-7301 125 C dswanagan@shorter.edu
SWANCHAK, Lori, E ... 570-961-4711 389 D swanchak@marywood.edu
SWANGER, Rachel ... 310-393-0411.. 56 C rachel_swanger@rand.org
SWANGLER, Jennifer ... 701-777-6374 345 B jennifer.swangler@und.edu
SWANK, Angela, P ... 919-209-2024 335 F apswank@johnstoncc.edu

SYKES, Dianne .... 434-832-7602 473 E sykesd@centralvirginia.edu
SYKES, Eric .... 203-582-7644.. 88 G eric.sykes@quinnipiac.edu
SYKES, Ethan .... 417-873-7654 252 G esykes@drury.edu
SYKES, Heather .... 610-341-4361 383 B hsykes@eastern.edu
SYKES, Jonah .... 413-236-2116 214 A jsykes@berkshirecc.edu
SYKES, Kristen .... 863-669-4933 106 A ksykes@polk.edu
SYKES, Laura, A .... 603-526-3760 272 H laura.sykes@colby-sawyer.edu
SYKES, Reggie .... 251-405-7130.... 1 E rsykes@bishop.edu
SYLER-JONES, Tracy ..... 817-257-7811 448 F t.syler-jones@tcu.edu
SYLJEBECK, Susan .... 517-264-7876 230 H ssyljebe@sienaheights.edu
SYLVE, Howard .... 903-923-1643 458 F hsylve@wileyc.edu
SYLVESTER, Douglas, J 480-965-6188.. 10 J douglas.sylvester@asu.edu
SYLVESTER, Joshua ...... 508-999-8133 212 A jsylvester@umassd.edu
SYLVESTER, Kenneth ..... 810-766-3383 232 A kenms@umich.edu
SYLVESTER-CAESAR, Jemma .... 713-221-2791 453 A caesarj@uhd.edu
SYLVIA, Hillary .... 508-999-8531 212 A hillary.sylvia@umassd.edu
SYLVIA, Lynn .... 910-362-7679 332 H lbsylvia845@mail.cfcc.edu
SYLWESTER, Breana ...... 541-383-7260 372 A bsylwester@cocc.edu
SYMICEK, Alan .... 715-425-4655 496 F alan.symicek@uwrf.edu
SYMINGTON, Paul .... 740-283-6643 352 I psymington@franciscan.edu
SYMONDS, Lisa .... 518-891-2915 310 A lsymonds@nccc.edu
SYMS, Deirdre .... 586-445-7862 227 B symsd@macomb.edu
SYNAKOWSKI, Edmund 307-766-5353 501 I esynakow@uwyo.edu
SYNAN, Sharon .... 706-245-7226 118 D ssynan@ec.edu
SYNDAB, Ricky .... 803-780-1025 414 B rsyndab@voorhees.edu
SYNDER, Brittany .... 305-809-3233.. 97 O brittany.snyder@cfk.edu
SYNDER, Deanna .... 816-604-4507 255 C deanna.synder@mcckc.edu
SYNDER, Tamara .... 352-638-9764.. 96 B tsnyder@beaconcollege.edu
SYNER, Alicia .... 304-205-6746 488 D alicia.syner@bridgevalley.edu
SYNODI, George, S ...... 203-832-7273.. 89 H gsynodi@newhaven.edu
SYOEN, Elise .... 423-869-6433 421 A elise.syoen@lmunet.edu
SYPNIEWSKI, Holly .... 601-974-1000 247 B sypnih@millsaps.edu
SYRMOS, Vassilis, L ..... 808-956-5006 129 C syrmos@hawaii.edu
SYVERTSON, Krisi .... 406-353-2607 262 H ksyvertson@ancollege.edu
SYVERUD, Kent .... 315-443-2235 321 G chancellor@syr.edu
SZABAT, Sandy .... 505-438-8884 288 F sandy@acupuncturecollege.edu
SZABO, Mihaela .... 304-336-8270 490 B mszabo@westliberty.edu
SZABO, Shari .... 863-680-4900 100 H sszabo@flsouthern.edu
SZAFRAN, Zvi .... 315-386-7204 320 B president@canton.edu
SZAJ, Christine .... 651-290-6362 242 L christine.szajv@mitchellhamline.edu
SZAKALY, CSC, Anthony .... 508-565-1343 219 A aszakaly@stonehill.edu
SZAKAS, Joseph, S .... 207-621-3198 196 H szakas@maine.edu
SZALDA, Katie .... 518-782-6767 315 E kszalda@siena.edu
SZALKOWSKI, Denise, M .... 716-673-3456 316 D denise.szalkowski@fredonia.edu
SZANI, Phyllis .... 201-200-3350 279 D pszani@njcu.edu
SZANTON, Sarah .... 410-502-2361 199 G sarah.szanton@jhu.edu
SZAREK, Michael .... 201-559-6047 277 J szarekm@felician.edu
SZARLETA, Ellen .... 219-980-6698 157 C eszarlet@iun.edu
SZAROLETTA, Betti .... 906-524-8301 226 C betti.szaroletta@kbocc.edu
SZARVAS, Tibor .... 318-797-5371 190 A tibor.szarvas@lsus.edu
SZARZYNSKI, Lori .... 414-382-6329 491 F lori.szarzynski@alverno.edu
SZATARAY, Balint .... 209-946-2654.. 71 E bsztaray@pacific.edu
SZATKO, Judi .... 402-280-2709 266 H judiszatko@creighton.edu
SZCZEPANEK, Charlene, L .... 401-456-8130 405 A cszczepanek@ric.edu
SZCZERBACKI, David .... 617-333-2233 208 G dszczerbacki@curry.edu
SZCZYS, Patricia .... 860-465-5295.. 85 H szczysp@easternct.edu
SZE TO, Pau Ping .... 215-572-5511 402 E pszeto@wts.edu
SZEFINSKI, Colleen ...... 201-761-6416 283 A cszefinski@saintpeters.edu
SZEJKO, Thomas .... 724-503-1001 402 B tszejko@washjeff.edu
SZELEST, Bruce .... 518-956-8058 316 A bszelest@albany.edu
SZELISTOWSKI, Warren 410-532-5110 201 D wszelistowski@ndm.edu
SZENTMIKLOSI, Jill, M . 407-582-4142 113 I jszentmiklosi@valenciacollege.edu
SZEP, Chris Ann .... 410-287-1028 198 E caszep@cecil.edu
SZEPIWDYCZ, Valerie ... 617-585-1139 217 E
SZESZYCKI, Donald, J .. 319-335-3565 163 H donald-szeszycki@uiowa.edu
SZKODNEY, Robert .... 908-526-1200 281 A bob.szkodny@raritanval.edu
SZKREDKA, Slawomir ... 805-482-2755.. 59 G sszkredka@stjohnsem.edu
SZMYT, Anne-Marie ...... 413-585-2262 218 H aszmyt@smith.edu
SZOLYGA, Chris .... 608-249-6611 492 H
SZOSTAK, Maja .... 607-778-5001 317 D szostakmm@sunybroome.edu
SZOTT, Kelly .... 541-552-7672 376 B
SZPARAGOWSKI, George .... 610-785-6205 397 E gszparagowski@scs.edu
SZROMBA, Matthew, P . 920-923-8505 493 D mpszromba93@marianuniversity.edu
SZTAJN, Paola .... 919-515-5900 342 A psztajn@ncsu.edu
SZUCS, Peter .... 503-491-6904 374 B peter.szucs@mhcc.edu
SZUKALSKI, SVD, John, A .... 563-876-3353 165 H jszukalski@dwci.edu
SZUPKA, Jennifer .... 803-774-3339 406 I szupkajl@cctech.edu
SZUR, Katalin .... 212-237-8041 294 D kszur@jjay.cuny.edu
SZWEDKO, Emmalee ..... 801-832-2553 461 F eszwedko@westminstercollege.edu
SZYMANKSI, David .... 904-620-2500 111 B david.szymanski@unf.edu
SZYMANSKI, Lynda ...... 563-387-1005 168 B szymly01@luther.edu
SZYMANSKI, Nicholas .. 330-263-2198 351 A nszymanski@wooster.edu
SZYMKOWICZ, Caitlin, B .... 413-585-4944 218 H cszymkowicz@smith.edu
SZYMURSKI, Tish .... 770-720-5527 124 G pss@reinhardt.edu

T

TA, Jennie .... 626-350-1500.. 28 F
TA, Minh-hoa .... 626-656-2101.. 73 E mhta@uwest.edu
TAAFAKI, Irene, J .... 692-625-3394 504 G
TABACHOW, Daisy .... 407-303-9203.. 95 B daisy.tabachow@ahu.edu
TABAK, Lorie .... 713-798-6649 431 D tabak@bcm.edu
TABAK, Rachel .... 716-896-0700 324 E rtabak@villa.edu
TABAKMAN, Jenna .... 713-221-8001 453 A tabakmanj@uhd.edu
TABAN, Faruk .... 832-230-5350 440 E faruk@na.edu
TABATABAI, Habib .... 405-974-2865 370 I htabatabai@uco.edu
TABB, Brian .... 612-455-3420 234 E brian.tabb@bcsmn.edu
TABB, Iris .... 314-340-3541 254 A tabbi@hssu.edu
TABB, Winston, G .... 410-516-8328 199 G wtabb@jhu.edu
TABCHOURI, Debbie ..... 337-521-8916 188 I debbie.tabchouri@solacc.edu
TABER, Charles, S .... 785-532-6224 175 C ctaber@ksu.edu
TABER, Samara .... 907-474-5526.. 10 A setaber@alaska.edu
TABER DOUGHTY, Teresa .... 817-272-2591 454 I teresa.doughty@uta.edu
TABERNER, Ian .... 617-585-0200 207 A ian.taberner@the-bac.edu
TABERSKI, Michael .... 585-245-5618 318 B mtaberski@geneseo.edu
TABING, Karla .... 618-985-3741 140 H karlatabing@jalc.edu
TABOADA, Luz, E .... 915-831-7796 436 A ltaboad2@epcc.edu
TABOR, Anne .... 207-973-1090 194 F tabora@husson.edu
TABOR, Pamela .... 615-687-6896 417 F registrar@abcnash.edu
TABOR, Tammy .... 620-276-9508 174 B tammy.tabor@gcccks.edu
TABRON-GIDDINGS, Jasmine .... 570-208-5898 386 G jasminetabron@kings.edu
TACCONE, Al .... 760-757-2121.. 52 F ataccone@miracosta.edu
TACK, Eric .... 678-466-4085 117 D erictack@clayton.edu
TACKETT, Lake .... 304-697-7550 487 E ltackett@huntingtonjuniorcollege.edu
TACZANOWSKY, Amy ... 724-589-2155 399 D ataczanowsky@thiel.edu
TADAMY, Everett, L ...... 412-268-1018 380 C et19@andrew.cmu.edu
TADAO, Tchuzie .... 680-488-2471 505 B
TADEO, Joseph .... 352-588-8244 107 D joseph.tadeo@saintleo.edu
TADEO ORBIK, Kelly .... 402-280-1293 266 H kellytadeoorbik@creighton.edu
TADEPALLI, Raghu .... 336-278-6000 328 J rtadepalli@elon.edu
TADESSE, Berhanu .... 657-278-8748.. 31 C btadesse@fullerton.edu
TADLOCK, Katherine ..... 740-593-2860 358 K tadlockk@ohio.edu
TADLOCK, Martin .... 727-873-4151 111 C mtadlock@mail.usf.edu
TADTMAN, Jeff .... 620-223-2700 173 I jeffta@fortscott.edu
TAFFORA, Raymond, P . 608-263-7400 495 D ray.taffora@wisc.edu
TAFOYA, Christina .... 760-355-6215.. 45 K christina.tafoya@imperial.edu
TAFOYA, Michelle .... 213-738-5500.. 66 B housing@swlaw.edu
TAFOYA, Yvette .... 562-860-2451.. 35 H ytafoya@cerritos.edu
TAFT, Tamara Jo .... 701-845-7227 345 G tammyjo.taft@vcsu.edu
TAGA, Brendon .... 360-475-7474 481 I btaga@olympic.edu
TAGAREL, Lyndsay .... 734-462-4400 230 G ltagarel@schoolcraft.edu
TAGAWA, Helen .... 510-809-1444.. 45 M
TAGGART, Julie .... 614-222-6171 351 B jtaggart@ccad.edu
TAGGART, Sean .... 541-956-7061 376 A staggart@roguecc.edu
TAGGART, Thomas .... 904-256-7000 102 H ttaggar@ju.edu
TAGLIALATELA, Giulio ... 409-772-1679 456 E gtaglial@utmb.edu
TAGUINOD, Bradley ...... 808-369-8594 128 F btaguinod@hmi.edu
TAHA, Dianne .... 516-726-5837 503 H tahad@usmma.edu
TAHMASSEBI, Debbie ... 801-832-2585 461 F dtahmassebi@westminstercollege.edu
TAICHMAN, Russell ...... 205-934-4720.... 8 A taichman@uab.edu
TAILLON, Gretchen .... 603-342-3003 273 C gtaillon@ccsnh.edu
TAILOR, Bhavna .... 201-327-8877 277 F btailor@eastwick.edu
TAILOR, Bhavna .... 973-661-0600 277 E btailor@eastwick.edu
TAIRA, Lora .... 217-234-5253 142 C ltaira@lakelandcollege.edu
TAIT, Melissa .... 847-214-7365 137 F mtait@elgin.edu
TAIT, Michelle .... 828-898-8785 330 E taitm@lmc.edu
TAIT, Tamara .... 866-680-2756 459 G studentlife@midwifery.edu
TAITANO, Carlos .... 671-735-2600 504 F ctaitano@triton.uog.edu
TAKAC, Jeff .... 478-301-2687 122 E takac_j@mercer.edu
TAKACS, Audrey .... 586-445-7314 227 B takacsa@macomb.edu
TAKACS, Sarolta, A .... 718-982-2315 293 E sarolta.takacs@csi.cuny.edu
TAKADA, Junko .... 714-744-2110.. 36 B takada@chapman.edu
TAKAGISHI-ALMEIDA, Michelle .... 213-738-6886.. 66 B publicservice@swlaw.edu
TAKAHASHI, Jack .... 800-754-1009 494 B
TAKAHASHI, Lucy .... 909-621-8142.. 57 K
TAKAHASHI, Sandra ..... 208-535-5372 131 B sandra.takahashi@cei.edu
TAKAHASHI, Tomoko .... 949-480-4047.. 64 G ttakahashi@soka.edu
TAKAI, Helio .... 718-636-3570 311 F htakai@pratt.edu
TAKAKI, Leslie .... 503-251-2840 377 B ltakaki@uws.edu
TAKATA, George .... 559-638-0300.. 67 D george.takata@reedleycollege.edu
TAKAYAMA-PEREZ, Amy .... 843-805-5507 408 C
TAKEDA, Sharon .... 916-278-3922.. 32 D sharon.takeda@csus.edu
TAKEDA-TINKER, Becky 303-534-6290.. 79 M becky.takeda-tinker@colostate.edu
TAKEMOTO, Mary Ann .. 562-985-2208.. 31 D maryann.takemoto@csulb.edu
TAKES, Faith, A .... 518-786-0855 306 H faith.takes@mildred-elley.edu
TAKSAR, Stephen .... 413-572-8424 213 F staksar@westfield.ma.edu
TALAVERA, Karla .... 661-255-1050.. 28 G talavera@calarts.edu
TALAVINIA, Phillip .... 419-358-3226 348 F talaviniap@bluffton.edu
TALBERT, Charles .... 773-907-4864 135 C ctalbert@ccc.edu
TALBERT, Cynthia .... 850-474-2636 111 F ctalbert@uwf.edu
TALBERT, Katie .... 828-898-2489 330 E talbertk@lmc.edu
TALBERT, Kelly .... 208-426-3844 130 H kellytalbert@boisestate.edu
TALBOT, Bill .... 607-844-8222 322 D bt021@tompkinscortland.edu
TALBOT, Reuben .... 970-675-3238.. 79 H reuben.talbot@cncc.edu
TALBOT, Scott .... 214-887-5191 435 F stalbot@dts.edu
TALBOTT, Everett Shane .... 615-230-3357 425 E everett.talbott@volstate.edu
TALBOTT, Jeffrey .... 909-748-8888.. 72 F jeff_talbott@redlands.edu
TALBOTT, Robert .... 650-543-3714.. 51 G rtalbott@menlo.edu
TALBOTT, Sherry .... 540-828-5369 464 L stalbott@bridgewater.edu
TALENTINO, Andrea ...... 585-389-2010 307 F atalent0@naz.edu
TALESH, Rameen, A ...... 949-824-5181.. 69 D rtalesh@uci.edu
TALIAFERRO, Kevin .... 301-243-2118 502 L kevin.taliaferro@dodiis.mil
TALIENTO, Tamela, K .... 931-431-9700 422 G ttaliento@nci.edu
TALLARIDA, Ronald, J .. 856-256-5413 281 F tallarida@rowan.edu
TALLCHIEF, Russ .... 405-208-6288 367 E trtallchief@okcu.edu
TALLERICO, Betty, L ...... 724-458-3790 384 G bltallerico@gcc.edu
TALLEY, Braque .... 870-575-8000.. 22 D

TALLEY, Chestley ... 903-730-4890 438 D
ctalley@jarvis.edu
TALLEY, Denise ... 540-891-3040 473 I
dguest@germanna.edu
TALLEY, Frederico, J ... 240-895-2185 202 B
fjtalley@smcm.edu
TALLEY, Lauren ... 770-533-7034 122 B
larmour@laniertech.edu
TALLEY, Nina ... 937-481-2299 364 A
nina_talley@wilmington.edu
TALLEY, Sue Lane ... 646-378-6186 310 D
sue.talley@nyack.edu
TALLMAN, Lawrence, J . 304-457-6247 486 E
tallmanlj@ab.edu
TALLON, Philip ... 281-649-3403 437 B
ptallon@hbu.edu
TALOSI, Mary ... 928-776-2359.. 16 J
mary.talosi@yc.edu
TALTON, Angela, L ... 626-256-4673.. 37 A
altalton@coh.org
TALWAR, Malvika ... 607-844-8222 322 D
mt056@tompkinscortland.edu
TAM, Victor ... 707-527-4246.. 63 D
vtam@santarosa.edu
TAMADA, Mike ... 503-788-6613 375 G
tamadam@reed.edu
TAMAN, Chris ... 760-757-2121.. 52 F
TAMANAHA, David ... 808-984-3253 130 D
davidt@hawaii.edu
TAMANAHA, Stephen ... 714-432-5809.. 38 B
stamanaha@occ.cccd.edu
TAMANDL, Salisha ... 480-994-9244.. 15 R
salishat@swiha.edu
TAMARES, Shanalee ... 909-558-4581.. 48 E
stamares@llu.edu
TAMARISK, Nancy ... 707-256-7782.. 53 E
ntamarisk@napavalley.edu
TAMASCO, Mary ... 973-353-5541 282 B
tamasco@rutgers.edu
TAMAYO, Yvonne ... 503-370-6391 377 F
ytamayo@willamette.edu
TAMBEAU, Renee ... 248-204-2208 227 A
rtambeau@ltu.edu
TAMBURRINO, Amanda 901-843-3030 423 A
tamburrino@rhodes.edu
TAMBURRO, Karen ... 847-467-3024 146 E
karen.tamburro@northwestern.edu
TAMMARO, Susan ... 717-867-6205 388 C
tammaro@lvc.edu
TAN, Amy ... 713-718-7814 437 C
amy.tan@hccs.edu
TAN, Kelsey ... 801-524-1972 459 E
TAN, Ming ... 619-876-4252.. 68 H
TAN, Sok Leng ... 218-282-8442 244 A
tans@crk.umn.edu
TAN, Susan ... 213-262-3939.. 46 D
TANABE, Clifton ... 915-747-5572 455 C
cstanabe@utep.edu
TANAKA, Andrew, Y ... 860-685-2607.. 90 B
atanaka@wesleyan.edu
TANAKA, Elizabeth ... 254-295-4949 453 D
etanaka@umhb.edu
TANAKA, Randy ... 731-352-4065 418 C
tanakar@bethelu.edu
TANAKA, Yasuo ... 510-666-8248.. 24 D
ytanaka@aimc.edu
TANBARA, Sabrina ... 212-799-5000 303 E
TANCHEL, Susie ... 617-559-8847 210 F
stanchel@hebrewcollege.edu
TANCHEVA, Kornelia ... 412-648-7705 400 H
tancheva@pitt.edu
TANCK, Buddy Jo ... 913-294-4178 173 I
buddyt@fortscott.edu
TANDAN, Lisa ... 828-251-6600 342 B
ltandan@unca.edu
TANDE, Brian ... 701-777-2335 345 B
brian.tande@und.edu
TANDON, Suteesh ... 563-336-3345 165 K
standon@eicc.edu
TANDONGFOR, William 510-215-4809.. 40 B
wtandongfor@contracosta.edu
TANDY, Joshua ... 765-641-4204 153 G
jjtandy@anderson.edu
TANDY, Paulette ... 702-895-3226 271 D
paulette.tandy@unlv.edu
TANEJA, Amit ... 508-793-3009 208 D
ataneja@holycross.edu
TANEJA, Ayush ... 334-244-3224.... 4 E
ataneja@aum.edu
TANG, Danny ... 573-341-4111 261 D
TANG, Meiling ... 707-638-5880.. 68 B
meiling.tang@tu.edu
TANG-RITCHIE, Leng ... 619-574-6909.. 55 E
lritchie@pacificcollege.edu
TANGALAKIS, Christina 818-240-1000.. 43 G
ctangalakis@glendale.edu
TANGEMAN, Bruce ... 402-323-3408 269 C
btangeman@southeast.edu
TANGENBERG, Katy ... 206-281-2759 483 G
tangenbergk@spu.edu
TANGQUIST, Jason ... 218-281-8424 244 A
jtangqui@crk.umn.edu
TANI, Sharolyn ... 808-735-4845 128 E
sharolyn.tani@chaminade.edu
TANIGAWA, Shane ... 909-687-1454.. 43 D
shanetanigawa@gs.edu
TANIS, Cleophat ... 239-732-1300 104 B
TANJI, Lorelei, A ... 949-824-5212.. 69 D
ltanji@uci.edu
TANKERSLEY, Holley ... 843-349-2949 408 A
htankers@coastal.edu
TANKERSLEY, Melody ... 330-672-0072 354 A
mtankers@kent.edu
TANKERSLEY,
Richard, A ... 704-687-8428 342 D
rtankers@uncc.edu
TANKING, Tony ... 913-360-7485 171 J
ttanking@benedictine.edu
TANKSLEY, Ashley ... 601-481-1357 247 A
atanksl1@meridiancc.edu
TANKSLEY, Jake ... 484-365-7402 388 H
jtanksley@lincoln.edu
TANKSLEY, Rick ... 323-259-2599.. 54 I
rtanksley@oxy.edu
TANKSLEY, Wallace ... 614-222-6165 351 B
wtanksley@ccad.edu
TANNER, Audrey ... 510-430-2376.. 52 E
atanner@mills.edu
TANNER, Audrey ... 410-669-9200 200 D
TANNER, Buffy ... 530-242-7714.. 64 C
btanner@shastacollege.edu
TANNER, Doug ... 912-260-4286 125 D
doug.tanner@sgsc.edu
TANNER, Douglas, R ... 229-333-5935 127 E
dtanner@valdosta.edu
TANNER, Elizabeth ... 210-486-3933 429 A
etanner@alamo.edu
TANNER, Greg ... 912-260-4259 125 D
greg.tanner@sgsc.edu
TANNER, J.B ... 304-724-3700 486 F
TANNER, Jason ... 770-528-3758 117 B
jtanner@chattahoocheetech.edu
TANNER, Jeff, F ... 757-683-3520 469 B
jtanner@odu.edu
TANNER, Jonathan ... 801-689-2160 459 I
jtanner@nightingale.edu
TANNER, Margaret ... 479-788-7519.. 21 G
margaret.tanner@uafs.edu
TANNER, Nicole ... 414-297-6556 499 C
tannern@matc.edu
TANNER, Norma ... 251-460-6141.... 9 A
ntanner@southalabama.edu
TANNER, Patrick ... 208-562-3247 131 E
patricktanner@cwi.edu
TANNER, Ray ... 803-777-4202 413 A
rtanner@mailbox.sc.edu
TANNER, Tyrone ... 713-790-7213 446 C
tytanner@pvamu.edu
TANNEY, Matt ... 765-361-6233 163 B
tanneym@wabash.edu
TANONA, Mary ... 508-373-5893 216 D
mary.tanona@mcphs.edu
TANOUYE, Allyson, M .. 808-956-7927 129 E
atanouye@hawaii.edu
TANSEY, John, G ... 603-646-1202 273 D
john.g.tansey@dartmouth.edu
TANTILLO, Astrida, O ... 312-413-7329 151 G
tantillo@uic.edu
TANYEL, Faruk ... 864-503-5587 414 A
ftanyel@uscupstate.edu
TANZILLI, Steve ... 412-392-4742 396 G
stanzilli@pointpark.edu
TANZOSCH, James ... 919-530-5063 341 E
jtanzosc@nccu.edu
TAO, Eric ... 408-733-1878.. 71 B
president@uewm.edu
TAO, Eric ... 888-488-4968.. 46 F
etao@itu.edu
TAOKA, Yasuko ... 402-375-7394 268 F
yataoka1@wsc.edu
TAORMINA, Melanie ... 570-321-4036 389 B
taormina@lycoming.edu
TAPHORN, Joseph, C ... 651-962-5775 244 E
jctaphorn@stthomas.edu
TAPHORN, Rick ... 731-661-5204 426 F
rtaphorn@uu.edu
TAPIA, Damaris ... 773-442-4208 146 A
d-tapia1@neiu.edu
TAPIA, Daniel ... 630-960-3195 144 F
dtapia@midwestern.edu
TAPIA, Giselle ... 787-766-1717 510 G
TAPIA, Juan ... 305-821-3333 100 E
jetapia@fnu.edu
TAPIA-MALDONADO,
Luis ... 787-894-6050 511 F
luis.tapia@upr.edu
TAPIA MALDONADO,
Luis, A ... 787-894-2828 513 C
luis.tapia@upr.edu
TAPLEY, Robyn ... 321-674-8050 100 C
rtapley@fit.edu
TAPP, Beth ... 612-624-5255 243 F
bethtapp@umn.edu
TAPP, Matthew ... 909-599-5433.. 48 A
mtapp@lifepacific.edu
TAPPAN, Charlene ... 860-512-2912.. 86 G
ctappan@manchestercc.edu
TAPPE, Diane ... 563-387-1045 168 B
tappdi01@luther.edu
TAPPEN, Mitch ... 575-835-5900 286 K
mitch.tappen@nmt.edu
TAPPER, Michelle ... 657-278-4207.. 31 C
mtapper@fullerton.edu
TAPSCOTT, Michael, R .. 202-994-1463.. 92 D
tapscott@gwu.edu
TARANGO, McKenzie ... 760-245-4271.. 74 D
mckenzie.tarango@vvc.edu
TARANTO, John, A ... 816-501-3630 250 F
john.taranto@avila.edu
TARASKEWICH,
Georgina ... 718-482-5100 294 F
gcapetanakis@lagcc.cuny.edu
TARAZI, Hilari ... 760-471-1316.. 72 H
htarazi@usk.edu
TARAZON, Mayte ... 844-922-8228.. 91 G
TARBELL, Donald, R ... 843-661-1119 409 G
dtarbell@fmarion.edu
TARBOX, James ... 619-594-4379.. 33 D
jtarbox@sdsu.edu
TARBOX, Norm ... 801-626-6003 461 A
ntarbox@weber.edu
TARBOX, Sandra ... 703-993-2353 467 E
starbox@gmu.edu
TARBUTTON, Ron ... 405-744-7147 367 G
ron.tarbutton@okstate.edu
TARBY, Jay ... 216-397-1703 353 O
tarby@jcu.edu
TARBY, Wendy ... 315-498-2742 310 F
tarbyw@sunyocc.edu
TARBY, Wendy ... 315-498-2622 310 F
TARDIFF, Robin ... 207-947-4591 194 B
rtardiff@bealcollege.edu
TARENCE, Elaine, P ... 334-387-3877.... 4 B
elainetarence@amridgeuniversity.edu
TARGONSKI, Conrad, A 608-796-3804 497 O
catargonski@viterbo.edu
TARHINI, Kassim, M ... 860-444-8334 503 G
kassim.m.tarhini@uscg.mil
TARHULE, Aondover ... 309-438-7018 140 D
tarhule@ilstu.edu
TARIN, Lucille ... 570-577-3661 379 C
lucille.tarin@bucknell.edu
TARLING, Mary ... 630-844-7802 133 D
mtarling@aurora.edu
TARNOWSKI, Jeff ... 706-867-3050 127 A
jeff.tarnowski@ung.edu
TAROLI, Stacie ... 570-342-8000 383 H
staroli@fortisinstitute.edu
TAROMINA, Katherine ... 206-517-4541 483 F
ktaromina@sieam.edu
TAROPE, Marji ... 670-237-6771 505 A
marji.tarope@marianas.edu
TARPEY, Andrea ... 413-755-4847 216 A
tarpey@stcc.edu
TARRANT, Carole ... 540-857-6281 475 G
ctarrant@virginiawestern.edu
TARRANT, Christopher .. 305-628-6656 107 F
ctarrant@stu.edu
TARRANT, Fredrick, A ... 770-720-9221 124 G
fkt@reinhardt.edu
TARRANT, Kaneesha ... 951-372-7877.. 59 C
kaneesha.tarrant@norcocollege.edu
TARRATS RIVERA, Jean 281-649-3026 437 B
jtarrats@hbu.edu
TARRER, Jerry ... 312-369-7060 136 D
jtarrer@colum.edu
TARSKI, Anne ... 830-591-7294 444 G
ahtarski@swtjc.edu
TART, Kathryn, M ... 832-842-8218 452 D
kmtart@uh.edu
TART, Marla, L ... 919-866-5901 338 G
mltart@waketech.edu
TART, Stuart ... 240-567-7494 200 G
stuart.tart@montgomerycollege.edu
TARTT, Tom ... 205-652-3533.... 9 B
ttartt@uwa.edu
TARVER, Eunice ... 918-595-7524 370 C
eunice.tarver@tulsacc.edu
TARVER, III, Walter, L .. 609-652-4804 283 E
walter.tarver@stockton.edu
TARVER-BEHRING,
Shari, A ... 818-677-2590.. 32 C
starver-behring@csun.edu
TARVER-ROSS,
Cassandra ... 470-639-0703 123 D
cassandra.ross@morehouse.edu
TARVER-ROSS,
Cassandra ... 404-639-0999 123 D
cassandra.tarver-ross@morehouse.edu
TARWATER, Anne ... 615-383-3230 417 G
tarwatera@dominicancampus.org
TARWATER, Lisa ... 865-573-4517 420 E
ltarwater@johnsonu.edu
TARY, Keely ... 423-236-2736 423 F
ktary@southern.edu
TASKE, Matt ... 513-244-4892 356 F
matt.taske@msj.edu
TASSAVA, Christopher .. 507-222-4047 234 G
ctassava@carleton.edu
TASSON, Dana ... 503-725-4429 375 E
tassond@pdx.edu
TAST, Maryellen ... 307-778-1146 501 E
mtast@lccc.wy.edu
TASTAD, Renee ... 413-552-2592 214 F
rtastad@hcc.edu
TATAR, Greg ... 310-434-4305.. 63 C
tatar_greg@smc.edu
TATARKA, Donna ... 973-328-5098 276 J
dtatarka@ccm.edu
TATE, Amy ... 414-229-3844 496 B
lensing@uwm.edu
TATE, Bernessa ... 312-553-3213 135 B
btruvillion@ccc.edu
TATE, Brad ... 513-745-5700 362 A
brad.tate@uc.edu
TATE, Celeste ... 541-278-5780 371 H
cetate@bluecc.edu
TATE, David ... 307-382-1882 501 J
dtate@westernwyoming.edu
TATE, Don ... 864-587-4227 412 F
tated@smcsc.edu
TATE, Edward ... 404-962-3263 127 D
edward.tate@usg.edu
TATE, Helen ... 401-456-8043 405 A
htate@ric.edu
TATE, James ... 507-537-6256 241 D
jim.tate@smsu.edu
TATE, Janene ... 225-771-4545 191 A
janene_tate@sus.edu
TATE, Janene ... 225-771-3216 191 B
janene_tate@sus.edu
TATE, Thomas ... 575-624-8400 287 B
tate@nmmi.edu
TATE, IV, William, F ... 225-578-2111 189 E
TATE, IV, William, F ... 225-578-2111 189 D
TATELA, Joseph ... 410-386-8327 198 D
jtatela@carrollcc.edu
TATEVOSIAN, Emil ... 213-613-2200.. 65 E
TATNALL, Amber ... 207-216-4392 195 J
atatnall@yccc.edu
TATOM, Monte ... 256-766-6610.... 5 E
mtatom@hcu.edu
TATRO, Clayton ... 620-227-9269 173 D
ctatro@dc3.edu
TATRO, Donna, E ... 609-258-2845 280 D
tatro@princeton.edu
TATRO, Fred ... 617-364-3510 207 B
ftatro@boston.edu
TATRO, Kim ... 920-832-6888 493 B
kimberly.n.tatro@lawrence.edu
TATRO, Lois ... 316-978-5890 178 D
lois.tatro@wichita.edu
TATSAK, Jenny ... 248-689-8282 232 C
jtatsak@walshcollege.edu
TATTON, Edward ... 914-606-8060 325 A
edward.tatton@sunywcc.edu
TATUM, Alfred, W ... 303-615-1900.. 81 M
atatum1@msudenver.edu
TATUM, Andrea ... 757-352-4127 470 B

TATUM, Ashley 940-668-7323 440 F atatum@nctc.edu
TATUM, Jeff 620-276-0606 174 B jeffrey.tatum@gcccks.edu
TATUM, Lance 334-670-3104 7 C ltatum@troy.edu
TATUM, Tanya 850-599-3777 109 I tanya.tatum@famu.edu
TATUM, Veronda 870-864-7133 21 A vtatum@southark.edu
TAUB, Alexander 215-477-1000 399 A
TAUBENFELD, Aviva 914-251-6550 319 B aviva.taubenfeld@purchase.edu
TAUBER, Hendy 323-937-3763 76 H htauber@yoec.edu
TAUBER, Yitzchok, M 845-425-9565 305 F
TAUBMAN, Mark, B 585-275-0017 323 M mark_taubman@urmc.rochester.edu
TAUER, Jackie 507-537-7157 241 D jackie.tauer@smsu.edu
TAUER, Ritamarie 281-649-3702 437 B rtauer@hbu.edu
TAUPIER, Andrea, S 413-748-3609 218 I ataupier@springfield.edu
TAURIAC, Jesse 617-243-2173 211 B jtauriac@lasell.edu
TAURIELLO, Claire, M 301-447-5202 201 B tauriello@msmary.edu
TAUSSI, Lee 845-398-4013 314 G altaussi@stac.edu
TAUZIN, Kristie, R 985-448-4509 192 F kristie.tauzin@nicholls.edu
TAVARE, Kristel 715-858-1833 498 E ktavare@cvtc.edu
TAVARES, Kim 513-529-5990 356 A kim.tavares@miamioh.edu
TAVARES, Rosemary 201-200-2595 279 D rtavares@njcu.edu
TAVARES, Shirley, A 787-725-8120 506 M investigacion@eap.edu
TAVARES, Stephen 860-465-4521 85 H tavaresst@easternct.edu
TAVAREZ, Alex 671-734-1812 504 E atavarez@piu.edu
TAVAREZ, Elisabeth, W 845-575-3000 305 D elisabeth.tavarez@marist.edu
TAVAREZ, Jason 805-565-6633 76 A jtavarez@westmont.edu
TAVE, Stephen 815-967-7329 148 C stave@rockfordcareercollege.edu
TAVELLI, Nancy, J 509-527-5297 486 B tavelln@whitman.edu
TAVERA, Deborah, T 610-660-1276 397 G dtavera@sju.edu
TAVERNER, Melissa, P 870-307-7201 19 I provost@lyon.edu
TAVERNER, Melissa, P 870-307-7202 19 I provost@lyon.edu
TAWNEY, Amy 210-567-2590 456 C tawney@uthscsa.edu
TAWNEY, Andrea 915-215-4850 451 B andrea.tawney@ttuhsc.edu
TAXTER, Marianne 619-265-0107 57 I mtaxter@platt.edu
TAYEH, Raja 402-826-6776 267 A raja.tayeh@doane.edu
TAYLOE, John 252-398-1232 328 C tayloj@chowan.edu
TAYLOR, Adam 864-388-8195 410 A ataylor@lander.edu
TAYLOR, Alison 501-450-3377 23 H ataylor45@uca.edu
TAYLOR, Allana 703-284-1530 468 H allana.taylor@marymount.edu
TAYLOR, Allen 304-696-6195 489 M taylor@marshall.edu
TAYLOR, Allison, S 402-280-3189 266 H allisontaylor@creighton.edu
TAYLOR, Amanda 202-885-3827 91 F ataylor@american.edu
TAYLOR, Amanda 864-379-6606 409 E taylor@erskine.edu
TAYLOR, Amy 203-392-6800 86 A taylora28@southernct.edu
TAYLOR, Andy 712-749-2226 164 C taylora@bvu.edu
TAYLOR, Angela 757-388-5133 470 F ataylor@sentara.edu
TAYLOR, Ann 765-361-6186 163 B taylora@wabash.edu
TAYLOR, Ann 314-516-5109 261 C taylorann@umsl.edu
TAYLOR, Anna 770-233-5560 125 H anna.taylor@sctech.edu
TAYLOR, AnnMarie 561-803-2500 105 C annmarie_taylor@pba.edu
TAYLOR, April 912-201-8000 125 F ataylor@southuniversity.edu
TAYLOR, Audra 254-442-5117 432 I audra.taylor@cisco.edu
TAYLOR, Baishakhi 413-585-4900 218 H btaylor44@smith.edu
TAYLOR, Beck, A 205-726-2727 6 E president@samford.edu
TAYLOR, Bill 408-741-2642 75 E bill.taylor@westvalley.edu
TAYLOR, Blythe 252-399-6541 326 K mbtaylor@barton.edu
TAYLOR, Bonnie 404-270-5132 126 B bonnie.taylor@spelman.edu
TAYLOR, Brad 843-792-7526 410 C taylobra@musc.edu
TAYLOR, Bradley, G 336-841-9548 329 F btaylor@highpoint.edu
TAYLOR, Brandy 912-871-1616 123 J btaylor@ogeecheetech.edu
TAYLOR, Brantley 716-884-9120 292 B bctaylor@bryantstratton.edu
TAYLOR, Brett 949-854-8002 39 K
TAYLOR, Brian 808-956-6182 129 E taylorb@hawaii.edu
TAYLOR, Brian 660-263-3900 251 D briantaylor@cccb.edu
TAYLOR, Cameron, P 202-441-0058 118 E cameron.taylor@emory.edu
TAYLOR, Carmen 308-398-7335 266 A carmentaylor@cccneb.edu
TAYLOR, Cathy 847-214-7238 137 F ctaylor@elgin.edu
TAYLOR, Cathy 615-460-6781 418 B cathy.taylor@belmont.edu
TAYLOR, Cathy, N 618-650-5176 150 C cattayl@siue.edu
TAYLOR, Caughman 803-434-2069 413 A caughman.taylor@uscmed.sc.edu
TAYLOR, Celya 870-230-5358 19 D taylorc@hsu.edu
TAYLOR, Charles 817-735-0268 454 B charles.taylor@unthsc.edu
TAYLOR, Charlie, M 205-348-5205 7 F ctaylor@uasystem.edu
TAYLOR, Cherie, O 713-646-1856 443 I ctaylor@stcl.edu
TAYLOR, Chris 937-775-4240 364 E chris.taylor@wright.edu
TAYLOR, Christopher 843-661-8231 409 F christopher.taylor@fdtc.edu
TAYLOR, Courtney 662-243-1929 246 B ctaylor@eastms.edu
TAYLOR, Craig 251-981-3771 5 A craig.taylor@columbiasouthern.edu
TAYLOR, Crystal 252-940-6219 332 C crystal.taylor@beaufortccc.edu
TAYLOR, Daniel 304-358-2000 487 D dtaylor@future.edu
TAYLOR, Darrell 304-896-7432 488 I darrell.taylor@southernwv.edu
TAYLOR, David 203-576-4644 89 C davtaylo@bridgeport.edu
TAYLOR, David, A 718-289-5598 293 B david.taylor@bcc.cuny.edu
TAYLOR, David, F 336-758-5000 344 C taylordf@wfu.edu
TAYLOR, David, R 540-568-3720 468 C taylordr@jmu.edu
TAYLOR, Dean 617-420-1820 218 F
TAYLOR, Debbie 864-231-2000 406 F dtaylor@andersonuniversity.edu
TAYLOR, Debora, W 512-448-8450 442 I deboraw@stedwards.edu
TAYLOR, Deborah 562-903-4703 27 A deborah.taylor@biola.edu
TAYLOR, Deshun 718-517-7730 314 F
TAYLOR, Donald 610-902-8200 379 G donald.taylor@cabrini.edu
TAYLOR, Dub 803-376-5723 406 D dtaylor@allenuniversity.edu
TAYLOR, Dustin 740-374-8716 363 F dtaylor@wscc.edu
TAYLOR, Ed 206-616-7175 485 A edtaylor@uw.edu
TAYLOR, Edward 608-663-2333 492 F etaylor@edgewood.edu
TAYLOR, Edward 608-663-2333 492 F edtaylor@edgewood.edu
TAYLOR, Endalyn 336-770-3207 343 D taylore@uncsa.edu
TAYLOR, Faye 732-247-5241 279 C ftaylor@nbts.edu
TAYLOR, G. Christine 205-348-2053 7 G christine.taylor@ua.edu
TAYLOR, JR., G. Don 540-231-3270 476 C taylorgd@vt.edu
TAYLOR, Gene 410-532-5324 201 D gtaylor@ndm.edu
TAYLOR, Gene 785-532-6912 175 C ksuad@ksu.edu
TAYLOR, Geoffrey 912-525-5000 124 gtaylor@scad.edu
TAYLOR, Gina 321-433-7000 98 I taylorg@easternflorida.edu
TAYLOR, Ginny 513-244-4432 356 F ginny.taylor@msj.edu
TAYLOR, Giselle 913-971-3381 176 C
TAYLOR, Goldie 404-752-1500 123 E gtaylor@msm.edu
TAYLOR, Greg 910-898-9605 336 D taylorg@montgomery.edu
TAYLOR, Greg 307-742-3776 502 E gtaylor@wyotech.edu
TAYLOR, Gregory 914-251-6485 319 E gregory.taylor@purchase.edu
TAYLOR, Gwen 706-771-4175 115 J gtaylor@augustatech.edu
TAYLOR, Hal 800-443-9266 503 D
TAYLOR, Heather 304-829-7408 487 A htaylor@bethanywv.edu
TAYLOR, Helen 318-797-5374 190 A helen.taylor@lsus.edu
TAYLOR, Hunter 252-398-6505 328 C tayloh1@chowan.edu
TAYLOR, Ivy, R 662-252-2491 248 G irtaylor@rustcollege.edu
TAYLOR, J. Kevin 805-756-1503 29 I jktaylor@calpoly.edu
TAYLOR, Jacob 814-472-3009 397 F jtaylor@francis.edu
TAYLOR, Jaime 304-696-3716 489 M jaime.taylor@marshall.edu
TAYLOR, Jaime, R 409-880-8405 449 G jtaylor81@lamar.edu
TAYLOR, James 410-777-2318 197 G jmtaylor@aacc.edu
TAYLOR, James 470-578-6033 121 M jtayl378@kennesaw.edu
TAYLOR, James 801-626-6055 461 A jamestaylor8@weber.edu
TAYLOR, James, E 202-646-1337 93 B
TAYLOR, Jan 865-981-8057 421 C jan.taylor@maryvillecollege.edu
TAYLOR, Jana 918-557-5356 365 C taylorj@bacone.edu
TAYLOR, Janelle, L 260-519-2891 156 C jtaylor@huntington.edu
TAYLOR, Janet 815-921-4324 148 B j.taylor@rockvalleycollege.edu
TAYLOR, Janie 817-461-8741 430 B jtaylor@abu.edu
TAYLOR, Jay 704-216-7116 337 F jay.taylor@rccc.edu
TAYLOR, Jeannie 800-280-0307 153 E jeannie.taylor@ace.edu
TAYLOR, Jeff 910-275-6342 335 E jtaylor@jamessprunt.edu
TAYLOR, Jeffrey 814-871-7213 384 A taylor030@gannon.edu
TAYLOR, Jeffrey, D 315-268-5978 295 F jdtaylor@clarkson.edu
TAYLOR, Jennifer 575-674-2281 285 L jetaylor@burrell.edu
TAYLOR, Jennifer 479-575-2254 21 F taylorj@uark.edu
TAYLOR, Jennifer 931-372-3897 426 B jennifertaylor@tntech.edu
TAYLOR, Jessica, L 503-255-0332 374 C jltaylor@multnomah.edu
TAYLOR, John 714-432-5935 38 B jtaylor174@occ.cccd.edu
TAYLOR, John 719-587-7382 77 G jhtaylor@adams.edu
TAYLOR, John 585-785-1300 299 F john.taylor@flcc.edu
TAYLOR, Joseph 804-342-1484 476 F jdtaylor@vuu.edu
TAYLOR, Joy 703-993-5270 467 E jtaylo16@gmu.edu
TAYLOR, Juanyce 601-984-1010 249 E jdtaylor@umc.edu
TAYLOR, Judith, M 240-567-7337 200 G judith.taylor@montgomerycollege.edu
TAYLOR, Julie, Y 256-765-4680 8 E jayates@una.edu
TAYLOR, Justin 785-833-4444 175 E justin.taylor@kwu.edu
TAYLOR, Karen 914-606-6963 325 A karen.taylor@sunywcc.edu
TAYLOR, Karina 414-297-8425 499 C taylorkl@matc.edu
TAYLOR, Kathryn 618-664-6833 138 F kathy.taylor@greenville.edu
TAYLOR, Kathy 504-816-4304 186 I ktaylor@dillard.edu
TAYLOR, Kathy 918-631-2051 371 C kathy-taylor@utulsa.edu
TAYLOR, Keith 814-871-7609 384 A ktaylor@gannon.edu
TAYLOR, Kelley, G 334-844-4794 4 D taylokg@auburn.edu
TAYLOR, Kelli, W 910-630-7157 331 E ktaylor@methodist.edu
TAYLOR, Kenneth 870-230-5216 19 D taylorke@hsu.edu
TAYLOR, Kent 575-624-8235 287 B kent@nmmi.edu
TAYLOR, Kevin 718-862-7825 304 M ktaylor02@manhattan.edu
TAYLOR, Kevin 303-615-1223 81 M ktaylo79@msudenver.edu
TAYLOR, Kevin, L 864-242-5100 406 H
TAYLOR, Kim 773-702-7749 151 E kimtaylor@uchicago.edu
TAYLOR, Kimberly 859-323-7311 185 F kta254@uky.edu
TAYLOR, Kimberly 518-292-1854 313 A taylok3@sage.edu
TAYLOR, Kirsten 217-786-2258 143 B kirsten.taylor@llcc.edu
TAYLOR, Kristen 817-257-4161 448 F kristen.taylor@tcu.edu
TAYLOR, Kristy 740-389-4636 355 F taylork@mtc.edu
TAYLOR, Kyle 217-420-6717 144 G kataylor@millikin.edu
TAYLOR, Kyle 405-789-7661 369 I kyle.taylor@swcu.edu
TAYLOR, Ladd 601-928-6299 247 E ladd.taylor@mgccc.edu
TAYLOR, Laura 706-290-2163 116 B lataylor@berry.edu
TAYLOR, Lauren, M 205-726-2956 6 E lmtaylor@samford.edu
TAYLOR, Laurna 615-361-7555 419 F lataylor@daymarcollege.edu
TAYLOR, Laurna 615-361-7555 419 F lataylor@daymarinstitute.edu
TAYLOR, Lee 334-387-3877 4 B leetaylor@amridgeuniversity.edu
TAYLOR, Leslie 970-491-1128 79 N leslie.taylor@colostate.edu
TAYLOR, Leslie, W 501-686-8998 22 B taylorlesliew@uams.edu
TAYLOR, Linda 610-499-1039 402 G lmtaylor@widener.edu
TAYLOR, Lindsey 706-236-2207 116 B ltaylor@berry.edu
TAYLOR, Lois, J 740-412-0687 358 A lotaylor@ohiochristian.edu
TAYLOR, Lora 910-938-6211 333 F taylorl@coastalcarolina.edu
TAYLOR, Loralyn 740-593-1059 358 K taylorl4@ohio.edu
TAYLOR, Lori 501-812-2224 23 B ltaylor@uaptc.edu
TAYLOR, Marcia 302-857-7823 90 E mtayor@desu.edu
TAYLOR, Marcia 918-781-7271 365 C taylorm@bacone.edu
TAYLOR, Marcie 765-641-4495 153 G mjtaylor@anderson.edu
TAYLOR, Margaret 315-786-2250 303 C mtaylor@sunyjefferson.edu
TAYLOR, Margaret, W 870-575-8733 22 D taylorm@uapb.edu
TAYLOR, Maria 704-233-8126 344 F m.taylor@wingate.edu
TAYLOR, Marilyn 520-621-3876 16 D taylorm@arizona.edu
TAYLOR, Mark 513-529-9203 356 A mataylor@miamioh.edu
TAYLOR, Mark, P 314-935-6344 262 A mark.p.taylor@wustl.edu

TAYLOR, Martha, M 334-844-4438 4 D taylomm@auburn.edu
TAYLOR, Mary 208-535-5303 131 B mary.taylor@cei.edu
TAYLOR, Mary 828-898-8763 330 E taylorm@lmc.edu
TAYLOR, Mary 330-325-6728 357 D mtaylor4@neomed.edu
TAYLOR, Matthew, A 410-651-7800 203 D mataylor3@umes.edu
TAYLOR, Melanie 562-903-4800 27 A melanie.taylor@biola.edu
TAYLOR, Michael 617-449-7037 219 D michael.taylor@urbancollege.edu
TAYLOR, Mike 330-263-2143 351 A mitaylor@wooster.edu
TAYLOR, Mischia 704-406-2260 329 A mataylor@gardner-webb.edu
TAYLOR, Misty 386-752-1822 100 B misty.taylor@fgc.edu
TAYLOR, Molly 214-333-5960 434 C molly@dbu.edu
TAYLOR, Monique 408-498-5106 73 B mtaylor@cogswell.edu
TAYLOR, Monique 802-860-2700 462 A mtaylor@champlain.edu
TAYLOR, Morris 618-650-2536 150 C mortayl@siue.edu
TAYLOR, Nancy, K 716-375-2317 313 C nktaylor@sbu.edu
TAYLOR, Nicolle 310-506-6464 56 G nicolle.taylor@pepperdine.edu
TAYLOR, Orlando, L 805-898-4038 42 D otaylor@fielding.edu
TAYLOR, Pamela 630-844-5262 133 D phtaylor@aurora.edu
TAYLOR, Pamela, L 781-283-3694 219 E ptaylor@wellesley.edu
TAYLOR, Patty, L 920-565-1000 493 A taylorpl@lakeland.edu
TAYLOR, OSB, Paul 724-805-2271 397 I paul.taylor@stvincent.edu
TAYLOR, Quintin 225-922-2391 187 F quintintaylor@lctcs.edu
TAYLOR, R 503-399-6566 372 B r.taylor@chemeketa.edu
TAYLOR, Rachelle 718-270-6966 294 G rachellet@mec.cuny.edu
TAYLOR, Ramona 804-524-5370 470 C rtaylor@vsu.edu
TAYLOR, Ranea 660-543-4255 260 G rtaylor@ucmo.edu
TAYLOR, Reagan 512-492-3037 430 A rtaylor@aoma.edu
TAYLOR, Robert 850-561-2644 109 I robert.taylor@famu.edu
TAYLOR, Robert 321-674-7384 100 C rotaylor@fit.edu
TAYLOR, Robert 712-722-6077 165 I robert.taylor@dordt.edu
TAYLOR, Rochelle 313-317-4138 225 B rtaylor33@hfcc.edu
TAYLOR, Roderick 509-543-1480 479 A rtaylor@columbiabasin.edu
TAYLOR, Ronald, K 304-462-6451 489 L ronald.taylor@glenville.edu
TAYLOR, Russell 828-398-7900 332 B russellgtaylor@abtech.edu
TAYLOR, Russell 828-398-7302 332 B rtaylor@abtech.edu
TAYLOR, Sabrina 818-252-5225 76 E sarina.taylor@woodbury.edu
TAYLOR, Sandi 661-395-4266 46 L staylor@bakersfieldcollege.edu
TAYLOR, Sarah 386-312-4190 107 C sarahtaylor@sjrstate.edu
TAYLOR, Sarah 847-628-2023 141 C sarah.skorburg@judsonu.edu
TAYLOR, Sarah 336-744-0900 327 E librarian@carolina.edu
TAYLOR, Scott 402-280-5104 266 H scotttaylor@creighton.edu
TAYLOR, Shawn 805-765-9300 62 N
TAYLOR, Shawn 863-638-7655 114 A shawn.taylor@warner.edu
TAYLOR, Sherri 334-291-4928 1 H sherri.taylor@cv.edu
TAYLOR, Stacey 617-732-2790 216 D stacey.taylor@mcphs.edu
TAYLOR, Stefanie 601-977-7778 249 C sltaylor@tougaloo.edu
TAYLOR, Stephanie 704-637-4470 327 I sataylor@catawba.edu
TAYLOR, Stephen 321-433-7509 98 I taylorm@easternflorida.edu
TAYLOR, Steven 334-670-3399 7 C sltaylor@troy.edu
TAYLOR, Steven, P 262-243-5700 492 E steve.taylor@cuw.edu
TAYLOR, Steven, T 303-963-3138 78 H staylor@ccu.edu
TAYLOR, Sue 972-825-4768 444 J staylor@sagu.edu
TAYLOR, Susan 719-255-3566 84 C staylor@uccs.edu
TAYLOR, Tavaris 706-588-8693 124 E tavaris.taylor@point.edu
TAYLOR, Tavaris 740-392-6868 356 G tavaris.taylor@mvnu.edu
TAYLOR, Teresa 479-619-4188 20 C ttaylor19@nwacc.edu
TAYLOR, Tim 618-634-3200 149 G
TAYLOR, Timothy 313-583-6500 231 I taylortd@umich.edu
TAYLOR, Tommy 205-726-2020 6 E ttaylor9@samford.edu
TAYLOR, Traki, L 850-245-0466 109 H traki.taylor@flbog.edu
TAYLOR, Vorley 740-366-9443 349 F taylor.1051@osu.edu
TAYLOR, Warren 717-391-7285 399 C
TAYLOR, Whitney 270-706-8604 181 G whitney.taylor@kctcs.edu
TAYLOR, William 419-559-2266 361 C wtaylor@terra.edu
TAYLOR-BENNS, Kimberly 484-365-7218 388 H ktaylorbenns@lincoln.edu
TAYLOR-BOUCHIE, Donna 812-888-4811 162 F dtbouchie@vinu.edu
TAYLOR-BROWNE, Wintlett 563-387-1486 168 B brownewi@luther.edu
TAYLOR DUPREE, Lesa 318-678-6000 187 H ltaylordupre@bpcc.edu
TAYLOR HEARD, Janice 216-987-5556 351 E janice.taylor-heard@tri-c.edu
TAYLOR-HICKEY, Brenda 229-391-5001 114 F
TAYLOR JARELL, Tracey 225-771-4680 191 B tracey_taylorjarell@sus.edu
TAYLOR-LAWTON, Cheri 708-709-7949 147 D ctaylorlawton@prairiestate.edu
TAYLOR-MINNIEFIELD, Cherilyn, Y 803-536-8698 411 G ctaylo37@scsu.edu
TAYLOR-SAWYER, Sandra 575-769-4138 285 O sandra.sawyer@clovis.edu
TAYLOR-YEAPLE, Sarah 865-981-8404 421 C sarah.yeaple@maryvillecollege.edu
TCHAKARIAN, Nazig 646-216-2860 308 G ntchakarian@nycda.edu
TEACHEY, Virginia 910-521-6000 343 B
TEACHMAN, Stephanie 425-640-1495 480 A stephanie.teachman@edcc.edu
TEACHOUT, David, J 336-334-4759 343 A djteacho@uncg.edu
TEAGLE, Natalie 336-285-3216 341 D ntteagle@ncat.edu
TEAGUE, Adrienne, L 540-887-7236 468 G alteague@marybaldwin.edu
TEAGUE, Brad 501-450-3150 23 H bteague@uca.edu
TEAGUE, Connie 801-883-8336 459 A
TEAGUE, Craig 319-895-4210 164 G cteague@cornellcollege.edu
TEAGUE, Delise 662-685-4771 245 C dteague@bmc.edu
TEAGUE, Donna 812-488-2212 161 G dt52@evansville.edu
TEAGUE, Edward 845-938-5569 503 I edward.teague@westpoint.edu
TEAGUE, Geni 425-640-1484 480 A geni.teague@edcc.edu
TEAGUE, Jeff 262-945-1259 492 B jteague@carthage.edu
TEAGUE, Randle 606-546-1202 185 D rteague@unionky.edu
TEAGUE, Rebecca 951-487-3072 53 A rteague@msjc.edu
TEAGUE, Sharyn, J 910-221-2224 331 B steague@manna.edu
TEAGUE, Tracie 805-969-3626 55 J tteague@pacifica.edu
TEAHEN, Rebecca, M 231-995-1855 229 A rteahen@nmc.edu
TEAL, Holly 970-248-1977 78 J hteal@coloradomesa.edu
TEAL, Kurtis 866-457-2828 171 I tealk@bartonccc.edu
TEALER, Eddie 972-860-7001 434 H etealer@dcccd.edu
TEASDALE, David 661-336-5100 46 K
TEASLEY, Martell, L 801-581-6194 459 O martell.teasley@utah.edu
TEAT, Jonathan 214-333-5128 434 C jonathan@dbu.edu
TEATER, Kristian 314-792-6100 254 F teater@kenrick.edu
TEBALDI, Edinaldo 401-232-6901 404 A etebaldi@bryant.edu
TEBAY, John 714-992-7035 54 C jtebay@fullcoll.edu
TEBBE, Robert 618-235-2700 150 E robert.tebbe@swic.edu
TEBERIAN, Shahan, G 610-917-1506 401 G sgteberian@valleyforge.edu
TEBRUGGE, Kimberly 719-333-1738 503 D kimberly.tebrugge@usafa.edu
TECHAIRA, David 831-755-6752 44 G dtechair@hartnell.edu
TECUN, Marianne 203-332-5139 86 F mtecun@housatonic.edu
TEDAMRONGWANISH, Jessica 414-277-7163 494 D
TEDDER, Charles 651-793-1854 238 I charles.tedder@metrostate.edu
TEDDER, Holly 212-854-8466 291 A htedder@barnard.edu
TEDDER, Tracey 863-680-4177 100 H ttedder@flsouthern.edu
TEDDERS, Stuart 912-478-1922 120 C stedders@georgiasouthern.edu
TEDESCO, Jonathan 440-375-7352 354 K jtedesco@lec.edu
TEDESCO, Joseph, W 713-743-4207 452 D jtedesco@uh.edu
TEDESCO, Stephanie 732-987-2252 278 A stedesco@georgian.edu
TEDJESKE, David 610-519-6979 401 K david.tedjeske@villanova.edu
TEDRICK, Charles 760-480-8474 75 J ctedrick@wscal.edu
TEED, Deborah 239-489-9248 101 A deborah.teed@fsw.edu
TEEGARDEN, Ellen 859-442-1687 181 H ellen.teegarden@kctcs.edu
TEEL, Gay 619-216-6670 66 A gteel@swccd.edu
TEERINK, Susan, M 414-288-1583 493 E susan.teerink@marquette.edu
TEETERS, Rebecca 617-585-1311 217 E rebecca.teeters@necmusic.edu
TEETS, Andrew 814-871-5856 384 A teets001@gannon.edu
TEETSEL, Craig, M 260-399-7700 162 B cteetsel@sf.edu
TEEVEER, Mikk 510-628-8010 48 C
TEFFT, Joshua 617-984-1700 218 C
TEFFT, Joshua 508-830-6687 213 D jtefft@maritime.edu
TEGAN, Jason 864-644-5143 412 D jtegen@swu.edu
TEGELER, Alyssa 765-983-1881 155 A tegelal@earlham.edu
TEGGATZ, Susan 312-355-6320 151 G steggatz@uic.edu
TEHRANI, Nader 212-353-4220 297 E ntehrani@cooper.edu
TEICHERT, Scott 801-626-7670 461 A scottteichert@weber.edu
TEICHMAN, Carl, F 309-556-3429 140 F cteich@iwu.edu
TEICHMAN, Shlomo 516-255-4700 311 J teichman@mlb.edu
TEICHMANN, Chase 813-988-5131 99 R teichmanc@floridacollege.edu
TEIG, Kathy 563-588-6385 164 E kathy.teig@clarke.edu
TEIJEIRO, Mike 650-949-7380 42 I teijeiromike@foothill.edu
TEINTZE, Martin 406-994-6515 264 C mteintze@montana.edu
TEIS, Lawrence, B 512-245-2114 450 C lt10@txstate.edu
TEITELBAUM, Aharon 845-783-0994 324 A
TEITLBAUM, Zalman 718-963-9770 323 L ed@utsny.edu
TEIXEIRA, Alberto 719-502-3256 82 E alberto.teixeira@ppcc.edu
TEJADA, Melinda, L 630-466-7900 152 K mtejada@waubonsee.edu
TEJADA, Michael 808-675-3935 128 D michael.tejada@byuh.edu
TEJEDA, Kary 570-422-2828 394 A ktejeda@esu.edu
TEJERA-ROCAFORT, Antonio 787-767-0445 511 F antonio.tejera@upr.edu
TEKALAN, Serif, A 832-230-5552 440 E satekalan@na.edu
TEKELY, Angela 610-647-4400 385 L atekely@immaculata.edu
TELANDER, Brittany 419-517-8971 355 C btelander@lourdes.edu
TELBERG, Tamara 845-758-7433 290 I telberg@bard.edu
TELFER, Lisa 954-322-1612 99 F
TELIHA, James, K 315-792-3111 324 B jkteliha@utica.edu
TELIME, Armenohy 818-710-1310 27 H
TELL, Mary 847-578-8537 148 F mary.tell@rosalindfranklin.edu
TELLA, Nicholas 401-598-1000 404 D nicholas.tella@jwu.edu
TELLEI, Patrick, U 680-488-1669 505 B tellei@palau.edu
TELLER, Ryan 402-486-2538 269 F ryan.teller@ucollege.edu
TELLES, Nick 505-428-1161 288 E nick.telles@sfcc.edu
TELLEZ, Laura 915-831-6359 436 A ltellez8@epcc.edu
TELLO, Ashley 254-659-7813 437 A atello@hillcollege.edu
TELLO, Steven 978-934-4240 212 B steven_tello@uml.edu
TELLO, Zaynna 408-924-1105 34 A zaynna.tello@sjsu.edu
TELLY, Nicole 408-727-1060 45 L
TELOKI, M.T 212-752-1530 304 A mteloki@limcollege.edu
TEMBY, Megan 800-686-1883 222 G mtemby@cleary.edu
TEMES, Marlene, M 407-582-4186 113 I mtemes@valenciacollege.edu
TEMEYER, Travis 734-487-1024 223 K ttemeyer@emich.edu
TEMKIN, Aron 802-485-2624 462 F atemkin@norwich.edu
TEMORES, Sandra 619-594-4766 33 D stemores@sdsu.edu
TEMPEL, Courtney 575-769-2811 285 O courtney.tempel@clovis.edu
TEMPERINO, Steven, H 603-535-2848 275 A stemperi@plymouth.edu
TEMPLE, Glena, G 708-524-6819 137 C president@dom.edu
TEMPLE, Jack 334-387-3877 4 B jacktemple@amridgeuniversity.edu
TEMPLE, James 661-362-3535 38 D james.temple@canyons.edu
TEMPLE, Kristen 816-235-8840 261 B templek@umkc.edu
TEMPLE, Lori 702-895-3628 271 D lorit@unlv.edu
TEMPLE, Melanie 252-862-1242 337 C metemple7181@roanokechowan.edu
TEMPLE, Troy 434-592-4653 468 E twtemple@liberty.edu
TEMPLE, Vicki 318-678-6000 187 H vtemple@bpcc.edu
TEMPLER, Lisa 979-230-3208 431 I lisa.templer@brazosport.edu
TEMPLETON, Chelneca 561-803-2353 105 C chelneca_templeton@pba.edu
TEMPLETON, Erin 864-596-9099 408 F erin.templeton@converse.edu
TEMPLETON, Jenna 412-365-1168 380 G jtempleton@chatham.edu
TEMPLETON, Joanna 516-877-3909 289 I jtempleton@adelphi.edu
TEMPLETON, Kelli 509-420-4545 480 E kelli@gather4him.net
TEMPLETON, Lisa 541-737-2676 375 A ecampus@oregonstate.edu
TEMPLETON, Lisa 541-737-0123 375 A

TEMPLETON, Mary .... 334-670-3189.... 7 C
mtempleton@troy.edu
TEMPLETON, Mary, A ... 318-675-7652 189 I
mary.templeton@lsuhs.edu
TEMPLIN, Kellly .... 979-458-6000 446 B
ktemplin@tamus.edu
TEN NAPEL, Karmen ..... 712-274-5191 168 E
tennapel@morningside.edu
TENA, Lydia .... 915-831-8818 436 A
lpere121@epcc.edu
TENA, Theresa .... 916-691-7252.. 50 H
theresa.tena@crc.losrios.edu
TENBUS, Eric .... 478-445-4441 119 B
eric.tenbus@gcsu.edu
TENCHER, Donald, E ..... 401-456-8007 405 A
dtencher@ric.edu
TENCZAR, Bob .... 909-537-5007.. 32 E
robert.tenczar@csusb.edu
TENENBAUM, Elchonon 707-638-5507.. 68 B
rabbi@tu.edu
TENER, Brent, B .... 615-343-1422 428 A
b.tener@vanderbilt.edu
TENG, Anthony .... 949-582-4895.. 65 D
ateng@saddleback.edu
TENGLIN, Ingrid, K .... 773-244-5601 145 G
itenglin@northpark.edu
TENGLUND, Ann .... 716-375-2378 313 C
ateng@sbu.edu
TENHOUSE, Mike .... 217-641-4558 141 A
mtenhouse@jwcc.edu
TENIENTE, Yvonne .... 805-922-6966.. 24 I
yteniente@hancockcollege.edu
TENIENTE-MATSON,
Cynthia .... 210-784-1600 447 E
cmatson@tamusa.edu
TENNANT, Ashley .... 304-367-4692 488 H
ashley.tennant@pierpont.edu
TENNANT, Cassie .... 989-463-7156 221 B
tennant@alma.edu
TENNANT, Leslie, A ...... 724-480-3552 381 H
leslie.tennant@ccbc.edu
TENNANT, Otto .... 270-789-5034 180 A
otennant@campbellsville.edu
TENNENT, Timothy, C ... 859-858-2202 179 C
TENNER, Katangela .... 601-877-6147 245 A
ksampson@alcorn.edu
TENNERELLI, Logan ...... 559-323-2100.. 61 F
ltennerelli@sjcl.edu
TENNEY, David .... 713-348-8036 442 F
dtenney@rice.edu
TENNEY, Randall .... 304-473-8099 491 D
tenney_r@wvwc.edu
TENNIE, Jameia .... 336-285-4110 341 D
jatennie@ncat.edu
TENNISON, Allen .... 612-343-4762 242 M
datennis@northcentral.edu
TENNY, Elissa .... 312-899-5100 149 F
president@saic.edu
TENORIO, Jessica .... 918-495-6813 368 F
jtenorio@oru.edu
TENSMEYER, Anna .... 509-543-1486 479 A
atensmeyer@columbiabasin.edu
TENTES, Theresa .... 650-738-4331.. 62 L
tentes@smccd.edu
TENUTA, Bob .... 815-455-8585 143 I
btenuta@mchenry.edu
TEPPER, Steven, J .... 480-965-6536.. 10 J
steven.tepper@asu.edu
TER MOLEN, Matthew ... 315-443-9161 321 G
termolen@syr.edu
TERCERO, Lorinda .... 432-552-2673 456 F
tercero_l@utpb.edu
TERDIMAN, David .... 201-684-7179 280 H
dterdima@ramapo.edu
TEREF, Steven .... 773-907-4361 135 C
steref@ccc.edu
TERENZIO, Marion .... 518-255-5111 319 C
terenzma@cobleskill.edu
TERESA, Daniel .... 831-755-6840.. 44 G
dteresa@hartnell.edu
TERESH, Tonia .... 619-388-7270.. 61 A
tteresh@sdccd.edu
TERHAAR, Jody, L .... 320-363-5601 235 F
jterhaar@csbsju.edu
TERHARK, Troy .... 715-836-2637 495 E
TERHUNE, James .... 610-328-8365 398 G
jterhun1@swarthmore.edu
TERHUNE, Jason .... 626-646-6518 494 F
jterhune@nashotah.edu
TERHUNE, Jason .... 262-646-6518 494 F
jterhune@nashotah.edu
TERKLA, Dawn, G .... 617-627-3274 219 C
dawn.terkla@tufts.edu
TERMOTT, Kenneth .... 732-247-5241 279 C
ktermott@nbts.edu
TERMUHLEN, Paula ...... 218-726-7572 243 G
ptermuhl@d.umn.edu
TERP, Cheryl .... 920-693-1134 498 H
cheryl.terp@gotoltc.edu
TERP, Douglas, C .... 207-859-4774 194 D
douglas.terp@colby.edu
TERPACK, Sallie, A .... 814-732-1024 394 B
terpack@edinboro.edu
TERPIS, Katherine .... 575-646-3279 287 C
kterpis@nmsu.edu
TERPSTRA, Joylita, W ... 423-478-7731 422 J
jterpstra@ptseminary.edu
TERPSTRA, Phil .... 620-276-9554 174 B
philip.terpstra@gcccks.edu
TERRANCE, Teah .... 585-385-8198 313 F
tterrance@sjfc.edu
TERRAZAS, Denise .... 951-372-7016.. 59 C
denise.terrazas@norcocollege.edu
TERRAZAS, Lissete .... 575-492-2122 289 F
lterrazas@usw.edu
TERRAZAS, Susan .... 909-760-3476.. 75 I
sterrazas@westernu.edu
TERRAZAS, Susan .... 909-706-2476.. 75 I
sterrazas@westernu.edu
TERRELL, Beth, M .... 260-399-7700 162 B
bterrell@sf.edu
TERRELL, Charles .... 304-434-8001 488 E
charles.terrell@easternwv.edu
TERRELL, David, R .... 765-285-2201 153 H
drterrell@bsu.edu
TERRELL, Jonathan .... 985-448-7079 192 F
jonathan.terrell@nicholls.edu
TERRELL, Mark .... 814-866-6641 387 D
mterrell@lecom.edu
TERRELL, Mark, A .... 252-399-6528 326 K
materrell@barton.edu
TERRELL, Patrice .... 478-825-4284 118 F
terrellp@fvsu.edu
TERRELL, Rita .... 512-492-3032 430 A
rterrell@aoma.edu
TERRELL LEACH,
Monica .... 910-672-1111 341 C
TERRELL-POWELL,
Yvonne .... 425-640-1456 480 A
yvonneterrellpowell@edcc.edu
TERRILL, Brian .... 410-209-2270 198 B
bterrill@bccc.edu
TERRILL, Kimberly .... 310-954-4135.. 52 I
kterrill@msmu.edu
TERRIO, Dan, M .... 509-527-4981 486 B
terrio@whitman.edu
TERRIO, Paul .... 612-238-4552 243 C
pterrio@smumn.edu
TERRONEZ, Danny .... 979-532-6465 458 E
terronezd@wcjc.edu
TERRY, Carolyn .... 240-567-4366 200 G
carolyn.terry@montgomerycollege.edu
TERRY, Catherine .... 615-966-1964 421 B
catherine.terry@lipscomb.edu
TERRY, Chihoko .... 910-410-1821 337 B
ckterry@richmondcc.edu
TERRY, Christopher ...... 607-735-1938 298 H
cterry@elmira.edu
TERRY, Colin .... 303-273-3000.. 79 J
cterry@mines.edu
TERRY, Cynthia .... 205-934-8152.... 8 A
cterry@uab.edu
TERRY, Daniel Scott ..... 304-637-1273 487 C
terrys@dewv.edu
TERRY, Denise, A .... 574-372-5100 155 F
terryda@grace.edu
TERRY, Edward .... 828-726-2202 332 G
eterry@cccti.edu
TERRY, Emily .... 252-398-6204 328 C
evterry@chowan.edu
TERRY, Gina .... 501-686-2923.. 21 E
gterry@uasys.edu
TERRY, James .... 573-876-2363 260 B
jterry@stephens.edu
TERRY, James, E .... 304-696-2486 489 M
terry@marshall.edu
TERRY, Laura, C .... 423-439-4210 419 G
terryl@etsu.edu
TERRY, Linda .... 512-223-7503 430 I
lkluck@austincc.edu
TERRY, SR.,
Matthew, L .... 972-524-3341 445 B
terry.matthew@swcc.edu
TERRY, Melissa .... 503-554-2101 373 A
terrym@georgefox.edu
TERRY, Melissa, D .... 503-554-2101 373 A
terrym@georgefox.edu
TERRY, Neil, W .... 806-651-2042 448 B
nterry@wtamu.edu
TERRY, Sandra .... 678-331-4368 122 C
sandra.terry@life.edu
TERRY, Scott .... 304-357-4363 487 J
scottterry@ucwv.edu
TERRY, Stephen .... 913-288-7685 175 B
sterry@kckcc.edu
TERRY, Toni .... 205-652-3400.... 9 B
tterry@uwa.edu
TERRY, Troy, M .... 864-294-2213 409 H
troy.terry@furman.edu
TERRY, Willa, J .... 662-252-2491 248 G
wterry@rustcollege.edu
TERRY-JACKSON,
Tonishea .... 773-602-5000 135 D
TERRY-SHARP,
Kathleen .... 901-321-4299 418 G
katerry@cbu.edu
TERRYN, Dottie .... 850-872-3801 101 N
dterryn@gulfcoast.edu
TERVORT, Syd .... 801-832-2148 461 F
stervort@westminstercollege.edu
TERWILLIGER, Brandi ... 208-885-3008 132 F
brandit@uidaho.edu
TESAR, Kathleen .... 212-799-5000 303 E
TESKE, Paul .... 303-315-2805.. 84 D
paul.teske@ucdenver.edu
TESKE, Yolanda, K .... 252-334-2029 331 F
yolanda.teske@macuniversity.edu
TESLUK, Paul, E .... 716-645-3221 316 C
ptesluk@buffalo.edu
TESORIERO, Cristine ..... 516-876-3033 318 C
tesorieroc@oldwestbury.edu
TESSIER, Dorita .... 509-527-2646 485 C
dorita.tessier@wallawalla.edu
TESSIER, Michael, A ..... 812-488-2956 161 G
mt28@evansville.edu
TESSIER-LAVIGNE,
Marc .... 650-723-2481.. 66 E
president@stanford.edu
TESSLER, Chani .... 773-973-0241 138 I
tessler@htc.edu
TESSLER, Faith .... 213-884-4133.. 24 A
ftessler@ajrca.edu
TESSLER, Lisa .... 845-437-5439 324 C
litessler@vassar.edu
TESSMAN, Brock .... 406-449-9129 263 J
btessman@montana.edu
TESTA, Ashley .... 412-536-1194 386 H
ashley.testa@laroch.edu
TESTA, Michael .... 610-892-1548 393 B
mtesta@pit.edu
TESTANI, Joe .... 585-275-2366 323 M
j.testani@rochester.edu
TESTI, Andrea .... 541-881-5761 376 F
atesti@tvcc.cc
TESTORI, Peter .... 413-565-1000 206 D
ptestori@baypath.edu
TETEN, Ryan, L .... 308-865-8995 269 I
tetenrl@unk.edu
TETER, Ayana .... 412-924-1398 396 F
ateter@pts.edu
TETI, Polly .... 215-242-7777 381 A
tetip@chc.edu
TETLOW, Tania .... 504-865-2011 190 C
pres@loyno.edu
TETREAULT, Jules .... 203-392-5556.. 86 A
tetreaultj4@southernct.edu
TETREAULT, Patricia, L . 570-941-7767 401 F
patricia.tetreault@scranton.edu
TETTEH, Edem .... 856-222-9311 281 C
etetteh@rcbc.edu
TETZLAFF, Christian ...... 770-533-6966 122 E
ctetzlaff@laniertech.edu
TEUTSCHEL, Linda .... 650-543-3744.. 51 G
linda.teutschel@menlo.edu
TEVAGA, Laura .... 808-675-3669 128 D
laura.tevaga@byuh.edu
TEVES, Erin .... 859-846-5494 184 E
eteves@midway.edu
TEVES, Frances .... 909-869-3503.. 30 A
fteves@cpp.edu
TEW, Keith .... 252-399-6361 326 K
ktew@barton.edu
TEW, Michael .... 734-487-3200 223 K
mtew@emich.edu
TEWART, Terri .... 505-428-1836 288 E
terri.tewart@sfcc.edu
TEWELL, Jodie .... 620-276-9533 174 B
jodie.tewell@gcccks.edu
TEWES, Matt .... 402-465-2102 268 G
mtewes@nebrwesleyan.edu
TEXIDOR, Migdalia .... 787-250-1912 508 D
mtexidor@metro.inter.edu
TEXTER, Lynne, A .... 215-951-1043 387 A
texter@lasalle.edu
TEYMOURTASH,
Janet, L .... 415-422-5898.. 72 J
janet@usfca.edu
TEZENO, Albert .... 972-599-3151 433 I
atezeno@collin.edu
THACHENKARY,
Sebastian .... 414-277-7141 494 D
thachenkary@msoe.edu
THACKABERRY, Sasha .. 225-578-3202 189 E
thackaberry@lsu.edu
THACKER, Allison .... 713-348-4818 442 F
invest@rice.edu
THACKER, Karen, S .... 610-796-8306 378 C
karen.thacker@alvernia.edu
THACKER, Linda .... 314-529-9308 255 B
lthacker@maryville.edu
THACKER, Samantha ..... 517-264-7172 230 H
sthacker@sienaheights.edu
THACKER, Tiffany .... 606-218-5953 186 B
tiffanythacker@upike.edu
THACKERAY, Rosemary . 801-422-4919 458 H
rosemary_thackeray@byu.edu
THADEN, Mark .... 540-654-2160 471 N
mthad2zw@umw.edu
THAKURIAH,
Piyushimita .... 848-932-2714 282 A
mhanniga@ejb.rutgers.edu
THALACKER, Karen .... 319-352-8225 170 J
karen.thalacker@wartburg.edu
THAMES, Brenda, A ...... 310-660-3111.. 41 E
rmahowald@elcamino.edu
THAMES, James, H .... 214-887-5013 435 F
jthames@dts.edu
THAMES, Judith .... 317-813-2301 158 C
jthames@ibcindianapolis.edu
THANKI, Sandip .... 702-992-2618 271 B
sandip.thanki@nsc.edu
THAO-SCHUCK, May ..... 651-690-6511 243 A
mthaoschuck644@stkate.edu
THARAKUNNEL, Kurian . 708-456-0300 151 D
kuriantharakunnel@triton.edu
THARCHIN, Jinpa .... 925-473-7342.. 40 D
jtharchin@losmedanos.edu
THARP, Brent .... 912-478-5444 120 C
btharp@georgiasouthern.edu
THARP, Glen .... 602-242-6265.. 11 C
glen.tharp@brooklinecollege.edu
THARP, Karen .... 931-598-1270 423 D
kmtharp@sewanee.edu
THARP, Katie .... 630-844-5449 133 D
ktharp@aurora.edu
THARP, Michael .... 845-341-4742 310 G
mike.tharp@sunyorange.edu
THARPE, Barbara .... 615-327-6827 421 D
btharpe@mmc.edu
THARPE, Brad .... 909-621-8519.. 57 E
brad_tharpe@pitzer.edu
THARRINGTON, Sally .... 434-949-1061 475 B
sally.tharrington@southside.edu
THARRINGTON,
Sterling .... 910-892-3178 329 E
stharrington@heritagebiblecollege.edu
THATCHER, Derek .... 740-366-9453 349 F
thatcher.42@cotc.edu
THATCHER, Kathleen ..... 406-657-2204 264 D
kathleen.thatcher@msubillings.edu
THATCHER, Rene .... 315-323-1550 314 D
rene@stlawu.edu
THAXTON, Deron .... 318-473-6409 189 F
dthaxton@lsua.edu
THAYER, Jainen .... 641-269-3500 166 G
thayerja@grinnell.edu
THAYER, Janet .... 518-956-8050 316 A
jthayer@albany.edu
THAYER, Scott .... 909-384-8992.. 60 F
sthayer@sbccd.cc.ca.us
THAYER, Tammy .... 608-246-6451 499 A
tthayer2@madisoncollege.edu
THAYER-MENCKE,
Laura .... 402-552-3470 266 E
thayermenckelaura@clarksoncollege.
edu
THE, Cheryl .... 817-202-6323 444 I
cthe@swau.edu
THE, James .... 817-202-6719 444 I
jthe@swau.edu
THEARD-GRIGGS,
Carolyn .... 773-995-3764 134 K
cthear20@csu.edu

THOMAS, London .... 864-388-8310 410 A
lthomas@lander.edu
THOMAS, Lori .... 732-987-2275 278 A
lthomas@georgian.edu
THOMAS, Marcia .... 501-623-2272.. 18 I
THOMAS, Marcia, R ...... 312-460-0600 133 A
mthomas@aaart.edu
THOMAS, Marcus .... 501-279-4332.. 19 C
mathomas@harding.edu
THOMAS, Margo .... 904-819-6474.. 99 E
mthomas@flagler.edu
THOMAS, Maria .... 515-650-3198 163 E
mariathomas@theartofeducation.edu
THOMAS, Mariette .... 504-864-7550 190 C
mlthoma1@loyno.edu
THOMAS, Mark .... 863-638-2345 114 A
mark.thomas@warner.edu
THOMAS, Mark .... 863-638-7228 114 A
mark.thomas@warner.edu
THOMAS, Mark .... 608-246-6301 499 A
mthomasjr@madisoncollege.edu
THOMAS, Mary Beth ..... 617-735-9766 209 D
thomasmb@emmanuel.edu
THOMAS, Maxcie .... 870-575-7029.. 22 D
thomasm@uapb.edu
THOMAS, Melinda .... 281-998-6150 443 A
melinda.thomas@sjcd.edu
THOMAS, Melissa .... 503-554-2218 373 A
mthomas@georgefox.edu
THOMAS, Meshia .... 804-257-5851 476 F
clthomas@vuu.edu
THOMAS, Micah .... 888-488-4968.. 46 F
mthomas@itu.edu
THOMAS, Michael .... 410-986-3220 198 B
mdthomas@bccc.edu
THOMAS, Michael .... 618-985-3741 139 E
thomasm@iecc.edu
THOMAS, Michael .... 484-581-1272 383 B
mthoma11@eastern.edu
THOMAS, Michael, A .... 949-214-3201.. 39 K
michael.thomas@cui.edu
THOMAS, Michael, D .... 802-443-5551 462 E
THOMAS, Mike, R .... 618-235-2700 150 E
michael.thomas@swic.edu
THOMAS, Nancy .... 423-472-7141 424 B
nthomas@clevelandstatecc.edu
THOMAS, Natalie .... 703-329-9100.. 93 H
THOMAS, Nathan .... 309-677-3140 134 A
nthomas@fsmail.bradley.edu
THOMAS, Nichole .... 315-268-3854 295 F
nthomas@clarkson.edu
THOMAS, Nishanth .... 973-803-5000 280 B
nthomas@pillar.edu
THOMAS, Patricia .... 334-229-4406.... 4 A
pthomas@alasu.edu
THOMAS, Patricia .... 412-323-4000 378 H
pthomas@manchesterbidwell.org
THOMAS, Patricia, A ..... 202-274-7257.. 94 B
pthomas@udc.edu
THOMAS, Paul .... 337-482-2976 193 B
paul.thomas@louisiana.edu
THOMAS, R. Brent .... 620-341-5278 173 F
rthomas2@emporia.edu
THOMAS, Rachel .... 504-520-5732 193 E
rthomas18@xula.edu
THOMAS,
Randi Malcolm .... 513-529-4151 356 A
thomasrm@miamioh.edu
THOMAS, Ray .... 616-988-3677 226 E
rthomas@kuyper.edu
THOMAS, Rebecca .... 859-233-8121 185 C
rthomas@transy.edu
THOMAS, Renard .... 661-362-3469.. 38 D
renard.thomas@canyons.edu
THOMAS, Renee .... 276-223-4752 476 A
rthomas@wcc.vccs.edu
THOMAS, Richard .... 304-293-7173 490 E
richard.thomas@mail.wvu.edu
THOMAS, Rick .... 414-277-7300 494 D
THOMAS, Rikki .... 757-727-5250 467 G
rikki.thomas@hamptonu.edu
THOMAS, Robbin .... 225-771-2552 191 E
rthomas@sulc.edu
THOMAS, Roberta .... 870-460-1453.. 22 C
thomasr@uamont.edu
THOMAS, Rosalyn .... 417-873-6827 252 G
rthomas005@drury.edu
THOMAS, Rosemary, M 304-637-1337 487 C
thomasr@dewv.edu
THOMAS, Roy .... 410-951-4231 204 B
rothomas@coppin.edu
THOMAS, Ryan .... 760-480-8474.. 75 J
rthomas@wscal.edu
THOMAS, S. Marjorie ... 941-487-4504 110 D
smthomas@ncf.edu
THOMAS, Sam .... 901-251-7100.. 93 H
THOMAS, Samantha ...... 214-768-3603 444 D
thomassa@smu.edu
THOMAS, Sandi .... 760-252-2411.. 26 G
sthomas@barstow.edu
THOMAS, Sandra .... 580-745-3172 369 G
sthomas@se.edu
THOMAS, Sapada .... 662-252-8093 248 G
sthomas@rustcollege.edu
THOMAS, Shannon .... 952-995-1626 238 C
shannon.thomas@hennepintech.edu
THOMAS, Shawn .... 806-291-3750 457 I
shawn.thomas@wbu.edu
THOMAS, Shiloa .... 610-526-1000 378 D
shiloa.thomas@theamericancollege.edu
THOMAS, Shirman .... 615-898-2516 422 C
shirman.thomas@mtsu.edu
THOMAS, Stacey .... 765-455-9391 157 B
stathoma@iuk.edu
THOMAS, Stacy .... 276-739-2429 475 F
sthomas@vhcc.edu
THOMAS, Steve .... 432-685-4520 440 B
steve@midland.edu
THOMAS, Steven .... 360-417-6235 482 C
sthomas@pencol.edu
THOMAS, Suresh .... 706-769-1472 115 E
THOMAS, Susan, L .... 660-785-4100 260 F
suethomas@truman.edu
THOMAS, Suzanne .... 843-792-1533 410 C
thomass@musc.edu
THOMAS, Tamara .... 909-558-4481.. 48 E
tthomas@llu.edu
THOMAS, Teresa .... 903-875-7315 440 D
teresa.thomas@navarrocollege.edu
THOMAS, Teresa, W ..... 615-898-2603 422 C
teresa.thomas@mtsu.edu
THOMAS, Teri .... 479-979-1448.. 23 I
tthomas@ozarks.edu
THOMAS, Terri .... 607-436-2020 316 F
terri.thomas@oneonta.edu
THOMAS, Tiffany .... 602-489-5300.. 10 F
tiffany.thomas@arizonachristian.edu
THOMAS, Timothy .... 315-792-5611 306 K
tthomas@mvcc.edu
THOMAS, Todd .... 423-652-6045 420 F
tthomas@king.edu
THOMAS, Tommy .... 423-869-6216 421 A
tommy.thomas@lmunet.edu
THOMAS, Tony .... 718-951-3118 293 C
tony.thomas@brooklyn.cuny.edu
THOMAS, Toyarna, Y .... 804-342-3565 476 F
tythomas@vuu.edu
THOMAS, Tracy .... 217-732-3168 142 G
THOMAS, Tyrone .... 843-355-4152 414 C
thomast@wiltech.edu
THOMAS, Vadim .... 518-276-8531 312 C
thomav@rpi.edu
THOMAS, Valerie, A ...... 410-455-3142 203 B
valerie.thomas@umbc.edu
THOMAS, Vanessa .... 909-384-8904.. 60 F
vthomas@sbccd.cc.ca.us
THOMAS, Vanessa .... 701-766-4415 344 G
THOMAS, Victoria .... 812-288-8878 159 M
vthomas@mid-america.edu
THOMAS, Victoria Lee .. 860-723-0011.. 85 F
thomasv@ct.edu
THOMAS, Von .... 402-643-3651 266 G
von.thomas@cune.edu
THOMAS, Wanda, S ...... 318-675-5190 189 I
wanda.thomas@lsuhs.edu
THOMAS, Wayne .... 423-636-7300 426 E
wthomas@tusculum.edu
THOMAS, Wendy .... 410-777-1309 197 G
wcthomas2@aacc.edu
THOMAS, Wilbert, L ..... 757-727-5356 467 G
bill.thomas@hamptonu.edu
THOMAS, Willie .... 423-472-7141 424 B
wthomas01@clevelandstatecc.edu
THOMAS-ANDERSON,
Tricia .... 972-860-7396 434 H
triciathomas-anderson@dcccd.edu
THOMAS-LITTLE,
Jill, M .... 586-445-7576 227 B
littlej@macomb.edu
THOMAS-STARCK,
Jennifer .... 781-283-3532 219 E
jthomass@wellesley.edu
THOMAS-WILLIAMS,
Regina .... 912-443-5708 125 B
rthomas@savannahtech.edu
THOMAS-WOOD,
Roberta .... 864-578-8770 411 F
rthomas@sherman.edu
THOMASON, Anne .... 309-341-7491 141 G
athomason@knox.edu
THOMASON, Chris .... 205-652-3533.... 9 B
cthomason@uwa.edu
THOMASON, Chris .... 205-652-5467.... 9 B
cthomason@uwa.edu
THOMASON,
Christopher .... 501-686-2940.. 21 E
cthomason@uasys.edu
THOMASON, Daniel ...... 405-491-6339 369 H
danny.thomason@snu.edu
THOMASON, Justin .... 989-837-4151 229 B
thomaso@northwood.edu
THOMASON, Mary .... 817-554-5950 439 H
mthomason@messengercollege.edu
THOMASON, Troy .... 407-628-6317 106 L
tthomason@rollins.edu
THOMBS, Dennis .... 817-735-5439 454 B
dennis.thombs@unthsc.edu
THOME, Jennifer .... 419-267-1223 357 E
jthome@northweststate.edu
THOMEN, Karlee .... 217-709-0920 142 D
kthomen@lakeviewcol.edu
THOMES, Chris .... 386-506-4499.. 98 D
chris.thomes@daytonastate.edu
THOMPSON, A. Renee .. 609-835-6000.. 93 H
THOMPSON, Adelia, P .. 757-594-7571 465 M
adelia.thompson@cnu.edu
THOMPSON, Al .... 715-346-2481 497 A
al.thompson@uwsp.edu
THOMPSON, Alanna ...... 256-306-2601.... 1 F
alanna.thompson@calhoun.edu
THOMPSON, Albert .... 757-822-1715 475 E
bthompson@tcc.edu
THOMPSON, Alfreda ..... 601-635-2111 246 A
athompson@eccc.edu
THOMPSON, Allen .... 360-867-6851 480 C
allen.thompson@evergreen.edu
THOMPSON, Allison, L . 318-342-6917 193 C
althompson@ulm.edu
THOMPSON, Amanda .... 937-393-3431 360 H
athompson@sscc.edu
THOMPSON, Amber ...... 254-710-3828 431 E
amber_thompson@baylor.edu
THOMPSON, Ameer .... 650-306-3322.. 62 J
thompsona@smccd.edu
THOMPSON, Amy .... 718-940-5713 314 A
althompson@sjcny.edu
THOMPSON, Angela ...... 310-954-5080.. 27 B
THOMPSON, Ann .... 814-393-1784 393 G
athompson@cuf-inc.org
THOMPSON, Annette ..... 210-283-5091 453 C
athompson@uiwtx.edu
THOMPSON, April .... 814-332-4356 378 A
THOMPSON, Ash .... 706-542-2273 126 G
contact@uhs.uga.edu
THOMPSON, Bart .... 225-578-3231 189 E
bthompson@lsu.edu
THOMPSON, Blake .... 601-925-3200 247 C
bthompson@mc.edu
THOMPSON, Bradley ..... 901-751-8453 421 G
bthompson@mabts.edu
THOMPSON, Brenda ...... 512-863-1956 445 C
thompso2@southwestern.edu
THOMPSON, Brian, L .... 904-819-6249.. 99 E
bthompson@flagler.edu
THOMPSON, Carey .... 901-843-3000 423 A
thompsonc@rhodes.edu
THOMPSON, Carey .... 717-337-6582 384 D
carthomp@gettysburg.edu
THOMPSON, Carleen .... 520-206-4637.. 15 B
cthompson57@pima.edu
THOMPSON, Cesarina ... 860-768-4648.. 89 G
cthompson@hartford.edu
THOMPSON, Chad .... 650-738-7035.. 62 L
thompsonc@smccd.edu
THOMPSON, Chandler .. 336-278-7423 328 J
cthompson39@elon.edu
THOMPSON, Cheryl ...... 505-387-7432 286 I
cthompson@navajotech.edu
THOMPSON, Chet .... 724-480-3558 381 H
chet.thompson@ccbc.edu
THOMPSON, Chris .... 803-705-4730 406 G
chris.thompson@benedict.edu
THOMPSON, Chris .... 919-761-2100 340 D
cthompson@sebts.edu
THOMPSON,
Christopher, J .... 651-962-5966 244 E
cjthompson@stthomas.edu
THOMPSON, Chuck ...... 909-621-8026.. 37 B
chuck.thompson@claremont.edu
THOMPSON, Cindy .... 816-235-1511 261 B
thompsoncym@umkc.edu
THOMPSON, Clare .... 563-884-5611 169 F
clare.thompson@palmer.edu
THOMPSON, Cora .... 912-358-4145 125 A
thompsonc@savannahstate.edu
THOMPSON,
Corinne, B .... 802-656-7898 463 A
corinne.thompson@uvm.edu
THOMPSON, Cory .... 703-323-4220 474 F
cthompson@nvcc.edu
THOMPSON, Cory .... 404-297-9522 120 B
THOMPSON, Craig .... 208-282-2120 131 G
thomcra2@isu.edu
THOMPSON, Craig, B ... 646-888-6639 304 J
thompsonc@mskcc.org
THOMPSON, Cynthia .... 217-206-4762 152 A
thompson.cynthia@uis.edu
THOMPSON, Danielle .... 904-632-3356 101 B
danielle.thompson@fscj.edu
THOMPSON, Dave .... 714-546-7600.. 37 J
THOMPSON, David .... 256-782-5455.... 6 A
dthompson@jsu.edu
THOMPSON, David .... 214-860-2342 434 I
davidthompson@dcccd.edu
THOMPSON, Dawn, G ... 503-777-7502 375 G
dthomp@reed.edu
THOMPSON, Deborah ... 252-794-4861 335 H
deborah.thompson@martincc.edu
THOMPSON,
Deborah, L .... 904-819-6302.. 99 E
dthompson@flagler.edu
THOMPSON,
Deborah, L .... 269-337-7318 225 F
debbie.roberts@kzoo.edu
THOMPSON, Deidre ...... 408-727-1060.. 45 L
THOMPSON, Desiree ..... 207-454-1021 195 I
dthompson@wccc.me.edu
THOMPSON, Dewayne .. 423-614-8160 420 H
dthompson@leeuniversity.edu
THOMPSON, Dixie .... 865-974-2475 427 B
dixielee@utk.edu
THOMPSON, Doug .... 507-933-7538 236 A
thompson@gustavus.edu
THOMPSON, Dreama .... 740-283-6264 352 I
dthompson@franciscan.edu
THOMPSON, Edward, J . 516-323-4600 306 M
ethompson@molloy.edu
THOMPSON, Elizabeth .. 423-869-6844 421 A
elizabeth.thompson@lmunet.edu
THOMPSON, Elizabeth .. 352-245-4119 112 E
elizabeth.thompson@taylorcollege.edu
THOMPSON, Erik .... 410-337-6000 199 B
erik.thompson@goucher.edu
THOMPSON, Erik .... 202-274-5600.. 94 B
elthompson@udc.edu
THOMPSON, Gabrielle .. 315-786-6560 303 C
gthompson@sunyjefferson.edu
THOMPSON, Garrett ...... 480-222-9219.. 15 Q
g.thompson@scnm.edu
THOMPSON, Gerene, M 727-816-3264 105 F
thompsg@phsc.edu
THOMPSON,
Gregory, T .... 843-349-2758 408 A
gtthomps@coastal.edu
THOMPSON, H. Paul ..... 864-977-7768 410 I
paul.thompson@ngu.edu
THOMPSON, Hailee .... 405-789-6400 369 H
hthompson@mail.snu.edu
THOMPSON, Heather .... 616-632-2959 221 E
THOMPSON, Heather .... 715-394-8593 497 C
hthomps9@uwsuper.edu
THOMPSON, Henry, L ... 724-266-3838 400 B
THOMPSON, Herbert ..... 386-481-2661.. 96 D
thompsoh@cookman.edu
THOMPSON, Howard ..... 563-425-5307 170 H
thompsonh@uiu.edu
THOMPSON, Ingrid .... 814-234-7755 398 E
ithompson@southhills.edu
THOMPSON, Jack .... 479-619-4140.. 20 C
jthompson19@nwacc.edu
THOMPSON, Jack .... 304-293-9416 490 E
jack.thompson@mail.wvu.edu
THOMPSON, Jacquelyn . 904-633-5960 101 B
jacquelyn.thompson@fscj.edu
THOMPSON, James ...... 662-472-9164 246 D
jathompson@holmescc.edu
THOMPSON, James, P .. 865-974-7262 427 B
jthompson@utk.edu
THOMPSON, Jamie .... 210-999-8820 451 E
jamie.thompson@trinity.edu

THORPE, Paul .... 610-341-5865 383 B
pwthorpe@eastern.edu
THORPE, Stephen, W .... 610-499-4117 402 G
swthorpe@mail.widener.edu
THORPE, Terry .... 229-928-1360 120 D
terry.thorpe@gsw.edu
THORSEN, Michelle ...... 425-640-1428 480 A
mthorsen@edcc.edu
THORSETT, Stephen ...... 503-370-6209 377 F
president@willamette.edu
THORSON, Andrea .... 661-395-4610.. 46 L
athorson@bakersfieldcollege.edu
THORSON, Carola .... 937-327-6360 364 D
thorsonc@wittenberg.edu
THORSON, Kip .... 507-372-3460 239 F
kip.thorson@mnwest.edu
THORSON, Phil .... 320-308-5396 240 I
pthorson@stcloudstate.edu
THORSTAD, Todd, M .... 320-222-5572 240 F
todd.thorstad@ridgewater.edu
THORTON, Toni .... 703-878-2800.. 93 H
THOTA, Vykuntapathi .... 804-524-5024 476 D
vthota@vsu.edu
THOURSON, Peter .... 541-485-1780 374 E
peterthourson@newhope.edu
THRAILKILL, James ...... 619-260-4558.. 72 I
jthrailkill@sandiego.edu
THRAILKILL, Krystal ...... 479-394-7622.. 23 C
kthrailkill@uarichmountain.edu
THRANE, Linda .... 713-348-6281 442 F
thrane@rice.edu
THRASH, Carrie .... 740-374-8716 363 F
cthrash@wscc.edu
THRASH, Rhone .... 304-829-7299 487 A
rthrash@bethanywv.edu
THRASHER, Kevin .... 303-333-4224.. 78 A
THRASHER, Lee .... 251-405-7072.... 1 E
lthrasher@bishop.edu
THREATT, Cindy .... 609-896-5101 281 B
cthreatt@rider.edu
THREATT, Norda .... 256-761-6119.... 7 B
nthreatt@talladega.edu
THREET, Ali .... 435-879-4469 460 B
threet@dixie.edu
THREET, Dwight .... 910-695-3831 337 H
threetd@sandhills.edu
THRELKELD, Aubry .... 978-232-2408 209 E
athrelke@endicott.edu
THRIFT, Jack .... 858-653-3000.. 29 D
THRO, Donna .... 314-256-8886 250 D
thro@ai.edu
THRO, William, E .... 859-257-2936 185 F
william.thro@uky.edu
THROCKMORTON,
Hunter .... 903-510-2586 452 A
jthr@tjc.edu
THROCKMORTON, Julie 412-809-5161 396 E
throckmorton.julie@ptcollege.edu
THRONSON, Howard ..... 360-491-4700 482 I
THRONSON, Jodean ..... 651-779-5837 237 H
jodean.thronson@century.edu
THROOP, Victoria .... 337-550-1410 189 G
vthroop@lsue.edu
THROWER, Jabe .... 870-850-4821.. 21 B
jthrower@seark.edu
THRUMAN, Michelle ..... 815-588-3575 139 A
michelle.thruman@highland.edu
THRUSH, Anne, R .... 989-774-3166 222 E
pybus1a@cmich.edu
THRUSH, Claudia .... 570-389-4012 393 D
cthrush@bloomu.edu
THRUSH, Claudia .... 570-389-4000 393 D
THUER, Rachel .... 856-225-6005 281 G
rmt84@camden.rutgers.edu
THUESON, Mike, B .... 208-496-2316 130 I
thuesonm@byui.edu
THULIN, Andrew .... 805-756-2161.. 29 I
athulin@calpoly.edu
THUM, Dennis, L .... 605-331-6777 417 C
dennis.thum@usiouxfalls.edu
THUM, Maureen .... 810-424-5605 232 A
mthum@umich.edu
THUM, Scott, W .... 260-422-5561 156 E
swthum@indianatech.edu
THUMITH, Robert, B ..... 618-650-2190 150 C
rthumit@siue.edu
THUMM MOORE, Kelly . 303-722-5724.. 81 L
kmoore@lincolntech.edu
THURBER, Darla .... 501-760-4113.. 20 A
darla.thurber@np.edu
THURBER, John, P .... 609-984-1155 284 C
jthurber@tesu.edu

THURINGER, Chris .... 859-257-2000 185 F
chris.thuringer@uky.edu
THURLOW, David .... 802-831-1064 463 C
dthurlow@vermontlaw.edu
THURMAN, Connie .... 319-398-5466 167 J
connie.thurman@kirkwood.edu
THURMAN, David .... 206-254-1904 217 I
THURMAN, Erik, J .... 651-962-6691 244 E
erik.thurman@stthomas.edu
THURMAN, Jill .... 765-998-5123 161 C
jill_thurman@taylor.edu
THURMAN, Kathy .... 615-898-5792 422 C
kathy.thurman@mtsu.edu
THURMAN, Katie .... 731-989-6672 419 K
knixon@fhu.edu
THURMAN, Kerri, L .... 217-443-8850 136 G
kthurman@dacc.edu
THURMAN, Kevin .... 573-431-4593 256 D
kthurman@mineralarea.edu
THURMAN, Quint .... 575-492-2123 289 F
qthurman@usw.edu
THURMAN, JR.,
Robert, D .... 314-773-0083 250 I
rthurman@brookesbible.org
THURMER, Anne .... 218-299-6506 239 C
anne.thurmer@minnesota.edu
THURMOND, Pat .... 866-492-5336 244 F
patricia.thurmond@mail.waldenu.edu
THURSTON, Emily .... 206-934-6925 483 C
emily.thurston@seattlecolleges.edu
THURSTON, Katie, S ..... 256-824-6042.... 8 B
katie.thurston@uah.edu
THURSTON, Michael ..... 413-585-3000 218 H
mthursto@smith.edu
THUSWALDNER, Gregor 509-777-3755 486 C
gthuswaldner@whitworth.edu
THWAITE, Sapna .... 810-766-6878 232 A
sapnav@umich.edu
THYGERSON, John .... 256-824-2870.... 8 B
john.thygerson@uah.edu
THYNNE, Sara .... 336-506-4186 332 A
sara.thynne@alamancecc.edu
THYREEN, Timothy, R ... 724-852-7777 402 C
thyreen@waynesburg.edu
TIAGI, Olesia .... 914-632-5400 307 A
otiagi@monroecollege.edu
TIAHRT, Cheryl .... 605-658-6026 416 D
cheryl.tiahrt@usd.edu
TIAPO, Bernadette .... 607-436-2830 316 F
bernadette.tiapo@oneonta.edu
TIAPO, Bernadette .... 607-436-2513 316 F
bernadette.tiapo@oneonta.edu
TIBBETTS, Bill .... 612-343-4181 242 M
wetibbet@northcentral.edu
TIBBITTS, Laura .... 512-463-1808 449 E
laura.tibbitts@tsus.edu
TIBBS, Terri .... 910-672-1696 341 C
ttibbs@uncfsu.edu
TIBERI, Tom, R .... 716-645-2171 316 C
tiberi@buffalo.edu
TIBERIO, Amy .... 401-254-5450 405 C
atiberio@rwu.edu
TICE, Jared .... 704-637-4410 327 I
jrtice18@catawba.edu
TICE, Jessica .... 304-558-0699 489 H
jessica.tice@wvhepc.edu
TICE, Laura, L .... 850-263-3261.. 95 P
lltice@baptistcollege.edu
TICHENOR, Kristin .... 617-989-4590 219 F
TICHENOR, Kristin, R .... 508-831-6720 220 F
tichenor@wpi.edu
TICK, Michael .... 315-443-7671 321 G
mtick1@syr.edu
TIDEMAN, Susan .... 816-415-7550 262 F
tidemans@william.jewell.edu
TIDWELL, Brandon .... 309-794-7141 133 C
brandontidwell@augustana.edu
TIDWELL, James, H ...... 502-597-8104 183 D
james.tidwell@kysu.edu
TIE, Peter .... 408-433-2280.. 36 H
TIEFENTHALER, Jay .... 515-964-6612 165 A
jmtiefenthaler3@dmacc.edu
TIEKEN, Scott, K .... 812-877-8604 160 F
tieken1@rose-hulman.edu
TIENSVOLD, Melissa ..... 406-275-4978 265 F
melissa_tiensvold@skc.edu
TIERCE, Meghan .... 559-730-3745.. 39 B
meghant@cos.edu
TIERNAN, Bernadette .... 973-720-2463 284 J
tiernanb@wpunj.edu
TIERNEY, Joan .... 815-280-2661 141 B
jtierney@jjc.edu

TIERNEY, Kathleen .... 610-526-5364 379 B
ktierney01@brynmawr.edu
TIET, Kien .... 626-350-1500.. 28 F
TIETJE, Brian .... 361-825-6045 447 C
brian.tietje@tamucc.edu
TIETJEN, Carl .... 585-275-2008 323 M
carl_tietjen@urmc.rochester.edu
TIETJEN, Rick .... 845-451-1380 297 G
rick.tietjen@culinary.edu
TIETZ, Leah Jo .... 406-449-9156 263 J
ltietz@montana.edu
TIFFANY, Beth .... 518-388-6286 323 J
TIFFIN, Doug .... 972-708-7340 435 E
president@diu.edu
TIFFT, Allison .... 918-595-7923 370 C
allison.tifft@tulsacc.edu
TIGER, Andrew .... 325-942-2337 450 E
andrew.tiger@angelo.edu
TIGHE, Charles .... 732-987-2612 278 A
ctighe@georgian.edu
TIGHE, Roger .... 254-442-5034 432 I
roger.tighe@cisco.edu
TIGNER, Terrell .... 816-604-3175 255 G
terrell.tigner@mcckc.edu
TIGNOR, Mia .... 772-462-7590 102 F
mtignor@irsc.edu
TIJERINA, Denise .... 806-742-2984 450 F
denise.tijerina@ttu.edu
TIKALSKY, Paul, J .... 405-744-5140 367 G
paul.tikalsky@okstate.edu
TILDEN, Kevin .... 949-214-3127.. 39 K
kevin.tilden@cui.edu
TILDEN, Marsha, A .... 740-368-3163 359 G
matilden@owu.edu
TILGHMAN, Justin .... 252-527-6223 335 G
jgtilghman38@lenoircc.edu
TILGHMAN, Patricia, E . 410-651-6449 203 D
petilghman@umes.edu
TILL, Kimberly, B .... 214-887-5061 435 F
ktill@dts.edu
TILLEMAN, Suzanne ...... 406-243-6195 263 K
suzanne.tilleman@umontana.edu
TILLEN, Dawn .... 270-824-1830 182 D
dawn.tillen@kctcs.edu
TILLERY, Sarah .... 971-722-6268 375 D
sarah.tillery@pcc.edu
TILLEY, Blake .... 636-481-3104 254 C
btilley@jeffco.edu
TILLEY, Genoria .... 225-216-8292 187 G
tilleyg@mybrcc.edu
TILLEY, Laurie .... 918-595-7000 370 C
laurie.tilley@tulsacc.edu
TILLINGHAST, David ...... 508-531-6140 212 D
dtillinghast@bridgew.edu
TILLIS, Antonio .... 856-225-6095 281 G
chancellor@camden.rutgers.edu
TILLMAN, Harry, J .... 757-446-7073 466 D
tillmahj@evms.edu
TILLMAN, Mark .... 904-256-7282 102 H
mtillma3@ju.edu
TILLMAN, Shalita .... 909-384-8659.. 60 F
scunningh@sbccd.cc.ca.us
TILLOTSON, Christina .... 720-496-1370.. 81 D
ctillotson@holmesinstitute.edu
TILLOTSON, James, R .... 515-964-0601 166 D
tillotsonj@faith.edu
TILLOTSON, Jeanette ..... 607-778-5195 317 D
tillotsonjo@sunybroome.edu
TILSON, Heather .... 505-454-3562 286 J
htilson@nmhu.edu
TILSON, Vincent .... 704-233-8011 344 F
tilson@wingate.edu
TILSTRA, Doug .... 509-527-2511 485 C
doug.tilstra@wallawalla.edu
TILTON, Abigail .... 940-898-3326 451 D
atilton@twu.edu
TILTON, James .... 401-863-2721 403 J
james_tilton@brown.edu
TIMBERMAN, Amy .... 812-877-8006 160 F
timberm1@rose-hulman.edu
TIMBERS, Tammy .... 301-860-5000 204 A
ttimbers@bowiestate.edu
TIMBY, Tracy .... 215-968-8225 379 D
tracy.timby@bucks.edu
TIMKO, Michael, A .... 724-503-1001 402 B
mtimko@washjeff.edu
TIMLIN, Kevin .... 573-986-6863 259 H
kjtimlin@semo.edu
TIMLIN, Laynee, H .... 757-455-2137 477 C
etimlin@vwu.edu
TIMM, Randy .... 619-594-5221.. 33 D
deanofstudents@sdsu.edu

TIMMER, Amy .... 517-371-5140 233 C
timmera@cooley.edu
TIMMER, JR., James .... 616-526-6037 222 C
jrt3@calvin.edu
TIMMER, Jeff .... 708-293-4597 151 A
jeff.timmer@trnty.edu
TIMMERMAN, Beth, J ... 989-774-2317 222 E
timme1bj@cmich.edu
TIMMERMAN, Candace . 402-375-7034 268 F
catimme1@wsc.edu
TIMMERMAN, David ..... 262-551-5813 492 B
dtimmerman@carthage.edu
TIMMERMAN, Melanie .. 740-392-6868 356 G
mtimmerman@mvnu.edu
TIMMERMANS, Dana ..... 714-992-7094.. 54 C
dtimmermans@fullcoll.edu
TIMMINS, Paul .... 541-346-1000 376 H
ptimmins@uoregon.edu
TIMMIS, Jerry .... 215-887-5511 402 E
jtimmis@wts.edu
TIMMONS,
Charles (Chip) .... 765-361-6054 163 B
timmonsc@wabash.edu
TIMMONS, Daren .... 803-641-3458 413 B
TIMMONS, George .... 518-828-4181 297 B
george.timmons@sunycgcc.edu
TIMMONS, Noelle .... 212-966-0300 308 B
TIMMONS, Tim .... 708-239-4787 151 A
tim.timmons@trnty.edu
TIMMS, Samara .... 619-849-2722.. 57 J
stimms@pointloma.edu
TIMONER, OP, Gerard .. 202-495-3820.. 93 D
TIMPONE, Peter .... 802-828-8554 463 B
peter.timpone@vcfa.edu
TIMPSON, Natalie .... 714-895-8992.. 38 A
ntimpson@gwc.cccd.edu
TIMS, Tiffany .... 740-753-6589 353 H
timst@hocking.edu
TIMSON, Joe .... 816-802-3419 254 D
jtimson@kcai.edu
TIMUR, Aysegul .... 239-590-1069 109 K
atimur@fgcu.edu
TINDALL, Amanda .... 502-213-2255 182 C
amanda.tindall@kctcs.edu
TINDALL, David .... 810-762-7981 226 B
dtindall@kettering.edu
TINDALL, Regina, A ...... 973-720-2954 284 J
tindallr@wpunj.edu
TINDELL, Jennifer .... 254-867-4891 449 D
jennifer.tindell@tstc.edu
TINDELL, Jodi .... 254-299-8686 439 E
jtindell@mclennan.edu
TINDOL, Chad .... 205-348-8123.... 7 G
chad.tindol@ua.edu
TINER, Scott .... 207-786-6396 194 A
stiner@bates.edu
TINGELSTAD, Erik .... 425-352-8277 478 D
etingelstad@cascadia.edu
TINGKANG, Monique ..... 808-844-2398 130 A
monique4@hawaii.edu
TINGLE, Caroline, D ..... 386-312-4270 107 C
carolinetingle@sjrstate.edu
TINGSON-GATUZ,
Connie .... 734-432-5883 227 C
ctingson-gatuz@madonna.edu
TINKER, Devon .... 509-359-2529 479 G
dtinker@ewu.edu
TINKEY, Danya .... 412-536-1029 386 H
dayna.tinkey@laroche.edu
TINKEY, Jim .... 412-536-1011 386 H
jim.tinkey@laroche.edu
TINKHAM, Brenda, S .... 252-398-6437 328 C
tinkhb@chowan.edu
TINKLEPAUGH, Eugene . 252-536-7248 335 B
etinklepaugh@halifaxcc.edu
TINKLEPAUGH, Megan . 330-385-1070 359 F
megan.tinklepaugh@ovct.edu
TINLEY, Jeffrey, J .... 865-354-3000 425 C
tinleyjj@roanestate.edu
TINLING, Walter .... 301-295-3083 503 C
walter.tinling@usuhs.edu
TINNEN, Lupita, M .... 972-881-5807 433 I
ltinnen@collin.edu
TINNEY, Tina, M .... 504-278-6468 188 G
ttinney@nunez.edu
TINSLEY, Ann, H .... 205-391-2251.... 3 E
atinsley@sheltonstate.edu
TINSLEY, Joseph .... 785-670-1288 178 C
joseph.tinsley@washburn.edu
TIOGANGCO, Sherise .... 808-934-2710 129 I
sherise@hawaii.edu
TIOGANGCO, Sherise .... 808-956-8010 129 E

TOMAS, Don, L 828-339-4242 338 B
d_tomas@southwesterncc.edu
TOMASELLI, Gordon, F 718-430-2000 290 A
TOMASELLO, Ronald 856-227-7200 276 E
rtomasello@camdencc.edu
TOMASZEWSKI, Lynn 215-568-4012 390 E
TOMASZKIEWICZ, Ed 815-226-3372 148 D
etomaszkiewicz@rockford.edu
TOMASZKIEWICZ, Teri 630-844-5511 133 D
ttomaszk@aurora.edu
TOMBARGE, Chuck 612-625-8510 243 F
tombarge@umn.edu
TOMBARI, Chris 303-340-7504 80 E
chris.tombari@ccaurora.edu
TOMBERLIN, Daniel, D 423-478-7713 422 J
dtomberlin@ptseminary.edu
TOMBES, Robert, M 804-827-5600 473 B
rtombes@vcu.edu
TOMBLESON, Shelly 719-336-1572 81 K
shelly.tombleson@lamarcc.edu
TOMBLIN, Debra 334-244-3250 4 E
dtomblin@aum.edu
TOMBLIN, John, S 316-978-5234 178 D
john.tomblin@wichita.edu
TOMCZAK, Patricia 217-228-5432 147 F
tomczpa@quincy.edu
TOMCZAK, Timothy 585-345-6831 300 F
tptomczak@genesee.edu
TOMCZYK, Christie 304-357-4944 487 J
christinetomczyk@ucwv.edu
TOMEK, Beverly 361-570-4200 453 B
tomekb@uhv.edu
TOMEK, Mary 804-333-6738 475 A
mtomek@rappahannock.edu
TOMES, Shawn 270-852-3203 183 E
stomes@kwc.edu
TOMESCU, Cosmin 212-592-2718 315 C
ctomescu@sva.edu
TOMEY, Dawn 785-594-8362 171 F
TOMFOHRDE, Tammy 423-869-6465 421 A
tammy.tomfohrde@lmunet.edu
TOMHAVE, Brian 909-599-5433 48 A
btomhave@lifepacific.edu
TOMLIN, Kathy, H 540-464-7323 476 B
tomlinkh@vmi.edu
TOMLIN, Ross, L 503-842-8222 376 E
rosstomlin@tillamookbaycc.edu
TOMLINSON, Ann 310-660-3593 41 E
atomlinson@elcamino.edu
TOMLINSON, Doug 972-883-2141 455 B
douglas.tomlinson@utdallas.edu
TOMLINSON, Elise 907-796-6300 10 B
emtomlinson@alaska.edu
TOMLINSON, Jan 740-364-9510 349 F
tomlinson.88@cotc.edu
TOMLINSON, Jason 940-898-3505 451 D
jtomlinson1@twu.edu
TOMLINSON, Jennifer 407-582-1908 113 I
jtomlinson2@valenciacollege.edu
TOMLINSON, Jessica 207-699-5016 195 A
jtomlinson@meca.edu
TOMLINSON, Jon 740-474-8896 358 A
jtomlinson@ohiochristian.edu
TOMLINSON, Karen 706-864-1948 127 A
karen.tomlinson@ung.edu
TOMLINSON, Kathryn 229-259-5178 128 B
kathryn.tomlinson@wiregrass.edu
TOMLINSON, Leslie 256-331-8040 3 C
ltomlinson@nwscc.edu
TOMLINSON, Rob 573-840-9649 260 E
rtomlinson@trcc.edu
TOMLINSON, Sandra 386-752-1822 100 B
sandra.tomlinson@fgc.edu
TOMLINSON, Tim 865-938-8186 419 B
tim.tomlinson@thecrowncollege.edu
TOMLINSON, Virginia 509-963-2001 478 E
virginia.tomlinson@cwu.edu
TOMLINSON-CLARKE,
Saundra 848-932-0815 282 A
saundra.tomlinson-clarke@gse.rutgers.edu
TOMLJANOVICH,
Marc, I 717-871-4435 395 A
marc.tomljanovich@millersville.edu
TOMMASINO, Joseph 631-665-1600 322 F
joseph.tommasino@touro.edu
TOMMASINO, Joseph 631-665-1600 322 G
joseph.tommasino@touro.edu
TOMMEY, Dale 870-574-4512 21 D
dtommey@sautech.edu
TOMOSER, T. Paul 402-280-3026 266 H
ptomoser@creighton.edu
TOMPKINS,
Anthony (Tony) 913-288-7150 175 B
atompkins@kckcc.edu
TOMPKINS, OSB,
John-Mary 724-805-2771 398 A
johnmary.tompkins@stvincent.edu
TOMPKINS, Kevin 252-492-2061 338 F
tompkinsk@vgcc.edu
TOMPKINS, Michael 845-758-7523 290 I
tompkins@bard.edu
TOMPKINS, Page 603-678-4888 275 B
TOMPKINS, Patrick 757-789-1748 473 H
ptompkins@es.vccs.edu
TOMPKINS, Ricky 479-619-4325 20 C
rtompkins1@nwacc.edu
TOMPKINS, Stefanie 303-273-3000 79 J
stompkins@mines.edu
TOMPOS, Betty 717-391-6947 399 C
tomposb@stevenscollege.edu
TOMPOS, Mike 651-523-2800 236 B
TOMS, David, E 401-456-8803 405 A
dtoms@ric.edu
TOMS, Debbie 605-718-2958 417 D
deborah.toms@wdt.edu
TOMS, Lisa 660-543-8059 260 G
toms@ucmo.edu
TOMSHINSKY, Ida 305-821-3333 100 E
itomshinsky@fnu.edu
TOMSO, Gregory 850-474-2934 111 F
gtomso@uwf.edu
TONCHE, Carlos 718-862-7313 304 M
ctonche01@manhattan.edu
TONCIC, JR.,
Andrew, A 724-458-2170 384 G
aatoncic@gcc.edu
TONDER, Rick 701-777-4270 345 A
rick.tonder@ndus.edu
TONDIGLIA, Dean 330-672-3111 354 A
u347@police.kent.edu
TONDREAU, Rebecca 401-598-1000 404 D
rebecca.tondreau@jwu.edu
TONEV, Simon, T 610-330-5783 387 C
tonevs@lafayette.edu
TONEY, Glenn 706-245-7226 118 D
gtoney@ec.edu
TONEY, Jeffrey 908-737-3452 278 E
jefftoney@kean.edu
TONEY, Pamela 800-462-7845 80 A
TONEY, RJ 970-943-2312 85 C
rjtoney@western.edu
TONG, Hui 425-235-2352 482 H
htong@rtc.edu
TONG, Ray 909-687-1513 43 D
raytong@gs.edu
TONG, Vincent 203-332-5220 86 F
vtong@gcc.commnet.edu
TONG, Vincent, P 203-285-2415 86 E
vtong@gatewayct.edu
TONG-CHING WU, Tom 508-531-2324 212 D
twu@bridgew.edu
TONI, Keith 508-678-2811 214 B
keith.toni@bristolcc.edu
TONKOWICH, Jonathan 307-332-2930 502 A
jtonkowich@wyomingcatholic.edu
TONNESON, Julie, A 612-626-9278 243 F
tonne001@umn.edu
TONONO, Hiroko 949-480-4116 64 G
htonono@soka.edu
TOOEY, Mary, J 410-706-2693 203 A
mjtooey@hshsl.umaryland.edu
TOOKE-RAWLINS, Dixie 540-231-4000 466 K
dtrawlins@vcom.vt.edu
TOOKE-RAWLINS, Dixie 540-231-6059 466 K
dtrawlins@vcom.vt.edu
TOOLE, Genesis 623-845-3000 13 C
genesis.toole@gccaz.edu
TOOLE, Michael 419-530-8000 363 B
michael.toole@utoledo.edu
TOOLE, Raymond, L 610-359-5330 382 A
rtoole@dccc.edu
TOOLIN, Cynthia 860-796-3468 88 C
ctoolin@holyapostles.edu
TOOMES, Christopher 409-772-3565 456 E
cwtoomes@utmb.edu
TOOMEY, Christopher 213-740-1638 73 D
ctoomey@usc.edu
TOOMEY, Marcia, D 978-232-2060 209 E
mtoomey@endicott.edu
TOOMSEN, Corbett 414-847-3335 494 C
corbetttoomsen@miad.edu
TOON, Kellie 865-694-6523 425 B
kltoon@pstcc.edu
TOONE, Rachel 828-669-8012 331 K
rachel.toone@montreat.edu
TOONG, Kenneth, K 413-545-1504 211 G
ktoong@mail.aux.umass.edu
TOOSI, Mori 863-297-1000 106 A
mtoosi@polk.edu
TOOTHMAN, Charles 434-797-8409 473 G
charles.toothman@danville.edu
TOOTOONCHI, Ahmad 731-881-7225 427 D
atootoon@utm.edu
TOOTOONCHI, Ahmad 509-828-1224 479 G
tootoonchi@ewu.edu
TOPHAM, Susan 619-388-6922 60 H
stopham@sdccd.edu
TOPIC, Miloš 616-331-2035 224 G
topicm@gvsu.edu
TOPLIFF, Donald, R 325-942-2165 450 E
don.topliff@angelo.edu
TOPOL, Eric 858-784-8469 64 A
TOPOLSKI, Virginia 201-559-6055 277 J
topolskiv@felician.edu
TOPOUSIS, Dana 530-752-9841 69 B
dtopousis@ucdavis.edu
TOPP, Joelle 517-371-5140 233 C
toppj@cooley.edu
TOPPE, Michele 503-725-4422 375 E
toppem@pdx.edu
TOPPER, Maria, L 301-447-5211 201 B
mtopper@msmary.edu
TOPPIN, Ian 404-225-4502 115 H
itoppin@atlantatech.edu
TOPPLE, Dianne 518-828-4181 297 B
dianne.topple@sunycgcc.edu
TOPSHE, Joyce 860-685-3757 90 B
jtopshe@wesleyan.edu
TORABI, Shouka 949-582-4565 65 D
storabi@saddleback.edu
TORAIN, Martarash 919-516-4000 339 I
TORAIN, Mirian 301-546-5259 201 E
torainml@pgcc.edu
TORAIN, Wes 256-306-2965 1 F
wes.torain@calhoun.edu
TORBET, Linda 734-384-4245 228 C
ltorbet@monroeccc.edu
TORBITZKY, Nichole 636-949-4651 254 H
ntorbitzky@lindenwood.edu
TORCHIA, Richard 215-572-2131 378 E
torchia@arcadia.edu
TORDELLA, Tina 304-243-2081 491 E
ttordella@wheeling.edu
TORELLO, Tom 518-445-3208 289 K
ttore@albanylaw.edu
TORGERSON, Jane 817-257-7940 448 F
j.torgerson@tcu.edu
TORGUSON, Kirsten 909-607-9313 37 F
kirsten_torguson@kgi.edu
TORIBIO, Rica 805-969-3626 55 J
rtoribio@pacifica.edu
TORINO, Frank 212-659-7200 303 H
ftorino@tkc.edu
TORMEY, Susan 315-498-2764 310 F
tormeys@sunyocc.edu
TORNABENE, Meredith 315-445-4185 303 I
tornabmm@lemoyne.edu
TORNO, Keith 616-222-3000 226 E
itdirector@kuyper.edu
TORNQUIST, Kristi 605-688-5106 417 A
kristi.tornquist@sdstate.edu
TORNQUIST, Susan 541-737-6943 375 A
susan.tornquist@oregonstate.edu
TORNQUIST, Wade 734-487-0042 223 K
wtornquis@emich.edu
TORO, Dan 619-849-2571 57 J
dantoro@pointloma.edu
TORO, Sofia 909-607-0121 37 F
sofia_toro@kgi.edu
TORO, Sofia 909-607-8587 37 F
storo@kgi.edu
TORO, Zulma, R 860-832-3000 85 G
toro@ccsu.edu
TORO-ZAPATA, Rogelio 787-264-1912 508 F
rtoro@intersg.edu
TOROK, Kate, M 585-385-3801 313 F
ktorok@sjfc.edu
TOROS, Orkun 972-883-4735 455 B
ont130030@utdallas.edu
TOROSYAN, Roben 508-531-2435 212 D
roben.torosyan@bridgew.edu
TORRANCE, Peggy, L 218-299-3339 235 H
torrance@cord.edu
TORRE, Patrick 203-932-7224 89 H
ptorre@newhaven.edu
TORRE, Scott 201-761-7403 283 A
storre@saintpeters.edu
TORREGOSA, Marivic 956-326-2574 446 E
mtorregosa@tamiu.edu
TORREGROSSA, Tom 318-342-5353 193 C
torregrossa@ulm.edu
TORRENCE, Michael 931-393-1682 424 F
mtorrence@mscc.edu
TORRENS, Michael 435-797-0220 460 C
michael.torrens@usu.edu
TORRES, Abigail 787-878-5475 507 L
atorres@arecibo.inter.edu
TORRES, Ana, D 787-834-9595 510 D
atorres@uaa.edu
TORRES, Angela 787-751-1912 509 A
atorres@juris.inter.edu
TORRES, Anna 860-512-3382 86 G
atorres1@manchestercc.edu
TORRES, Anna 330-941-3675 364 H
amtorres@ysu.edu
TORRES,
Antoinette (Toni) 212-353-4251 297 E
atorres@cooper.edu
TORRES, Arlene 646-664-3252 292 K
arlene.torres@cuny.edu
TORRES, Aurelio 956-364-4255 449 D
aurelio.torres@tstc.edu
TORRES, Betania 863-667-5463 108 K
btorres@seu.edu
TORRES, Carmelo 787-751-0178 510 E
ctorresr@uagm.edu
TORRES, Carmelo 787-751-0178 510 G
ctorresr@uagm.edu
TORRES, Carmen, Z 787-841-2000 509 J
admisiones@pucpr.edu
TORRES, Carmencita 787-766-1717 510 G
ctatorres@uagm.edu
TORRES, Cathy 305-809-3250 97 O
cathy.torres@cfk.edu
TORRES, Chanda 407-823-5001 110 E
chanda.torres@ucf.edu
TORRES, Cristobal 305-899-3836 96 A
ctorres@barry.edu
TORRES, Damaris 787-840-2575 509 I
dtorres@psm.edu
TORRES, Darlin 787-250-1912 508 D
djtorres@metro.inter.edu
TORRES, Donna, K 225-578-2111 189 D
TORRES, Edwin 310-954-4348 52 I
eotorres@msmu.edu
TORRES, Eliseo, S 505-277-0952 288 J
cheo@unm.edu
TORRES, Evelyn 787-264-1912 508 F
evetorre@intersg.edu
TORRES, Evelyn 787-882-2065 510 C
etorres@unitecpr.edu
TORRES, Frank 623-845-3904 13 C
frank.torres@gccaz.edu
TORRES, Gaile 406-395-4875 265 G
gtorres@stonechild.edu
TORRES, Geissa 787-815-0000 511 H
geissa.torres@upr.edu
TORRES, Graciela 787-761-0640 511 E
jefebiblioteca@utcpr.edu
TORRES, Gricelie 787-780-0070 505 F
grtorres@caribbean.edu
TORRES, Henry 501-660-1000 17 C
htorres@astate.edu
TORRES, Henry 870-972-3033 17 E
htorres@astate.edu
TORRES, Ivette 787-841-2000 509 J
itorres@pucpr.edu
TORRES, Jaclynn 432-685-6474 440 B
jtorres@midland.edu
TORRES, Jeannette 787-665-7910 506 D
jeannette.torres@columbiacentral.edu
TORRES, Jorge 787-743-3484 509 N
jtorres@sanjuanbautista.edu
TORRES, Jose 909-388-6900 60 D
jtorres@sbccd.cc.ca.us
TORRES, Juan, L 787-864-2222 508 C
juan.torres@guayama.inter.edu
TORRES, Justo 919-515-8008 342 A
jtorres3@ncsu.edu
TORRES, Kareen 954-201-7493 96 F
ktorres@broward.edu
TORRES, Leanne 765-641-4197 153 G
lmtorres@anderson.edu
TORRES, Lizandra 787-263-3770 512 C
lizandra.torres1@upr.edu
TORRES, Maribel 787-884-6000 507 D
mtorres@icprjc.edu

TRAPP, Lori ... 734-973-3529 232 D ltrapp@wccnet.edu
TRAPP, Ray ... 336-285-2436 341 D rtrapp@ncat.edu
TRAPP, Rodney ... 202-274-5930.. 94 B rodney.trapp@udc.edu
TRASKA, Anthony ... 216-687-2020 350 J a.traska@csuohio.edu
TRATARIS, Kat ... 415-351-3512.. 61 C ktrataris@sfai.edu
TRAUBE, David ... 304-357-0014 487 J davidtraube@ucwv.edu
TRAUGH, Cecelia ... 212-875-4668 290 H ctraugh@bankstreet.edu
TRAUPMAN-CARR, Carol ... 610-861-1348 390 F traupman-carrc@moravian.edu
TRAUSCH, Diane, M ... 312-261-3230 145 D diane.trausch@nl.edu
TRAUTH, Denise, M ... 512-245-2121 450 C president@txstate.edu
TRAUTMAN, Karla ... 605-688-4792 417 A karla.trautman@sdstate.edu
TRAUTMAN, Stewart ... 352-854-2322.. 97 N trautmas@cf.edu
TRAUTWEILER, Courtney ... 471-667-8181 252 B ctrautweiler@cottey.edu
TRAUTWEIN, Paul ... 310-434-4204.. 63 C trautwein_paul@smc.edu
TRAVENICK, Ron ... 707-638-5342.. 68 B ron.travenick@tu.edu
TRAVENY, Carol ... 267-502-2547 379 A carol.traveny@brynathyn.edu
TRAVER, Michele ... 810-762-0242 228 F michele.traver@mcc.edu
TRAVERNICHT, Marcia .. 585-475-7292 312 F mstwml@rit.edu
TRAVERS, Lesley ... 307-532-8202 501 B lesley.travers@ewc.wy.edu
TRAVERS, Nan ... 518-587-2100 320 E nan.travers@esc.edu
TRAVERSE, Marshall ... 425-558-0299 479 F
TRAVERSO, Susan ... 724-589-2100 399 D straverso@thiel.edu
TRAVIS, Antonio ... 404-756-4023 115 G atravis@atlm.edu
TRAVIS, Artie ... 301-687-4311 204 C altravis@frostburg.edu
TRAVIS, Brittany ... 718-779-1499 311 E btravis@plazacollege.edu
TRAVIS, David ... 715-425-3700 496 F david.travis@uwrf.edu
TRAVIS, Frederick ... 641-472-1209 168 C ftravis@miu.edu
TRAVIS, Rick ... 662-325-2646 247 F travis@ps.msstate.edu
TRAVIS, Scott ... 616-395-7251 225 D travis@hope.edu
TRAVIS, Theresa ... 610-499-4123 402 G ttravis@widener.edu
TRAVIS, Thomas ... 210-299-8501 503 C thomas.travis@usuhs.edu
TRAVIS-TEAGUE, Dianne ... 805-969-3626.. 55 J dtravis-teague@pacifica.edu
TRAVISANO, Jacqueline 305-284-6100 113 C jtravisano@miami.edu
TRAWICK, Michelle ... 402-554-2596 270 A mtrawick@unomaha.edu
TRAWICK, Rebecca ... 909-652-6493.. 35 L rebecca.trawick@chaffey.edu
TRAWICK, Travis, H ... 817-921-8833 445 A ttrawick@swbts.edu
TRAXLER, Pete ... 907-796-6139.. 10 B pbtraxler@alaska.edu
TRAXLER, Rebecca ... 937-775-7032 364 E rebecca.traxler@wright.edu
TRAXLER, Roxy ... 507-389-7470 241 C roxy.traxler@southcentral.edu
TRAXLER, Roxy ... 507-389-7200 241 C roxy.traxler@southcentral.edu
TRAXLER, Suzanne ... 715-232-2501 497 B traxlers@uwstout.edu
TRAYLOR, Angela ... 502-895-3411 183 H atraylor@lpts.edu
TRAYNHAM, Cynthia ... 919-546-8334 340 B cynthia.traynham@shawu.edu
TRAYNOR, Thomas, L ... 937-775-4859 364 E thomas.traynor@wright.edu
TRAYWICK, Deaver ... 828-251-6001 342 B traywick@unca.edu
TREACY, Margaret ... 845-569-3355 307 D margaret.treacy@msmc.edu
TREADWAY, Barbara ... 402-399-2474 266 F btreadway@csm.edu
TREADWAY, Chris ... 304-558-1112 489 H chris.treadway@wvhepc.edu
TREADWELL, Andrew ... 772-462-4804 102 F atreadwe@irsc.edu
TREADWELL, Dartell ... 662-252-8000 248 G dtreadwell@rustcollege.edu
TREADWELL, Melinda ... 603-358-2000 274 H president@keene.edu
TREADWELL, Orlando ... 202-274-5050.. 94 B
TREAGER-HUBER, Carey ... 317-921-4882 158 D ctreagerhuber@ivytech.edu
TREANOR, Ellen ... 657-278-4475.. 31 C etreanor@fullerton.edu
TREANOR, Laura ... 812-888-4262 162 F provost@vinu.edu
TREANOR, William, M .. 202-662-9030.. 92 E wtreanor@georgetown.edu
TREAT, Tod ... 509-682-6605 485 H ttreat@wvc.edu
TREBER, Karen, A ... 410-548-2330 204 D katreber@salisbury.edu
TRECARTIN, Ralph ... 269-471-3622 221 D rtrecartin@andrews.edu
TRECARTIN, JR., Ralph . 707-965-6211.. 55 I president@puc.edu
TRECHTER, Sara ... 530-898-4767.. 30 D strechter@csuchico.edu
TREDENNICK, Linda ... 509-313-6790 480 F tredennick@gonzaga.edu
TREDUP, Fred ... 702-895-3201 271 D fred.tredup@unlv.edu
TREECE, Richard ... 661-763-7768.. 67 G rtreece@taftcollege.edu
TREEN, Debbie ... 206-726-5020 479 E dtreen@cornish.edu
TREFF, Shaya ... 732-370-3360 285 I
TREFF, Yisroel Meir ... 732-370-3360 285 I
TREFT, Paul ... 712-274-5221 168 E treft@morningside.edu
TREFZ, Steve, A ... 605-336-6588 416 A strefz@sfseminary.edu
TREGEMBO, Tara ... 906-932-4231 224 D tarat@gogebic.edu
TREIBER, John ... 708-656-8000 145 C john.treiber@morton.edu
TREICHEL, Johnny ... 806-874-3571 432 J johnny.treichel@clarendoncollege.edu
TREISCH, Chad ... 630-829-6461 133 E ctreisch@ben.edu
TREJO, Alanna ... 805-437-2757.. 30 C alanna.trejo@csuci.edu
TREJO, Sam ... 909-387-1642.. 60 F strejo@sbccd.cc.ca.us
TREKELL, Eric ... 425-388-9273 480 B etrekell@everettcc.edu
TRELLES, Sofia ... 305-348-2797 110 A sofia.trelles@fiu.edu
TREMBLAY, Britni ... 785-243-1435 172 L btremblay@cloud.edu
TREMBLAY, Matthew ... 858-784-8469.. 64 A
TREMBLAY, Pamela ... 706-880-8313 122 A ptremblay@lagrange.edu
TREMBLAY, Paul ... 212-410-8142 308 E ptremblay@nycpm.edu
TREMBLAY, Rocky ... 203-285-2185.. 86 E rtremblay@gatewayct.edu
TREMBLE, Gayle ... 843-355-4133 414 C trembleg@wiltech.edu
TREML, Colleen ... 216-397-1595 353 O ctreml@jcu.edu
TREMPER, Michael ... 315-268-6789 295 F mtremper@clarkson.edu
TRENGOVE, Matthew ... 831-770-6854.. 44 G mtrengove@hartnell.edu
TRENIS, Neva, S ... 540-654-1055 471 N ntrenis@umw.edu
TRENKLE, Catheryne ... 970-521-6619.. 82 C catheryne.trenkle@njc.edu
TRENKLE, Lizza ... 254-659-7601 437 A ltrenkle@hillcollege.edu
TRENT, Dietra, Y ... 703-993-8730 467 E dtrent@gmu.edu
TRENT, Malissa ... 423-354-2521 425 A mbtrent@northeaststate.edu
TRENT-BROWN, Sonja .. 616-395-6829 225 D trentbrown@hope.edu
TRENTACOSTE, Peter ... 225-578-5388 189 E pjt@lsu.edu
TRENTHEM, Richard ... 901-843-3890 423 A trenthem@rhodes.edu
TRENUM, Gary ... 301-687-3174 204 C gtrenum@frostburg.edu
TREPAC, Letisha ... 309-268-8000 138 H
TREPAL, Michael, J ... 212-410-8067 308 E mtrepal@nycpm.edu
TREROTOLA, Michael, R ... 718-817-3185 300 C trerotola@fordham.edu
TRESSEL, James, P ... 330-941-3101 364 H jptressel@ysu.edu
TRESSELT, Thomas ... 212-353-4119 297 E
TRESSLER-GELOK, Thomas ... 718-390-3420 324 F thomas.gelok@wagner.edu
TRETHEWEY, Angela ... 530-898-4015.. 30 D atrethewey@csuchico.edu
TRETTER, April ... 502-272-7329 179 H atretter@bellarmine.edu
TREUNER, Mary ... 660-596-7249 259 M mtreuner@sfccmo.edu
TREUTING, Mary ... 318-473-6482 189 F maryt@lsua.edu
TREVARTHEN, Josie, B . 931-424-2055 427 E jtrev@utsouthern.edu
TREVETT-SMITH, Matthew ... 302-831-2027.. 91 C mtrevett@udel.edu
TREVIER, Tim ... 815-226-4107 148 D ttrevier@rockford.edu
TREVINO, Beth ... 618-374-5202 147 E beth.trevino@principia.edu
TREVINO, Cori ... 940-898-3273 451 D ctrevino@twu.edu
TREVINO, Crispin ... 361-593-4036 447 D crispin.trevino@tamuk.edu
TREVINO, Cynthia ... 806-291-3401 457 I trevinoc@wbu.edu
TREVINO, Leonard ... 412-365-1650 380 G ltrevino@chatham.edu
TREVINO, Monica ... 405-224-3140 371 B mtrevino@usao.edu
TREVINO, Nicole, G ... 512-428-1037 442 I nicoleg@stedwards.edu
TREVINO, Oscar ... 802-831-1348 463 C otrevino@vermontlaw.edu
TREVIRANUS, Lisa, A ... 651-696-6220 236 I
TREVIS, Michael ... 310-660-3101.. 41 E mtrevis@elcamino.edu
TREVISAN, Michael ... 509-335-4853 485 D trevisan@wsu.edu
TREVISANELLO, Lisa ... 352-591-5385.. 97 D lisa@chiu.edu
TREVOR, Tyler ... 406-449-9145 263 J ttrevor@montana.edu
TREVOR, Will ... 518-445-2311 289 K wtrev@albanylaw.edu
TREWARTHA, Robert ... 651-423-8275 238 E robert.trewartha@dctc.edu
TREZEVANT, Latitia ... 803-822-3597 410 D trezevantl@midlandstech.edu
TREZZA, Frank ... 240-567-5031 200 G frank.trezza@montgomerycollege.edu
TRI, Sandjaya ... 714-535-3886.. 64 I santri@southbaylo.edu
TRIANA, Alisha ... 765-983-1211 155 A trianal@earlham.edu
TRIANTIS, Alexander ... 410-234-9214 199 G atriantis@jhu.edu
TRIBBEY, Ann ... 804-330-0111 465 H
TRIBBLE, SR., Jeffery, L ... 404-687-4586 117 G tribblej@ctsnet.edu
TRIBBLE, Kenyetta ... 925-551-6204.. 40 C ktribble@dvc.edu
TRIBBLE, Sherman, R ... 919-267-1640 330 B
TRIBLE, JR., Paul, S ... 757-594-7002 465 M ptrible@cnu.edu
TRIBLEY, Walter ... 307-675-0505 501 G
TRICE, Matt ... 229-430-6618 114 I mtrice@albanytech.edu
TRICHE, Casie ... 985-448-4077 192 F casie.triche@nicholls.edu
TRIER, Vicki ... 406-247-3003 264 D vicki.trier@msubillings.edu
TRIERWEILER, John, K . 585-475-4727 312 F jktcmo@rit.edu
TRIETLEY, Rick ... 608-796-3001 497 O rctrietley@viterbo.edu
TRIEZENBERG, Steven, J ... 616-234-5708 232 B
TRIGALO, Ophir ... 312-567-3290 140 A trigalo@iit.edu
TRIGG, Debra ... 510-723-6716.. 35 J dtrigg@chabotcollege.edu
TRIGG, Latokia ... 864-592-4158 412 E triggl@sccsc.edu
TRIGONIS, Marina ... 760-471-1316.. 72 H mkaravokiris@usk.edu
TRIHUS, Meg ... 972-708-7379 435 E dean-students@diu.edu
TRIMARCHI, Valarie ... 912-201-8007 125 F vtrimarchi@southuniversity.edu
TRIMBLE, Ashtin ... 309-796-5143 133 G trimblea@bhc.edu
TRIMBLE, Celeste ... 360-491-4700 482 I
TRIMBLE, Jodene ... 208-535-5489 131 B jodene.trimble@cei.edu
TRIMBLE, LaDonna ... 661-722-6300.. 26 A ltrimble@avc.edu
TRIMBLE, Lisa ... 307-778-1603 501 E lisatrimble@lcccfoundation.edu
TRIMBLE, Michele ... 406-874-6305 263 H trimblem@milescc.edu
TRIMBOLI, Dana ... 718-262-2350 295 E dtrimboli@york.cuny.edu
TRIMBOLI, James ... 716-614-6202 309 G trimboli@niagaracc.suny.edu
TRINH, Dat, Q ... 909-469-5613.. 75 I dtrinh@westernu.edu
TRINH, Steven ... 650-574-6161.. 62 K
TRINH, SVD, Vinh ... 563-876-3353 165 H vtrinh@dwci.edu
TRINIDAD, Angel ... 787-878-5475 507 L atrinidad@arecibo.inter.edu
TRINIDAD, Vanessa ... 787-884-6000 507 D vtrinidad@icprjc.edu
TRINIDAD, Ysabel, D ... 909-869-3019.. 30 A ydtrinidad@cpp.edu
TRINN, Dune ... 858-653-3000.. 29 D dtrinn@calmu.edu
TRINOSKEY, Jessica ... 317-955-6730 159 K jtrinoskey@marian.edu
TRIOLO, John ... 718-631-6320 295 C jtriolo@qcc.cuny.edu
TRIPATHI, Satish, K ... 716-645-2901 316 C president@buffalo.edu
TRIPLETT, Jennifer ... 660-359-3948 257 D jtriplett@mail.ncmissouri.edu
TRIPLETT, Kevin ... 865-471-4369 418 E ktriplett@cn.edu
TRIPLETT ELLIS, Jill ... 901-843-3745 423 A ellisj@rhodes.edu
TRIPODI, Michael, A ... 201-684-6975 280 H mtripodi@rmapo.edu
TRIPP, Vanessa ... 252-789-0293 335 H vanessa.tripp@martincc.edu
TRIPPETT, William ... 262-472-1130 497 D trippetw@uww.edu
TRIPSAS, Zachary ... 617-585-0200 207 A zachary.tripsas@the-bac.edu
TRIPURANENI, Vinaya, L ... 909-448-4300.. 71 C vtripuraneni@laverne.edu
TRISCHMAN, Jackie ... 760-750-7204.. 33 A trischma@csusm.edu
TRISLER, Chad ... 208-562-2106 131 E chadtrisler@cwi.edu
TRITES, Roberta ... 309-438-5703 140 D seeling@ilstu.edu
TRITT, Lindsey ... 731-424-3520 424 E ltritt2@jscc.edu
TRIVEDI, Kalpen ... 413-545-2710 211 G ktrivedi@ipo.umass.edu
TRIVEDI, Sara ... 310-568-6105.. 51 A strivedi@lmu.edu
TRIVUNOVICH, Nick ... 813-974-7220 111 C ntrivuno@usf.edu
TROCHE, Albert ... 718-368-5109 294 E
TROCHIM, Shawn ... 254-299-8811 439 E strochim@mclennan.edu
TROCHUCK, Michael, S 708-239-4836 151 A mike.trochuck@trnty.edu
TROENDLE, Laura ... 909-621-8243.. 57 E laura_troendle@pitzer.edu
TROGDON, Joel ... 336-633-0200 337 A
TROGISCH, Colleen, M . 845-431-8974 298 D trogisch@sunydutchess.edu
TROHA, Amy, M ... 409-880-7011 449 G atroha@lamar.edu
TROHA, James, A ... 814-641-3101 386 E trohaj@juniata.edu
TROIANO, Laura ... 973-353-3905 282 B ltroiano@rutgers.edu
TROILO, David ... 212-938-5659 319 E dtroilo@sunyopt.edu

TUCKER, Sandra .... 386-481-2106.. 96 D
tuckers@cookman.edu
TUCKER, Sarah .... 304-558-0699 489 H
sarah.tucker@wvhepc.edu
TUCKER, Sarah .... 304-558-0265 489 H
tucker@wvctcs.org
TUCKER, Sarah, A .... 304-558-0265 488 B
tucker@wvctcs.org
TUCKER, Shawn .... 201-200-2222 279 D
stucker2@njcu.edu
TUCKER, Shawna .... 580-349-1534 367 F
shawna.tucker@opsu.edu
TUCKER, Sheryl .... 405-744-6368 367 G
sheryl.tucker@okstate.edu
TUCKER, Stacy .... 602-412-9003.. 16 G
stacy.tucker@phoenix.edu
TUCKER, Stacy .... 913-288-7239 175 B
stucker@kckcc.edu
TUCKER, Tommy .... 870-307-7324.. 19 I
thomas.tucker@lyon.edu
TUCKER, William, T ...... 631-451-4760 321 C
tuckerw@sunysuffolk.edu
TUCKER, Zack .... 501-882-4491.. 17 D
zatucker@asub.edu
TUCKMAN, Eric .... 626-289-7719.. 24 H
TUDELA, Virginia, C ..... 671-735-5590 504 D
virginia.tudela@guamcc.edu
TUDINI, Kathryn, E .... 716-645-2258 316 C
katietud@buffalo.edu
TUDOR, Amanda .... 859-985-3316 179 I
tudora@berea.edu
TUDOR, Colin .... 909-607-3679.. 37 B
colin.tudor@claremont.edu
TUDOR, David .... 859-276-4357 185 A
dtudor@sullivan.edu
TUDOR, Jarrod .... 740-654-6711 358 K
tudorg@ohio.edu
TUDOR, Lauren .... 412-365-2731 380 G
l.tudor@chatham.edu
TUDOR, Lisa .... 239-489-9350 101 A
ltudor@fsw.edu
TUDOR, Marie .... 314-392-2348 256 E
marie.tudor@mobap.edu
TUDOR, Robert .... 304-876-5294 490 A
rtudor@shepherd.edu
TUDOR-LOCKE, Catrine . 704-687-7917 342 D
ctudorlo@uncc.edu
TUDORIE,
Ionut Alexandru .... 914-961-8313 314 H
iatudorie@svots.edu
TUDRYN, Jonathan .... 413-755-4420 216 A
jtudryn@stcc.edu
TUEDIO, James, A .... 209-667-3531.. 33 B
jtuedio@csustan.edu
TUELL, David .... 865-471-2020 418 E
dtuell@cn.edu
TUELLER, David .... 801-422-3861 458 H
david_tueller@byu.edu
TUELLER, Steve, W .... 808-675-3705 128 D
steve.tueller@byuh.edu
TUESCHER-GILLE, Heidi 608-342-1125 496 E
tuescheh@uwplatt.edu
TUFAU-AFRIYIE,
Michelle .... 508-854-2300 215 F
mtufau@qcc.mass.edu
TUFEL, Peter .... 212-686-9244 290 C
TUGGLE, Andrew .... 530-226-4140.. 64 E
atuggle@simpsonu.edu
TUIA, Jennifer .... 360-596-5369 484 D
jtuia@spscc.edu
TUITASI, Michael .... 310-434-4389.. 63 C
tuitasi_michael@smc.edu
TUITASI, Sifagatogo ...... 684-699-9155 504 B
s.tuitasi@amsamoa.edu
TUITE, Jayme .... 724-222-5330 391 F
jtuite@penncommercial.edu
TUITE, Kathleen .... 973-618-3534 276 D
ktuite@caldwell.edu
TUITE, Marie .... 408-924-1200.. 34 A
marie.tuite@sjsu.edu
TUITT, Franklin, A .... 860-486-2422.. 89 D
franklin.tuitt@uconn.edu
TUKEL, Oya, I .... 973-596-6262 279 E
oya.i.tukel@njit.edu
TULAK, William .... 318-487-5443 187 J
williamtulak@cltcc.edu
TULBERG, Clark .... 805-525-4417.. 67 K
ctulberg@thomasaquinas.edu
TULINO, Michael .... 520-206-4625.. 15 B
mtulino@pima.edu
TULLEY, Nickolas, B ..... 240-895-3149 202 B
nbtulley@smcm.edu
TULLEY, Ronald .... 419-434-4445 362 D
rtulley@findlay.edu
TULLIER, Michael .... 334-724-4553.... 7 D
mtullier@tuskegee.edu
TULLOS, Casey .... 704-687-7501 342 D
kctullos@uncc.edu
TULLY, Greg, J .... 815-772-7218 145 B
gtully@morrisontech.edu
TULLY, John .... 860-832-1608.. 85 G
tullyj@ccsu.edu
TULLY, John, J .... 610-566-1776 403 B
jtully@williamson.edu
TULLY-DARTEZ,
Stephanie .... 870-862-8131.. 21 A
stully-dartez@southark.edu
TUMA, Tiffany .... 919-516-4101 339 I
tctuma@st-aug.edu
TUMBLIN, Tom .... 859-858-3581 179 C
TUMEO, Michael, D ...... 214-768-2808 444 D
mtumeo@smu.edu
TUMER, Irem .... 541-737-3467 375 A
TUMEY, Terrance .... 559-278-3178.. 31 B
TUMIEL, John .... 207-221-4628 197 E
jtumiel@une.edu
TUMILTY, Meredith .... 847-543-2946 136 A
mtumilty@clcillinois.edu
TUMINEZ, Astrid .... 801-863-3000 460 D
president@uvu.edu
TUNE, Kathie .... 434-791-7106 464 I
ktune@averett.edu
TUNG, Lisa .... 617-879-7335 213 B
ltung@massart.edu
TUNGSETH, Margaret .... 651-523-2203 236 B
mtungseth01@hamline.edu
TUNHEIM, Kathi .... 507-933-6540 236 A
ktunheim@gustavus.edu
TUNK, Chana .... 973-267-9404 280 F
TUNNING, Michael .... 563-884-5865 169 F
michael.tunning@palmer.edu
TUNSTILL, Hilda .... 931-393-1573 424 F
htunstill@mscc.edu
TUPOU, Candace .... 808-675-3777 128 D
candace.tupou@byuh.edu
TUPPER, Barb .... 319-399-8662 164 F
btupper@coe.edu
TUPPER, Rick .... 605-274-4499 414 G
rick.tupper@augie.edu
TUPUA, Tiare .... 684-699-9155 504 B
t.tupua@amsamoa.edu
TUPUOLA, Tafaimamao . 684-699-9155 504 B
t.tupuola@amsamoa.edu
TURBAN, Stephanie ...... 218-285-2242 240 E
stephanie.turban@rainyriver.edu
TURBEVILLE, Donna ...... 910-788-6203 338 A
donna.turbeville@sccnc.edu
TURBEVILLE, John .... 315-470-6660 319 D
jturbev@esf.edu
TURBIDE, Gerard .... 315-364-3358 324 I
gturbide@wells.edu
TURBIVILLE, Alice .... 610-957-6040 398 G
aturbiv1@swarthmore.edu
TURCHETTA, Greg .... 239-489-9061 101 A
gregory.turchetta@fsw.edu
TURCHI, Marissa .... 610-526-5151 379 B
mturchi@brynmawr.edu
TURCIOS, Mirna .... 661-726-1911.. 68 J
mirna.turcios@uav.edu
TURCOTT, Scott .... 765-677-2246 158 B
scott.turcott@indwes.edu
TURCOTTE, Amanda .... 859-233-8111 185 C
aturcotte@transy.edu
TURCOTTE, Jim .... 601-925-3809 247 C
turcotte@mc.edu
TURCOTTE, Paul .... 254-501-5817 447 A
ira@tamuct.edu
TUREK, John, G .... 714-879-3901.. 45 G
jgturek@hiu.edu
TURGEON, Pennie .... 516-686-7744 308 I
pturgeon@nyit.edu
TURICO, Michael .... 602-538-9396.. 10 D
TURK, David .... 903-813-2408 430 H
dturk@austincollege.edu
TURK, David, F .... 646-378-6153 310 D
david.turk@nyack.edu
TURK, Laura .... 540-831-5248 469 D
lturk@radford.edu
TURK, Matthew .... 773-834-2493 150 K
TURK, Stella .... 845-257-3105 316 E
turks@newpaltz.edu
TURK, Thomas .... 714-997-6819.. 36 B
turk@chapman.edu
TURK FIECOAT,
Heather .... 775-682-8081 271 E
hturk@unr.edu
TURKS, Stacie .... 209-946-2225.. 71 E
sturks@pacific.edu
TURLEY, Jo Lynn .... 660-596-7222 259 M
jturley@sfccmo.edu
TURLEY, Melissa .... 530-226-4941.. 64 E
mturley@simpsonu.edu
TURLEY, Patty .... 802-224-3000 463 D
TURLEY, Scott .... 479-575-6601.. 21 F
lturley@uark.edu
TURLEY-AMES, Kandi .... 208-282-3053 131 G
turlkand@isu.edu
TURLINGTON, Lisa .... 910-592-8081 337 G
lturlington@sampsoncc.edu
TURMAN, Paul, D .... 402-471-2505 268 C
pturman@nscs.edu
TURMAN, Thad .... 254-459-5336 446 D
tturman@tarleton.edu
TURNAGE, Craig, A .... 936-468-3407 445 E
turnagecraig@sfasu.edu
TURNAGE, Tyrone .... 252-493-7777 336 H
tturnage@email.pittcc.edu
TURNBOW, Eboni .... 707-826-3504.. 33 C
eboni.turnbow@humboldt.edu
TURNBULL, Donna .... 216-221-8584 357 C
donna.turnbull@thencc.edu
TURNER, Andrea .... 812-749-1248 159 O
aturner@oak.edu
TURNER, Angela .... 434-797-8438 473 G
angela.turner@danville.edu
TURNER, B, P .... 334-387-3877.... 4 B
businessoffice@amridgeuniversity.edu
TURNER, Brooke .... 850-973-1674 104 L
turnerb@nfc.edu
TURNER, Dawn .... 252-985-5124 339 D
dturner@ncwc.edu
TURNER, Debra .... 706-737-1431 116 A
debturner@augusta.edu
TURNER, Deidra .... 817-515-1280 445 F
deidra.turner@tccd.edu
TURNER, Donna, A .... 252-246-1240 339 C
daturner@wilsoncc.edu
TURNER, Donnell .... 617-243-2125 211 B
dturner@lasell.edu
TURNER, Elaine .... 404-727-7631 118 E
elaine.turner@emory.edu
TURNER, Elisabeth .... 805-493-6577.. 29 C
bethturner@callutheran.edu
TURNER, Eric, M .... 617-243-2071 211 B
eturner@lasell.edu
TURNER, Fraser, S .... 773-508-7591 143 C
fturner1@luc.edu
TURNER, Ginny Rae ...... 678-839-6592 127 C
vturner@westga.edu
TURNER, Heather .... 803-376-5801 406 D
hturner@allenuniversity.edu
TURNER, J. Fidel .... 404-880-6126 117 C
jturner@cau.edu
TURNER, Janet, K .... 503-943-7311 377 A
turnerj@up.edu
TURNER, Jeffrey .... 573-681-5087 254 G
turnerj@lincolnu.edu
TURNER, Jere .... 603-206-8165 272 L
jturner@ccsnh.edu
TURNER, John .... 979-830-4316 431 H
john.turner@blinn.edu
TURNER, Jonna .... 580-581-2218 365 D
jbrown@cameron.edu
TURNER, June .... 760-921-5558.. 56 A
june.turner@paloverde.edu
TURNER, K. B .... 601-979-7036 246 F
kb.turner@jsums.edu
TURNER, Kandy .... 610-499-4498 402 G
kkturner@widener.edu
TURNER, Kara .... 443-885-3126 201 A
kara.turner@morgan.edu
TURNER, Kay .... 718-817-1000 300 C
kturner27@fordham.edu
TURNER, Keith .... 320-762-4693 237 C
keith.turner@alextech.edu
TURNER, Keith .... 218-733-6940 238 G
keith.turner@lsc.edu
TURNER, Kim .... 806-742-3220 450 D
TURNER, Kirsten .... 859-257-1911 185 F
kirsten.turner@uky.edu
TURNER, Kyle .... 303-964-5724.. 83 E
kturner005@regis.edu
TURNER, Kyle .... 806-720-7779 439 D
kyle.turner@lcu.edu
TURNER, Lauren .... 978-934-1804 212 B
lauren_turner@uml.edu
TURNER, Louise .... 406-586-3585 263 I
louise.turner@montanabiblecollege.edu
TURNER, Marietta .... 217-351-2505 147 C
mturner@parkland.edu
TURNER, Matt .... 304-558-4016 489 H
matt.turner@wvhepc.edu
TURNER, Michael .... 843-953-5145 407 C
mturner7@citadel.edu
TURNER, Michael, C ...... 334-387-3877.... 4 B
mcturner@amridgeuniversity.edu
TURNER, Monica .... 575-769-4948 285 O
monica.sanchez@clovis.edu
TURNER, Natalie, T .... 502-597-6373 183 D
natalie.turner@kysu.edu
TURNER, Nicole .... 401-254-3886 405 C
nturner@rwu.edu
TURNER, Paaige, K .... 765-285-6000 153 H
pkturner@bsu.edu
TURNER, Pamela .... 502-213-2110 182 C
pamela.turner@kctcs.edu
TURNER, Phyllis .... 903-233-4170 439 A
phyllisturner@letu.edu
TURNER, Preston .... 731-425-2619 424 E
pturner@jscc.edu
TURNER, R. Elaine .... 352-392-1961 111 A
returner@ufl.edu
TURNER, R. Gerald .... 214-768-3300 444 D
cleggl@smu.edu
TURNER, Rebecca .... 727-341-3241 107 E
turner.rebecca@spcollege.edu
TURNER, Rebecca .... 812-941-2547 157 F
rebeturn@ius.edu
TURNER, Rebecca, E ..... 256-782-5485.... 6 A
bturner@jsu.edu
TURNER, Reginald .... 678-466-5115 117 D
reginaldturner@clayton.edu
TURNER, Rich .... 904-632-5112 101 B
rich.turner@fscj.edu
TURNER, Rick .... 714-997-6658.. 36 B
raturner@chapman.edu
TURNER, Robert, L .... 757-823-8670 469 A
rlturner@nsu.edu
TURNER, Ronne, P .... 314-935-5685 262 A
ronne.turner@wustl.edu
TURNER, Sarah .... 304-384-5348 489 J
slturner@concord.edu
TURNER, Savonda .... 706-754-7870 123 G
savonda@northgatech.edu
TURNER, Shane .... 541-463-5115 373 D
turners@lanecc.edu
TURNER, Sharisse .... 850-201-8582 112 C
sharisse.turner@tcc.fl.edu
TURNER, Sherry .... 901-843-3083 423 A
turners@rhodes.edu
TURNER, Shirley .... 603-375-7130 372 H
sturner@corban.edu
TURNER, Stephen .... 219-989-2232 160 D
sturner@pnw.edu
TURNER, Steve .... 760-872-2000.. 40 I
sturner@deepsprings.edu
TURNER, Steve .... 918-444-2000 366 G
turner@nsuok.edu
TURNER, Susan .... 203-932-7478.. 89 H
sturner@newhaven.edu
TURNER, Teresa .... 719-336-1591.. 81 K
teresa.turner@lamarcc.edu
TURNER, Teriann .... 870-512-7754.. 18 A
teriann_turner@asun.edu
TURNER, Tinicia .... 225-768-1774 187 B
tinicia.turner@franu.edu
TURNER, Toi .... 830-372-8019 449 A
tturner@tlu.edu
TURNER, Toni .... 516-255-4707 311 J
TURNER, Tony .... 843-863-7050 407 B
tturner@csuniv.edu
TURNER, Tonya .... 937-376-6018 349 J
tturner@centralstate.edu
TURNER, Tracy .... 213-738-5736.. 66 B
tturner@swlaw.edu
TURNER, Trey .... 936-468-5406 445 E
turnertrey@sfasu.edu
TURNER, William, L ...... 615-966-7153 421 B
william.turner@lipscomb.edu
TURNER, Yvonne .... 706-721-0211 116 A
yvturner@augusta.edu
TURNER CORTEZ,
Carlos, O .... 619-388-6957.. 60 H
ccortez@sdccd.edu
TURNER-FREDERICK,
Athena .... 718-420-4212 324 F
a.turner-frederick@wagner.edu
TURNER-TOLLEY, Robin 610-807-9221 386 B

U

ULMER, Robert, R .... 702-895-0628 271 D
robert.ulmer@unlv.edu
ULOZAS, Catherine, B .. 215-895-6685 382 F
catherine.b.ulozas@drexel.edu
ULREY, Burke .... 828-641-0259 327 B
ulreydb@brevard.edu
ULRICH, Jesse .... 515-576-7201 167 A
ULRICH, John .... 570-662-4804 394 F
julrich@mansfield.edu
ULRICH, John .... 570-662-4046 394 F
julrich@mansfield.edu
ULRICH, Mary .... 575-527-7526 287 F
mulrich@nmsu.edu
ULRICH, Trey, P .... 215-951-1671 387 A
ulrich@lasalle.edu
ULRICHSEN, Borre .... 509-313-6455 480 F
ulrichsen@gonzaga.edu
ULSES, Randy .... 513-556-3511 361 J
ulsesrj@ucmail.uc.edu
ULSHAFER, Kevin, L ..... 478-757-5125 127 F
kulshafer@wesleyancollege.edu
UMAN, Deborah .... 801-626-6424 461 A
deborahuman@weber.edu
UMANS, Dorothy .... 240-567-3820 200 G
dorothy.umans@montgomerycollege.edu
UMBERGER, Jennifer .... 570-389-5150 393 D
jumberger@bloomu.edu
UME, Ebere .... 815-740-3492 152 H
eume@stfrancis.edu
UMEHIRA, Ron .... 808-455-0228 130 C
umehira@hawaii.edu
UMEZU, Kodo .... 510-809-1444.. 45 M
UMFRESS, Jason, W ..... 912-279-5970 117 F
jumfress@ccga.edu
UMHOLTZ, Lynn .... 316-322-3144 172 D
lumholtz@butlercc.edu
UMIDI, Joseph .... 757-352-4404 470 B
joseumi@regent.edu
UMONTUEN, Nicholas .. 615-329-8763 419 H
numontuen@fisk.edu
UMPHREY, Monique ..... 713-718-8085 437 C
monique.umphrey@hccs.edu
UMSTATTD, Rustin .... 816-414-3700 256 C
rumstattd@mbts.edu
UNBEHAGEN, Leonard .. 504-278-6438 188 G
lunbehagen@nunez.edu
UNDA, Viviana .... 310-660-3515.. 41 E
vunda@elcamino.edu
UNDERCOFFER, Anita ... 909-652-6032.. 35 L
anita.undercoffer@chaffey.edu
UNDERCOFLER,
Jennifer .... 914-251-6707 319 B
jennifer.undercofler@purchase.edu
UNDERHILL, Terri .... 304-357-4980 487 J
terriunderhill@ucwv.edu
UNDERWOOD, Alex ...... 520-621-3432.. 16 D
aunderwood@arizona.edu
UNDERWOOD, Anita ..... 646-378-3090 310 D
anita.underwood@nyack.edu
UNDERWOOD, Cloris ... 954-486-7728 113 B
UNDERWOOD, Jeanette 972-775-7250 440 D
jeanette.underwood@navarrocollege.edu
UNDERWOOD, Jeffrey ... 323-343-3793.. 31 E
jeffrey.underwood@calstatela.edu
UNDERWOOD,
Kathy, A .... 702-895-0283 271 D
kathyunderwood@unlv.edu
UNDERWOOD, Kristen .. 563-387-1536 168 B
k.underwood@luther.edu
UNDERWOOD, Lori, J .. 757-594-7052 465 M
underwoo@cnu.edu
UNDERWOOD, Mark ..... 830-591-7286 444 G
meunderwood@swtjc.edu
UNDERWOOD,
Michelle, W .... 229-931-2627 120 D
michelle.underwood@gsw.edu
UNDERWOOD, Ruth ...... 478-289-2134 118 C
runderwood@ega.edu
UNDERWOOD, Tara ...... 478-471-2734 122 F
tara.underwood@mga.edu
UNDERWOOD, Tiffani ... 276-656-0281 474 G
tunderwood@patrickhenry.edu
UNDERWOOD,
Timothy, J .... 304-462-6432 489 L
timothy.underwood@glenville.edu
UNDERWOOD, Von, E .. 580-581-2491 365 D
vonu@cameron.edu
UNDERWOOD,
William, D .... 478-301-2500 122 E
underwood_wd@mercer.edu
UNEBASAMI, Lloyd .... 808-983-4100 128 H
UNEBASAMI,
Michael, T .... 808-956-6280 129 G
mune@hawaii.edu
UNGAR, Samuel, D ...... 718-384-5460 325 L
UNGAR, Shaya .... 732-370-3360 285 I
UNGER, Bradley .... 847-543-2477 136 A
bunger@clcillinois.edu
UNGER, Candace .... 619-574-6909.. 55 E
cunger@pacificcollege.edu
UNGER, Jacob .... 845-362-3053 291 B
junger@byts.edu
UNGER, Karen .... 845-758-7434 290 I
kunger@bard.edu
UNGER, Leigh .... 562-908-3415.. 58 L
lunger@riohondo.edu
UNGER, Maggie .... 952-446-4323 235 J
ungerm@crown.edu
UNGER, Sue .... 630-889-6565 145 E
sunger@nuhs.edu
UNGERANK, Stephanie . 501-882-8842.. 17 D
ssungerank@asub.edu
UNGERER, Dorothy .... 413-755-4438 216 A
daungerer@stcc.edu
UNIS, Corry, D .... 203-254-4000.. 87 I
cunis@fairfield.edu
UNKE, James, M .... 507-354-8221 236 J
unkejm@mlc-wels.edu
UNNAVA, H. Rao .... 530-752-4600.. 69 B
runnava@ucdavis.edu
UNNITHAN, Shashi .... 970-204-8607.. 81 A
shashi.unnithan@frontrange.edu
UNREIN, Ashley .... 970-521-6741.. 82 C
ashley.unrein@njc.edu
UNRUH, David, L .... 215-895-1261 382 F
dlu23@drexel.edu
UNRUH, John, A .... 530-898-5844.. 30 D
jaunruh@csuchico.edu
UNRUH, Nancy .... 620-276-9571 174 B
nancy.unruh@gcccks.edu
UNSWORTH, John, M ... 434-924-7849 472 D
jmu2m@virginia.edu
UNTARTO, SSPS,
Aprilia .... 563-876-3353 165 H
auntarto@dwci.edu
UNZICKER, Ted .... 208-792-2223 132 A
tounzicker@lcsc.edu
UPAH, Jesse .... 319-399-8000 164 F
UPCHURCH, Linda .... 478-289-2188 118 C
lupchurch@ega.edu
UPCHURCH, Luke .... 704-922-6513 334 G
upchurch.luke@gaston.edu
UPCHURCH, Luke .... 704-923-8405 334 G
upchurch.luke@gaston.edu
UPCHURCH, Rick .... 601-968-8942 245 B
rupchurch@belhaven.edu
UPDIKE, Jeremy .... 507-923-4210 234 A
updike@augsburg.edu
UPHOLD, Kimberly .... 253-680-7025 477 I
kuphold@batestech.edu
UPLINGER, Matthew ..... 920-206-2318 493 C
matthew.uplinger@mbu.edu
UPNEJA, Arun .... 617-358-6744 207 E
aupneja@bu.edu
UPSHAW, Kim .... 267-359-5598 382 F
kim.p.upshaw@drexel.edu
UPSHAW, Tyler .... 352-395-8516 107 D
tyler.upshaw@saintleo.edu
UPTON, Brian .... 417-865-2815 253 D
uptonb@evangel.edu
UPTON, Ed .... 817-921-8846 445 A
eupton@swbts.edu
UPTON, Michael .... 662-862-8035 246 E
maupton@iccms.edu
UPTON-GARVIN, Barbra 816-501-4555 258 I
barbra.uptongarvin@rockhurst.edu
UQDAH, Aesha .... 502-852-6585 186 A
aesha.uqdah@louisville.edu
URAN, Mike, T .... 320-308-2116 240 I
mturan@stcloudstate.edu
URBAITIS, Carol, S .... 585-785-1212 299 F
carol.urbaitis@flcc.edu
URBAN, Chad, H .... 843-577-5245 406 E
URBAN, David, J .... 615-898-2764 422 C
david.urban@mtsu.edu
URBAN, Kristi .... 979-830-4141 431 H
kristi.urban@blinn.edu
URBAN, Nathan, N .... 610-758-3605 388 E
nnu220@lehigh.edu
URBANCZYK, Allison .... 219-464-5212 162 D
allison.urbanczyk@valpo.edu
URBANEK, Lauren .... 617-585-1113 217 E
lauren.urbanek@necmusic.edu
URBANEK, Philip .... 251-405-7006.... 1 E
purbanek@bishop.edu
URBANEK-MUELLER,
Mary .... 314-256-8855 250 D
urbanek@ai.edu
URBANIAK, Kellene ...... 773-371-5400 134 D
kurbaniak@ctu.edu
URBANO, George .... 863-297-1086 106 A
gurbano@polk.edu
URDAN, Joely, B .... 414-229-4730 496 B
jurdan@uwm.edu
URDANETA, Marta .... 903-434-8367 440 G
murdaneta@ntcc.edu
URDIALES, Juan .... 323-260-8133.. 48 J
urdialjr@elac.edu
URDIALEZ, Christine ..... 210-366-2701 441 J
curdialez@questcollege.edu
URETSKY, Stewart .... 781-736-4403 208 A
suretsky@brandeis.edu
UREY, Denise .... 724-589-2009 399 D
durey@thiel.edu
URGO, Joseph, R .... 330-972-8379 361 H
jurgo@uakron.edu
URIBE, Kimberly .... 323-259-2523.. 54 I
kuribe@oxy.edu
URIBE NITTI, Christina . 507-457-1492 243 C
curibeni@smumn.edu
URICK, Cindy .... 610-372-4721 396 H
curick@racc.edu
URIEGAS, Samantha ..... 956-872-6763 443 H
sbmunoz@southtexascollege.edu
URLA, Jacqueline .... 413-545-2869 211 G
jurla@umass.edu
URQUIDEZ,
Kasandra, K .... 520-621-3705.. 16 D
kurquidez@arizona.edu
URQUIOLA, Angel .... 305-821-3333 100 E
aurquiola@fnu.edu
URRABAZO, Gloria .... 210-528-7047 441 B
gaurrabazo@ollusa.edu
URSCHEL, Kris .... 574-284-4542 160 I
kurschel@saintmarys.edu
URSO, David .... 540-453-2376 473 D
ursod@brcc.edu
URSUY, Andrea .... 989-686-9222 223 J
alnadols@delta.edu
URSUY, Andrea, L .... 989-686-9222 223 J
alnadols@delta.edu
URTZ, Anastasia .... 315-498-2692 310 F
urtza@sunyocc.edu
URTZ, Anastasia .... 315-498-2622 310 F
URTZ, Mike .... 607-753-4953 318 A
mike.urtz@cortland.edu
URY, Erica .... 573-334-6825 259 G
eury@sehcollege.edu
USATCH, Jeri .... 518-255-5227 319 C
usatchj@cobleskill.edu
USCHER, Nancy .... 702-895-4210 271 D
nancy.uscher@unlv.edu
USDAN, Stuart .... 205-348-6250.... 7 G
susdan@ches.ua.edu
USHER, Diane .... 401-254-3039 405 C
dusher@rwu.edu
USHER, John .... 251-460-6140.... 9 A
jusher@southalabama.edu
USINA, Phyllis .... 707-527-4547.. 63 D
pusina@santarosa.edu
UTASH, Sheree .... 316-677-9400 178 E
sutash@watc.edu
UTECH, Tracy .... 313-577-9278 232 K
tracy.utech@wayne.edu
UTER, Joe .... 202-806-6131.. 92 F
UTHOFF, Jay, L .... 563-387-1012 168 B
uthoffja@luther.edu
UTLEY, Danya .... 501-882-4509.. 17 D
dlutley@asub.edu
UTPADEL, Justin .... 715-232-2200 497 B
utpadelj@uwstout.edu
UTSCHIG, Theresa .... 414-930-3000 494 E
utschigt@mtmary.edu
UTSUKI, Melissa .... 626-914-8872.. 36 J
mutsuki@citruscollege.edu
UTT, Heather .... 580-349-1399 367 F
heather.utt@opsu.edu
UTTER, Alan .... 870-972-2030.. 17 E
autter@astate.edu
UVERO, Marilyn .... 562-988-2278.. 25 L
muvero@auhs.edu
UVIN, Peter .... 909-621-8117.. 37 D
peter.uvin@cmc.edu
UWONO, Dee .... 808-956-2299 129 E
deeuwono@hawaii.edu
UWONO, Dee, E .... 808-956-7077 129 C
deeuwono@hawaii.edu
UYENO, Sandra .... 808-956-7038 129 G
uyeno@hawaii.edu
UZMAN, James, C .... 713-221-8019 453 A
uzmana@uhd.edu
UZNANSKI, Laurel .... 360-867-6366 480 C
uznanski@evergreen.edu
UZORUO, Petra .... 409-984-6151 449 I
petra.uzoruo@lamarpa.edu
UZZELL, Janet, F .... 202-994-7377.. 92 D
janetuzzell@gwu.edu
UZZI, Jeannine .... 207-780-4485 197 D
jeannine.uzzi@maine.edu
U'REN, Brian .... 859-858-2298 179 C

V

VABRE, Bert .... 201-761-7834 283 A
bvabre@saintpeters.edu
VACA, Margarita .... 773-878-5824 149 A
mvaca@staugustine.edu
VACCARELLI, Rebecca ... 212-799-5000 303 E
VACCARO, Anne .... 718-862-7409 304 M
anne.vaccaro@manhattan.edu
VACCARO, Paul .... 508-849-3482 205 H
pvaccaro@annamaria.edu
VACEK, Heather .... 610-861-1516 390 F
vacekh@moravian.edu
VACEK, Kris .... 816-501-4819 258 I
kris.vacek@rockhurst.edu
VACIK, Stephen .... 601-857-3352 246 C
stephen.vacik@hindscc.edu
VAD, Aram .... 417-862-9533 253 F
VADEN, David .... 716-250-7500 292 A
dvaden@bryantstratton.edu
VADGAMA, Jadutt .... 323-563-9397.. 36 C
jayvadgama@cdrewu.edu
VAGLIENTI, Kendra .... 972-860-4332 434 F
kvaglienti@dcccd.edu
VAGNERINI, Beverly ...... 910-962-7422 343 C
vagnerinib@uncw.edu
VAHEY, Karen .... 516-686-7742 308 I
karen.vahey@nyit.edu
VAHLKAMP, Laura .... 618-545-3070 141 E
lvahlkamp@kaskaskia.edu
VAIDYA, Ashish .... 859-572-5123 184 E
vaidya@nku.edu
VAIDYA, Sameer .... 817-531-4840 451 C
svaidya@txwes.edu
VAINNER, Joseph .... 810-762-3300 232 A
jvainner@umich.edu
VAITHYLINGAM,
Mugunth .... 702-651-5900 270 K
mugunth.vaithylingam@csn.edu
VAKALAHI, Halaevalu ... 808-236-5812 128 G
hvakalahi@hpu.edu
VAKALIS, Marianne .... 212-986-4343 291 E
mpv@berkeleycollege.edu
VAKALIS, Marianne .... 973-278-5400 275 I
mpv@berkeleycollege.edu
VAKAMUDI, Ramesh ...... 404-413-0721 120 E
fmdrkv@gsu.edu
VAKIL, David .... 714-484-7152.. 54 B
dvakil@cypresscollege.edu
VAKNIN, Lauren .... 619-660-4295.. 44 D
lauren.vaknin@gcccd.edu
VALADAO, Christopher . 508-999-8772 212 A
cvaladao@umassd.edu
VALADEZ, Martin .... 509-865-8624 481 A
valadez_m@heritage.edu
VALADEZ, Roberto .... 619-388-3525.. 60 I
rvaladez@sdccd.edu
VALADEZ, Roberto .... 630-942-2481 135 I
valadezr@cod.edu
VALANIA, Joy .... 303-245-4804.. 82 A
VALCANA, Gary .... 256-216-5359.... 4 C
gary.valcana@athens.edu
VALCKE, Catherine .... 765-455-9561 157 B
chightow@iuk.edu
VALDERRAMA, Jesus .... 787-815-0000 511 H
VALDES, Debbie .... 786-391-1167.. 95 G
VALDES, Eduardo .... 409-772-8780 456 E
pvaldes@utmb.edu
VALDES, Jose, L .... 305-821-3333 100 E
jvaldes@fnu.edu
VALDES, Michael .... 734-487-2031 223 K
mvaldes@emich.edu
VALDEZ, Al .... 951-785-2115.. 47 C
avaldez@lasierra.edu
VALDEZ, Alex .... 956-665-7105 455 D
alex.valdez@utrgv.edu
VALDEZ, Anna .... 707-527-4527.. 63 D
avaldez@santarosa.edu

VAN NOORT, Kimberly . 919-843-8347 340 H
kpvannoort@northcarolina.edu
VAN NORMAN, Karen ... 973-761-9076 283 C
karen.vannorman@shu.edu
VAN NORT, Ella .... 213-624-1200.. 42 B
evanort@fidm.edu
VAN NOSTRAND, Chris 619-239-0391.. 34 G
cvannostrand@cwsl.edu
VAN NOSTRAND,
Robert .... 934-420-2700 320 F
foundation@farmingdale.edu
VAN NOY, Karla .... 785-749-8467 174 D
kvannoy@haskell.edu
VAN NOY, Vielane .... 435-222-1256.. 83 G
vvannoy@rvu.edu
VAN OMMEREN,
Andrew .... 712-707-7000 169 D
andrew.vanommeren@nwciowa.edu
VAN OMMEREN, Ryan .. 805-493-3211.. 29 C
rvommere@callutheran.edu
VAN OOT, Amy .... 860-701-5019.. 88 D
vanoot_a@mitchell.edu
VAN ORMAN, Kit .... 315-364-3317 324 I
kit@wells.edu
VAN PATTEN, Paul, G .. 615-898-2613 422 C
greg.vanpatten@mtsu.edu
VAN PELT, Donna .... 515-294-1280 163 G
dvanpelt@foundation.iastate.edu
VAN PROOYEN, Traci ... 309-268-8288 138 H
traci.vanprooyen@heartland.edu
VAN PUFFELEN,
Sara Kaitlin .... 706-419-1439 118 A
sarak.vanpuffelen@covenant.edu
VAN RENSBURG,
Deryck .... 310-506-5689.. 56 G
deryck.rensburg@pepperdine.edu
VAN RIJN, Paul .... 610-917-1450 401 G
p_vanrijn@valleyforge.edu
VAN RIPER, Lisa, K ...... 309-341-7760 141 G
lkvanriper@knox.edu
VAN ROOYEN, Pieter .... 313-883-8623 230 C
vanrooyen.pieter@shms.edu
VAN SCOTT, Mike .... 252-328-9479 341 A
vanscottmi@ecu.edu
VAN SICKLE, Fred .... 607-254-7150 297 F
fmv7@cornell.edu
VAN SICKLE, Fred .... 607-255-5142 297 F
fmv7@cornell.edu
VAN STAVERN, Becky ... 417-328-1815 259 I
bvanstavern@sbuniv.edu
VAN STRATEN, Amy ..... 920-831-4355 498 F
vanstrat@fvtc.edu
VAN TASSEL, Kristin ..... 785-227-3380 172 A
vantasselk@bethanylb.edu
VAN TASSELL, TOR,
Malachi .... 814-472-3001 397 F
mvantassell@francis.edu
VAN TIL, Seth, J .... 724-458-3887 384 G
sjvantil@gcc.edu
VAN UUM, Elizabeth ..... 314-516-5774 261 C
vanuum@umsl.edu
VAN VLERAH, Abby, L . 260-982-5132 159 J
alvanvlerah@manchester.edu
VAN VLIET, Krystyn ...... 617-253-3315 216 B
VAN VOORHIS, Sue, N . 612-625-8098 243 F
vanvo002@umn.edu
VAN VREEDE, LeeAnn .. 608-796-3808 497 O
levanvreede@viterbo.edu
VAN WAGNER, Molly ... 715-425-3195 496 F
molly.van-wagner@uwrf.edu
VAN WAGNER, Thomas 301-243-2211 502 L
thomas.vanwagner@dodiis.mil
VAN WAGONER,
Randall, J .... 315-792-5333 306 K
rvanwagoner@mvcc.edu
VAN WICKLIN, Robert .. 716-375-2331 313 C
bvanwick@sbu.edu
VAN WINKLE, Ken .... 575-234-9210 287 E
kvanwink@nmsu.edu
VAN WINKLE, Ken .... 575-646-2036 287 D
kvanwink@nmsu.edu
VAN WINKLE, Ken .... 575-646-9874 287 C
kvanwink@nmsu.edu
VAN WINKLE, Robin ...... 541-440-4668 376 G
robin.vanwinkle@umpqua.edu
VAN WOERT, Timothy .. 802-865-6499 462 A
tvanwoert@champlain.edu
VAN WORMER,
Laura, A .... 330-569-5249 353 G
vanwormerla@hiram.edu
VAN WYK, Natalie .... 610-361-5418 391 A
vanwykn@neumann.edu
VAN WYLEN, David, G . 616-395-7317 225 D
vanwylend@hope.edu

VAN WYNGARDEN,
Doug .... 708-239-4828 151 A
doug.vanwyngarden@trnty.edu
VAN ZEE, Carolina .... 909-537-7576.. 32 E
quinterc@csusb.edu
VAN ZEELAND, Kathy ... 414-930-3552 494 E
vanzeek@mtmary.edu
VANABLE, Peter .... 315-443-2543 321 G
pvanable@syr.edu
VANACORE, Gina .... 940-565-2282 453 E
gina.vanacore@unt.edu
VANAKEN, Troy .... 630-617-3100 137 G
president@elmhurst.edu
VANALSBURG,
Teresa, D .... 304-457-6380 486 E
vanalsburgtd@ab.edu
VANANDEN, Ian, C .... 301-447-5310 201 B
vananden@msmary.edu
VANASSE, Dennis .... 508-849-3372 205 H
dvanasse@annamaria.edu
VANBOCKSTAELE,
Elisabeth .... 215-762-4359 382 F
elisabeth.vanbockstaele@drexelmed.edu
VANBUREN, Tina .... 610-799-1510 388 D
tvanburen@lccc.edu
VANCAMP, Connie .... 412-809-5309 396 E
vancamp.connie@ptcollege.edu
VANCE, Gina, K .... 928-523-6747.. 14 H
gina.vance@nau.edu
VANCE, Gina, M .... 724-946-7110 402 D
vancegm@westminster.edu
VANCE, Justin .... 208-562-3449 131 E
justinvance@cwi.edu
VANCE, Karen .... 814-865-3917 391 G
ksv21@psu.edu
VANCE, Kristie .... 828-689-1353 331 C
kvance@mhu.edu
VANCE, Lara .... 859-622-3436 180 E
lara.vance@eku.edu
VANCE, Laura .... 828-641-0354 327 B
VANCE, Mickey .... 601-635-6338 246 A
mvance@eccc.edu
VANCE, Samantha .... 334-291-4974.... 1 H
samantha.vance@cv.edu
VANCE, Shawn .... 225-771-2552 191 E
svance@sulc.edu
VANCHHAWNG,
Stephen .... 260-422-5561 156 E
svanchhawng@indianatech.edu
VANDAL, Mike .... 701-477-7862 346 J
mvandal@tm.edu
VANDALL,
Christopher, P .... 608-258-2448 499 A
cvandall@madisoncollege.edu
VANDALOVSKY, Emily .. 201-879-7066 275 H
evandalovsky@bergen.edu
VANDE YACHT, Daniel .. 920-465-2111 495 F
vandeyad@uwgb.edu
VANDE ZANDE,
Carleen .... 608-262-5089 495 C
cvandezande@uwsa.edu
VANDEL, Laurie .... 406-496-4119 265 A
lvandel@mtech.edu
VANDEMEULEBROEKE,
Leon .... 973-761-9454 283 C
leon.vandemeulebroeke@shu.edu
VANDEN BOOGAARD,
Brad .... 806-874-3571 432 J
brad.vandenboogaard@clarendoncollege.edu
VANDEN BOUT,
David, A .... 512-232-0677 455 A
cnsdean@austin.utexas.edu
VANDEN BRANDEN,
Tara .... 815-226-4010 148 D
tvandenbranden@rockford.edu
VANDEN HOUTEN, Art .. 904-819-6274.. 99 E
vandena@flagler.edu
VANDENAVOND, Steve . 906-227-6767 228 I
svanden@nmu.edu
VANDENAVOND, Steve . 906-227-2190 228 I
svanden@nmu.edu
VANDENBERG,
Christine .... 908-852-1400 276 G
christine.vandenberg@centenaryuniversity.edu
VANDENBOSCH,
Kathryn .... 608-262-4930 495 D
kate.vandenbosch@cals.wisc.edu
VANDENELZEN, Brad .... 715-346-3693 497 A
VANDER FEEN, Aimee .. 605-331-6602 417 C
aimee.vanderfeen@usiouxfalls.edu

VANDER HART,
Mark, D .... 219-864-2400 159 N
VANDER HEIDEN,
Michael .... 920-498-6306 499 G
michael.vanderheiden@nwtc.edu
VANDER HOEK, Nancy . 605-229-8545 415 I
nancy.vanderhoek@presentation.edu
VANDER HOOVEN,
James, L .... 978-632-0001 215 C
jvanderhooven@mwcc.mass.edu
VANDER MAAS,
Brittany .... 256-766-6610.... 5 E
bvandermaas@hcu.edu
VANDER MOLEN,
Lori, L .... 402-280-1798 266 H
lorivandermolen@creighton.edu
VANDER STOEP,
Scott, D .... 616-395-7903 225 D
vanderstoep@hope.edu
VANDER VALK, Frank ... 518-587-2100 320 E
frank.vandervalk@esc.edu
VANDER VEER, Lisa ..... 815-939-5256 147 A
lvanderv@olivet.edu
VANDER WAL, Jennifer 605-688-4491 417 A
jennifer.vanderwal@sdstate.edu
VANDER WEELE,
Dennis, A .... 845-368-7206 314 I
dennis.vanderweele@use.salvationarmy.org
VANDER WERF, Dave .... 712-722-6020 165 I
dave.vanderwerff@dordt.edu
VANDER ZWAAG, Lora . 712-274-6400 171 B
lora.vanderzwaag@witcc.edu
VANDERBILT, Jonas ...... 903-927-3291 458 F
jvanderbilt@wileyc.edu
VANDERBILT, Robin ..... 937-298-3399 354 J
robin.vanderbilt@kc.edu
VANDERBILT, William ... 616-395-7850 225 D
vanderbilt@hope.edu
VANDERBURGH,
Paul, M .... 937-229-2345 362 C
pvanderburgh1@udayton.edu
VANDERGHEYNST, Jean 508-999-8539 212 A
jvandergheynst@umassd.edu
VANDERGIFF, Ronda .... 360-438-4356 482 I
rvandergriff2@stmartin.edu
VANDERGRIFF, Rhonda 573-334-6825 259 G
rvandergriff@sehcollege.edu
VANDERGRIFT, Donna .. 856-222-9311 281 C
dvandergrift@rcbc.edu
VANDERGRIFT, Paul ..... 919-516-4014 339 I
pvandergrift@st-aug.edu
VANDERHART, Mark ..... 219-864-2400 159 N
mvanderhart@midamerica.edu
VANDERHEIDE, Peter .... 801-863-8818 460 D
peter.vanderheide@uvu.edu
VANDERHILL, Dan .... 517-750-1200 231 C
danv@arbor.edu
VANDERHOOF, Doug .... 620-241-0723 172 J
doug.vanderhoof@centralchristian.edu
VANDERHOOF, Karen ... 973-328-5012 276 J
kvanderhoof@ccm.edu
VANDERKAR, Caroline .. 805-756-2945.. 29 I
cmoore36@calpoly.edu
VANDERMARK, Sarah ... 435-652-7500 460 B
sarah.vandermark@dixie.edu
VANDERMAUSE,
Roxanne, K .... 314-516-7067 261 C
vandermauserk@umsl.edu
VANDERMOLEN, Geoff .. 616-957-6045 222 B
gav016@calvinseminary.edu
VANDERPOOL, Molly .... 765-973-8415 157 A
moberry@iue.edu
VANDERPUYE,
Archibald, W .... 512-505-3076 438 A
awvanderpuye@htu.edu
VANDERSANDEN,
Susan .... 608-663-3367 492 F
svandersanden@edgewood.edu
VANDERSLICE,
Ronna, J .... 580-581-2250 365 D
rvanderslice@cameron.edu
VANDERSPOEL, James .. 906-932-4231 224 D
jimv@gogebic.edu
VANDERVEEN, Kathleen 616-331-2662 224 G
vandervk@gvsu.edu
VANDERVEEN, Sara ...... 269-927-8611 226 F
svanderveen@lakemichigancollege.edu
VANDERWOUDE,
Katrina .... 213-763-7000.. 49 F
VANDERZANDEN,
Ann Marie .... 515-294-7184 163 G
vanderza@iastate.edu

VANDERZEE, Lenore ..... 315-386-7109 320 B
vanderzeel@canton.edu
VANDERZWAAG,
George .... 585-275-4301 323 M
george.vanderzwaag@rochester.edu
VANDEURSEN,
Marianne .... 908-835-2430 284 H
vandeursen@warren.edu
VANDEVEN, Alissa .... 573-651-2206 259 H
avandeven@semo.edu
VANDEVERE, John, D ... 570-326-3761 392 W
jdv7@pct.edu
VANDEVILLE, Denise ..... 906-487-7379 224 B
denise.vandeville@finlandia.edu
VANDEWALKER,
Richard .... 409-984-6520 449 I
vandewalkerre@lamarpa.edu
VANDEWEERT, Lisa ...... 616-632-2885 221 E
lhv001@aquinas.edu
VANDIJK, Cindee .... 319-385-6495 167 H
cindee.vandijk@iw.edu
VANDIVERE, Julie .... 570-389-4713 393 D
jvandive@bloomu.edu
VANDORN, Cody .... 805-756-1131.. 29 I
cvandorn@calpoly.edu
VANDREHLE, Michael .... 507-537-6257 241 D
michael.vandrehel@smsu.edu
VANDUSER, Trisha .... 817-735-2508 454 B
trisha.vanduser@unthsc.edu
VANDUYN, Janet, A ...... 570-561-1818 397 H
VANDYKE, Diane .... 215-461-1143 390 C
dvandyke@mc3.edu
VANDYKE, John .... 541-885-1452 374 I
john.vandyke@oit.edu
VANDYKE, Ross .... 254-710-3555 431 E
ross_vandyke@baylor.edu
VANECEK, Frank .... 802-485-2135 462 F
vanecek@norwich.edu
VANEGAS, Jorge, A ...... 979-845-1230 446 F
jvanegas@tamu.edu
VANEK, Marian, S .... 412-383-1863 400 H
msv8@pitt.edu
VANEMAN, Christopher 864-596-9038 408 F
chris.vaneman@converse.edu
VANG, Chia .... 414-229-1101 496 B
vangcy@uwm.edu
VANG, Koue .... 916-484-8484.. 50 G
vangk@arc.losrios.edu
VANG, Mary .... 651-403-4147 241 B
mary.vang@saintpaul.edu
VANG, Tou .... 828-448-6041 339 A
tvang5@wpcc.edu
VANG, Touger .... 910-898-9651 336 D
vangt@montgomery.edu
VANGEL, Darcy .... 508-213-2111 217 H
darcy.vangel@nichols.edu
VANGELE, Jim .... 650-738-4455.. 62 L
vangelej@smccd.edu
VANGILDER, JT .... 785-539-3571 176 A
jt.vangilder@mccks.edu
VANGNESS FRISCH,
Jane .... 701-671-2627 346 D
jane.vangsness@ndscs.edu
VANGORDER, Karen ...... 260-481-6016 160 C
vangordk@pfw.edu
VANGSGARD, Mark, D .. 651-962-6095 244 E
mdvangsgard@stthomas.edu
VANGSNESS FRISCH,
Jane .... 701-671-2627 346 D
jane.vangsness@ndscs.edu
VANHECKE, JoNes, R ... 507-933-7526 236 A
jvanheck@gustavus.edu
VANHOOK, Jayson .... 423-614-8695 420 H
jvanhook@leeuniversity.edu
VANHORN, Amy .... 304-829-7115 487 A
avanhorn@bethanywv.edu
VANHORN, Amy .... 304-829-7150 487 A
avanhorn@bethanywv.edu
VANKO, David .... 410-704-2121 204 E
dvanko@towson.edu
VANLAECKEN, Erik .... 605-367-7624 417 B
erik.vanlaecken@southeasttech.edu
VANLANDINGHAM,
Taylor .... 479-524-1527.. 19 H
tvanlandingham@jbu.edu
VANLONDEN, April .... 800-287-8822 154 A
vanloap@earlham.edu
VANMETER, Mark .... 951-343-4323.. 27 G
mvanmeter@calbaptist.edu
VANN, Charlcie, P .... 256-782-8434.... 6 A
diversity@jsu.edu
VANN, Krista .... 585-582-8265 298 F
kristavann@elim.edu

VANN, JR., Linnie .... 410-334-2936 205 D
lvann@worwic.edu
VANN, Steve .... 607-735-1777 298 H
svann@elmira.edu
VANN, Wendy .... 252-862-1234 337 C
wpvann6919@roanokechowan.edu
VANN, Wendy, P .... 252-862-1234 337 C
wpvann6919@roanokechowan.edu
VANNAMEE, Christine ... 315-792-5497 306 K
cvannamee@mvcc.edu
VANNESTE, Ray .... 731-661-5534 426 F
rvaneste@uu.edu
VANNEY, Pete .... 715-365-4484 499 E
pvanney@nicoletcollege.edu
VANNOY, Sandra .... 828-262-2058 340 I
vannoysa@appstate.edu
VANNUCCI, Kristina .... 530-741-6986.. 77 E
kvannucc@yccd.edu
VANO, OSF, Barbara ..... 419-824-3703 355 C
bvano@lourdes.edu
VANORMAN, Chris .... 517-607-2506 225 C
cvanorman@hillsdale.edu
VANOSDALL,
Frederick, P .... 615-898-2874 422 C
rick.vanosdall@mtsu.edu
VANOVER, Johnna .... 405-789-6400 369 H
jvanover@snu.edu
VANOVER, Kathryn .... 918-540-6388 366 F
kathryn.vanover@neo.edu
VANPELT, Mark .... 928-681-5621.. 14 F
mvanpelt@mohave.edu
VANSCHOELANDT,
Debbie .... 949-367-8310.. 65 C
dvanschoelandt@ivc.edu
VANSCOY, Irma, J .... 803-777-6728 413 A
ivanscoy@mailbox.sc.edu
VANSCOY, Scott .... 909-869-3065.. 30 A
sgvanscoy@cpp.edu
VANSELOW, Kristen ...... 239-590-7040 109 K
kvanselow@fgcu.edu
VANSICKLE, Lisa .... 314-367-8700 260 H
lisa.vansickle@stlcop.edu
VANSKIKE, Kathryn .... 509-313-6128 480 F
vanskike@gonzaga.edu
VANSKIVER, Donnell ..... 301-687-4111 204 C
dhvanskiver@frostburg.edu
VANSTEEN, John .... 631-656-3187 300 B
john.vansteen@ftc.edu
VANSTEENBERGEN,
Sara .... 920-748-8715 494 J
vansteenbergens@ripon.edu
VANSUMEREN, Hans ..... 231-995-1793 229 A
hvansumeren@nmc.edu
VANT HUL, Tammy ...... 951-222-8000.. 59 D
VANTERPOOL, Elaine ..... 256-726-8355.... 6 C
dmerriweather@oakwood.edu
VANTRIESTE, Emilie ...... 215-204-8760 399 B
emilie.vantrieste@temple.edu
VANVALIN, Dana .... 626-584-5215.. 43 B
danavanvalin@fuller.edu
VANVALKENBURG,
Gretchen, R .... 334-844-1134.... 4 D
gzv0007@auburn.edu
VANVREEDE, Meredyth . 215-489-2267 382 B
meredyth.vanvreede@delval.edu
VANWEY, Leah .... 401-863-3184 403 J
leah_vanwey@brown.edu
VANWINGERDEN, Luke . 864-646-1474 412 H
lvanwing@tctc.edu
VANWORMER, Lisa .... 920-403-3272 495 B
lisa.vanwormer@snc.edu
VANZANTEN, Andy .... 605-367-5769 417 B
andrew.vanzanten@southeasttech.edu
VANZANTEN, Susan ...... 219-464-5022 162 D
susan.vanzanten@valpo.edu
VARAHRAMYAN, Kody .. 207-581-1506 196 G
varahramyan@maine.edu
VARAS, Elaine, P .... 215-898-1404 400 F
varas@upenn.edu
VARBERG, Peggy .... 701-777-4802 345 B
peggy.varberg@und.edu
VARBLE, Susan .... 504-280-6171 190 B
sfvarble@uno.edu
VARDAMAN, Lee .... 334-808-6319.... 7 C
vardaman@troy.edu
VARDANYAN,
Rouzanna .... 641-472-1154 168 C
rvardanyan@miu.edu
VAREBROOK, Cathy ...... 414-277-4523 494 D
varebrook@msoe.edu
VARELA, Donna .... 954-492-5353.. 97 G
dvarela@citycollege.edu
VARELA, Julio .... 956-340-8531 442 G
jvarela@riogrande.edu
VARELA, Legna .... 787-834-9595 510 D
lvarela@uaa.edu
VARELA, Lorell .... 787-834-9595 510 D
lovarela@uaa.edu
VARELA, Rebecca .... 870-307-7324.. 19 I
rebecca.varela@lyon.edu
VARELA, Susie .... 323-343-3694.. 31 E
svarela@cslanet.calstate.edu
VARELA LLAVONA,
Angélica .... 787-767-2040 513 B
angelica.varela@upr.edu
VARELAS, Nikos .... 312-413-9461 151 G
varelas@uic.edu
VARGA, Elizabeth .... 864-250-8454 409 I
elizabeth.varga@gvltec.edu
VARGAS, Adrienne .... 619-594-4562.. 33 D
avargas4@sdsu.edu
VARGAS, Amy .... 562-977-6091.. 42 K
amy.vargas@fremont.edu
VARGAS, Carlos .... 573-651-2222 259 H
president@semo.edu
VARGAS, Christina .... 631-451-4950 321 C
vargasc@sunysuffolk.edu
VARGAS, Dominique ..... 715-232-1181 497 B
vargasd@uwstout.edu
VARGAS, German .... 912-279-5918 117 F
gvargas@ccga.edu
VARGAS, Gineen .... 847-628-2524 141 C
gineen.vargas@judsonu.edu
VARGAS, Ingrid .... 650-738-4454.. 62 L
vargasi@smccd.edu
VARGAS, Jorge .... 401-841-7008 503 A
jorge.vargas@usnwc.edu
VARGAS, Jose .... 714-628-4886.. 58 G
vargas_jose@sccollege.edu
VARGAS, Julia .... 816-501-4545 258 I
julia.vargas@rockhurst.edu
VARGAS, Julio, R .... 787-765-1915 509 B
jvargas@opto.inter.edu
VARGAS, Karen .... 336-758-5000 344 C
VARGAS, Lizzette .... 787-753-6335 507 D
lvargas@icpruc.edu
VARGAS, Magda .... 787-841-2000 509 J
mivargas@pucpr.edu
VARGAS, Mary .... 616-632-2881 221 E
mcv005@aquinas.edu
VARGAS, Paloma .... 619-388-2795.. 60 J
pvargas@sdccd.edu
VARGAS, Phillip .... 210-431-4181 441 B
pvargas@ollusa.edu
VARGAS, Roy, M .... 561-862-4410 105 D
vargasr@palmbeachstate.edu
VARGAS, Silvia .... 610-799-1711 388 D
smaldonadovargas@lccc.edu
VARGASON, Kristen ...... 607-871-2010 290 B
vargason@alfred.edu
VARGHESE, Sara .... 619-644-7600.. 44 E
sara.varghese@gcccd.edu
VARGO, Michael .... 616-234-4690 224 F
mvargo@grcc.edu
VARGO, Michael .... 503-399-5144 372 B
michael.vargo@chemeketa.edu
VARGO, Valoree .... 330-672-2222 354 A
vvargo2@kent.edu
VARHOLAK, Mark .... 203-582-8613.. 88 G
mark.varholak@quinnipiac.edu
VARI, April .... 215-489-2413 382 B
april.vari@delval.edu
VARLEY, Steve .... 910-521-6000 343 B
VARLOTTA, Lori, E .... 805-493-3100.. 29 C
varlotta@callutheran.edu
VARMA, Mrinal .... 334-244-3600.... 4 E
varma@aum.edu
VARMA, Shanta .... 334-244-3272.... 4 E
svarma@aum.edu
VARNADO, Krystyna ..... 601-266-4050 249 F
krystyna.varnado@usm.edu
VARNELL, Jon .... 704-687-0513 342 D
jvarnell@uncc.edu
VARNER, David .... 402-472-3926 269 J
dave.varner@unl.edu
VARNER, Donica, T ...... 607-255-3903 297 F
dtv26@cornell.edu
VARNER, Donna, A .... 757-594-8816 465 M
dvarner@cnu.edu
VARNER, Jenny, M .... 336-249-8186 334 B
jmvarner@davidsondavie.edu
VARNER, Mary Helen ... 662-846-4011 245 G
mvarner@deltastate.edu
VARNER, Monica .... 918-631-3263 371 C
mkv4629@utulsa.edu
VARNER, Robin .... 859-280-1242 183 F
rvarner@lextheo.edu
VARNER, Stuart .... 731-989-6073 419 K
svarner@fhu.edu
VARNER, Tiffany .... 318-670-9692 191 D
twilliams@susla.edu
VARNER, Winship .... 775-831-1314 272 D
wvarner@sierranevada.edu
VARONA, Alina, R .... 415-883-2211.. 39 A
arvarona@marin.edu
VARSALONA, Jack, P .... 302-356-6818.. 91 E
officeofthepresident@wilmu.edu
VARSALONA, Jacque, R 302-295-1168.. 91 E
jacqueline.r.varsalona@wilmu.edu
VARSEK, Tamara, B ...... 814-393-1653 393 G
tvarsek@clarion.edu
VARSHNEY, Amitabh ..... 301-405-2316 202 H
varshney@umd.edu
VARSO, Shawn, V .... 330-941-3527 364 H
svvarso@ysu.edu
VARTANIAN, David, P .. 218-370-2374 229 I
vartania@oakland.edu
VARTANIAN, Lee .... 256-216-6608.... 4 C
lee.vartanian@athens.edu
VARY KEELE, Renee ...... 404-364-8868 123 K
rvary@oglethorpe.edu
VASALLO, Maria .... 617-873-0120 208 B
maria.vasallo@cambridgecollege.edu
VASAUSKAS, Audrey ..... 334-699-2266.... 1 B
avasauskas@acom.edu
VASCONCELLOS, Tina ... 510-748-2205.. 57 A
tvasconcellos@peralta.edu
VASCURA, Jacquelyn, L 740-826-8084 356 H
jkent@muskingum.edu
VASHAW, Tammy .... 603-342-3049 273 C
tvashaw@ccsnh.edu
VASILATOS-YOUNKEN,
Regina .... 814-865-2516 391 G
rxv@psu.edu
VASILE, Daniel .... 585-395-2226 317 E
dvasile@brockport.edu
VASINA, Mark .... 402-878-2380 267 D
mark.vasina@littlepriest.edu
VASKO, Genevieve .... 908-835-3135 284 H
vasko@warren.edu
VASKO, Tyler .... 307-532-8235 501 B
tyler.vasko@ewc.wy.edu
VASQUEZ, Amanda .... 973-720-2929 284 J
vasqueza@wpunj.edu
VASQUEZ, Amanda .... 915-747-5544 455 C
avasquez6@utep.edu
VASQUEZ, Becky, L ...... 386-226-6948.. 99 A
vasquezb@erau.edu
VASQUEZ, Diana .... 415-749-4534.. 61 C
dvasquez@sfai.edu
VASQUEZ, Francine ...... 602-286-8000.. 13 B
VASQUEZ, Graciela .... 562-860-2451.. 35 H
gvasquez@cerritos.edu
VASQUEZ, James .... 718-260-5604 295 A
jvazquez@citytech.cuny.edu
VASQUEZ, Jim .... 646-592-4416 326 D
jim.vasquez@yu.edu
VASQUEZ, John .... 616-234-5116 232 B
john.vasquez@vai.edu
VASQUEZ, Lisa, R .... 972-758-3894 433 I
lvasquez@collin.edu
VASQUEZ, Patrick .... 214-860-2094 434 I
patrick.vasquez@dcccd.edu
VASQUEZ, Richard, R ... 208-467-8499 132 E
rrvasquez@nnu.edu
VASQUEZ, Sandra .... 909-607-2821.. 57 E
VASQUEZ, Sandy .... 915-747-7873 455 C
svasquez@utep.edu
VASQUEZ, Vanessa .... 956-295-3605 449 C
vanessa.vasquez@tsc.edu
VASQUEZ, Wendy .... 510-628-8010.. 48 C
wvasquez@lincolnuca.edu
VASQUEZ-BROOKS,
Marie, E .... 407-582-5687 113 I
mvasquezbrooks@valenciacollege.edu
VASQUEZ DE VELASCO,
Guillermo .... 773-325-1858 136 H
gvv@depaul.edu
VASQUEZ HEILIG,
Julian .... 859-257-2000 185 F
jhe344@uky.edu
VASQUEZ-LEVY, David .. 510-849-8223.. 55 G
president@psr.edu
VASQUEZ-PORITZ,
Justin .... 718-260-5008 295 A
jvazquez-poritz@citytech.cuny.edu
VASQUEZ-SKILLINGS,
Rebecca .... 440-775-6453 357 G
rebecca.skillings@oberlin.edu
VASS, Dianna, J .... 410-951-3000 204 B
VASS, Mary-Hope .... 540-568-7487 468 C
vassmg@jmu.edu
VASSALLO, Thomas ...... 718-405-3722 296 F
thomas.vassallo@mountsaintvincent.edu
VASSAR, John .... 254-295-4505 453 D
jvassar@umhb.edu
VASSAR, Pam .... 913-469-8500 174 I
pvassar@jccc.edu
VASSELLI, John .... 713-718-5690 437 C
john.vasselli@hccs.edu
VATAN, Deanna .... 937-481-2242 364 A
deanna.vatan@wilmington.edu
VATANARTIRAN, Sinem 844-922-8228.. 91 G
VATANDOOST, Cyrus .... 615-514-2787 422 H
cyrus@nossi.edu
VATANDOOST, Nossi .... 615-514-2787 422 H
nossi@nossi.edu
VATH, Carrie .... 541-552-7672 376 B
VATISTAS, Vatistas .... 847-543-2375 136 A
vvatistas@clcillinois.edu
VATTEROTT, JR., John .. 314-423-1900 250 C
johnjr@stltrades.com
VAUCLIN, Danielle .... 985-448-5943 188 C
danielle.vauclin@fletcher.edu
VAUGHAN, Anthony ...... 212-678-8816 303 D
anvaughan@jtsa.edu
VAUGHAN, Cathy, A ..... 270-824-1705 182 D
cathy.vaughan@kctcs.edu
VAUGHAN, Chris .... 309-794-7292 133 C
chrisvaughan@augustana.edu
VAUGHAN, Chris .... 443-334-2690 202 E
cvaughan@stevenson.edu
VAUGHAN, Icer .... 316-942-4291 176 E
vaughani@newmanu.edu
VAUGHAN, John .... 626-914-8581.. 36 J
jvaughan@citruscollege.edu
VAUGHAN, John .... 360-475-7700 481 I
jvaughan@olympic.edu
VAUGHAN, Joseph .... 909-621-8613.. 44 H
joseph_vaughan@hmc.edu
VAUGHAN, K.T .... 540-458-8589 477 D
kvaughan@wlu.edu
VAUGHAN, Larry, F ...... 615-547-1222 419 C
lvaughan@cumberland.edu
VAUGHAN, Michael ...... 302-831-2401.. 91 C
vaughan@udel.edu
VAUGHAN, Renicka ...... 252-862-1308 337 C
rnvaughan@roanokechowan.edu
VAUGHAN, Steffanie ..... 336-506-4243 332 A
snvaughan776@alamancecc.edu
VAUGHAN, Timothy, S . 715-836-2500 495 E
vaughats@uwec.edu
VAUGHAN, William .... 303-384-2555.. 79 J
wvaughan@mines.edu
VAUGHAN-TUCKER,
Daenel .... 318-487-5443 187 J
dvaughantucker@cltcc.edu
VAUGHN, Andy .... 415-955-2001.. 24 J
VAUGHN, Bryan .... 903-886-5865 447 B
bryan.vaughn@tamuc.edu
VAUGHN, Caitlin .... 615-547-1307 419 C
cvaughn@cumberland.edu
VAUGHN, Chris .... 917-493-4486 305 A
cme@msmnyc.edu
VAUGHN, Debra .... 706-721-0211 116 A
dvaughn@augusta.edu
VAUGHN, Evan .... 843-383-8082 408 B
VAUGHN, Gary .... 806-291-3549 457 I
vaughng@wbu.edu
VAUGHN, James .... 405-224-3140 371 B
jvaughn@usao.edu
VAUGHN, Joyce .... 870-575-8188.. 22 D
vaughnj@uapb.edu
VAUGHN, Katie .... 501-882-8826.. 17 D
klvaughn@asub.edu
VAUGHN, Kellie .... 270-789-5173 180 A
kpvaughn@campbellsville.edu
VAUGHN, Lamont .... 773-442-4044 146 A
l-vaughn@neiu.edu
VAUGHN, Laura .... 865-882-4553 425 C
vaughnlp@roanestate.edu
VAUGHN, Patricia .... 336-757-7381 334 F
pvaughn@forsythtech.edu
VAUGHN, Patti .... 617-585-0200 207 A
patti.vaughn@the-bac.edu
VAUGHN, Robert .... 323-856-7661.. 25 G
rvaughn@afi.com
VAUGHN, Ronald, L ..... 813-253-6201 113 H
president@ut.edu
VAUGHN, Sheila .... 508-362-2131 214 D
VAUGHN, Woodrow ...... 256-726-7306.... 6 C
wvaughn@oakwood.edu

VAUGHT, Patrick .... 423-869-6241 421 A
patrick.vaught@lmunet.edu
VAUGHT, Wayne .... 801-863-8048 460 D
wvaught@uvu.edu
VAULTZ, Patrica .... 504-520-5237 193 E
pvaultz@xula.edu
VAUPEL, Christian, P .... 718-990-2781 313 G
vaupelc@stjohns.edu
VAVRA, Deborah .... 979-830-4241 431 H
dvavra@blinn.edu
VAZ, Pam .... 508-286-3485 220 B
vaz_pamela@wheatoncollege.edu
VAZ, Tammy .... 203-287-3036.. 88 E
VAZQUEZ, Adela .... 787-620-2040 505 C
avazquez@aupr.edu
VAZQUEZ, Airlyn .... 787-882-2065 510 C
avazquez@unitecpr.edu
VAZQUEZ, Carlo .... 412-237-3108 381 D
cvazquez@ccac.edu
VAZQUEZ, David .... 760-245-4271.. 74 D
david.vasquez@vvc.edu
VAZQUEZ, David .... 239-590-1121 109 K
dvazquez@fgcu.edu
VAZQUEZ, Dharma .... 787-758-2525 512 F
dharma.vazquez@upr.edu
VAZQUEZ, Edwin .... 787-738-2161 512 C
edwin.vazquez4@upr.edu
VAZQUEZ, Emsley .... 787-840-2575 509 I
evazquez@psm.edu
VAZQUEZ, Estrella .... 787-725-8120 506 M
evazquez@biblioteca.eap.edu
VAZQUEZ, Felice .... 908-737-7000 278 E
fvazquez@kean.edu
VAZQUEZ, Fermin .... 305-237-1152 104 E
fvazque2@mdc.edu
VAZQUEZ, Héctor .... 787-765-3560 506 K
hectorvazquez@edpuniversity.edu
VAZQUEZ, Harry .... 787-779-2500 506 B
VAZQUEZ, Heber .... 787-834-9595 510 D
heberv@uaa.edu
VAZQUEZ, Ingrid .... 787-850-9374 512 D
ingrid.vazquez1@upr.edu
VAZQUEZ, Ismael .... 787-864-2222 508 C
VAZQUEZ, Jose .... 347-964-8600 291 J
jvazquez@boricuacollege.edu
VAZQUEZ, Juan .... 559-730-3700.. 39 B
juanv@cos.edu
VAZQUEZ, Julia .... 213-738-6608.. 66 B
jvazquez@swlaw.edu
VAZQUEZ, Katherine ..... 787-738-2161 512 C
katherine.vazquez1@upr.edu
VAZQUEZ, Maria .... 787-725-8120 506 M
mvazquez0060@eap.edu
VAZQUEZ, Marie .... 531-622-2430 267 G
mvazquez@mccneb.edu
VAZQUEZ, Nelly .... 787-738-2161 512 C
nelly.vazquez1@upr.edu
VAZQUEZ, Obed .... 925-969-2423.. 40 C
ovazquez@dvc.edu
VAZQUEZ, Patricia .... 617-745-3851 209 B
patty.vazquez@enc.edu
VAZQUEZ, Respicio .... 847-214-7760 137 F
rvazquez@elgin.edu
VAZQUEZ, Rita .... 312-915-7221 143 C
rvazquez@luc.edu
VAZQUEZ, Robert .... 719-336-6653.. 81 K
robert.vazquez@lamarcc.edu
VAZQUEZ, Rosabel .... 787-620-2040 505 C
rvazquez@aupr.edu
VAZQUEZ, Rosalyn .... 518-861-2580 305 C
rvazquez@mariacollege.edu
VAZQUEZ, Sheila .... 787-622-8000 511 D
svazquez@pupr.edu
VAZQUEZ, Silvio, E ...... 630-752-5562 153 C
silvio.vazquez@wheaton.edu
VAZQUEZ, Vilmaris .... 787-878-5475 507 L
vvazquez@arecibo.inter.edu
VAZQUEZ, Vivian .... 787-758-2525 512 F
vivian.vazquez4@upr.edu
VAZQUEZ-BARQUET,
Ernesto .... 787-754-8000 511 D
evazquez@pupr.edu
VAZQUEZ-MARTINEZ,
Ernesto .... 787-622-8000 511 D
evazquezjr@pupr.edu
VAZQUEZ MEDINA,
Edwin .... 787-890-2681 511 G
edwin.vazquez7@upr.edu
VAZQUEZ-SOTOMAYOR,
Mariely .... 787-998-8997 509 M
mvazquez@eeapr.org
VAZSONYI, Nicholas ...... 864-656-3084 407 E
vazsony@clemson.edu

VEACH, Jason .... 816-268-5436 257 C
jveach@nts.edu
VEAL, Don-Terry .... 443-885-3035 201 A
don-terry.veal@morgan.edu
VEALE, Natasha .... 336-272-7102 329 C
VEARA, Dennis .... 248-218-2018 230 B
dveara@rochesteru.edu
VEARIL, Matt .... 303-494-7988.. 78 B
VEASLEY, Quintin .... 202-274-7254.. 94 B
quintin.veasley@udc.edu
VEATCH, John .... 818-667-2305.. 32 C
john.veatch@csun.edu
VEATCH, Laird .... 901-678-5395 426 G
lfveatch@memphis.edu
VEAZ, María, G .... 787-257-7373 510 F
m_veaz@uagm.edu
VECCHIO, Paul .... 607-871-2193 290 B
vecchio@alfred.edu
VECCHIO, Terry .... 508-854-4294 215 F
tvecchio@qcc.mass.edu
VECCHIONE, Tom .... 209-932-3042.. 71 E
tvecchione@pacific.edu
VEDDER, Kevin .... 931-372-3034 426 B
kvedder@tntech.edu
VEDDER, Kevin, A .... 410-546-6213 204 D
kavedder@salisbury.edu
VEDDER, Lori .... 810-762-3444 232 A
lvedder@umich.edu
VEDDERS, Michael .... 651-638-6094 234 D
vedmic@bethel.edu
VEDIA, Liliana .... 703-526-6922 468 H
lvedia@marymount.edu
VEEDER, Samantha .... 585-275-3226 323 M
sveeder2@finaid.rochester.edu
VEEGER, Anne .... 401-874-4408 405 E
veeger@uri.edu
VEER, Chelly .... 701-766-1302 344 G
chelly.veer@littlehoop.edu
VEGA, Aixa .... 787-834-9595 510 D
avega@uaa.edu
VEGA, Andre .... 617-570-4842 219 B
avega2@suffolk.edu
VEGA, Barbara .... 432-837-8810 450 B
bvega@sulross.edu
VEGA, Erlinda .... 787-264-1912 508 F
linvega@intersg.edu
VEGA, Evelyn .... 787-250-1912 508 D
evega@metro.inter.edu
VEGA, Fabian .... 713-718-2445 437 C
fabian.vega@hccs.edu
VEGA, Francesca .... 415-476-1000.. 70 D
francesca.vega@ucsf.edu
VEGA, Fredrick .... 787-250-1912 508 D
fredrickvega@metro.inter.edu
VEGA, Gregory .... 619-660-4030.. 44 D
gregory.vega@gcccd.edu
VEGA, Javier .... 212-592-2031 315 C
jvega@sva.edu
VEGA, Jesus .... 805-289-6507.. 74 B
jesusvega@vcccd.edu
VEGA, Magdalena .... 787-878-6000 507 D
mvega@icprjc.edu
VEGA, Manfredo .... 787-620-2040 505 C
mvega@aupr.edu
VEGA, Michelle .... 909-607-0821.. 37 F
michelle_vega@kgi.edu
VEGA, Natalie .... 303-273-3569.. 79 J
nvega@mines.edu
VEGA, Victor .... 734-973-3722 232 D
vvega@wcccnet.edu
VEGA, Waleska .... 787-761-0640 511 E
presidencia@utcpr.edu
VEGA, Zaida .... 787-766-1717 510 G
zvega@uagm.edu
VEGA-GONZALEZ,
Melvin .... 787-480-2426 506 C
melvega@sanjuan.pr
VEGA-LA SERNA,
Jennifer .... 559-730-3823.. 39 B
jenniferl@cos.edu
VEGERANO, George ...... 702-567-1920 270 I
gvegerano@lvcollege.edu
VEIL, Shari .... 402-472-3041 269 J
veil@unl.edu
VEIL-EHNERT, Jillain ..... 218-299-3556 235 H
ehnert@cord.edu
VEILLEUX, John, M ...... 989-774-3197 222 E
veill1jm@cmich.edu
VEIT, Kathy .... 650-723-2300.. 66 E
VEIT, Kenneth, J .... 215-871-6770 395 G
kenv@pcom.edu
VEIT, Linda .... 315-464-4513 317 C
veitl@upstate.edu

VEIT, Richard .... 732-571-3419 279 A
rveit@monmouth.edu
VEITCH, Dionne .... 814-824-3315 389 G
dveitch@mercyhurst.edu
VELA, Cesar .... 956-721-5142 438 H
cvela@laredo.edu
VELA, Eddie .... 530-898-6171.. 30 D
evela@csuchico.edu
VELA, Jason .... 307-675-0889 501 G
jvela@sheridan.edu
VELA, III, Manuel .... 956-326-1300 446 E
manuel_vela@tamiu.edu
VELA, Robert .... 210-486-0959 428 G
rvela63@alamo.edu
VELA, Robert, H .... 210-486-0959 429 C
rvela63@alamo.edu
VELAR-PRIETO, Jorge ... 787-993-8869 512 A
jorge.velar@upr.edu
VELASCO, Amy .... 805-756-2982.. 29 I
aevelasc@calpoly.edu
VELASCO, Anna .... 858-653-6740.. 46 H
avelasco@jpcatholic.edu
VELASCO, Debbie .... 612-767-7064 233 H
debbie.velasco@alfredadler.edu
VELASCO, Steven, C ..... 805-893-2434.. 70 E
steven.velasco@ucsb.edu
VELASCO, Ulises .... 707-467-1037.. 51 F
uvelasco@mendocino.edu
VELASQUEZ, Andrea ..... 540-458-8700 477 D
velasqueza@wlu.edu
VELASQUEZ, Ashleigh ... 708-293-4624 151 A
ashleigh.velasquez@trnty.edu
VELASQUEZ, Crystal ..... 432-685-4675 440 B
crystalv@midland.edu
VELÁZQUEZ, Ginger ...... 217-333-9634 152 B
gmayol@uillinois.edu
VELAZQUEZ, Jonathan .. 787-279-1912 508 A
jvelazquez@bayamon.inter.edu
VELAZQUEZ, Julio .... 787-850-9367 512 D
julio.velazquez1@upr.edu
VELAZQUEZ, Leida .... 787-864-2222 508 C
leida.velazquez@guayama.inter.edu
VELAZQUEZ, Marisol .... 787-864-2222 508 C
marisol.velazquez@guayama.inter.edu
VELAZQUEZ, Marisol .... 708-656-8000 145 C
marisol.velazquez@morton.edu
VELAZQUEZ, Monica, A 972-599-3144 433 I
mvelazquez@collin.edu
VELAZQUEZ, Tania .... 631-451-4475 321 C
velazqt@sunysuffolk.edu
VELAZQUEZ, Tania .... 631-451-4475 321 D
velazqt@sunysuffolk.edu
VELAZQUEZ-OLIVER,
Yoel, A .... 787-725-6500 505 G
yvelazquez@albizu.edu
VELDHEER, Kristine ...... 773-371-5460 134 D
kveldheer@ctu.edu
VELDKAMP, David .... 407-278-4484 248 F
dveldkamp@rts.edu
VELEZ, Ada .... 787-878-5475 507 L
avelez@arecibo.inter.edu
VELEZ, Angel .... 787-250-1912 508 D
avelez@metro.inter.edu
VELEZ, Arlene .... 787-725-6500 505 G
arvelez@albizu.edu
VELEZ, Ashley .... 787-841-2000 509 J
avelez@pucpr.edu
VELEZ, Carlos .... 319-399-8000 164 F
cvelez@coe.edu
VELEZ, Carlos .... 802-443-5745 462 E
velezbla@middlebury.edu
VELEZ, Glenis .... 787-710-8999 506 G
glenis.velez@dewey.edu
VELEZ, Joel .... 787-841-2000 509 J
joel_velez@pucpr.edu
VELEZ, Larissa .... 214-648-2668 457 A
larissa.velez@utsouthwestern.edu
VELEZ, Luis .... 787-728-1515 513 D
luis.velez@sagrado.edu
VELEZ, Rosa .... 787-264-1912 508 F
rosa_velez@intersg.edu
VELEZ, Vanessa .... 787-844-8181 513 A
vanessa.velez@upr.edu
VELEZ, Wanda .... 646-378-6181 310 D
wanda.velez@nyack.edu
VELEZ, Wilda .... 787-743-4041 506 D
wilda.velez@columbiacentral.edu
VELEZ AROCHO,
Jorge, I .... 787-841-2000 509 J
jivelezarocho@pucpr.edu
VELEZ-LUCE, Melissa .... 773-244-4796 145 G
mvelezluce@northpark.edu

VELEZ RIVERA,
Bienvenido .... 787-265-3822 512 E
decano.ingenieria@upr.edu
VELEZ-RUBIO, Miguel ... 787-993-8850 511 F
rectoria.uprb@upr.edu
VELEZ-RUBIO, Miguel ... 787-993-8850 512 A
miguel.velez@upr.edu
VELEZ-VENDRELL,
Norma .... 210-486-4516 428 I
nvelez-vendrell@alamo.edu
VELGUTH, Peter .... 989-317-4629 228 B
pvelguth@midmich.edu
VELIKY, Dawn .... 252-536-7227 335 B
rveliky004@halifaxcc.edu
VELKAVRH, Nick .... 562-907-4245.. 76 B
nvelkavrh@whittier.edu
VELKOFF, Townsend ..... 570-321-4258 389 B
velkoff@lycoming.edu
VELLECA, Kim .... 405-682-7595 367 D
kvelleca@occc.edu
VELLIOS, Kathryn .... 908-709-7062 284 D
kathryn.vellios@ucc.edu
VELLUZZI, Nicholas ...... 509-527-3685 485 B
nicholas.velluzzi@wwcc.edu
VELONI, Mary .... 888-777-7675 480 D
mveloni@faithseminary.edu
VELORIA, Ruth .... 602-557-1544.. 16 G
ruth.veloria@phoenix.edu
VELTRI, Linda .... 541-684-7338 371 I
lveltri@bushnell.edu
VELTSOS, Jennifer .... 507-389-1334 239 D
jennifer.veltsos@mnsu.edu
VELVEL, Lawrence, R .... 978-681-0800 216 C
velvel@mslaw.edu
VELZY, Kevin .... 315-312-5555 318 D
kevin.velzy@oswego.edu
VENABLE, James, E ...... 901-722-3260 423 G
jvenable@sco.edu
VENABLE, Margaret .... 706-272-4436 118 B
mvenable@daltonstate.edu
VENABLE, Margo .... 856-227-7200 276 E
mvenable@camdencc.edu
VENCAK, Denise .... 718-990-1435 313 G
vencakd@stjohns.edu
VENCILL, Jason .... 276-964-7251 475 C
jason.vencill@sw.edu
VENDERLEY, Emily .... 260-481-6322 160 C
emily.venderley@pfw.edu
VENDIOLA, Rudy .... 360-676-2772 481 F
rvendiola@nwic.edu
VENDITTELLI, Deborah .. 734-462-4400 230 G
dventitt@schoolcraft.edu
VENDITTI, Ferdinand ..... 518-262-5376 289 L
venditf@amc.edu
VENDRELY, Ann .... 574-535-7503 155 E
dean@goshen.edu
VENDRICK, Baxter .... 757-594-8987 465 M
baxter.vendrick@cnu.edu
VENEGAS, Clare .... 972-721-5179 452 B
cvenegas@udallas.edu
VENEGAS, Kristan .... 909-448-4995.. 71 C
kvenegas2@laverne.edu
VENEGAS, Stephanie ..... 575-624-7000 286 C
VENEGAS, Valerie, A .... 714-892-7711.. 38 A
vvenegas@gwc.cccd.edu
VENEKLASE, Dave .... 616-732-1195 223 E
dveneklase@davenport.edu
VENEMA, Cornelius ...... 219-864-2400 159 N
cvenema@midamerica.edu
VENERO, Sherri .... 715-682-1841 494 G
svenero@northland.edu
VENERO, Sherri .... 715-682-1824 494 G
svenero@northland.edu
VENETO, Dominic .... 904-256-7715 102 H
dveneto@ju.edu
VENEZIA, Shannon .... 806-742-3681 450 F
shannon.venezia@ttu.edu
VENKAT, Rama .... 702-895-1094 271 D
rama.venkat@unlv.edu
VENKATACHALAM,
Venky .... 605-658-6517 416 D
venky.venkatachalam@usd.edu
VENKATARAMAN, Latha 212-854-2255 297 C
lv2117@columbia.edu
VENKATARAMANAN,
Munirpallam, A .... 812-855-9011 156 G
vpfs@indiana.edu
VENKATESH, Karthik ..... 866-492-5336 244 F
karthik.venkatesh@laureate.net
VENKATESWARAN,
Anuradha .... 937-708-5633 363 G
a1venkateswaran@wilberforce.edu
VENN, Martha .... 404-962-3097 127 D
martha.venn@usg.edu

VENTI, Kimberly, A ... 716-888-8220 292 F ventik@canisius.edu
VENTIMIGLIA, Phil ... 404-413-4701 120 E pventimiglia@gsu.edu
VENTO, Jaclyn ... 516-628-5021 318 C ventoj@oldwestbury.edu
VENTO-CIFELLI, Lauren ... 732-571-3562 279 A lvento@monmouth.edu
VENTURA, Elizabeth, E ... 301-243-2045 502 L elizabeth.ventura@dodiis.mil
VENTURA, Heidi ... 615-248-1529 426 D hrventura@trevecca.edu
VENTURA, Jamey ... 802-635-1285 463 G jamey.ventura@northernvermont.edu
VENTURA, Sid ... 757-401-6125 477 G
VENTURA, Valerie ... 617-573-8120 219 B vventura@suffolk.edu
VENTURA, Yoav ... 626-264-8880 71 F
VENTURA-MENDOZA, Oscar ... 703-284-5711 468 H oscar.ventura-mendoza@marymount.edu
VENUGOPALAN, Devarajan ... 414-323-9790 496 B dv@uwm.edu
VENUTI, John, A ... 804-828-1210 473 B javenuti@vcu.edu
VENUTO, Mary Clare ... 856-225-6756 281 G maryclare.venuto@rutgers.edu
VER BERKMOES, John ... 616-945-5300 223 C john.verberkmoes@cornerstone.edu
VER STEEG, Jennie, E ... 515-643-6612 168 D jversteeg@mercydesmoines.org
VERA, David ... 617-449-7070 219 D
VERA-MORALES, Sheila 787-480-2451 506 C svera01@sanjuan.pr
VERBECK, Susan ... 308-635-6101 270 C sverbeck@wncc.edu
VERBOSH, Kyle ... 717-871-7871 395 A kyle.verbosh@millersville.edu
VERBOSH, Kyle, W ... 717-871-7871 395 A kyle.verbosh@millersville.edu
VERCH, Christopher ... 507-457-1709 243 C cverch@smumn.edu
VERCHER, Kathy ... 318-678-6000 187 H kvercher@bpcc.edu
VERCHER, Kevin ... 318-473-6497 189 F kvercher@lsua.edu
VERDERAME, Michael ... 847-982-2500 138 I verderame@htc.edu
VERDERBER, Carl ... 845-752-3000 323 I carlv@uts.edu
VERDEROSA, Patricia, K ... 717-337-6225 384 D pverdero@gettysburg.edu
VERDICCHIO, James ... 718-289-5923 293 B james.verdicchio@bcc.cuny.edu
VERDICCHIO, James ... 914-323-6001 315 A jverdicchio@sarahlawrence.edu
VERDILE, Vincent, P ... 518-262-6008 289 L verdilv@amc.edu
VERDIN, Regina ... 985-448-5908 188 C regina.verdin@fletcher.edu
VERDUCE, Cynthia, P ... 260-422-5561 156 E cpverduce@indianatech.edu
VERDUGO, Jason ... 651-523-2035 236 B jverdugo@hamline.edu
VERDUZCO, Oscar ... 509-574-4937 486 D overduzco@yvcc.edu
VERES, Joe ... 602-639-7500 12 J
VERES, Karen ... 610-861-5344 391 C kveres@northampton.edu
VERES, Madalina ... 215-596-8800 401 E
VERGARA, Derek ... 714-432-5741 38 B dvergara2@occ.cccd.edu
VERGNETTI, Stephenie ... 570-702-8944 386 D svergnetti@johnson.edu
VERHASSELT, Holly ... 706-867-3281 127 A holly.verhasselt@ung.edu
VERHOEVEN, Martin ... 707-621-7000 41 A
VERHOFF, Monica ... 419-448-2452 353 E mverhoff@heidelberg.edu
VERITY, Melena ... 301-696-3413 199 E verity@hood.edu
VERKAMP, Brian ... 270-809-2154 184 D bverkamp@murraystate.edu
VERKENNES, Joseph ... 734-384-4207 228 C jverkennes@monroeccc.edu
VERKRUYSE, Peter ... 217-732-3168 142 G pverkruyse@lincolnchristian.edu
VERLANIC, Amy ... 406-496-4289 265 A averlanic@mtech.edu
VERLENGIA, Andrew ... 515-271-3077 165 J andrew.verlengia@drake.edu
VERMA, Neena ... 617-353-2230 207 E neenav@bu.edu
VERMEER ELLIOTT, Julie ... 712-707-7200 169 D julie.elliott@nwciowa.edu
VERMEULEN, Jeffrey ... 717-815-6601 403 F jvermuel@ycp.edu
VERMEYCHUK, Janice ... 609-771-2483 276 I vermeyj@tcnj.edu
VERMILLION, Laurel ... 701-854-8014 346 H laurel.vermillion@sittingbull.edu
VERMUND, Sten ... 203-785-2867 90 C sten.vermund@yale.edu
VERNAZA, Karinna ... 814-871-7912 384 A vernaza001@gannon.edu
VERNI, Christine ... 716-286-8124 309 H cverni@niagara.edu
VERNON, Andrea ... 406-243-5159 263 K andrea.vernon@umontana.edu
VERNON, Brian ... 203-837-8851 86 B vernonb@wcsu.edu
VERNON, David ... 973-655-4227 279 B vernond@montclair.edu
VERNON, Marc, T ... 757-825-2851 475 D vernonm@tncc.edu
VERNON, Mitzi ... 859-257-7619 185 F vernon@uky.edu
VERNON, Sonja ... 513-721-7944 353 C svernon@gbs.edu
VERNON WHITE, Marisa ... 440-366-7622 355 B
VERRECCHIA, Lynn ... 508-793-2011 208 D
VERRET, C. Reynold ... 504-520-7541 193 E president@xula.edu
VERRILL, Tom ... 423-236-2816 423 F tverrill@southern.edu
VERRY SIDORAN, Laura ... 321-632-1111 98 I
VERSLUYS, Susan ... 512-472-4133 443 F susan.versluys@ssw.edu
VERSTANDIG, Kimberly ... 860-439-2408 87 H kimberly.verstandig@conncoll.edu
VERSTEEG, Deanna ... 605-274-4191 414 G deanna.versteeg@augie.edu
VERTA, Larissa, M ... 610-799-1517 388 D lverta@lccc.edu
VERTHEIN, Matt ... 602-243-8072 13 F matthew.verthein@phoenixcollege.edu
VERTIN, Diane ... 218-723-6012 235 G dvertin@css.edu
VERTREES, Larry ... 314-719-8024 253 E lvertrees@fontbonne.edu
VERWOERD, Fred ... 706-419-1129 118 A fred.verwoerd@covenant.edu
VERYSER, Joseph, C ... 248-204-2818 227 A jveryser@ltu.edu
VERZINSKI, Becky ... 301-860-3501 204 A bverzinski@bowiestate.edu
VERZYL, Scott ... 803-777-7700 413 A verzyl@mailbox.sc.edu
VESCIO, Sara, L ... 716-888-8285 292 F vescio11@canisius.edu
VESEI, Charles ... 440-826-3579 348 D cvesei@bw.edu
VESELY, Mark ... 910-521-6375 343 B mark.vesely@uncp.edu
VESELY, Pamela ... 828-898-8734 330 E veselyp@lmc.edu
VESHI, Susan ... 508-213-2227 217 H susan.veshi@nichols.edu
VESPASIAN, Bill ... 828-835-4211 338 E bvespasian@tricountycc.edu
VESPER, Josh ... 308-635-6185 270 C vesperj@wncc.edu
VESPERMAN, Katie ... 608-663-3224 492 F kvesperman@edgewood.edu
VESS, Paula ... 704-669-4101 333 E vessp750@clevelandcc.edu
VESSELLA, Thomas ... 562-988-2278 25 L tvessella@auhs.edu
VEST, Ann ... 502-456-6509 185 A avest@sullivan.edu
VEST, Eric ... 479-619-4345 20 C evest@nwacc.edu
VEST, Kevin ... 903-510-2178 452 A kevin.vest@tjc.edu
VEST, Rick ... 334-514-5070 2 F rick.vest@istc.edu
VESTAL, Amber ... 406-994-2343 264 C amber.vestal1@montana.edu
VESTER, Jonathan, S ... 252-451-8364 336 E jsvester529@nashcc.edu
VETERI, Kathleen ... 646-745-8361 291 A kveteri@barnard.edu
VETETO, Steve ... 303-779-6431 43 D stephenveteto@gs.edu
VETRANO, Dawn ... 718-779-1499 311 E dvetrano@plazacollege.edu
VETTER, Charlene, J ... 716-878-4436 317 F vettercj@buffalostate.edu
VETTER, Chris ... 503-589-8180 372 H cvetter@corban.edu
VETTER, Kay ... 502-852-3551 186 A kay.vetter@louisville.edu
VETTER, Phyllis, J ... 801-585-7002 459 O phyllis.vetter@legal.utah.edu
VETTER, Shaun ... 559-934-2234 74 N shaunvetter@whccd.edu
VETTICKAL, Jay ... 866-294-3974 154 H jay.vettickal@ccr.edu
VEUM, David ... 218-739-3375 236 H dveum@lbs.edu
VEVE, Mia ... 210-567-2648 456 C veve@uthscsa.edu
VEYL, Traci ... 209-384-6034 52 A traci.veyl@mccd.edu
VEZINA, Michelle ... 859-344-3380 185 B vezinam@thomasmore.edu
VIA, Sandra ... 540-365-4394 467 B svia@ferrum.edu
VIAL, Theodore, M ... 303-765-3166 81 G tvial@iliff.edu
VIALA, Linda ... 212-686-9244 290 C
VIANDEN, Becky ... 608-785-8515 496 A bvianden@uwlax.edu
VIANO, Gavin ... 508-286-5699 220 B viano_gavin@wheatoncollege.edu
VIAR, David ... 818-240-1000 43 G dviar@glendale.edu
VIAUD, Cindy ... 713-525-2162 454 G viaudc@stthom.edu
VIBBERTS, Richard ... 860-528-4111 88 A rvibberts@goodwin.edu
VIBOCH, Paul ... 304-263-6262 487 F pviboch@martinsburgcollege.edu
VIBROCK, Randy, G ... 662-329-7436 248 A rgvibrock@muw.edu
VICARS, Ron ... 276-523-7478 474 D rvicars@mecc.edu
VICE, David ... 916-900-2850 26 C dvice@asher.edu
VICENS, Catalina ... 787-622-8000 511 D cvicens@pupr.edu
VICENTE, Edward ... 787-279-1912 508 A evicente@bayamon.inter.edu
VICHALES, Kevin ... 210-832-2198 453 C vichcales@uiwtx.edu
VICHOREK, Jestina ... 218-733-7677 238 G jestina.vichorek@lsc.edu
VICK, Dustin ... 205-453-6300 93 H
VICKER, Kevin ... 816-584-6517 258 C kevin.vicker@park.edu
VICKERMAN, Pat ... 309-438-8901 140 D pvicker@ilstu.edu
VICKERS, Haley ... 580-559-5203 365 K hvickers@ecok.edu
VICKERS, Kelly, G ... 706-886-6831 126 D registrar@tfc.edu
VICKERS, LouAnn ... 503-838-8888 377 D vickersl@wou.edu
VICKERS, Neil, W ... 512-223-1098 430 I nvickers@austincc.edu
VICKERS, Selwyn, M ... 205-934-1111 8 A smv@uab.edu
VICKERS, Tonya ... 912-871-7295 123 J tvickers@ogeecheetech.edu
VICKERY, Ann Marie ... 267-341-3211 385 J amvickery@holyfamily.edu
VICKERY, Joseph ... 334-386-7274 5 C jvickery@faulkner.edu
VICKERY, Julia ... 432-685-4503 440 B jvickery@midland.edu
VICKOUS, Natalie ... 270-384-8065 183 G vickousn@lindsey.edu
VICORY, John ... 425-889-5321 481 H john.vicory@northwestu.edu
VICTOR, Paula, T ... 562-903-6000 27 A paula.victor@biola.edu
VICTORIN-VANGERUD, Nancy, M ... 651-523-2878 236 B nvictorinvangerud01@hamline.edu
VICTORINE, Jon ... 978-934-5060 212 B jon_victorine@uml.edu
VICTORINO, Christine ... 951-827-7883 70 B christine.victorino@ucr.edu
VICTORY, Gregory, J ... 919-660-1050 328 F gregory.victor@duke.edu
VIDAL, Betsy ... 787-704-1020 506 D bvidal@columbiacentral.edu
VIDAL, Karyn, J ... 561-202-6333 102 G
VIDEKA, Lynn ... 734-764-5347 231 H lvideka@umich.edu
VIDLER, Lynn ... 719-255-4550 84 C lvidler@uccs.edu
VIDMAR, Anthony ... 940-397-4782 440 C anthony.vidmar@msutexas.edu
VIDRINE, Tammy ... 225-768-1773 187 B tammy.vidrine@franu.edu
VIEIRA, Elvira ... 973-877-3062 277 G vieira@essex.edu
VIEIRA, Stephen ... 413-236-3003 214 A svieira@berkshirecc.edu
VIEIRA, Stephen ... 615-366-4451 423 H stephen.vieira@tbr.edu
VIELBIG, Matthew ... 425-235-7836 482 H mvielbig@rtc.edu
VIEN, Michele ... 518-694-7216 289 J michele.vien@acphs.edu
VIENNE, Charlie ... 936-294-1840 450 A cvienne@shsu.edu
VIENNE, Kristy ... 936-294-2274 450 A klv002@shsu.edu
VIENS, Rob ... 425-564-3158 477 J rob.viens@bellevuecollege.edu
VIERA, Eddie ... 561-868-3390 105 D vierae@palmbeachstate.edu
VIERBICKAS, Adam ... 660-543-4001 260 G avierbickas@ucmo.edu
VIERECK, Shannon ... 605-668-1467 415 F shannon.viereck@mountmarty.edu
VIERS, Christopher ... 812-855-9086 156 G cviers@iu.edu
VIERTEL, Cynthia, S ... 920-748-8312 494 J viertelc@ripon.edu
VIETEN, Shaun ... 323-860-1137 53 D shaunv@mi.edu
VIETHS, Brad ... 218-733-7600 238 G brad.vieths@lsc.edu
VIEWEG, Johannes ... 954-262-1506 105 A jvieweg@nova.edu
VIG, Megan ... 701-788-5254 345 D megan.vig@mayvillestate.edu
VIGDOR, Corey ... 908-737-4782 278 E cvigdor@kean.edu
VIGESAA, Linda ... 503-491-6928 374 B linda.vigesaa@mhcc.edu
VIGGERS, Victoria ... 915-831-6465 436 A vviggers@epcc.edu
VIGIL, Amanda ... 719-846-5011 83 L
VIGIL, Cynthia ... 509-533-3682 479 D cynthia.vigil@sfcc.spokane.edu
VIGIL, Julie ... 907-796-6494 10 B jlvigil@alaska.edu
VIGIL, Michael, J ... 303-369-5151 82 I michael.vigil@plattcolorado.edu
VIGIL, Renee ... 719-587-7526 77 G reneevigil@adams.edu
VIGIL, Vincent ... 657-278-4941 31 C vincentvigil@fullerton.edu
VIGIL, Virginia, P ... 505-467-6823 288 H vpvigil@swc.edu
VIGNATO, Linda ... 718-687-2671 314 A lvignato@sjcny.edu
VIGNES, Beau ... 251-981-3771 5 A beau.vignes@columbiasouthern.edu
VIGO-VERESTÍN, Milka ... 787-763-6700 507 A mvigo@se-pr.edu
VIGOREAUX, Jim ... 802-656-4627 463 A jim.vigoreaux@uvm.edu
VIGUERIA, Joseph, R ... 719-333-3205 503 D joseph.vigueria@usafa.edu
VIJAY MUNSHI, Natasha ... 502-272-8000 179 H
VIJITHA-KUMARA, Kanaka ... 309-467-6434 138 A kumara@eureka.edu
VILA, Cheryl, T ... 692-625-3394 504 G cvila@cmi.edu
VILA, Dendy ... 787-765-3560 506 K dmvila@edpuniversity.edu
VILACRUZ, Geraldo, G ... 608-246-6442 499 A gvilacruz@madisoncollege.edu
VILANOVA, Mayra ... 787-710-8999 506 G mayra.vilanova@dewey.edu
VILARDI, Robert ... 334-241-5919 7 C rvilardi@troy.edu

VILCHIZ, Victor .... 678-359-5197 120 F
vvilchiz@gordonstate.edu
VILE, John, R .... 615-898-2596 422 C
john.vile@mtsu.edu
VILEGI PAYNE,
Deborah .... 570-740-0232 389 A
dvilegi@luzerne.edu
VILELLE, Luke .... 540-362-6592 467 H
lvilelle@hollins.edu
VILKINA, Galina .... 212-616-7270 301 C
galina.vilkina@helenefuld.edu
VILLA, Cynthia .... 805-756-2171.. 29 I
cvvilla@calpoly.edu
VILLA, Gary 561-237-7025 103W
gvilla@lynn.edu
VILLAFANIA, John, A .... 692-625-5427 504 G
javillafania@cmi.edu
VILLAGOMEZ, Maria ..... 707-256-7156.. 53 E
mvillagomez@napavalley.edu
VILLAGOMEZ, Rosita .... 718-405-3275 296 F
rosita.villagomez@mountsaintvincent.edu
VILLALBA, Tabitha .... 559-442-8281.. 67 B
tabitha.villalba@fresnocitycollege.edu
VILLALOBOS, Alfredo .... 305-266-7678 104 A
a.villalobos@miuniversity.edu
VILLALOBOS, Bobbi ...... 310-233-4028.. 49 B
villalb@lahc.edu
VILLALOBOS, Joshua, I 915-831-7002 436 A
jvillal6@epcc.edu
VILLALONGA, Maria .... 787-720-1022 505 E
VILLALPANDO, Octavio . 323-343-3800.. 31 E
ovillal9@calstatela.edu
VILLALPANDO, Raoul .... 209-946-7337.. 71 E
rvillalpando@pacific.edu
VILLALVA, Maribel .... 915-747-6463 455 C
mvillalva2@utep.edu
VILLAMARIA, Paul .... 303-282-3318.. 83 H
paul.villamaria@archden.org
VILLANI, Jenna .... 973-720-2175 284 J
villanij3@wpunj.edu
VILLANO, Steven .... 713-226-5244 453 A
villanos@uhd.edu
VILLANUEVA, Ana, M ... 787-284-1912 508 E
avillanu@ponce.inter.edu
VILLANUEVA, Arelis ...... 787-766-1717 510 G
avillanueva@suagm.edu
VILLANUEVA, Celeste ... 510-879-9262.. 60 C
cvillanueva@samuelmerritt.edu
VILLANUEVA, Christina . 210-431-6789 442 J
cvillanueva@stmarytx.edu
VILLANUEVA, Daniel ..... 713-221-8136 453 A
villanuevad@uhd.edu
VILLANUEVA,
Donna-Mae .... 818-719-6444.. 49 D
villandm@piercecollege.edu
VILLANUEVA, Gil .... 804-289-8640 472 C
gvillanu@richmond.edu
VILLANUEVA,
Guillermo .... 415-239-3994.. 36 K
gvillanu@ccsf.edu
VILLANUEVA, Lynda ..... 281-425-6550 438 I
lvillanueva@lee.edu
VILLANUEVA, Naomi ..... 505-426-2138 286 J
naomivillanueva@sodexo.com
VILLANUEVA, Rebecca .. 432-264-5190 437 F
rvillanueva@howardcollege.edu
VILLANUEVA, Sandra .... 847-543-2419 136 A
svillanueva3@clcillinois.edu
VILLANUEVA,
Tammy, M .... 518-562-4100 296 A
tammy.villanueva@clinton.edu
VILLANUEVA-RUSSELL,
Yvonne .... 903-468-8225 447 B
yvonne.vrussell@tamuc.edu
VILLARE, Kathryn .... 978-681-0800 216 C
kvillare@mslaw.edu
VILLAROSE, Lesley .... 704-406-4373 329 A
lvillarose@gardner-webb.edu
VILLARREAL, Elisabeth .. 210-829-2736 453 C
villaret@uiwtx.edu
VILLARREAL, James ...... 210-431-4312 442 J
jvillarreal12@stmarytx.edu
VILLARREAL, Jose .... 323-265-8755.. 48 J
villarj@elac.edu
VILLARREAL, Luis .... 956-295-3802 449 C
luis.villarreal@tsc.edu
VILLARREAL, Mary Ann 801-581-7569 459 O
maryann.villarreal@utah.edu
VILLARREAL, Natalie ..... 361-698-1230 435 G
nvillarreal7@delmar.edu
VILLARREAL, Oscar .... 559-925-3347.. 75 B
oscarvillarreal@whccd.edu

VILLARREAL, Pete .... 530-741-6853.. 77 E
pvillarreal@yccd.edu
VILLARREAL, Sarah .... 760-750-4141.. 33 A
svillarr@csusm.edu
VILLARREAL, Velda .... 210-485-0735 428 G
vvillarreal@alamo.edu
VILLARREAL COOPER,
Tina .... 361-991-9403 445 D
VILLARRUEL, Antonia .... 215-898-8283 400 F
nursingdean@nursing.upenn.edu
VILLARUZ, Arlene .... 714-449-7437.. 51 B
avillaruz@ketchum.edu
VILLASENOR, Javier .... 562-938-4268.. 48 F
jvillasenor@lbcc.edu
VILLASENOR, Leslie ...... 312-261-3912 145 D
lvillasenor1@nl.edu
VILLASENOR, Marybel .... 956-665-2957 455 D
marybel.villasenor@utrgv.edu
VILLAVERDE, Cynthia .... 202-994-7618.. 92 D
cvillaverde@gwu.edu
VILLEGAS, Elias .... 503-316-3259 372 B
ellias.villegas@chemeketa.edu
VILLEGAS, Kevin .... 717-766-2511 389 H
kvillega@messiah.edu
VILLEGAS, Lucille .... 310-954-4010.. 52 I
lvillegas@msmu.edu
VILLEGAS, Michael .... 909-607-8509.. 37 C
mike.villegas@sodexo.com
VILLEGAS, Richard .... 925-473-7605.. 40 D
rvillegas@losmedanos.edu
VILLEGAS GOLD,
Robert .... 602-285-7397.. 13 F
robert.villegas.gold@phoenixcollege.edu
VILLEGAS-VIDAL, Ludi .. 818-364-7643.. 49 C
villegl@lamission.edu
VILLELLA, John .... 610-436-3111 395 D
jvillella@wcupa.edu
VILLELLA, Theresa .... 814-732-1297 394 B
tvillella@edinboro.edu
VILLENEUVE, Martha ..... 603-897-8260 273 I
mvilleneuve@rivier.edu
VILLETT, Steve .... 207-947-4591 194 B
svillett@bealcollege.edu
VILLOLDO, Sergio .... 787-754-8000 511 D
svilloldo@pupr.edu
VINAL, Alicia .... 978-232-2271 209 E
avinal@endicott.edu
VINCE, Morris .... 812-866-7039 155 G
morris@hanover.edu
VINCE, Savannah .... 919-866-5142 338 G
svince@waketech.edu
VINCENT, Alisha .... 605-995-2933 415 A
alisha.vincent@dwu.edu
VINCENT, Amanda .... 479-248-7236.. 19 B
registrar@ecollege.edu
VINCENT, Andrew .... 502-897-4785 184 G
avincent@sbts.edu
VINCENT, Angela .... 814-732-2921 394 B
vincent@edinboro.edu
VINCENT, Christine, L .. 815-835-6376 149 E
christine.l.vincent@svcc.edu
VINCENT, Danny, E .... 740-826-8110 356 H
dvincent@muskingum.edu
VINCENT, Deborah, S ... 708-239-4793 151 A
deborah.vincent@trnty.edu
VINCENT, Jennifer .... 508-678-2811 214 B
jennifer.vincent@bristolcc.edu
VINCENT, Jessica .... 304-473-8397 491 D
vincent_j@wvwc.edu
VINCENT, Peter .... 518-262-5253 289 L
vincenp@amc.edu
VINCENT, Renee .... 806-934-7221 429 E
lrvincent@actx.edu
VINCENT, Sara .... 860-512-3213.. 86 G
svincent@manchestercc.edu
VINCENT-DUNN, James 317-738-8075 155 D
jvincent-dunn@franklincollege.edu
VINCITORE, Rachel .... 757-631-8101 464 H
rachel.vincitore@atlanticuniv.edu
VINE, Scott .... 717-358-3843 383 I
scott.vine@fandm.edu
VINES, Andrew .... 562-860-2451.. 35 H
avines@cerritos.edu
VINES, Erin, E .... 661-722-6300.. 26 A
evines@avc.edu
VINES, Robert .... 239-590-7044 109 K
rvines@fgcu.edu
VINEYARD, George .... 314-454-8929 253 G
george.vineyard@barnesjewishcollege.edu
VINEYARD, Rusty .... 208-885-6246 132 F
vineyard@uidaho.edu

VINGER, Christopher .... 212-472-1500 309 D
christopher.vinger@nysid.edu
VINGOM, Troy .... 610-683-4000 394 D
vingom@kutztown.edu
VINH, Dan .... 845-451-1494 297 G
dan.vinh@culinary.edu
VINIK, Frank .... 202-319-4177.. 92 A
vinik@cua.edu
VINING, Caroline .... 479-356-2071.. 18 C
cvining@atu.edu
VINING, Robert .... 563-884-5690 169 F
robert.vining@palmer.edu
VINK, Cher .... 715-675-3331 499 F
vink@ntc.edu
VINLOVE, Amy .... 907-474-6440.. 10 A
alvinlove@alaska.edu
VINROE, Richard .... 316-295-5911 174 A
vinroer@friends.edu
VINSON, III, Ben .... 216-368-4346 349 D
ben.vinson@case.edu
VINSON, Bonita .... 940-872-4002 440 F
bvinson@nctc.edu
VINSON, Daniel .... 414-930-3494 494 E
vinsond@mtmary.edu
VINSON, Richard .... 336-721-2619 340 A
richard.vinson@salem.edu
VINTINNER, David, P .... 212-998-8014 309 F
david.vintinner@nyu.edu
VINYARD, Lisa .... 636-481-3101 254 C
lvinyard@jeffco.edu
VINZE, Ajay, S .... 573-882-6688 261 A
vinze@missouri.edu
VIOLA, JR., Frank, J ..... 610-917-1409 401 G
fjviola@valleyforge.edu
VIOLA, Joe .... 541-383-7776 372 A
jviola@cocc.edu
VIOLA, Michael .... 925-631-4286.. 59 I
mviola@stmarys-ca.edu
VIOLANTE, Janice .... 401-341-2441 405 D
janice.violante@salve.edu
VIOLETT, Adrienne .... 406-477-6215 263 C
VIOLETT, Edward .... 225-768-1711 187 B
edward.violett@franu.edu
VIRAG, Amanda .... 901-678-2295 426 G
avirag@memphis.edu
VIRAMONTES, Angel ...... 310-287-4473.. 49 H
viramoa@wlac.edu
VIRAMONTES, Melanie . 505-224-3588 285 N
mviramontes@cnm.edu
VIRASAWMI, Errol .... 516-364-0808 308 D
errol@nycollege.edu
VIRES, Charles .... 731-989-6004 419 K
cvires@fhu.edu
VIRGIN, Richard, P .... 619-260-4770.. 72 I
rvirgin@sandiego.edu
VIRJEE,
Framroze (Fram) .... 657-278-8678.. 31 C
presidentvirjee@fullerton.edu
VIRK, Surinder .... 718-997-5760 295 B
surinder.virk@qc.cuny.edu
VIRTANEN, B. Louise .... 906-524-8313 226 C
dean@kbocc.edu
VIRTUE, Alicia .... 805-437-8911.. 30 C
alicia.virtue@csuci.edu
VISCHER, Robert, K ...... 651-962-4838 244 E
rkvischer@stthomas.edu
VISCONAGE,
Elizabeth, L .... 410-864-4261 202 C
bvisconage@stmarys.edu
VISCONTI, Charlene ...... 212-662-7100 323 K
VISCUSI, Peter .... 641-784-5115 166 E
viscusi1@graceland.edu
VISEL, OSB, Jeana .... 812-357-6721 161 A
jvisel@saintmeinrad.edu
VISENTIN, Héline .... 413-585-3913 218 H
hvisenti@smith.edu
VISGARDA, Stacia .... 610-372-4721 396 H
svisgarda@racc.edu
VISKOZKI, Lynette .... 318-869-5137 186 F
lviskozk@centenary.edu
VISOT, Cynthia, S .... 813-974-6442 111 C
cvisot@usf.edu
VISSER, Erik .... 707-864-7000.. 64 H
erik.visser@solano.edu
VISSER, Jen .... 319-895-4167 164 G
jvisser@cornellcollege.edu
VISSER, Sandra, L .... 616-395-7748 225 D
visser@hope.edu
VISSER, Sarah .... 616-526-6454 222 C
sav36@calvin.edu
VISUANO, Denise .... 503-838-8349 377 D
visuanod@wou.edu

VISWANATHAN, K.G ..... 516-463-5676 301 G
k.g.viswanathan@hofstra.edu
VISWANATHAN, Suresh 212-938-5592 319 E
sviswanathan@sunyopt.edu
VITA, Claudine .... 610-647-4400 385 L
cvita@immaculata.edu
VITA, Paul .... 314-977-2500 259 F
paul.vita@slu.edu
VITAL, Allen .... 256-372-5230.... 1 A
allen.vital@aamu.edu
VITALE, John .... 847-578-8638 148 F
john.vitale@rosalindfranklin.edu
VITALE, JR., Joseph ..... 440-775-5573 357 G
jvitale@oberlin.edu
VITALE, Michael .... 352-365-3520 103 U
vitalem@lssc.edu
VITALE, Sandy .... 860-773-1424.. 87 G
svitale@tunxis.edu
VITALOS, Mark .... 610-606-4642 380 D
mavitalo@cedarcrest.edu
VITANGCOL REGOSO,
Aimee .... 269-471-3375 221 D
aimeev@andrews.edu
VITANGELI, Kory, M ...... 317-788-3485 161 H
kvitangeli@uindy.edu
VITATOE, David .... 216-397-1984 353 O
dvitatoe@jcu.edu
VITATOE, Steve .... 216-397-4277 353 O
svitatoe@jcu.edu
VITEK, Melissa .... 215-780-1527 398 B
mvitek@salus.edu
VITELLI, Chris .... 209-384-6101.. 52 A
chris.vitelli@mccd.edu
VITELLI, Kelly .... 814-732-1965 394 B
kvitelli@edinboro.edu
VITELLI, Mary .... 407-628-6303 106 L
mvitelli@rollins.edu
VITELLO, Joan .... 508-856-5081 212 C
joan.vitello@umassmed.edu
VITIELLO, Joseph .... 973-443-8891 277 I
joseph_vitiello@fdu.edu
VITO, Christine .... 304-760-1700.. 93 H
VITO, Christine .... 704-499-9200.. 93 H
VITRANO, Judy .... 504-314-2783 191 F
jvitrano@tulane.edu
VITTEK, Jeremy .... 740-695-9500 348 E
jvittek@belmontcollege.edu
VITTETOE, Stanley .... 727-791-2475 107 E
vittetoe.stan@spcollege.edu
VITUCCI, Tom .... 954-262-7304 105 A
tomv@nova.edu
VITZELIO, Tom .... 951-571-6383.. 59 B
tom.vitzelio@mvc.edu
VIVANCO, Nayeli .... 617-746-1990 210 H
nayeli.vivanco@hult.edu
VIVEIROS, Derek .... 508-678-2811 214 B
derek.viveiros@bristolcc.edu
VIVERETTE, Maggie, J ... 229-333-5463 127 E
mviveret@valdosta.edu
VIVIAN, Daniel, T .... 716-645-4540 316 C
dtvivian@buffalo.edu
VIVIAN, Richard .... 773-256-0710 143 F
richard.vivian@lstc.edu
VIVIANO-BRODERICK,
Tamara .... 352-854-2322.. 97 N
vivianot@cf.edu
VIZENOR, Andrea .... 650-738-7124.. 62 L
vizenora@smccd.edu
VIZOSO, Elisabet .... 305-237-2222 104 E
evizoso@mdc.edu
VIZZIELLO, Daniella .... 203-582-7806.. 88 G
daniella.vizziello@quinnipiac.edu
VIZZUSI, Brian .... 530-749-3879.. 77 E
bvizzusi@yccd.edu
VLACH, Erin .... 614-222-4000 351 B
evlach@ccad.edu
VLADESCU, Bogdana ..... 914-674-7697 306 C
bvladescu@mercy.edu
VLAHAKIS, Stacy .... 312-261-3724 145 D
svlahakis@nl.edu
VLAHOS, John .... 408-741-4606.. 75 D
john.vlahos@westvalley.edu
VLAHOS, John .... 408-741-4606.. 75 E
john.vlahos@westvalley.edu
VLASIE, Schemamonk ... 530-467-3544.. 60 A
fv@spots.edu
VLASTOS, Elizabeth ...... 610-372-1722 378 G
elizabeth.vlastos@berks.edu
VO, Alexander .... 212-812-4090 308 G
avo@nycda.edu
VO, Khoi .... 912-525-5000 124 I
kvo@scad.edu

WADE, Charles .... 810-762-0409 228 F
chuck.wade@mcc.edu
WADE, Damon .... 941-487-5000 110 D
dwade@ncf.edu
WADE, Doug .... 503-517-1043 377 C
dswade@warnerpacific.edu
WADE, Elisabeth .... 707-664-2880.. 34 B
WADE, Gourjoine .... 830-372-8060 449 A
gwade@tlu.edu
WADE, Gwen .... 404-880-8290 117 C
gwade@cau.edu
WADE, H. Keith .... 863-638-2940 114 B
wadehk@webber.edu
WADE, Janice .... 386-481-2882.. 96 D
wadej@cookman.edu
WADE, Jennifer, G .... 901-843-3850 423 A
goodloe@rhodes.edu
WADE, John .... 510-215-3804.. 40 B
jwade@contracosta.edu
WADE, John .... 847-635-2602 146 G
jwade@oakton.edu
WADE, Juli .... 860-486-2713.. 89 D
juli.wade@uconn.edu
WADE, Kevin, J .... 252-335-3271 341 B
kjwade@ecsu.edu
WADE, Kristi .... 310-338-5334.. 51 A
kristi.wade@lmu.edu
WADE, Kyle .... 864-587-4387 412 F
wadek@smcsc.edu
WADE, Landon .... 253-879-3651 484 G
lwade@pugetsound.edu
WADE, Latasha .... 410-651-6508 203 D
lwade@umes.edu
WADE, Lisa .... 901-722-3265 423 G
lwade@sco.edu
WADE, MaryAlice .... 785-628-4539 173 H
mawade2@fhsu.edu
WADE, Noreen .... 516-572-7780 307 E
noreen.wade@ncc.edu
WADE, Raymond .... 417-447-4818 257 G
wader@otc.edu
WADE, Tamara .... 706-507-8800 117 H
WADE, Veronica .... 206-934-5216 483 D
veronica.wade@seattlecolleges.edu
WADE, William .... 662-621-4126 245 D
wwade@coahomacc.edu
WADE JOHNSON,
Regina .... 314-719-3627 253 E
rwadejohnson@fontbonne.edu
WADFORD, Alton .... 252-493-7745 336 H
awadford@email.pittcc.edu
WADLINGTON, Corey ... 270-534-3413 183 B
corey.wadlington@kctcs.edu
WADLINGTON, Derek ... 717-264-2062 403 C
derek.wadlington@wilson.edu
WADSWORTH, Andrea .. 413-236-3001 214 A
awadsworth@berkshirecc.edu
WADSWORTH, Michael . 248-370-3352 229 I
wadsworth@oakland.edu
WADY, Andrea .... 972-686-7878 442 B
WAECHTER, Carolyn ..... 563-876-3353 165 H
waechter@dwci.edu
WAER, Amy, L .... 979-436-9051 446 F
waer@tamu.edu
WAERS, Stephen .... 706-385-1348 124 E
stephen.waers@point.edu
WAGEMESTER, Doug .... 319-398-4909 167 J
dwageme@kirkwood.edu
WAGENBLAST, Thomas . 973-290-4265 282 I
twagenblast@steu.edu
WAGENER, Melanee ...... 513-244-4381 356 F
melanee.wagener@msj.edu
WAGENHEIM,
Christopher .... 717-396-7833 392 U
cwagenheim@pcad.edu
WAGER, Lisa .... 212-217-4700 299 D
lisa_wager@fitnyc.edu
WAGERS, Karen, C .... 859-280-1236 183 F
kwagers@lextheo.edu
WAGES, Charlene .... 843-661-1140 409 G
cwages@fmarion.edu
WAGES, Kelli, E .... 419-434-6954 362 D
wages@findlay.edu
WAGESTER,
Kimberly, A .... 989-774-7388 222 E
wages1ka@cmich.edu
WAGGONER, Earl .... 303-963-3485.. 78 H
ewaggoner@ccu.edu
WAGGONER, Jon, G ..... 334-844-4866.... 4 D
waggojg@auburn.edu
WAGGONER, Julia ...... 715-682-1279 494 G
jwaggoner@northland.edu
WAGGONER, Reneau .... 270-831-9625 182 A
reneau.waggoner@kctcs.edu
WAGGONER, Todd .... 417-862-9533 253 F
twaggoner@globaluniversity.edu
WAGGONER, Wes, K .... 214-768-2110 444 D
wwaggoner@smu.edu
WAGLEY, Spencer .... 903-675-6282 451 F
spencer.wagley@tvcc.edu
WAGNAC, Evens .... 973-877-3000 277 G
WAGNER, Alexander ...... 617-349-8509 211 C
alex.wagner@lesley.edu
WAGNER, Anthony, E ... 864-656-2421 407 E
wagnera@clemson.edu
WAGNER, Claire, M ...... 513-529-7592 356 A
wagnercm@miamioh.edu
WAGNER, Craig .... 715-422-5308 499 B
craig.wagner@mstc.edu
WAGNER, Dan .... 605-995-2145 415 A
dan.wagner@dwu.edu
WAGNER, Daniel .... 419-755-4817 357 B
dwagner@ncstatecollege.edu
WAGNER, Daniel, O ...... 419-755-4817 357 B
dwagner@ncstatecollege.edu
WAGNER, David .... 715-394-8596 497 C
dwagne13@uwsuper.edu
WAGNER, David, H .... 336-334-7880 341 D
dhwagner@ncat.edu
WAGNER, Deanna .... 614-236-6904 349 B
dwagner1453@capital.edu
WAGNER, OSB,
Francis DeSales .... 812-357-6611 161 A
fwagner@saintmeinrad.edu
WAGNER, James, M ..... 214-648-2168 457 A
james.wagner@utsouthwestern.edu
WAGNER, Jeff .... 320-308-2286 240 I
jswagner@stcloudstate.edu
WAGNER, Jodi .... 509-527-2772 485 C
jodi.wagner@wallawalla.edu
WAGNER, Katherine ...... 516-572-7487 307 E
katherine.wagner@ncc.edu
WAGNER, Kevin, J .... 740-826-6129 356 H
kevinw@muskingum.edu
WAGNER, Kimberly .... 260-481-6103 160 C
kimberly.wagner@pfw.edu
WAGNER, Kimberly .... 847-214-7124 137 F
kwagner@elgin.edu
WAGNER, Kurt .... 732-571-4401 279 A
kwagner@monmouth.edu
WAGNER, Kyle .... 843-921-6901 411 A
kwagner@netc.edu
WAGNER, Linda .... 305-628-6699 107 F
lwagner@stu.edu
WAGNER, Marci, K .... 724-450-4089 384 G
mkwagner@gcc.edu
WAGNER, Mark .... 312-329-4131 144 I
mark.wagner@moody.edu
WAGNER, Mary .... 803-777-7700 413 A
mary.wagner@sc.edu
WAGNER, Megan .... 863-667-5205 108 K
mmwagner@seu.edu
WAGNER, Michael, F .... 603-646-0459 273 D
michael.f.wagner@dartmouth.edu
WAGNER, Mike .... 309-556-3561 140 F
mwagner@iwu.edu
WAGNER, Nicholas, J ... 989-964-2468 230 E
njwagner@svsu.edu
WAGNER, Patrick .... 620-229-6210 177 G
patrick.wagner@sckans.edu
WAGNER, Rich .... 612-381-3099 235 K
rwagner@dunwoody.edu
WAGNER, Richard .... 413-782-1288 220 A
richard.wagner@wne.edu
WAGNER, Richard, T .... 240-895-3421 202 B
rtwagner@smcm.edu
WAGNER, Rick .... 812-357-6378 161 A
rwagner@saintmeinrad.edu
WAGNER, Robert .... 607-274-3860 302 G
rwagner1@ithaca.edu
WAGNER, Robert .... 212-563-6647 323 I
r.wagner@uts.edu
WAGNER, Robert .... 435-797-0945 460 C
robert.wagner@usu.edu
WAGNER, Robin .... 717-337-7000 384 D
rowagner@gettysburg.edu
WAGNER, Russell .... 361-825-2352 447 C
russell.wagner@tamucc.edu
WAGNER, Sam .... 814-886-6465 390 G
swagner@mtaloy.edu
WAGNER, Sharon .... 513-244-4273 356 F
sharon.wagner@msj.edu
WAGNER, Susan .... 520-795-0787.. 10 I
financialaid@asaom.edu
WAGNER, Todd .... 618-545-3259 141 E
twagner@kaskaskia.edu
WAGNER, Tonya .... 608-796-3376 497 O
WAGNER, Tracy, A .... 941-309-4376 106 J
twagner@ringling.edu
WAGNER DAVIS,
Jennifer (J.J.) .... 434-924-3252 472 D
jwd3n@virginia.edu
WAGNER-FOSSEN,
Dena .... 406-771-4312 264 F
dfossen@gfcmsu.edu
WAGNER-SCHULTZ,
Jessica .... 715-634-4790 492 L
jwschultz@lco.edu
WAGNON, Bill .... 601-635-6242 246 A
bwagnon@eccc.edu
WAGNON, Shelley .... 313-993-1588 231 E
wagnonsm@udmercy.edu
WAGNON, Stan .... 405-974-2500 370 I
swagnon1@uco.edu
WAGONER, Dale .... 510-723-6618.. 35 J
dwagoner@chabotcollege.edu
WAGONER, Faye .... 304-485-5487 487 G
WAGONER, Jessica, M . 909-869-3147.. 30 A
jmwagoner@cpp.edu
WAGONER, Natalie .... 301-687-4406 204 C
nmwagoner@frostburg.edu
WAGONER, Zandra, L ... 909-593-3511.. 71 C
zwagoner@laverne.edu
WAGSTAFF, Jennifer ..... 434-791-5624 464 I
jwagstaff@averett.edu
WAGUESPACK, Bruce .... 225-743-8500 188 H
bwaguespack@rpcc.edu
WAHAB, R. Lizzie .... 518-564-2000 318 E
WAHFELDT, Tracy .... 217-373-3789 147 C
twahlfeldt@parkland.edu
WAHL, Anne, G .... 585-475-7688 312 F
agwvpa@rit.edu
WAHL, Lynette .... 651-523-3000 236 B
lwahl@hamline.edu
WAHL, Shawn, T .... 417-836-5247 256 G
shawnwahl@missouristate.edu
WAHL, Todd .... 812-749-1242 159 O
twahl@oak.edu
WAHLBECK, Paul, J ...... 202-994-6130.. 92 D
ccasdean@gwu.edu
WAHLROOS-RITTER,
Ingalill .... 818-252-5185.. 76 E
ingalill.wahlroos-ritter@woodbury.edu
WAHLS, Dustha .... 217-234-5210 142 C
dwahls@lakeland.cc.il.us
WAHLSTROM, David, A 617-989-4552 219 F
wahlstromd@wit.edu
WAHLSTROM, Tomi ...... 251-626-3303.... 7 E
twahlstrom@ussa.edu
WAHLSTROM HELGREN,
Elizabeth .... 312-567-6917 140 A
ewahlstr@iit.edu
WAHR, David .... 567-661-7401 359 I
david_wahr@owens.edu
WAHR, Linda .... 312-329-2213 144 I
linda.wahr@moody.edu
WAIAMAU-ARIOTA,
Kawika .... 425-235-2352 482 H
kwaiamau-ariota@rtc.edu
WAIBEL, Janet .... 573-882-2011 260 I
waibelj@umsystem.edu
WAID, Monica, K .... 941-359-7514 106 J
mwaid@ringling.edu
WAID, Patti .... 562-951-4000.. 29 H
pwaid@calstate.edu
WAIDE, Michael, P .... 304-367-4284 488 H
michael.waide@pierpont.edu
WAIKART, Elise .... 801-626-5050 461 A
elisewaikart@weber.edu
WAINWRIGHT,
Christopher .... 386-506-3162.. 98 D
christopher.wainwright@daytonastate.edu
WAINWRIGHT, Philip .... 404-727-7504 118 E
pwainwr@emory.edu
WAINWRIGHT,
William, S .... 985-545-1500 188 E
WAIS, Marc, L .... 212-998-4401 309 F
marc.wais@nyu.edu
WAISMAN, Dov .... 213-738-5733.. 66 B
academicaffairs@swlaw.edu
WAIT, Julianna, M .... 757-594-7385 465 M
julianna.wait@cnu.edu
WAITE, Dan .... 848-932-7787 282 B
dwaite@global.rutgers.edu
WAITE, Dan .... 848-932-7787 282 A
dwaite@global.rutgers.edu
WAITE, Lucy .... 716-896-0700 324 E
lwaite@villa.edu
WAITE, Michelle .... 402-472-2116 269 J
mwaite1@unl.edu
WAITE, Peter .... 801-626-8957 461 A
pwaite@weber.edu
WAITE, Zauyah .... 413-559-5751 210 D
zwaite@hampshire.edu
WAITHAKA, Maina .... 847-970-4904 152 I
mwaithaka@usml.edu
WAITS, Laura .... 713-221-5026 453 A
waitsl@uhd.edu
WAITSMAN, Eileen .... 410-209-6050 198 B
ewaitsman@bccc.edu
WAITZ, Ian, A .... 617-253-0218 216 B
WAIWAIOLE, Evelyn ...... 254-298-8766 445 G
evelyn.waiwaiole@templejc.edu
WAJDA, Phillip, J .... 518-388-6131 323 J
wajdap@union.edu
WAJERT, Susan .... 419-251-1314 355 G
susan.wajert@mercycollege.edu
WAKEFIELD, Sarah .... 425-235-2285 482 H
swakefield@rtc.edu
WAKEM, Jake .... 651-641-8228 235 I
wakem@csp.edu
WAKEMAN, Roger, F .... 315-859-4506 300 H
rwakeman@hamilton.edu
WAKIMOTO, Roger .... 310-825-7943.. 69 E
rwakimoto@conet.ucla.edu
WAKSDAHL, Robert, B .. 715-394-8017 497 C
rwaksdah@uwsuper.edu
WALBORN, Ronald .... 646-378-6171 310 D
ronald.walborn@nyack.edu
WALCERZ, Douglas .... 281-425-6305 438 I
dwalcerz@lee.edu
WALCHER, Sheldon ...... 847-543-2551 136 A
swalcher@clcillinois.edu
WALCHESKI, Michael .... 651-603-6184 235 I
walcheski@csp.edu
WALCHLE, John .... 740-392-6868 356 G
john.walchle@mvnu.edu
WALCK, Barbara .... 716-614-5902 309 G
bwalck@niagaracc.suny.edu
WALCOTT, Rom .... 706-542-6392 126 G
rwalcott@uga.edu
WALCROFT, Marie, B .... 215-699-5700 387 H
mwalcroft@lsb.edu
WALCZYK, Christine ..... 619-298-1829.. 65 K
WALD, Cara .... 651-638-6400 234 D
c-wald@bethel.edu
WALDBILLIG, Amy .... 513-569-1414 350 F
amy.waldbillig@cincinnatistate.edu
WALDEN, Daniel, W ..... 760-245-4271.. 74 D
daniel.walden@vvc.edu
WALDEN, David .... 315-859-4340 300 H
dwalden@hamilton.edu
WALDEN, Lisa .... 505-277-7494 288 J
lwalden@unm.edu
WALDEN, Michelle .... 910-678-8400 334 E
WALDEN, Stacey .... 906-248-3354 221 M
WALDEN, Wendy .... 864-250-8125 409 I
wendy.walden@gvltec.edu
WALDHOF, Kenneth ...... 718-862-7362 304 M
kenneth.waldhof@manhattan.edu
WALDMAN, Chaim, A ... 718-259-5600 299 A
WALDMAN, Elisa .... 916-469-8500 174 I
ewaldman@jccc.edu
WALDMAN, Martin .... 718-853-8500 322 E
WALDMANN, Robert, G 718-429-6600 324 D
robert.waldmann@vaughn.edu
WALDNER, Louann .... 559-688-3027.. 39 B
louannw@cos.edu
WALDO, Hilary .... 678-916-2625 115 I
hwaldo@johnmarshall.edu
WALDON, James .... 609-896-5029 281 B
jwaldon@rider.edu
WALDON, Russell .... 650-738-7099.. 62 L
waldonr@smccd.edu
WALDRON, David, E ..... 512-448-8453 442 I
dwaldron@stedwards.edu
WALDRON, Donna .... 910-893-1576 327 D
waldron@campbell.edu
WALDRON, Gregory, T . 401-865-2290 404 F
gregory.waldron@providence.edu
WALDRON, Jennifer ...... 319-273-2748 164 A
jennifer.waldron@uni.edu
WALDRON, Jerry .... 410-651-8200 203 D
jwaldron@umes.edu
WALDRON, John .... 270-706-8545 181 G
jwaldron0004@kctcs.edu
WALDRON, Kim .... 719-389-6704.. 78 I
kwaldron@coloradocollege.edu

WALLACE, Christa .... 409-944-1314 436 E
cwallace@gc.edu
WALLACE, Christine .... 810-762-9575 226 B
cwallace@kettering.edu
WALLACE, Darcie .... 770-426-2925 122 C
darcie.wallace@life.edu
WALLACE, David .... 562-985-5381.. 31 D
david.wallace@csulb.edu
WALLACE, David .... 270-534-3859 183 B
david.wallace@kctcs.edu
WALLACE, David .... 909-607-8095.. 57 K
david.wallace@pomona.edu
WALLACE, Debbie .... 870-543-5996.. 21 B
dwallace@seark.edu
WALLACE, Deborah .... 310-243-3750.. 30 E
dwallace@csudh.edu
WALLACE, Denise .... 850-599-3591 109 I
denise.wallace@famu.edu
WALLACE, Donald .... 760-921-5499.. 56 A
donald.wallace@paloverde.edu
WALLACE, Douglas, J ... 864-833-8312 411 D
dwallace@presby.edu
WALLACE, Elaine .... 954-262-1407 105 A
ewallace@nova.edu
WALLACE, Eric, C .... 806-356-3682 429 E
ecwallace@actx.edu
WALLACE, G. Brent .... 940-668-4230 440 F
bwallace@nctc.edu
WALLACE, Glenn .... 912-525-5000 124 I
gwallace@scad.edu
WALLACE, Greg .... 617-879-7000 213 B
greg.wallace@massart.edu
WALLACE, Harold .... 931-221-6274 417 H
wallaceh@apsu.edu
WALLACE, JR., James .. 219-980-6601 157 C
jamewall@iun.edu
WALLACE, Jason .... 303-282-3423.. 83 H
father.wallace@archden.org
WALLACE, Jeff .... 765-998-5396 161 C
jfwallace@taylor.edu
WALLACE, Jeremy .... 303-963-3237.. 78 H
jerwallace@ccu.edu
WALLACE, Jermaine ...... 217-735-7350 142 H
jermaine.wallace@lincolncollege.edu
WALLACE, Jerry .... 402-461-2400 266 A
jerrywallace@cccneb.edu
WALLACE, Jerry .... 910-893-1880 327 D
wallace@campbell.edu
WALLACE, Joel .... 817-202-6333 444 I
jwallace@swau.edu
WALLACE, John, M .... 412-624-5749 400 H
johnw@pitt.edu
WALLACE, Justin .... 661-259-7800.. 38 D
justin.wallace@canyons.edu
WALLACE, Kim .... 303-404-5671.. 81 A
kim.wallace@frontrange.edu
WALLACE, Kim .... 303-404-5316.. 81 K
kim.wallace@frontrange.edu
WALLACE, Kimberly ...... 239-590-1087 109 K
kwilliam@fgcu.edu
WALLACE, Laura, J .... 434-592-7330 468 E
jwallac@liberty.edu
WALLACE, Laurie .... 314-744-5321 256 E
wallace@mobap.edu
WALLACE, Leigh .... 229-217-4143 126 A
lwallace@southernregional.edu
WALLACE, Lynn .... 610-526-1327 378 D
lynn.wallace@theamericancollege.edu
WALLACE, Matthew, L .. 603-931-4369 275 A
mlwallace@plymouth.edu
WALLACE, Mike, J .... 408-554-4981.. 63 B
mjwallace@scu.edu
WALLACE, Miriam .... 941-487-4360 110 D
mwallace@ncf.edu
WALLACE, Nancy .... 716-888-2768 292 F
wallacen@canisius.edu
WALLACE, Nick .... 651-423-8307 238 A
nick.wallace@dctc.edu
WALLACE, Paula .... 912-525-5000 124 I
pwallace@scad.edu
WALLACE, Ray .... 812-941-2200 157 F
raywall@ius.edu
WALLACE, Robert .... 903-657-6543 448 D
rwallace@tbi.edu
WALLACE, Robert .... 718-982-2635 293 E
robert.wallace@csi.cuny.edu
WALLACE, Robert .... 650-723-2300.. 66 E
WALLACE, Robert .... 304-766-4114 490 D
wallacer@wvstateu.edu
WALLACE, Sally .... 404-413-0046 120 E
swallace@gsu.edu
WALLACE, Sam, G .... 318-257-2769 192 D
wallace@latech.edu

WALLACE, Scott .... 985-867-2235 190 K
swallace@sjasc.edu
WALLACE, Scott .... 706-737-1411 116 A
scwallace@augusta.edu
WALLACE, Steve .... 501-977-2086.. 23 A
wallace@uaccm.edu
WALLACE, Suzanne .... 608-663-8334 492 F
suzwallace@edgewood.edu
WALLACE, Tamara .... 540-831-6374 469 D
twallace8@radford.edu
WALLACE, Tami .... 615-230-3573 425 E
tami.wallace@volstate.edu
WALLACE, Thomas .... 661-654-2161.. 30 B
twallace4@csub.edu
WALLACE, Tom .... 615-898-2137 422 C
tom.wallace@mtsu.edu
WALLACE, Tracy .... 229-430-3867 114 I
twallace@albanytech.edu
WALLACK, Jessica .... 253-589-5734 478 J
jessica.wallack@cptc.edu
WALLEN, Jillian .... 402-280-5061 266 H
jillianwallen@creighton.edu
WALLENMEYER, Mark ... 479-619-4310.. 20 C
mwallenmeyer@nwacc.edu
WALLER, Caroline .... 870-235-4129.. 21 C
carolinewaller@saumag.edu
WALLER, Cynthia, G ..... 615-353-3645 424 G
cynthia.waller@nscc.edu
WALLER, Edward .... 281-283-3100 452 E
waller@uhcl.edu
WALLER, J. Kerry .... 706-778-8500 124 D
WALLER, J.J .... 912-525-5000 124 I
jwaller@scad.edu
WALLER, Janet .... 256-824-7777..... 8 B
janet.waller@uah.edu
WALLER, Karen .... 615-230-3500 425 E
karen.waller@volstate.edu
WALLER, Lorie .... 919-735-5151 338 H
loriew@waynecc.edu
WALLER, Louise .... 434-395-2358 468 F
wallermw@longwood.edu
WALLER, Matthew .... 479-575-5949.. 21 F
mwaller@uark.edu
WALLER, Michelle .... 318-473-6443 189 F
cwaller001@lsua.edu
WALLER, Rhonda .... 336-278-5185 328 J
rwaller3@elon.edu
WALLER, Stephen .... 661-395-4642.. 46 L
swaller@bakersfieldcollege.edu
WALLESHAUSER,
Linda, M .... 716-888-2244 292 F
walleshl@canisius.edu
WALLETT, Robert .... 215-248-7163 381 A
wallett@chc.edu
WALLEY, Jennifer .... 559-251-4215.. 27 I
jwalley@calchristiancollege.edu
WALLEY, Jim .... 601-477-4173 246 G
jim.walley@jcjc.edu
WALLEY, Katrina .... 575-769-4034 285 O
katrina.walley@clovis.edu
WALLEY, Trent .... 559-251-4215.. 27 I
twalley@calchristiancollege.edu
WALLHAUSSER, Karl ..... 606-546-1424 185 D
kwallhausser@unionky.edu
WALLIN, Cynthia .... 434-832-7707 473 E
wallinc@centralvirginia.edu
WALLIN, Gail .... 254-519-8025 447 A
gwallin@tamuct.edu
WALLIN, John .... 603-862-1234 274 F
john.wallin@unh.edu
WALLIN, Jon .... 540-261-4095 471 B
jon.wallin@svu.edu
WALLIN, Jonathan .... 540-261-8400 471 B
jon.wallin@svu.edu
WALLIN, Julie .... 917-493-4595 305 A
jwallin@msmnyc.edu
WALLIN, Kimberly .... 701-231-7411 345 F
kimberly.wallin@ndsu.edu
WALLIN, William .... 303-329-6355.. 79 L
director@cstcm.edu
WALLING, Lisa .... 931-526-3660 419 I
lisaq.walling@fortisinstitute.edu
WALLING, Ray .... 785-594-8389 171 F
ray.walling@bakeru.edu
WALLINGA, Michael .... 712-707-7108 169 D
mwalling@nwciowa.edu
WALLINGA, Willem .... 617-670-4457 209 G
wwallinga@fisher.edu
WALLINGTON, Jamison 323-668-7555.. 25 B
WALLINGTON-HARRIS,
Danielle .... 773-907-6834 135 C
dwallington-harris@ccc.edu

WALLIS, Donna .... 931-372-3492 426 B
dwallis@tntech.edu
WALLIS, OSB,
Jonathan .... 985-867-2287 190 K
WALLIS, Matthew .... 817-257-5808 448 F
matthew.wallis@tcu.edu
WALLIS, Sherry, L .... 660-263-3900 251 D
sherrywallis@cccb.edu
WALLMAN, Coree .... 415-771-7020.. 61 C
cwallman@sfai.edu
WALLMAN, Eric .... 407-582-2814 113 I
ewallman@valenciacollege.edu
WALLMAN, Marc .... 701-231-8640 345 F
marc.wallman@ndsu.edu
WALLNER, Heidi .... 715-346-2926 497 A
hwallner@uwsp.edu
WALLNER, Steve .... 262-595-2451 496 D
wallner@uwp.edu
WALLS, Caitlin .... 907-319-8755.... 9 H
caitlin.walls@ilisagvik.edu
WALLS, Eric, R .... 210-562-6201 456 C
wallse@uthscsa.edu
WALLS, Harry .... 661-362-2620.. 51 D
hwalls@masters.edu
WALLS, Keith .... 610-921-6619 377 G
kwalls@albright.edu
WALLS, Maryanna .... 301-962-5111 205 E
mwalls@yeshiva.edu
WALLS, Renee .... 870-230-5640.. 19 D
wallsr@hsu.edu
WALLS-MCKAY,
Maureen, J .... 434-395-2409 468 F
wallsmckaymj@longwood.edu
WALLSTEADT, Nicholas . 863-667-5493 108 K
ndwallsteadt@seu.edu
WALMSLEY, Fran .... 215-713-4171 391 A
walmesf@neumann.edu
WALPIN, Edward .... 505-984-6050 288 C
edward.walpin@sjc.edu
WALPOLE, Tommy .... 318-342-5419 193 C
walpole@ulm.edu
WALROND, LaKeesha .... 212-870-1222 309 E
lwalrond@nyts.edu
WALSH, Beth .... 630-752-5072 153 C
beth.walsh@wheaton.edu
WALSH, Brendan .... 845-451-1616 297 G
brendan.walsh@culinary.edu
WALSH, Carolyn .... 815-479-7837 143 I
cwalsh97@mchenry.edu
WALSH, Clifton .... 915-747-6636 455 C
cwalsh@utep.edu
WALSH, Debra .... 323-469-3300.. 24 P
dwalsh@amda.edu
WALSH, Denise .... 516-299-2000 304 E
denise.walsh@liu.edu
WALSH, Elizabeth, K ..... 610-660-1000 397 G
lkwalsh@sju.edu
WALSH, Eric .... 603-524-3207 272 K
ewalsh@ccsnh.edu
WALSH, Jack .... 724-266-3838 400 B
jwalsh@tsm.edu
WALSH, Jay .... 217-244-2119 151 F
jaywalsh@uillinois.edu
WALSH, Jennifer .... 808-544-0216 128 G
provost@hpu.edu
WALSH, Jennifer .... 516-877-4687 289 I
jenwalsh@adelph.edu
WALSH, Jill .... 484-664-3165 390 H
jillwalsh@muhlenberg.edu
WALSH, Joe .... 256-782-5616.... 6 A
ejwalsh@jsu.edu
WALSH, Julie .... 845-257-2632 316 E
walshj@newpaltz.edu
WALSH, Kate, D .... 607-255-5106 297 F
kmw33@cornell.edu
WALSH, Kenneth .... 617-573-8111 219 B
kwalsh4@suffolk.edu
WALSH, Kenneth .... 703-993-1000 467 E
WALSH, Kimberly, A ..... 563-588-7417 168 A
kimberly.walsh@loras.edu
WALSH, Konrad .... 336-734-7495 334 F
kwalsh@forsythtech.edu
WALSH, Lenore, J .... 516-876-4974 318 C
walshle@oldwestbury.edu
WALSH, Mark .... 813-974-2660 111 C
mwalsh@usf.edu
WALSH, Mary .... 785-864-4999 177 J
marywalsh@ku.edu
WALSH, Megan .... 716-375-2447 313 C
mwalsh@sbu.edu
WALSH, Meghan .... 414-382-6089 491 F
meghan.walsh@alverno.edu

WALSH, Melissa .... 610-526-6197 385 D
mwalsh@harcum.edu
WALSH, Michael .... 518-631-9846 295 F
mwalsh@clarkson.edu
WALSH, Michael, D ...... 540-568-6022 468 C
walshmd@jmu.edu
WALSH, Michelle .... 845-437-7452 324 C
miwalsh@vassar.edu
WALSH, Patrick .... 541-684-7244 371 I
pwalsh@bushnell.edu
WALSH, Peter, J .... 512-448-8441 442 I
peterjw@stedwards.edu
WALSH, Robert .... 718-862-7741 304 M
rob.walsh@manhattan.edu
WALSH, SJ, Robert .... 310-338-4264.. 51 A
robert.walsh@lmu.edu
WALSH, Susan .... 541-552-6114 376 B
walsh@sou.edu
WALSH, Susan, E .... 609-258-6207 280 D
swalsh@princeton.edu
WALSH, Suzanne, E ...... 336-273-4431 327 A
WALSH, Tammi .... 706-802-5134 119 D
twalsh@highlands.edu
WALSH, Tammy, S .... 941-359-7505 106 J
twalsh@ringling.edu
WALSH, Teresa .... 732-255-0400 279 F
twalsh@ocean.edu
WALSH-DAVIS,
Nicholas .... 818-785-2726.. 35 E
WALSH FITZPATRICK,
Mary .... 518-445-2377 289 K
mfitz@albanylaw.edu
WALSHOK, Mary, L ...... 858-534-3411.. 70 C
mwalshok@ucsd.edu
WALSINGHAM, Kelli ...... 850-873-3514 101 N
kwalsingham@gulfcoast.edu
WALSON, Christopher .. 336-517-2193 327 A
cwalson@bennett.edu
WALSTAD, Annette .... 406-447-5434 263 B
awalstad@carroll.edu
WALSTEAD, Brenda .... 360-992-2474 478 I
bwalstead@clark.edu
WALSTON, Angie .... 252-399-6313 326 K
amwalston@barton.edu
WALSTON, Dustin .... 910-275-6252 335 E
dwalston@jamessprunt.edu
WALSTON, Tim .... 660-785-4248 260 F
tdwalston@truman.edu
WALSTON, Valerie .... 419-530-7262 363 B
valerie.simmonswalston@utoledo.edu
WALTENBERGER, Don ... 641-683-5154 166 I
don.waltenberger@indianhills.edu
WALTER, Ally, P .... 515-574-1140 167 A
walter@iowacentral.edu
WALTER, Almar .... 614-287-2735 351 C
awalter3@cscc.edu
WALTER, Carla .... 510-466-7200.. 56 H
WALTER, George .... 610-902-8554 379 G
gw10130@cabrini.edu
WALTER, Jim .... 706-355-5120 115 F
jwalter@athenstech.edu
WALTER, Joey .... 850-201-6038 112 C
joey.walter@tcc.fl.edu
WALTER, Joey .... 509-682-6614 485 H
jwalter@wvc.edu
WALTER, Josh .... 503-768-7921 373 E
jwalter@lclark.edu
WALTER, Kelly, A .... 617-353-3530 207 E
kwalter@bu.edu
WALTER, Kristy .... 617-243-2147 211 B
kwalter@lasell.edu
WALTER, Margaret .... 530-752-2300.. 69 B
matrout@ucdavis.edu
WALTER, Mary Beth ...... 937-327-7517 364 D
walterm@wittenberg.edu
WALTER, Robyn .... 636-584-6601 253 B
robyn.walter@eastcentral.edu
WALTER, Shulem .... 718-855-4092 311 K
swalter@rcosy.org
WALTER, Tiffany .... 912-443-5711 125 B
twalter@savannahtech.edu
WALTER, Willis, W .... 804-524-6869 476 D
wwalter@vsu.edu
WALTERREIT, Jay .... 989-358-7215 221 C
walterrj@alpenacc.edu
WALTERS, Bramdon ...... 865-539-7027 425 B
bwalters@pstcc.edu
WALTERS, Briana .... 907-474-6239.. 10 A
bdwalters@alaska.edu
WALTERS, Candie .... 229-931-2299 125 E
cwalters@southgatech.edu
WALTERS, Carmen, J .... 601-977-7730 249 C
cjwalters@tougaloo.edu

WARD, Denise .... 651-696-6385 236 I
ward@macalester.edu
WARD, Denitta, D .... 303-735-6624.. 84 B
denitta.ward@colorado.edu
WARD, Diane .... 865-882-4513 425 C
wardd@roanestate.edu
WARD, Donna .... 517-265-5161 220 G
dward2@adrian.edu
WARD, Doris .... 662-252-8000 248 G
dward2@rustcollege.edu
WARD, Elizabeth .... 914-594-4846 309 B
elizabeth_ward@nymc.edu
WARD, Emily .... 718-489-5249 313 E
eward2@sfc.edu
WARD, Faith, W .... 334-670-3318.... 7 C
alumdev@troy.edu
WARD, Farrah, J .... 252-335-3849 341 B
fjward@ecsu.edu
WARD, Gary, L .... 573-882-4097 261 A
wardga@missouri.edu
WARD, Gayle, B .... 312-942-2285 148 G
gayle_ward@rush.edu
WARD, Glen .... 508-373-5616 216 D
glenn.ward@mcphs.edu
WARD, Heather .... 316-322-3121 172 D
hmward@butlercc.edu
WARD, Heather .... 919-962-1051 342 C
heather.ward@unc.edu
WARD, IV, James .... 207-581-2201 196 G
jsward@maine.edu
WARD, Jamie .... 417-455-5636 252 E
jamieward@crowder.edu
WARD, Jeff .... 617-732-2896 216 D
jward@mcphs.edu
WARD, Jenifer, K .... 563-387-1001 168 B
president@luther.edu
WARD, John .... 610-683-4253 394 D
ward@kutztown.edu
WARD, John .... 831-626-3143 502 M
john.ward@nps.edu
WARD, John, A .... 513-529-4634 356 A
wardja2@miamioh.edu
WARD, Joseph .... 435-797-1195 460 C
joe.ward@usu.edu
WARD, Joy, K .... 216-368-4437 349 D
joy.ward@case.edu
WARD, Kathryn .... 510-879-7303.. 60 C
kward@samuelmerritt.edu
WARD, Kathy .... 501-882-8836.. 17 D
kward@asub.edu
WARD, Kris .... 575-624-8319 287 B
wardk@nmmi.edu
WARD, Laurie .... 301-696-3803 199 E
ward@hood.edu
WARD, Lawrence, P .... 781-239-5346 206 B
lward@babson.edu
WARD, Leah .... 712-279-1682 164 B
leah.ward@briarcliff.edu
WARD, Leslie Colis .... 802-828-8631 463 B
leslie.ward@vcfa.edu
WARD, Lynne .... 801-321-7157 459 N
lward@utahsbr.edu
WARD, Marcus, D .... 601-877-6296 245 A
mdward@alcorn.edu
WARD, Mark .... 563-589-3115 170 G
WARD, Mary .... 581-803-2013 105 C
mary_ward@pba.edu
WARD, Matthew .... 805-493-3481.. 29 C
mward@callutheran.edu
WARD, Melissa .... 703-284-1500 468 H
melissa.ward@marymount.edu
WARD, Michael .... 314-362-9155 253 G
michael.ward@barnesjewishcollege.edu
WARD, Michael .... 973-408-3000 277 A
mward@drew.edu
WARD, Michael .... 336-838-6489 339 B
mrward284@wilkescc.edu
WARD, Michael, S .... 334-833-4463.... 5 G
mward@hawks.huntingdon.edu
WARD, Mike .... 270-686-9572 179 J
mike.ward@brescia.edu
WARD, Monica .... 770-426-2611 122 C
monica.ward@life.edu
WARD, Nayamka .... 718-818-6470 314 F
WARD, Patricia .... 510-666-8248.. 24 D
pward@aimc.edu
WARD, Paul, J .... 214-768-3233 444 D
paulw@smu.edu
WARD, Randall .... 617-364-3510 207 B
rward@boston.edu
WARD, Rhonda .... 740-725-4017 355 F
wardr@mtc.edu
WARD, Robert .... 714-564-6319.. 58 F
ward_robert@sac.edu
WARD, Robert, A .... 585-385-8310 313 F
bward@sjfc.edu
WARD, Roger, J .... 410-706-2477 203 A
rward@umaryland.edu
WARD, Russ .... 606-759-7141 182 E
russ.ward@kctcs.edu
WARD, Ryan .... 406-586-3585 263 I
ryan.ward@montanabiblecollege.edu
WARD, Scott .... 231-843-5802 233 A
scward@westshore.edu
WARD, Shenika .... 910-695-3952 337 H
wards@sandhills.edu
WARD, Stephen .... 808-544-0289 128 G
stward@hpu.edu
WARD, Steve .... 605-658-3600 416 D
steve.ward@usd.edu
WARD, Susan .... 864-455-7902 413 F
wardse@mailbox.sc.edu
WARD, Susan .... 208-496-7720 130 I
wards@byui.edu
WARD, Susie .... 402-354-7063 268 B
susie.ward@methodistcollege.edu
WARD, Suzanne .... 870-584-1403.. 22 F
sward@cccua.edu
WARD, Tamica .... 925-424-1542.. 35 K
tward@laspositascollege.edu
WARD, Theresa .... 518-454-2147 296 G
wardt@strose.edu
WARD, Thomas .... 212-563-6647 323 I
ward@uts.edu
WARD, JR., Thomas, J ...... 516-877-3131 289 I
tward@adelphi.edu
WARD, Tim .... 718-862-7307 304 M
tim.ward@manhattan.edu
WARD, Todd .... 970-675-3257.. 79 H
todd.ward@cncc.edu
WARD, Tony .... 334-727-8364.... 7 D
tward@tuskegee.edu
WARD, Tony .... 605-455-6057 415 H
tward@olc.edu
WARD, Tracy .... 951-343-4552.. 27 G
tward@calbaptist.edu
WARD, Tracy .... 910-275-6376 335 E
tward@jamessprunt.edu
WARD, Vicki .... 979-830-4347 431 H
vicki.ward@blinn.edu
WARD, Virginia .... 617-427-7293 210 C
vward@gordonconwell.edu
WARD, Wanda, E .... 217-265-0451 152 B
weward@illinois.edu
WARD, William .... 360-867-6115 480 C
wardw@evergreen.edu
WARD-JOHNSON,
Frances .... 336-334-7806 341 D
fward@ncat.edu
WARD-PERADOZA,
Marianne .... 512-448-8446 442 I
mperadoz@stedwards.edu
WARD-ROOF, Jeanine .... 231-591-3578 224 A
jeaninewardroof@ferris.edu
WARDE, Robin, T .... 401-232-6253 404 A
rwarde@bryant.edu
WARDEN, Chris .... 510-659-7382.. 54 J
cwarden@ohlone.edu
WARDEN, Joel .... 718-522-2300 313 E
WARDEN, Ken .... 479-788-7721.. 21 G
ken.warden@uafs.edu
WARDINSKY, Ken .... 208-769-3377 132 D
kmwardinsky@nic.edu
WARDLAW, Debra .... 803-786-3723 408 D
dwardlaw@columbiasc.edu
WARDLAW,
Theodore, J .... 512-404-4824 430 J
twardlaw@austinseminary.edu
WARDLE, Marianne .... 307-766-1121 501 I
WARDWELL, Melissa .... 717-871-7655 395 A
melissa.wardwell@millersville.edu
WARDZALA, Ellen .... 419-559-2408 361 C
ewardzala01@terra.edu
WARE, Amy .... 901-321-3331 418 G
aware1@cbu.edu
WARE, Bob .... 870-222-5360.. 22 C
wareb@uamont.edu
WARE, Charles .... 713-785-5995 432 L
charles.ware@cbshouston.edu
WARE, Cynthia .... 310-506-6373.. 56 G
cynthia.ware@pepperdine.edu
WARE, Larry .... 304-647-6220 490 C
lware@osteo.wvsom.edu
WARE, Lisa .... 864-587-4295 412 F
warel@smcsc.edu
WARE, Mamie .... 770-426-2718 122 C
mamie.ware@life.edu
WARE, Monique .... 317-955-6040 159 K
mware@marian.edu
WARE, Paige .... 214-768-3754 444 D
pware@smu.edu
WARE, Peggy, J .... 309-341-7211 141 G
pjware@knox.edu
WARE, Shelby .... 903-233-4070 439 A
shelbyware@letu.edu
WARE, Shunda .... 843-525-8307 412 G
sware@tcl.edu
WARE, Thomas .... 606-759-7141 182 E
thomas.ware@kctcs.edu
WARE-CARLTON,
Rachel, J .... 920-565-1000 493 A
carltonrj@lakeland.edu
WARE JOSEPH, Caran .... 303-765-3198.. 81 G
cwarejoseph@iliff.edu
WARE-ROBERTS,
Vonnie .... 405-466-2999 366 C
vonnie.w.roberts@langston.edu
WAREJAYE, Hollie .... 773-907-4456 135 C
hwarejaye@ccc.edu
WARFEL, Robert .... 513-745-2000 364 G
warfelr@xavier.edu
WARFIELD, Aimee, S .... 518-381-1207 315 B
warfieas@sunysccc.edu
WARFIELD, Tara .... 706-233-7247 125 C
twarfield@shorter.edu
WARGO, Kurt, A .... 864-938-3901 411 D
kawargo@presby.edu
WARGO, Melissa .... 828-227-3082 343 E
wargo@wcu.edu
WARING, Jennifer .... 215-248-7150 381 A
sm8127@bncollege.com
WARING, Stacie .... 646-717-9761 300 E
registrar@gts.edu
WARK, Maureen .... 978-921-4242 217 B
maureen.wark@montserrat.edu
WARK, Mike .... 253-964-6232 482 E
mwark@pierce.ctc.edu
WARK, Ryan .... 907-796-6100.. 10 B
mrwark@alaska.edu
WARKENTIN, Bettina .... 615-547-1374 419 C
bwarkentin@cumberland.edu
WARKENTIN, Liz .... 262-554-2010 494 A
liz.warkentin@acupuncture.edu
WARLEY, Russell, L .... 812-877-8046 160 F
warley@rose-hulman.edu
WARMACK, Dwaun, J .... 803-535-5412 407 D
WARMAN, Cassie .... 503-352-2905 375 C
warman@pacificu.edu
WARMANN, Cheryl .... 847-635-1719 146 G
cwarmann@oakton.edu
WARN, Dara .... 480-947-6644.. 14 N
dara.warn@pennfoster.edu
WARNEKE, Kent .... 402-844-7244 268 H
kent@northeast.edu
WARNER, Amy, C .... 317-274-7400 157 D
awarner@iupui.edu
WARNER, Angela .... 314-529-9300 255 B
awarner@maryville.edu
WARNER, Ann .... 337-475-5820 192 E
awarner@mcneese.edu
WARNER, OP,
Cecilia Anne .... 615-297-7545 417 G
president@aquinascollege.edu
WARNER, Charles .... 740-351-3468 360 F
cwarner@shawnee.edu
WARNER, Charles .... 610-436-2117 395 D
cwarner@wcupa.edu
WARNER, Corrina .... 706-721-2161 116 A
cwarner1@augusta.edu
WARNER, Dan .... 610-758-3100 388 E
daw318@lehigh.edu
WARNER, David .... 240-500-2231 199 C
cdwarner@hagerstowncc.edu
WARNER, Donald, D .... 406-874-6201 263 H
warnerd@milescc.edu
WARNER, Gail .... 760-355-6275.. 45 K
gail.warner@imperial.edu
WARNER, Isiah, M .... 225-578-7230 189 E
iwarner@lsu.edu
WARNER, Janice .... 732-987-2314 278 A
jwarner@georgian.edu
WARNER, Jason .... 214-768-4379 444 D
jasonw@smu.edu
WARNER, John .... 214-648-9794 457 A
john.warner@utsouthwestern.edu
WARNER, Kathleen .... 410-888-9048 200 E
kwarner@muih.edu
WARNER, Kelly, M .... 419-434-5184 362 D
kelly.warner@findlay.edu
WARNER, Kyle .... 989-463-7359 221 B
warnerka@alma.edu
WARNER, Linda .... 913-288-7194 175 B
lwarner@kckcc.edu
WARNER, Lynn .... 518-442-3300 316 A
lwarner@albany.edu
WARNER, Maleese .... 707-527-4828.. 63 D
mwarner@santarosa.edu
WARNER, Ryan .... 740-351-3127 360 F
rwarner@shawnee.edu
WARNER, Sandra .... 913-469-8500 174 I
swarner@jccc.edu
WARNER, Somerset .... 801-818-8900 459 J
swarner@provocollege.edu
WARNER, Susan, T .... 440-826-2476 348 D
swarner@bw.edu
WARNER, Timothy, R .... 650-723-4567.. 66 E
trw@stanford.edu
WARNES, Jamie, E .... 716-878-4822 317 F
warnesje@buffalostate.edu
WARNES, Taylor .... 218-879-0820 238 B
taylor.warnes@fdltcc.edu
WARNICK, Benjamin .... 508-588-9100 215 A
bwarnick@massasoit.mass.edu
WARNICK, Lorin, D .... 607-253-3030 297 F
ldw3@cornell.edu
WARNICK, Mark .... 870-248-4000.. 18 F
mark.warnick@blackrivertech.edu
WARNOCK, Bonnie .... 432-837-8201 450 B
bwarnock@sulross.edu
WARR, Annie .... 831-582-3595.. 32 B
awarr@csumb.edu
WARR, Jason .... 303-765-3185.. 81 G
jwarr@iliff.edu
WARREM, Beth .... 619-594-7985.. 33 D
bwarrem@sdsu.edu
WARREN, Aileen .... 402-559-8992 270 A
aileen.warren@unmc.edu
WARREN, Aileen .... 402-559-8992 269 K
aileen.warren@unmc.edu
WARREN, Ann .... 310-233-4250.. 49 B
warrenal@lahc.edu
WARREN, Ashley .... 432-335-6411 441 A
awarren@odessa.edu
WARREN, A'Lelianne .... 704-216-3617 337 F
alelianne.warren@rccc.edu
WARREN, Beverly .... 619-388-3209.. 60 I
bewarren@sdccd.edu
WARREN, Carolyn .... 901-722-3215 423 G
cwarren@sco.edu
WARREN, Charlotte, J ...... 217-786-2273 143 B
charlotte.warren@llcc.edu
WARREN, Cher .... 601-484-8614 247 A
cwarren@meridiancc.edu
WARREN, Cleve .... 904-357-8896 101 B
clwarren@fscj.edu
WARREN, Daniel .... 912-449-7534 125 D
daniel.warren@sgsc.edu
WARREN, Derrick .... 225-771-5380 191 B
derrick_warren@sus.edu
WARREN, Ester .... 434-592-6468 468 E
ejwarren@liberty.edu
WARREN, Gabriel .... 218-755-2756 237 F
gabriel.warren@bemidjistate.edu
WARREN, Gordon .... 325-203-5014 441 K
gwarren@rangercollege.edu
WARREN, Jacquelyn .... 314-516-6877 261 C
warrenja@umsl.edu
WARREN, James .... 212-410-8063 308 E
jwarren@nycpm.edu
WARREN, Jason, D .... 270-827-1867 182 A
jason.warren@kctcs.edu
WARREN, Joan, D .... 212-779-5000 303 E
WARREN, Kathi, D .... 713-348-6090 442 F
kdwarren@rice.edu
WARREN, Katie .... 507-786-3316 243 D
warren2@stolaf.edu
WARREN, Kayla .... 260-665-4105 161 E
warrenk@trine.edu
WARREN, Kelly .... 806-291-1022 457 I
warrenk@wbu.edu
WARREN, Kerry .... 256-216-5343.... 4 C
kerry.warren@athens.edu
WARREN, Layne .... 804-862-6100 470 C
lwarren@rbc.edu
WARREN, Leslie, A .... 906-227-2117 228 I
lwarren@nmu.edu
WARREN, Marty .... 903-923-2314 435 H
mswarren@etbu.edu
WARREN, Mary .... 601-643-8442 245 F
mary.warren@colin.edu
WARREN, Matt .... 918-631-4602 371 C
matt-warren@utulsa.edu

WARREN, Michelle 218-935-0417 244 G michelle.warren@wetcc.edu
WARREN, Mike 601-925-3204 247 C mjwarren@mc.edu
WARREN, Monica 615-297-7545 417 G
WARREN, Pamela, C 920-923-8530 493 D pcwarren17@marianuniversity.edu
WARREN, Reuben 334-725-2314 7 D rwarren@tuskegee.edu
WARREN, Robert 909-706-8424 75 I rjwarren@westernu.edu
WARREN, Russ 724-266-3838 400 B rwarren@tsm.edu
WARREN, Samantha 207-621-3024 196 G samantha.warren@maine.edu
WARREN, Samantha, C 207-621-3024 196 F samantha.warren@maine.edu
WARREN, Sara 410-225-2264 200 D swarren@mica.edu
WARREN, Shannon 304-645-6382 490 C swarren@osteo.wvsom.edu
WARREN, Shannon, N 410-651-6144 203 D snwarren@umes.edu
WARREN, Shauna 773-896-2400 134 L shauna.warren@ctschicago.edu
WARREN, Sydney 270-686-6417 179 J sydney.warren@brescia.edu
WARREN, Teresa 479-936-5171 20 C twarren4@nwacc.edu
WARREN, Thomas 207-941-7786 194 F warrent@husson.edu
WARREN, Todd, W 504-865-3434 190 C twwarren@loyno.edu
WARREN, William 202-319-6925 92 A warrenw@cua.edu
WARREN, William, J 801-581-6773 459 O william.warren@utah.edu
WARRENFELTZ, Jason 717-262-2013 403 C jason.warrenfeltz@wilson.edu
WARRICK, Cynthia 205-366-8808 7 A cwarrick@stillman.edu
WARRICK, Vicky 919-658-7832 340 G vwarrick@umo.edu
WARRINGTON, Adam 802-654-0505 463 F acw11030@ccv.vsc.edu
WARRINGTON, Amy 800-747-2687 144 H awarrington@monmouthcollege.edu
WARRINGTON, Myrna 800-567-2344 492 C mwarrington@menominee.edu
WARSHAUER, Wanda 860-515-3820 85 E wwarshauer@charteroak.edu
WARSHAWER, Elizabeth, B 215-972-2056 392 T
WARSHEL, Chad 315-568-3297 310 B cwarshel@nycc.edu
WARTERS, Alissa 843-661-1616 409 G twarters@fmarion.edu
WARTHEN, Diane 406-496-4400 265 A dwarthen@mtech.edu
WARUSZEWSKI, Stephen 814-472-3391 397 F swaruszewski@francis.edu
WARYCK, Susan 802-860-2702 462 A swaryck@champlain.edu
WASAN, Darsh, T 312-567-3001 140 A wasan@iit.edu
WASCALUS, Jaime 612-626-1616 243 F
WASCHULL, Stefanie 352-395-5175 108 A stefanie.waschull@sfcollege.edu
WASHBURN, Brian 408-551-1993 63 B bwashburn@scu.edu
WASHBURN, Dava 903-464-8634 436 G washburnd@grayson.edu
WASHBURN, Jillehn 802-322-1711 462 B jillehn.washburn@goddard.edu
WASHBURN, Kevin 319-335-9034 163 H kevin-washburn@uiowa.edu
WASHBURN, Marina 805-922-6966 24 I marina.washburn@hancockcollege.edu
WASHBURNE, Anne 207-221-4914 197 E awashburne@une.edu
WASHINGTON, A. Eugene 919-684-2255 328 F eugene.washington@duke.edu
WASHINGTON, Adrienne, J 610-758-5834 388 E ajw416@lehigh.edu
WASHINGTON, Andre 859-442-4176 181 H andre.washington@kctcs.edu
WASHINGTON, Angela 919-747-0031 338 G aewashington@waketech.edu
WASHINGTON, August, J 615-343-9750 428 A august.j.washington@vanderbilt.edu
WASHINGTON, Brandon 903-823-3232 446 A brandon.washington@texarkanacollege.edu
WASHINGTON, Carla, A 919-497-3306 330 I cwashington@louisburg.edu
WASHINGTON, Chelsea 386-481-2543 96 D shellc@cookman.edu
WASHINGTON, Cheryl 334-872-2533 6 F
WASHINGTON, Christopher 614-947-6129 352 J christopher.washington@franklin.edu
WASHINGTON, Craig 410-295-4089 504 A craig.washington@usna.com
WASHINGTON, Crystal 773-838-7535 135 F cwashington59@ccc.edu
WASHINGTON, Dana 815-802-8962 141 D dwashington@kcc.edu
WASHINGTON, Dennis 724-738-4832 395 C dennis.washington@sru.edu
WASHINGTON, DeSandra 910-678-0037 334 E washingd@faytechcc.edu
WASHINGTON, Dwight 301-546-7422 201 E washindx@pgcc.edu
WASHINGTON, Eddie, L 734-763-8216 231 H washine@umich.edu
WASHINGTON, Eric 718-960-8812 294 A eric.washington@lehman.cuny.edu
WASHINGTON, Felicia 213-740-2311 73 D felicia.washington@usc.edu
WASHINGTON, Geovette, E 412-624-4747 400 H gew@pitt.edu
WASHINGTON, Germaine 816-322-0110 251 B germaine.washington@calvary.edu
WASHINGTON, Gregory 703-993-1000 467 E
WASHINGTON, Ingrid 859-442-1148 181 H ingrid.washington@kctcs.edu
WASHINGTON, Isaiah 623-845-3996 13 C isaiah.washington@gccaz.edu
WASHINGTON, J. Leon 610-519-4002 401 K jleon.washington@villanova.edu
WASHINGTON, Jaleen 912-260-4200 125 D jaleen.washington@sgsc.edu
WASHINGTON, Jennifer 860-515-3820 85 E jwashington@charteroak.edu
WASHINGTON, Kaye, L 318-670-9474 191 D kwashington@susla.edu
WASHINGTON, Kimberly 814-886-6320 390 G kwashington@mtaloy.edu
WASHINGTON, L. Marshall 269-488-4200 225 G lmwashington@kvcc.edu
WASHINGTON, Lakeisha 573-681-5248 254 G washingtonl@lincolnu.edu
WASHINGTON, Lloyd 251-405-4060 1 E lwashington@bishop.edu
WASHINGTON, Lonnie 773-602-5000 135 D
WASHINGTON, Marcus 704-637-4382 327 I mjwashin18@catawba.edu
WASHINGTON, Marlowe 585-385-8236 313 F mwashington@sjfc.edu
WASHINGTON, Michael 731-881-7845 427 D mwashi24@utm.edu
WASHINGTON, Mona 901-435-1477 420 I mona_washington@loc.edu
WASHINGTON, Nakia 470-639-0434 123 D nakia.washington@morehouse.edu
WASHINGTON, Rikki 214-638-0484 438 E financialaid@kdstudio.com
WASHINGTON, Sadie 404-297-9522 120 B
WASHINGTON, Shawn 509-777-4330 486 C swashington@whitworth.edu
WASHINGTON, Sherrea 773-481-8061 135 G swashington@ccc.edu
WASHINGTON, Sherry 973-720-2222 284 J washingtons24@wpunj.edu
WASHINGTON, Shirley 240-965-2465 198 C sbwashington@captechu.edu
WASHINGTON, Tasha 205-247-8121 7 A twahington@stillman.edu
WASHINGTON, Timothy, L 301-736-3631 200 C twashington@msbbcs.edu
WASHINGTON, Tonia, T 803-934-3175 410 G twashington@morris.edu
WASHINGTON, Troy, W 937-229-2554 362 C twashington1@udayton.edu
WASHINGTON, Victoria 410-532-5370 201 D vwashington@ndm.edu
WASHINGTON, Willie 803-705-4734 406 G willie.washington@benedict.edu
WASHINGTON-LACY, Bonita 765-983-1311 155 A washibo@earlham.edu
WASHINGTON WHITE, Kendal, H 520-621-7057 16 D kwashing@arizona.edu
WASHINGTON-WHITE, Robin 817-515-7602 445 F robin.washington-white@tccd.edu
WASHKO, Mary Jo 804-523-5345 474 A mwashko@reynolds.edu
WASHO, Kevin 412-624-4200 400 H
WASHUT, Kyle 307-332-2930 502 A kwashut@wyomingcatholic.edu
WASIELEWSKI, Dan 641-472-1156 168 C dwasielewski@miu.edu
WASIELEWSKI, Laura 603-656-6051 274 A lwasielewski@anselm.edu
WASIELEWSKI, Matt 303-762-6955 80 I matt.wasielewski@denverseminary.edu
WASIELEWSKI, Matt 704-847-5600 340 F mwasielewski@ses.edu
WASILENKO, William, J 757-446-8480 466 D wasilewj@evms.edu
WASILESKI, Suzanne 603-342-3010 273 C swasileski@ccsnh.edu
WASKIEWICZ, Rhonda 207-992-4913 194 F waskiewiczr@husson.edu
WASMER, Tanya 920-693-1858 498 H tanya.wasmer@gotoltc.edu
WASS, Melissa 301-387-3746 199 A melissa.wass@garrettcollege.edu
WASSBERG, Catherine 651-523-2616 236 B cwassberg01@hamline.edu
WASSENMILLER, Angie 402-643-3651 266 G angela.wassenmiller@cune.edu
WASSERMAN, David 718-631-6697 295 C dwasserman@qcc.cuny.edu
WASSERMAN, Ed 510-642-3383 69 A ed.wasserman@berkeley.edu
WASSERMAN, Mona 718-489-5305 313 E mwasserman@sfc.edu
WASSERMAN, Noam 646-592-4905 326 D noam.wasserman@yu.edu
WASSILAK, Kristin, R 708-209-3136 136 E kristin.wassilak@cuchicago.edu
WASSMER, Dana 916-691-7514 50 H wassmed@crc.losrios.edu
WASSON, Dan 231-995-1164 229 A dan@nmc.edu
WASSON, Leslie 800-607-6377 60 C lwasson@samuelmerritt.edu
WASSON, Tanlee 859-622-8663 180 E tanlee.wasson@eku.edu
WASSUM, Elizabeth 910-755-7300 332 F
WASTVVEDT, Ross 507-537-6246 241 D provost@smsu.edu
WATANABE, Byron 808-455-0493 130 C byronw@hawaii.edu
WATANABE, Jerry 808-932-7941 129 D jerrywat@hawaii.edu
WATERFIELD, James, R 757-683-5070 469 B rwater@odu.edu
WATERFIELD, Steven 248-370-3131 229 I waterfield@oakland.edu
WATERMAN, Matthew 510-430-3246 66 G mwaterman@sksm.edu
WATERMOLEN, Jean, C 602-243-8124 14 A jean.watermolen@southmountaincc.edu
WATERS, Barry, D 989-774-7493 222 E water1b@cmich.edu
WATERS, Candace, R 864-488-4448 410 B cwaters@limestone.edu
WATERS, Chris 336-668-3869 343 A cawaters@uncg.edu
WATERS, Christopher, C 336-278-5055 328 J cwaters@elon.edu
WATERS, Gloria 617-353-2595 207 E gwaters@bu.edu
WATERS, Jennifer 205-226-4912 4 F jwaters@bsc.edu
WATERS, Jennifer 903-566-7380 456 A jwaters@uttyler.edu
WATERS, Jennifer, K 718-409-7200 320 G
WATERS, Jessica 202-885-3724 91 F waters@american.edu
WATERS, Joan 212-854-1234 297 C jwaters@columbia.edu
WATERS, Jon 434-544-8498 471 L waters.j@lynchburg.edu
WATERS, Kyndall 205-226-7795 4 F kwaters@bsc.edu
WATERS, Marlo 503-517-1012 377 C mwaters@warnerpacific.edu
WATERS, Melissa 770-426-2826 122 C mwaters@life.edu
WATERS, Michelle 252-335-0821 333 G michelle_waters@albemarle.edu
WATERS, Sarah 785-864-4560 177 J sarah.waters@ku.edu
WATERS, Taylor 410-626-2512 202 A taylor.waters@sjc.edu
WATERS-BAILEY, Stacy 336-757-3852 334 F swatersbailey@forsythtech.edu
WATERSTONE, Julie, K 213-738-5727 66 B jwaterstone@swlaw.edu
WATERSTONE, Michael 213-736-8154 51 A michael.waterstone@lls.edu
WATESKA, Alison 412-383-4066 400 H alw122@pitt.edu
WATESKA, Mark 402-826-8583 267 A mark.wateska@doane.edu
WATFORD, John 229-931-2150 125 E jwatford@southgatech.edu
WATHEN, Cory 949-582-4872 65 D cwathen@saddleback.edu
WATHINGTON, Deanna 386-481-2485 96 D wathingtond@cookman.edu
WATKINS, Adam 217-786-2323 143 B adam.watkins@llcc.edu
WATKINS, Brenda 708-456-0300 151 D brendawatkins@triton.edu
WATKINS, Bryce 717-796-1800 389 H bwatkins@messiah.edu
WATKINS, Dan 805-652-5577 73 I dwatlkins@vcccd.edu
WATKINS, Diana 580-628-6905 366 J diana.watkins@noc.edu
WATKINS, Elizabeth 415-514-2310 70 D graduate.dean@ucsf.edu
WATKINS, Elizabeth 415-476-2310 70 D graduate.dean@ucsf.edu
WATKINS, Elizabeth 951-827-1129 70 B provost@ucr.edu
WATKINS, Faye 850-599-3370 109 I faye.watkins@famu.edu
WATKINS, Frank 772-462-7475 102 F fwatkins@irsc.edu
WATKINS, James 478-387-4819 119 F jwatkins@gmc.edu
WATKINS, Jameson 509-452-5100 482 B jmwatkins@pnwu.edu
WATKINS, Janine 817-735-0295 454 B janine.watkins@untsystem.edu
WATKINS, Jeremi 252-335-4850 341 B jwwatkins@ecsu.edu
WATKINS, Jim 262-256-0982 494 F jwatkins@nashotah.edu
WATKINS, Joe 619-849-2650 57 J joewatkins@pointloma.edu
WATKINS, Kathryn, A 330-972-7666 361 H kwatkin@uakron.edu
WATKINS, Lydia 912-279-5906 117 F lwatkins@ccga.edu
WATKINS, Margaret 724-805-2814 397 I margaret.watkins@stvincent.edu
WATKINS, Mark 620-421-6700 175 F markw@labette.edu
WATKINS, Mark 502-852-1947 186 A mark.watkins@louisville.edu
WATKINS, Michael 818-354-5673 28 J michael.watkins@jpl.nasa.gov
WATKINS, Nicolette 801-618-0438 458 G nwatkins@ameritech.edu
WATKINS, Ophelia 575-646-4251 287 C owatkins@nmsu.edu
WATKINS, Pat, E 727-864-8854 98 J watkinpe@eckerd.edu
WATKINS, Rebecca, R 828-398-7151 332 B bwatkins@abtech.edu
WATKINS, Renee 973-596-3106 279 E renee.watkins@njit.edu
WATKINS, Ronnie 806-716-2246 443 G rwatkins@southplainscollege.edu
WATKINS, RoseMary 334-291-4913 1 H rosemary.watkins@cv.edu
WATKINS, Rusty 270-789-5005 180 A rdwatkins@campbellsville.edu

WATKINS, Sonya .... 405-974-2605 370 I
sewatkins@uco.edu
WATKINS, Suzanna .... 336-770-1432 343 D
watkinss@uncsa.edu
WATKINS, Tracy .... 903-233-4356 439 A
tracywatkins@letu.edu
WATKINS, William .... 818-677-2391.. 32 C
william.watkins@csun.edu
WATLAND, Kathleen ...... 260-422-5561 156 E
khwatland@indianatech.edu
WATLING, Robert .... 972-721-5236 452 B
rwatling@udallas.edu
WATNEY, Laurel .... 620-278-4233 177 H
lwatney@sterling.edu
WATSON, Allyson .... 850-561-2989 109 I
allyson.watson@famu.edu
WATSON, Alyssa .... 734-432-5633 227 C
abwatson@madonna.edu
WATSON, Andrew .... 870-759-4120.. 23 J
awatson@williamsbu.edu
WATSON, Andrew .... 870-759-4112.. 23 J
awatson@williamsbu.edu
WATSON, Angela .... 270-831-9671 182 A
angie.watson@kctcs.edu
WATSON, Angie .... 864-977-7018 410 I
angie.watson@ngu.edu
WATSON, Anthony .... 212-961-4322 293 A
awatson@bmcc.cuny.edu
WATSON, Ben .... 308-432-6366 268 D
bwatson@csc.edu
WATSON, Billy .... 864-977-7123 410 I
jw.watson@ngu.edu
WATSON, Bret .... 650-949-7777.. 42 I
WATSON, Bret .... 650-949-7777.. 42 I
watsonbret@fhda.edu
WATSON, Brett .... 760-480-8474.. 75 J
bwatson@wscal.edu
WATSON, Brian .... 217-234-5253 142 C
bwatson@lakelandcollege.edu
WATSON, Camille .... 800-818-6136.. 55 L
cwatson@paloaltou.edu
WATSON, Christopher ... 847-491-4100 146 E
christopher-watson@northwestern.edu
WATSON, Christopher ... 903-730-4890 438 D
cwatson@jarvis.edu
WATSON, Darah .... 870-236-6901.. 18 J
dwatson@crc.edu
WATSON, Darius .... 573-681-5216 254 G
watsond@lincolnu.edu
WATSON, David .... 937-529-2201 361 G
dwatson@united.edu
WATSON, Donna .... 914-395-2204 315 A
dwatson@sarahlawrence.edu
WATSON, Douglas .... 402-941-6519 267 L
watson@midlandu.edu
WATSON, Drew .... 863-667-5192 108 K
dwatson@seu.edu
WATSON, Edward .... 601-979-3950 246 F
edward.o.watson@jsums.edu
WATSON, Eric .... 713-353-3621 430 E
erwatson@aii.edu
WATSON, Erica .... 207-795-2843 195 B
watsoner@mchp.edu
WATSON, Frederica .... 713-718-5103 437 C
frederica.watson@hccs.edu
WATSON, George, E ..... 678-839-6000 127 C
nwatson@westga.edu
WATSON, Harold .... 630-829-6129 133 E
hwatson@ben.edu
WATSON, Hope .... 803-786-3763 408 D
hwatson@columbiasc.edu
WATSON, Jack .... 304-293-0826 490 E
jack.watson@mail.wvu.edu
WATSON, James .... 559-278-8400.. 31 B
jwatson@csufresno.edu
WATSON, Jeff .... 618-468-3800 142 E
jwatson@lc.edu
WATSON, Jeff .... 903-729-0256 451 F
jwatson@tvcc.edu
WATSON, John .... 972-273-3353 435 B
jwatson@dcccd.edu
WATSON, Jonelle .... 701-858-3577 345 E
jonelle.watson@minotstateu.edu
WATSON, Julia .... 678-664-0530 128 A
julia.watson@westgatech.edu
WATSON, Kathryn, J ...... 727-864-8474.. 98 J
watsonkj@eckerd.edu
WATSON, Kelly .... 513-875-3344 350 C
kelly.watson@chatfield.edu
WATSON, Kim .... 419-251-1852 355 G
kim.watson@mercycollege.edu
WATSON, Kimberly .... 301-405-5837 202 H
watsonk@umd.edu

WATSON, Lisa .... 409-933-8674 433 H
lwatson5@com.edu
WATSON, Lisa .... 307-754-6098 501 H
lisa.watson@nwc.edu
WATSON, Loree .... 281-649-3221 437 B
lwatson@hbu.edu
WATSON, Loretta .... 912-583-3224 116 E
lwatson@bpc.edu
WATSON, Lori .... 503-943-7393 377 A
duax@up.edu
WATSON, Lynda .... 903-434-8204 440 G
lwatson@ntcc.edu
WATSON, Maria .... 909-621-8192.. 57 K
maria.watson@pomona.edu
WATSON, Mary .... 212-229-5613 308 A
watsonm@newschool.edu
WATSON, OP,
Mary Grace .... 615-297-7545 417 G
srmgrace@aquinascollege.edu
WATSON, Michael, W ... 920-424-2184 496 C
watson@uwosh.edu
WATSON, Mindy .... 575-769-4065 285 O
mindy.watson@clovis.edu
WATSON, Monica .... 701-483-2592 345 C
monica.watson@dickinsonstate.edu
WATSON, Nailah .... 773-291-6100 135 E
WATSON, Nancy .... 712-279-5416 164 B
nancy.watson@briarcliff.edu
WATSON, Nevon .... 562-938-4023.. 48 F
nwatson@lbcc.edu
WATSON, Nick .... 573-642-3361 262 E
WATSON, Nyemma .... 856-225-6738 281 G
ncwatson@camden.rutgers.edu
WATSON, Paul .... 269-965-3931 225 H
watsonp@kellogg.edu
WATSON, Phyllis .... 850-599-3474 109 I
phyllis.watson@famu.edu
WATSON, Rachael .... 425-388-9578 480 B
rwatson@everettcc.edu
WATSON, Rebecca .... 334-670-3608.... 7 C
bvwatson@troy.edu
WATSON, Renee .... 702-895-5308 271 D
renee.watson@unlv.edu
WATSON, Rick .... 607-274-3958 302 G
rwatson@ithaca.edu
WATSON, Ron .... 936-468-3206 445 E
rewatson@sfasu.edu
WATSON, Sally .... 307-532-8303 501 B
sally.watson@ewc.wy.edu
WATSON, Samuel .... 803-533-3603 411 G
swatson2@scsu.edu
WATSON, III,
Samuel, E .... 940-397-4746 440 C
samuel.watson@msutexas.edu
WATSON, Sherry .... 207-509-7201 196 E
swatson@unity.edu
WATSON, Sonja, S .... 817-257-7160 448 F
sonja.watson@tcu.edu
WATSON, Steve .... 773-508-2560 143 C
swatson4@luc.edu
WATSON, Stevie .... 502-597-6290 183 D
stevie.watson@kysu.edu
WATSON, Susan, V .... 301-546-7011 201 E
watsonsv@pgcc.edu
WATSON, Terri .... 630-752-5762 153 C
terri.watson@wheaton.edu
WATSON, Todd .... 512-863-1508 445 C
tkw@southwestern.edu
WATSON, Tracey .... 882-354-3000 425 C
watsontl@roanestate.edu
WATSON, W. Clark .... 205-726-4503.... 6 E
wcwatson@samford.edu
WATSON, William .... 408-918-5106.. 62 F
william.watson@sjecc.edu
WATSON, William .... 770-794-3050 122 C
william.watson@life.edu
WATSON, Wyatt .... 479-964-3213.. 18 C
wwatson@atu.edu
WATSON, Yvonne .... 510-841-1905.. 26 I
ywatson@absw.edu
WATSON-BLAISDELL,
Kerri .... 207-834-7558 197 A
kerri.watson@maine.edu
WATSON-HALL,
Sherrell .... 848-445-6625 282 A
sherrell.watsonhall@ofa.rutgers.edu
WATSTEIN, Sara .... 206-296-6201 484 A
watsteins@seattleu.edu
WATT, James, R .... 814-641-3110 386 E
wattj@juniata.edu
WATT, Robert .... 209-934-2950 483 C
robert.watt@seattlecolleges.edu
WATTERS, James, H ..... 585-475-2378 312 F
jhwbgt@rit.edu

WATTS, Aimee .... 850-729-4957 104 M
wattsa@nwfsc.edu
WATTS, Barbara .... 434-381-6151 471 I
bwatts@sbc.edu
WATTS, Bill .... 402-472-3145 269 J
bill.watts@unl.edu
WATTS, Bruce .... 312-567-3253 140 A
bwatts1@iit.edu
WATTS, Christine .... 504-398-2177 192 A
cwatts@uhcno.edu
WATTS, Christopher ...... 817-257-7316 448 F
c.watts@tcu.edu
WATTS, Connie .... 606-487-3184 181 I
connie.watts@kctcs.edu
WATTS, Derek .... 309-298-1949 153 A
dj-watts@wiu.edu
WATTS, Eda .... 763-424-0944 240 A
WATTS, Janelle .... 601-877-6479 245 A
jswatts@alcorn.edu
WATTS, John .... 828-327-7000 333 B
WATTS, Jon, C .... 308-865-8205 269 I
wattsjc@unk.edu
WATTS, Katherine, K ..... 336-917-5563 340 A
katherine.watts@salem.edu
WATTS, Laurie, S .... 504-816-8180 190 F
lawatts@nobts.edu
WATTS, Monica .... 205-348-5411.... 7 G
monica.watts@ua.edu
WATTS, Nakisha .... 662-621-4205 245 D
nwatts@coahomacc.edu
WATTS, Ray, L .... 205-934-4636.... 8 A
rlwatts@uab.edu
WATTS, Robert .... 601-877-6470 245 A
rwatts@alcorn.edu
WATTS, Tracee .... 979-230-3163 431 I
tracee.watts@brazosport.edu
WATTS-MARTINEZ,
Evanda .... 804-862-6100 470 C
ewatts@rbc.edu
WATWOOD, Maribeth ..... 928-523-9322.. 14 H
maribeth.watwood@nau.edu
WATZKE, John, L .... 503-943-7135 377 A
watzke@up.edu
WAUGH,
Christopher, A .... 563-333-6259 169 G
waughchristophera@sau.edu
WAUGH, Susan .... 760-591-3012.. 72 G
swaugh@usa.edu
WAUGH, Wendy .... 308-432-6277 268 D
wwaugh@csc.edu
WAURIO, Laura .... 920-924-3229 499 D
lwaurio@morainepark.edu
WAUTLET, Heather .... 321-693-5256 100 C
hcudmore@fit.edu
WAVLE, Dana, C .... 812-941-2202 157 F
dwavle@ius.edu
WAWERS, Stephanie ..... 701-231-7211 345 F
stephanie.wawers@ndsu.edu
WAWRZUSIN, Andrea ... 513-745-3009 364 G
wawrzusina@xavier.edu
WAX, Shawn .... 312-369-7605 136 D
swax@colum.edu
WAXLER, Melanie .... 727-816-3259 105 F
waxlerm@phsc.edu
WAXMAN, Barbara .... 918-595-7872 370 C
barbara.waxman@tulsacc.edu
WAXMAN, Deborah .... 215-576-0800 396 I
officeofthepresident@rrc.edu
WAXTER, Catherine, A .. 412-359-1000 400 A
WAY, Christopher .... 617-253-2808 216 B
WAY, Joshua .... 646-378-6100 310 D
joshua.way@nyack.edu
WAY, Julie .... 414-277-4517 494 D
WAY, Kimera, K .... 715-836-5180 495 E
waykk@uwec.edu
WAY, Lauren .... 413-565-1000 206 D
lway@baypath.edu
WAY, Lori Beth .... 415-405-4034.. 33 E
lbway@sfsu.edu
WAY, Pete .... 315-655-7266 292 H
pmway@cazenovia.edu
WAY, Philip, K .... 256-233-8201.... 4 C
philip.way@athens.edu
WAY, Winmar .... 562-902-3388.. 65 I
winmarway@scuhs.edu
WAY BOLT, Mary .... 410-287-1025 198 E
mbolt@cecil.edu
WAYBRIGHT, Greg .... 630-752-5087 153 C
chaplains.office@wheaton.edu
WAYE, Katharine .... 315-279-5602 303 G
kwaye@keuka.edu
WAYLAND, David .... 432-552-2764 456 F
wayland_d@utpb.edu

WAYLAND, Marilina, L . 787-250-1912 508 D
mwayland@metro.inter.edu
WAYNE, William .... 315-568-3025 310 B
bwayne@nycc.edu
WAYNE, William, R ...... 405-325-2700 370 K
wwayne@ou.edu
WAYTON, Cristina .... 216-523-7415 350 J
c.sanchez17@csuohio.edu
WEARDEN, Stanley, T ... 910-630-7005 331 E
swearden@methodist.edu
WEARN, Mary .... 478-471-2730 122 F
mary.wearn@mga.edu
WEARY, Tanya .... 252-492-2061 338 F
wearyt@vgcc.edu
WEATHERALL, Maureen 310-338-5171.. 51 A
maureen.weatherall@lmu.edu
WEATHERBEE, Caroline 617-243-2407 211 B
cweatherbee@lasell.edu
WEATHERBY, Susan ..... 315-364-3208 324 I
accounting@wells.edu
WEATHERFORD,
Charles .... 850-412-5102 109 I
charles.weatherford@famu.edu
WEATHERFORD, Claire . 619-206-2719.. 72 I
cweatherford@sandiego.edu
WEATHERFORD,
Michael .... 831-656-2511 502 M
michael.weatherford@nps.edu
WEATHERLY, Megan ..... 936-468-1735 445 E
msweatherly@sfasu.edu
WEATHERS, Lisa .... 863-638-7244 114 A
lisa.weathers@warner.edu
WEATHERS, Mark .... 845-938-2517 503 I
christopher.weathers@westpoint.edu
WEATHERS, Melonie ..... 336-386-3207 338 D
weathersm@surry.edu
WEATHERSBY, Aaron .... 323-563-3432.. 36 C
aaronweathersby@cdrewu.edu
WEATHERSPOON,
Bridget .... 937-529-2201 361 G
bweatherspoon@united.edu
WEATHERSPOON,
David .... 847-543-2138 136 A
dweatherspoon@clcillinois.edu
WEAVER, Amy .... 501-505-2966.. 19 E
weaver@hendrix.edu
WEAVER, Andrea .... 910-962-7631 343 C
weavera@uncw.edu
WEAVER, Angela .... 618-468-5300 142 E
aweaver@lc.edu
WEAVER, Anne .... 504-865-5490 190 C
asweaver@loyno.edu
WEAVER, Benjamin .... 518-956-8030 316 A
bweaver@albany.edu
WEAVER, Bradley, K ..... 765-361-6308 163 B
weaverb@wabash.edu
WEAVER, Carol .... 304-457-6331 486 E
weaverc@ab.edu
WEAVER, Carolyn .... 515-271-1426 165 G
carolyn.weaver@dmu.edu
WEAVER, Catherine, B .. 540-568-3141 468 C
weavercb@jmu.edu
WEAVER, Charlie .... 478-822-1042 118 F
weaverc@fvsu.edu
WEAVER, Darlene .... 412-396-4020 383 A
weaverd1@duq.edu
WEAVER, David .... 907-786-7212.... 9 J
dweaver@alaska.edu
WEAVER, Deirdre .... 310-434-4791.. 63 C
weaver_deirdre@smc.edu
WEAVER, Ernestine .... 860-723-0114.. 85 F
weavere@ct.edu
WEAVER, Gina .... 585-345-6811 300 F
gmweaver@genesee.edu
WEAVER, Greg .... 713-920-1120 121 I
gweaver@ict.edu
WEAVER, Greg .... 713-920-1120 438 B
gweaver@ict.edu
WEAVER, Harry .... 909-687-1520.. 43 D
harryweaver@gs.edu
WEAVER, James, R .... 210-458-4992 455 E
james.weaver@utsa.edu
WEAVER, James, S .... 740-376-4611 355 E
jim.weaver@marietta.edu
WEAVER, Jeff .... 870-460-1028.. 22 C
weaver@uamont.edu
WEAVER, John .... 813-988-5131.. 99 R
weaverj@floridacollege.edu
WEAVER, JR.,
Joseph, B .... 405-744-2690 367 G
joe.weaver@okstate.edu
WEAVER, Kali .... 423-869-6057 421 A
kali.weaver@lmunet.edu

WEEKS, Adam .... 816-322-0110 251 B
adam.weeks@calvary.edu
WEEKS, Ashley .... 352-262-2745 125 F
aweeks@southuniversity.edu
WEEKS, David .... 626-969-3434.. 26 F
dweeks@apu.edu
WEEKS, Elizabeth .... 706-542-9389 126 G
weeksleo@uga.edu
WEEKS, Flora, E .... 870-230-5062.. 19 D
weeksf@hsu.edu
WEEKS, Michael .... 843-953-7416 407 C
mweeks@citadel.edu
WEEKS, Patricia .... 609-652-4826 283 E
patty.weeks@stockton.edu
WEEKS, Sandy .... 620-343-4600 173 G
WEEKS, Susan, M .... 817-257-7519 448 F
s.weeks@tcu.edu
WEEMES, Marcus .... 925-631-8631.. 59 I
mdw3@stmarys-ca.edu
WEEMS, Heather .... 320-308-3102 240 I
hlweems@stcloudstate.edu
WEEMS, Sherryl .... 386-506-3924.. 98 D
sherryl.weems@daytonastate.edu
WEEMS, William, A .... 713-500-5224 456 B
william.a.weems@uth.tmc.edu
WEENICK, Meredith .... 617-495-0908 210 E
meredith_weenick@harvard.edu
WEER, Christy, H .... 410-677-6571 204 D
chweer@salisbury.edu
WEERASURIYA, Yasith .. 949-794-9090.. 66 D
yasithw@stanbridge.edu
WEERHEIM, Revalee .... 307-742-3776 502 B
rweerheim@wyotech.edu
WEERS, Lee .... 641-628-7675 164 D
weersl@central.edu
WEESE, Brian .... 912-279-4564 117 F
bweese@ccga.edu
WEESE, Lacey .... 423-746-5262 426 C
lweese@tnwesleyan.edu
WEETER, Mark .... 918-335-6803 368 E
mweeter@okwu.edu
WEGENER, David .... 414-930-3506 494 E
wegenerd@mtmary.edu
WEGER, Brandon .... 618-393-2982 139 E
wegerb@iecc.edu
WEGHORST, Leasa .... 573-681-5970 254 G
weghorstl@lincolnu.edu
WEGHORST, Michelle ... 309-694-5505 139 B
michelle.weghorst@icc.edu
WEGLARZ, Donna, M ... 630-515-6064 144 F
dwegla@midwestern.edu
WEGLARZ, Joseph, R ... 845-575-3000 305 D
joseph.weglarz@marist.edu
WEGLICKI, Linda .... 843-792-3941 410 C
weglicki@musc.edu
WEGMAN, Barbara, A .... 260-452-2153 154 I
barb.wegman@ctsfw.edu
WEGNER, Janis .... 320-629-5123 240 D
janis.wegner@pine.edu
WEGNER, John .... 325-942-2596 450 E
john.wegner@angelo.edu
WEGNER, Laurie .... 828-327-7000 333 B
lwegner@cvcc.edu
WEGNER, Trisha .... 402-878-2380 267 D
trisha.wegner@littlepriest.edu
WEGRZYN, David .... 401-232-6261 404 A
dwegrzyn@bryant.edu
WEHBY, Laura .... 513-585-1426 350 D
laura.wehby@thechristcollege.edu
WEHBY, Rose .... 775-831-1314 272 D
rwehby@sierranevada.edu
WEHLBURG, Catherine . 256-233-8120.... 4 C
catherine.wehlburg@athens.edu
WEHLE, Arlean .... 504-568-4815 189 H
awehle@lsuhsc.edu
WEHLING, Adam .... 715-852-1394 498 E
awehling@cvtc.edu
WEHMEIER, Teresa .... 620-417-1603 177 F
teresa.wehmeier@sccc.edu
WEHMEIER, Wendall ..... 620-417-1181 177 F
wedall.wehmeier@sccc.edu
WEHNER, STD,
James, A .... 504-866-7426 190 G
jwehner@nds.edu
WEHNER, Jonathan, D .. 216-687-2054 350 J
j.d.wehner@csuohio.edu
WEHR, David Allen .... 412-396-6082 383 A
wehr@duq.edu
WEHRING, Matthew ...... 979-830-4138 431 H
matthew.wehring@blinn.edu
WEHRLEY, James, B ..... 336-841-4560 329 F
jwehrley@highpoint.edu
WEHRUNG, Nancy .... 509-335-4782 485 D
wehrung@wsu.edu
WEI, Mei .... 740-593-1479 358 K
weim@ohio.edu
WEIBEL, Melanie .... 515-271-4451 165 G
melanie.weibel@dmu.edu
WEIBLE, JR., Raymond . 814-262-3816 393 A
rweible@pennhighlands.edu
WEICH, Ronald .... 410-837-4458 204 F
rweich@ubalt.edu
WEICHEL, Brianna .... 402-461-7393 267 C
broncobookstore@hastings.edu
WEICHELT, Shelly .... 715-422-5504 499 B
shelly.weichelt@mstc.edu
WEICHOLD, Mark, H ..... 979-845-4016 446 F
provost@tamu.edu
WEICHOLD, Nelson .... 601-984-1010 249 E
nweichold@umc.edu
WEIDELL, Charleen .... 405-974-3772 370 I
cweidell@uco.edu
WEIDER, Susan, L .... 425-602-3014 477 H
sweider@bastyr.edu
WEIDNER, Bill .... 806-291-3801 457 I
weidnerb@wbu.edu
WEIDNER, Catherine ..... 607-274-3306 302 G
cweidner@ithaca.edu
WEIDNER, John, W .... 513-556-4450 361 J
weidnejw@ucmail.uc.edu
WEIDNER, Karen, K ...... 402-844-7330 268 H
karenkw@northeast.edu
WEIDNER, Penny, L ...... 717-901-5165 385 H
pweidner@harrisburgu.edu
WEIER, Gary, M .... 864-242-5100 406 H
WEIGEL, Kathleen 561-237-7441 103W
kweigel@lynn.edu
WEIGEL, Susan .... 816-926-4400 253 I
WEIGELT, Nicole .... 917-493-4270 305 A
nweigelt@msmnyc.edu
WEIGHILL, Dale .... 810-762-0456 228 F
dale.weighill@mcc.edu
WEIKEL, Bridget, K .... 757-683-4283 469 B
bweikel@odu.edu
WEIL, David .... 607-274-1530 302 G
dweil@ithaca.edu
WEIL, David .... 781-736-3883 208 A
davweil@brandeis.edu
WEIL, Denis .... 312-595-4900 140 A
dweil@id.iit.edu
WEIL, Valerie, P .... 215-596-8800 401 E
WEILAND-ZALEZNAK,
Carla .... 914-251-6046 319 B
carla.weiland@purchase.edu
WEILER, Eric .... 319-398-1281 167 J
eric.weiler@kirkwood.edu
WEILER, Phil .... 509-335-4742 485 D
phil.weiler@wsu.edu
WEILL, Lawrence .... 845-434-5750 321 E
WEILMINSTER, Deirdre . 301-846-2610 198 I
dweilminster@frederick.edu
WEIMER, Brian .... 573-882-5923 261 A
weimerb@missouri.edu
WEIMER, Jean .... 414-847-3272 494 C
jeanweimer@miad.edu
WEIMER, Rebecca .... 479-524-7493.. 19 H
bweimer@jbu.edu
WEIMER, Theresa .... 718-390-3122 324 F
tweimer@wagner.edu
WEIMER, Tresa .... 304-367-4826 489 K
tresa.weimer@fairmontstate.edu
WEIN, Kory, G .... 608-342-1151 496 E
weink@uwplatt.edu
WEIN, Mitchell, L .... 610-896-1223 385 I
mwein@haverford.edu
WEINACKER, Emily .... 928-776-2217.. 16 J
emily.weinacker@yc.edu
WEINBENDER, Sue .... 503-352-2123 375 C
weinbender@pacificu.edu
WEINBERG, Adam, S ..... 740-587-6281 352 A
weinberga@denison.edu
WEINBERG, Jerry, B ..... 618-650-3010 150 C
jweinbe@siue.edu
WEINBERGER, Jayne ..... 718-522-9073 290 E
jweinberger@asa.edu
WEINBERGER, Judah .... 212-463-0400 322 F
judah.weinberger6@touro.edu
WEINBERGER, Judah .... 212-463-0400 322 G
judah.weinberger6@touro.edu
WEINDLLING, Lauren ... 203-576-2400.. 89 C
lweindli@bridgeport.edu
WEINDORF, David, C .... 989-774-3094 222 E
weind1dc@cmich.edu
WEINER, Daniel .... 860-486-3152.. 89 D
dan.weiner@uconn.edu
WEINER, David .... 312-369-7816 136 D
dweiner@colum.edu
WEINER, Gregory .... 508-767-7312 206 A
gs.weiner@assumption.edu
WEINER, Marc .... 212-247-3434 304 L
mweiner@mandl.edu
WEINER, Melvyn, P ...... 212-247-3434 304 L
melweiner2@mandl.edu
WEINER, Michael .... 949-480-4337.. 64 G
mweiner@soka.edu
WEINER, Nettie .... 212-247-3434 304 L
nweiner@mandl.edu
WEINER, Steven, A .... 650-543-3927.. 51 G
steven.weiner@menlo.edu
WEINER, Stuart .... 212-247-3434 304 L
stuweiner@mandl.edu
WEINERT, Daniel, J ...... 563-884-5761 169 F
dan.weinert@palmer.edu
WEINERT, Daryl .... 412-268-2000 380 C
WEINERT, Rick .... 218-751-8670 242 O
rickweinert@oakhills.edu
WEINGARD, Cyndi .... 510-879-9200.. 60 C
cweingard@samuuelmerritt.edu
WEINGART, Brian .... 304-558-4618 489 H
brian.weingart@wvhepc.edu
WEINGART, Chedva ...... 626-585-7454.. 56 D
cweingart@pasadena.edu
WEINGART, Stephen, T . 260-359-4067 156 C
sweingart@huntington.edu
WEINGARTEN, Andrew .. 503-943-7205 377 A
weingart@up.edu
WEINGARTEN, Isreal ..... 845-426-3488 291 H
WEININGER, Melissa ..... 419-448-3416 361 D
weiningerm@tiffin.edu
WEINKAUF, Donald, H . 651-962-5762 244 E
weinkauf@stthomas.edu
WEINKOPF,
Christopher .... 805-525-4417.. 67 K
cweinkopf@thomasaquinas.edu
WEINMAN, Kevin, C ..... 413-542-2325 205 G
kweinman@amherst.edu
WEINMAN, Todd .... 615-322-2571 428 A
todd.weinman@vanderbilt.edu
WEINMAN, Todd, N ...... 802-656-3340 463 A
todd.weinman@uvm.edu
WEINMANN, Heather ..... 858-513-9240.. 68 K
heather.weinmann@ashford.edu
WEINMEISTER, Nick ...... 641-782-1432 170 F
weinmeister@swcciowa.edu
WEINS, Ben .... 605-331-6700 417 C
ben.weins@usiouxfalls.edu
WEINS, Sean, A .... 918-595-7916 370 C
sean.weins@tulsacc.edu
WEINSHEIM, Leslie .... 970-521-6714.. 82 C
leslie.weinsheim@njc.edu
WEINSHEL, Seth, D ...... 202-994-2552.. 92 D
sdweingw@gwu.edu
WEINSTEIN, Cindy, A ... 626-395-6249.. 28 J
caw@hss.caltech.edu
WEINSTEIN, Cindy, A ... 626-395-3600.. 28 J
caw@caltech.edu
WEINSTEIN, Daniel .... 718-997-4105 295 B
daniel.weinstein@qc.cuny.edu
WEINSTEIN, Heather ..... 802-828-2800 463 F
haw09010@ccv.vsc.edu
WEINSTEIN, Mark .... 937-766-8800 349 E
mweinstein@cedarville.edu
WEINSTEIN, Sara .... 804-752-3749 469 F
saraweinstein@rmc.edu
WEINSTOCK, Austin ...... 708-456-0300 151 D
austinweinstock@triton.edu
WEINTRAUB, Brandon .. 352-371-2833.. 98 G
it@dragonrises.edu
WEINTRAUB, Susan ...... 603-641-7600 274 A
sweintraub@anselm.edu
WEINTRAUB, Yitzchok .. 732-985-6533 280 E
WEINZAPFEL-SMITH,
Tami .... 812-237-4115 156 D
WEINZIMMER, Julianne 937-775-4818 364 E
julianne.weinzimmer@wright.edu
WEIPPERT, Linda .... 620-229-6175 177 G
linda.weippert@sckans.edu
WEIR, Amy .... 765-361-6078 163 B
weira@wabash.edu
WEIR, Catherine .... 310-434-8208.. 63 C
weir_catherine@smc.edu
WEIR, Dustin .... 323-860-0789.. 50 B
WEIR, Lljuna .... 601-877-6700 245 A
weir@alcorn.edu
WEIR, Paul .... 575-562-2153 286 B
WEIRICK, Chad .... 740-755-7327 349 F
weirick.7@cotc.edu
WEIS, Charlene .... 701-255-3285 347 A
cweis@uttc.edu
WEIS, Ed .... 516-299-2000 304 E
ed.weis@liu.edu
WEIS, Lisa .... 918-293-4768 368 B
lisa.weis@okstate.edu
WEISBERG, Bradley ...... 408-741-4012.. 75 E
bradley.weisberg@westvalley.edu
WEISBORD, Aviva .... 410-358-3144 205 C
WEISBORD, Beryl .... 410-484-7200 201 C
rbw@nirc.edu
WEISBORD, Dano, J ..... 413-585-2427 218 H
dweisbor@smith.edu
WEISE, Brittany .... 217-228-5432 147 F
ellerbr@quincy.edu
WEISENBERGER, Clare .. 602-275-7133.. 15M
WEISENBERGER, Sheila 310-338-2775.. 51 A
sheila.weisenberger@lmu.edu
WEISENBURGER, Leigh 207-786-6000 194 A
lweisenb@bates.edu
WEISENBURGER, Perk .. 231-591-2863 224 A
perkweisenburger@ferris.edu
WEISER, Bridget, R .... 785-833-4325 175 E
bridget@kwu.edu
WEISER, Kent, L .... 620-341-5350 173 F
kweiser@emporia.edu
WEISGERBER,
James (Chip), E .... 412-536-1765 386 H
chip.weisgerber@laroche.edu
WEISHAAR, Mary .... 618-650-3785 150 C
mweisha@siue.edu
WEISHNER, Stephanie .. 910-898-9645 336 D
weishners@montgomery.edu
WEISKOPF, Lee .... 662-325-1008 247 F
lee.weiskopf@pres.msstate.edu
WEISMAN, Susan, E ..... 718-489-5388 313 E
sweisman@sfc.edu
WEISMANTEL, David, P 517-355-2488 227 F
weismant@msu.edu
WEISNER, Christina ...... 252-335-0821 333 G
christina_weisner@albemarle.edu
WEISPFENNING, John .. 714-438-4888.. 37 I
johnw@cccd.edu
WEISS, Aaron .... 440-366-4866 355 B
WEISS, Andrea .... 212-824-2248 301 B
aweiss@huc.edu
WEISS, Beth .... 440-775-8413 357 G
beth.weiss@oberlin.edu
WEISS, David .... 210-567-3709 456 C
weissd@uthscsa.edu
WEISS, Deborah .... 334-844-5001.... 4 D
weissds@auburn.edu
WEISS, H .... 732-364-1220 275 F
WEISS, Johanna .... 804-594-4187 474 B
jweiss@jtcc.edu
WEISS, Joshua .... 413-565-1000 206 D
jweiss@baypath.edu
WEISS, Karen .... 618-252-5400 149 I
karen.weiss@sic.edu
WEISS, Kay .... 909-389-3362.. 60 E
kweiss@sbccd.cc.ca.us
WEISS, Lora, G .... 814-865-6332 391 G
lgw1@psu.edu
WEISS, Loriann .... 303-722-5724.. 81 L
lweiss@lincolntech.edu
WEISS, Mary Jane .... 978-998-7749 209 E
mweiss@endicott.edu
WEISS, Michael .... 843-208-8055 413 C
mcweiss@uscb.edu
WEISS, Toni .... 504-862-8342 191 F
tweiss@tulane.edu
WEISS, Valerie .... 313-664-7852 222 H
vweiss@collegeforcreativestudies.edu
WEISS-COOK, Laura ...... 785-320-4541 175 G
lauraweiss-cook@manhattantech.edu
WEISSBERG, Erik .... 617-587-5750 217 D
weissberge@neco.edu
WEISSENFLUH, Anji ...... 541-962-3236 372 I
aweissen@eou.edu
WEISSMAN, Neil, B ...... 717-245-1321 382 D
weissmne@dickinson.edu
WEISSMAN, Rebecca .... 315-267-2118 319 A
weissmr@potsdam.edu
WEISSMANN,
Kristopher, E .... 803-938-3763 413 G
weissmak@uscsumter.edu
WEIST, Barbara .... 253-879-2691 484 G
bweist@pugetsound.edu
WEIST, Ronald, D .... 301-546-0074 201 E
weistrd@pgcc.edu
WEISZ, Brett .... 406-247-5701 264 D
brett.weisz@msubillings.edu

WENTHE, Andrew .... 563-425-5348 170 H
wenthea@uiu.edu
WENTHOLD, Kathy .... 563-425-5394 170 H
wentholdk@uiu.edu
WENTHOLD, Marsha ..... 563-387-1415 168 B
mwenthold@luther.edu
WENTWORTH, Gail .... 518-255-5413 319 C
wentwoge@cobleskill.edu
WENTWORTH, Monica .. 615-966-6296 421 B
monica.wentworth@lipscomb.edu
WENTWORTH, Renae .... 864-242-5100 406 H
WENTZ, Deb .... 701-858-3301 345 E
deb.wentz@minotstateu.edu
WENTZ, Elizabeth, A ..... 480-965-7279.. 10 J
wentz@asu.edu
WENTZ, Meridith .... 715-232-5312 497 B
wentzm@uwstout.edu
WENTZ, Sheila, D .... 478-289-2380 118 C
swentz@ega.edu
WENTZ, Sheree, D .... 304-457-6386 486 E
wentzsd@ab.edu
WENYIKA, Reggies .... 785-248-2353 176 I
reggies.wenyika@ottawa.edu
WENZ, Donald, A .... 718-951-5511 293 C
donald@brooklyn.cuny.edu
WENZ, Michael .... 773-442-5117 146 A
m-wenz@neiu.edu
WENZEL, Claudia .... 216-397-4270 353 O
cwenzel@jcu.edu
WENZEL, Leslie .... 620-275-3220 174 B
leslie.wenzel@gcccks.edu
WENZLER, John .... 510-885-3664.. 31 A
john.wenzler@csueastbay.edu
WEPNER, Shelley .... 914-323-3153 305 B
shelley.wepner@mville.edu
WERBEL DASHEFSKY,
Linda .... 718-489-5370 313 E
lwerbel@sfc.edu
WERCHOUSKI, Kat .... 715-394-8415 497 C
kwerchou@uwsuper.edu
WERDANN, Frank .... 607-431-4340 301 A
werdannf@hartwick.edu
WERDELIN, Dorna .... 404-225-4593 115 H
dwerdelin@atlantatech.edu
WERKHEISER, Amber .... 919-718-7311 333 C
aconnor@cccc.edu
WERLING, Abigail .... 812-488-2361 161 G
am275@evansville.edu
WERLING, Karen .... 229-931-2902 125 E
kwerling@southgatech.edu
WERMUTH, Thomas, S . 845-575-3000 305 D
thomas.wermuth@marist.edu
WERNE, Stanley, J .... 812-888-6999 162 F
swerne@vinu.edu
WERNER, Anthony .... 920-465-2018 495 F
wernera@uwgb.edu
WERNER, Claudia .... 865-981-8035 421 C
claudia.werner@maryvillecollege.edu
WERNER, Jackie .... 312-553-5838 135 B
jwerner9@ccc.edu
WERNER, Kathleen .... 301-369-2322 198 C
kwerner@captechu.edu
WERNER, Keith, E .... 919-962-1000 340 H
WERNER, Lauren .... 620-235-4105 177 A
lwerner@pittstate.edu
WERNER, Renee .... 561-683-1400.. 94 F
rwerner@anho.edu
WERNER, Sarah .... 914-961-8313 314 H
swerner@svots.edu
WERNER, Tony .... 920-465-2018 495 F
wernera@uwgb.edu
WERNETTE, Judy .... 313-993-1582 231 E
wernetjm@udmercy.edu
WERNICKE, Rachel .... 703-993-2884 467 E
rwernick@gmu.edu
WERNICKI, Abigail .... 267-341-3237 385 J
awernicki@holyfamily.edu
WERNON, Michael .... 478-289-2148 118 C
mwernon@ega.edu
WERNOSKI, Rick .... 919-962-1668 342 C
wernoski@email.unc.edu
WERNSMAN, Scott .... 618-985-3741 140 H
scottwernsman@jalc.edu
WEROSH, Keith .... 219-473-4375 154 D
kwerosh@ccsj.edu
WERREMEYER, Nathan .. 601-857-3330 246 C
WERTH, Lori .... 606-218-5830 186 B
loriwerth@upike.edu
WERTHEIMER, Eric .... 631-632-7035 317 A
eric.wertheimer@stonybrook.edu
WERTZ, Joan .... 309-457-2384 144 H
jwertz@monmouthcollege.edu

WERTZ, Lori, N .... 915-747-8858 455 C
lnwertz@utep.edu
WERTZ, Melissa .... 412-809-5358 396 E
wertz.melissa@ptcollege.edu
WERTZ, Miriam .... 574-807-7209 154 B
miriam.wertz@betheluniversity.edu
WESCOAT, Bonna .... 404-727-6279 118 E
bwescoa@emory.edu
WESCOAT, Megan .... 308-635-6017 270 C
wescoatm@wncc.edu
WESCOTT, Abigail .... 276-244-1234 464 E
awescott@asl.edu
WESCOTT, Jon, D 570-326-3761 392W
jdw18@pct.edu
WESCOTT, Phebe .... 434-947-8288 469 E
pwescott@randolphcollege.edu
WESLEY, Artanya .... 262-472-1172 497 D
WESLEY, Homer .... 719-502-3563.. 82 E
homer.wesley@ppcc.edu
WESLOW, Suzanne .... 414-229-4503 496 B
sweslow@uwm.edu
WESNER, Katrin .... 910-962-4126 343 C
wesnerk@uncw.edu
WESNER, Samantha ...... 610-921-7611 377 G
swesner@albright.edu
WESS, Byron .... 215-953-5999.. 93 H
WESSEL, Tonya .... 816-584-7406 258 C
tonya.wessel@park.edu
WESSEL KREJCI, Janet .. 414-288-3812 493 E
janet.krejci@marquette.edu
WESSELL, Charlotte .... 212-353-4252 297 E
charlotte.wessell@cooper.edu
WESSELS, Gus .... 979-532-6505 458 E
gusw@wcjc.edu
WESSNER, Val .... 610-372-1722 378 G
WESSON, Cameron .... 717-358-3986 383 I
cwesson@fandm.edu
WESSON, G. Dale .... 404-880-8754 117 C
gwesson@cau.edu
WEST, Adrian .... 803-780-1269 414 B
west@voorhees.edu
WEST, Allen .... 903-693-1171 441 C
awest@panola.edu
WEST, Amy .... 731-425-2621 424 E
awest12@jscc.edu
WEST, Amy .... 731-425-2643 424 E
awest12@jscc.edu
WEST, Amy .... 419-372-2704 348 G
amywest@bgsu.edu
WEST, April .... 877-954-1500 421 F
WEST, Cathy .... 361-698-1265 435 G
cwest@delmar.edu
WEST, Chotsani .... 516-877-3000 289 I
WEST, Christina, D .... 202-216-4370 428 A
christina.d.west@vanderbilt.edu
WEST, Cynthia, L .... 731-881-7125 427 D
cwest@utm.edu
WEST, Dana .... 865-882-4657 425 C
westdk2@roanestate.edu
WEST, David .... 575-624-8014 287 B
west@nmmi.edu
WEST, David, L .... 901-722-3210 423 G
dwest@sco.edu
WEST, Debra .... 870-733-6722.. 17 F
dwest@asumidsouth.edu
WEST, Detra, E .... 330-569-5237 353 G
westde@hiram.edu
WEST, Dominique .... 718-960-8000 294 A
WEST, Greg .... 262-691-5417 500 B
gwest@wctc.edu
WEST, J. Cameron .... 334-833-4409.... 5 G
camwest@hawks.huntingdon.edu
WEST, Jeff .... 801-957-4250 461 C
jeff.west@slcc.edu
WEST, Jennifer, L .... 434-924-0311 472 D
WEST, Jody .... 212-280-1373 323 K
jwest@uts.columbia.edu
WEST, John .... 703-416-1441 466 A
jwest@divinemercy.edu
WEST, Judy .... 216-373-6396 357 F
jwest@ndc.edu
WEST, Junette .... 602-639-7500.. 12 J
WEST, Kevin .... 330-672-2220 354 A
kwest32@kent.edu
WEST, Kevin .... 828-689-1585 331 C
kwest@mhu.edu
WEST, Kristie .... 916-691-7199.. 50 H
westk@crc.losrios.edu
WEST, Lance 304-696-6440 489M
west24@marshall.edu
WEST, Linda, J .... 304-697-7550 487 E
lwest@huntingtonjuniorcollege.edu

WEST, Marc .... 440-826-3483 348 D
mwest@bw.edu
WEST, Mark, D .... 734-764-7409 231 H
markwest@umich.edu
WEST, Matthew .... 937-327-7946 364 D
counseling@wittenberg.edu
WEST, Maurice .... 214-379-5514 441 F
mwest@pqc.edu
WEST, Mickey .... 615-329-8680 419 H
mwest@fisk.edu
WEST, Molly .... 601-974-1063 247 B
molly.west@millsaps.edu
WEST, Monica .... 301-445-1937 202 G
mwest@usmd.edu
WEST, Peter .... 914-674-7803 306 C
pwest@mercy.edu
WEST, Peter .... 571-633-9651 472 A
peter.west@uona.edu
WEST, Randall .... 206-543-0521 485 A
randallw@uw.edu
WEST, Raymond .... 951-222-8000.. 59 D
WEST, JR., Reginald ..... 949-376-6000.. 47 D
rwest@lcad.edu
WEST, Rodney, A .... 808-237-5144 128 F
awest@hmi.edu
WEST, Ryan .... 503-399-5018 372 B
ryan.west@chemeketa.edu
WEST, Sue .... 303-444-0202.. 82 A
WEST, Susan .... 615-460-5602 418 B
susan.west@belmont.edu
WEST, Susan, H .... 615-460-6435 418 B
susan.west@belmont.edu
WEST, Tom .... 323-856-7680.. 25 G
twest@afi.com
WEST, Tom .... 954-262-4994 105 A
twest@nova.edu
WEST, Tracy .... 909-884-8891.. 39 I
WEST, William .... 512-404-4804 430 J
wwest@austinseminary.edu
WESTARY, Kenneth .... 443-840-3213 198 H
kwestary@ccbcmd.edu
WESTBERG, Caleb .... 773-995-3561 134 K
cwestber@csu.edu
WESTBROCK, Theresa ... 319-273-7868 164 A
theresa.westbrock@uni.edu
WESTBROOK, Ashley .... 706-245-7226 118 D
adenny@ec.edu
WESTBROOK, Sara .... 503-943-7161 377 A
westbroo@up.edu
WESTBROOK, Velma, S 985-448-4013 192 F
sue.westbrook@nicholls.edu
WESTBROOK, Velma, S 985-448-4687 192 F
sue.westbrook@nicholls.edu
WESTBROOKS, Elaine .... 919-962-1301 342 C
elainelw@email.unc.edu
WESTBY, Christopher .... 914-606-6810 325 A
christopher.westby@sunywcc.edu
WESTCOTT, James .... 605-367-5675 417 B
james.westcott@southeasttech.edu
WESTDYKE, Anne, E ..... 512-492-3147 442 I
anneew@stedwards.edu
WESTENBROEK, Steve ... 402-399-2465 266 F
swestenbroek@csm.edu
WESTER, Ken .... 479-968-0218.. 18 C
kwester@atu.edu
WESTER, Richard, J ...... 860-444-8286 503 G
richard.j.wester@uscg.mil
WESTERBERG, Sarah ...... 801-422-4668 458 H
sarah_westerberg@byu.edu
WESTERFIELD,
Mary Ann, K .... 302-356-6936.. 91 E
maryann.k.westerfield@wilmu.edu
WESTERGAARD,
Patricia .... 979-209-7446 431 H
pat.westergaard@blinn.edu
WESTERGAARD, Tricia .. 248-370-4585 229 I
westerga@oakland.edu
WESTERHOUSE, Joni, L 314-286-0120 262 A
westerhousej@wustl.edu
WESTERIK, Robin .... 406-604-4321 262 I
rwesterik@apollos.edu
WESTERLINK, Dafne ...... 432-837-8559 450 B
der14mw@sulross.edu
WESTERLUND, Richard . 517-321-0242 225 A
rwesterlund@glcc.edu
WESTERMANN, Jorg ..... 866-492-5336 244 F
jorg.westermann@mail.waldenu.edu
WESTERMEYER,
Susan, M .... 317-940-9135 154 C
swesterm@butler.edu
WESTERN, Lindajean ..... 330-823-2568 362 E
westerlh@mountunion.edu

WESTERSTANL STENPORT,
Anna .... 585-475-2935 312 F
llmgcj@rit.edu
WESTERVELT, Rob .... 636-949-1438 254 H
rwestervelt@lindenwood.edu
WESTERVELT, Wayne ..... 315-312-2265 318 D
wayne.westervelt@oswego.edu
WESTFALL, Anita, C ...... 540-568-6868 468 C
westfaac@jmu.edu
WESTFALL,
Christopher, T .... 501-686-5150.. 22 B
westfallchristophert@uams.edu
WESTFALL, Michael ...... 248-364-6152 229 I
mwestfall@oakland.edu
WESTFALL, Sarah, B ..... 269-337-7209 225 F
sarah.westfall@kzoo.edu
WESTFIELD,
Nancy Lynne .... 765-361-6434 163 B
westfiel@wabash.edu
WESTHOFF, James .... 207-992-4909 194 F
westhoffj@husson.edu
WESTHOFF, Randy .... 218-755-2016 237 F
randall.westhoff@bemidjistate.edu
WESTHOFF, Tom .... 620-235-4232 177 A
tmwesthoff@pittstate.edu
WESTLAKE,
Christopher, J .... 850-872-3212 101 N
cwestlake@gulfcoast.edu
WESTLEY, Chris .... 239-590-7090 109 K
cwestley@fgcu.edu
WESTLUND, Amy .... 530-242-7648.. 64 C
awestlund@shastacollege.edu
WESTLUND, Julie, A ..... 218-726-7985 243 G
jwestlun@d.umn.edu
WESTMAN, Andrea .... 425-739-8223 481 C
andrea.westman@lwtech.edu
WESTMAN, Craig .... 856-225-6510 281 G
craig.westman@rutgers.edu
WESTMAN, Dennis .... 580-745-2148 369 G
dwestman@se.edu
WESTMAN, Jennifer .... 307-332-2930 502 A
jwestman@wyomingcatholic.edu
WESTMAN, Lee Ann ..... 856-225-6671 281 G
leeann.westman@rutgers.edu
WESTMORELAND,
Andrew .... 205-726-2727.... 6 E
tawestmo@samford.edu
WESTMORELAND, Tim .. 830-372-8065 449 A
twestmoreland@tlu.edu
WESTON, Alison .... 540-674-3685 474 E
aweston@nr.edu
WESTON, Brenna .... 607-735-1830 298 H
bweston@elmira.edu
WESTON, Brian .... 619-388-6750.. 60 H
bweston@sdccd.edu
WESTON, Earl .... 970-207-4500.. 85 A
WESTON, Jackie .... 405-945-3310 368 C
jackie.weston@okstate.edu
WESTON, Jerri .... 318-473-6424 189 F
jweston@lsua.edu
WESTON, Laurie .... 252-493-7439 336 H
lweston@email.pittcc.edu
WESTON, Scott .... 304-357-4879 487 J
gradyweston@ucwv.edu
WESTOVER, Jon .... 919-515-5036 342 A
jrwestov@ncsu.edu
WESTOVER, Kristen .... 276-523-7490 474 D
kwestover@mecc.edu
WESTPHAL, Donald, M . 507-344-7320 234 C
don.westphal@blc.edu
WESTPHAL, Judith .... 920-424-3089 496 C
westphaj@uwosh.edu
WESTPHAL, Matt .... 918-540-6249 366 F
mwestphal@neo.edu
WESTPHAL, Wendy .... 317-955-6026 159 K
wwestphal@marian.edu
WESTRA, Amy .... 712-722-6024 165 I
amy.westra@dordt.edu
WESTRA, Kayla .... 507-372-3435 239 F
kayla.westra@mnwest.edu
WESTWATER, Julia .... 508-289-3379 220 E
jwestwater@whoi.edu
WETHERBEE, Scott .... 734-487-1050 223 K
scott.wetherbee@emich.edu
WETHERINGTON, Kitty .. 252-328-9882 341 A
wetheringtonk@ecu.edu
WETHERINGTON, Lee .... 252-527-6223 335 G
lwetherington@lenoircc.edu
WETHINGTON, Charles . 252-638-7350 334 A
wethingc@cravencc.edu
WETSELL, Linda, S .... 814-332-4790 378 A
lwetsell@allegheny.edu
WETSTEIN, Ken, A .... 217-581-5129 137 E
kawetstein@eiu.edu

WHITE, Anne .... 253-964-6716 482 E
awhite@pierce.ctc.edu
WHITE, Annette .... 804-751-9191 465 K
awhite@ccc-va.com
WHITE, Annita .... 770-467-4488 125 H
annita.white@sctech.edu
WHITE, Anthony .... 540-831-5095 469 D
awhite173@radford.edu
WHITE, April, D .... 260-982-5888 159 J
adwhite@manchester.edu
WHITE, Barbara .... 720-872-5608.. 78 H
bwhite@ccu.edu
WHITE, Belva .... 404-727-1408 118 E
bdwhite@emory.edu
WHITE, Bill .... 321-433-7400.. 98 I
whiteb@easternflorida.edu
WHITE, Billy .... 704-637-4565 327 I
wtwhite@catawba.edu
WHITE, BJ .... 847-735-5027 142 A
bwhite@lakeforest.edu
WHITE, Bo .... 254-710-2657 431 E
bo_white@baylor.edu
WHITE, Bradley .... 615-963-5817 426 A
bwhite2@tnstate.edu
WHITE, Brent .... 520-621-1900.. 16 D
brentwhite@arizona.edu
WHITE, Brian .... 561-297-3199 109 J
whiteb@fau.edu
WHITE, Brian .... 785-864-3276 177 J
brian-white@ku.edu
WHITE, Brian .... 617-287-5611 211 H
brian.white@umb.edu
WHITE, Brian .... 503-768-7307 373 E
bdwhite@lclark.edu
WHITE, Byron .... 704-687-6193 342 D
bwhite93@uncc.edu
WHITE, Caleb .... 608-822-2446 500 A
cwhite@swtc.edu
WHITE, Carolee .... 315-781-3337 301 F
cwhite@hws.edu
WHITE, Carolyn .... 908-526-1200 281 A
carolyn.white@raritanval.edu
WHITE, Carolyn .... 504-398-2149 192 A
cwhite@uhcno.edu
WHITE, Carrie .... 304-293-9391 490 E
cwhite17@mail.wvu.edu
WHITE, Catherine, D ..... 256-765-4291.... 8 E
cdwhite1@una.edu
WHITE, Cecil .... 479-619-3121.. 20 C
cwhite24@nwacc.edu
WHITE, Chelsea .... 713-785-5995 432 L
WHITE, Christopher ...... 815-836-5584 142 F
cwhite10@lewisu.edu
WHITE, Claudette .... 757-401-6125 477 G
WHITE, Courtney .... 435-652-7534 460 B
cwhite@dixie.edu
WHITE, Courtney .... 864-646-1484 412 H
cwhite12@tctc.edu
WHITE, Craig .... 217-424-6344 144 G
ccwhite@millikin.edu
WHITE, Craig .... 225-768-0804 187 B
craig.white@franu.edu
WHITE, Curtis .... 210-436-3622 442 J
cdwhite@stmarytx.edu
WHITE, Cynthia, L .... 972-758-3871 433 I
clwhite@collin.edu
WHITE, Damian .... 401-454-6580 405 B
dwhite01@risd.edu
WHITE, Daniel .... 865-974-6484 427 B
dwhite79@utk.edu
WHITE, Daniel, M .... 907-474-7112.. 10 A
uaf.chancellor@alaska.edu
WHITE, Daniel, R .... 606-474-3111 181 B
dwhite@kcu.edu
WHITE, Danielle, M ...... 607-587-3930 319 F
whitedm@alfredstate.edu
WHITE, David .... 903-586-2518 438 C
dwhite@jacksonville-college.edu
WHITE, David .... 252-737-3004 341 A
whited@ecu.edu
WHITE, Dawne .... 770-824-5245 128 A
dawne.white@westgatech.edu
WHITE, Debbie .... 402-872-2224 268 E
dwhite@peru.edu
WHITE, Deborah .... 252-246-1216 339 C
dwhite@wilsoncc.edu
WHITE, Debra .... 954-486-7728 113 B
dwhite@uftl.edu
WHITE, Dennis .... 618-985-3741 140 H
denniswhite@jalc.edu
WHITE, DeWayne .... 615-675-5255 428 C
dewayne@welch.edu

WHITE, Diane .... 678-407-5610 119 C
dwhite9@ggc.edu
WHITE, Diane .... 513-936-1664 362 A
diane.white@uc.edu
WHITE, Dominique .... 870-972-3964.. 17 E
dowhite@astate.edu
WHITE, Donald .... 318-274-6298 192 C
whited@gram.edu
WHITE, Donald .... 915-995-3100.. 93 H
WHITE, Elaine, T .... 718-429-6600 324 D
elaine.white@vaughn.edu
WHITE, Emily .... 256-782-8393.... 6 A
ehwhite@jsu.edu
WHITE, Erin .... 612-343-4457 242 M
erwhite@northcentral.edu
WHITE, Erin .... 910-672-1347 341 C
ewhite@uncfsu.edu
WHITE, Ernie .... 919-739-6805 338 H
ewhite@waynecc.edu
WHITE, Gary, R .... 805-893-2182.. 70 E
gary.white@sa.ucsb.edu
WHITE, Gene .... 870-543-5949.. 21 B
gwhite@seark.edu
WHITE, George .... 718-262-2804 295 E
gwhite@york.cuny.edu
WHITE, Georgia .... 775-445-4284 271 F
georgia.white@wnc.edu
WHITE, Gina .... 318-342-3002 193 C
ewhite@ulm.edu
WHITE, Greg .... 650-508-3500.. 54 G
provost@ndnu.edu
WHITE, Greg .... 650-508-3436.. 54 G
gwhite@ndnu.edu
WHITE, Heather .... 352-392-1261 111 A
heatherw@dso.ufl.edu
WHITE, Ian, K .... 973-618-3236 276 D
iwhite@caldwell.edu
WHITE, Jacqueline, M .. 401-865-2811 404 F
jwhite@providence.edu
WHITE, Jama .... 423-266-4574 423 B
WHITE, James .... 201-200-2597 279 D
jwhite4@njcu.edu
WHITE, James .... 501-332-0252.. 18 B
jwhite@asutr.edu
WHITE, James .... 303-492-7294.. 84 B
james.white@colorado.edu
WHITE, James .... 509-313-6568 480 F
whitej@gonzaga.edu
WHITE, Jared .... 334-242-2688.... 4 D
jrw0020@auburn.edu
WHITE, Jerry .... 574-807-7877 154 B
jerry.white@betheluniversity.edu
WHITE, Jessica .... 651-201-1845 237 B
jessica.white@minnstate.edu
WHITE, Jessie .... 254-659-7841 437 A
jwhite@hillcollege.edu
WHITE, Jim .... 218-755-3868 237 F
jim.white@bemidjistate.edu
WHITE, John .... 413-748-3895 218 I
jawhite@springfield.edu
WHITE, John .... 404-752-1734 123 E
jwhite@msm.edu
WHITE, John .... 760-565-4827.. 38 E
jowhite@collegeofthedesert.edu
WHITE, John .... 843-953-6810 408 C
whitej@cofc.edu
WHITE, John, E .... 609-497-7880 280 C
john.white@ptsem.edu
WHITE, Joy .... 470-639-0985 123 D
joy.white@morehouse.edu
WHITE, Julie .... 813-259-6586 102 B
jwhite66@hccfl.edu
WHITE, Julie .... 253-964-6776 482 E
juwhite@pierce.ctc.edu
WHITE, Julie, R .... 315-464-4816 317 C
whitejul@upstate.edu
WHITE, Juls .... 914-323-5217 305 B
juls.white@mville.edu
WHITE, Justin .... 479-619-4123.. 20 C
jwhite35@nwacc.edu
WHITE, Karen .... 703-526-6803 468 H
karen.white@marymount.edu
WHITE, Karol .... 319-363-1323 168 F
kwhite@mtmercy.edu
WHITE, Katie .... 760-757-2121.. 52 F
kwhite@miracosta.edu
WHITE, Katie .... 972-825-4636 444 J
kwhite@sagu.edu
WHITE, Kenneth, L .... 435-797-2201 460 C
ken.white@usu.edu
WHITE, Kevin .... 646-378-6103 310 D
kevin.white@nyack.edu

WHITE, Kimberly .... 256-782-5180.... 6 A
ksgwhite@jsu.edu
WHITE, Kyle .... 918-766-5512 368 E
kwhite@okwu.edu
WHITE, Lamar, J .... 803-793-5241 408 G
whitel@denmarktech.edu
WHITE, Lauren .... 361-698-1641 435 G
lwhite16@delmar.edu
WHITE, Linda .... 901-435-1477 420 I
linda_white@loc.edu
WHITE, Lindsay .... 918-595-7869 370 C
lindsay.white@tulsacc.edu
WHITE, Lindsey .... 479-619-4191.. 20 C
lwhite13@nwacc.edu
WHITE, London .... 918-465-1818 366 A
lwhite@eosc.edu
WHITE, Lori .... 765-658-4220 154 J
president@depauw.edu
WHITE, Mallory .... 731-989-6916 419 K
mwhite@fhu.edu
WHITE, Marcia .... 518-454-5121 296 G
marcia.white@strose.edu
WHITE, Mark, D .... 806-371-5143 429 E
mdwhite@actx.edu
WHITE, Marlene .... 908-709-7041 284 D
marlene.white@ucc.edu
WHITE, Mary Jo .... 206-934-5378 483 D
maryjo.white@seattlecolleges.edu
WHITE, Mary Kate .... 304-724-5000 487 B
mwhite@cdu.edu
WHITE, Mason, M .... 410-543-6165 204 D
mmwhite@salisbury.edu
WHITE, Matthew .... 757-727-5253 467 G
matthew.white@hamptonu.edu
WHITE, Maureen .... 860-439-2541.. 87 H
mwhite4@conncoll.edu
WHITE, Maureen .... 516-726-5632 503 H
whitem@usmma.edu
WHITE, Melea .... 319-399-8843 164 F
meleawhite@coe.edu
WHITE, Michael .... 972-860-8232 434 G
mwhite@dcccd.edu
WHITE, Michael .... 401-841-7560 503 A
michael.white@usnwc.edu
WHITE, Michael .... 401-863-2648 403 J
michael_p_white@brown.edu
WHITE, Michele, M ...... 540-568-6281 468 C
whitemm@jmu.edu
WHITE, Michelle .... 918-647-1399 365 E
mwhite@carlalbert.edu
WHITE, Michelle, R ...... 212-986-4343 275 I
michelle-white2@berkeleycollege.edu
WHITE, Michelle, R ...... 212-986-4343 291 E
michelle-white2@berkeleycollege.edu
WHITE, Mona .... 337-475-5501 192 E
mwhite@mcneese.edu
WHITE, Monica .... 504-816-4374 186 I
mwhite@dillard.edu
WHITE, Nicole .... 615-687-6904 417 F
nwhite@abcnash.edu
WHITE, O, I .... 903-923-2421 458 F
oiwhite@wileyc.edu
WHITE, O. Ivan .... 903-927-3384 458 F
oiwhite@wileyc.edu
WHITE, Odawa .... 715-634-4790 492 L
owhite@lco.edu
WHITE, Pamela .... 413-755-4452 216 A
pjwhite@stcc.edu
WHITE, Pamela .... 803-327-7402 407 F
pwhite@clintoncollege.edu
WHITE, Patricia .... 615-460-6524 418 B
patricia.white@belmont.edu
WHITE, Paul, M .... 920-565-1000 493 A
whitepm@lakeland.edu
WHITE, Randy .... 850-729-6404 104 M
whiter3@nwfsc.edu
WHITE, Ray .... 334-241-9537.... 7 C
grwhite@troy.edu
WHITE, Renée, T .... 646-909-2374 308 A
whitert@newschool.edu
WHITE, Rhonda .... 205-726-4371.... 6 E
rwhite7@samford.edu
WHITE, Robert .... 816-654-7616 254 E
rwhite@kcumb.edu
WHITE, Ronald .... 706-245-7226 118 D
rwhite@ec.edu
WHITE, Roslyn, M .... 601-877-6384 245 A
rmwhite@alcorn.edu
WHITE, Ryan .... 309-796-5194 133 G
whitery@bhc.edu
WHITE, Ryan .... 972-883-5561 455 B
ryan.white@utdallas.edu

WHITE, Sarah .... 412-536-1177 386 H
sarah.white@laroche.edu
WHITE, Sarah Beth .... 276-739-2472 475 F
swhite@vhcc.edu
WHITE, Shakeena .... 910-275-6362 335 E
swhite@jamessprunt.edu
WHITE, Shanice .... 601-979-0373 246 F
shanice.n.white@jsums.edu
WHITE, Shanna .... 315-386-7333 320 B
whites@canton.edu
WHITE, Shannan .... 251-460-6110.... 9 A
skwhite@southalabama.edu
WHITE, Shelley, Y .... 828-627-4516 335 C
sywhite@haywood.edu
WHITE, Sherron, D .... 252-335-3660 341 B
sdwhite@ecsu.edu
WHITE, Sloan .... 817-531-4414 451 C
swhite@txwes.edu
WHITE, Stephen .... 718-862-7548 304 M
stephen.white@manhattan.edu
WHITE, Stephen, E .... 401-254-3681 405 C
swhite@rwu.edu
WHITE, Stephen, F .... 615-898-2422 422 C
stephen.white@mtsu.edu
WHITE, Steven .... 316-978-3782 178 D
steven.white@wichita.edu
WHITE, Susan, K .... 913-627-4125 175 B
swhite@kckcc.edu
WHITE, Susannah .... 415-701-7040.. 61 D
swhite@sfcm.edu
WHITE, Tamara .... 303-404-5103.. 81 A
tamara.white@frontrange.edu
WHITE, Tamisia .... 212-870-1229 309 E
finaid@nyts.edu
WHITE, Tammy, S .... 205-652-3651.... 9 B
thw@uwa.edu
WHITE, Tanya .... 757-823-2886 469 A
tswhite@nsu.edu
WHITE, Theodore .... 816-235-1330 261 B
whitetc@umkc.edu
WHITE, Thomas .... 937-766-3200 349 E
thomaswhite@cedarville.edu
WHITE, Timothy, L .... 352-846-0850 111 A
tlwhite@ufl.edu
WHITE, Travis .... 918-595-7601 370 C
travis.white@tulsacc.edu
WHITE, Trisha .... 918-465-1708 366 A
twhite@eosc.edu
WHITE, Troy .... 903-923-2060 435 H
tgwhite@etbu.edu
WHITE, Wayman .... 252-335-0821 333 G
waywhite@albemarle.edu
WHITE, Wendy .... 252-638-7271 334 A
whitew@cravencc.edu
WHITE, Wendy, S .... 215-746-5240 400 F
wendy.white@ogc.upenn.edu
WHITE, William .... 215-248-7118 381 A
whitew@chc.edu
WHITE-FARNHAM,
Jamie .... 715-394-8233 497 C
jwhitefa@uwsuper.edu
WHITE HOWARD,
Demetria .... 601-977-7774 249 C
dhoward@tougaloo.edu
WHITE NEGLEY, Angela 304-696-2599 489 M
negley4@marshall.edu
WHITE PUGH, April ...... 864-644-5002 412 D
awhite@swu.edu
WHITE-SHOOK, Nadine . 757-455-3213 477 C
nwhiteshook@vwu.edu
WHITE-SMITH,
Kimberly .... 909-448-4583.. 71 C
kwhite-smith@laverne.edu
WHITE THUNDER,
Ellen .... 605-455-6076 415 H
ewhitethunder@olc.edu
WHITECAVAGE,
Michele .... 714-449-7404.. 51 B
mwhitecavage@ketchum.edu
WHITED, Jimmy, R .... 540-375-2308 470 E
whited@roanoke.edu
WHITEFIELD, Joe .... 615-904-8375 422 C
joe.whitefield@mtsu.edu
WHITEFORD, Aaron ...... 503-768-7944 373 E
ahw@lclark.edu
WHITEFORD, Craig .... 410-287-1914 198 E
cwhiteford@cecil.edu
WHITEHEAD, Amy .... 501-852-0871.. 23 H
amyw@uca.edu
WHITEHEAD, Debbie ..... 503-255-0332 374 C
debbiew@multnomah.edu
WHITEHEAD, JaRenae ... 757-683-4564 469 B
jwhitehe@odu.edu

WIDERGREN, James ..... 909-607-0107.. 37 F
WIDMER, Jocelyn .... 979-845-4016 446 F
widmerj@tamu.edu
WIDMER, Roger, H .... 972-985-3741 433 I
rwidmer@collin.edu
WIDNER, Kenneth .... 662-329-7021 248 A
kwidner@muw.edu
WIDOM, Jennifer .... 650-723-2300.. 66 E
WIEBE, John .... 915-747-5725 455 C
jwiebe@utep.edu
WIEBE, Weston, T .... 417-690-2211 251 H
wiebe@cofo.edu
WIECHMAN, Jeffery, P .. 507-354-8221 236 J
wiechmjp@mlc-wels.edu
WIECKI, Lisa .... 864-388-8035 410 A
lwiecki@lander.edu
WIED, Christine .... 979-830-4224 431 H
cwied@blinn.edu
WIEDEFELD, Kimberley . 585-594-6201 312 E
wiedefeld_kimberley@roberts.edu
WIEDENHOEFT,
Margaret .... 269-337-7133 225 F
margaret.wiedenoeft@kzoo.edu
WIEDERHOLT, Mark ...... 660-944-2968 251 J
markw@conception.edu
WIEDMAIER, Anne, E ... 715-365-4415 499 E
awiedmaier@nicoletcollege.edu
WIEDMAN, Sara .... 636-949-4943 254 H
swiedman@lindenwood.edu
WIEDMER, Shannon ...... 785-442-6009 174 F
swiedmer@highlandcc.edu
WIEGAND, Mark .... 502-272-8368 179 H
mwiegand@bellarmine.edu
WIEGAND, Mark .... 502-272-8000 179 H
WIEGAND, Randall, V ... 671-735-2930 504 F
wiegandr@triton.uog.edu
WIEGANDT, Scott, P ..... 502-272-8496 179 H
swiegandt@bellarmine.edu
WIEGEL, Lisa .... 563-288-6003 166 A
lwiegel@eicc.edu
WIEHE, Fred .... 408-727-1060.. 45 L
WIEHE, Kim .... 607-735-1707 298 H
kwiehe@elmira.edu
WIEJAK, Julie .... 219-989-2370 160 D
jwiejak@pnw.edu
WIELAND, Curtis .... 715-232-5446 497 B
wielandc@uwstout.edu
WIELENGA, Jay .... 712-707-7111 169 D
jayw@nwciowa.edu
WIENCEK, John .... 330-972-7593 361 H
johnw@uakron.edu
WIENS, Ann .... 415-703-9360.. 28 B
awiens@cca.edu
WIERDA, Bruce .... 231-777-0657 228 G
bruce.wierda@muskegoncc.edu
WIERDA, Kire .... 989-328-1268 228 D
kire.wierda@montcalm.edu
WIERSCH, Linda .... 704-878-3302 336 C
lwiersch@mitchellcc.edu
WIERSEMA, Kent .... 712-707-7121 169 D
kent.wiersema@nwciowa.edu
WIERSMA, Noelle .... 509-777-4874 486 C
nwiersma@whitworth.edu
WIERTEL, Anthony .... 716-926-8818 301 E
twiertel@hilbert.edu
WIERZBICKI, Andrzej .... 251-460-6280.... 9 A
awierzbicki@southalabama.edu
WIES, Jennifer .... 859-622-1646 180 E
jennifer.wies@eku.edu
WIESCHHORSTER,
Craig .... 616-331-2831 224 G
wieschhc@gvsu.edu
WIESE, Al .... 620-450-2132 177 B
allenw@prattcc.edu
WIESE, Bonnie .... 801-581-5701 459 O
bonnie.wiese@utah.edu
WIESE, Dennis .... 704-687-0330 342 D
dwiese@uncc.edu
WIESE, Joelle, D .... 202-687-7150.. 92 E
jdw237@georgetown.edu
WIESE, Karen .... 712-274-5159 168 E
wiesek@morningside.edu
WIESE, Trent .... 308-535-3612 267 J
wieset@mpcc.edu
WIESEHAN, Terry .... 765-973-8221 157 A
twiesaha@iue.edu
WIESEN, Liz .... 207-893-6601 196 C
lwiesen@sjcme.edu
WIESER, Jocelyn .... 440-366-7548 355 B
WIESER, Michelle .... 507-457-1451 243 C
mwieser@smumn.edu
WIEST, Courtney .... 352-588-8015 107 D
courtney.wiest@saintleo.edu
WIEST, Kresha .... 701-252-3467 347 B
kresha.wiest@uj.edu
WIETFELDT, Matthew .... 260-452-2278 154 I
matthew.wietfeldt@ctsfw.edu
WIEWEL, Wim .... 503-768-7680 373 E
president@lclark.edu
WIGBOLDY, Kyle .... 616-392-8555 233 E
kylew@westernsem.edu
WIGFALL, Arthur .... 212-463-0400 322 G
arthur.wigfall@touro.edu
WIGGETT, Janette, T ..... 603-535-2206 275 A
jtwiggett@plymouth.edu
WIGGINS, Adrian .... 609-652-4378 283 E
adrian.wiggins@stockton.edu
WIGGINS, Amy, F .... 252-862-1225 337 C
afwiggins7415@roanokechowan.edu
WIGGINS, Charles .... 828-395-1306 335 D
cpwiggins@isothermal.edu
WIGGINS, Debbie .... 757-490-1241 464 B
dwiggins@auto.edu
WIGGINS, Devon .... 903-510-2646 452 A
dwig@tjc.edu
WIGGINS, Erin .... 740-362-3366 355 H
ewiggins@msto.edu
WIGGINS, Gloria .... 910-275-6198 335 E
gwiggins@jamessprunt.edu
WIGGINS, Jessica .... 256-782-8041.... 6 A
jdwiggins@jsu.edu
WIGGINS, John .... 215-751-8000 381 I
jtwiggins@ccp.edu
WIGGINS, Michaele ...... 336-334-7593 341 D
sm8093@bncollege.com
WIGGINS, Sara .... 252-451-8313 336 E
swwiggins208@nashcc.edu
WIGGINS, Shelia .... 252-527-6223 335 G
slwiggins45@lenoircc.edu
WIGGINS, Symphoni ...... 706-821-8103 124 B
recordsofficestaff@paine.edu
WIGGINS, Vincent, D ... 773-907-4839 135 C
vwiggins1@ccc.edu
WIGGINTON, Nicholas .. 734-763-1290 231 H
nwigg@umich.edu
WIGGINTON, Van .... 281-542-2000 442 K
van.wigginton@sjcd.edu
WIGGINTON, Van, A ..... 281-542-2000 443 A
van.wigginton@sjcd.edu
WIGHT, Charles, A .... 410-543-6011 204 D
cawight@salisbury.edu
WIGHT, Erica .... 417-625-3188 256 F
wight-e@mssu.edu
WIGHT, Erica .... 801-957-6321 461 C
erica.wight@slcc.edu
WIGHT, Randall .... 870-245-5107.. 20 D
wight@obu.edu
WIGHTKIN, Joe .... 763-488-2518 238 C
joe.wightkin@hennepintech.edu
WIGHTMAN, Beth, A ..... 818-677-3434.. 32 C
beth.wightman@csun.edu
WIGHTMAN, James .... 614-236-6264 349 B
jwightman@capital.edu
WIGHTMAN, Todd .... 208-535-5440 131 B
todd.wightman@cei.edu
WIGINTON, Chad .... 580-477-7700 371 D
chad.wiginton@wosc.edu
WIGINTON, Joey .... 334-386-7402.... 5 C
jwiginton@faulkner.edu
WIGINTON, Melissa ...... 512-404-4862 430 J
mwiginton@austinseminary.edu
WIGLE, Derick .... 585-385-8281 313 F
dwigle@sjfc.edu
WIGNALL, Eric .... 815-740-3444 152 H
ewignall@stfrancis.edu
WIGNALL, Scott, D .... 724-946-7135 402 D
wignalsd@westminster.edu
WIGNES, David, R .... 608-785-9140 500 C
wignesd@westerntc.edu
WIJEWARDANE,
Johnnie Sue .... 540-831-7703 469 D
jwijewardane@radford.edu
WIKAN, Cory .... 318-869-5175 186 F
cwikan@centenary.edu
WIKLE, Karen .... 360-475-7133 481 I
kwikle@olympic.edu
WIKOFF, Karin .... 607-274-1364 302 G
kwikoff@ithaca.edu
WIKSTROM,
Christopher .... 276-656-0253 474 G
cwikstrom@patrickhenry.edu
WILBANKS, Jennifer ..... 660-596-7229 259 M
jwilbanks@sfccmo.edu
WILBANKS, Jennifer ..... 843-349-5208 409 J
jennifer.wilbanks@hgtc.edu
WILBANKS, Laura .... 734-487-6540 223 K
laura.wilbanks@emich.edu
WILBANKS, Scott .... 864-250-8281 409 I
scott.wilbanks@gvltec.edu
WILBORN, Colin .... 254-295-8642 453 D
cwilborn@umhb.edu
WILBUR, Gregg .... 518-736-3622 300 D
gwilbur@fmcc.suny.edu
WILBUR, Gregory .... 615-815-8360 422 F
WILBUR, Kathleen .... 517-353-9000 227 F
schlage6@msu.edu
WILBUR, Marcia .... 706-769-1472 115 E
mwilbur@acmin.org
WILBUR, Rachael .... 276-944-6232 466 L
rwilbur@ehc.edu
WILBUR, Shelley .... 941-487-4100 110 D
mwilbur@ncf.edu
WILBURN, Roberta .... 509-777-1000 486 C
rwilburn@whitworth.edu
WILCHER, Cheryl .... 305-626-9404 100 D
cwilcher@fmuniv.edu
WILCOTS, Barbara .... 303-458-4086.. 83 E
bwilcots@regis.edu
WILCOTS, Eric .... 608-263-2303 495 D
eric.wilcots@wisc.edu
WILCOX, Aviva .... 510-430-2262.. 52 E
awilcox@mills.edu
WILCOX, Bonnie .... 417-873-7201 252 G
bwilcox@drury.edu
WILCOX, Christin .... 775-831-1314 272 D
cwilcox@sierranevada.edu
WILCOX, Cindee .... 231-591-3900 224 A
cindeewilcox@ferris.edu
WILCOX, Cordelia, A .... 919-658-7494 340 G
cwilcox@umo.edu
WILCOX, Denise .... 909-469-5393.. 75 I
dwilcox@westernu.edu
WILCOX, Jerome .... 203-837-8242.. 86 B
wilcoxj@wcsu.edu
WILCOX, Kevin .... 518-956-8120 316 A
kwilcox@albany.edu
WILCOX, Kim .... 970-351-2496.. 84 F
kim.wilcox@unco.edu
WILCOX, Kim, A .... 951-827-5201.. 70 B
chancellor@ucr.edu
WILCOX, Laurie .... 603-535-3278 275 A
lrwilcox@plymouth.edu
WILCOX, Madeleine ...... 215-951-2815 399 E
wilcoxm@philau.edu
WILCOX, Mark .... 412-536-1104 386 H
mark.wilcox@laroche.edu
WILCOX, Ralph .... 813-974-8347 111 C
rcwilcox@usf.edu
WILCOX, Reed, N .... 540-261-4100 471 B
reed.wilcox@svu.edu
WILCOX, Robbin .... 419-267-1460 357 E
rwilcox@northweststate.edu
WILCOX, Tamera .... 785-309-3183 177 E
tamera.wilcox@salinatech.edu
WILCOXEN, Andrica ...... 913-288-7652 175 B
awilcoxen@kckcc.edu
WILCOXSON,
Douglas, A .... 517-750-1200 231 C
dwilcoxs@arbor.edu
WILCOXSON, Jesse .... 559-737-6281.. 39 B
jessew@cos.edu
WILD, Beth .... 918-595-8804 370 C
beth.wild@tulsacc.edu
WILD, Jeffrey .... 320-762-4594 237 C
jeffrey.wild@alextech.edu
WILD, Larry .... 847-628-2036 141 C
lwild@judsonu.edu
WILD, Robert, M .... 314-935-8081 262 A
rob.wild@wustl.edu
WILD, Shawn .... 215-968-8306 379 D
shawn.wild@bucks.edu
WILDA, Christine, M .... 413-545-2148 211 G
cwilda@umass.edu
WILDE, Jerry .... 765-973-8554 157 A
jwilde@iue.edu
WILDE, Sue .... 573-651-2175 259 H
swilde@semo.edu
WILDEMANN,
Leonard Walter .... 401-841-3780 503 A
wildemal@usnwc.edu
WILDER, Aliza .... 860-486-8478.. 89 D
aliza.wilder@uconn.edu
WILDER, Carrie .... 706-649-1888 117 I
cwilder@columbustech.edu
WILDER, Diane .... 610-896-1209 385 I
dwilder@haverford.edu
WILDER, Jason .... 928-523-5344.. 14 H
jason.wilder@nau.edu
WILDER, Jennifer .... 850-599-3651 109 I
jennifer.wilder@famu.edu
WILDER, Lesley .... 512-472-4133 443 F
lesley.wilder@ssw.edu
WILDER, Leslie .... 910-755-7324 332 F
wilderl@brunswickcc.edu
WILDER, Linda .... 860-515-3862.. 85 E
lwilder@charteroak.edu
WILDER, Marita .... 541-956-7139 376 A
mwilder@roguecc.edu
WILDER, Melanie .... 912-443-5717 125 B
mwilder@savannahtech.edu
WILDER, Michael .... 630-752-5818 153 C
michael.wilder@wheaton.edu
WILDER, Michael, S ..... 817-921-8689 445 A
mwilder@swbts.edu
WILDER, Paul, J .... 407-582-1818 113 I
pwilder1@valenciacollege.edu
WILDER, Ronald .... 575-769-4127 285 O
ronald.wilder@clovis.edu
WILDER, Stanley .... 225-578-2217 189 E
wilder@lsu.edu
WILDER, Sterly .... 919-684-5114 328 F
sterly.wilder@daa.duke.edu
WILDER, W. Mark .... 662-915-5756 249 D
acwilder@olemiss.edu
WILDER-BYRD,
Ellen, M .... 803-323-2236 414 D
wilderbyrde@winthrop.edu
WILDERMUTH, Amy, J . 412-648-1401 400 H
amy.wildermuth@pitt.edu
WILDEY, Diane .... 518-743-2337 320 A
daltod@sunyacc.edu
WILDHACK, John .... 315-443-8705 321 G
jwildhac@syr.edu
WILDING, Jody .... 281-649-3070 437 B
jwilding@hbu.edu
WILDING, Tim .... 205-226-4643.... 4 F
trwildin@bsc.edu
WILE, Kim .... 304-865-6141 487 H
kim.wile@ovu.edu
WILES, Duane .... 865-974-2425 427 B
dwiles@utfi.org
WILES, Mari, E .... 252-398-6268 328 C
wilesm@chowan.edu
WILEY, Carolyn .... 662-562-3200 248 D
WILEY, Casey .... 864-455-8204 413 F
wileyc@greenvillemed.sc.edu
WILEY, David .... 907-260-7422.... 9 D
WILEY, Diane .... 585-594-6381 312 E
wiley_diane@roberts.edu
WILEY, Ellen .... 717-947-6089 392 V
ewiley@pacollege.edu
WILEY, Fran, K .... 864-941-8351 411 C
wiley.f@ptc.edu
WILEY, Jeanelle .... 314-968-7123 262 C
jeanellewiley10@webster.edu
WILEY, Jeffrey .... 315-786-2248 303 C
jwiley@sunyjefferson.edu
WILEY, Karen .... 815-455-8547 143 I
kwiley@mchenry.edu
WILEY, Marilyn .... 940-565-4874 453 E
marilyn.wiley@unt.edu
WILEY, Mark .... 562-985-4121.. 31 D
mark.wiley@csulb.edu
WILEY, Matt .... 361-582-2468 457 E
matt.wiley@victoriacollege.edu
WILEY, Nina .... 937-328-7936 350 G
wileyn@clarkstate.edu
WILEY, Paul, G .... 931-598-1731 423 D
pwiley@sewanee.edu
WILEY, Stacey .... 814-824-2311 389 G
swiley@mercyhurst.edu
WILEY, Stephen .... 918-360-3763 365 C
wileys@bacone.edu
WILEY-HARRIS,
Courtney .... 585-340-9648 296 D
cwiley-harris@crcds.edu
WILFERTH, Joe .... 503-883-2662 373 F
jwilferth@linfield.edu
WILFONG, MacKenzie ... 918-595-7995 370 C
mackenzie.wilfong@tulsacc.edu
WILGENBUSCH, Sandy . 563-876-3353 165 H
wilgenbu@dwci.edu
WILGUS, Robynne .... 541-440-4622 376 G
robynne.wilgus@umpqua.edu
WILHELM, Alma .... 815-455-8781 143 I
awilhelm759@mchenry.edu
WILHELM, Cori .... 315-386-7873 320 B
wilhelmc@canton.edu
WILHELM, Jane .... 608-663-2203 492 F
jwilhelm@edgewood.edu
WILHELM, Jennifer .... 617-236-5470 209 G
jwilhelm@fisher.edu

WILLIAMS, Cathy .... 315-781-3696 301 F cwilliams@hws.edu
WILLIAMS, Cathy .... 299-500-2352 114 H cathy.williams@asurams.edu
WILLIAMS, JR., Cecil, L .... 501-429-8395.. 19 F
WILLIAMS, Chad .... 336-633-0049 337 A gcwilliams@randolph.edu
WILLIAMS, Channa .... 410-462-7461 198 B cwilliams@bccc.edu
WILLIAMS, Cheree .... 404-297-9522 120 B
WILLIAMS, Chris .... 217-234-5253 142 C
WILLIAMS, Chris, C .... 417-268-6017 250 G cwilliams@gobbc.edu
WILLIAMS, Christal .... 913-469-8500 174 I cwill216@jccc.edu
WILLIAMS, Christi .... 580-581-6712 365 D eo-tix@cameron.edu
WILLIAMS, Christine ..... 603-513-1150 274 G christine.williams@granite.edu
WILLIAMS, Cindy .... 406-243-2573 263 K cindy.williams@umontana.edu
WILLIAMS, Claire .... 925-631-4812.. 59 I cmw9@stmarys-ca.edu
WILLIAMS, Connie .... 803-536-0311 411 B
WILLIAMS, Corey .... 661-909-5626.. 51 D cwilliams@tms.edu
WILLIAMS, Corey .... 225-490-1617 187 B corey.williams@franu.edu
WILLIAMS, Corey .... 708-235-6810 138 E cwilliams43@govst.edu
WILLIAMS, Cornelius ..... 504-286-5205 191 C
WILLIAMS, Crystal, A .... 617-353-2230 207 E provost@bu.edu
WILLIAMS, D. Newell .... 817-257-7231 432 A n.williams@tcu.edu
WILLIAMS, Damon .... 919-530-7775 341 E damon.williams@nccu.edu
WILLIAMS, Dana .... 202-806-6800.. 92 F
WILLIAMS, Daniel, C .... 563-876-3353 165 H dwilliams@dwci.edu
WILLIAMS, Danielle ...... 845-431-8686 298 D danielle.williams4@sunydutchess.edu
WILLIAMS, Danisha .... 662-254-3345 248 B danisha.williams@mvsu.edu
WILLIAMS, Darlene .... 318-357-6100 192 G darlene@nsula.edu
WILLIAMS, Darnell .... 501-370-5273.. 20 F williams.darnell@philander.edu
WILLIAMS, Darryl, A ..... 845-938-4041 503 I
WILLIAMS, Daryle .... 951-827-1012.. 70 B
WILLIAMS, David .... 606-546-1624 185 D dwilliams@unionky.edu
WILLIAMS, David .... 707-864-7000.. 64 H david.williams@solano.edu
WILLIAMS, David .... 704-461-6010 326 L davidwilliams@bac.edu
WILLIAMS, David .... 814-472-3017 397 F dwilliams@francis.edu
WILLIAMS, David, K ..... 908-737-5326 278 E d1willia@kean.edu
WILLIAMS, David, S ..... 706-542-3240 126 G dwilliam@uga.edu
WILLIAMS, Dawn .... 202-806-7340.. 92 F dgwilliams@howard.edu
WILLIAMS, Deanna .... 314-889-4503 253 E dwilliams@fontbonne.edu
WILLIAMS, Debra .... 313-577-1031 232 K dr9780@wayne.edu
WILLIAMS, Debra, A ..... 404-880-6412 117 C dwilliams@cau.edu
WILLIAMS, Debra, J ..... 724-925-4200 402 F williamsdeb@westmoreland.edu
WILLIAMS, Demarcus ... 919-516-4000 339 I
WILLIAMS, Denise .... 586-445-7897 227 B williamsdl@macomb.edu
WILLIAMS, Dennis .... 405-789-6400 369 H dwilliam@snu.edu
WILLIAMS, Dereck .... 937-708-5808 363 G dwilliams@wilberforce.edu
WILLIAMS, Derrien .... 304-590-9079 490 D derrien.williams@wvstateu.edu
WILLIAMS, Desha .... 610-436-2408 395 D dwilliams2@wcupa.edu
WILLIAMS, Digna .... 787-834-9595 510 D dwilliams@uaa.edu
WILLIAMS, Donald, J .... 540-231-5991 476 C dowilli3@vt.edu
WILLIAMS, Donna, M .... 610-799-1107 388 D dwilliams@lccc.edu
WILLIAMS, Dorothy ...... 404-756-4016 115 G dwilliams@atlm.edu
WILLIAMS, Douglass .... 931-598-1349 423 D dwilliam@sewanee.edu
WILLIAMS, Dwayne .... 541-278-5904 371 H dwilliams@bluecc.edu
WILLIAMS, Elizabeth ..... 803-778-7873 406 I williamsel@cctech.edu
WILLIAMS, Elmer .... 787-850-9345 512 D elmer.williams@upr.edu
WILLIAMS, Emili .... 865-573-4517 420 E ewilliams@johnsonu.edu
WILLIAMS, Emma .... 478-825-4350 118 F emma.williams@fvsu.edu
WILLIAMS, Eric .... 310-434-3455.. 63 C williams_eric@smc.edu
WILLIAMS, Ericka .... 773-838-7783 135 F ewilliams249@ccc.edu
WILLIAMS, Erin .... 678-839-3801 127 C erint@westga.edu
WILLIAMS, Erin .... 309-794-7000 133 C erinwilliams@augustana.edu
WILLIAMS, Eugene .... 770-531-3172 116 D ewilliams4@brenau.edu
WILLIAMS, Eunice .... 315-498-2565 310 F williame@sunyocc.edu
WILLIAMS, F. Clark .... 615-343-3808 428 A f.clark.williams@vanderbilt.edu
WILLIAMS, Falecia, D ... 301-546-0400 201 E williafd@pgcc.edu
WILLIAMS, Forrest, G .... 801-863-8494 460 D forrest.williams@uvu.edu
WILLIAMS, Frances .... 716-851-1698 299 B williams@ecc.edu
WILLIAMS, Frank .... 585-389-2525 307 F fwillia7@naz.edu
WILLIAMS, JR., Frank .. 318-670-6681 191 D fwilliams@susla.edu
WILLIAMS, JR., Frantz .. 860-685-2000.. 90 B
WILLIAMS, Fred .... 714-808-4746.. 54 A fwilliams@nocccd.edu
WILLIAMS, Fred .... 714-808-4797.. 54 A fwilliams@nocccd.edu
WILLIAMS, Freddie .... 334-229-4291.... 4 A fwilliams@alasu.edu
WILLIAMS, Freddie .... 334-229-5631.... 4 A fwilliams@alasu.edu
WILLIAMS, Frederick .... 502-597-6891 183 D frederick.williams1@kysu.edu
WILLIAMS, Gabrielle .... 620-242-0488 176 B williamsg@mcpherson.edu
WILLIAMS, Gail, B .... 239-513-1122 102 D gwilliams@hodges.edu
WILLIAMS, Gail, C .... 757-446-5869 466 D williamsgc@evms.edu
WILLIAMS, JR., George, A .... 210-431-5521 441 B gawilliams6@ollusa.edu
WILLIAMS, Georgeann .. 843-525-8203 412 G gwilliams@tcl.edu
WILLIAMS, Georgia, E .. 252-398-6439 328 C willig@chowan.edu
WILLIAMS, Gerald .... 401-874-2901 405 E gman1@uri.edu
WILLIAMS, Gloria .... 817-722-1700 438 G
WILLIAMS, Goldie, C .... 606-783-2123 184 C gcwilliams@moreheadstate.edu
WILLIAMS, Greg .... 719-255-3292.. 84 C gwillia5@uccs.edu
WILLIAMS, Gregory, D .. 432-335-6410 441 A gwilliams@odessa.edu
WILLIAMS, Grimes .... 207-755-5290 195 D gwilliams@cmcc.edu
WILLIAMS, Gwenda .... 501-205-8879.. 18 H gwilliams@cbc.edu
WILLIAMS, H. James .... 513-244-4232 356 F president@msj.edu
WILLIAMS, Hans, M ..... 936-468-3304 445 E hwilliams@sfasu.edu
WILLIAMS, Helen, E .... 310-568-5615.. 56 G helen.williams@pepperdine.edu
WILLIAMS, Ingrid .... 415-338-1872.. 33 E icwilliams@sfsu.edu
WILLIAMS, Iwan .... 641-628-7686 164 D williamsi@central.edu
WILLIAMS, Jacqueline .. 201-216-5207 283 D jacqueline.williams@stevens.edu
WILLIAMS, Jalisa, D .... 413-572-8670 213 F jdwilliams@westfield.ma.edu
WILLIAMS, James, E .... 620-341-5267 173 F jwilliam@emporia.edu
WILLIAMS, Janelle .... 619-216-6661.. 66 A jwilliams@swccd.edu
WILLIAMS, Janelle, D ... 817-202-6510 444 I janellew@swau.edu
WILLIAMS, Janet .... 620-947-3121 177 I janetw@tabor.edu
WILLIAMS, Janet .... 336-278-5434 328 J jwilliams132@elon.edu
WILLIAMS, Janet .... 601-318-6568 249 H jwilliams@wmcarey.edu
WILLIAMS, Jason .... 815-740-6222 152 H jwilliams@stfrancis.edu
WILLIAMS, Jason .... 214-333-6978 434 C jasonw@dbu.edu
WILLIAMS, Jason, R ..... 208-496-4406 130 I williamsja@byui.edu
WILLIAMS, Jeff .... 903-983-8669 438 F jwilliams@kilgore.edu
WILLIAMS, Jennifer ...... 502-597-6486 183 D jennifer.williams@kysu.edu
WILLIAMS, Jennifer ...... 501-977-2009.. 23 A williams@uaccm.edu
WILLIAMS, Jennifer ...... 312-850-7016 135 H jwilliams416@ccc.edu
WILLIAMS, Jennifer ...... 334-229-4507.... 4 A jwilliams@alasu.edu
WILLIAMS, Jennifer ...... 434-544-8337 471 L williams_ja1@lynchburg.edu
WILLIAMS, Jenny .... 864-592-4940 412 E williamsj@sccsc.edu
WILLIAMS, Jermaine ...... 334-347-2623.... 2 A jlwilliams@escc.edu
WILLIAMS, Jermaine, F 516-572-7205 307 E jermaine.williams@ncc.edu
WILLIAMS, Jessica .... 712-324-5061 169 C jwilliams@nwicc.edu
WILLIAMS, Jessica, C .. 913-667-5709 172 I jwilliams@cbts.edu
WILLIAMS, Joan .... 319-208-5049 170 D jwilliams@scciowa.edu
WILLIAMS, Joan .... 336-370-8639 327 A jwilliams@bennett.edu
WILLIAMS, Joan, J .... 410-548-4503 204 D jjwilliams@salisbury.edu
WILLIAMS, Joanne .... 207-780-4020 197 D joanne.williams@maine.edu
WILLIAMS, JoAnne .... 203-773-8550.. 85 D
WILLIAMS, Joanne .... 804-862-6100 470 C jwilliams@rbc.edu
WILLIAMS, Joel .... 605-692-9337 415 B jwilliams@ilt.edu
WILLIAMS, Joey .... 512-232-3716 455 A joeywilliams@utexas.edu
WILLIAMS, John .... 508-999-8421 212 A john.williams@umassd.edu
WILLIAMS, John .... 607-587-4611 319 F williajc@alfredstate.edu
WILLIAMS, John, D ..... 903-813-2220 430 H jwilliams@austincollege.edu
WILLIAMS, John, H ...... 713-313-7310 449 B williams_jh@tsu.edu
WILLIAMS, John, M ..... 517-750-1200 231 C jwilliam@arbor.edu
WILLIAMS, John, W ..... 618-374-5148 147 E president@principia.edu
WILLIAMS, Jonathan ..... 212-998-1212 309 F
WILLIAMS, Joni .... 404-225-4602 115 H jwilliam@atlantatech.edu
WILLIAMS, Jordan .... 443-412-2449 199 D jowilliams@harford.edu
WILLIAMS, Joseph .... 540-674-3600 474 E jawilliams@nr.edu
WILLIAMS, Joshua .... 573-681-5128 254 G williamsj3@lincolnu.edu
WILLIAMS, Joshua .... 616-828-8804 224 E jwilliams@gracechristian.edu
WILLIAMS, Joyce .... 323-343-3615.. 31 E jwilli109@calstatela.edu
WILLIAMS, Julia .... 229-732-5920 115 B juliawilliams@andrewcollege.edu
WILLIAMS, Julian, R ..... 803-777-7000 413 A julian.williams@sc.edu
WILLIAMS, Juliana .... 215-780-1443 398 B jwilliams@salus.edu
WILLIAMS, Julie, E ...... 615-353-3346 424 G julie.williams@nscc.edu
WILLIAMS, Julie, R .... 712-362-7912 167 B jrwilliams@iowalakes.edu
WILLIAMS, Kallan .... 706-754-7724 123 G kwilliams@northgatech.edu
WILLIAMS, Karen .... 718-262-2415 295 E kwilliams29@york.cuny.edu
WILLIAMS, Karla, R ...... 718-289-5809 293 B karla.williams@bcc.cuny.edu
WILLIAMS, Kas .... 605-688-5585 417 A kas.williams@sdstate.edu
WILLIAMS, Katara, A .... 225-771-4680 191 B katara_williams@sus.edu
WILLIAMS, Kathleen ..... 770-426-2688 122 C kathleen.williams@life.edu
WILLIAMS, Kathy .... 903-223-3182 448 A kathy.williams@tamut.edu
WILLIAMS, Katraya .... 318-675-5049 189 I katraya.williams@lsuhs.edu
WILLIAMS, Katraya .... 318-670-9221 191 D kwilliams@susla.edu
WILLIAMS, KC .... 850-729-5298 104 M williamk@nwfsc.edu
WILLIAMS, Keena .... 517-629-0501 221 A kwilliams@albion.edu
WILLIAMS, Keith .... 404-756-4003 115 G kwilliams@atlm.edu
WILLIAMS, Kelley .... 316-295-5864 174 A kwilliams@friends.edu
WILLIAMS, Kelley .... 610-409-3698 401 H kwilliams@ursinus.edu
WILLIAMS, Kellyn .... 570-702-8940 386 D knolan@johnson.edu
WILLIAMS, Ken .... 202-685-4080 502 K kenneth.r.williams.mil@ndu.edu
WILLIAMS, Ken, M .... 248-232-4210 229 C kmwillia@oaklandcc.edu
WILLIAMS, Kenneth ...... 229-430-0919 114 I kwilliams@albanytech.edu
WILLIAMS, Kenneth ...... 802-258-3565 462 H ken.williams@sit.edu
WILLIAMS, Kent .... 316-322-3103 172 D kwilliams@butlercc.edu
WILLIAMS, Kevin .... 518-956-8030 316 A graduate@albany.edu
WILLIAMS, Kevin, H ..... 615-898-2424 422 C kevin.williams@mtsu.edu
WILLIAMS, Kim .... 870-850-4815.. 21 B kwilliams@seark.edu
WILLIAMS, Kimberlee, S .... 973-353-5262 282 B kimberlee.williams@rutgers.edu
WILLIAMS, Kimberly ..... 615-898-2088 422 C kimberly.williams@mtsu.edu
WILLIAMS, Kimberly ..... 708-239-4528 151 A kim.williams@trnty.edu
WILLIAMS, Kimberly ..... 919-890-7500.. 93 H
WILLIAMS, Kimberly ..... 918-444-5000 366 G willi204@nsuok.edu
WILLIAMS, Kristen .... 973-408-3788 277 A kwilliams3@drew.edu
WILLIAMS, Kristen .... 801-524-8106 459 E kwilliams@ldsbc.edu
WILLIAMS, Kristi .... 706-778-8500 124 D
WILLIAMS, Kristin .... 706-507-8848 117 H williams_kristin@columbusstate.edu
WILLIAMS, Kristin .... 859-256-3100 181 C kris.williams@kctcs.edu
WILLIAMS, Kristopher ... 402-826-8255 267 A kristopher.williams@doane.edu
WILLIAMS, Kyle .... 940-397-4730 440 C kyle.williams@msutexas.edu
WILLIAMS, Kyle, R .... 208-496-2510 130 I williamsk@byui.edu
WILLIAMS, Kyra .... 503-842-8222 376 E kyrawilliams@tillamookbaycc.edu
WILLIAMS, Lakeshia ..... 318-473-6495 189 F ldalton@lsua.edu
WILLIAMS, LaNeeca ...... 931-221-7690 417 H williamslr@apsu.edu
WILLIAMS, Larry .... 316-942-4291 176 E williamsl@newmanu.edu
WILLIAMS, Lashon .... 361-570-4128 453 B williamslb@uhv.edu
WILLIAMS, LaShonda ... 936-261-1591 446 C lrwilliams@pvamu.edu
WILLIAMS, LaTonda ..... 501-916-3180.. 22 A lwwilliams@ualr.edu
WILLIAMS, LaToya .... 713-623-2040 430 E lrwilliams@aii.edu
WILLIAMS, Laura .... 707-664-2153.. 34 B laura.williams@sonoma.edu
WILLIAMS, Laura, M .... 217-443-8878 136 G lwms@dacc.edu
WILLIAMS, Lauren .... 706-355-5023 115 F lwilliams@athenstech.edu
WILLIAMS, Lee .... 870-338-6474.. 22 G
WILLIAMS, Lee .... 903-823-3016 446 A lee.williams@texarkanacollege.edu
WILLIAMS, Leslie .... 559-325-3600.. 28 D lwilliams@chsu.edu
WILLIAMS, Leslie .... 661-654-2544.. 30 B lwilliams8@csub.edu

WILLIAMS, Leslie .... 831-582-4091.. 32 B
lewilliams@csumb.edu
WILLIAMS, Linda .... 916-660-7310.. 64 D
lwilliams@sierracollege.edu
WILLIAMS, Lindsay .... 254-298-8241 445 G
lindsay.williams@templejc.edu
WILLIAMS, Lisa .... 419-448-3444 361 D
lwilliam@tiffin.edu
WILLIAMS, Lisa .... 858-653-6740.. 46 H
lwilliams@jpcatholic.com
WILLIAMS, Lisa .... 216-987-2004 351 E
WILLIAMS, Lisa, L .... 325-793-3821 439 F
lwilliams@mcm.edu
WILLIAMS, Lisa, M .... 256-782-8186.... 6 A
lwilliam@jsu.edu
WILLIAMS, Lois, H .... 910-522-5800 343 B
lois.williams@uncp.edu
WILLIAMS, Lonnie .... 870-972-3081.. 17 E
lonniew@astate.edu
WILLIAMS, Loretta .... 706-233-7278 125 C
lwilliams@shorter.edu
WILLIAMS, Lorette .... 361-698-1351 435 G
lwilliams25@delmar.edu
WILLIAMS, Lori .... 713-798-4951 431 D
WILLIAMS, Lorie .... 574-520-4492 157 E
lojewill@iusb.edu
WILLIAMS, Lucille, W ... 803-934-3258 410 G
lwilliams@morris.edu
WILLIAMS, LuWanna ..... 478-822-1354 118 F
williamsl@fvsu.edu
WILLIAMS, Lyn .... 610-606-4666 380 D
lcwillia@cedarcrest.edu
WILLIAMS, Lynell .... 956-872-2114 443 H
lwillia5@southtexascollege.edu
WILLIAMS, Lynn .... 803-641-3385 413 B
lynnw@usca.edu
WILLIAMS, Lynne .... 218-726-6141 243 G
lwilliam@d.umn.edu
WILLIAMS, Lyrae .... 719-389-6699.. 78 I
lyrae.williams@coloradocollege.edu
WILLIAMS, Maisha .... 212-517-0400 305 E
WILLIAMS,
Marchetta, L .... 803-938-3721 413 G
mlwillia@uscsumter.edu
WILLIAMS, Marcia .... 757-455-3335 477 C
mwilliams@vwu.edu
WILLIAMS,
Marianne, R .... 518-262-5422 289 L
willimr@amc.edu
WILLIAMS, Marie .... 251-981-3771.... 5 A
marie.williams@columbiasouthern.edu
WILLIAMS, Mark .... 501-686-7000.. 22 B
mlw@uams.edu
WILLIAMS, Mark .... 706-379-3111 128 C
mark.williams@sodexo.com
WILLIAMS, Marrianne ... 530-242-7648.. 64 C
mewilliams@shastacollege.edu
WILLIAMS, Martinique .. 336-285-2979 341 D
mcwilli2@ncat.edu
WILLIAMS, Marvin .... 516-726-5753 503 H
williamsm@usmma.edu
WILLIAMS, Mary .... 510-374-6305.. 20 G
mary.williams@shortercollege.edu
WILLIAMS, Mary Beth .. 717-262-2006 403 C
marybeth.williams@wilson.edu
WILLIAMS, Matthew, W 404-527-7702 121 L
mwwilliams@itc.edu
WILLIAMS, Melanie, K .. 269-337-7220 225 F
williams@kzoo.edu
WILLIAMS, Melissa .... 916-608-6585.. 50 I
william@flc.losrios.edu
WILLIAMS, Melissa .... 254-295-4020 453 D
mwilliams@umhb.edu
WILLIAMS, Melva .... 318-670-9314 191 D
mwilliams@susla.edu
WILLIAMS, Melva, D .... 504-520-7453 193 E
mewillia@xula.edu
WILLIAMS, Melvenia ..... 803-535-5412 407 D
mwilliams@claflin.edu
WILLIAMS, Melvin .... 803-535-5575 407 D
mewilliams@claflin.edu
WILLIAMS, Michael .... 207-768-2712 195 G
mwilliams@nmcc.edu
WILLIAMS, Michael ...... 229-333-2100 128 B
michael.williams@wiregrass.edu
WILLIAMS, Michael ...... 850-644-7351 110 C
mswilliams@admin.fsu.edu
WILLIAMS, Michael ...... 609-984-1130 284 C
mwilliams@tesu.edu
WILLIAMS, Michael ...... 734-462-4400 230 G
mwilliam@schoolcraft.edu
WILLIAMS, Michael, D . 334-386-7103.... 5 C
mwilliams@faulkner.edu
WILLIAMS, Michael, R .. 817-735-2555 454 B
president@unthsc.edu
WILLIAMS, Michelle, A . 617-495-1000 210 E
mawilliams@hsph.harvard.edu
WILLIAMS, Michelle, H 610-566-1776 403 B
mwilliams@williamson.edu
WILLIAMS, Michelle, M 724-458-2216 384 G
mmwilliams@gcc.edu
WILLIAMS, Misty, B ..... 302-295-1121.. 91 E
misty.b.williams@wilmu.edu
WILLIAMS, Mitzi .... 404-756-4047 115 G
mwilliams@atlm.edu
WILLIAMS, Monica .... 313-993-1028 231 E
leonarmj@udmercy.edu
WILLIAMS, Murray, J .... 252-862-1308 337 C
mjwilliams@roanokechowan.edu
WILLIAMS, Nailah .... 202-274-5618.. 94 B
nawilliams@udc.edu
WILLIAMS, Nakeshia ..... 540-362-6000 467 H
williamsnn1@hollins.edu
WILLIAMS, Natasha ...... 512-863-1233 445 C
williamn@southwestern.edu
WILLIAMS, Nichelle ...... 661-722-6300.. 26 A
nwilliams@avc.edu
WILLIAMS, Nikisha ...... 646-745-8367 291 A
nwilliam@barnard.edu
WILLIAMS, Owen Scott . 985-448-4780 192 F
scott.williams@nicholls.edu
WILLIAMS, Paige .... 513-562-8777 347 I
pwilliams@artacademy.edu
WILLIAMS, Pamela .... 860-215-9306.. 87 F
pwilliams@threerivers.edu
WILLIAMS, Pamela .... 301-295-3185 503 C
pamela.williams@usuhs.edu
WILLIAMS, Patricia, A .. 515-263-2912 166 F
pwilliams@grandview.edu
WILLIAMS, Paul .... 229-391-4900 114 F
pwwilliams@abac.edu
WILLIAMS, Paulita, N ... 336-322-2170 336 G
tasha.williams@piedmontcc.edu
WILLIAMS, Peter .... 317-940-9700 154 C
williams@butler.edu
WILLIAMS, Peter .... 503-338-2442 372 D
pwilliams@clatsopcc.edu
WILLIAMS, Philip, J ..... 805-756-2706.. 29 I
pjw@calpoly.edu
WILLIAMS, Pilar .... 671-735-5590 504 D
pilar.williams@guamcc.edu
WILLIAMS, Princess ..... 410-822-5400 198 F
pwilliams@chesapeake.edu
WILLIAMS, Quinn .... 608-263-6105 495 C
qwilliams@uwsa.edu
WILLIAMS, R. Sanders . 919-681-6438 328 F
r.s.williams@duke.edu
WILLIAMS, Ramona ...... 423-636-7300 426 E
rwilliams@tusculum.edu
WILLIAMS, Randy .... 336-278-7919 328 J
rwilliams32@elon.edu
WILLIAMS, Randy .... 816-802-3527 254 D
rwilliams@kcai.edu
WILLIAMS, Raven .... 410-617-5424 200 B
rdwilliams@loyola.edu
WILLIAMS, Raymond .... 973-618-3295 276 D
rwilliams@caldwell.edu
WILLIAMS, Regina .... 713-313-7175 449 B
regina.williams@tsu.edu
WILLIAMS, Regine .... 504-286-5000 191 C
WILLIAMS, Renee .... 936-261-1744 446 C
rrwilliams@pvamu.edu
WILLIAMS, Rich .... 775-674-7979 271 C
rwilliams@tmcc.edu
WILLIAMS, Richard .... 781-239-2756 214 G
rwilliams@massbay.edu
WILLIAMS, Richard .... 770-426-2771 122 C
richard.williams@life.edu
WILLIAMS, Richard .... 724-805-2084 397 I
richard.williams@stvincent.edu
WILLIAMS, Richard, B .. 435-652-7502 460 B
president@dixie.edu
WILLIAMS, Robert .... 510-885-3942.. 31 A
robert.williams@csueastbay.edu
WILLIAMS, Robin .... 661-362-3240.. 38 D
robin.williams@canyons.edu
WILLIAMS, Robin .... 814-871-5615 384 A
williams171@gannon.edu
WILLIAMS, Robyn, A .... 920-923-8112 493 D
rawilliams61@marianuniversity.edu
WILLIAMS, Ron .... 706-507-8725 117 H
williams_ronald4@columbusstate.edu
WILLIAMS, Rosemary ... 718-270-5104 294 G
rosemary@mec.cuny.edu
WILLIAMS, Russ .... 478-445-5650 119 B
russ.williams@gcsu.edu
WILLIAMS, Ruth .... 847-635-7090 146 G
rwilliam@oakton.edu
WILLIAMS, Ryan .... 845-569-3105 307 D
ryan.williams@msmc.edu
WILLIAMS, Ryan, A .... 309-624-9268 149 B
ryan.a.williams@osfhealthcare.org
WILLIAMS, Sabrina, R .. 252-335-3969 341 B
srwilliams3@ecsu.edu
WILLIAMS, Sam .... 503-883-2575 373 F
swilliams2@linfield.edu
WILLIAMS, Scott .... 270-686-4508 182 F
scott.willliams@kctcs.edu
WILLIAMS, Scott, E ...... 276-944-6242 466 L
swilliams@ehc.edu
WILLIAMS, Scott, T ...... 706-542-3375 126 G
scottw@uga.edu
WILLIAMS, Scottie .... 630-617-3031 137 G
scottie.williams@elmhurst.edu
WILLIAMS, Sharaf .... 909-384-8988.. 60 F
swilliams@sbccd.cc.ca.us
WILLIAMS, Sharonda .... 504-865-7082 190 C
shwillia@loyno.edu
WILLIAMS, Shaun .... 817-515-5154 445 F
shaun.williams@tccd.edu
WILLIAMS, Shelitha ...... 585-345-6886 300 F
swwilliams@genesee.edu
WILLIAMS,
Shemetric, T .... 903-434-8102 440 G
swilliams@ntcc.edu
WILLIAMS, Sheree .... 502-585-4425 182 C
sheree.williams@kctcs.edu
WILLIAMS, Sonja .... 314-918-2538 253 C
swilliams@eden.edu
WILLIAMS, Sonya .... 212-229-5600 308 A
williasy@newschool.edu
WILLIAMS, Sonya .... 847-543-2635 136 A
swilliams20@clcillinois.edu
WILLIAMS, Sophia .... 414-297-6288 499 C
wills12@matc.edu
WILLIAMS, Steffani .... 315-498-6062 310 F
williast@sunyocc.edu
WILLIAMS, Stelfanie ..... 919-684-3711 328 F
stelfanie.williams@duke.edu
WILLIAMS, Stephanie ... 585-385-8010 313 F
swilliams@sjfc.edu
WILLIAMS, Stephen, R . 419-755-4811 357 B
swilliam@ncstatecollege.edu
WILLIAMS, Steve .... 414-277-7420 494 D
williams@msoe.edu
WILLIAMS, Steve .... 256-840-4174.... 3 F
steve.williams@snead.edu
WILLIAMS, Susan .... 919-760-8262 331 D
williams@meredith.edu
WILLIAMS, Susan .... 828-448-3178 339 A
swilliams@wpcc.edu
WILLIAMS, Susan 516-323-3030 306M
swilliams@molloy.edu
WILLIAMS, Susan .... 304-255-0793 489 J
swilliams@concord.edu
WILLIAMS, Susan, L ..... 302-831-8436.. 91 C
susanlyn@udel.edu
WILLIAMS, Suzanne ...... 213-477-2861.. 52 I
swilliams@msmu.edu
WILLIAMS, Suzanne ...... 803-780-1077 414 B
swilliams@voorhees.edu
WILLIAMS, Sydney .... 404-527-7761 121 L
swilliams@itc.edu
WILLIAMS, Sylvester ..... 570-422-3589 394 A
swilliams@esu.edu
WILLIAMS, Tamara, R ... 253-531-7203 482 A
williatr@plu.edu
WILLIAMS, Tamara, S ... 757-822-1184 475 E
tswilliams@tcc.edu
WILLIAMS, Tamika .... 615-460-6407 418 B
tamika.williams@belmont.edu
WILLIAMS, Tanisha .... 704-922-6537 334 G
williams.tanisha@gaston.edu
WILLIAMS, Tara .... 205-348-5506.... 7 G
tara_williams@ua.edu
WILLIAMS, Tara, A .... 336-633-0279 337 A
tawil@randolph.edu
WILLIAMS, Tasha .... 708-596-2000 149 H
twilliams@ssc.edu
WILLIAMS, Tasha .... 570-577-2000 379 C
natasha.williams@bucknell.edu
WILLIAMS, Teresa, G .... 704-233-8010 344 F
tgwilliams@wingate.edu
WILLIAMS, Teressa .... 907-852-1720.... 9 H
teressa.williams@tuzzy.org
WILLIAMS, Terria, C ..... 803-535-5720 407 D
twilliams@claflin.edu
WILLIAMS, Thelma, R ... 252-335-3471 341 B
trwilliams@ecsu.edu
WILLIAMS, Thomas ...... 501-450-5137.. 23 H
twilliams73@uca.edu
WILLIAMS, Thomas ...... 617-243-2499 211 B
twilliams@lasell.edu
WILLIAMS, Thomas ...... 303-352-3194.. 80 F
thomas.williams@ccd.edu
WILLIAMS, Tiffany .... 337-521-8971 188 I
tiffany.williams@solacc.edu
WILLIAMS, Tim .... 618-985-3741 140 H
timwilliams@jalc.edu
WILLIAMS, Tim .... 502-895-3411 183 H
twilliams@lpts.edu
WILLIAMS, Timera .... 202-408-2400.. 93 H
WILLIAMS, Todd, J .... 215-702-4861 380 A
president@cairn.edu
WILLIAMS, Tom .... 601-925-3844 247 C
twilliams@mc.edu
WILLIAMS, Tonjua, L .... 727-341-3241 107 E
williams.tonjua@spcollege.edu
WILLIAMS, Tony .... 928-226-4334.. 11 O
tony.williams@coconino.edu
WILLIAMS, Tonya .... 901-381-3939 428 B
tonya@visible.edu
WILLIAMS, Tonya .... 610-399-2278 393 F
twilliams@cheyney.edu
WILLIAMS, Tracey .... 903-510-2041 452 A
twil@tjc.edu
WILLIAMS, Traci .... 423-697-2659 424 A
traci.williams@chattanoogastate.edu
WILLIAMS, Tracy .... 229-500-3433 114 H
tracy.williams@asurams.edu
WILLIAMS, Tracy .... 651-523-2651 236 B
twilliams05@hamline.edu
WILLIAMS, Travis .... 707-826-5038.. 33 C
tjw17@humboldt.edu
WILLIAMS, Travis .... 919-761-2100 340 D
twilliam@sebts.edu
WILLIAMS, Treby .... 609-258-7097 280 D
trebyw@princeton.edu
WILLIAMS, Trevor .... 305-348-2107 110 A
trevor.williams@fiu.edu
WILLIAMS, Trudy .... 412-392-8085 396 G
twilliams@pointpark.edu
WILLIAMS, Valarie .... 706-385-1015 124 E
valarie.williams@point.edu
WILLIAMS, Vera, M ...... 478-289-2196 118 C
vwilliams@ega.edu
WILLIAMS, Verna, L ..... 513-556-0121 361 J
verna.williams@uc.edu
WILLIAMS, Vicki .... 501-420-1329.. 16 L
vicki.williams@arkansasbaptist.edu
WILLIAMS, Vicki .... 501-492-0570.. 16 L
vicki.williams@arkansasbaptist.edu
WILLIAMS, Vickie .... 334-214-4803.... 1 H
vickie.williams@cv.edu
WILLIAMS, Vicky .... 731-352-6405 418 C
williamsv@bethelu.edu
WILLIAMS, Victoria .... 610-796-5511 378 C
victoria.williams@alvernia.edu
WILLIAMS, Virginia, M . 530-221-4275.. 64 B
vwilliams@shasta.edu
WILLIAMS, Wendell ...... 618-453-1440 150 B
wendell.williams@siu.edu
WILLIAMS, Wendell ...... 713-313-7446 449 B
wendell.williams@tsu.edu
WILLIAMS, Wendy, E .... 843-953-5506 408 C
williamsw@cofc.edu
WILLIAMS, Winifred ...... 312-915-6175 143 C
wwilliams5@luc.edu
WILLIAMS-BRYANT,
Deanne .... 386-481-2871.. 96 D
williamsbryantd@cookman.edu
WILLIAMS DANDRIDGE,
Gwen .... 804-524-5000 476 D
WILLIAMS-EDMUND,
Junea .... 646-909-8911 308 A
williaej@newschool.edu
WILLIAMS-GAGE,
Sheila .... 845-368-7220 314 I
WILLIAMS-GOLDSTEIN,
Brittany, A .... 201-684-7609 280 H
bwillia1@ramapo.edu
WILLIAMS-HARMON,
Arlitha .... 559-791-2374.. 47 A
arlitha.williams@portervillecollege.edu
WILLIAMS-LESSANE,
Patricia .... 443-885-3350 201 A
patricia.lessane@morgan.edu
WILLIAMS LOSTON,
Adena .... 210-486-2900 428 G
aloston@alamo.edu
WILLIAMS-MIZE,
Amanda .... 405-682-7537 367 D
amanda.williams-mize@occc.edu

WILLIAMS-MOORE, Linda ... 412-648-1074 400 H lwmoore@pitt.edu
WILLIAMS-PEREZ, Kendra ... 319-226-2040 163 C kendra.williams-perez@allencollege.edu
WILLIAMS-SMITH, Rachel ... 423-236-2740 423 F rwilliamssmith@southern.edu
WILLIAMSON, Aletta ... 256-549-8200 2 B
WILLIAMSON, Angela ... 417-690-2208 251 H awilliamson@cofo.edu
WILLIAMSON, Ashley ... 334-222-6591 2 I abass@lbwcc.edu
WILLIAMSON, Carol ... 641-628-7667 164 D williamsonc@central.edu
WILLIAMSON, Cathy ... 641-673-1700 171 C williamsonc@wmpenn.edu
WILLIAMSON, Clarence 864-231-2000 406 F cwilliamson@andersonuniversity.edu
WILLIAMSON, Dan ... 860-528-4111 88 A
WILLIAMSON, David ... 601-266-1000 249 F david.williamson@usm.edu
WILLIAMSON, Dean ... 936-261-2188 446 C cdwilliamson@pvamu.edu
WILLIAMSON, Elaine ... 413-369-4044 208 F williamson@csld.edu
WILLIAMSON, Emily ... 406-243-5504 263 K emily1.williamson@umontana.edu
WILLIAMSON, Fred ... 510-549-4713 66 G fwilliamson@sksm.edu
WILLIAMSON, George ... 619-849-2610 57 J georgewilliamson@pointloma.edu
WILLIAMSON, Graciela . 858-513-9240 68 K graciela.williamson@ashford.edu
WILLIAMSON, Ian ... 505-454-3342 286 J iwilliamson@nmhu.edu
WILLIAMSON, James ... 660-263-3900 251 D jameswilliamson@cccb.edu
WILLIAMSON, James ... 931-526-3660 419 I
WILLIAMSON, James, R ... 858-784-8469 64 A gradprgm@scripps.edu
WILLIAMSON, Jeff ... 507-372-3408 239 F jeff.williamson@mnwest.edu
WILLIAMSON, Jennifer . 610-921-7668 377 G jwilliamson@albright.edu
WILLIAMSON, Jeremy ... 612-343-4450 242 M jdwillia@northcentral.edu
WILLIAMSON, Jeremy ... 407-646-2137 106 L jwilliamson@rollins.edu
WILLIAMSON, Jessica .. 912-623-2400 118 C jwilliamson@ega.edu
WILLIAMSON, Jon ... 214-648-1500 457 A jon.williamson@utsouthwestern.edu
WILLIAMSON, Jonathan 606-218-5300 186 B jonathanwilliamson@upike.edu
WILLIAMSON, Jordan, H ... 336-633-0156 337 A jhwilliamson@randolph.edu
WILLIAMSON, Kathleen 614-234-5950 356 E kwilliamson@mccn.edu
WILLIAMSON, Keith ... 207-326-4311 196 A
WILLIAMSON, Keith ... 940-397-4231 440 C keith.williamson@msutexas.edu
WILLIAMSON, Kimberly 252-493-7217 336 H kwilliamson@email.pittcc.edu
WILLIAMSON, Kip ... 256-228-6001 3 B williamsonkep@nacc.edu
WILLIAMSON, Laurel ... 281-998-6182 443 C laurel.williamson@sjcd.edu
WILLIAMSON, Laurel ... 281-998-6182 442 K laurel.williamson@sjcd.edu
WILLIAMSON, Laurel ... 281-998-6182 443 B laurel.williamson@sjcd.edu
WILLIAMSON, Laurel ... 281-998-6182 443 A laurel.williamson@sjcd.edu
WILLIAMSON, Lisa ... 706-245-7226 118 D lwilliamson@ec.edu
WILLIAMSON, Lisa ... 715-682-1678 494 G lwilliamson@northland.edu
WILLIAMSON, Margaret 504-280-7054 190 B mswilli4@uno.edu
WILLIAMSON, Margaret, L ... 806-742-3171 450 F margaret.l.williams@ttu.edu
WILLIAMSON, Marty ... 661-654-2677 30 B mwilliamson@csub.edu
WILLIAMSON, Michael 843-383-8140 408 B
WILLIAMSON, P. Kevin 336-285-3061 341 D pkwilliamson@ncat.edu
WILLIAMSON, Robin ... 501-450-3416 23 H rwilliamson@uca.edu
WILLIAMSON, Stephen . 605-367-7464 417 B stephen.williamson@southeasttech.edu
WILLIAMSON, Thomas . 612-659-6791 239 A thomas.williamson@minneapolis.edu
WILLIAMSON, Tracey ... 660-263-3900 251 D bookstore@cccb.edu
WILLIAMSON-LOTT, Joy ... 206-543-7468 485 A joyann@uw.edu
WILLIARD, Stacey ... 724-266-3838 400 B swilliard@tsm.edu
WILLIBY, Jason ... 785-628-4728 173 H jjwilliby3@fhsu.edu
WILLIE, Lisa ... 215-951-1011 387 A willie@lasalle.edu
WILLIE LEBRETON, Sarah ... 610-690-2044 398 G swillie1@swarthmore.edu
WILLIFORD, Andrea, G . 478-757-5131 127 F awilliford@wesleyancollege.edu
WILLIFORD, Brent ... 979-830-4146 431 H brent.williford@blinn.edu
WILLIFORD, Darryl ... 301-860-4186 204 A dwilliford@bowiestate.edu
WILLIFORD, David ... 615-675-5302 428 C dwilliford@welch.edu
WILLIFORD, G. Craig ... 503-255-0332 374 C cwilliford@multnomah.edu
WILLIFORD, Lynn, E ... 919-962-1500 342 C lynn_williford@unc.edu
WILLIFORD, Mickey ... 706-721-6544 116 A shwillif@augusta.edu
WILLING, Cindy ... 517-607-4315 225 C cwilling@hillsdale.edu
WILLINGHAM, Nathan .. 256-765-4607 8 E cnwillingham@una.edu
WILLINGHAM, Paul ... 281-655-3712 439 C paul.willingham@lonestar.edu
WILLINGHAM, Tynisha . 540-887-7030 468 G twillingham@marybaldwin.edu
WILLIS, Amy ... 229-391-5007 114 F apwillis@abac.edu
WILLIS, Bessie ... 757-727-5331 467 G bessie.willis@hamptonu.edu
WILLIS, Brian ... 828-398-7929 332 B bwillis@abtech.edu
WILLIS, Carla ... 352-588-8644 107 D carla.willis@saintleo.edu
WILLIS, Daria ... 425-388-9573 480 B dwillis@everettcc.edu
WILLIS, David ... 575-492-2173 289 F dwillis@usw.edu
WILLIS, Doug, G ... 972-378-8790 433 I dwillis@collin.edu
WILLIS, Eric, R ... 319-352-8470 170 J rick.willis@wartburg.edu
WILLIS, Gabe ... 985-549-3645 193 A gabe.willis@selu.edu
WILLIS, Gerry ... 401-341-2159 405 D willisg@salve.edu
WILLIS, Harvey ... 973-328-5232 276 J hwillis@ccm.edu
WILLIS, Howard ... 707-256-7355 53 E hwillis@napavalley.edu
WILLIS, Howard ... 408-274-7900 62 G
WILLIS, Jeff ... 337-550-1287 189 G jwillis@lsue.edu
WILLIS, Jeff ... 270-384-8097 183 G willisj@lindsey.edu
WILLIS, Kathy ... 618-468-5700 142 E kwillis@lc.edu
WILLIS, Kimberley ... 585-395-2501 317 E kwillis@brockport.edu
WILLIS, Leonard ... 410-462-8052 198 B lwillis@bccc.edu
WILLIS, Lesia ... 718-522-9073 290 E lwillis@asa.edu
WILLIS, Lisa ... 312-850-7131 135 H lwillis01@ccc.edu
WILLIS, Marc ... 918-647-1464 365 E mwillis@carlalbert.edu
WILLIS, Mary ... 559-278-4207 31 B mwillis@csufresno.edu
WILLIS, Michaela ... 605-688-4493 417 A michaela.willis@sdstate.edu
WILLIS, Richard ... 205-929-1776 6 B
WILLIS, Sarina ... 936-261-2173 446 C srphillips@pvamu.edu
WILLIS, Steve ... 434-947-8383 469 E swillis@randolphcollege.edu
WILLIS, Susan ... 918-343-6802 369 B swillis@rsu.edu
WILLIS, Tori ... 919-719-1890 340 B twillis@shawu.edu
WILLIS-BARKSDALE, Ava ... 610-409-3005 401 H awillisbarksdale@ursinus.edu
WILLIS KRAUSS, Michelle ... 252-249-1851 336 F mwillis@pamlicocc.edu
WILLITS, Rick ... 937-294-0592 356 D rick.willits@themodern.edu
WILLLIAMS, Venetia, C . 865-539-7266 425 B vcwilliams@pstcc.edu
WILLLIS, Howard ... 707-256-7355 53 E hwillis@napavalley.edu
WILLMARTH, Ephraim ... 315-858-0945 302 A ejwillmarth@hts.edu
WILLOUGHBY, Dan ... 714-992-7037 54 C dwilloughby@fullcoll.edu
WILLOUGHBY, G. Case 724-287-8711 379 E case.willoughby@bc3.edu
WILLOUGHBY, Karen ... 412-536-1201 386 H karen.willoughby@laroche.edu
WILLOUGHBY, Karen, P ... 412-536-1201 386 H karen.willoughby@laroche.edu
WILLOWBY, Nathan ... 765-641-4529 153 G njwillowby@anderson.edu
WILLS, Barbara ... 850-201-6060 112 C barbara.wills@tcc.fl.edu
WILLS, Helen ... 618-374-5189 147 E helen.wills@principia.edu
WILLS, Jeremiah ... 704-337-2506 339 F willsj@queens.edu
WILLS, Mark ... 213-252-5100 23 K mwills@alu.edu
WILLS, Mark ... 423-798-7970 425 F mark.wills@ws.edu
WILLS, Mike ... 417-836-7635 256 G mikewills@missouristate.edu
WILLS, Scott, D ... 419-772-2705 358 C s-wills@onu.edu
WILLS, Tim ... 618-437-5321 147 I wills@rlc.edu
WILLSON, Dawn ... 714-241-6186 37 J dwillson1@coastline.edu
WILLY, Randy ... 785-442-6005 174 F rwilly@highlandcc.edu
WILLYARD, Paula ... 918-595-2067 370 C paula.willyard@tulsacc.edu
WILMARTH, Constance . 541-684-7292 371 I cwilmarth@bushnell.edu
WILMER, Elizabeth ... 540-857-7313 475 G ewilmer@virginiawestern.edu
WILMES, David ... 724-738-2003 395 C david.wilmes@sru.edu
WILMESHERR, Jon ... 828-766-1360 336 A jwilmesherr@mayland.edu
WILMONTH, Charlie ... 918-540-6224 366 F charlie.wilmonth@neo.edu
WILMOT, Lynne ... 507-222-5500 234 G lwilmot@carleton.edu
WILMOTH, Dirk ... 828-398-7111 332 B dirkwilmoth@abtech.edu
WILMOTH, Wendy ... 404-297-9522 120 B
WILMOTT, Robert ... 314-977-9801 259 F robert.wilmott@health.slu.edu
WILMOUTH, Robert ... 406-657-1015 265 E president@rocky.edu
WILMS, Amy ... 909-748-8109 72 F amy_wilms@redlands.edu
WILROY, Claudia ... 805-378-1409 73 J cwilroy@vcccd.edu
WILSHUSEN, Lauren ... 617-879-7226 213 B lwilshusen@massart.edu
WILSKE, Don ... 517-483-1765 226 H wilsked@lcc.edu
WILSON, Adam ... 540-636-2900 465 L adam.wilson@christendom.edu
WILSON, Alan ... 706-385-1059 124 E alan.wilson@point.edu
WILSON, Allen, T ... 757-683-3144 469 B a3wilson@odu.edu
WILSON, Allyson ... 954-763-9840 95 J
WILSON, Amanda ... 317-921-4949 158 D amanda.wilson@ivytech.edu
WILSON, Amanda ... 918-647-1326 365 E adwilson@carlalbert.edu
WILSON, Amy ... 608-363-2699 491 H wilsonae@beloit.edu
WILSON, Amy, R ... 740-245-7382 363 A awilson@rio.edu
WILSON, Andy ... 252-398-6343 328 C aawilson@chowan.edu
WILSON, Angela ... 618-252-5400 149 I angela.wilson@sic.edu
WILSON, Anne ... 706-290-2667 116 B awilson@berry.edu
WILSON, Annette ... 312-362-6214 136 H awilso49@depaul.edu
WILSON, Annette ... 336-517-2302 327 A annette.wilson@bennett.edu
WILSON, Arthur, L ... 260-359-4031 156 C alwilson@huntington.edu
WILSON, Asif ... 312-553-5600 135 B awilson@ccc.edu
WILSON, Barbara ... 770-534-6203 116 D bwilson@brenau.edu
WILSON, Barbara, J ... 319-335-3565 163 H
WILSON, Betsyann ... 928-536-6245 14 J betsy.wilson@npc.edu
WILSON, Bill ... 406-683-7509 264 A william.wilson@umwestern.edu
WILSON, Blake ... 864-424-8022 413 H bentleyt@mailbox.sc.edu
WILSON, Bradley ... 724-738-2003 395 C bradley.wilson@sru.edu
WILSON, Breanna ... 828-652-6021 336 B
WILSON, Bryan ... 307-778-1179 501 E bwilson@lccc.wy.edu
WILSON, Carlos ... 601-979-8895 246 F carlos.d.wilson@jsums.edu
WILSON, Carlton, E ... 919-530-6794 341 E cwilson@nccu.edu
WILSON, Charles ... 704-922-6454 334 G wilson.charles@gaston.edu
WILSON, Charles ... 859-371-9393 179 G cwilson@beckfield.edu
WILSON, Cheri ... 256-726-7204 6 C cwilson@oakwood.edu
WILSON, Cheryl ... 443-334-2579 202 E cawilson@stevenson.edu
WILSON, Chip ... 740-397-9000 356 G chip.wilson@mvnu.edu
WILSON, Christina ... 618-374-5148 147 E christina.wilson@principia.edu
WILSON, Christine ... 310-206-1911 69 E cwilson@saonet.ucla.edu
WILSON, Christine ... 785-243-1435 172 L cwilson@cloud.edu
WILSON, Christine ... 207-778-7087 196 I christine.wilson@maine.edu
WILSON, Christopher ... 701-231-6409 345 F christopher.s.wilson@ndsu.edu
WILSON, Cleveland ... 803-535-1419 411 B wilsonc@octech.edu
WILSON, Craig ... 315-228-6941 296 E cawilson@colgate.edu
WILSON, Cynthia ... 251-928-8133 9 A cwilson@southalabama.edu
WILSON, Cynthia, L ... 713-348-5048 442 F clwilson@rice.edu
WILSON, Dani ... 714-992-7040 54 C dwilson@fullcoll.edu
WILSON, Daniel ... 252-398-6260 328 C dowilson@chowan.edu
WILSON, Daniel, B ... 740-826-8165 356 H dwilson@muskingum.edu
WILSON, Darlene ... 310-338-7725 51 A dwilson@lmu.edu
WILSON, David ... 207-974-4853 195 E dwilson@emcc.edu
WILSON, David ... 443-885-3200 201 A david.wilson@morgan.edu
WILSON, David ... 615-966-6219 421 B david.wilson@lipscomb.edu
WILSON, Dayton ... 304-766-3181 490 D dayton.wilson@wvstateu.edu
WILSON, De Lisa ... 404-880-6136 117 C dwilson@cau.edu
WILSON, Debra, J ... 906-248-8442 221 M dwilson@bmcc.edu
WILSON, Delfina ... 913-288-7618 175 B dwilson@kckcc.edu
WILSON, Dena, L ... 301-546-0167 201 E wilsondl@pgcc.edu
WILSON, Diana ... 307-432-1798 501 E dwilson@lccc.wy.edu
WILSON, Don ... 863-297-1000 106 A dhw@bosdun.com
WILSON, Donna ... 717-720-4000 393 C
WILSON, Doug ... 251-442-2406 8 C dwilson@umobile.edu
WILSON, Douglas ... 205-726-4266 6 E dwilson@samford.edu
WILSON, Elaine ... 606-451-6915 182 G elaine.wilson@kctcs.edu

WILSON, Elaine .... 410-827-5835 198 F
ewilson@chesapeake.edu
WILSON, Elighie .... 708-709-7767 147 D
ewilson@prairiestate.edu
WILSON, Elisabeth .... 952-996-1470 234 B
elisabeth.wilson@bethanygu.edu
WILSON, Elise .... 530-226-4718.. 64 E
ewilson@simpsonu.edu
WILSON, Erin .... 214-388-5466 435 D
erinwilson@dallasinstitute.edu
WILSON, Evan .... 217-245-3272 139 C
evan.wilson@ic.edu
WILSON, Fleetwood, L .. 206-934-3789 483 B
fleetwood.wilson@seattlecolleges.edu
WILSON, Fred .... 251-377-9281.... 8 C
fwilson@umobile.edu
WILSON, Fred .... 714-816-0366.. 68 E
fred.wilson@trident.edu
WILSON, Gary .... 828-726-2264 332 G
gwilson@cccti.edu
WILSON, Gena .... 229-931-2000 120 D
gena.wilson@gsw.edu
WILSON, Gordon, N ..... 801-581-3079 459 O
gordon.wilson@utah.edu
WILSON, Grant .... 308-635-6003 270 C
wilsong7@wncc.edu
WILSON, Heather .... 915-747-5555 455 C
hwilson@utep.edu
WILSON, Holly .... 318-473-6581 189 F
hwilson@lsua.edu
WILSON, Howard .... 712-722-6007 165 I
howard.wilson@dordt.edu
WILSON, Jackie .... 907-796-6389.. 10 B
jmwilson17@alaska.edu
WILSON, Jacqueline ...... 334-683-2309.... 3 A
jwilson@marionmilitary.edu
WILSON, Jamar .... 212-616-7200 301 C
WILSON, Jamelle .... 804-289-8135 472 C
jwilson9@richmond.edu
WILSON, JR.,
James, D .... 302-295-1194.. 91 E
jim.d.wilson@wilmu.edu
WILSON, Jamie, B .... 601-974-1086 247 B
jamie.wilson@millsaps.edu
WILSON, Janice .... 860-465-4466.. 85 H
wilsonj@easternct.edu
WILSON, Jason .... 810-762-0200 228 F
jason.wilson@mcc.edu
WILSON, JD .... 901-381-3939 428 B
jd@visible.edu
WILSON, Jennifer .... 212-229-5600 308 A
wilsonj@newschool.edu
WILSON, Jennifer .... 641-683-5174 166 I
jennifer.wilson@indianhills.edu
WILSON, Jessi .... 901-843-3850 423 A
wilsonj@rhodes.edu
WILSON, Jessica, D ...... 512-448-8414 442 I
jwilso12@stedwards.edu
WILSON, Jessica, J ...... 717-245-1554 382 D
wilsonje@dickinson.edu
WILSON, Jessica, L ...... 210-829-3931 453 C
jewilso1@uiwtx.edu
WILSON, Jimmy .... 212-686-9244 290 C
WILSON, Joani .... 309-298-2515 153 A
jm-wilson3@wiu.edu
WILSON, Jocelyn .... 516-671-2215 324 G
jwilson@webb.edu
WILSON, Jocelyn, M .... 516-671-2215 324 G
jwilson@webb.edu
WILSON, Joe .... 972-883-4995 455 B
joe.wilson@utdallas.edu
WILSON, John .... 404-270-5376 126 B
john.wilson@spelman.edu
WILSON, John .... 843-863-7102 407 B
jewilson@csuniv.edu
WILSON, John, R .... 804-278-4330 471 J
jwilson@upsem.edu
WILSON, Jon .... 913-234-0815 172 K
jon.wilson@cleveland.edu
WILSON, Jonathan .... 601-984-1010 249 E
jwilson5@umc.edu
WILSON, Joseph .... 706-641-5665 117 I
jwilson@columbustech.edu
WILSON, Josh .... 706-272-2473 118 B
jwilson@daltonstate.edu
WILSON, Joshua .... 870-368-2060.. 20 E
josh.wilson@ozarka.edu
WILSON, Judge .... 859-985-3131 179 I
wilsonju@berea.edu
WILSON, Judi .... 706-667-4368 116 A
jwilso24@augusta.edu
WILSON, Julie .... 304-829-7130 487 A
jwilson@bethanywv.edu
WILSON, Kamesha .... 252-527-6223 335 G
knwilson59@lenoircc.edu
WILSON, Katelyn .... 660-263-4100 257 B
katelynw@macc.edu
WILSON, Kathi .... 865-981-8211 421 C
kathi.wilson@maryvillecollege.edu
WILSON, Kathryn .... 585-395-2137 317 E
kwilson@brockport.edu
WILSON, Katrin .... 323-241-5200.. 49 E
wilsonk3@lasc.edu
WILSON, Keisha .... 704-330-1455 330 D
kwilson@jcsu.edu
WILSON, Kelly .... 619-398-4902.. 45 C
WILSON, Kenneth .... 205-247-8071.... 7 A
kwilson@stillman.edu
WILSON, Kenny .... 636-481-3356 254 C
kwilso20@jeffco.edu
WILSON, Kent .... 304-205-6689 488 D
kent.wilson@bridgevalley.edu
WILSON, Kevin .... 573-681-5412 254 G
wilsonk2@lincolnu.edu
WILSON, Kim .... 661-362-2844.. 51 D
kwilson@masters.edu
WILSON, Kim .... 870-368-2300.. 20 E
kwilson@ozarka.edu
WILSON, Kimberly, P ... 859-257-4751 185 F
kwilson@email.uky.edu
WILSON, Kristina .... 361-698-1137 435 G
kmwilson@delmar.edu
WILSON, Lana .... 765-998-5267 161 C
lnwilson@taylor.edu
WILSON, Laura .... 937-376-6254 349 J
lwilson@centralstate.edu
WILSON, Laura, L .... 650-723-9633.. 66 E
laura.wilson@stanford.edu
WILSON, Leah .... 585-582-1230 298 F
leahwilson@elim.edu
WILSON, Leana .... 850-474-2244 111 F
lwilson2@uwf.edu
WILSON, Leon, C .... 601-977-7735 249 C
lcwilson@tougaloo.edu
WILSON, Leslie, K .... 319-273-6240 164 A
leslie.wilson@uni.edu
WILSON, Lindsay .... 217-581-3413 137 E
lpwilson@eiu.edu
WILSON, Lisa, M .... 951-827-3486.. 70 B
lisa.wilson@ucr.edu
WILSON, Locord .... 601-979-3354 246 F
locord.d.wilson@jsums.edu
WILSON, Lori, J .... 570-577-3334 379 C
lwilson@bucknell.edu
WILSON, Lucy .... 919-546-8322 340 B
lwilson@shawu.edu
WILSON, M. Roy .... 313-577-2230 232 K
president@wayne.edu
WILSON, Marcus .... 954-201-6974.. 96 F
mwilson2@broward.edu
WILSON, Marcus .... 806-743-6443 451 A
marcus.wilson@ttuhsc.edu
WILSON, Mardell, A ..... 402-280-4076 266 H
mardellwilson@creighton.edu
WILSON, Margaret .... 660-626-2354 250 A
mwilson@atsu.edu
WILSON, Mark .... 931-372-3961 426 B
mwilson@tntech.edu
WILSON, Mark .... 423-472-7141 424 B
mwilson@clevelandstatecc.edu
WILSON, Mark .... 605-995-3024 415 E
mark.wilson@mitchelltech.edu
WILSON, Martha .... 207-221-4514 197 E
mwilson13@une.edu
WILSON, Martha .... 530-891-6900.. 27 E
WILSON, Mary .... 931-598-1860 423 D
mewilson@sewanee.edu
WILSON, Matt .... 817-722-1775 438 G
matt.wilson@tku.edu
WILSON, Matthew .... 734-462-4400 230 G
mwilson@schoolcraft.edu
WILSON, Matthew .... 215-204-7405 399 B
matthew.wilson@temple.edu
WILSON, Matthew, J ..... 302-356-6970.. 91 E
matthew.j.wilson@wilmu.edu
WILSON, Melanie .... 808-934-2519 129 I
mfwilson@hawaii.edu
WILSON, Melissa .... 270-706-8727 181 G
mwilson0132@kctcs.edu
WILSON, Michael .... 503-517-1261 377 C
mewilson@warnerpacific.edu
WILSON, Michael, D ..... 714-556-3610.. 73 H
mdwilson@vanguard.edu
WILSON, Michele .... 304-424-8355 490 F
michele.wilson@wvup.edu
WILSON, Michelle .... 870-633-4480.. 19 A
rwilson@eacc.edu
WILSON, Mindy .... 518-743-2252 320 A
wilsonm@sunyacc.edu
WILSON, Molly .... 937-229-1000 362 C
WILSON, Monica .... 603-646-2215 273 D
monica.wilson@dartmouth.edu
WILSON, Monica .... 304-434-8000 488 E
monica.wilson@easternwv.edu
WILSON, Nakeenya, S .. 512-505-3070 438 A
nswilson@htu.edu
WILSON, Nancy .... 205-929-3451.... 2 H
nwilson@lawsonstate.edu
WILSON, Natalie, L .... 412-578-6171 380 B
nlwilson@carlow.edu
WILSON, Natasha .... 660-248-3391 251 E
nwilson@centralmethodist.edu
WILSON, Nate .... 208-882-1566 132 C
nwilson@nsa.edu
WILSON, Nathan .... 317-931-2316 154 G
nwilson@cts.edu
WILSON, Nicole .... 757-822-7152 475 E
nwwilson@tcc.edu
WILSON, Oceana .... 802-440-4606 461 G
owilson@bennington.edu
WILSON, Patricia .... 256-306-2743.... 1 F
patricia.wilson@calhoun.edu
WILSON, Patrick .... 505-891-6908 286 J
patrickwilson@nmhu.edu
WILSON, Phillip .... 479-394-7622.. 23 C
pwilson@uarichmountain.edu
WILSON, Piper .... 417-477-7428 257 G
wilsonp@otc.edu
WILSON, Qiana .... 478-445-2037 119 B
qiana.wilson@gcsu.edu
WILSON, Qiana, N .... 706-542-7912 126 G
qiana.wilson@uga.edu
WILSON, Rebeka .... 402-375-7239 268 F
rewilso1@wsc.edu
WILSON, Reggie, L .... 352-797-5001 105 F
wilsonr@phsc.edu
WILSON, Robert .... 207-893-7750 196 C
WILSON, Robert, A .... 610-606-4637 380 D
rwilson@cedarcrest.edu
WILSON, Ronalyn .... 518-629-7622 302 C
r.wilson@hvcc.edu
WILSON, Ryan .... 859-622-8939 180 E
ryan.wilson@eku.edu
WILSON, Samantha .... 979-845-5139 446 F
samantha@tamu.edu
WILSON, Sandra .... 313-664-7471 222 H
sandra@collegeforcreativestudies.edu
WILSON, Scott .... 651-846-1694 241 B
scott.wilson@saintpaul.edu
WILSON, Scott .... 931-598-1173 423 D
swilson@sewanee.edu
WILSON, Scott, L .... 314-935-2656 262 A
scott.l.wilson@wustl.edu
WILSON, Sharntae .... 860-253-3006.. 86 C
swilson@asnuntuck.edu
WILSON, Shawn .... 989-964-7147 230 E
swilson@svsu.edu
WILSON, Shawna .... 517-264-7142 230 H
swilson@sienaheights.edu
WILSON, Sheila .... 252-399-6309 326 K
spwilson@barton.edu
WILSON, Sheila .... 330-263-2580 351 A
swilson@wooster.edu
WILSON, Shirley .... 213-624-1200.. 42 B
swilson@fidm.edu
WILSON, Sonali, B .... 216-687-3860 350 J
s.b.wilson@csuohio.edu
WILSON, Stacey .... 636-481-3207 254 C
swilson@jeffco.edu
WILSON, Stephan, M .... 405-744-9805 367 G
stephan.m.wilson@okstate.edu
WILSON, Stephen .... 478-445-5331 119 B
steve.wilson@gcsu.edu
WILSON, Steve .... 785-833-4410 175 E
steve.wilson@kwu.edu
WILSON, Steven .... 231-773-9131 228 G
WILSON, Steven .... 540-868-7132 474 C
stevenwilson@lfcc.edu
WILSON, Steven, H .... 610-758-3200 388 E
shw516@lehigh.edu
WILSON, TaJuan .... 912-478-5018 120 C
tajuanwilson@georgiasouthern.edu
WILSON, Tara, K .... 808-544-1460 128 G
tkwilson@hpu.edu
WILSON, Ted, H .... 270-707-3865 182 B
ted.wilson@kctcs.edu
WILSON, Thad, R .... 816-995-2815 258 G
thad.wilson@researchcollege.edu
WILSON, Thalia .... 910-672-2852 341 C
twilson@uncfsu.edu
WILSON, Tim .... 865-694-6666 425 B
trwilson@pstcc.edu
WILSON, Tim .... 412-391-4100 396 G
WILSON, Tomeka .... 210-486-2551 429 B
tcross13@alamo.edu
WILSON, Tommy .... 706-649-1894 117 I
twilson@columbustech.edu
WILSON, Torrey .... 317-788-6126 161 H
twilson@uindy.edu
WILSON, Travis .... 606-539-4002 185 E
travis.wilson@ucumberlands.edu
WILSON, Tricia .... 717-560-8200 387 E
twilson@lbc.edu
WILSON, Valarie .... 205-860-7845.... 7 A
vwilson@stillman.edu
WILSON, Valeri .... 619-660-4221.. 44 D
valeri.wilson@gcccd.edu
WILSON, Valerie .... 870-574-4514.. 21 D
vwilson@sautech.edu
WILSON, Valla, F .... 214-648-6066 457 A
valla.wilson@utsouthwestern.edu
WILSON, Valvia .... 601-977-7844 249 C
vwilson@tougaloo.edu
WILSON, Vicki .... 724-852-3375 402 C
vwilson@waynesburg.edu
WILSON, Vicky, W .... 864-833-8219 411 D
vwwilson@presby.edu
WILSON, Victor, K .... 706-542-3564 126 G
wilsonv@uga.edu
WILSON, Wendy .... 229-500-3503 114 H
wendy.wilson@asurams.edu
WILSON, Wes .... 404-627-2681 116 C
wes.wilson@beulah.edu
WILSON, Wes, C .... 404-627-2681 116 C
wes.wilson@beulah.edu
WILSON, Wesley .... 670-237-6834 505 A
wesley.wilson@marianas.edu
WILSON, William .... 423-354-2541 425 A
wrwilson@northeaststate.edu
WILSON, William, M .... 918-495-6175 368 F
president@oru.edu
WILSON, Yolanda .... 336-838-6128 339 B
yswilson142@wilkescc.edu
WILSON-ALLAM,
Deborah .... 315-792-3259 324 B
dlwilson@utica.edu
WILSON-BYRD, Holly ... 405-382-9204 369 F
h.wilsonbyrd@sscok.edu
WILSON-FENNELL,
Nicole .... 734-462-4400 230 G
nwilson@schoolcraft.edu
WILSON-LOGGINS,
Jennifer .... 770-534-6134 116 D
jloggins@brenau.edu
WILSON-PARKER,
Sharnita, I .... 252-335-3747 341 B
slwilson@ecsu.edu
WILSON PICKETT,
Clyde .... 651-201-1472 237 B
WILSON PICKETT,
Clyde .... 412-624-7860 400 H
cwp19@pitt.edu
WILSON RAMEY,
Melinda .... 916-278-4796.. 32 D
WILSON-SPARROW,
Sarah .... 518-595-1101 315 B
wilsons@sunysccc.edu
WILSON-SYKES, Jean .... 205-247-8145.... 7 A
jwilson-sykes@stillman.edu
WILSON-TAYLOR,
Sharon .... 312-369-7221 136 D
swilson-taylor@colum.edu
WILSTERMANN, Amy .... 616-526-7620 222 C
amw26@calvin.edu
WILT, Darrell .... 717-815-1288 403 F
dwilt1@ycp.edu
WILTERDING, James ..... 505-277-1068 288 J
jameswilterding@salud.unm.edu
WILTFONG, Justin .... 620-242-0400 176 B
WILTGEN, JR., Jim .... 501-450-1222.. 19 E
wiltgen@hendrix.edu
WILTROUT, Deborah ..... 239-590-1089 109 K
dwiltrout@fgcu.edu
WILTSHIRE, Rolly .... 718-289-5186 293 B
rolly.wiltshire@bcc.cuny.edu
WILTZ, Alex .... 413-775-1299 214 E
wiltza@gcc.mass.edu
WILTZIUS, Pierre .... 805-893-5024.. 70 E
mlpsdean@ltsc.ucsb.edu
WIMBERLY, Carey .... 478-471-2700 122 F
carey.wimberly@mga.edu

WIMBERLY, Chuck .... 478-289-2036 118 C
cwimberly@ega.edu
WIMBERLY, Frances ..... 706-396-8102 124 B
fwimberly@paine.edu
WIMBERLY, Yvette .... 501-374-6305.. 20 G
yvette.wimberly@shortercollege.edu
WIMBUSH, James, C .... 812-855-2739 156 F
jwimbush@iu.edu
WIMBUSH, James, C .... 812-856-5700 156 G
dema@indiana.edu
WIMER, Aaron .... 843-953-1658 407 C
awimer@citadel.edu
WIMER, Valinda .... 386-822-8850 112 A
vwimer@stetson.edu
WIMMER, Angela .... 501-686-7950.. 22 B
awimmer@uams.edu
WIMS, Daniel, K .... 256-372-5275.... 1 A
daniel.wims@aamu.edu
WIMS, Lois, A .... 508-929-8038 213 G
lwims@worcester.edu
WIN, Wambli .... 918-913-2755 365 C
winw@bacone.edu
WINBORNE, Malverne .. 734-487-2086 223 K
mwinborne@emich.edu
WINBUSH, Chauncey .... 304-876-5155 490 A
cwinbush@shepherd.edu
WINBUSH, Larkisha ...... 251-442-2250.... 8 C
lwinbush@umobile.edu
WINCH, Eric .... 908-709-7150 284 D
eric.winch@ucc.edu
WINCHELL, Brooks .... 617-873-0499 208 B
brooks.winchell@cambridgecollege.edu
WINCHELL, Lynne .... 303-361-7367.. 80 E
lynne.winchell@ccaurora.edu
WINCHESTER, Sara .... 732-255-0400 279 F
swinchester@ocean.edu
WINCKELMAN, Stephen 952-358-8597 239 G
stephen.winckelman@normandale.edu
WIND-NORTON, Laura .. 715-365-4578 499 E
lwindnorton@nicoletcollege.edu
WINDER, Katie .... 541-917-4547 373 G
winderk@linnbenton.edu
WINDER, Mark .... 319-895-4518 164 G
mwinder@cornellcollege.edu
WINDER, Wendy .... 801-618-0438 458 G
wwinder@ameritech.edu
WINDERS, Tim .... 219-989-2417 160 D
winders@pnw.edu
WINDES, Deborah, L .... 708-239-4844 151 A
deborah.windes@trnty.edu
WINDHAM, Adam .... 916-484-8216.. 50 G
windhaa@arc.losrios.edu
WINDHAM, Don .... 772-462-7357 102 F
dwindham@irsc.edu
WINDHAM, Greg .... 662-720-7210 248 C
jgwindham@nemcc.edu
WINDHAM, Jameka, A .. 305-628-6632 107 F
jwindham@stu.edu
WINDHAM, Joel .... 205-726-2011.... 6 E
jwindham@samford.edu
WINDHOLZ, Kevin .... 405-208-5600 367 E
kwindholz@okcu.edu
WINDHOLZ, Mindy .... 405-208-7902 367 E
mbwindholz@okcu.edu
WINDLE, Frank, H .... 215-871-6750 395 G
frankwi@pcom.edu
WINDLE, Lawrence, B ... 956-380-8100 442 G
lwindle@riogrande.edu
WINDMEYER, Sarah .... 785-442-6000 174 F
jnorth@highlandcc.edu
WINDOKUN, Prema ...... 805-898-4010.. 42 D
pwindokun@fielding.edu
WINDROW, Vincent, L .. 615-898-2338 422 C
vincent.windrow@mtsu.edu
WINDSOR, Michael, H .. 757-479-3706 472 F
mwindsor@vbts.edu
WINDY BOY, Helen ...... 406-395-4875 265 G
hwindyboy@stonechild.edu
WINE, David .... 815-939-5254 147 A
dwine@olivet.edu
WINEBRAKE, James ...... 910-962-3389 343 C
winebrakej@uncw.edu
WINEGARD, Tanya, C ... 402-280-2775 266 H
tanyawinegard@creighton.edu
WINEY, Mark .... 530-752-6778.. 69 B
mwiney@ucdavis.edu
WINFIELD-THOMAS,
Evelyn, B .... 269-387-6316 233 B
evelyn.winfield@wmich.edu
WINFREY GRIFFIN,
Polly .... 609-258-6191 280 D
polly@princeton.edu
WING, Jeanette, M .... 212-854-1754 297 C

WING, Seth .... 319-895-4150 164 G
swing@cornellcollege.edu
WINGARD, Ed .... 830-792-7234 443 E
facilitiesservices@schreiner.edu
WINGARD, Jason .... 215-204-7405 399 B
president@temple.edu
WINGARD, Jason, M .... 212-854-3771 297 C
jason.wingard@columbia.edu
WINGARD, Julia .... 757-823-8200 469 A
jbwingard@nsu.edu
WINGE, Jennifer .... 330-263-2118 351 A
jwinge@wooster.edu
WINGEIER-RAYO,
Philip .... 202-885-8611.. 94 D
pwingeier@wesleyseminary.edu
WINGENBACH, Edward . 413-559-5521 210 D
president@hampshire.edu
WINGER, Davin .... 580-349-1460 367 F
dwinger@opsu.edu
WINGER, Steven .... 563-876-3353 165 H
swinger@dwci.edu
WINGERT, Nancy .... 785-242-5200 176 I
nancy.wingert@ottawa.edu
WINGERT, Timothy .... 210-883-1190 453 C
optometry@uiwtx.edu
WINGFIELD, Erin .... 559-791-2332.. 47 A
ewingfield@portervillecollege.edu
WINGFIELD, Joy .... 865-573-4517 420 E
jwingfield@johnsonu.edu
WINGLER, Mike .... 336-838-6178 339 B
mswingler068@wilkescc.edu
WINGO, Tad .... 573-221-3675 253 J
WINGROVE,
Thurman, D .... 412-624-6028 400 H
twingrove@pitt.edu
WINGS, Arron .... 319-398-5624 167 J
arron.wings@kirkwood.edu
WINIGER, Brent .... 701-858-3331 345 E
brent.winiger@minotstateu.edu
WINISTORFER, Paul, M 540-231-5481 476 C
pwinisto@vt.edu
WINITZKY-STEPHENS,
Jessie .... 801-957-4090 461 C
jessie.winitzky-stephens@slcc.edu
WINKELBAUER, Brian ... 303-273-3140.. 79 J
bwinkelb@mines.edu
WINKELFOOS, Natalie ... 440-775-6463 357 G
natalie.winkelfoos@oberlin.edu
WINKELMAN, Andrew ... 708-209-3529 136 E
andrew.winkelman@cuchicago.edu
WINKELSTEIN, Beth, A . 215-898-7225 400 F
winkelst@seas.upenn.edu
WINKER, Amy .... 231-591-3823 224 A
amywinker@ferris.edu
WINKLEPLECK, Kari, L .. 712-274-5450 168 E
bull@morningside.edu
WINKLER, Fred, R .... 314-977-2401 259 F
fred.winkler@slu.edu
WINKLER, Katelyn .... 541-962-3512 372 I
winklekn@eou.edu
WINKLER, Nicole .... 434-961-5427 474 I
nwinkler@pvcc.edu
WINKLER, Yitzchak .... 305-534-7050 112 D
ywinkler@talmudicu.edu
WINKLERPRINS,
Vince, C .... 202-687-3220.. 92 E
vjw6@georgetown.edu
WINKLEY, Robert .... 617-585-1310 217 E
robert.winkley@necmusic.edu
WINN, Emmett .... 334-844-5771.... 4 D
winnjoh@auburn.edu
WINN, Lori .... 870-972-3454.. 17 E
lwinn@astate.edu
WINN, Matt .... 214-333-6923 434 C
mattw@dbu.edu
WINN, Regina .... 318-670-9411 191 D
rwinn@susla.edu
WINN, Rob .... 906-227-2700 228 I
rwinn@nmu.edu
WINN, Rose .... 559-453-7150.. 43 A
rose.winn@fresno.edu
WINN, Terry .... 405-425-5157 367 C
terry.winn@oc.edu
WINNEY, Maureen .... 518-587-2100 320 E
maureen.winney@esc.edu
WINNINGHAM, Rob ...... 503-838-8271 377 D
winninr@wou.edu
WINOKUR, Ted .... 802-383-6613 462 A
twinokur@champlain.edu
WINQUIST, Melissa ...... 480-858-9100.. 15 Q
m.winquist@scnm.edu
WINS, Cedric, T .... 540-464-7311 476 B
winsct@vmi.edu

WINSEMAN, Jeffrey .... 518-262-5511 289 L
winsemj@amc.edu
WINSETT, Kim .... 812-488-2940 161 G
kw83@evansville.edu
WINSLOW, Gregory ...... 614-236-6714 349 B
gwinslow@capital.edu
WINSLOW, SR., Kellen . 734-432-5345 227 C
kwinslowsr@madonna.edu
WINSLOW, Maggie .... 415-561-6555.. 58 B
WINSLOW, Mark .... 405-789-6400 369 H
mwinslow@snu.edu
WINSLOW-SCHABER,
Deborah, J .... 585-389-2066 307 F
dwinslo1@naz.edu
WINSOR, Robert .... 508-286-8213 220 B
winsor_robert@wheatoncollege.edu
WINSTEAD, Chris .... 601-266-4883 249 F
chris.winstead@usm.edu
WINSTEAD, Christopher 207-974-4810 195 E
cwinstead@emcc.edu
WINSTEAD, James .... 323-860-0789.. 50 B
WINSTEAD, Mel .... 704-847-5600 340 F
mwinstead@ses.edu
WINSTON, Leslie .... 804-627-5300 464 K
leslie_winston@bshsi.org
WINSTON, Mike .... 541-888-7292 376 C
michael.winston@socc.edu
WINSTON-MUIR,
Jeanni .... 301-846-2489 198 I
jwinston-muir@frederick.edu
WINT, Ayana .... 212-938-5654 319 E
awint@sunyopt.edu
WINT, Errol, L .... 317-274-0838 157 D
ewint@iupui.edu
WINTCH, Wesley .... 701-845-7234 345 G
wesley.wintch@vcsu.edu
WINTEMUTE, Mike .... 512-463-4862 449 E
mike.wintemute@tsus.edu
WINTER, Barbara, J ...... 620-235-4152 177 A
bwinter@pittstate.edu
WINTER, Cheryl .... 816-604-6748 255 D
cheryl.winter@mcckc.edu
WINTER, Cheryl .... 816-604-6748 255 E
cheryl.winter@mcckc.edu
WINTER, Christoph .... 415-955-2100.. 24 J
WINTER, Karla, R .... 844-642-2338 169 A
winterk@nicc.edu
WINTER, Kim .... 828-227-7311 343 E
kkruebel@wcu.edu
WINTER, Stacey, O .... 701-231-8954 345 F
stacey.winter@ndsu.edu
WINTER, Tara .... 319-352-8475 170 J
tara.winter@wartburg.edu
WINTER, Tara .... 518-255-5418 319 C
wintertl@cobleskill.edu
WINTER, Walter .... 212-217-3630 299 D
walter_winter@fitnyc.edu
WINTER, JR.,
William, F .... 618-650-5380 150 C
wwinter@siue.edu
WINTERBURN, Scott ..... 909-448-4393.. 71 C
rwinterburn@laverne.edu
WINTERHALTER, Teresa 678-407-5601 119 C
twinterhalter@ggc.edu
WINTERLING,
Stephen, A .... 727-816-3340 105 F
winters@phsc.edu
WINTERMEYER,
Stephen, F .... 317-278-2603 157 D
swinterm@iu.edu
WINTERS, Amy .... 845-687-5124 323 H
wintersa@sunyulster.edu
WINTERS, Amy .... 308-635-6195 270 C
winters4@wncc.edu
WINTERS, J. Chris .... 504-568-2243 189 H
cwinte@lsuhsc.edu
WINTERS, Jeremy, G .... 641-422-4990 168 G
jeremy.winters@niacc.edu
WINTERS, John .... 918-781-7241 365 C
wintersj@bacone.edu
WINTERS, Michael .... 314-256-8854 250 D
winters@ai.edu
WINTERS, Nick .... 509-682-6473 485 H
nwinters@wvc.edu
WINTERS, Stephanie ..... 719-219-9636.. 78 G
swinters@cavt.edu
WINTERS, Teresa .... 413-265-2210 208 E
winterst@elms.edu
WINTERS, Terri, S .... 603-862-4639 274 F
terri.winters@unh.edu
WINTERS, Todd, A .... 731-881-7250 427 D
winters@utm.edu
WINTERS, Vicky, L .... 253-535-7110 482 A
winters@plu.edu

WINTERSTEEN, Wendy .. 515-294-2042 163 G
wwinters@iastate.edu
WINTON, Diana .... 847-628-2532 141 C
diana.winton@judsonu.edu
WINZELER, Isabelle ...... 352-335-2332.. 94 E
isabelle.winzeler@acupuncturist.edu
WINZENREID,
Misty Anne .... 206-876-6100 483 H
mwinzenreid@theseattleschool.edu
WIPPERT, Lola .... 406-338-5441 263 A
WIPPMAN, David .... 315-859-4105 300 H
dwippman@hamilton.edu
WIRGAU, Linda .... 269-337-7175 225 F
linda.wirgau@kzoo.edu
WIRLEY, Eileen, M .... 585-292-3041 307 B
ewirley1@monroecc.edu
WIRT, Jonathan .... 919-532-5663 338 G
jawirth@waketech.edu
WIRTH, Eric .... 802-258-3511 462 H
WIRTH, Jack .... 513-562-8758 347 I
jwirth@artacademy.edu
WIRTH-CAUCHON, Alex 413-538-2797 217 C
awirthca@mtholyoke.edu
WIRTHLIN, James .... 319-656-2447 170 A
WIRTZ, Amy, M .... 920-565-1000 493 A
wirtzam@lakeland.edu
WIRTZ, Denis .... 410-516-8094 199 G
wirtz@jhu.edu
WIRTZ, Hilary .... 617-585-1100 217 E
WISBY, Heidi .... 248-689-8282 232 C
hwisby@walshcollege.edu
WISCHMANN, Teresa .... 309-779-7708 151 B
teresa.wischmann@trinitycollegeqc.edu
WISCHMEIER, Gordon ... 928-523-9011.. 14 H
WISCOMBE, Tom .... 213-613-2200.. 65 E
tom_wiscombe@sciarc.edu
WISCOTT, Richard .... 401-598-5156 404 D
richard.wiscott@jwu.edu
WISDOM, Ami .... 816-584-6542 258 C
ami.wisdom@park.edu
WISDOM, Bryan .... 706-865-2134 126 E
bwisdom@truett.edu
WISE, Adam .... 617-287-5335 211 H
adam.wise@umb.edu
WISE, Ashley .... 724-852-7625 402 C
awise@waynesburg.edu
WISE, Brittany .... 310-360-8888.. 26 K
WISE, Colleen .... 518-743-2306 320 A
wisec@sunyacc.edu
WISE, David .... 509-865-0717 481 A
wise_d@heritage.edu
WISE, Diane, K .... 301-696-3855 199 E
wise@hood.edu
WISE, Ginny .... 504-865-5259 191 F
gwise@tulane.edu
WISE, Jessica .... 740-333-5115 360 H
jwise@sscc.edu
WISE, John .... 716-926-8846 301 E
jwise@hilbert.edu
WISE, JR., L. Anthony .. 865-694-6616 425 B
lawise@pstcc.edu
WISE, Lance .... 404-225-4082 115 H
lwise@atlantatech.edu
WISE, Ryan .... 515-271-2082 165 J
ryan.wise@drake.edu
WISE, Sharon, H .... 315-792-3120 324 B
swise@utica.edu
WISE, Stephen .... 585-343-0055 300 F
spwise@genesee.edu
WISE, Steve .... 858-653-6740.. 46 H
WISE, Teresa .... 205-348-5256.... 7 G
teresa.wise@ua.edu
WISECUP, Mike .... 207-859-4000 194 D
WISELEY, Mark .... 563-884-5691 169 F
mark.wiseley@palmer.edu
WISELL, Teresita .... 914-606-6585 325 A
teresita.wisell@sunywcc.edu
WISEMAN, Chris .... 504-861-5431 190 C
cwiseman@loyno.edu
WISEMAN, James .... 414-930-3445 494 E
wisemanj@mtmary.edu
WISEMAN, Marcie .... 630-844-5416 133 D
mwiseman@aurora.edu
WISEMAN, Tina .... 573-288-6306 252 F
twiseman@culver.edu
WISENOR, Tad .... 509-777-4401 486 C
twisenor@whitworth.edu
WISER, Devin .... 801-626-7834 461 A
devinwiser@weber.edu
WISER, Hayes .... 843-525-8271 412 G
hwiser@tcl.edu
WISER, James .... 325-674-2476 428 F
jaw2ob@acu.edu

WOLFERSBERGER, Mark ... 808-675-3886 128 D
mark.wolfersberger@byuh.edu
WOLFF, Asaf ... 626-264-8880.. 71 F
WOLFF, Holly ... 563-425-5221 170 H
wolffh@uiu.edu
WOLFF, Holly, D ... 563-425-5221 170 H
wolffh@uiu.edu
WOLFF, Mark, S ... 215-898-1038 400 F
mswolff@upenn.edu
WOLFF, Robert ... 860-832-2807.. 85 G
wolffr@ccsu.edu
WOLFF, Susan, M ... 815-928-5776 147 A
swolff@olivet.edu
WOLFINGER, Jim ... 309-438-5415 140 D
jdwolfi@ilstu.edu
WOLFKILL, John ... 303-360-4833.. 80 E
john.wolfkill@ccaurora.edu
WOLFMAN, Jeffrey ... 978-665-4933 212 E
jwolfman@fitchburgstate.edu
WOLFORD, April ... 937-767-1286 347 G
WOLFORD, Emma ... 585-245-5716 318 B
ewolford@geneso.edu
WOLFORD, Tulio ... 719-389-6000.. 78 I
WOLFORD, Wendy ... 607-255-0157 297 F
www43@cornell.edu
WOLGAST, Brad ... 302-831-2141.. 91 C
bradw@udel.edu
WOLK, Joseph ... 508-531-1229 212 D
joseph.wolk@bridgew.edu
WOLKEN, Julie ... 713-798-8990 431 D
jwolken@bcm.edu
WOLKING, Daryl ... 540-338-1776 469 C
WOLLARD, Jason ... 480-212-1704.. 15 O
WOLLAS, Robyn ... 615-550-3164 428 E
robyn@williamsoncc.edu
WOLLENBERG, Chad ... 434-949-1033 475 B
chad.wollenberg@southside.edu
WOLLENBURG, Doug ... 912-525-5000 124 I
dwollenbu@scad.edu
WOLLER, Megan ... 814-871-7510 384 A
woller001@gannon.edu
WOLLMAN, Julie, E ... 610-499-4101 402 G
jewollman@widener.edu
WOLLMER, Keli ... 414-288-7184 493 E
keli.wollmer@marquette.edu
WOLLMERING, Jerry ... 660-785-4236 260 F
jerryw@truman.edu
WOLMA, Stephen ... 574-535-7784 155 E
swolma@goshen.edu
WOLMA, Steve ... 574-535-7784 155 E
swolma@goshen.edu
WOLMARK, Mordechai . 845-352-3431 326 A
WOLNIAK, Alexander ... 617-449-7039 219 D
alexander.wolniak@urbancollege.edu
WOLOHAN, Laurie ... 216-687-3606 350 J
l.wolohan@csuohio.edu
WOLOSON, Wendy ... 856-225-2711 281 G
ww207@camden.rutgers.edu
WOLOSZYNOWSKI, Daniel ... 757-594-7777 465 M
daniel.woloszynowski@cnu.edu
WOLPE, Paul, R ... 404-727-3150 118 E
pwolpe@emory.edu
WOLPERN, Kevin ... 952-887-1394 242 N
kwolpern@nwhealth.edu
WOLPIN, Aryeh ... 718-232-7800 325 H
WOLPIN, OBM, Chaim . 718-232-7800 325 H
WOLSEY, Timothy ... 480-732-7125.. 12 O
timothy.wolsey@cgc.edu
WOLTERS, Daniel ... 406-657-1161 265 E
woltersd@rocky.edu
WOLTERS-FREDLUND, Bernita ... 616-526-6203 222 C
bw24@calvin.edu
WOLTMANN, Tanya ... 847-543-2443 136 A
twoltmann@clcillinois.edu
WOLVAARDT, Bennie ... 210-446-6719 457 B
WOMACK, Cameron ... 828-328-7334 330 F
cameron.womack@lr.edu
WOMACK, Joseph ... 541-684-7241 371 I
jwomack@bushnell.edu
WOMACK, Larry ... 510-215-3836.. 40 B
lwomack@contracosta.edu
WOMACK, Sheila ... 304-384-6298 489 J
swomack@concord.edu
WOMACK, Tonya ... 727-864-7737.. 98 J
womacktm@eckerd.edu
WOMACK, Veronica ... 478-445-1382 119 B
veronic.womack@gcsu.edu
WOMACK, Wayne ... 479-788-7407.. 21 G
wayne.womack@uafs.edu
WOMBLE, Jeff ... 910-672-1474 341 C
jwomble@uncfsu.edu
WOMBLE, Lynn, Z ... 903-813-2891 430 H
lwomble@austincollege.edu
WOMBLE, Scott ... 314-837-6777 258 K
swomble@stlchristian.edu
WOMELSDUFF, Gary, E . 206-281-2678 483 G
womelg@spu.edu
WOMICK, Jason ... 864-587-4217 412 F
womickj@smcsc.edu
WONDERLY, Jennifer ... 312-341-3558 148 E
jwonderl@roosevelt.edu
WONDERS, Christopher 717-477-1251 395 B
cawonders@ship.edu
WONG, Adrianus Hilman ... 213-487-0110.. 41 D
WONG, Aliza ... 806-742-1828 450 F
aliza.wong@ttu.edu
WONG, Asia ... 504-865-3835 190 C
awong@loyno.edu
WONG, Bill ... 903-510-3158 452 A
bill.wong@tjc.edu
WONG, David, W ... 920-923-8576 493 D
dwwong@marianuniversity.edu
WONG, Erwin ... 212-220-8321 293 A
ewong@bmcc.cuny.edu
WONG, Eve ... 703-591-7042 466 M
ewong@fxua.edu
WONG, Gene ... 978-232-2311 209 E
gwong@endicott.edu
WONG, James ... 718-405-3733 296 F
james.wong@mountsaintvincent.edu
WONG, Jane ... 609-771-2277 276 I
wong@tcnj.edu
WONG, Jeannie ... 916-278-2067.. 32 D
jwong@csus.edu
WONG, Julie ... 847-317-7152 151 C
jwong@tiu.edu
WONG, Julie ... 818-299-5500.. 74 L
jwong@westcoastuniversity.edu
WONG, Keaton ... 718-990-2505 313 G
wongk1@stjohns.edu
WONG, Lam ... 216-987-4265 351 E
lam.wong@tri-c.edu
WONG, Leslie ... 202-885-2143.. 91 F
lawyers@american.edu
WONG, Martin ... 315-228-7203 296 E
mswong@colgate.edu
WONG, Michael ... 310-338-7760.. 51 A
michael.wong@lmu.edu
WONG, Michael Paul ... 951-571-6251.. 59 B
michaelpaul.wong@mvc.edu
WONG, Noel ... 504-865-5000 191 F
WONG, Richard ... 804-278-4240 471 J
rwong@upsem.edu
WONG, Rita ... 703-284-5982 468 H
rita.wong@marymount.edu
WONG, Rita ... 770-831-9500 126 F
WONG, Theresa ... 480-857-5118.. 12 O
theresa.wong@cgc.edu
WONG, Tony ... 562-809-5100.. 42 K
tony.wong@fremont.edu
WONG, Walter ... 415-254-6033.. 69 A
WONG, Yong Gao ... 312-368-0900 134 I
WONG (LAU), Kathleen 408-924-1187.. 34 A
kathleen.wonglau@sjsu.edu
WONG-DAVIS, Kris ... 765-494-4600 160 B
WONG-KIM, Evaon ... 323-343-4737.. 31 E
ewongkim@calstatela.edu
WONG NICKERSON, Agnes ... 619-594-5631.. 33 D
awongnickerson@sdsu.edu
WONGSAROJ, Ben ... 305-623-4100 100 D
ben.wongsaroj@fmuniv.edu
WONSEY, Jacquelyn ... 410-951-6367 204 B
jwonsey@coppin.edu
WOO, Donna ... 800-867-2243.. 55 D
dwoo@pacific-college.edu
WOO, Jang Hoon ... 562-926-1023.. 58 A
admin.online@ptsa.edu
WOO, Lina ... 650-543-3996.. 51 G
lina.woo@menlo.edu
WOO, Matthew, D ... 714-995-9988.. 47 B
WOO, Melissa ... 517-355-1855 227 F
mwoo@msu.edu
WOO, Melissa ... 517-355-1855 227 F
WOO, Meredith ... 434-381-6210 471 I
president@sbc.edu
WOO, Minah, C ... 443-518-4724 199 F
mwoo@howardcc.edu
WOO, Priscilla, M ... 714-995-9988.. 47 B
WOOD, Amy ... 828-328-7728 330 F
amy.wood@lr.edu
WOOD, Amy ... 419-448-3372 361 D
woodar@tiffin.edu
WOOD, Amy, B ... 615-963-7548 426 A
awood@tnstate.edu
WOOD, Ana, I ... 319-656-2447 170 A
chiqui.wood@shilohuniversity.edu
WOOD, Andy ... 662-472-9024 246 D
awood@holmescc.edu
WOOD, Anne ... 814-641-5310 386 E
wood@juniata.edu
WOOD, Becky ... 317-274-4417 157 D
rewood@iupui.edu
WOOD, Beth ... 256-260-2451.... 1 F
beth.wood@calhoun.edu
WOOD, Bobby ... 864-242-5100 406 H
WOOD, Caroline ... 540-868-7000 474 C
WOOD, Carolline ... 540-351-1516 474 C
cwood@lfcc.edu
WOOD, Casey ... 570-662-4078 394 F
cmwood@mansfield.edu
WOOD, Chris ... 903-693-2009 441 C
cwood@panola.edu
WOOD, Chris, A ... 304-637-1243 487 C
chris.wood@dewv.edu
WOOD, Christy ... 305-595-9500.. 94 G
WOOD, Dale ... 931-431-9700 422 G
dwood@nci.edu
WOOD, Darlene ... 620-223-2700 173 I
darlenew@fortscott.edu
WOOD, David, H ... 906-227-2112 228 I
dwood@nmu.edu
WOOD, Dawn ... 319-398-5443 167 J
dawn.wood@kirkwood.edu
WOOD, Derek ... 206-281-2955 483 G
woodd1@spu.edu
WOOD, Douglas, M ... 717-796-1800 389 H
dwood@messiah.edu
WOOD, Emily ... 856-225-2867 281 G
emily.wood@camden.rutgers.edu
WOOD, Emily, S ... 317-738-8283 155 D
ewood@franklincollege.edu
WOOD, Eric ... 817-257-7863 448 F
e.c.wood@tcu.edu
WOOD, Erin ... 701-662-1598 346 C
erin.wood@lrsc.edu
WOOD, Faye ... 843-863-7502 407 B
fwood@csuniv.edu
WOOD, Frank ... 305-809-3287.. 97 O
frank.wood@cfk.edu
WOOD, Fred, E ... 562-951-4000.. 29 H
fwood@calstate.edu
WOOD, Gary ... 262-595-2364 496 D
woodg@uwp.edu
WOOD, Gayle, E ... 865-539-7160 425 B
gwood@pstcc.edu
WOOD, Gretchen, D ... 585-292-3685 307 B
gwood9@monroecc.edu
WOOD, J. Luke ... 619-594-5211.. 33 D
luke.wood@sdsu.edu
WOOD, J. Luke ... 619-594-0167.. 33 D
luke.wood@sdsu.edu
WOOD, Jane ... 419-358-3324 348 F
woodj@bluffton.edu
WOOD, Jason ... 479-394-7622.. 23 C
jwood@uarichmountain.edu
WOOD, Jason, S ... 608-822-2300 500 A
jwood@swtc.edu
WOOD, Jill, H ... 314-516-5811 261 C
woodjh@umsl.edu
WOOD, John ... 307-855-2162 501 A
jwood@cwc.edu
WOOD, Jon ... 937-766-7871 349 E
jonwood@cedarville.edu
WOOD, Josh ... 812-535-5213 160 H
josh.wood@smwc.edu
WOOD, Joyce ... 765-998-5117 161 C
jywood@taylor.edu
WOOD, Judith ... 312-322-1780 150 F
jwood@spertus.edu
WOOD, Julia, H ... 865-694-6530 425 B
jwood@pstcc.edu
WOOD, Kathryn ... 909-748-8479.. 72 F
kathryn_wood@redlands.edu
WOOD, Kelly ... 417-836-8346 256 G
kellywood@missouristate.edu
WOOD, Laura ... 903-923-8207 441 C
lwood@panola.edu
WOOD, Laura, L ... 641-422-4355 168 G
woodlaur@niacc.edu
WOOD, Lee ... 850-872-3866 101 N
lwood10@gulfcoast.edu
WOOD, Lindsay, S ... 732-923-4589 279 A
lwood@monmouth.edu
WOOD, Lisa ... 208-282-2777 131 G
woodlis2@isu.edu
WOOD, Lynette ... 919-546-8344 340 B
lynette.wood@shawu.edu
WOOD, Marcus ... 662-476-5025 246 B
mwood@eastms.edu
WOOD, Martin ... 719-255-3438.. 84 C
mwood@uccs.edu
WOOD, Melinda ... 559-297-4500.. 45 N
mwood@iot.edu
WOOD, Michael ... 570-408-4500 403 A
mike.wood@wilkes.edu
WOOD, Mike ... 253-680-7301 477 I
mwood@batestech.edu
WOOD, Nicolle ... 978-542-6991 213 E
nicole.wood@salemstate.edu
WOOD, Pamela, R ... 919-658-7753 340 G
pwood@umo.edu
WOOD, Paul ... 530-226-2953.. 64 E
pwood@simpsonu.edu
WOOD, Phillip ... 423-478-7993 422 J
pwood@ptseminary.edu
WOOD, Phoebe ... 773-481-8525 135 G
pwood3@ccc.edu
WOOD, Pia ... 940-565-4941 453 E
pia.wood@unt.edu
WOOD, Robert ... 314-977-3718 259 F
robert.wood@slu.edu
WOOD, Robert, B ... 757-446-6137 466 D
woodrb@evms.edu
WOOD, Rodney ... 740-376-4791 355 E
rlw006@marietta.edu
WOOD, Roy ... 918-449-6101 366 G
wood40@nsuok.edu
WOOD, Scott ... 801-863-8516 460 D
scott.wood@uvu.edu
WOOD, Shane ... 417-626-1234 257 F
wood.shane@occ.edu
WOOD, Sharmay ... 906-635-2676 226 G
swood@lssu.edu
WOOD, Sharon, L ... 512-471-1166 455 A
swood@utexas.edu
WOOD, Shelia ... 504-286-5368 191 C
swood@suno.edu
WOOD, Steve ... 501-686-2941.. 21 E
spwood@uasys.edu
WOOD, Steve ... 828-835-4254 338 E
swood@tricountycc.edu
WOOD, Stewart ... 734-432-5645 227 C
swood@madonna.edu
WOOD, Susan ... 928-428-8261.. 12 F
susan.wood@eac.edu
WOOD, Tommy ... 785-594-6451 171 F
WOOD, Vicky ... 740-374-8716 363 F
president@wscc.edu
WOOD, Wende ... 843-377-2156 407 A
wwood@charlestonlaw.edu
WOOD-WILLIAMS, Danielle, L ... 479-575-4019.. 21 F
dlw11@uark.edu
WOODALL, Andy ... 540-665-4581 470 G
awoodall@su.edu
WOODALL, Betty, C ... 919-209-2019 335 F
bcwoodall@johnstoncc.edu
WOODALL, Eric ... 703-993-5442 467 E
ewoodall@gmu.edu
WOODALL, Marsha ... 270-824-1802 182 D
marsha.woodall@kctcs.edu
WOODALL, Stephen ... 404-756-4000 115 G
WOODARD, Bobby, R ... 334-844-8880.... 4 D
brw0016@auburn.edu
WOODARD, Brandyn ... 763-433-1253 237 E
brandyn.woodard@anokaramsey.edu
WOODARD, Brandyn ... 763-433-1253 237 D
brandyn.woodard@anokaramsey.edu
WOODARD, Emory ... 610-519-7093 401 K
emory.woodard@villanova.edu
WOODARD, Jeffrey ... 716-673-4002 316 D
jeffrey.woodard@fredonia.edu
WOODARD, Joanne ... 940-565-2711 453 E
joanne.woodard@unt.edu
WOODARD, Randall ... 352-588-8239 107 D
randall.woodard@saintleo.edu
WOODARD, Stephanie .. 309-341-5272 134 B
swoodard@sandburg.edu
WOODARD, Steve ... 425-640-1020 480 A
steve.woodard@edcc.edu
WOODARD, Thelma ... 336-334-7500 341 D
WOODARD, Tim ... 919-658-7756 340 G
twoodard@umo.edu
WOODARD-MINK, Lisa . 916-278-3852.. 32 D
lisa.woodard-mink@csus.edu

WORDEN, Michael .... 845-341-4901 310 G
michael.worden@sunyorange.edu
WORDEN, Michelle .... 585-245-5157 318 B
worden@geneseo.edu
WORDEN, Natalia .... 858-566-1200.. 40 J
nworden@disd.edu
WORDEN, Randy .... 815-226-3398 148 D
rworden@rockford.edu
WORDLOW-WILLIAMS,
Tamika .... 401-456-8061 405 A
twordlow@ric.edu
WORK, AJ .... 661-362-2333.. 51 D
awork@masters.edu
WORK, Christine .... 845-341-4763 310 G
christine.work@sunyorange.edu
WORK, Patricia .... 202-495-3835.. 93 D
assistant@dhs.edu
WORKMAN, Amanda .... 432-837-8226 450 B
ajw21ck@sulross.edu
WORKMAN, Andrew, A . 610-499-4106 402 G
aaworkman@widener.edu
WORKMAN, Aurora .... 914-606-6880 325 A
aurora.workman@sunywcc.edu
WORKMAN, Christine ... 843-953-5312 408 C
workmancl@cofc.edu
WORKMAN, Erin .... 626-568-8850.. 48 H
erin@lacm.edu
WORKMAN, Jennifer, L 302-356-6843.. 91 E
jennifer.l.workman@wilmu.edu
WORKMAN, Mark .... 979-209-7403 431 H
mark.workman@blinn.edu
WORKMAN, RaSheda ... 205-366-8817.... 7 A
rworkman@stillman.edu
WORKMAN, RaSheda ... 205-366-8817.... 7 A
rworkman@stillman.edu
WORKMAN, Sue, B ...... 216-368-5899 349 D
sue.workman@case.edu
WORKMAN, Tamora ..... 618-453-2973 150 B
tworkman@siu.edu
WORLEY, Alan .... 806-716-2338 443 G
aworley@southplainscollege.edu
WORLEY, John .... 510-659-6113.. 54 J
jworley@ohlone.edu
WORLEY, Karen .... 423-305-7783 418 F
WORLEY, Louise .... 717-815-1446 403 F
lworley@ycp.edu
WORLEY, Mark .... 972-241-3371 434 D
mworley@dallas.edu
WORLEY, Mary Beth ..... 575-527-7728 287 F
mbworley@nmsu.edu
WORLEY, Mike .... 864-388-8350 410 A
mworley@lander.edu
WORLEY, Paul .... 828-835-9564 338 E
pworley@tricountycc.edu
WORLEY, Phillip .... 419-372-3905 348 G
pworley@bgsu.edu
WORLEY, Rene .... 931-598-1123 423 D
rworley@sewanee.edu
WORM, Lori, M .... 920-424-3033 496 C
worm@uwosh.edu
WORMACK, Janet .... 410-543-6050 204 D
jewormack@salisbury.edu
WORMLEY, Antoinette .... 703-416-1441 466 A
financialaid@divinemercy.edu
WORMLEY, JR.,
Floyd, L .... 817-257-4320 448 F
floyd.wormley@tcu.edu
WORMSER, Jennifer ..... 909-621-8973.. 63 F
WORNALL, Robyn .... 707-256-7192.. 53 E
rwornall@napavalley.edu
WORNAT, Judy .... 225-578-5255 189 E
mjwornat@lsu.edu
WOROBEC, Sophia .... 312-942-6857 148 G
sophia_worobec@rush.edu
WORRALL, Dorothy .... 716-827-2469 323 G
worralld@trocaire.edu
WORRELL, Erick .... 405-682-1611 367 D
WORRELL, Mike .... 304-829-7240 487 A
mworrell@bethanywv.edu
WORRELS, Derrick .... 254-267-7010 441 K
dworrels@rangercollege.edu
WORSHAM, Thomas ..... 318-487-7498 187 E
thomas.worsham@lacollege.edu
WORSLEY, Christine ..... 925-969-2747.. 40 C
cworsley@dvc.edu
WORTH, Benjamin .... 540-863-2933 473 F
bworth@dslcc.edu
WORTH, Murtis .... 910-678-8294 334 E
worthm@faytechcc.edu
WORTH, Tiffany .... 217-735-7226 142 H
tworth@lincolncollege.edu
WORTHAM, Rachal .... 706-385-1463 124 E
rachal.wortham@point.edu
WORTHAM, Stanton ...... 617-552-3902 207 C
stanton.wortham@bc.edu
WORTHAM, Timothy ...... 610-341-1712 383 B
twortham@eastern.edu
WORTHEN, Kevin, J ...... 801-422-2521 458 H
kevin_worthen@byu.edu
WORTHINGTON, Leslie . 256-549-8256.... 2 B
lworthington@gadsdenstate.edu
WORTHINGTON,
Phyllis .... 870-512-7842.. 18 A
phyllis_worthington@asun.edu
WORTHLEY, Kristin .... 732-224-2133 276 B
kworthley@brookdalecc.edu
WORTHY, Mark .... 225-752-4233 187 D
mworthy@iticollege.edu
WOTTON, Heather .... 203-773-8558.. 85 D
hwotton@albertus.edu
WOUDENBERG, Robert . 315-866-0300 301 D
woudenbra@herkimer.edu
WOUGHTER, Kerrey ...... 231-995-1063 229 A
kwoughter@nmc.edu
WOUGHTER, Laura .... 740-389-4636 355 F
woughterl@mtc.edu
WOULFE, Rebecca .... 303-404-5497.. 81 A
rebecca.woulfe@frontrange.edu
WOVKANECH, Jason ..... 603-271-6484 273 A
WOYAK, Amber .... 847-578-8350 148 F
amber.woyak@rosalindfranklin.edu
WOZNIAK, Andrew .... 630-889-6878 145 E
awozniak@nuhs.edu
WOZNIAK, Danielle ...... 646-592-6275 326 D
danielle.wozniak@yu.edu
WOZNIAK, Jim .... 423-636-7300 426 E
jwozniak@tusculum.edu
WOZNICKI, John .... 609-984-1130 284 C
jwoznicki@tesu.edu
WOZNICKI, John .... 215-489-4889 382 B
john.woznicki@delval.edu
WRAGE, Rebecca .... 308-535-3679 267 J
wrager@mpcc.edu
WRAGG, Tunisia .... 212-517-0561 305 E
twragg@mmm.edu
WRAITH, Jon, M .... 603-862-2468 274 F
jon.wraith@unh.edu
WRASE, Micah .... 830-792-7206 443 E
mkwrase@schreiner.edu
WRAY, Donald, W .... 318-795-2392 190 A
donald.wray@lsus.edu
WRAY, Kimberli .... 701-774-4500 346 E
kimberli.wray@willistonstate.edu
WRAY, Kyle .... 405-744-4366 367 G
kyle.wray@okstate.edu
WRAY, Larry .... 910-962-3241 343 C
wrayl@uncw.edu
WRAY, Lee .... 931-372-3893 426 B
lwray@tntech.edu
WRAY, Rachel .... 207-786-6240 194 A
rwray@bates.edu
WRAY, Roger .... 434-949-1040 475 B
roger.wray@southside.edu
WREN, Jan .... 606-539-4328 185 E
jan.wren@ucumberlands.edu
WREN, Pam .... 865-524-8079 420 B
pam.wren@huhs.edu
WREN,
Rebecca-Greathouse ... 432-837-8203 450 B
rebecca.wren@sulross.edu
WREN, Sheryl .... 731-661-5202 426 F
swren@uu.edu
WRENN, Christy .... 318-869-5057 186 F
cwrenn@centenary.edu
WRENN, Gloria .... 239-513-1122 102 D
gwrenn@hodges.edu
WRENN, Patrick .... 920-403-3255 495 B
pat.wrenn@snc.edu
WRICE, Sheldon, B .... 330-972-6023 361 H
swrice1@uakron.edu
WRIGHT, Adam .... 214-333-5930 434 C
adam@dbu.edu
WRIGHT, Andrea, A ...... 252-862-1302 337 C
aawright1560@roanokechowan.edu
WRIGHT, Andrew .... 562-985-8410.. 31 D
andrew.wright@csulb.edu
WRIGHT, Andrew .... 218-755-2040 237 F
andrew.wright@bemidjistate.edu
WRIGHT, Andrew, R ...... 503-517-1582 377 C
arwright@warnerpacific.edu
WRIGHT, Angelina .... 325-942-2017 450 E
angie.wright@angelo.edu
WRIGHT, Angie .... 478-757-5192 127 F
awright@wesleyancollege.edu
WRIGHT, Ann .... 501-450-3808.. 19 E
wright@hendrix.edu
WRIGHT, Ann .... 864-250-8719 409 I
ann.wright@gvltec.edu
WRIGHT, Ariana .... 757-683-3141 469 B
a1wright@odu.edu
WRIGHT, Beatrice, V ..... 410-651-8387 203 D
bvwright@umes.edu
WRIGHT, Betsy .... 816-271-4237 257 A
bwright3@missouriwestern.edu
WRIGHT, Bo .... 706-379-3111 128 C
dbwright@yhc.edu
WRIGHT, Bob .... 262-742-4444 500 T
drbob@wrightgrad.edu
WRIGHT, Brandon .... 205-934-4324.... 8 A
btwright@uab.edu
WRIGHT, Brant .... 706-778-8500 124 D
bwright@piedmont.edu
WRIGHT, Brian .... 276-964-7207 475 C
brian.wright@sw.edu
WRIGHT, Cameron .... 307-766-6104 501 I
chgw@uwyo.edu
WRIGHT, Carlecia .... 281-655-3701 439 C
carlecia.wright@lonestar.edu
WRIGHT, Cary .... 276-326-4280 464 J
cwright@bluefield.edu
WRIGHT, Cathleen .... 830-372-8078 449 A
cwright@tlu.edu
WRIGHT, Chantelle .... 212-237-8754 294 D
cwright@jjay.cuny.edu
WRIGHT, Charles .... 609-771-2393 276 I
wrightc@tcnj.edu
WRIGHT, Charles .... 704-330-6257 333 D
charles.wright@cpcc.edu
WRIGHT, Charles, D ..... 405-325-3411 370 K
cwright@ou.edu
WRIGHT, Chatt, G .... 808-544-0203 128 G
cwright@hpu.edu
WRIGHT, Chris .... 575-624-8070 287 B
wright@nmmi.edu
WRIGHT, Christy .... 620-450-2133 177 B
christya@prattcc.edu
WRIGHT, Chuck, W ...... 803-938-3867 413 G
wrightcw@uscsumter.edu
WRIGHT, Colleen .... 269-965-3931 225 H
wrightc@kellogg.edu
WRIGHT, Constance ..... 864-977-7064 410 I
constance.wright@ngu.edu
WRIGHT, Cory .... 716-614-6897 309 G
cwright@niagaracc.suny.edu
WRIGHT, Craig, J .... 516-572-7121 307 E
craig.wright@ncc.edu
WRIGHT, Curits .... 504-520-7357 193 E
cwrigh14@xula.edu
WRIGHT, Cynthia .... 509-777-3244 486 C
cwright@whitworth.edu
WRIGHT, Dale .... 585-567-9321 302 B
dale.wright@houghton.edu
WRIGHT, Dave .... 253-879-3818 484 G
dwright@pugetsound.edu
WRIGHT, David .... 303-273-2120.. 79 J
dwright1@mines.edu
WRIGHT, David .... 303-384-2120.. 79 J
dwright1@mines.edu
WRIGHT, David .... 316-978-7157 178 D
david.wright@wichita.edu
WRIGHT, David .... 765-677-2100 158 B
iwupresident@indwes.edu
WRIGHT, David, W .... 213-740-4218.. 73 D
dwwright@usc.edu
WRIGHT, Deborah .... 828-398-7937 332 B
deborahdwright@abtech.edu
WRIGHT, Debra .... 951-785-2011.. 47 C
dwright@lasierra.edu
WRIGHT, Dewayne .... 931-372-3215 426 B
dawright@tntech.edu
WRIGHT, Donna .... 718-270-4911 294 G
dwright@mec.cuny.edu
WRIGHT, Duane .... 678-916-2609 115 I
dwright@johnmarshall.edu
WRIGHT, Edward .... 610-459-0905 391 A
wrighte@neumann.edu
WRIGHT, Edwin, R .... 717-867-6180 388 C
wright@lvc.edu
WRIGHT, Elizabeth .... 276-739-2440 475 F
ewright@vhcc.edu
WRIGHT, Ethel, B .... 404-413-1306 120 E
ebrown@gsu.edu
WRIGHT, George .... 949-214-3379.. 39 K
george.wright@cui.edu
WRIGHT, George .... 859-257-9293 185 F
gcwright@uky.edu
WRIGHT, Georgia .... 303-762-6995.. 80 I
georgia.wright@denverseminary.edu
WRIGHT, Germaine, A .. 718-960-8000 294 A
WRIGHT, Heather, H ..... 937-327-7992 364 D
hwright@wittenberg.edu
WRIGHT, Howard .... 770-426-2712 122 C
howard.wright@life.edu
WRIGHT, Ida .... 386-481-2281.. 96 D
wrighti@cookman.edu
WRIGHT, Jamel .... 309-467-6322 138 A
jwright@eureka.edu
WRIGHT, Jeannie .... 301-891-4010 205 A
jjwright@wau.edu
WRIGHT, Jeff .... 207-326-2253 196 A
jeff.wright@mma.edu
WRIGHT, Jeffrey .... 765-641-4544 153 G
jewright@anderson.edu
WRIGHT, Jerry .... 517-265-5161 220 G
jwright@adrian.edu
WRIGHT, Jill .... 309-694-5173 139 B
jwright@icc.edu
WRIGHT, Jimmy .... 606-886-3863 181 E
jimmy.wright@kctcs.edu
WRIGHT, Joanne .... 408-924-2250.. 34 A
joanne.wright@sjsu.edu
WRIGHT, Joel .... 229-500-3502 114 H
joel.wright@asurams.edu
WRIGHT, Jonas .... 415-503-6251.. 61 D
aharmon@sfcm.edu
WRIGHT, Jonathan .... 504-816-4222 186 I
jwright@dillard.edu
WRIGHT, Judith .... 262-742-4444 500 T
drjudith@wrightgrad.edu
WRIGHT, Julia .... 740-826-6159 356 H
julias@muskingum.edu
WRIGHT, Julie .... 480-732-7313.. 12 O
julie.wright@cgc.edu
WRIGHT, Karen, F .... 270-384-7313 183 G
wrightk@lindsey.edu
WRIGHT, Karl, S .... 803-535-5401 407 D
kawright@claflin.edu
WRIGHT, Kathy .... 707-256-7000.. 53 E
WRIGHT, LeAnne .... 903-223-3078 448 A
leanne.wright@tamut.edu
WRIGHT, Leroy .... 517-629-0222 221 A
lwright@albion.edu
WRIGHT, Leslie .... 651-227-9171 242 L
leslie.wright@mitchellhamline.edu
WRIGHT, Lydia .... 518-327-6061 311 C
lwright@paulsmiths.edu
WRIGHT, Mandy .... 406-268-3713 264 F
mandy.wright@gfcmsu.edu
WRIGHT, Martin .... 317-931-2330 154 G
mwright1@cts.edu
WRIGHT, Matthew .... 916-608-6687.. 50 I
wrightm@flc.losrios.edu
WRIGHT, Melissa .... 662-562-3277 248 D
WRIGHT, Michael .... 601-925-7713 247 C
mwright@mc.edu
WRIGHT, Michael .... 229-928-1378 120 D
michael.wright@gsw.edu
WRIGHT, Michael, G .... 313-577-8155 232 K
m.wright@wayne.edu
WRIGHT, Michael, G .... 330-325-6622 357 D
mwright2@neomed.edu
WRIGHT, Natalie .... 386-752-1822 100 B
natalie.wright@fgc.edu
WRIGHT, Nikki .... 313-577-2280 232 K
nikki.wright@wayne.edu
WRIGHT, Norman .... 801-863-8239 460 D
norman.wright@uvu.edu
WRIGHT, Nova .... 540-863-2868 473 F
nwright@dslcc.edu
WRIGHT, O'Neil .... 815-455-3700 143 I
WRIGHT, Paul .... 906-227-2480 228 I
sm8194@bncollege.com
WRIGHT, Paul .... 541-485-1780 374 E
paulwright@newhope.edu
WRIGHT, Paul .... 541-684-7250 371 I
pwright@bushnell.edu
WRIGHT, Peter .... 920-206-2327 493 C
peter.wright@mbu.edu
WRIGHT, Peter .... 920-206-2369 493 C
peter.wright@mbu.edu
WRIGHT, Quentin .... 281-260-3551 439 C
quentin.a.wright@lonestar.edu
WRIGHT, Rachel .... 585-567-9200 302 B
rachel.wright@houghton.edu
WRIGHT, Raymond, M . 401-874-2186 405 E
rmwright@uri.edu
WRIGHT, Rebekah .... 417-328-2077 259 I
rwright@sbuniv.edu
WRIGHT, Regina .... 212-875-4595 290 H
rwright@bankstreet.edu
WRIGHT, Rena .... 800-785-0585.. 39 D
rena.wright@columbiacollege.edu

YAFAR, Jorge 212-220-8033 293 A
jyafar@bmcc.cuny.edu

YAGER, David 215-717-6030 400 E
dyager@uarts.edu

YAGER, Ellice 662-720-7584 248 C
leyager@nemcc.edu

YAGER, Julia 413-584-2700 218 H

YAGER, Laura 559-278-6114 31 B
lyager@csufresno.edu

YAHNG, Charles 314-529-9312 255 B
cyahng@maryville.edu

YAHYAZADEH, Bizhan 802-485-2617 462 F
bizhan@norwich.edu

YAKIMOVICH, Andrew 470-578-6000 121 M

YAKOVLEV, Ilya 717-815-2254 403 F
iyakovlev@ycp.edu

YAKOWICZ, William 201-612-5253 275 H
wyakowicz@bergen.edu

YAKSHE, Patti, L 412-281-2600 396 B
pyakshe@pci.edu

YALE, Amanda, A 724-738-2011 395 C
amanda.yale@sru.edu

YALE, Jacob 814-886-6739 390 G
jyale@mtaloy.edu

YAM, Marylou 410-532-5300 201 D

YAMADA, Emiko 650-508-3749 54 G
eyamada@ndnu.edu

YAMADA, Emiko 650-508-3721 54 G
eyamada@ndnu.edu

YAMAGATA-NOJI,
Audrey 909-274-4505 52 J
ayamagat@mtsac.edu

YAMAGUCHI, Ryan 808-956-8975 129 E
rtyamagu@hawaii.edu

YAMAKAWA, Lynn 310-233-4387 49 B
yamakalm@lahc.edu

YAMAMOTO, Catherine 402-472-7749 269 J
cyamamoto1@unl.edu

YAMAMOTO, Cindy 808-984-3288 130 D
cindy@hawaii.edu

YAMAMOTO, Greg 626-396-2200 26 B

YAMAMOTO, Jessica 808-934-2688 129 I
jpky@hawaii.edu

YAMAMOTO, Kirk 213-924-4032 49 E
yamamokm@email.laccd.edu

YAMAMOTO, Lance 808-956-5148 129 G
lance@hawaii.edu

YAMAMURA, Whitney 916-608-6572 50 I
yamamuw@flc.losrios.edu

YAMAOKA, Seigen 510-809-1444 45 M

YAMASAKI, Erika 310-954-4412 52 I
eyamasaki@msmu.edu

YAMBA, A. Zachary 973-877-3022 277 G
yamba@essex.edu

YAMBO, Marc 630-889-6517 145 E
myambo@nuhs.edu

YAMEEN, Deanna 508-588-9100 215 A
dyameen@massasoit.mass.edu

YAMENTOU, Lionnel 714-533-3946 34 C
library@calums.edu

YAMPOLSKY, Chana 212-964-2830 306 F

YAMRICK, Eammalyn 212-517-0400 305 E
emmalyn@mmm.edu

YAMRICK, Emmalyn 212-774-0751 305 E
eyamrick@mmm.edu

YAN, Penny 765-983-1390 155 A
yanpe@earlham.edu

YAN, Ruth 319-226-2080 163 C
ruth.yan@allencollege.edu

YAN, Song 248-370-4146 229 I
songyan@oakland.edu

YANAI, Carolyn 702-463-2122 272 G
accounting@wongu.org

YANCEY, Amanda 706-385-1201 124 E
ayancey@point.edu

YANCEY, Amy 617-552-3146 207 C
amy.yancey@bc.edu

YANCEY, Laurica 919-658-7750 340 G
lyancey@umo.edu

YANCHAK, Frank 614-947-6723 352 J
frank.yanchak@franklin.edu

YANCY, Chad 205-929-3497 2 H
cyancy@lawsonstate.edu

YANDELL, April 817-257-7490 448 F
a.yandell@tcu.edu

YANES, Kenneth 212-484-1339 294 D
kyanes@jjay.cuny.edu

YANEZ, Katy 602-827-2552 14 H
katy.yanez@nau.edu

YANEZ, Mary, A 915-831-7803 436 A
myanez22@epcc.edu

YANEZ, Mercy 310-233-4342 49 B
yanezm@lahc.edu

YANEZ, Mercy 310-233-4447 49 B
yanezm@lahc.edu

YANEZ, Robert 413-748-3104 218 I
ryanez@springfield.edu

YANG, Alice 831-459-2328 71 A
ayang@ucsc.edu

YANG, Angela 949-582-4602 65 D
lyang26@saddleback.edu

YANG, Anthony 973-618-3605 276 D
ayang@caldwell.edu

YANG, Blia 831-459-4179 71 A
blyang@ucsc.edu

YANG, Catherine 916-686-7400 29 E

YANG, Eun Soon 951-372-8080 45 D

YANG, Henry, T 805-893-2231 70 E
henry.yang@ucsb.edu

YANG, Hong 401-232-6885 404 A
hyang@bryant.edu

YANG, Jasmine, X 315-859-4084 300 H
jxyang@hamilton.edu

YANG, K. Wayne 858-822-2824 70 C
kwayne@ucsd.edu

YANG, Kha, A 651-962-5219 244 E
yang8741@stthomas.edu

YANG, Lykos 408-260-0208 42 E
sjextension@fivebranches.edu

YANG, Michael 909-895-7138 45 H
michael@huca.edu

YANG, Nicole 920-693-1120 498 H
nicole.yang@gotoltc.edu

YANG, Olivia 509-335-5571 485 D
olivia.yang@wsu.edu

YANG, Pakou 651-779-3288 237 H
pakou.yang@century.edu

YANG, Paul Zhaohui 628-448-0023 46 G

YANG, Philip 408-532-5567 34 E

YANG, Phong 559-278-2048 31 B
pyang@csufresno.edu

YANG, Tony 269-471-3354 221 D
tonyy@andrews.edu

YANG, Xong Sony 309-794-8274 133 C
xongsonyyang@augustana.edu

YANG, Yixin 908-737-3459 278 E
yyang@kean.edu

YANKELEWITZ, Yoel 718-846-1940 325 O

YANKELITIS, Wendy 570-348-6201 389 D
yankelitis@marywood.edu

YANKEY, Terry, L 606-474-3222 181 B
tly@kcu.edu

YANNI, Stephen 906-248-8478 221 M
syanni@bmcc.edu

YANNICK, Lisa 610-436-3075 395 D
lyannick@wcupa.edu

YANNIELLO, Kristin 718-405-3252 296 F
kristin.yanniello@mountsaintvincent.
edu

YANNUZZI, Leigh 518-587-2100 320 E

YAO, Chunmei 910-521-6295 343 B
chunmei.yao@uncp.edu

YAO, Marian 408-924-2012 34 A
marian.sofish@sjsu.edu

YAO, Min 562-985-5459 31 D
min.yao@csulb.edu

YAO, Richard 805-437-8410 30 C
richard.yao@csuci.edu

YAP, Michael 213-252-5100 23 K
myap@alu.edu

YAQUB, Samia 530-895-2484 27 C
yaqubsa@butte.edu

YARABECK, John 936-294-1785 450 A
slo_jxy@shsu.edu

YARBROUGH, Boyd 864-388-8239 410 A
byarbrough@lander.edu

YARBROUGH, Breanna 334-386-7476 5 C
byarbrough@faulkner.edu

YARBROUGH, David 337-482-1015 193 B
yarbrough@louisiana.edu

YARBROUGH, Denise 585-275-4321 323 M
dyarbrough@admin.rochester.edu

YARBROUGH, Erin, A 405-325-0206 370 K
eyarbrough@ou.edu

YARBROUGH, John 706-865-2134 126 E
jyarbrough@truett.edu

YARBROUGH, Kenny 262-472-1918 497 D

YARBROUGH, Laura 870-508-6263 17 G
lyarbrough@asumh.edu

YARBROUGH, Laura, L 336-249-8186 334 B
laura_yarbrough@davidsondavie.edu

YARBROUGH, Mark, M 214-887-5011 435 F
myarbrough@dts.edu

YARBROUGH, Rachel 812-749-1399 159 O
ryarbrough@oak.edu

YARBROUGH, Scott 843-863-7563 407 B
syarbrou@csuniv.edu

YARLOTT, JR., David 406-638-3107 263 G
davidyarlott@lbhc.edu

YAROFAISUG, Faustino 691-320-2481 504 C
yaro@comfsm.fm

YARRITU, Daniel 979-230-3441 431 I
daniel.yarritu@brazosport.edu

YARROW, Lisa 713-646-1893 443 I
lyarrow@stcl.edu

YASIN, Dawood 510-356-4760 77 F

YASINSAC, Alec 251-460-6390 9 A
yasinsac@southalabama.edu

YASSERI, Darioush 405-945-6761 368 C
yasseri@okstate.edu

YASUDA, Cathy 541-881-5585 376 F
cyasuda@tvcc.cc

YATER, Ann 317-917-5915 158 D
aniebrug@ivytech.edu

YATES, Brian 434-592-4108 468 E
bcyates@liberty.edu

YATES, Deanna 270-706-8658 181 G
dyates0031@kctcs.edu

YATES, Deirdre 973-275-2191 283 C
deirdre.yates@shu.edu

YATES, Dorothy 407-823-3028 110 E
dorothy.yates@ucf.edu

YATES, Emilie 308-632-6933 269 E

YATES, Frances 765-973-8470 157 A
fyates@iue.edu

YATES, Jacob 606-337-4524 180 C
registrar@ccbbc.edu

YATES, James 870-864-7156 21 A
jyates@southark.edu

YATES, Jamie 717-337-6000 384 D
jyates@gettysburg.edu

YATES, Kristin 402-472-5242 269 H
kyates@nebraska.edu

YATES, Michelle 207-859-1405 196 D
registrar@thomas.edu

YATES, Randy 670-237-6724 505 A
randy.yates@marianas.edu

YATES, Shannon 910-486-3630 334 E
yatess@faytechcc.edu

YATES, Stephanie, L 217-554-1628 136 G
syates@dacc.edu

YATES, Vivian 216-987-4468 351 E
vivian.yates@tri-c.edu

YATES-MATTINGLY,
Shelia 513-875-3344 350 C
shelia.yates-mattingly@chatfield.edu

YATES SEAMAN, Liz 610-861-1505 390 F
yatese@moravian.edu

YATIN, Servet 617-984-1719 218 C
syatin@quincycollege.edu

YATS, Kirk, M 989-774-3674 222 E
yats1km@cmich.edu

YAUN, John 662-915-7348 249 D
jyaun@olemiss.edu

YAUNEY, Katherine, A 518-388-6013 323 J

YAVAS, Debora 310-377-5501 51 C
dyavas@marymountcalifornia.edu

YAVAS, Debra 310-377-5501 51 C
dyavas@marymountcalifornia.edu

YAVNEH KLOS, Naomi 509-359-2822 479 G
nyavnehklos@ewu.edu

YAVOR, Susan 610-341-4363 383 B
syavor@eastern.edu

YAVORSKI, Ginger 484-664-3190 390 H
gingeryavorski@muhlenberg.edu

YAZDANI, Linda 303-914-6536 83 C
linda.yazdani@rrcc.edu

YAZDI, Aliakbar, R 205-853-1200 2 G
ayazdi@jeffersonstate.edu

YAZEDJIAN, Ani 309-438-7018 140 D
ayazedj@ilstu.edu

YAZZIE, Lambert 480-732-7205 12 O
lambert.yazzie@cgc.edu

YBARRA, David 910-522-5793 343 B
david.ybarra@uncp.edu

YBARRA, Kathy 206-296-2810 484 A
ybarrak@seattleu.edu

YBARRA, Paul 916-577-2200 76 D
pybarra@jessup.edu

YDOYAGA, Shannon 817-515-4507 445 F
shannon.ydoyaga@tccd.edu

YDRACH, Gloriana 787-728-1515 513 D
gloriana.ydrach@sagrado.edu

YE, Eugene 602-285-7134 13 F
eugene.ye@phoenixcollege.edu

YEADON, Steven, W 503-777-7764 375 G
yeadons@reed.edu

YEAGER, Andrew 716-880-2336 305 G
ayeager@medaille.edu

YEAGER, Daphne 601-477-4151 246 G
daphne.yeager@jcjc.edu

YEAGER, Deonne 843-208-8723 413 C
deonne@uscb.edu

YEAGER, Edward 480-732-7177 12 O
ed.yeager@cgc.edu

YEAGER, Jason 304-462-6131 489 L
jason.yeager@glenville.edu

YEAGER, Kathrine, H 928-523-4036 14 H
kathy.yeager@nau.edu

YEANY, Ron 617-353-1701 207 E
ryeany@bu.edu

YEAP, Soon Beng 303-765-3110 81 G
syeap@iliff.edu

YEARBY, Annette 386-481-2364 96 D
yearbya@cookman.edu

YEARNS, Ellie, P 336-272-7102 329 C
ellie.yearns@greensboro.edu

YEAROUT, Teresa, A 276-964-7266 475 C
teresa.yearout@sw.edu

YEARTA, Charles, S 803-323-3499 414 D
yeartac@winthrop.edu

YEARWOOD, Burl 201-360-4651 278 C
byearwood@hccc.edu

YEARWOOD,
George (Rocky), A 919-508-2035 344 E
ryearwood@peace.edu

YEARWOOD, Jody 478-387-4392 119 F
jyearwood@gmc.edu

YEATER, Mike 432-264-5111 437 F
myeater@howardcollege.edu

YEATS, John Mark 816-414-3700 256 C
jmyeats@mbts.edu

YEATTS, Debra 910-630-7385 331 E
dyeatts@methodist.edu

YEBEI, Philemon 574-520-4218 157 E
pyebei@iu.edu

YECK, Alan 607-735-1825 298 H
ayeck@elmira.edu

YECKLEY, Trae 814-332-4368 378 A
tyeckley@allegheny.edu

YEE, David 415-239-3669 36 K
dyee@ccsf.edu

YEE, Ellen 617-585-0200 207 A
ellen.yee@the-bac.edu

YEE, Gary 402-559-5108 269 K
gcyee@unmc.edu

YEE, Helen 614-825-6255 347 E
hyee@aiam.edu

YEE, Jill 415-239-3174 36 K
jyee@ccsf.edu

YEE, Penny 315-859-4720 300 H
pyee@hamilton.edu

YEE-BULLOCK,
Calandria 772-466-4822 95 N

YEH, David 773-907-4071 135 C
dyeh@ccc.edu

YEH, Lisa 212-870-2530 291 A
lyeh@barnard.edu

YEHUDAH, Shoshana 646-565-6000 322 F
shoshana.yehudah@touro.edu

YEHUDAH, Shoshana 646-565-6000 322 G
shoshana.yehudah@touro.edu

YEKOVICH, Robert 713-348-4837 442 F
yekovr@rice.edu

YELDELL JONES,
Andrain 256-686-5850 93 H

YELKUR, Rama 940-898-2105 451 D
ryelkur@twu.edu

YELLIN, Dina 732-367-1060 275 K
dyellin@bmg.edu

YELTON, David 704-406-3522 329 A
dyelton@gardner-webb.edu

YELTON, Jennifer 573-642-3361 262 E

YEN, Charlie 310-434-3002 63 C
yen_charlie@smc.edu

YEN, Debbie 870-733-6764 17 F
dyen@asumidsouth.edu

YEN, Johanna, C 954-763-9840 95 J
atom@atom.edu

YENCER, Kristen 302-857-1401 91 A
kristen.yencer@dtcc.edu

YENCHA, Patricia 570-740-0200 389 A

YENCHO, Thomas 610-409-3491 401 H
tyencho@ursinus.edu

YENCO, Andrea 212-229-5671 308 A
yencoa@newschool.edu

YENDOL-HOPPEY,
Diane 904-620-2520 111 B
diane.yendol-hoppy@unf.edu

YOUNG, Jed .... 832-813-6521 439 C
jed.t.young@lonestar.edu
YOUNG, Jennifer, C ..... 412-397-5452 397 B
youngj@rmu.edu
YOUNG, Jill .... 570-389-4950 393 D
jyoung@bloomu.edu
YOUNG, Joanne .... 603-888-1311 273 I
YOUNG, John .... 315-781-3748 301 F
jyoung@hws.edu
YOUNG, John .... 303-360-4707.. 80 E
john.young@ccaurora.edu
YOUNG, John, O .... 248-370-2946 229 I
joyoung@oakland.edu
YOUNG, Johnny, W ...... 757-683-3442 469 B
jwyoung@odu.edu
YOUNG, Jon .... 805-565-6037.. 76 A
joyoung@westmont.edu
YOUNG, Justn .... 618-842-3711 139 F
youngj11@iecc.edu
YOUNG, Kaitlin .... 845-431-3700 298 D
kaitlin.young@sunydutchess.edu
YOUNG, Kalbert, K .... 808-956-8903 129 C
kalbert@hawaii.edu
YOUNG, Kelly .... 315-781-3783 301 F
keyoung@hws.edu
YOUNG, Kelsey .... 717-262-2003 403 C
conferences@wilson.edu
YOUNG, Ken 516-323-4501 306M
kyoung@molloy.edu
YOUNG, Kerry, A .... 315-786-2279 303 C
kyoung@sunyjefferson.edu
YOUNG, Kim .... 760-252-2411.. 26 G
kyoung@barstow.edu
YOUNG, Kimberly .... 540-286-8076 471 N
kyoung@umw.edu
YOUNG, Kirk .... 716-338-1023 303 A
kirkyoung@mail.sunyjcc.edu
YOUNG, Kristina .... 425-352-8550 478 D
kyoung@cascadia.edu
YOUNG, Kristine .... 775-881-7509 272 D
kyoung@sierranevada.edu
YOUNG, Kristine, M ..... 845-341-4700 310 G
president@sunyorange.edu
YOUNG, Lauren .... 716-888-2436 292 F
youngb@canisius.edu
YOUNG, Leah .... 717-245-1308 382 D
youngle@dickinson.edu
YOUNG, Leah .... 919-508-2319 344 E
YOUNG, Lee .... 281-283-3011 452 E
youngl@uhcl.edu
YOUNG, Linda, C .... 334-556-2234.... 2 C
lyoung@wallace.edu
YOUNG, Linda, K .... 715-836-5287 495 E
younglk@uwec.edu
YOUNG, Lindsay .... 361-570-4492 453 B
youngle@uhv.edu
YOUNG, Mark, S .... 303-762-6902.. 80 I
president@denverseminary.edu
YOUNG, Mary .... 203-773-8521.. 85 D
myoung@albertus.edu
YOUNG, Mary .... 713-313-7733 449 B
mary.young@tsu.edu
YOUNG, Mary .... 402-562-1492 266 A
myoung@cccneb.edu
YOUNG, Mary, E .... 903-823-3369 446 A
maryellen.young@texarkanacollege.edu
YOUNG, MaryAnne .... 941-487-4801 110 D
myoung@ncf.edu
YOUNG, Megan .... 918-333-6830 368 E
myoung@okwu.edu
YOUNG, Michael .... 508-531-1295 212 D
myoung@bridgew.edu
YOUNG, Michael, A ...... 215-707-7336 399 B
michael.young@tuhs.temple.edu
YOUNG, Michael, W ...... 212-327-8000 312 G
michael.young@rockefeller.edu
YOUNG, Michaela, J .... 315-386-7204 320 B
youngm@canton.edu
YOUNG, Michelle, D .... 310-338-2700.. 51 A
YOUNG, Michelle, L .... 315-268-4268 295 F
myoung@clarkson.edu
YOUNG, Misty .... 573-681-5580 254 G
youngm@lincolnu.edu
YOUNG, Monica .... 336-334-4822 335 A
mwyoung@gtcc.edu
YOUNG, Nanci .... 319-399-8000 164 F
YOUNG, Nancy .... 410-455-2393 203 B
nyoung@umbc.edu
YOUNG, Nancy .... 816-960-2008 251 G
newstudents@cityvision.edu
YOUNG, Nikki .... 940-898-3188 451 D
nyoung1@twu.edu
YOUNG, Norman .... 860-768-7819.. 89 G
young@hartford.edu
YOUNG, Patricia .... 707-864-7124.. 64 H
patricia.young@solano.edu
YOUNG, Patty, R .... 972-860-8354 434 H
pyoung@dcccd.edu
YOUNG, Quentin .... 606-539-3527 185 E
YOUNG, Randy .... 660-359-3948 257 D
ryoung@mail.ncmissouri.edu
YOUNG, Remmele .... 713-718-7452 437 C
remmele.young@hccs.edu
YOUNG, Rena .... 270-707-3732 182 B
rena.young@kctcs.edu
YOUNG, Rhett .... 740-284-5007 352 I
ryoung@franciscan.edu
YOUNG, Rob .... 937-327-7009 364 D
youngr11@wittenberg.edu
YOUNG, Robert .... 410-386-8261 198 D
ryoung@carrollcc.edu
YOUNG, Robert .... 540-453-2500 473 D
youngb@brcc.edu
YOUNG, Robert .... 814-472-3119 397 F
ryoung@francis.edu
YOUNG, Robert .... 501-370-5365.. 20 F
ryoung@philander.edu
YOUNG, Robert .... 423-236-2805 423 F
ryoung@southern.edu
YOUNG, Robert, F .... 843-349-2277 408 A
ryoung@coastal.edu
YOUNG, Samuel .... 714-449-7481.. 51 B
syoung@ketchum.edu
YOUNG, Sarah .... 309-457-2300 144 H
syoung@monmouthcollege.edu
YOUNG, Sarah, M .... 716-878-4619 317 F
youngsm@buffalostate.edu
YOUNG, Scott .... 816-235-1154 261 B
youngsc@umkc.edu
YOUNG, Scott .... 317-788-3306 161 H
syoung@uindy.edu
YOUNG, Scott .... 360-650-2593 485 I
scott.young@wwu.edu
YOUNG, Sean, B .... 262-243-5700 492 E
sean.young@cuw.edu
YOUNG, Shane .... 731-424-3520 424 E
syoung18@jscc.edu
YOUNG, Shane .... 216-373-5274 357 F
syoung@ndc.edu
YOUNG, Shawna .... 707-826-3961.. 33 C
shawna.young@humboldt.edu
YOUNG, Shawna .... 603-366-5266 272 K
syoung@ccsnh.edu
YOUNG, Sheri .... 401-598-1872 404 D
sheri.young@jwu.edu
YOUNG, Sherry .... 610-921-6639 377 G
syoung@albright.edu
YOUNG, Sonia .... 803-981-7372 414 F
syoung@yorktech.edu
YOUNG, Stacie, G .... 704-687-7203 342 D
sgyoung@uncc.edu
YOUNG, Stacy .... 989-328-1221 228 D
stacy.young@montcalm.edu
YOUNG, Stephanie .... 713-798-4951 431 D
YOUNG, Steve .... 850-718-2203.. 97 E
youngs@chipola.edu
YOUNG, Steven .... 828-694-1891 332 E
sd_young@blueridge.edu
YOUNG, Stuart .... 701-766-1321 344 G
stuart.young@littlehoop.edu
YOUNG, Sunya .... 803-376-5716 406 D
syoung@allenuniversity.edu
YOUNG, Susan .... 864-242-5100 406 H
YOUNG, Tangar .... 803-533-3712 411 G
tyoung15@scsu.edu
YOUNG, Ted .... 850-484-1794 105 H
fyoung@pensacolastate.edu
YOUNG, Teresa .... 806-291-3427 457 I
teresa.young@wbu.edu
YOUNG, Terrance, J ..... 484-365-7451 388 H
tyoung2@lincoln.edu
YOUNG, Terry .... 276-656-0315 474 G
tyoung@patrickhenry.edu
YOUNG, Terry .... 276-656-0287 474 G
tyoung@patrickhenry.edu
YOUNG, Terry .... 325-793-4683 439 F
tyoung@mcm.edu
YOUNG, Thelathia, N .... 570-577-1928 379 C
nikki.young@bucknell.edu
YOUNG, Thomas, W ..... 507-933-7551 236 A
tyoung3@gustavus.edu
YOUNG, Tim .... 714-556-3610.. 73 H
tyoung@vanguard.edu
YOUNG, Timothy .... 269-337-7321 225 F
timothy.young@kzoo.edu
YOUNG, Tina .... 319-385-6361 167 H
tina.young@iw.edu
YOUNG, Todd .... 541-654-5885 371 F
YOUNG, Troy .... 267-341-3494 385 J
tyoung2@holyfamily.edu
YOUNG, Wayne .... 402-280-2775 266 H
waynejr@creighton.edu
YOUNG, William .... 334-290-3254.... 2 F
william.young@istc.edu
YOUNG, William, D ...... 302-225-6297.. 91 B
youngd@gbc.edu
YOUNG WON, Duck ..... 323-643-0301.. 25 F
YOUNGBAUER, Mara .... 260-982-5250 159 J
mlyoungbauer@manchester.edu
YOUNGBLADE, Lise ...... 970-491-5841.. 79 N
lise.youngblade@colostate.edu
YOUNGBLOOD, Amy .... 713-522-7911 454 G
youngbah@stthom.edu
YOUNGBLOOD, Cecil ... 608-363-2660 491 H
youngblc@beloit.edu
YOUNGBLOOD, Jason .. 270-809-6859 184 D
jyoungblood@murraystate.edu
YOUNGBLOOD,
Jeanette .... 870-612-2022.. 22 H
jeanette.youngblood@uaccb.edu
YOUNGBLOOD, Joseph 908-737-7030 278 E
jyoungblood@kean.edu
YOUNGBLOOD, II,
Joseph .... 607-777-4351 284 C
jyoungblood@tesu.edu
YOUNGBLOOD,
Krisshunn .... 337-475-5426 192 E
kyoungblood@mcneese.edu
YOUNGBLOOD, Pamela 979-532-6542 458 E
pamy@wcjc.edu
YOUNGBLOOD,
Richard .... 504-526-4745 190 E
YOUNGBLOOD, Rick ..... 601-477-4014 246 G
rick.youngblood@jcjc.edu
YOUNGBLOOD, Robert . 256-766-6610..... 5 E
ryoungblood@hcu.edu
YOUNGBLOOD GILES,
Nikki .... 212-854-2033 291 A
nyoungbl@barnard.edu
YOUNGDAHL, Marcy .... 210-999-8111 451 E
myoungda@trinity.edu
YOUNGE, Jeffrey, W ..... 507-344-7328 234 C
jeff.younge@blc.edu
YOUNGEN, Audra .... 330-823-2072 362 E
youngeau@mountunion.edu
YOUNGER, Allan .... 336-757-3804 334 F
ayounger@forsythtech.edu
YOUNGER, James .... 859-442-1719 181 H
james.younger@kctcs.edu
YOUNGER, Kyle .... 662-243-1975 246 B
kyounger@eastms.edu
YOUNGER, Toyia .... 515-294-1909 163 G
tyounger@iastate.edu
YOUNGLOVE, Theodore 909-652-6402.. 35 L
ted.younglove@chaffey.edu
YOUNGMAN, Paul .... 540-458-8418 477 D
youngmanp@wlu.edu
YOUNGREN, Malcolm ... 212-982-3456.. 55 E
myoungren@pacificcollege.edu
YOUNGREN, Malcolm ... 929-436-3851.. 55 E
myoungren@pacificcollege.edu
YOUNGS, Samuel, J ..... 423-775-7514 418 D
syoungs2721@bryan.edu
YOUNGS, JR.,
Thomas, E .... 412-624-8785 400 H
tyoungs@cfo.pitt.edu
YOUNGS-MAHER,
Pamela .... 315-464-8561 317 C
youngsmp@upstate.edu
YOUNGSTRAND, Keri .... 218-281-8395 244 A
kyoungst@umn.edu
YOUNT, John, T .... 610-917-1818 401 G
jtyount@valleyforge.edu
YOUNT, Rebecca, H ...... 401-333-7159 404 C
byount@ccri.edu
YOUNTS, Philip .... 405-613-2536 369 I
philip.younts@swcu.edu
YOUSE, Lauren .... 573-629-3122 253 J
lauren.youse@hlg.edu
YOUSIF, Amar .... 713-486-2227 456 B
amar.yousif@uth.tmc.edu
YOUSIF, Bassam .... 812-237-2785 156 D
bassam.yousif@indstate.edu
YOVANOVICH, Michele . 239-433-6950 101 A
michele.yovanovich@fsw.edu
YOWE, Benita .... 864-592-4338 412 E
yoweb@sccsc.edu
YOWELL, Kristi .... 410-337-6000 199 B
kristi.yowell@goucher.edu
YPMA, Heidi .... 360-752-8433 478 A
hypma@btc.edu
YRUEGAS, Jennifer ...... 503-352-2236 375 C
jennifer.yruegas@pacificu.edu
YRUEGAS, Jennifer .... 503-352-2814 375 C
jyruegas@pacificu.edu
YSAIS, David .... 213-763-7063.. 49 F
ysaisdp@lattc.edu
YSURSA, JR., Bernie, J 618-235-2700 150 E
bernard.ysursa@swic.edu
YU, Allison .... 512-444-8082 448 H
yu@thsu.edu
YU, Bin .... 401-456-8160 405 A
byu@ric.edu
YU, Ellen .... 518-388-6293 323 J
yue@union.edu
YU, Fen .... 870-972-3027.. 17 E
fyu@astate.edu
YU, Hongtao .... 443-885-3333 201 A
hongtao.yu@morgan.edu
YU, Jenny .... 562-947-8755.. 65 I
jennyyu@scuhs.edu
YU, Paul, K .... 858-534-1571.. 70 C
pyu@ucsd.edu
YU, Regan .... 626-455-0312.. 58 J
YU, Tyler .... 678-407-5396 119 C
tyu@ggc.edu
YU, Zhanjing (John) ..... 530-242-7962.. 64 C
zyu@shastacollege.edu
YUCHA, James, B .... 804-828-2234 473 B
jyucha@vcu.edu
YUDIN, Lee, S .... 671-735-2002 504 F
lyudin@triton.uog.edu
YUDT, Angela, L .... 312-413-3470 151 G
ayudt@uic.edu
YUEH, Yir Gloria .... 623-572-3239 144 F
gyuehx@midwestern.edu
YUEN, Dan .... 212-924-5900 321 F
dyuen@swedishinstitute.edu
YUHAS, Meredith .... 860-231-5366.. 90 A
myuhas@usj.edu
YUHAS, Trevor .... 765-658-4268 154 J
trevoryuhas@depauw.edu
YUKECH, James .... 330-941-3001 364 H
jayukech@ysu.edu
YUKNA, Jennifer .... 314-529-6858 255 B
jyukna@maryville.edu
YUNITS, Sarah .... 508-588-9100 215 A
syunits@massasoit.mass.edu
YUNKE, Laurie .... 215-955-1756 399 E
laurie.yunke@jefferson.edu
YUNKER, Kristin, L .... 585-343-0055 300 F
klyunker@genesee.edu
YURACHEK, Hunter .... 479-575-7641.. 21 F
athldir@uark.edu
YURAN, Mark .... 218-726-6326 243 G
myuran@d.umn.edu
YURASEK, Kevin .... 352-365-3526 103 U
yurasekk@lssc.edu
YURECKO, Michele .... 973-290-4036 282 I
myurecko@steu.edu
YUSEN, Sandy .... 802-865-5727 462 A
syusen@champlain.edu
YUSOV-BALDONI,
Alexis .... 860-297-2119.. 89 B
alexis.baldoni@trincoll.edu
YUST, Rob .... 417-625-9395 256 F
yust-r@mssu.edu
YUSUF, Hamza .... 510-356-4760.. 77 F
YUTUC, Lloyd .... 301-891-4477 205 A
ylloyd@wau.edu
YVON, Karalee .... 413-265-2294 208 E
yvonk@elms.edu

Z

ZAAS, David .... 843-792-6788 410 C
zaas@musc.edu
ZABALA, Juan .... 409-880-8419 449 G
juan.zabala@lamar.edu
ZABATTA, Lori .... 401-598-4462 404 D
lori.zabatta@jwu.edu
ZABEL, Amy .... 815-939-5221 147 A
aezabel@olivet.edu
ZABLOUDIL, Darren ...... 319-398-7610 167 J
darren.zabloudil@kirkwood.edu
ZABOROWSKI, Barbara . 814-262-6425 393 A
bzabor@pennhighlands.edu
ZABOROWSKI, Shelley . 402-472-2841 269 J
szaborowski3@unl.edu
ZABOSKI, Gerald, C ..... 570-941-7900 401 F
gerald.zaboski@scranton.edu
ZABRISKIE, Mark .... 541-737-5774 375 A
mark.zabriskie@oregonstate.edu

ZEIGLER, Keri 410-857-2714 200 F kzeigler@mcdaniel.edu
ZEIGLER, Letherio 662-254-3335 248 B letherio.zeigler@mvsu.edu
ZEIGLER, Michael 803-535-5340 407 D mike.zeigler@claflin.edu
ZEIGLER, Michael, C 717-867-6060 388 C zeigler@lvc.edu
ZEIGLER, Sara 859-622-2222 180 E sara.zeigler@eku.edu
ZEIHER, Laura 218-299-6522 239 C laura.zeiher@minnesota.edu
ZEILBERGER, Yeruchom 845-207-0330 290 F
ZEILENGA, Jeffrey, R 573-882-5397 261 A zeilengaj@missouri.edu
ZEIMET, Dan, L 563-333-6202 169 G zeimetdaniell@sau.edu
ZEIND, Caroline 617-732-2874 216 D caroline.zeind@mcphs.edu
ZEISER, Richard, A 860-768-4181 89 G zeiser@hartford.edu
ZEITLOW, Terry 903-233-3835 439 A terryzeitlow@letu.edu
ZEKAN, Ingrid 352-245-4119 112 E ingrid.zekan@taylorcollege.edu
ZELASKO, Sandra 360-538-4000 480 G szelasko@ghc.edu
ZELAYA, Marjorie 702-567-1920 270 I
ZELAYA-LEON, Tricia 269-337-7183 225 F tricia.zelaya-leon@kzoo.edu
ZELENSKI, Paul 517-371-5140 233 C zelenskp@cooley.edu
ZELENY, Michael 402-472-2116 269 J mike.zeleny@unl.edu
ZELESKY, Jason 978-630-9139 215 C jzelesky@mwcc.mass.edu
ZELESNIK, Kelly 440-366-7028 355 B
ZELEZNIK, Matthew 724-480-3357 381 H matthew.zeleznik@ccbc.edu
ZELEZNY, Lynnette 661-654-2243 30 B lzelezny@csub.edu
ZELIG, Kaylah 303-352-6787 80 F kaylah.zelig@ccd.edu
ZELINKA, Yhara 860-343-5868 87 A yzelinka@mxcc.edu
ZELINSKI, Bob 352-854-2322 97 N zelinskb@cf.edu
ZELINSKI, Debbie 312-329-4231 144 I debbie.zelinski@moody.edu
ZELL, Jennifer 845-687-5049 323 H zellj@sunyulster.edu
ZELLAR, Nel 507-433-0832 240 G nel.zellar@riverland.edu
ZELLER, John, H 215-898-5169 400 F jzeller@upenn.edu
ZELLERS, Victoria 215-751-8913 381 I vzellers@ccp.edu
ZELLET, Jennifer 209-575-6058 77 A zelletj@mjc.edu
ZELLI, Brian 716-614-6731 309 G bzelli@niagaracc.suny.edu
ZELLMER, Jill, A 617-627-3298 219 C jill.zellmer@tufts.edu
ZELLNER, Wayne 719-632-8116 81 J wzellner@intellitec.edu
ZELTINGER, Jacquelyn 701-627-4738 346 F
ZEMAN, Ellen 802-651-5912 462 A zeman@champlain.edu
ZEMAN, Mark 315-464-5825 317 C zemanm@upstate.edu
ZEMAN, Mary Beth 973-720-2966 284 J zemanm@wpunj.edu
ZEMBA, Bethany, C 203-582-7430 88 G bethany.zemba@quinnipiac.edu
ZEMBA, Jennifer 724-838-4216 398 C jzemba@setonhill.edu
ZENDEJAS, Raul 210-805-3006 453 C rzendeja@uiwtx.edu
ZENDMAN, Ellen 914-606-6733 325 A ellen.zendman@sunywcc.edu
ZENELIS, John, G 703-993-2491 467 E jzenelis@gmu.edu
ZENG, Amy 617-573-8300 219 B azeng@suffolk.edu
ZENG, Xiangwu 201-216-3893 283 D xiangwu.zeng@stevens.edu
ZENGER, John 208-496-4632 130 I zengerj@byui.edu
ZENGER, Sheahon 203-932-7020 89 H szenger@newhaven.edu
ZENK, Leslie 704-687-5766 342 D lzenk@uncc.edu
ZENKER, James 865-938-8186 419 B james.zenker@thecrowncollege.edu
ZENN, Michael 312-355-5706 151 G mbzenn@uic.edu
ZENNER, Jami 970-223-2669 81 E jzenner@ibmc.edu
ZENNER FORD, Chandra 208-885-1205 132 F chandra@uidaho.edu
ZENNERMANN, Ewa 678-839-5331 127 C ezenner@westga.edu
ZENO, Mark 419-448-2058 353 E mzeno@heidelberg.edu
ZENTMEYER, James, R 248-370-3570 229 I zentmeye@oakland.edu
ZENTMIRE, Deborah 361-825-3918 447 C deborah.zentmire@tamucc.edu
ZENTNER, Aeron 714-241-6413 37 J azentner@coastline.edu
ZEONE, Alicia 507-280-3509 240 H alicia.zeone@rctc.edu
ZEPEDA, Lillian 718-997-5591 295 B lillian.zepeda@qc.cuny.edu
ZEPEDA, Milani 408-855-5123 75 D milani.zepeda@missioncollege.edu
ZEPEDA, Ofelia 520-383-0067 16 A ozepeda@tocc.edu
ZEPPOS, Nicholas 615-322-1813 428 A nick.zeppos@vanderbilt.edu
ZERBE, Bryan 415-565-4623 69 C zerbeb@uchastings.edu
ZERBE, Linda 610-282-1100 382 C linda.zerbe@desales.edu
ZERCHER, Charles, K 603-862-1781 274 F chuck.zercher@unh.edu
ZERILLO, Barbara 617-521-2000 218 G
ZERMENO, Zulema 530-741-6707 77 E zzermeno@yccd.edu
ZERO, Paula 540-654-1231 471 N pzero@umw.edu
ZERTUCHE, Ramon 210-431-6598 441 B rzertuche@ollusa.edu
ZERWAS, John, M 512-579-5149 454 H jzerwas@utsystem.edu
ZERWIC, Julie 319-335-7009 163 H julie-zerwic@uiowa.edu
ZEWE, Beth 814-732-1420 394 B zewe@edinboro.edu
ZEYNEP LEUENBERGER, Deniz 508-531-6125 212 D dleuenberger@bridgew.edu
ZGODA, Karen 716-896-0700 324 E kzgoda@villa.edu
ZHADKO, Olena 718-960-1172 294 A olena.zhadko@lehman.cuny.edu
ZHAI, Meihua 313-577-2001 232 K gy2460@wayne.edu
ZHANG, Ara 562-988-2278 25 L achang@auhs.edu
ZHANG, Cheryl 908-737-3199 278 E chzhang@kean.edu
ZHANG, Chunsheng 256-765-4898 8 E czhang@una.edu
ZHANG, James 810-762-7949 226 B jzhang@kettering.edu
ZHANG, Jiajie, W 713-500-3922 456 B jiajie.zhang@uth.tmc.edu
ZHANG, Jie 201-216-3743 283 D jie.zhang@stevens.edu
ZHANG, Ling 408-260-0208 42 E sjadmin@fivebranches.edu
ZHANG, Ling 408-260-0208 42 F sjadmin@fivebranches.edu
ZHANG, Ming 360-650-4454 485 I ming.zhang@wwu.edu
ZHANG, Shali, L 334-844-1714 4 D slz0002@auburn.edu
ZHANG, Shouhong 605-688-6312 417 A shouhong.zhang@sdstate.edu
ZHANG, William, B 336-334-5559 343 A wbzhang@uncg.edu
ZHANG, Xiao, Y 716-673-4806 316 D xiao.zhang@fredonia.edu
ZHANG, Yang 808-956-5877 129 E yz6@hawaii.edu
ZHAO, Jinhua 607-255-2000 297 F jz638@cornell.edu
ZHAO, Joanna 408-260-0208 42 E dean@fivebranches.edu
ZHAO, Joanna 831-476-9424 42 F dean@fivebranches.edu
ZHAO, Jun 708-534-8046 138 E jzhao@govst.edu
ZHAO, Lianna 949-451-5450 65 C lzhao@ivc.edu
ZHAO, Lincoln, Z 407-888-8689 100 A zzhao@fcim.edu
ZHAO, Rong Yuan 510-763-7787 24 C
ZHAO, Yanru 352-591-5385 97 D yanru@chiu.edu
ZHAO, Yiping 516-739-1545 308 F clinicmanager@nyctcm.edu
ZHAO, Zhen 352-591-5385 97 D zhen@chiu.edu
ZHARNEST, Marc 646-592-4440 326 D zharnest@yu.edu
ZHENG, John 662-254-3452 248 B zheng@mvsu.edu
ZHONG, Baisong 713-780-9777 429 G bzhong@acaom.edu
ZHOU, Chenn 219-989-2665 160 D czhou@pnw.edu
ZHOU, Jiangyuan 609-626-5593 283 E jy.zhou@stockton.edu
ZHOU, Lin 212-229-5300 308 A linzhou@newschool.edu
ZHOU, Lin 253-680-7105 477 I lzhou@batestech.edu
ZHOU, Sharon 408-733-1878 71 B sharon@uewm.edu
ZHOU, Wei 301-985-7705 203 E institutional-planning@umuc.edu
ZHOU, Wendy 303-384-2181 79 J wzhou@mines.edu
ZHOU, Xunhang (Hank) 734-487-0159 223 K xzhou2@emich.edu
ZHOU, Ying 252-737-1912 341 A zhouy14@ecu.edu
ZHU, Hong 574-631-3229 162 A hzhu1@nd.edu
ZHU, Jake 909-537-8101 32 E jzhu@csusb.edu
ZHU, Li 718-939-5100 304 C lzhu@libi.edu
ZHU, Lizhi (Frank) 718-522-9073 290 E lzhu@asa.edu
ZHU, WeiDong 201-761-6037 283 A wzhu@saintpeters.edu
ZHUANG, Miao 361-593-2244 447 D miao.zhuang@tamuk.edu
ZIA, Rashid 401-863-2573 403 J rashid_zia@brown.edu
ZIADY, Nicola 513-556-3015 361 J ziadyna@ucmail.uc.edu
ZIAVRAS, Sotirios, G 973-596-3462 279 E sotirios.g.ziavras@njit.edu
ZIBBY-DAMRON, Kathleen 618-437-5321 147 I zibbyk@rlc.edu
ZIBELL, Tammy 509-533-8135 479 C tammy.zibell@scc.spokane.edu
ZIC, Anthony 516-759-2040 324 G azic@webb.edu
ZICK, Brittney 815-825-2086 141 F bzick@kish.edu
ZIDEK, Steve 724-938-4194 393 E zidek@calu.edu
ZIEBARTH, Timothy, J 574-372-5100 155 F ziebartj@grace.edu
ZIEG, Michael 724-738-2489 395 C michael.zieg@sru.edu
ZIEGENGEIST, Roy, P 860-701-6509 503 G roy.p.ziegengeist1@uscg.mil
ZIEGLER, Alycia 860-215-9292 87 F aziegler@threerivers.edu
ZIEGLER, Amanda 866-776-0331 54 D aziegler@ncu.edu
ZIEGLER, SND, Carol 216-373-5238 357 F cziegler@ndc.edu
ZIEGLER, Jennifer 402-465-2149 268 G jziegle2@nebrwesleyan.edu
ZIEGLER, John 805-969-3626 55 J jziegler@pacifica.edu
ZIEGLER, John 724-738-9000 395 C john.ziegler@sru.edu
ZIEGLER, Mark 510-780-4500 47 K mzeigler@lifewest.edu
ZIEGLER, William 607-777-3583 316 B ziegler@binghamton.edu
ZIELASKOWSKI, Cynthia 518-381-1271 315 B zielascd@sunysccc.edu
ZIELINSKI, Deborah, M 401-825-2188 404 C dmzielinski@ccri.edu
ZIELINSKI SLENSKI, Amanda 989-463-7465 221 B slenskiar@alma.edu
ZIEMAK, Kellie 727-341-4245 107 E ziemak.kellie@spcollege.edu
ZIEMBA, David 508-362-2131 214 D dziemba@capecod.edu
ZIEMBA, Kerri 212-752-1530 304 A bookstore@limcollege.edu
ZIEMER, Katherine 603-862-3290 274 F
ZIEMKOWSKI, Peter 269-337-4400 233 D
ZIEMNICK, Tom 540-338-1776 469 C
ZIENTEK, Rita, M 716-878-4698 317 F zientekm@buffalostate.edu
ZIERFUSS-HUBBARD, Pamm 559-325-5420 67 A pamm.hubbard@cloviscollege.edu
ZIEROTH, Gary 260-452-2152 154 I gary.zieroth@ctsfw.edu
ZIESLER, Yasmine 802-224-3000 463 D yasmine.ziesler@vsc.edu
ZIEZIULA, Amy 607-778-5307 317 D zieziulaaj@sunybroome.edu
ZIGAS, Paul 252-328-6940 341 A zigasp@ecu.edu
ZIGLAR, Toby 678-839-1390 127 C tziglar@westga.edu
ZIGLER, Scott 336-770-3236 343 D ziglers@uncsa.edu
ZIKE, Jason 803-641-3581 413 B jasonz@usca.edu
ZILDZIC, Ines 925-229-6873 40 A izildzic@4cd.edu
ZILE, Heather 269-782-1238 231 A hzile@swmich.edu
ZIMECKI-FENNIMORE, Danielle 856-415-2138 281 D dzimecki@rcsj.edu
ZIMMANN, Angela 717-262-2010 403 C angela.zimmann@wilson.edu
ZIMMEL, Dana 352-294-4219 111 A zimmeld@ufl.edu
ZIMMER, Eric, A 260-399-7700 162 B ezimmer@sf.edu
ZIMMER, Joseph, E 716-375-2121 313 C jezimmer@sbu.edu
ZIMMER, Tim 618-262-8641 139 I zimmert@iecc.edu
ZIMMER, Timothy, P 217-581-3520 137 E tpzimmer@eiu.edu
ZIMMERHANZEL, Kathryn 432-686-4227 440 B kzimmerhanzel@midland.edu
ZIMMERMAN, AJ 626-815-6000 26 F
ZIMMERMAN, Angela 516-323-4723 306 M azimmerman@molloy.edu
ZIMMERMAN, Bill 320-589-6397 244 B billz@morris.umn.edu
ZIMMERMAN, Brian 765-983-1256 155 A zimmebr@earlham.edu
ZIMMERMAN, Christine 315-229-5394 314 D christinezimmerman@stlawu.edu
ZIMMERMAN, Darin, T 843-953-7796 407 C dzimmer1@citadel.edu
ZIMMERMAN, Eileen, P 207-753-6970 194 A ezimmerm@bates.edu
ZIMMERMAN, Ellen 508-626-4582 213 A ezimmerman@framingham.edu
ZIMMERMAN, Gail 276-376-1004 472 E gzimmerman@uvawise.edu
ZIMMERMAN, Jean 269-467-9945 224 C jzimmerman@glenoaks.edu
ZIMMERMAN, Jeff 417-625-9703 256 F zimmerman-j@mssu.edu
ZIMMERMAN, Jill 661-722-6300 26 A jzimmerman@avc.edu
ZIMMERMAN, Joanna 281-476-1859 443 B joanna.zimmerman@sjcd.edu
ZIMMERMAN, Karen 928-536-6272 14 J karen.zimmerman@npc.edu
ZIMMERMAN, Kevin 507-344-7797 234 C kevin.zimmerman@blc.edu
ZIMMERMAN, Kris 713-221-5054 453 A zimmermank@uhd.edu
ZIMMERMAN, Matthew 509-335-0899 485 D
ZIMMERMAN, Melanie 828-327-7000 333 B mzimmerman@cvcc.edu
ZIMMERMAN, Michael 586-445-7159 227 B zimmermanm@macomb.edu
ZIMMERMAN, Michael, A 916-339-4360 53 C mzimmerman@mticollege.edu

Accreditation Index of Institutions by Regional, National, Professional and Specialized Agencies

Degree levels are shown by the following symbols: (C) diploma/certificate; (A) associate; (B) baccalaureate; (M) master's; (S) beyond master's but less than doctorate; (FP) first professional; (D) doctorate.

AA: Commission on Accreditation of Allied Health Education Programs: anesthesiologist assistant (M)

AAB: Aviation Accreditation Board International: aviation (A,B,M,D)

AAFCS: American Association of Family and Consumer Sciences: family and consumer science (B)

AAQEP: Association for Advancing Quality in Educator Preparation: professional educators (C,B,M)

ABAI: Association for Behavior Analysis International Accreditation Board: behavior analysis (M,D)

ABHES: Accrediting Bureau of Health Education Schools: allied health (C,A,B,M)

ACAE: Accreditation Commission for Audiology Education: audiology (D)

ACATE: Commission on Accreditation of Allied Health Education Programs: art therapy (M)

ACBSP: Accreditation Council for Business Schools and Programs: business administration, management, accounting and related business fields (A,B,M,D)

Alabama State University ... AL ... 4
Athens State University ... AL ... 4
Bishop State Community College ... AL ... 1
George Corley Wallace State Community College - Selma ... AL ... 2
Jefferson State Community College ... AL ... 2
Lawson State Community College ... AL ... 2
Miles College ... AL ... 6
Oakwood University ... AL ... 6
Troy University ... AL ... 7
University of Mobile ... AL ... 8
University of West Alabama, The ... AL ... 9
Wallace State Community College - Hanceville ... AL ... 3
#University of Alaska Southeast ... AK ... 10
American InterContinental University ... AZ ... 10
Grand Canyon University ... AZ ... 12
Northern Arizona University ... AZ ... 14
University of Phoenix ... AZ ... 16
Cossatot Community College of the University of Arkansas ... AR ... 22
Harding University Main Campus ... AR ... 19
John Brown University ... AR ... 19
National Park College ... AR ... 20
North Arkansas College ... AR ... 20
NorthWest Arkansas Community College AR ... 20
Philander Smith College ... AR ... 20
Phillips Community College of the University of Arkansas ... AR ... 22
University of Arkansas at Pine Bluff ... AR ... 22
Alliant International University-San Diego CA ... 24
Biola University ... CA ... 27
California Baptist University ... CA ... 27
California Lutheran University ... CA ... 29
California Southern University ... CA ... 29
California State University Channel Islands ... CA ... 30
International Technological University ... CA ... 46
Mount Saint Mary's University ... CA ... 52
Northcentral University ... CA ... 54
Notre Dame de Namur University ... CA ... 54
Point Loma Nazarene University ... CA ... 57
Riverside City College ... CA ... 59
San Diego Miramar College ... CA ... 61
Skyline College ... CA ... 62
University of Redlands ... CA ... 72
Westcliff University ... CA ... 75
Woodbury University ... CA ... 76
Colorado State University Global ... CO ... 80
Colorado Technical University ... CO ... 80
Post University ... CT ... 88
Tunxis Community College ... CT ... 87
University of Bridgeport ... CT ... 89
Goldey-Beacom College ... DE ... 91
Gallaudet University ... DC ... 92
Strayer University ... DC ... 93
University of the District of Columbia ... DC ... 94
Bethune Cookman University ... FL ... 96
Embry-Riddle Aeronautical University-Daytona Beach ... FL ... 99
Florida Agricultural and Mechanical University ... FL ... 109
Florida Memorial University ... FL ... 100
Florida State College at Jacksonville ... FL ... 101
Keiser University ... FL ... 103
Palm Beach State College ... FL ... 105
Saint Leo University ... FL ... 107
Seminole State College of Florida ... FL ... 108
Southeastern University ... FL ... 108
Albany State University ... GA .. 114
Athens Technical College ... GA .. 115
Atlanta Metropolitan State College ... GA .. 115
Brenau University ... GA .. 116
LaGrange College ... GA .. 122
Piedmont University ... GA .. 124
South University ... GA .. 125
West Georgia Technical College ... GA .. 128
Kapiolani Community College ... HI ... 129
University of Hawaii - West Oahu ... HI ... 129
College of Western Idaho ... ID ... 131
Northwest Nazarene University ... ID ... 132
Chicago State University ... IL ... 134
City Colleges of Chicago Harold Washington College ... IL ... 135
#Concordia University Chicago ... IL ... 136
DeVry University - Chicago Campus ... IL ... 137
Harper College ... IL ... 138
Joliet Junior College ... IL ... 141
Lewis University ... IL ... 142
Millikin University ... IL ... 144
Northwestern College ... IL ... 146
Roosevelt University ... IL ... 148
Trinity Christian College ... IL ... 151
Triton College ... IL ... 151
University of St. Francis ... IL ... 152
Anderson University ... IN ... 153
Indiana University East ... IN ... 157
Indiana Wesleyan University ... IN ... 158
Ivy Tech Community College of Indiana-Indianapolis ... IN ... 158
Purdue University Global ... IN ... 160
Taylor University ... IN ... 161
Trine University ... IN ... 161
University of Indianapolis ... IN ... 161
University of Saint Francis ... IN ... 162
Vincennes University ... IN ... 162
St. Ambrose University ... IA ... 169
Baker University ... KS .. 171
Johnson County Community College ... KS .. 174
Kansas City Kansas Community College KS .. 175
MidAmerica Nazarene University ... KS .. 176
Neosho County Community College ... KS .. 176
Ottawa University ... KS .. 176
Pratt Community College ... KS .. 177
Kentucky State University ... KY .. 183
Thomas More University ... KY .. 185
West Kentucky Community and Technical College ... KY .. 183
Baton Rouge Community College ... LA ... 187
Delgado Community College ... LA ... 188
Dillard University ... LA ... 186
L.E. Fletcher Technical Community College ... LA ... 188
Louisiana College ... LA ... 187
Louisiana State University at Alexandria . LA ... 189
Louisiana State University at Eunice ... LA ... 189
Xavier University of Louisiana ... LA ... 193
Kennebec Valley Community College ... ME .. 195
Northern Maine Community College ... ME .. 195
University of New England ... ME .. 197
Baltimore City Community College ... MD .. 198
Bowie State University ... MD .. 204
College of Southern Maryland ... MD .. 198
Community College of Baltimore County, The ... MD .. 198
Coppin State University ... MD .. 204
Hood College ... MD .. 199
Notre Dame of Maryland University ... MD .. 201
Lasell University ... MA .. 211
Lesley University ... MA .. 211
Regis College ... MA .. 218
Cornerstone University ... MI ... 223
Ferris State University ... MI ... 224
Kettering University ... MI ... 226
Lake Superior State University ... MI ... 226
Madonna University ... MI ... 227
Mott Community College ... MI ... 228
Northwood University ... MI ... 229
Walsh College of Accountancy and Business Administration ... MI ... 232
Anoka-Ramsey Community College ... MN .. 237
#Augsburg University ... MN .. 234
Bethel University ... MN .. 234
Capella University ... MN .. 234
Hennepin Technical College ... MN .. 238
Inver Hills Community College ... MN .. 238
Metropolitan State University ... MN .. 238
Normandale Community College ... MN .. 239
North Hennepin Community College ... MN .. 240
Rochester Community and Technical College ... MN .. 240
St. Catherine University ... MN .. 243
Saint Paul College-A Community & Technical College ... MN .. 241
University of Minnesota-Crookston ... MN .. 244
Walden University ... MN .. 244
Alcorn State University ... MS .. 245
Delta State University ... MS .. 245
Jones County Junior College ... MS .. 246
Mississippi University for Women ... MS .. 248
Mississippi Valley State University ... MS .. 248
Evangel University ... MO . 253
Fontbonne University ... MO . 253
Harris-Stowe State University ... MO . 254
Lincoln University ... MO . 254
Lindenwood University ... MO . 254
Maryville University of Saint Louis ... MO . 255
Missouri Southern State University ... MO . 256
Northwest Missouri State University ... MO . 257
Park University ... MO . 258
Ranken Technical College ... MO . 258
Southwest Baptist University ... MO . 259
Webster University ... MO . 262
Westminster College ... MO . 262
William Woods University ... MO . 262
Chadron State College ... NE .. 268
Metropolitan Community College ... NE .. 267
Southeast Community College ... NE .. 269
College of Southern Nevada ... NV .. 270
Colby-Sawyer College ... NH .. 272
Great Bay Community College ... NH .. 272
Manchester Community College ... NH .. 272
Nashua Community College ... NH .. 272
Plymouth State University ... NH .. 275
River Valley Community College ... NH .. 273
Rivier University ... NH .. 273
Southern New Hampshire University ... NH .. 274
Caldwell University ... NJ ... 276
County College of Morris ... NJ ... 276
Essex County College ... NJ ... 277
Georgian Court University ... NJ ... 278
New Jersey City University ... NJ ... 279
Rowan College of South Jersey ... NJ ... 281
Thomas Edison State University ... NJ ... 284
Central New Mexico Community College NM .. 285
Eastern New Mexico University Main Campus ... NM .. 286
Luna Community College ... NM .. 286
New Mexico Highlands University ... NM .. 286
New Mexico State University Dona Ana Community College ... NM .. 287
Northern New Mexico College ... NM .. 287
Western New Mexico University ... NM .. 289
City University of New York Bronx Community College ... NY .. 293
City University of New York Medgar Evers College ... NY .. 294
City University of New York Queensborough Community College ... NY .. 295
College of Mount Saint Vincent ... NY .. 296
College of Saint Rose, The ... NY .. 296
Fashion Institute of Technology ... NY .. 299
LIM College ... NY .. 304
Metropolitan College of New York ... NY .. 306
Monroe College ... NY .. 307
Orange County Community College ... NY .. 310
Sullivan County Community College ... NY .. 321
SUNY Morrisville ... NY .. 321
Utica College ... NY .. 324
Wagner College ... NY .. 324
Campbell University ... NC .. 327
Catawba College ... NC .. 327
Craven Community College ... NC .. 334
Gardner-Webb University ... NC .. 329
Gaston College ... NC .. 334
Greensboro College ... NC .. 329
Guilford College ... NC .. 329
Lenoir-Rhyne University ... NC .. 330
Methodist University ... NC .. 331
#Pfeiffer University ... NC .. 339
University of Mount Olive ... NC .. 340
Wingate University ... NC .. 344
Ashland University ... OH .. 347
Capital University ... OH .. 349
Cedarville University ... OH .. 349
Central Ohio Technical College ... OH .. 349
Central State University ... OH .. 349
Columbus State Community College ... OH .. 351
Heidelberg University ... OH .. 353
Hocking College ... OH .. 353
Malone University ... OH .. 355
#Mount St. Joseph University ... OH .. 356
Mount Vernon Nazarene University ... OH .. 356
North Central State College ... OH .. 357
Northwest State Community College ... OH .. 357
Ohio Dominican University ... OH .. 358
Owens Community College ... OH .. 359
Rhodes State College ... OH .. 360
Sinclair Community College ... OH .. 360
Stark State College ... OH .. 360
Tiffin University ... OH .. 361
University of Findlay, The ... OH .. 362
University of Mount Union ... OH .. 362
University of Northwestern Ohio ... OH .. 362
Zane State College ... OH .. 365
Cameron University ... OK .. 365
East Central University ... OK .. 365
Langston University ... OK .. 366
Northeastern State University ... OK .. 366
Northern Oklahoma College ... OK .. 366
Northwestern Oklahoma State University OK .. 367
Oklahoma Baptist University ... OK .. 367
Oklahoma Christian University ... OK .. 367
Oklahoma City Community College ... OK .. 367
Oral Roberts University ... OK .. 368
Southern Nazarene University ... OK .. 369
Southwestern Oklahoma State University. OK .. 370
George Fox University ... OR .. 373
#Pacific University ... OR .. 375
Southern Oregon University ... OR .. 376
Alvernia University ... PA .. 378
Arcadia University ... PA .. 378
Bucks County Community College ... PA .. 379
Butler County Community College ... PA .. 379
#Cabrini University ... PA .. 379
California University of Pennsylvania ... PA .. 393
Cedar Crest College ... PA .. 380
Delaware Valley University ... PA .. 382
DeSales University ... PA .. 382
#Eastern University ... PA .. 383
Edinboro University ... PA .. 394
Elizabethtown College ... PA .. 383
Gannon University ... PA .. 384
Geneva College ... PA .. 384
Grove City College ... PA .. 384
HACC, Central Pennsylvania's Community College ... PA .. 385
Holy Family University ... PA .. 385
Immaculata University ... PA .. 385
La Roche University ... PA .. 386
Lebanon Valley College ... PA .. 388
Lehigh Carbon Community College ... PA .. 388
Lock Haven University ... PA .. 394
Luzerne County Community College ... PA .. 389
Manor College ... PA .. 389
Mansfield University of Pennsylvania ... PA .. 394
Marywood University ... PA .. 389
Messiah University ... PA .. 389
Millersville University of Pennsylvania ... PA .. 395
Moravian College ... PA .. 390
Mount Aloysius College ... PA .. 390
Neumann University ... PA .. 391
Northampton Community College ... PA .. 391
Peirce College ... PA .. 391
Pennsylvania College of Technology ... PA .. 392
Saint Vincent College ... PA .. 397
Thomas Jefferson University ... PA .. 399
University of the Sciences in Philadelphia PA .. 401
Wilkes University ... PA .. 403
York College of Pennsylvania ... PA .. 403
Inter American University of Puerto Rico Bayamon Campus ... PR .. 508
Universidad Ana G. Mendez Carolina Campus ... PR .. 510
Universidad Ana G. Mendez Cupey Campus ... PR .. 510
University of Puerto Rico-Aguadilla ... PR .. 511
University of Puerto Rico at Arecibo ... PR .. 511
University of Puerto Rico at Bayamon ... PR .. 512
University of Puerto Rico at Cayey ... PR .. 512
University of Puerto Rico at Ponce ... PR .. 513
University of Puerto Rico at Utuado ... PR .. 513
University of Puerto Rico-Carolina ... PR .. 512
University of Puerto Rico-Humacao ... PR .. 512
University of Puerto Rico-Mayaguez Campus ... PR .. 512
University of Puerto Rico-Rio Piedras Campus ... PR .. 513
Community College of Rhode Island ... RI ... 404
Aiken Technical College ... SC .. 406
Anderson University ... SC .. 406
Benedict College ... SC .. 406
Claflin University ... SC .. 407
Denmark Technical College ... SC .. 408
Greenville Technical College ... SC .. 409
Limestone University ... SC .. 410
Midlands Technical College ... SC .. 410
Morris College ... SC .. 410
Orangeburg-Calhoun Technical College .. SC .. 411

ACCSC: Accrediting Commission of Career Schools and Colleges: occupational, trade, and technical education (C,A,B,M)

ACFEI: American Culinary Federation, Inc.: culinary arts and culinary management (C,A,B)

ACICS: Accrediting Council for Independent Colleges and Schools: business and business related programs (C,A,B,M)

ACUP: Accreditation Commission for Acupuncture and Oriental Medicine: acupuncture (C,M,D)

ADNUR: Accreditation Commission for Education in Nursing: nursing (A)

New York City College of Technology/City University of New York .... NY .. 295
Niagara County Community College .... NY .. 309
Onondaga Community College .... NY .. 310
Orange County Community College .... NY .. 310
Phillips School of Nursing at Mount Sinai Beth Israel .... NY .. 311
Rockland Community College .... NY .. 312
St. Elizabeth College of Nursing .... NY .. 313
Saint Joseph's College, New York .... NY .. 314
Samaritan Hospital School of Nursing .... NY .. 314
State University of New York College of Technology at Delhi .... NY .. 320
Suffolk County Community College .... NY .. 321
SUNY Adirondack .... NY .. 320
SUNY Broome Community College .... NY .. 317
SUNY Canton-College of Technology .... NY .. 320
SUNY Corning Community College .... NY .. 320
SUNY Morrisville .... NY .. 321
Swedish Institute-College of Health Sciences .... NY .. 321
Tompkins Cortland Community College .. NY .. 322
Trocaire College .... NY .. 323
Ulster County Community College .... NY .. 323
Westchester Community College .... NY .. 325
Cabarrus College of Health Sciences .... NC .. 327
Caldwell Community College and Technical Institute .... NC .. 332
Cape Fear Community College .... NC .. 332
Carolinas College of Health Sciences .... NC .. 327
Carteret Community College .... NC .. 333
Catawba Valley Community College .... NC .. 333
Central Piedmont Community College .... NC .. 333
College of the Albemarle .... NC .. 333
Davidson-Davie Community College .... NC .. 334
Durham Technical Community College .... NC .. 334
Edgecombe Community College .... NC .. 334
Fayetteville Technical Community College .... NC .. 334
Gardner-Webb University .... NC .. 329
Gaston College .... NC .. 334
Johnston Community College .... NC .. 335
Mitchell Community College .... NC .. 336
Rowan-Cabarrus Community College .... NC .. 337
Sampson Community College .... NC .. 337
Wake Technical Community College .... NC .. 338
Wayne Community College .... NC .. 338
Western Piedmont Community College .... NC .. 339
Bismarck State College .... ND .. 346
Lake Region State College .... ND .. 346
North Dakota State College of Science .... ND .. 346
Aultman College of Nursing and Health Sciences .... OH .. 348
Central Ohio Technical College .... OH .. 349
Cincinnati State Technical and Community College .... OH .. 350
Clark State College .... OH .. 350
Columbus State Community College .... OH .. 351
Cuyahoga Community College .... OH .. 351
Edison State Community College .... OH .. 352
Fortis College .... OH .. 352
Good Samaritan College of Nursing and Health Science .... OH .. 353
Hocking College .... OH .. 353
Lakeland Community College .... OH .. 354
Lorain County Community College .... OH .. 355
Marion Technical College .... OH .. 355
Mercy College of Ohio .... OH .. 355
North Central State College .... OH .. 357
Northwest State Community College .... OH .. 357
Ohio University Main Campus .... OH .. 358
Owens Community College .... OH .. 359
Rhodes State College .... OH .. 360
Shawnee State University .... OH .. 360
Sinclair Community College .... OH .. 360
Southern State Community College .... OH .. 360
Stark State College .... OH .. 360
Terra State Community College .... OH .. 361
University of Cincinnati Blue Ash College. OH .. 362
University of Rio Grande .... OH .. 363
Carl Albert State College .... OK .. 365
Connors State College .... OK .. 365
Eastern Oklahoma State College .... OK .. 366
Murray State College .... OK .. 366
Northeastern Oklahoma Agricultural and Mechanical College .... OK .. 366
Northern Oklahoma College .... OK .. 366
Oklahoma City Community College .... OK .. 367
Oklahoma State University Institute of Technology-Okmulgee .... OK .. 368
Oklahoma State University - Oklahoma City .... OK .. 368
Redlands Community College .... OK .. 369
Rose State College .... OK .. 369
Seminole State College .... OK .. 369
Tulsa Community College .... OK .. 370
Central Oregon Community College .... OR .. 372
Chemeketa Community College .... OR .. 372
Portland Community College .... OR .. 375
Treasure Valley Community College .... OR .. 376
Bucks County Community College .... PA .. 379
Butler County Community College .... PA .. 379
Community College of Allegheny County PA .. 381
Community College of Beaver County .... PA .. 381
Community College of Philadelphia .... PA .. 381
Delaware County Community College .... PA .. 382
HACC, Central Pennsylvania's Community College .... PA .. 385
Harcum College .... PA .. 385
La Roche University .... PA .. 386
Lehigh Carbon Community College .... PA .. 388
Lock Haven University .... PA .. 394
Luzerne County Community College .... PA .. 389
Mercyhurst University .... PA .. 389
Montgomery County Community College PA .. 390
Mount Aloysius College .... PA .. 390
Northampton Community College .... PA .. 391
Pennsylvania College of Health Sciences PA .. 392
Pennsylvania College of Technology .... PA .. 392
Reading Area Community College .... PA .. 396
Westmoreland County Community College .... PA .. 402
Atenas College .... PR .. 505
Colegio Universitario de San Juan .... PR .. 506
EDP University of Puerto Rico .... PR .. 506
Inter American University of Puerto Rico / Metropolitan Campus .... PR .. 508
Inter American University of Puerto Rico Aguadilla Campus .... PR .. 507
National University College .... PR .. 509
Universidad Ana G. Mendez Carolina Campus .... PR .. 510
Universidad Ana G. Mendez Cupey Campus .... PR .. 510
University of Puerto Rico at Arecibo .... PR .. 511
Community College of Rhode Island .... RI 404
New England Institute of Technology .... RI 404
Aiken Technical College .... SC .. 406
Central Carolina Technical College .... SC .. 406
Florence - Darlington Technical College .. SC .. 409
Greenville Technical College .... SC .. 409
Horry-Georgetown Technical College .... SC .. 409
Midlands Technical College .... SC .. 410
Orangeburg-Calhoun Technical College .. SC .. 411
Piedmont Technical College .... SC .. 411
Spartanburg Community College .... SC .. 412
Technical College of the Lowcountry .... SC .. 412
Tri-County Technical College .... SC .. 412
Trident Technical College .... SC .. 412
York Technical College .... SC .. 414
Southeast Technical College .... SD .. 417
Chattanooga State Community College .. TN .. 424
Cleveland State Community College .... TN .. 424
Columbia State Community College .... TN .. 424
Dyersburg State Community College .... TN .. 424
Jackson State Community College .... TN .. 424
Lincoln Memorial University .... TN .. 421
Motlow State Community College .... TN .. 424
Nashville State Community College .... TN .. 424
Northeast State Community College .... TN .. 425
Pellissippi State Community College .... TN .. 425
Roane State Community College .... TN .. 425
Southern Adventist University .... TN .. 423
Southwest Tennessee Community College .... TN .. 425
Walters State Community College .... TN .. 425
Alvin Community College .... TX ... 429
Amarillo College .... TX ... 429
Austin Community College District .... TX ... 430
Baptist Health System School of Health Professions .... TX ... 430
Blinn College .... TX ... 431
Central Texas College .... TX ... 432
College of the Mainland .... TX ... 433
Collin College .... TX ... 433
Dallas College, Brookhaven Campus .... TX ... 434
Dallas College, El Centro Campus .... TX ... 434
Dallas College, Mountain View Campus .. TX ... 435
Del Mar College .... TX ... 435
El Paso Community College .... TX ... 436
Galveston College .... TX ... 436
Grayson College .... TX ... 436
Howard College .... TX ... 437
Kilgore College .... TX ... 438
Laredo College .... TX ... 438
Lee College .... TX ... 438
Lone Star College System .... TX ... 439
McLennan Community College .... TX ... 439
Navarro College .... TX ... 440
North Central Texas College .... TX ... 440
Odessa College .... TX ... 441
Panola College .... TX ... 441
Paris Junior College .... TX ... 441
San Antonio College .... TX ... 429
San Jacinto College Central .... TX ... 443
San Jacinto College South .... TX ... 443
South Plains College .... TX ... 443
South Texas College .... TX ... 443
Tarrant County College District .... TX ... 445
Temple College .... TX ... 445
Texarkana College .... TX ... 446
Trinity Valley Community College .... TX ... 451
Victoria College .... TX ... 457
Weatherford College .... TX ... 457
Ameritech College of Healthcare .... UT .. 458
Dixie State University .... UT .. 460
Salt Lake Community College .... UT .. 461
Snow College .... UT .. 461
Utah Valley University .... UT .. 460
Weber State University .... UT .. 461
Blue Ridge Community College .... VA .. 473
Dabney S. Lancaster Community College VA .. 473
Germanna Community College .... VA .. 473
J. Sargeant Reynolds Community College .... VA .. 474
John Tyler Community College .... VA .. 474
Lord Fairfax Community College .... VA .. 474
Mountain Empire Community College .... VA .. 474
Northern Virginia Community College .... VA .. 474
Patrick Henry Community College .... VA .. 474
Paul D. Camp Community College .... VA .. 474
Piedmont Virginia Community College .... VA .. 474
Rappahannock Community College .... VA .. 475
Riverside College of Health Careers .... VA .. 470
Southside College of Health Sciences .... VA .. 471
Southside Virginia Community College .... VA .. 475
Southwest Virginia Community College .... VA .. 475
Thomas Nelson Community College .... VA .. 475
Tidewater Community College .... VA .. 475
Virginia Highlands Community College .... VA .. 475
Virginia Western Community College .... VA .. 475
Wytheville Community College .... VA .. 476
Bellingham Technical College .... WA . 478
Big Bend Community College .... WA . 478
Clark College .... WA . 478
Columbia Basin College .... WA . 479
Everett Community College .... WA . 480
Grays Harbor College .... WA . 480
Highline College .... WA . 481
Lake Washington Institute of Technology WA . 481
Lower Columbia College .... WA . 481
Olympic College .... WA . 481
Pierce College District .... WA . 482
Seattle Central College .... WA . 483
Shoreline Community College .... WA . 484
Skagit Valley College .... WA . 484
Spokane Community College .... WA . 479
Tacoma Community College .... WA . 484
Walla Walla Community College .... WA . 485
Wenatchee Valley College .... WA . 485
Whatcom Community College .... WA . 486
Yakima Valley College .... WA . 486
Blue Ridge Community and Technical College .... WV . 488
Bluefield State College .... WV . 489
BridgeValley Community & Technical College .... WV . 488
Davis & Elkins College .... WV . 487
Eastern West Virginia Community and Technical College .... WV . 488
Fairmont State University .... WV . 489
Marshall University .... WV . 489
Southern West Virginia Community and Technical College .... WV . 488
University of Charleston .... WV . 487
West Virginia Northern Community College .... WV . 488
West Virginia University at Parkersburg .. WV . 490
Blackhawk Technical College .... WI ... 498
Chippewa Valley Technical College .... WI ... 498
Fox Valley Technical College .... WI ... 498
Gateway Technical College .... WI ... 498
Lakeshore Technical College .... WI ... 498
Madison Area Technical College .... WI ... 499
Mid-State Technical College .... WI ... 499
Milwaukee Area Technical College .... WI ... 499
Moraine Park Technical College .... WI ... 499
Nicolet Area Technical College .... WI ... 499
Northcentral Technical College .... WI ... 499
Northeast Wisconsin Technical College .. WI ... 499
Northwood Technical College .... WI ... 499
Southwest Wisconsin Technical College . WI ... 500
Waukesha County Technical College .... WI ... 500
Western Technical College .... WI ... 500
Casper College .... WY . 500
Central Wyoming College .... WY . 501
Laramie County Community College .... WY . 501
Northern Wyoming Community College District .... WY . 501
Northwest College .... WY . 501
Western Wyoming Community College ... WY . 501

AIJS: Association of Institutions of Jewish Studies: Jewish studies (C, A,B)

Women's Institute of Torah Seminary .... MD .. 205
Bais Medrash Mayan Hatorah .... NJ ... 275
Rabbinical Seminary M'kor Chaim .... NJ ... 280
Yeshiva Bais Aharon .... NJ ... 285
Yeshiva Chemdas Hatorah .... NJ ... 285
Yeshiva Gedolah Keren Hatorah .... NJ ... 285
Yeshiva Gedolah Tiferes Boruch .... NJ ... 285
Yeshivas Be'er Yitzchok .... NJ ... 285
Bais Medrash Ateres Shlomo .... NY .. 290
Central Yeshiva Tomchei Tmimim Lubavitch America .... NY .. 292
Mechon L'Hoyroa .... NY .. 305
Mesivta Torah Vodaath Seminary .... NY .. 306
Yeshiva Ohr Naftoli .... NY .. 325
Yeshiva Shaarei Tōrah of Rockland .... NY .. 326
Yeshivath Zichron Moshe .... NY .. 326

ANEST: Council on Accreditation of Nurse Anesthesia Educational Programs: nurse anesthesia (C, M,D)

Samford University .... AL 6
University of Alabama at Birmingham .... AL 8
University of Mobile .... AL 8
University of Arizona .... AZ 16
Arkansas State University-Jonesboro .... AR 17
University of Arkansas for Medical Sciences .... AR 22
California State University-Fullerton .... CA 31
Loma Linda University .... CA 48
National University .... CA 53
Samuel Merritt University .... CA 60
University of Southern California .... CA 73
Central Connecticut State University .... CT 85
Fairfield University .... CT 87
Quinnipiac University .... CT 88
Georgetown University .... DC 92
AdventHealth University .... FL 95
Barry University .... FL 96
Florida Gulf Coast University .... FL ... 109
Florida International University .... FL ... 110
Florida State University .... FL ... 110
University of Miami .... FL ... 113
University of North Florida .... FL ... 111
University of South Florida .... FL ... 111
Augusta University .... GA .. 116
Emory University .... GA .. 118
DePaul University .... IL ... 136
Millikin University .... IL ... 144
Rosalind Franklin University of Medicine & Science .... IL ... 148
Rush University .... IL ... 148
Southern Illinois University Edwardsville . IL ... 150
Marian University .... IN ... 159
University of Evansville .... IN ... 161
University of Saint Francis .... IN ... 162
University of Iowa .... IA ... 163
Newman University .... KS .. 176

ARCPA: Accreditation Review Commission on Education for the Physician Assistant: physician assisting programs (A,B,M)

ART: National Association of Schools of Art and Design: art and design (C,A,B,M,D)

- Radford University ... VA .. 469
- Virginia Commonwealth University ... VA .. 473
- Virginia Polytechnic Institute and State University ... VA .. 476
- Virginia State University ... VA .. 476
- Cornish College of the Arts ... WA .. 479
- Western Washington University ... WA .. 485
- Shepherd University ... WV .. 490
- West Virginia University ... WV .. 490
- Milwaukee Institute of Art & Design ... WI ... 494
- University of Wisconsin-Green Bay ... WI ... 495
- University of Wisconsin-Madison ... WI ... 495
- University of Wisconsin-Milwaukee ... WI ... 496
- University of Wisconsin-Stevens Point ... WI ... 497
- University of Wisconsin-Stout ... WI ... 497
- University of Wisconsin-Whitewater ... WI ... 497
- Casper College ... WY .. 500
- Northwest College ... WY .. 501

AT: Commission on Accreditation of Allied Health Education Programs: anesthesia technology (A)

- #College of DuPage ... IL 135
- Wayne County Community College District ... MI ... 232
- Milwaukee Area Technical College ... WI ... 499

ATECH: Commission on Accreditation of Allied Health Education Programs: assistive technology (C,M)

- University of Illinois at Chicago ... IL 151
- University of Pittsburgh ... PA .. 400
- University of Wisconsin-Milwaukee ... WI ... 496

AUD: American Speech-Language-Hearing Association: audiology (D)

- Auburn University ... AL 4
- @Samford University ... AL 6
- University of South Alabama ... AL 9
- Arizona State University ... AZ 10
- University of Arizona ... AZ 16
- University of Arkansas for Medical Sciences ... AR 22
- @California State University-Sacramento ... CA 32
- San Diego State University ... CA 33
- @San Jose State University ... CA 34
- University of California-San Diego ... CA 70
- University of the Pacific ... CA 71
- University of Colorado Boulder ... CO 84
- University of Northern Colorado ... CO 84
- University of Connecticut ... CT 89
- Gallaudet University ... DC 92
- Nova Southeastern University ... FL ... 105
- University of Florida ... FL ... 111
- University of South Florida ... FL ... 111
- Idaho State University ... ID ... 131
- Illinois State University ... IL 140
- Northern Illinois University ... IL 146
- Northwestern University ... IL 146
- Rush University ... IL 148
- University of Illinois Urbana-Champaign .. IL 152
- #Ball State University ... IN 153
- Indiana University Bloomington ... IN 156
- Purdue University Main Campus ... IN 160
- University of Iowa ... IA 163
- Wichita State University ... KS .. 178
- University of Louisville ... KY .. 186
- Louisiana State University Health Sciences Center-New Orleans ... LA ... 189
- Louisiana Tech University ... LA ... 192
- Towson University ... MD .. 204
- University of Maryland College Park ... MD .. 202
- University of Massachusetts ... MA .. 211
- Central Michigan University ... MI ... 222
- @Grand Valley State University ... MI ... 224
- Wayne State University ... MI ... 232
- Western Michigan University ... MI ... 233
- University of Minnesota ... MN .. 243
- University of Southern Mississippi ... MS .. 249
- Missouri State University ... MO .. 256
- Washington University in St. Louis ... MO .. 262
- University of Nebraska - Lincoln ... NE .. 269
- Montclair State University ... NJ ... 279
- Adelphi University ... NY .. 289
- City University of New York Brooklyn College ... NY .. 293
- City University of New York Graduate Center ... NY .. 293
- City University of New York Hunter College ... NY .. 294
- Hofstra University ... NY .. 301
- St. John's University ... NY .. 313
- Syracuse University ... NY .. 321
- University at Buffalo-SUNY ... NY .. 316
- East Carolina University ... NC .. 341
- University of North Carolina at Chapel Hill ... NC .. 342
- Kent State University Kent Campus ... OH .. 354
- Ohio State University Main Campus, The. OH .. 358
- Ohio University Main Campus ... OH .. 358
- University of Akron, Main Campus, The .. OH .. 361
- University of Cincinnati Main Campus ... OH .. 361
- Pacific University ... OR .. 375
- Bloomsburg University of Pennsylvania ... PA .. 393
- Salus University ... PA .. 398
- University of Pittsburgh ... PA .. 400
- University of Puerto Rico-Medical Sciences Campus ... PR .. 512
- University of South Dakota, The ... SD .. 416
- East Tennessee State University ... TN .. 419
- University of Memphis, The ... TN .. 426
- Vanderbilt University ... TN .. 428
- Lamar University ... TX .. 449
- Texas Tech University Health Sciences Center ... TX .. 451
- University of North Texas ... TX .. 453
- University of Texas at Austin ... TX .. 455
- University of Texas at Dallas, The ... TX .. 455
- University of Utah, The ... UT .. 459
- Utah State University ... UT .. 460
- James Madison University ... VA .. 468
- @Western Washington University ... WA .. 485
- West Virginia University ... WV .. 490
- University of Wisconsin-Madison ... WI ... 495
- University of Wisconsin-Stevens Point ... WI ... 497

BBT: Commission on Accreditation of Allied Health Education Programs: blood bank technology (C,M)

- Rush University ... IL 148
- University of Texas Medical Branch, The TX .. 456

BI: Association for Biblical Higher Education: bible college education (C,A,B,M,FP,D)

- Heritage Christian University ... AL 5
- Huntsville Bible College ... AL 5
- #Selma University ... AL 6
- Alaska Bible College ... AK 9
- Alaska Christian College ... AK 9
- Indian Bible College ... AZ 12
- Ecclesia College ... AR 19
- America Evangelical University ... CA 25
- Bethesda University of California ... CA 26
- Eternity Bible College ... CA 41
- @Ezra University ... CA 41
- Grace Mission University ... CA 43
- @Hayfield University ... CA 44
- Henry Appenzeller University ... CA 45
- Hope International University ... CA 45
- International Reformed University and Seminary ... CA 46
- Latin American Bible Institute ... CA 47
- Life Pacific University ... CA 48
- #Olivet University ... CA 55
- Presbyterian Theological Seminary in America ... CA 58
- Saint Photios Orthodox Theological Seminary ... CA 60
- SUM Bible College and Theological Seminary ... CA 67
- World Mission University ... CA 76
- Nazarene Bible College ... CO 82
- Hobe Sound Bible College ... FL ... 102
- Robert E. Webber Institute for Worship Studies, The ... FL ... 106
- South Florida Bible College ... FL ... 108
- Trinity College of Florida ... FL ... 112
- Beulah Heights University ... GA .. 116
- @Hudson Taylor University ... GA .. 121
- Luther Rice College and Seminary ... GA .. 122
- Pacific Rim Christian University ... HI 129
- Boise Bible College ... ID 130
- Lincoln Christian University ... IL 142
- Moody Bible Institute ... IL 144
- Faith Bible Seminary ... IN 155
- Horizon University ... IN 156
- Union Bible College ... IN 161
- Emmaus Bible College ... IA 166
- Faith Baptist Bible College and Seminary IA 166
- Barclay College ... KS .. 171
- Kansas Christian College ... KS .. 175
- Manhattan Christian College ... KS .. 176
- Clear Creek Baptist Bible College ... KY .. 180
- Kentucky Mountain Bible College ... KY .. 183
- Simmons College of Kentucky ... KY .. 184
- @Bridges Christian College ... LA 186
- Northpoint Bible College ... MA .. 218
- Grace Christian University ... MI 224
- Kuyper College ... MI 226
- Bethany Global University ... MN .. 234
- Bethlehem College & Seminary ... MN .. 234
- Oak Hills Christian College ... MN .. 242
- Southeastern Baptist College ... MS .. 249
- Baptist Bible College ... MO .. 250
- Brookes Bible College ... MO .. 250
- Calvary University ... MO .. 251
- @Carver Baptist Bible College, Institute & Theological Seminary ... MO .. 251
- Central Christian College of the Bible ... MO .. 251
- Heartland Christian College ... MO .. 254
- Midwest University ... MO .. 256
- Ozark Christian College ... MO .. 257
- Saint Louis Christian College ... MO .. 258
- Montana Bible College ... MT .. 263
- Yellowstone Christian College ... MT .. 265
- Summit Christian College ... NE .. 269
- Pillar College ... NJ 280
- Davis College ... NY .. 298
- Carolina Christian College ... NC .. 327
- Carolina College of Biblical Studies ... NC .. 327
- Lumbee River Christian College ... NC .. 331
- Manna University ... NC .. 331
- Trinity Bible College & Graduate School . ND .. 346
- Allegheny Wesleyan College ... OH .. 347
- God's Bible School and College ... OH .. 353
- Rosedale Bible College ... OH .. 360
- Tri-State Bible College ... OH .. 361
- Valor Christian College ... OH .. 363
- Family of Faith Christian University ... OK .. 366
- New Hope Christian College ... OR .. 374
- Pacific Bible College ... OR .. 375
- Cairn University ... PA .. 380
- Clarks Summit University ... PA .. 381
- Lancaster Bible College|Capital Seminary & Graduate School ... PA .. 387
- Universidad Pentecostal Mizpa ... PR .. 511
- Universidad Teologica Del Caribe ... PR .. 511
- Columbia International University ... SC .. 408
- Institute of Lutheran Theology ... SD .. 415
- @All Saints Bible College ... TN .. 417
- American Baptist College ... TN .. 417
- @Institute for G.O.D., The ... TN .. 420
- Johnson University ... TN .. 420
- Mid-South Christian College ... TN .. 422
- Welch College ... TN .. 428
- Williamson College ... TN .. 428
- Arlington Baptist University ... TX .. 430
- Baptist University of the Americas ... TX .. 431
- B.H. Carroll Theological Institute ... TX .. 431
- Christ Mission College ... TX .. 432
- College of Biblical Studies-Houston ... TX .. 432
- Dallas Christian College ... TX .. 434
- King's University, The ... TX .. 438
- @Regional Christian University ... TX .. 442
- Rio Grande Bible Institute ... TX .. 442
- @Southern Bible Institute and College ... TX .. 444
- @Southern Reformed College and Seminary ... TX ... 444
- Stark College & Seminary ... TX ... 445
- @Texas Baptist Institute and Seminary ... TX ... 448
- @Veritas College International Graduate School ... TX ... 457
- Ascent College ... VA .. 464
- Faith Bible College ... VA .. 467
- Virginia Christian University ... VA .. 473
- Wave Leadership College ... VA .. 477
- Appalachian Bible College ... WV .. 486

CAATE: Commission on Accreditation of Athletic Training Education: athletic training (B,M,D)

- Troy University ... AL 7
- University of Alabama, The ... AL 7
- University of West Alabama, The ... AL 9
- Grand Canyon University ... AZ 12
- Northern Arizona University ... AZ 14
- Arkansas State University-Jonesboro ... AR 17
- #Southern Arkansas University ... AR 21
- University of Arkansas Main Campus ... AR 21
- #University of Central Arkansas ... AR 23
- Azusa Pacific University ... CA 26
- California Baptist University ... CA 27
- California State University-Fullerton ... CA 31
- California State University-Long Beach ... CA 31
- #California State University-Northridge ... CA 32
- Point Loma Nazarene University ... CA 57
- San Diego State University ... CA 33
- San Jose State University ... CA 34
- #University of La Verne ... CA 71
- University of the Pacific ... CA 71
- Colorado Mesa University ... CO 78
- Metropolitan State University of Denver .. CO 81
- University of Colorado Colorado Springs . CO 84
- University of Northern Colorado ... CO 84
- Central Connecticut State University ... CT 85
- Quinnipiac University ... CT 88
- Sacred Heart University ... CT 89
- #Southern Connecticut State University ... CT 86
- University of Connecticut ... CT 89
- University of Delaware ... DE 91
- Barry University ... FL 96
- Bethune Cookman University ... FL 96
- Florida Gulf Coast University ... FL ... 109
- Florida International University ... FL ... 110
- Palm Beach Atlantic University ... FL ... 105
- University of Central Florida ... FL ... 110
- University of Miami ... FL ... 113
- University of North Florida ... FL ... 111
- University of South Florida ... FL ... 111
- University of Tampa ... FL ... 113
- #University of West Florida ... FL ... 111
- Emory University ... GA .. 118
- Georgia College & State University ... GA .. 119
- Georgia Southern University ... GA .. 120
- Mercer University ... GA .. 122
- #Piedmont University ... GA .. 124
- University of Georgia ... GA .. 126
- University of North Georgia ... GA .. 127
- Valdosta State University ... GA .. 127
- #University of Hawaii at Manoa ... HI 129
- Boise State University ... ID 130
- Idaho State University ... ID 131
- University of Idaho ... ID 132
- Aurora University ... IL 133
- #Eastern Illinois University ... IL 137
- Illinois State University ... IL 140
- McKendree University ... IL 144
- #Millikin University ... IL 144
- North Central College ... IL 145
- North Park University ... IL 145
- #Olivet Nazarene University ... IL 147
- University of Illinois Springfield ... IL 152
- #Anderson University ... IN 153
- Ball State University ... IN 153
- Franklin College of Indiana ... IN 155
- Indiana State University ... IN 156
- Indiana University Bloomington ... IN 156
- Indiana Wesleyan University ... IN 158
- Manchester University ... IN 159
- Purdue University Main Campus ... IN 160
- University of Evansville ... IN 161
- University of Indianapolis ... IN 161
- Central College ... IA 164
- Clarke University ... IA 164
- Drake University ... IA 165
- Grand View University ... IA 166
- Iowa State University ... IA 163
- Loras College ... IA 168
- #Luther College ... IA 168
- University of Iowa ... IA 163
- University of Northern Iowa ... IA 164
- Emporia State University ... KS .. 173
- Fort Hays State University ... KS .. 173
- Sterling College ... KS .. 177
- University of Saint Mary ... KS .. 178

CACREP: Council for Accreditation of Counseling & Related Educational Programs: counseling and its specialties (M,D)

CAEP: Council for the Accreditation of Educator Preparation: teacher education (B, M,D)

CAEPN: Council for the Accreditation of Educator Preparation: teacher education (B, M,D)

CAEPT: Council for the Accreditation of Educator Preparation: teacher education (B, M,D)

CAHIIM: Commission on Accreditation for Health Informatics and Information Management Education: health information management and health informatics (A,B,M)

Alabama State University — AL — 4
Bishop State Community College — AL — 1
Shelton State Community College — AL — 3
University of Alabama at Birmingham — AL — 8
Wallace State Community College - Hanceville — AL — 3
University of Alaska Southeast — AK — 10
Bryan University — AZ — 11
Central Arizona College — AZ — 11
Phoenix College — AZ — 13
Arkansas Tech University — AR — 18
National Park College — AR — 20
NorthWest Arkansas Community College — AR — 20
Bakersfield College — CA — 46
City College of San Francisco — CA — 36
Cosumnes River College — CA — 50
Cypress College — CA — 54
East Los Angeles College — CA — 48
Fresno City College — CA — 67
Loma Linda University — CA — 48
Saddleback College — CA — 65
San Diego Mesa College — CA — 60
Santa Barbara City College — CA — 63
Shasta College — CA — 64
University of Arizona Global Campus — CA — 68
Arapahoe Community College — CO — 77
Front Range Community College — CO — 81
Pueblo Community College — CO — 82
Regis University — CO — 83
Charter Oak State College — CT — 85
Middlesex Community College — CT — 87
Broward College — FL — 96
College of Central Florida — FL — 97
Daytona State College — FL — 98
Florida Agricultural and Mechanical University — FL — 109
Florida Gateway College — FL — 100
Florida International University — FL — 110
Florida SouthWestern State College — FL — 101
Florida State College at Jacksonville — FL — 101
Indian River State College — FL — 102
Keiser University — FL — 103
Miami Dade College — FL — 104
Nova Southeastern University — FL — 105
Palm Beach State College — FL — 105
Pensacola State College — FL — 105
St. Johns River State College — FL — 107
St. Petersburg College — FL — 107
Santa Fe College — FL — 108
Seminole State College of Florida — FL — 108
University of Central Florida — FL — 110
Valencia College — FL — 113
Albany State University — GA — 114
Athens Technical College — GA — 115
Atlanta Technical College — GA — 115
Augusta Technical College — GA — 115
Augusta University — GA — 116
Georgia Northwestern Technical College — GA — 120
Georgia Piedmont Technical College — GA — 120
Gwinnett Technical College — GA — 121
Lanier Technical College — GA — 122
Ogeechee Technical College — GA — 123
West Georgia Technical College — GA — 128
Wiregrass Georgia Technical College — GA — 128
University of Hawaii - Leeward Community College — HI — 130
Idaho State University — ID — 131
Blessing-Rieman College of Nursing & Health Sciences — IL — 133
Chicago State University — IL — 134
College of DuPage — IL — 135
College of Lake County — IL — 136
Danville Area Community College — IL — 136
DeVry University - Chicago Campus — IL — 137
Harper College — IL — 138
Illinois State University — IL — 140
Joliet Junior College — IL — 141
Malcolm X College, One of the City Colleges of Chicago — IL — 135
McHenry County College — IL — 143
Moraine Valley Community College — IL — 145
Northwestern College — IL — 146
Oak Point University — IL — 146
Oakton Community College — IL — 146
Richland Community College — IL — 148
Southern Illinois University Edwardsville — IL — 150
Southwestern Illinois College — IL — 150
University of Illinois at Chicago — IL — 151
Waubonsee Community College — IL — 152
Indiana Tech — IN — 156
Indiana University Northwest — IN — 157
Indiana University-Purdue University Indianapolis — IN — 157
Indiana University Southeast — IN — 157
Ivy Tech Community College of Indiana-Indianapolis — IN — 158
Purdue University Global — IN — 160
Vincennes University — IN — 162
Indian Hills Community College — IA — 166
Northeast Iowa Community College — IA — 169
Northwest Iowa Community College — IA — 169
Scott Community College — IA — 166
Hutchinson Community College — KS — 174
Neosho County Community College — KS — 176
University of Saint Mary — KS — 178
Washburn University — KS — 178
Eastern Kentucky University — KY — 180
Gateway Community and Technical College — KY — 181
Jefferson Community and Technical College — KY — 182
Sullivan University — KY — 185
Western Kentucky University — KY — 186
Delgado Community College — LA — 188
Louisiana Tech University — LA — 192
Southern University at New Orleans — LA — 191
Southern University at Shreveport-Louisiana — LA — 191
University of Louisiana at Lafayette — LA — 193
Beal University — ME — 194
Kennebec Valley Community College — ME — 195
Saint Joseph's College of Maine — ME — 196
Baltimore City Community College — MD — 198
Community College of Baltimore County, The — MD — 198
Coppin State University — MD — 204
Montgomery College — MD — 200
Prince George's Community College — MD — 201
University of Maryland Global Campus — MD — 203
Boston University — MA — 207
Bristol Community College — MA — 214
Fisher College — MA — 209
Springfield Technical Community College — MA — 216
Davenport University — MI — 223
Ferris State University — MI — 224
Grand Valley State University — MI — 224
Macomb Community College — MI — 227
Schoolcraft College — MI — 230
Southwestern Michigan College — MI — 231
University of Detroit Mercy — MI — 231
Anoka Technical College — MN — 237
College of Saint Scholastica, The — MN — 235
Minnesota State Community and Technical College — MN — 239
Rasmussen University - St. Cloud — MN — 242
Ridgewater College — MN — 240
Rochester Community and Technical College — MN — 240
Saint Cloud Technical and Community College — MN — 241
Saint Paul College-A Community & Technical College — MN — 241
Hinds Community College — MS — 246
Itawamba Community College — MS — 246
Meridian Community College — MS — 247
Southwest Mississippi Community College — MS — 249
University of Mississippi Medical Center — MS — 249
William Carey University — MS — 249
East Central College — MO — 253
Jefferson College — MO — 254
Metropolitan Community College - Penn Valley — MO — 255
Missouri Western State University — MO — 257
Ozarks Technical Community College — MO — 257
St. Charles Community College — MO — 258
Saint Louis University — MO — 259
State Fair Community College — MO — 259
Stephens College — MO — 260
Great Falls College Montana State University — MT — 264
Central Community College — NE — 266
Clarkson College — NE — 266
Metropolitan Community College — NE — 267
Northeast Community College — NE — 268
Western Nebraska Community College — NE — 270
College of Southern Nevada — NV — 270
Manchester Community College — NH — 272
Southern New Hampshire University — NH — 274
Camden County College — NJ — 276
Passaic County Community College — NJ — 280
Raritan Valley Community College — NJ — 281
Rowan College at Burlington County — NJ — 281
Central New Mexico Community College — NM — 285
San Juan College — NM — 288
Alfred State College — NY — 319
City University of New York Borough of Manhattan Community College — NY — 293
City University of New York Graduate Center — NY — 293
Erie Community College — NY — 299
Medaille College — NY — 305
Mohawk Valley Community College — NY — 306
Monroe Community College — NY — 307
Nassau Community College — NY — 307
Onondaga Community College — NY — 310
Plaza College — NY — 311
Suffolk County Community College — NY — 321
SUNY Broome Community College — NY — 317
SUNY Polytechnic Institute — NY — 321
Trocaire College — NY — 323
Brunswick Community College — NC — 332
Catawba Valley Community College — NC — 333
Central Carolina Community College — NC — 333
Central Piedmont Community College — NC — 333
Craven Community College — NC — 334
Davidson-Davie Community College — NC — 334
Durham Technical Community College — NC — 334
East Carolina University — NC — 341
Edgecombe Community College — NC — 334
Forsyth Technical Community College — NC — 334
Guilford Technical Community College — NC — 335
McDowell Technical Community College — NC — 336
Pitt Community College — NC — 336
Southwestern Community College — NC — 338
North Dakota State College of Science — ND — 346
Cincinnati State Technical and Community College — OH — 350
Columbus State Community College — OH — 351
Cuyahoga Community College — OH — 351
Eastern Gateway Community College - Jefferson County Campus — OH — 352
Franklin University — OH — 352
Lakeland Community College — OH — 354
Marion Technical College — OH — 355
Mercy College of Ohio — OH — 355
Ohio State University Main Campus, The — OH — 358
Owens Community College — OH — 359
Sinclair Community College — OH — 360
Stark State College — OH — 360
Terra State Community College — OH — 361
University of Cincinnati-Clermont College — OH — 362
University of Cincinnati Main Campus — OH — 361
University of Northwestern Ohio — OH — 362
University of Toledo — OH — 363
Zane State College — OH — 365
Rose State College — OK — 369
Southwestern Oklahoma State University — OK — 370
Tulsa Community College — OK — 370
Central Oregon Community College — OR — 372
Chemeketa Community College — OR — 372
Lane Community College — OR — 373
Oregon Health & Science University — OR — 374
Portland Community College — OR — 375
Community College of Allegheny County — PA — 381
Drexel University — PA — 382
Lehigh Carbon Community College — PA — 388
Peirce College — PA — 391
Pennsylvania College of Technology — PA — 392
Slippery Rock University of Pennsylvania — PA — 395
South Hills School of Business and Technology — PA — 398
Temple University — PA — 399
University of Pittsburgh — PA — 400
Huertas College — PR — 507
University of Puerto Rico-Medical Sciences Campus — PR — 512
Florence - Darlington Technical College — SC — 409
Greenville Technical College — SC — 409
Medical University of South Carolina — SC — 410
Trident Technical College — SC — 412
University of South Carolina Columbia — SC — 413
University of South Carolina Upstate — SC — 414
Dakota State University — SD — 416
National American University — SD — 415
Chattanooga State Community College — TN — 424
Concorde Career College — TN — 419
Dyersburg State Community College — TN — 424
Roane State Community College — TN — 425
Tennessee State University — TN — 426
Volunteer State Community College — TN — 425
Walters State Community College — TN — 425
Austin Community College District — TX — 430
Blinn College — TX — 431
College of the Mainland — TX — 433
Collin College — TX — 433
Del Mar College — TX — 435
El Paso Community College — TX — 436
Houston Community College — TX — 437
Lamar Institute of Technology — TX — 449
Lee College — TX — 438
Lone Star College System — TX — 439
McLennan Community College — TX — 439
Midland College — TX — 440
Panola College — TX — 441
Parker University — TX — 441
St. Philip's College — TX — 429
San Jacinto College North — TX — 443
South Texas College — TX — 443
Tarrant County College District — TX — 445
Texas Southern University — TX — 449
Texas State Technical College Waco — TX — 449
Texas State University — TX — 450
Tyler Junior College — TX — 452
University of Texas Health Science Center at Houston (UTHealth), The — TX — 456
Wharton County Junior College — TX — 458
Weber State University — UT — 461
Western Governors University — UT — 461
American National University — VA — 464
George Mason University — VA — 467
Lord Fairfax Community College — VA — 474
Mountain Empire Community College — VA — 474
Northern Virginia Community College — VA — 474
Tidewater Community College — VA — 475
Shoreline Community College — WA — 484
Spokane Community College — WA — 479
Tacoma Community College — WA — 484
University of Washington — WA — 485
American Public University System — WV — 486
Blue Ridge Community and Technical College — WV — 488
Marshall University — WV — 489
Mountwest Community and Technical College — WV — 488
Pierpont Community & Technical College — WV — 488
West Virginia Northern Community College — WV — 488
Chippewa Valley Technical College — WI — 498
Fox Valley Technical College — WI — 498
Gateway Technical College — WI — 498
Lakeshore Technical College — WI — 498
Mid-State Technical College — WI — 499
Milwaukee Area Technical College — WI — 499
Moraine Park Technical College — WI — 499
Northeast Wisconsin Technical College — WI — 499
Northwood Technical College — WI — 499
Southwest Wisconsin Technical College — WI — 500
University of Wisconsin-Green Bay — WI — 495
University of Wisconsin-Parkside — WI — 496
University of Wisconsin-Stevens Point — WI — 497
Waukesha County Technical College — WI — 500
Western Technical College — WI — 500
Laramie County Community College — WY — 501

CAMPEP: Commission on Accreditation of Medical Physics Education Programs, Inc.: medical physics (C,M,D)

University of Alabama at Birmingham — AL — 8
University of Arizona — AZ — 16
University of Arkansas at Little Rock — AR — 22
Loma Linda University — CA — 48
San Diego State University — CA — 33
Stanford University — CA — 66
University of California-Davis — CA — 69

University of California-Irvine ... CA ... 69
University of California-Los Angeles ... CA ... 69
University of California-San Diego ... CA ... 70
University of California-San Francisco ... CA ... 70
University of Colorado Denver I Anschutz Medical Campus ... CO ... 84
Yale University ... CT ... 90
Georgetown University ... DC ... 92
Florida Atlantic University ... FL ... 109
University of Florida ... FL ... 111
University of Miami ... FL ... 113
University of South Florida ... FL ... 111
Augusta University ... GA ... 116
#Emory University ... GA ... 118
Georgia Institute of Technology ... GA ... 119
Loyola University Chicago ... IL ... 143
Rush University ... IL ... 148
University of Chicago ... IL ... 151
Indiana University-Purdue University Indianapolis ... IN ... 157
Purdue University Main Campus ... IN ... 160
University of Iowa ... IA ... 163
University of Kentucky ... KY ... 185
University of Louisville ... KY ... 186
Louisiana State University and Agricultural and Mechanical College ... LA ... 189
Johns Hopkins University ... MD ... 199
University of Maryland, Baltimore ... MD ... 203
Harvard University ... MA ... 210
University of Massachusetts Lowell ... MA ... 212
University of Michigan-Ann Arbor ... MI ... 231
Wayne State University ... MI ... 232
University of Minnesota ... MN ... 243
Creighton University ... NE ... 266
University of Nebraska Medical Center ... NE ... 269
University of Nevada, Las Vegas ... NV ... 271
Dartmouth College ... NH ... 273
University of New Mexico Main Campus ... NM ... 288
Columbia University in the City of New York ... NY ... 297
Hofstra University ... NY ... 301
Icahn School of Medicine at Mount Sinai ... NY ... 302
New York University ... NY ... 309
Stony Brook University ... NY ... 317
University at Buffalo-SUNY ... NY ... 316
Duke University ... NC ... 328
East Carolina University ... NC ... 341
University of North Carolina at Chapel Hill ... NC ... 342
Case Western Reserve University ... OH ... 349
Cleveland State University ... OH ... 350
Ohio State University Main Campus, The ... OH ... 358
University of Cincinnati Main Campus ... OH ... 361
University of Toledo ... OH ... 363
Oregon Health & Science University ... OR ... 374
Thomas Jefferson University ... PA ... 399
University of Pennsylvania ... PA ... 400
University of Pittsburgh ... PA ... 400
Brown University ... RI ... 403
University of Rhode Island ... RI ... 405
Medical University of South Carolina ... SC ... 410
University of Tennessee, Knoxville ... TN ... 427
Vanderbilt University ... TN ... 428
University of Texas Health Science Center at Houston (UTHealth), The ... TX ... 456
University of Texas Health Science Center at San Antonio ... TX ... 456
University of Texas MD Anderson Cancer Center, The ... TX ... 456
University of Texas Southwestern Medical Center ... TX ... 457
University of Utah, The ... UT ... 459
University of Virginia ... VA ... 472
Virginia Commonwealth University ... VA ... 473
University of Washington ... WA ... 485
Medical College of Wisconsin ... WI ... 493
University of Wisconsin-Madison ... WI ... 495

CAPRT: Council on Accreditation of Parks, Recreation, Tourism and Related Professions: recreation, park resources, and leisure studies (B)

Arizona State University ... AZ ... 10
Northern Arizona University ... AZ ... 14
Arkansas Tech University ... AR ... 18
California Polytechnic State University-San Luis Obispo ... CA ... 29
California State University-Chico ... CA ... 30
California State University-Fresno ... CA ... 31
California State University-Long Beach ... CA ... 31
California State University-Northridge ... CA ... 32
California State University-Sacramento ... CA ... 32
San Francisco State University ... CA ... 33
San Jose State University ... CA ... 34
Georgia Southern University ... GA ... 120
University of Idaho ... ID ... 132
Chicago State University ... IL ... 134
Eastern Illinois University ... IL ... 137
Illinois State University ... IL ... 140
University of St. Francis ... IL ... 152
Western Illinois University ... IL ... 153
Indiana University Bloomington ... IN ... 156
University of Northern Iowa ... IA ... 164
Pittsburg State University ... KS ... 177
Eastern Kentucky University ... KY ... 180
Western Kentucky University ... KY ... 186
Grambling State University ... LA ... 192
Frostburg State University ... MD ... 204
Springfield College ... MA ... 218
Central Michigan University ... MI ... 222
Minnesota State University, Mankato ... MN ... 239
University of Mississippi ... MS ... 249
Missouri State University ... MO ... 256
Northwest Missouri State University ... MO ... 257
Southeast Missouri State University ... MO ... 259
University of Missouri - Columbia ... MO ... 261
University of New Hampshire ... NH ... 274
Ithaca College ... NY ... 302
Saint Joseph's College, New York ... NY ... 314
State University of New York College at Cortland ... NY ... 318
State University of New York, The College at Brockport ... NY ... 317
Appalachian State University ... NC ... 340
East Carolina University ... NC ... 341
North Carolina Central University ... NC ... 341
North Carolina State University ... NC ... 342
University of North Carolina at Greensboro ... NC ... 343
Winston-Salem State University ... NC ... 344
Kent State University Kent Campus ... OH ... 354
Ohio University Main Campus ... OH ... 358
University of Toledo ... OH ... 363
California University of Pennsylvania ... PA ... 393
Lock Haven University ... PA ... 394
Temple University ... PA ... 399
York College of Pennsylvania ... PA ... 403
Clemson University ... SC ... 407
Middle Tennessee State University ... TN ... 422
University of Tennessee, Knoxville ... TN ... 427
Texas State University ... TX ... 450
Brigham Young University ... UT ... 458
University of Utah, The ... UT ... 459
George Mason University ... VA ... 467
Longwood University ... VA ... 468
Old Dominion University ... VA ... 469
Radford University ... VA ... 469
Virginia Wesleyan University ... VA ... 477
Eastern Washington University ... WA ... 479
Western Washington University ... WA ... 485
Shepherd University ... WV ... 490
University of Wisconsin-La Crosse ... WI ... 496

CARTE: Commission on Accreditation of Recreational Therapy Education: recreational therapy (B,M)

Grand Valley State University ... MI ... 224
University of New Hampshire ... NH ... 274
East Carolina University ... NC ... 341
University of North Carolina Wilmington ... NC ... 343
Western Carolina University ... NC ... 343
Oklahoma State University ... OK ... 367
Slippery Rock University of Pennsylvania ... PA ... 395
Temple University ... PA ... 399
Clemson University ... SC ... 407

CEA: Commission on English Language Program Accreditation: english language (C)

University of Alabama at Birmingham ... AL ... 8
University of Alabama, The ... AL ... 7
University of Arizona ... AZ ... 16
Arkansas State University-Jonesboro ... AR ... 17
California State Polytechnic University-Pomona ... CA ... 30
California State University-Long Beach ... CA ... 31
Grossmont College ... CA ... 44
Learnet Academy ... CA ... 47
Los Angeles Pacific College ... CA ... 50
Northwestern Polytechnic University ... CA ... 54
San Jose State University ... CA ... 34
University of California-Irvine ... CA ... 69
University of California-San Diego ... CA ... 70
University of San Diego ... CA ... 72
University of the Pacific ... CA ... 71
Colorado State University ... CO ... 79
University of Colorado Boulder ... CO ... 84
University of Denver ... CO ... 84
University of Northern Colorado ... CO ... 84
Sacred Heart University ... CT ... 89
University of Connecticut ... CT ... 89
University of Delaware ... DE ... 91
Gallaudet University ... DC ... 92
Georgetown University ... DC ... 92
Atlantis University ... FL ... 95
Aviator College of Aeronautical Science & Technology ... FL ... 95
Embry-Riddle Aeronautical University-Daytona Beach ... FL ... 99
Florida State University ... FL ... 110
Full Sail University ... FL ... 101
Saint Leo University ... FL ... 107
St. Petersburg College ... FL ... 107
University of Central Florida ... FL ... 110
University of Florida ... FL ... 111
University of Miami ... FL ... 113
University of South Florida ... FL ... 111
Valencia College ... FL ... 113
Georgia Central University ... GA ... 119
Georgia Institute of Technology ... GA ... 119
Georgia State University ... GA ... 120
Mercer University ... GA ... 122
University of Georgia ... GA ... 126
University of Hawaii at Manoa ... HI ... 129
University of Idaho ... ID ... 132
Illinois Institute of Technology ... IL ... 140
Midwestern Career College ... IL ... 144
Southern Illinois University Carbondale ... IL ... 150
University of Illinois at Chicago ... IL ... 151
University of Illinois Urbana-Champaign ... IL ... 152
Western Illinois University ... IL ... 153
Ball State University ... IN ... 153
Indiana University Bloomington ... IN ... 156
Purdue University Northwest ... IN ... 160
Taylor University ... IN ... 161
University of Southern Indiana ... IN ... 162
Iowa State University ... IA ... 163
University of Iowa ... IA ... 163
University of Northern Iowa ... IA ... 164
Emporia State University ... KS ... 173
Kansas State University ... KS ... 175
Pittsburg State University ... KS ... 177
University of Kansas Main Campus ... KS ... 177
Washburn University ... KS ... 178
Mount St. Mary's University ... MD ... 201
Notre Dame of Maryland University ... MD ... 201
University of Maryland College Park ... MD ... 202
Boston University ... MA ... 207
Bunker Hill Community College ... MA ... 214
Middlesex Community College ... MA ... 215
Central Michigan University ... MI ... 222
Eastern Michigan University ... MI ... 223
Michigan State University ... MI ... 227
Saginaw Valley State University ... MI ... 230
University of Michigan-Dearborn ... MI ... 231
Wayne State University ... MI ... 232
Western Michigan University ... MI ... 233
University of Minnesota ... MN ... 243
University of Mississippi ... MS ... 249
Missouri State University ... MO ... 256
Missouri University of Science & Technology ... MO ... 261
St. Charles Community College ... MO ... 258
Saint Louis University ... MO ... 259
Southeast Missouri State University ... MO ... 259
University of Central Missouri ... MO ... 260
University of Missouri - Columbia ... MO ... 261
University of Missouri - Kansas City ... MO ... 261
College of Southern Nevada ... NV ... 270
Rutgers University - New Brunswick ... NJ ... 282
Columbia University in the City of New York ... NY ... 297
Rochester Institute of Technology ... NY ... 312
Durham Technical Community College ... NC ... 334
East Carolina University ... NC ... 341
University of North Carolina at Charlotte ... NC ... 342
University of North Carolina Wilmington ... NC ... 343
Cleveland State University ... OH ... 350
Ohio University Main Campus ... OH ... 358
University of Dayton ... OH ... 362
University of Findlay, The ... OH ... 362
University of Toledo ... OH ... 363
Oregon State University ... OR ... 375
Portland State University ... OR ... 375
University of Oregon ... OR ... 376
Willamette University ... OR ... 377
Drexel University ... PA ... 382
Duquesne University ... PA ... 383
Gannon University ... PA ... 384
Penn State University Park ... PA ... 391
University of Pennsylvania ... PA ... 400
University of Pittsburgh ... PA ... 400
Wilkes University ... PA ... 403
University of South Carolina Columbia ... SC ... 413
Tennessee State University ... TN ... 426
Dallas Baptist University ... TX ... 434
San Antonio College ... TX ... 429
University of Houston ... TX ... 452
University of North Texas ... TX ... 453
University of Texas at Arlington, The ... TX ... 454
University of Texas at Austin ... TX ... 455
University of Texas at San Antonio, The ... TX ... 455
University of Utah, The ... UT ... 459
Utah State University ... UT ... 460
Utah Valley University ... UT ... 460
George Mason University ... VA ... 467
Virginia Commonwealth University ... VA ... 473
Virginia Polytechnic Institute and State University ... VA ... 476
Gonzaga University ... WA ... 480
Washington State University ... WA ... 485
West Virginia University ... WV ... 490
University of Wisconsin-Milwaukee ... WI ... 496
University of Wisconsin-Stout ... WI ... 497

CGTECH: National Accrediting Agency for Clinical Laboratory Sciences: cytogenetic technologist (B)

University of Connecticut ... CT ... 89
Kennesaw State University ... GA ... 121
Northern Michigan University ... MI ... 228
University of Texas MD Anderson Cancer Center, The ... TX ... 456

CHIRO: Council on Chiropractic Education: chiropractic education (FP,D)

Life Chiropractic College West ... CA ... 47
Southern California University of Health Sciences ... CA ... 65
University of Bridgeport ... CT ... 89
Life University ... GA ... 122
National University of Health Sciences ... IL ... 145
Palmer College of Chiropractic ... IA ... 169
Cleveland University - Kansas City ... KS ... 172
Northwestern Health Sciences University ... MN ... 242
Logan University ... MO ... 255
D'Youville College ... NY ... 298
Northeast College of Health Sciences ... NY ... 310
University of Western States ... OR ... 377
Universidad Central Del Caribe ... PR ... 511
Sherman College of Chiropractic ... SC ... 411
Parker University ... TX ... 441
Texas Chiropractic College ... TX ... 448

CIDA: Council for Interior Design Accreditation: interior design (B,M)

Auburn University ... AL ... 4
Samford University ... AL ... 6
University of Alabama, The ... AL ... 7
University of North Alabama ... AL ... 8
Arizona State University ... AZ ... 10
Northern Arizona University ... AZ ... 14
Harding University Main Campus ... AR ... 19
University of Arkansas Main Campus ... AR ... 21
University of Central Arkansas ... AR ... 23
Academy of Art University ... CA ... 24
California State Polytechnic University-Pomona ... CA ... 30
California State University-Fresno ... CA ... 31
California State University-Northridge ... CA ... 32

CLPSY: American Psychological Association: clinical psychology (D)

CNCE: Accrediting Council for Continuing Education and Training: continuing education (C,A)

COARC: Commission on Accreditation for Respiratory Care: respiratory care (A,B,M)

- Indiana University of Pennsylvania ... PA .. 394
- Laurel Business Institute ... PA .. 388
- Laurel Technical Institute ... PA .. 388
- Luzerne County Community College ... PA .. 389
- Mansfield University of Pennsylvania ... PA .. 394
- Marywood University ... PA .. 389
- Mercyhurst University ... PA .. 389
- Millersville University of Pennsylvania ... PA .. 395
- Pennsylvania College of Health Sciences PA .. 392
- Pittsburgh Career Institute ... PA .. 396
- Reading Area Community College ... PA .. 396
- West Chester University of Pennsylvania PA .. 395
- York College of Pennsylvania ... PA .. 403
- #YTI Career Institute ... PA .. 403
- #Universidad Adventista de las Antillas ... PR .. 510
- Community College of Rhode Island ... RI ... 404
- New England Institute of Technology ... RI ... 404
- Florence - Darlington Technical College .. SC .. 409
- Greenville Technical College ... SC .. 409
- #Horry-Georgetown Technical College ... SC .. 409
- Midlands Technical College ... SC .. 410
- Piedmont Technical College ... SC .. 411
- Spartanburg Community College ... SC .. 412
- Trident Technical College ... SC .. 412
- Dakota State University ... SD .. 416
- Baptist Health Sciences University ... TN .. 418
- Chattanooga State Community College .. TN .. 424
- Columbia State Community College ... TN .. 424
- Concorde Career College ... TN .. 419
- East Tennessee State University ... TN .. 419
- #Jackson State Community College ... TN .. 424
- Roane State Community College ... TN .. 425
- Tennessee State University ... TN .. 426
- Volunteer State Community College ... TN .. 425
- Walters State Community College ... TN .. 425
- Alvin Community College ... TX .. 429
- Amarillo College ... TX .. 429
- Angelina College ... TX .. 429
- Cisco College ... TX .. 432
- Collin College ... TX .. 433
- Dallas College, El Centro Campus ... TX .. 434
- Del Mar College ... TX .. 435
- El Paso Community College ... TX .. 436
- Houston Community College ... TX .. 437
- Howard College ... TX .. 437
- Lamar Institute of Technology ... TX .. 449
- Lone Star College System ... TX .. 439
- McLennan Community College ... TX .. 439
- Midland College ... TX .. 440
- Midwestern State University ... TX .. 440
- St. Philip's College ... TX .. 429
- San Jacinto College Central ... TX .. 443
- South Plains College ... TX .. 443
- South Texas College ... TX .. 443
- Tarrant County College District ... TX .. 445
- Temple College ... TX .. 445
- Texas Southern University ... TX .. 449
- Texas Southmost College ... TX .. 449
- Texas State University ... TX .. 450
- Tyler Junior College ... TX .. 452
- University of Texas Health Science Center at San Antonio ... TX ... 456
- University of Texas Medical Branch, The TX ... 456
- Victoria College ... TX ... 457
- Weatherford College ... TX ... 457
- Dixie State University ... UT ... 460
- #Salt Lake Community College ... UT ... 461
- #Utah Valley University ... UT ... 460
- Weber State University ... UT ... 461
- Vermont Technical College ... VT ... 464
- Central Virginia Community College ... VA .. 473
- J. Sargeant Reynolds Community College ... VA .. 474
- Liberty University ... VA .. 468
- Mountain Empire Community College ... VA .. 474
- Northern Virginia Community College ... VA .. 474
- Radford University ... VA .. 469
- Tidewater Community College ... VA .. 475
- Highline College ... WA .. 481
- Seattle Central College ... WA .. 483
- Spokane Community College ... WA .. 479
- Tacoma Community College ... WA .. 484
- BridgeValley Community & Technical College ... WV .. 488
- Marshall University ... WV .. 489
- #Pierpont Community & Technical College WV .. 488
- Southern West Virginia Community and Technical College ... WV .. 488
- Chippewa Valley Technical College ... WI ... 498
- Madison Area Technical College ... WI ... 499
- Mid-State Technical College ... WI ... 499
- Milwaukee Area Technical College ... WI ... 499
- Moraine Park Technical College ... WI ... 499
- Northeast Wisconsin Technical College .. WI ... 499
- Western Technical College ... WI ... 500
- Casper College ... WY . 500

COARCP: Commission on Accreditation for Respiratory Care: polysomnography (C)

- Stony Brook University ... NY .. 317
- Rhodes State College ... OH .. 360
- Gannon University ... PA .. 384
- #Tyler Junior College ... TX ... 452

COE: Council on Occupational Education: occupational, trade, and technical education (C,A)

- J.F. Ingram State Technical College ... AL ... 2
- Reid State Technical College ... AL ... 3
- Advanced College ... CA 24
- #ATA College ... CA 26
- Healthcare Career College ... CA 44
- Los Angeles Pacific College ... CA 50
- Mayfield College ... CA 51
- San Francisco Film School ... CA 61
- Spartan College of Aeronautics and Technology ... CA 66
- #Colorado Academy of Veterinary Technology ... CO 78
- Saint Michael College of Allied Health ... DC 93
- Academy for Nursing and Health Occupations ... FL 94
- Florida Career College ... FL 99
- NRI Institute of Health Sciences ... FL ... 105
- Praxis Institute, The ... FL ... 106
- Saber College ... FL ... 107
- Universal Career School ... FL ... 113
- Gwinnett College-Marietta ... GA .. 121
- Interactive College of Technology ... GA .. 121
- Midwestern Career College ... IL ... 144
- Morrison Institute of Technology ... IL ... 145
- Central Louisiana Technical & Community College-Huey P. Long Campus ... LA ... 188
- Central Louisiana Technical College Avoyelles Campus ... LA ... 187
- Central Louisiana Technical Community College ... LA ... 187
- Delta College of Arts & Technology ... LA ... 186
- Louisiana Culinary Institute ... LA ... 189
- Northwest Louisiana Technical Community College ... LA ... 188
- Career Quest Learning Center ... MI ... 222
- Jersey College ... NJ ... 278
- Ohio Business College ... OH ... 357
- Lancaster County Career and Technology Center ... PA .. 387
- Trinity College of Puerto Rico ... PR .. 510
- Concorde Career College ... TN .. 419
- North Central Institute ... TN .. 422
- William Moore College of Technology ... TN .. 428
- Auguste Escoffier School of Culinary Arts TX ... 430
- Center for Advanced Legal Studies ... TX ... 432
- Interactive College of Technology ... TX ... 438
- Peloton College ... TX ... 441
- Quest College ... TX ... 441
- Southern Careers Institute ... TX ... 444
- Vista College ... TX ... 457
- Chester Career College ... VA .. 465
- Columbia College ... VA .. 465
- Eastern Virginia Career College ... VA .. 466

COMTA: Commission on Massage Therapy Accreditation: massage therapy, bodywork, aesthetics/ esthetics and skin care (C,A)

- Gadsden State Community College ... AL ... 2
- Idaho State University ... ID 131
- Elgin Community College ... IL 137
- Harper College ... IL 138
- National University of Health Sciences ... IL 145
- Community College of Baltimore County, The ... MD .. 198
- Lansing Community College ... MI ... 226
- Northwestern Health Sciences University MN .. 242
- Central Oregon Community College ... OR .. 372
- Community College of Rhode Island ... RI ... 404
- Technical College of the Lowcountry ... SC .. 412
- Roane State Community College ... TN .. 425
- Parker University ... TX ... 441

CONST: American Council for Construction Education: construction education (A,B,M)

- Auburn University ... AL ... 4
- Jefferson State Community College ... AL ... 2
- Tuskegee University ... AL ... 7
- University of Alaska Anchorage ... AK ... 9
- Arizona State University ... AZ 10
- Northern Arizona University ... AZ 14
- John Brown University ... AR 19
- University of Arkansas at Little Rock ... AR 22
- California Baptist University ... CA 27
- California Polytechnic State University-San Luis Obispo ... CA 29
- California State University-Chico ... CA 30
- California State University-Fresno ... CA 31
- California State University-Long Beach ... CA 31
- California State University-Northridge ... CA 32
- California State University-Sacramento ... CA 32
- Colorado State University ... CO 79
- Central Connecticut State University ... CT 85
- Florida Institute of Technology ... FL ... 100
- Florida International University ... FL ... 110
- Santa Fe College ... FL ... 108
- University of Florida ... FL ... 111
- University of North Florida ... FL ... 111
- Georgia Southern University ... GA .. 120
- Gwinnett Technical College ... GA .. 121
- Kennesaw State University ... GA .. 121
- Boise State University ... ID ... 130
- Bradley University ... IL ... 134
- Illinois State University ... IL ... 140
- Southern Illinois University Edwardsville . IL ... 150
- Ball State University ... IN ... 153
- Indiana State University ... IN ... 156
- Indiana University-Purdue University Indianapolis ... IN ... 157
- Purdue University Main Campus ... IN ... 160
- Kansas State University ... KS .. 175
- Eastern Kentucky University ... KY .. 180
- Northern Kentucky University ... KY .. 184
- Baton Rouge Community College ... LA ... 187
- Louisiana State University and Agricultural and Mechanical College ... LA ... 189
- University of Louisiana at Monroe ... LA ... 193
- University of Maryland Eastern Shore ... MD .. 203
- Wentworth Institute of Technology ... MA .. 219
- Eastern Michigan University ... MI ... 223
- Ferris State University ... MI ... 224
- Lansing Community College ... MI ... 226
- Michigan State University ... MI ... 227
- Michigan Technological University ... MI ... 228
- Minnesota State University Moorhead ... MN .. 239
- Minnesota State University, Mankato ... MN .. 239
- Mississippi State University ... MS .. 247
- University of Southern Mississippi ... MS .. 249
- Missouri State University ... MO . 256
- State Fair Community College ... MO . 259
- University of Nevada, Las Vegas ... NV . 271
- Central New Mexico Community College NM .. 285
- Alfred State College ... NY .. 319
- State University of New York College of Technology at Delhi ... NY .. 320
- Utica College ... NY .. 324
- East Carolina University ... NC .. 341
- North Carolina Agricultural and Technical State University ... NC .. 341
- North Dakota State University Main Campus ... ND .. 345
- Bowling Green State University ... OH .. 348
- Cincinnati State Technical and Community College ... OH ... 350
- Columbus State Community College ... OH .. 351
- Kent State University Kent Campus ... OH .. 354
- Ohio State University Main Campus, The. OH .. 358
- University of Cincinnati Main Campus ... OH .. 361
- University of Oklahoma Norman Campus. OK .. 370
- Oregon State University ... OR .. 375
- Drexel University ... PA .. 382
- Pennsylvania College of Technology ... PA .. 392
- Roger Williams University ... RI ... 405
- Clemson University ... SC .. 407
- Dallas College, North Lake Campus ... TX ... 435
- Lamar University ... TX ... 449
- Tarrant County College District ... TX ... 445
- Texas A & M University ... TX ... 446
- Texas State University ... TX ... 450
- University of Houston ... TX ... 452
- University of Texas at San Antonio, The . TX ... 455
- Virginia Polytechnic Institute and State University ... VA .. 476
- Central Washington University ... WA . 478
- Edmonds Community College ... WA . 480
- University of Washington ... WA . 485
- Washington State University ... WA . 485
- University of Wisconsin-Stout ... WI ... 497

COPSY: American Psychological Association: counseling psychology (D)

- Auburn University ... AL ... 4
- Arizona State University ... AZ ... 10
- University of Central Arkansas ... AR 23
- Colorado State University ... CO 79
- University of Denver ... CO 84
- University of Northern Colorado ... CO 84
- Howard University ... DC 92
- University of Florida ... FL ... 111
- University of Miami ... FL ... 113
- Georgia State University ... GA .. 120
- University of Georgia ... GA .. 126
- Loyola University Chicago ... IL ... 143
- Southern Illinois University Carbondale ... IL ... 150
- University of Illinois Urbana-Champaign .. IL ... 152
- Ball State University ... IN ... 153
- Indiana University Bloomington ... IN ... 156
- Purdue University Main Campus ... IN ... 160
- Iowa State University ... IA ... 163
- University of Iowa ... IA ... 163
- University of Kansas Main Campus ... KS .. 177
- University of Kentucky ... KY .. 185
- University of Louisville ... KY .. 186
- Louisiana Tech University ... LA ... 192
- University of Maryland College Park ... MD .. 202
- Boston College ... MA .. 207
- Boston University ... MA .. 207
- Northeastern University ... MA .. 217
- Springfield College ... MA .. 218
- University of Massachusetts Boston ... MA .. 211
- Andrews University ... MI ... 221
- Western Michigan University ... MI ... 233
- Saint Mary's University of Minnesota ... MN .. 243
- University of Saint Thomas ... MN .. 244
- University of Southern Mississippi ... MS .. 249
- University of Missouri - Columbia ... MO . 261
- University of Missouri - Kansas City ... MO . 261
- University of Nebraska - Lincoln ... NE .. 269
- Felician University ... NJ ... 277
- Saint Elizabeth University ... NJ ... 282
- Seton Hall University ... NJ ... 283
- New Mexico State University Main Campus ... NM .. 287
- Fordham University ... NY .. 300
- New York University ... NY .. 309
- Teachers College, Columbia University ... NY .. 322
- University at Albany, SUNY ... NY .. 316
- University of North Dakota ... ND .. 345
- Cleveland State University ... OH .. 350
- University of Akron, Main Campus, The .. OH .. 361
- Oklahoma State University ... OK .. 367
- University of Oklahoma Norman Campus. OK .. 370
- University of Oregon ... OR .. 376
- Carlow University ... PA .. 380
- Chatham University ... PA .. 380
- Lehigh University ... PA .. 388
- Universidad Ana G. Mendez Gurabo Campus ... PR .. 510
- Tennessee State University ... TN .. 426
- University of Memphis, The ... TN .. 426
- University of Tennessee, Knoxville ... TN .. 427
- Our Lady of the Lake University ... TX ... 441
- Texas A & M University ... TX ... 446
- Texas Tech University ... TX ... 450
- Texas Woman's University ... TX ... 451
- University of Houston ... TX ... 452
- University of North Texas ... TX ... 453
- University of Texas at Austin ... TX ... 455
- Brigham Young University ... UT .. 458
- University of Utah, The ... UT .. 459
- Radford University ... VA .. 469
- Virginia Commonwealth University ... VA . 473
- Northwest University ... WA . 481
- Washington State University ... WA . 485

West Virginia University ... WV . 490
Marquette University ... WI ... 493
University of Wisconsin-Madison ... WI ... 495
University of Wisconsin-Milwaukee ... WI ... 496

COSMA: Commission on Sports Management: sports management (B,M,D)

Troy University ... AL ... 7
Arkansas State University-Jonesboro ... AR ... 17
Metropolitan State University of Denver ... CO ... 81
Saint Leo University ... FL ... 107
University of North Florida ... FL ... 111
University of Tampa ... FL ... 113
Shorter University ... GA .. 125
University of Indianapolis ... IN ... 161
University of Southern Indiana ... IN ... 162
Wichita State University ... KS .. 178
University of Louisville ... KY .. 186
Louisiana State University and Agricultural and Mechanical College ... LA ... 189
Southeastern Louisiana University ... LA ... 193
Endicott College ... MA .. 209
Lasell University ... MA .. 211
Nichols College ... MA .. 217
Northeastern University ... MA .. 217
Western New England University ... MA .. 220
Central Michigan University ... MI ... 222
Davenport University ... MI ... 223
Southeast Missouri State University ... MO . 259
St. John Fisher College ... NY .. 313
SUNY Canton-College of Technology ... NY .. 320
Bowling Green State University ... OH .. 348
Ohio University Main Campus ... OH .. 358
University of Mount Union ... OH .. 362
Wilmington College ... OH .. 364
East Stroudsburg University of Pennsylvania ... PA .. 394
Kutztown University of Pennsylvania ... PA .. 394
Lancaster Bible College|Capital Seminary & Graduate School ... PA .. 387
Slippery Rock University of Pennsylvania. PA .. 395
York College of Pennsylvania ... PA .. 403
North Greenville University ... SC .. 410
Winthrop University ... SC .. 414
Liberty University ... VA .. 468

CR: Commission on Accreditation of Allied Health Education Programs: clinical researcher (C, A,M)

Arizona State University ... AZ ... 10
Durham Technical Community College ... NC .. 334

CSHSE: Council for Standards in Human Services Education: human services (A,B,M)

University of Alaska Anchorage ... AK ... 9
California State University-Fullerton ... CA ... 31
Community College of Denver ... CO ... 80
Metropolitan State University of Denver ... CO ... 81
Delaware Technical Community College, Terry Campus ... DE ... 91
University of Delaware ... DE ... 91
Hillsborough Community College ... FL ... 102
Kennesaw State University ... GA .. 121
University of North Georgia ... GA .. 127
College of DuPage ... IL ... 135
Elgin Community College ... IL ... 137
Ivy Tech Community College of Indiana-Indianapolis ... IN ... 158
University of Maine at Augusta ... ME .. 196
Allegany College of Maryland ... MD .. 197
Anne Arundel Community College ... MD .. 197
Stevenson University ... MD .. 202
Fitchburg State University ... MA .. 212
Northern Essex Community College ... MA .. 215
Quinsigamond Community College ... MA .. 215
Baker College of Owosso ... MI ... 221
St. Charles Community College ... MO . 258
Metropolitan Community College ... NE .. 267
Southeast Community College ... NE .. 269
Wayne State College ... NE .. 268
Great Basin College ... NV .. 271
Brookdale Community College ... NJ ... 276
New York City College of Technology/ City University of New York ... NY .. 295
Central Piedmont Community College ... NC .. 333
Montgomery Community College ... NC .. 336
Pitt Community College ... NC .. 336
Vance-Granville Community College ... NC .. 338
Central Ohio Technical College ... OH .. 349
Columbus State Community College ... OH .. 351
Rhodes State College ... OH .. 360
Clarion University of Pennsylvania ... PA .. 393
HACC, Central Pennsylvania's Community College ... PA .. 385
Lehigh Carbon Community College ... PA .. 388
Montgomery County Community College PA .. 390
University of Scranton, The ... PA .. 401
Central Carolina Technical College ... SC .. 406
Florence - Darlington Technical College .. SC .. 409
Midlands Technical College ... SC .. 410
Trident Technical College ... SC .. 412
University of South Carolina Beaufort ... SC .. 413
East Tennessee State University ... TN .. 419
Wharton County Junior College ... TX ... 458
Old Dominion University ... VA .. 469
Blackhawk Technical College ... WI ... 498
Gateway Technical College ... WI ... 498
Madison Area Technical College ... WI ... 499
University of Wisconsin Oshkosh ... WI ... 496

CVT: Commission on Accreditation of Allied Health Education Programs: cardiovascular technology (C,A,B)

Grossmont College ... CA ... 44
Loma Linda University ... CA ... 48
Orange Coast College ... CA ... 38
Florida SouthWestern State College ... FL ... 101
Florida State College at Jacksonville ... FL ... 101
International College of Health Sciences . FL ... 102
Nova Southeastern University ... FL ... 105
Polk State College ... FL ... 106
Santa Fe College ... FL ... 108
Valencia College ... FL ... 113
Augusta Technical College ... GA .. 115
Central Georgia Technical College ... GA .. 116
Georgia Southern University ... GA .. 120
Gwinnett Technical College ... GA .. 121
Piedmont University ... GA .. 124
Southern Crescent Technical College ... GA .. 125
South Suburban College ... IL ... 149
Louisiana State University Health Sciences Center-New Orleans ... LA ... 189
Southern Maine Community College ... ME .. 195
Howard Community College ... MD .. 199
MCPHS University ... MA .. 216
Grand Valley State University ... MI ... 224
Kirtland Community College ... MI ... 226
Saint Cloud Technical and Community College ... MN .. 241
Bryan College of Health Sciences ... NE .. 265
Eastern International College ... NJ ... 277
Eastwick College ... NJ ... 277
Molloy College ... NY .. 306
Central Piedmont Community College ... NC .. 333
Forsyth Technical Community College ... NC .. 334
Tulsa Community College ... OK .. 370
HACC, Central Pennsylvania's Community College ... PA .. 385
Pennsylvania College of Health Sciences PA .. 392
Clemson University ... SC .. 407
Piedmont Technical College ... SC .. 411
Southeast Technical College ... SD .. 417
Northeast State Community College ... TN .. 425
Dallas College, El Centro Campus ... TX .. 434
Hill College ... TX ... 437
St. Philip's College ... TX ... 429
Sentara College of Health Sciences ... VA .. 470
Spokane Community College ... WA .. 479
Milwaukee Area Technical College ... WI ... 499

CYTO: Commission on Accreditation of Allied Health Education Programs: cytotechnology (C,B,M)

University of Arkansas for Medical Sciences ... AR ... 22
Loma Linda University ... CA ... 48
University of California-Los Angeles ... CA ... 69
Indiana University-Purdue University Indianapolis ... IN ... 157
University of Nebraska Medical Center ... NE .. 269
Albany College of Pharmacy and Health Sciences ... NY .. 289
City University of New York Hunter College ... NY .. 294
Daemen College ... NY .. 298
Central Piedmont Community College ... NC .. 333
Duke University ... NC .. 328
Thomas Jefferson University ... PA .. 399
University of Puerto Rico-Medical Sciences Campus ... PR .. 512
University of Rhode Island ... RI ... 405
University of Texas MD Anderson Cancer Center, The ... TX ... 456
Old Dominion University ... VA .. 469

DA: American Dental Association: dental assisting (C,A)

Calhoun Community College ... AL ... 1
Coastal Alabama Community College ... AL ... 1
Lawson State Community College ... AL ... 2
Trenholm State Community College ... AL ... 3
Wallace State Community College - Hanceville ... AL ... 3
University of Alaska Anchorage ... AK ... 9
Phoenix College ... AZ ... 13
Pima Community College ... AZ ... 15
Arkansas Northeastern College ... AR ... 17
University of Arkansas - Pulaski Technical College ... AR ... 23
Cerritos College ... CA ... 35
Chaffey College ... CA ... 35
Citrus College ... CA ... 36
City College of San Francisco ... CA ... 36
College of Alameda ... CA ... 57
College of Marin ... CA ... 39
College of San Mateo ... CA ... 62
Cypress College ... CA ... 54
Diablo Valley College ... CA ... 40
Foothill College ... CA ... 42
Moreno Valley College ... CA ... 59
Orange Coast College ... CA ... 38
Palomar College ... CA ... 56
Pasadena City College ... CA ... 56
Redwoods Community College District ... CA ... 58
Sacramento City College ... CA ... 50
San Diego Mesa College ... CA ... 60
San Jose City College ... CA ... 62
Front Range Community College ... CO ... 81
Pikes Peak Community College ... CO ... 82
Manchester Community College ... CT ... 86
Tunxis Community College ... CT ... 87
Broward College ... FL ... 96
College of Central Florida ... FL ... 97
Daytona State College ... FL ... 98
Eastern Florida State College ... FL ... 98
Florida State College at Jacksonville ... FL ... 101
Gulf Coast State College ... FL ... 101
Hillsborough Community College ... FL ... 102
Indian River State College ... FL ... 102
Northwest Florida State College ... FL ... 104
Palm Beach State College ... FL ... 105
Santa Fe College ... FL ... 108
South Florida State College ... FL ... 108
Tallahassee Community College ... FL ... 112
Albany Technical College ... GA .. 114
Athens Technical College ... GA .. 115
Atlanta Technical College ... GA .. 115
Augusta Technical College ... GA .. 115
Columbus Technical College ... GA .. 117
Georgia Northwestern Technical College GA .. 120
Gwinnett Technical College ... GA .. 121
Lanier Technical College ... GA .. 122
Ogeechee Technical College ... GA .. 123
Savannah Technical College ... GA .. 125
Southern Crescent Technical College ... GA .. 125
Wiregrass Georgia Technical College ... GA .. 128
Kapiolani Community College ... HI ... 129
College of Western Idaho ... ID ... 131
Elgin Community College ... IL ... 137
Illinois Valley Community College ... IL ... 140
John A. Logan College ... IL ... 140
Kaskaskia College ... IL ... 141
Lewis and Clark Community College ... IL ... 142
Indiana University Northwest ... IN ... 157
Indiana University-Purdue University Indianapolis ... IN ... 157
International Business College ... IN ... 158
University of Southern Indiana ... IN ... 162
Des Moines Area Community College ... IA ... 165
Hawkeye Community College ... IA ... 166
Indian Hills Community College ... IA ... 166
Iowa Western Community College ... IA ... 167
Kirkwood Community College ... IA ... 167
Marshalltown Community College ... IA ... 167
Northeast Iowa Community College ... IA ... 169
Scott Community College ... IA ... 166
Western Iowa Tech Community College . IA ... 171
Flint Hills Technical College ... KS .. 173
Labette Community College ... KS .. 175
Salina Area Technical College ... KS .. 177
Wichita State University Campus of Applied Sciences and Technology ... KS .. 178
Big Sandy Community and Technical College ... KY .. 181
West Kentucky Community and Technical College ... KY .. 183
University of Maine at Augusta ... ME .. 196
Hagerstown Community College ... MD .. 199
Massasoit Community College ... MA .. 215
Middlesex Community College ... MA .. 215
Mount Wachusett Community College ... MA .. 215
Northern Essex Community College ... MA .. 215
Quinsigamond Community College ... MA .. 215
Springfield Technical Community College MA .. 216
Delta College ... MI ... 223
Grand Rapids Community College ... MI ... 224
Lake Michigan College ... MI ... 226
Mott Community College ... MI ... 228
Northwestern Michigan College ... MI ... 229
Washtenaw Community College ... MI ... 232
Wayne County Community College District ... MI ... 232
Central Lakes College ... MN .. 237
Century College ... MN .. 237
Dakota County Technical College ... MN .. 238
Hennepin Technical College ... MN .. 238
Hibbing Community College, A Technical and Community College ... MN .. 238
Minneapolis Community and Technical College ... MN .. 239
Minnesota State Community and Technical College ... MN .. 239
Minnesota West Community and Technical College ... MN .. 239
Northwest Technical College ... MN .. 240
Rochester Community and Technical College ... MN .. 240
Saint Cloud Technical and Community College ... MN .. 241
South Central College ... MN .. 241
Hinds Community College ... MS .. 246
Meridian Community College ... MS .. 247
Pearl River Community College ... MS .. 248
Metropolitan Community College - Penn Valley ... MO . 255
Ozarks Technical Community College ... MO . 257
State Technical College of Missouri ... MO . 260
Great Falls College Montana State University ... MT .. 264
Salish Kootenai College ... MT .. 265
Central Community College ... NE .. 266
Metropolitan Community College ... NE .. 267
Mid-Plains Community College ... NE .. 267
Southeast Community College ... NE .. 269
College of Southern Nevada ... NV .. 270
Truckee Meadows Community College ... NV .. 271
NHTI-Concord's Community College ... NH .. 273
Camden County College ... NJ ... 276
Central New Mexico Community College NM .. 285
Luna Community College ... NM .. 286
New Mexico State University Dona Ana Community College ... NM .. 287
Santa Fe Community College ... NM .. 288
University at Buffalo-SUNY ... NY .. 316
Alamance Community College ... NC .. 332
Asheville - Buncombe Technical Community College ... NC .. 332
Cape Fear Community College ... NC .. 332
Central Carolina Community College ... NC .. 333
Central Piedmont Community College ... NC .. 333
Coastal Carolina Community College ... NC .. 333
Davidson-Davie Community College ... NC .. 334
Fayetteville Technical Community College ... NC .. 334
Forsyth Technical Community College ... NC .. 334
Guilford Technical Community College ... NC .. 335
Montgomery Community College ... NC .. 336
Pitt Community College ... NC .. 336
Rowan-Cabarrus Community College ... NC .. 337

Wake Technical Community College .. NC .. 338
Wayne Community College .. NC .. 338
Western Piedmont Community College .. NC .. 339
Wilkes Community College .. NC .. 339
North Dakota State College of Science .. ND .. 346
Eastern Gateway Community College - Jefferson County Campus .. OH .. 352
Rose State College .. OK .. 369
Central Oregon Community College .. OR .. 372
Chemeketa Community College .. OR .. 372
Lane Community College .. OR .. 373
Linn-Benton Community College .. OR .. 373
Portland Community College .. OR .. 375
Umpqua Community College .. OR .. 376
HACC, Central Pennsylvania's Community College .. PA .. 385
Harcum College .. PA .. 385
Manor College .. PA .. 389
Westmoreland County Community College .. PA .. 402
University of Puerto Rico-Medical Sciences Campus .. PR .. 512
Community College of Rhode Island .. RI .. 404
Aiken Technical College .. SC .. 406
Florence - Darlington Technical College .. SC .. 409
Greenville Technical College .. SC .. 409
Horry-Georgetown Technical College .. SC .. 409
Midlands Technical College .. SC .. 410
Spartanburg Community College .. SC .. 412
Tri-County Technical College .. SC .. 412
Trident Technical College .. SC .. 412
York Technical College .. SC .. 414
Lake Area Technical College .. SD .. 415
Chattanooga State Community College .. TN .. 424
Northeast State Community College .. TN .. 425
Volunteer State Community College .. TN .. 425
Amarillo College .. TX .. 429
Del Mar College .. TX .. 435
El Paso Community College .. TX .. 436
Grayson College .. TX .. 436
Houston Community College .. TX .. 437
San Antonio College .. TX .. 429
Tyler Junior College .. TX .. 452
Germanna Community College .. VA .. 473
J. Sargeant Reynolds Community College .. VA .. 474
Northern Virginia Community College .. VA .. 474
Bates Technical College .. WA .. 477
Clover Park Technical College .. WA .. 478
Renton Technical College .. WA .. 482
South Puget Sound Community College .. WA .. 484
Spokane Community College .. WA .. 479
Blackhawk Technical College .. WI .. 498
Fox Valley Technical College .. WI .. 498
Gateway Technical College .. WI .. 498
Northeast Wisconsin Technical College .. WI .. 499
Northwood Technical College .. WI .. 499
Western Technical College .. WI .. 500

DANCE: National Association of Schools of Dance: dance (C,A,B,M,D)

University of Alabama, The .. AL .. 7
University of Arizona .. AZ .. 16
California Institute of the Arts .. CA .. 28
California State University-Fullerton .. CA .. 31
California State University-Long Beach .. CA .. 31
Chapman University .. CA .. 36
Loyola Marymount University .. CA .. 51
San Jose State University .. CA .. 34
University of Hartford .. CT .. 89
Florida State University .. FL .. 110
Jacksonville University .. FL .. 102
Miami Dade College .. FL .. 104
University of Florida .. FL .. 111
University of South Florida .. FL .. 111
University of Georgia .. GA .. 126
University of Illinois Urbana-Champaign .. IL .. 152
Ball State University .. IN .. 153
Butler University .. IN .. 154
University of Iowa .. IA .. 163
Wichita State University .. KS .. 178
Western Kentucky University .. KY .. 186
Community College of Baltimore County, The .. MD .. 198
Towson University .. MD .. 204
University of Maryland Baltimore County .. MD .. 203
University of Maryland College Park .. MD .. 202
Hope College .. MI .. 225
Oakland University .. MI .. 229
University of Michigan-Ann Arbor .. MI .. 231
Wayne State University .. MI .. 232
Western Michigan University .. MI .. 233
St. Olaf College .. MN .. 243
University of Minnesota .. MN .. 243
Belhaven University .. MS .. 245
University of Southern Mississippi .. MS .. 249
Southeast Missouri State University .. MO .. 259
University of Missouri - Kansas City .. MO .. 261
University of Nebraska - Lincoln .. NE .. 269
Montclair State University .. NJ .. 279
Rutgers University - New Brunswick .. NJ .. 282
University of New Mexico Main Campus .. NM .. 288
City University of New York Queensborough Community College .. NY .. 295
State University of New York, The College at Brockport .. NY .. 317
Appalachian State University .. NC .. 340
University of North Carolina at Charlotte .. NC .. 342
University of North Carolina at Greensboro .. NC .. 343
Kent State University Kent Campus .. OH .. 354
Ohio State University Main Campus, The .. OH .. 358
Ohio University Main Campus .. OH .. 358
University of Akron, Main Campus, The .. OH .. 361
University of Cincinnati Main Campus .. OH .. 361
Mercyhurst University .. PA .. 389
Point Park University .. PA .. 396
Slippery Rock University of Pennsylvania .. PA .. 395
Temple University .. PA .. 399
Coker University .. SC .. 408
Columbia College .. SC .. 408
University of South Carolina Columbia .. SC .. 413
Winthrop University .. SC .. 414
Southern Methodist University .. TX .. 444
Texas Christian University .. TX .. 448
Texas Tech University .. TX .. 450
Texas Woman's University .. TX .. 451
University of Texas at Austin .. TX .. 455
Brigham Young University .. UT .. 458
Southern Utah University .. UT .. 460
University of Utah, The .. UT .. 459
James Madison University .. VA .. 468
Radford University .. VA .. 469
Virginia Commonwealth University .. VA .. 473
University of Wisconsin-Madison .. WI .. 495
University of Wisconsin-Milwaukee .. WI .. 496
University of Wisconsin-Stevens Point .. WI .. 497
Casper College .. WY .. 500

DEAC: Distance Education Accrediting Commission: home study schools (A,B,M,D)

Columbia Southern University .. AL .. 5
Acacia University .. AZ .. 10
Cummings Gaduate Institute for Behavioral Health Studies .. AZ .. 12
Dunlap-Stone University .. AZ .. 12
Harrison Middleton University .. AZ .. 12
National Paralegal College .. AZ .. 14
Paralegal Institute at Brighton College, The .. AZ .. 14
Penn Foster College .. AZ .. 14
Sessions College for Professional Design .. AZ .. 15
Sonoran Desert Institute .. AZ .. 15
University of Arkansas System eVersity .. AR .. 22
Abraham Lincoln University .. CA .. 23
American Graduate University .. CA .. 25
Anaheim University .. CA .. 25
California Coast University .. CA .. 28
California Intercontinental University .. CA .. 29
California Miramar University .. CA .. 29
College of Exercise Science, International Sports Sciences Association, LLC .. CA .. 38
Hawthorn University .. CA .. 44
Laurus College .. CA .. 47
Taft Law School .. CA .. 67
Union University of California .. CA .. 68
University of the People .. CA .. 71
Viridis Graduate Institute .. CA .. 74
William Carey International University .. CA .. 76
Aspen University .. CO .. 78
Holmes Institute of Consciousness Studies .. CO .. 81
Taft University System, The .. CO .. 83
U.S. Career Institute .. CO .. 85
Moreland University .. DC .. 93
Quantic School of Business and Technology .. DC .. 93
Chi University .. FL .. 97
Doral College .. FL .. 98
Naaleh College .. FL .. 104
Sarasota University .. FL .. 108
Ashworth College .. GA .. 115
College of Court Reporting, Inc. .. IN .. 154
Antioch School of Church Planting and Leadership Development .. IA .. 163
Art of Education University, The .. IA .. 163
Shiloh University .. IA .. 170
Grantham University .. KS .. 174
NationsUniversity .. LA .. 190
WorldQuant University .. LA .. 193
American Business & Technology University .. MO .. 250
City Vision University .. MO .. 251
Rockbridge Seminary .. MO .. 258
Apollos University .. MT .. 262
EC-Council University .. NM .. 286
Southwest University of Naprapathic Medicine .. NM .. 288
Grace Communion Seminary .. NC .. 329
Lakewood University .. OH .. 355
American College of Healthcare Sciences .. OR .. 371
American Denturist College .. OR .. 371
Huntington University of Health Sciences .. TN .. 420
Bottega University .. UT .. 459
American National University .. VA .. 464
Atlantic University .. VA .. 464
University of Fairfax .. VA .. 471
University of Management & Technology .. VA .. 471
Catholic Distance University .. WV .. 487
Martinsburg College .. WV .. 487
Wright Graduate University for the Realization of Human Potential .. WI .. 500

DENT: American Dental Association: dentistry (FP,D)

University of Alabama at Birmingham .. AL .. 8
University of Arkansas at Little Rock .. AR .. 22
California Northstate University .. CA .. 29
Loma Linda University .. CA .. 48
University of California-Los Angeles .. CA .. 69
University of California-San Francisco .. CA .. 70
University of Southern California .. CA .. 73
University of the Pacific .. CA .. 71
Western University of Health Sciences .. CA .. 75
United States Air Force Academy .. CO .. 503
University of Colorado Denver I Anschutz Medical Campus .. CO .. 84
Howard University .. DC .. 92
Jacksonville University .. FL .. 102
Nova Southeastern University .. FL .. 105
University of Florida .. FL .. 111
University of Miami .. FL .. 113
Augusta University .. GA .. 116
Emory University .. GA .. 118
Idaho State University .. ID .. 131
Loyola University Chicago .. IL .. 143
Midwestern University .. IL .. 144
Southern Illinois University Edwardsville .. IL .. 150
University of Illinois at Chicago .. IL .. 151
Indiana University-Purdue University Indianapolis .. IN .. 157
University of Iowa .. IA .. 163
Wichita State University .. KS .. 178
University of Kentucky .. KY .. 185
University of Louisville .. KY .. 186
Louisiana State University Health Sciences Center at Shreveport .. LA .. 189
Louisiana State University Health Sciences Center-New Orleans .. LA .. 189
University of New England .. ME .. 197
Uniformed Services University of the Health Sciences .. MD .. 503
University of Maryland, Baltimore .. MD .. 203
Boston University .. MA .. 207
Harvard University .. MA .. 210
Tufts University .. MA .. 219
University of Detroit Mercy .. MI .. 231
University of Michigan-Ann Arbor .. MI .. 231
University of Minnesota .. MN .. 243
University of Mississippi Medical Center .. MS .. 249
A. T. Still University of Health Sciences .. MO .. 250
Saint Louis University .. MO .. 259
University of Missouri - Kansas City .. MO .. 261
Creighton University .. NE .. 266
University of Nebraska Medical Center .. NE .. 269
Roseman University of Health Sciences .. NV .. 272
University of Nevada, Las Vegas .. NV .. 271
University of New Mexico Main Campus .. NM .. 288
Columbia University in the City of New York .. NY .. 297
Icahn School of Medicine at Mount Sinai .. NY .. 302
New York Medical College .. NY .. 309
New York University .. NY .. 309
State University of New York Upstate Medical University .. NY .. 317
Stony Brook University .. NY .. 317
University at Buffalo-SUNY .. NY .. 316
University of Rochester .. NY .. 323
East Carolina University .. NC .. 341
University of North Carolina at Chapel Hill .. NC .. 342
Wake Forest University .. NC .. 344
Case Western Reserve University .. OH .. 349
Ohio State University Main Campus, The .. OH .. 358
University of Cincinnati Main Campus .. OH .. 361
University of Toledo .. OH .. 363
Oregon Health & Science University .. OR .. 374
Seton Hill University .. PA .. 398
Temple University .. PA .. 399
Thomas Jefferson University .. PA .. 399
University of Pennsylvania .. PA .. 400
University of Pittsburgh .. PA .. 400
University of Puerto Rico-Medical Sciences Campus .. PR .. 512
Medical University of South Carolina .. SC .. 410
Meharry Medical College .. TN .. 421
University of Tennessee, Knoxville .. TN .. 427
Vanderbilt University .. TN .. 428
Texas A & M University .. TX .. 446
Texas Tech University Health Sciences Center at El Paso .. TX .. 451
University of Texas Health Science Center at Houston (UTHealth), The .. TX .. 456
University of Texas Health Science Center at San Antonio .. TX .. 456
University of Texas MD Anderson Cancer Center, The .. TX .. 456
University of Texas Medical Branch, The .. TX .. 456
University of Utah, The .. UT .. 459
University of Vermont .. VT .. 463
University of Virginia .. VA .. 472
Virginia Commonwealth University .. VA .. 473
University of Washington .. WA .. 485
West Virginia University .. WV .. 490
Marquette University .. WI .. 493

DH: American Dental Association: dental hygiene (C,A,B,M)

Calhoun Community College .. AL .. 1
Fortis Institute .. AL .. 5
Wallace State Community College - Hanceville .. AL .. 3
University of Alaska Anchorage .. AK .. 9
Mesa Community College .. AZ .. 13
Mohave Community College .. AZ .. 14
Northern Arizona University .. AZ .. 14
Phoenix College .. AZ .. 13
Pima Community College .. AZ .. 15
Rio Salado College .. AZ .. 13
University of Arkansas at Fort Smith .. AR .. 21
University of Arkansas for Medical Sciences .. AR .. 22
Cabrillo College .. CA .. 27
Carrington College - Sacramento .. CA .. 34
Cerritos College .. CA .. 35
Chabot College .. CA .. 35
Concorde Career College .. CA .. 39
Cypress College .. CA .. 54
Diablo Valley College .. CA .. 40
Foothill College .. CA .. 42
Fresno City College .. CA .. 67
Loma Linda University .. CA .. 48
Moreno Valley College .. CA .. 59
Oxnard College .. CA .. 74
Pasadena City College .. CA .. 56
Sacramento City College .. CA .. 50
San Joaquin Valley College, Inc. - Visalia .. CA .. 61
Santa Rosa Junior College .. CA .. 63
Shasta College .. CA .. 64
Southwestern College .. CA .. 66
Taft College .. CA .. 67
University of Southern California .. CA .. 73
University of the Pacific .. CA .. 71

West Los Angeles College CA 49
Colorado Northwestern Community College CO 79
Community College of Denver CO 80
Concorde Career College CO 80
Pueblo Community College CO 82
Goodwin University CT 88
Tunxis Community College CT 87
University of Bridgeport CT 89
University of New Haven CT 89
Howard University DC 92
Broward College FL 96
Concorde Career Institute FL 98
Daytona State College FL 98
Eastern Florida State College FL 98
Florida SouthWestern State College FL 101
Florida State College at Jacksonville FL 101
Gulf Coast State College FL 101
Hillsborough Community College FL 102
Indian River State College FL 102
Miami Dade College FL 104
Palm Beach State College FL 105
Pasco-Hernando State College FL 105
Pensacola State College FL 105
St. Petersburg College FL 107
Santa Fe College FL 108
South Florida State College FL 108
State College of Florida, Manatee-Sarasota FL 109
Tallahassee Community College FL 112
Valencia College FL 113
Albany State University GA 114
Athens Technical College GA 115
Atlanta Technical College GA 115
Augusta University GA 116
Central Georgia Technical College GA 116
Clayton State University GA 117
Columbus Technical College GA 117
Georgia Highlands College GA 119
Georgia State University GA 120
Lanier Technical College GA 122
Savannah Technical College GA 125
Southeastern Technical College GA 125
West Georgia Technical College GA 128
Wiregrass Georgia Technical College GA 128
University of Hawaii at Manoa HI 129
University of Hawaii Maui College HI 130
College of Southern Idaho ID 131
Idaho State University ID 131
North Idaho College ID 132
Carl Sandburg College IL 134
College of DuPage IL 135
College of Lake County IL 136
Harper College IL 138
Illinois Central College IL 139
Lake Land College IL 142
Lewis and Clark Community College IL 142
Malcolm X College, One of the City Colleges of Chicago IL 135
Parkland College IL 147
Prairie State College IL 147
Rock Valley College IL 148
Southern Illinois University Carbondale IL 150
Indiana University Northwest IN 157
Indiana University-Purdue University Indianapolis IN 157
Indiana University South Bend IN 157
University of Southern Indiana IN 162
Des Moines Area Community College IA 165
Hawkeye Community College IA 166
Indian Hills Community College IA 166
Iowa Central Community College IA 167
Iowa Western Community College IA 167
Kirkwood Community College IA 167
Flint Hills Technical College KS 173
Johnson County Community College KS 174
Wichita State University KS 178
Big Sandy Community and Technical College KY 181
Bluegrass Community and Technical College KY 181
University of Louisville KY 186
Western Kentucky University KY 186
Louisiana State University Health Sciences Center-New Orleans LA 189
Southern University at Shreveport-Louisiana LA 191
University of Louisiana at Monroe LA 193
University of Maine at Augusta ME 196
University of New England ME 197
Allegany College of Maryland MD 197
Baltimore City Community College MD 198
Community College of Baltimore County, The MD 198
Hagerstown Community College MD 199
Howard Community College MD 199
University of Maryland, Baltimore MD 203
Bristol Community College MA 214
Cape Cod Community College MA 214
MCPHS University MA 216
Middlesex Community College MA 215
Mount Wachusett Community College MA 215
Quinsigamond Community College MA 215
Regis College MA 218
Springfield Technical Community College MA 216
Delta College MI 223
Ferris State University MI 224
Grand Rapids Community College MI 224
Jackson College MI 225
Kalamazoo Valley Community College MI 225
Kellogg Community College MI 225
Lansing Community College MI 226
Mott Community College MI 228
Oakland Community College MI 229
University of Detroit Mercy MI 231
University of Michigan-Ann Arbor MI 231
Wayne County Community College District MI 232
Century College MN 237
Lake Superior College MN 238
Minnesota State University, Mankato MN 239
Normandale Community College MN 239
Rochester Community and Technical College MN 240
Saint Cloud Technical and Community College MN 241
University of Minnesota MN 243
Meridian Community College MS 247
Mississippi Delta Community College MS 247
Northeast Mississippi Community College MS 248
Pearl River Community College MS 248
University of Mississippi Medical Center MS 249
Concorde Career College MO 251
Missouri Southern State University MO 256
Ozarks Technical Community College MO 257
State Fair Community College MO 259
University of Missouri - Kansas City MO 261
Great Falls College Montana State University MT 264
Central Community College NE 266
University of Nebraska Medical Center NE 269
College of Southern Nevada NV 270
Truckee Meadows Community College NV 271
NHTI-Concord's Community College NH 273
Bergen Community College NJ 275
Camden County College NJ 276
Eastern International College NJ 277
Middlesex College NJ 278
Rowan College at Burlington County NJ 281
New Mexico State University Dona Ana Community College NM 287
San Juan College NM 288
University of New Mexico Main Campus NM 288
Erie Community College NY 299
Farmingdale State College NY 320
Hostos Community College-City University of New York NY 294
Hudson Valley Community College NY 302
Monroe Community College NY 307
New York City College of Technology/ City University of New York NY 295
New York University NY 309
Orange County Community College NY 310
Plaza College NY 311
SUNY Broome Community College NY 317
Asheville - Buncombe Technical Community College NC 332
Cape Fear Community College NC 332
Catawba Valley Community College NC 333
Central Carolina Community College NC 333
Central Piedmont Community College NC 333
Coastal Carolina Community College NC 333
Fayetteville Technical Community College NC 334
Forsyth Technical Community College NC 334
Guilford Technical Community College NC 335
Halifax Community College NC 335
University of North Carolina at Chapel Hill NC 342
Wake Technical Community College NC 338
Wayne Community College NC 338
North Dakota State College of Science ND 346
Columbus State Community College OH 351
Cuyahoga Community College OH 351
Hocking College OH 353
Lakeland Community College OH 354
Lorain County Community College OH 355
Ohio State University Main Campus, The. OH 358
Owens Community College OH 359
Rhodes State College OH 360
Shawnee State University OH 360
Sinclair Community College OH 360
Stark State College OH 360
University of Cincinnati Blue Ash College. OH 362
Youngstown State University OH 364
Rose State College OK 369
Tulsa Community College OK 370
Lane Community College OR 373
Mt. Hood Community College OR 374
Oregon Institute of Technology OR 374
Pacific University OR 375
Portland Community College OR 375
Community College of Philadelphia PA 381
Fortis Institute PA 383
HACC, Central Pennsylvania's Community College PA 385
Harcum College PA 385
Lancaster County Career and Technology Center PA 387
Luzerne County Community College PA 389
Manor College PA 389
Montgomery County Community College PA 390
Northampton Community College PA 391
Pennsylvania College of Technology PA 392
University of Pittsburgh PA 400
Westmoreland County Community College PA 402
Community College of Rhode Island RI 404
Florence - Darlington Technical College SC 409
Greenville Technical College SC 409
Horry-Georgetown Technical College SC 409
Midlands Technical College SC 410
Trident Technical College SC 412
York Technical College SC 414
University of South Dakota, The SD 416
Chattanooga State Community College TN 424
Concorde Career College TN 419
East Tennessee State University TN 419
Roane State Community College TN 425
Tennessee State University TN 426
Tennessee Wesleyan University TN 426
Amarillo College TX 429
Austin Community College District TX 430
Blinn College TX 431
Coastal Bend College TX 432
Collin College TX 433
Concorde Career Institute TX 433
Dallas College, El Centro Campus TX 434
Del Mar College TX 435
El Paso Community College TX 436
Houston Community College TX 437
Howard College TX 437
Lamar Institute of Technology TX 449
Lone Star College System TX 439
Midwestern State University TX 440
Tarrant County College District TX 445
Temple College TX 445
Texas A & M University TX 446
Texas State Technical College Waco TX 449
Texas Woman's University TX 451
Tyler Junior College TX 452
University of Texas Health Science Center at Houston (UTHealth), The TX 456
University of Texas Health Science Center at San Antonio TX 456
Wharton County Junior College TX 458
Dixie State University UT 460
Salt Lake Community College UT 461
Utah College of Dental Hygiene at Careers Unlimited, The UT 459
Utah Valley University UT 460
Weber State University UT 461
Vermont Technical College VT 464
Northern Virginia Community College VA 474
Old Dominion University VA 469
Thomas Nelson Community College VA 475
Virginia Commonwealth University VA 473
Virginia Western Community College VA 475
Wytheville Community College VA 476
Bellingham Technical College WA 478
Clark College WA 478
Columbia Basin College WA 479
Eastern Washington University WA 479
Lake Washington Institute of Technology WA 481
Pierce College District WA 482
Seattle Central College WA 483
Shoreline Community College WA 484
Yakima Valley College WA 486
BridgeValley Community & Technical College WV 488
West Liberty University WV 490
West Virginia University WV 490
Chippewa Valley Technical College WI 498
Fox Valley Technical College WI 498
Madison Area Technical College WI 499
Milwaukee Area Technical College WI 499
Northcentral Technical College WI 499
Northeast Wisconsin Technical College WI 499
Waukesha County Technical College WI 500
Laramie County Community College WY 501
Northern Wyoming Community College District WY 501

DIETC: Academy of Nutrition and Dietetics: coordinated dietetics programs (B,M)

@University of Alabama at Birmingham AL 8
University of Alabama, The AL 7
University of Montevallo AL 8
University of Alaska Anchorage AK 9
@Northern Arizona University AZ 14
University of Arizona AZ 16
Arkansas State University-Jonesboro AR 17
@Harding University Main Campus AR 19
Loma Linda University CA 48
University of Southern California CA 73
@University of the Pacific CA 71
Colorado State University CO 79
@Fairfield University CT 87
University of Connecticut CT 89
University of New Haven CT 89
Delaware State University DE 90
Howard University DC 92
Nova Southeastern University FL 105
Georgia State University GA 120
University of Idaho ID 132
Bradley University IL 134
Dominican University IL 137
@Southern Illinois University Edwardsville IL 150
University of Illinois at Chicago IL 151
Indiana State University IN 156
@Indiana University-Purdue University Indianapolis IN 157
Purdue University Main Campus IN 160
University of Saint Francis IN 162
Iowa State University IA 163
@University of Iowa IA 163
Kansas State University KS 175
University of Kentucky KY 185
@University of New England ME 197
Johns Hopkins University MD 199
Framingham State University MA 213
@Merrimack College MA 216
University of Massachusetts Lowell MA 212
Eastern Michigan University MI 223
Grand Valley State University MI 224
Wayne State University MI 232
University of Minnesota MN 243
Delta State University MS 245
University of Mississippi MS 249
Fontbonne University MO 253
@Logan University MO 255
Southeast Missouri State University MO 259
@University of Central Missouri MO 260
University of Missouri - Columbia MO 261
University of Nebraska - Lincoln NE 269
University of Nebraska Medical Center NE 269
Rowan University NJ 281
City University of New York Hunter College NY 294
D'Youville College NY 298
Long Island University - LIU Post NY 304
@Pace University NY 311
State University of New York at Oneonta NY 316

DIETD: Academy of Nutrition and Dietetics: didactic dietetics programs (B,M)

DIETI: Academy of Nutrition and Dietetics: dietetic post-baccalaureate internships

DIETT: Academy of Nutrition and Dietetics: dietetic technician (A)

DMOLS: National Accrediting Agency for Clinical Laboratory Sciences: diagnostic molecular scientist (C,B,M)

DMS: Commission on Accreditation of Allied Health Education Programs: diagnostic medical sonography (C,A,B,M)

BridgeValley Community & Technical College ... WV 488
Marshall University ... WV 489
West Virginia University ... WV 490
Bellin College, Inc. ... WI 491
Blackhawk Technical College ... WI 498
Chippewa Valley Technical College ... WI 498
Concordia University Wisconsin ... WI 492
Northeast Wisconsin Technical College ... WI 499
University of Wisconsin-Madison ... WI 495
University of Wisconsin-Milwaukee ... WI 496
Laramie County Community College ... WY 501

DNUR: Accreditation Commission for Education in Nursing: nursing (C)

Camden County College ... NJ 276

DT: American Dental Association: dental laboratory technology (C,A)

Pima Community College ... AZ 15
Los Angeles City College ... CA 49
Pasadena City College ... CA 56
Indiana University-Purdue University Indianapolis ... IN 157
Kirkwood Community College ... IA 167
Louisiana State University Health Sciences Center-New Orleans ... LA 189
Middlesex Community College ... MA 215
Erie Community College ... NY 299
New York City College of Technology/ City University of New York ... NY 295
Durham Technical Community College ... NC 334
Bates Technical College ... WA 477

DTH: American Dental Association: dental therapy (A)

Ilisagvik College ... AK 9

EH: New England Commission of Higher Education

Albertus Magnus College ... CT 85
Asnuntuck Community College ... CT 86
Capital Community College ... CT 86
Central Connecticut State University ... CT 85
Charter Oak State College ... CT 85
Connecticut College ... CT 87
Eastern Connecticut State University ... CT 85
Fairfield University ... CT 87
Gateway Community College ... CT 86
Goodwin University ... CT 88
Hartford Seminary ... CT 88
Holy Apostles College and Seminary ... CT 88
Housatonic Community College ... CT 86
Manchester Community College ... CT 86
Middlesex Community College ... CT 87
Mitchell College ... CT 88
Naugatuck Valley Community College ... CT 87
Northwestern Connecticut Community-Technical College ... CT 87
Norwalk Community College ... CT 87
Post University ... CT 88
Quinebaug Valley Community College ... CT 87
Quinnipiac University ... CT 88
Sacred Heart University ... CT 89
Southern Connecticut State University ... CT 86
Three Rivers Community College ... CT 87
Trinity College ... CT 89
Tunxis Community College ... CT 87
United States Coast Guard Academy ... CT 503
University of Bridgeport ... CT 89
University of Connecticut ... CT 89
University of Hartford ... CT 89
University of New Haven ... CT 89
University of Saint Joseph ... CT 90
Wesleyan University ... CT 90
Western Connecticut State University ... CT 86
Yale University ... CT 90
Bates College ... ME 194
Bowdoin College ... ME 194
Central Maine Community College ... ME 195
Colby College ... ME 194
College of the Atlantic ... ME 194
Eastern Maine Community College ... ME 195
Husson University ... ME 194
Institute for Doctoral Studies in the Visual Arts ... ME 194
Kennebec Valley Community College ... ME 195
Maine College of Art ... ME 195
Maine College of Health Professions ... ME 195
Maine Maritime Academy ... ME 196
@Maine Media College ... ME 196
Northern Maine Community College ... ME 195
Saint Joseph's College of Maine ... ME 196
Southern Maine Community College ... ME 195
Thomas College ... ME 196
Unity College ... ME 196
University of Maine ... ME 196
University of Maine at Augusta ... ME 196
University of Maine at Farmington ... ME 196
University of Maine at Fort Kent ... ME 197
University of Maine at Presque Isle ... ME 197
University of New England ... ME 197
University of Southern Maine ... ME 197
Washington County Community College ... ME 195
York County Community College ... ME 195
American International College ... MA 205
Amherst College ... MA 205
Anna Maria College ... MA 205
Assumption University ... MA 206
Babson College ... MA 206
Bay Path University ... MA 206
Bay State College ... MA 206
Benjamin Franklin Institute of Technology ... MA 206
Bentley University ... MA 206
Berklee College of Music ... MA 206
Berkshire Community College ... MA 214
Boston Architectural College ... MA 207
Boston College ... MA 207
Boston Graduate School of Psychoanalysis ... MA 207
Boston University ... MA 207
Brandeis University ... MA 208
Bridgewater State University ... MA 212
Bristol Community College ... MA 214
Bunker Hill Community College ... MA 214
Cambridge College ... MA 208
Cape Cod Community College ... MA 214
Clark University ... MA 208
College of Our Lady of the Elms ... MA 208
College of the Holy Cross ... MA 208
Conway School of Landscape Design ... MA 208
Curry College ... MA 208
Dean College ... MA 209
Eastern Nazarene College ... MA 209
Emerson College ... MA 209
Emmanuel College ... MA 209
Endicott College ... MA 209
Fisher College ... MA 209
Fitchburg State University ... MA 212
Framingham State University ... MA 213
Franklin W. Olin College of Engineering ... MA 210
Gordon College ... MA 210
Gordon-Conwell Theological Seminary ... MA 210
Greenfield Community College ... MA 214
Hampshire College ... MA 210
Harvard University ... MA 210
Hebrew College ... MA 210
Hellenic College-Holy Cross Greek Orthodox School of Theology ... MA 210
Holyoke Community College ... MA 214
Hult International Business School ... MA 210
Laboure College ... MA 211
Lasell University ... MA 211
Lesley University ... MA 211
Massachusetts Bay Community College ... MA 214
Massachusetts College of Art and Design ... MA 213
Massachusetts College of Liberal Arts ... MA 213
Massachusetts Institute of Technology ... MA 216
Massachusetts Maritime Academy ... MA 213
Massachusetts School of Law at Andover ... MA 216
Massasoit Community College ... MA 215
MCPHS University ... MA 216
Merrimack College ... MA 216
MGH Institute of Health Professions ... MA 217
Middlesex Community College ... MA 215
Montserrat College of Art ... MA 217
Mount Holyoke College ... MA 217
Mount Wachusett Community College ... MA 215
New England College of Optometry ... MA 217
New England Conservatory of Music ... MA 217
Nichols College ... MA 217
North Shore Community College ... MA 215
Northeastern University ... MA 217
Northern Essex Community College ... MA 215
Quincy College ... MA 218
Quinsigamond Community College ... MA 215
Regis College ... MA 218
Roxbury Community College ... MA 215
Saint John's Seminary ... MA 218
Salem State University ... MA 213
Simmons University ... MA 218
Smith College ... MA 218
Springfield College ... MA 218
Springfield Technical Community College ... MA 216
Stonehill College ... MA 219
Suffolk University ... MA 219
Tufts University ... MA 219
UMass Chan Medical School ... MA 212
University of Massachusetts ... MA 211
University of Massachusetts Boston ... MA 211
University of Massachusetts Dartmouth ... MA 212
University of Massachusetts Lowell ... MA 212
Urban College of Boston ... MA 219
Wellesley College ... MA 219
Wentworth Institute of Technology ... MA 219
Western New England University ... MA 220
Westfield State University ... MA 213
Wheaton College ... MA 220
William James College ... MA 220
Williams College ... MA 220
Woods Hole Oceanographic Institution ... MA 220
Worcester Polytechnic Institute ... MA 220
Worcester State University ... MA 213
Colby-Sawyer College ... NH 272
Dartmouth College ... NH 273
Franklin Pierce University ... NH 273
Granite State College ... NH 274
Great Bay Community College ... NH 272
Keene State College ... NH 274
Lakes Region Community College ... NH 272
Magdalen College of the Liberal Arts ... NH 273
Manchester Community College ... NH 272
Nashua Community College ... NH 272
New England College ... NH 273
NHTI-Concord's Community College ... NH 273
Plymouth State University ... NH 275
River Valley Community College ... NH 273
Rivier University ... NH 273
Saint Anselm College ... NH 274
Southern New Hampshire University ... NH 274
Thomas More College of Liberal Arts, The ... NH 274
University of New Hampshire ... NH 274
@Upper Valley Educators Institute ... NH 275
White Mountains Community College ... NH 273
Brown University ... RI 403
Bryant University ... RI 404
College Unbound ... RI 404
Community College of Rhode Island ... RI 404
Johnson & Wales University ... RI 404
Naval War College ... RI 503
New England Institute of Technology ... RI 404
Providence College ... RI 404
Rhode Island College ... RI 405
Rhode Island School of Design ... RI 405
Roger Williams University ... RI 405
Salve Regina University ... RI 405
University of Rhode Island ... RI 405
Bennington College ... VT 461
Castleton University ... VT 463
Champlain College ... VT 462
Community College of Vermont ... VT 463
Goddard College ... VT 462
Landmark College ... VT 462
Middlebury College ... VT 462
Northern Vermont University-Johnson ... VT 463
Norwich University ... VT 462
Saint Michael's College ... VT 462
School for International Training (SIT) ... VT 462
Sterling College ... VT 462
University of Vermont ... VT 463
Vermont College of Fine Arts ... VT 463
Vermont Law School ... VT 463
Vermont Technical College ... VT 464

EMT: Commission on Accreditation of Allied Health Education Programs: emergency medical technician-paramedic (C, A,B)

Bevill State Community College ... AL 1
Calhoun Community College ... AL 1
Coastal Alabama Community College ... AL 1
Gadsden State Community College ... AL 2
George C. Wallace Community College - Dothan ... AL 2
Jefferson State Community College ... AL 2
Lurleen B. Wallace Community College ... AL 2
Northeast Alabama Community College ... AL 3
Northwest - Shoals Community College ... AL 3
Southern Union State Community College ... AL 3
Trenholm State Community College ... AL 3
University of South Alabama ... AL 9
Wallace State Community College - Hanceville ... AL 3
University of Alaska Anchorage ... AK 9
University of Alaska Fairbanks ... AK 10
Arizona Western College ... AZ 11
Central Arizona College ... AZ 11
Eastern Arizona College ... AZ 12
Glendale Community College ... AZ 13
Mesa Community College ... AZ 13
Mohave Community College ... AZ 14
Northland Pioneer College ... AZ 14
Paradise Valley Community College ... AZ 13
Phoenix College ... AZ 13
Pima Community College ... AZ 15
Yavapai College ... AZ 16
Arkansas Northeastern College ... AR 17
Arkansas State University-Beebe ... AR 17
Arkansas State University-Jonesboro ... AR 17
Arkansas State University-Mountain Home ... AR 17
Black River Technical College ... AR 18
East Arkansas Community College ... AR 19
National Park College ... AR 20
North Arkansas College ... AR 20
NorthWest Arkansas Community College ... AR 20
South Arkansas Community College ... AR 21
Southeast Arkansas College ... AR 21
University of Arkansas at Monticello ... AR 22
University of Arkansas Community College at Batesville ... AR 22
University of Arkansas Community College Hope-Texarkana ... AR 22
University of Arkansas - Pulaski Technical College ... AR 23
American River College ... CA 50
Bakersfield College ... CA 46
Butte College ... CA 27
California State University-Sacramento ... CA 32
City College of San Francisco ... CA 36
College of the Siskiyous ... CA 39
Crafton Hills College ... CA 60
Cuesta College ... CA 40
Foothill College ... CA 42
Imperial Valley College ... CA 45
Las Positas College ... CA 35
Moreno Valley College ... CA 59
Mt. San Antonio College ... CA 52
Napa Valley College ... CA 53
Palomar College ... CA 56
Point Loma Nazarene University ... CA 57
Redwoods Community College District ... CA 58
Saddleback College ... CA 65
Santa Rosa Junior College ... CA 63
Southwestern College ... CA 66
University of Antelope Valley ... CA 68
University of California-Los Angeles ... CA 69
Ventura College ... CA 74
Victor Valley College ... CA 74
West Hills College Lemoore ... CA 75
Aims Community College ... CO 77
Arapahoe Community College ... CO 77
Colorado Mountain College ... CO 78
Community College of Aurora ... CO 80
Pikes Peak Community College ... CO 82
Pueblo Community College ... CO 82
Capital Community College ... CT 86
Delaware Technical Community College, Terry Campus ... DE 91
Broward College ... FL 96
Chipola College ... FL 97
City College ... FL 97
College of Central Florida ... FL 97
Daytona State College ... FL 98
Eastern Florida State College ... FL 98
Florida Gateway College ... FL 100
Florida SouthWestern State College ... FL 101
Florida State College at Jacksonville ... FL 101
Gulf Coast State College ... FL 101
Hillsborough Community College ... FL 102

- Northern Virginia Community College VA 474
- Patrick Henry Community College VA 474
- Piedmont Virginia Community College VA 474
- Radford University VA 469
- Rappahannock Community College VA 475
- Southside Virginia Community College VA 475
- Southwest Virginia Community College VA 475
- Tidewater Community College VA 475
- Virginia Commonwealth University VA 473
- Central Washington University WA 478
- Columbia Basin College WA 479
- Tacoma Community College WA 484
- University of Washington WA 485
- Blue Ridge Community and Technical College WV 488
- Mountwest Community and Technical College WV 488
- New River Community and Technical College WV 488
- Pierpont Community & Technical College WV 488
- Southern West Virginia Community and Technical College WV 488
- Chippewa Valley Technical College WI 498
- Fox Valley Technical College WI 498
- Gateway Technical College WI 498
- Lakeshore Technical College WI 498
- Madison Area Technical College WI 499
- Mid-State Technical College WI 499
- Milwaukee Area Technical College WI 499
- Moraine Park Technical College WI 499
- Northcentral Technical College WI 499
- Northeast Wisconsin Technical College WI 499
- Waukesha County Technical College WI 500
- Western Technical College WI 500
- Casper College WY 500
- Laramie County Community College WY 501

EXSC: Commission on Accreditation of Allied Health Education Programs: exercise science (C,A,B,M)

- Northern Arizona University AZ 14
- Metropolitan State University of Denver CO 81
- Central Connecticut State University CT 85
- Southern Connecticut State University CT 86
- Barry University FL 96
- University of North Florida FL 111
- University of West Florida FL 111
- Clayton State University GA 117
- Georgia State University GA 120
- Valdosta State University GA 127
- Southern Illinois University Edwardsville IL 150
- Indiana Wesleyan University IN 158
- University of Indianapolis IN 161
- University of Southern Indiana IN 162
- Baker University KS 171
- Murray State University KY 184
- University of Louisville KY 186
- University of Louisiana at Monroe LA 193
- University of New England ME 197
- University of Southern Maine ME 197
- Frostburg State University MD 204
- Salisbury University MD 204
- Lasell University MA 211
- Springfield College MA 218
- Westfield State University MA 213
- Central Michigan University MI 222
- Wayne State University MI 232
- St. Catherine University MN 243
- Missouri Baptist University MO 256
- City University of New York York College NY 295
- Mercy College NY 306
- State University of New York, The College at Brockport NY 317
- Gardner-Webb University NC 329
- North Carolina Wesleyan College NC 339
- University of North Carolina at Charlotte NC 342
- North Dakota State University Main Campus ND 345
- University of Mary ND 347
- Baldwin Wallace University OH 348
- Bowling Green State University OH 348
- Kent State University Kent Campus OH 354
- Ohio Northern University OH 358
- Wright State University Main Campus OH 364
- Youngstown State University OH 364
- University of Central Oklahoma OK 370
- Bloomsburg University of Pennsylvania PA 393
- East Stroudsburg University of Pennsylvania PA 394
- Eastern University PA 383
- Gannon University PA 384
- Grove City College PA 384
- Indiana University of Pennsylvania PA 394
- Saint Francis University PA 397
- Seton Hill University PA 398
- Slippery Rock University of Pennsylvania PA 395
- University of Scranton, The PA 401
- West Chester University of Pennsylvania PA 395
- University of Rhode Island RI 405
- Winthrop University SC 414
- South Dakota State University SD 417
- George Mason University VA 467
- Liberty University VA 468
- Longwood University VA 468
- Old Dominion University VA 469
- University of Lynchburg VA 471

FEPAC: American Academy of Forensic Sciences: forensic science (B,M)

- University of Alabama at Birmingham AL 8
- University of New Haven CT 89
- George Washington University DC 92
- Florida International University FL 110
- University of Central Florida FL 110
- University of Tampa FL 113
- Albany State University GA 114
- Loyola University Chicago IL 143
- University of Illinois at Chicago IL 151
- Indiana University-Purdue University Indianapolis IN 157
- Eastern Kentucky University KY 180
- Towson University MD 204
- Boston University MA 207
- Madonna University MI 227
- Michigan State University MI 227
- University of Mississippi MS 249
- Alfred State College NY 319
- City University of New York John Jay College of Criminal Justice NY 294
- State University of New York College at Buffalo NY 317
- Syracuse University NY 321
- Fayetteville State University NC 341
- Ohio University Main Campus OH 358
- University of Central Oklahoma OK 370
- Arcadia University PA 378
- Cedar Crest College PA 380
- Duquesne University PA 383
- Penn State University Park PA 391
- West Chester University of Pennsylvania PA 395
- Sam Houston State University TX 450
- Texas A & M University TX 446
- University of North Texas TX 453
- Liberty University VA 468
- Virginia Commonwealth University VA 473
- Marshall University WV 489
- West Virginia University WV 490

FUSER: American Board of Funeral Service Education: funeral service education (C,A,B)

- Jefferson State Community College AL 2
- University of Arkansas Community College Hope-Texarkana AR 22
- American River College CA 50
- Cypress College CA 54
- Arapahoe Community College CO 77
- Goodwin University CT 88
- University of the District of Columbia DC 94
- Florida State College at Jacksonville FL 101
- Miami Dade College FL 104
- St. Petersburg College FL 107
- Columbus Technical College GA 117
- Gupton Jones College of Funeral Service GA 121
- Ogeechee Technical College GA 123
- Carl Sandburg College IL 134
- Malcolm X College, One of the City Colleges of Chicago IL 135
- Southern Illinois University Carbondale IL 150
- Worsham College of Mortuary Science IL 153
- Ivy Tech Community College of Indiana-Indianapolis IN 158
- Mid-America College of Funeral Service IN 159
- Vincennes University IN 162
- Des Moines Area Community College IA 165
- Kansas City Kansas Community College KS 175
- Delgado Community College LA 188
- Community College of Baltimore County, The MD 198
- Cape Cod Community College MA 214
- FINE Mortuary College MA 209
- Wayne State University MI 232
- University of Minnesota MN 243
- East Mississippi Community College MS 246
- Northwest Mississippi Community College MS 248
- Eastwick College NJ 277
- Mercer County Community College NJ 278
- #American Academy McAllister Institute of Funeral Service NY 290
- Hudson Valley Community College NY 302
- Nassau Community College NY 307
- SUNY Canton-College of Technology NY 320
- Fayetteville Technical Community College NC 334
- Cincinnati College of Mortuary Science OH 350
- University of Central Oklahoma OK 370
- Mt. Hood Community College OR 374
- Northampton Community College PA 391
- Pittsburgh Institute of Mortuary Science PA 396
- Piedmont Technical College SC 411
- John A. Gupton College TN 420
- Commonwealth Institute of Funeral Service TX 433
- Dallas Institute of Funeral Service TX 435
- Northeast Texas Community College TX 440
- San Antonio College TX 429
- Salt Lake Community College UT 461
- John Tyler Community College VA 474
- Tidewater Community College VA 475
- Lake Washington Institute of Technology WA 481
- Milwaukee Area Technical College WI 499

HLC: Higher Learning Commission, North Central Association

- American InterContinental University AZ 10
- Arizona Christian University AZ 10
- Arizona State University AZ 10
- Arizona Western College AZ 11
- Central Arizona College AZ 11
- Chandler-Gilbert Community College AZ 12
- Cochise College AZ 11
- Coconino Community College AZ 11
- Diné College AZ 12
- Eastern Arizona College AZ 12
- Estrella Mountain Community College AZ 13
- GateWay Community College AZ 13
- Glendale Community College AZ 13
- Grand Canyon University AZ 12
- Mesa Community College AZ 13
- Mohave Community College AZ 14
- Northern Arizona University AZ 14
- Northland Pioneer College AZ 14
- Paradise Valley Community College AZ 13
- Phoenix College AZ 13
- Phoenix Seminary AZ 15
- Pima Community College AZ 15
- Prescott College AZ 15
- Rio Salado College AZ 13
- School of Architecture, The AZ 15
- Scottsdale Community College AZ 13
- South Mountain Community College AZ 14
- Southwest College of Naturopathic Medicine & Health Sciences AZ 15
- Tohono O'odham Community College AZ 16
- University of Advancing Technology AZ 16
- University of Arizona AZ 16
- University of Phoenix AZ 16
- Yavapai College AZ 16
- #Arkansas Baptist College AR 16
- Arkansas Colleges of Health Education AR 17
- Arkansas Northeastern College AR 17
- Arkansas State University-Beebe AR 17
- Arkansas State University-Jonesboro AR 17
- Arkansas State University Mid-South AR 17
- Arkansas State University-Mountain Home AR 17
- Arkansas State University-Newport AR 18
- Arkansas State University-Three Rivers AR 18
- Arkansas Tech University AR 18
- Black River Technical College AR 18
- Central Baptist College AR 18
- Cossatot Community College of the University of Arkansas AR 22
- Crowley's Ridge College AR 18
- East Arkansas Community College AR 19
- Harding University Main Campus AR 19
- Henderson State University AR 19
- Hendrix College AR 19
- John Brown University AR 19
- Lyon College AR 19
- National Park College AR 20
- North Arkansas College AR 20
- NorthWest Arkansas Community College AR 20
- Ouachita Baptist University AR 20
- Ozarka College AR 20
- Philander Smith College AR 20
- Phillips Community College of the University of Arkansas AR 22
- South Arkansas Community College AR 21
- Southeast Arkansas College AR 21
- Southern Arkansas University AR 21
- Southern Arkansas University Tech AR 21
- University of Arkansas at Fort Smith AR 21
- University of Arkansas at Little Rock AR 22
- University of Arkansas at Monticello AR 22
- University of Arkansas at Pine Bluff AR 22
- University of Arkansas Community College at Batesville AR 22
- University of Arkansas Community College at Morrilton AR 23
- University of Arkansas Community College Hope-Texarkana AR 22
- University of Arkansas for Medical Sciences AR 22
- University of Arkansas Main Campus AR 21
- University of Arkansas - Pulaski Technical College AR 23
- University of Arkansas Rich Mountain AR 23
- University of Central Arkansas AR 23
- University of the Ozarks AR 23
- Williams Baptist University AR 23
- Adams State University CO 77
- Aims Community College CO 77
- Arapahoe Community College CO 77
- College for Financial Planning CO 78
- Colorado Christian University CO 78
- Colorado College CO 78
- Colorado Mesa University CO 78
- Colorado Mountain College CO 78
- Colorado Northwestern Community College CO 79
- Colorado School of Mines CO 79
- Colorado State University CO 79
- Colorado State University Global CO 80
- Colorado State University-Pueblo CO 80
- Colorado Technical University CO 80
- Community College of Aurora CO 80
- Community College of Denver CO 80
- Denver College of Nursing CO 80
- Denver Seminary CO 80
- Fort Lewis College CO 80
- Front Range Community College CO 81
- Iliff School of Theology CO 81
- Lamar Community College CO 81
- Metropolitan State University of Denver CO 81
- Morgan Community College CO 81
- Naropa University CO 82
- Nazarene Bible College CO 82
- Northeastern Junior College CO 82
- Otero Junior College CO 82
- Pikes Peak Community College CO 82
- Pueblo Community College CO 82
- Red Rocks Community College CO 83
- Regis University CO 83
- Rocky Mountain College of Art & Design CO 83
- Rocky Vista University CO 83
- Trinidad State Junior College CO 83
- United States Air Force Academy CO 503
- University of Colorado Boulder CO 84
- University of Colorado Colorado Springs CO 84
- University of Colorado Denver | Anschutz Medical Campus CO 84
- University of Denver CO 84
- University of Northern Colorado CO 84
- Western Colorado University CO 85
- Adler University IL 132
- American Academy of Art College IL 133
- @American Islamic College IL 133
- Augustana College IL 133
- Aurora University IL 133

HSA: Commission on Accreditation of Healthcare Management Education: healthcare management (M)

HT: National Accrediting Agency for Clinical Laboratory Sciences: histologic technology (C,A,B)

IACBE: International Accreditation Council for Business Education: business programs, accounting and business related (A,B,M,D)

IFSAC: International Fire Service Accreditation Congress Degree Assembly: fire and emergency related programs (A,B,M)

IPSY: American Psychological Association: doctoral internships in health service psychology

JOUR: Accrediting Council on Education for Journalism and Mass Communications: journalism and mass communications (B,M)

KIN: Commission on Accreditation of Allied Health Education Programs: kinesiotherapy (B)

LAW: American Bar Association: law (FP,D)

LC: Commission on Accreditation of Allied Health Programs: lactation consultant (C,A,B,M)

LIB: American Library Association: library and information studies (M)

LSAR: American Society of Landscape Architects: landscape architecture (B,M)

M: Middle States Commission on Higher Education

MAAB: Accrediting Bureau of Health Education Schools: medical assisting (C,A)

MAC: Commission on Accreditation of Allied Health Education Programs: medical assisting (C,A)

MACTE: Montessori Accreditation Council for Teacher Education: Montessori teacher education (C)

MEAC: Midwifery Education Accreditation Council: midwifery education (C,A,B,M,D)

MED: Liaison Committee on Medical Education: medicine (FP,D)

MFCD: American Association for Marriage and Family Therapy: marriage and family therapy (M,D)

Mount Mercy University .... IA 168
University of Iowa .... IA 163
Friends University .... KS .. 174
Kansas State University .... KS .. 175
Campbellsville University .... KY .. 180
Louisville Presbyterian Theological Seminary .... KY .. 183
University of Kentucky .... KY .. 185
University of Louisville .... KY .. 186
University of Louisiana at Monroe .... LA ... 193
University of Maryland College Park .... MD .. 202
Michigan State University .... MI ... 227
Bethel University .... MN .. 234
Capella University .... MN .. 234
Saint Mary's University of Minnesota .... MN .. 243
University of Minnesota .... MN .. 243
University of Southern Mississippi .... MS .. 249
Saint Louis University .... MO . 259
University of Nebraska - Lincoln .... NE .. 269
University of Nevada, Las Vegas .... NV .. 271
University of New Hampshire .... NH .. 274
Seton Hall University .... NJ .. 283
Iona College .... NY .. 302
Nyack College .... NY .. 310
Syracuse University .... NY .. 321
University of Rochester .... NY .. 323
Appalachian State University .... NC .. 340
East Carolina University .... NC .. 341
Pfeiffer University .... NC .. 339
Antioch University .... OH .. 347
Ohio State University Main Campus, The. OH .. 358
University of Akron, Main Campus, The .. OH .. 361
Oklahoma State University .... OK .. 367
Lewis and Clark College .... OR .. 373
University of Oregon .... OR .. 376
Drexel University .... PA .. 382
Evangelical Theological Seminary .... PA .. 383
La Salle University .... PA .. 387
Seton Hill University .... PA .. 398
Thomas Jefferson University .... PA .. 399
University of Rhode Island .... RI ... 405
Converse College .... SC .. 408
Lee University .... TN .. 420
Lipscomb University .... TN .. 421
Abilene Christian University .... TX .. 428
Our Lady of the Lake University .... TX .. 441
St. Mary's University .... TX .. 442
Texas Tech University .... TX .. 450
Texas Wesleyan University .... TX .. 451
Texas Woman's University .... TX .. 451
University of Houston - Clear Lake .... TX .. 452
Brigham Young University .... UT .. 458
Utah State University .... UT .. 460
Virginia Polytechnic Institute and State University .... VA .. 476
Pacific Lutheran University .... WA . 482
Seattle Pacific University .... WA . 483
Seattle University .... WA . 484
Whitworth University .... WA . 486
Edgewood College .... WI ... 492
University of Wisconsin-Stout .... WI ... 497

MIDWF: Accreditation Commission for Midwifery Education: nurse midwifery (C,M,D)

California State University-Fullerton .... CA 31
University of California-San Francisco .... CA 70
University of Colorado Denver I Anschutz Medical Campus .... CO 84
Fairfield University .... CT 87
Yale University .... CT 90
Georgetown University .... DC 92
Emory University .... GA .. 118
@Georgia College & State University .... GA .. 119
University of Illinois at Chicago .... IL 151
Frontier Nursing University .... KY .. 180
University of Michigan-Ann Arbor .... MI ... 231
Wayne State University .... MI ... 232
Bethel University .... MN .. 234
University of Minnesota .... MN .. 243
University of New Mexico Main Campus . NM .. 288
Columbia University in the City of New York .... NY .. 297
New York University .... NY .. 309
Stony Brook University .... NY .. 317
SUNY Downstate Health Sciences University .... NY .. 317
East Carolina University .... NC .. 341
Case Western Reserve University .... OH .. 349
Ohio State University Main Campus, The. OH .. 358
University of Cincinnati Main Campus .... OH .. 361
Oregon Health & Science University .... OR .. 374
Thomas Jefferson University .... PA .. 399
University of Pennsylvania .... PA .. 400
@University of Pittsburgh .... PA .. 400
Vanderbilt University .... TN .. 428
Baylor University .... TX .. 431
Texas Tech University .... TX ... 450
University of Utah, The .... UT .. 459
Shenandoah University .... VA .. 470
Seattle University .... WA . 484
University of Washington .... WA . 485
Marquette University .... WI ... 493

MIL: Commission on Accreditation of Allied Health Education Programs: medical illustrator (M)

Augusta University .... GA .. 116
University of Illinois at Chicago .... IL .. 151
Johns Hopkins University .... MD .. 199

MLTAB: Accrediting Bureau of Health Education Schools: medical laboratory technician (C,A)

Quinebaug Valley Community College .... CT 87
Rockford Career College .... IL 148
Stautzenberger College .... OH .. 361

MLTAD: National Accrediting Agency for Clinical Laboratory Sciences: medical laboratory technician (C,A)

Calhoun Community College .... AL 1
Fortis Institute .... AL 5
Gadsden State Community College .... AL 2
Jefferson State Community College .... AL 2
Wallace State Community College - Hanceville .... AL 3
Brookline College .... AZ 11
Central Arizona College .... AZ 11
Phoenix College .... AZ 13
Pima Community College .... AZ 15
Arkansas State University-Beebe .... AR 17
Arkansas State University-Jonesboro .... AR 17
National Park College .... AR 20
North Arkansas College .... AR 20
Phillips Community College of the University of Arkansas .... AR 22
College of the Canyons .... CA 38
De Anza College .... CA 42
Folsom Lake College .... CA 50
San Diego Miramar College .... CA 61
Southwestern College .... CA 66
Arapahoe Community College .... CO 77
Colorado Mesa University .... CO 78
Otero Junior College .... CO 82
Eastern Florida State College .... FL 98
Florida State College at Jacksonville .... FL ... 101
Indian River State College .... FL ... 102
Keiser University .... FL ... 103
Miami Dade College .... FL ... 104
Albany State University .... GA .. 114
Central Georgia Technical College .... GA .. 116
Chattahoochee Technical College .... GA .. 117
Dalton State College .... GA .. 118
Georgia Piedmont Technical College .... GA .. 120
North Georgia Technical College .... GA .. 123
Southeastern Technical College .... GA .. 125
Southern Regional Technical College .... GA .. 126
West Georgia Technical College .... GA .. 128
Kapiolani Community College .... HI ... 129
North Idaho College .... ID 132
Blessing-Rieman College of Nursing & Health Sciences .... IL 133
Elgin Community College .... IL 137
Illinois Central College .... IL 139
John A. Logan College .... IL 140
Kankakee Community College .... IL 141
Oakton Community College .... IL 146
Shawnee Community College .... IL 149
Southwestern Illinois College .... IL 150
University of Saint Francis .... IN 162
Des Moines Area Community College .... IA 165
Hawkeye Community College .... IA 166
Indian Hills Community College .... IA 166
Iowa Central Community College .... IA 167
Kirkwood Community College .... IA 167
Barton County Community College .... KS .. 171
Coffeyville Community College .... KS .. 173
Manhattan Area Technical College .... KS .. 175
Seward County Community College .... KS .. 177
Henderson Community College .... KY .. 182
Jefferson Community and Technical College .... KY .. 182
Madisonville Community College .... KY .. 182
Maysville Community and Technical College .... KY .. 182
Somerset Community College .... KY .. 182
West Kentucky Community and Technical College .... KY .. 183
Delgado Community College .... LA ... 188
Fortis College .... LA ... 187
L.E. Fletcher Technical Community College .... LA ... 188
Louisiana State University at Alexandria . LA ... 189
South Louisiana Community College .... LA ... 188
Southern University at Shreveport-Louisiana .... LA ... 191
University of Maine at Presque Isle .... ME .. 197
Allegany College of Maryland .... MD .. 197
Anne Arundel Community College .... MD .. 197
College of Southern Maryland .... MD .. 198
Community College of Baltimore County, The .... MD .. 198
Howard Community College .... MD .. 199
Bristol Community College .... MA .. 214
Bunker Hill Community College .... MA .. 214
Middlesex Community College .... MA .. 215
Mount Wachusett Community College .... MA .. 215
Quincy College .... MA .. 218
Springfield Technical Community College MA .. 216
Ferris State University .... MI ... 224
Northern Michigan University .... MI ... 228
Alexandria Technical & Community College .... MN .. 237
Hibbing Community College, A Technical and Community College .... MN .. 238
Lake Superior College .... MN .. 238
Minnesota State Community and Technical College .... MN .. 239
Minnesota West Community and Technical College .... MN .. 239
North Hennepin Community College .... MN .. 240
Northwestern Health Sciences University MN .. 242
Saint Paul College-A Community & Technical College .... MN .. 241
South Central College .... MN .. 241
Copiah-Lincoln Community College .... MS .. 245
Hinds Community College .... MS .. 246
Meridian Community College .... MS .. 247
Mississippi Delta Community College .... MS .. 247
Mississippi Gulf Coast Community College .... MS .. 247
Northeast Mississippi Community College MS .. 248
Pearl River Community College .... MS .. 248
East Central College .... MO . 253
Mineral Area College .... MO . 256
Moberly Area Community College .... MO . 257
North Central Missouri College .... MO . 257
Ozarks Technical Community College .... MO . 257
State Fair Community College .... MO . 259
Three Rivers College .... MO . 260
Flathead Valley Community College .... MT .. 263
Central Community College .... NE .. 266
Mid-Plains Community College .... NE .. 267
Southeast Community College .... NE .. 269
Western Nebraska Community College .... NE .. 270
College of Southern Nevada .... NV .. 270
River Valley Community College .... NH .. 273
Mercer County Community College .... NJ .. 278
Central New Mexico Community College NM .. 285
City University of New York Bronx Community College .... NY .. 293
Dutchess Community College .... NY .. 298
Erie Community College .... NY .. 299
Monroe Community College .... NY .. 307
Nassau Community College .... NY .. 307
Orange County Community College .... NY .. 310
SUNY Broome Community College .... NY .. 317
Alamance Community College .... NC .. 332
Asheville - Buncombe Technical Community College .... NC .. 332
Beaufort County Community College .... NC .. 332
Central Piedmont Community College .... NC .. 333
Coastal Carolina Community College .... NC .. 333
College of the Albemarle .... NC .. 333
Davidson-Davie Community College .... NC .. 334
Halifax Community College .... NC .. 335
Sandhills Community College .... NC .. 337
Southeastern Community College .... NC .. 338
Southwestern Community College .... NC .. 338
Stanly Community College .... NC .. 338
Wake Technical Community College .... NC .. 338
Wayne Community College .... NC .. 338
Western Piedmont Community College .... NC .. 339
Bismarck State College .... ND .. 346
Turtle Mountain Community College .... ND .. 346
Cincinnati State Technical and Community College .... OH .. 350
Clark State College .... OH .. 350
Columbus State Community College .... OH .. 351
Cuyahoga Community College .... OH .. 351
Edison State Community College .... OH .. 352
Hocking College .... OH .. 353
Lakeland Community College .... OH .. 354
Lorain County Community College .... OH .. 355
Marion Technical College .... OH .. 355
Shawnee State University .... OH .. 360
Sinclair Community College .... OH .. 360
Stark State College .... OH .. 360
Washington State Community College .... OH .. 363
Youngstown State University .... OH .. 364
Zane State College .... OH .. 365
Northeastern Oklahoma Agricultural and Mechanical College .... OK .. 366
Rose State College .... OK .. 369
Seminole State College .... OK .. 369
Southwestern Oklahoma State University. OK .. 370
Tulsa Community College .... OK .. 370
Portland Community College .... OR .. 375
Bucks County Community College .... PA .. 379
Community College of Allegheny County PA .. 381
Community College of Philadelphia .... PA .. 381
HACC, Central Pennsylvania's Community College .... PA .. 385
Harcum College .... PA .. 385
Mercyhurst University .... PA .. 389
Montgomery County Community College PA .. 390
Mount Aloysius College .... PA .. 390
Reading Area Community College .... PA .. 396
Community College of Rhode Island .... RI 404
New England Institute of Technology .... RI 404
Florence - Darlington Technical College .. SC .. 409
Greenville Technical College .... SC .. 409
Midlands Technical College .... SC .. 410
Spartanburg Community College .... SC .. 412
Tri-County Technical College .... SC .. 412
Trident Technical College .... SC .. 412
York Technical College .... SC .. 414
Lake Area Technical College .... SD .. 415
Mitchell Technical College .... SD .. 415
Western Dakota Technical College .... SD .. 417
Columbia State Community College .... TN .. 424
Concorde Career College .... TN .. 419
Fortis Institute .... TN .. 419
Jackson State Community College .... TN .. 424
Motlow State Community College .... TN .. 424
Northeast State Community College .... TN .. 425
Southwest Tennessee Community College .... TN .. 425
Volunteer State Community College .... TN .. 425
Amarillo College .... TX ... 429
Austin Community College District .... TX ... 430
Central Texas College .... TX ... 432
Dallas College, El Centro Campus .... TX ... 434
Del Mar College .... TX ... 435
El Paso Community College .... TX ... 436
Grayson College .... TX ... 436
Houston Community College .... TX ... 437
McLennan Community College .... TX ... 439
Navarro College .... TX ... 440
Northeast Texas Community College .... TX ... 440
Panola College .... TX ... 441
St. Philip's College .... TX ... 429
San Jacinto College Central .... TX ... 443
Tarleton State University .... TX ... 446
Texas Southmost College .... TX ... 449
Tyler Junior College .... TX ... 452
Weber State University .... UT .. 461
Central Virginia Community College .... VA .. 473
J. Sargeant Reynolds Community College .... VA .. 474
Northern Virginia Community College .... VA .. 474
Tidewater Community College .... VA .. 475
Virginia Western Community College .... VA .. 475

Wytheville Community College ... VA . 476
Clover Park Technical College ... WA . 478
Shoreline Community College ... WA . 484
Wenatchee Valley College ... WA . 485
BridgeValley Community & Technical College ... WV . 488
Marshall University ... WV . 489
New River Community and Technical College ... WV . 488
Pierpont Community & Technical College WV . 488
Southern West Virginia Community and Technical College ... WV . 488
Blackhawk Technical College ... WI ... 498
Chippewa Valley Technical College ... WI ... 498
Fox Valley Technical College ... WI ... 498
Madison Area Technical College ... WI ... 499
Milwaukee Area Technical College ... WI ... 499
Moraine Park Technical College ... WI ... 499
Northcentral Technical College ... WI ... 499
Northeast Wisconsin Technical College .. WI ... 499
Southwest Wisconsin Technical College . WI ... 500
Western Technical College ... WI ... 500
Casper College ... WY . 500

MPCAC: Masters in Psychology and Counseling Accreditation Council: counseling and psychology (M)

University of Denver ... CO 84
University of West Florida ... FL ... 111
Augusta University ... GA .. 116
Brenau University ... GA .. 116
Clayton State University ... GA .. 117
University of Georgia ... GA .. 126
University of Hawaii at Hilo ... HI 129
Western Illinois University ... IL 153
Indiana University Bloomington ... IN 156
University of Indianapolis ... IN 161
University of Kansas Main Campus ... KS .. 177
Morehead State University ... KY .. 184
Murray State University ... KY .. 184
Frostburg State University ... MD .. 204
Towson University ... MD .. 204
Assumption University ... MA .. 206
Boston College ... MA .. 207
Bridgewater State University ... MA .. 212
University of Massachusetts Boston ... MA .. 211
University of Southern Mississippi ... MS .. 249
Avila University ... MO .. 250
University of Missouri - Kansas City ... MO .. 261
Felician University ... NJ ... 277
William Paterson University of New Jersey ... NJ ... 284
New Mexico Highlands University ... NM .. 286
College of Staten Island CUNY ... NY .. 293
Fordham University ... NY .. 300
New York University ... NY .. 309
Russell Sage College ... NY .. 313
Teachers College, Columbia University ... NY .. 322
University at Albany, SUNY ... NY .. 316
University at Buffalo-SUNY ... NY .. 316
#University of Central Oklahoma ... OK .. 370
Pacific University ... OR .. 375
Arcadia University ... PA .. 378
Chatham University ... PA .. 380
Chestnut Hill College ... PA .. 381
Delaware Valley University ... PA .. 382
Eastern University ... PA .. 383
Lehigh University ... PA .. 388
Robert Morris University ... PA .. 397
Citadel, The Military College of South Carolina, The ... SC .. 407
Francis Marion University ... SC .. 409
University of South Carolina Aiken ... SC .. 413
Midwestern State University ... TX ... 440
Texas A & M International University ... TX ... 446
University of Utah, The ... UT .. 459
Whitworth University ... WA . 486
University of Wisconsin-Milwaukee ... WI ... 496

MT: National Accrediting Agency for Clinical Laboratory Sciences: medical technology/laboratory scientist (C,B)

Auburn University at Montgomery ... AL 4
University of Alabama at Birmingham ... AL 8
University of Alaska Anchorage ... AK 9
Arizona State University ... AZ 10
Brookline College ... AZ 11
Arkansas State University-Jonesboro ... AR 17
Baptist Health College Little Rock ... AR 18
University of Arkansas for Medical Sciences ... AR 22
California State University-Dominguez Hills ... CA 30
California State University-Los Angeles ... CA 31
Loma Linda University ... CA 48
San Francisco State University ... CA 33
San Jose State University ... CA 34
University of California-Davis ... CA 69
University of California-Irvine ... CA 69
University of California-San Diego ... CA 70
Metropolitan State University of Denver .. CO 81
University of Bridgeport ... CT 89
University of Connecticut ... CT 89
University of Delaware ... DE 91
George Washington University ... DC 92
Howard University ... DC 92
Barry University ... FL 96
Florida Gulf Coast University ... FL ... 109
Florida Southern College ... FL ... 100
Hillsborough Community College ... FL ... 102
Santa Fe College ... FL ... 108
University of Central Florida ... FL ... 110
University of West Florida ... FL ... 111
Augusta University ... GA .. 116
Georgia Southern University ... GA .. 120
Thomas University ... GA .. 126
University of Hawaii at Manoa ... HI 129
Idaho State University ... ID 131
Illinois State University ... IL 140
Loyola University Chicago ... IL 143
Northern Illinois University ... IL 146
Rush University ... IL 148
University of Illinois Springfield ... IL 152
Indiana University-Purdue University Indianapolis ... IN 157
Indiana University South Bend ... IN 157
Allen College ... IA 163
Mercy College of Health Sciences ... IA 168
St. Luke's College ... IA 169
Wichita State University ... KS .. 178
Bellarmine University ... KY .. 179
Eastern Kentucky University ... KY .. 180
University of Kentucky ... KY .. 185
Franciscan Missionaries of Our Lady University ... LA ... 187
Louisiana State University at Alexandria . LA ... 189
Louisiana State University Health Sciences Center at Shreveport ... LA ... 189
Louisiana State University Health Sciences Center-New Orleans ... LA ... 189
Louisiana Tech University ... LA ... 192
McNeese State University ... LA ... 192
University of Louisiana at Monroe ... LA ... 193
Morgan State University ... MD .. 201
Salisbury University ... MD .. 204
Stevenson University ... MD .. 202
University of Maryland, Baltimore ... MD .. 203
University of Massachusetts Dartmouth .. MA .. 212
University of Massachusetts Lowell ... MA .. 212
Andrews University ... MI ... 221
Eastern Michigan University ... MI ... 223
Ferris State University ... MI ... 224
Grand Valley State University ... MI ... 224
Lake Superior State University ... MI ... 226
Michigan State University ... MI ... 227
Michigan Technological University ... MI ... 228
Northern Michigan University ... MI ... 228
Saginaw Valley State University ... MI ... 230
Wayne State University ... MI ... 232
Northwestern Health Sciences University MN .. 242
St. Cloud State University ... MN .. 240
University of Minnesota ... MN .. 243
University of Mississippi Medical Center . MS .. 249
University of Southern Mississippi ... MS .. 249
Saint Louis University ... MO . 259
Southeast Missouri Hospital College of Nursing and Health Sciences ... MO . 259
Montana State University ... MT .. 264
University of Nebraska Medical Center ... NE .. 269
College of Southern Nevada ... NV .. 270
University of New Hampshire ... NH .. 274
University of New Mexico Main Campus . NM .. 288
Albany College of Pharmacy and Health Sciences ... NY .. 289
City University of New York York College NY .. 295
College of Staten Island CUNY ... NY .. 293
Farmingdale State College ... NY .. 320
Long Island University - LIU Post ... NY .. 304
Marist College ... NY .. 305
Mercy College ... NY .. 306
Nazareth College of Rochester ... NY .. 307
St. John's University ... NY .. 313
State University of New York Upstate Medical University ... NY .. 317
Stony Brook University ... NY .. 317
University at Buffalo-SUNY ... NY .. 316
University of Rochester ... NY .. 323
Carolinas College of Health Sciences ... NC .. 327
East Carolina University ... NC .. 341
University of North Carolina at Chapel Hill ... NC .. 342
Winston-Salem State University ... NC .. 344
University of North Dakota ... ND .. 345
Bowling Green State University ... OH .. 348
Ohio Northern University ... OH .. 358
Ohio State University Main Campus, The. OH .. 358
University of Cincinnati Main Campus ... OH .. 361
University of Toledo ... OH .. 363
Wright State University Main Campus ... OH .. 364
Youngstown State University ... OH .. 364
Northeastern State University ... OK .. 366
Oklahoma Christian University ... OK .. 367
Oregon Health & Science University ... OR .. 374
Oregon Institute of Technology ... OR .. 374
Neumann University ... PA .. 391
Pennsylvania College of Health Sciences PA .. 392
Thomas Jefferson University ... PA .. 399
Inter American University of Puerto Rico / Metropolitan Campus ... PR .. 508
Inter American University of Puerto Rico San German Campus ... PR .. 508
Universidad Ana G. Mendez Gurabo Campus ... PR .. 510
University of Puerto Rico-Medical Sciences Campus ... PR .. 512
South Dakota State University ... SD .. 417
Austin Peay State University ... TN .. 417
Baptist Health Sciences University ... TN .. 418
Lincoln Memorial University ... TN .. 421
University of Tennessee, Knoxville ... TN .. 427
Vanderbilt University ... TN .. 428
East Texas Baptist University ... TX ... 435
Tarleton State University ... TX ... 446
Texas A & M University - Corpus Christi . TX ... 447
Texas Southern University ... TX ... 449
Texas State University ... TX ... 450
Texas Tech University Health Sciences Center ... TX ... 451
University of Texas at El Paso ... TX ... 455
University of Texas Health Science Center at San Antonio ... TX ... 456
University of Texas MD Anderson Cancer Center, The ... TX ... 456
University of Texas Medical Branch, The TX ... 456
University of Texas Rio Grande Valley, The ... TX ... 455
Brigham Young University ... UT .. 458
Dixie State University ... UT .. 460
University of Utah, The ... UT .. 459
Weber State University ... UT .. 461
University of Vermont ... VT ... 463
Old Dominion University ... VA .. 469
Radford University ... VA .. 469
Virginia Commonwealth University ... VA .. 473
Heritage University ... WA .. 481
University of Washington ... WA .. 485
Marshall University ... WV . 489
West Liberty University ... WV . 490
West Virginia University ... WV . 490
Marquette University ... WI ... 493
University of Wisconsin-Milwaukee ... WI ... 496
University of Wisconsin-Parkside ... WI ... 496
University of Wisconsin-Stevens Point ... WI ... 497
University of Wyoming ... WY . 501

MUS: National Association of Schools of Music: music (C,A,B, M,D)

Alabama State University ... AL 4
Auburn University ... AL 4
Birmingham-Southern College ... AL 4
Huntingdon College ... AL 5
Jacksonville State University ... AL 6
Samford University ... AL 6
Troy University ... AL 7
University of Alabama at Birmingham ... AL 8
University of Alabama in Huntsville ... AL 8
University of Alabama, The ... AL 7
University of Mobile ... AL 8
University of Montevallo ... AL 8
University of North Alabama ... AL 8
University of South Alabama ... AL 9
University of Alaska Anchorage ... AK 9
Arizona State University ... AZ 10
Northern Arizona University ... AZ 14
University of Arizona ... AZ 16
Arkansas State University-Jonesboro ... AR 17
Arkansas Tech University ... AR 18
Harding University Main Campus ... AR 19
Henderson State University ... AR 19
Ouachita Baptist University ... AR 20
University of Arkansas at Fort Smith ... AR 21
University of Arkansas at Little Rock ... AR 22
University of Arkansas at Monticello ... AR 22
University of Arkansas at Pine Bluff ... AR 22
University of Arkansas Main Campus ... AR 21
University of Central Arkansas ... AR 23
Azusa Pacific University ... CA 26
Biola University ... CA 27
California Baptist University ... CA 27
California College of Music ... CA 28
California Jazz Conservatory ... CA 29
California Polytechnic State University-San Luis Obispo ... CA 29
California State Polytechnic University-Pomona ... CA 30
California State University-Bakersfield ... CA 30
California State University-Dominguez Hills ... CA 30
California State University-East Bay ... CA 31
California State University-Fresno ... CA 31
California State University-Fullerton ... CA 31
California State University-Long Beach ... CA 31
California State University-Los Angeles ... CA 31
California State University-Northridge ... CA 32
California State University-Sacramento ... CA 32
California State University-San Bernardino ... CA 32
California State University-Stanislaus ... CA 33
Chabot College ... CA 35
Chapman University ... CA 36
Colburn School, The ... CA 38
Concordia University Irvine ... CA 39
Humboldt State University ... CA 33
La Sierra University ... CA 47
Los Angeles College of Music ... CA 48
Loyola Marymount University ... CA 51
Master's University & Seminary, The ... CA 51
Musicians Institute ... CA 53
Pacific Union College ... CA 55
Pepperdine University ... CA 56
Point Loma Nazarene University ... CA 57
San Francisco State University ... CA 33
San Jose State University ... CA 34
Sonoma State University ... CA 34
University of Redlands ... CA 72
University of the Pacific ... CA 71
Vanguard University of Southern California ... CA 73
Westmont College ... CA 76
Adams State University ... CO 77
Colorado Christian University ... CO 78
Colorado Mesa University ... CO 78
Colorado State University ... CO 79
Colorado State University-Pueblo ... CO 80
Fort Lewis College ... CO 80
Metropolitan State University of Denver .. CO 81
University of Colorado Boulder ... CO 84
University of Denver ... CO 84
University of Northern Colorado ... CO 84
Western Colorado University ... CO 85
Central Connecticut State University ... CT 85
Manchester Community College ... CT 86
Southern Connecticut State University ... CT 86
University of Connecticut ... CT 89
University of Hartford ... CT 89
Western Connecticut State University ... CT 86
University of Delaware ... DE 91
American University ... DC 91
Catholic University of America, The ... DC 92
Howard University ... DC 92
Baptist College of Florida, The ... FL 95
Bethune Cookman University ... FL 96

NAEYC: National Association for the Education of Young Children: early childhood education (A,B,M)

Spartanburg Community College ... SC .. 412
Tri-County Technical College ... SC .. 412
Trident Technical College ... SC .. 412
Williamsburg Technical College ... SC .. 414
York Technical College ... SC .. 414
Chattanooga State Community College .. TN .. 424
Cleveland State Community College ... TN .. 424
Dyersburg State Community College ... TN .. 424
East Tennessee State University ... TN .. 419
Nashville State Community College ... TN .. 424
Northeast State Community College ... TN .. 425
Pellissippi State Community College ... TN .. 425
Roane State Community College ... TN .. 425
Southwest Tennessee Community College ... TN .. 425
Walters State Community College ... TN .. 425
Austin Community College District ... TX ... 430
Collin College ... TX ... 433
Dallas College, Brookhaven Campus ... TX ... 434
Del Mar College ... TX ... 435
Grayson College ... TX ... 436
Houston Community College ... TX ... 437
St. Philip's College ... TX ... 429
San Antonio College ... TX ... 429
San Jacinto College Central ... TX ... 443
University of Texas at San Antonio, The . TX ... 455
Wharton County Junior College ... TX ... 458
Weber State University ... UT .. 461
Danville Community College ... VA .. 473
Northern Virginia Community College ... VA .. 474
Thomas Nelson Community College ... VA .. 475
Tidewater Community College ... VA .. 475
Bates Technical College ... WA . 477
Highline College ... WA . 481
Chippewa Valley Technical College ... WI ... 498
Milwaukee Area Technical College ... WI ... 499
Waukesha County Technical College ... WI ... 500
Casper College ... WY . 500

NAIT: The Association of Technology, Management, and Applied Engineering: technology, applied technology, engineering technology and technology-related programs (A,B,M)

Jacksonville State University ... AL ... 6
Arkansas State University-Beebe ... AR 17
University of Arkansas at Fort Smith ... AR 21
University of Arkansas at Pine Bluff ... AR 22
California State University-Chico ... CA 30
California State University-Fresno ... CA 31
Rio Hondo College ... CA 58
San Jose State University ... CA 34
Central Connecticut State University ... CT 85
Idaho State University ... ID 131
University of Idaho ... ID 132
Illinois State University ... IL 140
Northern Illinois University ... IL 146
Southern Illinois University Carbondale ... IL 150
Indiana State University ... IN 156
Ivy Tech Community College of Indiana-Indianapolis ... IN 158
Purdue University Main Campus ... IN 160
Purdue University Northwest ... IN 160
Iowa State University ... IA 163
Fort Hays State University ... KS .. 173
Eastern Kentucky University ... KY .. 180
Morehead State University ... KY .. 184
Western Kentucky University ... KY .. 186
Baton Rouge Community College ... LA ... 187
Bossier Parish Community College ... LA ... 187
Delgado Community College ... LA ... 188
L.E. Fletcher Technical Community College ... LA ... 188
Louisiana Delta Community College ... LA ... 188
Nicholls State University ... LA ... 192
Northwest Louisiana Technical Community College ... LA ... 188
Nunez Community College ... LA ... 188
River Parishes Community College ... LA ... 188
South Louisiana Community College ... LA ... 188
Southeastern Louisiana University ... LA ... 193
SOWELA Technical Community College . LA ... 188
University of Louisiana at Lafayette ... LA ... 193
University of Southern Maine ... ME .. 197
Bemidji State University ... MN .. 237
Minnesota State University Moorhead ... MN .. 239
St. Cloud State University ... MN .. 240
Alcorn State University ... MS .. 245
Jackson State University ... MS .. 246
East Central College ... MO . 253
Ozarks Technical Community College ... MO . 257
Southeast Missouri State University ... MO . 259
State Technical College of Missouri ... MO . 260
University of Central Missouri ... MO . 260
University of Nebraska at Kearney ... NE . 269
Rowan College at Burlington County ... NJ ... 281
State University of New York College at Buffalo ... NY .. 317
East Carolina University ... NC .. 341
North Carolina Agricultural and Technical State University ... NC .. 341
Bowling Green State University ... OH .. 348
Kent State University Kent Campus ... OH .. 354
Ohio Northern University ... OH .. 358
Ohio University Main Campus ... OH .. 358
Owens Community College ... OH .. 359
Southwestern Oklahoma State University. OK .. 370
Millersville University of Pennsylvania ... PA .. 395
Pennsylvania College of Technology ... PA .. 392
Cleveland State Community College ... TN .. 424
Columbia State Community College ... TN .. 424
Jackson State Community College ... TN .. 424
Middle Tennessee State University ... TN .. 422
Motlow State Community College ... TN .. 424
Nashville State Community College ... TN .. 424
Northeast State Community College ... TN .. 425
Pellissippi State Community College ... TN .. 425
Tennessee State University ... TN .. 426
Walters State Community College ... TN .. 425
Texas A & M University - Kingsville ... TX ... 447
Texas Southern University ... TX ... 449
Texas State University ... TX ... 450
University of Houston ... TX ... 452
University of Texas at Tyler ... TX ... 456
Norfolk State University ... VA .. 469
Pierpont Community & Technical College WV . 488
University of Wisconsin-Platteville ... WI .. 496

NATUR: Council on Naturopathic Medical Education: naturopathic medical education (FP,D)

Southwest College of Naturopathic Medicine & Health Sciences ... AZ 15
University of Bridgeport ... CT 89
National University of Health Sciences ... IL 145
National University of Natural Medicine ... OR .. 374
Universidad Ana G. Mendez Gurabo Campus ... PR .. 510
Bastyr University ... WA . 477

NDT: Commission on Accreditation of Allied Health Education Programs: neurodiagnostic technology (C,A)

GateWay Community College ... AZ 13
Concorde Career College ... CA 39
Orange Coast College ... CA 38
Lincoln Land Community College ... IL 143
Kirkwood Community College ... IA 167
Johnson County Community College ... KS .. 174
University of Holy Cross ... LA ... 192
Laboure College ... MA .. 211
Kellogg Community College ... MI ... 225
Lansing Community College ... MI ... 226
Central New Mexico Community College NM .. 285
Catawba Valley Community College ... NC .. 333
Pamlico Community College ... NC .. 336
Cuyahoga Community College ... OH .. 351
Sinclair Community College ... OH .. 360
Southeast Technical College ... SD .. 417
Baptist Health Sciences University ... TN .. 418
Vanderbilt University ... TN .. 428
Alvin Community College ... TX ... 429
Concorde Career Institute ... TX ... 433
University of Utah, The ... UT .. 459
Bellevue College ... WA . 477
Fox Valley Technical College ... WI ... 498

NMT: Joint Review Committee on Education Programs in Nuclear Medicine Technology: nuclear medicine technology (C,A,B,M)

University of Alabama at Birmingham ... AL ... 8
GateWay Community College ... AZ 13
Baptist Health College Little Rock ... AR 18
University of Arkansas for Medical Sciences ... AR 22
Kaiser Permanente School of Allied Health Sciences ... CA 46
Loma Linda University ... CA 48
Gateway Community College ... CT 86
AdventHealth University ... FL 95
Broward College ... FL 96
Hillsborough Community College ... FL ... 102
Miami Dade College ... FL ... 104
Santa Fe College ... FL ... 108
Augusta University ... GA .. 116
Georgia Southern University ... GA .. 120
College of DuPage ... IL 135
Indiana University-Purdue University Indianapolis ... IN 157
University of Iowa ... IA 163
Delgado Community College ... LA ... 188
Johns Hopkins University ... MD .. 199
Prince George's Community College ... MD .. 201
MCPHS University ... MA .. 216
Regis College ... MA .. 218
Salem State University ... MA .. 213
Ferris State University ... MI ... 224
Saint Mary's University of Minnesota ... MN .. 243
University of Mississippi Medical Center . MS .. 249
Saint Louis University ... MO . 259
University of Missouri - Columbia ... MO . 261
Rowan College of South Jersey ... NJ ... 281
University of New Mexico Main Campus . NM .. 288
City University of New York Bronx Community College ... NY .. 293
#Manhattan College ... NY .. 304
Molloy College ... NY .. 306
University at Buffalo-SUNY ... NY .. 316
Caldwell Community College and Technical Institute ... NC .. 332
Forsyth Technical Community College ... NC .. 334
University of North Carolina at Chapel Hill ... NC .. 342
Cuyahoga Community College ... OH .. 351
University of Cincinnati Main Campus ... OH .. 361
University of Findlay, The ... OH .. 362
Community College of Allegheny County PA .. 381
Pennsylvania College of Health Sciences PA .. 392
Robert Morris University ... PA .. 397
University of Puerto Rico-Medical Sciences Campus ... PR .. 512
Midlands Technical College ... SC .. 410
Baptist Health Sciences University ... TN .. 418
Chattanooga State Community College .. TN .. 424
South College ... TN .. 423
Vanderbilt University ... TN .. 428
Amarillo College ... TX ... 429
Galveston College ... TX ... 436
Houston Community College ... TX ... 437
Tarrant County College District ... TX ... 445
University of the Incarnate Word ... TX ... 453
University of Utah, The ... UT .. 459
Old Dominion University ... VA .. 469
Virginia Commonwealth University ... VA .. 473
Bellevue College ... WA . 477
West Virginia University ... WV . 490
University of Wisconsin-La Crosse ... WI ... 496

NUR: Accreditation Commission for Education in Nursing: nursing (B,M,D)

Oakwood University ... AL ... 6
Troy University ... AL ... 7
Tuskegee University ... AL ... 7
University of Alaska Anchorage ... AK ... 9
Arkansas State University-Jonesboro ... AR 17
Arkansas Tech University ... AR 18
Ouachita Baptist University ... AR 20
Southern Arkansas University ... AR 21
University of Arkansas at Little Rock ... AR 22
Pacific Union College ... CA 55
Colorado Mountain College ... CO 78
Colorado State University-Pueblo ... CO 80
Denver College of Nursing ... CO 80
Metropolitan State University of Denver .. CO 81
Platt College ... CO 82
Post University ... CT 88
Delaware State University ... DE 90
Delaware Technical Community College, Terry Campus ... DE 91
University of the District of Columbia ... DC 94
Ave Maria University ... FL 95
Bethune Cookman University ... FL 96
Chipola College ... FL 97
College of Central Florida ... FL 97
Daytona State College ... FL 98
Florida Agricultural and Mechanical University ... FL ... 109
Florida SouthWestern State College ... FL ... 101
Florida State College at Jacksonville ... FL ... 101
Hodges University ... FL ... 102
Indian River State College ... FL ... 102
International College of Health Sciences . FL ... 102
Lake-Sumter State College ... FL ... 103
Miami Dade College ... FL ... 104
Miami Regional University ... FL ... 104
North Florida College ... FL ... 104
Palm Beach State College ... FL ... 105
Pensacola State College ... FL ... 105
Polk State College ... FL ... 106
St. Johns River State College ... FL ... 107
Seminole State College of Florida ... FL ... 108
South Florida State College ... FL ... 108
State College of Florida, Manatee-Sarasota ... FL ... 109
Tallahassee Community College ... FL ... 112
Abraham Baldwin Agricultural College ... GA .. 114
Albany State University ... GA .. 114
College of Coastal Georgia ... GA .. 117
Dalton State College ... GA .. 118
East Georgia State College ... GA .. 118
Georgia Highlands College ... GA .. 119
Gordon State College ... GA .. 120
LaGrange College ... GA .. 122
Middle Georgia State University ... GA .. 122
Piedmont University ... GA .. 124
South Georgia State College ... GA .. 125
Thomas University ... GA .. 126
University of North Georgia ... GA .. 127
University of Guam ... GU .. 504
University of Hawaii at Hilo ... HI 129
Chicago State University ... IL 134
Governors State University ... IL 138
Rockford University ... IL 148
St. John's College ... IL 149
Bethel University ... IN 154
Indiana State University ... IN 156
Indiana University East ... IN 157
Indiana University Kokomo ... IN 157
Indiana University Northwest ... IN 157
Purdue University Northwest ... IN 160
University of Evansville ... IN 161
Vincennes University ... IN 162
Iowa Wesleyan University ... IA 167
Emporia State University ... KS .. 173
Grantham University ... KS .. 174
Campbellsville University ... KY .. 180
Frontier Nursing University ... KY .. 180
Galen College of Nursing ... KY .. 180
Kentucky State University ... KY .. 183
Midway University ... KY .. 184
Thomas More University ... KY .. 185
University of Pikeville ... KY .. 186
Dillard University ... LA ... 186
Franciscan Missionaries of Our Lady University ... LA ... 187
Grambling State University ... LA ... 192
Louisiana State University at Alexandria . LA ... 189
University of Holy Cross ... LA ... 192
University of Maine at Augusta ... ME .. 196
University of New England ... ME .. 197
Bowie State University ... MD .. 204
Anna Maria College ... MA .. 205
Endicott College ... MA .. 209
Regis College ... MA .. 218
Andrews University ... MI ... 221
St. Catherine University ... MN .. 243
Alcorn State University ... MS .. 245
Lincoln University ... MO . 254
Missouri Southern State University ... MO . 256
Southwest Baptist University ... MO . 259
Webster University ... MO . 262
Montana State University - Northern ... MT .. 264
Salish Kootenai College ... MT .. 265
Bryan College of Health Sciences ... NE .. 265
Clarkson College ... NE .. 266
College of Saint Mary ... NE .. 266
Midland University ... NE .. 267
Great Basin College ... NV .. 271
Franklin Pierce University ... NH .. 273

NURSE: Commission on Collegiate Nursing Education: nursing (C,B, M,D)

NW: Northwest Commission on Colleges and Universities

NY: New York State Board of Regents

OPD: Commission on Opticianry Accreditation: opticianry (A)

OPE: Commission on Accreditation of Allied Health Education Programs: orthotics and prosthetics (C,B,M)

OPT: American Optometric Association: optometry (FP,D)

OPTR: American Optometric Association: optometric residency programs

OPTT: American Optometric Association: optometric technician (C)

OSTEO: American Osteopathic Association, Office of Osteopathic Education: osteopathic medicine (FP,D)

OT: American Occupational Therapy Association: occupational therapy (M,D)

OTA: American Occupational Therapy Association: occupational therapy assistant (A,B)

PA: National Accrediting Agency for Clinical Laboratory Sciences: pathologist's assistant (C,M)

PAST: Association for Clinical Pastoral Education: clinical pastoral education

- University of Rochester NY 323
- Duke University NC 328
- University of North Carolina at Chapel Hill NC 342
- Kettering College OH 354
- Thomas Jefferson University PA 399
- University of Pennsylvania PA 400
- University of Tennessee, Knoxville TN 427
- #Vanderbilt University TN 428
- Oblate School of Theology TX 440
- University of Texas MD Anderson Cancer Center, The TX 456
- University of Texas Southwestern Medical Center TX 457
- Eastern Mennonite University VA 466
- University of Virginia VA 472
- Virginia Commonwealth University VA 473
- University of Washington WA 485
- West Virginia University WV 490

PCSAS: Psychological Clinical Science Accreditation System: psychological clinical science (D)

- Arizona State University AZ 10
- University of Arizona AZ 16
- University of California-Berkeley CA 69
- University of California-Los Angeles CA 69
- University of Southern California CA 73
- Yale University CT 90
- University of Delaware DE 91
- University of South Florida FL 111
- Emory University GA 118
- University of Georgia GA 126
- Northwestern University IL 146
- University of Illinois Urbana-Champaign IL 152
- Indiana University Bloomington IN 156
- Purdue University Main Campus IN 160
- University of Iowa IA 163
- University of Kentucky KY 185
- University of Maryland College Park MD 202
- Boston University MA 207
- Harvard University MA 210
- Michigan State University MI 227
- University of Michigan-Ann Arbor MI 231
- University of Minnesota MN 243
- University of Missouri - Columbia MO 261
- Washington University in St. Louis MO 262
- Rutgers University - New Brunswick NJ 282
- University of New Mexico Main Campus NM 288
- Stony Brook University NY 317
- University at Buffalo-SUNY NY 316
- Duke University NC 328
- University of North Carolina at Chapel Hill NC 342
- Ohio State University Main Campus, The. OH 358
- Oklahoma State University OK 367
- University of Oregon OR 376
- Penn State University Park PA 391
- Temple University PA 399
- University of Pennsylvania PA 400
- University of Pittsburgh PA 400
- Vanderbilt University TN 428
- University of Texas at Austin TX 455
- University of Virginia VA 472
- Virginia Polytechnic Institute and State University VA 476
- University of Washington WA 485
- University of Wisconsin-Madison WI 495

PDPSY: American Psychological Association: post-doctoral residency in health service psychology

- Stanford University CA 66
- University of California-San Diego CA 70
- University of Southern California CA 73
- University of Michigan-Ann Arbor MI 231
- University of Rochester NY 323
- Brown University RI 403
- Virginia Commonwealth University VA 473
- University of Washington WA 485
- Medical College of Wisconsin WI 493

PERF: Commission on Accreditation of Allied Health Education Programs: perfusionist (C,B,M)

- University of Arizona AZ 16
- Quinnipiac University CT 88
- Barry University FL 96
- Rush University IL 148
- University of Iowa IA 163
- University of Nebraska Medical Center NE 269
- Hofstra University NY 301
- State University of New York Upstate Medical University NY 317
- Thomas Jefferson University PA 399
- Medical University of South Carolina SC 410
- Vanderbilt University TN 428
- University of Texas Health Science Center at Houston (UTHealth), The TX 456
- Milwaukee School of Engineering WI 494

PH: Council on Education for Public Health: public health (B, M,D)

- University of Alabama at Birmingham AL 8
- University of Alaska Anchorage AK 9
- University of Arizona AZ 16
- University of Arkansas for Medical Sciences AR 22
- University of Arkansas Main Campus AR 21
- California Baptist University CA 27
- California State University-Fresno CA 31
- California State University-Fullerton CA 31
- California State University-Long Beach CA 31
- California State University-Northridge CA 32
- California State University-San Bernardino CA 32
- California State University-San Marcos CA 33
- Charles R. Drew University of Medicine & Science CA 36
- Claremont Graduate University CA 37
- Loma Linda University CA 48
- National University CA 53
- San Diego State University CA 33
- San Francisco State University CA 33
- San Jose State University CA 34
- Touro University California CA 68
- University of California-Berkeley CA 69
- University of California-Davis CA 69
- University of California-Irvine CA 69
- University of California-Los Angeles CA 69
- University of San Francisco CA 72
- University of Southern California CA 73
- Colorado State University CO 79
- University of Colorado Denver I Anschutz Medical Campus CO 84
- University of Northern Colorado CO 84
- Southern Connecticut State University CT 86
- Western Connecticut State University CT 86
- Yale University CT 90
- American University DC 91
- George Washington University DC 92
- Bethune Cookman University FL 96
- Florida Agricultural and Mechanical University FL 109
- Florida International University FL 110
- Florida State University FL 110
- Nova Southeastern University FL 105
- University of Florida FL 111
- University of Miami FL 113
- University of North Florida FL 111
- University of South Florida FL 111
- University of West Florida FL 111
- Augusta University GA 116
- Emory University GA 118
- Georgia Southern University GA 120
- Georgia State University GA 120
- Mercer University GA 122
- Morehouse School of Medicine GA 123
- University of Georgia GA 126
- University of Hawaii at Manoa HI 129
- Idaho State University ID 131
- Benedictine University IL 133
- DePaul University IL 136
- Illinois State University IL 140
- Loyola University Chicago IL 143
- Northern Illinois University IL 146
- Northwestern University IL 146
- Southern Illinois University Carbondale IL 150
- Southern Illinois University Edwardsville IL 150
- University of Illinois at Chicago IL 151
- University of Illinois Urbana-Champaign IL 152
- Indiana University Bloomington IN 156
- Indiana University-Purdue University Indianapolis IN 157
- Purdue University Fort Wayne IN 160
- Des Moines University IA 165
- University of Iowa IA 163
- Kansas State University KS 175
- University of Kansas Main Campus KS 177
- Eastern Kentucky University KY 180
- University of Kentucky KY 185
- University of Louisville KY 186
- Western Kentucky University KY 186
- Louisiana State University Health Sciences Center at Shreveport LA 189
- Louisiana State University Health Sciences Center-New Orleans LA 189
- Louisiana State University Shreveport LA 190
- Tulane University LA 191
- University of New England ME 197
- University of Southern Maine ME 197
- Johns Hopkins University MD 199
- Morgan State University MD 201
- Salisbury University MD 204
- Uniformed Services University of the Health Sciences MD 503
- University of Maryland College Park MD 202
- University of Maryland, Baltimore MD 203
- Boston University MA 207
- Harvard University MA 210
- MCPHS University MA 216
- Northeastern University MA 217
- Simmons University MA 218
- Tufts University MA 219
- University of Massachusetts MA 211
- Andrews University MI 221
- Grand Valley State University MI 224
- Oakland University MI 229
- University of Michigan-Ann Arbor MI 231
- University of Michigan-Flint MI 232
- Wayne State University MI 232
- St. Catherine University MN 243
- University of Minnesota MN 243
- Jackson State University MS 246
- University of Southern Mississippi MS 249
- A. T. Still University of Health Sciences MO 250
- Missouri State University MO 256
- Saint Louis University MO 259
- University of Missouri - Columbia MO 261
- Washington University in St. Louis MO 262
- University of Montana - Missoula MT 263
- University of Nebraska Medical Center NE 269
- University of Nevada, Las Vegas NV 271
- University of Nevada, Reno NV 271
- Dartmouth College NH 273
- University of New Hampshire NH 274
- Montclair State University NJ 279
- Rutgers University - New Brunswick NJ 282
- William Paterson University of New Jersey NJ 284
- New Mexico State University Main Campus NM 287
- University of New Mexico Main Campus NM 288
- Albany College of Pharmacy and Health Sciences NY 289
- City University of New York Graduate Center NY 293
- Columbia University in the City of New York NY 297
- Cornell University NY 297
- Hofstra University NY 301
- Icahn School of Medicine at Mount Sinai NY 302
- New York Medical College NY 309
- New York University NY 309
- State University of New York College at Cortland NY 318
- State University of New York College at Old Westbury NY 318
- State University of New York Upstate Medical University NY 317
- Stony Brook University NY 317
- SUNY Downstate Health Sciences University NY 317
- Syracuse University NY 321
- Teachers College, Columbia University NY 322
- University at Albany, SUNY NY 316
- University at Buffalo-SUNY NY 316
- University of Rochester NY 323
- Appalachian State University NC 340
- Campbell University NC 327
- East Carolina University NC 341
- Lenoir-Rhyne University NC 330
- University of North Carolina at Chapel Hill NC 342
- University of North Carolina at Charlotte NC 342
- University of North Carolina at Greensboro NC 343
- University of North Carolina Wilmington NC 343
- North Dakota State University Main Campus ND 345
- University of North Dakota ND 345
- Case Western Reserve University OH 349
- Cleveland State University OH 350
- Kent State University Kent Campus OH 354
- Northeast Ohio Medical University OH 357
- Ohio State University Main Campus, The. OH 358
- Ohio University Main Campus OH 358
- University of Akron, Main Campus, The OH 361
- University of Cincinnati Main Campus OH 361
- University of Toledo OH 363
- Wright State University Main Campus OH 364
- Youngstown State University OH 364
- Oregon Health & Science University OR 374
- Oregon State University OR 375
- Portland State University OR 375
- Arcadia University PA 378
- Drexel University PA 382
- East Stroudsburg University of Pennsylvania PA 394
- La Salle University PA 387
- Temple University PA 399
- Thomas Jefferson University PA 399
- University of Pennsylvania PA 400
- University of Pittsburgh PA 400
- West Chester University of Pennsylvania PA 395
- Ponce Health Sciences University PR 509
- University of Puerto Rico-Medical Sciences Campus PR 512
- Brown University RI 403
- Clemson University SC 407
- Coastal Carolina University SC 408
- University of South Carolina Columbia SC 413
- South Dakota State University SD 417
- University of South Dakota, The SD 416
- East Tennessee State University TN 419
- Meharry Medical College TN 421
- Tennessee State University TN 426
- University of Memphis, The TN 426
- University of Tennessee, Knoxville TN 427
- Vanderbilt University TN 428
- Baylor University TX 431
- Texas A & M University TX 446
- Texas Tech University Health Sciences Center TX 451
- University of North Texas Health Science Center at Fort Worth TX 454
- University of Texas at El Paso TX 455
- University of Texas Health Science Center at Houston (UTHealth), The TX 456
- University of Texas Medical Branch, The TX 456
- Brigham Young University UT 458
- University of Utah, The UT 459
- Westminster College UT 461
- University of Vermont VT 463
- Eastern Virginia Medical School VA 466
- George Mason University VA 467
- Old Dominion University VA 469
- University of Virginia VA 472
- Virginia Commonwealth University VA 473
- Virginia Polytechnic Institute and State University VA 476
- Eastern Washington University WA 479
- University of Washington WA 485
- Western Washington University WA 485
- American Public University System WV 486
- Marshall University WV 489
- West Virginia University WV 490
- Medical College of Wisconsin WI 493
- University of Wisconsin-La Crosse WI 496
- University of Wisconsin-Madison WI 495
- University of Wisconsin-Milwaukee WI 496

PHAR: Accreditation Council for Pharmacy Education: pharmacy (FP,D)

- Auburn University AL 4
- Samford University AL 6
- University of Arizona AZ 16
- Harding University Main Campus AR 19
- University of Arkansas for Medical Sciences AR 22

PLNG: Planning Accreditation Board: certified planning (B,M)

PNUR: Accreditation Commission for Education in Nursing: practical nursing (C)

Fox Valley Technical College .... WI ... 498
Lakeshore Technical College .... WI ... 498
Milwaukee Area Technical College .... WI ... 499
Northeast Wisconsin Technical College .. WI ... 499

POD: American Podiatric Medical Association: podiatry (FP,D)

Samuel Merritt University .... CA 60
Western University of Health Sciences .... CA 75
Barry University .... FL 96
Rosalind Franklin University of Medicine & Science .... IL 148
Des Moines University .... IA 165
New York College of Podiatric Medicine . NY .. 308
Kent State University Kent Campus .... OH .. 354
Temple University .... PA .. 399

POLYT: Commission on Accreditation of Allied Health Education Programs: polysomnographic technologist education (C,A)

Wallace State Community College - Hanceville .... AL 3
GateWay Community College .... AZ 13
Baptist Health College Little Rock .... AR 18
Concorde Career College .... CA 39
Orange Coast College .... CA 38
Santa Fe College .... FL ... 108
Central Georgia Technical College .... GA .. 116
Moraine Valley Community College .... IL 145
Delgado Community College .... LA 188
Community College of Baltimore County, The .... MD .. 198
Montgomery College .... MD .. 200
Northern Essex Community College .... MA .. 215
Minneapolis Community and Technical College .... MN .. 239
Coahoma Community College .... MS .. 245
Southeast Community College .... NE .. 269
Thomas Edison State University .... NJ .. 284
City University of New York Kingsborough Community College .... NY .. 294
Hudson Valley Community College .... NY .. 302
Catawba Valley Community College .... NC .. 333
Central Piedmont Community College ..... NC .. 333
Lenoir Community College .... NC .. 335
Pitt Community College .... NC .. 336
University of North Carolina at Charlotte . NC .. 342
Lakeland Community College .... OH .. 354
Mercy College of Ohio .... OH .. 355
Concorde Career College .... OR .. 372
Linn-Benton Community College .... OR .. 373
Oregon Institute of Technology .... OR .. 374
Concorde Career College .... TN .. 419
Roane State Community College .... TN .. 425
Volunteer State Community College .... TN .. 425
Alvin Community College .... TX ... 429
Collin College .... TX ... 433
Concorde Career Institute .... TX ... 433

PSPSY: American Psychological Association: combined professional-scientific psychology (D)

University of South Alabama .... AL 9
Northern Arizona University .... AZ 14
University of California-Santa Barbara ..... CA 70
Florida State University .... FL ... 110
Rivier University .... NH .. 273
Kean University .... NJ ... 278
Pace University .... NY .. 311
Roberts Wesleyan College .... NY .. 312
University at Buffalo-SUNY .... NY .. 316
Yeshiva University .... NY .. 326
University of Houston - Clear Lake .... TX ... 452
Utah State University .... UT .. 460
James Madison University .... VA .. 468
University of Virginia .... VA .. 472

PTA: American Physical Therapy Association: physical therapy (D)

Alabama State University .... AL 4
@Faulkner University .... AL 5
Samford University .... AL 6
University of Alabama at Birmingham ...... AL 8
University of South Alabama .... AL 9
Northern Arizona University .... AZ 14
@Arkansas Colleges of Health Education .. AR 17
Arkansas State University-Jonesboro ...... AR 17
Harding University Main Campus .... AR 19
University of Arkansas for Medical Sciences .... AR 22
University of Central Arkansas .... AR 23
Azusa Pacific University .... CA 26
California State University-Fresno .... CA 31
California State University-Long Beach ... CA 31
California State University-Northridge ...... CA 32
California State University-Sacramento ... CA 32
Chapman University .... CA 36
Loma Linda University .... CA 48
Mount Saint Mary's University .... CA 52
Samuel Merritt University .... CA 60
San Diego State University .... CA 33
San Francisco State University .... CA 33
University of California-San Francisco ..... CA 70
University of St. Augustine for Health Sciences .... CA 72
University of Southern California .... CA 73
University of the Pacific .... CA 71
West Coast University .... CA 74
Western University of Health Sciences .... CA 75
Regis University .... CO 83
University of Colorado Denver I Anschutz Medical Campus .... CO 84
Quinnipiac University .... CT 88
Sacred Heart University .... CT 89
University of Connecticut .... CT 89
University of Hartford .... CT 89
University of Delaware .... DE 91
George Washington University .... DC 92
#Howard University .... DC 92
AdventHealth University .... FL 95
Florida Agricultural and Mechanical University .... FL ... 109
Florida Gulf Coast University .... FL ... 109
Florida International University .... FL ... 110
@Florida Southern College .... FL ... 100
Nova Southeastern University .... FL ... 105
University of Central Florida .... FL ... 110
University of Florida .... FL ... 111
University of Miami .... FL ... 113
University of North Florida .... FL ... 111
University of South Florida .... FL ... 111
Augusta University .... GA ... 116
Brenau University .... GA ... 116
Emory University .... GA ... 118
Georgia Southern University .... GA ... 120
Georgia State University .... GA ... 120
Mercer University .... GA ... 122
University of North Georgia .... GA ... 127
Idaho State University .... ID 131
Bradley University .... IL 134
Governors State University .... IL 138
Midwestern University .... IL 144
Northern Illinois University .... IL 146
Northwestern University .... IL 146
Rosalind Franklin University of Medicine & Science .... IL 148
University of Illinois at Chicago .... IL 151
@Hanover College .... IN 155
Indiana State University .... IN 156
Indiana University-Purdue University Indianapolis .... IN 157
Indiana Wesleyan University .... IN 158
Trine University .... IN 161
University of Evansville .... IN 161
University of Indianapolis .... IN 161
@Allen College .... IA 163
Briar Cliff University .... IA 164
Clarke University .... IA 164
Des Moines University .... IA 165
St. Ambrose University .... IA 169
University of Iowa .... IA 163
University of Saint Mary .... KS .. 178
Wichita State University .... KS .. 178
Bellarmine University .... KY .. 179
University of Kentucky .... KY .. 185
Western Kentucky University .... KY .. 186
Franciscan Missionaries of Our Lady University .... LA ... 187
Louisiana State University Health Sciences Center at Shreveport .... LA ... 189
Louisiana State University Health Sciences Center-New Orleans .... LA ... 189
Husson University .... ME .. 194
University of New England .... ME .. 197
University of Maryland Eastern Shore ..... MD .. 203
University of Maryland, Baltimore .... MD .. 203
American International College .... MA .. 205
Boston University .... MA .. 207
MCPHS University .... MA .. 216
MGH Institute of Health Professions .... MA .. 217
Northeastern University .... MA .. 217
Simmons University .... MA .. 218
Springfield College .... MA .. 218
@Tufts University .... MA .. 219
University of Massachusetts Lowell .... MA .. 212
Andrews University .... MI ... 221
Central Michigan University .... MI ... 222
Grand Valley State University .... MI ... 224
Oakland University .... MI ... 229
University of Michigan-Flint .... MI ... 232
Wayne State University .... MI ... 232
@Western Michigan University .... MI ... 233
College of Saint Scholastica, The .... MN .. 235
Concordia University, St. Paul .... MN .. 235
St. Catherine University .... MN .. 243
University of Minnesota .... MN .. 243
University of Mississippi Medical Center . MS .. 249
William Carey University .... MS .. 249
Maryville University of Saint Louis .... MO .. 255
Missouri State University .... MO .. 256
Rockhurst University .... MO .. 258
Saint Louis University .... MO .. 259
Southwest Baptist University .... MO .. 259
University of Missouri - Columbia .... MO .. 261
Washington University in St. Louis .... MO .. 262
University of Montana - Missoula .... MT .. 263
@College of Saint Mary .... NE .. 266
Creighton University .... NE .. 266
University of Nebraska Medical Center ... NE .. 269
University of Nevada, Las Vegas .... NV .. 271
Franklin Pierce University .... NH .. 273
Plymouth State University .... NH .. 275
Kean University .... NJ ... 278
Rutgers University - Camden .... NJ ... 281
Seton Hall University .... NJ ... 283
Stockton University .... NJ ... 283
University of New Mexico Main Campus . NM .. 288
City University of New York Hunter College .... NY .. 294
Clarkson University .... NY .. 295
College of Staten Island CUNY .... NY .. 293
Columbia University in the City of New York .... NY .. 297
Daemen College .... NY .. 298
Dominican College of Blauvelt .... NY .. 298
D'Youville College .... NY .. 298
Ithaca College .... NY .. 302
Marist College .... NY .. 305
Mercy College .... NY .. 306
Nazareth College of Rochester .... NY .. 307
New York Institute of Technology .... NY .. 308
New York Medical College .... NY .. 309
New York University .... NY .. 309
Russell Sage College .... NY .. 313
State University of New York Upstate Medical University .... NY .. 317
Stony Brook University .... NY .. 317
SUNY Downstate Health Sciences University .... NY .. 317
Touro College Main Campus .... NY .. 322
University at Buffalo-SUNY .... NY .. 316
Utica College .... NY .. 324
Campbell University .... NC .. 327
Duke University .... NC .. 328
East Carolina University .... NC .. 341
Elon University .... NC .. 328
High Point University .... NC .. 329
Methodist University .... NC .. 331
University of North Carolina at Chapel Hill .... NC .. 342
Western Carolina University .... NC .. 343
Wingate University .... NC .. 344
Winston-Salem State University .... NC .. 344
University of Jamestown .... ND .. 347
University of Mary .... ND .. 347
University of North Dakota .... ND .. 345
Cleveland State University .... OH .. 350
Mount St. Joseph University .... OH .. 356
Ohio State University Main Campus, The. OH .. 358
Ohio University Main Campus .... OH .. 358
University of Cincinnati Main Campus ..... OH .. 361
University of Dayton .... OH .. 362
University of Findlay, The .... OH .. 362
University of Mount Union .... OH .. 362
University of Toledo .... OH .. 363
Walsh University .... OH .. 363
Youngstown State University .... OH .. 364
Langston University .... OK .. 366
@Oklahoma City University .... OK .. 367
George Fox University .... OR .. 373
Pacific University .... OR .. 375
Alvernia University .... PA .. 378
Arcadia University .... PA .. 378
Chatham University .... PA .. 380
DeSales University .... PA .. 382
Drexel University .... PA .. 382
Duquesne University .... PA .. 383
Gannon University .... PA .. 384
Lebanon Valley College .... PA .. 388
@Messiah University .... PA .. 389
Misericordia University .... PA .. 390
@Moravian College .... PA .. 390
Neumann University .... PA .. 391
Saint Francis University .... PA .. 397
Seton Hill University .... PA .. 398
Slippery Rock University of Pennsylvania. PA .. 395
Temple University .... PA .. 399
Thomas Jefferson University .... PA .. 399
University of Pittsburgh .... PA .. 400
University of Scranton, The .... PA .. 401
University of the Sciences in Philadelphia PA .. 401
Widener University .... PA .. 402
University of Puerto Rico-Medical Sciences Campus .... PR .. 512
University of Rhode Island .... RI 405
@Anderson University .... SC .. 406
Medical University of South Carolina .... SC .. 410
University of South Carolina Columbia .... SC .. 413
University of South Dakota, The .... SD .. 416
Belmont University .... TN .. 418
East Tennessee State University .... TN .. 419
Lincoln Memorial University .... TN .. 421
South College .... TN .. 423
Tennessee State University .... TN .. 426
University of Tennessee at Chattanooga TN .. 427
Angelo State University .... TX ... 450
Baylor University .... TX ... 431
Hardin-Simmons University .... TX ... 436
Texas State University .... TX ... 450
Texas Tech University Health Sciences Center .... TX ... 451
Texas Woman's University .... TX ... 451
University of Mary Hardin-Baylor .... TX ... 453
University of North Texas Health Science Center at Fort Worth .... TX ... 454
University of Texas at El Paso .... TX ... 455
University of Texas Health Science Center at San Antonio .... TX ... 456
University of Texas Medical Branch, The TX ... 456
University of Texas Southwestern Medical Center .... TX ... 457
University of the Incarnate Word .... TX ... 453
Rocky Mountain University of Health Professions .... UT ... 459
University of Utah, The .... UT ... 459
University of Vermont .... VT ... 463
Emory & Henry College .... VA .. 466
Hampton University .... VA .. 467
Mary Baldwin University .... VA .. 468
Marymount University .... VA .. 468
#Old Dominion University .... VA .. 469
Radford University .... VA .. 469
Shenandoah University .... VA .. 470
University of Lynchburg .... VA .. 471
Virginia Commonwealth University .... VA .. 473
Eastern Washington University .... WA . 479
University of Puget Sound .... WA . 484
University of Washington .... WA . 485
Marshall University .... WV . 489
West Virginia University .... WV . 490
Wheeling University .... WV . 491
Carroll University .... WI ... 492
Concordia University Wisconsin .... WI ... 492
Marquette University .... WI ... 493
University of Wisconsin-La Crosse .... WI ... 496
University of Wisconsin-Madison .... WI ... 495
University of Wisconsin-Milwaukee .... WI ... 496

PTAA: American Physical Therapy Association: physical therapy assistant (A)

Bishop State Community College .... AL 1

RABN: Association of Advanced Rabbinical and Talmudic Schools: rabbinical and Talmudic education (A,B,M,D)

RAD: Joint Review Committee on Education in Radiologic Technology: radiography (C,A,B)

RADDOS: Joint Review Committee on Education in Radiologic Technology: medical dosimetry (C, B,M)

RADMAG: Joint Review Committee on Education in Radiologic Technology: magnetic resonance (C,A,B)

RTT: Joint Review Committee on Education in Radiologic Technology: radiation therapy (C, A,B,M)

SC: Southern Association of Colleges and Schools, Commission on Colleges

SCPSY: American Psychological Association: school psychology (D)

SP: American Speech-Language-Hearing Association: speech-language pathology (M)

SPAA: Network of Schools of Public Policy, Affairs and Administration: public affairs and administration (M)

SURGA: Commission on Accreditation of Allied Health Education Programs: surgical assistant (C,A)

SURGT: Commission on Accreditation of Allied Health Education Programs: surgical technology (C,A)

Temple College ... TX ... 445
Texas State Technical College Waco ... TX ... 449
Trinity Valley Community College ... TX ... 451
Tyler Junior College ... TX ... 452
Vernon College ... TX ... 457
Dixie State University ... UT ... 460
Salt Lake Community College ... UT ... 461
Lord Fairfax Community College ... VA ... 474
Piedmont Virginia Community College ... VA ... 474
Radford University ... VA ... 469
Riverside College of Health Careers ... VA ... 470
Sentara College of Health Sciences ... VA ... 470
Bellingham Technical College ... WA ... 478
Clover Park Technical College ... WA ... 478
Columbia Basin College ... WA ... 479
Renton Technical College ... WA ... 482
Seattle Central College ... WA ... 483
Spokane Community College ... WA ... 479
Yakima Valley College ... WA ... 486
Southern West Virginia Community and Technical College ... WV ... 488
West Virginia Northern Community College ... WV ... 488
West Virginia University at Parkersburg ... WV ... 490
Blackhawk Technical College ... WI ... 498
Chippewa Valley Technical College ... WI ... 498
Gateway Technical College ... WI ... 498
Madison Area Technical College ... WI ... 499
Mid-State Technical College ... WI ... 499
Milwaukee Area Technical College ... WI ... 499
Moraine Park Technical College ... WI ... 499
Northcentral Technical College ... WI ... 499
Northeast Wisconsin Technical College ... WI ... 499
Waukesha County Technical College ... WI ... 500
Western Technical College ... WI ... 500
Laramie County Community College ... WY ... 501

SURTEC: Accrediting Bureau of Health Education Schools: surgical technology (C,A)

Baptist Health College Little Rock ... AR ... 18
American Career College-Los Angeles ... CA ... 25
CBD College ... CA ... 35
CNI College ... CA ... 37
Glendale Career College ... CA ... 43
Valley College of Medical Careers ... CA ... 73
City College ... FL ... 97
Southern Technical College ... FL ... 109
Rockford Career College ... IL ... 148
Fortis College ... LA ... 187
Midwest Institute-Earth City ... MO ... 256
Mandl School - The College of Allied Health ... NY ... 304
Mohawk Valley Community College ... NY ... 306
Stautzenberger College ... OH ... 361
Meridian Institute of Surgical Assisting ... TN ... 421
Baptist Health System School of Health Professions ... TX ... 430
College of Health Care Professions, The ... TX ... 433
Riverside College of Health Careers ... VA ... 470
Sentara College of Health Sciences ... VA ... 470
Milwaukee Career College ... WI ... 494

SW: Council on Social Work Education: social work (B,M)

Alabama Agricultural and Mechanical University ... AL ... 1
Alabama State University ... AL ... 4
Auburn University ... AL ... 4
Jacksonville State University ... AL ... 6
Miles College ... AL ... 6
Oakwood University ... AL ... 6
Samford University ... AL ... 6
Talladega College ... AL ... 7
Troy University ... AL ... 7
Tuskegee University ... AL ... 7
University of Alabama at Birmingham ... AL ... 8
University of Alabama, The ... AL ... 7
University of Montevallo ... AL ... 8
University of North Alabama ... AL ... 8
University of South Alabama ... AL ... 9
University of Alaska Anchorage ... AK ... 9
University of Alaska Fairbanks ... AK ... 10
Arizona State University ... AZ ... 10
@Grand Canyon University ... AZ ... 12
Northern Arizona University ... AZ ... 14
@University of Phoenix ... AZ ... 16
Arkansas State University-Jonesboro ... AR ... 17
Harding University Main Campus ... AR ... 19
Philander Smith College ... AR ... 20
Southern Arkansas University ... AR ... 21
University of Arkansas at Fort Smith ... AR ... 21
University of Arkansas at Little Rock ... AR ... 22
University of Arkansas at Monticello ... AR ... 22
University of Arkansas at Pine Bluff ... AR ... 22
University of Arkansas Main Campus ... AR ... 21
Azusa Pacific University ... CA ... 26
California Baptist University ... CA ... 27
California State University-Bakersfield ... CA ... 30
California State University-Chico ... CA ... 30
California State University-Dominguez Hills ... CA ... 30
California State University-East Bay ... CA ... 31
California State University-Fresno ... CA ... 31
California State University-Fullerton ... CA ... 31
California State University-Long Beach ... CA ... 31
California State University-Los Angeles ... CA ... 31
California State University-Monterey Bay ... CA ... 32
California State University-Northridge ... CA ... 32
California State University-Sacramento ... CA ... 32
California State University-San Bernardino ... CA ... 32
California State University-San Marcos ... CA ... 33
California State University-Stanislaus ... CA ... 33
Fresno Pacific University ... CA ... 43
Humboldt State University ... CA ... 33
La Sierra University ... CA ... 47
Loma Linda University ... CA ... 48
@Northcentral University ... CA ... 54
@Pacific Oaks College ... CA ... 55
Pacific Union College ... CA ... 55
Point Loma Nazarene University ... CA ... 57
San Diego State University ... CA ... 33
San Francisco State University ... CA ... 33
San Jose State University ... CA ... 34
@Touro University Worldwide ... CA ... 68
University Massachusetts Global ... CA ... 71
University of California-Berkeley ... CA ... 69
University of California-Los Angeles ... CA ... 69
University of Southern California ... CA ... 73
@University of the Pacific ... CA ... 71
Whittier College ... CA ... 76
Colorado Mesa University ... CO ... 78
Colorado State University ... CO ... 79
Colorado State University-Pueblo ... CO ... 80
Metropolitan State University of Denver ... CO ... 81
@University of Colorado Colorado Springs ... CO ... 84
University of Denver ... CO ... 84
Central Connecticut State University ... CT ... 85
Eastern Connecticut State University ... CT ... 85
@Fairfield University ... CT ... 87
Quinnipiac University ... CT ... 88
Sacred Heart University ... CT ... 89
Southern Connecticut State University ... CT ... 86
University of Connecticut ... CT ... 89
University of Saint Joseph ... CT ... 90
Western Connecticut State University ... CT ... 86
Delaware State University ... DE ... 90
Catholic University of America, The ... DC ... 92
Gallaudet University ... DC ... 92
Howard University ... DC ... 92
University of the District of Columbia ... DC ... 94
Barry University ... FL ... 96
Florida Agricultural and Mechanical University ... FL ... 109
Florida Atlantic University ... FL ... 109
Florida Gulf Coast University ... FL ... 109
Florida International University ... FL ... 110
Florida Memorial University ... FL ... 100
Florida State University ... FL ... 110
Saint Leo University ... FL ... 107
Southeastern University ... FL ... 108
University of Central Florida ... FL ... 110
University of North Florida ... FL ... 111
University of South Florida ... FL ... 111
University of West Florida ... FL ... 111
Warner University ... FL ... 114
Albany State University ... GA ... 114
Augusta University ... GA ... 116
Clark Atlanta University ... GA ... 117
Dalton State College ... GA ... 118
Fort Valley State University ... GA ... 118
Georgia State University ... GA ... 120
Kennesaw State University ... GA ... 121
@Middle Georgia State University ... GA ... 122
@Point University ... GA ... 124
Savannah State University ... GA ... 125
Thomas University ... GA ... 126
University of Georgia ... GA ... 126
Valdosta State University ... GA ... 127
University of Guam ... GU ... 504
Brigham Young University Hawaii ... HI ... 128
Hawaii Pacific University ... HI ... 128
University of Hawaii at Manoa ... HI ... 129
Boise State University ... ID ... 130
Brigham Young University-Idaho ... ID ... 130
Idaho State University ... ID ... 131
Lewis-Clark State College ... ID ... 132
Northwest Nazarene University ... ID ... 132
Aurora University ... IL ... 133
Bradley University ... IL ... 134
@Chamberlain University-Addison ... IL ... 134
Chicago State University ... IL ... 134
DePaul University ... IL ... 136
Dominican University ... IL ... 137
Erikson Institute ... IL ... 137
Governors State University ... IL ... 138
Greenville University ... IL ... 138
Illinois State University ... IL ... 140
Lewis University ... IL ... 142
Loyola University Chicago ... IL ... 143
Methodist College ... IL ... 144
Northeastern Illinois University ... IL ... 146
Olivet Nazarene University ... IL ... 147
St. Augustine College ... IL ... 149
Southern Illinois University Carbondale ... IL ... 150
Southern Illinois University Edwardsville ... IL ... 150
Trinity Christian College ... IL ... 151
University of Chicago ... IL ... 151
University of Illinois at Chicago ... IL ... 151
University of Illinois Springfield ... IL ... 152
University of Illinois Urbana-Champaign ... IL ... 152
University of St. Francis ... IL ... 152
Western Illinois University ... IL ... 153
Anderson University ... IN ... 153
Ball State University ... IN ... 153
Goshen College ... IN ... 155
Huntington University ... IN ... 156
Indiana State University ... IN ... 156
Indiana University-Purdue University Indianapolis ... IN ... 157
Indiana Wesleyan University ... IN ... 158
Manchester University ... IN ... 159
@Marian University ... IN ... 159
Purdue University Northwest ... IN ... 160
Saint Mary's College ... IN ... 160
Taylor University ... IN ... 161
University of Indianapolis ... IN ... 161
University of Saint Francis ... IN ... 162
University of Southern Indiana ... IN ... 162
Valparaiso University ... IN ... 162
Briar Cliff University ... IA ... 164
Buena Vista University ... IA ... 164
Clarke University ... IA ... 164
Dordt University ... IA ... 165
Grand View University ... IA ... 166
Loras College ... IA ... 168
Luther College ... IA ... 168
Mount Mercy University ... IA ... 168
Northwestern College ... IA ... 169
St. Ambrose University ... IA ... 169
University of Iowa ... IA ... 163
University of Northern Iowa ... IA ... 164
Wartburg College ... IA ... 170
Bethel College ... KS ... 172
Fort Hays State University ... KS ... 173
Kansas State University ... KS ... 175
@Kansas Wesleyan University ... KS ... 175
Newman University ... KS ... 176
Pittsburg State University ... KS ... 177
Tabor College ... KS ... 177
University of Kansas Main Campus ... KS ... 177
Washburn University ... KS ... 178
Wichita State University ... KS ... 178
Asbury University ... KY ... 179
Brescia University ... KY ... 179
Campbellsville University ... KY ... 180
Eastern Kentucky University ... KY ... 180
Kentucky Christian University ... KY ... 181
Kentucky State University ... KY ... 183
Morehead State University ... KY ... 184
Murray State University ... KY ... 184
Northern Kentucky University ... KY ... 184
Spalding University ... KY ... 184
University of Kentucky ... KY ... 185
University of Louisville ... KY ... 186
University of Pikeville ... KY ... 186
Western Kentucky University ... KY ... 186
Grambling State University ... LA ... 192
Louisiana College ... LA ... 187
Louisiana State University and Agricultural and Mechanical College ... LA ... 189
Northwestern State University ... LA ... 192
Southeastern Louisiana University ... LA ... 193
Southern University and A&M College ... LA ... 191
Southern University at New Orleans ... LA ... 191
Tulane University ... LA ... 191
University of Louisiana at Monroe ... LA ... 193
Saint Joseph's College of Maine ... ME ... 196
University of Maine ... ME ... 196
University of Maine at Presque Isle ... ME ... 197
University of New England ... ME ... 197
University of Southern Maine ... ME ... 197
Bowie State University ... MD ... 204
Coppin State University ... MD ... 204
Frostburg State University ... MD ... 204
Hood College ... MD ... 199
McDaniel College ... MD ... 200
Morgan State University ... MD ... 201
Salisbury University ... MD ... 204
University of Maryland Baltimore County ... MD ... 203
University of Maryland, Baltimore ... MD ... 203
Anna Maria College ... MA ... 205
Boston College ... MA ... 207
Boston University ... MA ... 207
Bridgewater State University ... MA ... 212
College of Our Lady of the Elms ... MA ... 208
Eastern Nazarene College ... MA ... 209
Gordon College ... MA ... 210
@Lesley University ... MA ... 211
Regis College ... MA ... 218
Salem State University ... MA ... 213
Simmons University ... MA ... 218
Smith College ... MA ... 218
Springfield College ... MA ... 218
Western New England University ... MA ... 220
Westfield State University ... MA ... 213
Adrian College ... MI ... 220
Andrews University ... MI ... 221
Calvin University ... MI ... 222
Central Michigan University ... MI ... 222
Cornerstone University ... MI ... 223
Eastern Michigan University ... MI ... 223
Ferris State University ... MI ... 224
Grand Valley State University ... MI ... 224
Hope College ... MI ... 225
Kuyper College ... MI ... 226
Madonna University ... MI ... 227
Michigan State University ... MI ... 227
Northern Michigan University ... MI ... 228
Oakland University ... MI ... 229
Saginaw Valley State University ... MI ... 230
Siena Heights University ... MI ... 230
Spring Arbor University ... MI ... 231
University of Detroit Mercy ... MI ... 231
University of Michigan-Ann Arbor ... MI ... 231
University of Michigan-Flint ... MI ... 232
Wayne State University ... MI ... 232
Western Michigan University ... MI ... 233
Augsburg University ... MN ... 234
Bemidji State University ... MN ... 237
Bethel University ... MN ... 234
Capella University ... MN ... 234
College of Saint Scholastica, The ... MN ... 235
Concordia College ... MN ... 235
Metropolitan State University ... MN ... 238
Minnesota State University Moorhead ... MN ... 239
Minnesota State University, Mankato ... MN ... 239
North Central University ... MN ... 242
St. Catherine University ... MN ... 243
St. Cloud State University ... MN ... 240
@Saint Mary's University of Minnesota ... MN ... 243
St. Olaf College ... MN ... 243
Southwest Minnesota State University ... MN ... 241
University of Minnesota ... MN ... 243
University of Minnesota Duluth ... MN ... 243
University of Saint Thomas ... MN ... 244
Walden University ... MN ... 244
Winona State University ... MN ... 241
Alcorn State University ... MS ... 245
Belhaven University ... MS ... 245
Delta State University ... MS ... 245

THEA: National Association of Schools of Theatre: theatre (C,A,B, M,D)

THEOL: The Association of Theological Schools: theology (M, FP,D)

TRACS: Transnational Association of Christian Colleges and Schools: christian studies education (C,A,B, M,D)

VET: American Veterinary Medical Association: veterinary medicine (FP,D)

WC: Western Association of Schools and Colleges, Senior College and University Commission

WJ: Western Association of Schools and Colleges, Accrediting Commission for Community and Junior Colleges

Index of FICE Numbers

Code	Institution	State	Page
002292	Michigan Technological University	MI	228
002293	Lake Superior State University	MI	226
002294	Monroe County Community College	MI	228
002295	Montcalm Community College	MI	228
002297	Muskegon Community College	MI	228
002299	North Central Michigan College	MI	228
002301	Northern Michigan University	MI	228
002302	Northwestern Michigan College	MI	229
002303	Oakland Community College	MI	229
002307	Oakland University	MI	229
002308	Olivet College	MI	229
002310	St. Clair County Community College	MI	230
002311	Kuyper College	MI	226
002313	Sacred Heart Major Seminary	MI	230
002314	Saginaw Valley State University	MI	230
002315	Schoolcraft College	MI	230
002316	Siena Heights University	MI	230
002317	Southwestern Michigan College	MI	231
002318	Spring Arbor University	MI	231
002322	Finlandia University	MI	224
002323	University of Detroit Mercy	MI	231
002325	University of Michigan-Ann Arbor	MI	231
002326	University of Michigan-Dearborn	MI	231
002327	University of Michigan-Flint	MI	232
002328	Washtenaw Community College	MI	232
002329	Wayne State University	MI	232
002330	Western Michigan University	MI	233
002331	Western Theological Seminary	MI	233
002332	Anoka-Ramsey Community College	MN	237
002334	Augsburg University	MN	234
002335	Riverland Community College	MN	240
002336	Bemidji State University	MN	237
002337	Bethany Lutheran College	MN	234
002339	Central Lakes College	MN	237
002340	Carleton College	MN	234
002341	College of Saint Benedict	MN	235
002342	St. Catherine University	MN	243
002343	The College of Saint Scholastica	MN	235
002345	University of Saint Thomas	MN	244
002346	Concordia College	MN	235
002347	Concordia University, St. Paul	MN	235
002350	Vermilion Community College	MN	241
002353	Gustavus Adolphus College	MN	236
002354	Hamline University	MN	236
002355	Hibbing Community College	MN	238
002356	Itasca Community College	MN	238
002357	Luther Seminary	MN	236
002358	Macalester College	MN	236
002360	Minnesota State University, Mankato	MN	239
002361	Martin Luther College	MN	236
002362	Minneapolis Cmty & Tech College	MN	239
002365	Minneapolis College of Art & Design	MN	237
002367	Minnesota State University Moorhead	MN	239
002369	North Central University	MN	242
002370	North Hennepin Community College	MN	240
002371	University of Northwestern St. Paul	MN	244
002373	Rochester Community & Tech College	MN	240
002375	Southwest Minnesota State Univ	MN	241
002377	St. Cloud State University	MN	240
002379	Saint John's University	MN	243
002380	St Mary's University of Minnesota	MN	243
002382	St. Olaf College	MN	243
002383	Crown College	MN	235
002385	Northland Community & Tech College	MN	240
002386	United Theol Seminary-Twin Cities	MN	243
002388	University of Minnesota Duluth	MN	243
002389	University of Minnesota-Morris	MN	244
002391	Mitchell Hamline School of Law	MN	242
002393	Minnesota State College Southeast	MN	239
002394	Winona State University	MN	241
002396	Alcorn State University	MS	245
002397	Belhaven University	MS	245
002398	Blue Mountain College	MS	245
002401	Coahoma Community College	MS	245
002402	Copiah-Lincoln Community College	MS	245
002403	Delta State University	MS	245
002404	East Central Community College	MS	246
002405	East Mississippi Community College	MS	246
002407	Hinds Community College	MS	246
002408	Holmes Community College	MS	246
002409	Itawamba Community College	MS	246
002410	Jackson State University	MS	246
002411	Jones County Junior College	MS	246
002413	Meridian Community College	MS	247
002414	Millsaps College	MS	247
002415	Mississippi College	MS	247
002416	Mississippi Delta Community College	MS	247
002417	Mississippi Gulf Coast Cmty College	MS	247
002422	Mississippi University for Women	MS	248
002423	Mississippi State University	MS	247
002424	Mississippi Valley State University	MS	248
002426	Northeast Mississippi Cmty College	MS	248
002427	Northwest Mississippi Cmty College	MS	248
002430	Pearl River Community College	MS	248
002433	Rust College	MS	248
002435	Southeastern Baptist College	MS	249
002436	Southwest Mississippi Cmty College	MS	249
002439	Tougaloo College	MS	249
002440	University of Mississippi	MS	249
002441	University of Southern Mississippi	MS	249
002447	William Carey University	MS	249
002449	Avila University	MO	250
002450	Calvary University	MO	251
002453	Central Methodist University	MO	251
002454	University of Central Missouri	MO	260
002456	Columbia College	MO	251
002457	Concordia Seminary	MO	252
002458	Cottey College	MO	252
002459	Crowder College	MO	252
002460	Culver-Stockton College	MO	252
002461	Drury University	MO	252
002462	Eden Theological Seminary	MO	253
002463	Evangel University	MO	253
002464	Fontbonne University	MO	253
002466	Harris-Stowe State University	MO	254
002467	Conception Seminary College	MO	251
002468	Jefferson College	MO	254
002471	St Louis Cmty College-Cosand Center	MO	259
002473	Kansas City Art Institute	MO	254
002474	Kansas City Univ of Med & BioSci	MO	254
002476	Kenrick-Glennon Seminary	MO	254
002477	A. T. Still Univ of Health Sciences	MO	250
002479	Lincoln University	MO	254
002480	Lindenwood University	MO	254
002482	Maryville University of Saint Louis	MO	255
002484	Metropolitan Cmty Col-Penn Valley	MO	255
002485	Midwestern Baptist Theol Seminary	MO	256
002486	Mineral Area College	MO	256
002488	Missouri Southern State University	MO	256
002489	Missouri Valley College	MO	256
002490	Missouri Western State University	MO	257
002491	Moberly Area Community College	MO	257
002494	Nazarene Theological Seminary	MO	257
002495	Truman State University	MO	260
002496	Northwest Missouri State University	MO	257
002498	Park University	MO	258
002499	Rockhurst University	MO	258
002500	College of the Ozarks	MO	251
002501	Southeast Missouri State University	MO	259
002502	Southwest Baptist University	MO	259
002503	Missouri State University	MO	256
002504	Univ Hlth Sci & Pharm in St Louis	MO	260
002506	Saint Louis University	MO	259
002509	Saint Paul School of Theology	KS	177
002512	Stephens College	MO	260
002514	North Central Missouri College	MO	257
002515	Univ of Missouri System Admin	MO	260
002516	University of Missouri - Columbia	MO	261
002517	Missouri Univ of Science Tech	MO	261
002518	Univ of Missouri - Kansas City	MO	261
002519	Univ of Missouri - Saint Louis	MO	261
002520	Washington University in St. Louis	MO	262
002521	Webster University	MO	262
002523	Westminster College	MO	262
002524	William Jewell College	MO	262
002525	William Woods University	MO	262
002526	Carroll College	MT	263
002527	University of Providence	MT	265
002528	Miles Community College	MT	263
002529	Dawson Community College	MT	263
002530	Montana State University Billings	MT	264
002531	Montana Technological University	MT	265
002532	Montana State University	MT	264
002533	Montana State University - Northern	MT	264
002534	Rocky Mountain College	MT	265
002536	University of Montana - Missoula	MT	263
002537	The University of Montana Western	MT	264
002539	Chadron State College	NE	268
002540	College of Saint Mary	NE	266
002541	Concordia University	NE	266
002542	Creighton University	NE	266
002544	Doane University	NE	267
002548	Hastings College	NE	267
002551	University of Nebraska at Kearney	NE	269
002553	Midland University	NE	267
002554	University of Nebraska at Omaha	NE	270
002555	Nebraska Wesleyan University	NE	268
002557	Mid-Plains Community College	NE	267
002559	Peru State College	NE	268
002560	Western Nebraska Community College	NE	270
002563	Union College	NE	269
002565	University of Nebraska - Lincoln	NE	269
002566	Wayne State College	NE	268
002567	York College	NE	270
002568	University of Nevada, Reno	NV	271
002569	University of Nevada, Las Vegas	NV	271
002572	Colby-Sawyer College	NH	272
002573	Dartmouth College	NH	273
002575	Franklin Pierce University	NH	273
002579	New England College	NH	273
002580	Southern New Hampshire University	NH	274
002581	NHTI-Concord's Community College	NH	273
002582	Manchester Community College	NH	272
002583	Great Bay Community College	NH	272
002586	Rivier University	NH	273
002587	Saint Anselm College	NH	274
002589	University of New Hampshire	NH	274
002590	Keene State College	NH	274
002591	Plymouth State University	NH	275
002595	Assumption College for Sisters	NJ	275
002596	Atlantic Cape Community College	NJ	275
002597	Bloomfield College	NJ	276
002598	Caldwell University	NJ	276
002599	Centenary University	NJ	276
002600	Saint Elizabeth University	NJ	282
002603	Drew University	NJ	277
002607	Fairleigh Dickinson University	NJ	277
002608	Georgian Court University	NJ	278
002609	Rowan University	NJ	281
002610	Felician University	NJ	277
002613	New Jersey City University	NJ	279
002615	Middlesex College	NJ	278
002616	Monmouth University	NJ	279
002617	Montclair State University	NJ	279
002619	New Brunswick Theological Seminary	NJ	279
002621	New Jersey Institute of Technology	NJ	279
002622	Kean University	NJ	278
002624	Ocean County College	NJ	279
002625	William Paterson University of NJ	NJ	284
002626	Princeton Theological Seminary	NJ	280
002627	Princeton University	NJ	280
002628	Rider University	NJ	281
002629	Rutgers University - New Brunswick	NJ	282
002631	Rutgers University - Newark	NJ	282
002632	Seton Hall University	NJ	283
002638	Saint Peter's University	NJ	283
002639	Stevens Institute of Technology	NJ	283
002642	The College of New Jersey	NJ	276
002643	Union County College	NJ	284
002650	University of the Southwest	NM	289
002651	Eastern New Mexico University	NM	286
002653	New Mexico Highlands University	NM	286
002654	New Mexico Inst of Mining & Tech	NM	286
002655	New Mexico Junior College	NM	287
002656	New Mexico Military Institute	NM	287
002657	NM State University-Main Campus	NM	287
002658	NM State University-Alamogordo	NM	287
002659	NM State University-Carlsbad	NM	287
002660	San Juan College	NM	288
002661	Eastern New Mexico Univ - Roswell	NM	286
002663	Univ of New Mexico Main Campus	NM	288
002664	Western New Mexico University	NM	289
002665	Vaughn Col of Aeronautics & Tech	NY	324
002666	Adelphi University	NY	289
002668	Alfred University	NY	290
002669	Bank Street College of Education	NY	290
002670	Clarks Summit University	PA	381
002671	Bard College	NY	290
002674	New York Theological Seminary	NY	309
002677	Brooklyn Law School	NY	291
002678	Bryant & Stratton College	NY	292
002681	Canisius College	NY	292
002685	Cazenovia College	NY	292
002687	CUNY Brooklyn College	NY	293
002688	CUNY City College	NY	293
002689	CUNY Hunter College	NY	294
002690	CUNY Queens College	NY	295
002691	CUNY Borough of Manhattan CC	NY	293
002692	CUNY Bronx Community College	NY	293
002693	CUNY John Jay Col Criminal Justice	NY	294
002694	CUNY Kingsborough Cmty College	NY	294
002696	NYC Col of Tech/City Univ of NY	NY	295
002697	CUNY Queensborough Cmty Col	NY	295
002698	College of Staten Island CUNY	NY	293
002699	Clarkson University	NY	295
002700	Colgate Roch Crozer Divinity School	NY	296
002701	Colgate University	NY	296
002703	College of Mount Saint Vincent	NY	296
002705	The College of Saint Rose	NY	296
002707	Columbia University in City of NY	NY	297
002708	Barnard College	NY	291
002710	Cooper Union	NY	297
002711	Cornell University	NY	297
002712	D'Youville College	NY	298
002713	Dominican College of Blauvelt	NY	298
002718	Elmira College	NY	298
002722	Fordham University	NY	300
002726	General Theological Seminary	NY	300
002728	Hamilton College	NY	300
002729	Hartwick College	NY	301
002731	Hobart and William Smith Colleges	NY	301
002732	Hofstra University	NY	301
002733	Holy Trinity Orthodox Seminary	NY	302
002734	Houghton College	NY	302
002735	Hilbert College	NY	301
002737	Iona College	NY	302
002739	Ithaca College	NY	302
002740	Jewish Theol Seminary of America	NY	303
002741	American Jewish University	CA	25
002742	The Juilliard School	NY	303
002744	Keuka College	NY	303
002748	Le Moyne College	NY	303
002749	New York Col of Podiatric Medicine	NY	308
002751	Long Island University	NY	304
002754	Long Island University-LIU Post	NY	304
002758	Manhattan College	NY	304
002759	Manhattan School of Music	NY	305
002760	Manhattanville College	NY	305
002763	Maria College of Albany	NY	305
002765	Marist College	NY	305
002769	Marymount Manhattan College	NY	305
002772	Mercy College	NY	306
002775	Molloy College	NY	306
002777	Medaille College	NY	305
002778	Mount Saint Mary College	NY	307
002779	Nazareth College of Rochester	NY	307

Index of Universities, Colleges and Schools